Preface

In the preface to the previous, twelfth, edition of *The Chambers Dictionary* we noted the 'The English language continues to develop at an astonishing rate.' This development seems to have accelerated in the intervening three years, with the internet playing a key part not just in providing new words (such as tweet and hashtag) but also in enabling neologisms to spread around the world at unprecedented speed.

This thirteenth edition has therefore required the most comprehensive update to *The Chambers Dictionary* in recent years, with over five hundred new words added, and all the existing words and definitions thoroughly checked and, where necessary, modified. In a new innovation for Chambers, many of these words were first submitted by our Facebook friends and Twitter followers as part of a social media campaign which we ran in 2013. All these submitted words were considered by an editorial board of John Murray Press, and many have ended up in the dictionary.

Yet this focus on new words does not mean that we ever lose sight of the features that make *The Chambers Dictionary* unique. As always, we have resisted the temptation to discard rare, literary and historical words. The new Word Lover's Ramble, written by Trevor Barnes with access to a copy of every edition going back to 1871, also brings into focus many fascinating historical words which in many cases have seen their meanings change considerably over the time that Chambers has been in print.

The twelfth edition of *The Chambers Dictionary* received widespread praise. However, the editors of Chambers have always prided themselves on responsiveness to feedback from users, and three changes may be particularly noticeable to those who 'upgrade' to this latest edition: firstly, the two-colour section now sits at the end of the dictionary rather than in the middle; secondly, the list of first names has been reinstated (and updated), at the request of crossword fans; and thirdly, additional folds have been added to the jacket to improve its durability.

The Chambers Dictionary is also now available in ebook and app formats. The latter may particularly appeal to crossword lovers, due to features such as anagram solving and suggesting solutions to partial words. Chambers remains the dictionary of choice for crossword fans, word lovers and curious people everywhere. Whichever group you fall into, we hope you enjoy this new thirteenth edition.

A short history of English

Introduction

English is now used as a first language by about 700 million speakers, and is a second language for many millions more. It appears in many guises, ranging from the 'new' Englishes of Africa and Asia, eg Indian English, through the usages of North America to the oldest established varieties (the English of England, Hiberno-English and Scots in Lowland Scotland). English is now a world language, the most widespread in linguistic function and geographical extent that the world has ever seen.

The modern varieties of English have emerged over the last five or six centuries through contact with other languages and through dynamic interaction with each other. All, however, derive from one ultimate source: the Germanic language-variety which was brought to Britain from northern Germany by Anglo-Saxon invaders in the fifth century AD. The people who spoke this variety supplanted the Romano-British inhabitants, who gradually retreated to the northern and western parts of the island where, in North Wales and the Gaelic-speaking areas of Scotland, they remain. The invaders' language subsequently became a distinct language, English, which developed and spread within the British Isles up to the sixteenth century. English was subsequently taken beyond these islands with the imperial expansions of the seventeenth, eighteenth and nineteenth centuries.

During these centuries the structure of the English language changed radically. Our evidence for these changes comes, of course, not from the direct analysis of speech – for sound-recordings of English only began to be made at the end of the nineteenth century – but from comparative study of other languages and through the painstaking analysis by scholars of the written records which have come down to us continuously from the seventh century onwards.

A Germanic language

All Germanic languages derive from a common ancestor known as Proto-Germanic. English is a member of the Western branch of the Germanic languages, which also includes German, Dutch, Afrikaans, and (its closest Germanic relative) Frisian, this last being a language-variety spoken in what is now part of the Netherlands. Other branches of Germanic which are traditionally identified include North Germanic (Danish, Norwegian, Swedish, Faroese, Icelandic) and East Germanic (now extinct, and recorded for the most part in the fourth-century Gothic Bible translation of Bishop Ulfilas).

The Germanic languages are themselves part of a much larger language family: the Indo-European group, which includes such diverse languages as Bengali and Brythonic, Russian and Romany, Sanskrit and Spanish. This group stems ultimately from Proto-Indo-European, which was probably originally spoken in what is now Southern Russia.

English shares a number of characteristics with its Germanic relations. Probably the best-known of these is the Germanic modification of inherited consonantal sounds known as Grimm's Law, so-called after the philologist and folklorist J Grimm (1785–1863). Grimm showed that there was a regular set of consonantal differences bet ween the Germanic languages and the others of the Indo-European family, which dated from the period of divergence of Proto-Germanic from the other Indo-European varieties. The effects of Grimm's Law in Old English can be seen through comparing groups of cognates, ie words in different languages with a common ancestor (c f Latin *co-* + *gnātus* 'born together '). Thus, for instance, *p* in other Indo-European languages corresponds to *f/v* in Germanic languages, eg father (German *Vater*, but Latin *pater*, French *pere*, Italian *padre*, Sanskrit *pitar-*), foot (Dutch *voet* , but Latin *pes*, *ped-*, French *pied*, Sanskrit *padam* 'footstep'), etc.

The discovery of such shared linguistic features has made it possible to reconstruct the relationships of the languages which derive from Proto-Indo-European. However, it is worth remembering that, just as children derive some of their linguistic behaviour from their parents but are also strongly influenced by their peer group, so language-varieties borrow usages from those language-varieties with which they come into contact and transmit these acquired characteristics to future generations. Indeed, without such contacts the processes of linguistic change would have been much slower in operation: such a pattern is observable in languages which have little contact with others (for instance Icelandic, which has been an isolated language for much of the last thousand years, has barely changed during this period). The history of English is not one of internal evolution, hermetically sealed from outside influence. Rather, its history is one of constant and dynamic interaction between inherited usage and the languages with which it came into contact .

It is traditional to distinguish between 'external history', ie the changing functions of varieties of the vernacular in relation to other languages and to broader developments in society, and 'internal history', ie the changing forms of the language. This distinction is adopted here.

External history

The earliest forms of English were very different from those in present-day use, and the modern configuration has taken many centuries to emerge. The history of English is traditionally divided into a sequence of epochs distinguished by certain language-external events and characterized by language-internal differences.

The following broad periods are generally recognized, although there is a good deal of scholarly debate about the precise boundaries bet ween them.

The
Chambers
Dictionary

13th Edition

The Chambers Dictionary

13th Edition

This thirteenth edition published in 2014 by Chambers Harrap Publishers Ltd.

First published as *Chambers's Twentieth Century Dictionary* in 1901; published as *Chambers English Dictionary* in 1988; first published as *The Chambers Dictionary* in 1993.

An HachetteUK company.

British Library Cataloguing in Publication Data: a catalogue record for this title is available from the British Library.

ISBN 9781473602250

10 9 8 7 6 5 4 3 2 1

Fonts featured in letter openers published by the following foundries: Adobe, Apple, ATF, Berthold, Bitstream, Elsner&Flake, Garamond, International TypeFounders Inc, ITC, Linotype, Microsoft, Stempel, T.26, URW++, Wagner.

Typeset by Cenveo® Publisher Services.

Hodder & Stoughton policy is to use papers that are natural, renewable and recyclable products and made from wood grown in sustainable forests. The logging and manufacturing processes are expected to conform to the environmental regulations of the country of origin.

Chambers Harrap Publishers Ltd
338 Euston Road
London NW1 3BH
www.chambers.co.uk

Designed by Chambers Harrap Publishers Ltd
Letter openers and Miscellany designed by Sharon McTeir
Typeset in Optima and Arial by Cenveo

Additional typesetting by Mac Bride
Printed in India

Contents

Contributors to this edition

Publisher
Sam Richardson

Consulting Editors and Chief Lexicographers
Ian Brookes
Michael Munro

Editorial Board of John Murray Press authors and staff
Eleanor Birne
Gyles Brandreth
Nick Davies
Rosie Gailer
Henry Hitchings
Georgina Laycock
John Julius Norwich
Harry Ritchie
Ben Schott
David Swarbrick

Writer of Miscellany Section
Trevor Barnes

Production Controller
Christopher Watkins

Acknowledgements

The Publishers of this thirteenth edition are grateful to the many members of the public who have written to us with comments and suggestions.

In addition, we would like to thank all of the people whose suggestions have proved helpful in compiling this and past editions of the dictionary, our many, valued subject consultants, and the many individuals and organizations who have responded to requests for information.

Finally, we would like to acknowledge our debt to all the lexicographers who have worked on the previous editions of this dictionary.

A short history of English

Prehistoric Old English ('pre-Old English'): the period before written records, roughly 450–650/700AD. During this period English diverged from the other members of the Germanic group to become a distinct language.

Old English: often referred to as Anglo-Saxon after the Germanic tribes who used it : the period from the appearance of written records in English to the Norman Conquest of 1066. During this period, English was used nationally for the documentary purposes of Anglo-Saxon government. It also had a literary function: the epic poem *Beowulf* was copied in a manuscript dating from circa 1000, and the end of the period saw the emergence of a formidable native prose tradition with the composition of the *Anglo-Saxon Chronicle* and the religious homilies of Aelfric and Wulfstan. Most Old English which has come down to us is written in the West-Saxon dialect, since the national focus of power for much of the period lay in the south-western kingdom of Wessex. However, the Old English written record provides evidence for at least three other dialect-groupings : Old Mercian in the Midlands, Old Northumbrian in Northern England and in what later became Lowland Scotland to the south of the Clyde-Forth line, and Kentish in South-East England.

Towards the end of the Anglo-Saxon period, large numbers of North Germanic (Scandinavian) peoples settled in northern England. Their language, in part because it seems to have been to a degree mutually intelligible with local varieties of Old English, had a profound effect on the subsequent history of English beyond the area of primary Scandinavian settlement. However, Scandinavian left little mark on the written record until after the Norman Conquest of 1066.

Middle English: the period from the Norman Conquest to the arrival of printing in Britain in 1476. The Conquest saw the large-scale replacement of the old Anglo-Saxon aristocracy with a French-speaking and European-centred elite. Although English remained in widespread use in speech, it lost its national status; documentary functions were taken over by Latin, which was undergoing a revival in Western Europe, while many literary functions were taken over by varieties of French. The French-speaking elite seems to have shifted quite quickly to the regular use of English in speech, but French remained in prestigious use until at least the end of the fourteenth century. Written English, for much of the Middle Ages, was of solely local significance, primarily used for initial education and for the production of texts with a local readership; it was thus strongly marked by dialectal variation in writing. This situation changed towards the end of the period. Geoffrey Chaucer's *Canterbury Tales*, written for an aristocratic and metropolitan audience around 1390–1400, marks one stage in the emergence of the vernacular as having a national significance, as does the translation of the Bible into English associated with the proto-Protestant Wycliffite movement at the end of the fourteenth century.

Towards the end of the Middle English period, distinct varieties of the language emerged outside England: Older Scots in Lowland Scotland, and Hiberno-English in eastern Ireland.

Early Modern English: the period from 1476 to the early eighteenth century. Caxton's introduction of printing to England at the end of the fifteenth century coincided with the elaboration of English as a vernacular capable of being used for all linguistic functions. The role of English was given impetus by the Protestant Reformation, which placed a religious duty of literacy on all, and provided national texts for the purpose : the vernacular Bible and Prayer-Book. This national role coincided with the standardization of written English and with the emergence during the sixteenth century of a prestigious form of pronunciation. Evolving class-structures in society, notably the rise of a powerful London bourgeoisie, provided audiences for sophisticated vernacular texts, such as the dramas of Elizabethan and Jacobean England, and the prestige of the vernacular was reinforced by the victories of the rising middle classes in the mid-seventeenth-century Civil Wars.

The foundation of the modern British state following the Act of Union between England, Wales and Scotland (1707) may be taken as an external marker of the end of the Early Modern period. Older Scots continued to be used up to this date, although it underwent severe competition from the forces of Anglicization, particularly in religious discourse. During this period, new varieties of English/Scots appeared in overseas settlements such as the Plantations in Ulster from the end of the sixteenth century, and in the British Colonies in North America.

Later Modern English: the period from the early eighteenth century to the present day. Tendencies already prefigured in earlier centuries, such as the development of mass literacy and of urban varieties, came to fruition during this period. It is also the period when overt pride in English was most clearly signalled, notably with the arrival of large-scale codifications of the language such as Samuel Johnson's *Dictionary* of 1755. Above all, the defining linguistic characteristic of this period is the spread of English beyond its place of origin, to the various parts of the Empire and later, with the cultural hegemony of the United States, to the new electronic media.

After 1707 Older Scots developed into Modern Scots, but became much more restricted in register, to non-prestigious speech and to specialized usages, eg in the verse of Robert Burns. Subsequent attempts to reinstate Scots as a national, ie Scottish, vernacular rather than as a collection of local varieties have met so far with mixed success. Other varieties within the English-language continuum have emerged as elaborated usages in their own right , eg Indian English, where a special variety with its own distinctive grammatical, lexical and accentual properties has emerged as a national prestigious usage.

Internal history

The developments in the social function of English described above all left their mark on the internal evolution of the language, at every level: in pronunciation and spelling, in grammar and in vocabulary.

Towards the end of the Old English period, **spelling** became standardized on the basis of West Saxon, for reasons already given; but during the Middle English period it became usual for dialectal variation to be manifested in spelling. There are therefore, for instance, no fewer than 500 ways of spelling the simple word 'through' in Middle

English, ranging from fairly recognizable *thurgh*, *thorough* and *þorowe* to exotic-seeming *drowȝ*, *yhurght*, *trghug* and *trowffe*. As long as English was used simply on a local basis this practice was comparatively unproblematic, since the phonic conventions of each locality could be accepted comparatively easily within that locality as an appropriate reflection of pronunciation. However, the inconvenience of not having a national system became much more apparent when English started to take on national functions once again. By the beginning of the fifteenth century, the usage developed in London was starting to take on a national role, and London spelling of this period is in its essentials the basis of the present-day English pattern. During the sixteenth century, a parallel standardized Scottish system competed for a while with London spelling in Scotland, and a slightly modified form of the system appeared in the United States at the end of the eighteenth century (thus distinctions of the *coloured* – *colored* type) and has been subsequently sustained there and elsewhere.

The reconstruction of **pronunciation** during the Old and Middle English periods is based upon a mixture of evidence of greater or lesser value: the interpretation of spellings, the analysis of rhyming practice in verse, comparison with other languages and with later states of the language. The major development in the history of English is a phenomenon called the Great Vowel Shift, which affected the 'long vowels' of later Middle English. This sound-change, which probably arose in London as a result of complex processes of social interaction, may be dated to the period between 1400 and 1600 by the evidence of words coming into the language. Thus *doubt* and *guile*, French words which entered the language before 1400, were subjected to the diphthongization-processes of the Shift, while *soup* and *tureen*, later adoptions, were not so subjected.

The evidence for a standard form of pronunciation is uncertain until the sixteenth century. In 1589, George Puttenham, in *The Arte of English Poesie*, advises the accomplished poet to adopt the accentual usage of 'the better brought vp sort ':

> 'ye shall therfore take the vsuall speach of the Court , and that of London and the shires lying about
> London within lx. myles, and not much aboue.'

The history of standard pronunciation is a complex matter, and the evolution of present-day prestigious accents is a matter of quite complex interaction bet ween varieties rather than a simple process of descent. However, broadly speaking, Puttenham's description still holds for England at least, although other prestigious accents are found widely throughout the English-speaking world. Thus the accent-component of Scottish Standard English is prestigious in Scotland, and the variety known as General American is prestigious in the United States.

In **grammar**, the major change between Old and Present-Day English is the shift from synthesis to analysis in expressing grammatical relations.Whereas the relationships within and between phrases in Present-Day English are largely expressed by word-order, in Old English, these relationships are expressed to a much greater extent by special endings attached to words. These endings are called inflections.

The Old English inflectional system means that Old English word-order can be much more flexible than that of its descendant. Thus, in Present-Day English

> 1. *The lord binds the servant.*

and 2. *The servant binds the lord.*

mean very different things. The word-order indicates the relative functions of the phrases 'the lord' and 'the servant'. This was not necessarily the case in Old English. Sentence 1. above can be translated into Old English as

> 3. *Se hlāford bint þone cnapan.*

However, it could also be translated as

> 4. *Þone cnapan bint se hlāford.*

or 5. *Se hlāford þone cnapan bint.*

and so on. In sentences 3. – 5. above, the phrase *se hlāford*, because it is in the so-called nominative case, with a nominative form of the definite article the (*se*) is always the subject of the clause in whatever position it appears. And, because it is in the so-called accusative case, with an accusative form of the definite article (*þone*) and an accusative inflection on the accompanying noun (*-an*), *þone cnapan* is always the direct object of the clause. The cases, not the word-order, here determine the relationship between the two phrases. There were conventions in Old English that placed the subject in initial position, but these conventions could easily be departed from for stylistic effect .

This system did not survive intact into the Middle English period; it appears that interaction with Scandinavian encouraged the loss of inflections, and the conventions of word-order, whereby subject/object positioning had become stylistically formalized, became more fixed to take over the task originally performed by inflections. The Present-Day English pattern resulted. However, it is wrong to describe Present-Day English as wholly uninflected: a few inflections remain in Present-Day English, even if we do not call them such (cf *Tom*, *Tom's*, *pig*, *pig's*, *pigs*, etc).

Perhaps most obviously, there have been changes in the lexicon between Old and Present-Day English, and these changes reflect the kinds of linguistic contacts which the language has undergone. Although much of the core vocabulary of English is derived from Old English – eg *hand*, *head*, *wife*, *child*, *stone*, *name*, *man*, *fish*, *ride*, *choose*, *bind*, *love*, etc – the lexicon in general has been greatly augmented by borrowings from other languages.

Scandinavian has affected some of the most basic features of the language, such as the pronoun system – *they*, *their* and *them* are all from Scandinavian – and the system of grammatical inflection, eg the -s endings on some parts of the verb-paradigm in *loves* etc. Further, some items of core vocabulary are Scandinavian in origin, eg *take*, *ill*, *egg*, *skin*. More subtly, cognate items in Scandinavian and English have developed distinct meanings, eg *skirt*, *shirt*, and many Scandinavian words are found only in some varieties, eg *kirk*.

French has had a massive effect on the range of lexical items available in the language. To exemplify from the noun alone: words such as *action, bucket, calendar, courtesy, damage, envy, face, grief, honour, joy, labour, marriage, noise, opinion, people, quality, rage, reason, sound, spirit, task, use, vision, waste,* all of which are common in Present-Day usage, are all derived from French. Many French words are found in high-register contexts, and this means that their meanings in English diverge from those in French, eg *commence,* which has high-register connotations in English which are not shared by the French original *commencer.*

Of course, numerous other languages have had an effect on English, reflecting various cultural and imperial developments. Latin learning , sometimes mediated through French, has given English words such as *arbiter, pollen, junior, vertigo, folio,* etc. Contact with the world beyond Western Europe has given most of the European languages such words as *harem* (Arabic), *steppe* (Russian), *taboo* (Tongan), *chocolate* (Nahuatl), but it seems likely that imperial expansion in India gave English such items as *thug, pyjama, gymkhana, mulligatawny.*

The hospitality of English to foreign words has often been commented on; indeed, borrowing is the characteristic method whereby English expands its vocabulary, something which marks English off from its near-relatives such as German. Old English, like modern German, created new words through compounds, eg *sciprāp* 'cable' (lit . 'ship-rope'); cf German *Fernseher* 'television' (lit . 'far-seer '). However, this is no longer a marked feature of Present-Day English. One reason for this change must be to do with the grammatical structure of the later forms of English: there is no need to fit borrowed items into a complex inflectional system. Another reason is probably to do with custom: the more English borrowed, the more borrowing became customary; the more borrowing became customary, the more English borrowed.

© Jeremy J. Smith 1998

Jeremy J. Smith is Professor of English Philology at the University of Glasgow. He is the author of many articles and books on the history of English.

Examples of Earlier English

The Lord's Prayer in Old, Middle and Early Modern English, and in Older Scots

Old English (West Saxon, late ninth century)

> 'Þū ūre fæder þe eart on heofonum, sīe þīn nama gehālgod. Cume þīn rīce. Sīe þīn wylla on eorþan swā swā on heofonum. Syle ūs tōdæg ūme dæghwāmlican hlāf. And forgief ūs ūre gyltas swā swā wē forgiefaþ þm þe wið ūs āgyltaþ. And ne læd þū nā ūs on costnunge, ac ālīes ūs fram yfele.

Middle English (Kentish, 1340)

> Vader oure þet art ine heuenes, yhalȝed by þin name. Cominde þi riche. Yworþe þi wil ase ine heuene and ine erþe. Bread oure echedayes yef ous today. And uorlet ous oure yeldinges ase and we uorleteþ oure yelderes. And ne ous led naȝt into uondinge, ac vri ous uram queade.

Middle English (Central Midlands, c. 1380)

> Oure fadir, þat art in heuenys, halewid be þi name. 'Pi kyngdom come to. Be hi wile don ase in heuene and in erþe. Ȝiue to us þis day oure breed ouer oþer substaunse. And forȝiue to us oure dettes, as and we forȝiuen to oure dettouris. And leede us not into temptaciouns, but delyuere us from yuel.

Older Scots (c. 1520)

> Our fader, that art in heuenis, hallewit be thi name. Thi kingdom cum to. Thi wil be done in erde as in heuen. Gefe to vs this day our breid ouer vthir substaunce. And forgif to vs our dettis, as we forgef to our dettouris. And leid vs nocht into temptacioun, bot deliuer vs fra euile.

Early Modern English (Book of Common Prayer, 1549)

> Our Father, which art in heaven, Hallowed be thy Name. Thy kingdom come. Thy will be done, in earth as it is in heaven. Give us this day our daily bread. And forgive us our trespasses, As we forgive them that trespass against us. And lead us not into temptation ; But deliver us from evil.

Varieties of English

This dictionary is written with the British speaker of English in mind. However, English exists in many varieties in the world today. Some of the differences between the forms of English spoken and written in The United Kingdom and in the rest of the world are shown below.

American English

The characteristic American spellings of a number of individual words (eg *manoeuvre/maneuver, defence/defense, practise/practice*) are noted in the dictionary. Some spelling differences involving groups of similar words are as follows :

Brit   US

-ogue	*-og*	American English simplifies words such as *catalogue* and *pedagogue* to *catalog* and *pedagog*.
-our	*-or*	American English has *-or* in words such as *color* and *humor. Glamour* and *saviour*, however, are generally written -our.
-re	*-er*	Eg *center, meter, theater*. But to show the hard sound of c or g : *acre, massacre, ogre*, etc ; however, *meager* not *meagre*.
ll	*l*	In inflections and derivatives of words ending in *l* not immediately preceded by a single stressed vowel, American English does not double the *l* (cf page xxiv): *canceled, counselor, disheveled, equaled, marvelous, traveler*, etc. (Note also *woolen*.)
pp	*p*	Similarly, *kidnaper, worshiping*, etc.
tt	*t*	And also *carburetor* (but eg *formatting*).
l	*ll*	Eg *enroll, fulfill, instill, skillful* and *willful*.
ae, oe or *e*	*e*	The tendency to replace ae and oe with e in words derived from Latin and Greek is more strongly developed in the US than in Britain, eg *esophagus, hemoglobin*.
-ize or *-ise*	*-ize*	In verbs that may be spelt *-ize* or *-ise*, the use of *-ize* is now standard in American English. Note also *analyze, paralyze*, etc.

As a rule, hyphens are used less frequently in American English than in British English, although there is an increasing tendency to omit hyphens in Britain as well.

Generally speaking , American pronunciation differs from British English as follows :

Brit   US

ä	In many words, eg *ask, dance, half* and *rather*, American English has a shorter, more front vowel than that of standard British English.
i	Where British English has /i/ in final position in words such as *happy* and *city*, American English has /ē/.
ö	An alternative pronunciation /ä/ is common in words such as *haunt , launch, saunter, taunt* and *vaunt*.
o	In American English, words such as *block, got, pond, probable* and *top* are pronounced with an /ä/ sound. In words in which the vowel is followed by f, s, th, r, g or ng , eg *coffee, dog, cross, forest* and *long*, a longer vowel similar to /ö/ is also common.

ū	After the sounds *t, d, n, l* and *s*, American English has /oo/ rather than /ū/, eg in *new* and *tune*.
ī	In most words ending in *-ile*, such as *agile, fertile, fragile* and *hostile*, American English pronounces the final syllable as /-il/ rather than /-īl/.
t	In words such as *latter, metal* and *writing*, the *-tt-/-t-* is pronounced with the same sound as that of the *-dd- -/-d-* in *ladder, medal* and *riding*.
r	In most accents of American English *r* is pronounced at the end of a word and before a consonant.

There are a number of differences between the American pronunciation of vowels followed by r and the British pronunciation of the corresponding vowels :

Brit   US

a	Some Americans tend to make a sound approaching /e/, so that , for example, *marry* approximates to *merry*.
ā	This is commonly pronounced as a diphthong before r, the first element of which is close to a lengthened /e/. The second element of the diphthong, /ə/, is sometimes not pronounced when the vowel occurs in initial or medial position; eg the usual pronunciation of *Maryland* is /mer'i-lənd /.
är spelt *-er-*	In words such as *clerk* and *Derby*, where British speech preserves an older pronunciation /är/, American speech has /ûr/.
-ə-ri	American English tends to give greater prominence than British English does to the suffixes *-ary* and *-ory*, and often also *-ery* ; for example, *monetary* (Brit /-tə-ri or -tri /, US /-te-ri /), *confectionery* (Brit /-nə-ri /, US /-ne -ri /) and *obligatory* (Brit /-tə-ri / or *-tri* /, US /-tö-ri /).

In addition to the above, many differences between American and British English pronunciation are noted in the entries for particular words and prefixes in the dictionary. See for example *anti-, schedule, simultaneous* and *tomato*.

Many differences between British and American usage with regard to vocabulary and meaning are noted in the dictionary, eg *bonnet/hood, coffin/casket, curtains/drapes, estate agent/realtor, motorway/expressway, pavement/sidewalk, sweets/candy* and *windscreen/windshield*.

Canadian English

In spelling, Canadian usage stands midway between American English and British English. The usage is, however, far from uniform and varies from province to province and even from person to person. Hence spellings such as *color, traveler* and *center*, and *colour, traveller* and *centre*, are to be found alongside each other.

In pronunciation, Canadian English exhibits features found in both American and British English, although it more commonly follows American English: eg speakers of Canadian English pronounce *tomato* with an /ā/.

Brit Can

r   Like American English, Canadian English pronounces *r* in word-final position and before a consonant.

t   In the pronunciation of many Canadians, words such as *matter* and *madder* rhyme, as in American English.

i   The sound heard in *squirrel*, etc approaches /*û*/.

īl   Of the words which end in /*īl*/ in British English, most, eg *docile*, *textile*, *fragile*, end in /*īl*/ as in British English, but some such as *missile* and *fertile* may end in /-*il* / as in American English.

ī, ow In Canadian English, the vowels in eg *loud* and *ride* do not rhyme with those of *lout* and *write*.

English in Australia and New Zealand

Although there are differences between the English of Australia and that of New Zealand, the two varieties are sufficiently similar to be treated together. Vocabulary that is peculiar to this region includes: names of local flora and fauna (*bowerbird*, *galah*, *wallaby*); words to do with local topography and everyday life, some imported in extended use into British English (*black stump*, *bush*, *outback*, *walkabout*); general words that do not exist in British English in the same meaning (*bullock* = 'to work very hard', *king-hit* = 'knockout blow '); and many colourful colloquialisms and idioms (*beaut*, *bludge*, *crook*, *dinkum*, *she's apples*).

The spelling of Australian and New Zealand English traditionally follows that of British English but American spelling is now sometimes also found.

Features of pronunciation that can be noted are :

Brit Aust , NZ

r   As in British English, *r* is not pronounced before a consonant or at the end of a word, except by speakers in the southern part of the South Island of New Zealand.

i   Australian and New Zealand English have /*ē*/ in words such as *happy* and *very*, where British English has /*i*/. In closed unstressed syllables, where British English has /*i*/, Australian and New Zealand English have /*ə*/, as for example in *mistake*, *defeat*, *ticket*, etc.

oor   The pronunciation /*ŭə*/ of words like *sure*, *pure*, etc has been almost entirely superseded by either /*ö*/ or /*ooə*/.

a   In many words in which British English has /*ä*/, Australian and New Zealand English have /*a*/. In words ending in *-ance*, New Zealand English has /*ä*/ where Australian English has /*a*/ or /*ä*/. In Australian English *lather* is pronounced with /*a*/, but in New Zealand with /*ä*/.

ō   Before *l*, this is usually pronounced as /*o*/.

A feature of Australian English which seems to be increasingly gaining a foothold in British usage is the 'high rising terminal' (HRT) which is marked by a rising intonation pattern in the final syllable or syllables of an utterance. If the Chambers mailbag is anything to go by this is a habit which seems to cause considerable irritation, not least because it is associated with certain imported soap operas!

English in South Africa

In the nineteenth century, varieties of English were developed by the Dutch (influenced by Afrikaans), by the black population (influenced by local African languages) and by Indian immigrants who arrived in the country in

the second half of the century. English has been an official language of South Africa since 1910; Afrikaans replaced Dutch as an official language in 1925. During the apartheid era, Afrikaans was spoken by the white population and was regarded as the language of authority and government, whereas English, although a minority language, was spoken by many blacks, both as a language of political protest and as a means of attaining an international voice. At the end of the apartheid era, many African languages were also accepted as official languages.

The English of South Africa is therefore not a homogeneous variety, and the influences on it have been diverse. Many of the loan words from Afrikaans and African languages relate to local flora and fauna and other aspects of everyday life (some imported into British English): *aardvark* (an animal), *baas* (master), *backveld* (remote country), *dikkop* (a type of bird), *donga* (Zulu; gully), *fundi* (Nguni; an expert), *induna* (Zulu; a tribal leader), *jukskei* (an outdoor game), *koppie* (a low hill), *mossie* (a type of bird), *poort* (a mountain pass), *sjambok* (a whip), *snoek* (a fish) and *springbok* (an animal). A number of terms have permeated world consciousness for historical reasons, notably *apartheid*, *commando*, *trek* and *veld*. Words of English derivation include *pig-lily* (a kind of local lily) and *square-face* (gin), and words of mixed origin include *kingklip* (a fish). In other cases, words known in British English have special meanings in South African English, eg *bioscope* (a cinema), *camp* (a fenced-off area of pasture), *canteen* (a public house), *lay -by* (a down payment), *robot* (a traffic signal), *stamp* (pounded maize) and *township* (a black urban settlement).

Apart from relatively few and minor peculiarities of vocabulary, the standard English of South Africa is very similar to that of British English. South African pronunciation of English is characterized by a clipped accent with tight vowel sounds and more strongly articulated consonants /*p*/, /*t*/ and /*k*/. Other features are as follows:

Brit S Afr

r   The South African English treatment of *r* word-finally and before consonants is the same as that of British English.

i   South African English has /*ē*/ where British English has /*i*/ in *very*, *secretary*, etc. In other positions, /*i*/ is pronounced more centrally than in British English, with a vowel close to /*ə*/.

a, e, ä, etc There is a tendency to raise these vowels to values approaching /*e*/, /*i*/, /*o*/ or /*ö*/, etc so giving /*de'dē*/ for *daddy*, /*kit'l*/ for *kettle*, and so on.

är   This is normally pronounced as a long /*e*/ or /*ā*/ sound in words like *bear*, *fair*, etc.

English in the Indian Subcontinent

The use of English in the Indian Subcontinent dates from the first British contacts with the region in the seventeenth century; between then and independence in 1947 English developed into the language of government and education. Today, Hindi is the official language of India, and English has 'associate' status, although it has no such status beside Urdu in Pakistan and Bengali in Bangladesh.

English in India, Pakistan and Bangladesh is normally learned as a second language, and is often greatly influenced by the speaker's first language. Thus no homogeneous Indian English can be described here but only a number of features about which one may make some general remarks.

Two common features of Indian English are the use of retroflex *ṭ*, *ḍ*, etc for British English *t*, *d*, etc, and the substitution of *p, t, d* for *f, th, dh*. Speakers whose native language is Hindi or Urdu tend to insert an *i* before the initial consonant clusters in words such as *speech* and *school*, because these consonant groups do not occur in initial position in Hindi or Urdu.

Indian English pronounces word-final and pre-consonantal *r*.

Vowels in unstressed syllables are often pronounced in the way they would be in stressed syllables, where British English has /ə/ or / i /.

British contact with the peoples and languages of the Indian Subcontinent has resulted in a number of English loan words, including the familiar *bungalow* (from Hindi), *guru* (from Hindi), *jodhpurs* (from a place-name) and *pyjamas* (from Hindustani). Some English words and expressions are used in special ways: *demit* means 'to resign' (as in Scottish English) and *prepone*, meaning 'to bring forward to an earlier date', has a wider currency than it does in British English.

English in South-East Asia

The use of English in South-East Asia dates from the end of the eighteenth century and beginning of the nineteenth, when the British East India Company established settlements at Penang and Singapore in the country then called Malaya; these two places, together with Malacca, had been formed into the Straits Settlements by 1867. In 1898, Britain bought from China a 99-year lease on the New Territories of Hong Kong, and other territories in the region became British protectorates.

Malaysia became independent in 1957, and the Federation of Malaysia was formed in 1963. Singapore achieved self-governance in 1959 and (after a brief period of incorporation in the Federation) full independence in 1965. The principal languages of the area (in addition to English) are Chinese, Tamil and Malay, reflecting the ethnic mix of the populations. Hong Kong was returned to China on expiry of the lease in 1997.

The situation today is that British English is the dominant influence in Singapore, Malaysia and Hong Kong, while American English is more influential in the Philippines and other areas of the South Pacific, as a legacy of the American acquisition of these territories after the Spanish-American War of 1898. In Singapore, English continued as the language of government , but education was based on a bilingual system of English and one of the three ethnic languages. In Malaysia, Malay (or, more accurately, Bahasa Malaysia) has been the official language since 1957, although more recently English has been actively promoted as a second language.

In the light of these historical facts, it is more realistic to speak of Singaporean English than of Malaysian English, although this is likely to change with time. Some linguists, however, prefer to regard the forms of English used in Singapore and in Malaysia as sub-varieties of a larger distinct variety, which they call Singaporean and Malaysian English (SME). In Singapore, since three-quarters of the population are ethnically Chinese, Mandarin and other Chinese languages are likely to exert a strong influence on the development of Singaporean English.

The vocabulary of English in SE Asia includes a few items that are also familiar in British English, such as *lychee* and *yin* and *yang*. Then there are words of English origin that are used mainly by Singaporean and Malaysian speakers as a part of their culture or lifestyle, such as *airflown* (denoting freshly imported food) and *red packet* (a red envelope containing money, given on ceremonial occasions), and more informal uses (sometimes disparagingly called Singlish) such as *to cut* ('to overtake') and *to zap* ('to photocopy'). Other words, such as *sarabat* (a strong-tasting drink made of ginger and sugar) and *silat* (the Malay equivalent of *kung fu*) are not English in origin, and represent concepts for which no other word exists. Finally and (in the context of SE Asian usage) more controversially, there are slang words of non-English origin, such as *chim* ('profound'), *malu* ('shameful') and others that are less easy to translate, such as *kiasu* (roughly, 'afraid to lose out ').

Differences in pronunciation of English in SE Asia are largely affected by the influence of the other principal languages of the area, Chinese, Tamil and Malay. The principal features are (1) some consonants (notably /p/, /t/ and /k/) are not aspirated, (2) the last consonant of two at the end of a word (eg *lamp, first*) will often be silent, (3) there are considerable differences in vowel quality in words such as *bid, cot , stuff* and *pull* (in which the vowel tends to be longer) and in the articulation of diphthongs, as in *bait, boat* and *bare* (which tend to be shorter and closer to the first sound of the diphthong).

Using the dictionary

Order of entries

All entries are listed alphabetically, each entry having as a basic pattern the following elements :

(1) Headword
(2) Pronunciation
(3) Part of speech label
(4) Definition(s)
(5) Etymology

Entries may also contain subheads – words that are derived from the headword by the addition of a suffix (derivatives) or another word (compounds) or idiomatic phrases that include the headword or one of its derivatives. This grouping of related words within an entry preserves and explains their etymological 'family' link.

Where, however, such grouping is felt to be less helpful to the user we have separated the words into independent entries, as at **intention** and **shutter**, showing their relationships to **intend** and **shut** by means of the etymologies.

Structure

1.   Headword

The word (in bold type) projecting at the head of an entry is referred to as the headword. Headwords are listed in alphabetical order.

Superscript numbers are added to headwords where necessary to indicate homographs (words of identical spelling but of different origin).

cape [1]

cape [2]

Included in the headword list, in alphabetical order, are cross references, words of which the full entry, or on which further information, is to be found elsewhere in the dictionary. Also included in the alphabetical headword sequence are **abbreviation** and **symbol** entries, which follow full-word entries of identical spelling.

Where an abbreviation includes a number, eg **MP3**, this is ordered as if the numeral represents a word, eg

MPS
MP3
MPV

2.   Pronunciation

A respelling system has been used in this dictionary. It is a method that is intelligible to people who are not familiar with phonetic symbols, and one that allows for more than one interpretation – so that each user of the dictionary may choose a pronunciation in keeping with his or her speech.

A quick guide to some common vowel sounds is given on the line at the foot of right- hand pages of the dictionary. A detailed guide to the system is provided on pages xx and xxi.

Guidance on stress patterns in words of more than one syllable is given by the use of the stress mark ('), which follows the syllable that has the main accent, both in respelling and in subheads for which no full or partial respelling is required.

Pronunciation guidance (inside oblique lines) follows the headword, and is given elsewhere in an entry where helpful. Where a word may be pronounced in more than one way, alternative pronunciations are linked by the word 'or ', or by a comma in a string of alternatives. The main, current British pronunciations of a word are given, and also significant and commonly encountered US, Australian, etc variants as applicable.

afebrile /ā-fē'bril, -feb'r|ī or -ril/

Alternative pronunciations may be expressed as partial pronunciations, simply giving the syllable or syllables that may be pronounced differently, rather than respelling the word in full. That part of a word not included in the respelling is to be assumed unchanged from the main pronunciation.

3.   Part of speech label

Following the pronunciation at the head of an entry is a label to indicate the headword's part of speech (eg *adj* for adjective, *n* for noun). A further part of speech label, indicated by ✦ , may follow a set of definitions, to show that the preceding bold word is also used with another grammatical function. Eg

gash[1] *vt* to cut deeply into. ✦ *n* a deep, open cut.

Part of speech labels are given after all headwords, derivatives and compounds, except some foreign phrases. Phrases in entries are not labelled.

4.   Definition(s)

Definitions in the dictionary entries are ordered and grouped with a view to clarity, ease of comprehension and use. Normally the most common meanings are given first, unless an earlier, perhaps more specific, sense serves to clarify or explain its subsequent use.

In abbreviation and symbol entries, definitions are listed alphabetically.

Definitions are separated by semicolons.

5.   Etymology

The etymology is given in square brackets at the end of the definition and before any subheads.

[From OE *brand* (see **brand**) and *isen* iron]

If no etymology is shown, this indicates that the origin and history of the headword is unknown or uncertain or that the word has been arbitrarily coined. A bold word given as an etymology directs the reader to that word entry as the derivation; other etymologies may direct the reader directly to another etymology. A bold prefix given as an etymology indicates that the headword is formed from that prefix plus the remaining word-item; both elements may be found at their separate dictionary entries.

For abbreviations used in etymologies and elsewhere in the dictionary, see pages xxii – xxiv.

6. Subheads

Subheads are bold-print items not listed as separate entries, but listed and explained within an entry. Subheads may fall into one of three categories :

(a) Direct derivatives

These are words which are formed by adding a suffix or ending either to the headword or to the root word. They are listed in alphabetical order and introduced by ■. Their pronunciation basically follows that of the headword, with vowels marked for length and stress marks placed *after* the syllable with the main accent. Where necessary, fuller respelling guidance is given. If the meaning of a direct derivative is readily deducible, it may be undefined.

■ **chicā'ner** *n* a person who chicanes; a quibbler.

(b) Compounds

Compound words (ie those made up of two or more words, the first being the entry headword or one of its derivatives) follow any direct derivatives and are introduced by ◻. They may be hyphenated, one-word or multi-word compounds. If the compound's meaning is evident from its two parts, it may be undefined.

◻ **door'bell** *n.* **door'case** *n* the frame that encloses a door.

(c) Phrases

Following any direct derivatives and any compound words, all phrasal items relating to the headword are listed alphabetically and introduced by ■. These may be phrases, phrasal verbs or idioms.

7. Alternative forms

Words spelt or formed in more than one way, but sharing the same meaning(s) and use, are shown in the dictionary linked by the word 'or'. Where a number of such alternatives are shown, strict alphabetical order may be waived in order to list the most commonly used form first.

pizzazz, pizazz, pazazz, or **pazazz**

At headwords, alternative forms that have different pronunciations are each followed immediately by their appropriate pronunciation(s). If the pronunciation follows both headword forms, it applies to both.

In hyphenated compound words, alternative forms may be shown only by the alternative element of the compound (eg **hunt'ing-box** , **-lodge** or **-seat**).

8. Hyphenation

To save possible confusion, hyphens are never used to split a headword or subhead over two lines. Thus any hyphens that do occur at the end of a line may be taken to be integral to the spelling of the words.

9. Inflections

Inflected forms of words are shown in parentheses after the part of speech label. Where no explanation of the inflected forms of a verb is given, the first word is the present participle and the second is a past tense and past participle of the verb. Plural forms and verb participles, etc are shown only if they are irregular in formation, or warrant special clarification. Comparative and superlative forms of adjectives are given (again by the same criteria).

wag 1 */wag/ vi* (**waggfiing**; **wagged**)

10. Classification labels

A label in italic relating to the classification (eg *offensive, dialect, psychol*) of a word or meaning precedes the list of meanings where it applies to all of the meanings given.

Where a label applies to only one definition in a list , it immediately follows that definition:

a person or thing that bounces; a cheque that bounces (*inf*);

A label which precedes the part of speech label at the head of an entry applies to all meanings of the word and to its derivatives and their meanings unless it is cancelled by a further classification label. This applies also where there is only one sense and one meaning of a word.

A bracketed language classification label (eg *Fr, Ger*) preceding the part of speech label at the head of an entry signifies that the word is still regarded as a foreign word, rather than as a naturalized English word. German nouns have been spelt with a capital letter, as they are in their country of origin.

Sittlichkeit */zitfilihh-k|t/* (*Ger*) *n* morals, morality

11. Grammatical information

Definitions may be preceded by grammatical notes in brackets. These give information about the spelling form and usage of a word. They may indicate that , for example, an adjective is restricted to a particular position or a verb is used reflexively.

(*esp in passive*) to publish the work of (an author);

12. Prefix , suffix and combining forms

These entries are treated as ordinary word entries except in the respects specified below.

In the respelling given at a prefix or similar headword, no stress pattern is specified, as it varies according to the words formed with that element.

Different senses covered by prefixes, suffixes and combining forms are separated by semicolons. Where these senses are used for reference in other parts of the dictionary, they have been numbered.

All words listed as subheads in entries for prefix , suffix and combining forms are treated as derivatives of the headword.

13. Panels

Words formed using the prefixes **anti-**, **non-**, **out-**, **over-**, **post-**, **pre -**, **re -**, **sub-**, **super-**, **un -**, **under-** and **up-** which do not require any explanation in the dictionary are listed in panels at the foot of relevant pages.

The parts of speech and stress patterns of these words are shown; their meanings can be easily derived by referring to the numbered senses at the relevant prefix entry, and if necessary to the word to which the prefix has been attached.

Spelling rules

The most important spelling rules are explained in this article; an understanding of these is assumed for all entries in the dictionary where no inflected form (plural, past tense, etc) is given. Inflected forms are given for words that have inflections with un-predictable spellings (eg *tangos* and *mangoes*), inflections with spellings that do not follow the general rules (*paid* and *laid* as opposed to *played*), or inflections that are regular but about which there is often uncertainty (eg *monkeys*, not '*monkies*').

In general, derivatives (eg nouns and adverbs based on adjectives, such as *brightness* and *brightly* from *bright*, or adjectives formed from nouns, such as *noisy* from *noise*) are spelt out in full in the dictionary, but since the rules for the formation of such derivatives are much the same as for inflections, they are covered here also.

The rules given here are those that apply in British English. See also page xii for the rules of American spelling, where these differ from the British norm.

The basic rules of inflection and derivation:

(i)   Plural nouns are normally formed by adding -s to the singular form:

cat   cats

dog   dogs

horse   horses

(NB There should be no apostrophe before the *s* in a plural noun; forms like *bag's of potato's* are commonly seen but are quite wrong. *Do's* is an exception, though *dos* is also correct .)

Verbs are generally inflected by adding -s, -ing and -ed to the base form:

follow follows following followed

If a word ends in *s, z, x, sh* or *ch*, -es is added rather than -s :

kiss   kisses

box   boxes

push   pushes

However, if the *ch* is pronounced / k / or / hh /, -s alone is added:

stomachs   lochs   psychs

(ii)   Comparative and superlative **adjectives** (and some adverbs) are formed by the addition of -er and -est to the base form:

black blacker blackest

(iii)   Derivatives of nouns, verbs and adjectives are generally formed by the simple addition of a suffix to the stem:

sing   singer

move   movement

red   redness

cruel   cruelty

Adjectives which end in *ic* form adverbs in -*ally*:

economic   economically

(The only common exception is *publicly*)

Inflection of words ending in *o*:

(i)   Most nouns ending in *o* add -s to form the plural :

zoo   zoos

radio   radios

albino   albinos

A small group of words add -es, eg *cargoes, echoes, goes, heroes, potatoes*. A number of words, such as *banjo, fiasco* and *halo*, may add either -s or -es. These are indicated in the dictionary.

(ii)   For the 3rd person singular of the present tense of the **verb**, the rule for adding - s or - es can be stated in terms of the noun rules :

if the noun takes only -s, or if there is no related noun, add -s :

two radios → *she radios*

if the noun takes -es in the plural, or may take either -s or -es, add -es to the verb :

two echoes → *it echoes*

(The main exception to this is *do*, plural *do's* or *dos*, 3rd person singular *does*.)

Words ending in *y*:

(i)   A noun ending in *y* preceded by a consonant generally has a plural in - *ies* :

fly   flies

country   countries

Proper nouns are an exception (eg the four *Marys*), as are words in which the final *y* belongs to the adverbial part of a compound (eg *lay-bys, stand-bys*).

If the final *y* is preceded by a vowel, it does not change to *ie* in the plural :

day   days

donkey   donkeys

(but see *money* for the exceptional plural *monies*).

(ii)   The rules for verb inflections are much the same as for nouns. If the *y* follows a consonant , it changes to *ie* before -*s*, but if it follows a vowel, it does not :

cry   cries

deny   denies

but

stay   stays

enjoy   enjoys

buy   buys

Similarly, in the past tense:

cry   cried

deny   denied

but

stay   stayed

enjoy   enjoyed

(*Said, paid* and *laid* are exceptions.)

(iii) **Adjectives** ending in y preceded by a consonant generally change the y to i in the comparative and superlative :

happy   happier   happiest

The only exceptions are a few one -syllable words in which the final y is pronounced /ī/: see the dictionary entries for *dry*, *shy*, *sly*, etc. If the final y is preceded by a vowel, it generally does not change in the comparative and superlative :

grey   greyer   greyest
coy   coyer   coyest

However, a number of adjectives ending in ey (mostly ones based on nouns, eg *clayey* from *clay*) change the ey to i:

clayey   clayier   clayiest

(iv) **Derivatives** follow similar rules as those for inflections, ie a y following a consonant changes to an i before a following suffix (except -ing), whereas one following a vowel does not :

happy   happily   happiness
merry   merriment
deny   denier
envy   enviable
comply   compliant
but
coy   coyly   coyness
employ   employment
play   player
enjoy   enjoyable
buoy   buoyant

Words which are exceptions to the inflectional rules tend to be exceptions also to the derivational rules, but the irregularities are not always predictable. See the dictionary entries for *dry*, *shy*, *sly*, etc. (Note also the spelling of *busyness*, to distinguish it from *business*.)

Words ending in e:

Before a suffix beginning with a vowel, the final e is generally dropped:

smile   smiling   smiled   smiler
white   whiter   whitest   whiten
pale   palish
ice   icy
use   usable
escape   escapism

Before a consonant, the e is retained:

move   movement
use   useful   useless

There are, however, exceptions:

(i) Verbs ending in ee, oe and ye do not drop the e before -ing :

hoe   hoeing
dye   dyeing

(ii) Verbs ending in ie change the ie to y before -ing :

die   dying
tie   tying

(iii) A few verbs retain the final e in order to show the correct pronunciation and to be distinguishable from similar words with no e :

sing   singing
but
singe   singeing
swing   swinging
but
swingeing

(Note also the adjective *holey* = full of holes, as opposed to *holy*.)

(iv) Before an a or o, the e is retained after a soft c or g:

notice   noticing   but   noticeable
advantage   advantageous

(v) Adverbs formed from adjectives ending in le preceded by a consonant simply replace the final e with y:

simple   simply
single   singly

(vi) Words ending in dge may correctly retain or drop the final e in derivatives; thus *judgment* and *judgement*, *abridgment* and *abridgement* are equally correct.

(vii) Common exceptions to all the above rules are *argument*, *awful*, *daily*, *duly*, *eerily*, *gaily*, *truly* and *wholly*.

Doubling of a final consonant:

If a word ends in a single consonant which is preceded by a single vowel written with a single letter and the stress of the word is on the final syllable of the word (or if there is only one syllable), the final consonant is doubled before a suffix beginning with a vowel:

drum   drumming   drummed   drummer
omit   omitting   omitted
refer   referring   referred   referral
red   redder   reddest   redden
ton   tonnage
but
dream   dreaming   dreamed   dreamer
profit   profiting   profited
enter   entering   entered
refer   reference (note the change in stress)
green   greener   greenest

A few words double the final consonant contrary to the above rule:

worship worshipping worshipped worshipper (and also *format*, *handicap*, *hobnob*, *humbug*, *kidnap*, *leapfrog* and *zigzag*)

A final l preceded by a single - letter vowel generally doubles regardless of the position of the stress, as in:

signal   signalling   signalled   signaller
rebel   rebelling   rebellion   rebellious
cancel   cancelling   cancellation

but not before the suffixes -ize /-ise, -ism, -ist and -ity, as in:

equal   equality   equalize
final   finalist

though again there are exceptions, such as *medallist*, *tranquillity* and *crystallize*.

Note also *paralleling* and *paralleled* (where one would expect a double ll before the suffix) and *woolly* and *woollen* (where one would expect a single l).

A few words allow both single and double consonants: see the dictionary entries for eg *benefit*, *bias*, *bus*, *focus*, *gas*, *leaflet* , *plus* and *yes*.

Words ending in c :

When a suffix beginning with a vowel is added, and the consonant still has the hard / k / sound, the c becomes ck:

picnic picnicking   picnicked   picnicker

Two exceptions are arc and talc :
arcing /arcking, arced/arcked
talcing/talcking, talced/talcked

The forms without *k* are the commoner. No *k* is added when the final *c* becomes a soft sound (/sh/ or /s/) in the derivative:

> *magic magicking magicked* but *magician*
>
> *electric electricity*

-ie - or - ei-?

The rule '*i* before *e* except after *c*' applies only to words in which the vowel has the long /ē/ sound :

> *believe belief*
>
> *siege*

> *pier*
>
> but
>
> *deceive deceit*
>
> *ceiling*

(Common exceptions are *seize*, *weir* and *weird*, scientific words such as *protein*, *caffeine* and *codeine*, and proper names such as *Keith*, *Neil*, *Sheila*, *Reid* and *Madeira*.)

If a word is pronounced with the sound /a/, *ei* is always the correct spelling :

> *eight heir neighbour reign weight*

Characters used in other languages

Some foreign words included in the etymologies in this dictionary include characters that are not used in English. A brief guide to the pronunciation of the non-English characters which appear most frequently is given below. The pronunciations given are necessarily approximate as it is not always possible to convey the exact phonetic values intended by means of respelling symbols or verbal explanations.

Vowels

Symbol	Sound
ā, ē, ī, ū	In Latin, Old English, etc, these are long vowels with the sounds (or approximately the sounds) represented by the respelling symbols *a* or *ä*, *ā* or *e*, *ē*, and *oo* respectively; in the pinyin transcription of Chinese, these are vowels with a first (level) tone.
ō	This represents a long *o* or *ö* sound or a monophthongal pronunciation of the respelling character *ō*; in the pinyin transcription of Chinese, this is a vowel with a first (level) tone.
ȳ	A long *ü* sound.
ǣ	A long vowel similar in sound to the RP pronunciation of respelling symbol *a*.
a, e, etc, ă, ě, etc	Short vowels corresponding to *ā*, *ē*, etc, with values, varying from language to language, similar to those of the corresponding long vowels or those of the short vowels of English.
ă, ě, etc	In the pinyin transcription of Chinese, these are vowels with a third (falling, then rising) tone; in Romanian, *ă* has the sound *ə*.
â, ê, î, ô, û	In some languages, eg Middle High German, these symbols are used for long vowels with the values *ä*, *ā*, *ē*, *ō*, *oo* respectively; in Romanian, *â* and *î* represent a sound midway between *ē* and *oo*.
á, é, etc	In the pinyin transcription of Chinese, these are vowels with a second (rising) tone.
à, è, etc	In the pinyin transcription of Chinese, these are vowels with a fourth (falling) tone.
ä, ö	These have the values of respelling symbols *e*/*ā* and *ø*/*œ* respectively.
ĩ, etc	The diacritic [˜] is used, as in the respelling, to show nasalization of vowels.

Consonants

Symbol	Sound
ḍ, ṇ, ṣ, ṭ	These are retroflex counterparts of *d*, *n*, etc.
ṛ	In Sanskrit, a vowel rather than a consonant; in Hindi, etc, a consonant formed by the tongue moving from a retroflex position to strike against the alveolar ridge.
ḥ	The normal *h* sound of English.
ṁ	This marks nasalization of the preceding vowel or the following consonant in Sanskrit.
ñ	A sound similar to *ny*, as in Spanish *cañon*.
ṅ	The sound written *ng* in the respelling and in English orthography.
c	In Sanskrit, etc, a sound midway between *k* and *ch*; in Turkish, the sound of *j* as in *judge*.
ç	In French, Arabic and Portuguese, this represents the sound *s*; in Turkish, *ch*.
č, ć	In Serbo-Croat , *č* represents the sound *ch*, and *ć* represents *ty*.
ş	In Turkish, the sound *sh*.
ś	In Sanskrit, etc, a sound similar to *sh*.
q	In Arabic, a sound similar to *k* but pronounced slightly farther back in the mouth; in Chinese, a sound like *ch* ; in Gothic, *kw*.
ğ	This marks a lengthening of the preceding vowel in Turkish.
gg	In Gothic, the sound *ng*.
'	In Russian words, this represents a 'soft sign', marking a y-like palatalization of the preceding consonant ; in Chinese words, it is a mark of strong aspiration; in Arabic, Hebrew and Hawaiian, a glottal stop.
'	In Arabic and Hebrew, a sound like *hh* but produced rather deeper in the throat .

Detailed chart of pronunciation

Vowels and diphthongs in accented syllables

Symbol		Examples	Pronunciation
ā	as in	name, aid, rein, tare, wear, hair, heir, fairy	*nām, ād, rān, tār, wār, hār, ār, fār′i*
ä	"	grass, path, palm, harm, heart	*gräs, päth, päm, härm, härt*
a	"	sat , bad, have, marry	*sat, bad, hav, mar′i*
ē	"	lean, keel, dene, chief, seize, gear, sheer, here, bier, query	*lēn, kēl, dēn, chēf, sēz, gēr, shēr, hēr, bēr, kwē′ri*
e	"	red, thread, said, bury	*red, thred, sed, ber′i*
ī	"	side, shy, dye, height , hire, byre, fiery	*sīd, shī, dī, hīt, hīr, bīr, fīr′i*
i	"	pin, busy, hymn	*pin, biz′i, him*
ō	"	bone, road, foe, low, dough, more, soar, floor, port , Tory	*bōn, rōd, fō, lō, dō mōr, sōr, flōr, pōrt, tōr′i*
		(For alternative pronunciation of port , more, etc, see ö)	
ö	"	haul, lawn, fall, bought , swarm, more, soar, floor, port , Tory	*höl, lön, föl, böt, swörm, mör, sör, flör, pört, tör′i*
		(For alternative pronunciation of port , more, etc, see ō)	
o	"	got , shot , shone	*got, shot, shon*
oo	"	fool, sou, boor, tour	*fool, soo, boor, toor*
ŭ	"	good, full, would	*gŭd, fŭl, wŭd*
ū	"	tune, due, newt , view, endure, fury	*tūn, dū, nūt, vū, in-dūr′, fū′ri*
u	"	bud, run, love	*bud, run, luv*
û	"	heard, bird, word, absurd	*hûrd, bûrd, wûrd, ab-sûrd′*
ow	"	mount , frown, sour	*mownt, frown, sowr*
oi	"	toy, buoy, soil	*toi, boi, soil*

Stress

In words of more than one syllable, the syllable with the main accent is shown by a stress mark ′ following that syllable, both in the respellings (eg *äf′ter, bi-gin′*) and in entries in bold type (eg **af′ters, beginn′er**).

Note the difference in pronunciation, as shown by the position of the stress mark, between **blessed′** (*blest*) and **bless′ed** (*bles′id*), **refined′** (*re-fīnd′*) and **refin′edly** (*ri-fīn′id-li*).

Vowels in unaccented syllables

Neutral vowels in unaccented syllables are usually shown by ə (schwa)

eg *el′ə-mənt, in′fənt, ran′dəm, pre′shəs* (precious), *nā′chər* (nature).

In certain cases, they are more exactly represented by *i*

eg *ē′vil, bi-hōld′, bles′id, man′ij, di-ment′*.

Vowels followed by r

In certain accents, for example in Scots, Irish, General American, **r** is pronounced wherever it occurs in the spelling and this is the form adopted in the dictionary.

In certain other accents, for example Received Pronunciation or what is sometimes called the BBC accent, it is pronounced only when it occurs before a vowel. Elsewhere the following rules apply:

ār	is pronounced as		eə		ör	is pronounced as		ö or öə
är	"	"	"	ä		oor	"	"	"	ŭə
ēr	"	"	"	iə		ūr	"	"	"	ūə
er	"	"	"	eə		ûr	"	"	"	û
īr	"	"	"	īə		owr	"	"	"	owə

Consonants

Symbol		Examples	Pronunciation
b	as in	hob, rabbit	*hob, rab'it*
ch	"	church, much, match	*chûrch, much, mach*
d	"	ado, dew	*ə-doo', dū*
dh	"	then, father	*dhen, fä'dhər*
f	"	faint, phase, rough	*fānt, fāz, ruf*
g	"	gold, guard, ghastly	*gōld, gärd, gäst'li*
gz	"	exact	*igz-akt'*
h	"	happy, home	*hap'i, hōm*
hh	"	loch, Taoiseach	*lohh, tē'shohh*
hl	"	(Welsh) pennill	*pen'ihl*
(h)w	"	whale, which	*(h)wāl, (h)wich*
j	"	jack, gentle, ledge, region	*jak, jen'tl, lej, rē'jən*
k	"	keep, cat, chorus	*kēp, kat, kōr'əs (kör')*
ks	"	lax, vex	*laks, veks*
kw	"	quite, coiffeur	*kwīt, kwä-fœr*
l	"	lamp, collar	*lamp, kol'ər*
m	"	meat, palm, stammer	*mēt, päm, stam'ər*
n	"	net, gnome, knee, dinner	*net, nōm, nē, din'ər*
ng	"	fling, longing	*fling, long'ing*
ngg	"	single, longer, languor	*sing'gl, long'gər, lang'gər*
ngk	"	monkey, precinct	*mungk'i, prē'singkt*
p	"	peat, apple	*pēt, ap'l*
r	"	rest, wreck, arrive	*rest, rek, ə-rīv'*
s	"	sad, city, circuit, scene, mass, psalm	*sad, sit'i, sûr'kit, sēn, mas, säm*
sh	"	shine, machine, sure, militia, acacia	*shīn, mə-shēn', shoor, mi-lish'ə, ā-ka'sh(y)ə*
t	"	tape, nettle, thyme	*tāp, net'l, tīm*
th	"	thin, three	*thin, thrē*
v	"	valid, river	*val'id, riv'ər*
w	"	was, one, twig	*woz, wun, twig*
y	"	young, bastion	*yung, bast'yə n*
z	"	zoo, was, roads	*zoo, woz, rōdz*
zh	"	azure, measure, conge, lesion	*azh'ər (or ā'zhūr), mezh'ə r, kɔ̃-zhā, lē'zhə n*

Additional sounds in foreign and dialect words

Symbol		Examples	Pronunciation
ø	as in	*Fr* deux , feu, peu	*dø, fø, pø*
œ	"	*Fr* fleur, leur, cœur	*flœr, lœr, kœr*
ü	"	(1) *Fr* sur, luminaire	*sür, lü-mē-ner*
		(2) *Ger* über, Führer	*ü'bər, fü'rər*
		(3) *Scots* bluid, buik	*blüd, bük*

Nasalized vowels

ã	as in	*Fr* sang , temps, dent	*sã, tã, dã*
ɛ̃	"	*Fr* faim, vin, plein	*fɛ̃ , vɛ̃ , plɛ̃*
ɔ̃	"	*Fr* tomber, long , sonde	*t ɔ̃-ba, lɔ̃, sɔ̃d*
	"	*Fr* lundi, humble, un	*lœ̃-de, œ̃bl', œ̃*
ɑ̃	"	*Port* são	*sɑ̃oo*

An apostrophe is used in words such as timbre (*tɛ̃br'*), maître (*metr'*) and humble (*œbl'*) in the pronunciation of which a final *ə* (eg *tɛ̃brə*) is possible.

Vowels in bold entries

The long vowels ā, ē, ī, ō, ū, have the values ā , ē, ī, ō, ū; ȳ is to be pronounced ī.

Abbreviations used in the dictionary

The following abbreviations are used in the dictionary. They are shown here in italic type, but are also found in the dictionary in roman type.

Many of the abbreviations are used as labels, but other, unabbreviated, labels are also found in the dictionary, all of which should be self-explanatory. It should be noted that the label Bible, unless it is qualified, refers to the Authorized Version.

abbrev	abbreviation		*Du*	Dutch
account	accounting			
AD	Anno Domini		*E*	east, eastern
adj	adjective		*E Afr*	East Africa(n)
adv	adverb		*E Anglia*	East Anglia(n)
Afr	Africa(n)		*econ*	economics
Afrik	Afrikaans		*educ*	education
agric	agriculture		*eg*	(L *exempli gratia*) for example
Am	America(n)		*Eg yp*	Egyptian
am	(L *ante meridiem*) before noon		*elec*	electricity, electrical
Am Sp	American Spanish		*embryol*	embryology
anat	anatomy		*Eng*	England, English
Anglo-Chin	Anglo-Chinese		*eng*	engineering
Anglo-Fr	Anglo-French		*esp*	especially
Anglo-Ind	Anglo-Indian		*etc*	(L *et cetera*) and so on, and the rest
Anglo-L	Anglo-Latin		*ety*	etymology
anthrop	anthropology		*EU*	European Union
appar	apparently		*euphem*	euphemistic
approx	approximately			
Ar	Arabic		*fem*	feminine
archaeol	archaeology		*ff*	following pages
archit	architecture		*fig*	figurative(ly)
astrol	astrology		*Finn*	Finnish
astron	astronomy		*fl*	(L *floruit*) flourished
atomic no	atomic number		*Flem*	Flemish
attrib	attributive(ly)		*fortif*	fortification
Aust	Australia(n)		*Fr*	France, French
Aust rules	Australian rules football		*Fris*	Frisian
			ft	foot, feet
bacteriol	bacteriology			
BC	before Christ		*g*	gram(s)
biochem	biochemistry		*gen*	generally
biol	biology		*geog*	geography
bot	botany		*geol*	geology
Brit	Britain, British		*geom*	geometry
			Ger	Germany, German
c	century		*Gmc*	Germanic
c.	(L *circa*) about		*Gr*	Greek
Can	Canada, Canadian		*gym*	gymnastics
cap(s)	capital(s)			
cf	(L *confer*) compare		*ha*	hectare(s)
chem	chemistry, chemical		*Heb*	Hebrew
Chin	Chinese		*HGer*	High German
cinematog	cinematography		*hist*	history, historical
cm	centimetre(s)		*hortic*	horticulture
C of E	Church of England		*Hung*	Hungarian
compar	comparative			
comput	computing		*Icel*	Icelandic
conj	conjunction		*ie*	(L *id est*) that is
cry stallog	crystallography		*imit*	imitative
cu	cubic		*immunol*	immunology
cwt	hundredweight(s)		*impers*	impersonal
			in	inch(es)
			incl	including
Dan	Danish		*Ind*	India(n)
derog	derogatory		*indic*	indicative
dimin	diminutive		*inf*	informal
dm	decimetre(s)			

infl	influenced	*OIr*	Old Irish
intens	intensive, intensifier	*OLGer*	Old Low German
interj	interjection	*ON*	Old Norse
interrog	interrogative	*ONFr*	Old Northern French
Ir	Ireland, Irish	*OPers*	Old Persian
irreg	irregular(ly)	*ophthalmol*	ophthalmology
Ital	Italy, Italian	*opp*	opposite, opposed
IVR	International Vehicle Registration	*orig*	originally
		ornithol	ornithology
Jap	Japanese	*OSax*	Old Saxon
joc	jocular(ly)	*OSlav*	Old Slavonic
		OWelsh	Old Welsh
kg	kilogram(s)	*oz*	ounce(s)
km	kilometre(s)		
		Pak	Pakistan(i)
L	Latin	*palaeog*	palaeography
lb	pound(s) (weight)	*palaeontol*	palaeontology
LGer	Low German	*pap*	past participle
Lincs	Lincolnshire	*pat*	past tense
lit	literal(ly)	*pathol*	pathology
LL	Low (or Late) Latin	*perf*	perfect
		perh	perhaps
m	metre(s)	*Pers*	Persian
masc	masculine	*pers*	personal, person
maths	mathematics	*pfx*	prefix
MDu	Middle Dutch	*pharm*	pharmacy
ME	Middle English	*pharmacol*	pharmacology
mech	mechanics	*philos*	philosophy
Med	medieval	*photog*	photography
med	medicine, medical	*phys*	physics
meteorol	meteorology	*physiol*	physiology
Mex	Mexican	*pl*	plural
Mex Sp	Mexican Spanish	*pm*	(L *post meridiem*) after noon
MFlem	Middle Flemish	*Pol*	Polish
MFr	Middle French	*Port*	Portuguese
MHGer	Middle High German	*poss*	possible, possibly
milit	military	*prep*	preposition
MLGer	Middle Low German	*pres*	present
mm	millimetre(s)	*prob*	probably
Mod	modern	*prp*	present participle
Mod Du	Modern Dutch	*prt*	present tense
Mod Fr	Modern French	*pseudo-Fr*	pseudo-French
Mod Gr	Modern Greek	*pseudo-Ital*	pseudo-Italian
Mod L	Modern Latin (= New Latin)	*pseudo-L*	pseudo-Latin
mph	miles per hour	*psychol*	psychology
myth	mythology		
		qv, qqv	(L *quod vide*) which see
N	north, northern		
n	noun	®	registered trademark
N Am	North America(n)	*radiog*	radiography
naut	nautical	*radiol*	radiology
NE	north- east, north- eastern	*RAF*	Royal Air Force
neg	negative	*RC*	Roman Catholicism, Roman Catholic
New L	New Latin	*relig*	religion
N Ireland	Northern Ireland	*Russ*	Russian
N Irish	Northern Irish		
Norw	Norwegian	*S*	south, southern
n pl	plural noun	*S Afr*	South Africa(n)
n sing	singular noun	*Sans*	Sanskrit
NW	north-west, north-western	*Scand*	Scandinavian
NZ	New Zealand	*sci-fi*	science fiction
		Scot	Scotland, Scottish
obs	obsolete	*sculpt*	sculpture
ODu	Old Dutch	*SE*	south-east , south-eastern
OE	Old English	*Serb*	Serbian
OFr	Old French	*sfx*	suffix
OFris	Old Friesian	*Shakesp*	Shakespeare
OHGer	Old High German	*sing*	singular

sl	slang		*ult*	ultimately
Slav	Slavonic		*US*	United States (of America)
sociol	sociology		*USSR*	Union of Soviet Socialist Republics
Sp	Spanish		*usu*	usually
Sp Am	Spanish American			
specif	specifically		*v*	verb
sq	square		*vet*	veterinary medicine
St	Saint		*vi*	intransitive verb
stats	statistics		*Viet*	Vietnamese
superl	superlative		*vt*	transitive verb
surg	surgery			
SW	south-west, south-western		*W*	west, western
Swed	Swedish		*W Afr*	West Africa(n)
			W Indies	West Indies
technol	technology		*WSax*	West Saxon
telecom	telecommunications			
theol	theology		*yd*	yard(s)
transl	translation, translating, translated		*Yorks*	Yorkshire
Turk	Turkish			
T V	television		*zool*	zoology
UK	United Kingdom			

Aa

a b c d e f g h i j k l m n o p q r s t u v w x y z

Arial Designed by Robin Nicholas and Patricia Saunders in 1982. UK.

A¹ or **a** /ā/ *n* the first letter in the modern English alphabet as in the Roman, etc (see **aleph** and **alpha**), with various sounds, as in name, path, bad; the sixth note of the diatonic scale of C major (*music*); the key or scale having that note for its tonic (*music*); one of the four blood types in the ABO blood group system; the designation of the principal series of paper sizes, ranging from A0 (841 × 1189mm) to A10 (26 × 37mm); in road-classification, followed by a number, the designation of a major or trunk road, as in the *A60*; in hexadecimal notation, 10 (decimal) or 1010 (binary); the highest in a category or range; something or someone of the first class or order, or of a class arbitrarily designated A; anything shaped like the letter A.
□ **A'-line** *adj* (of clothing) narrow at the top and widening evenly to a full hemline. **A'-list** *adj* (*inf*) belonging to the most important or famous group (of celebrities, etc). **A'-lister** *n*. **A1** /ā wun/ *adj* indicating a first-class vessel in Lloyd's Register of Shipping; hence first-rate or excellent. **A'-road** *n* a principal or trunk road. **A'-side** *n* (*music*) the side of a single which holds the principal track being marketed.
■ **from A to B** from one point or place to another. **from A to Z** from beginning to end; right through.

A² /ā or ə/ *pronoun* a dialect form of **I**.

A *abbrev*: absolute (temperature); Academician; Academy; ace (*cards*); acre(s); adult, formerly used to designate a motion picture at a showing of which any child under 14 should be accompanied by an adult, superseded by **PG**; advanced; alto (*music*); amateur; America; American; ammeter; angstrom; answer; area; argon (now **Ar**; *chem*); Associate (of a society, etc); Athletic; atomic; atomic weight; Australia; Australian; Austria (IVR).
□ **A'-bomb** *n* atomic bomb. **A-effect** see under **alien**. **A level** or **Advanced** (or **advanced**) **level** *n* (a pass in) an examination generally taken after seven years of secondary education, *esp* in England and Wales (also *adj*, often with *hyphen*).

A *symbol*: (as a medieval Roman numeral) 50 or 500; ampere (SI unit).

Å *symbol*: Ångström or angstrom.

Ā *symbol*: (medieval Roman numeral) 5000.

a¹ /ə/, also (*esp emphatic*) /ā/ *adj* the indefinite article, a broken down form of **an¹** used before a consonant sound. [OE *ān* one]

a² /ā, ə/ (*dialect*) *pronoun* he; she; it; they. [OE *hē* he, *hēo* she, and *hīe* they]

a *abbrev*: about; absent; acceleration; accepted; acre; acreage; acting; active; adjective; advance; advanced; afternoon; alto; *anno* (*L*), in the year; *annus* (*L*), year; anonymous; answer; *ante* (*L*), before; anterior; are (metric measure); atto-.

a' /ö or ā/ a Scot and N Eng form of **all**.
■ **a''body** *pronoun* everybody. **a''gate** *adv* every way. **a''thing** *pronoun* everything. **a''where** *adv* everywhere.

à /ə/ *prep* from, of, as in *Thomas à Kempis* (Thomas from Kempen). [L *ab*]

ā see **AA**.

@ *symbol*: at (a rate of); (*esp* in email) at (a certain address).

a-¹ /ə-/ *pfx* a reduced form of the OE preposition *an* or *on*, on, in or at, as in *abroad*, *afire*, *afloat*, *asleep*, *a-begging*, *a-hunting*, and occasionally used separately as a preposition, as in *once a year*.

a-² /ə- or a-/ or **an-** /ən- or an-/ *pfx* without, not, opposite to, as in *amoral*, *anaemia* or *anodyne*. [Gr privative *a-* without or not]

AA *abbrev*: Alcoholics Anonymous; anti-aircraft; Architectural Association; Associate of Arts; Australian Army; Automobile Association; formerly used to designate a cinema film at a showing of which children under 14 were not admitted, superseded by **15**.

ĀĀ, **aa** or **ā** *symbol*: (in prescriptions, etc) in equal quantities of each. [LL *ana*, from Gr, again]

aa /ä'ä/ *n* a type of scoriaceous volcanic rock with a rough surface and many jagged fragments. [Hawaiian]

AAA *abbrev*: Amateur Athletic Association; American Automobile Association; anti-aircraft artillery; Australian Automobile Association.

AAAS *abbrev*: American Academy of Arts and Sciences; American Association for the Advancement of Science.

AAC *abbrev*: Amateur Athletic Club; *anno ante Christum* (*L*), in the year before Christ; Army Air Corps.

AAEW *abbrev*: Atlantic Airborne Early Warning.

aah /ä/ *interj* expressing satisfaction, pleasure, etc (also *n* and *vi*). [Imit]

AAM *abbrev*: air-to-air missile.

A&B *abbrev*: Arts & Business, an organization that develops links between the arts and industry.

A&E *abbrev*: accident and emergency (hospital department).

A&M *abbrev*: Agricultural and Mechanical; (Hymns) Ancient and Modern.

A&R *abbrev*: artists and recording; artists and repertoire.

AAP *abbrev*: Australian Associated Press.

AAQMG *abbrev*: Assistant Adjutant and Quartermaster General.

aar *abbrev*: against all risks (*commerce*); average annual rainfall.

aardvark /ärd'värk or (*S Afr*) ärt'färk/ *n* the antbear, a long-nosed African edentate that feeds on termites, etc. [Afrik, from Du *aarde* earth, and *vark* (now *varken*) pig]

aardwolf /ärd'wülf or (*S Afr*) ärt'volf/ *n* (*pl* **aard'wolves**) the earthwolf, a hyena-like African mammal that feeds mainly on termites and carrion. [Afrik, from Du *aarde* earth, and *wolf* wolf]

aargh, also **argh** /a, ä/ *interj* expressing pain, dismay, etc.

Aaronic /ā-ron'ik/ or **Aaronical** /-ik-l/ *adj* relating to Aaron, the Jewish high priest (*Bible*); relating to the priesthood; pontifical.
□ **Aaron's beard** *n* a saxifrage, often grown dangling from pots; the great St John's wort; ivy-leaved toadflax, or a similar plant. **Aaron's rod** *n* mullein, goldenrod, or a similar plant, with tall straight flowering stem.

AAS *abbrev*: *Academiae Americanae Socius* (*L*), Fellow of the American Academy.

A'asia *abbrev*: Australasia.

aasvogel /äs'fō-gəl or (*S Afr*) äs'fool/ *n* a S African vulture. [Du *aas* carrion, and *vogel* bird]

AAT *abbrev*: alpha-1 antitrypsin, a tissue-protecting blood protein.

AB /ā-bē'/ *n* one of the four blood types in the ABO blood group system.

AB *abbrev*: able-bodied (seaman); Advisory Board; Alberta (Canadian province); *Artium Baccalaureus* (*L*), Bachelor of Arts (*US*); Autobahn.

Ab /ab/ or **Av** /av/ *n* the eleventh civil or fifth ecclesiastical month of the Jewish Calendar (parts of July and August). [Syriac]

ab /ab/ (*inf*) *n* (*usu* in *pl*) an abdominal muscle.

ab-¹ /ab-/ *pfx* opposite to, from or away from, as in *abnormal* or *abreaction*. [L *ab* from]

ab-² /ab-/ *pfx* used to indicate an electromagnetic unit in the centimetre-gram-second system (eg **abam'pere** and **ab'volt** equivalent respectively to 10 amperes and 10^{-8} volts). [**absolute**]

a/b *abbrev*: airborne.

ABA *abbrev*: Amateur Boxing Association; American Bar Association.

aba or **abba** /a'bə/ or **abaya** /a-bä'yə/ *n* a Syrian cloth of goat's or camel's hair, *usu* striped; an outer garment made of it; a covering outer garment, *usu* black, worn by women in some Arab countries. [Ar '*abā*, '*abāya*]

abac /ā'bak/ *n* a nomogram (qv under **nomography**). [Fr *abaque*, from L *abacus*]

abaca /ab'ə-kə/ *n* a plantain grown in the Philippine Islands; its fibre, called Manila hemp. [Tagálog]

---

fāte; fär; mē; fûr; mīne; mōte; för; mūte; pŭt; dhen (then); *el'ə-mənt* (element) • For other sounds see detailed chart of pronunciation

abaci see **abacus**.

aback /ə-bak'/ adv backwards; said of sails pressed backward against the mast by the wind (naut). [OE on bæc on back; see **a-**[1]]
■ **taken aback** taken by surprise.

abactinal /ab-ak-tī'nəl/ or /ab-ak'ti-nəl/ (zool) adj remote from the actinal area; without rays. [**ab-**[1]]
■ **abacti'nally** (or /-ak'/) adv.

abactor /ab-ak'tər/ (obs) n a cattle thief. [LL]

abacus /ab'ə-kəs/ n (pl **ab'aci** /-sī/ or **ab'acuses**) a counting frame, consisting of horizontal rods along which movable beads can be slid; a level tablet on the capital of a column, supporting the entablature (archit). [L abacus, from Gr abax, abakos]

Abaddon /ə-bad'ən/ n Apollyon; hell (Milton). [Heb ābaddōn, from ābad to be lost]

abaft /ə-bäft'/ (naut) adv and prep behind. [**a-**[1] and OE bæftan after, from **be-** and æftan (see **aft**)]

abalone /ab-ə-lō'nē/ n an edible shellfish, the sea-ear, esp a richly coloured variety found on the Pacific coast of N America, a source of mother-of-pearl. [Am Sp abulón. Origin uncertain]

abampere /ab-am'pār/ (elec) n a unit equivalent to 10 amperes. [**ab-**[2] and **ampere**]

abandon /ə-ban'dən/ vt to give up; to desert; to leave a place, not intending to return; to give (oneself) without restraint; to give up all claims to; to banish (Shakesp). ◆ n (sometimes as Fr /ä-bä-dɔ̃/) the condition of letting oneself go; careless freedom of action. [OFr abandoner to put at one's disposal or in one's control (à bandon), or to the ban; see **ban**[1]]
■ **aband'** vt (Spenser) to abandon. **aban'doned** adj completely deserted; given up, as to a vice; profligate, dissolute; very wicked. **aban'donedly** adv. **abandonee'** n (law) an insurer to whom a wreck has been abandoned. **aban'donment** n.
❏ **aban'donware** n (comput sl) software that is no longer distributed by its original publisher.
■ **abandon ship** the order to take to the lifeboats when a ship is in danger.

à bas /a bä/ (Fr) interj down, down with!

abase /ə-bās'/ vt to humble; to degrade, belittle; to lower, put down; to cast down. [OFr abaissier to bring low, from L ad to, and LL bassus low]
■ **abased'** adj. **abase'ment** n.

abash /ə-bash'/ vt to strike with shame or embarrassment; to disconcert; to astound (archaic); to confound (archaic). [OFr esbahir, from pfx es- (L ex out), and bahir to astound, from interj bah]
■ **abashed'** adj. **abash'edly** adv. **abash'less** adj (obs) shameless; unabashed. **abash'ment** n.

abask /ə-bäsk'/ adv in genial warmth. [**a-**[1]]

abate[1] /ə-bāt'/ vi to grow less; to subside; to be abated (law). ◆ vt to put an end to (law); to nullify, to bring down (law); to lessen or reduce; to deduct (with of); to mitigate; to blunt; to curtail (Shakesp); to except (Shakesp); to demolish (obs). [OFr abatre to beat down, from L ab from, and LL batere, for L batuere to beat]
■ **abāt'able** adj. **abāt'ed** adj blunted; diminished; lowered; subdued; beaten down or cut away, as the background of sculptures, etc carved in relief. **abate'ment** n the act or process of abating; the sum or quantity abated; the state of being abated; the interruption of an action on the defender's plea that it should not continue at the present time or in the present form (law); the reduction of a legacy (law); a supposed mark of dishonour on a coat of arms (heraldry) appar never actually used.

abate[2] /ə-bāt'/ vi and vt (reflexive) to intrude on a freehold and take possession before the heir. [OFr enbatre to thrust in]
■ **abate'ment** n. **abāt'or** n.

abatis or **abattis** /ab'ə-tis, ə-bat'ē or -is/ (fortif) n (pl **abatis** or **abattis** /-ēz/) a rampart of felled trees with branches outward; a similar arrangement of barbed wire. [Fr; see **abate**[1]]

abat-jour /a-ba-zhoor'/ (Fr) n a skylight; a screen or shutter.

abattis see **abatis**.

abattoir /ab'ə-twär/ n a slaughterhouse. [Fr; see **abate**[1]]

abattu /a-bat-ü'/ (Fr) adj cast down or dejected.

abature /ab'ə-chər/ n in hunting, the trail through underwood beaten down by a stag. [Fr; see **abate**[1]]

abat-voix /a-ba-vwä'/ (Fr) n a sounding-board.

abaxial /ab-ak'si-əl/ (bot) adj away from the axis. [**ab-**[1] and **axis**[1]]

abaya see **aba**.

Abb. abbrev: Abbess; Abbey; Abbot.

abb /ab/ n properly, woof- or weft-yarn, but sometimes warp yarn. [OE āb, āweb, from pfx ā out, and webb web]

abba[1] /ab'ə/ n father (applied to God) (Bible); a Syriac or Coptic bishop. [Aramaic abbā, retained in the Greek New Testament and its translations]

abba[2] see **aba**.

abbacy /ab'ə-si/ n the office or jurisdiction of an abbot or abbess; the time during which someone is abbot or abbess; an abbey. [Appar orig Scot; LL abbātia abbey]
■ **abbatial** /ab-ā'shl/ adj relating to an abbey, abbot or abbess.

Abbasid /a-bas'id or ab'ə-sid/ or **Abbaside** /-sīd/ n any member of the later (750–1258) of the two great dynasties of caliphs, descendants of Abbas, uncle of Mohammed. ◆ adj of or relating to this dynasty.

abbatial see under **abbacy**.

abbé /ab'ā/ n esp in France, a courtesy title for a priest, an ecclesiastic in minor orders, or for a tutor or holder of a benefice, even if a layman. [Fr, orig abbot]

abbess /ab'is/ n a woman who is head of an abbey. [LL abbātissa, fem of abbās abbot]

abbey /ab'i/ n (pl **abb'eys**) a convent under an abbot or abbess, or (loosely) a prior or prioress; the church now or formerly attached to such an abbey; a name often retained by an abbatial building that has become a private house. [OFr abaiè (Fr abbaye), from LL abbātia (see **abba**[1] and **abbacy**)]
❏ **abb'ey-counter** or **abb'ey-piece** n a pilgrim's token, evidence of a visit to an abbey. **abb'ey-laird** n (hist) a debtor in sanctuary in the precincts of Holyrood Abbey. **abb'ey-lubber** n a lazy monk, a term much used by the Reformers.

abbot /ab'ət/ n (also fem **abb'ess**) a person in charge of an abbey. [LL abbās, abbātis, from Aramaic abbā; see **abba**[1]]
■ **abb'otship** n.

abbr. or **abbrev.** abbrev: abbreviated; abbreviation.

abbreviate /ə-brē'vi-āt/ vt to shorten; to contract; to abridge. ◆ adj shortened. [L abbreviāre, -ātum, from ab (intensive), and brevis short]
■ **abbrevia'tion** n an act of shortening; a shortened form; part of a word written or printed instead of the whole. **abbrē'viātor** n. **abbrē'viatory** /-ə-tor-i/ adj. **abbrē'viature** n (obs) an abbreviation; an abridgement.

ABC /ā-bē-sē'/ also (obs) **abcee** or **absey** /ab'si/ n the alphabet, so named from its first letters; a first reading-book; hence, the rudiments or the basics; anything arranged alphabetically, such as an acrostic or a railway guide.
❏ **absey book** n (Shakesp) a primer or hornbook.

ABC abbrev: American Broadcasting Company; Arab Banking Corporation; Associated British Cinemas; Audit Bureau of Circulations; Australian Broadcasting Corporation (formerly, Commission).

abd abbrev: abdicated; abridged.

abdabs see **habdabs**.

Abderian /ab-dē'ri-ən/ adj of Abdera, a town in Thrace, notorious for the stupidity of its inhabitants and birthplace of Democritus, 'the laughing philosopher' (also n).
■ **Abderite** /ab'dər-īt/ n a native or citizen of Abdera; a simpleton.

abdicate /ab'di-kāt/ vt and vi formally to renounce or give up (office or dignity); to fail to fulfil (one's duties or responsibilities). [L ab from or off, and dicāre, -ātum to proclaim]
■ **ab'dicable** adj. **ab'dicant** adj (rare). **abdica'tion** n. **ab'dicator** n.

abdomen /ab'də-mən or ab-dō'mən/ n the belly; in mammals, the part between diaphragm and pelvis; in arthropods, the hind-body. [L abdōmen, -inis]
■ **abdominal** /-dom'/ adj. **abdom'inally** adv. **abdom'inoplasty** n a plastic surgery procedure for the stomach (also inf **tummy tuck**). **abdom'inous** adj pot-bellied.

abduce /ab-dūs'/ vt an earlier form of **abduct**. [L abducere, from ab from, and ducere, ductum to draw or lead]
■ **abdūc'ent** adj (anat) (of a muscle) drawing back; separating.

abduct /ab-dukt'/ vt to take away by deception or violence; to kidnap; (of a muscle) to cause abduction in (a part of the body). [L abductus, pap of abducere (see **abduce**)]
■ **abductee'** n a person who is abducted. **abduction** /-duk'shən/ n the carrying away, esp of a person by deception or force; separation of parts of the body after a wound or fracture (surg); muscular action drawing one part of the body (such as an arm or finger) away from another or away from the median axis of the body; a syllogism whose minor premise is only probable (logic). **abduc'tor** n a person who abducts; a muscle that abducts (anat).

abeam /ə-bēm'/ (naut) adv in a line at right angles to a vessel's length, on the beam. [**a-**[1]]

---

abear /ə-bār'/ vt (pat **abore'**; pap **aborne'**) to bear, comport or behave (obs); (only as infinitive) to endure or tolerate (dialect). [OE āberan]

abecedarian /ā-bi-sē-dā'ri-ən/ adj relating to the ABC; rudimentary; arranged in the manner of an acrostic. ◆ n a learner of the ABC, a beginner; a teacher of the ABC; an Anabaptist of a sect that rejected all learning. [ABC (noun)]

abed /ə-bed'/ adv in bed. [a-¹ and bed¹]

abeigh /ə-bēhh'/ (Scot) adv aloof. [Origin obscure]

abele /ə-bēl'/ or ā'bl/ n the white poplar-tree. [Du abeel, from OFr abel or aubel, from LL albellus, from L albus white]

abelia /ə-bēl'i-ə/ n a plant of the genus Abelia, shrubs of the honeysuckle family (Caprifoliaceae) with pink or white flowers. [Clarke Abel (1780–1826), English physician and botanist]

Aberdeen /ab-ər-dēn', sometimes ab'/ adj of or originating in Aberdeen or Aberdeenshire (abbrev **Aber**, usu in the designation of the Bishop of Aberdeen and Orkney). ◆ n (in full **Aberdeen terrier**) a coarse-haired kind of Scottish terrier.
■ **Aberdō'nian** adj of Aberdeen; (traditionally) parsimonious (facetious). ◆ n a person from Aberdeen.
❏ **Aberdeen Angus** /ang'gəs/ n a breed of hornless cattle descended from Aberdeenshire humlies and Angus doddies.

aberdevine /ab-ər-di-vīn'/ n a bird-fancier's name for the siskin. [Ety uncertain]

Aberdonian see under **Aberdeen**.

Aberglaube /ä'bər-glow-bə/ (Ger) n superstition.

Abernethy biscuit /ab-ər-neth'i bis'kit, also -nē'thi, also ab'/ n a hard biscuit, appar orig with caraway seeds. [Poss after Dr John Abernethy (1764–1831) who was interested in diet]

aberrate /ab'ə-rāt/ vi to wander or deviate from the right way. [L aberrāre, -ātum, from ab from, and errāre to wander]
■ **aberrance** /-er'/ or **aberr'ancy** n. **aberr'ant** adj wandering or straying; having characteristics not strictly in accordance with type (bot and zool). **aberr'antly** adv. **aberrā'tion** /-ər-/ n a deviation from the usual, normal or right course, direction or behaviour; a wandering of the intellect, mental lapse; a non-convergence of rays, owing to difference in refrangibility of different colours (**chromatic aberration**) or to difference of focus of the marginal and central parts of a lens or mirror (**spherical aberration**); an apparent displacement of a star, owing to the finite ratio of the velocity of light to that of the earth (**aberration of light**; astron). **aberra'tional** adj.

abessive /ab-es'iv/ (grammar) adj denoting absence or lack. ◆ n the abessive case. [L abesse to be absent]

abet /ə-bet'/ vt (**abett'ing**; **abett'ed**) to incite by encouragement or aid (usu to commit an offence; see also **aid and abet** under **aid**); to back up (Spenser); to make good. ◆ n (Spenser) abetting. [OFr abeter, from à (L ad to), and beter to bait; see **bait**]
■ **abet'ment** or **abett'al** n. **abett'er** or (esp law) **abett'or** n.

ab extra /ab ek'strä/ (L) from the outside.

abeyance /ə-bā'əns/ or **abeyancy** /-ən-si/ n a state of suspension or temporary inactivity; the state of being without a claimant (eg of a peerage). [OFr abeance, from à (L ad to), and beer or baer to gape or open wide; origin uncertain]
■ **abey'ant** adj.

ABF abbrev : Actors' Benevolent Fund; Army Benevolent Fund.

ABFM abbrev : American Board of Foreign Missions (now defunct).

ABH and **abh** abbrev : actual bodily harm.

abhominable see **abominable** under **abominate**.

abhor /ab-hör'/ vt (**abhorr'ing**; **abhorred'**) to detest; to loathe; to shrink from with horror; to protest against, to reject (Shakesp); to fill with horror (Shakesp). [L abhorrēre, from ab from, and horrēre to bristle or shudder]
■ **abhorr'ence** /-hor'/ n extreme hatred; something that is abhorred. **abhorr'ency** n (obs). **abhorr'ent** adj (esp with to) detesting; repugnant; strongly opposed; out of keeping; detestable; detested. **abhorr'ently** adv. **abhorr'er** n someone who abhors; (with cap) a member of the court party in England in 1679, who abhorred the Petitioners, a Tory (hist). **abhorr'ing** n repugnance; an object of abhorrence.

ABI abbrev : Association of British Insurers.

Abib /ā'bib/ n an earlier name for the month of Nisan in the Jewish calendar. [Heb ābīb, literally, an ear of corn]

abide¹ /ə-bīd'/ vt (pat **abōde'**, also **abīd'ed**, (Spenser) **abid'**; pap **abōde'** or **abīd'ed**, also **abidd'en**) to bide or wait for; (usu with negatives and questions) to meet, face or sustain; to endure; to tolerate. ◆ vi to remain; to dwell or stay; to conform to, adhere to, comply with or obey (with by). [OE ābīdan, from pfx ā-, and bīdan to wait]

■ **abīd'ance** n. **abīd'ing** adj continual, permanent or lasting. ◆ n (archaic) a continuance. **abīd'ingly** adv.

abide² /ə-bīd'/ (Shakesp; Milton) vt to aby. [**aby**, confused with **abide**¹]

à bientôt /a byẽ-tō'/ (Fr) see you again soon.

abies /ab'i-ēz/ n a tree of the genus Abies, the genus of the true firs.

abigail /ab'i-gāl/ (archaic) n a lady's-maid. [From Abigail, in Beaumont and Fletcher's Scornful Lady, or Bible, 1 Samuel 25]

ability /ə-bil'i-ti/ n the quality or fact of being able (to); power (physical and mental); strength; talent, skill. [OFr ableté (Fr habileté), remodelled after its source, L habilitās, -ātis, from habēre to have or hold; see **able**]

ab initio /ab in-ish'i-ō or -it'i-ō/ (L) from the beginning (abbrev **ab init** /ab in-it'/).

ab intra /ab in'tra/ (L) from the inside.

abiogenesis /ab-i-ō-jen'is-is or ā-bī-/ n the origination of living by non-living matter, spontaneous generation. [Coined by TH Huxley in 1870; Gr a- (privative), bios life, and genesis birth]
■ **abiogenetic** /-ji-net'ik/ adj. **abiogenet'ically** adv. **abiogenist** /-oj'ə-nist/ n a believer in abiogenesis.

abiosis /ā-bī-ō'sis/ (med) n absence of life. [Gr a- (privative), and biotikos, from bios life]
■ **ābiot'ic** adj without life; inanimate.

abiturient /a-bi-tū'ri-ənt/ n in Germany, a pupil leaving school for a university having passed the final-year school examinations (**abitur**). [New L abituriēns, -entis, prp of abiturīre, desiderative of L abīre to go away, from ab from, and īre to go]

abject /ab'jekt/ adj mean, wretched; worthless; grovelling; base or contemptible; cast away. ◆ n an outcast; a base slave; someone in more servile subjection than a subject. ◆ vt (obs) /ab-jekt'/ to throw or cast down or away. [L abjicere, abjectum, from ab from, and jacere to throw]
■ **abjec'tion** n abjectness; casting out; forcible expulsion of spores (bot). **ab'jectly** adv. **ab'jectness** n.

abjoint /ab-joint'/ (bot) vt to cut off by forming a septum. [L ab from, and **joint**]
■ **abjunction** /-jungk'shən/ n.

abjure /ab-j(y)oor'/ vt to renounce solemnly or on oath; to recant; to repudiate. [L ab from, and jurāre, -ātum to swear]
■ **abjurā'tion** n. **abjur'er** n.
■ **abjure the realm** (hist) to swear an oath to leave a country and never return.

abl. abbrev : ablative.

ablactation /ab-lak-tā'shən/ n weaning or the cessation of the production of milk; grafting by inarching (hortic). [L ab from, and lactāre to suckle, from lac milk]

ablation /ab-lā'shən/ n removal, esp surgical removal of an organ or body tissue, etc; loss or removal caused by melting, evaporation, weathering or (space technol) by heat friction on re-entering the atmosphere. [L ab from, and lātum used as supine of ferre to take]
■ **ablate** /ab-lāt'/ vt to remove or decrease by ablation. **ablatitious** /-lə-tish'əs/ adj. **ablatī'val** adj. **ab'lative** /-lə-tiv/ adj relating to ablation; in or belonging to a case which in Indo-European languages originally expressed direction from or time when, later extended to other functions (grammar). ◆ n the ablative case; a word in the ablative. **abla'tor** n a substance or material undergoing ablation, esp the heat shield of a spacecraft.
❏ **ablative absolute** n in Latin, a phrase generally comprising a noun or pronoun coupled with another noun, an adjective or a participle, both in the ablative case and usu indicating the time or cause of an event.

ablaut /äp'lowt or ab'lowt/ (philology) n a variation in root vowel, as in sing, sang, song, sung, explained by former accentuation (also called **gradation**). [Ger ab off, and Laut sound]

ablaze /ə-blāz'/ adv and adj in a blaze or on fire; brightly lit; feeling (an emotion) with great intensity (usu with with). [a-¹ and **blaze**¹]

able /ā'bl/ adj (**ā'bler**; **ā'blest**) having enough strength, power or means (to do a thing); clever, skilful. ◆ vt to enable (obs); to warrant (Shakesp). [See **ability**]
■ **a'bled** adj able-bodied (cf **differently abled** under **differ**). **a'bleism** n discrimination in favour of able-bodied people. **a'bleist** adj. **a'bly** adv. **aiblins** or **ablins** /ā'blinz/ or **yibbles** /yib'lz/ adv (Scot) perhaps. ❏ **able-bod'ied** adj having a strong body; free from disability, etc; robust. **able seaman**, **able-bodied seaman** or **able rating**, also (fem) **able seawoman** or **able-bodied seawoman** n a seaman able to perform all the duties of seamanship and having a higher rating than the ordinary sailor (abbrev **AB**).

-able /-ə-bl/ *adj sfx* combining with verbs to convey any of various passive senses (now the chief use as a living suffix), such as 'capable of being', 'able to be', 'worthy of being', 'likely to be', 'that must be'; combining with verbs to convey any of various active senses, such as 'capable of', 'able to', 'worthy of', 'suitable to', 'likely to'; combining with nouns to convey such meanings as 'worthy of', 'suitable for', 'in accordance with', 'causing'. See also **-ible**. [OFr, from L *-ābilis*, from *-bilis* as used with a 1st-conjugation verb]
  ■ **-ability** *n sfx*. **-ably** *adv sfx*.

ablet /ab'lit/ *n* the freshwater fish, the bleak. [Fr *ablette*, from LL *a(l)bula* dimin of *alba* white]

abloom /ə-bloom'/ *adv* and *adj* in a blooming state. [**a-¹** and **bloom¹**]

ablow /ə-blō'/ *adv* and *adj* in a blowing state. [**a-¹** and **blow¹,³**]

ablush /ə-blush'/ *adv* and *adj* in a blushing state. [**a-¹**]

ablution /ə-bloo'shən/ *n* (often in *pl*) the act of washing, *esp* the body; ceremonial washing; (often in *pl*) the wine and water used to rinse the chalice, drunk by the officiating priest (*RC church*); (in *pl*) a room or building for washing oneself (*milit sl*). [L *ablūtiō, -ōnis*, from *ab* away, and *luere* to wash]
  ■ **ablu'tionary** *adj*. **ablutomane** /ə-bloo'tō-mān/ *n* (Fr *-mane*, from Gr, see **mania**) a person who is obsessed with cleanliness.

ably see under **able**.

ABM *abbrev*: antiballistic missile.

abnegate /ab'ni-gāt/ *vt* to deny; to renounce. [L *ab* away, and *negāre* to deny]
  ■ **abnega'tion** *n*. **ab'negator** *n*.

abnormal /ab-nör'ml/ *adj* not normal; departing from what is normal or usual; of a branch of medicine or psychology dealing with the abnormal. ◆ *n* (*finance*) an item not occurring regularly. [Fr *anormal*, from LL *anormalus*, from Gr *anōmalos* (see **anomaly**); influenced by L *norma* rule, and *ab* from]
  ■ **abnor'malism** *n*. **abnormality** /-nör-mal'i-ti/ *n*. **abnor'mally** *adv*. **abnor'mity** *n*. **abnor'mous** *adj* (rare).
  □ **abnormal load** *n* (*usu* of road transport) a larger or heavier load than is generally carried.

Abo /ab'ō/ (*Aust; offensive*) *n* (*pl* **Ab'ōs**) an Aboriginal or Aborigine. ◆ *adj* Aboriginal. [Short form]

aboard /ə-börd'/ *adv* or *prep* on board; in or into a ship, railway train, etc; alongside (*naut*); on base (*baseball*). [**a-¹**]

ABO blood group system /ā-bē-ō' blud groop sis'təm/ (*med*) *n* a system by which human blood is classified into four groups (O, A, B, AB) according to the antigens carried by the red blood cells.

abode¹ /ə-bōd'/ *n* a dwelling-place or home; a stay. ◆ *vt* and *vi*, *pat* and *pap* of **abide¹**.
  ■ **of no fixed abode** (*law*) having no regular or habitual address.

abode² /ə-bōd'/ (*obs*) *n* a presage. ◆ *vt* (*Shakesp*) to presage. [OE *ābodian* to proclaim; cf **bode¹** and **forebode**]
  ■ **abode'ment** *n* (*obs*) a foreboding; an omen.

a'body see under **a'**.

ab officio et beneficio /ab o-fish'i-ō (or *-fik'*) et ben-e-fish'i-ō (or *-fik'*)/ (*LL*) (literally, from office and benefice, (of a member of the clergy) suspended from office.

aboideau /ab'ə-dō/ or **aboiteau** /-tō/ *n* a tide gate. [Can Fr]

aboil /ə-boil'/ *adv* and *adj* in a boiling state. [**a-¹** and **boil¹**]

aboiteau see **aboideau**.

abolish /ə-bol'ish/ *vt* to put an end to (*esp* a practice or institution). [L *abolēre, -itum*, partly through Fr *abolir*]
  ■ **abol'ishable** *adj*. **abol'ishment** *n* (rare). **aboli'tion** *n*. **aboli'tionary** *adj*. **aboli'tionism** *n*. **aboli'tionist** *n* a person who seeks to abolish anything, *esp* slavery or capital punishment.

abolla /ə-bol'ə/ (*hist*) *n* a Roman military cloak. [L]

abomasum /ab-ō-mā'səm/ *n* (*pl* **aboma'sa**) the fourth or true stomach of ruminants, lying close to the omasum (also **abomā'sus** (*pl* **abomā'si**)). [L *ab* away from, and *omāsum* tripe, paunch (a Gallic word)]
  ■ **abomā'sal** *adj*.

abominate /ə-bom'in-āt/ *vt* to abhor; to detest, loathe. [L *abōmināri, -ātus* to turn from as being of bad omen; see **omen**]
  ■ **abom'inable** or (*obs*) **abhom'inable** *adj* hateful; detestable; very bad (*inf*). **abom'inableness** *n*. **abom'inably** *adv*. **abomina'tion** *n* extreme aversion; anything detested or abominable. **abom'inator** *n*.
  □ **abominable snowman** *n* a mythical hairy manlike creature supposed to live in the Himalayas (also called the **yeti**).

abondance see **abundance**.

à bon droit /a bɔ̃ drwä'/ (Fr) with justice.

à bon marché /a bɔ̃ mar-shä'/ (Fr) at a good bargain, cheap.

abonnement /a-bon-mä'/ (Fr) *n* a subscription.

aboral /ab-ö'rəl/ (*zool*) *adj* away from the mouth. [L *ab* from, and *oral*]

abord¹ /ə-börd'/ (*archaic*) *vt* to accost. ◆ *n* approach. [Fr *aborder*, from *à bord* to the side]

abord² /ə-börd'/ (*Spenser*) *adv* astray. [Perh for **abroad**]

aborigine /ab-ə-rij'i-nē or -ni/ *n* an original or native inhabitant of a country (also (rare) **aborigin** or **aborigen** /ə-bor'i-jin/); (with *cap*) one of the original inhabitants of Australia. [L (*pl*) *aborīginēs*, from *ab* from, and *orīgō, -inis* beginning; in English, *aborigines* orig had no singular form]
  ■ **aborig'inal** *adj* (often with *cap*) earliest, primitive or indigenous; of the Australian Aborigines. ◆ *n* (now often, and in Australia always, with *cap*) an aborigine; (with *cap*) an Australian Aboriginal language. **aborig'inalism** *n* due recognition of native peoples. **aboriginality** /-al'i-ti/ *n* (also with *cap*) the fact of being aboriginal. **aborig'inally** *adv*.

ab origine /ab ō-rij'in-ē or -rēg'in-e/ (*L*) from the very first, from the source.

aborning /ə-börn'ing/ (*US*) *adv* while being born, produced, etc, as in *die aborning*. [**a-¹** and **born**]

abort /ə-bört'/ *vi* to miscarry in birth; (of a baby) to be lost in this way; to fail before getting fully under way or reaching a viable stage of development; to come to nothing. ◆ *vt* to cause to abort; to check or call off (an attack, mission, etc) at an early stage; to stop (eg the flight of a rocket) in emergency before completion of mission; to abandon (a computer activity), *usu* because an error has been made or because there has been a program or system failure. ◆ *n* an instance of abortion (*esp* of a rocket launch). [L *aborīrī, abortus*, from **ab-¹** (reversing the meaning), and *orīrī* to rise]
  ■ **abortee'** *n* a woman who has an abortion. **aborticide** /ə-bört'i-sīd/ *n* the killing of a fetus in the womb; a drug or agent causing this, an abortifacient. **abortifa'cient** /-i-fā'shənt or -shi-ənt/ *adj* causing abortion. ◆ *n* a drug or other means of causing abortion. **abor'tion** *n* the premature expulsion of an embryo or a fetus, either occurring naturally (**spontaneous abortion**) or by artificial means (**induced abortion**), *esp* in the first three months of pregnancy; the procuring of an induced abortion; arrest of development; the result of such arrest; anything that fails in the course of coming into being; a misshapen or ill-contrived thing (*offensive sl*). **abor'tional** *adj* relating to abortion; dreadful or terrible (*inf*). **abor'tionist** *n* a person who performs abortions, *esp* illegally; a person who is in favour of abortion on demand. **abor'tive** *adj* born before due time; unsuccessful; brought out or produced in an imperfect condition; abortifacient; checked in development. **abort'ively** *adv*. **abort'iveness** *n*. **abortuary** /ə-bört'ū-ə-ri/ *n* (from *abort*ion and mort*uary*) an anti-abortion term for an abortion clinic.
  □ **abortion pill** *n* a drug taken orally that brings about abortion.
  ■ **contagious abortion** contagious bacterial infections of cattle and of horses, causing abortion.

abought /ə-böt'/ *pat* and *pap* of **aby**.

aboulia or **abulia** /a-boo'li-ə, -bow' or -bū'-/ *n* loss of willpower; inability to make decisions. [Gr *a-* (privative), and *boulē* will]

abound /ə-bownd'/ *vi* to exist in great plenty; to be rich (in); to be filled (with). [OFr *abunder*, from L *abundāre* to overflow, from *ab* from, and *unda* a wave]
  ■ **abound'ing** *adj*.

about /ə-bowt'/ *prep* round on the outside of; around; here and there in; near in place, time, size, etc; on the person of; connected with; concerning; engaged in. ◆ *adv* around; halfway round, in the opposite direction (eg *to face about*); nearly; here and there; on the opposite tack (*naut*); in motion or activity, on the go. [OE *onbūtan*, from *on* in (cf **a-¹**), and *būtan* without, from *be* by, and *ūtan*, orig a locative, from *ūt* out]
  ■ **abouts'** *prep* (*Spenser*) about.
  □ **about'-face** *n* (orig used in US as a military command) the act of turning to face in the opposite direction; a complete change of opinion, attitude, etc. ◆ *vi* to perform an about-face. **about'-ship'** *vt* and *vi* to put (the ship) on the opposite tack. **about'-sledge** *n* a blacksmith's heavy hammer. **about'-turn** *n* and *vi* same as **about-face** above.
  ■ **about to** on the point of (doing, etc; also **just about to**); (in *neg*) not likely or keen (to do something) (*inf*). **be about** to be up and on the go after sleep or rest. **bring about** see under **bring**. **come about** to happen in the course of time. **go about** see under **go¹**. **put about** see under **put¹**. **turn about** see under **turn**.

above /ə-buv'/ *prep* over; in or to a position higher than that of; beyond in degree, amount, number, importance, etc; too magnanimous, respectable or proud for. ◆ *adv* overhead; in a higher position, order or power; in an earlier passage (of text, etc); in heaven. ◆ *adj* mentioned, stated, or given in an earlier passage. ◆ *n* (with *the*) that which has been mentioned, stated, or given earlier. [Late OE ābufan, from OE ā-on (cf **a-¹**), and bufan above, from be by, and ufan above]

□ **above'-board** adj open, without deception. **above'-ground** adj alive; not buried. **above'-mentioned** adj. **above'-named** adj. **above-the-line'** adj of or relating to the Government's expenditure and revenue allowed for in its original estimates and provided for by taxation; of or relating to the expenditure and revenue detailed in a company's profit and loss account. **above-the-line advertising** n advertising using conventional media such as television, radio, newspapers, cinemas and posters. **above-the-line costs**, **transactions**, etc n pl (econ; also without hyphens) items in the balance of payments accounts which record total payments and receipts on visible and invisible trade and on investment and capital transactions.

■ **above all** notably, more than anything else. **above and beyond** in addition to, more than is required. **above oneself** elated; conceited. **above par** see under **par¹**.

ab ovo /ab ō'vō or -wō/ (L, literally, from the egg) from the beginning.

ABP abbrev : arterial blood pressure.

Abp or **abp** abbrev : Archbishop.

abr. abbrev : abridged; abridgement.

abracadabra /ab-rə-kə-dab'rə/ interj used as a magic word in a spell or in conjuring. ◆ n gibberish; a magic word, used as a charm (obs). [Found in a poem traditionally attributed to the 2c physician Q Serenus Sammonicus]

abrade¹ /ə-brād'/ vt to wear down or off. [L ab from, and rādere, rāsum to scrape]
■ **abrā'dant** adj and n abrasive.

abrade² see **abraid**.

Abrahamic /ā-brə-ham'ik/ adj denoting any of the three major religions (Judaism, Christianity and Islam) that arose from the traditions believed to have been established by the patriarch Abraham.

Abraham-man /ā'brə-həm-man'/ or **Abram-man** /ā'brəm-man'/ n orig a Bedlam inmate let out to beg; an unruly beggar, esp one shamming insanity (archaic). [Said to be from an Abraham Ward in old Bedlam, a psychiatric hospital in London]
■ **sham Abraham** to feign sickness.

abraid, **abrade** /ə-brād'/ or (Spenser) **abray** /ə-brā'/ (obs) vt to awake or rouse. ◆ vi to start; to awake. [OE ābregdan, from intens pfx ā-, and bregdan; see **braid¹**]

abram /ā'brəm/ (Shakesp) adj an obsolete form of **auburn**.

abranchiate /ə-brang'ki-āt or -ət/ or **abranchial** /ə-brang'ki-əl/ (zool) adj without gills. [Gr a- (privative), and branchia gills]

abrasion /ə-brā'zhən/ n a wearing away; a worn-down or grazed place; a graze on the skin. [See **abrade¹**]
■ **abrā'sive** /-ziv or -siv/ adj tending to abrade; harsh; (of a person) tending to irritate or offend. ◆ n a substance used to clean, smoothe, etc by scratching and grinding. **abrā'sively** adv. **abrā'siveness** n.

à bras ouverts /a brä-zoo-ver'/ (Fr) with open arms.

abraxas /ə-braks'əs/ n a mystic word, or a gem engraved with such a word, often bearing a mystical figure of combined human and animal form, used as a charm; (with cap) the genus of the gooseberry or magpie moth. [Said to have been coined by the 2c Egyptian Gnostic Basilides to express 365 by addition of the numerical values of the Greek letters]

abray see **abraid**.

abrazo /ə-brä'sō/ n (pl **abra'zos**) in Central and S America, an embrace, esp in greeting. [Sp]

abreaction /ab-rē-ak'shən/ (psychol) n the resolution of a neurosis by reviving forgotten or repressed ideas of the event first causing it. [L ab from, and **reaction**]
■ **abreact'** vi. **abreact'ive** adj.

abreast /ə-brest'/ adv with fronts in line; side by side; (with of) keeping pace with. [**a-¹**]

abrégé /a-brā-zhā'/ (Fr) n an abridgement.

abricock /ab'ri-kok/ an obsolete form of **apricot**.

abridge /ə-brij'/ vt to shorten; to epitomize; to curtail (rights, etc) (law). [OFr abregier (Fr abréger), from L abbreviāre]
■ **abridg'able** or **abridge'able** adj. **abridge'ment** (sometimes **abridg'ment**) n contraction; shortening; a compendium of a larger work; an epitome or synopsis; a curtailment (law); (probably) a pastime (Shakesp). **abridg'er** n.

abrim /ə-brim'/ adv and adj in a brimming state, up to the brim. [**a-¹**]

abrin see under **Abrus**.

abroach /ə-brōch'/ (obs) adv and adj in a condition to let the liquor run out; in a state to be diffused, afloat or astir. [**a-¹**]

abroad /ə-bröd'/ adv in or to a foreign country; over a wide area; in full breadth; out of doors; at large; in the field; current; wide of the mark (archaic); astray (archaic). ◆ n anywhere foreign, foreign places. [**a-¹**]

abrogate /ab'rō-gāt/ vt to annul or rescind (a law, agreement, etc). [L ab away, and rogāre, -ātum to ask, or to propose a law]
■ **abrogā'tion** n. **ab'rogātive** adj. **ab'rogātor** n.

Abroma /a-brō'mə/ n a genus of East Indian sterculiaceous fibre-yielding trees. [Gr a- (privative), and brōma food]

abrooke /ə-brŭk'/ (Shakesp) vt to brook, bear or endure. [Pfx a- (intens), and **brook²**]

ABRSM abbrev : Associated Board of the Royal Schools of Music.

abrupt /ə-brupt'/ adj sudden; unexpected; precipitous; steep; passing with sudden transitions, disjointed; (of manners) short or rude; truncated; as if broken off. ◆ n (Milton) an abyss. [L abruptus broken away, from ab from, and rumpere, ruptum to break]
■ **abrup'tion** /-shən/ n a breaking off. **abrupt'ly** adv. **abrupt'ness** n.

Abrus /a'brəs or ā'/ n a tropical genus akin to the bean. [Gr habros graceful]
■ **ā'brin** n a poisonous protein contained in the seeds of the jequirity (Abrus precatorius).

ABS abbrev : anti-lock braking system.

abs. abbrev : absence; absent; (also **absol.**) absolute; (also **absol.**) absolutely; absorbent; (also **abstr.**) abstract.

abscess /ab'ses or -sis/ n a collection of pus in a cavity, usu causing an inflamed swelling. [L abscessus, from abs from, and cēdere, cēssum to go or retreat]
■ **ab'scessed** adj.

abscind /ab-sind'/ vt to cut off. [L abscindere, abscissum to cut off, from ab from, and scindere to cut]
■ **abscissa** /-sis'ə/, also **absciss** or **abscisse** /ab'sis/ n (pl **abscissae** /ab-sis'ē or -sis'ī/, **absciss'as** or **ab'scisses**) (maths) the intercept between a fixed point and the foot of an ordinate; the x-co-ordinate in analytical geometry. **absciss'in** n same as **abscisin** (see under **abscise**). **abscission** /-sizh'ən/ n an act of cutting off, or the state of being cut off; a figure of speech in which words demanded by the sense are left unsaid, the speaker stopping short suddenly (rhetoric); organic shedding of a part (eg a leaf or fruit) (bot); liberation of a fungal spore by breakdown of part of its stalk (bot).
□ **absciss layer** or **abscission layer** n (bot) a layer of parenchymatous cells through which a leaf, branch or bark scale separates off.

abscise /ab-sīz'/ (bot) vi to fall off by abscission. ◆ vt to cause to separate by abscission. [L abscīsus, pap of abscīdere, from abs away, and caedere to cut]
■ **abscisin** /-sis'in/ n any of a number of plant hormones which promote abscission.
□ **abscisic acid** n an abscisin that promotes abscission in leaves and dormancy in buds and seeds.

abscissa, **abscission** see under **abscind**.

abscond /ab-skond'/ vi to hide, or leave quickly and secretly, esp to escape a legal process. [L abscondere, from abs from or away, and condere to hide]
■ **abscond'ence** n. **abscond'er** n.

abseil /ab'sāl, ap'zīl, ab-sīl'/ vi to let oneself down a rock face using a double rope. ◆ n an act of abseiling. [Ger ab down, and Seil rope]
■ **ab'seiling** n.

absent /ab'sənt/ adj being away; not present; inattentive or dreamy. ◆ vt /ab-sent'/ (usu reflexive) to keep away. [L absēns, -sentis, prp of abesse, from ab away from, and esse to be]
■ **ab'sence** n the state of being away or not present; want or lack; non-existence; abstraction, inattention; sudden loss of consciousness of which the sufferer is later unaware (med). **absentee'** n a person who is absent on any occasion; a person who makes a habit of being away from his or her position, office, school, etc. **absentee'ism** n the practice of absenting oneself from duty or position; the persistent habit of being absent from work, school, etc. **ab'sently** adv inattentively or dreamily.
□ **absent healing** see **distant healing** under **distant**. **absent-mind'ed** adj inattentive to surroundings; preoccupied. **absent-mind'edly** adv. **absent-mind'edness** n.

absente reo /ab-sent'ē rē'ō or -te rä'ō/ (L) in the absence of the accused (abbrev **abs re**).

absey see **ABC** (n).

absinthe or **absinth** /ab'sinth/ n the wormwood plant or other species of Artemisia; a bitter, green, aniseed-flavoured liqueur containing (orig, at least) extract of wormwood. [Fr absinthe, from L absinthium, from Gr apsinthion wormwood]

■ **absinth'iated** adj impregnated with absinth. **ab'sinthism** n (pathol) illness caused by drinking too much absinthe.

absit /ab'sit/ n leave to pass one night away from college. [L, let him, her or it be absent, from abesse, from ab away from, and esse to be] ■ **absit invidia** /ab'sit in-vid'i-a or -wid'/ no offence, (literally) may there be no ill-will. **absit omen** /ab'sit ō'mən/ touch wood, (literally) may there be no (ill) omen (as in a word just used).

absolute /ab'səl-oot or -ūt/ adj free from limits, restrictions or conditions; certain, positive; complete; unlimited; free from mixture, pure; independent of relation to or comparison with other things; peremptory; unrestricted by constitutional checks; out of ordinary syntactic relation, standing as an independent construction, such as the Latin ablative absolute and Greek genitive absolute (grammar); existing in and by itself without necessary relation to anything else (philos); capable of being conceived independently of anything else. ◆ n (with the; often with cap) that which is absolute, self-existent or uncaused. [L absolūtus, pap of absolvere; see **absolve**] ■ **ab'solutely** adv separately, by itself; unconditionally; positively; /-loot'li or -lūt'/ completely, as a colourless but emphatic affirmative (abbrev **abs.** or **absol.**). **ab'soluteness** n. **absolu'tion** n release from punishment or guilt; acquittal; remission of sins, declared officially by a priest, or the formula by which it is expressed. **ab'solutism** n government or theory of government by a ruler with unrestricted power; adherence to the doctrine of the Absolute. **ab'solutist** n a supporter of absolute government, or of a philosophy of the Absolute (also adj). **absolutory** /ab-sol'ū-tər-i/ adj of, or giving, absolution. ❑ **absolute address** n the code designating a specific memory location determined by a computer. **absolute age** n (geol) see **radiometric** under **radio-**. **absolute alcohol** n water-free alcohol. **absolute ceiling** n the altitude above sea level, in standard atmospheric conditions, at which the rate of ascent of an aircraft would be zero (cf **service ceiling** under **service**[1]). **absolute humidity** n humidity expressed as grams of water per cubic metre of air. **absolute magnitude** n the magnitude that a star would have at a standard distance of 10 parsecs. **absolute majority** n a vote gained by a candidate which is greater than the total number of votes for all other candidates. **absolute monopoly** n (econ) a situation in which a single organization has total control over the output of a product, commodity or service for which there is no substitute. **absolute music** n music which does not attempt to illustrate or describe (cf **programme music**). **absolute pitch** n the pitch of a note as determined by the number of vibrations per second, perfect pitch; a sense of or memory for absolute pitch. **absolute privilege** n (law) a privilege that protects speakers in a parliament, law court, etc in making (even malicious) statements from the floor, from possible charges under the laws of slander. **absolute temperature** n temperature measured on the Kelvin scale or Rankine scale. **absolute undertaking** n (commerce) a promise by a party to a contract that he or she shall take absolute responsibility for something which is necessary for the performance of the contract, eg obtaining a licence to sell the goods. **absolute units** n pl those derived directly from fundamental units and not based on arbitrary numerical definitions. **absolute value** n the magnitude of a numerical value, irrespective of its relation to other values. **absolute zero** n the zero of the absolute scale of temperature ($-273.15°C$), the lowest temperature theoretically possible, at which entropy is zero.

absolve /ab-zolv' or -solv'/ vt to release or set free from guilt; to pardon; to give absolution to or for; to acquit without blame; to discharge (from); to accomplish, finish off (Milton). [L absolvere, from ab from, and solvere to loose] ■ **absolv'er** n. **absolv'itor** n (L, let him be absolved; Scots law) a decision absolving a defender at the conclusion of legal proceedings.

absonant /ab'sə-nənt/ adj discordant; abhorrent; unnatural; contrary to reason (with to or from), opp to consonant. [L ab from, and sonāns, -antis, prp of sonāre to sound]

absorb /ab-sörb' or -zörb'/ vt to suck in; to swallow up; to imbibe; to take in; to incorporate; to reduce or lessen (the force, impact, etc of something); to take up and transform (energy) instead of transmitting or reflecting (phys); to engage wholly or engross. [L ab from, and sorbēre, sorptum to suck in] ■ **absorbabil'ity** n. **absorb'able** adj. **absorb'ate** n an absorbed substance. **absorbed'** adj swallowed or soaked up; entirely occupied or engrossed. **absorb'edly** adv. **absorbefacient** /-i-fā'shənt or -shi-ənt/ adj causing or promoting absorption. ◆ n a medicine, etc, which causes or promotes absorption. **absorb'ency** n. **absorb'ent** adj absorbing; able to absorb. ◆ n something that absorbs. **absorb'er** n something that absorbs; material for capturing neutrons without generating more neutrons (nuclear phys). **absorb'ing** adj engrossing the attention. **absorb'ingly** adv. **absorp'tance** n (phys) the ratio of the radiant flux absorbed by a body to that incident on it (formerly **absorptiv'ity**). **absorptiometer** /-sörp-shi-om'i-tər/ n an apparatus for determining the solubility of gases in liquids. **absorptiomet'ric** adj. **absorptiom'etry** n. **absorp'tion** n the act of absorbing; the entire

occupation of the mind. **absorp'tive** adj capable of absorbing. **absorp'tiveness** or **absorptiv'ity** n. ❑ **absorbent cotton** n (N Am) cotton wool. **absorption bands** or **lines** n pl dark bands or lines interrupting a spectrum, due to absorption of light in the medium traversed. **absorption coefficient** n (phys) the fraction of energy absorbed at a surface; (in a medium) the natural logarithm of the ratio of incident and emergent energy. **absorption costing** n product costing that takes account of overheads. **absorption spectrum** n a system of absorption lines and bands.

abs re or **abse re** abbrev: absente reo (L), the accused being absent.

abstain /ab-stān'/ vi to hold or refrain (from, specif from voting or from drinking alcohol). ◆ vt (Spenser) to restrain. [Fr abstenir, from L abs from, and tenēre to hold] ■ **abstain'er** n a person who abstains, esp from alcoholic drinks. **absten'tion** n. **absten'tionism** n the policy of not using one's vote, esp in a political election. **absten'tionist** n and adj. **absten'tious** adj.

abstemious /ab-stē'mi-əs/ adj temperate; restrained in relation to food, drink, or other pleasures. [L abstēmius, from abs from, and tēmētum strong wine] ■ **abstē'miously** adv. **abstē'miousness** n.

abstention, abstentious see under **abstain**.

absterge /ab-stûrj'/ (med) vt to wipe; to cleanse; to purge. [L abstergēre, -tersum to wipe away, from abs from, and tergēre to wipe] ■ **absterg'ent** adj cleansing or purging. ◆ n a cleansing agent. **abster'sion** n a cleansing or purging process. **abster'sive** adj having the quality of cleansing; purgative. ◆ n an abstersive substance.

abstinent /ab'sti-nənt/ adj abstaining; temperate or self-restrained in one's appetites. [L abstinēns, -entis, prp of abstinēre; see **abstain**] ■ **ab'stinence** n abstaining or refraining, esp from some indulgence (with from). **ab'stinency** n the quality of being abstinent. **ab'stinently** adv.

abstract /ab-strakt'/ vt to draw away; to separate; to remove quietly; to purloin; to summarize; to form a general concept from consideration of particular instances. ◆ n /ab'strakt/ that part or thing which represents the essence; an abstraction; an abstract painting, sculpture, photograph, etc; a summary or abridgement; in Shakespeare, Antony and Cleopatra I.4.9, explained by some as an abridgement of time of separation, while others conjecture obstruct. ◆ adj /ab'strakt/ abstracted; apart from actual material instances, existing only as a mental concept, opp to concrete; away from practice, theoretical; (of terms) denoting a quality of a thing apart from the thing, eg 'redness'; representing ideas in geometric and other designs, not the forms of nature (art); (of verse) using words primarily for their auditory and rhythmic qualities. [L abs away from, and trahere, tractum to draw] ■ **abstract'ed** adj drawn off (with from); removed; absent-minded. **abstract'edly** adv. **abstract'edness** n. **abstrac'ter** n or formerly in the Civil Service **abstrac'tor** n a person who makes abstracts. **abstrac'tion** n the act of abstracting; the state of being abstracted; abstract quality or character; withdrawal from worldly things; absent-mindedness; a purloining; the process of abstracting by the mind; a thing existing only in idea; a theory or visionary notion; an abstract term; an abstract composition (art). **abstrac'tional** adj. **abstrac'tionism** n. **abstrac'tionist** n a person dealing in abstractions or unrealities (also adj). **abstrac'tive** adj able or tending to abstract; formed by or relating to abstraction. ◆ n anything abstractive; an abstract. **abstrac'tively** adv. **ab'stractly** adv. **ab'stractness** n. ❑ **abstract expressionism** n a development in art that began in America in the 1940s in which the expression of the artist's feelings informs his or her abstract representations. **abstract of title** n (law) a summary of facts concerning ownership; a document giving evidence, in shortened form, of the ownership of property or land. ■ **in the abstract** as an abstraction; in theory.

abstrict /ab-strikt'/ (biol; obs) vt to set free (spores, etc), esp by constriction of the stalk. [L abs from, and stringere, strictum to tie] ■ **abstric'tion** n.

abstruse /ab-stroos'/ adj difficult to understand; remote from apprehension; hidden (archaic). [L abstrūsus thrust away, from abs away, and trūdere, trūsum to thrust] ■ **abstruse'ly** adv. **abstruse'ness** n.

absurd /ab-sûrd'/ adj senseless or meaningless; opposed to reason; ridiculous. [L absurdus, from ab from, and surdus deaf, inaudible, indistinct, harsh, out of fashion, not to the purpose] ■ **absurd'ism** n the belief that mankind lives in a world that is essentially meaningless (see **theatre of the absurd** under **theatre**). **absurd'ist** n and adj (a person) following this belief. **absurd'ity** or **absurd'ness** n. **absurd'ly** adv.

ABTA /ab'tə/ abbrev: Association of British Travel Agents.

abthane /ab'thān/ n a monastic territory of the Columban church. [LL abthania, from Gaelic abdhaine abbacy]

abulia see **aboulia**.

abuna /ə-boo'nə/ n an Ethiopian patriarch. [Amharic, from Arabic, our father]

abundance /ə-bun'dəns/ n ample sufficiency; great plenty; a call of nine tricks (solo whist; also **abondance** /-bund'/); (also **abundance ratio** or **relative abundance** the proportion of one isotope to the total (for a specified element) (phys). [See **abound**]
■ **abund'ancy** n. **abund'ant** adj. **abund'antly** adv in large quantities; very, completely.

abune /ə-bün'/ a Scots form of **above**.

ab urbe condita /ab ûr'be kon'di-ta or ŭr'be kon'di-tä/ (L) from the founding of the city (of Rome) 753BC (abbrev **AUC**).

aburst /ə-bûrst'/ adv and adj in a bursting condition. [a-[1]]

abuse /ə-būz'/ vt to misuse (eg drugs); to take undue advantage of; to betray (eg a confidence); to misrepresent; to deceive; to revile or swear at; to maltreat; to violate, esp sexually. ♦ n /ə-būs'/ wrong use; an evil or corrupt practice; deceit; hurt or maltreatment; undue advantage; betrayal (of confidence); ill usage, maltreatment; (esp sexual) violation; reviling, insulting language. [L ab from, and ūti, ūsus to use]
■ **abusage** /ə-bū'sij/ n wrong use, esp of words or grammar. **abuser** /ə-bū'zər/ n. **abū'sion** /-zhən, Spenser also -zi-ən/ n (now rare) misuse; deception; wrong; outrage; reviling. **abū'sive** /-siv/ adj containing, giving, or of the nature of, abuse; (of speech) coarse, rude or insulting; wrong; (of a word) wrongly applied, catachrestical (archaic). **abū'sively** adv. **abū'siveness** n.

abut /ə-but'/ vi (**abutt'ing**; **abutt'ed**) to join, end or lean (on, upon or against). ♦ vt to border. [OFr abouter to touch by an end, and OFr abuter to touch at the end; cf also Fr aboutir to end at, from à to, and bout or but end; see **butt**[2]]
■ **abut'ment** n an endwise meeting or junction; the structure on which each side of an arch ends or rests (archit); a place of abutting. **abutt'al** n an abutment; (in pl) boundaries. **abutt'er** n (law) a person whose property abuts. **abutt'ing** adj confronting.

abutilon /ə-bū'ti-lon/ n a plant of the showy-flowered genus Abutilon of the mallow family (Malvaceae), some species yielding fibres. [Ar aubūtilūn]

abutment, **abuttal**, etc see under **abut**.

abuzz /ə-buz'/ adv and adj in a buzz. [a-[1] and **buzz**[1]]

abvolt /ab'vōlt/ or -volt/ n 10⁻⁸ volts. [ab-[2] and **volt**[1]]

aby or **abye** /ə-bī'/ (archaic) vt (pat and pap **abought** /ə-böt'/) to pay the penalty for; to pay as a penalty. ♦ vi to atone; to endure or continue. [OE abycgan, from pfx a- back, and bycgan to buy; merging and confused with **abide**[1]]

abysm /ə-bizm'/ n (archaic and poetic) an abyss. [OFr abisme, from a LL superl of abyssus; see **abyss**]
■ **abys'mal** adj very bad; bottomless; unfathomable; very deep; abyssal. **abys'mally** adv.

abyss /ə-bis'/ n a bottomless gulf; primal chaos; the supposed water-filled cavity under the earth; hell; anything very deep; the depths of the sea; a measureless or apparently measureless chasm. [Gr abyssos bottomless, from a- (privative), and byssos depth, bottom]
■ **abyss'al** adj very deep or bottomless, esp of ocean depths. **abyssopelagic** /ə-bis-ō-pi-laj'ik/ adj relating to the deepest regions of the ocean.

Abyssinian /ab-i-sin'i-ən or -sin'yən/ adj of or relating to Abyssinia, the former name of Ethiopia.
❑ **Abyssinian cat** n a small domestic cat of African origin, greyish or brownish marked with darker colour.

AC abbrev : Aero Club; air-conditioned or air-conditioning; Air Corps; aircraft(s)man; Alpine Club; alternating current (elec); ante Christum (L), before Christ; appellation (d'origine) contrôlée (Fr); athletic club; Companion of the Order of Australia.

Ac (chem) symbol : actinium.

ac abbrev : acre (N Am); alternating current (elec); in medical prescriptions, etc, ante cibum (L), before food.

a/c abbrev : account; account current.

ACA abbrev : Associate Chartered Accountant.

acacia /ə-kā'sh(y)ə/ n (pl **aca'cias** or **aca'cia**) a wattle, any plant of the genus Acacia, related to the sensitive plants; also applied to the false acacia of the genus Robinia. [L, from Gr akakiā]

academe /a-kə-dēm' or ak'ə-dēm/ (formal or literary) n the world of scholars; academic life; an academic, esp if pedantic; an academy (poetic). [Ety as for **academy**]
■ **academ'ia** n the academic life or world.

academy /ə-kad'ə-mi/ n a specialized (eg military) school, or a university; orig Plato's school of philosophy and hence his followers and his philosophical system; a secondary school (esp in Scotland); a riding school; a society for the promotion of the arts, science or fine art; the annual exhibition of the Royal Academy or of the Royal Scottish Academy. [Gr Akadēmeia Plato's school of philosophy, from the name of the garden outside Athens where Plato taught]
■ **academic** /-dem'ik/ adj of an academy or university; sceptical; scholarly; formal; theoretical only, of no practical importance or consequence; orig of the philosophical school of Plato. ♦ n a person studying or teaching at a university, esp one who has scholarly tastes (sometimes derog); orig a Platonic philosopher; (in pl) academic studies (US). **academ'ical** adj academic. ♦ n in Scotland, a pupil or former pupil of an academy; (in pl) formal university dress, usu cap, gown, etc. **academ'icalism** n close adherence to formal academic teaching. **academ'ically** adv. **academician** /ə-kad-ə-mish'ən/ n a member of an academy, esp of the French Academy or the Royal Academy of Arts (London) or Royal Scottish Academy (Edinburgh). **academ'icism** or **acad'emism** n academicalism. **acad'emist** n an academic; an academician.
❑ **Academy Award** n a formal name for an **Oscar**[1].

Acadian /ə-kā'di-ən/ adj of or relating to the Acadians or their dialect of French, or to Acadia, former name for part of E Canada including Nova Scotia and New Brunswick. ♦ n one of the French-speaking early settlers of Acadia, or one of their descendants, including the Cajuns (qv). [Fr Acadie Acadia, from Micmac ākade abundance]

açaí or **assai** /ə-sə-ē' or a-sī'/ n the small, purple fruit of a S American tree of the genus Euterpe, valued for its nutritional qualities. [Port açaí, from Tupí assaí]

acajou /ak'ə-zhoo or -zhoo'/ n the cashew tree or its fruit or gum; a kind of mahogany. [See **cashew**]

acalculia /ā-kal-kū'li-ə/ (psychol) n the inability to make simple mathematical calculations (also **dyscalculia**). [a-[2] and L calculāre to count]

acaleph or **acalephe** /ak'ə-lef, -lēf or -le'fə/ n a jellyfish of the class **Acale'pha** or **Acale'phae**, which also includes medusas. [Gr akalēphē a nettle, sea-anemone]
■ **acale'phan** n and adj.

acamprosate /ə-kam'prə-sāt/ n a drug thought to be beneficial in maintaining abstinence in alcohol-dependent patients.

acanaceous /ak-ə-nā'shəs/ (bot) adj prickly. [L acanus a kind of thistle, from Gr akanos, from akē a point]

acanthus /ə-kan'thəs/ n (pl **acanth'uses** or **acanth'i** /-ī/) any plant of the prickly-leaved genus Acanthus, esp A. spinosus or A. mollis; a conventionalized representation of an acanthus leaf, as in Corinthian capitals. [Gr akanthos, from akē point]
■ **acanth'** n (obs) acanthus. **acanth'a** n a thorn, prickle; a spiny growth or body part. **Acanthā'ceae** /ak-/ n pl the acanthus family, related to the figworts. **acanthā'ceous** adj prickly; of the Acanthaceae. **Acanthamoe'ba** n (med) a protozoan living in tapwater, which may cause keratitis in contact lens wearers. **acanth'ine** adj of, like or ornamented with acanthus. **Acanthoceph'ala** n pl (Gr kephalē head) a division of parasitic worms with spiny proboscis and no mouth or alimentary canal. **acanthoceph'alan** adj. **acanth'oid** adj like acanthus; spiny. **acanthopterygian** /ak-an-thop-tər-ij'yən/ adj (Gr pteryx, -ygos wing, fin) spiny-finned. **acanth'ous** adj spiny.

acapnia /ā- or ə-kap'ni-ə/ n deficiency of carbon dioxide. [Gr a- (privative), and kapnos smoke]

a cappella /a kə-pel'ə or ä käp-pel'lä/ (music) adj and adv (of choral music) sung without accompaniment or with accompaniment merely doubling the voice parts (also **alla cappella**). [Ital, in the church style]

acari, **acarian**, etc see **acarus**.

acarpellous or (chiefly US) **acarpelous** /ā-kär'pə-ləs/ (bot) adj (of flowers) having no carpels. [Gr a- (privative), and karpos fruit]

acarpous /ā- or a-kär'pəs/ (bot) adj sterile, not bearing fruit. [Gr a- (privative), and karpos fruit]

acarus /ak'ə-rəs/ n (pl **ac'arī**) a mite. [Gr akari a mite, from akarēs too short to cut, from a- in privative sense, and keirein to cut]
■ **acā'rian** adj. **acarī'asis** n disease due to or infestation by mites. **acaricide** /a-kar'i-sīd/ n a mite killer. **ac'arid** n one of the Acarida. **Acar'ida** n pl the order of Arachnida to which mites and ticks belong. **acar'idan**, **acarid'ean** or **acarid'ian** adj and n. **Acarī'na** n pl Acarida. **ac'arine** adj. **acarodomatium** or **acaridomatium** /-dō-mā'shyəm/ n (pl **acarodomā'tia** or **acaridomā'tia**) a habitat for mites provided by certain plants that benefit from their presence. **ac'aroid**

adj mite-like. **acarol'ogist** *n*. **acarol'ogy** *n* the study of mites. **acaroph'ily** *n* symbiotic association of plants with mites.
❑ **acarine disease** *n* a disease of bees due to mites in the spiracles.

ACAS /ā'kas/ *abbrev* : Advisory, Conciliation and Arbitration Service, an independent organization set up by the British government in 1974 to help avoid or resolve industrial disputes and improve industrial relations.

acatalectic /ǝ-ka-tǝ-lek'tik/ (*prosody*) *adj* (of a line of verse) having the full number of syllables. ◆ *n* an acatalectic verse or line. [Gr *akatalēktos*, from a- (privative); see **catalectic**]

acatalepsy /ǝ-kat'ǝ-lep-si/ (*philos*) *n* the unknowableness to a certainty of all things. [Gr *akatalēpsiā*, from a- (privative), *kata* thoroughly, and *lēpsis* a seizing]
■ **acatalep'tic** *adj* and *n*.

acatamathesia /ǝ-kat-ǝ-mǝ-thē'zi-ǝ or -zhǝ/ (*psychol*) *n* the inability to comprehend data (objects, language, etc) presented to the senses. [Gr a- (privative), and *katamanthanein* to observe, understand, from *kata* (intens), and *manthanein* to learn]

acates /ǝ-kāts'/ (*obs*) *n pl* bought provisions. [OFr *acat*, from LL *accaptāre* to acquire, from L *ad* to, and *captāre* to seize; cf **cate**, **cater**[1]]
■ **acāt'er** or **acāt'our** *n* (*obs*) an officer who buys provisions, a caterer; a ship's chandler.

acathisia see **akathisia**.

acaudal /ā-kö'dǝl/ *adj* tailless (also **acau'date**). [Gr a- (privative), and **caudal**]

acaulescent /ak-ö-les'ǝnt/ *adj* having a very short stem. [Gr a- (privative), L *caulis* stem, and sfx *-escent*]
■ **acaul'ine** /-līn or -lin/ or **acaulose** /-lōs'/ *adj* stemless.

ACC *abbrev* : Accident Compensation Corporation (*NZ*).

acc. *abbrev* : acceptance (*commerce*); accompanied; according; account (also **acct** or **a/c**); accountant; accusative (also **accus.**; *grammar*).

ACCA *abbrev* : (Associate of the) Association of Chartered Certified Accountants.

accablé /a-ka-blä'/ (*Fr*) *adj* depressed or overwhelmed.

ACCAC *abbrev* : Awdurdod Cymwysterau, Cwricwlwm ac Asesu Cymru (*Welsh*), the Qualifications, Curriculum and Assessment Authority for Wales.

Accadian same as **Akkadian**.

accede /ak- or ak-sēd'/ *vi* to come forward; to arrive (with *to*); to come to an office or honour; to join up or become a party, hence to agree or assent (with *to*). [L *accēdere*, *accēssum* to go near, from *ad* to, and *cēdere* to go; see **cede**]
■ **accēd'ence** *n*. **accēd'er** *n*.

accelerando /ak-se-lǝ-ran'dō or (*Ital*) ät-che-le-rän'dō/ (*music*) *adj* and *adv* with increasing speed (*abbrev* **accel**). [Ital]

accelerate /ak-sel'ǝ-rāt/ *vt* to increase the speed of; to hasten the progress or occurrence of. ◆ *vi* to become faster. [L *accelerāre, -ātum*, from *ad* to, and *celer* swift]
■ **accel'erant** *n* an accelerating agent (also *adj*). **accelerā'tion** *n* increase of speed; rate of change of velocity; a cumulative advance ahead of the normal or theoretical; the power or means of accelerating. **accel'erative** *adj* quickening. **accel'erātor** *n* any person or thing that accelerates, *esp* a substance that accelerates chemical action, a nerve or muscle that increases rate of action, an apparatus or device for increasing the speed of a machine, computer, etc, or one for imparting high energies to atomic particles. Devices for accelerating charged particles include the **cyclotron** type (for accelerating the heavier particles, such as protons; used in the treatment of cancer), and modifications of this, such as the **synchrocyclotron** type and the **synchrotron** type (for accelerating electrons). Other types of accelerators are the **proton synchrotron** (of which examples are the **cosmotron** and the **bevatron**), the **betatron** (for accelerating electrons; used in medicine and industry), **linear accelerators** and **electron ring accelerators**. **accel'eratory** *adj*. **accelerom'eter** *n* an instrument for measuring acceleration of aircraft, etc. ❑ **accelerated aging test** *n* (*elec eng*) a test for the stability of cables, using twice the normal voltage. **accelerated fatigue tests** *n pl* (*engineering*) the repeated application to a machine or component of simulated operating loads to determine its safe fatigue life before it is reached in service. **acceleration** or **accelerator principle** *n* in Keynesian economic analysis, the relationship between a sustained rise in the sales of an item and the increase in the ordering by firms of the extra factory equipment made necessary by the increased output. **accelerator board** or **card** *n* (*comput*) an additional circuit board to speed up some aspect of the operation of a computer.

accend /ak- or ak-send'/ (*obs*) *vt* to kindle. [L *accendere, accēnsum* to kindle]
■ **accen'sion** *n*.

accent /ak'sǝnt/ *n* modulation of the voice; tone of voice; stress on a syllable, word, or note; a mark used to direct this stress; a mark over a letter to indicate differences of stress, pitch, length, quality of sound, etc; intensity; any way of pronouncing speech characteristic of a region, a class or an individual; a distinguishing mark; a distinctive mode of expression, such as that of an artist; a significant word (*poetic*); a highlight or other touch bringing out some particular effect (*art*); (in *pl*) speech, language (*poetic*). ◆ *vt* /ak-sent'/ to express or mark the accent of; to utter; to accentuate. [L *accentus*, from *ad* to, and *cantus* song]
■ **ac'centless** *adj*. **accent'ūal** *adj* according to or characterized by accent. **accentūal'ity** *n*. **accent'ūally** *adv*. **accent'ūate** *vt* to mark, play or pronounce with accent; to make prominent or emphasize. **accentūā'tion** *n* emphasis or stress; see **pre-emphasis** (*telecom*).

accentor /ak-sen'tör or -tǝr/ *n* a bird of the hedge sparrow genus formerly called *Accentor*, but now *Prunella*. [L, one who sings with another, from *ad* to, and *cantor* singer]

accept /ǝk-sept'/ *vt* (*old* or *formal*, *vi* with *of*) to take (something offered); to receive (with approval, favour, consent, resignation or passivity); to reply to, suggesting agreement or compliance; to reply to in the affirmative, say yes to; to view favourably or to tolerate; to promise to pay (a bill of exchange); to understand, take on board. [L *acceptāre*, from *accipere, acceptum*, from *ad* to, and *capere* to take]
■ **accept'able** *adj* worth accepting; welcome, pleasing; capable of being accepted, tolerable; satisfactory, adequate. **acceptabil'ity** *n*. **accept'ableness** *n*. **accept'ably** *adv*. **accept'ance** *n* accepting; favourable reception; favour; acceptableness; an agreeing to terms; an agreement to enter into a contract; agreement to pay a bill of exchange, *usu* by signing it; an accepted bill; acceptation. **accept'ancy** *n*. **accept'ant** *n* someone who accepts. ◆ *adj* ready to receive. **acceptā'tion** *n* a kind reception; the sense in which a word, etc, is understood. **accept'ed** *adj* customary or usual; generally approved or agreed; established. **accept'edly** *adv*. **accept'er** *n*. **accept'ive** *adj* ready to receive. **acceptiv'ity** *n*. **accept'or** *n* someone who accepts something, *esp* a bill of exchange; any molecule or ion that accepts electrons from a donor; an impurity in semiconductor material which increases the conductivity of the material by attracting electrons; a horse which has its entry for a race confirmed.
❑ **accepting house** *n* a financial institution, such as a merchant bank, which accepts bills of exchange.

acceptilation /ǝk-sep-ti-lā'shǝn/ *n* the remission of a debt without payment or by accepting a nominal payment only (*Roman* and *Scots law*); Christ's atonement (on the theory that only God's acceptance made his sacrifice sufficient) (*theol*). [L *acceptīlātiō*, verbal release from debt, literally bringing of receipt]

access /ak'ses/ *n* approach; admittance; a way of opportunity, approach or entrance; addition, accession; onset or attack of illness; a fit (of illness or passion); permission to log on to a computer system, and to read and alter files held; the possibility of transferring data to and from memory (*comput*). ◆ *vt* to locate or retrieve information; to retrieve information from (a computer), or from a computer in (a particular location); to gain access to in any sense. [See **accede**]
■ **access'ary** *n* and *adj* accessory (*esp* in legal senses). **accessibil'ity** *n*. **access'ible** *adj* within reach; approachable; easily comprehensible. **access'ibly** *adv*. **accession** /ak-sesh'ǝn/ *n* the act or event of acceding; a coming, *esp* to an office or honour, or as an addition or new member; that which is added; an addition by nature or industry to existing property (*law*); acquisition of such an addition by the owner of the existing property (*law*); assent; an access or fit (*obs*). ◆ *vt* to enter in a book as an accession to a library. **accessor'ial** *adj*. **access'orily** *adv*. **access'orize** or **-ise** *vt* to add accessories to. **access'ory** *adj* additional; subsidiary, present along with something more important; occurring by accident; contributing; aiding or participating in a crime (*law*) or misdeed, but not as a principal. ◆ *n* anything, *esp* an item of equipment, that is secondary, additional or non-essential; someone who helps or allows others to commit a crime. ❑ **access broadcasting**, **access television**, etc *n* radio and television programmes put out independently by groups of people, not professionally involved in broadcasting, who want to bring their points of view to public notice. **access charge** *n* a charge for access to a computer or telecommunications network. **access course** *n* a course preparing those without formal qualifications for further education. **access eye** *n* (*building*) a plug provided in soil, waste and drain pipes that can be unscrewed for easy access to a blockage. **accessory minerals** *n pl* minerals whose presence or absence is not considered when a type of rock is given a name. **accessory pigments** *n pl* pigments found in chloroplasts and blue-green algae that transfer their absorbed energy to *chlorophyll a* (the primary pigment) during

---

■ words derived from main entry word; ❑ compound words; ■ idioms and phrasal verbs

photosynthesis. **accessory shoe** same as **hot shoe** (see under **hot**[1]). **access road** *n* a minor road built to give access to a house, locality, motorway, etc. **access television** see **access broadcasting** above. **access time** *n* the time needed for information stored in a computer to be retrieved.

■ **accessary before** (or **after**) **the fact** someone who helps a criminal before (or after) the committing of a crime. **deed of accession** (*Scots law*) one by which a bankrupt's creditors accede to a settlement privately, ie by trust deed.

acciaccatura /ät-chä-ka-too'rə/ (*music*) *n* a short grace note, written with a stroke through the tail and played very quickly. [Ital *acciaccare* to crush]

accidence /ak'si-dəns/ *n* the part of grammar dealing with the inflections of words. [Ety as for **accident**]

accident /ak'si-dənt/ *n* anything that happens; an unforeseen or unexpected event; a chance; a mishap; an unessential quality or property; unevenness of surface. [L *accidēns, -entis*, prp of *accidere* to happen, from *ad* to, and *cadere* to fall]

■ **accidental** /-dent'-/ *adj* happening by chance; not essential. ◆ *n* a sharp, flat, or natural not in the key signature (*music*); (in *pl*) the strong chance effects of light (*art*); a non-essential feature; item. **accident'alism** *n* the state or quality of being accidental; chance manner; a system based on symptoms rather than on causes (*med*); use of accidentals (*art*); the theory that events happen without a cause (*philos*). **accidental'ity** *n*. **accident'ally** *adv*. **accident'ed** *adj* uneven; varied.

□ **ac'cident-prone** *adj* (*usu* predicative) more than normally liable to have accidents.

■ **a chapter of accidents** an unforeseen course of events; a series of accidents.

accidie /ak'si-di/ *n* acedia. [OFr *accide*, from LL *acēdia* (see **acedia**)]

accinge /ak-sinj'/ (*fig*) *vt* to gird. [L *ad* to, and *cingere* to gird]

accipitrine /ak-sip'i-trīn or -trin/ *adj* relating to or associated with hawks. [L *accipiter* a hawk]

■ **accip'iter** *n* any bird belonging to the *Accipiter* genus of hawks having short broad wings adapted for woodland.

accite /ak-sīt'/ *vt* to cite; to summon; to excite (*Shakesp*). [LL *accitāre*, from *ad* to, and *citāre* to cite or call]

acclamation /ak-lə-mā'shən/ *n* a shout of applause or assent; enthusiastic approval or welcome. [L *acclāmāre*, from *ad* to, and *clāmāre, -ātum* to shout; see **claim**]

■ **acclaim** /ə-klām'/ *vt* to hail or declare by acclamation (*usu* with *as*); to welcome with enthusiasm. ◆ *n* acclamation. **acclamatory** /ə-klam'ə-tər-i/ *adj*.

■ **by acclamation** with enthusiastic vocal assent rather than a formal vote.

acclimatize or **-ise** /ə-klī'mə-tīz/, also (*US*) **acclimate** /ə-klī'mət or ak'lī- or -li-/, **climatize** or **-ise** /klī'mə-tīz/ *vt* to accustom (a person, animal, plant, etc) to a new climate or environment. ◆ *vi* to become acclimatized. [Fr *acclimater*, from *à* to, and *climat* climate]

■ **acclī'matizable** or **-s-** *adj*. **acclīmatizā'tion** or **-s-**, also **acclīmatā'tion** or **acclīmā'tion** /ak-lī- or -li-/ *n*. **acclī'matizer** or **-s-** *n*.

acclivity /ə-kliv'i-ti/ *n* an upward slope. [L *ad* to, and *clīvus* a slope]

■ **accliv'itous** or **acclī'vous** *adj*.

accoast /ə-kōst'/ an older form of **accost**.

accoied see **accoy**.

accoil /ə-koil'/ (*rare*) *n* reception. ◆ *vi* (*pat* **accoyld'**) (*Spenser*) to assemble. [OFr *acoil* (Fr *accueil*)]

accolade /ak'ə-lād or a-kə-lād', also -ko-/ *n* a high award, honour or praise publicly given; the action used in conferring knighthood, formerly an embrace or kiss, now a tap on each shoulder with the flat of a sword; an embrace; a brace or other line connecting staves (*music; rare*); a brace-like ornament (*archit*). [Fr, from L *ad* to, and *collum* neck]

accommodate /ə-kom'ə-dāt/ *vt* to adapt; to make suitable; to adjust; to harmonize or make consistent; to furnish or supply (with); to find or provide room, etc, for; to provide with a loan; to oblige. ◆ *vi* (*rare*) to come to terms; to make adjustment. [L *accommodāre, -ātum*, from *ad* to, and *commodus* fitting]

■ **accomm'odable** *adj*. **accomm'odāting** *adj* ready to make adjustment; obliging; pliable; easily corrupted. **accomm'odātingly** *adv*. **accommodā'tion** *n* adaptation; adjustment, *esp* of the eye to change of distance; the adaptation or twisting of language to a sense not intended; obligingness; settlement or compromise; the supplying of needs (*esp* housing or refreshment); a help towards satisfaction of a need; a convenience; lodgings, living quarters (formerly or *N Am* sometimes *pl*); space for what is required; adaptation of revelation by way of compromise with human ignorance or weakness (*theol*); a loan of money. **accomm'odātive** *adj*. **accomm'odātiveness** *n*. **accomm'odātor** *n*.

□ **accommodation address** *n* an address to which mail may be sent but which is not that of the addressee's home or office. **accommodation bill** *n* a bill drawn, accepted or endorsed by one or more persons as security for a sum advanced to another by a third party, such as a banker. **accommodation ladder** *n* a stairway on the outside of a ship allowing access to and from small boats, etc, alongside. **accommodation rig** *n* an offshore oil rig with sleeping, supply, and recreational facilities. **accommodation road** *n* a road giving access to buildings, etc, off the public road. **accommodation train** *n* (*US*) one stopping at all or most stations on the way.

accompany /ə-kum'pə-ni/ *vt* to go or be in company with; to attend; to go along with; to perform an accompaniment to or for (*music*); to associate, join, or couple. [Fr *accompagner*; see **company**]

■ **accom'panier** *n*. **accom'paniment** *n* something which accompanies; a subsidiary part or parts supporting a solo (*music*). **accom'panist** (also **accom'panyist**) *n* a person providing musical accompaniment.

accomplice /ə-kom'plis or -kum'-/ *n* a person who helps another or others to commit a crime (*of* or *with* a person, *in* or *of* the crime); an associate (*Shakesp*). [L *complex, -icis* joined; prefix unexplained]

accomplish /ə-kom'plish or -kum'-/ *vt* to complete; to fulfil; to achieve; to equip (*obs*); to finish off, complete, in culture and acquirements. [OFr *acomplir*, from L *ad* to, and *complēre* to fill up; see **complete**]

■ **accom'plishable** *adj*. **accom'plished** *adj* complete, finished or highly skilled; expert; polished. **accom'plisher** *n*. **accom'plishment** *n* completion; an achievement; making accomplished; an acquired skill, *esp* in matters of culture or social behaviour, sometimes superficial or merely ornamental.

accompt, accomptable and **accomptant** obsolescent spellings of **account, accountable** and **accountant** with the same pronunciation.

accorage see **accourage**.

accord /ə-körd'/ *vi* to agree; to correspond (with). ◆ *vt* to give or grant (to a person); to cause to agree; to reconcile. ◆ *n* agreement; harmony; the set of notes to which an instrument is tuned; assent (*obs*). [OFr *acorder*, from L *ad* to, and *cor, cordis* the heart]

■ **accord'able** *adj*. **accord'ance** or **accord'ancy** *n* agreement; conformity; a granting. **accord'ant** *adj* agreeing; corresponding. **accord'antly** *adv*. **accord'er** *n*. **accord'ing** *adj* in accordance; agreeing; harmonious. **accord'ingly** *adv* agreeably (*obs*); suitably; in agreement (with what precedes); therefore.

■ **accord and satisfaction** (*commerce*) the process by which a party agrees to release the other party from contractual obligations (the *accord*) in exchange for a consideration given for the release (the *satisfaction*). **according as** in proportion as; depending on whether. **according to** in accordance with, or agreeably to; as asserted by; in proportion to. **as accords** (*formal*) as may be appropriate. **of one's own accord** spontaneously; voluntarily. **with one accord** with spontaneous unanimity.

accordion /ə-kör'di-ən/ *n* a musical instrument with folding bellows that cause free metal reeds to vibrate, the notes being determined by pressing on studs or a keyboard. [**accord**]

■ **accord'ionist** *n*.

□ **accord'ion-pleating** or **accordion pleats** *n* pleating with very narrow folds like the bellows of an accordion.

accost /ə-kost'/ earlier **accoast** /-kōst'/ *vt* to approach and speak (often threateningly) to; to speak first to; to solicit as a prostitute. ◆ *vi* (*Spenser*) to lie alongside, border; to fly along near the ground. ◆ *n* address; greeting. [OFr *acoster*, from LL *accostāre* to be side by side, from L *ad* to, and *costa* a rib, a side]

■ **accost'able** *adj*.

accouchement /a-koosh'mä or -mənt or a-koosh-mä'/ *n* delivery in childbirth. [Fr]

■ **accoucheur** /-shær'/, *fem* **accoucheuse** /-shæz'/ *n* a person who assists women in childbirth, ie a midwife.

account /ə-kownt'/ *vt* to reckon; to judge, value; to recount (*obs*). ◆ *vi* to count; to reckon; to keep accounts; to give a reason or explanation; to give a statement of money dealings; to answer as someone responsible; to have the responsibility or credit (of killing or otherwise disposing of anything or anybody; with *for*). ◆ *n* counting; reckoning; a business relationship; a reckoning of money or other responsibilities; (in *pl*) the statement of a company's financial affairs, containing the profit and loss account and the balance sheet; a record of business transacted between two people or people and organizations; a section of a ledger in which a record is made of every transaction relating to the same activity (*bookkeeping*); a statement of money owing; a continuing facility for the purchase of goods and services on credit; a facility with a bank, building society, etc for carrying out financial transactions and storing money; the period of time (*usu* a fortnight) allowed before accounts are settled (*stock exchange*); the client of an advertising agency, public relations consultancy, etc; advantage; value (as in *of no account*); estimation; consideration; sake; a descriptive report; a statement; a narrative; a performance. [OFr *acconter*, from L *ad* to, and *computāre* to reckon; see **compute** and **count**[1]]

■ **accountabil'ity** *n*. **account'able** *adj* liable to account, responsible; explicable. **account'ableness** *n*. **account'ably** *adv*. **account'ancy** *n* the office, work or profession of an accountant. **account'ant** *n* a person whose work involves the preparation, recording, analysis and interpretation of the accounts of a company, etc. **account'antship** *n*. **account'ing** *n* the setting up, maintaining and analysing of financial records. ♦ *adj* relating to the keeping of accounts.

❑ **account book** *n* a book for keeping accounts in. **account day** *n* a designated day on which accounts are settled on the London Stock Exchange. **account executive** *n* the person in an advertising agency who is responsible for looking after a client's requirements (*abbrev* **AE**).

■ **bring** or **call to account** to demand of someone an explanation or justification of what they have done; to reprimand. **by all accounts** according to general opinion. **find one's account** to derive advantage. **for account of** on behalf of. **for the account** for settlement on the regular settling day. **give a good** (or **bad**) **account of oneself** to give a good (or bad) performance; to do well (or badly). **go to one's** (**long**) **account** to go to the last judgement, die. **hold to account** to hold responsible. **in account with** in business relations requiring the keeping of an account with. **leave out of account** not to consider as a factor. **make account of** to set value upon. **on** or **to account** as an instalment or interim payment. **on account of** because of. **on no account** not for any reason or consideration. **on one's own account** for one's own sake; on one's own responsibility. **on someone's account** on behalf or to the advantage of someone. **put to good account** to put to good use, take advantage of. **settle accounts** or **square accounts** (or **an account**) **with** to complete financial transactions with; to revenge oneself against (*fig*). **take into account** or **take account of** to take into consideration. **take no account of** to overlook or fail to take into consideration. **turn to** (**good**) **account** to turn to advantage.

accourage /a-kur'ij/ or **accorage** /a-ko-rāj'/ (*Spenser*) *vt* to encourage. [OFr *acorager*, from *à* to, and *corage* courage]

accourt /a-kört'/ *vt* to entertain. [An invention of Spenser's, from **court**]

accoutre or (*US*) **accouter** /a-koo'tar/ *vt* (**accou'tring** (or *US* **accoutering** /a-koo'tar-ing/); **accou'tred** (or *US* **accou'tered** /-tard/)) to dress or equip (*esp* a warrior). [Fr *accoutrer*, earlier *accoustrer*; origin doubtful]

■ **accou'trement** (or *US* **accou'terment**; /-tar- or -tra-/), also (*obs*) **accus'trement** or **accous'trement** *n* equipping; (*usu* in *pl*) dress or other items for a particular activity; military equipment apart from clothing and weapons.

accoy /a-koi'/ (*Spenser*) *vt* (*pap* **accoied'** or **accoyed'**) to still; to soothe; to subdue. [OFr *acoyer*, from *à* to, and *coi* quiet, from L *quiētus*; see **coy**]

accoyld see **accoil**.

accredit /a-kred'it/ *vt* to bring into credit, show to be true or correct; to accept as true; to provide with or send with credentials; to certify as meeting official requirements; to attribute (to); to ascribe to (*with* the thing attributed); to accept (a student) for university entrance on the basis of work done in school as opposed to an examination (*NZ*). [Fr *accréditer*, from *à* to, and *crédit* credit]

■ **accredita'tion** *n*. **accred'ited** *adj* provided with credentials; certified officially; accepted as valid; (of livestock) certified free from a particular disease, eg brucellosis.

accrescent /a-kres'ant/ *adj* growing; ever-increasing; enlarged and persistent (*bot*). [L *accrēscere, accrētum*, from *ad* to, and *crēscere* to grow]

■ **accresc'ence** *n*. **accrète'** *vi* to grow together; to become attached. ♦ *vt* to unite; to form or gather round itself. **accrē'tion** *n* continued growth, *esp* as a result of a gradual accumulation of layers; the growing together of parts that are usually separate; something which has grown in such a way; an extraneous addition. **accrē'tive** *adj*.

❑ **accretion disc** *n* (*astron*) a flat disc formed by matter in orbit around a celestial body.

accrue (or *Spenser* **accrew**) /a-kroo'/ *vi* to come as a natural result or development of something, or as an addition or product; to fall (to someone) by way of advantage; to fall due; to increase (*Spenser*). ♦ *vt* (*Spenser*) to accumulate. [OFr *acrewe* what grows up to the profit of the owner, from *acreistre*, from L *accrēscere*]

■ **accru'al** *n*.

acct *abbrev* : account.

accubation /ak-ū-bā'shan/ *n* a lying or reclining on a couch. [L *ad* to, and *cubāre* to lie down]

acculturation /a-kul-cha-rā'shan/ *n* the process or result of assimilating, through continuous contact, features (such as customs, beliefs, etc) of another culture. [L *ad* to, and **culture**]

■ **accul'tural** *adj*. **accul'turate** *vt* and *vi*.

accumbent /a-kum'bant/ *adj* lying down or reclining on a couch; having the radicle lying along the edges of the cotyledons (*bot*). [L *ad* to, and *cumbere* to lie]

■ **accumb'ency** *n*.

accumulate /a-kū'mū-lāt/ or -*mya*-/ *vt* to heap or pile up; to amass. ♦ *vi* to increase greatly; to go on increasing; to take university, etc degrees by accumulation, ie to take a higher degree at the same time as a lower, or at a shorter interval than usual (also *vt*). ♦ *adj* heaped up; amassed. [L *ad* to, and *cumulus* a heap]

■ **accūmūlā'tion** *n* heaping up; a heap or mass. **accum'ūlative** *adj* heaping up or growing by progressive addition; cumulative; tending to accumulate, acquisitive. **accum'ulatively** *adv*. **accum'ulativeness** *n*. **accum'ūlātor** *n* a thing or person that accumulates; a means of storing energy, *esp* an electric battery that can be recharged by sending a reverse current through it; in a computer, etc, a device that performs arithmetical operations and stores the results; (also **accumulator bet**) a bet on at least two, and *usu* four or more, races with the original stake and winnings from each race being, by previous arrangement, laid on the next race, so that the gambler either wins a large amount or loses all.

accurate /ak'ū-rat/ or -*ya*-/ *adj* exact; done carefully and precisely; lacking errors. [L *accūrātus* performed with care, from *ad* to, and *cūra* care]

■ **acc'ūracy** /-a-si/ *n* correctness; exactness. **acc'ūrately** *adv*. **acc'ūrateness** *n*.

accurse /a-kûrs'/ *vt* to curse; to condemn to misery or destruction. [OE pfx *ā*-, and *cursian* to curse]

■ **accurs'ed** (or /-kûrst'/) or (*poetic*) **accurst'** *adj* subjected to a curse; doomed; worthy of a curse, hated. **accur'sedly** *adv*. **accur'sedness** *n*.

accus. *abbrev* : accusative (also **acc.**).

accuse /a-kūz'/ *vt* to bring a charge against (with *of*). ♦ *n* (*Shakesp*) accusation. [L *accūsāre, -ātum*, from *ad* to, and *causa* cause, partly through OFr *accuser*.]

■ **accūs'able** *adj*. **accūs'al** *n* accusation. **accūsā'tion** *n* the act of accusing; a charge brought. **accūsati'val** *adj*. **accūs'ative** *adj* accusing; in or belonging to a grammatical case which expresses the direct object of transitive verbs, primarily expressing destination or the goal of motion. ♦ *n* (*grammar*) the accusative case; a word in the accusative case. **accus'atively** *adv*. **accūsatō'rial** *adj* of an accuser; denoting a judicial procedure in which the judge is not the same person as the prosecutor. **accūs'atory** *adj* containing accusation. **accused'** *n* (*sing* or *pl*) the person or persons accused (also *adj*). **accuse'ment** *n* (*Spenser*) a charge. **accūs'er** *n*. **accus'ing** *adj*. **accus'ingly** *adv*.

accustom /a-kus'tam/ *vt* to make familiar by custom (with *to*); to habituate. [OFr *acostumer* (Fr *accoutumer*), from *à* to, and *costum* or *coustume*; see **custom**]

■ **accus'tomary** *adj*. **accus'tomed** *adj* usual; frequent; habituated; in the habit. **accus'tomedness** *n*.

accustrement see under **accoutre**.

AC/DC /ā'sē-dē'sē/ *abbrev* : (*elec*) alternating current/direct current. ♦ *adj* (*sl*) bisexual.

ACE /ās/ *abbrev* : Advisory Centre for Education; Allied Command Europe; angiotensin converting enzyme; Architects' Council of Europe; Arts Council England; Association for the Conservation of Energy.

❑ **ACE inhibitor** *n* a substance that interferes with the production of angiotensin converting enzyme, used to treat high blood pressure, kidney disease, etc.

ace /ās/ *n* a unit; the one in dice, cards, dominoes, etc; a single point; a winning serve, *esp* one which the opponent fails to touch (*tennis*); a hole in one (see under **hole**[1]; *golf*); a jot; a person of the highest character (*Burns*); a person of distinguished achievement, an expert (*orig* an airman) (*inf*). ♦ *adj* (*inf*) of highest quality; outstanding. ♦ *vt* to serve an ace against (an opponent) (*tennis*); to play (a hole) in one stroke (*golf*); to pass (an examination) with the highest available mark (*US inf*). [Fr *as*, from L *as* unity, from *as* Tarentine Doric form of Gr *heis* one]

■ **an ace up one's sleeve** or **an ace in the hole** a decisive but hidden advantage. **hold all the aces** to have all the advantages, be in a winning position. **play one's ace** to use one's best weapon, resource, etc. **within an ace of** within a hair's-breadth of.

-acea /-ā-sē-a/ *n pl sfx* used in names of zoological divisions, *esp* orders or classes.

-aceae /-ā-sē-ē/ *n pl sfx* used in names of plant families.

■ words derived from main entry word; ❑ compound words; ■ idioms and phrasal verbs

acedia /ə-sē'di-ə/ n listlessness; torpor; sloth. [Gr akēdiā, akēdeia, from a- (privative), and kēdos care. See **accidie**]

acellular /ā-sel'ū-lər or -yə-lər/ (biol) adj not containing cells; not made up of cells. [Gr a- (privative), and **cell**]

acentric /ā-sen'trik/ adj lacking a centre. [Gr a- (privative), and kentron centre]

-aceous /-ā-shəs/ sfx relating or related to, resembling, etc.

acephalous /a-, ā- or ə-sef'ə-ləs/ adj headless; without a ruler, leader, etc (fig); lacking a syllable or syllables in the first foot (prosody). [Gr akephalos, from a- (privative), and kephalē head]

ACER /ā'sər/ abbrev : Australian Council for Educational Research.

acer /ā'sər or ā'kər/ n a plant of the maple genus Acer, which gives its name to the family **Acerā'ceae** /as-/. [L acer maple]
■ **acerā'ceous** adj.

acerate same as **acerose**.

acerb /a-sûrb'/ or **acerbic** /ə-sûr'bik/ adj bitter and sour. [L acerbus]
■ **acerbate** /as'ər-bāt/ vt to embitter; to irritate. **acerb'ically** adv. **acerb'ity** n.

acerose /as'ə-rōs/ adj chaffy (obs); needle-pointed (bot). [L acerosus, from acus, -eris chaff, confused with acus, -ūs needle, or acer sharp]

acerous /ə-sē'rəs/ adj without horns, antennae or tentacles. [Gr a- (privative), and keras horn]

acervate /ə-sûr'vāt/ adj heaped. [L acervāre, -ātum to heap]
■ **acer'vately** adv. **acervā'tion** n.

acescence /ə-ses'əns/ or **acescency** /-ən-si/ n souring; turning (of milk). [L acēscere to sour, from acēre to be sour]
■ **acesc'ent** adj.

acesulfame K /a-si-sul'fām kā/ n an artificial sweetener, 130 times sweeter than sugar. [K for potassium, and sulfamic acid]

acet- or **aceto-** /a-sit- or -set-, ə- or a-se-tō- or -sē- or -si-/ combining form denoting vinegar; acetic acid. [L acētum vinegar]
■ **ac'etal** n a liquid formed by oxidation of alcohol, etc; any of a class of compounds of which this is the type. **acetal'dehyde** n a liquid of characteristic smell, acetic aldehyde. **acet'amide** n the amide of acetic acid. **acē'taminophen** (or /-min'/) n the US name for **paracetamol**. **ac'etate** n an ester of acetic acid; short form of **acetate rayon** an artificial fibre made from cellulose acetate; a (piece of) transparent film on which information, diagrams, etc may be written for display by overhead projector, etc (**acetate film** film of low flammability, whose photographic emulsion is coated on cellulose acetate (also called **non-flam film**, **safety film**)). **acetic** /-sēt' or -set'/ adj of, of the nature of or producing **acetic acid**, CH₃COOH (also known as ethanoic acid), or its diluted form, vinegar. **acetificā'tion** /-set-/ n. **acet'ify** vt and vi to turn into vinegar. **ac'etone** n the simplest of the ketones; any ketone. **acē'etose** adj acetous. **acē'tous** adj like or producing vinegar; sour. **acetyl** /as'i-til, -tīl or a-sē'/ n the radical (CH₃CO) of acetic acid (**acetyl-salicylic acid** aspirin). **acetylcholine** /-kō'lēn (also -ko', -lēn or -lin)/ n a substance secreted at the ends of nerve fibres when they activate muscles. **acetylcholinesterase** /-es'tər-ās/ n an enzyme that breaks down acetylcholine, thought to be a factor in Alzheimer's disease. **acetylene** /-set'/ n a gas (C₂H₂), produced from calcium carbide and water, used in welding, synthesizing acetic acid, illumination, etc (also **ethyne**). **acetylen'ic** /-len' or -lēn'/ adj.

acetabulum /a-si-tab'ū-ləm or -sē-/ (zool) n (pl **acetab'ūla**) the hollow that receives the head of the thigh bone; one of the cotyledons of the placenta of ruminants; the cavity that receives a leg in the body of insects; (in various invertebrates) a sucker. [L acētabulum a vinegar cup]
■ **acetab'ūlar** adj.

acetate, **acetic**, etc, **acetone**, **acetyl**, **acetylene** see under **acet-**.

ACGB abbrev : Arts Council of Great Britain (now replaced by **ACE**, **ACW** and **SAC**).

ACGI abbrev : Associate of the City and Guilds Institute.

ach interj same as **och**.

Achaean /ə-kē'ən/ or **Achaian** /-kī' or -kā'/ adj belonging to Achāiā in the Peloponnese, or to Greece generally (also n).

achaenium, etc see **achene**.

achar /ə-chär'/ n a spicy pickle made primarily from mango, used in Indian cooking. [Hindi acar, from Persian]

acharné /a-shär-nā'/ (Fr) adj (esp of battles) furious or desperate.
■ **avec acharnement** /a-vek a-shär-nə-mā/ obstinately, furiously, rancorously or with gusto.

acharya /ä-chär'yə/ n a Hindu teacher or learned man. [Hindustani āchārya, from Sans]

Achates /ə-kā'tēz/ n an intimate and trusty comrade. [From Aeneas's friend in Virgil's Aeneid]

■ **fidus Achates** /fē'dəs/ (L, faithful Achates) a close and reliable friend.

achates /ə-chāts'/ (Spenser) same as **acates**.

ache¹ /āk/ n a persistent, dull pain. ◆ vi to be in or be the site of persistent, dull pain; to long (for). [The verb was properly ake, the noun ache, as in speak and speech, from OE acan (verb) and æce (noun)]
■ **ach'age** n (Tennyson). **ach'ing** n and adj. **ach'ingly** adv. **ach'y** adj.

ache² /āch/ (Shakesp) same as **aitch**.

achene /ə-kēn'/, **achaenium** or **achenium** /ə-kē'ni-əm/ n a dry, indehiscent, one-seeded fruit, formed of one carpel, the seed separate from the fruit wall, as in the buttercup. [From Gr a- (privative), and chainein to gape]
■ **achae'nocarp** n any dry, indehiscent fruit, esp an achene. **achē'nial** adj.

Achernar /ā'kər-när/ n a first-magnitude star in the constellation Eridanus. [Ar ākhir al nahr end of the river (Eridanus)]

Acheron /ak'ə-ron/ (Gr myth) n one of the rivers of Hades. [Gr Acherōn]
■ **Acheron'tic** adj gloomy, dark or forbidding.
□ **Acherontis pabulum** n (L) (of a bad person) food for Acheron.

Acheulean or **Acheulian** /ə-shoo'li-ən/ adj belonging to an early Palaeolithic culture above the Chellean and below the Mousterian. [Saint Acheul near Amiens, France, where implements of this period are found in river deposits]

à cheval /a shə-val'/ (Fr) adv (of a bet) laid on two adjacent numbers or cards. [Literally, on horseback]

achieve (obs **atchieve**) /ə-chēv'/ vt to bring to a successful outcome; to perform; to accomplish; to win; to end (obs). [Fr achever, from à chief (venir), from LL ad caput to a head; see **chief** and **hatchment**]
■ **achieve'able** adj. **achieve'ment** n achieving; something achieved; an exploit; an escutcheon or armorial shield granted in memory of some achievement (heraldry); escutcheon, armour, etc, hung over a tomb; a hatchment. **achiev'er** n.
□ **achievement age** n the level of an individual's educational achievement as determined by comparing his or her score in a test with the average score of others of the same age. **achievement quotient** n ratio of achievement age to chronological age (usu × 10; abbrev **AQ**).

achillea /a-kil'i-ə/ n a plant of the yarrow genus Achillea of perennial plants (family Compositae). [L achillea, achilleos, from Gr achilleios, from Achilleus Achilles]

Achillean /ak-i-lē'ən/ adj like Achilles, the great Greek hero in the Trojan war, invulnerable except in the heel, by which his mother held him when she dipped him in the river Styx.
□ **Achilles' heel** or **heel of Achilles** n a person's weak or most vulnerable point. **Achilles' tendon** n the attachment of the soleus and gastrocnemius muscles of the calf of the leg to the heel-bone.

achimenes /a-kim'ən-ēz or -ki-men'/ n (pl **achimenes**) a plant of the genus Achimenes of herbaceous perennial plants (family Gesneriaceae) of tropical S America. [L]

Achitophel or **Ahithophel** /ə-kit'ō-fel or -hit'/ n a cautious person (Shakesp); (after Dryden's application to Shaftesbury) an able but unprincipled counsellor. [From King David's counsellor who abetted the rebellion of Absalom]

achkan /äch'kən/ n a knee-length coat with a high collar, buttoned all the way down, worn by men in India. [Hindustani ackan]

achlamydeous /ak-lə-mid'i-əs/ (bot) adj without perianth. [Gr a- (privative), and chlamys, -ydos a mantle]

achondroplasia /ā- or a-kon-drō-plā'zhi-ə or -zi-ə/ n dwarfism characterized by shortness of the arms and legs. [Gr a- (privative), chondros cartilage, and plassein to make]
■ **achondroplastic** /-plas'tik/ adj.

achromatic /ak-rō-mat'ik/ adj (of a lens) transmitting light without much chromatic aberration; without colour. [Gr a- (privative), and chrōma, -atos colour]
■ **a'chromat** n an achromatic lens. **achromat'ically** adv. **achromatic'ity** n. **achrō'matin** n the part of a cell nucleus that does not stain with basic dyes. **achrō'matism** n the state of being achromatic. **achromatiza'tion** or **-s-** n. **achrō'matize** or **-ise** vt to make achromatic. **achromatopsia** /ə-krō-mə-top'si-ə/ n (Gr ops eye) total colour blindness. **achrō'matous** adj having little or no colour.

Achtung /ahh'tŭng/ (Ger) interj look out!

achy see under **ache**¹.

ACIB abbrev : Associate of the Chartered Institute of Bankers.

---

aciclovir see under **acyclic**.

acicular /a-sik'ū-lər/ adj needle-shaped; slender and sharp-pointed. [L acicula, dimin of acus a needle]
■ **acic'ulate** or **acic'ulated** adj marked as if with needle-scratches.

acid /as'id/ n a substance with a sour taste; any of a class of substances which turn vegetable blues (eg litmus) red, and combine with bases, certain metals, etc, to form salts (chem); any of a class of substances that dissolve in water with the formation of hydrogen ions (chem); any of a class of substances that can transfer a proton to another substance, etc (chem); something harsh, biting, or sarcastic (fig); LSD (sl); short form of **acid house** (see below). ◆ adj relating to, of the nature of, or having the properties of an acid (chem); sharp; sour; (of soil) having an acid reaction; biting, keen (fig); ill-natured, morose (fig); containing a large proportion of silica (geol); relating to acid house. [L acidus sour, from acēre to be sour]
■ **acid'ic** adj. **acid'ically** adv. **acidifi'able** adj. **acidifica'tion** n. **acid'ifier** n. **acid'ify** vt to make acid; to convert into an acid. ◆ vi to become acid. **acidim'eter** n an apparatus for performing acidimetry. **acidim'etry** n measurement of the concentration of acids by titration with a standard solution of alkali. **acid'ity** n the quality of being acid or sour; the extent to which a solution is acid (see **pH**). **ac'idly** adv. **ac'idness** n. **acid'ophil** n an acidophilic cell. **acidophilic** /-fil'ik/ adj (of a cell) easily stained with acid dyes; (of micro-organisms or plants) flourishing in an acidic environment. **acidō'sis** n (med) the presence of acids in the blood beyond normal limits. **acid'ūlate** vt to make slightly acid. **acid'ūlous** or **acid'ūlent** adj slightly sour; subacid; (of eg mineral waters) containing carbonic acid; caustic or sharp (fig). **ac'idy** adj resembling acid; sharp, bitter.
❑ **acid drop** n a sweet flavoured with tartaric acid. **acid dye** n a dyestuff with acid properties. **acid freak** or **ac'id-head** n (drug sl) a person who takes LSD habitually. **acid house** n (sometimes with caps) a youth movement originating in the 1980s, involving large gatherings of people to dance under bright flashing lights to loud repetitive music featuring complex percussion patterns, and often associated with the use of certain drugs, esp Ecstasy. **acid-house'** adj. **acid jazz** n a form of jazz influenced by acid rock. **acid rain** n rain or other forms of precipitation containing sulphur and nitrogen compounds and other pollutants released by the combustion of fossil fuels in industrial processes. **acid reflux** n the regurgitation of acid from the stomach into the oesophagus. **acid rock** n a type of rock music featuring bizarre electronic and instrumental effects supposedly influenced by, or suggestive of the effects of, hallucinogenic drugs. **acid salt** n a salt in which only part of the replaceable hydrogen is replaced by a metal. **acid soil complex** n (bot) a combination of aluminium and/or manganese toxicity with calcium deficiency which has a detrimental effect on calcicole plants. **acid test** n a test for gold by acid; a searching test (fig).
■ **put the acid on** (inf; Aust and NZ) to pressurize (a person).

acidanthera /a-si-dan'thə-rə/, also a-ki-/ n a plant of the genus Acidanthera of white-flowered plants of NE Africa (family Iridaceae). [Gr akis pointed object, and anthēra (see **anther**)]

acidophilus /a-si-dof'i-ləs/ n a bacterium, Lactobacillus acidophilus, used to counter intestinal imbalance and in making yoghurt. [**acid**, and **-philus** (see under **phil-**)]

acierate /as'i-ə-rāt/ vt to turn into steel. [Fr aciérer, from acier steel, from LL aciārium (ferrum), literally edging (iron), from L aciēs edge]
■ **ac'ierage** n the covering of a metal plate with a film of iron. **acierā'tion** n.

aciform /as'i-förm/ adj needle-shaped. [L acus needle, and **-form**]

ACII abbrev : Associate of the Chartered Insurance Institute.

acinaciform /as-i-nas'i-förm/ (bot) adj scimitar-shaped. [Gr akīnakēs a short sword (a Persian word), and **-form**]

acinus /as'i-nəs/ n (pl **ac'ini**) one of the small fruits that make up an aggregate fruit, like the raspberry; an aggregate fruit; a pip; a racemose gland. [L acinus berry, pip]
■ **acinā'ceous** adj full of pips; berry-like; like a cluster of grapes. **acin'iform** adj berry-like. **ac'inous** or **ac'inose** (or /-ōs'/) adj consisting of acini; like a cluster of berries.

ACIS abbrev : Associate of the Institute of Chartered Secretaries and Administrators (formerly known as the Chartered Institute of Secretaries).

ack-ack /ak'ak'/ adj anti-aircraft. ◆ n anti-aircraft fire. [Formerly military signallers' name for the letters AA]

ackee see **akee**.

ack emma /ak em'ə/ (milit sl) adv ante meridiem, before midday (cf **pip emma**). [Formerly signallers' name for the letters AM]

ackers /ak'ərz/ (sl) n pl money (also **akk'as**). [Origin uncertain]

acknow /ak-nō'/ (obs) vt (pat **acknew'**; pap **acknown'** or **acknowne'**) to recognize; to acknowledge. [OE on in, on, and cnāwan to know]
■ **acknowne'** adj (Shakesp) confessedly cognizant.

acknowledge /ək-nol'ij/ vt to admit a knowledge or awareness of; to admit to or recognize as true, genuine, valid, or one's own; to confess; to express gratitude or thanks; to admit or intimate receipt of. [From **acknow**; see **knowledge**]
■ **acknowl'edgeable** adj capable of being acknowledged or suitable for acknowledgement. **acknowl'edgeably** adv. **acknowl'edgement** (sometimes **acknowl'edgment**) n recognition; admission; confession; thanks; a notification of having received something.

ACL abbrev : anterior cruciate ligament.

aclinic /ə-klin'ik/ adj without inclination or magnetic dip. [Gr aklinēs horizontal, from a- (privative), and klīnein to tilt]
❑ **aclinic line** n the magnetic equator (qv under **magnet**).

ACLU abbrev : American Civil Liberties Union.

ACM abbrev : Air Chief Marshal.

ACMA abbrev : Associate of the Chartered Institute of Management Accountants (formerly known as the Institute of Cost and Management Accountants).

acme /ak'mi/ n the top or highest point; the culmination or perfection in the career of anything; the crisis, eg of a disease (archaic). [Gr akmē, from akē a point]
■ **Ac'meism** n a movement in Russian poetry, active about 1910 to 1917. **Ac'meist** n. **ac'mite** n a soda pyroxene whose crystals often show a steep pyramid.

ACMI abbrev : Associate of the Chartered Management Institute.

acne /ak'ni/ n a skin disease caused by inflammation of the sebaceous follicles, esp on the face, neck, and shoulders. [Perh Gr akmē a point]
■ **ac'ned** adj.
❑ **acne rosacea** /rō-zā'shi-ə/ n (old) a chronic disease of the skin of the nose, cheeks and forehead, characterized by flushing and redness of the skin, pimples and pustules (also called **rosacea**).

ACNI abbrev : Arts Council of Northern Ireland.

acock /ə-kok'/ adv in a cocked manner; defiantly. [**a-**[1] and **cock**[1]]
❑ **acock'-bill** adv (naut) (of an anchor ready for dropping or yards topped up (a sign of mourning)) having the end pointing upward.

acoelomate /ā-sē'lə-māt/ adj without a coelom. ◆ n an acoelomate animal. [Gr a- (privative), and **coelom**]

acoemeti /a-sem'i-tī/ n pl an Eastern order of monks (5–6c), who by alternating choirs kept divine service going on day and night. [Latinized pl of Gr akoimētos sleepless, from a- (privative), and koimaein to put to sleep]

Acol /ak'ol/ n a system of bidding in the game of bridge. [After Acol Road in London, where the system was devised]

acold /ə-kōld'/ (Shakesp) adj chilled. [Prob OE ācōlod pap of ācōlian, from pfx ā- (intens), and cōlian to cool]

acolouthos /a-kə-loo'thos/ (hist) n the head of the Varangian guard of the Byzantine emperors. [Gr akolouthos an attendant, from akoloutheein to follow]
■ **acolou'thic** or **acoluth'ic** adj relating to or associated with an after-image or sensation following upon the immediate effect of a stimulus. **acolou'thite** n (obs) an acolyte.

acolyte /ak'ə-līt/ or (obs) **acolyth** /-lith/ n a faithful follower; an attendant or assistant; a person in minor orders, next below subdeacon (RC church); a junior church officer, esp one who bears a candle in a procession. [Ety as for **acolouthos**]

à compte /a kõt'/ (Fr) on account; in part payment.

aconite /ak'ə-nīt/ n any plant of the ranunculaceous genus Aconitum, esp wolf's-bane or monk's-hood; poison obtained from it, or (poetic) deadly poison in general (often **aconī'tum**). [L aconītum, from Gr akonīton]
■ **aconit'ic** adj. **aconitine** /-kon'-/ n a poisonous alkaloid obtained from aconite.
■ **winter aconite** an early-flowering ranunculaceous plant (Eranthis hyemalis).

à contre coeur /a kõtr' kœr'/ (Fr) reluctantly.

Acorn® /ā'körn/ abbrev : A Classification of Residential Neighbourhoods, a type of socio-economic classification that identifies the area and housing in which people live and can be used for direct mail or market research.

acorn /ā'körn/ n the fruit of the oak. [OE æcern; form influenced by confusion with **corn**[1] and perh **oak** (Scot and N Eng aik, OE āc)]
■ **ā'corned** adj.
❑ **a'corn-cup** n the woody cup-shaped part of an acorn that holds the nut. **a'corn-shell** or **a'corn-barnacle** n a sedentary crustacean of the genus Balanus. **acorn worm** n any of various wormlike sea-animals (enteropneusts) of the Hemichordata which have a proboscis and collar somewhat like an acorn in shape.

à corps perdu /a kor per-dü'/ (Fr) desperately, with might and main.

Acorus /ak'ə-rəs/ n the sweet-flag genus of the arum family. [Latinized from Gr akoros]

acosmism /ə-koz'mi-zm/ n disbelief in the existence of an eternal world, or of a world distinct from God. [Gr a- (privative), and kosmos the world]
■ **acos'mist** n.

acotyledon /ə-kot-i-lē'dən/ n a cryptogam. [Gr a- (privative), and cotyledon]
■ **acotylē'donous** adj.

acouchy or **acouchi** /ə-koo'shē/ n a kind of small S American rodent, an agouti. [Tupí acuchy]

à coup sûr /a koo sür'/ (Fr) to a certainty.

acoustic /ə-koo'stik/ or **acoustical** /-sti-kəl/, (formerly) -kow'/ adj of or relating to the sense of hearing or to the theory of sound; used in hearing, auditory; operated by sound vibrations, eg an acoustic mine; (of musical instruments) not electric, eg an acoustic guitar or piano; (made of material) intended to reduce the disturbance caused by excessive noise. ◆ n (**acoustic**) acoustic properties. [Gr akoustikos, from akouein to hear]
■ **acous'tically** adv. **acoustician** /-ti'shən/ n a person who studies or has studied the science of acoustics; a person who makes or repairs acoustic instruments, etc. **acous'tics** n (sing) the science of sound; (pl) acoustic properties.
❑ **acoustic coupler** n a device which converts electrical pulses to sound (acoustic waves) for transmission and reception along telephone lines to and from a computer, allowing computers to be connected to a terminal via a modem and telephone handset; any device used to convert electrical signals to sound signals or vice versa. **acoustic phonetics** n sing the scientific study of vibrations and air movements made by speech sounds. **acoustic shock** n an injury to the ear caused by a sudden loud noise, esp via a telephone. **acousto-elec'tric** adj of or relating to electroacoustics.

à couvert /a koo-ver'/ (Fr) adj and adv under cover, protected.

ACP abbrev: African, Caribbean and Pacific.

ACPO abbrev: Association of Chief Police Officers (of England, Wales and Northern Ireland).

ACPOS abbrev: Association of Chief Police Officers in Scotland.

acpt. (commerce) abbrev: acceptance.

ACPU abbrev: auxiliary computer power unit.

acquaint /ə-kwānt'/ vt to let know; to inform. ◆ adj (Scot and N Eng) acquainted. [OFr acointer, from LL accognitāre, from L ad to, and cognitus known]
■ **acquaint'ance** n knowledge, esp when falling short of intimacy; a person (or sometimes persons) known slightly. **acquaint'anceship** n slight knowledge. **acquaint'ed** adj (usu with with) personally known to and on at least nodding terms with; having personal knowledge of. ❑ **acquaintance rape** n rape committed by a person known to the victim.
■ **make someone's acquaintance** to meet and become familiar with a person one has not met before.

acquest /ə-kwest'/ n acquisition; a thing acquired. [OFr; see acquire]

acquiesce /a-kwi-es'/ vi to rest satisfied or without making opposition; to assent (with in). [L acquiēscere, from ad to, and quiēs rest]
■ **acquiesc'ence** n quiet assent or submission. **acquiesc'ent** adj acquiescing. ◆ n a person who acquiesces. **acquiesc'ently** or **acquiesc'ingly** adv.

acquight see acquit.

acquire /ə-kwīr'/ vt to gain or get; to attain to, achieve. [L acquīrere, -quīsītum, from ad to, and quaerere to seek]
■ **acquīrabil'ity** n. **acquīr'able** adj that may be acquired. **acquīr'al** n. **acquired'** adj. **acquire'ment** n acquisition; something learned or obtained by effort, not a gift of nature. **acquisition** /ak-wi-zish'ən/ n the act of acquiring; something which is acquired. **acquisitive** /ə-kwiz'/ adj able, desiring or eager to acquire usu possessions. **acquis'itively** adv. **acquis'itiveness** n a desire or propensity to acquire possessions. **acquist** /ə-kwist'/ n acquisition.
❑ **acquired behaviour** or **character** n behaviour or character originating in the adaptation of an organism to its environment, not inherited. **Acquired Immune Deficiency Syndrome** or **Acquired Immunodeficiency Syndrome** see AIDS. **acquired immunity** n (immunol) immunity resulting from exposure to foreign substances or micro-organisms (cf natural immunity). **acquired taste** n a liking for something that comes after some experience; a thing so liked (often ironic). **acquisition accounting** n an accounting procedure in which a company's assets are changed from the book value to the fair market value following a takeover. **acquisitive award** or **prize** n (Aust) a

prize put up by the sponsor of an art competition who in return becomes the owner of the winning entry or entries.
■ **target acquisition** a fighter or bomber pilot's sighting of his target, either visually or by radar.

acquit /ə-kwit'/, (obs) **acquite** or **acquight** /ə-kwīt'/ vt (**acquitt'ing**; **acquitt'ed** or (obs) **acquit'**) to free; to release; to discharge (eg a debt); to discharge (oneself of a duty); hence, to behave or conduct (oneself); to prove (oneself); to release from an accusation. [OFr aquiter, from L ad to, and quiētāre to quiet, settle; see quit]
■ **acquit'ment** n (obs). **acquitt'al** n a judicial discharge from an accusation; performance of a duty. **acquitt'ance** n a discharge from an obligation or debt; a receipt in evidence of such a discharge. ◆ vt (Shakesp) to acquit or clear.

acrasia /ə-krā'zi-ə/ n weakness of will, by which a person acts against usual or expected judgement. [Gr a- (privative), and kratos power]
■ **acratic** /-krat'ik/ adj.

acrawl /ə-kröl'/ adv crawling (with with). [a-1 and crawl1]

ACRE /ā'kər/ abbrev: Advisory Committee on Releases to the Environment, a public body that advises on the effect on health and the environment of the release of genetically modified organisms.

acre /ā'kər/ n a measure of land equivalent to 4840 sq yd (approx 0.4 ha; also Scottish acre 6150.4 sq yd, Irish 7840 sq yd, both obs); (in pl) lands or estates; (in pl) a very large area or amount (inf). [OE æcer field; Ger Acker, L ager, Gr agros, Sans ajra a plain]
■ **acreage** /ā'kər-ij/ n area in acres. **acred** /ā'kərd/ adj landed. ❑ **a'cre-breadth** n (archaic) 22 yards. **acre-foot** n a unit of volume of water equivalent to covering an acre one foot deep, ie 43560 cu ft (approx 1200 cu m). **a'cre-length** n (archaic) 220 yards.

acrid /ak'rid/ adj pungent; (of speech, manner, etc) biting. [L ācer, ācris sharp or keen; noun suffix perh in imitation of acid]
■ **acrid'ity** n. **ac'ridly** adv.

acridine or **acridin** /ak'ri-dēn or -dīn or -din/ n a compound found in coal tar, a parent substance of dyes and antibacterial drugs. [**acrid**, and noun sfx -ine]
■ **acriflavine** /-flā'vēn/ or **acriflavin** /ak-ri-flā'vin/ n (acridine and flavin(e)) an antiseptic.

Acrilan® /ak'ri-lan/ n a type of acrylic fibre (rather like wool).

acrimony /ak'ri-mə-ni/ n bitterness of feeling or language. [L ācrimōnia, from ācer sharp]
■ **acrimō'nious** adj. **acrimō'niously** adv. **acrimō'niousness** n.

acro- /a-krō-/ combining form denoting tip, point or summit. [Gr akron tip, end, and akros highest, outermost]

acroamatic /ak-rō-ə-mat'ik/ or **acroamatical** /-mat'i-kəl/ adj esoteric. [Gr akroāmatikos, from akroāma anything to be listened to, from akroaesthai to listen]

Acrobat® /ak'rə-bat/ (comput) n a computing language for text and graphics, designed for use with different operating systems.

acrobat /ak'rə-bat/ n a performer of gymnastic feats; a person who performs balancing acts on a tightrope; a tumbler. [Gr akrobatēs acrobat, or akrobatos walking on tiptoe, from akron point, and the root of bainein to go]
■ **acrobat'ic** adj. **acrobat'ically** adv. **acrobat'ics** n pl acrobatic performances (often fig). ◆ n sing the art of the acrobat. **ac'robatism** n the art of the acrobat.

acrocentric /ak-rō-sen'trik/ (biol) adj (of chromosomes) having the centromere at the end. ◆ n a rod-shaped chromosome. [Gr akron point, and **centric**]

acrocyanosis /ak-rō-sī-ə-nō'sis/ n a bluish discoloration of the hands and feet resulting from lack of oxygen in the blood. [Gr akron point, and **cyanosis**]

acrogen /ak'rə-jən or -jen/ n a non-flowering plant with the growing-point at the tip, a fern or moss. [Gr akron point, and -genēs born]
■ **acrogen'ic** or **acrogenous** /ə-kroj'i-nəs/ adj. **acrog'enously** adv.

acrolein /ə-krō'lē-in/ (chem) n the aldehyde of allyl alcohol, a pungent-smelling colourless liquid (also **acrylal'dehyde** and **prō'penal**). [L ācer, ācris sharp, and olēre to smell]

acrolith /ak'rō-lith or -rə-/ n a wooden statue with stone extremities. [Gr akrolithos, from akron point, and lithos stone]
■ **acrolith'ic** adj.

acromegaly /ak-rō-meg'ə-li/ n a disease characterized by excessive growth, esp of the face, hands and feet. [Gr akron point, and megas, megalos great]
■ **acromegal'ic** adj suffering from acromegaly.

acromion /ə-krō'mi-on or -ən/ n (pl **acromia**) a process of the spine of the scapula (also **acromion process**). [Gr akros outermost, and ōmos shoulder]
■ **acro'mial** adj.

acronychal, acronycal or (US) **acronical** /ə-kron'i-kəl/ adj (of the rising or setting of stars) occurring at nightfall. [Gr akronychos at nightfall, from akron point, and nychos, -eos night]
■ **acron'ychally** adv.

acronym /ak'rə-nim/ n a word formed from or based on the initial letters or syllables of other words, such as radar. [acro-, and Gr onyma, onoma name]
■ **acronym'ic** or **acron'ymous** adj.

acropetal /ə-krop'i-təl/ (bot) adj in the direction of the tip of the plant. [Gr akron tip, and L petere to seek]
■ **acrop'etally** adv.

acrophobia /ak-rō-fō'bi-ə/ n fear of heights. [Gr akros highest, and phobos fear]

acrophony /ə-krof'ən-i/ n the use of a symbol (derived from an ideogram) to represent the initial sound only of the name of the object for which the ideogram stood. [acro-, and Gr phōnē sound]
■ **acrophonet'ic** or **acrophonic** /-fon'/ adj.

acropolis /ə-krop'ə-lis/ n a citadel, esp that of Athens. [Gr akropolis, from akros highest, and polis a city]

acrosome /ak'rə-sōm/ n a structure containing enzymes, found at the tip of the sperm, associated with the penetration process into the egg cell. [acro- and -some[2]]

acrospire /ak'rō-spīr/ (bot) n the first leaf that sprouts from a germinating seed. [ME akerspire, from OE æhher (see **icker**) ear, and **spire**[1]]

across /ə-kros'/ prep and adv from side to side (of); on or to the other side (of); crosswise. [**a-**[1]]
□ **across'-the-board'** adj (of wage increases, etc) applying in all cases (**across the board** adv). **across'-the-ta'ble** adj (of a discussion, conference, etc) face to face.
■ **come across** to find or meet by chance; to hand over information, a confession, money, etc, in answer to demand or inducement (inf). **get** or **come across** to take effect (on the audience across the footlights, and so generally). **get it across** to make acceptable or to bring to a successful issue; to explain. **put it across (someone)** to deceive (him or her).

acrostic /ə-kros'tik/ n a poem or puzzle in which the first (or last) letters of each line spell a word or sentence; an acronym. [Gr akros extreme, and stichos a line]
■ **acros'tically** adv.

acroterion /ak-rō-tē'ri-on/ (archit) n (pl **acrotē'ria**) a pedestal or ornament at the top or side angle of a pediment (also **acrotē'rium** and **acrō'ter** (or /ak'/)). [Gr akrōtērion extremity, from akros extreme]
■ **acrotē'rial** adj.

acrotism /ak'rə-ti-zm/ (med) n absence of pulsation. [Gr a- (privative), and krotos sound made by striking]

acrylic /ə-kril'ik/ n a synthetic fibre; acrylic resin; a paint containing acrylic resin. ♦ adj of or relating to an acrylic or acrylic resin. [acrolein, and Gr hȳlē matter]
■ **acryl'amide** n a highly toxic amide, $CH_2=CHCONH_2$, which polymerizes while melting and has many industrial uses.
□ **acrylamide gel electrophoresis** (biol) electrophoretic separation of proteins or RNA according to their molecular weight. **acrylic acid** n a very reactive acid belonging to the series of oleic acids, obtainable from acrolein by oxidation. **acrylic resins** n pl thermoplastic resins formed by the polymerization of esters, amides, etc, derived from acrylic acid, and used in making paints, plastics, etc.

acrylonitrile /ak-ri-lō-nī'trīl/ n vinyl cyanide, obtained by polymerization and used in making synthetic fibres for carpets, etc, and synthetic rubbers.

ACS abbrev : active control system; Association for Commonwealth Studies.

ACT abbrev : Australian Capital Territory.

act /akt/ vi to produce an effect, to do something; to behave in a specified way; to perform, eg on the stage; to feign; to exert force or influence; to be suitable for performance. ♦ vt to perform; to imitate or play the part of. ♦ n something done, a deed; an exploit; the process (of doing); a pretence; a decree; a legislative enactment; a written instrument in verification; a short prayer (RC); a distinct main section of a play, opera, etc; an individual performance or turn such as in a variety show; the person or people performing this; a public disputation or lecture maintained for a degree (archaic). [L āctus, -ūs an action, doing, āctum a thing done, and āctor a doer or actor; agere, āctum to drive or drive]

■ **actabil'ity** n. **act'able** adj. **act'ant** n (grammar) a noun phrase functioning as the agent of the verb. **act'ing** n action; the act or art of performing an assumed or a dramatic part; feigning. ♦ adj performing some duty temporarily, or for another. **act'or, fem act'ress** n a person who acts on the stage, in films, etc. **act'orish, act'orly** or (fem) **act'ressy** adj affectedly theatrical. **act'ure** n (Shakesp) action or performance.
□ **act curtain** or **act drop** n a curtain for closing the proscenium arch between acts or scenes. **act of contrition** n (RC) a prayer expressing penitence. **act of God** n a result of natural forces, unexpected and not preventable by human foresight. **act of grace** n a favour, esp a pardon granted by a sovereign. **act of parliament** see under **parliament**.
■ **act as** to perform the duties of. **act for** to substitute for; to represent legally or contractually. **act on** to exert an influence on; to act in accordance with. **act out** to play as an actor; to express in behaviour (one's fears, etc). **act up** (inf) to behave badly; (of a machine) to malfunction. **act up to** to come in practice up to the standard of; to fulfil. **catch someone in the act** to come upon someone in the process of doing something they should not be doing. **clean up one's act** (inf) to regulate one's activities, put one's affairs in good or proper order. **get in on** or **get into the act** (inf) to start participating in something apparently profitable already taking place in order to share in the benefits. **get one's act together** (inf) to get oneself organized. **hard act to follow** (inf) an outstanding person, or something outstanding another person has done, regarded as difficult to equal. **put on an act** to make a pretence; to show off.

act. abbrev : acting; active.

acta /ak'tə/ n pl official minutes of proceedings; official proceedings or acts. [L, records]
□ **acta sanctorum** /ak'ta sangk-tō'rəm, -tō' or -rūm/ n pl (L) deeds of the saints.

Actaeon /ak-tē'ən/ n a hunter transformed into a stag by Artemis; hence someone with horns implanted upon him, a cuckold. ♦ vt to cuckold. [L Actaeōn, from Gr Aktaiōn]

acte gratuit /akt gra-twē'/ (Fr) an impulsive act lacking motive.

actg abbrev : acting.

ACTH abbrev : adrenocorticotrophic hormone, a hormone secreted by the pituitary gland which stimulates the adrenal cortex; also produced synthetically and used as a treatment eg for rheumatoid arthritis and skin diseases.

actin /ak'tin/ n a protein found in muscle, active in muscular contraction. [act]

actin- or **actino-** /ak-tin or ak-ti-no/ combining form denoting a ray. [Gr aktīs, aktīnos ray]
■ **actinal** /ak-tī'nəl or ak'ti-nəl/ adj belonging to the radiating bands on the body of an echinoderm where the tube-like feet are, or to the region of the mouth and tentacles in Anthozoa. **actī'nally** (or /ak'/) adv. **actinia** /-tin'/ n (pl **actin'iae** or **actin'ias**) a sea-anemone (properly, of the genus Actinia). **actin'ian** n and adj. **actin'ic** adj of or showing actinism (**actinic glass** glass that impedes actinic rays; **actinic rays** those rays (esp ultraviolet) that have a marked chemical action). **actin'ically** adv. **ac'tinide** or **ac'tinoid** n a member of the **actinide series**, a group of radioactive metallic elements from atomic number 89 (actinium) to 103. **ac'tinism** n the chemical action of radiant energy. **actin'ium** n a radioactive metallic element (symbol **Ac**; atomic no 89) found in pitchblende. **actinobacillus** /-bə-sil'əs/ n (pl **actinobacill'i**) a bacillus of the genus of bacteria Actinobacillus, one of which causes **actinobacillō'sis**, woody-tongue (qv). **actin'olite** n (Gr lithos a stone) a green amphibole. **actinom'eter** n an instrument for measuring the heat-intensity or the actinic effect of light rays. **actinomor'phic** adj (Gr morphē form; biol) radially symmetrical. **actinomor'phy** n. **Actinomyces** /-mī'sēz/ n (Gr mykēs fungus) the ray fungus, a genus of minute fungi, often pathogenic, with radiating mycelium. **actinomycosis** /-kō'sis/ n lumpy jaw in cattle, etc, and a chronic infection in man, caused by different species of Actinomyces. **ac'tinon** n actinium emanation, an isotope of radon. **actinother'apy** n the treatment of disease by exposure to rays, esp ultraviolet rays. **Actinozo'a** n pl a former name for the Anthozoa.

action /ak'shən/ n acting; activity; behaviour; a deed; an operation; a gesture; fighting; a battle; a lawsuit, or proceedings in a court; a mode of moving the legs; the movement of events in a drama, novel, etc; the mechanism, esp of a keyboard instrument. ♦ vt to carry out or put into effect. ♦ interj an instruction from a film director to begin a scene. [Fr, from L āctiō, -ōnis]

■ **ac'tionable** adj giving ground for a lawsuit. **ac'tionably** adv. **ac'tioner** n (sl) a film or story which has plenty of action. **ac'tionist** n an activist.
□ **action committee** or **group** n members of an organization who are chosen to take active measures. **action figure** n a toy consisting of a small model of a character from a film, television programme,

comic, etc. **ac'tion-packed** adj full of exciting activity. **action painting** n an American version of tachism in which paint is dripped, spattered, smeared, etc onto the canvas. **action plan** or **sheet** n a written plan detailing the various stages of a project and the length of time each will take. **action point** n an agreed point of action or procedure. **action potential** n (med) the voltage pulse(s), produced in a nerve by a stimulus or stimuli, which when rapidly repeated can lead in motor nerves to continuous muscular response. **action radius** n the distance a ship or aircraft can go without running out of fuel before reaching its base or starting-point again. **action replay** n on television, the repeating of a piece of film, eg the scoring of a goal in football, usu in slow motion. **action spectrum** n (bot) the relationship between the rate of a light-dependent physiological process (eg photosynthesis) and the wavelength of light. **action stations** n pl posts to be manned during or preparatory to battle (often fig). **ac'tion-taking** n (Shakesp) resorting to law instead of resorting to fighting. ■ **a piece of the action** (inf) participation in an enterprise, etc, often including a share in the profits. **industrial action** see under **industry**. **out of action** not working; temporarily unfit to participate.

active /ak'tiv/ adj acting; in actual operation; given to action; brisk; busy; nimble; practical, opp to speculative; effective; (of a volcano) liable to erupt, not extinct; (of bacteria, etc) potent; radioactive; of that voice in which the subject of the verb represents the doer of the action (grammar). ◆ n (grammar) the active voice or an active construction. [L āctīvus]
■ **ac'tivate** vt to make active; to increase the energy of; to increase the capacity for adsorption in (carbon); to increase the biological activity of (sewage, etc) by aeration; to stimulate; to make radioactive. **activā'tion** n. **ac'tivātor** n a person or thing, substance, etc that activates. **ac'tively** adv. **ac'tiveness** n. **ac'tivism** n a policy of direct, vigorous and sometimes militant action; a philosophy of creative will, esp the practical idealism of Rudolf Eucken (1846–1926). **ac'tivist** n a person who supports a policy of vigorous action; a person who plays a special part in advancing a project or in strengthening the hold of political ideas; a believer in the philosophy of activism. **activ'ity** n quality, state, or fact of being active; occupation, esp recreational pursuit; a training exercise designed to teach through practical experiment, research, and discussion; (esp in pl) doings; the rate at which atoms of a radioactive substance disintegrate per unit of time. ❏ **activated charcoal** n charcoal treated eg with acid to increase its adsorptive power. **active birth** n childbirth in which the mother chooses her own position and has a greater than usual freedom of movement. **active control system** n (aeronautics) an advanced automatic flight control system, integrating aerodynamics, structure and electronic design. **active immunity** n immunity due to the making of antibodies within the organism. **active life** n life, esp within a religious order, devoted to good works as opposed to contemplation. **active list** n a list of full-pay officers engaged in or available for military service. **active matrix** n a liquid crystal display system in which each pixel is controlled individually, giving a high colour resolution. **active service** n service in the battle area, or (orig US) in the army, navy or air force even in time of peace. **activity holiday** n a holiday offering participation (and usu training or coaching) in a particular occupation, esp sport.

ActiveX® /ak'ti-veks'/ (comput) n a set of software controls enabling the use of Java applets in an Internet browser.

acton /ak'tən/ n a stuffed jacket worn under a coat of mail (also **hacqueton** or **haqueton**). [OFr auqueton, from Sp, from Ar al qūtun the cotton]

actor, **actress** see under **act**.

ACTS /akts/ abbrev : Action of Churches Together in Scotland.

ACTU abbrev : Australian Council of Trade Unions.

actual /ak'tū-əl or ak'chū-əl/ adj real; existing in fact; at the time being or current; of the nature of an action (Shakesp). [Fr actuel, from LL āctuālis]
■ **ac'tualist** n a person who deals with or considers actual facts. **actualité** /ak-tü-al'ē-tā/ n (joc) the truth. **actuality** /-al'i-ti/ n the fact or state of being actual; realism; something that really exists; a newsreel or current affairs programme (also **actualités** /ak-tü-al-ē-tā/; Fr). **actuali'zā'tion** or **-s-** n. **ac'tualize** or **-ise** vt to make actual; to realize in action. **ac'tually** adv as a matter of fact; truly, however little one might expect it; really, in fact.
❏ **actual bodily harm** n (law) minor injuries inflicted during an attack, considered less serious than grievous bodily harm.
■ **in actual fact** actually.

actuary /ak'tū-ə-ri/ n a registrar or clerk (mainly hist; still in the Convocation of Canterbury); a person whose profession is to assess financial and business problems, esp insurance risks, and to calculate premiums using mathematical and statistical techniques. [L āctuārius (scriba) an amanuensis or a clerk]
■ **actuarial** /-ā'ri-əl/ adj. **actuā'rially** adv.

actuate /ak'tū-āt or ak'choo-āt/ vt to put into, or incite to, action. ◆ vi to act. [L āctus action; see **act**]
■ **actuā'tion** n. **ac'tūātor** n.

acture see under **act**.

actus reus /ak'təs rē'əs or ak'tūs rā'ŭs/ (law) n (pl **actus** /-toos/ **rei** /-ī or -ē/) the act which is necessary for the crime to be constituted. [Mod L, guilty act]

ACU abbrev : Association of Commonwealth Universities.

acuity /ə-kū'i-ti/ n sharpness (eg of mind, vision, etc). [LL acuitās, -ātis, from L acus needle]

aculeate /ə-kū'li-āt or -ət/ adj (also **acū'leated**) pointed; prickly; having a sting; stinging. ◆ n a stinging insect. [L aculeātus, from aculeus a sting or goad, dimin of acus needle]
■ **acu'leus** n a thorn or prickle (bot); a sting (zool); an ovipositor (zool).

acumen /ak'ū-mən or ə-kū'men/ n sharpness; quickness of perception; penetration. [L acūmen, -inis a point]
■ **acū'minate** vt to sharpen; to give a point to. ◆ vi (rare) to taper. ◆ adj (bot) tapering in long hollow curves to a point (also **acū'minated**). **acūminā'tion** n. **acu'minous** adj.

acupressure /ak'ū-presh-ər/ n the arrest of a haemorrhage by a needle pressing across the artery; in acupuncture or related treatments, pressure (as opposed to a needle) applied to an acupoint. [L acus needle, and **pressure**]

acupuncture /ak'ū-pungk-chər/ n the complementary therapy (traditional Chinese and medical) of puncturing the skin with needles at specified points (**ac'upoints**) in order to cure illness, relieve symptoms, or effect anaesthesia. [L acus needle, and **puncture**]
■ **ac'upuncturist** n.

acushla /ə-koosh'lə/ (Anglo-Irish) n darling. [Ir a chuisle, vocative of cuisle vein]

acute /ə-kūt/ adj sharp; sharp-pointed; ending in an acute angle (bot); keen; mentally penetrating; piercing; finely discriminating; keenly perceptive; shrewd; urgently pressing; (of a disease) coming to a crisis, opp to chronic. ◆ n an acute accent. [L acūtus, pap of acuere to sharpen]
■ **acut'ance** n a physical measure of the sharpness of a photographic image. **acute'ly** adv. **acute'ness** n.
❏ **acute accent** n a mark (´) over a letter in ancient Greek indicating a rising pitch, now used for various purposes in indicating pronunciation in various languages. **acute angle** n an angle of less than 90°. **acute rheumatism** n rheumatic fever.

ACW abbrev : aircraft(s)woman; Arts Council of Wales.

acyclic /ā- or ə- or a-sī'klik, also -sik'lik/ adj not periodic; not whorled (bot); with open-chain structure, aliphatic (chem). [Gr a- (privative), and kyklos a wheel]
■ **aci'clovir** (formerly **acy'clovir**) /-klō-vīr/ n a drug used in the treatment of forms of herpes and of HIV.

acyl /ā'sil or as'il/ (chem) n and adj (denoting) the carboxylic acid RCO–. [acid and -yl]

AD abbrev : active duty (milit); air defence; Alzheimer's Disease; anno domini (L), in the year of the Lord, now used in numbering the years since Christ was thought to have been born (also **A.D.**); Dame of the Order of Australia, discontinued in 1986.

ad /ad/ (inf) n an advertisement. [Short form]
❏ **ad'ware** n computer software that is bundled with another program and displays advertising while the other program is running.

ad abbrev : after date; ante diem (L), before the day.

ad. /ad/ (tennis, N Am) abbrev : advantage.

-ad[1] /-ad/ (biol) combining form denoting towards, as in caudad (towards the tail) or cephalad (towards the head). [L ad to or towards]

-ad[2] /-ad/ sfx used in (1) names for nymphs, etc (naiad, dryad or hamadryad); (2) titles of epic poems, etc (Iliad or Dunciad); (3) words for numerical groups (triad, decad(e), myriad or Olympiad). [Gr -as, -ados]

ADA or **Ada** /ā'də/ n a computer-programming language orig devised for military use, one of its applications being simultaneous control of diverse operations. [Named after Ada Lovelace (1816–52), daughter of Byron and assistant to C Babbage]

ADA abbrev : adenosine deaminase.

ad absurdum see **reductio ad absurdum**.

adactylous /ā-dak'ti-ləs/ adj without fingers or toes. [Gr a- (privative), and daktylos a finger]

adage /ad'ij/ n an old saying; a proverb. [Fr, from L adagium, from ad to, and root of āiō I say]

adagio /ə-dä'j(y)ō or -ji-ō/ (*music*) *adv* slowly. ◆ *adj* slow. ◆ *n* (*pl* **ada'gios**) a slow movement; a piece in adagio time. [Ital, from *ad agio* at ease]

Adam /ad'əm/ *n* the first man, according to the Book of Genesis; unregenerate human nature; a gaoler (*perh* as wearing buff) (*Shakesp*). ◆ *adj* applied to an 18c style of architecture, interior decoration and furniture designed by Robert and James *Adam*. [Heb *Adām*]
■ **Adamic** or **Adamical** /ə-dam'ik, -əl/ *adj* of or like Adam; naked. **Ad'amite** *n* a descendant of Adam; a person who goes about naked, *esp* a member of a 2c sect in N Africa. **Adamit'ic** or **Adamit'ical** *adj*. **Ad'amitism** *n*.
❑ **Adam's ale** or **wine** *n* water. **Adam's apple** *n* the projection of the thyroid cartilage in front of the throat, traditionally supposed to be part of the forbidden fruit stuck in Adam's throat; forbidden fruit (see **forbid**). **Adam's flannel** *n* mullein. **Adam's needle** *n* a species of *Yucca*.
■ **Adam and Eve** (*Cockney rhyming sl*) to believe. **not know someone from Adam** (*inf*) not to know someone, or who someone is.

adamant /ad'ə-mənt or -mant/ *n* a name applied by the ancients to various hard substances, eg steel; an imaginary rock with fabulous properties; diamond (*obs*); lodestone (*obs*). ◆ *adj* unyielding. [Gr *adamas, -antos*, prob orig steel, also diamond, from *a-* (privative), and *damaein* to tame or overcome]
■ **adamantē'an** *adj* (*Milton*) hard as adamant. **adaman'tine** *adj* unbreakable; impregnable; impenetrable; magnetically attractive (*obs*). **ad'amantly** *adv*.
❑ **adamantine lustre** *n* (*mineralogy*) a lustre similar to the metallic but without opacity.

Adamite, etc see under **Adam**.

Adansonia /a-dən-sō'ni-ə/ *n* the baobab genus. [Michel *Adanson* (1727–1806), French botanist]

ad aperturam libri /ad ap-er-tū'ram lib'rī or -tū'am lib'rē/ (*L*) as the book opens.

adapt /ə-dapt'/ *vt* to make fit or suitable; to modify; to adjust. ◆ *vi* to adjust to new conditions. [Fr *adapter*, from L *adaptāre*, from *ad* to, and *aptāre* to fit]
■ **adaptabil'ity** *n*. **adapt'able** *adj*. **adapt'ableness** *n*. **adaptation** /ad-əp-tā'shən/ *n* the fact, act, process or result of adapting; a character by which anything is adapted to conditions; adjustment. **adapt'ative** *adj*. **adapt'ed** *adj* modified to suit; suitable. **adapt'er** or **adapt'or** *n* someone who or something which adapts; an attachment or accessory enabling a piece of apparatus to be used for a purpose, or in conditions, other than that or those for which it was originally intended, *esp* a device that will connect two parts of different sizes, or a device that enables one to connect two electrical devices (eg a plug and socket) that have incompatible terminals, or that allows more than one electrical appliance to be powered from one socket. **adap'tion** *n* adaptation. **adapt'ive** *adj*. **adapt'ively** *adv*. **adapt'iveness** *n*. **adapt'ogen** *n* (in herbal medicine) a natural substance which helps the body to cope with stress and other adverse circumstances.
❑ **adaptive radiation** *n* (*ecology*) evolutionary diversification of species from a common ancestral stock, filling available ecological niches (also **divergent radiation**).

Adar /ä'där or ā'där/ *n* in the Jewish calendar, the twelfth month of the ecclesiastical year, the sixth of the civil year (part of February and March). [Heb *adār*]
❑ **Adar Sheni** /shä'nē/ *n* Veadar, literally Adar the second.

ad arbitrium /ad är-bit'ri-əm or -ūm/ (*L*) at pleasure.

ADAS *abbrev* : Agricultural Development and Advisory Service.

ad astra /ad as'tra/ (*L*) to the stars.

ad avizandum /ad a-vi-zan'dəm or a-vē'zän'dūm/ (*Scots law*; *L*) for further consideration; see **avizandum**.

adaw /ə-dö'/ (*Spenser*) *vt* to daunt; to subdue. ◆ *vi* to subside. [Appar a 16c misunderstanding of the ME *adv adaw* out of life, from OE *of dagum* from days (dative pl)]

adaxial /a-dak'si-əl/ (*bot*) *adj* next to or towards the axis. [L *ad* next to]

adays /ə-dāz'/ (*obs*) *adv* by day; daily (*Spenser*). [OE *dæges*, genitive of *dæg* day, with prep *a* (see **a-¹**) added later]

ADC *abbrev* : advice of duration and charge, a telephone service by which the operator advises the caller of the cost of the call he or she has just made, now called Charge Advice (also **AD and C**); aide-de-camp; analogue-to-digital converter (*comput*).

ad Calendas Graecas /ad ka-len'däs grī'käs/ (*L*) at the Greek calends, ie never, as the Greeks had no calends.

ad captandum /ad kap-tan'dəm or -dūm/, also **ad captandum vulgus** /vul'gəs or wūl'gŭs/ (*L*) (used as *adv* or *adj*) with the intention of pleasing or appealing to the emotions of the crowd.

ad clerum /ad kler'əm or klā'rŭm/ (*L*) to the clergy.

ad crumenam /ad kroo'mə-nam or krŭ-mā'nam/ (*L*) to the purse.

ADD *abbrev* : attention deficit disorder.

add /ad/ *vt* to put, join or annex (to something else); to sum up or compute the sum of; to say further. ◆ *vi* to make an addition; to increase (with *to*); to find the total of numbers, etc. [L *addere, additum*, from *ad* to, and *dare* to put]
■ **add'er** *n* a person who adds; a machine for adding; a basic component of a chip, consisting of a number of switches which add digital signals (*comput*). **additament** /ə-dit'ə-mənt or ad'/ *n* something added (*archaic*); an additional ornament external to the shield, eg supporters or symbols of office (*heraldry*). **addi'tion** *n* the act of adding; a person or thing added; the part of arithmetic or algebra that deals with adding; a person's title or designation (*Shakesp*). **addi'tional** *adj* added. **additional'ity** *n* the principle (*orig* applied to EU funding of projects) that funding should be additional to, not a replacement for, funding from the beneficiary; the principle that grants, credits, etc should be awarded only to promote activity that would not occur without the presence of such an incentive. **addi'tionally** *adv*. **additi'tious** *adj* increasing. **add'itive** *adj* of the nature of an addition; characterized by addition; to be added. ◆ *n* a substance added to foodstuffs or other commodities for a special purpose, eg as a colorant or preservative.
❑ **add'-in** *n* (*pl* **add'-ins**) (*esp comput*) an additional device or piece of software installed internally in a system to extend its capabilities. **adding machine** *n* an obsolete apparatus for performing basic arithmetical calculations. **additional member system** *n* an electoral system, used eg in the Scottish Parliament and the National Assembly for Wales, in which parties whose share of the vote is not reflected in the number of successful candidates are allowed to nominate further representatives. **addition compound** or **product** *n* (*chem*) one formed by the direct union of two or more substances. **addition reaction** *n* (*chem*) the union of two molecules to form a larger molecule with no by-products. **additive-free'** *adj* of food, containing no chemical additives. **add'-on** *n* (*pl* **add'-ons**) (*esp comput*) an additional unit, a peripheral; an additional charge. **add-to system** *n* a hire-purchase arrangement by which a customer obtains a series of articles, making a down payment on the first only.
■ **add up** to calculate by addition; to be consistent, or satisfactory to the mind; to point to a reasonable conclusion. **add up to** to amount to; to come to as result or conclusion. **in addition** (**to**) as well (as), besides.

add. *abbrev* : addendum; addition; additional; address.

addax /ad'aks/ *n* a large African antelope with long slightly twisted horns. [L, from an African word]

addebted /a-det'id/ (*obs except Scot*) *adj* indebted; owed. [ME *endetted*, from OFr *endetter* or *endeter* to get into debt, from LL *indebitāre*]

addeem /ə-dēm'/ (*obs*) *vt* to adjudge; to award. [Pfx *ad-*, and **deem**]

addend /ad'end or ə-dend'/ *n* a number or quantity added to another. [**addendum**]

addendum /ə-den'dəm/ *n* (*pl* **adden'da**) a thing to be added, such as supplementary material to a book, etc; the distance between the centre and the outer edge of a tooth on a gear or of the thread of a screw (*engineering*). [L gerundive of *addere* ; see **add**]

adder¹ /ad'ər/ *n* the only venomous snake found in Britain, a viper. [OE *nædre* (*an adder* for *a nadder* ; cf obs Ger *Atter* for *Natter*)]
❑ **add'erstone** *n* a prehistoric spindle-whorl or bead, popularly attributed to the agency of adders. **ad'der's-tongue** *n* a genus (*Ophioglossum*) of ferns whose spore cases grow on a spike resembling a snake's tongue; dog's-tooth violet (*N Am*). **ad'der's-wort** or **add'erwort** *n* the bistort or snakeweed, supposed to cure snake-bite.

adder² see under **add**.

addict /ə-dikt'/ *vt* (*usu* in passive with *to*) to make (someone) dependent on (*esp* a drug). ◆ *adj* (*obs*) addicted. ◆ *n* /ad'ikt/ a slave to a habit or vice, *esp* a drug; a fanatical devotee of an activity or thing. [L *addīcere, addictum*, from *ad* to, and *dīcere* to declare]
■ **addict'ed** *adj* inclined or given up (to); dependent on. **addict'edness** *n*. **addic'tion** *n* the state of being addicted; a habit that has become impossible to break. **addict'ive** *adj* tending to cause addiction; habit-forming.

addio /a-dē'o/ *interj* goodbye. [Ital *a Dio* to God]

Addison's disease /ad'i-sənz di-zēz'/ *n* a disease in which there is progressive destruction of the suprarenal cortex, accompanied by wasting, weakness, low blood pressure and pigmentation of the skin (bronzed skin). [Dr Thomas *Addison* (1793–1860), who investigated it]

additament, **addition**, **additive**, etc see under **add**.

addle /ad'l/ *n* (now *dialect*) liquid filth. ♦ *adj* putrid; bad (eg of an egg); barren, empty; muddled. ♦ *vt* and *vi* to make or become confused, muddled; to make or become rotten. [OE *adela* mud]
■ **add'led** *adj*. **add'lement** *n*.
❑ **add'le-brained**, **add'le-headed** or **add'le-pated** *adj* muddle-headed.

addoom /ə-doom'/ (*Spenser*) *vt* to adjudge, award. [Pfx *ad*-, and **doom**]

addorsed /ə-dörst'/ (*heraldry*) *adj* turned back to back. [L *ad* to, and *dorsum* back]

address /ə-dres'/ *vt* to apply or devote (oneself; with *to*); to apply oneself to; to direct; to aim; to direct one's words to or speak directly to; to send; to put a written or printed direction or indication of destination upon; to woo (*archaic*); to arrange (*obs*); to prepare (*obs*); to take one's stance in preparation for striking (a golf ball); to dress (*obs*); to don (*archaic*). ♦ *vi* to direct one's words (towards) (*Shakesp*); to prepare oneself (*Shakesp*). ♦ *n* act or mode of addressing; deportment; adroitness; preparation, a move or incipient act (*Milton*); a formal communication in writing; a speech; a direction, eg of a letter or mail; a place to which letters, etc may be directed; a place where a person, organization, etc may be found; the place where a person lives; a name, label or number that identifies the location of a stored item of data, etc (*comput*); a location within a computer's memory in which data is stored; (in *pl*) attentions of the nature of courtship. [Fr *adresser*, from LL *addirectiāre*, from L *ad* to, and *directum* straight; see **dress** and **direct**]
■ **addressabil'ity** *n*. **address'able** *adj*. **addressed'** *adj* aimed; directed. **addressee'** *n* the person to whom a letter, etc is addressed. **address'er** or **address'or** *n*. **Addressograph**® /ə-dres'ō-gräf/ *n* an obsolete machine for printing addresses automatically on envelopes, etc. **addrest'** or **addressed'** *adj* (*obs*) arrayed; equipped; set up (*Spenser*); ready or prepared (*Shakesp*).
❑ **address bar** *n* (*comput*) the area in a web browser which displays the address of the website being accessed. **address book** *n* a notebook, *usu* with alphabetical thumb-index, in which names and addresses can be entered; a facility on a computer, mobile phone, etc for storing details of email addresses, phone numbers, etc. **address bus** *n* (*comput*) a pathway within the processor linking the memory address register to the memory, enabling it to determine where a read or write operation will take place.

adduce /ə-dūs'/ *vt* to bring forward in discussion, to cite or quote. [L *addūcere*, *adductum*, from *ad* to, and *dūcere* to bring]
■ **addūc'ent** *adj* drawing inward or together, as a muscle does. **addūc'er** *n*. **addūc'ible** *adj*. **adduct** /ə-dukt'/ *vt* to draw inward or together, *esp* a muscle. **adduc'tion** *n* the act of adducing or of adducting. **adduc'tive** *adj* tending to bring forward. **adduc'tor** *n* an adducent muscle.

-ade /-ād/ *combining form* indicating: (1) an action (such as *escapade*); (2) the product of an action (such as *masquerade*, *lemonade*). [L *-ata*, participial ending, often via Fr *-ade*]

adeem /ə-dēm'/ (*law*) *vt* to cancel (a bequest) by destruction or sale of the thing bequeathed, or otherwise. [L *ad* to, and *emere*, *emptum* to take]
■ **ademption** /-dem'shən/ *n*.

adelantado /a-de-lan-tä'dō/ (*Sp*) *n* (*pl* **adelanta'dos**) a grandee; a provincial governor.

Adélie penguin /ə-dā'li peng'gwin/ *n* a medium-sized penguin with a white ring around the eye. [Named after *Adélie*, wife of the 19c French explorer Jules Dumont d'Urville]

à demi /a də-mē'/ (*Fr*) by halves or half.

aden- /a-dən-/ *combining form* denoting gland. [Gr *adēn* gland]
■ **adenec'tomy** *n* surgical removal of a gland. **adenine** /ad'ən-ēn* or *ad'ən-īn/ *n* a substance found in all glandular tissues, one of the four bases in deoxyribonucleic acids, in close association with thymine. **adenitis** /ad-ən-ī'tis/ *n* inflammation of glands. **adenocarcinoma** /-ō-kär-si-nō'mə/ *n* (*pl* **adenocarcinō'mata** or **adenocarcinō'mas**) a malignant tumour of glandular origin or gland-like structure. **adenohypophysis** /-ō-hī-poph'i-sis/ *n* (*pl* **adenohypoph'yses** /-sēz/) the anterior lobe of the pituitary gland. **ad'enoid** *adj* gland-like; glandular. ♦ *n* (*usu* in *pl*) glandular tissue at the back of the nose. **adenoid'al** *adj* of adenoids; affected by or as if by adenoids (such as a voice). **adenoidec'tomy** *n* surgical removal of adenoids. **adenō'ma** *n* (*pl* **adenō'mata** or **adenō'mas**) a benign tumour like, or originating in, a gland. **adenō'matous** *adj*. **adenosine** /ad'ə-nō-sin*, also *ə-den'/ *n* a nucleoside made up of adenine and ribose, one of its compounds being **adenosine triphosphate**, which is present in all cells and stores energy for muscle contraction. **adenovī'rus** *n* any of a group of

viruses that attack the upper respiratory tract, and may produce malignancy.

Adeni /ä'di-ni/ *n* and *adj* (a citizen) of Aden.

adept /ad'ept, ə-dept' or a-dept'/ *adj* completely skilled (at or in). ♦ *n* an expert; an alchemist who has attained the great secret (of the philosopher's stone) (*obs*). [L *adeptus* (*artem*) having attained (an art), pap of *adipīscī* to attain]
■ **adept'ly** *adv*. **adept'ness** *n*.

adequate /ad'i-kwit* or *-kwət/ *adj* sufficient; competent. [L *adaequātus* made equal, from *ad* to, and *aequus* equal]
■ **ad'equacy** /-kwə-si/ *n*. **ad'equately** *adv*. **ad'equateness** *n*. **ad'equative** *adj*.

adermin /ə-dûr'min/ *n* a former name of pyridoxine. [Gr *a*- (privative), and *derma* skin, because deprivation of this vitamin was shown to cause dermatitis in rats]

Ades /ä'dēz/ (*Milton*) *n* variant of **Hades**.

à dessein /a de-sĕ'/ (*Fr*) on purpose.

adessive /a-des'iv/ (*grammar*) *adj* (of a case, found eg in Finnish) denoting place where. ♦ *n* the adessive case. [L *adesse* to be at a place or to be present]

ad eundem /ad ē-un'dəm* or *ā-oon'dem/ (*L*) to or at the same level or status (as already attained, *esp* at another university). [Short for L *ad eundem gradum*]

à deux /a dø/ (*Fr*) of two, between two, two-handed.
■ **à deux mains** /mĕ/ with both hands; for two hands.

ADF *abbrev* : automatic direction-finder.

ad finem /ad fī'nəm* or *fē'/ (*L*) at, to, or towards the end (*abbrev* **ad fin.**).

ADH *abbrev* : antidiuretic hormone.

adharma /ə-där'mä* or *ə-dûr'mə/ *n* unrighteousness, *opp* to *dharma*. [Sans]

ADHD *abbrev* : attention deficit hyperactivity disorder.

adhere /əd- or *ad-hēr'/ *vi* to stick (to); to remain fixed or attached (to); to remain faithful (eg to a party, leader, or doctrine); to be consistent (*Shakesp*); to agree; to affirm a judgement (*Scots law*). [L *ad* to, and *haerēre*, *haesum* to stick]
■ **adhēr'ence** *n* state of adhering; the growing together of unlike parts (*bot*). **adhēr'ent** *adj* sticking; grown together and unlike. ♦ *n* someone who adheres; a follower; a partisan; a person who is loosely associated with a body, group, party, etc without being a member. **adhēr'er** *n*.

adhesion /ad- or *əd-hē'zhən/ *n* the act of adhering or sticking; strong, firm contact; steady attachment; the intermolecular force which holds matter together, particularly closely contiguous surfaces (*phys*); growing together of unlike parts (*bot*); reunion of separated surfaces (*surg*); abnormal union of parts that have been inflamed (*pathol*); (often in *pl*) a band of fibrous tissue joining such parts. [See **adhere**]
■ **adhē'sive** /-siv* or *-ziv/ *adj* sticky; likely or tending to adhere. ♦ *n* a substance such as glue used for sticking things together. **adhē'sively** *adv*. **adhē'siveness** *n*.

adhibit /əd-hib'it/ *vt* to apply; to attach; to admit; to administer. [L *adhibēre*, *-itum*, from *ad* to, and *habēre* to hold]
■ **adhibi'tion** *n*.

ad hoc /ad hok/ (*L*) *adj* and *adv* for this special purpose.
■ **ad hocery** /hok'ə-ri/ *n* (*facetious*) the use of ad hoc measures, improvisation or pragmatism.

ad hominem /ad hom'in-em/ (*L*) addressed to the feelings or prejudices of the hearer or reader; dealing with an opponent by attacking their character instead of answering their argument. [Literally, to the man]

ADI *abbrev* : approved driving instructor.

adiabatic /ad-i-ə-bat'ik/ *adj* without transference of heat. [Gr *a*- (privative), *dia* through, and *batos* passable]
■ **adiabat'ically** *adv*.

Adiantum /a-di-an'təm/ *n* the maidenhair genus of ferns. [Gr *adiantos*, from *a*- (privative), and *diantos* capable of being wetted]

adiaphoron /a-di-af'ə-ron/ (*theol* and *ethics*) *n* (*pl* **adiaph'ora**) a matter of indifference, which is neither approved nor disapproved in the religion or ethical system; any tenet or usage considered non-essential. [Gr, from *a*- (privative), and *diaphoros* differing, from *dia* apart, and *pherein* to carry]
■ **adiaph'orism** *n* tolerance or indifference in regard to non-essential points in theology; latitudinarianism. **adiaph'orist** *n*. **adiaphoris'tic** *adj*. **adiaph'orous** *adj*.

adiathermic /ad-i-ə-thûr'mik/ *adj* impervious to radiant heat. [Gr *a*- (privative), *dia* through, and *thermē* heat]
■ **adiather'mancy** *n* impermeability to radiant heat (also **ather'mancy**). **adiather'manous** *adj*.

---

fāte; fär; mē; fûr; mīne; mōte; för; mūte; pŭt; dhen (then); *el'ə-mənt* (element) • For other sounds see detailed chart of pronunciation

adieu /ə-dū'/ *interj* farewell, goodbye. ◆ *n* (*pl* **adieus** or **adieux** /ə-dūz'/) a farewell. [Fr *à Dieu* (I commend you) to God]

Adi-Granth /u-dhē'grunt'/ *n* another name for the **Granth**. [Hindi, the first scripture]

ad infinitum /ad in-fi-nī'təm or -nē'tŭm/ (*L*) to infinity (*abbrev* **ad inf.**).

ad init. /ad i-nit'/ *abbrev*: *ad initium* (*L*), at or to the beginning.

ad inquirendum /ad in-kwīr-en'dəm or in-kwēr-en'dŭm/ (*law*) *n* the name of a writ commanding an inquiry. [LL, literally, for making inquiry]

ad interim /ad in'tə-rim/ (*LL*) for or in the meantime (*abbrev* **ad int.**).

adiós /a-dē-os' or -ōs'/ *interj* goodbye. [Sp, literally, to God]

adipic /ə-dip'ik/ *adj* of fat, only in **adipic acid** $C_6H_{10}O_4$, an acid obtained by treating fat with nitric acid (also **butanedicarboxylic acid**). [L *adeps, adipis* soft fat]
■ **adiponec'tin** *n* a hormone secreted by fat tissue. **adipose** /ad'i-pōs/ *adj* fatty. **adiposity** /-pos'i-ti/ *n*.
□ **adipose tissue** *n* the vesicular structure in the animal body which contains fat.

adipocere /ad'i-pō-sēr or -sēr'/ *n* a fatty, waxy substance resulting from the decomposition of animal bodies in moist places or under water, but not exposed to air. [L *adeps, adipis* soft fat, and *cēra* wax]

adipocyte /ad'i-pō-sīt/ *n* (*biol*) a fat-storing cell. [L *adeps, adipis* soft fat, and **-cyte**]

adipose, etc see under **adipic**.

adit /ad'it/ *n* an opening or passage, *esp* into a mine. [L *aditus*, from *ad* to, and *ire*, *itum* to go]

adj. *abbrev*: adjective; adjourned; adjustment; adjutant (also with *cap*).

adjacent /ə-jā'sənt/ *adj* lying near or next (to). [L *ad* to, and *jacēns, -entis*, prp of *jacēre* to lie]
■ **adja'cency** *n*. **adja'cently** *adv*.
□ **adjacent angles** *n pl* (*geom*) a pair of angles that have the same vertex and one side in common.

adjective /aj'ik-tiv/ *n* a word added to a noun to qualify it, or to limit its denotation by reference to quality, number or position. ◆ *adj* added; dependent; subsidiary; (of dyes) requiring a mordant. [L *adjectīvum* (*nōmen*) added (word), from *adjicere, -jectum* to add, from *ad* to, and *jacere* to throw]
■ **adjectival** /-tī'v'l/ *adj* of an adjective; using many adjectives; used facetiously as a euphemism (eg *What adjectival nonsense this is!*). **adjecti'vally** *adv*. **ad'jectively** *adv*.

adjoin /ə-join'/ *vt* to join on; to lie next to. ◆ *vi* to be in contact. [Through Fr *adjoign-* prp stem, and *adjoint* pap of *adjoindre*, from L *adjungere*, from *ad* to, and *jungere* to join]
■ **adjoin'ing** *adj*. **adjoint** /aj'oint or (Fr) ad-zhwẽ/ *n* a civil officer who assists a French mayor; an assistant professor in a French college.

adjourn /ə-jûrn'/ *vt* to put off to another day; to postpone; to discontinue (a meeting) in order to reconstitute it at another time or place. ◆ *vi* to suspend proceedings and disperse, either for any time specified, or (*sine die*) without such time being specified. [OFr *ajorner*, from LL *adiurnāre*, from L *ad* to, and LL *jurnus*, L *diurnus* daily; cf **journal¹**]
■ **adjourn'ment** *n*.
□ **adjournment debate** *n* a brief parliamentary debate, immediately before the adjournment of the House, allowing members to raise issues which would otherwise not be discussed.
■ **Acts of Adjournal** (*Scots law*) procedural rules of the High Court.

Adjt or **adjt** *abbrev*: adjutant.
□ **Adjt-Gen.** *n* Adjutant-General.

adjudge /ə-juj'/ *vt* to decide; to assign; to award. [OFr *ajuger*, from L *adjūdicāre*; cf **judge**]
■ **adjudge'ment** (sometimes **adjudg'ment**) *n* the act of adjudging; sentence.

adjudicate /ə-joo'di-kāt/ *vt* to determine judicially; to pronounce; to award. ◆ *vi* to pronounce judgement; to act as judge in a competition in one of the arts, eg music. [L *adjūdicāre, adjūdicātum*]
■ **adjudi'ca'tion** *n* the act or process of adjudicating; an order of the Bankruptcy Court, adjudging a debtor to be a bankrupt and transferring his or her property to a trustee (*Eng law*); a form of diligence (qv) by which a creditor attaches land (*Scots law*). **adju'dicative** *adj*. **adju'dicator** *n*.

adjunct /aj'ung(k)t/ *adj* joined or added. ◆ *n* a thing joined or added, but subordinate or not essentially a part; a person (*usu* subordinate) joined to another in office or service; any word or clause enlarging the subject or predicate (*grammar*); any accompanying quality or non-essential attribute (*logic*). [L *adjunctus*, pap of *adjungere* to join]
■ **adjunction** /ə-jungk'shən/ *n*. **adjunct'ive** *adj* forming an adjunct. **adjunct'ively** *adv*. **ad'junctly** (or /-jungkt'/) *adv*.

adjure /ə-joor'/ *vt* to charge on oath; to command or request solemnly; to make swear (*obs*). [L *adjūrāre*, from *ad* to, and *jūrāre, -ātum* to swear]
■ **adjurā'tion** /aj-/ *n*. **adjur'atory** *adj*. **adjur'ing** *adj*.

adjust /ə-just'/ *vt* to regulate; to adapt or put in proper relation; to alter; to settle. ◆ *vi* to adapt oneself (to). [Obs Fr *adjuster*, from LL *adjuxtāre* to put side by side, from L *juxtā* near; confused by association with *jūstus* right]
■ **adjustabil'ity** *n*. **adjust'able** *adj*. **adjust'ably** *adv*. **adjust'er** *n* a person or thing that adjusts; see under **average** and **loss**. **adjust'ment** *n*. **adjust'or** *n* an organ or faculty that determines behaviour in response to stimuli.

adjutage or **ajutage** /aj'(y)ŭ-tij or -oo- or -ū-/ *n* a nozzle, as in a fountain. [Fr *ajutage*; cf **adjust**]

adjutant /aj'ŭ-tənt/ *n* an officer specially appointed to assist a commanding officer; (*usu* **adjutant bird**) a large stork or crane of India and SE Asia (from its stalking gait). [L *adjūtāns, -antis*, prp of *adjūtāre*, frequentative of *adjuvāre*, from *ad* to, and *juvāre* to assist]
■ **ad'jutancy** *n* the office of an adjutant; assistance (*rare*).
□ **adjutant-gen'eral** *n* (*pl* **adjutants-gen'eral**) the head of a department of the general staff; the executive officer of a general.

adjuvant /aj'ə-vənt/ *adj* helping. ◆ *n* a help; a substance added eg to a medicine, vaccine, etc to increase its effectiveness. [Fr, from L *ad* to, and *juvāre* to help]
■ **ad'juvancy** *n*.

ADL *abbrev*: Activity of Daily Living, one of a number of pre-defined activities used to measure the extent of a person's incapacity, eg for insurance purposes.

adland see under **advertise**.

ad libitum /ad lib'i-təm or -tŭm/ (*L*) at will, at pleasure; extempore, impromptu (*abbrev* **ad lib.**).
■ **ad-lib** /ad-lib'/ *adv* spontaneously or freely. ◆ *adj* impromptu, extemporized. ◆ *vt* and *vi* to extemporize or speak without preparation, *esp* to fill up time. ◆ *n* an improvised speech; a spontaneous (often humorous) remark. **ad-libb'er** *n*. **ad-libb'ing** *n*.

ad litem /ad lī'təm or lē'tem/ (*L*) (of a guardian, etc) appointed for a lawsuit.

ad loc. *abbrev*: *ad locum* (*L*), at the place.

Adm. *abbrev*: Admiral.

ad-man or **adman** see under **advertise**.

ad manum /ad mā'nəm or mä'nŭm/ (*L*) at or to hand, ready.

ad-mass or **admass** see under **advertise**.

admeasure /ad-mezh'ər/ *vt* to measure or measure out; to apportion. [OFr *amesurer*, from LL *admēnsūrāre*, from L *ad* to, and *mēnsūra* measure]
■ **admeas'urement** *n*.

admin see under **administer**.

adminicle /əd-min'i-kl/ *n* anything that aids or supports; an auxiliary; any corroborative evidence (*law*). [L *adminiculum* a support, from *ad* to, and *manus* hand]
■ **adminic'ular** *adj*. **adminic'ulate** *vt* and *vi*.

administer /əd-min'i-stər/ *vt* to govern; to manage or control as a manager, steward, substitute or executor; to dispense (justice or rites); to supervise the swearing of (an oath); to give (medicine or treatment). ◆ *vi* to minister. [L *administrāre, -ātum*, from *ad* to, and *ministrāre* to minister]
■ **admin'istrable** *adj*. **admin'istrant** *adj* and *n*. **admin'istrate** *vt* to administer. **administrā'tion** (*inf* short form **ad'min**) *n* the act of administering; management; the organization of a business; the people whose job it is to carry out such organization; dispensation of sacraments; the government; the state of being subject to an administrative order. **admin'istrative** *adj* concerned with administration. **admin'istratively** *adv*. **admin'istrātor** *n* a person who manages or directs; the person to whom is committed, under a commission entitled **letters of administration**, the administration or distribution of the personal estate of a deceased person, in default of an executor; someone empowered to act for a person legally incapable of acting for themselves (*Scots law*). **admin'istrātorship** *n*. **admin'istrātrix** *n* a female administrator.
□ **administrative order** *n* a court order allowing an administrator to freeze the debts of a company in financial difficulties.

admirable, etc see under **admire**.

admiral /ad'm(ə-)rəl/ *n* the chief commander of a navy; a naval officer ranking with a general in the army (**admiral of the fleet** ranking with field marshal); an admiral's flagship; the chief ship in a fleet of merchant ships or fishing-boats; a cone shell; a butterfly of certain kinds (see **red¹** and **white**). [OFr *a(d)miral*, from Ar *amīr-al-bahr* a lord of the sea, confused with L *admīrābilis* (see **admire**)]
■ **ad'miralship** *n* the office or art of an admiral.

■ words derived from main entry word; □ compound words; ■ idioms and phrasal verbs

■ **Lord High Admiral** an office dating from the 15c, William IV (when Duke of Clarence) being the last holder until the office was taken over by Elizabeth II in 1964. **the Ad'miralty** or **the Admiralty Board** the board administering the Royal Navy (since 1964 under the British Ministry of Defence); the building where it transacts business.

admire /əd-mīr'/ vt to have (or express) a high opinion of; to wonder at (archaic). ◆ vi (obs) to wonder. [Fr admirer, from L ad at, and mīrāri to wonder]
■ **admirable** /ad'mə-rə-bl/ adj worthy of being admired. **ad'mirableness** n. **ad'mirably** adv. **admirā'tion** n the act of admiring; wonder, together with esteem, love, or veneration; astonishment (Bible, Shakesp and Milton); admirableness (Shakesp); an object of admiration (Shakesp); a wonder (Shakesp). **ad'mirative** adj (archaic). **admīr'a(u)nce** n (Spenser) admiration. **admīr'er** n a person who admires; a romantic adorer. **admīr'ing** adj. **admīr'ingly** adv.
■ **Admirable Crichton** /krī'tən/ someone who excels in many things, from James Crichton (1560–82), Scottish athlete, Latin poet, polymath.

ad misericordiam /ad mi-ze-ri-kŏr'di-am/ (L) (of an argument, etc) appealing to pity.

admissible, etc see under **admit**.

admit /əd-mit'/ vt (**admitt'ing**; **admitt'ed**) to allow to enter (with into or to); to let in; to concede; to acknowledge; to confess; to be capable of. ◆ vi (with of) to be capable of; to allow as possible or valid. [Partly through Fr, from L admittere, -missum, from ad to, and mittere, missum to send]
■ **admissibil'ity** or **admiss'ibleness** n. **admiss'ible** adj that may be admitted or allowed (generally, or specifically as legal proof). **admission** /-mish'ən/ n the act of admitting; anything admitted or conceded; permission to enter; the price charged for entry. **admiss'ive** adj. **admitt'able** adj that may be admitted. **admitt'ance** n admission; acceptability or acceptance (Shakesp); the property of an electric circuit by virtue of which a current flows under the action of a potential difference. **admitt'ed** adj acknowledged or conceded; (of a law clerk) qualified to practise as a solicitor, having been admitted to the Law Society's roll of solicitors. **admitt'edly** adv.

admix /əd- or ad-miks'/ vt to mix with something else. [L ad to, and mix]
■ **admix'ture** n the action of mixing; what is added to the chief ingredient of a mixture; a mixture.

ad modum /ad mŏ'dəm or mod'ŭm/ (L) after the manner (of).

admonish /əd-mon'ish/ vt to warn; to reprove mildly; to counsel earnestly. [OFr amonester, from LL admonestāre, from L admonēre, from ad to, and monēre to warn]
■ **admon'ishment** n admonition.

admonition /ad-mo-nish'ən or -mə-/ n reproof; counsel; warning; advice; ecclesiastical censure. [L admonitiō, -ōnis; cf **admonish**]
■ **admonitive** /-mon'/ or **admon'itory** adj containing admonition. **admon'itor** n.

adnascent /ad-nas'ənt or -nā'sənt/ adj growing together with or upon something else. [L adnāscēns, -entis, prp of adnāscī, from ad to, and nāscī to be born]

adnate /ad'nāt or ad-nāt'/ (bot) adj attached (esp by the whole length) to a different kind of organ. [L adnātus, usu agnātus, from ad to, and (g)nātus born]
■ **adnation** /-nā'shən/ n.

ad nauseam /ad nö'zi-am, -shi- or now'si-/ (L) to the point of producing disgust.

adnexa /ad-nek'sə/ (anat) n pl the organs that are attached to a particular organ. [New L, from L adnexus, pap of adnectere to bind to]
■ **adnex'al** adj.

adnoun /ad'nown/ (grammar) n an adjective used as a noun.
■ **adnom'inal** adj.

ado /ə-doo'/ n (pl **ados'**) a to-do; bustle; trouble; difficulty; stir or fuss. [at do, N Eng infinitive with **at¹** instead of **to**, borrowed from Scand]
■ **without further** (or **more**) **ado** immediately, promptly.

adobe /ə-dō'bi/ n a sun-dried brick; a house made of such bricks; (also **adobe clay**) a name for any kind of mud which, when mixed with straw, can be sun-dried into bricks. ◆ adj made of adobe. [Sp, from adobar to plaster]

adobo /ə-dō'bō/ n a Filipino dish of meat cooked in soy sauce and vinegar. [Sp, marinade]

adolescent /a-də-les'ənt/ adj growing from childhood to maturity; between puberty and full maturity; belonging to or typical of this state; immature. ◆ n a young person between childhood and adulthood. [L adolēscēns, -entis, prp of adolēscere to grow up]
■ **adolesc'ence** n the state or time of being adolescent.

Adonai /a-dō'nī or a-do-nā'ī/ n a name of God in the Old Testament, usu translated 'Lord' (see also **Jehovah**). [Heb adōnāi my lord]

Adonis /ə-dō'nis or -don'is/ n a young man beloved by Aphrodite (Gr myth); a particularly handsome youth or young man; a beau or dandy. [Gr Adōnis, from Phoenician adōn lord]
■ **Adō'nia** n pl the festival of mourning for Adonis. **Adonic** /ə-don'ik/ n (prosody) a verse of a dactyl and a spondee (or a trochee), said to have been used in the Adonia (also adj). **ad'onize** or **-ise** vt and vi to adorn (oneself).

adoors /ə-dörz'/ (obs) adv at doors; at the door. [a-¹ at, and **door**]

adopt /ə-dopt'/ vt to take voluntarily as one's own child, with the rights of one's own child (also vi); to take into any relationship; to take as one's own; to take up; to take over; to take (a precaution, etc); to choose formally (eg a candidate); to endorse or approve (eg a resolution or minutes). [L adoptāre, from ad to, and optāre to choose]
■ **adopt'ed** adj taken by adoption. **adoptee'** n an adopted child. **adopt'er** n. **Adoptianism** or **Adoptionism** /ə-dop'shən-izm/ (often without cap) n the doctrine that Christ, as man, is the adopted son of God. **adop'tianist** or **adop'tionist** n. **adop'tion** n. **adop'tious** /-shəs/ adj (Shakesp) adopted. **adopt'ive** adj that adopts or is adopted.

adore /ə-dör'/ vt to worship; to love or revere intensely; to adorn (Spenser). [L ad to, and ōrāre to pray]
■ **ador'able** adj. **ador'ableness** n. **ador'ably** adv. **adorā'tion** n. **ador'er** n. **ador'ing** adj. **ador'ingly** adv.

adorn /ə-dörn'/ vt to deck or dress; to embellish. ◆ n (Spenser) adornment. ◆ adj (Milton) adorned, ornate. [OFr äorner, adorner, from L adōrnāre, from ad to, and ōrnāre to furnish]
■ **adorn'ment** n ornament; decoration.

adown /ə-down'/ (archaic or poetic) adv and prep same as **down¹**. [**a-¹**]

ADP abbrev: adenosine diphosphate (biochem); automatic data processing (comput).

ad patres /ad pā'trēz or pat'rās/ (L) (gathered) to his or her fathers, dead.

adpress see **appress**.

adrad /ə-drad'/ or **adred** /ə-dred'/ (Spenser) adj afraid. [OE ofdrǣd, from pfx of-, and drǣdan to dread; see also **adread**]

adread /ə-dred'/ (obs) vt (pat adrad' (Spenser)) to fear. [OE ondrǣdan, from pfx on-, and- against, and drǣdan to dread]

ad referendum /ad re-fe-ren'dum or -dŭm/ (L) to be further considered.

ad rem /ad rem/ (L) to the point; to the purpose.

adreno- or **adren-** /ə-dre-nō- or -drē-nō- or -dren or -drēn/ combining form denoting adrenal, adrenal glands, adrenalin. [L ad to, and rēnēs kidneys]
■ **adrenal** /ə-drē'nəl/ adj beside the kidneys; of or relating to the adrenal glands, two small ductless glands over the kidneys, which secrete adrenaline and steroids (**adrenal cortex** the secreting outer part of the adrenal glands). ◆ n an adrenal gland. **adrenaline** or **adrenalin** /ə-dren'ə-lin/ n a hormone secreted by the adrenal glands that causes constriction of the arteries, so increasing blood pressure and stimulating the heart muscle (also (N Am) **epinephrine**); also produced synthetically (as **Adrenalin®**) for this property. **adrener'gic** adj (of the sympathetic nerve fibres) releasing (a substance resembling) adrenaline; activated by adrenaline; (of an agent) having the same effect as adrenaline. **adrenocorticotrophic** or **-tropic** /-kŏr'tik-ō-trof'ik or -trop'ik/ adj (**cortex** and Gr trophē food) stimulating the activity of the adrenal cortex (**adrenocorticotrop(h)ic hormone** or **adrenocorticotrop(h)in** /-trof'in, -trop'in or -trō'/ see **ACTH**). **adrenoleukodys'trophy** n an inherited, fatal, degenerative disease of the nervous system, affecting young boys (abbrev **ALD**).

Adriamycin® /ā-dri-ə-mī'sin/ n a proprietary name for **doxorubicin**.

adrift /ə-drift'/ adj or adv drifting; loose from moorings; left to one's own resources, without help, guidance or contacts; cut loose; off course or inaccurate (inf). [**a-¹**]

adroit /ə-droit'/ adj dexterous; skilful; ingenious. [Fr à droit according to right, from L directus straight; see **direct**]
■ **adroit'ly** adv. **adroit'ness** n.

à droite /a drwät'/ (Fr) to the right.

adry /ə-drī'/ (archaic or poetic) adj and adv in a state of thirst or dryness. [After athirst, acold, etc]

ADS abbrev: American Depositary Share.

adscititious /ad-si-ti'shəs/ adj added or assumed; additional. [L adscīscere, -scītum to take or assume, from ad to, and scīscere to inquire, from scīre to know]
■ **adscitit'iously** adv.

adscript /ad'skript/ (hist) adj attached to the soil. ◆ n a feudal serf so attached. [L adscrīptus, from ad to, and scrībere to write]
■ **adscrip'tion** n.

ADSL *abbrev*: Asymmetric Digital Subscriber Line, a fast Internet connection over an analogue phone line, in which traffic moves more quickly in one direction than in the other.

adsorb /ad-sörb'/ *vt* of a solid or a liquid, to accumulate on its surface a thin film of the molecules of a gas or liquid that is in contact with it (cf **absorb**). [L *ad* to, and *sorbēre* to suck in]
■ **adsorbabil'ity** *n*. **adsorb'able** *adj*. **adsorb'ate** *n* the vapour or liquid adsorbed. **adsorb'ent** *n* a solid (such as charcoal) that adsorbs a gas, etc in contact with it. **adsorp'tion** *n*. **adsorp'tive** *adj*.

adsuki bean see **adzuki bean**.

adsum /ad'sum or -sŭm/ (L) I am present; here.

ad summum /ad sum'um or sŭm'ŭm/ (L) to the highest point.

aduki bean see **adzuki bean**.

adularia /ad-ū-lā'ri-ə/ (*mineralogy*) *n* a transparent orthoclase feldspar. [From the *Adula* group in the Alps]

adulate /ad'ū-lāt/ *vt* to fawn upon or flatter; to praise excessively. [L *adūlārī, adūlātus* to fawn upon]
■ **adūlā'tion** *n*. **ad'ūlator** *n*. **ad'ūlatory** *adj*.

Adullamite /ə-dul'ə-mīt/ *n* John Bright's name for a Whig seceder from the Liberal party (1866) (*hist*); hence someone who withdraws their allegiance from any political or intellectual group. [From the cave of *Adullam*, Bible, 1 Samuel 22.1–2]

adult /ad'ult or ə-dult'/ *adj* fully grown; mature; of or for adults; suitable for the mature person only, *esp* of pornographic material. ◆ *n* a fully grown person, animal or plant. [L *adultus*, pap of *adolēscere* to grow up; see **adolescent**]
■ **ad'ulthood** *n*.

adulterate /ə-dul'tə-rāt/ *vt* to debase or falsify, by mixing with something inferior or spurious; to commit adultery with (*obs*). ◆ *vi* (*Shakesp*) to commit adultery. ◆ *adj* defiled by adultery; spurious; corrupted by base elements. [L *adulterāre, -ātum*, prob from *ad* to, and *alter* another. Some forms come from Fr, remodelled later on Latin]
■ **adult'erant** *n* something with which anything is adulterated (also *adj*). **adultera'tion** *n* the act of adulterating; the state of being adulterated. **adult'erātor** *n* a person who adulterates a commodity.

adulterer /ə-dul'tə-rər/ *n* (also *fem* **adult'eress**) a person guilty of adultery. [**adulterate**]
■ **adult'erine** *adj* resulting from adultery; spurious; illegal (*hist*). ◆ *n* the offspring of adultery. **adult'erize** or **-ise** *vi* (*archaic*) to commit adultery. **adult'erous** *adj* relating to, of the nature of, or guilty of, adultery. **adult'erously** *adv*. **adult'ery** *n* voluntary sexual intercourse between a married person and someone who is not that person's legal partner; lack of chastity generally (*Bible*); applied *esp* by theologians to marriages disapproved of, expressing reproach or scorn; image worship; adulteration or falsification (*obs*).

adumbrate /ad'um-brāt or ə-dum'/ *vt* to give a faint shadow of; to outline faintly; to foreshadow; to overshadow. [L *adumbrāre, -ātus*, from *ad* to, and *umbra* a shadow]
■ **adumbrā'tion** *n*. **adum'brative** *adj*. **adum'bratively** *adv*.

adunc /ə-dungk'/ *adj* hooked (also **adunc'ate**, **adunc'ated** or **adunc'ous**). [L *aduncus, aduncātus*, from *ad* to, and *uncus* a hook]
■ **aduncity** /ə-dun'si-ti/ *n*.

ad unguem /ad ung'gwem or oong'/ (L) to a nicety, (literally, to the nail).

ad unum omnes /ad ū'nəm om'nēz or oo'nŭm om'nās/ (L) everyone to the last man.

adust /ə-dust'/ *vt* (*Milton*) to scorch. ◆ *adj* burnt up or scorched (*obs*); browned with the sun (*obs*); sallow and melancholy (from medieval notions of dryness of body) (*archaic*). [L *adūstus*, pap of *adūrere* to burn up]

adv. *abbrev*: advent; adverb; *adversus* (L), against; advisory; advocate.

ad valorem /ad va-lö'rəm, -lō'rəm or wa-lö'rem/ (L) according or in proportion to value; depending on the value of goods, as opposed to weight, content or quantity (*abbrev* **ad val.**).

advance /əd-väns/ *vt* to put forward; to promote; to further; to supply beforehand; to pay before due time; to lend, *esp* on security; to raise (*Shakesp*); to raise in price; to extol (*obs*). ◆ *vi* to move or go forward; to approach *esp* aggressively (with *on*); to make progress; to rise in rank or in value. ◆ *n* a forward move; progress; an increase; a rise in price, value, or wages; payment beforehand; a loan; an approach, overture, move towards agreement, favour, etc. ◆ *adj* forward (of position); made, given, etc ahead of time. [OFr *avancer*, from LL *abante* (Fr *avant*), from L *ab ante* from before; the prefix refashioned later as if from *ad*]
■ **advanced'** *adj* at or appropriate to a far-on stage (of education, thought, emancipation, life, etc). **advance'ment** *n* promotion; furthering; payment in advance.

❑ **advanced gas-cooled reactor** *n* a nuclear reactor in which carbon dioxide is used as a coolant (*abbrev* **AGR**). **Advanced Higher** *n* an examination taken in Scotland at a more advanced level than Highers (also *adj*). **advance directive** *n* another name for **living will** (see under **living**). **advanced level** see **A level** under **A** (*abbrev*). **advanced passenger train** *n* a lightweight type of train, electrically powered, designed to run at 250km/h (156mph) and to tilt at curves (*abbrev* **APT**). **advanced skills teacher** *n* an experienced teacher paid to help train other teachers while continuing to teach classes rather than seek promotion to a management post. **Advanced Subsidiary level** see **AS level**. **advance factory** *n* one built to encourage development, in the belief that a firm will take it over. **advance** or **advanced guard** *n* a guard or party in front of the main body. **advance man** *n* (*N Am*) a person who travels in advance of a public figure to organize publicity, security, etc. **advance note** *n* an order for (generally) a month's wage given to a sailor on engaging. **advance workings** *n pl* (*mining*) workings in which the whole face is carried forward, no support pillars being left.
■ **in advance** beforehand; in front.

advantage /əd-vänt'ij/ *n* superiority over another; a favourable condition or circumstance; gain or benefit; the first point after deuce (*tennis*). ◆ *vt* and *vi* to benefit or profit. [Fr *avantage*, from *avant* before; see **advance**]
■ **advan'tageable** *adj* (*rare*) profitable; convenient. **advan'taged** *adj* having the benefit of a good social or financial situation. **advantageous** /ad-vənt-ā'jəs/ *adj* of advantage; useful (with *to* and *for*). **advanta'geously** *adv*. **advanta'geousness** *n*.
❑ **advantage court** *n* (often shortened to **ad court**) the left side of a tennis court, from which the serve is made and received at odd-numbered points. **advantage rule** *n* in games, a rule under which an infringement and its penalty are overlooked when this is to the advantage of the non-offending side.
■ **have the advantage of** to recognize without being recognized. **take advantage of** to avail oneself of; to make undue use of an advantage over; to seduce. **take at advantage** to use favourable conditions against; to take by surprise. **to advantage** so that the merits are clearly perceived. **turn something to advantage** to use circumstances or a situation to one's benefit.

advection /ad-vek'shən/ (*meteorol*) *n* movement horizontally of air or atmospheric conditions. [L *advectio*, from *ad* to, and *vehere* to carry]

advene /ad-vēn'/ (*archaic*) *vi* to be superadded. [Ety as for **advent**]

advent /ad'vənt or -vent/ *n* a coming or arrival; (with *cap*) the first or the second coming of Christ; the period immediately before the Christian festival of the Nativity, including four Sundays. [L *advenīre, adventum* to approach, happen, from *ad* to, and *venīre* to come; *adventus* arrival]
■ **Ad'ventism** *n*. **Ad'ventist** *n* someone who expects an imminent second coming of Christ; a millenarian, who expects a golden age after the second coming of Christ. **adventive** /-vent'/ *adj* accidental; not permanently established in a habitat (*bot*). ◆ *n* a thing or person coming from outside.

adventitious /ad-vən-tish'əs/ *adj* accidental; additional; foreign; appearing casually; developed out of the usual order or place. [L *adventīcius* extraneous]
■ **adventi'tia** *n* (*anat*) the outermost covering of an organ or part, *esp* of a blood vessel. **adventi'tiously** *adv*.

adventure /əd-ven'chər/ *n* an exciting experience; the spirit of enterprise; a remarkable incident; an enterprise; risk; a commercial speculation; a chance (*obs*); trial of the issue (*obs*). ◆ *vt* to risk; to dare; to venture; to put forward as a venture; to venture to say or utter. ◆ *vi* to risk oneself; to take a risk. [L *adventūrus* future participle of *advenire* to approach or happen, from *ad* to, and *venire* to come; partly through Fr]
■ **adven'turer** *n* (also *fem* **adven'turess**) someone who engages in hazardous enterprises; a soldier of fortune, or speculator; someone who pushes his or her fortune, *esp* by unscrupulous means. **adven'turesome** *adj* adventurous. **adven'turism** *n* the practice of engaging in hazardous and ill-considered enterprises; in foreign policy, opportunism employed in the service of expansionism. **adven'turist** *n* and *adj*. **adventuris'tic** *adj*. **adven'turous** *adj* enterprising; daring; ready to incur risk. **adven'turously** *adv*. **adven'turousness** *n*.
❑ **adventure game** *n* an elaborate or complex computer game, often involving role playing. **adventure playground** *n* a playground with objects that can be used by children for building, to climb on, etc.

adverb /ad'vûrb/ *n* a word added to a verb, adjective or other adverb to express some modification of the meaning or an accompanying circumstance. [L *adverbium*, from *ad* to, and *verbum* a word (transl Gr *epirrēma*, literally, that which is said afterwards)]
■ **adverb'ial** /əd-/ *adj*. **adverb'ialize** or **-ise** *vt* to give the character of an adverb to. **adverb'ially** *adv*.

■ words derived from main entry word; ❑ compound words; ■ idioms and phrasal verbs

ad verbum /ad vûr'bəm/ or /wer'bŭm/ (L) word for word (literally, to a word).

adversaria /ad-vər-sā'ri-ə/ n pl miscellaneous notes; a commonplace book. [L adversāria]

adversarial /ad-vər-sā'ri-əl/ adj combative; antagonistic; hostile, esp on party lines in politics; involving opposing parties or interests (law). [Ety as for **adversary**]

adversary /ad'vər-sə-ri/ n an opponent. [L adversus, from ad to, and vertere, versum to turn]
■ **adversative** /əd-vûrs'/ adj denoting opposition, contrariety or variety. **ad'verse** /-vûrs/ adj contrary (with to); opposed; unfavourable; hurtful; facing the main axis (bot). **ad'versely** adv. **ad'verseness** n. **advers'ity** n adverse circumstances; misfortune; perversity (Shakesp).
■ **the Adversary** Satan.

advert[1] /ad'vərt or -vûrt/ (inf) n an advertisement. [Short form]

advert[2] /ad-vûrt'/ vi (with to) to turn one's attention; to refer. [L advertere, from ad to, and vertere to turn]
■ **advert'ence** or **advert'ency** n attention; heedfulness; regard. **advert'ent** adj attentive; heedful. **advert'ently** adv.

advertise or (esp US) **advertize** /ad'vər-tīz or -tīz'/, formerly (Shakesp) -vûrt'iz/ vt to give notice of; to give public information about merits claimed for; to draw attention to; to offer for sale by public notice, printed or broadcast; to inform or give notice to (archaic). ♦ vi to issue advertisements; to ask (for) by means of public notice, eg in a newspaper. [Fr avertir, avertiss-, from L advertere to turn towards; see **advert**[2]]
■ **advertisement** /əd-vûr'tis-mənt or -tiz-/ or (esp US) **advertizement** /-tiz- or -tīz'/ n the act of advertising; a public notice, usu with the purpose of informing and/or changing public attitudes and behaviour (inf short form **ad** or **ad'vert**); a short performance recorded for radio, TV, etc to advertise goods or services (inf short form **ad** or **ad'vert**); news (obs). **advertiser** /ad' or -tīz'/ n someone who advertises; often part of a newspaper's title. **ad'vertising** n the business of producing advertisements. ♦ adj (Shakesp) attentive.
□ **ad'land** n (facetious) the imaginary and usu idealized world portrayed in advertisements; the advertising industry. **ad-man** or **adman** /ad'man/ n someone who takes part in advertising, esp advertising addressed to the ad-mass. **ad'-mass** or **ad'mass** n advertising intended to appeal to a mass public; the mass aimed at by such advertising. **advertising agency** n an organization which helps a company to sell its products or services by undertaking market research, creating advertising material, and buying space in newspapers, TV schedules, etc.
■ **Advertising Standards Authority** an independent group established in the UK in 1962 to ensure that the self-regulating system of advertising works effectively in the public interest (abbrev **ASA**).

advertorial /ad-vər-tö'ri-əl/ (orig US) n an advertisement presented in the guise of editorial material (also adj). [advertisement and editorial]

advew /ad-vū'/ (Spenser) vt to view. [L ad to, and **view**]

advice /əd-vīs'/ n counsel; information (usu in pl); formal official intelligence about anything; specially skilled opinion, eg of a physician or lawyer. [OFr advis (Fr avis), from L ad visum according to what is seen or seems best]
■ **advice'ful** (Spenser avize'full) adj (obs) watchful; attentive; skilled in advising.
□ **advice'-boat** n (obs) a swift vessel employed in conveying despatches. **advice note** n a document sent by the supplier of goods to the buyer advising that the goods ordered have been despatched.
■ **take advice** to ask for advice, esp in legal matters; to act on advice.

advise /əd-vīz'/ vt to counsel; to recommend; to inform; to announce; to view (obs); to take thought of or consider (obs); to take to avizandum (Scots law). ♦ vi to reflect or deliberate (obs); to consult (with). [OFr aviser, and LL advisāre; cf **advice**]
■ **advisabil'ity** n. **advīs'able** adj to be recommended; expedient; open to advice. **advīs'ableness** n. **advīs'ably** adv. **advīs'atory** adj (rare) advisory. **advīsed'** adj having duly considered; considered; deliberate; apprised; amenable to advice. **advīs'edly** /-id-li/ adv after consideration; intentionally; wisely or prudently. **advīs'edness** n deliberate consideration; prudent procedure. **advīse'ment** n (obs or archaic or N Am) counsel, deliberation. **advīs'er** or **advīs'or** n someone who advises; a teacher appointed by a British education authority to advise on the teaching and development of a particular subject. **advīs'ership** n. **advīs'ing** n (Shakesp) counsel, advice. **advīs'orate** n the body of advisers appointed by an education authority. **advīs'ory** adj having the attribute or function of advising. ♦ n a statement providing advice.
■ **Advisory, Conciliation and Arbitration Service** see **ACAS**.

ad vivum /ad vī'vum or wē'wŭm/ (L) to the life, lifelike.

advocaat /ad'vō-kät or -kä/ n a liqueur containing raw eggs and flavourings; a medicinal drink of eggs, rum or brandy, and lemon juice. [Du advokaatenborrel advocate's dram, as a clearer of the throat]

advocate /ad'və-kit or -kät or -kət/ n an intercessor or defender; someone who pleads the cause of another; in Scotland and some other countries, a person who is qualified to plead before the higher courts of law, a member of the Bar (corresponding to a barrister in England); a person who recommends or urges something, eg a certain reform, method, etc; (with cap) the Holy Spirit (New English Bible); (only in Aberdeen) a solicitor. ♦ vt and vi to act as an advocate (for). [OFr avocat and L advocātus, from advocāre, -ātum to call in, from ad to, and vocāre to call]
■ **ad'vocacy** /-kə-si/ n the function of an advocate; a pleading for; defence. **advocā'tion** n. **ad'vocātor** n. **ad'vocātory** adj.
□ **advocate-dep'ute** n a salaried Scottish law-officer appointed as public prosecutor by the **Lord Advocate**, the chief law-officer of the Crown and public prosecutor of crimes for Scotland.

advocatus diaboli /ad-və-kä'təs dī-ab'ə-lī or ad-wō-kä'tŭs dē-ab'o-lē/ (L) n the devil's advocate (qv).

advoutrer /əd-vow'trər/ and **advoutry** /-tri/ obsolete forms intermediate between **avoutrer** and **adulterer**, etc.

advowson /əd-vow'zən/ n the right of appointing a clergyman to a church benefice. [OFr avoeson, from LL advocātiō, -ōnis, from L advocātus]

advt abbrev : advertisement.

adward (Spenser) same as **award**.

adware see under **ad** (n).

adynamia /a-di-nā'mi-ə/ n helplessness, lack of strength accompanying a disease. [Gr a- (privative), and dynamis strength]
■ **adynamic** /-am'/ adj without strength; characterized by the absence of force (phys).

adytum /ad'i-təm/ n (pl **ad'yta**) the most sacred part of a temple; the chancel of a church. [Latinized from Gr adyton, from a- (privative), and dyein to enter]

adze or (US) **adz** /adz/ n a cutting tool with an arched blade which is set at right angles to the handle. [OE adesa]

adzuki bean /ad-zoo'ki bēn/ n a type of kidney bean grown esp in China and Japan (also **adsuki bean** /ad-soo'ki/ and **aduki bean** /a-doo'ki/). [Jap azuki]

AE abbrev : Account Executive; Air Efficiency Award.

ae /ā, yā or ye/ (Scot) adj one; very or same. [Scot form of OE ān one, used attributively]
■ **ae'fald**, **ae'fauld**, **ā'fald** or **a'fawld** adj one-fold or single; single-minded; faithful; simple; sincere; honest.

ae. or **aet.** abbrev : aetatis (L), of his or her age, aged (so many years).

AEA abbrev : Atomic Energy Authority.

aecidium /ē-sid'i-əm/ or **aecium** /ē'si-əm/ (bot) n (pl **aecid'ia** and **aec'ia**) a cup-shaped fructification in rust fungi. [Gr (dimin of) aikiā injury]
■ **aecid'iospore** or **aec'iospore** n spore produced in it.

aedes /ā-ē'dēz/ n a member of the Aedes genus of mosquitoes, which includes Aedes aegypti, the species that carries yellow fever and dengue fever. [Gr aedes distasteful]

aedile /ē'dīl/ n a magistrate in ancient Rome who had responsibility for public buildings, games, markets, police, etc. [L aedīlis, from aedēs, -is a building]
■ **ae'dileship** n.

aefald, etc see under **ae**.

aegirine /ē'ji-rēn/ or **aegirite** /ē'ji-rīt/ (mineralogy) n a green pleochroic pyroxene. [Ægir Norse sea-god or giant]

aegis /ē'jis/ n protection; patronage. [Gr aigis in Gr mythology a shield belonging to Zeus or to Pallas]

aeglogue /ēg'log/ (archaic) n an eclogue (qv). [From the mistaken belief that the word meant goat-herd discourse, from Gr aix, aigos goat, and logos discourse]

aegrotat /ē-grō'tat or ē'/ (archaic) n in universities, a medical certificate of illness, or a degree granted when illness has prevented the taking of examinations, etc. [L aegrōtat he or she is sick, 3rd pers sing present indicative of aegrōtāre, from aeger sick]

Aegyptian an archaic spelling of **Egyptian**.

AELTC abbrev : All England Lawn Tennis and Croquet Club.

aelur(o)- see **ailuro-**.

aemule /ē'mūl/ (Spenser) vt to emulate. [L aemulārī]

aeneous /ā-ī'ni-əs/ *adj* (*rare*) of a shining bronze colour. [L *aēneus* made of bronze]

■ **Aeneolithic** /ā-ē-ni-ō-lith'ik/ *adj* (Gr *lithos* stone) belonging to a transitional stage at the end of the Neolithic age, when copper was already in use.

Aeolian /ē-ō'li-ən/ *adj* of Aeolis or Aeolia, in NW Asia Minor, or its ancient Greek colonists. ◆ *n* an Aeolian Greek.

■ **Aeolic** /-ol'ik/ *n* the Greek dialect of the Aeolians.

❑ **Aeolian mode** *n* in ancient Greek music, the same as the Hypodorian or Hyperphrygian; in old church music, the authentic (qv) mode with A for its final.

aeolian /ē-ō'li-ən/ *adj* relating to, acted on by, or due to the agency of, the wind; aerial. [L *Aeolus*, from Gr *Aiolos* god of the winds]

❑ **aeolian deposits** *n pl* (*geol*) sediments deposited by wind, as desert sands, loess, etc. **aeolian** (or **Aeolian**) **harp** *n* a soundbox with strings tuned in unison, sounding harmonics in a current of air.

aeolipile or **aeolipyle** /ē-ol'i-pīl/ *n* a hollow ball turned by the escape of steam through valves set at a tangent. [L *Aeolus* god of the winds, and *pila* ball; or Gr *Aiolou pylai* Gates of Aeolus]

aeolotropy /ē-ə-lot'rə-pi/ *n* variation in physical properties according to direction. [Gr *aiolos* changeful, and *tropē* a turn]

■ **aeolotrop'ic** *adj*.

aeon or **eon** /ē'on/ *n* a vast age; eternity; the largest, or a very large division of geological time; a thousand million years (*astron*); in Gnosticism, a power emanating from the supreme deity, with its share in the creation and government of the universe. [L *aeon*, from Gr *aiōn*]

■ **aeō'nian** *adj* eternal.

Aepyornis /ē-pi-ör'nis/ *n* a gigantic Holocene fossil wingless bird of Madagascar. [Gr *aipys* tall, and *ornis* bird]

aequo animo /ē- or ī-kwō an'i-mō/ (L) with an equable mind.

AER *abbrev* : annual equivalent rate.

aerate /ā'(ə-)rāt/ *vt* to put air into; to charge with air or with carbon dioxide or other gas (as in the production of **aerated waters**); to excite or perturb (*inf*). [L *āēr* air]

■ **aerā'ted** *adj*. **aerā'tion** *n* exposure to the action of air; mixing or saturating with air or other gas; oxygenation of the blood by respiration. **ā'erātor** *n* an apparatus for the purpose of aeration.

❑ **aerated concrete** *n* lightweight concrete made by a process which traps gas bubbles in the mix. **aerating root** *n* a root that rises erect into the air, a breathing organ in mud plants.

AERE *abbrev* : formerly, Atomic Energy Research Establishment.

aerenchyma /ā(-ə)-reng'ki-mə/ (*bot*) *n* respiratory tissue. [Gr *āēr* air, *en* in, and *chyma* that which is poured]

■ **aerenchymatous** /-kī'/ *adj*.

aerial /ā'ri-əl/ or *ā-ē'*, or *ā-er'i-əl/ adj* of, in or belonging to the air; airy; unreal; lofty; (for the following meanings *usu* /ā'(ə-)ri-əl/) atmospheric; elevated; performed high above the ground, eg *aerial acrobatics*; connected with aircraft, eg used in or against aircraft; using aircraft (eg *aerial support*); carried out from aircraft; growing in air (*biol*). ◆ *n* (always /ā'(ə-)ri-əl/) a wire, rod, etc exposed to receive or emit electromagnetic waves; an antenna. [L *aerius*, from *āēr* air]

■ **aer'ialist** *n* someone who performs on the high wire or trapeze; a skier who performs gymnastic manoeuvres in midair. **aeriality** /-al'i-ti/ *n*. **aer'ially** *adv*.

❑ **aerial perspective** *n* (*art*) a technique of indicating relative distance through gradation of tone, colour, etc. **aerial railway** or **ropeway** *n* one for overhead conveyance. **aerial surveying** *n* surveying by photographs taken from the air.

aerie[1] see **eyrie**.

aerie[2] see **aery**[1].

aeriform /ā'(ə-)ri-förm/ *adj* gaseous; unreal. [L *āēr* air, and *fōrma* form]

aero- /ā(-ə)-rō-/ *combining form* denoting: air; aircraft. [Gr *āēr* air]

■ **ae'ro** *adj* of or relating to aircraft or aeronautics. **aerobat'ic** *adj*. **aerobat'ics** *n sing* (Gr *bateein* to tread) the art of performing stunts in an aircraft. ◆ *n pl* aerial acrobatics. **a'erobe** *n* (Gr *bios* life) an organism that requires free oxygen for respiration. **aerobic** /-ōb' or -ob'/ *adj* requiring free oxygen for respiration; biochemical change, eg effected by aerobes; involving the activity of aerobes; of or relating to aerobics. **aerob'ically** *adv*. **aerob'ics** *n sing* exercising by means of such rhythmic activities as walking, swimming, cycling, etc in order to reduce fat and improve physical fitness; a system intended to increase fitness and improve body-shape, consisting of fast, repeated and strenuous gymnastic exercises (also **Aerobics**®). **aerobiolog'ical** /-bī-ō-loj'/ *adj*. **aerobiolog'ically** *adv*. **aerobiol'ogist** *n*. **aerobiol'ogy** *n* the study of airborne micro-organisms. **aerobī'ont** *n* an aerobe. **aerobiō'sis** *n* life in the presence of oxygen. **aerobiotic** /-ot'ik/ *adj*. **aerobiot'ically** *adv*. **a'erobomb** *n* a bomb for dropping from aircraft. **aerobot'** *n* an unmanned gas-filled craft used to conduct experiments in planetary atmospheres. **a'erobrake** *vi* and *n*. **a'erobraking** or **aerodynamic braking** *n* the use of a planet's atmosphere to reduce

the speed of space vehicles. **A'erobus**® *n* a type of suspended monorail system. **a'erodart** *n* an arrow-headed missile of steel dropped from aircraft in warfare. **a'erodrome** *n* (Gr *dromos* running) an area, with its buildings, etc, used for the take-off and landing of aircraft; an early type of flying machine (*hist*). **aerodynam'ic** or **aerodynam'ical** *adj*. **aerodynam'ically** *adv*. **aerodynam'icist** *n* a person concerned with aerodynamics. **aerodynam'ics** *n sing* (Gr *dynamis* power) the dynamics of gases; the science or study of the forces acting upon bodies in a flow of air or gas (**aerodynamic braking** see **aerobraking** above). ◆ *n pl* the properties of a body required for efficient movement through air. **a'erodyne** /-dīn/ *n* a heavier-than-air aircraft. **aeroelas'tic** *adj* able to be deformed by aerodynamic forces. **aeroelastic'ian** *n* a person who studies flutter and vibration in high-speed aircraft. **aeroelastic'ity** *n*. **aeroem'bolism** *n* an airman's condition similar to caisson disease, caused by rapid ascent to high altitudes. **a'ero-engine** *n* an aircraft engine. **a'erofoil** *n* a body (eg wing or tail plane) shaped so as to produce an aerodynamic reaction (lift) normal to its direction of motion, for a small resistance (drag) in that plane. **a'erogel** *n* any of various extremely light and porous solid materials containing small pockets of gas, a foam. **aerogen'erator** *n* a generator driven by wind. **a'erogram** *n* a message by wireless telegraphy; a message sent by telegram (or telephone) and aeroplane; an aerogramme; an aerograph record. **a'erogramme** or **a'érogramme** *n* an air letter; a sheet of thin, *usu* blue paper, with postage stamp imprinted, to be folded and sent by airmail at a special low rate. **a'erograph** *n* a meteorograph; an airborne automatic recording instrument. **aerog'raphy** *n* meteorology. **aerohy'droplane** *n* a winged hydroplane or flying-boat. **a'erolite** or **a'erolith** *n* (Gr *lithos* a stone) a meteoric stone or meteorite. **aerolithol'ogy** *n* the science of aerolites. **aerolit'ic** *adj*. **aerolog'ical** *adj*. **aerol'ogist** *n*. **aerol'ogy** *n* the branch of science that deals with the atmosphere. **a'eromancy** *n* (Gr *manteiā* divination) divination by atmospheric phenomena; weather forecasting. **aerom'eter** *n* an instrument for measuring the weight or density of air and gases. **aeromet'ric** *adj*. **aerom'etry** *n* pneumatics. **a'eromotor** *n* an engine for aircraft. **a'eronaut** *n* (Gr *nautēs* a sailor) a balloonist or airman. **aeronaut'ic** or **aeronaut'ical** *adj*. **aeronaut'ically** *adv*. **aeronaut'ics** *n sing* the science or art of aerial travel. **aeroneuros'is** *n* flight fatigue, a nervous disorder of airmen, with emotional and physical symptoms. **aeron'omist** *n*. **aeron'omy** *n* the science of the earth's atmosphere. **aeroph'agy** *n* (Gr *phagein* to eat) spasmodic swallowing of air, leading to belching, stomach pain, etc. **a'erophobe** *n* a person suffering from aerophobia, *esp* as fear of flying. **aeropho'bia** *n* (Gr *phobos* fear) morbid fear of draughts; (loosely) morbid fear of flying. **aerophob'ic** (or /-fob'/) *adj*. **a'erophone** *n* any wind instrument. **a'erophyte** *n* (Gr *phyton* a plant; *bot* or *pathol*) an epiphyte. **a'eroplane** *n* any heavier-than-air power-driven flying machine, with fixed wings; a small plane for aerostatic experiments (see **plane**[1]). **aeroplank'ton** *n* minute organisms carried in the air. **a'eroshell** *n* a form of parachute enabling a spacecraft to make a soft landing. **aerosid'erite** *n* (Gr *sidēros* iron) an iron meteorite. **a'erosol** *n* a colloidal system, such as a mist or a fog, in which the dispersion medium is a gas; a liquid, eg insecticide, in a container under pressure; the container. **a'erosolize** or **-ize** *vt* to reduce (a liquid or solid) to an aerosol. **a'erospace** *n* the earth's atmosphere together with space beyond; the branch of technology or of industry concerned with the flight of spacecraft through this. ◆ *adj* of or belonging to, or capable of operating in, air and/or space (**aerospace-plane** an aircraft-like vehicle that can take off and land on runways, manoeuvre in the atmosphere, operate in space, and re-enter the atmosphere). **a'erospike** *n* see **linear aerospike engine** under **line**[1]. **a'erostat** *n* (Gr *statos* standing) a balloon or other aircraft lighter than air; a balloonist; an air-sac (*zool*). **aerostat'ic** or **aerostat'ical** *adj*. **aerostat'ics** *n sing* the science of the equilibrium and pressure of air and other gases; the science or art of ballooning. **aerostation** /-stā'shən/ *n* ballooning. **aerotac'tic** *adj* (Gr *taxis* arrangement; *adj taktikos*) relating to or showing aerotaxis. **aerotax'is** *n* (*biol*; *obs*) movement towards or from oxygen. **a'erotone** *n* a type of deep bath equipped with a mechanism to direct compressed air at the body as a form of massage. **a'erotrain** *n* a train driven by an aircraft engine, riding on a cushion of air. **aerotrop'ic** *adj* (Gr *tropē* turning). **aerot'ropism** *n* (*bot*) curvature in response to concentration of oxygen.

aeruginous /ē-roo'ji-nəs or i-roo'jə-/ *adj* relating to or like copper-rust or verdigris. [L *aerūginōsus*, from *aerūgō* rust of copper, from *aes*, *aeris* brass or copper]

aery[1] or **aerie** /ā'(ə-)ri/ (*poetic*) *adj* aerial; incorporeal; spiritual; visionary. [L *āerius*; see **aerial**]

❑ **aerie light** *adj* (*Milton*) light as air.

aery[2] same as **eyrie**.

aes alienum /ēz al-i-ē'nəm/ or *īs al-i-ā'nŭm/ (L) *n* debt, (literally) another's copper or brass.

æsc /ash/ n the rune (ᚠ) for a, used in Old English for æ; the ligature æ used in Old English for the same sound (that of a in Mod Eng RP cat). [OE æsc ash tree, the name of the rune]

Aeschna /esk'nə/ n a genus of large, usu colourful dragonflies.

Aesculapian /ē-skū-lā'pi-ən or es-kū-/ adj to do with or relating to the art of healing (also **Escula'pian**). [L Aesculāpius, Gr Asklēpios, the god of healing]

Aesculus /ēs'kū-ləs/ n the horse-chestnut genus of the family Hippocastanaceae. [L aesculus a species of oak]
■ **aes'cūlin** n a glucoside in horse-chestnut bark.

aesir see **as**[2].

aesthesia or (US) **esthesia** /ēs- or es-thē'zi-ə/ or **aesthesis** /-thē'sis/ n feeling; sensitivity. [Gr aisthesis, from aisthanesthai to feel or perceive]
■ **aesthēs'iogen** n something producing sensation, esp a stimulus or suggestion producing a sensory effect on a subject under hypnosis. **aesthēsiogen'ic** adj.

aesthete or (US) **esthete** /ēs' or es'thēt/ n a professed disciple of aestheticism; a person who affects an extravagant love of art. [Gr aisthētikos perceptive, from aisthanesthai to feel or perceive]
■ **aesthetic** /es-thet'ik, is- or ēs-/ adj relating to, possessing, or pretending to possess, a sense of beauty; artistic or affecting to be artistic; relating to perception by the senses (obs). **aesthet'ical** adj of or relating to aesthetics. **aesthet'ically** adv. **aesthetician** /-tish'ən/ n someone devoted to or knowledgeable or skilled in aesthetics; a beautician (N Am). **aesthet'icism** n the principles of aesthetics; the cult of the beautiful, applied esp to a late 19c movement to bring art into life, which developed into affectation. **aesthet'icist** n. **aesthet'icize** or **-ise** /-sīz/ vt to make aesthetic. **aesthet'ics** n sing the principles of taste and art; the philosophy of the fine arts.

aestival or (US) **estival** /e- or ē-stī'vəl/ adj of summer. [L aestīvus, aestīvālis relating to summer, and aestīvāre to pass the summer, from aestās summer]
■ **aestivā'tion** or (US) **estivā'tion** n a spending of the summer; manner of folding in the flower-bud (bot); arrangement of foliage leaves relative to one another in the bud (bot); dormancy during the dry season (zool and bot).

aes triplex /ēz trī'pleks or īs trip'leks/ (L) n a strong defence, (literally) triple brass.

aet abbrev : after extra time.

aet. see **ae**.

aetatis suae /ē-tat'is sū'ē or ī-tä'tis sū'ī/ (L) of his or her age.

aether /ē'thər/ n same as **ether** (but not generally used in the chemical sense).

Aethiopian see **Ethiopian**.

aethrioscope /ē'thri-ō-skōp or -ə-/ n an instrument for measuring the minute variations of temperature due to the condition of the sky. [Gr aithriā the open sky, and skopeein to look at]

aetiology or (US) **etiology** /ē-ti-ol'ə-ji/ n the science or philosophy of causation; an inquiry into the origin or causes of anything; the medical study of the causation of disease. [Gr aitiologiā, from aitiā cause, and logos discourse]
■ **aetiolog'ical** adj. **aetiolog'ically** adv.

Aetnean see under **etna**.

AEW abbrev : airborne early warning.

AF abbrev : Admiral of the Fleet; Anglo-French; Associate Fellow; audio-frequency.

AFA abbrev : Amateur Football Association.

AFAIK or **afaik** abbrev : as far as I know.

afald, afawld see under **ae**.

afar /ə-fär'/ adv from a far distance (usu, from afar); at or to a distance (usu, afar off). [**of** and **on**, with **far**]

afara /ə-fär'ə/ n a type of W African tree having a light-coloured, straight-grained wood. [Yoruba]

AFC abbrev : Air Force Cross; Association Football Club; automatic flight control.

afear, affear or **affeare** /ə-fēr'/ (Spenser) vt to frighten. [Pfx a- (intensive), and OE fǣran to frighten]
■ **afeard'** or **affeard'** adj (Shakesp) afraid.

afebrile /ā-fē'bril, -feb'ril or -ril/ adj without fever. [**a-**[2] and **febrile**]

affable /af'ə-bl/ adj easy to speak to; courteous, esp towards inferiors; pleasant or friendly. [Fr, from L affābilis, from affārī to speak to, from ad to, and fārī to speak]
■ **affabil'ity** n. **aff'ably** adv.

affair /ə-fär'/ n something which is to be done; business; any matter, occurrence, etc; a minor battle; a matter of intimate personal concern; a thing (inf); a romantic intrigue, love affair, affaire; (in pl) transactions

in general; (in pl) public concerns. [OFr afaire (Fr affaire), from à and faire, from L ad to, and facere to do; cf **ado**]

affaire /a-fer' / (Fr) n liaison or intrigue; (usu with name of chief person involved) an episode or incident arousing speculation and scandal; (also **affaire d'amour** /dam-oor/) a love affair.
□ **affaire de cœur** /a-fer də kœr/ n an affair of the heart. **affaire d'honneur** /a-fer do-nœr/ n an affair of honour (a duel).

affear, affeare, affeard or **affear'd** see **afear** and **affeer**.

affect[1] /ə-fekt'/ vt to act upon; to infect or attack as or like a disease; to influence; to move the feelings of; (in passive only) to assign or allot. ◆n /af'ekt/ the emotion that lies behind action (psychol); pleasantness or unpleasantness, or complex of ideas involved in, an emotional state (psychol); disposition of body or mind (obs); affection or love (obs). [L afficere, affectum, from ad to, and facere to do]
■ **affect'ed** adj. **affect'ing** adj having power to move the emotions. **affect'ingly** adv. **affect'ive** adj of, arising from or influencing emotion. **affect'ively** adv. **affectivity** /af-ek-tiv'i-ti/ n. **affect'less** adj. **affect'lessness** n.
□ **affective disorders** n pl (psychol) a group of disorders whose primary characteristic is a disturbance of mood.

affect[2] /ə-fekt'/ vt to make a show of preferring; to do, wear or inhabit by preference; to assume; to assume the character of; to make a show or pretence of; to aim at or aspire to (obs); to have a liking for (archaic). ◆ vi to incline or tend. [L affectāre, -ātum, frequentative of afficere ; see **affect**[1] above]
■ **affectā'tion** /af-/ n assumption of or striving after an appearance of what is not natural or real; pretence. **affect'ed** adj full of affectation; feigned. **affect'edly** adv. **affect'edness** n. **affect'er** n.

affection /ə-fek'shən/ n love; attachment; the act of influencing; emotion; disposition; inclination; affectation (Shakesp); an attribute or property; a disease. ◆ vt (rare) to love. [L affectiō, -ōnis]
■ **affec'tional** adj. **affec'tionate** adj full of affection; loving; eager, keen, passionate or well inclined (obs). **affec'tionately** adv. **affec'tionateness** n. **affec'tioned** adj disposed (Bible); full of affectation (Shakesp).

affeer /ə-fēr'/ (archaic) vt to assess; to reduce to a certain fixed sum. [OFr affeurer, from L afforāre, from L ad to, and forum a market]
■ **affeered'** (Shakesp **affear'd'**) adj confirmed. **affeer'ment** n.

affenpinscher /af'en-pinsh-ər/ n a small dog related to the Brussels griffon, having tufts of hair on the face. [Ger, from Affe monkey, and Pinscher terrier]

afferent /af'ə-rənt/ (physiol) adj bringing inwards, as the nerves that convey impulses to the central nervous system. [L afferēns, -entis, from ad to, and ferre to carry]

affettuoso /äf-fet-too-ō'sō/ (music) adj tender. ◆ adv tenderly. [Ital]

affiance /ə-fī'əns/ vt to betroth. ◆n faith pledged (obs); contract of marriage (archaic); trust (obs); affinity (obs). [OFr afiance ; see **affy**]
■ **affi'anced** adj betrothed.

affiant /ə-fī'ənt/ (US) n someone who makes an affidavit.

affiche /a-fēsh' / (Fr) n notice or placard.

afficionado see **aficionado**.

affidavit /a-fi-dā'vit/ n a written declaration on oath. [LL affīdāvit, 3rd pers sing perf of affīdāre to pledge one's faith; see **affy**]

affied see **affy**.

affiliate /ə-fil'i-āt/ vt to adopt or attach as a member or branch; to attribute the paternity of; to assign the origin of. ◆ vi to become closely connected; to associate; to fraternize. ◆n /ə-fil'i-ət/ an affiliated person, an associate; a branch, unit, or subsidiary of an organization. [L affīliātus adopted, from ad to, and fīlius a son]
■ **affil'iable** adj. **affilia'tion** n.
□ **affiliation order** n a court order requiring that the putative father of an illegitimate child should contribute to its support.

affine /a-fīn' or af'īn/ n a relation, esp by marriage. ◆ adj related; (in mathematics) preserving finiteness, as in **affine geometry** the geometry associated with affine transformations, and **affine transformation** the composition of a reversible linear mapping followed by a translation. [OFr affin, from L affīnis neighbouring, from ad to or at, and fīnis a boundary]
■ **affīn'al** adj denoting a relationship by marriage. **affined'** adj related; bound by some tie.

affinity /ə-fin'i-ti/ n relationship by marriage; relationship of sponsor and godchild; natural or fundamental relationship, esp common origin; attraction; a spiritual attraction between two people; a person whose attraction for another is supposed to be of this kind; nearness (obs); the extent to which a compound of a functional group is reactive with a given reagent (chem); a measure of the strength of interaction between antigen and antibody or between a receptor and its ligand (immunol). [Ety as for **affine**]
■ **affin'itive** adj.

❑ **affinity card** n a credit card linked to a particular charity, to which the issuing bank pays a fee on issue and subsequent donations according to the credit level. **affinity group** n a group of people with a common aim or interest.

affirm /ə-fûrm'/ vt to assert confidently or positively; to ratify (a judgement); to confirm or stand by (one's own statement); to declare one's commitment to; to state in the affirmative (logic); to declare formally, without an oath (law). ◆ vi to make an affirmation. [OFr afermer, from L affirmāre, from ad to, and firmus firm]
■ **affirm'able** adj. **affirm'ance** n affirmation; assertion; confirmation. **affirm'ant** adj and n. **affirmation** /af-ər-mā'shən or -ûr-/ n assertion; something which is affirmed; a positive judgement or proposition; a solemn declaration in lieu of an oath. **affirm'ative** adj affirming or asserting; positive, not negative; (of an answer, etc) agreeing, saying 'yes'; dogmatic. ◆ n the affirmative mode; an affirmative word, proposition or utterance. **affirm'atively** adv. **affirm'atory** adj. **affirm'er** n. **affirm'ingly** adv.
❑ **affirmative action** n (chiefly N Am) positive steps taken to ensure that minority groups and women are not discriminated against, esp as regards employment.

affix /ə-fiks'/ vt to fix to something; to subjoin; to attach; to append; to add (to something). ◆ n /af'iks/ an addition to a root, stem, or word, whether prefix, suffix or infix, to produce a derivative or an inflected form (grammar); any appendage or addition. [L affīgere, -fīxum, from ad to, and fīgere to fix]

afflated /ə-flā'tid/ adj inspired. [L afflāre, -flātum (verb), and afflātus, -ūs (noun), from ad to, and flāre to breathe]
■ **afflā'tion** or **afflā'tus** n inspiration (often divine).

afflict /ə-flikt'/ vt to distress severely; to harass; to humble (Bible); to vex. [L afflīgere, -flīctum to overthrow, cast down, from ad to, and flīgere to dash to the ground]
■ **afflict'ed** adj harassed by disease of body or mind (with with); suffering; overthrown (Milton); humble (Spenser). **afflict'ing** n and adj distressing. **afflic'tion** n state or cause of severe distress. **afflict'ive** adj causing distress.

affluent /af'loo-ənt or -lū-/ adj wealthy; abounding; inflowing. ◆ n an inflowing stream. [L affluere, from ad to, and fluere, fluxum to flow]
■ **aff'luence** n wealth; abundance; inflow. **aff'luently** adv. **aff'luentness** n. **aff'lux** or **affluxion** /ə-fluk'shən/ n an inflow, an accession.
❑ **affluent society** n a society in which the ordinary person can afford many things once regarded as luxuries.

affluenza /a-floo-en'zə/ n a malaise said to affect affluent young people, characterized by feelings of guilt and isolation. [**affluence** and **influenza**]

affogato /af-ə-gä'tō/ n (pl **affoga'tos**) a dessert made by pouring espresso coffee over ice cream. [Ital, drowned]

afforce /ə-förs'/ (law; hist) vt to strengthen (eg a jury by addition of skilled people). [OFr aforcer, from LL exfortiāre, from L ex out, and fortis strong]
■ **afforce'ment** n.

afford /ə-förd'/ vt to yield, give or provide; to bear the expense, or disadvantage of (having the necessary money or other resources, or security of position); (Spenser **aafford**) to consent. [ME aforthen, from OE geforthian to further or cause to come forth]
■ **affordabil'ity** n. **afford'able** adj.

afforest /a- or ə-for'ist/ vt to cover with forest; to convert into hunting ground (hist). [LL afforēstāre, from L ad to, and LL forēsta forest]
■ **affor'estable** adj. **afforestā'tion** n.

affranchise /a-, ə-fran'chīz or -shīz/ vt to free from slavery, or from some obligation. [OFr afranchir, afranchiss-, from à to, and franchir to free, from franc free]
■ **affran'chisement** /-chiz- or -shiz-/ n.

affrap /a-frap'/ (Spenser) vt and vi to strike. [Ital affrappare, from pfx af- (L ad to), and frappare to strike; or directly from **frap**]

affray /ə-frā'/ n a disturbance or breach of the peace; a brawl, fight or fray; fear (Spenser). ◆ vt (archaic) to disturb or startle; to frighten; to scare away. [OFr afrayer, esfreer (Fr effrayer), from LL exfridāre to break the king's peace, from L ex out of, and OHGer fridu (Ger Friede) peace]
■ **affrayed'** adj (archaic) alarmed (now **afraid**).

affreightment /ə-frāt'mənt/ n the hiring of a vessel; the contract governing such a hire. [Fr affrètement (formerly affrétement), remodelled on **freight**]

affrended /a-fren'did/ (Spenser) adj reconciled. [**friend**]

affret /a-fret'/ (Spenser) n a furious onset. [Prob from Ital affrettare to hasten]

affricate /af'ri-kət or -kāt/ (phonetics) n a consonant sound beginning as a plosive and passing into the corresponding fricative. [L affricāre, -ātum to rub against, from ad to, and fricāre to rub]
■ **aff'ricāted** adj. **africā'tion** n. **affric'ative** n affricate (also adj).

affright /ə-frīt'/ vt to frighten. ◆ n sudden terror. [OE āfyrhtan, from ā-, (intensive), and fyrhtan to frighten]
■ **affright'ed** adj. **affright'edly** adv. **affright'en** vt. **affright'ened** adj. **affright'ful** adj (archaic) frightful. **affright'ment** n sudden fear.

affront /ə-frunt'/ vt to meet face to face; to face; to confront; to throw oneself in the way of (Shakesp); to insult to one's face. ◆ n a contemptuous treatment; an open insult; indignity. [OFr afronter to slap on the forehead, from LL affrontāre, from L ad to, and frōns, frontis forehead]
■ **affronté, affrontée** or **affrontee** /ä-fron'tā or ə-frun'tē/ adj facing each other; looking frontwise, or towards the beholder (heraldry). **affront'ed** adj insulted or offended, esp in public. **affront'ing** n and adj. **affront'ingly** adv. **affront'ive** adj.

affusion /ə-fū'zhən/ n pouring on (esp in baptism). [L affūsiō, -ōnis, from affundere, from ad to, and fundere, fūsum to pour]

affy /ə-fī'/ (obs) vt (**affy'ing**; **aff ied'** (Spenser **affyde'**)) to trust; to assure on one's faith; to betroth; to repose or put (trust). ◆ vi to trust or confide. [OFr afier, from LL affīdāre, from L ad to, and fidēs faith; cf **affiance**]

AFG abbrev : Afghanistan (IVR).

Afghan /af'gan/ n a native or citizen, or the main language (Pashto), of Afghanistan, a republic in central Asia; (without cap) a heavy knitted or crocheted woollen blanket or shawl. ◆ adj belonging or relating to Afghanistan or its inhabitants.
❑ **Afghan coat** n a coat made of sheepskin and often embroidered, as orig worn in Afghanistan. **Afghan hound** n an ancient hunting and sheep dog of Afghanistan and N India, kept as a pet in the West.

afghani /af-gä'ni/ n the standard monetary unit of Afghanistan (100 puls). [Pashto afghānī Afghan]

aficionado or sometimes **afficionado** /a-fish-yo-nä'dō or a-fē-thyō-nä'dhō/ n (pl **aficiona'dos** or **afficiona'dos**) an ardent follower, fan; an amateur. [Sp]

afield /ə-fēld'/ adv to or at a distance; to, in, or on the field. [a-¹]

afire /ə-fīr'/ adj and adv on fire; in a state of inflammation. [a-¹]

aflaj see **falaj**.

aflame /ə-flām'/ adj and adv in flames; burning; on fire with an emotion. [a-¹]

aflatoxin /af-lə-tok'sin/ n a (possibly carcinogenic) toxin produced in foodstuffs by species of the mould Aspergillus. [Aspergillus flavus, from L aspergere to sprinkle, and flavus yellow, and **toxin**]

AFL-CIO abbrev : American Federation of Labor and Congress of Industrial Organizations.

afloat /ə-flōt'/ adv and adj floating; at sea; unfixed; in circulation; out of debt (fig). [a-¹]

aflutter /ə-flut'ər/ adv in a flutter. [a-¹]

AFM abbrev : Air Force Medal; audio-frequency modulation.

à fond /a fõ/ (Fr) fundamentally; thoroughly.

afoot /ə-fūt'/ adv and adj astir; actively in existence; on foot. [a-¹]

afore /ə-för'/ prep (archaic or dialect) before. ◆ combining form denoting in front of or before. ◆ adv beforehand or previously. [OE onforan, from on and foran; see **before**]
■ **afore'hand** adv beforehand; before the regular time for accomplishment; in advance. **afore'mentioned** adj previously mentioned, aforesaid. **afore'said** adj said or named before. **afore'thought** adj (usu after n) thought of or meditated before; premeditated. ◆ n premeditation. **afore'time** adv in former or past times.

a fortiori /ā för-ti-ö'rī, -shi- or ä för-ti-ö'rē/ (L) with stronger reason.

afoul /ə-fowl'/ adj and adv in entanglement; in collision (with of). [a-¹]

AFP abbrev : Agence France Presse; alpha-fetoprotein.

AFPC abbrev : Advanced Financial Planning Certificate (see **FPC**).

Afr abbrev : Africa; African.

afraid /ə-frād'/ adj struck with fear, fearful (with of); timid; reluctantly inclined to think (that); regretfully admitting. [Pap of **affray**]

afreet see **afrit**.

afresh /ə-fresh'/ adv anew, once more. [Pfx a- of, and **fresh**]

African /af'ri-kən/ adj of Africa. ◆ n a native of Africa; a person of African descent. [L Africānus]
■ **Af'ric** n (poetic) Africa. ◆ adj African. **African'der** n a S African breed of cattle. **Af'ricanism** n an African characteristic. **Af'ricanist** n someone who is learned in matters relating to Africa. **Africanizā'tion** or **-s-** n. **Af'ricanize** or **-ise** vt and vi to make African; to exclude

people of other races (from), replacing them with Africans. **Af'ricanoid** *adj* of African type.
❑ **Af'rican-American** *n* an American of African origin. ◆ *adj* of or relating to African-Americans. **African coast fever** see **East Coast fever** under **east**. **African grey parrot** *n* a grey parrot (*Psittacus erithacus*). **African mahogany** *n* a W African hardwood, from the genus *Khaya*, which seasons easily. **African violet** *n* (also without *cap*) a plant from tropical Africa (*Saintpaulia ionantha*), commonly with violet-coloured flowers but not related to the violet.

Afrikaans /a-fri-käns'/ *n* one of the official languages of South Africa, having developed from 17c Dutch. [Du, African]
■ **Afrikan'er** *n* (formerly **African'er**, **African'der** or **Afrikan'der**) a person born in South Africa of white parents (*esp* of Dutch descent). ◆ *adj* of or relating to Afrikaners. **Afrika'nerdom** *n* the Afrikaners in South Africa; their nationalistic feeling or political ascendancy.
❑ **Afrikander Bond** *n* a South African nationalist league (1881–1911).

afrit or **afreet** /ä-frēt'/ or /af'rēt/ (*Arab myth*) *n* an evil demon. [Ar '*ifrīt* a demon]

Afro /af'rō/ *n* and *adj* (sometimes without *cap*) (relating to) a hairstyle characterized by thick, bushy curls standing out from the head; short for **African**.

Afro- /a-frō-/ *combining form* denoting African.
■ **Afro-Amer'ican** *adj* of or relating to African-Americans (also *n*). **Afro-Asian** /-āzh'yən/ *adj* of or consisting of Africans and Asians; of Asian origin but African citizenship; of mixed Asian and African blood; (of language) belonging to a group spoken in SW Asia and N Africa. **Afro-Asiat'ic** *adj* relating to Afro-Asian languages. **Afro-Caribbē'an** *adj* of or relating to (the culture, music, dance, etc of) people of African descent in or from the Caribbean (also *n*). **Afrocen'tric** or **Afrocen'tric** *adj* in US education, etc, emphasizing African history and culture, with the aim of providing African-American students, etc with a sense of cultural identity. **Afrocent'rism** *n*. **Afrojazz'** *n* jazz showing evidence of influence of African music. **Afrorock'** *n* rock music showing evidence of influence of African music.

afront /ə-frunt'/ *adv* in front (*obs*); abreast (*Shakesp*). [**a-**[1]]

afrormosia /af-rör-mō'zi-ə/ *n* a very durable W African wood used as an alternative to teak; the tree yielding this timber. [**Afro-** and *Ormosia*, genus name from Gr *hormos* necklace]

aft /äft/ *adj* or *adv* (*compar* **after** (qv); *superl* **aft'ermost** or **aft'most** (qqv)) behind; near or towards the stern of a vessel or aircraft. [OE *æftan*]

after /äf'tər/ *prep* and *adv* behind in place; later in time than; following in search of; in imitation of; in proportion to, or in agreement with; following in importance, order, etc; concerning; subsequent to or subsequently, afterwards; in the style or manner of; according to; in honour of; with the name, or a name derived from the name, of; past (an hour) (*N Am*). ◆ *adj* behind in place; later in time; more towards the stern (in this sense the *compar* of **aft**). ◆ *conj* later than the time when. [OE *æfter*, in origin a compar from *af* (*æf*) off, of which **aft** is orig a superl, but itself compared *æfter*, *æfterra*, *æftemest*, and tending to be regarded as compar of **aft**; see **of** and **off**.]
■ **af'terings** *n pl* (*archaic* or *dialect*) the last milk drawn in milking a cow. **af'ters** *n pl* (*inf*) in a meal, the dessert or other course following a main course. **af'terward** (chiefly *US*) or **af'terwards** *adv* at a later time; subsequently.
❑ **af'terbirth** *n* the placenta and membranes expelled from the uterus after a birth; a posthumous birth. **af'terburner** *n* the device used in afterburning. **af'terburning** *n* reheat, the use of a device to inject fuel into the hot exhaust gases of a turbojet in order to obtain increased thrust. **af'tercare** *n* care subsequent to a period of treatment, corrective training, etc; aftersales service (qv). **af'ter-clap** *n* (*archaic*) an unexpected sequel, after an affair is supposed to be at an end. **af'ter-crop** *n* a second crop from the same land in the same year. **af'ter-damp** *n* chokedamp, arising in coal mines after an explosion of firedamp. **af'terdeck** *n* (*naut*) the deck behind a ship's bridge. **after-dinn'er** *n* the time following dinner. ◆ *adj* belonging to that time, *esp* before leaving the table. **af'tereffect** *n* an effect that comes after an interval. **aftereye'** *vt* (*Shakesp*) to gaze after. **af'tergame** *n* a second game played in the hope of reversing the issue of the first; means employed after the first turn of affairs. **af'terglow** *n* a glow remaining after a light source has faded, *esp* that in the sky after sunset; pleasant residual feelings following an experience (*fig*). **af'tergrass** *n* the grass that grows after mowing or reaping. **af'tergrowth** *n* a later growth; an aftermath. **af'ter-guard** *n* (*naut*) the men on the quarterdeck and poop who work the after sails, many of them unskilled; hence a drudge or person with a menial job; a merchant ship's officers. **af'terheat** *n* (*nuclear eng*) the heat from fission products in a nuclear reactor after it has been shut down. **af'ter-image** *n* an image that persists for a time after one looks at an object. **af'terlife** *n* a future life; later life; a life after death. **af'ter-light** *n* the light of later knowledge. **af'termarket** *n* the service offered to consumers after the purchase of goods and services (also *adj*). **af'termath** *n* later consequences (of a particular

incident or occurrence), *esp* if bad; a second mowing of grass in the same season. **af'ter-mentioned** *adj* mentioned subsequently. **afternoon'** *n* the time between noon and evening. ◆ *adj* /af'/ happening at this time. **af'terpains** *n pl* the pains after childbirth, as the uterus contracts. **af'ter-party** *n* an informal party arranged to follow a more formal event. **af'terpiece** *n* a minor piece after a play. **af'tersales** *adj* after a sale has been completed, *usu* with reference to servicing the goods, installation, etc. **aftersales service** *n* service offered by a retailer to a customer following the purchase of goods, eg repair, provision of spare parts, advice on installation. **af'tershaft** *n* a second shaft arising from the quill of a feather. **af'tershave** *n* a lotion for men, for use after shaving. **af'tershock** *n* one of several minor shocks following the main shock of an earthquake. **af'tershow** *adj* occurring after a musical or theatrical performance. **af'tersun** *n* a lotion applied to damaged skin after sunbathing. **af'tersupper** *n* the time between supper and bedtime (*obs*); *prob* a dessert at the end of a supper, *poss* a rere-supper (*Shakesp*). ◆ *adj* in the time after supper. **af'terswarm** *n* a second swarm or cast (qv) of bees. **af'tertaste** *n* a taste that remains or comes after eating or drinking. **af'ter-tax** *adj* (of profit) remaining after (*esp* income) tax has been paid; (of a price) inclusive of VAT. **af'terthought** *n* a thought or thing thought of after the occasion; a later thought or reflection or modification. **af'tertime** *n* later time. **af'terword** *n* an epilogue. **af'terworld** *n* the world inhabited by the souls of the dead.
■ **after a fashion** see under **fashion**. **after all** when everything is taken into account; in spite of everything. **be after doing** (*Irish*) to have just done.

aftermost /äf'tər-mōst/ or /-məst/ or **aftmost** /äft'/ *adj* (*superl* of **aft**) nearest the stern; hindmost. [OE *æftemest*, a double superl]

afterward, **afterwards** see under **after**.

AFV *abbrev* : armoured fighting vehicle.

AG *abbrev* : Adjutant-General; *Aktiengesellschaft* (*Ger*), joint stock company; (also **A-G**) Attorney-General.

Ag (*chem*) *symbol* : silver. [L *argentum*]

AGA *abbrev* : air-ground-air.

Aga /ä'gə/ *n* a large, permanently-lit iron stove with multiple ovens, used for cooking and heating. [Shortened form of the name of the original Swedish manufacturer]
❑ **Aga saga** *n* a popular novel in a semi-rural middle-class setting.

aga or **agha** /ä'gə or ä-gä'/ *n* a Turkish commander or chief officer. [Turk *aga, aghā*]
❑ **Aga Khan** /kän/ *n* the title of the head of the Ismaili Muslims.

agaçant /a-ga-sä'/, *fem* **agaçante** /-sät'/ (*Fr*) *adj* provoking or alluring.
■ **agacerie** /-s(ə-)rē/ *n* allurement, coquetry.

Agadah, **Agadic** see **Haggadah**.

again /ə-gen' or ə-gān'/ *adv* once more; in return; in response or consequence; back (to a previous condition, situation, etc); further; on the other hand; to the same amount in addition; at some future time (*dialect*). ◆ *prep* (*dialect*) against. [OE *ongēan, ongegn*; Ger *entgegen*]
■ **again and again** repeatedly.

against /ə-genst' or ə-gänst'/ *prep* opposite to; in opposition or resistance to; in protection from; in or into contact or collision with or pressure upon; towards the time of (*obs*); in anticipation of; in contrast or comparison with; in exchange for; instead of. ◆ *conj* in readiness for the time that. [**again**, with genitive ending *-es*, and *-t* as in *whilst*, *betwixt* and *amongst*]
■ **have something against** to dislike or disapprove of.

agalactia /ag-ə-lak'shi-ə or -ti-ə/ *n* failure to secrete milk. [Gr *a-* (privative), and *gala, galaktos* milk]

agalloch /ə-gal'ək/ *n* eaglewood. [Gr *agallochon*, from an Asian language; see **eaglewood**]

agalmatolite /a-gal-mat'ə-līt/ *n* material of various kinds (steatite, pyrophyllite, etc) from which Chinese figures are carved. [Gr *agalma*, *-atos* a statue (of a god), and *lithos* stone]

Agama /ag'ə-mə/ *n* an Old World genus of thick-tongued lizards giving name to the family **Agamidae** /a-gam'i-dē/. [Carib name of another lizard]
■ **ag'amid** *n* and *adj* (a lizard) of this family. **ag'amoid** *n* and *adj* (a lizard) having the features of an agamid.

Agamemnon /a-ga-mem'non/ *n* the leader of the Greeks in the Trojan war, king of Mycenae; generic name for a king.

agami /ag'ə-mi/ *n* the golden-breasted trumpeter, a crane-like bird of S America. [Carib name]

agamic /ə-gam'ik/ or **agamous** /ag'ə-məs/ *adj* asexual; parthenogenetic; cryptogamous (*obs*). [Gr *a-* (privative), and *gamos* marriage]

■ **agamogenesis** /-jen'/ n reproduction without sex, as in lower animals and in plants. **ag'amospermy** n the formation of seeds without fertilization.

agamid, agamoid see under **Agama**.

agamous see **agamic**.

Aganippe /ag-ə-nip'ē/ n a fountain on Mount Helicon, sacred to the Muses (Gr myth); poetic inspiration. [Gr Aganippē]

agapanthus /a-gə-pan'thəs/ n any of several plants, with clusters of blue flowers, of the Agapanthus genus of lily native to S Africa. [Gr agape love, and anthos flower]

agape[1] /ə-gāp'/ adj or adv with gaping mouth. [a-[1]]

agape[2] /ag'ə-pē/ n (pl **ag'apes** or **ag'apae** /-pē/) selfless Christian love; the love of God for man; a feast in token and celebration of such love, modelled on that held by the early Christians at communion time, when contributions were made for the poor. [Gr agapē love]
■ **Agapemone** /-pēm' or -pem'ə-nē/ n a religious community of men and women whose 'spiritual marriages' were in some cases not strictly spiritual, founded in 1849 at Spaxton, near Bridgwater; any similar community, esp with reference to its delinquencies.

agar /ā'gär/ or **agar-agar** /ā'gär-ā'gär/ n a jelly prepared from seaweeds of various kinds used in bacteria-culture, medicine, glue-making, silk-dressing, and cooking; any of the seaweeds concerned. [Malay]

agaric /ag'ə-rik or ə-gar'ik/ n a fungus, properly one of the mushroom family, but loosely applied. [Gr agarikon]
■ **agar'ic** adj.

agast see **aghast**.

agate[1] /ag'ət or -āt/ n a banded variegated chalcedony, used as a semiprecious stone; a marble used in games, made of this material or of variegated glass; a dwarfish person (as if a figure cut in agate) (Shakesp); ruby type (printing). [Fr, from Gr achātēs, said to be so called because first found near the river Achates in Sicily]
■ **ag'ateware** n a form of ceramic made to look like agate.

agate[2] /ə-gāt'/ (archaic or dialect) adv agoing, on the way; astir; afoot; astray. [a-[1] and gate[2]; a Scot and N Eng word]

a'gate see under **a'**.

agathodaimon /a-ga-thō-dī'mon/ n a benevolent guardian spirit. [Gr agathos good, and daimōn spirit]

à gauche /a gōsh'/ (Fr) to the left; on the left.

agave /ə-gā'vē/ n a plant of the aloe-like American genus Agave (family Amaryllidaceae), in Mexico usu flowering about the seventh year, in hothouse conditions requiring 40–60 (popularly 100) years (also called **American aloe, maguey** and **century plant**). [L Agāvē, Gr Agauē, daughter of Cadmus, fem of agauos illustrious]

agaze /ə-gāz'/ (archaic) adj and adv at gaze or gazing. [a-[1]]

agazed /ə-gāzd'/ (Shakesp) adj struck with amazement. [Prob a variant of **aghast**]

AGC abbrev : automatic gain control.

age /āj/ n duration of life; the time during which a person or thing has lived or existed; the time of life reached; mature years; legal maturity; the age or fact of being old; equivalence in development to the average of an actual age; a period of time; any great division of world, human, or individual history; a generation; a century; (esp in pl) a long time, however short (inf). ◆ vi (**aging** or **ageing** /āj'ing/; **aged** /ājd/) to grow old; to develop the characteristics of old age; to mature. ◆ vt to make to seem old or to be like the old; to determine the age of. [OFr aäge (Fr âge), from L aetās, -ātis, for aevitās, from L aevum age]
■ **aged** /āj'id/ adj advanced in age, old; /ājd/ of the age of; subjected to aging, eg aged timbers. ◆ n pl /āj'id/ (usu with the) old people. **agedness** /āj'id-nis/ n the condition of being aged. **age'ism** n discrimination on grounds of age. **age'ist** n and adj. **age'less** adj never growing old, perpetually young; timeless. **age'lessness** n. **age'long** adj lasting an age. **ag'ing** or **age'ing** n the process of growing old or developing qualities of the old; maturing; change in properties that occurs in certain metals at atmospheric temperature after heat treatment or cold-working.
□ **age'-bracket** n the people between particular ages, taken as a group. **age group** n a group of people of a similar age. **age hardening** n hardening of metals by spontaneous structural changes over time. **age limit** n the age under or over which one may not do something. **age'-long** adj having been in existence for a long time. **age of consent** see under **consent. age of discretion** see under **discretion. age'-old** adj very old, ancient.
■ **be** or **act your age!** don't be childish. **be ages with** (Scot) to be the same age as. (**come**) **of age** (to become) old enough to be considered legally mature (with respect to voting, crime, contracts, marriage, etc). **of an age** of the same or similar age. **over age** too old. **under age** too young; not yet of age.

-age /-ij/ sfx forming nouns denoting: a collection, group, eg baggage ; an action, process, eg slippage ; the result of an action, eg wreckage ; a condition, eg bondage ; a home or place, eg parsonage ; cost or charge, eg postage ; rate, eg mileage.

agee see **ajee**.

agen (poetic) same as **again**.

agency see under **agent**.

agenda /ə- or a-jen'də/ n pl (often treated as n sing) (a list of) things to be done; a programme of business for discussion at a meeting. [L neuter pl of agendus to be done, gerundive of agere to do]
■ **hidden agenda** see under **hide**[1]. **on the agenda** requiring attention.

agene or (US) **Agene**® /ā'jēn/ n nitrogen trichloride, formerly widely used as a whitening agent in flour.

agent /ā'jənt/ n a person or thing that acts or exerts power; any natural force acting on matter; a person (or company) authorized or delegated to transact business for another; a person who acts on behalf of another in effecting a legal relationship between that other person and a third party; a sales representative for a business; formerly, a bank manager; formerly, the representative of the government in a group of Indian states; a paid political party worker; a secret agent or spy; a computer program capable of performing a sequence of operations without repeated user intervention; the doer of an action, the subject of an active verb or noun (grammar). ◆ vt to conduct as a law agent (Scot); to act as an agent to. ◆ adj acting; of an agent. [L agēns, -entis, prp of agere to do]
■ **agency** /ā'jən-si/ n the operation or action of an agent; instrumentality, operation; the office or business of an agent; such a business putting employers and those requiring employment in contact with each other (eg a recruitment agency or nursing agency); a government department (N Am); formerly, a group of Indian states assigned to an agent. **agen'tial** /-shəl/ adj relating to an agent or agency; agentive (grammar). **a'gentive** adj (grammar) of an affix, etc, signifying the agent of a verb, eg the suffix -er in speaker. ◆ n a grammatical case denoting this. **agentiv'ity** n.
□ **agency nurse, secretary**, etc n one employed through an agency. **agency shop** n (N Am) an establishment in which the union, usu by agreement with the management, represents all workers whether they are members of it or not. **agent-gen'eral** n (pl **agents-gen'eral**) a representative in England of an Australian state or Canadian province. **agentive noun** or (non-technical) **agent noun** n (grammar) a noun denoting the person, machine, etc doing something, eg writer, accelerator. **Agent Orange** n a defoliant containing dioxin.
■ **law agent** see under **law**[1].

agent provocateur /a-zhä prō-vo-ka-tœr'/ (Fr) n a person employed to lead others, by pretending sympathy with them, into committing unlawful acts.

ageratum /ā-jə-rā'təm/ n any plant of the tropical American genus Ageratum, having clumps of long-lasting purple flowers. [New L, ult from Gr agēraton something which does not grow old, from a- (privative), and gērat-, stem of gēras old age]

agflation /ag-flā'shən/ n an economic situation in which increased demand causes an increase in the price of food products, and a potential rise in general inflation. [agriculture and inflation]

agger /aj'ər or ag'ər/ (Roman hist) n a mound, esp one of wood or earth for protection or other military purpose; any elevation, esp artificial. [L]

aggiornamento /a-jör-na-men'tō/ (Ital) n modernizing.

agglomerate /ə-glom'ə-rāt/ vt to make into a ball; to collect into a mass. ◆ vi to grow into a mass. ◆ adj /-rat or -rāt/ agglomerated; clustered; gathered in a head (bot). ◆ n /-rat or -rāt/ a mass of things; a volcanic rock consisting of irregular fragments. [L agglomerāre, -ātum, from ad to, and glomus, glomeris a ball]
■ **agglom'erated** adj. **agglomerā'tion** n. **agglom'erative** adj.

agglutinate /ə-gloo'ti-nāt/ vt to glue together; to cause to stick together or clump. ◆ vi to stick as if glued; to clump. ◆ adj /-nat or -nāt/ agglutinated. [L agglūtināre, from ad to, and glūten, -inis glue]
■ **agglut'inable** adj. **agglut'inant** adj. ◆ n an agglutinating agent. **agglut'inated** adj. **agglutinā'tion** n the act of agglutinating; an agglutinated mass; the clumping of bacteria, cells, protozoa, etc (biol); a type of word-formation process in which words are inflected by the addition of one or more meaningful elements to a stem, each of which elements expresses one single element of meaning (linguistics). **agglut'inative** adj tending, or having power, to agglutinate. **agglut'inin** n an antibody causing agglutination of bacteria, cells, etc. **agglut'inogen** n the substance in bacteria or in blood cells that stimulates the formation of, and unites with, agglutinin.
□ **agglutinating** (or **agglutinative**) **languages** n pl languages in which words are inflected by agglutination.

---

aggrace /ə-grās'/ (*Spenser*) *vt* (*pat* **aggraced'** or **agraste'**) to grace; to favour. ◆ *n* kindness; favour. [**grace**, after Ital *aggratiare* (now *aggraziare*)]

aggrade /ə-grād'/ (*geol*) *vt* to raise the level of (a surface) through the deposition of detritus. ◆ *vi* to build up in this way. [L *ad* to, and *gradus* a step, in imitation of **degrade**]
■ **aggradation** /ag-rəd-ā'shən/ *n*.

aggrandize or **-ise** /ə-gran'dīz or ag'rən-/ *vt* to make or seem to make greater. [Fr *agrandir*, *agrandiss-*, from L *ad* to, and *grandis* large]
■ **aggrandizement** or **-s-** /ə-gran'diz-mənt/ *n*.

aggrate /ə-grāt'/ (*obs*) *vt* to gratify or please; to thank. [Ital *aggratare*, from L *ad* to, and *grātus* pleasing]

aggravate /ag'rə-vāt/ *vt* to make more distressing, more troublesome, or worse; to irritate or annoy (*inf*). [L *aggravāre*, *-ātus*, from *ad* to, and *gravis* heavy]
■ **agg'ravated** *adj* (*law*) of an offence, made more serious (eg by violence). **agg'ravating** *adj*. **agg'ravatingly** *adv*. **aggravā'tion** *n*.

aggregate /ag'ri-gāt/ *vt* to collect into a mass or whole; to assemble; to add as a member to a society; to amount to (*inf*). ◆ *vi* to accumulate. ◆ *adj* /-gət or -gāt/ formed of parts that combine to make a whole; gathered into a mass or whole; formed from an apocarpous gynaeceum (*bot*); formed into a single mass or cluster (*bot*). ◆ *n* /-gət or -gāt/ an assemblage; a mass; a total; any material mixed with cement to form concrete; a collection of elements having a common property that identifies the collection (*maths*). [L *aggregāre*, *-ātum* to bring together, as a flock, from *ad* to, and *grex*, *gregis* a flock]
■ **agg'regately** *adv*. **aggregā'tion** *n*. **agg'regative** *adj*. **agg'regātor** *n* (*comput*) a piece of software that allows a computer user to view data from various web pages in a single window.
■ **in the aggregate** taken as a whole. **on aggregate** in total.

aggress /ə-gres'/ *vi* to make a first attack; to begin a quarrel; to intrude. [L *aggredī*, *-gressus*, from *ad* to, and *gradī* to step]
■ **aggression** /-gresh'ən/ *n* a first act of hostility or injury *esp* without provocation; the use of armed force by a state against the sovereignty, territorial integrity or political independence of another state; self-assertiveness, either as a good characteristic or *usu* as a sign of emotional instability. **aggress'ive** *adj* making the first attack, or prone to do so; discourteously hostile or self-assertive, now often contrasted with *assertive*; offensive as opposed to defensive; showing energy and initiative. **aggress'ively** *adv*. **aggress'iveness** *n*. **aggress'or** *n* the person who or force which attacks first.

aggri or **aggry** /ag'ri/ *adj* applied to ancient W African variegated glass beads. [Origin unknown]

aggrieve /ə-grēv'/ *vt* to press heavily upon; to cause pain or injure; to distress. [OFr *agrever*, from L *ad* to, and *gravis* heavy]
■ **aggrieved'** *adj* injured or distressed; having a grievance.

aggro /ag'rō/ (*sl*) *n* aggressive behaviour or trouble-making, *esp* between gangs, racial groups, etc; problems or difficulties. [Short form of **aggravation**, also associated with **aggression**]

aggry see **aggri**.

agha see **aga**.

aghast, earlier (or eg *Milton*) **agast**, /ə-gäst'/ *adj* stupefied with horror. [Pap of obs *agast*, from OE intensive pfx *ā-*, and *gǣstan* to terrify]

agila /ag'i-lä/ *n* eaglewood. [Port *águila* eaglewood, or Sp *águila* eagle; see **eaglewood**]

agile /aj'īl or (*US*) -əl/ *adj* nimble or active; quick-moving and supple. [Fr, from L *agilis*, from *agere* to do or act]
■ **ag'ilely** *adv*. **agility** /ə-jil'i-ti/ *n* nimbleness; swiftness and suppleness.
❑ **agile development** *n* (*comput*) a method of developing computer systems that is characterized by rapid responsiveness to changing requirements.

agin /ə-gin'/ *prep* (*dialect* or *facetious*) against. [**again**]
■ **aginn'er** *n* (*inf*) an opponent (eg of change); a rebel, a malcontent.

agio /aj'(i-)ō or ā'j(i-)ō/ *n* (*pl* **ag'ios**) the sum payable for the convenience of exchanging one kind of money for another, eg silver for gold, paper for metal; the difference in exchange between worn or debased coinage and coinage of full value; the amount of deviation from the fixed par of exchange between the currencies of two countries; the discount on a foreign bill of exchange; money-changing, agiotage. [The word used in Ital is *aggio*, a variant of *agio* convenience]
■ **agiotage** /aj'ə-tij/ *n* speculative manoeuvres in stocks and shares; stock-jobbing; money-changing; agio.

agist /ə-jist'/ *vt* to take in to graze for payment; to charge with a public burden. [OFr *agister*, from *à* (L *ad*) to, and *giste* resting place, from *gésir*, from a frequentative of L *jacēre* to lie]
■ **agist'ment** *n* the action of agisting; the price paid for cattle pasturing on the land; a burden or tax. **agist'or** or **agist'er** *n* an officer in charge of cattle agisted.

agitate /aj'i-tāt/ *vt* to keep moving; to stir violently; to disturb; to perturb; to excite; to discuss, or keep up the discussion of. ◆ *vi* to stir up public feeling. [L *agitāre*, frequentative of *agere* to put in motion]
■ **ag'itāted** *adj*. **ag'itātedly** *adv*. **agitā'tion** *n*. **ag'itātive** *adj*. **ag'itātor** *n* a person who excites or keeps up a social or political agitation; an agent, *esp* for the private soldiers in the Parliamentary army (*hist*); an apparatus for stirring.

agitato /ä-ji-tä'tō/ (*music*) *adj* agitated; restless and wild. ◆ *adv* agitatedly. [Ital, from L *agitāre* to agitate]

agitprop /aj'it-prop/ *n* (often *cap*; also **ag'it-prop**) agitation and political propaganda, *esp* of a pro-communist nature (also *adj*). [Russ *Agitpropbyuro* office of *agitatsiya* agitation and *propaganda*]

Aglaia /ä-glī'a/ *n* one of the Graces. [Gr *aglaiā* splendour, triumph]

agleam /ə-glēm'/ *adj* and *adv* gleaming. [**a-¹**]

aglee see **agley**.

aglet, **aiglet** /ag'lit or ā'glit/ or **aiguillette** /ā-gwi-let'/ *n* the metal or plastic tag of a lace or string; an ornamental tag or other metal appendage; anything dangling; (*usu* **aiguillette**) a tagged point of braid hanging from the shoulder in some uniforms. [Fr *aiguillette*, dimin of *aiguille* a needle, from L *acūcula* dimin of *acus* a needle]
❑ **aglet babie** /bā'bi/ *n* (*Shakesp*) *prob* a small figure forming the tag of a lace.

agley or **aglee** /ə-glī' or ə-glē'/ (*Scot*) *adv* askew; awry. [**a-¹**, and Scot *gley* squint]

aglimmer /ə-glim'ər/ *adj* and *adv* glimmering. [**a-¹** and **glimmer¹**]

aglitter /ə-glit'ər/ *adj* and *adv* glittering, sparkling. [**a-¹**]

aglow /ə-glō'/ *adj* and *adv* glowing. [**a-¹**]

AGM or **agm** *abbrev* : air-to-ground missile; annual general meeting.

agma /ag'mə/ *n* (the phonetic symbol *F* for) a velar nasal consonant, as the *ng* in *thing* or the *n* in *think* (see also **eng**). [Gr, fragment, nasalized g]

agnail /ag'nāl/ *n* a torn shred of skin beside the nail (also **hangnail**). [OE *angnægl* a corn, from *ange*, *enge* compressed, painful, and *nægl* nail (for driving in), confused with *hang*, and (finger-)*nail*]

agname /ag'nām/ *n* a name over and above the ordinary name and surname. [**name**; after LL *agnōmen*]
■ **ag'named** *adj*.

agnate /ag'nāt/ *adj* related on the father's side or (*Roman law*) through a male ancestor; related generally; allied. ◆ *n* a person related in this way. [L *agnātus*, from *ad* to, and (g)*nāscī* to be born. See **cognate**]
■ **agnatic** /-nat'-/ or **agnat'ical** *adj*. **agnat'ically** *adv*. **agnā'tion** *n*.

agnize or **-ise** /ag- or ə-gnīz'/ (*archaic*) *vt* to acknowledge or confess. [L *agnōscere*, from *ad* to, and (g)*nōscere* to know; modelled on **cognize**, etc]

agnomen /ag- or ə-gnō'mən/ *n* a name added to the family name, generally on account of some great exploit, as *Africanus* to Publius Cornelius Scipio. [L, from *ad* to, and (g)*nōmen* a name]
■ **agnom'inal** *adj*.

agnosia /ag-nō'zi-ə or -si-ə or -zhə/ (*psychol*) *n* inability to recognize familar things or people, *esp* after brain damage. [Gr *a-* (privative), and *gnōsis* knowledge, recognition]

agnostic /ag- or ə-gnos'tik/ *n* and *adj* (a person) believing that we know nothing of things beyond material phenomena, that a Creator, creative cause and an unseen world are things unknown or unknowable; (a) sceptic. [Coined by English biologist TH Huxley in 1869 from Gr *agnostos* unknown or unknowable, from *a-* (privative), *gnostos* known or knowable, and *-ic*]
■ **agnos'ticism** *n*.

agnus castus /ag'nəs kas'təs/ *n* a species of *Vitex*, a verbenaceous tree. [Gr *agnos*, the name of the tree, and L *castus*, a translation of Gr *hagnos* chaste, with which *agnos* was confused]

Agnus Dei or **agnus dei** /ag'nəs or än'yŭs dā'ē/ *n* a part of the Roman Catholic mass beginning with these words; a musical setting of this; a figure of a lamb emblematic of Christ, bearing the banner of the cross; a cake of wax stamped with such a figure, and blessed by the Pope. [L *agnus Deī* lamb of God]

ago /ə-gō'/ or (*archaic*) **agone** /ə-gon'/ *adv* gone; past; since. [OE *āgān*, pap of *āgān* to pass away, from intensive pfx *ā-*, and *gān* to go]

agog /ə-gog'/ *adj* and *adv* in excited eagerness. [Perh connected with OFr *en gogues* frolicsome, of unknown origin]

agoge /a-gō'jē/ n in ancient Greek music, tempo; sequence in melody. [Gr *agōgē* leading]
■ **agogic** /a-goj'ik/ adj giving the effect of accent by slightly dwelling on a note. **agog'ics** n sing.

à gogo or **à go-go** /ə gō'gō/ in abundance, to one's heart's content; used in names of nightclubs, etc. See also **go-go**. [Fr]

agoing /ə-gō'ing/ (archaic or dialect) adj and adv in motion. [**a-**[1] and **going**[2]]

agon see under **agony**.

agone see **ago**.

agonic /ə-gon'ik/ adj making no angle. [Gr *agōnos*, from a- (privative), and *gōniā* angle]
❑ **agonic line** n (geol) the line of no magnetic variation, along which the magnetic needle points directly north and south.

agonize, etc see under **agony**.

agonothetes /ə-gō-nə-thē'tēz or a-gō'no-thet-ās/ (Gr) n a judge or director of public games.

agony /ag'ə-ni/ n extreme suffering; a violent mental struggle, anguish; the death struggle; Christ's anguish in Gethsemane; conflict in games (obs). [Gr *agōniā* contest, agony, from *agōn* meeting, contest]
■ **ag'on** n in ancient Greece, a conflict between two protagonists; a struggle. **ag'onist** n in ancient Greece, a competitor in public games; someone engaged in a struggle, whether physical or spiritual (rare); a chief character in a literary work; (in the following senses, a back-formation from **antagonist**) a muscle whose action is opposed by another action (the *antagonist*); a chemical substance (eg a drug) which produces an observable inhibitory or excitatory response in a body tissue (eg a muscle or nerve). **agonistes** /a-gon-is'tēz/ n someone in the grip of inner conflict. **agonis'tic** adj of or relating to a chemical agonist; of or relating to a broad class of behaviour patterns including attack, threat, appeasement and flight; (also **agonist'ical**) relating to athletic contests; combative. **agonist'ically** adv. **agonist'ics** n sing (archaic) the art and theory of games and prize-fighting. **ag'onize** or **-ise** vi to struggle or contend; to suffer agony; to worry intensely (inf). ◆ vt to subject to agony. **ag'onized** or **-s-** adj suffering or expressing anguish. **ag'onizedly** or **-s-** /-īz-id-li/ adv. **ag'onizing** or **-s-** adj causing agony; intensely painful. **ag'onizingly** or **-s-** adv.
❑ **agony aunt** n (sometimes with caps) a person, usu a woman, who gives advice in an agony column or in a radio or television programme of similar nature; any female adviser (inf). **agony column** n the part of a newspaper or magazine in which readers submit, and receive advice about, personal problems; the part of a newspaper containing special advertisements, eg for missing friends, etc. **agony uncle** n.

agood /ə-gŭd'/ (Shakesp) adv in good earnest, heartily. [**a-**[1]]

agora[1] /ag'ə-rə/ n (pl **ag'orae** /-ī/ or **ag'oras**) in ancient Greece, an assembly, place of assembly or marketplace. [Gr *agorā*]
■ **ag'oraphobe** n a person who suffers from agoraphobia. **agorapho'bia** n morbid fear of (crossing) open places. **agorapho'bic** (or /-fob'/) adj and n.

agora[2] /ag-ə-rä'/ n (pl **agorot** /-rot'/) an Israeli monetary unit, $\frac{1}{100}$ of a shekel. [Heb *agōrāh*, from *āgōr* to collect]

agouta /ə-goo'tə/ n a solenodon. [Taino *aguta*]

agouti, **agouty** or **aguti** /ə-goo'tē/ n (pl **agou'tis**, **agou'ties** or **agu'tis**) a small S American rodent related to the guinea-pig; a pattern of fur characterized by irregular stripes. [Fr, from Sp *aguti*, from Guaraní *acuti*]

AGR abbrev : advanced gas-cooled reactor (see under **advance**).

agr. or **agric.** abbrev : agriculture.

agraffe /ə-graf'/ n a hooked clasp used by stonemasons to hold blocks together. [Fr *agrafe*, from à to, and *grappe*, from LL *grappa*, from OHGer *krapfo* hook]

agrammatism /ə-gram'ə-ti-zm/ n inability to form sentences with the correct structure, esp following brain damage.

à grands frais /a grã fre'/ (Fr) at great expense.

agranulocytosis /a-gran-ū-lō-sī-tō'sis/ n a blood disorder in which there is a marked decrease in granulocytes, with lesions of the mucous membrane and skin (also **agranulō'sis**). [Gr ā- (privative), **granule** or **granulocyte**, and **-osis**]

agrapha see **agraphon**.

agraphia /ə-graf'i-ə/ n loss of the power to write, from brain disease or injury. [Gr a- (privative), and *graphein* to write]
■ **agraph'ic** adj.

agraphon /a'gra-fon/ n (pl **a'grapha** /-fa/) a traditional utterance ascribed to Jesus, not in the canonical Gospels. [Gr, unwritten]

agrarian /ə-grā'ri-ən/ adj relating to land, or its management, uses or distribution. [L *agrārius*, from *ager* a field]
■ **agrā'rianism** n equitable division of lands; a political movement in favour of change in conditions of property in land.

agraste (Spenser) pat of **aggrace**.

agravic /ā- or ə-grav'ik/ adj of or relating to a condition or place where the effect of gravity is zero.

agree /ə-grē'/ vi (**agree'ing**; **agreed'**) to be, or come to be, of one mind (with); to suit, do well or be compatible (with); to concur (with *with* and *in*, *on* or *about*); to accede or assent (to); to be consistent (with); to harmonize; to get on together; to take the same gender, number, case, or person (with *with*; *grammar*); to make friends again (obs or dialect). ◆ vt to concede (that); to decide jointly (to do, that); to consent (to do); to please or satisfy (obs); to reconcile (people; obs); to settle (a dispute or a difference; obs); to arrange with consent of all (obs for a time, but in recent use). [OFr *agréer* to accept kindly, from L *ad* to, and *grātus* pleasing]
■ **agreeabil'ity** n. **agree'able** adj suitable; pleasant or affable; in harmony; conformable; willing or consenting (inf). ◆ adv in accordance. **agree'ableness** n. **agree'ably** adv. **agree'ment** n concord; conformity; harmony; a compact, contract, or treaty; the taking of the same gender, number, case, or person (grammar); an embellishment (obs).
❑ **agreement to agree** n (commerce) an agreement that both parties are interested in entering into a contract at some future date.

agrégé /a-grā-zhā'/ (Fr) n a successful candidate in a competitive university examination for teaching posts.
■ **agrégation** /a-grā-ga-sjɔ̃/ n the examination.

agrément /a-grā-mã'/ (Fr) n the approval by a state of a diplomatic representative sent to it.
■ **agréments** n pl amenities (also **agrémens**); courtesies, charms or blandishments; embellishments, such as grace notes and trills (music).

agrestal, **agrestial** see under **agrestic**.

agrestic /ə-gres'tik/ adj of the fields; rural; unpolished. [L *agrestis*, from *ager* a field]
■ **agrestial** /ə-gres'ti-əl/, also **agres'tal** adj growing, etc in the open country; growing wild in cultivated ground, such as weeds (bot).

agri- /a-gri-/ or **agro-** /a-grō-/ combining form denoting fields, land use, or agriculture. [L *ager*, Gr *agros* field]
■ **ag'ribusiness** or **ag'robusiness** n all the operations of supplying the market with farm produce taken together, including growing, provision of farm machinery, distribution, etc. **agrichem'ical** adj (of fruit and vegetables) treated with chemicals after being harvested. **agrimon'etary** adj relating to the finances of agricultural businesses. **ag'riproduct** n a commodity for the use of farmers, eg fertilizer or animal feed. **ag'riscience** n science as applied to agriculture. **agritour'ism** n the business of providing holidays in a rural setting. **agriturismo** /ag-ri-toor-iz'mō/ n (pl **agrituris'mos** or **agrituris'mi**) (in Italy) a place offering holiday accommodation in a rural setting. **agrobiolog'ical** adj. **agrobiol'ogist** n. **agrobiol'ogy** n the study of plant nutrition and soil yields. **agrochem'ical** n a chemical intended for agricultural use (also adj). **agroec'osystem** n an ecosystem on cultivated land. **agrofor'estry** n any system of land use which integrates the cultivation of trees and shrubs and the raising of agricultural crops and/or animals on the same land, whether at the same time or sequentially, taking economic, ecological and cultural factors into account. **agroindust'rial** adj. **agroind'ustry** n the area of production that serves the needs of both agriculture and industry. **agrolog'ical** adj. **agrol'ogist** n. **agrol'ogy** n the study of the structure, history, etc of soils, esp as they affect agriculture. **agroterr'orism** or **ag'roterror** n the use of disease-carrying organisms in the agricultural sector for purposes of terrorism. **agroterr'orist** n.

agric. see **agr.**

agriculture /ag'ri-kul-chər/ n the art or practice of cultivating the land. [L *ager* (Gr *agros*) field, and *cultūra* cultivation]
■ **agricult'ural** adj. **agricult'urally** adv. **agricult'urist** or **agricult'uralist** n someone skilled in agriculture; a farmer.

agrimony /ag'ri-mə-ni/ n a perennial herb of a genus (*Agrimonia*) of the rose family, with small yellow flowers and bitter taste and a rootstock which provides a yellow dye; extended to other plants, esp **hemp agrimony** (*Eupatorium cannabinum*), a composite. [L *agrimōnia* (a blunder or misreading), from Gr *argemōnē* long prickly-headed poppy]

agrin /ə-grin'/ (archaic) adv in the act of grinning. [**a-**[1]]

agriology /a-gri-ol'ə-ji/ n the comparative study of the customs found among primitive peoples. [Gr *agrios* wild, from *agros* field, and *logos* a discourse]

agrise, **agrize** or **agryze** /ə-grīz'/ (obs) vt to terrify (Spenser); to horrify; to disfigure. [OE *āgrīsan* to dread]
■ **agrised'** adj.

agro-, agrobiology, etc see **agri-**.

agronomy /ə-gron'ə-mi/ n rural economy. [Fr agronomie]
■ agronō'mial adj. agronom'ic or agronom'ical adj. agronom'ics n sing the science dealing with the management and productivity of land. agron'omist n.

agrostology /a-gra-stol'ə-ji/ n the study of grasses. [Gr agrōstis dog's-tooth grass]
�« p agrostological /-tə-loj'i-kl/ adj. agrostol'ogist n.

aground /ə-grownd'/ adv in or to a stranded condition; on the ground. [a-¹]

agryze see **agrise**.

AGT abbrev : advanced gas turbine.

Agt or **agt** abbrev : agent; agreement.

aguacate /ä-gwä-kä'tā/ n the avocado pear. [Sp, from Nahuatl ahuacatl]

aguardiente /ä-gwär-dyen'tā/ n a brandy made in Spain and Portugal; any spirituous liquor. [Sp, from agua ardiente burning water, from L aqua water, and ardēns, -entis, from ardēre to burn]

ague /ā'gū/ n a burning fever (Bible); a fever with hot and cold fits; malaria; a shivering fit. [OFr (fièvre) ague, from L (febris) acūta sharp (fever)]
■ agued /ā'gūd/ adj struck with ague; shivering; cold. ā'gūish adj. ā'gūishly adv.
❑ a'gue-cake n (obs) a swelling on the spleen, caused by ague. a'gue-fit n. a'gue-proof adj.

aguise or **aguize** /ə-gīz'/ (obs) vt to dress or equip (Spenser); to adorn; to fashion. [Pfx a-, and **guise**]

aguna or **agunah** /ə-goo'nə/ (Judaism) n (pl agu'not) a woman whose husband has abandoned her but fails to provide an official divorce. [Heb, chained woman]

aguti see **agouti**.

AGW abbrev : actual gross weight.

AH abbrev : (in dates) anno Hegirae (L), in the year of Hegira (ie from the flight of Mohammed on 13 September in 622AD).

Ah or **ah** abbrev : ampere hour.

ah /ä/ interj expressing surprise, joy, pity, complaint, objection, etc. ◆ vi to make such an interjection. [Perh OFr ah]

AHA abbrev : alpha-hydroxy acid.

aha /ə-hä'/ or /-hä/ interj expressing exultation, pleasure, surprise or contempt. [ah and ha¹]

à haute voix /a ōt vwä'/ (Fr) aloud.

ahead /ə-hed'/ adv further on; in advance; forward; headlong. [a-¹]

aheap /ə-hēp'/ (obs) adv in a heap. [a-¹]

aheight /ə-hīt'/ (archaic) adv on high or aloft. [a-¹]

ahem /ə-h(e)m'/ interj used to draw attention to oneself or to express a reservation, as though clearing the throat. [A lengthened form of hem²]

ahent /ə-hent'/ Scot and N Eng form of **ahint**.

ahi /ä'hē/ n another name for the yellowfin tuna. [Hawaiian, literally, fire]

ahigh /ə-hī'/ (obs) adv on high. [a-¹]

ahimsa /ə-him'sə/ n the duty of sparing animal life; non-violence. [Sans ahiṁsā]

ahint /ə-hint'/ or **ahind** /ə-hin(d)'/ (dialect, esp Scot) adv and prep behind. [OE æthindan]

ahistorical /ā-hi-stor'i-kəl/ adj not historical; taking no account of, or not related to, history. [Gr a- (privative), and **historical**]

Ahithophel see **Achitophel**.

ahl abbrev : ad hunc locum (L), at this place.

ahold /ə-hōld'/ adv at or to grips, or a condition of holding; near the wind (ie so as to hold there) (obs naut; Shakesp). [a-¹ and hold¹]

-aholic or **-oholic** /-ə-ho-lik/ (facetious) adj and n sfx (someone) having an addiction to (something) as in workaholic, clothesoholic. [By analogy, from alcoholic]
■ -aholism or -oholism /-lizm/ n sfx.

ahorse /ə-hörs'/ or **ahorseback** /-bak/ (archaic) adv on horseback. [a-¹]

ahoy /ə-hoi'/ (naut) interj used to hail another vessel, etc. [ah and hoy²]

AHQ abbrev : Allied Headquarters; Army Headquarters.

AHRC abbrev : Arts and Humanities Research Council.

Ahriman /ä'ri-män/ n in Zoroastrianism, the evil spirit, opp to Ormuzd. [Pers Ahrīman, Zend anro mainyus dark spirit]

AHS abbrev : anno humanae salutis (L), in the year of human salvation.

à huis clos /a wē klō'/ (Fr) with closed doors.

ahull /ə-hul'/ (naut) adv with sails furled, and helm lashed to the lee-side. [a-¹ and hull¹]

ahungered /ə-hung'gərd/ or **ahungry** /-gri/ (both archaic) adj oppressed with hunger (also, from confusion of prefixes, anhung'(e)red, an-hung'ry or an hungry). [Prob OE of-hyngred]

Ahura Mazda /ä'hoor-ä maz'dä/ n the chief god of the ancient Persians, the creator and lord of the whole universe. [See **Ormuzd**]

ahv abbrev : ad hanc vocem (L), at this word.

AI abbrev : Amnesty International; artificial insemination; artificial intelligence.

ai¹ /ä'ē/ n the three-toed sloth. [Tupí ai, representing the animal's cry]

ai² see **ayu**.

AIA abbrev : Associate of the Institute of Actuaries.

aia same as **ayah**.

AIB abbrev : formerly, Associate of the Institute of Bankers.

AIBA abbrev : Association Internationale de Boxe Amateur (Fr), International Amateur Boxing Association.

aiblins see under **able**.

AICC abbrev : All-India Congress Committee.

aichmophobia /āk-mə-fō'bi-ə/ n abnormal fear of sharp or pointed objects. [Gr aichmē point of a spear, and phobos fear]

aich whow see **whow**.

AID abbrev : artificial insemination by donor (now known as **DI**).

aid /ād/ vt to help. ◆ n help; succour; assistance, eg in defending an action; something which helps; an auxiliary; a helper; an apparatus, etc that gives help, eg hearing aid, navigational aid; a feudal tax for certain purposes, eg paying the lord's ransom, the expense of knighting his son, his daughter's marriage; subsidy or money grant to the sovereign (hist); money, etc donated to relieve poor or disaster-stricken countries. [OFr aider, from L adjūtāre, frequentative of adjuvāre, from juvāre, jūtum to help]
■ aid'ance n aid, help or support. aid'ant adj (archaic) aiding or helping. aid'ed adj. aid'er n. aid'ful adj. aid'ing adj. aid'less adj.
❑ aid climbing n rock climbing using spikes, ladders or other fixed aids, opp to free climbing.
■ aid and abet (law) to assist and encourage, esp in committing a crime. in aid of (inf) intended to achieve; in support of.

aida /ä'də/ n a finely-meshed cotton fabric used for cross-stitch embroidery. [Origin unknown]

aide /ād/ n a confidential assistant to a person of senior rank, eg an ambassador or president; an aide-de-camp. [Fr, assistant]
❑ aide-de-camp /ed'/ or /äd'də-kä'/ n (pl aides-de-camp /ed'/ or /äd'/) (Fr, of the field) an officer who attends a general, governor, etc and acts as a personal assistant; an officer attending a monarch (usu hist).

aide-mémoire /ād-me-mwär'/ n an aid to the memory; a reminder; a memorandum-book; a written summary of a diplomatic document. [Fr]

aidos /ī'dōs/ (Gr) n shame, modesty.

AIDS /ādz/ n a condition brought about by a virus which causes the body's immune system to become deficient, leaving the sufferer very vulnerable to infection. [Acronym for acquired immune deficiency syndrome]
❑ AIDS-related complex n a viral condition, marked esp by fever and swollen lymph nodes, that may develop into AIDS.

aiery a variant of **eyrie**.

AIFA abbrev : Association of Independent Financial Advisers.

aiglet same as **aglet**.

aigre-doux /egr'-doo'/ (fem **aigre-douce** /-doos'/) (Fr) adj bitter-sweet, sourish.

aigrette or **aigret** /ā'gret or ā-gret'/ n an egret; an egret plume; any ornamental feather plume; a spray of jewels; a tuft; a pappus (bot); a savoury cooked in deep fat. [Fr aigrette]

aiguille /ā-gwēl'/ n a sharp, needle-like peak of rock; a slender boring tool. [Fr]
■ aiguillette' n see **aglet**.

AIH abbrev : artificial insemination by husband.

aikido /ī-kē'dō or (Jap) ī-ki-dō/ n a Japanese martial art using locks and pressure against joints. [Jap, from ai to harmonize, ki breath, spirit, and dō way, doctrine]

aikona /ī'ko-nə/ (Bantu) interj it is not; no.

ail /āl/ vt (impers) to trouble, afflict, be the matter with; to have the matter with one. ◆ vi to be sickly or indisposed. ◆ n trouble; indisposition. [OE eglan to trouble]

■ **ail'ing** adj unwell; in poor health. **ail'ment** n indisposition; disease, esp if not very serious; pain.
■ **what ails him at?** (Scot) what is his objection to?

ailanto /ā-lan'tō/ or **ailanthus** /ā-lan'thəs/ n (pl **ailan'tos** or **ailan'thuses**) the tree of heaven (genus Ailantus, family Simarubaceae), a tall and beautiful Asiatic tree. [Amboina (Moluccas) name aylanto tree of the gods]

aileron /ā'lə or el'ə-rō, or -ron/ n a flap on an aeroplane wing tip for lateral balancing; a half-gable, eg on a penthouse (archit). [Fr, dimin of aile, from L āla a wing]
■ **ailette** /ā-let'/ n a plate of armour for the shoulder.

ailes de pigeon /el də pē-zhõ/ (Fr) n pl powdered side-curls of hair, known as 'pigeon's wings'.

ailette see under **aileron**.

ailment see under **ail**.

ailuro- /ī-loor-ə-/ or **ailur-** /ī-loor-/, also **ailour(o)-** and **aelur(o)-** /ī- or ē-loor-/ combining form denoting cat. [Gr ailouros cat]
■ **ailur'ophile** or **ailour'ophile** /-fīl/ n a cat lover or fancier. **ailurophilia** or **ailourophilia** /-fil'i-ə/ n love of cats. **ailurophil'ic** or **ailourophil'ic** adj. **ailur'ophobe** or **ailour'ophobe** /-fōb/ n a cat hater; someone with an abnormal fear of cats. **ailuropho'bia** or **ailouropho'bia** n. **ailuropho'bic** or **ailouropho'bic** adj.

AIM /ām/ abbrev : Alternative Investment Market.

aim /ām/ vt to point, level or direct (a weapon or blow); to intend or try (to do); to estimate or guess (obs); to place. ◆ vi to direct a course; to level a weapon; to direct a blow or missile; to direct a remark with personal or special application; to direct one's intention and endeavours with a view to attaining (with at); to conjecture (obs). ◆ n an act or manner of aiming; an object or purpose aimed at; design; intention; a guess or estimate (Shakesp); a shot (Shakesp). [Prob partly OFr esmer (Picardian amer), from L aestimāre, partly OFr aesmer, from L adaestimāre; cf **esteem** and **estimate**]
■ **aim'er** n someone who aims. **aim'less** adj without a fixed aim. **aim'lessly** adv. **aim'lessness** n.
■ **aim off** to aim slightly off the target to allow for wind or other factors (shooting); to allow for the possible bias, exaggeration or eccentricity inherent in a statement, opinion, etc. **cry aim** (archaic) to encourage by calling out 'aim', hence, to applaud. **give aim** (archaic) to guide by reporting the result of previous shots. **take aim** to aim deliberately.

ain /ān/ (Scot) adj own. [ON eiginn or OE ǽgen a variant of āgen]

aîné (fem **aînée**) /e-nā'/ (Fr) adj elder or senior.

ain't /ānt/ (inf) contracted form of are not, used also for am or is not ; also for have not and has not.

Ainu /ī'noo/ n a people of Japan, taller and with more abundant body-hair than most Japanese; their language. ◆ adj of the Ainu or their language.

aioli or **aïoli** /ī-ō'lē/ n a garlic-flavoured mayonnaise. [Provençal ai garlic, from L allium, and oli oil, from L oleum]

air /ār/ n the gaseous mixture (chiefly nitrogen and oxygen) of which the earth's atmosphere is composed; the medium through which sound waves travel (radio); the medium in which aircraft operate; the distance between the ground and a leaping athlete, a ball sent into the air, etc (sport; inf); any gas (obs); a light breeze; breath (obs); effluvium; the aura or atmosphere surrounding or created by anything; bearing, outward appearance, manner, look; an assumed or affected manner; (in pl) an affectation of superiority; exposure or publicity; a melody or tune (see also **ayre**); the chief, usually upper, part or tune (music). ◆ adj of or relating to the air; affecting or regulating (the) air; by means of (the) air; operated by air; of aircraft; carried out or conveyed by aircraft. ◆ vt to expose to the air; to ventilate; to warm and dry; to give an airing to, to voice; to wear openly, display; to make public knowledge, to spread. ◆ vi to take an airing; to become aired; to be broadcast (TV and radio). [OFr (and Fr) air, from L āēr, āeris, from Gr āēr, āeros air]
■ **air'er** n someone who airs; a frame on which clothes are dried. **air'ily** adv in an airy manner; jauntily. **air'iness** n. **air'ing** n exposure to air or heat, to general notice or to open debate; a short excursion in the open air. **air'less** adj without air; without free communication with the outer air; without wind; stuffy. **air'lessness** n. **air'ward** or **air'wards** adv up into the air. **air'worthiness** n. **air'worthy** adj in fit condition for safe flying. **air'y** adj consisting of or relating to air; open to the air; having sufficient (fresh) air; like air; unsubstantial; sprightly, jaunty; offhand.
❑ **air ambulance** n an aircraft used to take patients from remote places to hospital. **air'-arm** n the branch of the fighting services that uses aircraft. **air'bag** n a safety device in a motor-car, etc consisting of a bag that inflates to protect the occupants in a collision; an air-filled bag for another purpose, eg raising sunken craft. **air'ball** n (sport) a shot that completely fails to touch the target. **air'base** n a base of operations for aircraft. **air'-bath** n exposure of the body to air; an

apparatus for the therapeutic application of compressed or rarefied air, or for drying substances in air. **air'-bed** n an inflated mattress. **air'-bell** n an air-bubble. **air'-bends** n pl aeroembolism. **air'-bladder** n a sac containing gas, such as those that buoy up certain seaweeds; a fish's swim bladder, serving to regulate buoyancy, etc. **air'boat** n a swamp boat. **air'borne** adj carried by air; borne up in the air. **Airborne Warning and Control System** see **AWACS**. **air'-brake** n a brake worked by compressed air; a means of reducing the speed of an aircraft. **air'-breathing** adj (of a means of propulsion) which needs to take in air for combustion. **air'-brick** n a block with holes for ventilation. **air'-bridge** n a link by air transport between two points. **air'brush** n a device for spraying paint, etc, powered by compressed air, or for touching up or toning down a photograph; a tool for achieving a similar effect in computer graphics. ◆ vt to treat or alter with an airbrush; to remove (a person) from a story or account (often with out). **air'brushed** adj. **air'-bubble** n a bubble of air, specif one causing a spot on a photograph. **air'-built** adj built in air; having no solid foundation. **air'burst** n the explosion of a bomb, etc in the air (also vi). ◆ adj designed to explode in the air. **air'-car** n one made to ride on a cushion of air. **air'-cavity** or **air'-cell** n (bot) an intercellular space containing air. **air'-chief-mar'shal** n a Royal Air Force officer of equivalent rank to an admiral or general (abbrev **ACM**). **air cleaner** n an air filter. **air-comm'odore** n a Royal Air Force officer of equivalent rank to a commodore or brigadier. **air'-compressor** n a machine which draws in air at atmospheric pressure, compresses it, and delivers it at higher pressure. **air'-condition** vt to equip eg a building with devices for air-conditioning. **air'-conditioned** adj. **air'-conditioner** n. **air'-conditioning** n (devices for) the bringing of air to the desired state of purity, temperature and humidity (often shortened to **air'con'**). **air'-cool** vt. **air'-cooled** adj. **air'-cooling** n cooling by means of air. **air'-corridor** n in an area where flying is restricted, a narrow strip along which flying is allowed. **air'-cover** n protection given by fighter aircraft to other forces during a military operation; the protecting aircraft. **air'craft** n (pl **air'craft**) any structure or machine for travelling in the air. **air'craft-carrier** n a vessel from which aircraft can take off and on which they can land. **air'craftman** or **air'craftsman** n (RAF) a member of the lowest rank. **air'craftwoman** or **air'craftswoman** n (someone of) the lowest rank in the WRAF. **air'crew** n the crew of an aircraft. **air curtain** n a current of air directed across a doorway or other opening to prevent draughts, maintain temperature, etc. **air'-cushion** n a cushion that can be inflated; a protective barrier, eg between a hovercraft and land or water, formed by down-driven air. **air dam** n on a motor vehicle, a front spoiler. **air'-drain** n a cavity in the external walls of a building to prevent damp from getting through to the interior. **air'drawn** adj drawn in air; visionary; imaginary (Shakesp). **air'drome** n (chiefly US) an aerodrome. **air'drop** n (milit) a landing of men or supplies by parachute (also vt). **air'-dry** vt to dry by exposing to the air. **air'-engine** n an engine driven by heated or compressed air. **air'field** n an open expanse where aircraft may land and take off. **air filter** n a filter preventing dust, etc from entering the air-intake of an internal-combustion engine. **air'flow** n the flow of air past a moving vehicle or in a wind tunnel. **air'foil** n (N Am) an aerofoil. **air force** n a force organized for warfare in the air, often with caps when referring to a national force. **Air Force** or **air'-force** adj (**air-force blue** a greyish-blue such as is used for Royal Air Force uniforms). **air'frame** n the body of an aircraft as opposed to its engines. **air freight** n transport of freight by air; the cost of this. **air'-freight** vt. **air frost** n (meteorol) an air (not ground) temperature of below 0°C. **air'gap** n a gap in the magnetic circuit of a piece of electrical apparatus, eg the gap between the rotor and stator of an electric machine. **air'-gas** n producer gas. **air'glow** n a faint light in the night sky, produced by radiation from the upper atmosphere. **air'graph** n a letter photographically reduced for sending by air. **air'-grating** n a grating admitting air for ventilation. **air guitar** n the playing of an imaginary guitar to music, esp rock music. **air'gun** n a gun that discharges missiles by means of compressed air. **air'head** n an idiot, feather-brain (sl); a forward base for aircraft in enemy territory. **air hockey** n a game, similar to table football, in which players use paddles to shoot a puck resting on a cushion of air through the opponent's goal. **air'hole** n a hole for the passage of air; a hole in ice where animals come up to breathe; an air-pocket. **air hostess** n an earlier word for a stewardess or flight attendant. **air'-house** n an inflatable building of nylon or Terylene coated with polyvinyl chloride which can be used by industrial firms for storage, etc. **airing cupboard** n a large cupboard used for drying and storing clothes and linen. **air'-intake** n a valve or other opening through which air is drawn in, esp to an engine; the amount of air so drawn in. **air'-jacket** n a casing containing air to reduce loss or gain of heat; a garment with airtight cavities to buoy up in water. **air kiss** n (inf) a greeting in which a person performs a simulated kiss but does not touch the other person's face. **air-kiss** vt. **air'-lane** n a route normally taken by aircraft because of steady winds. **air layering** n (hortic) the layering of shoots, not by bending them down to root in the soil but by enclosing in compost, etc at their current place of growth. **air letter** n a letter sent by airmail. **air letter form** *n* a prestamped sheet of paper used for sending correspondence by air. **air lieutenant** *n* a rank in the Zimbabwean Air Force equivalent to a flying officer in the Royal Air Force. **air'lift** *n* a transport operation carried out by air, *esp* in an emergency (also *vt*); transportation by air. **air'line** *n* a route or system of traffic by aircraft (also *adj*); a company operating such a system; a hose carrying air under pressure. **air'liner** *n* a large passenger aircraft; an aircraft operating in an airline. **air loadmaster** *n* one of a team of *usu* three men in charge of winching operations on a helicopter. **air'lock** *n* a small chamber in which the pressure of air can be raised or lowered, through which communication is made between a caisson where the air is compressed and the outer air (*civil eng*); a bubble in a pipe obstructing the flow of liquid. **air'mail** *n* mail conveyed by air (also *adj*). ◆ *vt* to send by airmail. **air'man** *n* or **air'woman** *n* a person who flies; an aircraft pilot, technician or navigator, *specif* in the Royal Air Force someone below officer rank. **air'manship** *n* the art of handling aircraft. **air-mar'shal** *n* a Royal Air Force officer of equivalent rank to a vice-admiral or a lieutenant-general. **air mass** *n* a vast horizontally uniform body of air. **air'-mechanic** *n* someone who tends and repairs aircraft. **air mile** *n* a nautical mile used to measure distance by air; (*usu pl*) a point gained by a purchaser of air tickets or other products, allowing free air travel to a certain distance as points are accumulated. **air'-minded** *adj* having one's thoughts continually and favourably directed towards flying. **air miss** see **airprox** below. **air'-officer** *n* a Royal Air Force officer above the rank of air-commodore. **air'-passage** *n* the passage by which air enters and leaves the lungs; a journey to a particular destination by air. **air-pir'acy** *n* the hijacking of an aircraft. **air pistol** and **air rifle** *n* guns that fire missiles by means of compressed air. **air'plane** *n* (chiefly *N Am*) an aeroplane. **air'-plant** *n* (*bot*) a non-parasitic plant growing on another, an epiphyte. **air play** *n* the broadcasting of a song, singer, record, etc on the radio. **air'-pocket** *n* a region of rarefied or down-flowing air, in which aircraft lose height. **air pollution** *n* contamination of the air by noxious substances such as exhaust fumes and industrial waste. **air'port** *n* an aerodrome, *usu* with a custom house, used as a station for transport of passengers and cargo; an opening for the passage of air. **airport fiction** *n* a style of fiction that makes few demands on the reader, considered suitable for reading on holiday. **air'-power** *n* military power in terms of aircraft. **air'prox** or **air miss** *n* a near collision between aircraft in flight. **air'-pump** *n* an instrument for pumping air out or in. **air quotes** *n pl* (*inf*) a gesture, made by holding up and bending the index (and/or middle) fingers when speaking, to draw an interlocutor's attention to the fact that a word is being used ironically or incorrectly. **air rage** *n* (*inf*) uncontrolled anger or aggression on an aeroplane, *esp* endangering the safety of fellow-passengers. **air'-raid** *n* an attack on a place by aircraft. **air'-rail** *n* a rail on which a road vehicle is carried overhead for part of its course. **air rifle** see **air pistol** above. **air'-sac** *n* an alveolus, or the cluster of alveoli, at the termination of a bronchiole in the lungs; an outgrowth of the lung in birds, helping respiration or lightening the body; in insects, a dilatation of the trachea. **Air Scout** *n* a member of a branch of the Scouts with special interest in air activities. **air'screw** *n* the propeller of an aircraft. **air-sea rescue** *n* the combined use of aircraft and high-speed launches in sea rescue. **air'shaft** *n* a passage for air into a mine, building, etc. **air'ship** *n* a mechanically driven dirigible aircraft, lighter than air. **air shot** *n* in golf, cricket or other sports, a stroke that fails to connect with the ball. **air'show** *n* a flying display, *usu* at an airbase. **air shower** *n* a flash of light created after a cosmic ray enters the earth's atmosphere. **air'sick** *adj*. **air'-sickness** *n* nausea affecting travellers by air. **air'side** *adj*, *adv* and *n* (of, in or relating to) that part of an airport having direct access to the apron, and off-limits to non-travelling public and unauthorized personnel, the area *usu* controlled by an airport authority (**go** or **pass airside** to enter this restricted area). **air sign** *n* any of the three signs of the zodiac (Gemini, Libra and Aquarius) believed to have an affinity with air. **air'space** *n* the part of the atmosphere above a particular territory, state, etc; the space used or required by an aircraft in manoeuvring; cubic contents available for respirable air; an air-cell. **air'speed** *n* the speed of an aircraft, missile, etc in relation to the air through which it is moving. **air'-splint** *n* a contrivance zipped up and inflated for giving temporary support to an injured limb. **air station** *n* an airfield, *esp* a military one, with facilities for aircraft maintenance. **air'stop** *n* a stopping-place for helicopters. **air'stream** *n* a flow of air. **airstream mechanism** *n* the part(s) of the body, eg the lungs, which can produce a flow of air on which speech sounds, etc may be produced. **air strike** *n* an attack with aircraft. **air'strip** *n* a temporary or emergency landing-place for aircraft; a runway. **air support** *n* support given by fighter aircraft to other forces during a military operation; the supporting aircraft involved in such an operation. **air taxi** *n* a *usu* small aeroplane or a helicopter making short trips, often to and from an airport. **air**

terminal *n* a terminus in a town to or from which passengers are conveyed from or to an airport; the terminal building(s) of an airport. **air'tight** *adj* impermeable to air; impenetrable (*fig*). **air'time** *n* the amount of broadcasting time on radio or television allotted to a particular topic, type of material, commercial advertisement, etc; the time at which the broadcasting of a programme, etc is due to begin. **airtime provider** *n* an organization that provides access to mobile phone services. **air'-to-air** *adj* from one aircraft to another. **air-traffic control** *n* the organized control, by visual and radio means, of the traffic into and out of aerodromes and on air routes (*abbrev* **ATC**). **air-traffic controller** *n*. **air'-trap** *n* a device to prevent the escape of foul air. **air'-umbrella** *n* strong air-cover. **air vice-marshal** *n* a Royal Air Force officer of equivalent rank to a rear-admiral or major-general (*abbrev* **AVM**). **air'wave** *n* a channel for broadcasting. **air'way** *n* a passage for air; a radio channel; an organized route for air travel; used in *pl* to form names of airline companies. **air'woman** *n* see **airman** above. **air'y-fair'y** *adj* fanciful; delicate, flimsy or insubstantial.

■ **by air** in an aircraft. **change of air** change in routine, circumstances, etc. **give oneself airs** to put on a superior manner. **give the air** to dismiss. **go up in the air** to become excited or angry (see also below). **in the air** prevalent in a vague or indefinite form. **off the air** not broadcasting or being broadcast for a period of time. **on the air** in the act of broadcasting; broadcast by radio. **take air** to get wind or become known. **take the air** to have an airing. **up in the air** undecided; excited or angry.

Airedale /ār'dāl/ or **Airedale terrier** /ter'i-ər/ *n* a large terrier of a breed *orig* from *Airedale* in Yorkshire.

airn /ārn/ Scots form of **iron**.

airt /ārt/ (*Scot*) *n* direction, quarter. ◆ *vt* to direct. [Perh Gaelic *aird* point (of compass)]

aisle /īl/ *n* a side division of the nave or other part of a church or similar building, generally separated off by pillars; (loosely) any division of a church, or a small building attached; a passage between rows of seats eg in an aircraft, theatre, cinema, etc; a passageway in a supermarket on either side of which products are displayed; a passageway (*N Am*); the corridor of a railway train or aircraft. [OFr *ele* (Fr *aile*), from L *āla* a wing; confused with **isle** and **alley¹**]

■ **aisled** /īld/ *adj* having aisles.

■ **lead up the aisle** to marry. **rolling in the aisles** in a state of uncontrollable laughter.

aisling /ī'shling or ash'ling/ *n* (a poetic description of) a vision or dream. [Ir]

ait¹ or **eyot** /āt/ *n* a small island. [Cf OE *ēgath*, *īgeoth* appar connected with *īeg* island; the phonology is obscure]

ait² /āt/ Scots form of **oat**.

AITC *abbrev* : Association of Investment Trust Companies.

aitch /āch/ *n* the eighth letter of the modern English alphabet (H or h). [OFr *ache*, from which LL *ahha* is inferred]

■ **drop one's aitches** to fail to pronounce initial aitches on words.

aitchbone /āch'bōn/ *n* in cattle, the bone of the rump; the cut of beef over it. [*an aitchbone* is for *a nachebone*, from OFr *nache*, from L *natis* buttock; and **bone**]

AITO *abbrev* : Association of Independent Tour Operators.

aitu /ī'too/ *n* in Polynesia, a demigod. [Polynesian]

aizle see **easle**.

Aizoon /ā-ī-zō'on/ *n* an African genus of plants giving name to the family **Aizoā'ceae**, related to the goosefoots. [Appar Gr *āei* ever, and *zōos* living]

à jamais /a zha-me'/ (Fr) for ever.

ajar¹ /ə-jär'/ *adv* and *adj* partly open. [OE *on* on, and *cerr* a turn]

ajar² /ə-jär'/ (*archaic*) *adj* jarring, out of tune or harmony. [**a-¹** and **jar²**]

Ajax /ā'jaks/ *n* a Greek hero in the Trojan war; a privy, by a pun on *a jakes* (*obs*). [L from Gr *Aiās*]

ajee or **agee** /ə-jē'/ (*Scot* and *dialect*) *adv* off the straight; ajar. [**a¹**, and **gee¹**, **jee²**]

ajowan /aj'ō-wən/ or **ajwan** /aj'wən/ *n* a plant of the caraway genus yielding ajowan oil and thymol. [Origin uncertain]

ajutage see **adjutage**.

AK *abbrev* : Alaska (US state); Knight of (the Order of) Australia.

aka or **AKA** *abbrev* : also known as.

akaryote /ā-kar'i-ōt/ (*zool*) *n* a cell that does not have a nucleus. [Gr *ā* (privative), and *karyon* a kernel]

akathisia or **acathisia** /a-kə-thiz'i-ə or -this-/ *n* a psychological condition characterized by agitation and a frequent desire to alter the posture. [Gr *a-* (privative), and *kathizein* to sit down]

ake /āk/ old spelling of the verb **ache**[1].

akedah /ə-kä'dä or a-kä-dä/ (*Heb*) *n* the binding of Isaac in the Bible, Genesis 22.

akee or **ackee** /a-kē'/ *n* a small African sapindaceous tree, now common in the West Indies; its edible fruit, often used in Caribbean cookery. [Kru *ā-kee*]

Akela /ə-kā'lə/ *n* the adult leader of a group, or pack, of Cub Scouts. [From a character in Kipling's *The Jungle Book*]

akene /a-kēn'/ *n* same as **achene**.

AK-47 *abbrev*: Automatic Kalashnikov 47, a type of sub-machine gun.

akimbo /ə-kim'bō/ *adj* and *adv* with hand on hip and elbow out. [ME *in kenebow* (possibly) in a keen (sharp) bow or bend; other suggestions are *can-bow* (ie can-handle), and ON *kengboginn* bent into a crook, from *kengr* kink, and *boginn* bowed]

akin /ə-kin'/ *adv* by kin; of nature. ◆ *adj* related by blood; of a similar nature. [**a**[1] and **kin**[1]]

akinesia /a- or ā-ki-nē'zi-ə or -si-ə or -shə/ or **akinesis** /a- or ā-ki-nē'sis/ (*pathol*) *n* the lack, loss, or impairment of the power of voluntary movement. [Gr *akinesia* lack of motion; *a-* (privative), and *kinein* to move]
  ■ **akinet'ic** *adj*.

akita /ə-kē'tə/ *n* a large, powerful Japanese breed of dog. [*Akita*, prefecture in Japan]

Akkadian /ə-kā'di-ən/ *n* the Semitic language of the ancient Middle-Eastern kingdom of Akkad; a native of this kingdom. ◆ *adj* of the Akkadians or their language. [City of *Agade*]

akkas see **ackers**.

akolouthos, **akoluthos**, etc same as **acolouthos**, etc.

akrasia same as **acrasia**.

AKST *abbrev*: Alaska Standard Time.

akvavit see **aquavit**.

AL *abbrev*: Alabama (US state); Albania (IVR); Anglo-Latin.

Al (*chem*) *symbol*: aluminium.

ALA *abbrev*: alpha-linolenic acid, an essential fatty acid; Associate of the Library Association (now replaced by **MCLIP**).

Ala. *abbrev*: Alabama (US state).

ala /ā'lə/ *n* (*pl* **alae** /ā'lē/) a membranous outgrowth on a fruit (*bot*); a side petal in the pea family (*bot*); a large side sepal in the milkworts (*bot*); a leafy expansion running down the stem from a leaf (*bot*); any flat winglike process, *esp* of bone (*zool*). [L *āla* wing]
  ■ **ā'lar** or **ā'lary** *adj* relating to a wing. **ā'late** or **ā'lated** *adj* winged, having an ala.

à la /a la/ *prep* in the manner of, eg *à la James Joyce*; in cooking, prepared with or in the manner of (a person or place), eg **à la Dubarry** with cauliflower, **à la Florentine** with spinach, etc. [Fr, from contraction of *à la mode de*]

alaap see **alap**.

alabamine /a-la-bä'mēn/ *n* a name once proposed for element number 85, now called **astatine**. [*Alabama*, where its discovery in nature was claimed]

alabandine see **almandine**.
  ■ **alaband'ite** *n* a cubic mineral, manganese sulphide.

à l'abandon /a la-bā-dō'/ carelessly, recklessly. [Fr, neglected, uncared-for]

alabaster /al'ə-bä-stər, also -bä'/ (*Spenser, Shakesp, Milton, etc* **alablaster**) *n* a soft, semi-transparent massive gypsum, widely used for ornamental purposes. ◆ *adj* of or like alabaster. [Gr *alabastros*, said to be from *Alabastron* a town in Egypt]
  ■ **alabas'trine** *adj*.
  ■ **oriental alabaster** stalactitic calcite.

à la belle étoile /a la be-lā-twäl'/ (*Fr*) in the open air.

à la bonne heure /a la bo-nær'/ (*Fr*) well done! that is right.

à l'abri /a la-brē'/ (*Fr*) under shelter.

à la campagne /a la kä-pan'y'/ (*Fr*) in the country.

à la carte /a la kärt' or ä lä kärt'/ with each dish charged individually at the price shown on the menu; with the freedom to pick and choose (*fig*). [Fr, according to the bill of fare]

alack /ə-lak'/ (*archaic*) *interj* denoting regret. [Prob **ah** and **lack**[1]]
  ❑ **alack'-a-day** *interj* woe be to the day; alas.

alacrity /ə-lak'ri-ti/ *n* briskness; cheerful readiness; promptness. [L *alacritās, -ātis*, from *alacer, alacris* brisk]

Aladdin /ə-lad'in/ *n* a character in the *Arabian Nights*.
  ❑ **Aladdin's cave** *n* (*fig*) a place full of wonderful treasures. **Aladdin's lamp** *n* a magic object able to grant all one's desires.

à la dérobée /a la dā-ro-bā'/ (*Fr*) by stealth.

alae see **ala**.

à la hauteur de /a la ō-tær' də/ (*Fr*) on a level with or abreast of; able to understand or to deal with.

alaiment old spelling of **allayment** (see under **allay**[1]).

à la lanterne /a la lā-tern'/ (*Fr*) away with them and hang them (as in the French Revolution); literally, to the lamp(-chain).

alalia /ə-lā'li-ə/ *n* loss of speech. [Gr *a-* in privative sense, and *laleein* to talk]

à la main /a la mē'/ (*Fr*) in hand and ready; by hand.

à la maître d'hôtel /a la metr' dō-tel'/ in major-domo fashion; in cooking, served plain with a parsley garnish. [Fr, in the style of a house-steward or hotel-keeper]

alameda /a-la-mā'dä/ *n* a public walk, *esp* between rows of poplars. [Sp *álamo* poplar]

à la mode /a la mod'/ *adv* and *adj* (also **alamode** /a-lə-mōd'/) according to the fashion, fashionable; of beef, larded and stewed with vegetables (*cookery*); of desserts, served with ice cream (*N Am*). [Fr *à la mode*]
  ■ **al'amode** *n* a light glossy silk.

alamort /a-lə-mört'/ *adj* half-dead; dejected. [Fr *à la mort* to the death; see also **amort**]

aland /ə-land'/ (*archaic*) *adv* ashore. [**a-**[1] and **land**[1]]

alang /ä'läng/ or **alang-alang** /ä'läng-ä'läng/ same as **lalang**.

alanine /al'ə-nēn or -nīn/ *n* an amino acid, a common constituent of proteins. [Ger *Alanin*]

alannah /ə-lä'nə/ *n* (used as term of endearment) my child. [Ir *a* O, and *leanbh* child]

alap /ə-läp'/ *n* in Indian music, the introductory section of a raga (also **alaap'** or **alap'a**). [Sans]

à la page /a la päzh'/ (*Fr*) up to date, au courant.

à la Portugaise see under **Portugaise**.

à la poupée /a la poo-pā'/ (*Fr*) of the printing of an engraving or etching, with inks of different colours being spread on the plate with paper or cloth pads (*poupées*) before the impression is taken.

Alar® /ā'lär/ *n* the chemical daminozide, formerly used as a spray to prevent blemishes and to delay the ripening of apples, but withdrawn when discovered to be carcinogenic.

alar, **alary** see under **ala**.

alarm /ə-lärm'/ *n* a state of (*esp* sudden) fear; apprehension of danger; a warning of danger; a mechanical contrivance for arousing, warning, or giving notice; the noise made by such a device; *orig* a call to arms; a din (*obs*). ◆ *vt* to strike with fear; to arouse, startle or agitate; to give notice of danger; to fit or switch on an alarm; to call to arms (*obs*). [OFr *alarme*, from Ital *all'arme* to (the) arms]
  ■ **alarmed'** *adj*. **alarm'edly** *adv*. **alarm'ing** *adj*. **alarm'ingly** *adv*. **alarm'ism** *n*. **alarm'ist** *n* a scaremonger or someone who is easily alarmed (also *adj*). **alarum** /ə-la'rəm, -lä' or -lā'/ *n* and *vt* alarm (now *archaic* except of a warning mechanism or sound).
  ❑ **alarm'-bell** *n* a bell warning of danger. **alarm call** *n* a telephone service by which a subscriber can arrange to be called at a particular time, eg to wake him or her in the morning. **alarm clock** *n* a clock that can be set to ring an alarm at a chosen time. **alarm'-radio** *n* a clock radio.
  ■ **alarms** (or **alarums**) **and excursions** a stage direction for a sketchy conventionalized representation of skirmishing or the outskirts of a battle; hence, vague hostilities or confused activity. **give, raise** or **sound the alarm** to give the signal to prepare for an emergency.

alarum see under **alarm**.

Alas. *abbrev*: Alaska (US state).

alas /ə-las'/ *interj* (now rather *archaic* or *mock-heroic*) expressing grief or misfortune. [OFr *ha las, a las* (Mod Fr *hélas*); *ha* ah, and *las, lasse* wretched, weary, from L *lassus* wearied]
  ■ **alas the day** or **alas the while** (*archaic* or *poetic*) ah! unhappy day or time.

Alaskan malamute see **malamute**.

Alaska Standard Time or **Alaska Time** /ə-las'kə (stan'dərd) tīm/ *n* one of the standard times used in N America, being 9 hours behind Greenwich Mean Time (*abbrev* **AKST** or **AST**).

alastrim /ə-las'trim/ *n* a mild form of smallpox or a similar disease. [Port]

alate[1] /ə-lāt'/ *adv* (*archaic*) lately. [**of** and **late**]

alate[2], **alated** see under **ala**.

a latere /ā la'tə-rē or ä la'tə-rä/ (L) (of a legate sent by the Pope) confidential, (literally) from the side.

à la volée /a la vo-lā'/ (Fr) on the flight (said of any quick return).

Alawite /al'ə-wīt/ n a member of a Shiite Muslim sect, based chiefly in Syria. [Ar 'Alawi follower of Ali]

alay old spelling of **allay**[1].

Alb. abbrev: Albania.

alb /alb/ n a priest's long white sleeved vestment. [OE albe, from LL alba, from L albus white]

albacore, also **albicore** /al'bə-kōr or -kör/ n a large tuna with long pectoral fins; a species of mackerel (S Afr). [Port albacor, from Ar al the, and bukr young camel]

Alban /al'bən/, **Albany** /-i/ or **Albion** /-bi-ən/ n ancient names for the island of Great Britain, now used poetically for Britain, England, or esp Scotland; (**Alban**) the ancient kingdom of the Picts and (Celtic) Scots, which the addition of Lothian and Strathclyde transformed into Scotland. [Celtic]
■ **Al'bany** n a Scottish dukedom first conferred in 1398.
□ **Albany herald** n one of the Scottish heralds.

Alban. /öl'bən/ abbrev: Albanensis (L), of St Albans.

Albanian /al-bā'ni-ən/ adj of or relating to the SE European Republic of Albania. ◆ n a native or citizen of Albania; the language of the Albanians.

albarello /al-bə-rel'ō or al-ba-rel'lō/ n (pl **albarell'os** or **albarel'li** /-lē/) a majolica jar used for dry drugs. [Ital]

albata /al-bā'tə/ n a variety of German silver. [L albāta (fem) whitened, from albus white]

albatross /al'bə-tros/ n a large, long-winged seabird with remarkable powers of flight; a score of three strokes less than par on a hole (golf); used symbolically to mean an oppressive and inescapable fact, influence, etc (from the dead bird hung round the neck of the sailor in Coleridge's Ancient Mariner). [See **alcatras**; perh influenced by L albus white]

albe, **albee** or **all-be** /öl-bē' or öl'bē/ (archaic) conj albeit. [**all** and **be**]

albedo /al-bē'dō/ n (pl **albe'dos**) orig whiteness; a measure of the reflecting power of an object (eg a planet), expressed as the proportion of incident light it reflects (phys). [L albēdō whiteness, from albus white]

albeit /öl-bē'it/ conj even if, although; although it be (that). [ME all be it]

albergo /al-ber'gō/ (Ital) n (pl **alber'ghi**) an inn, auberge.

albert /al'bərt/ n a short kind of watch chain. [After Queen Victoria's husband]

Alberti bass /al-bûr'ti bās/ n a type of bass accompaniment consisting of broken chords. [Domenico Alberti (1710–40), an exponent of this]

albertite /al'bər-tīt/ n a pitch-black solid bitumen. [Discovered at the Albert mine, New Brunswick, Canada]

albescent /al-bes'ənt/ adj becoming white; whitish. [L albēscēns, -entis, prp of albēscere to grow white, from albus white]
■ **albesc'ence** n.

albespyne or **albespine** /al'bə-spīn/ (archaic) n hawthorn. [OFr albespine (Fr aubépine), from L alba spīna white thorn]

albicore see **albacore**.

Albigensian /al-bi-jen'si-ən/ adj of the town of Albi or its district (the Albigeois), in S France; of a Catharist or Manichaean sect or of the 13c crusade (beginning in the Albigeois) by which, along with the Inquisition, the Catholic Church savagely suppressed it (also n). [LL Albigēnsēs]
■ **Albigen'sēs** n pl. **Albigen'sianism** n.

albino /al-bē'nō or (N Am) -bī'/ n (pl **albi'nos**) a person or other animal with abnormally white skin and hair and pink irises; a plant lacking in pigment. [Port, from L albus white]
■ **albiness** /al'bin-es/ n (archaic) a female albino. **albin'ic** or **albinis'tic** adj. **al'binism** /-bin-/ or **albinoism** /-bē'/ n. **albinotic** /al-bin-ot'ik/ adj.

Albion see **Alban**.

albite /al'bīt/ n a white plagioclase feldspar, sodium and aluminium silicate. [L albus white]
■ **albit'ic** adj. **al'bītize** or **-ise** vt to turn into albite.

albugo /al-bū'gō/ n (pl **albu'gos**) leucoma. [L albūgō, -inis whiteness, from albus white]
■ **albugineous** /-jin'i-əs/ adj like the white of an egg or of the eye.

album /al'bəm/ n (pl **al'bums**) a blank book for the insertion of photographs, autographs, poetical extracts, scraps, postage-stamps, etc; a printed book of selections, esp of music; a book-like container for recorded discs; a long-playing disc; in ancient Rome, a white tablet or register on which the praetor's edicts and such public notices were recorded; a visitors' book (US). [L neuter of albus white]
□ **al'bum-leaf** n (transl Ger Albumblatt) a short musical composition.

albumen /al-bū'mən, -min or al'/ n the white of an egg, the nutritive material surrounding the yolk in the eggs of higher animals, a mixture of proteins; any tissue within the seed coat other than the embryo itself, endosperm and perisperm, a store of food for the young plant, no matter what its chemical nature (bot); an albumin (obs). [L albūmen, -inis, from albus white]
■ **albū'menize**, **albū'minize**, or **-ise** vt (photog) to cover or impregnate with albumen or an albuminous solution. **albū'min** (or /al'/) n a protein of various kinds soluble in pure water, the solution coagulable by heat. **albū'minate** n an alkali compound of an albumin. **albū'minoid** adj like albumen. ◆ n an old name for a protein in general; any one of a class of substances including keratin and chondrin. **albū'minous** adj like or containing albumen or albumin; insipid. **albūminūr'ia** n presence of albumin in the urine.

album Graecum /al'bum grē'kum or al'būm grī'kŭm/ (LL) n the dried dung of dogs, formerly used for inflammation of the throat.

albumin, **albuminize**, etc see under **albumen**.

alburnum /al-bûr'nəm/ n sapwood, the soft wood between inner bark and heartwood. [L albus white]
■ **alburn'ous** adj.

alcahest see **alkahest**.

Alcaic /al-kā'ik/ adj of or relating to the Greek lyric poet Alcaeus (fl 600BC), or of the kind of verse invented by him. ◆ n (esp in pl) Alcaic verses.
□ **Alcaic strophe** n a verse form much used by Horace, consisting of two eleven-syllable Alcaics: ∪−∪−−/−∪∪−∪, followed by a nine-syllable: ∪−∪−−∪−∪, and a ten-syllable: −∪∪−∪∪−∪−∪; imitated by Tennyson in 'O mighty-mouth'd inventor of harmonies'.

alcaicería /al-kī-the-rē'a/ (Sp) n a bazaar.

alcaide or **alcayde** /al-kād' or äl-kī'dhä or -dä/ n the governor of a Spanish fortress; a Spanish gaoler. [Sp alcaide, from Ar al-qā'īd, from al the, and qā'īd leader, from qāda to lead]

alcalde /äl-käl'dä/ n formerly, a Spanish judge or magistrate; a Spanish mayor. [Sp from Ar al-qādī, from qada to judge]

Alcantara® /al-kan-tä'rə/ n a synthetic fabric resembling suede, used in clothing, interior decoration, etc. [Ar al-qantara the bridge]

alcarraza /al-kə-rä'ze or -thə/ (Sp) n a porous vessel for cooling water.

alcatras /al'kə-tras/ n a name applied to several large water birds, such as the pelican, gannet, frigate bird and albatross. [Sp alcatraz pelican]

alcayde see **alcaide**.

alcázar /al-ka-zär' or -kä'thär/ (Sp) n a palace, fortress or bazaar.

Alcelaphus /al-sel'ə-fəs/ n a genus of antelopes, the hartebeests. [New L]

alchemy or **alchymy** /al'ki-mi or -kə-/ n the infant stage of chemistry, aimed chiefly towards transmuting of other metals into gold, and discovering the elixir of life; a transmuting power (fig); a gold-like substance (eg brass) (obs); a trumpet made of it (obs). [Ar al-kīmīā, from al the, and kīmīā, from late Gr chēmeiā, chymeiā, variously explained as the Egyptian art (Khēmiā 'black-land' or Egypt, from the Egyptian name), the art of Chymēs (its supposed inventor), or the art of pouring (chyma fluid; cf cheein to pour)]
■ **alchemic** /-kem'ik/ or **alchem'ical** adj. **al'chemist** n. **al'chemize** or **-ise** vt to transmute; to change by alchemy.

alcheringa /al-chə-ring'gə/ or **alchera** /al'chə-rə/ n dreamtime. [Australian Aboriginal words]

alchymy see **alchemy**.

Alcidae /al'si-dē/ n pl the auk family. [New L]

Alcides /al-sī'dēz/ n a patronymic of Hercules, from Alcaeus, father of Amphitryon. [L, from Gr]

ALCM abbrev: air-launched cruise missile.

alcohol /al'kə-hol/ n a liquid generated by the fermentation of sugar or other saccharine matter and forming the intoxicating element of fermented liquors; any drink containing this; a general term for a class of hydrocarbon compounds analogous to common (or ethyl) alcohol, in which a hydroxyl group is substituted for an atom of hydrogen; a fine powder, esp a sublimate (obs); hence (obs) an essence, a distillate. [Ar al-koh'l, from al the, and koh'l antimony powder used in the East to stain the eyelids]
■ **alcohol'ic** adj of, like, containing or due to alcohol; relating to alcoholism. ◆ n someone addicted to excessive drinking of alcohol. **al'coholism** n alcoholic poisoning; the condition suffered by an alcoholic. **alcoholīzā'tion** or **-s-** n. **al'coholīze** or **-ise** vt to convert

into or saturate with alcohol. **alcoholom'eter** n an instrument for measuring the proportion of alcohol in solutions. **alcoholom'etry** n. ❑ **al'cohol-free** adj containing little or no alcohol. **alcoholic fermentation** n (biol) a fermentation in the absence of oxygen in which sugar is converted to alcohol and carbon dioxide.

alcolock /al'kō-lok/ n a breath-testing device fitted in a car that locks the ignition if the driver's breath contains more than the permitted amount of alcohol. [From **alcohol** and **lock**¹]

al conto /al kon'tō/ (Ital) à la carte.

al contrario /al kon-trä'ri-ō/ (Sp) on the contrary.

alcopop /al'kō-pop/ (inf) n a commercially sold drink containing alcohol but packaged and tasting like a soft drink. [From **alcohol** and **pop**¹]

Alcoran /al-ko-rän'/ (archaic) n the Koran. [Fr, from Ar al the, and **Koran**]

alcorza /al-kör'tha/ (Sp) n a kind of sweet; icing.

alcove /al'kōv/ n a recess in a room, eg for a bed, seating, shelving, etc; any recess, eg a covered outdoor shelter in a wall; a shady retreat (archaic). [Sp alcoba a place in a room railed off to hold a bed, from Ar al the, and qobbah a vault]

Alcyonium /al-si-ō'ni-əm/ n a genus of Anthozoa growing as masses of polyps, dead men's fingers. [Gr alkyoneion an organism said to resemble a halcyon's nest, from alkyōn halcyon, kingfisher] ■ **Alcyonā'ria** n pl the group to which Alcyonium, sea pens, sea fans, red coral and organ-pipe coral belong. **alcyonā'rian** n and adj.

ALD abbrev: adrenoleukodystrophy.

Ald. abbrev: Alderman.

aldea /al-dā'a/ (Sp) n a village or hamlet.

Aldebaran /al-deb'a-ran/ n a first-magnitude red star of the Hyades. [Ar al-dabarān the follower (of the Pleiades)]

aldehyde /al'di-hīd/ n a volatile fluid with a suffocating smell, obtained by the oxidation of alcohol; a compound differing from an alcohol in having two fewer hydrogen atoms. [Contraction of alcohol dēhydrogenātum, alcohol deprived of hydrogen] ■ **aldehydic** /aldihīd'ik/ adj.

al dente /al den'tā/ (cookery) adj and adv of food, esp pasta and vegetables, firm to the bite. [Ital, to the tooth]

alder /öl'dər/ n any tree of the genus **Al'nus**, related to the birches, usu growing in moist ground; extended to various other trees or shrubs; an artificial fishing fly. [OE alor; Ger Erle; L alnus]. ■ **al'dern** adj made of alder. ❑ **al'der-buck'thorn** n a species of buckthorn (Rhamnus frangula). **al'der-fly** n a riverside neuropterous insect of the order Megaloptera. **al'der-leaved** adj.

alder-liefest /öl-dər-lē'fist/ (Shakesp) adj most beloved of all. [OE alra (WSax ealra), genitive pl of al (eal) all, and superl of **lief**]

alderman /öl'dər-mən/ n (pl **al'dermen**) in Anglo-Saxon times a nobleman of highest rank, a governor of a shire or district, a high official; later, head of a guild; in English boroughs, a civic dignitary next in rank to the mayor, elected by fellow councillors (chiefly hist); a superior member of an English county council (chiefly hist); a member of the governing body of a borough or of its upper house, elected by popular vote (N Am). [OE aldorman (WSax ealdorman) from aldor (ealdor) a chief, from ald (eald) old, and noun-forming sfx -or] ■ **aldermanic** /öl-dar-man'ik/ adj. **alderman'ity** n. **al'dermanlike** or **al'dermanly** adj pompous and portly. **al'dermanry** n. **al'dermanship** n.

Alderney /öl'dər-ni/ n a small dairy cow, orig of a breed kept in Alderney in the Channel Islands.

Aldine /öl'dīn/ adj from the press, or named in honour, of Aldus Manutius of Venice and his family (15–16c).

Aldis lamp /ol'dis lamp/ n a portable lantern with a movable device for sending messages by Morse code. [ACW Aldis (1878–1953), its British inventor]

aldose /al'dōs/ (chem) n any of a class of monosaccharide sugars which contain an aldehyde group. [aldehyde] ❑ **aldo-** combining form denoting a sugar which belongs to this class, such as glucose (an **aldohex'ose**) or ribose (an **aldopen'tose**).

aldrin /al'drin/ n a chlorinated hydrocarbon, used as a contact insecticide. [K Alder (1902–58), German chemist]

ale /āl/ n an alcoholic beverage made from an infusion of malt by fermentation, applied to beers made without the use of hops as a flavouring; a feast or festival, from the liquor drunk (archaic). [OE (Anglian) alu (WSax ealu); ON öl] ❑ **ale'bench** n (archaic) a bench in or in front of an alehouse. **ale'-berry** n (archaic) a beverage made from ale and bread sops with flavouring. **ale'-bush**, **ale'-pole** or **ale'-stake** n (hist) a bush, pole or stake used as an alehouse sign. **ale'-conner** n (hist) a civic officer

appointed to test the quality of the ale brewed. **ale'cost** n the costmary plant (used in flavouring ale). **ale'-draper** n (obs) a tavern-keeper. **ale'-hoof** n (OE hōfe) ground-ivy. **ale'house** n a place at which ale is sold. **ale'washed** adj (Shakesp) affected by drinking beer. **ale'wife** n (pl **ale'wives**) a woman who sells ale (archaic); a fish related to the herring, common off the NE coast of America (perhaps from its corpulent shape, but perhaps a different word).

aleatory /ā'li-ə-tə-ri/ adj depending on contingencies; used of the element of chance in poetic composition, etc; aleatoric (music). ◆ n aleatory music. [L āleātōrius, from āleātor a dicer, from ālea a die] ■ **aleatoric** /ā-li-ə-tör'ik/ adj in which chance influences the choice of notes (music); aleatory.

Alec, **alec** or **Aleck** see under **smart**.

alecost see under **ale**.

Alecto /a-lek'tō/ n one of the Furies. [Gr Alēktō (literally) unceasing]

alee /ə-lē'/ (naut) adv on or toward the lee-side. [ON ā on, and hlē lee]

aleft /ə-left'/ adv on or to the left hand. [**a-**¹ and **left**¹]

alegar /al'i- or ā'li-gər/ n sour ale, or vinegar made from it. [**ale**, with termination as **vinegar**]

alegge, **aleggeaunce** see **allege**².

Alemaine see under **Almain**.

Alemannic /a-lə-man'ik/ adj of the Alemannen, an ancient people of SW Germany, or their dialect. ◆ n the High German dialect of Switzerland, Alsace, etc.

alembic /ə-lem'bik/ n old-fashioned type of distilling apparatus. [Ar al the, and anbīq, from Gr ambix cap of a still] ■ **alem'bicated** adj over-refined. **alembica'tion** n.

alembroth /ə-lem'broth/ same as **sal alembroth** (see under **sal**¹).

alemtuzumab /a-lem-tuz'ū-mab/ n a therapeutic antibody that triggers the immune system to eliminate malignant cells, used in the treatment of some forms of leukaemia. [alem (arbitrarily coined), tumour, zu (denoting a humanized antibody), and monoclonal antibody]

alendronate /ə-len'drə-nāt/ n a synthetic drug that inhibits the resorption of bone, used esp in the prevention and treatment of osteoporosis (also **alendronate sodium**).

alength /ə-length'/ or **-lenth'**/ adv at full length. [**a-**¹]

à l'envi /a lä-vē'/ (Fr) emulously; in emulation.

aleph /ä'lef or ā'lef/ n the first letter of the Phoenician and Hebrew alphabets, resembling an ox's head, representing a glottal stop but adopted by the Greeks for a vowel sound. See **A**¹ and **alpha**. [Heb āleph ox]

alepine /al'i-pēn/ n a mixed fabric of wool and silk or mohair and cotton. [Perh Aleppo]

à l'époque /a lā-pok'/ (Fr) at the time.

alerce /ə-lûrs'/ or /ä-ler'thā/ n the wood of the sandarach tree; the Chilean arbor vitae. [Sp, larch, from L larix, -icis larch, perh confused with Ar al'arza the cedar]

alerion or **allerion** /ə-lē'ri-ən/ (heraldry) n an eagle displayed, without feet or beak. [Fr]

alert /ə-lûrt'/ adj watchful; wide awake; brisk, sharp or lively. ◆ n a danger warning; the time for which it lasts; a condition of readiness or expectancy; a sudden attack or surprise. ◆ vt to make alert. [Fr alerte, from Ital all'erta on the erect, from erto, from L ērēctus erect] ■ **alert'ly** adv. **alert'ness** n. ❑ **alert box** n (comput) a box appearing on the screen of a computer to warn the user of a problem. ■ **on** or **upon the alert** on the watch; wakefully attentive.

alethic /ə-leth'ik/ (philos) adj relating to or concerning truth or possibility. [Gr alētheia truth]

Aleurites /al-ū-rī'tēz/ n a genus of plants of the spurge family, yielding tung oil and candlenut oil. [Gr aleuron flour]

aleurone /a-lū'rōn/ n a protein found in some seeds (also **aleu'ron** /-on or -ən/). [Gr aleuron flour]

alevin /al'ə-vin/ n a young fish, esp a salmonid. [Fr, from OFr alever to rear, from L ad to, and levāre to raise]

alew /ə-loo'/ or **-lū'**/ (Spenser) n same as **halloo**.

alewashed, **alewife** see under **ale**.

alexanders /a-lig-zän'dərz/ n an umbelliferous plant (genus Smyrnium) the stems of which were formerly eaten as celery is now. [OE alexandre; L olus atrum, olusatrum, literally, 'black herb, vegetable', has been suggested as source]

Alexander technique /a-lig-zän'dər tek-nēk'/, also -läg-/ n a technique of exercise, manipulation, etc designed to improve posture and so avoid physical strain. [FM *Alexander* (1869–1955), its Australian originator]

Alexandrian /a-lig-zän'dri-ən, also -ləg-/ adj relating to *Alexandria* in Egypt, its Hellenistic school of philosophy, its poetry, or the general character of its culture and taste, erudite and critical rather than original in inspiration, sometimes with a suggestion of decadence (also n); relating to *Alexander* the Great or another person of the same name.
■ **Alexan'drine** n and adj Alexandrian. **alexan'drine** n a verse of six iambs (in English), or in French of twelve and thirteen syllables in alternate couplets (perhaps from a poem on *Alexander* the Great by *Alexandre* Paris) (also adj). **alexan'drite** n a dark green mineral, a kind of chrysoberyl (discovered on the day of majority of the Tsarevich later *Alexander* II).

alexia /ə-lek'si-ə/ n loss of power to read; word blindness. [New L, from Gr a- (privative), and *legein* to speak, confused with L *legere* to read]
■ **alex'ic** adj.

alexin /ə-lek'sin/ (*immunol*) n an obsolete term for complement (qv). [Gr *alexein* to ward off]
■ **alexipharmic** /-si-fär'mik/ adj (Gr *pharmakon* drug) acting against poison. **alexiphar'mic** or **alexiphar'makon** n an antidote to poison.

aleye see allay[1].

ALF abbrev: Animal Liberation Front, an organization dedicated to freeing animals from captivity considered to be cruel or exploitative.

Alf /alf/ n a classic example of a narrow-minded, ignorant and male-chauvinist man (also adj). [Shortening of Alfred]

alfa see halfa.

alfalfa /al-fal'fə/ n a variety of, or (*esp US*) another name for, the fodder plant, lucerne. [Sp *alfalfa*, from Ar *alfaçfçah*]

alfaquí /al-fa-kē'/ (Sp) n a Muslim expounder of the law.

alférez /al-fā'rāth/ (Sp) n a standard-bearer.

Alford plea /öl'fərd plē/ (*US law*) n a plea by a defendant in court to accept a conviction without admitting guilt. [After the case of Henry *Alford* in 1970]

alforja /al-för'hha/ (Sp) n a saddlebag; a baboon's cheekpouch.

alfresco /al-fres'kō/ adv and adj in the fresh or cool air; on fresh or moist plaster (*art*). [Ital; see **fresco** and **fresh**]

Alg. abbrev : Algeria.

alga /al'gə/ n (pl algae /al'jē/ or -gē/) a seaweed; any member of the Algae. [L *alga* seaweed]
■ **Al'gae** n pl (*bot*) a group (*usu* classified separately from other plants) of prokaryotic and eukaryotic photosynthetic organisms without roots, stems or leaves, the seaweeds and related forms. **al'gal** /-gəl/ adj. **al'gicide** /-ji-sīd/ n a substance used to destroy algae. **al'gin** /-jin/ n sodium alginate, a gummy nitrogenous organic compound obtained from seaweeds. **al'ginate** n a salt of alginic acid. **algin'ic** adj (**alginic acid** an acid obtained from certain seaweeds, used in plastics, medicine, as a food-thickening agent, etc). **al'goid** /-goid/ adj of the nature of or resembling an alga. **algolog'ical** adj. **algolog'ically** adv. **algol'ogist** n. **algol'ogy** n the study of algae.
❑ **algae poisoning** n a form of often fatal poisoning affecting livestock, etc, caused by the ingestion of toxins in decomposing algae and characterized by nervous symptoms.

algarroba /al-ga-rō'bə/ n (also **algarō'ba** or **algarro'bo** (pl **algarro'bos**)) the carob; the mesquite; the fruit of either. [Sp *algarroba*, *algarrobo*, from Ar *al kharrūbah*; cf **carob**]

algate or **algates** /öl'gāt(s)/ adv always, at all events, nevertheless (*obs*); altogether (*Spenser*). [**all** and **gate**[2]; orig dative, with -s on the analogy of *always*, etc]

algebra /al'jə-brə or -ji-/ n a method of calculating by symbols, by means of letters employed to represent quantities, and signs to represent their relations, thus forming a kind of generalized arithmetic; in modern mathematics, any of a number of systems using symbols and involving reasoning about relationships and operations. [Ital and Sp, from Ar *al-jebr* resetting (of anything broken), hence combination, from *jabara* to reunite]
■ **algebraic** /-brā'ik/ or **algebrā'ical** adj. **algebrā'ically** adv. **algebrā'ist** n a person skilled in algebra.

Algerian /al-jē'ri-ən/ adj of or relating to *Algeria* or *Algiers* in N Africa. ◆n a native or citizen of Algeria.
■ **Algerine** /al'jə-rēn/ n an Algerian (*archaic*); (without *cap*) a pirate (*hist*).

algesia /al-jē'zi-ə or -si-/ n sensitivity to pain. [New L, from Gr *algēsis*, from *algein* to suffer]
■ **algē'sis** n the sensation of pain.

-algia /-al-ji-ə/ n *combining form* denoting pain (in a particular part or because of a particular thing). [Gr *algos* pain]
■ **-algic** adj *combining form*.

algicide see under **alga**.

algid /al'jid/ adj cold or chill, *esp* applied to a cold fit in disease. [L *algidus* cold]
■ **algid'ity** n.

algin, **alginate**, **algology**, etc see under **alga**.

Algol[1] /al'gol/ n a variable star in the constellation Perseus. [Ar *al ghūl* the ghoul]

Algol[2] or **ALGOL** /al'gol/ n a type of computer programming language first developed in Europe in the 1950s, used *esp* for scientific and mathematical applications. [*Algorithmic language*]

algolagnia /al-gō-lag'ni-ə/ n sexual pleasure obtained from inflicting or suffering pain. [Gr *algos* pain, and *lagneiā* lust]

Algonquian /al-gong'kwi-ən/ or **Algonkian** /-ki-/ n and adj (of) a family of Native American languages, including Natick, Shawnee, Ojibwa, Cheyenne, etc, spoken over a wide area; (a member) of a tribe speaking one of these languages. [Am Eng, from **Algonquin**]

Algonquin /al-gong'kwin/ or **Algonkin** /-kin/ n a leading group of Native American tribes in the valley of the Ottawa and around the northern tributaries of the St Lawrence; a member of this group; their language. ◆adj of the Algonquin or their language. [Micmac *algoomaking* at the place of spearing fish]

algophobia /al-gō-fō'bi-ə/ n obsessive fear of pain. [Gr *algos* pain, and **phobia**]

algorism /al'gə-ri-zm/ n the Arabic system of numeration; arithmetic; an algorithm. [LL *algorismus*, from Ar *al-Khwārazmi* the native of Khwārazm (Khiva), ie the 9c mathematician Abu Ja'far Mohammed ben Musa]

algorithm /al'gə-ri-dhm/ n a rule for solving a mathematical problem in a finite number of steps; a set of instructions or steps designed to provide a method of solving a problem or achieving a result (*comput*); a step-by-step method for solving a problem, often in the form of a flow chart. [**algorism**]
■ **algorith'mic** adj. **algorith'mically** adv.
❑ **algorithmic language** or **algorithmic orientated language** see **Algol**[2].

alguazil /al-gwa-zil'/ or **alguacil** /äl-gwä-thēl'/ n in Spain, an officer who makes arrests, etc. [Sp (now) *alguacil*, from Ar *al-wazīr*. See **vizier**]

algum /al'gəm/ (*Bible*) n a wood imported into ancient Palestine, *prob* red sandalwood (also **al'mug**). [Heb *algūm*]

Alhagi /al-hā'jī or -hä'jē/ n a papilionaceous manna-yielding genus of desert shrubs. [Ar *al-hāj*]

Alhambra /al-ham'brə/ n the palace of the Moorish kings of Granada in Spain. [Ar *al-hamrā'* the red (house)]
■ **Alhambresque** /-bresk'/ adj.

alias /ā'li-əs/ adv otherwise known as. ◆n (pl **a'liases**) an assumed name. [L *aliās* at another time, otherwise, from *alius* other]
■ **a'liasing** n (*image technol*) image imperfections resulting from limited detail in eg a raster display, resulting in a diagonal line appearing stepped.

alibi /al'i-bī/ n the plea in a criminal charge of having been elsewhere at the relevant time; the fact of being elsewhere; an excuse for failure (*inf*). ◆vt to provide an alibi for. [L *alibī* elsewhere, orig locative, from *alius* other]

alicant /al-i-kant'/ n wine made near *Alicante* in Spain.

Alice /al'is/ n the main character in the children's fantasies *Alice's Adventures in Wonderland* (1865) and *Through the Looking-glass* (1872) by Lewis Carroll.
❑ **Alice band** n a wide hairband of coloured ribbon or other material (as worn by Alice in Tenniel's illustrations to *Through the Looking-glass*). **Al'ice-in-Won'derland** adj as if happening in a dream or fantasy; unreal.

alicyclic /a-li-sī'klik or -sī'/ adj having properties of aliphatic organic compounds but containing a ring of carbon atoms instead of an open chain. [**aliphatic** and **cyclic**]

alidad /al'i-dad/ or **a-li-dad'**/ or **alidade** /-dād/ (*surveying*) n a revolving index for reading the graduations of an astrolabe, quadrant, or similar instrument, or for taking the direction of objects. [Ar *al 'idādah* the revolving radius, from '*adid* humerus]

alien /ā'li-ən or -lyən/ adj belonging to something else; foreign; from elsewhere; extraneous; repugnant or offensive; inconsistent (with *to*); incompatible or irreconcilable; estranged. ◆n a foreigner; a resident neither native-born nor naturalized; an outsider; an extraterrestrial; a plant introduced to a locality by man but maintaining itself. ◆vt to alienate (*archaic*); to transfer (*rare*); to estrange (*archaic*). [L *aliēnus*, from *alius* other]

■ **alienabil'ity** n. **a'lienable** adj (law) capable of being transferred to another. **a'lienage** n the state of being an alien. **a'lienate** vt to transfer; to estrange or to distance by taking away friendship or contact. ◆ adj (obs) withdrawn; estranged. **alienā'tion** n estrangement; mental or emotional detachment; the state of not being involved; the critical detachment with which, according to Bertolt Brecht, audience and actors should regard a play, considering action and dialogue and the ideas in the drama without emotional involvement; the transfer of property to another, or the right to dispose of property (law). **a'lienātor** n. **al'iened** adj made alien; estranged. **alienee'** n (law) a person to whom property is transferred. **al'ienism** n the position of being a foreigner; the study and treatment of mental diseases. **a'lienist** n a person who specially studies or treats mental diseases; a psychiatrist specializing in the legal aspects of mental illness (N Am). **a'lienor** n (law) a person who transfers property.
□ **alienation effect** or **A-effect** n Brecht's theory of alienation (see above).

aliform /ā'li-förm or al'i-/ adj wing-shaped. [L āla wing, and forma shape]

aligarta see **alligator**.

alight[1] /ə-līt'/ vi (pat and pap **alight'ed** (or **alit'**)) to dismount, descend; to perch, settle; to land; to come to rest; to come by chance (upon something); to fall, strike. [OE ālīhtan (see **light**[2])]

alight[2] /ə-līt'/ adj on fire; lit up. [**a-**[1] and **light**[1]]

align (N Am **aline**) /ə-līn'/ vt to arrange in line; to make (eg a view or policy) fit or tally (with with); to regulate by a line. ◆ vi to agree or fall into line; to be arranged on or in a line. [Fr aligner, from L ad to, and līneāre to line]
■ **align'ment** (N Am **aline'ment**) n setting in a line or lines; a row arranged in this way, such as of standing-stones; the ground-plan of a railway or road (archaic); the taking of a side, or the side taken, politically, etc.
□ **alignment chart** n a nomogram, esp one comprising three scales in which a line joining values on two determines a value on the third.

alike /ə-līk'/ adj the same in appearance or character. ◆ adv equally. [OE gelīc, combined with ON ālīkr, OE onlīc; see **like**[1]]

aliment /al'i-mənt/ n nourishment; food; provision for maintenance, alimony (Scots law). ◆ vt to support, sustain; to provide aliment for. [L alimentum, from alere to nourish]
■ **alimental** /-ment'l/ adj supplying food. **aliment'ary** adj relating to aliment; nutritive. **alimentā'tion** n. **aliment'ative** adj. **aliment'iveness** n a phrenologist's word for the instinct to seek food or drink.
□ **alimentary canal** n the internal passage from the mouth to the anus.

alimony /al'i-mə-ni/ n an allowance for support made by one spouse to the other pending or after their divorce or legal separation. [L alimōnia, from alere to nourish]

à l'improviste /a lē-prō-vēst'/ (Fr) suddenly; unexpectedly; unawares.

A-line see under **A**[1].

aline, alinement see **align**.

alineation see **allineation**.

aliped /al'i-ped/ adj (zool) having winged feet, used eg of the bat, whose toes are connected by a winglike membrane. ◆ n an animal with winged feet. [L ālipes, -pedis, from āla wing, and pēs, pedis foot]

aliphatic /a-li-fat'ik/ (chem) adj fatty; belonging to the open-chain class of organic compounds, or methane derivatives (cf **aromatic**). [Gr aleiphar, aleiphatos oil]

aliquant /al'i-kwənt/ (maths) adj such as will not divide a number without a remainder (eg 5 is an aliquant part of 12). [L aliquantum somewhat]

aliquot /al'i-kwot/ (maths) adj such as will divide a number without a remainder; of equal quantities. ◆ n an aliquot part. [L aliquot some or several]

alisma /ə-liz'mə/ n a plant of the water-plantain genus Alisma of monocotyledons, giving name to the family **Alismā'ceae**. [Gr alisma water plantain]
■ **alismā'ceous** adj.

alit see **alight**[1].

aliterate /ā-lit'ə-rət or -rit/ adj unwilling or disinclined to read. ◆ n an aliterate person. [**a-**[2] and **literate**]
■ **alit'eracy** n.

aliunde /ā-li-un'de or -di/ (law) adv from another source (also adj). [L, from elsewhere]

alive /ə-līv'/ adj living; vigorous; existing; lively or animated; (of a wire, etc) live; sensitive, cognizant (with to). [OE on līfe (dative of līf life), in life]
■ **alive'ness** n.

■ **alive and kicking** strong and active; full of vigour. **alive and well** still existing, esp despite rumours to the contrary. **alive with** swarming with. **come alive** to become animated; to gain interest or relevance. **look alive** be brisk; hurry up.

aliyah or **aliya** /a-lē'yä/ n immigration to Israel; the honour of being called to read from the Torah. [Heb, literally, a going up or ascent]

alizari /a-li-zä'rē/ n an eastern Mediterranean name for the madder root. [Sp and Fr, prob from Ar al the, and 'açārah juice pressed out]
■ **alizarin** /a-liz'ə-rin/ or **alizarine** /a-liz'ə-rēn/ n the colouring matter of madder root ($C_{14}H_8O_{14}$) now made synthetically.

alkahest or **alcahest** /al'kə-hest/ n the universal solvent of the alchemists. [Appar a sham Ar coinage of Paracelsus]

alkali /al'kə-lī or -li/ (chem) n (pl **al'kalis** or **al'kalies**) a substance which, dissolved in water, forms a solution containing hydroxyl ions and with a pH of more than 7. ◆ adj of, relating to, containing or forming an alkali. [Ar alqalīy the calcined ashes]
■ **alkalesc'ence** or **alkalesc'ency** n. **alkalesc'ent** adj tending to become alkaline; slightly alkaline. **alkal'ic** adj (of igneous rocks) containing large amounts of alkalis. **alkalify** /al'kəl-i-fī or al-kal'i-fī/ vt and vi. **alkalim'eter** n an instrument for measuring the concentration of alkalis. **alkalim'etry** n. **al'kaline** /-līn or -lin/ adj having the properties of an alkali; containing a high proportion of alkali. **alkalinity** /-lin'/ n the quality of being alkaline; the extent to which a substance is alkaline. **al'kalize** or **-ise** vt to make alkaline (also **al'kalinize** or **-ise**). **al'kaloid** n any of various nitrogenous organic bases found in plants, having specific physiological action. ◆ adj relating to or resembling alkali. **alkalosis** /al-kə-lō'sis/ n an illness in which the blood or tissues of the body become too alkaline.
□ **alkali metals** n pl the univalent metals of the first group of the periodic system, lithium, sodium, potassium, rubidium, caesium, francium, forming strong basic hydroxides. **alkaline earth** n an oxide of any of the alkaline earth metals; an alkaline earth metal. **alkaline earth metals** n pl the bivalent metals of the second group of the periodic system, calcium, strontium, barium, and sometimes magnesium and radium.

alkane /al'kān/ n the general name for a hydrocarbon of the series beginning with methane, of general formula C_nH_{2n+2}. [alkyl and methane]

alkanet /al'kə-net/ n a Mediterranean plant (genus Alkanna) of the borage family; a red dye obtained from its root; extended to various related plants (genus Anchusa, etc). [Sp alcaneta, dimin, from Ar alhennā the henna]

alkene /al'kēn/ n the general name for an unsaturated hydrocarbon of the ethylene series, of general formula C_nH_{2n}. [alkyl and ethene]

alkie or **alky** /al'ki/ (inf) n an alcoholic.

Alkoran same as **Alcoran**.

alkyd /al'kid/ n (also **alkyd resin**) any of a group of synthetic thermosetting resins used in paints and protective coatings and in adhesives. [alkyl and acid]

alkyl /al'kil/ n a general name for monovalent hydrocarbon radicals of formula C_nH_{2n+1}, often denoted R; a compound with one or more such radicals in it, such as lead alkyl. [Ger Alkohol alcohol and **-yl**]
■ **al'kylating** adj (of a drug) killing cells by damaging DNA and interfering with cell replication. **alkylā'tion** n the substitution of an alkyl group into a compound.

alkyne /al'kīn/ n a general name for aliphatic hydrocarbons with a triple bond, of formula C_nH_{2n-2}, the simplest being acetylene. [alkyl and ethyne]

all /öl/ adj comprising every individual one (eg all men, all roads, all instances); comprising the whole extent, etc of (eg all winter); any whatever; (preceding 'the') as many as there are, or as much as there is (eg all the men, all the cheese); also used following pl pers pronoun or sometimes n pl (eg we all laughed, the guests all came); the greatest possible (eg with all haste, in all sincerity); every. ◆ n the whole; everybody; everything; the totality of things; the universe; one's whole possessions or utmost efforts (formerly often in pl). ◆ adv wholly; entirely; quite or completely; without limit, infinitely; on all sides; on each side, apiece; even or just (passing into a mere intensive, eg all on a summer's day, or almost into a conjunction by omission of if or though). ◆ combining form denoting infinite, infinitely; universal; completely; wholly; by all; having all for object. [OE (Anglian) all, (WSax eall); Ger all]
■ **all'ness** n the condition of being all.
□ Possible compounds are without limit and only a selection can be given: **all'-Amer'ican** adj representative of the whole of America, esp in some admirable quality; typically American (in behaviour, appearance, etc); chosen to represent the United States; consisting entirely of US or American members. **All Blacks** n pl the New Zealand international rugby team. **all'-building** adj (Shakesp) poss on

---

■ words derived from main entry word; □ compound words; ■ idioms and phrasal verbs

which all is built, but *prob* a misprint. **all-cheer'ing** *adj* giving cheerfulness to all. **all'-clear** *n* a signal that the reason for sheltering, or (*fig*) for inactivity, is past. **all'comers** *n pl* everyone who arrives or is present. **all'-day** *adj* lasting all day. **all-dread'ed** *adj* dreaded by all. **all'-elec'tric** *adj* using only electricity for heating and lighting. **all'-embracing** *adj* encompassing everything. **all-end'ing** *adj*. **All'-father** *n* Woden; Zeus; God. **all'-fired** *adj* (*inf, orig US*) (as an intensifier) infernal (*perh* for hell-fired). **all'-firedly** *adv*. **all-fives'** *n* a game of dominoes in which the aim is to make the end pips sum a multiple of five. **All Fools' Day** *n* April Fools' Day, 1 April. **all-fours'** *n* a card game in which there are four chances that score a point (see also **four**). **all-giv'er** *n* (*Milton*) the giver of all, God. **all'-good** *n* the plant good-King-Henry. **all-good'** *adj* infinitely good. **all-hail'** *interj* (*archaic*) a greeting (literally, all health). ◆ *n* (*archaic*) a salutation of 'All hail'. ◆ *vt* (*archaic*) to greet with 'All hail'. **All-hall'owmass** *n* the feast of All Saints. **all'hall'own, all'hall'owen, all'holl'own** or **all'hall'ond** *adj* (*orig* genitive pl of noun; *obs*) (*Shakesp* **al-hallown summer** a spell of fine weather about All Hallows). **All Hall'ows Day** *n* All Saints' Day, 1 November. **All-hall'owtide** *n* the season of All Hallows. **all'heal** *n* a panacea (*obs*); the great valerian or other plant thought to have healing properties, eg self-heal. **all-hid'** *n* (*archaic*) hide-and-seek. **all-import'ant** *adj* essential; crucial. **all-in'** *adj* including everything (also **all-inclu'sive**; see also **all in** below); (of a school, etc) comprehensive; (of wrestling) freestyle, with no restrictions on holds. **all'-in-one** *adj* and *n* (something) combining two or more functions in a single item. **all'night** *adj* lasting, open, etc all night. **allnight'er** *n* any event, activity, party, etc that lasts all night. **all-obey'ing** *adj* (*Shakesp*) obeyed by all. **all'-or-noth'ing** (or **-none'**) *adj* that must be gained, accepted, etc completely or not at all. **all'-out** *adj* using maximum effort; (of a strike) with everyone participating. **all'-ov'er** *adj* over the entire surface, body, etc. **all-o'verish** *adj* (*inf*) having an indefinite sense of indisposition, discomfort, or malaise. **all-o'verishness** *n* (*inf*). **all-par'ty** *adj* involving all the parties to a dispute, political action, etc. **all'-pervading** *adj* spreading or filtering through the whole of. **all'-play-all'** *adj* of a competition, in which every competitor plays against every other in turn. **all'-points bulletin** *n* (*N Am*) a report giving details of a wanted person, crime, etc issued by one police station and transmitted to all others in the region or state. **all-pow'erful** *adj* supremely powerful; omnipotent. **all'-pro'** *n* (*American football*) a player who has been selected to a team consisting of the best professional players in each playing position (also *adj*). **all-pur'pose** *adj* that can be used for any purpose, in any circumstances, etc. **all-red'** *adj* (*obs*) exclusively on British territory (from the conventional colouring of maps). **all-risks'** *adj* (of insurance) covering all risks except a number specifically excluded (eg war risks). **all'-round** *adj* including, applying to all (also *adv*); adequate, complete, or competent on all sides. **all-round camera** *n* a camera able to make a strip picture of the whole periphery of an object revolved before it. **all-round'er** *n* someone who shows ability in many sports or many aspects of a particular sport, *esp* a cricket player who can both bat and bowl; someone who shows an ability in or who has an involvement in many kinds of work, etc (also *adj*). **all-round'ness** *n*. **all-rul'ing** *adj*. **All Saints' Day** *n* 1 November, a Christian festival in honour of the saints collectively. **all'-seat'er** *n* a venue at which standing is not permitted or possible (also *adj*). **all'seed** *n* a weed (genus *Radiola*) of the flax family, or other many-seeded plant. **all-see'ing** *adj*. **all-se'er** *n* (*Shakesp*) one who sees all, ie God. **all'sorts** *n pl* things of various odd shapes, sizes, colours, etc (also *fig*). **All Souls' Day** *n* (*RC*) 2 November, a day of prayer for souls in Purgatory. **all'spice** *n* pimento or Jamaica pepper, supposed to combine the flavours of cinnamon, nutmeg and cloves (see also **calycanthus** under **calyx**). **all'-star** *adj* having a cast or team all of whom are stars. **all-tell'ing** *adj* (*Shakesp*) revealing all. **all'-terrain** *adj* (of vehicles) designed for use on rough terrain. **all'-thing** *adv* (*Shakesp*) every way. **all'-tick'et** *adj* (of an event) for which tickets must be obtained in advance. **all'-time** *adj* of all time to date. **all-time high** or **low** *n* a high or low level never before reached. **all-time record** *n* a record exceeding all others in all times. **all'-up** *n* and *adj* (of loaded aircraft) total (weight). **all-up service** *n* (*old*) a service carrying first-class mail by air at regular postage rates. **all'-weather** *adj* capable of use in all kinds of weather; weatherproof. **all-wheel drive** *n* a type of four-wheel drive in which each wheel can rotate at a different speed. **all'-wheel-drive'** *adj*. **all-wing' aeroplane** *n* an aeroplane with no fuselage, the cabin being in the wings. **all'-work** *n* all kinds of work (*esp* domestic).

■ **after all** when everything has been considered; in spite of all that; nevertheless. **all along** everywhere along; all the time. **all and some** (*obs*) one and all. **all at once** suddenly. **all but** everything short of, almost. **all for** (*inf*) strongly in favour of. **all found** (*usu* of a price) all in, with everything included. **all in** exhausted; everything included. **all in all** all things considered, all or everything together; something which someone is wholly wrapped up in. **all of** (*inf*) as long or as far, etc as; the whole distance, time, etc of. **all out** at full power or speed; completely exhausted. **all over** everywhere; over the whole of;

covered with (*inf*); thoroughly, entirely; very characteristically; excessively attentive towards. **all over the place** all awry, or in a disorganized muddle. **all over with** finished, done with, completely at an end with. **all right** unhurt, safe; adequate, suitable; acceptable (also *US inf* **all-right**); yes, fine, ok; you can be sure of that!; (also **a bit of all right**) very good, or *esp* of a young woman, very attractive (*sl*). **all-singing, all-dancing** (*inf*) incorporating a full range of features and elaborations. **all's one** it is just the same. **all square** (of debts, etc) settled; (in games) having equal scores. **all systems go** everything (is) in working order, starting up, etc (also *fig*). **all that** (*usu* after a negative or a question) so, especially, as ... as all that. **all the best** a phrase used to wish someone good luck, etc. **all there** completely sane; of normal intelligence, not stupid (*inf*); alert. **all the same** see under **same**. **all the way** completely, as in *I'm with you all the way*; a euphemistic expression for full sexual intercourse, as in *go all the way* (*with someone*). **all told** including every person, thing, etc; taking everything into account. **all to one** (*obs*) altogether. **all up with** at an end with; beyond any hope for. **and all** as well as the rest. **and all that** and all the rest of it, et cetera. **as all that** to that extent. **at all** in the least degree; in any way; in any circumstances; used also merely to give emphasis. **be all over someone** to be excessively and sometimes irritatingly friendly and attentive to someone. **be all things to all men** to alter one's approach, behaviour, attitude, etc to suit the person one is dealing with; to be (*usu* excessively) affable. **for all** notwithstanding. **for good and all** finally. **in all** all told; in total. **once and for all** once and once only, finally. **when all is said and done** after all; all things considered.

alla breve /ä'lə or äl'lä, brä'vä or brev/ (*music*) in quick common time; with 2 or 4 minims to the bar. *n* a piece of music played alla breve. [Ital, according to the breve, there being *orig* a breve to the bar]

alla cappella /ä'lə ka-pel'ə or äl'lä käp-pel'lä/ see **a cappella**.

alla Franca /ä'lə frang'kə or äl'lä frängk'ä/ (*Ital*) in the French style.

Allah /al'ä or -ə or -ə/ (*Islam*) *n* the name of God. [Ar *allāh*, from *alilāh*, the God]

■ **Allahu akbar** /äl-lä-hoo äk-bär/ (*Arab*) God is great.

alla marcia /ä'lə mär'chə or äl'lä mär'chä/ *adv* (*music*) in the manner of a march. [Ital]

allanite /al'ə-nīt/ *n* a cerium-bearing aluminium iron silicate occurring as an accessory mineral in igneous and other rocks, also containing lanthanum and other rare-earth metals. [T *Allan* (1777–1833), Scottish mineralogist]

allantois /a-lan'tō-is/ *n* a membranous sac-like appendage for effecting oxygenation in the embryos of mammals, birds and reptiles. [Irregularly formed from Gr *allās*, *-āntos* a sausage, and *eidos* form] ■ **allanto'ic** *adj*. **allan'toid** /*-toid*/ *adj* sausage-shaped; relating to the allantois. ◆ *n* the allantois. **allanto'in** *n* a white crystalline powder produced by the oxidation of uric acid, used in the treatment of wounds, skin irritation, etc.

alla prima /ä'lə prē'mə or äl'lä prē'mä/ (*Ital*) a technique of painting in which only one layer of pigment is applied to the surface to complete the canvas.

allargando /a-lär-gan'dō/ (*music*) *adj* and *adv* slowing and broadening. [Ital *allargare* to broaden]

alla stoccata /ä'lə sto-kat'ə or äl'lä sto-kä'tä/ (*Ital*) thrusting with a pointed weapon.

alla Tedesca /ä'lə te-des'kə or äl'lä te-des'kä/ (*Ital*) in the German style.

allative /al'ə-tiv/ (*grammar*) *adj* describing a case denoting movement to or towards. ◆ *n* (a word in) the allative case. [L *allatum*, supine of *afferre*, from *ad* to, and *ferre* to bear]

alla vostra salute /äl'lä vōs'trä sa-loo'tä/ (*Ital*) to your health.

allay[1], earlier **aleye, alay**, etc. /ə-lā'/ *vt* to put down; to quell; to calm; to alleviate; to abate, lessen; to reduce; to alloy or temper. ◆ *vi* to abate. [OE *ālecgan*, from pfx *ā-* (intensive), and *lecgan* to lay. This verb in ME became indistinguishable in form in some of its parts from **allay**[2] or **alloy**, and from **allege**[2], and the meanings also overlapped] ■ **allay'er** *n*. **allay'ing** *n*. **allay'ment** *n*.

allay[2] /ə-lā'/ *vt* to alloy; to mix with something inferior; to dilute; to debase; to lessen or detract from the goodness of. ◆ *n* alloy; alloying; dilution; lessening; impairment. [See **alloy** and the etymological note to **allay**[1]]

all-be see **albe**.

alledge old spelling of **allege**[1,2].

allée /a-lā'/ (*Fr*) *n* an avenue, walk or garden path.

allege[1] /ə-lej'/ *vt* to assert with a view to subsequent proof, hence without proof; to bring forward in argument or plea; to cite or quote in discussion; to declare in court upon oath (*obs*); to cite (*archaic*). [OFr *esligier* to clear at law, from L *ex* from, and *lītigāre* to sue]

■ **allegation** /al-i-gā'shən/ n the act of alleging; that which is alleged; an unproved or unaccepted assertion; citation. **alleged** /ə-lejd'/ adj. **allegedly** /-lej'əd-li/ adv. **alleg'er** n.

allege² (Spenser **allegge** or **alegge**) /ə-lej'/ (obs) vt to alleviate; to allay. [OFr aleger, from L alleviāre (see **alleviate**) fused with OE ālecgan (see **allay¹**)]
■ **allege'ance** /ə-lej'əns/ (Spenser **aleggeaunce** /a-lej'i-ans/) n alleviation.

allegiance /ə-lē'j(i-)əns/ n the relation or obligation of subject to sovereign or state or of liegeman to liege-lord (hist); loyalty (to a person or cause). [L ad to, and **liege**]
■ **alle'giant** adj (Shakesp).

allegory /al'i-gə-ri or -gö-/ n a narrative, picture or other work of art intended to be understood symbolically; symbolical narration. [Gr allēgoriā, from allos other, and agoreuein to speak]
■ **allegoric** /-gor'ik/ or **allegor'ical** adj. **allegor'ically** adv. **all'egorist** n. **allegoriza'tion** or **-s-** n. **all'egorize** or **-ise** vt to put in the form of an allegory; to treat as allegory. ◆ vi to use allegory. **all'egorizer** or **-s-** n.

allegro /a-lā'grō or ə-leg'rō/ (music) adv and adj with brisk movement; lively and rather fast. ◆ n (pl **alle'gros**) an allegro piece or movement. [Ital, from L alacer brisk]
■ **allegret'to** adv and adj somewhat brisk (less so than allegro). ◆ n (pl **allegret'tos**) an allegretto piece or movement.

allele or **allel** /a-lēl'/ n short forms of **allelomorph** /al-ēl'ō-mörf/ any one of the two or more possible forms of a gene; a gene considered as the means of transmission of an allele. [Gr allēlōn of one another, and morphē form]
■ **allel'ic** adj. **allelomor'phic** adj. **allelomor'phism** n.

allelopathy /a-li-lop'ə-thi/ (biol) n an adverse influence exerted either by one individual plant over another by the production of a chemical inhibitor, or by one strain over another of the same species. [Fr allélopathie, from Gr allēlos each other, and pathos suffering]

alleluia or **alleluiah** /al-i-loo'yä/ same as **hallelujah**.

allemande /al'(i-)mand or al-mäd/ (music) n a smooth-running movement of moderate tempo, in common time, coming after the prelude in a classical suite; a Swabian dance in triple time; a German dance in 2–4 time; a movement effecting change of position in a dance. [Fr allemande (fem) German]

allenarly /a-le'nər-li/ (obs except Scots law) adv solely, only. [**all** and anerly]

Allen screw /a'lən skroo/ n a screw with a hexagonal recess in the head, turned by an **Allen key**, an L-shaped hexagonal rod (also called **socket head screw**). [Orig a trademark]

allergy /al'ər-ji/ n an altered or acquired state of sensitivity; an abnormal reaction of the body to substances normally harmless; hypersensitivity to certain antigens or other excitant substances; antipathy, dislike or repugnance (inf). [Gr allos other, and ergon work]
■ **all'ergen** n any substance that induces an allergic reaction. **allergen'ic** adj causing an allergic reaction. **allergic** /ə-tûr'jik/ adj (of the body) reacting in an abnormally sensitive manner; suffering from an allergy (to). ◆ n an allergic person. **all'ergist** n a doctor specializing in diseases and conditions caused by allergies.
❑ **allergic rhinitis** n hay fever.

allerion see **alerion**.

alleviate /ə-lē'vi-āt/ vt to make light; to mitigate. [LL alleviāre, -ātum, from L ad to, and levis light]
■ **allēvia'tion** n. **allēv'iative** adj. **allēv'iātor** n. **allēviā'tory** adj.

alley¹ /al'i/ n (pl **all'eys**) a passage; a narrow lane; a back lane; a walk in a garden or shrubbery; a long narrow enclosure or rink for bowls or skittles; the space between the parallel lines at the side of a tennis court (N Am). [OFr alee (Fr allée) a passage, from aller to go]
■ **alleyed** /al'id/ adj having alleys or the form of an alley.
❑ **all'eycat** n a stray cat living in alleys and backstreets. **all'eyway** n a narrow passage; a corridor.

alley² or **ally** /al'i/ n (pl **alleys** or **allies** /-iz/) a choice taw or large marble. [Prob orig made of **alabaster**]
❑ **all'(e)y-taw'** or **all'(e)y-tor'** n.

alley-oop /a-lā-oop' or -li-/ n a manoeuvre in basketball, etc in which the ball is thrown high in the air so that a player running into space may catch it and score; in skateboarding and snowboarding, a spin made in the opposite direction to that in which the boarder is travelling. [Alley Oop, character created by American cartoonist VT Hamlin (1900–93)]

allez-vous-en /a-lā-voo-zä'/ (Fr) away with you; begone.

allheal see under **all**.

alliaceous /a-li-ā'shəs/ adj garlic-like. [L allium garlic]

alliance see under **ally¹**.

allice or **allis** /al'is/ n a species of shad (also **allis shad**). [L alōsa, alausa shad]

allicholy or **allycholly** /al'i-kol-i/ (Shakesp; joc) n and adj melancholy.

allicin /al'i-sin/ n a powerful antibiotic obtained from garlic. [L allium garlic]

alligarta see **alligator**.

alligate /al'i-gāt/ (obs) vt to conjoin; to perform alligation. [L alligāre, -ātum, from ad to, and ligāre to bind]
■ **alligation** /-gā'shən/ n binding together (rare); conjunction; calculation of values or properties of a mixture (maths).

alligator /al'i-gā-tər/ earlier **aligarta** or **alligarta** /-gär'tə/ n a reptile of a mainly American family related to the crocodile but with a shorter, broader snout and non-protruding teeth. [Sp el the (L ille), and lagarto lizard (L lacertus)]
❑ **alligator apple** n a fruit and tree of the custard apple genus. **alligator clip** n a clip with strong toothed grips, esp for electrical connections. **alligator pear** n (N Am) the avocado pear.

allineation or **alineation** /ə-lin-i-ā'shən/ n position in a straight line; alignment. [L ad to, and līneāre, -ātum to draw a line, from līnea line]

allis see **allice**.

alliteration /ə-lit-ə-rā'shən/ n the recurrence of the same initial sound (not necessarily letter) in words in close succession, such as 'the low last edge of the long lone land' (Swinburne); head-rhyme, the characteristic structure of versification of Old English and other Old Germanic languages, each line having three accented syllables (two in the first half) with the same initial consonant or with different initial vowels. [L ad to, and lītera, littera a letter]
■ **allit'erate** vi to begin with the same sound; to constitute alliteration; to practise alliteration. **allit'erative** adj. **allit'eratively** adv.

allium /al'i-əm/ n a plant of the Allium genus to which onions, leeks, garlic, etc belong. [L, garlic]

allo- /a-lō- or a-lə-/ combining form denoting other; one of a group constituting a structural unit; different; from outside. [Gr allos other]
■ **all'ocarpy** n (Gr karpos fruit; bot) fruiting after cross-fertilization. **allocheiria** or **allochiria** /-kī'ri-ə or -kī'/ n (Gr cheir hand; bot) attribution of a sensation to the wrong part of the body, eg to the other hand when one is painful. **allochthonous** /al-ok'thən-əs/ adj (Gr chthon ground) of a rock, having moved or been moved from another environment, away from its native location (also **exotic**). **allodynia** /-din'i-ə/ n (Gr odynē pain) the experience of severe pain as a result of a stimulus that would not normally cause it. **allog'amous** adj. **allog'amy** n (Gr gamos marriage; bot) cross-fertilization. **all'ograft** n (immunol) a graft from one individual to another of the same species. **all'ograph** n (Gr graphē writing) a writing made by one person on behalf of another; one of two or more symbols constituting a grapheme (linguistics). **allomet'ric** adj. **allom'etry** n (Gr metron measure) (the study of) the growth of a part of the body relative to that of other parts or of the whole body, in one organism or comparatively in a number of different organisms. **all'omorph** /-mörf/ n (Gr morphē form; linguistics) one of two or more forms of the same morpheme. **allomorph'ic** adj. **all'oparent** n (zool) an animal that exhibits parental behaviour towards a young animal other than its natural offspring. **allopat'ric** adj (Gr patra fatherland; bot) of two species or populations not growing in the same area and therefore unable to breed because of distance or geographical barrier, opp to **sympatric**. **allop'atry** n. **all'ophone** /-fōn/ n (Gr phōnē sound; linguistics) one of two or more forms of the same phoneme. **allophonic** /-fon'/ adj. **all'oplasm** n (obs) protoplasm differentiated to perform a special function. **alloplas'tic** adj (Gr plastikos; see **plastic**) affected by or affecting external factors. **allopurinol** /-pūr'in-ol/ n (**purine** and **-ol²**) a drug, $C_5H_4N_4O$, used in the treatment of gout, reducing the formation of uric acid. **all'osaur** /-sör/ n (Gr sauros lizard) a member of the genus **Allosaur'us**, large, lizard-hipped, carnivorous dinosaurs. **allosteric** /-ster' or -stēr'/ adj (biol; see **steric**) relating to proteins, particularly enzymes, which change their three-dimensional shape on binding with a smaller molecule which is not a substrate, often leading to altered activity. **allos'tery** n. **all'otheism** n (Gr theos god) the worship of other gods or other people's gods. **allotrope** /al'ə-trōp/ n (Gr tropos turn, habit) an allotropic form. **allotrop'ic** adj (of a chemical element) existing in more than one form. **allot'ropism** n. **allot'ropous** adj having nectar accessible to all kinds of insects (bot); of insects, eg those that visit allotropous flowers, short-tongued. **allot'ropy** n the property (esp in chemical elements such as carbon) of existing in more than one form.

allocarpy see under **allo-**.

allocate /al'ə-kāt or al'ō-kāt/ vt to place; to locate; to apportion or assign. [L allocāre, from ad to, and locāre, -ātum to place, from locus a place]

■ words derived from main entry word; ❑ compound words; ■ idioms and phrasal verbs

■ **all'ocable** or **allocāt'able** adj. **allocā'tion** n the act of allocating; a share allocated; allotment; apportionment; an allowance made upon an account.

allocheiria...to...**allochthonous** see under **allo-**.

allocution /a-lō-kū'shən/ n an exhortation, esp (Roman hist) of a general to his troops; a formal address, esp of the Pope to the cardinals. [L allocūtiō, -ōnis, from ad to, and loquī, locūtus to speak]

allodium or **alodium** /a- or ə-lō'di-əm/ n an estate not subject to a feudal superior (also **allod** or **alod** /al'od/). [LL allōdium, from a Gmc word meaning complete ownership; cf **all** and OE ēad wealth, prosperity]
■ **allō'dial** or **alō'dial** adj.

allodynia...to...**allograph** see under **allo-**.

alloiostrophos /a-loi-o'stro-fos/ (classical prosody) adj irregularly divided, not in alternate strophe and antistrophe.

allometric, **allometry**, **allomorph** see under **allo-**.

allonge /a-lōzh'/ n a piece of paper attached to a bill of exchange for further endorsement. [Fr]

allons /a-lɔ̃'/ (Fr) interj let us go; come on; come.

allonym /al'ə-nim/ or -ō-/ n another person's name adopted as a pseudonym by a writer. [Fr, from Gr allos other, and onyma, onoma name]
■ **allon'ymous** adj.

alloparent, **allopatric** see under **allo-**.

allopathy /a-lo'pə-thi/ n orthodox medical practice, treatment of diseases by drugs, etc, whose effect on the body is the opposite of that of the disease, distinguished from homeopathy. [Ger Allopathie, coined by Hahnemann (1755–1843), from Gr allos other, and pathos suffering]
■ **all'ōpath** or **allop'athist** n a person who practises allopathy. **allopathic** /al-ō-path'ik/ adj. **allopath'ically** adv.

allophone...to...**allostery** see under **allo-**.

allot /ə-lot'/ vt (**allott'ing**; **allott'ed**) to distribute in portions; to parcel out; to assign; to divide as by lot. [OFr aloter, from à to, and the Gmc root of **lot**]
■ **allot'ment** n the act of allotting; a part or share allotted; a piece of ground let out for spare-time cultivation usu under a public scheme; the distribution of shares to individuals who have applied to purchase them; the number of shares distributed; a portion of a field assigned to a cottager to labour for himself (hist). **allottee'** n someone to whom something is allotted. **allott'ery** n (Shakesp) a share allotted.

allotheism see under **allo-**.

allotriomorphic /a-lot-ri-ō-mör'fik/ adj crystalline in internal structure but not in outward form. [Gr allotrios alien, and morphē form]

allotrope, **allotropy**, etc see under **allo-**.

allow /ə-low'/ vt to permit; to assign; to grant or give, esp periodically; to concede or acknowledge; to assume as an element in calculation or as something to be taken into account; to admit or agree as due; to conclude, hence to assert (US); to abate; to praise (obs); to pass, sanction, accept (archaic); to indulge (Shakesp). ◆ vi to permit; to make allowance for. [OFr alouer to praise or bestow, of double origin: (1) L allaudāre, from ad to, and laudāre to praise; (2) L ad, and locāre to place]
■ **allowabil'ity** n. **allow'able** adj that may be allowed; permissible; excusable. **allow'ableness** n. **allow'ably** adv. **allow'ance** n that which is allowed; a limited portion or amount allowed, allotted or granted; a ration or stint; an amount that can be deducted when calculating taxable income; money allowed to meet expenses or in consideration of special conditions (also **allowable expense**); abatement; a sum periodically granted; a taking into account in calculation or excuse, eg in make allowances for; approbation (archaic); admission, acknowledgement or permission (Shakesp). ◆ vt to put upon an allowance; to supply in limited quantities. **allowed'** adj permitted; licensed; acknowledged. **allow'edly** adv.

alloy /al'oi or ə-loi'/ n a mixture of metals; extended to a mixture of metal with non-metal; the baser ingredient in such a mixture (esp in gold or silver); anything added in a mixture that impairs or debases the main ingredient; the fineness or standard of gold or silver; a metal with improved properties due to additional material eg stainless steel. ◆ vt to mix (metal); to mix with a less valuable metal; to impair or debase by being present; to temper or qualify. ◆ vi to become alloyed. [Fr aloi (noun), aloyer from OFr alei, aleier, from L alligāre, from ad to, and ligāre to bind; **allay²** is from the corresponding Norman Fr alai, confused with **allay¹**]

allseed, **allspice** see under **all**.

all-to, **alto** or **all to** /öl'tu/ adv and pfx a spurious word arising from the wrong division of **all** and a word with the pfx to- asunder, such as

altto brake, all to brake for all tobrake: hence, altogether, eg altoruffled (Milton all to ruffld).

allude /ə-lood' or -lūd'/ vi (with to) to convey an indirect reference in passing; to refer without explicit mention, or with suggestion of further associations; to refer. [L allūdere, from ad at, and lūdere, lūsum to play]
■ **allu'sion** /-zhən/ n indirect reference. **allu'sive** /-siv/ adj alluding; hinting; referring indirectly; canting (heraldry). **allu'sively** adv. **allu'siveness** n.

allure¹ /ə-lūr' or -loor'/ vt to entice, seduce or attract; to draw on as by a lure (obs). [OFr alurer, from à to, and lurer to lure]
■ **allure'** or **allure'ment** n. **allur'er** n. **allur'ing** adj. **allur'ingly** adv.

allure² /a-lür'/ (Fr) n mien, gait or air.

allusion, etc see under **allude**.

alluvia, **alluvial** see **alluvium**.

alluvion /ə-loo'vi-ən or -lū'/ n land gradually gained from a river or the sea by the washing up of sand and earth; the formation of such land; a flood; alluvium. [L alluviō, -ōnis; see **alluvium**]

alluvium /ə-loo'vi-əm or -lū'/ n (pl **allu'via**) matter transported in suspension and deposited by rivers or floods. [L neuter of alluvius washed up, from ad to, and luere to wash]
■ **allu'vial** adj.

ally¹ /ə-lī'/ vt (**ally'ing**; **allied'**) to join by marriage, friendship, treaty, co-operation or assimilation. ◆ n /al'ī/ (formerly, and still by some /ə-lī'/) (pl **all'ies** (or /-īz'/)) a member of or someone who is party to an alliance; a state or sovereign joined in league for co-operation in a common purpose; a person that co-operates or helps, a supporter; a kinsman (Shakesp); anything near to another in classification or nature. [OFr alier, from L alligāre; see **alligate**]
■ **allī'ance** n the state of being allied; union, or combination by marriage, treaty, etc; kinship; a group of allies or kindred; a subclass or group of families (bot). **all'ied** (or /-īd'/) adj.

ally², **ally-taw** see **alley²**.

allycholly see **allicholy**.

allyl /al'il/ (chem) n an organic radical (C_3H_5) whose sulphide is found in oil of garlic. [L allium garlic, and Gr hȳlē matter]

alma¹ or **almah** /al'ma/ n an Egyptian dancing-girl (also **al'me** or **al'meh** /-me/). [Ar 'almah learned (in dancing and music), from 'alama to know]

alma² /äl'mä/ (Ital) n soul, essence.

almacantar /al-mə-kan'tər/ or **almucantar** /al-mū-kan'tər/ (astron) n a circle of altitude, parallel to the horizon; an instrument for determining a star's passage across an almacantar. [Ar almuqantarāt the sundials, from al the, and qantarah bridge]

Almagest /al'mə-jest/ n a great treatise by the Alexandrian astronomer Ptolemy (c.150AD); extended to other great medieval works on astronomy, etc. [Ar al-majistē, from al the, and Gr megistē (syntaxis), greatest (systematic treatise)]

Almain /al'mān/ (obs) n and adj German. [Fr allemand German, and Allemagne Germany, from L Alemanni or Alamanni a people of SW Germany]
■ **al'main** n the allemande. **Al'maine**, **Al'many** or **Al'emaine** n Germany.

alma mater /al'mə mā'tər or al'ma mä'ter/ (L) n benign mother, applied by alumni to their university, school or college.

almanac /öl'mə-nak/ n a register of the days, weeks and months of the year, with astronomical events, anniversaries, etc, published annually; an annual publication containing a variety of factual information. [Appar from an Ar word al-manākh]

almandine /al'mən-dīn or -dēn/ n (earlier **alaban'dine**) precious (red iron-alumina) garnet. [LL alabandīna, from Alabanda a town in Caria, where it was found]

alme, **almeh** see **alma¹**.

almery see **ambry**.

almighty /öl-mī'ti/ adj omnipotent; irresistible; invincible; mighty. ◆ adv exceedingly. [OE ælmihtig]
■ **the Almighty** God. **the almighty dollar** (Washington Irving) money, esp as all-powerful.

almirah /al-mī'rə/ n a cupboard, wardrobe or cabinet. [Hindi almārī, from Port almario, from L armārium; see **ambry**]

almond /öl'- or ä'mənd/ n the fruit, and esp the kernel, of a tree related to the peach, with a dry husk instead of flesh; anything of the shape of an almond (an ellipse pointed at one end), eg a tonsil or a rock-crystal ornament. [OFr almande (Fr amande), from L amygdala, from Gr amygdalē]
❑ **al'mond-blossom** n. **al'mond-eyed** adj with apparently almond-shaped eyes. **al'mond-oil** n. **almond paste** n marzipan. **al'mond-tree** n.

almoner /ä'mə-nər or al'/ n a medical social worker attached to a hospital (no longer an official title); a distributor or giver of alms (*archaic*). [OFr *aumoner, aumonier* (Fr *aumónier*), from LL *eleēmosynārius* (adj); see **alms**]
■ **al'monry** n (*archaic*) a place of distribution of alms.

almost /öl'möst or -məst/ adv very nearly. [**all** and **most** (in sense of nearly)]

almous /ä'məs or ö'məs/ (*obs* or *dialect*) n same as **awmous**.

alms /ämz/ n (*sing* or *pl*) relief given out of charity to the poor; a good or charitable deed (*obs*). [OE *ælmysse*, through LL from Gr *eleēmosynē*, from *eleos* compassion; see also **awmous**]
◻ **alms'-deed** n (*archaic*) a charitable deed. **alms'-dish** n (*archaic*) a dish for receiving alms. **alms'-drink** n (*Shakesp*) leavings of drink. **alms'-fee** n (*archaic*) Peter's pence. **alms'-folk** n pl (*archaic*) people supported by alms. **alms'giving** n the act of making charitable donations. **alms'house** n a house endowed for the support and lodging of the poor. **alms'-man** n (*archaic*) a man who lives by alms. **alms'-woman** n (*archaic*).

almucantar see **almacantar**.

almuce see **amice**[2].

almug /al'mug/ (*Bible*) n algum. [Heb *almūg*, prob for *algūm*]

alnage /öl'nij/ (*obs*) n measurement by the ell; inspection of cloth. [OFr *aulnage*, from *aulne* ell]
■ **al'nager** n an official inspector of cloth.

Alnico® /al'ni-kō/ n an alloy of iron, nickel, aluminium, cobalt and copper. [*aluminium*, *nickel* and *cobalt*]

Alnus see **alder**.

alodial same as **allodial** (see under **allodium**).

alodium (also **alod**) same as **allodium**.

aloe /al'ō/ n any member of a mainly S African genus *Aloe*, consisting mostly of trees and shrubs of the family Aloeaceae, extended to the so-called **American aloe** (see **agave**), also (often in *pl*) to aloes-wood or its resin; (*usu* in *pl* form but treated as *sing*; also **bitter aloes**) a bitter purgative drug, condensed from the juice of the leaves of various species of *Aloe*. [Directly and through OE *aluwan, alewan* (pl), from L *aloē*, from Gr *aloē*; the application to eaglewood comes from the Septuagint translation of Heb *ahālīm, ahālōth* agalloch]
■ **aloed** /al'ōd/ adj planted, shaded, mixed or flavoured with aloes. **aloet'ic** /-ō-et'ik/ n a medicine containing a great proportion of aloes. ◆ adj of or relating to aloes.
◻ **al'oes-wood** n the heartwood of eaglewood. **aloe vera** /ver'a or vē'ra/ n (also with *caps*) a species of aloe plant or *esp* the juice of its leaves (thought to have healing and other qualities) used in cosmetics, etc.

aloft /ə-loft'/ adv on high; overhead; above; on the top; high up; up the mast (*naut*); in or to heaven. ◆ prep (*Shakesp*) on the top of. [ON ä *lopt* (pronounced /loft/; of motion) and ä *lopti* (of position) in the sky, from ä on, in or to, and *lopt* (see **loft**)]

alogia /ə-lō'ji-ə/ n inability to speak, due to brain lesion. [Gr ä (privative), and *logos* speech]

alogical /a- or ä-lö'i-kəl/ adj outside the domain of logic. [Gr a- (privative), and **logical**]

aloha /ə- or ä-lö'hä or -ə/ interj greetings; farewell. [Hawaiian, love or kindness]
◻ **aloha shirt** n a brightly-coloured loose-fitting shirt.

alone /ə-lōn'/ adj single; solitary; unaccompanied; without any other; by oneself; unique. ◆ adv singly. [**all** and **one**]
■ **alone'ly** adv (*obs* or *archaic*). **alone'ness** n.
■ **go it alone** (*inf*) to act on one's own, without help.

along[1] /ə-long'/ adv by or through the length; lengthwise; at full length; throughout; onward; together, in company or conjunction. ◆ prep lengthwise by, through, or over; by the side of. [OE *andlang*, from pfx *and*- against, and *lang* long (see **long**[1])]
■ **alongshore** adj see **longshore**. **alongshore'man** n. **along'side** prep and adv beside; side by side (with); close to the side (of).
■ **along with** in addition to; in conjunction with. **I**, etc **will be along I**, etc will arrive.

along[2] /ə-long'/ (*archaic* and *dialect*) adj on account (of or on). [OE *gelang*; see **long**[2]]

alongst /ə-longst'/ (*obs* and *dialect*) adv and prep along; by the length (of). [OE *andlanges*, from *andlang* along, with adv genitive ending -*es* and -*t* as in **amidst, betwixt**, etc]

aloo, also **alu** /ä- or a-loo'/ (*Ind cookery*) n potato. [Hindi and Urdu *ālū*]

aloof /ə-loof'/ adv with avoidance or detachment; reserved and haughty; apart; some way off (from); without participation; to windward (*obs*). ◆ adj distant or withdrawn. ◆ prep (*Milton*) aloof from. [**a-**[1] and **loof**[1]]
■ **aloof'ly** adv. **aloof'ness** n.

alopecia /a-lō-pē'si-ə or -shə/ n baldness, hair loss. [Gr *alōpekiā* fox-mange or a bald spot, from *alōpēx* fox]
■ **alopecoid** /al-ō-pē'koid or al-op'i-koid/ adj fox-like.
◻ **alopecia areata** /ar-ē-ä'tə or ar-ē-ä'tə/ n baldness occurring in patches on the scalp.

aloud /ə-lowd'/ adv loudly; audibly. [**a-**[1]]

à l'outrance /a loo-trãs'/ (*Fr*) same as **à outrance**.

alow[1] /ə-lō'/ (*naut*) adv to a lower position; in the lower part of a ship. [**a-**[1] and **low**[1]]

alow[2] or **alowe** /ə-low'/ (*Scot*) adv ablaze. [**a-**[1] and **low**[4]]

ALP abbrev : Australian Labor Party; automated language processing.

alp /alp/ n a high mountain; a mountain pasture; (in *pl*; with *cap*) the mountain ranges of Switzerland and neighbouring countries. [L *Alpēs* the Alps; perh Celtic]
■ **Alp'ine** or **alp'ine** /-īn/ adj of the Alps or other mountains; growing on mountain tops. ◆ n an alpine plant; a member of the Alpine race. **alp'inism** /-in-/ n the art or practice of mountain-climbing. **alp'inist** n.
◻ **alp'englow** n a reddish light seen on snow-capped peaks at sunrise or sunset. **alp'enhorn** or **alp'horn** n a long powerful horn made of wood and bark, used chiefly by Alpine cowherds. **alp'enstock** n a mountain traveller's long spiked staff. **Alpine orogeny** n (*geol*) the earth movements during the Tertiary period which led to the development of the Alps and associated mountain chains. **Alpine race** n one of the principal Caucasian physical types, characterized by broad head, sallow skin and moderate stature. **Alpine skiing** n competitive skiing involving downhill and slalom events.

ALPA abbrev : Air Line Pilots Association.

alpaca /al-pak'ə/ n a domesticated animal related to the llama; cloth made of its long silky wool. [Sp, prob from Aymara]

alpargata /äl-pär-gä'tä/ n a light sandal with rope or hemp sole. [Sp]

al pasto /äl pä'stō/ (*Ital*) according to a fixed rate (said of meals in a restaurant).

alpeen /al'pēn/ n a cudgel. [Ir *ailpín*]

alpenglow, alpenhorn and **alpenstock** see under **alp**.

Alpha or **alpha** /al'fə/ n (in international radio communication) a code word for the letter *a*.

alpha /al'fə/ n the first letter of the Greek alphabet (A or α); the first or brightest star of a constellation; the beginning; in classification, the first or one of the first grade; as an ancient Greek numeral α' = 1 ,α = 1000. ◆ adj short for alphabetical (*inf* or *comput*); in chemical classification, designating one of two or more isomeric forms of a compound; being the most powerful or influential member of a group. [Gr *alpha*, from Heb *āleph*; see **aleph** and **A**[1]]
■ **alphamet'ic** n a popular mathematical puzzle in which numbers are replaced by letters forming words.
◻ **al'pha-blocker** n a drug used to make blood vessels dilate, *esp* in muscle. **alpha-chlor'alose** n a narcotic poison used in bait, eg to control vermin. **alpha decay** n radioactive decay involving the emission of alpha particles. **alpha-fētōprō'tein** n a protein whose presence in excessive quantities in amniotic fluid has been found to correlate with certain fetal abnormalities, eg those leading to spina bifida. **alpha-hydroxy acid** n any of various weak organic acids used in cosmetics. **alphanūmer'ic** or **alphanūmer'ical** adj consisting of, or (of a machine) using, both letters and numbers (also **alphamer'ic** or **alphamer'ical**). **alphanūmer'ically** or **alphamer'ically** adv. **alpha particle** n (*phys*) a helium nucleus given off by radioactive substances. **alpha radiation** or **rays** n (*phys*) a stream of alpha particles. **alpha rhythm** or **wave** n one of the principal slow waves recorded on an electroencephalogram indicating normal relaxed brain activity. **al'phasort** vt (*comput*) to sort, *esp* into alphabetical order (also n). **al'phatest** vt to perform an alpha test on. **alpha test** n an initial test (cf **beta test**) of a product (eg new computer software) by its developers. **alpha wave** see **alpha rhythm** above.
■ **alpha and omega** beginning and end.

alphabet /al'fə-bet or -bit/ n a system of letters, *esp* when arranged in conventional set order; first elements or basics; an index (*obs*). ◆ vt (*US*) to arrange alphabetically. [Gr *alphabētos*, from *alpha* and *bēta*, the first two Greek letters]
■ **alphabetä'rian** n someone learning the alphabet, a beginner; a person who studies alphabets. **alphabet'ic** or **alphabet'ical** adj relating to or in the order of an alphabet. **alphabet'ically** adv. **alphabet'iform** adj shaped like letters. **alphabetiza'tion** or **-s-** n. **al'phabetize** or **-ise** vt to arrange alphabetically.
◻ **alphabet soup** n a confusing or off-putting series or mass of strings of letters, *esp* the abbreviations of names of official bodies (after a type of soup with letter-shaped noodles in it).

Alphonsine /al-fon'sīn or -sin or -zin/ adj of Alphonso X (the Wise), king of Castile, or his planetary tables, completed in 1252.

■ words derived from main entry word; ◻ compound words; ■ idioms and phrasal verbs

alphorn, **alpine**, etc see under **alp**.

Alpini /äl-pē'nē/ *n pl* (*sing* **Alpi'no**) Italian troops for mountain warfare. [Ital, Alpine]

al più /äl pū/ (*Ital*) at most.

already /ol- or öl-red'i/ *adv* previously, or by the time in question. [**all** and **ready**]

alright /öl-rīt/ *an* alternative, less acceptable, spelling of **all right**, much used in informal contexts.

ALS *abbrev* : amyotrophic lateral sclerosis.

als /äls or öls/ *an* obsolete form of **also** and **as**[1].

Alsatia /al-sā'sh(y)ə/ *n* a former name for the district of *Alsace* in NE France; (until 1697) a sanctuary for debtors and criminals at Whitefriars, London.
■ **Alsa'tian** *adj* of Alsatia. ◆ *n* a person from Alsatia; a German sheepdog of wolflike breed, often used by police and security officers because of its strength and fierceness (*usu* called **German Shepherd**, **German Shepherd dog** or **German Police dog**).

alsike /al'sik/ *n* a white or pink-flowered clover. [From *Alsike*, Sweden, where it grows]

also /öl'sō/ *adv* likewise; further. [OE *all* (WSax *eall*) *swā* all so]
❑ **al'so-ran** *n* a horse that *also ran* in a race but did not get a 'place'; a person of a similar degree of importance.

alsoon or **alsoone** /al-soon'/ (*Spenser*) *adv* as soon. [**as**[1] and **soon**]

alstroemeria /al-strə-mē'ri-ə/ *n* a plant of the S American genus *Alstroemeria*, with inverted leaves. [C *Alströmer* (1736–94), Swedish botanist]

alt[1] /alt/ (*music*) *n* a high tone, in voice or instrument. [L *altus* high]
■ **in alt** in the octave beginning on the G an octave and a fifth above middle C; in an exalted and high-flown mood.

alt[2] /alt/ (*Milton*) *n* halt, rest. [Fr *alte* or Sp *alto*, from Ger *Halt*]

alt.[1] *abbrev* : alternate; altitude; alto.

alt.[2] /alt/ *combining form* denoting a style of popular music regarded as outside the mainstream, as in *alt.country*, *alt.rock*. [Short for **alternative**]

Altaic /al-tā'ik/ *n* a family of languages, forming one branch of Ural-Altaic, and consisting of Turkic, Mongolic and Tungusic (also *adj*). [Fr *altaïque* relating to the Altai mountains of Central Asia]

Altair /äl-tā'ir or al-tär'/ *n* a first-magnitude star in the constellation Aquila. [Ar *al ta'ir* the bird]

altaltissimo /al-tal-tis'i-mō/ *n* the very highest summit. [Reduplicated compound of Ital *alto* high, and *altissimo* highest]

alta moda /äl'tä mo'dä/ (*Ital*) *n* high fashion, the art of designing and making exclusive, fashionable clothes.

altar /öl'tər/ *n* a block or table for making sacrifices on; the table used for mass or the Eucharist; a place where worship or the marriage ceremony is carried out (*fig*); a ledge on a dry-dock wall. [L *altāre*, from *altus* high]
■ **al'tarage** *n* offerings made upon the altar during the offertory, for the maintenance of the priest. **al'tarwise** *adv* in the position of an altar at the east end of the chancel.
❑ **altar boy** *n* a boy assisting the priest at the altar, an acolyte. **al'tar-cloth** *n* the covering of the altar, often including the frontal and the superfrontal. **al'tarpiece** *n* a work of art placed above and behind an altar. **al'tar-rails** *n pl* in a church or chapel, rails separating the presbytery from the rest of the chancel. **al'tar-stone** *n* a stone serving as an altar; a consecrated slab forming or inserted in the top of an altar. **al'tar-tomb** *n* a monumental memorial, in form like an altar, often with a canopy.
■ **family altar** the symbol or place of family worship. **high altar** the principal altar. **lead to the altar** to marry (a woman).

altazimuth /al-taz'i-məth/ *n* an instrument devised by British astronomer George Airy (1801–92) for determining *alt*itude and *azim*uth.

alter[1] /ol- or öl'tər/ *vt* to make different; to modify; to castrate (*archaic*). ◆ *vi* to become different. [L *alter* one of two or the other of two, from the root of *alius* other, and the old compar sfx *-ter*]
■ **alterabil'ity** *n*. **al'terable** *adj*. **al'terant** *adj* altering; having the power of producing changes. ◆ *n* an alternative. **alterā'tion** *n*. **al'terative** *adj* able to cause change. ◆ *n* a medicine or treatment that changes bodily functions. **al'tered** *adj* (of a rock) changed in mineral composition by natural forces. **alterity** /öl- or al-ter'i-ti/ *n* otherness.

alter[2] /al'tər/ *adj* (*psychol*) other, distinct from oneself, used of people or things seen in contrast with the ego. [L, other]
❑ **alter ego** /al'tər eg'ō, ē'gō, öl'tər ē'gō or al'ter eg'ō/ *n* (*pl* **alter egos**) one's second self (see **second**[1]); a trusted, intimate friend.

altercate /öl'tər-kāt/ *vi* to dispute heatedly, argue. [L *altercārī, -ātus*, from *alter* other]
■ **altercā'tion** *n*. **al'tercative** *adj*.

altern /öl- or al-tûrn'/ (*archaic*) *adj* alternate. ◆ *adv* alternately. [L *alternus*]

alternat /al-ter-na'/ (*Fr*) *n* the diplomatic practice of determining precedence among powers of equal rank by lot or of otherwise avoiding the difficulty.

alternate /ol' or öl'tər-nāt, also al', formerly (eg Milton) -tûr'/ *vt* to cause to follow by turns or one after the other (properly, of two things). ◆ *vi* to follow or interchange (with each other; properly, of two things); to happen by turns, change by turns. ◆ *n* a deputy, substitute; an alternative. ◆ *adj* /-tûr' or (N Am) öl'/ arranged or coming one after the other by turns; every other or second; sometimes used with the sense 'alternative'; (of leaves) placed singly with change of side at each node; (of parts of a flower) each placed opposite the space between other parts of the flower; (of angles) placed one after the other on either side of a line (*geom*). [L *alternāre, -ātum*, from *alter* one or other of two]
■ **alter'nance** (or /al' /) *n* alternation, interchange or variation; training by alternate periods of theoretical and practical work. **alter'nant** or **al'ternant** *adj* alternating. ◆ *n* a spelling or sound variant that does not affect meaning (allomorph or allophone); a type of determinant (*maths*); an alternative proposition, eg one of the components in an alternation (*logic*). **alter'nately** *adv*. **al'ternating** *adj*. **alternā'tion** *n* the act of alternating; alternate succession; interchange; the type of disjunction in which 'or' is used inclusively (*logic*); reading or singing antiphonally. **al'ternātor** *n* a generator of alternating current.
❑ **alternate energy** see **renewable energy** under **renew**. **alternate host** *n* (*biol*) one of the two or more hosts of a parasite which has the different stages of its life cycle in unrelated hosts (cf **alternative host**). **alternating current** *n* an electric current that periodically reverses its direction. **alternation of generations** *n* (*biol*) the occurrence in a life cycle of two or more different forms in successive generations, the offspring commonly reproducing by a different method.

alternatim /ol- or öl-tər-nä'təm/ (*music*) *adv* alternating between polyphonic harmonization of plainsong and unadorned plainsong. [L *alternātim* alternately]

alternative /ol- or öl-tûr'nə-tiv/ *n* either of a pair, or any of a set, of possibilities; a choice between them; one of them, *esp* other than the one in question. ◆ *adj* possible as an alternative; disjunctive; alternate (*obs*); considered by some as preferable to the existing state or form of something, very often with the connotation of being less conventional, less materialistic, more in harmony with the environment and the natural order of things, etc, as *alternative society*, *alternative technology*, etc. [**alternate**]
■ **alter'natively** *adv* with an alternative; by way of alternative.
❑ **alternative birth** *n* a method of childbirth favouring home delivery and minimal medical involvement. **alternative comedy** *n* comedy that seeks to avoid stereotypes, often relying on black humour and ironic wit and taking a particular left-wing political position. **alternative energy** *n* energy derived from renewable resources. **alternative fuel** *n* a fuel for motor vehicles other than petrol. **alternative host** *n* (*biol*) one of two or more possible hosts in the life cycle of a parasite (cf **alternate host**). **alternative medicine** *n* treatments and therapies, including acupuncture, homeopathy, etc, used as alternatives to conventional medicine (cf **complementary medicine**). **Alternative Service Book** a modernized version of the liturgy of the Church of England, used as an alternative to the Book of Common Prayer. **alternative society** *n* a form of society that eschews conventional values. **alternative technology** *n* a form of technology intended to protect the environment and conserve natural resources. **alternative vote** *n* a system of voting whereby, if a voter's favourite candidate is out of the running, the vote is transferred to the candidate marked next in order of preference.

alterne /al-tûrn' or al'tûrn, also öl-/ (*bot*) *n* one of two or more plant communities adjoining but differing greatly. [Fr *alterne* alternate, from L *alternus*]

alternis vicibus /al-tûr'nis vī'si-bus or al-ter'nēs vē'ki-bŭs, also wē'/ (*L*) alternately.

alterum tantum /al'tə-rum tan'tum or al'te-rŭm tan'tŭm/ (*L*) as much more.

altesse /al-tes'/ (*Fr*), **alteza** /al-tā'tha/ (*Sp*), or **altezza** /al-tet'sa/ (*Ital*) *n* highness.

althaea or (*esp N Am*) **althea** /al-thē'ə/ *n* a plant of the marshmallow and hollyhock genus *Althaea* (or *Althea*), sometimes extended to the *Hibiscus* genus and applied *esp* to the Rose of Sharon. [Gr *althaiā* marshmallow]

Althing /öl'thing/ *n* the Icelandic parliament. [ON and Icel]

althorn /alt'hörn/ *n* a tenor saxhorn. [**alt**[1]]

although /öl-dhō'/ *conj* though (*esp* but not necessarily, in stating matter of fact). [**all** and **though**]

altimeter /al-tim'i-tər or al'ti-mē-tər, also öl' or ol'/ n an instrument for measuring height, by means of differences in atmospheric pressure, or (**radio altimeter**) by means of a time taken for a radio wave from an aircraft to be reflected back. [L altus high, and **meter**[1]]
■ **altimet'rical** adj. **altimet'rically** adv. **altim'etry** n.

Altiplano /al-ti-plä'nō/ n a plateau in the Bolivian and Peruvian part of the Andes, containing Lake Titicaca. [Sp, plateau]

altisonant /al-tis'ə-nənt/ adj high-sounding. [L altus high, and sonāns, -antis, prp of sonāre to sound]

altissimo /al-tis'(s)i-mō/ (music) adj very high. [Ital, superl of alto high]
■ **in altissimo** in the octave beginning on the G two octaves and a fifth above middle C.

altitonant /al-tit'ə-nənt/ adj thundering on high or loudly. [L altus high, and tonāns, -antis, prp of tonāre to thunder]

altitude /al'ti-tūd/ n height, esp above sea level; angle of elevation of a star, etc above the horizon; length of the perpendicular from apex to base of a triangle; high rank or eminence; a high point or position; (in pl) exalted mood, passion or manner. [L altitūdō, -inis, from altus high]
■ **altitūd'inal** adj relating to altitude; found at high level. **altitūdinā'rian** n someone tending to loftiness in doctrine or belief (also adj). **altitūd'inous** adj high.
❑ **altitude sickness** same as **mountain sickness** (see under **mountain**).

Alt key /olt' kē/ (comput) n a key used, in conjunction with others, to access alternative keyboard functions.

alto[1] /al'tō/ (music) n (pl **al'tos**) a high falsetto male voice; (properly countertenor) the highest male voice; contralto, the lowest female voice; the part sung by a countertenor or contralto; an instrument of corresponding range; a person with a countertenor or contralto voice; a viola (archaic). ◆ adj of the alto range. [Ital, from L altus high]
❑ **alto clef** n (music) the clef in which middle C is placed on the middle line of the stave, used esp for viola music.

alto[2] see **all-to**.

altocumulus /al-tō-kū'mū-ləs/ n (pl **altocu'muli** /-lī/) cumulus cloud forming at 2400–6000m (8000–20000ft). [New L, from altus high, and **cumulus**]

altogether /öl-tə-gedh'ər/ adv all together (obs or by confusion); wholly; completely; without exception; in total; all things considered. [**all** and **together**]
■ **for altogether** (rare) for all time, for good and all. **the altogether** (inf) the nude.

alto-rilievo /äl'tō-rēl-yā'vō/ (art) n (pl **alto-rilie'vos**) high relief; figures projected by at least half their thickness from the background on which they are sculptured. [Ital. See **relief**]

altostratus /al-tō-strä'təs or -strä'təs/ n (pl **altostra'ti** /-tī/) cloud forming a continuous layer at 2400–6000m (8000–20000ft). [New L, from altus high, and **stratus** (see under **stratum**)]

altrices /al-trī'sēz/ n pl birds whose young are hatched very immature and have to be fed in the nest by the parents. [L altrīcēs (pl of altrix) feeders or nurses]
■ **altricial** /-trish'l/ adj and n.

altruism /al'troo-i-zm/ n the principle of living and acting for the interest of others. [Fr altruisme, formed by French philosopher Auguste Comte (1798–1857) from Ital altrui someone else, from L alterī huīc to this other]
■ **al'truist** n. **altruist'ic** adj. **altruist'ically** adv.

altum silentium /al'tum si-len'sh(y)um or al'tŭm si-len'ti-ŭm/ (L) profound silence.

ALU (comput) abbrev: arithmetic logic unit.

alu see **aloo**.

aludel /al'ū-dəl or -oo-dəl/ (chem) n a pear-shaped pot used in sublimation. [Sp, from Ar al-uthāl]

alula /al'ū-lə/ n (pl **al'ulae** /-ī/ or **al'ulas**) in birds, the bastard wing. [L dimin of āla wing]

alum /al'əm/ n double sulphate of aluminium and potassium, with 24 molecules of water, crystallizing in transparent octahedra; any similar compound of a trivalent metal (esp aluminium) and a univalent metal or radical. [L alūmen, -inis alum]
■ **al'umish** adj having the character or taste of alum.
❑ **al'um-root** n an American plant of the saxifrage family with astringent root. **al'um-shale** or **al'um-slate** n a slate consisting mainly of clay, iron pyrites and coaly matter, from which alum is obtained. **al'um-stone** n alunite.

aluminium /al-ū-min'i-əm, al-ū'-/ or (N Am) **aluminum** /ə-loo'mi-nəm/ n a light silvery malleable and ductile metallic element (symbol **Al**; atomic no 13), first named (though not then isolated) **alu'mium** by Sir Humphry Davy, then (as still N Am) **alum'inum**. [Ety as for **alum**]

■ **alumina** /ə-lū' or ə-loo'mi-nə/ n oxide of aluminium. **alu'minate** n a salt whose acid is aluminium hydroxide. **aluminif'erous** or **alu'minous** adj bearing or containing aluminium or alumina. **alum'inize** or **-ise** vt to treat (a metal) so as to form an aluminium alloy on its surface; to coat (eg glass) with aluminium.
❑ **aluminium bronze** n an alloy of aluminium and copper, of lighter weight than gold, but like it in colour. **alumino-sil'icates** n pl compounds of alumina, silica and bases.

alumnus /a-lum'nəs/ n (pl **alum'nī**) a former pupil or student. [L, foster-son or pupil, from alere to nourish]
■ **alum'na** n (pl **alum'nae** /-nē/) a female alumnus.

alunite /al'ū-nīt or -yə-/ n alum-stone, a hydrous sulphate of aluminium and potassium. [Fr alun alum]

alure /al'yər/ (obs) n a walk behind battlements; a gallery; a passage. [OFr aleure, from aller to go]

alveolus /al-vē'ə-ləs or al'vi-/ n (pl **alveolī**) a pit, small depression or dilatation; a tooth socket; one of the clustered cells at the termination of a bronchiole in the lungs. [L alveolus, dimin of alveus a hollow]
■ **alve'olar** (or /-öl', or al'/) adj of an alveolus; produced with the tongue against the roots of the upper teeth (phonetics); pitted. ◆ n an alveolar consonant. **alvē'olate** (or /al'vi-/) adj pitted; honeycombed; inserted in an alveolus. **al'veole** n an alveolus. **alveolitis** /al-vi-ə-lī'tis/ n inflammation of the alveoli in the lungs.
❑ **alveolar arch** n the part of the jaw in which the teeth are embedded.

alvine /al'vīn/ adj of the belly. [L alvīnus from alvus belly]

always /öl'wāz/ adv every time; ever; continually; in any case; still (Scot); from the beginning (inf). [**all** and **way**[2], from OE ealne weg (accusative) and ME alles weis (genitive)]
■ **alway** /öl'wā/ adv (archaic) through all time; always.

alycompaine same as **elecampane**.

alyssum /al'i-səm or ə-lis'əm/ n a plant of the Alyssum genus of low-growing, cruciferous plants with white, yellow or mauve flowers, grown eg in rock-gardens; a mass of such plants. [Gr alysson a plant reputed to cure madness, from **a-**[2] and Gr lyssa madness]
■ **sweet alyssum** a white scented perennial of a related genus.

Alzheimer's disease /alts'hī-mərz di-zēz'/ n an illness affecting the brain and causing dementia in the middle-aged or elderly. [Alois Alzheimer (1864–1915), German neurologist]

AM abbrev: Albert Medal; amplitude modulation; Anno Mundi (L), in the year of the world; Armenia (IVR); Artium Magister (L), Master of Arts (US); Assembly Member (of the National Assembly for Wales); Associate Member; ave Maria (L), hail Mary; Member of the Order of Australia.

Am (chem) symbol: americium.

Am. abbrev: amateur; America; American.

am /am or əm/ used as 1st person sing of the verb to be. [OE (Anglian) am, eam (WSax eom), a relic of the verbs in -mi, from the root es-; cf Gr eimi (for esmi), L sum and Sans asmi]

a.m. or **am** abbrev: ante meridiem (L), before noon, ie in the morning.

AMA abbrev: American Medical Association; Australian Medical Association.

amabile /a-mä'bi-lā/ (Ital) adj of wines, etc, sweet.

amadavat see **avadavat**.

amadou /am'ə-doo/ n tinder made from fungi (genus Polyporus) growing on trees, used also as a styptic. [Fr, of doubtful origin]

amah /ä'mə/ (E Asia) n a native maidservant or child's nurse, esp wet nurse. [Port]

amain /ə-mān'/ (archaic or poetic) adv with main force; violently; at full speed; exceedingly. [**a-**[1] and **main**[1]]

à main armée /a mē-när-mā'/ (Fr) by force of arms, with mailed fist.

a majori /ā mə-jö'rī or ä mī-ö'rē/, also **a majori ad minus** /ad mī'nus or ad mi'nŭs/ (L) from the greater (to the less).

amakosi a plural of **inkosi**.

amalgam /ə-mal'gəm/ n a mixture of mercury with other metal; any soft mixture; a mixture or blend; an ingredient. [LL amalgama, perh from Gr malagma an emollient]
■ **amal'gamate** vt to mix with mercury; to merge. ◆ vi to unite in an amalgam; to come together as one; to blend. **amalgamā'tion** n a blending or merging; a union of diverse elements; the joining together of two or more separate businesses to form one business. **amal'gamative** adj.

amandine /a-man'din, -dīn, -dēn or am'an-/ n a protein in sweet almonds; a candle or a cosmetic which is prepared from them. [Fr amande almond]

amanita /a-mə-nī'tə/ n a mushroom of the Amanita genus, including the fly agaric (qv) and other poisonous kinds. [Gr amānītai (pl) a kind of fungus]

---

amantadine /ə-man'tə-dēn/ n a drug used in the treatment of influenza and Parkinson's disease.

amanuensis /ə-man-ū-en'sis/ n (pl **amanuen'sēs**) a literary assistant, esp one who writes to dictation or copies from manuscript. [L āmanuēnsis, from ā from, and manus hand]

amaracus /ə-mar'ə-kəs/ n marjoram. [L amāracus, from Gr amārakos]

amarant /am'ə-rant/ or **amaranth** /am'ə-ranth/ n a fabled never-fading flower, emblem of immortality; any species of **Amarant'us** or **Amaran'thus**, the love-lies-bleeding genus, with richly coloured long-lasting spikes, giving name to the family **Amarantā'ceae** or **Amaranthā'ceae**, related to the goosefoots; (**amaranth**) a highly nutritious S American cereal (also **grain amaranth**); a type of dye used for colouring foodstuffs. [Gr amarantos, from a- (privative), and marainein to wither; the th forms from confusion with anthos flower] ■ **amarantā'ceous** or **amaranthā'ceous** adj. **amarant'in** adj (Milton) of or like amaranth; fadeless; immortal; purple. **amarant'ine** or **amaran'thine** /-īn/ adj.

amaretto /am-ə-ret'ō/ n (pl **amarett'os**) an Italian liqueur flavoured with almonds. [Ital, from amaro bitter] ■ **amaret'ti** /-tē/ n pl almond-flavoured biscuits, eaten as a dessert.

amaryllis /a-mə-ril'is/ n the belladonna lily, forming the genus Amaryllis which gives name to the narcissus and snowdrop family **Amaryllidā'ceae**, differing from lilies in the inferior ovary. [Amaryllis, a girl's name in the Gr and L poets and others] ■ **amaryll'id** n any member of the family. **amaryllidā'ceous** adj.

amass /ə-mas'/ vt and vi to gather in great quantity; to accumulate. [Fr amasser, from L ad to, and massa a mass] ■ **amass'able** adj. **amass'ment** n.

amate[1] /ə-māt'/ (Spenser) vt to match. [a-[1] (intens), and mate[1]]

amate[2] /ə-māt'/ (archaic) vt to daunt; to dismay. [OFr amatir to subdue; cf **checkmate**, **mat**[2] and **mate**[2]]

amateur /am'ə-tər, -tūr or a-mə-tûr'/ n an enthusiast or admirer; a person who practises something for the love of it, not as a profession; someone whose understanding of, or ability in, a particular art, etc is superficial, trifling, or inexpert; a person who takes part in sport for pleasure, opp to professional; a dilettante. ◆ adj of or relating to an amateur. [Fr, from L amātor, -ōris a lover, from amāre to love] ■ **am'ateurish** adj done imperfectly and defectively, the work of an amateur rather than a professional hand, performed without professional skill. **am'ateurishly** adv. **am'ateurishness** or **am'ateurism** n. **am'ateurship** n.

Amati /ə-mä'tē/ n a violin or cello made by the Amati family (c.1550–1700) of Cremona.

amation /a-mä'shən/ (rare) n love-making. [L amatio, amationis, from amāre to love]

amative /am'ə-tiv/ adj inclined towards love. [L amāre, -ātum to love] ■ **am'ativeness** n propensity to love or to sexuality.

amatol /am'ə-tol/ n a high explosive composed of ammonium nitrate and trinitrotoluene.

amatory /am'ə-tə-ri/ adj relating to or causing love; amorous. [L amātōrius] ■ **amato'rial** /-tö'/ adj. **amato'rially** adv. **amato'rian** adj. **amato'rious** adj.

amaurosis /am-ö-rō'sis/ n blindness caused by disease of the optic nerves, usu without outward change in the eye. [Gr amaurōsis, from amauros dark] ■ **amaurotic** /-rot'ik/ adj.

amaze /ə-māz'/ vt to overwhelm with astonishment or wonder; to daze (obs); to bewilder (obs); to stun (obs); to strike with fear (obs). ◆ n bewilderment (obs); panic (obs); extreme astonishment (archaic). [OE āmasian (found in the pap āmasod)] ■ **amaz'edly** adv. **amaz'edness** n amazement (rare); stupefaction (obs); bewilderment (obs); panic, terror (obs). **amaze'ment** n astonishment mingled with wonder; incredulity; bewilderment (rare). **amaz'ing** adj. **amaz'ingly** adv. ❑ **amaze'balls** adj (facetious) unusually good, amazing.

Amazon /am'ə-zon, -zən or formerly a-mā'zon/ n in Greek mythology, one of a nation of women warriors, located near the Black Sea; one of a legendary race of female warriors of S America; the great river of S America (Port Amazonas Amazons, perh based on a misunderstood Tupí-Guaraní word amassona, amaçunu tidal bore, connected with records of Amazons living on its banks); a native of the Amazons; (the following usu without cap) a female soldier; a strong, vigorous or aggressive woman; a tropical American green parrot; an amazon ant. ◆ adj (also **Amazō'nian**) of or relating to the River Amazon in S America; (also without cap) of, relating to or resembling an Amazon. [Gr Amāzōn, -onos, in folk etymology referred to a- (privative), and māzos breast, with the explanation that Amazons cut off the right breast lest it should get in the way of the bowstring]

■ **am'azonite** n amazon-stone. **Ama'zon-like** adj and adv. ❑ **amazon ant** n a European and American ant (genus Polyergus) which enslaves the young of other species. **am'azon-stone** n a green microcline, said to be given by the Brazilian Amazons to the men who visited them.

ambages /am-bā'jēz/ n pl windings; roundabout ways; delays. [L ambāgēs (pl), from ambi- about, and agere to drive or lead] ■ **ambage** /am'bij/ n tortuousness; circumlocution. **ambagious** /-bā'jəs/ adj tortuous; circumlocutory. **ambagitory** /-baj'i-tər-i/ adj (Walter Scott).

amban /am'ban/ n a Chinese resident official in a dependency. [Manchu, minister]

Ambarvalia /am-bär-vā'li-ə/ n pl an ancient Roman festival with processions round the cornfields. [L Ambarvālia, from ambi- around, and arvum field]

ambassador /am-bas'ə-dər/, fem **ambassadress** /am-bas'ə-drəs/ n a diplomat of the highest rank, sent by one sovereign or state to another as a permanent representative; a messenger or agent. [Fr ambassadeur, from L ambactus a slave or servant, generally thought to be of Celtic origin] ■ **ambassadorial** /-dö'ri-əl/ adj. **ambass'adorship** n. **am'bassage** /-bəs-ij/ or **am'bassy** n forms of **embassage** and **embassy**. ❑ **ambass'ador-at-large'** n an ambassador not accredited to any particular foreign government. **ambassador extraordinary** n an ambassador sent on a special occasion, as distinguished from the resident ambassador. **ambassador plenipotentiary** n a high-ranking ambassador with treaty-signing powers.

ambatch /am'bach/ n a pith-tree. [Appar an African name]

amber /am'bər/ n a yellowish fossil resin; a clear brownish-yellow colour; the orange traffic light, which acts as a cautionary signal between red (stop) and green (go); ambergris (obs). ◆ adj made of amber; of the colour of amber. [Fr ambre, from Ar 'anbar ambergris] ■ **am'bered** adj (obs) embedded in amber; flavoured with ambergris. **am'berite** n an amberlike smokeless powder. **am'berous** or **am'bery** adj. **am'broid** or **am'beroid** n pressed amber, a synthetic amber formed by heating and compressing pieces of natural amber too small to be of value in themselves, sometimes along with other resins. ❑ **am'ber-fish** n a golden or greenish fish (genus Seriola) of the horse-mackerel family (Carangidae), abundant in warm seas. **amber gambler** n (inf) a reckless driver who speeds through a traffic light after it has changed from green to amber. **am'berjack** n (the species Seriola dumerili of) the amber-fish, a large Atlantic game fish having golden markings when young. **amber liquid** (or **fluid**) n (Aust inf) beer.

AMBER alert /am'bər ə-lûrt'/ (US) n a statewide bulletin giving a description of an abducted child. [Acronym of America's Missing: Broadcast Emergency Response; coined in memory of Amber Hagerman, a 9-year-old child abducted and murdered in 1996]

ambergris /am'bər-grēs/ n an ash-grey strongly-scented substance, originating in the intestines of the spermaceti whale and used in the manufacture of perfumes. [Fr ambre gris grey amber]

ambi- /am-bi-/ pfx round, both, on both sides. [L, from ambo both]

ambiance see under **ambient**.

ambidextrous /am-bi-dek'strəs/, (archaic) **ambidexterous** /am-bi-deks'tər-əs/ and **ambidexter** /-dek'stər/ adj able to use both hands equally well; on both sides; double-dealing. [**ambi-** and L dexter right] ■ **ambidex'ter** n (archaic) someone who is ambidextrous. **ambidexterity** /-ter'i-ti/ or **ambidex'trousness** n the quality of being ambidextrous. **ambidex'trously** adv.

ambient /am'bi-ənt/ adj going round; (of eg air temperature) surrounding; enveloping; (of music) intended to be restful and relaxing, and played at a low volume to provide an atmosphere. ◆ n something which encompasses; the air or sky. [L ambiēns, -entis, prp of ambīre, from pfx ambi- about, and īre to go] ■ **ambience** /am'bi-əns/ or **ambiance** /ã-bē-ãs/ n environment; surrounding influence; atmosphere; the use or disposition of accessories in art. ❑ **ambient illumination** n (image technol) the level of uncontrollable background light at a location. **ambient noise** n (acoustics) the noise existing in a room or any other environment.

ambiguous /am-big'ū-əs/ adj doubtful; undetermined; of intermediate or doubtful nature; indistinct; wavering; having more than one possible meaning; equivocal. [L ambiguus, from ambigere to go about or waver, from pfx ambi- both ways, and agere to drive] ■ **ambigū'ity** n doubtful or double meaning; an equivocal expression. **ambig'uously** adv. **ambig'uousness** n.

ambilateral /am-bi-lat'ə-rəl/ adj relating to or involving both sides. [**ambi-** and L latus, lateris side]

ambisexual /am-bi-sek'sū-əl/ or -shoo-əl/ adj (esp of sexual characteristics, eg pubic hair) common to both sexes; of or relating to both sexes. [**ambi-**]

Ambisonics® /am-bi-son'iks/ n sing a system of high-fidelity sound reproduction using multiple channels, which electronically reproduces ambient sound as perceived by the human ear. [**ambi-**]

ambit /am'bit/ n circuit; scope; compass; precincts; confines. [L ambitus a going round, from pfx ambi- round, and itus going, from īre, itum to go]

ambition /am-bish'ən/ n aspiration after success or advancement; the object of aspiration. [L ambitiō, -ōnis canvassing, from pfx ambi- about, and īre, itum to go]
 ■ **ambi'tionless** adj. **ambitious** /am-bish'əs/ adj full of ambition; strongly desirous (of or to do); aspiring; indicating ambition; pretentious. **ambi'tiously** adv. **ambi'tiousness** n.

ambitty /am-bit'i/ adj (of glass) devitrified. [Fr ambité, of obscure origin]

ambivalence /am-biv'ə-ləns/ or **ambivalency** /-lən-si/ n coexistence in one person of opposing emotional attitudes towards the same object. [**ambi-** and L valēns, -entis, prp of valēre to be strong]
 ■ **ambiv'alent** adj. **ambiv'alently** adv.

ambivert /am'bi-vûrt/ n someone who is neither an extravert nor an introvert. [**ambi-** and L vertere to turn]
 ■ **ambiver'sion** /-shən/ n.

amble /am'bl/ vi to move at an easy pace; (of a horse, etc) to move by lifting together both legs on one side alternately with those on the other side; to move like an ambling horse; to ride an ambling animal. ◆ n an ambling pace. [Fr ambler, from L ambulāre to walk about]
 ■ **am'bler** n. **am'bling** n and adj.

amblyopia /am-bli-ō'pi-ə/ n impaired sight without any apparent damage to the eye. [Gr amblyōpiā, from amblys dull, and ops eye]
 ■ **amblyo'pic** adj.

Amblyopsis /am-bli-op'sis/ n the blindfish of the Mammoth Cave in Kentucky. [Gr amblys dull, and opsis sight]

Amblystoma same as **Ambystoma**.

ambo /am'bō/ n (pl **am'bōs** or **ambō'nes** /-nēz/) an early Christian raised reading-desk or pulpit. [LL ambō, from Gr ambōn, -ōnos crest of a hill or pulpit]

amboceptor /am'bə-sep-tər/ (biochem) n in immunization, an antibody acting as a double receptor, linking both with the antigen and with the complement. [L ambo both, and **receptor**]

Amboina-wood (also **Amboyna-**) /am-boi'nə-wūd/ n the finely coloured knotty wood of Pterocarpus indicus, a papilionaceous tree. [Island of Amboina in the Moluccas, Indonesia]
 ❑ **Amboina pine** n a tree (Agathis alba), a source of resin.

ambroid see under **amber**.

ambrosia /am-brō'z(h)i-ə or -zhə/ n the food (later, the drink) of the Greek gods, which conferred everlasting youth and beauty; the anointing oil of the gods; any fragrant or delicious food or beverage; something sweet and pleasing; bee-bread; fungi cultivated for food by certain bark-beetles (**ambrosia beetles**) of the Scolytidae; (with cap) a genus of Compositae, a common cause of hay fever, known in N America as ragweeds. [Gr ambrosiā, from ambrotos immortal, from a- (privative), and brotos (orig mortos) mortal; cf Sans amṛta immortal]
 ■ **ambrō'sial** adj fragrant; sweet; delicious; immortal; heavenly. **ambrō'sially** adv. **ambrō'sian** adj.

Ambrosian /am-brō'z(h)ən or -z(h)yən/ adj relating to St Ambrose, 4c bishop of Milan, to his liturgy, to the form of plainsong introduced by him, to various religious orders and to the public library at Milan (founded 1602–9 by Cardinal Federigo Borromeo) named in his honour. ◆ n a member of any of these orders.

ambrotype /am'brə-tīp/ n an early kind of photograph made by backing a glass negative with black varnish or paper so that it appears as a positive. [Gr ambrotos immortal, and **type**]

ambry, **aumbry** or **almery**, (Scot) **awmry** or **awmrie** /am' or öm'(b)ri/ n a recess for church vessels; a cupboard; a pantry; a dresser; a safe. [OFr almerie, from L armārium a chest or safe, from arma arms or tools]

ambs-ace or **ames-ace** /ām' or am'zās/ n double ace, the lowest possible throw at dice; bad luck; worthlessness. [OFr ambes as, from L ambōs assēs both aces]

ambulacrum /am-bū-lā'krəm or -lak'rəm/ n (pl **ambulā'cra**) a radial band in the shell of an echinoderm, bearing rows of pores through which the tube-feet protrude. [L ambulācrum a walk, from ambulāre to walk]
 ■ **ambulā'cral** adj.

ambulance /am'bū-ləns/ or -byə-/ n a vehicle or (**air ambulance**) helicopter, etc for conveying the sick or injured; a movable field hospital. [L ambulāre, -ātum to walk about]
 ■ **am'bulant** adj walking; able to walk; moving from place to place; unfixed (rare); allowing or calling for walking. ◆ n a walking patient. **am'bulate** vi to walk. **ambulā'tion** n. **am'bulātor** n a walker; a wheel for road-measuring. **am'bulatory** /-ə-tər-i/ adj of or for walking; moving from place to place, not stationary; subject to change (law; hist). ◆ n a covered walk, eg an aisle, cloister, portico or corridor.
 ❑ **ambulance broker** n a broker specializing in the affairs of crashed companies. **am'bulance-chaser** n a lawyer on the lookout for accidents in order to instigate actions for damages (US); a person or firm offering to pursue a claim on behalf of an accident victim in return for a percentage of the sum obtained. **am'bulanceman** or **am'bulancewoman** n a male or female member of the crew of an ambulance.

ambuscade /am-bə-skād'/ n an ambush. ◆ vt and vi to ambush. [Fr embuscade or Sp emboscada; see **ambush**]
 ■ **ambuscā'do** n (pl **ambuscā'dos** or **ambusca'does**) (esp 16–17c; would-be Sp) an ambuscade.

ambush /am'būsh/ n a lying or laying in wait in order to attack by surprise; an attack made in this way; a place of lying in wait; a person or troop lying in wait. ◆ vt and vi to attack from ambush. [OFr embusche (Fr embûche), from embuscher, from LL imboscāre, from im in, and boscus (see **bush**[1])]
 ■ **am'bushment** n (archaic) ambush.
 ❑ **ambush bug** n (US) any of several insects of the Phymatidae that prey on other insects from a place of concealment, eg within a flower.

Ambystoma /am-bis'tə-mə/, also **Amblystoma** /-blis'/ n a genus of tailed amphibians in the gill-less or salamandroid suborder, called axolotl in the larval stage. [Origin disputed; poss an erroneous formation from Gr amblys blunt, and stoma mouth]

AMCS abbrev : Airborne Missile Control System.

AMD abbrev : age-related macular degeneration.

AMDG abbrev : ad majorem Dei gloriam (L), to the greater glory of God.

am-dram /am'dram/ (inf) n (usu sing) amateur dramatics (also adj).

âme /äm/ (Fr) n a soul.
 ❑ **âme damnée** /da-nā/ n a tool or agent blindly devoted to one's will (literally, a damned soul). **âme de boue** /də bū/ n a low-minded person (literally, a soul of mud). **âme perdue** /per-dü/ n a desperate character (literally, a lost soul).

amearst a Spenserian spelling of **amerced** (pat and pap of **amerce**).

ameba, **amebic**, etc US spelling of **amoeba**, **amoebic**, etc.

ameer see **amir**.

ameiosis /ā-mī-ō'sis/ (biol) n (pl **ameio'ses** /-sēz/) non-pairing of the chromosomes in meiosis. [**a-**[2]]

Amelanchier /am-ə-lang'ki-ər or -lan'chi-ər/ n the shadbush genus of the rose family. [Fr amélanchier]

amelcorn /am'əl-körn/ n a kind of wheat, emmer. [Ger Amelkorn, Du amelkorn; cf **amylum**, **corn**[1]]

amelia /ə-mē'li-ə or -mel'i-ə/ n a congenital condition in which one or more limbs are completely absent. [**a-**[2] and Gr melos limb]

ameliorate /ə-mē'li-ə-rāt or -lyə-/ vt to make better; to improve. ◆ vi to grow better, to improve. [Fr améliorer, from L ad to, and melior better]
 ■ **ameliorā'tion** n improvement; the process by which the meaning of a word gradually becomes less pejorative (linguistics). **ame'liorātive** adj. **ame'liorātor** n.

amen /ä-men' or ā-men'/ interj so let it be, said esp at the end of a prayer. ◆ n an expression of assent, by saying 'amen'; the last word. ◆ vt to say amen to; to ratify solemnly; to approve; to conclude. [Heb āmēn true, truly, retained in Gr and Eng translations]
 ❑ **Amen glass** n a type of drinking-glass engraved with a Jacobite inscription, esp 'God save the king. Amen'.

amenable /ə-mē'nə-bl or (esp US) ə-men'ə-bl/ adj ready to be led or won over; liable or subject. [Fr amener to lead, from à, from L ad to, and mener to lead, from LL mināre to lead or drive (eg cattle), from L minārī to threaten]
 ■ **amenabil'ity** or **amen'ableness** n. **amen'ably** adv.

amenage /am'e-nāj/ (Spenser) vt to tame. [OFr ame(s)nager, from à to, and mesnage household]

amenaunce /am'ə-nöns/ (Spenser) n bearing. [OFr amenance; see **amenable**]

amend /ə-mend'/ vt to free from fault or error; to correct; to improve; to alter in detail, with a view to improvement, (eg a bill before parliament); to rectify; to cure; to mend. ◆ vi to grow or become better; to reform; to recover. [Fr amender, from L ēmendāre, from ē out of, and mendum a fault]

■ **amend'able** adj. **amend'atory** adj corrective. **amend'er** n. **amend'ment** n correction; improvement; an alteration or addition to a document, agreement, etc; an alteration proposed on a bill under consideration; a counter-proposal or countermotion put before a meeting.
■ **make amends** to supply a loss; to compensate (for).

amende /a-mãd'/ (Fr) n a fine or penalty.
❑ **amende honorable** /o-nor-äbl'/ n orig, an ignominious public confession; now, a frank admission of wrong satisfying the honour of the injured.

amenity /ə-mē'ni-ti/ or /ə-men'i-ti/ n pleasantness, eg in situation, climate, manners or disposition; a pleasing feature, object or characteristic; a facility (usu in pl); civility. [L amoenus pleasant]
■ **amene** /ə-mēn'/ adj (rare) pleasant.
❑ **amenity bed** n a hospital bed, the occupant of which pays for amenities such as privacy while still receiving free medical treatment. **amenity kit** n a small bag of toiletries given to airline passengers for use during a flight.

amenorrhoea or (esp N Am) **amenorrhea** /a- or ā-men-ə-rē'ə/ n failure or absence of menstruation. [a-², Gr mēn month, and rhoiā a flowing]

ament¹ /ā'mənt or ə-ment'/ (psychiatry) n a person who fails to develop mentally; a sufferer from amentia. [L āmēns, -entis, from ā from, and mēns, mentis mind]
■ **amentia** /a- or ā-men'shi-ə/ n mental deficiency.

ament² see **amentum**.

amentum /ə-men'təm/ n (pl **amen'ta**) a catkin (also **a'ment**). [L, thong]
■ **amentā'ceous** or **amen'tal** adj. **amentif'erous** adj catkin-bearing.

Amer. abbrev : America; American.

Amerasian /am-ə-rā'zhən/ n anyone of mixed American and Asian parentage, esp a person fathered by an American serviceman in Vietnam or Korea. ◆ adj of mixed American and Asian parentage. [American and **Asian**]

amerce /ə-mûrs'/ vt to fine (esp with a discretionary fine); to deprive; to punish. [Anglo-Fr amercier, from à merci at mercy]
■ **amerc'eable** or **amerc'iable** adj. **amerce'ment** or **amerc'iament** n infliction of a fine; a fine.

American /ə-mer'i-kən/ adj relating to America, esp to the United States. ◆ n a native or citizen of America; the English language as spoken in America. [From America, perh so called from Richard Ameryk, Sheriff of Bristol, who financed John Cabot's voyage; also said to be from Amerigo (L Americus) Vespucci]
■ **Americana** /ə-mer-i-kä'nə/ n pl things characteristic of America, esp old books, paintings, furniture, etc; (as sing) a style of American popular music that combines elements of country, rock and folk music. **Amer'icanism** n a custom, characteristic, word, phrase or idiom characteristic of Americans; the condition of being an American citizen; (advocacy of) American policies, political attitudes, etc; devotion to American institutions. **Amer'icanist** n a person who studies American biology, archaeology, etc. **Americaniza'tion** or **-s-** n. **Amer'icanize** or **-ise** vt to make American. **Americano** /-kä'nō/ n (pl **America'nos**) coffee made by adding hot water to one or two shots of espresso; a cocktail made with Campari, vermouth and soda water.
❑ **American aloe** n agave. **American blackbird** n a grackle. **American blight** n a plant louse pest of apple trees. **American bowls** n sing tenpin bowling, a game like skittles. **American chameleon** n an anole. **American cloth** n cloth with a glazed coating. **American eagle** n the bald eagle. **American Express**® **card** n a type of credit card issued by a commercial company (abbrev **Amex**). **American football** n an American game of football, somewhat resembling rugby, played with an elliptical ball between teams of eleven players (unlimited substitution being allowed), scoring being by points won for touchdowns and goals. **American Indian** n a member of the indigenous peoples of America, thought on discovery to be Indian. **American-In'dian** adj. **American organ** n an instrument resembling the harmonium, in which air is sucked inwards to the reeds. **American pit bull terrier** n an American breed of pit bull terrier (qv under **pit**¹). **American plan** n in a hotel, etc, the system of including meals in the charge for a room (see also **European plan** under **European**). **American Sign Language** n the form of sign language used by deaf people in N America (abbrev **ASL**). **American smooth** n a ballroom dance incorporating steps from the foxtrot, tango and waltz. **American tiger** n a jaguar. **American tournament** see round robin under **round**¹.
■ **American standard code for information interchange** (comput) ASCII. **the American Dream** the idea that the American way of life offers the possibility of unlimited economic, social, etc success to every individual.

americium /a-mə-rish'i-əm or -ris'/ n an artificially produced radioactive transuranic metallic element (symbol **Am**; atomic no 95). [First produced in America]

Amerind /am'ə-rind/ n and adj American Indian (also **Amerind'ian**).
■ **Amerin'dic** adj.

à merveille /a mer-ve'y'/ (Fr) wonderfully, perfectly.

ames-ace see **ambs-ace**.

Ameslan /am'(ə-)slan/ n American Sign Language.

Ames test /āmz test/ n a test for determining the carcinogenicity of a substance by measuring its mutational effect on specific salmonella bacteria. [Bruce Ames (born 1928), US biochemist]

Ametabola /a-me-tab'ə-lə/ n pl in some classifications, the lowest insects, with little or no metamorphosis. [a-² and Gr metabolē change]
■ **ametabol'ic** /-ə-bol'ik/ or **ametab'olous** adj. **ametab'olism** n.

amethyst /am'ə-thist/ n a bluish violet quartz used as a gemstone, anciently supposed to prevent drunkenness; its colour. ◆ adj of or coloured like amethyst. [Gr amethystos, from a- (privative), and methyein to be drunken, from methy wine; cf **mead**¹ and Sans madhu sweet]
■ **amethyst'ine** /-īn/ adj.
■ **oriental amethyst** a purple corundum.

Amex /am'eks/ abbrev : American Express® (card); American Stock Exchange.

Amharic /am-har'ik/ n a Semitic language, the official language of Ethiopia (also adj). [Amhara district of Ethiopia]

ami /a-mē'/ (Fr) n a friend.
■ **amie** /a-mē/ n a female friend; a mistress.
❑ **ami de cour** /də koor/ n a court friend, ie an untrustworthy friend. **ami du peuple** /dü pœpl'/ n friend of the people (esp Marat, French revolutionist).

amiable /ā'mi-ə-bl/ adj of sweet and friendly disposition; lovable; friendly (Shakesp); love-inspiring (Shakesp). [OFr amiable friendly, from L amīcābilis, from amīcus friend; confused in meaning with OFr amable (Fr aimable), from L amābilis, from amāre to love]
■ **āmiabil'ity** or **ām'iableness** n. **ām'iably** adv.

amianthus /a-mi-an'thəs/ or more correctly **amiantus** /-təs/ n the finest fibrous asbestos, which can be made into cloth unaffected by fire. [Gr amiantos (lithos) undefiled (stone), from a- (privative), and miainein to soil]

amicable /am'i-kə-bl/ adj in friendly spirit. [L amīcābilis, from amīcus friend, from amāre to love]
■ **amicabil'ity** or **am'icableness** n. **am'icably** adv.
❑ **amicable numbers** n pl (maths) see **friendly numbers** under **friend**.

amice¹ /am'is/ n a strip of fine linen, worn formerly on the head, now on the shoulders, by a priest at mass; a cloak or wrap. [OFr amit, from L amictus cloak, from amb- about, and jacere to throw]

amice² /am'is/ or **almuce** /al-mūs'/ n a furred hood with long ends hanging down in front, originally a cap or covering for the head, afterwards a hood or cape with a hood and later a college hood, worn by certain religious orders. [OFr aumuce, of doubtful origin]

Amicus /am'i-kəs/ n a British trade union for workers in manufacturing industries (now part of Unite).

amicus curiae /a-mī'kus kū'ri-ē or a-mē'kŭs koo'ri-ī/ n (pl **ami'cī** (or /-mē'kē/)) formerly, in Scots law, a disinterested adviser, not a party to the case; a person or group not directly involved in a case who may be represented by request or permission of the court; counsel representing such; (wrongly) a friend in high quarters. [L, a friend of the lawcourt]

amid /ə-mid'/ prep in the midst of; among. ◆ adv (archaic) in the midst. [OE on middan (dative of adj), in middle]
■ **amid'most** adv and prep in the very middle (of). **amid'ships** adv in, near or towards the middle of a ship lengthwise (from genitive of ship). **amidst'** adv and prep amid.

amide /am'īd/ n a derivative of ammonia in which an acid radical takes the place of one or more of the three hydrogen atoms; any of various inorganic compounds in which a metal takes the place of one of these three atoms. [From **ammonia**]

Amidol® /am'i-dol/ n a colourless chemical $(C_6H_3(NH_2)_2(OH).2HCl)$ used as a photographic developer.

amidships see under **amid**.

amie see under **ami**.

amigo /ə-mē'gō/ (Sp) n (pl **ami'gos**) a friend.

amildar /am'il-där/ n a factor or manager in India; a collector of revenue amongst the Mahrattas. [Hindustani 'amaldār, from Ar 'amal work, and Pers dār holder]

amine /am'īn or -ēn/ n a derivative of ammonia (NH₃) in which one or more hydrogen atoms are replaced by organic radicals. [From **ammonia**]
□ **amino acid** /a-mē'nō/ n any of a group of organic compounds containing at least one from both the amino and the carboxyl groups (eg **amino-acetic acid**, glycine), some of which (**essential amino acids**) cannot be synthesized by the body and must be supplied in the diet. **amino group** n the group NH₂ in an amine.

aminobutene /ə-mē-nō-bū'tēn/ n a drug once used for pain relief as a less addictive alternative to morphine. [**amine** and **butene**]

a minori /ā mi-nö'rī or ä mi-nö'rē/, also **a minori ad majus** /ad mā'jus or ad mī'ūs/ (L) from the less (to the greater).

amir or **ameer** /a- or ə-mēr'/ n the title borne by certain Muslim princes. [Ar amīr ; see **admiral** or **emir**]

amis (Spenser) same as **amice**[1].

Amish /ā' or ä'mish, or am'ish/ adj of or belonging to a strict US Mennonite sect (also n pl). [Ger amisch, after J Amman or Amen (c.1645–c.1730), Swiss bishop]

amiss /ə-mis'/ adv astray; wrongly; improperly; faultily. ◆ adj out of order; wrong; unsuitable; to be objected to. ◆ n (obs) an evil; a misdeed. [**a-**[1] and **miss**[1]]
■ **come amiss** to be unwelcome or untoward. **not go amiss** to be beneficial or advantageous. **take amiss** to take offence at (strictly, by misinterpretation).

amissible /ə-mis'i-bl/ adj liable to be lost. [L āmittere, āmissum to lose, from ā from, and mittere to send]
■ **amissibil'ity** n.

amissing /ə-mis'ing/ (Scot) adj wanting; lost. [**a-**[1]]

amitosis /a-mi-tō'sis/ (biol) n (pl **amito'ses** /-sēz/) cell division without mitosis. [**a-**[2] and Gr mitos thread]
■ **amitotic** /-tot'ik/ adj. **amitot'ically** adv.

amitriptyline /a-mi-trip'tə-lēn/ n an antidepressant drug, also used to treat enuresis. [From amino, tryptamine (a hallucinogenic substance) and methyl, with ending -ine]

amity /am'i-ti/ n friendship; goodwill; friendly relations. [Fr amitié, from L amicus a friend]

amla /äm'lə/ n an East Indian tree, the emblic.

amman see **amtman**.

ammeter /am'i-tər/ n an instrument for measuring electric current usu in amperes. [From **ampere** and Gr metron measure]

ammiral an old form (Milton) of **admiral**.

ammo /am'ō/ n a familiar contraction of **ammunition**.

Ammon /am'on/ n the ancient Egyptian ram-headed god Amún or Amen, identified by the Greeks with Zeus, famous for his temple and oracle in the Libyan oasis of Siwa; (without cap) the Asian wild sheep, the argali (from its gigantic horns). [Gr Ammōn, -ōnos]

ammonal /am'ə-nal/ n a high explosive made from ammonium nitrate and aluminium.

ammonia /a- or ə-mō'ni-ə/ n a pungent compound of nitrogen and hydrogen (NH₃) first obtained in gaseous form from sal ammoniac; its solution in water, containing ammonium hydroxide (liquid ammonia, formerly called spirits of hartshorn). [New L, back-formation from Eng sal ammoniac, from L sal salt, and ammoniacus of Ammon; see **Ammon**]
■ **ammō'niac** or **ammonī'acal** adj of ammonia; of the region of the temple of Ammon (applied only to gum ammoniac, and to sal ammoniac, which is said to have been first made in that district from camel-dung). **ammoniacum** /am-ə-nī'ə-kəm/ n gum ammoniac. **ammō'niated** adj combined, impregnated, with ammonia. **ammō'nium** n a univalent radical, NH₄, resembling the alkali metals in chemical behaviour.
□ **ammonium nitrate** n a white crystalline solid used in explosives and as a fertilizer.
■ **gum ammoniac** a gum resin used in medicine.

ammonite /am'ə-nīt/ n a fossil cephalopod of many kinds, with a coiled chambered shell resembling a ram's horn. [New L ammōnītes, from Ammon]
■ **amm'onoid** n a member of the order Ammonoidea, to which the ammonites and related cephalopods belong.

ammophilous /a-mo'fi-ləs/ adj sand-loving. [Gr ammos sand, and phileein to love]

ammunition /a-mū-nish'ən/ n orig military stores generally; things used for charging firearms, such as missiles or propellants (inf **am'mo**); explosive military devices; anything that can be used in fighting (lit and fig). ◆ adj for ammunition; supplied from army stores. ◆ vt to supply with ammunition. [Obs Fr amunition, appar from l'amunition for la munition; see **munition**]

amnesia /am-nē'zh(y)ə or -zi-ə/ n loss of memory. [Gr amnēsiā]

■ **amne'siac** n someone who suffers from amnesia (also adj). **amne'sic** adj and n.
□ **amnesic shellfish poisoning** n severe, sometimes fatal, poisoning caused by the ingestion of domoic acid from contaminated shellfish.

amnesty /am'nə-sti/ n a general pardon; a period during which offenders may admit to certain crimes or infringements without penalty; an act of oblivion. ◆ vt to give amnesty to. [Gr amnēstiā forgetfulness]

amnio- /am-ni-ō-/ combining form denoting amnion; amniotic. [**amnion**]
■ **amniocentesis** /-sin-tē'sis/ n (pl **amniocente'ses** /-sēz/) the insertion of a hollow needle into the uterus of a pregnant woman to withdraw a sample of the amniotic fluid to test for fetal abnormalities, etc (inf short form **am'nio**). **amniotomy** /-ot'/ n surgical rupture of the amnion during, or in order to induce, labour.

amnion /am'ni-ən/ n (pl **am'nia**) the innermost membrane enveloping the embryo of reptiles, birds and mammals. [Gr]
■ **am'niote** n any vertebrate animal that possesses an amnion, chorion and allantois during fetal development. **amniot'ic** adj.
□ **amniotic cavity** n the space between the embryo and the amnion. **amniotic fluid** n the fluid within the amnion in which the embryo is suspended.

amn't /am'ənt/ a Scots contraction of **am not**.

amobarbital /ā- or a-mō-bär'bit-əl/ n a white crystalline powder used as a sedative. [From amylobarbitone, its chemical name]

amoeba or (US) **ameba** /ə-mē'bə/ n (pl **amoe'bae** /-bē or -bī/ or **amoe'bas**) a protozoan of ever-changing shape. [Gr amoibē change]
■ **amoebī'asis** n infection (esp of the colon) by amoebae. **amoe'bic** adj. **amoe'biform** adj. **amoe'boid** adj.

amoebaean /a-mē-bē'ən/ adj answering alternately, responsive, as often in pastoral poetry. [L amoebaeus, from Gr amoibaios, from amoibē alternation]

à moitié /a mwa-tyā'/ (Fr) half; by halves.

amok /ə-mok'/ or **amuck** /ə-muk'/ adj and adv in a frenzy, esp in the phrase **run amok** to rush about wildly, attacking anyone in one's path (also fig). [Malay amoq frenzied]

amomum /ə-mō'məm/ n a plant of the genus Amomum of the ginger family, including cardamoms and grains of Paradise. [Latinized from Gr amōmon prob cardamom]

à mon avis /a mo-na-vē'/ (Fr) in my opinion.

amontillado /ə-mon-ti-l(y)ä'dō/ n (pl **amontilla'dos**) a light medium-dry sherry orig from Montilla. [Sp]

amoove (Spenser) same as **amove**[1].

amoral /ā-mor'əl, also a-/ adj non-moral, outside the domain of morality. [**a-**[2] and **moral**]
■ **amor'alism** n refusal to recognize the validity of any system of morality. **amor'alist** n. **amoral'ity** n. **amor'ally** adv.

amorance /am'ə-rəns/ (psychol) n the state of being in love; romantic love. [L amor love]
■ **am'orant** adj.

amorce /ə-mörs'/ n a percussion cap for a toy pistol. [Fr, priming]

amorist /am'ə-rist/ n a lover; a ladies' man; one who writes of love; a seeker of sexual adventures or experiences. [L amor love]
■ **am'orism** n.

amornings /ə-mör'ningz/ (obs or dialect) adv of a morning. [**a-**[1] and **morning**, with genitive ending added]

amoroso /a-mə-rō'sō/ adj tender (music; also adv); (of sherry) sweet, full-bodied. ◆ n (pl **amoro'sos**) (also fem **amoro'sa**) a lover; a ladies' man; a dark sweet sherry. [Ital and Sp]

amorous /am'ə-rəs/ adj inclined to esp sexual love; in love; fond; amatory; relating to love. [OFr amorous (Fr amoureux), from LL amōrōsus, from amor love]
■ **amorosity** /-os'i-ti/ n (rare). **am'orously** adv. **am'orousness** n.

amor patriae /ā'mör pä'tri-ē or ä'mor pa'tri-ī/ (L) love of country.

amorphous /ə-mör'fəs/ adj without definite shape or structure; shapeless; without crystalline structure. [Gr amorphos shapeless, from a- (privative), and morphē form]
■ **amor'phism** or **amor'phousness** n. **amor'phously** adv.

amort /ə-mört'/ (obs or archaic) adj spiritless, dejected. [Fr à to, and mort death; but partly from **alamort** wrongly understood as all amort]

amortize or **-ise** /ə-mör'tīz or -tiz/ (law) vt to alienate in mortmain or convey to a corporation (obs); to pay off (a debt), esp through a

sinking-fund; to write off a wasting asset. [LL a(d)mortizāre, from Fr à to, and mort death]
■ amortiza'tion or -s- n. amort'izement or -s- n.

amosite /am'ə-sīt/ n brown asbestos, a form of asbestos mined only in South Africa. [Asbestos Mines of South Africa, and -ite]

amount /ə-mownt'/ vi to come in total (to); to come in meaning or substance (with to); to go up (Spenser). ◆ n the whole sum; principal and interest together; quantity; value, import, equivalence. [OFr amonter to ascend, from L ad to, and mōns, montis a mountain]
■ any amount of a great deal of. no amount of not even an infinite quantity of.

amour /ə-moor'/ n a love affair (now usu discreditable); a loved one; love or friendship (obs); love-making (usu in pl; archaic). [Fr, from L amor, amōris love]
■ amourette /a-moo-ret'/ n a petty amour; an amoretto.

amour courtois /a-moor koor-twä'/ (Fr) n courtly love.

amour fou /a-moor foo'/ (Fr) n a passionate love affair. [Literally, mad love]

amour-propre /a-moor-pro'pr'/ (Fr) n self-esteem; sometimes, excessive self-esteem, as shown by readiness to take offence at slights.

amove[1] /ə-moov'/ vt to stir up (obs); to affect (obs); to rouse (Spenser). [OFr amover, from L admovēre, from ad to, and movēre to move]

amove[2] /ə-moov'/ (law; hist) vt to remove. [L āmovēre, from ā from, and movēre to move]

amoxicillin /ə-mok'si-sil-in/ n an antibiotic drug, a type of semi-synthetic penicillin.

AMP abbrev : adenosine monophosphate.

amp /amp/ n short form of ampere and amplifier.
■ amped adj (sl; often with up) excited.
■ amp up (sl) to increase in intensity.

ampassy see ampersand.

ampelo- /am-pe-lo-/ or ampeli- /am-pe-li-/ combining form denoting of the vine, vine-like. [Gr ampelos vine]
■ ampelography /am-pel-og'rə-fi/ n the botany of the vine.

ampelopsis /am-pi-lop'sis/ n (pl ampelop'ses /-sēz/) a plant of the genus of climbing shrubs Ampelopsis; (formerly and rarely) any of certain related plants such as the Virginia creeper. [Gr ampelos vine, and opsis appearance]

ampere or ampère /am'pār or -pär', or ä-per'/ n a base SI unit, the unit of electric current (symbol A), defined as that which, flowing in two straight parallel conductors of infinite length and negligible circular cross-section, one metre apart in a vacuum, will produce a force between the conductors of 2×10^{-7} newtons per metre length. [AM Ampère (1775–1836), French physicist]
■ am'perage n current in amperes.
❑ ampere hour n unit of charge = 3600 coulombs, or one ampere flowing for one hour.
■ international ampere a unit formerly defined by means of the rate of deposition of silver from a solution of silver nitrate, which was slightly less than the practical unit in use; now defined as having the same value as an ampere.

ampersand /am'pər-sand/ n the character & (orig ligatured E and T, for Latin et) representing and (also am'perzand, am'pussy-and and am'passy /amp'ə-si/). [and per se, and, ie & by itself means 'and'; cf a-per-se]

Ampex® /am'peks/ n an old system of magnetic recording of television signals. ◆ vt to record by Ampex.

amphetamine /am-fet'ə-mēn/ n C₉H₁₃N, or its sulphate or phosphate, a synthetic, potentially habit-forming drug used as an appetite suppressant and in the treatment of narcolepsy. [alpha methyl phenethyl amine]

amphi- /am-fi-/ pfx denoting both, on both sides (or ends) or around. [Gr]

amphibian /am-fi'bi-ən/ adj amphibious; of the Amphi'bia, a class of cold-blooded vertebrates, typically gill-breathing in the larval state and lung- or skin-breathing as adults, including frogs, toads, newts, salamanders and caecilians. ◆ n a member of the Amphibia; an aeroplane designed to alight on land or water; a vehicle for use on land or water. [New L amphibia, from Gr; see amphibious]

amphibious /am-fib'i-əs/ adj living, or adapted to life or use, both on land and in or on water; of military operations, in which troops are conveyed across the sea or other water in landing barges, assault-craft, etc, and land on enemy-held territory; of double, doubtful or ambiguous nature; leading two lives (archaic). [Gr amphibios, from amphi on both sides, and bios life]
■ amphib'iously adv. amphib'iousness n.

amphibole /am'fi-bōl/ (mineralogy) n any mineral of a group of dark-coloured, rock-forming silicates differing from the pyroxenes in cleavage angle (about 56° instead of about 87°), silicates of calcium, magnesium, and other metals, including hornblende, actinolite, tremolite, etc. [Gr amphibolos ambiguous, on account of the resemblance between hornblende and tourmaline]
■ amphib'olite n a rock composed essentially of amphibole.

amphibology /am-fi-bol'ə-ji/ n a phrase or sentence ambiguous not in its individual words but in its construction; the use of such ambiguities. [Gr amphibolos, from amphi on both sides, and ballein to throw]
■ amphibol'ic or amphibological /-bə-loj'/ adj. amphib'olous /-ə-ləs/ adj. amphib'oly n amphibology.

amphibrach /am'fi-brak/ (prosody) n a foot of three syllables, a long between two short, or stressed between two unstressed. [L amphibrachus, Gr amphibrachys short at both ends, from amphi on both sides, and brachys short]
■ amphibrach'ic adj.

amphictyon /am-fik'ti-on/ (Gr hist) n a delegate to a council of an amphic'tyony, a league of neighbouring communities connected with a temple and cult, esp of Delphi. [Gr amphiktyones, appar for amphiktiones dwellers around, from amphi around, and ktizein to dwell]
■ amphictyon'ic adj.

amphigastrium /am-fi-gas'tri-əm/ n (pl amphigas'tria) a scale-like leaf on the ventral side of some liverworts. [amphi-, and Gr gastēr belly]

amphigory /am'fi-gə-ri/ n nonsense verse. [Fr amphigouri, of unknown origin]

amphimacer /am-fim'ə-sər/ (prosody) n a foot of three syllables, a short between two long. [Gr amphimakros, from amphi on both sides, and makros long]

amphimixis /am-fi-mik'sis/ n the fusion of gametes; sexual reproduction; combination of characteristics from both parents. [amphi- and Gr mīxis intercourse, mixing]
■ amphimic'tic adj.

Amphineura /am-fi-nū'rə/ n pl a class of molluscs with two ventral and two lateral nerve-cords, including the Chiton genus. [amphi-, and Gr neuron nerve]

amphioxus /am-fi-ok'səs/ n a lancelet of the genus Branchiostoma (formerly Amphioxus). [amphi-, and Gr oxys sharp]

amphipathic /am-fi-path'ik/ adj another word for amphiphilic. [amphi-, and Gr pathos feeling]

amphiphilic /am-fi-fil'ik/ (chem and phys) adj of an unsymmetrical molecular group of which one end is hydrophilic and the other end hydrophobic. [amphi-, and Gr philos loving]

amphipod /am'fi-pod/ n one of the Amphip'oda, an order of small sessile-eyed crustaceans with swimming feet and jumping feet, eg sandhoppers, etc. [amphi-, and Gr pous, podos a foot]
■ amphip'odous adj.

amphiprostyle /am-fip'rə-stīl/ adj (Gr archit) having a portico at either end but not at the sides. [amphi- and prostyle]

amphiprotic /am-fi-prō'tik/ (chem) adj having both protophilic (basic) and protogenic (acidic) properties. [amphi- and proto-]

amphisbaena /am-fis-bē'nə/ n (pl amphisbae'nae /-nē/ or amphisbae'nas) a fabulous two-headed snake; (with cap) a genus of snake-like lizards, chiefly tropical American, whose rounded tails give the appearance of a head at each end. [Gr amphisbaina, from amphis both ways, and bainein to go]
■ amphisbae'nic adj.

amphiscian /am-fish'i-ən/ n an inhabitant of the torrid zone, whose shadow is thrown both ways, ie northwards one part of the year, and southwards the other part (also adj). [Gr amphiskios, from amphi both ways, and skiā a shadow]

amphistomous /am-fis'tə-məs/ adj having a sucker at either end, as some worms. [Gr amphistomos with double mouth, from amphi on both sides, and stoma mouth]

amphitheatre /am'fi-thē-ə-tər/ n a building with rows of seats one above another, around an open space; a similar configuration of hill slopes; one of the galleries in a theatre. [Gr amphitheātron, from amphi on both sides, and theātron theatre]
■ amphithe'atral, amphitheat'ric or amphitheatrical /-at'ri-kl/ adj. amphitheat'rically adv.

amphitropous /am-fit'rə-pəs/ (bot) adj (of an ovule) bent into a V-shape and attached to its stalk near the middle of its concave side. [amphi- and tropos a turning]

Amphitryon /am-fit'ri-ən/ n in Greek mythology, the husband of Alcmene (Hercules being the son of Alcmene and Zeus disguised as Amphitryon); a hospitable entertainer, esp of doubtful identity (in allusion to the line in Molière's play, 'Le véritable Amphitryon est l'Amphitryon où l'on dîne'). [Gr Amphitryōn]

ampholyte /am'fə-līt/ n an amphoteric electrolyte.

amphora /am'fə-rə/ n (pl **am'phorae** /-rē or -rī/ or **am'phoras**) a two-handled jar used by the Greeks and Romans for holding liquids. [L amphora, from Gr amphoreus, amphiphoreus, from amphi on both sides, and phoreus a bearer]
■ **amphor'ic** /-for'/ adj (med) like the sound produced by blowing into a bottle.

amphoteric /am-fō-ter'ik or -fə-/ adj of both kinds; acting both ways, eg as acid and base, electropositive and electronegative. [Gr amphoteros both]

ampicillin /am-pi-sil'in/ n an antibiotic drug, a type of semi-synthetic penicillin. [amino and penicillin]

ample /am'pl/ adj spacious; wide; large enough; abundant; liberal; copious; full or rather bulky in form. [Fr ample, from L amplus]
■ **am'pleness** n. **amplia'tion** n enlarging; an enlargement. **am'pliative** adj (rare). **am'ply** /-pli/ adv.

amplexus /am-plek'səs/ n (pl **amplexus**) the clasping of the female of certain amphibians by the male as part of the mating process; the period of this. [L amplexus, amplexūs embrace or encircling]
■ **amplexicaul** /am-plek'si-köl/ adj (L caulis stem; bot) clasping the stem by a dilated base.

ampliation, etc see under **ample**.

amplify /am'pli-fī/ vt (**am'plifying**; **am'plified**) to make more copious in expression; to add to; to increase loudness of (sound), strength of (current), etc. ♦ vi to enlarge (on an utterance, etc). [Fr amplifier, from L amplificāre]
■ **amplifica'tion** n enlargement. **am'plifier** n someone who amplifies; a lens that enlarges the field of vision; a device for giving greater loudness.

amplitude /am'pli-tūd/ n largeness; abundance; width; range; extent of vibratory movement (from extreme to extreme, or from mean to extreme); the angular distance from the east point of the horizon at which a heavenly body rises, or from the west point at which it sets. [Fr amplitude, from L amplitūdō]
❏ **amplitude modulation** n (telecom) modulation in radio transmission by varying the amplitude of the carrier wave (cf **frequency modulation**).

amplosome /am'plə-sōm/ n the short or stocky type of human figure. [L amplus large, and Gr sōma body]

amply see under **ample**.

ampoule or (US) **ampule** /am'pūl, also -pool/ n a small sealed glass, etc container for a hypodermic dose, etc (also **am'pul** /-pūl/). [Fr; see **ampulla**]

AMPS abbrev : Advanced Mobile Phone Service; automated message-processing system.

ampulla /am-pūl'ə/ n (pl **ampull'ae** /-ē/) a small two-handled ancient Roman flask; a pilgrim's bottle; a vessel for holy oil, as at coronations; a cruet for the wine and water used at the altar; any small membranous vesicle (biol); the dilated end of a semicircular canal in the ear. See also **ampoule**. [L irregular dimin of amphora a flagon; partly directly from L, partly through OE ampulle, OFr ampo(u)le and Ital ampolla]
■ **ampullos'ity** n (Browning) turgidity or bombast.

ampussy-and see **ampersand**.

amputate /am'pū-tāt/ vt to cut off (eg a limb). [L amputāre, -ātum, from amb- around, and putāre, -ātum to lop]
■ **amputa'tion** n. **am'putātor** n. **amputee'** n.

AMR abbrev : automatic message routeing.

AMRAAM abbrev : advanced medium-range air-to-air missile.

amrit /am'rət/ n a sacred sweetened water used in the Sikh baptismal ceremony; the ceremony itself. [Punjabi, from Sans amṛta immortal]

amrita /am-rē'tə/ n the drink of the Hindu gods. [Sans amṛta immortal; cf Gr ambrotos]
■ **amritattva** /am-rē-tät'vä/ n immortality.

AMSL abbrev : above mean sea level.

amt abbrev : amount.

amtman /ämt'män/ or **amman** /am'an/ n in Germany, Switzerland, the Netherlands and Scandinavia, a district magistrate. [Ger Amtmann, Amman, Dan and Norw amtmand, from amt office or administration (from the same root as **ambassador**) and Ger Mann, Dan mand man]

amtrack /am'trak/ n an amphibious tracked military motor landing-vehicle. [am for amphibious, and **track**¹]

Amtrak /am'trak/ n a US corporation (the National Railroad Passenger Corporation) managing passenger rail-travel between major US cities. [American Travel and Track]

amu abbrev : atomic mass unit.

amuck see **amok**.

amulet /am'yū-lət or -lit/ n a charm worn to ward off evil, disease, etc; a medicine supposed to operate magically. [L amulētum]
■ **amulet'ic** adj.

amuse /ə-mūz'/ vt to occupy pleasantly; to entertain or divert; to provoke mirth in; to beguile with expectation; to occupy the attention of; to put in a muse (obs); to beguile (archaic). [Fr amuser, from à to, and muser to stare; see **muse**¹]
■ **amus'able** adj. **amused'** adj. **amus'edly** adv. **amuse'ment** n distraction of attention; a beguiling thing; idle wasting of time; a pleasant feeling of the ludicrous; something which amuses; a mechanical or other device for amusement at a fairground, amusement arcade, etc; recreation; pastime. **amus'er** n. **amusette** /am-ū-zet'/ n a light 18c field gun invented by Marshal Saxe of France. **amus'ing** adj mildly funny; diverting; entertaining. **amus'ingly** adv. **amus'ive** adj deceptive (obs); recreational (obs); interesting; entertaining; amusing. **amus'iveness** n.
❏ **amusement arcade** n a public hall, or open area off the street, with mechanical gambling machines, video games, etc. **amusement park** n a public park with fairground rides, sideshows, etc.

amuse-bouche or **amuse-gueule** /ə-mooz'boosh or -gül, or a-müz-boosh' or -gœl'/ (Fr) n (pl **amuse-bouche** or **amuse-bouches**, **amuse-gueule** or **amuse-gueules**) a small savoury item of food served as an appetizer. [Literally, amuse-mouth]

amygdal /ə-mig'dəl/ n (obs) an almond. [L amygdala, from Gr amygdalē almond]
■ **amyg'dala** n (pl **amyg'dalae** /-ē/) (zool) a lobe of the cerebellum; one of the palatal tonsils. **amygdalā'ceous** or **amyg'dalate** adj related to the almond. **amyg'dale** /-dāl/ n an amygdule. **amyg'dalin** n a poisonous glucoside found in cherry kernels, bitter almonds, etc, at one time thought useful in treating cancer in the drug Laetrile. **amyg'daloid** adj almond-shaped; having amygdules. ♦ n an igneous rock in which almond-shaped steam-cavities have been filled with minerals. **amygdaloid'al** adj having amygdules. **Amyg'dalus** n the almond genus, or section of Prunus. **amyg'dule** n a mineral-filled steam-cavity in a lava.

amyl /am'il/ n an alcohol radical, C_5H_{11}. [From the first syllable of Gr amylon starch, fine meal, and hȳlē matter, from having been first obtained from fusel-oil made from starch]
■ **am'ylase** /-ās/ n any of the enzymes that play a part in hydrolysis of starch and similar substances. **am'ylene** n a hydrocarbon of composition C_5H_{10}.
❏ **amyl alcohol** n $C_5H_{11}OH$, the fraction of fusel-oil that distils at about 131°C (also called **pentanol**). **amyl nitrate** n a liquid added to diesel fuel to improve its ignition quality; amyl nitrite (non-standard). **amyl nitrite** n a fruity-smelling, amber-coloured liquid, once used medicinally as a vasodilator, now inhaled as a recreational drug.

amylum /am'i-ləm/ (chem) n starch. [Gr amylon the finest flour, starch; literally, unmilled, from a- (privative), and mylē a mill]
■ **amylā'ceous** adj. **am'yloid** adj. ♦ n in any of several pathological conditions, an intercellular deposit of starch-like material in the tissues. **amyloid'al** adj. **amyloidō'sis** n the condition of the body in which amyloid is deposited in the tissues. **amylopec'tin** n the major component of starch (about 80 per cent), consisting of branched polysaccharide chains. **amylop'sin** n an enzyme in pancreatic juice that converts starch into sugar. **am'ylose** n the minor component of starch (about 20 per cent), consisting of long unbranched polysaccharide chains.

amyotrophy /a-mi-ot'rə-fi/ n atrophy of the muscles. [Gr a- (privative), mys muscle, and trophē nourishment]
■ **amyotroph'ic** adj.
❏ **amyotrophic lateral sclerosis** n the most common form of motor neurone disease (abbrev **ALS**).

Amytal® /am'i-təl/ n a proprietary name for **amobarbital**.

AN abbrev : Anglo-Norman; Angola (IVR).

an¹ /an or ən/ adj one; the indefinite article, used before a vowel sound, and by some (now rarely) before an unstressed syllable beginning with a sounded h. [OE ān; see **one**]

an² /an or ən/ (archaic) conj if. [A form of **and**¹]
■ **an'** n and.

an³ /an or ən/ (obs) prep a form of **on**.

an symbol : actinon.

an. abbrev : anno (L), in the year; anonymous; ante (L), before.

an- see **a-²**.

-an see **-ian**.

ana /ä'nə or a'nə/ written a̅a̅ or a̅ (in recipes and prescriptions) in equal quantities. [LL, from Gr, (literally) throughout]

-ana /-ä-nə or -ā-nə/ or **-iana** /-i-ä-nə or -ā-nə/ sfx denoting things belonging to or typical of (a specified person), such as sayings,

anecdotes, small objects, etc, eg *Johnsoniana* or *Victoriana* (the latter generally used in reference to the time of Queen Victoria rather than to Victoria herself). [L neuter pl ending of adjs in -*anus*]
■ **a'na** *n pl* (or *collective sing* with *pl* **a'na's** or **a'nas**) a collection of someone's table talk or of gossip, literary anecdotes or possessions.

anabaptist /a-nə-bap'tist/ *n* a name given by opponents to a person who holds that baptism should be of adults only and therefore that those baptized in infancy must be baptized again; (with *cap*) one of a Protestant sect of German origin (1521) rejecting infant baptism and seeking establishment of a Christian communism. ◆ *adj* of the anabaptists. [Gr *ana-* again, and *baptizein* to dip]
■ **anabapt'ism** *n.* **anabaptist'ic** *adj.* **anabaptize'** or **-ise'** *vt* to baptize again; to rename.

anabas /an'ə-bas/ *n* a fish of the genus *Anabas*, including the climbing perch, an East Indian fish that often leaves the water. [Gr *anabās*, aorist participle of *anabainein* to climb, from *ana* up, and *bainein* to go]

anabasis /a-na'bə-sis/ *n* a going up, ascent; a military advance up-country, such as that of Cyrus the younger (401BC) described (with the subsequent katabasis or retreat of the 10000) by Xenophon in his *Anabasis*. [Gr, from *ana* up, and *basis* going]
■ **anabatic** /-bat'ik/ *adj* upward-moving.

anabiosis /an-ə-bī-ō'sis/ *n* returning to life after apparent death; the ability to do this; a state of suspended animation. [Gr *anabiōsis*, from *ana* up or back, and *bios* life]
■ **anabiot'ic** *adj.*

anableps /an'ə-bleps/ *n* a fish of the genus *Anableps* of bony fishes with open air-bladders and projecting eyes divided in two for vision in air and water. [Gr *ana* up, and *blepein* to look]

anabolism /ə-nab'ə-li-zm/ *n* chemical synthesis of complex substances in living matter, *opp* to *catabolism*. [Gr *anabolē* a heaping up, from *ana* up, and *bolē* a throw]
■ **anabolic** /an-ə-bol'ik/ *adj.* **anab'olite** *n* a product of anabolism. **anabolit'ic** *adj.*
❑ **anabolic steroids** *n pl* steroids used to increase the build-up of body tissue, *esp* muscle, illegally used by some athletes.

anabranch /an'ə-bränch/ (*esp Aust*) *n* a stream that leaves a river and re-enters lower down. [For *anastomosing branch*]

anacardium /a-nə-kär'di-əm/ *n* a plant of the cashew-nut genus *Anacardium*, giving name to a family **Anacardiā'ceae** related to the hollies and maples. [Gr *ana* according to, and *kardiā* heart (from the shape of the fruit)]
■ **anacardiā'ceous** *adj.*

anacatharsis /a-nə-kə-thär'sis/ *n* vomiting. [Gr *anakatharsis* clearing up, from *ana* up, throughout, and *katharsis* (see **catharsis**)]
■ **anacathar'tic** *n* and *adj.*

anacharis /ə-nak'ə-ris/ *n* a plant of the genus *Anacharis* of water plants including *Anacharis helodea* or *Elodea canadensis*, a N American weed found in Britain in 1842, soon clogging canals and rivers by vegetative growth. [Gr *ana* up, and *charis* grace]

anachronism /ə-nak'rə-ni-zm/ *n* an error assigning a thing to an earlier or (less strictly) to a later age than it belongs to; anything out of keeping with chronology. [Gr *ana-* backwards, and *chronos* time]
■ **anachron'ic** *adj.* **anachron'ically** *adv.* **anachronist'ic** *adj.* **anachronist'ically** *adv.* **anach'ronous** *adj.* **anach'ronously** *adv.*

anaclastic /an-ə-klas'tik/ *adj* refractive. [Gr *anaklastos* bent back, from *ana-* back, and *klaein* to break]

anaclitic /a-nə-klit'ik/ (*psychiatry*) *adj* characterized by strong emotional dependence on others. [Gr *anaklitos* leaning back, from *ana* back, and *klinein* to lean]

anacoluthia /a-nə-kə-loo'thi-ə or -lū-/ *n* a non-sequential syntactic construction in which the latter part of a sentence does not grammatically fit the earlier. [Gr *anakolouthiā*, *anakolouthon*, from *an-* (privative), and *akolouthos* following]
■ **anacolu'thic** *adj.* **anacolu'thon** *n* (*pl* **anacolu'tha**) an instance of anacoluthia; anacoluthia.

anaconda /a-nə-kon'də/ *n* a gigantic S American snake, a water boa, *Eunectes murinus*. [Perhaps from a Sinhalese name for another snake in Sri Lanka]

anacoustic zone /a-nə-koo'stik zōn/ *n* a zone of absolute silence in space. [**an-** and **acoustic**]

Anacreontic /ə-nak-ri-on'tik/ *adj* after the manner of the Greek poet Anacreon, free, convivial or erotic. ◆ *n* a poem in this vein. [From the Gr poet *Anakreōn* (fl 6c BC)]
■ **anacreont'ically** *adv.*

anacrusis /a-nə-kroo'sis/ *n* (*pl* **anacru'ses** /-sēz/) one or more short syllables introductory to the normal rhythm of a line (*prosody*); one or more unstressed notes immediately preceding the first bar line (*music*).

[Gr *anakrousis* a pushing back, striking up a tune, from *ana* up, back, and *krouein* to strike]
■ **anacrustic** /-krus'tik/ *adj.*

anadem /an'ə-dem/ *n* a fillet, chaplet, or wreath. [Gr *anadēma*, from *ana* up, and *deein* to bind]

anadiplosis /an-ə-di-plō'sis/ *n* rhetorical repetition of an important word (or sometimes phrase). [Gr *anadiplōsis*, from *ana* back, and *diploein* to double]

anadromous /ə-nad'rə-məs/ *adj* of fish, ascending rivers periodically to spawn, *opp* to *catadromous*. [Gr *anadromos* running up, from *ana* up, and *dromos* a run]

anadyomene /a-nə-dī-om'ə-nē/ *adj* coming up or emerging (*esp* of Aphrodite from the sea). [Gr *anadyomenē*]

anaemia or (*US*) **anemia** /ə-nē'mi-ə/ *n* bloodlessness; lack of red blood corpuscles or of haemoglobin, a condition marked by paleness and weakness. [Gr *anaimiā*, from *an-* (privative), and *haima* blood]
■ **anae'mic** *adj* suffering from anaemia; sickly, spiritless, washed-out, lacking in body (*fig*). **anae'mically** *adv.*
■ **pernicious anaemia** a severe form of anaemia characterized by abnormalities in the red blood corpuscles, etc.

anaerobe /an'ā(-ə)-rōb or an'ə-rōb/ *n* an organism that lives in absence of free oxygen (also **anaero'biont**). [Gr *an-* (privative), *āēr* air, and *bios* life]
■ **anaerobic** /-ob'ik or -ōb'ik/ or **anaerobiotic** /-ō-bī-ot'ik/ *adj* living in the absence of free oxygen; (of a process, etc) requiring the absence, or not requiring the presence, of free oxygen; effected by anaerobes, as a biochemical change; involving the activity of anaerobes. **anaerob'ically** or **anaerobiot'ically** *adv.* **anaerobio'sis** *n* life in the absence of oxygen.

anaesthesia or (*US*) **anesthesia** /a-nəs-thē'zi-ə or -zh(i-)ə/, also **anaesthesis** /-sis/ *n* loss of feeling; insensibility, general or local. [Gr *anaisthēsiā* insensibility, *anaisthētos* insensible, from *an-* (privative), and *aisthanesthai* to perceive]
■ **anaesthesiol'ogist** (*usu* **anesthesiol'ogist**) *n.* **anaesthesiol'ogy** (*usu* **anesthesiol'ogy**) *n* (*N Am*) the science of administering anaesthetics. **anaesthetic** /-thet'ik or -thēt'ik/ *adj* producing or connected with insensibility. ◆ *n* an anaesthetic drug or agent. **anaesthet'ically** *adv.* **anaesthet'ics** *n sing* the science of anaesthesia. **anaesthetist** /-ēs'thə-tist or -es'/ *n* a person who administers anaesthetics. **anaesthetizā'tion** or **-s-** *n.* **anaes'thetize** or **-ise** *vt.*
■ **general anaesthetic** one which produces insensibility in the whole body, *usu* causing unconsciousness. **local anaesthetic** one producing insensibility in only the relevant part of the body.

anaglyph /an'ə-glif/ *n* an ornament in low relief; a picture composed of two prints, in complementary colours, seen stereoscopically through spectacles of these colours. [Gr *anaglyphos*, *anaglyptos* in low relief, from *ana* up or back, and *glyphein* to engrave, carve]
■ **anaglyph'ic** *adj.* **Anaglypta®** /an-ə-glip'tə/ *n* a type of plain white wallpaper that has a heavily embossed pattern (also *adj*). **anaglyp'tic** *adj.*

anagnorisis /a-nag-nor'i-sis or -nō'ri-/ (*literary*) *n* (*pl* **anagnō'rises** /-sēz/) recognition leading to dénouement. [Gr *anagnōrisis*]

anagoge or **anagogy** /a-nə-gō'ji/ *n* mystical interpretation. [Gr *anagōgē* leading up, elevation, from *ana* up, and *agein* to lead]
■ **anagogic** /-goj'ik/ *adj* relating to mystical interpretation; of the strivings in the unconscious towards morally high ideals. **anagog'ical** *adj.* **anagog'ically** *adv.*

anagram /an'ə-gram/ *n* a word or phrase formed by the letters of another in different order. ◆ *vt* and *vi* to anagrammatize. [Gr *ana* back, and *gramma* letter]
■ **anagrammat'ic** or **anagrammat'ical** *adj.* **anagrammat'ically** *adv.* **anagram'atism** *n* the practice of constructing anagrams. **anagramm'atist** *n* a maker of anagrams. **anagramm'atize** or **-ise** *vt* and *vi* to transpose so as to form an anagram.

anal, **anally** see under **anus**.

anal. *abbrev*: analogous; analogy; analysis; analytic or analytical.

analcime /a-nal'sīm/ or **analcite** /a-nal'sīt/ *n* a cubic zeolite, a hydrated sodium aluminium silicate. [Gr *an-* (privative), and *alkimos*, *alkis* strong, because weakly electrified by friction]

analects /an'ə-lekts/ or **analecta** /a-nə-lek'tə/ *n pl* collected literary fragments. [Gr (*pl*) *analekta*, from *ana* up, and *legein* to gather]
■ **analec'tic** *adj.*

analemma /a-nə-lem'ə/ *n* a scale showing the daily declination of the sun, in the shape of a figure 8; (loosely) a sundial. [Gr, (the pedestal of) a sundial, from *ana* up, and *lambanein* to take]
■ **analemmat'ic** *adj* relating to the seasonal difference between time as shown by clocks and by the sun.

analeptic /a-nə-lep'tik/ adj restoring vigour; restoring to consciousness, esp after anaesthesia; comforting. ◆ n a restorative medicine. [Gr analēptikos restorative, from ana up, and lambanein to take]

analgesia /an-al-jē'zi-ə/ n painlessness; insensibility to pain. [Gr analgēsiā, from an- (privative), and algeein to feel pain]
■ **analgesic** /-jē'sik/ n an anodyne. ◆ adj producing analgesia.

analogue or (US) **analog** /an'ə-log/ n that which is analogous to something else, eg protein substances prepared to resemble meat; that which has a similar function (distinguished from a homologue) (biol); a variable physical quantity which is similar to some other variable in that variations in the former are in the same proportional relationship as variations in the latter, often being used to record or represent such changes (also adj); a device which measures continuously varying quantities, eg temperature and time; a watch with the traditional face and hands, opp to digital (also adj). [Gr analogon, from analogos proportionate]
❑ **analogue computer** n a type of computer in which continuously varying electrical currents or voltages, etc are used to represent proportionally other quantities (eg forces or speeds) in working out problems about these qualities. **analogue transmission** n (telecom) the transmission of signals and messages by means of radio waves, without first converting them to a computerized form as in digital transmission.
▥ **analogue-to-digital** (**A/D**) **converter** (comput) an integrated circuit which enables a digital computer to accept data from an analogue device (also called **digitizer**).

analogy /ə-nal'ə-ji/ n an agreement or correspondence in certain respects between things otherwise different; a resemblance of relations; parallelism; relation in general; a likeness; proportion, or the equality of ratios (maths); likeness in function but not in evolutionary origin, as distinguished from homology (biol); a resemblance by virtue of which a word may be altered on the model of another class of words, as strove, striven, remodelled upon drove, driven, throve, thriven, etc (philology). [Gr analogiā, from ana according to, and logos ratio]
■ **analogic** /an-ə-loj'ik/ (rare) or **analog'ical** adj. **analog'ically** adv. **anal'ogist** n someone who sees, follows, or uses analogies. **anal'ogize** or **-ise** vt to explain or consider by analogy. **anal'ogon** /-gon/ n (Gr) analogue. **anal'ogous** /-gəs/ adj having analogy; bearing some correspondence or resemblance; similar in certain circumstances or relations (with to); (of organs) similar in function but different in evolutionary origin (biol). **anal'ogously** adv. **anal'ogousness** n.

analphabet /an-al'fə-bet/ or **analphabete** /-bēt/ adj ignorant of the alphabet (also n). [Gr analphabētos, from an- (privative); see **alphabet**]
■ **analphabet'ic** adj totally illiterate; not alphabetic.

analysand see under **analysis**.

analyse or (N Am) **analyze** /an'ə-līz/ vt to resolve or separate a thing into its elements or component parts; to ascertain those parts; to trace a thing or things to the source or cause; to discover the general principles underlying individual phenomena by doing this; to resolve a sentence into its syntactic elements (grammar); to psychoanalyse. [Gr analȳein to unloose, from ana up, and lȳein to loose]
■ **an'alysable** or (N Am) **-z-** adj. **an'alyser** or (N Am) **-z-** n a person who analyses; in a polariscope the nicol (or substitute) through which the polarized light passes; a device that analyses.

analysis /ə-nal'ə-sis or -i-sis/ n (pl **anal'yses** /-sēz/) the action or process of analysing; a table or statement of the results of analysis; the examination of market research data and information (commerce); analytical chemistry; formerly, proof by assuming the result and reasoning back to principles, opp to synthesis (maths); use of algebraical methods; psychoanalysis. [Gr analysis, from analȳein to unloose, from ana up, and lȳein to loose]
■ **analysand** /ə-nal'i-zand/ n a person undergoing psychoanalysis. **an'alyst** /-list/ n someone skilled in or practising analysis, esp chemical or economic; a psychoanalyst.
❑ **analysis situs** /sīt'əs/ n (maths) older name for topology (maths meanings).
▥ **in the final** (or **last**) **analysis** when all inessentials are excluded from the problem or the situation.

analytic /a-nə-lit'ik/ adj relating to, performing, or inclined to analysis; resolving into first principles. ◆ n (often pl in form) analytical logic; analytical geometry. [analyse]
■ **analyt'ical** adj. **analyt'ically** adv. **analytic'ity** n.
❑ **analytical chemistry** n (loosely, **analysis**) chemistry concerned with determination of the constituents of chemical compounds, or mixtures of compounds. **analytical engine** n a data-processing machine invented by British mathematician Charles Babbage in 1833, the precursor of the modern computer. **analytical geometry** n co-ordinate geometry. **analytical languages** n pl those that use separate words instead of inflections. **analytical logic** n logic which is concerned with analysis. **analytical philosophy** n a school of philosophy of the first half of the 20c, which sought to resolve philosophical problems through analysis of language, esp in terms of formal logic.

anamnesis /a-nam-nē'sis/ n (pl **anamnē'ses** /-sēz/) the recalling to memory of things past; the recollection of the Platonic pre-existence; a patient's account of his or her medical history. [Gr anamnēsis, from ana up, back, and mimnēskein to remind, recall to memory]
■ **anamnes'tic** adj. **anamnes'tically** adv.

anamorphosis /a-nə-mör'fə-sis or -fō'/ n (pl **anamorphoses** /-fə-sēz or -fō'sēz/) a deformed figure appearing in proportion when rightly viewed, eg in a curved mirror, or in a particular direction. [Gr anamorphōsis a forming anew, from ana back or anew, and morphōsis a shaping, from morphē shape, form]
■ **anamor'phic** or **anamor'phous** adj.
❑ **anamorphic lens** n a device in a film projector for converting standard 35mm film images into widescreen format.

anan /ə-nan'/ (obs or dialect) interj expressing failure to understand. [**anon**]

ananas /ə-nä'nəs or -nä-/ n (also **an'ana**) the pineapple (Ananas sativus); the pinguin (Bromelia pinguin), or its fruit. [From a Native American language]

anandamide /ə-nan'də-mīd/ n a neurotransmitter that is released naturally from neurons and is thought to be associated with the pleasurable effect of certain drugs. [Sans ananda bliss, and **amide**]

anandrous /a-nan'drəs/ (bot) adj without stamens. [Gr anandros lacking men, from an- (privative), and anēr, andros a man]

Ananias /a-nə-nī'əs/ n a liar. [From the story in Bible, Acts 5.1–5]

ananke /a-nang'kē/ n necessity. [Gr anankē]

ananthous /a-nan'thəs/ (bot) adj without flowers. [Gr ananthēs, from an- (privative), and anthos a flower]

anapaest or (N Am) **anapest** /an'ə-pēst or (N Am) an'ə-pest/ (prosody) n a foot of two short (or unstressed) syllables followed by a long (or stressed) syllable, a dactyl reversed. [Gr anapaistos struck back, from ana back, and paiein to strike]
■ **anapaes'tic** or **anapaes'tical** adj.

anaphase /an'ə-fāz/ (biol) n the stage of mitosis at which the daughter chromosomes move towards the poles of the spindle. [Gr ana up, back, and **phase**]

anaphora /ə-naf'ə-rə/ n the rhetorical device of beginning successive sentences, lines, etc with the same word or phrase; the use of a word (such as it or do) to avoid repetition of a preceding word or group of words; the offering of the Eucharistic elements. [Gr anaphorā a carrying back or reference, from ana back, and pherein to bear]
■ **an'aphor** n a word used to begin successive sentences, lines, etc. **anaphoric** /an-ə-for'ik/ or **anaphor'ical** adj referring to a preceding word or group of words. **anaphor'ically** adv.

anaphrodisiac /an-af-rō-diz'i-ak/ adj tending to diminish sexual desire. ◆ n an anaphrodisiac agent. [Gr an- (privative), and aphrodīsiakos sexual]

anaphylaxis /an-ə-fi-lak'sis/ n an increased susceptibility to injected foreign material, protein or non-protein, brought about by a previous introduction of it (also **anaphylax'y**). [Gr ana back, and phylaxis protection]
■ **anaphylac'tic** or **anaphylac'toid** adj having a resemblance to anaphylaxis.
❑ **anaphylactic shock** n a sudden and very severe instance of anaphylaxis.

anaplasty /an'ə-plä-sti/ n the repairing of superficial lesions by the use of adjacent healthy tissue, as by transplanting a portion of skin. [Gr ana again, and plassein to form]
■ **anaplas'tic** adj.

anaplerosis /an-ə-pli-rō'sis/ n the filling up of a deficiency. [Gr anaplērōsis, from ana up, and plēroein to fill]
■ **anaplerot'ic** adj.

anaptyxis /a-nəp-tik'sis/ (phonetics) n the development of a vowel between consonants. [Gr anaptyxis gape, from ana back, and ptyssein to fold]
■ **anaptyc'tic** adj.

anarcho- /ə-när-kō-/ combining form denoting an anarchic style or philosophy, as in anarcho-punk. [**anarchy**]
■ **anarch'o-syn'dicalism** n syndicalism. **anarch'o-syn'dicalist** n and adj.

anarchy /an'ər-ki/ n complete absence of law or government; a harmonious condition of society in which government is abolished as unnecessary; utter lawlessness; chaos; complete disorder. [Gr anarchiā leaderlessness, lawlessness, from an- (privative), and archē government]

■ **anarch** /an'ärk/ *n* (*archaic*) an author, promoter or personification of lawlessness. **anarchal** /an-ärk'l/ *adj* (*rare*). **anarch'ial** *adj* (*rare*). **anarch'ic** or **anarch'ical** *adj*. **anarch'ically** *adv*. **an'archism** *n* the principles or practice of the anarchists. **an'archist** *n* a person whose ideal of society is one without government of any kind; a person who seeks to bring about such a condition by terrorism; a person who causes disorder and upheaval. ◆ *adj* promoting anarchy. **anarchist'ic** *adj*. **anarchist'ically** *adv*. **anarchize** or **-ise** /an'ər-kīz/ *vt* to make anarchic.

anarthrous /an-är'thrəs/ *adj* used without the article (of Greek nouns); without distinct joints (*biol*). [Gr *an-* (privative), and *arthron* a joint or article]

■ **anar'thrously** *adv*. **anar'throusness** *n*.

anasarca /a-nə-sär'kə/ *n* diffused dropsy in the skin and subcutaneous tissue. [Gr phrase *ana sarka* throughout the flesh]

anastasis /a-nas'tə-sis/ *n* in Byzantine art, the Harrowing of Hell; convalescence; resurrection. [Gr *anastasis* rising or raising up or again, from *ana* up, again, and *stasis* a setting or standing]

■ **anastatic** /an-ə-stat'ik/ *adj* of anastasis; with characters raised in relief.

anastigmat /an-ə-stig'-mat or ən-as'tig-mat/ *n* a lens specially designed to avoid the focusing defect of astigmatism. [Gr *an-* (privative), and **astigmatic**]

■ **anastigmat'ic** /an-ə-/ *adj* free from astigmatism. **anastig'matism** *n*.

anastomosis /ə-nas-tə-mō'sis/ *n* (*pl* **anastomō'ses** /-sēz/) communication by cross-connections to form a network. [Gr *anastomōsis* outlet, from *ana* back, and *stoma* mouth]

■ **anas'tomose** *vi* to intercommunicate in such a way. **anastomot'ic** *adj*.

anastrophe /ə-nas'trə-fi/ (*rhetoric*) *n* inversion. [Gr *anastrophē*, from *ana* back, and *strephein* to turn]

anastrozole /ə-nas'trə-zōl/ *n* a drug that inhibits the production of oestrogen, used *esp* in the treatment of advanced breast cancer.

anat. *abbrev* : anatomic; anatomy.

anatase /an'ə-tās/ *n* a mineral consisting of titanium oxide. [Gr *anatasis* a stretching, from its long crystals]

anathema /a- or ə-nath'i-mə or -na-thē-mə/ *n* (*pl* **anath'emas**) an object of abhorrence; a solemn ecclesiastical curse or denunciation involving excommunication; a curse or execration; a person or thing cursed ecclesiastically or generally. [Gr *anathema* a thing dedicated or accursed, for *anathēma* a votive offering, from *ana* up, and the root of *tithenai* to place]

■ **anathematical** /-mat'i-kl/ *adj*. **anathematization** or **-s-** /-mə-tī-zā'shən/ *n*. **anath'ematize** or **-ise** *vt* and *vi*.

■ **anathema maranatha** /ma-rə-na'thə/ (Aramaic *māranāthā*, come, Lord) words happening to occur together in Bible, 1 Corinthians 16.22, wrongly understood as an intensified curse.

Anatolian /a-nə-tō'li-ən/ *adj* of Anatolia, now the major part of Turkey; of or denoting any or all of an extinct family of languages belonging to or closely related to the Indo-European family. ◆ *n* a native or inhabitant of Anatolia; the Anatolian family of languages.

anatomy /ə-nat'ə-mi/ *n* the science of the physical structure of an animal or plant learned by dissection; the art of dissecting any organized body; a subject for dissection (*obs*); a skeleton, a shrivelled and shrunken body, alive or dead, or mummy (*archaic*); physical frame or structure; the human body (*inf*); dissection; analysis (*fig*). [Gr *anatomē* dissection, from *ana* up, and *tomē* a cutting]

■ **anatomic** /an-ə-tom'ik/ or **anatom'ical** *adj*. **anatom'ically** *adv*. **anat'omist** *n* a person skilled in anatomy. **anat'omize** or **-ise** *vt* to dissect; to lay open minutely (*fig*).

anatropous /a- or ə-nat'rə-pəs/ (*bot*) *adj* of an ovule, inverted so that the micropyle is next to the stalk. [Gr *ana* back, up, and *tropē* a turning]

■ **anat'ropy** *n*.

anatta, **anatto** see **annatto**.

a natura rei /ä na-tū'rə rē'ī or na-too'rä rā'ē/ (*L*) from the nature of the case.

anax andron /a'naks an'drōn/ (*Gr*) *n* lord of men (*esp* applied to Agamemnon).

anaxial /an-ak'si-əl/ (*zool*) *adj* asymmetrical. [**a-²**]

anbury /an'bə-ri/ *n* a soft bloody wart on horses, etc (also **angleberry** /ang'gl-bər-i/); a disease in turnips, cabbages, etc, due to a slime-fungus. [Perh for *angberry*, from OE *ange* narrow, painful, and **berry¹**]

ANC *abbrev* : African National Congress.

ance /äns/ Scot and N Eng form of **once**.

-ance /-əns/ *sfx* forming nouns denoting an action, condition, or quality, as in *surveillance*, *protuberance*, *repugnance*.

ance-errand see under **errand**.

ancestor /an'se-stər/ *n* (also *fem* **an'cestress**) someone from whom a person is descended, a forefather; a plant or animal from which another type has evolved; a person or thing regarded as the forerunner of another. [OFr *ancestre*, from L *antecēssor*, from *ante* before, and *cēdere*, *cēssum* to go]

■ **ancestorial** /-ses-tō'ri-əl/ *adj*. **ances'tral** *adj* of or relating to ancestors; inherited or derived from ancestors. **ances'trally** *adv*. **an'cestry** *n* a line of ancestors; lineage.

□ **an'cestor-worship** *n*.

ancho /än'chō/ *n* a type of dried chilli pepper, used in Mexican cookery. [Sp, wide]

anchor /ang'kər/ *n* an implement for mooring a ship by holding it to the bottom, for holding a balloon to the ground, or for any similar purpose; anything that gives stability or security (*fig*); (in *pl*) the brakes of a vehicle (*inf*); a short form of **anchor man**. ◆ *vt* to fix by an anchor; to fasten; to act as anchor man in (an activity). ◆ *vi* to cast anchor; to stop or rest. [OE *ancor*, from L *ancora*; cf Gr *ankȳra*, from *ankos* a bend; connected with **angle¹**]

■ **anch'orage** *n* the act of anchoring; a place of or for anchoring; a set of anchors (*Shakesp*); rest or support to the mind (*fig*); duty imposed for anchoring. **anch'orless** *adj*.

□ **Anchor Boys** *n pl* the most junior section of the Boys' Brigade. **anchor buoy** *n* a buoy indicating the position of an anchor. **anchor escapement** or **recoil escapement** *n* a clock escapement in which the pallets push the escape wheel slightly backwards at the end of each swing, causing a recoil of the pendulum. **anch'or-hold** *n* the hold of an anchor upon the ground; security (*fig*). **anch'or-ice** *n* ground ice. **anchor leg** *n* the last stage of a relay race. **anchor man** or **anchor** *n* the man at the back of a team in a tug-of-war; the man who runs the last stage of a relay race; (also **anch'or-man**) a person on whom the success of an activity depends, *esp*, on television, the person responsible for smooth running of a dialogue or discussion between or among others. **anchor plate** *n* a heavy, *usu* steel, plate set into the ground or foundations to which bracing for a structure is fixed. **anch'or-ring** *n* a solid generated by the revolution of a circle about an axis in its plane but not cutting it and not passing through its centre. **anch'or-stock** *n* the crossbar of an anchor, which causes one or other of the flukes to turn to the bottom. **anchor string** *n* (*mining*) a length of casing run into the top of wells and often cemented in to prevent a blow-out.

■ **at anchor** anchored. **cast anchor** to let down the anchor. **ride at anchor** to be anchored. **weigh anchor** to take up the anchor.

anchorite /ang'kə-rīt/, **anchoret** /-ret/ or (*Shakesp*) **anchor** /ang'kər/ *n* a man or woman who has withdrawn from the world, *esp* for religious reasons; a recluse. [Gr *anachōrētēs*, from *ana* apart, and *chōreein* to withdraw]

■ **anch'orage** *n* a recluse's cell. **anch'oress** or **anc'ress** *n* a female anchorite. **anchorit'ic**, **anchorit'ical**, **anchoret'ic** or **anchoret'ical** *adj*.

anchovy /an'chō-vi, -chə- or an-chō'vi/ *n* a small edible Mediterranean fish (*Engraulis encrasicholus*) of the herring family, often used for pickling, and making sauce, paste, etc. [Sp and Port *anchova*; of doubtful etymology]

■ **anchoveta** /-vet'ə/ *n* (*Am Sp*) a small Pacific anchovy, used for bait. □ **an'chovy-pear** *n* the fruit of a West Indian lecythidaceous tree (*Grias cauliflora*), often pickled.

anchusa /an-kū'sə or an-choo'sə/ *n* any Eurasian plant of the boraginaceous genus *Anchusa*, having rough, hairy stems and leaves and bright blue flowers.

anchylosis, etc see **ankylosis**, etc.

ancienne noblesse /ã-syen nob-les'/ (*Fr*) the old nobility; the nobility of the ancien régime.

ancien régime /ã-syẽ rā-zhēm'/ (*Fr*) the old order (*esp* before the French Revolution).

ancient¹ /ān'shənt or sometimes -chənt/ *adj* very old; of former times; of long standing; belonging or relating to times long past, *esp* before the downfall of the Western Roman Empire (476AD). ◆ *n* an aged man; an elder or senior; someone who lived in ancient times, *usu* in *pl* and applied *esp* to the Greeks and Romans. [Fr *ancien*, from LL *antiānus* former, old, from L *ante* before]

■ **an'ciently** *adv*. **an'cientness** *n*. **an'cientry** *n* (*archaic*) antiquity; seniority; ancestry; dignity of birth; old people (*Shakesp*).

□ **ancient Greek** *n* the Greek language until the death of Alexander the Great. **ancient history** *n* the history of Ancient Greece and Rome; information, news or gossip which, contrary to the expectations of the teller, one is already well aware of (*inf*, *fig*); something no longer of importance. **ancient lights** *n* the legal right to receive in perpetuity, by certain windows, a reasonable amount of daylight. **ancient monument** *n* an old and historic building, etc scheduled for preservation, *esp* if in the care of the government.

■ **the Ancient of days** (*Bible*) the Almighty, God.

---

ancient² /ān'shənt/ (obs) n a flag; a standard-bearer; an ensign. [See **ensign**]

ancile /an-sī'lē or an-kē'lā/ (L) n in ancient Rome, the shield believed to have fallen from heaven in the reign of Numa Pompilius, on the safety of which the prosperity of Rome depended.

ancillary /an-sil'ə-ri or an'si-lə-ri/ adj auxiliary; supplementary; subsidiary; subordinate; (of computer equipment) additional in any way, not a necessary part of the computing process; subserving; ministering. ◆ n an ancillary thing. [L ancilla a maid-servant]

ancipitous /an-sip'i-təs/ or **ancipital** /an-sip'i-təl/ (bot) adj two-edged and flattened. [L anceps, -cipitis two-edged or double, from ambi- on both sides, and caput, capitis head]

ancle an archaic spelling of **ankle**.

ancome /an'kəm/ (obs or dialect) n a sudden inflammation; a whitlow. [Cf **oncome** and **income**]

ancon /ang'kon/ n (pl **ancones** /-kō'nēz/) the elbow; a console to support a door cornice; a breed of sheep with very short legs. [Latinized from Gr ankōn a bend or elbow]

Ancona /ang-kō'nə/ n a breed of laying poultry with speckled plumage. [Ancona in Italy]

ancora /ang-kō'rä or -kō'/ adv encore. [Ital]

ancress see under **anchorite**.

AND /and/ (comput) n a logic circuit that has two or more inputs and one output, the output signal being 1 if all its inputs are 1, and 0 if any of its inputs is 0. [**and¹**]

AND abbrev : Andorra (IVR).

and¹ /and, ənd, ən or n/ conj indicating addition; also; also of another kind; used to introduce a consequence or aim; used to introduce a question expressive of surprise, realization, wonder, incredulity, etc; used to join identical words to indicate repetition, progression or continuity; used after some verbs to indicate intent (inf); sometimes appar meaningless ('When that I was and a little tiny boy'); as a conditional conjunction (from ME times only; often in Shakesp; now archaic; also **an, an if**) if; even if, although; as if. [OE and, ond; cf Ger und, and L ante before, Gr anti against]
■ **and all** not without. **and how!** see under **how¹**. **and/or** either or both. **and then some** (inf) and even more. **but and** see under **but¹**.

and² /and/ n the symbol ampersand; a use of the word 'and'; something added.

and³ /ən/ (dialect and Shakesp) conj than. [Perh ON an, en, enn than]

Andalusian /an-də-loo'z(h)i-ən or -s(h)i-ən/ n a native of Andalusia (Sp Andalucía), in Spain (also adj); a breed of laying poultry with blue plumage.
■ **andalu'site** /-sīt/ n a silicate of aluminium, first found in Andalusia.

andante /an-dan'tā/ (music) adv and adj moving with moderately slow, even expression. ◆ n a movement or piece to be played in andante time. [Ital, prp of andare to go]
■ **andantino** /an-dan-tē'nō/ adj, adv and n (pl **andanti'nos**) (a movement, etc) somewhat slower than andante; now more usu intended for somewhat quicker.

Andean /an-dē'ən/ or **Andine** /an'dīn/ adj of or like the Andes Mountains.
■ **andesine** /an'diz-ēn or -in/ n (mineralogy) a feldspar intermediate between albite and anorthite. **an'desite** n a volcanic rock with plagioclase and some ferromagnesian mineral as phenocrysts in a microlithic groundmass (both found in the Andes). **andesitic** /-it'ik/ adj.

Anderson shelter /and'ər-sən shel'tər/ n a small air-raid shelter consisting of an arch of corrugated iron, built partially underground, used in Britain during World War II (also **And'erson**). [Sir John Anderson, Home Secretary 1939–40]

andesine, andesite see under **Andean**.

andiron /an'dī-ərn or -ī'/ n an iron bar to support the end of a log in a fire, a firedog. [OFr andier (Fr landier = l'andier); perh from a Gaulish word for a bullock, because early examples were decorated with animal heads; form influenced by early confusion with **iron**]

Andorran /an-dö'rən/ adj of or relating to the Principality of Andorra in the Pyrenees, or its inhabitants. ◆ n a native or citizen of Andorra.

andouillette /ã-doo-yet'/ n a small chitterling sausage. [Fr]

andradite /an'drə-dīt/ n a yellowish, green or brownish-black garnet, a silicate of calcium and iron, used as a gemstone. [JB d'Andrada e Silva (1763–1838), Brazilian mineralogist]

Andrew Ferrara /an'droo fi-rä'rä/ n a make of sword-blade highly esteemed in Scotland from c.1600 (also **An'dro** or **Andrea** /-drä'ä or an'/ **Ferrara**). [According to some from Andrea dei Ferrari of Belluno, to others Andrew Ferrars or Ferrier of Arbroath, poss as a native of Ferrara, or from L ferrārius smith]

andro- or **andr-** /an-dr(ō)-/, also an-dro-/ combining form denoting man; male. [Gr anēr, andros man, male]
■ **androcentric** /an-drō-sent'rik/ adj centred around men or males. **androcephalous** /-sef'ə-ləs/ adj (Gr kephalē head) man-headed. **androdioecious** /-dī-ē'shəs/ adj having hermaphrodite and male flowers on separate plants (see **dioecious**). **androdioe'cism** n. **androecial** /an-drē'shi-əl/ adj. **androecium** /an-drē'shi-əm or -si-əm/ n (pl **androe'cia**) (Gr oikion house) stamens collectively. **androgen** /an'drō-jən/ n any one of the male sex hormones; a synthetic compound with similar effect. **androgen'ic** adj relating to an androgen. **androg'enous** adj having only male offspring. **an'drogyne** /-jīn/ n and adj (a) hermaphrodite. **androgynous** /an-droj'i-nəs or -drog'/ adj having the characteristics of both male and female in one individual; hermaphrodite; having both male and female flowers (bot). **androg'yny** n (Gr gynē woman) hermaphroditism. **an'droid** n a robot in human form; (**Android**®) a computer operating system used mainly on mobile devices. **androl'ogy** n the branch of medicine which deals with functions and diseases specific to males. **andromonoecious** /an-drō-mon-ē'shəs/ adj having hermaphrodite and male flowers on the same plant (see **monoecious**). **andromonoe'cism** n. **an'dropause** n another name for the **male menopause** (see under **male**). **an'drophore** /-för/ n (Gr phoros a bearing) a prolongation of the receptacle carrying the stamens. **androsterone** /an-dros'tə-rōn or an-dro-stē'rōn/ n (from sterol) a male sex hormone, found in the testes and in urine.

andromeda /an-drom'i-də/ n a plant of the genus Andromeda of shrubs of the family Ericaceae; (with cap) a northern constellation lying between Cassiopeia and Pegasus. [After Andromeda, in Greek mythology, a maiden delivered by Perseus from a sea-monster]
■ **andromedotoxin** /an-drom'i-dō-tok'sin/ n a toxic substance obtained from andromeda which lowers blood pressure.
❑ **Andromeda galaxy** or **Andromeda nebula** n a spiral galaxy in Andromeda, visible to the naked eye.

andvile (Spenser) same as **anvil**.

ane /yin, ān/ (Scot and obs) adj, n and pronoun one; an, a. [OE ān]

anear /ə-nēr'/ (archaic) adv nearly; near. ◆ prep near. ◆ vt to approach or come near to. [of and near]

aneath /ə-nēth', or (Scot) ə-neth' or ə-nāth'/ (chiefly Scot) adv and prep beneath. [**a-¹** and the root of **beneath**]

anecdote /an'ik-dōt or -ək-/ n a short narrative of an incident of private life; anecdotes collectively. [Gr an- (privative), and ekdotos published, from ek out, and didonai to give]
■ **an'ecdotage** n anecdotes collectively; garrulous old age (with pun on dotage). **anecdot'al** adj. **anecdot'alist** n a person who relates anecdotes. **anecdot'ally** adv. **anecdot'ical** adj. **an'ecdotist** n an anecdotalist.

anechoic /an-ə-kō'ik or -e-/ adj echoless; (of a material) preventing echo. [Gr an- (privative), and **echoic**]

anelace see **anlace**.

anele /ə-nēl'/ vt to anoint (archaic); to administer extreme unction to. [OE an on, and ele oil; used in reminiscence of Shakespeare; see **unaneled**]

anelli /ə-nel'i/ n pl ring-shaped pieces of pasta, used esp in soups. [Ital, from L anellus a little ring]

anemia, anemic US spellings of **anaemia, anaemic**.

anemo- /ə-ne-mō- or ə-ni-mo-/ combining form denoting wind. [Gr anemos wind; cf L animus and anima]
■ **anemogram** /ə-nem'o-gram/ n an anemographic record. **anem'ograph** /-gräf/ n an instrument for measuring and recording the pressure and velocity of the wind. **anemographic** /-graf'ik/ adj. **anemograph'ically** adv. **anemog'raphy** n. **anemology** /an-i-mol'ə-ji/ n the study of the winds. **anemometer** /-mom'i-tər/ n a wind gauge. **anemometric** /-mō-met'rik/ or **anemomet'rical** adj. **anemom'etry** n. **anemoph'ilous** adj wind-pollinated. **anemoph'ily** n. **anemopho'bia** n fear of wind or draughts.

anemone /ə-nem'ə-nē/ n any member of the genus Anemone of the crowfoot family; a sea-anemone. [Gr anemōnē, from anemos wind]
❑ **anemone fish** n any of various damselfishes of the genus Amphiprion.

anencephaly /an-ən-sef'ə-li or -kef'/ n congenital absence of all or part of the brain (also **anencephal'ia** /-āl'yə/). [Gr an- (privative), and see **encephalon**]
■ **anencephal'ic** adj.

an-end /ən-end'/ adv to the end, continuously (Shakesp); upright (Shakesp); straight ahead (naut). [**an³** and **end**]
■ **most an end** (obs) almost always.

anent /ə-nent'/ (mainly Scot) prep in a line with; against; towards; in regard to, concerning, about. [OE on efen on even]

■ words derived from main entry word; ❑ compound words; ■ idioms and phrasal verbs

anergy /an'ər-jē/ n absence of energy; reduction or lack of immunity to an antigen. [New L *anergia*, from Gr *an-* (privative), and *ergon* work]
■ **anergia** /an-ûr'jē-ə/ n. **aner'gic** adj.

anerly /an'ər-li/ (*archaic Scot*) adv only. [**ane**; *r* perh on analogy of some other word]

aneroid /an'ə-roid/ adj dispensing with the use of liquid. ◆ n an aneroid barometer. [Fr *anéroïde*, from Gr *a-* (privative), *nēros* wet, and *eidos* form]

anesthesia, etc US spelling of **anaesthesia**, etc.

anestrus, etc US spelling of **anoestrus**, etc.

anetic /ə-net'ik/ (*med*) adj soothing. [L *aneticus*, from Gr *anetikos* abating sickness]

aneuploid /an'ū-ploid/ (*biol*) n a cell or individual with missing or extra chromosomes or part of them. [Gr *an-* (privative), *eu* well, and **-ploid**]
■ **an'euploidy** n.

aneurin /an'ū-rin or ə-nū'rin/ n vitamin B$_1$, deficiency of which affects the nervous system (also called **thiamine**). [Gr *a-* (privative), and *neuron* nerve]

aneurysm or **aneurism** /an'ū-ri-zm/ n dilatation of an artery (*pathol*); any abnormal enlargement. [Gr *aneurysma*, from *ana* up, and *eurys* wide]
■ **aneurys'mal** or **aneuris'mal** adj.

anew /ə-nū' or (*US*) -noo'/ adv afresh; again. [**of** and **new**]

ANFO or **anfo** abbrev : ammonium nitrate (and) fuel oil, an explosive.

anfractuous /an-frak'tū-əs/ adj winding, involved or circuitous. [L *anfractuōsus*, from *ambi-* about, and *frangere* to break]
■ **anfractuosity** /-os'i-ti/ n.

Ang. abbrev : *Anglice* (L), in English.

Angaraland /ang-gä-rä'land/ (*geol*) n an ancient landmass which later formed NE Asia. [*Angara* River]

angary /ang'gə-ri/ (*law*) n a belligerent's right to seize and use neutral or other property (subject to compensation). [Gr *angareiā* forced service, from *angaros* a courier, from a Persian word, from Assyrian *agarru* hired labourer]

angekok or **angekkok** /ang'gi-kok/ n an Inuit sorcerer or shaman. [Inuit]

angel /ān'jəl/ n a divine messenger; a ministering spirit; an attendant or guardian spirit; a person possessing the qualities attributed to these, ie gentleness, purity, etc; a dead person regarded as received into heaven; someone supposed to have a special commission, such as the head of the Church in the Bible, Revelation 2 and 3; a messenger generally (*poetic*); a former English coin bearing the figure of an angel; a radar echo of unknown origin; a financial backer or adviser, *esp* one who finances theatrical ventures (*inf*); a rich person who is an easy victim for those in search of money (*inf*); a nurse (*inf*); a hell's angel. [Gr *angelos* a messenger]
■ **ān'gelhood** n. **angelic** /an-jel'ik/ or **angel'ical** adj. **angel'ically** adv. **āngelol'atry** n angel-worship. **āngelol'ogy** n doctrine regarding angels. **āngeloph'any** n the manifestation of an angel to a human. ❑ **an'gel-cake** or **an'gel-food-cake** n a light cake made of flour, sugar and egg white. **angel dust** n (*inf*) the drug phencyclidine, a hallucinogen. **an'gelfish** n a kind of shark (genus *Squatina*), with large winglike pectoral fins (also **an'gelshark**); a tropical American river-fish (genus *Pterophyllum*) of the family Cichlidae, with a much-compressed, almost circular body but crescent-shaped owing to the long fin filaments, the whole banded with changing black vertical stripes; applied also to *Pomacanthus* and several other fishes of the Chaetodontidae. **angel hair** n pasta shaped in very thin strips. **angel shot** n (*hist*) cannonballs linked by a chain, intended to destroy ships' rigging. **angels on horseback** n pl oysters and bacon on toast. **an'gel-water** n a perfumed liquid, at first made largely from angelica, then from ambergris, rose-water, orange-flower water, etc.
■ **on the side of the angels** basically in sympathy with traditional virtues and virtuous aims. **the Angelic Doctor** St Thomas Aquinas.

Angeleno /an-je-lē'nō/ n (pl **Angele'nos**) a native or citizen of Los Angeles. [Am Sp *Angeleño*]

angelica /an-jel'i-kə/ n (with *cap*) a genus of umbelliferous plants with large leaves and double-winged fruit, once regarded as a defence against poison and pestilence; a garden plant by some included in the genus as *A. archangelica*, by others called *Archangelica officinalis*; its candied leaf-stalks and midribs, used as a decoration for cakes, etc. [Med L *herba angelica* angelic herb]
❑ **angel'ica-tree** n an American aralia.

angelus /an'jə-ləs/ (*Christianity*) n a short devotional exercise in honour of the Incarnation, repeated three times daily; the bell rung in Roman Catholic countries at morning, noon, and sunset, to invite the faithful to recite the angelus. [From the introductory words, '*Angelus Domini nuntiavit Mariae*']

anger /ang'gər/ n hot displeasure provoked by some action, incident, situation, etc, often involving hostility and a desire for retaliation; wrath; inflammation (now *dialect*); affliction (*obs*). ◆ vt to make angry; to irritate. [ON *angr* ; cf **agnail**, **anbury**, **angina**, **anguish**]
■ **an'gerless** adj. **an'gerly** (*archaic*) or **ang'rily** adv. **ang'riness** n. **ang'ry** adj excited with anger; feeling or directing anger towards (with *at* or *with*); (of a sore, etc) inflamed; (of the sky, or a person's facial expression, etc) of threatening or lowering aspect. ◆ n an angry young man; an angry person.
❑ **angry young man** n a young man loud in disgust at what his elders have made of society (popularized by *Look Back in Anger*, play (1956) by John Osborne, one of a group of writers of the period to whom the term was subsequently applied).

Angevin /an'ji-vin/ adj of Anjou, in France; of or relating to the Plantagenet house that reigned in England from 1154 to 1485, descended from Geoffrey, Count of Anjou. ◆ n a native of Anjou; a member of the house of Anjou (by some reckoned only down to the loss of Anjou (1204), by others, until the deposition of Richard II in 1399).

angico /an'ji-kō/ n (pl **an'gicos**) a S American tree of the mimosa family (genus *Piptadenia*); its gum. [Port, from Tupí]

angina /an-jī'nə or (*rare*) an'ji-nə/ (*med*) n short for angina pectoris; any inflammatory disease of the throat, such as quinsy, croup, etc; any of various diseases involving sudden intense pain. [L *angīna* ; cf **anguish**]
■ **anginal** /an-jī'nl or an'ji-nl/ adj.
❑ **angina pectoris** n a disease of the heart marked by paroxysms of intense pain, radiating from the breastbone mainly towards the left shoulder and arm.

angio- /an-ji-ō- or sometimes an-ji-o-/ combining form denoting: a case or vessel; the blood vessels (*med* and *zool*); the seed vessels (*bot*). [Gr *angeion* a case, vessel]

angiocarpous /an-ji-ō-kär'pəs/ (*bot*) adj having the fruit (or in fungi the hymenium) within a special covering. [Gr *angeion* a case, and *karpos* fruit]

angiogenesis /an-ji-ō-jen'ə-sis/ n the development of blood vessels in an organ or tumour. [**angio-**]

angiogram /an'ji-ō-gram/ n a photograph made by angiography. [**angio-**]
■ **angiog'raphy** n the process of making X-ray photographs of blood vessels by injecting the vessels with a substance opaque to the rays.

angioma /an-ji-ō'mə/ (*med*) n (pl **angiō'mas** or **angiō'mata**) a benign tumour composed of blood or lymph vessels. [New L from Gr *angeion* vessel, and **-oma**]

angioplasty /an'ji-ō-plas-ti/ n surgery of the blood vessels; a non-surgical procedure to widen, clean out, etc the blood vessels using balloon dilatation or laser. [**angio-**]

angiosarcoma /an-ji-ō-sär-kō'mə/ (*pathol*) n a malignant tumour of the vascular endothelia, occurring in the liver and other sites. [**angio-**]

angiosperm /an'ji-ō-spûrm/ n a plant of the **Angiosperm'ae**, one of the main divisions of flowering plants, in which the seeds are in a closed ovary, not naked as in gymnosperms. [Gr *angeion* case, and *sperma* seed]
■ **angiosperm'al** or **angiosperm'ous** adj.

angiostatin /an-ji-ō-stat'in/ n a protein that occurs naturally in plasminogen, believed to be effective in limiting the growth of cancerous tumours. [**angio-**, **-stat** and **-in** (1)]

angiostomous /an-ji-os'tə-məs/ or **angiostomatous** /an-ji-ō-stō'mə-təs/ (*zool*) adj narrow-mouthed; with a mouth that is not distensible. [Gr *angeion* a vessel, case, confused with L *angere* to compress, and Gr *stoma, stomatos* mouth]

angiotensin /an-ji-ō-ten'sin/ n a protein that causes a rise in blood pressure. [**angio-** and **hypertension**]

angklung /ang'kləng/ n a musical instrument of SE Asia, consisting of bamboo tubes suspended on a frame which is shaken to sound the chosen note(s) (also **anklong** or **anklung**). [Javanese *angklung*]

Angle /ang'gl/ n a member or descendant of the German tribe (OE *Engle*) from Schleswig that settled in Northumbria, Mercia and East Anglia during the 5c. [L *Anglus*, from the Germanic name for the people of *Angul*, district of Schleswig (cf ety for **angle²**)]
■ **Ang'lian** adj of the Angles. ◆ n an Angle; the English dialect of the Angles.

angle¹ /ang'gl/ n a corner; the distance or change in direction between two lines or surfaces diverging from the same point, measured in degrees (°), radians, right angles or (of angular velocity) revolutions; a measurement of such a change in direction, etc; the inclination of two straight lines, or of two curves measured by that of their tangents, or of two planes measured by that of perpendiculars to their intersection (*geom*); the spread of a cone, a number of meeting planes or the like,

measured by the area on the surface of a sphere subtending it at the centre (*geom*); an outlying corner or nook (*archaic*); a point of view, a way of looking at something (*inf*); a scheme, a plan devised for profit (*sl*); a sharply curving direction (of a shot or kick) (*sport*); a frame (*snooker*, etc); an angle shot (*squash*); an angle iron. ◆ *vt* to move, drive, direct, turn, adjust or present at an angle; to present (news, etc) in such a way as to serve a particular end; to corner, put in a corner; to put in the jaws of a billiard pocket. ◆ *vi* to proceed at an angle or by an angular course. [Fr, from L *angulus*, cognate with Gr *ankylos*; both from root *ank-* to bend, seen also in **anchor** and **ankle**]
■ **ang'led** *adj* having angles; biased. **ang'lewise** *adv*.
❑ **angle bracket** *n* a bracket with a pointed shape, W or o. **angled deck** or (*US*) **canted deck** *n* the flight deck of an aircraft-carrier prolonged diagonally from one side of the ship, so that aircraft may take off and land without interference from or with aircraft parked at the bows. **ang'ledozer** *n* a bulldozer whose blade may be angled or tilted to the left or right. **angle grinder** *n* an electric tool with an abrasive disc for grinding or sanding. **angle iron** *n* (also **angle** or **angle bar**) an L-shaped piece of iron or steel used in structural work, etc. **angle of attack** *n* (*aeronautics*) the angle between the chord line of an aerofoil and the relative airflow, normally the immediate flight path of the aircraft. **angle of deviation** *n* (*phys*) the angle between the paths of a ray of light before and after passing through a prism or other optical device. **angle of incidence** see under **incident**. **angle of reflection** see under **reflect**. **angle of refraction** see under **refract**. **angle shot** *n* a shot taken with a camera tilted above or below the horizontal (*cinematog*); a shot which hits first the side wall and then the front wall, without touching the floor (*squash*).

angle² /*ang'gl*/ *vi* to fish with rod and line (for); to try to gain by some artifice (with *for*). ◆ *vt* to angle for. ◆ *n* a fish-hook or fishing-tackle (*obs*); an act of angling (*esp fig*). [OE *angul* a hook]
■ **ang'ler** *n* a person who fishes with rod and line, *esp* for sport; the devilfish or fishing-frog, a wide-mouthed voracious fish (*Lophius piscatorius*) that attracts its prey by waving filaments attached to its head (also **angler fish**); extended to related kinds, some of them remarkable for the dwarf males parasitic on the female. **ang'ling** *n*.
❑ **ang'leworm** *n* any worm used as bait by anglers.

angleberry see **anbury**.

Anglepoise® /*ang'gl-poiz*/ *n* a brand of reading lamp with a jointed stand that can be moved into a variety of different positions.

anglesite /*ang'gli-sīt*/ *n* orthorhombic lead sulphate, a common lead ore, first found in *Anglesey*.

Anglican /*ang'gli-kən*/ *adj* of or characteristic of the Church of England and churches in communion with it; English (*esp US*). ◆ *n* a member of the Anglican Church. [Med L *Anglicanus*, from L *Anglus* Angle]
■ **Ang'licanism** *n* the principles of the Church of England; attachment to English institutions, *esp* the English Church.

Anglice /*ang'gli-sē*/ or (L) *ang'gli-kā*/ (also without *cap*) *adv* in English. [Med L]

anglicize or **-ise** /*ang'gli-sīz*/ *vt* to make English (also **ang'lify**). ◆ *vi* to assume or conform to English ways.
■ **ang'licism** /*-sizm*/ *n* an English idiom or peculiarity; English principles. **ang'licist** or **ang'list** *n* a person who has a scholarly knowledge of the English language, literature and culture. **angliciza'tion** or **-s-** *n*. **anglist'ics** *n sing* the study of English language, literature and culture.

Anglo /*ang'glō*/ (*inf*) *adj* and *n* (*pl* **Ang'los**) (a person) of British extraction; (an) Anglo-American (*esp US*).

Anglo- /*ang-glō-*/ *combining form* denoting English or British, *esp* jointly English or British and something else. [L *Anglus*]
■ **Anglo-Amer'ican** *adj* English in origin or birth, American by settlement or citizenship; (*esp US*) having English as one's mother tongue and sharing a cultural outlook of British origin; (*esp US*) non-Hispanic; of England or Britain and America. ◆ *n* an Anglo-American person. **Anglo-Cath'olic** *n* a person who regards himself or herself as a Catholic of Anglican pattern; a High-Church Anglican (also *adj*). **Anglo-Cathol'icism** *n*. **Anglocen'tric** *adj* taking English or British affairs, institutions, culture, etc as a norm, focus, etc in one's outlook or behaviour. **Anglo-French'** *adj* of England or Britain and France. ◆ *n* the form of the French language spoken in medieval England. **Anglo-In'dian** *adj* of England or Britain and India; of India under the British; of the English or British in India; of British birth but (formerly or presently) long resident in India; of English as spoken in India; Eurasian. ◆ *n* a person of British birth long resident (formerly or presently) in India; an Indian Eurasian. **Anglo-I'rish** *n* the English language as spoken in Ireland; Irish people of English descent; people of mixed English and Irish descent. ◆ *adj* of England or Britain and Ireland; of the Anglo-Irish people or speech (**Anglo-Irish agreement** an agreement between the British and Irish governments, *esp* the document signed in 1985 agreeing to regular consultation on political, legal and security matters with respect to Northern Ireland).

angloma'nia *n* (also with *cap*) a craze, or indiscriminate admiration, for what is English. **angloma'niac** *n* (also with *cap*). **Anglo-Nor'man** *n* (the French dialect of) any of the Normans in England after the Norman Conquest (also with *cap*). (All the following also with *cap*) **ang'lophile** or **ang'lophil** *n* (Gr *philos* friend) a friend and admirer of England and all things English (also *adj*). **anglophil'ia** *n*. **anglophil'ic** *adj*. **ang'lophobe** *n* (Gr *phobos* fear) a person who fears or dislikes England and all things English (also *adj*). **anglophō'bia** *n*. **anglophō'biac** or **anglophobic** /*-fōb*/ or *-fob*/ *adj*. **Ang'lophone** *adj* (sometimes without *cap*) of a state, person, etc, speaking or using English (*esp* as opposed to French), in everyday affairs. ◆ *n* an English-speaking (*esp* as opposed to French-speaking) person, *esp* in a state, etc where English is not the only language spoken. **Anglophon'ic** *adj* (sometimes without *cap*). **Anglo-Ro'mani** *n* a modified form of Romany with English syntax, as used by Romanies in Britain, and also in the USA, etc. **Anglo-Sax'on** *n* Old English, the language before 1100 or 1150AD; plain English, often implying forthright use of English words that are usually taboo in ordinary conversation (*inf*); one of the Germanic settlers in England and Scotland, including Angles, Saxons and Jutes, or one of their descendants; a Saxon of England, distinguished from the Old Saxons of the Continent; a white native speaker of English. ◆ *adj* of or relating to the Anglo-Saxons or their language; of or relating to Britain and N America, as opposed to continental Europe. **Anglo-Sax'ondom** *n*.

Angola /*ang-gō'lə*/ *adj* relating to *Angola* in Africa; (sometimes without *cap*) Angora.
■ **Ango'lan** *n* and *adj* (a native or inhabitant) of Angola.

angophora /*ang-gof'ə-rə*/ *n* any of several trees of E Australia belonging to the *Angophora* genus closely related to the eucalypts. [Gr *angos* vessel, jar (from shape of fruits), and *phoros* bearing]

Angora /*ang-gō'rə* or *-gō'rə*/ *adj* of *Angora* a town of ancient Galatia, now (as Ankara since 1930) capital of Turkey; (sometimes without *cap*) of an Angora breed or yarn, etc. ◆ *n* (in all meanings sometimes without *cap*) an Anatolian goat; its long silky wool (the true mohair); cloth made from it; a silky-haired rabbit; an Angora cat; yarn or material made partly or wholly of Angora rabbit hair. [Gr *Ankÿra*, in later times *Angora*, now *Ankara*]
❑ **Angora cat** *n* a silky-haired kind of cat similar to the Persian but with a more pointed head, longer body and full tail; a term treated by some as obsolete for Persian cat.

Angostura /*ang-go-stū'rə*/ *n* an aromatic bitter bark from certain trees of the family Rutaceae (*esp Cusparia*), formerly used in medicine. [Named after the town of *Angostura* (now Ciudad Bolívar) on the narrows (Sp *angostura*) of the Orinoco in Venezuela]
❑ **Angostura bitters**® *n* a brand of aromatic bitters, first made in Angostura, used as a flavouring in cocktails and other drinks, etc.

angry see under **anger**.

angst /*ängst*/ *n* (often *cap*) anxiety, *esp* a general feeling of anxiety produced by awareness of the uncertainties and paradoxes inherent in the state of being human. [Ger *Angst*, Dan *angst* fear, anxiety]
■ **angst'y** *adj* (*inf*).
❑ **angst'-ridden** *adj*.

Ångström or **angstrom** /*ang'* or *ong'strəm*/ *n* a unit (10^{-10} metres) used in expressing wavelengths of light, ultraviolet rays, X-rays, molecular and atomic distances. [Anders J *Ångström* (1814–74), Swedish physicist]

Anguilla /*ang-gwil'ə*/ *n* the common eel genus. [L *anguīlla*, dimin of *anguis* snake]
■ **anguill'iform** *adj* eel-like. **Anguill'ūla** *n* the paste-eel genus of nematode worms.

Anguis /*ang'gwis*/ *n* the generic name not of a snake but of the blindworm. [L *anguis* snake]
■ **ang'uifauna** *n* fauna of snakes. **ang'uiform** *adj* snake-shaped. **anguine** /*ang'gwin*/ *adj* of or like a snake. **anguiped** or **anguipede** /*-ped* or *-pēd*/ *adj* having feet or legs in the form of snakes, as used of mythological giants or the like.

anguish /*ang'gwish*/ *n* excessive suffering of body or mind; agony. ◆ *vt* to afflict with anguish. ◆ *vi* to suffer anguish. [OFr *angoisse* choking, from L *angustia* tightness, narrowness]
■ **ang'uished** *adj*.

angular /*ang'gū-lər* or *-gyə-*/ *adj* having an angle or corner; measured by an angle; stiff in manner, the opposite of easy or graceful; bony and lean in figure. [L *angularis*, from *angulus* **angle**²]
■ **angular'ity** /*-lar'i-*/ *n*. **ang'ularly** *adv*. **ang'ulate** *adj* (also **ang'ulated**) formed with angles. ◆ *vt* and *vi* to make or become angular. **angulā'tion** *n* the action of making angulate; an angular formation, angle; the measurement of angles.
❑ **angular acceleration** *n* the acceleration of a spacecraft round an axis. **angular momentum** *n* the product of a rotating body's moment of inertia and its angular velocity. **angular velocity** *n* the rate at which an object rotates round a fixed point or axis, measured as the rate of

---

change in the angle turned through by the line between the object and the point or axis.

angusti- /ang-gu-sti-/ (biol; rare) combining form signifying narrow. [L angustus narrow]
■ **angustifo'liate** adj narrow-leaved. **angustiros'trate** adj narrow-beaked.

angwantibo /ang-wän'ti-bō/ n (pl **angwan'tibos**) a small, golden brown, tailless W African lemur (Arctocebus calabarensis). [W African word]

anharmonic /an-här-mon'ik/ (maths, phys, electronics) adj not harmonic. [Gr an- (privative), and harmonikos harmonic]
❑ **anharmonic ratio** n the cross-ratio of four numbers, four points on a straight line or four lines in a pencil (harmonic when = −1).

anhedonia /an-hi-dō'ni-ə/ (psychol) n the inability to feel pleasure; the loss of interest in formerly pleasurable pursuits. [Gr an- (privative), and hēdonē pleasure]
■ **anhedon'ic** adj.

anhedral /an-hē'drəl or -hed'rel/ adj allotriomorphic (chem); having a downward (negative) dihedral angle (aeronautics). [Gr an- (privative), and adj combining form -hedral, ult from Gr hedrā seat]

an-heires (Shakesp) an obscure word in Merry Wives of Windsor II.1.196, variously conjectured to be an error for **on here**, for **mynheers**, or for **ameers**.

anhelation /an-hi-lā'shən/ (med) n shortness of breath, or difficult breathing. [L anhēlātiō, -ōnis, from anhēlāre to gasp]

anhung(e)red see **ahungered**.

anhydride /an-hī'drīd/ n a compound representing in its composition an acid minus water (ie obtainable from an acid by the elimination of water, or combinable with water to form an acid). [Gr an- (privative), and hydōr water]
■ **anhy'drite** n a mineral, anhydrous calcium sulphate. **anhy'drous** adj free from water.

ani /ä'nē/ n (pl **an'is**) a tropical American bird, a black cuckoo (genus Crotophaga) with a curved bill and long tail. [Sp or Port ani', from Tupí]

ani- see **ano-**.

aniconic /an-ī-kon'ik/ adj symbolizing without aiming at resemblance; relating to aniconism. [Gr an- (privative), and eikōn image]
■ **ani'conism** /-kən-izm/ n worship or veneration of an object that represents a deity without being an image. **ani'conist** n.

anicut or **annicut** /an'i-kut/ (Anglo-Ind) n a dam. [Tamil anaikaṭṭu dam-building]

anigh /ə-nī'/ (literary or pseudo-archaic) prep and adv nigh. [a-, as in anear, afar, and **nigh**; a modern formation]

anight /ə-nīt'/ (Shakesp) adv of nights, by night, at night. [**of** and **night**]

anil /an'il/ n indigo (plant or dye). [Port anil, from Ar an-nil the indigo plant, from Sans nīlī indigo]

anile /an'īl or ā'nīl/ adj old-womanish; imbecile. [L anus, -ūs an old woman]
■ **anility** /a- or ə-nil'i-ti/ n old-womanishness; imbecile dotage.

aniline /an'i-lēn, -lin or -līn/ n a product of coal tar extensively used in dyeing and other industrial and manufacturing processes, first obtained from anil (also adj).
❑ **aniline dyes** n pl a general term for all synthetic dyes having aniline as their base.

anima /an'i-mə/ n the soul, the innermost part of the personality; in Jungian psychology, the female component of the male personality. [L]
❑ **anima mundi** /mun'di or mŭn'dē/ n the soul of the world.

animadvert /an-i-mad-vûrt'/ vi to take cognizance (law; usu with on or upon); to take note; to comment critically (on); to express censure. ◆ vt (obs) to consider, to observe. [L animus the mind, ad to, and vertere to turn]
■ **animadver'sion** n. **animadvert'er** n.

animal /an'i-məl/ n an organism having life, sensation and voluntary motion (typically distinguished from a plant, which is organized and has life, but apparently not sensation or voluntary motion); often, a lower animal, ie one below man; a mammal; a brutish or sensual man; a person, thing, organization, etc, as in there's no such animal (inf). ◆ adj of, of the nature of, derived from, or belonging to an animal or animals; brutal, sensual. [L animal, from anima air, breath, life, soul]
■ **animal'ic** adj (rare) of or relating to animals. **an'imalism** n physicality; the state of being actuated by mere animal appetites; brutishness, sensuality; the theory that man is a mere animal being. **an'imalist** n a person who practises or believes in animalism; a person who paints, carves, or writes stories about animals. **animalist'ic** adj. **animality** /-al'i-ti/ n animal nature or life; the status of an animal or of a lower animal. **animaliza'tion** or **-s-** n. **an'imalize**

or **-ise** vt to represent or conceive in animal form (rare); to endow with animal life or the properties of animal matter; to convert into animal matter; to brutalize, sensualize. **an'imally** adv physically.
❑ **animal bipes** /an'i-mal bī'pēz or bi'pās/ n (L) a two-footed animal, man. **animal husbandry** n the business of rearing livestock. **animal implume** /an'i-mal im-ploo'mē or -me/ n (L) a featherless animal. **animal kingdom** n a category of living organisms comprising all animals. **animal liberationist** n a member or supporter of any body dedicated to ending the exploitation of animals by man. **animal magnetism** see under **magnet**. **animal pole** n (zool) the apex of the upper hemisphere of the developing ovum, containing little or no yolk. **animal rationale** /an'i-mal rā-shi-ō-nä'lē or ra-ti-ō-nä'le/ n (L) a reasoning animal. **animal rights** n pl the rights of animals to exist without being exploited by humans. **animal risibile** /an'i-mal rī-si'bi-lē or rē-si'bi-le/ n (L) an animal able to laugh. **animal spirits** n pl (orig **spirit**) formerly, a supposed principle formed in the brain out of vital spirits and conveyed to all parts of the body through the nerves; nervous force; exuberance of health and life; cheerful buoyancy of temper; the spirit or principle of volition and sensation (Milton). **an'imal-worship** n. **an'imal-worshipper** n.

animalcule /a-ni-mal'kūl/ n (pl **animal'cūles** or **animal'cūla**) a microscopic animal, one that cannot be seen by the naked eye; a small animal (obs). [L animalculum, dimin of animal]
■ **animal'cūlar** adj. **animal'cūlist** n a believer in the former biological theory (**animal'cūlism**) that the spermatozoon contains all future generations in germ.

animate /an'i-māt/ vt to give life to; to enliven; to put spirit into; to actuate; to record still drawings, etc on film or videotape in such a way that the images appear to move. ◆ adj /-mət/ living; having animal life. [L animāre, -ātum, from anima air, breath, life]
■ **an'imated** adj lively; full of spirit; endowed with life; moving as if alive. **an'imatedly** adv. **animat'ic** n (advertising, cinematog, etc) a section of animation in or for a TV commercial, film, etc; a rough simulation of a TV commercial, etc, produced from a storyboard with a voice-over. **an'imating** adj. **an'imatingly** adv. **anima'tion** n the act of animating; the state of being alive; liveliness; vigour; the creation of the illusion of movement, esp in an animated cartoon; the technique or craft of this; the creation of moving images on a screen (comput). **an'imatism** n the primitive attribution of life to natural phenomena and natural objects, but not (as in animism) belief that spirits reside in them. **an'imātor** n (also, chiefly US, **an'imāter**) a person who enlivens or animates something; an artist who makes drawings for animated cartoons, films, etc. **animatron'ic** adj of or like something animated by animatronics. **animatron'ics** n sing the art of animating a lifelike figure of a person, animal, etc on a computer screen.
❑ **animated cartoon** n a motion picture produced from drawings, each successive drawing showing a very slight change of position so that a series of them gives the effect of an actual movement.

animato /a-ni-mä'tō/ (music) adv and adj in a lively manner. [Ital]

anime /an'i-mā/ n a style of animated film or television programme, originating in Japan, featuring futuristic stories with explicit content. [Jap]

animé or **anime** /an'i-mā or -mē/ n the resin of the West Indian locust tree; extended to other gums and resins. [Said to be Fr animé living, from the number of insects in it; but perhaps a native name]

animism /an'i-mi-zm/ n the attribution of a soul to natural objects and phenomena; the theory of German chemist GE Stahl (1660–1734) that the soul is the vital principle and source of the phenomena of animal life. [L anima the soul]
■ **an'imist** n. **animis'tic** adj.

animo et fide /an'i-mō et fī'dē or fi'dā/ (L) by courage and faith.

animosity /a-ni-mos'i-ti/ n strong dislike; enmity. [L animōsitās fullness of spirit]

animus /an'i-məs/ n sing intention; actuating spirit; hostility; in Jungian psychology, the male component of the female personality. [L animus spirit, soul]

anion /an'ī-ən/ n an ion that seeks the anode; an electronegative ion. [Gr ana up, and ion going, prp neuter of ienai to go]
■ **anion'ic** adj.

aniridia /an-i-rid'i-ə/ n a congenital condition in which the eye is incompletely formed. [Gr an- (privative) and īris, -idos iris]
■ **anirid'ic** adj.

anise /an'is/ n an umbelliferous plant (genus Pimpinella) whose aromatic seeds, of a flavour similar to liquorice, are used in making cordials, liqueurs, etc, and in baking, etc; (Gr anēthon) a plant mentioned in the Bible (Matthew 23), believed to be dill. [Gr anīson anise]
■ **an'iseed** n the seed of anise; anisette. **anisette** /an-i-zet'/ n a cordial or liqueur prepared from anise seed.
❑ **aniseed ball** n a boiled sweet flavoured with aniseed.
■ **star-anise** see under **star**[1].

aniso- /a-nī-sō- or -so-/ *combining form* denoting unequal. [Gr *anisos* unequal, from *an-* (privative), and *isos* equal]
■ **anisocercal** /-sûr'kl/ *adj* (of fishes) with unequal tail-lobes. **anisodac'tylous** *adj* (of birds) with three toes turned forward, one backward. **anisog'amy** *n* (*biol*) the sexual fusion of gametes that differ in size. **anisom'erous** *adj* (*bot*) with unequal numbers of parts in the floral whorls. **anisophyll'ous** *adj* (*bot*) with differently formed leaves on different sides of the shoot. **anisotrop'ic** *adj* not isotropic, showing differences of property or of effect in different directions. **anisotrop'ically** *adv*. **anisot'ropy** *n*.

anker /ang'kər/ *n* an old measure for wines and spirits used in N Europe, varying considerably (that of Rotterdam 8½ imperial gallons). [Du]

ankerite /ang'kə-rīt/ *n* a mineral, a rhombohedral carbonate of calcium, iron, magnesium and manganese. [Professor MJ *Anker* (1772–1843), Austrian mineralogist]

ankh /angk/ *n* an ansate cross, ie T-shaped with a loop above the horizontal bar, the symbol of life. [Egyp, life]

ankle or (*obs*) **ancle** /ang'kl/ *n* the joint connecting the foot and leg; the part of the leg between this and calf. [OE *anclēow*; cf Ger *Enkel*, and **angle**[1]]
■ **ank'led** *adj* having ankles. **ank'let** /-lit/ *n* an ornamental or supporting ring or chain for the ankle.
❑ **ank'le-biter** or **ank'le-nipper** *n* (*Aust sl*) a child. **ank'le-boot** or **ank'le-jack** *n* a boot reaching above the ankle. **ank'le-chain** *n* a chain worn as decoration round the ankle. **ankle sock** *n* a sock reaching to and covering the ankle. **ankle strap** *n* (a shoe with) a strap which fastens round the ankle.

anklong, **anklung** see **angklung**.

Ankole /ang-kō'lē/ *n* a breed of large cattle with long horns. [*Ankole*, plateau region in Uganda]

ankus /ang'kəs/ *n* an elephant goad. [Hindustani]

ankylosaur /ang'kə-lə-sör/ *n* any of the **Ankylosauria** /-sör'i-ə/ a suborder of bird-hipped plant-eating dinosaurs of the Cretaceous period, with short legs and flattened heavily-armoured bodies, including **Ankylosaur'us** which gave name to the suborder. [New L, from Gr *ankylos* crooked, and *sauros* lizard]

ankylosis or **anchylosis** /ang-ki-lō'sis/ (*pathol*) *n* the fusion of bones or skeletal parts; the fixation of a joint by fibrous bands or union of bones. [Gr *ankylōsis* stiffening of a joint, from *ankyloein* to crook]
■ **ank'ylose** or **anch'ylose** *vt* and *vi* to stiffen or fuse, as a joint or bones. **ank'ylosed** or **anch'ylosed** *adj*.
❑ **ankylosing spondylitis** *n* rheumatoid arthritis of the spine.

ankylostomiasis or **anchylostomiasis** /ang-ki-lō-sto-mī'ə-sis or -stō-/ (*pathol*) *n* a disease characterized by anaemia, caused by infestation with a parasitic nematode (*Ankylostomum duodenale* or other). [Gr *ankylos* crooked, and *stoma* mouth]

ANL *abbrev* : Anti-Nazi League.

anlace or **anelace** /an'las or -ləs/ (*hist*) *n* a short two-edged tapering dagger. [Ety unknown]

anlage /an' or än'lä-gə/ (*biol*) *n* (*pl* **an'lagen** /-gən/ or **an'lages**) the primordium or first discernible rudiment of an organ. [Ger]

anme *abbrev* : *anonyme* (*Fr*), limited liability.

ann /an/ (*Scot; obs*) *n* see under **annates**.

anna /an'ə/ *n* a former coin of India, Pakistan and Bangladesh, one sixteenth of a rupee. [Hindi *ānā*]

annabergite /an'ə-bûr-gīt/ *n* an apple-green mineral, hydrous nickel arsenate. [*Annaberg* in Saxony, eastern Germany]

annal /an'əl/ *n* a year's entry in a chronicle; (in *pl*) records of events under the years in which they happened; (in *pl*) historical records generally; (in *pl*) yearbooks. [L *annālis* yearly, from *annus* a year]
■ **ann'alist** *n* a writer of annals. **annalist'ic** *adj*. **ann'alize** or **-ise** *vt* (*obs*) to record.

annates /an'āts or -əts/ (*hist*) *n pl* (*obs sing* **annat** /an'ət/) the first-fruits, or one year's income of a benefice, paid to the Pope (in England from 1535 to the crown, from 1703 to Queen Anne's bounty and extinguished or made redeemable in 1926). [LL *annāta*, from L *annus* a year]
■ **ann'at** or **ann** *n* (*Scots law*; *obs*) from 1672 to 1925 the half-year's stipend payable after a parish minister's death to his widow or next of kin.

annatto or **anatto** /a- or ə-nat'ō/, also **annatta**, **anatta** /-ə/ or **arnotto** /är-not'ō/ *n* (*pl* **annatt'os** or **anatt'os**, etc) a bright orange colouring matter obtained from the fruit pulp of a tropical American tree, *Bixa orellana* (family Bixaceae), etc. [Supposed to be of Carib origin]

anneal /ə-nēl'/ *vt* and *vi* to heat and cool gradually (glass, metals), *esp* in order to temper or toughen; to heat (eg glass) in order to fix colours

on (*archaic*); to strengthen, toughen; to reform the duplex structure of (a nucleic acid) (*biochem*). [OE pfx *an-* on (cf **an**[3]), and *ælan* to burn]
■ **anneal'er** *n*. **anneal'ing** *n*.

annectent /ə-nek'tənt/ (*biol*; *obs*) *adj* connecting, linking or having characteristics that are intermediate between those of two other species, genera, etc. [L *annectere*, from *ad* to, and *nectere* to tie]

annelid /an'ə-lid/ *n* a member of the **Annelida** /ə-nel'i-də/, a class comprising the red-blooded worms, having a long body composed of numerous rings. [L *annellus*, *ānellus*, dimin of *ānulus* a ring]
■ **annel'idan** *n* and *adj*.

annex /ə-neks'/ *vt* to add to the end; to join or attach; to take permanent possession of; to purloin, appropriate (*inf*); to affix; to append. ◆ *n* /an'eks/ something added, now only as a documentary appendix or addendum; an annexe (*esp US*). [L *annectere*, *annexum*, from *ad* to, and *nectere* to tie]
■ **annexā'tion** /an-/ *n*. **annexā'tionist** *n* and *adj*. **ann'exe** *n* a supplementary building, built as an extension to the main building; an annex to a document. **annexion** /ə-nek'shən/ *n* the act of annexing (*archaic*); something annexed (*Shakesp*). **annex'ment** *n* (*rare*) addition (*Shakesp*); the thing annexed. **annexure** /a-nek'shər/ *n* something added, *esp* an addition to a public document.

annicut see **anicut**.

annihilate /ə-nī'(h)i-lāt/ *vt* to reduce to nothing; to put out of existence; to crush or wither by look or word (*fig*); to defeat completely (*inf*); to cause (a subatomic particle) to undergo annihilation (*phys*). ◆ *vi* (*phys*) to undergo annihilation. [L *annihilāre*, *-ātum*, from *ad* to, and *nihil* nothing]
■ **annīhilā'tion** *n* reduction to nothing; a crushing defeat; the destruction of soul as well as body (*theol*); the process by which a particle and its corresponding antiparticle (eg an electron and a positron) combine and are spontaneously transformed into radiation (**annihilation radiation**) (*phys*). **annīhilā'tionism** *n* the belief that the soul (*esp* of the unrepentant wicked) dies with the body. **annī'hilātive** *adj*. **annī'hilātor** *n*.

anniversary /a-ni-vûr'sə-ri/ *n* the day of the year on which an event happened or is celebrated as having happened in a previous year; the celebration proper to such a recurrence, *esp* a mass or religious service. ◆ *adj* returning, happening or commemorated about the same date every year; relating to annual recurrence or celebration. [L *anniversārius*, from *annus* a year, and *vertere*, *versum* to turn]

anno /an'ō/ (*L*) in the year.
■ **anno Christi** /kris'tī or -tē/ in the year of Christ. **anno Domini** /an'ō dom'in-ī or -in-ē/ in the year of our Lord (also *n* (*inf*) advancing old age). **anno mundi** /mun'dī or mŭn'dē/ in the year of the world (used in reckoning dates from the supposed time of creation). **anno regni** /reg'nī or -nē/ in the year of the reign. **anno salutis** /sal-ū'tis or -oo'/ in the year of redemption. **anno urbis conditae** /ûr'bis kon'dit-ē or ŭr'bis kon'dit-ī/ in the year of the founding of the city (ie Rome, 753BC).

Annona see **Anona**.

annotate /an'ō-tāt or -ə-/ *vt* to supply (a literary work, etc) with notes. ◆ *vi* to append notes. [L *annotāre*, from *ad* to, and *notāre*, *-ātum* to mark]
■ **ann'ōtatable** *adj*. **annōtā'tion** *n* the making of notes; a note of explanation; comment. **ann'ōtative** *adj*. **ann'ōtātor** *n*.

announce /ə-nowns'/ *vt* to declare; to give public notice of; to make known. ◆ *vi* (*US*) to make known one's intention to run as a candidate. [OFr *anoncer*, from L *annuntiāre*, from *ad* to, and *nuntiāre* to report]
■ **announce'ment** *n*. **announc'er** *n* a person who announces; a person who reads the news and announces other items in the programme (*TV* and *radio*).

annoy /ə-noi'/ *vt* and *vi* to trouble, to vex; to aggravate, irritate; to tease; to harm or injure (*esp* in military sense). ◆ *n* (*archaic* and *poetic*) annoyance. [OFr *anoier* (noun *anoi*, Mod Fr *ennui*), from LL *inodiāre*, from L phrase *in odiō*, hateful; Ital *annoiare*]
■ **annoy'ance** *n* that which annoys; the act of annoying; the state of being annoyed. **annoyed'** *adj* (with *at* or *with*). **annoy'er** *n*. **annoy'ing** *adj*. **annoy'ingly** *adv*.

annual /an'ū-əl/ *adj* yearly; coming every year; lasting or living for a year; requiring to be renewed every year; performed in a year; being, or calculated as, the total for one year. ◆ *n* a plant that lives for one year only; a publication that is produced yearly, *esp* a reference book or an illustrated gift-book; a yearbook. [LL *annuālis*, from *annus* a year]
■ **ann'ualize** or **-ise** *vt* to convert to a yearly rate, amount, etc. **ann'ually** *adv*.
❑ **annual accounts** *n pl* a company's yearly financial statements, *incl* profit and loss account, balance sheet, cash flow statement and notes. **annual equivalent rate** *n* an interest percentage rate calculated as if it were paid and compounded once a year (*abbrev* **AER**). **annual**

---

general meeting *n* (*abbrev* **AGM** or **agm**) a meeting of the directors and shareholders of a company, at which the annual accounts (qv) are presented and discussed and directors and auditors are elected, and which limited companies are legally required to hold once a year; a similar yearly meeting held by any group or society. **annual** or **annualized percentage rate** *n* an interest percentage rate (as for hire-purchase and loan agreements) calculated and expressed on an annual basis (*abbrev* **APR**). **annual report** *n* the report, including the annual financial statements, audit report and formal directors' report, presented by a company to its shareholders each year. **annual rings** *n pl* rings, as seen in cross-section, in a branch or trunk of a tree, each representing generally a year's growth of wood.

annuity /ə-nū'i-ti/ *n* a guaranteed payment (generally of uniform amount) falling due in each year during a given term (such as a period of years or the life of an individual), *usu* purchased from an insurance company by payment of a lump sum which is not returnable. [Fr *annuité*, from LL *annuitās, -ātis*, from L *annus* year]
■ **annū'itant** *n* a person who receives or holds an annuity.
❑ **annuity due** *n* one whose first payment is due in advance. **annuity share** *n* a share in a split capital trust that is highly geared towards income.
■ **certain annuity** one for a fixed term of years, subject to no contingency whatever. **complete annuity** one of which a proportion is payable up to the day of death. **contingent annuity** one that depends on the continuance of some status, such as the life of a person. **curtate annuity** one payable only at the end of each year survived. **deferred** or **reversionary annuity** one whose first payment is not to be made until a certain number of years have expired.

annul /ə-nul'/ *vt* (**annull'ing**; **annulled'**) to make null; to reduce to nothing; to abolish. [Fr *annuler*, from LL *annūllāre*, from L *ad* to, and *nūllus* none]
■ **annul'ment** *n*.

annular /an'ū-lər/ *adj* ring-shaped; cutting in a ring; ring-bearing. ◆ *n* the ring finger. [L *annulāris*, for *ānulāris*, from *ānulus* a ring, dimin of *ānus* a ring]
■ **annūlarity** /-lar'i-ti/ *n*. **Annūlā'ta** *n pl* (*obs*) the Annelida. **ann'ūlate** *n* (*obs*) an annelid. **ann'ūlate** or **ann'ūlated** *adj* ringed. **annūlā'tion** *n* a ring- or belt-like structure; the process of forming rings; a circular formation. **ann'ūlet** *n* a little ring; a small flat fillet encircling a column, etc (*archit*); a little circle borne as a charge (*heraldry*). **ann'ūlose** *adj* ringed. **ann'ūlus** *n* (*pl* **ann'ūli**) any ring-shaped structure, *esp* a ring of cells that brings about dehiscence of a moss sporogonium or a fern capsule (*biol*); the area between two concentric circles.
❑ **annular eclipse** *n* one in which a ring-shaped part of the sun remains visible.

annunciate or (now *obs*) **annuntiate** /ə-nun's(h)i-āt/ *vt* to proclaim. [Med L *annunciāre*, from L *annuntiāre, -ātum*, from *ad* to, and *nuntiāre*, from *nuntius* a messenger; cf **announce**]
■ **annunciā'tion** /-si-/ *n* proclamation; *esp* (with *the* and *cap*) that of the angel to the Virgin Mary (Bible, Luke 1.26–38), or its anniversary, 25 March (**Annunciation Day** Lady Day). **annun'ciative** *adj*. **annun'ciātor** *n* a device giving audible or visual information, eg indicating where a bell or telephone is being rung, now often operated by closed-circuit television; an announcer, someone who annunciates.
❑ **Annunciation lily** *n* the white lily (*Lilium candidum*) often seen in pictures of the Annunciation.

annus horribilis /an'əs or an'ŭs ho-ri'bi-lis/ (L) *n* literally, a year of horrors, *esp* applied by Queen Elizabeth II to 1992, a year of ill fortune for the British royal family. [By analogy with **annus mirabilis**]

annus mirabilis /an'əs mi-ra'bi-lis or an'ŭs mē-rä'bi-lis/ (L) *n* literally, a year of wonders, *esp* applied to 1666 (year of plague and fire of London), or to other years of remarkable or catastrophic, etc event.

ano- /ā-nō-/ or **ani-** /ā-ni-/ (*med, pathol*, etc) *combining form* denoting anus. [*anus*]
■ **anorec'tal** *adj* of or relating to the anus and rectum.

anoa /a- or ə-nō'ə/ *n* the sapi-utan, or wild ox of Sulawesi in Indonesia, like a small buffalo. [Native name]

Anobium /a-nō'bi-əm/ *n* a genus of small beetles of the family **Anobiidae** /a-nō-bī'i-dē/, a number of species of which bore in dry wood. [New L, from Gr *ano* upwards, and *bios* life]

anode /an'ōd/ *n* the electrode of an electrolytic cell by which current enters the electrolyte or gas; in valves and tubes, the electrode to which electrons flow. Cf **cathode**. [Gr *anodos* way up, from *ana* up, and *hodos* way]
■ **anōd'al** (or /an'od-al/) or **anodic** /an-od'ik/ *adj*. **an'odize** or **-ise** *vt* to form a protective or decorative coat on (a metal) by using it as an anode in electrolysis.

❑ **anodic protection** *n* a system for protecting metal against corrosion by making it the anode (positive electrode) in a circuit (cf **cathodic protection**).

anodyne /an'ō-dīn or -ə-/ *n* a medicine that allays pain; something that relieves mental distress; something that prevents, soothes or avoids argument, criticism or controversy. ◆ *adj* allaying pain or mental distress; preventing, soothing or avoiding argument, criticism, or controversy; harmless, bland, innocent. [Gr *anōdynos*, from *an-* (privative), and *odynē* pain]

anoesis /a-nō-ē'sis/ *n* (*pl* **anoe'ses**) sensation or emotion not accompanied by understanding of it. [Gr *anoia* lack of understanding]
■ **anoet'ic** *adj*.

anoestrus or (*US*) **anestrus** /a-nē'strəs/ (*zool*) *n* a (sometimes prolonged) period of sexual inactivity between periods of oestrus (also **anoes'trum**). [Gr *an-* (privative), and **oestrus**]
■ **anoes'trous** *adj*.

anoint /ə-noint'/ *vt* to smear with ointment or oil; to consecrate with oil; to mark as an intended successor; (ironically) to drub, beat thoroughly (*dialect*). [Fr *enoint*, pap of *enoindre*, from L *inungere, inunctum*, from *in* on, and *ung(u)ere* to smear]
■ **anoint'er** *n*. **anoint'ment** *n*.
■ **the Anointed** the Messiah. **the Lord's anointed** (in royalist theory) king by divine right.

anole /ə-nōl'/ *n* any small arboreal lizard of the tropical American genus *Anolis* (also called **American chameleon**). [Carib]

anomaly /ə-nom'ə-li/ *n* irregularity; deviation from the rule, or from the strict characteristics of type, etc; something displaying such irregularity or deviation, something anomalous; the angle measured at the sun between a planet in any point of its orbit and the last perihelion (*astron*). [Gr *anōmalos*, from *an-* (privative), and *homalos* even, from *homos* same]
■ **anomalis'tic** or (now *rare*) **anomalis'tical** *adj* anomalous; departing from established rules; irregular. **anomalis'tically** *adv*. **anom'alous** *adj* irregular; deviating from rule; (of vision) relatively insensitive to one or more colours. **anom'alously** *adv*. **anom'alousness** *n*.
❑ **anomalistic month** see under **month**. **anomalistic year** see under **year**. **anomalous water** *n* polywater.

anomie /an'ə-mē/ *n* (in society or in an individual) a condition of hopelessness caused or characterized by breakdown of rules of conduct and loss of belief and sense of purpose (also **an'omy**). [Fr, from Gr *anomia*, or *-iē* lawlessness, from *ā-* (privative), and *nomos* law]
■ **anomic** /ə-nom'ik/ *adj*.

anon /ə-non'/ (*archaic* or *literary*) *adv* in one (instant); immediately; soon; at another time; coming (in reply to a call). ◆ *interj* expressing failure to hear or understand. [OE *on* in, and *ān* one]

anon. *abbrev* : anonymous.

Anona or **Annona** /ä-nō'nə/ *n* a tropical genus of dicotyledons, including custard apple, sweet-sop, and other edible fruits, giving its name to the family **Anonā'ceae**, related to the magnolias. [Latinized from Sp *anón*, from Taino]
■ **anonā'ceous** *adj*.

anonyma /ə-non'i-mə/ (*obs*) *n* a showy woman of easy morals. [Latinized Gr]

anonymous /ə-non'i-məs/ *adj* lacking a name; without name of author, real or feigned; lacking distinctive features or individuality. [Gr *anōnymos*, from *an-* (privative), and *onyma, onoma* name]
■ **anonym** /an'/ *n* a person whose name is not given; a pseudonym. **anonym'ity** *n*. **anon'ymize** or **-ise** *vt* to remove the name(s) and any other identifying feature(s) from; to make anonymous. **anon'ymously** *adv*. **anon'ymousness** *n*.

anopheles /a-nof'ə-lēz/ *n* a member of the *Anopheles* genus of germ-carrying mosquitoes. [Gr *anōphelēs* hurtful, from *an-* (privative), and *ophelos* help]
■ **anoph'eline** *adj* relating to Anopheles. ◆ *n* a mosquito of this genus.

Anoplura /a-nō-ploo'rə/ *n pl* an order or suborder of wingless insects, the bugs, and *esp* sucking lice. [Gr *anoplos* unarmed, and *ourā* tail]

anorak /an'ə-rak/ *n* a *usu* hooded waterproof outer jacket; a Greenlander's fur coat; someone who follows a pursuit or interest that is regarded as dull and unsociable (*inf*); someone who has an obsessive interest in the statistics and trivia associated with a subject (*sl*); a socially inept person (*inf*). [Inuit]

anorectal see under **ano-**.

anorexia /a-ə-rek'si-ə/ also (formerly) **anorexy** /an'o-rek-si or -rek'/ *n* lack of appetite; anorexia nervosa. [Gr *an-* (privative), and *orexis* longing, from *oregein* to reach out]
■ **anorec'tic** *adj* causing a lack of appetite; relating to, or suffering from, anorexia (nervosa). ◆ *n* an anorectic substance. **anoret'ic** *n* and *adj* (an) anorectic. **anorex'ic** *adj* relating to, or suffering from, anorexia

(nervosa); relating to anorexics. ◆ *n* a person suffering from anorexia (nervosa).

❑ **anorexia nervosa** /nər-vō'sə or -zə/ *n* (*psychol* or *med*) a condition characterized by loss of appetite and aversion to food due to emotional disturbance, normally leading to marked emaciation, etc and sometimes death.

anorthic /a-nör'thik/ (*crystallog*) *adj* triclinic, referable to three unequal oblique axes. [Gr *an-* (privative), and *orthos* right]
■ **anor'thite** *n* a plagioclase feldspar, calcium aluminium silicate (from the oblique angles between the prism faces).

anorthosite /a-nör'thō-sīt/ *n* a coarse-grained rock consisting almost entirely of plagioclase feldspar. [Fr *anorthose* (from Gr *an-* (privative), and *orthos* right) and **-ite** (3)]

anosmia /a-noz'mi-ə/ (*med*) *n* the partial or complete loss of sense of smell. [Gr *an-* (privative), *osmē* smell, and **-ia** (1)]
■ **anosmat'ic** or **anos'mic** *adj*.

AN Other /ā en udh'ər/ *n* a name added to a list (of a sports team, etc) to represent a person still to be announced. [Humorous version of **another**, as if a person's name]

another /ə-nudh'ər/ *adj* and *pronoun* a different or distinct (thing or person); one more; a second; one more of the same kind; any other. [Orig *an other*]
❑ **anoth'erguess** *adj* (*archaic*) see **othergates**.
■ **another place** used in the House of Commons to refer to the House of Lords and vice versa. **one another** a compound reciprocal pronoun *usu* regarded as interchangeable with 'each other', but by some restricted to cases where more than two individuals are involved. **one with another** taken all together, taken on an average.

anough same as **enough** (*sing*).

anourous see **anurous**.

anovulant /a-nov'ū-lənt or -nō'vū-/ *adj* inhibiting ovulation. ◆ *n* an anovulant drug. [Gr *an-* (privative), and **ovulate**]
■ **anovulāt'ory** *adj* (of a menstrual cycle) without ovulation.

anow (*Milton*) see **enow**[1], **enough** (*pl*).

anoxia /a-nok'si-ə/ (*med*) *n* deficient supply of oxygen to the tissues. [Gr *an-* (privative), oxygen, and **-ia** (1)]
■ **anox'ic** *adj*.

ANPR *abbrev*: automatic number plate recognition.

ANS *abbrev*: autonomic nervous system.

ans. *abbrev*: answer.

Ansafone® /an'sə-fōn/ *n* an answerphone (qv).

ansate /an'sāt/ or **ansated** /-id/ *adj* having a handle or hand-like shape. [L *ansātus*, from *ansa* handle]
❑ **ansate cross** see **ankh**.

Anschauung /an-show'ŭng/ *n* direct perception through the senses (*psychol* or *philos*); an attitude or point of view. [Ger *Anschauung* perception, intuition, view]

Anschluss /an'shlŭs/ (*Ger*) *n* union, *esp* the political union of Germany and Austria in 1938.

anserine /an'sə-rīn/ *adj* of the goose or the goose family; stupid. [L *anserīnus*, from *anser* goose]

ANSI /an'si/ *abbrev*: American National Standards Institute, an organization that establishes US standards for computer software and hardware.

answer /än'sər/ *n* that which is said, written or done in meeting a charge, combating an argument, objection or attack; that which is called for by a question or questioning state of mind; the solution of a problem; an acknowledgement; a return in kind; anything given, sent or said in return; an immediate result or outcome in definite relation to the act it follows; a repetition or echo of a sound; restatement of a theme by another voice or instrument (*music*). ◆ *vt* to speak, write or act in answer to or against; to say or write as an answer; to give, send, afford or be an answer to; to behave in due accordance with; to be in proportion to or in balance with; to give a conclusive or satisfactory answer to; to serve the purpose of; to fulfil; to recompense satisfactorily (*obs*); to be punished for (*inf*). ◆ *vi* to give an answer; to behave in answer; to be responsible (with *for*); to suffer the consequences (with *for*); to be in conformity (with *for*); to serve the purpose (with *to*), to succeed; to react (*usu* with *to*). [OE *andswaru* (noun), *andswarian* (verb), from *and-* against, and *swerian* to swear]
■ **answerabil'ity** *n*. **an'swerable** *adj* capable of being answered; accountable; suitable (*archaic*); equivalent (*archaic*); in due proportion (*archaic*). **an'swerably** *adv*. **an'swerer** *n*. **an'swerless** *adj*.
❑ **answer back code** *n* an individual set of characters by which each telex machine can identify itself and be identified. **answering service** *n* a commercial service which answers telephone calls, takes messages, etc for its clients when they are not available. **answerphone** /än'sər-fōn/ or **answering machine** *n* a device that

automatically answers incoming telephone calls, plays a pre-recorded message to the callers and records their messages on audiotape.
■ **answer back** (*inf*) to answer someone who expects silent submission; to answer pertly. **answer to** to give an indication of accepting as one's name; to have as one's name (*inf*); to be accountable to. **have** (or **know**) **all the answers** to be in complete command of the situation with no chance of being caught out (a statement *usu* made with reference to another person who is too self-confident).

ant /ant/ *n* a small, hymenopterous, scavenging (or sometimes predacious) social insect (family Formicidae), of proverbial industry, living in organized colonies; loosely, a termite. [OE *æmete*; cf **emmet**]
■ **ant'ing** *n* the introduction by birds of live ants or other stimulants into their plumage, possibly as a pleasurable means of cleaning it and their skin.
❑ **ant'bear** *n* the great anteater, the largest species of anteaters, found in swampy regions in S America; the aardvark of S Africa. **ant'bird** *n* a S American ant thrush. **ant cow** *n* an aphis kept and tended by ants for its honeydew. **ant'eater** *n* any one of a Central and S American family of edentates, adapted for feeding on ants and termites; a pangolin; an aardvark; an echidna. **ant'-** or **ants''-eggs** *n pl* pupae of ants. **ant'-hill** *n* a hillock raised as a nest in wood, soil, etc by ants or by termites; anything like an ant-hill in terms of crowdedness, bustle, etc (*fig*). **ant'lion** *n* a neuropterous insect (*esp* genus *Myrmeleon*) similar to a damselfly, whose larvae trap ants in a funnel-shaped sand-hole. **ant'pitta** *n* any of several S American birds related to the ant thrushes. **ant thrush** *n* any bird of the northern S American family Formicariidae which feeds on insects disturbed by travelling ants, or of the long-legged thrush-like Asian and Australian family Pittidae.
■ **have ants in one's pants** (*inf*) to be restless, impatient, needlessly hurrying.

an't /änt/ (*archaic* or *dialect*) a contraction of **are not**, **am not**, **has not**, or /ant/ **on it**, **and it** (= if it).

ant- see **anti-**.

-ant /-ənt/ *sfx* (1) forming adjectives denoting attribution of an action or condition, eg *sonorant*, *pleasant*; (2) forming nouns denoting the agent of an action, eg *suppressant*, *accountant*. [L *-ans*, *-antis*, present participle ending in the 1st conjugation]

anta[1] /an'tə/ (*archit*) *n* (*pl* **an'tae** /-tē/) a pilaster at either side of a doorway or the corner of a flank wall. [L]
■ **in antis** (*L*) literally, between the antae; (of a portico) not framed by columns but having antae terminating the side walls; (of a portico) recessed in a façade.

anta[2] /än'ta/ *n* a tapir. [Port, from Sp, elk]

Antabuse® /an'tə-būs/ or -būz/ *n* a drug in tablet form containing disulfiram, used in the treatment of alcoholism.

antacid /an-tas'id/ *adj* counteracting acidity of the stomach. ◆ *n* a medicine that counteracts acidity. [**anti-**]

antagonist /an-tag'ə-nist/ *n* a person who contends or struggles with another; an opponent; a muscle that opposes the action of another; in an organism, something that has an opposite effect; a drug acting against another drug or other chemical or hormone. ◆ *adj* acting against. [Gr *antagōnistēs*, from *anti* against, and *agōn* contest. See **agony**]
■ **antag'onism** *n* opposition; hostility; production of opposing effects, eg in a living body; interference with the growth of another organism, eg by using up the food supply or producing an antibiotic substance. **antagonist'ic** *adj*. **antagonis'tically** *adv*. **antagoniza'tion** or **-s-** *n*. **antag'onize** or **-ise** *vt* to arouse opposition in; to struggle violently against; to counteract the action of.

antaphrodisiac /an-ta-frō-diz'i-ak or -frə-/ *adj* counteracting sexual desire. ◆ *n* an antaphrodisiac agent. [**anti-**]

antar /an'tər/ (*Shakesp*) *n* a cave. [Fr *antre*, from L *antrum*, from Gr *antron*]

antara /an-tar'ə/ *n* a type of Andean Pan-pipes. [Am Sp, from Quechua]

Antarctic /an-tärk'tik/ *adj* opposite the Arctic; of, near, or relating to the south pole. ◆ *n* the south polar regions. [Gr *antarktikos*, from *anti* opposite, and *arktikos* (see **Arctic**)]
❑ **Antarctic Circle** *n* the parallel of latitude 66°32′S, bounding the region of the earth surrounding the south terrestrial pole.

Antares /an-tā'rēz or -tä'/ *n* a first-magnitude red star, the brightest in the Scorpius constellation. [Gr *Antarēs*, from pfx *anti-* like, and *Arēs* Mars]

antarthritic /an-tär-thrit'ik/ (*med*) *adj* counteracting arthritis. ◆ *n* an agent that counteracts arthritis (also **antiarthrit'ic**). [**anti-**]

antasthmatic, also **antiasthmatic** /an-tas(th)-mat'ik, also *an-ti-as(th)-mat'ik/* (*med*) *adj* counteracting asthma. ◆ *n* an agent that counteracts asthma. [**anti-**]

■ words derived from main entry word; ❑ compound words; ■ idioms and phrasal verbs

ante /an'ti/ (*orig* and *esp US*) *n* a fixed stake put down by a poker player, *usu* before the deal; advance payment. ◆ *vt* to stake (*poker*); to pay (*usu* with *up*). [L, before]
■ **up** (or **raise**) **the ante** (*inf*, *fig*) to increase the costs or risks involved in, or the demands requiring to be met before, some action.

ante- /an-ti-/ *pfx* signifying before. [L *ante*, old form *anti*; connected with Gr **anti-**]

antebellum /an-ti-bel'əm/ *adj* and *n* (happening in) the time before the war (whichever is in mind). [L *ante bellum* before the war]

antecedent /an-ti-sē'dənt/ *adj* going before in time; prior. ◆ *n* that which precedes in time; an ancestor; the noun or its equivalent to which a relative pronoun refers (*grammar*); the conditional part of a hypothetical proposition (*logic*); the numerator term of a ratio (*maths*); (in *pl*) previous principles, conduct, history, etc. [L *antecēdēns*, *-entis*, from *ante* before, and *cēdere* to go]
■ **antecēde'** *vt* to go before in time, rank, etc. **antece'dence** *n*. **antece'dently** *adv*.

antecessor /an'ti-ses-ər/ or *-ses'/ *n* a predecessor (*rare*); an ancestor (*obs*). [L; cf **antecedent** and **ancestor**]

antechamber /an'ti-chām-bər/ *n* a chamber or room leading to a more important apartment. [Fr *antichambre*, from L *ante* before, and *camera* a vault]

antechapel /an'ti-chap-əl/ *n* the outer part of the west end of a college chapel. [**ante-**]

antechoir /an'ti-kwīr/ *n* the space in front of the choir in a church. [**ante-**]

antedate /an'ti-dāt/ *n* a date assigned which is earlier than the actual date. ◆ *vt* to date before the true time; to assign to an earlier date; to bring about at an earlier date; to be of previous date to; to accelerate; to anticipate. [**ante-** and **date**[1]]

antediluvian /an-ti-di-loo'vi-ən/ or *-lū'/ *adj* existing or happening before Noah's Flood; resembling the state of things before the Flood; very old-fashioned, primitive. ◆ *n* an antediluvian thing or person; a person who lived before the Flood; someone who lives to be very old. [**ante-** and L *dīluvium* flood]
■ **antedilu'vial** *adj* (*geol*; *rare*). **antedilu'vially** *adv*.

antefix /an'ti-fiks/ *n* (*pl* **an'tefixes** or **antefix'a**) (*usu* in *pl*) an ornament concealing the ends of roofing tiles and protecting the rafters of classical temples, etc. [L *ante* before, in front, and *figere*, *fixum* to fix]
■ **antefix'al** *adj*.

antelope /an'ti-lōp/ or *-tə-/ *n* (since the 17c) any one of a group of hollow-horned, hoofed, ruminant mammals closely related to goats; a pronghorn; a fabulous fierce horned beast (*Spenser*). [OFr *antelop*, from Med L *antalopus*, from Late Gr *antholops*, of unknown origin]

antelucan /an-ti-loo'kən/ or *-lū'/ (*archaic*; *literary*) *adj* (of eg worship) before dawn or daylight. [L *antelūcānus*, from *ante* before, and *lūx* light]

ante lucem /an'te lū'səm or loo'/, or /loo'kəm/ (*L*) before light.

antemeridian /an-ti-mə-rid'i-ən/ *adj* occurring before midday. [L *antemerīdiānus*, from *ante merīdiem* before noon]

ante meridiem /an'te me-rid'i-em or me-rē'di-em/ (*L*) before noon.

ante mortem /an'te mör'tem/ (*L*) before death.
❏ **ante-mortem inspection** *n* an inspection of livestock by a vet immediately before slaughter, to ensure that the animal meets required standards of fitness, health, etc.

antemundane /an-ti-mun'dān/ (*archaic*; *literary*) *adj* before the existence of the world. [**ante-** and L *mundānus*, from *mundus* world]

antenatal /an-ti-nā'təl/ *adj* before birth; of, or relating to, the health and care, etc of women during pregnancy. ◆ *n* a medical examination for pregnant women. [**ante-** and L *nātālis* natal, or *nātus* born]
■ **antena'tally** *adv*. **antenā'tī** (or */-nā'tē/*) *n pl* those born before a certain time, used of Scots born before 1603 and Americans before the Declaration of Independence (1776) (cf **postnati**).
❏ **antenatal clinic** *n* a clinic for the purpose of treating and giving advice to pregnant women.

ante-Nicene /an-ti-nī'sēn/ *adj* before the first council of *Nicaea* in Bithynia, 325AD.

antenna /an-ten'ə/ *n* (*pl* **antenn'ae** /-ē/ or (*TV* and *radio*) **antenn'as**) a feeler or horn in insects, crustaceans and myriapods; in TV and radio communication, a structure for sending out or receiving electromagnetic signals; an aerial. [L *antemna*, *antenna* yard (of a mast)]
■ **antenn'al** or **antenn'ary** *adj*. **antennif'erous** *adj* bearing or having antennae. **antenn'iform** *adj*. **antenn'ūle** *n* one of a first or smaller pair of antennae in crustaceans.

antenuptial /an-ti-nup'shəl/ *adj* before marriage. [**ante-**]

anteorbital /an-ti-ör'bi-təl/ *adj* situated in front of the eyes. [L *ante* before]

antepast /an'ti-pāst/ (*obs*) *n* something to whet the appetite; a foretaste. [L *ante* before, and *pāscere*, *pāstum* to feed]

antependium /an-ti-pen'di-əm/ *n* a hanging for the front of an altar, a frontlet or forecloth; a frontal. [L *ante* before, and *pendēre* to hang]

antepenult /an-ti-pe-nult' or *-pi-/ *n* the last syllable but two (of a word). [L *ante* before, and **penult**]
■ **antepenult'imate** *adj* last but two.

ante-post /an'ti-pōst/ *adj* (of betting) beginning before the runners' numbers are posted; occurring during the time before the runners come under starter's orders. [**ante** and **post**[1]]

anteprandial /an-ti-pran'di-əl/ *adj* before dinner. [L *ante* before, and *prandium* dinner]

anterior /an-tē'ri-ər/ *adj* before, in time or place; in front; towards the front of the body (*anat*); of or near the head (*zool*); towards the bract or away from the axis (*bot*). [L *anterior* (*compar*), from *ante* before]
■ **anteriority** /-or'i-ti/ *n*. **antē'riorly** *adv*.

anterograde amnesia /an'tə-rō-grād am-nē'zhə or *-zyə*/ (*behaviourism*) *n* loss of memory for events after injury to the brain or mental trauma, with little effect on information acquired previously. [L *anterior* previous, and *gradī*, *gressus* to go; **amnesia**]

anteroom /an'ti-room/ *n* a room leading into another larger room; a waiting room; an officers' mess sitting room. [**ante-**; modelled on Fr *antichambre* (see **antechamber**)]

anteversion /an-ti-vûr'shən/ (*med*) *n* the abnormal tipping forward of a bodily organ, *esp* the uterus. [L *ante* before, and *vertere*, *versum* to turn]
■ **antevert'** *vt*.

anthelion /an-thē'li-ən or *-lyən*/ *n* (*pl* **anthe'lia**) a luminous coloured ring seen on a cloud or fog bank opposite the sun; a white spot on the parhelic circle seen opposite the sun. [Gr *ant(h)ēlios*, *-on*, from *anti* opposite, and *hēlios* the sun]

anthelix see **antihelix**.

anthelminthic /an-thel-min'thik/ or **anthelmintic** /-tik/ *adj* destroying or expelling worms, *esp* parasitic intestinal worms. ◆ *n* a drug used for that purpose. [Gr *anti* against, and *helmins*, *helminthos* a worm]

anthem /an'thəm/ *n* a composition for a church choir, commonly with solo passages, *usu* set to a passage from the Bible; any song of praise or gladness; loosely, an officially recognized national hymn or song (such as a *national anthem*); a song or tune that provokes a powerful response from an audience; an antiphon (*obs*). ◆ *vt* to praise in an anthem. [OE *antefn*, from Gr *antiphōna* (pl) sounding in answer, from *anti* in return, and *phōnē* voice. See **antiphon**]
■ **anthem'ic** *adj* (*esp* of popular music) provoking a powerful response from an audience. **an'themwise** *adv* (*Bacon*) in the manner of an antiphonal anthem.

anthemion /an-thē'mi-ən/ *n* (*pl* **anthē'mia**) the so-called honeysuckle ornament in ancient art, a conventionalized plant-form more like a palmetto. [Gr *anthemion*, dimin of *anthos* a flower]

anther /an'thər/ (*bot*) *n* the part of a stamen that produces the pollen. [Gr *anthēra* a medicine made from flowers, *esp* their inner parts, from *anthos* flower]
■ **antherid'ial** *adj*. **antherid'ium** *n* (*pl* **antherid'ia**) the gametangium in which male gametes are produced. **antherozō'oid** or **antherozō'id** *n* (Gr *zōoeidēs* like an animal, from *zōion* animal, and *eidos* shape) a motile male gamete produced in an antheridium.
❏ **an'thersmut** *n* a fungus (*Ustilago violacea*) causing a disease affecting plants of the carnation and pink family, in which the anthers produce the fungus spores instead of pollen.

anthesis /an-thē'sis/ (*bot*) *n* the opening of a flower-bud; the lifetime of a flower from opening to setting of seed. [Gr *anthēsis* flowering, from *anthos* flower]

Anthesteria /an-the-stē'ri-ə/ *n pl* the Athenian spring festival of Dionysos, held in the month of *Anthestērion* (February–March). [Gr *ta Anthestēria* (Feast of Flowers), *Anthestērion* (the month), from *anthos* flower]

antho- /an-tho- or an-thə-/ *combining form* denoting flower. [Gr *anthos* flower]
■ **anthocarp** /an'thō-kärp/ *n* (Gr *karpos* fruit) a fruit resulting from many flowers, such as the pineapple; a fruit of which the perianth or the torus forms part. **anthocarp'ous** *adj*. **an'thochlore** /-klōr or -klör/ *n* (Gr *chlōros* green, yellow) a yellow pigment in flowers. **anthocyan** /-sī'ən/ or **anthocy'anin** *n* (Gr *kyanos* blue) a glucoside plant pigment, violet in neutral, red in acid, blue in alkaline cell-sap. **an'thoid** *adj* (Gr *eidos* shape) flower-like. **anthol'ogy** *n*, etc see separate entry. **anthomā'nia** *n* (Gr *mania* madness) a craze for flowers. **anthomā'niac** *n*. **Anthonomus** /an-thon'ə-məs/ *n* (Gr *nomos*

herbage, food) the genus of the cotton-boll weevil. **anthophilous** /an-thof'i-las/ adj loving, frequenting or feeding on flowers. **an'thophore** /-thō-fōr or -fŏr/ n (bot) an elongation of the receptacle between calyx and corolla. **anthophyllite** /an-thō-fil'īt, or -tha- or sometimes -thof'/ n (New L anthophyllum clove, from Gr phyllon leaf) an orthorhombic amphibole, usu massive and occurring in metamorphic rocks. **anthoxan'thin** n (Gr xanthos yellow) a yellow pigment in plants. **Anthozō'a** n pl (Gr zōia animals) a class of coelenterates including sea anemones, corals, etc.

anthology /an-tho'lə-ji/ n a choice collection of writings, (esp poems), songs or paintings, etc; literally, a flower-gathering. [Gr, a collection of epigrams, literally, a flower-gathering, from anthos flower, and -logia gathering (from leigein to collect)]
■ **anthol'ogist** n a person who compiles an anthology. **anthol'ogize** or **-ise** vt and vi.

Anthony /an'tə-ni/ n a 4c Egyptian saint, patron saint of swineherds; (also **tantony** /tan'/, **St Anthony pig** or **tantony pig**) the smallest pig in a litter; an obsequious follower.
■ **St Anthony's cross** a tau cross. **St Anthony's fire** (popularly) erysipelas. **St Anthony's nut** earth-nut or pignut. **tantony bell** a small bell.

anthophilous see under **antho-**.

anthracene /an'thrə-sēn/ n a product of coal-tar distillation ($C_{14}H_{10}$) consisting of three benzene rings condensed together, a source of dyestuffs. [Ety as for **anthrax**, with sfx -ene (chem)]

anthracite /an'thrə-sīt/ n hard lustrous coal that burns nearly without flame or smoke, consisting almost entirely of carbon. [Gr anthrakitēs a kind of coal; cf **anthrax**]
■ **anthracitic** /-sit'ik/ adj of or of the nature of anthracite.

anthracnose /an-thrak'nōs/ n any of several plant diseases caused by a fungus and characterized by the appearance of dark, sunken spots. [Ety as for **anthrax**, and Gr nosos disease]

anthracoid see under **anthrax**.

anthracosis /an-thrə-kō'sis/ n a diseased state of the lung due to breathing in coal dust. [Ety as for **anthrax**, with -osis]

anthraquinone /an-thrə-kwin'ōn/ n a yellow crystalline solid ($C_{14}H_8O_2$) used in the manufacture of dyes (also **diphenylene diketone**). [Ety as for **anthrax**, and **quinone**]

anthrax /an'thraks/ n a deadly disease due to a bacillus, most common in sheep and cattle but communicable to humans (also known as **malignant pustule** or **wool-sorter's disease**); the bacillus that causes the disease; a sore caused by the disease; a carbuncle or malignant boil. [Gr anthrax, -akos charcoal, coal, carbuncle (stone or boil)]
■ **anthracic** /-thras'ik/ adj. **anthracoid** /an'thrə-koid/ adj like anthrax.

anthrop- /an-throp-/ or **anthropo-** /an-thro-pō-, -pə- or -po-/ combining form denoting man, human. [Gr anthrōpos man (in general sense)]
■ **anthrop'ic** or **anthrop'ical** adj human. **anthropobiol'ogy** n human biology. **anthropocentric** /an-thrō-pō-sent'rik/ adj (Gr kentron centre) regarding the human race as the centre of, or central to, the universe. **anthropocent'rically** adv. **anthropocent'rism** n. **anthropogenesis** /-jen'/ n. **anthropogen'ic** adj. **anthropogeny** /-oj'ən-i/ n (Gr genos race, birth) the study of man's origin. **anthrōpogeog'raphy** n the geography of the races of man. **anthropogony** /-og'ə-ni/ n (Gr gonē, gonos birth, begetting) the study, or an account, of the origin of man. **anthropography** /-og'rə-fi/ n the study of the geographical distribution of human races. **an'thropoid** (or /-thrōp'/) adj (Gr eidos form) manlike, applied esp to the highest apes (gorilla, chimpanzee, orang-utan, gibbon) but also to the higher Primates generally, ie man, apes, monkeys, but not lemurs. ◆ n an anthropoid ape. **anthropoid'al** adj. **anthropol'atry** n (Gr latreiā worship) man-worship, the giving of divine honours to a human being. **anthrōpological** /-loj'/ adj. **anthrōpolog'ically** adv. **anthropol'ogist** n. **anthropol'ogy** n the scientific study of human beings and their way of life, the science of man in its widest sense. **anthropomet'ric** adj. **anthropometry** /-om'i-tri/ n (Gr metreein to measure) measurement of the human body. **anthrō'pomorph** n (Gr morphē shape) a representation, esp conventionalized, of the human form in art. **anthropomorph'ic** adj. **anthropomorph'ically** adv. **anthropomorph'ism** n conception or representation of a god as having the form, personality or attributes of man; ascription of human characteristics to what is not human, esp an

animal. **anthropomorph'ist** n. **anthropomorph'ite** n a person who ascribes human form, personality or attributes to God. **anthropomorphit'ic** adj. **anthropomorph'itism** n. **anthropomor'phize** or **-ise** vt to regard as or render anthropomorphic. **anthropomorphō'sis** (or /-mörf'ə-sis/) n transformation into human shape. **anthropomorph'ous** adj formed like or resembling man. **anthropopathic** /-path'ik/ adj. **anthropopath'ically** adv. **anthropopathism** /-op'ə-thizm/ or **anthropop'athy** n (Gr pathos suffering, passion) ascription of human passions and affections (to God, nature, etc). **anthropophagi** /-of'ə-jī or -gē/ n pl (Gr phagein to eat) man-eaters, cannibals. **anthropophaginian** /-jin'i-ən/ n (Shakesp) a cannibal. **anthropoph'agite** /-ə-jīt/ n. **anthropoph'agous** /-ə-gəs/ adj. **anthropoph'agy** /-ə-ji/ n cannibalism. **anthropophō'bia** n a morbid fear of people or society. **anthropophō'bic** n and adj. **anthropoph'ūism** n (Gr phyē nature) the ascription of a human nature to the gods. **anthrop'ophyte** n a plant introduced incidentally in the course of cultivation. **Anthropopithē'cus** n (Gr pithekos ape) the chimpanzee. **anthropopsy'chic** /-sī'kik or -psī'kik/ adj. **anthropopsy'chically** adv. **anthropopsy'chism** n (Gr psychē soul) ascription to nature or God of a soul or mind like man's. **anthroposoph'ical** adj. **anthropos'ophist** n. **anthropos'ophy** n (Gr sophiā wisdom) the knowledge of the nature of men; human wisdom; specif the spiritualistic doctrine of Austrian philosopher Rudolf Steiner (1861–1925). **anthropot'omy** n (Gr tomē a cut) human anatomy.

anthurium /an-thū'ri-əm/ n a member of the Anthurium genus of tropical American plants with showy leaves and flowers. [Gr anthos flower, and oura tail]

anti /an'ti, also (N Am) an'tī/ prep opposed to, against. ◆ n and adj (a person who is) opposed to anything. [Gr anti against, instead of, etc]

anti- /an-ti-, also (US) an-tī-/ or often before a vowel **ant-** /ant-/ pfx denoting: (1) acting against, counteracting, resisting, resistant to; (2) opposed to; (3) opposite or reverse. [Gr anti against]

> Words with the prefix **anti-** are listed in the following text or in the separate panels.

antiaditis /an-ti-ə-dī'tis/ (med) n tonsillitis. [Gr antias, -ados tonsil]

anti-aircraft /an-ti-ār'krāft or (US) -tī-/ adj intended for use against hostile aircraft. [**anti-** (1)]

antiar /an'chär or an'ti-är/ n the upas-tree; its poisonous latex. [Javanese antjar]

antiarrhythmic /an-ti-ə-ridh'mik/ (med) adj counteracting, or capable of controlling, arrhythmia. ◆ n an antiarrhythmic agent or drug. [**anti-** (1)]

antibacchius /an-ti-bə-kī'əs/ (prosody) n a foot of two long (or stressed) syllables followed by a short (or unstressed) one. [**anti-** (3) and **bacchius** (see under **bacchanal**)]

antiballistic /an-ti-bə-lis'tik/ adj (of a missile, etc) designed to destroy a ballistic missile. [**anti-** (1)]

antibarbarus /an-ti-bär'bä-rus/ (LL) n a list of words and sayings to be avoided in the classical usage of a language.

antibiosis /an-ti-bī-ō'sis/ (biol) n a state of mutual antagonism between associated organisms, opp to symbiosis; inhibition of growth by a substance produced by another organism. [**anti-** (1) and Gr biosis way of life, from bios life]
■ **antibiotic** /-ot'ik/ adj inimical to life; inhibiting the growth of another organism, used esp of a substance produced by micro-organisms which, in dilute solution, has the capacity to inhibit the growth of, or to destroy, micro-organisms causing infectious diseases; relating to antibiosis. ◆ n an antibiotic substance.
❑ **antibiotic resistance** n (biol) a property of certain micro-organisms or cells which enables them to survive high concentrations of a normally lethal agent, usu acquired by the selection of a rare resistant mutant in the presence of low concentrations of the agent.

antibody /an'ti-bo-di/ (biol) n a substance which inactivates a foreign body such as a protein, bacterium, virus or toxin by combining with it. [**anti-** (1)]

Antiburgher /an-ti-bûr'gər/ (hist) n a member of that section of the Scottish Secession Church which parted from the main body (the Burghers) in 1747, interpreting the reference in the oath administered

---

Some words formed with the prefix **anti-**; the numbers in brackets refer to the numbered senses in the entry for **anti-**.

anti-abor'tion adj (2).	**anticorrō'sive** adj (1).	**anti-Gall'ican** adj and n (2).
antibactēr'ial adj (1).	**antidīūret'ic** adj and n (1).	**anti-Gall'icanism** n (2).
antibil'ious adj (1).	**antifric'tion** adj (1).	**anti-inflamm'atory** adj (1).

■ words derived from main entry word; ❑ compound words; ■ idioms and phrasal verbs

to burgesses in Edinburgh, Glasgow and Perth to 'the true religion presently professed within this realm' to mean the Established Church (also *adj*). [**anti-** (2)]

antic, also (*obs*) **antick**, **anticke** or sometimes **antique** /*an'tik*/ *n* (*usu* in *pl*) an extraordinary action or trick, a caper; an extraordinary figure or ornament (*obs*); a grotesque pageant (*Shakesp*); a buffoon, clown, mountebank (*archaic*). ♦ *adj* (*archaic*) grotesque, fantastic. ♦ *vt* (**ant'icking**; **ant'icked**) (*Shakesp*) to make grotesque. ♦ *vi* (*archaic*) to cut capers. —See also **antique**. [Ital *antico* ancient, from L *antíquus*; orig used of the fantastic decorations found in the remains of ancient Rome]
■ **anticize** /*ant'i-sīz*/ *vi* (*Browning*) to play antics.

anticapitalist /*an-ti-kap'i-tə-list*/ *n* and *adj* (a person) opposed to capitalism or its influence. [**anti-** (2)]

anticathode /*an-ti-kath'ōd*/ *n* the target of an X-ray tube, on which the cathode rays are focused and from which X-rays are emitted. [**anti-** (3)]

anticatholic /*an-ti-kath'(ə-)lik*/ *adj* opposed to the Catholic or the Roman Catholic Church, to Catholics, or to what is catholic. [**anti-** (2)]

anti-chip /*an-ti-chip'*/ *adj* (of paint, etc) resistant to chipping. [**anti-** (1)]

antichlor /*an'ti-klör*/ *n* any substance used in paper- or textile-making to free the pulp from the last traces of free chlorine. [**anti-** (1)]

anticholinergic /*an-ti-kō-li-nûr'jik*/ (*med*) *adj* counteracting the effect of acetylcholine; blocking parasympathetic nerve impulses. ♦ *n* a drug which blocks these impulses. [**anti-** (1)]

Antichrist /*an'ti-krīst*/ *n* an opponent of Christ; the great opposer of Christ and Christianity expected by the early Church, later applied by some (eg Protestant extremists) to the Pope and others. [Gr *Antichristos*, from *anti-* against, and *Christos* Christ]
■ **antichristian** /*-kris'-*/ *adj* relating to Antichrist; opposed to Christianity. **antichris'tianism** *n*. **antichris'tianly** *adv*.

Antichthon /*an-tik'thōn*/ *n* the supposed second earth thought by Pythagoreans to exist on the other side of the sun; the southern hemisphere (*obs*). [Gr *anti* opposite to, and *chthōn* earth]
■ **antich'thones** /*-thon-ēz*/ *n pl* (*obs*) the antipodeans.

anticipate /*an-tis'i-pāt*/ *vt* to forestall (a person or thing); to use, spend, deal with in advance or before the due time; to realize beforehand; to foresee or count upon as certain; to expect; to precede (*rare*); to advance to an earlier time, bring on sooner. ♦ *vi* to do anything, or take action, before the appropriate, expected or due time; to be before the normal time (*obs*). [L *anticipāre*, *-ātum*, from *ante* before, and *capere* to take]
■ **antic'ipant** *adj* anticipating, anticipative (also *n*). **anticipā'tion** *n* an act of anticipating; imagining beforehand; expectation; assignment to too early a time; the introduction of a tone or tones of a chord before the whole chord (*music*); intuition; foretaste; previous notion; presentiment; prejudice (*obs*). **anti'cipative** or **anti'cipatory** *adj*. **anti'cipatively** or **anti'cipatorily** *adv*. **antic'ipator** *n*.

anticivic /*an-ti-siv'ik*/ *adj* opposed to citizenship, *esp* the conception of it engendered by the French Revolution. [**anti-** (2)]
■ **anticiv'ism** *n*.

antick, **anticke** obsolete forms of **antic**, **antique**.

anticlerical /*an-ti-kler'i-kəl*/ *adj* opposed to the clergy or their (political) power. ♦ *n* a member of an anticlerical party. [**anti-** (2)]
■ **anticler'icalism** *n*.

anticlimax /*an-ti-klī'maks*/ *n* the opposite of climax; a ludicrous drop in impressiveness after a progressive rise; a disappointing, weak or dull outcome or follow-up, in sudden contrast to preceding events, expectations, etc. [**anti-** (3)]
■ **anticlimac'tic** *adj*. **anticlimac'tically** *adv*.

anticline /*an'ti-klīn*/ (*geol*) *n* an arch-like fold dipping outwards from the fold-axis. [**anti-** (1), and Gr *klinein* to lean]
■ **anticlin'al** *adj* sloping in opposite directions; perpendicular to the surface near the growing-point (*bot*). ♦ *n* an anticline. **anticlinō'rium** /*-klin-* or *-klīn-*/ *n* (Gr *oros* mountain) a series of folds which as a whole is anticlinal.

anticlockwise /*an-ti-klok'wīz*/ *adv* in the opposite direction to that in which the hands of a clock travel. [**anti-** (3)]

anticoagulant /*an-ti-kō-ag'ū-lənt*/ *n* and *adj* (a drug) that hinders normal clotting of blood. [**anti-** (1)]

anticonvulsant /*an-ti-kən-vul'sənt*/ *n* and *adj* (a drug) used to control convulsions in epilepsy, etc (also **anticonvul'sive**). [**anti-** (1)]

anticous /*an-tī'kəs*/ (*bot*) *adj* on the anterior side, or away from the axis. [L *antícus* in front, from *ante* before]

anticyclone /*an-ti-sī'klōn*/ (*meteorol*) *n* a rotatory outflow of air from an area of high pressure. [**anti-** (3)]
■ **anticyclonic** /*-klon'ik*/ *adj*.

antidepressant /*an-ti-di-pres'ənt*/ *n* a drug used to counteract depression (also *adj*). [**anti-** (1)]

antidesiccant /*an-ti-des'i-kənt*/ *n* a chemical which prevents or inhibits the drying-out of a plant, etc. [**anti-** (1)]

anti-devolutionist /*an-ti-dē-və-loo'shə-nist*, *-de-* or *-lū'*/ *n* a person who is opposed to devolution. [**anti-** (2)]

antidisestablishmentarianism /*an-ti-di-sə-stab-lish-mən-tā'ri-ə-ni-zm*/ *n* a movement against the removing of state recognition of an established church, *esp* the Anglican Church in the 19c. [**anti-** (2)]
■ **antidisestablishmenta'rian** *adj*.

antidiuretic /*an-ti-dī-e-ret'ik*/ *adj* inhibiting the formation of urine. ♦ *n* an antidiuretic drug. [**anti-** (1)]
❑ **antidiuretic hormone** *n* vasopressin.

antidote /*an'ti-dōt*/ *n* something which counteracts a poison; anything that prevents an evil or something unwanted (with *against*, *for* or *to*) (*fig*). [Gr *antidotos*, from *anti* against, and *didonai* to give]
■ **antido'tal** *adj*.

antidromic /*an-ti-drom'ik*/ (*med*) *adj* (of nerve fibres) conducting or able to conduct impulses in the opposite direction to normal. [**anti-** (1) and Gr *dromos* a course, run]

antiemetic /*an-ti-i-met'ik*/ *adj* preventing vomiting. ♦ *n* an antiemetic drug. [**anti-** (1)]

antient an obsolete spelling of **ancient**[1,2].

anti-establishment /*an-ti-e-stab'lish-mənt* or *-i-*/ *adj* opposed to the opinions and values of the establishment in society. ♦ *n* the people who are opposed to such opinions, etc. [**anti-** (2)]

anti-fade /*an-ti-fād'*/ *adj* resistant to fading. [**anti-** (1)]

anti-federal /*an-ti-fed'ə-rəl*/ *adj* opposed to federalism; applied to the former US party afterwards called Democratic. [**anti-** (2)]
■ **anti-fed'eralism** *n*. **anti-fed'eralist** *n*.

anti-feedant /*an-ti-fē'dənt*/ *n* any of a number of substances present in some species of plants which make the plants resistant to insect pests. [**anti-** (1)]

anti-flash /*an-ti-flash'*/ *adj* protecting against the flash of explosions, etc. [**anti-** (1)]

antifouling /*an-ti-fow'ling*/ *adj* intended to prevent fouling of ships' bottoms by marine growths, eg barnacles. ♦ *n* an antifouling substance applied in paint form to ships' bottoms, etc. [**anti-** (1)]

antifreeze /*an'ti-frēz*/ *n* a substance (eg ethylene glycol) with low freezing point put into water to lower its freezing point, *esp* used in the radiator of an internal-combustion engine to prevent freezing up. [**anti-** (1)]

antifungal /*an-ti-fung'gl*/ *adj* preventing the growth of fungi. ♦ *n* an antifungal agent. [**anti-** (1)]

anti-g /*an-ti-jē*/ *adj* resistant to the effects of high acceleration, *esp* of an astronaut's equipment. [**anti-** (1) and *g* for **gravity**]

antigay /*an-ti-gā'*/ *adj* opposed or hostile to homosexuals or gay rights movements, activities, organizations, etc. [**anti-** (2)]

antigen /*an'ti-jən* or *-jen*/ (*biol*) *n* any substance that stimulates the production of an antibody. [**anti-** (1) and Gr *gennaein* to engender]
■ **antigen'ic** *adj*. **antigen'ically** *adv*.
❑ **antigenic determinant** *n* (*immunol*) a small part of an antigen which has a structure complementary to a part of its corresponding antibody (also **epitope**). **antigenic variation** *n* (*immunol*) the development of new antigenic determinants by many viruses, bacteria and protozoa through genetic mutation and selection.

antihalation /*an-ti-hə-lā'shən*/ (*photog*) *n* the prevention of halation, *usu* by placing a layer of dye on the back of the film to absorb light which has passed through the emulsion on it. [**anti-** (1)]

Some words formed with the prefix **anti-**; the numbers in brackets refer to the numbered senses in the entry for **anti-**.

anti-inflā'tionary *adj* (1).	**anti-mod'ernist** *adj* and *n* (1), (2).	**anti-na'tional** *adj* (2).
antimalā'rial *adj* (1).	**antimonarch'ical** *adj* (2).	**antinoise'** *adj* (1).
antimicrō'bial *adj* (1).	**antimon'archist** *n* (2).	**antiperistal'tic** *adj* (3).

antihelix /*an-ti-hē'liks*/ or **anthelix** /*an'thi-liks* or *an-thē'liks*/ (*anat*) *n* (*pl* **antihelices** /*-li-sēz*/ or **anthel'ices**) the inner curved ridge of the external ear. [Gr *anthelix*, from *helix* a coil]

anti-hero /*an'ti-hē-rō*/ *n* (also *fem* **anti-heroine** /*-her-ō-in*/) a principal character (in a novel, play, etc) who lacks noble qualities and whose experiences are without tragic dignity. [**anti-** (3)]
∎ **anti-heroic** /*-hi-rō'ik*/ *adj*.

antihistamine /*an-ti-his'tə-mēn*/ *n* any of a group of drugs that prevents the action of histamines in allergic conditions. [**anti-** (1)]

antihypertensive /*an-ti-hī-pər-ten'siv*/ *adj* (of a drug or other measure) used to lower the blood pressure. ◆ *n* an antihypertensive drug. [**anti-** (1)]

anti-icer /*an-ti-ī'sər*/ *n* a chemical substance that prevents ice forming, eg on roads or aircraft parts. [**anti-** (1)]

anti-Jacobin or sometimes **antijacobin** /*an'ti-jak'ə-bin*/ (*hist*) *adj* opposed to the Jacobins and to the French Revolution or to democratic principles. ◆ *n* a person opposed to the Jacobins; (with *cap*) a weekly paper started in England in 1797 by Canning and others to refute the principles of the French Revolution. [**anti-** (2)]
∎ **anti-Jac'obinism** *n*.

antijamming /*an-ti-jam'ing*/ *n* a technique designed to prevent or reduce deliberate jamming of radio signals, radar communications, etc (also *adj*). [**anti-** (1)]

antiknock /*an-ti-nok'*/ *n* a substance that prevents knock or detonation in internal-combustion engines (also *adj*). [**anti-** (1)]

antilegomena /*an-ti-le-go'mi-nə*/ *n pl* (often with *cap*) those books of the New Testament not at first universally accepted but ultimately admitted into the Bible (2 Peter, James, Jude, Hebrews, 2 and 3 John, and Revelation), *opp* to *homologoumena*. [Gr, spoken against]

anti-lock /*an-ti-lok'*/ *adj* (of a braking system) designed to prevent the wheels of a vehicle locking when the brakes are applied. [**anti-** (1)]

antilogarithm /*an-ti-log'ə-ridhm* or *-rithm*/ *n* a number of which a particular number is the logarithm (short form **an'tilog**). [**anti-** (3)]

antilogy /*an-til'ə-ji*/ *n* a contradiction. [Gr *antilogiā* contradiction]
∎ **antil'ogous** /*-gəs*/ *adj* of the contrary kind; negatively electrified by heating.

Antilope /*an-til'ō-pē*/ *n* the Indian antelope genus. [Form of **antelope**, adopted by PS Pallas (1741–1811), German naturalist]
∎ **antil'opine** /*-pīn*/ *adj* of antelopes.

antilymphocyte serum /*an-ti-lim'fə-sīt sē'rəm*/ (*immunol*) *n* serum used to prevent defensive action of lymphocytes, eg in cases where they would reject an organ transplanted into the body. [**anti-** (1)]

antimacassar /*an-ti-mə-kas'ər*/ *n* a covering for chair-backs, etc (*orig* to protect against soiling from macassar oil or other grease in the hair). [**anti-** (1)]

anti-magnetic /*an-ti-mag-net'ik*/ *adj* (of a material) having or causing resistance to magnetism. [**anti-** (1)]

anti-marketeer /*an-ti-mär-ki-tēr'*/ *n* a British person who opposed Britain's entry into or British membership of the European Common Market. [**anti-** (2)]

antimasque or **antimask** /*an'ti-mäsk*/ *n* a farcical interlude dividing the parts of, or preceding, the more serious masque. [**anti-** (3)]

antimatter /*an'ti-mat'ər*/ *n* matter which consists of particles (antiparticles) similar to those of terrestrial matter but of opposite electrical charge or, in the case of the neutron, reversed magnetic polarity. [**anti-** (3)]

antimere /*an'ti-mēr*/ *n* (in symmetrical organisms) a body part that corresponds to a similar structure on the other side of the body. [**anti-** (3), and Gr *meros* part]
∎ **antimeric** /*an-ti-mer'ik*/ *adj*. **antimerism** /*an-tim'ər-izm*/ *n*.

antimetabole /*an-ti-mə-tab'ə-li*/ (*rhetoric*) *n* a figure of speech in which the same words or ideas are repeated in inverse order, as in Quarles's 'Be wisely worldly, but not worldly wise'. [Gr]

antimetabolite /*an-ti-me-tab'ə-līt*/ *n* a drug that inhibits normal cell growth. [**anti-** (1)]

antimetathesis /*an-ti-mə-tath'ə-sis* or *-mi-*/ (*rhetoric*) *n* inversion of the members of an antithesis, as in Crabbe's 'A poem is a speaking picture; a picture, a mute poem'. [Gr]

antimnemonic /*an-ti-ni-mon'ik*/ *adj* tending to weaken the memory (also *n*). [**anti-** (1)]

antimony /*an'ti-mə-ni*/ *n* a brittle bluish-white element (symbol **Sb**; atomic no 51) of metallic appearance; type (*obs printing sl*). [LL *antimōnium*, of unknown origin, prob from an Arabic word]
∎ **an'timonate** /*-mən-*/ or **antimō'niate** *n* a salt of any antimonic acid. **antimonial** /*-mō'ni-əl*/ *adj* relating to, or containing, antimony. ◆ *n* a drug containing antimony. **antimonic** /*-mon'ik*/ *adj* containing pentavalent antimony. **an'timonide** *n* a binary compound with antimony as one of its constituents. **antimō'nious** *adj* containing trivalent antimony. **an'timonite** *n* a salt of antimonious acid; the mineral stibnite (not chemically an antimonite).

antimutagen /*an-ti-mū'tə-jən*/ (*biol*) *n* a compound that inhibits the action of a mutagen. [**anti-** (1)]

antinephritic /*an-ti-ne-frit'ik*/ (*med*) *adj* and *n* (a drug) acting against diseases of the kidney. [**anti-** (1)]

antineutrino /*an-ti-nū-trē'nō*/ (*phys*) *n* the antiparticle of the neutrino. [**anti-** (3)]
∎ **antineu'tron** /*-tron*/ *n* an uncharged particle that combines with the neutron with mutual annihilation and emission of energy.

anting see under **ant**.

antinode /*an'ti-nōd*/ (*phys*) *n* a point of maximum disturbance midway between nodes. [**anti-** (3)]
∎ **antinōd'al** *adj*.

antinomian /*an-ti-nō'mi-ən*/ *n* and *adj* (a person) denying the obligatoriness of moral law; (a person) believing that Christians are emancipated by the gospel from the obligation to keep the moral law, faith alone being necessary. [**anti-** (1) and Gr *nomos* law]
∎ **antinō'mianism** *n*. **antinomic** /*-nom'ik*/ or **antinom'ical** *adj* relating to, of the nature of, or involving, antinomy. **antinomy** /*an-tin'ə-mi*/ *n* a contradiction in a law; a conflict of authority; conclusions discrepant though apparently logical.

anti-novel /*an'ti-nov-l*/ *n* a type of novel originating in the mid-20c which largely discards plot and character and concerns itself with tiny inner dramas on the border of consciousness. [**anti-** (3)]

antinuclear /*an-ti-nū'kli-ər*/ *adj* opposed to the development or use of nuclear weapons. [**anti-** (2)]

Antiochene /*an-tī'ō-kēn*/ or **Antiochian** /*an-ti-ō'ki-ən*/ *adj* of the Syrian city of *Antioch*; of the eclectic philosophy of *Antiochus* of Ascalon; of any of the Seleucid kings of that name.
∎ **Antio'chianism** *n* a school of theology in the 4c and 5c in revolt against allegorizing of Scripture by the Alexandrian school.

antiodontalgic /*an-ti-ō-don-tal'jik*/ (*med*) *adj* and *n* (a substance) of use against toothache. [**anti-** (1), Gr *odous*, *odontos* tooth, and *algeein* to suffer pain]

antioxidant /*an-ti-ok'si-dənt*/ *n* a substance that prevents or inhibits oxidation; a substance, such as vitamin C, that counters the deleterious effects of oxidizing agents in the human body (also *adj*). [**anti-** (1)]

antipapal /*an-ti-pā'pəl*/ *adj* opposed to the Pope or the papal system (see also **antipope**). [**anti-** (2)]

antiparallel /*an-ti-par'ə-lel*/ (*geom*) *adj* making with a transverse line an internal angle equal to the external angle made by another line (also *n*). [**anti-** (3)]

antiparticle /*an'ti-pär-ti-kl*/ *n* the 'pair' of an elementary particle, particle and antiparticle being mutually destructive, having the same mass and spin but having opposite values for their other properties (eg charge, baryon number, strangeness). [**anti-** (3)]

antipasto /*an-ti-päs'tō*/ (*Ital*) *n* (*pl* **antipas'ti** /*-tē*/) an hors d'œuvre, an appetizer. [Cf **antepast**]

antipathy /*an-tip'ə-thi*/ *n* aversion, dislike, negative feeling; repugnance; animosity, hostility; an object of antipathy; opposition in feeling (*obs*); incompatibility (*obs*); mutual opposition (*obs*). [**anti-** (1), and Gr *pathos* feeling]
∎ **antipathet'ic** or **antipathet'ical** *adj*. **antipathet'ically** *adv*. **antipathic** /*an-ti-path'ik*/ *adj* belonging to, displaying or feeling antipathy; opposite; contrary. **antip'athist** *n* a person possessed by an antipathy.

antiperiodic /*an-ti-pē-ri-od'ik*/ (*med*) *adj* destroying the periodicity of diseases; antimalarial. ◆ *n* a drug with such an effect. [**anti-** (1)]

Some words formed with the prefix **anti-**; the numbers in brackets refer to the numbered senses in the entry for **anti-**.

anti-pred'ator *adj* (1).	**antirust'** *adj* (1).	**antisub'marine** *adj* (1).
antiri'ot *adj* (1).	**antiship'** *adj* (1).	**antispam'** *adj* (1).
anti-roll' *adj* (1).	**antiskid'** *adj* (1).	**anti-tank'** *adj* (1).

∎ words derived from main entry word; ◻ compound words; ∎ idioms and phrasal verbs

antiperistalsis /an-ti-per-i-stal'sis/ (med and zool) n action of intestinal waves of contraction contrary to normal, from anus to mouth, forcing contents of the intestine upwards. [**anti-** (3)]
- **antiperistal'tic** adj.

antiperistasis /an-ti-pər-ist'ə-sis/ (archaic) n opposition of circumstances; resistance or reaction. [Gr, surrounding, interchange, from anti against, and peristasis a circumstance, from peri around, and stasis a setting, stand]

anti-personnel /an'ti-pûr-sə-nel'/ adj intended to destroy military personnel and other persons, but not necessarily equipment, etc. [**anti-** (1)]

antiperspirant /an-ti-pûr'spi-rənt/ n a substance that helps to stop perspiration when applied to the skin (also adj). [**anti-** (1)]

antipetalous /an-ti-pet'ə-ləs/ (bot) adj opposite a petal. [**anti-** (3)]

antiphiloprogenitive /an-ti-fi-lō-prō-jen'i-tiv/ adj intended to prevent the production of offspring. [**anti-** (1)]

antiphlogistic /an-ti-flə-jis'tik/ adj acting against heat, or (med) inflammation. ◆ n a medicine to allay inflammation. [**anti-** (1)]

antiphon /an'ti-fən/ n alternate chanting or singing; a type of church music sung by two parties each responding to the other (also called **antiph'ony** /-ən-i/). [Gr anti in return, and phōnē voice, a doublet of **anthem**]
- **antiph'onal** n a book of antiphons or of anthems (also called **antiph'onary** and **antiph'oner**). ◆ adj sung or recited in alternation. **antiph'onally** adv. **antiphonic** /-fon'/ or (obs) **antiphon'ical** adj (rare) mutually responsive. **antiphon'ically** adv.

antiphrasis /an-tif'rə-sis/ (rhetoric) n the use of words in a sense opposite to the literal one. [Gr, from anti against, and phrasis speech]
- **antiphrastic** /an-ti-fras'tik/ or (obs) **antiphras'tical** adj involving antiphrasis; ironical. **antiphras'tically** adv.

antipodes /an-tip'ə-dēz or an'ti-pō-dēz/ n pl (sing (rare) **antipode** /an'ti-pōd/) (also sing; sometimes with cap) Australia and New Zealand, as being diametrically opposite to Great Britain or Europe on the surface of the globe; orig those who live on the other side of the globe, or on opposite sides (literally, standing feet to feet; obs); a point or place diametrically opposite to another on the surface of the earth or of any globular body or sphere; a pair of points or places so related to each other; the exact opposite of a person or a thing. [Gr antipodes, pl of antipous with feet opposite, from pous, podos a foot]
- **antip'odal** or (esp of Australia and New Zealand, sometimes with cap) **antipode'an** adj.
- ❏ **antipodal cells** n pl (bot) in flowering plants, three cells in the embryo-sac at the end remote from the micropyle, representing the prothallus.

antipole /an'ti-pōl/ n the opposite pole; direct opposite. [**anti-** (3)]

antipope /an'ti-pōp/ n a pontiff set up in opposition to one asserted to be canonically chosen, eg one of those who resided at Avignon in the 13c and 14c (see also **antipapal**). [**anti-** (3)]

antiproton /an-ti-prō'ton/ (phys) n a short-lived particle comparable to the proton but negatively charged. [**anti-** (3)]

antipruritic /an-ti-prū-rit'ik/ (med) n and adj (a substance) that reduces itchiness. [**anti-** (1)]

antipsychotic /an-ti-sī-kot'ik/ (med) adj (of a drug) alleviating psychosis. ◆ n an antipsychotic drug. [**anti-** (1)]

antipyretic /an-ti-pī-ret'ik/ (med) adj counteracting fever. ◆ n an antipyretic agent. [Gr anti- against, and pyretos fever, from pȳr fire]

antiq. abbrev : antiquarian; antiques; antiquities.

antiquark /an'ti-kwärk or -kwörk/ (phys) n the antiparticle corresponding to the quark. [**anti-** (3)]

antiquary /an'ti-kwə-ri/ n a person who studies, collects or deals in relics of the past, but not usually very ancient things. ◆ adj (Shakesp) ancient. [L antīquārius, from antīquus old]
- **antiquarian** /-kwā'ri-ən/ adj connected with the study of antiquities; (of books) old and rare. ◆ n an antiquary; before metrication, a size of drawing paper (53 × 31in). **antiqua'rianism** n.

antique /an-tēk' or formerly an'tik/ (and sometimes written **antick**, now obs) adj ancient; of a good old age, olden (now archaic or rhetorical in a good sense); (of articles or furniture) made in an earlier period and sought by collectors; relating to, or dealing in, antiques; old-fashioned; having an air of bygone times; after the manner of the ancients. ◆ n anything very old; an old relic; a piece of old furniture or other object sought by collectors; a type of thick and bold face with lines of equal thickness (printing). ◆ vt to alter the appearance of (wood, leather, etc) so that it seems very old. ◆ vi (US) to collect or shop for antiques. —See also **antic**. [L antīquus old, ancient, from ante before; influenced by Fr antique]
- **antiquate** /an'ti-kwāt/ vt to make antique, old or obsolete; to put out of use. **an'tiquated** adj. **antiqua'tion** n. **antique'ly** adv. **antique'ness** n. **antiquitarian** /an-tik-wi-tā'ri-ən/ n a person attached to old ways or beliefs. **antiq'uity** n ancient times, esp the times of the ancient Greeks and Romans; great age; old age, seniority (Shakesp); ancient style; the people of ancient times; (now usu in pl) a relic of the past; (in pl) manners, customs, etc of ancient times.
- **the antique** ancient work in art; the style of ancient art.

antirachitic /an-ti-rə-kit'ik/ (med) adj tending to prevent or cure rickets. ◆ n an antirachitic agent. [**anti-** (1)]

anti-racism /an-ti-rā'si-zm/ n opposition to prejudice and persecution on grounds of race, and support for policies that promote equality among and tolerance between groups of different racial origins. [**anti-** (2)]
- **anti-ra'cist** adj and n.

antiretroviral /an-ti-ret'rō-vī-rəl/ (med) adj acting to counteract or control a retrovirus. ◆ n an antiretroviral agent or drug. [**anti-** (1)]

anti-roll bar /an-ti-rōl' bär/ n a crosswise bar in the suspension of a motor vehicle that increases stability when cornering, etc. [**anti-** (1)]

antirrhinum /an-ti-rī'nəm/ n any plant of the snapdragon genus Antirrhinum. [Latinized from Gr antirrhīnon snapdragon, from anti like, mimicking, and rhīs, rhīnos nose]

antiscian /an-tish'i-ən/ n a dweller on the same meridian on the other side of the equator, whose shadow at noon falls in the opposite direction (also adj). [**anti-** (3) and Gr skiā shadow]

antiscorbutic /an-ti-skör-būt'ik/ (med) adj acting against scurvy. ◆ n a remedy or preventive for scurvy. [**anti-** (1)]

antiscriptural /an-ti-skrip'chə-rəl/ adj opposed to the authority of the Bible. [**anti-** (2)]

anti-Semite /an-ti-sem'īt or -sē'mīt/ n a hater of Semites, esp Jews, or of their influence. [**anti-** (2)]
- **anti-Semitic** /-sim-it'/ adj. **anti-Semitism** /-sem'/ or -sēm'/ n.

antisense /an'ti-sens/ adj (of a drug, etc) designed to treat diseases and infection by inhibiting the production of pathogenic proteins. [**anti-** (1)]

antisepalous /an-ti-sep'ə-ləs/ (bot) adj opposite a sepal. [**anti-** (3)]

antisepsis /an-ti-sep'sis/ (med) n destruction, or inhibition of growth, of bacteria by a chemical agent. [Gr anti- against, and sēpsis putrefaction]
- **antisep'tic** adj relating to or effecting antisepsis; emotionless and bland, clinical (inf). ◆ n an antiseptic agent. **antisep'tically** adv. **antisep'ticism** /-sizm/ n antiseptic treatment. **antisep'ticize** or **-ise** /-sīz/ vt.

antiserum /an'ti-sēr-əm/ (med and biochem) n (pl **an'tiserums** or **an'tisera**) a serum which contains antibodies. [antibody and serum]

antisexist /an-ti-sek'sist/ adj opposed to or preventing sexism (also n). [**anti-** (2)]
- **antisex'ism** n.

antisocial /an-ti-sō'shəl/ adj opposed to the good of society, or the principles of society; disinclined to mix in society; without social instincts. [**anti-** (2)]
- **antiso'cialism** n. **antiso'cialist** n formerly, an unsociable person; an opponent of socialism. **antisociality** /-shi-al'i-ti/ n unsociableness; opposition to the principles of society. **antiso'cially** adv.

antispasmodic /an-ti-spaz-mod'ik/ (med) adj preventing or alleviating spasms or convulsions. ◆ n a remedy, or alleviating agent, for spasms. [**anti-** (1)]

antispast /an'ti-spast/ (prosody) n a foot composed of an iambus and a trochee. [Gr antispastos, from antispaein to draw back, from spaein to draw]
- **antispast'ic** adj.

Some words formed with the prefix **anti-**; the numbers in brackets refer to the numbered senses in the entry for **anti-**.

antiterr'or adj (1).	**antitheft'** adj (1).	**antivī'ral** adj (1).
antiterr'orism n (1).	**antitrinitā'rian** adj and n (2).	**antivī'rus** adj (2).
antiterr'orist adj (1).	**antitrinitā'rianism** n (2).	**antiwar'** adj (2).

---

antistatic /an-ti-stat'ik/ adj (also **antistat** /an' or -stat'/) having the property of counteracting static electricity; not attracting positively charged ions, eg dust. ◆ n an antistatic substance. [**anti-** (1)]
❑ **antistatic agent** n (textiles) a substance applied to a textile to prevent its becoming charged with static electricity by friction during processing or wear. **antistatic fluid** n a fluid applied to prevent the effects of static electricity on vinyl discs (from dust) and sound film (from scratches on the track).

antistrophe /an-tis'trə-fi/ n the returning dance in Greek choruses, reversing the movement of the strophe (qv); the stanza answering the strophe in the same metre; repetition in reverse order (rhetoric); retortion of an argument (rhetoric); an inverse relation. [Gr antistrophē, from strophē a turning]
■ **antistrophic** /an-ti-strof'ik/ adj. **antistroph'ically** adv. **antis'trophon** n (rhetoric) an argument retorted on an opponent.

antisyzygy /an-ti-si'zi-ji/ n union of opposites. [Gr antisyzygiā, from anti- against, opposite, and syzygiā union, coupling from sy-, syn- with, together, and zygon a yoke]

antithalian /an-ti-thə-lī'ən or -thā-li-ən/ adj opposed to mirth or fun. [**anti-** (1), and Gr Thaleia, the comic muse]

antitheism /an-ti-thē'i-zm/ n doctrine antagonistic to theism; denial of the existence of a God; opposition to God. [**anti-** (1), and Gr theos a god]
■ **antithē'ist** n. **antitheist'ic** adj.

antithesis /an-ti'thə-sis/ n (pl **antith'eses** /-sēz/) a figure of speech in which thoughts or words are balanced in contrast (rhetoric); a thesis or proposition opposing another; opposition; the direct opposite (of or to). [Gr, from anti- against, opposite, and thesis placing]
■ **an'tithet** /-thet/ n (rare) an instance of antithesis. **antithet'ic** or **antithet'ical** adj. **antithet'ically** adv.

antithrombin /an-ti-throm'bin/ (med and biochem) n a substance produced by the liver which prevents clotting of the blood in the veins. [**anti-** (1), and Gr thrombos a clot]

antitoxin /an-ti-tok'sin/ (med and immunol) n a substance that neutralizes toxin formed in the body. [**anti-** (1)]
■ **antitox'ic** adj.

antitrade /an'ti-trād/ n (usu in pl) a wind that blows in the opposite direction to the trade wind, ie in the northern hemisphere from the north-east and in the southern hemisphere from the south-east. [**anti-** (3)]

antitragus /an-ti-trā'gəs/ (anat) n (pl **antitrā'gī**) a prominence of the external ear, opposite the tragus. [**anti-** (3)]

antitrust /an-ti-trust'/ (mainly US) adj (of legislation, etc) directed against the adverse effects of trusts or other such monopolies on commerce. [**anti-** (1)]

antitussive /an-ti-tus'iv/ (med) adj tending to alleviate or suppress coughing. ◆ n an antitussive agent. [**anti-** (1) and L tussis a cough]

antitype /an'ti-tīp/ n that which corresponds to the type; that which is prefigured by the type; a contrary type. [**anti-** (3)]
■ **antityp'al**, **antitypic** /-tip'ik/ or **antityp'ical** adj.

antivaccinationist /an-ti-vak-si-nā'shə-nist/ n an opponent of vaccination. [**anti-** (2)]
■ **antivaccinā'tionism** n.

antivenin /an-ti-ven'in/ or **antivenene** /-ēn'/ n an antitoxin counteracting (esp snake) venom. [**anti-** (1)]

antivitamin /an'ti-vit-ə-min or -vī-tə-/ (med) n a substance with a chemical structure very similar to a vitamin, which prevents that vitamin from having its effect. [**anti-** (1)]

antivivisection /an-ti-viv-i-sek'shən/ n opposition to vivisection. [**anti-** (2)]
■ **antivivisec'tionism** n. **antivivisec'tionist** n and adj.

antler /an'tlər/ n one of a pair of bony outgrowths from the frontal bone of a deer; orig the lowest branch of a stag's horn, then any branch, then the whole. [OFr antoillier; assumed derivation from LL ant(e)oculāris in front of the eyes, is unlikely]
■ **ant'lered** adj.
❑ **ant'ler-moth** n a noctuid moth (Charaeas graminis), with antler-like markings on the wings, its larvae very destructive to pastures.

antlia /an'tli-ə/ n (pl **ant'liae** /-ē/) the suctorial proboscis of insects of the Lepidoptera order; (with cap) the Air Pump, a small southern constellation. [L antlia a pump, from Gr antliā bilge-water]
■ **ant'liate** adj.

antoninianus /an-tə-ni-ni-ā'nəs/ n a Roman coin equal to two denarii in value. [Antoninus, official name of the 3c emperor Caracalla]

antonomasia /an-tə-no-mā'zi-ə/ n the use of an epithet, or the name of an office or attributive, for a person's proper name (eg his lordship for an earl); and conversely (eg a Napoleon for a great conqueror). [Gr, from antonomasiā, from onomazein to name, from onoma a name]

Anton Piller /an'ton pil'ər/ or **Anton Piller order** /ör'dər/ (law) n in English law (esp in copyright cases), a High Court order by which a plaintiff (or his or her representatives) may enter and search a defendant's premises, and seize material evidence. [Anton Piller, plaintiff to whom in 1976 such an order was granted]

antonym /an'tə-nim/ n a word opposite in meaning to another. [Gr onyma, onoma a name]
■ **antonym'ic** or **anton'ymous** adj. **anton'ymy** n.

antre /an'tər/ (poetic) n a cave (also (Shakesp) **an'tar**). [Fr; L antrum, from Gr antron a cave]

antrorse /an-trörs'/ (biol) adj turned up or forward. [From anterus (hypothetical positive of L anterior front) and L versus turned]

antrum /an'trəm/ (esp anat) n (pl **an'tra**) a cavity. [L, cave]
■ **an'tral** adj.

antsy /an'tsi/ (sl) adj eager, excited; nervous. [From the phrase have ants in one's pants; see under **ant**]

ANU abbrev : Australian National University (in Canberra).

Anubis /a-nū'bis or -noo'/ n the ancient Egyptian jackal-headed god of the dead. [L, from Gr Anoubis, from Egyp Anup]

anucleate /ā-nū'kli-āt/ or **anucleated** /ā-nū-kli-ā'tid/ adj without a nucleus. [Gr a- (privative), and **nucleate**]

anuria /a-nū'ri-ə/ (med) n inhibition of urine formation. [Gr an- (privative), and ouron urine]
■ **anuresis** /an-ū-rē'sis/ n failure of the body to secrete urine.

anurous /ə-nū'rəs or an'yə-rəs/ or **anourous** /ə-noo'rəs/ (zool) adj tailless. [Gr an- (privative), and ourā tail]
■ **Anu'ra** or **Anou'ra** n pl the Salientia or tailless amphibians, frogs and toads.

anus /ā'nəs/ (anat and zool) n the opening at the end of the alimentary canal by which undigested residues are excreted. [L ānus, -ī a ring]
■ **ā'nal** adj of or relating to the anus; in Freudian psychology, of or relating to the second stage of psychosexual development, in which the child's interest and gratification is concentrated on the excretory function; (of an adult) categorized as having personality traits such as obsessiveness, attention to detail, and obstinacy, thought to result from fixation at the anal stage (psychol). **ā'nally** adv.
❑ **anal retentive** adj and n (of or relating to) a person having anal personality traits.

anvil /an'vil or -vəl/ n an iron block on which metal can be hammered into shape; the incus of the ear. [OE anfilte, onfilti]
❑ **anvil secateurs** n pl secateurs with two straight blades, the cutting blade closing against a blunt flat blade.
■ **on** or **upon the anvil** in preparation, under discussion.

anxious /ang(k)'shəs/ adj uneasy with fear and desire regarding something doubtful; solicitous; eager (for something, or to do something). [L anxius, from angere to press tightly. See **anger**, **anguish**]
■ **anxiety** /ang-(g)zī'i-ti/ n a state of being anxious; a state of chronic apprehension as a symptom of mental disorder. **anxiolytic** /angk-si-ō-lit'ik/ adj and n (med) (a drug) reducing anxiety and tension. **an'xiously** adv. **an'xiousness** n.

any /en'i/ adj and pronoun one (unspecified); some; whichever, no matter which. ◆ adv (usu with a compar adj) at all, to an appreciable extent. [OE ǣnig, from ān one]
■ **an'ybody** n and pronoun any single person; a person of any account. **an'yhow** adv in any way whatever; in any case; at least; indifferently, carelessly. **an'yone** (or **any one**) n and pronoun anybody at all; anybody whatever. **an'yplace** adv (N Am inf) anywhere. **an'yroad** adv (dialect) anyway. **an'ything** n and pronoun a thing (unspecified), as opposed to nothing. ◆ adv to any extent. **anythinga'rian** n a person with no beliefs in particular. **anythinga'rianism** n. **an'ytime** adv at any time. **an'yway** or (dialect, esp US) **an'yways** adv anyhow; in any case; in any manner (archaic). **an'ywhen** adv (rare or dialect). **an'ywhere** adv in or to any place; in any range, to any extent, eg anywhere near, anywhere between. **an'ywheres** adv (N Am dialect) anywhere. **an'ywhither** adv (archaic; rare). **an'ywise** adv (now chiefly US) in any manner, to any degree.
■ **any amount** (inf) a lot. **any day** in any circumstances. **any more** any longer. **any old** any, with connotations of indifference, lack of thought, etc (**any old how** without any special care; **any old thing** anything at all). **anyone else** any other person. **anything but** certainly not, by no means. **anything goes** any sort of behaviour, dress, person, etc is tolerated or accepted. **as ... as anything** to a very great extent. **at any rate** whatever may happen; at all events. **be anybody's** to be sexually available to all. **if anything** used to introduce a contradiction

or qualification to an earlier statement. **like anything** very much; with great vigour.

ANZAAS /an'zəs or an'zas/ abbrev : Australian and New Zealand Association for the Advancement of Science.

Anzac /an'zak/ n an Australian or New Zealand soldier, esp a member of the Australian and New Zealand Army Corps during World War I (also adj).
❑ **Anzac biscuit** n a biscuit made with oats and syrup, orig sent to Anzac forces during World War I. **Anzac Day** n 25 April, a public holiday in Australia and New Zealand in memory of the Anzac landing in Gallipoli (1915).

anziani /an-tsē-ä'nē/ (Ital) n pl councillors, senators.

Anzus /an'zəs/ (also **ANZUS**) abbrev : (the alliance between) Australia, New Zealand and the United States.

AO abbrev : Army Order; Officer of (the Order of) Australia.

AOB or **aob** abbrev : any other business.

AOC abbrev : Air Officer Commanding; (of wine) appellation d'origine contrôlée (qv).

AOCB abbrev : any other competent business.

ao dai /ow dī/ n a traditional Vietnamese, long, high-necked tunic for women, slit to the waist at the sides, worn over trousers. [Viet]

AOK (inf) abbrev : all items satisfactory.

AOL (comput) abbrev : America Online, an Internet service provider.

AONB abbrev : Area of Outstanding Natural Beauty (protected area).

A1 see under **A¹**.

Aonian /ā-ō'ni-ən/ adj relating to Aonia in Boeotia in Greece, or to the Muses supposed to dwell there.
❑ **Aonian fount** n the fountain Aganippe, on a slope of Mount Helicon (the Aonian mount).

AOR abbrev : adult-oriented rock; album-oriented rock (or radio).

aor. abbrev : aorist.

aorist /ā'ə-rist/ (grammar) n a tense, esp in Greek, expressing simple past time, with no implications of continuance, repetition or the like (also adj). [Gr aoristos indefinite, from a- (privative), and horistos limited]
■ **aorist'ic** adj. **aorist'ically** adv.

aorta /ā-ör'tə/ n (anat and zool) the main arterial vessel that carries blood from the heart. [Gr aortē, from aeirein to raise up]
■ **aor'tal** or **aor'tic** adj. **aorti'tis** n (pathol) inflammation of the aorta.

aoudad /ä'ŭ-dad/ n a N African wild sheep. [Native name in French spelling]

à outrance /a ŭ-träs'/ (Fr) to the utmost; to the death; to the bitter end.

AP abbrev : Air Police (US); American plan; anti-personnel; Associated Press.

ap abbrev : additional premium; ante prandium (L), before a meal (on prescriptions); author's proof.

ap. abbrev : apothecary; apparent(ly).

APA abbrev : Australian Publishers' Association.

apace /ə-pās'/ adv literally, at a quick pace; swiftly. [**a-¹** and **pace¹**]

Apache /ə-pach'ē/ n a Native American of a group of tribes in Arizona, New Mexico, etc; (**apache** /ə-pash'/) a lawless ruffian or hooligan in Paris or elsewhere. [Perh Zuñi āpachu enemy]

APACS abbrev : Association for Payment Clearing Services.

apadana /a-pə-dä'nə/ n the great hall or throne room of an Ancient Persian palace, free-standing, with many columns and often a portico. [OPers apadāna palace]

apage /ap'ə-jē/ or ap-a-ge/ or **apage Satanas** /sat'a-nas/ (Gr) away, depart (Satan).

apagoge /a-pə-gō'jē/ n reduction to absurdity, indirect proof by showing the falsehood of the opposite. [Gr apagōgē leading away, from apagein to lead off]
■ **apagogic** /-goj'ik/ or **apagog'ical** adj. **apagog'ically** adv.

apaid see **apay**.

apanage see **appanage**.

apart /ə-pärt'/ adv separately; aside; asunder, parted; separate; out of consideration. [Fr à part, from L ad partem to the side]
■ **apart'ness** n.
■ **apart from** except.

apartheid /ə-pärt'hāt or -pär'tīd/ n segregation and separate development (of races), esp as formerly practised in South Africa; any system of segregation (fig). [Afrik, literally, separateness]

apartment /ə-pärt'mənt/ n (now usu in pl) a separate room in a house, used or occupied by a particular person or party; a flat, a set of rooms usu on one floor of a building (usu used as a dwelling; mainly N Am); a compartment (obs). [Fr appartement a suite of rooms forming a

complete dwelling, from L ad to, and partīre, partīrī to divide, from pars, partis part]
■ **apartmental** /-ment'əl/ adj.

apatetic /a-pə-tet'ik/ (zool) adj of an animal's coloration or marking which closely resembles that of another species or of its surroundings. [Gr apatētikos deceitful]

apathaton /ə-path'i-tən/ a Shakespearean form of **epitheton**.

apathy /ap'ə-thi/ n lack of feeling, passion or interest; indifference. [Gr apatheia, from a- (privative), and pathos feeling]
■ **apathet'ic** or **apathet'ical** adj. **apathet'ically** adv.

apatite /ap'ə-tīt/ n a mineral consisting of calcium phosphate and fluoride (or chloride, hydroxyl or carbonate ions), a major constituent of the bones and teeth of vertebrates, and of sedimentary phosphate rocks. [Gr apatē deceit, from its having been confused with other minerals]

Apatosaurus /ə-pat-ə-sö'rəs/ n the scientific name for the Brontosaurus genus. [Gr apatē deceit, and sauros lizard]

apay or **appay** /ə-pā'/ vt (pap and pat **apaid'**, **apayd'**, **appaid'** or **appayd'**) to satisfy (archaic); to repay (obs). [OFr apayer, from L ad, and pācāre, from pāx peace]

APB (N Am) abbrev : all-points bulletin.

APC abbrev : armoured personnel carrier (milit); aspirin, phenacetin and caffeine (pharm); automatic public convenience.

APE abbrev : alkylphenol ethoxylate, a chemical used in cleaning products.

ape /āp/ n a monkey; specif an anthropoid primate; a large monkey without a tail or with a very short one; a mimic; an imitator, a coarse, clumsy or stupid person (chiefly N Am). ◆ vt to mimic; to imitate. [OE apa; Ger Affe]
■ **ape'dom** n. **ape'hood** n. **ap'ery** n the conduct of someone who apes; any ape-like action; a colony of apes (rare). **ap'ish** adj like an ape; imitative; foppish, silly. **ap'ishly** adv. **ap'ishness** or (Carlyle) **ap'ism** n.
❑ **ape'man** n any of several extinct primates thought to have been intermediate in development between man and the higher apes. **ape'shit** adj (vulgar sl) berserk; destructively crazy; extremely excited (see also **go ape** below).
■ **go ape** (or vulgar **apeshit**; sl) to go crazy (with over or for). **God's ape** (obs) a born fool. **make someone one's ape** or **put an ape in someone's hood** (obs) to make a fool of someone.

apeak or **apeek** /ə-pēk'/ (naut) adv vertical. [**a-¹**]

APEC /ā'pek/ abbrev : Asia-Pacific Economic Co-operation.

apepsia /a-pep'si-ə/ (med) n (also **apep'sy**) failure or absence of digestive function; weakness of digestion (obs). [Gr apepsia indigestion; a- (privative), and peptein to digest]

aperçu /a-per-sü'/ n a summary exposition; a brief outline; a glimpse; an immediate intuitive insight. [Fr aperçu survey, sketch; literally (pap of apercevoir), perceived]

aperient /ə-pē'ri-ənt/ adj (med) laxative. ◆ n an aperient drug. [L aperīre, apertum to open]
■ **aperitive** /ə-per'i-tiv/ adj (med) laxative. ◆ n same as **apéritif**; an aperitive medicine.

aperiodic /ā-pē-ri-od'ik/ adj not periodic; highly damped and coming to rest without oscillation (phys). [Gr a- (privative), and **periodic**]
■ **aperiodicity** /-ə-dis'i-ti/ n.

apéritif or **aperitif** /ə-pe-ri-tēf', -per'i- or (Fr) a-pā-rē-tēf'/ n a drink taken as an appetizer. [Fr, from LL aperitīvus, from aperīre to open]

a-per-se /ā'pər-sē/ n the letter a by itself, making the word **a¹,²** (archaic); anything unique in excellence (fig). [L a per sē a by itself; cf **ampersand**]

apert /ə-pûrt'/ (archaic) adj open, public. [OFr, from L apertus open]
■ **apert'ness** n.

aperture /ap'ər-chər or -tūr/ n an opening; a hole; the diameter of the opening through which light passes in an optical instrument such as a camera; the effective area over which an antenna extracts power from an incident wave (radar and telecom). [L apertura, from aperīre to open]
❑ **aperture priority** n a facility enabling a camera to select the shutter speed automatically once the aperture has been selected by the photographer.

apery see under **ape**.

apetalous /ə-pet'ə-ləs/ (bot) adj without petals. [Gr a- (privative), and petalon a leaf]
■ **apet'aly** n.

à peu près /a pə pre'/ (Fr) nearly.

APEX or **Apex** /ā'peks/ abbrev : (in full **Apex Trust**) Advancement of the Employment Prospects of Ex-offenders; advance purchase excursion (a reduced airline or long-distance rail fare).

apex /ā'peks/ n (pl **ā'pexes** or **apices** /āp'- or ap'i-sēz/) the summit, tip or point; a vertex (geom); the culminating point or climax of anything. [L apex, apicis a tip]

Apgar test /ap'gär test/ (med) n a system used to assess the health of a newborn baby immediately (usu at one and five minutes) after birth, the **Apgar score** (maximum total 10) comprising points for heart rate, muscle tone, colour, respiratory effort and response to stimulation. [Virginia Apgar (1909–74), US anaesthetist]

aphaeresis see **apheresis**.

aphagia /ə-fā'j(i-)ə/ (med and zool) n inability or unwillingness to swallow or eat; (of the imago of certain insects) inability to feed. [Gr a- (privative), and phagia, from phagein to eat]

aphakia /ə-fā'ki-ə/ (ophthalmol) n the absence of a lens in the eye. [Gr a- (privative), and phakos lentil, lens]

Aphaniptera /af-ə-nip'tə-rə/ n pl the flea order (or suborder) of wingless, bloodsucking insects with well-developed hindlegs for jumping. [Gr aphanēs invisible, and pteron wing]
■ **aphanip'terous** adj.

aphanite /af'ə-nīt/ n any rock of such close texture that separate minerals contained within it cannot be distinguished by the naked eye. [Gr aphanēs invisible]

aphasia /ə-fā'zi-ə or -zhə/ (pathol) n inability to express thought in words, or inability to understand thought as expressed in the spoken or written words of others, caused by brain disease or damage. [Gr a- (privative), and phasis speech, from phanai to speak]
■ **apha'siac** n and adj. **aphasic** /a-fā'zik or a-faz'ik/ adj.

aphelion /ə-fē'li-ən or ap-hē'-/ (astron) n (pl **aphē'lia**) a planet's furthest point in its orbit from the sun. [Gr apo from, and hēlios sun]
■ **aphē'lian** adj (rare).

apheliotropic /a-fē-li-ə-trop'ik or ap-hē-, also -ō-/ (bot, etc) adj (eg of leaves, roots) turning away from the sun. [Gr apo from, hēlios sun, and tropikos relating to turning]
■ **apheliot'ropism** n.

apheresis /a-fē'ri-sis/ n a process in which blood from a donor is separated into its constituent parts, so that those that are required may be used for transfusion and the remainder returned to the donor; (also **aphae'resis**) the taking away of a sound or syllable at the beginning of a word (grammar). [Gr apo away, and pherein to carry]

aphesis /af'i-sis/ n the gradual and unintentional loss of an unaccented vowel at the beginning of a word (as in squire from esquire), a special form of apheresis. [Gr aphesis letting go, from apo from, and hienai to send]
■ **aphetic** /ə-fet'ik/ adj. **aphet'ically** adv. **aph'etize** or **-ise** vt.

aphis /af'is, ā'fis/ or **aphid** /af'id, ā'fid/ n (pl **aph'ides** /-i-dēz/ or **aph'ids**) a plant louse (eg greenfly or blackfly), a small homopterous insect that sucks plant juices. [Ety unknown]
■ **aph'icide** or **aphid'icide** /-sīd/ n a substance or agent that kills aphids. **aphid'ian** adj and n. **aphid'ious** adj.

aphonia /ə-fō'ni-ə/ or **aphony** /af'ə-ni/ (pathol) n loss of voice from hysteria, disease of larynx or vocal cords, etc. [Gr a- (privative), and phōnē voice]
■ **aphonic** /-fon'-/ adj non-vocal, having no sound. **aphonous** /af'ə-nəs/ adj voiceless.

aphorism /af'ə-ri-zm/ n a concise statement of a principle in any science; a brief, pithy saying; an adage. [Gr aphorizein to define, from apo from, and horos a limit]
■ **aph'orist** n. **aphoris'tic** adj. **aphorist'ically** adv. **aph'orize** or **-ise** vi. **aph'orizer** or **-s-** n.

aphotic /ə-fō'tik/ adj able to grow without light (bot); lightless (eg of a deep-sea region). [Gr a- (privative), and phōs, phōtos light]

aphrodisiac /a-frō-diz'i-ak or -frə-/ adj exciting sexually. ◆n something that arouses sexual desire, eg a food or a drug. [Gr aphrodīsiakos, from Aphrodītē the goddess of love]
■ **aphrodis'ia** n (med) sexual desire, esp violent. **aphrodis'iacal** adj. **Aphrodis'ian** adj belonging to Aphrodite, dedicated to sexual love.

aphtha /af'thə/ (pathol) n (pl **aph'thae** /-thē/) a small ulceration on the surface of a mucous membrane, as in the disease thrush. [Gr aphtha, mostly in pl aphthai]
■ **aph'thous** adj.
❑ **contagious aphthae** foot-and-mouth disease.

aphyllous /a-fil'əs/ (bot) adj without foliage, leafless. [Gr a- (privative), and phyllon a leaf]
■ **aphyll'y** n.

API (comput) abbrev : Applications Programming Interface.

a piacere /ä pē-a-chā'rā/ (Ital) at pleasure.

apian /ā'pi-ən/ adj of or relating to bees. [L apis a bee, and apiārium a bee-house]
■ **āpiarian** /-ā'ri-ən/ adj relating to beehives or beekeeping. **ā'piarist** n a beekeeper. **ā'piary** /-ar-i/ n a place where bees are kept. **āpicul'tural** adj. **ā'piculture** n beekeeping. **āpicul'turist** n. **apither'apy** n the therapeutic use of bee products, such as royal jelly and propolis. **āpiv'orous** adj feeding on bees.

apical /ap'i- or ā'pi-kəl/ adj of or at the apex; denoting a sound articulated with the tip of the tongue (phonetics). [See **apex**]
■ **ap'ically** adv. **ap'ices** n pl see **apex**. **apicūlate** /ap-ik'-/ adj (bot) with a short sharp point on an otherwise blunt end.
❑ **apical meristem** n (bot) a group of dividing cells at the tip of a stem or root.

Apician or **apician** /ə-pish'(y)ən/ adj luxurious and expensive in diet. [From Apicius, 1c AD Roman gourmet]

apiculture, etc see under **apian**.

apiece /ə-pēs'/ adv for each piece, thing or person; to each individually. [**a¹** and **piece**]

apiezon oils /a-pī'zən oilz/ n pl the residue of almost zero vapour pressure left by vacuum distillation of petroleum products. [Gr a- (privative), and piezein to press]

apiol /ā'pi-ol or ap'i-/ n an organic substance derived from parsley seeds, used (esp formerly) as an agent to increase menstrual flow, or to bring about abortion of a fetus. [L apium parsley, and **-ol²**]

apish, etc see under **ape**.

apivorous see under **apian**.

APL (comput) abbrev : A Programming Language, a language widely used in scientific and mathematical work.

aplacental /a-plə-sen'təl/ adj without a placenta. [Gr a- (privative), and **placental**]

aplanatic /a-plə-nat'ik/ adj (esp of a lens) free from spherical aberration. [Gr a- (privative), and planaein to wander]
■ **a'planat** n an aplanatic lens or instrument. **aplanatism** /ə-plan'ə-tizm/ n. **aplan'ogamete** n a non-motile gamete. **aplan'ospore** n a non-motile spore.

aplasia /ə-plā'zi-ə or -zhə/ (med) n imperfect development or absence of an organ or part. [Gr a- (privative), and New L -plasia, from Gr plasis moulding]
■ **aplastic** /-plas'-/ adj.
❑ **aplastic anaemia** n a form of anaemia caused by malfunctioning of the bone marrow.

aplenty /ə-plen'ti/ adv in plenty. [**a-¹** and **plenty**]

aplite /ap'līt/ n a fine-grained, light-coloured igneous rock containing mainly quartz and feldspar. [Ger Aplit, from Gr haploos simple]

aplomb /ə-plom' or (Fr) a-plɔ̃'/ n literally, perpendicularity; self-possession, coolness. [Fr aplomb, from à plomb according to a plummet]

aplustre /a-plus'tər/ n the ornament on the stern of a ship in ancient Greece and Rome. [L āplustre, aplustre, from Gr aphlaston]

apnoea or (esp N Am) **apnea** /ap-nē'ə/ (pathol) n a cessation of breathing, asphyxia; a temporary cessation of breathing, eg (**sleep apnoea**) occurring in certain adults during sleep, or in newborn infants. [Gr apnoia, from a- (privative), and pno(i)ē breath]

apo. abbrev : apogee.

Apoc. abbrev : Apocalypse; Apocrypha; Apocryphal.

apocalypse /a-pok'ə-lips/ n (with the and cap) the last book of the New Testament, also known as the Revelation of St John; the end of the world; any book purporting to reveal the future or last things; a revelation or disclosure. [Gr apokalypsis an uncovering, from apo from, and kalyptein to cover]
■ **apocalypt'ic** adj relating to the Apocalypse; prophetic of disaster or of the end of the world. **apocalypt'ical** adj. **apocalypt'ically** adv.
❑ **apocalyptic number** n the number of the Beast, the mystical number 666, spoken of in the Bible, Revelation 13.18, supposed to be the sum of the numerical values of the Greek and Hebrew letters of a name, for which many solutions have been offered.

apocarpous /a-pō-kär'pəs/ (bot) adj (of the ovaries of flowering plants) having the carpels separate. [Gr apo from, and karpos fruit]

apocatastasis /ap-ō-kə-tas'tə-sis/ n the final restitution of all things at the appearance of the Messiah, an idea extended by Origen (185–254) to the final conversion and salvation of all created beings, the Devil and his angels not excepted (theol); the process of return to previous or normal condition (med). [Gr apokatastasis, from *apo-* again, back, and *katastasis* establishment; cf **catastasis**]

apochromatic /ap-ə-krō-mat'ik/ (*phys* and *photog*) *adj* (of a lens, particularly a microscope objective) corrected for chromatic aberration for three wavelengths. [Gr *apo* from, and *chrōma, -atos* colour]
■ **apochro'mat** *n* an apochromatic lens or instrument. **apochro'matism** *n*.

apocope /ə-pok'ə-pē/ *n* the cutting off of the last sound or syllable of a word. [Gr *apokopē*, from *apo* off, and *koptein* to cut]
■ **apoc'opate** *vt.* **apocopā'tion** *n*.

apocrine /ap'ə-krīn* or *-krin/ (*biol*) *adj* (of a gland) whose product is formed by the breakdown of part of its active cells. [Gr *apo* off, and *krīnein* to separate]

apocrypha /ə-pok'ri-fə/ *n pl* (*sing* **apoc'ryphon**) (*usu* with *cap*) those books or parts of books included in the Septuagint and Vulgate translations of the Old Testament but not accepted as canonical by Jews or Protestants, and also later books (Apocrypha of the New Testament) never accepted as canonical or authoritative by any considerable part of the Christian Church; hidden or secret things (*rare*). [Gr, things hidden, from *apo* from, and *kryptein* to hide]
■ **apoc'ryphal** *adj* of the Apocrypha; of doubtful authority; spurious; fabulous. **apoc'ryphally** *adv*.

Apocynum /ə-pos'i-nəm/ *n* the dogbane genus of plants, giving name to the periwinkle family **Apocynā'ceae**, closely related to the asclepiads. [Gr *apokynon* an asclepiad poisonous to dogs, from *apo* off, and *kyōn, kynos* a dog]
■ **apocynā'ceous** *adj* of that family.

apod /ap'od/ or **apode** /ap'ōd/ (*zool*) *n* an animal without feet or ventral fins. ◆ *adj* (also **ap'odal** or **ap'odous**) footless. [Gr *a-* (privative), and *pous, podos* a foot]

apodictic /a-pə-dik'tik/ or **apodeictic** /-dīk'-/ *adj* necessarily true; true by demonstration; beyond contradiction. [Gr *apodeiktikos*, from *apodeiknynai* to demonstrate, from *apo* back, and *deiknynai* to show]
■ **apodic'tical** or **apodeic'tical** *adj* (*archaic*). **apodic'tically** or **apodeic'tically** *adv*.

apodosis /ə-pod'ə-sis/ (*grammar*) *n* the clause in a conditional sentence that indicates the consequence if the condition applies (cf **protasis**). [Gr *apodosis*, from *apo* back, and *didonai* to give]

apodous see **apod**.

apodyterium /a-pə-di-tē'ri-əm/ *n* an undressing-room at a Roman bath; a dressing-room (*archaic*). [Gr *apodytērion*, from *apodyein* to undress, from *apo* from, and *dyein* to get into, put on]

apoenzyme /ap-ō-en'zīm/ (*biochem*) *n* a protein component which combines with a coenzyme (qv) to form an enzyme. [Gr *apo* from, and **enzyme**]

apogaeic see under **apogee**.

apogamy /ə-pog'ə-mi/ (*bot*) *n* omission of the sexual process in the life history, whereby the sporophyte develops either from an unfertilized egg cell or some other cell. [Gr *apo* from, and *gamos* marriage]
■ **apogam'ic** or **apog'amous** *adj*. **apog'amously** *adv*.

apogee /ap'ō-jē/ *n* the point in the orbit of a heavenly body or an artificial satellite when it is furthest from the earth, *opp* to **perigee**; highest point; culmination (*fig*); the sun's greatest meridional altitude (*obs*). [Gr *apogaion*, from *apo* from, and *gaia* or *gē* the earth]
■ **apogaeic** /-jē'ik/, **apogē'al** or **apogē'an** *adj*. **apogeotrop'ic** *adj* (*biol*) turning against the direction of gravity. **apogeotrop'ically** *adv*. **apogeotropism** /-ot'-/ *n*.

apograph /ap'ə-gräf/ *n* an exact copy. [Gr *apographon* a copy, from *apo* from, and *graphein* to write]

à point /a pwɛ̃'/ (*Fr*) to a nicety; (of food) done to a turn, perfectly.

apolipoprotein /a-pə-lip-ə-prō'tēn* or *-līp-/ *n* any of a class of proteins, some of which are believed to be connected with the onset of Alzheimer's disease. [Gr *apo* from, and **lipoprotein**]

apolitical /ā-pə-lit'i-kəl/, also *a-/ *adj* indifferent to political affairs; uninvolved in politics. [Gr *a-* (privative), and **political**]
■ **apolitical'ity** or **apolit'icism** *n*. **apolit'ically** *adv*.

Apollinarian[1] /ə-pol-i-nā'ri-ən/ *adj* of *Apollinaris* (died c.390AD), Bishop of Laodicea in Syria, or of his doctrine that in Christ the Logos took the place of a soul. ◆ *n* a follower of Apollinaris.
■ **Apollinā'rianism** *n*.

Apollinarian[2] see under **Apollo**.

Apollinaris /ə-po-li-nā'ris/ *n* (also **Apollinaris water**) a mineral water rich in sodium bicarbonate and carbon dioxide, from the *Apollinaris* spring in the Ahr valley of Germany.

Apollo /ə-pol'ō/ *n* the Greek sun-god, patron of poetry and music, medicine, archery, etc; (sometimes without *cap*; *pl* **apoll'os**) an extremely handsome young man; (without *cap*) a Eurasian mountain butterfly. [Gr *Apollōn, -ōnos*, L *Apollō, -inis*]
■ **Apollinarian** /-i-nā'ri-ən/ *adj* sacred to Apollo. **Apoll'ine** /-īn/ *adj* of Apollo. **Apollōnian** /ap-ə-lō'ni-ən/ *adj* of Apollo; having the characteristics of Apollo, controlled, harmonious, rational, often *opp* to *Dionysian*. **apollonicon** /-on'i-kən/ *n* (*music*) a gigantic barrel organ, partly automatic.

Apollonian[1] /a-pə-lō'ni-ən/ *adj* of the mathematician *Apollonius* of Perga (3c BC), or another Apollonius.

Apollonian[2] see under **Apollo**.

Apollyon /a-pol'yən/ *n* the Destroyer or Devil (Bible, Revelation 9.11). [Gr *apollyōn*, prp of *apollyein* to destroy utterly, from *apo-* (indicating completeness), and *ollyein* or *ollynai* to destroy]

apologetic /ə-pol-ə-jet'ik/ *adj* regretfully acknowledging fault; *orig* serving as a defence or vindication. ◆ *n* (*formal*) a vindication, defence. [Gr *apologia* defence, *apologos* a tale, from *apo* off, and *logos* speaking]
■ **apologet'ical** *adj*. **apologet'ically** *adv*. **apologet'ics** *n sing* the defensive argument or method, *esp* the defence of Christianity. **apologia** /ap-ə-lō'ji-ə/ *n* a written defence or vindication. **apol'ogist** /-jist/ *n* a defender by argument. **apologize** or **-ise** /ə-pol'ə-jīz/ *vi* to express regret for a fault; to put forward a defence. **apologue** /ap'ə-log/ *n* a fable, *esp* one involving animals. **apology** /ə-pol'ə-ji/ *n* an explanation with expression of regret; a regretful acknowledgement of a fault; a poor specimen hardly worthy of its name (*usu* with *for*); a defence, justification, apologia; an apologue (*obs*).

apolune /ap'ə-lūn* or *-loon/ *n* the point in a spacecraft's orbit round the moon where it is furthest from it, *opp* to *perilune*. [Gr *apo* from, and Fr *lune*, from L *luna* moon]

apomixis /a-pə-mik'sis/ (*biol*) *n* omission of sexual fusion in reproduction, as in parthenogenesis, or in apogamy. [Gr *apo* from, and *mixis* mingling, intercourse]
■ **ap'omict** or an organ produced by apomixis. **apomictic** /-mik'tik/ or **apomic'tical** *adj*. **apomic'tically** *adv*.

apomorphine /ap-ə-mör'fēn/ or **apomorphia** /-fi-ə/ *n* an alkaloid prepared by dehydrating morphine (morphia), used in the treatment of Parkinson's disease. [Gr *apo* from, and **morphine**, **morphia**]

aponeurosis /ap-ō-nū-rō'sis/ (*anat*) *n* (*pl* **aponeuro'ses**) a broad, flat, sheetlike tendon, to which a muscle attaches. [Gr *aponeurōsis*, from *apo* off, and *neuron* tendon]
■ **aponeurotic** /-rot'ik/ *adj*.

apoop /ə-poop'/ (*naut*) *adv* on the poop, astern. [**a-**[1] and **poop**[1]]

apopemptic /a-pə-pemp'tik/ (*rare*) *adj* valedictory. [Gr *apopemptikos*, from *apo* away from, and *pempein* to send]

apophasis /ə-pof'ə-sis/ (*rhetoric*) *n* effectively saying something by stating that you will not mention it. [L, from Gr, denial, from *apo* away from, and *phanai* to say]
■ **apophat'ic** *adj* (*theol*) (of a description of God) using negatives, ie saying what God is not.

apophlegmatic /ap-ō-fleg-mat'ik/ (*med*) *adj* promoting the discharge of mucus. ◆ *n* an apophlegmatic agent. [Gr *apophlegmatikos*, from *apo* off; see **phlegm**]

apophthegm or **apothegm** /ap'ə-them* or *-ō-/ *n* a pithy saying, more short, pointed and practical than the aphorism need be. [Gr *apophthegma*, from *apo* forth, and *phthengesthai* to utter]
■ **apophthegmatic** or **apothegmatic** /ap-ə-theg-mat'ik* or *ap-ō-/, **apophthegmat'ical** or **apothegmat'ical** *adj*. **apophthegmat'ically** or **apothegmat'ically** *adv*. **apophtheg'matist** or **apotheg'matist** *n*. **apophtheg'matize**, **apotheg'matize** or **-ise** *vi* to speak in apophthegms.

apophyge /ə-pof'i-jē/ (*archit*) *n* the curve where a column merges in its base or capital. [Gr *apophygē* escape]

apophyllite /ə-pof'i-līt* or *ap-ō-fil'īt/ *n* a mineral, hydrated calcium potassium silicate, that exfoliates on heating. [Gr *apo* off, and *phyllon* leaf]

apophysis /a-pof'i-sis* or *-zis/ *n* (*pl* **apoph'yses** /-sēz/) an outgrowth or protuberance, *esp* on a bone, on the end of a pine-cone scale, or on a moss stalk below the capsule (*biol*); a vein-like offshoot from an igneous intrusion (*geol*). [Gr, offshoot, from *apo* off, and *phyein* to grow]
■ **apophys'eal** or **apophys'ial** *adj*.

apoplectic, etc see under **apoplexy**.

apoplexy /ap'ə-plek-si/ n sudden loss of sensation and motion, generally the result of haemorrhage or thrombosis in the brain (pathol); such a fit of infuriation that one appears to be on the point of bursting a blood vessel (inf). [Gr apoplēxiā, from apo- (expressing completeness) and plēssein to strike]
■ **apoplec'tic** adj of apoplexy (also (archaic) **apoplec'tical**); infuriated (inf). ◆ n a person with apoplexy. **apoplec'tically** adv. **ap'oplex** n (archaic) apoplexy. ◆ vt (archaic; Shakesp) to affect with apoplexy.

apoprotein /ap'ə-prō-tēn/ (biochem) n the protein component of a conjugated protein. [Gr apo from, and **protein**]

apoptosis /ap-əp-tō'sis/ n the natural destruction of cells in a growing organism. [Gr apoptōsis, from apo- off, away, and ptōsis falling]
■ **apoptotic** /-tot'ik/ adj.

aporia /a-pō'ri-a or -pō'/ n a professed doubt of what to say or to choose (rhetoric); a difficulty. [Gr]

aport /ə-pört'/ (naut) adv and adj on or towards the port side. [**a-**[1] and **port**[2]]

à portée /a por-tā'/ (Fr) within reach or range.

aposematic /ap-ə-sē-mat'ik/ (zool) adj (of animal coloration) serving as a warning. [Gr apo away from, and sēma, sēmatos sign]
■ **aposematism** /-sē'mə-tizm/ n.

aposiopesis /ə-pos-i-ŏ-pē'sis or ap-ō-sī-/ n (pl **aposiope'ses** /-sēz/) a sudden breaking off in the midst of a sentence, eg Shakespeare, Macbeth I.7.58, 'If we should fail—'. [Gr aposiōpēsis, from apo off, and siōpē silence]
■ **aposiopetic** /-pet'/ adj.

apositia /a-pō-sish'i-ə/ (obs; med) n an aversion to food. [Gr apo away from, and sītos bread, food]
■ **aposit'ic** adj.

apospory /ə-pos'pə-ri/ (bot) n omission of spore-formation in the life history, when the gametophyte develops without meiosis from the sporophyte. [Gr apo away from, and **spore**]
■ **apos'porous** adj.

apostasy /ə-pos'tə-si/ n abandonment of one's religion, principles or party; a revolt from ecclesiastical obedience, from a religious profession, or from holy orders (RC); defection. [Gr apostasiā a standing away, from apo from, and stasis a standing]
■ **apost'ate** /-āt or -it/ n a person who has abandoned their religion, principles, etc; a renegade, deserter from any allegiance. ◆ adj having abandoned one's religion, etc. **apostatic** /ap-ō-stat'ik/ or **apostat'ical** adj. **apostatize** or **-ise** /ə-pos'tə-tīz/ vi.

a posteriori /ā po-stē-ri-ō'rī, -ō'rī or ä po-ster-i-ō'rē/ adj and adv applied to reasoning from experience, from effect to cause, opp to a priori; inductive(ly); empirical(ly); gained from experience. [L ā from, and posteriōrī, ablative of posterior coming after]

apostil or **apostille** /ə-pos'til/ n a marginal note. [Fr apostille. See **postil**; origin of a- uncertain]

apostle /ə-pos'l/ n a person sent to preach the gospel; esp (and usu with cap) one of Christ's twelve chosen followers; a first introducer of Christianity in a country, eg Augustine, the apostle of the English; a principal champion or supporter of a new system, or of a cause; one of the twelve officials forming a presiding high council in the Mormon Church. [Gr apostolos one sent away, from apo away, and stellein to send]
■ **apos'tleship** n. **apostolate** /ə-post'ə-lāt/ n the office of an apostle; leadership in a Propaganda (qv). **apostolic** /ap-əs-tol'ik/ or **apostol'ical** adj. **apostol'ically** adv. **apostol'icism** /-i-sizm/ or **apostolicity** /ə-post-ə-lis'i-ti/ n the quality of being apostolic. **apos'tolize** or **-ise** vi to preach. ◆ vt to proclaim.
❑ **Apostles' Creed** n the oldest form of Christian creed that exists, from early times ascribed to the Apostles. **apostle spoons** n pl silver spoons with handles ending in figures of the Apostles, once a common baptismal present. **apostolic fathers** n pl the immediate disciples and fellow labourers of the Apostles, more especially those who have left writings (Barnabas, Clement of Rome, Ignatius, Hermas, Polycarp). **apostolic see** n the see of Rome. **apostolic succession** n the derivation of holy orders by unbroken chain of transmission from the Apostles through bishops, the theory of the Catholic Church; the assumed succession of a ministry so ordained to apostolic powers and privileges. **apostolic vicar** n the cardinal representing the Pope in extraordinary missions.

apostrophe[1] /ə-pos'trə-fi/ n a mark (') showing (among other uses) the omission of a letter or letters in a word; a sign of the modern English genitive or possessive case (orig marking the dropping of e). [Gr apostrophos turning away, elision; confused with **apostrophe**[2]]

apostrophe[2] /ə-pos'trə-fi/ n a sudden turning away from the ordinary course of a speech to address some person or object present or absent (explained by Quintilian as addressed to a person present, but extended by modern use to the absent or inanimate); the ranging of chloroplasts along the side walls of the cell in intense light (bot). [Gr apo from, and strophē a turning]
■ **apostrophic** /ap-ə-strof'ik/ adj. **apos'trophize** or **-ise** vt to address in or by apostrophe.

apostrophus /ə-pos'trə-fəs/ n the symbol Ɔ, used in Roman numerals (IƆ = 500, IƆƆ = 5000, IƆƆƆ = 500000).

apothecary /ə-poth'ə-kə-ri/ n a legal description for a licentiate of the Society of Apothecaries, licensed to dispense prescribed drugs; a druggist or pharmacist (archaic); a medical practitioner of an inferior branch, who often kept a shop for drugs (obs). [LL apothēcarius, from Gr apothēkē a storehouse, from apo away, and tithenai to place]
❑ **apothecaries' measure** n liquid units of capacity (fluid ounce, etc) used by pharmacists before 1969. **apothecaries' weight** n a pre-1969 system based on the troy ounce.

apothecium /a-pə-thē's(h)i-əm/ (bot) n (pl **apothe'cia**) an open fructification in Discomycetes and lichens, often cup- or saucer-shaped. [Latinized dimin of Gr apothēkē a storehouse]
■ **apothe'cial** adj.

apothegm, etc see **apophthegm**.

apothem /ap'ə-them/ (maths) n the perpendicular from the centre to any of the sides of a regular polygon. [Gr apo away from, and thema that which is placed]

apotheosis /ə-poth-i-ō'sis/ n (pl **apotheo'ses** /-sēz/) a deification; glorification; a perfect example of its type. [Gr apotheōsis, from apo- (expressing completion), and theos a god]
■ **apoth'eosize** or **-ise** (or /a-pə-thē'ə-sīz/) vt.

apotropaic /ap-ə-trō-pā'ik/ adj turning aside (or intended to turn aside) evil. [Gr apo from, and tropē turning]
■ **apotropa'ism** n an apotropaic practice or custom, a superstition or magic ritual. **apot'ropous** adj (bot) anatropous with a ventral raphe.

apozem /ap'ə-zem/ (med) n a decoction. [Gr apozema, from apo off, and zeein to boil]

app /ap/ (comput) n a short form of **application** (program).

app. abbrev: apparent; apparently; appendix; applied; apprentice; approved; approximate.

appaid see **apay**.

appair /ə-pār'/ an obsolete form of **impair**[1].

appal /ə-pöl'/ vt (**appall'ing**; **appalled'**) to horrify, dismay; to weaken, dim, fade (obs); to abate (Spenser). ◆ vi to grow or become pale, flat or flavourless (obs); to become faint (Spenser). [Perh from OFr apalir, apallir to become pale, make pale. See **pall**[2] and **pale**[2]]
■ **appall'ing** adj. **appall'ingly** adv.

Appaloosa /a-pə-loo'sə/ n a N American breed of horse, usu white or grey with dark spots. [Prob the Palouse Indians]

appalto /a-päl'tō/ (Ital) n (pl **appal'ti** /-tē/) a contract or monopoly.

appanage or **apanage** /ap'ə-nij/ n a provision for maintenance, esp of a king's younger child; dependent territory; a perquisite; an adjunct or attribute. [Fr apanage, from L ad, and panis bread]
■ **app'anaged** or **ap'anaged** adj endowed with an appanage.

apparat /a'pə-rät/ n the political machine of a Communist party. [Russ, apparatus]
■ **apparatchik** /ä-pə-räch'ik/ n (pl **apparat'chiks** or **apparat'chiki**) a member of a Communist bureaucracy or party machine; a Communist agent; an official in any large organization, esp a political party.

apparatus /a-pə-rā'təs or -rä'təs/ n (pl **appara'tuses** or **appara'tus**) things prepared or provided, material; a set of instruments, tools, natural organs, etc; a machine or piece of equipment with a particular purpose; materials (such as variant readings) for the critical study of a document (in full **apparatus criticus** /ap-ə-rā'təs krit'i-kəs or ap-a-rä'tŭs krit'i-kŭs/); a system that enables something to function. [L appārātus, -ūs, from ad to, and pārāre, -ātum to prepare]

apparel /ə-par'əl/ n attire, dress (archaic); ecclesiastical embroidery (archaic); rigging (archaic); equipment (obs). ◆ vt (**appar'elling**; **appar'elled**) to dress, clothe (archaic); to adorn (formal or obs); to equip (obs). [OFr apareiller, from L ad to, and pār equal]
■ **appar'elment** n.

apparent /ə-par'ənt or -pā'rənt/ adj that may be seen; obvious; conspicuous; seeming; obtained by observation without correction (distinguished from true or from mean). ◆ n (Shakesp) heir apparent. [L appārens, -entis, prp of appārēre; see **appear**]

■ **appar'ency** *n* (*archaic*) apparentness; the position of being heir apparent. **appar'ently** *adv*. **appar'entness** *n*.

❑ **apparent horizon** see **horizon**. **apparent magnitude** *n* the apparent brightness of a celestial body expressed on a numerical scale. **apparent solar time** or **apparent time** *n* time as measured by the apparent position of the sun in the sky (as shown eg on a sundial), *opp* to **mean** (*solar*) time.

apparition */a-pə-rish'ən/ n* an appearing; that which appears (*esp* suddenly or unexpectedly); a phantom; a ghost; an appearance, aspect; reappearance (eg of a celestial body) after occultation. [See **appear**]

■ **appari'tional** *adj*.

apparitor */ə-par'i-tər/ n* an officer in attendance on a court, to execute orders (*obs*); such an officer in an ecclesiastical court; a university beadle; someone who appears (*rare*). [L *appāritor*. See **appear**]

appartement */a-par-tə-mã'/* (*Fr*) *n* a set of rooms in a house for an individual or a family.

appay, appayd see **apay**.

appeach */ə-pēch'/* (*Shakesp*) *vt* to accuse, censure or impeach. [OFr *empechier* ; see **impeach**]

■ **appeach'ment** *n*.

appeal */ə-pēl'/ vi* to call upon, have recourse to (with *to*); to refer (to a witness or superior authority); to make supplication or earnest request (to a person for a thing); to ask for (aid, charity, etc) by making a demand on people's feelings; to resort for verification or proof (to some principle or person); to attract one's interest or enjoyment; to demand another judgement by a higher court; to remove to another court; to ask for the umpire's decision *esp* as to whether a player is out (*cricket*). ◆ *vt* to call on a higher court to review (a case, conviction, etc) (*esp US*); to accuse (*Spenser, Shakesp*); to offer up (prayers) (*Spenser*). ◆ *n* recourse; an act of appealing; a supplication; a process by which a party may have a decision reviewed by a higher court or authority (*law*); a case under such a process (*law*); an evocation of sympathetic feeling, interest or enjoyment; (in advertising) an element designed to meet a particular desire of consumers; an impeachment (*Shakesp*); a challenge (to defend one's honour) (*obs*). [OFr *apeler*, from L *appellāre*, *-ātum* to address, call by name; also to appeal to, impeach]

■ **appeal'able** *adj* (of a decision) that can be appealed against or referred to a superior tribunal. **appeal'ing** *adj* making an appeal; imploring; arousing sympathy; attractive, enticing. **appeal'ingly** *adv*. **appeal'ingness** *n*.

❑ **appeal court** *n* a court of law which has jurisdiction to hear appeals on points of law from the decisions of inferior courts.

■ **appeal to the country** to seek approval by a general election. **Court of Appeal** a section of the English Supreme Court of Judicature that hears appeals on all High Court and most county court judgements, etc. **Court of Criminal Appeal** (from 1907 to 1966) an English court for appeal in criminal cases.

appear */ə-pēr'/ vi* to become visible; to present oneself formally before an authority, court, etc; to act as the legal representative or counsel for another; to come into view, to come before the public; to perform (on stage or on film, etc); to be published; to be manifest; to seem. [OFr *apareir*, from L *appārēre*, from *ad* to, and *pārēre, pāritum* to come forth]

■ **appear'ance** *n* the act of appearing, eg in court to prosecute or answer a charge; the action of seeming to be, looking like; the publication of a book, etc; the effect of appearing conspicuously; show, parade; the condition of that which appears, form, aspect; outward look or show; a naturally observable phenomenon; an apparition. **appear'er** *n*.

❑ **appearance money** *n* a fee paid to a celebrity to secure his or her presence at an event.

■ **keep up appearances** to keep up an outward show, *esp* one that belies, or is intended to disguise, the inward reality. **put in** or **make an appearance** to appear in person, *esp* if only briefly. **to all appearances** so far as appears to anyone.

appease */ə-pēz'/ vt* to pacify; to placate by making or effecting concessions; to satisfy; to quiet; to allay. [OFr *apeser* to bring peace, from L *ad* to, and *pāx, pācis* peace]

■ **appeas'able** *adj*. **appease'ment** *n* the action of appeasing; the state of being appeased. **appeas'er** *n*. **appeas'ing** *adj*. **appeas'ingly** *adv*.

❑ **appeasement behaviour** *n* (*animal behaviour*) submissive behaviour of an animal in an attempt to inhibit attack by a potential aggressor.

appel */a-pel'/* (*fencing*) *n* a stamp of the front foot in false attack, in order to create an opening for a hit; a sharp blow with the épée, also as a feint. [Fr, challenge, from *appeler* to call, appeal]

appel au peuple */a-pel ō pœ'pl'/* (*Fr*) a plebiscite.

appellant */ə-pel'ənt/ n* a person who appeals, *specif* (*law*) against a decision of the first court or tribunal to a higher body; a person who impeaches (*obs*); a challenger to single combat (*obs*); a person who in the Jansenist controversy appealed against the bull Unigenitus (1713) to a pope 'better informed', or to a general council (*church hist*). [L *appellāre* to call]

■ **appell'ate** *adj* relating to appeals; (of a tribunal) having the power to review cases on appeal and reverse decisions of inferior courts. **appellation** */ap-ə-lā'shən/ n* a name, *esp* one attached to a particular person; the act of naming. **appella'tional** *adj*. **appell'ative** */ə-pel'ə-tiv/ n* a common noun or common name (as distinguished from a proper name); a designation. ◆ *adj* (of nouns) common (as distinguished from proper); of or relating to the giving of names. **appell'atively** *adv*. **appellee** */ap-el-ē'/ n* (*law*) a person accused or appealed against.

appellation contrôlée */a-pel-a-syɔ̃ kɔ̃-trō-lā'/* or **appellation d'origine** */dor-ē-zhēn'/* **contrôlée** (*Fr*) (in the labelling of French wines, etc) a guarantee that the product conforms to certain specified conditions of origin, strength, etc (also *abbrev* **AOC**).

append */ə-pend'/ vt* to hang on or attach (to something); to add. [L *ad* to, and *pendere* to hang]

■ **append'age** *n* something appended; *esp* one of the paired jointed structures (antennae, jaws or legs) of arthropods; any external outgrowth which does not appear essential to growth or reproduction of a plant (*bot*). **append'ant** *adj* attached, annexed, consequent. ◆ *n* a person or thing added; an adjunct, quality (*archaic*).

appendectomy */ap-en-dek'tə-mi/* or **appendicectomy** */ə-pen-di-sek'tə-mi/ n* a surgical removal of the vermiform appendix. [Ety as for **append**, with Gr *ektomē* cutting out]

appendicitis */ə-pen-di-sī'tis/ n* inflammation of the vermiform appendix. [**appendix** and **-itis**]

appendicular see under **appendix**.

Appendicularia */a-pən-dik-ū-lār'i-ə/ n* a genus of ascidians that retains the larval vertebrate characteristics which are lost in the more or less degenerate sea-squirts. [NL; see **appendix**]

■ **appendiculār'ian** *n* and *adj*.

appendiculate */a-pən-dik'yə-lət* or *-ū-lət/* (*biol*) *adj* having small appendages attached. [L *appendicula*, dimin of **appendix**]

appendix */ə-pen'diks/ n* (*pl* **append'ixes** or **append'ices** */-sēz, -siz/*) something appended or added; a supplement; an addition to a book or document, containing explanatory matter, not essential to its completeness; a process, prolongation or projection from an organ (*anat*); *specif* the vermiform appendix (*anat*). [L, from *appendere* to hang, append; see **append**]

■ **appendicular** */ap-en-dik'ū-lər/ adj* of the nature of, or belonging to, an appendix.

❑ **appendix vermiformis** or **vermiform appendix** *n* (*anat* and *zool*) the distal remains of the caecum of the intestine, in humans, a narrow, blind tube.

apperception */a-pər-sep'shən/ n* the mind's perception of itself as a conscious agent; an act of voluntary consciousness, merged with self-consciousness; the conscious assimilation of a new sense-experience to others already in the mind. [L *ad* to, and **perception** (see under **perceive**)]

■ **apperceive** */-sēv'/ vt*. **appercep'tive** *adj*. **appercipient** */-sip'i-ənt/ adj*.

apperil or **apperill** */ə-per'il/* (*Shakesp*) *n* peril. [L *ad*, and **peril**]

appertain */a-pər-tān'/ vi* to belong (to), as a possession, a right or attribute; to pertain or relate (to). [OFr *apartenir, apertenir*, from L *ad* to, and *pertinēre* to belong]

■ **appertain'ance** *n* (*obs*) appurtenance. **appertain'ing** *adj* proper, appropriate (with *to*). **appertain'ment** *n* (*Shakesp*) appurtenance. **apper'tinent** *adj* appertaining. ◆ *n* (*Shakesp*) appurtenance.

appestat */ap'i-stat/* (*med*) *n* a neural centre in the hypothalamus believed to control (food) appetite. [*appetite*, and **-stat**]

appetent */ap'i-tənt/ adj* eagerly desirous; craving; longing. [L *appetēns, -entis*, prp of *appetere*, from *ad* to, and *petere* to seek]

■ **app'etence** or **app'etency** *n*.

appetite */ap'ə-tīt* or *-i-/ n* a strong physical desire to satisfy a bodily need (eg for food, drink or sex); natural desire; inclination, enthusiasm; desire for food; hunger (with *for*). [OFr *apetit*, from L *appetitus*, from *appetere* ; see **appetent**]

■ **app'etible** *adj* (*obs*) attractive, desirable. **appetise'ment** *n* (*Walter Scott* **appeteeze'ment**). **appetition** */-tish'ən/ n* (*archaic*) direction of desire. **app'etitive** (or */a-pet'i-tiv/*) *adj* having or giving an appetite. **app'etize** or **-ise** *vt* (*rare*) to create or whet the appetite in. **app'etizer** or **-s-** *n* something, *esp* food or drink, to whet the appetite. **app'etizing** or **-s-** *adj*. **appetiz'ingly** or **-s-** (or */ap'/*) *adv*.

applaud */ə-plöd'/ vt* to express approval of by clapping the hands or suchlike; to extol, praise greatly; to commend, express approval of in words. ◆ *vi* to clap the hands or express approval in some other way.

[L *applaudere*, *-plausum*, from *ad* to, and *plaudere* to clap; cf **explode**]

■ **applaud'er** *n*. **applaud'ing** *adj*. **applaud'ingly** *adv*. **applause** /*-plöz'*/ *n* clapping of hands or some other sign of approval; general approbation; loud praise; acclamation. **applausive** /*ə-plös'iv*/ *adj*. **applaus'ively** *adv*.

apple /*ap'l*/ *n* a tree (*Malus domestica*) of the rose family, closely related to the pear-tree; the firm round edible fruit of this tree; any of various other fruits (eg pineapple, custard apple) or even galls (oak-apple); the wood of the apple tree; the fruit of the forbidden tree in the Garden of Eden (*Bible*). [OE *æppel*, cf Ger *Apfel*; ON *epli*; Ir *ubhall*; Welsh *afal*]

□ **app'le-blight** *n* American blight, a woolly substance produced by an aphid that infests apple trees. **app'le-blossom** *n*. **apple butter** *n* a kind of spread made from stewed apples, sugar and spices. **app'le-cart** *n*. **apple-cheeked'** *adj* having full red cheeks. **app'le-jack** *n* (*US*) apple brandy, distilled from fermented apple juice. **app'le-John** *n* (*Shakesp*, etc) a variety of apple considered to be in perfection when shrivelled and withered (also **John-app'le**). **app'le-knocker** *n* (*N Am inf*) a picker or seller of apples; a coarse or dull-witted person. **apple of discord** *n* any cause of envy and contention, after the golden apple (in Greek mythology) inscribed 'for the fairest', thrown among the gods by Eris, goddess of discord, and claimed by Aphrodite, Pallas and Hera. **apple of Sodom** or **Dead Sea apple** *n* a fruit described by the ancients as fair to look upon but turning to ashes when touched, variously thought to be a gall, or the fruit of an asclepiad *Calotropis procera*; by botanists applied to the poisonous green-pulped fruit of *Solanum sodomaeum*; any fair but disappointing thing. **apple of the eye** *n* the pupil of the eye; something or someone especially dear. **apple-pie'** *n* a pie made with apples and *usu* a pastry crust. ♦ *adj* expressing, containing, or typical of, traditionally-upheld and revered American values. **apple-pie bed** *n* a bed prepared as a practical joke, eg with sheets doubled up, so as to be impossible or painful to get into. **apple-pie order** *n* perfect order. **apple polisher** *n* (*N Am inf*) a sycophant. **apple sauce** *n* a sauce of stewed apples served *esp* with roast pork. **app'le-squire** *n* (*obs*) a prostitute's attendant; a man kept by a woman as a concubine. **apple strudel** /*stroo'dl*/ *n* a sweet pastry containing apples, spices, etc. **app'le-wife** or **app'le-woman** *n* (*archaic*) a woman who sells apples at a stall.

■ **apples and pears** (*rhyming sl*; often shortened to **apples**) stairs. **bad** (or **rotten**) **apple** a person likely to have a negative influence on others in a group. **she's apples** (*Aust inf*) everything is just fine, in good order. **the Big Apple** (also **the Apple**) see under **big[1]**. **upset the apple-cart** to throw plans into confusion.

appleringie /*ap-l-ring'gi*/ (*Scot*) *n* southernwood (*Artemisia abrotanum*). [Anglo-Fr *averoine*, from L *abrotanum*, from Gr *abrotanon*]

applet /*ap'lət*/ (*comput*) *n* a small program, *usu* written in Java, that runs within another application. [*appl*ication, and dimin sfx *-let*]

appletini /*ap-l-tē'ni*/ *n* a cocktail made with vodka and apple juice. [*Apple* martini]

Appleton layer /*ap'l-tən lā'ər*/ (*phys*) *n* an ionized region in the atmosphere, about 150 miles up, that acts as a reflector of radio waves. [Sir Edward *Appleton* (1892–1965), British physicist]

appliance...to...**applied** see under **apply**.

appliqué /*a-plē'kā, -kā'* or (*Fr*) *ä-plē-kā'*/ *n* work applied to, or laid on, another material, either of metalwork or of lace, etc (also *adj* and *vt*). [Pap of Fr *appliquer* to apply]

apply /*ə-plī'*/ *vt* (**apply'ing**; **applied'**) to lay or put in contact; to administer; to bring to bear; to put to use; to show the relevance or relevance of; to assign; to ascribe (*obs*); to wield or ply; to direct; to devote (to a pursuit); to adapt (*obs*); to lay on as appliqué; to cover with appliqué. ♦ *vi* to suit or agree; to have recourse; to offer oneself as a candidate; to make or lodge a request; to be relevant; to hold good; to give close attention; to betake oneself (*obs*). [OFr *aplier*, and its source, L *applicāre*, *-ātum*, from *ad* to, and *plicāre* to fold]

■ **applī'able** *adj* (*obs*) applicable; compliant. **applī'ance** *n* application; an instrument or tool used for a particular purpose; apparatus; a fire engine (*old*); compliance (*Shakesp*). **applicability** /*ap-li-kə-bil'i-ti*/ *n*. **app'licable** *adj* (now also /*-plik'*/ in *adj* and *adv*) that may be applied; suitable; relevant. **app'licably** *adv*. **app'licant** *n* a person who applies; a petitioner; a candidate for a post. **app'licate** *adj* put to practical use, applied. **applicā'tion** *n* the act of applying, administering or using; a thing applied; a formal request for a post, etc; an appeal or petition; diligence; close thought or attention; employment, use of anything in special regard to something else; a particular type of problem or process (*comput*); an application program (*comput*, *inf*); a bringing to bear; the lesson or moral of a fable; employment of a word with assignment of meaning; a kind of needlework, appliqué (*archaic*); compliance (*obs*). **app'licative** *adj* put into actual use in regard to anything; practical. **app'licator** *n* a

device or tool for applying something. **app'licatory** /*-kə-tər-i*/ *adj* having the property of applying. **applied** /*ə-plīd'*/ *adj* placed with a flat surface against or close to something; turned to use; (of an academic subject) put to use for a purpose rather than studied for its own sake, (opp to *pure* or *theoretical*). **appli'er** *n*.

□ **applications** (or **application**) **package**, **program** or **software** *n* (*comput*) a package, program or software designed to cope with a particular job or perform a specific function. **applied arts** see **useful** under **use[2]**.

appoggiatura /*äp-pod-jä-too'rä*/ (*music*) *n* (*pl* **appoggiatū'ras** or **appoggiature** /*-too'rā*/) a grace note written in smaller size taking its time at the expense of the following note. [Ital, from *appoggiare* to lean on; same root as **appui**]

appoint /*ə-point'*/ *vt* to fix, settle; to select for a position, assign to a job or office; to assign, grant; to ordain, prescribe; to fix the time of (*archaic*); to engage to meet (*archaic*); to destine, devote (*archaic*); to equip (*obs* except in *pap*); to blame, arraign (*Milton*). [OFr *apointer*, from *à point* to (the) point]

■ **appoint'ed** *adj* fixed; furnished; equipped. **appointee'** *n* a person appointed to a job, position or office. **appoint'er** *n*. **appoint'ive** *adj* (*US*) filled by appointment. **appoint'ment** *n* an engagement, between two or more people, *esp* for a meeting, consultation, etc, at a predetermined time; an office, position, to which one is or may be nominated; direction, ordinance; nomination; (now *usu* in *pl*) equipment; an article of equipment (*archaic*); allowance paid to a public officer (*obs*). **appoint'or** *n* (*law*) a person who is given (by the owner) the power to appoint property to other persons.

□ **appointment book** *n* a book in which a person's prearranged engagements are recorded.

■ **by appointment** at a predetermined time. **by appointment to** (added to the name of a product, service, etc) expressing approval, *esp* by royalty.

apport /*ə-pört'*/ *n* in psychical research, the (supposed) transport of material objects without material agency; (*usu* in *pl*) an object brought on the scene at a spiritualistic séance by no visible agency. [Fr, from L *apportāre* to bring]

apportion /*ə-pör'shən*/ *vt* to portion out; to divide into fair shares or portions; to adjust in due proportion. [L *ad* to, and **portion**]

■ **appor'tionable** *adj*. **appor'tionment** *n*.

appose[1] /*a-pōz'*/ *vt* to apply, eg a seal to a document; to place side by side. [Fr *apposer*, from L *ad* to, and *pausāre* to cease, rest; confused and blended in meaning with words from *pōnere*, *positum* to put]

appose[2] /*a-pōz'*/ *vt* (*obs*) to confront; to examine, question (*Spenser* etc). [Variant of **oppose**]

■ **appos'er** *n* (*obs*). **apposition** /*ap-ə-zish'ən*/ *n* a public examination, a disputation, as on Speech Day at St Paul's School, London.

apposite /*ap'ə-zit*/ *adj* apt; to the purpose. [L *appositus*, pap of *appōnere* to put to, from *ad* to, and *pōnere* to put]

■ **app'ositely** *adv*. **app'ositeness** *n*. **apposition** /*-zish'ən*/ *n* application; juxtaposition; the position of a word parallel to another in syntactic relation (*grammar*); growth of a cell wall by deposition on the surface next to the plasma membrane (*bot*). **apposi'tional** *adj*. **appositive** /*ə-poz'*/ *adj* placed in apposition.

appraise /*ə-prāz'*/ *vt* to estimate the worth of; to set a price on; to value with a view to sale or (in USA) payment of customs duty; to assess the performance of (an employee). [Later form of **apprize**]

■ **apprais'able** *adj*. **apprais'al** or **appraise'ment** *n* a valuation; estimation of quality; a formal assessment of an employee's performance. **appraisee'** *n* an employee undergoing appraisal. **apprais'er** *n* a person who values property; a person who estimates quality. **apprais'ingly** *adv*. **apprais'ive** *adj*. **apprais'ively** *adv*.

□ **appraisal drilling** *n* the drilling of wells (**appraisal wells**) in a newly discovered oilfield to assess the size of the field and the characteristics of the oil.

appreciate /*ə-prē'shi-āt* or *-si-*/ *vt* to estimate justly; to be fully sensible of all the good qualities in; to estimate highly; to perceive, be aware of; to raise in value, to advance the quotation or price of, opp to *depreciate*. ♦ *vi* to rise in value. [LL *appretiāre*, *-ātum*, from *ad* to, and *pretium* price]

■ **apprē'ciable** *adj* capable of being estimated or measured; considerable; significantly large; perceptible. **apprē'ciably** *adv*. **apprēciā'tion** *n* the act of setting a value, especially on a work of literature, music or art; awareness, perception; just, and also favourable, estimation; a sympathetic critical essay; increase in value (eg of an asset or commodity). **apprē'ciative** *adj* characterized by, expressing or implying appreciation. **apprē'ciatively** *adv*. **apprē'ciativeness** *n*. **apprē'ciātor** *n* a person who appreciates, or estimates highly or justly. **apprē'ciatory** /*-shyə-tər-i*/ *adj*.

apprehend /*a-pri-hend'*/ *vt* to lay hold of; to arrest; to become conscious of through the senses; to become aware of through the intellect, recognize; to catch the meaning of, to understand; to consider, conceive; to look forward to, anticipate, *esp* with fear (*formal*). [L *appraehendere*, from *ad* to, and *praehendere, -hēnsum* to lay hold of]

■ **apprehensibil'ity** *n*. **apprehens'ible** *adj*. **apprehen'sion** *n* the act of apprehending or seizing; arrest; fearful anticipation, dread; conscious perception (*archaic*); conception, becoming aware of through the intellect; ability to understand. **apprehens'ive** *adj* having an apprehension or notion; fearful; anticipating something adverse; relating to perception through the mind and senses; intelligent, clever (*archaic*). **apprehens'ively** *adv*. **apprehens'iveness** *n*.

apprentice /ə-*pren'tis*/ *n* a person bound by formal agreement to a skilled person to learn a craft or trade; a novice. ◆ *adj* working or acting as an apprentice. ◆ *vt* to bind by formal agreement, or to place as an apprentice. ◆ *vi* (*N Am*) to serve as an apprentice. [OFr *aprentis*, from *aprendre* to learn, from L *appraehendere* ; see **apprehend**]

■ **apprent'icehood** *n* (*Shakesp*) apprenticeship. **apprent'icement** (*rare*) or **apprent'iceship** *n* the state of an apprentice; a time of training for a trade, or for any activity; hence, a period of seven years (*archaic*).

■ **serve an apprenticeship** to undergo the training of an apprentice.

appress /ə-*pres'*/ or **address** /*ad-*/ *vt* to press together. [L *apprimere, -pressum*, from *ad* to, and *premere* to press]

■ **appressed'** or **addressed'** *adj* (*bot*) closely pressed together but not united. **appressorium** /*a-pres-ör'i-əm*/ *n* (*pl* **appressor'ia**) (*bot*) a flattened outgrowth which attaches a parasite to its host.

apprise /ə-*prīz'*/ *vt* to give notice to; to inform (of). [Fr *apprendre*, pap *appris* ; see **apprehend**]

apprize or **apprise** /ə-*prīz'*/ (*archaic*) *vt* to put a selling price on (*Scots law*); to value, appreciate; to have sold for payment of debt (*Scots law*). [OFr *appriser, aprisier*, from *à* to, and *prisier* to price, prize. See **appraise**]

■ **appriz'er** or **-s-** *n* (*Scots law*) a creditor for whom property is apprized. **appriz'ing** or **-s-** *n* (*Walter Scott ; archaic*) the sheriff's sentence directing property to be apprized.

appro see **on appro** under **approbation** and **approve¹**.

approach /ə-*prōch'*/ *vt* to come near to in any sense; to come into personal relations or seek communication with; to resemble; to bring near. ◆ *vi* to come near; to make an approach. ◆ *n* a drawing near; the stroke by which a player puts or attempts to put the ball onto the green (also **approach stroke, shot**, etc; *golf*); access (*archaic*); an avenue or means of access; the course or process of bringing an aircraft near to the airport, the stage prior to landing (*aeronautics* ; also *adj*); approximation; attitude towards, way of dealing with; (*usu* in *pl*) advances towards personal relations; (in *pl*) trenches, etc by which besiegers strive to reach a fortress, or routes into any area of military importance. [OFr *aprochier*, LL *adpropiāre*, from L *ad* to, and *prope* near]

■ **approachabil'ity** *n*. **approach'able** *adj* capable of being approached, accessible; (of a person) agreeable, kind, open.
❑ **approach road** *n* a slip road leading onto a motorway.

approbation /a-*prə-bā'shən*/ *n* a formal act of support or endorsement; approval; confirmation (*Shakesp*); probation, trial (*Shakesp*). [L *approbāre, -ātum* ; see **approve¹**]

■ **app'robate** *vt* to approve authoritatively (*US*); to accept as valid (*Scots law*). **app'robative** (*archaic*) or **approbatory** /*ap'rə-bə-tər-i* or *ə-prō'*/ *adj*.

■ **approbate and reprobate** (*Scots law*) at once to accept and reject the same deed or instrument (a forbidden practice). **on approbation** (or *inf* **on appro** /*ap'rō*/) on approval.

approof /ə-*proof'*/ (*archaic*) *n* trial, proof; sanction, approval. [OFr *approve* ; see **approve¹**]

appropinque /*a-prō-pingk'*/ or **appropinquate** /*-ping'kwāt*/ (*archaic*) *vt* and *vi* to approach. [L *appropinquāre* to approach, from *ad* to, and *propinquus*, from *prope* near]

■ **appropinquā'tion** *n* approach. **appropinq'uity** *n* nearness.

appropriate /ə-*prō'pri-ət*/ *adj* suitable (with *to* or *for*); set apart for a purpose; peculiar, specific (with *to*). ◆ *vt* /*-pri-āt*/ to make the private property of someone; to take to oneself as one's own; to steal; to set apart for a purpose, assign (*formal* or *archaic*); to suit (with *to*; *archaic*). [LL *appropriatus*, from L *appropriāre, -ātum*, from *ad* to, and *proprius* one's own; see **proper**]

■ **apprō'priately** *adv*. **apprō'priateness** *n*. **apprōpriā'tion** *n* the act of appropriating; the taking of and/or dividing of assets (*account*, etc); the use of a company's after-tax earnings to pay a dividend (*finance*); the making over of a benefice to a monastery or other corporation; the assigning of supplies granted by parliament to particular specified objects; the sum of money allocated for spending (eg on a sales promotion); sometimes used loosely for *impropriation*. **apprō'priative** *adj*. **apprō'priativeness** *n*. **apprō'priator** *n*.

❑ **appropriate technology** *n* (the development, adaption or upgrading of) local or locally appropriate industries (eg spinning, weaving, pottery, etc in developing countries) as an alternative to expensive and inappropriate imported technologies. **appropriation account** *n* an account in a partnership or company which is used to show allocation of profits. **appropriation bill** *n* a bill stating in some detail how the revenue is to be spent.

approve¹ /ə-*proov'*/ *vt* to think well of, to be pleased with; to commend; to confirm, sanction or ratify; to show, demonstrate (*esp reflexive* ; *obs*); to test (*Shakesp*); to convict (*Shakesp*). ◆ *vi* to judge favourably, to be pleased (with *of*). [OFr *aprover*, from L *approbāre*, from *ad* to, and *probāre* to test or try, from *probus* good]

■ **approv'able** *adj* deserving approval. **approv'al** or (*archaic*) **approv'ance** *n* favourable judgement; commendation; an act of approving. **approv'er** *n* a person who approves; an accomplice in crime admitted to give evidence against a prisoner, an informer (*Eng law* ; *hist*). **approv'ing** *adj*. **approv'ingly** *adv*.
❑ **approved school** *n* (between 1933 (Scotland 1937) and 1969) a state boarding school for young people who had broken the law or who were pronounced to be in need of care and protection.

■ **seal** (or **stamp**) **of approval** formal commendation or ratification. **on approval** (or *inf* **on appro** /*ap'rō*/) subject to approval; without obligation to buy.

approve² /ə-*proov'*/ (*law*) *vt* to turn to one's profit, increase the value of (*orig* and *esp* common land). [OFr *aproer, approuer*, from *à* to (L *ad*), and *pro, prou* advantage; see **prowess**; confused with **approve¹**]

approx. *abbrev* : approximate; approximately; approximation.

approximate /ə-*prok'si-mət*/ *adj* nearly exact, approaching correctness (**very approximate** very nearly exact; but now widely used to mean very rough); close together; nearest or next. ◆ *vt* /*-āt*/ to bring near; to come or be near to. ◆ *vi* to come near (to), approach. [L *approximāre, -ātum*, from *ad* to, and *proximus* nearest, superl *adj*, from *prope* near]

■ **approx'imal** *adj* (*anat*) close together; next to. **approx'imately** *adv*. **approximā'tion** *n* an approach (*lit* and *fig*); an imprecise account, calculation, etc; a result in mathematics not rigorously exact, but so near the truth as to be sufficient for a given purpose. **approx'imative** /*-i-mā-tiv* or *-i-mə-tiv*/ *adj* approaching closely.

appui, also **appuy** /*a-pwē'*/ *n* defensive support for a military force; any kind of support (*obs*); the reciprocal action between a horse's mouth and a rider's hand. ◆ *vt* (**appuy'ing** ; **appuied'**) to support; *specif* to place beside a *point d'appui* (*milit*). [Fr, from OFr *apuyer*, from assumed LL *appodiāre*, from L *ad* to, and *podium* support]

■ **point d'appui** see separate entry.

appulse /ə-*puls'*/ *n* a striking against something; (of two celestial objects) an apparent coming to conjunction or to the meridian as perceived by an observer (*astron*); *specif* the close approach of a planet or asteroid to a star without the occurrence of an eclipse. [L *appulsus, -ūs*, from *appellere*, from *ad* towards, and *pellere* to drive]

appurtenance /ə-*pûr'tə-nəns*/ *n* something that appertains; an appendage or accessory; a right belonging to a property (*law*). [Anglo-Fr *apurtenance*, from OFr *apertenance*, from *apertenir*. See ety for **appertain**]

■ **appur'tenant** *adj* and *n*.

appuy see **appui**.

APR *abbrev* : annual (or annualized) percentage rate.

Apr. *abbrev* : April.

apraxia /ə-*prak'si-ə*/ (*pathol*) *n* an inability, not due to paralysis, to perform voluntary purposeful movements of parts of the body, caused by brain lesion. [Gr, inaction]

■ **aprax'ic** or **apract'ic** *adj*.

APRC *abbrev* : *anno post Romam conditam* (*L*), in the year after the founding of Rome (753BC).

après /*a-pre'*/ (Fr) *prep* after.

❑ **après-goût** /*-goo*/ *n* an aftertaste.

■ **après coup** /*koo*/ too late, after the event.

après-ski or **apres-ski** /*a-pre-skē'* or *-prä-*/ *n* (the evening period of, or clothes, etc suitable for) amusements after the day's skiing (also *adj*). [Fr]

apricot /*ā'pri-kot*, also *a'*/, formerly **apricock** /*-kok*/ *n* an Asian fruit (*Prunus armeniaca*), roundish, orange-coloured, with a downy skin, and of a rich aromatic flavour; its colour; the tree that bears it. [Port *albricoque*, from Ar *al-birqūq*, from *al* the, Late Gr *praikokion*, from L *praecoquum* or *praecox* early ripe; the form is perh due to a fancied connection with L *aprīcus* sunny; assimilated to Fr *abricot* ; see **precocious**]

April /*ā'pril* or *-prəl*/ *n* the fourth month of the year. [L *Aprīlis*]

■ **April'ian** or **A'prilish** *adj*.

❑ **A'pril-fish** *n* an April fool's hoax, deception or errand (translation of Fr *poisson d'avril*). **April fool** *n* a person who is hoaxed, deceived, or made a fool of on 1 April (in Scotland also called a **gowk**, as in the phrase *hunt-the-gowk* (qv)); a hoax or trick played on that day. **April Fools' Day** *n* 1 April, the day on which tricks are traditionally played and fools made.

a prima vista /a prē'ma vēs'ta/ (*Ital*) at first sight.

a priori /ā prī-ō'rī, -ō' or ä prē-ō'rē/ *adj* and *adv* the term applied to reasoning from what is prior (logically or chronologically), eg reasoning from cause to effect, from a general principle to its consequences, or even from observed fact to another fact or principle not observed, or to arguing from pre-existing knowledge, or even cherished prejudices; from the forms of cognition independent of experience (*Kant*). [L *ā* from, and *priōrī* (ablative) preceding]

■ **apriō'rism** *n*. **apriō'rist** *n* a person who believes in Kant's view of a priori cognition. **apriority** /-or'i-ti/ *n*.

apron /ā'prən/ *n* a piece of cloth, leather, etc worn in front, *esp* to protect clothes from dirt or damage; a ceremonial garment worn by Freemasons and some clergymen; anything resembling an apron in shape or use, such as a leg-covering for use in an open vehicle; a stage or part of stage in front of the proscenium arch, projecting to a greater or lesser extent into the auditorium (also **a'pron-stage**); that part of a boxing ring that extends beyond the ropes; a rim, border, etc; an area of ground surface at the entrance to a hangar, lock, airport terminal, etc; an extent of eg gravel or sand, spread outward from a source (*geol*); a flat, horizontal piece of the framework of a chair, table, etc acting to strengthen the legs; a protective plate, shielding the operator, on various machines and mechanisms; a continuous conveyor belt made up of metal, rubber, etc plates; a timber behind the stem of a ship (*shipbuilding*). ◆ *vt* to cover with, or as if with, an apron. [ME *napron*, from OFr *naperon*, from *nappe* cloth, tablecloth, from L *mappa* a napkin (*an apron from a napron*; cf **adder**)]

■ **ā'pronful** *n* an amount capable of being carried in one's upturned apron.

❑ **a'pron-man** *n* (*Shakesp*) a man who wears an apron, a workman. **a'pron-string** *n* a string by which an apron is tied.

■ **tied to a woman's apron-strings** ruled by and dependent on a woman (*esp* one's wife or mother).

apropos /a-prō-pō' or -prə-/ *adv* to the purpose; appropriately; in reference to (with *of*); by the way, incidentally. ◆ *adj* to the purpose, pertinent. [Fr *à propos*. See **propose** and **purpose**]

à propos de bottes /a prō-pō də bot'/ (*Fr*) literally, apropos of boots, ie without real relevancy; by the way.

à propos de rien /a prō-pō də ryē'/ (*Fr*) apropos of nothing.

apsaras /up'sə-rəs/ *n* (*pl* **ap'sarases** /-sēz/) a divine water sprite (*Hindu myth*); such a being represented as a voluptuous female figure in Hindu temple carvings, paintings, etc. [Sans]

apse /aps/ *n* a semicircular or polygonal recess, *esp* at the east end of a church choir, and where, in the Roman basilica, the praetor's chair stood; an apsis (*astron*). [L *apsis*, *-īdis*, from Gr *hapsis* (*apsis*), *-īdos* a felloe, wheel, arch, loop, from *haptein* to fit, connect. See **apt**]

■ **ap'sidal** *adj* of an apse or apsis. **apsid'iole** *n* (*archit*) a subsidiary apse. **aps'is** *n* (*pl* **aps'ides** /-dēz/ (or *ap-sī'dēz*)/) in an orbit, the point of greatest or least distance from the central body (*astron*); an apse.

Apso see **Lhasa Apso**.

APT *abbrev*: advanced passenger train.

apt /apt/ *adj* fitting; suitable; apposite, appropriate; tending (to); liable, ready or prone; open to impressions, ready to learn (often with *at*); likely (to). ◆ *vt* (*obs*) to fit, adapt. [L *aptus* fit, suitable]

■ **ap'titude** *n* natural ability, readiness to learn (with *for*); tendency (with *to*); fitness. **apt'ly** *adv*. **apt'ness** *n*.

apt *abbrev*: apartment.

aptamer /ap'tə-mər/ *n* any of various artificially created RNA-based molecules with therapeutic properties. [L *aptus* fit, suitable, because they attach themselves to targeted molecules]

apterous /ap'tə-rəs/ *adj* (*biol*) wingless. [Gr *a-* (privative), and *pteron* feather, wing, side-wall]

■ **ap'teral** *adj* wingless (*zool*); without columns along the sides (*archit*). **ap'terism** *n* (*zool*) winglessness. **apterium** /ap-tē'ri-əm/ *n* (*pl* **apte'ria**) (*ornithol*) a bare patch on a bird's skin.

apteryx /ap'tə-riks/ *n* (*pl* **ap'teryxes**) a member of the flightless genus of birds, *Apteryx*, the kiwis, found in New Zealand, having vestigial wings, no tail, reddish-brown feathers that lack aftershafts, and being about the size of a large hen. [Gr *a-* (privative), and *pteryx*, *-ygos* wing]

■ **apterygial** /-tər-ij'i-əl/ *adj* (*zool*) lacking paired limbs. **Apterygota** /ap-ter-i-gō'tə/ *n pl* a class of primitive insects, wingless, without metamorphosis (ie bristle-tails, silverfish, springtails, but see **collembolan**).

aptitude, **aptly**, **aptness** see under **apt**.

aptote /ap'tōt/ (*grammar*) *n* an indeclinable noun. [Gr *aptōtos*, from *a-* (privative), and *ptōsis* case]

■ **aptotic** /-tot'ik/ *adj* uninflected.

apyrexia /a-pi-rek'si-ə/ (*med*) *n* absence or intermission of fever. [Gr *apyrexiā*, from *a-* (privative), and *pyressein* to be feverish]

■ **apyret'ic** *adj*.

AQ *abbrev*: achievement quotient.

aq. *abbrev*: *aqua* (*L*), water, solution, liquid (*chem* and *pharm*); aqueous.

AQA *abbrev*: Assessment and Qualifications Alliance.

AQPS (*horse-racing*) *abbrev*: *autre que pur sang* (*Fr*), other than pure blood, non-thoroughbred.

aqua /ak'wə/ *n* water; a pale blue colour, aquamarine. ◆ *adj* aquamarine. [L *aqua* water]

❑ **aqua caelestis** /sē-les'tis or kī-/ *n* (L *caelestis* coming from heaven) rain water; rectified spirits; cordial. **aqua fontana** /fon-tän'ə/ *n* (L *fontānus* of a spring) spring water. **aqua fortis** or **aquafor'tis** *n* (L *fortis* strong) (ancient name for) concentrated nitric acid; etching with nitric acid. **aquafor'tist** *n* an etcher or engraver who uses aquafortis. **aqua mirabilis** *n* (L *mīrābilis* wonderful; *obs*) a preparation distilled from cloves, nutmeg, ginger, and spirit of wine. **aqua pura** /pū'ra/ *n* pure water. **aqua regia** /rē'jya or rā'gi-a/ *n* (L *rēgius* royal) a mixture of nitric and hydrochloric acids, which dissolves the royal metal, gold. **aqua Tofana** /tō-fä'na/ *n* a secret poison (probably arsenical) made by a 17c Sicilian woman Tofana. **aqua vitae** /vī'tē or wē'tī/ *n* (L, of life) alcohol; brandy, whisky, etc.

aqua- /a-kwə- or a-kwa-/, also **aqui-** /a-kwi-/ *combining form* denoting water. [L *aqua* water]

■ **aquabat'ic** *adj*. **aquabat'ics** *n sing* or *n pl* spectacular feats in water. **a'quaboard** *n* a board for riding on the surface of water. **a'quacade** *n* (*N Am*) an exhibition of swimming, diving, etc, *usu* accompanied by music. **a'quaculture** or **a'quiculture** *n* the practice of using the sea, lakes, rivers, etc for fish farming, shellfish cultivation, the growing of plants, etc. a'quadrome *n* a leisure facility specializing in aquatic pursuits. **a'quafer** *n* see **aquifer**. **a'quafit** *n* a type of aerobic exercise performed in water. **a'qualeather** *n* leather made from fishskin. **a'qualung** *n* a lightweight, self-contained diving apparatus with compressed-air supply carried on the back. **a'quanaut** *n* a skin-diver; someone who explores and/or lives in the sea at considerable depth. **aquanaut'ics** *n sing* or *n pl*. **a'quaphobe** *n* a person suffering from an extreme fear of water. **aquaphō'bia** *n*. **aquaphō'bic** *adj* and *n*. **a'quaplane** *n* a board on which a person stands and is towed behind a motorboat. ◆ *vi* to ride on an aquaplane; (of a car, etc) to travel or skid on a film of water which has built up between the tyres and the road surface. **a'quaplaner** *n*. **a'quaplaning** *n*. **aquarō'bic** *adj*. **aquarō'bics** or **aquaerō'bics** *n sing* a system of exercises, similar to aerobics, performed to music in chest-high water.

aquamanile /ak-wə-mə-nī'lē, -nē'lā/ or **aquamanale** /-nä'lē/ *n* a medieval jug, often in the form of a human or animal figure; a basin in which the priest washes his hands during the celebration of mass (*relig*). [Through LL, from L *aquae* of water, and *mānālis* flowing, or *manus* hand]

aquamarine /ak-wə-mə-rēn'/ *n* a pale bluish-green variety of beryl, a gemstone; its colour. ◆ *adj* bluish-green. [L *aqua marīna* sea water, from *mare* the sea]

aquanaut, **aquaphobe**, **aquaplane**, etc see under **aqua-**.

aquarelle /ak-wə-rel'/ *n* watercolour painting; a painting in (transparent) watercolours. [Fr, from Ital *acquerella*, *acquarella*, from *acqua*, from L *aqua* water]

■ **aquarell'ist** *n*.

aquarium /ə-kwā'ri-əm/ *n* (*pl* **aquā'riums** or **aquā'ria**) a tank or (a building containing) a series of tanks for keeping aquatic animals or plants. [Ety as for **Aquarius**]

■ **aquā'rian** *adj* of or relating to aquariums. ◆ *n* (*archaic*) an aquarist. **aquā'rist** (or /ak'wə-/) *n* a person who keeps, or is curator of, an aquarium (also (now *obs*) **aquar'iist**).

Aquarius /ə-kwār'i-əs/ *n* the Water Bearer, a constellation giving its name to, and formerly coinciding with, a sign of the zodiac (*astron*); the eleventh sign of the zodiac, between Capricorn and Pisces (*astrol*); a person born between 21 January and 19 February, under the sign of Aquarius (*astrol*; *pl* **Aquā'rius** or **Aquā'riuses**). [L *aquārius*, adj from *aqua* water]

■ **Aquar'ian** *n* and *adj* (relating to or characteristic of) a person born under the sign of Aquarius.

aquarobics see under **aqua-**.

aquatic /ə-kwat'ik or -kwot'/ *adj* living, growing, practising sports, or taking place, in or on water. ◆ *n* an aquatic plant, animal or sportsperson. [L *aquāticus*, from *aqua* water]

■ **aquat'ics** *n sing* or *n pl* water sports.

aquatint /akʹwə-tint/ n (also **aquatint'a**) a method of etching on copper by the use of resin and nitric acid; a print produced by such a method. ◆ vt and vi to engrave in aquatint. [Ital acqua tinta dyed water, from L aqua water, and tingere, tinctum to dye]

à quatre /a kaʹtr'/ (Fr) of or between four; four together. ■ **à quatre mains** /mē/ for four hands.

a quattr'occhi /a kwat-rokʹē/ (Ital) face to face, tête-à-tête.

aquavit /akʹwə- or äʹkwə-vēt/ n a Scandinavian spirit made from potatoes or grain, flavoured with caraway seeds (also **akʹvavit**). [Dan, Swed and Norw akvavit, from Med L aqua vītae]

aqueduct /akʹwi-dukt/ n an artificial channel or pipe for conveying water, most commonly understood to mean a bridge across a valley; a bridge carrying a canal; a small passage in an animal body (zool). [L aqua water, and dūcere, ductum to lead]

aqueous /äʹkwi-əs/ adj of water; watery; deposited by water. [L aqua water]
❑ **aqueous humour** n (med and zool) the watery fluid between the cornea and the lens in the eye.

aqui- see **aqua-**.

aquiculture see **aquaculture** under **aqua-**.

aquifer /akʹwi-fər/ (geol) n (also **aʹquafer**) any rock formation containing water in recoverable quantities (sufficient to supply wells, etc). [New L, from L aqua water, and ferre to carry]

Aquifoliaceae /ak-wi-fō-li-āʹsi-ē/ n pl the holly family. [L aquifolium holly, from acus, -ūs needle, and folium leaf]
■ **aquifoliāʹceous** /-shəs/ adj.

Aquila /akʹwi-lə/ n the golden eagle genus; the Eagle, a constellation north of Sagittarius. [L aquila eagle]
■ **aqʹuiline** /-līn/ adj of the eagle; hooked like an eagle's beak.

aquilegia /ak-wi-lēʹjyə/ n a plant of the columbine genus Aquilegia, native to Europe, N Africa and Asia. [Prob L aquila eagle]

aquiline see under **Aquila**.

Aquilon /akʹwi-lon/ (Shakesp; also without cap) n the north wind. [L aquilō, -ōnis]

aquiver /ə-kwivʹər/ adv or adj in a quivering state. [**a-1**]

a quoi bon? /a kwa bõ/ (Fr) what's the good of it?

AR abbrev: airman recruit (US); annual return (finance); Arkansas (US state); army regulation; autonomous region (or republic); augmented reality (comput).

Ar (chem) symbol: argon.

Ar. abbrev: Arab; Arabia; Arabian; Arabic; Aramaic.

ar /är/ n the eighteenth letter of the modern English alphabet (R or r).

ARA abbrev: Aircraft Research Association; Amateur Rowing Association; Associate of the Royal Academy.

Arab /arʹəb/ n one of the Semitic people inhabiting Arabia and neighbouring countries; a horse of a native Arabian breed popular for its grace and speed; a neglected or homeless boy or girl (usu **street Arab**; offensive). ◆ adj Arabian. [L Arabs, Arabis, from Gr Araps, Arabos]
■ **Arabian** /ə-rāʹbi-an or -byən/ adj of or belonging to Arabia or the Arabs. ◆ n a native of Arabia; an Arabian horse (see **Arab**). **Arabic** /arʹəb-ik/ adj relating to Arabia, or to its language, numerals or script. ◆ n the language or script of the Arabs; see also **gum arabic** under **gum²**. **Arʹabism** n an Arabic idiom. **Arʹabist** n a person learned in, or studying, Arabic culture, history, language, etc. **arabizāʹtion** or **-s-** n. **arʹabize** or **-ise** vt to make Arab. **Arʹaby** n a poetical name for Arabia. ❑ **Arabian camel** n a one-humped camel. **Arabic** (or **Arabian**) **numerals** n pl the numerals in ordinary use in arithmetic, eg 1,2,3,4 transmitted from India to Europe by the Arabs (cf **Roman numerals**). **Arab Spring** n a period of mass protest and democratic reform occurring across many Arab countries from 2010.

Arab. abbrev: Arabia; Arabian; Arabic.

araba /ə-räʹbə/ n a Central Asian wheeled carriage (also **arʹba** or **arōʹba**). [Ar and Pers ʹarābah]

arabesque /a-rə-beskʹ/ adj after the manner of Arabian designs; of or in the style of an arabesque. ◆ n painted, sculptured or metalwork ornament, known esp from Islamic art and that of the Spanish Moors, consisting of foliage and other plant forms curiously and intricately intertwined; a piece of such artwork; a short musical composition with analogous decorative qualities; a posture in ballet-dancing in which one leg is stretched out backwards parallel with the ground and the body is bent forward from the hips. [Fr, from Ital arabesco; -esco corresponding to Eng -ish]
■ **arabesquedʹ** adj ornamented with arabesques.

Arabian, Arabic see under **Arab**.

arabica /ə-rabʹi-kə/ n coffee produced from the shrub Coffea arabica, originating in Ethiopia and now widely grown esp in S America.

arabin /arʹə-bin/ (chem) n the essential principle of gum arabic (qv under **gum²**). [Arabic and **-in**]
■ **arʹabinose** (or /-abʹ/) n a sugar produced from arabin, used as a culture medium for certain bacteria.

arabis /arʹə-bis/ n any member of a large genus, Arabis, of trailing plants (family Cruciferae), including rockcress, wall cress, etc. [LL Arabis Arabian, perh from its dry habitats]

Arabism, arabize, etc see under **Arab**.

arable /arʹə-bl/ adj (of land) fit for ploughing or crop production; relating to the use of such land. ◆ n arable land or farming. [L arābilis, from arāre, cognate with Gr aroein to plough, OE erian, Eng **ear³** (vt), and Ir araim]

Araby see under **Arab**.

Araceae, araceous see under **arum**.

arachidonic acid see under **arachis**.

arachis /arʹə-kis/ n any plant of the Brazilian genus Arachis of the family Leguminosae, including the monkey nut, groundnut, or peanut, which ripens its pods underground. [Gr arachos and arakis, names of leguminous plants]
❑ **arachidonʹic acid** n an unsaturated fatty acid ($C_{19}H_{31}COOH$) occurring in animal cells (also **eicosatetraenoic acid**). **arachis oil** n peanut oil.

Arachnida /a-rakʹni-də/ n pl the large class of arthropods that includes spiders, scorpions, mites, etc. [Gr arachnē spider]
■ **arachʹnid** n any member of the class. **arachʹnidan** n and adj. **arachʹnoid** adj of or like the Arachnida; like a cobweb, formed of or covered with fine interwoven hairs or fibres (bot and zool). ◆ n (anat and zool) the arachnoid membrane. **arachnoiʹdal** adj. **arachnoidīʹtis** n (med) inflammation of the arachnoid membrane. **arachnologʹical** adj. **arachnolʹogist** n a person who studies the Arachnida. **arachnolʹogy** n. **arachʹnophobe** n a person suffering from an extreme fear of spiders. **arachnophōʹbia** n. **arachnophōʹbic** adj. ❑ **arachnoid membrane** n (anat and zool) one of the three coverings of the brain and spinal cord, between the dura mater and pia mater, non-vascular, transparent and thin.

araeometer or **areometer** /a-ri-omʹə-tər or -i-tər/ (hist) n an instrument for determining specific gravity, a hydrometer. [Gr araios thin, and metron measure]
■ **araeometric** or **araeometrical** /-metʹ/ adj. **araeomʹetry** n the measuring of specific gravity.

araeostyle or **areostyle** /ə-rēʹō-stīl or arʹē-/ (archit) adj having columns four diameters or more apart. ◆ n a building or colonnade so built. [Gr araios thin, sparse, and stŷlos column]
■ **araeosystyle** or **areosystile** /-sisʹtīl/ adj alternately araeostyle and systyle (also n).

aragonite /arʹə-gə-nīt or ə-ragʹə-nīt/ n an orthorhombic mineral composed of calcium carbonate. [Aragon, in Spain]

araise or **arayse** /ə-rāzʹ/ (obs) vt to raise; to raise from the dead (Shakesp). [Pfx a- (intens), and **raise**]

arak once obs, now the more usual spelling of **arrack**.

Araldite® /aʹrəl-dīt/ n an epoxy resin used as a strong glue.

aralia /ə-rāʹli-ə/ n a plant of the Aralia genus of the ivy family, **Araliāʹceae**, much grown as decorative plants. [Perh Native American origin]
■ **araliāʹceous** adj.

Aramaic /a-rə-māʹik/ adj relating to Aramaea, or Aram (roughly, modern Syria), or to its language (also **Aramaean** /-mēʹən/). ◆ n any of a group of Semitic languages (including that spoken by Christ) once used in this and neighbouring areas, esp in commerce and government, still spoken by some small communities in SW Asia. [Gr Aramaios]
■ **Aramāʹism** n an Aramaic idiom.

arame /ə-räʹmi or (Jap) a-ra-me/ n a type of edible seaweed, looking like black bootlaces. [Jap]

aramid fibre /arʹə-mid fīʹbər/ n an exceptionally strong lightweight synthetic fibre much used in composite materials. [aromatic polyamide **fibre**]

Aran /arʹən/ adj (of knitwear) made in a style or with a pattern that originated in the Aran Islands, off the west of Ireland; of or relating to the Aran islands.

Aranea /ə-rāʹni-ə/ n the garden spider genus (also called **Epeira**). [L arānea spider]
■ **Arāʹneae** /-ē/, **Araneida** /ar-ə-nēʹi-də/ or **Araneidae** /-dē/ n pl spiders as a class or order. **arāʹneid** /-ni-id/ n a spider. **arāʹneous** adj cobwebby.

Arapaho /ə-rapʹə-hō/ n (pl **Arapʹaho** or **Arapʹahos**) a member of Native American people now living in Oklahoma and Wyoming; the

Algonquian language of this people. ◆*adj* of the Arapaho or their language. [Crow *allapaho* many tattoo marks]

arapaima /*a-rə-pī'mə*/ *n* a gigantic S American river-fish, chief food-fish of the Amazon, reaching sometimes 200kg (4cwt), the pirarucu (*Arapaima* (or *Sudis*) *gigas*; family Osteoglossidae). [Of Tupí origin]

arapunga /*a-rə-pung'gə*/ or **araponga** /*-pong'gə*/ *n* the campanero or S American bell-bird. [Tupí *araponga*]

arar /*ä'rär*/ *n* the sandarac tree. [Moroccan name]

araroba /*ä-rä-rō'bə*/ *n* Goa powder, a bitter yellow powder obtained from cavities in a papilionaceous Brazilian tree (*Andira*, or *Vataireopsis*, *araroba*), and introduced to Goa from Brazil, formerly used medicinally, yielding chrysarobin; the tree itself. [Prob Tupí]

araucaria /*a-rö-kā'ri-ə*/ *n* a tree of the monkey puzzle genus *Araucaria*, evergreen coniferous trees of S America and Australasia. [*Arauco*, in S Chile]

à ravir /*a ra-vēr'*/ (*Fr*) ravishingly.

arayse see **araise**.

ARB *abbrev* : Architects Registration Board.

arb /*ärb*/ (*inf*; *stock exchange*) *n* short form of **arbitrageur**.

arba see **araba**.

arbalest /*är'bə-lest* or *-list*/ (*esp hist*) *n* (also **ar'balist**, **ar'blast** or **ar'cubalist**) a medieval crossbow; a cross-staff; an arbalester. [L *arcuballista*, from *arcus* bow, and *ballista* (see **ballista**); partly through OE *arblast*, from OFr *arbaleste*]
■ **ar'balester**, **ar'balister** or **ar'blaster** *n* a crossbowman.

arbiter /*är'bi-tər*/ *n* (also *fem* **ar'bitress**) a judge; an umpire, or a person chosen by parties to decide between them; a person who has absolute control, or right to judge. [L]
■ **ar'bitrable** *adj*. **ar'bitrage** /*-trij*/ *n* arbitration; the exploitation of market imperfections to make a profit, eg by buying stocks and shares in one country or market and selling them in another (also *vi*). **ar'bitrager** or *usu* **arbitrageur** /*-tra-zhœr'*/ *n* a person who carries out arbitrage (*inf* short form **arb**). **ar'bitral** *adj* (mainly *Scots law*). **arbit'rament** (now less *usu* **arbit'rement**) *n* the decision of an arbiter; determination; power of decision. **ar'bitrate** *vi* and *vt* to decide, determine (*archaic*); to refer to arbitration; to judge as arbiter or arbitrator. **arbitrā'tion** *n* (submission to) the decision of an arbiter; in industrial relations and law, a method of settling a dispute by referring it to an independent body or arbitrator, both parties having agreed beforehand to abide by its decision. **ar'bitrātor** *n* an arbiter; a person who is appointed to determine a dispute or difference (*law*, etc). **ar'bitrātrix** *n* (*archaic*) a female arbitrator.
❑ **Arbitration Court** *n* (*Aust* and *NZ*) a tribunal for the settlement of industrial disputes.

arbiter elegantiarum /*är'bi-ter e-le-gan-shi-ä'rəm* or *e-le-gan-ti-ä'rŭm*/ (*L*) *n* a judge on matters of taste.

arbitrary /*är'bi-trə-ri*/ *adj* arising from accident rather than from rule; capricious; not bound by rules; (of a penalty, etc) dependent upon the discretion of an arbiter, judge or court (rather than upon a set law or statute); (of a ruler or power) despotic, absolute; not representing any specific value (*maths*). [L *arbitrārius*, from *arbiter*]
■ **ar'bitrarily** (or /*-tra'*/) *adv*. **ar'bitrariness** (or /*-tra'*/) *n*.

arbitrate, **arbitration**, etc see under **arbiter**.

arbitrium /*ar-bit'ri-əm* or *-ŭm*/ (*L*) *n* power of decision.

arblast see **arbalest**.

arbor[1] /*är'bər*/ *n* a tree, *esp* in scientific use. [L]
■ **arborā'ceous** *adj* tree-like; wooded. **arboreal** /*är-bö'ri-əl*/ *adj* of, or of the nature of, trees; tree-dwelling. **arbo'reous** *adj* of or belonging to trees; tree-like; in the form of a tree; wooded. **arboresc'ence** *n* a tree-like growth; a tree-like crystalline formation. **arboresc'ent** *adj* growing, formed or branched like a tree. **ar'boret** *n* a shrubbery (*obs*); an arboretum (*obs*); a little tree, shrub (*Milton*). **arborē'tum** (or /*är-bor-ä'tŭm*/) *n* (*pl* **arborē'ta**) a botanic garden of trees and shrubs. **arboricul'tural** *adj*. **ar'boriculture** *n* the cultivation of trees, *esp* for ornamental and scientific purposes. **arboricul'turist** *n*. **ar'borist** *n* a person who studies trees. **arborīzā'tion** or **-s-** *n* an arborescence. **ar'borous** *adj* of, or formed by, trees.
❑ **Arbor Day** *n* in USA, Canada, Australia, New Zealand, etc, a day set apart every year for the general planting of trees. **arbor vitae** /*vī'tē* or *wē'tī*/ *n* (L, tree of life) an evergreen coniferous tree of the genus *Thuja*, related to cypress; the tree-like branching in the vertical cross-section of the human cerebellum (*anat*).

arbor[2] *n* a cylindrical or conical shaft, beam, spindle or axis in a mechanical device. [**arbor**[1]]

arbor[3] see **arbour**.

arborio /*är-bö'ri-ō*/ *n* a round-grained rice, used in making risotto. [Ital, ult from L *arbor* tree]

arbour or (now *N Am*) **arbor** /*är'bər*/ *n* a lawn, garden, herb garden or orchard (*obs*); a grassy place (*obs*); a retreat or bower of trees or climbing plants; a pergola (*esp N Am*); a shaded walk (*Milton*). [Anglo-Fr *herber*, from L *herbārium*, from *herba* grass, herb; meaning changed through confusion with L *arbor* tree]
■ **ar'boured** *adj* having, or in, an arbour.

arbovirus /*är'bō-vī-rəs*/ *n* any of a group of viruses carried by mosquitoes or other insects, causing diseases such as yellow fever. [From *ar*thropod-*bo*rne *virus*]

Arbroath smokie /*är-brōth' smō'ki*/ *n* an unsplit smoked haddock, produced at *Arbroath* in Scotland.

arbutus /*är-bū'təs* or *är'*/ *n* a shrub or tree of the genus *Arbutus* (strawberry-tree), ornamental evergreens native to S Europe; a N American ericaceous plant (also known as **trailing arbutus** or **mayflower**), with fragrant pink or white flower clusters.
■ **ar'bute** *n* (*archaic*) the strawberry-tree or other arbutus.

ARC *abbrev* : AIDS-related complex.

arc /*ärk*/ *n* a part of the circumference of a circle or other curve (*maths*, *astron*, etc); anything of a similar shape; a luminous discharge of electricity (of low voltage and high current) across a gap between two conductors or terminals; an arch (*Milton*). ◆*adj* (*maths*) denoting an inverse hyberbolic or trigonometrical function (as in *arc sine* or *arc tangent*). ◆*vi* (**arc'ing** or **arck'ing**; **arced** or **arcked**) to form an arc. [L *arcus* a bow]
■ **arc'ing** or **arck'ing** *n*.
❑ **arc'-lamp** or **arc'-light** *n* a lamp whose source of light is an electric arc between carbon electrodes. **arc'minute** *n* a unit of angular measurement, $\frac{1}{60}$ of a degree. **arc'second** *n* a unit of angular measurement, $\frac{1}{3600}$ of a degree. **arc welding** see **weld**[1].

arcade /*är-kād'*/ *n* a row of arches, open or closed, on columns or pilasters; a walk with an arch over it; a covered passageway lined with shops; an amusement arcade. [Fr, from LL *arcāta* arched; see **arch**[1]]
■ **arcād'ed** *adj*. **arcād'ing** *n*.

Arcadian /*är-kā'di-ən*/ *adj* of Arcadia, a district in Greece whose people were traditionally idealized as having a simple rural lifestyle, with much music and dancing; pastoral; simple, innocent. ◆*n* an inhabitant of Arcadia.
■ **Arcād'ianism** *n*. **Arcady** /*är'kə-di*/ *n* a poetical name for Arcadia.

arcane /*är-kān'*/ *adj* secret; mysterious. [L *arcānus* secret, from *arca* a chest]
■ **arcane'ly** *adv*. **arcane'ness** *n*. **arcan'ist** /*-kān'*/ *n* a person who has knowledge of a secret manufacturing process (*esp* in ceramics).

arcanum /*är-kā'nəm*/ *n* (*pl* **arca'na**) a secret or mystery; a secret remedy or elixir. [L, neuter of *arcānus* (see ety for **arcane**)]

arccos /*ärk-kos'* or *-koz'*/ *abbrev* : arc cosine (see **arc**).

arc de triomphe /*ärk də trē-ɔ̃f'*/ (*Fr*) *n* triumphal arch.

arc-en-ciel /*ärk-ã-syel'*/ (*Fr*) *n* a rainbow.

arch[1] /*ärch*/ *n* a structure of wedge-shaped stones or other pieces supporting each other by mutual pressure and able to sustain an overlying weight; anything of a similar form; an archway; an arched gateway; the bony structure of the foot between the heel and toes, normally having an upward curve; a curved or arch-shaped skeletal structure supporting, covering or enclosing an organ or organs (*anat* and *zool*); one of the basic patterns of the human fingerprint; (*usu* in *pl*) used in collectors' names for moths of different kinds, with markings like arcading, as in *silvery arches*. ◆*vt* to cover or provide with an arch. ◆*vt* and *vi* to bend in the form of an arch. [OFr *arche*, from L *arcus* bow (as if *arca*)]
■ **arched** *adj* having the form of an arch; covered with an arch. **arch'let** *n* a little arch. **arch'wise** *adv* in the manner of an arch.
❑ **arch'stone** *n* a voussoir (qv). **arch'way** *n* an arched or vaulted passage or entrance.
■ **Court of Arches** (also known as **the Arches**) the ecclesiastical court of appeal for the province of Canterbury, formerly held at the church of St Mary-le-Bow (so called from the arches that support its steeple). **dropped** or **fallen arch** a flattened foot arch.

arch[2] /*ärch*/ *adj* chief, principal (now *esp* in compounds; see **arch-**); waggish, mischievous; roguish; cunning, shrewd; finished, accomplished, pre-eminent, *esp* in evil (*Bunyan*). ◆*n* (*Shakesp*) chief. [From **arch-**, in words such as *arch*-rogue, etc]
■ **arch'ly** *adv*. **arch'ness** *n*.

arch. *abbrev* : archaic; archaism; archery; archipelago; architect; architectural; architecture.

arch- /*ärch-*/ (or *ärk-* in direct borrowings from Greek)/ *pfx* first or chief, often used to give further emphasis to an already critical or disparaging epithet. [OE *arce-*, *ærce-*, through L from Gr *archi*, from *archos* chief]

-arch /*-ärk* or *-ärk*/ *combining form* denoting chief, ruler, as in *matriarch*, *monarch*. [Gr *archē* rule]

archae- *combining form* see **archaeo-**.

Archaea /är-kē'ə or är'/ *n pl* a domain of living organisms containing prokaryotic micro-organisms. [Gr *archaios* ancient, from *archē* beginning]
■ **Archae'an** *adj* and *n*.

Archaean or (*US*) **Archean** /är-kē'ən/ (*geol*) *adj* of or belonging to the first eon of geological time, between *approx* 4500 and 2500 million years ago (also *n*). [Gr *archaios* ancient, from *archē* beginning]

archaeo- or (*esp N Am*) **archeo-** /är-ki-ō- or -o-/, **archae-** or (*esp N Am*) **arche-** /är-ki-/ *combining form* denoting ancient, primitive; relating to archaeology. [Gr *archaios* ancient, from *archē* beginning]
■ **Archaebacter'ia** *n pl* a former name for **Archaea**. **archaeoastron'omy** *n* the study of prehistoric (eg megalithic) monuments with a view to establishing their possible astronomical significance. **archaeomag'netism** *n* the process of ascertaining magnetic intensity and direction in a prehistoric object (the date at which there was a corresponding intensity and direction in the earth's magnetic field being the date also of the object). **archaeometall'urgy** *n* the study of archaeological metal objects and methods of metal production, etc. **archaeozool'ogist** *n*. **archaeozool'ogy** *n* the study of zoological remains in archaeology.

archaeol. *abbrev* : archaeology.

archaeology or (*esp N Am*) **archeology** /är-ki-ol'ə-ji/ *n* the study of ancient people through their material remains, *usu* as discovered by excavation. [LL, from Gr *archaiologia* the study of antiquity]
■ **archaeolog'ical** *adj*. **archaeolog'ically** *adv*. **archaeol'ogist** *n*.

archaeometry /är-ki-om'ə-tri/ *n* the use of scientific methods in archaeology (also **archeom'etry**). [**archaeo-**]
■ **archaeomet'ric** *adj*. **archaeom'etrist** *n*.

archaeopteryx /är-ki-op'tə-riks/ *n* a Jurassic fossil bird of the *Archaeopteryx* genus, with a long bony tail, sharp-toothed jaws, and wings bearing three clawed digits. [**archaeo-** and Gr *pteryx* wing]

Archaeornithes /är-ki-ör'ni-thēz/ *n pl* a subclass of primitive reptile-like fossil birds, the Saururae, including the archaeopteryx and similar birds. [**archaeo-** and Gr *ornithes*, pl of *ornīs*, *ornīthos* bird]

Archaeus see **Archeus**.

archaic /är-kā'ik/ *adj* (of a word, phrase, etc) not absolutely obsolete but no longer in general use; antiquated, savouring of the past; old-fashioned. [Gr *archaikos*, from *archaios* ancient, from *archē* beginning]
■ **archā'ically** *adv*. **archā'icism** *n* (an) archaic quality or style. **ar'chāism** *n* an archaic word or phrase; a tendency to archaize. **ar'chāist** *n*. **archāist'ic** *adj* affectedly or imitatively archaic. **ar'chaize** or **-ise** *vi* to imitate the archaic; to use archaisms. **ar'chaizer** or **-s-** *n*.

archangel /ärk'ān-jəl or -ān'/ *n* an angel of the highest order; garden angelica; dead-nettle; a kind of pigeon. [Gr *archangelos*, from *archos* chief, and *angelos* messenger]
■ **archangelic** /-an-jel'/ *adj*.

archbishop /ärch-bish'əp or ärch'/ *n* a metropolitan bishop who superintends the bishops in his province, and also exercises episcopal authority in his own diocese. [OE *ærcebiscop*; see **arch-** and **bishop**[1]]
■ **archbish'opric** *n* the office or jurisdiction of, or area governed by, an archbishop.

arch-chimic /ärch-kim'ik/ (*Milton*) *adj* supreme in alchemy. [See **arch-** and **chemic**]

Archd. *abbrev* : Archdeacon; Archduke.

archdeacon /ärch-dē'kən or ärch'/ *n* a chief deacon; the ecclesiastical dignitary having the chief supervision of a diocese or part of it, next under the bishop. [OE *ærcedīacon*; see **arch-** and **deacon**]
■ **archdea'conry** *n* the office, jurisdiction or residence of an archdeacon.

archdiocese /ärch-dī'ə-sis or -sēs/ *n* an archbishop's diocese or jurisdiction. [**arch-** chief, and **diocese**]
■ **archdiocesan** /-dī-os'i-sn/ *adj*.

archdruid /ärch-droo'id/ *n* a chief or presiding druid. [**arch-**]

archduke /ärch'dūk or -dūk'/ (*hist*) *n* a chief duke, *esp* (after 1453) a son of the Emperor of Austria. [**arch-** chief, and **duke**]
■ **archdū'cal** *adj*. **archduchess** /ärch-duch'is/ *n* a princess of the Austrian imperial family; a wife or widow of an archduke. **archduch'y** or **archduke'dom** *n*.

arche- *combining form* see **archaeo-**.

archegonium /är-ki-gō'ni-əm/ (*bot*) *n* (*pl* **archego'nia**) the flask-shaped female reproductive organ of mosses and ferns, and (in a reduced form) of flowering plants. [Gr *archegonos* founder of a race]
■ **archego'nial** *adj*. **Archegoniā'tae** *n pl* formerly, a main division of the vegetable kingdom, the bryophytes and pteridophytes. **archego'niate** *adj* having archegonia.

arch-enemy /ärch-en'ə-mi/ *n* a chief enemy; Satan (also **arch-fel'on**, **arch-fiend'**, **arch-foe'**). [**arch-**]

archenteron /ärk-en'tə-ron/ (*zool*) *n* in the developing embryo, the primitive gut. [Gr pfx *arch-*, and *enteron* gut]

archeology, etc see **archaeology**, etc.

archer /är'chər/ *n* a person who shoots with a bow and arrows (*fem* (*archaic*) **arch'eress**); (with *cap* and *the*) Sagittarius. [OFr *archier*, from L *arcārius*, from *arcus* a bow]
■ **arch'ery** *n* the art or sport of shooting with the bow; a company of archers; a collection of bows and arrows, etc.
□ **arch'erfish** *n* a small spiny-finned fish of (*esp* SE) Asia and Australia that catches insects by shooting water at them from its mouth.

archetype /ärk'i-tīp/ *n* the original pattern or model, prototype; a perfect or typical example. [Gr *archetypon*, from *archē* beginning, and *typos* a model]
■ **archetȳp'al** or **archetyp'ical** *adj*. **archetȳp'ally** or **archetyp'ically** *adv*.

Archeus or **Archaeus** /är-kē'əs/ (*hist*; also without *cap*) *n* the personification of a spirit supposed by Paracelsus to dwell in and control all living things and processes, residing primarily in the stomach. [New L *archaeus*, from Gr *archaios* original]

arch-flamen /ärch-flā'mən/ *n* a chief flamen or priest. [**arch-**]

archgenethliac /ärch-jə-neth'li-ak/ (*Browning*; *derog*) *n* the greatest of genethliacs or astrologers. [**arch-**]

arch-heretic /ärch-her'ə-tik/ *n* a leader of heresy. [**arch-**]

Archibald /är'chi-bəld or -böld/ or in short form **Archie** /är'chi/ (*milit sl*, esp from World War I and II) *n* an anti-aircraft gun. [Arbitrary name]

Archichlamydeae /är-ki-klə-mid'i-ē/ (*bot*) *n pl* one of the main divisions of the dicotyledons, in which the petals, if present, are in general not united. [Gr pfx *archi-* denoting primitiveness, and *chlamys*, *-ydos* mantle]
■ **archichlamyd'eous** *adj*.

archidiaconal /är-ki-dī-ak'ə-nəl/ *adj* of an archdeacon, his office or his jurisdiction. [Gr *archidiākonos*; see **deacon**]

archiepiscopal /är-ki-i-pis'kə-pəl/ *adj* of an archbishop. [Gr *archiepiskopos* archbishop]
■ **archiepis'copacy** or **archiepis'copate** *n* the rank or province of an archbishop.
□ **archiepiscopal cross** *n* a patriarchal cross.

archil /är'chil or -kil/ *n* (also called **orchel** /ör'chəl/, **orchella** /-chel'ə/, **or'chil** or **orchill'a**) a red or violet dye made from various lichens; a lichen that yields it, *esp* a species of *Roccella*. [OFr *orchel*, *orseil* (Fr *orseille*), from Ital *orcello* (origin undetermined)]

Archilochian /är-ki-lō'ki-ən/ *adj* of, relating to or derived from *Archilochus* of Paros (c.714–676BC), Greek poet, reputed originator of iambic metre, and proverbially bitter and satirical. ◆ *n* an Archilochian verse, ie dactylic tetrameter catalectic, dactylic trimeter catalectic (*lesser Archilochian*), or dactylic tetrameter combined with trochaic tripody (*greater Archilochian*).

archilowe /är'hhi-lō/ (*obs Scot*) *n* a treat given in return. [Origin unknown]

archimandrite /är-ki-man'drīt/ *n* in the Greek Church, an abbot, the head of a monastery or convent. [Late Gr *archimandrītēs*, from pfx *archi-* first, and *mandrā* an enclosure, a monastery]

Archimedean /är-ki-mē-dē'ən or -mē'di-ən/ *adj* relating to *Archimedes*, a celebrated Greek mathematician of Syracuse (c.287–212BC).
□ **Archimedean drill** *n* a drill in which to-and-fro movement of a nut on a helix causes alternating rotary motion of the bit. **Archimedean screw** *n* a machine for raising water, etc, in its simplest form a tube bent spirally turning on its axis. **Archimedean spiral** *n* the curve described by a point moving uniformly along a uniformly revolving radius vector, its polar equation being $r = \alpha\theta$.
▩ **principle of Archimedes** or **Archimedes' principle** the principle that a body weighed when immersed wholly or partly in a fluid shows a loss of weight equal to the weight of fluid it displaces.

archipelago /är-kə-pel'ə-gō or -ki-/ *n* (*pl* **archipel'agoes** or **archipel'agos**) *orig* (with *cap*) the Aegean Sea; a sea abounding in islands, such as the Aegean, hence a group of islands. [An Italian compound *arcipelago*, from Gr pfx *archi-* chief, and *pelagos* sea, with prefix restored to Gr form]
■ **archipelagic** /-pi-laj'ik/ *adj*.

archit. *abbrev* : architect; architectural; architecture.

architect /är'ki-tekt/ *n* a designer of buildings, *specif* someone professionally qualified as such; a designer of ships (**naval architect**); a maker or planner (of something). ◆ *vt* to plan or design as an architect. [Gr *architektōn* master-builder, from pfx *archi-* chief, and *tektōn* a builder]
■ **architecton'ic** *adj* relating to architecture; constructive; controlling, directing; relating to the arrangement of knowledge (*philos*). ◆ *n* (often **architecton'ics**) the science of architecture; the systematic

arrangement of knowledge (*philos*). **architec'tural** /-*chər-əl*/ *adj*. **architec'turally** *adv*. **arch'itecture** *n* the art or science of building; structure; *specif* one of the fine arts, the art of designing buildings; style of building; structures or buildings collectively; the overall design of the software and *esp* the hardware of a computer, or of a local network; organization, framework, structure.

architrave /*är'ki-trāv*/ (*archit*) *n* the lowest division of the entablature resting immediately on the abacus of the column; the collective name for the various parts, jambs, lintels, etc, that surround a door or window; the moulding round an arch. [Ital *architrave*, from Gr pfx *archi-* chief, and L *trabs, trabis* a beam]
■ **arch'itraved** *adj*.

architype /*är'ki-tīp*/ (*zool*) *n* a primitive type from which others may be derived. [Gr pfx *archi-* first, and **type**]

archive /*är'kīv*/ *n* (*usu* in *pl*) a repository of public records or of records generally; public records; (*rare* in *sing*) a historical document; files of old data stored on tape or disk (*comput*). ◆ *vi* and *vt* to keep archives or store in archives. [Fr, from LL *archī(v)um*, from Gr *archeion* office of chief magistrates, from *archē* government]
■ **archīv'al** (or /*ärk'i-vəl*/) *adj*. **archivist** /*ärk'i-vist*/ *n* a keeper of archives or records.

archivolt /*är'ki-vōlt*/ (*archit*) *n* the under-curve of an arch, intrados; an ornamental moulding on it. [Ital *archivolto*, from *arco* (L *arcus* an arch), and *volta* vault]

archlute /*ärch'loot* or *-lūt*/ *n* a large double-necked bass lute, popular *esp* in the 17c. [**arch-** and **lute¹**]

arch-mock /*ärch-mok'*/ *n* (*Shakesp*) the height of mockery. [**arch-**]

archology /*är-kol'ə-ji*/ (*rare*) *n* a doctrine of the origin of things; the science of government. [Gr *archē* beginning, rule, and *logos* discourse]

archon /*är'kon, -kōn* or *-kən*/ (*hist*) *n* one of nine chief magistrates of ancient Athens. [Gr *archōn, -ontos*, prp of *archein* to be first, to rule]
■ **arch'onship** *n* the office of an archon. **arch'ontate** *n* an archon's tenure of office. **archontic** /*-ont'ik*/ *adj*.

arch-pirate /*ärch-pī'rət*/ *n* a chief pirate. [**arch-**]

arch-poet /*ärch-pō'it*/ *n* a chief poet; a poet laureate (*obs*). [**arch-**]

arch-prelate /*ärch-prel'it*/ *n* a chief prelate. [**arch-**]

arch-priest /*ärch-prēst'*/ *n* a chief priest; in early times, a kind of vicar to the bishop; later, a rural dean; a superior appointed by the Pope to govern the secular priests sent into England from the foreign seminaries during the period 1598–1621; in the Eastern Orthodox Church, the highest title among the secular clergy. [**arch-**]

arch-traitor /*ärch-trā'tər*/ *n* a chief traitor, greatest of traitors, sometimes applied *esp* to the Devil, or to Judas. [**arch-**]

arch-villain /*ärch-vil'ən*/ *n* a supremely villainous person. [**arch-**]

-archy /*-är'ki* or *-ər'ki*/ *combining form* denoting government of a particular type, as in *oligarchy, monarchy*. [Gr *archē* rule]

ARCIC *abbrev*: Anglican-Roman Catholic International Commission.

arco /*är'kō*/ (*music*) *adv* (also **coll'ar'co**) with the bow (a direction marking the end of a pizzicato passage). ◆ *n* the bow of a stringed instrument. [Ital]
❑ **arco saltando** /*säl-tän'dō*/ *adv* with rebounding bow. ◆ *n* a quick staccato.

arcology /*är-kol'ə-ji*/ *n* a system of architecture that integrates buildings with the natural environment; a city built according to this system. [**architecture** and **ecology**]

arcsin /*ärk-sin'*/ *abbrev*: arc sine (see **arc**).

arctan /*ärk-tan'*/ *abbrev*: arc tangent (see **arc**).

Arctic or **arctic** /*ärk'tik*/ *adj* relating to the Arctic, north pole or to the north; extremely cold (*inf*); *orig* of or relating to the (Great) Bear. ◆ *n* (*usu* **the Arctic**) the area lying north of the Arctic Circle or north of the timber line; (**arctic**) a waterproof overshoe (*N Am*). [L *arcticus* north, of or relating to the (northern constellation) the Great Bear, from Gr *arktikos*, from Gr *arktos* a bear]
❑ **arctic char** *n* a fish (*Salvelinus alpinus*) of Arctic waters. **Arctic Circle** *n* the parallel of latitude 66°32′N, bounding the region of the earth surrounding the north terrestrial pole. **arctic fox** *n* a small fox (*Alopex lagopus*) of Arctic regions. **arctic hare** *n* a large hare (*Lepus arcticus*) of the Canadian Arctic. **arctic tern** *n* a black-capped tern (*Sterna paradisea*) that breeds in the Arctic and migrates south.

Arctiidae /*ärk-tī'i-dē*/ *n pl* the family of medium-sized nocturnal moths, the tiger moths, whose hairy caterpillars are known as woolly bears. [New L, ult from Gr *arktos* bear]
■ **arc'tiid** /*-ti-*/ *n* a moth of this family.

Arctogaea /*ärk-tō-jē'ə*/ *n* a zoological region including all lands outside of Notogaea and Neogaea. [Gr *arktos* bear, and *gaia* earth]
■ **Arctogae'an** or **Arctogae'ic** *adj*.

arctoid /*ärk'toid*/ *adj* bear-like. [Gr *arktos* a bear]

arctophile /*ärk'tə-fīl*/ *n* a lover or collector of teddy-bears (also **arc'tophil**). [Gr *arktos* bear, and **-phile**]
■ **arctophil'ia** *n*. **arctoph'ilist** *n*. **arctoph'ily** *n*.

Arctostaphylos see **bearberry** under **bear²**.

Arcturus /*ärk-tū'rəs* or *-too'*/ *n* the brightest star in the northern sky, a red giant in the constellation Boötes. [Gr *Arktouros*, from *arktos* bear, and *ouros* guard]

arcuate /*är'kū-āt*/ or **arcuated** /*-id*/ *adj* arched, bow-shaped (*esp* in scientific use). [L *arcuātus*, pap of *arcuāre* to bend like a bow, from *arcus* a bow]
■ **arcua'tion** *n*.

arcubalist /*är'kū-bə-list*/ *n* see **arbalest**.

ARCUK *abbrev*: Architects' Registration Council of the United Kingdom (now replaced by **ARB**).

arcus /*är'kəs*/ or **arcus senilis** /*sē-nī'lis*/ (*pathol*) *n* a bow-shaped or ring-shaped greyish fatty deposit in the cornea (*esp* common in old people). [L *arcus* a bow, and *senilis* of old people]

ARD (*med*) *abbrev*: acute respiratory disease (of any type).

ard /*ärd*/ (*archaeol*) *n* a primitive type of plough, used to scratch the top layer of soil. [ME, from ON *arthr* plough]

Ardas /*ur-das'*/ *n* in the Sikh religion, a short direct prayer to God (similar in status to the Lord's Prayer in Christianity). [Punjabi, supplication]

Ardea /*är'di-ə*/ *n* the heron and bittern genus. [L *ardea* heron]

ardeb /*är'deb*/ *n* an Egyptian dry measure of $5\frac{1}{2}$ bushels. [Ar *irdab*]

ardent /*är'dənt*/ *adj* burning, fiery; zealous, burning with emotion; combustible, inflammable (*obs* except in **ardent spirits**, distilled alcoholic liquors, whisky, brandy, etc). [L *ardēns, -entis*, prp of *ardēre* to burn]
■ **ard'ency** *n*. **ard'ently** *adv*. **ard'our** or (*N Am*) **ard'or** *n* warmth of passion or feeling; eagerness; enthusiasm (with *for*).

ardentia verba /*ar-den'shi-ə vûr'bə* or *ar-den'ti-a wer'ba*/ (*L*) words that burn, glowing language.

ardor, ardour see under **ardent**.

ard-ri, ard-righ, ardri or **ardrigh** /*örd'rē* or *-rē'*/ (*Irish hist*) *n* a head king. [Ir *ārd* noble, and *rī* king]

ARDS *abbrev*: acute respiratory distress syndrome.

arduous /*är'dū-əs*/ *adj* steep, difficult to climb; difficult to accomplish; laborious. [L *arduus* steep, high]
■ **ard'uously** *adv*. **ard'uousness** *n*.

are¹ /*är*/ used as plural and also the second person singular of the present indicative of the verb *to be*. [Old Northumbrian *aron*, which ousted the usual OE *sind, sindon*; both from the root *es-*]

are² /*är*/ *n* the unit of the metric land measure, 100 sq m. [Fr, from L *ārea* a site, space, court]

area /*ā'ri-ə*/ *n* a space or piece of ground; a portion of surface; a region (*lit* and *fig*); part of a building, city, etc designated for a special purpose or character; the floor of a theatre, etc; a sunken space around or alongside the basement of a building (*N Am* **a'reaway**, *esp* as a passageway); a measure of the size of any surface. [L *ārea* an open empty place, etc]
■ **ā'real** *adj*.
❑ **area code** *n* (*N Am*) a three-digit number used before the local telephone number when dialling long-distance telephone calls. **area sampling** *n* a marketing technique in which a number of people or organizations within particular geographical areas are sampled at random. **ā'rea-sneak** *n* (*obs*) a thief who sneaks in by basement doors. **areaway** see above.

areach /*a-rēch'*/ (*obs*) *vt* (*pat Spenser*) **arraught** /*a-röt'*/) to reach, get at; to seize. [OE *ārǣcan*, from *ā-* (intensive), and *rǣcan* to reach]

aread, arede or **arreede** /*ə-rēd'*/ *vt* (*pat* and *pap* **ared'** or **aredd'**) to declare, utter (*obs*); to guess (*archaic*); to interpret, explain (*archaic*); to adjudge (*obs*); to decide (*obs*); to counsel (*Milton* and *Spenser*). [OE *ārǣdan*; see **read**]

areal see under **area**.

arear, arere Spenserian spellings of **arrear** (*adv*).

à rebours /*a rə-boor'*/ (*Fr*) against the grain; contrarily.

areca /*är'i-kə* or *ə-rē'kə*/ *n* a tree of the betel nut genus of palms, *Areca*, native to SE Asia and the Indian subcontinent. [Port, from Malayalam *adekka*]
❑ **ar'eca-nut** *n* betel nut, the nut of *Areca catechu*, which stains the teeth and gums bright red, traditionally chewed in S Asia for its intoxicating effects.

ared, aredd, arede see **aread**.

arefaction /*a-ri-fak'shən*/ (*obs*) *n* drying. [L *ārefacere* to make dry, from *ārēre* to dry, and *facere* to make]
■ **ar'efy** *vt* and *vi* to dry up, wither.

areg see **erg**².

arena /ə-rē'nə/ n an area enclosed by seating, in which public sporting contests or entertainments take place; *orig* part of an ancient amphitheatre covered with sand for combats; any sphere of action. [L *arēna* sand]
■ **arenaceous** /ar-i-nā'shəs/ adj sandy; composed of sand or quartz grains (*geol*); with shell(s) composed of agglutinated sand grains (*zool*); sand-growing (*bot*). **Arenā'ria** n the sandwort genus, related to chickweed; a genus of birds, the turnstones. **arenā'tion** n remedial application of (hot) sand. **arenic'olous** adj (*zool*) sand-dwelling.
□ **arena stage** n a stage which can have an audience all round it (see **theatre-in-the-round** under **theatre**).

aren't /ärnt/ contraction of **are not** or (*inf*, as interrogative) **am not**.

areography /ar-i-og'rə-fi/ n description of the physical features of the planet Mars. [Gr *Arēs* Mars, and *graphein* to write]
■ **areograph'ic** adj.

areola /ə-rē'ə-lə/ n (pl **arē'olae** /-lē/ or **arē'olas**) a small space marked off by lines, or a slightly sunken spot (*biol*); an interstice in a tissue (*physiol*); the dark-coloured area surrounding the nipple (*physiol*); the part of the iris of the eye bordering on the pupil (*physiol*). [L *āreola*, dimin of *ārea* (see **area**)]
■ **arē'olar** adj. **arē'olate** or **arē'olated** adj divided into small areas. **arēolā'tion** n division into areolae. **areole** /ar'i-ōl/ n (*bot*) an areola; a spiny or hairy spot on a cactus.

areometer see **araeometer**.

Areopagus /a-ri-op'ə-gəs/ n the hill on which the supreme court of ancient Athens was held; the court itself; any important tribunal. [Latinized from Gr *Areios pagos* hill of Ares (Greek god of war)]
■ **Areop'agite** /-gīt or -jīt/ n a member of the Areopagus. **Areopagitic** /-git' or -jit'/ adj relating to the Areopagus.

areostyle, **areosystile** see **araeostyle**.

arere see **arear**.

aret or **arett** /a-ret'/ (*obs*) vt to entrust, commit (*Spenser*); to assign, allot; to adjudge, award. [OFr *areter*, from *a-* to, and *reter*, from L *reputāre* to reckon]

arête /a-ret'/ n a sharp ridge; *esp* in French Switzerland, a rocky edge on a mountain. [Fr, from L *arista* an ear of corn, fish-bone, spine]

Aretinian /a-ri-tin'i-ən/ adj relating to Guido of Arezzo, Italian monk and music theorist (died 1050). [L *Arētīnus*, *Arrētinus* of Arrētium or Arezzo]
□ **Aretinian syllables** n pl (*music*) the initial syllables of the half-lines of a hymn to John the Baptist, which, falling on successive notes of the diatonic scale, were used (apparently by Guido, and still in Italy and France) as names for the notes: *Ut* queant laxis *re*sonare fibris *Mi*ra gestorum *fa*muli tuorum, *Sol*ve polluti *la*bii reatum, Sancte Ioannes. Thus C in the bass is *C fa ut*, being the fourth note (fa) of the first hexachord (on G) and the first note (ut) of the second hexachord (on C). See **gamut**.

arett see **aret**.

arew /a-roo'/ (*Spenser*) adv a-row, in a row.

arfvedsonite /är'ved-sə-nīt/ (*mineralogy*) n a sodium-rich amphibole. [JA *Arfvedson* (1792–1841), Swedish mineralogist]

Arg (*chem*) symbol: arginine.

argal /är'gl/ adv in Shakespeare's *Hamlet*, the gravedigger's bungled attempt to say the Latin word *ergō* therefore.

argala /är'gə-lə/ n the adjutant stork of India. [Hindustani *hargīla*]

argali /är'gə-li/ n (pl **argali**) the great wild sheep (*Ovis ammon*) of Asia. [Mongolian]

argan /är'gan/ n a Moroccan timber tree of the family Sapotaceae; its oil-bearing seed. [N African pronunciation of Ar *arjān*]

argand /är'gand/ n a gas- or oil-lamp admitting air to both the inside and outside of the flame. [Invented by Aimé *Argand* (1755–1803), French physicist]

Argathelian /är-gə-thē'li-ən/ (*hist*) adj of the party in 18c Scotland that approved of the political influence of the house of Argyle. [LL *Argathelia* Argyle]

argemone /är-je-mō'nē/ n a plant of the prickly poppy genus *Argemone*, with showy white or yellow flowers and prickly leaves. [Gr *argemōnē* a kind of poppy]

argent /är'jənt/ adj and n silver (*archaic* or *poetic*); silvery-white or white (*heraldry*). [Fr, from L *argentum* silver]
■ **argentif'erous** adj (*geol*) silver-bearing. **ar'gentine** /-tīn/ adj of or like silver. ◆n white metal coated with silver; spongy tin; a small marine fish (family **Argentin'idae**) with silvery sides. **ar'gentite** n silver-glance, native sulphide of silver.

argent comptant /ar-zhä kõ-tä'/ (*Fr*) n ready money.

Argentine /är'jən-tīn/ or **Argentinian** /är-jən-tin'i-ən/ adj of or relating to the Republic of *Argentina* in S America, or its people. ◆n a native or citizen of Argentina (also **Argentino** /-tē'nō/). [*Argentina* named from the Rio de la Plata (silver river)]

argentine, **argentite** see under **argent**.

Argestes /är-jes'tēz/ (*Milton*) n the north-west wind personified. [Gr *Argestēs*]

argh see **aargh**.

arghan /är'gan/ n pita fibre, or the plant yielding it. [Origin unknown]

argie-bargie see under **argue**.

argil /är'jil/ n potter's clay; pure clay or alumina. [L *argilla*, Gr *argillos* white clay, from *argēs* white]
■ **argillā'ceous** adj (*geol*) clayey. **ar'gillite** n (*geol*) an indurated clay rock.

arginine /är'ji-nīn/ n one of the essential amino acids. [Origin obscure]

Argive /är'gīv or -jīv/ adj belonging to the ancient Greek city of *Argos* (*hist*); Greek (*literary*). ◆n a person from Argos; a Greek (*literary*).

argle-bargle see under **argue**.

Argo /är'gō/ n a large southern constellation consisting of four separate constellations. [After the ship the Argonauts sailed in]

argol¹ /är'gəl/ n dried dung used as fuel. [Mongolian]

argol² /är'gəl/ n a (*usu* reddish) hard crust formed on the sides of wine-vessels, from which cream of tartar and tartaric acid are obtainable. [Prob connected with Gr *argos* white]

argon /är'gon/ n a colourless odourless inert gaseous element (symbol **Ar**; atomic no 18) discovered in the atmosphere in 1894 by Rayleigh and Ramsay. It constitutes about 1% by volume of the atmosphere, from which it is obtained by fractionation of liquid air, and is used in gas-filled electric lamps, radiation counters and fluorescent tubes. [Gr *ārgon* (neuter) inactive, from *a-* (privative), and *ergon* work]
□ **argon laser** n a laser using argon, which gives strong emission at 488.0, 514.5, and 496.5 nm.

Argonaut /är'gə-nöt/ n one of those who sailed in the ship *Argo* in search of the golden fleece (*Gr myth*); (without *cap*) the paper nautilus (genus *Argonauta*). [Gr *Argō*, and *nautēs* a sailor]
■ **argonaut'ic** adj.

argosy /är'gə-si/ (*hist*; also *fig* and *poetic*) n a great merchant ship, *esp* of Ragusa (modern Dubrovnik) or Venice. [Ital *Ragusea* Ragusan (ship)]

argot /är'gō/ n slang, *orig* that of thieves and vagabonds; the language of a particular group or sect. [Fr; of unknown origin]

argue /är'gū/ vt to discuss with reasoning; to persuade or bring by reasoning (into or out of a course of action); to seek to show by reasoning; to give reason to believe; to prove or indicate; to accurse (*obs*). ◆vi to contend with reasoning; to contradict, dispute; to offer reasons. [Fr *arguer*, from L *argūtāre* (frequentative of *arguere* to show, accuse); *argūmentum* proof, accusation, summary of contents]
■ **ar'guable** adj capable of being disputed; capable of being maintained. **ar'guably** adv. **ar'guer** n. **ar'gufier** n. **ar'gufy** vi (*inf*) to bandy arguments; to wrangle. ◆vt to harass with arguments or wrangling. **ar'gument** n a reason or series of reasons offered or available as proof or inducement (with *for* or *against*); exchange of such reasons; debate; matter of debate or contention; an unfriendly discussion; a summary of subject-matter; hence contents (*Shakesp*); proof, evidence (*archaic*); a variable upon which another depends, or a quantity or element to which a function, operation, etc applies (*maths, comput, logic*); the angle between a vector and its axis of reference (*maths*). **argūmentā'tion** n reasoning; sequence or exchange of arguments. **argūment'ative** adj fond of, prone to or addicted to arguing; controversial. **argūment'atively** adv. **argūment'ativeness** n.
□ **ar'gy-bar'gy**, **ar'gie-bar'gie** or **ar'gle-bar'gle** vi (*inf, orig Scot*) to argue tediously or vexatiously. ◆n a lively dispute.
■ **argue the toss** see under **toss**. **argument from design** see under **design**.

argulus /är'gū-ləs/ n (pl **ar'gulī**) a fish louse of the genus *Argulus*, extremely destructive to fish life. [Dimin of **argus**]

argument, etc see under **argue**.

argumentum /är-gū-men'tum, also -goo- and -tŭm/ (*L*; *rhetoric* and *logic*) n argument, proof.
□ **argumentum ad baculum** see **argumentum baculinum** below. **argumentum ad crumenam** /ad krŭ'mən-əm or -mān-am/ n argument addressed to the purse (ie to the desire for money). **argumentum ad hominem** /hom'in-em/ n an appeal to the known prejudices and preferences or previous admissions of an opponent; argument relying upon personal abuse, or attack upon the opponent's character, rather than his or her viewpoint. **argumentum ad ignorantiam** /ig-nōr-an'shi-əm or ig-nōr-an'ti-am/ n argument founded on the ignorance of an opponent. **argumentum ad invidiam**

/in-vid'i-am or -wid'/ n an appeal to prejudices. **argumentum ad judicium** /joo-dish'i-əm or ū-dik'i-ŭm/ n an appeal to common sense or judgement. **argumentum ad rem** /rem/ n argument to the purpose, directed at the real issue. **argumentum ad verecundiam** /ve-re-kun'di-am or -kŭn'/ n an appeal to awe or reverence (towards a prestigious or authoritative name or figure). **argumentum baculinum** /ba-kŭl-īn'um or ba-kŭl-ēn'ŭm/ or **argumentum ad baculum** n the argument of the stick or rod, ie of force. **argumentum per impossibile** /per im-po-sib'il-ē or -ā/ n the proof from the absurdity of a contradictory supposition.
■ **argumenti causa** /är-gū-men'tī kö'zə or ar-goo-men'tē kow'za/ for the sake of argument.

argus /är'gəs/ n (pl **ar'guses**) (with cap) in Greek mythology, Io's guardian, whose hundred eyes Hera transferred to the peacock's tail; (with cap) a vigilant watcher; a pheasant of SE Asia (**argus pheasant**) of the genus Argusianus, with a long colourful tail with eye-spots; a butterfly with many eye-spots on the wings (as some Lycaenidae and Satyridae); an ophiuroid with much-divided coiling arms. [Gr Argos, literally, bright]
□ **Ar'gus-eyed** adj keen-sighted, vigilant. **argus tortoise beetle** n a black-spotted, reddish, tortoise-shaped beetle that feeds on plants of the convolvulus family.

argute /är-gūt'/ adj shrill; keen; shrewd. [L argūtus]
■ **argute'ly** adv. **argute'ness** n.

argy-bargy see under **argue**.

argyle or **Argyll** /är-gīl'/ n a vessel for containing gravy and keeping it hot, designed by John, 4th Duke of Argyll, in early 1770s; (a sock or sweater knitted in) a lozenge pattern adapted from Campbell of Argyll tartan (also adj).

argyria /är-jir'i-ə/ n (med) skin pigmentation caused by long exposure to or use of preparations of silver. [Gr argyros silver]
■ **ar'gyrite** n same as **argentite** (see under **argent**). **ar'gyrodite** n a mineral composed of silver, germanium and sulphur.

arhythmia, arhythmic see **arrhythmic**.

aria /ä'ri-ə/ (music) n an air or melody, esp an accompanied vocal solo in a cantata, oratorio or opera; a regular strain of melody followed by another in contrast and complement, and then repeated da capo. [Ital, from root of **air**]

Arian[1] /ā'ri-ən/ adj of, relating to, or following, Arius of Alexandria (died 336AD), or Arianism. ◆ n a person who adheres to the doctrines of Arius; a Unitarian.
■ **A'rianism** n the heretical doctrine of Arius, that Christ was not consubstantial (qv) with God the Father, but only the first and highest of all finite beings. **A'rianize** or **-ise** vt and vi.

Arian[2] see under **Aries**.

ariary /är-i-ar'i/ n (pl **ariar'y**) the standard monetary unit of Madagascar (5 iraimbilanja). [Malagasy]

Aricept® /ar'i-sept/ n a drug (donepezil hydrochloride, $C_{24}H_{29}NO_3HCl$) that increases the level of acetylcholine, used in the treatment of Alzheimer's disease.

ARICS abbrev: Associate of the Royal Institution of Chartered Surveyors.

arid /ar'id/ adj dry; parched; barren; (of a region or climate) having so little rainfall as to support only desert or semi-desert vegetation (see **arid zone** below); meagre, lifeless. [L aridus]
■ **arid'ity** or **ar'idness** n. **ar'idly** adv.
□ **arid zone** n (ecology) a zone of latitude 15°–30°N and S in which the rainfall is so low that only desert and semi-desert vegetation occur.

Ariel /ā'ri-əl/ n a man's name in the Old Testament; in later demonology, a water spirit; an angel; a spirit of the air (such as Shakespeare's Ariel, also a sylph in Pope); (without cap) species of swallow, petrel and toucan; the third largest of the satellites of Uranus. [Heb Ariel, with meaning influenced by **air**]

ariel /ā'ri-əl/ n a kind of mountain gazelle native to Arabia. [Ar aryil]

Aries /ā'rēz/ n the Ram, a constellation giving its name to, and formerly coinciding with, a sign of the zodiac (astron); the first sign of the zodiac, between Pisces and Taurus (astrol); a person born between 21 March and 20 April, under the sign of Aries (astrol; pl **A'ries** or **A'rieses**). [L ariēs, -etis ram]
■ **A'rian** or **A'rien** n and adj (relating to or characteristic of) a person born under the sign of Aries.
■ **first point of Aries** the intersection of celestial equator and ecliptic passed by the sun in spring in the northern hemisphere, now actually in Pisces.

arietta /är-i-et'ə/ (music) n a little aria or air (also (Fr) **ariette** /-et'/). [Ital arietta, dimin of aria]

aright /ə-rīt'/ adv in a right way; rightly; on or to the right (archaic). [**a-**[1] and **right**[1]]
■ **a-rights'** n (Spenser) rightly.

aril /a'ril/ (bot) n (also **arill'us** (pl **arill'ī**)) a covering or appendage of some seeds, an outgrowth of the funicle; sometimes, a caruncle (false aril). [LL arillus raisin]
■ **ar'illary, ar'illate** or **ar'illated** adj having an aril. **ar'illode** n a caruncle or false aril, from near the micropyle. **ar'illoid** adj.

Arimaspian /a-ri-mas'pi-ən/, also **Arimasp** /ar'i-masp/ (Gr myth) adj relating to the Arimaspi, described by Herodotus as a one-eyed people of the extreme north, warring perpetually with griffins for gold hoards (also n).

arioso /ar-i-ō'sō/ (music) adj and adv in the melodious manner of an aria, or between aria and recitative. ◆ n (pl **ario'sos** or **ario'si** /-sē/) a piece in this style. [Ital aria]

ariot /ə-rī'ət/ adv in riot, riotously. [**a-**[1]]

aripple /ə-rip'l/ adv in a ripple. [**a-**[1]]

aris /ar'is/ (Cockney sl) n arse. [Short for 'Aristotle', rhyming slang for 'bottle', which is in turn short for 'bottle and glass', rhyming slang for 'arse']

arise /ə-rīz'/ vi (pat **arose** /ə-rōz'/; pap **arisen** /ə-riz'n/) to rise up; to take rise, originate (with from or out of); to come into being, view, or activity. [Pfx **a-** up, out, and **rise**]

arish see **arrish**.

arista /ə-ris'tə/ (biol) n (pl **aris'tae** /-ī/) a bristly process from the glume of certain grasses, an awn; a bristle-like appendage on some insects' antennae. [L, an awn]
■ **aris'tate** (or /ar'/) adj awned.

Aristarch /ar'i-stärk/ n a severe critic. [Aristarchus, Alexandrian grammarian (c.160BC)]

aristate see under **arista**.

Aristides /a-ri-stī'dēz/ n an embodiment of justice. [L, from Aristeidēs, Athenian statesman (5c BC)]

Aristippus /a-ri-stip'əs/ n an embodiment of self-indulgence. [L, from Aristippos, the founder of the Cyrenaic school of philosophy (c.435–c.356BC)]

aristocracy /a-ri-stok'rə-si/ n government by, or political power of, a privileged order; a state governed in this way; a nobility or privileged class; a class of people holding privileged status in any field. [Gr aristokratiā, from aristos best, and kratos power]
■ **aristocrat** /ar'is-tə-krat or ə-ris'/ n (sometimes (inf) shortened to **aristo** /a'ris-tō or ə-ris'tō/ (pl **aristos**)) a member of an aristocracy; a person who has the characteristics of or attributed to an aristocracy; a haughty person; one of the best (or the best) of its kind. **aristocrat'ic** adj (also **aristocrat'ical**) belonging to an aristocracy; having the character that belongs to, or is thought to befit, aristocracy. **aristocrat'ically** adv. **aristocratism** /-tok'rə-tizm/ n the spirit of, practices of, or belief in, aristocracy.

aristolochia /ar-i-stō-lō'ki-ə/ n any plant of the birthwort genus Aristolochia, herbs and climbers, especially abundant in tropical S America, giving name to the family **Aristolochiā'ceae**. [Gr aristolocheia, from aristos best, and locheiā childbirth, from the former reputation of birthwort]

ariston metron /a-ris'ton met'ron/ (Gr) the middle (or moderate) course is the best; the golden mean.

Aristophanic /ar-i-sto-fan'ik/ adj relating to or characteristic of the Greek comic dramatist Aristophanes (c.448–c.388BC).

Aristotelian /ar-i-sto-tē'li-ən/ or **Aristotelean** /ar-i-sto-ti-lē'ən/ adj relating to the Greek philosopher Aristotle (384–322BC) or to his philosophy. ◆ n a follower of Aristotle.
■ **Aristote'lianism** or **Aristot'elism** n.
□ **Aristotelian logic** n the logical theories of Aristotle as developed in the Middle Ages, concerned mainly with syllogistic reasoning. **Aristotle's lantern** n a chewing apparatus in sea urchins, the framework of muscles and ossicles supporting the teeth and enclosing the lower oesophagus (compared by Aristotle to a ship's lantern).

Arita /ə-rē'tə/ n a Japanese porcelain manufactured from the early 17c at Arita near Nagasaki.

arith. abbrev: arithmetic; arithmetical.

arithmetic /ə-rith'mə-tik/ n the science of numbers, incl addition, subtraction, division, multiplication; the art of calculating by numbers; a treatise on calculation by numbers (obs). [Gr arithmētikē (technē) (art) of numbers, from arithmos number]
■ **arithmetic** /ar-ith-met'ik/ or **arithmet'ical** adj. **arithmet'ically** adv. **arithmetician** /-mə-tish'n or ar'/ n a person skilled in arithmetic.
□ **arithmetical progression** or **sequence** n a series increasing or diminishing by a common difference, eg 7, 10, 13, 16, 19, 22, or 12, $10\frac{1}{2}$, 9, $7\frac{1}{2}$, 6. **arithmetic logic unit** n (comput) the part of a central processing unit that carries out arithmetic and logical operations (abbrev **ALU**). **arithmetic** (or **arithmetical**) **mean** see **mean**[3].

arithmo- /a-rith-mo-/ combining form denoting number or numbers. [Gr arithmos number]

■ **arithmomā′nia** *n* (*psychiatry*) an obsessive preoccupation with numbers, characterized by a compulsion to count people or objects. **arithmom′eter** *n* (*obs*) a calculating machine. **arithmophō′bia** *n* fear of numbers.

Ariz. *abbrev*: Arizona (US state).

Ark. *abbrev*: Arkansas (US state).

ark /ärk/ *n* a chest or coffer; in Jewish history, the wooden coffer in which the Tables of the Law were kept; a large floating vessel, as *esp* (*usu* with *cap*) Noah's in the biblical Flood (Genesis 6–8); a toy representing Noah's ark. ◆ *vt* (*obs*) to put in an ark. [OE *arc* (*earc*), from L *arca* a chest, from *arcēre* to guard]
■ **ark′ite** *adj* and *n*.
□ **ark′-shell** *n* a box-like bivalve mollusc shell (genus *Arca*).
■ **out of the Ark** (*inf*) utterly old-fashioned, antediluvian.

arkose /är-kōs′/ *n* a sandstone rich in feldspar grains, formed from granite, etc. [Fr]

ARLA *abbrev*: Association of Residential Letting Agents.

arles /ärlz/, also *ārlz*/ (*archaic*; *dialect*) *n pl* a preliminary payment, *esp* in confirmation of a bargain, or an engagement of a servant. [Scot and N Eng; ME *erles*, appar through OFr from a dimin of L *arrha*]
■ **arle** *vt* to give a preliminary payment to or for.
□ **arle′-penny** or **arles′-penny** *n*.

Arm. *abbrev*: Armenian; Armoric.

arm¹ /ärm/ *n* the human forelimb from shoulder to hand; an upper limb in other bipedal mammals; a similar member in other animals, eg a tentacle; a narrow projecting part; an inlet; a branch; a subdivision of a large company, organization, etc, *esp* one specializing in a certain area, service or resource; a rail or support for the arm, eg on a chair; (in clothing) a sleeve; power (*fig*); ability to throw (*sport*). ◆ *vt* (*obs*) to take in the arms; to conduct arm in arm. [OE *arm* (*earm*); cognate with L *armus* the shoulder joint, and with Gr *harmos* a joint]
■ **armed** *adj* (*usu* in compounds) having an arm or arms, as in *one-armed*. **arm′ful** *n* (*pl* **arm′fuls**). **arm′less** *adj*. **arm′let** *n* a little arm; a ring or band round the arm.
□ **arm′band** *n* a band of cloth worn round the sleeve; an inflatable plastic cuff worn on the upper arm as a buoyancy aid. **arm candy** *n* (*inf*) someone who is invited as a partner to a social event more to add to the glamour of the occasion than for his or her sparkling conversational skills. **arm′chair** *n* a chair with arms. ◆ *adj* amateur; stay-at-home; doctrinaire, theoretical; conducted from (the security or comfort of) home; comfortable. **arm′-chancing** *n* and *adj* see **chance one's arm** under **chance**. **arm′hole** *n* the hole in a garment through which the arm is put. **arm′lock** *n* (in wrestling, etc; also *fig*) a hold by the arms (also *vt*). **arm′pit** *n* the hollow under the shoulder. **arm′rest** *n* the arm of a chair. **arm wrestling** *n* a test of strength whereby two people with their elbows resting on a flat surface each grip the other's hand and try to force it down until the arm touches the surface.
■ **arm in arm** with arms interlinked. **as long as one's arm** (of a list, etc) extremely long. **at arm's length** at a distance (*lit* and *fig*); not showing friendliness or familiarity but careful detachment; (of negotiations, etc) in which each party preserves its independent ability to bargain (**arms′-length** *adj*, eg in shareholding, having broad and ultimate control, without involvement in policy decisions, etc). **cost an arm and a leg** (*inf*) to be prohibitively expensive. **give one's right arm** to give or do anything in one's power. **in arms** carried as a child; (of a child) young enough for this. **put the arm on** (*N Am inf*) to try to coerce. **right arm** someone's main support or assistant. **secular arm** the civil authority, as opposed to the spiritual or ecclesiastical. **the long arm of the law** the far-reaching power and influence of the law, *esp* the police force. **twist someone's arm** see under **twist**. **within** (or **in**) **arm's reach** able to be reached easily, ie from where one is sitting. **with open arms** with a hearty welcome.

arm² /ärm/ *n* a weapon; a branch of the fighting forces; (in *pl*) weapons of offence and defence; (in *pl*) hostilities; (in *pl*) fighting, soldiering; (in *pl*) heraldic insignia, coat of arms. ◆ *vt* to provide with weapons, means of protection, armature, or (*fig*) equipment; to make (a bomb, etc) ready to explode; to strengthen (a vehicle, etc) with a metal plate or similar. ◆ *vi* to take arms. [Fr *armes*, from L *arma* (pl)]
■ **armed** *adj* supplied with arms; provided with means of defence; (of an animal, etc) having a protective armour; (of a plant) thorny, prickly, barbed; with beak, claws, etc, of a particular tincture (*heraldry*).
□ **armed eye** *n* the eye aided eg with a magnifying glass (cf **naked eye**). **armed forces** or **armed services** *n pl* the combined military forces of a country. **arms control** *n* agreement among nations not to build up armaments. **arms race** *n* competition among nations in building up armaments.
■ **armed to the teeth** see under **tooth**. **bear arms** to serve as a soldier; (also (*obs*) **give arms**) to show or have armorial bearings (*heraldry*). **call to arms** an appeal or warning to prepare to fight. **in arms** armed; ready to fight; quartered (*heraldry*). **lay down one's arms** to surrender, submit. **of all arms** of every kind of troops. **take arms** or

take up arms to resort to fighting. **under arms** armed. **up in arms** in readiness to resist; protesting hotly.

armada /är-mä′də (sometimes, *esp* formerly, -mā′)/ *n* a fleet of armed ships, *esp* that sent by Philip II of Spain against England in 1588. [Sp, fem pap of *armar*, from L *armāre* to arm]

armadillo /är-mə-dil′ō/ *n* (*pl* **armadill′os**) an American mammal with long snout, tubular ears and large front claws, an edentate whose body is covered with bands of bony plates. [Sp, dimin of *armado* armed; see **armada**]

Armageddon /är-mə-ged′ən/ *n* the great symbolical battlefield of the Apocalypse, scene of the final struggle between the powers of good and evil (*Bible*); a great, or *esp* the ultimate, war or battle of nations. [*Harmagedōn* or *Armageddōn*, given as Heb name in Bible, Revelation 16.16; perh suggested by the famous battlefield of *Megiddo*, in the plain of Esdraelon]

Armagnac /är′mä-nyak/ *n* a dry brandy distilled in SW France. [Name of district]

Armalite® /är′mə-līt/ *n* a low-calibre, high-velocity assault rifle with an automatic and semi-automatic facility. [**arm²** and **lite¹**]

armament /är′mə-mənt/ *n* munitions, *esp* for warships; defensive equipment; a force equipped for war; total means of making war. [L *armāmenta* tackle, equipment]

armamentarium /är-mə-men-tā′ri-əm/ *n* (*pl* **armamenta′ria** or **armamenta′riums**) the collective equipment, medicines, etc available to a doctor or other medical practitioner. [L, arsenal, armoury]

armature /är′mə-tūr or -chər/ *n* armour; any defensive apparatus; a wooden or wire support around which a sculpture, model, etc, is constructed; a piece of ferromagnetic material, eg an iron bar, set across the poles of a magnet; a moving part in a magnetic circuit to indicate the presence of electric current; a rotor, the metal part (wound with current-carrying wire) that, in a generator, turns to produce a current, and in a motor, provides the current that produces torque. [L *armātūra* armour]

Armenian /är-mē′nyən/ *adj* belonging to *Armenia*, in W Asia, or its people or language, or their branch of the Christian Church. ◆ *n* a native of Armenia; one of the Armenian people; the language of the Armenians.
■ **Armē′noid** *adj* of the eastern branch of the Alpine race (also *n*).

armes parlantes /ärm par-lät′/ (*Fr*) used of arms that indicate the name of the family that bears them, such as a press and a tun for Preston. [Literally, talking arms]

armet /är′mit/ (*hist*) *n* a helmet introduced about 1450 in place of the basinet, consisting of an iron cap, spreading over the back of the neck, having in front the visor, beaver and gorget. [Fr]

armgaunt /ärm′gönt/ (*Shakesp*) *adj perh* with gaunt limbs, or *perh* worn with armour, but *prob* an error.

armiger /är′mi-jər/ (*heraldry* or *hist*) *n* a person entitled to a coat of arms; an esquire. [L, an armour-bearer, from *arma* arms, and *gerere* to bear]
■ **armig′eral** *adj*. **armig′ero** *n* (*Shakesp*, *Merry Wives of Windsor*) Slender's blunder for **armiger**. **armig′erous** *adj* bearing, or entitled to bear arms.

armilla /är-mil′ə/ *n* a bracelet (also **ar′mil**; *archaeol*); a frill on a mushroom stalk (*bot*). [L *armilla* an armlet, dimin of *armus* the upper arm, the shoulder]
■ **armill′ary** (or /är′/) *adj* of bracelets or hoops.
□ **armillary sphere** *n* (*astron*) a skeleton sphere made up of hoops to show the motions of the celestial bodies.

armillaria /är-mi-lā′ri-ə/ *n* any fungus of the genus *Armillaria*, *esp* the honey fungus (qv), also known as **shoestring fungus** or **bootlace fungus**.

Arminian /är-min′i-ən/ *n* a follower of the Dutch theologian *Arminius* (1560–1609), who denied the Calvinistic doctrine of absolute predestination, as well as that of irresistible grace (also *adj*).
■ **Armin′ianism** *n*.

armipotent /är-mip′ə-tənt/ (*archaic* or *literary*) *adj* powerful in arms. [L *arma* arms, and *potēns*, *-entis* powerful]

armistice /är′mi-stis/ *n* a suspension of hostilities; a truce. [Fr, from LL *armistitium*, from L *arma* arms, and *sistere* to stop]
□ **Armistice Day** *n* 11 November 1918, the day fighting ended in World War I, kept since as an anniversary, from 1946 as Remembrance Sunday (qv under **remember**).

armlet see under **arm¹**.

armoire /är-mwär′/ (*antiques*, etc) *n* a large, decorative wardrobe or cupboard. [Fr]

armorial see under **armour**.

Armoric /är-mor'ik/ adj of Armorica (Brittany), or its people. ◆ n the Breton language. [L Armoricus, from Gallic are-morici dwellers by the sea]
∎ **Armor'ican** n and adj.

armour or (N Am) **armor** /är'mər/ n defensive clothing, esp of metal, chain mail, etc; protective covering; armoured vehicles; heraldic insignia. ◆ vt to equip with armour. [OFr armure, from L armātūra, from arma arms]
∎ **armo'rial** adj of heraldic arms. ◆ n a book of coats of arms. **ar'morist** n a person skilled in heraldry. **ar'mory** n heraldry; armorial bearings (archaic); armoury (US); a drill hall and headquarters of an army unit (N Am); an arsenal (US). **ar'moured** adj protected by armour, armour-plate, etc, as in armoured car, armoured personnel carrier; (of glass, etc) strengthened, protective. **ar'mourer** n a maker, repairer or custodian of arms and armour. **ar'mourless** adj. **ar'moury** n a collection of arms and armour; a place where arms are kept; a place where arms are manufactured (US); a place where soldiers perform drill (US); armour collectively (archaic).
❑ **armorial bearings** n pl the design in a coat of arms. **ar'mour-bearer** n a person who carries another's armour, a squire. **ar'mour-clad** adj clad in armour. ◆ n an armoured ship. **ar'mour-plate** n a defensive metal plate for a ship, tank, etc. **ar'mour-plated** adj. **ar'mour-plating** n.

armozeen or **armozine** /är-mə-zēn'/ n a kind of taffeta or plain silk (usu black), used for clerical gowns. [Fr armoisin]

armure /är'mūr/ n a type of fabric with a pebbled surface. [Fr]

army /är'mi/ n a large body of people armed for war and under military command; a body of people banded together in a special cause, sometimes (eg the 'Salvation Army') in imitation of military methods; a host, multitude (eg of people, insects, etc); a great number. [Fr armée, pap fem of armer, from L armāre, -ātum to arm]
❑ **army ant** n any of several kinds of stinging ants which move about in vast numbers. **army corps** /kōr/ n a miniature army comprising all arms of the service. **army list** n a list of all commissioned officers. **army worm** n the larva of a small fly (genus Sciara) that collects in vast armies and can move in multitudes from field to field destroying crops; the larva of any of several (esp N American and E African) types of moth that can move in multitudes from field to field destroying crops.

arna /är'nä/ n the Indian water buffalo (Bubalus bubalis). [Hindi]

Arnaut or **Arnaout** /är-nowt'/ n an Albanian, formerly applied esp to one in the Turkish Army. [Turk]

arnica /är'ni-kə/ n a tincture of the flowers of a composite plant (Arnica montana or mountain tobacco) which is applied to sprains and bruises (but not to open wounds). [Origin unknown]

arnotto see annatto.

arnut /är'nət/ same as earth-nut (see under earth).

aroba see araba.

aroid see under arum.

aroint or **aroynt** /ə-roint'/ (archaic) vt (Browning) to drive or frighten away. [Origin unknown]
∎ **aroint thee** (Shakesp) away, begone.

arolla /ə-rol'ə/ n the Swiss stone pine or Siberian cedar (Pinus cembra). [Fr arolle]

aroma /ə-rō'mə/ n a spicy or distinctive fragrance; flavour or peculiar charm (fig). [L, from Gr arōma, -atos spice]
∎ **aro'matase** /-tāz/ n an enzyme that converts androgens into oestrogens. **aromatic** /ar-ō-mat'ik/ adj fragrant; spicy; belonging to the closed-chain class of organic compounds, or benzene derivatives, opp to fatty or aliphatic (chem). ◆ n an aromatic substance. **aromat'ically** adv. **aromatic'ity** n. **arōmatizā'tion** or **-s-** n. **arō'matize** or **-ise** vt to render aromatic; to perfume.
❑ **aromatherapeu'tic** adj. **aromather'apist** n. **aromather'apy** n a method of treating bodily ailments using essential plant oils, esp in combination with massage.

arose see arise.

around /ə-rownd'/ prep on all sides of; round or round about; somewhere near. ◆ adv on every side; in a circle; round about, on the move; in existence or circulation (inf). [a-¹ and round¹]
∎ **get around to** (inf) to reach the point of (doing something). **have been around** (inf) to be experienced or sophisticated.

arouse /ə-rowz'/ vt and vi to rouse; to stimulate. ◆ n (rare) an act of arousing, an alarm. [Pfx a- (intensive), and rouse¹]
∎ **arous'al** n. **arous'er** n.

a-row or **arow** /ə-rō'/ adv in a row; one following the other (obs). [a-¹ and row¹]

aroynt see aroint.

ARP abbrev : air-raid precautions.

ARPANET /är'pə-net/ n a computer network developed by the US Defense Department in 1969, a forerunner of the Internet. [Advanced Research Projects Agency Network]

arpeggio /är-ped'j(y)ō/ (music) n (pl **arpegg'ios**) a chord of which the notes are performed, not simultaneously, but in rapid (normally upward) succession; the notes of a chord played or sung, esp as an exercise, in rapid ascending or descending progression, according to a set pattern. [Ital arpeggiare to play the harp, from arpa harp]
∎ **arpegg'iate** /-ji-āt/ vt to perform or write in arpeggios. **arpeggia'tion** n. **arpeggione** /är-pej-i-ōn'ā/ n an early 19c bowed stringed instrument.

arpent /är'pənt or är-pä'/ n an old French measure for land (still used in Quebec and Louisiana) varying from about 50 to 35 ares (1¼ acres to ⅚ of an acre). [Fr, from L arepennis, said to be a Gallic word]

arquebus /är'kwi-bus/ or **harquebus** /här'/ (hist) n a portable long-barrelled gun. [Fr arquebuse, from Du haakbus, from haak hook, and bus box, barrel of a gun; Ger Hakenbüchse]
∎ **arquebusade'** n a lotion for shotgun wounds. **arquebusier** /-bus-ēr'/ n a soldier armed with an arquebus.

ARR abbrev : anno regni regis (or reginae) (L), in the year of the king's (or queen's) reign.

arr. abbrev : arranged (by); arranger; arrival; arrived, arrives, arriving, etc.

arracacha /a-rə-kä'chə/ n an umbelliferous plant (genus Arracacia) of northern S America, with edible tubers. [Quechua aracacha]

arrack or now usu **arak** /ar'ak/ n a strong alcoholic drink made in Asian countries from toddy, or the fermented juice of the coco and other palms, as well as from rice and jaggery sugar. [Ar 'araq juice]

arragonite another spelling of aragonite.

arrah /ar'ə/ interj Anglo-Irish expression of emotion, wonder, mild expostulation, etc.

arraign /ə-rān'/ vt to put on trial; to accuse publicly; to call to account (obs). [OFr aresnier, from LL arratiōnāre, from L ad to, and ratiō, -ōnis reason]
∎ **arraign'er** n. **arraign'ing** n. **arraign'ment** n.

arrange /ə-rānj'/ vt to set in a rank or row; to put in order; to settle or work out; to adapt for other instruments or voices, or for a different setting or style (music); to adapt (a play, etc) for broadcasting. ◆ vi to come to an agreement (with to); to make plans (with to or for). [OFr arangier, from à to, and rangier, rengier; see range]
∎ **arrange'able** adj. **arrange'ment** n. **arrang'er** n.
❑ **arranged marriage** n a match decided by the families of the bride and groom, rather than the couple themselves.

arrant /ar'ənt/ adj downright, unmitigated, out-and-out; notorious; rascally. [A variant of errant]
∎ **arr'antly** adv.

arras /ar'əs/ n rich tapestry (as formerly made at Arras in France); a hanging screen of tapestry for a wall.
∎ **arr'ased** adj covered with arras. **arr'asene** n an embroidery material, of wool and silk.

arraught see areach.

array /ə-rā'/ n order, arrangement; an imposing, purposeful or significant arrangement; an arrangement of terms in rows and columns, (esp if square) a matrix (maths); a set of storage locations, etc referenced by one or more identifiers (comput); a panel of jurors (law); dress or equipage (archaic or poetic). ◆ vt to empanel (jurors) (law); to dress, adorn or equip (archaic or poetic); to put in order, arrange. [Anglo-Fr arrai, OFr arei, array, equipage, from L ad, and the Gmc root found in Eng ready, Ger bereit]
∎ **array'al** n. **array'er** n. **array'ment** n the act of arraying; clothing (obs).

arrear /ə-rēr'/ n that which remains unpaid or undone (usu in pl); (in pl) total unpaid debt, debts not paid by the due date; that which is in the rear or behind (archaic); (in sing or now usu pl) the condition of being behindhand. ◆ adv (obs) backward, behind. [OFr arere, ariere (Fr arrière), from L ad to, and retrō back, behind]
∎ **arrear'age** n arrear, arrears.
∎ **in arrears** behindhand, esp in the payment of debts, rent, etc.

arrect /a-rekt'/ adj (of an animal's ears) upright, pricked up; on the alert. [L arrēctus]

arrectis auribus /a-rek'tēs ow'ri-bŭs/ (L) with ears pricked up.

arreede see aread.

arrest /ə-rest'/ vt to bring to a standstill, check; to seize; to catch, fix (eg the attention); to apprehend and take into custody (a person) by legal authority; to seize by warrant; to take as security (Shakesp). ◆ vi to suffer a cardiac arrest. ◆ n the act of arresting; seizure by warrant; stoppage, failure (eg of an organ or mechanism). [OFr arester, from L ad to, and restāre to stand still]
∎ **arrest'able** adj (of an offence) such that the offender may be arrested without warrant; liable to arrest. **arrestation** /ar-es-tā'shən/ n

the act of arresting; arrest. **arrestee'** *n* a person prevented by arrestment from making payment or delivery to another until the arrester's claim upon that other is secured or satisfied (*Scots law*); a person legally arrested (*N Am*). **arrest'er** *n* a person who, or thing which, arrests; a lightning-arrester (qv under **lightning**); (also **arrest'or**) a person who makes an arrestment (*Scots law*). **arrest'ing** *adj* striking. **arrest'ingly** *adv*. **arrest'ive** *adj* tending to arrest. **arrest'ment** *n* a checking, stopping; detention of a person arrested until liberated on bail, or by security (*law*); a process which prohibits a debtor from handing over to his or her creditor money or property until a debt due by that creditor to a third party, the arrester, is paid or secured (*Scots law*). ❑ **arrester gear** *n* shock-absorbing transverse cables on an aircraft-carrier's deck for the arrester hook of an alighting aircraft to catch on. **arrester hook** *n* a hook put out from an aircraft alighting on an aircraft-carrier, to catch on the arrester gear. **arrest of judgement** *n* (*law*) a delay between conviction and sentence because of possible error. ◼ **cardiac arrest** a heart attack; heart failure. **under arrest** having been apprehended by legal authority, held in custody.

arrêt /a-ret', ä're' or ä-rā'/ *n* a decision; the judgement of a tribunal. [Fr, from OFr *arester* ; see **arrest**]

arrhenotoky /a-rə-not'ə-ki/ (*biol*) *n* parthenogenetic production of males alone, by virgin females. [Gr *arrēn* male, and *tokos* offspring]

arrhythmic /ə- or ā-rith'mik or -ridh'/ *adj* having an irregular or interrupted rhythm. [Gr *a-* (privative)] ◼ **arrhyth'mia** or **arhyth'mia** *n* (*med*) irregularity of the heartbeat. **arrhyth'mically** or **arhyth'mically** *adv*.

arriage /ar'ij/ (*hist*) *n* a former feudal service in Scotland, said to have been rendered by the tenant with his beasts of burden. [See **average** and **aver²**]

arride /ə-rīd'/ (*archaic*) *vt* to please, gratify. [L *arrīdēre*]

arriéré /a-rē-ā-rā'/ (*Fr*) *adj* backward, old-fashioned.

arrière-ban /ar-ē-er-ban' or -bā'/ (*hist*) *n* a feudal sovereign's summons to all freemen to take up arms; the army thus collected. [OFr *ariereban*, from OHGer *hari* army, and *ban* public proclamation; confused with Fr *arrière*]

arrière-garde /a-rē-er-gärd'/ (*Fr*) *n* rearguard.

arrière-pensée /a-rē-er-pä-sā'/ (*Fr*) *n* a mental reservation; a subsidiary or concealed aim.

arriero /a-ri-ā'rō/ (*Sp*) *n* (*pl* **arrie'ros**) a muleteer.

arris /ar'is/ (*building, etc*) *n* a sharp edge on stone, metal, etc at the meeting of two surfaces. [See **arête**] ❑ **arris gutter** *n* a V-shaped gutter *usu* of wood. **arris rail** *n* a wooden, etc rail of triangular section. **arris tile** *n* an angular roof-tile for use where hips or ridges intersect.

arrish or **arish** /ä'rish/ (*dialect*) *n* a stubble field. [OE *ersc* (in compounds)]

arrive /ə-rīv'/ *vi* to reach any place; to attain to any object (with *at*); to achieve success or recognition; to happen, come about (*obs*); to reach shore or port (*obs*). ◆ *vt* (*obs*) to reach. [OFr *ariver* to reach shore, from LL *adrīpāre*, from L *ad* to, and *rīpa* shore] ◼ **arriv'al** *n* the act of arriving; a person or thing that arrives; the attainment of a position or state; (in *pl*) the part of an airport or terminal where passengers report on arrival. **arriv'ance** or **arriv'ancy** *n* (*Shakesp*) a group of arrivals.

arrivederci or **a rivederci** /ä-rē-və-der'chē/ (*Ital*) *interj* goodbye until we meet again.

arriviste /a-rē-vēst'/ *n* a person who is on the make; a parvenu, upstart; a self-seeker. [Fr] ◼ **arr'ivisme** *n*.

arroba /ə-rō'bə or ä-ro'bä/ *n* a (regionally variable) weight of 25 pounds (11.35kg) or more, used in Spanish, Portuguese and Spanish American regions. [Sp and Port from Ar *ar-rub'* the quarter]

arrogance /ar'ə-gəns/ *n* undue assumption of importance; conceit, self-importance. [Fr, from L *arrogāntia* ; see **arrogate**] ◼ **arr'ogant** *adj* claiming too much; overbearing; conceited, self-important. **arr'ogantly** *adv*.

arrogate /ar'ə-gāt/ *vt* to claim as one's own; to claim proudly or unduly; to ascribe, attribute or assign (to another). [L *arrogāre*, from *ad* to, and *rogāre*, *-ātum* to ask, to claim] ◼ **arroga'tion** *n* act of arrogating; undue assumption.

arrondissement /ä-rɔ̃-dēs-mã'/ *n* in France, a subdivision of a department, or a municipal subdivision of some large cities, *esp* Paris. [Fr, from *arrondir* to make round]

arrow¹ /ar'ō/ *n* a straight, pointed missile, made to be shot from a bow; any arrow-shaped mark or object; (in *pl*) darts (*inf*); the chief shoot of a plant (*obs*); *specif* the flowering stem of the sugar-cane. ◆ *vt* to

indicate or show the position of, by an arrow. [OE *arwe* ; prob cognate with L *arcus* bow] ◼ **arr'owed** *adj* marked or patterned with arrow shapes. **arr'owy** *adj* of or like arrows. ❑ **arr'ow-grass** *n* a grass of the genus of marsh plants (genus *Triglochin*) whose burst capsule is like an arrowhead. **arr'owhead** *n* the head or pointed part of an arrow; anything resembling this in shape; an aquatic plant (*Sagittaria sagittifolia*) of the Alismaceae, with arrow-shaped leaves. **arr'ow-headed** *adj* shaped like the head of an arrow. **arr'ow-poison** *n* poison smeared on arrowheads. **arr'owroot** *n* a West Indian plant, *Maranta arundinacea* or other species; its rhizome, *orig* used in S America as an antidote to arrow-poison; a nutritious starch from the rhizome, now *esp* in powdered form used as a thickener, etc; extended to other plants and their starch (see **Portland**). **arr'ow-shot** *n* the range of an arrow. **arr'owwood** *n* species of the genus *Viburnum* (*esp V. dentatum*) or other shrubs or trees formerly used by Native Americans to make arrows. **arr'owworm** *n* any of various small wormlike marine animals of the phylum Chaetognatha with an arrow-shaped, finned transparent body.

arrow² see **ary**.

arroyo /ə-roi'ō/ (*US*) *n* (*pl* **arroy'os**) a rocky ravine; a dry watercourse. [Sp]

'Arry /ar'i/ (*old inf*) *n* (also *fem* **'Arr'iet**) a jovial vulgar Cockney. [Cockney pronunciation of *Harry*, *Harriet*] ◼ **'Arr'yish** *adj*.

ARSA *abbrev* : Associate of the Royal Society of Arts (officially the Royal Society for encouragement of Arts, Manufactures and Commerce).

arse /ärs/ or (*N Am*) **ass** /as/ (now *vulgar sl*) *n* the buttocks; impudence, cheek (*Aust*); a foolish or annoying person; sexual intercourse. [OE *ærs* (ears); Ger *Arsch*, Swed *ars* ; cognate with Gr *orros* (for *orsos*)] ◼ **ars'ey** or **ars'y** *adj* irritable, bad-tempered, argumentative; lucky (*Aust*). ❑ **arse bandit** *n* (*offensive*) a male homosexual. **arse'hole** (*N Am* **ass'hole**) *n* the anus; a worthless, contemptible, etc person. **arse'holed** *adj* very drunk. **arse kisser** or **licker** *n* an extremely obsequious person. **arse kissing** or **licking** *n*. **ars'y-vers'y** *adv* and *adj* backside foremost, contrary. ◼ **arse about face** back to front. **arse around** or **about** to mess around, do nothing in particular or nothing of any value. **get one's arse into gear** to get organized (to do something). **go arse over tit** to stumble or fall in spectacular fashion. **I, etc can't be arsed** I, etc can't be bothered (to do something). **kick arse** or **ass** to act forcefully; to be extremely dynamic and powerful. **not know one's arse from one's elbow** to be extremely ignorant.

arsenal /är'si-nəl or ärs-nəl/ *n* a magazine or factory for naval and military weapons and ammunition; a stock of anything considered of analogous power or potential; a storehouse (*fig*); a dockyard (*hist*). [Ital *arzenale*, *arsenale* (Sp, Fr *arsenal*), from Ar *dār çinā'ah* workshop, from (*dār* house), *al* the, and *çinā'ah* art]

arsenic /är'sənik or ärs-nik/ *n* a chemical element (symbol **As**; atomic no 33); a poison, the trioxide of the element (As_2O_3) (also called **white arsenic**). ◆ *adj* /-sen'ik/ containing arsenic in the pentavalent state. [Gr *arsenikon* yellow orpiment, fancifully associated with Gr *arsēn* male, and the alchemists' notion that metals can be of male or female gender] ◼ **ar'senate** or **arseniate** /-sē'ni-āt/ *n* a salt of arsenic acid. **arsen'ical** *adj* composed of or containing arsenic. **ar'senide** *n* a compound of arsenic with a metal. **arsē'nious** *adj* containing arsenic in the trivalent state. **ar'senite** *n* a salt of arsenious acid. **arsenopyrī'tēs** *n* mispickel, a mineral composed of iron, arsenic and sulphur. **arsine** /är'sēn, -sin or -sīn/ *n* the poisonous gas, hydride of arsenic (AsH_3); (in *pl*) any compound in which one or more hydrogen atoms of AsH_3 are replaced by an alkyl radical, a halogen, etc (also **arsenic (III) hydride**).

arses plural of **arse** and **arsis**.

arshin, **arshine** or **arsheen** /är-shēn'/ *n* an old measure of length, about 28in (71cm) in Russia, about 30in (76cm, but legally a metre) in Turkey. [Turkish]

arsine see under **arsenic**.

arsis /är'sis/ (*classical prosody* and *music*) *n* (*pl* **ar'sēs**) literally, a lift, an up-beat; hence the weak position in a bar or foot; understood by the Romans as the strong position; used in English in both senses, *opp* to *thesis*; elevation of the voice to higher pitch *obs*. [L, from Gr *arsis*, from *airein* to lift]

arsmetrick /ärz-met'rik/ *n* an obsolete form of **arithmetic**. [False ety from L *ars metrica* art of measuring]

arson¹ /är'sən/ *n* the crime of maliciously and feloniously setting fire to property. [OFr *arson*, from L *arsiō*, *-ōnis*, from *ardēre*, *arsum* to burn] ◼ **ar'sonist** or (*rare*) **ar'sonite** *n*.

arson² /ˈär'sən/ (obs) n a saddlebow. [OFr arçun, from L arcus a bow]

arsphenamine /ärs-fen'ə-mēn or -mīn/ n salvarsan (qv), a synthetic compound of arsenic. [arsenic, phene and amine]

arsy-versy see under **arse**.

art¹ /ärt/ n practical skill, or its application, guided by principles; human skill and agency, opp to nature; application of skill to production of beauty (esp visible beauty) and works of creative imagination, as in the fine arts; (in general use) the visual arts, drawing and painting, and usu sculpture; a branch of learning, esp one of the liberal arts (see **trivium** under **trivia, quadrivium** under **quadri-**), as in faculty of arts, master of arts; skill or knowledge in a particular department; a skilled profession or trade, craft, or branch of activity; magic or occult knowledge or influence; a method or knack of doing a thing; cunning, artifice, crafty conduct; a wile, trick. ◆ adj of, for or concerned with painting, sculpture, etc (as in art gallery, art historian); intended to be decorative or artistic; produced with studied artistry, not arising spontaneously or by chance; following artistic aims at the expense of commercial considerations, as in art cinema. [L ars, artis]
■ **art'ful** adj cunning; skilful, masterly; produced by art; dexterous, clever (archaic). **art'fully** adv. **art'fulness** n. **art'iness** n the quality or state of being arty. **art'less** adj simple; guileless, unaffected; inartistic (rare). **art'lessly** adv. **art'lessness** n. **art'y** (inf) or less commonly **art'sy** adj artistic, or affectedly aspiring to be. ◆ n (inf) an arty person. □ **art autre** /är-tō-tr'/ n a post-World War II movement in painting, including tachisme. **art brut** n the primitive (literally, raw), unrefined or naïve art of non-professional or untrained artists (eg children, mental patients, prisoners, etc). **art deco** /ärt dek'ō/ n the style of decorative art characteristic of the 1920s and 1930s, developing the curvilinearity of art nouveau into more streamlined geometrical forms. **art form** n a set form or arrangement in poetry or music; an accepted medium of artistic expression. **art'house** n a cinema that shows films regarded as artistic as distinct from popular, incl cult and foreign, subtitled films (also adj). **art nouveau** /är noo-vō'/ n a decorative form of art (c.1890–1910) in which curvilinear forms are important and fundamentally unrelated images are often combined in a single design. **art paper** n a type of paper for illustrations, coated with a composition containing china clay. **arts centre** n a building for practising, performing or exhibiting various arts and art forms. **arts'man** n a craftsman (obs); a scholar (obs). **art'-song** n a song whose words and music are the product of conscious art, the music reflecting every turn of meaning (distinguished from a folk song). **art therapy** n art used as a means of communication, or a creative activity, to assist personal development, diagnosis and rehabilitation. **art union** n (Aust and NZ) a lottery. **art'work** n the illustrations and other decorative material in a publication; production of or work in creating, artistic objects; work(s) of art. **arty-craft'y** adj to do with, or esp involved in, arts and crafts; self-consciously artistic. **arty-fart'y** or **artsy-farts'y** adj (derog, inf) arty, arty-crafty.
■ **art and part** (orig law, etc) concerned in either by art in contriving or by part in actual execution, now loosely used in the sense of participating, sharing. **fine art** the aesthetically significant forms of art (now usu defined as architecture, painting, sculpture and some graphic arts) as distinct from applied and decorative art; loosely, (a college course combining) art history and practical art tuition; sometimes, the fine arts (see below); an operation or practice requiring special skill or craftsmanship (inf). **get something down to a fine art** to become very skilled at something through practice. **soft art** (and **soft sculpture**) works of art (and sculpture) constructed from textiles or other soft materials. **term of art** a technical word. **the fine arts** painting, poetry, music, etc.

art² /ärt/ (archaic, esp church, formal or poetic) used as 2nd pers sing present indicative of the verb to be. [OE (WSax) eart, (Mercian) earth, (Northumbrian) arth; from the root es- seen in **is, are¹**]

art. abbrev : article; artificial; (also **arty**) artillery.

artal see **rotl**.

artefact or **artifact** /är'ti-fakt/ n (esp archaeol) a thing made by human workmanship; any non-natural feature accidentally introduced, eg during a scientific study. [L arte, by art (ablative of ars), and factum made]
■ **artefac'tual** adj.

artel /är-tel'/ n a Russian workers' guild. [Russ]

Artemis /är'tə-mis/ (Gr myth) n the Greek virgin goddess of the moon, identified by the Romans with Diana. [Gr]

artemisia /är-tə-miz'i-ə/ n any plant of the Artemisia genus of composites including wormwood, southernwood, mugwort, sagebrush, etc. [Gr artemisiā]
■ **artemis'inin** n see **qinghaosu**.

artery /är'tə-ri/ n a tube or vessel that conveys blood from the heart to the body (anat and zool); any main channel of communication or movement. [L artēria, from Gr artēriā windpipe, artery]

arterial /-tē'ri-əl/ adj. **artērializā'tion** or **-s-** n. **artēr'ialize** or **-ise** vt to make arterial. **arteriog'raphy** n (radiol) the radiological examination of arteries following direct injection of a contrast medium. **artē'riole** n (anat and zool) a very small artery. **artēriosclerō'sis** n (Gr sklērōsis hardening; med) hardening of the arteries. **artēriosclerotic** /-ot'ik/ adj. **artēriot'omy** n (Gr tomē a cut; obs med) the cutting or opening of an artery, to let blood. **artēriovē'nous** adj relating to an artery and a vein. **arterī'tis** n (med) inflammation of an artery.
□ **arterial road** n a main traffic road from which lesser routes branch.

artesian /är-tē'zyən or -zh(y)ən/ (sometimes with cap) adj denoting a type of well in which water rises in a borehole by hydrostatic pressure from a basin-shaped aquifer (**artesian basin**) whose outcrop is at a higher level. [Artesian of Artois (LL Artesium) in N France where such wells were in early use]

Artex® /är'teks/ n a plaster coating for walls and ceilings giving a textured finish. [**art¹** and **texture**]

artful see under **art¹**.

arthralgia /är-thral'ji-ə/ (pathol) n pain in a joint. [Gr arthron a joint, and algos pain]
■ **arthral'gic** adj.

arthritis /är-thrī'tis/ n inflammation of a joint, associated with swelling, pain, stiffness, etc; (such inflammation caused by) gout. [Gr arthron a joint, and **-itis**]
■ **arthritic** /-thrit'ik/ adj of, relating to, or of the nature of, arthritis. ◆ n a person suffering from arthritis; a gouty person.

arthrodesis /är-thrō-dē'sis/ (med) n the immobilizing of a joint in the body by the surgical fusion of the bones. [Gr arthron joint, and desis binding together]

arthromere /är'thrō-mēr/ (zool) n a body segment of an articulated animal, a somite. [Gr arthron a joint, and meros part]

arthropathy /är-throp'ə-thi/ (med) n a disease of the joints. [Gr arthron joint, and patheia suffering]

arthroplasty /är'thro-pla-sti/ (med) n surgical repair of a joint; replacement of a joint by an artificial joint. [Gr arthron joint, and plastos moulded]

arthropod /är'thrə-pod or -thrō-/ n any member of the **Arthropoda** /är-throp'od-ə/ a major division of the animal kingdom, with segmented bodies and jointed appendages (crustacea, arachnids, peripatuses, millipedes, centipedes, insects, tardigrades, etc). [Gr arthron joint, and pous, podos a foot]
■ **arthrop'odal** adj.

arthroscopy /är-thros'kə-pi/ (med) n examination of a joint with an endoscope. [Gr arthron joint, and skopeein to look]
■ **arthroscope** /är'thrə-skōp/ n a fibre-optic endoscope used in arthroscopy. **arthroscopic** /-skop'ik/ adj.

arthrosis /är-thrō'sis/ (med) n connection by a joint, articulation; degenerative, non-inflammatory, disease of the joints. [Gr arthrōsis, from arthron a joint]

arthrospore /är'thrō-spör/ (bot) n a conidium; (inappropriately) a vegetative cell that has passed into a resting state. [Gr arthron joint, and sporā seed]

Arthurian /är-thū'ri-ən/ adj relating to King Arthur, a 6c ruler of the Britons, whose court is the centre of many legends, but who himself probably had real existence; relating to the legends.
■ **Arthurian'a** n pl stories, etc connected with the court of King Arthur.

artic see **articulated lorry** under **article**.

artichoke /är'ti-chōk/ n a thistlelike perennial plant (Cynara scolymus) with large fleshy scaly head and bracts and edible receptacle; the grey-green flower-head of the artichoke, served as a vegetable (also **globe artichoke**). [N Ital articiocco (Ital carciofo), from OSp alcarchofa, from Ar al-kharshōfa, al-kharshūf]
■ **Jerusalem artichoke** a totally different plant (Helianthus tuberosus), a species of sunflower with edible tubers like potatoes (Jerusalem being a corruption of Ital girasole sunflower); the white-fleshed tuber with knobbly brownish or reddish skin, served as a vegetable.

article /är'ti-kl/ n a separate element, member or part of anything; a particular object or commodity; an item; a single clause or term; a distinct point in an agreement, or (in pl) an agreement regarded as made up of such (as in articles of apprenticeship, etc); (in pl) rules or conditions generally; a section, paragraph or head; a literary composition in a newspaper, periodical, encyclopedia, etc, dealing with a subject distinctly and independently; the adjective the (definite article), a or an (indefinite article) or the equivalent in another language (grammar); a joint, segment (obs); a juncture, critical moment, nick of time (obs). ◆ vt to bind by articles of apprenticeship; to set forth as a charge (that); to indict; to stipulate (obs); to arrange by agreement, etc (obs). ◆ vi (obs) to bring specific charges (against).

[L *articulus* a little joint, *articulāre*, *-ātum* to provide with joints, to utter distinctly, from *artus* joint]

■ **ar'ticled** *adj* bound as apprentice (eg in a legal office). **artic'ūlable** *adj* that can be articulated. **artic'ulacy** *n* articulateness. **artic'ūlar** *adj* belonging to the joints; at or near a joint. **Articūlā'ta** *n pl* in Cuvier's obsolete classification, the arthropods and higher worms. **artic'ūlate** /-*lət*/ *adj* jointed; composed of distinct parts; (eg of human speech) composed of recognizably distinct sounds; clear; able to express one's thoughts with ease. ◆ *vt* /-*lāt*/ to attach by a joint; to connect by joints; to form into distinct sounds, syllables or words; to express coherently. ◆ *vi* to form a joint (with; *lit* and *fig*); to speak distinctly; to come to terms (*Shakesp*). **artic'ūlated** *adj*. **artic'ūlately** *adv*. **artic'ūlateness** *n*. **articūlā'tion** *n* jointing; a joint; a segment; distinctness, or distinct utterance; a consonant. **artic'ūlātor** *n* a person who articulates or speaks; a person who articulates bones and mounts skeletons; an apparatus, etc that articulates. **artic'ūlatory** *adj*.

□ **articulated lorry**, etc *n* a lorry, etc made easier to manœuvre by having its (sometimes detachable) front section flexibly attached to the rear section so that it can move at an angle to it (*inf* short form **artic'** (or /*är'*/)).

■ **articles of association** (a document containing) the internal regulations and conditions for the business of a joint-stock company registered under the Companies Acts. **articles of faith** the binding statement of points of belief of a Church, etc. **articles of war** the code of regulations for the government and discipline of armed services. **in the article of death** (L *in articulō mortis*; *archaic*) at the point of death. **Lords of the Articles** (*hist*) a standing committee of the Scottish parliament who drafted the measures to be submitted. **of great article** (*Shakesp*) of great importance. **the genuine article** the real thing, not a counterfeit. **Thirty-nine Articles** the articles of religious belief finally agreed upon by the bishops and clergy of the Church of England in 1562.

artifact see **artefact**.

artifice /*är'ti-fis*/ *n* contrivance or trickery; an ingenious expedient; a crafty trick, machination; skill, craft, resource; handicraft (*Milton*); workmanship (*obs*). [L *artificium*, from *artifex*, *-ficis* an artificer, from *ars*, *artis* art, and *facere* to make]

■ **artif'icer** *n* a mechanic (*esp army* and *navy*); a person who creates skilfully; a craftsman; a contriver; (with *cap*) the Creator; a trickster (*obs*).

artificial /*är-ti-fish'əl*/ *adj* contrived, *opp* to *spontaneous*; made by man; synthetic, *opp* to *natural*; fictitious, factitious, feigned, made in imitation, *opp* to *real*; affected in manners; (of classifications) based on superficial structural features rather than on natural relationships (*biol*); ingenious (*obs*); *perh* creative, playing the artificer, or *perh* merely skilful (*Shakesp*); technical (*obs*). [ME, from L *artificialis*, from *artificium* (see **artifice**)]

■ **artificiality** /-*fish-i-al'i-ti*/ *n*. **artific'ialize** or **-ise** *vt*. **artific'ially** *adv*. **artific'ialness** *n*.

□ **artificial horizon** *n* a gyroscopic device indicating an aircraft's attitude in relation to the horizontal. **artificial insemination** *n* the injection of semen into the uterus or vagina by other means than sexual union (*abbrev* **AI**). **artificial intelligence** *n* the use of computers in such a way that they perform functions normally associated with human intelligence, such as learning, adapting, self-correction and decision-taking (*abbrev* **AI**). **artificial kidney** *n* a kidney machine. **artificial language** *n* an invented language functioning not as the native speech of its users but as a computer language or means of international communication. **artifical life** *n* simulation of the behaviour of living organisms by computers. **artificial porcelain** *n* soft-paste porcelain. **artificial radioactivity** *n* radiation from isotopes after high-energy bombardment in an accelerator by alpha particles, protons, or neutrons. **artificial respiration** *n* stimulation of respiration manually or mechanically by forcing air in and out of the lungs. **artifical satellite** *n* a man-made spacecraft designed to orbit a celestial body. **artificial selection** see **select**. **artificial silk** see **silk**. **artificial sunlight** *n* light from lamps rich in ultraviolet rays.

■ **artificial insemination by donor** former name for **donor insemination** (see under **donation**), discontinued because of the similarity of its commonly used abbreviation **AID** to **AIDS**.

artillery /*är-til'ə-ri*/ *n* offensive weapons of war, formerly in general, now the heavier kinds (ancient ballistas, catapults, modern cannon, etc); a branch of the military service using these; the science of handling guns, gunnery; missiles (*obs*). [OFr *artillerie*, from *artiller* to arm, of doubtful origin]

■ **artill'erist** *n* a person skilled in artillery; a gunner.

□ **artill'eryman** *n* a soldier of the artillery. **artill'ery-plant** *n* a tropical American plant (genus *Pilea*) of the nettle family that ejects its pollen in puffs.

artiness see under **art**[1].

artiodactyl /*är-ti-ō-dak'til*/ (*zool*) *adj* even-toed. ◆ *n* a member of the **Artiodac'tyla** or even-toed ungulates, in which the third and fourth digit form a symmetrical pair and the hindfoot bears an even number of digits (cf **perissodactyl**). [Gr *artios* even in number, and *daktylos* finger or toe]

artisan /*är'ti-zən*/ or *-sən*/ *n* a handicraftsman or mechanic, a skilled manual worker. [Fr, from Ital *artigiano*, ult from L *artitus* skilled, from *ars*, *artis* art]

■ **artis'anal** (or /*ärt'*/) *adj*.

artist /*är'tist*/ *n* a person who practises or is skilled in an art, now *esp* a fine art; a person who has the qualities of imagination and taste required in art; a painter or draughtsman; a performer, *esp* in music; a person good at, or given to, a particular activity, such as *booze artist* (*sl*); a learned man (*obs*); someone who professes magic, astrology, alchemy, etc, or chemistry (*obs*). [Fr *artiste*, from L *ars*, *artis* art]

■ **artist'ic** or (now *rare*) **artist'ical** *adj*. **artist'ically** *adv*. **art'istry** *n* artistic pursuits; artistic workmanship, quality or ability.

□ **artistic temperament** *n* the emotional and capricious temperament ascribed to artists. **artist's proof** *n* an unnumbered proof (now *esp* a first impression) of a print made and/or kept for the artist's own use or record.

artiste /*är-tēst'*/ *n* a public performer, entertainer; someone adept in a manual art. [Fr]

Artium Baccalaureus /*är'shi-um ba-ka-lö'rē-us* or *är'ti-ŭm ba-ka-low'rä-ŭs*/ (L) *n* Bachelor of Arts.

Artium Magister /*är'shi-um ma-jis'tər* or *är'ti-ŭm ma-gis'ter*/ or **Magister Artium** (L) *n* Master of Arts.

artless see under **art**[1].

artocarpus /*är-tō-kär'pəs*/ *n* a plant of the genus *Artocarpus* of the family Moraceae, including breadfruit and jack-fruit. [Gr *artos* bread, and *karpos* fruit]

artsy, **arty**, **arty-farty** see under **art**[1].

arugula /*ə-roo'gə-lə* or *-gyə-*/ *n* rocket, a Mediterranean herb used in salads. [Ital dialect, ult from L *eruca* a colewort]

arum /*ā'rəm*/ *n* a perennial plant of the cuckoo pint or wake-robin genus *Arum*; any of several related plants, *esp* the **arum lily** (see below). [L *arum*, from Gr *aron*]

■ **Arā'ceae** /*a-*/ *n pl* the family of spadiciflorous monocotyledons to which they belong. **araceous** /*a-rā'shəs*/ or **aroid** /*ā'roid*/ *adj* of the Araceae; like an arum. **ā'roid** *n* any plant of the family.

□ **arum lily** *n* a plant with large leaves, a fleshy stem and a large ornamental white spathe with yellow spadix (also called **calla lily**, **zantedeschia**).

■ **Titan arum** see under **Titan**.

arundinaceous /*ə-run-di-nā'shəs*/ (*bot*) *adj* of or like a reed. [L *arundināceus*, from *arundō*, *-inis* a reed]

ARV *abbrev* : antiretroviral; armoured recovery vehicle.

arval /*är'vəl*/ *adj* relating to ploughed land. [L *arvālis*, from *arāre* to plough]

□ **Arval Brethren** *n pl* in ancient Rome, a college of priests who sacrificed to the field deities.

Arvicola /*är-vik'ō-lə*/ *n* the water-rat genus of voles. [L *arvum* a field, and *colere* to inhabit]

■ **ar'vicole** *n* a member of the genus. **arvic'oline** *adj*.

arvo /*är'vō*/ (Aust *inf*) *n* (*pl* **ar'vos**) afternoon.

ary /*ā'ri* or *e'ri*/ or (*obs*) **arrow** /*ar'ō*/ (*dialect*) *adj* any. [From *e'er a*, *ever a*; cf **nary**]

Aryan /*ā'* or *ā'ri-ən*/ *adj* Indo-Germanic, Indo-European; of the Indian, or Indian and Iranian, branch of the Indo-European languages; speaking one of these languages; (in Nazi politics) Caucasian, *esp* of N European type and *esp* as opposed to Jewish. ◆ *n* a member of the prehistoric people belonging to the Indo-European language family, or a descendant; the parent Indo-European language; a speaker of an Aryan language; (in Nazi politics) a person of Aryan descent. [Sans *ārya* noble]

■ **Ar'yanize** or **-ise** *vt*.

Arya Samaj /*är'yä sä-mäj'*/ *n* a reformed Hindu religious body or school, founded by Dayananda Saraswati (1824–83), based on the Vedas, and opposing idolatry, caste, and child-marriage. [Hindi *ārya samāj* noble association]

aryballos /*a-ri-bal'os*/ *n* an ancient Greek globular oil-flask with a neck. [Gr]

■ **aryball'oid** *adj*.

aryl /*ar'il*/ (*chem*) *n* any aromatic univalent hydrocarbon radical. [**aromatic**, and Gr *hylē* matter]

arytaenoid or **arytenoid** /*a-ri-tē'noid*/ (*anat* and *zool*) *adj* pitcher-shaped. ◆ *n* one of a pair of cartilages or muscles of the larynx. [Gr *arytainoeidēs*, from *arytaina* a cup, and *eidos* form]

AS *abbrev* : Advanced Subsidiary (examination); air speed; air staff; all sections (*insurance*); Anglo-Saxon; *anno salutis* (*L*), in the year of salvation; antisubmarine; Assistant Secretary.

As (*chem*) *symbol* : arsenic.

as[1] /az or əz/ *adv* in whatever degree, proportion or manner; to whatever extent; in that degree; to that extent; so far; (passing into *conj* or almost *prep*) for instance; in the manner, character, part, aspect, of; in so far as; whereas. ◆ *conj* because, since; while, when; as if; that (consequence) (*Milton*); than (*non-standard* or *dialect*). ◆ *pronoun* who, which, that (after *such, so, same,* or where a statement is treated as antecedent; in *Shakesp* after a demonstrative pronoun; otherwise *dialect* or *non-standard*). [OE *all-swā* (*eall-swā*) all so, wholly so]
■ **as also** likewise. **as ... as** or **... as** no matter how .... **as and when** at an appropriate future time. **as concerning, as for, as regards** or **as to** for the matter of. **as from** or **as of** from (a specified time). **as how** that (with noun clause) (*non-standard* or *dialect*); introducing a question (similarly **as why**) (*obs*). **as if** or **as though** as it would be if. **as if!** an interjection expressing incredulity. **as is** (*inf*) as it stands; unaltered. **as it were** so to speak; in a kind of way. **as many as** all who. **as much** the same; just that. **as now** or **as then** just as at this or that, time. **as was** formerly; in a former state. **as well** also; in addition; equally well, suitably, happily, etc. **as yet** up to the moment; until now (also **as-yet**). **as you were** a military order to return to the former position; in general use, countermanding an instruction. **so as to** with the purpose or consequence specified. **when as** (*archaic*) at what time.

as[2] /äs/ (*Norse myth*) *n* (*pl* **aesir** /es'ir/) a Norse god, an inhabitant of Asgard. [ON *āss* a god (pl *æsir*); cf OE *ōs*, seen in such proper names as *Oswald, Osric*]

as[3] /as/ (*ancient Rome*) *n* (*pl* **ass'es**) a Roman unit of weight, a pound of 12 ounces; a Roman copper coin, *orig* a pound in weight, ultimately half an ounce. [L *ās, assis*]

ås /ōs/ (*geol*) *n* (*pl* **åsar** /ōs'är/) a kame or esker. [Sw]

ASA *abbrev* : Advertising Standards Authority; Amateur Swimming Association; American Standards Association (now known as **ANSI**, but still used to denote the speed of photographic film).

asafoetida /a-sə-fet'i-də or -fē'ti-/ *n* a foul-smelling gum resin, obtained from the root latex of some species of *Ferula*, formerly used medicinally, now in Indian cooking (also **asafet'ida, assafoet'ida** or **assafet'ida**). [Pers *azā* mastic, and L *fētida* (fem) stinking]

a salti /ä säl'tē/ (*Ital* literally, in jumps) by fits and starts.

asana /ä'sə-nə/ *n* any of the positions taught in yoga. [Sans *āsana*]

Asante /ə-san'tē/ *n* and *adj* same as **Ashanti**; (of) the language of the Ashanti.

ASAP or **asap** *abbrev* : as soon as possible.

åsar see **ås**.

asarum /as'ə-rəm/ *n* the dried root of the wild ginger (*Asarum canadense*). [L *asarum* (from Gr *asaron*) asarabacca]
■ **asarabacca** /as-ə-rə-bak'ə/ *n* (L *bacca* berry) a plant (*Asarum europaeum*), of the birthwort family, formerly used in medicine.

ASB *abbrev* : Accounting Standards Board.

asbestos /az-bes'tos/ *n* a fine fibrous form of certain minerals capable of being woven into incombustible cloth or felted sheets for insulation, etc; (commercially) chrysotile, a fibrous serpentine. ◆ *adj* of or like asbestos, *esp* in being resistant to heat. [Gr, literally, unquenchable, from *a-* (privative), and *sbestos* extinguished]
■ **asbes'tic, asbes'tiform, asbes'tine** or **asbes'tous** *adj* of or like asbestos. **asbestō'sis** *n* a lung disease with scarring and carcinoma caused by inhaling asbestos dust over long periods.
❑ **asbestos cement** *n* cement containing asbestos fibres, used to make thin slabs for various purposes in building.

ASBM *abbrev* : air-to-surface ballistic missile.

ASBO /az'bō/ *abbrev* : Anti-Social Behaviour Order, a court order that places restrictions on a person who has been found guilty of antisocial acts.

ascarid /as'kə-rid/ or **ascaris** /-ris/ *n* (*pl* **as'carids** or **ascarides** /-kar'i-dēz/) any nematode worm of the parasitic genus *Ascaris* (family **Ascar'idae**) infesting the small intestines, a roundworm. [Gr *askaris*, pl *askarides*]
■ **ascariasis** /as-kə-rī'ə-sis/ *n* infestation with, or disease caused by, ascarids (*esp Ascaris lumbricoides*).

ascaunt see under **askance**.

ascend /ə-send'/ *vi* to go up, mount, rise; to go back in time or ancestry. ◆ *vt* to go up, mount, climb; to trace back in time or ancestry; to go up to (*Shakesp*). [L *ascendere, ascēnsum*, from *ad* to, and *scandere* to climb]
■ **ascend'ance** or **ascend'ence** (both *rare*), now *usu* **ascend'ancy** or **ascend'ency** *n* dominating influence. **ascend'ant** or less commonly **ascend'ent** *n* the part of the ecliptic just risen or about to

rise above the horizon at any instant (a planet in the ascendant is supposed to influence a person born at the time) (*astrol*); a position of pre-eminence; an ancestor or relative in the ascending line; a person who rises or mounts (*obs*); a rise, up-slope (*obs*). ◆ *adj* rising; just risen above the horizon; predominant. **ascend'er** *n* a person or thing that ascends; (the upper part of) a letter such as b, d, h, k (*printing*, etc); a metal grip threaded on a rope as a foothold or aid to climbing (*mountaineering*). **ascend'able** or **ascend'ible** *adj* scalable. **ascend'ing** *adj* rising; curving up from a prostrate to an erect position (*bot*). **ascension** /-sen'shən/ *n* ascent (a Gallicism when used of a mountain ascent); an ascent to heaven, *esp* Christ's. **ascen'sional** *adj*. **ascen'sive** *adj* moving or tending upwards. **ascent'** *n* a going up; advancement; a going back in time or ancestry; a way up; an up-slope.
❑ **Ascension Day** or **Ascen'sion-day** *n* (*Christianity*) a festival, ten days before Whitsunday, commemorating Christ's Ascension. **Ascen'siontide** *n* the period from Ascension Day to Whitsunday.
■ **ascend the throne** to become king or queen. **in the ascendant** increasing in influence, prosperity, etc. **right ascension** (*astron*) a coordinate of the position of a celestial body measured (*usu* in terms of time) eastwards along the celestial equator from the First Point of Aries, the other co-ordinate being the declination.

ascertain /a-sər-tān'/ *vt* to find out for certain; to verify, prove; to apprise (*obs*); to assure (*obs*); to make certain, prove (*obs*). [OFr *acertener* to make certain, from *à* to, and *certain* certain]
■ **ascertain'able** *adj*. **ascertain'ment** *n*.
❑ **ascertained goods** *n pl* (*business law*) goods which are identified and agreed upon after the contract is made.

ascesis /ə-sē'sis/ *n* the practice of disciplining oneself; asceticism. [Gr *askēsis* exercise, training]

ascetic /a- or ə-set'ik/ *n* a person who rigidly abstains from ordinary bodily gratifications for conscience's sake; a person who aims to achieve holiness through mortification of the flesh; a strict hermit; a person who lives a life of austerity. ◆ *adj* (also **ascet'ical**) rigorous in mortifying the flesh; of asceticism; austere. [Gr *askētikos*, from *askētēs*, a person in training, from *askeein* to work, exercise, train]
■ **ascet'ically** *adv*. **ascet'icism** /-sizm/ *n*.

asci see **ascus**.

ascian /ash'i-ən/ *n* an inhabitant of the torrid zone, shadowless when the sun is right overhead. [Gr *askios* shadowless, from *a-* (privative), and *skiā* a shadow]

ascidium /ə-sid'i-əm/ *n* (*pl* **ascid'ia**) (*bot*) a pitcher-shaped leaf or part of a leaf, such as the pitcher of the pitcher plants, the bladder of the bladderwort. [Gr *askidion*, dimin of *askos* a leather bag, wineskin]
■ **ascid'ian** *n* (*zool*) a sea-squirt, or tunicate, a member of the Urochordata, a subphylum of the Chordata, shaped like a double-mouthed flask.

ASCII /as'ki/ (*comput*) *abbrev* : American Standard Code for Information Interchange, a binary code representing characters and used by VDUs, printers, etc.

ascites /ə-sī'tēz/ (*pathol*) *n* dropsy of the abdomen. [Gr *askītēs*, from *askos* belly]
■ **ascit'ic** /-sit'ik/ or **ascit'ical** *adj*.

ascititious same as **adscititious**.

asclepiad[1] /a-sklē'pi-ad/ *n* a verse used by the Greek poet *Asclepiades* (3c BC) made up of a spondee, two (in the *Greater Asclepiad* three) choriambi, and an iambus (--/-∪∪-/-∪∪-/∪-).
■ **Asclepiadē'an** or **Asclepiad'ic** *n* and *adj*.

asclepiad[2] /a-sklē'pi-ad/ or **asclepias** /-əs/ *n* a plant of the chiefly American genus *Asclepias* of the swallow-wort family, milkweed. [Gr *asklēpias, -ados* swallow-wort]
■ **Asclepiadā'ceae** *n pl* the milkweed and swallow-wort family, closely related to the periwinkle family. **asclepiadaceous** /-ā'shəs/ *adj*.

Asclepius or **Asclepios** /a-sklē'pi-əs/ (*Gr myth*) *n* a mortal who became the god of healing (also called (*L*) **Aesculā'pius**).

ascomycete, ascospore see under **ascus**.

asconce or (*Shakesp*) **a sconce** obsolete forms of **askance**.

ascorbic /ə-skör'bik/ *adj* antiscorbutic, only in **ascorbic acid** vitamin C ($C_6H_8O_6$). [Gr *a-* (privative), and **scorbutic**]
■ **ascor'bate** *n* a salt of ascorbic acid.

ascot /as'kot/ *n* a type of necktie with broad ends that are tied to lie one across the other. [The racecourse at *Ascot*, England, well-known for the fashionable dress of spectators]

ascribe /ə-skrīb'/ *vt* to attribute, impute or assign (to). [L *ascrībere*, from *ad* to, and *scrībere, scrīptum* to write]
■ **ascrib'able** *adj*. **ascription** /-skrip'shən/ *n* the act, expression or formula of ascribing or imputing, eg that ascribing glory to God at the end of a Christian sermon.

■ words derived from main entry word; ❑ compound words; ■ idioms and phrasal verbs

ascus /as'kəs/ (bot) n (pl **asci** /as'ī or as'kī/) an enlarged cell, commonly elongated, in which usually eight spores are formed. [Gr askos bag]
■ **ascomycete** /as-kō-mī'sēt/ n any one of the **Ascomycetes** /-sē'tēz/, one of the main divisions of the fungi, characterized by formation of asci. **ascomycē'tous** adj. **as'cospore** n a spore formed in an ascus.

Asdic /as' or az'dik/ n an apparatus for detecting and locating a submarine or other underwater object by means of ultrasonic waves echoed back from the submarine, etc. [Allied (or Anti-) Submarine Detection Investigation Committee]

ASE abbrev : Association for Science Education.

-ase /-āz or -ās/ (chem) sfx denoting an enzyme, specif one that hydrolyses the prefixed substance (thus fructase, amylase, protease). [diastase, from Gr diastasis separation]

ASEAN or **Asean** /as'i-ən/ abbrev : Association of Southeast Asian Nations.

aseismic /a-, ā- or ə-sīz'mik/ adj free from earthquakes; (of buildings) able to withstand earthquakes. [Gr a- (privative), and **seismic**]

aseity /a- or ā-sē'i-ti/ (philos) n the condition of deriving from, or originating in, itself. [L ā from, and sē (ablative) oneself]

asepalous /a-, ā- or ə-sep'ə-ləs/ (bot) adj without sepals. [Gr a- (privative), and **sepal**]

asepsis see under **aseptic**.

aseptate /a-, ā- or ə-sep'tāt/ (bot) adj not partitioned by septa. [Gr a- (privative), and **septum**]

aseptic /a-, ā- or ə-sep'tik/ adj not liable to, or preventing, decay or putrefaction; involving or accompanied by measures to exclude micro-organisms. ◆ n an aseptic substance. [Gr asēptos, from a- (privative), and sēpein to cause to decay]
■ **asep'sis** n (pl **asep'ses**) freedom from sepsis or blood poisoning; the process of rendering, or condition of being, aseptic; exclusion of micro-organisms. **asep'ticism** /-sizm/ n aseptic treatment. **asep'ticize** or **-ise** /-ti-sīz/ vt to make aseptic; to treat with aseptics.

asexual /ə- or ā-sek'sū-əl or -shoo-əl/ adj without sex; neither male nor female; not involving sexual activity; vegetative. [Gr a- (privative), and **sexual**]
■ **asexūality** /-al'i-ti/ n. **asex'ūally** adv.

Asgard /äs'gärd/ n the heaven of Norse mythology, abode of the twelve gods and twenty-six goddesses, and of heroes slain in battle. [ON Āsgarthr, from āss a god, and garthr an enclosure]

ASH abbrev : Action on Smoking and Health.

ash[1] /ash/ n (often in pl) the dust or remains of anything burnt; (also **volcanic ash** or **ashes**) volcanic dust, or a rock composed of it; a light silver-grey colour; (in pl) the remains of a human body when burnt; (in pl) a dead body (fig; poetic). [OE asce ; ON aska]
■ **ash'en** adj resembling ash; of the colour of ash; (of the face) very pale. **ash'ery** n a place where potash or pearl ash is made. **ash'y** adj. ❑ **ash'-bin**, **-bucket** or **-can** n a receptacle for ashes and other household refuse. **ash-blond'** or (fem) **ash-blonde'** adj (of hair) of a pale, silvery blond colour; having hair of this colour (also n). **ash'en-grey** adj of the colour of wood ashes. **ash'-heap** n a heap of ashes and household refuse. **ash'-hole** or **-pit** n a hollow, esp under a fireplace, to receive ashes. **ash'-leach** n a tub in which alkaline salts are dissolved from wood ashes. **ash'-pan** n a tray fitted underneath a grate to receive the ashes. **ash'tray** n a small tray or saucer for tobacco ash (also **ash'-stand**). **Ash Wednesday** n (Christianity) the first day of Lent, named from the custom of sprinkling ashes on the head to show penance and mourning. **ash'y-grey** adj.
■ **the Ashes** a trophy in the form of a small urn competed for by the cricket teams of England and Australia (from a mock obituary of English cricket after the Australian victory in 1882, after which the trophy purporting to contain the ashes of English cricket was devised); a series of test matches for this trophy; a series of matches between Australia and Great Britain at any other sport.

ash[2] /ash/ n a well-known timber tree (Fraxinus excelsior, or other species) of the olive family; its white, tough, hard wood; an ashen spear-shaft or spear (obs). [OE æsc ; Ger Esche, ON askr]
■ **ash'en** adj made of, or relating to, the ash tree.
❑ **ash'-key** n the winged fruit of the ash. **ash'-plant** n an ash sapling; a whip, staff or walking-stick made from an ash sapling.

ash[3] same as **æsc**.

ashake /ə-shāk'/ (archaic) adv or adj in a shaking state. [**a-**[1]]

ashamed /ə-shāmd'/ adj feeling or affected with shame (with of an action or person; with for, meaning on behalf of, a person; also with to do, or that). [Pfx a- (intensive), and OE sc(e)amian to shame]
■ **ashame'** vi (obs) to feel shame. ◆ vt (archaic) to put to shame. **ashamed'ly** (or /-id-li/) adv. **ashamed'ness** (or /-id-nes/) n. **asham'ing** adj (archaic).

Ashanti /ə-shan'tē/ n a Ghanaian people (also adj).

ashen, etc see under **ash**[1,2].

ashet /ash'it/ (now chiefly Scot; also N Eng) n a large meat-plate or flat serving-dish. [Fr assiette]

ashine /ə-shīn'/ (archaic or poetic) adv or adj in a shining state. [**a-**[1]]

ashiver /ə-shiv'ər/ (archaic or poetic) adv or adj in a shivering or quivering state. [**a-**[1] and **shiver**[1]]

Ashkenazim /äsh-kə-nä'zim/ n pl the Polish and German Jews (as distinguished from the Sephardim, the Spanish and Portuguese Jews). [Heb Ashkenaz a northern people (Genesis 10) by later Jews identified with Germany]
■ **Ashkenaz'i** n a member of the Ashkenazim; the pronunciation of Hebrew used by them. ◆ adj of the Ashkenazim.

ashlar or **ashler** /ash'lər/ n a squared or dressed stone used in building or facing a wall; finely-jointed masonry of such stones. ◆ adj made of ashlar. ◆ vt to face with ashlar. [OFr aiseler, from L axillāris, from axilla, dimin of axis axle, plank]
■ **ash'laring** or **ash'lering** n ashlar masonry or facing; a vertical timber between the floor-joists and rafters.
❑ **ash'lar-work** n ashlar masonry.

ashore /ə-shōr'/ adv on, or onto, the shore or land (from the sea). [**a-**[1] and **shore**[1]]

ashram /ä'shrəm/ (Hinduism) n usu in India, a hermitage for a holy man, or a place of retreat for a religious community; such a community. [Sans āśrama]
■ **ash'rama** n any one of the four stages of life which a man of the upper three castes should ideally pass through: pupil, householder, hermitage-dweller, and wanderer who has renounced the world. **ash'ramite** n a person living in an ashram.

ashtanga /ash-tang'gə/ n a form of yoga aiming to synchronize breathing and posture (also called **ashtanga vinyasa yoga**). [Sans, eight-limbed, referring to the eight stages of classical yoga]

Ashtaroth, **Ashtoreth** see **Astarte**.

Ashura /ash'ŭ-rä/ (Islam) n a fast-day observed on the tenth day of Moharram (qv), esp among Shiite Muslims, in commemoration of the death of Imam Hosain. [Ar 'Ashūrā]

Asian /ā'zhən, ā'shən/ or (often offensive) **Asiatic** /-si-at'ik/ adj belonging to Asia (esp Asia Minor); formerly in literature or art, florid. ◆ n a native of Asia, or person of Asian descent.
■ **Asianic** /-an'ik/ adj Asian, esp of a group of non-Indo-European languages of Asia and Europe. **Asiat'icism** /-i-sizm/ n imitation of Asiatic or Eastern manners.
❑ **Asian pear** n any of several varieties of pear with firm, crisp flesh (also called **nashi**); a tree which yields this fruit.

aside /ə-sīd'/ adv on or to one side; privately; apart. ◆ n words spoken in an undertone, so as not to be heard by some person present; words spoken by an actor which the other persons on the stage are supposed not to hear; an indirect effort of any kind. ◆ adj (US) private, apart. ◆ prep (now only Scot) beside. [**a-**[1] and **side**[1]]
■ **aside from** apart from. **set aside** to quash (a judgement); to put to one side (lit and fig).

asinico /a-si-nē'kō/ (Shakesp) n a stupid fellow. [Sp asnico, dimin of asno, from L asinus ass]

asinine /as'i-nīn/ adj of or like an ass; idiotic. [L asinīnus, from asinus ass]
■ **as'ininely** adv. **asininity** /-in'i-ti/ n.

ASIO /ā'zi-ō or az'i-ō/ abbrev : Australian Security Intelligence Organization.

ask[1] /äsk/ vt to beg, request, seek; to make a request of; to inquire; to inquire of; to invite (esp with out, over or along); to proclaim (archaic). ◆ vi to make a request (for); to inquire (after a person or their welfare, etc, about a matter, etc). ◆ n something requested or demanded of someone, as in a tough ask. [OE ascian, acsian ; Ger heischen, ON æskja]
■ **ask'er** n.
❑ **asking price** n the price set by the seller of an article before bargaining has begun; the asking rate.
■ **ask for it** (inf) to behave in a way likely to bring trouble on oneself. **don't ask me!** I haven't the faintest idea! **for the asking** freely available on request. **I ask you!** would you believe it, don't you agree (usu expressing criticism). **if you ask me** in my opinion.

ask[2] /ask/ (dialect) n a newt (also **ask'er**). [Appar OE āthexe ; cf Ger Eidechse lizard]

askance /ə-skäns'/ adv (also **askant**) sideways; awry; obliquely; quizzically, sceptically. ◆ vt (Shakesp) to turn aside. [Ety very obscure]
■ **ascaunt'** (folio reading **aslant**) prep (Shakesp) slantwise across.

■ **look**, **eye** or **view askance** to look (at) with disdain, disapproval, envy, or (now *usu*) suspicion.

askari /as'kə-rē/ or *a-skä'rē*/ *n* (*pl* **askaris**) an E African soldier or policeman. [Ar *'askarī* soldier]

asker see **ask**[1,2].

askesis same as **ascesis**.

askew /ə-skū'/ *adv* or *adj* at or to an oblique angle; awry. [Appar **a-**[1] and **skew**[1]]

asklent see **aslant**.

ASL *abbrev*: American Sign Language.

aslake /ə-slāk'/ *vt* to slake (*obs*); to mitigate (*archaic*); to appease (*obs*). [OE *āslacian*; see **slake**[1]]

aslant /ə-slänt'/, also (*Scot*) **asklent** /əs-klent'/ *adv* or *adj* on the slant, slantwise. ◆ *prep* slantwise across, athwart. [**a-**[1] and **slant**[1]]

asleep /ə-slēp'/ *adv* or *adj* in or to a sleeping state; inattentive; dead (*euphem*); (of limbs) numbed, sometimes with tingling or prickly feeling. [**a-**[1]]

ASLEF /az'lef/ or *as'lef*/ *abbrev*: Associated Society of Locomotive Engineers and Firemen.

AS level /ā-es' lev'əl/ *n* (a pass in) an Advanced Subsidiary level GCE examination, one which is designed to be taken by students studying for the Advanced level after one year of study (also *adj*).

ASLIB or **Aslib** *abbrev*: Association for Information Management (formerly the Association of Special Libraries and Information Bureaux).

aslope /ə-slōp'/ (*archaic*) *adv* or *adj* on the slope. [OE *āslopen*, pap of *āslūpan* to slip away]

ASM *abbrev*: air-to-surface missile; assistant stage manager.

-asm see **-ism**.

asmear /ə-smēr'/ (*archaic*) *adj* smeared over. [**a-**[1]]

Asmodeus /as- or *az-mə-dē'əs*/ or **Asmoday** /-dā'/ *n* an evil spirit of Semitic mythology. [L, from Gr *Asmodaios*, from Heb *Ashmadai*]

asmoulder /ə-smōl'dər/ (*archaic*) *adv* in a smouldering state. [**a-**[1]]

asocial /ā-sō'shəl/ *adj* not social; antisocial. [Gr *a-* (privative)]

asp[1] /asp or *äsp*/ *n* a venomous snake of various kinds, including *Vipera aspis* of southern Europe, Cleopatra's asp (*prob* the horned viper), the biblical asp (*prob* the Egyptian juggler's snake, *Naja haje*), and the cobra de capello (also (*archaic* and *poetic*) **asp'ic** or **asp'ick**). [L, from Gr *aspis*]

asp[2] /asp or *äsp*/ (*archaic*) *n* an aspen.

asparagus /ə-spar'ə-gəs/ *n* any plant of the *Asparagus* genus of the family **Asparagaceae** /-ā'si-ē/, with leaves reduced to scales, some cultivated as ornamental plants, and one species (*A. officinalis*) for its young shoots eaten as a delicacy. [L, from Gr *asp(h)aragos*]
■ **asparag'inase** /-aj'/ *n* an enzyme that causes asparagine to hydrolyse to aspartic acid and ammonia. **aspar'agine** /-jin or -jēn/ *n* an amino acid found in asparagus and other vegetables.
❑ **asparagus bean** *n* a tropical American bean (*Vigna sesquipedalis*) with very long pods. **asparagus fern** *n* a fern-like decorative species of asparagus, *A. plumosus*. **asparagus pea** *n* the Goa bean. **aspar'agus-stone** *n* a pale yellowish-green apatite.

aspartic acid /ə-spär'tik as'id/ *n* an amino acid found in young sugar-cane, etc, and formed by the hydrolysis of asparagine (also **2-aminobutanedioic acid**). [Irreg coinage from *aspar*agine, and **acid**]
■ **aspartame** /ə-spär'tām/ *n* an artificial sweetener, *approx* 200 times sweeter than sucrose, derived from aspartic acid and phenylalanine.

Aspasia /a-spā'zyə or *a-spä'zi-a*/ *n* a gifted Athenian courtesan, mistress of Pericles (*Gr hist*); any charming and accomplished woman of easy morals.

aspect /as'pekt/ (in Spenser, Shakesp, Milton, etc *a-spekt'*) *n* a view in a specific direction; a direction of facing; an appearance presented; way of viewing; a part or feature; a surface facing a particular direction, face, side, elevation; the situation of one planet with respect to another, as seen from the earth (*astrol*); in some languages, a verbal form expressing such features as simple action, repetition, beginning, duration, etc (*grammar*); attitude (*aeronautics*); a look, a glance (*obs*). ◆ *vt* /-pekt'/ (*obs*) to look at or for. [L *aspectus*]
■ **as'pectable** *adj* (*archaic*) visible; worth looking at. **aspec'tual** *adj* (*grammar* and *astrol*) of or relating to aspect.
❑ **aspect ratio** *n* the ratio of the width to the height of a reproduced image (also **picture ratio**; *TV*); the ratio of the span of an aerofoil to its mean chord (*aeronautics*).

aspen /as'pən/, also *ä'spən* or *-spin*/ (or Spenser **aspine**) *n* the trembling poplar. ◆ *adj* made of, or like, the aspen; tremulous; timorous. [OE *æspe*; Ger *Espe*]
■ **as'pen-like** *adj*.

asper[1] /as'pər/ *n* a former Turkish monetary unit, worth $\frac{1}{120}$ of a piastre. [Gr *aspron* rough, later white]

asper[2] /as'pər/ *adj* (*obs*) rough, harsh. ◆ *n* (in ancient Greek) a rough breathing (qv). [L]
■ **as'perate** *vt* to roughen. **asperatus** /-rä'təs/ *adj* (of a cloud formation) having a roughened appearance. **as'perous** *adj* rough with short hairs.

asperge /a-spûrj'/ *vt* to sprinkle. ◆ *n* a sprinkler for holy water. [L *aspergere*, from *ad* to, and *spargere* to sprinkle]
■ **aspergation** /-gā'/ *n*. **asper'ger** /-jər/ *n*. **asper'ges** *n* (*RC*) a short service introductory to the mass, so called from the words *Asperges me, Domine, hyssopo et mundabor* (Psalm 51). **aspergill** /as'pər-jil/ *n* a holy-water sprinkler (also **aspergillum** /-jil'əm/ (*pl* **aspergill'a** or **aspergill'ums**)). **aspergillō'sis** *n* a disease, fatal to birds and also occurring in domestic animals and man, caused by any of various moulds, *esp* species of *Aspergillus*. **Aspergill'um** *n* a genus of boring Lamellibranch molluscs in which the shell forms an elongated cone, ending in a disc pierced with numerous small tubular holes. **Aspergill'us** *n* a genus of minute moulds occurring on decaying substances.

Asperger's syndrome /as'pûr-gərz sin'drōm/ (*med*) *n* a mild psychiatric disorder characterized by poor social interaction and obsessive behaviour. [Hans *Asperger* (1906–80), Austrian psychiatrist]

asperity /a-sper'i-ti/ *n* roughness; harshness; bitter coldness; (in *pl*) excrescences, rough places. [L *asperita_s*, *-a_tis*, from *asper* (see **asper**[2])]

aspermia /ə-spûr'mi-ə/ *n* failure to produce sperm. [Gr *a-* (privative), and *sperma*, *-atos* seed, semen]

asperous see under **asper**[2].

asperse /ə-spûrs'/ *vt* to slander or accuse falsely; to bespatter. [L *aspergere*, *aspersum*, from *ad* to, and *spargere* to sprinkle]
■ **asper'sion** *n* calumny; slander; a shower or spray (*Shakesp*); sprinkling with holy water (*RC*). **aspers'ive** *adj*. **aspersoir** /äs-per-swär/ *n* (*Fr*) an aspergill. **aspersō'rium** /-ri-əm/ *n* (*L*) a holy-water vessel. **aspers'ory** *adj* (*rare*) tending to asperse; defamatory. ◆ *n* an aspergill; an aspersorium.
■ **cast aspersions** to criticize, slander.

asphalt /as'falt or *-folt*/ *n* (also **asphal'tum**) a black or dark-brown, hard, bituminous substance, occurring naturally, and obtained as a residue in petroleum distillation, etc, anciently used as a cement; a mixture of this with rock chips or other material, used for paving, roofing, etc. ◆ *vt* to lay, cover or impregnate with asphalt. [Gr *asphaltos*, from an Asian language]
■ **as'phalter** *n* a person who lays asphalt. **asphalt'ic** *adj*.

aspheric /ə- or *ā-sfer'ik*/ or **aspherical** /-i-kəl/ *adj* not spherical; (of a surface) not forming part of a sphere. [**a-**[2]]

aspheterism /as-fet'ə-ri-zm/ *n* (*Southey*) denial of the right of private property. [Gr *a-* (privative), and *spheteros* one's own]
■ **asphet'erize** or **-ise** *vt* (*Coleridge*).

asphodel /as'fə-del or *-fō-*/ *n* a plant of the lily family with spikes of clustered flowers and narrow grasslike leaves (in Greek mythology, the plant of the dead); applied to other plants, *esp* **bog asphodel**. [Gr *asphodelos*; cf **daffodil**]

asphyxia /as-fik'si-ə/ (*med*) *n* (literally) stoppage of the pulse; stoppage or suspension of the vital functions owing to any cause which interferes with respiration and prevents oxygen from reaching the body tissue (also (formerly) **asphyx'y**). [Gr *asphyxiā*, from *a-* (privative), and *sphyxis* pulse]
■ **asphyx'ial** *adj*. **asphyx'iant** *n* and *adj* (a chemical substance) producing asphyxia. **asphyx'iate** *vt* to produce asphyxia in. ◆ *vi* to die of asphyxia. **asphyx'iated** *adj*. **asphyxiā'tion** *n* the action of asphyxiating or condition of being asphyxiated. **asphyx'iātor** *n*.

aspic[1] /as'pik/ *n* a clear savoury meat- or fish-jelly used as a glaze or a mould for fish, game, hard-boiled eggs, etc. [Fr, perh from *aspic* (asp) because it is 'cold as an aspic' (French proverb)]

aspic[2] /as'pik/ *n* the broad-leaved lavender (*Lavandula spica* or *latifolia*). [Fr, from L *spīca* spike]

aspic[3], **aspick** see **asp**[1].

aspidistra /a-spi-dis'trə/ *n* an evergreen plant of the *Aspidistra* genus of the family Convallariaceae, often grown indoors, having long, tough leaves and brownish-purple flowers. [Perh Gr *aspis* a shield]

aspidium /a-spid'i-əm/ (*bot*) *n* (*pl* **aspid'ia**) any one of the shield-fern genus (*Aspidium*) of ferns (including those *usu* divided between the genera *Dryopteris*, *Polystichum* and *Tectaria*), having a shield-shaped or kidney-shaped indusium. [Gr *aspidion*, dimin of *aspis* shield]
■ **aspid'ioid** *adj*.

aspine see **aspen**.

aspire /ə-spīr'/ vi (with to, after, or an infinitive) to desire eagerly; to aim at, or strive for, high things; to tower up. [L aspīrāre, -ātum, from ad to, and spīrāre to breathe]

■ **aspīr'ant** (or /as'pir-/) n a person who aspires (with after or for); a candidate. ◆ adj ambitious; mounting up. **aspirate** /as'pir-āt/ vt and vi to pronounce with a full breathing, ie the sound of h, as in house (phonetics); to follow (a stop) by an audible breath (phonetics); to replace (a consonant) by another sound, normally a fricative, when there is a combination with the sound h or the letter h (grammar, phonetics, etc); to draw (gas, fluid, etc) out of a cavity, eg (med) a body cavity, by suction; to supply air to an internal-combustion engine. ◆ n /-it or -ət/ the sound represented by the letter h; a consonant sound, a stop followed by an audible breath, such as bh in Sanskrit; sometimes extended to a fricative; a mark of aspiration, the rough breathing (') in Greek; a letter representing an aspirate sound. ◆ adj of or relating to an aspirate. **aspirā'tion** n eager desire; (usu in pl) lofty hopes or aims; pronunciation of a sound with a full breathing; an aspirated sound; drawing a gas, liquid or solid, in, out or through; breathing (obs). **aspirā'tional** adj relating to the aspirations or aims of a person or of people. **as'pirator** n an apparatus for drawing air or other gases through bottles or other vessels; an instrument for removing fluids or solids from cavities of the body (med). **aspīr'atory** /-ə-tə-ri or as'pir-/ adj relating to breathing. **aspīr'ing** adj desiring, aiming at, etc. **aspīr'ingly** adv. **aspīr'ingness** n.

■ **drop one's aspirates** to omit to pronounce the sound of h.

aspirin /as'pə-rin/ n a drug (acetyl-salicylic acid) used for relieving rheumatic pains, neuralgia, etc, and as an anti-coagulant. [Ger, from A(cetyl) and Spir(säure) spiraeic (now salicylic) acid, and **-in** (3)]

asplenium /a-splē'ni-əm/ n spleenwort, any fern of a widely-distributed genus of ferns, Asplenium, with long or linear sori whose indusia arise from a vein (eg wall rue). [Gr asplēnon, (literally) spleenless, from a- (privative), and splēn spleen, reputedly a cure for spleen]

asport /a-spört'/ (rare) vt to carry away, esp wrongfully. [L asportāre, from abs away, and portāre to carry]

■ **asportā'tion** n.

aspout /ə-spowt'/ (archaic) adv spoutingly. [**a-¹**]

asprawl /ə-spröl'/ (archaic) adv in a sprawl. [**a-¹**]

aspread /ə-spred'/ (archaic) adv in or into a spreading state. [**a-¹**]

asprout /ə-sprowt'/ (archaic) adv in a sprouting state. [**a-¹**]

asquat /ə-skwot'/ (archaic) adv squattingly. [**a-¹**]

asquint /ə-skwint'/ adv and adj towards the corner of the eye; obliquely. [Appar **a-¹**, and some such word as Du schuinte slant]

ASR abbrev : airport surveillance radar; air-sea rescue; automatic send and receive (or answer, send and receive).

Ass. or **Assoc.** abbrev : Associate; Associated; Association.

ass¹ /as or äs/ n a small, usu grey, long-eared animal of the genus Equus; a dull, stupid person, a fool (inf). [OE assa, from L asinus; cf Gr onos ass]

ass² see **arse**.

assafetida see **asafoetida**.

assagai see **assegai**.

assai¹ /äs-sä'ē/ (music) adv very. [Ital, from L ad to, and satis enough]

assai² see **açaí**.

assail /ə-sāl'/ vt to attack. [OFr asaillir, from L assilīre, from ad upon, and salīre to leap]

■ **assail'able** adj. **assail'ant** n a person who attacks. **assail'er** n. **assail'ment** n.

Assam /a-sam'/ n a full-bodied tea produced in Assam in NE India.

■ **Assamese** /as-ə-mēz'/ adj of Assam, its people or their language. ◆ n (pl **Assamese'**) a native or citizen of Assam; the official language of Assam.

assart /a-särt'/ (legal hist) vt to reclaim for agriculture by grubbing. ◆ n a forest clearing; assarted land; the grubbing up of trees and bushes. [Anglo-Fr assarter, from LL exsartāre, from L ex out, and sar(r)īre to hoe, weed]

assassin /ə-sas'in/ n a person who, usu for a fee or reward, or for political reasons, kills by surprise or secretly; orig a follower of the Old Man of the Mountains, a member of his military and religious order in Persia and Syria (11c–13c), notorious for secret murders. [Through Fr or Ital from Ar hashshāshīn hashish-eaters]

■ **assass'inate** vt to murder by surprise or secret assault; to murder (esp a prominent person) violently, often publicly; to destroy (eg a person's reputation) by treacherous means; to maltreat (Milton). ◆ n (obs) a person who assassinates. **assassinā'tion** n. **assass'inātor** n.

❑ **assassin bug** n any of a family (Reduviidae) of hemipteran insects that kill and suck the vital juices from other insects.

assault /ə-sölt' or -solt'/ n a sudden violent attack; a storming, eg of a town; rape, attempted rape, indecent attack; in English law, unlawful attempt to apply force to the person of another (when force is actually applied, the act amounts to battery); an attack of any sort by arguments, appeals, abuse, etc. ◆ vt to make an assault or attack upon; to attack indecently, rape, or attempt to rape. ◆ adj used in attack; preparing, or prepared, for attack. [OFr asaut, from L ad upon, and saltus a leap, from salīre to leap. See **assail**]

■ **assault'er** n. **assault'ive** adj.

❑ **assault boat** n a portable boat for landing on beaches or crossing rivers. **assault course** n a course laid out with obstacles that must be negotiated, used for training soldiers, etc (also fig).

■ **assault at** or **of arms** a display of attack and defence in fencing.

assay /a- or ə-sā'/ vt to put to the proof, to make trial of; to test; to determine the proportion of a metal, or other component, in; to give or yield as result; to test fatness of (a killed stag) by a trial cut (obs); to taste before presenting to a dignitary, etc (as guarantee against poison) (hist); to put to proof in action; to afflict (Spenser); to tempt (obs); to affect (Spenser); to experience (Shakesp); to endeavour (now usu essay); to assail (Spenser and Shakesp); to challenge (Shakesp); to accost (Shakesp). ◆ vi to venture, make an attempt; to carry out assaying (of ores, etc). ◆ n (sometimes /as'ā/) a test, trial; a determination of proportion of metal in an ore, or of a certain constituent in a substance; a specimen used for the purpose; the quality or standard of a metal as found by assaying; determination of the fatness of a stag (obs); experiment (obs); experience (obs); endeavour, attempt, tentative effort (usu essay); an assault (Spenser and Shakesp, etc); proof, temper, quality or standard, such as might be found by assaying (obs; Spenser and Shakesp). [OFr assayer and assai; see **essay**]

■ **assay'able** adj. **assay'er** n a person who assays metals. **assay'ing** n.

❑ **assay'-master** n an officer who determines the amount of gold or silver in coin or bullion. **assay office** n (often with caps) a (government) department in which gold and silver articles are assayed and hallmarks assigned. **assay'-piece** n a sample chosen for assay; an example of excellence.

■ **cup of assay** (hist) a small cup for trial tasting before offering to a dignitary, etc.

assegai or **assagai** (Afrik **assegaai**) /as'ə-gī/ n a slender spear of hard wood tipped with iron, either for hurling or for thrusting with, used in S Africa. ◆ vt to kill or wound with an assegai. [Through Fr or Port from Ar azzaghāyah, from az = al the, and zaghāyah, a Berber word]

assemble /ə-sem'bl/ vt to call or bring together; to collect; to put together the parts of; to convert (a program) to machine code from assembly language (comput). ◆ vi to meet together. [Fr assembler, from LL assimulāre to bring together, from ad to, and simul together]

■ **assem'blage** n a collection of persons or things; the whole collection of remains found on an archaeological site; all the flora and fauna of one type in an ecosystem (biol); the act of assembling; the putting together of parts (technical); (also /a-sä-bläzh/) (putting together) a sculptural or other work of art consisting in whole or in part of selected objects, usu objects made for another purpose. **assem'blance** or **assem'blaunce** n (Spenser) an assembling. **assem'bler** n someone who or or something that assembles; a program that converts a program in assembly language into one in machine code (comput); assembly language (see below). **assem'bly** n the act of assembling; the putting together of parts; a company assembled; a formal ball or meeting for dancing and social intercourse (hist); a reception or at-home (hist); a meeting for religious worship or the like; a deliberative or legislative body, esp in some legislatures a lower house; a drumbeat, esp a signal for striking tents (milit).

❑ **assembly hall** n a hall, eg in a school, in which assemblies are held. **assembly language** n (comput) a low-level programming language, generally using symbolic addresses, which is translated into machine code by an assembler (see above). **assembly line** n a serial arrangement of workers and apparatus for passing on work from stage to stage in assembling a product. **assem'blyman** n and **assem'blywoman** n a member of an assembly or lower house. **assembly room** n a public ballroom or room for entertainments or formal gatherings; an assembly shop. **assembly shop** n a place where components are assembled.

■ **General Assembly** the highest court of the Presbyterian Church or the United Reformed Church. **Legislative Assembly** or **House of Assembly** the lower or only house of some legislatures. **National Assembly** (also **Constituent Assembly**) the first of the revolutionary assemblies in France (1789–91); (also **Church Assembly**) a deliberative body of the Church of England set up in 1920, consisting of houses of Bishops, Clergy, and Laity, superseded in 1970 by the General Synod (see **synod**).

assemblé /ä-sä-blä'/ (ballet) n a leap with extended leg followed by a landing with both legs together. [Fr assembler to bring together]

assembly see under **assemble**.

assent /ə-sent'/ vi to express agreement or acquiescence (with to). ♦ n an agreeing or acquiescence; compliance. [L assentīrī to assent, agree and also its frequentative assentārī to flatter]
■ **assentaneous** /as-ən-tā'ni-əs/ adj (rare) ready to agree. **assentā'tion** n obsequious assent, adulation. **ass'entātor** n (obs). **assent'er** n. **assentient** /ə-sen'shənt/ or **assent'ive** adj. **assent'ingly** adv. **assent'iveness** n. **assent'or** n a person who subscribes a candidate's nomination paper in addition to proposer and seconder.
■ **royal assent** the sovereign's formal acquiescence in a measure which has passed the Houses of Parliament.

assert /ə-sûrt'/ vt to declare positively; to lay claim to; to insist upon; to affirm; to vindicate or defend by arguments or measures (now used only with cause as object, or reflexively); to bear evidence of (obs; rare). [L asserere, assertum to lay hands on, claim, from ad to, and serere to join]
■ **assert'able** adj. **assert'er** or **assert'or** n a champion, defender; a person who makes a positive statement. **asser'tion** /-shən/ n affirmation, averment; a positive statement or declaration; that which is averred or declared; the act of claiming one's rights; vindication or championship (archaic). **assert'ive** adj asserting or confirming confidently; positive, dogmatic; self-assertive. **assert'ively** adv. **assert'iveness** n. **assert'ory** adj affirmative.
■ **assert oneself** to defend one's rights or opinions, sometimes with unnecessary zeal; to thrust oneself forward.

assess /ə-ses'/ vt to fix the amount of (eg a tax); to tax or fine; to fix the value or profits of, for taxation (with at); to estimate, judge, evaluate (eg a person's work, performance, character). [L assidēre, assessum to sit beside (esp of judges in a court) from ad to, at, and sedēre to sit]
■ **assess'able** adj. **assess'ment** n the act of assessing; the examining of revenue and costs to calculate the amount of tax to be paid; the valuing of property to calculate liability to taxation; (the amount of) a tax or charge assessed. **assess'or** n a person who assesses; a legal adviser who sits beside a magistrate; a person appointed as an associate in office with another; a person who assesses taxes, or value of property, income, etc for taxation; someone who shares another's rank or position (archaic). **assessō'rial** /as-/ adj. **assess'orship** n.
❑ **assessment centre** a place where candidates for a job or a university place may be evaluated.

asset /as'et/ n an item of property; something advantageous or well worth having; an item of value belonging to a business or organization (categorized for accounting purposes as current assets and fixed assets, which may themselves be intangible, tangible or financial); (in pl) the property of a deceased or insolvent person, considered as chargeable for all debts, etc; (in pl) the entire property of all sorts belonging to a merchant or to a trading association. [From assets, orig singular, from the Anglo-Fr law phrase aver assetz to have enough, from OFr asez enough, from L ad to, and satis enough]
❑ **ass'et-stripper** n. **ass'et-stripping** n (now usu derog) the practice of acquiring control of a company and selling off its assets for financial gain.

asseverate /ə-sev'ə-rāt/ vt to declare solemnly (formerly, now archaic, **assev'er**). [L asseverāre, -ātum, from ad to, and sevērus serious; see severe]
■ **assev'erating** adj. **assev'eratingly** adv. **asseverā'tion** n.

assez bien /a-sā byẽ'/ (Fr) pretty well.

asshole see under **arse**.

assibilate /a- or ə-sib'i-lāt/ (phonetics) vt to sound as a sibilant. [L ad to, and sībilāre to hiss]
■ **assibilā'tion** n.

assiduity /a-si-dū'i-ti/ n persistent application or diligence; (in pl) constant attentions. [L assiduus, from ad to, at, and sedēre to sit]
■ **assiduous** /ə-sid'ū-əs/ adj constant or unwearied in application; unflagging, unremitting. **assid'uously** adv. **assid'uousness** n.

assiege /ə-sēj'/ (Spenser) vt to besiege. [See **siege**]

assiento /a-sē-en'tō/ (hist) n (pl **assien'tos**) a treaty (esp that between Spain and Britain, 1713) for the supply of African slaves for Spanish American dominions. [Sp (now asiento) seat, seat in a court, treaty]

assign /ə-sīn'/ vt to allot, share out; to designate, appoint; to put forward, adduce; to make over, transfer; to ascribe, refer; to specify; to fix, determine. ♦ n a person to whom any property or right is made over, an assignee (law); (in pl) appendages (Shakesp). [Fr assigner, from L assignāre to mark out, from ad to, and signum a mark or sign]
■ **assign'able** adj that may be assigned. **assignation** /as-ig-nā'shən/ n an appointment to meet, used chiefly of clandestine meetings between lovers and mostly with disapproval; the making over of any right to another (Scots law). **assignee** /as-īn-ē'/ n a person to whom any right or property is assigned; a person who receives a contractual right or liability under an assignment; a trustee of a sequestrated estate. **assignment** /-sīn'/ n the act of assigning; anything assigned; a legal process whereby contractual rights and liabilities may be transferred from an original contracting party to a third person; the writing by which such a transfer is made; a task, piece of work, etc allotted; (Spenser altered in 1596 to **dessignment**) design, enterprise. **assign'er** n. **assignor** /as-i-nör'/ n (law) a person who transfers a right or asset under an assignment.
❑ **assigning authority** n a national body authorized to assign load-lines to ships.

assignat /as'ig-nat or a-sēn-yä'/ (hist) n one of the paper bonds first issued in 1789 by the French government on the security of the appropriated church lands, and later (1790–97) accepted as notes of currency. [Fr]

assignation...to...assignor see under **assign**.

assimilate /ə-sim'i-lāt/ vt to make similar or like (with to or with); to convert into a substance similar to itself, as the body does to food; to take fully into the mind, experience effects of (eg knowledge); to receive and accept fully within a group, absorb; to modify (a speech sound), making it more like a neighbouring sound in a word or sentence (phonetics). ♦ vi to become like (with to); to be incorporated or absorbed (into). [L assimilāre, -ātum, from ad to, and similis like]
■ **assim'ilable** adj. **assimilā'tion** n. **assimilā'tionist** n a person who advocates a policy of assimilation, esp of racial groups (also adj). **assim'ilātive** or **assimilā'tory** adj having the power or tendency to assimilate. **assim'ilātor** n.

assist /ə-sist'/ vt to help (with work, etc, in a matter, etc); to work as an assistant to; to accompany or attend (Shakesp). ♦ vi to help (with or in); to be present at a ceremony, etc (now a Gallicism). ♦ n (chiefly N Am) an act that assists; help; a play that helps to make a goal possible (sport); a play that makes it possible for a batter or runner to be put out (baseball). [Fr assister, from L assistere to stand by, from ad to, and sistere to set, take one's stand]
■ **assis'tance** n help; relief. **assis'tant** adj helping. ♦ n a person who assists; a helper. **assis'tantship** n the post of assistant. **assis'ted** adj for which help (eg financial aid, additional power) is supplied. **assis'ter** n.
❑ **assistant referee** n (in football) one of the two officials who assist the referee, adjudicating on offsides and throw-ins (formerly called **linesman**). **assisted area** n an area within the European Union that is eligible for additional funds to generate economic activity. **assisted-liv'ing facility** n (US) a residential establishment where elderly, disabled, etc people receive regular care but maintain a degree of independence. **assisted place** n a place at an independent school, funded by the state. **assisted take-off** n a take-off in which the full power of an aircraft's normal engines is supplemented by eg turbojet, rocket motor units, or liquid rockets.

assize /ə-sīz'/ n (in pl) periodical sittings of judges on circuit, in England and Wales, with a jury (until 1972, when Crown Courts replaced them); a legislative sitting (hist); a statute settling the weight, measure, or price of anything (hist); a trial by jury (Scot); a jury (Scot); judgement, sentence (obs). ♦ vt (obs) to assess; to set or fix the quantity or price of. [OFr assise assembly of judges, set rate, from asseoir, from L assidēre, from ad to, and sedēre to sit]
■ **assiz'er** n an officer with responsibility for weights and measures; a juror (hist; Scots law).

Assoc. same as **Ass.**

associate /ə-sō'shi-āt or -si-/ vt to join, connect, link; to connect in one's mind; to make a colleague or partner; to accompany (Shakesp). ♦ vi to consort, keep company (with with); to combine or unite. ♦ adj /-ət or -āt/ associated; connected; confederate; joined as colleague or junior colleague; joined without full membership. ♦ n /-ət or -āt/ a person joined or connected with another; a colleague, companion, friend, partner or ally; a person admitted to a society without full membership. [L associāre, -ātum, from ad to, and socius a companion]
■ **associabil'ity** n. **asso'ciable** /-shi-ə-bl or -shə-bl/ adj capable of being associated. **asso'ciated** adj connected; (usu with caps) denoting a company that is amalgamated with another company. **asso'ciateship** n. **associā'tion** /-si- or -shi-/ n an act of associating; union or combination; a society of persons joined to promote some object; a plant or animal community, usu occupying a wide area, consisting of a definite population of species (biol); loose aggregation of molecules (chem); an old name for **association football** (see below); connection of thoughts or of feelings; (usu in pl) thought, feeling or memory, more or less permanently connected with eg a place, an occurrence, or something said; a relationship between the EU and certain other countries, eg in Africa and the Caribbean, being more than just a trade agreement but with the associated members not enjoying membership of the EU. **associa'tional** adj. **associa'tionism** n (psychol) the theory which considers association of ideas to be the basis of all mental activity. **asso'ciātive** adj tending to association; such that $(a*b)*c = a*(b*c)$, where * denotes a binary operation (maths). **associativity** /-ə-tiv'/ n. **asso'ciator** n.

❏ **associate professor** *n* in N America, Australia and New Zealand, a university or college teacher immediately below professor in rank. **association copy** *n* a copy of a book deriving additional interest from some association, eg a copy inscribed as given to or by some person of note. **association football** *n* (also **soccer**) a form of football, using a round ball, with 11 players on each side. **associative learning** *n* learning based on association of ideas (qv below). **associative memory** *n* (*comput* and *psychol*) a memory system in which a particular input is associated with a particular output. **associative storage** *n* (*comput*) a storage device in which information is identified by content rather than by address.

■ **association of ideas** mental linkage that facilitates recollection, eg by similarity, contiguity or repetition.

assoil[1] /ə-soil'/ *vt* to absolve, acquit (with *of* or *from*; *archaic*); to discharge, release (with *of* or *from*; *archaic*); to solve (*obs*); to dispel (*obs*); to determine (*obs*). [Anglo-Fr *assoilier*, from L *ab* from, and *solvere* to loose]

■ **assoil'ment** *n* (*archaic*) absolution. **assoilzie** /ə-soil'i or -yi/ *vt* to absolve (*obs Scot*); to free (a defender or accused) of a claim or charge (*Scots law*).

assoil[2] /ə-soil'/ (*archaic*; *non-standard*) *vt* to soil, sully, dirty.

assonance /as'ə-nəns/ *n* a correspondence in sound; vowel-rhyme, coincidence of vowel sound without regard to consonants, as in *mate* and *shape*, *feel* and *need*; extended to correspondence of consonants with different vowels; resemblance, correspondence. [L *assonāre*, *-ātum*, from *ad* to, and *sonāre* to sound]

■ **ass'onant** *adj*. **assonantal** /-ant'əl/ *adj*. **ass'onate** *vi* to correspond in vowel sound; to practise assonance.

assort /ə-sört'/ *vt* to distribute in classes, classify; to class, rank. ◆ *vi* to agree or be in accordance; to suit well; to keep company (*archaic*). [Fr *assortir*, from L *ad* to, and *sors*, *sortis* a lot]

■ **assort'ative** /-ə-tiv/ *adj*. **assort'ed** *adj* classified, arranged in sorts; made up of various sorts. **assort'edness** *n*. **assort'er** *n*. **assort'ment** *n* the act of assorting; a quantity or number of things assorted; a variety.

❏ **assortative mating** *n* (*bot*) non-random mating, resulting from eg pollinating insects.

assot /ə-sot'/ (*obs*) *vt* to befool, or besot. [OFr *asoter*, from *à* to, and *sot* fool; see **sot**[1]]

■ **assott'** or **assott'ed** *adj* (*Spenser*, etc) infatuated.

ASSR *abbrev*: Autonomous Soviet Socialist Republic (an administrative division within the former Soviet Union).

Asst or **asst** *abbrev*: Assistant or assistant.

assuage /ə-swāj'/ *vt* to soften, mitigate or allay. ◆ *vi* (*archaic*) to abate or subside; to diminish. [OFr *assouager*, from L *ad* to, and *suāvis* mild]

■ **assuage'ment** *n*. **assuag'ing** *n* and *adj*. **assuā'sive** /-siv/ *adj* soothing; mitigating.

assubjugate /ə-sub'jŭ-gāt/ (*Shakesp*) *vt* to reduce to subjection. [*a-*, intensive pfx, and **subjugate**]

assuefaction /ə-swi-fak'shən/ (*obs*) *n* habituation. [L *assuēfacere*, from *assuētus* accustomed, and *facere* to make]

assuetude /as'wi-tūd/ *n* accustomedness; habit. [L *assuētūdo*]

assume /ə-sūm' or -soom'/ *vt* to adopt, take in; to take up, take upon oneself; to take for granted; to claim without justification; to pretend to possess. ◆ *vi* to make undue claims; to be arrogant. [L *assūmere*, *assūmptum*, from *ad* to, and *sūmere* to take]

■ **assum'able** *adj*. **assum'ably** *adv*. **assumed'** *adj* appropriated, usurped; pretended, simulated; taken as the basis of argument. **assum'edly** *adv*. **assum'ing** *adj* haughty; arrogant. ◆ *n* assumption; arrogance; presumption. ◆ *conj* (often with *that*) if it can be taken for granted that. **assum'ingly** *adv*. **assumpsit** /ə-sump'sit/ *n* an action at common law, the historical basis of the modern law of contract, in which the plaintiff asserts that the defendant undertook (L *assūmpsit*) to perform a certain act and failed to fulfil his or her promise. **assumption** /-sum'- or -sump'-/ *n* an act of assuming; taking upon oneself; arrogance; taking for granted; supposition; that which is taken for granted or supposed; the minor premise in a syllogism (*logic*); a taking up bodily into heaven, *esp* the **Assumption of the Virgin**, celebrated on 15 August (declared a dogma of the Roman Catholic Church in 1950); reception, incorporation (*archaic*). **Assump'tionist** *n* a member of the Roman Catholic congregation (**Augustinians of the Assumption**) founded at Nîmes in 1843 (also *adj*). **assump'tive** *adj* of the nature of an assumption; gratuitously assumed; apt, or too apt, to assume.

■ **deed of assumption** (*Scots law*) a deed executed by trustees under a trust deed assuming a new trustee or settlement.

assure /ə-shoor'/ *vt* to make sure or secure; to give confidence; to tell positively; to insure; to betroth (*obs*). [OFr *aseürer* (Fr *assurer*), from LL *adsēcūrāre*, from *ad* to, and *sēcūrus* safe; see **sure**[1]]

■ **assur'able** *adj*. **assur'ance** *n* confidence; feeling of certainty; subjective certainty of one's salvation (*theol*); composure; self-confidence; unabashedness; audacity; a positive, confidence-giving declaration; insurance which provides for a future certainty rather than a possibility, now *esp* life insurance; security; the securing of a title to property (*law*); a promise; a surety, warrant; a betrothal (*obs*). **assured'** *adj* certain; confident; beyond doubt; insured; self-confident; over-bold; brazen-faced; secured; pledged; betrothed (*obs*). ◆ *n* a person whose life or property is insured; the beneficiary of an insurance policy. **assur'edly** *adv* certainly, in truth, undoubtedly (also *interj*); confidently (*archaic*). **assur'edness** *n*. **assur'er** *n* a person who gives assurance; an insurer or underwriter; a person who insures his or her life.

assurgent /ə-sûr'jənt/ *adj* rising, ascending; rising in a curve to an erect position (*bot*); depicted as rising from the sea (*heraldry*). [L *ad* to, and *surgere* to rise]

■ **assur'gency** *n* the tendency to rise.

asswage an obsolete spelling of **assuage**.

Assyrian /ə- or ə-sir'i-ən/ *adj* of or relating to the vast, ancient empire of *Assyria* in W Asia or the civilization, art, culture or language of the Assyrians. ◆ *n* an inhabitant or native of Assyria; the Semitic language of ancient Assyria; a modern form of an Aramaic dialect still spoken, Syriac.

■ **Assyriol'ogist** *n*. **Assyriol'ogy** *n* the science of Assyrian antiquities.

assythment /ə-sīth'mənt or -sīdh'/ (*Scots law*; now *hist*) *n* indemnification, or reparation, by someone who has caused a death, etc. [ME *aseth* amends, from OFr *aset*, adv mistaken for objective of nominative *asez*; see **asset**]

AST *abbrev*: advanced skills teacher; advanced supersonic transport; Alaska Standard Time; Atlantic Standard Time; automatic station tuning (*radio*).

astable /ā-stā'bl/ *adj* not stable; oscillating between two states (*elec*). [Gr *a-* (privative), and **stable**[1]]

astacology /a-stə-kol'ə-ji/ *n* the science of the crayfish or of breeding it. [Gr *astakos* lobster, crayfish, and **-logy**]

■ **astacological** /-loj'-/ *adj*. **astacol'ogist** *n*.

astarboard /ə-stär'börd/ (*naut*) *adv* on or towards the starboard. [**a-**[1]]

astare /ə-stär'/ (*archaic*) *adv* in a state of staring. [**a-**[1] and **stare**[1]]

astart /ə-stärt'/ (*Spenser*) *vi* to start up; to befall. ◆ *adv* with a start, suddenly. [Pfx *a-* up, and **start**]

Astarte /a-stär'ti/ (*myth*) *n* the Phoenician goddess of love, whose attributes symbolize the notion of productive power, identified with the Semitic goddess **Ashtaroth** /ash'tar-oth/ or **Ash'toreth** (*Bible*, etc) and the Assyrian and Babylonian **Ish'tar**, goddess of love and war. [L and Gr form of the name, from Phoenician '*strt*, related to Heb '*Ashtoreth*]

astatic /ā- or ə-stat'ik/ *adj* having no tendency to stand in a fixed position; without polarity, as a pair of magnetic needles set in opposite directions (*phys*). [Gr *astatos* unstable, from *a-* (privative), and *statos*, verbal adj of *histanai* to make to stand]

■ **astatine** /as'tə-tēn/ *n* a radioactive chemical element (symbol **At**; atomic no 85) of the halogen series.

astatki /a-stat'kē/ *n* the residue of petroleum-distillation, used as fuel. [Russ *ostatki*, pl of *ostatok* residue]

asteism /as'tē-i-zm/ (*rhetoric*) *n* refined irony. [Gr *asty*, *asteōs* a town (seen as a place of refinement)]

astely /a-stē'li/ (*bot*) *n* absence of a central cylinder or stele. [Gr *a-* (privative), and *stēlē* column]

■ **astē'lic** *adj*.

aster /as'tər/ *n* a plant of the *Aster* genus of Compositae, with showy radiated heads, white to lilac-blue or purple, flowering in late summer and autumn (hence often called Michaelmas daisies), or a related form; extended to the similar **China aster** (*Callistephus hortensis*) brought from China to France by a missionary in the 18c; a group of radiating fibrils, seen immediately prior to and during cell division (*biol*); a star (*obs*). [Gr *astēr* star]

-aster /-ə-stər/ *combining form* denoting: a poor imitation of; a person who has pretensions to being, as in *criticaster*, *poetaster*, *politicaster*. [L]

asteria see under **asterism**.

Asterias /ə-stēr'i-as/ *n* the common crossfish or fivefinger genus of sea urchins. [New L, from Gr, starred, from *astēr* star]

■ **as'terid** or **asterid'ian** *n* a starfish.

asterisk /as'tə-risk/ *n* a star-shaped mark (*) used as a reference to a note, as a mark of omission, as a mark of a word or root inferred to have existed but not recorded, and for other purposes. ◆ *vt* to mark with an asterisk. [LL *asteriscus* a small star, from Gr *asteriskos*, dimin of *astēr* a star]

■ **as'terisked** *adj*.

asterism /as'tə-ri-zm/ n a group of stars; three asterisks placed to direct attention to a passage; in some gemstones and minerals, the property of showing by reflected or transmitted light a star-shaped luminous figure due to inclusions or tubular cavities. [Gr *asterismos* a constellation]
■ **asteria** /as-tēr'i-ə/ n a precious stone that shows asterism when cut *en cabochon*. **astēr'iated** adj (*mineralogy*) showing asterism.

astern /ə-stûrn'/ (*naut*) adv in or towards the stern; behind. [**a-¹**]

asteroid /as't(ə-)roid/ n any of the thousands of rocky objects found generally in orbits between those of Mars and Jupiter (also, *esp* formerly, called a **minor planet**); a starfish, a member of the Asteroidea. ◆ adj resembling a star, star-shaped; of the Asteroidea. [Gr *asteroeidēs* star-like]
■ **asteroid'al** adj. **Asteroid'ea** n pl a class of echinoderms, the starfishes.

astert /ə-stûrt'/ (*obs*) vi same as **astart**.

asthenia /as-thē'ni-ə or -thi-nī'ə/ n (*med*) debility, loss of muscular strength. [Gr *astheneia*, from a- (privative), and *sthenos* strength]
■ **asthenic** /-then'ik/ adj of or relating to asthenia; lacking strength; of a slender body type, narrow-chested, with slight muscular development (*anthrop*); (of, or characteristic of, a person) belonging to a type thought prone to schizophrenia, having a small, light trunk and disproportionately long limbs (*psychol*). ◆ n a person of asthenic type. **asthenosphere** /-then'ə-sfēr/ n (*geol*) the upper mantle of the earth, a shell lying below, and softer and more readily able to yield to persistent stress than, the lithosphere.

asthma /as'mə, also asth', ast', and in N Am usu az'/ n a chronic disorder of the organs of respiration, characterized by difficulty of breathing, wheezing, and a tightness in the chest. [Gr *asthma, -atos*, from *aazein* to breathe with open mouth]
■ **asthmatic** /-mat'/ adj of or suffering from asthma. ◆ n a person suffering from asthma. **asthmat'ical** adj (*old*). **asthmat'ically** adv.

asthore /as-thōr'/ (*Anglo-Irish*) n darling. [Ir a *stóir*, vocative of *stór* treasure]

Asti /as'tē/ n an Italian white wine made round about *Asti* in the Monferrato hills in Piedmont.

astichous /as'ti-kəs/ (*bot*) adj not in rows. [Gr a- (privative), and *stichos* a row]

astigmatism /ə-stig'mə-ti-zm/ n a defect in an eye, lens or mirror, by which rays from a single point are focused as two short focal lines at right angles to each other and at different distances (also **astig'mia** /-mi-ə/). [Gr a- (privative), and *stigma, -atos* a point]
■ **astigmatic** /a-stig-mat'ik/ adj and n. **astigmat'ically** adv.

astilbe /a-stil'bi/ n a plant of the *Astilbe* genus of perennial plants of the family Saxifragaceae, with clusters of *usu* red or white flowers. [Gr a- (privative), and *stilbos* glittering]

astir /ə-stûr'/ adv on the move; out of bed, up and about; excited, roused; in motion. [**a-¹** and **stir¹**]

ASTM abbrev : American Society for Testing and Materials.

astomatous /a-stom'ə-təs or -stō'mə-/ (*bot* and *zool*) adj mouthless, or without a mouthlike opening (also **astomous** /as'tə-məs/). [Gr a- (privative), and *stoma, -atos* mouth]

astonish /ə-ston'ish/ vt to impress with sudden surprise or wonder; to amaze or shock; to daze or stun (*Shakesp*). —Earlier forms **astone**/ə-stun'/, **astony**/-ston'i/ and **astun'**. [Ult from L *ex* out, and *tonāre* to thunder]
■ **aston'ied** adj (*obs*) astonished. **aston'ished** adj amazed; dazed; stunned (*obs*). **aston'ishing** adj very wonderful, amazing; very surprising, extraordinary. **aston'ishingly** adv. **aston'ishment** n amazement; wonder; a cause for astonishment.

astoop /ə-stoop'/ (*archaic*) adv in a stooping position. [**a-¹** and **stoop¹**]

astound /ə-stownd'/ vt to amaze, to strike dumb with astonishment. ◆ adj (*archaic*) astounded. [From *astoned*, pap of **astone** (see **astonish**)]
■ **astound'ed** adj stunned; dazed; amazed. **astound'ing** adj. **astound'ingly** adv. **astound'ment** n (*archaic*).

astr. or **astron.** abbrev : astronomer; astronomical; astronomy.

astraddle /ə-strad'l/ adv with legs wide apart and *usu* on each side of something. [**a-¹**]

astragal /as'trə-gəl/ n a small semicircular moulding (often a beading) round a column or elsewhere (*archit*); a round moulding near the mouth of a cannon; a glazing bar in a window (*archit*; *Scot*); (in *pl*) dice (*obs*). [Gr *astragalos* a vertebra, ankle-bone, moulding, milk vetch, in *pl* (knucklebones used as) dice]
■ **astragalus** /as-trag'əl-əs/ n (*pl* **astrag'ali** /-ī/) one of the ankle-bones (*zool*); (with *cap*) the tragacanth and milk vetch genus.

astrakhan /as-trə-kan'/ n lambskin with curled wool from the Middle East; a rough fabric made in imitation of it. ◆ adj made of astrakhan; (of a lamb) of the type suitable for astrakhan production. [*Astrakhan*, a Russian city on the Caspian Sea]

astral /as'trəl/ adj belonging to the stars; starry; star-shaped; belonging to a mitotic aster (*biol*); in theosophy, of a supersensible substance supposed to pervade all space and enter into all bodies. [L *astrālis*, from *astrum* a star]
❑ **astral body** n (*theosophy*) an astral counterpart of the physical body; a ghost or wraith. **astral spirits** n pl spirits supposed to animate the heavenly bodies, forming, as it were, their souls.

astrand /ə-strand'/ adv on the strand. [**a-¹** and **strand¹**]

astrantia /ə-stran'shi-ə/ n a plant of the *Astrantia* genus of hardy, perennial umbelliferous plants with showy petal-like bracts. [Gr *astron* star]

astraphobia /a-strə-fō'bi-ə/ or **astrapophobia** /-strə-pə-fō'bi-ə/ n a morbid fear of (thunder and) lightning. [Gr *astrapē* lightning, and *phobos* fear]

astray /ə-strā'/ adv out of the right way, off course; out of the correct place; away from correct behaviour, wrong; in a lost state. [OFr *estraié*, from *estrayer*, from L *extravāgarī* to wander abroad]

Astrex see **Rex**.

astrict /ə-strikt'/ (*archaic*) vt to bind, to compress; to constipate (*med*); to restrict (*Scots law*). [L *astringere, astrictum*, from *ad* to, and *stringere* to draw tight]
■ **astric'tion** /-shən/ n constipation (*med*); obligation, binding (*obs*). **astric'tive** adj astringent (*med*); binding (*obs*).

astride /ə-strīd'/ adv in a striding position; with a leg on each side. ◆ prep astride of; on either side of. [**a-¹**]

astringe /ə-strinj'/ vt to draw together or tight, to compress (*med*); to constipate (*med*); to bind, oblige (*obs*). [Ety as for **astrict**]
■ **astrin'gency** n. **astrin'gent** adj having power to contract organic tissues (*med*); styptic (*med*); contracting, drawing together; (of eg manner) sharp, austere, severe; (of eg words, criticism) caustic, biting. ◆ n an astringent agent, eg a medical preparation, or a cosmetic lotion to tone the skin. **astrin'gently** adv.

astringer see **austringer**.

astro- /a-strō- or -strо-/ combining form denoting: star; celestial body; outer space; star-shaped; astrology. [Gr, from *astron* a star]

astrobiology /as-trō-bī-ol'ə-ji/ n the study of life in space. [**astro-**]
■ **astrobiol'ogist** n.

astrobleme /a'strō-blēm/ n a depression in the earth's surface caused by an ancient meteorite or comet. [**astro-** and Gr *blema* shot, wound]

astrochemistry /as-trō-kem'i-stri/ n the study of molecules and radicals in outer space. [**astro-**]

astrocompass /as'trō-kum-pəs/ n an instrument for determining the direction of an aircraft by taking readings from a star. [**astro-**]

astrocyte /as'trə-sīt/ n (*anat* and *zool*) a much-branched, star-shaped neuroglia cell. [**astro-**]
■ **astrocytō'ma** n (*pl* **astrocytō'mas** or **astrocytō'mata**) a tumour of the central nervous system, composed largely of astrocytes.

astrodome /as'trə-dōm/ n a small transparent observation dome on the top of the fuselage of an aeroplane, for astronomical observations; a sports centre covered by a huge translucent dome, *orig* one at Houston, Texas. [**astro-**]

astrodynamics /as-trō-dī-nam'iks/ n sing the science of the motion of bodies in outer space and the forces that act on them. [**astro-**]
■ **astrodynam'icist** n.

astrofell see **astrophel**.

astrogeology /as-trō-jē-ol'ə-ji/ n the study of the geology of the moon, etc. [**astro-**]
■ **astrogeol'ogist** n.

astroid /as'troid/ (*maths*) n a hypocycloid with four cusps. [**astro-** and **-oid**]

astrol. abbrev : astrological; astrology.

astrolabe /as'trə-lāb/ n an ancient instrument for showing the positions of the sun and bright stars at any given time, or for taking altitudes above the horizon. [**astro-** and *-labe*, from *lab-*, root of Gr *lambanein* to take]

astrolatry /ə-strol'ə-tri/ n star-worship. [**astro-** and Gr *latreia* worship]

astrology /ə-strol'ə-ji/ n the study of the supposed influence of the movements and positions of the stars and planets on human and terrestrial affairs (formerly called **judicial astrology**); *orig* practical astronomy (*obs*). [L *astrologia* (early) astronomy, from Gr *astron* star, and *logos* discourse]
■ **astrol'oger** or **astrol'ogist** n. **astrolog'ic** or **astrolog'ical** adj. **astrolog'ically** adv.

astrometeorology /as-trō-mēt-i-ə-rol'ə-ji or -mēt-yə-/ n the study of the influence, or supposed influence, of the stars, planets, etc on climate and weather. [**astro-**]

astrometry /a-strom'ə-tri/ n the precise measurement of position in astronomy. [**astro-**]
■ **astrōmet'ric** adj. **astrōmet'rical** adv.

astron. see **astr.**

astronaut /as'trə-nöt/ n a person engaged in space travel. [**astro-** and -**naut**, from Gr nautēs a sailor]
■ **astronaut'ic** or **astronaut'ical** adj. **astronaut'ically** adv. **astronaut'ics** n sing the science of travel in space.

astronavigation /as-trō-na-vi-gā'shən/ n the navigation of aircraft, spacecraft or sailing craft by means of observation of the stars. [**astro-**]

astronomy /ə-stron'ə-mi/ n the scientific study of the celestial bodies and the heavens. [astronomia, from Gr astron star, and nomos law]
■ **astron'omer** n. **astronom'ical** or **astronom'ic** adj relating to astronomy; prodigiously great, like the distance of the stars (inf). **astronom'ically** adv. **astron'omize** or **-ise** vi to study astronomy.
❑ **Astronomer Royal** n an honorary title awarded to a distinguished British astronomer; until 1972, the director of the Royal Greenwich Observatory. **astronomical time** see **time**. **astronomical unit** n the earth's mean distance from the sun, about 92.9 million miles, used as a measure of distance within the solar system (abbrev **AU**). **astronomical year** see under **year**.

astrophel or **astrofell** /as'trō-fel/ (Spenser) n an unidentified bitter starlike plant, suggested to be the seaside aster. [Poss Gr astron star, and phyllon leaf]

astrophotography /as-trō-fə-tog'rə-fi/ n photography of celestial bodies for astronomical study. [**astro-**]
■ **astrophotographic** /-fō-tə-graf'ik/ adj.

astrophysics /as-trō-fiz'iks/ n sing the branch of astronomy which applies the laws of physics to the study of the stars and interstellar matter. [**astro-**]
■ **astrophys'ical** adj. **astrophys'icist** n.

AstroTurf® /as'trō-tûrf/ n an artificial surface for sports pitches, etc, having a woven, grass-like pile on a rubber base. [From its use in the Houston Astrodome]

astrut /ə-strut'/ (archaic) adv protrudingly; distendedly. ◆ adj protruding; distended. [**a-¹** and **strut¹**]

astucious, astuciously, astucity see under **astute**.

astun see **astonish**.

astute /a- or ə-stūt' or (US) -stoot'/ adj shrewd; perceptive, sagacious; wily. [L astūtus, from astus craft]
■ **astucious** /-tū'shəs/ adj (Walter Scott) astute. **astu'ciously** adv (Walter Scott). **astucity** /-tū'si-ti/ n. **astute'ly** adv. **astute'ness** n.

astylar /a-stī'lər/ (archit) adj without columns. [Gr a- (privative), and stȳlos a column]

asudden /ə-sud'ən/ (archaic) adv suddenly. [**a-¹**]

asunder /ə-sun'dər/ adv apart; into parts; separately. [**a-¹**]

ASW abbrev : antisubmarine warfare.

aswarm /ə-swörm'/ adv in swarms. [**a-¹**, and **swarm¹**]

asway /ə-swā'/ adv swayingly. [**a-¹**]

aswim /ə-swim'/ (archaic) adv afloat. [**a-¹**]

aswing /ə-swing'/ (archaic) adv swingingly; in a swing. [**a-¹**]

aswirl /ə-swûrl'/ adv in a swirl. [**a-¹**]

aswoon /ə-swoon'/ (archaic) adv in a swoon. [Poss for on or in swoon; or orig a pap, ME iswowen, from OE geswōgen swooned (not known in other parts of speech)]

asylum /ə-sī'ləm/ n (pl **asy'lums**) a place of refuge for debtors and for those accused of crime; an institution for the care or relief of the unfortunate, such as the blind or (old) mentally ill; (any place of) refuge or protection; political asylum. [L asylum, from Gr asylon (neuter) inviolate, from a- (privative), and sȳlon, sȳlē right of seizure]
■ **asylee'** n (chiefly US) a person who has been granted asylum.
❑ **asylum seeker** n a person who migrates to another country seeking political asylum.
■ **political asylum** protection given to a person by one country from arrest in another; refuge provided by a country to a person leaving his or her own without the permission of its government.

asymmetry /ā- or a-sim'ə-tri/ n lack of symmetry, irregularity of form or arrangement. [Gr asymmetriā, from a- (privative), and symmetriā symmetry]
■ **asymmetric** /-et'rik/ or **asymmet'rical** adj. **asymmet'rically** adv. **Asymmetron** /-sim'ə-tron/ n one of the genera of marine organisms making up the lancelets.

❑ **asymmetrical warfare** n warfare between forces with different military capabilities, in which the weaker force uses tactics such as guerrilla attacks.

asymptomatic /ā- or a-sim(p)'tə-ma-tik/ adj having, displaying or producing no symptoms. [**a-²**]
■ **asymptomat'ically** adv.

asymptote /a'sim(p)-tōt/ (maths) n a line (usu straight) that continually approaches a curve but never meets it. [Gr asymptōtos, from a- (privative), syn together, and ptōtos apt to fall, from piptein to fall]
■ **asymptotic** /-tot'ik/ or **asymptot'ical** adj. **asymptot'ically** adv.

asynartete /a-sin'är-tēt/, also **asynartetic** /-tet'ik/ (prosody) adj not connected, consisting of parts having different rhythms. ◆ n a verse of such a kind. [Gr asynartētos, from a- (privative), syn together, and artaein to knit]

asynchronism /ā- or ə-sing'krə-ni-zm/ n lack of synchronism or correspondence in time (also **asyn'chrony**). [Gr a- (privative), syn together, and chronos time]
■ **asyn'chronous** adj. **asyn'chronously** adv.
❑ **asynchronous transmission** n transmission of electronic data along communication lines, in which the end of the transmission of one character or packet of data initiates the transmission of the next.

asyndeton /ə-sin'də-ton/ (rhetoric; grammar) n (pl **asyn'deta**) a sentence or construction in which the conjunctions are omitted. [Gr asyndeton, from a- (privative), and syndetos bound together, from syn together, and deein to bind]
■ **asyndet'ic** adj.

asynergy /ə- or ā-sin'ər-ji/ (med) n lack of co-ordination in action, eg of muscles (also **asyner'gia**). [Gr a- (privative), syn together, and ergon work]

asyntactic /ā- or a-sin-tak'tik/ adj loosely put together, irregular, ungrammatical. [Gr asyntaktikos, from a- (privative), and syntaktos, from syntassein to put in order together]

asystole /a-sis'to-lē or ā-/ (med) n inability of the heart to pump out blood (also **asys'tolism**). [Gr a- (privative), and systolē contraction]

AT abbrev : administrative trainee; alternative technology; anti-tank; appropriate technology; Atlantic Time.

At (chem) symbol : astatine.

at¹ /at or ət/ prep denoting (precise) position in space or time, or some similar relation, such as amount, response, occupation, aim, activity. [OE æt ; cf Gothic and ON at, L ad, Sans adhi]
❑ **at-bat'** or **at bat** n (baseball) a player's turn to bat. **at-home'** n a reception held in a person's own house. **at it** occupied in a particular way, doing a particular thing; up to some criminal activity (inf); having sexual intercourse (inf). **at that** see under **that**.
■ **get someone at it** to make someone excited, worked up or agitated. **where it's at** see under **where**.

at² /at/ n a monetary unit of Laos, $\frac{1}{100}$ of a kip. [Thai]

ATA abbrev : Air Transport Association (US); Air Transport Auxiliary.

atabal /at'ə-bal or ä-tä-bäl'/ n a Moorish kettledrum. [Sp, from Ar at-tabl the drum]

atabeg /ä-tä-beg'/ or **atabek** /-bek'/ (hist) n a Turkish ruler or high official. [Turk atabeg, from ata father, and beg prince]

atabrin or **atebrin** /at'ə-brin/ n mepacrine.

atacamite /ə-tak'ə-mīt/ n a mineral, a basic chloride of copper. [Atacama, in Chile]

atactic see under **ataxia**.

ataghan same as **yatagan**.

atalaya /ä-tä-lä'yä/ n a watchtower. [Sp, from Ar]

ataman /at'a-man/ n (pl **at'amans**) a Cossack headman or general, a hetman. [Russ, from Ger Hauptmann, from Haupt head, and Mann man]

AT&T abbrev : American Telephone and Telegraph Company.

atap or **attap** /at'ap/ n the nipa palm; its leaves used for thatching. [Malay]

ataraxia /a-tə-rak'si-ə/ or **ataraxy** /a'tə-rak-si/ n tranquillity, the freedom from anxiety orig aspired to by the Epicureans, Stoics and Sceptics; a state of calmness, tranquillity (med). [Gr ataraxiā, from a- (privative), and tarassein to disturb]
■ **atarac'tic** or **atarax'ic** adj and n (a) tranquillizing (drug).

à tâtons /a tä-tɔ̃'/ (Fr) gropingly.

atavism /at'ə-vi-zm/ n the reappearance of ancestral, but not parental, characteristics; reversion to an ancestral, or to a primitive, type. [L atavus a great-great-great-grandfather, an ancestor, from avus a grandfather]
■ **atavist'ic** adj. **atavist'ically** adv.

ataxia /a-tak'si-ə/ or **ataxy** /a-tak'si or at'ak-si/ n inability to co-ordinate voluntary movements (med; see **locomotor ataxia** under

locomotive); lack of order (obs). [Gr ataxiā disorder, from a-
(privative), and taxis order]
■ **atact'ic** or **atax'ic** adj.

at-bat see under **at¹**.

ATC abbrev : air-traffic control; Air Training Corps; automatic train
control.

atchieve see **achieve**.

ATD abbrev : actual time of departure.

Ate /ā'tē, ä'tē or ä'tā/ n the Greek goddess of mischief and of all rash
actions and their results.

ate /et or āt/ pat of **eat**.

-ate /-āt or -at/ adj sfx indicating possession of a characteristic, as in
affectionate, roseate. ◆ n sfx denoting: office, rank, or group, as in
inspectorate ; the product of a chemical process, as in condensate ; a
salt, as in phosphate. [L -atus, ending of the past participle in the 1st
conjugation]

atebrin see **atabrin**.

atelectasis /a-te-lek'tə-sis or a-ti-/ (med) n incomplete inflation of a
lung at birth; the collapse of a lung in an adult. [Gr atelēs incomplete,
and ektasis stretching out]
■ **atelectatic** /-tat'ik/ adj.

ateleiosis /ə-te-lī-ō'sis, -li- or -tē-/ (med) n dwarfism without
disproportion. [Gr ateleiōtos insufficient, from a- (privative), and telos
an end]

atelier /at'ə-lyā/ n a workshop, esp an artist's studio. [Fr]

a tempo /ä tem'pō/ (music) in time, ie revert to the previous or original
tempo. [Ital]

atemporal /ā-tem'pə-rəl/ adj without consideration of time. [a-² and
temporal¹]
■ **atemporal'ity** n.

à terre /a ter'/ (Fr) on the ground; with the foot (usu both feet) flat on
the ground (ballet).

ATF (US) abbrev : Bureau of Alcohol, Tobacco and Firearms.

Athabascan or **Athabaskan** /a-thə-bas'kən/ n a group of Native
American languages including Apache and Navajo; a speaker of one
of these languages (also **Athapasc'an** or **Athapask'an**). ◆ adj of or
relating to this group of languages. [Cree Athapaskaaw scattered grass
or reeds]

athame /ə-thä'mä or a'thə-/ n a double-sided dagger used in pagan
rituals. [Origin uncertain]

Athanasian /a-thə-nā'sh(y)ən or -z(h)yən/ adj relating to Athanasius
(c.296–373AD), Archbishop of Alexandria, or to the Christian creed
erroneously attributed to him.

athanasy /ə-than'ə-si/ n deathlessness. [Gr athanasiā, from a-
(privative), and thanatos death]

Atharvaveda /ä-tär'vä-vä'dä/ (Hinduism) n one of the Vedas,
comprising spells, charms and exorcistic chants. [Sans, from atharvan
fire-priest, and veda knowledge]

atheism /ā'thē-i-zm/ n disbelief in the existence of a god. [Gr atheos,
from a- (privative), and theos god]
■ **a'theist** n. **atheist'ic** or **atheist'ical** adj. **atheist'ically** adv. **a'theize**
or **-ise** vi to talk or write as an atheist. ◆ vt to render godless; to make
an atheist of. **a'theous** adj (Milton) atheistic; godless.

atheling /ath'ə-ling/ (hist) n a member of a noble family; later, a prince
of the blood-royal, or the heir apparent. [OE ætheling, from æthele
noble; cf Ger Adel]

athematic /a- or ā-thi-mat'ik/ adj without a thematic vowel (grammar
and linguistics); not using themes as a basis (music). [a-²]
■ **athemat'ically** adv.

Athene /a-thē'nē/ or **Athena** /-nə/ n the Greek goddess of wisdom,
born from the head of Zeus, tutelary goddess of Athens, identified by
the Romans with Minerva.
■ **Athenaeum** /ath-ə-nē'əm/ n a temple of Athene; an ancient
institution of learning, or literary university; a name sometimes taken
by a literary institution, library, or periodical.

Athenian /ə-thē'ni-ən/ adj of Athens, the capital of Greece. ◆ n a native
or citizen of Athens or Attica.

atheology /ā-thē-ol'ə-ji/ n opposition to theology. [a-²]
■ **atheological** /-ə-loj'i-kl/ adj.

atherine /ath'ə-rīn/ adj belonging or relating to a genus (Atherina)
of small fishes of a family (**Atherinidae** /-in'i-dē/) similar to the
grey mullets, sometimes sold as smelt. ◆ n an atherine fish. [Gr
atherīnē]

athermancy /ə-thûr'mən-si/ (phys) n impermeability to radiant heat.
[Gr a- (privative), and thermainein to heat]
■ **ather'manous** adj.

atheroma /a-thə-rō'mə/ (pathol) n (pl athero'mas or athero'mata) a
cyst with contents of a porridge-like consistency; atherosclerosis. [Gr
athērōma, from athērē and athare porridge]
■ **atherogen'esis** n. **atherogen'ic** adj causing atheroma.
athero'matous adj. **atherosclero'sis** /-ō'sis/ n the thickening of
the inner coat of arteries by deposition of cholesterol and
other substances, the most significant form of arteriosclerosis.
atherosclerotic /-ot'ik/ n and adj.

athetesis /a-thi-tē'sis/ n rejection (of a passage of text) as spurious. [Gr
athetēsis rejection, from a- (privative), and the root of tithenai to set]
■ **ath'etize** or **-ise** vt to reject.

athetosis /a-thi-tō'sis/ (pathol) n slow, involuntary writhing
movement of fingers and toes due to a lesion of the brain. [Gr athetos
without position, set aside, and **-osis** (2)]
■ **ath'etoid** adj. **athetos'ic** or **athetot'ic** adj.

a'thing see under **a'**.

athirst /ə-thûrst'/ adj thirsty; (with for) eager, avid. [OE ofthyrst ; see
thirst]

athlete /ath'lēt/ n a person who takes part in vigorous physical
exercise, orig and esp in contests of strength, speed, endurance or
agility; a person who is active and vigorous in body or mind. [Gr
athlētēs, from athlos contest]
■ **athlē'ta** n (obs) an athlete. **athletic** /-let'ik/ adj relating to athletics;
of, like or suitable for an athlete; strong, vigorous; of a long-limbed,
large-chested muscular type of body (anthrop). **athlet'ically** adv.
athlet'icism /-i-sizm/ n practice of, training in, or devotion to,
athletics; vigorous strength. **athlet'ics** n pl or n sing athletic sports. ◆ n
sing the practice of athletic sports.
❏ **athlete's foot** n a contagious disease of the foot, caused by a
fungus. **athletic support** n (a more formal word for) a jockstrap.

at-home see under **at¹**.

-athon /-ə-thon/ or **-thon** /-thon/ combining form denoting something
long in terms of time and endurance, usu a prolonged fund-raising
event, eg telethon, talkathon, walkathon. [After marathon]

athrill /ə-thril'/ (archaic) adv in a thrill, thrilling. [a-¹]

athrob /ə-throb'/ adj and adv with throbs, throbbing. [a-¹]

athrocyte /ath'rə-sīt or -rō-/ (biol; obs) n a cell having the ability to
absorb and store foreign matter. [Gr athroos in a group, crowded, and
-cyte]
■ **athrocytō'sis** n (pl **athrocytō'sēs**).

athwart /ə-thwört'/ prep across. ◆ adv sideways; transversely; awry;
wrongly; perplexingly. [a-¹]

atilt /ə-tilt'/ adv on a tilt; as a tilter (hist). [a-¹ and **tilt¹**]

atimy /at'i-mi/ n loss of honour; in ancient Athens, loss of civil rights,
public disgrace. [Gr atimiā, from a- (privative), and timē honour]

atingle /ə-ting'gl/ adj and adv in a tingle. [a-¹ and **tingle¹**]

a-tishoo or **atishoo** /ə-tish'oo/ (inf) n and interj (an imitation of) the
sound of a sneeze.

Ativan® /at'i-van/ n a proprietary name for lorazepam, a drug used to
treat anxiety or insomnia, a tranquillizer for short-term use.

Atkins see **Tommy Atkins** under **tommy**.

Atkins diet /at'kinz dī'ət/ n a high-protein, low-carbohydrate diet
intended to cause rapid weight loss. [Dr Robert Atkins (1930–2003),
US physician who devised it]

ATL abbrev : Association of Teachers and Lecturers.

Atlantean, **Atlantes** see **Atlas**.

Atlantic /ət- or at-lan'tik/ adj of, bordering on or relating to the Atlantic
Ocean; of or relating to Atlas, Atlantean (obs). ◆ n the Atlantic Ocean,
extending from the Arctic to the Antarctic, separating the continents of
Europe and Africa from N and S America. [L atlanticus, from Gr
atlantikos of Atlas (see **Atlas**)]
■ **Atlan'ticism** n the policy of close co-operation between N America
and W Europe. **Atlan'ticist** n. **Atlan'tis** n a legendary vanished island
in the Atlantic Ocean.
❏ **Atlantic Charter** n an Anglo-American declaration during the
Second World War of eight common principles of right in future
peace. **Atlantic seal** n the grey seal. **Atlantic Standard Time** or
Atlantic Time n one of the standard times used in N America, being 4
hours behind Greenwich Mean Time (abbrev **AST** or **AT**).

Atlantosaurus /ət-lan'tə-sö-rəs/ n a gigantic lizard-hipped, four-
footed, herbivorous Jurassic dinosaur of Colorado and Wyoming.
[New L, from Gr Atlas, Atlantos (see **Atlas**), and sauros lizard]

ATLAS /at'ləs/ abbrev : automated telephone line address system, a
memory store in which the operator can store programmed telephone
numbers for calls required later in the day; automatic tabulating, listing
and sorting package, a software package for these purposes.

Atlas /at'ləs/ n the Titan who held up the heavens on his shoulders (Gr
myth); the African mountain range into which Atlas was transformed

(*Gr myth*); a figure of a man serving as a column in a building (*pl* **Atlantes** /at-lan'tēz/). [Gr *Atlas, Atlantos*]

■ **Atlante'an** *adj* of Atlas; gigantic; of Atlantis.

atlas[1] /at'ləs/ *n* (*pl* **at'lases**) a book containing maps and often geographical information; the first cervical vertebra, supporting the skull (*anat*); before metrication, a size of drawing paper. [From **Atlas**, whose figure used to appear on title pages of atlases]

atlas[2] /at'ləs/ (*obs*) *n* a satin manufactured in Asia. [Ar]

atlatl /at'ə-lā-təl/ or /at'la-tl/ *n* a Native American throwing stick; an ancient Mexican spear-thrower. [Nahuatl, spear-thrower]

ATM *abbrev* : anti-tank missile; asynchronous transfer mode (*comput*); automated (or automatic) teller machine.

atm. *abbrev* : atmosphere (unit of pressure); atmospheric.

atman /ät'mən/ (*Hinduism*) *n* the divine within the self, the essential self. [Sans *ātman* self, soul]

atmology /at-mol'ə-ji/ (*phys*) *n* the science of the phenomena of aqueous vapour. [Gr *atmos* vapour, and *logos* discourse]

■ **atmol'ogist** *n*.

atmolysis /at-mol'i-sis/ (*phys* and *chem*) *n* a method of separating mixed gases by their different rates of passage through a porous septum. [Gr *atmos* vapour, and *lysis* loosing, from *lyein* to loose]

■ **at'molyse** or (*N Am*) **-yze** /-līz/ *vt*.

atmometer /at-mom'i-tər/ (*phys* and *bot*) *n* an instrument for measuring the rate of evaporation from a moist surface. [Gr *atmos* vapour, and *metron* measure]

atmosphere /at'məs-fēr/ *n* the gaseous envelope that surrounds the earth or any of the celestial bodies; any gaseous medium; a unit of atmospheric pressure equal to the pressure exerted by a column of mercury 760 millimetres in height at 0°C, practically the same as standard atmosphere (see under **standard**); the air or climate in a place; a feeling of space and distance in a picture; any surrounding influence or pervading feeling (*fig*). [Gr *atmos* vapour, and *sphaira* a sphere]

■ **atmospher'ic** /-fer'ik/ or **atmospher'ical** *adj* of or depending on the atmosphere; having a perceptible atmosphere (eg of a place, music, etc). **atmospher'ically** *adv*. **atmospher'ics** *n pl* noises interfering with radio reception, due to electric disturbances in the ether. □ **atmospheric engine** *n* an early variety of steam engine in which the steam is admitted only to the underside of the piston. **atmospheric hammer** *n* a hammer driven by compressed air. **atmospheric perspective** *n* aerial perspective. **atmospheric pollution** *n* harmful concentrations of gases and aerosols in the atmosphere. **atmospheric pressure** *n* the pressure exerted by the atmosphere at the surface of the earth due to the weight of the air.

at. no. or **at. numb.** *abbrev* : atomic number.

ATOC *abbrev* : Association of Train Operating Companies.

atoc see **atok**.

atocia /a-tō'shi-ə/ (*zool*) *n* sterility in a female. [Gr *atokiā*, from *a-* (privative), and *tokos* birth, offspring]

■ **atoke** /at'ōk/ *n* the sexless part in certain polychaete worms. **atokous** /at'ə-kəs/ or **at'okal** *adj* without offspring.

atok or **atoc** /a-tok'/ *n* a species of skunk. [Quechua]

atoke, etc see under **atocia**.

atoll /at'ol or ə-tol'/ *n* a coral island consisting of a circular belt of coral enclosing a central lagoon. [Name in Maldive Islands]

atom /at'əm/ *n* the smallest particle in an element which can take part in a chemical reaction, consisting of a nucleus and one or more orbiting electrons (*chem*); a hypothetical particle of matter so small as to be incapable of further division, according to atomic philosophy (see below); anything very small. [Gr *atomos*, from *a-* (privative), and *tomos*, verbal adj of *temnein* to cut]

■ **atomic** /ə-tom'ik/ *adj* relating to atoms; obtained by means of atomic fission, as *atomic energy* or *atomic power*; driven by atomic power, as *atomic aircraft-carrier, submarine*, etc; heated by atomic power, as *atomic radiator*. **atom'ical** *adj*. **atom'ically** *adv*. **atomicity** /at-əm-is'i-ti/ *n* (*chem*) the state or fact of being composed of atoms; the number of atoms in a molecule; valency. **at'omism** *n* the doctrine that atoms arranged themselves into the universe; atomic philosophy; the atomic theory; a theory that mental processes and psychological states can be analysed into simple elements (*psychol*). **at'omist** *n* a person who believes in atomism. **atomis'tic** *adj*. **atomist'ically** *adv*. **atomizā'tion** or **-s-** *n* the reduction of liquids to the form of spray; reduction into small units, splintering, fragmentation. **at'omize** or **-ise** *vt* to reduce to atoms; to reduce (a liquid or solid) to a fine spray or minute particles; to destroy by atomic weapons. **atomi'zer** or **-s-** *n* an instrument for discharging liquids in a fine spray. **at'omy** *n* (*archaic*) an atom, or mote; a pygmy (*Shakesp*).

□ **atom** (or **atomic**) **bomb** *n* a nuclear device in which quantities of uranium-235 or plutonium are forced to become critical with the result that their nuclei are bombarded by neutrons and split with explosive transformation of part of their mass into energy. **atomic clock** *n* a clock in which, to achieve greater accuracy, the oscillations of a quartz crystal (qv) are regulated by the vibration of certain atoms such as a caesium atom. **atomic energy** *n* nuclear energy. **atomic mass unit** *n* $\frac{1}{12}$ of the mass of an atom of carbon-12. **atomic number** *n* the number of units of charge of positive electricity on the nucleus of an atom of an element. **atomic philosophy** *n* a system of philosophy enunciated by Democritus, which taught that the ultimate constituents of all things are indivisible particles, differing in form and in their relations to each other. **atomic pile** *n* an early name for a device for the controlled release of nuclear energy, eg a lattice of small rods of natural uranium embedded in a mass of pure graphite which serves to slow down neutrons. **atomic power, atomic radiator** see **atomic** above. **atomic second** *n* a time interval whose measurement uses the frequency of radiation emitted or absorbed during transition from one energy state to another of a chosen atom. **atomic theory** *n* the hypothesis that all atoms of the same element are alike and that a compound is formed by union of atoms of different elements in some simple ratio. **atomic time** *n* time whose unit is the atomic second. **atomic transmutation** *n* the change of one type of atom to another as a result of a nuclear reaction. **atomic volume** *n* the atomic weight of an element divided by its density. **atomic warfare** *n* warfare using atomic weapons. **atomic weight** *n* relative atomic mass (qv under **relate**). **a'tom-smasher** *n* (*inf*) an apparatus for breaking up the atom, an accelerator.

■ **Atomic Energy Authority** and **Atomic Energy Commission** the respective bodies in Britain and the USA responsible for the development and control of atomic energy. **primeval atom** a hypothetical dense conglomerate from whose explosion 60 thousand million years ago the universe was (according to one theory) gradually formed.

atomy[1] /at'ə-mi/ (*Shakesp*) *n* a skeleton or walking skeleton. [Formerly also *atamy* and *natomy*, for **anatomy**, mistakenly divided *an atomy*]

atomy[2] see under **atom**.

atonal, etc see under **atony**.

atone (or *obs* **attone**) /ə-tōn'/ *vi orig* to make *at one*, to reconcile (*obs*); to give satisfaction or make reparation (*for*); to make up for deficiencies; to agree, be in accordance (*Shakesp*). ◆ *vt* to appease, to expiate; to harmonize, or reconcile (*obs*). ◆ *adv* (*obs*) at one, at once, together. [*at one*]

■ **atone'ment** *n* the act of atoning; expiation; reparations; the reconciliation of God and man by means of the incarnation and death of Christ (*theol*); reconciliation (*obs*). **aton'er** *n*. **aton'ingly** *adv*. **attonce** /ə-tons'/ or **attones** /ə-tōnz'/ *adv* (both *Spenser*) at once; together.

atony /at'ə-ni/ *n* lack of muscle tone, energy or strength, debility (*med*); lack of stress or accent (*prosody*). [Gr *atoniā*, from *a-* (privative), and *tonos* tone, strength]

■ **atonal** /ā-tō'nl/ or *a-/ adj* (*music*) not referred to any scale or tonic. **atō'nalism** *n*. **atō'nalist** *n*. **atonality** /at-ə-nal'i-ti/ *n*. **atō'nally** *adv*. **atonic** /a-ton'ik/ *adj* without tone (*prosody*); unaccented (*prosody*); (of a muscle) relaxed, lacking tone (*med*); debilitated (*med*). **atonic'ity** /-is'/ *n* atony.

atop /ə-top'/ *adv* on or at the top. ◆ *prep* on top of. [**a-**[1] and **top**[1]]

atopy /at'ə-pi* or *ā'tə-pi/ (*med*) *n* hypersensitivity with an inherited tendency to acute allergic reaction, but without predisposition to any particular type of allergic reaction. [Gr *atopia* strangeness, from *a-* (privative), and *topos* place]

■ **atopic** /-top'/ *adj*.

à tort et à travers /a tor' ā a tra-ver'/ (*Fr*) at random.

atorvastatin /ə-tör-və-stat'in/ *n* a statin drug used to lower the amount of fatty substances, *esp* cholesterol, in the blood.

à toute force /a toot fors'/ (*Fr*) by all means, absolutely.

à tout hasard /a too a-zār'/ (*Fr*) on the off chance.

à tout prix /a too prē'/ (*Fr*) at any price.

à tout propos /a too prō-pō'/ (*Fr*) on every occasion.

ATP *abbrev* : adenosine triphosphate; advanced turboprop; Automatic Train Protection.

atrabilious /a-trə-bil'yəs or -i-əs/ (*archaic*) *adj* having a melancholy temperament; hypochondriac; splenetic, acrimonious. [L *āter, ātra* black, and *bīlis* gall, bile]

■ **atrabil'iousness** *n*.

atracurium /a-trə-kū'ri-əm/ *n* a muscle-relaxing drug used in surgery.

atrament /at'rə-mənt/ (*archaic*) *n* blacking; ink; any black fluid, such as that emitted by the octopus. [From L *ātrāmentum* ink, from *āter* black]

■ **atrament'al** or **atrament'ous** adj.

à travers /a tra-ver'/ (Fr) across, through.

atrazine /at'rə-zēn/ n a widely used chemical weedkiller ($C_8H_{14}N_5Cl$), a white crystalline compound. [amino triazine]

atremble /ə-trem'bl/ (archaic or poetic) adv in a tremble. [**a-¹**]

atresia /ə-trē'zh(y)ə/ (anat) n absence of, or closure of, a passage in the body. [Formed from Gr trēsis perforation]

atrioventricular /ā-tri-ō-ven-trik'ū-lər/ adj of or affecting both the atria and the ventricles of the heart. [**atrium** and **ventricle**]

atrip /ə-trip'/ (naut) adv (of an anchor when it is just drawn out of the ground) in a perpendicular position; (of a sail) when it is hoisted from the cap, sheeted home and ready for trimming. [**a-¹**]

atrium /ā' or ā'tri-əm or -ūm/ n (pl **a'tria** or sometimes **a'triums**) the entrance hall or chief apartment of an ancient Roman house; a church forecourt or vestibule; a central courtyard (archit); a cavity or entrance (zool and anat); specif either of the two upper cavities of the heart into which blood passes from the veins. [L ātrium]

■ **a'trial** adj.

atrocious /ə-trō'shəs/ adj extremely cruel or wicked; awful, heinous; very grievous; appalling, execrable. [L ātrōx or atrōx cruel]

■ **atro'ciously** adv. **atro'ciousness** n. **atrocity** /ə-tros'i-ti/ n atrociousness; an atrocious act.

Atropa see under **Atropos**.

atrophy /at'rə-fi/ n wasting away; degeneration; diminution of size and functional activity by disuse; emaciation. ◆ vt and vi (lit and fig) to (cause to) suffer atrophy; to starve, to waste away. [Gr a- (privative), and trophē nourishment]

■ **atroph'ic** adj. **at'rophied** adj.

atropin /at'rə-pin/ or **atropine** (also /-pīn/) n a poisonous alkaloid found in deadly nightshade, used in medicine eg for premedication (also **atropia**). [New L Atropa belladonna, from **Atropos**; see also **belladonna**]

■ **at'ropism** n.

Atropos /at'rō-pos/ (Gr myth) n the Fate that cuts the thread of life. [Gr]

■ **At'ropa** n the deadly nightshade genus of the potato family.

atropous /at'rə-pəs or -rō-/ (bot) adj (of an ovule) orthotropous. [Gr a- (privative), and tropos turning]

ATS abbrev : anti-tetanus serum; Auxiliary Territorial Service (replaced by **WRAC** in 1949).

■ **Ats** /ats/ n pl women of the Auxiliary Territorial Service.

ats (law) abbrev : at the suit of.

Att. abbrev : Attorney (also **Atty**).

attaboy /at'ə-boi/ (inf) interj expressing encouragement or approval. [Poss corruption of that's the boy]

attach /ə-tach'/ vt to bind or fasten; to connect or associate; to join in action, function or affection; to seize or arrest (law); to seize, lay hold of (obs). ◆ vi to adhere, to be fastened; to be attributable or incident (to); to come into effect (rare). [OFr atachier, from a (from L ad to), and perhaps the root of **tack¹**]

■ **attach'able** adj. **attached'** adj. **attach'ment** n an act or means of fastening; a bond of fidelity or affection; seizure of goods or person by virtue of a legal process; a piece, etc that is to be attached; temporary secondment; an electronic file sent with an email message (comput).

❑ **attachment order** n (law) a court order prohibiting a debtor from selling off his or her assets until a particular claim has been settled. **attachment theory** n (behaviourism) a theory which proposes that the emotional bond between human infants and their parents has an evolutionary history and that various attachment behaviours enhance survival.

■ **attachment of earnings** (law) arrestment of an employee's wages by a court order to honour financial commitments.

attaché /ə-tash'ā/ n a junior member of an ambassador's staff; a specialist attached to a diplomatic department; an attaché-case. [Fr, attached]

❑ **atta'ché-case** n a small rigid rectangular case for documents, etc.

attack /ə-tak'/ vt to act against with violence; to assault; to criticize severely; to begin (a task or activity) vigorously; to begin to affect or act destructively upon. ◆ vi to take the initiative in attempting to score (sport); to launch an attack. ◆ vt and vi (music) to perform sharply and vigorously. ◆ n an assault or onset; the offensive part in any contest; the beginning of active operations on anything, even dinner; severe criticism or calumny; a sudden onset or episode of illness; a performer's approach to a piece, dance, etc, or their style of beginning in terms of crispness, verve, and precision (music, ballet, etc); used collectively (with the) to designate the players in a team who are in attacking positions, eg the forwards in football or hockey; in lacrosse,

the name of certain positions between centre and the opponents' goal. [Fr attaquer ; a doublet of **attach**]

■ **attack'able** adj. **attack'er** n.

attagirl /at'ə-gûrl/ (inf) interj expressing encouragement or approval to a woman. [Fem form of **attaboy**]

attain /ə-tān'/ vt to reach or gain by effort; to accomplish; to reach, arrive at (archaic). ◆ vi (archaic) to come or arrive. [OFr ataindre, from L attingere, from ad to, and tangere to touch]

■ **attainabil'ity** or **attain'ableness** n. **attain'able** adj that may be reached, achievable. **attain'ment** n an act of attaining; the thing attained; acquisition; (in pl) acquirements in learning.

attainder /ə-tān'dər/ n the action of attainting; the loss of civil rights through conviction for high treason (hist ; law). [OFr ataindre (see **attain**)]

■ **attaint'** vt to convict (obs); to deprive of rights by conviction for treason (hist ; law); to accuse (archaic); to disgrace, stain (from a fancied connection with taint ; archaic). ◆ n the act of touching, esp a hit (in tilting) (archaic); infection (Shakesp); attainder; a stain, disgrace. ◆ adj (Shakesp) corrupted, tainted. **attaint'ment** or **attaint'ure** n.

attap see **atap**.

attar /at'ər/ n a very fragrant essential oil made in Bulgaria and elsewhere, chiefly from the damask rose (also **ott'o**, **ott'ar**). [Pers atar]

attask /ə-täsk'/ (obs) vt to take to task (only in the pap **attaskt'** a doubtful reading in Shakespeare's King Lear). [Pfx a- (intensive)]

attemper /ə-tem'pər/ (archaic) vt to mix in due proportion; to modify or moderate; to adapt. [L attemperāre, from ad to, and temperāre to regulate]

■ **attem'pered** adj.

attempt /ə-temt'/ vt to try, endeavour (to do, or with n of action); to try to obtain (obs); to tempt, entice (archaic); to make an attack upon (archaic or obs). ◆ vi to make an attempt or trial. ◆ n an effort; a personal assault (now usu on someone's life); any intentional act that can fairly be described as one of a series which, if uninterrupted and successful, would constitute a crime (law); temptation (Milton). [OFr atempter, from L attentāre, from ad to, and temptāre, tentāre to try, from tendere to stretch]

■ **attemptabil'ity** n. **attempt'able** adj that may be attempted. **attempt'er** n a person who attempts; a tempter (Milton).

attend /ə-tend'/ vt to wait on; to accompany (archaic); to be present at (a meeting, etc); to go regularly to (a school, etc); to wait for (obs); to give attention to (obs); to hold (the flag) while a player is putting so that it can be removed as the ball approaches the hole (golf). ◆ vi to listen (to); to apply oneself, direct one's mind and efforts (with to); to act as an attendant or companion (with on or upon; archaic); to wait, be consequent (with on or upon; archaic). [L attendere, attentum]

■ **attend'ance** n the act of attending; presence; number of persons attending; attention, careful regard (Bible). **attend'ancy** n (obs) attendance, a retinue; relative position. **attend'ant** adj giving attendance; accompanying. ◆ n a person who attends or accompanies; a servant; (with on or upon) what accompanies or follows, a consequence; a person who owes a duty or service to another (law). **attendee'** n used in the sense of 'attender', of a person attending a conference, attendance centre, etc. **attend'er** n a person who pays attention or is attentive; a person who attends; a companion (archaic). **attend'ment** n (obs, rare) accompaniments; (Spenser) **atten'dement** intention.

❑ **attendance allowance** n a non-contributory benefit paid to an invalid who requires constant attendance or supervision. **attendance centre** n a non-residential centre where a young offender may be required to attend regularly, instead of serving a prison sentence.

attent see under **attention**.

attentat /a-tä-tä'/ (Fr) n an (esp unsuccessful) attempt at an (esp political) crime of violence.

attention /ə-ten'shən/ n the act of attending; steady application of the mind; care, consideration; notice, observation; civility, courtesy; the position of standing rigidly erect with hands by the sides and heels together (milit); (in pl) courtship (archaic). ◆ interj used in calling for someone's, or esp a crowd's, attention; an order to come to attention, in readiness to execute a command (milit). [L attentiō, -ōnis]

■ **attent'** adj (Spenser and Shakesp) giving attention. ◆ n (Spenser) attention. **atten'tional** adj (psychol, etc) relating to attention or concentration. **attent'ive** adj full of attention; courteous, mindful; alert, observant. **attent'ively** adv. **attent'iveness** n.

❑ **attention deficit (hyperactivity) disorder** n an abnormal inability to concentrate for more than very short periods of time. **attention line** n a line in a letter used to indicate the particular employee of an organization to whom the document is addressed. **attention span** *n* the length of time for which a person can concentrate. **attention value** *n* (*advertising*) the degree to which an advertisement has been noticed or remembered by a reader or viewer.

■ **draw (someone's) attention to** to direct (someone's) notice towards. **pay attention** to listen or concentrate carefully; to take particular notice. **selective attention** (*behaviourism*) the aspect of perception that implies a readiness to respond to a particular stimulus or aspects of it.

attenuate /ə-ten'ū-āt/ *vt* to make thin or lean; to break down into finer parts; to reduce in density; to reduce in strength or value. ◆ *vi* to become thin or fine; to grow less. ◆ *adj* attenuated. [L *attenuāre*, *-ātum*, from *ad* to, and *tenuis* thin]

■ **atten'uant** *n* anything that attenuates (also *adj*). **atten'uated** *adj* thin; thinned; dilute, rarefied; tapering. **attenuā'tion** *n* the process of making slender; reduction of intensity, density, force, or (of bacteria) virulence; in homeopathy, the reduction of the active principles of medicines to minute doses; reduction in magnitude, amplitude or intensity, arising from absorption or scattering (*nuclear eng* and *telecom*). **atten'uator** *n*.

❑ **attenuated vaccine** *n* (*immunol*) live bacterial or virus vaccine in which the microbes have a greatly diminished capacity to cause disease but are still able to evoke protective immunity.

attercop /at'ər-kop/ (*obs* or *dialect*) *n* a spider; an ill-natured person. [OE *attorcoppa*, from *attor*, *ātor* poison and perh *cop* head, or *copp* cup]

attest /ə-test'/ *vt* to testify or bear witness to; to affirm by signature or oath; to give proof of, to manifest; to call to witness (*obs*). ◆ *vt* and *vi* (*old*) to enrol for military service. ◆ *vi* to bear witness (to). ◆ *n* (*Shakesp*) witness, testimony. [L *attestārī*, from *ad* to, and *testis* a witness]

■ **attest'able** *adj*. **attestā'tion** /at-/ *n* an act of attesting; administration of an oath. **attest'ative** *adj*. **attest'ed** *adj* vouched for; certified free from disease, *specif* the tubercle bacillus. **attest'er** or **attest'or** *n*.

Att.-Gen. *abbrev* : Attorney-General (also **AG**, **A-G**, **Atty-Gen.**).

Attic /at'ik/ *adj* of Attica, the region around Athens; refined, classical, pure (in taste, language, etc). ◆ *n* the dialect of Ancient Greek used in Athens.

■ **Att'icism** /-sizm/ *n*. **Atticize** or **-ise** /at'i-sīz/ *vt* to make conformable to the language or idiom of Attica. ◆ *vi* to use the idioms of the Athenians; to side with the Athenians; to affect Attic or Greek style or manners.

❑ **Attic salt** *n* wit of a dry, delicate and refined quality.

attic /at'ik/ (*archit*) *n* a low storey or structure above the cornice of the main part of an elevation, *usu* of the so-called **Attic order**, ie with square columns or pilasters instead of pillars; a room in the roof of a house. [The structure was supposed to be in the Athenian manner; see **Attic**]

attire /ə-tīr'/ *vt* to dress, array or adorn; to prepare. ◆ *n* dress, clothing; any kind of covering (*obs*). [OFr *atirer* to put in order, from *à tire* in a row, from *à* (L *ad*) to, and *tire*, *tiere* order, dress; see **tier**]

■ **attire'ment** *n* (*obs*). **attir'ing** *n*.

attitude /at'i-tūd/ *n* posture, or position; a posture or position expressing some thought or feeling; a habitual mode of thought or feeling; a studied or affected posture; a position on one leg with the other leg extended behind, modelled on the position of the *Flying Mercury* of Giovanni Bologna (1524–1608) (*ballet*); of an aircraft in flight, or on the ground, the angles made by its axes with the relative airflow, or with the ground, respectively; the tilt of a vehicle measured in relation to the surface of the earth as horizontal plane (*space flight*); a personal viewpoint of or to a product or organization (*marketing*); antagonistically insolent manner, posture, and *esp* style and tone of speech (*sl*); individuality, *esp* being confidently unconventional (*sl*). [Fr *attitude* or Ital *attitudine*, from L *aptitūdō*, *-inis*, from *aptus* fit]

■ **attitud'inal** *adj*. **attitudinā'rian** *n* a person who studies attitudes. **attitud'inize** or **-ise** *vi* to assume affected attitudes. **attitud'inizer** or **-s-** *n*. **attitud'inizing** or **-s-** *n*.

❑ **attitude angle** *n* in a cornering motor vehicle, the slight angle between the track of the vehicle and the direction in which the tyres are pointing.

■ **strike an attitude** to assume a position or figure indicative of a feeling or emotion not really felt.

attn *abbrev* : for the attention of.

atto- /a-tō-/ *combining form* denoting 10^{-18}. [Dan and Norw *atten* eighteen]

attollent /ə-tol'ənt/ *adj* lifting up, raising; (*usu* **attoll'ens**; of a muscle) involved in raising or lifting up (*med*, *anat*). ◆ *n* (*usu* **attoll'ens**) a muscle that raises. [L *attollēns*, *-entis*, prp of *attollere* to lift up, from *ad* to, and *tollere* to lift]

attonce, attone see **atone**.

attorn /ə-tûrn'/ (*law*) *vt* to transfer to another. ◆ *vi* to accept tenancy under a new landlord. [LL *attornāre* to assign; see **turn**]

■ **attorn'ey** *n* (*pl* **attor'neys**) (OFr pap *atorné*) a person legally authorized to act for another; a person legally qualified to manage cases in a court of law (*esp N Am*); a solicitor, lawyer, attorney at law (*esp N Am*). ◆ *vt* (*Shakesp*) to perform by proxy; to employ as a proxy. **attor'neydom** *n*. **attor'neyism** *n*. **attor'neyship** *n*. **attorn'ment** *n* acknowledgement of a new landlord.

❑ **Attorney-Gen'eral** *n* (*pl* **Attorneys-General** or **Attorney-Generals**) the chief law officer for England, the Republic of Ireland, a dominion, colony, etc, the English one being a member of the government, representing the Crown in important civil and criminal matters, and leader of the English Bar; the Crown's attorney in the duchies of Lancaster and Cornwall, and the county palatine of Durham; in the United States, one of the seven officials who constitute the president's cabinet, the head of the Department of Justice; also (without *caps*) the legal adviser of a State governor. **attorney at law** or **public attorney** *n* a professional and duly qualified legal agent. **attorney in fact** or **private attorney** *n* a person duly appointed by power of attorney to act for another in matters of contract, money payments, and the like.

■ **letter, power** or **warrant of attorney** a formal instrument by which one person authorizes another to perform specific acts on his or her behalf.

attract /ə-trakt'/ *vt* to cause to approach by means of unseen forces; to draw (a crowd, attention, financial investment, etc); to allure or entice; to be attractive to; to be liable to (tax) (*law*, etc). [L *attrahere*, *attractum*, from *ad* to, and *trahere* to draw]

■ **attract'able** *adj* that may be attracted. **attract'ant** *n* something that attracts, *esp* that effects communication in insects and animals. **attract'ing** *adj*. **attract'ingly** *adv*. **attrac'tion** *n* the act of attracting; an attracting force (*phys*); that which attracts; the influence of one linguistic element on the form of another by proximity (*grammar*). **attract'ive** *adj* having the power of attracting; alluring or appealing. **attract'ively** *adv*. **attract'iveness** *n*. **attract'or** *n*.

■ **Great Attractor** a powerful gravitational force of uncertain origin pulling certain galaxies, including our own, towards its source.

attrahent /at'rə-hənt or ə-trā'ənt/ *adj* attracting or drawing; (*usu* **att'rahens**) (eg of a muscle) that draws towards (*med* or *anat*); (of a substance) acting as an attractant (*biol*; *obs*). ◆ *n* that which attracts. [L *attrahēns*, *-entis*, prp of *attrahere* ; see **attract**]

attrap /ə-trap'/ (*Spenser*) *vt* to adorn with trappings; to dress or array. [L *ad* to, and **trap**⁴]

attrib. *abbrev* : attributed; attributive; attributively.

attribute /ə-trib'ūt or (*Milton*) at'ri-būt/ *vt* to ascribe, assign, or consider as belonging (to). ◆ *n* /at'/ that which is attributed; that which is inherent in, or inseparable from, anything; that which can be predicated of anything; a quality or property; a virtue; an accessory; (in art) a conventional symbol; a word added to another to denote an attribute (*grammar*); an item of information about the status of a file stored by the operating system (*comput*). [L *attribuere*, *-tribūtum*, from *ad* to, and *tribuere* to give]

■ **attrib'utable** *adj*. **attribution** /at-ri-bū'shən/ *n* the act or an act of attributing; that which is attributed. **attrib'utive** *adj* expressing an attribute; (of an adjective) placed immediately before or immediately after the noun it qualifies (*grammar*). ◆ *n* (*grammar*) a word added to another to denote an attribute. **attrib'utively** *adv*. **attrib'utiveness** *n*.

❑ **attribution theory** *n* (*psychol*) the theory explaining how people link actions and emotions to particular causes in order to understand behaviour.

attrist /ə-trist'/ (*obs*) *vt* to sadden. [Fr *attrister*, from L *ad* to, and *tristis* sad]

attrite /ə-trīt'/ *adj* worn by rubbing or friction (*obs*); repentant through fear of punishment rather than from the love of God (*theol*). ◆ *vt* (*US milit*) to wear down, gradually diminish (enemy forces, strength, morale or resources); to destroy, kill (*euphem*). [L *attrītus*, from *atterere*, from *ad* to, and *terere*, *trītum* to rub]

■ **attrit'** *vt* to attrite. ◆ *n* (*euphem*) the wearing down of enemy forces; a death (among enemy personnel). **attrition** /a- or ə-trish'ən/ *n* rubbing together; wearing down, as by friction; a defective or imperfect sorrow for sin (*theol*); the wearing down of an adversary, resistance, resources, etc (*fig*, *esp milit*); gradual decrease in a workforce by natural wastage (qv). **attrit'ional** *adj*.

attuition /a-tū-ish'ən/ (*psychol*) *n* a mental operation intermediate between sensation and perception. [L *ad* to, and *tuērī* to attend to]

■ **att'uent** *adj* performing the function of attuition. **att'uite** /-īt/ *vt* to be conscious of by attuition. **attui'tional** *adj*. **attu'itive** *adj*. **attu'itively** *adv*.

attune /ə-tūn' or (US) -toon'/ vt to put in tune; to make (one's voice, song, etc) tuneful; to make (something) harmonize or accord; to accustom or acclimatize. [L ad to, and **tune**]
■ **attune'ment** n.

Atty abbrev : Attorney.

ATV abbrev : all-terrain vehicle; Associated Television, now replaced by Central Television.

atwain /ə-twān'/ (archaic) adv in(to) two parts; asunder. [**a-¹**]

atweel /ə-twēl'/ (Scot) adv or interj well; indeed. [wat weel, ie wot well]

atween /ə-twēn'/ (archaic or dialect) adv at intervals. ◆ prep between.
■ **atwixt'** adv and prep betwixt.

atwitter /ə-twit'ər/ adv in a state of twittering. [**a-¹** and **twitter¹**]

at. wt. abbrev : atomic weight.

atypical /ā- or ā-tip'i-kəl/ adj not typical. [**a-²** and **typical**]
■ **atyp'ically** adv.

AU abbrev : African Union; Ångström unit (also **ÅU**, now usu **Å**); astronomical unit.

Au (chem) symbol : gold. [L aurum]

aubade /ō-bäd'/ n a musical announcement of dawn; a sunrise song. [Fr, from aube dawn, from Provençal alba dawn]

auberge /ō-berzh'/ n an inn. [Fr, of Gmc origin; see **harbour**]
■ **aubergiste** /ō-ber-zhēst'/ n an innkeeper.

aubergine /ō'bər-jēn or -zhēn/ n the egg-shaped fruit of an Asian annual plant (Solanum melongena); its purple colour. ◆ adj of this colour. [Fr, from Catalan alberginia; ult from Sans vātingana]

aubrieta /ō-bri-et'ə/, **aubrietia** or (popularly) **aubretia** /ō-brē' or ō-bri-ē'sh(y)ə/ n a plant of the purple-flowered Mediterranean genus Aubrieta of trailing cruciferous plants, much grown in rock-gardens, etc. [Claude Aubriet (c.1665–1742), naturalist-painter]

auburn /ö'bûrn/ adj reddish brown; orig light yellow. [LL alburnus whitish, from L albus white]

AUC abbrev : anno urbis conditae (or ab urbe condita) (L) in the year from the building of the city (used to reckon dates in Roman history, starting from 753BC).

auceps /ö'seps/ (Walton) n a hawker. [L, bird-catcher, fowler, from avis bird, and capere to catch]

au contraire /ō kɔ̃-trer'/ (Fr) on the contrary.

au courant /ō koo-rä'/ (Fr) well-informed; well up in the facts or situation. [Literally, in the current or stream]

auction /ök'shən/ n a public sale at which goods are sold to the highest bidder; a method of selling goods or property by inviting bids; auction bridge. ◆ vt to sell by auction (also with off). [L auctiō, -ōnis an increasing, from augēre, auctum to increase]
■ **auc'tionary** adj. **auctioneer'** n a person who sells or is licensed to sell by public auction. ◆ vt to sell by auction (also with off).
❑ **auction bridge** n an early form of the game of bridge, in which all tricks won counted towards winning a game.
■ **auction by reserve** an auction in which the auctioneer may not withdraw the lot once the first bid is made, and the lot is sold to the highest bidder. **Dutch auction** a kind of auction at which the salesperson starts at a high price, and comes down until a bid is made; any of several other unconventional or informal types of auction.

auctorial /ök-tö'ri-əl or -tö'/ adj of an author or his or her trade. [L auctor, -ōris author]

aucuba /ö'kū-bə or -kū'/ n any plant of the Japan laurel genus Aucuba. [Jap]

audacious /ö-dā'shəs/ adj daring; bold; impudent. [Fr audacieux, from L audāx, from audēre to dare]
■ **audā'ciously** adv. **audā'ciousness** or **audacity** /ö-das'i-ti/ n.

audax et cautus /ö'daks et kö'təs or ow'daks et kow'tŭs/ (L) bold and cautious.

au désespoir /ō dā-zes-pwär'/ (Fr) in despair.

audial /ö'di-əl/ adj relating to hearing or sounds. [L audīre to hear]

audible /ö'di-bl/ adj able to be heard. ◆ n (American football) a tactic or game plan called out in coded form by the quarterback at the line of scrimmage to replace the previously arranged play. ◆ vi (American football) to call an audible. [Med L audibilis, from L audīre to hear]
■ **audibil'ity** or **aud'ibleness** n. **aud'ibly** adv.

audience /ö'di-əns/ n an assembled group of hearers or spectators; the listeners to a radio programme, viewers of a television programme, or even readers of a book, magazine, author, etc; the people exposed to a particular medium (esp TV, radio or cinema); the act of hearing; a formal or ceremonial interview; a judicial

hearing (archaic); admittance to a hearing; (also **audiencia** /ow-di-en-thē'ə or -sē'ə/) a court of government or justice in the Spanish-American Empire; the territory administered by it. [L audientia, from audire to hear]
■ **aud'ient** adj listening; paying attention. ◆ n (formal, esp church hist) a hearer.
❑ **audience participation** n involvement by members of the audience in a theatrical performance, television or radio programme, etc esp by direct appeals to them from performers. **audience research** n the discovery of facts about an audience (esp of radio or TV programmes) such as age and behaviour patterns.

audile /ö'dīl or -dīl/ adj relating to hearing. ◆ n a person inclined to think in terms of sound. [auditory and sfx -ile, following **agile**, **fragile**, etc]

audio /ö'di-ō/ n (pl aud'ios) reproduction of recorded or broadcast sounds (also adj); sound, as opposed to vision (inf); an acoustic device by which a pilot returning to an aircraft-carrier knows when the aircraft is at a proper speed for landing; short for **audiotypist** or **audiotyping**. [Ety as for **audio-**]
❑ **audio book** n a book in recorded form, eg on audio cassette. **audio cassette** n a cassette of audiotape. **audio disc** (or **disk**) n a disc on which sound is recorded. **aud'io-engineer'** n a person whose job concerns the transmission and reception of broadcast sound. **audio-frequency** /ö'di-ō-frē'kwən-si/ n a frequency of oscillation which, when the oscillatory power is converted into a sound pressure, is perceptible by the ear. **aud'iotape** n magnetic tape for recording and reproducing sound; a sound recording on tape, an audio cassette. **aud'iotyping** n. **aud'iotyp'ist** n a typist able to type directly material reproduced by a dictating machine.

audio- /ö-di-ō-/ combining form denoting sound, esp denoting recorded and broadcast sound; relating to, using, or involving, audio-frequencies. [1st pers sing of prt of L audīre to hear]
■ **aud'iogram** n a tracing produced by an audiograph. **aud'iograph** n a machine used to test a patient's hearing by transmitting sound waves directly to the inner ear. **audio-loca'tion** n echo location. **audiolog'ical** adj. **audiol'ogist** n. **audiol'ogy** n the science of hearing, esp with reference to the diagnosis and treatment of hearing defects. **audiom'eter** n an instrument for measuring differences in hearing; one for measuring minimum intensities of sounds which, for specified frequencies, are perceivable by the ear. **audiomet'ric** adj. **audiomet'rically** adv. **audiometrician** /-mi-trish'ən/ n. **audiom'etrist** n. **audiom'etry** n the measurement of differences in hearing. **aud'iophil** /-fil/ or **audiophile** /-fīl/ n an enthusiast for the true reproduction of recorded or broadcast sound. **audiovis'ual** adj concerned simultaneously with seeing and hearing; of a device or method that uses both sound and vision (**audiovisual aids** material such as pictures, video recordings, etc used in the classroom). **audiovis'ually** adv. **aud'iphone** n an instrument which, pressed against the teeth, communicates sounds through the bones to the ears.

audit /ö'dit/ n an examination of accounts by an authorized person or persons; a statement of account; a check or examination; an evaluation of a specified quantity or quality, as in energy audit, efficiency audit; a calling to account generally; a periodical settlement of accounts (obs); audience, hearing (obs). ◆ vt to examine and officially verify, etc (the accounts of a company); to attend (a course or class) without intending to take any examination (N Am and Aust). [L audītus a hearing, from audīre to hear]
■ **aud'itable** adj. **aud'itor** n a person who audits accounts; a hearer (fem **aud'itress**); a person who audits a course or class (N Am and Aust). **auditor'ial** adj. **aud'itorship** n.
❑ **audit ale** n an ale of special quality brewed for some Oxford and Cambridge colleges (orig for use on the day of audit). **Audit Commission** n the body responsible for the auditing of local authorities and NHS bodies in England and Wales. **audit committee** n a subcommittee of a company's board of directors with responsibility for liaising with external auditors. **audit trail** n (comput) the record of the file updating that takes place during a specific transaction.

audita querela /ö-dī'tə kwə-rē'lə or ow-dē'tä kwe-rā'lä/ (L; law) the name of a writ giving leave to appeal (literally, the suit having been heard).

audition /ö-dish'ən/ n a trial performance by an applicant for an acting, musical, etc part, place or position (also vt and vi with for); the sense, or an act, of hearing; mode of hearing; something heard (rare). [L audītiō, -ōnis a hearing, from audīre to hear]
■ **aud'itive** adj of, or related to, hearing.

auditor, etc see under **audit**.

auditorium /ö-di-tö'ri-əm/ n (pl audito'riums or audito'ria) in a theatre or the like, the space allotted to the audience; a public hall, for concerts, meetings, etc (N Am); the reception room of a monastery. [L audītōrium, from audītōrius concerning hearing or hearers]

■ words derived from main entry word; ❑ compound words; ■ idioms and phrasal verbs

auditory /ö'di-tə-ri/ adj relating to the sense, process or organs of hearing. ◆ n (archaic) an audience; a place where lectures, etc are heard. [L auditōrius]

auf /öf/ (obs) n an elf's child, an oaf. [ON ālfr elf]

au fait /ō fe'/ (Fr) well-acquainted with a matter; well-informed, expert (with with).

aufgabe /owf'gä-bə/ (psychol) n a task set as an experiment, etc. [Ger]

Aufklärung /owf-klä'rŭng or (Ger) -kle'/ (Ger) n enlightenment, esp the 18c intellectual movement.

Aufl. abbrev : Auflage (Ger), edition.

au fond /ō fɔ̃'/ (Fr) at bottom.

au fromage /ō fro-mäzh'/ (Fr) with cheese.

auf Wiedersehen /owf ve'dər-zā(-ə)n/ (Ger) goodbye until we meet again.

Aug. abbrev : August; Augustine.

aug. abbrev : augmentative.

Augean /ö- or ow-je'ən/ adj filthy; difficult. [From Augeas, in Greek legend the king of Elis the cleaning of whose filthy stables was one of the labours of Hercules]

auger /ö'gər/ n a carpenter's boring tool; an instrument for boring holes in the ground. [From nauger (an auger for a nauger), from OE nafugār, from nafu a nave of a wheel, and gār a piercer; see **nave**² and **gore**²]
❑ **au'ger-bit** n an auger that fits into a carpenter's brace. **au'ger-hole** n. **au'ger-shell** n Terebra. **au'ger-worm** n the goat-moth larva, which bores trees.

Auger effect /ō-zhä i-fekt'/ (phys) n the non-radiative transition of an atom from an excited state to one of lower energy with emission of an electron (**Auger electron**). [Pierre Auger (1899–1993), French physicist]

aught /öt/ n anything, anything at all; a whit, jot. [OE ā-wiht contracted to āht (whence **ought**²), and shortened to aht (whence **aught**); ā-wiht is from ā, ō ever, and wiht creature, whit, wight]

augite /ö-jīt or -gīt/ n one of the pyroxene group of minerals, very similar to hornblende, usu greenish, an essential component of many igneous rocks. [Gr augē brightness]
■ **augitic** /-jit' or -git'/ adj.

augm. abbrev : augmentative; augmenté (Fr), enlarged.

augment /ög-ment'/ vt to increase; to make larger. ◆ vi to grow larger. ◆ n /ög'mənt/ increase (obs); the prefixed vowel or initial vowel-lengthening in some past tenses of the verb in Sanskrit and Greek; sometimes applied also to such inflectional prefixes as the ge- of the German perfect participle. [L augēre to increase]
■ **augment'able** adj. **augmenta'tion** n increase; addition; an additional charge in a coat of arms bestowed as a mark of honour (heraldry); the repetition of a melody in notes of greater length than the original (music); an increase of stipend obtained by a parish minister by an action raised in the Court of Teinds against the titular and heritors, or an increase in a feu-duty, rent, etc (Scots law). **augment'ative** adj having the quality or power of augmenting; (of an affix or derivative) increasing the force of the original word (grammar; also n). **augment'ed** adj made larger; increased; a semitone higher than perfect or major (music). **augment'er** n. **augment'or** n (biol) a nerve that increases the rate of activity of an organ.
❑ **augmented reality** n an environment in which computer-generated elements are added in real time to the real environment (abbrev **AR**). **Augmented Roman Alphabet** n earlier name for Initial Teaching Alphabet (qv).

Augmentin® /ög-men'tin/ n a drug used as an antibiotic against a wide range of infections.

au grand sérieux /ō grã sä-ryø'/ (Fr; now **très au sérieux** /tre-zō/) in all seriousness.

au gratin /ō gra-tē'/ (Fr) cooked covered with breadcrumbs or grated cheese, or with both.

augur /ö'gər/ n among the ancient Romans, a person who sought knowledge of secret or future things by observing the flight and the cries of birds; a diviner; a soothsayer; appar an augury or portent (Shakesp). ◆ vt to foretell from signs. ◆ vi to guess or conjecture; to bode or portend. [L; prob from avis bird]
■ **au'gural** /-gū-rəl or -gyər-əl/ adj. **au'gurer** n (Shakesp) an augur. **au'gurship** n. **au'gūry** n the art or practice of auguring; an omen.
■ **augur well** (or **ill**) **for** to be an encouraging (or discouraging) sign with respect to.

August /ö'gəst/ n the eighth month of the year. [After the Roman emperor Augustus]

august¹ /ö-gust'/ adj venerable; imposing; sublime; majestic. [L augustus, from augēre to increase, honour]
■ **august'ly** adv. **august'ness** n.

august² or usu **auguste** /ow-goost'/ (also with cap) n a circus clown of the white-faced, bungling type. [Ger, Augustus]

Augustan /ö-gus'tən/ adj relating to the Emperor Augustus, or to the brilliant literature of his reign (31BC–14AD); hence relating to any similar age, such as the reign of Anne in English literature, and that of Louis XIV in French; classic; refined. ◆ n a writer of an Augustan age.

auguste see **august**².

Augustine /ö'gə-stin or ö-gus'tin/ or **Augustinian** /-tin'i-ən/ n a person belonging to any order of friars or nuns whose rule is based on the writings of St Augustine (354–430AD); a person who holds the opinions of St Augustine, esp on predestination (theol).
■ **Augustin'ian** adj of or relating to St Augustine. **Augustin'ianism** n.
❑ **Augustinian** (or **Austin**) **canons** see **canon**². **Augustinian** (or **Austin**) **friars** or **hermits** n pl the fourth order of mendicant friars, wearing a black habit, but not to be confused with the Black Friars or Dominicans.

AUI (comput) abbrev : Attachment Unit Interface.

Aujeszky's disease /ow-yes'kiz di-zēz'/ n a notifiable disease of pigs, cattle, sheep, dogs, cats and rats, caused by a herpes virus, with symptoms similar to those of rabies. [A Aujeszky (1869–1933), Hungarian scientist, who identified it]

au jour le jour /ō zhoor lə zhoor'/ (Fr) from hand to mouth (literally, from day to day).

auk /ök/ n a short-winged, black-and-white, heavy-bodied seabird of the family Alcidae. [ON ālka]
■ **auk'let** n one of the smaller birds of the family.
■ **great auk** a large, flightless auk, the garefowl (extinct c.1844). **little auk** an auk (Plautus alle) of the N Atlantic and Arctic Oceans, the rotche or dovekie.

aula /ö'lə/ n (L) a hall. [L aula, Gr aulē court, courtyard, hall]
■ **aula'rian** adj relating to a hall, esp one in a collegiate university. ◆ n at Oxford University, a member of a hall, as distinguished from a collegian. **au'lic** adj (formal or archaic) of or relating to a royal court; courtly.
❑ **Aula Regis** or **Curia Regis** n (hist) a feudal assembly of tenants-in-chief; the Privy Council; the Court of King's Bench. **Aulic Council** n (Ger Reichshofrat; hist) a court or personal council of the Holy Roman Empire, established in 1501 by Maximilian I, and co-ordinate with the Imperial Chamber (Reichskammergericht).

auld /öld/ (Scot) adj old. [OE ald]
❑ **auld-farr'ant** adj (ie old-favouring) old-fashioned (archaic); precocious. **auld'-warld** adj (archaic) old-world, ancient.
■ **auld lang syne** long ago (literally, old long since). **Auld Reekie** Edinburgh (literally, old smoky). **the Auld Kirk** (archaic) the Church of Scotland; whisky.

aulic see under **aula**.

aulnage, aulnager variant spellings of **alnage, alnager**.

aulos /ö'los or ow'los/ n (pl **aul'oi** /-oi or -ē/) an ancient Greek wind instrument, a double pipe with double reeds. [Gr]

aumail /ö-māl'/ (archaic; rare) vt to enamel; to figure or variegate (Spenser). [See **enamel**]

aumbry /öm'bri/ n same as **ambry**.

au mieux /ō myø'/ (Fr) on the best of terms (literally, at the best).

aumil /ö'mil or ä'mil/ n an amildar.

au naturel /ō na-tü-rel'/ (Fr) adv cooked plainly, or uncooked; served without dressing (cookery); in an unadorned state; naked. [Literally, in the natural state]

aune /ōn/ (obs) n an old French measure of length (esp of fabric), approx 119cm (47in). [OFr aulne; related to **alnage**, **ell**¹]

aunt /änt/ n a father's or mother's sister, or an uncle's wife or a great-aunt (used with cap as a title either before a woman's first name or independently); a woman to whom one can turn for advice, sympathy, practical help, etc (fig); an old woman (obs); a gossip (obs); a procuress (obs). [OFr ante, from L amita a father's sister]
■ **aunt'ie** or **aunt'y** n dimin for **aunt**; a title sometimes used by children for female friends of their parents; (**Aunt'ie**) a facetious name for the BBC. **aunt'ly** adj.
❑ **Aunt Sally** n a fairground or pub game, in which sticks or balls are thrown to smash a pipe in the mouth of a wooden figure; any of several variations of the game; a target for abuse, criticism or blame (fig).

aunter /ön'tər/ (obs) n adventure. [OFr aventure]

au pair /ō per'/ *n* a young person who comes from abroad (*esp* to learn the language) and perform light domestic duties, baby-sitting, etc for a family in exchange for board and lodging and pocket-money. ♦ *adj* relating to an au pair or such an arrangement; *orig* meaning by mutual service without payment. [Fr]

au pied de la lettre /ō pyā də la let'r'/ (*Fr*) exactly, literally. [Literally, to the foot of the letter]

au pis aller /ō pē-za-lā'/ (*Fr*) at the worst; as a last resort.

au poids de l'or /ō pwa də lor'/ (*Fr*) very dear (literally, at its weight in gold).

au premier /ō prə-myā'/ (*Fr*) on the first (floor).

aura /ö'rə/ *n* (*pl* **aur'ae** /-ē/ or **aur'as**) a supposed subtle emanation, *esp* that essence which is claimed to emanate from all living things and to provide an atmosphere for occult phenomena, invisible to most people but *appar* seen by some as a luminous or coloured glow; air, distinctive character (*fig*); the peculiar sensations that precede an attack of epilepsy, hysteria, or certain other ailments (*pathol*). [L *aura* a breeze]
■ **aur'al** *adj* relating to the air, or to the aura.

aural[1] /ö'rəl/ *adj* of, relating to, or received by, the ear. [L *auris* ear]
■ **aur'ally** *adv*. **aur'iform** *adj* ear-shaped. **aur'iscope** *n* (*med*) an instrument for examining the ear, an otoscope. **aur'ist** *n* a specialist in diseases of the ear, an otologist.

aural[2] see under **aura**.

aura popularis /ö'rə po-pū-la'ris or ow-ra po-pū-lä'ris/ (*L*) *n* popular favour (literally, the popular breeze).

aurar see **eyrir**.

aurate /ö'rāt/ *n* a salt of auric acid. [L *aurum* gold]
■ **au'rated** *adj* compounded with auric acid (*obs*); gold-coloured. **aureate** /ö'ri-ət/ *adj* gilded; golden; floridly rhetorical. **au'reately** *adv*. **au'reateness** *n*. **aure'ity** *n* the peculiar properties of gold. **au'reus** /ö'ri-əs or ow'rā-ūs/ *n* (*pl* **au'rei** /-ī or -ē/) a gold coin of the Roman Empire. **au'ric** *adj* relating to gold; containing trivalent gold (*chem*). **aurous** /ö'rəs/ *adj* containing univalent gold.
❑ **auric acid** *n* a hypothetical acid of composition HAuO$_2$, *usu* applied to auric hydroxide (Au(OH)$_3$) or *esp* auric oxide (Au$_2$O$_3$).

aurea mediocritas /ö'rē-a mē-dē-ok'ri-tas or ow'rā-a me-di-ok'ri-täs/ (*L*) *n* the golden (or happy) mean.

aureate, **aureity** see under **aurate**.

aurelia /ö-rē'li-ə/ *n* a jellyfish of the large *Aurelia* genus of common jellyfishes, or of a related genus; formerly a chrysalis or pupa (from its golden colour). [New L, from L *aurum* gold]
■ **aure'lian** *adj* golden; of an aurelia. ♦ *n* (*obs*) a lepidopterist.

aureola /ö-rē'ə-lə/ or **aureole** /ö'rē-ōl/ *n* a crown, or an increment to the ordinary blessedness of heaven, gained by virgins, martyrs, and doctors (*hist* and *RC theol*); the gold or coloured disc or ring represented around the head in à religious picture, symbolizing glory; a glorifying halo (*fig*); a halo or corona around the sun or moon, or the clear space within it (*meteorol*); the coloured rings around the Brocken spectre (*meteorol*); (erroneously) a halo surrounding the whole figure (eg a vesica piscis); any halo-like appearance. [L, fem of *aureolus* golden, dimin of *aureus* of gold]
■ **au'reoled** *adj* encircled with an aureole.

Aureomycin® /ö-rē-ə-mī'sin/ or -ö-/ *n* a tradename for chlortetracycline, an antibiotic used to treat skin and eye infections. [From *Streptomyces aureofaciens*, from which it is obtained]

au reste /ō rest'/ (*Fr*) as for the rest; besides.

aureus see under **aurate**.

au revoir /ō rə-vwär'/ (*Fr*) goodbye until we meet again.

auric see under **aurate**.

auricle /ö'ri-kl/ *n* the external ear (*zool*); an ear-like appendage to an atrium in the heart, or the atrium itself (*anat*); an ear-like lobe of a leaf, etc (*bot*). [L *auricula*, dimin of *auris* the ear]
■ **aur'icled** *adj* having appendages like ears. **auric'ūla** *n* a species of *Primula* (also called **bear's-ear**, or **dusty-miller**); (with *cap*) a genus of gastropod molluscs. **auric'ūlar** *adj* relating to the ear or hearing; auricle-shaped; known by hearing, or by report; told privately. **auric'ūlarly** *adv*. **auric'ūlate** /-lət/ or **auric'ūlated** *adj* ear-shaped; having auricles or appendages like ears.
❑ **auricular confession** *n* confession to a priest. **auricular therapy** *n* acupuncture treatment using points on the ear that are physically related to specific parts of the body.

auriferous /ö-rif'ə-rəs/ *adj* bearing or yielding gold. [L *aurifer*, from *aurum* gold, and *ferre* to bear]
■ **au'rify** *vt* and *vi* to turn into gold.

auriform see under **aural**[1].

aurify see under **auriferous**.

Auriga /ö-rī'gə/ *n* a prominent northern constellation. [L *auriga* charioteer]

Aurignacian /ö-rig-nā'sh(y)ən/ *adj* belonging to an upper Palaeolithic culture that succeeded the Mousterian and preceded the Solutrean. [*Aurignac*, in Haute-Garonne, SW France, where objects of this culture have been found]

auriscope, **aurist** see under **aural**[1].

aurochs /ö' or ow'roks/ *n* (*pl* **aur'ochs**) the urus or wild ox (extinct 1627); the European bison (*obs*; *non-standard*). [OHGer *ûr-ohso*, from *ûr* (adopted into L as *ūrus*, into Gr as *ouros* wild ox), and *ohso* ox]

aurora /ö-rö'rə/ *n* (*pl* **auro'ras** or **auro'rae**) (often with *cap*) the dawn; (with *cap*) the (Roman) goddess of dawn (*poetic*); a rich orange colour; a luminous atmospheric phenomenon of electrical character seen in and towards the Polar regions, with a tremulous motion, and streamers of light. [L *Aurōra*]
■ **auro'ral** or **auro'rean** *adj* relating to the dawn; rosy; fresh and beautiful; (**auroral**) of or relating to the aurora. **auro'rally** *adv*.
❑ **aurora australis** /ös-trā'lis or os- or -ä'lis/ *n* the southern lights, a phenomenon in the southern hemisphere, similar to the aurora borealis (also with *caps*). **aurora borealis** /bö-ri-ā'lis, -ä'lis or bö-/ or (*rare*) **septentrionalis** /sep-ten-tri-on-ā'lis or -ä'lis/ *n* the northern aurora or northern lights (also with *caps*). **auroral zones** *n pl* the two regions (around the north and south geomagnetic poles) in which the aurora is most and most frequently seen, and electrical disturbances occur.

aurous see under **aurate**.

aurum potabile /ö'rum po-tab'i-lē or ow'rŭm pö-tä'bi-le/ (*L*) *n* a former medicine or cordial containing a small quantity of gold, (literally, drinkable gold).

AUS *abbrev* : Australia (also IVR).

auscultation /ös-skəl-tā'shən/ *n* listening to internal bodily sounds (eg of the heart, lungs, abdomen, fetal heart, etc) as an aid to diagnosis, *usu* with a stethoscope. [L *auscultāre* to listen]
■ **aus'cultate** *vt* and *vi* to examine by auscultation. **auscul'tative** *adj*. **aus'cultātor** *n* a person who practises auscultation; an instrument for the purpose; formerly in Germany, a person who had passed their first public examination in law, and who was merely retained, not yet employed or paid by government. **auscultatory** /-kul'tə-tə-ri/ *adj*.

au second /ō sə-gɔ̃'/ (*Fr*) on the second (floor).

au secours /ō sə-koor'/ (*Fr*) a call for help.

au sérieux /ō sā-ryo'/ (*Fr*) seriously.

Ausgleich /ows'glīhh/ (*Ger*) *n* a settlement; an arrangement; the agreement establishing a dual monarchy for Austria and Hungary in 1867.

Ausländer /ows'len-dər/ (*Ger*) *n* a foreigner.

Auslese /ows'lā-zə/ (*Ger*) *n* choice, selection; wine made from selected bunches of grapes.

Ausonian /ö-sö'ni-ən/ (*poetic*) *adj* Italian. [L *Ausonia* a poetical name for Italy]

auspice /ö'spis/ *n* *orig* an omen drawn from observing birds; an omen, *esp* a good one, a prognostic; augury; (in *pl*) patronage. [Fr, from L *auspicium*, from *auspex*, *auspicis* a bird-seer, from *avis* bird, and *specere* to look, to observe]
■ **auspicate** /ös'pi-kāt/ *vt* to foreshow; to initiate or inaugurate with hopes of good luck. ♦ *vi* to augur. **auspicious** /-pish'əs/ *adj* having good auspices or omens of success; favourable, fortunate, propitious. **auspi'ciously** *adv*. **auspi'ciousness** *n*.
■ **under the auspices of** with the aid, guidance or protection of.

Aussichtspunkt /ows'zihhts-pŭngkt/ (*Ger*) *n* (*pl* **Aussichtspunkte** /-tə/) a selected position for admiring scenery, a vantage point.

Aussie /oz'i or os'i/ (*sl*) *n* and *adj* Australian.

Aussiedler /ows'zēd-lər/ (*Ger*) *n* an immigrant. [Literally, out-settler]

Aust. or **Austr.** *abbrev* : Australia; Australian.

austenite /ö'stə-nīt/ (*chem*) *n* a solid solution of carbon or other substance in one of the forms of iron. [WC Roberts-*Austen* (1843–1902), English metallurgist]
■ **austenit'ic** *adj* (of stainless steels) composed chiefly of austenite.

Auster /ös'tər/ (*literary*) *n* the south wind. [L]

austere /ö-stēr'/ *adj* sour and astringent; harsh; severe, stern; grave; severe in self-discipline; severely simple, without luxury. [L *austērus*, from Gr *austēros*, from *auein* to dry]
■ **austere'ly** *adv*. **austere'ness** *n*. **austerity** /-ter'/ *n* the quality of being austere; severity of manners or life; harshness; asceticism; severe simplicity of style, dress or habits; a lower standard of living associated with the curtailment of government spending. ♦ *adj* demonstrating or adopted in austerity.

■ words derived from main entry word; ❑ compound words; ■ idioms and phrasal verbs

Austin see under **Augustine**.

Austr. same as **Aust.**

austral /ö'strəl/ adj (also with cap) southern. ♦ n (pl **austral'es** /-trä'läz/) a former unit of currency in Argentina (100 centavos). [L australis southern, from Auster the south wind]

Australasian /o-strə-lä'zhən or -zi-ən/ adj relating to Australasia, or the lands that lie south-east of Asia. ♦ n a native or colonist of one of these lands. [L australis southern, and **Asian**]

Australian /ö- or o-strä'li.ən/ adj of, or relating to, Australia, the largest island in the world and the smallest continent, an independent member of the Commonwealth (formerly a British colony). ♦ n a person native to or resident in Australia. [L australis southern, from Auster the south wind]
■ **Austrā'lianism** n an Australian idiom; a characteristically Australian attitude. **aus'tralite** n a tektite found in the interior of Australia. **Aus'traloid** adj of or relating to an ethnic group that includes the Australian Aborigines and certain other S Asian peoples. ♦ n a member of this group. **Aus'tralorp** n an Australian breed of black hen (Australian and Orpington).
❑ **Australia Day** n (a public holiday celebrating) the anniversary of the founding of the colony of New South Wales on 26 January 1788. **Australian crane** see **brolga**. **Australian rules football** or **Australian rules** n an Australian version of football played by eighteen a side with an oval ball (also Aust inf **Rules**). **Australian salmon** n the kahawai. **Australian terrier** n a small wire-haired terrier similar to the cairn terrier.

Australopithecus /o-strə-lō-pith'i-kəs or -trä- or ö-strə-/ n a genus of extinct human-like primates, known from fossil skulls, etc found in southern Africa, and belonging to the subfamily **Australopitheci'nae**. [New L, from L australis southern, and Gr pithēkos ape]
■ **australopith'ecine** /-sēn/ adj and n.
❑ **Australopithecus robustus** n a proto-human species that lived between two and three million years ago.

Austrian /ö'stri.ən/ or /os'tri.ən/ adj of or relating to Austria, a federal republic in central Europe. ♦ n a native or citizen of Austria.
❑ **Austrian blind** n a fabric window blind with several vertical lines of shirring, giving a decorative gathered effect, esp when the blind is raised.

Austric /ö'strik/ adj belonging to a family of languages divided into **Austrōāsiat'ic** (in India and Indo-China, including the Munda or Kolarian, Mon-Khmer and Khasi groups, and the languages of the Semang and Sakai) and **Austrōnē'sian** (including the Indonesian, or Malay, Polynesian, Micronesian and Melanesian groups). [L Auster south wind]

austringer /ö'strin-jər/ n a keeper of goshawks (also **a'stringer** or **ostreger** /os'tri-jər/). [OFr ostruchier]

Austro-¹ /o-strō-/ combining form denoting: Australian; southern. [L australis southern]

Austro-² /o-strō-/ combining form denoting Austrian.

Austroasiatic, Austronesian see **Austric**.

AUT abbrev: Association of University Teachers (now replaced by UCU).

aut- see **auto-**.

autacoid /ö'tə-koid/ (med) n an internal secretion that excites or inhibits action in various tissues; a hormone or chalone. [Gr autos self, and akos drug]

autarchy /ö'tär-ki/ n absolute power; autocracy. [Gr autos self, and archein to rule]
■ **autar'chic** or **autar'chical** adj. **aut'archist** n.

autarky /ö'tär-ki/ n self-sufficiency; the economic situation of a country which is a closed economy conducting no international trade (econ). [Gr autarkeia, from autos self, and arkeein to suffice]
■ **autar'kic** or **autar'kical** adj. **aut'arkist** n.

autecology /ö-tə-kol'ə-ji/ n (the study of) the ecology of an individual organism or species. [**auto-** (1)]
■ **autecolog'ic** or **autecolog'ical** adj.

auteur /ö-tœr'/ n a film-director, esp thought of as the creator of a particular genre, and showing a unique personal stamp. [Fr, (literally) author]
■ **au'teurism** n. **au'teurist** n and adj.

authentic /ö-then'tik/ adj genuine; authoritative; true, entitled to acceptance, of established credibility; (of writing) trustworthy, as setting forth real facts; own, proper (Milton); applied in music to medieval modes (eg Gregorian chants) having their sounds within the octave above the final (qv) (cf **plagal**); in existentialism, used to describe the way of living of someone who takes full cognizance of the meaninglessness of the world yet deliberately follows a consistent course of action. [Gr authentikos warranted, from autos self]
■ **authen'tical** adj (archaic or formal) authentic. **authen'tically** adv. **authen'ticate** vt to make authentic; to prove genuine; to give legal validity to; to certify the authorship of. **authentica'tion** n. **authen'ticātor** n. **authenticity** /ö-thən-tis'i-ti/ n the quality of being authentic; the state of being true or in accordance with fact; genuineness.
❑ **authentic cadence** n (music) a perfect cadence.

author /ö'thər/ n a person who brings anything into being; a beginner of any action or state of things; the original writer of a book, article, etc (also fem **auth'oress**); elliptically, an author's writings; one's authority for something (obs). ♦ vt to create as an author. [Through Fr from L auctor, from augēre, auctum to increase, to produce]
■ **authorial** /-thö' or -thö'/ adj. **auth'oring** n. **auth'orish** adj. **auth'orism** n the state or quality of being an author. **authoriz'able** or **-s-** adj. **authoriza'tion** or **-s-** n. **auth'orize** or **-ise** vt to give authority to; to sanction; to justify; to establish by authority. **auth'orizer** or **-s-** n. **auth'orless** adj anonymous. **auth'orship** n.
❑ **auth'orcraft** n. **authorized capital** n the maximum amount of money that a company is allowed to raise by issuing shares to the public if it desires to do so. **Authorized Version** n the English translation of the Bible completed in 1611 (also called **King James Bible** or **Version**).

authority /ö-thor'i-ti/ n legal power or right; power derived from office or character or prestige; weight of testimony; permission; a person or body holding power; an expert; a passage or book referred to in witness of a statement; the original bestower of a name (biol). [L auctōritās, -ātis, from auctor (see **author**)]
■ **authorita'rian** adj setting authority above freedom; relating to, governed by, or stressing the importance and power of authority, or of a small group representing it; domineering, disciplinarian. ♦ n an authoritarian person. **authorita'rianism** n. **authoritative** /ö-thor'it-āt-iv or ö-thor'it-ət-iv/ adj having the sanction or weight of authority; accepted, approved; definitive, reliable; dictatorial. **author'itatively** adv. **author'itativeness** n.
■ **have on good authority** to be confident of the truth of a statement.

authorize, etc see under **author**.

Autif or **AUTIF** abbrev: Association of Unit Trusts and Investment Funds (now replaced by **IMA**).

autism /ö'ti-zm/ (psychiatry) n absorption in imaginative activity directed by the thinker's wishes, with loss of contact with reality; an abnormality of childhood development affecting language and social communication. [Gr autos self]
■ **autis'tic** adj and n. **autis'tically** adv.

auto¹ /ö'tō/ (chiefly N Am) n (pl **au'tos**) short form of **automobile**.

auto² /ä'ü-tō/ n (pl **au'tos**) a drama, esp a short religious one; an auto-da-fé. [Sp and Port, from L actus an act]

auto- /ö-tō-/ or sometimes before a vowel **aut-** /öt-/ combining form denoting: (1) self; (2) same; (3) self-caused; (4) automobile; (5) automatic. [Gr autos self, same]

autoantibody /ö-tō-an'ti-bo-di/ (med) n an antibody produced in reaction to an antigenic constituent of the body's own tissues. [**auto-** (1)]

Autobahn /ow'tō-bän or ö'tə-/ (Ger) n a motorway.

autobiography /ö-tō-bī-og'rə-fi or -bi-/ n an account of a person's life written by the subject; this as literary genre. [Gr autos self, bios life, and graphein to write]
■ **autobiog'rapher** n. **autobiographic** /-ō-graf'ik/ adj of the nature of autobiography. **autobiograph'ical** adj of, or relating to, autobiography; autobiographic. **autobiograph'ically** adv.

autobus /ö'tō-bus/ n a motor-bus. [**auto-** (4)]

autocade same as **motorcade** (see under **motor**). [**auto-** (4)]

autocar /ö'tō-kär/ n a motor car. [**auto-** (4)]

autocarp /ö'tō-kärp/ n a fruit produced by self-fertilization. [Gr autos self, and karpos fruit]

autocatalysis /ö-tō-kə-tal'i-sis/ n the catalysis of a reaction by a product of that reaction (chem); reaction or disintegration of a cell or tissue due to the influence of one of its own products (zool). [**auto-** (1, 3)]
■ **autocatalyse** or (N Am) **-yze** /-kat'ə-līz/ vt. **autocatalytic** /-lit'ik/ adj.

autocephalous /ö-tō-sef'ə-ləs/ (church) adj having its own head; independent. [Gr autos self, and kephalē head]
■ **autoceph'aly** n condition of being autocephalous.

autochanger /ö'tō-chān-jər/ n (a record player having) a device by means of which records are dropped from a stack one at a time onto the turntable. [**auto-** (5)]

autochthon /ö-tok'thon/ n (pl **autoch'thons** or **autoch'thonēs**) one of the primitive inhabitants of a country; an aboriginal. [Gr *autochthōn* sprung from the soil, from *autos* self, and *chthōn*, *chthonos* soil, from the myth that the original Athenians actually sprang from the soil]

■ **autoch'thonism** or **autoch'thony** n the condition of being autochthonous. **autoch'thonous** adj (of flora, fauna) indigenous; formed in the region where found (*geol*); originating in the organ in which it is found (*pathol*); (of an idea) coming into the mind with no apparent connection to the subject's train of thought (*psychol*).

autoclave /ö'tō-klāv/ n a strong, sealed vessel for carrying out chemical reactions under pressure and at high temperatures, or one in which superheated steam under pressure is used for sterilizing or cooking. ◆ vt and vi to sterilize in an autoclave. [Fr, self-fastening apparatus, from Gr *autos* self, and perhaps L *clāvis* key or *clāvus* nail]

autocoprophagy /ö-tō-ka-prof'ə-ji/ (*zool*) n the act of eating one's own faeces, refection. [**auto-** (1) and **coprophagy**]

autocorrelation /ö-tō-ko-ri-lā'shən/ (*stats*) n correlation between successive items in a series such that their covariance is not zero and they are not independent. [**auto-** (2)]

autocrat /ö'tō-krat/ or -tə-/ n a person who rules by his or her own power; an absolute sovereign; a dictatorial person. [Gr *autokratēs*, from *autos* self, and *kratos* power]

■ **autocracy** /-tok'rə-si/ n an absolute government by one person; a country, society, etc ruled by an autocrat; despotism. **autocrat'ic** adj. **autocrat'ically** adv.

autocrime /ö'tō-krīm/ n theft of, or from, a motor vehicle. [**auto-** (4)]

autocritique /ö-tō-krē-tēk'/ (Fr) self-criticism, esp political.

autocross /ö'tō-kros/ n motor racing round a rough grass track. [**auto-** (4)]

autocue /ö'tō-kū/ n a device showing a speaker the text of what he or she has arranged to say. [**auto-** (5)]

autocycle /ö'tō-sī-kl/ n a motorcycle. [**auto-** (4)]

auto-da-fé /ö'tō-da-fā'/ n (pl **autos-da-fé**) the public declaration of the judgement passed on heretics in Spain and Portugal by the Inquisition; the infliction of the punishment that immediately followed, esp the public burning of the victims. [Port *auto da fé* (Sp *auto de fe*); *auto*, from L *actum* act; *da* of the, from L *de* of; and *fé*, from L *fidēs* faith]

autodestruct /ö-tō-di-strukt'/ adj (of a craft, missile, etc) capable of destroying itself; relating to the function of self-destruction. ◆ vi (of a missile, machine, etc) to destroy itself. [**auto-** (1)]

autodidact /ö-tō-dī'dakt or ö'tō-di-dakt/ n a self-taught person. [Gr *autodidaktos*, from *autos* self, and *didaktos* taught]

■ **autodidact'ic** adj. **autodidact'ically** adv. **autodidact'icism** n.

auto-digestion /ö-tō-dī-jes'tyən or -jən, also -di-/ n autolysis. [**auto-** (1)]

autodyne /ö'tō-dīn/ (radio) adj of an electrical circuit in which the same elements and valves are used both as oscillator and detector. [**auto-** (2) and (**hetero**)**dyne**]

autoerotic /ö-tō-ə-rot'ik or -i-/ adj relating to sexual excitement or gratification gained from one's own body, with or without external stimulation. [**auto-** (1)]

■ **autoerot'icism** or **autoer'otism** n.

autoexposure /ö-tō-ek-spō'zhər/ n a system for automatically adjusting the aperture and/or shutter speed of a camera according to the lighting conditions. [**auto-** (5)]

autoflare /ö'tō-flār/ n an aircraft automatic landing system operating from an altitude of 50 feet and dependent on a very accurate radio altimeter. [**auto-** (5)]

autofocus /ö'tō-fō-kəs/ n a device that automatically focuses a camera lens on the subject being photographed (also adj). [**auto-** (5)]

autogamy /ö-tog'ə-mi/ (bot and zool) n self-fertilization. [Gr *autogamos* breeding alone, from *autos* self, and *gamos* marriage]

■ **autog'amous** or **autogamic** /ö-tō-gam'ik/ adj.

autogenous /ö-to'jə-nəs/ adj self-generated; independent; (of a graft or vaccine) produced from tissue, bacteria, from the patient's own body (*med*); (of a joint) made without flux, etc, by melting edges together (*metalwork*); capable of autogenesis (*zool*). [Gr *autogenēs*, from *genos* offspring]

■ **autogen'esis** n spontaneous generation. **autogen'ic** adj self-generated or produced from the subject's own body, autogenous. **autogen'ics** n sing (also **autogenic training**) a system of relaxation teaching voluntary control of bodily tension, etc. **autog'enously** adv. **autog'eny** n autogenesis.

autogiro or **autogyro** /ö-tō-jī'rō/ n (pl **autogi'ros** or **autogy'ros**) a rotating-wing aircraft whose chief support in flight is derived from the reaction of the air upon freely-revolving unpowered rotors. [Orig trademark; invented by Juan de la Cierva in 1923; Sp, from Gr *autos* self, and *gyros* circle]

autograft /ö'tō-gräft/ (surg) n a graft from one part to another of the same body (also vt). [**auto-** (2) and **graft**[1]]

autograph /ö'tə-gräf/ n one's own handwriting; a signature, esp that of a famous person, kept as a collector's item; an original manuscript, handwritten by the author. ◆ vt to write with one's own hand; to write one's signature in or on, to sign. ◆ adj handwritten by the author; (of painting, sculpture, etc) done by the artist, not by a pupil or follower. [Gr *autographos* written with one's own hand, from *autos* self, and *graphein* to write]

■ **autographic** /-graf'ik/ adj. **autograph'ically** adv. **autography** /ö-tog'rə-fi/ n the act of writing with one's own hand; something handwritten; reproduction of the outline of a writing or drawing by facsimile.

❑ **autograph album** or **book** n one in which to collect signatures (of friends, famous personalities, etc) and often rhymes or epigrams, etc.

autogravure /ö-tō-gra-vūr' or ö'/ n a process of photo-engraving similar to autotype. [**auto-** (2)]

autoguide /ö'tō-gīd/ adj and n (of) a system whereby information on traffic conditions is collected by road-side sensors and relayed to drivers via receivers in their vehicles. [**auto-** (4) or (5)]

autogyro see autogiro.

autoharp /ö'tō-härp/ n a kind of zither, with button-controlled dampers, which produces chords. [**auto-** (5)]

autohypnosis /ö-tō-hip-nō'sis/ n a self-induced hypnotic state, or the process of bringing it on. [**auto-** (1)]

■ **autohypnotic** /-not'ik/ adj.

auto-immunity /ö-tō-i-mū'ni-ti/ n the production by a living body of antibodies which attack constituents of its own tissues, the cause of certain serious diseases (**auto-immune diseases**). [**auto-** (1)]

■ **auto-immune'** adj. **auto-immuniza'tion** or **-s-** n.

auto-intoxication /ö'tō-in-tok-si-kā'shən/ n poisoning caused by substances produced within the body. [**auto-** (1, 3)]

■ **auto-intox'icant** n and adj.

autokinesis /ö-tō-ki-nē'sis or -kə-/ n spontaneous motion, esp the apparent movement of a stationary object. [Gr *autokinesis* self-motion]

■ **autokinet'ic** adj.

autolatry /ö-tol'ə-tri/ n worship of oneself. [Gr *autos* self, and *latreiā* worship]

autologous /ö-to'lə-gəs/ adj making use of blood or tissue obtained from (and stored for re-use in the treatment of) the same patient, prior to or during an operation or transfusion; derived from the same individual. [**auto-** (2) and *-logous* (on the model of **homologous**)]

autology /ö-tol'ə-ji/ n scientific study of oneself. [**auto-** (1)]

Autolycus /ö-tol'i-kəs/ n a thief; a plagiarist. [From the character in Shakespeare's *Winter's Tale*, or in Greek mythology]

autolysis /ö-tol'i-sis/ n the breaking down of dead tissue by enzymes produced in the organism's own cells. [Gr *autos* self, and *lysis* loosening]

■ **aut'olyse** or (N Am) **-yze** /-līz/ vt and vi to (cause to) undergo autolysis. **autolyt'ic** adj.

❑ **autolysed yeast powder** n a flavour-enhancer derived from yeast.

automagic or **automagical** /ö-tə-maj'ik(-əl)/ (sl) adj performing a task with astonishing ease and speed. [Blend of **automatic** and **magic**]

■ **automag'ically** adv.

automat /ö'tə-mat/ n a restaurant or shop where dishes, hot or cold, are obtained from slot machines (chiefly US); a vending machine, esp for food and drink; an automaton (archaic). [From trademark; after **automatic**]

automate see under **automation**.

automatic /ö-tə-mat'ik/ adj working by itself without direct and continuing human operation; (of a firearm) reloading itself from an internal magazine, or able to continue firing as long as there is pressure on the trigger; (of a motor vehicle or its gears) operated by automatic transmission; (of a telephone system) worked by automatic switches; (of behaviour, reactions, etc) done, etc without thinking, mechanical; (of a process) carried out by an automatic machine; occurring as a matter of course, inevitable. ◆ n an automatic firearm, machine, etc; the position of the switches, etc on a machine, etc that allows it to operate automatically. [Gr *automatos* self-moving, from *autos* self]

■ **automat'ical** *adj* (*archaic*). **automat'ically** *adv*. **automaticity** /-*tis'i-ti*/ *n*. **autom'atism** *n* automatic or involuntary action; an automatic act done without the full co-operation of the personality, which may even be totally unaware of its existence (*biol*); the self-acting power of the muscular and nervous systems, by which movement is effected without intelligent determination (*med* and *zool*); action without conscious volition; the doctrine that animals are automata, their movements, etc being the result of mechanical laws; suspension of control by the conscious mind, so that ideas may be released from the unconscious, a technique of surrealism (*art*). **autom'atist** *n* a person who holds the doctrine of automatism; a person who acts automatically. **autom'atize** or **-ise** *vt* to make automatic.

❑ **automatic data processing** *n* the automated handling and processing of information by computers. **automatic defibrillator** *n* a small battery-powered device implanted in the body which senses and corrects abnormal heart rhythms. **automatic drive** *n* automatic transmission. **automatic gain control** *n* a system in amplifiers that compensates for a wide range of input signals to give a more uniform level of output. **automatic pilot** *n* (also **au'topilot**) a device which can be set to guide and control an aircraft or a ship on a chosen course; used *fig* of an automatism that takes over one's actions or behaviour in fatigue, abstraction, etc. **automatic teller** or **automatic teller machine** *n* an electronic panel set into the exterior wall of a bank, etc from which (on the insertion of a card and the keying of a personal identification number) customers are able to obtain cash, information about their accounts, etc (*abbrev* **ATM**). **Automatic Train Protection** *n* a system which automatically stops or slows down a train in response to a signal or speed restriction (*abbrev* **ATP**). **automatic transmission** *n* (in a motor vehicle) power transmission by fluid drive, allowing gears to change automatically; the transmission of (*usu*) computer data between two points via a telephone system. **Automatic Vehicle Identification** *n* a system for toll roads which recognizes electronically-tagged vehicles and automatically charges the owner's account (*abbrev* **AVI**). **automatic vending** *n* the sale of products (eg cigarettes, confectionery) by means of coin-operated slot-machines. **automatic writing** *n* writing performed without the volition of the writer.

automation /ö-tə-mā'shən/ *n* a high degree of mechanization in manufacture, the handling of material between processes being automatic and the whole system being automatically controlled. [Irreg formation from **automatic**]

■ **aut'omate** *vt* to apply automation to. **aut'omated** *adj*.
❑ **automated teller machine** same as **automatic teller machine** (see under **automatic**).

automaton /ö-tom'ə-tən/ *n* (*pl* **autom'atons** or **autom'ata**) a machine that imitates the movement of a living creature, activated by a concealed mechanism such as clockwork; such a machine as a toy, amusement or decoration; a living being regarded as without consciousness; a person who acts by routine, without intelligence or feeling. [Gr, neuter of *automatos* (see **automatic**)]

automobile /ö'tə-mō-bēl/ *n* a motor car. ♦ *adj* /ö-tō-mō'bīl/ self-moving. [Gr *autos* self, and L *mōbilis* mobile]

■ **automobil'ia** *n pl* collectable items of motoring interest. **automō'bilism** *n*. **automō'bilist** *n*.

automorphism /ö-tō-mör'fizm/ *n* ascription to others of one's own characteristics; isomorphism of an algebraic system with itself (*maths*). [Gr *autos* self, and *morphē* form]

■ **automor'phic** *adj* marked by automorphism; idiomorphic. **automor'phically** *adv*.

automotive /ö-tə-mō'tiv/ *adj* self-propelling; of or relating to automobiles; of or relating to the motor car trade. [Gr *autos* self, and LL *motivus* causing to move]

autonomy /ö-ton'ə-mi/ *n* the power or right of self-government, *esp* partial self-government; an autonomous state or region; independence from others; the Kantian doctrine that the human will carries its guiding principle within itself (*philos*). [Gr *autonomos*, from *autos* self, and *nomos* law]

■ **autonomic** /ö-tō-nom'ik/ *adj* self-governing; relating to the autonomic nervous system (*zool*); spontaneous (*bot* and *zool*). **autonom'ical** *adj*. **autonom'ically** *adv*. **autonom'ics** *n sing* the study of self-regulating systems for process control. **auton'omist** *n*. **auton'omous** *adj* (of a country, region, etc) (partially) self-governing; independent (of the will) guided by its own principles (*philos*); autonomic (*bot* and *zool*). **auton'omously** *adv*.
❑ **autonomic nervous system** *n* (*zool* and *med*) in vertebrates, a system of nerve fibres, innervating muscles, glands, etc, whose actions are automatic (*abbrev* **ANS**).

autonym /ö'tə-nim/ *n* a writing published under the author's real name; an author's real name. [Gr *autos* self, and *onyma, onoma* name]

autophagous /ö-to'fə-gəs/ *adj* self-devouring; (of a bird) capable of feeding itself from the moment of hatching. [Gr *autos* self, and *phagein* to eat]

■ **autopha'gia** or **autophagy** /-ə-ji/ *n* sustenance by self-absorption of the tissues of the body, eg during starvation (*med*); in a lysosome, the intracellular digestion of material of the cell (*biochem*); eating or biting of part of one's own body (*psychiatry*).

autophanous /ö-to'fə-nəs/ *adj* self-luminous. [Gr *autos* self, and *phānos* bright]

autophony /ö-to'fə-ni/ (*med*) *n* in the diagnosis of thoracic disease, observation of the resonance of one's own voice by speaking with the ear on the patient's chest; a condition in which the patient is aware of increased resonance of his or her voice, pulse, etc in the head, as in certain diseases of the middle ear, etc. [Gr *autos* self, and *phōnē* sound]

autopilot see **automatic pilot** under **automatic**.

autopista /ö' or ow'tō-pē-sta/ (*Sp*) *n* a motorway.

autoplasty /ö'tō-pla-sti/ (*surg*) *n* grafting of healthy tissue from another part of the same body. [Gr *autos* self, and *plastos* formed]
■ **autoplas'tic** *adj*.

autopoint /ö'tō-point/ *n* a point-to-point (qv under **point**[1]) over rough country in motor vehicles. [**auto-** (4)]

autopsy /ö'top-si or -top'/ *n* (also **autop'sia**) a post-mortem examination of a corpse; personal inspection (*obs*). ♦ *vt* to perform an autopsy on. [Gr *autos* self, and *opsis* sight]
■ **autopt'ic** or **autopt'ical** *adj*. **autopt'ically** *adv*.

autoradiography /ö-tō-rā-di-og'rə-fi/ *n* a technique used to show the distribution of radioactively labelled molecules in cells or tissues. [**auto-** (1)]
■ **autora'diograph** *n* an autoradiographic record. **autoradiograph'ic** *adj*.

autoreply /ö-tō-ri-plī'/ *n* a facility which allows a previously-written response to be sent automatically in reply to incoming email (also called **autorespon'der**); a message sent by this. [**auto-** (5)]

auto-reverse /ö-tō-ri-vûrs'/ *n* and *adj* (a facility provided in a cassette player for) reversing the tape direction so as to play the following side on completion of the first, without turning the tape over manually. [**auto-** (5)]

autorickshaw /ö-tō-rik'shö/ *n* a light, three-wheeled vehicle powered by a motorcycle engine, used in India, etc. [**auto-** (4)]

autoroute /ö- or ō-tō-root'/ (*Fr*) *n* a motorway.

autosave /ö'tō-sāv/ (*comput*) *n* a facility which automatically saves newly-recorded data at regular intervals (also *vi* and *vt*). [**auto-** (5)]

autoschediasm /ö-tō-sked'i-a-zm or -skē'di-/ *n* anything which is extemporized. [Gr *autoschediasma* improvisation, *autoschediazein* to extemporize, from *autoschedon* on the spot, from *autos* self, and *schedios* off-hand]
■ **autoschedias'tic** *adj*. **autosched'iaze** /-āz/ *vt*.

autoscopy /ö-to'skə-pi/ (*psychol*) *n* hallucination of an image of one's body. [Gr *autos* self, and *skopeein* to see]
■ **autoscop'ic** *adj*.

autosome /ö'tō-sōm/ (*biol*) *n* a chromosome other than a sex-chromosome. [Gr *autos* self, and *sōma* body]
■ **autosom'al** *adj*.

autostrada /ö'tō- or ä'oo-tō-strä-də/ (*Ital*) *n* a motorway.

auto-suggestion /ö-tō-sə-jes'chən/ (*psychol*) *n* a mental process similar to suggestion, but originating in a belief in the subject's own mind. [**auto-** (3)]
■ **auto-sugges'tive** *adj*.

autotelic /ö-tō-tel'ik or -tə-/ *adj* being an end in itself, or its own justification. [Gr *autotelēs*, from *autos* self, and *telos* end]

autoteller /ö'tō-tel-ər/ *n* an automatic cash dispenser. [**auto-** (5)]

autotest /ö'tō-test/ *n* a competition in which drivers race standard road cars around a circuit. [**auto-** (4)]

autotheism /ö-tō-thē'i-zm/ *n* assumption of divine powers; the doctrine of the self-subsistence of God, *esp* of the second person in the Trinity (*theol*). [Gr *autos* self, and *theos* a god]
■ **autothe'ist** *n*.

autotimer /ö'tō-tī-mər/ *n* a device on a cooker, etc that can be adjusted in advance to turn the apparatus on or off at a desired time. [**auto-** (5)]

autotomy /ö-tot'ə-mi/ (*zool*) *n* the reflex casting off of part of its body by an animal attempting to escape. [Gr *autos* self, and *tomē* cut]

autotoxin /ö-tō-tok'sin/ *n* a poisonous substance formed within the organism against which it acts. [**auto-** (1)]
■ **autotox'ic** *adj*.

autotransformer /ö-tō-trans-för'mər/ *n* a transformer having at least part of the windings common to both the primary and secondary circuits. [**auto-** (2)]

autotransplantation /ö-tō-trans-plän-tā'shən (or -plan-)/ (*surg*) *n* the reinsertion of a transplant or graft from a particular individual in the same individual. [**auto-** (1)]

autotrophic /ö-tō-trof'ik/ (*biol*) *adj* (of an organism) able to generate all its chemical constituents from simple, inorganic compounds (*esp* all its carbon compounds from carbon dioxide). [Gr *autos* self, and *trophē* food]
■ **au'totroph** *n* an autotrophic organism. **autotroph'ism** or **au'totrophy** *n*.

autotype /ö'tō-tīp/ *n* a true impression or copy of the original; a process of printing from a photographic negative in a permanent pigment. ◆ *vt* to reproduce by such a process. [**auto-** (2)]
■ **autotypog'raphy** *n* a process by which drawings made on gelatine are transferred to a plate from which impressions may be taken.

autovac /ö'tō-vak/ *n* a vacuum mechanism in a motor car for raising petrol to a higher tank so that it may flow by gravity to the carburettor. [**auto-** (4)]

autowinder /ö'tō-wīn-dər/ (*photog*) *n* a device for advancing the film in a camera automatically. [**auto-** (5)]

autoxidation /ö-tok-si-dā'shən/ (*chem*) *n* the oxidation of a substance by exposure to air. [**auto-** (5)]
■ **autox'idative** *adj*.

autrefois acquit, **attaint** or **convict** /ō-trə-fwä a-kē', a-tē' or kō-vē'/ (*law*) three defence pleas, arguing that a defendant cannot be charged a second time with an offence of which he or she has been acquitted, or a (capital) offence of which he or she has been found guilty. [Fr]

autre temps, autre moeurs /o-trə tä', o-trə mær'/ (*Fr*) other times, other manners (or customs).

autumn /ö'təm/ *n* the season of the year when fruits are gathered in, lasting approximately from September to November in the northern hemisphere and from March to May in the southern hemisphere; in the astronomical year, the period of time between the autumnal equinox and the winter solstice; a period of harvest or of maturity. [L *autumnus*]
■ **autum'nal** /ö-tum'nəl/ *adj* relating to autumn; blooming in autumn; beyond the prime (*fig*); withering or withered (*fig*). **autum'nally** *adv*. **au'tumny** /-tə-mi/ *adj* (*inf*) autumn-like.
❑ **autumn crocus** *n* a species of *Colchicum*, meadow-saffron.

autunite /ö'tu-nīt or -tə-/ *n* a mineral composed of a hydrous phosphate of uranium and calcium. [*Autun* in France, where it is found]

auxanometer /ök-sə-no'mi-tar/ *n* an instrument for measuring plant-growth. [Gr *auxanein* to grow, and *metron* measure]

aux armes /ö-zärm'/ (*Fr*) to arms.

auxesis /ök-sē'sis/ *n* increase in size; hyperbole; growth resulting from an increase in cell size (*biol*; *obs*). [Gr *auxēsis* increase]
■ **auxet'ic** *adj* involving increase in size. ◆ *n* something that promotes auxesis.

auxiliary /og- or ög-zil'(y)ə-ri or -ē'ri/ *adj* helping; subsidiary; peripheral (*comput*). ◆ *n* a helper; a subordinate or assistant person or thing; an auxiliary verb (*grammar*); (*esp* in *pl*) a soldier serving with another, allied, nation; a naval vessel not used for combat. [L *auxiliāris*, from *auxilium* help, from *augēre* to increase]
■ **auxil'iar** *n* and *adj* (*archaic*) (an) auxiliary.
❑ **auxiliary language** *n* a language, such as English or Esperanto, used by speakers of other languages to aid communication. **auxiliary verb** *n* (*grammar*) a verb that helps to form the mood, tense or voice of another verb.

auxin /ök'sin/ (*bot*) *n* any of a number of growth-promoting substances present in minute quantities in plants. [Gr *auxein* to increase]

auxometer /ök-som'i-tər/ (*optics*) *n* an instrument for measuring magnifying power. [Gr *auxein* to increase, and *metron* measure]

auxotroph /ök'sō-trof/ *n* a mutant organism requiring an unusually large supply of nutritional substances owing to an inability to produce a certain enzyme. [Gr *auxein* to increase, and *trophe* food]

AV *abbrev* : Alternative Vote; audiovisual; (also **A.V.**) Authorized Version (*Bible*).

Av a variant spelling of **Ab**.

Av. *abbrev* : Avenue (in street names); *Avocat* (*Fr*), lawyer; *Avril* (*Fr*), April.

av *abbrev* : *annos vixit* (*L*), lived (so many) years.

av. same as **ave.**

AVA *abbrev* : audiovisual aid(s).

ava¹ or **ava'** /ə-vö'/ (*Scot*) *adv* at all. [For *of all*]

ava² /ä'vä/ same as **kava.**

avadavat /av-ə-də-vat'/ or **amadavat** /am-ə-/ *n* an Indian songbird related to the weaver birds. [From *Ahmadabad*, whence they were sent to Europe as cage-birds]

avail¹ /ə-vāl'/ *vt* to be of value or service to; to benefit; (reflexively with *of*) to make use, take advantage; to give (someone) the benefit (of), inform (someone of) (*esp US*; *archaic*). ◆ *vi* to be of use; to answer the purpose; to draw advantage, be the better (*Shakesp*). ◆ *n* effectual advantage (*archaic* except in phrases such as *of* or *to no avail*, *of any avail*); (in *pl*) profits, proceeds (*obs*). [L *ad* to, and *valēre* to be worth, to be strong; appar modelled on **vail³**]
■ **avail'ful** *adj* (*obs*) of avail; serviceable. **avail'ing** *adj*. **avail'ingly** *adv*.

avail², **availe** see **avale.**

available /ə-vā'lə-bl/ *adj* at one's disposal, that one may avail oneself of; accessible; within reach; obtainable; to be had or drawn upon; valid (*law*); profitable (*obs*). [**avail¹** and **-able**]
■ **availabil'ity** *n* the quality of being available; power of effecting or promoting an end; the possession of qualities, other than merit, which predispose a candidate to success in an election (*esp US politics*; *archaic*). **avail'ableness** *n*. **avail'ably** *adv*.
❑ **available market** *n* (*business*) a market where goods can be sold and bought freely, the price being fixed by the law of supply and demand.

aval /ä'vəl/ *adj* relating to a grandparent. [L *avus* grandfather]

avalanche /av'ə-länsh, -länch, -lansh, -lanch or -lönsh/ *n* a hurtling mass of snow, with ice and rock, descending a mountainside; a landslip; a snowslip, eg from a roof; an overwhelming influx (*fig*); a shower of particles resulting from the collision of a high-energy particle with matter (*nucleonics*). ◆ *vt* and *vi* to carry or come down as or like an avalanche. [Fr dialect, from *avaler* ; see **avale**]

avale, **avail** or **availe** /ə-vāl'/ (*obs*) *vt* to lower (*Spenser*); to doff. ◆ *vi* (*Spenser*) to come down; to alight. [Fr *avaler* to descend, from *à* (L *ad*) to, and *val* (L *vallis*) valley]

avant /a-vä'/ (*Fr*) before.
❑ **avant-goût** /-goo/ *n* a foretaste. **avant-propos** /-prō-pō/ *n* preliminary matter; a preface.

avant-courier /a-vä-kŭr'i-ər' or -kŭ-ryä'/ *n* a person who runs or is sent ahead; (in *pl*) scouts or advance guard (*hist*). [Fr *avant-coureur* forerunner, scout; *avant-courrier* forerunner]

avant-garde /av-ä-gärd'/ *n* those who create or support the newest ideas and techniques in an art, etc. ◆ *adj* of or relating to the avant-garde; daringly innovative or unconventional. [Fr, vanguard]
■ **avant-gard'ism** *n* avant-garde theory or practice, or support of these. **avant-gard'ist** or **avant-gard'iste** *n* a member of the avant-garde.

avanti /a-vän'tē/ (*Ital*) *interj* forward.

avanturine see **aventurine.**

avarice /av'ə-ris/ *n* eager desire for wealth; covetousness. [Fr, from L *avāritia*, from *avārus* greedy, from *avēre* to pant after]
■ **avaricious** /-ish'əs/ *adj* extremely covetous, grasping, mercenary; greedy for gain. **avari'ciously** *adv*. **avari'ciousness** *n*.

avascular /ə-vas'kū-lər or ā-/ (*med*) *adj* not having blood vessels. [Gr *a-* (privative), and **vascular**]

avast /ə-väst'/ (*naut*) *interj* hold fast! stop! [Prob Du *houd vast* hold fast]

avatar /av'ə-tär/ *n* the manifestation of a Hindu deity in a visible form; incarnation; supreme glorification of any principle (*fig*); a movable image used to represent someone in cyberspace (*comput*). [Sans *ava* away, down, and root *tar-* to pass over]

avaunt¹ /ə-vönt'/ *interj* (*archaic*) move on; begone. ◆ *n* (*Shakesp*) dismissal. ◆ *vi* (*obs*) to advance (*Spenser*); to depart. [Fr *avant* before, from L *ab* from, and *ante* before]

avaunt² /ə-vönt'/ (*obs*) *vt* and *vi* to boast. ◆ *n* a boast. [OFr *avanter*, from LL *vānitāre* to boast, from L *vānus* vain]

AVC *abbrev* : additional voluntary contribution (to a pension scheme); automatic volume control.

■ words derived from main entry word; ❑ compound words; ■ idioms and phrasal verbs

avdp. or **avoir.** *abbrev* : avoirdupois.

ave /ä'vē, ä'vi or ä'vā/ (*formal, archaic,* or *esp RC church*) *interj* be well and happy; hail. ◆ *n* (*RC*) a recitation of the ave Maria (see below). [Imperative of L *avēre* to be well. See **angelus**]
◻ **ave Maria** /ä'vä mə-rē'ə/ *n* (*RC*) an address or prayer to the Virgin Mary (Bible, Luke 1.28) (also called **ave Mary, hail Mary, angelic salutation**).
■ **ave atque vale** /ä'vē at'kwi va'lē or ä'vä (-wä) at'kwe vä'lä (wä')/ (*L*) hail and farewell.

ave. or **av.** /av/ *abbrev* : avenue; average.

avec plaisir /a-vek ple-zēr'/ (*Fr*) with pleasure.

Avena /a-vē'nə/ *n* the oat genus of grasses. [L *avēna* oats]
■ **avenaceous** /av-i-nā'shəs/ *adj* of the nature of oats; belonging to the Avena genus.

avenge /ə-venj'/ or *-venzh'/ vt* to take vengeance on someone on account of; to requite or repay. ◆ *n* (*obs*) revenge. [OFr *avengier,* from L *ad* to, and *vindicāre* to claim. See **vengeance**]
■ **avenge'ful** *adj.* **avenge'ment** *n* (*archaic*). **aveng'er** *n.* **aveng'eress** *n* (*rare*) a female avenger. **aveng'ing** *adj.*

avenir /a-və-nēr'/ (*Fr*) *n* future.

avens /av'ənz/ *n* any plant of the hardy rosaceous genus *Geum* (eg **water avens** *Geum rivale,* with pinkish flowers; **wood avens** herb bennet, with yellow flowers); also the related sub-alpine **mountain avens** (*Dryas octopetala*), an evergreen dwarf shrub that bears white flowers. [OFr *avence*]

aventail or **aventaile** /av'ən-tāl/ (*hist*) *n* the flap or movable part of a helmet in front, for admitting air. [OFr *esventail* airhole, from L *ex* out, and *ventus* wind]

aventre /a-ven'tr/ (*Spenser*) *vt* (*appar*) to thrust, direct. [Origin unknown]

aventure /ə-ven'chər/ obsolete form of **adventure.**

aventurine /a-ven'chə-rin/ or **avanturine** /-van'/ *n* a brown, spangled kind of Venetian glass; a kind of quartz enclosing spangles of mica or haematite (also **gold'stone**). ◆ *adj* shimmering or spangled, eg of certain kinds of feldspar or sealing wax. [Ital *avventura* chance, because of the accidental discovery of the glass]

avenue /av'ə-nū or (*N Am*) -noo/ *n* the principal approach to a country house, *usu* bordered by trees; a double row of trees, with or without a road; a wide and handsome street, with or without trees; (with *cap*) used in street names generally; any passage or entrance into a place; means of access or attainment (*fig*). [Fr, from L *ad* to, and *venīre* to come]

aver[1] /ə-vûr'/ *vt* (**averr'ing; averred'**) to declare to be true; to affirm or declare positively; to allege in a pleading in a court action (*law*). [Fr *avérer,* from L *ad* and *vērus* true]
■ **aver'ment** *n* positive assertion; an allegation in a pleading in a court action (*law*).

aver[2] /ä'vər/ (*obs*) *n* possessions; cattle; a draught animal, *esp* an old or worthless cart-horse (*Scot*). [OFr *aveir, aver* (Fr *avoir*) possessions, stock, from L *habēre* to have]

average /av'(ə-)rij/ *n* the arithmetical mean value of any quantities (see under **mean**[3]); estimation of such a mean; loosely, an ordinary or typical value, common run; *orig* a customs duty or similar charge (*obs*); any expense other than freight payable by the owner of shipped goods; expense or loss by damage of ship or cargo; equitable distribution of expense or loss; assessment of compensation in the same proportion as amount insured bears to actual worth. ◆ *adj* mean, medial; prevailing, typical, ordinary; mediocre. ◆ *vt* to obtain the average of; to amount to on an average; to do or achieve on an average. ◆ *vt* and *vi* to even out to an average. [Cf Fr *avarie,* Ital *avaria* duty on goods, from Ar *'awārīyah* damaged goods; poss connected with **aver**[2]]
■ **av'eragely** *adv.*
◻ **average adjuster** *n* an assessor employed by an insurance company in marine claims. **average costing** *n* (*business*) a method of calculating the average cost of producing one unit by taking the total manufacturing costs for a period and dividing by the number of units produced.
■ **law of averages** popularly, a proposition stating that the mean of a situation is maintained by the averaging of its extremes. **on average** typically.

Avernus /a-vûr'nəs or a-ver'nŭs, or -wer'/ (*poetic*) *n* the (entrance to the) infernal regions (*Roman myth*); any abyss (after Lake Avernus in Campania). [L, from Gr *aornos* (*limnē*) birdless (lake), from the tradition that birds were killed by the lake's poisonous exhalations]

Averroism or **Averrhoism** /a-və-rō'i-zm/ *n* the doctrine of the Arab philosopher *Averrhoës* (1126–98), that the soul is perishable, the only

immortal soul being the world-soul from which individual souls went forth, and to which they return.
■ **Averro'ist** or **Averrhō'ist** *n.*

averse /ə-vûrs'/ *adj* disinclined (with *to* or sometimes pedantically *from*); reluctant; turned away or backward (*obs*); turned away from the main axis (*bot*). [L *āvertere, āversus,* from *ab* from, and *vertere* to turn]
■ **averse'ly** *adv.* **averse'ness** *n.* **aver'sion** *n* turning aside; dislike; hatred; the object of dislike. **aver'sive** *adj* showing aversion; with the purpose, or result, of averting. **avert'** *vt* to turn aside; to prevent; to ward off. **avert'ed** *adj.* **avert'edly** *adv.* **avert'ible** or (*rare*) **avert'able** *adj* capable of being averted.
◻ **aversion therapy** *n* treatment of a person suffering from an undesirable habit or a compulsive form of behaviour by associating his or her thoughts about it with something unpleasant such as the administration of an electric shock.

avert see under **averse.**

avertiment /ə-vûr'ti-ment/ (*Milton*) *n* advertisement.

Avertin® /ə-vûr'tin/ *n* tradename of the anaesthetic *tribromoethanol.*

Aves /ä'vēz, ä'vās or -wäs/ *n pl* birds as a class of vertebrates. [L *avis* bird]
■ **ā'vian** *adj* of or relating to birds. **ā'viarist** *n* a person who keeps an aviary. **ā'viary** *n* a large cage or enclosure, etc for keeping birds. **ā'viculture** (or /av'/) *n* bird-rearing; bird-fancying. **āvifau'na** (or /av-/) *n* the bird-life found in a region. **āvifau'nal** *adj.* **ā'viform** (or /av'/) *adj* birdlike in form or structure. **ā'vine** *adj* avian.
◻ **avian flu** or **avian influenza** see **bird flu** under **bird.**

Avesta /ə-ves'tə/ *n* the Zoroastrian holy Scriptures. [Pehlevi *Avîstâk* lore]
■ **Aves'tan** or **Aves'tic** *adj* of the Avesta or its East-Iranian language. ◆ *n* the language of the Avesta (also called **Zend**).

avgas /av'gas/ (*US*) *n* any kind of aviation gasoline.

avgolemono /av-gə-lem'ə-nō/ (*Gr*) *n* a soup or sauce made from chicken stock, lemon juice and egg yolks. [Mod Gr *avgo* egg, and *lemono* lemon]

AVI *abbrev* : Automatic Vehicle Identification.

avian, aviary, etc see under **Aves.**

aviate /ā'vi-āt/ *vi* to fly mechanically, navigate the air. [Back-formation from **aviation**; ult from L *avis* a bird]
■ **āviā'tion** *n* the art or practice of mechanical flight; the production, design, operation, etc of aircraft; the aircraft industry; (*usu military*) aircraft collectively (*US*). **ā'viator** *n* a pilot who flies aircraft, an airman or airwoman. **ā'viatress** or **aviatrix** /ā-vi-ā'triks/ *n* a female pilot.
◻ **aviation spirit** *n* a motor fuel with a low initial boiling point and complying with a certain specification, for use in aeroplanes.

Avicula /ə-vik'ū-lə/ *n* a genus of pearl oysters, so named from their winglike shape, giving the name to the family **Avicūl'idae.** [New L, from L *avicula* little bird]

Avicularia /ə-vik-ū-lār'i-ə/ *n* the bird-catching spider genus, giving the name to the family **Avicularī'idae.** [New L, from L *aviculārius* bird-keeper]

aviculture see under **Aves.**

avid /av'id/ *adj* greedy; eagerly desirous (for). [L *avidus*]
■ **avid'ity** *n* greed; desire, eagerness; a measure of the strength of binding between an antigen and an antibody (*immunol*). **av'idly** *adv.* **av'idness** *n.*

avidin /av'i-din/ *n* a protein found in egg white which combines with biotin and prevents its absorption. [From **avid** and biot*in*]

aviette /ā-vi-et'/ (*hist*) *n* an aeroplane driven by man-power; a type of glider. [Fr, from **avion** and dimin sfx *-ette*]

avifauna, aviform, avine see under **Aves.**

avion /av-yɔ̃'/ (*Fr*) *n* an aeroplane.
■ **par avion** /par av-yɔ̃/ by air; by airmail.

avionics /ā-vi-on'iks/ *n sing* the science concerned with the development and use of electronic and electrical devices for aircraft and spacecraft; (*usu pl*) the electronic equipment on an aircraft or spacecraft. [aviation and electr*onics*]
■ **avion'ic** *adj.*

avirulent /ā-vir'ū-lənt or a-/ *adj* not causing infection or disease. [**a-**[2] and **virulent**]

avisandum see **avizandum.**

avis au lecteur /a-vē ō lek-tœr'/ (*Fr*) notice to the reader.

avise, avize or **avyze** /ə-vīz'/ obsolete forms (*Spenser,* etc) of **advise.**
■ **avise'ment** *n* (*obs*). **avize'full** *adj* (*Spenser*) watchful.

avised see **black-a-vised** under **black.**

aviso /ə-vī'zō/ n (pl **avi'sos**) an advice-boat (hist); a notification (obs). [Sp, advice, advice-boat, from L ad visum (see **advice**)]

avital /ə-vī'təl or av'i-təl/ (obs) adj of a grandfather; ancestral. [L avītus, from avus a grandfather]

avitaminosis /ā-vi-tə-mi-nō'sis or ə- or -vī-/ (med) n (pl **avitaminoses** /-ēz/) lack of vitamins or a condition due to this. [**a-²**, **vitamin** and **-osis**]

avizandum /a-vi-zan'dəm/ (Scots law) n private consideration of a case by a judge before giving judgement (also **avisan'dum**). [Gerund of LL avizāre, avisāre to advise]

avize, **avizefull** see **avise**.

AVM abbrev : Air Vice-Marshal; automatic vending machine.

avo /av'ō/ n (pl **av'os**) a monetary unit in Macau, 1/100 of a pataca. [Port]

avocado /a-və-kä'dō/ n (pl **avoca'dos**) a tropical evergreen tree of the laurel family; (also **avocado pear** /pär/) its pear-shaped fruit, with buttery-textured, bland-flavoured flesh around a single large stone (also **alligator pear**); the colour of the skin of the fruit, blackish-green; the colour of the flesh of the fruit, yellowish green (also adj). [Sp aguacate, from Aztec ahuacatl]

avocat consultant /a-vō-kä kõ-sül-tä'/ (Fr) n consulting lawyer, chamber counsel.

avocation /a-vō-kā'shən or -və-/ n properly, a diversion or distraction from one's regular employment; improperly used for **vocation**, business which calls for one's time and attention; diversion of the thoughts from any employment (archaic); the calling of a case to a higher court (law; hist). [L āvocātiō, -ōnis a calling away, from ab from, and vocāre to call]

avocet or **avoset** /av'ə-set/ n a wading bird (genus Recurvirostra) with webbed feet and long, slender, curved, elastic bill. [Fr avocette, Ital avosetta]

Avogadro's constant or **number** /a-və-gä'drōz kon'stənt or num'bər/ (phys) n the number of specified elementary units (eg molecules, atoms, ions) in a mole of any substance. [A Avogadro (1776–1856), Italian physicist]

Avogadro's law, **rule** or **hypothesis** /a-və-gä'drōz lö, rool or hī-poth'ə-sis/ (phys) n the law that at equal temperature and pressure equal volumes of gases contain the same number of molecules. [Ety as for **Avogadro's constant**]

avoid /ə-void'/ vt to evade, escape; to shun, shirk; to empty (obs); to invalidate (law); to leave, quit (Shakesp); to dismount from (obs). ♦ vi (obs) to take oneself off. [Anglo-Fr avoider, OFr esvuidier, from L ex out, and root of **void**]
 ■ **avoid'able** adj. **avoid'ably** adv. **avoid'ance** n the act of avoiding or shunning; an act of annulling (law); the shunning of certain relatives among primitive peoples (anthrop). **avoid'er** n.
 □ **avoidable costs** n pl (econ) costs which arise exclusively from investment or production decisions and which would not be incurred if no output took place.

avoirdupois /av-ər-də-poiz', av' or av-wär-dü-pwä'/ n a system of weights in which the pound (lb) equals 16 ounces (oz) (abbrev **avdp.** or **avoir.**); weight, esp heaviness or stoutness (facetious). ♦ adj of the system of weights. [OFr aveir de pes to have weight, from L habēre to have, dē from, and pēnsum that which is weighed]

avoision /ə-voi'zhən/ n a portmanteau word coined by the Institution of Economic Affairs in 1979 to represent a compromise, and blurring of the moral distinction, between tax avoidance (which is legal) and tax evasion (which is illegal).

à volonté /a vo-lõ-tā'/ (Fr) at pleasure.

avoparcin /ā-vō-par'sin/ n an antibiotic, formerly used to promote growth in farm animals, but banned by the European Union in 1997 as being possibly responsible, through the food chain, for human resistance to the chemically similar antibiotic vancomycin (qv).

avoset see **avocet**.

a vostro beneplacito /a vos'trō bā-nā-plä'chē-tō/ (Ital) at your pleasure, at your will.

à votre santé /a votr' sä-tā'/ (Fr) to your health.

avouch /ə-vowch'/ (archaic) vt to avow or to acknowledge; to vouch for; to assert positively, to maintain; to guarantee; to own to; to appeal to (obs). ♦ vi to give assurance. ♦ n (Shakesp) evidence. [OFr avochier, from L advocāre to call to one's aid. See **vouch**, **advocate**]
 ■ **avouch'able** adj. **avouch'ment** n.

avoure /a-vowr'/ (Spenser) n avowal. [See **avow**]

avoutrer /a-voo'trər/ or **avouterer** /-tə-rər/ and **avoutry** /-tri/ obsolete forms of **adulterer** and **adultery**.

avow /ə-vow'/ vt to declare; to acknowledge, own to; to maintain or affirm. ♦ vi (law) to justify an act done. ♦ n (archaic) a solemn promise; a vow. [OFr avouer, orig to swear fealty to, from L ad to, and LL vōtāre, from L vōtum a vow: with sense affected by L advocāre. See **vow** and **avouch**]
 ■ **avow'able** adj. **avow'ableness** n. **avow'al** n a positive declaration; an acknowledgement; a frank confession. **avowed'** adj. **avow'edly** adv. **avow'er** n. **avow'ry** n the act of avowing and justifying in one's own right the distraining of goods (law; hist); advocacy considered as personified in a patron saint (obs).

avoyer /a-vwa-yā'/ (Fr) n formerly, the chief magistrate in some Swiss cantons.

AVR abbrev : Army Volunteer Reserve.

a vuestra salud /a vŭ-äs'tra sä-loodh'/ (Sp) to your health.

avulse /ə-vuls'/ vt to pluck or tear away by force. [L āvellere, āvulsum]
 ■ **avul'sion** n forcible separation; a tearing away, out of or off (eg med, of part of the body); the sudden removal of land by change of a river's course or flooding, whereby it remains the property of the original owner, opp to alluvion.

avuncular /ə-vung'kū-lər/ adj of or suitable to an uncle; benign, kindly. [L avunculus an uncle]

avvogadore /a-vō-ga-dō'rä/ (Ital) n an official criminal prosecutor in Venice.

avyze see **avise**.

aw /ö/ (chiefly Scot and N Am) interj expressing disappointment, sympathy, disgust, etc.

awa or **awa'** /ə-wo' or -wä'/ (Scot) adv away.

AWACS /ā'waks/ abbrev : airborne warning and control system (a radar system mounted on an aircraft, used to detect enemy planes, and to control weapons or planes directed against them).

await /ə-wāt'/ vt to wait or look for; to be in store for; to attend (obs); to lie in wait for, to watch for (obs). ♦ n (Spenser) an ambush, watch. [ONFr awaitier, from à to and waitier (see **wait¹**)]

awake /ə-wāk'/ vt (pat usu **awoke'**, sometimes **awaked'**; pap **awōk'en**, also (archaic) **awaked'** or **awoke'**) to rouse from sleep; to rouse from inaction, cause to be active or alert. ♦ vi to cease sleeping; to rouse oneself from sleep, inattention or indifference. ♦ adj not asleep; vigilant; alert, aware, cognizant (with to). [OE āwǣcnan (pat āwōc, pap āwacen), confused with āwacian (pat āwacode). See **wake¹**, **watch**]
 ■ **awak'en** vt to awake; to rouse into interest or attention; to call to a sense of sin (theol). ♦ vi to awake; to spring into being. **awak'ening** adj becoming awake; rousing; revivifying, reanimating. ♦ n a becoming awake, aware or active; a throwing off of indifference or ignorance; a rousing. **awak'ing** n and adj.
 ■ **be awake to** to be fully aware of.

awanting /ə-won'ting/ (chiefly Scot; archaic) adj wanting; missing. [**a-¹**, and the gerund of **want¹**]

award /ə-wörd'/ vt to give officially as a payment or prize; to determine such payment, etc; to adjudge; to grant. ♦ n that which is awarded; a prize; judgement or final decision, esp of arbitrators. [OFr ewarder, eswarder to determine or ordain after examination, from L ex thoroughly, and the root of **ward** and **guard**]
 ■ **awardee'** n. **award'er** n.

aware /ə-wār'/ adj informed or conscious (usu with of or that); wary (obs). [OE gewær wary, watchful, from wær cautious. See **ware³**]
 ■ **aware'ness** n state of being aware; consciousness, esp a vague or indistinct form.

awarn /ə-wörn'/ (Spenser) vt to warn. [Pfx a- (intensive) and **warn¹**]

awash /ə-wosh'/ adv on a level with the surface of the water; afloat at the mercy of the waves. ♦ adj having the surface covered with water; full of (with with). [**a-¹**]

awatch /ə-woch'/ (archaic) adv on the watch. [**a-¹**]

awave /ə-wāv'/ (archaic) adv in a wave; in waves. [**a-¹**]

away /ə-wā'/ adv onward; continuously; without hesitation, stop or delay; forthwith; out of the place in question; not at home; on the opponents' ground (sport; also adj); at or to a distance; off; in or into an averted direction; out of existence, life or consciousness; with effect of removal or elimination; far; about (after here, there or where; now dialect); (with omission of verb; usu acting as an imperative) = go away or (with with) take away; (with omission of verb; usu acting as an infinitive after can, may, etc) to endure (with with; archaic). ♦ n (football pools) a match won by a team playing on the opponents' ground. ♦ interj begone; get out. [OE aweg, onweg, from on on, and weg way]
 ■ **aways'** (obs, Spenser **awayes'**) adv away.
 □ **away'day** n an occasion when members of an organization meet in a place other than their usual premises (also adj).

■**away from it all** in or into a place which is remote from the bustle of life. **away you go!** or **away with you** an expression of disbelief or scepticism. **make away with** to steal, run off with; to destroy (*archaic*).

AWD *abbrev:* all-wheel drive.

awdl /ow'dl/ (*Welsh*) *n* a Welsh ode conforming to the strict metrical, alliterative and internal rhyming conventions of traditional bardic verse.

AWE *abbrev:* Atomic Weapons Establishment.

awe /ö/ *n* reverential wonder or fear; dread; power to inspire awe (*archaic*). ♦ *vt* to strike with or influence by awe or fear. [ON *agi;* cf OE *ege* fear; Gr *achos* distress]
■**awed** /öd/ *adj* awe-stricken; expressive of awe. **awe'less** *adj* without awe; fearless; regarded without awe (*Shakesp*). **awe'lessness** *n*. **awe'some** (or *obs* **aw'some**) *adj* awed; awe-inspiring; dreadful; amazing, great, impressive (*sl*). **awe'somely** *adv*. **awe'someness** *n*. ❑ **awe'-inspiring** *adj* causing or deserving a sense of awe; astonishing, breathtaking. **awe'-stricken** or **awe'-struck** *adj* struck with awe. **awe'-strike** *vt*.

aweary /ə-wē'ri/ (*archaic*) *adj* weary. [Pfx *a-* (intensive) and **weary**[1]]
■**awea'ried** *adj* weary.

a-weather /ə-wedh'ər/ (*naut*) *adv* towards the weather or windward side, *opp* to *alee*. [**a-**[1]]

a-week /ə-wēk'/ *adv* in the week. [**a-**[1]]

aweel /ə-wēl'/ (*Scot*) *interj* well; well then. [*ah well*]

aweigh /ə-wā'/ (*naut*) *adv* in the process of being raised, as an anchor just raised from the bottom. [**a-**[1] and **weigh**[1]]

aweto /ə-wā'tō or (*Maori*) ä-fe'tō/ *n* (*pl* **awe'tos**) the so-called vegetable caterpillar, the body of the caterpillar filled with a parasitic fungus, used to obtain a pigment. [Maori *aweheto*]

awful /ö'fəl/ *adj* very bad, thoroughly unpleasant; tiresomely great (*inf*); inspiring awe, causing dread (*archaic*); filled with awe (*obs*). ♦ *adv* (*inf*) very. [**awe**, with sfx *-ful*]
■**aw'fully** *adv* very, thoroughly (*inf*); badly, dreadfully; so as to fill with awe or terror, in an awe-inspiring manner (*archaic*); in an awe-struck manner (*archaic*). **aw'fulness** *n*.

awfy /ö'fi/ (*Scot*) *adv* awfully; extremely. [Dialect form of **awfully**]

awhape /ə-(h)wāp'/ (*Spenser*) *vt* to confound or amaze. [Cf Gothic *af-hwapjan* to choke]

awheel (*obs* **awheels**) /ə-(h)wēl(s)'/ *adv* on wheels, *esp* on a bicycle. [**a-**[1]]

a'where see under **a'**.

awhile /ə-(h)wīl'/ *adv* for some time; for a short time. [OE *āne hwīle* a while (dative); combined as early as 13c]

a-wing /ə-wing'/ *adv* on the wing. [**a-**[1] and **wing**[1]]

AWK or **awk** /ök/ *n* a computer-programming language used for data processing. [From the initials of its developers Alfred Aho, Peter Weinberger, and Brian Kernighan]

awkward /ök'wərd/ *adj* clumsy; ungraceful; embarrassed; difficult to deal with; embarrassing; oblique, inverted, backhanded (*obs*); froward (*obs*); adverse (*Shakesp*). [Prob ON *afug* turned the wrong way, and sfx *-ward*]
■**awk'wardish** *adj*. **awk'wardly** *adv*. **awk'wardness** *n* clumsiness; embarrassing or inharmonious quality or condition.

awl /öl/ *n* a pointed instrument for boring small holes. [OE *æl;* ON *alr,* Ger *Ahle*]
❑ **awl'bird** *n* (*dialect*) the green woodpecker; the avocet.

awmous /ö'məs/ (*Scot*) *n* alms. [ON *almusa;* cf OE *ælmysse* alms]

awmrie, awmry see **ambry**.

awn[1] /ön/ *n* the beard of barley, or similar bristly growth or structure from a glume, etc. [ON *ögn,* or a lost OE cognate; Ger *Ahne*]
■**awned** *adj*. **awn'er** *n* a machine for removing the awns from grain. **awn'less** *adj*. **awn'y** *adj*.
❑ **awn hair** *n* one of the bristly hairs which form the intermediate layer of fur in certain mammals.

awn[2] see under **awning**.

awning /ö'ning/ *n* a covering (*esp* of canvas) to shelter eg a window, door or patio from the sun or weather. [Origin unknown; Fr *auvent* window-shade, may be connected]
■**awn** *vt* to shelter with an awning.

awny see under **awn**[1].

awoke /ə-wōk'/ *pat* of **awake**.

AWOL /ā'wol/ (*milit*) *abbrev*: absent (or absence) without official leave.

awork /ə-wûrk'/ (*archaic*) *adv* at work. [**a-**[1]]

awrack /ə-rak'/ (*obs*) *adv* in a state of wreck. [**a-**[1], and **wrack**[1,2]]

awrong /ə-rong'/ (*obs*) *adv* wrongly. [**a-**[1]]

awry /ə-rī'/ *adj* twisted to one side; distorted, crooked; wrong, amiss. ♦ *adv* askew; unevenly; perversely; erroneously. [**a-**[1]]
■**look awry** to look askance at anything. **walk awry** (*archaic*) to go wrong.

AWU /ā'woo/ *abbrev*: atomic weight unit.

ax. *abbrev*: axiom.

axe or (*N Am*) **ax** /aks/ *n* (*pl* **ax'es**) a tool for cutting or chopping, having its edge and handle in the same plane; a pointed stone-dressing hammer (*building*); the ruthless cutting down of expenditure (*fig*); dismissal from one's job (with *the; inf*); a musical instrument, eg (in jazz) a saxophone or (*esp* in rock music) a guitar (*sl*). ♦ *vt* to cut or strike with an axe; to dismiss as superfluous (*inf*); to cut down, reduce (*fig*); to dispense with (*fig*). [OE *æx;* cf Gr *axīnē*]
❑ **axe'-breaker** *n* (*Aust*) any of several kinds of hard-wooded tree. **axe'-head** *n*. **axe'man** (*US usu* **ax'man**) *n* a man who carries or uses an axe; a man who plays a guitar or (*esp* jazz) other musical instrument (*sl*); a ruthless cutter of costs (*inf*). **axe'-stone** *n* a kind of jade used for making axes.
■**axe to grind** a personal reason for getting involved.

axel /ak'səl/ (*ice skating*) *n* a jump from one skate to the other, incorporating one and a half or (**double axel**) two and a half turns in the air. [*Axel* Paulsen (1855–1938), Norwegian skater]

axenic /ā-zen'ik/ *adj* (of a biological culture) not contaminated. [Gr *a-* (privative), and *xenos* strange, foreign]

axerophthol /ak-sə-rof'thol/ *n* vitamin A, a pale yellow crystalline substance, deficiency of which causes xerophthalmia. [**a-**[2] and **xerophthalmia** (see under **xero-**)]

axes plural of **axe** and **axis**[1].

axial, axile see under **axis**[1].

axilla /ak-sil'ə/ *n* (*pl* **axill'ae** /-ē/) the armpit (*anat*); the axil (*bot*). [L *āxilla* the armpit]
■**ax'il** *n* (*bot*) the upper angle between leaf and stem or branch and trunk. **ax'illar** or **ax'illary** *adj*.

axinite /ak'si-nīt/ *n* a brilliant brown mineral with axe-shaped crystals, containing calcium, aluminium, boron, silicon, etc. [Gr *axīnē* an axe]
■**axin'omancy** *n* (Gr *manteiā* divination) divination from the motions of an axe poised upon a stake, or of an agate placed upon a red-hot axe.

axiology /ak-si-ol'ə-ji/ (*philos*) *n* the science of the ultimate nature, reality and significance of values. [Gr *axia* worth, value, from *axios* worthy, and **-logy**]
■**axiological** /-ə-loj'i-kl/ *adj*. **axiolog'ically** *adv*. **axiologist** /-ol'ə-jist/ *n*.

axiom /ak'si-əm/ *n* a self-evident truth; a universally received principle; an assumption made for the purpose of argument. [Gr *axiōma, -atos,* from *axioein* to think worthy, to take for granted, from *axios* worthy]
■**axiomat'ic** or **axiomat'ical** *adj*. **axiomat'ically** *adv*. **axiomat'ics** *n sing* the study of axioms and axiom systems. **axiomatize** or **-ise** /-om'ə-tīz/ *vt*.

axioma medium /ak-si-ō'ma mē'di-əm or med'i-ŭm/ (L) *n* a generalization from experience.

axion /ak'si-on/ (*phys*) *n* a hypothetical elementary particle. [*axial* and **-on** (1)]

axis[1] /ak'sis/ *n* (*pl* **axes** /ak'sēz/) a line about which a body rotates, or about which a figure is conceived to revolve; a straight line about which the parts of a figure, body or system are symmetrically or systematically arranged; a fixed line adopted for reference in co-ordinate geometry, curve-plotting, crystallography, etc; an axle (*obs*); the second vertebra of the neck in higher vertebrates (*zool*); the main stem or root, or a branch in relation to its own branches and appendages (*bot*); an alliance of powers, as if forming together an axis of rotation, *esp* the political alliance of Germany and Italy (1936). [L *axis* an axle; cf Gr *axōn,* Sans *aksa,* OE *eax*]
■**ax'ial** *adj* relating to, or of the nature of, an axis. **axial'ity** *n*. **ax'ially** *adv*. **ax'ile** /ak'sīl/ *adj* (*bot*) coinciding with an axis. **ax'oid** *n* a curve generated by the revolution of a point round an advancing axis.
❑ **axial skeleton** *n* (in vertebrates) the skull, vertebral column, sternum and ribs. **axial tomography** *n* (*med*) a technique of tomography using a camera that rotates on an axis. **axis cylinder** *n* (*anat*) the excitable core of a medullated nerve-fibre. **axis of incidence** *n* the line passing through the point of incidence of a ray perpendicularly to the refracting surface. **axis of refraction** *n* the continuation of the same line through the refracting medium. **axis of the equator** *n* the polar diameter of the earth which is also the axis of rotation.

axis[2] /ak'sis/ *n* (*pl* **ax'ises**) a white-spotted deer of India. [L *axis,* Pliny's name for an Indian animal]

axle /ak'sl/ n the pin or rod in the nave of a wheel on or by means of which the wheel turns; a rounded spindle end of an axle-tree; a pivot or support of any kind (*fig*); an axis (*obs*). [More prob ON *öxull* than a dimin from OE *eax*]
□ **ax'le-box** n the box (eg on a railway carriage) in which the axle end turns. **ax'le-guard** n a pedestal (qv) or pillow-block. **ax'le-tree** n a crossbar or shaft fixed across the underside of a cart or similar vehicle, on each rounded end of which a wheel rotates; an axle (*obs*).

Axminster /aks'min-stər/ n a variety of cut-pile carpet, the tufts of pile each being inserted separately into the backing during its weaving (also *adj*). [*Axminster* in Devon, where it originated]

axoid see under **axis¹**.

axolotl /ak'sə-lo-tl/ n a type of Mexican salamander (genus *Ambystoma*) commonly retaining its larval character throughout life, though capable of breeding. [Aztec]

axon /ak'son/ (*anat* and *zool*) n an extension of a nerve cell or neuron which transmits impulses away from the cell. [New L, from Gr *axōn* axis]
■ **ax'onal** adj. **ax'oplasm** n the cytoplasm of an axon. **axoplas'mic** adj.

axonometric /ak-sə-nō-met'rik/ adj of an architectural or other projection in which a drawing of a three-dimensional object has all lines to exact scale, with all parallel lines remaining parallel, so that it appears distorted. [Gr *axōn* (see **axon**), -*o*- and -**metric** (see -**meter**)]

ay¹ /ä/ interj ah, oh; alas, *esp* in ay me. [ME *ey, ei*, perh from Fr *ahi, ai*; cf Sp *ay de mi*]

ay² see **aye¹**.

ay³ see **aye²**.

ayah /ī'ə/ n in India and other former British territories, a waiting-maid or nursemaid (also **aia**). [Hindi *āyā*; from Port *aia* nurse]

ayahuasca /a-ya-(h)was'kə/ or **ayahuasco** /-kō/ n (pl **ayahuas'cas** or **ayahuas'cos**) a S American vine of the family Malpighiaceae; a drink made from the roots of the vine, having hallucinatory effects. [Am Sp *ayahuasca*, from Quechua *ayawáskha*]

ayatollah /a-yə-tol'ə or -tō'lə/ n (sometimes with *cap*) a Muslim religious leader of the Shiah sect; (loosely) an ideological leader or policy maker. [Pers, from Ar, sign of God, from *āyat* sign, and *allāh* God]

aye¹ or **ay** /ī/ adv yes; indeed. ◆ n (in parliamentary use and generally **aye**) a vote in the affirmative; a person who votes in the affirmative. ◆ interj (*naut*; *usu* **aye aye**) expressing affirmation, agreement, compliance with an order. [Perh a dialect form of **aye²**; perh a variant of **yea**]
■ **the ayes have it** (in parliament) affirmative votes are in the majority.

aye² or **ay** /ā/ (now Scot and N Eng or archaic) adv ever; always; for ever. ◆ combining form denoting ever, as in Shakespeare's **aye'remaining**, etc. [ON *ei* ever; OE *ā*; connected with **age** and **ever**]
■ **for aye** or **for ever and aye** for ever, to all eternity.

aye-aye /ī'ī/ n an arboreal squirrel-like nocturnal lemur of Madagascar, with very long thin fingers. [Malagasy *aiay*]

ayelp /ə-yelp'/ adv in a state of yelping. [**a-¹**]

ayenbite /ä-yen'bīt/ (*obs*) n remorse, as in the book-title *Ayenbite of Inwyt* (remorse of conscience). [ME *ayen* again, and **bite**]

aygre /ā'gər/ (*Shakesp*) same as **eager¹**.

ayin /ä'yēn/ n the sixteenth letter of the Hebrew alphabet. [Heb]

Aylesbury /ālz'bə-ri/ n a breed of ducks much valued as food. [A market town in Bucks]

Aymara /ī-mə-rä'/ n (pl **Aymaras'** or (collectively) **Aymara'**) a people of S America; a member of the Aymara people; their language (of the Andean-Equatorial family), now confined to Bolivia, Peru and parts of N Chile. [Sp *aimara*]
■ **Aymaran'** adj and n.

ayont /ə-yont'/ (Scot and N Eng) adv and prep beyond. [Pfx *a*-, and **yond**]

ayre /ār/ n an old spelling of **air**, *esp* as a tune or song, in particular an Elizabethan or Jacobean song for solo voice.

ayrie same as **eyrie**.

Ayrshire /ār'shər/ n a breed of reddish-brown and white dairy cattle. [The former Scottish county, where they originated]

ayu /ä'ū, ī'(y)oo/ or **ai** /ī/ n a small edible Japanese fish (*Plecoglossus altevis*) (also called **sweet'fish**). [Jap]

ayuntamiento /a-yoon-ta-mē-än'tō/ (*Sp*) n (pl **ayuntamien'tos**) a municipal council.

ayurveda /ī-oor- or ī-ə-vā'də/ (also with *cap*) n the traditional Indian medicine system, in which good health is seen as a balance of energies, achieved through detoxification, meditation, diet, yoga, astrology and herbal medicine. [Sans, knowledge of long life]
■ **ayurve'dic** (also with *cap*) adj.

ayword /ā'wûrd/ (*Shakesp*) n a byword, proverbial reproach. [Origin obscure]

AZ abbrev : Arizona (US state); Azerbaijan (IVR).

azalea /ə-zā'li-ə/ n a plant of the group of deciduous shrubs, *Azalea*, (formerly a separate genus, now a subgenus of *Rhododendron* with five stamens and annual leaves) popular for their many showy flowers. [Gr *azaleos* dry; reason for name uncertain]

azan /ä-zän'/ n the Muslim call to public prayer made five times a day by a muezzin. [Ar '*adhan* invitation]

Azania /ə-zā'ni-ə or -zä'/ n a name given to South Africa by supporters of Black majority rule during apartheid. [Origin uncertain]
■ **Aza'nian** n and adj.

Azapo /a-za'pō/ abbrev : Azanian People's Organization.

azathioprine /a-zə-thī'ə-prēn/ n a synthetic drug used in transplant surgery to suppress the body's immune system. [**azo-, thio-** and **purine**]

azeotrope /a-zē'ə-trōp/ (*chem*) n any liquid mixture which distils without a change in the proportion(s) of its components at a boiling point which *usu* differs from that of any component. [Gr *a*- (privative), *zeein* to boil, and *tropos* a turn]
■ **azeotrop'ic** /-trop'/ adj.

Azerbaijani /a-zər-bī-jä'ni or -zhä'ni/ adj of or relating to the republic of *Azerbaijan* in E Transcaucasia, its people or its language. ◆ n (pl **Azerbaija'nis** or **Azerbaija'ni**) a native or inhabitant of Azerbaijan; the Turkic language of Azerbaijan; an Iranian who speaks Azerbaijani as his or her native tongue.
■ **Azer'i** n an Azerbaijani (also *adj*).

azide /ā'zīd or az'īd/ (*chem*) n a salt or an ester derived from hydrazoic acid. [**azo-** and chem sfx -*ide*]
■ **azidothy'midine** n AZT (qv), a derivative of thymidine.

Azilian /ə-zil'i-ən/ (*archaeol*) adj belonging to a period of transition between Palaeolithic and Neolithic. [Mas d'*Azil*, Ariège, where objects of this culture have been found in a cave]

azimuth /az'i-məth/ (*astron, surveying*, etc) n the arc of the horizon between the meridian of a place and a vertical circle passing through any celestial body. [Ar *as-sumūt*, from *as* = *al* the, and *sumūt*, pl of *samt* direction. See **zenith**]
■ **az'imuthal** (or /-mūdh' or -mūth'/) adj of or relating to the azimuth. □ **azimuthal projection** a zenithal projection.

azine /ā'zēn or -zin/ (*chem*) n any six-membered organic compound containing one or more nitrogen atoms. [**azo-**]

azione /a-tsi-ö'nā/ (*music*) n a composition performed as a drama. [Ital]
□ **azione sacra** /sak'ra/ n an azione that is like an oratorio in form. **azione teatrale** /tā-ä-tral'ā/ n a type of stylized music theatre.

azo- or **az-** /ā- or a-zō, āz or az/ combining form denoting nitrogen. [**azote**]
■ **azo-com'pound** n a compound in which two nitrogen atoms are each attached to (*usu*) a carbon atom, eg **azoben'zene** $C_6H_5N:NC_6H_5$. **azo dye** n a dye (*usu* yellow, red or brown) containing an azo-compound.

Azobacter same as **Azotobacter** (see under **azote**).

azoic /ə-zō'ik/ adj without life; before the existence of animal life; (of rocks, etc) formed when there was no animal life on the Earth, containing no organic traces. [Gr *a*- (privative), and *zōē* life]

azole /ā'zōl, az'ōl/ n any of various organic compounds with a five-membered ring. [**azo-**]

azolla /ə-zol'ə/ n a tiny water fern of the genus *Azolla*, native to tropical or subtropical areas, able to fix nitrogen and used as a green manure. [New L, appar formed from Gr *azein* to dry, and *ollynai* to destroy]

azonal /ə-zō'nəl or ā-/ adj not arranged in zones or regions. [Gr *a*- (privative), and *zōnē* a belt]
■ **azonic** /a-zon'ik/ adj not limited to a zone, not local.

azoospermia /ā- or ā-zō-ō-spûr'mi-ə/ n absence of spermatazoa in semen, causing infertility. [**a-²** and **zoosperm**]
■ **āzōösper'mic** adj.

azote /a-zōt'/ n an old name for nitrogen, so called because it does not sustain animal life. [Gr *a*- (privative), and *zaein* to live]
■ **azot'ic** /a-zot'ik/ adj nitric. **az'otize** or -**ise** vt to combine with nitrogen. **Azōtobac'ter** (or **Azōbacter**) n a genus of nitrogen-fixing bacteria. **azō'tous** adj nitrous. **azotur'ia** n an excess of urea or other

nitrogenous substances in the urine (*med*); muscle weakness occurring in horses during or after training (*vet*).

azoth /ā'zoth/ *n* the alchemists' name for mercury; Paracelsus's universal remedy. [From Ar *az-zāūg*, from *al* the, and *zāūg*, from Pers *zhīwah* quicksilver]

Azrael or **Azrail** /az'rā-əl/ (*Jewish* and *Islamic myth*) *n* the angel of death.

AZT *abbrev* : azidothymidine, a drug used in the treatment of AIDS.

Aztec /az'tek/ *n* one of a people dominant in Mexico before the Spanish conquest; the Aztec language, Nahuatl. ◆ *adj* of the Aztecs or their language.
◻ **Aztec two-step** *n* (*sl*) Montezuma's revenge, diarrhoea.

azulejo /a-thoo-lā'hhō/ (*Sp*) *n* (*pl* **azule'jos**) a painted and glazed pottery tile.

azure /azh'ər, ā'zhər or ā'zhūr/ *adj* of a delicate blue; sky-coloured; blue (represented in engraving, etc by horizontal lines) (*heraldry*). ◆ *n* a delicate blue colour; the sky. [OFr *azur*, from

LL *azura*, from Ar *al* the, and *lazward*, Pers *lājward* lapis lazuli, blue colour]
■ **azurē'an** or **az'urine** /-īn/ *adj* azure. **az'urine** *n* a blue-black aniline dye; a freshwater fish, the blue roach. **az'urite** *n* blue basic carbonate of copper, chessylite. **az'urn** *adj* (*Milton*) azure. **az'ury** *adj* bluish.

azygous /az'i-gəs/ *adj* not yoked or joined with another (*biol*); not having a paired structure (*anat*). [Gr *azygos*, from *a-* (privative), and *zygon* a yoke]
■ **az'ygos** *n* (*biol*) an unpaired structure. **az'ygously** *adv*. **azygy** /az'i-ji/ *n*.

azymous /az'i-məs/ *adj* unfermented; unleavened. [Gr *azmos*, from *a-* (privative), and *zȳmē* leaven]
■ **az'ym** /-im/ or more usually **az'yme** /-īm or -im/ *n* unleavened bread. **az'ymite** *n* (also with *cap*) a member of any church using unleavened bread in the Eucharist.

B or **b** /bē/ n the second letter in the modern English alphabet as in the Roman, corresponding to the Greek *beta* (B, β), its sound a voiced bilabial stop; the seventh note of the diatonic scale of C major (H in German notation, B being used for B flat) (*music*); the key or scale having that note for its tonic (*music*); one of the four blood types in the ABO blood group system; the designation of the subsidiary series of paper sizes (used for posters), ranging from B0 (1000 × 1414mm) to B10 (31 × 44mm); in road-classification, followed by a number, the designation of secondary roads; in hexadecimal notation, 11 (decimal) or 1011 (binary); the second highest in a category or range; something or someone of the second class or order, or of a class arbitrarily designated B; a designation indicating lesser importance, secondary billing, etc such as the **B'-side** of a record or a **B'-movie**; anything shaped like the letter B.
  ❑ **B flat** or **B** n a 19c euphemism for a domestic bedbug. **B'-list** *adj* (*inf*) not belonging to the most important or famous group (of celebrities, etc). **B'-lister** n. **B lymphocyte** or **B cell** n a type of lymphocyte or cell, originating (in mammals) in the bone marrow, which manufactures antibodies, present on the cell surface, in response to stimulation by an antigen. **B quadratum**, **quadrate B** or **square B** n in old music, B natural. **B rotundum** or **round B** n in old music, B flat. **B'-school** n business school.

B or **B.** *abbrev*: Bachelor; Baron; bass (*music*); Belgium (IVR); bishop (in chess); Britain; British.

B *symbol*: (as a medieval Roman numeral) 300; baryon number (*phys*); black (on lead pencils to indicate softness); boron (*chem*).

B *symbol*: magnetic flux density.

B̄ *symbol*: (medieval Roman numeral) 3000.

B- (*aeronautics*) *pfx* used to designate a bomber plane.

b or **b.** *abbrev*: barrel(s); bastard; billion; book; born; bowled (*cricket*).

b *abbrev*: breadth.

BA *abbrev*: Bachelor of Arts; Booksellers Association (of the United Kingdom and Ireland); British Academy, a body promoting literary and social studies; British Airways; British Association for the Advancement of Science.

Ba (*chem*) *symbol*: barium.

ba /bä/ n in ancient Egyptian religion, the soul, represented as a bird with a human head. [Egypt]

ba' /bö/ n Scots form of **ball**[1,2].
  ■ **ba'ing** and **ba'spiel** n see under **ball**[1].

baa /bä/ n the cry of a sheep. ◆ *vi* to bleat. [Imit]
  ■ **baa'ing** n.

Baal /bä'əl/ n (*pl* **Bä'alim**) a god of the Phoenicians, *orig* probably a fusion of many local gods; a false god generally. [Heb]
  ■ **Bä'alism** n. **Bä'alite** n.

baas /bäs/ (*S Afr*) n master, overseer, sir (*esp* as used by a black or coloured South African addressing a white). [Afrik, from Du]
  ■ **baas'skap** n the condition in which one section of the population is treated as a master race; the theory used to justify this.

Baathist or **Ba'athist** /bä'thist/ n a member of the socialist or reformist party of various Arab countries, *esp* Syria and Iraq (also *adj*). [Ar *baath* renaissance]
  ■ **Baa'thism** or **Ba'a'thism** n.

baba /bä'bä/ n a small cake, leavened with yeast, with or without fruit, soaked in a rum syrup (also **rum baba** or **baba au rhum** /ō rom/). [Fr, from Pol *baba* old woman]

babaco /bə-bak'ō/ n a subtropical five-sided fruit related to papaya, *orig* from Ecuador.

babacoote /bab'ə-koot/ n a large lemur, the indri or a closely related species. [Malagasy *babakoto*]

baba ghanouzh, **baba ganoush** or **baba ganouj** /bä'ba gə-noosh' or -noozh'/ n a purée made with aubergines and tahini, flavoured with garlic and lemon juice, used in Middle-Eastern cookery. [Ar]

babassu /bab-ə-soo'/ n a Brazilian palm (genus *Attalea*) or its oil-yielding nut. [Prob Tupí]

Babbitt /bab'it/ n a conventional middle-class businessman (or other person) who esteems success and has no use for art or intellectual pursuits. [Eponymous hero of novel (1922) by Sinclair Lewis]
  ■ **Babb'ittry**, **Babb'itry** or **Babb'ittism** n.

babbitt /bab'it/ vt to fit with **Babbitt**, **Babbit** or **Babbitt's metal**, a soft anti-friction alloy (tin, with copper, antimony, and *usu* lead). [Isaac *Babbitt* (1799–1862), the Massachusetts inventor]

babble /bab'l/ vi to speak like a baby; to make a continuous murmuring sound like a brook, etc; to talk incoherently or irrelevantly; to talk incessantly; to divulge secrets. ◆ vt to say in a confused, uncontrolled or unthinking way; to divulge by foolish talk. ◆ n idle senseless talk; disturbance caused by interference from other conversations (*telecom*); confused murmuring, as of a stream. [Prob imit, from the repeated syllable *ba*; cf Du *babbelen*, Ger *pappelen*, Fr *babiller*, perh influenced by *Babel*]
  ■ **babb'lative** *adj*. **babb'lement** n. **babb'ler** n someone who babbles; (also **babbling brook**) a cook (*Aust rhyming sl*); any of a large group of noisy, chattering, thrush-like birds (also **babbling thrush**). **babb'ling** n and *adj*. **babb'ly** *adj*.

babe /bāb/ n a form of **baby** (especially in literary use); an affectionate term of address (*inf*); a girl or girlfriend (*inf*); a stunningly attractive woman or man (*inf*).
  ■ **babeli'cious** *adj* (*sl*) stunningly attractive.

Babee see **Babi**.

Babel /bā'bl/ n (also without *cap*) a confused sound of voices; (also without *cap*) a scene of confusion; a foolishly conceived lofty structure. [Heb *Bābel*, prob Assyrian *bāb-ili*, gate of God, associated in the Bible (Genesis 11.9) with confusion]
  ■ **bā'beldom** n. **bā'belish** or **bab'elesque** *adj*. **bā'belism** n.

babesiasis /ba-bi-zī'ə-sis/ or **babesiosis** /ba-bē-zē-ō'sis/ n redwater, a cattle infection caused by the parasite **Babesia** /ba-bē'zh(y)ə/. [Victor *Babès* (died 1926), Romanian bacteriologist]

Babi or **Babee** /bä'bē/ n a member of an eclectic Persian sect, followers of *Bab*-ed-Din 'the Gate of Righteousness' (Mirza Ali Mohammed, 1819/20–50), who claimed to be a prophet bringing a new revelation from God (also **Ba'bist**).
  ■ **Ba'bism**, **Ba'biism** or **Ba'beeism** n.

babiche /ba-bēsh'/ n rawhide used for strapping and laces. [Fr-Can, from Algonquian]

babingtonite /bab'ing-tə-nīt/ n a pyroxene, ferrous silicate with admixtures, sometimes worked as an iron ore. [William *Babington* (1756–1833), mineralogist]

Babinski effect or **reflex** /bə-bin'ski i-fekt' or rē'fleks/ (*physiol*) n a reflex curling upwards of the toes when the sole of the foot is stroked, normal in babies but abnormal in others. [Joseph *Babinski* (1857–1932), French neurologist]

babiroussa, **babirusa** or **babirussa** /bä-bi-roo'sə/ n a wild hog found *esp* in Sulawesi, Indonesia, with great upturned tusks in the male. [Malay *bābi* hog, and *rūsa* deer]

Babism see under **Babi**.

bablah /bab'lə/ or **babul** /bä'bool or -bool'/ n a species of acacia (*A. arabica*) from which gum arabic is obtained; the pods of that and other species, used for tanning. [Hindi and Pers *babūl*]

baboo see **babu**.

baboon /bə-boon'/ n a large monkey of various species, with long muzzle, dog-like tusks, large lips, a tail, and buttock-callosities; a clumsy, uncouth person of low intelligence. [ME *babewyn* grotesque figure, baboon, from OFr *babuin*, poss from *baboue* grimace]
  ■ **baboon'ery** n. **baboon'ish** *adj*.

■ words derived from main entry word; ❑ compound words; ■ idioms and phrasal verbs

babouche, **babuche** or **baboosh** /bə-boosh'/ n an Oriental heelless slipper. [Fr, from Ar *bābūsh*, from Pers *pā* foot, and *pūsh* covering]

babu or **baboo** /bä'boo/ n a title for Hindus in some parts of India corresponding to Mr; an Indian clerk; an Indian with a superficial English education (*esp hist*). ♦ *adj* superficially learned. [Hindi *bābū*]
■ **ba'budom** n. **ba'buism** n.

babuche see **babouche**.

babul see **bablah**.

babushka /bə-boosh'kə/ n a triangular headscarf tied under the chin (chiefly *US*); a grandmother, granny, elderly woman. [Russ *bābushka* grandmother, dimin of *baba* old woman]

baby /bā'bi/ n an infant, young child; an unborn child; the youngest or smallest member of a family or group; a young animal; a babyish person; a thing small of its kind, as varieties of grand piano, car, etc; a small incandescent spotlight used in film and television production (*image technol*); a girl, girlfriend, often as an affectionate term of address (*inf*); an inexperienced person; one's pet project, invention, machine, etc; one's own responsibility; a doll (*obs*); the reflection of oneself in the pupil of another's eye (*obs*). ♦ *vt* (**ba'bying**; **ba'bied**) to treat like a baby; to pamper. ♦ *adj* of or relating to babies; being the smallest member of a family or group. [Prob imit. See **babble**]
■ **ba'byhood** n. **ba'byish** adj.
❑ **ba'by-batterer** n an adult who makes frequent violent assaults on an infant. **ba'by-battering** n. **baby beef** n beef from calves which are fattened for slaughter on a diet of roughage and high protein concentrates. **Baby Bell** n (*US inf*) a regional telephone company. **baby blue** n a pale shade of blue. **baby blues** n pl (*inf*) postnatal depression; blue eyes. **baby bond** n (*inf*) a special savings scheme for children. **baby bonus** n (*inf*, chiefly *Can* and *Aust*) family allowance. **baby boom** n (*inf*) a sudden sharp increase in the birth rate. **baby boomer** n a person born during a baby boom, *esp* that which followed World War II. **ba'by-bouncer** (*Brit*) or **ba'by-jumper** (*US*) n a harness or seat suspended from springs, elastic straps, etc in which a young baby can amuse itself. **Baby Buggy**® n a light, collapsible pushchair for a baby or toddler. **baby carriage** n (*N Am*) a baby's pram. **baby daddy** or **baby father** n (*inf*) a man who has fathered a child but who is not regarded by the mother as a permanent partner. **baby doll** n a doll in the form of a baby; a woman with an innocent childlike appearance and personality. **baby-doll pyjamas** n pl women's pyjamas with a loose top and very short bottoms with elasticated legs. **baby face** n a young-looking face, *esp* one plump and smooth like a baby's; someone with such a face. **ba'by-farming** n (*obs*) looking after infants for pay. **ba'byfood** n any of various foods specially prepared, eg by straining, blending, etc, for babies. **baby grand** n a small grand piano, about 5 feet in length. **Ba'bygro**® n an all-in-one stretch-fabric suit for a baby. **baby house** n a doll's house. **ba'by-minder** n a person who takes in young children to look after for pay. **baby oil** n an emollient oil for the skin, *esp* of babies. **ba'by-ribbon** n a very narrow ribbon. **baby's breath** n a variety of gypsophila with fragrant flowers. **ba'by-sit** vi and (*esp N Am*) vt to act as baby-sitter (to). **ba'by-sitter** n a person who looks after a baby, child or children to relieve the usual carer. **ba'by-sitting** n. **ba'by-snatcher** n a person marrying or having as a lover someone who is much younger (*usu derog*; also **cradle-snatcher**); a person who steals a baby, eg from its pram (*inf*). **ba'by-snatching** n. **baby talk** n the speech of babies learning to talk, or an adult's imitation of it. **baby tooth** n a milk tooth. **ba'by-walker** n a wheeled frame with a canvas, etc seat for supporting a baby learning to walk.
■ **be left holding the baby** to be left in the lurch with an irksome responsibility. **throw the baby out with the bathwater** to get rid of the essential along with the superfluous.

babycino or **babyccino** /bā'bi-chē-nō/ n (*pl* **ba'bycinos** or **ba'byccinos**) a drink of frothy steamed milk, often served with a sweet topping. [**baby** and **cappuccino**]

Babylon /bab'i-lon/ n a place of sorrowful exile; a place, etc of luxury and decadence, used (*derog*) formerly by Protestants in reference to the Roman Catholic Church, more recently by Rastafarians of Western culture, or generally by one group of another group which they consider to be corrupt. [*Babylon*, city of ancient Mesopotamia]
■ **Babylō'nian** adj of Babylon; huge, gigantic; Romish, popish (*obs*; from the identification with Rome of the scarlet woman of the Bible, Revelation 17); Babel-like, confused in language; luxurious, decadent. ♦ n an inhabitant of Babylon; the ancient language of Babylonia, Akkadian. **Babylon'ish** adj.
❑ **Babylonian** or **Babylonish captivity** n the exile of the Jews deported to Babylon in 597 and 586BC, lasting until c.538; the exile of the popes at Avignon, 1309–77.

BAC *abbrev*: formerly, British Aircraft Corporation.

bac /bak/ (*inf*) n short form of **baccalaureate**.

Bacardi® /bə-kär'di/ n a type of rum, *orig* produced in the West Indies.

bacca /bak'ə/ (*bot*) n a berry. [L *bacca* a berry]
■ **bacc'ate** adj having berries; berry-like; pulpy. **bacciferous** /bak-sif'ər-əs/ adj bearing berries. **bac'ciform** adj of the shape of a berry. **bacciv'orous** adj living on berries.

baccalaureate /ba-kə-lö'ri-ət/ n the university degree of bachelor, or a diploma of lesser status awarded by a college, etc. [LL *baccalaureus*, altered from *baccalārius*. See **bachelor**]
■ **baccalau'rean** adj.

baccarat or **baccara** /bak'ə-rä/ n a French card game in which players bet money against the banker; a type of crystal made at *Baccarat*, France. [Fr]

baccare see **backare**.

baccate see under **bacca**.

Bacchus /bak'əs/ n the (chiefly Roman) god of wine. [L *Bacchus*, Gr *Bakchos*]
■ **Bacchae** /bak'ē/ n pl priestesses or female followers of Bacchus. **bacchanal** /bak'ə-nəl/ n a worshipper, priest or priestess of Bacchus; a drunken reveller; a dance, song or revel in honour of Bacchus. ♦ *adj* relating to drinking or drunken revels. **bacchanā'lia** or **bacch'anals** n pl orgiastic feasts in honour of Bacchus; drunken revels. **bacchanalian** /-nā'li-ən/ n a drunken reveller. ♦ *adj* bacchanal. **bacchanā'lianism** n. **bacchant** /bak'ant/ n (*pl* **bacch'ants** or **bacchant'es**) a priest, priestess or votary of Bacchus; a reveller; a drunkard. ♦ *adj* engaged in wild revelry. **bacchante** /bə-kant'/ or **bak'ant**, or (*after Italian baccante*) **ba-kant'i**/ n a priestess of Bacchus; a female bacchanal. **bacchiac** /bak-ī'ak/ adj relating to the bacchius. **Bacchian** /bak'i-ən/ or **Bacchic** /bak'ik/ adj relating to Bacchus; (often without *cap*) jovial; (often without *cap*) drunken. **bacchī'us** n (*pl* **bacchī'ī**) (*classical prosody*) a foot of two long syllables preceded by one short.

bacciferous, etc see under **bacca**.

baccy /bak'i/ or **bacco** /-ō/ informal short forms of **tobacco**.

Bach. or **bach.** *abbrev* : Bachelor or bachelor.

bach /bähh/ (*Welsh*) n affectionate term of address (chiefly used after a person's name).

bacharach /bak'ər-ak or bähh'ə-rähh/ n a wine from *Bacharach*, on the Rhine.

bachata /bə-chä'tə/ n a type of Latin American music played with guitar and percussion; a dance performed to this music. [Am Sp]

bachelor /bach'əl-ər/ n an unmarried man; one who has taken his or her first degree at a university; a young knight who follows the banner of another, as too young to display his own (*hist*); a young unmated bull-seal or other male animal. [OFr *bacheler*, from LL *baccalārius*; of doubtful origin]
■ **bach** or **batch** n (*Aust* or *NZ inf*) a bachelor. ♦ *vi* (or *vt* with *it*) to live as a bachelor; to do for oneself. **bach'elordom** or **bach'elorhood** n. **bachelorette'** n (*N Am*) an unmarried woman. **bach'elorism** n the habit or condition of a bachelor. **bach'elorship** n the degree of bachelor.
❑ **bachelorette party** n (*N Am*) a hen party. **bachelor flat** or (*sl*) **pad** n a flat or other residence for an unmarried person. **bachelor girl** n a young unmarried woman who supports herself. **Bachelor of Arts** n a university or college degree conferred upon a student who has successfully completed an undergraduate course in the arts or humanities; a man or woman who has received such a degree (*abbrev* **BA**). **Bachelor of Science** n a university or college degree conferred upon a student who has successfully completed an undergraduate course in the sciences or social sciences; a man or woman who has received such a degree (*abbrev* **BSc**). **bachelor party** n (*N Am*) a stag party. **bachelor's-butt'ons** n a double-flowered yellow or white buttercup; also applied to double feverfew, species of *Centaurea*, and many other plants. **bachelor's wife** n an ideal woman with none of the shortcomings of married men's wives.
■ **knight-bachelor** see **knight**.

Bach flower remedy /bähh flowr rem'ə-di/ n one of a number of tinctures extracted from the flowers of wild plants, used to alleviate stress and other emotional disorders. [Named after the British physician and homeopath, Edward *Bach* (1887–1936)]

Bach trumpet /bähh trum'pit/ n a small modern trumpet for playing the complex high-pitched parts in Bach and other baroque music. [Johann Sebastian *Bach*, German composer (1685–1750)]

bacillus /bə-sil'əs/ n (*pl* **bacill'ī**) (with *cap*) a genus of aerobic rod-shaped bacteria (family Bacillaceae); a member of the genus; (loosely) any rod-shaped bacterium; (*popularly*) any disease-causing bacterium. [LL *bacillus*, dimin of *baculus* a rod]

■ **Bacillā'ceae** *n pl* a family (order Eubacteriales) of endospore-producing bacteria. **bacillaemia** or (*US*) **bacillemia** /-ē'mi-ə/ *n* (*med*) the presence of bacilli in the blood. **bacill'ar** or **bacill'ary** (also /bas'/) *adj* of the shape or nature of a bacillus, rodlike. **bacill'icide** *n* something which destroys bacilli. **bacill'iform** *adj*.

bacitracin /ba-si-trā'sin/ *n* an antibiotic obtained from a certain bacterium and used against Gram-positive bacteria, *esp* in skin infections. [LL *bacillus*, and Margaret *Tracy*, an American child in whom the substance was found]

back[1] /bak/ *n* the rear part of the body in humans (*specif* between the neck and buttocks), and the upper part in other creatures; the rear part, the side opposite to the front, or the side remote from that *usu* presented or seen; the underside of a leaf or of a violin; part of the upper surface of the tongue opposite the soft palate; the convex side of a book, opposite to the opening of the leaves; the thick edge of a knife, etc; the upright rear part of a chair, bench, etc; something added to the rear or far side; the surface of the sea, or of a river; the keel and keelson of a ship; one of the players positioned behind the forwards (*rugby*, etc); the side of a sloping vein nearest the surface (*mining*); the earth between one level and the one above (*mining*). ◆ *adj* rearward, situated at or towards the back of; (of a road) not main, not direct; remote; reversed; made by raising the back of the tongue (*phonetics*); belonging to the past. ◆ *adv* to or towards the back; to or towards the place from which one came; to a former state or condition; behind; behind in time; in return, reply or retaliation; in check; again; ago. ◆ *vt* to help or support; to support (a horse, an opinion, etc) by placing a wager or bet; to countersign or endorse; to provide a back or backing for; to lie at the back of; to form the back of; to cause to move backwards or in the opposite direction; to write or print at the back of (a parliamentary bill, etc); to mount or ride (now *rare*). ◆ *vi* to move or go back or backwards; (with *on* or *onto*) to have the back facing; (of the wind) to change counter-clockwise. [OE *bæc*; Swed *bak*, Dan *bag*]

■ **backed** *adj* having a back. **back'er** *n*. **back'ing** *n* support at the back; support for an enterprise; musical accompaniment, *esp* of a popular song; the action of putting or going back; a body of helpers; anything used to form a back or line the back; counter-clockwise change of wind. **back'less** *adj* lacking or not requiring a back. **back'most** *adj* farthest to the back. **backward** /bak'wərd/ *adj* and *adv* towards the back; on the back; towards the past; from a better to a worse state; in a direction opposite to the normal; (of a fielder in cricket) standing in a position behind the batsman's wicket, eg *backward point*. ◆ *adj* keeping back; shy, bashful; unwilling; less advanced than normal in mental, physical or intellectual development; late. ◆ *n* (*poetic*) the past portion of time. **backwardā'tion** *n* (*stock exchange*) the percentage paid by a seller of stock for keeping back its delivery until the following account; the postponement of delivery of stock. **back'ward-looking** *adj* having more regard to the past than the future; conservative, reactionary. **back'wardly** *adv*. **back'wardness** *n*. **back'wards** *adv* backward.

□ **back'ache** *n* pain in the back. **back'band** *n* a rope, strap or chain passing over a horse's back and holding up the shafts of a vehicle (also **back'-chain** and **back'-rope**). **back'beat** *n* (*music, orig jazz*) one of the normally unstressed beats in a bar, used as a secondary syncopated beat; breakbeat. **back'-bench** *adj* of or sitting on the **back benches**, the seats in parliament occupied by members who do not hold office. **back'bench'er** *n*. **back'bite** *vt* to speak ill of or unkindly of (someone) in his or her absence (also *vi*). **back'biter** *n*. **back'biting** *n* (also *adj*). **back'-block** *adj* of the back-blocks. **back'-blocker** *n*. **back'-blocks** *n pl* (*Aust* and *NZ*) remote, sparsely populated country; the back part of a station, far from water. **back'board** *n* a board at the back of a cart, boat, etc; a board fastened across the back to straighten the body; a board laid under a mattress, to support the back while sleeping; a rigid vertical panel placed above and behind the basket to deflect the ball (*basketball*). **back boiler** *n* a hot-water boiler behind and heated by a domestic fire. **back'bond** same as **backletter** below. **back'bone** *n* the spinal column; a main support or axis; something similar to the spinal column in appearance and function; the keel and keelson; the spine of a book (chiefly *US*); firmness of character; a high-speed line to which smaller channels are attached (*comput*). **back'boned** *adj*. **back'boneless** *adj*. **back'breaker** *n* a very heavy job; a hold in which one's opponent is pressed down on his or her back over one's knee or shoulder (*wrestling*). **back'breaking** *adj* exhausting. **back burner** *n* the rear burner on a stove, used *esp* for keeping a pot simmering that needs no immediate attention. **back'-burner** *adj* (*fig*) not requiring immediate attention. **back-cal'culate** *vi* and *vt* to make a calculation as to an earlier condition, situation, etc (*esp* as to the level of a person's intoxication) based on data recorded at a later time. **back'-calcula'tion** *n*. **back'cast** *vi* to make a backward movement with a fishing-line prior to casting; to formulate a strategy by fixing a goal and working backwards to determine what steps must be taken to achieve it. ◆ *n* the act of backcasting. **back**

catalogue the recordings already made by a musician. **back-chain** see **backband** above. **back channel** *n* a covert means of passing information. **back'chat** *n* answering back; impertinence, repartee. ◆ *vi* to answer impertinently. **back'-cloth** or **back'drop** *n* the painted cloth or curtain at the back of the stage; the background to any situation, activity, etc. **back'-comb** *vi* and *vt* to give (the hair) a puffed-out appearance by combing the underlying hairs towards the roots and smoothing the outer hairs over them. **back'-country** *n* remote, thinly populated districts (also *adj*). **back'court** *n* (*tennis*) that part of the court lying behind the service-line (also *adj*); in other games, that part of the court nearest the baseline. **back'-crawl** *n* (*swimming*) the crawl stroke, performed on the back (now *usu* called **back'stroke**). **back'-cross** *n* a cross between a hybrid and a parent; the process or act of back-crossing. ◆ *vt* to cross (a hybrid) with a parent. **back'-crossing** *n*. **back-date'** *vt* to put an earlier date on; to count as valid retrospectively from a certain date. **back door** *n* a door in the back part of a building; clandestine or illicit means. **back'door** *adj* unworthily secret; clandestine. **backdown** see **back down** below. **back'-draught** *n* a backward current. **backdrop** see **back-cloth** above. **back'-end'** *n* the rear end; the later part of a season (*dialect*); the late autumn (*dialect*); the aspects of the running of an operation, eg a website, that do not involve interaction with the public. **back'fall** *n* an obsolete term for an acciaccatura (*music*); a fall on the back as in wrestling (often *fig*); a lever in the coupler of an organ. **back'field** *adj* (*American football*, etc) of or in the position of a back or the backs. ◆ *n* (*American football*) the backs collectively. **back'file** *n* the back numbers of a newspaper, journal, etc. **back'fill** *n* the material used in backfilling. ◆ *vt* and *vi* to refill (eg foundations or an excavation) with earth or other material. **back'filling** *n*. **back'fire** *n* ignition of gas in an internal-combustion engine's cylinder at the wrong time, or inside eg a Bunsen burner instead of at the outlet; a controlled forest or prairie fire started in order to create a bare space, to stop a major fire spreading further (*N Am*). ◆ *vi* /bak-fīr'/ (of a plan, etc) to go wrong and have a bad effect on the originator; to have a backfire; to start a backfire (*N Am*). **back'fitting** *n* (*nuclear eng*) making changes to nuclear (and other) plants already designed or built eg to cater for changes in safety criteria. **back'flip** *n* a backward aerial somersault. **back-formā'tion** *n* the making of a word from another that is, wrongly or humorously, taken to be a derivative, as the verb *sidle* from the adverb *sideling* treated as if it were a participle; a word made in this way. **back'-friend** *n* a pretended friend (*obs*); a backer, a friend who stands at one's back. **back'-ganging** *adj* (*Scot*) in arrears. **back garden** or (*Scot*) **back green** *n* a garden or green at the back of a house. **back'ground** *n* the space behind the principal figures of a picture; that against which anything is, or ought to be, seen (*fig*); upbringing and previous history; environment; an inconspicuous or obscure position, the shadows; ground at the back. ◆ *adj* in the background (*lit* or *fig*); (of music, light, etc) complementary to and unobtrusively accompanying something else such as a film or social activity. **background heating** *n* heating which provides a low level of warmth but requires supplementing for complete comfort. **background processing** *n* (*comput*) processing carried out non-interactively, when work placed in a **background queue** is attended to as computing resources become available. **background radiation** *n* low-level radiation from substances present in the environment. **background tasks** *n pl* (*comput*) tasks such as printing which a computer can carry out simultaneously with tasks involving user input. **back'-hair** *n* the hair at the back of the head. **back'hand** *n* a stroke made with the back of the hand turned in the direction of the stroke (*tennis*, etc); the part of the court to the left of a right-handed player, or the right of a left-handed (*tennis*); handwriting with the letters sloping backwards. ◆ *adj* (of a shot in tennis, etc) played with the back of the hand turned in the direction of the stroke. ◆ *vt* to play a backhand shot. **back'handed** *adj* backhand; (of a blow) carried out with the back of the hand; (of a compliment, etc) indirect, dubious, sarcastic, derogatory in effect. **back'-hander** *n* a blow with the back of the hand; a backhand stroke; a bribe (*inf*); an extra glass of wine out of turn, the bottle being passed back. **back'-heel** *vt* (*football*) to kick (the ball) backwards with the heel (also *n*). **back'hoe** *n* (also **backhoe loader**) (a tractor equipped with) a shovel at the end of a mechanical arm, for making minor excavations. **back'ing-down** *n* abandonment of one's position; shirking. **backing storage** *n* (*comput*) the storage of data externally from the computer in a backing store. **backing store** *n* (*comput*) a large-capacity computer data store supplementary to a computer's main memory. **backing track** *n* a recorded accompaniment to a live singer. **back issue** *n* a back number of a publication. **back'land** *n* a piece of land at the back of an established property, *specif* when viewed or used as an area for building development; back-country. **back lane** *n* a lane to the rear of a building or buildings. **back'lash** *n* reaction or consequence, *esp* if violent; the jarring or recoiling motion of ill-fitting machinery. **back'letter** *n* (*Scots law*) a deed attaching a qualification or condition to the terms of a conveyance or other instrument. **back'lift** *n* (*cricket* or *football*, etc) a backward lifting of the bat (or leg) before the stroke is played (or ball is kicked). **back'-light** n (*photog*) light falling on a subject from the rear. ◆ vt to illuminate something from the rear. **back'-lighting** n. **back'-lill** (*Scot*) sometimes (*non-standard*) **-lilt** n the left-hand thumb hole at the back of a bagpipe chanter. **back'list** n books previously published which a publisher keeps in print, as opposed to newly published books. **back'-load** n a load taken on by a lorry for a return journey. ◆ vi to obtain a back-load. **back'-loading** n. **back'log** n a reserve or accumulation of business, stock, work, etc that will keep one going for some time; a log at the back of a fire (chiefly N Am). **back'lot** n (*film*, *TV*) the outdoor area, often next to the studio, used for exterior scenes. **back'marker** n a person who starts a race with the least advantageous handicap; a competitor at the back of the field. **back-mutā'tion** n (*biol*) see **reversion** under **reverse. back number** n a copy or issue of a newspaper or magazine of a previous date; a person or thing out of date, old-fashioned or no longer useful. **back'-office** adj of staff, etc who work in banks, the Civil Service, etc, behind the scenes out of the public view. **back'-of-the-en'velope** adj (of a calculation) performed quickly and without scrupulous regard to accuracy. **back'pack** n a pack carried on the back, a rucksack. ◆ vi to carry a pack on the back, esp as a hiker. **back'packer** n. **back'packing** n. **back pass** n (*football*) a pass from a player to his or her own goalkeeper, which the goalkeeper is not allowed to handle. **back passage** n a passageway at or towards the rear of a building; the rectum (*inf*). **back pay** n pay that is overdue; pay for work that was done in the past, often resulting from a back-dated pay increase. **back-ped'al** vi to push the pedals backwards, as in slowing a fixed-wheel bicycle; to hold back; to reverse one's course of action; to retreat from an opponent while still facing him or her (*boxing*). **back-ped'alling** n. **back'piece** or **back'plate** n a piece or plate of armour for the back. **back pressure** n (*engineering*) the pressure opposing the motion of the piston of an engine on its exhaust stroke; the exhaust pressure of a turbine. **back'-projection** n the projection of film onto the back of a special screen so as to be seen from the other side as a background to action taking place in front of the screen. **back rest** n the part of a seat which supports the sitter's back. **back room** n a place where secret work is done. **back'room** adj (of people) doing important work behind the scenes, esp in secret. **back-rope** see **backband** above. **back row** n (*rugby*) the line of forwards at the back of a scrum. **back'-row** adj. **back'saw** n a saw stiffened by a thickened back. **back'scatter** n (*phys*) the deflection of radiation or particles by scattering through angles greater than 90° with reference to the original direction of travel. ◆ vt to scatter in this way. **back'scratch** vi. **back'scratcher** n a long-handled instrument for scratching the back; a person who practises backscratching. **back'scratching** n doing favours in return for favours, for the advantage of both parties; servile flattery. **back-seat driver** n someone free of responsibility but full of advice; someone controlling from a position from which he or she ought not to control. **back'set** n a setting back, reverse; an eddy or counter-current. **backsey** /bak'sī'/ n (*Scot*) sirloin. **back'-shift** n a group of workers whose time of working overlaps or comes between the day shift and the night-shift; the time this group is on duty. **back'side** n the back or rear side or part of anything; the rear part of an animal; the buttocks (*inf*); the premises at the rear of a house (*Scot*). **back'sight** n a sight taken back towards a previous fixed point (*surveying*); the sight of a rifle nearer the stock. **back'-slang** n slang in which every word is pronounced as if spelt backwards. **back'-slapping** adj vigorously and demonstratively cheery. ◆ n such an approach, manner or behaviour towards associates. **back'slash** n (*comput*) a character consisting of a line sloping from top left to bottom right. **back'slide** vi to slide or fall back in faith, morals or work, etc. **back'slider** n. **back'sliding** n. **back'space** (or /-spās'/) vi to move the cursor of a computer or the carriage of a typewriter one or more spaces back by means of a particular key. ◆ n the key used for backspacing (also **back'spacer** or **backspace key**); the act of backspacing. **back'-spaul** or **-spauld** n (*Scot*) the back of the shoulder; the hindleg. **backspeir'** or **backspeer'** vt and vi (*Scot*) to cross-question. **back'spin** n (*sport*) a rotary movement against the direction of travel of a ball imparted to reduce its momentum on impact. **back'stabbing** n the act of treacherously criticizing someone to whom one poses as a friend. **back'stabber** n. **backstage'** adj and adv (*lit* and *fig*) behind the scenes, unobserved by the public. **back'stairs** n pl servants' or private stairs of a house. ◆ adj secret or underhand. **back'stall** n a garrotter's confederate on the lookout behind. **backstart'ing** adj (*Spenser*) starting back. **back'stays** n pl ropes or stays extending from the topmast-heads to the sides of a ship, and slanting a little backwards (*naut*); any stay or support at the back. **back'stitch** n (*needlework*) a stitch in which the needle enters behind, and comes out in front of, the end of the previous stitch (also vi and vt). **back'stop** n a screen, wall, etc acting as a barrier in various sports or games, eg shooting, baseball, etc; (the position of) a player, eg in rounders, who stops the ball; something providing additional support, protection, etc; something preventing excessive backward movement. **back story** n the events supposed to have happened before the incidents portrayed

in a film, novel, etc. **back straight** n the straight part of a racecourse or track farthest from the finish. **back'street** n a street away from the main road in a town or city, esp as part of a poorer, less fashionable area; a back lane. **backstreet abortion** n an abortion performed by an unqualified person operating illicitly. **back stretch** n a back straight. **back'stroke** n a blow or stroke in return; back-crawl, a swimming stroke with alternate backward circular movements of each arm and scissors movements of the legs, performed on the back; formerly a swimming stroke with simultaneous backward circular movements of both arms, and the breaststroke kick, performed on the back (also called **English backstroke**). **back'swimmer** n an aquatic insect of the Notonectidae family which swims on its back, propelled by its back legs. **back'swing** n (*sport*) the first stage in a swing of a club, racket, etc, in which it is swung back and away from the ball. **back'sword** n a sword with a back or with only one edge; a fencing stick with a basket-hilt, a singlestick. **backsword'man** n. **back talk** n (N Am) backchat. **back-to-back'** adj with backs facing and usu close up against each other; (of houses) built thus (also n); following in close sequence (*inf*). **back'track** vi to go back on one's course; to reverse an opinion or course of action. ◆ n a return track to the starting point; a retracing of steps. **back'tracking** n. **back translation** n the re-translation of a translated text into the original language to test the quality of the original translation. **back'up** or **back'-up** n a standby, support or reserve; a copy taken of data being worked on, stored on another disk against the possibility of damage to or loss of the working disk (*comput*); the overflow from an obstructed pipe, etc. **backup file** n (*comput*) a copy of a computer file to be used in the event of the original file being lost or corrupted. **backup light** n (N Am) reversing light. **back'veld** /-felt/ n (S Afr) country remote from towns. ◆ adj remote, rustic, primitive. **backvel'der** /-dər/ n. **back'ward-looking** adj having more regard to the past than the future; conservative, reactionary. **back'wards-compatible** adj (*comput*) of an operating system, able to run software designed for earlier versions of itself; of hardware, able to run earlier versions of software. **back'wash** n a receding wave; a backward current; a reaction, repercussion or aftermath. ◆ vt to affect with backwash; to clean the oil from (wool) after combing. **back'water** n a pool or belt of water connected with a river but not in the line of its present course or current; a place regarded as dull and isolated from important events; water held back by a dam; water thrown back by the turning of a water wheel; a backward current of water; swell of the sea caused by a passing ship. **back'woods** n pl the forest beyond the cleared country; a remote region. **backwoods'man** n a person who lives in the backwoods; a person of uncouth manners; a peer who seldom attends the House of Lords. **back'word** n a withdrawal of a promise, etc; a retort. **back'work** n (*mining*) work done underground but not at the coalface. **back'worker** n. **back'-wounding** adj (*Shakesp*) backbiting. **backyard'** n a yard behind a house; one's home territory. ◆ adj (of a person) operating a small business from domestic premises, or practising unofficially or illegally.

■ **back and fill** (*naut*) to trim sails so that the wind alternately presses them back and fills them; to vacillate. **back and forth** to and fro. **back down** to abandon one's opinion or position; to move (a boat) backwards by pushing the oars (*rowing*) (**back'down** n). **back of** (US) behind. **back off** to move backwards or retreat; back down. **back out** to move out backwards; to evade an obligation or undertaking. **back to front** the wrong way round, with the back where the front should be; reversed, in mirror image; in the wrong order, with matters that should be deferred being discussed or dealt with first; completely, thoroughly. **back to nature** back to a simple way of life (also often **back'-to-na'ture** adj). **back up** to give support to; (of water) to accumulate behind an obstruction; to make a backup of (data) (*comput*). **backward and forward** to and fro. **back water** to row or turn the paddle wheels backwards. **bend**, **fall** or **lean over backwards** (*inf*) to try very hard to be accommodating or to please. **break the back of** to overburden; to accomplish the hardest part of. **get off someone's back** to stop pestering or bothering someone. **get someone's back up** (*inf*) to annoy or irritate someone. **give** or **make a back** to take up position for leapfrog. **have one's back to the wall** to be in a very difficult or desperate situation. **have someone's back** (chiefly US *inf*) to protect someone. **keep**, **place** or **put on the back burner** to set aside, postpone work on, or keep in reserve for later consideration or action. **know something backwards** to have a thorough knowledge of something. **on the back of** close behind; just after (*Scot*). **put one's back into** to put great effort into. **ring bells backward** to begin with the bass bell, in order to raise the alarm. **see the back of** to be rid of or finished with. **set one's** or **put someone's back up** to show or arouse resentment, irritation or anger. **take a back seat** to withdraw into an inconspicuous or subordinate position. **talk through the back of one's neck** see under **neck**. **the Backs** the grounds of Cambridge colleges backing onto the River Cam. **to the backbone** through and through.

back² /bak/ n a large vat or tub. [Fr *bac* trough, dimin *baquet*, perh partly through Du *bak*]

■ **back'et** n (Scot) a shallow wooden trough for ashes, coals, etc.

backare or **baccare** /bak'ār or bak-ā'ri/ (Shakesp) interj back; stand back. [Perh for back there; or sham Latin]

backgammon /bak-gam'ən or bak'/ n a board game for two players with dice and 15 men or pieces each; a triple game scored by the winner bearing off all 15 men while the loser still has a man in the winner's inner table. ◆ vt to defeat in such a way. [back, because the pieces are sometimes taken up and obliged to go back, that is, re-enter at the table, and ME gamen play]

backra /bak' or buk'rə/ (W Indies) n a white man or woman; white people. [Ibo, Efik mbakára white man]

backronym or **bacronym** /bak'rə-nim/ n an acronym formed using the initial letters or syllables of an existing word. [From backward and acronym]

backsheesh, **backshish** see **baksheesh**.

backward, **backwards**, etc see under **back**[1].

baclava see **baklava**.

bacon /bā'kn/ n pig's flesh (now the back and sides) salted or pickled and dried, and used as food; a rustic (Shakesp). [OFr bacon, of Gmc origin; cf OHGer bahho, bacho; Ger Bache]
■ **ba'coner** n a pig suitable for bacon production.
□ **ba'con-and-eggs'** n birdsfoot trefoil.
■ **bring home the bacon** (inf) to achieve an object, successfully accomplish a task; to provide material support. **save (some)one's bacon** (inf) (to enable someone) to come off unscathed from a difficult situation.

Baconian /bā-kō'ni-ən/ adj relating to Francis Bacon (1561–1626), or his inductive philosophy, or to Roger Bacon (died c.1292) or his teaching, or to the theory that Francis Bacon wrote Shakespeare's plays (also n).
■ **Baco'nianism** n.

BACS abbrev : Bankers Automated Clearing Service.

bacteria /bak-tē'ri-ə/ n pl (sing **bactē'rium** or (non-standard) **bactē'ria**) a group of unicellular or filamentous micro-organisms belonging to the Schizomycetes, saprophytic, parasitic or autotrophic, agents in putrefaction, nitrogen fixation, etc and the cause of many diseases. [Gr baktērion, dimin of baktron a stick]
■ **bactē'rial**, **bactē'rian** or **bacteric** /-ter'ik/ adj. **bactē'rioid** or **bac'teroid** n a swollen bacterium living symbiotically in the root-nodules of beans and other plants. **bac'terize** or **-ise** vt to treat with bacteria. **bac'teroid** n see **bacterioid** above.
□ **bacteria bed** n a filter bed. **bacterial leaching** n (mining) see under **leach**[1]. **bacterial recovery** n see **microbiological mining** under **microbe**.

bacterio- /bak-tē-ri-ō-/, **bacteri-** /bak-tē-ri-/ or **bacter-** /bak-tər-/ combining form relating to bacteria. [bacteria]
■ **bacteraemia** or (US) **bacteremia** /-ē'mi-ə/ n the presence of bacteria in the blood. **bacterae'mic** or (US) **bactere'mic** adj. **bactērīcī'dal** adj. **bactē'ricide** n a substance that destroys bacteria. **bactēriochlorophyll** /-klor'- or -klōr'ō-fil/ n in some bacteria, a substance related to the chlorophyll of green plants. **bactēriolog'ical** adj. **bactēriol'ogist** n. **bactēriol'ogy** n the scientific study of bacteria. **bactērioly'sin** (or /-ol'i-/) n an antibody that destroys bacteria. **bactēriol'ysis** n (Gr lysis dissolution) destruction of bacteria by an antibody. **bactēriolyt'ic** adj. **bacteriophage** /bak-tē'ri-ō-fāj/ or /-fāzh/ n (Gr phagein to eat) any of a large number of viruses, present in the atmosphere, soil, water, living things, etc, whose function is to destroy bacteria. **bactērio'sis** n any bacterial plant disease. **bactērios'tasis** n (Gr stasis standing) inhibition of the growth of bacteria. **bactē'riostat** n an agent that inhibits the growth of bacteria. **bactēriostat'ic** adj.

Bactrian /bak'tri-ən/ adj belonging to Bactria (now nearly corresponding to Balkh, a district of N Afghanistan), esp applied to a two-humped camel native to central Asia. ◆ n a two-humped camel.

baculiform /bə-kū'li-förm or bak'ū-li-/ (biol) adj rod-shaped. [L baculum a stick, and **-form**]

baculine /bak'ū-līn/ adj relating to the stick or cane, or to punishment by flogging. [L baculum a stick]

baculite /bak'ū-līt/ n a fossil of the genus Baculites /-īt'ēz/, allied to the ammonites, with a straight, tapering shell. [L baculum a stick]

baculovirus /bak'ū-lō-vī-rəs/ n a type of virus found only to attack insects. [L baculus a rod, and **virus**]

baculum /bak'ū-ləm/ n (pl **bac'ula**) the bone in the penis of certain mammals. [L baculum a stick]

bad /bad/ adj (compar **worse** or (sl) **badd'er**; superl **worst** or (sl) **badd'est**) ill or evil; wicked, naughty; hurtful; incorrect, faulty; rotten; poor; unskilful; worthless; unfavourable; painful; injured; unwell; spurious; severe; harmful; offensive, disagreeable; having serious effects; good, attractive (sl, orig US). ◆ adv (N Am inf) badly; hard. ◆ n something evil, wicked, hurtful, etc. [Ety very obscure. The ME badde

is perh from OE bæddel a hermaphrodite, bædling an effeminate fellow]
■ **badd'ie** or **badd'y** n (inf) a criminal person or villain, esp as portrayed in films, television or radio shows. **badd'ish** adj somewhat bad; not very good. **bad'ly** adv in a bad way; severely; to a marked extent, very much. ◆ adj (N Eng) unwell. **bad'ness** n.
□ **bad'ass** (US sl) n an aggressive or difficult person. ◆ adj (also **bad'assed**) touchy, difficult; tough, intimidating; excellent. **bad bank** n a bank set up to administer unprofitable assets. **bad blood** n angry or hostile feeling (also **bad feeling**). **bad boy** (chiefly US inf) any impressive thing. **bad debt** n a debt that cannot be recovered and is therefore written off as a loss. **bad hair day** n (inf) a day that starts badly (characterized by difficulty with one's hair) and gets worse, a day one would rather not have to face. **bad'lands** n pl greatly eroded wasteland in South Dakota; any similar eroded region. **bad language** n swearing. **badly off** adj poorly provided esp with money. **bad'man** n (chiefly US) an outlaw. **bad'mouth** vt (inf) to criticize, malign. **bad news** n pl any unwelcome, upsetting or irritating event, or a report of such; someone or something troublesome, irritating, etc (sl). **bad shot** n a wrong guess. **bad-tem'pered** adj easily annoyed, sulky. **bad trip** n (inf) an episode of terrifying hallucinations and physical discomfort resulting from taking a drug, esp LSD. **bad'ware** n same as **malware**.
■ **big bad** see under **big**[1]. **feel bad about** (inf) to be sorry about, regret. **from bad to worse** into an even worse situation. **go bad** to decay, become mouldy or putrid. **go to the bad** to go to moral ruin. **in a bad way** (inf) ill; in trouble. **in someone's bad books** unpopular with someone. **make the best of a bad job** (inf) to do the best one can in unfavourable circumstances. **my bad** (US sl) a phrase used to acknowledge that one has made a mistake. **not bad** fairly good. **not half bad** (inf) pretty good, excellent. **take the bad with the good** to accept unpleasant things along with pleasant ones. **too bad** (inf) what a pity!; regrettable, a shame. **to the bad** in deficit. **with a bad grace** ungraciously.

baddeleyite /bad'ə-li-īt/ n a mineral yielding zirconium, consisting of 90% zirconium dioxide, found in beach sands, in Sri Lanka and Brazil. [Joseph Baddeley, who brought specimens to Europe in 19c]

badderlock /bad'ər-lok/ (Scot) n an edible seaweed (genus Alaria) resembling tangle (also **balderlocks** /böl'dər-loks/). [Poss for Balder's locks, from Balder, the Norse god]

bade /bad or (poetic) bād/ pat of **bid**[1,2].

badge /baj/ n a mark or emblem showing rank, membership of a society, etc; any distinguishing mark or symbol. ◆ vt to call by a distinguishing name, mark or symbol. [ME bage. Origin obscure]
□ **badge engineering** n (motoring) the bringing out of a new model that is only marginally, if at all, different from one already existing under a different marque.

badger /baj'ər/ n a burrowing, nocturnal, hibernating animal of the otter and weasel family; applied to other animals, such as hyrax, wombat, ratel; a paintbrush or other brush (made of badger's hair); (with cap) a member of the junior section of the St John's ambulance brigade. ◆ vt to pester or worry. [Prob from **badge** and the noun-forming sfx -ard, in reference to the white mark like a badge on its forehead]
■ **badg'erly** adj like a badger; greyish-haired, elderly.
□ **badg'er-baiting** or **-drawing** n the sport of setting dogs to draw out a badger from a barrel or artificial earth, etc. **badg'er-dog** n the dachshund, a long-bodied and short-legged dog used in badger-baiting. **badg'er-legged** adj having legs of unequal length, as the badger was commonly supposed to have.

badging-hook see **bagging-hook**.

badinage /ba-di-näzh' or bad'i-nij/ n light playful talk; banter. [Fr badinage, from badin playful or bantering]

badious /bā'di-əs/ (bot) adj chestnut-coloured. [L badius]

badmash or **budmash** /bud'mash/ (Ind) n an evil-doer. ◆ adj dishonest; badly behaved. [Pers]

badminton /bad'min-tən/ n a game played with rackets and a shuttlecock on a court with a high net, with the object of making the shuttlecock strike the ground in the opponent's court; a cooling summer drink of claret, sugar and soda-water. [Badminton in Gloucestershire, a seat of the Dukes of Beaufort]

BAe abbrev : British Aerospace (now known as BAE Systems).

Baedeker /bā'di-kər/ n any of the series of travellers' guidebooks published by Karl Baedeker (1801–59) or his successors; any similar guidebook; any handbook or vade-mecum.
□ **Baedeker raid** n one of the series of raids on historic places in Britain by the Luftwaffe in 1942.

bael, **bel** or **bhel** /bel/ n a thorny Indian rutaceous tree (Aegle marmelos); its edible fruit, the Bengal quince. [Hindi]

baetyl /bē'til/ n a magical or holy meteoric stone. [Gr baitylos]

BAF *abbrev* : British Athletics Federation (replaced by UK Athletics).

baff /baf/ (*golf*; *old*) *vt* to strike the ground with the sole of the club, and so to send the ball up in the air. [Perh imit]
■ **baffy** /baf'i/ *n* a club like a brassy, but with a slightly shorter shaft and a more sloping face.

baffle /baf'l/ *vt* to frustrate, confound, bewilder, or impede perplexingly; to regulate or divert (liquid, gas, sound waves, etc); to provide with a baffle; to cheat, hoodwink (*obs*); to disgrace publicly (*obs*). ◆ *n* a plate or similar device for regulating or diverting the flow of liquid, gas, sound waves, etc (also **baff'le-board, baff'le-plate** or **baff'ler**); confusion, check (*obs*). [Perh Scot and connected with *bauchle* to treat contemptuously; but cf Fr *bafouer*, or earlier *beffler*, from OFr *befe* mockery]
■ **baff'lement** *n*. **baff'ler** *n* a baffle. **baff'ling** *adj*. **baff'lingly** *adv*.
❑ **baffle wall** *n* a wall that acts as a baffle, *esp* for sound.

baft[1] /bäft/ *n* a coarse fabric, *orig* Oriental, later made in and shipped from England. [Pers *baft* woven]

baft[2] /bäft/ (*archaic*) *adv* and *prep* behind; abaft, astern (*naut*). [OE *beæftan*, from *be* by, and *æftan* behind]

BAFTA /baf'tə/ *abbrev* : British Academy of Film and Television Arts.

bag /bag/ *n* a sack, pouch, receptacle for carrying or containing; a handbag; a bagful; a measure of various quantities; a game bag, hence the quantity of fish or game secured, however great; (in *pl*) plenty, lots (*inf*); an udder; an unattractive, slovenly or immoral woman (*offensive sl*); (in *pl*) trousers (*inf*); a quantity of drugs, *esp* heroin in a paper or other container (*drug sl*); a person's particular interest or speciality (*old sl*); a base (*baseball sl*). ◆ *vi* (**bagg'ing; bagged**) to bulge, swell out; to sag; to drop away from the right course (*naut*). ◆ *vt* to put (*esp* game) into a bag; hence to kill (game); to cram full; to seize, secure or steal; to claim or reserve for oneself (*inf*); to denigrate or criticize (*Aust* and *US*). [ME *bagge*, from ON *baggi* a bundle]
■ **bag'ful** *n* (*pl* **bag'fuls**) as much as a bag will hold. **bagged** /bagd/ *adj* in a bag; hanging slackly or in bags. **bagg'ies** *n pl* baggy shorts; soft fabric shoes. **bagg'ily** *adv* in a baggy fashion. **bagg'iness** *n*. **bagg'ing** *n* cloth or material for bags. **bagg'it** *adj* (*Scot*) bagged; full of spawn, etc. ◆ *n* a ripe female salmon that has failed to shed her eggs. **bagg'y** *adj* loose like a bag; bulged. **bag'less** *adj*.
❑ **bag lady** *n* a homeless woman who carries her possessions, accumulated scavengings, etc around with her in a carrier bag (or *usu* several). **bag'man** *n* a man who carries a bag; an old-fashioned name for a commercial traveller; a man who collects or distributes money as part of racketeering (*US*); a swagman (*Aust*). **bag'-net** *n* a bag-shaped net for catching fish. **bag'wash** *n* (a laundry offering) a laundry service in which only basic washing is done. **bag'wig** *n* an 18c wig with back-hair enclosed in an ornamental bag.
■ **bag and baggage** with all one's belongings, completely, as in *to clear out bag and baggage*. **bag of bones** an emaciated living being. **bag of nerves** (*inf*) a very agitated and apprehensive person. **bag of tricks** the whole outfit. **bags** (**l**) (*sl*; *orig children's sl*) I lay claim to. **in the bag** secured or as good as secured. **let the cat out of the bag** see under **cat**[1].

bagarre /ba-gär'/ (*Fr*) *n* a scuffle, brawl, rumpus.

bagasse /bə-gas'/ *n* dry refuse in sugar-making. [Fr; Sp *bagazo* husks of grapes or olives after pressing]
■ **bagassō'sis** *n* an industrial disease caused by inhaling bagasse.

bagatelle /bag-ə-tel'/ *n* a trifle, trinket; a piece of music in a light style; a game played on a board with balls, *usu* nine, and a cue or spring, the object being to put the balls into numbered holes or sections. [Fr, from Ital *bagattella* a conjuror's trick, a trifle]

bagel /bā'gəl/ *n* a hard leavened ring-shaped roll; a score of zero games in a set of tennis (*inf*). ◆ *vt* (*inf*) in tennis, to defeat by six games to love. [Yiddish *beygel*, from Ger *Beugel*, from Gmc root *bug-* to bend]

baggage /bag'ij/ *n* travellers' luggage; the tents, provisions, etc of an army; opinions, feelings, etc brought forward from earlier experience, *usu* either irrelevant to or adversely affecting the present situation (*esp* in the phrase *emotional baggage*); an immoral woman (*obs*); a cheeky young woman (*obs*). [OFr *bagage*, from *baguer* to bind up]
❑ **bagg'age-animal** *n*. **bagg'age-car** *n* (*US*) a railway luggage van. **baggage reclaim** *n* the process whereby (*esp* long-distance) travellers collect their baggage on arrival at their destination; the area in an airport terminal, etc where travellers collect their baggage after arrival. **bagg'age-train** *n* a train of baggage-animals, wagons, etc.

bagging-hook /bag'ing-hŭk/ (*dialect*) *n* a type of sickle (also **badging-hook** /baj'/). [Ety uncertain]

bagh /bäg/ *n* (*Ind*) a garden. [Hindi]

bagnio /ban'yō/ *n* (*pl* **bagn'ios**) an Oriental prison; a brothel; a bathing-house, *esp* one with hot baths (*obs*). [Ital *bagno*, from L *balneum* a bath]

bagpipes /bag'pīps/ *n pl* (also *n sing* **bag'pipe**) a wind instrument consisting of a *bag* fitted with *pipes*, *usu* consisting of a chanter and some drones.
■ **bag'piper** *n*. **bag'piping** *n*.

BAgr or **BAgric** *abbrev* : Bachelor of Agriculture.

baguette /bə-get'/ *n* a long narrow French loaf of white bread with a thick crust; a precious stone cut in the shape of a long rectangle; a small moulding like an astragal (*archit*). [Fr dimin, from L *baculum* rod]

baguio /bä-gē'ō/ *n* (*pl* **bagui'os**) a hurricane. [Philippine Islands Sp]

bah /bä/ *interj* expressing disgust or contempt. [Fr]

bahada see **bajada**.

Bahadur /bə-hä'dər or -hö'/ (*Ind*) *n* a title of respect often added to the names of officers and officials. [Hindi *bahādur* hero]

Bahai or **Baha'i** /bə- or bä-hä'ē/ *n* an adherent of an *orig* Persian religion, a development of Babism (see **Babi**), following the teaching of *Baha*-Ullah, 'the Glory of God' (Mirza Husain Ali, 1817–92), and emphasizing world unity and peace; the religion itself. ◆ *adj* relating to or following this religion.
■ **Baha'ism** *n*. **Baha'ist** or **Baha'ite** *n*.

Bahamian /bə-hā'mi-ən or -hä'mi-ən/ *adj* of or relating to the Commonwealth of the *Bahamas* in the Caribbean, or its inhabitants. ◆ *n* a native or inhabitant of the Bahamas; a descendant of such.

Bahasa /bə-hä'sə/ *n* a variety of Malay used in Indonesia (**Bahasa Indonesia**) and Malaysia (**Bahasa Malaysia**). [Malay *bahasa* language]

bahookie /bə-hook'i/ (*Scot*) *n* the buttocks. [Perh from *behind* and **hock**[1]]

Bahraini /bä-rä'nē/ *adj* of or relating to the state of *Bahrain* in the Arabian Gulf, or its inhabitants. ◆ *n* a native or citizen of Bahrain.

baht /bät/ *n* the standard monetary unit of Thailand (100 satang). [Thai *bāt*]

bahut /ba-hü', bä-ü/ *n* an ornamented, *usu* round-topped, chest or cabinet. [Fr]

bahuvrihi /bä-hŭ-vrē'hē or -hoo-/ *n* a class of compound words in which the first element governs or describes the second, but the qualified element cannot be substituted for the whole (eg *turncoat*, *hunchback*, *bluestocking*). [Sans, from *bahu* much and *vrihi* rice, together forming such a compound]

BAI *abbrev* : *Baccalaureus in Arte Ingeniaria* (L), Bachelor of Engineering.

baignoire /ben-wär/ *n* a theatre box on a level with the stalls. [Fr, bath]

bail[1] /bāl/ *n* the (*usu* monetary) security given to procure the release of an accused person by assuring his or her subsequent appearance in court; release from custody on the strength of such security; the person or persons giving or becoming that security; jurisdiction, custody (*Spenser*). ◆ *vt* to set (someone) free by giving security for them; to release on such security being given; to deliver (goods) in trust upon a contract (*law*). [OFr *bail* custody, handing over, *baillier* to control, guard, hand over, from L *bājulāre* to bear a burden, carry, carry on]
■ **bail'able** *adj*. **bailee'** *n* (*law*) a person to whom goods are bailed. **bail'er** *n* (*US*) a variant spelling of **bailor**. **bail'ment** *n* (*law*) a delivery of goods in trust; the action of bailing a prisoner. **bail'or** *n* (*law*) a person who bails goods to a bailee.
❑ **bail'bond** *n* a bond given by a prisoner as surety upon being bailed. **bail'-dock** or **bale'-dock** *n* a room at the Old Bailey, London, in which prisoners were formerly kept during the trials. **bail-out** see **bail out** below. **bails'man** *n* a person who gives bail for another.
■ **accept**, **admit to** or **allow bail** are all said of the magistrate; the prisoner **offers** or **surrenders to bail**. **bail out** (*inf*) to stand bail for (a prisoner); to assist out of (financial) difficulties (**bail'out** *n*). **forfeit** or (*inf*) **jump bail** to fail to reappear in court at the designated time after being released on bail. **give leg bail** to run for it. **on bail** released once bail money has been received by a court. **stand**, **go** or **give bail** to provide the bail (for a prisoner).

bail[2], also **bale** /bāl/ *vt* to clear (a boat, etc) of water with bails; to ladle (water) (often with *out*; see also **bail out** below). ◆ *n* a bucket or other container for ladling out water from a boat. [Fr *baille* bucket, perh from LL *bacula*, dimin of *baca* a basin]
■ **bail'er** *n*.
■ **bail out** (*usu* **bale out**) to escape from an aeroplane by parachute; to escape from a potentially difficult situation; see also under **bail**[1].

bail³ /bāl/ (cricket) n one of the crosspieces that lie on top of the stumps to form the wicket. [Prob connected with **bail**⁵]

bail⁴ /bāl/ n on a typewriter, teleprinter, etc, a hinged bar that holds the paper against the platen. [Prob connected with **bail**⁵]

bail⁵ /bāl/ n (also **bayle**) a barrier; a pole separating horses in an open stable; a frame for holding a cow's head during milking (*Aust* and *NZ*). ♦ vt (also (*Shakesp*) **bale**) to confine. [OFr *baile*, perh from *baillier* to enclose; or L *baculum* a stick]
■ **bail up** to secure (a cow's head) in a bail (*Aust* and *NZ*); to stop and disarm in order to rob (*Aust*); to put one's hands up in surrender (*Aust*); to bring or be brought to bay, to corner or be cornered (*Aust*).

bail⁶ /bāl/ n a hoop; a semicircular handle, as of a kettle, etc. [Prob ON *beygla* hoop, from the Gmc root *bug-* to bend]

bailey /bā'li/ n the outer wall of a feudal castle; hence the outer court, or any court within the walls. [Fr *baille* palisade, enclosure, from LL *ballium*]
■ **motte and bailey** see under **motte**². **the Old Bailey** the Central Criminal Court in London in what was the ancient bailey between Ludgate and Newgate.

Bailey bridge /bā'li brij/ n a prefabricated bridge which can be constructed speedily for emergency use. [Designed during World War II by Sir Donald *Bailey*]

bailie (also **baillie**) /bāl'i/ n in Scotland, the title of a magistrate who presides in a burgh court and is elected by the town council from among the councillors (now *hist*); a sheriff's officer (*obs*); the chief magistrate of a Scottish barony or part of a county (*obs*); a land-steward (*obs*). [OFr *bailli* and *baillif*; see **bailiff**]
■ **bail'ieship** (also **baill'ieship**) n.

bailiff /bā'lif/ n an agent or land-steward; a sheriff's officer; the first civil officer in Jersey and in Guernsey; a court official (chiefly *US*); formerly any king's officer, eg sheriff, mayor, etc, *esp* the chief officer of a hundred (county division), surviving in certain cases as a formal title; a foreign magistrate (*hist*). [OFr *baillif*, from LL *bājulivus*, from *bājulus* carrier, administrator. See **bail**¹]
■ **bail'iwick** n the jurisdiction of a bailiff (*law*); jurisdiction in general (*law*); someone's area of interest (*joc*).

bailli /bī-yē'/ (Fr) n a magistrate.
■ **bailliage** /-äzh/ n his or her jurisdiction.

baillie see **bailie**.

Baily's beads /bā'liz bēds/ (astron) n pl bright spots, resembling a string of beads, visible during the seconds before and after a total eclipse of the sun. [Detected in 1836 by the astronomer F *Baily*]

bainin /bā-nēn'/ n a type of wool produced in Ireland that is only partially scoured and therefore retains some natural oil (also *adj*). [Ir *báiníń* homespun]

bainite /bā'nīt/ n a constituent of a certain stage in the heat treatment of steel. [EC *Bain* (1891–1971), US metallurgist]

bain-marie /ban-ma-rē'/ or /bĕ-ma-rē'/ n a vessel of hot or boiling water into which another vessel is placed to cook slowly or keep hot (*cookery*); a water bath (*chem*). [Fr *bain-marie* bath of Mary, from L *balneum Mariae*; origin uncertain, perh from *Mary* or *Miriam*, sister of *Moses*, who reputedly wrote a book on alchemy]

Bairam /bī'räm or bī-räm'/ n the Turkish name for the festivals of Eid al-Adha (the **Greater Bairam**) and Eid al-Fitr (the **Lesser Bairam**). [Pers]

bairn /bārn/ (Scot and N Eng) n a child. [OE *bearn*, from *beran* to bear]
■ **bairn'like** or **bairn'ly** adj.
□ **bairn's'-part** see **legitim**. **bairn'-team** or **bairn'-time** n a brood of children.

Baisakhi /bī-sak'i/ n a Sikh festival commemorating the founding of the Khalsa brotherhood, held at the Hindu New Year. [Hindi *Baisakh* the month April, from Sans *Vaiś'ākha*]

baisemain /bāz'mĕ/ (obs) n chiefly in *pl*, a compliment paid by kissing the hand. [Fr *baiser* to kiss, and *main* hand]

bait /bāt/ n food put on a hook to attract fish or make them bite; any allurement or temptation; a rage (*sl*); a refreshment, *esp* on a journey (*archaic* or *dialect*); a stop for that purpose (*archaic*). ♦ vt to set (a trap, etc) with food; to tempt; to feed (a horse, etc), *esp* on a journey (*archaic*); to set dogs on (a bear, bull, etc); to persecute, harass; to exasperate, *esp* with malice, tease. ♦ vi (*archaic*) to take, or stop for, refreshment on a journey. [ME *beyten*, from ON *beita* to cause to bite, from *bita* to bite]
■ **bait'er** n. **bait'ing** n.
□ **bait'fish** n fish used as bait; fish that may be caught with bait.
■ **bait and switch** another name for **switch selling** (see under **switch**). **rise to the bait** to do what someone else intends or suggests one should do.

baiza /bī'zä/ n (pl **bai'za** or **bai'zas**) a monetary unit in Oman, $\frac{1}{1000}$ of a rial. [Ar, from Hindi *paisā*; cf **paisa**]

baize /bāz/ n a coarse, *usu* green, woollen cloth with a long nap, used mainly for coverings, linings, etc; a table cover of such cloth, *esp* the covering of card- and snooker-tables, etc. ♦ vt to cover or line with baize. [Fr *baies*, pl (fem) of *bai*, from L *badius* bay-coloured]

bajada or **bahada** /ba-hä'də/ (geol) n a slope formed by the deposition of rock debris. [Sp *bajada* a slope]

Bajan /bā'jən/ (inf) adj Barbadian. [Variant short form]

bajan /bā'jən/ (Aberdeen) or **bejant** /bē'jənt/ (St Andrews) n a freshman (so formerly at several continental universities). [Fr *béjaune* novice, from *bec jaune* yellow bill, unfledged bird]

Bajau /bə-jow'/ adj of or relating to a people of Sabah, a state of E Malaysia. ♦ n a member of this people.

bajillion /bə-jil'yən/(sl) n an unspecified but extremely large number. [Coinage based on **billion**]

Bajocian /ba-jō'si-ən or -shən/ (geol) adj of a division of the Middle Jurassic (also n). [L *Bajocassēs* a people living in Bayeux]

bajra /bäj'rə or -rä/, also **bajri** or **bajree** /bäj'rē/ n a kind of Indian millet. [Hindi]

baju /bä'joo/ n a short jacket traditionally worn in Malaysia. [Malay]

bake /bāk/ vt (prp **bāk'ing**; pap **baked** /bākt/ or (archaic) **bāk'en**) to dry, harden or cook by the heat of the sun or fire; to make or cook in an oven; to harden by cold (*Shakesp*); to cake (*Shakesp*). ♦ vi to cook or become firm through heat; (of persons, weather, etc) to be very hot (*inf*); to work as a baker. ♦ n a baking; a party at which the food is baked (N Am); a kind of biscuit (*Scot*). [OE *bacan*; cognate with Ger *backen* to bake, Gr *phōgein* to roast]
■ **bāk'er** n a person who bakes or sells bread, etc; an artificial fly used in salmon-fishing. **bāk'ery** n a bakehouse; a baker's shop. **bāk'ing** adj extremely hot. ♦ n the process by which bread (or cake, etc) is baked; a quantity baked at one time.
□ **bake'apple** n (Can) the fruit of the cloudberry. **bake'board** n (Scot) a board for kneading dough on. **baked Alaska** n a pudding consisting of ice cream, and *usu* cake, covered with meringue, baked rapidly. **baked beans** n pl beans boiled and baked, now generally applied to a variety tinned in tomato sauce. **bake'house** n a house or place used for baking in. **bake'meat** n (Bible) pastry, pies. **bake'off** n a cake-making contest; (*esp* in the computer industry) a public test of several similar products in order to establish which one performs best. **baker's dozen** see **dozen**¹. **bake'stone** n a flat stone or plate of iron on which cakes are baked in the oven. **bake'ware** n heat-resistant dishes suitable for use in baking. **baking powder** n a mixture (eg tartaric acid and sodium bicarbonate) giving off carbon dioxide, used as a raising agent in baking. **baking soda** n sodium bicarbonate.

Bakelite® /bā'kə-līt/ n a synthetic resin with high chemical and electrical resistance, made by condensation of cresol or phenol with formaldehyde. [LH *Baekeland* (1863–1944), its American inventor]

Baker day /bā'kər dā/ (inf) n a periodic in-service training day for teachers, on which students do not attend school. [Kenneth *Baker*, Secretary of State for Education 1986–9]

Bakewell pudding or **tart** /bāk'wel pŭd'ing or tärt/ n a flan consisting of a pastry base spread with jam and a filling made of eggs, sugar, butter and ground almonds. [*Bakewell*, Derbyshire]

bakkie /bak'i/ (S Afr) n a pick-up truck. [Afrik, dimin of *bak* back]

baklava or **baclava** /bak'lə-və/ n a Middle-Eastern dessert made of layers of filo pastry, honey, nuts, etc. [Turk]

baksheesh, **bakhshish**, **backsheesh** or **backshish** /bak' buk'shēsh/ n a gift or present of money in various Asian or N African countries, a gratuity or tip. ♦ vt to give money to, tip. [Pers *bakhshīsh*]

BAL abbrev : blood alcohol level.

bal. (bookkeeping) abbrev : balance.

Balaam /bā'lam/ n a prophet who strives to mislead, like *Balaam* in the Bible, Numbers 22–24; unimportant paragraphs kept in readiness to fill up a newspaper (press sl).
■ **Bā'laamite** n. **Bālaamit'ical** adj.
□ **Ba'laam-box** or **-basket** n a place in which such paragraphs are kept in readiness.

Balaclava /ba-lə-klä'və/ or **Balaclava helmet** /hel'mit/ (also without cap) n a knitted hat covering the head and neck, with an opening for the face. [*Balaklava* in Crimea]

baladin /ba-la-dĕ'/ (Fr) n a theatrical dancer (also *fem* **baladine** /-dēn/).

balalaika /ba-lə-lī'kə/ n a Russian musical instrument, like a guitar, with triangular body and *usu* three strings. [Russ]

balance /bal'əns/ n equilibrium; what is needed to produce equilibrium, a counterpoise; harmony among the parts of anything; stability of body or mind; equality or just proportion of weight or power; the sum required to make the two sides of an account equal, hence the surplus, or the sum due (*bookkeeping*); the process of balancing an account, or the tabular representation of this (*bookkeeping*); the remainder; the act of weighing two things; an instrument for weighing, *usu* formed of two dishes or scales hanging from a beam supported in the middle; (with *cap* and *the*) Libra; a contrivance that regulates the speed of a clock or watch. ◆ *vt* to set or keep in equilibrium; to counterpoise; to compare; to weigh in a balance; to settle (eg an account); to examine and test so as to make the debt and credit sides of an account agree (*bookkeeping*). ◆ *vi* to have equal weight or power, etc; to be or come to be in equilibrium; to hesitate or fluctuate; in dancing, to match one's partner's steps to and fro; (of accounts) to have the credit and debit sides equal (*bookkeeping*). [Fr, from L *bilanx* having two scales, from *bis* double, and *lanx, lancis* a dish or scale]

■ **bal'anced** *adj* poised so as to preserve equilibrium; stable, well-adjusted; fair, unbiased; (of a meal, diet, etc) containing a combination of the types of food necessary for good health. **bal'ancer** *n* a person who, or that which, balances; an acrobat; a fly's rudimentary hindwing (see also **halteres**).

▫ **balanced flue** *n* a sealed unit which both takes its air for combustion from outside the building and discharges the gases produced to the outside. **balanced pair** *n* (*telecom*) two wires which are electrically balanced to each other and earth. **balance sheet** *n* a statement which shows the assets and liabilities of a company on a specified date; a summary and balance of accounts. **balance wheel** *n* a wheel in a watch or chronometer which regulates the beat or rate. **balancing act** *n* an entertainment in which someone performs a feat of keeping himself or herself or objects in equilibrium; an attempt to keep several tasks in progress at once or reconcile various different demands.

■ **balance of mind** sanity. **balance of nature** ecological equilibrium caused by interdependence. **balance of payments** the difference over a stated period between a nation's total receipts (in all forms) from foreign countries and its total payments to foreign countries. **balance of power** a state of equilibrium of forces in which no nation or group of nations has the resources to go to war with another or others with likelihood of success; potentially decisive power held by a third party when two others are in equilibrium. **balance of trade** the difference in value between a country's imports and exports. **in the balance** unsettled; undecided. **off balance** unstable, *esp* mentally or emotionally; in a state of unreadiness to respond to an attack, challenge, etc. **on balance** having taken everything into consideration. **strike a balance** to choose a middle-of-the-road decision.

balancé /bal-ä-sä'/ (*Fr*; *ballet*) *n* a rocking step taking the weight from one foot to the other.

Balanus /bal'ə-nəs/ *n* the acorn-shell genus. [Gr *balanos* acorn]
■ **balanitis** /bal-ə-nī'tis/ *n* inflammation of the glans penis in mammals. **Balanogloss'us** *n* (Gr *glōssa* tongue) a genus of wormlike animals of the Hemichordata.

balas /bal'əs/ *n* a rose-red spinel (*usu* **balas ruby**). [OFr *balais* (Ital *balascio*), from LL *balascus*, from Pers *Badakhshān*, a place near Samarkand where they are found]

balata /bal'ə-tə/ *n* (also **bull'y-tree**) a tropical American sapotaceous tree (*Manilkara bidentata*); its gum, used as a substitute for rubber and gutta-percha. [Prob Tupí]

balboa /bäl-bō'ə/ *n* the standard monetary unit of Panama (100 centésimos). [Vasco Nuñez de *Balboa*, c.1475–1517]

Balbriggan /bal-brig'ən/ *n* a knitted cotton fabric like that *orig* made at *Balbriggan*, Ireland; underclothing made of it.

balbutient /bal-bū'sh(y)ənt/ *adj* stammering. [L *balbūtiēns, -entis,* from *balbūtīre* to stutter]

balcony /balk'ə-ni (or 18c bal-kō'ni)/ *n* a platform, with a balustrade or railing, projecting from the wall of a building, supported by pillars or consoles, and with access *usu* from a door or window; in theatres, *usu* the gallery immediately above the dress circle (*N Am* the dress circle itself). [Ital *balcone*, from *balco*, of Gmc origin; OHGer *balcho* (Ger *Balken*), Eng **balk**]
■ **balconet** or **balconette** /bal-kə-net'/ *n* a miniature balcony. **bal'conied** *adj.*

bald /böld/ *adj* without hair, feathers, etc on the head (or on other parts of the body); (of a bird or animal) having white markings on the face; bare, unadorned; (of a tyre) having a worn tread (*inf*); lacking in grace or charm, blunt; undisguised, obvious; paltry, trivial (*archaic*). [Perh **balled** rounded]

■ **bald'ing** *adj* going bald. **bald'ish** *adj* somewhat bald. **bald'ly** *adv* plainly, without tactful circumlocution. **bald'ness** *n.* **bald'y**, also **bald'ie** *n* (*inf*) a bald-headed person (also *adj*); an over-short haircut (*Scot*).

▫ **bald'-coot** or **bald'icoot** *n* the coot, from its pure white wide frontal plate. **bald eagle** *n* the American white-headed eagle, used as the national emblem. **bald'-faced** *adj* (of a lie, etc) shameless, out-and-out; (of a bird or animal) having white markings on the face. **bald'-head** *n* a person with a bald head. **bald'-headed** *adj* having a bald head. ◆ *adj* and *adv* (*sl*) without restraint, without regard for the consequences; out and out. **baldicoot** see **bald-coot** above. **bald'pate** *n* a person destitute of hair; a kind of wild duck. ◆ *adj* (also **bald'pated**) bald.

■ **bald as a coot** see under **coot**[1].

baldachin, baldaquin /bal' or böl'də-kin/ or **baldacchino** /-kē'nō/ *n* a canopy over a throne, pulpit, altar, etc; in Roman Catholic processions, a canopy carried over the priest who carries the host; silk brocade. [Ital *baldacchino*, Fr *baldaquin* a canopy, from Ital *Baldacco* Baghdad, from where the material of which they were made came]

balderdash /böl'dər-dash/ *n* senseless talk; anything jumbled together without judgement; obscene language or writing (*dialect*); a jumbled mixture of liquids (*obs*). [Origin unknown]

balderlocks see **badderlock**.

baldicoot see under **bald**.

baldmoney /böld'mu-ni/ *n* spignel; gentian of various kinds. [Ety unknown]

baldric or **baldrick** /böld'rik/ *n* a warrior's belt or shoulder sash, for supporting a sword, etc; (*Spenser* **baudricke**) the zodiac. [Cf MHGer *balderich* girdle]

Baldwin /böld'win/ (*US*) *n* a variety of apple. [Personal name]

bale[1] /bāl/ *n* a bundle, or package of goods; a measure, *esp* (*US*) 500lb of cotton; a group (of turtles); the set of dice for any special game (*obs*). ◆ *vt* to make into bales. [ME *bale*, perh from OFr *bale*, from OHGer *balla, palla* ball. See **ball**[1]]
■ **bal'er** *n* a machine for baling hay, etc.

bale[2] see **bail**[2].

bale[3] /bāl/ *n* evil, injury, mischief (*archaic*); misery, woe (*archaic*). [OE *bealu*; OHGer *balo*; ON *böl*]
■ **bale'ful** *adj* malignant, hurtful, of evil influence; painful (*obs*); sorrowful, lugubrious (*archaic*). **bale'fully** *adv*. **bale'fulness** *n.*

Balearic /ba-lē-ar'ik/ *adj* of or relating to the *Balearic* Islands in the W Mediterranean, which consist of Majorca, Minorca, Ibiza, Formentera and several smaller islands.

balection see **bolection**.

baleen /ba- or ba-lēn'/ *n* whalebone, horny plates growing from the palate of certain whales (also *adj*). [OFr *baleine*, from L *balaena* whale]

bale-fire /bāl'fīr/ *n* a bonfire; a beacon-fire (*Scot*); a funeral pyre (*obs*). [OE *bæl*; cf ON *bāl* bale, Gr *phalos* bright, white]

Balfour declaration /bal'fər dek-lə-rā'shən/ *n* the statement made in November 1917 by Arthur *Balfour*, the then British Foreign Secretary, that the British Government was in favour of the establishment of a national home for the Jewish people in Palestine.

balibuntal /ba-li-bun'tl/ *n* (a hat made of) fine, closely woven straw. [From *Baliuag* in the Philippines, and *buntal*, Tagálog for the straw of the talipot palm]

Balinese /bä-lə-nēz'/ *adj* relating to the island of *Bali* (east of Java), its people, or their language. ◆ *n* (*pl* **Balinese'**) a native or inhabitant of Bali; their language.

balise /ba-lēz'/ *n* a device mounted on a railway track that transmits information to (and sometimes receives information from) passing trains by telegraphy. [Fr, beacon, signal]

balista see **ballista**.

balk or **baulk** /bö(l)k/ *vi* to pull up or stop short; to refuse a jump, etc; to jib (at something) (*fig*); to lie out of the way (*Spenser*); to bandy words (*obs*). ◆ *vt* to shirk, avoid; to decline; to ignore, pass over; to let slip; to put a stumbling-block in the way of; to thwart, frustrate, foil, check; to chop (logic) (*Shakesp*). ◆ *n* a check, frustration; a disappointment; a failure to take a jump or the like; the part of a snooker table marked off by the balkline; an illegal action made by the pitcher to deceive a baserunner (*baseball*); a squared timber; a tie-beam of a house, stretching from wall to wall, *esp* when laid so as to form a loft (**the balks**); an unploughed ridge; a place overlooked, an omission (*obs*); a ridge (*obs*); the beam of a balance (*obs*); a rope to connect fishing-nets. [OE *balca* ridge; OHGer *balcho* beam]
■ **balk'd** *adj* (*Shakesp*) *prob* heaped in balks. **balk'er** *n.* **balk'iness** *n.* **balk'ing** *n* and *adj*. **balk'ingly** *adv*. **balk'y** *adj* apt to balk; perverse, refractory.

▫ **balk'line** *n* a line drawn across a snooker table; a boundary line for the preliminary run in a jumping competition.

Balkan /böl'kən or bol'/ *adj* belonging or relating to the *Balkan* peninsula in SE Europe, or to its peoples or its countries.

■ **Balkanizā'tion** or **-s-** n. **Bal'kanize** or **-ise** vt (also without cap) to reduce to the condition of the Balkan peninsula, which was divided in the late 19th and early 20th centuries into a number of mutually hostile territories.

ball[1] /böl/ n anything spherical or nearly so; a rounded or matted mass; any rounded protuberant part of the body, eg the ball of the foot; a round or oval object used in sports (of varying size, shape and composition according to the sport); a pass of the ball in sports such as soccer and rugby; a delivery of the ball at cricket; a pitch thrown out of the strike zone (baseball); a game played with a ball, esp (US) baseball or football; a bullet or solid missile projected from a gun, cannon, etc; a spherical mass of wound yarn, string, etc; (usu pl) a testicle (vulgar sl); the eyeball; a bolus for a horse; a spherical cake of soap (obs); (in pl) nonsense (also interj; vulgar); (in pl) a balls-up (vulgar sl); (in pl) guts, courage (sl, esp US). ◆ vt to form into a ball; to clog; to entangle; (of swarming bees) to cluster round (the queen); (usu of a man) to have sexual intercourse with (vulgar sl, orig US). ◆ vi to gather into a ball; to clog. [ME bal, from ON böllr; OHGer ballo, pallo]

■ **balled** adj formed into a ball. **ball'ing** n forming into a ball; snowballing; (Scot **ba'ing** /bö'ing/, also **ba'spiel** /bö'spēl/) a periodical game of football played by the population of a town in the streets and sometimes in the river. **ball'siness** n. **ballsy** /böl'zi/ adj (sl, esp US) gutsy, tough and courageous.
❑ **ball'-and-claw** see **claw-and-ball** under **claw**. **ball'-barrow** n a wheelbarrow with a ball-shaped wheel. **ball-bear'ing** n a device for lessening friction by making a revolving part turn on loose steel balls; one of the balls so used. **ball'-boy** or **ball'-girl** n (sport) a boy or girl who collects balls that are out of play, supplies balls to the players, etc. **ball'-breaker** or (US) **ball'-buster** n (vulgar sl) a person, task or job, etc that is excessively demanding; a woman who is ruthless, demanding or demoralizing in her treatment of men. **ball'-breaking** or **-busting** n and adj. **ball'clay** n (geol) a fine-textured highly plastic clay used for ceramics. **ball'cock** n the stopcock of a cistern regulated by a floating ball that rises and falls with the water. **ball'-flower** n (archit) an ornament in Decorated Gothic, resembling a ball within a globular flower. **ball game** n any game played with a ball, esp (US) baseball or football; a situation, as in a whole new ball game (inf). **ball'hawk** n (N Am inf) a sportsman who has a talent for gaining possession of the ball. **ball lightning** n a slowly moving luminous ball occasionally seen during a thunderstorm. **ball mill** n (engineering) a horizontal cylindrical container in which a substance is ground by rotation with steel or ceramic balls. **ball park** n (chiefly US) a baseball field; a sphere of activity; the area designated for the landing of a spacecraft (**in the right ball park** (inf and fig) more or less correct). **ball'park** adj (orig US) approximate, esp in the phrase ballpark figures. **ball'peen hammer** n a hammer with a rounded peen, used esp for beating metal. **ball'-player** n a player (esp of football) with outstanding ball-control skills; a baseball player (N Am). **ball'point** or **ballpoint pen** n a fountain pen with a tiny ball rotating against an inking cartridge as its writing tip. **ball'-proof** adj proof against balls discharged from firearms. **balls'-aching** adj (sl) tedious. **ballsed-up**, **balls-up** see **balls up** below. **balls-out'** adj (sl) performed in an aggressive and uncompromising manner. **ball valve** n a non-return valve closed by a ball forced into an aperture.
■ **ball and chain** a means of hobbling a prisoner consisting of an iron ball chained to an ankle; a severe encumbrance; one's wife (sl). **ball-and-socket joint** (physiol and engineering) a joint formed of a ball partly enclosed in a cup-shaped cavity, allowing rotation on various axes. **ball of fire** a lively, dynamic person; a glass of brandy (inf). **balls up** (vulgar sl) to make a muddle or mess of; to throw into confusion (**balls'-up** n; **ballsed'-up** adj). **ball up** to clog; to make a mess of (sl; **ball'up** n (US); **balled'-up** adj). **have someone by the balls** (vulgar sl) to have someone at one's mercy or in a helpless state. **keep the ball rolling** to keep things going. **make a balls** or **balls-up of** (vulgar sl) to do badly, make a thorough mess of. **on the ball** (inf) properly in touch with the situation; on the alert. **play ball** (inf) to co-operate. **set**, **start** or **get the ball rolling** to make the first move; to start things going. **the ball at one's feet** success within one's grasp; an opportunity ready to be taken. **the ball's in your court** the responsibility for the next move is yours. **the whole ball of wax** (N Am sl) the whole lot. **three balls** the sign of a pawnbroker.

ball[2] /böl/ n a (usu formal) gathering for dancing. ◆ vi (N Am sl) to enjoy oneself, have a ball. [OFr bal, from baller to dance, from LL ballāre, perh from Gr ballizein to dance]
■ **ball'ing** n.
❑ **ball'-dress** n. **ball'-gown** n. **ball'room** n. **ballroom dancing** n recreational formal dancing.
■ **have a ball** (inf) to enjoy oneself very much. **open the ball** to begin operations.

ballabile /ba-lä'bi-lā/ n (pl **balla'biles** or **balla'bili** /-lē/) a part of a ballet danced by the whole corps de ballet, with or without the

principal dancers. [Ital, fit to be danced, from ballare to dance, from LL ballāre]

ballad /bal'əd/ (hist **ballet** /-ət/, archaic Scot **ballat** /-ət/ or **ballant** /bal'ənt/) n a slow, sentimental song; a simple narrative poem in short stanzas (usu of four lines, of eight and six syllables alternately); a popular song, often scurrilous, referring to contemporary persons or events (chiefly hist); formerly a drawing-room song, usu sentimental, in several verses sung to the same melody; orig a song accompanying a dance; (**ballet** /bal'ət/) a form of madrigal (hist). ◆ vt (obs) to make ballads about. [OFr ballade, from LL ballāre to dance; see **ball**[2]]
■ **balladeer'** n a person who sings ballads (also vi). **ball'adist** n a writer or singer of ballads. **ball'adry** n ballads collectively; ballad-making.
❑ **ballad concert** n a concert of drawing-room ballads. **ball'admonger** n a dealer in, or composer of, ballads. **ballad opera** n (hist) an opera with spoken dialogue, and songs set to existing popular tunes.

ballade /ba-läd'/ n a poem of one or more triplets of stanzas, each of seven, eight or ten lines, including refrain, followed by an envoy, the whole on three (or four) rhymes; sometimes (loosely) any poem in stanzas of equal length; an ill-defined form of instrumental music, often in six-eight or six-four time. [An earlier spelling of **ballad**, with old pronunciation restored]
❑ **ballade royal** n rhyme royal (James I's **ballat royal** has an additional line and rhymes ababbcbc).

balladin and **balladine** same as **baladin** and **baladine**.

ballan /bal'ən/ n a species of wrasse (also **ball'anwrasse**). [Perh Ir ball spot]

ballant a Scots form of **ballad**.

ballast /bal'əst/ n heavy material used to weigh down and steady a ship or balloon; broken stone or other material used as the bed of a road or railway; anything which provides steadiness or stability; something which maintains or stabilizes the current in a circuit (electronics). ◆ vt (pap **ball'asted** (Shakesp **ball'ast**)) to load with ballast; to make or keep steady; to load (Shakesp). [Prob Old Swed barlast, from bar bare, and last load]
❑ **ball'ast-heaver** n.
■ **in ballast** carrying ballast only.

ballat see **ballad** and **ballade**.

ballerina /ba-lə-rē'nə/ n (pl **balleri'nas**; formerly also **balleri'ne** /-nā/) a female ballet-dancer. [Ital]

ballet[1] /bal'ā or ba-lā'/ n a theatrical performance of formalized dancing with set steps, mime and fluid graceful movements; the art or activity of dancing in this way; (a suite of) music for it; a troupe giving such performances; in skiing, skating, etc, a balletic performance; a dance (obs). [Fr, from dimin of bal a dance]
■ **balletic** /bal-et'ik/ adj of the art of ballet; in or similar to the style of ballet. **ballet'ically** adv. **balletomane** /-et'ō-mān/ n an enthusiast for ballet. **balletomā'nia** n.
❑ **ball'et-dancer** n. **ball'et-dancing** n. **ball'et-girl** n. **ball'et-master** or **ball'et-mistress** n a man or woman who directs or teaches ballet.

ballet[2] see **ballad**.

ballista or **balista** /bə-lis'tə/ n a Roman military weapon in the form of a crossbow for projecting heavy missiles. [L, from Gr ballein to throw]

ballistic /bə-lis'tik/ adj projectile; relating to projectiles. [ballista]
■ **ballis'tics** n sing the science of projectiles; the study of firearms. **ballis'tite** n a smokeless powder composed of guncotton and nitroglycerine. **ballistōcar'diogram** n a record produced by a **ballistōcar'diograph**, an instrument for detecting the movements in the body caused by each heartbeat. **ballistōcardiog'raphy** n.
❑ **ballistic missile** n a missile which is initially guided but drops to its target under the force of gravity. **ballistic pendulum** n a suspended block for finding the velocity of projectiles.
■ **go ballistic** (sl) to lose one's temper or become violently angry.

ballium /bal'i-əm/ n the Late Latin form of **bailey**.

ballocks see **bollocks**.

ballon /ba-lõ'/ (ballet) n bounciness of step. [Fr, ball]

ballon d'essai /ba-lõ de-sā'/ (Fr) n an experimental balloon; a feeler or preliminary sounding of opinion.

balloon /bə-loon'/ n an apparatus for travel in the air, or for carrying weather-recording instruments, etc, supported by buoyancy rather than mechanically driven, consisting of a large bag that is filled with gas, and a cabin or basket beneath; a toy consisting of an inflatable rubber bag; something inflated or hollow, usu coloured (fig); a large globular wineglass; a round-bottomed flask (chem); an ornamental ball on a pillar, etc (archit); a balloon-shaped outline enclosing the words or thoughts of a strip cartoon character; a balloon-shaped outline enclosing words, etc for insertion into text (proofreading, etc);

a person both foolish and opinionated (*Scot*); (also **ballon** /ba-lō or ba-lōn'/) a game played with a large inflated ball, or the ball itself (*obs*). ◆ *adj* of or like a balloon; (of a loan, mortgage, etc) involving a final payment much larger than preceding ones. ◆ *vt* to inflate; to send high in the air. ◆ *vi* to ascend or travel in, or as if in, a balloon; to puff out like a balloon; (of an aeroplane) to rise up in the air (as a result of landing on a firm surface, or increased airspeed, etc). [Ital *ballone*, augmentative of *balla* ball]

■ **ballonet** /bal-o-net'/ *n* in a balloon or dirigible, a small bag from which air is allowed to escape, and into which air is forced, to compensate for changes of pressure in the gasbag. **balloon'ing** *n*. **balloon'ist** *n*.

❑ **balloon angioplasty** *n* angioplasty using a balloon catheter (see below). **balloon'-back'** *adj* (of a dining-room chair) having a circular or oval-shaped back-support. **balloon barrage** *n* a system of balloons attached to each other and to the ground, as a protection against hostile aircraft. **balloon catheter** *n* a catheter inserted into a bodily vessel and inflated to dilate it. **balloon tyre** *n* a large pneumatic tyre of low pressure. **balloon'-vine'** *n* heartsease, a tropical American climber with bladdery pods. **balloon whisk** *n* a whisk made of wire loops.

■ **when the balloon goes up** when the trouble starts; when proceedings begin.

ballot /bal'ət/ *n* a ticket or paper (formerly a small ball) used in registering a secret vote; a secret vote registered or method of voting by putting a ballot into a box; in the USA extended to open voting; the total number of votes cast in an election. ◆ *vt* to take the vote or ballot of. ◆ *vi* (**ball'oting; ball'oted**) to vote by ballot; to draw lots. [Ital *ballotta*, dimin of *balla* ball. See **ball**[1]]

■ **ballotee'** *n*.

❑ **ballot box** *n* a box into which ballots are put in voting; the system of voting by secret ballot. **ballot paper** *n* a paper on which a ballot vote is recorded. **ball'ot-rigging** *n* dishonest manipulation of a ballot.

ballow /bal'ō/ (*Shakesp*) *n* a cudgel (other readings are **bat** and **battero**). [Perh a misprint for **baton**]

ballsy see under **ball**[1].

bally /bal'i/ (*old sl*) *adj* a euphemism for bloody, but almost meaningless.

ballyhoo /ba-li-hoo'/ (*sl*) *n* noisy publicity; fuss, commotion. ◆ *vt* (**ballyhoo'ing; ballyhoo'ed**) to create loud publicity, make a ballyhoo, about.

ballyrag see **bullyrag**.

balm /bäm/ *n* an aromatic substance; a fragrant and healing ointment; aromatic fragrance; anything that heals or soothes pain; a tree yielding balm; a labiate plant (*Melissa officinalis*) with an aroma similar to that of lemon; extended to *Melittis* (**bastard balm**) and other garden herbs. ◆ *vt* to embalm (*archaic*); to anoint with fragrant oil (*Shakesp*); to soothe (*archaic*). [OFr *basme*, from L *balsamum*. See **balsam**]

■ **balm'ily** *adv*. **balm'iness** *n*. **balm'y** *adj* (of the air) warm and soft; fragrant; mild and soothing; bearing balm.

■ **balm** (or **balsam**) **of Gilead** the resinous exudation of trees of the genus *Commiphora* or *Balsamodendron*, from the belief that it is the substance mentioned in the Bible (Jeremiah 8.22) as found in Gilead; the balsam fir.

balmacaan /bal-mə-kän'/ *n* a man's loose overcoat with raglan sleeves. [From *Balmacaan*, near Inverness, Scotland]

bal masqué /bal ma-skä'/ (*Fr*) *n* a masked ball.

balm-cricket /bäm-krik'it/ (*Tennyson*) *n* a cicada. [Ger *Baum* tree, and **cricket**[2]]

Balmer series /bal'mər sē'rēz or -riz/ (*phys*) *n* a group of lines in the hydrogen spectrum. [J J *Balmer* (1825–98), Swiss mathematician]

balmoral /bal-mor'əl/ *n* a round flat Scottish bonnet with a pompom; a figured woollen petticoat; a kind of boot lacing in front. [*Balmoral*, royal residence in Aberdeenshire built in Queen Victoria's reign]

balmy[1] see under **balm**.

balmy[2] a variant of **barmy**.

balneal /bal'ni-əl/ *adj* of baths or bathing. [L *balneum*, from Gr *balaneion* bath]

■ **bal'neary** *n* a bath; a bathing-place; a medicinal spring. ◆ *adj* of or for bathing. **balnea'tion** *n* bathing. **balneol'ogist** *n*. **balneol'ogy** *n* the scientific medical study of bathing and mineral springs. **balneother'apy** *n* treatment of disease by baths.

balneum Mariae /bal'ni-əm ma-rī'ē or bal'ne-ūm ma-rē'ī/ (L) *n* a bain-marie.

baloney or **boloney** /ba-lō'ni/ (*sl*) *n* deceptive talk; nonsense; (chiefly *US*) Bologna sausage. [Thought to be from **Bologna sausage**]

baloo or **balu** /bä'loo/ *n* in India, a bear. [Hindi *bhālū*]

BALPA *abbrev* : British Air Line Pilots Association.

bal paré /bal pa-rä'/ (*Fr*) *n* a dress ball.

balsa /böl'sə or bal'sə/ *n* corkwood, a tropical American tree (*Ochroma lagopus*) of the family Bombacaceae, with very light wood (also **bal'sawood**); a raft or float. [Sp, raft]

balsam /böl'səm/ *n* a plant of the genus *Impatiens* (family Balsaminaceae); a liquid resin or resinous oily substance, *esp* balm of Gilead; any healing ointment or preparation (*fig*). ◆ *vt* to heal; to embalm (*rare*). [L *balsamum*, from Gr *balsamon*; prob of Semitic origin]

■ **balsamic** /-sam'ik/ *adj*. **balsamif'erous** *adj* producing balsam. **Balsami'na** *n* a discarded synonym of the genus *Impatiens*, giving name to the balsam family **Balsaminaceae** /-in-ā'si-ē/, closely related to the geraniums. **bal'samy** *adj* fragrant.

❑ **balsam fir** *n* an American fir (*Abies balsamea*). **balsamic vinegar** *n* a rich-flavoured, dark Italian vinegar matured in wooden barrels. **balsam of Peru** see under **Peruvian**. **balsam of Tolu** see **Tolu**. **balsam poplar** *n* an American species of poplar.

■ **Canada balsam** a turpentine from the balsam fir.

Balt /bölt/ *n* a native or inhabitant of the Baltic provinces or states; a speaker of a Baltic language; a member of the former land-owning class (of German origin) in the Baltic provinces or states; an immigrant to Australia from the Baltic or (loosely) Europe generally (*Aust inf*, often *derog*). [From the *Baltic Sea*, from L *Baltia* Scandinavia]

■ **Balt'ic** *adj* of the sea separating Scandinavia from the mainland of NE Europe; of, denoting or relating to a Balt or Balts; belonging or relating to Estonia, Latvia or Lithuania; (also without *cap*) extremely cold (*inf*). ◆ *n* the Baltic languages, Lithuanian, Latvian and (extinct) Old Prussian.

❑ **Balt'o-slav', Balt'o-slav'ic** or **Balto-slavon'ic** *adj* of a family of Indo-European languages comprising the Slavonic and Baltic languages.

balthazar or **balthasar** /bal'thə-zär/, also **belshazzar** /bel-shaz'ər/ (also with *cap*) *n* a very large wine bottle, in capacity *usu* taken to equal 16 ordinary bottles (12.80 litres or 2.75 gallons). [Coined in reference to the King of Babylon in the Bible, Daniel 5.1]

balti /böl'ti/ *n* a kind of Indian cookery originating in Britain, in which food is cooked in a wok-like dish and eaten out of the same dish; this dish. [Hindi *balti* bucket, scoop, from the shape of the dish]

Baltimore /böl'tə-mör/ *n* a common orange and black N American bird of the hangnest family, also called **fire-bird**, **Baltimore oriole**, etc. [From Lord *Baltimore*, whose livery was orange and black]

balu see **baloo**.

Baluch or **Baluchi** /ba-looch' or -loo'chi/ *n* a native or inhabitant of Baluchistan; the language of the people of this region. ◆ *adj* of this region or its people. [Pers *Balūchī*]

■ **Baluchitherium** /-thē'ri-əm/ *n* (Gr *therion* wild beast) a gigantic Tertiary fossil rhinoceros, paraceratherium, found in this region.

balun /bal'ən/ *n* a transformer used to connect a *balanced* circuit and an *unbalanced* one.

baluster /bal'ə-stər/ *n* a small pillar supporting a stair rail or a parapet coping, often circular in section and curvaceous in outline; a balustrade (*archaic*). ◆ *adj* (of a vessel, its stem or handle) like a baluster in shape. [Fr *balustre*, from LL *balaustium*, from Gr *balaustion* pomegranate flower; from its shape]

■ **bal'ustered** *adj*. **bal'ustrade** *n* a row of balusters joined by a rail or coping.

balzarine /bal'zə-rēn/ *n* a light dress material of mixed cotton and worsted. [Fr *balzorine*]

bam /bam/ (*inf*) *n* a hoax; a false tale. ◆ *vt* (**bamm'ing; bammed**) to cheat or hoax. [See **bamboozle**]

bambino /bam-bē'nō/ *n* (*pl* **bambi'nos** or **bambi'ni** /-nē/) a child; a picture or image of the child Jesus. [Ital]

bamboo /bam-boo'/ *n* a gigantic tropical and subtropical grass (genus *Bambusa*) with hollow-jointed woody stem and edible young shoots (**bamboo shoots**); the stem, used *esp* for making furniture; bamboo-coloured bisque porcelain. [Perh Malay *bambu*]

❑ **bamboo curtain** *n* the impenetrable political barrier of Asian, *esp* Chinese, communism (cf **iron curtain**).

bamboozle /bam-boo'zl/ (*inf*) *vt* to deceive; to confound or mystify. [Origin unknown; first appears about 1700]

■ **bamboo'zlement** *n*. **bamboo'zler** *n*.

bampot /bam'pot/ (*Scot inf*) *n* an idiot, fool (also **bamm'er**). [Ety uncertain; cf **barmpot**]

Ban /ban/ (*hist*) *n* the governor of a **Ban'at** (also **Ban'ate** or **Bann'at**), a military district on the boundaries of the Hungarian kingdom. [Pers *bān* lord]

ban[1] /ban/ *n* a prohibition; sentence of banishment; outlawry; anathematization; a denunciation; a curse; a condemnation by society, etc; a proclamation (*obs*). ◆ *vt* (**bann'ing; banned**) to forbid or prohibit; to curse (*archaic* and *dialect*); to anathematize. ◆ *vi* (*archaic*) to curse. [OE *gebann* proclamation, *bannan* to summon; cf **ban³** and **banns**]

ban² /ban/ n (pl **bani** /bän'i/) a Romanian and Moldovan monetary unit, $\frac{1}{100}$ of a leu. [Romanian]

ban³ /ban/ (*hist*) n in feudal England, the calling of the younger vassals for military service; those so called; in the Prussian Army, each of two divisions of the army reserve. [OFr, of Gmc origin; cf **ban¹**]
■ **arrière-ban** /ar-i-ār-ban/ or (Fr) ar-yer-bä/ in feudal England, the reserve or older vassals liable for military service.

banal /bə-näl'/ adj commonplace, trivial, flat. [Fr]
■ **banal'ity** n cliché, triviality, triteness. **banaliza'tion** or **-s-** n. **banal'ize** or **-ise** vt to make banal. **banal'ly** adv.

banana /bə-nä'nə/ n a gigantic tree-like herbaceous plant (*Musa sapientum*) or its nutritious yellow fruit which grows in hanging bunches. [Sp or Port, from the native name in Guinea]
❑ **bana'na-bender** n (*Aust inf*) a Queenslander. **bana'na-fingered** adj clumsy, all thumbs. **banana kick** n (*football*) a sharply curving shot hit with the outside of the foot. **Bana'naland** n (*Aust*) Queensland. **Bana'nalander** n (*Aust*) a Queenslander. **banana liquid**, **oil** or **solution** n a solution with the odour of bananas, used for various purposes, eg in photography, as a solvent for paint, etc. **banana plug** n (*elec eng*) an electrical plug with one conductor, with a spring metal tip in the shape of a banana. **banana republic** n (*derog*) any of the small republics in the tropics which depend on exports of fruit and on foreign investment; hence any small country dependent on foreign capital. **banana skin** n (*fig*) something which causes a slip-up or a downfall. **banana split** n a dish composed of a banana halved lengthways, ice cream, and other ingredients.
■ **be** or **go bananas** (*sl*) to be or go crazy. **top banana** (*inf*) the star entertainer in a line-up (*esp* of comedians); the most important person in a group, organization, etc.

Banat, Banate see **Ban**.

banausic /ba-nö'sik/ (*formal*) adj (also **banau'sian**) merely mechanical; really or apparently appropriate to an artisan; vulgar; materialistic. [Gr *banausikos*, from *banausos* a handicraftsman]

Banbury cake /ban'bər-i käk/ n a kind of mince pie made in *Banbury*, Oxfordshire.

banc /bangk/ (*law*) n the judges' bench. [Fr]
■ **in banc** or **in banco** in full court.

bancassurance /bang'kə-shoo-rəns/ n the provision of financial services spanning both banking and insurance. [**bank¹** and **assurance**]
■ **banc'assurer** n.

banco /bang'kō/ n the standard money in which a bank keeps its accounts, as distinguished from the current money of the place. [Ital; see **bank¹,²**]

Band /bant/ (Ger) n (pl **Bände** /ben'də/) a volume of a book or journal.

band¹ /band/ n a flat strip (of cloth, rubber, metal, etc) to bind round or reinforce anything, as a hat-band, waistband, rubber band, etc; a stripe of contrasting colour, texture, etc; a flat strip between mouldings, or dividing a wall surface; a finger-ring; a belt for driving machinery; the neck-band or collar of a shirt, also the collar or ruff worn in the 17c (termed a **falling-band** when turned down); (in *pl*) the pair of linen strips hanging down in front from the collar, worn by some Protestant clergymen and by barristers and advocates, formerly by others; a group or range of frequencies or wavelengths between two specified limits (*radio, electronics*); in sound reproduction, a separately recorded section of a record or tape; a group of close-set lines *esp* in a molecular spectrum (*phys*); a particular range, between an upper and lower limit, of eg intelligence, wealth, etc. ◆ vt to mark with a band; to ring (a bird) (*N Am*). [ME *bande*, from OFr *bande*, of Gmc origin; cf OE *bindan*; Ger *Binde* a band; Eng **band³**, **bind**]
■ **band'ed** adj fastened as with a band; striped with bands; arranged in or into bands. **band'ing** n the division of children preparing to enter secondary education into groups according to ability, in order to obtain an even spread in the mixed-ability classes usual in comprehensive schools.
❑ **band'-box** (or /ban'boks/) n a light kind of box for holding (*orig*) bands, caps, millinery, etc. ◆ adj (*esp US*) very neat and tidy, spruce; delicate, flimsy. **band'brake** or **band'-clutch** n a brake or clutch in the form of a flexible band that can be tightened about a wheel or drum. **band'fish** n a bright-red Mediterranean fish (genus *Cepola*), or other ribbon-shaped fish. **band-pass filter** n (*telecom*) a filter which freely passes currents having frequencies within specified nominal limits, and highly attenuates currents with frequencies outside these limits. **band'-saw** n an endless saw, a toothed steel belt. **band'-string** n an ornamental string for fastening bands or a collar. **band'-wheel** n a wheel on which a strap or band runs. **band'width** n the width of a band of radio or TV frequencies; the range of frequencies in a

communications channel; the informational capacity of a link between computers.

band² /band/ n a group of people bound together for any common purpose; a troop of conspirators, confederates, etc; a group of instrumentalists, *esp* brass, wind and percussion players, often attached to a regiment; a group of players of music other than classical music; an orchestra (*inf*); a group of native people on a reservation with elected chiefs (*Can*); a herd or flock (*N Am*). ◆ vt to form into a band. ◆ vi to associate, assemble, confederate. [Fr *bande*, of Gmc origin, with changed sense; cf **band¹,³**, **bend¹**, **bind**]
❑ **band'-call** n a rehearsal. **band'master** n the conductor of a band (also **band'leader**). **band'mate** n a member of the same band of musicians. **Band of Hope** n a 19c–20c association of young people pledged to lifelong abstinence from alcoholic drinks. **band'shell** n a bandstand with a concave rear wall. **bands'man** n a member of a band of musicians. **band'stand** n a structure for accommodating a band of musicians. **band'wagon** n the car that carries the band in a circus procession; a fashionable movement, a trend enjoying current success.
■ **beat the band** (*inf*) to be the best (*esp* in the phrase **to beat the band** so as to beat everything). **get**, **jump** or **leap on the bandwagon** to join in any popular and currently successful movement in the hope of gaining advantage from it.

band³ /band/ n that by which loose things are held together; a moral bond of restraint or of obligation (*fig*); a tie or connecting piece; (in *pl*) shackles, bonds, fetters; an agreement or promise given (*archaic*); security given (*archaic*); a banding together, a confederacy (*Scot*); a pledge (*Spenser*). [ME *band*, *bond*, from ON *band*. See **band¹**, **bind**, **bond¹**]
■ **band'ster** n (*hist*) a binder of the sheaves after the reapers.
❑ **band'-stone** n a stone set transversely in a wall to bind the structure.

band⁴ /band/ (Spenser) vt to ban or banish.

band⁵ an obsolete *pat* of **bind**.

banda /ban'də/ (Afr) n a thatched hut. [Native word]

bandage /ban'dij/ n a strip of cloth for winding round an injured part of the body; an adhesive plaster for protecting a wound or cut; a piece of cloth used to blindfold the eyes. ◆ vt to bind with a bandage. [MFr *bandage*; see also ety at **band¹**]

Band-aid® /ban'dād/ n a type of sticking-plaster for covering minor wounds. ◆ adj (*usu* without *cap*; of policies, etc) makeshift, temporary.

bandalore /ban'də-lör/ (*obs*) n an 18c toy resembling a yo-yo which, through the action of a coiled spring, returned to the hand when thrown down. [Origin unknown]

bandana or **bandanna** /ban-dan'ə/ n a silk or cotton square, with spots or diamond prints, *orig* from India, worn on the head or round the neck. [Hindi *bādhnū*, a mode of dyeing]

bandar /bun'där/ n a rhesus monkey. [Hindi]

B and B, **b. and b.**, **B&B** or **b&b** abbrev : bed and breakfast (see under **bed¹**).

bandeau /ban'dō or ban-dō'/ n (pl **bandeaux** /ban'dōz or -dōz'/) a band to bind the hair, worn around the head; a band inside a hat; a bandage for the eyes. [Fr]

bandeirante /bə-dā-ē-rät'/ (Port) n a pioneer, explorer or adventurer, *esp* one who took part in expeditions (**bandeiras**) in search of gold and slaves in 17c Brazil.

bandelet /ban'də-let/ (*archit*) n a small flat moulding around a column. [Fr *bandelette*]

bandelier /ban-də-lēr'/ a form of **bandoleer**.

banderilla /ban- or bän-dā-rēl'yä/ n a dart with a streamer, stuck by bullfighters in the bull's neck. [Sp, dimin of *bandera* banner]
■ **banderillero** /ban- or bän-dā-rēl-yä'rō/ n (pl **banderille'ros**) a bullfighter who uses banderillas.

banderol, **banderole** /ban'də-rōl/, **bandrol** /ban'drōl/ or **bannerol** /ban'ə-rōl/ (Spenser **bannerall** /-röl/) n a small banner or streamer, like that on a masthead; a flat band with an inscription, common in Renaissance buildings (*archit*). [Fr]

bandersnatch /ban'dər-snach/ n a monster invented by Lewis Carroll.

bandh /bund/ (Ind) n a general strike. [Hindi, a tying up]

bandicoot /ban'di-koot/ n a member of the genus *Perameles* of small marsupials; the largest species of rat, found in India and Sri Lanka, also called **Malabar-rat** and **pig-rat**. ◆ vt (*Aust*) to remove (potatoes) from the ground leaving the tops undisturbed. [Telugu *pandikokku* pig-rat]

bandit /ban'dit/ n (pl **ban'dits** or **banditti** /ban-dit'ē/, also loosely used as *sing*, a body of bandits) an outlaw; a brigand; an enemy plane (*RAF sl*). [Ital *bandito*, pl *banditi*, from LL *bannīre*, *bandīre* to proclaim. See **ban¹**]
■ **ban'ditry** n.

■ words derived from main entry word; ❑ compound words; ■ idioms and phrasal verbs

■ **one-armed bandit** a fruit machine, so called from the similarity to an arm of the lever pulled to operate it, and the heavy odds against the user.

bandmaster see under **band²**.

bandobast or **bundobust** /*bun'dō-bust*/ (*Ind*) *n* an arrangement, settlement. [Hindi and Pers *band-o-bast* tying and binding]

bandog /*ban'dog*/ *n* an aggressive dog kept chained or tied up; a cross between an American pit bull terrier and a mastiff, rottweiler or Rhodesian ridgeback, bred for exceptional ferocity. [ME *band-dogge*; **band³** and **dog¹**]

bandoleer or **bandolier** /*ban-də-lēr'*/ *n* a shoulder belt, *esp* for carrying ammunition. [OFr *bandouillere*, from Ital *bandoliera*, from *banda* a band]
■ **bandoleer'ed** or **bandolier'ed** *adj* wearing a bandoleer.

bandoleon see **bandoneon**.

bandolero /*ban-dō-lā'rō*/ *n* (*pl* **bandole'ros**) a highwayman. [Sp]

bandoline /*ban'dō-lēn*/ *n* a gummy substance formerly used for stiffening the hair. ♦ *vt* to stiffen (the hair) with bandoline. [Prob from **band³**]

bandoneon /*ban-dō'nē-ən* or *ban-don'i-ən*/ *n* a kind of button accordion popular in S America, *esp* for playing tango music (also **bandon'ion, bandol'eon**). [S American Sp, from H *Band*, its German inventor]

bandook see **bundook**.

bandore /*ban-dör'*/ *n* an Elizabethan wire-stringed instrument like a cittern (also **bando'ra**). [Sp *bandurria*, Fr *mandore*; L *pandura*, Gr *pandourā* a three-stringed lute]

bandrol see **banderol**.

bandsman, bandstand see under **band²**.

bandura /*ban-doo'rə*/ *n* a Ukrainian twelve-stringed instrument of the lute family. [Ukrainian, from Pol, from Ital, from L *pandura* (cf **bandore**)]

bandwagon see under **band²**.

bandwidth see under **band¹**.

bandy¹ /*ban'di*/ *vt* (**ban'dying; ban'died**) to beat to and fro; to toss from one another (eg words *with* someone); to pass (a story, information, etc) from mouth to mouth (with *about*); to give and take (blows or reproaches); to fight, strive (*Shakesp*). [Origin obscure]
■ **ban'dying** *n*.

bandy² /*ban'di*/ *adj* bent wide apart at the knee; having such legs or crooked legs. [Poss **bandy³**]
□ **ban'dy-legged'** *adj*.

bandy³ /*ban'di*/ *n* a club bent at the end for striking a ball; a ball game played with such a club, an early form of hockey (also **ban'dy-ball**); a game played on ice, similar to ice-hockey but played with a ball and curved sticks; a version of tennis (*obs*); a tennis stroke (*obs*). [Origin obscure]

bandy⁴ /*ban'di*/ (*Ind*) *n* a carriage or (bullock) cart. [Telugu *bandi*]
□ **ban'dyman** *n*.

bandy-bandy /*ban'di-ban'di*/ *n* a small, venomous, ringed Australian snake (*Vermicella annulata*). [From an Aboriginal language]

bane /*bān*/ *n* a source or cause of evil, misery, etc; poison; destruction, death; mischief, harm (*archaic*). ♦ *vt* to harm (*archaic*); to poison (*Shakesp*). [OE *bana* a murderer; ON *bani* death]
■ **bane'ful** *adj* destructive; pernicious; poisonous. **bane'fully** *adv.* **bane'fulness** *n*.
□ **bane'berry** *n* a black poisonous berry, the fruit of the ranunculaceous plant *Actaea spicata*; the plant itself.
■ **the bane of one's life** something which causes one enormous trouble or misery.

bang¹ /*bang*/ *n* a heavy blow; a sudden loud noise; an explosion; a thrill, burst of activity, sudden success (*fig*); an act of sexual intercourse (*sl*); an injection of a drug (*sl*). ♦ *vt* to beat; to strike violently; to slam (eg a door); to have sexual intercourse with (*sl*); to beat or surpass. ♦ *vi* to make a loud noise; to slam; to inject a drug (*sl*); to dash, bounce (*dialect*). ♦ *adv* with a bang; abruptly; absolutely (as in *bang up-to-date, bang in the middle*). ♦ *adj* complete, total (used for emphasis, as in *the whole bang lot*). [ON *banga* to hammer; cf Ger *Bengel* a cudgel]
■ **bang'er** *n* something that bangs; an explosive firework; a decrepit old car (*inf*); a sausage (*inf*). **bang'ing** *adj* dealing blows; overwhelming, very great (*inf*); (also **bang'in'**) great, very good (*sl*). **bang'ster** *n* (*obs Scot*) a violent person; a braggart; a victor.
□ **bang'-up** *adj* (*archaic sl*) in the height of excellence or fashion.
■ **bang goes** (*inf*) that's the end of. **bang off** (*inf*) immediately. **bang on** (*inf*) right on the mark; to speak at length, *esp* assertively and repetitiously. **bang one's head against a brick wall** to waste one's time in unproductive effort. **bang out** to produce in a hurry (eg a

piece of writing); of printers, to mark someone's retirement or the end of someone's apprenticeship by banging tables, etc with mallets, etc. **bang to rights** *orig*, caught red-handed (*criminal sl*); certainly, absolutely, no doubt (*inf*). **bang up** (*sl*) to imprison, *specif* to shut up in a cell; to knock about, beat up (*US*). **Big Bang** the hypothetical explosion of a small dense mass which most scientists believe (the **Big Bang theory**) to have been the origin of the universe; the changes in the system and rules of the British Stock Exchange instituted on 27 October 1986, in effect deregulating many of its practices and abolishing the distinction between jobbers and brokers. **go with a bang** to go well, be a success.

bang² /*bang*/ *n* a fringe, hair cut square across the brow (often in *pl*). ♦ *vt* to cut (hair) square across. [Orig an Americanism, poss from the phrase *bang off* (see under **bang¹**)]
■ **banged** *adj* wearing the hair in such a way.
□ **bang'-tail** *n* a tail with the end tuft squared; an animal whose tail-hair is banged. **bang-tail muster** *n* (*Aust*) a cattle round-up in which the tail-hair is banged as each animal is counted.

bang³ same as **bhang**.

Bangalore torpedo /*bang'gə-lör tör-pē'dō*/ *n* an explosive device for blowing gaps in barbed-wire obstacles, etc, invented by sappers and miners of the Indian Army at *Bangalore*.

Bangla see **Bengali** under **Bengal**.

bangle /*bang'gl*/ *n* a circular bracelet worn on the arm or leg. [Hindi *barigrī, barigrī*]
■ **ban'gled** *adj* wearing bangles.

bangsring see **banxring**.

bani see **ban²**.

banian see **banyan**.

banish /*ban'ish*/ *vt* to condemn to exile; to drive away; to expel. [Fr *bannir, baniss-*, from LL *bannīre* to proclaim]
■ **ban'ishment** *n* exile.

banister or **bannister** /*ban'i-stər*/ *n* a stair-rail with its supports (often in *pl*). [*baluster*]

banjax /*ban-jaks'*/ or *ban'*/ (*sl*) *vt* to ruin, destroy; to thwart. [Anglo-Irish; poss combination of **bang¹** and **smash**]

banjo /*ban'jō*/ or *ban-jō'*/ *n* (*pl* **ban'jos** or **ban'joes**) a musical instrument played with the fingers or with a plectrum, having a long neck, a circular body of stretched parchment like a drum, and *usu* five strings of catgut and wire; applied to various tools or devices shaped like a banjo. [Southern US black pronunciation of **bandore**]
■ **ban'joist** /*-ist*/ *n*.

banjulele /*ban-jū-lā'li*/ *n* a small banjo with gut strings. [*banjo* and *ukulele*]

bank¹ /*bangk*/ *n* an institution for the keeping, lending and exchanging, etc of money; a moneybox for savings; a stock of money, fund or capital; in games of hazard, the money held by the proprietor or the person who plays against all; in card games, etc, a pool to draw cards, tokens, etc from; the person who holds this supply; any store of material or information, eg *blood bank* and *databank*; any supply, reserve or pool (of workers, resources, etc); bank paper. ♦ *vt* to deposit in a bank. ♦ *vi* to have a bank account; to count, rely (on) (*inf*). [Fr *banque*, from Ital *banca*; of Gmc origin, cognate with **bank²,³**]
■ **bank'ability** *n.* **bank'able** *adj* able to be received by a bank; reliable; *esp* of a film star, likely to ensure profitability (*US*). **bank'er** *n* a person who keeps a bank; a person employed in banking business; a betting card game; a certainty, something that can be banked on or betted on; a result forecast the same in all the entries on a coupon as being a certainty (*football pools*). **bank'ing** *n* the business or services of a bank. ♦ *adj* relating to a bank.
□ **bank account** *n* an account set up by a customer depositing money in a bank; the business record of the money deposited in a bank. **bank'-agent** *n* formerly in Scotland, the head of a branch bank (now **bank manager**). **bank balance** *n* the amount of money by which a bank account is in credit or debit. **bank'-bill** *n* formerly, a banknote; a bank draft. **bank book** or **bank pass book** *n* a book in which a record is kept of money deposited in or withdrawn from a bank. **bank card** see **banker's card** below. **bank charge** *n* a bank's periodic charge to a customer for handling transactions. **bank cheque** *n* an order to pay issued upon a bank. **bank draft** *n* a bill drawn by one bank upon another. **banker's card** *n* a cheque card or debit card (also **bank card**). **banker's draft** *n* a bill of exchange obtained from a bank by one of its customers, enabling the purchase of goods, etc by the presentation of the draft to the seller, the bank debiting the customer's account with that amount. **banker's envelope** *n* an envelope *usu* approx the same width as A4 paper, with the flap on the long edge. **banker's order** *n* a standing order (qv under **stand**). **bank giro** *n* a credit clearing system which enables transfer of money between accounts in UK banks. **bank holiday** *n* a weekday on which banks are legally closed, bills falling due on these being payable the

following day, in England and Wales observed as a general holiday. **bank interest** *n* an amount paid by a bank to a depositor; an amount charged by a bank to a borrower. **bank loan** *n* an amount lent by a bank to a borrower for a specific period at an agreed rate of interest. **bank'note** *n* a note issued by a bank, which passes as money, being payable to the bearer on demand. **bank'-paper** *n* banknotes in circulation. **bank paper** *n* a thin strong paper similar to but lighter than bond paper. **bank pass book** see **bank book** above. **bank rate** *n* until 1972 the rate at which the Bank of England was prepared to discount bills, replaced by minimum lending rate (qv), itself replaced in 1981 by the base rate. **bank reserves** *n pl* the cash reserve kept readily available by a bank for ordinary demands. **bank'roll** *n* money resources. ◆ *vt* to finance. **bank statement** *n* a summary, provided by the bank, of the transactions on a customer's account. **bank'-stock** *n* a share or shares in the capital stock of a bank. **bank switching** *n* (*comput*) the process of switching between one bank of memory and another to increase available memory.
■ **bank of issue** one that issues its own notes or promises to pay. **break the bank** in gambling, to win from the management the sum fixed as the limit it is willing to lose on any one day. **central bank** a national bank (eg in UK the Bank of England), which deals mainly with its own government and with other banks, eg regulating interest rates and managing the national debt. **clearing bank** a bank which is a member of the London Clearing House. **joint-stock bank** one whose capital is subscribed by a large number of shareholders. **laugh** (or **cry**) **all the way to the bank** to be delighted (or (*ironic*) sorry) to be making a lot of money, *esp* undeservedly or as a result of sharp practice. **merchant bank** one whose functions include financing transit of goods and providing financial and commercial advice. **private bank** one carried on by fewer than ten persons.

bank² /bangk/ *n* a mound or ridge; an upward slope; the edge of a river, lake, etc; the raised border of a road, railway cutting, etc; the surface at a pit-mouth; the coalface in a mine; a shoal or shallow; a bed of shellfish; a mass of cloud or mist; the tilt of an aircraft; a cushion of a snooker or billiard table. ◆ *vt* to enclose with a bank; to deposit or pile (up); to cover (a fire) with ashes, etc, so as to make it burn more slowly (often with *up* or *down*); (usu with *down*) to restrain (passions, etc likely to erupt at any moment); to propel a snooker or billiard ball against the cushion. ◆ *vt* and *vi* (of aircraft) to tilt in turning. [ME *banke*, prob Scand; cognate with **bank¹,³**, **bench**]
■ **bank'er** *n* a locomotive used to help push a heavy load up a steep slope (also **bank(ing) engine**); a fishing-vessel on the Bank of Newfoundland, or a fisherman in such a vessel; a river full to the top of its banks (*Aust* and *NZ*). **bank'erly** *adj* like a banker. **bank'ing** *n* the elevation of the outside of bends in a road, railway or sports track; an embankment.
❑ **bank barn** *n* (*N Am*) a barn built into the side of a slope. **bank'-high** *adv* up to the top of the bank. **bank shot** *n* (*basketball*) a shot that sends the ball off the backboard and into the basket. **banks'man** *n* an overseer at a pit-mouth, building site, etc.
■ **from bank to bank** from the time the collier begins to descend for his spell of work until he reaches the top again. **run a banker** (*Aust* and *NZ*; of a river) to be full to the top of its banks.

bank³ /bangk/ *n* a tier or rank, eg of oars, keys on a typewriter, etc; a bench for the rowers in a galley; the bench on which judges sat; a set of apparatus or equipment laid out together; a working table in various crafts; a pottery. [OFr *banc*, of Gmc origin; cognate with **bank¹,²**]
■ **bank'er** *n* a mason's bench; a builder's board on which cement, etc is mixed.
❑ **bank'er-mark** *n* a mason's mark on a stone.

banket /bang-ket'/ (*S Afr*; *geol*) *n* a gold-bearing pebbly conglomerate. [Du *banketje* almond rock]

bankrupt /bang'krupt/ *n* a person who fails in business; an insolvent person; a person who is or becomes deficient or lacking in a specified quality (eg a *moral bankrupt*). ◆ *adj* insolvent; destitute (with *of*); deficient or lacking in a specified quality (eg *spiritually bankrupt*). ◆ *vt* to make bankrupt; to have (a person) declared bankrupt; to ruin or impoverish (*fig*). [Fr *banque-route*, Ital *banca rotta*, from *banca* bank, and *rotto*, *-a*, from L *ruptus* broken]
■ **bank'ruptcy** /-si/ *n* the state of being or act of becoming bankrupt.
❑ **bankruptcy order** *n* an order adjudging a debtor bankrupt.

Banksia /bangk'si-ə/ *n* a genus of Australian Proteaceae; (without *cap*) a shrub or tree of the genus. [Sir Joseph *Banks* (1744–1820), botanist]

banlieue /bä-lyə'/ (*Fr*) *n* a suburb.

Bannat see **Ban**.

banner /ban'ər/ *n* strictly, a square flag bearing a coat of arms; a military standard; a flag bearing some device, often carried on two poles, used in processions, etc; something which represents one's beliefs; a banner headline; a banner ad; a military subdivision, *esp* in the Manchu Army (*hist*). ◆ *adj* especially good or significant, as in *a banner year*. [OFr *banere*, from LL *bandum*, *bannum*; cognate with **band³** and **bind**]

■ **bann'ered** *adj* furnished with banners.
❑ **banner ad** *n* an advertisement positioned across the top of a page on the Internet. **banner cloud** *n* a stationary cloud that forms on the lee side of some mountains. **banner headline** *n* a large-type headline running right across a newspaper page.

banneret /ban'ə-ret or -rit/ (*hist*) *n* a knight of higher grade, *orig* one bringing vassals under his own banner, later, one dubbed on the field of battle (often confused with **baronet**). [OFr *baneret*, literally, bannered]

bannerol, **bannerall** see **banderol**.

bannister see **banister**.

bannock /ban'ək/ (chiefly *Scot*) *n* a flat (*orig* home-made) cake of oatmeal, barley or pease-meal, *usu* baked on a griddle. [OE *bannuc*]

banns /banz/ *n pl* a proclamation of intended marriage. [**ban¹**]
■ **forbid the banns** to make formal objection to a projected marriage.

banoffee pie /bə-nof'ē pī/ *n* a dessert consisting of a sweet pastry case filled with bananas and soft toffee or caramel and topped with cream. [*banana* and *toffee*]

banquet /bang'kwit/ *n* a feast; now *esp* a lavish formal meal followed by speeches; a course of sweetmeats, fruit and wine, separate, or after a meal (*obs*). ◆ *vt* (**banq'ueting**; **banq'ueted**) to give a feast to or in honour of. ◆ *vi* to feast. [Fr, from *banc* bench]
■ **banqueteer'** *n*. **banq'ueter** *n*. **banq'ueting** *n*.
❑ **banq'ueting-hall** *n*. **banq'ueting-house** *n*.

banquette /bang-ket'/ *n* a raised way inside a parapet; a footway, *esp* on a bridge; a built-in wall-sofa used instead of individual seats, eg in a restaurant; the long seat behind the driver in a French diligence. [Fr; Ital *banchetta*, dimin of *banca* seat]

bansela see **bonsela**.

banshee /ban'shē/ (*orig* Irish folklore) *n* a female spirit who wails and shrieks before a death in a household. [Ir *bean sídhe*, Old Ir *ben síde* woman of the fairies]

bant¹ see under **banting¹**.

bant² /bant/ (*dialect*) *n* vigour, strength, springiness. [Cf **bent¹** and MDu *bant* power, force]

bantam /ban'təm/ *n* a small variety of the common domestic fowl; a small man, *esp* a soldier. ◆ *adj* of bantam breed; little and combative. [Prob *Bantam* in Java]
❑ **ban'tamweight** *n* a weight category, applied *esp* in boxing; a sportsperson of the specified weight for the category (eg in professional boxing above flyweight, **junior bantamweight** or **super flyweight** (maximum 52kg/115lb), **ban'tamweight** (maximum 54kg/118lb), and **super bantamweight** or **junior featherweight** (maximum 55kg/122lb)).

banteng /ban'teng/ or **banting** /-ting/ *n* a wild ox of the East Indies. [Malay]

banter /ban'tər/ *vt* to make fun of; to joke at; to impose upon, trick (*archaic*). ◆ *n* humorous ridicule; joking; a joke (*archaic*). [Ety unknown]
■ **bant'erer** *n*. **bant'ering** *n* and *adj*. **bant'eringly** *adv*.

banting¹ /ban'ting/ (*obs*) *n* weight-reduction by avoiding fat, sugar and starch. [W *Banting* (1797–1878), a London cabinetmaker, who recommended it to the public in 1863]
■ **bant** *vi* (back-formation) to diet. **bant'ingism** *n*.

banting² see **banteng**.

bantling /bant'ling/ (*archaic* and *derog*) *n* a young child, a brat. [Prob Ger *Bänkling* bastard, from *Bank* bench]

Bantu /ban'too/ (also without *cap*) *n* a name given to a large group of African languages and the peoples speaking them in southern and central Africa; a former, now offensive, name for a black person in South Africa. ◆ *adj* of or relating to these languages and peoples. [*Bantu*, people]
■ **Ban'tustan** *n* (*offensive*) any of the partially self-governing regions, or homelands, of South Africa populated and administered by black people before the end of apartheid in 1994.

banxring or **bangsring** /bangks'ring/ *n* a tree-shrew. [Javanese *bangsring*]

banya /bän'ya/ *n* a Russian sauna-type bath. [Russ]

banyan, **banian** /ban'yən or -yan/ or **bania** /ban'yə/ *n* an Indian fig tree with vast rooting branches; (also with *cap*) a Hindu trader, *esp* from Gujarat; loosely, outside India, any Hindu; an Indian broker or financier; a loose jacket, gown, or undergarment worn in India. [Port *banian*, perh through Ar *banyān*, from Hindi *baniyā*, from Sans *vāṇija*, from *vaṇij* a merchant]
❑ **banyan days** *n pl* (*obs*) days on which no meat was served, hence days of short commons generally, from the abstinence from flesh of the Banyan merchants.

■ words derived from main entry word; ❑ compound words; ■ idioms and phrasal verbs

banzai /ban'zī/ *n* a Japanese battle-cry and salute to the emperor; a Japanese exclamation of joy. ♦ *adj* (of Japanese parties) rollicking; (of Japanese military attacks) kamikaze. [Jap *banzai* 10000 years, forever]

baobab /bā'ō-bab/ *n* a gigantic tropical African and Australian tree, the monkey bread tree (genus *Adansonia*; family Bombacaceae). [Prob African]

BAOR *abbrev*: (until 1994) British Army of the Rhine.

Bap. or **Bapt.** *abbrev*: Baptist.

bap /bap/ (*Scot* and *N Eng*) *n* a large, flat, elliptical breakfast roll; (*usu* in *pl*) a female breast (*sl*). [Ety uncertain]

bap. or **bapt.** *abbrev*: baptized.

Baphomet /baf'ō-met/ *n* a mysterious idol the Templars were accused of worshipping. [For *Mahomet*]
- **baphomet'ic** *adj*.

Bapt. see **Bap.**

baptize or **-ise** /bap-tīz'/ *vt* to administer baptism to; to christen, give a name to; to name at launching and break a bottle of wine on the bow of (a ship). [Gr *baptizein*, from *baptein* to dip]
- **bapt'ism** /-izm/ *n* immersion in or sprinkling with water as a religious ceremony; an experience regarded as initiating one into a society, group, etc. **baptis'mal** *adj*. **baptis'mally** *adv*. **bapt'ist** *n* a person who baptizes; (with *cap*) a member of a Christian sect which approves only of baptizing by immersion, and that only of persons who profess their faith in Christ. **bap'tistery** or **bap'tistry** *n* a place for administration of baptism, whether a separate building or part of a church; a tank of water for baptisms in a Baptist church.
  □ **baptismal name** *n* one given at baptism, a Christian name. **baptismal regeneration** *n* the doctrine of the remission of sin original and actual, and of the new birth into the life of sanctifying grace, in and through the sacrament of baptism. **baptism by desire** *n* the grace held to be given to a believer who ardently desires baptism, but dies before receiving it. **baptism for the dead** *n* the vicarious baptism of a living for an unbaptized dead Christian. **baptism of blood** *n* martyrdom of the unbaptized Christian. **baptism of fire** *n* the gift of the Holy Spirit; martyrdom by fire regarded as an equivalent to baptism; any trying ordeal, such as a first experience of being under fire.
- **clinical baptism** baptism administered to the sick. **conditional** (or **hypothetical**) **baptism** baptism administered conditionally when it is doubtful whether the person was previously baptized validly or at all. **private baptism** baptism elsewhere than in church.

bapu /bä'poo/ (*Ind*) *n* spiritual father. [Hindi]

Bar. *abbrev*: Barrister; (the Apocryphal Book of) Baruch (*Bible*).

bar[1] /bär/ *n* a rod, strip or oblong block of any solid substance; formerly, any of various standards of weight or value; a pound, sovereign (*esp* **half a bar** ten shillings or fifty pence) (*obs sl*); a strong rod or long piece used as a lever, door fastening, barrier, part of a gate or grate, etc; a crossbar; a bolt; a barrier; an obstruction or impediment; that which completely puts an end to an action or claim; in salary statements, a level beyond which one cannot rise unless certain conditions, concerning eg the amount of advanced work one does, are met; a bank or shoal as at the mouth of a river or harbour; a counter across which liquor or food is served; (one room in) a public house; a counter at which one particular article of food, clothing, etc, is sold, or one particular service is given; a rail or similar structure marking off a space, as in a house of parliament, or that at which prisoners are arraigned in court; (*usu* with *cap*) barristers or advocates collectively, or (loosely) the legal profession; a court; an authority appealed to; a ballet-dancer's exercise rail (*usu* **barre**); an addition to a medal, a strip of metal below the clasp, showing that it has been won twice; a ridge between a horse's teeth; a stripe, *esp* transverse; a heating element in an electric fire; a horizontal band across a shield (*heraldry*); a rhythmic unit in music, consisting of a certain number of beats in either simple or compound time, marked by the time signature; a bar line (*music*) (see also **double bar** under **double**); (in *pl*) the game of (prisoners'-)base (but see **base**[1]). ♦ *vt* (**barr'ing**; **barred**) to fasten, secure, shut (out or in), furnish or mark with a bar or bars; to hinder; to obstruct; to exclude the possibility or validity of; to preclude; to divide into bars. ♦ *prep* except, but for. [OFr *barre*, from LL *barra*]
- **bar'ful** (*Shakesp* **barre'full**) *adj* full of obstructions. **barr'ing** *n* the action of the verb. ♦ *prep* except for; leaving out of consideration.
  □ **bar'bell** *n* a bar weighted at the ends for weightlifting exercises. **bar billiards** *n sing* a small-scale version of billiards played in bars. **bar chart** or **bar graph** *n* a graph showing comparative quantities by means of rectangular blocks of varying proportional height. **bar'code** *n* an arrangement, readable by computer, of thick and thin parallel lines, eg printed on, and giving coded details of, goods at a point of sale, library books, etc. **bar'coded** *adj*. **barcode reader** or **scanner** *n* an optical device which can read barcode data and translate them into digital signals for processing. **Bar Council** *n* the governing professional body of English barristers. **bar'fly** *n* (*old inf*) a drinker who spends his or her time in bars. **barfly jumping** *n* the sport of jumping onto a Velcro-covered wall and sticking there. **bar graph** see **bar chart** above. **bar'-iron** *n* iron in malleable bars. **bar'keep** *n* (*US*) a person who serves drinks at a bar. **bar'keeper** *n* the keeper of a refreshment bar or toll-bar. **bar line** *n* (*music*) a vertical line across the staff between each bar. **bar lunch** or **bar meal** *n* a light meal or snack available in a bar. **bar magnet** *n* a permanent magnet in the form of a straight bar. **bar'maid**, **bar'man** or **bar'person** *n* a woman, man or person who serves at a bar in a public house, etc. **bar'-parlour** *n* a small room adjoining a bar in a public house. **barred code** *n* (*telecom*) any dialled code that automatic exchange apparatus is primed to reject by connecting the caller no further than the number unobtainable tone. **barring-out'** *n* (*obs*) the shutting out of a schoolmaster from school by the pupils, to enforce demands. **bar'-room** *n* (chiefly *US*) a room in which there is a bar, taproom (also *adj*). **bar-sin'ister** see **baton-sinister** under **baton**. **bar slide** *n* a bar-shaped hair ornament. **bar stool** *n* a high stool suitable for sitting at a bar. **bar supper** *n* a bar meal available in the evening. **bar tack** *n* a straight stitch made at right angles to a buttonhole or other weak spot to strengthen it. **bar'tender** *n* a barman or barmaid. **bar'wood** *n* a red dyewood imported in bars from Africa.
- **at the bar** in court; in practice as a barrister or advocate. **bar none** (*inf*) with no exceptions. **behind bars** in prison. **called to the bar** admitted as barrister or advocate. **called within the bar** made Queen's (or King's) Counsel in the UK.

bar[2] /bär/ (*meteorol*) *n* (*pl* **bar** or **bars**) a unit used in expressing atmospheric pressure (1 bar = 10^5 N/m^2). [Gr *baros* weight]
- **bar'ic** *adj* barometric.

bar[3] /bär/, **baur** or **bawr** /bör/ (*Scot*) *n* a joke; an amusing incident or story. [Poss Scot *bar* (the game of tossing the) caber]

bar[4] /bär/ *n* a fish, the maigre. [Fr]

bar. *abbrev*: baritone.

bara brith /bar'ə brith/ *n* a spiced tea bread containing fruit. [Welsh, speckled bread]

baracan see **barracan**.

baragouin /bä-rä-gwē or -gwin'/ *n* any jargon or unintelligible language. [Fr; from Breton *bara* bread, and *gwenn* white, said to have originated in the Breton soldiers' astonishment at white bread]

barasingha or **barasinga** /ba-ra-sing'gə/ (*Ind*) *n* the swamp deer, *Cervus duvauceli*. [Hindi *bārah singā*, literally, twelve horn]

barathea /ba-rə-thē'ə/ *n* a soft fabric of worsted, or of worsted and silk, etc. [Origin unknown]

barathrum /ba-rath'rŭm/ *n* an abyss; an insatiable person. [L, from Gr *barathron*]

baraza /ba-ra'za/ (*E Afr*) *n* a public meeting-place; a meeting. [Swahili]

BARB or **Barb** /bärb/ *abbrev*: Broadcasters' Audience Research Board.

barb[1] /bärb/ *n* a subsidiary backward-facing projection near the point of an arrow, fish-hook, etc; one of the filaments of a feather's web; a small freshwater fish of the genus *Barbus*, often kept in aquariums; a sting (*fig*); a wounding or wittily pointed remark; a woven linen covering for the throat and breast (and sometimes the lower part of the face) worn by women in the Middle Ages, still part of the habit of certain orders of nuns. ♦ *vt* to arm with barbs; to pierce, as with a barb; to shave, trim, mow (*obs*). [L *barba* a beard]
- **barb'ate** *adj* bearing a hairy tuft. **barb'ated** *adj* barbed; bearded. **barbe** *n* a Waldensian teacher. **barbed** *adj* having a barb or barbs; wounding, spiteful; (by confusion) barded. **barb'el** *n* a freshwater fish of the carp family with beard-like appendages at its mouth; such an appendage. **barb'ellate** *adj* (*bot*) having barbed or bearded bristles. **barb'et** *n* a tropical bird with bristly beak; a kind of poodle. **barbicel** /bär'bi-sel/ *n* a tiny hook on the barbule of a feather. **barb'ule** *n* a small barb; a fish's barbel; a hairlike structure on the barb of a feather.
  □ **barbed wire** *n* (also (*US*) **barb'wire**) wire with short sharp points twisted on at intervals, used for fences, etc.

barb[2] /bärb/ *n* a horse of a racing breed related to the Arab; a dark-coloured fancy pigeon. [From *Barbary*, where the breeds originated]

Barbados or **Barbadoes** /bär-bā'dōs, -dos or -dōz/ *adj* of the West Indian island of *Barbados*.
- **Barbā'dian** *n* and *adj*.
  □ **Barbados cherry** *n* the cherry-like fruit of West Indian trees of the genus *Malpighia*. **Barbados earth** *n* an earthy marl found in Barbados. **Barbados gooseberry** *n* the edible fruit of a West Indian climbing cactus (*Pereskia aculeata*). **Barbados leg** *n* elephantiasis. **Barbados pride** *n* a West Indian shrub, peacock-flower (*Caesalpinia* or *Poinciana pulcherrima*); an Asiatic ornamental tree (*Adenanthera pavonina*) naturalized in the West Indies, also called **red sandalwood**.

barbarous /bär'bə-rəs/ adj falling short of the standard of correctness, classical purity, and good taste; unscholarly; corrupt, ungrammatical or unidiomatic; uncultured; uncivilized; brutal; harsh. [Gr *barbaros* foreign, literally, stammering, from the unfamiliar sound of foreign tongues]
■ **barbār'ian** n someone without taste or refinement; a somewhat uncivilized person; a cruel person; *orig* someone who was not a Greek, later neither a Greek nor a Roman; a foreigner. ♦ adj (also **barbar'ic** /bär-bar'ik/) uncivilized; characteristic of barbarians; rude; tastelessly ornate and ostentatious; wild and harsh; foreign. **bar'barism** n savagery, brutal or uncivilized behaviour; rudeness of manners; a form of speech offensive to scholarly taste. **barbar'ity** /bär-bar'i-ti/ n savageness; cruelty. **barbarization** or **-s-** /bär-bər-ī-zā'shən/ n. **bar'barize** or **-ise** vt to make barbarous; to corrupt, as a language. **bar'barously** adv. **bar'barousness** n.

Barbary /bär'bə-ri/ n the country of the *Berbers*, in N Africa. [**Berber**]
■ **barbaresque** /-esk'/ adj.
❑ **Barbary ape** n the magot, a kind of macaque, native to N Africa and Gibraltar, the only European monkey. **Barbary coast** n the N African coast in the Mediterranean. **Barbary sheep** n a N African wild sheep.

barbasco /bär-bas'kō/ n (pl **barbas'cos**) any of a variety of S American plants, the juice of whose roots is used in the preparation of fish-poisons, synthetic hormones, etc. [Sp]

barbastelle or **barbastel** /bär-bə-stel' or bär'/ n a hairy-lipped bat. [Fr]

barbe see under **barb¹**.

barbecue, barbeque or (inf) **bar-b-q** /bär'bi-kū or -bə-/ vt to grill over an open fire, *usu* of charcoal, often adding a highly seasoned sauce to the food; to roast whole (obs); to cure on a barbecue (obs). ♦ n a framework for barbecuing food over an open fire; a portable grill for cooking thus; food cooked in this way; a party, *esp* held out of doors, where food is so cooked; an open floor on which coffee beans and the like are spread out to dry. [Sp *barbacoa*, from Haitian *barbacòa* a framework of sticks set upon posts]
❑ **barbecue sauce** n a spicy sauce added to barbecued food.

barbel, barbellate see under **barb¹**.

barber /bär'bər/ n a person who shaves beards, cuts and styles men's hair, etc. ♦ vt to shave or cut the hair of. [OFr *barbour*, from L *barba* a beard]
❑ **barb'er-monger** n (Shakesp) a man decked out by his barber, a fop. **barber's block** n a round block on which wigs are made. **bar'bershop** or **bar'bershop** n a barber's premises; a type of music originating in the USA, played, or *esp* sung, in close chromatic harmony, *usu* in quartets (also adj). **barber's pole** n the barber's sign, a pole striped spirally, *gen* red and white. **barber's rash** or **itch** n an infection by the fungus *Tinea barbae*, causing a scaly rash in the bearded area as well as sycosis. **barb'er-surgeon** n (hist) one who let blood and drew teeth as well as shaved.

barberry /bär'bə-ri/ n a thorny shrub (genus *Berberis*) of various species, most with yellow flowers and red berries, common in ornamental hedges. [LL *berberis*; the Ar *barbārīs* is borrowed; not connected with **berry¹**]

Barberton daisy /bär'bər-tən dā'zi/ n (a plant of) the *Gerbera* genus of composites native to South Africa, flourishing *esp* in the *Barberton* district of Transvaal.

barbet see under **barb¹**.

barbette /bär-bet'/ n an earthen terrace inside the parapet of a rampart, serving as a platform for heavy guns; a fixed cylinder which encloses and protects the rotating part of an armoured turret in a warship. [Fr]

barbican /bär'bi-kən/ n a projecting watchtower over the gate of a castle or fortified town; *esp* the outwork intended to defend the drawbridge. [OFr *barbacane*; origin unknown]

barbicel see under **barb¹**.

barbie /bär'bi/ (Aust inf) n a barbecue.

Barbie doll® /bär'bi dol/ n a teenage doll with separately purchasable clothing and accessories; (also **barbie**) a woman resembling a Barbie doll in glamour, fashion sense and colourful style (inf); (also **barbie**) a physically attractive but empty-headed young woman (inf, derog).

barbituric /bär-bi-tū'rik/ (chem) adj applied to an acid got from malonic acid and urea, source of important sedatives. [From the lichen *Usnea barbata* and *uric* acid]
■ **barb'itone** n (also (US) **barb'ital**) a derivative of barbituric acid used as a sedative and hypnotic. **barbit'urate** (or /-tūr'/) n a salt or ester of barbituric acid, used as a source of sedative and hypnotic drugs.

Barbizon School /bär'bi-zon skool/ (art) n a mid-19th-century group of French painters. [From *Barbizon* a village near Paris where they often worked]

barbola /bär-bō'lə/ or **barbola work** /wûrk/ n ornamentation with small flowers, fruit, etc made of plastic paste and coloured. [Orig proprietary term, from **barbotine**]

barbotine /bär'bə-tin/ n a fine clay used for ornamenting pottery; pottery ornamented with this. [Fr, from *barboter* to dabble about noisily]

Barbour® /bär'bər/ or **Barbour**® **jacket** /jak'ət/ (also **Barbour**® **coat** /kōt/) n a strong waterproof jacket (or coat), *esp* one made of waxed cotton.

bar-b-q see **barbecue**.

barbs /bärbz/ (inf) n pl barbiturates.

barbule see under **barb¹**.

barca /bär'ka/ (Ital) n a boat, barge.

barcarolle or **barcarole** /bär'kə-rōl, -rōl' or -rol'/ n a gondolier's song; a musical composition of a similar character. [Ital *barcarola* a boat-song, from *barca* a boat]

Barcelona nut /bär-sə-lō'nə nut/ n a type of hazelnut exported from Spain, *usu* kiln-dried to retain its flavour.

BArch abbrev : Bachelor of Architecture.

barchan(e) see **barkhan**.

Barclaycard /bär'kli-kärd/ n a cheque guarantee and credit card issued by *Barclays* Bank.

bard¹ /bärd/ n one of the ancient Celtic order of formal poets and singers; a strolling minstrel (archaic; Scot); a poet (literary); a poet whose work has won a competition at the Eisteddfod. [Scot Gaelic and Ir *bard*]
■ **bard'ic** adj. **bard'ling** n a poetaster. **bardol'atrous** adj. **bardol'atry** n (Gr *latreiā* worship) Shakespeare-worship. **bard'ship** n. **bard'y** adj (Scot) insolent; impudent.
❑ **bard'-craft** n.
■ **the Bard** the poet regarded by a country as its national poet, eg Shakespeare, Burns.

bard² /bärd/ n a piece of bacon or pork fat used to cover meat or game during cooking to prevent drying-out; (in pl) a protective or ornamental covering for a warhorse (obs). ♦ vt to cover (a piece of meat or game) with bards; to provide (a horse) with bards (obs). [Fr *barde*, from Sp *albarda* packsaddle, perh from Ar *al-barda'ah*, from *al* the, and *barda'ah* mule's packsaddle]
■ **bard'ed** adj caparisoned.

bard³ an old spelling of **barred** (see **bar¹**); also short for **barded**.

bardash /bär-dash'/ (obs) n a homosexual male, a catamite. [Fr *bardache*]

bardo /bär'dō/ (Tibetan Buddhism) n the intermediate stage between death and rebirth. [Tibetan, between two]

Bardolino /bär-dō-lē'nō/ n an Italian dry red wine made around the village of *Bardolino* in the Veneto region.

bare¹ /bär/ adj naked; open to view; uncovered, bareheaded (obs); without the usual covering; unarmed (obs); unfurnished, empty; threadbare, worn; unprovided or scantily provided; poor; scanty; mere; basic; unadorned, unpolished (obs); paltry (Shakesp); laid waste (Shakesp; Milton). ♦ vt to strip or uncover. [OE *bær*; Ger *baar*, *bar*; ON *berr*]
■ **bare'ly** adv hardly, scarcely; just and no more; not quite; nakedly (obs); plainly, explicitly, openly (obs). **bare'ness** n. **bär'ish** adj somewhat bare.
❑ **bare'back** adj and adv without a saddle. **bare'backed** adj with bare back; unsaddled. **bare'boat** adj in shipping, used of a charter or hire in which the chartering company is totally responsible for manning, supplies, maintenance and insurance. **bare'bone** n (Shakesp) a very lean person. **bare bones** n pl the barest essentials or facts. **bare'-breached** adj (Scot) trouserless. **bare'faced** adj with the face uncovered; beardless; avowed (Shakesp); shameless; impudent. **barefacedly** /-fäst'li or -fās'id-li/ adv. **bare'facedness** n. **bare'foot** or **barefoot'ed** adj and adv having the feet bare; discalced. **barefoot doctor** n *orig* in China, an agricultural worker trained in the basic principles of health, hygiene and first aid in order to treat fellow workers. **barehand'ed** adj and adv with no weapon. **barehead'ed** adj and adv without a hat. **bareknuck'le** or **bareknuck'led** adj and adv without boxing gloves on; fiercely aggressive. **bareland croft** n a croft with no croft house. **bare'legged** adj and adv.
■ **with one's bare hands** with no weapon or tool.

bare² /bär/ old pat of **bear¹**.

barege or **barège** /bä-rezh'/ n a light, silky dress fabric. [*Barèges* in Hautes-Pyrénées, where it was first made]
■ **baregine** /bar'i-jēn/ n a gelatinous mass of bacteria and sulphur found in mineral waters.

baresark a non-standard form of **berserk**.

barf /bärf/ (*N Am sl*) *vi* to vomit. ◆ *n* vomited matter; an act of vomiting. [Prob imit]

bargain /bär'gin/ *n* a contract or agreement; any transaction or deal (*stock exchange*); something acquired by bargaining; something for sale at an advantageously low price; haggling, discussion about terms of purchase, etc (*Shakesp*); strife, struggle (*obs*; *Scot and N Eng*). ◆ *vi* to make a contract or agreement; to haggle; to count on; to strive (*obs*; *Scot*). ◆ *vt* to lose by bad bargaining (with *away*). [OFr *bargaine*]
■ **bar'gainer** *n*.
❑ **bar'gain-basement** or **-counter** *n* places in a shop where bargains are sold (also *adj*). **bar'gain-hunter** *n* a person who goes shopping for bargains. **bargaining chip** (*US*) or **counter** (*Brit*) *n* an advantage or asset possessed by one party which can be used to extract a concession in negotiations.
■ **bargain and sale** in law, a mode of conveyance whereby property may be assigned or transferred for valuable consideration. **bargain for** to count on, make allowance for, expect. **bargain on** to rely on, expect. **drive a hard bargain** to bargain vigorously and uncompromisingly before coming to an agreement. **into the bargain** as well, in addition. **make the best of a bad bargain** to do one's best in an adverse situation. **sell someone a bargain** (*Shakesp*) to make a fool of someone. **strike a bargain** to agree on terms.

bargander see **bergander**.

barge /bärj/ *n* a flat-bottomed freight boat, with or without sails, used on rivers and canals; a lighter; a large pleasure-boat; the second boat of a man-of-war; a small sailing vessel (*obs*). ◆ *vi* to move clumsily; to bump (with *into*); to push one's way rudely. [OFr *barge*, from LL *barga*; cf **bark²**]
■ **barg'ee** *n* a bargeman.
❑ **barge'man** *n* manager of a barge. **barge'master** *n* proprietor of a barge. **barge'pole** *n* a pole for propelling a barge.
■ **barge in** to intrude; to interrupt. **not touch with a bargepole** to refuse to have anything to do with.

bargeboard /bärj'börd/ *n* a board along the edge of a gable to cover the rafters and keep out rain. [Perh LL *bargus* a gallows]
❑ **barge'-couples** *n pl* gable rafters. **barge'-stones** *n pl* the stones making up the sloping edge of a gable.

bargello /bärje-lō/ *n* (*pl* **bar'gellos**) a type of needlepoint or tapestry stitch that produces a zigzag pattern. [The *Bargello*, a Florentine museum, having examples of this stitch]

barghest, **bargest** or **barghaist** /bär'gest or -gäst/ *n* a dog-like goblin portending death. [Perh connected with Ger *Berggeist* mountain-spirit]

bargoose /bär'goos/ (*S Eng dialect*) *n* (*pl* **bar'geese**) the barnacle-goose; the shelduck. [First sense a contraction; second sense poss from the band of brown on its shoulders, and its goose-like movement]

bariatric /ba-ri-at'rik/ *adj* relating to the medical treatment of obesity. [Gr *baros* weight, and *iātros* physician]
■ **bariat'rics** *n sing*.

baric see under **bar²** and **barium**.

barilla /ba-ril'ə/ *n* an impure sodium carbonate produced by burning certain seaside plants; a seaside plant (*Salsola soda*) common in Spain and Sicily. [Sp]

barista /bä-rē'sta/ *n* a person who is employed to make coffee in a coffee shop. [Ital, bartender]

barite see under **barium** and **baryta**.

baritone or **barytone** /bar'i-tōn/ *n* a deep-toned male voice between bass and tenor; a singer with such a voice (in these senses now *usu* **baritone**); any of several low-pitched musical instruments, *esp* the baritone saxophone; (**barytone**, also **bar'yton**) a musical instrument like the viola da gamba with sympathetic strings added. ◆ *adj* of the pitch and range of a baritone or barytone; (**barytone**) (*Gr grammar*) not having an acute accent on the last syllable. [Gr *barytonos* deep-sounding, not accented, from *barys* heavy, deep, and *tonos* a tone]

barium /bā'ri-əm/ *n* a metallic element (symbol **Ba**; atomic no 56) present in baryta. [See **baryta**]
■ **bā'ric** *adj*. **bā'rite** *n* (*N Am*) barytes.
❑ **barium meal** *n* a mixture of barium sulphate swallowed to render the alimentary canal opaque to X-rays.

bark¹ /bärk/ *n* the abrupt cry of a dog, wolf, etc; the report of a gun; a cough (*inf*). ◆ *vi* to utter a bark; to clamour; to advertise wares noisily; to cough (*inf*). ◆ *vt* to utter with a bark (*Spenser*); to utter abruptly and peremptorily; to advertise (wares) noisily. [OE *beorcan*]
■ **bark'er** *n* a dog; a barking dog; a tout advertising wares, a show, etc in a loud voice to attract custom; a pistol or cannon (*obs sl*). **bark'ing** *adj* (*sl*) barking mad.
❑ **barking deer** *n* the muntjac. **barking iron** *n* (*sl*) a pistol. **barking mad** *adj* (*sl*) crazy, raving mad.

■ **bark up the wrong tree** to act, speak, proceed, etc under a misapprehension, mistakenly to take inappropriate action. **chief barker** the title of the president of the Variety Club of Great Britain. **his bark is worse than his bite** his words may be bad-tempered or fierce, but his actual deeds are not so bad.

bark² /bärk/ *n* the rind or covering of the trunk and branches of a tree; that used in tanning or dyeing; that used in medicine (cinchona); an outer covering or skin. ◆ *vt* to scrape or rub the skin from; to strip or peel bark from; to tan (leather); to cover with or as if with bark, encrust. ◆ *vi* (*obs*) to form a bark. [ON *börkr*; Dan *bark*]
■ **bark'en** *vt* and *vi* to dry up into a barky crust. ◆ *adj* (*poetic*) made or composed of bark. **bark'less** *adj*. **bark'y** *adj*.
❑ **bark'-bed** *n* a hotbed of spent bark. **bark'-beetle** *n* any beetle of the family Scolytidae, tunnellers in and under bark. **bark'-bound** *adj* prevented from growing by failure to shed the bark. **bark'-cloth** *n* a thin papery kind of cloth made by soaking and beating the inner bark of some trees, *esp* tapa. **bark'-louse** *n* any of various aphids that infest the bark of trees.

bark³, **barkentine** see **barque**.

barkan see **barkhan**.

Barker's mill /bär'kərz mil/ *n* a device rotated by water, invented by a 17c Dr *Barker*.

barkhan, **barkan**, **barchan** or **barchane** /bär-kän'/ *n* a crescent-shaped sand-dune, of the type found in central Asian deserts. [Native word in Turkmenistan]

barley¹ /bär'li/ *n* a hardy grass (*Hordeum vulgare* and other species); its grain used for food, and for making malt liquors and spirits. [OE *bærlic* of barley, from root of **bear³**, and sfx *-līc*]
❑ **bar'ley-bree**, **-broo** or **-broth** *n* (*Scot*) strong ale; whisky. **bar'leycorn** *n* (personified as **John Barleycorn**) the grain from which malt is made; a single grain of barley; a measure of length = $\frac{1}{3}$ of an inch (*obs*); a V-shaped sight on a gun. **barley sugar** *n* a sweet made by melting and cooling sugar (formerly by boiling it with a decoction of barley). **bar'ley-sugar** *adj usu* (eg of furniture legs, etc) referring to the twisted spiral shape of a barley-sugar stick. **barley water** *n* a liquid produced by boiling down pearl barley in water, *usu* sweetened and flavoured as a cold drink. **barley wine** *n* a strong English beer.
■ **pearl barley** the grain stripped of husk and pellicle, and completely rounded by grinding. **pot barley** the grain deprived by milling of its outer husk, used in making broth, etc.

barley² /bär'li/ (*Scot and N Eng dialect*) *interj* in games, a call for truce. ◆ *n* a truce; a breathing space. [Perh **parley¹**]

barley-brake or **-break** /bär'li-brāk/ *n* an old country game, *orig* played by three couples, in which one pair had to catch the others. [Perh because often played in a *barley*-field; or perh from **barley²**]

barm /bärm/ *n* froth of fermenting liquor; yeast. [OE *beorma*, Dan *bärme*, Ger *Bärme*]
■ **barm'iness** *n*. **barm'y** *adj* frothy; fermenting; mentally unsound (also **balmy** /bä'mi/; *sl*).
❑ **barm cake** *n* (*Eng dialect*) a soft round bread roll. **barm'y-brained** *adj*.

barmbrack /bärm'brak/ (*Irish*) *n* a fruit loaf, *usu* made with yeast. [Ir *bairigen* or *bairsín*, and *breac* speckled cake]

barm-cloth /bärm'kloth/ (*archaic*) *n* an apron. [OE *barm* (WSax *bearm*) bosom, and **cloth**]

bar mitzvah or **bar mitsvah** /bär mits'və/ *n* (sometimes *caps*; also with *hyphen* or as one word) in the Jewish religion, a boy attaining the age (*usu* 13 years) of religious responsibility; the ceremony marking this event, with accompanying festivities. [Heb, son of the law]

barmkin /bärm'kin/ (*archaic*; *Scot and N Eng*) *n* a battlement, or a turret, on the outer wall of a castle; the wall itself. [Origin obscure]

barmpot /bärm'pot/ (*N Eng*) *n* an idiot, fool. [Ety uncertain; prob related to **barm**. Cf **bampot**]

barn¹ /bärn/ *n* a building in which grain, hay, etc are stored; a stable or cattle shed (*N Am*); a large bare building; a large garage for buses, trucks, etc (*N Am*). ◆ *vt* to store in a barn. [OE *bere-ern*, contracted *bern*, from *bere* barley, and *ern* a house]
❑ **barn dance** *n* a social gathering at which square-dances and other traditional country dances are danced; a progressive dance. **barn door** *n* the door of a barn; an adjustable flap in front of a light source, eg a studio lamp for controlling the light; a cricketer who blocks every ball (*old*; *facetious*); a target too broad to be missed (*humorous*). **barn owl** *n* a species of owl, generally buff-coloured above and white below. **barns'breaking** *n* (*Scot*) a boisterous frolic; an injurious or mischievous activity. **barn'storm** *vi* to tour *usu* country areas giving theatrical performances; to travel about speaking at meetings, *usu* for election purposes; to give a highly energetic performance. ◆ *vt* to give such performances at (a place). **barn'stormer** *n*. **barn'storming** *n* and *adj*. **barn swallow** *n* (*N Am*) the swallow. **barn'yard** *n* and *adj*.

barn² /bärn/ (*nuclear phys*) *n* a unit of effective cross-sectional area of a nucleus for the capture of neutrons, $10^{-28}m^2$. [Appar from 'as big as a *barn*']

Barnaby /bär'nə-bi/ *n* a form of *Barnabas*.
■ **Bar'nabite** *n* a member of the Congregation of Regular Clerics of St Paul, founded at Milan in 1530, so called from their church of St Barnabas there.
□ **Barnaby Day** or **Barnaby Bright** *n* St Barnabas's Day, 11 June, in Old Style reckoned the longest day.
■ **Long Barnaby** same as **Barnaby Day** above.

barnacle¹ /bär'nə-kl/ *n* a barnacle-goose; a cirripede crustacean that adheres to rocks and ship bottoms; a companion not easily shaken off. [OFr *bernaque*, from LL *bernaca*]
□ **bar'nacle-goose** or **ber'nicle-goose** *n* a wild black-and-white goose of N Europe (*Branta leucopsis*), once believed to develop from a barnacle (the **goose'-bar'nacle**) that attaches itself, *esp* to floating wood, by a thick stalk.

barnacle² /bär'nə-kl/ *n* an instrument put on a restless horse's nose to keep him quiet; (in *pl*) spectacles (*obs inf*). [OFr *bernac*]
■ **bar'nacled** *adj*.

barnet /bär'nit/ (*inf*) *n* hair, hairstyle. [Cockney rhyming slang from *Barnet Fair*, a famous horse fair once held at Barnet, Hertfordshire]

barney /bär'ni/ (*inf*) *n* a rough noisy quarrel; humbug; a prizefight.

barocco, barock see **baroque**.

barodynamics /bar-o-dī-nam'iks/ *n sing* mechanics applied to heavy structures, such as dams and bridges, which may collapse under their own weight. [Gr *baros* weight, and **dynamics**]

barogram /bar'ō-gram/ or -ə-/ *n* a tracing produced by a barograph. [Gr *baros* weight, and **-gram**]

barograph /bar'ə-gräf/ *n* a recording barometer. [Gr *baros* weight, and **-graph**]

Barolo /ba-rō'lō/ *n* an Italian fine red wine made in the *Barolo* area of Piedmont.

barometer /bə-rom'i-tər/ *n* an instrument for measuring atmospheric pressure; a weather glass; an indicator of change (eg in public opinion; *fig*; also *adj*). [Gr *baros* weight, and *metron* measure]
■ **barometric** /bar-ō-met'rik/ or **barometrical** /-met'ri-kl/ *adj*. **baromet'rically** *adv*. **barometry** /ba-rom'ət-ri/ *n*.

barometz /ba'rō-mets/ *n* the Scythian lamb, a plant at one time supposed to be also animal, growing on a stalk but eating grass like a lamb, near the Caspian Sea; a tree fern (*Cibotium* or *Dicksonia barometz*), of the East Indies and Pacific islands, whose woolly rootstock and leaf bases looked somewhat like a lamb. [Russ *baranets* club moss, dimin of *baran* ram]

baron /bar'ən/ *n* a title of rank, the lowest in the British peerage; a foreign noble of similar grade; the head of any organization or institution who is regarded as wielding despotic power (eg a *press baron*); formerly a title of the judges of the Court of Exchequer; in feudal times, a tenant-in-chief of the crown; later a peer or great lord of the realm generally; the owner of a freehold estate, whether titled or not (*Scot hist*); a husband, as opposed to **feme** wife (*heraldry* and *Eng law*); until 1832, the name for the parliamentary representatives of the Cinque Ports. [OFr *barun, -on*, from LL *barō, -ōnis* man]
■ **bar'onage** *n* the whole body of barons; a list or book of barons. **bar'oness** *n* the wife or widow of a baron; a woman holding a baronial title in her own right. **baronial** /bə-rō'ni-əl/ *adj* relating to a baron or barony; applied to a turreted style of architecture formerly popular for country houses in Scotland. **baronne** /ba-ron/ *n* (*Fr*) a baroness. **bar'ony** *n* the territory of a baron; in Ireland, a division of a county; in Scotland, a large freehold estate, or manor; the rank of baron; the sphere of influence of a press baron, etc.
□ **baron bailie** *n* (*Scot hist*) a magistrate appointed by the lord superior in a burgh of barony. **baron of beef** *n* a joint consisting of two sirloins left uncut at the backbone. **bar'on-off'icer** *n* (*Walter Scott*) an estate official.

baronet /bar'ə-net/ *n* now the lowest British hereditary title (*of England*, now of *Great Britain*, since 1611; *of Scotland*, or of *Nova Scotia*, since 1625; *of Ireland*, since 1619); a lesser baron (*obs*; confused with **banneret**); a baron's substitute (*obs*). [Dimin of **baron**]
■ **bar'onetage** *n* the whole body of baronets; a list or book of baronets. **bar'onetcy** *n* the rank or title of baronet. **bar'onetess** *n* the wife or widow of a baronet. **baronet'ical** *adj*.

barong /ba-rong'/ *n* a broad-bladed Philippine knife. [Moro]

barony see under **baron**.

baroque /bə-rok' or -rōk'/ *n* (also **barock'** or **barocco** /bə-rok'ō/ (*pl* **barocc'os**)) a bold, vigorous, exuberant style in architecture, decoration, and art generally, that arose with the Counter-Reformation and prevailed in Louis XIV's time, degenerating into tasteless extravagance in ornament; a comparable style in music, or literature;

the period dominated by this style; *orig* a jeweller's term applied to a rough pearl. ◆ *adj* in baroque style; whimsical; flamboyant; rococo. [Fr from Port and Sp; of architecture, from Ital]

baroreceptor /bar-ō-ri-sep'tər/ (*med*) *n* a sensory receptor sensitive to a pressure stimulus. [Gr *baros* weight, and **receptor**]

baroscope /bar'ō-skōp/ or *ba'rə-*/ *n* an instrument for indicating changes in the density of the air. [Gr *baros* weight, and *skopeein* to look at]

barostat /bar'ō-stat/ *n* an automatic device for regulating pressure, eg in an aircraft. [Gr *baros* weight, and **-stat**]

barotitis /bar-ō-tī'tis or *-təs*/ *n* inflammation and pain in the ear caused by pressure changes, *esp* during air travel. [Gr *baros* weight, and **-itis**]

barotrauma /bar'ō-trö-mə/ *n* injury to the ears, lungs, etc caused by changes in atmospheric pressure. [Gr *baros* weight, and **trauma**]

Barotse /bə-rot'si/ *n* a member of an African people living mainly in Zambia; their language.

barouche /ba- or bə-roosh'/ *n* a four-wheeled carriage with two bench-seats and a retractable hood. [Ger *Barutsche*, from Ital *baroccio*, from L *bis* twice, and *rota* a wheel]

barp /bärp/ (*Scot dialect*) *n* a mound or cairn. [Gaelic *barpa* a burial cairn]

barque or **bark** /bärk/ *n* a ship of small size, square-sterned, without headrails; technically, a three-masted vessel whose mizzenmast is fore-and-aft-rigged (instead of being square-rigged like the fore- and mainmasts); any boat or sailing ship (*poetic*). [Fr *barque*, from LL *barca*; poss from Gr *bāris* a Nile barge]
■ **barqu'entine** or **bark'entine** /-ən-tēn/ *n* a three-masted vessel, with the foremast square-rigged, and the mainmast and mizzenmast fore-and-aft-rigged.

barracan or **baracan** /bar'ə-kan/ (*obs*) *n* a thick, strong fabric resembling camlet. [Fr *barracan*, from Ar *barrakān* camlet, Pers *barak* a fabric made of camel's hair]

barrace /bar'as/ (*obs*) *n* the lists in a tournament. [OFr *barras*, from *barre* bar]

barrack¹ /bar'ək/ *n* (*usu* in *pl*, often behaving as *sing*) a building for soldiers, *esp* in a garrison; a huge, plain, often bleak, building, *esp* for housing many persons. ◆ *vt* and *vi* to lodge in barracks. [Fr *baraque*, from Ital *baracca*, or Sp *barraca* tent]
□ **barr'ack-room** *adj* (of humour, etc) somewhat coarse. **barrack-room lawyer** *n* an argumentative soldier given to disputing military procedure; hence any insistent but unqualified giver of advice. **barrack square** *n* a military drilling yard; strictness, rigorous training. ◆ *adj* strict, rigorous.
■ **confined to barracks** of soldiers, not allowed out of the barracks when off duty, as a punishment; extended to general use, *esp* of children, confined to the house or school as a punishment.

barrack² /bar'ək/ *vt* and *vi* to make a hostile demonstration (against), *esp* by cheering ironically. ◆ *vi* (*Aust* and *NZ*; with *for*) to support, shout encouragement to. [Prob N Ir dialect *barrack* to brag]
■ **barr'acker** *n*. **barr'acking** *n* and *adj*.

barracoon /ba-rə-koon'/ *n* a depot for slaves. [Sp *barracón*, augmentative of *barraca* tent]

barracouta /bar-ə-koo'tə/ *n* an edible fish (genus *Thyrsites*) of the hairtail family, from the southern hemisphere, called snoek in S Africa and elsewhere. [**barracuda**]

barracuda /bar-ə-koo'də/ *n* a voracious tropical fish (genus *Sphyraena*) similar to the grey mullets. [Sp *baracuta*]

barrage /bar-äzh' or bar'äzh or bar'ij/ *n* an artificial bar across a river; the forming of such a bar; a barrier formed by a continuous shower of projectiles along a fixed or a moving line (curtain-fire), or by captive balloons, or mines, or otherwise; a heavy or continuous fire, as of questions, criticisms, etc; in sport, a heat or round to select contestants, or decide a dead-heat. ◆ *vt* to assail with a barrage. [Fr, from *barre* bar]
□ **barr'age-balloon** *n*. **barr'age-fire** *n* curtain-fire.

barramundi /bar-ə-mun'di/ *n* any of several Australian river-fish (eg *Lates calcarifer*) valued as a food, a fish of the genus *Scleropages* (family Osteoglossidae), and the Australian lungfish of the *Neoceratodus* genus. [From an Aboriginal language]

barranca /ba-rang'kə/ (*US*) *n* a deep gorge (also **barran'co** (*pl* **barran'cos**)). [Sp *barranco*]

barrat /bar'ət/ *n* (*obs*) deceit, strife or trouble. [OFr *barat* deceit; traced by some to Gr *prattein* to do, by others to a Celtic or a Scand origin]
■ **barr'ator** *n* a person who vexatiously stirs up lawsuits, quarrels, etc. **barr'atrous** *adj*. **barr'atrously** *adv*. **barr'atry** *n* fraudulent practices on the part of the master or mariners of a ship to the prejudice of the owners (*maritime law*); the stirring up of suits and quarrels, forbidden under penalties to lawyers; the purchase or sale of offices of church or state.

■ words derived from main entry word; □ compound words; ■ idioms and phrasal verbs

Barr body /bär bod'i/ *n* an inactive X-chromosome in the cell nuclei of females. [Murray L *Barr* (1908–95), Canadian anatomist]

barre /bär/ *n* a horizontal rail fixed to the wall at waist level, which ballet-dancers use to balance themselves while exercising (sometimes **bar**); a capo on a guitar, lute, etc; the placing of the left forefinger across the strings of a guitar, etc to act as a capo. [Fr]
■ **barré** /ba-rā'/ *adj* of a chord on a guitar, etc, played with the left forefinger laid across the strings.

barrefull see **barful** under **bar**[1].

barrel /bar'əl/ *n* a wooden container made of curved staves bound with hoops; its contents or its capacity (36 imperial gallons of ale and beer; 35 imperial gallons, 42 US gallons, of oil; various weights or quantities of other goods); a revolving drum; a cylinder eg of a capstan; a hollow cylinder eg of a pen or quill; a tube eg of a gun; a toggle-button; the trunk of a horse, etc; a roly-poly person (*inf*); a large quantity, a lot (eg of fun) (*inf*). ◆ *vt* (**barr'elling**; **barr'elled**) to put in barrels. ◆ *vi* (*N Am*) to travel or move very quickly, drive very fast. [OFr *baril*; perh connected with **bar**[1]]
■ **barr'elage** *n* a quantity of barrels. **barr'elful** *n* (*pl* **barr'elfuls**) as much as a barrel will hold. **barr'elled** *adj* having a barrel or barrels; put in barrels.
□ **barr'el-bulk** *n* a measure of capacity of 5 cubic feet. **barrel-chest'ed** *adj* having a large, rounded, projecting ribcage. **barr'elhouse** *n* (*N Am*) a cheap saloon. ◆ *adj* (of jazz) crude and rough in style. **barrel organ** *n* a mechanical instrument for playing tunes by means of a revolving drum set with pins and turned by a handle. **barrel roll** *n* (*aerobatics*) a complete revolution on the longitudinal axis. **barrel vault** *n* a vault with a simple semi-cylindrical roof. **barr'el-vaulted** *adj*.
■ **have someone over a barrel** to be in a position to get whatever one wants from someone. **on the barrelhead** (*US*) on the spot, without delay, as payment. **scrape the (bottom of the) barrel** to utilize the very last of one's resources; to turn to something or someone as a last resort, reluctantly and perhaps not without humiliation.

barren /bar'ən/ *adj* incapable of bearing offspring; not producing fruit, seed, crops, vegetation, etc; infertile; unproductive, unfruitful (*lit* and *fig*); arid, jejune; lacking in, devoid of (with *of*); dull, stupid (*Shakesp*). ◆ *n* (in *pl*) in N America, plateaux with shrubs, etc but no timber. [OFr *barain, brahain, brehaing*]
■ **barr'enness** *n*.
□ **barren strawberry** *n* a plant (*Potentilla fragariastrum*) very like the wild strawberry, but with inedible fruit. **barr'enwort** *n* a herb (genus *Epimedium*) of the barberry family.

barret /bar'it/ *n* a flat cap; a biretta. [Fr *barrette*; cf **beret**, **biretta**]
□ **barr'et-cap** *n*.

barrette /ba-ret'/ *n* a bar-shaped hairclip or hair ornament. [Dimin of Fr *barre* bar]

barretter /bə-re'tər/ (*electronics*) *n* a resistor capable of variation and used for a number of purposes such as detecting radio waves or stabilizing electric current. [Perh from OFr *barateor* exchanger]

barricade /bar'i-kād/ *n* a temporary defensive barrier, eg to block a street; a barrier. ◆ *vt* to block; to close or enclose with a barricade. — Earlier form **barricā'do** (*pl* **barricā'dos** or **barricā'does**). [Fr *barricade* or Sp *barricada*, perh from Fr *barrique* or Sp *barrica* cask, the first street barricades being casks filled with stones, etc; or from LL *barra* bar]

barrico /ba-rē'kō/ *n* (*pl* **barri'cos** or **barri'coes**) a small cask. [Sp *barrica*]

barrier /bar'i-ər/ *n* a defensive stockade or palisade; a fence or other structure to bar passage or prevent access; a separating or restraining obstacle; (in *pl*) lists; (in *pl*) a martial exercise of the 15c–16c in which the combatants were on opposite sides of a low fence. ◆ *vt* to shut by means of a barrier. [OFr *barriere*, from LL *barrāria*, from *barra*]
□ **Barrier Act** *n* an act of the General Assembly of the Church of Scotland (1697) decreeing that changes in the law of the Church, even when approved by the Assembly, should not become law until approved by a majority of presbyteries. **barrier cream** *n* a dressing for the skin, *esp* of the hands, used as a protection against dirt, oils and solvents. **barrier layer** (*electronics*) see **depletion layer** under **deplete**. **barrier method** *n* the method of contraception in which a physical barrier is placed between the sperm and the ovum, such as a condom or diaphragm. **barrier nursing** *n* the nursing of patients in isolation from other patients for fear of cross-infection. **barrier reef** *n* a coral reef fringing a coast with a navigable channel inside.

barrio /bar'i-ō/ *n* (*pl* **barr'ios**) a Spanish-speaking, *usu* poor, community or district. [Sp, district, quarter]

barrister /bar'i-stər/ *n* a person who is qualified to plead at the bar in a lawcourt (in Scotland called **advocate**). [From LL *barra* bar (ie orig of the Inns of Court)]
■ **barristerial** /-tē'ri-əl/ *adj*. **barr'istership** *n*.
□ **barr'ister-at-law'** *n*.

■ **revising barrister** a barrister formerly appointed to revise the voters' lists.

barrow[1] /bar'ō/ *n* a small *usu* hand-propelled cart for carrying a load; a larger cart, with two or four wheels, from which goods are sold in the street; a similar structure without any wheels, to be carried by two people. [OE *bearwe*, from *beran* to bear]
□ **barrow boy** *n* a street trader with wares displayed on a barrow. **barr'owload** *n* as much as a barrow will hold; a great amount. **barr'ow-tram** *n* the shaft of a barrow.

barrow[2] /bar'ō/ *n* a hill or hillock (*obs* except in place names); an ancient earth-built grave-mound, tumulus. [OE *beorg*; cf Ger *Berg*]

barrow[3] /bar'ō/ (now only *dialect*) *n* a castrated boar. [OE *bearg*]

barrulet /bar'ū-lit/ (*heraldry*) *n* a horizontal band one-quarter the width of a bar. [Dimin of *barrule*, assumed dimin of OFr *barre*; cf **bar**[1]]

Barsac /bär'sak/ *n* a sweet white wine made in the commune of *Barsac* in Bordeaux.

Bart *abbrev*: Baronet.

bartender see under **bar**[1].

barter /bär'tər/ *vt* to give in exchange (with *for* or *away*). ◆ *vi* to trade by exchange of commodities; to bargain over the terms of such an exchange. ◆ *n* trade by direct exchange of goods. [Prob OFr *barat*; see **barrat**]
■ **bar'terer** *n*.
□ **barter trading** *n*.

Bartholin's glands /bär'tə-linz glandz/ (*physiol*) *n pl* a pair of mucus-secreting glands in the vagina. [Discovered by Caspar *Bartholin* (1655–1738), Danish anatomist]

Bartholomew /bär-thol'ə-mū/ or (*obs*) **Bartholmew, Bartlemew** /-t(h)l-mū/ or **Bartlemy** /-tl-mi/ *adj* relating to the Apostle *Bartholomew*, his day (24 August), or the fair held about that time at West Smithfield, London (1133–1855); sold at Bartholomew Fair.
□ **Barthol'omew-tide** *n* the time about St Bartholomew's Day.
■ **Black Bartholomew** 24 August 1662, when the Act of Uniformity came into force in England.

bartizan or **bartisan** /bär'ti-zan or -zan'/ *n* a parapet or battlement; a projecting gallery on a wall-face; a corbelled corner turret (*non-standard*). [Appar first used by Sir Walter Scott, who found a reading *bertisene*, for **bratticing**; see **brattice**]
■ **bar'tizaned** (or /bär-ti-zand'/) *adj*.

barton /bär'tən/ *n* a farmyard. [OE *bere-tūn* yard, from *bere* barley, and *tūn* enclosure]

Bart's /bärts/ *abbrev*: St Bartholomew's Hospital, London.

bartsia /bärt'si-ə/ *n* a herbaceous plant of the family Scrophulariaceae, with some varieties parasitic on the roots of other plants. [Johann *Bartsch* (1709–38), Prussian botanist]

barycentric /ba-ri-sen'trik/ *adj* relating to the centre of gravity. [Gr *barys* heavy, and *kentron* centre]

barye /bä'rē/ *n* a unit of atmospheric pressure, equivalent to 10^{-6} bars (also **mī'crobar**).

baryon /bar'i-on/ *n* a heavy subatomic particle involved in strong interactions with other subatomic particles and composed of three quarks bound together by gluon. [Gr *barys* heavy]
□ **baryon number** *n* the number of baryons minus the number of antibaryons (antiparticles of baryons) in a system.

Baryonyx /ba-rē-on'iks/ *n* a rare genus of flesh-eating dinosaurs with large, hook-like claws. [Gr *baros* heavy, and *onyx* claw]

barysphere /bar'i-sfēr/ *n* the heavy core of the earth within the lithosphere. [Gr *barys* heavy, and *sphaira* sphere]

baryta /bə-rī'tə/ *n* barium monoxide. [Gr *barys* heavy]
■ **bary'tes** /bə-rī'tēz/ *n* heavy spar, barium sulphate (also **barite** /bā'rīt/); (loosely) baryta. **barytic** /ba-rit'ik/ *adj* of or containing baryta or barium.
□ **baryta paper** *n* paper coated on one side with an emulsion of barium sulphate and gelatine, used in moving-pointer recording apparatus and for photographic printing papers.

baryton, barytone see **baritone**.

BAS *abbrev*: Bachelor of Agricultural Science; British Antarctic Survey.

basal see under **base**[1].

basalt /bas'ölt or ba-sölt'/ *n* a dark-coloured igneous rock composed essentially of plagioclase and pyroxene, and commonly olivine and magnetite or titaniferous iron; *esp* a compact rock of this kind; a type of pottery similar in appearance to the rock. [L *basaltēs*, from Gr *basanītēs* (*lithos*) touchstone]
■ **basalt'ic** *adj*.

basan /ba'zən/ *n* a sheepskin roughly tanned and undressed. [Ar *bitanah* lining]

basanite /bas'ə-nīt/ n a black jasper that serves as a touchstone; a variety of basalt containing nepheline, leucite, or analcime. [Gr *basanos* touchstone]

basant /bas'ant/ n a Pakistani spring festival. [Urdu, spring]

bas-bleu /bä-blø'/ (Fr) n a bluestocking.

bascule /bas'kūl/ n an apparatus one end of which rises as the other sinks. [Fr *bascule* seesaw]
□ **bascule bridge** n a bridge with one or more sections that rise when a counterpoise sinks in a pit.

base[1] /bās/ n that on which something rests; the foot, bottom; a foundation, support; the part, eg of an organ of a plant or animal, nearest the place of attachment; the foot of a pillar, on which the shaft rests (*archit*); the side or face on which a geometrical figure is regarded as standing; a number on which a system of numeration or of logarithms is founded; the chief ingredient; an ingredient of a mixture that plays a subsidiary but important part, such as giving bulk; in dyeing, a mordant; a starting point; a standard against which comparisons can be made; in make-up, the foundation or first layer of colour applied to the skin; a baseline; a fixed station in games such as baseball; an old game of which prisoners'-base and rounders are forms, and baseball a development (possibly a different word; see **bar[1]**); a place from which operations are conducted or on which they depend; home or headquarters eg of a fleet; a compound that reacts with an acid to form a salt, or dissolves in water forming hydroxyl ions (*chem*); the region between the emitter and collector of a transistor, into which minority carriers are injected (*electronics*); that element in words to which suffixes and prefixes are added, the stem (*philology*); the lower part of a shield (*heraldry*); (in *pl*) a knee-length pleated skirt worn by medieval knights (*Spenser*); a horse's housing (*Milton*). ◆ vt (**bās'ing**; **based** /bāst/) to make or form a base; to found or place on a base. [Fr *base*, from L *basis*, from Gr *basis*, from root of *bainein* to go]
■ **bās'al** adj relating to or situated at the base; at the lowest level; (loosely) fundamental. **base'less** adj without a base or foundation. **base'lessness** n. **base'ment** n the storey of a building beneath the ground floor; an underlying support; a complex of igneous and metamorphic rocks beneath sedimentary rock (*geol*). **basilar** /bas'il-ər/ adj situated at the base, *esp* of the skull.
□ **basal anaesthesia** n anaesthesia acting as a basis for further and deeper anaesthesia. **basal ganglia** n pl in vertebrates, ganglia connecting the cerebrum with other nerve centres. **basal metabolic rate** n the output of calories per square metre of body surface per hour by a fasting and resting individual. **basal metabolism** n the amount of energy required by a fasting and resting individual. **basal plane** n (*crystallog*) a crystal face or form parallel to the lateral or horizontal axes. **base'ball** n a team game, played nine-a-side with bat and ball, the players on the batting side attempting to score runs by progressing around four bases on the field; a ball used for this game. **baseball cap** n a tight-fitting cap with a long peak. **base'baller** n. **base'band** adj (telecom) applied to a device capable of operating only over a narrow range of frequencies. **base'board** n a board which forms a base for something; a skirting-board (*N Am*). **base'-burner** n (*N Am*) a stove in which fuel is fed automatically from a hopper. **base hospital** n (*Aust*) a hospital that serves a wide rural area. **base'-level** n (*geog*) the level to which land can be or is eroded by water. **base'-levelled** adj. **base'line** n an accurately measured line used as a base for triangulation; each of the lines at the back of the court (*tennis*); a line joining bases (*baseball*); the line on which the type stands, below which the descenders hang (*printing*); a starting point against which to measure something, a standard of comparison. **base'liner** n (*tennis*) a player who plays mainly from the baseline and rarely approaches the net. **base'-load** n (*elec eng*) the minimum demand of electricity on a power-station (cf **peak load** under **peak[1]**). **base'man** n (baseball) any of the three fielders stationed near first, second and third base (hence *first baseman*, etc). **base pair** n (biochem) a purine linked to a pyrimidine by hydrogen bonds, forming a link between complementary strands of DNA or RNA. **base pairing** n. **base'plate** n the foundation plate of a piece of heavy machinery. **base rate** n the rate, determined by a bank, on which it bases its lending rates of interest. **base ring** n a strengthening band of metal round the breech of a muzzle-loading cannon. **base'runner** n a baseball player attempting to perform a circuit of the bases. **base station** n (telecom) a radio and mobile phone service provider, relaying calls between systems and users. **base substitution** n (biol) a mutation in which a base in the DNA is replaced by a different base (cf **deletion mutation**). **base unit** n a fundamental unit from which other units in a system of measurement are derived.
■ **base out** (*US*) to bottom out. **get to** or **make first base** (*N Am inf*) to complete the first stage in a process. **off base** (*N Am inf*) wrong, mistaken. **touch base with** (*orig N Am*) to make contact with.

base[2] /bās/ adj low in place, value, estimation or principle; low in morals, reprehensible, vile; worthless; debased; counterfeit; servile as opposed to free (*law*); lowly, humble (*Bible* and *Shakesp*); illegitimate (*obs*); bass (*obs*). [Fr *bas*, from LL *bassus* thick, squat]
■ **base'ly** adv. **base'ness** n.
□ **base'born** adj (archaic) low-born; illegitimate. **base coin** n spurious coin. **base metal** n any metal other than the precious metals; any metal that alters on exposure to air (cf **noble metal**). **base'-minded** adj of a low mind or spirit; mean. **base'-spirited** adj mean-spirited.

base[3] /bās/ vt a form of **abase**.

baseball see under **base[1]**.

base-court /bās'kört/ (hist) n the outer court of a castle or mansion; an inferior court of justice. [Fr *basse-court* (now *basse-cour*)]

baseej or **basij** /bas'ēj/ n pl (with *the* ; also with *cap*) in Iran, volunteer vigilantes who enforce strict Islamic behaviour and dress code, *esp* on women. [Iranian]

base jumping /bās jum'ping/ n the recreational practice of parachuting from low-level objects and structures (*esp* landmarks), including specifically a building, an aerial, a span and an earthbound object (eg a mountain). [Acronymic]
■ **base jump** n. **base jumper** n.

baselard /bas'ə-lärd/ (obs) n a dagger or hanger. [Anglo-Fr]

basement see under **base[1]**.

basen a Spenserian spelling of **basin**.

basenji /bə-sen'jē/ n a smallish, erect-eared, curly-tailed African hunting dog that rarely barks. [Bantu, pl of *mosenji, musengi* native]

bases plural of **base[1]** and **basis**.

BASF abbrev: *Badische Anilin und Soda-Fabrik*, a multinational chemical company.

bash[1] /bash/ vt to beat, batter; to smash; to dent; to attack harshly or maliciously, physically or verbally. ◆ vi to crash (into) (*inf*); to become dented; to solicit as a prostitute (*sl*). ◆ n a heavy blow; the mark of a blow; a dent; a party (*inf*). [Prob Scand]
■ **bash'er** n a person who, or thing that, bashes (sometimes used as *sfx*); a straw hat (*sl*). **bash'ing** n the activity of making harsh or malicious physical or verbal attacks on individuals or (members of) groups one dislikes (often used as a *combining form*, as in *queer-bashing, union-bashing*). **bash'ment** n same as **dancehall** (see under **dance**). **bash'tag** n (*inf*) a hashtag (qv under **hash[3]**) used for critical or abusive comments.
■ **bash on** (*inf*) to persevere, carry on. **have a bash** (*inf*) to have a try; to make an attempt (at). **on the bash** (*sl*) on the spree; on the streets as a prostitute.

bash[2] see under **bashful**.

bashaw /ba-shö'/ n a pasha (archaic); a haughty person. [Turk *basa*; cf **pasha**]
■ **bashaw'ism** n. **bashaw'ship** n.

bashful /bash'fŭl/ adj modest; shy, lacking confidence; resulting from or indicating modesty or shyness. [See **abash**]
■ **bash** vi (Spenser) to be abashed. **bash'fully** adv. **bash'fulness** n. **bash'less** adj (obs) unashamed.

Bashi-Bazouk /bash-ē-bə-zook'/ n a Turkish irregular soldier. [Turk *basi-bozuk* wild head]
■ **Ba'shi-Bazouk'ery** n.

bashlik /bash'lik/ n a Russian hood with long ends. [Russ *bashlyk* a Caucasian hood, from Turk *bas* a head]

basho /bash'ō/ n (pl **bash'o**) in sumo wrestling, a tournament. [Jap]

BASIC /bā'sik/ abbrev : British American Security Information Council.

BASIC or **Basic** /bā'sik/ n a computer language using a combination of simple English and algebra. [*Beginners' All-purpose Symbolic Instruction Code*]

basic /bā'sik/ adj belonging to or of the nature of a base; fundamental; simple, plain, without extras; containing excess of a base (*chem, dyeing, steel-making*, etc); poor in silica, *opp* to *acid* (*geol*). ◆ n (in *pl*) fundamental principles. [**base[1]**]
■ **bas'ically** adv with reference to what is basic; fundamentally, essentially. **bāsicity** /bās-is'it-i/ n.
□ **Basic English** n a reduced English vocabulary of 850 words for teaching foreigners or for use as an auxiliary language; (without *cap*) English using few and simple words. **basic(-oxygen) process** n a steelmaking process in which oxygen is blown at high pressure through molten pig iron. **basic salt** n a salt having one or more hydroxyl groups in place of an acid radical or radicals. **basic slag** n a by-product of the basic process, rich in lime and used as manure.
■ **back to basics** a political slogan advocating a return to what are regarded as basic values of morality and behaviour.

basidium /ba-sid'i-əm/ (bot) n (pl **basid'ia**) a fungal fructification from which spores (*usu* four) are released. [Gr *basis* basis, and Gr dimin ending -*idion*]

■ **basid'ial** *adj.* **Basidiomycetes** /bə-sid-i-ō-mī-sē'tēz/ *n pl* one of the main groups of fungi, characterized by the possession of basidia, including the familiar toadstools as well as rusts and smuts. **basidiomycē'tous** *adj.* **basid'iospore** *n* a spore produced by a basidium.

basifixed /bā'si-fikst/ (*bot*) *adj* attached by the base. [**base**[1] and **fixed**]

basifugal /bā- or bə-sif'ū-gl/ (*bot*) *adj* developing in a direction away from the base. [**base**[1] and L *fugere* to flee]

basij see **baseej**.

basil[1] /baz'il/ *n* an aromatic labiate plant (*Ocimum*; also called **sweet basil**); extended to calamint and other labiates. [OFr *basile*, from L *basilisca*, representing Gr *basilikon*, literally, royal, perh with reference to *basiliskos* basilisk, cobra, as a reputed cure for snakebite]

basil[2] /baz'il/ same as **basan**.

basil[3] see **bezel**.

basilar see under **base**[1].

Basilian /ba-, bə-zil'i-ən or -sil'/ *adj* of St *Basil* (c.329–379AD). ◆ *n* a monk or nun following his rule.

basilica /bə-sil'i-kə/ *n* a large oblong hall, with double colonnades and commonly a semicircular apse, used for judicial and commercial purposes; a magnificent church formed out of such a hall, or built after its plan; a Roman Catholic church with honorific privileges; *orig* a royal palace. [Gr *basilikos* royal, from *basileus* king]
■ **basil'ical** *adj* royal. **basil'ican** *adj* of a basilica. **basil'icon** *n* an ointment of various kinds, as being of sovereign virtue.
□ **basilic vein** *n* (*physiol*) the large vein in the upper part of the arm.

basilisk /bas' or baz'i-lisk/ *n* a mythical serpent which could kill with a glance or breath, so named, according to Pliny, from its crown-like crest; a harmless crested lizard of tropical America; a brass cannon throwing a shot of about 200lb (*hist*). [Gr *basiliskos*, dimin of *basileus* a king]

basin (*archaic* **bason**) /bā'sən/ *n* a wide open container or dish; a sink, washbasin; a basinful; any hollow place containing water, such as a dock; the area drained by a river and its tributaries; a region of synclinal structure (*geol*). [OFr *bacin*, from LL *bachinus*, perh from *bacca* a vessel]
■ **ba'sinful** *n* (*pl* **ba'sinfuls**) as much as fills a basin. **ba'sin-wide** (*Spenser* **basen wide**) *adj* wide as a basin.
■ **have a basinful** (*inf*) to have more than enough (of).

basinet /bas'i-net/ or **basnet** /bas'net/ *n* a light close-fitting steel helmet worn alone with a visor, or with the great helm over it. [Dimin of **basin**]

basipetal /bā- or bə-sip'i-tl/ (*bot*) *adj* proceeding or developing in the direction of the base. [**base**[1] and L *petere* to seek]

basis /bā'sis/ *n* (*pl* **bas'es** /bās'ēz/) the foundation, or that on which a thing rests; the groundwork or first principle; the fundamental ingredient; a pedestal. [See **base**[1]]

bask /bäsk/ *vi* to lie in the warmth or sunshine; to enjoy and take great pleasure. [ON *bathask* to bathe]
□ **basking shark** *n* a large but harmless shark that shows its great dorsal fin as it basks.

Baskerville /bas'kər-vil/ *n* a printing typeface. [John *Baskerville* (1706–75), English printer]

basket /bäs'kit/ *n* a container made of plaited or interwoven twigs, rushes, canes or other flexible material; a basketful; the hoop with an open net attached, used as a goal at basketball; a goal scored in basketball; a collection of similar or related ideas or things; a group or collection, *esp* of foreign currencies used to calculate a standard exchange rate (*econ*); a bastard (*euphem*); the back part of a stagecoach outside; a basket-hilt. [Origin obscure]
■ **bas'ketful** *n* (*pl* **bas'ketfuls**) as much as fills a basket. **bas'ketry** *n* basketwork.
□ **bas'ketball** *n* a team game in which points are scored by throwing a ball into a raised horizontal net (*orig* a basket); the ball used in the game. **basket case** *n* (*sl*) a person with all four limbs amputated (*obs*); a nervous wreck, someone unable to cope; a country that cannot cope economically. **basket chair** *n* a wicker chair. **basket clause** *n* (*N Am*) a comprehensive clause in a contract. **bas'ket-hilt** *n* a sword hilt with a protective covering like basketwork. **bas'ket-maker** *n* (with *caps*; *archaeol*) a member of an ancient American culture of SW USA, known for their basketwork. **bas'ket-making** *n*. **bas'ket-stitch** *n* (*knitting*) groups of plain and purl stitches alternating vertically and horizontally, resembling basketwork in effect. **bas'ketweave** *n* a form of weaving using two or more strands in the warp and weft. **bas'ketwork** *n* articles made of interlaced twigs, canes, etc (also *adj*); the art of making these.

basmati rice /bas-mat'i rīs/ *n* a long-grain, naturally perfumed rice. [Hindi *basmati* fragrant]

bas mitzvah, etc see **bath mitzvah**.

basnet see **basinet**.

basoche /ba-sosh'/ (*Fr*) *n* a medieval guild of clerks of the parliament of Paris, performers of mystery plays.

bason see **basin**.

basophil /bā'sə-fil/ *adj* of *esp* white blood cells having an affinity for basic stains. ◆ *n* a cell of this kind. [*basic* and **-phil**]
■ **basophil'ic** *adj* basophil.

Basotho /ba-soo'tō/ *n* a Bantu people of Lesotho (formerly Basutoland); a member of this people (*pl* **Baso'thos**); their language (also **Sotho**). —Also **Basu'to, Basu'tu** /-*too*/.

ba'spiel see **balling** under **ball**[1].

Basque /bäsk or bask/ *n* a member of a people (in their own tongue **Euscara, Eskuara**) inhabiting the W Pyrenees, in Spain and France; their agglutinative non-Indo-European language; (without *cap*) a short-skirted jacket, or a continuation of a bodice a little below the waist; (without *cap*) on a skirt, a similar area extending shortly below the waist, to which pleats or gathers are often attached; (without *cap*) a close-fitting (under-)bodice. ◆ *adj* of the Basques or their language or country. [Fr *Basque*, from L *Vasconēs* a people of Gascony]
■ **basqued** /bäskt/ *adj* furnished with a basque. **basquine** /-kēn'/ *n* an outer petticoat worn by Basque and Spanish women.

bas-relief /bas-ri-lēf'/ or /ba'ri-lēf/ or (*Ital*) **basso-rilievo** /bäs'sō-rē-lyā'vō/, popularly **-relievo** /bas'ō-ri-lē'vō/ *n* sculpture in which the figures do not stand far out from the ground on which they are formed; this technique in sculpture. [Fr and Ital. See **base**[2] and **relief**]

bass[1] /bās/ *n* the lowest part in music; a bass singer (often in the Italian form **basso** /bäs'sō/ (*pl* **bas'sos** or **bas'si** /-si/)); a bass instrument, *esp* (*inf*) a bass guitar or double bass; low-frequency sound as output from an amplifier, etc; a knob or dial that adjusts this sound. ◆ *adj* low, deep; (of a musical instrument or voice) low in pitch and range. ◆ *vt* (*Shakesp*) to utter in a deep tone. [See **base**[2]]
■ **bass'ist** *n* a person who plays a double bass or a bass guitar. **bass'y** *adj* somewhat bass; predominantly bass.
□ **bass'-bar** *n* a strip of wood on the belly of a violin, etc, under the bass foot of the bridge, to distribute the vibrations. **bass clef** *n* (*music*) the clef in which the F a fifth below middle C is written on the fourth line of the stave. **bass compensation** *n* (*acoustics*) differential attenuation introduced into a sound-reproducing system to emphasize bass frequencies. **bass drum** *n* the large drum of an orchestra or band. **bass fiddle** *n* (*inf*) a double bass. **bass guitar** *n* an electric guitar similar in sound and range to the double bass. **bass horn** *n* an old wind instrument, a modification of the serpent. **bass'line** *n* the lowest line in a piece of jazz or popular music, provided by a bass instrument or electronically. **bass tuba** *n* the lowest instrument of the saxhorn class. **bass viol** *n* a six-stringed instrument, used for playing the lowest part in early music, the viola da gamba; the double bass (*inf, esp US*).

bass[2] or **basse** /bas/ *n* a European sea fish of the sea perch family (or *Dicentrarchus labrax*); extended to other sea and freshwater fishes. ◆ *vt* to fish for bass. [OE *bærs*; cf Ger *Bars* the perch]

bass[3] /bas/ *n* bast; any article made of bast or some similar material. [See **bast**]
□ **bass'wood** *n* an American lime-tree or its wood.

basset /bas'it/ *n* a low-set, smooth-coated hound with long ears (also **bass'et-hound** or **basset hound**); an old Venetian card game, resembling faro, widely popular in the 18c; an outcrop (*geol*). ◆ *vi* (*geol*) (of strata) to crop out. [Fr, from *bas* low]
□ **basset horn** *n* (Ital *corno di bassetto*) a low-pitched instrument of the clarinet family. **bass'et-hornist** *n*.

bassinet /bas'i-net/ *n* a kind of basket with a hood, used as a cradle; a similarly shaped pram; a bed in hospital, with necessary equipment, for care of a baby. [Fr dimin of *bassin* a basin]

basso see **bass**[1].

bassoon /bə-soon' or -zoon'/ *n* (Ital *fagotto*) a large woodwind instrument formed of a long jointed wooden pipe, with a range from B flat below the bass stave to C or F in the treble. The **double bassoon** (Ital *contrafagotto*) sounds an octave lower. [Ital *bassone*, augmentative of *basso* low, from root of **base**[2], **bass**[1]]
■ **bassoon'ist** *n*.

basso profundo or **basso profondo** /bä'sō prō-fun'dō or (Ital) prō-fūn'do/ (*music, esp opera*) *n* (*pl* **basso profundos**) an extremely deep bass voice or singer. [Ital]

basso-rilievo see **bas-relief**.

basswood see under **bass**[3].

bast /bast/, also **bass** /bas/ *n* phloem, the conductive material in a plant; inner bark, *esp* of lime; fibre; matting. See **bass**[3]. [OE *bæst*; Ger *Bast*]

basta /bas'tə/ (*Shakesp*) *interj* enough. [Ital and Sp]

bastard /bas'tərd or bä'stərd/ n a child born of parents not married to each other; a difficult or unpleasant person or thing, an unfortunate person, or neutrally, a chap (*offensive sl*); (also **baster** /bas'tər/) a person of mixed European and African parentage (*S Afr hist*); a sweet Spanish wine (*Shakesp*). ◆*adj* born out of wedlock; not genuine; resembling, but not identical with, the species bearing the name (*science, esp bot*); of abnormal shape or size; false. [OFr *bastard* (Fr *bâtard*) child of the packsaddle (OFr *bast*)]
■ **bast'ardism** n bastardy. **bastardizā'tion** or **-s-** n. **bas'tardize** or **-ise** vt to debase, corrupt; to pronounce to be or prove to be a bastard. ◆ vi to beget bastards (*Shakesp*); to degenerate. **bas'tardly** adj. **bas'tardy** n the state of being a bastard.
❑ **bas'tard-bar** n an inaccurate name for the baton-sinister in heraldry. **bastard file** n a file with teeth of a medium degree of coarseness. **bastard title** n an abbreviated title of a book on an otherwise blank page preceding the full title-page. **bastard types** n pl (*printing*) types cast with an extra deep bevel to avoid the use of leads, such as longprimer face on pica body. **bastard wing** n three, four or five feathers on the first digit (corresponding to the thumb) of a bird's wing.

baste¹ /bāst/ vt to keep (meat) moist when roasting by drizzling melted fat or butter over. [Ety unknown]

baste² /bāst/ (*needlework*) vt to tack. [OFr *bastir*, from OHGer *bestan* to sew]

baste³ /bāst/ vt to beat with a stick. [Prob connected with ON *beysta*, Dan *böste* to beat]
■ **bāst'ing** n.

bastel-house /bas'təl-hows/ (*Scot and N Eng*) n a fortified house, *usu* with vaulted ground-floor. [**bastille**]

baster see **bastard**.

bastide /ba-stēd'/ (*Fr*) n a fortified town in SW France; a country house in S France.

bastille /ba-stēl'/ n (with *cap*) an old fortress and state prison in Paris, demolished in the Revolution (July 1789); hence any prison, *esp* as a symbol of tyranny; a tower for the defence of a fortress (*hist*); a movable tower used by besiegers. [Fr, from OFr *bastir* (Fr *bâtir*) to build]
■ **Bastille Day** 14 July, a French national holiday.

bastinado /ba-sti-nā'dō or -nä'/ or **bastinade** /ba-sti-nād'/ vt (**bastinād'oing** or **bastinād'ing**; **bastinād'oed** or **bastinād'ed**) to beat with a baton or stick, *esp* on the soles of the feet. ◆ n (pl **bastinā'does** or **bastinādes'**) a beating performed in this way, as a punishment. [Sp *bastonada*, Fr *bastonnade*, from *baston* baton; cf **baton, batten¹**]

bastion /bast'yən or bast'i-ən/ n a kind of tower at the angle of a fortification; a defence, defender (*fig*). [Fr, from Ital *bastione*, from *bastire* to build]
■ **bast'ioned** adj.

bastle, bastle-house same as **bastel-house**.

bastnäsite or **bastnaesite** /bast-nä'sīt/ n a yellow to reddish-brown mineral, a fluorocarbonate of lanthanum and cerium. [Swed *bastnäsit*, from *Bastnäs*, in Sweden, where it was found]

basto /bä'stō/ n (pl **bas'tos**) in quadrille, the ace of clubs. [Sp, club]

basuco /bə-soo'kō/ n an addictive impure mixture of coca paste and cocaine. [Colombian Sp]

Basuto see **Basotho**.

BASW abbrev : British Association of Social Workers.

bat¹ /bat/ n a flattish club for striking the ball in cricket; a rounded club for baseball; in tennis, etc, a racket (*inf*); a turn at batting (*cricket*); a batsman; something shaped like a bat, eg the signalling devices used by a batman to guide aircraft; a heavy stick; the clown or harlequin's lath; a piece of brick; speed, rate (*sl*); a drunken spree (*sl*); a blow; a sheet of batting (also **batt**); a layer of felt used in hat-making (also **batt**). ◆ vt and vi (**batt'ing**; **batt'ed**) to hit with a bat in cricket, etc; to take a turn at batting in cricket, etc; to hit as with a bat. [Perh from OE *bat* (a doubtful form), prob Celtic *bat* staff]
■ **batt'er** n. **batt'ing** n the action or art of using a bat in cricket or baseball; cotton wadding prepared in sheets, for quilts, etc.
❑ **bat'fish** n any of several groups of fish with winglike projections, *esp* the Ogocephalidae or the Pacific Epippidae. **bat'fowling** n catching birds at night by using lights to confuse them. **bat'man** n a man on an airfield or aircraft-carrier who assists planes to taxi to position using a pair of lightweight bats (also **bats'man**). **bat printing** n a method of printing in which designs are transferred by means of a sheet of gelatine. **bats'man** or **bats'woman** n a player who bats in cricket; (**batsman**) see also **batman** above. **bats'manship** n.
■ **bat around** (*sl*) to wander; to go on a bat. **bat for both sides** (*sl*) to be bisexual; to be duplicitous. **bat for the other side** (*sl*) to be homosexual. **carry one's bat** (*cricket*) of an opening batsman, to remain not-out at the end of a completed innings. **go to bat for** (*N Am*

inf) to defend, take the side of. **off one's own bat** by one's own efforts; on one's own initiative. **right off the bat** (*N Am inf*) straight away.

bat² /bat/ n a flying mammal with wings attached mainly to its arms and hands, but extending along its sides to the hind-feet and tail. [ME *bakke*, appar from Scand; cf Dan *aftenbakke* evening-bat]
■ **bats** adj (*inf*) crazy. **batt'y** adj bat-like; bat-infested; crazy (*inf*).
❑ **bats'wing** adj shaped like a bat's wing, eg of the flame of a gas-burner. **batwing sleeve** n a sleeve that is very wide at the armhole and tight at the wrist.
■ **blind as a bat** completely blind. **have** (or **be**) **bats in the belfry** (*inf*) to be crazy or slightly mad. **like a bat out of hell** (*inf*) very quickly.

bat³ /bat/ vt (**batt'ing**; **batt'ed**) to flutter (*esp* an eyelid). [Cf **bate³**]
■ **not bat an eye** or **eyelid** to show no surprise or emotion; not to sleep a wink.

bat⁴ /bat/ n the informal speech of a foreign language, lingo. [Hindi, speech, word]
■ **sling the bat** to speak such a language.

bat. or **batt.** abbrev : battalion; battery.

batable /bāt'ə-bl/ adj short for **debatable**.

batata /bə-tä'tə/ n the sweet potato. [Sp from Haitian]

Batavian /bə-tā'vi-ən/ adj relating to the ancient *Batāvi* in the Low Countries, or to the modern Dutch, or to *Batavia* (Jakarta). ◆n a member of the Batavi; a Dutch person (*rare*).

batch¹ /bach/ n the quantity of bread baked, or of anything made or got ready, at one time; a set; a quantity of material required for one operation; a group of similar objects or people; a collection of computer transactions which are processed as a single unit. ◆ vt to collect into, or treat in, batches. [From the root of **bake**]
■ **batch'ing** adj and n.
❑ **batch file** n (*comput*) a file containing commands which are executed in order. **batch loaf** n a loaf baked touching others and pulled apart after baking, having hard top and bottom crusts and soft sides. **batch processing** n (*comput*) a method of processing data in which similar items of data are collected together for processing at one time. **batch production** n a type of production in which identical items are manufactured and processed in groups rather than singly.

batch² see **bach** under **bachelor**.

bate¹ /bāt/ vt and vi to abate; to lessen, diminish; to blunt. [Aphetic form of **abate¹**]
■ **bate'less** adj that cannot be blunted (*Shakesp*); not bated (*obs*). **bate'ment** n (*obs*) reduction.
❑ **batement light** n a window whose sill is not horizontal.
■ **with bated breath** (holding one's breath) in fear or suspense.

bate² /bāt/ n (*Spenser*) strife, contention. [Aphetic form of **debate**]
❑ **bate'-breed'ing** adj (*Shakesp*).

bate³ /bāt/ vi to beat the wings impatiently, to try to fly from the fist or perch when still attached by leash or jesses (*falconry*); to be impatient (*obs*). [OFr *batre*, from LL *batere*]

bate⁴ same as **bait**, a rage (*sl*).

bateau /bä-tō'/ n (pl **bateaux** /-tōz'/) a light riverboat, *esp* on Canadian rivers. [Fr]

bateleur /bat'(ə-)lər/ n a short-tailed African eagle. [Fr, mountebank, appar from its characteristic movements]

Batesian mimicry /bāt'si-ən mim'i-kri/ n mimicry in which an animal is protected from predators by its resemblance to another which is dangerous or unpalatable. [HW *Bates* (1825–92), English naturalist]

Bath /bäth/ n a famous city in SW England, with Roman *baths*.
■ **Bathō'nian** adj (*geol*) of a division of the Middle Jurassic (also n).
❑ **Bath bun** n a rich sweet bun. **Bath chair** n (also without *cap*) a large wheelchair for invalids. **Bath Oliver** n a plain biscuit invented by Dr W Oliver (1695–1764) of Bath. **Bath stone** n a building stone quarried at Bath.

bath¹ /bäth/ n (pl **baths** /bädhz/, also **bäths/**) water for immersing the body; an act of bathing; a receptacle or a house for bathing; (in *pl*) a building containing baths for the use of the public, and a swimming pool; a place for undergoing medical treatment by means of bathing; the act of exposing the body to vapour, mud, sunlight, etc; a liquid or other material (eg sand), or a receptacle, in which anything is immersed for heating, washing or steeping (*chem*). ◆ vt to give a bath to; to wash (oneself) in a bath. ◆ vi to take a bath. [OE *bæth*; Ger *Bad*]
❑ **bath'cube** n bath salts in the form of a solid cube. **bath'house** or **bath-house** n. **bath mat** n a mat placed beside a bath for someone to step out onto after having a bath. **bath'robe** n (*orig US*) a towelling loose-fitting garment worn *esp* before and after bathing or swimming. **bath'room** n a room containing a bath, and *usu* a washbasin and lavatory; (*esp N Am*) a lavatory. **bath salts** n pl a *usu* sweet-smelling substance used to soften and perfume bathwater. **bath sheet** n an extra-large bath-towel. **bath'-towel** n a large towel. **bath'tub** n a bath,

in UK often a movable tub, but in N America the permanent bathroom fixture.
■ **Order of the Bath** a British order of knighthood, so named from the bath taken before installation.

bath² /bäth/ n the largest Jewish liquid measure, containing about eight imperial gallons. [Heb]

bath-brick /bäth'brik/ n a preparation of siliceous silt, manufactured at Bridgwater in the form of blocks and used in cleaning knives. [Traditionally said to be named after the first maker, one *Bath*, or from its resemblance to *Bath stone*]

bathe /bādh/ vt to wash as in a bath; to wash or moisten, with any liquid; to moisten, suffuse, encompass. ◆ vi to take a dip or swim; to bask. ◆ n the act of bathing; a swim or dip. [OE *bathian*]
■ **bath'er** n someone who bathes; (in pl) a swimming costume.
□ **bathing beauty** or (old) **bathing belle** n an attractive woman in a swimsuit, esp when competing in a beauty contest. **bathing box** or **hut** n a small structure for bathers to change in. **bathing cap** n a tight rubber cap worn on the head to keep the hair dry and out of the way when swimming. **bathing costume** or **dress** n (old) a swimsuit. **bathing machine** n (hist) a wheeled bathing hut for transporting a bather into the sea. **bathing suit** n (old or N Am) a swimsuit.

bathetic see under **bathos**.

bathmism /bath'mi-zm/ n a supposed directive force in evolution or an inherent tendency to develop along divergent lines. [Gr *bathmos* step]
■ **bath'mic** adj.

bath mitzvah or **bath mitsvah** /bäth mits'və/ (also **bas mitzvah**, etc /bäs/) or **bat mitzvah** /bät/; sometimes with caps; also with hyphen or as one word; esp US) n a girl of the Jewish religion attaining the age (usu 12 years) of religious responsibility; the festivities held in recognition of this event. [Heb, daughter of the law]

bathochromic /bath-ō-krōm'ik/ adj changing to a longer wavelength in the absorption spectrum of a compound. [Gr *bathos* depth, and *chrōma* colour]

batholith /bath'ō-lith/ n a mass of igneous rock that has risen from a great depth (also **bath'olite**, **bath'ylith** or **bath'ylite**). [Gr *bathos* depth, or *bathys* deep, and *lithos* a stone]
■ **batholithic**, **batholitic**, **bathylithic** or **bathylitic** /-lith', -lit'/ adj.

bathometer /bə- or ba-thom'i-tər/ n a bathymeter. [Gr *bathos* depth, and *metron* measure]

Bathonian see under **Bath**.

bathophobia /bath-ō-fō'bi-ə/ n a morbid fear of falling from a high place. [Gr *bathos* depth, and *phobos* fear]

bathorse /bat'hörs, bät'- or formerly bä'hörs/ (hist) n a packhorse carrying an officer's baggage. [Fr *bât* packsaddle]

bathos /bā'thos/ n a ludicrous descent from the elevated to the ordinary in writing or speech. [Gr *bathos* depth]
■ **bathetic** /bə-thet'ik/ adj (irregularly formed on the analogy of *pathos*, *pathetic*).

bathy- /ba-thi-/ combining form denoting deep. [Gr *bathys* deep]
■ **bath'yal** /bath'i-əl/ adj of ocean depths of between 200 and 2000 metres. **bathyb'ius** n (Gr *bios* life) a substance on the sea bottom formerly thought to be living matter. **bathygraph'ical** adj (Gr *graphein* to write) of maps, representing the contours of the seabed. **bathylite** or **bathylith** n see **batholith**. **bathymeter** /bath-im'ət-ər/ n (Gr *metron* measure) a sounding instrument. **bathymet'ric** or **bathymet'rical** adj. **bathym'etry** n the science of sounding seas and lakes. **bathyorograph'ical** adj (Gr *oros* mountain) of maps, representing the contours of land height and water depth. **bathypelagic** /-əj'ik/ adj (Gr *pelagos* sea) found in the depths of the sea, down to 4000m below sea level. **bath'yscaphe** or **bath'yscape** n (Gr *skaphos* ship) an electrically powered crewed vessel with a spherical observation cabin on its underside, used for deep-sea exploration. **bath'ysphere** n (Gr *sphaira* sphere) a submersible observation chamber lowered and raised from a surface vessel.

batik /bat'ik or ba-tēk'/ n an orig Indonesian method of producing designs on cloth by covering with wax, for each successive dipping, those parts that are to be protected from the dye; fabric patterned by this method. [Malay]

bating /bā'ting/ prep excepting, except. [**bate¹**]

batiste /bə-tēst'/ n a fine fabric of linen, cotton or wool. [Fr, cambric, from *Baptiste*, the reputed original maker or from its use in wiping the heads of children after baptism]

batler /bat'lər/ (Shakesp) n a beetle for beating clothes (altered by some editors to **bat'let**). [**bat¹**]

batman¹ /bat'mən, formerly bä'mən/ n an officer's personal attendant; a person in charge of a bathorse (hist). [Fr *bât* packsaddle, and **man¹**]
□ **batwoman** /bat'-/ n an officer's female personal attendant.

batman² see under **bat¹**.

bat mitzvah, etc see **bath mitzvah**.

baton /bat'on or bat'n/, also (archaic) **batoon** /bə-toon'/ n a staff of office, eg that of a marshal; a policeman's truncheon; a short stick passed on from one runner to the next in a relay race; a light wand used by the conductor of an orchestra; a knobbed staff carried, tossed and twirled by a drum-major, etc at the head of a marching band, etc; a baton round. ◆ vt to strike with a baton. [Fr *bâton*]
□ **baton charge** n a swift forward movement of police against a hostile crowd, with truncheons drawn for use. **bat'on-charge** vt. **baton gun** n a gun which fires **baton rounds**, plastic bullets, used in riot control. **baton-sin'ister** n a heraldic indication of illegitimacy, a diminutive of a bend-sinister, not extending to the sides of the shield, so as to resemble a marshal's baton laid diagonally over the family arms from sinister to dexter (improperly called **bar-sin'ister**).
■ **under the baton of** (of choirs and orchestras) conducted by.

batrachia /bə-trā'ki-ə/ (sometimes with cap) n pl the Amphibia; the Salientia, tailless amphibia, or frogs and toads. [Gr *batrachos* a frog]
■ **batra'chian** adj and n. **batrachopho'bia** n an aversion to frogs, toads and newts. **batrachopho'bic** adj.

batsman see under **bat¹**.

batswing see under **bat²**.

batswoman see under **bat¹**.

batt see **bat¹**.

batt. see **bat**.

batta /bat'ə/ (Anglo-Ind) n an allowance in addition to ordinary pay; subsistence money. [Prob Kanarese *bhatta* rice]

battailous /ba-tā'ləs or -ti'/ (Spenser) adj warlike. [OFr *bataillos*; see **battle¹**]

battalia /bə-tā'lyə or -tā'/ n order of battle (archaic); the main body of an army in array (obs). [Ital *battaglia*; see **battle¹**]

battalia pie /bə-tal'yə pī/ n articles such as pincushions, embroidered by nuns in convents with scenes from the Bible; a pie containing sweetbreads, etc. [Fr *béatilles*, dimin from L *beātus* blessed, and perh L *pius* pious]

battalion /bə-tal'yən or -i-ən/ n a body of soldiers consisting of several companies; a body of men drawn up in battle array. [Fr *bataillon*, from Ital *battaglione*; see **battle¹**]

batteilant /bat'ā-lənt/ (Spenser) adj combatant. [Fr *bataillant*]

battels /bat'lz/ n pl (at Oxford and some other universities) accounts for provisions received from college kitchens and butteries; sums charged in college accounts generally. [Poss connected with **battle²**]
■ **batt'el** vi to have such an account. **batt'eler** n someone who battels; a student of rank below a commoner (obs).

battement /bat-mã/ (ballet) n a movement in which one leg is extended repeatedly to the front, side or back with a beating motion against the other leg. [Fr, beating, from *battre* to beat]

batten¹ /bat'ən/ n a piece of sawn timber used for flooring, support of laths, etc; a strip of wood fastened across parallel boards, or used to fasten down hatches aboard ship, etc; a row of electric lamps or a strip of wood carrying them. ◆ vt to fasten or furnish with battens. [**baton**]
■ **batt'ening** n battens forming a structure.
■ **batten down the hatches** to prepare for a crisis; orig to secure the hatches on a ship against bad weather.

batten² /bat'ən/ vi to thrive at the expense of (with on); to grow fat; to feed abundantly (on; lit and fig). ◆ vt (obs) to fatten. [ON *batna* to grow better, from *bati* advantage; cf Du *baten* to avail]

Battenberg, **Battenburg** or **Battonberg**, etc (**cake**) /bat'ən-bûrg (kāk)/ n a kind of cake usu made in pink and yellow squares and covered with marzipan. [Perh from *Battenberg*, a village in Germany]

Batten's disease /bat'ənz diz-ēz'/ n a severe progressive genetic disorder which causes blindness, deafness, loss of muscle control and early death. [FE Batten (1865–1918), British doctor]

batter¹ /bat'ər/ vt to hit with repeated blows; to damage or wear with beating or by use; to attack with artillery; to attack (people or ideas) (fig). [OFr *batre* (Fr *battre*), from LL *battere* (L *ba(t)tuere*) to beat]
■ **batt'ered** adj suffering frequent violent assaults; in particular **battered baby** (or **child**) a baby (or child) suffering such attacks at the hands of its parents, or **battered wife** a woman who suffers such attacks by her spouse. **batt'erer** n.
□ **batt'ering-ram** n a large beam used for battering down walls.
■ **battered baby** (or **child**) **syndrome** a collection of symptoms found in a baby or young child, caused by violence on the part of the parent or other adult suffering from social and psychological disturbance. **on the batter** (sl) on the bat, on a spree.

batter² /bat'ər/ n ingredients (usu flour and eggs) beaten along with some liquid (eg milk) into a paste (cookery); paste for sticking; a damaged piece of type (printing). [Prob from **batter¹**]
■ **batt'ered** adj covered or treated with batter.

batter³ see under **bat**¹.

batter⁴ /bat'ər/ (building) n a slope (eg of the face of a structure) upwards and backwards. ◆ vi to slope in this way. [Origin doubtful]

batterie /bat-(ə-)rē/ (ballet) n a jump in which the dancer beats the calves together. [Fr, from battre to beat; see **batter**¹]
 ❑ **batterie de cuisine** /də kwē-zēn/ n (Fr) a set of cooking utensils.

battero see **ballow**.

battery /bat'ə-ri/ n a series of two or more electric cells arranged to produce or store electricity; a single voltaic or solar cell; the act of battering; a wound (Shakesp); a number of cannon or other offensive weapons with their equipment; the place on which cannon are mounted; a unit of artillery or its personnel; a collection or set of equipment; a combination of Leyden jars, lenses, or other apparatus; a battery of tests; a series (of questions); an attack against a person, beating or wounding by touching clothes or body (law); an arrangement of tiers of cages in which hens are kept, the eggs they lay running down into wire containers outside the cages; an arrangement of similarly restrictive compartments for rearing pigs or cattle intensively; utensils for preparing or serving meals (cf **batterie de cuisine**); the pitcher and catcher (baseball); the percussion section of an orchestra. [OFr batterie]
 ■ **battery of tests** (psychol) a set of tests covering various factors relevant to some end purpose, eg job selection. **cross batteries** two weapon batteries commanding the same spot from different directions. **masked battery** a battery out of the enemy's view.

battill old spelling of **battle**².

batting see **bat**¹.

battle¹ /bat'l/ n a contest between opposing armies, navies, air forces, etc; a fight or encounter; conflict, struggle (fig); a battalion (archaic). ◆ vi to fight; to struggle; to contend (with against or with). ◆ vt to contest; to dispose in battalions (archaic). [Fr bataille, from L battuālia fighting]
 ■ **batt'ler** n someone who struggles, esp resolutely against difficult circumstances; someone who scrapes a living by any means available (Aust and NZ).
 ❑ **batt'le-axe** or **-ax** n (also without hyphen) a kind of axe once used in battle; a domineering, usu older woman (inf). **battle-axe block** or **section** n (Aust and NZ) a plot of land without a street frontage, with access to and from the street via a drive or lane. **batt'lebus** n a coach forming a mobile base for a politician on tour. **batt'le-cruiser** n a large warship, the same size as a battleship but faster and with fewer guns. **batt'le-cry** n a war cry; a slogan. **batt'ledress** n a soldier's ordinary uniform. **battle fatigue** n (psychol) a psychological disorder caused by stress of combat (also fig). **batt'lefield** or **batt'leground** n (lit and fig) the place on which a battle is or was fought. **batt'le-piece** n a picture or description of a battle. **batt'leplane** n (obs) a large fighting aeroplane. **battle royal** n a general mêlée; a fierce fight (also fig). **batt'le-scarred** adj scarred in battle; well-worn, looking well used. **batt'leship** n a warship of the first class.
 ■ **do battle** (often fig) to fight. **half the battle** anything that brings one well on the way to success. **join battle** to engage in fighting.

battle² /bat'l/ adj (dialect) nourishing; fertile. ◆ vt and vi (archaic) to feed; to fatten; to make or become fertile. [Perh connected with ON bati improvement; see **batten**²]

battle³ /bat'l/ (obs) vt to furnish with battlements (esp in pap). [OFr batailler movable defences]

battledore or **battledoor** /bat'l-dör/ n (obs or archaic) a light bat for striking a shuttlecock; the game played with this; a wooden bat used for washing, etc; a hornbook. [Perh Sp batidor a beater, a washing beetle]
 ■ **not to know a B from a battledore** to be thoroughly ignorant.

battlement /bat'l-mənt/ n a wall or parapet with embrasures. [Same as **battle**³]
 ■ **batt'lemented** adj.

battology /ba-tol'ə-ji/ n futile repetition in speech or writing. [Gr battologiā stuttering, said to be from Battos, who consulted the Delphic oracle about his defect of speech (Herodotus 4.155), and legein to speak]
 ■ **battolog'ical** adj.

battre la campagne /ba-tr' la kā-pan'y'/ (Fr) to scour the country, to beat the bush.

batts see **bot**¹.

battue /ba-too', ba-tū' or bä-tü/ n a hunt in which animals are driven into some place for the convenience of the shooters; indiscriminate slaughter. [Fr, from battre to beat]

battuta /bät-too'tä/ (Ital) n a beat.
 ■ **a battuta** in strict time.

batty¹ see under **bat**².

batty² /bat'i/ n a West Indian slang word for (a person's) bottom. [From a pronunciation of **botty**]
 ❑ **batty boy** n (derog sl) a male homosexual.

batwing see under **bat**².

batwoman see under **batman**¹.

bauble /bö'bl/ n a trifling piece of finery; a round coloured decoration for a Christmas tree; a child's plaything; a jester's sceptre, a stick surmounted by a head with an ass's ears; a piece of childish fooling; a foolish person (Shakesp). [OFr babel, baubel toy, trinket]
 ■ **bau'bling** adj (Shakesp) trifling.

bauchle /bö'hhl/ (Scot) n a loose, down-at-heel, or badly worn shoe; a worn-out, useless or clumsy person or thing. ◆ vi to shamble. ◆ vt to make shapeless; to bungle or spoil. [Origin obscure]

baud¹ or **baud rate** /böd (rāt)/ (telegraphy) n a unit of signalling speed, given as the number of signal events per second; the speed at which computers pass information (eg by telephone line) to other computers, etc, where one baud equals one bit per second (comput). [Fr inventor JME Baudot (died 1903)]

baud² see **bawd**².

baudekin /böd'i-kin/ same as **baldachin**.

baudric, baudrick or **baudricke** /böd'rik/ same as **baldric**.

baudrons or **Baudrons** /böd'rəns/ (Scot) n quasi-proper name for the cat; also for the hare. [Origin obscure]

bauera /bow'ə-rə/ n a plant of the Bauera genus of evergreen shrubs with pink flowers (family Cunoniaceae) found in Australia. [F and FA Bauer, 19c Austrian botanical painters]

Bauhaus /bow'hows/ n a German school of art and architecture (1919–33) having as its aim the integration of art and technology in design. [Literally, building-house]

bauhinia /bō-hin'i-ə/ n a plant of the Bauhinia genus of tropical trees of the subfamily Caesalpinioideae. [J and G Bauhin, 17c Swiss botanists]

bauk, baulk same as **balk**.

baur see **bar**³.

bausond /bö'sənd/ (obs, Scot and N Eng) adj of animals, having white spots, esp on the forehead, or a white stripe down the face. [OFr bausant black-and-white spotted]
 ❑ **baus'on-faced** adj.

bauxite or **beauxite** /bök'sīt, -zīt or bö'zīt/ n a clay-like compound, the main ore of aluminium. [From Les Baux, near Arles, and **-ite** (3)]
 ■ **bauxitic** /-it'ik/ adj.

bavardage /bä-vär-däzh'/ n chattering, prattle. [Fr bavard garrulous, from bave drivel]

bavarois /bä-vär-wä'/ n a dessert of thickened and flavoured whipped cream. [Fr, Bavarian]

bavin /bav'in/ n a bundle of brushwood. [Origin unknown]
 ❑ **bavin wits** n pl (Shakesp) wits that blaze and die like bavins.

bawbee /bö-bē'/ (Scot) n a halfpenny; orig a silver coin worth three Scots pennies; (usu in pl) money. [Prob from a Scottish mint master (1538), Alexander Orrok of Sillebawbe]

bawble same as **bauble**.

bawcock /bö'kok/ (Shakesp) n a fine fellow. [From Fr beau fine, and coq a cock]

bawd¹ /böd/ n a female brothel-keeper or procuress; formerly, a male pander. [Prob ME bawdstrot pander, from OFr baldestrot, prob from bald bold, gay, and the root of **strut**¹]
 ■ **bawd'ily** adv. **bawd'iness** n. **bawd'ry** n procuring (obs); unchastity (archaic); lewd talk or writing (archaic). **bawd'y** adj lewd, sexually explicit. ◆ n bawdy talk or writing.
 ❑ **bawd'-born** adj (Shakesp) born of a bawd. **bawd'y-house** n (archaic) a brothel.

bawd² (Shakesp **baud**) /böd/ n a hare. [Perh **baudrons**]

bawdkin same as **baldachin**.

bawl /böl/ vt and vi to shout or cry out very loudly; to weep noisily. ◆ n a loud cry or shout. [Perh LL baulāre to bark, but cf Icel baula to low like a cow, from ON baula a cow]
 ■ **bawl'er** n. **bawl'ing** n.
 ■ **bawl out** (inf) to reprimand loudly and angrily.

bawley /bö'li/ (Essex and Kent) n a small fishing-smack. [Origin obscure]

bawn /bön/ n a fortification round a house; an enclosure for cattle. [Ir bábhun enclosure]

bawr see **bar**³.

baxter /bak'stər/ (obs) n a baker. [**bake**]

bay¹ /bā/ n an inlet of the sea with a wider opening than a gulf; an inward bend of the shore; a similar recess in a land form, eg in a mountain range. [Fr baie, from LL baia a harbour]

■ words derived from main entry word; ❑ compound words; ■ idioms and phrasal verbs

◻ **bay salt** *n* coarse-grained salt, *orig* from seawater.

■ **the Bay State** Massachusetts.

bay[2] /bā/ *n* the space between two columns, timbers, walls, etc; any recess or stall; a space for a vehicle to park; a space where vehicles can be loaded and unloaded (also **loading bay**); a passing-place in a military trench; a side-line in a railway station (also **bay'-line**); a compartment or section of an aircraft (eg *bomb bay*) or ship (eg *sick bay*); the space under one house gable (*Shakesp*). [OFr *baée*, from *baer* to gape, be open; prob connected with **bay**[1]]

◻ **bay platform** *n* a railway platform where a line ends in a station which also has continuing lines. **bay window** *n* any window forming a recess. **bay-win'dowed** *adj*.

bay[3] /bā/ *adj* reddish brown inclining to chestnut (of horses, *usu* with a black mane and tail). ◆ *n* a bay horse. [Fr *bai*, from L *badius* chestnut-coloured]

bay[4] /bā/ *n* the laurel tree; extended to other trees and shrubs, species of *Magnolia, Myrica*, etc; (in *pl*) an honorary garland or crown of victory, *orig* of laurel; hence (in *pl*), literary renown (*archaic*). [OFr *baie* a berry, from L *bāca*]

◻ **bay'berry** *n* the berry of the bay tree, or of candleberry; a tree (*Pimenta acris*) related to allspice. **bay leaf** *n* the dried leaf of the laurel tree (*Laurus nobilis*) used as a flavouring agent in cooking. **bay rum** *n* an aromatic liquid prepared from the leaves of *Pimenta acris*, used medicinally and cosmetically; this liquid mixed with certain other substances.

bay[5] /bā/ *vi* to bark or howl (*esp* of large dogs); to complain or demand vociferously (often with *for*). ◆ *vt* to bark or howl at; to utter by baying; to chase with barking; to bring to bay. ◆ *n* barking, baying (*esp* of a dog in pursuit); the combined cry of hounds in conflict with a hunted animal; the last stand of a hunted animal when it faces the hounds at close quarters (also *fig*). [Partly OFr *abai* barking, *bayer* to bark, partly OFr *bay* open-mouthed suspense, from LL *badāre* to open the mouth] ■ **bay (at) the moon** to make a futile gesture. **bring to bay** to force to make a stand. **keep at bay** to fight off; to prevent from coming closer. **stand** (or **be**) **at bay** to face the dogs at close quarters; to face one's pursuers.

bay[6] /bā/ or **bez** /bā or bāz/ *n* (in full **bay'-antler, -tine** or **bez'-antler, -tine**) the second tine of a deer's horn. [OFr *besantlier*, from *bes-* secondary (from L *bis* twice), and *antlier* antler]

bay[7] or **baye** /bā/ (*Spenser*) *vt* to bathe.

bayadère /bä-yä-der'/ *n* a Hindu dancing-girl; a woven, horizontally striped fabric. [Fr, from Port *bailadeira*]

Bayard[1] /bā'är(d)/ or Fr bä-yär/ *n* a type of knight 'without fear and without reproach'. [From the French knight *Bayard* (c.1473–1524)]

Bayard[2] /bā'ärd or -ərd/ *n* a horse famous in medieval legend; (without *cap*) a bay horse or a horse generally (*archaic*); a type of blind recklessness or bold ignorance.

baye see **bay**[7].

Bayes' theorem /bāz thē'ə-rəm/ *n* a statistical theorem of probability that enables estimates of probability to be continually revised with reference to observations of occurrences. [Thomas *Bayes* (1702–61), English mathematician] ■ **Bayes'ian** *adj*.

bayle see **bail**[5].

bayonet /bā'ə-nit or bä-ə-net'/ *n* a stabbing blade of steel that may be fixed to the muzzle of a firearm; military force; (in *pl*) soldiers armed with bayonets; (also **bayonet fitting**) a type of fitting for a light bulb, camera lens, etc, in which prongs on its side fit into slots to hold it in place. ◆ *vt* to stab with a bayonet; to force at the point of the bayonet. [Fr *baïonnette*, perh from *Bayonne* in France; or from OFr *bayon* arrow]

■ **bay'oneted** *adj* armed with a bayonet.

◻ **bayonet joint, socket**, etc *n* one with, or for, a bayonet fitting.

bayou /bī'oo/ (*US*) *n* the marshy offshoot of a lake or river. [Perh Fr *boyau* gut, or Choctaw *bāyuk* little river]

bayt a Spenserian spelling of **bate**[1]; also of **bait**.

bazaar or **bazar** /bə-zär'/ *n* an Eastern marketplace or exchange; a fair in imitation of an Eastern bazaar, often selling goods in aid of charity; a big shop. [Pers *bāzār* a market]

bazazz see **bezzazz**.

bazoo /bə-zoo'/ (*US sl*) *n* the mouth. [Du *bazuin* trumpet]

bazooka /bə-zoo'kə/ *n* an anti-tank gun for rocket-driven projectiles; *orig* a crude wind instrument with a slide, used for humorous purposes; a rocket launcher situated on the wing of an aeroplane. [Invented name]

bazouki see **bouzouki**.

bazzazz see **bezzazz**.

BB *abbrev*: Boys' Brigade.

BB or **2B** *symbol*: very black (on lead pencils).

bb *abbrev*: books.

BBA *abbrev*: British Bankers' Association.

BBB *symbol*: (on a pencil) blacker than a BB pencil.

BBBC or **BBB of C** *abbrev*: British Boxing Board of Control.

BBC *abbrev*: British Broadcasting Corporation.

BBFC *abbrev*: British Board of Film Classification.

BB gun /bē bē gun/ *n* a type of air-gun. [*BB*, grade of pellets that it fires]

bbl *abbrev*: barrels.

BBQ *abbrev*: barbecue.

BBS (*comput*) *abbrev*: Bulletin Board System, a computerized forum for mail and information, now generally obsolete.

BBSRC *abbrev*: Biotechnology and Biological Sciences Research Council.

BC *abbrev*: Battery Commander; (also **B.C.**) before Christ (used in dating to indicate the number of years before the year once thought to be that of Christ's birth); Board of Control; British Columbia (Canadian province); British Council.

BCC *abbrev*: British Chambers of Commerce.

bcc *abbrev*: blind carbon copy, used to denote a copy sent without the knowledge of the main recipient.

BCD see **binary-coded decimal** under **binary**.

BCE *abbrev*: before the Common Era, used (to be culturally neutral) instead of BC in numbering the years before the current era.

BCF *abbrev*: British Cycling Federation; bromochlorodifluoromethane, a compound formerly used in fire extinguishers.

BCG® *n* a strain of tubercle bacillus, used for inoculation against tuberculosis. [Initials of *Bacillus Calmette–Guérin*]

BCh *abbrev*: *Baccalaureus Chirurgiae* (*L*), Bachelor of Surgery.

BCL *abbrev*: Bachelor of Civil Law.

BCom or **BComm** *abbrev*: Bachelor of Commerce.

BCS *abbrev*: British Computer Society.

BD *abbrev*: Bachelor of Divinity; bank draft; Bangladesh (IVR); bills discounted.

bd *abbrev*: board; bond; bound.

BDA *abbrev*: British Deaf Association; British Dental Association; British Diabetic Association (also known as Diabetes UK); British Dyslexia Association.

Bde *abbrev*: Brigade.

bdellium /del'i-əm/ *n* a gum from trees of the genus *Commiphora*; used to translate, but *prob* unconnected with, Heb *b'dōlakh* (Bible, Genesis 2.12; meaning unknown). [L, from Gr *bdellion*]

BDI *abbrev*: *Bundesverband der Deutschen Industrie* (*Ger*), Federation of German Industries.

Bdr *abbrev*: bombardier.

BDS *abbrev*: Bachelor of Dental Surgery; Barbados (IVR).

bds *abbrev*: boards.

BE *abbrev*: Bachelor of Education; Bachelor of Engineering; bill of exchange; Board of Education.

Be (*chem*) *symbol*: beryllium.

be *abbrev*: bill of exchange.

be /bē/ *vi* (*prp* be'ing; *pap* been /bēn or bin/; *present subjunctive* be; *archaic* and *dialect present indicative* be (see am, art[2], is, are[1]); for *pat* see was, wast[1], were, wert) to live; to exist; to happen, take place; to occupy a position in space; to have the state or quality mentioned; to remain or continue without change; (with *infinitive*) must, need (to); 'be' also helps form some compound tenses, such as continuous and passive. [OE *bēon*; Ger *bin* (1st pers); Gaelic *bi* exist; Welsh *byw* live; Gr *phyein* produce, grow; L *fuī* I was, *fīō* I become; Sans *bhavati* he is; orig to grow]

◻ **be'-all** *n* (*Shakesp*) all that is to be. **be-all and end-all** *n* the supreme aim or issue.

■ **be that as it may** see under **may**[1].

be- /bi-/ *pfx* used (1) to form words with the sense of around, on all sides, in all directions, thoroughly, as in *besiege*; (2) to form verbs from adjectives and nouns (often in facetious modern coinages, eg *bejerseyed*); (3) formerly, to make intransitive verbs transitive, as in *bespeak*. [OE *bi-*, weak form of *bī* (see **by**[1])]

BEA *abbrev*: formerly, British European Airways.

BEAB *abbrev*: British Electrotechnical Approvals Board.

beach /bēch/ *n* the shore of a sea or of a lake, *esp* when sandy or pebbly; a marginal terrace formed by waves; the strand. ◆ *vt* to drive or haul up on a beach. [Orig a dialect word for shingle]

■ **beached** adj having a beach; driven on a beach. **beach'y** adj pebbly.
❏ **beach'-ball** n a large, usu inflatable, colourful ball for playing games on a beach. **beach boy** n a male beach attendant; a beach bum. **beach buggy** n an open vehicle with huge tyres, used for driving on beaches. **beach bum** n (inf) a young man who loafs about on the beach. **beach'comber** /-kōm-/ n someone who gathers jetsam, etc on beaches; a long rolling wave; a loafer about the wharfs in Pacific seaports; a settler on a Pacific island who maintains himself by pearl-fishing. **beach'combing** n. **beach'front** adj of property, facing the beach. **beach'head** n an area held on an enemy's shore for the purpose of landing. **beach'-master** n an officer in charge of disembarking troops. **beach plum** n a shrub related to the plum (*Prunus Maritima*) native to Atlantic coastal areas of N America; its edible fruit. **beach'side** adj. **beach'wear** n casual clothing designed for wearing on a beach.

beach-la-mar see **Bislama**.

beacon /bē'kən/ n a fire on high ground lit as a signal, eg to warn of danger; a hill on which it could be lit; a buoy, lighthouse, etc marking a rock or shoal in navigable waters; a light or other signal to guide aircraft; a sign marking a street crossing, eg a **Belisha** /bə-lē'shə or bə-lish'ə/ **beacon** (Leslie Hore-*Belisha*, British minister of transport who introduced it in 1934); a wireless transmitter in which the radiation is concentrated in one or more narrow beams, so as to act as a guide to shipping or aircraft; anything that warns of danger. ◆ vt to act as a beacon to; to light up; to mark by beacons. ◆ vi to shine like a beacon. [OE *bēacen* a beacon, a sign]
❏ **beacon school** n a school identified as a centre of excellence and providing guidance to other schools in its area.
■ **floating beacon** a lightship.

bead /bēd/ n a small ball strung with others in a rosary, for counting prayers; a prayer (obs); a small ball or similar ornament pierced for stringing to form a necklace, etc; a bead-like drop; the front sight of a gun; a narrow moulding orig of semicircular section, sometimes broken into bead-like parts, now in various shapes, used esp for edging, covering small gaps, etc; the flange of a tyre. ◆ vt to provide with beads or beading. ◆ vi to form a bead or beads. [OE *gebed* prayer; see **bid²**]
■ **bead'ed** adj having beads or a bead; in bead-like form. **bead'ing** n bead moulding; work in beads. **bead'y** adj bead-like, small and bright (as eyes); covered with beads or bubbles.
❏ **bead'-house** n orig a chapel; an almshouse whose inmates were required to pray for the founder's soul. **bead'-proof** adj of such proof or strength as to carry beads or bubbles after shaking, as alcoholic liquors. **bead'-roll** n orig a list of the dead to be prayed for, hence a list of names, a long series; a rosary. **beads'man**, **bedes'man** or **beads'woman** n a person bound or endowed to pray for others; a licensed beggar (Scot). **beady eye** n used to suggest distrustful attentiveness to another's behaviour (esp in the phrase *keep a beady eye on*). **bead'y-eyed** adj with small round bright eyes; observant, sharp-eyed.
■ **draw a bead on** (inf) to take aim at. **tell one's beads** to say one's prayers.

beadle /bē'dl/ n a mace-bearer, esp (Oxford and Cambridge Universities **bedel** or **bedell** /-del'* or *bēd'/) a vice-chancellor's; a minor official of a church, college, etc; formerly a parish officer with the power of punishing minor offenders; in Scotland, the church officer attending on the minister; a messenger or crier of a court (obs). [OE *bydel*, from *bēodan* to proclaim, to bid; affected by OFr form *bedel*]
■ **bead'ledom** or **bead'lehood** n stupid officiousness. **bead'leship**, **bed'elship** or **bed'ellship** n the office of beadle or bedel.

beadman, **bedeman** old forms of **beadsman** (see under **bead**).

beady see under **bead**.

beagle /bē'gl/ n a small hound; sometimes, a harrier (dog); a bailiff; a small kind of shark; a spy (obs). ◆ vi to hunt with beagles. [Ety unknown; poss OFr *beegueulle* clamourer, from *beer* to gape, and *gueule* throat]
■ **bea'gler** n. **bea'gling** n hunting with beagles.

beak /bēk/ n a bird's bill; a hard or sharp snout; a nose (joc); a pointed projection; in the ancient galley an iron point projecting from the bow for piercing the enemy's vessel; a magistrate, schoolmaster or schoolmistress (old sl). [OFr *bec*, from L *beccus* (recorded by Suetonius) a cock's bill]
■ **beaked** /bēkt/ adj. **beak'y** adj.
❏ **beak'-iron** same as **bick-iron**.

beaker /bē'kər/ n a large drinking bowl or cup, or its contents; a deep glass or other vessel used by chemists, generally with a lip for pouring; a usu plastic tumbler; one of a set of similar cylindrical-shaped objects, a child's toy. [ON *bikarr*, prob from LL *bicārium*, or *bīcārium*, appar from Gr *bīkos* a drinking bowl]

■ **beak'erful** n (pl **beak'erfuls**) as much as fills a beaker.
❏ **Beaker Folk** n pl a round-headed, heavy-browed, square-jawed people that appeared in Britain at the dawn of the Bronze Age, makers of round barrows in which bell-shaped pottery beakers are often found.

beam /bēm/ n a large and straight piece of timber or steel forming one of the main structural members of a building, etc; any of the transverse pieces of framing extending across a ship's hull; the part of a balance from which the scales hang; the stem, or main part of a deerhorn, an anchor or a plough; either of the two wooden cylinders in a loom; a raised horizontal bar on which gymnasts perform balancing exercises (gym); a great fault (fig; from the metaphor of the mote and the beam in the Bible, Matthew 7.3); a tree (obs except in *hornbeam*, *whitebeam*, etc); the greatest width of a ship or boat; breadth; a shaft or ray of light or other radiations; a gleam; a broad smile, lighting up the face. ◆ vt to send forth; to place on a beam; to transmit or direct, eg by beam system. ◆ vi to shine; to smile radiantly. [OE *bēam* tree, stock of a tree, ray of light; Ger *Baum* tree; perh related to Gr *phȳma* a growth, from *phyein* to grow]
■ **beam'er** n a workman or machine that puts yarn on the beam of a loom; a fast, head-high ball (cricket); a beam trawler. **beam'ily** adv radiantly. **beam'iness** n radiance; breadth. **beam'ing** n and adj. **beam'ingly** adv. **beam'ish** adj radiant. **beam'less** adj without beams; emitting no rays. **beam'let** n a little beam. **beam'y** adj shining; radiant; massive like a weaver's beam; broad.
❏ **beam compass** n an instrument consisting of a beam and adjustable legs, for drawing extra-large circles. **beam'-ends** n pl the ends of the transverse beams of a ship. **beam'-engine** n a steam-engine with a beam connecting the piston-rod and the crank of the wheel-shaft or the buckets of a pump. **beam sea** n one rolling against the ship's side. **beam splitter** n a device used to divide a beam of light, radiation, etc into two or more separate beams. **beam system** n a system whereby, with the aid of reflectors, short wireless waves are projected (like a lighthouse beam) in a particular direction, not radiated in all directions. **beam trawl** n a trawling net kept open by a beam along its upper lip, resting on runners. **beam trawler** n. **beam trawling** n. **beam tree** n a pleonastic name for the whitebeam. **beam weapon** n any weapon whose destructive force consists of a beam of energy such as subatomic particles.
■ **abaft** or **before the beam** behind or before a line across the greatest width of a ship. **broad in the beam** wide-hipped. **fly the beam** to fly an aircraft in the direction shown by a radio beam. **lee beam** the side away from, or towards, the wind. **off the beam** off the course shown by a radio beam; off the right track (fig). **on her beam-ends** of a ship, so much inclined to one side that the beams become nearly vertical. **on one's beam-ends** in acute distress, destitute. **on the beam** in the direction of a ship's beams, at right angles to her course; on the course shown by a radio beam; on the right track (fig). **on the port** (or **starboard**) **beam** applied to any distant point out at sea, at right angles to the keel, and on the left (or right) side. **ride the beam** same as **fly the beam** (see above). **weather beam** same as **lee beam** (see above).

BEAMA abbrev: British Electrotechnical and Allied Manufacturers' Association.

bean /bēn/ n the name of several kinds of leguminous plants and their seeds, esp the common or broad bean (*Vicia faba*) and the French, kidney or haricot bean (*Phaseolus vulgaris*); applied also to the seeds of other plants, from their bean-like form, such as coffee; a coin (obs except in **not a bean** (inf) not a cent, no money at all); (in pl) little or nothing at all (N Am inf); the head (inf); a component of a Java program that can be reused in other programs (comput). ◆ vt (inf) to hit on the head. [OE *bēan*, Ger *Bohne*]
■ **bean'ery** n (US sl) a cheap restaurant. **bean'ie** n (inf) a small, close-fitting hat. **bean'o** n (pl **bean'os**) (inf) a beanfeast, a rowdy jollification; bingo.
❏ **bean'bag** n a small cloth bag containing dried beans or the like, used in games, etc; a large cushion filled eg with chips or balls of plastic foam, used as seating (also **beanbag chair**). **bean caper** n a shrub (genus *Zygophyllum*) of steppe and desert whose flower-buds are used as capers. **bean counter** n (inf) an accountant, esp one considered parsimonious or unsupportive of creativity. **bean curd** n a soft paste made from soya beans, used in Chinese and vegetarian cookery. **bean'feast** n an annual dinner given by employers to their workers; a jollification. **bean'-king** n the king of the festivities on Twelfth Night, finder of a bean hidden in the Twelfth cake. **bean'pole** n a supporting pole up which a bean plant climbs; a tall, very thin person (inf). **bean sprout**, **bean shoot** n the young shoot of the mung bean or certain other beans, used as a vegetable esp in Chinese cookery. **bean'stalk** n the stem of a bean plant. **bean tree** n a name given to several trees, as Moreton Bay chestnut, carob tree, and catalpa.
■ **full of beans** (inf) energetic and in high spirits. **give someone beans** (archaic) to treat someone severely. **know how many beans make five** (inf) to be fully alert, know what's what. **old bean** (inf) an

affectionate form of address, *usu* to a man. **spill the beans** (*inf*) to divulge information, or a secret, whether inadvertently or not.

bear[1] /*bār*/ *vt* (**bear'ing**; **bore** (*archaic* **bare**); **borne** /*börn*/) to carry; to have; to convey; to remove from the board in the final stage of the game (*backgammon*); to sustain or support; to thrust or drive; to endure, tolerate; to admit of; to purport; to behave or conduct (oneself); to bring forth, give birth to (*pap* **born** /*börn*/ in passive uses except with *by*); to display on one's heraldic shield, to be entitled to (*heraldry*). ◆ *vi* to suffer; to be patient; (with *on* or *upon*) to have reference to; to press (*on* or *upon*); to lie in, or take, a direction; to be capable of sustaining weight; to be productive. ◆ *n* (*Spenser* **beare** /*bēr*/) a burden; also (*Spenser*) a bier (see **bier**). [OE *beran*; Gothic *bairan*, L *ferre*, Gr *pherein*; Sans *bharati* he carries]

■ **bear'able** *adj* able to be borne or endured. **bear'ableness** *n*. **bear'ably** *adv*. **bear'er** *n* a person who or that which bears; the actual holder of a cheque, etc; a person who helps to carry the coffin at a funeral, a pall-bearer; a carrier or messenger; formerly in India, a personal, household or hotel servant. **bear'ing** *n* demeanour; direction; a supporting surface; relation, relevance; a heraldic device or coat of arms; the part of a machine that bears friction, *esp* part of a shaft or axle and its support (sometimes in *pl*; see **ball-bearing** under **ball**[1]).

□ **bearer bill**, **bond**, **security**, etc *n* a bond, etc which has been made out to be payable to the person in possession of it. **bearing cloth** *n* (*hist*) a gown worn at a child's baptism. **bearing rein** *n* a fixed rein between the bit and the saddle, by which a horse's head is held up and its neck made to arch.

■ **bear a hand** see under **hand**. **bear away** to sail away; to carry away. **bear down** to overthrow; to press downwards; in childbirth, to exert downward muscular pressure; (with *upon* or *towards*) to sail with the wind (towards); (with *upon*) to approach (someone or something) rapidly and purposefully. **bear hard** (*Shakesp*) to have ill-will to. **bear hard** or **heavily upon** (*lit* and *fig*) to press heavily on; to oppress, afflict. **bear in hand** to make out, maintain (*archaic*); to keep in expectation, to flatter someone's hopes (*Shakesp*). **bear in mind** to remember (that); to think of, take into consideration. **bear in upon** (*usu* in *passive*) to impress upon, or to make realize, *esp* by degrees. **bear out** to corroborate. **bear up** to keep up one's spirits. **bear up for** to sail towards (a place). **bear with** to make allowance for, be patient with. **bear witness** see **witness**. **bring to bear** to bring into operation (*against* or *upon*). **find**, **get** (or **lose**) **one's bearings** to ascertain (or to become uncertain of) one's position or orientation.

bear[2] /*bār*/ *n* a heavy carnivorous animal with long shaggy hair and hooked claws; also applied to other unrelated animals, such as the koala; a teddy bear; a person who sells stocks for delivery at a future date, anticipating a fall in price, *opp* to *bull* (the old phrase *a bearskin jobber* suggests an origin in the proverbial phrase, *to sell the bearskin before one has caught the bear*; *stock exchange*); the name of two constellations, **the Great Bear** and **the Little Bear** (Ursa Major and Minor); any rude, rough or ill-mannered fellow. ◆ *vi* (*stock exchange*) to act as a bear. ◆ *vt* (*stock exchange*) to lower the price of (a stock) or depress (a market) by selling speculatively. [OE *bera*; Ger *Bär*; Du *beer*; appar from an Indo-European root *bhero-* brown]

■ **bear'ish** *adj* like a bear in manners; inclining towards, anticipating, a fall in price (*stock exchange*). **bear'ishly** *adv*. **bear'ishness** *n*.

□ **bear-animal'cule** *n* a tardigrade, a kind of minute arthropod with four pairs of stumpy legs. **bear'-baiting** *n* the former sport of setting dogs to attack a bear. **bear'berry** *n* a trailing plant (genus *Arctostaphylos*) of the family Ericaceae; extended to various plants. **bear'bine** *n* a bindweed. **bear'cat** *n* the lesser or red panda. **bear garden** *n* an enclosure for bear-baiting or for exhibiting bears; a turbulent assembly. **bear hug** *n* a hold in which one wraps one's arms tightly around one's opponent's arms and upper body (*wrestling*); a similar tight hug. **bear'-lead** *vt* to lead about, eg a performing bear, but also more *gen* to supervise, act as tutor to. **bear market** *n* (*stock exchange*) a market in which prices are falling. **bear pit** *n* an enclosure for bears. **bear's'-breech** *n* acanthus. **bear's'-ear** *n* auricula. **bear's'-foot** *n* black hellebore. **bear'skin** *n* the pelt of a bear; a shaggy woollen cloth for overcoats; the high fur cap worn by the Guards in the UK. **bear'ward** *n* a warden or keeper of bears.

bear[3] or **bere** /*bēr*/ *n* barley; in Scotland, now the little-grown four-rowed (really six-rowed) variety. [OE *bere*]

bear[4] see **bere**[2].

bearbine see under **bear**[2].

beard /*bērd*/ *n* the hair that grows on the chin and cheeks of a man's face; the tuft on the lower jaw of a goat, seal, etc; a fish's barbel; an awn or thread-like spike as on the ears of barley (*bot*); a tuft of hairs; a barb of a hook, an arrow, etc; the gills of an oyster, etc; a woman who escorts a homosexual man to give the impression that he is heterosexual (*sl*). ◆ *vt* to oppose resolutely or with effrontery; to take by the beard. [OE; Ger *Bart*, Russ *boroda*]

■ **beard'ed** *adj* having a beard; prickly; awned; barbed. **beard'ie** *n* (*inf*) a bearded person. **beard'less** *adj* having no beard; young, immature.

□ **bearded collie** *n* a breed of collie dog with a long coat and a tuft of hair on its chin. **bearded dragon** or **bearded lizard** *n* a large Australian lizard (*Amphibolus barbatus*) with an inflatable pouch beneath its jaw. **bearded tit** *n* a small bird that inhabits reed beds. **bearded vulture** *n* the lammergeier. **beard'-grass** *n* a kind of bearded grass (genus *Polypogon*).

beare see **bear**[1].

béarnaise /*bā-ar-nez'*/ or **béarnaise sauce** /*sös'*/ (also with *cap*) *n* a sauce made from egg yolks, butter, shallots, tarragon, chervil and wine vinegar. [Fr *béarnaise* (fem of *béarnais*) of Béarn, region of SW France]

bearward see under **bear**[2].

beast /*bēst*/ *n* an irrational animal, as opposed to a human being; a four-footed animal; a brutal person; anything beastly (*inf*); a police officer (*sl*). ◆ *vt* (*milit sl*) to subject (a recruit) to extreme tests of physical and mental stress. [OFr *beste* (Fr *bête*), from L *bestia*]

■ **beast'hood** *n* the state or nature of a beast. **beast'ie** *n* (*orig Scot*) a *dimin* form of **beast**, the four-footed animal; an insect, spider, etc (*inf*). **beast'ily** *adv* (*Shelley*) bestially. **beast'like** *adj* (also *adv*). **beast'liness** *n*. **beast'ly** *adj* vile, disagreeable (*inf*); like a beast in actions or behaviour, bestial. ◆ *adv* abominably, frightfully (*inf*); brutishly.

□ **beast fable** *n* a story in which animals behave like humans. **beast'ly-head** *n* (*Spenser*) personality or self of a beast. **beast of burden** *n* an animal, eg a donkey or bullock, used to carry or pull loads. **beast of prey** *n* one that devours other animals, *esp* higher animals, applied *usu* to the Carnivora.

■ **mark of the Beast** a stamp on the forehead or right hand of a worshipper of **the Beast** (Antichrist) as in the Bible, Revelation 13; hence a sign of whatever was considered to be of the Antichrist, or (loosely) evil or even bad manners. **number of the beast** 666, the apocalyptic number. **the beast with two backs** a man and a woman in the act of having sexual intercourse.

beastings same as **beestings**.

beat /*bēt*/ *vt* (**beat'ing**; **beat**; **beat'en** or now (rarely) **beat**) to strike repeatedly; to pound; to form (a path, track, etc) by frequent use of the same route; to batter; to whip up or switch; to flap; to strike (bushes, undergrowth, etc) in order to rouse game; to thrash; to defeat, to frustrate; to forestall; to be too difficult for; to outdo, excel; to drive or thrust (back, down, off, etc); to spread (eg gold) flat and thin by beating with a tool; to mark (time) with a baton, etc; to break or bruise (*Bible*). ◆ *vi* to give strokes repeatedly; to flap; to pulsate; to impinge; to mark time in music; to swindle (*US*); to sail as close as possible to directly into the wind. ◆ *n* a recurrent stroke, its sound, or its moment, eg of a watch, verse, the pulse, or a conductor's baton; the rhythmic base unit in music, *usu* grouped into bars; pulsation, *esp* that heard when two notes nearly in tune are sounded together; a round or course, such as a policeman's; an area of land or stretch of riverbank on which sportsmen hunt or fish; a place of resort; the act of beating in order to rouse game. ◆ *adj* worn-out, exhausted (*inf*); relating to beatniks (*inf*); affected with bursitis (eg *beat elbow* or *knee*). [OE *bēatan*, pat *bēot*]

■ **beat'able** *adj*. **beat'en** *adj* made smooth or hard by beating or treading; trite; worn by use; exhausted and dispirited. **beat'er** *n* a person who or thing which beats or strikes; a person who rouses or beats up game; a crushing or mixing instrument. **beat'ing** *n* the act of striking; a thrashing; a defeat; pulsation or throbbing; the rousing of game. **beatnik** /*bēt'nik*/ *n* one of the **beat generation** (*orig* in *US*), bohemian poets, etc who, in the 1950s, dissociated themselves from the aims of contemporary society; a young person whose behaviour, dress, etc is unconventional.

□ **beat'box** *n* (*inf*) an electronic drum machine; a ghetto-blaster. ◆ *vi* to imitate an electronic drum machine using the voice. **beat'-'em-up** *n* (*inf*) a type of computer game in which an unarmed character has to fight against several enemies. **beat music** *n* popular music with a very pronounced rhythm. **beat'-up** *adj* (*inf*) dilapidated through excessive use.

■ **beat about the bush** see under **bush**[1]. **beat a retreat** to retreat, *orig* to beat the drum as a signal for retreat (**beat the retreat** to perform the military ceremony (**beating the retreat**) consisting of marching and military music *usu* performed at dusk, *orig* marking the recall of troops to their quarters); to go away in a hurry, *esp* to avoid punishment or unpleasantness. **beat down** of a buyer, to try to reduce (the price of goods), to persuade (the seller) to settle for less. **beat it** (*sl*) to make off hastily or furtively; (often as *imperative*) go away! **beat off** to overcome or repel. **beat one's brains** or **beat one's brains out** to puzzle about something. **beat one's breast** to show extravagant signs of grief. **beat out** to flatten or reduce in thickness by beating. **beat someone's brains out** (*sl*) to kill by hitting repeatedly on the head; to subject to a vicious beating. **beat someone to it** to manage to do something before someone else can. **beat the air** to fight to no

purpose, or against an imaginary enemy. **beat the bounds** to trace out boundaries in a perambulation, certain objects in the line of journey being formally struck. **beat the clock** to do or finish something within the time allowed. **beat the pants** or **socks off** (inf) to defeat thoroughly. **beat the retreat** see **beat a retreat** above. **beat up** to pound or whip into froth, paste, a mixture, etc; to put up game, by beating the bushes, etc; to alarm by a sudden attack; (also in US **beat up on**) to thrash, to subject to a violent and brutal attack (inf); to disturb; to arouse; to go about in quest of anything; to make way against wind or tide. (**it**) **beats me** (inf) I have no idea what the answer is. **take a beating** (inf) to suffer physical or verbal chastisement. **take some** (or **a lot of**) **beating** (inf) to be of very high quality, ie to be difficult to surpass.

beatae memoriae /bi-ā'tē me-mō'ri-ē, also -mö', or be-ä'tī me-mo'ri-ī/ (L) of blessed memory.

beath /bēdh/ (Spenser) vt to bathe, heat. [OE bethian to foment]

beatify /bē-at'i-fī/ vt (**beat'ifying**; **beat'ified**) to make blessed or happy; to declare to be in the enjoyment of eternal happiness in heaven, and therefore entitled to public reverence (RC). [L beātus blessed, and facere to make]
■ **beatific** /bē-ə-tif'ik/ or **beatif'ical** adj making supremely happy; revealing supreme happiness. **beatif'ically** adv. **beatifica'tion** n the act of beatifying; a declaration by the Pope that a person is blessed in heaven, authorizing a certain definite form of public reverence payable to them, the first step to canonization (RC).
■ **beatific vision** a glimpse of the glory of heaven.

beati pacifici /bi-ā'tī pa-sif'i-sī or be-ä'tē pa-kif'i-kē/ (L) blessed are the peacemakers.

beatitude /bē-at'i-tūd/ n heavenly happiness; happiness of the highest kind; a title given to patriarchs in the Orthodox Churches; (in pl) the sayings of Christ in Matthew 5, declaring certain classes of person to be blessed (Christianity). [L beātitūdō, from beātus blessed]

beatnik see under **beat**.

beatus ille /bē-ā'tŭs or bā-ä'tŭs il'ā/ (L) happy the man (literally, happy he).

beau /bō/ n (pl **beaux** or **beaus** /bōz/) a man attentive to dress or fashion (old); a fop or dandy; a lover, boyfriend. Cf **belle**. [Fr beau, bel, from L bellus fine, gay]
■ **beau'ish** adj.
❏ **beau garçon** /gär-sɔ̄/ n a handsome man; a dandy. **beau geste** /zhest/ n a gracious gesture. **beau ideal** /ī-dē'əl or ē-dā-äl/ n ideal beauty; a type or embodiment of the highest excellence. **beau jour** /zhoor/ n a fine day, good times. **beau monde** /mɔ̄d/ n the world of fashion and high society. **beau-pere** /bū-pēr'/ n (Fr père father; obs) a term of courtesy for father, used esp of ecclesiastical persons; (OFr per equal, peer) a companion (Spenser). **beaux arts** /bō-zär/ n pl the fine arts; (with caps) a decorative classical style of architecture, especially popular in 19c France. **beaux esprits** /-zes-prē/ see **bel esprit**. **beaux yeux** /-zyø/ n pl fine eyes; a pretty woman.

beaufet or **beauffet** /bu-fet'/ n obsolete forms of **buffet**[1] (sideboard, cupboard).

beaufin an over-sophisticated spelling of **biffin**.

Beaufort scale /bō'fərt skāl/ n a scale of wind velocity, with 0 for calm, 12 to 17 for hurricane. [Devised by Sir Francis Beaufort (1774–1857), English admiral and hydrographer]

Beaujolais /bō'zho-lā/ n a red or white wine of east central France. [From Beaujolais, a subdivision of Lyonnais]

beaumontague or **beaumontage** /bō-mon-tāg' or -mon'tij/ n a composition for hiding cracks and holes in wood or iron. [Perh from Elie de Beaumont (1798–1874), French geologist]

Beaune /bōn/ n a red or white wine from Beaune in E France.

beauté du diable /bō-tā dü dyä'bl'/ (Fr) n an irresistible or overpowering beauty; an attractiveness which the charm and sparkle of youth give to an otherwise unattractive person.

beauty /bū'ti/ n the quality that gives pleasure to the sight, or aesthetic pleasure generally; a particular grace or excellence; a beautiful person (often ironic), esp a woman; beautiful women as a group (obs); a very fine specimen of its kind (inf); the good feature (of) (inf); (in pl) beautiful passages or extracts; another name for **bottomness** (see under **bottom**). ◆ vt (**beau'tying**; **beau'tied**; Shakesp) to make beautiful. ◆ interj (Aust and NZ) an enthusiastic expression of approval (also Aust, NZ and Scot **you beauty**). [OFr biaute (Fr beauté), from LL bellitās, -ātis, from L bellus]
■ **beaut** n (sl) someone or something exceptionally beautiful or remarkable. ◆ adj and interj (esp Aust) excellent, fine. **beau'teous** /bū'ti-əs/ adj a bookish word for beautiful. **beau'teously** adv. **beau'teousness** n. **beautician** /bū-tish'ən/ n a person professionally engaged in hairdressing, facial make-up, manicuring and other beauty treatments. **beautifica'tion** n. **beau'tifier** n a person who or something which beautifies or makes beautiful. **beau'tiful** adj good-

looking, attractive; with qualities that give pleasure or delight to the senses, esp the eye and ear, or which awaken admiration in the mind; very enjoyable, excellent (inf). **beau'tifully** adv. **beau'tify** vt to make beautiful; to grace; to adorn. ◆ vi (rare) to become beautiful, or more beautiful.
❏ **beauty contest** n a competition held for the selection of a beauty queen. **beauty parlour** or **salon** n an establishment which offers hairdressing, manicuring, face-massaging and other beauty treatments. **beauty queen** n a woman who is voted the most attractive or best-proportioned in a competition. **beauty sleep** n sleep, esp the sleep before midnight, considered the most refreshing. **beauty spot** n a patch placed on the face to heighten beauty; a birthmark resembling such a patch; a foil to set off something else; a scene of outstanding beauty.
■ **the beautiful people** (also with caps) the rich, attractive and fashionable members of a society.

beaux see **beau**.

beauxite see **bauxite**.

beaver[1] /bē'vər/ n an amphibious rodent (genus Castor); its valuable fur; a hat of beaver fur or a substitute material; a glove of beaver fur; a heavy woollen cloth; a boy belonging to the most junior branch of the scout movement (also **Beaver Scout**); the female pubic area or genitalia (vulgar sl, orig US). [OE befer, beofor; Du bever, Ger Biber, Gaelic beaghar, L fiber]
■ **beav'ery** n a place where beavers are kept.
❏ **beav'erboard** or (US) **Beaverboard**® n a building-board of wood fibre. **beaver lamb** n lambskin dyed to look like beaver fur. **beaver rat** n the coypu; the musquash; the Australian water rat of the genus Hydromys. **beav'er-tree** or **beav'er-wood** n a species of magnolia whose bark beavers eat.
■ **beaver away** (inf) to work very hard (at). **mountain beaver** the sewellel.

beaver[2] /bē'vər/ n in medieval armour, the covering for the lower part of the face, the visor being that for the upper part (later the movable beaver was confused with the visor); a beard or bearded man (sl). [OFr bavière child's bib, from bave slaver]
■ **beav'ered** adj.

bebeeru /bi-bē'roo/ n the greenheart tree of Guyana. [Native name]
■ **bebee'rine** /-rin or -rēn/ n an alkaloid yielded by its bark, a substitute for quinine.

bebop /bē'bop/ n a variety of jazz music, from about 1940, which added new harmonies, melodic patterns, and rhythms to accepted jazz characteristics (also vi). [Imit of two quavers in the rhythm; see also **bop**[1]]
■ **bē'bopper** n.

bebung /bā'bŭng/ (music) n a tremolo effect produced on the clavichord by fluctuating the pressure of the finger on the key. [Ger]

becall /bi-köl'/ vt to call names. [be- (1)]

becalm /bi-käm'/ vt to make calm, still or quiet. [be- (2)]
■ **becalmed'** adj motionless from lack of wind.

became /bi-kām'/ pat of **become**.

bécasse /bā-käs'/ (Fr) n a woodcock.

because /bi-koz' or bi-köz'/ adv and conj for the reason that; on account (of). [by and cause]

beccaccia /bāk-kä'chä/ (Ital) n a woodcock.

beccafico /be-ka-fē'kō/ n (pl **beccafi'cos**) a garden warbler or related bird, considered a delicacy esp by the Italians. [Ital, from beccare to peck, and fico a fig]

béchamel, béchamel sauce or **bechamel** /bā'shə-mel (sös) or besh'ə-mel/ n a white sauce, traditionally flavoured with onion and herbs and sometimes enriched with cream. [Fr; from the name of a steward of Louis XIV]

bechance /bi-chäns'/ (archaic) vi to happen by chance (to); to befall. ◆ adv by chance; accidentally. [be- (1), and chance (vi)]

becharm /bi-chärm'/ vt to charm; to enchant. [be- (1)]

bêche-de-mer /besh'də-mer/ n the trepang or sea-slug, a species of Holothuria, much esteemed in China as a food delicacy; beach-la-mar (qv). [Fr, from Port bicho do mar 'sea-worm', the sea-slug]

Becher's Brook /bē'cherz brŭk/ n a notoriously difficult jump in the Grand National steeplechase; a particularly difficult or critical obstacle, problem or possible stumbling-block.

beck[1] /bek/ n a sign with the finger or head; a nod; a bow or curtsey (Scot). ◆ vi to make such a sign. ◆ vt to call by a nod. [A contraction of **beckon**]
■ **at someone's beck** (**and call**) in attendance and subject to someone's will.

beck[2] /bek/ (N Eng dialect) n a stream. [ON bekkr; Ger Bach]

becke /bek/ (Spenser) n same as **beak**.

■ words derived from main entry word; ❏ compound words; ■ idioms and phrasal verbs

becket /bek'it/ (naut) n a loop of rope having a knot at one end and an eye at the other; a large hook, or a wooden bracket used to keep loose tackle or spars in a convenient place. [Perh Du bogt, bocht a bend of rope]

beck-iron same as **bick-iron**.

beckon /bek'n/ vt and vi to nod or (now usu) make a summoning sign (to). [OE bīecnan, from bēacen a sign. See **beacon**]

becloud /bi-klowd'/ vt to obscure by clouds; to dim, obscure. [**be-** (2)]

become /bi-kum'/ vi (pat **became'**; pap **become'**) to come to be; to be the fate of; to arrive, have got (to a place) (obs). ◆ vt to suit or befit; to grace or adorn fittingly; to look well in. [OE becuman; see **come**] ∎ **becom'ing** adj. **becom'ingly** adv. **becom'ingness** n.

becquerel /bek'ə-rel, -rəl or -rel'/ n a derived SI unit, the unit of radioactivity (symbol **Bq**), defined as the activity of a quantity of radioactive material in which one nucleus decays per second. [AH Becquerel (1852–1908), French physicist]

BECTU /bek'too/ abbrev : Broadcasting Entertainment Cinematograph and Theatre Union.

becurl /bi-kûrl'/ vt to curl. [**be-** (1)]

BEd abbrev : Bachelor of Education.

bed[1] /bed/ n a couch or place to sleep on; a mattress; a bedstead; a garden plot; a layer of oysters, etc; a place in which anything rests; conjugal union, sexual intercourse, the marriage-bed, matrimonial rights and duties; a place available for occupancy in a hospital, nursing home, etc; the channel of a river; a sea or lake bottom; a layer or stratum; the underside of something; an underlying surface; a flat surface on which something can be laid. ◆ vt (**bedd'ing**; **bedd'ed**) to put to bed; to provide, or make, a bed for; to have sexual intercourse with (inf); to plant in a bed; to lay in layers or on a surface; to embed. ◆ vi to go to bed; to cohabit. [OE bed(d); Ger Bett, ON bethr; prob related to L fodere to dig (as orig a hole)] ∎ **bedd'able** adj (inf) sexually attractive. **bedd'er** n a plant suitable for a flower-bed; a bedmaker in a Cambridge college (inf). **bedd'ing** n bedclothes, etc, with or without the mattress; litter for cattle; stratification (geol; **false bedding** see under **false**). **bed'ward** or **bed'wards** adv in the direction of bed; towards bedtime. ❑ **bed'bath** n the washing of a sick person in his or her bed, a blanket bath. **bed'-blocking** n a situation in which a hospital patient, though fit, cannot vacate a bed because there is no aftercare available. **bed'-bottle** n a bottle for bedridden males to urinate in. **bed'bug** n a brown flattened biting bug (Cimex lectularius). **bed'chamber** n (archaic) a bedroom. **bed'-closet** n a closet serving as a bedroom. **bed'clothes** n pl sheets, blankets, etc for a bed. **bed'cover** n an upper covering for a bed. **bedding plant** n a plant sufficiently well-grown for planting in a bed. **bedd'y-bye** or **-byes** n (used in speaking to children or facetious) bed, as a place to sleep. **bed'fast** adj (Scot and N Eng) confined to bed. **bed'fellow** n a sharer of a bed; a colleague (fig); something or someone that associates with another (fig). **bed'head** n the headboard of a bed; (also **bed hair**) the dishevelled appearance of the hair after sleeping (inf). **bed'-hopping** n (inf) having a series of casual sexual affairs. **bed'-jacket** n a light jacket worn when sitting up in bed. **bed'-key** n a tool for tightening a bedstead. **bed linen** n sheets and pillowcases. **bed'maker** n a person who makes the beds and cleans college rooms at Oxford, etc. **bed'pan** n a utensil into which a person confined to bed can urinate and defecate; a warming pan. **bed'plate** n (mech) the metal base to which the frame of a machine, engine, etc is attached. **bed'post** n a corner support of a bedstead. **bed'presser** n (Shakesp) a heavy, lazy fellow. **bed'-rest** n confinement to bed, usu on medical orders; a support for someone sitting up in bed. **bed'ridden** (also obs **bed'rid**) adj confined to bed by age or sickness; worn-out. **bed'right** or **bed'rite** n (Shakesp) the privilege or due of the marriage-bed. **bed'rock** n the solid rock underneath superficial formations; fundamental principles; the lowest state. ◆ adj bottom, lowest; basic, fundamental. **bed'roll** n a sleeping-bag or bedclothes rolled up so as to be easily carried by a camper, etc. **bed'room** n a room with a bed; a sleeping apartment; room in bed, sleeping space. ◆ adj (esp of a comedy or farce) involving or hinting at sexual activity between people in a bedroom, in night-clothes, etc. **bedroom tax** n (inf) in Britain, a financial penalty imposed on tenants if a property supplied by a local authority or housing association contains more rooms than is merited by the size of the household. **bed'-settee** n a sofa that converts into a bed. **bed'-sheet** n a cotton, nylon, etc sheet for a bed. **bed'side** n the space beside a bed (also adj). **bedside book** n one esp suitable for reading in bed. **bedside manner** n that assumed by a doctor, etc at a sickbed. **bedsitt'ing-room** n a combined bedroom and sitting room, eg in lodgings (shortened to **bed'sit** or **bed'sitter**). **bed'socks** n pl warm socks for wearing in bed. **bed'sore** n an ulcer, esp over the bony prominences, arising from long confinement to bed (also called **pressure sore**). **bed'spread** n a coverlet put over a bed by day. **bed'-staff** n a staff or lath formerly used for various purposes

in connection with beds; a handy weapon. **bed'stead** n a frame for supporting a bed. **bed'straw** n any plant of the genus Galium, esp (Our) Lady's bedstraw (G. verum), once used as stuffing for mattresses. **bed'-swerver** n (Shakesp) a person false to his or her marriage vow. **bed'-table** n a table for use by a person in bed. **bed'tick** n (old) the case into which stuffing is put to make a mattress. **bed'time** n the time for going to bed. ◆ adj to do with, or suitable for, bedtime. **bed'-warmer** n a warming pan. **bed'-wetting** n the accidental passing of urine in bed. **bed'-work** n (Shakesp) work easily performed, as if done in bed. **bed'-worthy** adj (inf) sexually attractive.

∎ **be brought to bed** (of) (archaic) to give birth (to). **bed and board** food and lodging; full connubial relations. **bed and breakfast** overnight accommodation with breakfast at a hotel, etc (**bed'-and-break'fast** adj (stock exchange) of deals in which shares are sold one day and rebought the next (also vt)). **bed down** to (cause to) settle down, esp in a makeshift bed, for sleep. **bed of down** a bed of roses. **bed of honour** the grave of a soldier who has fallen in battle. **bed of justice** (Fr lit de justice) the king's throne in the Parlement of Paris; a sitting at which the king was present, chiefly for the registration of his own decrees. **bed of nails** the board studded with nails on which fakirs lie; an extremely difficult and uncomfortable situation. **bed of roses** any easy or comfortable place. **bed out** to plant out in a flower-bed, etc. **get in bed with** (commercial jargon) to form an alliance with (another business). **get out of bed on the wrong side** to start the day in a bad mood. **go** or **put to bed** (of newspapers, magazines, etc) to go to or send to press. **go to bed with** to have sexual intercourse with. **keep one's bed** (archaic) to remain in bed. **lie in the bed one has made** to have to accept the consequences of one's own acts. **Lords** or **Ladies of the Bedchamber** officers in the royal household who wait upon a king or queen. **make a bed** to tidy and put in order the bedclothes on a bed. **take to one's bed** to go to bed because of illness, grief, age, etc.

bed[2] /bed/ (Spenser) same as **bid[2]**.

bedabble /bi-dab'l/ vt to dabble or wet. [**be-** (1)]

bedad /bi-dad'/ (Irish) interj an oath, = by God! [Variant of **begad**]

bedaggle /bi-dag'l/ vt to dirty by dragging along the wet ground. [**be-** (1)]

bedarken /bi-där'kn/ vt to cover with darkness. [**be-** (1)]

bedash /bi-dash'/ vt to bespatter, splash. [**be-** (1)]

bedaub /bi-döb'/ vt to daub over or smear. [**be-** (1)]

Bedawin same as **Bedouin**.

bedazzle /bi-daz'l/ or **bedaze** /bi-dāz'/ vt to dazzle or overpower by any strong light. [**be-** (1)] ∎ **bedazz'led** or **bedazed'** adj stupefied, besotted. **bedazz'lement** n.

beddable see under **bed[1]**.

bede (obs) same as **bead** a prayer.

bedeafen /bi-def'n/ vt to make deaf; to stun. [**be-** (1)]

bedeck /bi-dek'/ vt to deck or ornament. [**be-** (1)]

bedeguar /bed'i-gär/ n a soft spongy gall found on the branches of sweetbrier and other roses, also called **sweetbrier sponge**. [Fr bédeguar, from Pers and Ar bādā-war, literally, wind-brought]

bedel[1] or **bedell** old spellings of **beadle**, still used at Oxford and Cambridge Universities.

bedel[2] /bē'dl/ (Bridges) n appar bevel-wheel.

bedeman, **bedesman** same as **beadsman** (see under **bead**).

bederal see **bedral**.

bedevil /bi-dev'l/ vt (**bedev'illing**; **bedev'illed**) to throw into confusion; to torment; to play the devil with, make havoc with; to treat with devilish malignity; to possess as a devil would. [**be-** (2)] ∎ **bedev'ilment** n.

bedew /bi-dū'/ vt to moisten gently, as with dew. [**be-** (2)]

Bedford cord /bed'fərd körd/ n a heavy ribbed cloth similar to corduroy. [Bedford, town in central England]

bedide /bi-dīd'/ see **bedye**.

bedight /bi-dīt'/ (archaic or poetic) vt (pap and pat **bedight'**) to equip, array, furnish; to adorn. [**be-** (1)]

bedim /bi-dim'/ vt (**bedimm'ing**; **bedimmed'**) to make dim or dark. [**be-** (2)] ∎ **bedimm'ing** n and adj.

bedizen /bi-dī'zən or bi-diz'ən/ vt to dress gaudily. [**be-** (1)] ∎ **bediz'ened** adj. **bediz'enment** n.

bedlam /bed'ləm/ n a place of uproar, a madhouse; pandemonium; an asylum for lunatics (archaic); a madman (obs). ◆ adj fit for a madhouse. [From the priory St Mary of Bethlehem, in London, afterwards a madhouse (Bethlehem Royal Hospital)]

■ **bed'lamism** *n* anything characteristic of madness. **bed'lamite** *n* a madman.

Bedlington /bed'ling-tən/ or **Bedlington terrier** /ter'i-ər/ *n* a long-bodied lightly built terrier, swiftest of its kind. [*Bedlington*, in Northumberland, where it was first bred]

Bedouin or **Beduin** /bed'oo-in, -ēn/ or /bed'win/ (also without *cap*) *n* (*pl* **Bed'ouin** or **Bed'ouins**) a tent-dwelling nomadic Arab (*orig pl*). ◆ *adj* of or relating to the Bedouin. [Fr *bédouin*, from Ar *badāwin* dwellers in the desert]
   ■ **Bedu** /bed'oo/ *n* and *adj* (a) Bedouin.

bedraggle /bi-drag'l/ *vt* to soil by dragging in the wet or dirt. [**be-** (1)]
   ■ **bedragg'led** *adj* very wet and untidy.

bedral or **bederal** /bed'(ə-)rəl/ (*Scot*) *n* a beadle, church officer, or minister's attendant; a grave-digger. [**beadle**]

bedrench /bi-drench'/ or **-drensh'/** *vt* to drench or wet thoroughly. [**be-** (1)]

bedrop /bi-drop'/ *vt* to drop upon. [**be-** (3)]
   ■ **bedropped'** or **bedropt'** *adj* sprinkled as with drops; strewn.

Beds. *abbrev* : Bedfordshire.

Bedu see under **Bedouin**.

beduck /bi-duk'/ *vt* to duck or plunge under water. [**be-** (1)]

Beduin see **Bedouin**.

bedung /bi-dung'/ *vt* to manure; to befoul with dung. [**be-** (2)]

bedust /bi-dust'/ *vt* to cover with dust. [**be-** (2)]

bedwarf /bi-dwörf'/ *vt* to make dwarfish. [**be-** (2)]

bedye /bi-dī'/ *vt* (*pat* and *pap* **bedyed'** (*Spenser* **bedide'** or **bedyde'**)) to dye or stain. [**be-** (1)]

bee[1] /bē/ *n* any of various four-winged hymenopterous insects, typically making honey and living in social communities; a gathering of persons to unite their labour for the benefit of one individual or family, or for some joint amusement, exercise or competition (as in *quilting bee*, *spelling bee*); a busy person; (*usu* in *pl*) a lump of a type of yeast. [OE *bēo*; Ger *Biene*]
   ◻ **bee balm** *n* a species of *Monarda* or other sweet-smelling plant. **bee'-bread** *n* the pollen and honey mixture fed by bees to their young. **bee'-eater** *n* any bird of a brightly plumaged family (Meropidae) closely related to the kingfishers, which feed on bees. **bee'-flower** *n* a flower pollinated by bees. **bee fly** *n* a nectar-eating fly of the Bombyliidae family. **bee'-glue** *n* propolis. **bee'hive** *n* a case or box in which bees are kept, made of straw-work, wood, etc; a place bustling with activity; a beehive hairstyle. ◆ *adj* dome-shaped, like an old-fashioned beehive, as *beehive hairstyle, beehive tomb*. **bee'-house** *n*. **bee'keeper** *n*. **bee'keeping** *n*. **bee'-kite** *n* the honey buzzard. **bee'line** *n* the most direct route from one point to another (*esp* in **make a beeline for** below). **bee'-master** *n* a beekeeper. **bee'-moth** *n* a moth (*Aphomia sociella*) whose larvae are very destructive to bees' nests. **bee'-orchis** *n* an orchid of the genus *Ophrys*, whose flower resembles a bee. **bee'-skep** *n* a beehive, properly of straw. **beesting lips** or **beestung lips** *n pl* pouting lips. **bees'wax** *n* the wax secreted by bees and used by them in constructing their cells; this wax as used for various purposes, eg for polish, candles or cosmetics. ◆ *vt* to polish with beeswax. **bees'wing** *n* a filmy crust of tartar formed in port and some other wines after long keeping. **bees'winged** *adj* (of wine) so old as to show beeswing.
   ■ **a bee in one's bonnet** an obsession; a whimsical or crazy fancy on some point. **make a beeline for** to take the most direct way towards (like bees to a source of nectar). **the bee's knees** (*inf*) someone or something particularly good, admirable, etc.

bee[2] /bē/ *n* the second letter of the modern English alphabet (B or b).

Beeb /bēb/ (*inf*) *n* the BBC.

beech /bēch/ *n* a common forest-tree of the genus *Fagus* with smooth grey bark; extended to the related genus *Nothofagus* and to many trees not related; the wood of such a tree. [OE *boece, bēce*; Ger *Buche*, L *fāgus*, Gr *phēgos* (oak)]
   ■ **beech'en** *adj* (*archaic*).
   ◻ **beech'-drops** *n* cancer root, an American orobanchaceous plant parasitic on beech roots. **beech fern** *n* a fern of the family Thelypteridaceae (a mistranslation of *Phegopteris*; from Gr *phēgos*, a kind of oak). **beech marten** *n* the stone marten. **beech mast** *n* the mast or nuts of the beech tree, which yield a valuable oil, **beech'-oil**. **beech'wood** *n* a wood of beech trees; beech timber.

beedi, beedie see **bidi**.

beef /bēf/ *n* the flesh of adult domestic cattle as food; extended to that of some other animals, such as the horse; muscle (*inf*); vigorous muscular force (*inf*); a steer or cow, *esp* one fattened for the butcher (*archaic*; *pl* in this sense **beefs** or **beeves** /bēvz/); a complaint (*inf*); an argument or quarrel (*inf*). ◆ *adj* of beef. ◆ *vi* (*inf*) to grumble. [OFr *boef* (Fr *bœuf*), from L *bōs, bovis*; cf Gr *bous*, Gaelic *bò*, Sans *go*, OE *cū*]
   ■ **beef'y** *adj* like beef; fleshy, muscular (*inf*); stolid (*inf*).

◻ **beef'-brained** *adj* (*inf*) stupid. **beef'-brewis** (*obs*) or **beef broth** *n* broth made from beef. **beef'burger** *n* a round flat cake of minced meat, *usu* fried or grilled. **beef'cake** *n* (*inf*) very muscular men, considered sexually attractive; photographs of such; brawn as distinct from brain. **beef cattle** *n pl* cattle reared mainly for their meat (cf **dairy cattle**). **beef'eater** *n* the ox-bird or oxpecker; a consumer of beef; a yeoman of the guard; a warder of the Tower of London. **beef'-ham** *n* beef cured like ham. **beef olive** *n* a thin slice of beef rolled round a savoury stuffing and *usu* stewed. **beef'steak** *n* a thick lean slice of beef for grilling or frying. **beefsteak fungus** *n* an edible fungus *Fistulina hepatica*, which looks rather like beefsteak. **beef tea** *n* a hot drink made from beef stock. **beef tomato** *n* a particularly large fleshy variety of tomato. **beef Wellington** *n* a dish of beef covered in pâté and baked in pastry. **beef'-witted** *adj* .(*inf*) stupid. **beef'wood** *n* the wood of the casuarina and other trees.
   ■ **beef up** (*inf*) to add strength to, reinforce.

beefalo /bē'fə-lō/ *n* (*pl* **beef'aloes** or **beef'alos**) a cross between a cow and a N American buffalo. [*beef*, and *buffalo*]

beegah same as **bigha**.

Beelzebub /bē-el'zi-bub/ *n* a form of Baal worshipped by the Philistines at Ekron; the prince of the fallen angels; a devil or the Devil. [Heb *ba'al z'būb* fly-lord]

Beemer /bē'mər/ *n* (*inf*) a BMW® car or motorcycle.

been /bēn or bin/ *pap* of **be**; *present infinitive* and *pl present indicative* of **be** (*archaic*).

beenah /bē'nä/ *n* a form of marriage (in Sri Lanka, etc) in which the man goes to live with his wife's relatives and the children belong to her group. [Ar *bīnah* separate]

beep /bēp/ *n* the sound made by the horn of a car, etc, or by a pager or other electronic device. ◆ *vi* and *vt* to (cause to) make such a sound. ◆ *vt* to signal to with a car horn; to call with a pager or other electronic device. [*Imit*]
   ■ **beep'er** *n*.

beer[1] /bēr/ *n* an alcoholic drink made by fermentation from malted barley flavoured with hops; the generic name of malt liquor, including ale and porter; a glassful, etc of this to drink; applied to other fermented liquors such as ginger beer. [OE *bēor*; Ger *Bier*, Du *bier*, ON *bjorr*]
   ■ **beer'age** *n* brewers collectively, the brewing industry. **beer'iness** *n*. **beer'y** *adj* affected by beer; smelling or tasting of beer; in the habit of drinking beer.
   ◻ **beer'-barrel** *n*. **beer belly** *n* a protuberant belly caused, or considered so, by excessive beer-drinking. **beer bottle** *n*. **beer engine** or **beer pump** *n* a machine for drawing beer up from the casks to the bar. **beer garden** *n* a garden with tables where beer and other refreshments may be purchased. **beer goggles** *n pl* (*sl*) a supposed source of impaired vision due to drinking alcohol, causing potential sexual partners to appear more attractive than they really are. **beer gut** *n* (*inf*) a beer belly. **beer'hall** *n* (*S Afr*) a large public drinking-place formerly for non-white people only. **beer house** *n* a house where beer is sold. **beer'-mat** *n* a small, *usu* cardboard table mat for a beer glass, etc. **beer money** *n* money given in lieu of beer and spirits; a gratuity. **beer parlor** or **parlour** *n* (*Can*) a public room in a hotel, etc, where beer is served. **beer pong** *n* a drinking game involving the throwing of table-tennis balls into glasses of beer. **beer'-up** *n* (*Aust sl*) a drinking bout; a rowdy drunken party.
   ■ **beer and skittles** idle enjoyment. **bitter beer** pale ale, a highly hopped beer made from the very finest selected malt and hops (**mild** or **sweet ale** being comparatively lightly hopped). **black beer** a kind of beer made at Gdańsk, black and syrupy. **dry beer** see under **dry**. **small beer** weak beer; something trifling or unimportant, *esp* when compared with something else.

beer[2] see **bere**[2].

beesome /bē'səm/ (*Shakesp*) *adj* supposed to be for **bisson**.

beestings /bē'stingz/ *n* the first milk drawn from a cow after calving. [OE *bȳsting, bēost*; Ger *Biest*, Du *biest*]

beet[1] /bēt/ *n* a plant (genus *Beta*; *esp B. vulgaris*) of the family Chenopodiaceae, with a red or white succulent root, used as food (red; see **beetroot** below) and as a source of sugar (white). [OE *bēte*, from L *bēta*]
   ◻ **beet'-fly** *n* a fly (*Pegomyia hyoscyami*) whose larvae are injurious to beet and mangel-wurzel. **beet'root** *n* the dark-red root of the beet plant eaten as a vegetable. ◆ *adj* (of a person's complexion) florid, red through embarrassment. **beet sugar** *n*.

beet[2] or **bete** /bēt/ (*obs except dialect*) *vt* to improve; to mend (*esp* a fire); to relieve, assuage. [OE *bētan*; cf *bōt*, **boot**[2]]
   ■ **beet'mister** (*Walter Scott* **-master**) *n* a help in need.

beetle[1] /bē'tl/ *n* any insect of the Coleoptera, an order in which the forewings are reduced to hard and horny covers for the hindwings; a game in which a drawing of a beetle is made up gradually from its

component parts, body, head, etc, according to the throw of dice, the object being to produce a completed drawing; (*esp* with *cap*) a particular variety of small Volkswagen car with rounded roof and bonnet, resembling a beetle (*inf*); to jut, to overhang (first found in *Shakesp*); to scurry (*inf*). ◆ *adj* (always applied to brows) overhanging, scowling. [ME *bityl*, from OE *bitula, bitela*, from *bītan* to bite; the connection of beetle brows with the insect is not accepted by all]
■ **beet'ling** *adj* jutting; prominent; overhanging.
▫ **beet'le-browed** *adj* with overhanging or prominent brows. **beetle brows** *n pl*. **beet'le-crusher** *n* (*sl*) a big heavy foot or boot; a policeman; an infantryman. **beetle drive** *n* a progressive series of games of beetle. **beet'le-eyed** *adj* blind.
■ **beetle off** to hurry away like a beetle, scurry (*inf*); to fly (RAF *sl*). **black beetle** the cockroach (properly not a beetle).

beetle² /bē'tl/ *n* a heavy wooden mallet used for driving wedges, crushing or beating down paving-stones, or the like; a wooden pestle-shaped utensil for mashing potatoes, beating linen, clothes, etc. [OE *bīetl*, from *bēatan* to beat]
▫ **beet'lehead** or **beet'lebrain** *n* a heavy stupid person. **bee'tleheaded** or **beet'lebrained** *adj*.

beetroot see under **beet¹**.

beeves /bēvz/ *n pl* cattle, oxen. [See **beef**]

beezer /bē'zər/ (Scot *sl*) *adj* excellent, very good (also *interj*). ◆ *n* an excellent thing. [Origin unknown]

BEF *abbrev*: British Expeditionary Force.

bef. *abbrev*: before.

befall /bi-föl'/ (*archaic*) *vt* (**befall'ing**; **befell'**; **befall'en** (Spenser **befeld'**)) (also *vi* with *dative*) to fall or happen to; to occur to. ◆ *vi* to happen or come to pass; to befit; to fall in one's way (*Spenser*). [OE *bef(e)allan*; see **fall**]

befana or **beffana** /be-fä'nə/ *n* an Epiphany gift. [Ital *La Befana*, a toy-bringing old woman, a personification of Epiphany, Gr *epiphaneia*]

befinned /bi-find'/ *adj* having fins. [**be-** (2)]

befit /bi-fit'/ *vt* (**befit'ting**; **befit'ted**) to be fitting, or suitable to or for; to beseem. ◆ *vi* to be right. [**be-** (1)]
■ **befit'ting** *adj*. **befit'tingly** *adv*.

beflower /bi-flow'ər/ *vt* to cover or sprinkle all over with flowers. [**be-** (2)]

befoam /bi-fōm'/ (*archaic*) *vt* to bespatter or cover with foam. [**be-** (2)]

befog /bi-fog'/ *vt* to envelop in fog; to obscure. [**be-** (2)]

befool /bi-fool'/ *vt* to make a fool of or deceive; to treat as a fool. [**be-** (2)]

before /bi-för'/ *prep* in front of; ahead of; in the presence or sight of; under the consideration or cognizance of; previous to; previous to the expiration of; in preference to; superior to. ◆ *adv* in front; sooner; earlier; in the past; formerly. ◆ *conj* previous to the time when (sometimes with *that*); rather than that. ◆ *adj* (*Shakesp*) previous. [OE *beforan*. See **fore**]
■ **before'hand** *adv* before a particular time; in advance or anticipation; by way of preparation; in advance of one's needs; in credit, comfortably off (*archaic*).
▫ **before'-men'tioned** *adj*. **before'time** *adv* (*archaic*) in former time.
■ **be beforehand with** to forestall (a person). **before Christ** see **BC**. **before the mast** serving as an ordinary sailor. **before the wind** in the direction in which the wind is blowing, and hence helped along by it.

befortune /bi-för'tūn/ (Shakesp) *vi* (with *dative*) to happen to, to befall. [**be-** (3)]

befoul /bi-fowl'/ *vt* to make foul; to soil. [**be-** (2)]

befriend /bi-frend'/ *vt* to commence a friendship with; to act as a friend to; to favour. [**be-** (2)]
■ **befriend'er** *n*.

befringe /bi-frinj'/ *vt* to adorn with fringes. [**be-** (2)]

befuddle /bi-fud'l/ *vt* to reduce to a confused condition (*esp* through drink). [**be-** (1)]

beg¹ /beg/ *vi* (**begg'ing**; **begged** /begd/) to ask for alms or charity, *esp* habitually; (of a dog) to sit up on the hindquarters for a reward. ◆ *vt* to ask for earnestly; to beseech; to pray; to fail to answer or resolve. [Perh from **beghard**, the verb being a back-formation]
■ **beggar** /beg'ər/ *n* a person who begs; a person who lives by begging; a person who is in need, *esp* of money (*hyperbole*); an impoverished person; often used playfully and even affectionately. ◆ *vt* to reduce to beggary; to exhaust or impoverish; to go beyond the resources of (eg description or imagination). **begg'ardom** *n* the fraternity of beggars. **begg'arliness** *n*. **begg'arly** *adj* poor; mean; worthless. ◆ *adv* meanly. **begg'ary** *n* extreme poverty. **begg'ing** *n* and *adj*. **begg'ingly** *adv*.
▫ **begg'ar-man** *n*. **begg'ar-my-neigh'bour** *n* a game that goes on until one player has gained all the others' cards; profit-making at the expense of others (also *adj*). **beggar's lice**, **beggar's ticks** or **beggar ticks** *n pl* any of various plants with burrs; the burrs themselves. **begging bowl** *n* a bowl carried by beggars, *esp* certain orders of monks, to receive food, money, etc (often *fig*). **begging letter** *n* a letter soliciting charity, *esp* money.
■ **beg for a fool** (*obs*) to sue for the guardianship of, and administration of the estate of, a person on grounds of his or her mental deficiency. **beggar belief** to be impossible to believe. **beg off** to obtain another's release through entreaty; to seek remission of some penalty; to ask to be excused from some commitment. **beg the question** to avoid giving an answer; to assume that the thing to be proved is already true in one of the premises, or in part of the proof (*logic*); to raise an issue for debate (*non-standard*). **go begging** or **a-begging** to lack a purchaser, occupant, etc.

beg² same as **bey**.

begad /bi-gad'/ and **begar** /bi-gär'/ (*Shakesp*) *interj* by God! [Euphemistic alterations]

began /bi-gan'/ *pat* of **begin**.

begar¹ /bā'gär/ (*Ind*) *n* forced labour. [Hindi *begār*]

begar² see **begad**.

begat see **beget**.

begem /bi-jem'/ *vt* to adorn, as with gems. [**be-** (2)]

beget /bi-get'/ (*literary*) *vt* (**begett'ing**; **begot'** (or *archaic, esp Bible* **begat'**); **begott'en** (or **begot'**)) to produce or cause; (of humans, and commonly of the father) to produce (offspring); to produce as an effect, to cause. [OE *begitan* to acquire; see **get**]
■ **begett'er** *n* someone who begets; a father; the agent that occasions or originates anything (now often **only begetter**).

beggar see under **beg¹**.

beghard /beg'ärd/ *n* in Flanders or elsewhere from the 13c, a man living a monastic life without vows and with power to return to the world. [Flem *beggaert*; origin doubtful; cf **beguine**]

begift /bi-gift'/ *vt* to present with gifts. [**be-** (2)]

begild /bi-gild'/ *vt* to gild; to cover or overlay with gold leaf. [**be-** (1)]

begin /bi-gin'/ *vi* (**beginn'ing**; **began'** or (*rare*) **begun'**; **begun'**) to come into being; to originate; to perform the first act; to open or commence; to have an opening or commencement. ◆ *vt* to perform the first act of; to enter on; to start. [OE *beginnan* (less usual than *onginnan*), from pfx *be-* and *ginnan* to begin]
■ **beginne'** *n* (Spenser) beginning. **beginn'er** *n* someone who begins; a person who is in the early stages of learning or doing anything. **beginn'ing** *n* origin; a start; an entering upon action; an opening or first part; a rudiment. **beginn'ingless** *adj*.
▫ **beginner's luck** *n* apparently fortuitous success achieved by an inexperienced participant.
■ **to begin with** firstly; at first.

begird /bi-gûrd'/ (*archaic* or *poetic*) *vt* (*pat* and *pap* **begirt'** (or **begird'ed**)) to gird or bind with a girdle; to surround or encompass. [OE *begyrdan*; **be-** (1) and **gird¹**]

beglamour /bi-glam'ər/ or (US) **beglamor** *vt* to invest with glamour; to bedazzle, infatuate or impress with glamour. [**be-** (2)]

beglerbeg /beg'lər-beg/ *n* formerly, the governor of a Turkish province, in rank next to the grand vizier. [Turk, literally, bey of beys]

begloom /bi-gloom'/ *vt* to render gloomy. [**be-** (2)]

begnaw /bi-nö'/ *vt* to gnaw or bite, eat away. [**be-** (1)]

bego /bi-gō'/ *vt* to beset (*obs* except in compound **woebegone** (see under **woe**)). [OE *begān* to beset, surround]

begone /bi-gon'/ *interj* be gone; be off; get away.

begonia /bi-gō'ni-ə/ *n* a plant of the genus *Begonia* (giving name to a family **Begonià'ceae**) of tropical, *esp* American, plants cultivated for their waxy, brightly coloured flowers and their remarkable unequal-sided and often coloured leaves. [Named after Michel *Bégon* (1638–1710), French patron of botanical science]

begored /bi-görd'/ (Spenser) *adj* besmeared with gore. [**be-** (2)]

begorra or **begorrah** /bi-gor'ə/ *interj* (*esp facetious*; attributed to Irish speakers) by God! [Euphemistic alteration]

begot, **begotten** see **beget**.

begrime /bi-grīm'/ *vt* to soil with grime. [**be-** (2)]

begrudge /bi-gruj'/ *vt* to grudge; to envy the possession of. [**be-** (1)]
■ **begrudg'ingly** *adv*.

beguile /bi-gīl'/ *vt* to charm; to cheat or deceive; to spend (time) pleasantly; to trick into some course of action. [**be-** (1), and *obs* transitive verb **guile**]
■ **beguile'ment** *n*. **beguil'er** *n*. **beguil'ingly** *adv*.

beguine¹ /bə-gēn'/ *n* a dance of French West Indian origin or its music, in bolero rhythm. [Fr]

beguine² or **béguine** /bāˈgēn or begˈin/ n a member of a sisterhood living as nuns but without vows, and with power to return to the world. [Fr *béguine* ; cf **beghard**]
  ■ **beguin** or **béguin** /bāgˈ-ɛ̄ or begˈin/ n a beghard. **béguinage** /bāgˈēn-äzh or begˈin-ij/ n an establishment for beguines.

begum /bāˈ or bēˈgəm/ n (in India, Pakistan, etc) a Muslim woman of high rank; a deferential title given to any married Muslim woman. [Urdu *begam* ; cf **beg²**, **bey**]

begun /bi-gunˈ/ pap (sometimes pat) of **begin**.

begunk /bi-gungkˈ/ (Scot) vt to trick; to play a trick on; to cheat; to jilt. ◆ n a trick; a jilting. [Origin uncertain; Scot *gunk* jilt, trick, recorded later]

behalf /bi-häfˈ/ n interest, benefit; sake, account; part. [ME *behalve*, from OE *be healfe* by the side. See **half**]
  ■ **on** (N Am **in**) **behalf of**, or **on** (N Am **in**) **someone's behalf** speaking, acting, etc for (someone).

behappen /bi-hapˈn/ (Spenser) vt to happen to. [**be-** (1)]

behatted /bi-hatˈid/ adj wearing a hat. [**be-** (2)]

behave /bi-hāvˈ/ vt (pat and pap **behaved**ˈ) to conduct (oneself) well; to manage, conduct (often *oneself*) in a specified manner. ◆ vi to conduct oneself in a specified manner (often *towards*); to conduct oneself well; (of things) to function, handle, respond. [**be-** (1) and **have**; OE had *behabban* to detain, restrain]
  ■ **behaviour** or (N Am) **behavior** /bi-hāvˈyər/ n conduct; manners or deportment, esp good manners; general course of life; treatment of others; manner of action; the activity of an organism, esp as measurable for its effects; response to stimulus (*physiol* and *psychol*); the functioning, response or activity of an object or substance. **behavˈioural** or (N Am) **behavˈioral** adj of or relating to behaviour or behaviourism. **behavˈiourally** or (N Am) **behavˈiorally** adv. **behavˈiourism** or (N Am) **behavˈiorism** n the psychological theory that behaviour is governed by conditioning rather than internal processes and that by changing behaviour patterns it is possible to treat psychological disorders. **behavˈiourist** or (N Am) **behavˈiorist** n an upholder of behaviourism.
  ❑ **behavioural enrichment** n the creation of a mentally stimulating environment for a captive animal, eg in a zoo, with provision of objects for the animal to investigate and play with. **behavioural science** n a science (eg psychology, sociology) which studies the behaviour of human beings or other organisms. **behaviour therapy** n a means of treating a neurotic symptom (eg a phobia) by training the patient in new behaviour and gradually conditioning him or her to react normally.
  ■ **on** or **upon one's best behaviour** consciously trying to be as well-behaved as possible.

behead /bi-hedˈ/ vt to cut off the head of. [**be-** (1) meaning off or away]
  ■ **beheadˈal** n (rare). **beheadˈing** n.

beheld /bi-heldˈ/ pat and pap of **behold**.

behemoth /bə- or bi-hēˈmoth/ n an animal described in the Bible (Job 40.15–18), usually taken to be the hippopotamus; a great beast; something huge or gigantic. [Heb *b'hēmōth*, pl of *b'hēmāh* beast, or a Hebraistic form of the Egyptian *p-ehe-mout* water-ox]

behest /bi-hestˈ/ n a command; a request; a promise (obs). [OE *behǣs* a promise; see **hest**]

behight /bi-hītˈ/ or **behote** /bi-hōtˈ/ (obs) vt (pat and pap **behight**ˈ or **behote**ˈ) to vow; to promise; to warrant, to command, to name (Spenser). [OE *behātan* to vow, from *be-* and *hātan* to be called, to call, to command. For the confusion of tenses and voices and for reduplication, see **hight**]

behind /bi-hīndˈ/ prep in, to or at the back of (in position, or as a support); at the far side of; in the place or state left by; after (in time, rank or order); in the past compared with; later than; causing; supporting; inferior to, or less far advanced than. ◆ adv at the back, in or to the rear; backwards, less advanced; past; remaining after someone's departure; in arrears. ◆ n the rump, the buttocks (euphem); a score worth one point made in a number of ways (also adj) (Aust rules). [OE *behindan*; Ger *hinten*; see **hind³**]
  ❑ **behind**ˈ**-door** adj surreptitious, clandestine. **behind**ˈ**hand** adj and adv tardy, late; in arrears; out of date, behind the times; less well prepared or provided than others. **behind post** n (Aust rules) one of the two smaller posts on either side of the main goalposts.
  ■ **behind someone's back** without someone knowing (when he or she might feel entitled to know). **come from behind** to progress from the rear of a field of contestants or from a losing position into a winning position (also fig). **put something behind one** to resign something (usu unpleasant) to the past and consider it finished.

behold /bi-hōldˈ/ vt (pat and pap **beheld**ˈ) (literary or Bible) to look at; to view, see; to contemplate; perh, to restrain (Spenser). ◆ vi (literary or Bible) to look. ◆ interj (or imperative) (archaic) see; lo; observe. [OE

behaldan (WSax *behealdan*) to hold, observe, from *be-* and *h(e)aldan* to hold]
  ■ **behold**ˈ**en** adj bound in gratitude (to); under an obligation (to). **behold**ˈ**er** n a person who beholds; an onlooker. **behold**ˈ**ing** adj (Shakesp) beholden. ◆ n (Shakesp) sight, contemplation.

behoof /bi-hoofˈ/ n benefit; convenience. [OE *behōf*]

behote see **behight**.

behove or (esp US) **behoove** /bi-hoovˈ/ (unhistorically bi-hōvˈ)/ vt and vi (now only used impersonally with *it*) to be fit, right or necessary. [OE *behōfian* to be fit, to stand in need of]
  ■ **behove**ˈ**ful** adj (archaic). **behove**ˈ**ly** adj (obs) useful; profitable.

behowl /bi-howlˈ/ vt to howl at (emendation by William Warburton for 'beholds' in Shakesp, *Midsummer Night's Dream* V.1.361). [**be-** (3)]

beige /bāzh/ n a very pale pinkish-brown or yellowish-brown colour; a woollen fabric of undyed wool. ◆ adj pinkish- or yellowish-brown. [Fr]

beigel /bāˈgl/ n an alternative spelling of **bagel**.

beignet /benˈyā/ n a fritter; a deep-fried ball of choux pastry. [Fr]

bein, also **bien** /bēn/ adj and adv comfortable (Scot); well-off (Scot); good (criminal sl). [ME *bene*, of dubious origin; ON *beinn*, L *bene*, and Fr *bien*, all offer difficulties]
  ■ **bein**ˈ**ness** n (Scot).

being /bēˈing/ n existence; substance; essence; any person or living thing that exists or may exist; anything material or immaterial that can be conceived as existing (philos). ◆ adj existing or present. [Verbal noun and prp of **be**]
  ■ **bē**ˈ**ingless** adj. **bē**ˈ**ingness** n.
  ■ **the Supreme Being** God.

beinked /bē-ingktˈ/ adj smeared with ink. [**be-** (2)]

bejabers /bi-jāˈbərs/ interj (esp facetious; attributed to Irish speakers) by Jesus! [Euphemistic alteration]

bejade /bi-jādˈ/ (obs) vt to tire out. [**be-** (1)]

bejant see **bajan**.

bejesuit /bi-jezˈū-it/ vt to initiate or seduce into Jesuitism. [**be-** (2)]

bejewel /bi-jooˈəl/ vt to adorn with or as if with jewels. [**be-** (2)]
  ■ **bejew**ˈ**elled** adj.

bekah /bēˈkä/ (Bible) n a half-shekel. [Heb]

bekiss /bi-kisˈ/ vt to cover with kisses. [**be-** (1)]

beknave /bi-nāvˈ/ vt to call or treat as a knave. [**be-** (2)]

beknown /bi-nōnˈ/ (archaic or dialect) adj known. [**be-** (1)]

bel¹ /bel/ n a unit used to express a relationship between two power levels, the number of bels being the logarithm to the base 10 of the ratio between the two levels; cf **decibel**. [Alexander Graham *Bell* (1847–1922), inventor of the telephone]

bel² see **bael**.

belabour or (US) **belabor** /bi-lāˈbər/ vt to beat soundly; to assail verbally; to argue about or discuss at excessive length. [**be-** (1)]

bel-accoyle /bel-a-koilˈ/ (Spenser) n a favourable or kind reception. [OFr *bel acoil* fair welcome. See **accoil**]

belace /bi-lāsˈ/ vt to adorn with lace. [**be-** (2)]

belah /bēˈlä/ n an Australian tree of the *Casuarina* genus. [From an Aboriginal language]

bel air /be-lerˈ/ (Fr) n fine deportment.

belamoure or **bellamoure** /bel-a-mowrˈ/ (Spenser) n a beloved one; some kind of flower. [Fr *bel amour* fair love]

belamy /belˈə-mē/ (Spenser) n a good or intimate friend. [Fr *bel ami* fair friend]

Bel&Dr. (Bible) abbrev : (the Apocryphal Book of) Bel and the Dragon.

Belarussian /be-la-rushˈən/ adj of Belarus, a republic of the former Soviet Union; of its language or people. ◆ n a native or citizen of Belarus; the language of Belarus. [See **Belorussian**]

belate /bi-lātˈ/ vt (archaic) to make late; to retard. [**be-** (2)]
  ■ **belāt**ˈ**ed** adj coming too late; out of date; benighted (obs). **belāt**ˈ**edly** adv. **belāt**ˈ**edness** n.

belaud /bi-lödˈ/ vt to praise up. [**be-** (1)]

belay /bi-lāˈ/ vt (pat and pap **belayed**ˈ) to make fast; to secure by a turn (of a rope) around a cleat, belaying pin, point of rock, etc (naut and mountaineering); to desist from (naut); to set or overlay (with ornament) (Spenser); to beset, to besiege (obs); to waylay (obs). ◆ interj enough; hold. ◆ n (mountaineering) a turn of a rope in belaying; the rock, etc around which a belay is made. [OE *belecgan* ; Ger *belegen*, Du *beleggen*. See **lay¹**]
  ❑ **belaying pin** n (naut) a pin for belaying ropes around.

bel canto /bel kanˈtō/ (Ital) n a manner of operatic singing that cultivates beauty of tone (also adv).

belch /belch or belsh/ vt and vi to void (wind) from the stomach by the mouth; to eject violently; to pour forth, as the smoke from a volcano, chimney, etc. ◆ n an act of belching. [OE *bealcian*; Du *balken*]

belcher /bel'chər/ n a dark-blue neckerchief with blue-centred white spots. [From Jim *Belcher*, a famous English boxer]

beldam or **beldame** /bel'dəm/ n an old woman (formerly a term of address); a hag; a furious woman; a grandmother or remoter ancestress (obs). [Formed from **dam²** and *bel-*, used like *grand-*, from Fr *bel, belle*, but not a French use]

beleaguer /bi-lēg'ər/ vt to lay siege to; to pester. [Du *belegeren* to besiege, from *be-*, and *leger* camp. See **leaguer¹**]
■ **beleag'uerment** n.

belee /bi-lē'/ (Shakesp) vt to place on the lee side of something. [**be-** (2)]

belemnite /bel'əm-nīt/ n a fossil pointed like a dart, being the internal shell of a cephalopod mollusc, formerly known as *thunderbolt*, *thunderstone*, *elf-bolt*. [Gr *belemnitēs*, from *belemnon* a dart]

bel esprit /be-le-sprē'/ (Fr) n (pl **beaux esprits** /bō-zes-prē'/) a wit or genius.

bel étage /be-lā-täzh'/ (Ger Fr) n the best storey, the first floor.

belfry /bel'fri/ n the part of a steeple or tower in which bells are hung; a bell tower, sometimes a separate building; a movable wooden tower, used in the Middle Ages in attacking a fortification. [Orig and properly a watchtower, from OFr *berfroi*, from MHGer *berchfrit*, from *bergan* to protect and *frid, frit* a tower]
■ **bel'fried** adj having a belfry.

Belg. abbrev : Belgian; Belgium.

belga /bel'gə/ n a former currency unit of Belgium used in foreign exchange (from 1926 until the end of World War II), worth five paper francs. [L *Belga* a Belgian]

belgard /bel-gärd'/ (Spenser) n a fair or kind look. [Ital *bel guardo* lovely look]

Belgian /bel'jən/ adj of or relating to *Belgium* in N Europe, or its inhabitants. ◆ n a native or citizen of Belgium. [L *Belga, Belgicus*]
■ **Bel'gic** adj of the *Belgae*, a Celtic tribe which inhabited Belgium in Roman times, or of Belgium.
❑ **Belgian Blue** n a variety of cattle. **Belgian hare** n a hare-like breed of domestic rabbit.

Belgravian /bel-grā'vi-ən/ adj belonging to *Belgravia* (a fashionable part of London), or to fashionable life.

Belial /bēl'yəl or bi-lī'l/ n the Devil; in Milton, one of the fallen angels. Not a proper name in the Old Testament. [Heb *b'li-ya'al*, from *b'li* not, and *ya'al* use]

belie /bi-lī'/ vt (**bely'ing**; **belied'**) to show the untruth of; to present falsely, misrepresent or falsify; to contradict or reject as false or a lie; to be false to, fail to fulfil; to fill with lies (Shakesp); to fail to fulfil or justify. [**be-** (3)]
■ **belī'er** n.

belief /bə- or bi-lēf'/ n conviction of the truth of anything; faith; confidence or trust in a person, etc; an opinion or doctrine believed; intuition, natural judgement (as used by some philosophers). [Noun use of ME *bileven*; see ety at **believe**]
■ **belief'less** adj.
■ **the belief** (archaic) the Apostles' Creed. **to the best of my belief** as far as I know.

believe /bə- or bi-lēv'/ vt to regard as true; to accept as true what is said by (someone); to think (followed by a noun clause). ◆ vi to be firmly convinced; to have esp religious faith (in or on); (with in) to consider right or good; to judge. [ME *bileven*, from *bi-, be*, and *leven*, superseding OE *gelēfan*]
■ **believ'able** adj. **believ'er** n a person who believes; a person who is an adherent of Christianity, Islam, or any other religion. **believ'ing** adj trustful; having belief. **believ'ingly** adv.
■ **believe something of someone** to think someone capable of something. **be unable** or **hardly able to believe one's eyes** or **ears** to receive with incredulity what one has just seen or heard. **I (don't) believe so** I (don't) think so. **make believe** see under **make¹**. **would you believe it?** it seems incredible but it is true.

belike /bi-līk'/ (archaic) adv probably; perhaps. [OE pfx *be-* and **like¹**]

Belisha beacon see **beacon**.

belittle /bi-lit'l/ vt to make small; to make (something or someone) out to be insignificant or unimportant; to disparage. [**be-** (2)]
■ **belitt'lement** n. **belitt'ling** adj.

belive /bi-līv'/ (archaic and Scot) adv with speed; immediately. [ME *bi life* from *bī* by and *līfe* dative of *līf* life]

Belizean /bə-lē'zi-ən/ adj of or relating to the state of *Belize* in Central America, or its people. ◆ n a native or citizen of Belize.

bell¹ /bel/ n an instrument for giving a ringing sound, typically a hollow vessel of metal with flared mouth struck by a tongue or clapper, but taking many other forms; anything bell-shaped, as in *diving bell, bell-glass*, the open end of some wind instruments, etc; a flower corolla shaped like a bell; the body of a Corinthian or Composite capital, without the surrounding foliage (archit); the sound of a bell; a signal or intimation by bell; a stroke or double stroke of a bell to indicate the number of half-hours of the watch that have elapsed, **two bells**, **three bells**, etc, meaning that two, three, etc half-hours have passed, the end of the watch of four hours being **eight bells** (naut). ◆ vi to ring. ◆ vt to furnish with a bell, esp in **bell the cat** (see below). ◆ vt and vi to (cause to) flare out in the shape of a bell. [OE *belle* cognate with Du *bel*]
■ **belled** adj shaped like a bell.
❑ **bell beaker** n the distinctive wide-necked pottery vessel found (sometimes inverted) in the graves of Beaker Folk. **bell'bind** n (dialect) hedge or field bindweed. **bell'bird** n the S American campanero; any of several Australian and NZ birds with a bell-like call, such as either of the two species of honeyeater (*Manorina melanophrys* and *Anthornis melanura*) or the thickhead (*Oreoica gutturalis*); elsewhere, other birds with bell-like notes. **bell'-bottomed** adj (of trousers) widening greatly from knee to ankle. **bell'-bottoms** n pl. **bell'boy** n a hotel porter or page. **bell buoy** n a buoy carrying a bell, rung by the movement of the waves. **bell'cote** n (archit) an ornamental structure made to contain one or two bells, and often crowned by a small spire. **bell crank** n a lever with two arms, usu at right angles, and a common fulcrum at their junction. **bell end** n a rounded end part; (vulgar sl) the tip of the penis; an idiot or fool; someone despised. **bell'flower** n a campanula. **bell'-founder** n a person who casts bells. **bell'-foundry** n. **bell'-glass** n a bell jar. **bell'hanger** n a person who hangs and repairs bells. **bell'-heather** n a variety of erica with bell-shaped flowers. **bell'hop** n (chiefly N Am) a bellboy. **bell'-housing** n a tapered outer casing of part of a vehicle's transmission. **bell jar** n a bell-shaped glass cover, in laboratories placed over apparatus to confine gases, etc, or used to protect ornaments or flower arrangements. **bell magpie** n (Aust) the currawong. **bell'man** n a person who rings a bell, esp on the streets, before making public announcements; a town crier. **bell'-metal** n the metal of which bells are made, an alloy of copper and tin. **bell pull** n a cord or handle used in ringing a bell. **bell'-punch** n a ticket punch containing a bell. **bell push** n a button used in ringing an electric or spring bell. **bell'ringer** n a person who rings a bell on stated occasions; a performer on church bells or musical hand bells. **bell'ringing** n. **bell'-rope** n the rope by which a bell is rung. **bell'-shaped** adj. **bell'-siller** /-sil'ər/ n (Walter Scott) a fee for bellringing at a funeral. **bell tent** n a bell-shaped tent. **bell tower** n a tower built to contain one or more bells, a campanile. **bell'-turret** n a turret containing a chamber for a bell, usu crowned with a spire. **bell'wether** n the leading sheep of a flock, on whose neck a bell is hung; a ringleader; a setter of a standard, pattern or trend, a leader (econ, etc). **bell'wort** n any plant of the family Campanulaceae; a plant of the genus *Uvularia* (US).
■ **bear** or **carry off** (or **away**) **the bell** to have or gain the first place. **bell, book and candle** a phrase popularly used in reference to a form of excommunication ending, 'Do to (ie shut) the book, quench the candle, ring the bell'. **bells and whistles** (sl) additional, largely decorative rather than functional features. **bells of Ireland** an annual plant (*Moluccella laevis*) with white flowers and green bell-shaped calyxes, sometimes used in dried-flower arrangements. **bell the cat** to undertake the leading part in any hazardous enterprise, from the fable of the mice who proposed to hang a warning bell round the cat's neck. **clear as a bell** (of a sound) distinct and pure in tone. **give someone a bell** (sl) to telephone someone. **ring a bell** to begin to arouse a memory. **ring the bell** to achieve a great success (from the bell of a shooting-gallery bull's-eye). **ring the bells backward** to reverse the order of chimes. **sound as a bell** in perfect condition, health, etc.

bell² /bel/ vi to bellow, roar; to utter loudly. ◆ n the cry of a stag at rutting-time. [OE *bellan* to roar; cf Ger *bellen*]

bell³ /bel/ n a bubble formed in a liquid. [Ety doubtful; cf Du *bel* perh from L *bulla* a bubble in water]

belladonna /bel-ə-don'ə/ n the deadly nightshade or dwale (*Atropa belladonna*), all parts of which are narcotic and poisonous from the presence of atropine; the drug prepared from it. [Ital *bella donna* fair lady; one property of belladonna is to enlarge the pupil of the eye]
❑ **belladonna lily** n a pink-flowered S African amaryllis.

bella figura /be-la fi-goo'rə/ n a good impression and appearance. [Ital]

bellamoure see **belamoure**.

bellarmine /bel'är-mēn or -ər-/ n a greybeard, or large jug with a big belly, decorated with a bearded face, said to represent Cardinal *Bellarmine* (1542–1621), made in mockery by Dutch Protestants.

Bellatrix /be-lā'triks (L -ä'trēks)/ n a second-magnitude star in Orion, one of the corners of the quadrilateral. [L *bellātrix* female warrior]

belle /bel/ n a beautiful woman or girl; the chief beauty of a place or occasion. Cf **beau**. [Fr *belle* (fem), from L *bella* fine, gay]
❑ **belle amie** /be-la-mē/ n a female friend or mistress. **belle assemblée** /be-la-sã-blā/ n a fashionable gathering. **belle-de-nuit** /-də-nwē/ n (Fr, night beauty) marvel of Peru (qv). **belle laide** /bel led/ n a jolie laide. **belle-laide** adj. **belle-mère** /bel-mer/ n a mother-in-law. **belle passion** /pa-syɔ̃/ n the tender passion, love. **belle peinture** /pɛ̃-tür/ n naturalistic painting. **belle vue** /vü/ n a fine prospect.
■ **la belle époque** /la-bel-ā-pok/ (also with *caps*) 'the fine period', the time of security and gracious living for the well-to-do, ended by World War I.

belles-lettres /bel-let'r'/ n pl polite or elegant literature, including poetry, fiction, criticism, aesthetics, etc. [Fr, literally, fine letters]
■ **belletris'tic** or **belletris'tical** adj. **bellett'rist** or **bellet'rist** n.

belleter /bel'ə-tər/ n a bell-founder. [For *bellyetter*, from **bell**[1] and OE *gēotan* to pour]

bellibone /bel'i-bōn/ (*Spenser*) n a beautiful and good woman. [Appar Fr *belle* (et) *bonne*]

bellicose /bel'i-kōs/ adj contentious, warlike. [L *bellicōsus*]
■ **bell'icosely** adv. **bellicosity** /-kos'i-ti/ n.

bellied see **belly**.

belligerent /be-lij'ə-rənt/ adj aggressive; waging war; recognized legally as waging war. ◆ n a country, person, etc waging war; one recognized as so doing. [L *belligerāre* to wage war, from *bellum* war, and *gerere* to wage]
■ **bellig'erence** n. **bellig'erency** n. **bellig'erently** adv.

Bellini /be-lē'ni/ n a pink cocktail made with chilled champagne and peach nectar or peach schnapps. [Named after Giovanni *Bellini* (c.1430–1516), Venetian painter]

Bellona /be-lō'nə/ n the Roman goddess of war; a woman of great spirit and vigour.

bellow /bel'ō/ vi to roar like a bull; to make any violent outcry. ◆ vt to roar out. ◆ n the roar of a bull; any deep loud sound or cry. [ME *belwen*; OE *bylgian* to roar; cf **bell**[2]]
■ **bell'ower** n.

bellows /bel'ōz/ or (*old*) bel'us/ n pl or n sing an instrument for producing a current of air to blow up a fire, or sound an organ, accordion, etc (also **pair of bellows**); a telescopic sleeve connected between a camera body and lens, used when focusing on small close objects; something which fans the fire of hatred, jealousy, etc; the lungs. ◆ adj in the form of a bellows, allowing for expansion, as in a gusseted tongue of a boot, etc. [Ety as for **belly**; the singular form did not survive the 15c]
❑ **bell'ows-fish** n the trumpetfish.
■ **bellows to mend** (*esp* in sporting parlance) shortness of breath, eg in a horse.

Bell's palsy /belz pöl'zi/ n a sudden paralysis of the muscles of one side of the face, caused by damage to the facial nerve, which results in distortion of the features and may affect the senses of hearing and taste. [Sir Charles *Bell* (1774–1842), Scottish surgeon]

bellum internecinum /bel'əm or -ŭm in-tər-ne-sī'nəm or -ter-ne-kē'nŭm/ (L) n a war of extermination.

belly /bel'i/ n the part of the body between the breast and the thighs, containing the intestines, etc; the stomach, as the receptacle of the food; the bowels; the womb or uterus (*archaic*); the deep interior of anything; the bulging part of anything, as of a bottle, or any concave or hollow surface, as of a sail; the front or undersurface, as opposed to the back; in a violin or a leaf, the upper surface; a soundboard on a piano (*music*). ◆ adj ventral, abdominal; belonging to the flesh, carnal (*theol*). ◆ vi (*pat* and *pap* **bellied** /bel'id/) to swell or bulge out (often with *out*). [ME *bali, bely*, from OE *bælig, belig, bælg, belg* bag]
■ **bell'ied** adj with a belly, esp a big belly, pot-bellied; bulging; puffed out. **bell'yful** n (*inf*) a sufficiency; more than enough. **bell'ying** n and adj.
❑ **bell'yache** n a pain in the belly; a persistent complaint or whine (*sl*). ◆ vi (*sl*) to complain whiningly. **bell'yacher** n. **bell'y-band** n a saddle-girth; a band fastened to the shafts of a vehicle, and passing under the belly of the horse drawing it. **belly button** n (*inf*) the navel. **belly dance** n a sensuous Eastern dance, performed by a woman, with very pronounced movement of the abdomen and hips. ◆ vi to perform such a dance. **belly dancer** n. **belly flop** n an inexpert dive in which one lands face down, flat on the water; a belly landing. **bell'y-flop** vi. **bell'y-god** n a person who makes a god of his belly, a glutton. **belly landing** n (of an aircraft) a landing without using the landing wheels. **belly laugh** n a deep unrestrained laugh. **belly tank** n (*aeronautics*) see **ventral tank** under **venter**[1]. **bell'y-timber** n (*archaic*) provisions, food.
■ **belly up to** (*US sl*) to go directly or purposefully towards. **go belly up** (*sl*) to die, fail (as a dead fish, floating belly upwards); (of a business, etc) to fail.

belomancy /bel'ō-man-si/ n divination by means of arrows. [Gr *belos* a dart, and *manteiā* divination]

Belone /bel'ə-ni or -ō-/ n a genus of needle fish of the family **Belon'idae**, including the garfish. [Gr *belone* a needle, from *belos* a dart]

belong /bi-long'/ vi (in all senses *usu* with *to*) to pertain (to); to be the property (of; with *to*); to be a part or appendage (of), or in any way connected (with) (with *with* or *to*); to have a proper place (in); to be entirely suitable; to be a native or inhabitant, or member (of). [ME *bi-, belongen*, intensive of *longen*. See **long**[3]]
■ **belong'er** n (*sociol*) a person of conservative, middle-class values and lifestyle, conforming to social norms. **belong'ings** n pl possessions; personal effects; matters connected with any person (*obs*); persons connected, relatives (*obs*).

Belorussian or **Byelorussian** /be- or bje-lə-rush'ən/ (*hist*) adj of Belorussia, Byelorussia or White Russia, a region to the west of Moscow (cf **Belarussian**); of its language or people. ◆ n a native of this region; their language. [Russ *Belorussiya*, from *beliy* white]

belove /bi-luv'/ vt (*obs* except in *pap* **beloved** /bi-luvd'/) to love. [**be**-(1)]
■ **beloved** /bi-luv'id/ adj much loved, very dear, often compounded with *well-, best-*, etc. ◆ n /bi-luv'id/ a person who is much loved. **belov'ing** adj (*Shakesp*) loving.

below /bi-lō'/ prep beneath in place, rank or quality; underneath; not worthy of. ◆ adv in a lower place; farther on in a text; downstairs; on earth, or in hell. [ME *bilooghe*, from *bi* by, and *looghe* low]
■ **belowstairs'** adj and adv downstairs; in or belonging to the servants' quarters.
❑ **below-the-line** adj denoting an item in a financial statement that is different in nature from others and reported separately; of or relating to that part of the government's spending and revenue not allowed for in its original estimates; of or relating to marketing expenditure on items other than advertising, such as sponsorship or public relations.

bel paese /bel pä-ā'zē/ n a mild Italian cheese. [Formerly a trademark; Ital, literally, beautiful country]

bel sangue /bel sän'gwā/ (*Ital*) n gentle blood.

belshazzar see **balthazar**.

belt /belt/ n a band of leather or other material, esp one worn around the waist; a band of flexible material used to transmit motion in machinery; a broad stripe of anything, different in colour or material from whatever surrounds it; something which confines or restrains; a zone of country, a district (*geog*); a strait; a band for the waist awarded in recognition of a specific (grade of) achievement (see **black belt, Lonsdale belt**); a seat belt; a sharp blow, impact or shock (*inf*). ◆ vt to award a belt, or to invest formally with one, as in conferring knighthood; to encircle with a belt; to thrash with a belt; to hit hard (*inf*). ◆ vi (*sl*) to move very fast. [OE *belt*, from L *balteus*]
■ **belt'ed** adj wearing a belt, eg of a knight; marked with a band or bands of different colours. **belt'er** n (*inf*) something outstanding or strikingly good; a song for belting out; a singer who belts out songs. **belt'ing** n belts collectively; material for making belts; a beating (*inf*). ◆ adj (*inf*) outstandingly good.
❑ **belt-and-bra'ces** adj giving double security or double the chances of success. **belt bag** n another term for **bum bag** (see under **bum**[1]). **belt drive** n a system of transmitting power using an endless flexible belt. **belt'man** n (*Aust*) the member of a lifesaving team who swims out to the rescue, with a line tied to his belt. **belt'way** n (*US*) a ring road.
■ **belt out** (*inf*) to sing, play or send out vigorously or with great enthusiasm. **belt up** (*inf*) to be quiet; to fasten one's seat belt. **hit**, etc, **below the belt** to hit, etc, an opponent's body lower than the waist (forbidden in some sports); hence (*fig*) to deliver a mean blow, attack unfairly. **hold the belt** to hold the championship in wrestling, boxing, or the like. **tighten one's belt** to reduce one's demands or expenditure, to economize (**belt'-tightening** n). **under one's belt** (*fig*) firmly and irrevocably secured or in one's possession.

Beltane /bel'tān/ n an ancient Celtic festival, held at the beginning of May, when bonfires were lighted on the hills; the first day of May (*Old Style*), one of the four old quarter days of Scotland, the others being Lammas, Hallowmas and Candlemas. [Gaelic *beálltainn, beilteine,* appar bright fire. It has nothing to do with **Baal**]

beluga /bi-loo'gə/ n the great Russian sturgeon, a source of caviar, *Acipenser huso*, the white whale, closely allied to the narwhal, found in Arctic seas. [Russ *beliy* white]

belvedere /bel'vi-dēr or bel-vi-dēr'/ n a pavilion or raised turret or lantern on the top of a house, built to provide a view, or to admit the breeze; a summerhouse on high ground. [Ital *belvedere*, from *bel* beautiful, and *vedere* to see]

belying see **belie**.

BEM abbrev: British Empire Medal.

bema /bē'mə/ n the tribune or rostrum from which Athenian orators made their speeches; hence the apse or chancel of a basilica; a raised platform in a synagogue (*Judaism*). [Gr *bēma* a step]

bemad /bi-mad'/ (*archaic*) vt to madden. [**be-** (1)]

bemaul /bi-möl'/ (*archaic*) vt to maul thoroughly. [**be-** (1)]

bemazed /bi-māzd'/ (*archaic*) adj stupefied, bewildered. [**be-** (1)]

Bembex /bem'beks/ or **Bembix** /-iks/ n a genus of sand wasps, noted for their loud buzz; (without *cap*) a member of the genus. [Gr *bembix* a buzzing insect]

bemean[1] /bi-mēn'/ (*archaic*) vt to make mean, to lower or debase. [**be-** (2)]

bemean[2] /bi-mēn'/ (*obs*) vi to signify. [**be-** (1)]

bemedal /bi-med'əl/ (*archaic*) vt to cover with medals. [**be-** (2)]

bemete /bi-mēt'/ (*archaic*) vt to measure. [**be-** (1)]

bemire /bi-mīr'/ (*archaic*) vt to soil with mire; (in *passive*) to be stuck in the mire. [**be-** (2)]
■ **bemired'** adj.

bemoan /bi-mōn'/ vt to lament, bewail; to pity. ◆ vi to grieve. [**be-** (1)]
■ **bemoan'er** n. **bemoan'ing** n.

bemock /bi-mok'/ (*archaic*) vt to mock at, deride. [**be-** (1)]

bemoil /bi-moil'/ (*Shakesp*) vt to bemire, bedraggle. [**be-** (1)]

bemonster /bi-mon'stər/ (*archaic*) vt to make monstrous; to regard or treat as a monster. [**be-** (2)]

bemouth /bi-mowdh'/ (*archaic*) vt to mouth about. [**be-** (1)]

bemud /bi-mud'/ (*archaic*) vt to bespatter with mud; to confuse. [**be-** (2)]

bemuddle /bi-mud'l/ (*archaic*) vt to confuse or muddle completely. [**be-** (1)]

bemuffle /bi-muf'l/ (*archaic*) vt to wrap or muffle up completely. [**be-** (1)]

bemuse /bi-mūz'/ vt to put in confusion; to puzzle; to stupefy. [**be-** (1)]
■ **bemused'** adj. **bemuse'ment** n.

ben[1] /ben/ (*Scot* and *Irish*) n a mountain peak. [Gaelic *beinn*, oblique case of *beann*]

ben[2] /ben/ (*Scot*) prep and adv in or towards the inner or better room or rooms (of). ◆ n the inner or better room or rooms of a house, *opp* to *but*. [ME *binne*, from OE *binnan* within]
■ **a but and ben** a two-roomed house. **but and ben** backwards and forwards in the house (also *fig*); out and in; at opposite ends of a house or passage. **far ben** on terms of great intimacy or favour.

ben[3] /ben/ n any of several tropical trees of the *Moringa* genus, *esp* the horseradish tree, its seed (**ben'-nut**) yielding **ben'-oil** or **oil of ben**, used as a lubricant and in the preparation of perfumes and cosmetics. [Ar *bān*]

bename /bi-nām'/ vt (*pat* and *pap* **benamed'** (*archaic* **benempt'**)) to name, mention; to vow. [OE *benemnan*, from *nemnan* to name]

bench /bench or bensh/ n a long (*usu* wooden) seat with or without a back; a seat in a boat; a worktable or working place; a judge's seat; the body or assembly of judges; a tribunal; a seat for officials and reserve players at a match (*football, baseball,* etc); a level ledge in the slope of masonry or earthwork; a level tract between a river and nearby hills (*US*); a terrace (*geol*); in a greenhouse or conservatory, a raised bed or a platform with sides, for holding potted plants; a platform on which dogs are displayed at a dog show. ◆ vt to place on or provide with benches; to take (a player) out of a game; to put (plants) on greenhouse benches; to show (dogs); to bench-press (a specified weight). ◆ combining form used to denote the particular area in Parliament where MPs sit, and their respective prominence (as in *front bench, back bench*). [OE *benc*; cognate with Ger *Bank* and Du *bank*]
■ **bench'er** n a senior member of an inn of court; a person who sits on a bench in some official capacity. **bench'ership** n.
❑ **bench fees** n pl laboratory fees paid by scientific, medical and technical students. **bench'-hole** n (*Shakesp*) a latrine. **bench'mark** n a surveyor's mark cut on a rock, etc indicating a point of reference in levelling; something taken or used as a point of reference or comparison, a standard, criterion, etc (also *adj*); a standard program, used to compare the performance of different makes of computer hardware or software (*comput*). ◆ vt to test by means of a benchmark. **bench press** n a weightlifting exercise in which one lies on a bench with feet on the floor and raises a weight from chest level to arm's length. **bench'-press** vt to lift (a specified weight) in this manner. **bench test** n a test carried out on something before it is installed or released. **bench'-test** vt. **bench'-warmer** n (*sport sl*) a reserve player. **bench'-warrant** n one issued by a judge rather than a justice or magistrate.

■ **on the bench** holding the office of a judge or bishop; officiating as judge; acting as a reserve player. **raise to the bench** to make a judge or bishop.

bend[1] /bend/ vt (*pat* and *pap* **bent**; also **bend'ed**) to force into (or out of) a curved or angled form; to curve; to bow, turn (the body) downwards; to dispose or incline to a point of view; to aim or direct (one's attention, etc); to alter or disregard (rules) for one's own purposes; to subject (to one's will, etc); to fasten (*naut*); to drink hard at (*Scot*); to subject to tension (*obs*); to brace or bring to tension (*obs*; also *fig*). ◆ vi to curve; to stoop; to bow (down) the body; to give way, yield, or show flexibility; to turn in a given direction; to incline to a point of view; to drink hard (*Scot*). ◆ n a knot by which a line is tied to another, or to itself after passing through a ring, etc; a band, strip; a parallel band crossing a shield diagonally from top left to bottom right (a **bend-sin'ister** a supposed mark of illegitimacy, runs from top right to bottom left; *heraldry*); an act of bending; the state of being bent; a bent thing; a place of bending; a bow or stoop; half a butt of leather cut lengthwise; a directing of the eye (*Shakesp*); a strengthening band (*Spenser*); a pull of liquor, or a drinking bout (*Scot*). [OE *bendan* to constrain, bind, fetter, string (as a bow), *bend* bond, fetter]
■ **bend'able** adj. **bend'ed** adj (only in **on bended knee**). **bend'ee** adj (*heraldry*) bendy. **bend'er** n a person or machine which bends; a (drunken) spree (*sl*); a male homosexual (*sl*); a temporary shelter consisting of a shell of woven branches covered with tarpaulins or plastic sheeting (*inf*); a sixpence (*obs sl*); a thing very large or fine of its kind (*dialect*). **bend'ing** n and adj. **bend'ingly** adv. **bend'let** n (*heraldry*) a half-width bend. **bend'wise** adv (*heraldry*) diagonally. **bend'y** adj divided into bends (*heraldry*); full of or characterized by curves or bends; flexible (*inf*). **bent** n and adj see **bent**[1].
❑ **bend-sin'ister** n see above. **bent'wood** n wood artificially curved for chair-making, etc (also *adj*).
■ **bend over backwards** see under **back**[1]. **round the bend** (*inf*) crazy, mad. **the bends** decompression sickness, also known as **caisson disease**; aeroembolism.

bend[2] /bend/ (*Spenser*) n same as **band**[2].

bene[1] /bēn/ (*archaic; Wordsworth*) n a prayer; a boon. [OE *bēn*]

bene[2] an old spelling of **been**.

beneath /bi-nēth'/ adv and prep below; in a lower position so as to be under, or nearly so, or to be covered (by); inside, behind or at the back (of); at a lower level (relative to). ◆ prep in a manner or of a type not worthy of the dignity of or unbecoming to. ◆ adj (*Shakesp*) lower. [OE *beneothan*]

bene decessit /be'ne di-ses'it or dā-kā'sit/ (*LL*) n a leaving certificate given to a schoolboy, curate, etc (literally, he has left well).

benedicite /be-ni-dī'si-ti or -dis'i-ti, also (*L*) -dēk'i-te/ interj bless you (an old form of greeting). ◆ n a blessing; a grace at table; (with *cap*) the canticle beginning *Benedicite omnia opera* (All ye works of the Lord, bless ye) from *The Song of the Three Holy Children*. [L *benedīcite*, pl imperative of *benedīcere* to bless, from *bene* well, and *dīcere* to say, speak]

Benedick /ben'i-dik/ or **Benedict** /-dikt/ n a name for a newly married man, *esp* if formerly a confirmed bachelor. [From *Benedick* in Shakespeare's *Much Ado about Nothing*]

Benedict see **eggs Benedict** under **egg**[1].

benedict /ben'i-dikt/ (*obs*) adj blessed; benign. [L *benedīcere*, *benedictum*, from *bene* well, and *dicere* to say, speak]
■ **benedic'tion** /-shən/ n a blessing; a solemn invocation of the divine blessing on men or things; a blessing pronounced at the end of a religious service; a brief and popular service in the Roman Catholic Church; grace before or after a meal; blessedness. **benedic'tional** adj. **benedict'ive** adj. **benedict'ory** adj. **Benedict'us** n the canticle of Zacharias (Bible, Luke 1.68–79: Blessed be the Lord God of Israel), used in Roman Catholic and Anglican services; the fifth movement of the Mass (Blessed is he that cometh in the name of the Lord). **benedight** /-dīt'/ adj (*Longfellow*) blessed.
■ **apostolic benediction** that at the end of 2 Corinthians in the Bible.

Benedictine /be-ni-dik'tin or -tīn/ adj relating to St *Benedict* of Nursia (c.480–547), or his monastic rule. ◆ n a monk or nun of the order founded by him at Monte Cassino; /-tēn/ a cordial or liqueur resembling Chartreuse, distilled at Fécamp in Normandy, formerly by Benedictine monks.

Benedict's solution or **reagent** /ben'ə-dikts sə-loo'shən, -lū'shən or rē-ā'jənt/ n a chemical solution used to detect the presence of sugars, *esp* in urine as a test for diabetes. [SR *Benedict* (1884–1936), US chemist]

Benedictus see under **benedict**.

benefaction /be-ni-fak'shən/ n the act of doing good; a good deed done or benefit conferred; a grant or endowment. [L *benefactiō, -ōnis*; cf following entries]

■ **ben'efact** vt to confer a benefit on. **ben'efactor** or **ben'efactress** (also /-fak'/) n a person who confers a benefit; a person who aids eg an institution financially, a patron. **benefac'tory** adj.

benefic /bi-nef'ik/ adj kindly; benign; beneficent; favourable (astrol). [L beneficus kindly, beneficent, beneficium a service, benefit, from bene well, and facere to do]
■ **benefice** /ben'i-fis/ n a church living, an area from which an income is obtained, esp in return for the spiritual care of its inhabitants; the income so obtained; a fief (hist). **ben'eficed** adj possessing a benefice. **beneficence** /bi-nef'i-sans/ n active goodness; kindness; charity; a beneficent gift. **benef'icent** adj. **beneficential** /-sen'shl/ adj. **benef'icently** adv. **beneficial** /ben-i-fish'l/ adj useful; advantageous; enjoying the use of and profits from property (law). ◆ n (Spenser) appar a letter of presentation to a benefice. **benefici'ally** adv. **benefi'cialness** n. **benefi'ciary** n a holder of a benefice or a fief; a person who receives a gift or advantage; a person who enjoys, or has the prospect of enjoying, any interest or estate held in trust by others, eg under a will or insurance policy (law). ◆ adj of or being a beneficiary.

beneficiate /be-ni-fish'i-āt/ vt to treat (ores, etc) to get rid of impurities. [Sp beneficiar to benefit, from L beneficium a service, benefit]
■ **beneficia'tion** n treatment of ores, etc to get rid of impurities.

benefit /ben'i-fit/ n any advantage, natural or other; a performance, match, etc whose proceeds go to one of the company, a player, or other particular person or cause (also adj); money or services enjoyed as a right under social security or insurance schemes; a kindness; a favour. ◆ vt (**ben'efiting** (also **ben'efitting**); **ben'efited** (also **ben'efitted**)) to do good to; to be to the advantage of. ◆ vi to obtain advantage or good (with from or by). [ME benfet, from Anglo-Fr benfet, from L benefactum]
❑ **benefit of clergy** n originally an exemption of clergymen, in certain cases, from criminal process before a secular judge, but later covering the first offence of all who could read. **benefit of inventory** n (Scots law; hist) an heir's privilege of securing himself or herself against unlimited liability for his or her ancestor, by producing within a year an inventory of his or her heritage or real estate, to the extent of which alone he or she was liable. **benefit of the doubt** n presumption of innocence when culpability is uncertain. **benefit society** n a friendly society. **benefit tourism** n the practice of visiting a country in order to claim social security benefits without seeking work. **benefit tourist** n.

Benelux /ben'ə-luks/ n a name for (the economic union between) Belgium, the Netherlands and Luxembourg.

bene merentibus /be'ne me-rent'i-bus or -bŭs/ (L) to the well-deserving.

benempt see **bename**.

beneplacito /be-ne-plä'chē-tō/ (Ital) interj good pleasure; by your leave.

Benesh /ben'esh/ n a system of notation for detailing movements in dancing, introduced in 1955 by Joan and Rudolf Benesh.

benet¹ /bi-net'/ vt to catch in a net, to ensnare. [be- (1) or (2)]

benet² /ben'it/ n an exorcist, the third of the four lesser orders in the Roman Catholic Church. [OFr beneit, from L benedictus blessed]

bene vobis /be'ne vō'bis or wō'bēs/ (L) interj health to you.

benevolence /bi-nev'ə-lans/ n disposition to do good; an act of kindness; generosity; a gift of money, esp for support of the poor; a kind of forced loan or contribution, levied by kings without legal authority, first so called under Edward IV in 1473 (Eng hist). [OFr benivolence and L benevolentia]
■ **benev'olent** adj charitable, generous; kindly, well-disposed. **benev'olently** adv.

BEng abbrev : Bachelor of Engineering.

benga /ben'gə/ n a form of Kenyan popular music featuring guitars. [From an African language]

Bengal /ben- or beng-göl'/ n a striped cotton woven in the Bengal region, or an imitation of it. ◆ adj from Bengal, modern Bangladesh and the Indian state of West Bengal; made of Bengal.
■ **Bengalese** /ben-gə-lēz' or beng-/ n (pl **Bengalese'**) a person from Bengal (also adj). **Bengali** /ben-gö'li or beng-/ adj of or belonging to Bengal or Bengalis. ◆ n a person from Bengal; (also **Bangla** /bang'gla/) the language of Bengal, the official language of Bangladesh. **bengaline** /beng'gə-lēn/ n a fabric usu of silk and cotton or silk and wool, with a crosswise rib.
❑ **Bengal fire** or **Bengal light** n a brilliant, steady, blue light, used as a shipwreck signal, to illuminate country at night, and in fireworks.

beni see **benne**.

benight /bi-nīt/ vt (chiefly in passive) to be overtaken by night (ie before reaching one's destination); (active) to cover with darkness; to darken, cloud (fig; of sorrow, disappointment, etc). [be- (2)]

■ **benight'ed** adj overtaken by night; lost in intellectual or moral darkness; ignorant. **benight'en** vt (rare) to benight. **benight'ening** n. **benight'er** n. **benight'ing** n (also adj). **benight'ment** n.

benign /bi-nīn'/ adj favourable, esp in astrology, opp to malign; gracious and kindly; of a mild type, opp to malignant (med); (of weather or climate) mild, salubrious. [OFr benigne, from L benīgnus, prob from bene well, and root of genus birth, type]
■ **benignancy** /bi-nig'nən-si/ n benignant quality. **benig'nant** adj kind and gracious; beneficial, favourable; not malignant. **benig'nantly** adv. **benig'nity** n goodness or kindliness of disposition; a kindness, a kindly act; favourable circumstances, propitiousness, of climate, weather, disease, planets. **benign'ly** /-nīn'/ adv.

Beninese /be-ni-nēz'/ or **Beninois** /-nwä'/ adj of or relating to the Republic of Benin in W Africa, or its inhabitants. ◆ n (pl **Beninese'** or **Beninois'**) a native or citizen of Benin.

Benioff zone /ben'i-əf zōn/ (geol) n a seismic zone generated by collision between plates. [Hugo Benioff (1899–1968), American geophysicist]

beniseed see under **benne**.

benison /ben'i-sən or -zən/ n (literary) a benediction, blessing. [OFr beneiçun, from L benedictiō, -ōnis]

bénitier /bā-nē'tyā/ n a holy-water font, or stoup. [Fr, from LL benedictārium, from L benedictus]

benj /benj/ n bhang. [Ar]

Benjamin /ben'jə-min/ n a youngest son; a favourite child. [As in Bible, Genesis 42]

benjamin¹ /ben'jə-min/ n a kind of 19c overcoat. [Perh alluding to **Joseph**; or a tailor's name]

benjamin² /ben'jə-min/ n gum benzoin (also **gum benjamin**). [benzoin]
❑ **ben'jamin-tree** n a tree of the genus Styrax; the American spicebush; a kind of fig tree.

benne /ben'ē/, **benni** or **beni** /ben'i/ n sesame. [From (Sierra Leone) Mende bene]
❑ **benn'e-seed**, **benn'i-seed** or **ben'iseed** n sesame seed.

bennet¹ /ben'it/ see **herb bennet** under **herb**.

bennet² /ben'it/ (S Eng) n a dry grass stalk. [**bent²**]

benny¹ /ben'i/ (sl) n an amphetamine tablet. [Abbrev of **Benzedrine®**]

benny² /ben'i/ (sl) n an overcoat. [Prob abbrev of **benjamin¹**]

benomyl /ben'ə-mil/ n a pesticide and fungicide, with possible health risks, used on growing fruit and vegetables. [benzo and methyl]

bent¹ /bent/ pat and pap of **bend**. adj curved; having a bend; intent, determined (on or upon doing something); morally crooked, or criminal (sl); homosexual (sl); sexually deviant (sl); stolen (sl); obedient, governed (Spenser). ◆ n tendency, trend, inclination; direction; leaning or bias, natural inclination of the mind; the extent to which a bow may be bent or a spring wound; capacity of endurance; a piece of framework (building); curvature, curve (obs). [**bend¹**]
■ **to the top of one's bent** to the full measure of one's inclination.

bent² /bent/ n any stiff or wiry grass; the old dried stalks of grasses; a genus (Agrostis) of grasses, slender and delicate in appearance, some useful as pasture-grasses and for hay (also **bent grass**); a place covered with bents, a heath (Scot and N Eng); a hillside. [OE beonet, found in place names, as Beonetlēah Bentley]
■ **bent'y** adj.
■ **take to the bent** (Scot) to take flight.

Benthamism /ben'thə-mi-zm/ n the social and political teaching of Jeremy Bentham (1748–1832), the philosophical doctrine of utilitarianism.
■ **Ben'thamite** n.

benthos /ben'thos/ n the flora and fauna of the sea bottom or lake bottom (cf **plankton** and **nekton**). [Gr benthos depth]
■ **ben'thic** adj. **benthon'ic** or **benthoal** /ben-thō'əl/ adj living on the sea bottom. **benthopelagic** /-thō-pi-laj'ik/ adj (of marine fauna) living just above the seabed. **ben'thoscope** n a submersible sphere from which to study deep-sea life.

bento box /ben'tō boks/ n a container with several compartments, used orig in Japan for sushi or cold food. [Jap bento boxed meal]

bentonite /ben'tə-nīt/ n a valuable clay, consisting mainly of montmorillonite, widely used in industry as a bond, filler, etc. [Fort Benton, Montana, where it was found]

ben trovato /ben trō-vä'tō/ (Ital) adj apt but untrue.

bentwood see under **bend¹**.

benumb /bi-num'/ vt to make insensible or powerless; to stupefy (now chiefly with cold); to deaden the feelings of; to paralyse generally. [**be-** (2)]

■ **benumbed**' *adj.* **benumbed'ness** *n.* **benumb'ment** *n.*

ben venuto /ben ve-noot'ō/ (*Ital*) *interj* welcome.

Benzedrine® /ben'zi-drēn/ *n* a tradename for amphetamine.

benzene /ben'zēn/ *n* the simplest of the aromatic series of hydrocarbons, discovered by Faraday in 1825, now mostly prepared by destructive distillation of coal tar, its molecule consisting of a ring or closed chain of six carbon atoms each with a hydrogen atom attached, formerly called benzine or benzol, names now used differently (see below). [From **benzoin**] ■ **ben'zal** or **benzyl'idine** *n* a radical whose oxide is **benzal'dehyde** or oil of bitter almonds. **benz'idine** *n* a base used in preparing azo dyes. **ben'zil** *n* a double benzoyl radical. **benzine** /ben'zēn/ *n* a mixture of hydrocarbons obtained by destructive distillation of petroleum, used as a solvent, motor fuel, etc; improperly, benzene. **ben'zoate** /-zō-āt/ *n* a salt of benzoic acid. **benzocaine** /ben-zō-kā'in or ben'zō-kān/ *n* (**benzine** and **cocaine**) a drug used as a local anaesthetic. **benzodiazepine** /ben-zō-dī-az'ə-pēn, -pin or -pīn/ *n* one of a group of tranquillizing and soporific drugs. **ben'zol** or **ben'zole** *n* crude benzene, used as motor fuel; improperly, benzene. **ben'zoline** *n* benzine; impure benzene. **benzoquinone** /ben-zō-kwin'ōn/ see **quinone** under **quinol. benzoyl** /ben'zō-il/ *n* the radical C_6H_5:CO. **benzpyrene** /benz-pī'rēn/ *n* (**benzene** and **pyrene²**) a cancer-inducing hydrocarbon ($C_{20}H_{12}$) found in coal tar and present in small quantities in smoke, including tobacco smoke. **ben'zyl** /-zil/ *n* the radical $C_6H_5CH_2$. **benzyl'idine** *n* see **benzal** above. ◻ **benzene hexachloride** *n* (known as **BHC**) a chlorinated hydrocarbon, a very toxic insecticide. **benzene ring** *n* a ring of six linked carbon atoms, as in a molecule of benzene.

benzoin /ben'zō-in or -zoin/ *n* gum benjamin, the aromatic and resinous juice of *Styrax benzoin*, a tree of Java and Sumatra, used in perfumery, incense, etc and as an expectorant, inhalant and antiseptic, the chief constituent of friar's balsam; a former name for benzene. [In the 16c, benjoin, most prob through Ital from Ar *lubān jāwī* frankincense of Jawa (ie Sumatra)] ■ **benzo'ic** *adj* relating to benzoin, as in **benzoic acid**, C_6H_5COOH, found in benzoin and other gums.

bepaint /bi-pānt'/ (*archaic*) *vt* to paint over; to colour. [**be-** (1)]

bepat /bi-pat'/ (*archaic*) *vt* to pat frequently, to beat. [**be-** (1)]

bepatched /bi-pacht'/ (*archaic*) *adj* mended with patches; wearing patches on the face by way of adornment. [**be-** (1)]

bepearl /bi-pûrl'/ (*archaic*) *vt* to cover over with pearls. [**be-** (1)]

bepelt /bi-pelt'/ (*archaic*) *vt* to pelt vigorously. [**be-** (1)]

bepepper /bi-pep'ər/ (*archaic*) *vt* to pelt with a rain of shot or blows. [**be-** (1)]

bepester /bi-pest'ər/ (*archaic*) *vt* to vex or pester greatly. [**be-** (1)]

bepity /bi-pit'i/ (*archaic*) *vt* to pity greatly. [**be-** (1)]

beplaster /bi-plä'stər/ (*archaic*) *vt* to plaster thickly; to daub. [**be-** (1)]

beplumed /bi-ploomd'/ (*archaic*) *adj* adorned with feathers. [**be-** (2)]

bepommel /bi-pum'l/ (*archaic*) *vt* to pommel soundly. [**be-** (1)]

bepowder /bi-pow'dər/ (*archaic*) *vt* to powder over. [**be-** (1)]

bepraise /bi-prāz'/ (*archaic*) *vt* to lavish praise on. [**be-** (1)]

beprose /bi-prōz'/ (*archaic*) *vt* to reduce to prose; to discuss in prose and tediously. [**be-** (2)]

bepuff /bi-puf'/ (*archaic*) *vt* to puff out; to praise greatly. [**be-** (1)]

bequeath /bi-kwēdh'/ *vt* to leave by will to another person (strictly, personal property); to pass on to posterity, to leave behind; to commit or entrust to anyone (*obs*). [OE *becwethan*, from pfx *bi-, be-* and *cwethan* to say; see **quoth**] ■ **bequeath'able** *adj.* **bequeath'al** *n.* **bequeath'ment** *n.*

bequest /bi-kwest'/ *n* the act of bequeathing; that which is bequeathed, a legacy. [ME *biqueste*, from OE pfx *bi-, be-* and *cwethan* to say; see **quoth**]

berate /bi-rāt'/ *vt* to scold or chide severely. [**be-** (1)]

beray /bi-rā'/ (*obs*) *vt* to befoul (also (*non-standard*) **bewray'**). [**be-** (1) and **ray⁴**]

Berber /bûr'bər/ *n* a member of one of the Muslim peoples of N Africa; the language of the Berbers. ◆ *adj* of or relating to the Berbers. [Ar *barbar*; connection with Gr *barbaros* is doubtful]

berberis /bûr'bə-ris/ *n* any shrub of the barberry genus *Berberis*, giving name to the family **Berberidā'ceae**, related to the buttercup family. [Ety as **barberry**] ■ **berberidā'ceous** *adj.* **ber'berine** *n* an alkaloid obtained from barberry roots.

Berbice chair /bə-bēs' chär/ *n* an armchair whose arms extend to form leg-rests. [From *Berbice* a river and county in Guyana]

berceau /ber-sō'/ (*Fr*) *n* (*pl* **berceaux** /-sōz or -sō/) a cradle; a covered walk.

berceuse /ber-sœz'/ *n* a lullaby or cradlesong; a musical composition in similar rhythm. [Fr]

berdache or **berdash** /bər-dash'/ (*hist*) *n* a Native American transvestite, *usu* male, adopting not only the dress but also the status and role of the opposite sex. [Fr *bardache* male homosexual]

bere¹ another spelling of **bear³**.

bere², beer or **bear** /bēr/ *n* a pillowcase (*usu* **pill'ow-bere**). [Origin obscure; cf Ger *Bühre*]

Berean /be-rē'ən/ *n* a member of an 18c Scottish presbyterian sect (also *adj*). [*Beroea*, Gr *Beroia* in Macedonia, where the people searched the scriptures daily (Bible, Acts 17.11)]

bereave /bi-rēv'/ *vt* (*pat* and *pap* **bereaved'** (*usu* by death), **bereft'** (*usu* in general sense); *archaic pap* **bereav'en**) to widow, orphan, or deprive by death of some dear relative or friend; to deprive or rob of anything valued; to snatch away (*obs*). [OE *bereāfian* to plunder; see **reave**] ■ **bereaved'** *adj.* **bereave'ment** *n* loss by death of a relative or friend. **bereft'** *adj* deprived (of something), having had something taken away.

Beres drops /ber'es drops/ *n pl* a liquid dietary supplement, consisting of a mixture of trace elements. [Named after Dr Josef *Beres*, 20c Hungarian biochemist]

beret /be'rā or bə-rā'/ or **berret** /ber'et/ *n* a flat, round, woollen or felt cap worn by Basques and others. [Fr *béret*]

berg¹ /bûrg or berhh/ *n* (*S Afr*) a hill or mountain. [Ger *Berg*, Du *berg* hill; cognate with **barrow²**] ◻ **berg'-adder** *n* a venomous S African viper, living on hillsides. **berg'-cedar** *n* a rare conifer (*Widdringtonia juniperoides*) of the Cedarbergen in South Africa. **bergfall** /bûrg'föl or berk'fäl/ *n* (Ger, mountain fall) a fall of mountain rock. **berghaan** /berhh'hän or bûrg'hän/ *n* (Du, mountain cock; *S Afr*) the bateleur eagle. **bergmehl** /berk'māl or bûrg'/ *n* (Ger, mountain flour) a powdery deposit of diatom frustules. **bergschrund** /berk'shrunt/ *n* (Ger, mountain cleft) a crevasse formed at the head of a mountain glacier between the moving and stationary ice. **berg wind** *n* in S Africa, a hot, dry wind blowing from the mountains towards the coastal regions.

berg² /bûrg/ *n* short for **iceberg**.

bergamask, also **bergomask** /bûr'gə-mäsk/ *n* (also with *cap*) a native of *Bergamo* in Italy; a rustic dance associated with that district.

bergamot¹ /bûr'gə-mot/ *n* a (small citrus tree producing a) kind of citron or orange, whose aromatic rind yields oil of bergamot, used in perfumery; the essence extracted from this fruit; a mint of similar smell; a kind of woven tapestry made in Bergamo; a kind of rug made in Bergama (also **ber'gama**). [Said to be from *Bergamo* in Italy; or *Bergama* (Pergamum) in Asia Minor; or as **bergamot²**]

bergamot² /bûr'gə-mot/ *n* a fine dessert pear. [Fr, from Ital, from Turk *begarmudi* prince's pear]

bergander or **bargander** /bər-gan'dər/ *n* the shelduck. [Perh from **burrow** and **gander**]

bergen /bûr'gən/ *n* a large framed rucksack. [Ety uncertain; perh from *Bergen* in Norway]

bergenia /bər-gē'ni-ə/ *n* a plant of the *Bergenia* genus of perennial plants of the family Saxifragaceae, having red, purple or pink flowers. [KA von *Bergen* (1704–60), German botanist and physician]

bergère /ber-zher'/ *n* a type of easy chair or sofa with cane back and arms (also *adj*). [Fr, shepherdess]

berghaan, bergmehl see under **berg¹**.

bergomask see **bergamask**.

bergschrund see under **berg¹**.

Bergsonian /bûrg-sō'ni-ən/ *adj* relating to Henri *Bergson* (1859–1941) and his philosophy of creative evolution. ◆ *n* a follower of Bergson. ■ **Berg'sonism** /-sən-izm/ *n.*

bergylt /bûr'gilt/ *n* a red northern sea fish of the family Scorpaenidae. [Norw *berggylta* rock-pig]

beribboned /bi-rib'ənd/ *adj* decorated with ribbons. [**be-** (2)]

beri-beri /ber'i-be-ri/ *n* a mainly tropical disease caused by lack of thiamine which results in nerve inflammation, paralysis, oedema and heart failure. [Sinhalese *beri* weakness]

berk or **burk** /bûrk/ (*sl*) *n* a fool. [Short for Cockney rhyming slang *Berkeley Hunt*, for **cunt**]

Berkeleian /bär-klē'ən, bärk'li-ən or (US) bûr-klē'ən/ *adj* relating to Bishop *Berkeley* (1685–1753), who maintained that the world we see and touch depends for its existence on being perceived. ◆ *n* a follower of Berkeley. ■ **Berkelei'anism** (or /bärk'/) *n.*

berkelium /bər-kē'li-əm (earlier bûrk'li-əm)/ n an artificially produced radioactive transuranic metallic element (symbol **Bk**; atomic no 97). [First produced in a cyclotron at Berkeley, California]

Berks. /bärks/ abbrev : Berkshire.

berley or **burley** /bûr'li/ (Aust) n bait, groundbait; leg-pulling, humbug (inf). ◆ vt to scatter (bait) over water. [Origin unknown]

berlin /bûr'lin, bər-lēn/ or -lin'/ n an old four-wheeled covered carriage, with a seat at the rear covered with a hood (also **ber'line**); a closed motor car with the driver's seat partitioned off. [From the city of Berlin] ■ **Berlin'er** n a newspaper format between broadsheet and tabloid in size, typically measuring approx 31.5 × 47cm (about 12½ × 18½in); an iced doughnut with a jam filling. �‡ **Berlin blue** n Prussian blue. **Berlin wool** n a fine dyed wool for worsted-work, knitting, etc.

berm /bûrm/ n a wall of sand built as a defence in desert warfare; a narrow ledge or path beside a road, etc; the area of level ground between the raised mound of a barrow or other earthwork and the ditch surrounding it (archaeol). [Fr berme ; Ger Berme]

Bermudian /bər-mū'di-ən/ or **Bermudan** /-mū'dən/ adj and n (a native or inhabitant) of Bermuda, an island group in the NW Atlantic. ◼ **Bermuda grass** /bər-mū'də/ n a type of grass native to S Europe, now growing widely in warm countries, with wiry rootstock, used in lawns and for binding sand-dunes. **Bermuda petrel** same as **cahow**. **Bermuda rig** n a sailing rig in which there is a large fore-and-aft sail fixed directly to a tall mainmast. **Bermuda rigged** adj. **Bermuda shorts** n pl shorts, for men or women, reaching almost to the knee (also **Bermu'das**). **Bermuda Triangle** n the area between Florida, Bermuda and Puerto Rico where ships and aeroplanes are alleged to have mysteriously disappeared.

Bernardine /bûr'nər-din or -dēn/ adj Cistercian (also n). [From Bernard of Clairvaux, founder of the order]

bernicle-goose same as **barnacle-goose** (see under **barnacle¹**).

berob /bi-rob'/ (Spenser) vt to rob or plunder. [**be-** (1)]

BERR abbrev : (until 2009) (Department for) Business, Enterprise and Regulatory Reform.

berret see **beret**.

berry¹ /ber'i/ n any small succulent fruit; a simple fruit with pericarp succulent throughout (thus strictly excluding strawberry, raspberry and blackberry, which are aggregate fruits) (bot); a coffee bean; a cereal grain; a lobster's or crayfish's egg; a knob on a swan's bill. ◆ vi (**berr'ying**; **berr'ied**) to produce berries, swell; to gather berries. [OE berie] ■ **berr'ied** adj bearing berries; of lobsters, etc, having eggs. **berr'ying** n. ◼ **berry bug** n the harvest mite or chigger, of the genus Trombicula.

berry² /ber'i/ n a pottage or sop (as in ale-berry, breadberry). [OE brīw pottage, porridge]

bersaglieri /ber-sä-lyä'rē/ n pl the riflemen or sharpshooters of the Italian Army, first organized in the Sardinian Army in 1836. [Ital; pl of bersagliere, from bersaglio a target]

berserk /bər-zûrk' or -sûrk'/ adj violently frenzied or angry (usu with go). ◆ n (also **berserk'er**) a Norse warrior who on the battlefield was filled with a frenzied and irresistible fury. [ON berserkr frenzied warrior, literally, prob bear-shirt] ■ **berserk'ly** adv.

berth /bûrth/ n a sleeping-place in a ship, train or caravan, usu a narrow fixed bunk; a place allotted to a ship at anchor or at a wharf; room for a ship to manoeuvre; any allotted or assigned place; a situation or place of employment, usu a comfortable one. ◆ vt and vi to moor or dock (a ship). ◆ vt to provide with a berth. [Ety obscure] ■ **berth'age** n accommodation, or dues paid, for mooring or anchoring. ■ **give a wide berth to** to keep well away from, avoid.

bertha /bûr'thə/ n a woman's deep (usu lace) collar worn to cover a low neckline (also **berthe**); (with cap; often **Big Bertha**) a big German gun (from Frau Berta Krupp of the Krupp steelworks), first used of guns shelling Paris 1918. [Woman's name] ◼ **bertha army worm** n a type of cutworm of north central USA and Canada, destructive to crops.

Bertholletia /bûr-thō-lē'sh(i)ə/ n the Brazil-nut genus of Lecythidaceae. [Named in honour of the chemist CL Berthollet (1748–1822)]

Berthon-boat /bûr'thon-bōt/ n a type of collapsible boat. [Edward L Berthon (1813–99), its inventor]

bertillonage /ber-tē-yo-näzh'/ (Fr) n a system of criminal identification by detailed measurement, worked out by Alphonse Bertillon (1853–1914), a Paris police officer.

Berufsverbot /bə-roofs'fər-bōt/ (Ger) n in Germany, the policy of excluding political extremists from public service.

beryl /ber'il/ n a precious stone occurring in hexagonal crystals, of which emerald and aquamarine are varieties, a silicate of beryllium and aluminium, green, colourless, yellow or blue, once thought to have magic properties. ◆ adj pale greenish. [OFr beryl, from L bēryllus, from Gr bēryllos] ■ **beryll'ia** n the oxide of **beryll'ium**, a metallic element (symbol **Be**; atomic no 4), used for windows in X-ray tubes, and industrially to harden alloys, etc. **berylliō'sis** n a disease caused by exposure to the fumes or dust from beryllium salts, in which granulomata are formed esp in the lungs.

BES abbrev : Business Expansion Scheme.

besaint /bi-sānt'/ (archaic) vt to make a saint of. [**be-** (2)] ■ **besaint'ed** adj canonized; haunted with saints.

bescatter /bi-skat'ər/ (archaic) vt to scatter over. [**be-** (1)]

bescrawl /bi-skröl'/ (archaic) vt to scrawl or scribble over. [**be-** (1)]

bescreen /bi-skrēn'/ (archaic) vt to screen; to overshadow. [**be-** (1)]

bescribble /bi-skrib'l/ (archaic) vt to write in a scribbling hand; to scribble about, over or upon. [**be-** (3)]

besee /bi-sē'/ (obs) vt (pap **beseen'**) to look to; to provide for; to treat; to provide, furnish, apparel, adorn. [OE besēon, from be- (pfx) and sēon to see] ■ **beseen'** adj of (specified) appearance; (well, etc) furnished.

beseech /bi-sēch'/ (Spenser **beseeke** /bi-sēk'/) vt (pat and pap **besought** /bi-söt'/ or **beseeched'**) to entreat, implore; to ask or pray earnestly to (God, etc); to beg. ◆ n (Shakesp) entreaty. [**be-** (1) and ME sechen; see **seek**] ■ **beseech'er** n. **beseech'ing** n and adj. **beseech'ingly** adv. **beseech'ingness** n.

beseem /bi-sēm'/ vi to be fitting or becoming; to seem (obs). ◆ vt to be seemly for; to become; to be fit for or worthy of. [**be-** (1)] ■ **beseem'ing** n and adj. **beseem'ingly** adv. **beseem'ingness** n. **beseem'ly** adj (rare).

beseen see **besee**.

beset /bi-set'/ vt (**besett'ing**; **beset'**) to surround with hostile intentions, besiege; to assail mentally, perplex, endanger, with problems, temptations, obstacles, etc; to surround or set round with anything (now esp jewels; now only in pap); to occupy so as to allow no one to go out or in. [OE besettan, from settan to set] ■ **beset'ment** n. **besett'er** n. **besett'ing** adj constantly assailing; dominant.

beshadow /bi-shad'ō/ (archaic) vt to cast a shadow over. [**be-** (1)]

beshame /bi-shām'/ (archaic) vt to put to shame. [**be-** (1)]

beshine /bi-shīn'/ (archaic) vt to light up. [**be-** (1)] ■ **beshone** /-shon'/ adj.

beshrew /bi-shroo'/ (archaic) vt to wish evil on, curse (latterly only in oaths). [**be-** (1) and obs vt **shrew** to curse]

beside /bi-sīd'/ prep by or to the side of, next to, near; outside of; away from; as distinct from, compared with; over and above, besides (rare). ◆ adv nearby; besides; apart; to the side. [OE besīdan by the side (dative); the -s in besides is of the adverbial genitive] ■ **besides'** adv in addition; moreover; otherwise, else. ◆ prep over and above; other than, with the exception of; apart from; beside (obs); away from (obs). ■ **beside oneself** having lost self-control, irrational (with worry, anger, etc). **beside the mark**, **point** or **question** irrelevant (and therefore inconsequential).

besiege /bi-sēj'/ vt to attack violently with the intent of capturing; to surround with armed forces; to throng round in large numbers; to importune; to pester (inf). [**be-** (1)] ■ **besiege'ment** n. **besieg'er** n. **besieg'ing** n and adj. **besieg'ingly** adv (rare) urgently.

besigh /bi-sī'/ (archaic) vt to sigh over. [**be-** (3)]

besing /bi-sing'/ (archaic) vt to celebrate in song. [**be-** (3)] ■ **besung'** adj.

besit /bi-sit'/ (archaic) vt to besiege; to sit well on, to suit. [OE besittan, from sittan to sit] ■ **besitt'ing** adj (Spenser) becoming.

B ès L (Fr) abbrev : Bachelier ès Lettres, Bachelor of Letters.

beslave /bi-slāv'/ vt to make a slave of; to call slave. [**be-** (2)]

beslaver /bi-slav'ər/ (archaic) vt to slaver or slobber upon; to cover with fulsome flattery. [**be-** (1)]

beslubber /bi-slub'ər/ vt to bedaub or besmear. [**be-** (1)]

besmear /bi-smēr'/ vt to smear over; to bedaub; to pollute, besmirch. [**be-** (1)]

besmirch /bi-smûrch'/ vt to soil, eg with smoke or dirt (literary); to sully (a reputation, etc). [**be-** (1)]

besmut /bi-smut'/ vt (**besmutt'ing**; **besmutt'ed**) to blacken with soot. [**be-** (1)]
■ **besmutt'ed** adj.

besmutch /bi-smuch'/ (archaic) vt to besmirch. [**be-** (1)]

besognio /bi-zōn'yō/ n (pl **besogn'ios**) a beggar. [Ital; see **bezonian**]

besoin /bə-zwɛ̃'/ (Fr) n need, want, desire.

beso las manos /bā'sō läs mä'nōs/ (Sp) interj I kiss your hands.

besom[1] /bē'zəm/ n a bunch of twigs for sweeping or a broom made of twigs tied to a handle; (also (Scot) /biz'əm or buz'əm/) any broom; any cleansing or purifying agent. ◆ vt (**be'soming**; **be'somed**) to sweep (often with away or out). [OE besema; Ger Bezen, Du bezem]
□ **be'som-head** n a blockhead. **be'som-rider** n a witch.
■ **jump the besom** see under **broom**.

besom[2] or **bisom** /biz'əm or bē'zəm/ (Scot and N Eng) n a term of reproach esp for a woman, implying slatternliness, laziness, impudence, or unscrupulous energy. [Perh the same word as **besom**[1]; or perh connected with OE bysn, bisn example, or ON bȳsn wonder]

besonian see **bezonian**.

besort /bi-sört'/ (Shakesp) vt to match, befit, become. ◆ n suitable company. [**be-** (1)]

besot /bi-sot'/ vt (**besott'ing**; **besott'ed**) to make sottish, dull, or stupid; to make a sot of; to cause to dote; to infatuate. [**be-** (2)]
■ **besott'ed** adj infatuated; stupefied, stupid; intoxicated (obs). **besott'edly** adv. **besott'edness** n.

besought /bi-söt'/ pat and pap of **beseech**.

besouled /bi-sōld'/ (archaic) adj endowed with a soul. [**be-** (2)]

bespangle /bi-spang'gl/ vt to adorn with spangles, or with anything sparkling or shining. [**be-** (2)]

bespatter /bi-spat'ər/ vt to spatter or sprinkle with dirt or anything wet; to defame. [**be-** (1)]
■ **bespatt'ered** adj.

bespeak /bi-spēk'/ vt (pat **bespoke'** (or archaic **bespake'**); pap **bespōk'en**, also **bespoke'**) to engage in advance, to order or apply for; to request or ask for; to betoken, be evidence for; to foretell; to address (poetic). ◆ vi (obs) to speak, speak out; see also separate entry **bespoke**. ◆ n an actor's benefit, so called because his friends and patrons choose the piece to be performed; an application in advance. [**be-** (3)]

bespeckle /bi-spek'l/ vt to mark with speckles or spots. [**be-** (1)]
■ **bespeck'led** adj.

bespectacled /bi-spek'tə-kəld/ adj wearing, or as if wearing, spectacles. [**be-** (2)]

bespeed /bi-spēd'/ (archaic) vt (pat **besped'**) to help on. [**be-** (1)]
■ **besped'** adj having got on (well, etc).

bespice /bi-spīs'/ (Shakesp) vt to season with spice. [**be-** (2)]

bespit /bi-spit'/ (archaic) vt (pat and pap **bespit'** or **bespat'**; pap (Browning) **bespate'**) to spit upon, defile with spittle. [**be-** (1)]

bespoke /bi-spōk'/ adj (esp of clothes) specially tailored or designed to the client's measurements, requirements, etc; (of a tailor, etc) making clothes, etc, to order. [Pap of **bespeak**]

besport /bi-spört'/ vt to disport (oneself). [**be-** (1)]

bespot /bi-spot'/ vt to cover with spots. [**be-** (1)]
■ **bespott'ed** adj. **bespott'edness** n.

bespout /bi-spowt'/ vt to spout over; to declaim pompously. [**be-** (1)]

bespread /bi-spred'/ vt (**bespread'ing**; **bespread'**) to spread over; to cover. [**be-** (3)]

besprent /bi-sprent'/ (obs) adj sprinkled over; scattered. [OE besprengan; see **sprinkle**]

besprinkle /bi-spring'kl/ vt to sprinkle over. [**be-** (1)]

B ès S (Fr) abbrev: Bachelier ès Sciences, Bachelor of Sciences.

Bessarabian /bes-ə-rā'bi-ən/ adj of Bessarabia, a region in SE Europe, now mostly in Moldova and Ukraine. ◆ n a native or citizen of Bessarabia; a type of carpet from this region.

Bessemer /bes'ə-mər/ adj relating to the steelmaking process invented by Sir Henry Bessemer (1813–98).
□ **Bessemer converter** n a type of furnace used in the Bessemer process. **Bessemer iron** or **pig** n pig iron suitable for making Bessemer steel. **Bessemer process** n a process for making steel from molten pig iron.

Besserwisser /bes'ər-vis-ər/ (Ger; often facetious) n someone who (thinks he or she) always knows better or more than anyone else.

best /best/ adj (serving as superl of **good**) good in the highest degree; first; highest; most excellent in any way. ◆ n one's utmost endeavour, the limit of one's ability; the highest perfection; the most outstanding or finest example; the most advantageous or largest share, part,

success or lot (as in the best of the bargain, the best of three games); best wishes (inf); one's smartest clothing. ◆ adv (superl of **well**[1]) to the highest degree of quality, excellence, etc; better than anyone else. ◆ vt (inf) to win against, outdo or outwit. [OE betst, betest; see **better**]
■ **best'ie** n (sl) a best friend.
□ **best'-ball** adj (golf) applied to foursomes, etc in which it is the lowest score at individual holes that is counted. **best-before date** n the date (stamped, etc on a package esp with the wording 'best before (eg) 12 September') up to which a manufacturer can guarantee the good quality of a consumer (usu food) product. **best boy** n (esp N Am) the chief assistant to the head lighting electrician on a film or television production crew. **best boy** or **girl** n (inf) a favourite friend of the opposite sex, a boyfriend or girlfriend. **best buy** n the most highly recommended purchase from those available. **best end** n a cut of lamb, etc from the part of the neck nearest the ribs. **best maid** n (Scot) a bridesmaid. **best man** n the groom's (male) attendant and ring-keeper at a wedding. **best part** n the larger part. **bestsell'er** n a book, etc that has sold many copies, overall or in a given season; the writer of such a book. **bestsell'erdom** n bestsellers collectively, popular publishing. **bestsell'ing** adj of a book, etc or author that is a bestseller.
■ (**all**) **for the best** likely to have the best ultimate outcome. **all the best** see under **all**. **as best one can** as well as one can. **at best** assuming the most favourable conditions. **at the best of times** even in the most favourable circumstances. **for the best** done with the best of intentions or outcome; see (**all**) **for the best** above. **get** or **have the best of it** to gain the advantage in a contest. **give someone best** to concede the victory to someone. **had best** see under **have**. **make the best of** to obtain the best results from (a poor, unpromising, etc situation). **make the best of one's way** to go as fast as one can. **put one's best foot forward** see under **foot**. **six of the best** see under **six**. **to the best of one's knowledge** or **belief** or **ability** as far as one knows, believes or is able. **with the best** (**of them**) as successfully as anyone.

bestad(de) see **bestead**[2].

bestain /bi-stān'/ (archaic) vt to stain all over. [**be-** (1)]

bestar /bi-stär'/ (archaic) vt to cover with stars. [**be-** (2)]

bestead[1] /bi-sted'/ vt (pat **bestead'ed**; pap **bestead'** or **bested'**) to help, relieve; to be of use to, avail. ◆ vi to profit, be advantageous. [**be-** (1) and obs vt **stead**]

bestead[2] or **bested** /bi-sted'/ (Spenser **bestad** or **bestadde** /bi-stad'/) adj set about (with); beset (with by, foes; with with, dangers, etc); situated (usu with ill, hard, etc). [**be-** (2) and **stead** placed]

bestial /bes'ti-əl/ adj like an animal, brutish; sexually depraved; rude, unrefined. ◆ n (archaic Scot) a collective name for cattle. [L bestiālis, from bestia beast]
■ **best'ialism** n lack of the human capacity for reasoning. **bestiality** /-al'i-ti/ n behavioural likeness to animals; disgusting vice; copulation between a person and an animal. **best'ialize** or **-ise** vt to make bestial.

bestiary /bes'ti-ə-ri/ n a book of a type popular in the Middle Ages, describing animals, both real and fabled, allegorized for moral teaching purposes. [LL bestiārium a menagerie, from bestia a beast]

bestick /bi-stik'/ vt (pat and pap **bestuck'**) to cover all over; to transfix; to adorn. [**be-** (1)]

bestie see under **best**.

bestill /bi-stil'/ (archaic) vt to make quiet, to hush. [**be-** (1)]

bestir /bi-stûr'/ vt to cause to begin lively action; to arouse into activity. [**be-** (1)]

bestorm /bi-störm'/ (archaic) vt to assail with storms or tumult. [**be-** (1)]

bestow /bi-stō'/ vt to give or confer (a reward, distinction, etc); to endow with (a particular quality); to stow, place, or put by (archaic); to provide accommodation for (archaic); to apply, employ (resources, etc); to acquit (oneself) (Shakesp). [**be-** (1)]
■ **bestow'al** n act of bestowing; disposal. **bestow'er** n. **bestow'ment** n.

bestraddle /bi-strad'l/ vt to stand or sit with one leg on either side of; to straddle across. [**be-** (3)]

bestraught /bi-ströt'/ (obs) adj distraught; distracted; mad. [**distraught**, with change of prefix to **be-** (1)]

bestreak /bi-strēk'/ vt to overspread with streaks. [**be-** (1)]

bestrew /bi-stroo'/ vt (pap **bestrewed'** or **bestrown'** /-strōn'/ or **bestrewn'**) to cover loosely with something strewn or scattered over. [**be-** (1)]

bestride /bi-strīd'/ vt (pat **bestrode'** or (archaic) **bestrid'**; pap **bestridd'en** or (archaic) **bestrid'**) to stand or sit across in an imposing manner; to defend or protect; to stride over. [**be-** (3)]
■ **bestrīd'able** adj.

bestuck pat and pap of **bestick**.

bestud /bi-stud'/ vt to adorn as with studs, as the sky with stars. [**be-** (1)]

besuited /bi-soo'tid or -sū-/ adj wearing a suit. [**be-** (2)]

bet /bet/ n a prediction of the result of anything yet to be decided, often gambled on with money or other stakes; the stakes to be lost or won on the result of a doubtful outcome; opinion, guess. ◆ vt and vi (**bett'ing**; **bet** or **bett'ed**) to lay or stake (money, etc) as a bet; to predict. [Poss shortened from the noun **abet**]
■ **bett'er** n a person who bets (also **bett'or**). **bett'ing** n.
❏ **betting shop** n premises, not on a racecourse, licensed for the placing of bets and payment of winnings.
■ **a good** (**better** or **best**) **bet** a (more or most) hopeful proposition or possibility. **an even bet** an equal chance. **you bet** (sl) certainly.

bet. abbrev : between.

beta /bē'tə/ n the second letter (B, β) of the Greek alphabet; in the ancient Greek alphabetic numbering system β' = 2, ,β = 2000; in classification, the second or one of the second grade, the grade below alpha; in a constellation, a star second in brightness. ◆ adj in chemical classification, designating one of two or more isomeric forms of a compound; relating to electrons; denoting a version of a product (eg new computer software) being tested under working conditions. [Gr bēta; see **B**, **beth**]
■ **be'tacism** /-sizm/ n pronunciation of the sound of 'b' as that of 'v'. **be'tatron** n (Gr -tron agent sfx) see **accelerator** under **accelerate**.
❏ **be'ta-blocker** n a drug that reduces heart rate and interferes with the action of stress hormones such as adrenaline, used to treat eg high blood pressure and angina. **betacarotene** /-kar'ə-tēn/ n a nutrient found in yellow and orange fruits and vegetables. **beta decay** n radioactive decay in which a neutron in an atomic nucleus spontaneously breaks up into a proton (which remains within the nucleus) and an electron (which is emitted). **Beta fibre** n a high-fibre product of sugar beet used as a dietary supplement to aid the absorption of cholesterol. **beta interferon** n a drug used to treat multiple sclerosis. **beta rays** n pl streams of **beta particles** or electrons or positrons, given off by some radioactive substances. **beta rhythm** or **wave** n a wave recorded in an electroencephalogram representing the normal activity of the brain of someone who is awake with open eyes. **beta test** n a test, in normal working conditions (cf **alpha test**), of a product (eg new computer software) before it is marketed. **be'ta-test** vt. **beta-thalassaemia** /-tha-lə-sē'mi-ə/ n a genetic disorder of the haemoglobin.

Betacam® /bē'tə-kam/ n a high-quality format used for camcorders and video recorders; a camcorder or video recorder using this format.

betaine /bē'tə-in or -ēn/ n a crystalline, sweet-tasting alkaloid occurring in sugar beet and other plants, also found in animals. [L bēta beet, and -ine]

betake /bi-tāk'/ (literary) vt (pat **betook'**; pap **betāk'en**) (reflexive) to take oneself to, go; to apply or have recourse to. [**be-** (1)]

betcha /bech'ə/ a spelling of **bet you** representing colloquial pronunciation.

bete see **beet²**.

bête /bet/ (Fr) n a brute, stupid person.
■ **bêtise** /bet-ēz/ n stupidity; a blunder.
❏ **bête noire** /nwär/ n literally, black beast; a bugbear; a person or thing that one especially dislikes or fears.

beteem or **beteeme** /bi-tēm'/ (Spenser and Shakesp) vt to grant, vouchsafe, allow. [Perh from a lost OE word corresponding to Du betamen to beseem]

betel /bē'tl/ n the leaf of the **betel pepper** (Piper betle) which is chewed in the East along with the areca-nut and lime as a mild stimulant. [Through Port from Malayalam vettila]
❏ **betel nut** n the areca-nut.

Betelgeuse or **Betelgeux** /bēt' or bet'əl-jooz/ n a reddish first-magnitude star in Orion's shoulder. [Fr, from Ar bayt-al-jawzā' Orion]

beth /beth or bāth/ n the second letter of the Hebrew and Phoenician alphabets, resembling a house. [Heb bēth house; see **B**, **beta**]

bethankit /bi-thang'kit/ (Scot) interj elliptical for God be thanked. ◆ n a grace.

Beth Din /bāt dēn or beth din/ n a Jewish court, in London presided over by the Chief Rabbi. [Heb bēth house, and dīn judgement]

bethel /beth'əl/ n a Methodist or Baptist church; an old ship fitted as a place of worship for sailors. [Heb Bēth-ēl house of God]

Bethesda /be-thez'də/ (Heb) n a healing pool at Jerusalem; (usu without cap) a Nonconformist church building.

bethink /bi-thingk'/ (literary) vt (pat and pap **bethought** /bi-thöt'/) to think about or call to mind; to recollect, usu in the phrase bethink oneself of; to propose to (oneself). ◆ vi to consider. [OE bithencan; cf Ger bedenken. See **think¹**]

bethrall /bi-thröl'/ (Spenser) vt to enslave. [**be-** (2)]

bethumb /bi-thum'/ vt (pap **bethumbed'**) to mark with the thumbs. [**be-** (1)]

bethump /bi-thump'/ vt to thump or beat soundly. [**be-** (1)]

bethwack /bi-thwak'/ vt to thrash soundly. [**be-** (1)]

betide /bi-tīd'/ vt (pat **betī'ded** or **betid** /-tid'/; pap **betid'** (Spenser **betight** /-tīt'/)) to befall, happen to (orig with dative and formerly sometimes followed by to or unto); to betoken (non-standard and rare). [**be-** (1); see **tide²**]

betime /bi-tīm'/ (Shakesp) vi to betide. [**be-** (2)]

betimes /bi-tīmz'/ (literary) adv in good time; early; speedily, soon. [**be-** (1) and **time**, with adverbial genitive -s]

bêtise see under **bête**.

betitle /bi-tī'tl/ vt to give a name to. [**be-** (2)]

betoil /bi-toil'/ vt to weary with toil. [**be-** (1)]

betoken /bi-tō'kn/ vt to show by a sign; to be an omen of; to mean, symbolize (archaic). [**be-** (1)]

béton /bā-tɔ̃'/ (Fr) n lime concrete; concrete.

betony /bet'ə-ni/ n a common labiate plant (Stachys or Betonica officinalis) growing in woods, of great repute in ancient and medieval medicine; extended to various labiate and scrophulariaceous plants. [Fr bétoine, from L betonica, vettonica]

betook /bi-tŭk'/ pat of **betake**.

betoss /bi-tos'/ (Shakesp) vt to agitate. [**be-** (1)]

betray /bi-trā'/ vt to hand over or expose (a friend, one's country, etc) to an enemy; to give information about treacherously (to an enemy); to disclose in breach of trust; to deceive (someone innocent and trustful), seduce; to disappoint the hopes of; to reveal or show unintentionally; to show signs of. [**be-** (1) and OFr trair (Fr trahir), from L tradere to deliver up]
■ **betray'al** n the act of betraying. **betray'er** n a traitor; the seducer of a trustful female.

betread /bi-tred'/ vt (pat **betrod'**; pap **betrodd'en**) to tread over or walk upon. [**be-** (1)]

betrim /bi-trim'/ vt to trim or set in order, deck, dress. [**be-** (1)]

betroth /bi-trōdh' or -tröth'/ (old) vt to contract or promise to marry (a woman); to affiance (one person to another); to pledge (oneself) to. [**be-** (2), and **troth** or **truth**]
■ **betroth'al** or **betroth'ment** n an engagement to marry; a ceremonious declaration of such an engagement. **betrothed'** adj and n (a person) promised in marriage.

better /bet'ər/ adj (serving as compar of **good**) good in a greater degree; preferable; improved; more suitable; larger; kinder; stronger in health; completely recovered from illness, etc. ◆ adv (compar of **well¹**) well to a greater degree or extent; more fully, completely, expertly, etc; over or more. ◆ n a person superior in quality or rank (esp in pl). ◆ vt to make better; to surpass, to do better than. ◆ vi (rare) to grow better. [OE bet (adv), betera (adj) better; Gothic batiza, Ger besser; prob cognate with **boot²**]
■ **bett'ered** adj. **bett'ering** adj improving; surpassing. ◆ n amelioration; improvement. **bett'erment** n improvement, esp in standard of life, status or value of property. **bett'ermost** adj best. **bett'erness** n.
❏ **bett'er-ball** n a form of stroke-play golf between two teams of two players, in which only the lower score of each team is counted for each hole; a golf match in which one player competes against the best individual score of two or more players for each hole. **better half** n a jocular or patronizing term for a spouse, formerly applied seriously to a wife or husband, an intimate friend, and even the soul as opposed to the body.
■ **be** (**all**) **the better for** to be improved as a result of. **be better than one's word** to do more than one had promised. **better off** in superior circumstances; more fortunate; richer. **better oneself** to improve one's position or social standing. **for better** (**or**) **for worse** whatever the result may be. **for the better** in the way of improvement. **get the better of** to gain the advantage over, overcome. **go one better than** to outdo. **had better** see under **have**. **have seen** or **known better days** to be worse off or in worse condition now than formerly. **so much the better** that is, or would be, preferable. **the better part of** more than half of. **think better of** to revise one's decision about, esp to decide against; to have a higher opinion of.

bettong /bet'ong/ n an Australian rat-kangaroo of the genus Bettongia. [From an Aboriginal language]

betty /bet'i/ n a man who occupies himself with housework; a burglar's jemmy (old sl). [Dimin of Elizabeth]
■ **Betty Martin** an expression of disbelief, usu in the phrase all my eye and Betty Martin.

Betula /bet'ū-lə/ n the birch genus, giving name to the family **Betulā'ceae**, which includes hazel and hornbeam. [L betula]

---

betumbled /bi-tum'bəld/ (Shakesp) adj tumbled or disordered. [**be-** (1)]

between /bi-twēn'/ prep in, to, through or across the space that separates; intermediate to; indicating a choice of alternatives; indicating that both alternatives apply; by combined action or influence of; from one to another of; to and from; in joint possession of (gen of two). ◆ adv in or to an intermediate place; at spatial or temporal intervals. ◆ n an interval (Shakesp); an intermediate size of needle. [OE betwēonum and betwēon, from be by, and twēgen, twā twain, two]

■ **between'ity** n (playful) intermediateness. **between'ness** n the state or fact of being between.

□ **between'-decks** n the space between any two decks of a ship (also adv). **between'-maid** n a servant subsidiary to two others (esp cook and housemaid), a tweeny. **Between the Sheets** n a cocktail containing rum, brandy, Cointreau and lemon juice. **between'time**, **between'times** or **between'whiles** adv at intervals.

■ **between ourselves** or **between you and me** (sl and the cat or post or bedpost, etc), **between the two of us**, or **between us two** in confidence. **between the devil and the deep blue sea** in a desperate dilemma, faced with two undesirable alternatives. **go between** to act as a mediator (**go'-between** n).

betwixt /bi-twikst'/ prep and adv (archaic) between. [OE betweox, from twā two, and sfx -ix -ish, with added -t, as in **against** and **amidst**]

■ **betwixt and between** in a middling, undecided, or intermediate position.

Beulah /bū'lə/ n a name for the land of Israel in the Bible (Isaiah 62.4); a Nonconformist chapel. [Heb, literally, married woman]

beurre /bœr/ (Fr) n butter.

□ **beurre blanc** /blã/ n a sauce made with butter, shallots and vinegar, red wine or lemon juice, usu served with fish. **beurre manié** /ma-nyā/ n a butter and flour mixture for thickening sauces. **beurre noir** /nwär/ n butter heated until it browns.

beurré or **beurre** /bœ-rā'/ adj of delicate flavour and texture, applied to several varieties of pear (also n). [Fr, buttery]

BeV abbrev: billion electronvolts, where billion = one thousand million.

bevatron /bev'ə-tron/ n a type of proton accelerator (see under **accelerate**). [From **BeV** and Gr agent sfx -tron]

bevel /bev'l/ n a slant or inclination of a surface; a tool opening like a pair of compasses, and adjustable for measuring angles. ◆ adj having the form of a bevel; slanting. ◆ vt (**bev'elling**; **bev'elled**) to form so as to have a bevel or slant. ◆ vi to slant. [From the (unattested) older form of Fr beveau bevel (tool)]

■ **bev'elled** adj cut to an oblique angle, sloped off. **bev'eller** n. **bev'elling** n. **bev'elment** n.

□ **bevel gear** n (mech) a set of wheels (**bevel wheels**) working on each other in different planes, the cogs of the wheels being bevelled or at oblique angles to the shafts.

bever[1] see under **beverage**.

bever[2] an obsolete form of **beaver**[1] and **beaver**[2].

beverage /bev'ə-rij/ n any liquid for drinking, esp tea, coffee, milk, etc; a mixture of cider and water (obs); a drink or drink-money to celebrate an occasion (dialect). [OFr bevrage (Fr breuvage), beivre, from L bibere to drink]

■ **bever** /bēv'ər/ n a small snack between meals (dialect); a time for drinking (obs). **bevv'ied** adj (inf) drunk. **bevv'y** or **bev'y** n (inf) an alcoholic drink; a drinking session.

□ **beverage room** n (Can) a beer parlour.

Bevin boy /bev'in boi/ n a young man in the UK in World War II selected to work in a coalmine instead of doing the normal military service. [Ernest Bevin (1881–1951), Minister of Labour and National Service during the war]

bevue /bā-vū'/ n a blunder. [Fr bévue]

bevy[1] /bev'i/ n a company or flock (of larks, quails, swans, roes or ladies). [Origin obscure]

bevy[2] see under **beverage**.

bewail /bi-wāl'/ vt to lament; to mourn loudly over (esp the dead). ◆ vi to lament. [**be-** (1)]

■ **bewailed'** adj. **bewail'ing** n and adj.

beware /bi-wār'/ vi (usu with of, or with that or lest) to be on one's guard (against); to be careful (of); to take heed; to take care (of) (obs); to take warning by (obs). ◆ vt to be on one's guard against; to take care of (obs); to take care (with infinitive or clause) (archaic). Used normally only in infinitive and imperative; old writers have was ware, etc. [**be** and **ware**[2]]

beweep /bi-wēp'/ vt (pat and pap **bewept'**) to weep over, lament; to wet or disfigure by weeping. [**be-** (1)]

beweltered /bi-wel'tərd/ (archaic) adj besmeared by weltering in blood. [**be-** (1)]

bewet /bi-wet'/ (Shakesp) vt (pat and pap **bewett'ed** or **bewet'**) to wet or moisten. [**be-** (1)]

bewhiskered /bi-wis'kərd or -hwis'kərd/ adj having whiskers on the face. [**be-** (2)]

bewhore /bi-hōr'/ (Shakesp) vt to call a whore; to make a whore of. [**be-** (2)]

Bewick's swan /bū'iks swon/ n a small white swan (Cygnus bewickii) native to N Asia and NE Europe, that winters occasionally in W Europe. [T Bewick (1753–1828), English wood engraver, illustrator of History of British Birds]

bewig /bi-wig'/ vt to cover or dress in a wig. [**be-** (2)]

■ **bewigged'** adj.

bewilder /bi-wil'dər/ vt to perplex, confuse; to cause to get lost (archaic). [**be-** (1) and obs Eng wildern, from OE wilddēoren wilderness, from wild wild, and dēor beast]

■ **bewil'dered** adj confused in mind; lost (archaic); trackless, pathless (archaic); confused, mixed up (archaic). **bewil'dering** adj. **bewil'deringly** adv. **bewil'derment** n.

bewitch /bi-wich'/ vt to affect by witchcraft (mostly malignantly); to fascinate or charm. [**be-** (1)]

■ **bewitch'ery** n. **bewitch'ing** adj charming; enchanting. **bewitch'ingly** adv. **bewitch'ment** n.

bewray[1] /bi-rā'/ (archaic) vt to reveal, esp inadvertently; to betray; to divulge; to show up; to reveal the existence, presence or whereabouts of. [ME bewreien, from be-, and OE wrēgan to accuse]

bewray[2] see **beray**.

bey /bā/ n a Turkish governor (hist); a Turkish title of rank (hist); in modern Turkey, the usual term of address to adult males, corresponding to Mr. [Turk]

beyond /bi-yond'/ prep on the farther side of; farther on in comparison with; out of reach of; above, superior to, better than; apart from, in addition to. ◆ adv farther away; into the hereafter. ◆ n (with the) the unknown; the hereafter. [OE begeondan, from pfx be-, and geond across, beyond; see **yon**]

■ **beyond measure** too great to be measured; excessively. **beyond one** more than one is able to do; outside one's comprehension. **beyond seas** abroad. **go beyond** to surpass, go further than; to circumvent; to overreach (Bible; Shakesp). **the back of beyond** a place of extreme remoteness. **the** (**Great**) **Beyond** the afterlife.

bez, **bez-antler**, **bez-tine** see **bay**[6].

bezant /bez'ənt or bi-zant'/ n a gold coin first struck at Byzantium or Constantinople; a small yellow circle like a gold coin (heraldry).

bezazz see **bezzazz**.

bezel /bez'l/ n the part of the setting of a precious stone which encloses it; an oblique side or face of a cut gem; the grooved rim in which a watchglass, etc is set; a sloped cutting edge (eg of a chisel; usu **basil** /baz'l/); an indicator light on a car dashboard. [From an OFr word represented by Mod Fr biseau; ultimate origin uncertain]

Bézier curve /bez'i-ā kûrv/ n a curve, used eg in car body design, that is created from two fixed end points and two or more control points which can be moved to alter the shape of the curve. [Pierre Bézier (1910–99), French engineer]

bezique /bə-zēk'/ n a card game for two, three or four people, played with two packs, from which all cards below the seven have been removed; the winning combination at this game of the jack of diamonds and queen of spades. [Fr bésigue, of obscure origin]

bezoar /bē'zōr/ n a stony concretion found in the stomachs of goats, antelopes, llamas, etc, formerly thought to be an antidote to all poisons. [Through Sp bezoar and Ar bāzahr, from Pers pādzahr antidote, from zahr poison]

■ **bezoardic** /bez-ō-ärd'ik/ adj.

bezonian or **besonian** /bi-zō'nyən/ (Shakesp) n a beggar. [Ital bisogno need]

bezzazz, **bezazz**, **bazzazz**, **bazazz**, **bizzazz** or **bizazz** /bə-zaz'/ (inf) n variants of **pizzazz**.

bezzie /bez'i/ (Brit sl) n a person's best friend (also **bezzie mate**). [Altered form of **best**]

BF abbrev: Burkina Faso (IVR).

bf abbrev: bloody fool (inf); bold face (type); brought forward (as in accounts, etc).

BFBS abbrev: British Forces Broadcasting Service.

BFF (inf) abbrev: best friend forever.

BFI abbrev: British Film Institute.

BFPO abbrev: British Forces Post Office, a military postal service for troops serving overseas.

BG *abbrev* : Bulgaria (IVR).

BH *abbrev* : Belize (formerly British Honduras; IVR).

Bh (*chem*) *symbol* : bohrium.

Bhagavad Gita /bäg'ə-vəd gē'tə or bug'ə-/ *n* a sacred Hindu text, part of the Mahabharata. [Sans, song of the blessed one]

bhagee see **bhaji**.

Bhagwan /bug'wän/ (*Ind*) *n* God; a guru. [Sans]

bhai /bī/ (*Ind*) *n* brother; a form of address for a man. [Hindi]

bhajan /buj'ən/ *n* a Hindu religious song. [Sans]

bhaji, **bhajee** or **bhagee** /bä'jē/ *n* (in Indian cookery) an appetizer consisting of vegetables deep-fried in batter; a mild vegetable curry served as a side dish.

bhakti /buk'ti/ *n* (in Hinduism) devotion to a god, as a path to salvation; a form of yoga. [Sans, portion]

bhang /bang/ *n* a narcotic and intoxicant, the leaves and shoots of hemp. [Hindi *bhãg*; Pers *bang*; Sans *bhangā*]

bhangra /bang'grə/ *n* a combination of traditional Punjabi and Western pop music (also *adj*). [Punjabi, of uncertain origin]

bharal /bur'əl/ *n* the blue sheep of the Himalayas, *Pseudois nayaur* (also **burrel**, **burrell**, **burrhel** or **burhel**). [Hindi]

Bharat /bu'rut/ *n* Hindi name of the Republic of India. [*Bharata* legendary monarch]
■ **Bha'rati** *adj*.

Bharata Natyam /bur'ə-tə nat'yəm/ *n* a form of Hindu temple dance originating in the Tamil Nadu region of S India, first described by the sage *Bharata*.

bhavan /buv'ən/ (*Ind*) *n* a large house or official building. [Hindi]

BHC *abbrev* : benzene hexachloride.

bheestie, **bheesty** see **bhisti**.

bhel see **bael**.

bhelpuri /bāl'poo-ri/ *n* an Indian dish of puffed rice with onions. [Hindi]

bhindi /bin'di/ *n* okra as used in Indian cookery. [Hindi]

bhisti, **bheesty**, **bheestie** or **bhistee** /bēs'tē/ *n* an Indian water carrier. [Urdu *bhīstī*, from Pers *behistī*, from *bihisht* paradise]

bhoona see **bhuna**.

bhp *abbrev* : brake horsepower.

Bhs *abbrev* : British Home Stores.

bhuna or **bhoona** /boo'nə/ (*Ind cookery*) *adj* (of a dish) sautéed in oil and a mix of spices. ◆ *n* a dish cooked in this way. [Hindi and Urdu]

Bhutanese /boo-tə-nēz' or bū-/ *adj* of or relating to the Kingdom of Bhutan in the Himalayas, or its inhabitants. ◆ *n* (*pl* **Bhutanese'**) a native or citizen of Bhutan.

Bi (*chem*) *symbol* : bismuth.

bi¹ /bī/ (*inf*) *adj* and *n* (*pl* **bis**) (a) bisexual.

bi² /be/ *n* in traditional Chinese medicine, one of five responses (**bi syndromes**) that present as blockages in the circulation of chi in the meridians.

bi- /bī-/ or sometimes before a vowel **bin-** /bin-/ *pfx* two, twice, double. [L *bis* twice, two-, *bīnī* two by two, for *duis, duīnī*]

biannual /bī-an'ū-əl/ *adj* happening, etc twice a year, half-yearly. ◆ *n* (rarely) a biennial. [L *bi-* twice, two-, and *annus* year]
■ **biann'ually** *adv*.

bias /bī'əs/ *n* a one-sided mental inclination; a prejudice; any special influence that sways one's thinking; an unevenness or imbalance, *esp* in distribution or sampling of statistics; (in the game of bowls) a bulge or greater weight on one side of a bowl making it turn to one side; a turning to one side by a bowl; a slanting line or cut diagonally across the grain of a fabric; the voltage applied to certain electronic components to cause them to function in a given direction only. ◆ *adj* cut slantwise. ◆ *adv* slantwise. ◆ *vt* (**bī'asing** (also **bī'assing**); **bī'ased** (also **bī'assed**)) to prejudice or influence, *esp* unfairly; to affect so as to cause movement, etc in one direction rather than another; to cut on the slant. [Fr *biais* slant; of unknown origin]
■ **bī'asing** *n*.
❑ **bias binding** *n* (a long narrow folded piece of) material cut slantwise to provide stretch and used for binding *esp* curved edges in sewing. **bias crime** *n* (*N Am*) a crime committed for racial reasons. **bī'as-cut** *adj* cut on the bias. **bī'as-drawing** *n* (*Shakesp*) a turning awry.
■ **on the bias** diagonally, across the grain (of a fabric).

biathlon /bī-ath'lon/ (*sport*) *n* a competition in cross-country skiing and shooting. [L *bi-* two-, and Gr *athlon* a contest]
■ **biath'lete** *n*.

biaxial /bī-aks'i-əl/ *adj* having two (optic, etc) axes (also **biax'al**). [**bi-**]

Bib. *abbrev* : Bible.

bib /bib/ *n* a cloth or plastic shield put under a young child's chin; (of an apron, overalls, etc) the front part above the waist; a vest bearing their number worn by competing athletes, etc; the pout, a fish of the cod and haddock genus with a large chin barbel. ◆ *vt* and *vi* (**bibb'ing**; **bibbed**) to drink, to tipple. [Prob from L *bibere* to drink; perh partly imit]
■ **bibā'cious** *adj*. **bibā'tion** *n* tippling. **bibb'er** *n* a tippler; chiefly used as a *combining form*, eg (*Bible*) *winebibber*. **bib'ful** *n* see **spill a bibful** below.
❑ **bib'cock** *n* a tap with downturned nozzle.
■ **best bib and tucker** (*inf*) best clothes. **bib and brace** applied to overalls with a front bib and straps over the shoulders. **spill a bibful** (*sl*) to give away a secret, make an embarrassing revelation. **stick**, **poke** or **put one's bib in** (*Aust sl*) to interfere.

BIBA *abbrev* : British Insurance Brokers' Association.

bibble-babble /bib'l-bab'l/ (*Shakesp*) *n* idle talk. [Reduplication of **babble**]

Bibby /bib'i/ *n* a stateroom on a passageway in a ship. [Name of a shipping line]

bibelot /bib'lō or bēb'-/ *n* a knick-knack. [Fr]

bibl. *abbrev* : biblical; bibliographical; bibliography.

bible /bī'bl/ *n* (*usu* with *cap*) (the book containing) the Scriptures of the Old and New Testaments; (*usu* with *cap*) a comprehensive book regarded as the ultimate authority on its subject; the third stomach of a ruminant, with many folds like the leaves of a book. [Fr, from LL *biblia*, fem sing (earlier neuter pl) from Gr *biblia* books, esp the canonical books (sing *biblion* a book, dimin of *biblos* papyrus, paper)]
■ **biblical** /bib'li-kəl/ *adj* of, like or relating to the Bible. **bib'lically** *adv*. **bib'licism** /-sizm/ *n* biblical doctrine, learning or literature; literal interpretation and acceptance of the Bible. **bib'licist** or **bib'list** *n* a person skilled in biblical learning; a person who makes the Bible the sole rule of faith (*obs*); a person who interprets and accepts the Bible literally.
❑ **Bī'ble-basher**, **-pounder** or **-thumper** *n* (*inf*) a vigorous, aggressive or dogmatic Christian preacher. **Bī'ble-bashing**, **-pounding** or **-thumping** *n* and *adj*. **Bible belt** *n* those areas of the Southern USA of predominantly fundamentalist and puritanical Christian religious dogma. **Bible paper** *n* very thin strong paper for printing.

bibli- /bi-bli-/ *combining form* denoting book or books. [Gr *biblion* book; cf **bible**]
■ **bibliographer** /-og'rə-fər/ *n* a person versed in bibliography; the compiler of a bibliography. **bibliographic** /-ə-graf'ik/ or **bibliograph'ical** /-əl/ *adj*. **bibliog'raphy** *n* the study, description or knowledge of books, in regard to their outward form, authors, subjects, editions and history; a list of books on a particular subject or by a single author; a list of the works referred to in the process of writing a book, article, etc. **bibliolater** /-ol'ə-tər/ or **bibliol'atrist** *n* a person given to bibliolatry. **bibliol'atrous** *adj*. **bibliol'atry** *n* (Gr *latreiā* worship) a superstitious reverence for a book, *esp* the Bible. **bibliological** /-ō-loj'i-kəl/ *adj*. **bibliologist** /-ol'ə-jist/ *n*. **bibliol'ogy** *n* bibliography; booklore. **bib'liomancy** /-man-si/ *n* (Gr *manteiā* divination) divination by opening the Bible or other book at random. **bib'liomane** *n*. **bibliomā'nia** *n* (Gr *mania* madness) a mania for collecting or possessing books; love of books. **bibliomā'niac** *adj*. **bibliomaniacal** /-mə-nī'ə-kəl/ *adj*. **bibliopegic** /-pej'ik/ *adj* (Gr *pēgnynai* to fix). **bibliopegist** /-op'i-jist/ *n* a bookbinder; a fancier of bindings. **bibliop'egy** *n* the fine art of bookbinding. **bibliophagist** /-of'ə-jist/ *n* a voracious reader. **bib'liophil** or **bib'liophile** /-fil, -fīl/ *n* (Gr *philos* friend) a lover or collector of books (also *adj*). **biblioph'ilism** *n*. **biblioph'ilist** *n*. **biblioph'ily** *n*. **bibliophō'bia** *n* (Gr *phobeein* to fear) hatred of books. **bib'liopole** *n* (Gr *pōlēs* seller; *archaic*) a bookseller. **bibliopolic** /-pol'ik/ or **bibliopol'ical** /-əl/ *adj*. **bibliop'olist** *n*. **bibliop'oly** *n* (*archaic*) bookselling. **bibliothē'ca** *n* (Gr *bibliothēkē* from *thēkē* repository) a library; a bibliography; a series of books. **biblioth'ecary** *n* (*rare*) a librarian.

biblio. or **bibliog.** *abbrev* : bibliography.

bibulous /bib'ū-ləs or -ŭ-/ *adj* addicted to strong drink; absorbent of liquid. [L *bibulus*, from *bibere* to drink]
■ **bib'ulously** *adv*. **bib'ulousness** *n*.

bicameral /bī-kam'ə-rəl/ *adj* (of a legislative body) having two chambers. [L *bi-* two-, and *camera* chamber]
■ **bicam'eralism** *n* the system or principle of having two legislative chambers. **bicam'eralist** *n*.

bicarbonate /bī-kär'bə-nāt or -nət/ *n* an acid salt of carbonic acid, hydrogen carbonate. [**bi-** twice, and **carbonate**]
❑ **bicarbonate of soda** *n* sodium bicarbonate, used in baking powder or as an antacid digestive remedy (*inf* short form **bi'carb**).

biccy or **bickie** /bik'i/ (*inf*) *n* (*pl* **bicc'ies** or **bick'ies**) short form of **biscuit**.

■ words derived from main entry word; ❑ compound words; ■ idioms and phrasal verbs

bice /bīs/ n a pale blue or green paint. [Fr *bis*]

bicentenary /bī-sen-tē'nə-ri or -ten'ə-ri/ or (*esp N Am*) **bicentennial** /bī-sen-ten'i-əl/ adj happening every 200 years; relating to a 200th anniversary. ◆ n a 200th anniversary. [L *bi-* two-, and *centēnārius* relating to a hundred, from *centum* a hundred; or *bi-*, *centum* and *annus* a year]

bicephalous /bī-sef'ə-ləs/ adj having two heads. [**bi-**]

biceps /bī'seps/ n a muscle with two heads, *esp* that at the front of the upper arm or that at the back of the thigh. [L *biceps* two-headed, from *bi-* two-, and *caput* head]
- **bicipital** /-sip'l/ adj of or relating to the biceps; two-headed.

bichir /bich'ər or bī'kər/, also **birchir** /bûr'chər/ n any of various primitive African freshwater fishes of the genus *Polypterus*. [Origin unknown]

bichon frise /bē'shō frē-zā'/ n a modern breed of small dog with a curly white coat. [Fr *bichon* a breed of lapdog, and *frisé* curly]

bichord /bī'körd/ adj (of a musical instrument) having paired strings in unison for each note. [L *bi-* two-, and **chord**²]

bichromate /bī-krō'māt/ n a dichromate, or salt of dichromic acid. [**bi-**]

bicipital see under **biceps**.

bicker¹ /bik'ər/ vi to argue in a petty way, squabble; to quiver; to glitter; (of running water) to run quickly and noisily; to patter. ◆ n a fight, quarrel; a clattering noise; a rapid, noisy, short run (*Scot*). [Of unknown origin]

bicker² /bik'ər/ (*Scot*) n a bowl, *esp* of wood, for holding liquor; a vessel of wooden staves for porridge. [Scot form of **beaker**]

bickie see **biccy**.

bick-iron /bik'ī-ərn/ n a small anvil with two horns; the tapered end of an anvil. [From earlier *bickern*, a two-horned anvil, from Fr *bigorne*, from L *bicornis* two-horned]

bicoastal /bī-kō'stəl/ adj living or based simultaneously on two coasts, *esp* of N America. [**bi-**]

bicolour or (*US*) **bicolor** /bī-kul'ər/, also **bicoloured** or (*US*) **bicolored** /-kul'ərd/ adj composed of two colours, two-coloured. [**bi-**]

biconcave /bī-kon'kāv/ adj concave on both sides. [**bi-**]

biconvex /bī-kon'veks/ adj convex on both sides. [**bi-**]

bicorn or **bicorne** /bī'körn/ adj two-horned; two-cornered. ◆ n (*milit, formal* or *hist*) a hat with brim folded up on both sides, forming two corners (worn either front-to-back or side-to-side). [L *bicornis* two-horned, from *bi-* two-, and *cornū* a horn]

bicorporate /bī-kör'pə-rāt/ (*heraldry*) adj double-bodied, as the head of a lion to which two bodies are attached. [**bi-**]

bicultural /bī-kul'chə-rəl/ adj of, having, containing or consisting of two distinct cultures. [**bi-**]
- **bicul'turalism** n.

bi-curious /bī-kū'ri-əs/ adj considering experimenting in bisexuality.
- **bi-curiosity** n.

bicuspid /bī-kus'pid/ adj having two cusps. ◆ n a tooth located between the molars and the canine teeth, a premolar. [**bi-**]
- **bicusp'idate** adj.
- **bicuspid valve** n a mitral valve.

bicycle /bī'si-kl/ n a vehicle with two wheels, one directly in front of the other, driven by pedals or (**mo'tor-bicycle**) a motor. ◆ vi to ride a bicycle. [L *bi-* two-, and Gr *kyklos* a circle or wheel]
- **bī'cyclist** n.
- **bicycle chain** n the chain transmitting motion from the pedals to the wheels of a bicycle. **bicycle clip** n one of a pair of metal clips for holding a cyclist's trousers closely to his or her legs to avoid fouling the chain, etc. **bicycle kick** n (*football*) an overhead kick made with both feet off the ground. **bicycle polo** see under **polo**¹. **bicycle pump** n a hand pump for inflating bicycle tyres.

bicyclic /bī-sī'klik/ adj having two rings of atoms in a molecule. [**bi-**]

bid¹ /bid/ vt (**bidd'ing**; **bade** /bad/, also (*esp poetic*) *bād/* or **bid**; **bidd'en** or **bid**), *esp* to offer to pay at an auction; to propose (how many tricks one will win, eg in bridge); to proclaim (eg the banns of marriage). ◆ vi to make an offer or proposal, *esp* to state a price one will charge for work to be done; to make an attempt to win or achieve something. ◆ n an offer of a price; the amount offered; an attempt to win or achieve something (*press*); a call (*cards*). [OE *bēodan*; Gothic *biudan*, Ger *bieten* to offer]
- **bidd'able** adj tractable, easily persuaded or controlled; capable of or fit for bidding (*cards*). **bidd'er** n. **bidd'ing** n an offer, the offering of a price; the act or process of making bids (*cards*); the bids made (*cards*).
- **bid/offer spread** n in a financial market, the difference between the bid and offer prices, representing the dealer's margin. **bid price** n the

price at which a professional dealer is willing to buy shares or other items from the market.
- **bid fair** to seem likely. **bid in** (of an owner or his or her agent) in an auction, to overbid the highest offer. **bid up** to raise the market price of (something) artificially, by means of specious bids, etc.

bid² /bid/ vt (**bidd'ing**; **bade** /bad/, also (*esp poetic*) *bād/* or **bid**; **bidd'en** or **bid**) to invite; to command (*archaic*); to ask for (*archaic*); to pray (*obs*); to greet with, say as a greeting. [OE *biddan*; Gothic *bidjan*; Ger *bitten*. See **bead**]
- **bidd'ing** n someone's orders; a command; an invitation.
- **bidd'ing-prayer** n *orig* the praying, or saying, of a prayer, then by confusion with **bid**¹ taken to mean enjoining or inviting of prayer; a petitionary prayer said just before the sermon; a prayer for the living and the dead, said in English churches until the Reformation.

bidarka /bī-dār'kə/ n an Alaskan Inuit kayak. [Russ *baidarka*, dimin of *baidara* an umiak]

biddy /bid'i/ n a chicken, hen (*dialect*); in *Shakesp* applied to Malvolio; an old woman (*sl* and *derog*). [Poss the woman's name *Biddy* (short for *Bridget*), but perh the first meaning is another word]
- **red biddy** see under **red**¹.

bide /bīd/ vi (pat **bīd'ed**, **bode**, (*Shakesp*) **bid**, or (*Scot*) **bade** /bād/; pap **bīd'ed** or (*obs* and *Scot*) **bidd'en**) (*archaic* or *Scot*) to wait; to dwell; to remain. ◆ vt to await (*obs* except in **bide one's time** to await a favourable moment); to face unflinchingly (*poetic*); to endure. [OE *bīdan*; but sometimes for **abide**¹]
- **bīd'ing** n (*Shakesp*) residence, habitation.
- **bī'die-in** n (*Scot, inf*) a resident lover.

bident /bī'dənt/ n a two-pronged tool; a two-year-old sheep. [L *bi-* two, and *dēns, dentis* a tooth]
- **bidental** /bī-dent'l/ adj two-pronged; two-toothed. ◆ n (*ancient Rome*) a place struck by lightning (possibly consecrated by sacrifice of a sheep). **bīdent'āte** or **bīdentāt'ed** adj two-toothed.

bidet /bē'dā or bi-det'/ n a basin on a low pedestal, for washing the genital and anal areas, etc; a small horse (*archaic*). [Fr, pony]

bidi, **beedi** or **beedie** /bē'dē/ n a cheap thin Indian cigarette, sometimes fruit-flavoured. [Hindi, from Sans *vītika*]

bidirectional /bī-dī-rek'shə-nəl/ adj operating or passing signals in two directions; printing the lines of a text alternately left to right and right to left (*comput*, etc).

bidon /bē'dõ/ n a container for liquids, such as a wooden cup, water bottle, tin can or oil drum. [Fr]
- **bidonville** /bē'don-vēl or bē-dõ-/ n in a French-speaking country, a shanty town with dwellings made from oil drums.

BIDS abbrev : Bath Information and Data Services, an Internet service providing bibliographic information for academic users.

Biedermeier /bē'dər-mī-ər/ adj of a style of furniture derived from the French empire style, common in Germany in the first half of the 19c; (of German painting) of the Romantic Revival; bourgeois, hidebound (*derog*). [Name of a fictitious German poet]

bield /bēld/ (chiefly *Scot*) n shelter; protection. ◆ vt (*Walter Scott*) to shelter. [Scot and N Eng; OE *beldo* (WSax *bieldo*) courage; related to **bold**]
- **bield'y** adj.

bien¹ another spelling of **bein**.

bien² /byē/ (*Fr*) adv well.
- **bien-aimé** /byē-ne-mā/ adj well-beloved. **bien chaussé** /shō-sā/ adj well-shod. **bien élevé** /-nā-lav-ā/ adj well brought up, well-mannered. **bien entendu** /-nā-tã-dü/ interj of course; it goes without saying. **bien-être** /-netr/ n a sense of wellbeing. **bien pensant** /pā-sā/ adj right-thinking; orthodox. **bienséance** /-sā-ãs/ n propriety; (in *pl*) the proprieties.

Biennale /bē-ə-nä'lā/ n an international art festival held regularly in Venice since 1895. [Ital, biennial]

biennial /bī-en'i-əl or -en'yəl/ adj lasting two years; happening or appearing once in two years. ◆ n a plant that flowers and fruits only in its second year, then dies; an event taking place or celebrated every two years. [L *biennium* two years, from *bi-* two, and *annus* a year]
- **bienn'ially** adv.

bier /bēr/ n a stand or frame of wood for carrying a dead person to the grave. [OE *bǣr*; cf Ger *Bahre*, L *feretrum*. From root of verb **bear**¹]
- **bier right** n (*hist*) the ordeal of appearing before the corpse one was believed to have murdered (which was expected to bleed in the presence of the murderer).

bierkeller /bēr'ke-lər/ n a German or German-style bar, selling beer. [Ger, beer cellar]

biestings same as **beestings**.

bifacial /bī-fā'shl/ adj having two faces; having two dissimilar sides. [**bi-**]

bifarious /bī-fā'ri-əs/ adj in two rows (bot); double (obs). [L bifārius double]

■ **bifar'iously** adv.

biff /bif/ (inf) n a blow. ◆ vt to strike hard. [Imit]

biffin /bif'in/ n a variety of red cooking apple; such an apple slowly dried and flattened into a cake. [For beefing, from its colour of raw beef]

bifid /bif'id or bī'fid/ adj divided into two parts by a deep split. [L bifidus, from bi- two, and findere to cleave or split]

bifilar /bī-fī'lər/ adj having two threads. [L bi- two, and fīlum thread]

bifocal /bī-fō'kəl/ adj having two different focal lengths; having bifocal lenses. [**bi-**]

■ **bifo'cals** n pl spectacles with bifocal lenses, for far and near vision.

bifold /bī'fōld/ adj twofold; of two kinds (Shakesp). [**bi-**]

bifoliate /bī-fō'li-āt or -ət/ adj having two leaves or leaflets. [L bi- two-, and folium leaf]

■ **bifo'liolate** adj having two leaflets.

biform /bī'fōrm/ adj having two forms. [L biformis, from bi- two-, and fōrma form]

bifter /bif'tər/ or **biftah** /bif'tə/ (sl) n a hand-rolled cigarette, esp one containing cannabis. [Origin unknown]

BIFU abbrev : Banking, Insurance and Finance Union (replaced by **UNIFI**).

bifurcate /bī'fûr-kāt or -fûr'/ adj having two prongs or branches. ◆ vi to divide into two branches. [L bifurcus, from bi- two-, and furca a fork]

■ **bī'furcated** adj. **bifurca'tion** n.

big¹ /big/ adj (**bigg'er**; **bigg'est**) large or great; grown-up; older (as in big sister, big brother); magnanimous, generous (usu facetious); loud; pompous, pretentious, boastful; very important, as the Big Three, Big Four, etc, leaders, countries, organizations, etc; (of things) significant, considerable; (of wine) having an intense taste and colour; advanced in pregnancy (obs). ◆ adv (inf) boastfully or ambitiously, as in talk big; greatly or impressively; on a grand scale, as in think big. [ME big; origin obscure]

■ **bigg'ish** adj. **bigg'y** or **bigg'ie** n (inf) a large or important person or thing. **big'ness** n bulk, size.

❑ **big bad** n in a role-playing game, an evil character who creates problems which have to be overcome by the players of the game. **big band** n a large jazz or dance band. **big'-band** adj. **Big Bang** or **big bang** n see under **bang¹**. **Big Beat** n a type of electronic dance music combining aspects of hip-hop and rock. **big-bell'ied** having a big belly; pregnant (with). **Big Ben** n the bell in the clock tower of the Houses of Parliament, London; the tower itself; the clock itself. **Big Blue** n a nickname for the IBM computer company. **Big Board** n (US inf; also without caps) the New York Stock Exchange. **big-box'** adj (US inf) denoting a retail outlet in the style of a warehouse. **Big Brother** n a dictator, as in George Orwell's Nineteen Eighty-four (1949); a powerful leader or organization, regarded as ubiquitous and sinister. **Big Brotherism** n. **big bucks** n pl (sl) large amounts of money. **big'-bud** n a swelling of currant buds caused by a gall mite. **big business** n large business enterprises and organizations, esp collectively. **big cat** see under **cat¹**. **big cheese** n (old sl) an important person. **big Daddy** or **big White Chief** n (inf; both also **Big**) a paternalistic or domineering head of an organization, etc. **big data** n computer data sets that are so large and complex that specialist tools are required to process them. **big deal** n (inf) used as a scornful response to an offer, boast, etc. **big dipper** n a roller-coaster at an amusement park (orig US); (with caps) the constellation of the Plough (esp N Am). **big end** n in an internal-combustion engine, the larger end of the connecting rod. **Big-endian** see **Little-endian** under **little**. **big'eye** n a tropical or subtropical sea fish (family Priacanthidae) with very large eyes. **big fish** n a powerful person; such a person in a criminal organization thought worthy of capture. **Big'foot** n (also without cap; pl **big'feet**) in the USA and Canada, a hairy primate reputed to inhabit wilderness areas, and said to be between 6 and 15 feet tall. **Big Four** n a collective name for the four largest UK clearing banks: HSBC, Lloyds TSB, Barclays and the Royal Bank of Scotland. **big game** see under **game¹**. **big girl's blouse** n (inf) someone who behaves in a feeble or effeminate manner. **big government** n (chiefly US derog) a style of government in which there is high taxation and the state takes a prominent role in the provision of public services. **big guns** n pl (inf) the important, powerful persons in an organization, etc. **big hair** n hair in a bouffant style. **big'head** n (inf) a conceited person; conceit (N Am). **big'headed** adj. **big-heart'ed** adj generous. **big hitter** n (in cricket, baseball, etc) a player who hits the ball a long way; an important, influential, or successful person (inf). **big'horn** n a large-horned mountain-dwelling sheep (Ovis canadensis) of N America and Siberia. **big house** n prison (US sl); the house of the local landowner, a wealthy citizen, or the like. **big iron** n (comput sl) large, powerful mainframe computers. **big money** same as **big bucks**

above. **big'mouth** n (sl) a talkative and often boastful or indiscreet person. **big'mouthed** adj. **big name** n (inf) a celebrity. **big noise** n (inf) an important person. **big'-note** vt (Aust inf) to boast about oneself, try to make (oneself) seem important. **Big Pharma** n the major pharmaceutical companies, collectively. **big science** n scientific and technical research that requires large financial resources. **big screen** n the cinema, as opposed to television. **big'-screen** adj. **big shot** see **bigwig** below. **big society** n the political idea that more power and responsibility should be devolved from the state into the hands of local communities. **big stick** n (inf) a display of force, as a threat or means of persuasion. **big tent** n a political group or party that accommodates a broad range of views. **big'-tent'** adj. **big-tick'et** adj (US inf) expensive. **big time** n (inf) the top level in any pursuit, esp show business. **big'-time** adj at the top level; important. ◆ adv to a large extent, greatly. **big toe** see under **toe**. **big top** n a large circular tent used for circus performances. **big tree** n (N Am) the giant redwood. **big wheel** n a Ferris wheel. **big White Chief** n see **big Daddy** above; an important person (inf). **big'wig** or **big shot** n (inf) a powerful person, a person of some importance.

■ **be big on** (inf) to do a lot of, be strong in (a particular area of work, etc); to be enthusiastic about. **big up** (sl) to express approval and respect for. **go over big** (with) (inf) to impress greatly. **in a big way** to a large extent; vigorously, enthusiastically. **that's big of him**, etc (usu ironic) that action, etc is generous on his, etc part. **the Big Apple** (also **the Apple**) (inf) New York City. **the Big C** (inf) cancer. **the Big Smoke** see under **smoke**. **too big for one's boots** or **breeches** conceited, self-important. **what's the big idea?** what on earth is going on?

big² /big/ (Scot) vt (**bigg'ing**; **bigged**) to build, pile up. [ON byggja, cognate with OE būian]

■ **bigg'in** n anything built, a house.

biga /bī'gə or bē'ga/ (ancient Rome) n (pl **bi'gae**) a two-horse chariot. [L, earlier in pl, from bi- two-, and jugum yoke]

bigamy /big'ə-mi/ n the custom, crime or fact of having two wives or husbands at once; a second marriage (church law; obs). [L bi- two-, and Gr gamos marriage]

■ **big'amist** n a person who has committed bigamy. **big'amous** adj. **big'amously** adv.

bigarade /bē'ga-räd/ n a bitter Seville orange. [Fr]

❑ **bigarade sauce** n a sauce flavoured with these oranges.

bigener /bī'jin-ər/ (bot) n a hybrid between different genera. [L bigener a hybrid]

■ **bigeneric** /-er'ik/ adj.

❑ **bigeneric hybrid** n a hybrid resulting from a cross between individuals from two different genera.

bigg /big/ n four-rowed barley. [ON bygg]

biggin¹ /big'in/ (archaic) n a child's cap or hood; a nightcap; a serjeant-at-law's coif. [Fr béguin beguine's cap]

biggin² see under **big²**.

bigha /bē'gə/ n a land measure in India, locally $\frac{1}{3}$ to $\frac{2}{3}$ of an acre. [Hindi]

bight /bīt/ n a wide bay; a bend or coil (in a rope, etc). [OE byht; cf Dan and Swed bugt, Du bocht]

bignonia /big-nō'ni-ə/ n any member of the Bignonia genus of tropical plants with trumpet-shaped flowers, giving name to the family **Bignoniā'ceae**. [Named after the Abbé Bignon (1662–1743), Louis XIV's librarian]

■ **bignoniā'ceous** adj.

bigot /big'ət/ n a person blindly and obstinately devoted to a particular set of ideas, creed or political party, and dismissive towards others. [OFr; origin disputed]

■ **big'oted** adj having the qualities of a bigot. **big'otry** n blind or excessive zeal, esp in religious, political or racial matters.

biguanide /bī-gwä'nīd/ n one of a group of drugs used in the treatment of late-onset diabetes. [**bi-**, guanidine and **-ide**]

BIH abbrev : Bosnia-Herzegovina (IVR).

Bihari /bi-hä'ri/ n an inhabitant or native of Bihar in NE India; the language of this people. ◆ adj of or relating to Bihar, its people or language. [Hindi]

BIIBA abbrev : British Insurance and Investment Brokers' Association (now known as **BIBA**).

bijection /bī-jek'shən/ (maths) n a mapping function that is both an injection and a surjection. [**bi-**, and -jection from L jacere to throw]

■ **bijec'tive** adj.

bijou /bē'zhoo/ n (pl **bijoux** /bē'zhooz/) a trinket; a jewel. ◆ adj small and elegant. [Fr]

■ **bijouterie** /bē-zhoot'ər-ē/ n jewellery, esp trinkets.

bijwoner same as **bywoner**.

bike[1] /bīk/ *n* and *vi* short form of **bicycle** or **motorbike** (*inf*); a woman who regularly has casual sex with many different people (*derog sl*). ■ **bī'ker** or (*Aust* and *NZ inf*) **bī'kie** *n* a motorcycle rider, *esp* a member of a gang. **bī'king** *n*. ▫ **biker jacket** *n* a heavy leather jacket, typically worn by motorcyclists. **bike'way** *n* (*N Am*) a lane, road, etc exclusively for pedal cycles. ■ **get off one's bike** (*Aust sl*) to lose control of oneself. **get on one's bike** (*inf*) to start making an effort. **on your bike** (*sl*) a contemptuous expression of dismissal.

bike[2] or **byke** /bīk/ (*Scot*) *n* a nest of wasps, wild bees, etc; a swarm of people. ◆ *vi* to swarm. [Origin unknown]

bikini /bi-kē'ni/ *n* a brief swimming costume for women, in two separate parts; (*usu pl*) a pair of scantily cut briefs, *esp* for women. [From *Bikini*, an atoll of the Marshall Islands, scene of atom-bomb experiments in the late 1940s; the bikini's effects on men were reputed to be similar] ▫ **bikini line** *n* the limit on the lower abdomen normally reached by a bikini, beyond which the skin is exposed. **bikini wax** *n* a depilatory treatment, using wax, on areas exposed by bikini bottoms.

Bikram yoga /bik'ram yō'gə/ *n* a relatively strenuous form of yoga practised in a heated room (also **hot yoga**). [*Bikram* Choudhury (born 1946), Indian founder of the system]

bilabial /bī-lā'bi-əl/ (*phonetics*) *adj* produced by contact or approximation of the two lips, eg 'b' or 'w'. ◆ *n* a bilabial consonant. [L *bi-* two-, and *labium* a lip] ■ **bīlā'biate** *adj* (*bot*) two-lipped, like some corollas.

bilander /bī'land-ər/ *n* a two-masted cargo vessel used in Holland (also **by'lander**). [Du *bijlander*]

bilateral /bī-lat'ə-rəl/ *adj* having or involving two sides; affecting two parties or participants mutually. [L *bi-* two, and *latus, lateris* side] ■ **bilat'eralism** *n* two-sidedness; equality in value of trade between two countries. **bilat'erally** *adv*. ▫ **bilateral symmetry** *n* symmetry about a single plane.

bilberry /bil'bə-ri/ or *-be-/ n* a whortleberry shrub; its dark-blue berry. [Cf Dan *böllebær*]

bilbo /bil'bō/ *n* (*pl* **bil'boes** or **bil'bos**) a rapier or sword. [From *Bilbao*, in Spain]

bilboes /bil'bōz/ *n pl* a bar with sliding shackles for confining prisoners' ankles. [Perh connected with **bilbo**]

bilby /bil'bi/ *n* a burrowing Australian bandicoot with large ears and a long tail. [From an Aboriginal language]

Bildungsroman /bil'dŏŏngs-rō-män/ (*Ger*) *n* a novel concerning the early emotional or spiritual development or education of its hero.

bile /bīl/ *n* a thick bitter fluid secreted by the liver as an aid to digestion; excess or disturbance of its secretion; either of two (out of the four) humours of early physiology, of which **yellow bile** (also known as **choler**) was associated with anger, and **black bile** with melancholy; irritability, ill temper. [Fr, from L *bīlis*] ■ **biliary** /bil'yər-i/ *adj* of the bile, the bile ducts or the gall bladder. ◆ *n* short form of **biliary fever**, infectious canine jaundice. **bilious** /bil'yəs/ *adj* relating to or affected by bile; nauseated; irritable; bad-tempered; (of colours) very unpleasant, sickly. **bil'iously** *adv*. **bil'iousness** *n*. ▫ **bile ducts** *n pl* the ducts that convey the bile to the small intestine.

bi-level /bī-lev'əl/ *adj* having two levels; (of a house) divided vertically into two ground-floor levels (*N Am*). ◆ *n* (*N Am*) a bi-level house. [**bi-**]

bilge /bilj/ *n* the bulging part of a cask; the broadest part of a ship's bottom; the lowest internal part of the hull, below the floorboards (also in *pl*); filth, dirty water, etc such as collects there; rubbish, drivel (*sl*). ◆ *vi* (of a ship) to spring a leak in the bilge. ◆ *vt* to pierce the bilge of a ship. [Perh altered from **bulge**] ■ **bilg'y** *adj* having the appearance and disagreeable smell of bilge-water. ▫ **bilge keel** *n* a ridge along the bilge of a ship to prevent or reduce rolling. **bilge'-pump** *n*. **bilge'-water** *n*.

Bilharzia /bil-härt'si-ə/ or *-zi-ə/ n* a genus of parasitic worms with adhesive suckers, infesting human and other blood, with two larval stages, first in water-snails and then in man. [Theodor *Bilharz* (1825–62), German parasitologist] ■ **bilharz'ia, bilharzī'asis** or **bilharziō'sis** *n* a disease (also known as **schistosomiasis**) caused by these worms, common in tropical countries, *esp* Egypt and other parts of Africa.

bilian /bil'i-an/ *n* a heavy ant-proof lauraceous timber tree of Borneo. [Malay]

biliary see under **bile**.

bilimbi /bi-lim'bi/ *n* (also **bilim'bing, blim'bing**) an East Indian tree of the wood-sorrel family; its acid fruit. [Dravidian and Malay]

bilinear /bī-lin'i-ər/ *adj* of or involving two lines; (of a mathematical expression) containing two variables, each of which is linear. [**bi-**]

bilingual /bī-ling'gwəl/ *adj* expressed in two languages; speaking two languages, *esp* as mother tongues or with similar fluency. [L *bilinguis*, from *bi-* two-, and *lingua* tongue] ■ **bīling'ualism** *n*. **bīling'ually** *adv*. **bīling'uist** *n*.

bilious see under **bile**.

bilirubin /bi-li-roo'bin/ *n* an orange pigment in bile. [L *bīlis* bile, and *ruber* red] ■ **biliver'din** *n* (*verd* as in *verdure*) a green pigment in bile.

biliteral /bī-lit'ə-rəl/ *adj* of or involving two letters; written in two scripts. [L *bi-* two-, and *lītera, littera* a letter]

biliverdin see under **bilirubin**.

bilk /bilk/ *vt* to elude; to cheat; to avoid paying someone what is due. [Perh a form of **balk**; orig a term in cribbage] ■ **bilk'er** *n*.

Bill /bil/ (*sl*) *n* (with *the*) (members of) the police force. [**Old Bill** (see under **old**)]

bill[1] /bil/ *n* a written account of money owed; a draft of a proposed law; a bill of exchange, a promissory note; a banknote (*N Am*); a poster advertising an event, product, etc (often as a *combining form*, as in *playbill, handbill*); a slip of paper serving as an advertisement; a list of performers, etc in order of importance; a programme of entertainment; any written statement of particulars; a written accusation of serious crime (*Eng law*). ◆ *vt* to give or send a request for payment to; to announce or advertise; to enter (items) on a statement (*obs*). [LL *billa*, from L *bulla* a knob, a seal, hence a document bearing a seal, etc; cf **bull**[3]] ■ **billed** /bild/ *adj* named in a list or advertisement. **bill'ing** *n* the making out or sending of bills or invoices; the (total amount of) money received from customers or clients; advertising by poster; precedence of naming in an announcement or poster, eg *top billing, second billing*, etc. ▫ **bill'board** *n* (chiefly *N Am*) a board on which large advertising posters are stuck, a hoarding. **bill'book** *n* a book used in commerce in which an entry is made of all bills accepted and received. **bill'-broker** *n* a person who deals in bills of exchange and promissory notes. **bill'-chamber** *n* (until 1933) a department of the Scottish Court of Session dealing with summary business. **bill'-discounter** *n* a person who discounts or advances the amount of bills of exchange and notes which have some time to run. **bill'fold** *n* (*N Am*) a soft case or wallet for paper money. **bill'head** *n* a form used for business accounts, with name and address printed at the top. **bill'poster** or **bill'sticker** *n* a person who sticks up bills or posters. ■ **bill of adventure** a document produced by a merchant stating that goods shipped by him or her, and in his or her name, are the property of another, whose adventure or chance the transaction is. **bill of costs** an account of a solicitor's charges and outgoings in the conduct of the client's business. **bill of exceptions** a statement of objections by way of appeal against the ruling or direction of a judge. **bill of exchange** a document promising payment of a certain sum on a certain date by one party or another; a document employed by the parties to a business transaction whereby payment is made through a mutually convenient third party, thereby avoiding the cost and complications of foreign exchange. **bill of fare** a list of dishes or articles of food, a menu. **bill of health** an official certificate of the state of health on board ship before sailing. **bill of indictment** a statement of a charge made against a person. **bill of lading** a document signed by a ship's owner, master or the owner's agent, stating that specified goods have been shipped or received for shipment, and specifying the terms and conditions under which they are being transported. **bill of mortality** (*hist*) an official return of births and deaths in the London area (hence **within the bills of mortality** within the London district for which such returns were made). **bill of quantities** (*building, civil eng*) a list of items giving the quantities of material and brief descriptions of work comprised in an engineering or building works contract. **bill of rights** see under **right**[1]. **bill of sale** (*Eng law*) a formal deed transferring the ownership (but not the possession) of goods. **bill of sight** permission to land imported goods of which the merchant does not know the quantity or the quality. **bill of store** a licence from the customs authorities to reimport British goods formerly exported. **bill of victualling** a victualling-bill (qv under **victual**). **clean bill of health** a certificate stating that there is no illness on board a ship; a statement that a person is healthy; a statement that an organization, etc is in a good condition. **double** (or **triple**) **bill** a programme of entertainment consisting of two (or three) main items, *esp* films. **fill** (or **fit**) **the bill** to be adequate. **top the bill** to head the list of performers, be the star attraction.

bill[2] /bil/ *n* the beak of a bird, or anything similar in shape or function; a sharp promontory; the point of an anchor fluke (*naut*). ◆ *vi* to touch bills as doves do; hence, to caress or talk fondly. [OE *bile*, related to **bill**[3]]

■ **-billed** /-*bild*/ *combining form* having a bill of the stated type. **bill'ing** *n* and *adj*.

❑ **bill'board** *n* (*naut*) a board used to protect a ship's planking from damage by the bills when the anchor is weighed. **bill'fish** *n* (*N Am*) any of a number of fish with elongated jaws.

■ **bill and coo** (*inf*) (of lovers) to kiss and talk intimately together.

bill[3] /*bil*/ *n* a concave battle-axe with a long wooden handle; a billhook. [OE *bil*]

❑ **bill'hook** *n* a cutting tool with a long blade and wooden handle in the same line with it, often with a hooked tip, used in eg pruning. **bill'man** *n* a soldier armed with a bill.

billabong /*bil*'*ə-bong*/ (*Aust*) *n* a cut-off loop of a river, replenished only by floods; an offshoot from a river (strictly one that does not rejoin it). [Aboriginal words *billa* river, and *bung* dead]

billboard see **bill**[1,2].

billet[1] /*bil*'*it*/ *n* a note or letter assigning quarters to soldiers or others; the quarters requisitioned; an allocated sleeping- or resting-place; a job or occupation; a little note or document. ◆ *vt* (**bill'eting**; **bill'eted**) to quarter or accommodate (eg soldiers). [OFr *billette*, dimin of *bille*; see **bill**[1]]

billet[2] /*bil*'*it*/ *n* a small log of wood used as fuel; a piece of timber sawn on three sides and rounded on the fourth; a bar of metal; an ornament in Norman architecture in the form of short cylinders with spaces between; a bearing in the form of an upright rectangle (*heraldry*). [Fr *billette*, from *bille* the young trunk of a tree; origin unknown]

❑ **bill'et-head** *n* a piece of wood round which the harpoon-line runs.

billet-doux /*bi-li-doo'* or *bē-yā-doo'*/ *n* (*pl* **billets-doux** /*bil-i-dooz'* or *bē-yā-doo'*/) a love letter. [Fr *billet* letter, and *doux* sweet]

billiards /*bil'yərdz*/ *n sing* any of various games played with a cue and balls on a rectangular table, the table in the most common version having pockets at the sides and corners, into which the balls can be struck. [Fr *billard*, from *bille* a stick, hence a cue]

■ **bill'iard** *adj*.

❑ **billiard ball** *n*. **billiard cloth** *n* a green cloth for covering a billiard table. **billiard cue** *n*. **bill'iard-marker** *n* a person who marks the points made by the players. **billiard table** *n*.

billie see **billy**.

billingsgate /*bil'ingz-gāt*/ *n* foul and abusive language. [From *Billingsgate* the former London fish market]

Billings method /*bil'ingz meth'əd*/ *n* a rhythm method of contraception involving the examination of the discharge from the cervix. [Drs Evelyn and John *Billings*, Australian physicians who devised the method in the 1960s]

billion /*bil'yən*/ *n* a thousand millions (10^9); (*esp* formerly, in Britain) a million millions (10^{12}); (loosely; *esp* in *pl*) a very great number (*inf*); a billion pounds, dollars, etc. ◆ *adj* being a billion in number. [Fr, from L *bis* twice, two-, and **million**]

■ **billionaire** /-*ār'*/ *n* (also *fem* **billionair'ess**) a person with resources worth (more or less) a billion pounds, dollars, etc. **bill'ionfold** *adj* and *adv* (*usu* preceded by *a* or a numeral). **bill'ionth** *adj* and *n*.

billon /*bil'ən*/ *n* base metal; *esp* an alloy of silver with copper, tin, or the like. [Fr, from same root as **billet**[2]]

billow /*bil'ō*/ *n* a great wave or cloud; a wave, the sea (*poetic*). ◆ *vi* to roll or swell in great waves or clouds; to bulge (out), as a sail in the wind. [Appar ON *bylgja*; Swed *bölja*, Dan *bölge* wave]

■ **bill'owed** *adj*. **bill'owing** *adj*. **bill'owy** *adj*.

billy or **billie** /*bil'i*/ *n* (*pl* **bill'ies**) a cylindrical container with a wire handle and lid for boiling water, cooking, etc out of doors (also **bill'y-can**); a brother (*Scot*); a comrade, a companion-in-arms (*Scot*); a truncheon (*N Am*). [Prob from *Bill*, a familiar abbrev of William]

❑ **billy goat** *n* a he-goat.

billyboy /*bil'i-boi*/ *n* a cargo boat. [Prob connected with **bilander**]

Billy Bunter /*bil'i bun'tər*/ *n* the type of a fat, greedy, clumsy schoolboy. [Name of a character in stories by Frank Richards (pseudonym of Charles Hamilton, 1875–1961)]

billy-can see **billy**.

billycock /*bil'i-kok*/ *n* a hard felt hat. [Poss from *William Coke*, nephew of Earl (1837) of Leicester, or from 19c Cornish hatter *William Cock*]

billy-oh or **billy-o** /*bil'i-ō*/ *n* in phrase **like billy-oh** or **billy-o** vigorously, fiercely. [Origin obscure]

bilobar /*bī-lō'bər*/, **bilobate** /*bī-lō'bāt*/ or **bilobed** /*bī'lōbd*/ *adj* having two lobes. [L *bi-* two-, and **lobe** or **lobule**]

■ **bilobular** /*bī-lob'ū-lər*/ *adj* having two lobules.

bilocation /*bī-lō-kā'shən*/ *n* the power of being in two places at the same time. [Coined from L *bi-* two-, and **location**]

bilocular /*bī-lok'yv-lər*/ *adj* divided into two cells. [L *bi-* two-, and *loculus*, dimin of *locus* place]

biltong /*bil'tong*/ (*S Afr*) *n* sun-dried lean meat. [Du *bil* buttock, and *tong* tongue]

Bim /*bim*/ (*sl*) *n* an inhabitant of Barbados.

Bimana /*bim'ə-nə* or *bī-mā'nə*/ *n pl* two-handed animals, an obsolete name for mankind. [L *bi-* two-, and *manus* hand]

■ **bim'anal** or **bim'anous** *adj*.

bimanual /*bī-man'ū-əl*/ *adj* using or performed with both hands. [**bi-**]

■ **biman'ually** *adv*.

bimbashi /*bim-bä'shē*/ *n* a military officer (in Turkey or Egypt). [Turk *bin* thousand, and *bas* head]

bimbo /*bim'bō*/ (*sl*, *usu derog*) *n* (*pl* **bim'bos**) a person, now *usu* a woman, *esp* one who is young and physically very attractive but dim, naive or superficial; a youngster. [Ital, child]

■ **bimbette'** *n* (*sl*) a particularly dim, etc female bimbo.

bimestrial /*bī-mes'tri-əl*/ *adj* of two months' duration. [L *bimestris*, from *bi-*, and *mēnsis* a month]

bimetallic /*bī-mi-tal'ik*/ *adj* composed of, or using, two metals; (of a monetary system) in which gold and silver are used in fixed relative values.

■ **bimetallism** /*bī-met'əl-izm*/ *n* such a system. **bimet'allist** *n* and *adj*.

❑ **bimetallic strip** *n* a strip formed by bonding two metals one of which expands more than the other, so that it bends with change of temperature, used in thermostatic switches, etc.

bimillenary /*bī-mil'i-nə-ri*/ *n* a period of 2000 years; a 2000th anniversary. ◆ *adj* happening every 2000 years; relating to a 2000th anniversary. [**bi-**]

bimillennium /*bī-mi-len'i-əm*/ *n* (*pl* **bimillenn'iums** or **bimillenn'ia**) same as **bimillenary**. [**bi-**]

bimodal /*bī-mō'dəl*/ (*stats*) *adj* having two modes. [**bi-** and **mode**]

■ **bimodal'ity** *n*.

bimolecular /*bī-mə-lek'ū-lər* or *-mō-*/ (*chem*) *adj* involving two molecules. [**bi-** and **molecule**]

bimonthly /*bī-munth'li*/ *adj* or *adv* (happening, etc) once in two months; (happening, etc) twice a month. [**bi-** and **month**]

bin[1] /*bin*/ *n* a container for rubbish; a container for storing some kinds of food; a container for storing or displaying goods; a stand or case with compartments in which to store bottled wine in a wine cellar; the wine contained in it; short for **loony bin**; gaol (*sl*); a pocket (*sl*). ◆ *vt* (**binn'ing**; **binned**) to put (eg bottled wine) into a bin; to throw into a waste bin (*inf*); to reject, discard (*inf*). [OE *binn* a manger]

❑ **bin'-bag** *n* (*inf*) a large strong plastic bag for *esp* household rubbish; a bin-liner. **bin card** *n* a record card detailing the stock level in a storage bin. **bin'-end** *n* any of the last bottles of wine remaining from a bin, often sold at a reduced price. **bin'-liner** *n* a *usu* plastic bag for lining a rubbish bin or dustbin. **bin'man** *n* a dustman.

bin[2] /*bin*/ (*Shakesp*) used for **be** and **been**.

bin- see **bi-**.

binary /*bī'nə-ri*/ *adj* composed of or relating to two; twofold; expressed in binary notation; relating to two terms (*maths*, *logic*); describing the two-way division of British higher education into universities and the other institutions. ◆ *n* binary notation; a binary star. [L *bīnārius*, from compound *bīnī* two by two]

❑ **binary code** *n* (*comput*) a code of numbers that involves only two digits, 0 and 1. **binary-coded decimal** *n* (*comput*) a decimal number written in binary code such that each number is represented by a unique sequence of four bits (*abbrev* **BCD**). **bi'nary-compatible** *adj* (*comput*) denoting a file that is identical at the binary level but has a different header. **binary digit** *n* (*comput*, *telecom*) either of the two digits 0 and 1; the smallest unit of information (*usu* in short form **bit**). **binary fission** *n* (*biol*) the division of an organism or cell into two parts. **binary form** *n* (*music*) a form of a movement founded on two themes. **binary notation** *n* a system of numerical notation using the base 2 (instead of 10 as in the decimal system) in which numbers are expressed using only the binary digits. **binary number** *n* a number expressed in binary notation. **binary pulsar** *n* (*astron*) a system consisting of a pulsar and a small companion star rotating round each other. **binary star** *n* (*astron*) a double star revolving about their common centre of gravity. **binary system** *n* a system using binary notation. **binary weapon**, **munition**, etc *n* a bomb or shell loaded with two separate canisters of non-toxic chemicals, the chemicals combining at the time of firing to produce a lethal compound.

binate /*bī'nāt*/ (*bot*) *adj* growing in pairs; double; consisting of two leaflets. [New L *bīnātus*, from L *bīnī* two by two]

binaural /*bin-ö'rəl* or *bī-nö'rəl*/ *adj* having, employing, or relating to two ears; (of sound reproduction) using two sound channels. [**bin-**]

■ **binaur'ally** *adv*.

■ words derived from main entry word; ❑ compound words; ■ idioms and phrasal verbs

❏ **binaural effect** *n* the ability to tell the direction from which a sound is coming, as a result of the different arrival times of the sound at a person's two ears.

Binca® /bing'kə/ *n* an open-weave canvas fabric used for embroidery, etc.

bind /bīnd/ *vt* (*pat* and *pap* **bound** /bownd/) to tie or fasten together; to pass or put something round; to restrain; to fix; to sew a border on; to bandage or tie (*up*); to fasten the sections together and put a cover on (a book); to impose an obligation on; to oblige by oath or promise; to contract as an apprentice; to hold or cement firmly; to cause (dry ingredients) to cohere by adding a small amount of liquid (*cookery*); (of frost) to make (the earth) stiff and hard; to constipate; to bore (*old sl*). ◆ *vi* to become bound; to chafe, restrict free movement; to complain (*old sl*). ◆ *n* a tie (*music*); a difficult or annoying situation, a bore (*inf*); the indurated clay between layers of coal; capacity, measure (*Scot*); a stem of the hop or other twiner. —See also **bound**¹ and **bounden**. [OE *bindan*; cf Ger *binden*, Sans *badhnōti* he binds] ■ **bind'er** *n* a person who binds (books, sheaves, etc); anything that binds, such as a rope, a bandage, a cementing agent, a tie-beam, a header in masonry, or a case or file for binding loose papers in; an attachment to a reaping machine for tying the bundles of grain cut and thrown off; a reaping machine provided with such an attachment. **bind'ery** *n* a workplace where books are bound. **bind'ing** *adj* restraining; obligatory; (of specific foods, etc) likely to cause constipation. ◆ *n* the act of someone who binds; anything that binds; the covering of a book. ❏ **binder twine** *n* twine used in a binder. **binding energy** *n* (*nuclear phys*) the difference between the rest mass of a nucleus and that of its constituent protons and neutrons, which is always greater. **bind'weed** *n* any of various weeds that trail along the ground and twine themselves around other plants, trees, etc (*esp* one of the genus *Convolvulus*); also (**black bindweed**) a species of *Polygonum*. ■ **be bound up in** to be wholly devoted to or occupied with. **be bound up with** to be intimately or indissolubly connected with. **bind off** (chiefly *US*) to cast off (in knitting, etc). **bind over** to subject to legal constraint (*esp* not to disturb the peace). **I'll be bound** I'll bet, I'm certain.

bindi or **bindhi** /bin'dē/ *n* a *usu* red circular mark traditionally worn as a facial decoration by Indian women. [Hindi *bindi*, from Sans *bindu* point, dot]

bindi-eye /bin'di-ī/ *n* an Australian herbaceous plant, *esp* of the genus *Calotis*, with burr-like fruits. [From an Aboriginal language]

bindle /bin'dl/ (chiefly *US sl*) *n* a small paper packet containing an illegal drug. [Ger *Bündel* packet]

bine /bīn/ *n* the flexible stem of a climbing plant; the stem of the hop. [Orig dialect form of **bind**]

binervate /bī-nûr'vāt/ *adj* with two ribs or nerves. [**bi-** and **nerve**]

bing¹ /bing/ (*dialect*) *n* a heap or pile (*esp* of waste from a coalmine); a bin. [ON *bingr*]

bing² /bing/ (*obs sl*; *Walter Scott*) *vi* to go. [Perh Romany]

binge /binj/ or /binzh/ (*inf*) *n* a bout of overindulgence, *esp* in eating and drinking. ◆ *vi* to overindulge in this way. [Perh from dialect *binge* to soak] ◆ *adj* unrestrained, as in *binge drinking*. ■ **bin'ger** *n*. ❏ **binge drinking** *n* overindulgence in alcohol at regular intervals.

Binghi /bing'gī/ or -*gi*/ (*Aust sl, usu derog*; also without *cap*) *n* an Aboriginal; the archetypal Aboriginal. [From an Aboriginal word meaning 'brother']

bingle¹ /bing'gl/ (*Aust sl*) *n* a car-crash, smash. [From World War II slang *bingle* a skirmish]

bingle² /bing'gl/ *n* a hairstyle midway between *b*ob and *shingle* (also *vt*).

bingo¹ /bing'gō/ *n* a game in which numbers are called at random which may then be covered on players' cards, prizes being won by the first to cover all or certain of the numbers displayed on a card (cf **housey-housey** under **house**, **lotto** under **lottery**, **tombola**). ◆ *interj* the exclamation made by the first player to finish in this game; an exclamation expressing a sudden success, discovery, unexpectedness, etc. [Origin uncertain] ❏ **bingo hall** *n* a commercial establishment where bingo is played. **bingo wing** *n* (*usu* in *pl*; *sl*) a flap of loose skin that hangs down from the upper arm (so called because it is often displayed by people raising a hand to claim victory in bingo).

bingo² /bing'gō/ *n* a familiar name for brandy. [Prob *B*, for **brandy**, and **stingo**]

bingy /bin'ji/ (*Aust inf*) *n* the stomach. [From an Aboriginal language]

bink /bingk/ (*Scot*) *n* a bench, bank, shelf; a plate rack; a wasps' or bees' nest. [Scot and N Eng form of **bench**]

binnacle /bin'ə-kl/ (*naut*) *n* the casing in which a ship's compass is kept. [Formerly *bittacle*, from Port *bitácola*, from L *habitáculum* a dwelling-place, from *habitáre* to dwell]

binocle /bin'o-kl/ or -*ə*-/ *n* a telescope for use with both eyes at once, binoculars. [Ety as for **binocular**]

binocular /bi-nok'ū-lər/ *n* (*usu* **binoculars**) a binocular telescope; a binocular microscope. ◆ *adj* with two eyes; suitable for use with two eyes; stereoscopic. [L *bīnī* two by two, and *oculus* an eye] ■ **binoc'ularly** *adv*. ❏ **binocular vision** *n* the ability of animals with forward-facing eyes to focus both eyes simultaneously on an object to perceive a single three-dimensional image.

binomial /bī-nō'mi-əl/ *adj* consisting of two terms, as $a + b$ (*maths*); another term for **binominal**. ◆ *n* a binomial expression; the two-part Linnaean name of an animal or plant. [L *binōmius*] ❏ **binomial distribution** *n* (*stats*) the probability distribution of the total number of specified outcomes in a predetermined number of independent trials, each having a constant probability of outcome. **binomial theorem** *n* Newton's theorem giving any power of a binomial.

binominal /bī-nom'i-nəl/ *adj* making use of two names, as the Linnaean nomenclature which names every species by giving first the generic and then the specific name. [L *binōminis*, from *bi-* two- and *nōmen*, *-inis* name]

bins /binz/ (*inf*) *n pl* a short form of **binoculars**; spectacles.

bint /bint/ (*sl, usu derog*) *n* a girl, woman, girlfriend. [Ar, daughter]

binturong /bin'tū-rong/ *n* a SE Asian prehensile-tailed carnivore, related to the civet. [Malay]

binucleate /bī-nū'kli-āt/ *adj* (of a cell) having two nuclei. [**bi-**]

bio- /bī-ō-/ *combining form* signifying: life; living organisms; life or living organisms in relation to their biological environment; living tissue, as in eg the terms below. [Gr *bios* life] ■ **bioaccum'ulate** *vi* of a *usu* harmful substance, to build up in a living organism. **bioaccumula'tion** *n*. **bi'oactive** *adj* having an effect on living organisms. **bioassay** /bī-ō-ə-sā' or -as'ā/ *n* the assessment of the strength and effect of a drug or other substance by testing it on a living organism and comparing the results with the known results of another drug, etc. **bioastronaut'ics** *n sing* the science dealing with the effects of travel in space on living organisms. **bioavailabil'ity** *n* the extent to which a drug, etc, after administration (eg by mouth), is available to the tissue it is intended to act on. **bioavail'able** *adj*. **biobibliograph'ical** *adj* dealing with the life and writings of someone. **bi'oblast** *n* (Gr *blastos* germ) a hypothetical unit of living matter; a minute granule in protoplasm. **biocat'alyst** *n* a substance, eg an enzyme, that produces or speeds up a biochemical reaction. **biochem'ical** *adj* and *n*. **biochem'ically** *adv*. **biochem'ist** *n*. **biochem'istry** *n* the chemistry of living things, physiological chemistry (**biochemical oxygen demand** a measure of the amount of oxygen required by micro-organisms in a volume of water, used as a guide to the state of pollution of the water). **bi'ochip** *n* a silicon chip implanted into and functioning as part of a human body. **biocidal** /-sīd'/ *adj* killing living material, pesticidal. **bi'ocide** *n*. **bioclimatol'ogy** *n* same as **biometeorology** (see below). **biocoenology** /bī-ō-sēn-ol'ə-ji/ *n* the study of biocoenoses. **biocoenosis** /bī-ō-sēn-ō'sis/ *n* (*pl* **biocoenoses** /-nō'sēz/) (Gr *koinos* common) an association of organisms ecologically interdependent. **biocoenotic** /-not'ik/ *adj* ecological. **biocompat'ibility** *n*. **biocompat'ible** *adj* compatible with and not harmful to living tissue. **bi'ocomputer** *n* a computer with biological components, or modelled on the structure or function of biological molecules. **biocomput'ing** *n* computing using biocomputers; same as **bioinformatics** (see below). **biocontrol'** *n* biological control. **bioconver'sion** *n* the conversion of organic matter into usable energy, now *esp* by means of biological processes. **bioda'ta** *n pl* (*esp US* and *Anglo-Ind*) biographical information, curriculum or curricula vitae. **biodegradabil'ity** *n*. **biodegrad'able** *adj* (of substances) able to be broken down by bacteria. **biodegrada'tion** (also **biodeteriora'tion**) *n*. **biodegrade'** *vi*. **biodestruct'ible** *adj* biodegradable. **biodies'el** *n* a biofuel intended as a substitute for diesel fuel. **biodiverse'** *adj*. **biodiver'sity** *n* the diversity of the natural world, ecological variety and richness. **biodynam'ic** *adj* dealing with the activities of living organisms; (of a system of land cultivation) fertilizing with organic materials only. **biodynam'ics** *n sing*. **bioecol'ogy** *n* the branch of ecology dealing with the interrelationship of living organisms and the environment. **bioelec'tric** *adj*. **bioelectric'ity** *n* electrical phenomena in plants and animals. **bioelectrother'apy** *n* a form of physical therapy in which low-energy electric current is applied to the skin through a pad or membrane. **bioenerget'ics** *n sing* the biology of energy relationships in living organisms or energy changes produced by them; Reichian therapy. **bi'oenergy** *n* fuel or electricity produced from organic matter. **bioengineer'** *n*. **bioengineer'ing** *n* see **biological**

engineering under **biology**. **bioeth'anol** n ethanol produced from fermented plant material, used as a petrol additive or substitute. **bioeth'icist** n. **bioeth'ics** n sing the study of the ethical problems produced by medical and biological research, etc. **biofeed'back** n a technique for learning control of autonomic body functions in response to monitoring by electronic instruments such as an electrocardiograph. **bi'ofilm** n a thin surface layer of micro-organisms bound together by secreted polymer substances. **bioflā'vonoid** n (also called **citrin**) vitamin P, a vitamin that regulates the permeability of the capillary walls, found in citrus fruit, blackcurrants and rosehips. **bi'ofuel** n fuel produced from organic matter, whether directly or through burning or fermentation. **bi'ogas** n domestic or commercial gas obtained by bioconversion. **bi'ogen** /-jen/ n (Gr genos race, offspring) a hypothetical unit of protoplasm. **biogen'esis** n (Gr genesis production) the derivation of living things from living things only; biogeny. **biogenet'ic** or **biogen'ic** adj relating to biogens, biogeny, or biogenesis (**biogenetic law** the theory of recapitulation of the history of the race in the development of the individual). **biogenous** /-oj'/ adj parasitic; biogenic. **biog'eny** n the course of organic evolution or development of living organisms. **biogeochem'ical** adj. **biogeochem'istry** n the science of plants and animals in relation to chemicals in the soil. **biogeog'rapher** n. **biogeograph'ical** adj. **biogeog'raphy** n the geographical distribution of plants and animals. **bi'ograph** n (Gr graphein to write) a biography; a bioscope. ◆ vt (inf) to write a biography of. **biohaz'ard** n a danger of disease or pollution from living organisms, encountered eg during biological research. **bioinformati'cian** n. **bioinformat'ics** n sing the use of computers to process information in biology, esp to analyse the structure of genes. **bioluminesc'ence** n the emission of light by living organisms, such as certain insects, marine animals, bacteria, fungi. **bioluminesc'ent** adj. **biolysis** /bī-ol'i-sis/ n the disintegration of organic matter under the influence of bacteria. **biomagnet'ics** n sing a type of magnetic therapy in which small magnets are placed on acupuncture points. **bi'omarker** n a biological substance, the presence of which in serum may be an indication of disease (also **mark'er**); a physical characteristic whose changes may be used to monitor the progression of a condition. **bi'omass** n the quantity or weight of living material (animals, plants, etc) in a unit of area; living material as a source of energy. **biomatē'rial** n suitable synthetic material from which to produce artificial body parts that are to be in direct contact with living tissue. **biomathematic'ian** n. **biomathemat'ics** n sing mathematics as applied to the biological sciences. **biomechan'ical** adj. **biomechan'ics** n sing the mechanics of movements in living creatures. **biomed'ical** adj of or relating to both biology and medicine; applied to the study of the effects of stress, esp space travel, on living organisms. **biomed'icine** n. **biometeorolog'ical** adj. **biometeorol'ogy** n the effect of weather and climate on plants, animals and man. **biomet'ric** adj. **biometrician** /-trish'ən/ n. **biom'etry** n (Gr metron measure) the statistical or quantitative study of biology (also n sing **biomet'rics**). **biomimet'ic** adj. **biomimet'ics** n sing a branch of science that bases new technology on mechanisms, features, methods and accomplishments found in nature. **bi'omining** n (mining) same as **microbiological mining** (see under **microbe**). **bi'omolecule** n any chemical compound that occurs naturally in living organisms. **bi'omorph** n (Gr morphē form) a representation of a living thing as decoration. **biomorph'ic** adj. **bionom'ic** adj. **bionom'ics** n sing (Gr nomos law) the study of the relations between the organism and its environment, ecology. **bi'oparent** n a biological parent, not a step-parent or guardian. **biopharmaceut'ical** n a biological substance used as a drug, esp when manufactured (also adj). **biophor** or **biophore** /bī'ō-fōr/ n (Gr phoros carrying) a hypothetical unit of living matter proposed by AFL Weismann. **biophys'ical** adj. **biophys'icist** n. **biophys'ics** n sing a form of biology dealing with biological structures and processes in terms of physics. **biopīr'acy** n the development and often patented use by the more technically advanced countries of materials native to developing countries, eg medicinal plants, with no fair compensation to their country of origin. **bi'oplasm** n (Gr plasma form) protoplasm. **bioplas'mic** adj. **bi'oplast** n (Gr plastos moulded) a minute portion of protoplasm. **biopoiesis** /-poi-ēs'is/ n the creation of living from non-living material as an evolutionary process. **biopol'ymer** n a polymer produced in living organisms. **bi'oprospect** vi to investigate living organisms with the aim of discovering materials that can be exploited for commercial gain. **biopsycholog'ical** adj. **biopsychol'ogy** n the branch of psychology, or of biology, which deals with the interaction of mind and body, and the effects of this interaction. **biopsychosocial** /-sī-kō-sō'shl/ adj (of diseases, etc) combining a biological, psychological, and social dimension. **bioreac'tor** n a container in which micro-organisms are grown for industrial use. **biorefin'ery** n a facility that produces fuel, electricity and chemicals from organic matter. **bioremedia'tion** n the use of living organisms to decontaminate soil by absorbing pollutants (cf **phytoremediation** under **phyt-**). **bi'orhythm** n a periodic change in the behaviour or physiology of many animals and plants (eg hibernation and migration)

mediated by hormones which are in turn influenced by changes in day-length; a circadian rhythm associated eg with sleep, and independent of day-length; any of three physiological, emotional and intellectual rhythms or cycles, supposed to cause variations in mood or performance. **biorhyth'mics** n sing the study of biorhythms. **bi'osafety** n the control and containment of potentially harmful biological material. **biosat'ellite** n an artificial satellite containing living organisms to be studied during flight. **biosci'ence** n any one of the biological sciences. **bioscientif'ic** adj. **biosci'entist** n. **bi'oscope** n (Gr skopeein to look at) a cinematographic apparatus or theatre; a cinema (S Afr); the cinema (S Afr inf). **biosecūr'ity** n the protection of living organisms from harmful effects brought about by other species, esp the transmission of disease. **bi'osensor** n a living organism used to detect the presence of chemicals. **bi'osolids** n pl solid excrement. **bi'osphere** n the part of the earth and its atmosphere in which living things are found. **biospher'ic** adj. **biostā'ble** adj not affected by the biological environment. **biostratigraph'ic** or **biostratigraph'ical** adj. **biostratig'raphy** n the stratigraphy of sedimentary rocks. **biosyn'thesis** n the production of complex molecules by a living organism. **biosynthet'ic** adj. **biosystemat'ic** adj. **biosystemat'ics** n sing the study of relationships of organisms and of laws of classification. **biō'ta** n the flora and fauna of a region. **bi'otech** n biotechnology. **biotechnolog'ical** adj. **biotechnol'ogist** n. **biotechnol'ogy** n the utilization of living organisms (eg bacteria) in industry, etc, eg in the creation of energy, destruction of waste, and the manufacture of various products; ergonomics (N Am). **bioterr'orism** or **bi'oterror** n the use for purposes of terrorism of disease-carrying organisms and agricultural pests. **bioterr'orist** n. **bioturba'tion** n the disturbance of the soil by living organisms. **bi'otype** n within a species, a distinct sub-group. **bi'owarfare** n biological warfare (qv under **biology**). **bi'oweapon** n a disease-causing bacteria or toxic substance used as a weapon in war.

bio /bī'ō/ or **biog** /bī'og or -og'/ n (pl **bī'os** or **bī'ogs**) short forms of **biography**.

biog see **bio**.

biogas...to...**biograph** see under **bio-**.

biography /bī-og'rə-fi/ n a written account or history of the life of an individual; such accounts collectively; the art of writing such accounts. [**bio-** and Gr graphein to write]
■ **biographee** n the subject of biography. **biog'rapher** n a person who writes biography. **biograph'ic** or **biograph'ical** adj. **biograph'ically** adv.

biohazard, bioinformatics see under **bio-**.

biol. abbrev : biology.

biology /bī-ol'ə-ji/ n the science of living things; the life sciences collectively, including botany, anatomy and physiology, zoology, etc. [**bio-** and **-logy**]
■ **biological** or (US) **biologic** /-loj'/ adj of or relating to biology; physiological; produced by physiological means; effected by living organisms or by enzymes; (of washing powder, etc) using enzymes to clean clothes. **biolog'ically** adv. **biol'ogist** n.
❑ **biological clock** n a supposed in-built mechanism which regulates the physiological rhythms and cycles of living organisms. **biological control** n a method of reducing the numbers of a pest (plant, animal or parasite) by introducing or encouraging one of its enemies or interfering with its reproductive behaviour. **biological engineering** n the provision of (electrical, electronic, etc) aids for bodily functions, eg artificial limbs and joints, hearing aids, etc (also **bioengineering**); the engineering required in biosynthesis of animal and plant products, eg for fermentation processes (also **bioengineering**); the manipulation of living cells so as to promote their growth in a desired way. **biological warfare** n methods of warfare involving the use of disease bacteria or toxic substances.

bioluminescence...to...**biomathematics** see under **bio-**.

biome /bī'ōm/ n an extensive ecological community, usu with a dominant vegetation. [**bio-** + **-ome**]

biomechanics...to...**biomorphic** see under **bio-**.

bionic /bī-on'ik/ adj relating to or using bionics; superhuman, esp with parts of the body replaced with electronic devices (inf). [**bio-** and electronic]
■ **bion'ics** n sing another name for **biomimetics**; (loosely) the replacement of parts of the body by electronic or mechanical devices, such as powered limbs, heart valves, etc.

bionomic(s) see under **bio-**.

biont /bī'ont/ n a living organism. [Gr bios life, and ōn (stem ont-) from einai to be]
■ **-biont** combining form signifying an organism belonging to a specified habitat or environment. **-biontic** adj combining form.

bioparent...to...**biophysics** see under **bio-**.

biopic /bī'ō-pik/ n a film, usu an uncritically admiring one, telling the life-story of a celebrity. [biographical picture]

■ words derived from main entry word; ❑ compound words; ■ idioms and phrasal verbs

biopiracy...to...**bioprospect** see under **bio-**.

biopsy /bī'op-si/ n the surgical removal of tissue or fluid from a living body for diagnostic examination; such examination. [Fr *biopsie*, from Gr *bios* life, and *opsis* sight]

biopsychological...to...**biorhythmics** see under **bio-**.

BIOS /bī'os/ (*comput*) *abbrev* : Basic Input-Output System, an essential part of a computer operating system, *usu* stored as firmware (qv under **firm¹**), controlling input and output operations and on which more complex functions are based.

biosafety...to...**biosensor** see under **bio-**.

-biosis /-bi-ō-sis/ *combining form* signifying a (specified) way of living. [Gr *biōsis* way of life].
■ **-biotic** *adj combining form*.

biosolids...to...**bioterrorist** see under **bio-**.

biotic /bī-ot'ik/ *adj* relating to living organisms. [Gr *biōtikos*]
■ **biot'ically** *adv*.

biotin /bī'ō-tin/ n one of the members of the vitamin B complex (also known as **vitamin H**). [Gr *biotos* means of living]

biotite /bī'ō-tīt/ n a black or dark ferromagnesian mica. [JB *Biot* (1774–1862), French physicist and astronomer]

biotope /bī'ō-tōp/ n (*ecology*) a region uniform in its environmental conditions and its biota.

bioturbation...to...**biowarfare** see under **bio-**.

biparous /bip'ə-rəs/ *adj* producing offspring in twos; dichasial. [**bi-** and L *parere* to bring forth]

bipartisan /bī-pärt'i-zan/ *adj* relating to, supported by, or consisting of members of, two parties. [**bi-**]
■ **bipart'isanship** n.

bipartite /bī-pär'tīt/ *adj* divided into two parts; (of eg a document) having two corresponding parts; (of eg an agreement) affecting two parties. [L *bi-* two-, and *partītus* divided, from *partīre*, *-īrī* to divide]
■ **bipartition** /-tish'ən/ n division into two parts.

biped /bī'ped/ n an animal with two feet. [L *bipēs*, *-pedis*, from *bi-* two-, and *pēs*, *pedis* foot]
■ **bi'ped** or **bi'pedal** /bī-ped'əl or -pē'dəl/ *adj* having two feet; using two feet for walking. **biped'alism** n.

bipetalous /bī-pet'ə-ləs/ *adj* having two petals. [L *bi-* two-, and **petal**]

biphasic /bī-fā'zik/ *adj* having two phases. [**bi-** and **phase¹**]

biphenyl /bī-fen'l or -fē'nl/ n and *adj* same as **diphenyl**.

bipinnaria /bī-pin-ā'ri-ə/ n a starfish larva with two ciliated bands. [L *bi-* two-, and *pinna* a feather]

bipinnate /bī-pin'āt/ (*bot*) *adj* pinnate, with each pinna pinnate. [**bi-**]

biplane /bī'plān/ n an aeroplane with two sets of wings, one above the other. [L *bi-* two-, and **plane¹**]

BIPM *abbrev* : *Bureau International des Poids et Mesures* (Fr), International Bureau of Weights and Measures, an organization that ensures worldwide uniformity of measurements.

bipod /bī'pod/ n a two-legged stand. [L *bi-* two-, and Gr *pous*, *podos* foot]

bipolar /bī-pō'lər/ *adj* having two poles, extremities or extremes (*lit* and *fig*); relating to or occurring at both north and south poles; (of a transistor) using both positive and negative charge carriers (*electronics*); involving episodes of both mania and depression; suffering from bipolar disorder. [**bi-**]
■ **bipolar'ity** n.
❑ **bipolar disorder** n a form of mental illness characterized by phases of depression and elation with lucid intervals.

bipropellant /bī-pro-pel'ənt/ n rocket propellant made up of two liquids, the fuel and the oxidizer, kept separate prior to combustion. [**bi-**]

bipyramid /bī-pir'ə-mid/ n a crystal form of two pyramids base to base.

biquadratic /bī-kwo-drat'ik or -kwə-/ n a quantity twice squared, or raised to the fourth power. [L *bi-* twice, and *quadrātus* squared]
❑ **biquadratic equation** n an equation involving the fourth, and no higher, power of the unknown quantity. **biquadratic root** n the square root of the square root.

biquintile /bi-kwin'tīl/ n the aspect of planets when they are twice the fifth part of a great circle (ie 144 degrees) from each other. [L *bi-* twice, and *quintus* the fifth]

biracial /bī-rā'shl, -shyəl/ *adj* (chiefly *US*) of or relating to two races.

biramous /bī-rā'məs/ (*zool*) *adj* forked, with two branches, as some crustacean limbs.

birch /bûrch/ n a hardy forest-tree (genus *Betula*), with smooth white bark and very durable wood; its wood, valued for furniture-making; a rod for punishment, consisting of a birch twig or twigs. ◆ *vt* to flog. [OE *berc*, *bierce* ; ON *björk*, Sans *bhūrja*]

■ **birch** or **birch'en** *adj* made of birch.
❑ **birch'bark** n the bark of the paper-birch, formerly used by Native Americans to make canoes. **birch fly** see **black fly** under **black**. **birch rod** n a birch for punishment.

Bircher /bûr'chər/ n a member of the John *Birch* Society, an American right-wing anticommunist organization named after an intelligence officer and missionary killed by Chinese communists in 1945.

birchir see **bichir**.

bird /bûrd/ n a member of the *Aves*, a class of warm-blooded, egg-laying, feathered vertebrates with forelimbs modified into wings; a general name for a feathered animal (*orig* applied to the young); a person (*sl*; *usu* with *adj*, eg *rare bird*, *odd bird*); a prison sentence, prison (*sl*; from **bird-lime**, rhyming slang for 'time'); a girl, *esp* one's girlfriend (now *sl*; *orig* confused with **bride** or **burd¹**). ◆ *vi* to shoot at or seek to catch or snare birds. [OE *brid* the young of a bird, a bird]
■ **bird'er** n (*inf*) a birdwatcher. **bird'ie** n (*dimin*) a little bird; a score of one stroke less than par on a hole (also *vi* and *vt*). **bird'ing** n the hunting or snaring of birds; birdwatching. **bird'like** *adj*.
❑ **bird-alane** see under **burd²**. **bird'bath** n a basin set up for birds to bathe in. **bird'-bolt** n (*Shakesp*) a short thick blunted bolt or arrow for killing birds without piercing. **bird'brain** n (*inf*) a flighty, silly person. **bird'brained** *adj*. **bird'cage** n a cage of wire or wicker for holding birds; the paddock at a racecourse (*orig* that at Newmarket, now *Aust* and *NZ inf*). **bird'call** n a bird's song; an instrument for imitating birdsong. **bird'-catcher** n a professional catcher of birds. **bird'-catching** n and *adj*. **bird-catching spider** n a bird-spider. **bird'-cherry** n a small wild cherry tree (*Prunus padus*); its astringent fruit. **bird'-dog** n (*N Am*) a dog trained to find or retrieve birds for hunters. ◆ *vt* to watch closely. **bird'-eyed** *adj* quick-sighted. **bird'-fancier** n a person who breeds cagebirds, or keeps them for sale. **bird flu** n a highly contagious strain of influenza that affects poultry and can be transmitted to humans (also called **avian flu** or **avian influenza**). **bird'-hipped** *adj* (of dinosaurs) having a pelvis slightly similar to a bird's, the pubis extending backwards to lie parallel with the upper pelvis, ornithischian. **bird'-house** n (*N Am*) a nest box; an aviary. **bird impact** n bird strike. **bird'ing-piece** n a fowling-piece. **bird'-life** n birds collectively. **bird'-lime** n a sticky substance put on tree branches to catch birds; see also **bird** (n) above. **bird'-louse** n (*pl* **bird'-lice**) a louse-like insect of the order Mallophaga, parasitical on birds and mammals. **bird'-lover** n a person who likes birds and (often) who promotes their welfare. **bird'man** n an ornithologist or a person otherwise concerned with birds; a man who flies (or attempts flight) using his own muscle power (*usu sci-fi*); an airman (*obs inf*). **bird-nesting** see **bird's-nesting** below. **bird of paradise** n any bird of the family Paradiseidae, inhabitants chiefly of New Guinea, closely related to the crows but of very beautiful plumage. **bird-of-paradise flower** n any of various plants of the genus *Strelitzia*, found in S America and southern Africa, with flowers resembling birds' heads. **bird of prey** n one that devours other animals, applied *usu* to the Falconiformes. **bird'-pepper** n a species of *Capsicum*. **bird'-scarer** n a mechanical device for scaring birds away from growing crops. **bird'seed** n seed (hemp, etc) for feeding cagebirds; a thing trifling in amount, chickenfeed (*sl*). **bird's-eye** n a kind of primrose, of speedwell, or of tobacco. ◆ *adj* such as might be seen by a flying bird; having markings like birds' eyes. **bird's-eye maple** n the timber of any of various N American maples, with markings in the grain reminiscent of birds' eyes. **bird's-eye view** n a general view from above; a general view of a subject. **birds'foot** n a papilionaceous genus (*Ornithopus*) with clawlike pods. **birdsfoot trefoil** n a perennial plant (*Lotus corniculatus*) with flat-topped clusters of yellow flowers on stalks, often tinged with red (also **bacon-and-eggs**, **eggs-and-bacon**). **bird'shot** n pellets suitable for shooting birds. **bird'-skiing** n water-skiing with a winglike device that enables the skier to rise off the water. **bird's'-nest** n the nest in which a bird lays and hatches her eggs; a name given to several plants from their appearance, *esp Monotropa* and *Neottia* (bird's-nest orchid) and *Asplenium nidus* (bird's-nest fern). **bird's'-nesting** or **bird'-nesting** n seeking and robbing birds' nests. **bird's-nest soup** n (*Chinese cookery*) a soup made from swallows' nests. **bird'song** n a bird's or birds' musical vocalization. **bird'-spider** n any of various large spiders (genus *Mygale*) preying on small birds, found in tropical America; extended to others of the family Aviculariidae. **bird strike** n the collision of a bird or birds with an aircraft resulting in aircraft damage. **bird table** n a table, inaccessible to cats, for wild birds to feed on. **bird'watcher** n. **bird'watching** n the observation of birds in their natural habitat. **bird'wing** or **birdwing butterfly** n any of various very large brightly-coloured butterflies of SE Asia. **bird'-witted** *adj* flighty; incapable of sustained attention.
■ **a bird in the hand is worth two in the bush** a certainty is not to be thrown away for a poor chance of something better. **a little bird told me** I heard from a source I will not reveal. **birds of a feather** see under **feather**. **do bird** (*sl*; see **bird** (n) above) to serve a prison sentence. **get** (or **give someone**) **the bird** (ie the goose; *orig theatre sl*) to be hissed (or to hiss someone); hence to be dismissed (or to dismiss someone).

in **bird** (*sl*; see **bird** (*n*) above) in prison. **kill two birds with one stone** to accomplish one thing by the same means as, or by accomplishing, another. **like a bird** with alacrity. (**strictly**) **for the birds** (*sl*) not to be taken seriously, of little value. **the birds and the bees** (*inf*) the facts of life. **watch the birdie** (*inf*) a humorous instruction to look at the camera when one is about to be photographed.

birefringent /bī-rə-frin'jənt/ (*mineralogy*) *adj* doubly refracting, as Iceland spar is. [**bi-**]
■ **birefrin'gence** *n*.

bireme /bī'rēm/ *n* an ancient vessel with two banks of oars. [L *birēmis*, from *bi-* two-, and *rēmus* an oar]

biretta /bi-ret'ə/ *n* the square cap with three or four projections on the crown worn by Roman Catholic clergy, black for priests, purple for bishops, and red for cardinals. [Ital *berretta*, from LL *birretum* cap]

biriani see **biryani**.

birk /birk or bûrk/ (*Scot and N Eng*) *n* birch.
■ **birk'en** *adj* birchen.

birkie /bûrk'i or birk'i/ (*Scot*) *n* a strutting or swaggering fellow; a fellow generally. ◆ *adj* active. [Perh connected with ON *berkia*, OE *beorcan* to bark]

birl[1] /bûrl or birl/ *vt* and *vi* to spin round (*Scot*); to make a log spin by treading on it (*N Am*); to toss (a coin or coins) (*Scot*). [Appar onomatopoeic]

birl[2] or **birle** /bûrl or birl/ (*Scot and N Eng*) *vt* and *vi* to pour out; to ply with drink; to carouse. [OE *byrelian*, from *byrele* a cupbearer, from *beran* to bear]
■ **birl'er** *n*. **birl'ing** *n* the act of drawing liquor.

birlieman /bûr' or bir'li-mən/ (*Walter Scott*) *n* same as **byrlaw-man** (see under **byrlaw**).

birlinn /bir'lin/ (*hist*) *n* a chief's barge or galley in the Western Isles. [Gaelic *birlinn*, from ON *byrthingr*, from *byrthr* burden]

Biro® /bī'rō/ *n* (*pl* **Bi'ros**) a kind of ballpoint pen. [Laszlo *Biró* (1899–1985), Hungarian who designed it]

birostrate /bī-ros'trāt/ *adj* double-beaked. [L *bi-* twice, and *rōstrātus* beaked, from *rōstrum* a beak]

birr[1] /bûr or bir/ (*esp Scot and US*) *n* impetus, force, vigour; a violent push (*Scot*); emphasis, stress in speaking; any sharp whirring sound. ◆ *vi* to whirr. [ON *byrr* a favourable wind]

birr[2] /bûr or bēr/ *n* the standard monetary unit of Ethiopia (100 cents). [Amharic]

birse /bûrs or birs/ (*Scot*) *n* bristle. [OE *byrst*]
■ **bir'sy** *adj*.
■ **lick the birse** to draw a hog's bristle through the mouth, as in admission as a burgess (*souter*) in Selkirk. **set up someone's birse** to rouse the wrath of someone, from the bristling up of enraged animals.

birsle /birs'l or bə'sl/ (*Scot*) *vt* to scorch, to toast. [Origin unknown]

birth[1] /bûrth/ *n* the process of being born; the act of bearing young; coming into the world; dignity of family; origin; offspring (*archaic*). ◆ *vt* (*US*) to give birth to; to deliver (a baby). [Prob ON *byrthr*]
■ **birth'dom** *n* (*Shakesp*) birthright. **birth'ing** *n* (*esp* natural) childbirth (also *adj*).
❑ **birth certificate** *n* an official document giving the date and place of one's birth and the names of one's parents. **birth control** *n* the control of reproduction by contraception. **birthing pool** *n* a pool used in a water birth (qv). **birth'mark** *n* a mark, eg a pigmented area or spot, on one's body at birth; a distinguishing quality. **birth mother** *n* the mother who gives birth to the child (as contrasted with an adoptive or a genetic mother). **birth'night** *n* the night on which one is born, or the anniversary of that night; the evening of the sovereign's birthday (*obs*). **birth parent** *n* a natural parent (as contrasted with an adoptive parent); a birth mother or her partner (as contrasted with a genetic parent). **birth pill** *n* a contraceptive pill. **birth'place** *n* the place of one's birth. **birth rate** *n* the proportion of live births to population. **birth'right** *n* the right or privilege to which one is entitled by birth; native rights. **birth sign** *n* the sign of the zodiac under which one was born. **birth'stone** *n* a gemstone associated with one's birth sign. **birth'-strangled** *adj* (*Shakesp*) strangled at birth. **birth weight** *n* a baby's weight at birth. **birth'wort** *n* a plant (*Aristolochia clematitis*) formerly reputed to help parturition.
■ **give birth** of a mother, to bear or produce a baby.

birth[2] /bûrth/ *n* a place allotted to a ship at anchor. [Same as **berth**]

birthday /bûrth'dā/ *n* the day on which one is born; its anniversary, or a day officially recognized instead. ◆ *adj* relating to the day or anniversary of one's birth. [**birth**[1] and **day**]
❑ **birth'day-book** *n* a book in which to record the birthdays of one's friends. **birthday honours** *n pl* titles, etc, conferred on the sovereign's official birthday. **birthday suit** *n* (*joc*) a state of complete nakedness.
■ **official birthday** a day on which a sovereign's or ruler's birthday is officially celebrated.

biryani, **biriyani** or **biriani** /bi-ryä'ni or bi-ri-yä'ni/ *n* a spicy rice dish. [From Urdu]

BIS *abbrev*: Bank for International Settlements; Department for Business, Innovation and Skills.

bis /bis/ *adv* twice; a direction indicating that a section is to be repeated (*music*). [L]

biscacha same as **viscacha**.

Biscayan /bis'kā-ən or -kā'/ *adj* of or relating to *Biscay* in Spain, its people, or their language; Basque generally. ◆ *n* a native of Biscay; a long heavy musket, or its bullet (*obs*).

biscotto /bis-kot'ō/ *n* (*pl* **biscott'i** /-ē/) a small biscuit, flavoured with anise, almonds, etc. [Ital]

biscuit /bis'kit/ *n* a small, thin, crisp cake made of unleavened dough (*Brit*); an unsweetened scone eaten with meat or gravy (*N Am*); pottery that has been fired but not yet glazed; a square mattress (*milit sl*). ◆ *adj* pale brown in colour. [OFr *bescoit* (Mod Fr *biscuit*), from L *bis* twice, and *coquere*, *coctum* to cook or bake]
■ **bis'cuity** *adj* like a biscuit in flavour or texture.
❑ **bis'cuit-root** *n* camass.
■ **take the biscuit** (*ironic*) to surpass everything else.

bise /bēz/ *n* a cold north or north-east wind prevalent at certain seasons in and near Switzerland. [Fr]

bisect /bī-sekt'/ *vt* and *vi* to divide into two (*usu* equal) parts. [L *bi-* two-, and *secāre*, *sectum* to cut]
■ **bisec'tion** *n*. **bisec'tor** *n* a line that divides an angle or line into two equal parts.

biserial /bī-sē'ri-əl/ (*biol*) *adj* arranged in two series or rows. [**bi-**]

biserrate /bī-ser'āt/ (*biol*) *adj* doubly serrated. [**bi-**]

bisexual /bī-sek'sū-əl or -shoo-əl/ *adj* and *n* (a) hermaphrodite; (a person) attracted sexually to both sexes. [**bi-**]
■ **bisexual'ity** *n*. **bisex'ually** *adv*.

bish /bish/ (*inf*) *n* a blunder, mistake. [Origin obscure]

bishop[1] /bish'əp/ *n* in the Roman Catholic and Orthodox churches and in the Anglican Communion, a senior clergyman consecrated for the spiritual direction of a diocese, *usu* under an archbishop; in the early Christian, and certain modern Protestant, churches, a spiritual overseer of a local church or group of churches; in chess, any of four pieces, two on each side, *usu* with a top in the shape of a mitre, that can move in a diagonal line over any number of empty squares; a hot drink of mulled red wine flavoured with bitter oranges; any of several kinds of colourful African weaver bird (also **bish'op-bird**). ◆ *vt* to confirm (*joc*); to appoint to the office of bishop; to supply with bishops (*rare*); to let (milk, etc) burn while cooking (*N Eng dialect*). [OE *biscop*, from L *episcopus*, from Gr *episkopos* overseer, from *epi* upon, and *skopeein* to view]
■ **bish'opdom** *n* episcopal order; bishops collectively. **bish'opess** *n* a bishop's wife; a female bishop (*joc*). **bish'opric** *n* the office and jurisdiction of a bishop; a diocese.
❑ **bishop's cap** *n* a genus (*Mitella*) of the saxifrage family, with one-sided inflorescences. **bishop's court** *n* the court of a diocesan bishop. **bishop sleeve** *n* a full sleeve drawn in tightly at the wrist. **bish'opweed** or **bishop's weed** *n* goutweed.
■ **the bishop has put his foot in it** (*obs*) it has burnt while cooking.

bishop[2] /bish'əp/ *vt* to fill, or otherwise tamper with, the teeth of (a horse, to make it seem younger). [From a person of the name]

bisk see **bisque**[1,2].

Bislama /bis-lə-mä'/ or (*esp* formerly) **beach-la-mar** /bēch-lä-mär'/ *n* a Melanesian pidgin, the official language of Vanuatu. [Port *bicho do mar*, Fr *bêche-de-mer* sea-slug, the chief product of the area]

bismar /bis' or biz'mər/ (*Orkney and Shetland*) *n* a kind of steelyard. [ON *bismari*]

bismillah /bis-mil'a/ *interj* in the name of Allah. [Ar]

bismuth /bis' or biz'məth/ *n* a brittle reddish-white element (symbol **Bi**; atomic no 83). [Ger *Bismuth*, *Wissmuth* (now *Wismut*), origin unknown]

bisociation /bī-sō-si-ā'shən or -shi-/ *n* the simultaneous association of an idea or object with two quite different sets of facts or ideas, eg in a pun. [**bi-** and **association**]
■ **bisō'ciative** *adj*.

bisom see **besom**[2].

bison /bī'sən or -zən/ *n* a large wild ox with shaggy hair and a fatty hump, the European bison, almost extinct except in parks, and the American, commonly called buffalo in America. [From L *bisōn*, *-ontis*, prob of Gmc origin; cf OHGer *wisunt*, OE *wesend*]

Bispa /bis'pə/ *abbrev*: British Independent Steel Producers' Association (now known as the UK Steel Association).

bisphenol /bis-fē'nol/ *n* a hydrocarbon used in the manufacture of plastics and resins. [L *bis* twice, and **phenol**]

■ words derived from main entry word; ❑ compound words; ■ idioms and phrasal verbs

bisphosphonate /bis-fos'fǝ-nāt/ n any of a family of drugs primarily used to prevent and treat osteoporosis. [L *bis* twice, and **phosphate**]

bisque[1] or **bisk** /bisk/ n a rich shellfish soup, made with wine and cream. [Fr]

bisque[2] or **bisk** n a kind of unglazed white porcelain; pottery that has undergone the first firing before being glazed. [See **biscuit**]

bisque[3] /bisk/ n a term in some sports for the handicap whereby a player allows a weaker opponent (at the latter's choice of time) to score a point in a set, deduct a stroke at a hole, take an extra turn in croquet, etc. [Fr]

bissextile /bi-sek'stīl/ adj having an intercalary day. ◆ n leap year. [L *bisextilis*, from *bis* twice, and *sextus* sixth, the sixth day before the calends of March (24 February) being doubled]

bisson /bis'ǝn/ adj (*Shakesp* **bee'some**) blind, purblind; (*Shakesp* **biss'on**) *perh* blinding. [OE *bisene* blind]

bistable /bī'stā-bl/ adj (of a valve or transistor circuit) having two stable states. [**bi-**]

bistort /bis'tört/ n adderwort or snakeweed, a plant (*Polygonum bistorta*) with a twisted rootstock (also called **snakeweed**). [L *bistorta*, from *bis* twice, and *tortus* twisted]

bistoury /bis'tǝr-i/ n a narrow surgical knife for making incisions. [Fr *bistouri*]

bistre or **bister** /bis'tǝr/ n a pigment of a warm brown colour made from the soot of wood, *esp* beechwood, used for ink and paint. [Fr *bistre*; origin unknown]
■ **bis'tred** adj.

bistro /bē'strō/ n (pl **bis'tros**) a small bar or restaurant. [Fr slang, poss from Russ *bystro* quickly]

bisulcate /bī-sul'kāt/ adj cleft in two (*zool*); cloven-footed (*zool*); with two furrows (*bot*). [L *bi-* two-, and *sulcus* a furrow]

bisulphate /bī-sul'fāt/ n an acid sulphate.
■ **bīsulph'ide** n a disulphide.

bit[1] /bit/ n a bite, morsel; a small piece, a little; a coin; 12½ cents (*N Am*) (used only in **two**, **four** or **six bits**, ie a quarter, a half or three-quarters of a dollar); the smallest degree; a brief space of time; a small tool for boring (see **brace**); the boring-piece of a drilling machine; the cutting or biting part of various tools; the part of the bridle that the horse holds in its mouth; the part of a key that engages the lever of the lock; used with the effect of a diminutive, as in *a bit of a laddie*, *a bit laddie* (*dialect*, *esp Scot*); a girl, young woman (*inf*); an (area of) activity, an act, a role (*sl*). ◆ vt (**bitt'ing**; **bitt'ed**) to put the bit in the mouth of; to curb or restrain. [From **bite**]
■ **bit'less** adj without a bit. **bit'sy** adj (*inf*) prettily small. **bitt'ie** n (*Scot*) a small piece, short distance, or short time. **bitt'ock** n (*Scot*) a little bit. **bitt'y** adj scrappy, disjointed, made up of odds and ends; not forming an artistic whole.
□ **bit'-part** n a small part in acting. **bit player** n an actor who plays bit-parts.
■ **a bit** or **a bit of** somewhat, rather, as in *a bit of a fool*, *a bit stupid*. **a bit of all right** (*sl*) a person or thing highly approved of. **a bit off** (*inf*) in bad taste. **a bit on the side** (*sl*) (one's partner in) extramarital sexual relations. **bit by bit** piecemeal; gradually. **bits and bobs** or **bits and pieces** odds and ends. **champ at the bit** to be impatient to act. **do one's bit** to do one's due share. **every bit** just as much. **not a bit** or **not a bit of it** not at all. **off the bit** on a loose rein. **on the bit** on a tight rein. **take** (or **get**) **the bit in** (or **between**) **one's teeth** to throw off control; to take up or have a tenacious interest (in) or occupation (with something). **to bits** (to fall, etc) apart; very much (*inf*).

bit[2] /bit/ (*comput*) n a binary digit (see under **binary**).
□ **bit'coin** n a unit of digital currency held and exchanged for goods by means of computer software. **bit'map** n (*comput*) a method of organizing the screen display whereby each pixel is assigned to one or more bits in memory, depending on the level of shading or number of colours required. **bit'-mapped** adj. **bit'-mapping** n. **bit'-rate** n the rate of transmission of bits, *usu* measured in bits per second. **bit'-slice** n a now obsolete high-performance microprocessor of either 2, 4 or 8 bits, individually programmed and combined to form a customized CPU of any desired word size. **bit'stream** n a transmitted sequence of bits.
■ **bits per inch** a measurement for the density of data on a storage medium (*abbrev* **bpi**). **bits per second** a measurement for the rate of transmission of bits (*abbrev* **bps**).

bit[3] /bit/ pat and pap of **bite**.

bitch /bich/ n the female of the dog, wolf, and fox; a woman, very rarely a man (*abusive*); a malicious or arrogant woman (*sl*); an extremely difficult or unpleasant situation or problem (*sl*); an act of grumbling or complaining (*sl*); a person who undertakes demeaning tasks for another (*sl*). ◆ vi (*sl*) to complain, talk bitchily. ◆ vt (*sl*) to mess up, spoil (often with *up*); to behave bitchily towards. [OE *bicce*; ON *bikkja*]

■ **bitch'ery** n ill-tempered, malicious behaviour or talk. **bitch'ily** adv. **bitch'iness** n. **bitch'ing** or **bitch'in'** (*US sl*) adj outstandingly good. ◆ adv very. **bitch'y** adj catty, malicious; resembling or characteristic of a bitch.
□ **bitch'-slap** vt (*sl*) to slap in the face, *esp* with the back of the hand; to humiliate.
■ **the bitch goddess** material success as an object of worship.

bite /bīt/ vt and vi (pat **bit**; pap **bitt'en** or (*archaic*) **bit**) to seize or tear with the teeth; to puncture with the mouthparts, as an insect does; to cut or penetrate; to eat into chemically; to smart or cause to smart; to take effect; to grip, to take firm hold (of); to deceive, take in (now only in *passive*); to accept something offered as bait (also *fig*); to speak harshly against (*archaic*). ◆ n a grasp by the teeth; the manner or configuration in which the teeth come together; a puncture by an insect; the wound or sore caused by this; a nibble at the bait (*angling*); something bitten off; a mouthful; a snack; biting quality; grip; pungency; incisiveness; corroding action; a playful imposition, a swindling (*obs sl*). [OE *bītan*; Gothic *beitan*, ON *bīta*, Ger *beissen*]
■ **bit'er** n a person or thing that bites; an animal with a habit of biting; a fish apt to take the bait; a cheat (*obs* except in **the biter bit** the cheater cheated; the wrongdoer paid back). **bite'size** adj (of food) small enough to be eaten in one bite. **bit'ing** n the action of the verb. ◆ adj which bites; sharp, cold; sarcastic.
□ **biting louse** n a bird-louse. **biting midge** n a tiny fly which feeds on the blood of people and animals.
■ **bite and** (or **or**) **sup** something to eat and (or) drink. **bite back** to refrain from saying. **bite in** (*etching*) to eat out the lines of with acid. **bite off more than one can chew** to overestimate one's capacities; to undertake something one cannot achieve. **bite one's lip** to restrain one's anger or mirth. **bite someone's head off** to speak to someone unnecessarily angrily. **bite** (or **bite on**) **the bullet** to submit bravely to something unpleasant; to face up to an unpalatable fact or situation. **bite the dust** to fall down dead; (of plans, etc) to come to nothing. **bite the hand that feeds one** to show ingratitude, often with the likely result of losing the help one is receiving. **bite the thumb** (*obs*) to express defiance by knocking the thumb-nail against the teeth. **bitten off** abruptly cut short. **once bitten, twice shy** a bad experience makes one cautious on a second occasion. **put the bite on** to extort money from. **soundbite** see under **sound**[1]. **what's biting you**, etc? what is the matter with you, etc?, what is annoying you, etc?

bito /bē'tō/ n (pl **bi'tos**) a tree (*Balanites aegyptiaca*; family Zygophyllaceae) of dry tropical Africa and Asia; its oil-yielding fruit.

bitonal /bī-tō'nǝl/ adj using two musical keys simultaneously. [**bi-**]
■ **bitonal'ity** n.

bitser /bit'sǝr/ n (*Aust inf*) a mongrel dog. [From *bits of* this, *bits of* that]

bitt /bit/ (*naut*) n a post for fastening cables, etc (*usu* in *pl*). ◆ vt to fasten (a cable, etc) round the bitts. [Perh ON *biti* a crossbeam]
■ **bitt'er** n the turn of cable round the bitts, hence *perh* **the bitter end** the end of the rope; the end of a task, however long-drawn-out or difficult; final conclusive defeat or death.

bittacle same as **binnacle**.

bitte /bit'ǝ/ (*Ger*) interj please; don't mention it; I beg your pardon.

bitter[1] /bit'ǝr/ adj having a taste like that of quinine or hops; sharp; painful; acrimonious; broodingly resentful; extremely and painfully cold. ◆ n any substance having a bitter taste, *esp* a type of beer. [OE *biter*, from *bītan* to bite]
■ **bitt'erish** adj. **bitt'erly** adv. **bitt'erness** n. **bitt'ers** n pl a liquid prepared from bitter herbs or roots, and used to aid digestion or stimulate appetite, or to flavour drinks.
□ **bitter aloes** see **aloe**. **bitt'er-apple** n a type of cucumber, the colocynth. **bitt'er-cress** n cardamine. **bitt'er-earth** n magnesia. **bitt'er-king** n an intensely bitter shrub of the quassia family, growing in the Malay Archipelago. **bitter lemon** n a lemon-flavoured soft drink. **bitter orange** n the Seville orange, bitter when ripe, used for making marmalade, etc. **bitt'er-pit** n a disease of apples, etc, characterized by brown spots and depressions. **bitt'er-root** n an American xerophytic plant (*Lewisia rediviva*). **bitt'er-spar** n dolomite. **bitt'ersweet** n the woody nightshade (*Solanum dulcamara*), whose stems when chewed taste first bitter, then sweet; an apple that tastes both sweet and bitter (*Shakesp*); a mixture of sweet and bitter (also *fig*; also *adj*). **bitter vetch** see **vetch**. **bitt'erwood** n any of various trees, *esp* of the family Simarubaceae.
■ **a bitter pill to swallow** something which is difficult or unpleasant to accept, such as an unwelcome fact. **the bitter end** see **bitt**.

bitter[2] see under **bitt**.

bitterling /bit'ǝr-ling/ n a small brightly coloured fish (*Rhodeus amarus*).

bittern[1] /bit'ǝrn/ n a marsh bird of the heron family with a loud deep call. [ME *bittour*, *botor*, from OFr *butor*]

bittern² /bit'ərn/ n a bitter oily liquid remaining in salt-works after crystallization of the salt. [**bitter¹**]

bittock see under **bit¹**.

bittor, bittour or **bittur** /bit'ər/ (Spenser, Dryden) n the bittern.

bitty see under **bit¹**.

bitumen /bi-tū' or bit'yu-mən/ n the name applied to various inflammable impure mixtures of hydrocarbons, such as naphtha, petroleum, asphalt; one of these, a tarry substance used to surface roads and roofs. [L *bitūmen*, *-inis*]

■ **bitū'minate** vt to mix with or make into bitumen (also **bitū'minize** or **-ise**). **bituminiza'tion** or **-s-** n. **bitū'minous** or **bitūmed'** (also /bit'/) adj (Shakesp) impregnated with bitumen.
❑ **bituminous coal** n coal that flames in burning, being rich in volatile hydrocarbons.

bivalent /bī-vā'lənt or biv'ə-lənt/ adj having a valency of two (chem); relating to one of a pair of homologous chromosomes (also n). [**bi-** and **-valent**]

■ **biva'lence** or **biva'lency** n.

bivalve /bī'valv/ n an animal, esp a lamellibranch, having a shell in two valves or parts, such as the oyster; a seed vessel of a similar kind. ♦ adj having two valves. [L bi- two-, and valva a folding door]

■ **bivalv'ular** adj.

bivariant /bī-vā'ri-ənt/ (chem) adj having two independent variables (also n).

bivariate /bī-vā'ri-āt/ (stats) adj involving two variables (also n).

bivious /biv'i-əs/ adj (obs) leading two, or different, ways. [L bivius, from bi- two-, and via a way]

■ **biv'ium** n in echinoderms, the two rays enclosing the madreporite.

bivouac /biv'oo-ak/ n a makeshift camp or camping place without tents; the making of or staying in this. ♦ vi (**biv'ouacking**; **biv'ouacked**) to pass the night in the open air or in a makeshift camp; to make such a camp. [Fr, from Ger Beiwacht additional watch]

bivvy /biv'i/ (sl) n and vi a short form of **bivouac**.

bi-weekly /bī-wē'kli/ adj occurring or appearing once every two weeks, or twice a week (also adv). ♦ n a periodical issued twice a week, or once every two weeks.

Bixa /bik'sə/ n a tropical American genus of plants yielding anatta, giving name to the **Bixa'ceae**, a family of parietal Archichlamydeae. [Sp bixa, from Taino bixa]

bi-yearly /bī-yēr'li/ adj and adv (happening, issued, etc) twice a year, or every two years.

biz /biz/ slang for **business**.

bizarre /bi-zär'/ adj odd; fantastic; extravagant. [Fr, from Sp bizarro gallant, brave, poss from Basque bizarra beard]

■ **bizarre'ly** adv. **bizarr'erie** or **bizarre'ness** n.

bizazz see **bezzazz**.

bizcacha see **viscacha**.

bizone /bī'zōn/ n a unit or country formed of two zones, eg that comprising the British and US occupation zones in Germany after 1945.

■ **bizo'nal** adj.

bizzazz see **bezzazz**.

bizzy /biz'i/ (sl) n a policeman. [Perh from busybody]

BJP abbrev: Bharatiya Janata Party, an Indian political party that advocates Hindu nationalism.

Bk (chem) symbol: berkelium.

bk abbrev: bank; book.

bkg abbrev: banking.

bkpg abbrev: bookkeeping.

bks abbrev: barracks; books.

BL abbrev: Bachelor of Law; Bachelor of Letters; British Legion; formerly, British Leyland; British Library.

B/L or **b/l** abbrev: bill of lading.

bl abbrev: bale; barrel; bill of lading.

blab¹ /blab/ (inf) vi (**blabb'ing; blabbed**) to talk idly or indiscreetly; to tell tales. ♦ vt to let out (a secret). ♦ n a person who lets out secrets; a tattler (Milton); tattling. [ME blabbe; cf ON blabbra, Ger plappern]

■ **blabb'ing** n and adj.

blab² /blab/ n (obs) a blister. ♦ vt to swell. [**bleb**]

■ **blabb'er** adj swollen.

blabber /blab'ər/ (inf) vi to talk meaninglessly or idly, usu at length. ♦ n (also **blabb'ermouth**) a person who blabs or blabbers, esp one who reveals secrets. [**blab¹**]

black /blak/ adj of the darkest colour; reflecting no light; used as a classification of pencil leads to indicate softness in quality and darkness in use; obscure; dismal; sullen; bad-tempered; angry; horrible; grotesque, grimly humorous, making a joke of tragic or unpleasant aspects of life, as in black comedy or black humour; dusky; dirty; malignant; unlucky; dark-haired; wearing dark armour or clothes; (of coffee or tea) without milk or cream; illicit; (of income) not reported in tax returns; unofficial; under trade-union ban; (the following senses often with cap) dark-skinned, of African, West Indian or Australian Aboriginal descent; of African, Asian or mixed descent (esp S Afr); (of an area or state) inhabited or controlled by black people; of, belonging to, or relating to, black people. ♦ n black colour or absence of colour; (often with cap) a dark-skinned person, esp of African, West Indian or Australian Aboriginal descent; a black pigment; (usu with cap) in chess or draughts, the player with the black pieces; a smut; smut fungus; black clothes (formerly, still in Scotland, in pl). ♦ vt to make black; to punch (someone's eye) so as to produce a black eye; to soil or stain; to draw in black; to blackmail (sl); to put under trade-union ban, to boycott, ban. [OE blæc black]

■ **black'en** vt to make black; to defame. ♦ vi to become black. **black'ing** n a substance used for blacking leather, metal, etc. **black'ish** adj. **black'ly** adv in an angry or threatening way. **black'ness** n.
❑ **Black Africa** n Africa south of the Sahara, where the population is mainly black. **black'amoor** n (archaic) a dark-skinned or black person. **black-and-blue'** adj livid in colour because of bruising. **black-and-tan'** adj and n (a dog) having black hair on the back, and tan or yellowish-brown elsewhere; (usu **Black and Tan**) (of) an armed auxiliary policeman in Ireland in the 1920s (from his khaki uniform with black cap and armlet). ♦ n a drink that is a mixture of ale and stout or porter. **black and white** adj partly black, partly white; drawing or drawn in black on a white ground; not in colour (cinematog, photog, TV); consisting of extremes, not admitting any middle ground. **black art** n magic (perh a translation of L nigromantia, erroneously used for Gr nekromanteiā, see **necromancy** under **necro-**). **black-a-vised** /blak'ə-vīst or -vīzd/ adj (perh Fr à vis in the face) swarthy. **black'ball** vt to vote against (someone) by putting a black ball into a ballot box; to ostracize; to vote against, veto (a proposal). **black'balling** n. **black'band** n iron ore containing enough coal to calcine it. **black bass** /bas/ n a N American freshwater fish (genus Micropterus). **black bean** n an Australian tree, Castanospermum australe, with attractive wood; the wood of this tree; any black bean of the genus Phaseolus; a soya bean, the seed of the plant Glycine max, used in Asiatic cookery after fermenting, salting and seasoning. **black bear** n an American or Asiatic bear, usu black but sometimes brown. **black beetle** n a cockroach. **black belt** n a belt showing the highest grade of proficiency in various martial arts; a person who has attained this grade; an area with rich dark soil (US); a region of the Southern USA in which black people outnumber white people (US). **black'berry** n the bramble or its fruit; in some districts, the blackcurrant or the bilberry. **black'berrying** n gathering blackberries. **black'bird** n a species of thrush, the male of which is black with a yellow beak; a grackle or other bird of the family Icteridae (N Am); a Polynesian or black person recruited or kidnapped for labour (archaic sl). **black'birder** n a person or ship engaged in slave-trading. **black'birding** n. **black'board** n a board with a black surface, for writing on with chalk; a similar board of any colour. **black'-boding** adj of evil omen. **black body** n a body or surface that absorbs all incident radiation, reflecting none. **black body radiation** n that emitted by a black body. **black body temperature** n that at which a black body would emit the same radiation as is emitted by a given radiator at a given temperature. **black book** n an important book bound in black; a book recording the names of persons deserving punishment (see also **in someone's black books** below). **black bottom** n an American dance of the late 1920s. **black box** n a type of seismograph for registering underground explosions; a flight recorder; a device or unit, esp electronic, whose internal workings need not be understood by the user (comput, etc). **black'boy** n an Australian grass-tree. **black bread** n dark, coarse rye-bread. **black'-browed** adj having black eyebrows; sullen, scowling. **black'buck** n an Indian antelope, the male of which is dark-coloured. **black'-bull'y** n sapodilla. **black bun** n (Scot) a rich dark fruitcake in a pastry case, traditionally eaten at New Year. **black butt** n any of several Australian trees of the genus Eucalyptus, used for timber. **black cabbage** same as **cavolo nero**. **black'cap** n a warbler, the male of which has a black crown; an apple baked with a caramelized sugar coating; a black American raspberry. **black cap** n (hist) the cap put on by English judges to pronounce sentence of death. **black'-cat** n the pekan. **black cattle** n pl (archaic) cattle of any colour, orig from Wales or Scotland. **black chalk** n bluish-black clay-slate, used for drawing, and for making black paint. **black'-coated** adj wearing a black coat; of the professional class. **black'cock** n the male of the **black grouse** (see below). **Black Consciousness** n (also without caps) a Black movement promoting and publicizing the separate cultural traditions of black society. **Black Country** n a heavily industrialized area of the West Midlands. **blackcurr'ant** n the small black berry of the garden shrub Ribes nigrum of the gooseberry genus; this shrub. **black damp** n

air in a mine in which the oxygen has been displaced by carbon dioxide. **black death** *n* (with *the* and *usu* with *caps*) a deadly epidemic of bubonic plague that swept over Asia and Europe, reaching England in 1348. **black diamond** *n* same as **carbonado²**; (in *pl*) coal. **black dog** *n* (*inf*; with *the*) depression, melancholy. **black draught** *n* a purgative medicine, chiefly senna and Epsom salts. **black drop** *n* a liquid preparation of opium, vinegar, and sugar. **black earth** *n* a fertile deposit covering wide regions in S Russia and in central India. **black economy** *n* economic activity involving payment in kind or cash not declared for tax purposes. **Black English** *n* (*orig US*) any of the varieties of English spoken by (*esp* urban) black people. **black eye** *n* an eye with darkened bruised swollen skin around it, *usu* resulting from a blow; an eye of which the iris is dark. **black-eye(d) bean** or **pea** *n* the cowpea; (the seed of) a plant widely cultivated for its seed pods containing beans which are usually creamy-white with a 'black eye'. **black-eyed Susan** *n* a N American composite plant of the *Rudbeckia* genus, whose flowers have dark centres and yellow or orange rays; a tropical African climbing plant (*Thunbergia alata*) that has yellow flowers with purple centres. **blackʹface** *n* a breed of sheep with a black face; stage make-up for a white performer playing a black person; such a performer. **blackʹfaced** *adj*. **blackʹ-fellow** *n* (*Aust inf*) an Australian Aborigine. **blackʹ-figure** or **blackʹ-figured** *adj* (*ancient Greece*) having black painted figures on a plain (*usu* red) clay ground (*cf* **red-figure(d)**). **blackʹfish** *n* a name given to several kinds of fish, eg the black ruff, a kind of perch; the pilot whale; a salmon after spawning. **blackʹ-fisher** *n* a poacher of fish by night. **blackʹ-fishing** *n*. **black flag** *n* the flag of a pirate; the banner of anarchism; the flag hoisted at the execution of a criminal; the flag waved to call a driver in from a racing circuit. **black-flagʹ** *vt* to call in a driver by waving the black flag. **black fly** *n* a thrips or aphid that infests beans, etc; these insects collectively; any of several black- or grey-bodied insects of the family Simuliidae, hump-backed bloodsuckers (also known as **birch fly** and **buffalo gnat**) some of which carry the nematode that causes onchocerciasis. **Blackʹfoot** *n* (*pl* **Blackʹfoot** or **Blackʹfeet**) a member of a tribe of Algonquin Native Americans (also *adj*). **Black Forest gateau** or **cake** *n* an elaborate rich chocolate cake filled and topped with cherries and cream. **blackʹ-fox** *n* the pekan. **Black Friar** *n* (also without *caps*) a Dominican, from his black mantle (over a white woollen habit). **black Friday** *n* Good Friday; an unlucky Friday; (*US*) the Friday after Thanksgiving Day, regarded by retailers as the beginning of the highly profitable Christmas shopping season. **black frost** *n* frost without rime or snow. **blackʹgame** *n* black grouse. **black gold** *n* (*inf*) oil. **black gram** same as **urd**. **black grouse** *n* a large N European grouse, the male of which (**blackʹcock**) is black with a lyre-shaped tail, and the female of which is called a **greyʹhen**. **blackguard** /blagʹgärd/ *n* (somewhat *old*) a contemptible scoundrel (also *adj*). ◆ *vt* to vituperate. ◆ *vi* to play the blackguard. **blackʹguardism** *n*. **blackʹguardly** *adj* and *adv*. **black guillemot** *n* a guillemot native to N Atlantic coasts which has mainly black summer plumage. **black hand** *n* (*usu* with *caps*) a secret society or underground influence. **blackʹ-hat hacker** *n* a computer hacker who tries to break into a system to perform acts of sabotage (*cf* **white-hat hacker**). **blackʹhead** *n* an accumulation of sebum in a pore or hair follicle, a comedo; a bird of various kinds, such as the blackheaded gull; an infectious disease of turkeys, pheasants and other fowl. **blackʹheaded** *adj* having a black head. **blackʹheart** *n* a dark kind of cherry. **black-heartʹed** *adj* having an evil disposition. **black hole** *n* a punishment cell, *esp* (with *caps*) that at Calcutta in which 123 of 146 British prisoners were alleged to have died of suffocation in 1756; a region of space-time from which matter and energy cannot escape, inferred to exist where a massive star has collapsed (*astron*). **black house** *n* an obsolete type of house in the Scottish highlands and islands, built of turf. **black ice** *n* a thin layer of transparent ice on a road. **blackʹjack** *n* vingt-et-un, or a game like it; a combination of an ace and a face card in the game of blackjack; a large jug for holding drink, *orig* made of leather; a pirate flag; zinc blende; a short leather-covered club with weighted head (*N Am*). ◆ *vt* (*N Am*) to hit with a blackjack. **black knight** *n* (*stock exchange*) a person making an unwelcome bid to take over a company. **blackʹlead** *n* graphite used in making pencils, blacking grates, etc. **blackʹleg** *n* a worker continuing to work during a strike or one taking a striker's place (*derog*); the disease black-quarter; any of a number of diseases of vegetables; a swindler, *esp* at a racecourse. ◆ *vi* to work as a blackleg. **black letter** *n* the Old English typeface (also called **Gothic**). **black light** *n* invisible infrared or ultraviolet electromagnetic radiation. **blackʹlist** *n* a list of defaulters or persons convicted or suspected of something, disapproved of, or who are liable to loss of employment or lack of full recognition because of their (*usu* political) views. ◆ *vt* to put on a blacklist. **blackʹlisting** *n*. **black lung** *n* a lung disease that affects miners, pneumoconiosis. **black magic** see under **magic**. **black Maria** /mə-rīʹə/ *n* a van for transporting prisoners; hearts (the card game); a shell that emits dense black smoke, or a gun discharging it (*obs milit sl*). **black mark** *n* something known or noted to one's discredit. **black market** *n* buying and selling (*esp* of scarce products) that is against the

law or official regulations. **black-marketeerʹ** *n* a person who operates on the black market. **black mass** *n* a travesty of the Roman Catholic mass practised in devil-worship. **black Monday** *n* Easter Monday; (the day of) the international stock-market crash in October 1987; the day of return to school. **black money** *n* income not reported for tax purposes. **Black Monk** *n* a Benedictine (also without *caps*). **Black Muslim** *n* a member of a militant African-American Muslim sect. **black nationalism** *n* (also with *caps*) a movement aimed at increasing Black self-determination and reducing White influence in all areas with a black population. **black nationalist** *n*. **black op** *n* (*milit sl*) a covert operation. **blackʹout** *n* total extinction or concealment of lights; a failure or cut in electrical power; a sudden loss of consciousness, or failure of the mind to work; a complete stoppage or suppression (of news, communications, etc); a stoppage in the transmission of radio or television programmes; a break in radio communication. See also **black out** below. ◆ *adj* for blacking out windows, etc with. **Black Panther** *n* a member of a militant Black political movement formed in the 1960s with the aim of ending domination by white people. **black paper** *n* an unofficial document similar in form to a government white paper, criticizing official policy. **black pepper** *n* see **pepper**. **blackʹpoll** *n* a N American warbler with a black and white head. **Black Pope** *n* (*derog*) the head of the Jesuits. **black powder** *n* gunpowder used in quarry work. **Black Power** *n* (also without *caps*) a militant movement to increase the influence of black people, *esp* in the US. **black pudding** *n* a dark sausage made with pig's blood and other materials. **black-quartʹer** *n* an apoplectic disease of cattle and sheep. **black rat** *n* the smaller of the two British rats (*usu* brown). **black rhinoceros** *n* a two-horned African rhinoceros with a prehensile upper lip. **black robin** *n* an extremely rare NZ bird, *Petroica traversi*. **Black Rod** *n* the usher of the chapter of the Garter and of the House of Lords, who summons the Commons at the opening of the UK Parliament; a similar officer in Commonwealth parliaments. **black rot** *n* any disease of plants, vegetables or fruit in which parts turn black. **Black Russian** *n* a cocktail consisting of vodka and Kahlúa. **black sheep** *n* a disreputable member of a family or group. **Blackʹshirt** *n* a member of a Fascist organization, *esp* in the Nazi SS and in Italy during World War II. **blackʹsmith** *n* a smith who works in iron. **black smoker** *n* (*geol*) an underwater volcanic spring, a deep-sea vent that sends out water rich in chemicals and mineral particles. **black snake** *n* a large agile non-poisonous snake (*Coluber constrictor*) (*US*); a very venomous snake (*Pseudechis porphyriacus*), closely related to the cobra (*Aust*); a long whip. **black spot** *n* the name given to disease of various plants, eg roses; an area which has bad conditions or a bad record for a specified trouble. **Black Stone** *n* a piece of black basalt in the Kaaba, sacred to Muslims. **black stump** *n* (*Aust* and *NZ*) a mythical distance-marker on the edge of civilization (*esp* in **beyond the black stump** in the far outback). **black swan** *n* a swan with black plumage and a red beak, native to Australia; something rare or non-existent (*old*). **blackʹ-tailed deer** *n* the mule deer. **blackʹthorn** *n* a dark-coloured thornbush bearing sloes, with white flowers that appear before its leaves in March and April; a walking-stick made from its stem. **black tie** *n* a man's black bow tie worn with a dinner jacket. ◆ *adj* (of an occasion) formal, at which a dinner jacket should be worn. **blackʹtop** *n* (*esp N Am*) bituminous material used for surfacing roads, etc; a road so surfaced. ◆ *vt* to surface a road with blacktop. **black velvet** *n* champagne mixed with stout. **blackʹ-visaged** *adj* having a black visage or appearance. **black vomit** *n* vomit containing blood, *usu* being a sign of some disease, eg yellow fever. **blackʹwash** *n* a lotion of calomel and lime-water; anything that blackens. **Black Watch** see under **watch**. **black water** *n* waste water from toilets (*cf* **grey water**). **blackʹwater** *n* a cattle disease (*cf* **redwater** under **red¹**); (also **blackwater fever**) a fever in which the urine is dark-coloured. **black widow** *n* a very venomous spider, *esp* a N American species, the female of which has a black body and the habit of eating her mate. **blackʹwood** *n* the dark-coloured timber of several trees, including the American logwood, an Australian acacia, and the East Indian *Dalbergia labifolia*; any one of the trees themselves; (with *cap*) a bidding convention in bridge named after its American inventor.

■ **black in the face** purple through strangulation, passion, or effort. **black out** to obliterate with black; to extinguish or cover all lights; suddenly to lose consciousness; to suppress (news or radio communication). **black up** to apply black make-up to the face in order to play the role of a black person. **in black and white** in writing or in print; (in art, etc) in no colours but black and white; (*esp* to **see everything in black and white**) (to see things) only as one extreme or the other. **in someone's black books** (*inf*) having incurred someone's displeasure; in trouble or disgrace (in a certain person's eyes). **in the black** solvent, out of debt; making a profit. **put the black on** (*sl*) to blackmail.

BlackBerry® /blakʹbər-i/ *n* a proprietary brand of smartphone.

blackmail /blakʹmāl/ *n* payment made to robbers for protection (*hist*); hush-money extorted under threat of exposure, often baseless; such

extortion; the use of threats to compel. ◆ *vt* to extort money from (a person); to force by threats (into doing something). [**black** and *mail*, an obsolete term for payment of money]
  ■ **black'mailer** *n*.
  ❑ **blackmail selling** *n* the practice of refusing to further the sale of property unless the purchaser fulfils certain conditions, such as arranging the mortgage with a given company.

blad¹ /*blad*/ *n* a sample of a book produced as promotional material. [Poss ety as **blaud**; or *blurb* and *advertisement*]

blad² see **blaud**.

bladder /*blad'ər*/ *n* a thin distended or distensible bag; any such bag in the animal body, *esp* the receptacle for urine. [OE *blǣdre*, from *blāwan* to blow; OHGer *blā*(h)en, *blājen* to blow; Ger *Blatter*, from *blāhen*; cf L *flātus* breath]
  ■ **bladd'ered** *adj* having a bladder, *esp* of a specified kind (eg *weak-bladdered*); very drunk (*sl*). **bladd'ery** *adj*.
  ❑ **bladder campion** *n* a species of the genus *Silene* with inflated calyx. **bladder cherry** *n* the winter cherry or strawberry tomato. **bladder fern** *n* a small fern with bulbous sporangia, growing on rocks and walls. **bladder nut** *n* a genus (*Staphylea*) of shrubs with inflated capsule. **bladd'erworm** *n* the asexual state of a tapeworm or cestode. **bladd'erwort** *n* a genus (*Utricularia*) of floating plants with bladders that catch small animals. **bladd'erwrack** *n* a common brown seaweed with air-bladders.

blade /*blād*/ *n* the flat or expanded part of a leaf or petal, *esp* a leaf of grass or corn; the cutting part of a knife, sword, etc; a sword; a knife (*sl*); (in *pl*) hand-shears for shearing sheep (*Aust* and *NZ*); the flat part of an implement, not necessarily having a cutting edge; the flat part of an oar; an oar; the paddle-like part of a propeller; the runner of an ice-skate; the free outer part of the tongue behind the tip; a dashing fellow (*archaic*). [OE *blæd*; cf ON *blath*, Ger *Blatt*]
  ■ **blad'ed** *adj*. **blā'der** *n* (*inf*) a person who skates using Rollerblades.
  ❑ **blade'-bone** *n* the flat bone at the back of the shoulder, the scapula. **blade'work** *n* (*rowing*) management of the oars.

blae /*blā*/ (*Scot*) *adj* blackish or dark bluish; livid; bleak. [ON *blār* livid]
  ■ **blaes**, **blaize** or **blaise** /*blāz*/ *n* (*sing* or *pl*) hardened clay or somewhat carbonaceous shale, often blae (also red) in colour.
  ❑ **blae'berry** *n* the whortleberry or bilberry.

blag /*blag*/ (*sl*) *vt* and *vi* (**blagg'ing**; **blagged**) to rob, steal; to scrounge, wheedle. ◆ *n* a theft, robbery; a scrounge. [Ety uncertain]
  ■ **blagg'er** *n*.

blague /*bläg*/ *n* humbug, pretentious nonsense. [Fr]
  ■ **blagueur** /*blä-gœr'*/ *n* a person who talks pretentious nonsense.

blah /*blä*/, **blah-blah** /*blä'blä'*/ or **blah-blah-blah** /*blä'blä'blä'*/ (*sl*) *n* bunkum; pretentious nonsense. ◆ *vi* to talk stupidly or insipidly. ◆ *adj* (**blah**) dull, insipid. [Poss imit]

blain¹ /*blān*/ *n* a boil or blister. [OE *blegen*]

blain² /*blān*/ *n* a fish (*Gadus luscus*), the bib or pout.

Blairism /*blā'ri-zm*/ *n* the policies and style of government associated with Tony *Blair*, British prime minister 1997–2007.
  ■ **Blair'ite** *adj* of, relating to or representing the policies of Tony Blair and his associates (also *n*).

BLAISE or **Blaise** /*blāz*/ *abbrev*: British Library Automated Information Service (now replaced by **BLPC**).

blaise, **blaize** see under **blae**.

blame /*blām*/ *vt* to find fault with; to censure; to impute fault to; to accuse of being responsible *for*; to lay the responsibility *for* (something bad) *on*; to bring discredit upon (*Spenser, Bible*). ◆ *n* the imputation of a fault; culpability; responsibility for what is wrong, not as it should be; injury (*Spenser*). ◆ *adj* (*US*) confounded (also *adv*). [Fr *blâmer*, OFr *blasmer*, from Gr *blasphēmeein* to speak ill; see **blaspheme**]
  ■ **blā'mable** or **blame'able** *adj*. **blā'mableness** or **blame'ableness** *n*. **blā'mably** or **blame'ably** *adv*. **blamed** *adj* (*US sl*) damned, confounded (also *adv*). **blame'ful** *adj* deserving blame. **blame'fully** *adv*. **blame'fulness** *n*. **blame'less** *adj* without blame; guiltless; innocent. **blame'lessly** *adv*. **blame'lessness** *n*. **blame'worthy** *adj* deserving blame; culpable.
  ■ **be to blame** to be the cause of something bad.

blanc-de-Chine /*blä-də-shēn'*/ *n* a white porcelain made at Te-hua under the Ming dynasty. [Fr, white of China]

blanch /*blänch* or *blänsh*/ *vt* to whiten; to remove colour from; to prevent (celery, etc) from turning green by growing it in the dark; to immerse (fruit, vegetables, etc) briefly in boiling water (*cookery*). ◆ *vi* to grow white; to fade; to become pale. ◆ *adj* and *adv* see **blench²**. [Fr *blanchir*, from *blanc* white; see **blank**]

blanchisseuse /*blä-shē-sœz'*/ (*Fr*) *n* a laundress.

blancmange /*blə-mäzh'* or -*mönzh'*/ *n* a flavoured milk dessert thickened with cornflour or gelatine and set in a mould; *orig* fowl or other meat mixed with cream, etc (*obs*). [Fr *blancmanger*, from *blanc* white, and *manger* food]

blanco /*blang'kō*/ (*milit*) *n* an opaque white or khaki substance for treating uniform belts, etc. ◆ *vt* to treat with blanco. [*Blanco*, a trademark, from Fr *blanc* white]

bland¹ /*bland*/ *adj* gentle; mild; without distinctive characteristics, dull; not irritating or stimulating; polite, suave; unemotional, impassive; ironical. [L *blandus*]
  ■ **bland'ly** *adv*. **bland'ness** *n*.

bland² /*bland*/ *n* in Orkney and Shetland, buttermilk and water. [ON *blanda*]

blandish /*blan'dish*/ *vt* to flatter and coax, cajole. [Fr *blandir*, *blandiss-*, from L *blandīrī*]
  ■ **bland'ishment** *n* flattery, cajolery; (in *pl*) winning expressions or actions, attractions.

blank /*blangk*/ *adj* (of writing paper, etc) not written on; (of magnetic tape or another recording medium) with nothing recorded on it; (of a questionnaire, etc) printed with empty spaces for information to be inserted, or with these spaces still unfilled; empty; featureless; expressionless; nonplussed; sheer; unproductive; (of verse) unrhymed. ◆ *n* a blank space in a document; a card, sheet of paper, game tile, etc with no mark or writing on it; a lottery-ticket that brings no prize; emptiness, a void or vacancy; a lapse of memory or concentration; a type of document with blank spaces to be filled up (*archaic* except in *US*); a roughly shaped piece to be fashioned into a manufactured article; a dash in place of an omitted (*esp* taboo) word; a blank cartridge. ◆ *vt* to make blank; euphemistically used for damn, from the former convention of printing 'd—'; (*esp* with *off*) to seal (an opening) with a plug, etc; (*esp* with *out*) to blot out, cover up; to prevent (one's opponent in a game) from making any score (*N Am*); to ignore or pretend not to see (*inf*); to make pale (*obs*); to disconcert (*Milton*). ◆ *vt* and *vi* to produce blanks during a manufacturing process. [Fr *blanc*, from root of Ger *blinken* to glitter, from OHGer *blichen*; cf Gr *phlegein* to shine]
  ■ **blank'ing** *n*. **blank'ly** *adv*. **blank'ness** *n*.
  ❑ **blank cartridge** *n* one without a bullet. **blank cheque** *n* a signed cheque in which the sum is not filled in; complete freedom to act as one thinks best. **blank door** or **window** *n* a recess imitating a doorway or window. **blank'ety-blank'**, **blank'ety-blank'y** or **blankety blank blank** *n*, *adj* or *adv* euphemisms for damned, as in **blank** (*vt*) above. **blank verse** *n* unrhymed verse *esp* of five feet.
  ■ **draw a blank** (*inf*) to get no result, fail. **fire blanks** (*sl*) of a man, to be infertile. **go blank** or **go a complete**, etc **blank** (*inf*) to be unable to produce any response.

blanket /*blang'kit*/ *n* a covering, *usu* of wool or a similar synthetic fabric, for a bed, or used as a garment by Native Americans, etc; a covering generally; fertile material put round a nuclear reactor core to breed new fuel; a rubber or plastic sheet used in offset printing to transfer the image from the plate to the paper; coverage; something that conceals or obscures. ◆ *vt* to cover, obstruct, or extinguish with, or as if with, a blanket (*lit* and *fig*); to toss in a blanket; to cover (an area) totally, eg with publicity. ◆ *adj* applying generally or covering all cases; applied to Native Americans or black S Africans who retain the traditional tribal way of life. [OFr *blankete*, dimin of *blanc* white]
  ■ **blank'eting** *n* cloth for blankets; tossing in a blanket.
  ❑ **blanket bath** *n* the washing of a sick person in bed. **blanket bog** see **blanket mire** below. **blanket coverage** *n* advertising, etc that is directed at the public in general rather than a particular target audience. **blanket finish** *n* a very close finish to a race. **blanket mire** or **bog** *n* a continuous area of peat bog over a wide extent. **blanket spray** *n* a spray of pesticide, etc covering everything in a given area. **blanket stitch** *n* a stitch used *esp* for the edges of a blanket. **blank'etweed** *n* a rapidly spreading green filamentous alga that forms in ponds.
  ■ **on the wrong side of the blanket** illegitimately. **wet blanket** a damper of spirits; a killjoy.

blanquet /*blä-ke'*/ (*Fr*) *n* a variety of pear.

blanquette /*blä-ket'*/ (*Fr*) *n* a ragout of eg chicken or veal made with a white sauce.

blare /*blār*/ *vi* to roar; to sound loudly and *usu* harshly, as eg a trumpet does. ◆ *n* a loud harsh noise. [ME *blaren*, from MDu *blaren*]

blarney /*blär'ni*/ *n* flattery or cajoling talk. ◆ *vt* to cajole. [*Blarney* Castle, near Cork, where a stone difficult to reach is said to confer the gift of persuasive talk on those who kiss it]
  ❑ **blar'ney-land** *n* Ireland.

blasé /*blä'zā*/ *adj* indifferent to pleasure, etc because of familiarity; surfeited with enjoyments. [Fr pap of *blaser* to cloy]

blash /*blash*/ (*Scot*) *n* a dash or splash of liquid or semi-liquid; battering rain; watery stuff. [Imit]
  ■ **blash'y** *adj*.

■ words derived from main entry word; ❑ compound words; ■ idioms and phrasal verbs

blaspheme /blas-fēm'/ *vt* to speak impiously or contemptuously of (God or sacred things). ◆ *vi* to speak profanely or impiously; to curse and swear. [Gr *blasphēmiā*; see **blame**]

■ **blasphem'er** *n*. **blasphemous** /blas'fi-məs* or (*Spenser* and *Milton*) *-fē'*/ *adj*. **blas'phemously** (also (*Spenser*) /-fē'*/) *adv*. **blas'phemy** *n* (*Spenser* also /-fē'*/) impious or profane speaking or behaviour; contempt or indignity offered to God.

❑ **blasphemous libel** *n* (*law*) blasphemy against the Christian faith.

blast /bläst/ *n* a blowing or gust of wind; a forcible stream of air; a sound of a wind instrument, car horn, etc; an explosion or detonation; a shock-wave of air caused by this; an enjoyable or exciting event or occasion, *esp* a party (*sl*, *esp N Am*); a blight; a violent verbal outpouring; any scorching, withering or pernicious influence; an explosion shot (qv under **explode**). ◆ *vi* to emit blasts; to use explosives; to move swiftly and forcefully (*inf*); to swell (*dialect*); to wither (*obs*); to curse; to smoke marijuana (*sl*). ◆ *vt* to blow up, destroy or damage with explosives; to create (a cavity, etc) with explosives; to inflate (*dialect*); to strike powerfully; to strike with a blast; to blight, wither or scorch (crops, etc; also *fig*); to strike with a curse, to curse, to attack vituperatively. ◆ *interj* expressing irritation or annoyance. [OE *blǣst*; cf ON *blāsa*, Ger *blasen*]

■ **blast'ed** *adj* blighted; cursed, damned (often as an intensifier); thoroughly intoxicated by drink or drugs (*sl*). **blast'er** *n* a person or thing that blasts; a sand-wedge (*golf*). **blast'ing** *n* and *adj*. **blast'ment** *n* (*Shakesp*) blight.

❑ **blast'-freezing** *n* a process of freezing food by means of a current of intensely cold air. **blast furnace** *n* a smelting furnace into which hot air is blown. **blast'-furnaceman** *n*. **blast'-hole** *n* a hole in the bottom of a pump through which water enters. **blast'-off** *n* the (moment of) launching of a rocket-propelled missile or space capsule (**blast off** *vt* and *vi*). **blast'-pipe** *n* a pipe in a steam-engine, to convey the waste steam up the chimney.

■ **a blast from the past** (*inf*) an enjoyably nostalgic experience or thing. **at** or **in full blast** in a state of maximum activity.

-blast /-bläst/ (*biol*) *combining form* denoting: developing; budding; immature. [Gr *blastos* bud]

blastema /bla-stē'mə/ *n* primordial material; the primordium of an organ; the protoplasmic part of an ovum, distinguished from the yolk; the axial part of a plant embryo. [Gr *blastēma* sprout]

blasto- /blas-tō-/ (*biol*, *esp embryol*) *combining form* denoting sprout, bud, germ. [Ety as for **-blast**]

■ **blas'tocoel** or **blas'tocoele** /-sēl/ *n* the cavity inside a blastula. **blas'tocyst** *n* the blastula in mammals. **blas'toderm** *n* (Gr *derma* skin; *embryol*) the layer or layers of cells arising from the germinal disc, or the portion of a partially segmenting egg which undergoes division. **blastogenesis** /-jen'/ *n* transmission of hereditary characteristics by the germ-plasm; reproduction by budding. **blastogen'ic** *adj* relating to the germ-plasm. **blast'oid** *adj* and *n*. **Blastoid'ea** *n pl* (Gr *eidos* form) a group of bud-like calcareous fossil echinoderms. **blastō'ma** *n* (*pl* **blastō'mas** or **blastō'mata**) (*pathol*) a neoplasm composed of immature cells. **blas'tomere** *n* (Gr *meros* part) one of the cells formed in an early stage of the cleavage of a fertilized ovum. **blas'topore** *n* (Gr *poros* a passage) the orifice of a gastrula. **blas'tosphere** *n* (Gr *sphaira* a sphere) a blastula.

blastula /blas'tū-lə/ or -tyə-/ *n* (*pl* **blas'tulae** /-lē/ or **blastulas**) a hollow sphere of cells, one cell thick, formed in the cleavage of a fertilized ovum. [Ety as for **-blast**]

■ **blast'ular** *adj*. **blastulā'tion** *n*.

blat[1] /blat/ (*N Am*) *vi* (**blatt'ing**; **blatt'ed**) to cry like a sheep or calf; to make a lot of noise; to blab. ◆ *vt* to blurt out. [Imit]

blat[2] see **blatt**.

blatant /blā'tənt/ (*Spenser* also **blattant**, prob /blat'ənt/) *adj* clamorous, offensively noisy; offensively obtrusive; glaringly obvious; shameless; flagrant. [Prob a coinage of Spenser: for the *blatant beast*, see *Faerie Queene* V.12.37 onward]

■ **blat'antly** *adv*.

blate /blāt/ (*Scot*) *adj* bashful, timidly awkward. [Perh OE *blā* pale]

blather, blatherer, blatherskite see **blether**.

blatt or **blat** /blat/ (*sl*) *n* a newspaper. [Ger]

blattant see **blatant**.

blatter /blat'ər/ (chiefly *Scot*) *n* a clattering rainy blast; a clatter or torrent of words. ◆ *vi* to beat with clattering, like rain on a window. ◆ *vt* to utter volubly. [L *blaterāre* to babble, with sense prob modified by sound]

blaubok /blow'bok/ or *Afrik* **bloubok** /blō'bok/ *n* a small southern African antelope; a large extinct species of southern African antelope. [Du *blauw* blue, and *bok* goat]

blaud or **blad** /blöd/ (*Scot*) *n* a fragment; a broken-off slab; a screed or selection (of verse, etc). ◆ *vt* to strike; to disfigure. [Perh connected with OE *blāwan* to blow]

Blaue Reiter /blow'ə rī'tər/ *n* (with *Der*) the name given to an important art book published by two artists in Munich and transferred (1911) to the group of Expressionist painters formed round them. [Ger, The Blue Rider]

blawort /blä'/ or *blä'wərt/*, also **blewart** /bloo'ərt/ (*Scot*) *n* the harebell; the corn bluebottle. [*blae* and OE *wyrt* herb]

blaxploitation /blak-sploi-tā'shən/ *n* the commercial exploitation of Black culture, relying on stereotypes, in US cinema in the 1970s. [From **black** and **exploitation**]

blay or **bley** /blā/ *n* the bleak, a small fish. [OE *blǣge*]

blazar /blā'zär/ (*astron*) *n* a type of active galaxy that is a more energetic source of radiation than a quasar. [Poss from **blaze**[1], by analogy with **quasar**]

blaze[1] /blāz/ *n* a burst of light or of flame; a fire; an area of brilliant light or colour; a bursting out or active display (of a quality or feeling). ◆ *vi* to burn with a strong flame; to throw out a brilliant light; to be furious (*inf*). [OE *blǣse* torch]

■ **blaz'es** *n pl* the fires of hell, in imprecations like **to blazes**; also **like blazes** furiously, frenziedly. **blāz'ing** *adj* burning brightly; very angry (*inf*).

❑ **blazing star** *n* (*N Am*) any of several star-shaped flowers such as *Chamaelirium luteum* or *Liatris squarrosa*.

■ **blaze away** to fire a rapid and repeated stream of bullets; to work very hard (*inf*). **blaze up** to burst into flames; to become furious or very excited (*inf*).

blaze[2] /blāz/ *n* a white mark on an animal's face; a mark on a tree made by chipping the bark or otherwise. ◆ *vt* to mark (a tree or a track) with a blaze. [Perh Du *bles* or ON *blesi*; or **blaze**[1]]

■ **blazed** *adj*.

■ **blaze a** (or **the**) **trail** (*lit* and *fig*) to show the way as a pioneer.

blaze[3] /blāz/ *vt* (with *abroad*) to proclaim, spread (news). [MDu *blāsen*; cognate with ON *blāsa* to blow; confused with **blazon**]

■ **blaz'er** *n* (*Spenser*) a person who spreads or proclaims.

blazer[1] /blā'zər/ *n* a light jacket, often in the colours or with the badge of a club, school, etc. [**blaze**[1]]

■ **blaz'ered** *adj*.

blazer[2] see under **blaze**[3].

blazon /blā'zn, also (*heraldry*) blaz'n/ *vt* to make public; to display ostentatiously; to depict or to explain in heraldic terms (*heraldry*). ◆ *n* a coat of arms, heraldic bearings (also *fig*); the science or rules of coats of arms; a description or representation (of good qualities). [Fr *blason* a shield, confused with **blaze**[3]]

■ **blaz'oner** *n* a person who blazons; a herald. **blaz'onry** *n* the art of drawing or of deciphering coats of arms; heraldry.

bldg *abbrev* : building.

BLDSC *abbrev* : British Library Document Supply Centre.

bleach /blēch/ *vt* to make pale or white; to whiten (eg textile fabrics); to clean or disinfect with bleach. ◆ *vi* to grow white. ◆ *n* a process or act of bleaching; a bleaching agent. [OE *blǣcan*]

■ **bleach'er** *n* a person or thing that bleaches. **bleach'ers** *n pl* (*esp N Am*) cheap, open-air seats for spectators at a sports ground, etc; the people occupying such seats. ◆ *n sing* a tier of such seats. **bleach'ery** *n* a place for bleaching cloth. **bleach'ing** *n* and *adj*.

❑ **bleach'-field** *n* a place for bleaching cloth; a bleacher's office or works. **bleaching green** *n* a green for bleaching clothes on. **bleaching powder** *n* a compound of calcium, chlorine and oxygen ($CaOCl_2$), used as a bleaching agent.

bleak[1] /blēk/ *adj* dull and cheerless; cold, unsheltered; barren, desolate; hopeless; colourless (now only *dialect*). [Appar ON *bleikr*, cognate with OE *blǣc*, *blāc* pale, shining, black; cf **bleach**]

■ **bleak'ly** *adv*. **bleak'ness** *n*. **bleak'y** *adj* (*obs*) bleak.

bleak[2] /blēk/ *n* a small silvery river fish whose scales yield a pigment used in making artificial pearls. [ON *bleikja*, or a lost equivalent OE word]

blear /blēr/ *adj* (of the eyes) dim, watery; blurred as with inflammation; dim, indistinct. ◆ *vt* to dim (the eyes); to dim the sight of; to blur (the face); to hoodwink. [Cf Ger *Blerr* soreness of the eyes]

■ **bleared** *adj*. **blear'ily** *adv*. **blear'iness** *n*. **blear'y** *adj* (of the eyes) blurred, dim, watery; dull with sleep, drowsy.

❑ **blear'y-eyed** or **blear'-eyed** *adj*.

bleat /blēt/ *vi* to cry like a sheep; to complain, whine; to talk nonsense. ◆ *n* a sheep's cry or similar quavering sound; a complaint, grumble. [OE *blǣan*; imit; cf L *bālāre* to bleat; Gr *blēchē* a bleating]

■ **bleat'er** *n* (*inf*) a complainer. **bleat'ing** *n* and *adj*.

bleb /bleb/ *n* a transparent blister of the cuticle; a bubble, as in water. [Variant of **blob**]

bled /bled/ *pat* and *pap* of **bleed**.

blee /blē/ (*archaic*) *n* complexion, colour. [OE *blēo*]

bleed /blēd/ vi (pat and pap **bled**) to exude blood or sap; to be severely wounded or die in battle (archaic); to ooze or drop like blood; (of paint or dye) to run; (of printed matter) to overrun the edge of the page; to have money, etc extorted from one; to feel great pity. ◆ vt to draw blood from, esp therapeutically (hist); to draw sap from; to print or trim (the printed sheet) so that the text, etc runs off the page; to extort or extract from; to draw off (liquid or gas) from any closed system or container, eg hydraulic brakes or central heating radiators. ◆ n (printing) an illustration deliberately extended beyond the trimmed page. [OE blēdan. See **blood**]

■ **bleed'er** n a person who bleeds; a haemophiliac (inf); an extortionist (US sl); a (nasty) person (sl). **bleed'ing** n a discharge of blood or sap; the act or process of drawing off blood; the diffusion or running of colouring matter; traces of copper showing through worn silver-plate; the drawing off of liquid or gas from a closed system. ◆ adj emitting blood, sap or other liquid; terribly weakened by war; full of compassion; bloody (lit in Shakesp, fig as vulgar sl).

❑ **bleeding edge** n (inf) a part or area (of an organization, branch of study, etc) that generates extremely innovative ideas. **bleed'ing-edge** adj. **bleeding heart** n a name given to various plants of the genera Dicentra, Colocasia, etc; a contemptuous name for a do-gooder. **bleed nipple** or **valve** n a valve to enable liquid or gas to be drawn from a closed system or tank.

■ **bleed like a pig** or **a stuck pig** to bleed copiously. **my heart bleeds for you**, etc (often ironic) I am very sorry.

bleep /blēp/ vi to give out a short high sound or radio signal. ◆ vt to contact (a person) by activating his or her bleeper; (esp with out) to prevent a word in a broadcast from being heard by replacing it with a bleep. ◆ n a sound or signal given out by a bleeper; a bleeper. [Imit]

■ **bleep'er** n a device that bleeps on receiving a certain radio or other signal; such a device, carried by eg a doctor, police officer, etc, by which he or she can be contacted.

blemish /blem'ish/ n (lit and fig) a stain, defect or flaw. ◆ vt to spoil the beauty of, stain; to disfigure, damage, spoil (archaic); to tarnish; to defame; to disrupt (the peace) (law; hist). [OFr blesmir, blemir, prp blemissant to stain, of dubious origin]

■ **blem'ishment** n (Spenser).

blench[1] /blench or blensh/ vi to shrink or start back, flinch. ◆ n (Shakesp) a sideways look. [OE blencan]

blench[2] /blench or blensh/ (Scot hist) adj or adv (of feudal tenure) on the basis of payment of a merely nominal yearly duty (also **blanch**). [See **blanch**]

blend[1] /blend/ vt (pat and pap usu **blend'ed**, also (esp poetic) **blent**) to mix (components) together, esp so as to lose their individual identity; to pollute, vitiate (Spenser). ◆ vi to be mingled; to harmonize; to shade off. ◆ n a mixture; a portmanteau word. [ME blenden; cf OE blandan, ON blanda]

■ **blend'ed** adj mixed together; denoting a domestic arrangement which involves children living with the children of a step-parent (chiefly US). **blend'er** n a person or thing that blends, specif a kitchen device for mixing or liquidizing food. **blend'ing** n.

blend[2] /blend/ (obs) vt (pap **blent**' or **yblent**') to blind; to dazzle; to delude, beguile. [OE blendan]

blende /blend/ n a mineral, zinc sulphide. [Ger Blende, from blenden to deceive, from its confusible resemblance to galena]

Blenheim /blen'əm/ n a kind of spaniel named after the Duke of Marlborough's country house in Oxfordshire.

blennorrhoea /ble-nō-rē'ə/ n a discharge of mucus. [Gr blennos mucus, and rhoiā flow]

blenny /blen'i/ n a member of the genus Blennius or related genera of acanthopterygian fishes, usu slimy. [Gr blennos mucus]

blent /blent/ pat and pap of **blend**[1,2].

blepharism /blef'ə-ri-zm/ n spasm of the eyelid. [Gr blepharon eyelid]

■ **blephari'tis** n inflammation of the eyelid. **bleph'aroplasty** n plastic surgery of the eyelids. **bleph'arospasm** n blepharism.

blesbok /bles'bok/ n a S African antelope with a blaze on its forehead. [Du bles blaze, and bok goat]

bless[1] /bles/ vt (pap **blessed** /blest/ or **blest**) to consecrate; to make the sign of the cross over (Christianity); to extol as holy, pronounce holy or happy; to invoke divine favour upon; to wish happiness to; to make joyous, happy or prosperous; to glorify; to approve officially; to be thankful for. ◆ interj expressing (often ironic) affection for something regarded as delicate and pleasing. [OE blēdsian, blētsian, bletsian to bless, prob from blōd blood]

■ **bless'ed** or **blest** adj happy; prosperous; bringing relief or happiness; in heaven; beatified; accursed, confounded (euphemistic for **blasted**). **bless'edly** adv. **bless'edness** n. **bless'ing** n a wish or prayer for happiness or success; any means or cause of happiness; a gift from God (Bible); a prayer invoking the favour of God at a meal; official approval.

❑ **blessed sacrament** n (Christianity) the consecrated Host. **Blessed Virgin** n (RC) the Virgin Mary (also **BVM**).

■ **a blessing in disguise** something apparently unfortunate proving unexpectedly advantageous. **be blessed with** to have the good fortune to possess. **bless me!** or **bless my soul!** (old) an exclamation of surprise. **bless you!** for **God bless you!**, used superstitiously to someone who has just sneezed; an expression of gratitude or affection. **count one's blessings** to be grateful for what one has rather than bemoan what one lacks. **single blessedness** the unmarried state.

bless[2] /bles/ (Spenser) vt (pat **blest** or **blist**) to brandish. [Perh from **bless**[1] as if to make the sign of the cross; or from **bless**[3]; or poss connected with **blaze**[1]]

bless[3] /bles/ vt to wound; to thrash. [Fr blesser to wound]

blest /blest/ pap of **bless**[1] and pat of **bless**[2].

blet /blet/ n incipient internal decay in fruit without external sign; a part affected with this. ◆ vi (**blett'ing**; **blett'ed**) (of fruit) to become soft or sleepy. [Fr]

blether /bledh'ər/ (Scot) or **blather** /bladh'ər/ (US and dialect) vi to talk garrulous nonsense; to chat, gossip. ◆ n a person who blethers; (often in pl) garrulous nonsense; a chat. [ME blather from ON blathra talk foolishly, blathr nonsense]

■ **bletherä'tion** n. **bleth'erer** or **blath'erer** n. **bleth'ering** n and adj.

bleuâtre /blœ-ä'tr'/ (Fr) adj bluish.

blew[1] /bloo/ pat of **blow**[1,3].

blew[2] an old spelling (Spenser, Milton) of **blue**[1].

blewart see **blawort**.

blewits /blū'its/ n a kind of edible mushroom of the Tricholoma family, lilac-coloured when young. [Perh from **blue**]

bley /blā/ n same as **blay**.

blight /blīt/ n a disease in plants which shrivels or withers them; a fungus, insect, or other cause of blight; anything that injures, destroys, depresses or frustrates; a blighted state, decay, a setback, a check. ◆ vt to affect with blight; to shrivel; to frustrate. [Origin obscure; perh connected with **bleach**, **bleak**[1]]

■ **blight'ed** adj affected with blight; spoiled, ruined; (of a usu urban area) becoming a slum. **blight'er** n a term of (usu playful) abuse, scamp, beggar, wretch (inf); a cause of blighting. **blight'ing** n and adj. **blight'ingly** adv.

■ **planning blight** a fall in value, and consequent neglect, of property in an area, caused by uncertainty about its planned future.

blighty /blī'ti/ (milit sl) n home; the home country; a wound necessitating return home (World War I). [Hindi bilāyatī foreign, European, from Ar wilāyat province, country. Cf **vilayet**]

blimbing same as **bilimbi**.

blimey or **blimy** /blī'mi/ (sl) interj expressing surprise or annoyance (also **cor blimey** or **gorbli'mey**). [Corruption of God blind me]

blimp[1] /blimp/ n an incurably conservative elderly military officer, as Colonel Blimp of the cartoonist David Low (1891–1963), or any other person of similar views.

■ **blimp'ish** adj like Colonel Blimp. **blimp'ishness** n.

blimp[2] /blimp/ n a non-rigid dirigible lighter-than-air craft, used for observing, advertising, etc; a soundproof housing for a sound-film camera. [Poss from Type B-limp, distinguishing this sort of craft from Type A-rigid]

blimy see **blimey**.

blin /blin/ (Spenser) vt and vi (**blinn'ing**; **blinned**) to cease (from). ◆ n cessation; stoppage. [OE blinnan to cease, from be- (1) and linnan to cease]

blind /blīnd/ adj without sight; dark; obscure; invisible, hidden from view; not directed, or affording no possibility of being directed, by sight or by foresight; without previous or adequate knowledge; ignorant or undiscerning; unobserving; voluntarily overlooking; without an exit; (in flying) using instruments only, without seeing one's course or receiving radio directions; (of plants) failing to produce expected growth or flowers; of or intended for the blind, eg blind school; extremely drunk (inf). ◆ adv without seeing; without prior knowledge; relying on instruments only. ◆ n (with the) people without sight collectively; something intended to blind one to the facts; a window screen, either on a roller or made of slats; an awning; something which obstructs the light or the view; a screen behind which hunters hide (N Am); a stake put up without seeing one's cards (poker); a drinking spree, a binge (sl). ◆ vt to make blind; to darken, obscure or deceive; to dazzle; to make matt; to fill in cracks on (a newly made road) with grit, to scatter grit on (a tarry surface). ◆ vi to curse, swear (sl); to drive extremely fast and recklessly (sl). [OE blind; ON blindr]

■ **blind'age** n (milit) a temporary wooden screen faced with earth as a protection against splinters of shell, etc. **blind'ed** adj deprived of sight;

without intellectual discernment. **blind'er** *n* a person or thing that blinds; (*usu* in *pl*) a horse's blinkers (*N Am*); a spectacularly good performance (*inf*); a drinking spree (*inf*). **blind'ing** *n* the act of making blind. ◆ *adj* causing blindness; dazzling; incapacitatingly intense; excellent (*inf*). **blind'ingly** *adv.* **blind'less** *adj.* **blind'ly** *adv.* **blind'ness** *n.*

□ **blind alley** *n* a cul-de-sac; a situation, job, etc, which does not offer any prospect of improvement or advancement. **blind-all'ey** *adj.* **blind coal** *n* anthracite (as burning without flame); coal partly carbonized by an igneous intrusion. **blind date** *n* a social engagement arranged for one, *esp* by a third party, with someone one has not met previously, *esp* with a view to romance; the partner (to be) met in this way. **blind-drunk'** *adj* so drunk as to be like a blind person. **blind'fish** *n* an eyeless fish (genus *Amblyopsis*) of the Kentucky Mammoth Cave. **blind'fold** *adj* (earlier *blind-felled* struck blind) having the eyes bandaged so as not to be able to see; (of chess, etc) played without seeing the board; thoughtless; reckless. ◆ *adv* without being able to see; heedlessly. ◆ *vt* to cover the eyes of; to mislead. ◆ *n* a piece of fabric, handkerchief, etc used for covering up the eyes. **Blind Freddie** *n* (*Aust inf*) an imaginary epitome of imperceptiveness. **blind gut** *n* the caecum. **blindman's buff** *n* (ie **buffet**) a game in which a blindfold player tries to catch the others. **blind road** *n* a grassy track invisible to those that are on it. **blind'-side** *vt* (*N Am*) to exploit someone's blind side in surprising or taking advantage of them. **blind side** *n* the side on which a person is blind to danger; (one's) weak point; the part of the field between the scrum, etc and the touch-line nearer it (*rugby*). **blind'sight** *n* (*psychol*) a condition, caused by brain damage, in which a person is able to respond to visual stimuli without consciously perceiving them. **blind snake** *n* a non-venomous burrowing snake of tropical regions with small or vestigial eyes. **blind spot** *n* the spot on the retina where the optic nerve joins and where there are no visual cells; a point within the normal range of a transmitter at which the field strength is abnormally small (*radio*); a point on a road which is obscured from vision; an area in an auditorium where one cannot see or hear properly; a region of understanding in which one's intuition and judgement always fail. **blind'-stamped** *adj.* **blind stamping** or **tooling** *n* (*bookbinding*) making impressions on the covers without gilding. **blind'-storey** *n* a triforium. **blind summit** *n* a summit on a road whose slope is such as to prevent one from seeing approaching traffic. **blind tooling** see **blind stamping** above. **blind trust** *n* (chiefly *N Am*) a trust which manages a political public figure's private capital, so as to prevent conflict of interest. **blind'worm** *n* a slow-worm.

■ **bake blind** to bake (a pastry case) without a filling. **blind (someone) with science** to confuse (someone) with much complicated detail. **not a blind bit of** (*inf*) not any. **swear blind** (*inf*) to declare emphatically. **the blind leading the blind** the ignorant trying to instruct the ignorant. **turn a blind eye** to pretend not to have seen.

blindman's buff see under **blind**.

bling /bling/ or **bling bling** (*sl*) *n* jewellery, *esp* of a large and conspicuous style; conspicuous wealth. ◆ *adj* large and conspicuous in style. [Imit of the sound of rattling jewellery]
■ **bling'y** *adj.*

blini /blē′ni/ *n* (*pl* **bli'ni** or **bli'nis**) a small buckwheat pancake, *esp* as eaten with caviar and sour cream. [Russ; see **blintz**]

blink /blingk/ *vi* to close both eyes momentarily; to wink; to glance, peep; to look with the eyes half-closed; to look with amazement (*at*); to shine unsteadily or intermittently. ◆ *vt* to open and close (the eyes) rapidly; to flash (a light) off and on; to shut out of sight, to ignore or evade (*rare*). ◆ *n* a glimpse, glance or wink; a gleam, *esp* momentary. [Cf **blench**[1]]
■ **blink'ard** *n* (*archaic*) a person who blinks or has bad eyes. **blinked** *adj* affected with blinking. **blink'er** *n* (*usu* in *pl*) leather flaps to prevent a horse from seeing sideways or backwards; an intermittent flashing light. ◆ *vt* to obscure or limit the vision of (*lit* and *fig*); to put blinkers on (a horse). **blink'ered** *adj.* **blink'ing** *adj* or *adv* (*sl*) used as an intensifier, *prob* as a substitute for *bloody*. **blinks** *n* a mud or water weed (genus *Montia*) of the family Portulacaceae, with minute half-closed flowers.
■ **in the blink of an eye** quickly; suddenly. **on the blink** (*inf*) (of an electrical or electronic device) working intermittently or not working at all.

blintz or **blintze** /blints/ *n* a thin filled pancake. [Yiddish *blintse*, from Russ *blin* (*pl blini*) pancake; cf **blini**]

blip /blip/ *n* a sharp tap or blow; the image of an object on a radar screen, *usu* a bright spot or sudden sharp peak on a line; an unforeseen irregularity, setback or deviation claimed or expected to be temporary; the short, high sound made by a radar instrument. ◆ *vi* (**blipp'ing**; **blipped**) to produce a blip. ◆ *vt* to tap or hit sharply.

bliss /blis/ *n* the highest happiness; the special happiness of heaven. [OE *blīths*, from *blīthe* blithe]
■ **bliss'ful** *adj.* **bliss'fully** *adv.* **bliss'fulness** *n.* **bliss'less** *adj.*

□ **blissed'-out** *adj* (*sl*) affected by hallucinatory drugs; ecstatic.

blist /blist/ (*Spenser*) *pat* and *pap* of **bless**[1,2].

blister /blis′tər/ *n* a thin bubble or bladder on the skin, often containing watery matter; a similar spot elsewhere (eg on a leaf, metal or paint); a medication applied to raise a blister; the protective bulging outer hull of a double-hulled ship, to lessen risk of sinking (*naut*); a transparent bulge on the fuselage of an aeroplane, eg for observation; an irritating person, a pest (*sl*). ◆ *vt* to raise a blister or blisters on; to attack with scathing words; to ornament with puffs (*Shakesp*). ◆ *vi* to develop blisters. [ME; most prob OFr *blestre*, connected with ON *blāstr*, *blāsa* to blow; Ger *Blase*]
■ **blis'tering** *adj* (of criticism) virulent, cruel; painfully intense or strenuous; (of the weather) very hot; (of an action, pace, etc) hard, fast. **blis'tery** *adj.*

□ **blister beetle** or **blister fly** *n* an insect which secretes a substance that blisters skin, formerly used in medicine, *esp* Spanish fly (genus *Cantharis*). **blister card** or **pack** *n* a bubble pack. **blister copper** *n* copper at an intermediate stage of production, about 98% pure. **blister fly** see **blister beetle** above. **blister pack** see **blister card** above. **blis'ter-plaster** *n* a plaster made of Spanish flies, used to raise a blister. **blis'ter-steel** or **blis'tered-steel** *n* steel made from wrought iron with a blistered surface.

BLit see **BLitt**.

blit /blit/ (*comput*) *vi* (**blitt'ing**; **blitt'ed**) to transfer a large array of bits between different locations in a computer's memory. [From *block transfer*]
■ **blitt'er** *n* a chip or system that performs such transfers.

blite /blīt/ *n* a name for several plants of the goosefoot family. [Gr *bliton*]

blithe /blīdh/ *adj* cheerful; merry; joyfully heedless. [OE *blīthe* joyful. See **bliss**]
■ **blithe'ly** *adv.* **blithe'ness** *n.* **blithe'some** *adj* joyous. **blithe'somely** *adv.* **blithe'someness** *n.*

blither /blidh′ər/ *vi* to blether.
■ **blith'ering** *adj* used to express contempt.

BLitt or **BLit** /bē-lit′/ *abbrev* : *Baccalaureus Litterarum* (*L*), Bachelor of Literature; Bachelor of Letters.

blitz /blits/ *n* an attack or bombing from the air (also **blitzkrieg** /blits′krēg/); any sudden, overwhelming attack (also **blitzkrieg**); an intensive campaign (*inf*); a burst of intense activity, in order to achieve something (*inf*). ◆ *vt* to attack or damage (as if) by an air raid; to deal with or complete by a burst of intense activity. [Ger *Blitzkrieg* lightning war, the German method first used in Poland in 1939, from *Blitz* lightning and *Krieg* war]
■ **blitzed** *adj* (*sl*) highly intoxicated by drink or drugs.

blive /blīv/ (*Spenser*) *adv* same as **belive**.

blizzard /bliz′ərd/ *n* a blinding storm of wind and snow. [A 19c coinage, most prob onomatopoeic, on the analogy of *blow*, *blast*, etc]
■ **blizz'ardly** *adj.* **blizz'ardy** *adj.*

bloat /blōt/ *vt* to swell or puff out; to dry (fish) partially by smoke. ◆ *vi* to swell or grow turgid. ◆ *n* the cattle and sheep disease hoove (also **bloat'ing**); bloatedness; a drunkard. ◆ *adj* puffed up, swollen, *esp* with self-indulgence. [Cf ON *blautr* soft]
■ **bloat'ed** *adj* having been bloated; swollen (often as a result of gluttony); swollen with riches (*fig*). **bloat'edness** *n.* **bloat'er** *n* a herring partially dried in smoke, *esp* at Yarmouth.

□ **bloat'ware** *n* (*comput sl*) software with more facilities than most users need, making correspondingly large demands on system resources.

■ **bloated capitalists** a political catchphrase used by Marxists and other socialists (and also *joc* by others) to describe the ruling or managerial class.

blob /blob/ *n* a drop or globule; anything soft and round; a round spot; a score of zero, a duck (*cricket sl*). ◆ *vi* (**blobb'ing**; **blobbed**) to make a blob or blobs, to form into a blob or blobs. [Imit]
■ **blobb'y** *adj.*

bloc /blok/ *n* a combination of parties, nations or other units to achieve a common purpose. [Fr]

block /blok/ *n* a mass of wood or stone, etc, *usu* flat-sided; a piece of wood or other material used as a support (eg for chopping, beheading), shaped as a mould, engraved, etc for printing from, or used as a toy; (in *pl*) starting-blocks (often used in figurative phrases describing speed in starting on an enterprise); a pulley with its framework or the framework alone; a compact mass, group or set; a group of buildings bounded by intersecting streets; such a group regarded as a measure of distance (*N Am*); a large building containing individual units of accommodation, etc; a building lot (*esp Aust*); an extensive area of land for settlement, etc (*Aust* and *NZ*); an obstruction; the head (*esp* in the phrase *knock someone's block off*); an impassive person; a psychological barrier preventing intellectual

development, progress, etc; an instance of, or a cause of, blockage or blocking; an administrative unit in India; a bloc; a group of records or information units treated as a complete unit during the transfer or modification of data (*comput*); (also **license block**) a section of sea within which a company is licensed to explore for and extract oil or gas; a brake block; a cylinder block; a chopping-block; a pad of writing or drawing paper. ◆ *adj* in a block or lump; comprising a number grouped and dealt with together. ◆ *vt* to close or obstruct (a place) with obstacles; to obstruct (a person); to impede or prevent; to make inactive, bring to a standstill, interrupt; to shape as on a block, or to sketch out roughly (often with *in* or *out*); to stop (a ball) with a forward defensive shot (*cricket*); to hinder the play or the action of an opposing player (*sport*); to print (*usu* a fabric) from a block; to stamp a pattern, etc on (leather, a book cover, etc); (also with *out*) to plan or rehearse the movements of the actors in (a scene, etc) (*theatre*); see **select** (*comput*). [Fr *bloc*, prob Gmc in origin]
■ **blockade'** *n* a cutting off of a place by surrounding it with troops or ships (*milit*); an obstruction. ◆ *vt* to block up by troops or ships. **block'age** *n* something that obstructs; an act or instance of obstructing, or the state of being obstructed; resistance to understanding, learning, etc set up by existing habits of thought and action. **blocked** *adj*. **block'er** *n* a player who blocks (*sport*); a substance, used as a drug, that prevents the production, or the operation, of some other substance in the body (*med*). **block'ing** *n* the interruption of a train of thought, *esp* by unpleasant thoughts rising in the mind; the cut-off of anode current in a valve because of high negative voltage in the grid (*electronics*). **block'ish** *adj* like a block; stupid, dull. **block'y** *adj* block-shaped; in blocks; stocky, chunky.
❏ **blockade'-runner** *n* a person or ship that passes through a blockading force. **block and tackle** *n* a lifting device comprising a case (block) containing a pulley and its chains or ropes (tackle). **block'board** *n* plywood board made up of veneer enclosing thin strips of wood. **block'-book** *n* a book printed from engraved blocks, not movable types. **block'buster** *n* a bomb or explosive charge able to destroy a number of buildings simultaneously; a forceful or powerful thing or person; an expensively produced and commercially successful film, novel, etc. **block'busting** *n* and *adj*. **block capital** *n* a capital letter written in sanserif. **block'-chain** *n* an endless chain of blocks and links. **block'-coal** *n* coal that breaks into cuboidal blocks. **block diagram** *n* (*comput*) one made up of squares and rectangles representing different hardware and software components, with lines showing their interconnections. **blocked shoe** *n* a ballet dancer's dancing pump with a stiffened toe-piece, enabling dancing on points. **blocked style** *n* (*typing*) the display style, with all text beginning at the left margin without centring, indenting or underscoring. **block gauge** *n* a block of hardened steel with its opposite faces accurately ground and polished flat and parallel, used to check the accuracy of other gauges. **block grant** *n* a general grant made by the central government to a local authority for all its services. **block'head** *n* (*inf*) a stupid person; a woodenhead. **block'hole** *n* (*cricket*) the place where a batsman rests the end of his bat when batting. **block'house** *n* a small temporary fort; a house constructed of squared logs; a shelter of reinforced concrete, etc used as an observation post and control centre for rocket launches, etc. **blocking motion** *n* notice of intention to bring up a certain matter at a future date, thus preventing (or blocking) raising of the subject on a motion for adjournment. **block letter** *n* a block capital; block type. **block party** *n* a party given for all of the residents of a building or neighbourhood. **block plane** *n* a small very acute-angled plane for cutting across the grain at the end of a piece of wood. **block printing** *n* printing from hand-carved or engraved blocks, now used for specialist books, wallpaper and textiles. **block release** *n* release from employment for a period of weeks or more in order to follow a course of study. **block'ship** *n* a warship too old for action, but useful in port defence. **block'-system** *n* (*rail*) a system in which no train is allowed onto a section of line so long as any other is on it. **block'-tin** *n* tin in the form of blocks or ingots. **block type** *n* a heavy-letter type, without serifs. **block vote** *n* a vote by a delegate at a conference, counted as the number of people he or she represents. **block'work** *n* blocks of precast concrete used for building.
■ **do one's block** (*Aust* and *NZ inf*) to be very angry. **on the block** up for auction.

blog /*blog*/ *n* a document containing personal observations, often in the form of a journal, that is published on the World Wide Web. ◆ *vi* (**blogg'ing; blogged**) to write a blog. [Shortening of *weblog*]
■ **blogg'able** *adj* forming a suitable subject for a blog. **blogg'er** *n*. **blogg'ing** *n*. **blog'osphere** *n* (*inf*) the part of the World Wide Web that contains blogs.
❏ **blog'post** *n* a single entry in a blog. **blog'ring** *n* a set of blogs, *usu* on a common theme, which are connected by hyperlinks. **blog'roll** *n* a series of hyperlinks to recommended weblogs, often found on the sidebar of a blog.

blokart /*blō'kärt*/ *n* a lightweight three-wheeled vehicle, fitted with a sail, designed to be raced over a beach or other level area. [Blend of **blow¹** and **go-kart** (see under **go¹**)]
■ **blō'karting** *n*.

bloke /*blōk*/ (*inf*) *n* a man, chap (*inf*); the commander (*naut sl*). [Origin obscure]
■ **bloke'dom** *n* the world or lifestyle of blokes. **blok(e)'ish, blo'key** *adj* matey, hearty, like one of the blokes.

bloncket /*blong'ket*/ (*Spenser*) *adj* grey. [Fr *blanquet, blanchet* whitish, dimin of *blanc* white]

blond (*usu* in *fem* **blonde**) /*blond*/ *n* a person of fair complexion and light-coloured hair (cf **brunette**). ◆ *adj* (of hair) between pale gold and light chestnut in colour; having fair hair and *usu* a fair complexion; light-coloured. [Fr]
❏ **blond beast** *n* (also with *caps*) a blond type of N European man, admired, eg by Nietzsche, for his physical splendour; any predatory type of man. **blonde bombshell** *n* an extremely attractive blonde woman. **blonde moment** *n* (*sl*) a temporary period of stupidity, supposedly characteristic of women with blonde hair. **blond'-** or **blonde'-lace** *n* lace made of silk, *orig* raw silk.

blonde /*blond*/ *n* see under **blond**; (**Blonde**®) a floodlight with a variable beam for studio use (*image technol*). [**blond**]

blood /*blud*/ *n* the oxygenating fluid (red in the higher animals) circulating in the body; descent, birth; relationship, kinship; (elliptically) a blood horse, one of good pedigree; a swaggering dandy about town; the blood-royal (as in *princes of the blood*); temperament; bloodshed or murder; the juice of anything, *esp* if red; the supposed seat of passion, hence temper, anger (as *his blood is up*), etc; the sensual nature of man; (*sl*) a sensational or melodramatic tale, a penny-dreadful; a young man (also used as a term of address). ◆ *vt* to bleed; to smear with blood; to initiate into blood sports or to war (also *fig*). [OE *blōd*; cf OFris *blōd* and Ger *Blut*]
■ **blood'ed** *adj* having blood; of pure blood, pedigreed; initiated. ◆ *combining form* having blood or temperament of the specified kind. **blood'less** *adj* without blood; dead; anaemic, pale; happening without bloodshed; spiritless, lifeless; unemotional. **blood'lessness** *n*.
❏ **blood agar** *n* agar-agar for growing bacteria, to which blood has been added before the jelly set. **blood-and-thund'er** *adj* (of fiction, etc) violent, sensational, melodramatic. **blood bank** *n* a supply of blood plasma, or the place where it is kept. **blood'bath** *n* a bath in warm blood; a massacre (also *fig*). **blood'-bespotted** *adj* spotted or sprinkled with blood. **blood'-bird** *n* an Australian honeyeater, the male of which has scarlet plumage. **blood blister** *n* a blister with blood in it, caused eg by a bruise. **blood'-boltered** *adj* clotted or matted with blood. **blood'-bought** *adj* (*Shakesp*) bought at the expense of blood or life. **blood brother** *n* a brother by birth; a person who has entered a close and binding friendship with another, in some cultures by ceremonies involving the mixing of blood. **blood cell** *n* any of the cells that circulate in the blood. **blood'-consuming** *adj* (*Shakesp*). **blood corpuscle** *n* a cell normally contained in suspension in the blood. **blood count** *n* the number of red or white corpuscles in the blood. **blood'curdling** *adj* exciting horror with a physical feeling as if the blood had curdled. **blood'curdlingly** *adv*. **blood diamond** *n* a diamond mined in a war zone and sold to fund a military campaign. **blood donation** *n*. **blood donor** *n* a person who gives blood for use in transfusion. **blood doping** or **packing** *n* the practice of temporarily increasing the oxygen-carrying capacity of an athlete's blood by reinjecting red blood cells previously drawn off. **blood'-dust** *n* haemoconia. **blood'-feud** *n* a family feud arising out of an act of bloodshed, a vendetta. **blood'fin** *n* a small freshwater fish native to S America which has red fins. **blood'-fine** *n* a fine paid in compensation for a murder. **blood'-flower** *n* a plant of the genus *Haemanthus*; a species of *Asclepias*. **blood fluke** *n* a schistosome. **blood'-frozen** *adj* (*Spenser*) having the blood frozen or chilled. **blood group** *n* any of various types of blood identified and defined by their antigenetic structures, *esp* one of the four types of human blood (designated O, A, B, AB). **blood'-guilt** or **blood'-guiltiness** *n* the guilt of shedding blood, eg in murder. **blood'-guilty** *adj*. **blood heat** *n* the normal temperature of human blood (37°C or 98.4°F). **blood horse** *n* a horse of the purest and most highly prized blood, origin or stock, a thoroughbred. **blood'-hot** *adj* as hot or warm as blood. **blood'hound** *n* a large hound, noted for its powers of following a scent; a detective (*inf*). **blood'letter** *n*. **blood'letting** *n* drawing off blood by opening a vein (also *fig*); bloodshed. **blood libel** *n* a false accusation of murder or barbarism, *esp* the medieval slander that Jews sacrificed Christian children at Passover. **blood'line** *n* (of animals, etc) all the individuals in a family line over a number of generations, *esp* as considered with regard to some characteristic or other. **blood'lust** *n* desire for bloodshed. **blood money** *n* money earned by laying or supporting a capital charge against anyone, *esp* if the charge is false or made by an accomplice; money paid to a hired assassin; money paid

or accepted for doing something shameful; compensation formerly paid to the next of kin of a victim who has been killed. **blood oath** *n* (*Aust*) an interjection expressing surprise or anger. **blood orange** *n* a variety of orange with red or red-streaked pulp. **blood packing** see **blood doping** above. **blood plasma** *n* the almost colourless liquid left after the blood cells and platelets have been removed from blood. **blood'-plate** *n* a platelet. **blood poisoning** *n* a name popularly, but loosely, used of pyaemia and septicaemia. **blood pressure** *n* the pressure of the blood on the walls of the blood vessels, varying with age and physical condition. **blood pudding** *n* black pudding. **blood purge** *n* the massacre or execution of large numbers believed by a government or ruler to be disloyal. **blood'-rain** *n* rain coloured by red dust from the desert. **blood'-red** *adj* of the colour of blood. **blood relation** or **relative** *n* a person related by common ancestry. **blood'root** *n* a N American plant (*Sanguinaria canadensis*) of the poppy family with red rootstock and sap. **blood-roy'al** *n* royal descent. **blood'-sacrifice** *n* (*Shakesp*) a sacrifice made with bloodshed. **blood sausage** *n* a blood pudding. **blood'shed** *n* the shedding of blood; slaughter. **blood'shot** *adj* (of the eye) red or inflamed with blood. **blood'-sized** *adj* sized or smeared with blood. **blood'-spavin** *n* a disease of horses consisting of the swelling of a vein on the inside of the hock, from a checking of the blood. **blood sports** *n pl* those involving the killing of animals, fox hunting and the like. **blood'sprent** *adj* sprinkled with blood. **blood'stain** *n*. **blood'stained** *adj* stained with blood; guilty of murder. **blood'stock** *n* pedigree horses collectively; young men available as dance partners. **blood'stone** *n* a green chalcedony with blood-like spots of red jasper; haematite. **blood'stream** *n* the blood flowing through the body (also *fig*). **blood'sucker** *n* an animal that sucks blood, *esp* a leech; an extortionist; a person who sponges on another. **blood'sucking** *adj* that sucks or draws blood (also *fig*). **blood sugar** *n* the concentration of glucose in the blood. **blood'-tax** *n* (*derog*) conscription or universal military service. **blood test** *n* an analysis of a small specimen of blood. **blood'thirstily** *adv*. **blood'thirstiness** *n*. **blood'thirsty** *adj* eager to shed blood; depicting much violence. **blood transfusion** *n* the taking of blood from the veins of one person and subsequent injection of it into those of another. **blood type** *n* blood group. **blood typing** *n* the classification of blood according to blood groups, or the identification of the blood group to which a sample of blood belongs. **blood vessel** *n* a vein or artery. **blood'-wagon** *n* (*sl*) an ambulance. **blood'-wite** or **blood'-wit** *n* (*OE law*) a fine for shedding blood; the right to levy it. **blood'wood** *n* a name for various trees with red wood or juice, or their timber, eg a lythraceous tree of the East Indies (genus *Lagerstroemia*), eucalyptus of different kinds, or logwood. **blood'worm** *n* a red aquatic midge larva (genus *Chironomus*); a tubifex.

■ **after** or **out for** (**someone's**) **blood** having murderous intentions (towards someone) (*lit* and *fig*). **avenger of blood** the next of kin to a murdered person whose duty it was thought to be to avenge his or her death. **blood and iron** see **Blut**. **blood is thicker than water** family obligations take precedence over other ties. **blood on the carpet** resolution of a conflict by extreme and unpleasant measures. **first blood** the first drawing of blood in a fight (also *fig*). **fresh**, **new** (or **young**) **blood** new (or young) members in any association of people, to add vitality and new ideas. **in blood** in full vigour. **in hot** (or **cold**) **blood** in (or free from) excitement or sudden passion. **in one's blood** in one's character, inborn. **make someone's blood boil** (or **run cold**) to arouse someone's fury (or to horrify someone).

bloody /blud'i/ *adj* of the nature of blood; stained with blood; like or consisting of blood; marked by considerable bloodshed; murderous, cruel; thoroughly unpleasant (*old*). ◆ *adj* or *adv* as an intensifier, sometimes expressing anger, but often almost meaningless. ◆ *vt* (**blood'ying**; **blood'ied**) to make bloody.

■ **blood'ily** *adv*. **blood'iness** *n*.

□ **blood'y-bones** see **rawhead** under **raw**. **blood'y-eyed** *adj*. **blood'y-faced** *adj*. **bloody flux** *n* dysentery, in which the discharges from the bowels are mixed with blood. **bloody hand** see under **hand**. **bloody Mary** *n* (*pl* **bloody Marys**) a cocktail consisting of vodka, tomato juice and seasoning. **bloody-mind'ed** *adj* liking bloodshed, cruel; in a mood of, or inclined to show, aggressive obstinacy (*inf*). **bloody-mind'edness** *n*. **blood'y-nose** (or **blood'y-nosed**) **beetle** *n* a beetle (genus *Timarcha*) that exudes red liquid when disturbed. **blood'y-sweat** *n* a sweat accompanied by the discharge of blood.

blook /blook/ *n* a printed book reproducing the content of a blog. [From *blog* and *book*]

bloom¹ /bloom/ *n* a blossom or flower (also *collectively*); the state of being in flower; the prime or highest perfection of anything; the first freshness of beauty of anything; rosy colour; the glow on the cheek; a powdery, waxy or cloudy surface or appearance; a sudden rapid seasonal multiplication of phytoplankton, algae, etc (*bot*). ◆ *vi* to bear flowers; to come into flower; to be in a state of beauty or vigour; to flourish. ◆ *vt* to give a bloom to. [ON *blōm*; cf Gothic *blōma*, Ger *Blume*]

■ **bloom'ing** *adj* flowering; flourishing; fresh and youthful; bright; (as an intensifier) bloody (*inf*; *euphem*). **bloom'less** *adj* without bloom. **bloom'y** *adj* flowery; flourishing; covered with bloom.

bloom² /bloom/ *n* a mass or bar of iron or steel in an intermediate stage of manufacture, *esp* one thicker than a billet. [OE *blōma*]

■ **bloom'ery** *n* a furnace for making iron ore or iron into blooms.

bloomer¹ /bloo'mər/ *n* and *adj* an outfit for women, advocated by Mrs *Bloomer* of New York about 1849 (although not devised by her), consisting of a jacket with close sleeves, a skirt falling a little below the knee, and long (or short), loose, baggy trousers gathered at the ankle (or below the knee); (in *pl*) bloomer trousers; (in *pl*) a loose undergarment similar to knickers, with legs gathered above the knee.

bloomer² /bloo'mər/ *n* an embarrassing blunder (*inf*); a longish crusty loaf of white bread with rounded ends and a number of slashes across the top; a plant that blooms in a specified way, eg *perennial bloomer*; a floriated initial letter. [**bloom¹**]

bloomery see under **bloom²**.

Bloomsbury Group /bloomz'bə-ri groop/ *n* a group of literary and artistic friends, some living in the *Bloomsbury* district of London, who wrote during and after World War I, including Virginia Woolf, Lytton Strachey and EM Forster.

■ **Blooms'buryite** *n* a member of the Bloomsbury Group.

bloop /bloop/ (*esp N Am*) *n* a howling sound on a soundtrack or made by a radio. ◆ *vi* to make such a sound. ◆ *vt* to hit (a baseball) so that it only just clears the infield. [Imit]

■ **bloo'per** *n* a radio that makes such a sound; a stupid mistake (*sl*); an unintentionally comical out-take from a film, TV programme, etc, broadcast for entertainment; in baseball, a hit that carries the ball just clear of the infield (also **bloop**).

bloosme /bloom/ *n* and *vi* Spenser's form of **blossom**, modified by **bloom¹**.

blootered /bloo'tərd/ (*Scot sl*) *adj* drunk. [Pap of Scot dialect *blooter* to beat]

blore /blōr or blōr/ (*archaic*) *n* a violent gust of wind. [Prob related to **blare** and **blow¹**]

blossom /blos'əm/ *n* a flower or bloom, *esp* one that precedes edible fruit (also *collectively*); the state of being in flower (*lit* or *fig*). ◆ *vi* (often with *out*) to produce blossoms or flowers; to flourish. [OE *blōstm*, *blōstma*, from the same root as **bloom¹** and L *flōs*]

■ **bloss'oming** *n*. **bloss'omy** *adj* covered with flowers, flowery.

blot¹ /blot/ *n* a spot, as of a drop of ink; an obliteration; a stain in reputation; a blemish; see **blotting** below (*biol*). ◆ *vt* (**blott'ing**; **blott'ed**) to obliterate, destroy (*lit* and *fig*; often with *out*); to spot or smudge; to disgrace; to blemish; to remove excess (ink, lipstick, etc) with blotting-paper, paper tissue, etc. [Prob obscure]

■ **blott'er** *n* a person who blots; a sheet, pad or book of blotting-paper; a record of police-station activity (*US*). **blottesque** /-esk'/ *adj* (of painting) executed with heavy blot-like touches; (of writing) vigorously descriptive. ◆ *n* a daub. **blott'ing** *n* spotting as with ink; obliterating; smudging; drying with blotting-paper, etc; blotting-paper; the method for transferring biological molecules *usu* from a gel to a membrane filter (also **blot**; *biol*). **blott'o** *adj* (*sl*) helplessly drunk. **blott'y** *adj* blotted; smudged.

□ **blott'ing-pad** *n* a pad of blotting-paper. **blott'ing-paper** *n* unsized paper, used for absorbing ink.

■ **blot one's copybook** to blemish one's record, *esp* by an indiscretion.

blot² /blot/ *n* a piece liable to be taken at backgammon; exposure of a piece; a weak point in anything. [Cf Dan *blot*, Du *bloot* naked, exposed]

blot³ /blot/ (Spenser) *n* spawn. [Perh connected with **blow¹**]

blotch /bloch/ *n* an irregular discoloration; a pustule; any plant disease characterized by blotching. ◆ *vt* to mark or cover with blotches. [Prob formed on **blot¹**]

■ **blotched** *adj*. **blotch'iness** *n*. **blotch'ing** *n* and *adj*. **blotch'y** *adj*.

bloubok see **blaubok**.

blouse /blowz/ *n* a shirt-like garment for women; a short, loose jacket gathered into a waistband, part of a soldier's or airman's battledress; a loose belted outer garment worn by (*esp* French) workmen. ◆ *vt* to arrange in loose folds. ◆ *vi* to puff out loosely. [Fr]

blouson /bloo'zon/ *n* a loose outer garment gathered into a waistband. [Fr]

□ **blouson noir** /bloo-zō nwär'/ *n* (*old*) a rebellious young man, *usu* one of a group, so called from the black windcheaters worn by many of them.

bloviate /blō've-āt/ (*US sl*) *vi* to speak arrogantly or pompously. [**blow¹**, with pseudo-L suffix]

blow¹ /blō/ *vi* (*pat* **blew** /bloo/; *pap* **blown** /blōn/, in imprecations **blowed** /blōd/) to produce a current of air; (of air or wind) to move (often *impers*); to be carried along by air, etc; to breathe hard; (of a whistle or other signal, or a brass instrument) to sound; to take part in a jazz session; to spout, as whales do; to boast; to act as an informer (*sl*); (of insects) to deposit eggs; to explode, collapse (often with *up*, *down*, *in*, etc); of an electric fuse, to melt (also *vt*); to depart, *esp* hurriedly (*sl*). ◆ *vt* to force air on or into; to force air down (one's nose) in order to clear it; to shape (glass, etc) by blowing air into it; to make (air, etc) move; to drive by a current of air; to sound (eg a brass instrument); to destroy or force by explosive; to spread by report; to inform on; to fan or kindle; (of insects) to deposit eggs on; (in imprecations) to curse, confound, blast (*usu* with *me*, *it*); to squander (*sl*); to fail to succeed with or in when one has the chance (*sl*; *usu* with *it*); to depart from, *esp* hurriedly (*sl*); to perform fellatio on (*sl*). ◆ *n* a blast; a breath of fresh air; an insect egg; cannabis (*Brit sl*); cocaine (*US sl*). [OE *blāwan*; Ger *blähen*, *blasen*; L *flāre*]

■ **blow'er** *n* a person who blows; a mechanical device for producing a blast of air, etc; an escape of gas through a crack (*mining*); a speaking tube, telephone, or similar means of sending messages (*inf*); a communication system (*inf*). **blow'ie** *n* (*Aust* and *NZ inf*) a blowfly. **blown** *adj* out of breath, tired; swelled; stale, worthless. **blow'y** *adj* windy; gusty.

❑ **blow'back** *n* backward pressure of gases, eg in a boiler, engine or firearm; repercussions or consequences of an action (*fig*). **blow'ball** *n* the downy head of a dandelion in seed. **blow'down** *n* an accident in a nuclear reactor. **blow'-dry** *vt* to arrange (hair) by simultaneously brushing and drying it with a hand-held hairdryer. ◆ *n* an instance of this. **blow'-dryer** *n*. **blow'fish** *n* any globe fish. **blow'fly** *n* a flesh-fly (genus *Sarcophaga*); a bluebottle (genus *Calliphora*). **blow'gun** *n* a blowpipe (weapon). **blow'hard** *n* a boastful person (also *adj*). **blow'hole** *n* a whale's nostril; a hole in ice to which seals, etc come to breathe; a vent for escape of gas, etc; a bubble in metal; a natural vent from the roof of a cave up to the ground surface, through which air and water are forced by rising tides. **blow'-in** *n* (chiefly *Aust inf*) a recent arrival, newcomer. **blow'job** *n* (*sl*) an act of fellatio. **blow'lamp** *n* a portable lamp producing a jet of very hot flame. **blow'-moulding** *n* a process used in manufacturing plastic objects, the molten thermoplastic being blown against the sides of the mould. **blow'-off** see **blow off** below. **blow'-out** *n* a lavish meal or entertainment (*sl*); a tyre-burst (*inf*); a violent escape of oil and gas from an oil well. **blow-out preventer** *n* a stack of heavy-duty valves fitted in the wellhead of an oil well to prevent blow-outs. **blow'pipe** *n* a pipe through which air is blown onto a flame, to increase its heat, used in *blowpipe analysis*, etc; a long straight tube from which an arrow, pellet, etc is blown by the breath; a glass-blower's tube. **blow'torch** *n* (*N Am*) a blowlamp. **blow'-up** *n* an explosion; an enlargement of (part of) a photograph, illustration, etc. ◆ *adj* inflatable. **blow'-valve** *n* a snifting-valve.

■ **blow away** (*sl*) to kill, murder; to surprise or excite; to disprove (a theory, etc). **blow a well** (*mining*) temporarily to remove pressure at a wellhead to allow tubings and casings to be blown free of debris, water, etc. **blow hot and cold** to be favourable and unfavourable by turns, to be irresolute. **blow in** to turn up unexpectedly. **blow off** to allow (steam, etc) to escape; (of steam, etc) to escape forcibly; to break wind from the anus (*inf*); to fail to keep an appointment (with; *inf*) (**blow-off** *n* and *adj*). **blow on** or **upon** to take the bloom, freshness, or the interest off; to bring into discredit; to inform upon. **blow one's** (or **someone's**) **mind** (*sl*) to go (or cause to go) into a state of ecstasy under the influence of a drug or of an exhilarating experience. **blow one's stack** or **top** (*inf*) to explode in anger. **blow out** to extinguish by blowing; to become extinguished; to force outwards by an explosion; (of a tyre) to burst suddenly (*inf*); (of an oil well) to emit an uncontrolled jet of oil and gas; to fail to keep an appointment with (someone) (*inf*). **blow over** to pass away or die down, as a storm, a danger or a scandal. **blow** (**someone's** or) **one's brains out** (*inf*) to kill (someone or) oneself by shooting (him or her or) oneself in the head. **blow someone's cover** (*inf*) to reveal someone's identity. **blow the whistle on** (*inf*) to inform on (a person); to expose (an illegal practice, etc). **blow up** to come suddenly into prominence; to destroy by explosion; to explode; to finish in disaster; to inflate (*lit* and *fig*); to scold; to lose one's temper; to enlarge (eg an illustration); to go to pieces (*US sl*). **blow upon** see **blow on** above.

blow² /blō/ *n* a firm stroke or knock, *esp* with the fist or a striking tool; a sudden misfortune or calamity. [Found from the 15c; perh from **blow¹** or connected with Ger *bläuen* to beat]

❑ **blow'-by-blow** *adj* (of a story or description) very detailed.

■ **at a blow** by a single action, suddenly. **come to blows** (of people quarrelling) to start fighting.

blow³ /blō/ *vi* (**blow'ing**; blew /blōō/; **blown** /blōn/) to bloom or blossom. ◆ *vt* (*Milton*) to put forth (eg flowers). ◆ *n* blossom, bloom; a display of blossom. [OE *blōwan*; Ger *blühen*; cf **bloom¹**, **blossom**]

blowze or **blowse** /blowz/ *n* a ruddy, fat-faced young woman; a beggar girl (*obs*). [Perh related to **blush** or **blow³**, or of cant origin]

■ **blowzed** or **blowsed** *adj* blowzy.

blowzy or **blowsy** /blow'zi/ *adj* fat and ruddy, or flushed with exercise; dishevelled; coarse, rowdy. [**blowze**]

BLPC *abbrev* : British Library Public Catalogue.

BLT *abbrev* : bacon, lettuce and tomato (as a sandwich filling).

blub /blub/ (*inf*) *vi* (**blubb'ing**; **blubbed'**) to weep, sob. [Short for **blubber**]

blubber /blub'ər/ *n* the fat of whales and other sea animals; excessive fat; a jellyfish; a bout of weeping. ◆ *vi* to weep effusively. ◆ *vt* to utter while weeping. [ME *blober*, *bluber*; prob imit]

■ **blubb'ered** *adj* of a face, swollen with weeping. **blubb'ery** *adj* having a texture like blubber; swollen with fat.

blucher properly /blōō'hhər, often bloo'kər or bloo'chər/ (*obs*) *n* a strong leather half-boot or high shoe. [Marshal *Blücher*, the Prussian general at Waterloo]

blude /blüd/ *n* a Scots form of **blood**.

■ **blud'y** or **blud'ie** *adj*.

bludge /bluj/ (*sl*, *esp Aust* and *NZ*) *n* an easy job; a spell of loafing. ◆ *vi* and *vt* to scrounge. ◆ *vi* to loaf about; to evade work or other responsibility.

■ **bludg'er** *n*.

bludgeon /bluj'ən/ *n* a short stick with a heavy striking end; something or someone that is effective but heavy-handed. ◆ *vt* to beat with a bludgeon; to assail heavily (*fig*); to coerce (*inf*). [First in 18c; origin very obscure]

blue¹ /blōō/ *adj* of the colour of the unclouded sky; livid; greyish; dismal; depressed (*inf*); (of women) intellectual, pedantic (*obs*); indecent or obscene (*inf*); dressed in blue; symbolized by blue; politically conservative or right-wing; (of a US state) tending to vote Democrat. ◆ *n* the colour of blue things; a blue object; the sky; the sea; a blue pigment; (also **wash'ing-blue**) a blue powder or liquid (indigo, Prussian blue, etc) used in laundries; a member of a party whose colour is blue (eg *hist* the opponents of the Greens in ancient Constantinople, or the 17c Presbyterians, later (and currently) the Conservatives); a present or past representative of Oxford or Harrow (dark blue), Cambridge or Eton (light blue), in sports; a similar representative of any university; the badge awarded to him or her, or the honour of wearing it; blue clothes; a bluestocking (*obs*); a butterfly of the family Lycaenidae; a former squadron of the British fleet; an argument or fight (*Aust* and *NZ sl*); a mistake (*Aust* and *NZ sl*). ◆ *vt* to make blue; to treat with blue. ◆ *vi* to turn blue. [ME *blew*, from OFr *bleu*, of Gmc origin; ON *blā* gave ME *bla*, *blo* and **blae**]

■ **blue'ing** or **blu'ing** *n* the process of imparting a blue colour, *esp* to metal, or of neutralizing yellow laundry; blue-rot in wood; washing-blue (*US*). **blue'ish** or **blu'ish** *adj*. **blue'ly** *adv*. **blue'ness** *n*. **blues** *adj* of or relating to the blues. **blues'y** *adj* like the blues. **bluey** /blōō'i/ *adj* inclined towards blue (*esp* in compounds, eg *bluey-green*). ◆ *n* an airmail letter (*milit sl*); a bundle or swag, often in a blue cloth (*Aust*); a blanket (*Aust*); a summons, *usu* for a traffic offence (*Aust*); (with *cap*) someone with ginger hair (*Aust sl*).

❑ **blue asbestos** *n* crocidolite. **blue baby** *n* a baby with congenital cyanosis. **blue'back** *n* the sockeye, chief salmon of the N Pacific. **blue bag** *n* a barrister's bag; a small bag of washing-blue. **Blue'beard** *n* a villainous character in European folklore, who murdered his wives in succession; (also without *cap*) any similar wife-murderer. **blue'bell** *n* in S England, the wood hyacinth; /blōō'bel'/ in Scotland and N England, the harebell; also used to refer to various other plants in different parts of the world. **Blue Beret** *n* (*inf*) a soldier working for a United Nations peace-keeping force. **blue'berry** *n* the fruit of *Vaccinium vacillans* and other American species, a small blue-black berry. **blue'bird** *n* a small American bird (*Sialia sialis*) related to the warblers. **blue'-black** *n* and *adj* black with a tinge of blue; blue changing eventually to black. **Blue Blanket** *n* the banner of the Edinburgh craftsmen. **blue blood** *n* (Sp *sangre azul*) aristocratic blood. **blue'-blooded** *adj*. **blue-bonn'et** *n* a round flat blue woollen cap; a Scottish peasant, a Scotsman. **blue book** *n* a report or other paper printed by parliament (from its blue paper wrapper). **blue'bottle** *n* a large fly (genus *Calliphora*) with metallic blue abdomen, a blowfly; the blue cornflower; a policeman or beadle (*sl*); the Portuguese man-of-war (*Aust* and *NZ*). **blue box** *n* a blue container used for depositing items for recycling. **bluebreast** see **bluethroat** below. **blue'buck** *n* the blaubok. **blue'cap** *n* a one-year-old salmon, with blue-spotted head; the blue tit; a Scotsman (*Shakesp*). **blue cheese** *n* blue-veined cheese, eg Gorgonzola. **blue'-chip** *n* a term applied to the most reliable industrial shares, or to anything of high value or prestige (also *adj*). **blue'coat** *n* a serving-man, alms-man, or other wearing a blue coat (*archaic*); a pupil of Christ's Hospital or other **Bluecoat school**, whose uniform is a blue coat. **blue'-collar** *adj* relating to manual work or workers. **blue devil** *n* an evil demon; (in *pl*) the apparitions seen in delirium tremens, hence deep despondency. **blue duck** *n* a species of duck (*Hymenolaimus malacorhynchus*) found in the mountains of New Zealand. **blue ear disease** *n* (*vet*) a viral disease of pigs, affecting their respiratory and reproductive systems. **Blue Ensign** n a blue flag with the Union Jack in one corner, until 1864 the flag of the Blue squadron, now flown by the Naval Reserve and certain yachts and merchant vessels. **blue'-eye** n the Australian blue-faced honeyeater, a bird with blue eye-patches. **blue-eyed boy** n (inf) a favourite who can do no wrong. **blue-eyed grass** n a mainly N American iridaceous plant with blue flowers (genus Sisyrinchium). **blue-eyed soul** n soul music (written and) performed by white musicians. **blue film** or **movie** n (inf) a pornographic film. **blue'fin** n a large variety of tuna. **blue'fish** n a large voracious fish (Pomatomus saltatrix) of the family Serranidae, on the US Atlantic coast. **blue flag** n one awarded to beaches meeting European Union standards of cleanness. **blue fox** n the arctic fox; its fur. **blue funk** n (sl) a state of great terror. **blue'gill** n an American freshwater sunfish. **blue'gown** n one of a former class of licensed beggars in Scotland, a King's Bedesman. **blue'grass** n a slightly glaucous permanent grass (Poa pratensis, etc) of Europe and N America, esp Kentucky; a simple style of country music, originating in Kentucky and popular in the southern USA. **blue'-green** or **blue'-grey** adj between blue and green or grey. **blue-green algae** n the Cyanophyta. **blue ground** n a greyish-blue decomposed agglomerate in which diamonds are found. **blue gum** n any of several species of Eucalyptus (esp E. globulus). **blue hare** n the mountain hare. **blue heeler** n (Aust) a heeler (qv under **heel**[1]) with a dark speckled coat. **blue'jacket** n (inf) a seaman in the navy. **blue jay** n a N American jay (Cyanocitta cristata). **blue john** n ornamental fluorspar. **blue laws** n pl (US hist) puritanical 18c laws in Connecticut. **blue line** n (in ice hockey) a line marked off between the centre line and a goal line. **Blue Mantle** n one of the pursuivants of the English College of Arms. **blue mould** n a fungus that turns bread, cheese, etc blue. **blue movie** see **blue film** above. **blue murder** n (inf) used in phrases describing a terrible din or commotion. **blue'nose** n (N Am) a straitlaced or puritanical person (inf); (with cap) a nickname for a Nova Scotian. **blue note** n a flattened note, usu third or seventh, characteristic of the blues. **blue'-on-blue** adj (milit) involving accidental firing on one's allies. **blue pencil** n a pencil of the colour traditionally used for correcting, emending, etc. **blue-pen'cil** vt to correct, edit or censor. **Blue Peter** n a blue flag with a white rectangle, hoisted when a ship is about to sail; a call for trumps in whist. **blue pointer** n a large voracious shark found off the coast of Australia, the mako shark. **blue'print** n a photographic print, white on blue, on paper sensitized with ferric salts produced from a photographic negative or a drawing on transparent paper (also called **cyanotype, ferroprussiate print**); a detailed plan of work to be done, or a guide or model provided by agreed principles or rules or by conclusions from earlier experiment. ◆ vt to produce a blueprint of. **blue ribbon** or **riband** n the ribbon of the Order of the Garter; any very high distinction or prize (also adj, with hyphen); the badge of the teetotal **Blue Ribbon Army**, founded in America in 1878. **blue rinse** n (hairdressing) a bluish colouring for white or grey hair. **blue-rinse** or **blue-rinsed'** adj applied, usu disparagingly, to the supposed type of well-groomed, usu middle-class, older women (**blue rinsers**). **blue'-rot** n a blue discoloration in coniferous wood, caused by a fungus of the genus Ceratostomella. **blue ruin** n (sl) gin. **blue screen** n (in film, television, etc) a blue-coloured background against which material may be shot for superimposition elsewhere. **blue'-screen** adj. **blue shark** n a shark with a dark blue back (Prionace glauca). **blue sheep** n the bharal. **blue-sky** or **-skies** adj (of research, etc) having no immediate practical application; (of stocks, securities) financially unsound or fraudulent. **blue-sky laws** n pl (US) laws to prevent fraud in the sale of stocks (against capitalizing of the blue-skies stocks). **blues'man** n a blues musician. **blue-sky thinking** n creative thought that is not constrained by current thinking or practical considerations. **blue'stocking** n an intellectual woman. **blue'stone** n a blue-grey sandstone; blue vitriol. **blue streak** n something as rapidly moving and dramatic as lightning, esp applied to speech (often as **talk a blue streak**). **blue'throat** or **blue'breast** n a songbird of Europe and Asia, the male of which has a blue throat. **blue tit** n a small bird (Cyanistes caeruleus or Parus caeruleus) with blue wings and tail and a blue-topped head. **blue'tongue** n a viral disease of sheep and cattle transmitted by mosquitoes. **blue'-tongue** n (Aust) a rouseabout; a lizard of the genus Tiliqua. **Blue'tooth®** n a short-range radio technology that simplifies communication between computers, cellular phones, etc (after Harald Bluetooth, a 10c Danish king said to have preferred talking to fighting). **blue vitriol** n hydrated copper sulphate. **blue water** n open sea. **blue water gas** see under **water**. **blue'weed** n viper's bugloss (also **blue thistle**). **blue whale** n a large baleen whale (Balaenoptera musculus) the largest living animal. **blue whiting** n a fish of the cod family, found in northern seas. **blue'wing** n an American teal. ■ **burn blue** (of candles) to burn with a blue flame (eg as an omen of death or signifying the presence of the Devil). **full blues** (naval sl) full formal naval uniform. **into the blue** into the unknown. **once in a blue moon** very rarely (from the rare occasions when the moon appears to be blue because of dust particles in the atmosphere). **out of the blue** from the cloudless sky; entirely unexpectedly. **shout, scream** or **cry blue murder** to shout loudly in pain, alarm or rage. **the Blues** the Royal Horse Guards. **(the) blues** depression (inf); (usu construed as sing) a slow sad song, orig an African-American folk song, characteristically with three four-bar lines and blue notes, or any similar composition (sometimes neither slow nor sad). **true blue** a person unswervingly faithful, esp to a political party represented by the colour blue, orig used of Covenanters (see **blue** (n) above; **true'-blue** adj). **washing-blue** see **blue** (n) above.

blue² /bloo/ (inf) vt to squander. [Prob for **blow**[1]]

bluette /bloo- or blü-et'/ (Fr) n a spark, flash; a short playful piece of music.

bluff¹ /bluf/ vt or vi to deceive or seek to deceive by concealment of weakness or show of self-confidence or threats (orig poker to conceal poor cards). ◆ n a bluffing act or behaviour; a horse's blinker. [Perh Du bluffen to brag, boast]
■ **bluff'er** n.
■ **bluff it out** to maintain a show of confidence in a difficult situation. **call someone's bluff** to expose or challenge someone's show of strength, confidence, etc.

bluff² /bluf/ adj steep or upright in front; rough and hearty in a good-natured way; outspoken; (of the shape of a body) such that, when it moves through air or other fluid, it leaves behind it a large disorderly wake and experiences a large drag, opp to streamlined; blustering, surly (dialect). ◆ n a high steep bank, esp of a river; a clump of trees (Can dialect). [Perh Du blaf broad, flat; or MLGer blaff even, smooth]
■ **bluff'ly** adv. **bluff'ness** n.

bluid /blüd/ n a Scots form of **blood**.
■ **bluid'y** adj.

blunder /blun'dər/ vi to make a gross mistake; to flounder about. ◆ vt to utter thoughtlessly; to mismanage, bungle; to achieve, put or make by blundering. ◆ n a gross mistake. [ME blondren; prob connected with **blend²**]
■ **blun'derer** n. **blun'dering** n and adj. **blun'deringly** adv.

blunderbuss /blun'dər-bus/ (hist) n a short handgun with a wide bore. [Du donderbus, from donder thunder, bus a box, gun-barrel, gun; Ger Donnerbüchse]

blunge /blunj/ (pottery) vt to mix (clay or the like) with water. [From blend and plunge]
■ **blung'er** n a machine or person that blunges.

blunk /blungk/ (Scot) vt to spoil; to bungle.
■ **blunk'er** n (Walter Scott) a bungler, or according to Jamieson's Dictionary of the Scottish Language, someone who prints cloth.

blunt /blunt/ adj not having a sharp edge or point; rough, unrefined, ordinary; outspoken, abrupt, direct; dull; barren (Spenser). ◆ vt to make dull. ◆ vi to become dull. ◆ n a cigar filled with marijuana (sl); money, esp cash (obs sl). [Origin unknown]
■ **blunt'ish** adj. **blunt'ly** adv. **blunt'ness** n.
❑ **blunt instrument** n any heavy object used as a weapon. **blunt'-witt'ed** adj (Shakesp) dull, stupid.

blur /blûr/ n an ill-defined spot or smear; a confused impression. ◆ vt (**blurr'ing**; **blurred**) to blot; to make indistinct in outline; to blemish, disfigure (obs). ◆ vi to make blurs. [Perh a variant of **blear**]
■ **blurr'y** adj.

Blu-ray® /bloo'rā'/ n a method of storing data on high-capacity compact discs using a blue laser.

blurb /blûrb/ n a publisher's commendatory description of a book, usu printed on the jacket; any brief commendatory advertisement. ◆ vt (esp US inf) to praise, describe, state, etc in a blurb. [Attributed to Gelett Burgess (1866–1951), American author]

blurt /blûrt/ vt to utter suddenly or unadvisedly (with out). ◆ vi (Shakesp) to snort or puff in scorn. ◆ n (rare) an abrupt outburst. ◆ adv with a blurt. [Prob imit]
■ **blurt'ing** n and adj.

blush /blush/ n a red glow on the skin caused by shame, modesty, etc; any reddish colour or suffusion. ◆ adj pinkish. ◆ vi to grow red as a result of shame, modesty, etc; to grow red. ◆ vt to make red. [Cf OE blyscan to shine]
■ **blush'er** n a person who blushes; a cosmetic, usu pinkish, applied to the cheeks, etc to add colour to them. **blush'et** n (Jonson) a blushing girl. **blush'ful** adj. **blush'ing** n and adj. **blush'ingly** adv. **blush'less** adj. **blush'lessly** adv.
❑ **blush'-rose** n a pink variety of rose. **blush wine** n a rosé wine.
■ **at (the) first blush** at the first glance or sight; offhand. **put to the blush** (archaic) to cause to blush.

bluster /blus'tər/ vi to blow boisterously; to storm, rage; to bully or swagger. ◆ vt to utter loudly or boastfully; to bully by a show of temper. ◆ n a blast or roaring eg of the wind; bullying or boasting language; a storm of anger. [Cf E Frisian blüstern to bluster]

■ **blust'erer** n. **blus'tering** n and adj. **blus'teringly** adv. **blus'terous** (Shakesp **blus'trous**) adj noisy; boastful. **blus'tery** adj stormy; swaggering.

Blut /bloot/ (Ger) n blood.
■ **Blut und Eisen** /ŭnt ī'zən/ blood and iron (Bismarck), relentless force. Also **Eisen und Blut**.

Blu-Tack® /bloo'tak/ n a malleable solid adhesive used to fix paper temporarily to walls, noticeboards, etc. ◆ vt to attach with Blu-Tack.

blutwurst /bloot'vŭrst/ n blood pudding. [Ger]

Blvd abbrev : Boulevard.

BM abbrev : Bachelor of Medicine; British Midland (now known as **bmi**); British Museum.

BMA abbrev : British Medical Association.

BMATT (sometimes /bē'mat/) abbrev : British Military Advisory and Training Team.

BMEWS (sometimes /bē'mūz/) abbrev : ballistic missile early warning system.

BMI abbrev : body mass index.

bmi abbrev : British Midland (a UK airline).

BMJ abbrev : British Medical Journal.

BMus abbrev : Bachelor of Music.

BMW abbrev : Bayerische Motoren Werke (Ger), Bavarian motor works.

BMX /bē-em-eks'/ n cycle racing on a rough artificial track; a BMX bike. [Abbrev of bicycle motocross]
❑ **BMX bike** n a small bicycle designed for BMX racing, also used for stunt-riding.

Bn abbrev : Baron.

bn abbrev : battalion; billion.

BNB abbrev : British National Bibliography.

BNC abbrev : British National Corpus.

BNES abbrev : British Nuclear Energy Society.

BNFL abbrev : British Nuclear Fuels plc (orig Limited).

BNP abbrev : British National Party.

bo[1] see **boo**.

bo[2] see **bo tree**.

bo[3] /bō/ (US sl) n (pl **bos**) a familiar term of address for a man.

b.o. abbrev : body odour (also **B.O.**); box office; branch office; buyer's option.

boa /bō'ə/ n (with cap) a genus, mainly S American, of large snakes that kill their prey by squeezing; popularly any large constricting snake; a long, serpent-like coil of fur, feathers or the like worn round the neck by women. [L boa a kind of snake]
❑ **boa constrictor** n properly, the name of one species; popularly, any boa, python or similar snake.

boab /bō'ab/ (Aust) n a baobab.

BOAC abbrev : formerly, British Overseas Airways Corporation.

boak see **boke**.

Boanerges /bō-ə-nûr'jēz/ n a noisy preacher or shouting orator (sing and pl). [Sons of thunder, from Bible, Mark 3.17]

boar /bōr, bör/ n the male pig or its flesh. [OE bār ; Du beer]
■ **boar'ish** adj swinish; brutal.
❑ **boar'fish** n a fish (genus Capros) of the horse-mackerel family with hoglike snout. **boar'-hound** n a powerful dog used for hunting the wild boar, esp the great Dane or German mastiff. **boar'-spear** n a spear used in boar-hunting.
■ **wild boar** the wild pig of Europe and Asia, having prominent tusks.

board (Spenser, etc **bord, borde, boord** or **boorde**) /börd or börd/ n a long and wide, comparatively thin, strip of timber; a table; provision of meals (with or without lodging); a table around which committee meetings are held; a formal group or committee, esp one that administers a company, etc; a slab, etc prepared for playing a game (such as a chessboard) or other special purpose (such as a noticeboard, blackboard, surfboard); a printed circuit board; the side of a ship (naut); (in pl) the stage; (in pl) the wall around an ice-hockey rink; a sheet of stiff or laminated paper; a flat sheet of composite material, such as chipboard, plasterboard, etc; a rectangular piece forming the side of a book-binding; the distance sailed by a vessel in one tack (naut); (in duplicate bridge) a set of hands, or the board or set of pockets into which the set of hands is placed for passing on to the next group of players; conversation (Spenser); coast (Spenser). ◆ vt to cover with boards (often with up); to supply with food (and bed) at fixed terms; to place in lodgings; to go on board (a ship) with hostile intent; to enter (a ship or (orig US) a train, bus, etc); to accost, attack (Shakesp). ◆ vi to receive food (with or without lodging); to live as a

boarder (with); to border (Spenser). [OE bord board, the side of a ship; ON borth, connected either with bear[1] or with broad]
■ **board'er** n a person who receives board; a pupil at a boarding school; a person who boards a ship; a person engaged in skateboarding, snowboarding, etc. **board'ing** n the act of covering with boards; a structure or collection of boards; the act of boarding a ship, aircraft, etc; the provision of board.
❑ **board'-foot** n a unit of **board'-measure** for timber, a piece one inch thick by 12 inches square. **board game** n a game (eg chess, snakes-and-ladders) which is played with pieces, counters, etc on a specially designed board. **boarding card** or **pass** n a card allowing one to board an aircraft, ship, etc. **boarding house** n a house where boarders are kept. **boarding party** n a group of people who go on board a ship. **boarding pass** see **boarding card** above. **board'ing-pike** n a pike used in boarding a ship, or in defending it when attacked. **boarding school** n a school in which board and lodging are provided for pupils. **board'-measure** see **board-foot** above. **board meeting** n a meeting of the board of directors of an organization. **board of directors** n a group of individual directors appointed by a company and collectively responsible for the management of that company. **Board of Trade** n (Brit) a former government ministry concerned with trade and industry; (without caps; N Am) a chamber of commerce. **Board of Trade unit** n (elec) a kilowatt-hour (abbrev **BTU**). **board'room** n a room for meetings of a board of directors. ◆ adj taking place in a boardroom. **board'sailing** n sailboarding. **board'sailor** n. **board'-school** n formerly, a school under control of a school board. **board shorts** n pl loose-fitting knee-length shorts, worn esp by surfers. **board-wa'ges** n pl payment to a servant in lieu of food. **board'walk** n (N Am) a footpath made of boards.
■ **above board** openly. **board out** to have one's meals elsewhere than where one lives; to place in lodgings. **go by the board** to go over the side of a ship; to be discarded or ignored; to meet disaster. **on board** aboard; see also **take on board** below. **sweep the board** to win everything; to take all the cards. **take on board** to receive or accept (suggestions, new ideas, additional responsibilities, etc).

boart see **bort**.

boast[1] /bōst/ vi to talk conceitedly; to brag (with of). ◆ vt to brag of; to speak proudly or confidently of, esp justifiably; to possess with pride. ◆ n an expression of pride; a brag; the cause of boasting. [ME bōst ; origin unknown; appar Welsh bostio and Gaelic bòsd a bragging, are borrowed from English]
■ **boast'er** n. **boast'ful** adj given to bragging. **boast'fully** adv. **boast'fulness** n. **boast'ing** n. **boast'less** adj without boasting; simple, unostentatious.

boast[2] /bōst/ vt (in stone-cutting) to shape roughly. [Origin unknown]
■ **boast'er** n a broad steel chisel used for boasting.

boast[3] /bōst/ (squash) vt to make (the ball) first hit one of the side walls and then the end wall, or hit (a stroke) of this kind. ◆ vi to play a stroke like this. ◆ n such a stroke. [Perh Fr bosse the place where the ball hits the wall]
■ **boast'ed** adj. **boast'ing** n.

boat /bōt/ n a small rowing, sailing or motor vessel; loosely, a ship; a boat-shaped utensil (as sauce boat). ◆ vi to sail about in a boat. ◆ vt to put or convey in a boat; to ship (oars); (with it) to go in a boat. [OE bāt, cognate with ON beit]
■ **boat'er** n a person who boats; a straw hat. **boat'ie** n a boating enthusiast (Aust and NZ); a rowing enthusiast (university sl). **boat'ing** n.
❑ **boat'bill** n a bird of the heron family (from the shape of its bill). **boat'-builder** n a person or firm that constructs boats. **boat deck** n a ship's top deck, on which the lifeboats are carried. **boat'-fly** n a water bug (genus Notonecta), with boat-shaped body, that swims on its back. **boat'hook** n a hook fixed to a pole used for pulling or pushing off a boat. **boat'house** n a house or shed for a boat. **boat'load** n. **boat'man** n a man who is in charge of a boat; a rower. **boat neck** n a high slit-shaped neckline extending on to the shoulders. **boat'-necked** adj. **boat people** n pl refugees, esp from Vietnam, who set off in boats to find a country that will admit them. **boat race** n a race between rowing boats; (with the and caps) the annual boat race between Oxford and Cambridge Universities. **boat racing** n. **boat shoe** n a soft leather shoe like a moccasin. **boat'-song** n a song sung by a boatman. **boat'tail** n a grackle. **boat train** n a train run to connect with a ship.
■ **have an oar in another's boat** to meddle with someone else's affairs. **in the same boat** (of people) in the same unfavourable circumstances. **push the boat out** (inf) to entertain, celebrate, etc lavishly. **take to the boats** to escape in lifeboats from a sinking ship (also fig).

boatel see **botel**.

boatswain (often **bosun, bo'sun, bo's'n** or **bos'n**) /bō'sn/ n the foreman of a crew (warrant officer in the navy) who looks after a ship's

---

■ words derived from main entry word; ❑ compound words; ■ idioms and phrasal verbs

boats, rigging, flags, etc; the skua (*prob* from its aggressiveness). [**boat** and **swain**]

❑ **boat'swain-bird** *n* the tropicbird. **boatswain's call**, **pipe** or **whistle** see under **whistle**. **boatswain's chair** *n* (*naut*) a wooden seat slung from ropes, for a man working on a ship's side, rigging, etc. **boatswain's mate** *n* boatswain's assistant.

bob¹ /bob/ *vi* (**bobb'ing**; **bobbed**) to move quickly up and down or to and fro; to curtsy or bow quickly; (with *for*) to try to catch (a swinging or floating apple, etc) with one's teeth as a game; to ride a bobsleigh; to fish with a bob. ◆ *vt* to move in a short jerking manner; to tap; to perform, measure, do, etc (something) with a bob; to make a curtsy; to cut (hair) square across; to dock, to bobtail. ◆ *n* a short jerking motion; a quick curtsy; anything that moves with a bob or swing; the weight of a pendulum, plumb line, etc; a pendant (*archaic*); a knot of hair; a short straight haircut for women and girls; a bunch or cluster (eg of cherries) (*dialect*); a bunch of lobworms, used in catching eels; a bob-fly; any small roundish body; the refrain or burden of a song (*archaic*); a short line at or near the end of the stanza (*poetry*); a bobsleigh; (in *pl*) the runners for a bobsleigh (*N Am*); a dance (*Scot*); a slight blow (*obs*); a gibe (*obs*); (also **plain bob**) a term in bellringing, eg **bob minor** is rung on six bells, **bob major** on eight, **bob royal** on ten, **bob maximus** on twelve. [Poss Gaelic *baban*, *babag* tassel, cluster]
■ **bobb'er** *n* a float attached to a fishing-line. **bobb'ish** *adj* in good spirits.
❑ **bob'-apple** *n* the game of trying to catch a swinging or floating apple with one's teeth. **bob'cat** *n* a kind of lynx. **bob'-cherry** *n* the game of trying to catch a swinging cherry with one's teeth. **bob'-fly** *n* (*angling*) the top dropfly. **bob skate** *n* (*N Am*) an ice-skate with two parallel blades. **bob'sleigh** or **bob'sled** *n* a short sledge; a sleigh made up of two of these; a racing sledge for two or more people, with a continuous seat, steering mechanism, and brakes. ◆ *vi* to ride or race on a bobsleigh. **bob'tail** *n* a short or cut tail; an animal with a bobbed tail (also *adj*); applied in contempt to the rabble, as in *rag-tag and bobtail*. ◆ *vt* to cut short. **bob'tailed** *adj* with tail cut short. **bob'wheel** *n* (*poetry*) the bob with the lines following it. **bob'wig** *n* a wig with the ends turned up into short curls.
■ **bob up** to appear suddenly.

bob² /bob/ (*old sl*) *n* (*pl* **bob**) a shilling. [Prob not OFr *bobe* = 1½d]
■ **a bob or two** or **a few bob** a not inconsiderable sum of money.

bob³ /bob/ *n* (with *cap*) a familiar form or diminutive of Robert.
■ **bob's your uncle** (*sl*) an expression denoting the completion of a task or satisfaction with it.

bob⁴ /bob/ (*obs*) *vt* (**bobb'ing**; **bobbed**) to make a fool of; to take by cheating (*Shakesp*); to cheat (out of) (*Shakesp*). [OFr *bober*]

boba /bō'bə/ *n* another name for **yaws**. [Malay]

bobac see **bobak**.

Bobadil /bob'ə-dil/ *n* a swaggering boaster. [From the soldier in Ben Jonson's *Every Man in his Humour*]

bobak or **bobac** /bō'bak/ *n* a species of marmot. [Pol *bobak*]

bobbery /bob'ə-ri/ (*obs sl*) *n* a noisy row. [Perh Hindi *bāp re* O father]

bobbin /bob'in/ *n* a reel or spool for winding yarn, wire, etc; narrow cord. [Fr *bobine*]
❑ **bobbin lace** *n* pillow lace. **bobbin net** or **bobb'inet** *n* a fine machine-made netted lace.

bobbish see under **bob¹**.

bobbitt /bob'it/ *vt* to cut off the penis of (one's husband or lover). [Lorena *Bobbitt*, an American woman who did this]

bobble /bob'l/ *n* a bobbing action; the movement of disturbed water; a woolly ball for trimming clothes, etc; (*usu* in *pl*) pilling on the surface of cloth; a fumble or bungle (*orig US*). ◆ *vt* and *vi* to bob rapidly or continuously; to fumble or bungle (*orig US*). [**bob¹**]
■ **bobb'ly** *adj* (of cloth) pilled.
❑ **bobble hat** *n* a *usu* knitted tapering hat with a bobble at the top. **bobb'lehead** or **bobblehead doll** *n* (*N Am*) a small doll, *usu* depicting a famous personality, with a disproportionately large head mounted on a spring.

bobby /bob'i/ (*sl*) *n* a policeman. [Familiar form of *Robert*, from Sir Robert Peel, Home Secretary at the passing of the Metropolitan Police Act, 1828; cf **peeler**]

bobby calf /bob'i käf/ *n* a calf slaughtered before it has been weaned.

bobby-dazzler /bob-i-daz'lər/ (*old inf*) *n* anything or anyone overwhelmingly excellent, striking or showy; a young girl who sets out to make an impression.

bobby pin /bob'i pin/ (chiefly *US*) *n* a hairgrip.

bobbysock /bob'i-sok/ (*N Am inf*, *esp* formerly) *n* an ankle sock, *esp* as worn by teenage girls.
■ **bobb'ysoxer** *n* an adolescent girl, teenager.

bobcat see under **bob¹**.

bobol /bub' or bob'öl/ (*W Indies*) *n* corruption or fraud in public life. ◆ *vi* (**bob'olling**; **bob'olled**) to be engaged in corruption. [Perh from *Vaval*, traditional character in carnival]

bobolink /bob'ō-lingk or -ə-/ *n* a widespread N American songbird (*Dolichonyx oryzivorus*). [*Bob Lincoln*, imit of its note]

bobsled, **bobsleigh** see under **bob¹**.

bobstays /bob'stāz/ (*naut*) *n pl* ropes used to hold the bowsprit down to the stem, and counteract the strain of the foremast-stays.

bobtail see under **bob¹**.

bobwhite /bob-(h)wīt'/ *n* an American quail. [Imit]

bocage same as **boscage**.

bocca /bok'ka or bok'ə/ (*Ital*) *n* mouth.

bocce /boch'ā/ or **boccia** /boch'ə/ *n* an Italian form of bowls. [Ital]

boche or **bosche** /bosh/ (*derog World War I sl*; *orig Fr*; also with *cap*) *n* a German, *esp* a German soldier.

bock¹ /bok/ (*Fr*, from *Ger*) *n* a strong German beer; now often a glass or mug of beer (holding a quarter of a litre). [From *Einbocker bier*, *Eimbockbier* beer from Einbeck (Eimbeck)]

bock² see **boke**.

BOD *abbrev*: biochemical oxygen demand.

bod /bod/ (*orig milit sl*) *n* a person; a person's body. [Contraction of **body**]

bodach /bōd'əhh, bod' or (Gaelic) bot'əhh/ (*Scot*) *n* an old man, a churl; a goblin or spectre. [Gaelic]

bodacious /bə-dā'shəs/ (*sl*, *esp N Am*) *adj* extremely good, marvellous. [From **bold** and **audacious**]

boddle see **bodle**.

bode¹ /bōd/ *vt* to portend; to be a prediction of; to foretell; to have a presentiment of. ◆ *vi* to be a (good or bad) omen. ◆ *n* (*Scot*) a bid, offer. [OE *bodian* to announce, from (ge)*bod* a message; related to **bid¹,²**]
■ **bode'ful** *adj* boding, ominous. **bode'ment** *n* an omen, presentiment. **bod'ing** *adj* presaging. ◆ *n* an omen or portent.

bode² /bōd/ see **bide**.

bodega /bo-dē'gə or (Sp) bō-dā'ga/ *n* a wine shop; a warehouse for storing and maturing wine. [Sp, from L, from Gr *apothēkē* a storehouse]
■ **bodeguero** /-gā'rō/ *n* (*pl* **bodeguer'os**) (*Sp*) a man who owns or runs a bodega.

bodge /boj/ (*inf*) *vt* and *vi* variant of **botch**. ◆ *vi* (*Shakesp*) *prob* variant of **budge¹**. ◆ *n* a piece of poor or clumsy workmanship; a clumsy worker (also **bodg'er**).

bodger /boj'ər/ (*dialect*) *n* a travelling pedlar who turns beechwood to make chairs, etc; see also under **bodge**. [Origin uncertain]

bodgie /boj'i/ (*Aust and NZ*) *n* a young Australian male of the 1950s, similar in dress and behaviour to the British Teddy boy; something that is a fake, useless, or fraudulent (also *adj*). [Perh from *bodge* to botch]

Bodhisattva /bō-di-sat'wə or -və, or bo-/ (*Buddhism*) *n* a person who postpones entry into nirvana in order to help others; a future Buddha. [Sans *bodhi* enlightenment, and *sattva* existence]

bodhi tree see **bo tree**.

bodhrán /bow-rän' or bō'rən/ *n* a shallow one-sided drum, common in Irish and Scottish folk music. [Ir]

bodice /bod'is/ *n* a woman's tight-fitting outer waistcoat; the close-fitting upper part, from shoulder to waist, of a woman's dress; a stiffened inner garment (*orig pl* of **body**) (*archaic*).
❑ **bod'ice-ripp'er** *n* (*inf*) a romantic (historical) novel involving sex and violence.

bodikin /bod'i-kin/ *n* dimin of **body**, in *Od's bodikins* God's little body.

bodily see under **body**.

bodkin /bod'kin/ *n* a small pointed tool for pricking holes, for dressing the hair, for correcting type, etc; a large blunt needle for threading tape, etc; a small dagger (*obs*). [Poss connected with Welsh *bidog* dagger]
■ **sit** or **ride bodkin** to be wedged in tight between two others.

bodle or **boddle** /bod'l or bōd'l/ *n* a former Scottish copper coin, in the 17c worth about one-sixth of an English penny. [Origin unknown]

bodrag /bod'rag/ (*Spenser*) *n* a hostile attack, a raid (also **bord'raging**). [Perh Ir *buaidhreadh* a disturbance]

body /bod'i/ *n* (*pl* **bod'ies**) the whole frame of a human or a lower animal; the main part of an animal, as distinguished from the limbs; the main part of anything; the main text of a letter, advertisement, etc, excluding eg headings, address, etc; the part of a vehicle which carries the load or passengers; a garment or part of a garment covering the trunk, a bodice; a legless close-fitting garment for women or infants fastening at the crotch; a corpse; matter, as opposed to spirit; substance or substantial quality; fullness, as of flavour in a wine; solidity; a three-dimensional figure (*obs maths*); opacity of a paint or pigment; a mass; a solid object; a person (*inf*); a number of persons united by something they have in common; size of type. ◆ *vt* (**bod'ying; bod'ied**) (*usu* with *forth*) to give form to; to embody. [OE *bodig*]

■ **-bodied** *combining form* with a (certain type of) body. **bod'iless** *adj* without a body; incorporeal. **bod'ily** *adj* of the body, *esp* as opposed to the mind; actual, real (*Shakesp*). ◆ *adv* in the flesh; as a whole.

❑ **bodily function** *n* any of the processes or activities performed by or connected with the body, such as breathing, hearing and digesting. **body armour** *n* protective covering or clothing for the body. **body art** *n* the decoration of the human body by techniques such as tattooing and body piercing. **body bag** *n* a bag made of heavy material in which a dead body (*esp* that of a war casualty or accident victim) is transported. **body blow** *n* in boxing, a blow to the body; a serious setback. **body board** *n* a short surfboard on which the surfer lies. **bod'y-builder** *n* a person who by an exercise and dietary regime builds up the size and strength of the muscles; an apparatus for exercising muscles; a nutritious food; a person who makes vehicle bodies. **bod'y-building** *n* and *adj*. **body carpet** or **carpeting** *n* carpet manufactured in strips that are joined together to form the required size. **bod'y-cavity** *n* the cavity in which the viscera of the higher animals lie, the coelom. **bod'y-centred** *adj* of crystals, having an atom at each vertex of the unit cell and at its centre. **bod'y-check** *n* (*sport*) a deliberate obstruction of an opposing player's movements, permitted in eg lacrosse and ice-hockey, not in soccer (also *vt*). **bod'y-checking** *n*. **body clock** *n* the biological clock. **body colour** *n* the degree of consistency, substance and tingeing power of a paint; watercolour mixed with zinc or other white to give it body. **body corporate** *n* a corporation. **body count** *n* a count of the number of corpses, eg at the end of a violent act; a count of the number of people present. **bod'y-curer** *n* (*Shakesp*) a doctor. **body double** *n* (*cinematog*) a substitute for an actor during filming, *esp* in nude scenes and dangerous stunts. **body dysmorphic disorder** see **dysmorphia**. **body fascism** *n* (*sl*) an ardent and obsessive belief in the importance of strength and physical appearance over other personal characteristics. **body fascist** *n*. **bod'yguard** *n* a guard consisting of one person or several people, to accompany and give physical protection to someone. **body image** *n* (*psychol*) a person's subjective picture of his or her own body. **body language** *n* communication of information by means of conscious or unconscious gestures, attitudes, facial expressions, etc. **bod'yline**, **body-line bowling** or **bodyline bowling** *n* (*cricket*) intimidatory short-pitched fast bowling delivered at the batsman's body, *esp* directed towards the legside. **body mass index** *n* an index of obesity calculated by dividing weight in kilograms by the square of height in metres. **body packer** *n* (*sl*) someone who smuggles drugs by swallowing them or otherwise hiding them in his or her body. **body piercing** *n* the practice of piercing various parts of the body in order to insert decorative metal studs or rings. **body politic** *n* the collective body of the people in its political capacity. **bod'y-popper** *n*. **bod'y-popping** *n* a form of dancing with robot-like movements. **body scanner** *n* (*med*) an electronic X-ray or ultrasound scanner for the whole body. **body search** *n* a search of a person's body, *esp* for drugs and other concealable items. **body servant** *n* a personal attendant. **bod'yshell** *n* a vehicle's bodywork. **body shop** *n* a vehicle body repair or construction shop. **body snatcher** *n* (*hist*) a person who secretly disinters dead bodies (*usu* to sell them) for dissection. **body stocking** *n* a one-piece, skintight undergarment for women. **bod'ysuit** *n* a close-fitting one-piece garment for women. **bod'ysurf** *vi* to surf without a board by lying on a wave. **body swerve** *n* a swerving movement of the body made to avoid eg a sports opponent. **bod'y-swerve** *vi*. **bod'y-warmer** *n* a padded sleeveless jacket. **bod'ywork** *n* the metal outer shell of a motor vehicle; a form of alternative therapy which concentrates on releasing tension or balancing energies in the body. **bod'yworker** *n* a therapist using bodywork techniques. **body wrap** *n* a beauty treatment in which the body is wrapped in hot bandages to cleanse it and reduce fat.

■ **body and soul** one's entire self. **in a body** (acting) all together.

Boeotian /bē-ō'sh(i)ən/ *adj* of *Boeotia* in Greece, proverbial for the dullness of its inhabitants; hence, stupid, dull. ◆ *n* an inhabitant of Boeotia; a stupid person.

Boer /boor/ (chiefly *hist*) *n* a South African of Dutch descent, *orig* one engaged in farming (also *adj*). [Du; see **boor** and **bower**²]

❑ **boerbull** /boor'bŭl/ *n* (*S Afr*) a South African crossbred mastiff. **boeremusiek** /boor'ə-mŭ-zik/ *n* (*S Afr*) traditional Afrikaner dance music. **boerewors** /boor'ə-vörs/ *n* (*Afrik boere-* farmers', country-style, and *wors* sausage) a traditional South African sausage, *usu* containing a mixture of beef and pork. **Boer War** *n* either of two wars (1880–81 and 1899–1902) fought between Britain and South Africa.

boeuf bourguignon /bœf boor-gē-nyɔ̃'/ *n* a beef and vegetable casserole cooked in red wine. [Fr, Burgundy beef]

boff /bof/ (*sl; esp US*) *n* a punch; a hearty laugh; an entertainment. ◆ *vi* and *vt* to hit, slug; to have sexual intercourse (with). [Ety uncertain; perh in part imit]

boffin /bof'in/ (*orig milit sl*) *n* a research scientist, *esp* one employed by the armed forces or government; any expert or intellectual.

boffo /bof'ō/ (*inf*) *adj* highly successful; excellent. [From old US slang *boff* a great success]

Bofors gun /bō'förz or -förs gun/ *n* a single- or double-barrelled, quick-firing anti-aircraft gun. [From *Bofors*, Sweden, where *orig* made]

bog /bog/ *n* spongy, *usu* peaty, ground; a marsh; a type of vegetation growing on peat deficient in lime (*sl*). ◆ *vt* (**bogg'ing; bogged**) to sink (also *vi*). [Ir and Scot Gaelic *bogach*, from *bog* soft]

■ **bogg'iness** *n*. **bogg'y** *adj*.

❑ **bog asphodel** *n* a yellow-flowered bog-plant, *Narthecium ossifragum*. **bog'bean** *n* a marsh plant, *Menyanthes trifoliata* (also called **buck'bean**). **bog'-butter** *n* a butter-like substance found in Irish peat bogs. **bog cotton** *n* cotton grass. **bog iron** see **bog ore** below. **bog'land** *n*. **bog'-Latin** *n* Shelta. **bog moss** *n* sphagnum. **bog myrtle** *n* sweet-gale (*Myrica gale*), a bog-plant. **bog'oak** *n* trunks of oak embedded in bogs and preserved from decay. **bog ore** or **bog iron** *n* an iron ore found in boggy land, limonite. **bog spavin** see **spavin**. **bog standard** *adj* (*sl*) basic, ordinary. **bog'trotter** *n* (*derog sl*) an Irishman; (in Ireland) an uncultured rustic. **bog'trotting** *n* and *adj*.

■ **bog down** to encumber or be encumbered with an overwhelming amount of work, a difficult task, etc. **bog off** (*vulgar sl*) go away.

bogan /bō'gn/ (*N Am*) *n* a quiet tributary or backwater. [Algonquian *pokelogan*]

bogbean see under **bog**.

bogey¹ /bō'gi/ (*golf*) *n* a score of one stroke above the par for any hole; *orig* the score of an imaginary good player, Colonel *Bogey*, fixed as a standard, which may be higher than par or sometimes equivalent to it. ◆ *vt* to complete (a hole) in one above par. [Perh **bogy**]

■ **double**, **triple**, etc **bogey** a score of two, three, etc above par for any hole.

bogey² see **bogie** and **bogy**.

boggard /bog'ərd/, **boggart** /-ərt/ or **boggle** /bog'l/ see **bogle**.

boggle /bog'l/ *vi* to start, draw back with fright; to hesitate, demur; to equivocate; (of one's mind, *esp* in *the mind boggles*) to be unable to imagine or grasp something, to be astounded by something (*inf*). ◆ *n* a scruple, objection; a bungle. [**bogle**]

■ **bogg'ler** *n*.

bogie or **bogey** /bō'gi/ *n* a low heavy truck, a trolley; a small railway freight truck; a pivoted undercarriage, as in a railway locomotive or vehicle; a child's home-made racing cart (*Scot*). [Ety unknown; perh connected with **bogy**]

bogle /bō'gl/ *n* a spectre or goblin; (also **tattiebogle**) a scarecrow (*Scot*); a bugbear, or source of terror. —**bogg'le**, **bogg'ard** and **bogg'art** are N Eng forms. [Scot; poss connected with **bug**⁴]

■ **bogle about the bush** or **stacks** a kind of hide-and-seek.

BOGOF /bog'of/ *abbrev* : buy one get one free.

bogong /bō'gong/ or **bugong** /boo'-/ *n* a noctuid moth eaten by Australian Aborigines. [From an Aboriginal language]

bogus /bō'gas/ *adj* counterfeit, spurious; bad or disappointing (*N Am sl*). [An American cant word, of very uncertain origin, possibly ult related to **bogy**]

bogy or **bogey** /bō'gi/ *n* (*pl* **bō'gies** or **bō'geys**) a goblin; a bugbear or special object of dread; the Devil; a policeman (*sl*); a piece of nasal mucus (*sl*). [Perh a form of **bogle**]

■ **bō'gyism** or **bō'geyism** *n*.

❑ **bo'gyman** or **bo'geyman** *n* the Devil or other frightening being with whom to threaten children.

boh see **boo**.

bohea /bō-hē'/ *n* the lowest quality of black tea; black tea generally. [From the Wǔyí hills in Fujian province, China]

Bohemian /bō-hē'mi-ən/ *n* a native or inhabitant of Bohemia, formerly a kingdom, now part of the Czech Republic; a Gypsy; (also without *cap*) an artist or writer, or anyone, who sets social conventions aside; the Czech language. ◆ *adj* of or relating to Bohemia; (also without *cap*) *esp* of an artist or writer, following an unconventional lifestyle. [Fr *bohémien* a Gypsy, from the belief that they came from *Bohemia*]

■ **Bohē'mianism** *n* (also without *cap*).

❑ **Bohemian ruby** *n* rose quartz. **Bohemian topaz** *n* citrine.

boho /bō'hō/ (*inf*) *adj* and *n* (*pl* **bo'hos**) (a) bohemian.

bohrium /bō'ri-əm/ *n* an artificially produced radioactive transuranic element (symbol **Bh**; atomic no 107), formerly called **unnilseptium** and **nielsbohrium**. [Niels *Bohr* (1885–1962), Danish physicist]

bohunk /bō'hungk/ (*N Am sl*, *esp US*) *n* a Slav or Hungarian, *esp* an unskilled labourer; the language of such a labourer. [Perh *Bohemian Hungarian*]

boil[1] /boil/ *vi* to pass rapidly from liquid into vapour with violent and copious production of bubbles; to reach boiling point; (of a vessel) to contain boiling liquid; to bubble up as if from the action of heat; to be heated in boiling liquid; to be hot; to be very excited or angry. ◆ *vt* to heat to a boiling state; to cook, dress, clean or otherwise treat by boiling. ◆ *n* the act or condition of boiling; a swirling disturbance made at the surface of the water by a fish coming to the fly. [OFr *boillir*, from L *bullīre*, from *bulla* a bubble]
■ **boil'er** *n* a person who boils; that in which anything is boiled; a vessel in which steam is generated; a vessel in which water is heated for circulation; a (*usu* old) fowl, best cooked by boiling. **boil'ery** *n* a place for boiling, *esp* for obtaining salt. **boil'ing** *n* the act of causing to boil; the condition of being boiled or at boiling point; a quantity boiled at once; a boiled sweet (*Scot*); a collection, set (*inf*). ◆ *adj* at boiling point; very hot; bubbling; extremely angry.
▫ **boiled shirt** *n* a dress shirt. **boiled sweet** *n* a sweet of boiled sugar, flavouring, and often colouring. **boil'ermaker** *n* an industrial metalworker; a drink consisting of whisky with a beer chaser (*N Am sl*). **boil'erplate** *n* steel plate suitable for making boilers; cliche-ridden writing (*N Am*); (items of) standard formulaic text. ◆ *adj* formulaic or stereotypical. **boiler room** *n* a room in a building or ship that houses a boiler; a site of strenuous and important effort (*fig*); an operation involving the fraudulent sale by a broker to investors of shares that are overpriced or worthless (*stock exchange*). **boiler suit** *n* a one-piece overall with trousers, and *usu* long sleeves. **boiling point** *n* the temperature at which a liquid, *esp* water, boils, *esp* at atmospheric pressure; the point of emotion, *esp* anger, where control is lost. **boiling-water reactor** *n* a light-water reactor in which steam drives the turbines directly (see also **light-water reactor** under **light**[2], **pressurized water reactor** under **pressure**). **boil'over** *n* (*Aust inf*) a surprising result, *esp* in a sporting event.
■ **boil away** to evaporate (completely) by boiling. **boil down** to reduce in bulk by boiling; to extract the substance of (*lit* and *fig*). **boil down to** (*fig*) to mean, to signify when reduced to essentials. **boil off** to remove (impurities, etc) by boiling. **boil over** to bubble over the sides of the containing vessel; to break out into unrestrained indignation. **come to the boil** to reach boiling point; to reach a critical state. **go off the boil** to stop boiling, fall below boiling point; to subside from an active or critical state. **on the boil** boiling; active.

boil[2] /boil/ *n* an inflamed swelling, *esp* one caused by infection of a hair follicle. [OE *bȳl*; Ger *Beule*]

boing /boing/ or **boink** /boink/ *n* the sound of a bouncing impact. ◆ *interj* imitating this sound. ◆ *vi* to bounce or hit with such a sound. [Imit]

boisterous /boi'st(ə-)rəs/ *adj* noisy and exuberant; wild; turbulent; stormy. [ME *boistous*]
■ **bois'terously** *adv*. **bois'terousness** *n*.

boîte de nuit /bwät də nwē'/ (*Fr*) *n* a nightclub.

bok /bok/ (*S Afr*) *n* a goat; an antelope. [Du, goat]

bok choy /bok choi'/ *n* another name for **Chinese cabbage** (see under **china**[1]). [Variant of **pak choi**]

boke or **boak** /bōk/, also **bock** /bōk or bok/ (chiefly *Scot*) *vi* to belch; to retch, vomit; to gush, spurt. ◆ *vt* to vomit; (of a volcano, etc) to emit. ◆ *n* the act of boking; vomit. [Prob imit but cf Older Scot *bolk*, ME *bolken*, and **belch**]

Bokmål /book'mōl/ *n* one of the two official written varieties of modern Norwegian (the other being Nynorsk), based on the written Danish introduced when Norway and Denmark were united (formerly called Riksmål). [Norw, book language]

boko /bō'kō/ (*sl*) *n* (*pl* **bō'kos**) the nose. [Origin unknown]

BOL *abbrev*: Bolivia (IVR).

bolas /bō'las or -ləs/ *n* (properly *pl*) a S American missile, consisting of two or more balls or stones strung together, swung round the head and hurled so as to entangle an animal. [Sp, balls]
▫ **bolas spider** *n* a spider that catches its prey with a sticky drop on the end of a line thrown like a bolas.

bold /bōld/ *adj* daring; actively courageous; forward or impudent; presumptuous; executed vigorously; striking, noticeable, well-marked; steep or abrupt; (of eg currants) full-flavoured, mature, plump; (of type) boldfaced; naughty (*Irish*). ◆ *n* boldfaced type. [OE *bald*; OHGer *bald*, ON *ballr*]
■ **bold'en** *vt* (*obs*) to make bold. **bold'ly** *adv*. **bold'ness** *n*.
▫ **bold'face** *n* boldfaced type (also *adj*). **bold'faced** *adj* impudent; (of type) having a black heavy face.
■ **be so bold** (**as to**) to venture (to), take the liberty (of). **bold as brass** utterly unabashed. **make bold** to venture, take the liberty.

bold-beating /bōld'bēt'ing/ (*Shakesp*) *adj* possibly for 'bowl-beating' ie tub-thumping, or a conflation of **bold** and **browbeating**.

bole[1] /bōl/ *n* the trunk of a tree. [ON *bolr*; Ger *Bohle* a plank]

bole[2] /bōl/ *n* a friable earthy clay, *usu* red. [Gr *bolos* a clod]

bole[3] /bōl/ (*Scot*) *n* a recess in a wall; an opening to admit light and air (also **win'dow-bole**). [Origin unknown]

bolection or **balection** /bō- or bə-lek'shən/ (*archit*) *n* a moulding around a panel, projecting beyond the surface of the framing. [Origin unknown]

bolero /bə-lā'rō/ *n* (*pl* **boleros**) a Spanish dance; a tune to which it may be danced; (*usu* /bol'ə-rō/) a jacket or waistcoat not reaching the waist nor meeting in front. [Sp]

Boletus /bō-lē'təs/ *n* a genus of fungi, both edible and poisonous, with a pore-like surface instead of gills; (without *cap*; *pl* **bole'tuses** or **bole'tī**) a fungus of this genus. [L *bōlētus*, from Gr *bōlītēs* mushroom]

bolide /bō'līd/ *n* a large meteor, *esp* one that bursts; a fireball. [Fr, from L *bolis*, *-idis*, from Gr *bolis* missile]

bolivar /bol'i-vär or bo-lē'vär/ *n* the standard monetary unit of Venezuela (100 centimos). [Simón *Bolívar* (1783–1830), national hero]

Bolivian /bə-liv'i-ən/ *adj* of or relating to the Republic of *Bolivia* in S America, or its inhabitants. ◆ *n* a native or citizen of Bolivia.
■ **boliviano** /bol-ē-vi-ä'nō/ *n* (*pl* **bolivia'nos**) the standard monetary unit of Bolivia (100 centavos).

bolix see **bollocks**.

boll[1] /bōl/ *n* a swelling; a knob; a round seed-capsule, as in cotton, flax, poppy, etc. ◆ *vi* to swell, to form bolls. [A form of **bowl**[1], from OE *bolla*]
■ **bolled** /bōld/ *adj* swollen, podded. **bollen** /bō'lən or (*Shakesp*) bōln/ *adj* (*obs*) swollen.
▫ **boll weevil** *n* a weevil (*Anthonomus grandis*) whose larvae infest cotton bolls. **boll'worm** *n* a moth caterpillar that destroys cotton bolls, maize, tomatoes, etc, in USA *Chloridea obsoleta*, in Egypt and India *Earias insulana* and *E. fabia*.

boll[2] /bōl/ *n* a measure of capacity for grain, etc, used in Scotland and N England, in Scotland *usu* = 6 imperial bushels, in England varying from 2 to 6 bushels; also a measure of weight, containing, for flour, 140lb. [Prob ON *bolli*]

Bollandist /bol'ən-dist/ *n* any of the Jesuit writers who continued the *Acta Sanctorum* by John *Bolland* (1596–1665).

bollard /bol'ärd/ *n* a short post on a wharf or ship, etc, round which ropes are secured; one of a line of short posts preventing the passage of motor vehicles. [Prob **bole**[1]]

bollen see under **boll**[1].

bolletrie /bol'ə-trē/ same as **bully-tree**.

bollix see **bollocks**.

bollock /bol'ək/ (*sl*) *vt* to reprimand severely. [From **bollocks**]
■ **boll'ocking** *n*.

bollocks /bol'əks/, **ballocks**, **bollix** or **bolix** /bol' or bal'əks/ *n pl* (*vulgar sl*) testicles. ◆ *n sing* (*sl*) nonsense (also *interj*); a muddle, mess. ◆ *vt* (*US sl*) (*usu* with *up*) to make a botch of. [OE *beallucas* testicles]
▫ **boll'ock-naked** *adj* (*vulgar sl*) completely naked.

Bollywood /bol'i-wŏod/ *n* the Indian commercial film industry. [From *Bombay*, former name of Mumbai, and *Hollywood*]

bolo[1] /bō'lō/ (*esp US*) *n* (*pl* **bo'los**) in boxing, a long sweeping uppercut (also **bolo punch**). [Ety uncertain]

bolo[2] /bō'lō/ *n* (*pl* **bo'los**) a traditional long-bladed Philippine knife. [Sp]

Bologna /bo-lō'nyä/ *adj* of the town of *Bologna* in Italy. [L *Bonōnia*]
■ **Bologn'ese** (or /-äz'/) *adj* and *n*. **bologn'ese** /bol-on-yāz' or bol-ən-āz'/ *adj* and *n* (in) a meat and tomato sauce.
▫ **Bologna phial** *n* an unannealed bottle that shatters on scratching. **Bologna phosphorus** *n* barium sulphide. **Bologna sausage** *n* a large sausage made of mixed meats. **Bologna stone** *n* fibrous barytes.
■ **spaghetti (alla) bolognese** see under **spaghetti**.

bolometer /bō-lom'i-tər/ *n* an instrument for measuring radiant energy. [Gr *bolē* stroke, ray (from *ballein* to throw), and *metron* a measure]
■ **bolomet'ric** *adj*. **bolom'etry** *n*.

boloney see **baloney**.

bolo tie /bō'lō tī/ (*N Am*) *n* a length of cord worn around the neck as a tie, fastened by an ornamental clasp. [From **bolas**]

Bolshevik (or **bolshevik**) /bol'shə-vik/ *n* a member of the Russian Majority (or Extreme) Socialist party, *opp* to Menshevik (*hist*); a violent revolutionary Marxist communist; an anarchist, agitator, causer of trouble (used loosely as a term of disapproval). ◆ *adj* of or relating to the Bolsheviks. [Russ, from *bolshe* greater, from its more

thoroughgoing programme, or from its being in a majority (ie at the Russian Social Democratic Congress in 1903), and -*vik*, agent sfx]
■ **Bol'shevism** *n*. **Bol'shevist** *n* a Bolshevik (also *adj*). **Bol'shevize** or **-ise** *vt*. **bol'shie** or **bol'shy** *adj* and *n* (*inf*) (a person) behaving in an awkward or intractable manner; (a person) holding left-wing views.

bolster /*bōl'stər* or *bol'*/ *n* a long, sometimes cylindrical, pillow or cushion; a pad; anything resembling it in form or use, *esp* any piece of a mechanism acting as a support against pressure; a form of cold chisel; the jutting-out part of a knife which abuts on the handle. ◆ *vt* (also with *up*) to support as with a bolster; to hold up; to pad (*out*, etc). [OE *bolster*]
■ **bol'stered** *adj* supported; swelled out. **bol'stering** *n* and *adj* propping up or supporting.

bolt[1] /*bōlt* or *bolt*/ *n* a bar or rod that slides into a hole or socket to fasten a door, etc; a sliding mechanism in a firearm used to eject a spent cartridge and insert a new one; a heavy screw or pin with a head; an arrow, *esp* for a crossbow; a thunderbolt; a roll of a definite measure (of cloth, etc); the uncut edge of a sheet folded for a book; a rush, a sudden dash. ◆ *vt* to fasten with a bolt; to utter precipitately; to swallow hastily; to cause to rush out, run away or take flight; to connect or join (*fig*); to break away from, withhold support from (*US*); to make up (cloth) into bolts. ◆ *vi* to spring, dart; to run away, escape; (of a horse) to run out of control; to withhold support from one's party, its policy or nominee (*US*); (of a plant) to flower and run to seed; (of a biennial plant) to behave like an annual. ◆ *adv* like a bolt. [OE *bolt*; OHGer *bolz*]
■ **bolt'er** *n*.
❑ **bolt'-action** *adj* (of a firearm) having a bolt for ejecting or advancing cartridges. **bolt'head** *n* the head of a bolt. **bolt'hole** *n* a hole into which a bolt slides; a secret passage or way of escape; a refuge from danger; a secluded, private place. **bolt'-on** *adj* additional, supplementary. ◆ *n* an additional part which can be attached to a computer or other machine. **bolt rope** *n* a rope sewn round the edge of a sail to prevent it from tearing.
■ **a bolt from the blue** an unexpected event. **a fool's bolt is soon shot** a fool soon gives away the initiative, leaving himself or herself unprotected. **bolt upright** upright, and straight as an arrow. **have shot one's bolt** to be unable to do more than one has done.

bolt[2], **bolter**, **bolting** see **boult**.

Boltzmann constant /*bōlts'mən kon'stənt*/ (*phys*) *n* the ratio of the gas constant to Avogadro's constant. [Ludwig *Boltzmann* (1844–1906), Austrian physicist]

bolus /*bō'ləs*/ *n* (*pl* **bo'luses**) a rounded mass; a large pill; a drug dose injected quickly into a blood vessel. [L *bōlus*, from Gr *bōlos* a lump]

boma[1] /*bō'mə*/ (*E Afr*) *n* a fenced enclosure. [Swahili]

boma[2] /*bō'mə*/ *n* a boa or anaconda. [Congo; thence carried by Portuguese to Brazil]

bomb /*bom* or (*old*) *bum*/ *n* a hollow case containing explosive, incendiary, smoke-producing, poisonous, or other offensive material; (with *the*) nuclear weapons collectively; a great deal of money (*inf*); a piece of programming, inserted into software, that can be activated to sabotage the system (*comput*); (also **volcanic bomb**) a rounded mass of lava thrown out by a volcano; a ball that travels high in the air (*inf*; *sport*); an old worn-out car (*Aust* and *NZ inf*); (of a play, etc) a fiasco, a flop (*N Am sl*). ◆ *vi* to throw, discharge, or drop bombs; (sometimes with *out*) to be a flop, fail (*N Am inf*); to move very quickly, *esp* in a vehicle (*inf*). ◆ *vt* to attack, injure or destroy with bombs. [Fr *bombe*, prob from L *bombus*, from Gr *bombos* humming sound]
■ **bombed** *adj* devastated by bombs; intoxicated by drugs (*sl*). **bomber** /*bom'ər*/ *n* a person who bombs or plants bombs; a bombing aeroplane; a pill or capsule of an illicit drug, *esp* amphetamine (*sl*); a cigarette containing marijuana (*sl*). **bomb'ing** *n*. **bomb'let** *n* a small bomb; a part of a larger complex weapon.
❑ **bomb calorimeter** *n* an apparatus for determining the calorific value of fuels by ignition in a thick-walled steel vessel. **bomb disposal** *n* the act of removing and detonating previously unexploded bombs. **bomb** (**disposal**) **squad** *n* a group of soldiers or police officers trained in bomb disposal. **bomber jacket** *n* a short jacket with zipped front and elasticated waist. **bomb'-happy** *adj* in a state of mind for discharging bombs without compunction; with nerves shattered by exposure to bombing. **bomb-ketch** see **bomb-vessel** below. **bomb'proof** *adj* proof or secure against the force of bombs. ◆ *n* (*obs*) a bombproof structure. **bomb'shell** *n* a bomb; (now only *fig*) a sudden and surprising piece of news; a stunningly attractive young woman (*inf*). **bomb'sight** *n* a device for aiming and releasing bombs from a bomber. **bomb'site** *n* an area which has been laid waste by air-raid(s) (also *fig*). **bomb'-vessel** or **-ketch** *n* (*hist*) a vessel for carrying mortars used in bombarding from the sea.
■ **cost a bomb** (*inf*) to be very expensive. **go down a bomb** (*inf*) to be received with enthusiasm. **go like a bomb** to go very well or very quickly. **make a bomb** (*inf*) to make or earn a great deal of money.

bombacaceous see under **bombax**.

bombard /*bom-bärd'*/ *vt* to attack with artillery; to batter or pelt; to subject to a succession of blows or impingements; to assail, eg with questions (*fig*); to subject (eg an atom) to a stream of high-energy particles (*phys*). ◆ *n* /*bom'bärd*/ an early cannon for throwing stones, etc; a large liquor-jug, a blackjack (*Shakesp*); a bass reed stop on the organ; (also **bombarde**) a shawm. [OFr *bombard* an old cannon for firing stones or shot; see also ety of **bomb**]
■ **bombardier** /*bom-* or *bum-bər-dēr'*/ *n* the lowest non-commissioned officer in the British artillery; the person in a bomber who aims and releases the bombs. **bombardment** /*bom-bärd'mənt*/ *n*. **bombar'don** (or /*bom'*/) *n* the bass tuba.
❑ **bombardier beetle** *n* a beetle that explosively discharges an acrid volatile fluid.

bombasine or **bombazine** /*bom'bə-zēn* or formerly *bum'*/ *n* a twilled or corded fabric of silk and worsted, or of cotton and worsted. [Fr *bombasin*, from LL *bombȳcinus*, from Gr *bombȳkinos* silken, from *bombȳx* silkworm]

bombast /*bom'bast*/ *n* pompously inflated language; cotton wool, padding, stuffing (*obs*). ◆ *adj* (*Shakesp*) inflated. ◆ *vt* /*-bast'*/, also *bom'*/ (*archaic*) to pad, stuff; to inflate, make grandiose. [Variant of obs *bombace*, from OFr, from as **bombax**]
■ **bombas'tic** *adj* pompous; inflated. **bombas'tically** *adv*.

bombax /*bom'baks*/ *n* any tree of the *Bombax* genus of tropical, chiefly S American trees, giving name to the silk-cotton family, **Bombacā'ceae**. [LL *bombax* cotton, from Gr *bombȳx* silk]
❑ **bombacā'ceous** *adj*.

Bombay duck /*bom'bā duk*/ *n* a fish, the bummalo.

Bombay mix /*bom'bā miks*/ *n* a dry spiced mixture of fried lentils, peanuts, etc, eaten as a snack *orig* in Indian cookery.

bombazine see **bombasine**.

bombe /*bom* or *b3b*/ *n* a dessert, *usu* ice cream frozen in a round or melon-shaped mould. [Fr]

bombé /*bom'bā* or *b3-bā*/ *adj* (of furniture) having a rounded, convex front. [Fr, bulging, convex]

bomber see under **bomb**.

bombilate /*bom'bil-āt*/ or **bombinate** /*bom'bin-āt*/ *vi* to hum, buzz, drone, boom. [L *bombilāre*, *bombināre*]
■ **bombilā'tion** or **bombinā'tion** *n*.

bombo /*bom'bō*/ (*Aust inf*) *n* (*pl* **bom'bos**) cheap wine, plonk. [Ety uncertain]

bombora /*bom-bō'rə* or *-bō'rə*/ (*Aust*) *n* a submerged reef; a dangerous current or rough sea over such a reef. [From an Aboriginal language]

Bombyx /*bom'biks*/ *n* the silkworm moth genus, giving name to the family **Bombycidae** /*-bis'i-dē*/. [Gr *bombȳx*]
■ **bom'bycid** *n* an insect of the family (also *adj*).

bon /*b3*/ (*Fr*) *adj* good. [Fr, from L *bonus* good]
❑ **bon accueil** /*bo-na-kœy*/ *n* good reception, due honour. **bon ami** (*fem* **bonne amie**) /*bo-na-mē*/ *n* good friend; lover. **bon appetit** /*bo-na-pə-tē*/ *interj* good appetite, said politely to those who are (about to start) eating. **bon camarade** /*ka-ma-rad*/ *n* good comrade. **bon chrétien** /*krā-tyē*/ *n* (literally, good Christian) a kind of pear, the William. **bon diable** /*dē-äbl'*/ *n* a good-natured fellow. **bon goût** /*goo*/ *n* good taste. **bon gré, mal gré** /*grā, mal grā*/ *adv* willing or unwilling, willy-nilly. **bonjour** /*-zhoor*/ *interj* good day; good morning. **bon marché** /*mar-shā*/ *n* a bargain; cheapness. ◆ *adj* cheap. ◆ *adv* cheaply. **bon mot** /*mō*/ *n* (*pl* **bons mots**) a witty saying. **bonsoir** /*-swär*/ *interj* good evening. **bon ton** /*t3*/ *n* the height of fashion. **bon vivant** /*vē-vä*/ *n* a jovial companion; a person who lives well, *esp* one who enjoys fine food (*fem* **bonne vivante** is not used in Fr). **bon viveur** /*vē-vœr*/ *n* (not used in Fr) a bon vivant, *esp* a man-about-town. **bon voyage** /*vwä-yäzh*/ *interj* may you have a good journey.

bona /*bō'nə* or *bo'na*/ (*L*) *n pl* goods.
❑ **bona mobilia** /*mō-bi'li-ə* or *-a*/ *n pl* (*law*) movable goods. **bona peritura** /*per-i-tū'rə* or *-too'ra*/ *n pl* (*law*) perishable goods. **bona vacantia** /*va-kan'shi-ə* or *wa-kan'ti-a*/ *n pl* (*law*) unclaimed goods.

bona fide /*bō'nə fīd, fī'də, -di* or *bon'ä fī'dā*/ *adj* genuine; done or carried out in good faith. ◆ *adv* in good faith. ◆ *n* (*Irish inf*) a public house legally open outside normal licensing hours to serve travellers. [L, (in) good faith]
❑ **bona fides** /*fī'dēz* or *fid'ās*/ *n* good faith; genuineness; also (treated as *pl*) proofs of trustworthiness.

bonamano see **buonamano**.

bonamia /*bo-nā'mi-ə*/ *n* a parasite that causes bonamiasis.
■ **bonami'asis** *n* a fatal disease of oysters, attacking their immunological system.

---

bonanza /bə-nan'zə or bɒv- or bo-/ n a rich mine or vein of precious ore (N Am); a large amount of (usu) silver; any source of wealth or stroke of luck. ◆ adj very prosperous. [Sp, good weather (at sea)]

Bonapartean /bō-nə-pär'ti-ən/ adj of Napoleon Bonaparte or his family.
■ **Bō'napartism** n attachment to his dynasty or policy. **Bō'napartist** n and adj.

bona-roba /bō'nə-rō'bə/ (Shakesp) n a prostitute, courtesan. [Ital buona roba, literally, good stuff (or dress)]

bonasus or **bonassus** /bo-nas'əs/ n a bison. [L from Gr bonasos, bonassos]

bonbon /bon'bon or bɔ̃-bɔ̃/ n a confection, a sweet; a cracker (for pulling) (obs). [Fr, reduplication of bon good]
■ **bonbonnière** /bɔ̃-bon-yer'/ n a fancy box for holding sweets.

bonce /bons/ n a large marble; the head (sl). [Origin obscure]

bond[1] /bond/ n something that binds; a link, connection, union or (chem) attraction; a written obligation to pay a sum or to perform a contract; a debenture, a security issued by the government or a company when borrowing money; any adhesive or cementing force or material; in building, the overlapping connection of one course of stones or bricks with another, as in English bond or Flemish bond; (in pl) imprisonment, captivity; the status of goods retained in a **bonded warehouse** or **store** until duties are paid or the goods are exported; **bond paper**. ◆ vt to connect, secure or bind with a bond; to put in a bonded warehouse; to put in a condition of bond; to cause to adhere (to) (eg metal to glass or plastic). ◆ vi to adhere together securely; to form an emotional bond. [A variant of **band**[1], from OE bindan to bind]
■ **bond'ed** adj secured by bond. **bond'er** n a bondstone or header. **bond'ing** n an act of bonding; the forming of a close emotional attachment, esp between a mother and her newborn child (psychol).
❑ **bonded debt** n the debt of a corporation represented by the bonds it has issued, as contrasted with its floating debt. **bonded warehouse** see under n above. **bond energy** n the energy, in joules, released on the formation of a chemical bond between atoms and absorbed on its breaking. **bond'holder** n a person who holds bonds of a private person or public company. **bond paper** n a superior kind of paper, used esp as stationery, orig intended for bonds. **bonds'man** n a surety. **bond'stone** n a stone that reaches a considerable distance into or entirely through a wall, binding it together. **bond'-timber** n timber built into a wall for the purpose of binding it together lengthwise. **bond'-washing** n an illegal series of deals in bonds designed to avoid payment of tax.

bond[2] /bond/ adj in a state of servitude. [OE bonda a farmer, a householder, from ON bóndi, búandi a tiller, a husbandman, from búa to till, cognate with OE buan, the meaning having been affected by association with **bond**[1]]
■ **bond'age** n captivity; slavery; serfdom, villeinage; a sexual practice in which the partners derive additional pleasure through, or by applying, physical restraint or binding. ◆ adj (of usu black leather clothes or accessories) having chains, metal studs, buckles, etc for erotic or dramatic effect. **bond'ager** n (hist) a female outworker in the Borders and N England, one of whom every male farm worker had to provide for the farm work.
❑ **bond'maid**, **bond'woman** or **bonds'woman** n a female slave or serf. **bond'man** or **bonds'man** n a male slave or serf. **bond'manship** n. **bond'servant** n a slave. **bond'-service** n the condition of a bondservant; slavery. **bond'-slave** n a slave. **bonds'man**, **bonds'woman** see bondman, bondwoman above.

bondsman see under bond[1], [2].

bonduc /bon'duk/ n the nicker seed. [Ar bonduq a kind of nut]

bone /bōn/ n a hard substance forming the skeleton of the higher animals; a separate piece of the skeleton; a piece of whalebone or other material used for stiffening corsets, etc; a bobbin for lace-making; (in pl) the skeleton or anything resembling it in any way; (in pl) mortal remains; (in pl) pieces of bone or something similar held between the fingers of the hand and rattled together to keep time to music; (in pl) dice; (in pl) a nickname for a doctor (inf). ◆ vt to take the bones out of (eg meat); to provide (a corset, etc) with bones; to have sexual intercourse with (US vulgar sl); to seize, nab (sl). [OE bān; Ger Bein leg]
■ **boned** adj having bones; having the bones removed. **bone'less** adj lacking bones; spineless (fig). **bō'ner** n (sl) a howler, a blunder; an erection of the penis (vulgar). **bō'niness** n. **bō'ny** adj full of, consisting of, or like bones; thin.
❑ **bone'-ache** n pain in the bones. **bone ash** or **bone'-earth** n the remains of bones burned in air. **bone'-bed** n a deposit of fossil bones. **bone'-black** n the carbonaceous remains of bones heated in the absence of air. **bone'-brecc'ia** n rock formed of broken fossil bones. **bone'-cave'** n a cave containing deposits of fossil bones of animals

that lived in it or their prey. **bone china** n china in the making of which bone ash is used. **bone-dry** adj as dry as a bone; under total prohibition of alcohol. **bone'-dust** n ground or pulverized bones, used in agriculture. **bone-earth** see bone ash above. **bone'fish** n a game fish (family Albulidae) found in warm shallow waters. **bone'head** n (inf) a blockhead. **bone'-headed** adj. **bone-i'dle** adj utterly idle, idle to the bone. **bone'-lace** n lace woven with bobbins, formerly often made of bones. **bone marrow** see marrow[1]. **bone marrow grafting** n (med) grafting or transplantation of bone marrow to patients with bone marrow failure (used in aplastic anaemia or after therapeutic destruction of the bone marrow in leukaemia). **bone meal** n ground bones used as fertilizer and as animal feed. **bone'-mill** n a mill where bones are ground. **bone of contention** n something that causes strife. **bone'-oil** n a liquid produced by the destructive distillation of bones. **bone'set** n a N American species of hemp agrimony. **bone'setter** n a person who treats broken or dislocated bones, esp when not surgically qualified. **bone'shaker** n an inf name for earlier forms of bicycle; an old or unreliable vehicle with inadequate suspension. **bone spavin** see under spavin. **bonetired** see bone-weary below. **bone'-tur'quoise** n a blue fossil bone or tooth used as turquoise. **bone'-weary** or **bone'tired** adj utterly exhausted. **bone'yard** n (sl) a cemetery. **bony fishes** n pl the Teleostei, an order of fishes including most of the living forms. **bony pike** n the American (and fossil) garfish.
■ **a bone to pick** (inf) a difference to be cleared up (with somebody); something to occupy one (archaic). **bare bones** the essentials (of a subject). **bone up on** (inf) to study or collect information about (a subject). **close to the bone** same as near the bone (see below). **feel in one's bones** to know instinctively, without proof. **make no bones of** or **about** to have no scruples about; to make no fuss or difficulty about; to be quite open about. **near the bone** on the verge of being indecent; offensively pointed; mean; hard up, poor. **(never) make old bones** (not) to live to old age. **off** (or **on**) **the bone** (of meat or fish) with its bones (not) removed. **to the bone** to the inmost part; to the minimum. **work one's fingers to the bone** to work until one is exhausted.

bonfire /bon'fīr/ n a large fire in the open air on occasions of public celebration, for consuming garden refuse, etc, orig a fire in which bones were burnt. [bone and fire]
❑ **Bonfire night** n 5 November, Guy Fawkes night (see guy[2]).

bong[1] /bong/ n a deep hollow or ringing sound. ◆ vi to make such a sound (also vt). [Imit]

bong[2] /bong/ n a water pipe used for smoking cannabis, crack, etc. [Thai baung]

bongo[1] /bong'gō/ or **bongo drum** /drum/ n (pl bon'gos or bongo drums) a small Cuban drum, generally used in pairs, played with the fingers. [Am Sp bongó]

bongo[2] /bong'gō/ n (pl bong'os) a central African bushbuck. [Native name]

bongrace /bon'grās/ n a shade against the sun, worn on the front of women's hats in the Middle Ages; a broad-brimmed hat or bonnet. [Fr bonne (fem) good, and grâce grace]

bonheur-du-jour /bo-nœr-dü-zhoor'/ n a small desk or writing table popular esp in 18c France. [Fr, happiness of the day]

bonhomie or **bonhommie** /bon'o-mē/ n easy good nature. [Fr]
■ **bon'homous** adj.

bonibell see bonnibell.

bonie /bōn'i/ (Burns) adj a variant spelling of bonny.

boniface /bon'i-fās/ n an innkeeper. [From the hearty Boniface of Farquhar's Beaux' Stratagem, or the Bonifazio of Ariosto's La Scolastica]

bonilasse see bonnilasse.

boning /bō'ning/ n the process of estimating straightness by looking along a row of poles, as in boning-rod or boning-telescope.

bonism /bon'i-zm/ n the doctrine that the world is good, but not the best possible. [L bonus good]
■ **bon'ist** n.

bonito /bo-nē'tō/ n (pl boni'tos) any of several large fish of the mackerel family, somewhat smaller than the tunas. [Sp]

bonk /bongk/ n a blow or thump, or its sound (inf); an act of sexual intercourse (vulgar sl). ◆ vt and vi to hit or thump (inf); to have sexual intercourse (with) (vulgar sl). [Imit]
■ **bonk'ing** n.
❑ **bonk'buster** n (inf) a novel, film, etc featuring frequent and graphic scenes of sexual intercourse.
■ **the bonk** (inf) a state of fatigue that prevents a cyclist or a runner from continuing.

bonkers /bong'kərz/ (sl) adj crazy; slightly drunk (archaic).

---

bonne /bon/ *fem* of **bon** (*Fr*) *adj* good. ◆*n* a French maid or nursemaid.
□ **bonne bouche** /boosh'/ *n* (Fr *bouche* mouth) a delicious morsel. **bonne chance** /shãs/ *interj* good luck. **bonne compagnie** /kɔ̃-pa-nyē/ *n* good society. **bonne femme** /fam/ *adj* (*cookery*) of a dish, cooked simply and garnished with fresh vegetables and herbs. **bonne foi** /fwa/ *n* good faith. **bonne grâce** /gräs/ *n* good grace, gracefulness; (in *pl*) favour. **bonne mine** /mēn/ *n* good appearance, pleasant looks.

bonnet /bon'it/ *n* a woman's head-covering, tied on by ribbons, etc; a man's soft cap (now *Scot*); an additional part laced to the foot of jibs, or other fore-and-aft sails, to gather more wind (*naut*); a wire cowl over a chimney top; the cover of a motor-car engine, or of various parts of machinery, etc; the second stomach of a ruminant; a raised portion between guns at a salient (*fortif*); a decoy or pretended player or bidder at a gaming-table or an auction, the accomplice of a thimblerigger or other petty swindler. ◆ *vt* to put a bonnet on; to crush someone's own hat over the eyes of (someone). [OFr, from LL *bonnetum*, orig the name of a material]
■ **bonn'eted** *adj*.
□ **bonn'ethead** *n* the shovelhead shark. **bonnet laird** *n* (*Scot*) a small landowner (who wore a bonnet, not the hat of the gentry). **bonnet monkey** *n* an Indian macaque (from the appearance of the head). **bonn'et-piece** *n* a gold coin of James V of Scotland, on which the king wears a bonnet. **bonnet-rouge** /bon-ā-roozh/ *n* (*Fr*) the red cap of liberty of the French Revolution, in the form of a Phrygian cap.

bonnibell or **bonibell** /bo-ni-bel'/ (*Spenser*) *n* a good and fair maid. [Fr *bonne et belle* good and fair; or for *bonny belle*]

bonnilasse or **bonilasse** /bon'i-läs/ *n* (*Spenser*) for *bonny lass*.

bonny or **bonnie** /bon'i, also (*Scot*) bō'ni/ *adj* comely, pretty; plump; healthy-looking; as a general term expressing appreciation, fine, splendid, considerable, etc (often *ironic*); smiling, cheerful (*obs*); big and strong (*Shakesp*). ◆*n* a sweetheart. [Origin obscure]
■ **bonn'ily** *adv*. **bonn'iness** *n*.

bonobo /bon'ō-bō/ *n* (*pl* **bon'obos**) a species of chimpanzee (*Pan paniscus*) found in the Democratic Republic of Congo, considered to be the closest animal relative of human beings (also **pygmy chimpanzee**).

bonsai /bon'sī or bōn'sī/ *n* (*pl* **bon'sai**) a dwarf tree growing in a pot, produced by special methods of cultivation; the art of growing such trees. [Jap *bon* tray, bowl, and *sai* cultivation]

bonsella /bon-sel'ə/ or **bansela** /ban-/ (*S Afr*) *n* a gratuity to a black African. [Zulu *ibhansela* a gift]

bonspiel /bon'spēl/ *n* a curling tournament. [Appar from a Du compound of *spel* play; cf **ba'spiel** under **ball**[1]]

bontebok /bon'tə-bok/ *n* a S African antelope. [Du *bont* particoloured, and *bok* goat]

bonus /bō'nəs/ *n* something good or desirable gained or given with something else; a premium beyond the usual interest for a loan; an extra dividend to shareholders; a policyholder's share of profits; an extra payment to a workforce, salesmen, etc, eg for reaching specified targets or at special times of year such as Christmas; a bribe. [L *bonus* good]
□ **bonus issue** *n* an issue of additional shares (**bonus shares**) to a company's shareholders in proportion to their existing shareholding, representing a capitalization of reserves.

bonxie /bongk'si/ (*Shetland*) *n* the great skua. [ON *bunkie* heap]

bonze /bonz/ *n* a Buddhist priest. [Jap *bonzô* or *bonzi* a priest]

bonzer or **bonza** /bon'zə/ (*Aust* and *NZ inf*) *adj* very good. [Perh from Fr *bon* good, influenced by US *bonanza*]

boo /boo/ *n* and *interj* an exclamation used in fun to startle someone (also **bo** or **boh** /bō/); a sound expressing disapproval or contempt (also **booh**). ◆ *vt* and *vi* to show disapproval (of) by making such a sound.
□ **boo'-boy** *n* (*inf*) a person who jeers and heckles. **boo-hoo** /-hoo'/ *n* the sound of noisy weeping. ◆ *vi* to weep noisily. **boo'-word** *n* a word denoting something disliked, disapproved of, or feared.
■ **not say boo to a goose** to be extremely timid.

booay, **booai** or **boohai** /boo'ī/ (*NZ*) *n* a remote rural place. [Poss from *Puhoi* in the North Auckland district, once considered remote]
■ **up the booay** (*inf*) utterly lost or mistaken.

boob[1] /boob/ (*inf*) *vt* to bungle. ◆ *vi* to blunder. ◆*n* a blunder (also **booboo** /boo'boo/); a stupid fellow (*US*). [**booby**[1]]
□ **boob tube** *n* (*N Am sl*) a television set.

boob[2] /boob/ (*sl*) *n* (*usu* in *pl*) a female breast. [**booby**[2]]
□ **boob job** *n* (*inf*) cosmetic surgery performed on the breasts. **boob tube** *n* a woman's garment of stretch fabric covering the torso from midriff to armpit.

booboo see **boob**[1].

boobook /boo'book/ *n* an Australian owl (*Ninox boobook*). [From an Aboriginal language; from its cuckoo-like cry]

booby[1] /boo'bi/ *n* a stupid person; a pupil at the bottom of the class; a name for various kinds of gannet. [Perh Sp *bobo* a dolt]
■ **boo'byish** *adj* like a booby; stupid. **boo'byism** *n*.
□ **booby hatch** *n* (*N Am inf*) a psychiatric hospital. **booby prize** *n* a prize for the least successful in a competition, etc. **booby trap** *n* a harmless-looking object which on being touched sets off an explosion; a form of practical joke, by which something is made to fall upon someone entering a door, or the like. **boo'by-trap** *vt* to set up a booby trap in or on.

booby[2] /boo'bi/ (*sl*) *n* a female breast. [Obs Eng *bubby*]

boodie or **boodie-rat** /boo'di(-rat)/ *n* a now rare species of rat-kangaroo, found in the islands off W Australia. [From an Aboriginal language]

boodle[1] /boo'dl/ *n* counterfeit money; money obtained by political or official corruption; spoil; caboodle. [Perh Du *boedel* property]

boodle[2] /boo'dl/ (*sl*) *n* a stupid person.

boody /boo'di/ *vi* (**bood'ying**; **bood'ied**) to sulk or mope. [Fr *bouder* to pout]

boofhead /boof'hed/ (*Aust inf*) *n* a stupid person. [Prob from earlier *bufflehead*, from *buffle* buffalo]

boogaloo /boo-gə-loo'/ *n* a dance popular in the 1960s in which the dancer shuffles and swings the shoulders. ◆ *vi* to dance the boogaloo. [Poss from **boogie-woogie**]

booger /boo'gə/ (*N Am sl*) *n* a piece of nasal mucus. [Altered form of **bogy**]

boogie /boo'gi/ *n* boogie-woogie; dancing to pop music. ◆ *vi* (**boog'ieing**; **boog'ied**) (*inf*) to dance to pop music. [See **boogie-woogie**]
□ **boogie board** *n* (*inf*) a body board.

boogie-woogie /boo'gi-woo'gi/ *n* a jazz piano style with a repeated strongly rhythmic bass and melodic variations above. [Reduplicated from US slang *boogie* an African-American performer]

booh see **boo**.

boohai see **booay**.

book /book/ *n* a collection of sheets of paper, etc, bound or otherwise fastened together, either printed, written on, or blank; a large-scale literary composition; a division of a volume or composition; (with *the* and sometimes *cap*) the Bible; a record of bets made with different people; (with *the*) a telephone directory; any source of information or knowledge; a set of rules; a libretto; a script; the first six tricks gained by a side in whist, etc; a structure resembling a book; (in *pl*) formal accounts of transactions, eg minutes of meetings, records kept of a business. ◆ *vt* to engage or reserve in advance; (of the police, a traffic warden, etc) to take the name of, for an alleged offence; hence, to arrest; (of a referee) to enter a player's name in a notebook for an offence (*football*); to write or enter in a book (*archaic*). ◆ *vi* to make a reservation in advance. [OE *bōc* book, beech; cf Ger *Buche* beech, and *Buch* book, supposed to be from early Germanic use of beech boards]
■ **book'able** *adj*. **book'er** *n* one who engages entertainers in advance. **book'ful** *adj* full of information gathered from books. **book'ie** *n* (*inf*) a bookmaker. **book'ing** *n* a reservation of eg a room in a hotel, a theatre seat, a seat on a plane, train, etc; an engagement for the services of someone, *usu* a performer; the taking of a name for an offence. **book'ish** *adj* relating to books; fond of books, studious; acquainted only with, and experienced only through books. **book'ishness** *n*. **book'less** *adj* without books; unlearned. **book'let** *n* a little book, *esp* one of only a few pages, saddle-stitched, with paper covers. **book'sie** or **book'sy** *adj* by way of being literary. **book'y** *adj* bookish.
□ **book'-account** *n* an account of debt or credit in a book. **book'binder** *n* a person who binds books. **book'bindery** *n* (*US*) a place where books are bound. **book'binding** *n*. **book'-canvasser** *n* (*obs*) a person who goes around soliciting orders for a book. **book'case** *n* a piece of furniture with shelves for books. **book club** *n* a society that sells at reduced prices, buys, circulates on loan, or prints books for its members. **book'-debt** *n* a sum owing to a seller, as shown in the seller's business-books. **booked-out'** or **booked-up'** *adj* full up; unable to accept further reservations, bookings or appointments. **book'end** *n* one of a pair of props for the end of a row of books. ◆ *vt* to place between two other similar things. **book group** *n* a group of people who agree to read a particular book and then meet to discuss it (also called **reading group**). **book'-hand** *n* (*hist*) one of the writing styles used to produce copies of books in manuscript before the invention of printing. **book'-holder** *n* a prompter in the theatre. **booking clerk** *n* a person who sells tickets. **booking hall** *n*. **booking office** *n* an office where reservations are made or tickets sold. **book'keeper** *n*. **book'keeping** *n* the keeping of

accounts in a regular and systematic manner; the record of the financial transactions of a business. **book'land** n (OE bōcland) land taken from the folcland or common land, and granted by bōc or written charter to a private owner. **book'-learned** /-lûrn'id/ adj. **book'-learning** n learning acquired from books, as opposed to practical knowledge. **book'lore** (Scot **book'-lear** or **buik'-lear** /-lär/) n book-learning; bibliographical lore. **book'louse** n (pl **book'lice**) a wingless insect of the order Psocoptera, which damages books. **book lung** n the respiratory organ in spiders and other arachnids, formed of fine membranes like the leaves of a book. **book'maker** n a person who accepts bets at racecourses, etc, and pays out the winnings; a person who makes up books from the writings of others, a compiler. **book'making** n. **book'man** n a scholar, student. **book'mark** n a (decorative) strip of leather, fabric, paper, etc, or other object, for marking a particular opening or one's current place in a book (also **book'marker**); an electronic equivalent in the form of a record of the location of the Internet site, web page, etc. ♦ vt to make an electronic record of. **book'-mate** n (Shakesp) a companion in study, a schoolfellow. **book'-mindedness** n habitual direction of the mind towards books. **book'mobile** n (N Am) a mobile library. **book'-muslin** n muslin used in bookbinding. **book'-oath** n (Shakesp) an oath made on the Book or Bible. **Book of Changes** n the I Ching. **book of hours** see under **hour**. **Book of Life** n a personal identity document formerly used in South Africa. **book of words** n (inf) directions for use. **book'plate** n a label usually pasted inside the cover of a book, bearing the owner's name or other distinguishing information. **book'-post** n a former name for **Media Mail** (see under **medium**). **book price** or **value** n the officially recorded value, not necessarily the market value, of a commodity, etc. **book'rest** n a support for a book, a bookstand. **book'-scorpion** n a scorpion-like arachnid found in libraries, probably feeding on booklice. **book'seller** n a person who sells books; formerly a publisher. **book'selling** n. **book'shelf** n a shelf for books. **book'shop** n a shop where books are sold. **book'stall** n a stall or stand where books are sold. **book'stand** n a bookstall; a stand or support for holding up a book in reading. **book'store** n (N Am) a bookshop. **book token** n a voucher to be exchanged for books of a stated price, given as a gift. **book trade** n the trade of dealing in books. **book value** see **book price** above. **book'work** n study from books, theoretical as opposed to practical work; work on account books, etc. **book'worm** n a grub that eats holes in books, esp a beetle larva (genus Anobium); a person who is devoted to reading.

■ **be on the books** to have one's name on an official list; to be a member or client. **book in** to reserve a place or room; to register at a hotel. **book of original** (or **prime**) **entry** (bookkeeping) a book in which the first record of transactions is made, eg before entry in a ledger. **book out** to leave a hotel formally, by settling one's bill, handing in one's key, etc. **book through** to book as a whole (a journey to be made in parts). **bring to book** to bring to account. **by the book** strictly according to the rules. **closed book** a person or subject that is not known or understood at all (cf **open book** below). **close the book(s) on** to bring to a definite conclusion. **get one's books** to be dismissed. **in anyone's book** indeed, without any doubt. **in my** (etc) **book** in my (etc) view. **in someone's good** (or **bad**) **books** favourably (or unfavourably) regarded by someone. **open book** a person or subject that is well-known or clearly understood (cf **closed book** above). **read** (**someone**) **like a book** to understand thoroughly (usu a person's character or motives). **suit one's book** to be agreeable to or favourable to one. **take a leaf out of someone's book** to profit by someone's example. **talk like a book** to talk pedantically, or with precision and readiness. **throw the book at** (inf) to administer a lengthy and detailed reproof to; to punish severely. **without book** from memory; unauthorizedly.

bool see **bowl**².

Boolean /boo'li-ən/ adj relating to George Boole (1815–64), English mathematician, or his logical system.
□ **Boolean algebra** n a logical system which makes the algebraic manipulation of sets possible. **Boolean expression** n an expression containing the logical operators 'and', 'or', 'not', used extensively in computing.

boom¹ /boom/ vt to make a hollow sound or roar. ♦ n a hollow roar. [From a LGer root found in OE byme a trumpet, Du bommen to drum; like **bomb**, of imit origin]
■ **boom'y** adj.
□ **boom'box** n (sl) a powerful portable radio and cassette recorder with built-in speakers, a ghetto-blaster.

boom² /boom/ vi to become active or busy suddenly; to become suddenly prosperous; to increase sharply in value. ♦ vt to push into sudden prominence; to boost by advertising. ♦ n a sudden increase of activity in business, etc, a period of expansion of the economy; a sudden rise in price or value. [Prob from **boom**¹]
■ **boom'er** n a baby boomer (qv under **baby**). **boom'ing** n and adj. **boom'let** n a minor economic boom.

□ **boom town** n one which has expanded rapidly and prospered because of eg the arrival of a valuable new industry.
■ **boom and bust** alternate periods of economic expansion and recession.

boom³ /boom/ n a pole which controls the position of a sail; a chain or bar stretched across a harbour; a barrier of floating logs; an inflatable barrier used to contain oil from spillages, etc; a long beam; a movable and usu extendable beam which holds an overhead camera or microphone in a TV studio or on a film set; a tree (as combining form, eg kaffirboom, etc; S Afr). [Du boom beam, tree]
□ **boom'-iron** n a ring in which a ship's boom slides. **boom'slang** n (S and E Afr) a venomous tree snake.

boomer¹ /boo'mər/ (Aust and NZ) n a large male kangaroo, esp of the great grey species; anything large or very successful (inf). [Partly from **boom**¹, partly from Eng dialect boomer anything very large of its type]

boomer² see under **boom**².

boomerang /boo'mə-rang/ n a curved missile used by the Australian Aborigines, sometimes so balanced that it returns towards the thrower; an act that recoils upon the agent. ♦ vi to recoil in such a way, backfire. [From an Aboriginal language]

boomps-a-daisy see under **bump**¹.

boomslang see under **boom**³.

boon¹ /boon/ n a gift, favour; something to be thankful for, a blessing; a petition, request (obs). [ON bōn prayer, cognate with OE bēn]

boon² /boon/ adj jovial, convivial, or intimate (as a boon companion). [Fr bon, from L bonus good]

boondocks /boon'doks/ (N Am inf) n pl (with the; also **boo'nies**) wild or remote country; a dull provincial place. [Tagálog bundok mountain]

boondoggle /boon'dog-l/ (US) n a Scout's plaited cord of varicoloured leather strips; an article of simple handcraft; work, or a task, of little or no practical value, esp work officially provided as a palliative for unemployment. ♦ vi to do such work. [Scout coinage]
■ **boon'doggler** n.

boong /boong/ (Aust offensive) n an Aborigine; a New Guinea native; any black person. [From an Aboriginal language]

boonies /boo'niz/ see **boondocks**.

boor /boor/ n a coarse, ill-mannered person; a Dutch colonist in South Africa (hist); a countryman, a peasant (obs). [Du boer; perh partly OE būr, gebūr farmer]
■ **boor'ish** adj awkward or rude. **boor'ishly** adv. **boor'ishness** n.

boord or **boorde** /bōrd or börd/ old spellings of **board**.

boorka /bûr'kə/ same as **burka**.

boortree see **bourtree**.

boose see **booze**.

boost /boost/ vt to push up; to raise (eg price, morale); to advertise or promote; to supplement or increase (eg voltage or air supply); to increase the pressure of; to push (a spacecraft) into orbit by means of a booster. ♦ vi (US sl) to shoplift; to steal. ♦ n an act or instance of boosting; the amount by which the induction pressure of a supercharged engine exceeds the atmospheric pressure. [Orig US; ety unknown]
■ **boost'er** n a person or thing which boosts; a keen supporter (US); an auxiliary motor in a rocket, usu breaking away after delivery of its impulse; any device to increase the effect of another mechanism; an additional dose of a vaccine to increase or renew the effect of the original dose; a shoplifter (US sl). **boost'erism** n the practice of boosting or promoting a product or idea.
□ **booster seat** n a small seat or cushion placed on top of another seat to raise the level of a sitting child.

boot¹ /boot/ n a covering for the foot and at least the ankle, often the calf or even higher up the leg, made of leather, rubber, etc; a compartment in a motor car for luggage, etc; a kick (inf); the operation of booting a computer; a Denver boot (US); an instrument of torture for the leg (Scot hist); a box or receptacle in a coach (obs). ♦ vt to put boots on; to kick; to turn out, dismiss (with out; inf); to start up the initial programs on (a computer), to bootstrap, usu by transferring the disk-operating-system program from its storage on the disk into the computer's working memory (often with up); to attach a Denver boot to (US). [OFr bote (Mod Fr botte), from LL botta, bota, of doubtful origin]
■ **boot'able** adj having the necessary software to boot a computer. **boot'ed** adj having boots on, equipped for riding; (of birds, esp poultry) having feathered legs. **bootee** /boo'tē or -tē'/ n a short boot; an infant's knitted boot (also **boot'ie**); /boo'tē/ a Royal Marine (milit sl). **boot'ikin** n (obs) the boot for torture (Scot); a boot or mitten for the gouty; an infant's legging. **boots** n (old) a hotel servant who cleans boots, runs messages, etc.

❑ **boot'black** *n* a person whose job is to clean and polish shoes; a shoeblack. **boot boy** same as **bovver boy** (see under **bovver**). **boot camp** *n* (*sl, orig N Am*) a training centre for military recruits; a place for punishing and reforming young offenders. **boot'-catcher** *n* an inn servant who helped to pull off guests' boots. **boot'cut** *adj* of trousers, cut wide at the hem to allow for high heels or boots. **boot'-faced** *adj* with an unsmiling, expressionless face. **boot'-hook** *n* an instrument for pulling on long boots. **boot'hose** *n* (*pl* **boot'hose**) (*Shakesp*) a long over-stocking which covers the leg like a boot. **boot'-jack** *n* a device for pulling off boots. **boot'lace** *n* a lace for fastening boots. **bootlace fungus** *n* honey fungus. **bootlace tie** *n* a very thin stringlike necktie. **boot'last** or **boot'-tree** *n* the last or foot-like mould on which boots or shoes are made or stretched to keep their shape. **boot'leg** *n* the leg of a high boot. ◆ *vt* and *vi* to smuggle (alcoholic drink); to make or deal in (illicit goods such as alcoholic drink or illegally made recordings). ◆ *adj* made or sold illicitly. **boot'legger** *n*. **boot'legging** *n*. **boot'less** *adj* without boots. **boot'licker** *n* a toady (*US* **boot'lick**; also *vt*). **boot'licking** *n*. **boot'maker** *n*. **boot'making** *n*. **boot sale** same as **car boot sale** (see under **car**). **boot'strap** *n* a bootlace; a strap on the back of a boot to help in pulling it on; the piece of software that boots up (*comput*). ◆ *vt* (*comput*) to input initial data so as to enable the subsequent loading of a computer program. **boot'-topping** *n* the part of a ship's hull between the load-line and the waterline when the ship is without cargo; the act of coating this; paint, etc, for the purpose. **boot-tree** see **bootlast** above. **boot virus** *n* (*comput*) a virus in the sector of a disk used in booting up. ■ **bet one's boots** (*inf*) to be quite certain. **boot and saddle** (altered from Fr *boute-selle* place saddle) the signal for mounting (**boots and saddles** the bugle-call which formerly called the US cavalry to mount). **boots and all** (*Aust* and *NZ*) without reservation. **die in one's boots** or **with one's boots on** to die while still working, still in harness. **fill one's boots** (*inf*) to take as much of something as one wants; to do something to the fullest extent. **get the boot** (*inf*) to be dismissed. **have one's heart in one's boots** to have lost courage. **lick someone's boots** to try to ingratiate oneself with someone by obsequious behaviour. **like old boots** (*inf*) vigorously. **old boot** (*derog inf*) an unattractive older woman. **pull oneself up by one's** (**own**) **bootstraps** to get on by one's own efforts. **put the boot in** or **put in the boot** (*inf*) to resort to physical or verbal bullying; to attack unfairly; to bring a situation to an end brutally. **the boot is on the other leg** (*obs*) or **foot** responsibility (now) lies the other way, the situation is reversed. **too big for one's boots** conceited, bumptious. **tough as old boots** robust; indestructible.

boot² /boot/ *vt* to give profit or advantage to. ◆ *n* (*obs*) advantage; profit; any reparation or compensation paid (*OE law*); booty (*Shakesp*). [OE *bōt* compensation, amends, whence *bētan* to amend (see **beet²**)]
■ **boot'less** *adj* unprofitable, useless. **boot'lessly** *adv*. **boot'lessness** *n*.
■ **to boot** in addition.

Boötes /bō-ō'tēz/ *n* a constellation beside the Great Bear, containing the bright star Arcturus. [Gr *Boōtēs*, literally, an ox-driver]

booth /boodh or booth/ *n* a hut or small shop of simple construction; a stall at a fair or market; a partly enclosed compartment, such as one in which to vote, telephone, or eat in a restaurant. [ON *būth*, or a cognate word; cf Ger *Bude*]

bootless see under **boot¹,²**.

booty¹ /boo'ti/ *n* spoil taken in war or by force; plunder, a prize. [MLGer *bute*; cognate with ON *bȳti* share, from *bȳta* to divide]
■ **play booty** to join with others in order to cheat one player; to play a game with the intention of losing.

booty² /boo'ti/ (*N Am inf*) *n* a person's bottom.
■ **bootyli'cious** *adj* (of a woman's figure, *esp* the buttocks) attractively curvaceous.
❑ **booty call** *n* (*sl*) a telephone call, *esp* late at night, requesting a meeting for the sole purpose of sexual intercourse.

booze, (*obs*) **boose** /booz/ or (*archaic*) **bouse** /bowz/ (*inf*) *vi* to drink alcohol; *esp* to excess. ◆ *n* intoxicating liquor; a drinking bout. [Variant of **bouse¹**]
■ **boozed** *adj*. **booz'er** *n* a person who boozes; a public house (*sl*). **boozey** see **boozy** below. **booz'ily** *adv*. **booz'iness** *n*. **booz'ing** *adj* drinking; for drinking. **booz'y** or **booz'ey** *adj* inclined to booze; drunken.
❑ **booze cruise** *n* a foreign excursion for the purpose of buying cheap alcohol; a pleasure trip on a boat during which a lot of alcohol is consumed. **booze'hound** *n* (*sl*) a heavy or habitual drinker. **booze'-up** *n* a drinking bout.

bop¹ /bop/ *n* short for **bebop**, of which it was a development in the 1950s; a dance with (or to) pop music (*inf*). ◆ *vi* (**bopp'ing**; **bopped**; *inf*) to dance to pop music.
■ **bopp'er** *n*.

bop² /bop/ (*sl*) *n* a blow. ◆ *vt* (**bopp'ing**; **bopped**) to strike. [*imit*]

bo-peep /bō-pēp'/ *n* a children's game in which one peeps from behind something and cries 'Bo'; a quick look (*Aust* and *NZ inf*).

bor /bö(r)/ *n* neighbour, an East Anglian form of address to a man or a woman. [OE *būr*, usu *gebūr* farmer; cf **neighbour**]

bor. *abbrev* : borough.

bora¹ /bö'rə/ *n* a strong north-east wind in the upper Adriatic. [Venetian variant of Ital *borea*, from L *boreas*]

bora² /bö'rə/ *n* an Australian Aboriginal initiation rite. [From an Aboriginal language]

borachio /bo-rach'(i-)ō/ *n* (*pl* **borach'ios**) a Spanish wineskin; a drunken fellow. [Sp *borracha*, *borracho*]

boracic, boracite see under **borax¹**.

borage /bur'ij or bor'ij/ *n* a blue-flowered, bristly, aromatic herb, *Borago officinalis* (family **Boragina'ceae**), the leaves of which have a cucumber-like flavour and are used in salads and to flavour drinks. [LL *borrāgō*]
■ **boragina'ceous** *adj*.

borak /bö'rək/ or **borax** /bö'raks/ (*Aust* and *NZ sl*) *n* nonsense, banter. [From an Aboriginal language]
■ **poke borak at** to make fun of, jeer at.

borane see under **boron**.

borax¹ /bö'raks/ *n* a mineral, hydrated sodium tetraborate, found on alkaline lake shores. [Fr and LL *borax*, from Ar *būraq*]
■ **boracic** see **boric** below. **bo'racite** /-rə-sīt/ *n* a mineral composed of magnesium borate and chloride. **bo'rate** *n* a salt or ester of boric acid. **bo'ric** or **boracic** /bo-ras'ik/ *adj* of or relating to borax or boron; penniless, skint (*inf*; rhyming slang for *boracic lint*).
❑ **boric, boracic** or **orthoboracic acid** *n* an acid (H_3BO_3) obtained from borax, and also found native in mineral springs in Italy.

borax² see **borak**.

borazon see under **boron**.

borborygmus /bör-bə-rig'məs/ *n* (*pl* **borboryg'mī**) the sound of flatulence in the intestines. [Gr *borborygmos*]
■ **borboryg'mic** *adj*.

bord obsolete spelling of **board**.

bord and pillar /börd ənd pil'ər/ *n* a mining technique in which coal is extracted in two stages, first through a grid of parallel tunnels (**bords**) which when finished leave blocks (**pillars**) that are extracted in a second stage.

bordar /börd'ər/ (*hist*) *n* a villein who held his cottage at his lord's pleasure. [LL *bordārius* of Gmc origin. See **board**]

borde obsolete spelling of **board**.

Bordeaux /bör-dō'/ *n* claret, wine of the *Bordeaux* region of SW France.
❑ **Bordeaux mixture** *n* a mixture of lime and copper sulphate, used to kill fungus and insect parasites on plants.

bordello /bör-del'ō/ *n* (*pl* **bordell'os**) a brothel (also (*archaic*) **bordel** /bör'dəl/). [Ital, from OFr *bordel* a cabin, from LL *borda*]

border /bör'dər/ *n* the edge or margin of anything; the boundary of a country, etc, *esp* (with *cap*) that between England and Scotland; (in *pl* with *cap* and *the*) the area of Scotland bordering on England, *esp* the area between Northumberland and the Lothians; a flower-bed in a garden; a piece of ornamental edging or trimming. ◆ *adj* of or on the border. ◆ *vi* to come near or be adjacent (with *on*, *upon*, *with*); to verge on, be nearly the same as (with *on*). ◆ *vt* to provide with a border; to form a border to, be adjacent to. [OFr *bordure*; from root of **board**]
■ **bord'ered** *adj*. **bord'erer** *n* a person who lives or was born on the border of a country. **bord'erless** *adj*.
❑ **Border collie** *n* a breed of medium-sized, *usu* black and white, collie dog. **bordered pit** *n* (*bot*) a thin area in the secondary wall of a cell, surrounded by a thickened arched border. **border effect** *n* (*image technol*) a faint dark line on the denser side of a boundary between a lightly exposed and a heavily exposed region on a developed emulsion (also **edge effect** or **fringe effect**). **bord'erland** *n* a border region; the undefined margin between two things (also *adj*). **Border Leicester** *n* a sheep of a breed developed by crossbreeding Leicesters and Cheviots. **bord'erline** *adj* marginal, doubtfully or just coming within the definition of a quality, condition, etc (also *n*). **borderline personality disorder** *n* (*psychiatry*) a mental illness characterized by instability of mood and behaviour, problems with relationships and self-image, and sometimes dissociation and paranoia. **Border terrier** *n* a small rough-haired terrier, *orig* from the Borders.

bordereau /bor-d(ə-)rō'/ (*Fr*) *n* a memorandum or detailed statement.

bordraging /börd'rag-ing/ *n* see **bodrag**.

■ words derived from main entry word; ❑ compound words; ■ idioms and phrasal verbs

bordure /bör'dūr or -joor/ (heraldry) n a border surrounding a shield. [Ety as for **border**]

bore[1] /bōr/ vt to pierce (something) so as to form a hole; to produce (a hole) by drilling, etc; to weary or annoy with tediousness (perh a different word: not known before mid-18c). ◆ vi to form a hole or borehole by drilling or piercing; (of a racehorse or athlete) to push against other competitors (to gain advantage in a race) (also vt). ◆ n a hole made by boring; the cavity of a tube; the diameter of the cavity of a tube; an artesian well (Aust); a person, thing or activity that wearies; something that causes annoyance, a nuisance (inf). [OE borian to bore; cf Ger bohren; cognate with L forāre to bore, Gr pharynx the gullet]
■ **bored** adj wearied by tedious things. **bore'dom** n tedium. **bor'er** n a person or thing that bores; a name common to many animals, esp insects that pierce wood, rocks, etc. **bor'ing** adj causing boredom, tedious. ◆ n the act of making a hole in anything; a hole made by boring; (in pl) the chips produced by boring. **bor'ingly** adv. **bor'ingness** n.
❑ **bore'hole** n a bore made in the earth's crust for geological investigation or for water, oil, etc.

bore[2] /bōr/ n a tidal flood that rushes with great violence up the estuaries of certain rivers, an eagre. [ON bāra a wave or swell]

bore[3] /bōr/ pat of **bear**[1].

Boreas /bor'i- or bō'ri-as/ n the north wind. [L, from Gr]
■ **bo'real** /bo' or bō'/ adj of the north wind or the north; (with cap) of a biogeographical region consisting of the northern and mountainous parts of the northern hemisphere; (with cap) of a post-glacial period when the climate of Europe and N America resembled that of the present Boreal region.

borecole /bōr'kōl/ n kale. [Du boerenkool, literally, peasant's cabbage]

boree /bō'rē/ (Aust) n any of several species of acacia. [From an Aboriginal language]

boreen /bō-rēn'/ n a lane. [Ir bóithrín]

borel see **borrel**.

borgo /bōr'gō/ (Ital) n (pl **bor'gos**) a borough, a market-town.
■ **borghetto** /bor-get'tō/ n (pl **borghet'tos**) a big village.

boric see under **borax**[1].

boride see under **boron**.

borlotti bean /bōr-lot'i bēn/ n a variety of kidney bean with a pinkish speckled skin. [Ital, pl of borlotto kidney bean]

born /bōrn/ see **bear**[1].
❑ **born'-again** adj with renewed spiritual life; revitalized, transformed. n a person who has received new spiritual life. **born fool**, **born mimic**, etc n someone whose folly, mimic ability, etc, is innate.
■ **born to be** destined to be. **in (all) one's born days** in one's whole lifetime. **not born yesterday** not young in experience, not a fool.

borne /bōrn/ pap of **bear**[1].
■ **be borne in on** to be realized or grasped by.

borné /bor'nā/ adj limited, narrow-minded. [Fr pap of borner to limit]

Bornholm disease /bōrn'hōm diz-ēz'/ n epidemic pleurodynia, a rare infectious disease caused by a virus. [From the Baltic island Bornholm where it was first described]

bornite /bōr'nīt/ n a copper ore, sulphide of copper and iron. [I von Born (1742–91), Austrian mineralogist]

boro- /bö-ro-/ combining form denoting boron.

boron /bö'ron/ n a non-metallic element (symbol **B**; atomic no 5) present in borax and boric acid, obtained as an amorphous powder or impure in diamond-like crystals. [See **borax**[1]]
■ **borane** /bōr'ān/ n any boron hydride, efficient as high-energy fuel. **borazon** /bōr'a-zon/ n a man-made substance, a compound of boron and nitrogen, hard as diamond. **boride** /bōr'īd/ n any of a class of substances made by combining boron chemically with a metal, some of which are extremely hard and heat-resistant. **borosil'icate** n a salt of boric and silicic acids, used in making heat- and chemical-resistant glass.

boronia /bo-rō'ni-ə/ n an Australian scented shrub of the genus Boronia. [F Borone (1769–94), Italian botanist]

borough /bur'ə/ n a town with a corporation and special privileges granted by royal charter; a town that sends representatives to parliament; one of the local government divisions of a city such as London or New York; in some US states, a municipal corporation. [OE burg, burh a city, from beorgan, cognate with Ger bergen to protect]
❑ **borough court** n formerly, an inferior court dealing with minor offences, etc, presided over by local magistrates. **bor'ough-English** n a former custom in some S English boroughs (until 1925), by which estates descended to the youngest son. **bor'ough-monger** n a buyer or seller of the parliamentary seats of boroughs. **bor'ough-reeve** n the

chief municipal official in some unincorporated English towns prior to 1835.
■ **close** or **pocket borough** a borough, esp before 1832, whose parliamentary representation was in the nomination of some person. **county borough** until 1974, a borough (by Acts of 1888, 1926, 1958, respectively above 50000, 75000 and 100000 inhabitants) with some of the attributes of a county. **pocket borough** see **close borough** above. **rotten borough** one of the boroughs, all abolished in 1832, which still returned members to parliament although the constituency had disappeared. —See also the Scottish terms grouped under **burgh**.

borrel, **borrell** or **borel** /bor'əl/ (archaic) adj rustic, boorish. [OFr burel coarse cloth]

borrow /bor'ō/ vt and vi to obtain (money, etc) on loan or trust; to adopt (words, etc) from a foreign source; to derive from another (with from, of). ◆ vi (golf) to allow for slope or wind, esp by putting the ball uphill of the hole. ◆ n a pledge or surety (archaic); a borrowing (Shakesp); the allowance to be made for a slope on a green (golf). [OE borgian, from borg, borh a pledge, security]
■ **borr'owed** adj taken on loan; counterfeit; assumed. **borr'ower** n. **borr'owing** n and adj.
❑ **borrowed time** n an unexpected extension of life, or of the time allowed for some activity. **borrow hole** or **pit** n (civil eng) a pit formed by the excavation of material to be used elsewhere for embanking, etc. **borrowing days** n pl the last three days of March (Old Style), supposed in Scottish folklore to have been borrowed by March from April, and to be especially stormy. **borrow pit** see **borrow hole** above.
■ **to borrow** (obs) for a pledge or surety.

borsch or **borscht** /bōrsh(t)/ n a Russian and Polish beetroot soup (also **bortsch** /bōrch/, etc). [Russ borshch]

borstal or **borstall** /bōr'stəl/ n formerly, an establishment for the detention of young adult delinquents, now replaced by a range of more or less similar detention systems. [From the first reformatory of the kind at Borstal, a suburb of Rochester, Kent]

bort or **boart** /bōrt/ n diamond fragments or dust; a coarse diamond or crystalline form of carbon, used industrially for cutting or as an abrasive. [Ety doubtful]

bortsch see **borsch**.

borzoi /bōr'zoi/ n a dog like a huge greyhound, but with a long soft coat. [Russ borzii swift]

bosbok see **bushbuck** under **bush**[1].

boscage or **boskage** /bosk'ij/ n thick foliage; woodland. [Fr boscage, bocage, from LL boscus, cognate with Ger Busch, Eng **bush**[1]]

boschbok see **bushbuck** under **bush**[1].

bosche see **boche**.

Bosch process /bosh prō'ses/ n a process for obtaining hydrogen by reducing steam with carbon monoxide. [Carl Bosch (1874–1940), German chemist]

boschveld see **bushveld** under **bush**[1].

Bose-Einstein condensate /bō'zə-īn'stīn kon'dən-sāt/ (phys) n the state of atoms that have been cooled to just above absolute zero, and which behave as a single entity or pool. [SN Bose (see **boson**), and Albert Einstein (see **Einsteinian**)]

Bose-Einstein statistics see **boson**.

bosh /bosh/ (inf) n nonsense; foolish talk. [Turk bosh worthless]

boshta /bosh'tə/ or **boshter** /-tər/ (obs Aust inf) adj very good. [Perh a variant of **bonzer**]

bosie /bō'zi/ (Aust) n a googly. [BJT Bosanquet (1877–1936), English cricketer]

bosk /bosk/ (literary) n a thicket, a little wood. [Cf **bush**[1] and **boscage**]
■ **bosk'et** or **bos'quet** n (obs) a thicket; a plantation. **bosk'iness** n. **bosk'y** adj woody or bushy; shady; somewhat tipsy (inf).

boskage see **boscage**.

bosker /bos'kər/ (obs Aust inf) adj very good. [Perh a variant of **bonzer**]

Bosman /boz'mən/ (inf) n the free transfer of a footballer whose contract has expired to another club within the EU in accordance with the **Bosman ruling**, a decision of the European Court of Justice in 1995. [Jean-Marc Bosman (born 1964), Belgian footballer]

bo's'n, **bos'n** see **boatswain**.

Bosnian /boz'ni-ən/ adj of Bosnia-Herzegovina (formerly a constituent republic of Yugoslavia, now an independent republic) or its people; of Bosnia, the northern region of Bosnia-Herzegovina or its people. ◆ n a native or citizen of Bosnia-Herzegovina or Bosnia.

bosom /bŏŏz'əm/ n the breast of a human being; the part of the dress that covers it; (sometimes in pl) a woman's breasts; the imagined seat of the passions and feelings, the heart; desire (Shakesp); one's embrace, clasp; any close or secret receptacle. ◆ adj (used attrib) confidential; intimate. ◆ vt to enclose in the bosom; to carry in the bosom. [OE bōsm; cf Ger Busen]
■ **bos'omed** adj having a bosom; enclosed. ◆ combining form having a bosom of a specified kind. **bos'omy** adj (of a woman) having large breasts.
■ **Abraham's bosom** the abode of the blessed dead.

boson /bō'zon/ (phys) n any of a class of subatomic particles whose behaviour is governed by **Bose-Einstein statistics**, according to which, under certain conditions, particles of the same kind will accumulate in each low-energy quantum mechanical state. [SN Bose (1894–1974), Indian physicist]

bosquet see **bosket** under **bosk**.

boss[1] /bos/ (inf) n a chief or leader; a master, employer, manager or foreman; the person who pulls the wires in political intrigues. ◆ adj chief; excellent. ◆ vt to manage or control; to domineer over (sometimes with about or around). [New York Dutch baas master]
■ **boss'ily** adv. **boss'iness** n. **boss'ism** n (US) the domination of a political party by bosses. **boss'y** adj disagreeably domineering.
❑ **boss cocky** n (Aust inf) a boss. **boss'yboots** n sing (inf) a person who enjoys telling others what to do.

boss[2] /bos/ n a knob or stud; a thickened part of a shaft, for strengthening or to allow attachment of other parts (mech); a wheel or propeller hub; a raised ornament in wood or leatherwork, or (archit) at the intersection of ribs in a vault; a dome-shaped protuberance of igneous rock exposed by erosion. ◆ vt to ornament with bosses. [OFr boce (Fr bosse) from OHGer bōzan to beat]
■ **bossed** adj embossed.

boss[3] /bos/ or **bossy** /bos'i/ (US) n a calf or cow.

boss[4] /bos/ (Scot) adj hollow; empty. [Obscure]

boss[5] /bos/ (dialect and sl) vi to make a mess of. ◆ n a mistake. [Origin unknown]
❑ **boss'-eyed** adj with one good eye; squint-eyed; out of true. **boss shot** n a bungled shot or attempt.

bossa nova /bos'ə nō'və/ n a style of dancing originating in Brazil, or the music for it. [Port bossa trend, tendency, and nova new]

bossy see **boss**[1,3].

bostangi /bo-stan'ji/ (hist) n a Turkish palace guard. [Turk bostanji]

boston /bost'ən/ n a game of cards, somewhat similar to whist; a kind of waltz. [From Boston, USA]
❑ **Boston crab** n a wrestling hold in which a wrestler sits on a prone opponent's back and applies pressure to the legs. **Boston ivy** n a variety of Virginia creeper. **Boston terrier** n a breed of dog arising from crossbreeding between a bulldog and a bull-terrier.

bostryx /bos'triks/ (bot) n a cymose inflorescence in which each lateral axis arises on the same side (cyclically) of its parent axis. [Gr, curl]

bosun, bo'sun see **boatswain**.

Boswellian /boz-wel'i-ən/ adj after the hero-worshipping, detailed and intimate manner of James Boswell (1740–95) in his biography of Samuel Johnson.
■ **Bos'wellism** n. **Bos'wellize** or **-ise** /-wəl-īz/ vi to write like Boswell.

bot[1] or **bott** /bot/ n the maggot of a botfly, parasitic in the intestines of the horse and other animals; (in pl) the diseased condition caused by this; (Scot **batts**) colic; (only **bot**) a cadger (Aust inf). ◆ vi and vt (only **bot**; **bott'ing**; **bott'ed**; Aust inf) to cadge or borrow. [Origin unknown]
❑ **bot'fly** n a name for various flies of the family Oestridae that lay their eggs on horses, etc. **bot'hole** n a hole in a hide due to boring by a bot.
■ **on the bot** (Aust inf) cadging, trying to scrounge.

bot[2] /bot/ n a computer program designed to perform routine tasks, such as searching the Internet, with some autonomy. [Short form of **robot**]
❑ **bot'net** n a collection of bots that run on infected computers and are used to cause widespread damage to computing systems.

bot. abbrev : botanical; botany; bottle.

botany /bot'ə-ni/ n the science of plants; the plants of an area; the properties of a particular group of plants; fine wool, orig from Botany Bay (sometimes with cap; also adj). [Gr botanē grass, fodder]
■ **botan'ic(al)** adj. **botan'ical** n a drug made from vegetable matter. **botan'ically** adv. **bot'anist** n a person skilled in botany. **bot'anize** or **-ise** vi to seek for and collect plants for study. **bot'anomancy** n (obs) divination by means of plants, esp the leaves of sage and fig.
❑ **botanic(al) garden** n a garden containing a diverse collection of plants, maintained for educational, scientific and conservation

purposes. **Botany Bay** n an early convict settlement near what is now Sydney; a general name for a convict settlement.

botargo see **bottarga**.

BOTB abbrev : British Overseas Trade Board (now known as British Trade International).

botch /boch/ n a clumsy patch; badly finished work; a bungle; a swelling on the skin; a boil, pimple, or sore (Milton); a blemish. ◆ vt to patch or mend clumsily; to put together unsuitably or unskilfully; to bungle (often with up). ◆ vi to do repairs; to bungle. [Partly perh from ONFr boche (OFr boce) ulcer; verb prob from ME bocchen to bungle]
■ **botch'er** n a bungler; a repairer. **botch'ery** n. **botch'ing** n and adj. **botch'y** adj marked with or full of botches.

bote /bōt/ (law) n compensation for injury or damage to property. [ME; from **boot**[2]]

botel or **boatel** /bō-tel'/ (orig US) n a waterside hotel catering especially for boat-owners; a boat or ship which functions as a hotel. [From boat and hotel]

botfly see under **bot**[1].

both /bōth/ adj and pronoun the two; the one and the other. ◆ adv or conj as well (sometimes of more than two). [ON bāthar (superseding OE bēgen, bā); Ger beide ; cf L ambō, Gr amphō, Sans ubhau, orig ambha]

bothan /bo'han/ (Scot) n a booth, hut; an illegal drinking den. [Gaelic]

bother /bodh'ər/ vt to perplex or tease; to worry or concern; to fluster; to pester; to give pain or trouble to. ◆ vi to stir oneself; to worry or be concerned (about). ◆ n petty trouble, difficulty, or perplexity; a person or thing causing bother. ◆ interj expressing irritation. [First found in 18c Irish-born writers; poss Anglo-Irish for **pother** or from Ir bodhair to annoy or deafen]
■ **botherā'tion** n (inf) petty trouble or concern. ◆ interj (inf) expressing irritation. **both'ersome** adj.
■ **bother one's head about** to trouble oneself about. **I** or **they**, etc **cannot be bothered** I or they, etc consider it too much trouble (to do something); I or they, etc find (someone or something) annoying (with with).

bothy or **bothie** /both'i/ (chiefly Scot) n a humble cottage or hut; a one-roomed hut or temporary dwelling, often built as a shelter in a mountain; a barely furnished dwelling for farm-servants. [Cf **booth**]
❑ **bothy ballad** n a folk song dealing with country matters, usu bawdy. **both'yman** n.

botoné or **bottony** /bot'ə-ni/ (heraldry) adj having buds or knobs at the extremity, applied to a cross having each arm terminated in three buds, like trefoil. [OFr; see **button**]

Botox® **treatment** /bō'toks trēt'mənt/ n the injection of a botulinum toxin into the skin as a temporary treatment to make lines on the face less apparent. [Botulinum toxin type A]
■ **bo'toxed** adj having had this treatment.

bo tree /bō trē/ or **bodhi tree** /bōd'i/ n in India and Sri Lanka the pipal (Ficus religiosa), holy tree of the Buddhists, under which Buddha found enlightenment, planted close by every temple. [Sinhalese bo, from Pali bodhi perfect knowledge]

botryoid /bot'ri-oid/ or **botryoidal** /-oid'əl/ adj like a bunch of grapes. [Gr botrys a bunch of grapes]
■ **bot'ryose** adj botryoidal; racemose (bot). **Botrytis** /bə-trī'tis/ n a genus of fungi (family Moniliaceae), several of which cause plant diseases, and one of which (Botrytis cinerea) causes noble rot (qv).

Botswanan /bot-swä'nən/ adj of or relating to the southern African country of Botswana or its inhabitants. ◆ n a native or inhabitant of Botswana.

bott see **bot**[1].

bottarga /bo-tär'gə/ or **botargo** /bo-tär'gō or bō-/ n cured pressed mullet or tuna roe. [Ital, from Ar butarkhah]

botte /bot/ (Fr) n a pass or thrust in fencing.

bottega /bot-tā'gä/ (Ital) n a wine shop; the studio of an artist and his or her assistants or apprentices.

bottine /bot-ēn'/ n a high boot; a half-boot; a lady's boot; a small boot. [Fr, dimin of botte boot]

bottle[1] /bot'l/ n a narrow-necked hollow vessel, esp of glass or plastic, for holding liquids; a bottleful; a glass or plastic container with a teat for feeding milk to a baby; a hot-water bottle; (chiefly with the) alcoholic drink or drinking, a drinking bout; money collected from busking, the takings (sl); courage, firmness of resolve (sl). ◆ vt to enclose in a bottle or bottles; to preserve in bottles or jars; to attack using a bottle as a weapon (sl); (often with it) to fail to do or achieve something as a result of losing one's nerve (sl). ◆ vi (sl) to collect money from busking. [OFr bouteille, dimin of botte a vessel for liquids, from LL butis a vessel]

■ **bott'led** *adj* enclosed or preserved in bottles or jars; shaped or protuberant like a bottle; kept in restraint; drunk (*sl*). **bott'leful** *n* (*pl* **bott'lefuls**) as much as fills a bottle. **bott'ler** *n* a person or machine that bottles; an excellent person or thing (*Aust inf*).

□ **bottle bank** *n* a purpose-built container in which empty glass bottles, jars, etc may be deposited for collection for recycling. **bott'le-blond** or (*fem*) **bott'le-blonde** *n* someone whose blond(e) hair-colouring came out of a bottle (ie is artificial, not natural). **bott'lebrush** *n* a brush for cleaning bottles, with bristles standing out from a central axis; a name for various plants of similar appearance, such as horse-tail, mare's-tail, Banksia, and Callistemon. **bott'le-chart** *n* a chart showing currents from evidence of bottles thrown into the sea. **bott'le-coaster** *n* a bottle-slider. **bott'le-feed** *vt* to feed milk to (a baby) from a bottle rather than the breast. **bott'le-feeding** *n*. **bott'le-fish** *n* a fish (*Saccopharynx ampullaceus*) that can blow its body out like a bottle. **bottle gas** or **bottled gas** *n* liquefied butane or propane gas in containers for use in lighting, cooking, heating, etc. **bottle glass** *n* a coarse green glass used in the making of bottles. **bott'le-gourd** *n* a climbing, musky-scented Indian cucurbitaceous annual, with bottle-shaped fruit (also **false calabash**). **bott'le-green** *adj* and *n* dark green, like bottle glass. **bott'le-head** *n* a bottle-nosed whale. **bott'le-holder** *n* a boxer's attendant; a backer or supporter generally. **bott'le-imp** *n* an imp confined in a bottle. **bottle jack** *n* (*NZ*) a large jack for heavy lifting. **bott'leneck** *n* a narrow place in a road where traffic is apt to be congested (often *fig*); a traffic hold-up; a cause of obstruction or congestion; a style of guitar-playing in which a glissando effect is produced by sliding (*orig*) a bottleneck or (now *usu*) a tube fitted onto a finger along the strings (also **bottleneck guitar**). **bott'lenose** *n* a large swollen nose; a bottle-nosed toothed whale (*Hyperoodon planifrons*) or dolphin (*Tursiops truncatus* and others). **bott'le-nosed** *adj* with a nose or snout shaped like a bottle. **bott'le-o** or **-oh** *n* (*Aust*) a dealer in used bottles (from his cry). **bott'le-opener** *n* a device for opening bottles. **bottle party** *n* a more or less improvised drinking party where each person brings a bottle. **bottle shop** or **bottle store** *n* (*Aust* and *NZ*) a place where alcoholic drinks are sold for consumption off the premises only, an off-licence. **bott'le-shouldered** *adj* with sloping shoulders like a champagne bottle. **bott'le-slider** *n* a tray for passing a decanter round the table. **bottle store** see **bottle shop** above. **bottle tree** *n* an Australian sterculiaceous tree with swollen trunk. **bott'le-washer** *n* a person or machine that washes bottles; a factotum, dogsbody (*inf*).

■ **bottle off** to draw from the cask and put into bottles. **bottle out** (*sl*) to lose one's nerve and withdraw (from eg a contest). **bottle up** to enclose (as) in a bottle; to confine, keep contained (an army, etc); to hold back, restrain (emotions); to replenish the stock of bottles behind a bar. **bring up on the bottle** to rear by bottle-feeding rather than by breastfeeding. **pass the bottle of smoke** (*Dickens*) to acquiesce in some falsehood; to make pretence. **three-bottle man** a man able to drink three bottles of wine without seeming the worse for it.

bottle² /*bot'l*/ *n* a bundle (of hay). [OFr *botel*]

bottom /*bot'əm*/ *n* the lowest part or surface of anything; that on which anything rests or is founded; the part of the body one sits on, buttocks; the bed of the sea, a river, etc; the seat of a chair; the less dignified or important end (of a table, class, etc); the foot of a page, hill, etc; (often *pl*) the lower part of a two-piece garment; low land, eg by a river; the lower part of a ship, hence the ship itself; groundwork, foundation; the fundamental character or ingredient; staying power, stamina; solidity of character; financial resources; the portion of a wig hanging down over the shoulder; (*usu* in *pl*) the dregs or sediment resulting from various industrial processes; a ball of thread (*Shakesp*). ◆ *adj* undermost, lowest; fundamental; (of a quark) having bottomness (*phys*). ◆ *vt* to put a bottom on; to ground or base (*esp* with *on* or *upon*); to get to the bottom of, understand fully; to get to the bottom of (a mine, etc; *Aust*; also *vi*); to wind (*Shakesp*). ◆ *vi* to find bottom; to found, rest. [OE *botm*; Ger *Boden*; cognate with L *fundus* bottom, Gaelic *bonn* the sole]

■ **bott'omed** *adj*. **bott'omless** *adj* having no bottom; very deep; limitless. **bott'ommost** /-*mōst* or -*mast*/ *adj* nearest the bottom. **bott'omness** *n* a property that characterizes quarks and hadrons, conserved in strong and electromagnetic interactions between particles (also **beauty**). **bott'omry** *n* (*law*) the practice of obtaining a loan (to finance a sea voyage) using the ship as security.

□ **bottom dead centre** see **outer dead centre** under **outer**. **bottom drawer** *n* the drawer or any supposed place in which a young woman keeps articles for use after her marriage; a collection of articles kept for marriage. **bottom end** *n* the big end in a vertical internal combustion engine. **bottom feeder** *n* a fish that feeds on the bed of the sea, a lake, etc (also **bottom fish**); a despicable person (*sl*). **bottom fisher** *n* (*stock exchange sl*) an investor who seeks to buy shares in badly performing companies in the hope that they will increase in value. **bott'om-glade** *n* (*Milton*) a glade or open space in a bottom or valley. **bott'om-grass** *n* (*Shakesp*) grass growing on low ground. **bott'om-heav'y** *adj* having the lower part too heavy or large in proportion to

the upper. **bott'om-hole assembly** *n* (*mining*) the drilling string attached to the bottom of the drilling pipe, comprising the drill bit and collars to maintain direction. **bottom house** *n* (*W Indies*) the open area below a house that rests on pillars, sometimes enclosed and occupied. **bott'om-land** *n* (*US*) alluvial deposits. **bottomless pit** *n* a resource that can never be exhausted; (with *caps*; with *the*) Hell. **bottom line** *n* the final line of a financial statement, showing net profit or loss; the essential factor in a situation. **bott'om-sawyer** *n* the sawyer who works at the bottom of the saw-pit. **bott'om-up** *adj* (of eg business strategy, computer programming, etc) based on the requirements or desires of the users rather than on a centralized decision taken by the business managers or computer programmers.

■ **at bottom** fundamentally. **at the bottom of** the real origin or cause of. **bet one's bottom dollar on** (*inf*) to bet all one has on, be absolutely certain about. **bottom out** (*US* **base out**) of prices, etc, to reach and settle at the lowest level, *esp* just before a rise. **bottoms up** an interjection used when drinking a toast. **from the bottom of one's heart** with heartfelt sincerity. **get to the bottom of** to discover the explanation of. **stand on one's own bottom** (*obs*) to be independent. **the bottom has fallen out of the market** there has been a sudden reduction in the market demand (for something). **touch** or **hit bottom** to reach the lowest point.

bottony see **botoné**.

botty /*bot'i*/ *n* a child's or slang word for (a person's) **bottom**.

botulism /*bot'ū-li-zm*/ *n* severe, often fatal, poisoning by tinned or other food carrying a **botulinum toxin** or **botulin**, a powerful bacterial poison produced by the *Bacillus botulinus* (or *Clostridium botulinum*) organism. [L *botulus* sausage, from the shape of the bacteria]

boubou /*boo'boo*/ *n* any of various African shrikes of the genus *Laniarius*, the male and female of which often sing in pairs. [From an African name]

bouche /*boosh*/ (*Fr*) *n* the staff of cooks in a large house.

bouché /*boo-shā'*/ (*Fr*) *adj* stoppered; corked while still fermenting.

bouchée /*boo-shā'*/ (*Fr*) *n* a small sweet or savoury pastry.

bouclé /*boo-klā'*/ *adj* (of a yarn) having the threads looped to give a bulky effect. ◆ *n* such a yarn; a fabric made of such a yarn. [Fr, curled, looped]

bouderie /*boo-d(ə-)rē'*/ (*Fr*) *n* pouting, sulking.

boudoir /*boo'dwär*/ *n* a woman's private room. [Fr, from *bouder* to pout, to be sulky]

□ **boudoir grand** *n* a small grand piano, slightly bigger than a baby grand (qv).

bouffant /*boo'fã*/ *adj* (of a hairstyle or the style of an article of clothing) puffed out, full, bulging. [Fr]

bouffe see **opera bouffe** under **opera¹**.

bougainvillaea or **bougainvillea** /*boo-gən-vil'i-ə* or -*vi-lē'ə*/ *n* any member of a tropical American genus (*Bougainvillea*) of Nyctaginaceae, frequently trained over trellises, its triplets of flowers almost concealed by rosy or purple bracts (also **bougainvil'ia**). [From the first French circumnavigator of the globe, Louis Antoine de Bougainville (1729–1811)]

bouge a Shakespearean form of **budge¹**.

bouget a Spenserian form of **budget¹**.

bough /*bow*/ *n* a branch of a tree; the gallows. [OE *bōg*, *bōh* an arm, the shoulder; Ger *Bug* shoulder, the bow of a ship, from OE *būgan* to bend]

□ **bough'pot** *n* (*archaic*) a pot for boughs as an ornament; a flowerpot; a bunch of flowers.

bought¹, **boughten** see **buy**.

bought² /*bowt*/ (*obs*) *n* a bend or curve; a twist or coil (*Spenser*). [See **bight**]

bougie /*boo'zhē*/ *n* a wax candle; a medical instrument (*orig* of waxed linen) for distending contracted body passages, or for calibration, applying medication, etc. [Fr, a wax candle, from *Bougie* in Algeria]

bouillabaisse /*boo-ya-bes'* or -*bās'*/ *n* a Provençal spiced soup made of fish and vegetables. [Fr]

bouilli /*boo'yē*/ *n* boiled or stewed meat. [Fr; see **boil¹**]

■ **bouillon** /*boo'yõ*/ *n* a strong broth.

bouillotte /*boo-yot'*/ *n* a gambling card game resembling poker. [Fr]

bouk /*book*/ (*Scot*) *n* body; bulk. [OE *būc* belly, ON *būkr*, coalescing with **bulk¹**]

Boul. *abbrev* : Boulevard.

boulder /*bōl'dər*/ *n* a large stone rounded by the action of water; a mass of rock transported by natural agencies from its native bed (*geol*). ◆ *adj* containing boulders. [Origin obscure; Swed dialect *bullersten*, large stone in a stream, has been compared]

■ **bould'ering** n climbing carried out on large boulders.
❑ **boulder clay** n a stiff stony mass of finely ground rock, usu containing boulders and pebbles, deposited as a ground moraine under land-ice.

boule[1] see **buhl**.

boule[2] /boo'lē or -lā/ n the parliament of modern Greece; a council or senate in ancient Greece. [Gr boulē]

boules /bool/ n pl (but usu sing in construction) a French form of bowls played on rough surfaces, pétanque. [Fr]

boulevard /boo'lə-vär(d) or bool'vär(d)/ n a broad road, walk, or promenade bordered with trees; a broad main road; a strip of grass between pavement and road or the centre strip between two carriageways (chiefly Can). [Fr (orig applied to a road built on demolished town fortifications), from MDu bollewerc; see **bulwark**]
■ **boulevardier** /bool-vär'dyā/ n a frequenter of boulevards or promenades, chiefly of Paris; a man-about-town.

bouleversement /bool-vers-mä'/ n an overturning; overthrow, ruin. [Fr]

boulle see **buhl**.

boult or **bolt** /bōlt/ vt to sift through coarse cloth; to examine by sifting. [OFr bulter, from buleter, appar from bure, from LL burra a coarse reddish-brown cloth, from Gr pyrrhos reddish]
■ **boult'er** or **bolt'er** n a sieve; a machine for separating bran from flour. **boult'ing** or **bolt'ing** n.
❑ **boulting** or **bolting cloth** n a firm silk or nylon fabric with various mesh sizes used for boulting meal or flour, for embroidery, or for photographic enlargements. **boult'ing-hutch** or **bolt'ing-hutch** n a hutch or large box into which flour falls when it is boulted.

boun or **bowne** /boon or bown/ vt (used reflexively) and vi to prepare; to get ready; to dress; to set out. ◆ adj ready. [See **bound**[2]; revived by Sir Walter Scott]

bounce[1] /bowns/ vi to jump or spring suddenly; to spring up or back like a ball; to burst (into or out of a room, etc); (of a cheque) to come back to the payee unredeemed because of lack of funds in the drawer's account; (of an email message) to be returned to the sender without reaching the intended recipient; to boast, to exaggerate. ◆ vt to cause to rebound; (of a bank) to return (a cheque) to the payee unredeemed; to turn out, eject, dismiss; to hustle, force; to reprimand, bring to book (sl); to beat (obs). ◆ n a thud; a leap or spring; springiness; resilience, vitality; an improvement after a period of decline (inf); boasting, a bold lie; dismissal (US inf). ◆ adv and interj expressing sudden or bouncing movement or (formerly) the noise of a gun. [Du bonzen to strike, from bons a blow]
■ **bounc'er** n a person or thing that bounces; a cheque that bounces (inf); a short-pitched fast delivery bowled so as to bounce and rise sharply off the ground (cricket); a person employed to eject undesirable people from a club, dance hall, etc, or to prevent them from entering (inf); something big; a bully; a liar. **boun'cily** adv. **boun'ciness** n. **bounc'ing** adj large and heavy; energetic; hearty. **bounc'y** adj prone to bouncing or full of bounce; lively, cocky; vigorous, resilient.
❑ **bouncy castle** n an inflatable piece of play equipment consisting of a base and sides in the shape of a castle, for children to jump around in.
■ **bounce back** to recover quickly and easily. **on the bounce** (inf) in succession, without a break.

bounce[2] /bowns/ n the lesser spotted dogfish.

bound[1] /bownd/ pat and pap of **bind**. adj tied, fastened; (of books) provided with a binding; in linguistics, of a morpheme that cannot stand alone but only occurs as part of a word, eg the plural marker -s. ◆ combining form restricted to, or by, something specified, eg housebound, stormbound.
❑ **bound'-bailiff** n a sheriff's officer, so called from his bond given to the sheriff for the discharge of his duty.
■ **bound to** obliged to (a person, etc); certain to (do something) (perh partly from **bound**[2]). **bound up with** closely linked with.

bound[2] /bownd/ adj ready to start (for); on the way to (with for, or following an adv, eg homeward bound; also as combining form, eg in southbound); ready, prepared (obs). See also **bound**[1]. [ON búinn, pap of búa to prepare; cf **boun**]

bound[3] /bownd/ n a limit; the upper or lower value in a range of possible values (stats); (in pl) the limit of that which is reasonable or permitted; (in pl) a borderland, land generally within certain understood limits, the district. ◆ vt to set bounds to, to limit or restrain; to surround or form the boundary of. [OFr bonne, from LL bodina; cf Breton bonn, a boundary]
■ **bound'ed** adj restricted, cramped; surrounded. **bound'less** adj having no limit; vast. **bound'lessness** n.
❑ **bound water** n (bot) water held by colloidal interaction and capillary forces.

■ **out of bounds** not to be visited, entered, etc; in such a prohibited place.

bound[4] /bownd/ vi to spring or leap; to move or run with leaps; rebound. ◆ n a spring or leap. [Fr bondir to spring, in OFr to resound, from L bombitāre]
■ **bound'er** n a person who bounds; a person whose moral conduct is objectionable (old sl). **bound'ing** adj.
■ **by leaps and bounds** by startlingly rapid stages.

boundary /bown'də-ri or -dri/ n a limit; a border; termination, final limit; a line marking the limit of a cricket field; a hit to the limit of a cricket ground; a score for such a hit (four or six runs). [**bound**[3]]
❑ **boundary condition** n (maths) a condition that must be met for the solution of a set of differential equations. **boundary layer** n the very thin layer of air on the surface of an aircraft whose viscosity affects the aircraft's velocity, causing turbulence to build up and thereby increasing drag (**boundary-layer control** the removal of the boundary layer by a suction system or other means). **boundary rider** n (Aust) a person who is responsible for the maintenance of fences on a station.

bounden /bownd'n/ adj obligatory, esp in the phrase one's bounden duty. [Archaic pap of **bind**]

bountree /boon'tri/ see **bourtree**.

bounty /bown'ti/ n generosity in bestowing gifts; the gift bestowed; money offered as a reward or premium in general or, formerly, an inducement to enter the army, or (**king's** or **queen's bounty**) to a mother who has three or more children at a birth. [OFr bontet (Mod Fr bonté) goodness, from L bonitās, -ātis, from bonus good]
■ **boun'teous** or **boun'tiful** adj generous in giving; abundant, plentiful. **boun'teously** or **boun'tifully** adv. **boun'teousness** or **boun'tifulness** n. **boun'tyhed** n (Spenser).
❑ **bounty hunter** n a person who hunts down wanted criminals, or anything for which a reward has been offered.
■ **Lady Bountiful** the charitable great lady of a district; an ironic name for a patronizingly generous female do-gooder.

bouquet /boo-kā' or boo'kā/ n a bunch of flowers; the perfume given off by wine; a compliment, praise. [Fr bouquet, dimin of bois a wood; cf Ital bosco; see **boscage**, **bush**[1]]
■ **bouquetière** /boo-k(ə)-tyer'/ n a flower girl.
❑ **bouquet garni** /boo'kā gär-nē'/ n a bunch or sachet of herbs used as flavouring, removed before the dish is served (Fr, garnished bouquet).

Bourbon /boor'bon or bûr'/ n a member of the European royal family which ruled in France and elsewhere between the 16th and 20th centuries; a political reactionary (US); a hybrid variety of rose; (without cap; usu /bûr'bən/) maize whiskey (orig made in Bourbon County, Kentucky).
■ **Bour'bonism** n. **Bour'bonist** n an adherent of the Bourbons.
❑ **Bourbon biscuit** n two chocolate-flavoured pieces of biscuit with chocolate cream between.

bourd /boord/ (obs) n a jest, fun. [OFr bourde, of unknown origin]
■ **bourd'er** n a jester.

bourdon[1] /boor'dən/ n a drone bass of a bagpipe; a bass stop in an organ or harmonium; the bass accompaniment to a melody (obs). [See **burden**[2]]

bourdon[2] /boor'dən/ (obs) n a pilgrim's staff; a club. [Fr, from LL burdō, -ōnis a mule]

Bourdon gauge /bör' or boor'dən gāj/ n a type of gauge for measuring the pressure of gases or liquids. [E Bourdon (1808–84), French engineer]

bourg /boorg/ n a town, esp beside a castle; a market-town. [Fr]

bourgeois[1] /boorzh'wä/ n (pl bourg'eois) (also fem bourg'eoise) a member of the middle class; a merchant or shopkeeper; a person with capitalist, materialistic or conventional values. ◆ adj middle-class; conventional; humdrum; conservative; capitalist; materialistic. [Fr, a citizen]
■ **bourgeoisie** /boor'zhwä-zē or -zē'/ n the middle class of citizens, esp seen as capitalistic, materialistic, etc. **bourgeoisificā'tion** n. **bourgeois'ify** vt to convert to a bourgeois way of thinking or living.

bourgeois[2] /bûr-jois'/ n an old type size, larger than brevier and smaller than longprimer, approx 9-point. [Fr; perh from the name of the type founder]

bourgeon see **burgeon**.

bourguignon /boor-gē-nyõ'/ (cookery) adj (of meat dishes) stewed with onion, mushrooms and Burgundy wine. See also **boeuf bourguignon**. [Fr, Burgundian]

Bourignian /boo-rin'yən or -i-ən/ adj of or relating to Antoinette Bourignon (1616–80), a religious visionary for whom religion consisted in inward emotion, not in knowledge or practice.

bourkha same as **burka**.

─────────────────────

■ words derived from main entry word; ❑ compound words; ■ idioms and phrasal verbs

bourlaw see **byrlaw**.

bourn[1] or **bourne** /boorn, börn or bôrn/ (archaic) n a boundary, limit or goal; domain (Keats). [Fr borne a limit]

bourn[2] or **bourne** /boorn, börn or bôrn/ (S Eng) n a stream; a dry chalk bed that is liable to be flooded. [Ety as for **burn**[2]]

bourrée /boo'rā or -rā'/ n a brisk dance in duple time, from the Auvergne or the Basque provinces; a musical composition in the same rhythm. [Fr]

bourse /boors/ n an exchange where merchants meet for business; any European stock exchange, esp (with cap) that in Paris. [Fr; see **purse**]

boursier /boor-syā'/ (Fr) n a scholar maintained by a foundation; a speculator on the exchange.

bourtree or **boortree** /boor'tri/ (Scot) n the elder-tree (also **bountree** /boon'tri/). [Ety unknown]
□ **bour'tree-gun** n a popgun made of an elder twig.

bouse[1] /booz or bowz/ vi and n archaic form of **booze**. [ME busen, appar from MDu būsen to drink excessively]
■ **bous'ing** or **bous'y** adj. **bous'ingken** n (obs criminal sl) a low drinking-shop.

bouse[2] or **bowse** /bows/ (chiefly naut) vt and vi to haul with tackle. [Origin unknown]

boustrophedon /bow-stro-fē'don or boo-/ adj and adv (of ancient writing) alternately from right to left and from left to right. [Gr boustrophēdon turning like ploughing oxen, from bous ox, and strophē a turning]

bout /bowt/ n a turn or period of time doing something; a stint; in boxing or wrestling, a contest; a fit or attack (of an illness). [**bought**[2]]

boutade /boo-täd'/ (formal) n a sudden outburst. [Fr, from bouter to thrust]

boutique /boo-tēk'/ n a small shop; a department in a shop; in the 1960s, used esp for a small, expensive, exclusive dress shop for women; now, a small shop, or a department in a shop, selling fashionable clothes, etc; a small specialist business or agency operating within a larger business sphere, esp advertising, accountancy or investment services. ◆ adj small, specialist, exclusive. [Fr]
□ **boutique hotel** n a usu small hotel, with an intimate and individualistic atmosphere and style.

bouton /boo-tɔ̃'/ n an enlargement of the end of a nerve fibre in contact with part of another nerve fibre. [Fr, button]
■ **boutonné** or **boutonnée** /-ton-ā/ adj reticent, buttoned-up. **boutonnière** /-to-nyer/ n a flower for the buttonhole, etc.
□ **boutonnière deformity** n (med) a type of deformity in which a finger is bent down at the middle joint and bent back up at the end joint as the result of a buttonhole-shaped tear in a tendon.

bouts rimés /boo rē-mā'/ n pl rhyming words given out by someone as the line-endings of a stanza, for others to fill up the lines. [Fr, rhymed ends]

bouvier /boo'vyā or -vi-ā/ n a large rough-coated dog orig bred in Flanders to herd and guard cattle. [Fr]

bouzouki /boo-zoo'ki/ n a metal-stringed instrument like a large long-necked mandolin, used esp in Greece (also **bazou'ki** /bə-/). [Mod Gr]

bovate /bō'vāt/ (hist) n an oxgang. [LL bovāta, from bōs, bovis an ox]

bovid /bō'vid/ adj belonging to the family **Bo'vidae**, which includes not only cattle but also other ruminants such as sheep and goats (also n). [New L Bovidae, from L bōs, bovis an ox]

bovine /bō'vīn/ adj of or relating to cattle; stupid, dull. ◆ n an animal of the cattle family. [L bōs, bovis an ox or cow]
■ **bo'vinely** adv.
□ **bovine somatotrophin** n a hormone drug that increases milk production in cattle. **bovine spongiform encephalopathy** n an infectious degenerative brain disease of cattle, thought to be related to Creutzfeldt-Jakob disease, orig caused by cattle feed processed from scrapie-infected sheep remains (usu abbrev **BSE**).

Bovril® /bov'ril/ n a concentrated beef extract used to make drinks, to flavour meat dishes, etc. [L bōs, bovis ox, cow]

bovver /bov'ər/ (old sl) n rowdy or violent behaviour by street gangs (also adj). [Prob Cockney pronunciation of **bother**]
□ **bovver boy** n a member of a gang of hooligans in the habit of engaging in street fights using heavy, hobnailed boots (**bovver boots**) to kick their opponents; a troublemaker, esp one who uses rough methods.

bow[1] /bow/ vi to bend; to bend the neck or body in greeting, acknowledging a compliment, etc; to submit (to). ◆ vt to bend or incline downwards; to crush down; to usher with a bow; to express by a bow. ◆ n a bending of the neck or body as a formal or respectful greeting, or to acknowledge applause, etc. [OE būgan to bend; cognate with L fugere to flee, to yield]
■ **bowed** /bowd/ adj bent forward.
■ **a bowing acquaintance** a slight acquaintance. **bow and scrape** to kowtow, to ingratiate oneself sycophantically. **bow in** to make a first appearance in public. **bow out** to withdraw or retire from a place, situation, etc. **make one's bow** to retire ceremoniously; to leave the stage. **take a bow** to acknowledge applause or recognition.

bow[2] /bō/ n a piece of flexible wood or other material for shooting arrows, bent by means of a string stretched between its ends; anything of a bent or curved shape, such as the rainbow; a bow-shaped strip for collecting current from an overhead wire (elec eng); a yoke (Shakesp); a rod (orig curved but now nearly straight) strung with horsehair, by which the strings of a violin, etc are played; a ring of metal forming a handle; the frame surrounding the lenses, or the curved end of the leg of spectacles (US); a bowknot; a looped knot of ribbons; a bow tie; a single movement (up or down) or stroke of the bow in playing an instrument. ◆ vi to handle the bow in playing. ◆ vt to play (an instrument) with a bow; to mark (for stringed instruments) which notes should be played downbow and which upbow. [OE boga; cognate with Ger Bogen]
■ **bow'ing** n the technique of playing a stringed instrument with a bow; the marking of the upbows and downbows. **bow'yer** n a bowman; a maker of bows for archery.
□ **bow'-backed** adj with bent back. **bow'bent** adj (Milton) bent like a bow. **bow'-boy** n a boy archer; Cupid (Shakesp). **bow'-compasses** n pl a small pair of compasses, often with a bow-shaped spring instead of a hinge. **bow'fin** n a N American freshwater fish (genus Amia) of the order Holostei. **bow'-fronted** adj having a convex front. **bow'-hand** n the hand in which the bow is held, normally in archery, the left, in stringed instrument-playing, the right. **bow'head** n an Arctic right whale (Balaena mysticetus), with a large head and arched jaw. **bow'knot** n a (usu decorative) knot with one or two loops. **bow leg** n a bandy leg like a bow. **bow'-legged** /-legd or -leg-id/ adj. **bow'man** n an archer. **bow'saw** n a saw with a narrow blade stretched like a bowstring in a strong bow-shaped frame (also **log'-saw**); a saw with a narrow blade stretched in an H-shaped frame and held taut by tightening a cord at the opposite end of the frame. **bow'shot** n the distance to which an arrow can be shot from a bow. **bow'string** n the string by which a bow is drawn; a string with which the Turks strangled offenders (hist); a horizontal tie on a bridge or girder. ◆ vt (pat and pap **bow'stringed**, sometimes **bow'strung**) to strangle with a bowstring. ◆ adj of, for or having a bowstring. **bow'string-hemp** n the genus Sanseviera or its fibre. **bow tie** n a necktie tied in a two-looped bowknot, often for formal wear. **bow'-tied** adj wearing a bow tie. **bow window** n a window projecting in a curve; a pot-belly (obs sl). **bow-win'dowed** adj.
■ **draw the long bow** to make extravagant statements. **on the bow hand** wide of the mark. **two strings to one's bow** an alternative in reserve.

bow[3] /bow/ n the forepart of a ship or boat, often used in pl, the ship, etc being considered to have starboard and port bows, meeting at the stem; the rower nearest the bow (rowing). [From a LGer, Du or Scand word for shoulder; see **bough**]
■ **bow'er** or **bow'er-anchor** n an anchor at the bow (best-bower and small-bower).
□ **bow'man** n the rower nearest the bow. **bow'-oar** n the oar nearest the bow. **bow'-side** n (rowing) the rowers on the same side as bow. **bow wave** n the wave created by the bow of a moving vessel; a shock wave (fig).
■ **bold** or **bluff bow** a broad bow. **lean bow** a narrow bow. **on the (port** or **starboard) bow** within 45° (to port or starboard) of the point right ahead.

bowat, bowet or **buat** /boo'ət/ (Scot) n a lantern. [LL boeta box]
■ **MacFarlane's buat** (Walter Scott) the moon.

bowdlerize or **-ise** /bow'dlə-rīz/ vt to expurgate a book or writing, by removing whatever might be considered indelicate, esp to do so unnecessarily. [Dr T Bowdler (1754–1825), who published an expurgated Shakespeare in ten volumes in 1818]
■ **bowd'lerism** n. **bowdleriza'tion** or **-s-** n. **bowd'lerizer** or **-s-** n.

bowel /bow'əl/ n an interior part of the body, now esp the large intestine; (in pl) the entrails, intestines; (in pl) the innermost, interior part of anything; (in pl) feelings of pity, tenderness (obs, Bible and Shakesp). ◆ vt (**bow'elling; bow'elled**) (obs) to take out the bowels of. [OFr boel, from L botellus a sausage, an intestine]
□ **bowel movement** n an instance or act of excretion or defecation; faeces, excrement.

bower[1] /bow'ər/ n a shady enclosure or recess in a garden, an arbour; an inner apartment (archaic); a lady's private room, boudoir (poetic); a dwelling (poetic). ◆ vt to enclose; to embower (Shakesp). ◆ vi (Spenser) to lodge. [OE būr a chamber, from root of būan to dwell]
■ **bow'ery** adj leafy, shady.

❑ **bow'erbird** *n* a bird native to Australia and New Guinea that makes a bower adorned with colourful feathers, shells, etc; a person who collects useless bits and pieces (*Aust inf*). **bow'erwoman** *n* (*archaic*) a chambermaid, lady's maid.

bower² /*bow'ər*/ *n* the name in euchre for the two highest cards, the jack of trumps, and the other jack of the same colour, the **right bower** and **left bower** respectively. [Ger *Bauer* peasant, jack at cards]

bower³, bower-anchor see under **bow³**.

bowery /*bow'ə-ri*/ *n* (*archaic US*) a farm. [Du *bouwerij*]
■ **the Bowery** a street in New York frequented by tramps and drunks.

bowes a Miltonic spelling of **boughs** (*pl* of **bough**).

bowet see **bowat**.

bowget obsolete variant of **budget¹**.

bowie knife /*bō'i* or (*US*) *boo'i nīf*/ *n* a strong, one-edged dagger-knife with a blade about 12 inches long. [James Bowie (1790–1836), US colonel who popularized it, and perhaps invented it]

bowl¹ /*bōl*/ *n* a vessel, characteristically of approximately hemispherical shape, for domestic use; a round drinking cup, more wide than deep; drink, alcohol; a bowlful; the round hollow part of anything; a large bowl-shaped structure, stadium, etc. [OE *bolla*]
■ **bowl'ful** *n* (*pl* **bowl'fuls**) as much as fills a bowl.

bowl² /*bōl*/ *n* a heavy wooden ball with a bias (qv); (in *pl*, treated as *sing*) a game played by rolling such balls on a green towards a jack; (in *pl*, treated as *sing*) sometimes the game of skittles (ninepins) or American bowls (tenpins); a ball (*obs*); a marble; (in *pl*, treated as *sing*) the game of marbles. ◆ *vi* to play at ninepin or tenpin bowling; to roll or trundle (*esp* with *on* or *along*); to travel swiftly and smoothly in a wheeled vehicle (*usu* with *along*); to deliver a ball to the batsman at the wicket (*cricket*); to take one's turn at bowling. ◆ *vt* to roll or trundle; to deliver (a ball) to the batsman (*cricket*); to dismiss (a batsman) by hitting the wicket with a bowled ball (also with *out*). [Fr *boule* ball, from L *bulla*]
■ **bowled** *adj* (*cricket*) dismissed (by having one's wicket hit) when a specified person was the bowler. **bowl'er** *n* a person who plays at bowls or bowling, or who bowls in cricket. **bowl'ing** *n* and *adj*.
❑ **bowling alley** *n* a long narrow covered place for ninepin or tenpin bowling; a building where tenpin bowling is played. **bowling crease** see under **crease¹**. **bowling green** *n* a smooth grassy plot for bowls.
■ **bowl over** to knock down; to overwhelm, thoroughly impress or delight (*inf*).

bowlder /*bōl'dər*/ *n* same as **boulder**.

bowler¹ /*bō'lər*/ *n* a stiff felt hat with a round crown and narrow brim. [Said to be the name of a hatter who made it in 1850]
❑ **bowler hat** *n* a bowler. ◆ *vt* (with *hyphen*; *orig milit sl*) to discharge, dismiss.

bowler² see under **bowl²**.

bowline /*bō'lin* or *-līn*/ *n* a rope from the weather side of the square sails to the larboard or starboard bow, to keep the sail close to the wind (*naut*); (also **bowline knot**) a simple knot which makes a loop that will not slip at the end of a rope. [MLGer *bōline*, MDu *boechlijne*]

bowne see **boun**.

bowpot same as **boughpot** (see under **bough**).

bowr /*bowr*/ (*Spenser*) *n* a muscle. [**bow¹** to bend]

bowse see **bouse²**.

bowser /*bow'zər*/ *n* a light tanker for supplying fuel or water; a petrol pump (*old*; now *Aust* and *NZ*). [Orig a tradename]

bowsie /*bow'zi*/ (*Irish*) *n* a disreputable low-class person. [Origin uncertain]

bowsprit /*bō'sprit*/ (*naut*) *n* a strong spar projecting over the bows of a ship. [MLGer *bōgsprēt*, MDu *boechspriet*]

bowwow /*bow'wow*/ *n* a dog (*childish* or *facetious*); /*bow-wow'*/ a dog's bark. [Imit]

bowyang /*bō'yang*/ (*Aust inf*) *n* (*usu* in *pl*) straps or strings tied round each trouser-leg below the knee by outdoor labourers. ◆ *adj* limited in outlook, hick. [UK dialect variations may derive from the Australian; origin unknown]

bowyer see under **bow²**.

box¹ /*boks*/ *n* a case or receptacle (*usu* with four sides and a lid) for holding anything; a compartment or cubicle; a pigeonhole, *esp* a numbered one for mail; a small house or lodge, such as a *shooting-box*, etc; in a theatre, a small enclosure with several seats; an old square pew or similar enclosure, such as a *sentry-box*, *signal-box*, *witness box*, etc; the batter's standing-place (*baseball*); the penalty box (*football*); a coffin (*inf*); the driver's seat on a carriage; a case for protecting machinery, etc; a gearbox; the case of a ship's compass; a predicament; an accidental mixing of flocks of sheep (*Aust* and *NZ*); a light, *usu* padded shield covering the genitals (*sport, esp cricket*); part of a printed page enclosed within lines, etc; the contents of a box; a

fund; a (Christmas) present; a stock or package of units put together for unit trusts (*finance*); the vagina (*vulgar sl*). ◆ *vt* to put into or provide with a box or boxes; to enclose, confine (often with *in* or *up*); to overturn (a watchman) in his box (*obs sl*); to mix (eg flocks of sheep) (*Aust* and *NZ*); to make a cut in the trunk of (a tree) to collect the sap. [OE *box*, from L *buxem*, accusative of *buxis* from Gr *pyxis* a box]
■ **box'ful** *n* (*pl* **box'fuls**) as much as a box will hold. **box'iness** *n*. **box'y** *adj* shaped like a box; (of clothes) having a square appearance; (of reproduced music) sounding as if recorded in a box.
❑ **box and whisker plot** see **boxplot** below. **box beam** *n* a box girder. **box'-bed** *n* a kind of bed formerly common in Scotland, often in a living room or kitchen, with its ends, sides and roof of wood, and sometimes capable of being closed in front by two sliding panels. **box'board** *n* a sturdy cardboard used to make boxes. **box camera** *n* a simple box-shaped camera. **box canyon** *n* (*N Am*) a narrow canyon with almost vertical sides. **box'car** *n* (*N Am*) a box-wagon. **box'-cloth** *n* a heavy cloth for riding garments. **box'-coat** *n* a short loose coat; a heavy overcoat worn by those travelling on the outside of a coach (*obs*). **box cutter** *n* (*chiefly US*) a short knife with a renewable, sharp blade. **box'-day** *n* (*obs*) one of the Court of Session vacation days when papers ordered to be deposited in court had to be lodged. **boxed set** or **box set** *n* a collection of several similar items packaged as a single unit. **box file** *n* a box-shaped container with a spring clip for holding documents steady, capable of holding many or *esp* bulky items. **box'-fish** see **coffer-fish** under **coffer**. **box'-frame** *n* a box-shaped framework of a building. **box girder** *n* a hollow, square or rectangular girder, often used in bridge construction. **box'-haul** *vt* to veer (a square-rigged ship) hard round. **Boxing Day** *n* the day after Christmas, when boxes or presents were traditionally given to employees, etc; the first weekday after Christmas, observed as a public holiday. **box'-iron** *n* a hollow smoothing-iron in which a heater is placed. **box jellyfish** *n* (*Aust*) any of several tropical jellyfish with venomous tentacles. **box junction** *n* an area at a crossroads or other road junction, marked with yellow criss-cross lines, into which a vehicle may not move unless its exit is clear. **box'keeper** *n* (*obs*) an attendant who opens the doors of boxes at theatres, etc. **box kite** *n* a kite composed of open-ended boxes. **box'-lobby** *n* the lobby leading to the boxes in a theatre. **box number** *n* a number to which replies, eg to advertisements, may be sent either at a post office or a newspaper. **box office** *n* in a theatre, etc, the office at which seats may be booked; receipts from a play, etc; ability to draw an audience; an attraction as judged by the box office. **box'-office** *adj*. **box'-pleat** *n* a type of double pleat formed by folding the cloth under in both directions. **box'-pleated** *adj*. **box'plot** or **box and whisker plot** *n* a method of displaying statistical data by means of a box representing the values between the 25th and 75th percentile, divided by a horizontal line representing the median, and two terminated lines representing the maximum and minimum values respectively. **box profits** *n pl* profits made by financial managers when buying and selling units for unit trusts. **box'room** *n* a room (*esp* a small room without an outside window) in which boxes, etc, are stored, sometimes pressed into service as a bedroom. **box seat** *n* a driver's seat on a coach; a seat in a box in a theatre, etc; a commanding or favourable position (*inf*). **box set** see **boxed set** above. **box'-spanner** *n* a spanner consisting of a cylindrical piece of steel shaped at one or both ends into a hexagon to fit over the appropriate nut, and turned by a rod inserted through a hole at the opposite end. **box spring** *n* one of a set of spiral springs in an open box-shaped frame as part of a mattress. **box van** *n* a motor van with a box-shaped goods compartment. **box'-wagon** *n* a closed railway goods-wagon. **box'wallah** *n* (*Ind*) (see **wallah**) a pedlar; a businessman or shopkeeper (*derog*).
■ **box the compass** to name the 32 compass points in order in either or both directions; to make a complete turnaround in any opinion. **in the wrong box** in a false position, in a scrape. **the box** (*inf*) the television set; television. **the whole box and dice** (*Aust* and *NZ*) the whole lot. **think outside the box** to disregard conventional thinking in order to achieve an original solution to a problem.

box² /*boks*/ *n* a blow on the head or ear with the hand. ◆ *vt* to strike with the hand or fist, *esp* in a boxing match. ◆ *vi* to fight with the fists, *esp* in a boxing match. ◆ *vt* and *vi* (*Scot*) to butt. [Poss connected with Gr *pyx* with the fist]
■ **box'er** *n* a person who boxes or is skilled in boxing; a medium-sized, smooth-haired dog of a breed, with bulldog blood, developed in Germany; (with *cap*) a member of a Chinese society hostile to foreigners, the name arising from a Chinese phrase literally meaning 'righteous harmonious fist' (*hist*); (in *pl*) boxer shorts. **box'ing** *n* the act or art of fighting with the fists, *esp* now as a sport; a fight with the fists.
❑ **boxer shorts** *n pl* loose shorts as worn by boxers; loose-fitting underpants for men, with an elasticated waistband and front opening (also **box'ers**). **boxing glove** *n* a padded glove worn in boxing.
■ **box clever** to act in a clever or cunning way.

box 183 **brachy-**

box³ /boks/ n an evergreen shrub or small tree (*Buxus sempervirens*) with hard smooth yellowish wood, often used to border garden-walks and flower-beds (also **box'-tree** or **box'wood**); its wood (also **box'wood**); extended to various other plants, *esp* the *Eucalyptus* genus. [OE *box*, from L *buxus*, from Gr *pyxos* the box-tree]
■ **box'en** *adj* made of or like boxwood.
❏ **box elder** n a N American maple, *Acer negundo*. **box'thorn** n a solanaceous shrub with red berries.

Box and Cox /boks and koks/ n pl two people who never meet, or who alternate in a place, job, etc. ♦ *adj* and *adv* alternating. [From the play *Cox and Box* in which two men rent the same room by night and day respectively; adapted (1847) by JM Morton from French farce, and made into a comic opera (1867) by FC Burnand and AS Sullivan]

box-calf /boks'käf/ n a chrome-tanned calfskin with rectangular markings made by rolling. [Said to be named after Joseph *Box*, a shoemaker]

boxercise /bok'sər-sīz/ n exercises combining elements of aerobics with movements simulating boxing blows. [From **box²** and **exercise**]

boxty /bok'sti/ n an Irish dish of potato griddle-cakes, eaten with various fillings. [Ir *bacstai*, from *bac* hob and *stai* open fire]

boy /boi/ n a male child; a lad; a son; a young man generally; (in Ireland and elsewhere) a man; in some countries a native or black servant or labourer (*offens*); a slave (*obs*); (in *pl*) a group of men with whom a man is friendly or familiar (*inf*); a man with a particular function, skill, etc, as in *backroom boy*; a camp-follower (*Shakesp*); a knave (*obs*). ♦ *vt* (*Shakesp*) to play (a female part) as a boy. ♦ *interj* same as **oh boy!** below. [ME *boi* boy; Fris *boi*; Du *boef*, Ger *Bube*]
■ **boy'hood** n. **boy'ish** *adj*. **boy'ishly** *adv*. **boy'ishness** n.
❏ **boy band** n a pop group, targeting mainly the teenage market, composed of young males chosen because they look good and can dance and sometimes even sing. **boy bishop** n a mock bishop formerly elected by choirboys or schoolboys, in office from St Nicholas's to Holy Innocents' Day (6–28 December). **boy'friend** n a girl's favourite boy for the time being; a male lover in a romantic or sexual relationship. **boy'-girl** *adj* of a romantic relationship between a young boy and girl; romantically sentimental. **boy'-meets-girl'** *adj* (often of love stories) following the traditional romantic pattern. **boy racer** n (*inf*) a male driver with a juvenile need to impress others with the speed and aggression of his driving. **Boys' Brigade** n a Christian organization for boys that aims to promote obedience, reverence, discipline, and self-respect. **Boy Scout** see **scout¹**. **boy's love** n southernwood. **boy's play** n trifling.
■ **boys will be boys** one must expect and put up with foolish or childish behaviour from men. **oh boy!** an expression of pleasure, enthusiasm, etc. **the boy next door** an ordinary young man, *esp* when regarded as a romantic partner. **the boys in blue** (*inf*) the police.

boyar /bo-yär' or boi'är/ n a member of the old Russian aristocracy next in rank to the ruling princes, before the reforms of Peter the Great. [Russ *boyarin*]

boyau /bwo'yō, bwä'yō or boi'ō/ (*fortif*) n (*pl* **bo'yaux**) a communication trench. [Fr, bowel]

boycott /boi'kot/ vt to refuse to take part in, deal with, handle by way of trade, etc; to shut out from all social and commercial intercourse. ♦ n an act of boycotting. [From Captain *Boycott* (1832–97) of County Mayo, who was so treated by his neighbours in December 1880]
■ **boy'cotter** n.

boyf /boif/ (*sl*) n a person's boyfriend.

Boyle's law see under **law¹**.

boyo /boi'ō/ (*sl*; *orig Irish* and *Welsh*) n (*pl* **boy'os**) a boy, young man. [**boy**]

boysenberry /boi'sən-be-ri/ n a fruit growing on a bramble, a hybrid of certain raspberries and blackberries. [Rudolph *Boysen* (1895–1950), US horticulturalist]

bozo /bō'zō/ (*sl*, *orig US*) n (*pl* **bo'zos**) a man, fellow, now *esp* a rather dim-witted one. [Prob Sp dialect *boso*, from Sp *vosotros* you (pl)]

bozzetto /bot-set'tō/ (*Ital*) n (*pl* **bozzet'ti** /-tē/) a small model or sketch of a projected sculpture.

BP *abbrev* : (used in radiocarbon dating, with 1950 as 'present') before present; (also **B/P**) bills payable; blood pressure; British Petroleum; British Pharmacopoeia.

Bp *abbrev* : Bishop.

bp *abbrev* : base pair (*biol*); (also **b/p**) bills payable; birthplace; bishop; blood pressure; boiling point.

BPC *abbrev* : British Pharmaceutical Codex.

BPharm *abbrev* : Bachelor of Pharmacy.

BPhil *abbrev* : *Baccalaureus Philosophiae* (L), Bachelor of Philosophy.

bpi (*comput*) *abbrev* : bits (or bytes) per inch.

b.pl. *abbrev* : birthplace.

BPM *abbrev* : (also **bpm**) beats per minute (in dance music).

BPS *abbrev* : British Psychological Society.

bps (*comput*) *abbrev* : bits per second.

Bq *symbol* : becquerel (SI unit).

BR *abbrev* : (also **B/R**) bills receivable; Brazil (IVR); formerly, British Rail.

Br (*chem*) *symbol* : bromine.

Br. *abbrev* : Britain; British; Brother.

br *abbrev* : bank rate; bedroom; (also **b/r**) bills receivable.

br. *abbrev* : branch; bridge; bronze; brother; brown.

bra /brä/ n short for **brassière**.
■ **bra'less** *adj* not wearing a brassière.

braaivleis /brī'flās/ (S Afr) n a barbecue party, often shortened to **braai**. [Afrik *braai* to grill, and *vleis* meat]

brabble /brab'l/ (*archaic*) vi to babble or clamour; to brawl or wrangle. ♦ n a clamorous contest, a brawl (*Shakesp*); a quibble. [Du *brabbelen* to stammer, to jabber]
■ **brabb'lement** n.

braccate /brak'āt/ (*zool*) *adj* having feathered legs or feet. [L *brācātus* wearing breeches]

braccio /brät'chō/ n (*pl* **braccia** /brät'chä/) an obsolete Italian measure of length, more than half a metre. [Ital, literally, arm]

brace /brās/ n anything that draws together and holds tightly; an instrument of wood or iron used by carpenters and metalworkers for turning boring tools; a type of bracket, { or }, connecting words, lines, staves of music, indicating that they are taken together, and also used as a third level of bracket in algebra, after round and square brackets; a pair or couple (*esp* of game shot); (in *pl*) straps worn over the shoulders for supporting the trousers; (often in *pl*) an appliance made of wire fitted over the teeth to straighten them; (in *pl*) ropes for squaring or traversing horizontally the yards of a ship; armour for the arm (*Shakesp*). ♦ vt to tighten or strengthen, to give firmness to; to steady and make (oneself) ready for a blow, etc; to tone up; to embrace, encompass (*Spenser*). [OFr *brace* (Fr *bras*) the arm, power, from L *brāchum*, *bracchium*, Gr *brachīōn*]
■ **brāc'er** n a person who or thing that braces; a strong alcoholic drink intended to give someone strength (*inf*); a wristguard. **brāc'ing** *adj* giving strength or tone; stimulating.
❏ **brace-and-bit'** n a brace with the drilling bit in place.

bracelet /brā'slit/ n an ornament for the wrist or ankle; a handcuff (*inf*). [Fr dimin, from L *brāchiāle*, from *brāchium*; see **brace**]

brach /brach/ n a dog for the chase, a bitch hound. [OFr *brachet*, pl *brachès*, dimin of *brac*, from LL *braccō*, of Gmc origin]
■ **brach'et** or **bratch'et** n a brach; a whelp; a brat.

brachia, **brachial**, **brachiate** see **brachium**.

brachiocephalic /brak-i-ō-se-fal'ik/ (*anat*) *adj* relating to the arms and head. [Gr *brachīōn* an arm, and *kephalē* head]

brachiopod /brak'i-ō-pod/ n a member of a phylum **Brachiopoda** /-op'o-də/ of shelled sea creatures related to worms and Polyzoa, having usually two long arm-like processes serving to waft food particles to the mouth. [Gr *brachīōn* an arm, and *pous*, *podos* a foot]

Brachiosaurus /brak-i-ō-sö'rəs/ n a genus of huge lizard-hipped plant-eating dinosaurs, unusual in that their front legs were longer than their back legs; (without *cap*) a member of the genus. [Gr *brachīōn* an arm, and *sauros* a lizard]

brachistochrone /bra-kis'tə-krōn or -tō-/ (*maths*) n the curve along which a particle acted on by a force (eg gravity) will pass in the shortest time from one given point to another. [Gr *brachistos*, superl of *brachys* short, and *chronos* time]

brachium /brā'kē-əm or brä-ki-ūm/ n (*pl* **bra'chia**) (*anat*) the upper part of the arm or forelimb. [L *brāchium*; see **brace**]
■ **brachial** /brāk' or brak'i-əl/ *adj* of the arm. **brach'iāte** *adj* having branches in pairs at right angles to the stem (*bot*); having arms (*zool*). ♦ vi (*zool*) to use the arms as a supplementary means of locomotion. **brachiā'tion** n.
❏ **brachial artery** n the great arterial trunk supplying the arm between the armpit and the elbow, direct continuation of the axillary artery. **brachium civile** /si-vī'lē/ n (L) the civil arm. **brachium seculare** /sek-ū-lā'rē or sā-ku-lä're/ n (L) the secular arm.

brachy- /bra-ki-/ combining form signifying short. [Gr *brachys* short]
■ **brachyax'is** n (*crystallog*) brachydiagonal. **brachycephal** /-sef'əl/ n (Gr *kephalē* a head) a short-headed person. **brachycephalic** /-si-fal'ik/ or **brachycephalous** /-sef'ə-ləs/ *adj* short-headed, *esp* having a skull whose breadth is 80 per cent or more of its length. **brachyceph'aly** n short-headedness, *opp* to *dolichocephaly*. **brachydac'tyl**, **brachydactyl'ic** or **brachydac'tylous** *adj*. **brachydac'tyly** n (Gr *daktylos* finger, toe) abnormal shortness of

fingers and toes. **brachydiag'onal** *n* (*crystallog*) the shorter lateral axis. **brach'ydome** *n* a dome parallel to the brachydiagonal. **brachyg'raphy** *n* certain old systems of shorthand. **brachyl'ogy** *n* concise or shortened expression. **brachypin'akoid** or **brach'yprism** *n* a pinakoid or prism parallel to the brachydiagonal. **brachyp'terous** *adj* (Gr *pteron* wing) short-winged; short-finned. **brachyther'apy** *n* radiotherapy in which the radiation source is placed near or within the area requiring treatment. **Brachyura** /-ū'rə/ *n pl* (Gr *oura* a tail) a group of decapod crustaceans having the abdomen reduced and bent forward under the thorax, the crabs. **brachyū'ral** or **brachyū'rous** *adj*.

brack /brak/ *n* a flaw in cloth. [Related to **break**[1]]

bracken /brak'n/ *n* a fern, *esp Pteridium aquilinum*, the commonest British fern, abundant on hillsides, etc; a mass of such ferns. [Ety obscure]

bracket /brak'it/ *n* a projecting support; a small shelf fastened to a wall; a gas pipe projecting from a wall (*hist*); either of a pair of symbols used to enclose words or mathematical symbols, such as **round brackets** or parentheses, **square brackets**, and braces; one of the side pieces of a gun-carriage, supporting the trunnions; the space intervening between overestimated and underestimated shots at a target in range-finding (*artillery*); a bracketed group; a group or category defined and demarcated by certain limiting parameters, as in *income bracket*. ◆ *vt* to support by brackets; to enclose by brackets; to group together. ◆ *vt and vi* (*artillery*) to find the range. [Fr *braguette*, from Sp *bragueta*, from L *brāca*, sing of *brācae* breeches] �‒ **bracket clock** *n* a rectangular clock with an internal pendulum designed to stand on a table or wall-bracket. **brack'et-creep** *n* an inflationary phenomenon whereby a salary rise makes a taxpayer less well-off by pushing him or her into a higher tax bracket. **bracket fungus** *n* a fungus that forms shelf-like growths on tree trunks.

brackish /brak'ish/ *adj* saltish, rather salt. [Du *brak* brackish] ■ **brack'ishness** *n*.

bract /brakt/ *n* a leaf (often modified) that bears a flower in its axil. [L *bractea* a thin plate of metal, gold-leaf] ■ **bract'eal** *adj*. **bract'eate** *n* (*archaeol*) a thin-beaten plate of gold or silver. ◆ *adj* made of metal beaten thin; having bracts. **bract'eolate** *adj* having bracteoles. **bract'eole** *n* a small leaf on the axis of a flower. **bract'less** *adj*. **bract'let** *n* a bracteole.

brad /brad/ *n* a small tapering nail with a side projection instead of a head. [ON *broddr* spike] �‒ **brad'awl** *n* a small boring tool.

Bradbury /brad'bə-ri/ (*hist*) *n* (*pl* **Brad'burys** or **Brad'bury's**) a name for a d1 note. [JS *Bradbury*, Secretary to the Treasury 1913–19]

Bradshaw /brad'shō/ *n* a noted railway-guide, 1839–1961, first published by George *Bradshaw* (1801–53).

brady- /bra-di-/ combining form signifying slow. [Gr *bradys* slow] ■ **bradycard'ia** *n* (Gr *kardia* heart) slowness of heartbeat. **bradykinin** /-kīn'in/ *n* a chemical compound that forms in the blood to dilate blood vessels and contract smooth muscle. **bradypept'ic** *adj* (Gr *peptikos* digesting) slow of digestion (also *n*). **brad'yseism** /-sīzm/ *n* (Gr *seismos* a shake) a slow up-and-down movement of the earth's crust.

brae /brā/ (*Scot*) *n* a sloping bank of a river or seashore; a hill-slope. [ON *brā* eyelid; cf **brow**]

brag /brag/ *vi and vt* (**bragg'ing**; **bragged**) to boast or bluster. ◆ *n* a boast or boasting; a thing one boasts of or is proud of; a card game like poker. ◆ *adj* or *adv* (*Spenser*) proud, proudly. [Origin doubtful] ■ **bragg'ingly** *adv*. **brag'ly** *adv* (*Spenser*). �‒ **bragging rights** *n pl* a notional claim to superiority gained as a result of success against one's rivals.

bragadisme see under **braggart**.

braggadocio /bra-gə-dō'shi-ō or -chi-ō/ *n* (*pl* **braggado'cios**) a braggart or boaster (also with *cap*); empty boasting. [From *Braggadocchio* in Spenser's *Faerie Queene*]

braggart /brag'ərt/ *adj* boastful. ◆ *n* a vain boaster. [Fr *bragard* vain, bragging] ■ **bragg'artism** (*Shakesp* **brag'adisme**) *n* boastfulness. **bragg'artly** *adj*.

Brahma[1] /brä'mə or -mä'/ *n* the first god of the Hindu triad, the creator of the universe; (also **Brah'man**) the eternal impersonal Absolute principle. ■ **Brah'man** /-mən/ or **Brah'min** *n* one of the highest or priestly caste (*Hinduism*); (**Brahmin**; *derog, esp US*) a highly cultured or socially snobbish person, *esp* of the Boston upper class. **Brah'mana** *n* a sacred Hindu commentary on the Vedas. **Brahmanic** /-man'/, **Brahman'ical**, **Brahmin'ic**, **Brahmin'ical** or **Brah'minee** *adj* appropriated to the Brahmans. **Brah'manism** or **Brah'minism** *n* one of the religions of India, worship of Brahma; the religion and practices of the Brahmans. **Brahmi** /brä'mē/ *n* an ancient Indian alphabet.

◻ **Brahma Samaj** /su-mäj'/ or **Brahmo Somaj** *n* a reformed Hindu theistic society or church, founded in 1830. **brahmin** (*US* **Brahman**) **bull** or **cow** *n* the zebu, or a zebu cross.

Brahma[2] /brä'mə/ *n* a large, *orig* Chinese breed of fowl, modified in Europe and America, having feathered legs (also *adj*). [*Brahmaputra*, whence it is said to have been brought]

Brahms and Liszt /brämz ənd list/ (*sl*) *adj* drunk. [Rhyming slang for *pissed*]

braid[1] /brād/ *vt* to plait, intertwine; to arrange in plaits; to thread, wind about or through; to trim, bind, or outline with braid; to jerk, whip out (*obs*). ◆ *vi* (*obs*) to start; to change colour or appearance. ◆ *n* a plait, *esp* of hair (now chiefly *N Am*); a band for the hair; a fabric woven in a narrow band; an interweaving, plaiting; embroidery; a sudden movement, start (*obs*). [OE *bregdan* to move quickly, flash, change colour, plait, weave; ON *bregtha*] ■ **braid'ed** *adj* plaited; entwined; trimmed with braid; divided into several shallow interconnected channels; tarnished, faded (*obs*). **braid'ing** *n* plaiting; manufacture of braid; work in braid; embroidery; braids collectively.

braid[2] /brād/ (*Shakesp*) *vt* to upbraid, reproach. [Prob from **upbraid** or another meaning of **braid**[1] as in ON]

braid[3] /brād/ *adj* Scots form of **broad**.

braide /brād/ (*Shakesp*) *adj* dissembling, deceitful. [OE *brǣgd* falsehood, from *bregdan* to weave]

Braidism /brād'i-zm/ (*archaic*) *n* hypnotism. [From Dr James *Braid*, who practised it c.1842]

brail /brāl/ *n* one of the ropes used to truss up a sail (*naut*); a piece of leather to bind up a hawk's wing; (*in pl*) the feathers about a hawk's rump. ◆ *vt* to haul in (eg a sail) by pulling upon the brails. [OFr *brail*, from L *brācāle* a waistbelt, from *brācae* breeches]

Braille /brāl/ *n* a kind of raised type in relief for the blind, having arbitrary signs consisting of varying combinations of six dots on the following basic arrangement (∷). ◆ *adj* written in Braille. ◆ *vt* to transcribe, print or mark in Braille. [Louis *Braille* (1809–52), its French inventor] ■ **braill'er** or **braille'-writer** *n* a machine for writing in Braille. **Braill'ist** *n* a person who can transcribe Braille.

brain /brān/ *n* (sometimes in *pl*) in vertebrates, that part of the central nervous system that is contained within the skull; in invertebrates, the nervous ganglia near the head end of the body; the seat of the intellect and of sensation; the intellect; (in *pl*) intelligence, common sense (*inf*); a person of exceptional intelligence (*inf*); (in *pl*) a person or persons planning and controlling an enterprise; the controlling mechanism in an electronic device. ◆ *vt* to dash out the brains of; to hit hard over the head (*inf*); to conceive of (*Shakesp*). [OE *brægen*; Du *brein*, dialect Ger *Bregen*] ■ **brained** *adj* having brains (*esp* as combining form, as in *feather-brained*). **brain'iness** *n*. **brain'ish** *adj* (*Shakesp*) brainsick; hot-headed; furious. **brain'less** *adj* without brains or understanding; silly. **brain'lessly** *adv*. **brain'lessness** *n*. **brain'y** *adj* (*inf*) well-endowed with brains; intellectual. ◻ **brain'box** *n* (*inf*) the cranium; a very clever person. **brain'case** *n* the cranium. **brain'child** *n* (*pl* **brain'children**) an original thought or work. **brain coral** *n* a coral with brain-like convolutions. **brain damage** *n* a general term covering all injury or disease of the brain, temporary or permanent. **brain'-damaged** *adj*. **brain'-dead** *adj* (also *fig*). **brain death** *n* the cessation of function of the brain, thought by some doctors to be the true indication of death, rather than the cessation of the heartbeat (also called **cerebral** or **clinical death**). **brain drain** *n* the continuing loss of citizens of high intelligence and creativity through emigration. **brain fever** *n* encephalitis, inflammation of the brain. **brain-fever bird** *n* an Indian cuckoo (*Cuculus varius*) that sings repetitively in the night. **brain'pan** *n* the cranium. **brain'power** *n* intellectual ability. **brain'sick** *adj* diseased in the understanding, deranged. **brain'sickly** *adv* (*Shakesp*). **brain'sickness** *n*. **brain'stem** *n* the stem-like part of the brain connecting the spinal cord with the cerebral hemispheres, and controlling certain major functions, eg the operation of the heart and lungs and the ability to be conscious. **brain'storm** *n* (*inf*) a sudden disturbance of the mind; a sudden inspiration. **brain'storming** *n* (*orig US*) the practice of thrashing out a problem, developing a strategy, etc by intensive group discussion in which ideas are put forward in an extempore manner. **brains trust** *n* a committee of experts; a number of reputedly well-informed persons chosen to answer questions of general interest in public and without preparation, *usu* on radio or television. **brain'teaser** *n* (*inf*) a difficult puzzle or problem. **brain'wash** *vt* to subject (a person) to systematic indoctrination or mental pressure to make him or her change his or her views or confess to a crime, etc. **brain'washing** *n*. **brain'wave** *n* an electrical impulse produced by the brain; a sudden bright idea (*inf*).

■ words derived from main entry word; ◻ compound words; ■ idioms and phrasal verbs

■ **on the brain** (*inf*) as an obsession. **pick someone's brains** see under **pick**[1].

brainiac /brā′ni-ak/ (*N Am inf*) *n* an exceptionally intelligent person. [From a character in the *Superman* comic]

braird /brārd/ or **breer** /brēr/ *n* (*orig Scot*) the first shoots of corn or other crop. ◆ *vi* (of crops) to appear above ground. [OE *brerd* edge]

braise[1] /brāz/ *vt* to stew (*usu* portion-sized pieces of meat, whole vegetables, etc) slowly in a closed pan. [Fr *braiser*]

braise[2] or **braize** /brāz/ *n* a sea bream or porgy. [Perh connected with **bream**[1], or with **bass**[2]]

brak /brak/ (*S Afr*) *adj* brackish or alkaline. [Afrik]

brake[1] /brāk/ *n* a device for applying resistance to the motion of a body either to slow it down (eg a vehicle brake) or to absorb and measure the power developed by an engine, etc; any means of stopping or slowing down (*fig*); an instrument for breaking flax or hemp; a harrow; a kind of vehicle (see **break**[2]). ◆ *vt* to slow down or stop with, or as if with, a brake. ◆ *vi* to apply or operate a brake, *esp* on a vehicle; to be slowed down or stopped by a brake. [From root of **break**[1]; cf Du *braak* a flax-brake]
■ **brake′less** *adj*.
□ **brake block** *n* a block pressed against a wheel as a brake. **brake disc** *n* a disc on the wheel against which the brake pads are forced in a disc brake. **brake drum** *n* a metal drum attached to a wheel or shaft so as to retard motion by the application of brake shoes. **brake′-fade** *n* a decrease of efficiency in a brake sometimes resulting in complete absence of stopping-power. **brake fluid** *n* the fluid in a hydraulic brake system that transmits pressure from the brake pedal to the brake pistons. **brake horsepower** *n* the effective or useful power of a motor, measured by the brake applied to the driving shaft. **brake light** *n* a red light at the rear of motor vehicles to warn following drivers when the brakes are applied. **brake lining** *n* asbestos-base friction fabric riveted to brake shoes. **brakeman** see **brakesman** below. **brake pads** *n pl* the friction material in a disc brake, corresponding to the brake shoes in a drum brake. **brake parachute** *n* a parachute attached to the tail of some high-performance aircraft, used as a brake for landing. **brake shoe** *n* the rubbing part of a brake. **brakes′man** (*US* **brake′man**) *n* the man whose business it is to manage the brake of a railway train; the operator of a winch at a pithead. **brake van** *n* (*rail*) the carriage in which the brake is worked. **brake′-wheel** *n* the wheel to which a brake is applied.

brake[2] /brāk/ *n* a thicket. [Ety obscure]
■ **brāk′y** *adj*.

brake[3] /brāk/ archaic *pat* of **break**[1].

brake[4] /brāk/ *n* fern; bracken. [Perh **bracken**]

brake[5] /brāk/ *n* a handle, as of a pump; a lever for working a machine. [Prob through OFr *brac*, from L *brāchium* an arm]

brake[6] /brāk/ (*Shakesp*) *n* an obscure word in *Measure for Measure* II.1.39 (not made clearer by emendation of *ice* to *vice*).

Bramah-press /brā′mə-pres/ *n* a hydraulic press invented by Joseph Bramah (c.1748–1814), inventor also of the **Bram′ah-lock**, etc.

bramble /bram′bl/ *n* the blackberry bush, a wild prickly shrub of the raspberry genus (*Rubus*); any rough prickly shrub; a blackberry (*Scot*). ◆ *vi* to gather blackberries. [OE *brēmel*; Du *braam*, Ger *Brombeere*]
■ **bram′bling** *n* a bird closely related to the chaffinch. **bram′bly** *adj*.
□ **bram′ble-berry** *n*. **bram′ble-bush** *n* a blackberry bush or thicket. **bram′ble-finch** *n* the brambling.

brame /brām/ (*Spenser*) *n* fierce passion, longing. [Prob Ital *brama*]

Bramley /bram′li/ *n* a variety of large cooking apple. [M *Bramley*, English butcher who first grew it in mid-19c]

bran /bran/ *n* the husks of grain sifted from the flour; the coarsest part of the ground husks, formerly prescribed medically, now eaten generally as a health food; the coarser part or refuse of anything. [OFr *bran*, perh of Celtic origin]
■ **bran′fulness** *n*. **brann′y** *adj*.
□ **bran′-mash** *n*. **bran′-pie′** (*obs*) or **bran tub** *n* a tub of bran from which small presents, etc, are drawn eg at parties.

brancard /brang′kərd/ (*obs*) *n* a horse-litter. [Fr]

branch /brānch or bränsh/ *n* a shoot or arm-like limb of a tree; anything like a limb of a tree; any offshoot from a main trunk, such as a minor road, railway line, etc (also *adj*); a subdivision, a section or department of a subject; any subordinate division of a business, subsidiary factory, shop, office, etc (also *adj*); a tributary or (*rare*) brook (*US*); a departure from the sequential ordering of instructions into a different section of the program, because of a GOTO or an IF … THEN statement (*comput*). ◆ *vt* to divide into branches; to adorn with figures of branches, by embroidery or otherwise (*Spenser*, etc). ◆ *vi* to spread out as a branch or in branches (with *off* or *from*). [Fr *branche*, from LL *branca* an animal's paw]

■ **branched** *adj*. **branch′er** *n* a young hawk or other bird when it leaves the nest and begins to take to the branches. **branch′ery** *n* branches collectively (*lit* and *fig*). **branch′ing** *n* and *adj*. **branch′less** *adj*. **branch′let** *n* a little branch. **branch′y** *adj*.
□ **branch line** *n* a subsidiary railway line. **branch officer** *n* (*navy*) since 1949, any officer holding a warrant. **branch′-pilot** *n* one who holds the Trinity House certificate. **branch water** *n* (*US*) plain water, *esp* used to dilute alcoholic spirits in a drink. **branch′-work** *n* ornamental figured patterns.
■ **branch out** (of a business, etc) to expand, diversify.

branchia /brang′ki-ə/ *n* (*pl* **branch′iae** /-ē-ē/) a gill. [L *branchia*, from Gr *branchion* (*pl* -*a*)]
■ **branch′ial** *adj*. **branch′iate** *adj*.

Branchiopoda /brang-ki-op′ə-də/ *n pl* a subclass of Crustacea with numerous flattened, leaf-shaped, lobed swimming-feet that serve also as breathing organs. [Gr *branchia* gills, and *pous, podos* foot]
■ **branch′iopod** *n* and *adj*.

brand /brand/ *n* a trademark, tradename, design, etc by which a product or group of products is identified; a particular product or class of products; in general, a particular type or kind; a piece of wood burning or partly burned; an instrument for branding; a mark burned into anything with a hot iron; a flaming torch (*poetic*); a sword, from its glitter; a mark of infamy, stigma; a general name for the fungoid diseases or blights of grain crops (*bunt, mildew, rust* and *smut*). ◆ *vt* to burn or mark with a hot iron, or otherwise; to fix a mark of infamy upon, to stigmatize (sometimes with *as*); to label with a proprietary name; to fix indelibly in the memory. [OE *brand, brond*, ON *brandr*, from root of **burn**[1]]
■ **brand′ed** *adj*. **brand′er** *n* (*Scot*) a gridiron. ◆ *vt* to cook on the gridiron. **brand′ered** *adj*. **brand′ing** *n*. **brand′ling** *n* a salmon-parr; a type of worm, reddish with lighter bands, used eg as bait for fishing.
□ **brand awareness** *n* the level of public familiarity with a branded product. **branded goods** *n pl* goods sold under the proprietary name of their manufacturer. **brand′-image** *n* the impression that the public has of a product or (*fig*) a person. **brand′ing-iron** *n*. **brand′-iron** *n* a gridiron; an iron to brand with; a trivet or tripod to set a pot or kettle upon; (*Spenser* **brond′yron**, etc) a sword. **brand leader** *n* the brand of product with the largest share of the market. **brand loyalty** *n* continued support by consumers of a particular brand rather than its competitors. **brand name** *n* a tradename identifying a particular manufacturer's products. **brand′-new** *adj* completely new (as if newly from the fire) (also *obs* **bran′-new**).
■ **a brand from the burning** a person snatched out of a pressing danger (Bible, Amos 4.11).

brandade /brä-däd′/ *n* a Provençal dish made of salt fish cooked with olive oil, garlic and cream. [Fr]

brandise /bran′dīs/ *n* a trivet. [From OE *brand* (see **brand**) and *isen* iron]

brandish /bran′dish/ *vt* to wave or flourish (eg a brand or weapon). ◆ *n* a waving or flourish. [Fr *brandir, brandiss-*, from root of **brand**]
■ **brand′isher** *n*.

brandling see under **brand**.

brandreth /bran′dreth/ *n* or -*drith*/ *n* a stand of wood for a cask or hayrick; a gridiron (*dialect*); a rail round a well. [ON *brandreith*, from *brandr* (see **brand**), and *reith* carriage]

brandy /bran′di/ *n* an alcoholic spirit distilled from grape wine; a glass of this; (with modifier) an alcoholic spirit distilled from other fruits or their juices, or a liqueur made by steeping fruit in brandy, eg *peach brandy, cherry brandy*. (Formerly *brand-wine*, from Du *brandewijn*, from *branden* to burn, to distil, and *wijn* wine; cf Ger *Branntwein*]
■ **bran′died** *adj* heartened or strengthened with brandy.
□ **brandy Alexander** *n* a cocktail made with brandy, crème de cacao and cream. **brand′y-ball** *n* a kind of sweet. **brand′y-bottle** *n* (*dialect*) candock. **brandy butter** *n* butter with brandy and sugar beaten in, traditionally served with Christmas pudding. **brandy glass** *n* a short-stemmed drinking-glass with a globular bowl. **brand′y-pawnee** *n* (Hindi *pānī* water) brandy and water. **brandy snap** *n* a thin crisp biscuit flavoured with ginger and *orig* brandy.

brane /brān/ (*phys*) *n* a multi-dimensional surface embedded in a space with extra dimensions. [From **membrane**]

brangle /brang′gl/ (*archaic*) *vi* to wrangle. ◆ *n* a brawl. [Fr *branler*]
■ **brang′ling** *n* disputing.

brank[1] /brangk/ *n* buckwheat. [Pliny says *brance* (doubtful reading, perh *brace*) is the Gallic name of a kind of corn]

brank[2] /brangk/ *vi* to prance, toss the head; to strut or swagger. [Prob a variant of **prank**[2]]
■ **brank′y** *adj* (*Scot*) showy.

branks /brangks/ (*Scot*) *n pl* (rarely in *sing*) a bridle; a scold's bridle, with a hinged iron framework to enclose the head and a bit or gag.

[Ety very obscure; OFr *bernac* (see **barnacle**²); Ger *Pranger* pillory, Du *prang* fetter, have been compared]

brankursine /brangk'ər-sin or -ûr'/ *n* acanthus, or bear's-breech. [LL *branca ursīna* a bear's paw]

branle see **brawl**².

bran-new see **brand-new** under **brand**.

bransle see **brawl**².

brant goose see **brent goose**.

brantle see **brawl**².

bras a Spenserian spelling of **brass** (*n*).

brasero /brä-sā'rō/ *n* (*pl* **braser'os**) a brazier; a place for burning criminals or heretics. [Sp, from *brasa* a live coal]

brash¹ /brash/ *adj* forward, bumptious; crude, flashy; reckless, impetuous (*US*); (of wood) brittle (*US*). [Perh onomatopoeic] ■ **brash'ly** *adv.* **brash'ness** *n*.

brash² /brash/ *n* angular fragments of rock, which occasionally form the basement bed of alluvial deposits; fragments of crushed ice; clippings of hedges or trees. [Prob Fr *brèche*] ■ **brash'y** *adj*.

brash³ /brash/ *n* heartburn, water brash; a sudden burst of rain; a slight attack of illness (*Scot*); an attack or bout (*obs, Scot and N Eng*). ◆ *vt* (*obs*) to attack. [Prob onomatopoeic]

brasier same as **brazier** (see under **braze**²).

brass /bräs/ or (*Spenser*) **bras** *n* an alloy of copper and zinc; bronze (*obs*); effrontery (*sl*); money (*inf*); an article or fixture of brass; a renewable sleeve for a bearing (*engineering*); a memorial plate of brass in a church; (*collectively*) the brass wind instruments or their players in an orchestra or band; a prostitute (*sl*). ◆ *adj* made of brass. [OE *bræs*]

■ **brass'ily** *adv.* **brass'iness** *n.* **brass'y** *n* an old-fashioned club which had a brass sole, corresponding to a two-wood (also **brass'ie**; also *adj*); a bronze-coloured fish, the bib or pout. ◆ *adj* like brass in appearance, hardness, sound, or otherwise; brazen-faced; showy, loud.

❑ **brass band** *n* a band of players of (mainly) brass wind instruments; a small military band. **brass'-bounder** *n* (*obs*) a midshipman; a privileged apprentice on a ship for whom a premium is paid (so called from his gold braid). **brass'-faced** *adj* (*inf*) impudent, shameless. **brass farthing** *n* (*inf*) something of very little or no value. **brass'founder** *n* a person who casts objects in brass. **brass'founding** *n*. **brass hat** *n* (*milit sl*) a staff officer (with gold braid on his hat). **brass monkey(s)** *n* (*sl*) a term used variously to refer to extremely cold weather (in allusion to the expression *cold enough to freeze the balls off a brass monkey*). **brass neck** *n* (*inf*) effrontery. **brass plate** *n* a nameplate on a professional person's office door, usu made of brass, usu a symbol of membership of the professional class. **brass rubber** *n*. **brass rubbing** *n* the process of copying the design on a church memorial brass, etc onto paper by laying the paper over the brass and rubbing it with coloured wax, chalk, etc; the copy so obtained. **brass tacks** *n pl* (*inf*) details of practical business. **brass'ware** *n* ware or goods of brass.

■ **brass (someone) off** (*sl*) to make (someone) annoyed or fed up. **top brass** brass hats; those in authority at the top (also **the brass**).

brassard /bras'ärd/ *n* a piece of armour for the arm (also **brassart** /bras'ärt/ or **brass'et**; *hist*); an armband or armlet. [Fr, from *bras* arm]

brasserie /bras'(ə-)rē/ *n* a bar serving food; a simple restaurant. [Fr, brewery]

brassica /bras'i-kə/ *n* a plant of the turnip and cabbage genus (*Brassica*) of the family Cruciferae. [L, cabbage]

brassière or **brassiere** /bras'i-er, braz'/ or in N Am sometimes *brə-zēr'*/ *n* a woman's undergarment to support or cover the breasts, now usu shortened to **bra**. [Fr]

brast an obsolete or Scot and N Eng form of **burst** (*prt, pat,* and *pap*).

brat /brat/ *n* a contemptuous name for a child; a badly behaved child or (now) young person; any overgarment of coarse cloth (*obs* or *dialect*); a child's pinafore (*obs* or *dialect*); an apron (*obs* or *dialect*). [OE *bratt*, prob cognate with Olr *brat* plaid, Gaelic *brat* apron]

■ **brat'ling** *n* a little brat. **bratt'ish** *adj.* **bratt'y** *adj*.

❑ **brat pack** *n* (*inf, derog*) a group of successful and popular young (usu teenage male) stars working in a creative field, *esp* cinema, with a rowdy, high-spirited image. **brat'-pack** or **brat'pack** *adj.* **brat packer** *n* a member of the brat pack.

bratchet /brach'it/ see under **brach**.

brattice /brat'is/, **brattish** /brat'ish/ or **brettice** /bret'is/ *n* in medieval siege operations, a fixed tower of wood; a covered gallery on a castle wall, commanding the wall-face below (in these senses also **bretesse** /bri-tes'/ or **bretasche** /bri-tash'/); a wooden partition;

a wooden lining; a partition to control ventilation in a mine. ◆ *vt* to provide with a brattice. [OFr *breteshe*, from LL *bretachia*; cf **bartizan**] ■ **bratt'icing** or **bratt'ishing** *n* work in the form of brattices; cresting or ornamental work along a ridge, cornice or coping (*archit*). ❑ **bratt'ice-cloth** *n* strong tarred cloth used for mine brattices.

brattle /brat'l/ (chiefly *Scot*) *n* a clattering noise; a quarrel; tumult. ◆ *vi* to make a clattering noise. [Imit] ■ **bratt'ling** *n* and *adj*.

bratwurst /brat'voorst/ *n* a type of German pork sausage. [Ger]

braunch an old spelling of **branch**.

braunite /brow'nīt/ *n* an ore of manganese. [From AE *Braun*, German treasury official]

brava see **bravo**.

bravado /brə-vä'dō/ *n* (*pl* **brava'dos** or **brava'does**) a display of bravery; boastful threatening; a swaggerer (*obs*). ◆ *vi* to display bravado. [Sp *bravada*; see **brave**]

Bravais lattice /brav'ā or brə-vä' lat'is/ (*crystallog*) *n* one of the fourteen different lattices formed by the points of crystals. [From A *Bravais*, 19c French physicist]

brave /brāv/ *adj* daring, courageous; noble; making a fine appearance; finely dressed, showy, handsome; excellent. ◆ *vt* to meet boldly; to defy; to face (out). ◆ *n* a brave soldier, *esp* a Native American warrior; a bully, a bravo (*archaic*); bravado (*archaic*). ◆ *adv* (*poetic*) bravely. [Fr *brave*; Ital and Sp *bravo*; origin unknown; cf **braw**]

■ **brave'ly** *adv.* **brav'ery** *n* courage; heroism; finery, showy dress; bravado (*obs*).

❑ **brave new world** *n* a desirable or perfect future society (from Shakesp, *Tempest* V.1.182), *usu* used sardonically, specifically by Aldous Huxley as the title of his novel (1932) portraying a society where scientific, etc progress has produced a repressive, totalitarian regime rather than a utopia.

Bravo or **bravo** /brä'vō/ *n* (in international radio communication) a code word for the letter *b*.

bravo /brä'vō/ *interj* (also /brä-vō'/) well done; excellent (also **bra'va** when addressed to a woman, **bra'vi** /-vē/ to a number of persons). ◆ *n* (*pl* **bra'vos** or **bra'voes**) a call of 'bravo'; a daring villain; a hired assassin. [Sp and Ital]

bravura /brä-voo'rə/ *n* spirit and dash in execution (*music*); a florid air with difficult and rapid passages (*music*); a brilliant or daring display. ◆ *adj* performed with brilliance and daring. [Ital]

braw /brö/ (*Scot*) *adj* fine, splendid, beautiful; dressed finely. [Scot variant of **brave**] ■ **braw'ly** *adv.* **braws** *n pl* fine clothes.

brawl¹ /bröl/ *n* an unruly, rowdy punch-up. ◆ *vi* to fight rowdily; to make a disturbance; (of a stream) to murmur or gurgle. [ME *bralle*, of doubtful origin; perh connected with Du *brallen*, Ger *prahlen* to boast] ■ **brawl'er** *n.* **brawl'ing** *n* and *adj*.

brawl² /bröl/ *n* an old French dance or dance tune (also **branle**, **bransle** /bran'l/ or **brantle** /brant'l/). [Fr *branle*]

brawn /brön/ *n* muscle, *esp* of the arm or calf of the leg; thick flesh; muscular strength; a boar (*dialect*); a preparation of meat made from pig's head and ox-feet, cut up, boiled and pickled. [OFr *braon* flesh (for roasting); of Gmc origin, cf Ger *braten* to roast] ■ **brawned** *adj.* **brawn'iness** *n* the quality of being brawny; muscularity. **brawn'y** *adj* fleshy; muscular; strong.

braxy /brak'si/ (*Scot*) *n* a bacterial disease of sheep; applied loosely to various diseases of sheep; a sheep so infected; its flesh. ◆ *adj* infected with this disease. [Prob orig pl of *brack*, variant of **break**¹] ❑ **braxy mutton** *n* the flesh of a braxy sheep or generally of a sheep that has died of disease or accident.

bray¹ /brā/ *n* the cry of the ass, a heehaw; any harsh grating sound. ◆ *vi* to make a sound like an ass, to heehaw; to give out harsh sounds. ◆ *vt* to utter in a loud harsh voice. [OFr *brai, brait*; braire, from LL *bragīre*, perh of Celtic origin] ■ **bray'er** *n*.

bray² /brā/ *vt* to break, pound, or grind small, as in a mortar. [OFr *breier* (Fr *broyer*)] ■ **bray'er** *n* an instrument for grinding or spreading ink in printing.

braze¹ /brāz/ *vt* to join with hard solder. [OFr *braser* to burn; perh influenced by **brass**. Cf **braise**¹, **brasero**] ■ **braze'less** *adj* without soldering. **brazier** /brāz'yər or brāzh'(y)ər/ *n* a container or tray for hot coals.

braze² /brāz/ *vt* to cover with, or make like, brass. [**brass**] ■ **bra'zen** *adj* of or belonging to brass; impudent. ◆ *vt* to face (out) impudently. **bra'zenly** *adv.* **bra'zenness** or **bra'zenry** *n* effrontery. **brazier** /brāz'yər or brāzh'(y)ər/ *n* a worker in brass. ❑ **bra'zen-face** *n* a shameless, impudent person. **bra'zen-faced** *adj*.

■ words derived from main entry word; ❑ compound words; ■ idioms and phrasal verbs

brazier see under **braze**[1,2].

brazil /brə-zil'/ or **brazil-wood** /-wŭd/ n the hard reddish wood of the East Indian sappan tree or *esp* tropical American species of *Caesalpinia*, used in dyeing. [OFr *bresil* (Sp *brasil*, Ital *brasile*), from LL *brasilium* a red dyewood brought from the East. When a similar wood was discovered in S America, the country became known as *terra de brasil* land of red dyewood]
■ **brazilein** /-zil'i-in/ n a dyestuff obtained by the oxidation of brazilin. **Brazil'ian** n a native or citizen of Brazil, in S America; a Brazilian wax (see below). ◆ *adj* of or from Brazil. **braz'ilin** n a dyestuff obtained from brazil-wood.
❑ **Brazilian ruby** n not a true ruby, used for pink topaz (topaz that has become red after heating) or red tourmaline. **Brazilian wax** n the use of a waxing process to remove nearly all of a person's pubic hair; carnauba. **Brazil nut** n the white, oily, edible, hard-shelled seed of a large Brazilian tree (genus *Bertholletia*); the tree itself.

BRCS *abbrev* : British Red Cross Society (see **Red Cross** under **red**[1]).

BRE *abbrev* : Bachelor of Religious Education (chiefly *US*); Building Research Establishment.

breach /brēch/ n a break; an act of breaking; an opening or discontinuity; a breaking of a law, contract, covenant, promise, etc; a quarrel; a broken condition or part of anything; a gap made in a fortification; breakers (*obs*). ◆ *vt* to make a breach or opening in. ◆ *vi* (of a whale) to leap clear of the water. [ME *breche*, partly from OE *bryce*, but influenced by OFr *bresche* (Mod Fr *brèche*)]
❑ **breach of confidence** n the giving away of a secret or confidential information. **breach of contract** n failure to observe the terms of a contract. **breach of promise** n failure to carry out a promise to marry. **breach of the peace** n a disturbance of the public peace by violence, etc.
■ **step into the breach** to take the place of someone who is absent, *esp* in a crisis.

bread /bred/ n food made of a baked dough of flour or meal, *usu* with yeast or other raising agent; food; livelihood; money (*sl*). ◆ *vt* to cover (a cutlet, etc) with breadcrumbs before cooking. [OE *brēad*, prob from a Gmc root meaning a fragment; cf Scot use of **piece**]
■ **bread'ed** *adj*.
❑ **bread'-and-butt'er** n bread sliced and buttered; livelihood. ◆ *adj* connected with making a living or with the consumption of bread-and-butter; materialistic, practical; youthful, naive; ordinary, routine. **bread-and-butter letter** n a letter of thanks for hospitality. **bread-and-butter pudding** n a baked dessert made from buttered bread, dried fruit, eggs, milk and sugar. **bread'basket** n a basket for holding bread; a cereal-growing region; the stomach (*sl*). **bread'berry** n bread steeped in hot milk. **bread bin** n a container in which bread is stored. **bread'board** n a board on which bread is cut or dough kneaded; a board on which temporary or experimental electronic circuits may be laid out. ◆ *vt* to make an experimental version of (an electronic circuit). **bread'-chipper** n (*Shakesp*) a person who cuts the crusts off bread, an under-butler. **bread'-corn** n grain of which bread is made. **bread'crumb** n the inner parts of a loaf; (*usu* in *pl*) bread crumbled down, eg as a dressing (when commercially produced *usu* coloured orange) for fish, etc. ◆ *vt* to cover with breadcrumbs. **bread'fruit** n the fruit of a moraceous tree (*Artocarpus altilis*) of the South Sea Islands, which when roasted forms a good substitute for bread; the tree. **bread'head** n (*sl*) a drug dealer who is not an addict; someone motivated by money alone. **bread knife** n a large serrated knife for cutting bread. **bread'line** see **on the breadline** below. **bread'nut** n the fruit of a tropical American tree (*Brosimum alicastrum*) related to the breadfruit tree, used as bread when boiled or roasted. **bread pudding** n a baked pudding made with bread, milk, sugar, eggs and dried fruit. **bread'room** n an apartment in a ship's hold where the bread is kept. **bread'root** n the prairie-turnip, a N American papilionaceous plant (*Psoralea esculenta*) with an edible root; the yam. **bread sauce** n a thick milk-based sauce made with bread(crumbs). **bread'stick** n a long, thin stick of bread dough baked until crisp. **bread study** n any branch of study taken up as a means of gaining a living. **bread'stuff** n bread in any form; any material of which bread is made. **bread tree** n a name for various trees whose seeds or pith yield a substitute for bread, eg *Kaffir-bread*. **bread'winner** n the person who earns a living for a family.
■ **bread and circuses** translation of the Roman satirist Juvenal's *panem et circenses* (food and amusements at public expense). **bread buttered on both sides** very fortunate circumstances. **cast one's bread upon the waters** to be generous or charitable without expecting any reward. **know which side one's bread is buttered on** to know how to act for one's own best interests. **on the breadline** at subsistence level, with just enough to make ends meet (from **breadline**, a queue of poor or down-and-out people waiting for free food, *esp* from government sources). **take the bread out of someone's mouth** to deprive someone of the means of living.

breaded[1] see under **bread**.

breaded[2] see **brede**.

breadth /bredth/ n extent from side to side, width; an area or extent considered for its width; liberality of mind; in art, subordination of details to the harmony of the whole. [OE *brēdu*, from *brād* broad]
■ **breadth'ways** or **breadth'wise** *adv* in terms of breadth; broadside on.

break[1] /brāk/ vt (*pat* **broke**, *archaic* **brake**; *pap* **brō'ken** or, less *usu*, **broke**) to divide, part or sever, wholly or partially; to rupture, burst; to shatter, crush; to destroy the continuity or integrity of; to damage (something) so that it fails to work; to interrupt (a fall, journey, etc); to escape forcibly from (*inf*); to make a forced entry to; to bruise or penetrate the surface of; to break a bone in, or separate the bones of; to overcome or wear out; to tame or habituate to obedience (see also **break in** below); to crush the spirit of; to cure (of a habit); to violate (eg a law, promise, bounds or prison); to set aside (eg a will); to cut up (an animal's body); to unfurl; to decipher (a code); to impart (*esp* with delicacy); to make bankrupt; to demote or cashier; to improve on (a particular time, number of strokes, etc for a course or distance); to arpeggiate (*music*); to cause to change from a simple vowel to a diphthong (*linguistics*). ◆ *vi* to separate; to come apart, or go to pieces, *esp* suddenly; to give way; to start away, make a sudden burst of speed; to disperse; to burst forth (*usu* with *out*); to force a passage (with *out* or *through*); to pass suddenly into a condition or action (eg into laughter, revolt, sweat, spots; with *out*); (of flowers) in plant-breeding, to become variegated or striped; to pause for rest or refreshment; (of eg day, hope, a scene) to come into view, appear suddenly; (of news) suddenly to become generally known; to become bankrupt; (of a boy's voice at puberty) to change suddenly; to collapse; (of a wave) to burst into foam; to sever a connection, friendship (with); (of a ball) to change direction (*cricket, golf*); to break the balls (see below) (*snooker*, etc); to change from a simple vowel to a diphthong under influence of a neighbouring sound (*linguistics*); (of the weather) to change suddenly, *esp* after a settled period; (of cloud, etc) to disperse. ◆ *n* an act of breaking; the state of being broken; an opening or crack; a discontinuity; a breach in a relationship; a pause, interval or interruption; a pause for rest or refreshment; an instrumental passage or solo in jazz or pop music; a consecutive series of successful strokes (*snooker, croquet*, etc); the number of points so scored at snooker, etc; a continuous run of anything; the opening shot in snooker, billiards, etc; the start of a horse race; the deviation of a ball on striking the pitch (*cricket*); an instance of breaking service (*tennis*); onset (of the monsoon); a social blunder (*US*); a chance (as in *an even break*); a good chance, an opportunity; a piece of luck, good or bad. [OE *brecan*; Ger *brechen*]
■ **break'able** *adj* able to be (easily) broken. ◆ *n* (*esp* in *pl*) an item that can be (easily) broken. **break'ableness** n. **break'age** n the act of breaking or its consequences; the article or quantity broken. **break'er** n a person or machine that breaks something; a wave broken on rocks or on the shore; someone who broadcasts on Citizens' Band radio (*sl*). **break'ing** n and *adj*.
❑ **break'away** n revolt, defection; withdrawal, secession; an escape; a sudden attacking movement in various sports; an escape; a stampede or stampeding animal (*Aust*). ◆ *adj* having seceded, defected, etc. **break'back** *adj* crushing. **break bad** (*chiefly US sl*) to turn from a moral way of life to an immoral one. **break'beat** n in house music, etc, a short sample of drum beats or other rhythm taken from old soul or jazz records and repeated to make a new rhythm. **breakbone fever** n dengue. **break crop** n (*agric*) a crop grown in rotation with cereals. **break'dance** n a street dance, *usu* to sampled music, using some routines drawn from gymnastics. ◆ *vi* to perform such a dance. **break'dancer** n. **break'dancing** n. **break'down** n a stoppage through accident; collapse; a nervous breakdown; disintegration; a vigorous and noisy American dance; the sudden passage of current through an insulating material at a particular voltage (*elec eng*); an analysis, investigation of data under different headings. ◆ *adj* assisting after a breakdown, etc, eg **breakdown truck** or **breakdown gang** a vehicle or gang that clears and tows away a vehicle after a breakdown or wreckage after an accident. **breakdown voltage** n (*elec eng*) the potential difference at which breakdown (qv above) occurs. **break-even** see **break even** below. **break fee** n (*finance*) a payment made by one party in a financial agreement to another in order to escape from the terms of the agreement. **break'-front** n and *adj* (a bookcase, wardrobe, etc) having a centre section projecting beyond the two end sections. **break'-in** n an illegal (and sometimes violent) entering of a building. **breaking point** n the point at which a person, relationship, situation, etc breaks down under stress. **breaking stress** n (*engineering*) the stress necessary to break a material, either in tension or compression. **break'-jaw** *adj* very difficult to pronounce accurately. **break'neck** *adj* headlong, very fast, *usu* dangerously so. **break of day** n dawn. **break'off** n a discontinuation, abrupt cessation. **breakout** see **break out** below. **break point** n a point giving a player the opportunity to break service (*tennis*); (also **break'point**) a point at which a computer program will stop running to allow checking, etc.

break'-promise or **break'-vow** n (both Shakesp) a person who habitually breaks promises or vows. **break'through** n a forcible passage through a barrier; the solving of a problem, esp scientific, after much effort, opening the way to further developments; any comparable success. **breakthrough bleeding** n intermittent discharge of blood from the uterus between menstrual periods. **break'time** n (at school, etc) recess, break between work periods. **break'-up** n dissolution; dispersal; an ending of a relationship. **break-vow** see **break-promise** above. **break'water** n a barrier against the force of the waves. **break'-wind** n a windbreak.

■ **break a jest** to make a jest, crack a joke. **break a lance with** to enter into a contest with. **break a leg** (theatre) a phrase used to wish someone good luck. **break a record** see under **record**. **break a strike** see under **strike**. **break away** to make a breakaway; to be scattered, as clouds after a storm. **break bread** to have a meal (with); to administer or take part in Holy Communion (Christianity). **break bulk** to open the hold and take out a portion of the cargo; to begin to use goods supplied in bulk. **break camp** to dismantle and pack one's tents, etc. **break cover** (of eg a fox) to burst out from concealment; to come out of hiding. **break down** to demolish; to crush; to collapse; to be overwhelmed by one's emotions; to suffer a nervous breakdown; to fail completely; to analyse. **break even** to avoid making a loss but fail to make a profit; to reach the point at which revenue equals costs (**break'even** n and adj). **break forth** to burst out, issue. **break free** see **break loose** below. **break ground** see under **ground¹**. **break in** (also **break**) to tame or accustom (an animal) to obedience; to make (shoes, etc) less stiff by use. **break in**, **in on** or **into** to enter violently; to interpose abruptly. **breaking and entering** housebreaking, illegal entry into property. **break into** to begin to use up or spend (something held in reserve, a large denomination note, etc); to begin an activity suddenly; eg song, laughter. **break it down** (Aust inf) stop it! **break loose** or **free** to extricate oneself forcibly; to break through all restraint. **break no squares** to make no difference, do no harm, matter little. **break off** to detach by breaking; to put an abrupt end to; to leave off or stop abruptly. **break one's mind** (obs) to communicate one's thoughts to someone. **break out** to appear suddenly; to break through all restraint; to escape (**break'out** n); to become active suddenly; to become covered with (a rash, etc; with in). **break service** or **break someone's serve** (tennis, etc) to win a game in which one's opponent is serving. **break sheer** (of a ship riding at anchor) to be forced by wind or tide out of a position clear of the anchor. **break someone's heart** to crush someone emotionally, esp by failing them in love. **break the balls** (or simply **break**) to open the game by striking one of the red balls (snooker); to open the game by striking the red ball or giving a miss, or to continue the game this way when a similar position occurs (billiards). **break the ice** (fig) to get through first difficulties, esp restraint on first meeting. **break through** to make a breakthrough. **break up** to break open; to break in pieces; to go to pieces; to put an end to; to disperse, to part; to end a relationship; (of a school) to close for the holidays; to dig or plough up; to disconcert or upset (inf); to make helpless with laughter (inf). **break upon the wheel** (hist) to punish by stretching on a wheel and breaking the bones. **break wind** to let out flatulence from the bowels. **break with** to cease relations with, esp to quarrel with; to cease adherence to (tradition, a habit). **make a break for** to bolt towards.

break² or **brake** /brāk/ n a long wagonette; a carriage frame that is all wheels and no body, used in breaking in horses; an estate car. [**break¹**, perh by way of **brake¹** vt]

breaker¹ see under **break¹**.

breaker² /brā'kər/ n a small water cask, used on shipboard. [Prob Sp barrica barrel]

breakfast /brek'fəst/ n the first meal of the day (also adj); a break or breaking of fast. ◆ vi to take breakfast. ◆ vt to provide with breakfast. ❑ **breakfast bar** n a snack containing cereal and often dried fruit and nuts, eaten as a substitute for a conventional breakfast; a raised flat surface in a kitchen at which to sit and eat. **break'fast-room** n. **break'fast-set** n the crockery used at breakfast. **break'fast-table** n. **breakfast television** n television programmes broadcast in the early morning.

bream¹ /brēm/ n a freshwater fish of the carp family, with high-arched back; a fish of the family Sparidae (sea bream); a fish (Ray's bream, Brama brama) related to the mackerel; extended to other fishes. [OFr bresme (Fr brême), from OHGer brahsema (Mod Ger Brassen)]

bream² /brēm/ vt to clean (eg a ship's bottom) by burning off seaweed, shells, etc. [Prob connected with **broom**, Du brem]

breare /brēr/ (Spenser) n same as **brier¹**.

breaskit see **brisket**.

breast /brest/ n the front of the human body between the neck and the belly; one of the two mammary glands in women (or rudimentary in men), forming soft protuberances on the chest; the corresponding part of any animal; the part of a jacket, etc which covers the breast; a swelling slope; (the source of) the emotions, affections; singing voice (obs). ◆ vt to set the breast against, to push forward with the breast against; to surmount; to oppose manfully. [OE brēost; Ger Brust, Du borst]

■ **breast'ed** adj (usu as combining form) having (a certain type of) breast(s).

❑ **breast'bone** n the sternum, the bone running down the middle of the breast, to which the first seven ribs are attached. **breast cancer** n a malignant tumour of the breast. **breast-deep'** adv as deep as to reach to the breast. **breast'fed** adj. **breast'feed** vt to give milk to (a baby) from the breasts. **breast'feeding** n. **breast-high'** adv high as the breast; breast-deep. **breast'-knot** n a knot of ribbons worn on the breast. **breast'pin** n an ornamental pin for the breast. **breast'plate** n a plate or piece of armour for the breast; an embroidered square of linen with precious stones, worn on the breast of the Jewish high-priest (Bible). **breast'plough** n a kind of spade for cutting turf, with a crossbar against which the breast is pressed. **breast pump** n a pump for removing milk from the breasts. **breast'rail** n the upper rail of a breastwork. **breast screening** n mammography, as a diagnostic tool for breast cancer. **breast'stroke** n a swimming-stroke performed breast-down, with circling movements of the arms and a frog-like movement of the legs. **breastsummer** or **bressummer** /bres'ə-mər/ n a summer or beam supporting the whole, or a great part, of the front of a building in the manner of a lintel. **breast wall** n a retaining wall. **breast wheel** n a water wheel turned by water delivered upon it at about half its height. **breast'work** n (fortif) a hastily constructed earthwork.

■ **double-** and **single-breasted** see under **double** and **single**. **make a clean breast** to make a full confession.

breath /breth/ n the air drawn into and then expelled from the lungs; exhaled air as smell or vapour; the power of breathing; life; a single act of breathing; breathing without vibrating the vocal cords (phonetics); a sound so produced; a whisper; the time occupied by a single act of breathing; a very slight breeze; a slight suspicion. ◆ adj produced by breath without voice. [OE brǣth; Ger Brodem steam, breath]

■ **breath'alyse** or (N Am) **breath'alyze** vt to test with a breathalyser. **breath'alyser** or (N Am) **breath'alyzer** n a device which indicates the amount of alcohol in a person's breath, by means of a plastic bag containing alcohol-sensitive crystals which change colour when a certain concentration of alcohol vapour is blown through them. **breathed** /bretht/ adj having a breath (esp as combining form, eg long-breathed, and see also under **breathe**). **breath'ful** adj (Spenser) full of breath or air, also full of scent or odour. **breath'ily** adv. **breath'iness** n. **breath'less** adj out of breath; with the breath held or taken away, from excitement, interest, etc; breezeless, airless; dead. **breath'lessly** adv. **breath'lessness** n. **breath'y** adj (of a speaking voice) accompanied by much unvocalized breath; (of a singer or instrument-player) without proper breath control, causing impure sound.

❑ **breath'taking** adj astounding. **breath'takingly** adv. **breath test** n a test carried out on a person's breath, by breathalyser or other device, to determine how much alcohol that person has consumed.

■ **a breath of fresh air** a short excursion in the open air; any refreshing and invigorating change. **below** or **under one's breath** in a low voice. **catch one's breath** to rest until one is no longer out of breath; to stop breathing for an instant. **draw breath** to breathe; to be alive. **get one's breath back** to recover normal breathing after exertion; to recover from a surprise. **hold one's breath** to refrain from breathing temporarily; to wait in anxious expectation. **in the same breath** at the same time. **out of breath** having difficulty in breathing; panting from exertion, etc. **save one's breath** to refrain from pointless talk. **spend** or **waste one's breath** to talk to no avail or profitlessly. **take (one's) breath** to recover freedom of breathing; to stop for breath, rest, or refreshment. **take someone's breath away** to make someone breathless with astonishment, delight, etc. **with bated breath** with breath restrained out of suspense, fear or reverence.

breathe /brēdh/ vi to draw in or expel breath or air to or from the lungs or other respiratory organs; to respire; (of wind) to blow lightly; (of wine) to be exposed to the air so as to improve in flavour; (of fabric, leather, etc) to allow air, moisture, etc to pass through; to take breath, to rest or pause; to live, continue to draw breath. ◆ vt to draw into or expel from the lungs; to instil, imbue; to breathe out (fire, etc); to utter unvoiced (phonetics); to utter softly, whisper; to express, display; to give breathing space to, allow to rest; to tire by some brisk exercise. [From **breath**]

■ **breathable** /brēdh'ə-bl/ adj fit for breathing; (of fabric, leather, etc) allowing the passage of air, moisture, etc. **breathed** /brēdhd/ adj (phonetics) pronounced without voice (see also under **breath**). **breath'er** n someone who breathes or lives; a spell of exercise; a rest to recover breath (inf); a vent to release pressure or for ventilation. **breath'ing** n the act of breathing; an instance of breathing; aspiration, longing; respite; either of two signs (' and ') used in Greek to signify presence (rough breathing) or absence (smooth breathing) of the aspirate respectively. ◆ *adj* lifelike.

❑ **breathing hole** *n* (*Can*) an opening in the ice for a submerged animal to breathe. **breathing space** or (*obs*) **breath'ing-time** *n* space or time in which to breathe or rest; a brief respite. **breath'ing-while** *n* time sufficient for drawing breath; any very short period.

■ **breathe again** to be relieved after an anxious moment or time. **breathe down someone's neck** to keep too insistently close to someone, *esp* by way of supervision. **breathe easily** or **freely** to be at ease. **breathe one's last** to die. **breathe (up)on** (*obs*) to tarnish the name of.

breccia /brech'yə/ (*geol*) *n* a rock composed of angular fragments. [Ital]

■ **brecciated** /brech'i-ā-tid/ *adj* reduced to or composed of breccia.

brecham /brehh'əm/ (*Scot*) *n* a horse-collar. [OE *beorgan* to protect, and *hama* covering]

Brechtian /brehh'ti-ən/ *adj* relating to or suggestive of the writings or dramatic theories and techniques of the German playwright Bertolt Brecht (1898–1956).

bred /bred/ *pat* and *pap* of **breed**.

brede /brēd/ *n* and *vt* (*pat* and *pap* (*Spenser*) **bread'ed**) an archaic form of **braid**[1].

bree[1] /brē/ (*Scot*) *n* the eyebrow. [OE *bræw*, *brēaw*; cf Ger (*Augen*) *braue*; and **brae**]

bree[2] /brē/ (*Scot*) *n* the liquor in which anything has been boiled. [Perh OE *brīw*; cf **berry**[2], Ger *Brei*]

breech /brēch/ *n* (almost always in *pl*, **breeches** /brich'iz/; in N Am, etc also **britches**) a garment worn by men on the lower parts of the body: strictly, as distinguished from trousers, coming to just below the knee, but often used generally for trousers; (in *sing*) the lower back part of the body, the buttocks; breech birth or delivery (*obstetrics*); the lower or back part of anything, *esp* of a gun (*pl* in these senses pronounced /brēch'iz/). ◆ *vt* /brich, brēch/ (*obs*) to put into breeches; to flog. [OE *brēc*, pl of *brōc*; cf Ger *Bruch*, Du *broek*]

■ **breeched** *adj*. **breeching** /brich'ing/ *n* a part of a horse's harness attached to the saddle, coming round the breech and hooked to the shafts; a strong rope attached to the breech of a gun to secure it to a ship's side. ◆ *adj* (*Shakesp*) subject to whipping. **breech'less** *adj* trouserless.

❑ **breech birth** or **delivery** *n* one in which the buttocks, and sometimes also the feet, of the baby come first. **breech'block** *n* a part of a breech-loading firearm which is moved to introduce a charge. **breech delivery** see **breech birth** above. **Breeches Bible** *n* the Geneva Bible (qv), which uses the word 'breeches' for 'aprons' in Genesis 3.7. **breech'es-buoy** *n* a life-saving apparatus enclosing the person like a pair of breeches. **breeches part** or **role** *n* (*theatre*, *opera*) a part in which a woman plays a man or boy. **breech'-loader** *n* a firearm loaded by introducing the charge at the breech instead of the muzzle. **breech'-loading** *adj*.

■ **wear the breeches** (of the female in a (*usu* marital) relationship) to be in charge.

breed /brēd/ *vt* (*pat* and *pap* **bred**) to generate or bring forth; to cause or promote the generation of, or the production of breeds of; to train or bring up; to cause or occasion. ◆ *vi* to be pregnant (now *dialect*); to produce offspring; to be produced or brought forth; to be in training, to be educated (*Walter Scott*). ◆ *n* that which is bred, progeny or offspring; a strain, variety or race; a kind, type. [OE *brēdan* to cherish, keep warm; Ger *brüten* to hatch]

■ **breed'er** *n* a person or thing that breeds; a breeder reactor; a heterosexual (*derog sl*). **breed'ing** *n* the act or process of producing; ancestry, pedigree; upbringing; manners.

❑ **breed'-bate** *n* (*Shakesp*) a person who foments trouble or strife. **breeder reactor** *n* a nuclear reactor which creates more fissile material than it consumes. **breeding ground** *n* a place where animals, etc go to breed; an attitude, environment, etc which fosters or creates *esp* something considered undesirable.

■ **best of breed** a dog judged the outstanding animal of its type at a show; the best available product on the market (*commerce*).

breeks /brēks/ *n pl* Scots form of **breeches**.

breem see **breme**.

breer see **braird**.

breese see **breeze**[3].

breeze[1] /brēz/ *n* a light wind; a disturbance or quarrel (*inf*); a whispered rumour (*inf*); something delightfully easy (*inf*). ◆ *vi* to blow as or like a breeze; to go briskly and cheerily (*inf*); to do, achieve, etc something with ease (with *through*). [OSp *briz* NE wind]

■ **breeze'less** *adj*. **breez'ily** *adv*. **breez'iness** *n*. **breez'y** *adj* fanned with or subject to breezes; bright, lively, exhilarating.

❑ **breeze'way** *n* a roofed passage, *usu* open at the sides, connecting two buildings.

■ **breeze up** to freshen into a breeze. **breeze up sale** (*horse-racing*) a horse sale at which prospective purchasers can watch (*usu* young, untried) horses go through their paces over a short distance. **get the breeze up** to get the wind up (see **wind**[1]).

breeze[2] /brēz/ *n* furnace refuse used in making **breeze brick**, **breeze'blocks** or **breeze concrete** for building. [Perh OFr *brese*]

breeze[3], **breese** or **brize** /brēz/ (*archaic* or *dialect*) *n* a gadfly, botfly, or other dipterous pest of horses and cattle. [OE *briosa*]

bregma /breg'mə/ (*anat*) *n* (*pl* **breg'mata**) the part of the skull where the frontal and the two parietal bones join, sometimes divided into the right and left bregmata. [Gr]

■ **bregmat'ic** *adj*.

brehon /brē'hən/ (*Irish hist*) *n* a judge in medieval Ireland. [Ir *breitheamh*, pl *breitheamhuin*]

❑ **Brehon Law** or **Laws** *n* the system of jurisprudence in use among the Irish until near the middle of the 17c.

breloque /brə-lok'/ *n* an ornament attached to a watch chain. [Fr]

breme or **breem** /brēm/ (*Spenser*) *adj* fierce, keen. [Perh related to OE *brēman* to rage]

bremsstrahlung /bremz'shträ-lŭng/ (*phys*) *n* electromagnetic radiation emitted when a charged particle changes its velocity, as when an electron collides with, or is deflected by, a positively charged nucleus. [Ger *bremsen* to brake and *Strahlung* radiation]

Bren /bren/ or **Bren gun** /gun/ (also without *cap*) *n* a light machine-gun. [First manufactured in *Br*no (now in the Czech Republic), and then in *En*field, in England]

bren or **brenne** /bren/ (*obs*) *vt* and *vi* (*pat* and *pap* **brent**) to burn. [See ety for **burn**[1]]

■ **brent** *adj*.

brent /brent/ (*Scot*) *adj* lofty; steep; smooth, unwrinkled. [OE *brant* steep; ON *brattr*]

brent goose /brent goos/ *n* a small wild goose, mostly slaty-grey, but with a black head, neck, tail and long wing feathers and a white belly, often confused with the barnacle-goose (also **brant goose** or **brent barnacle**). [Prob *branded* brindled]

brer /brûr or brär/ (*Southern US dialect*) *n* brother (*usu* followed by a name).

brere /brēr/ (*Spenser*) *n* a form of **brier**[1].

bresaola /brə-zō'la/ *n* salt-cured, air-dried beef, served thinly sliced with oil, lemon juice and black pepper. [Ital, from *brasare* to cook slowly]

bressummer see **breastsummer** under **breast**.

bretasche, **bretesse** see **brattice**.

brethren /bredh'rən/ see **brother**.

Breton /bret'ən/ *n* a native of Brittany (*Bretagne*), France; the Celtic tongue of Brittany, Brezonek; (also without *cap*; also **Breton hat**) a hat with a rounded crown and turned-up brim. ◆ *adj* of Brittany; Armoric. [Fr]

brettice see **brattice**.

Bretwalda /bret-wŏl'də/ (*hist*) *n* a title of certain kings of Old English kingdoms, whose superiority over the others was more or less acknowledged. [Prob Lord of the *Britons*, or of *Britain*, from OE *walda* ruler]

breve /brēv/ *n* the mark of a short vowel (as in ĕ), *opp* to *macron*; an obsolescent note, (‖◌‖), twice as long as the longest now generally used (the semibreve), but half (or in perfect time one-third) as long as the obsolete long (*music*); a papal brief (see under **brief**). [L *brevis* short]

brevet /brev'it/ *n* a military commission entitling an officer to take rank above that for which he or she receives pay; a badge indicating such a commission. ◆ *vt* (**brev'eting**; **brev'eted**; those who pronounce it /bri-vet'/ write **brevett'ing** and **brevett'ed**) to confer such rank on. [Fr, from L *brevis* short]

brevet d'invention /brə-ve dĕ-vä-syõ'/ (*Fr*) *n* a patent.

breveté /brəv-tā'/ (*Fr*) *adj* patented.

breviary /brē'vi-ə-ri/ *n* a book containing the daily service of the Roman Catholic Church. [L *breviārium*, from *brevis* short]

breviate /brē'vi-āt or -ət/ *n* a short compendium; a lawyer's brief. [L *breviātus*, from *breviāre* to shorten]

brevier /brə-vēr'/ *n* an old type size (*approx* 8-point) between bourgeois and minion, said (doubtfully) to have been used for breviaries.

brevi manu /brē'vī mä'nū or bre'wē man'oo/ (*L*) *adv* offhand (literally, with a short hand).

brevipennate /bre-vi-pen'ət/ *adj* of birds, having short wings. [L *brevis* short, and *penna* wing]

brevity /brev'i-ti/ n shortness; conciseness. [Poss Anglo-Fr *breveté* shortness, infl by L *brevitās*, *brevitātis*, from L *brevis* short]
❑ **brevity code** n a code in which a single symbol is substituted for a group of words.

brew /broo/ vt to prepare by infusion, boiling and fermentation, as beer from malt and other materials, or by infusion, mixing or boiling, without fermentation, as for tea or punch; to contrive or plot. ♦ vi to perform the operation of brewing ale or beer, etc; (*esp* of tea) to be in the process of being brewed; to be in preparation, gathering or forming. ♦ n a brewing; a brewage; a variety of making of a brewed beverage; a drink of tea or coffee (*inf*); a concoction, mixture. [OE *brēowan*; cf Ger *brauen*]
■ **brew'age** n something brewed; the process of brewing. **brew'er** n a person who brews. **brew'ery** n a place used for brewing. **brew'ing** n the act or an instance of making liquor from malt; the quantity brewed at once. **brew'ster** n (now mainly *Scot*; *orig fem*) a brewer.
❑ **brewer's droop** n (*inf*) in a man, inability to get an erection when drunk. **brewers'** or **brewer's yeast** n a yeast used in brewing, *esp Saccharomyces cerevisiae*, also used medically as a source of the vitamin B complex vitamins. **brew'-house** n a brewery. **brew'master** n the supervisor of the brewing in a brewery. **brew'pub** n a combined pub and small-scale brewery, serving its own real ale.
■ **brew up** to make a drink, *esp* tea (**brew'-up** n).

brewis /broo'is/ (*archaic* and *dialect*) n broth, *esp* beef broth; bread soaked in broth, fat, gravy, or the like. [OFr *broez*, infl by OE *brīw* bree]

Brezhnev Doctrine /brezh'nev dok'trin/ n (*hist*) the Soviet doctrine which arose during the leadership of Leonid *Brezhnev* (died 1982), that the Soviet Union had the right to intervene in the internal affairs of another communist country to counter a supposed threat to socialism.

Brezonek /brez'ə-nek/ n see **Breton**.

briar see **brier**[1,2].

Briard /brē-är(d)/ n a large, heavy, hairy dog of a French breed. [*Brie*, district in NE France]

Briarean /brī-ā'ri-ən/ adj relating to *Briareus* (Gr *Briareōs*), a hundred-handed giant; many-handed. [Gr *briaros* strong]

bribe /brīb/ n something offered to someone to influence their judgement unduly or to persuade them to behave in a certain way; spoil, booty (*obs*). ♦ vt to influence by offering a bribe; to gain over or win over by bribery; to steal (*obs*). ♦ vi to practise bribery. [OFr *bribe* a lump of bread; origin doubtful]
■ **brib'able** adj. **brib'er** n. **brib'ery** n the act of giving or taking bribes.
❑ **brib'ery-oath** n an oath taken by an elector that he or she had not been bribed.

BRIC /brik/ abbrev: Brazil, Russia, India and China.

bric-à-brac or **bricabrac** /brik'ə-brak/ n old curiosities, knick-knacks, or other treasured odds and ends. [Fr]

brick /brik/ n baked clay; a shaped block of baked clay, generally rectangular in shape (the standard dimensions being about 21.5cm × 10.25cm × 6.5cm ($8\frac{1}{2}$ × 4 × $2\frac{1}{2}$in)); a brick-shaped block of other material, often compressed; a child's building block of wood, etc; a loaf or a bun more or less in the shape of a brick; the colour of brick, brick-red; (*inf*) an old-fashioned bulky mobile phone; a helpful, supportive, kind person. ♦ adj made of brick or bricks; of the colour of brick, brick-red. ♦ vt to fill or wall (in, up, etc) with brick; to cover with brick or an appearance of brick. [Fr *brique*, from the same root as **break**[1]]
■ **brick'en** adj (*obs*) made of brick. **brick'ie** n (*inf*) a bricklayer. **brick'ing** n brickwork; imitation brickwork. **brick'y** adj like or of brick.
❑ **brick'bat** n a piece of brick, *esp* if used as a missile; a critical remark. **brick'clay** n a clay containing sand and a good deal of iron; any clay, loam or earth used for brickmaking. **brick'-dust** n powdered brick; the colour of powdered red brick. **brick'-earth** n a clayey silt or loam used for brickmaking. **brick'field** n a place where bricks are made. **brick'fielder** n (*Aust*) a hot dry wind (*orig* one bringing dust from the brickfields of Sydney suburbs). **brick'-kiln** n a kiln in which bricks are made. **brick'layer** n in the building trade, a person who lays and builds with bricks. **brick'laying** n. **brick'maker** n. **brick'making** n. **brick'-nog** or **brick'-nogging** see **nog**[2]. **brick-red'** adj of the colour of an ordinary red brick. **bricks'-and-mor'tar** adj (of a commercial enterprise, etc) not using the Internet to conduct its business. **brick'-shaped** adj of the shape of a standard brick. **brick'-tea** n tea pressed into cakes. **brick'work** n work constructed in brick; bricklaying. **brick'works** n a factory producing bricks. **brick'yard** n a brickfield.
■ **drop a brick** to say or do something horrifyingly tactless or indiscreet. **like a ton of bricks** heavily and promptly. **like banging** (or **knocking**) **one's head against a brick wall** said of a laborious but unrewarding attempt, eg to persuade, inform, etc. **make bricks without straw** to try to do a piece of work without the materials

necessary for it; to make something that will not last. **see through a brick wall** to be unusually perspicacious.

brickle /brik'l/ (*Spenser* and *Scot*) adj apt to break; weak; troublesome. [Cf **bruckle**]

brickwall /brik'wöl/ a corruption of **bricole**.

bricolage /brik-ə-läzh'/ n a work of art or construction put together from whatever materials are available. [Fr]

bricole /brik'əl, -öl/ or /bri-kōl'/ n a medieval military catapult for hurling stones; the rebound of a ball from the wall of a real tennis court; a similar stroke in billiards; a rebound (*fig*). [Fr, from LL *briccola*]

bridal /brī'dəl/ n (*poetic* or *archaic*) a marriage feast; a wedding. ♦ adj belonging to or relating to a bride or a wedding; nuptial. [OE *brȳdealo*, literally, bride-ale; see **bride** and **ale** (feast)]
❑ **bridal suite** n a set of hotel rooms intended for a newly married couple. **bridal wreath** n any of various shrubs of the genus *Spiraea*, having sprays of white flowers.

bride /brīd/ n a woman about to be married or newly married. ♦ vi and vt (with *it*; *Shakesp*) to act the bride. [OE *brȳd*; ON *brúthr*, Ger *Braut*]
❑ **bride'-ale** n (*archaic*) the ale-drinking at a marriage feast (see **bridal**). **bride'-bed** n (*archaic*) the marriage bed. **bride'cake** or **bride's'-cake** n wedding cake. **bride'-chamber** n (*archaic*) a nuptial apartment; the room in which a wedding is performed. **bride'groom** n a man about to be married or newly married. **bride'maid**, **bride'maiden**, **bride's'-maid** or **brides'maid** n (all except **bridesmaid** *obs* or *dialect*) a young (traditionally unmarried) woman who attends the bride at a wedding. **bride'man**, **bride's'-man** or **brides'man** n (*obs* or *dialect*) a young unmarried man who attends the bridegroom at a wedding. **bride price** see **bridewealth** below. **bride's-cake** see **bridecake** above. **brides'maid**, **bride's-maid** see **bridemaid** above; a team or individual that is always runner-up or never quite makes it to the top (*sport sl*). **bride's-man**, **bridesman** see **brideman** above. **bride'wealth** or **bride price** in tribal societies, etc, a price paid (*usu* in kind) to a bride's family by the bridegroom. **bridezill'a** n (*sl*) a bride-to-be whose selfish and demanding behaviour in planning her wedding is regarded as monstrous (from the science-fiction film monster Godzilla).

bridewell /brīd'wəl/ n a house of correction; a gaol. [From a palace near *St Bride's Well* in London]

bridge[1] /brij/ n a structure spanning a river, road, etc giving communication across it by foot, road, rail, etc; the narrow raised platform from which the captain of a ship gives directions; a thin upright piece of wood supporting the strings in a violin or similar instrument; the bony upper part of the nose; a support for a snooker cue; a bridgelike structure by which false teeth are attached to natural teeth or roots; a connecting or transitional passage in music (also **bridge passage**); in the theatre, a platform (for stagehands) that rises above the stage; anything that connects across a gap (*lit* and *fig*); a piece of hardware that connects networks or parts of a network (*comput*); a type of electrical circuit for measuring resistance, etc. ♦ vt to be or build a bridge over; to connect the extremities of (a gap) (*fig*); to make an electrical connection between. [OE *bryg*; Ger *Brücke*, ON *bryggja*]
■ **bridge'able** or **bridg'able** adj. **bridge'less** adj. **bridg'ing** n the process of making, or the construction forming, a bridge; a brace or braces fixed between joists to strengthen them; provision of credit necessary for a business transaction; a method of climbing a rock chimney by straddling it.
❑ **bridge'board** n a notch-board. **bridge'-builder** n a person who builds bridges; a person who tries to reconcile hostile parties, etc, *esp* in diplomacy. **bridge'-building** n. **bridge'head** n a fortification covering the end of a bridge nearest to the enemy's position; a place suitable for such fortification; any advanced position seized in enemy territory. **bridge'-house** n a house at the end of a bridge. **bridge'work** n a dental bridge; the fitting of dental bridges. **bridging loan** n a short-term loan, *usu* for a fairly large sum and at a relatively high rate of interest, providing bridging for a business transaction, *esp* house purchase.
■ **bridge of boats** a bridge resting on boats moored abreast across a piece of water. **cross a bridge when one comes to it** to bother about a future problem only when it affects one.

bridge[2] /brij/ n any of various card games, for two pairs of players, developed from whist (see **auction bridge** under **auction** and **contract bridge** under **contract**); *orig* a variety (**bridge whist**) in which the dealer or dealer's partner chose the trump suit, or no-trumps, and the dealer played his or her partner's hand as a dummy. [Earlier known as *bridge whist*, *biritch*; ety unknown]
■ **Bridgera'ma** n an apparatus which shows on large electronically lit boards the steps of a bridge game in progress in another room.

❑ **bridge'-drive** n a tournament of bridge-playing. **bridge roll** n a long thin soft bread roll (said to be named from its consumption at bridge games but *poss* from **bridge**[1]).

bridie /brī'di/ (*Scot*) n a meat and onion turnover.

bridle /brī'dl/ n an apparatus on a horse's head by which to control it; any curb or restraint; a movement expressing resentment, scorn or vanity, a tossing back of the head, like a horse pulled up by the bridle; a mechanical device that limits movement between parts of a component. ◆ vt to put a bridle on; to manage by a bridle; to check or restrain. ◆ vi to toss the head (*up at* the thing taken amiss). [OE *brīdel*; OHGer *brittel*]

■ **brī'dled** adj wearing a bridle; (of a bird) with markings similar to a bridle. **brī'dler** n a person who governs or restrains with or as with a bridle.

❑ **bri'dle-hand** n the hand that holds the bridle in riding, the left hand. **bri'dlepath**, **bri'dle-road** or **bri'dleway** n a path or way for those riding or leading horses. **bri'dle-rein** n the strap of a bridle. **bri'dle-wise** adj (*US*; of a horse) obedient without requiring the use of the bridle.

■ **bite on the bridle** to be impatient, like a restive horse.

bridoon /bri-doon'/ n the light snaffle usual in a military bridle in addition to the ordinary bit, controlled by a separate rein. [Fr *bridon*, from *bride* a bridle]

Brie /brē/ n a white, soft cheese *orig* made in *Brie*, NE France.

brief /brēf/ adj short in duration; (now *usu* of clothing) short in length or extent, scanty, skimpy; concise; brusque in manner. ◆ n a summary of a client's case by a solicitor for the instruction of a barrister or counsel (*law*); a writ; a papal brief (qv below); a short statement of any kind; a statement of the aims of an advertising campaign, etc; instructions; a lawyer, *esp* a barrister (*sl*); (in *pl*) close-fitting legless underpants for men or women. ◆ vt to give information or issue instructions to; to instruct or retain (a barrister). ◆ vi (with *against*) to make known information that will be damaging to someone's reputation or career. [Fr *bref*, from L *brevis* short]

■ **brief'ing** n the action, or an instance, of making or giving a brief; instructions or information imparted. **brief'less** adj. **brief'ly** adv. **brief'ness** n.

❑ **brief'-bag** n the bag in which a barrister carries his or her briefs to and from court. **brief'case** n a small case for carrying briefs, or for documents in general.

■ **hold a brief** (*law*) to be retained as counsel; (with *for*) to argue for, to champion. **hold no brief for** not to support or advocate. **in brief** in few words. **king's brief** (*hist*) a royal mandate ordering collections to be made in churches for specified charitable purposes. **papal brief** a less severe papal document than a bull. **take a brief** to undertake a case. **the brief and the long** (*Shakesp*) the short and the long. **to be brief** in order to speak in few words.

brier[1] or **briar** /brīr or brī'ər/, also (*Spenser*, etc) **brere** /brēr/ n a prickly shrub; a wild rosebush. [OE (Anglian) *brēr* (WSax *brǣr*)]

■ **briered** or **briared** adj caught in or covered with briers. **brier'y** adj thorny; full of briers.

■ **sweetbrier** eglantine, a wild rose (*Rosa rubiginosa*) with scented leaves.

brier[2] or **briar** /brī'ər/ n the white heath (*Erica arborea*), a S European shrub; a tobacco pipe made out of its root (also **bri'er-root** or **bri'er-wood**). [Fr *bruyère* heath]

Brig. abbrev: Brigadier.

brig[1] /brig/ n a two-masted, square-rigged vessel; a place of detention on board ship (*US Navy*); a prison (*US sl*). [Short form of **brigantine**[1]]

brig[2] /brig/ n Scot and N Eng form of **bridge**[1]. [ON *bryggja*]

brigade /bri-gād'/ n a body of troops consisting of a group of battalions and supporting units commanded by a brigadier; a band of people more or less organized for a specific purpose. ◆ vt to form into brigades; to group (people) together, *esp* oppressively. [Fr *brigade*, from Ital *brigata*, from LL *briga* strife]

■ **brigadier** /brig-ə-dēr'/ n a field officer (in the British Army and Royal Marines) between colonel and major-general in rank, often having command of a brigade; a brigadier general (*US inf*) /brē-gä-dyä/ in the French Army, a corporal.

❑ **brigade major** n a staff-officer attached to a brigade as assistant to the brigadier. **brigadier general** n an officer ranking above colonel and below major-general (*US army*); a former name for a brigadier (*Brit army*).

brigalow /brig'ə-lō/ (*Aust*) n any of several species of acacia. [From an Aboriginal language]

brigand /brig'ənd/ n a bandit or highway robber, *esp* a member of a gang. [Fr, from Ital *brigante*, from LL *briga* strife]

■ **brig'andage** or **brig'andry** n. **brigandine** or **brigantine** /brig'ən-dēn, -tēn/ n a mail-coat of steel rings or plates sewn onto linen or leather.

brigantine[1] /brig'ən-tēn/ n a two-masted vessel, with the mainmast of a schooner and the foremast of a brig. [Fr *brigantin*, from Ital *brigantino* pirate ship]

brigantine[2] see under **brigand**.

Brig. Gen. abbrev: Brigadier General.

bright /brīt/ adj shining; full of light; vivid; clear; cheerful; vivacious; clever; illustrious; hopeful, having good prospects; beautiful (*archaic*). ◆ adv brightly; clearly. ◆ n a vivid colour; (in *pl*) a vehicle's headlights when on full beam (*N Am*). [OE *byrht*, *beorht*; cognate with Gothic *bairhts* clear]

■ **bright'en** vt and vi to make or grow bright or brighter; to clear up; to cheer up. **bright'ly** adv. **bright'ness** n. **bright'some** adj bright; brilliant.

❑ **brightening agent** n a compound that increases the brightness of a white or coloured textile by converting some of the ultraviolet radiation into visible light. **bright-field illumination** n a method of illumination in microscopy in which the specimen appears dark on a bright background. **bright'work** n polished metal on cars, etc.

■ **bright and early** very early; in good time. **bright-eyed and bushy-tailed** (*inf*) eager and alert. **bright young thing** a member of the young and fashionable social set in the 1920s and 1930s. **look on the bright side** to be hopeful. **the bright lights** the places of entertainment in a city centre; city life, *esp* as compared with the quiet life of the countryside.

Bright's disease /brīts diz-ēz'/ n a generic name for diseases of the kidneys with albumen in the urine. [Dr Richard *Bright* (1789–1858), English physician]

brigue /brēg/ vi to intrigue. ◆ n strife; intrigue. [Fr]

■ **briguing** /brēg'ing/ n canvassing.

brill[1] /bril/ n a fish related to the turbot, spotted with white. [Ety unknown]

brill[2] /bril/ (*inf*) adj short form of **brilliant**, excellent.

brilliant /bril'yənt/ adj sparkling; glittering; splendid; superlatively bright, having a dazzling hard lustre; of outstanding or conspicuous ability or intelligence; performing or performed in a showy manner or with great display of technical skill; (of musical tone) bright and clear, without many high harmonies; very good, excellent (*inf*); brilliant-cut. ◆ n a brilliant-cut diamond or other gem; a very small type (about 4-point). ◆ vt and vi to cut and polish the smaller triangular facets on a diamond. [Fr *brillant*, prp of *briller* to shine, which like Ger *Brille* eyeglass is from LL *beryllus* a beryl]

■ **brill'iance** or **brill'iancy** n. **brill'iantly** adv. **brill'iantness** n.

❑ **brill'iant-cut** (of gems) cut in a many-faceted form resembling two pyramids base to base, the upper one cut off square.

brilliantine /bril'yən-tēn/ n perfumed hair oil for making the hair glossy; a glossy cotton and mohair fabric. [Fr, from *brillant* shining]

brim /brim/ n the upper edge of a vessel or of a similarly shaped cavity; the margin or brink of a river or lake; the rim of a hat. ◆ vt (**brimm'ing**; **brimmed**) to fill to the brim. ◆ vi to be or become full to the brim. [ME *brymme*]

■ **brim'ful** or **brim-full'** adj full to the brim; brimming with tears. **brimful'ness** or **brimfull'ness** n. **brim'less** adj without a brim. **brimmed** adj brim-full; having a brim (also as *combining form*, eg *wide-brimmed*). **brimm'er** n a bowl, glass, etc full to the brim. **brimm'ing** adv and adj.

■ **brim over** to begin to overflow; (often with *with*) to be unable to contain (an emotion).

briming /brē'ming/ or **brim'ing** (*Cornwall*) n phosphorescence of the sea. [Origin unknown]

brimstone /brim'stən/ n sulphur (*archaic*); a virago, a scold (*obs*); (in full, **brimstone butterfly**) a common yellow butterfly (*Gonepteryx rhamni*), related to the cabbage whites. [Literally, burning stone; from OE *brȳne* a burning, from *byrnan* to burn, and **stone**; cf Ger *Bernstein*]

■ **brim'stony** adj.

brinded /brin'did/, **brindled** /brin'dld/ or **brindle** /brin'dl/ adj marked with spots or streaks. [See **brand**]

■ **brin'dle** n the state of being brindled.

brindisi /brin'di-zi or brēn-dē'zē/ (*Ital*) n a toast; a drinking-song.

brine /brīn/ n very salty water; the sea; any saline solution. ◆ vt to treat with brine. [OE *brȳne* a burning]

■ **brin'iness** n. **brin'ish** adj like brine; somewhat salt. **brīn'y** adj relating to brine or to the sea; salt.

❑ **brine'-pan** or **-pit** n a pan or pit in which brine is evaporated to obtain salt; a salt spring. **brine shrimp** n a small phyllopod crustacean of salt lakes and brine pools.

■ **the briny** (*inf*) the sea.

Brinell hardness test or **Brinell test** /bri-nel' (härd'nəs) test/ (metallurgy, etc) n a test to determine the hardness (**Brinell hardness**) of a substance, expressed in terms of its **Brinell (hardness) number**, by pressing a steel ball into the substance being tested under a given pressure. [JA *Brinell* (1849–1925), Swedish engineer who devised the test]

bring /bring/ vt (pat and pap **brought** /bröt/) to fetch; to cause to come; to persuade or force (oneself); to bring forward, cite or institute (eg an argument, charge, action). [OE *bringan* to carry, bring; perh related to **bear**[1]]
■ **bring'er** n. **bring'ing** n.
■ **bring about** to bring to pass or effect; to turn round. **bring and buy sale** a charity sale at which those who attend both bring items to be sold, and buy other items. **bring down** to overthrow; to lower; to humble; to shoot; to sadden. **bring forth** to give birth to or produce. **bring forward** to advance; to present or suggest (an idea, etc). **bring home** to prove; to impress, convince. **bring home the bacon** see under **bacon**. **bring in** to introduce; to yield as income; to pronounce (a verdict). **bringings forth** (Shakesp) the fruits of one's own actions. **bringing up** upbringing, rearing, training. **bring off** to bring away, eg by a boat from a ship; to rescue; to achieve, bring to a successful conclusion; to induce an orgasm in (vulgar sl). **bring on** to induce; to cause to advance; to advance the growth of (plants). **bring oneself to** to persuade or steel oneself to (do something unpleasant). **bring out** to make clear or prominent; to put (eg a book, play or singer) before the public; to introduce (a young woman) formally into society as a debutante; to encourage (a shy person) to be more outgoing; to cause (workers) to come out on strike; (of an allergy, etc) to make (a person) covered in (spots, etc). **bring over** to convert. **bring round** to restore from illness or unconsciousness; to win over. **bring the house down** to provoke or receive a general, enthusiastic burst of applause. **bring to** to restore to consciousness; to bring to a standstill (naut). **bring to bear** see under **bear**[1]. **bring under** to subdue. **bring up** to rear or educate; to introduce to notice; to make prominent; to vomit. **bring up short** to make stop suddenly. **bring up the rear** to come last. **brought forward** (bookkeeping) (of a subtotal) transferred to the head of the next column.

brinjal /brin'jäl or -jöl/ n in Indian cookery, the aubergine. [Sans vātiṅgaṇa, through Pers, Ar and Port]

brinjarry /brin-jä'ri/ n a travelling dealer in grain and salt in S India. [Hindi banjārā]

brink /bringk/ n the edge or border of a steep place or of a river (often fig). [Prob Dan brink declivity]
□ **brink'man** n a person who practises **brink'manship** or **brinks'manship**, the action or art of going to the very edge of, but not into, war or other disaster in pursuit of a policy.
■ **on the brink of** on the point of, very near.

brio /brē'ō/ n liveliness, vivacity, spirit. [Ital]

brioche /brē'osh/ n a type of light, soft loaf or roll rich with butter and eggs. [Fr]

briony same as **bryony**.

briquette or **briquet** /bri-ket'/ n a brick-shaped block made of compressed coal dust, charcoal, etc; a small brick-shaped slab. ♦ vt to form into briquettes. [Fr briquette, dimin of brique, **brick**]

bris /bris/ or **brith** /brith/ (Judaism) n a circumcision ceremony. [Heb, covenant]

brisé /brē-zā'/ (ballet) n a movement in which the dancer jumps off one foot, strikes the feet or legs together and lands on two feet. [Fr pap of briser to break]
□ **brisé volé** /vol-ā/ n (pl **brisés volés** /brē-zā vol-ā or vol-āz/) (Fr pap of voler to fly) a brisé performed with each leg alternately, completed by landing on one foot.

brise-soleil /brēz-so-lā'/ (Fr) n a louvred screen to keep sunlight from walls and windows of buildings. [Literally, sun-break]

brisk /brisk/ adj full of life and spirit, lively; promptly active; invigorating; sharp, effervescing; pert (obs); spruce (obs). ♦ vt and vi to make or become brisk; to move briskly. [First found in Shakespeare's time; poss Welsh brysg brisk of foot; perh Fr brusque]
■ **brisk'en** vt and vi to make or become brisk. **brisk'ish** adj. **brisk'ly** adv. **brisk'ness** n. **brisk'y** adj (Shakesp).

brisket /bris'kit/ (Walter Scott **breaskit** /bres'kit/) n the breast (Scot); the breast of an animal, esp the part next to the ribs; meat from this part of an animal. [Perh connected with Fr brechet, brichet]

brisling /bris'ling/ n a Norwegian sprat. [Norw, sprat]

brissel-cock /bris'l-kok/ (obs Scot) n a fowl conjectured to be the turkey. [Ety uncertain]

bristle /bris'l/ n a short stiff hair. ♦ vi (**brist'ling; brist'led**) to stand erect (like bristles); to be copiously provided, be full (with with); to have or set bristles erect; to show rage or resistance. ♦ vt to cover (as with bristles); to make bristly; to make (eg bristles) erect. [Connected with OE byrst; Scot birse; cognate with Ger Borste, ON burst]
■ **brist'led** adj having or fitted with bristles. **brist'liness** n. **brist'ling** adj thick and rough. **brist'ly** adj.
□ **brist'lebird** n any of several small Australian songbirds with bristles around the bill. **bristlecone pine** or **brist'lecone** n a W American pine (Pinus aristata) with bristle-like prickles on its cones, used in radiocarbon dating. **brist'le-fern** n a filmy fern (Trichomanes radicans) with a bristle on the receptacle. **bris'tle-grass** n a grass of the genus Setaria. **brist'letail** n any insect of the order Thysanura. **bristle worm** n a chaetopod.
■ **set up one's bristles** to show resistance.

Bristol /bris't(ə)l/ n a city in SW England.
■ **bris'tols** n pl breasts (Cockney rhyming sl from Bristol City, **titty**[1]).
□ **Bristol board** n a smooth cardboard. **Bristol-brick'** n an earthy material for scouring cutlery, like bath-brick. **Bristol-di'amond** n a kind of quartz crystal found near Bristol. **Bristol fashion** adv in good order, esp in the phrase shipshape and Bristol fashion.

brisure /brizh'yər or brē-zür'/ n any part of a rampart or parapet which breaks off at an angle from the general direction (fortif); a variation of a coat of arms showing the relation of a younger to the main line (heraldry). [Fr, from briser to break]

Brit /brit/ n (inf short form of **British**) a British person.

Brit. abbrev : Britain; Britannia; British; Briton.

Brit- /brit-/ combining form denoting contemporary British culture.
■ **Brit'art** n a movement in British modern art originating in the 1990s. **Brit'pop** n a type of guitar-based British popular music of the mid-1990s.

brit /brit/ n a young herring, sprat, or other fish. [Ety unknown]

Britannia /bri-tan'yə/ n a seated female figure with a trident and helmet, representing Britain or the British Commonwealth; the ancient Roman province occupying the south of what is now Great Britain. [L Britannia, Brittan(n)ia, Great Britain or the British Islands]
□ **Britannia metal** n an alloy, mainly tin with copper, antimony, lead or zinc or a mixture of these, similar to pewter.

Britannic /bri-tan'ik/ adj relating to Britannia or Britain (archaic, but surviving officially in Britannic majesty). [See **Britannia**]

Britart see under **Brit-**.

britches see **breech**.

brith see **bris**.

British /brit'ish/ adj relating to Britain, to its former or present inhabitants or citizens, or to its empire or commonwealth of nations; relating to the variety of English used in Britain; relating to the ancient Britons. ♦ n the British people; the language of the ancient Britons; Welsh (obs). [OE Brettisc, from Bret a Briton, Welshman]
■ **Brit'icize** or **-ise** vt and vi to make or become British or like the British. **Brit'isher** n (orig US) a native or citizen of Britain. **Brit'ishism** or **Brit'icism** /-sizm/ n an expression characteristic of the English spoken in Britain. **Brit'ishness** n.
□ **British bulldog** n a team game of chasing in which as the members of one team are caught, they join the other team. **British disease** n extreme militancy in industrial relations, esp excessive use of strikes. **British gum** n dextrin. **British plate** n a kind of German silver. **British Standards Institution** see BSI. **British Standard Time** n the time, one hour ahead of Greenwich Mean Time, used in Britain throughout the year from 1968 to 1971. **British Summer Time** n the time adopted in Britain during the summer, one hour ahead of Greenwich Mean Time (to give extra daylight in the evenings). **British thermal unit** n the amount of heat required to raise the temperature of 1lb of water by 1°F, equivalent to 1055.06 joules.
■ **British warm** see **warm**.

Briton /brit'ən/ n a native or citizen of the United Kingdom; one of the Brythonic inhabitants of Britain before and after the coming of the English, or one of their present representatives the Welsh; a Breton (obs). [L Brittō, -onis, or -ōnis; see **Brythonic**]
■ **Brit'oness** n (Spenser) a female Briton. **Britton'ic** adj Brythonic.

Britpop see under **Brit-**.

britschka, britska see **britzka**.

brittle /brit'l/ adj apt to break, easily broken; frail; curt, edgy, sensitive; unstable. ♦ n a type of hard toffee made with caramelized sugar and nuts. [OE brēotan to break]
■ **brittlely** /brit'l-li/ or **britt'ly** adv. **britt'leness** n.
□ **brittle bone disease** or **brittle bones** n an inherited disease, osteogenesis imperfecta, characterized by abnormal fragility of the bones; osteoporosis (non-standard). **britt'lestar** n a member of a class of echinoderms like starfish with long, snaky, sharply differentiated arms.

Brittonic /bri-ton'ik/ adj Brythonic.

britzka, **britzska**, **britska** /brits'kə/ or **britschka** /brich'kə/ n an open four-wheeled carriage with a folding top. [Pol *bryczka*]

Brix scale /briks skāl/ n a scale used in measuring the density of sugar in a solution at a given temperature. [AFW *Brix* (1798–1890), German scientist]

brize see breeze³.

BRN *abbrev* : Bahrain (IVR).

Bro. *abbrev* : Brother (*pl* **Bros.**).

bro¹ or **bro'** /brō/ n a contracted form of **brother** (often used in addressing a male).

bro² /brō/ n a place for which one feels great affinity because of birth, upbringing, long residence, etc there. [Welsh, locality]

broach /brōch/ vt to pierce (eg a cask), to tap; to open up or begin; to start to speak about. ◆ vi and vt to (cause a sailing-ship to) veer dangerously when running downwind, so as to lie beam on to the waves (also n). ◆ n a tapering, pointed instrument, used chiefly for boring or rounding holes; a spit; (also **broach'-spire**) a church spire, now restricted to one without parapets, consisting of a tall octagonal and a low square pyramid interpenetrating each other; a visible corner of the square pyramid in such a spire. [Fr *broche*; cf **brooch**]
■ **broach'er** n a broach or spit; a person who broaches or utters.
■ **broach the admiral** to steal some liquor from a cask in transit or in store. **broach to** (*naut*) to turn to windward.

broad /bröd/ adj wide; large, spacious, free or open; widely diffused; covering a wide range, spectrum, etc; giving prominence to main elements, or harmony of the whole, without insisting on detail; slow and full-toned; strongly marked in pronunciation or dialect; (of a vowel) open (*phonetics*); outspoken, obvious, unsubtle; coarse, vulgar; having liberal mind or outlook; (of money) denoting the less liquid categories (eg M2, M3, qqv under **M** (*symbol*)), such as that in an account, etc, realizable only with several months' notice. ◆ n the broad part; (in East Anglia) a lake-like expansion of a river; a broadpiece; a woman or, sometimes, a prostitute (*N Am offensive sl*). Also *adv*. [OE *brād*, Gothic *braiths*]
■ **broad'en** vt and vi to make or grow broad or broader. **broad'ish** adj. **broad'ly** adv. **broad'ness** n. **broad'ways** or **broad'wise** adv breadthwise.
❏ **broad arrow** n a mark (⬆) used on government property, or generally. **broad'band** adj across, involving, or designed to operate across, a wide range of frequencies (*telecom*); capable of accommodating data from a variety of input sources, as voice, telephone, television, etc (*comput*). **broad'-based** adj including a wide range of opinions, subjects, political groups, etc. **broad bean** n a plant (*Vicia faba*) of the family Leguminosae, or one of its large flat edible seeds which grow in pods. **broad'bill** n any of several birds with a broad bill, such as the spoonbill, the scaup (*US*), or a member of the tropical family Eurylaimidae. **broad'-brim** n a hat with a broad brim, such as those once worn by Quakers; a Quaker (*inf*). **broad'brush** adj rough; not worked out in detail (*inf*). **Broad Church** n a party within the Church of England favouring a broad and liberal interpretation of dogmatic definitions and creed subscription; (*esp without cap*) a political or other group, party, etc that is similarly liberal-minded or all-inclusive. **broad'-church** adj. **broad'cloth** n a fine, fulled woollen or worsted cloth. **broad day** or **daylight** n clear, open daylight. **broad'-gauge** see gauge. **broad jump** n (*N Am*) long jump. **broad'-leaf** n any broad-leaved tree; any tobacco plant with broad leaves. **broad'-leaved** adj (*esp* in classifying types of tree) having broad leaves, not needles; deciduous, hardwood. **broad'loom** adj (of carpet) woven on a wide loom. **broad-mind'ed** adj liberal; tolerant. **broad-mind'edly** adv. **broad-mind'edness** n. **broad'piece** n a 17c 20-shilling coin. **Broad Scots** (also formerly **Scotch**) n older or dialect forms of the Scottish tongue, a development of Old English. **broad'sheet** n any standard sheet of paper, unfolded and uncut; a large sheet of paper printed *usu* on one side only, containing eg an advertisement or (*hist*) a proclamation, ballad, popular song, etc; a newspaper of large format, measuring *approx* 40 × 60cm (about 16 × 24in); a quality newspaper. **broad'side** n the side of a ship; all the guns on one side of a ship of war; their simultaneous discharge; a strongly critical verbal attack; a broadsheet. ◆ vt to hit or collide with the side of (*N Am*). **broad'-spectrum** adj wide-spectrum. **broad'sword** n a cutting sword with a broad blade; a man armed with such a sword. **broad'tail** n fur prepared from the skin of very young karakul lambs; a karakul sheep. **broad'way** n a broad road, often the name of the chief thoroughfare of a town or district.
■ **as broad as it is long** six of one and half a dozen of the other.

broadcast /brōd'kāst/ n a radio or TV programme; the transmission of material by radio or TV for reception by the public; sowing by broadcasting; general dissemination. ◆ vt (*pat* and *pap* **broad'cast** or (now *rare*) **broad'casted**) to scatter, send out or disseminate freely by

any means, *esp* by radio or TV transmission. ◆ vi to transmit a broadcast; to take part in a broadcast. ◆ adj scattered or sown over the general surface; dispersed widely; communicated generally, by word of mouth, pamphlets, radio, TV, or any other means; by means of broadcast. ◆ adv in all directions. [Ety as for **broad**, and **cast** to throw]
■ **broad'caster** n. **broad'casting** n.
■ **Broadcasters' Audience Research Board** the group that commissions and publishes data on British TV audience research. **broadcast videotex** teletext.

Brobdingnagian /brob-ding-nag'i-ən/ n an inhabitant of the fabled region of *Brobdingnag* in Swift's *Gulliver's Travels*, where everything was gigantic. ◆ adj of Brobdingnag; (*usu without cap*) immense.
■ **Brob'dingnag** adj immense.

brocade /brō-kād'/ n a heavy silky fabric with a raised (or apparently raised) design on it. [Ital *broccato*, Fr *brocart*, from Ital *broccare*, Fr *brocher* to prick, stitch; from same root as **broach**]
■ **brocād'ed** adj woven or worked in the manner of brocade; dressed in brocade.

brocage see brokerage under broker.

brocard /brō'kärd or -kard/ n an elementary law or principle; a canon; /bro-kar/ a gibe (*Fr*). [Fr *brocard*, LL *brocarda*, from *Brocard* or *Burchard*, Bishop of Worms, who published a book of ecclesiastical rules]

Broca's area /brō'kəz ā'ri-ə/ n the region of the brain concerned with speech, found in the left frontal lobe in most right-handed people. [P *Broca* (1824–80), French surgeon]

brocatelle or (now *N Am*) **brocatel** /bro-kə-tel'/ n a stiff, *orig* silk-and-linen, heavy-figured fabric like brocade. [Fr, from Ital *broccatello* gold tinsel, from *broccato* brocade]

broccoli /brok'ə-li/ n (also **sprouting broccoli**) a type of cabbage cultivated for its green leafy stalks and branched heads of flower-buds, eaten while immature as a vegetable. [Ital; pl of *broccolo* a sprout, dimin of *brocco* a skewer, a shoot]
■ **Broccoli'ni**® n a green vegetable with long stalks and small florets, a hybrid of broccoli and gai lan.

broch¹, also **brogh** or **brough** /brohh/ n a dry-built circular tower of the late Iron Age with galleries in the thickness of the wall, common in Scotland, very rare elsewhere; a luminous ring around the moon. [Scot, from ON *borg*; OE *burh*]

broch² /brōch/ obsolete spelling of **broach**, **brooch**.

brochan /brohh'ən/ (*Scot*) n gruel; sometimes porridge. [Gaelic]

broché /brō'shā/ adj of fabrics, woven with a pattern like brocade. ◆ n such a fabric. [Fr pap of *brocher* to stitch]

brochette /bro-shet'/ n a small metal or wooden skewer for holding food together or steady while cooking; food cooked in this way. [Fr]

brochure /brō'shər or -shoor'/ n an information or publicity booklet. [Fr, from *brocher* to stitch, from *broche* a needle. See **broach**]
■ **bro'chureware** n (*comput sl*) pages on a company website produced by converting printed marketing materials into an online format.

brock¹ /brok/ n a badger; a dirty, stinking fellow. [OE *brocc*, from Celtic (eg Gaelic *broc*)]
■ **brocked** or **brock'it** adj (*Scot*) variegated, *esp* black and white.

brock² /brok/ (*Scot*) n food scraps; pigswill; rubbish. [OE (*ge*)*broc* fragment, from *brecan* to break]
■ **brock'age** n fragments of crockery, furniture, etc (*Scot*); a mis-struck coin.

Brocken spectre /brok'ən spek'tər/ n the shadow of an observer, enlarged and often surrounded by coloured lights, thrown onto a bank of cloud, a phenomenon sometimes encountered on mountain-tops. [*Brocken*, a peak in the Harz mountains of Germany]

brocket /bro'kit/ n a stag in its second year, with its first, dagger-shaped, horns; a small S American deer with short unbranched horns. [Fr *brocard*, from *broque* a spike]

brockit see under brock¹.

brockram /brok'rəm/ (*N Eng*) n breccia.

brod¹ /brod/ n a Scots form of **board**.

brod² /brod/ (*dialect*) n a goad; a spike; a kind of nail; a prick. ◆ vt (**brodd'ing**; **brodd'ed**) to prod. [OE *brord*; ON *broddr*; cf OIr *brot* and Gaelic *brod* a goad, sting]

brodekin or **brodkin** /brōd'kin/ (*obs*) n a buskin. [Fr *brodequin*]

broderie anglaise /brod-rē ã-glez' or brō'də-ri ã'glāz/ n openwork embroidery. [Fr, English embroidery]

Broederbond /broo' or brü'dər-bont/ (*S Afr*) n an organization of Nationalist Afrikaners, highly secret until recent years, with membership in key public and professional positions, etc. [Afrik from Du *broeder* brother, and *bond* band, fellowship]

brog /brog/ (*Scot*) *n* an awl. ◆ *vt* (**brogg'ing**; **brogged**) to prick. [Origin obscure]

brogh see **broch**[1].

brogue[1] /brōg/ *n* a stout shoe, *usu* with a decorative pattern of holes (also **brō'gan**); a rough shoe of untanned leather formerly worn in parts of Scotland and Ireland. [Ir *brōg*, dimin *brògan* and Gaelic *bròg* a shoe]

brogue[2] /brōg/ *n* a lilting Irish accent. [Perh **brogue**[1], but Ir *barróg* hold, grip, speech impediment, is also suggested]
■ **brogu'ish** or **brogue'ish** *adj* having a slight brogue.

broider /broi'dər/ (*archaic*) *vt* and *vi* to embroider. [OFr *brouder*, *broder*; see **embroider**]
■ **broid'erer** *n*. **broid'ering** *n*. **broid'ery** *n*.

broil[1] /broil/ *vt* to cook over hot coals; to grill (*esp N Am*). ◆ *vi* to be extremely hot, or (*N Am*) enraged. [OFr *bruillir* or *bruller* to burn]
■ **broil'er** *n* a very hot day; a quickly reared young chicken sold ready for broiling (also *adj*); a part of a cooker used for broiling (*N Am*).
❑ **broiler house** *n* a place where broiler chickens are reared.

broil[2] /broil/ *n* a noisy quarrel; a confused disturbance. —Also (*Scot*) **brulyie**, **bruilzie** or **brulzie** /brül'(y)i or brül'yi/. [Fr *brouiller* to trouble]
■ **broil'er** *n* a person who stirs up broils.

brokage see under **broker**.

broke /brōk/ *pat* and old *pap* of **break**[1]. *adj* (*inf*) bankrupt, without money; hard up.
■ **go for broke** to make an all-out bid or supreme effort, or to gamble everything (in order to gain something).

broken /brō'kən/ *pap* of **break**[1]. *adj* smashed, in pieces; incomplete, fragmentary; interrupted; altered in direction; (of flowers) in plant-breeding, variegated; with the surface interrupted; intermittent; humbled or crushed; shattered in health, spirit, estate or position; bankrupt; thrown into disorder; dispersed, routed; trained to saddle or bridle (also **broken-in**'); outlawed (*obs*); infringed, violated; (of a chord) played as an arpeggio (*music*); (of a language) spoken badly or haltingly, as by a learner.
■ **brōk'enly** *adv*. **brōk'enness** *n*.
❑ **brok'en-backed** *adj* having the back dislocated; (of a ship) so loosened in her frame as to droop at both ends. **brok'en-down** *adj* worn-out; ill; no longer functional; ruined in character or strength. **broken-heart'ed** *adj* crushed emotionally; greatly depressed or hurt, *esp* by disappointment in love. **broken-heart'edly** *adv*. **broken-heart'edness** *n*. **broken home** *n* the home of children whose parents are divorced or have separated. **broken man** *n* a man whose life is completely shattered; an outlaw, *esp* in the Scottish Highlands and Border country (*hist*). **broken meats** *n pl* the leavings of a banquet. **broken music** *n* (*Shakesp*) part-music. **broken-wind'ed** *adj* (of eg a horse) having short breath or disordered respiration.

broker /brō'kər/ *n* a person employed to buy and sell for others; a secondhand dealer; a go-between, negotiator or intermediary; a stockbroker; a pander, pimp (*obs*). [ME *brocour*, from Anglo-Fr *brocour*. The original meaning seems to be tapster; cf **broach**]
■ **broke** or (*US*) **brok'er** *vi* to bargain, negotiate; to act as broker. **brōk'erage**, **brōk'age** or (*obs*) **brōc'age** *n* the business of a broker; commission for transacting business for others; the act of procuring, pimping (*obs*). **brōk'ery** *n* (*obs*) the business of a broker; broker's wares. **brōk'ing** *n*.
❑ **brō'ker-dealer** *n* (*stock exchange*) since 27 October 1986, a firm or person officially combining the jobs of stockbroker and stockjobber, but only acting as one or the other in any single deal.

brolga /brol'gə/ *n* a large grey Australian crane (also **Australian crane** or **native companion**). [From an Aboriginal language]

brolly /brol'i/ (*inf*) *n* an umbrella.

brom- see **bromo-**.

bromance /brō'mans/ (*sl*) *n* a close, but not romantic or sexual, relationship between two men. [Blend of **bro**[1] and **romance**]

brome-grass /brōm'gräs/ *n* a grass (genus *Bromus*) strongly resembling oats. [Gr *bromos* a kind of oats]

bromelain /bro'mə-lān/ or **bromelin** /-lin/ *n* an enzyme, obtained from the juice of the pineapple plant, that breaks down proteins, used medically and in skin-care products, etc. [**bromelia**]

bromelia /brō- or brə-mē'lyə or -li-ə/ *n* any plant of the genus *Bromelia*, giving name to the pineapple family, **Bromēliā'ceae**, mainly epiphytic and xerophytic monocotyledons, with stiff leaves in rosettes. [Named in honour of the Swedish botanist Olaf Bromel (1639–1705)]
■ **bromēliā'ceous** *adj*. **bromēl'iad** *n* any plant of the family.

bromine /brō'mēn/, *-min* or *-mīn/ *n* a non-metallic chemical element (symbol **Br**; atomic no 35), a red liquid giving off an irritating poisonous brown vapour. [Gr *bromos* stink]

brō'mate *n* a salt of bromic acid. **brō'mic** *adj*. **brō'mide** *n* a salt of hydrobromic acid, HBr; a platitude; a dull platitudinous person (from the use of bromides as sedatives); a type of monochrome photographic print, loosely applied to other types. **brōmid'ic** *adj* conventionally commonplace. **brōmidrō'sis** or **brōmhidrō'sis** *n* osmidrosis. **brominā'tion** *n* the substitution by bromine in or the addition of bromine to organic compounds. **brō'mism** or **brō'minism** *n* poisoning by an overdose of bromine. **brō'moform** *n* a bromine compound analogous to chloroform.
❑ **bromic acid** *n* a compound of hydrogen, bromine and oxygen, $HBrO_3$. **bromide paper** *n* (*photog*) a paper with a sensitive surface containing silver bromide, used in printing from a negative.

brommer /brom'ər/ (*S Afr*) *n* the bluebottle fly. [Afrik; onomatopoeic]

bromo- /brō-mō-/ or before a vowel **brom-** /brōm-/ *combining form* denoting bromine.

bronchi, **bronchia**, etc see **bronchus**.

broncho see **bronco**.

broncho- /brong-kō-/ *combining form* relating to the bronchi. [Gr *bronchos* windpipe, and *bronchia* bronchia]
■ **bron'choconstrictor** or **bron'chodilator** *n* any drug that causes the bronchi to narrow or expand. **bronchog'raphy** *n* radiological examination of the trachea or bronchi. **bronchopneumō'nia** *n* inflammation of the lungs caused by infection of the bronchioles. **bronch'oscope** *n* an instrument which, when passed down into the bronchi, allows their examination, the removal of foreign bodies, etc. **bronchoscop'ic** or **bronchoscop'ical** *adj*. **bronchoscop'ically** *adv*. **bronchos'copy** *n*.

bronchus /brong'kəs/ *n* (*pl* **bronch'i** /-ī/) (*anat*) either of the main forks of the windpipe. [Gr *bronchos* windpipe, and *bronchia* bronchia]
■ **bronch'ia** *n pl* the small branches of the bronchi. **bronch'ial** *adj* relating to the bronchi, or to the bronchia. **bronchiectasis** /-ek'tə-sis/ *n* a chronic disease caused by dilated bronchi. **bronchiōl'ar** *adj*. **bronch'iole** /-ōl/ *n* any of the minute branches of the bronchi. **bronchioli'tis** *n* inflammation of the bronchioles, generally occurring in infants. **bronchitic** /-it'ik/ *adj* relating to or suffering from bronchitis. ◆ *n* a person suffering from bronchitis. **bronchitis** /-ī'tis/ *n* inflammation of the lining of the bronchial tubes.
❑ **bronchial tube** *n* either of the bronchi; a smaller branch of the bronchi.

bronco or **broncho** /brong'kō/ (*N Am*) *n* (*pl* **bron'cos** or **bron'chos**) a wild or half-tamed horse. [Sp *bronco* rough, sturdy]
❑ **bronc'obuster** *n* (*inf*) a person who breaks in broncos; a cowboy.

brond an obsolete form of **brand**.

brondyron see **brand-iron** under **brand**.

brontosaurus /bron-tə-sö'rəs/ *n* a member of the *Brontosaurus* genus, the popular (and formerly the technical) name for the *Apatosaurus* genus, lizard-hipped, quadripedal, herbivorous dinosaurs, found as fossils in Wyoming and Colorado (also **bront'osaur**). [Gr *brontē* thunder, and *sauros* lizard]

Bronx cheer /brongks chēr/ (*US*) *n* a vulgar sound of disapproval, a raspberry. [From the *Bronx* borough of New York City]

Bronx hat /brongks hat/ *n* a warm, *usu* woollen, brimless hat. [Ety as for **Bronx cheer**]

bronze /bronz/ *n* an alloy of copper and tin; now also applied to a copper alloy without tin; anything cast in bronze; the colour of bronze; a bronze medal; impudence (*obs*). ◆ *adj* made of bronze; coloured like bronze. ◆ *vt* and *vi* to make or become like bronze in colour or appearance; to harden (*fig, obs*). [Fr, from Ital *bronzo*, *bronzino*, perh from L (*aes*) *Brundusīnum* (brass) from Brindisi; or perh from Pers *birinj*, *pirinj* copper]
■ **bronzed** *adj* coated with bronze; bronze-coloured, suntanned; hardened (*fig, obs*). **bron'zen** *adj* (*rare*). **bron'zer** *n* a cosmetic applied to the skin to give the appearance of a suntan. **bron'zify** *vt* (*rare*) to make into bronze. **bron'zing** *n* the process of giving or assuming the appearance of bronze; the acquiring of a suntanned appearance. **bron'zite** *n* an enstatite with bronze-like lustre. **bronz'y** *adj*.
❑ **Bronze Age** *n* (*archaeol*) a prehistoric condition or stage of culture coming between the Stone Age and the Iron Age marked by the use of bronze as the material for tools and weapons. **bronzed skin** *n* Addison's disease. **bronze medal** *n* in athletics competitions, etc, the medal awarded as third prize. **bronze'-wing**, **bronze-wing pigeon** or **bronzed-wing(ed) pigeon** *n* any of various species of Australian pigeon with lustrous bronze markings on the wings.

broo[1] /broo or brü/ (*Scot*) *n* liquor that comes off from anything or in which anything has been boiled. [Prob OFr *bro*, *breu* broth]

broo[2] or **brow** /broo/ (*Scot*) *n* a brow in any sense; (*perh* a different word) a liking, good opinion (with *of*). [**brow**]

broo³ see **buroo**.

brooch /brōch/ n an ornamental clasp with a joined pin. ◆ vt (Shakesp) to adorn as with a brooch. [Fr broche a spit; see **broach**]

brood /brood/ n something bred; offspring, children, or family; the number hatched, produced or cherished at once; the condition of breeding or brooding; a race, kind, breed; parentage, extraction (archaic). ◆ adj for breeding (as in brood mare, etc). ◆ vt to sit on or cover in order to breed or hatch; to hatch; to cover, eg with wings; to cherish with care; to meditate moodily on. ◆ vi to sit as a hen on eggs; to hang envelopingly (over); to think anxiously for some time; to meditate silently (with on or over). [OE brōd; Du broed; cf **breed**]
■ **brood'er** n a person or animal that broods; a heated building or enclosure for rearing young chicks. **brood'ily** adv. **brood'iness** n thinking anxiously or resentfully; threatening, oppressive. **brood'ing** adj. **brood'ingly** adv. **brood'y** adj (of a hen) inclined to sit or incubate; (of a woman) wanting to have a baby (inf); prolific, fertile (obs); apt to brood, sullen, moody.
❑ **brood'-pouch** or **brood'-sac** n a body-cavity, eg in viviparous cockroaches, in which eggs or embryos are received and developed.

brook¹ /brŭk/ n a small stream. [OE brōc; Du broek, Ger Bruch]
■ **brook'let** n a little brook.
❑ **brook'lime** n a speedwell that grows in brooks and ditches. **brook trout** n an orig N American char introduced into Europe. **brook'weed** n water pimpernel (genus Samolus), a water plant of the primrose family superficially like a crucifer.

brook² /brŭk/ vt to enjoy (now chiefly Scots law or archaic); to bear or endure (formal). [OE brūcan to use, enjoy; Ger brauchen, L frui, fruct-]

brookite /brŭk'īt/ n a mineral, titanium oxide. [Henry James Brooke (1771–1857), English mineralogist]

brool /brool/ n a deep murmur. [Ger Brüll a roar]

broom /broom/ n a long-handled domestic sweeping brush; a yellow-flowered papilionaceous shrub, Cytisus scoparius, or a related plant; a besom made of its twigs or of anything similar. ◆ vt to sweep with a broom. [OE brōm]
■ **broom'y** adj covered with or consisting of broom.
❑ **broom'ball** n a team game played on ice, orig by British diplomatic staff in Moscow, using brooms and a plastic ball. **broom'-corn** n a kind of millet of whose stalks brooms are made. **broom'rape** n (L rapum a knob) a genus (Orobanche) of plants, parasitic on broom and other roots. **broom'staff** (archaic) or **broom'stick** n the handle of a broom.
■ **marry over the broomstick** or **jump the besom** or **broomstick** to go through an irregular form of marriage in which both jump over a broomstick. **new brooms sweep clean** people newly appointed to a position work very conscientiously, or try to sweep away abuses, old attitudes, old methods, etc. **not know a B from a broomstick** to be very ignorant.

broose (Walter Scott **brouze**) /brooz or brūz/ (Scot) n a race at a wedding. [Origin unknown]

Bros. (sometimes pronounced /bros or broz/) (commerce) abbrev: Brothers.

brose /brōz/ n a food made by pouring boiling water or milk on oatmeal or peasemeal, seasoned with salt and butter. [Scot; perh connected with **brewis**, **broo**¹]
■ **Athole** or **Atholl brose** a mixture of whisky and honey and sometimes oatmeal. **brose and bannock day** Shrove Tuesday.

broth /broth/ n water in which vegetables and meat, etc have been boiled, used as soup or (in laboratories, often with other substances added) as a medium for culture of bacteria. [OE broth, from brēowan to brew; see **brew**]
■ **a broth of a boy** (Irish) the quintessence of a good fellow.

brotha /brudh'ə/ (US sl) n an African-American man. [Altered form of **brother**]

brothel /broth'l/ n a house or establishment where prostitution is practised. [ME brothel worthless person, from OE brothen ruined, from brēothan to go to ruin; infl in meaning by bordel (see **bordello**)]
❑ **brothel creeper** n (inf) a man's soft, usu suede, shoe with thick crêpe sole.

brother /brudh'ər/ n (pl **broth'ers** or **breth'ren**; see below) a male in relation to another person of either sex born of the same parents or (half-brother) parent; anyone closely united with or resembling another who is associated in common interests, occupation, etc; a fellow member of a religious order, a trade union, etc; a fellow creature; a fellow citizen; someone of the same religion as another; a lay member of a male religious order; a kinsman (Bible); as a form of address to (usu) a stranger (esp US dialect or archaic, or, now also Brit, facetious). ◆ adj associated in any relation (also as a combining form,

as in brother-man). ◆ interj expressing surprise, disgust, etc. [OE brōthor, pl brēther; cognate with Ger Bruder, Gaelic brathair, L frāter, Sans bhrātr; Gr phrātēr fellow clansman]
■ **breth'ren** n pl brothers, used esp in the sense of fellow members and in the names of certain bodies, such as Christian Brethren, Moravian Brethren, Plymouth Brethren, etc. **broth'erhood** n the state of being a brother; a sense of companionship; an association of men for any purpose. **broth'erlike** adj. **broth'erliness** n. **broth'erly** adj like a brother; kind or affectionate.
❑ **brother-ger'man** n a full brother, one with whom one has both parents in common (cf **half-brother**). **broth'er-in-law** n (pl **broth'ers-in-law**) the brother of a husband or wife; a sister's husband; a husband's or wife's sister's husband.

Brotstudien /brōt'shtoo-dē-ən or -dyən/ (Ger) n pl studies by which one earns one's living, (literally, bread studies).

brough see **broch**¹.

brougham /broo'əm, brō'əm or broom/ n a one-horse closed carriage, named after Lord Brougham (1778–1868); an early motor car with uncovered driver's seat.

brought /brōt/ pat and pap of **bring**.

brouhaha /broo-hä'hä or broo'hä-hä/ n fuss, excitement, clamour, or an instance of this. [Fr; perh from Heb]

brouze see **broose**.

brow /brow/ n the eyebrow; the ridge over the eyes; the forehead; a person's aspect, appearance; the edge of a hill; a gallery in a coalmine running across the face of the coal; a ship's gangway (navy); a pit-head. [OE brū]
■ **brow'less** adj without eyebrows; without shame.
❑ **brow'-antler** or **brow'-tine** n the first tine of a deer's horn. **brow'band** n the bridle strap that goes over a horse's forehead. **brow'beat** vt to bear down on with stern looks or speech; to bully. **brow'beaten** adj. **brow'beater** n. **brow'beating** n. **brow'-bound** adj crowned. **brow-tine** see **brow-antler** above.

brown /brown/ adj of a dark, woody or dusky colour, tending towards red or yellow; dark-complexioned; tanned or sunburnt; formerly conventionally applied to a sword, perh burnished, perh rusty, perh bloodstained. ◆ n a dark-reddish earthy or woody colour; a brown pigment; a brown object or thing; a copper coin (obs sl); a close-flying number of game birds, esp (lit and fig) **fire into the brown** to shoot into an area without aiming at a particular target. ◆ vt to give a brown colour to; to roast until brown. ◆ vi to become brown. [OE brūn; Du bruin, Ger braun]
■ **brown'ie** n a benevolent creature who may secretly help with domestic work (folklore); (with cap; in full **Brownie Guide**) a member of the senior of two junior sections of the Guides, having a brown (since 1990 yellow) uniform; (a square piece of) a kind of rich, chewy chocolate cake containing nuts (orig N Am); a simple, early, mass-produced make of box camera (also **Brown'ie**®); a kind of currant bread (Aust and NZ). **brown'ing** n the process of making or becoming brown; a product for making gravy, etc brown. **brown'ish** adj. **brown'ness** n. **brown'y** adj of a brownish colour.
❑ **brown ale** n a dark-coloured mild beer. **brown algae** or **brown seaweeds** n pl the Phaeophyceae, one of the main divisions of the algae. **brown-bag** vt and vi (US) to bring (one's lunch, or alcohol) in a brown paper bag or something similar. **brown bear** n the common bear of Europe and Asia. **Brown Bess** n the old British flintlock musket (from its brown walnut stock). **Brown Betty** n (US) a baked pudding containing apples and other fruit. **brown bill** n a foot soldier's or watchman's halberd, painted brown. **brown bread** n any dark-coloured bread, esp that made of unbolted flour, eg wholemeal. ◆ adj (rhyming sl) dead. **brown coal** n lignite. **brown dwarf** see **dwarf**. **brown earth** n a type of soil with a rich brown surface layer, formed under deciduous forest in temperate humid regions. **brown fat** n heat-producing fat cells of a brownish colour, found in various parts of the body, eg between the shoulder-blades, thought to be activated by overeating and thus to have a bearing on weight gain. **brown'field** adj denoting a site that has previously been developed for urban or industrial use (cf **greenfield**). **brown George** n a hard biscuit; a brown earthenware vessel. **brown goods** n pl (commercial jargon) a term covering types of electrical equipment orig wooden-cased, such as audio and TV (as opposed to traditionally white kitchen appliances such as refrigerators and washing machines). **Brownie Guide** see brownie above. **Brownie Guider** see **brown owl** below. **brownie point** n (sometimes ironic, usu in pl) a notional good mark or commendation for doing well. **brown lung (disease)** n byssinosis. **brown'-nose** vt and vi (vulgar sl) to act obsequiously (towards), curry favour (with). ◆ n an extremely obsequious person (also **brown'-noser**). **brown'out** n (esp US) a reduction in electrical power, etc, a partial blackout. **brown owl** n the tawny owl; (with caps; now correctly **Brownie Guider**) the former official, now the popular, name for a woman who has charge of a group of Brownies. **brown paper** n coarse strong paper used chiefly for wrapping. **brown rat** n the larger

fāte; fär; mē; fûr; mīne; mōte; för; mūte; pŭt; dhen (then); el'ə-mənt (element) • For other sounds see detailed chart of pronunciation and commoner of the two British rats (often black). **brown rice** *n* rice hulled but not polished. **brown rot** *n* any of several plant diseases causing browning. **brown sauce** *n* any brown-coloured savoury sauce, now *esp* a sharp-flavoured commercially bottled variety. **brown seaweeds** see **brown algae** above. **Brown'shirt** *n* a member of Hitler's organization of storm troopers; a Nazi; a fascist. **brown spar** *n* a brownish variety of dolomite. **brown'stone** *n* (*US*) a dark-brown sandstone, regarded as the favourite building material of the prosperous classes; a building made of this. **brown stout** *n* a kind of dark ale. **brown study** *n* a reverie; absent-mindedness. **brown sugar** *n* unrefined or partially refined sugar. **brown'tail moth** *n* a brown and white European moth (*Euproctis chrysorrhoea*) that damages the leaves of trees. **brown trout** *n* a kind of trout common in Europe, dark-coloured on the back and lighter underneath.

■ **browned off** (*inf*) fed up; bored; downhearted, dispirited. **do brown** (*sl*) to deceive or take in completely.

Brownian /brow'ni-ən/ (*phys*) *adj* relating to Robert *Brown* (1773–1858), who drew attention to **Brownian movement** or **motion**, an agitation of particles in a colloid solution caused by the non-uniform impact of molecules in the surrounding medium.

Brownist /brow'nist/ *n* a person holding the church principles of Robert *Browne* (c.1550–1633), which were taken up and modified by the Independents or Congregationalists of England.
■ **Brown'ism** *n*.

brown jolly /brown jol'i/ *n* a corruption of **brinjal**.

browse /browz/ *vi* to feed on the rough shoots of plants; to read or look round a shop in a casual or haphazard way. ◆ *vt* to browse on. ◆ *vi* and *vt* (*comput*) to examine stored information (*in* or *on*). ◆ *n* young twigs and shoots; an act of browsing. [OFr *brouster* (Fr *brouter*), from *broust* a sprout]
■ **brows'able** *adj*. **brows'er** *n* a person, animal or thing that browses; (also **client**) software that acts as an interface between the user and the content on the Internet or on an internal network. **brows'ing** *n* the shoots and leaves of plants; fodder; the action of the verb browse. **brows'y** *adj*.

browst /browst/ (*Scot*) *n* a brewing. [**brew**]

brrr *interj* imitative of shivering with cold.

BRS *abbrev* : British Road Services.

BRU *abbrev* : Brunei (IVR).

brucellosis /broo-sə-lō'sis/ or -*se*-/ *n* a disease of animals, mainly cattle, communicable to humans as undulant fever (also called **contagious abortion**). [Sir David *Bruce* (1855–1931), Australian-born bacteriologist, Mod L -*ella*, and -**osis**]

bruchid /broo'kid/ *adj* and *n* (a beetle) of the family **Bru'chidae** whose larvae live on peas, beans, etc. [Gr *brouchos* locust]

brucine /broo'sēn/ *n* an alkaloid, less physiologically active than strychnine, obtained from nux vomica. [Wrongly thought to come from the simarubaceous genus *Brucea*, named after James *Bruce* (1730–94), Scottish traveller in Africa]

brucite /broo'sīt/ *n* a mineral, magnesium hydroxide. [Named after A *Bruce*, American mineralogist]

Brücke see **Die Brücke**.

bruckle /bruk'l/ (*Scot*) *adj* liable to break, brittle and unstable. [OE *brucol*, from *brecan* to break]

Bruges group /broozh groop/ *n* a group of British politicians opposed to the creation of a federal Europe. [From *Bruges*, Belgium, where Margaret Thatcher made a famous anti-federalist speech]

bruhaha a spelling of **brouhaha**.

bruilzie *n* Scots form of **broil**[2].

Bruin /broo'in/ *n* a name for a bear, *esp* in children's stories; the name of the bear in the epic *Reynard the Fox*. [Du, brown]

bruise /brooz/ *vt* to crush by beating or pounding without breaking the surface; to pound; to pulverize by pounding; to mark and discolour part of the surface of (eg the skin of a person, fruit, etc); to hurt by unkind words. ◆ *vi* to be marked with bruising; to be injured physically or in feelings; to ride recklessly along (*hunting sl*). ◆ *n* an injury with discoloration of the human skin made by anything blunt and heavy; a similar injury to fruit or plants. [OE *brȳsan* to crush, combined with OFr *brisier*, *bruiser*, *bruser* to break]
■ **bruis'er** *n* a person or thing that bruises; a prize-fighter, or a big, strong, aggressive person generally (*inf*). **bruis'ing** *n* and *adj*.

bruit /broot/ *n* something rumoured widely; a rumour or report; a murmur heard in auscultation (*med*); noise (*archaic*). ◆ *vt* to spread by rumour; to report; to make famous. [Fr *bruit*, from Fr *bruire*; cf LL *brugītus*; prob imit]

brûlé /broo-lā/ (*cookery*) *adj* with a coating of caramelized sugar. [Fr, burnt]

brulzie or **brulyie** *n* Scots forms of **broil**[2].

Brum /brum/ (*inf*) *n* Birmingham. [Contraction of **brummagem**]
■ **Brumm'ie** *n* a person from Birmingham. ◆ *adj* relating to Birmingham, its people or their accent.

Brumaire /brü-mer'/ *n* the second month in the French revolutionary calendar, about 22 October to 20 November. [Fr *brume* fog, from L *brūma* winter]

brumby /brum'bi/ (*Aust*) *n* a wild horse. [Origin unknown]

brume /broom/ (*literary*) *n* fog. [L *brūma* winter, contracted from *brevima* (not attested) the shortest day, from *brevis* short]
■ **brum'al** *adj* relating to winter. **brum'ous** *adj* foggy, wintry.

brummagem /brum'ə-jəm/ (*inf*) *n* (with *cap*) Birmingham; a thing made in Birmingham, *esp* something showy and worthless. ◆ *adj* showy and worthless, sham, counterfeit. [Old form of the name]

brummer /broo'mər/ (*S Afr*) *n* older form of **brommer**.

brumous see under **brume**.

brunch /brunch or brunsh/ *n* a meal combining *br*eakfast and l*unch*. [Portmanteau word]

Bruneian /broo-nī'ən/ *adj* of or relating to the state of *Brunei* in the Malay Archipelago, or its inhabitants. ◆ *n* a native or citizen of Brunei.

Brunella see **prunella**[1].

brunette (*masc* **brunet**) /broo-net'/ *n* a person with brown or dark hair. ◆ *adj* (of hair-colour) dark brown. [Fr dimin of *brun* brown]

Brunonian /broo-nō'ni-ən/ *adj* relating to the system of medicine founded by Dr John *Brown* of Edinburgh (c.1736–88) in which all diseases are categorized as *sthenic* or *asthenic*, depending on excess or deficiency of excitement. [*Brūnō, -ōnis*, Latinization of *Brown*]

brunt /brunt/ *n* the force of a blow; the chief stress or crisis of anything; the shock of an onset or contest. ◆ *vt* (*rare*) to bear the brunt of. [Origin obscure]

bruschetta /brü-sket'ə or -shet'/ *n* (*pl* **bruschett'as**, **bruschette** /-tā/) toasted ciabatta or other bread brushed with olive oil and topped with tomatoes, basil, olives, etc. [Ital]

brush /brush/ *n* an implement set with bristles or similar for grooming, cleansing, painting, applying friction or beating a soft rhythm; a tuft; a bushy tail, *esp* of the fox; a bundle of wires, strips, etc, making electrical contact between surfaces in relative motion; a brushlike electrical discharge of sparks or luminosity; any brushlike effect; an application of a brush; a grazing contact; a fleeting encounter; an skirmish, a clash; lopped or broken twigs; an area of shrubs and small trees, a thicket; thick forest (*Aust*); the backwoods; a brisk run or race (*US*). ◆ *vt* to pass a brush over, groom, sweep, paint, etc with a brush; to touch or rub as if with a brush; to apply or remove by a sweeping motion (with *on*, *off* or *away*). ◆ *vi* to use a brush; to pass with light contact; to move off abruptly, make off. [OFr *brosse* brushwood; prob connected with **bristle**]
■ **brushed** *adj* smoothed, rubbed, straightened, etc with a brush; (of cloth) with the surface roughened or raised. **brush'er** *n*. **brush'ing** *n* the action of the verb brush. ◆ *adj* lively, brisk. **brush'y** *adj* like a brush; covered with brush.
❑ **brush discharge** *n* an electrical discharge between conductors that is not intense enough to cause a spark. **brush fire** *n* a fire of dry bushes, etc, which usually spreads quickly and dangerously (also *fig* and as *adj*). **brush kangaroo** *n* (*Aust*) a wallaby (*esp* large). **brush'-off** *n* (*inf*) a curt or discourteous dismissal or act of ignoring; a rebuff. **brush turkey** *n* an E Australian mound-bird. **brush-up** see **brush up** below. **brush'wheel** *n* a revolving brush; a friction wheel with bristles on the rubbing surface. **brush'wood** *n* loppings and broken branches; underwood or stunted wood. **brush'work** *n* work done with a brush; a painter's individual manner of using the brush.
■ **brush aside** or **off** to ignore or dismiss, *esp* brusquely. **brush up** to freshen one's appearance; to clean and tidy; to renew one's knowledge of (a subject; sometimes with *on*) (**brush'-up** *n*).

brusque /broosk or brusk/ *adj* blunt and abrupt in manner. [Fr]
■ **brusque'ly** *adv*. **brusque'ness** *n*. **brusquerie** /broos'kə-rē/ *n*.

Brussels /brus'əlz/ *n* the capital of Belgium; (in full **Brussels carpet**) a kind of worsted carpet with heavy uncut pile on a linen backing.
❑ **Brussels lace** *n* a fine lace with appliqué sprigs on a net ground. **Brussels sprout** *n* (also without *cap*) a variety of the common cabbage with many heads, each like a miniature cabbage; an individual head from this.

brust /brust/ (*Spenser*) same as **burst**.

brut /broot or (*Fr*) brü/ (*Fr*) *adj* (of wines) unsweetened, dry.

brute /broot/ *n* a brutal person; one of the lower animals, *esp* the larger mammals; a large articulated goods trolley used on railway stations; a large high-intensity spotlight. ◆ *adj* belonging to the lower animals; irrational; stupid; coarse; grossly sensual; lacking in sophistication, crude; (of a thing) merely physical; unworked, in its natural or raw state. ◆ *vt* see **bruting** below. [Fr *brut* rough, crude, from L *brūtus* dull, irrational]

■ **brut'al** *adj* like a brute; unfeeling; coarse; inhuman, senselessly cruel; grossly sensual. **brut'alism** *n* deliberate crudeness of style in art, architecture, literature, etc. **brut'alist** *n* and *adj*. **brutal'ity** *n*. **brutalizā'tion** or **-s-** *n*. **brut'alize** or **-ise** *vt* to make like a brute, degrade; to treat with brutality. ◆ *vi* to become like a brute. **brut'ally** *adv*. **brute'like** *adj*. **brute'ness** *n* a brutelike state; brutality; stupidity (*Spenser*). **brut'ify** *vt* to make brutal, stupid or uncivilized. **brut'ing** *n* the process of shaping a diamond by rubbing it with another (**brute** *vt*; **brut'er** *n*). **brut'ish** *adj* brutal. **brut'ishly** *adv*. **brut'ishness** *n*.

❑ **brute fact** *n* a fact alone, presented without explanation. **brute force** *n* sheer physical strength.

brutum fulmen /broo'təm ful'men/ (*L*) *n* an ineffectual threat (literally, random thunderbolt).

Brutus /broo'təs/ *n* a kind of wig; a way of wearing the hair brushed back from the forehead, popular at the time of the French Revolution, when it was fashionable to admire the old Romans, such as *Brutus*.

bry- or **bryo-** /brī-(-ō)-/ *combining form* denoting moss. [Gr *bryon* moss, liverwort]

Brylcreem® /bril'krēm/ *n* a cream used by men for styling the hair.

bryology /brī-ol'ə-ji/ *n* the study of mosses. [Gr *bryon* moss, liverwort, and *logos* discourse]

■ **bryological** /-ə-loj'i-kl/ *adj*. **bryol'ogist** *n*.

bryony /brī'ə-ni/ *n* a wild climbing plant (*Bryonia dioica*, **white bryony**) of the family Cucurbitaceae, common in English hedgerows. [L *bryōnia*, from Late Gr *bryōniā*]

■ **black bryony** a climbing plant (*Tamus communis*) of the family Dioscoreaceae, similar to bryony in habit and disposition.

bryophyte /brī'ō-fīt/ *n* a member of the **Bryophyta** /-of'i-tə/, one of the main groups of the vegetable kingdom, mosses and liverworts. [Gr *bryon* moss, liverwort, and *phyton* plant]

bryostatin /brī-ō-stat'in/ *n* a complex lactone extracted from certain marine animals, believed to have properties useful in treating cancer. [**Bryozoa** and **statin**]

Bryozoa /brī-ō-zō'ə/ *n pl* an old name for the Polyzoa, from their resemblance to mosses. [Gr *bryon* moss, and *zōia* living things]

Brython /brith'on/ *n* a Celt of the group to which the Welsh, Cornish and Bretons belong, distinguished from Goidel. [Welsh *Brython* Briton, introduced in philological use by Sir John Rhys (1840–1915)]

■ **Brython'ic** *adj*.

BS *abbrev*: Bachelor of Science (*US*); Bachelor of Surgery; The Bahamas (IVR); British Standard(s); Building Society; bullshit (*US sl*).

bs *abbrev*: balance sheet; bill of sale; bullshit (*US sl*).

BSA (*comput*) *abbrev*: Business Software Alliance.

BSC *abbrev*: British Steel Corporation (now known as Corus); Broadcasting Standards Commission (now replaced by **Ofcom**); Building Societies Commission (now replaced by **FSA**).

BSc *abbrev*: Bachelor of Science.

BSE *abbrev*: bovine spongiform encephalopathy.

BSI *abbrev*: British Standards Institution, an organization which lays down minimum standards of quality and issues standard specifications for a wide range of manufactured goods.

BSL *abbrev*: British Sign Language.

BSM *abbrev*: British School of Motoring.

BST *abbrev*: bovine somatotrophin; British Standard Time; British Summer Time.

BT *abbrev*: British Telecommunications.

Bt *abbrev*: *Bacillus thuringiensis*, a naturally occurring insecticide used in pest control; Baronet.

BTA *abbrev*: British Tourist Authority.

BTCV *abbrev*: British Trust for Conservation Volunteers.

BTEC *abbrev*: Business and Technician Education Council (now replaced by **Edexcel**, but still used to denote some further education qualifications).

BTO *abbrev*: British Trust for Ornithology.

BTU *abbrev*: Board of Trade unit (1kWh); British thermal unit (also **Btu** or **btu**).

BTW or **btw** *abbrev*: by the way.

B2B *abbrev*: business-to-business.

B2C *abbrev*: business-to-consumer.

bu. *abbrev*: bushel(s).

buat see **bowat**.

buaze or **bwazi** /bū'āz or bwä'zi/ *n* an African fibre-yielding polygalaceous shrub (genus *Securidaca*). [Native name]

bub[1] /bub/ or **bubby** /bub'i/ *n* boy (as term of address) (*US*); a baby (*Aust* and *NZ inf*). [Cf Ger *Bube* boy]

bub[2] /bub/ (*archaic sl*) *n* strong drink. [Origin unknown]

buba /boo'bə/ (*med*) *n* another name for **yaws**.

bubalis /bū'bə-lis/ *n* a member of the *Bubalus* genus of bovids, including the buffalo (also **bubal** /bū'bəl/). [Gr *boubalis*, *boubalos* African antelope, Late Gr *boubalos* buffalo, from *bous* ox]

■ **bū'baline** *adj*. **Bū'balus** *n* the Asian buffalo genus.

bubble /bub'l/ *n* a globule of liquid or solidified liquid blown out with gas; a glass or plastic dome; anything empty and insubstantial; an unsound or fraudulent scheme; a bubbling noise. ◆ *adj* insubstantial; deceptive; fleeting, transient; like a bubble in shape and lightness. ◆ *vi* to rise in bubbles; to give off bubbles; to make sounds as of rising and bursting bubbles; (with *with*) to show (great joy, rage, etc); to blubber (*Scot*). ◆ *vt* (*archaic*) to cheat with bubble schemes. [Cf Swed *bubbla*, Du *bobbel*]

■ **bubb'ler** *n* (*US* and *Aust*) a drinking fountain. **bubb'ly** *adj* (*lit* and *fig*) having bubbles; bubble-like; cheerful and lively. ◆ *n* (*inf*) champagne.

❑ **bubble bath** *n* a cosmetic preparation that makes foam in bathwater. **bubble car** *n* a midget motor car resembling a bubble in its rounded line and windowed top. **bubble chamber** *n* (*phys*) a device for showing the path of a charged particle by the string of bubbles left in its track, a variant of the cloud chamber. **bubble gum** *n* a kind of chewing gum that can be blown into large bubbles. **bubb'le-headed** *adj* (*inf*) frivolous, flighty. **bubble-jet printer** *n* a kind of inkjet printer, in which droplets of heated ink are projected onto the paper by the expansion of the bubbles. **bubble memory** *n* (*comput*; *obs*) a memory composed of minute moving pockets of magnetism that represent, by their presence or absence in relation to fixed points, bits (qv) of digital information. **bubble pack** *n* a type of packaging in which goods are enclosed in a transparent bubble of plastic, etc backed by card. **bubb'le-shell** *n* a gastropod (genus *Bulla*) with thin globose shell. **bubble sort** *n* (*comput*) a method of sorting items of data in a list by repeatedly scanning the list and putting adjacent pairs of items in order. **bubble wrap** *n* plastic packing material consisting of small air-filled pockets. **bubb'ly-jock** *n* (*Scot*) a turkey cock.

■ **bubble and squeak** a British dish of leftover boiled potatoes and cabbage mashed together and fried, sometimes together with other leftovers. **bubble over** to show uncontrolled anger, mirth, etc. **bubble under** to hover just below a significant point or division, as on a scale.

bubby see **bub**[1].

bubinga /boo'bing-ə/ *n* a species of W African tree (*esp Didelotia africana*) or its hard wood, used in furniture-making. [Bantu]

bubkes, bubkis /bŭb'kəs/, **bupkes** or **bupkis** /bŭp'kəs/ *n* a trifling or insignificant amount. [Yiddish, literally, beans]

Bubo /bū'bō/ *n* a genus of large horned owls, including the eagle-owl. [L *bubo*, *-onis* a horned owl]

bubo /bū'bō/ (*med*) *n* (*pl* **bū'boes**) an inflammatory swelling of the lymph nodes, *esp* in the groin or armpit. [L *bubō*, from Gr *boubōn* the groin, a bubo]

■ **bubonic** /-bon'ik/ *adj* relating to or characterized by buboes. **bubonocele** /bū-bon'ō-sēl/ *n* (Gr *kēlē* tumour) a hernia in the groin, with related swelling. **bū'bukle** *n* (*Shakesp*) a ridiculous word of Fluellen's (*Henry V*, III.6.99) for a red pimple, made up from *bubo* and *carbuncle*.

❑ **bubonic plague** *n* a form of plague characterized by buboes.

bucardo /boo-kär'dō/ *n* (*pl* **bucar'dos**) a recently extinct species (*Capra pyrenaica pyrenaica*) of Spanish mountain goat. [Sp]

bucatini /boo-kə-tē'nē/ *n pl* pasta in the form of long thin hollow tubes. [Ital, dimin pl of *bucato*, from *buco* hole]

buccal /buk'əl/ *adj* of, towards or relating to the cheek; relating to the mouth, oral. [L *bucca* cheek]

buccaneer or **buccanier** /bu-kə-nēr'/ *n* one of the piratical adventurers in the West Indies during the 17c, who plundered chiefly Spanish ships; an unscrupulous opportunist. ◆ *vi* to act as a buccaneer. [Fr *boucanier*, from *boucan* a Carib wooden gridiron (used by French settlers in the West Indies)]

■ **buccaneer'ing** *n* and *adj*. **buccaneer'ish** *adj*.

buccina /buk'si-nə/ *n* a Roman curved trumpet. [L *būcina* trumpet, *būcinātor* trumpeter]

■ **buc'cinator** *n* (*anat*) a flat cheek muscle used in chewing and blowing. **buc'cinatory** *adj*. **Buc'cinum** *n* the whelk genus of molluscs, with trumpet-like shell.

bucellas /boo- or bū-sel'əs/ *n* a white wine from *Bucellas* near Lisbon.

Bucentaur /bū-sen'tör/ *n* the Venetian state barge used formerly in an Ascension-Day ceremony in which the doge dropped a ring into the sea, symbolizing the marriage of Venice with the Adriatic. [Ital *bucentoro*, *bucintoro*, of uncertain origin]

---

fāte; fär; mē; fûr; mīne; mōte; för; mūte; pūt; dhen (then); *el'ə-mənt* (element) ● For other sounds see detailed chart of pronunciation

Bucephalus /bū-sef'ə-ləs/ n Alexander the Great's famous warhorse; any horse (*familiar* or *facetious*). [Gr *Boukephalos*, from *bous* ox, and *kephalē* head]

Buchmanism /bŭk- or book'mə-ni-zm/ n the Oxford Group movement. [See **Oxford**]
■ **Buch'manite** /-īt/ adj and n.

buchu or **bucku** /boo'hhoo, -choo or -koo, also bu'-/ (*S Afr*) n a rutaceous shrub (genus *Barosma*) with leaves of medicinal value. [Khoikhoi]

buck[1] /buk/ n the male of eg the deer, goat, hare or rabbit (cf **doe**); a bok (qv); a lively young man (*archaic*); a dandy (*archaic*); a black man, male Native American, Aborigine, etc (*offensive*; often *adj*); a counter or marker (*cards*); a dollar (*N Am* and *Aust inf*); an act of bucking. ◆ vi (of a horse, etc) to jump repeatedly into the air, coming down with the back arched, head down, and forelegs stiff. ◆ vt to throw (a rider) by bucking; to resist, be in opposition to; to cheer, invigorate, tone up (*inf*; *usu* with *up*). [OE *buc*, *bucca*; Du *bok*, Ger *Bock* a he-goat]
■ **buckeen'** n an impoverished youthful member of the minor Irish aristocracy, or one aspiring to their way of life without the means to support it. **buck'er** n an animal that bucks. **buck'ish** adj lively, frisky; dandified; like a goat. **buck'ishly** adv.
□ **buck'eye** n the American horse-chestnut (genus *Aesculus*); a native of the state of Ohio (*US*); an automatic coupling for connecting railway vehicles. ◆ adj (*US*) flashy, showy; corny. **buck fever** n excitement or nervousness experienced by a novice hunter on first sighting game. **buck'horn** or **buck's'-horn** n the material of a buck's horn as used for handles, etc; a British plantain with leaves shaped like buck's horn (also **buck's horn plantain**). **buck'hound** n a small kind of staghound used for hunting bucks. **buck'-jumper** n an animal that bucks. **buck naked** adj (*US inf*) completely naked. **buck passing** see **pass the buck** below. **buck'-rabbit** n a male rabbit; Welsh rarebit with poached egg. **buck'rake** n a large agricultural rake, often attached to a tractor. **buck'saw** n a large saw consisting of a blade set in an H-shaped frame tightened by a cord, used with a sawhorse. **buck's-horn, buck's horn plantain** see **buckhorn** above. **buck'shot** n a large kind of shot, used in shooting deer. **buck'skin** n a soft leather made of deerskin or sheepskin; a strong twilled woollen cloth with cropped nap; a horse of buckskin (greyish-yellow) colour; a backwoods American; (in *pl*) breeches or a suit of buckskin. ◆ adj made of or like the skin of a buck. **buck's, bucks'** or **bucks party** n (*Aust inf*) a stag party for a man about to be married. **buck'thorn** n a genus (*Rhamnus*) of shrubs whose berry supplies the sap-green used by painters; see also **sea buckthorn** under **sea**. **buck'tooth** n a projecting front tooth. **buck'toothed** adj.
■ **bang for one's buck** (*inf*, chiefly *N Am*) value for money. **buck up** (*sl*) to hurry up, get going; to cheer up; to improve; to stimulate; to dress up (*dialect*). **make a fast buck** (*inf*) to earn some money quickly or easily but not necessarily honestly. **pass the buck** (*sl*) to shift the responsibility to someone else (from the practice of passing the marker to the next dealer in some forms of poker) (**buck'-passing** n). **the buck stops here** the final responsibility rests here.

buck[2] /buk/ n the body of a cart. [OE *būc* body]
□ **buck'board** n (*N Am*) a light horse-drawn vehicle consisting of a flexible board on four wheels, with a two-person seat. **buck'-wagon** n (*S Afr, archaic*) a large canvas-covered trek wagon.

buck[3] /buk/ (*archaic* or *dialect*) vt to soak or steep in lye, a process in bleaching. ◆ n lye in which clothes were steeped before bleaching. [Ety obscure: ME *bouken*; cognate words are Ger *bäuchen, beuchen*]
■ **buck'ing** n.
□ **buck'-basket** n a basket in which clothes were carried to be bucked. **buck'-wash** or **-washing** n.

buckaroo or **buckeroo** /buk'ə-roo or -roo'/ (*US*) n a cowboy (also **buckay'ro** (*pl* **buckay'ros**)). [Sp *vaquero*]

buckbean /buk'bēn/ n bogbean, a marsh plant. [Flem *bocks boonen* goat's beans]

buckeen see under **buck[1]**.

buckeroo see **buckaroo**.

bucket /buk'it/ n a vessel for drawing or holding water, etc; one of the compartments on the circumference of a water wheel; one of the scoops of a dredging machine; a wastepaper bin (*inf*); a subdivision of a data file, used to locate data (*comput*); something shaped like a bucket; an ice cream tub (*Aust inf*); (a glass of) alcoholic drink (*Scot inf*); a bucketful. ◆ vt to lift in a bucket. ◆ vt and vi to drive or ride very hard or bumpily; to push forward mercilessly; to swindle (*archaic*). ◆ vi (*inf*) (of rain) to pour heavily. [Prob connected with OE *būc* a pitcher, or OFr *buket* a pail. Not Gaelic *bucaid* a bucket]
■ **buck'etful** n (*pl* **buck'etfuls**) as much as a bucket will hold. **buck'eting** n.
□ **bucket list** n (*inf*) a list compiled by someone who is terminally ill of things they would like to do before dying. **buck'etload** n (*inf*) a

great amount. **bucket seat** n a round-backed, often forward-tipping, seat in a car, aeroplane, etc. **bucket shop** n (*inf*) the office of an unregistered stockbroker, a mere agent for bets on the rise or fall of prices of stock, etc (*orig US*); any not wholly reliable agency, eg one dealing in unsold airline tickets. **buck'et-wheel** n a contrivance for raising water by means of buckets attached to the circumference of a wheel.
■ **bucket and spade** a child's beach toy, comprising a small bucket and spade for playing with sand and water. **give the bucket** to dismiss. **kick the bucket** (*sl*) to die (*perh* from dialect *bucket* a beam from which slaughtered animals are hung).

buckeye, buckhorn, buckhound see under **buck[1]**.

buckie /buk'i/ (*Scot*) n a shellfish such as the whelk; an obstinate, awkward person. [Prob related to L *buccinum* a shellfish]

buckle /buk'l/ n a (*usu* metal or plastic) fastening for a strap or band, consisting of a rim and a tongue; a crisped, curled or warped condition. ◆ vt and vi to connect or fasten with a buckle; to bend or warp; to prepare (*esp* oneself) for action; to join closely eg in fight or marriage (*obs* or *dialect*). [Fr *boucle* the boss of a shield, a ring, from LL *buccula*, dimin of *bucca* a cheek]
■ **buck'ler** n a small shield used in parrying; a protector, protection. ◆ vt (*Shakesp*) to protect, shield.
□ **buck'le-beggar** n (*Scot hist*) a person who performed marriages without a licence. **buckler fern** n a European fern of the genus *Dryopteris*.
■ **buckle down** to apply oneself zealously (to). **buckle to** to buckle down to. **buckle under** to give in or collapse under strain.

Buckley's /buk'liz/ or **Buckley's chance** /chäns/ (*Aust inf*) no chance at all. [Origin doubtful]

buckling /buk'ling/ n a smoked Baltic herring. [Ger *Bückling*]

buckminsterfullerene /buk-min-stər-fŭl'ər-ēn/ n a ball-shaped molecule containing 60 carbon atoms linked together in hexagons and pentagons to form a closed, near spherical and very stable structure, the first discovered fullerene (also **buck'yball**). [*Buckminster Fuller* (1895–1983), US engineer who designed a geodesic dome for the 1967 Montreal Expo]

bucko /buk'ō/ n (*pl* **buck'oes**) a swaggerer, a domineering bully (*orig naut sl*); a young lad, chap (chiefly *Irish*). [**buck[1]**]

buckra /buk'rə/ n (used by West Indian and Southern US black people) a white man. [Calabar Efik *mbākara* a European]

buckrake see under **buck[1]**.

buckram /buk'rəm/ n a coarse open-weave fabric of jute, cotton or linen made very stiff with size; stiffness in manners and appearance (*formal*). ◆ adj made of buckram; stiff (*formal*); precise (*formal*). ◆ vt to give the quality of buckram to. [OFr *boquerant*]

Bucks. abbrev : Buckinghamshire.

bucksaw see under **buck[1]**.

Buck's fizz or **buck's fizz** /buks fiz/ n champagne (or sparkling white wine) and orange juice. [*Buck's Club* (in London) and **fizz**]

buckshish /buk'shēsh/ same as **baksheesh**. [See **baksheesh**, **bukshi**]
■ **buckshee'** adj (*inf*) free, gratuitous; spare, extra.

buckshot, buckskin see under **buck[1]**.

bucksom a Miltonic spelling of **buxom**.

buckthorn, bucktooth, bucktoothed see under **buck[1]**.

bucku see **buchu**.

buckwheat /buk'(h)wēt/ n a plant (*Polygonum* or *Fagopyrum*), its seed used *esp* in Europe for feeding horses, cattle and poultry, and *esp* in America for making into flour to make cakes for the breakfast-table, etc. [Prob Du *boekweit*, or Ger *Buchweizen* beech-wheat, from the shape of the seeds]

buckyball see **buckminsterfullerene**.

buckytube /buk'i-tūb/ n a tiny graphite tube, structurally similar to a buckyball. [**buckminsterfullerene** and **tube**]

bucolic /bū-kol'ik/ or (less often) **bucolical** /-əl/ adj relating to the tending of cattle; pastoral; rustic, rural. ◆ n (**bucolic**) a pastoral poem or poet; a rustic. [L *būcolicus*, from Gr *boukolikos*, from *boukolos* a herdsman]
■ **bucol'ically** adv.

bud[1] /bud/ n a rudimentary shoot of a plant; a flower while still not opened; in simple organisms, a protuberance that develops asexually into a new individual (*biol*); the first visible rudiment of a limb, horn, etc; something undeveloped or immature; a term of endearment to a young person (*obs*); a débutante (*obs US*). ◆ vt (**budd'ing; budd'ed**) to put forth as buds; to graft by inserting (a bud) under the bark of another tree. ◆ vi to put forth buds; to come as a bud; to be in or issue from the bud; to begin to develop. [ME *budde*; *perh* related to Du *bot* a bud]

■ words derived from main entry word; □ compound words; ■ idioms and phrasal verbs

■ **budd'ing** *n* the action of putting forth or inserting buds. ◆ *adj* in bud; beginning to develop or show talent in a particular way (as a *budding poet*). **budd'y** *adj.* **bud'less** *adj.*

❑ **bud'-scale** *n* a leaf specialized as a scale protecting a bud. **bud'worm** *n* a larva that feeds on plant or tree buds.

■ **in bud** putting forth buds. **nip in the bud** to destroy or put a stop to (something) at its very beginning.

bud² see **buddy¹**.

Buddha /boo'də or bŭd'ə/ *n* a title applied to Sakyamuni or Gautama, the N Indian founder (5c BC) of a religion of spiritual purity; a general name for any one of a series of teachers of whom he is one; (*usu* without *cap*) a statue or picture of the Buddha. [Sans *buddha* wise, from *bodhati* he understands]

■ **Budd'hism** *n* the religion founded by the Buddha. **Budd'hist** *n* a believer in Buddhism. ◆ *adj* (also **Buddhist'ic**) of or relating to Buddhism.

❑ **Buddhist cross** *n* a Greek cross with the arms bent clockwise, a form of swastika.

buddle /bud'l/ *n* a sloping container for washing ore. ◆ *vt* to wash in a buddle. [Origin unknown]

buddleia /bud'li-ə or bud-lē'ə/ *n* a plant of the genus *Buddleia*, shrubs and trees with opposite leaves and showy clusters of purple or orange flowers. [Named in honour of Adam *Buddle* (died 1715), English botanist]

buddy¹ /bud'i/ (*inf*; *orig US*) *n* brother, friend (as term of address; also **bud**); a pal, one's most constant companion; someone who volunteers to help and care for a person suffering from AIDS. [Prob from same root as **butty²**]

❑ **budd'y-budd'y** *n* a friend, pal. ◆ *adj* (*derog*) over-friendly. **buddy movie** *n* a film on the theme of camaraderie.

■ **buddy up** to make friends.

buddy² see under **bud¹**.

budge¹ /buj/ *vi* and *vt* to move or stir. [Fr *bouger*, from L *bullīre* to bubble]

■ **budg'er** *n.*

■ **budge up** (*inf*) to move closer together (eg along a bench) *usu* so as to make room for others.

budge² /buj/ *n* lambskin fur. ◆ *adj* pompous; stiff. [Origin obscure]

budge³ see **budgerigar**.

budgeree /buj'ə-ri or -rē/ (*obs Aust inf*) *adj* good. [Aboriginal word *budgeri*]

budgerigar /buj'ə-ri-gär/ *n* a small cage and aviary bird, an Australian parakeet (short form **budge** or **budgie** /buj'i/). [From an Aboriginal language]

❑ **budgie smugglers** *n pl* (*Aust inf*) close-fitting swimming trunks for men.

budgerow or **budgero** /buj'ə-rō/ (*Anglo-Ind*) *n* (*pl* **budg'erows** or **budg'eros**) a heavy keel-less barge. [Hindi *bajrā*]

budget¹ /buj'it/ *n* (often with *cap*) a financial statement and programme put before parliament by the Chancellor of the Exchequer; a plan of domestic or business expenditure; a restricted spending allowance; the overall expenditure allowed for a specific period or occasion; a sack or its contents (*obs*); a compact collection of things; news; a socket in which the end of a cavalry carbine rests (*archaic*). ◆ *adj* cheap, economical, inexpensive. ◆ *vi* (**budg'eting**; **budg'eted**) to prepare a budget. ◆ *vt* to provide for in a budget; to organize the spending of (money, etc). [Fr *bougette*, dimin of *bouge* a pouch, from L *bulga*]

■ **bud'getary** *adj.*

❑ **budget account** *n* a special bank account, into which money is paid regularly by the bank from a customer's main account and from which payment of previously agreed recurring expenses, eg fuel bills, TV licence, is made; an account with a shop, into which the customer makes regular payments to cover purchases at the shop. **budgetary control** *n* a system of financial control of a business by constantly monitoring the activities of the various departments in terms of the individual budgets assigned to each.

■ **budget deficit financing** a deliberate budgeted excess of government expenditure over income, with the object of stimulating economic growth, financed by borrowing. **budget for** to allow for, when planning one's expenditure.

budget² /buj'it/ *n* a fixed rudder on a barge. [Ety uncertain]

budgie see **budgerigar**.

budmash see **badmash**.

budo /boo'dō/ *n* (*pl* **bu'dos**) the system or philosophy of the martial art. [Jap, the way of the warrior]

buenas noches /bwen'as noch'es/ (*Sp*) goodnight.

buenas tardes /bwen'as tar'dhes/ (*Sp*) good afternoon.

buenos dias /bwen'os dē'as/ (*Sp*) good day, good morning.

buff¹ /buf/ *n orig* buffalo-hide; now white leather from which the grain surface has been removed, used for army accoutrements; a military coat; the colour of buff, a dull brownish yellow; the bare skin (*inf*); a buff-stick or buff-wheel; (in *pl*) certain regiments in the British Army, from their former buff-coloured facings (eg East Kent Regiment, Ross-shire Buffs); a member of a party whose colour is buff; an enthusiast, fan, expert (*orig* a keen attender at fires, so called from the buff uniform of the former New York volunteer firemen) (*inf*). ◆ *vt* to polish with a buff. ◆ *adj* brownish-yellow; having attractively well-developed muscles (*inf*). [Fr *buffle* a buffalo]

■ **buff'er** *n* a person or thing that buffs or polishes. See also **buffer¹**. **buff'ing** *n* the act or process of polishing.

❑ **buff'-coat** or **buff'-jerkin** *n* a strong, military coat; a soldier. **buff'-leather** *n.* **buff'-stick**, **buff'-wheel** or **buff'ing-wheel** *n* a stick or wheel covered with buff-leather or the like, and impregnated with an abrasive for polishing. **buff'-tip moth** *n* a European moth with buff wing tips.

■ **in the buff** (*inf*) naked.

buff² /buf/ *n* a dull blow or its sound; a buffet, blow or stroke (*obs*). ◆ *vt* to strike, *esp* with a dull sound; to burst out. [OFr *buffe* a blow]

■ **blindman's buff** see under **blind**.

buffa /bŭf'fa/ *n* (*pl* **buf'fe** /-fā/) a comic actress in an opera (*cf* **buffo**). [Ital]

buffalo /buf'ə-lō/ *n* (*pl* **buff'aloes**) a name for certain large animals of the cattle family, *esp* the tame, often domesticated, Asiatic buffalo, and the entirely wild and fierce Cape buffalo of southern Africa; the American bison (*N Am*). ◆ *vt* (*N Am inf*) to bewilder; to overawe. [Ital *buffalo*, through L from Gr *boubalos*]

❑ **buff'alo-berry** *n* a N American shrub of the family Elaeagnaceae, or its edible fruit. **buff'alo-bird** *n* an oxpecker. **buffalo chips** *n pl* dried buffalo dung used as fuel. **buffalo fish** *n* a N American freshwater cyprinoid fish with a humped back. **buffalo gnat** see **black fly** under **black**. **buff'alo-grass** *n* a short grass (*Buchloe dactyloides*) growing on the western prairies of the USA; any of various other American or African grasses. **buff'alo-nut** *n* a N American shrub of the sandalwood family; its oil-yielding nut. **buffalo robe** *n* a bison-hide rug or cloak. **Buffalo wings** *n pl* (*N Am*) deep-fried chicken wings served in a barbecue sauce.

buffe see **buffa**.

buffer¹ /buf'ər/ *n* a mechanical apparatus for deadening the force of a concussion, as in railway carriages or at the end of a railway line; a ship's fender; something or someone that acts as a protection against impact, shock or damage; a fellow, *esp* a dull or ineffectual fellow (as in *old buffer*); a boatswain's mate (*naut*); a substance or mixture which opposes change of hydrogen-ion concentration in a solution (*chem*); a temporary store into which data can go while awaiting transfer eg from computer to printer, acting as an adjusting mechanism between processes of different speeds (*comput*). ◆ *vt* to protect against shock (*lit* and *fig*); to store (data) in a buffer (*comput*); to add a buffer to (*chem*). ◆ *vi* to use, or be used as, a buffer. [**buff²**]

■ **buff'ered** *adj.*

❑ **buffer state** or **zone** *n* a neutral country or zone lying between two others whose relations are or may become strained. **buffer stock** *n* stock held in reserve to minimize the effect of price fluctuations or unreliable deliveries.

buffer² see under **buff¹**.

buffet¹ /bŭf'ā/ *n* a refreshment counter or bar; a meal set out on a table, etc, from which the diners serve themselves; /buf'it/ a sideboard, an ornamental side-table for the display of china; a low (*esp* rectangular) stool (*Scot and N Eng*). [Fr *buffet*; origin unknown]

❑ **buffet car** /bŭf'ā kär/ *n* a railway coach with light meal or snack service.

buffet² /buf'it/ *n* a blow with the fist; a slap; a stroke, *esp* heavy and repeated, eg of the wind, fortune, etc. ◆ *vt* to strike with the hand or fist; to knock or push about roughly, to batter; to struggle against, beat back. ◆ *vi* to deal heavy blows, to battle. [OFr *buffet*, from *buffe* a blow, esp on the cheek]

■ **buff'eting** *n* a striking with the hand, boxing; repeated blows; irregular oscillation of any part of an aircraft, caused and maintained by an eddying wake from some other part.

buffi see **buffo**.

bufflehead /buf'l-hed/ *n* a N American diving duck resembling the golden-eye; a stupid fellow. [From **buffalo** and **head**]

buffo /bŭf'fō/ *adj* comic. ◆ *n* (*pl* **buf'fi** /-fē/) a comic actor in an opera (*cf* **buffa**). [Ital]

buffoon /buf-oon'/ *n* a person who sets out to amuse others by jests, grimaces, etc; a fool. [Fr *bouffon*, from Ital *buffone*; *buffare* to jest]

■ **buffoon'ery** *n.*

---

bufo /bū'fō/ (*Jonson*) *n* a black tincture in alchemy. [L *bufo* toad]

bufotenine /bū-fō-ten'ēn or -īn/ *n* a poisonous paralysing hallucinogenic drug. [Fr, from L *bufo* toad (from the skin of which it is obtained), *ten*- hold, and **-ine**¹ (1)]

buftie or **bufty** /buf'ti/ (*Scot derog sl*) *n* a homosexual. [Origin unknown]

bug¹ /bug/ *n* a name applied loosely to certain insects, *esp* of the order Hemiptera (suborder Heteroptera), and *specif* to one (*Cimex lectularius*) that infests houses and beds; any insect or small animal (*N Am*); a disease-germ (*inf*); a viral disease (*inf*); a craze, obsession; an enthusiast (*inf*); a crazy person; an important person (**big bug**); a snag, a defect, a fault, now *esp* in a computer system or program (*inf*); a hidden microphone; a light vehicle stripped of everything inessential; a lunar excursion module (qv under **module**); the weight allowance given to an apprentice jockey (*US, racing*). ◆ *vt* (**bugg'ing**; **bugged**) to plant a concealed listening device in; to annoy, irritate, pester (*sl*). [Perh OE *budda* beetle; perh same as **bug**⁴]
　■ **bugged** *adj*. **bugg'ing** *n* and *adj*. **bugg'y** *adj* infested with bugs; crazy, batty (*US inf*).
　❑ **bug'bane** or **bug'wort** *n* a ranunculaceous plant (*Cimicifuga foetida*) related to baneberry, reputed to drive away insects. **bug'house** (*sl*) *n* a mental hospital (*US*); a cinema. ◆ *adj* insane. **bug'-hunter** *n* (*inf*) a collecting entomologist. **bugwort** see **bugbane** above.

bug² /bug/ (*N Am*) *vi* (**bugg'ing**; **bugged**) (with *out*) to desert or retreat, *esp* in panic. [Perh from **bugger** (**off**)]
　❑ **bug'-out** *n* desertion; a deserter.

bug³ /bug/ (*US inf*) *vi* (**bugg'ing**; **bugged**) (of the eyes) to start or bulge.
　❑ **bug'-eyed** *adj* with eyes protruding in astonishment, etc.

bug⁴ /bug/ *n* (*obs*) a bogy, or object of terror. [ME *bugge*, poss from Welsh *bwg* a hobgoblin]
　■ **bug'aboo** *n* a bogy, or object of terror; a cause of anxiety.
　❑ **bug'bear** *n* an object of terror, dislike or annoyance. **bug'-word** *n* (*obs*) a terrifying or threatening word.

bugbear see under **bug**⁴.

buggan /bug'ən/, **buggane** /-ān/ or **buggin** /-in/ (*dialect*) *n* an evil spirit, a hobgoblin. [**bug**⁴; cf **bogle**]

bugger /bug'ər/ *n* someone guilty of buggery; a term of abuse for a man or child, often quite colourless or even kindly (*vulgar sl*); a rogue, scamp, applied inoffensively to a child or animal (*US*); a difficult or unpleasant task, etc (*vulgar sl*). ◆ *vt* to practise buggery with; (the following all *vulgar sl*) to exhaust; to frustrate, ruin the plans of; to spoil, prevent success in (also with *up*). ◆ *vi* (with *off* ; *vulgar sl*) to go away quickly. ◆ *interj* (*vulgar sl*) used to express annoyance. [Fr *bougre*, from *Bulgarus* Bulgarian, with pejorative historical reference to Bulgarian heretics]
　■ **bugg'ery** *n* anal intercourse between a man and another man, a woman, a child or (*law*) an animal.
　❑ The following are all vulgar slang: **bugger all** *n* none, nothing. **bugg'er-all** *adj* no, none.
　■ The following are also vulgar slang: **bugger about** or **around** to potter about, do nothing useful; to mess (someone) about. **don't** or **couldn't give a bugger** couldn't care less. **like buggery** furiously, frenziedly; used to express strong disagreement. **play silly buggers** to behave foolishly.

Buggins's turn /bug'in-ziz tûrn/ (*inf*) *n* the assigning of promotion, etc in accordance with seniority, by rotation, etc, rather than on merit. [Origin unknown]

buggy¹ /bug'i/ *n* a light carriage or gig of several kinds: in N America, a one-horse, four-wheeled vehicle with one seat; in England, two-wheeled; in India, hooded; a light, very basic vehicle, as in *beach buggy*. [Ety unknown]

buggy² see under **bug**¹.

bugle¹ /bū'gl/ *n* orig a buffalo or wild ox; a bugle-horn, the musical instrument. ◆ *vi* to play or sound on a bugle; to make a sound like a bugle. [OFr *bugle*, from L *būculus*, dimin of *bōs* an ox]
　■ **bū'gler** *n* a person who plays the bugle. **bū'glet** *n* a small bugle.
　❑ **bū'gle-band** *n*. **bū'gle-call** *n*. **bū'gle-horn** *n* a horn used as a drinking vessel or hunting horn; a treble instrument with or without keys, *usu* made of copper, similar to the trumpet, but having the bell less expanded and the tube shorter and more conical, used more for signalling than music.

bugle² /bū'gl/ *n* a member of the genus (*Ajuga*) of labiate plants without upper lips. [Fr, Ital *bugola*, from LL *bugula*, *būgillō*]
　❑ **bū'gle-weed** *n* (*US*) a mint of the genus *Lycopus* of the labiate family.

bugle³ /bū'gl/ *n* a slender elongated bead, *usu* black, used as a decoration on clothing. ◆ *adj* (*Shakesp*) like bugles. [Poss connected with LL *bugulus* hair-pad, or with Du *beugel* ring]

bugler, **buglet** see under **bugle**¹.

bugloss /bū'glos/ *n* a name for several plants of the borage family, especially *Lycopsis arvensis*, a common cornfield weed, and viper's bugloss (qv). [Fr *buglosse*, from L *būglōssa*, from Gr *bouglōssos*, from *bous* ox, and *glōssa* tongue]

bugong see **bogong**.

bugwort see under **bug**¹.

buhl, also **boulle** or **boule** /bool/ *n* a complicated form of marquetry, using gold, silver, brass, pewter, ivory or mother-of-pearl inlaid in tortoiseshell, etc, forming panels for furniture decoration; furniture decorated with such marquetry. [From André Charles *Boulle* (1642–1732), a cabinetmaker in the service of Louis XIV]

buhrstone, also **burrstone** /bûr'stōn/ *n* a variety of quartz, containing many small empty cells, which give it a roughness of surface particularly adapted for millstones; a millstone made of this. [Perh connected with **burr**¹, from its roughness]

buik or **buke** /buk, bük or būk/ (*Scot*) *n* variants of **book** and **bouk**.

build /bild/ *vt* (*pat* and *pap* **built** or (*archaic*) **build'ed**) to erect (eg a house, bridge, etc); to construct (eg a railway, etc); to control the building of, to have built; to establish (*fig*); to base (eg hopes) (on); to form (combinations) (*cards*). ◆ *vi* to construct a building or buildings, to be a builder; to increase gradually; to depend (*on* or *upon*). ◆ *n* physical form; make, style of construction. [OE *gebyld*, pap of (not attested) *byldan* to build, from *bold* a dwelling]
　■ **build'er** *n* a person who builds, or controls the work of building; a substance added to soap, etc to increase its effectiveness. **build'ing** *n* the art, occupation or process of erecting houses, etc; a substantial structure for giving shelter, eg a house, office block; used as a collective noun for a gathering of rooks. **built** *adj* formed or shaped; constituted, naturally disposed; muscular (*inf*).
　❑ **builder's bottom** or **builder's bum** *n* (*sl*) the cleavage at the top of the buttocks revealed above low-hanging trousers when a person, *esp* a workman, bends down. **builders' merchant** *n* a trader who supplies building materials. **builder's tea** *n* tea brewed so as to be particularly strong, usually sugared. **building block** *n* a hollow or solid block made of concrete or other material, larger than a brick; a child's toy made of wood, etc; a component part (*fig*). **build'ing-board** *n* an artificial material made in panels for lining walls. **building line** *n* the line, fixed by a local authority, beyond which buildings must not project. **building paper** *n* any of several types of heavy-duty waterproof paper consisting of plastic impregnated paper or of bitumen sandwiched between layers of kraft paper, and used for insulation and damp-proofing of various kinds. **building society** *n* a society that advances money to its members as mortgages for homes, and provides interest-bearing accounts for savers. **build'out** *n* a process of expansion or growth. **build'-up** *n* a building up, increasing or strengthening; the amount of this; a working up of favourable publicity; preliminaries leading up to a climax in a story, speech, etc. **built'-in** *adj* formed as part of a main structure, *esp* if recessed; present as part of one's genetic inheritance; inherent; included (as part of a deal, etc); very firmly fixed. **built-in obsolescence** *n* the deliberate inclusion in a product of features which lead to deterioration or out-of-dateness before the end of the product's useful life. **built'-up** *adj* (of an area) covered with buildings; raised by adding something to the underside.
　■ **build in** to enclose or fix by building; to incorporate at the initial stage (*lit* and *fig*). **build up** to close up (eg a doorway) by building work; to cover with buildings; to raise the height of by adding something; to create, be created, or increase, gradually (eg a concentration of troops, a reputation, voltage, tension); to put together from parts already made; to strengthen (someone) physically; to praise; to edify spiritually (*obs*).

buirdly /bûrd'li/ (*Scot*) *adj* stalwart, large and well-made. [Poss a variant of **burly**]

buist /büst/ (*Scot*) *n* a box; a tar box; an owner's mark on sheep or cattle. ◆ *vt* to mark thus. [OFr *boiste* (Fr *boîte*) box]

buke see **buik**.

bukshi or **bukshee** /buk'shē/ *n* a paymaster, *esp* in India (cf **baksheesh**). [Pers *bakhshī*]

bulb /bulb/ *n* a subterranean bud with swollen leaf-bases in which reserve materials are stored; a flowering plant that grows from such; a protuberance or swelling; a bulb-shaped object; the medulla oblongata; a dilatation or expansion of a glass tube; a light bulb; a bulb-shaped rubber device for squeezing, as eg in an eye-dropper or bicycle horn. ◆ *vi* to form bulbs; to bulge out or swell. [L *bulbus*, from Gr *bolbos* an onion]
　■ **bulb'ar** *adj*. **bulbed** *adj*. **bulbif'erous** *adj* (of a plant) producing bulbs. **bulb'il** or **bulb'el** *n* a small bud that may grow into an independent plant. **bulbos'ity** *n*. **bulb'ous** *adj* bulging; swollen. **bulb'ously** *adv*. **bulb'ousness** *n*.

❏ **bulb fly** *n* a hoverfly whose larvae attack bulbs. **bulbourethral glands** see **Cowper's glands**.

■ **bulb of percussion** a raised cone on a worked flint, marking where a blow was struck.

bulbul /bŭl'bŭl/ *n* any bird of the family Pycnonotidae of Africa and Asia; in Persian poetry, the nightingale; a sweet singer. [Ar]

Bulg. *abbrev* : Bulgaria or Bulgarian.

Bulgarian /bul-gā'ri-ən/ *adj* of or relating to *Bulgaria*, a republic in SE Europe, its inhabitants or its language. ◆ *n* a native or citizen of Bulgaria; the Slavonic language of Bulgaria.

■ **Bul'gar** /-gär/ *n* a member of an ancient Finno-Ugrian tribe that settled in what is now Bulgaria and adopted the Slavonic language; a Bulgarian. ◆ *adj* of or relating to the Bulgars. **Bulgaric** /-gar'ik/ *adj* of the Bulgars. ◆ *n* the ancient language of the Bulgars. **Bul'garize** or **-ise** *vt* to make Bulgarian.

bulge /bulj/ *n* a protuberance, swelling; a salient (*milit*); a temporary increase. ◆ *vi* and *vt* to swell out. [OFr *boulge*, prob from L *bulga* a leather knapsack: a Gallic word; cf **bilge**]

■ **bul'ger** *n* (*obs*) a wooden golf club with a convex face. **bul'giness** *n*. **bul'ging** *adj* swelling out; overfull. **bul'gingly** *adv*. **bul'gy** *adj*.

■ **have** or **get the bulge on someone** (*old sl*) to have or get a decided advantage over someone.

bulgine see **bullgine**.

bulgur or **bulghur** /bŭl' or bul'gər/ *n* a form of cooked, broken wheat (also **bulg(h)ur wheat**). [Turk]

bulimia /bŭ-lim'i-ə/ (*med*) *n* abnormal hunger or appetite (also *fig*); bulimia nervosa. —Earlier forms **bul'imy**, **bulī'mus**. [Gr *boulīmiā*, from *bous* ox, and *līmos* hunger]

■ **bulim'ic** *adj* and *n*.

❏ **bulimia nervosa** /nər-vō'sə or -zə/ *n* a pathological condition, an eating disorder in which binge eating is followed by depression and guilt, self-induced vomiting and purging, etc.

bulk¹ /bulk/ *n* volume or size; great size; the greater part; any huge body or structure; a mass; a heap (now only of tobacco); roughage; the thickness of paper; the thickness of a book without its covers; a cargo; the belly, trunk or body; a hull or hold. ◆ *vi* to have bulk; to fill out (with *out* or *up*); to be of weight or importance; (of paper, etc) to be of (specified) bulk. ◆ *vt* to put or hold in bulk; to transport (several different consignments) together as a single load; (often with *out* but also with *up*) to cause to swell, make greater in size. [Prob ON *bulki* heap or cargo, confused with OE *buc* belly; see **bouk**]

■ **bulk'ily** *adv*. **bulk'iness** *n*. **bulk'y** *adj* having bulk; filling much space; unwieldy.

❏ **bulk'-buy'** *vt*. **bulk buying** *n* large-scale purchase of a commodity, *esp* on preferential terms and by a single buyer, sometimes on behalf of a body of consumers; guaranteed purchase by one country of all or most of another's output of a commodity. **bulk cargo** *n* cargo such as coal or wheat that is not packed in containers but loaded in bulk. **bulk carrier** *n* a vessel carrying bulk cargo. **bulk discount** *n* a reduction in a unit price when large quantities are purchased.

■ **break bulk** see under **break¹**. **bulk large** to be prominent or intrusive; to seem important. **load in bulk** to put cargo in loose. **sell in bulk** to sell cargo as it is in the hold; to sell in large quantities.

bulk² /bulk/ *n* a stall or framework built in front of a shop. [Ety doubtful; cf ON *bālkr* beam, OE *bolca* gangway of a ship]

■ **bulk'er** *n* (*archaic*) a street thief or prostitute.

bulkhead /bulk'hed/ *n* any of the partitions separating one part of the interior of a ship, aircraft, etc from another; a protecting barrier or structure; the roof of a shop's bulk; the bulk itself. [**bulk¹** and **bulk²**]

■ **collision bulkhead** that nearest the bow.

bull¹ /bŭl/ *n* an uncastrated male of the cattle family; a male whale, walrus, elephant, moose, etc; (with *cap* and *the*) Taurus; a person who seeks to raise the price of stocks, and speculates on a rise, *opp* to *bear* ; a bull's-eye ; (a shot that hits) the centre of a target; nonsense (*sl*); tediously excessive discipline, eg too much drill, polishing of kit, etc (*milit sl*); a policeman (*obs US sl*). ◆ *adj* male; massive, strong; (of the stock market), rising. ◆ *vt* to try to raise the price of; to polish over-zealously (*milit sl*); (of a bull) to copulate with (a cow). ◆ *vi* to brag (*sl*); to talk rubbish (*sl*); (of a cow) to be on heat, seek the bull. [ME *bole*, prob ON *bole, boli*; most prob related to **bellow**]

■ **bull'ing** *n* the mounting of cows by other cows, indicative of their being on heat. **bull'ish** *adj* like a bull; obstinate, aggressive; inclining towards rising prices (*stock exchange*); optimistic, upbeat (*inf*). **bull'ishly** *adv*. **bull'ishness** *n*. **bull'ock** *n* an ox or castrated bull. ◆ *vi* (*Aust* and *NZ*) to work very hard. ◆ *vt* to force (one's way). **bull'ocky** *n* (*Aust* and *NZ*) a bullock-driver.

❏ **bull ant** short for **bulldog ant** (see below). **bull'-baiting** *n* the former sport of baiting or exciting bulls with dogs. **bull'bars** *n pl* a strong metal framework on the front of a vehicle to protect it from damage if struck by an animal. **bull'bat** *n* (*US*) the nighthawk. **bull'-beef** *n* (*pl* **bull'-beeves**) (*obs; Shakesp*) an ox fattened for slaughter.

bull'-calf *n* a male calf; a stupid fellow, lout. **bull'-dance** *n* a dance of men only. **bull dike** same as **bull dyke** below. **bull'dog** *n* a breed of sturdy muscular dogs of great courage, formerly used for baiting bulls; a person of obstinate courage; a short-barrelled revolver of large calibre; a proctor's attendant at Oxford; (**Bulldog**®) a brand of stationery clip with a spring, used for holding papers, etc together or to a board. ◆ *vt* to attack like a bulldog; to wrestle with and throw (a steer, etc) (*US*). **bulldog ant** *n* a black or red Australian ant with a vicious sting. **bull'dust** *n* a euphemism for bullshit (*Aust* and *NZ*); fine dust, as on outback roads (*Aust*). **bull dyke** *n* (*offensive sl*) a lesbian of masculine appearance and manner. **bull fiddle** *n* (*US inf*) a double bass. **bull'fight** *n* a popular spectacle in Spain, Portugal, S France, and Latin America, in which a bull is goaded to fury by mounted men (picadors) armed with lances, and killed by a specially skilful unmounted swordsman (matador). **bull'fighter** *n*. **bull'fighting** *n*. **bull'finch** *n* a common European finch with red breast and thick neck; (*perh* for *bull-fence*) a kind of high, thick hedge hard to jump. **bull'frog** *n* a large frog. **bull'-fronted** *adj* having a forehead like a bull. **bull'head** *n* the miller's thumb, a small river fish with a large, flat head; extended to various similar fishes, eg the pogge (**armed bullhead**); a stupid person. **bull-head'ed** *adj* impetuous and obstinate. **bull-head'edness** *n*. **bull'-hoof** *n* a West Indian passion flower (from the shape of its leaf). **bull'horn** *n* (*N Am*) a loudhailer. **bull market** *n* (*stock exchange*) a market in which prices are rising. **bull'-mastiff** *n* a cross between a bulldog and a mastiff, the mastiff strain predominating. **bull'-necked** *adj* thick-necked. **bull'nose** *adj* and *n* (something) with a blunt nose or rounded edge. **bull'-nosed** *adj*. **bull'ock's-heart** *n* the custard apple. **bull'-of-the-bog'** *n* (*Scot*) the bittern. **bull pen** *n* a pen for a bull; a similar enclosure for prisoners (*US*); the part of a baseball ground where pitchers warm up; the pitchers on a baseball team who enter the game to relieve the starting pitcher. **bull point** *n* (*inf*) a key point, a salient point. **bull'-pup** *n* a young bulldog. **bull'ring** *n* the enclosure for bullfighting or bull-baiting; a ring for a bull's nose. **bull'-roarer** *n* an oblong slip of wood, whirled at the end of a string to give a loud whirring noise; a similar artefact used in an Australian Aboriginal ceremonial, the *turndun* ; the similar *rhombos* of the Greek mysteries. **bull session** *n* (*esp N Am*) an informal discussion *esp* between men. **bull's'-eye** *n* a round opening or window; the centre of a target; a shot that hits it (also *fig*); a big, round, hard peppermint sweet; the central boss formed in making a sheet of spun glass (*old*); a thick lens, or round piece of glass, as in a lantern; a lantern. **bull shark** *n* a heavy-bodied shark (*Carcharhinus leucas*), noted for its aggressive behaviour. **bull'shit** *n* (*vulgar sl*) nonsense; deceptive humbug; bull (*milit sl*). ◆ *vi* and *vt* to talk nonsense (to), often with the intention of deceiving; to polish over-zealously (*milit sl*). **bull'shitter** *n*. **bull'shitting** *n*. **bull'shot** *n* a cocktail of vodka, beef consommé and seasoning. **bull snake** *n* a gopher snake. **bull's wool** *n* (*Aust inf*) any fibrous bark; a euphemistic term for bullshit (see above). **bull terrier** *n* a breed of dog with a smooth, short-haired coat, *orig* a cross between a bulldog and a terrier. **bull trout** *n* a large variety of sea-trout (*Salmo trutto eriox*); a salmon that has re-entered fresh water after spawning. **bull'whip** or **bull'whack** *n* a heavy short-handled whip. ◆ *vt* to lash with a bullwhip.

■ **a bull in a china shop** a person who lacks the delicacy that the situation calls for. **bull into** to plunge hastily into. **not know a B from a bull's foot** to be very ignorant. **take the bull by the horns** to grapple boldly with a danger or difficulty.

bull² /bŭl/ *n* nonsense; pretentious talk; a ludicrous self-contradiction. [Prob OFr *boul* cheat]

bull³ /bŭl/ *n* an edict of the Pope with his seal affixed. [L *bulla* a knob, a lead seal]

■ **bull'ary** *n* a collection of papal bulls.

bull⁴ /bŭl/ *n* drink made by pouring water into a cask that formerly held alcohol. [Origin unknown]

bull⁵ /bŭl/ *n* a deck game in which pads are thrown at an inclined board, the **bull'-board**. [Origin unknown]

bulla /bŭl'ə/ *n* (*pl* **bull'ae** /-ē/) a seal attached to a papal document; a round metal ornament worn by children in ancient Rome; a blister; (with *cap*) the bubble-shell genus of molluscs. [L *bulla*]

■ **bull'ate** *adj* blistered or puckered, bubble-like, inflated.

bullace /bŭl'is/ *n* the fruit or tree of the wild plum (*Prunus insititia*), closely related to the damson. [Cf OFr *beloce*]

bullary see under **bull³**.

bullate see under **bulla**.

bull-board see **bull⁵**.

bulldoze /bŭl'dōz/ *vt* to intimidate, bully; to level and clear by bulldozer; to demolish as if by bulldozer; to force or push through against opposition (*fig*). [Origin obscure]

■ **bull'dozer** *n* a person who bulldozes; a powerful, heavy tractor with a vertical blade at the front, used for levelling and clearing land.

---

buller /bŭl'ər/ (Scot) n turbulence in water; a bubbling; a bellow. ◆ vi to seethe; to gurgle; to bellow. [Cf Dan bulder, Swed buller rumble, noise, roar; prob partly from or infl by OFr bullir, Icel bulla to boil]

bullet /bŭl'it/ n a little ball; a projectile, now esp a round or conical one fired from any kind of small arm; a plumb or sinker in fishing; (also **bullet point**) a solid dot used to highlight items in a list (printing); (with the) dismissal from employment (inf). [Fr boulette, dimin of boule a ball, from L bulla]
□ **bull'et-head** n a round head; an obstinate fellow (US). **bull'et-headed** adj. **bull'et-proof** adj proof against bullets (also fig). **bullet train** n a high-speed passenger train, esp in Japan.

bulletin /bŭl'i-tin/ n an official report of public news, or of a patient's progress; a periodical publication of a society, etc. [Fr, from Ital bullettino]
□ **bulletin board** n a noticeboard containing messages, advertisements, and interchange of information, esp (comput) an electronic one containing also programs and databases (**Bulletin Board System** see **BBS**).

bullet-tree, **bulletrie** same as **bully-tree**.

bullgine or **bulgine** /bŭl'jīn/ (US inf) n a steam locomotive. [Said to be **bull¹** and en**gine**]

bullion /bŭl'yən/ or /-i-ən/ n gold or silver in the mass and uncoined; gold or silver in general; a heavy twisted cord fringe, often covered with gold or silver wire. [Perh connected with LL bulliō, -ōnis a boiling]
■ **bull'ionist** n one in favour of metallic currency.

bullock see under **bull¹**.

bully¹ /bŭl'i/ n a person, often of superior strength or size, who distresses or persecutes others, eg with threats, cruel teasing, etc; a blustering, noisy, overbearing fellow; a ruffian hired to beat or intimidate anyone (archaic); a man who lives on the earnings of a prostitute (obs); a term of genial familiarity, esp to a man (obs). ◆ adj excellent, great (inf); blustering (archaic). ◆ vi (**bull'ying**; **bull'ied**) to bluster. ◆ vt to oppress cruelly; to threaten in a noisy way; to coerce. ◆ interj good. [Perh Du boel a lover; cf Ger Buhle]
■ **bull'yism** n.
□ **bully boy** n a ruffian hired to beat or intimidate someone. **bull'y-boy** adj intimidatory. **bull'y-rook** n (obs) a hired ruffian; a comrade. ■ **bully for you**, etc (often ironic) good for you, etc.

bully² /bŭl'i/ or **bully-beef** /bŭl'i-bēf/ n tinned or pickled beef. [Prob Fr bouilli boiled beef, infl by **bull¹**]

bully³ /bŭl'i/ n a scrimmage in Eton football; formerly in hockey, the opening or restarting move, where one player from each team struck the ground and the opponent's stick alternately three times in quick succession, before attempting to be the first to strike the ball lying between them (also **bull'y-off**; also vt and vi). [Origin uncertain]
■ **bully off** (obs) to restart a game of hockey with a bully.

bully⁴ /bŭl'i/ n a miner's hammer.

bullyrag /bŭl'i-rag/ or **ballyrag** /bal'i-rag/ vt to assail with abusive language or horseplay; to badger, intimidate. [Origin unknown; perh from **rag³**]

bully-tree /bŭl'i-trē/ n the balata tree (also **bull'et-tree**, **bull'etrie** or **boll'etrie**). [Perh from **bullace** or **balata**]

buln-buln /bŭl'n-bŭl'n/ (Aust) n a lyrebird. [From an Aboriginal language]

bulrush /bŭl'rush/ n a name given to two distinct tall marsh or water plants, the reedmace or cat's-tail, and clubrush, a plant of the sedge family; in the Bible, the plant papyrus. [Perh **bole¹**, or **bull¹** in sense of massive or coarse, and **rush²**]
■ **bul'rushy** adj.
□ **bulrush millet** n pearl millet.

bulse /buls/ n a small bag for or of diamonds, gold dust, etc. [Port bolsa, from LL bursa a purse. See **purse**]

bulwark /bŭl'wərk/ n a fortification or rampart; a breakwater or sea-wall; the side of a ship projecting above the deck; any means of defence or security. ◆ vt to defend; to fortify. [Cf Ger Bollwerk]

bum¹ /bum/ (inf) n the buttocks; the anus. ◆ vt (**bumm'ing**; **bummed**) (vulgar sl) to have anal intercourse with. [Cf **bump¹** in sense of swelling]
■ **bum'ster** adj of trousers, cut in a style low enough to show the cleavage at the top of the buttocks. **bum'sters** n pl trousers in this style.
□ **bum bag** or **bum'bag** n a small bag, usu worn on a belt round the waist, orig used by skiers, etc. **bum'bai'liff** (obs; Shakesp **bum'-bay'lie**) n a bailiff who comes behind to make arrests; a sheriff's officer. **bum'fluff** n (inf) downy hair growing on the chin of an adolescent male; nonsense. **bum'freezer** n (sl) an Eton jacket; a waist-length jacket. **bum roll** n a shaped pad or cushion worn below the waist to make a skirt stand out from the body. **bum'sucker** n (vulgar sl) a toady. **bum'sucking** n.
■ **bums on seats** (theatre) audiences, good houses.

bum² /bum/ (chiefly N Am sl) n a (drunken) spree; a dissolute fellow, tramp; a sponger; a devotee of a (specified) sport, etc to such an extent as to neglect other responsibilities. ◆ adj worthless; despicable; dud; wrong, false. ◆ vi (**bumm'ing**; **bummed**) to loaf; to sponge; to live dissolutely. ◆ vt to cadge. [Cf **bummel**]
■ **bummed** adj (US sl) disappointed; dejected. **bumm'er** n a plundering straggler or camp-follower (during the American Civil War); a dissolute fellow, a loafer, a sponger; a dismal failure (inf); something worthless (inf); a disappointment (inf); a bad trip on drugs (inf); a nasty experience (inf).
□ **bum rap** n (sl) a false criminal charge. **bum steer** n (sl) something misleading, false or worthless, a dud.
■ **bum around** to travel around rather aimlessly. **give someone the bum's rush** (sl) to eject someone by force; to dismiss someone summarily, esp from one's employment.

bum³ /bum/ vi (**bumm'ing**; **bummed**) to hum or make a murmuring sound, like a bee. ◆ vt (Scot) to toss, hurl. ◆ n a humming sound. [Imit]
■ **bumm'er** n a person or thing that bums.
□ **bum'-bee** n (dialect) a bumblebee. **bum'-clock** n (Scot) a flying beetle that drones.
■ **head'-bummer** /hēd'/ (Scot) a manager or person in authority.

bumalo see **bummalo**.

bumbaze /bum-bāz'/ (Scot) vt to perplex, bamboozle. [Origin obscure]

bumbershoot /bum'bər-shoot/ (US facetious) n an umbrella. [Alteration of umbrella, with para**chute**]

Bumble /bum'bl/ n a beadle; a self-important minor official. [From Mr Bumble in Dickens's Oliver Twist]
■ **Bum'bledom** n.

bumble or (Scot) **bummle** /bum'(b)l/ vi to utter indistinctly; to bungle; to make a buzzing sound, to drone; to bustle about blunderingly. ◆ n confusion; indistinct utterance; a bungler; an idler. [Frequentative of **bum³**]
■ **bum'bler** n a bungler. **bum'bling** n.
□ **bum'blebee** n a large wild loud-humming bee, a humble-bee. **bum'ble-foot** n cellulitis in a bird's foot, due to pus-forming organisms; club foot. **bum'ble-puppy** n the old game of nine-holes; unscientific whist or bridge; a racket game in which a string is wound round a post by hitting a slung ball or bag.

bumbo /bum'bō/ n (pl **bum'bos**) a mixture of rum or gin, water, sugar and nutmeg, or similar drink. [Perh Ital bombo, a child's word for drink]

bum-boat /bum'bōt/ n a Thames scavenger's boat (obs); a boat bringing vegetables, etc for sale to ships. [Origin doubtful]

bumf or **bumph** /bumf/ (inf) n lavatory paper; papers, official papers, documents (derog). [Short for bum-fodder, from **bum¹** and **fodder**]

Bumiputra /boo-mi-poot'rə/ n an indigenous inhabitant of Malaysia. [Malay, son of the earth]

bumkin or **bumpkin** /bum'kin/ n a short beam of timber projecting from each bow of a ship, for the purpose of extending the lower corner of the foresail to windward; a small outrigger over the stern of a boat, usually serving to extend the mizzen. [From **boom³** and dimin termination -kin]

bummalo or **bumalo** /bum'ə-lō/ n (pl **bumm'alo** or **bum'alo**) the Bombay duck, a small Indian fish of a family (Scopelidae) related to the salmon, dried and eaten as a relish (also **bummalō'ti** or **bumalō'ti**). [Marathi bombīl]

bummel /bum'əl/ n a stroll; a leisurely journey. [Ger Bummel]

bummer see under **bum²,³**.

bummle see **bumble**.

bummock /bum'ək/ (Orkney) n a brewing of ale for a feast. [Ety unknown]

bump¹ /bump/ vi to make a heavy or loud noise; to knock dully; to jolt; to move joltingly. ◆ vt to strike with a dull sound; to strike against; to dislodge, knock, shove; in bumping races (esp Oxford and Cambridge), to catch up with and touch (the boat in front), and consequently move up one place; (with out) to spread out (text) in printing so as to fill any desired number of pages (printing); to turn away (a passenger who holds a valid reservation for a seat on a flight) because the airline has allowed too many seats to be booked. ◆ n a dull heavy blow; a thump; (in pl) a customary series of thumps (administered in various ways in various parts of the country) esp to a child celebrating his or her birthday; the act of bumping in a bumping race; a jolt; a lump or swelling; a protuberance on the head associated by phrenologists with specific qualities or propensities of mind; hence (*inf*) faculty. [Imit]

■ **bump'er** *n* any thing or person that bumps; a bar on the front and back of a motor vehicle to lessen the shock of collision; a railway buffer (*US*); a pad fitted round the inside of a cot to stop a baby bumping itself; a bumping race; a cup or glass filled to the brim for drinking a toast; anything large or generous in measure; a crowded house at a theatre or concert; a bouncer (*cricket*). ◆ *adj* full to overflowing; unusually large or plentiful. ◆ *vi* to drink bumpers. **bump'ily** *adv*. **bump'iness** *n*. **bump'ing** *n*. **bumpol'ogy** *n* (*joc*) phrenology. **bump'y** *adj*.

□ **bump and run** *n* (*golf*) an approach shot played so that the ball runs a long distance after landing. **bumper car** *n* a Dodgem. **bumper sticker** *n* a small label bearing a slogan or advertisement affixed to the bumper of a motor vehicle. **bumping race** *n* a boat race in which the boats start at fixed intervals, and seek to bump, not to pass the boat in front. **bumps'adaisy** or **boomps'-a-daisy** *interj* exclamation on bumping into someone or something, or to a child on falling. **bump'-start** *vt* to start (a car) by pushing it and engaging the gears while it is moving (also *n*).

■ **bump and grind** to dance erotically with exaggerated movements of the hips. **bump into** to happen to meet (someone). **bump off** (*sl*) to kill, murder. **bump up** (*inf*) to raise (prices); to increase the size of. **with a bump** with an unpleasant suddenness.

bump² /*bump*/ (*obs*) *n* the booming cry of the bittern. ◆ *vi* to utter that cry. [Imit]

bumper¹ /*bum'pər*/ (*Aust inf*) *n* a cigarette butt. [Perh a conflation of **butt²** and **stump**]

bumper² see under **bump¹**.

bumph see **bumf**.

bumpkin¹ /*bum(p)'kin*/ *n* an awkward, clumsy rustic; a clown. [Prob Du *boomken* a log]

■ **bump'kinish** *adj*.

bumpkin² see **bumkin**.

bumptious /*bump'shəs*/ *adj* offensively self-important. [Prob formed from **bump¹**]

■ **bump'tiously** *adv*. **bump'tiousness** *n*.

bun¹ /*bun*/ *n* a kind of sweet roll or cake; hair formed into a rounded mass; (in *pl*) the buttocks (*US inf*). [Perh from OFr *bugne* a swelling]

□ **bun fight** *n* (*inf*) a tea party; a noisy occasion or assembly.

■ **have a bun in the oven** (*inf*) to be pregnant.

bun² /*bun*/ *n* a dry stalk (*dialect*); a hare's scut (*Scot and N Eng*). [Possibly Gaelic *bun* a root, a stump]

bun³ /*bun*/ *n* a playful name for a rabbit or a squirrel. [Origin unknown]

buna /*bū*- or *boo'nə*/ *n* an artificial rubber made by the polymerization of butadiene. [Orig a trademark]

BUNAC /*bū'nak*/ *abbrev* : British Universities North America Club, an organization arranging travel and work placements overseas for young people.

Bunbury /*bun'bə-ri*/ *n* the name of an invented person used as an excuse for sudden departures. ◆ *vi* (**Bun'burying**; **Bun'buried**) to make such an excuse or departure. [From the invented character in Wilde's *The Importance of Being Earnest*]

bunce /*buns*/ (*sl*) *n* profit or gain; money. ◆ *vi* to ring up wrongfully on every customer's bill the price of an item kept beside the till of a supermarket, etc, in order to defray losses by theft, etc. [Ety uncertain, perh altered from *bonus*]

bunch /*bunch* or *bunsh*/ *n* a number of things aggregated or fastened together; a definite quantity fastened together, as of linen yarn (180 000 yards), etc; a cluster; a handful, eg of flowers; a group (*inf*); something in the form of a tuft or knot; (in *pl*) a hairstyle in which the hair is pulled to both sides at the back of the head, and each tuft secured with a band or ribbon; a lump, hump, swelling (*obs*). ◆ *vi* to swell out in a bunch; to cluster, form a tight group. ◆ *vt* to make a bunch of; to concentrate. [Origin unknown]

■ **bunched** *adj* gathered into a bunch; humped, protuberant; lumpy. **bunch'iness** *n*. **bunch'ing** *n* the act of drawing together into a bunch; too close grouping together of cars on a motorway, etc (*esp* after a long gap), of ships arriving in port, etc. **bunch'y** *adj* growing in bunches or like a bunch; bulging.

□ **bunch'-backed** *adj* (*Shakesp*) hump-backed. **bunch grass** *n* any of several clumped W American grasses.

■ **bunch of fives** see under **five**.

bunco see **bunko**.

buncombe see **bunkum**.

Bund /*bunt*/ (*Ger*) *n* a league or confederacy.

□ **Bundesbank** /*bun'des-bangk*/ *n* the state bank of Germany. **Bundesrat** or formerly **Bundesrath** /*-rät*/ *n* the upper house of the parliaments of Germany and of Austria; the executive council of the federal republic of Switzerland. **Bun'destag** /*-tähh*/ *n* the lower house of the parliament of Germany. **Bun'deswehr** /*-vär*/ *n* the German armed forces.

bund /*bund*/ *n* (*orig* in India, etc) a man-made embankment or dam. ◆ *vt* to embank. [Hindi *band* from Pers]

bundle /*bun'dl*/ *n* a number of things loosely bound together; a bunch; a loose parcel; a strand of conducting vessels, fibres, etc (*biol, fibre optics*, etc); a definite measure or quantity, such as two reams of paper, twenty hanks of linen yarn, etc; computer software and hardware supplied together; a lot of money, *esp* in the phrase *make a bundle* (*sl*); a brawl (*sl*). ◆ *vt* to make into a bundle or bundles; (*usu* with *up*) to wrap up warmly; to put hastily or unceremoniously (away, etc); to hustle; to sell (*esp* specific computer software along with hardware) as a single package. ◆ *vi* to pack up one's things for a journey; to go hurriedly or in confusion (with *away, off* or *out*); to lie in bed together fully clad (an old custom in Wales, New England and parts of Scotland for sweethearts and others). [Related to **bind** and **bond¹**]

■ **bund'ler** *n*. **bund'ling** *n*.

■ **bundle of fun** an exuberant and entertaining person (sometimes *ironic* of one who is not). **bundle of laughs** (*orig US*, often *ironic*) an entertaining person or situation. **bundle of nerves** see under **nerve**. **drop one's bundle** (*Aust sl*) to lose one's nerve, to give up. **go a bundle on** (*sl*) to like or be enthusiastic about.

bundobust see **bandobast**.

bundook or **bandook** /*bun'dook*/ (*milit sl*) *n* a rifle. [Hindi *bandūq*]

bundu /*bun'doo*/ (*Southern Afr*) *n* a remote uncultivated region. [Bantu]

Bundy® /*bun'di*/ (*Aust*) *n* a time-clock in a factory, etc.

bung¹ /*bung*/ *n* the stopper of the hole in a barrel; a large cork. ◆ *vt* to stop (up) or enclose with a bung (also *fig*). [Ety uncertain]

□ **bung'hole** *n* a hole for a bung. **bung'-vent** *n* a small hole in a bung to let gases escape, etc.

bung² /*bung*/ (*Aust inf*) *adj* broken; dead (*obs*); useless (*obs*). [From an Aboriginal language]

■ **go bung** to die (*obs*); to fail, go bust (*obs*); to go phut.

bung³ /*bung*/ (*sl*) *n* a bribe, tip. ◆ *vt* to bribe, pay. [Ety unknown]

bung⁴ /*bung*/ (*sl*) *vt* to throw or shove carelessly and hurriedly. [Imit]

bung⁵ /*bung*/ *n* a purse (*obs criminal sl*); a cutpurse, pickpocket (*Shakesp*). [Cf OE *pung* purse]

■ **nip a bung** to pick a pocket.

bunga bunga /*bung'gə bung'gə*/ (*sl*) *n* a group sexual activity involving a strong element of primitive ritual. [Prob an invented phrase meant to evoke a primitive language]

bungalow /*bung'gə-lō*/ *n* a lightly built house, properly with a veranda and one storey; (loosely) a one-storey house; in some parts of Australia, a separate living structure in the garden. [Hindi *banglā* (house) in the style of Bengal]

■ **bung'aloid** *adj* and *n* (*facetious, usu derog*).

■ **dak bungalow** see **dak**.

bungee or **bungey** /*bun'ji*/ *n* a tension device using springs, elastic cable or rubber in such a way as to facilitate the movement of the controls in aircraft, etc; (also **bun'gie, bun'gy, bun'je, bun'jee, bun'jie** or **bun'jy**) india-rubber, a rubber or eraser (*sl*). [Ety unknown]

□ **bungee jumping** *n* the sport of jumping from a height with strong rubber ropes or cables attached to the ankles to ensure that the jumper bounces up before reaching the ground or other surface.

bungle /*bung'gl*/ *n* anything clumsily done; a gross mismanagement. ◆ *vi* to act in a clumsy manner. ◆ *vt* to make or mend clumsily; to mismanage grossly; to make a failure of because of a lack of skill. [Ety doubtful; cf Swed dialect *bangla* to work ineffectually]

■ **bung'ler** *n*. **bung'ling** *adj* clumsy, awkward; unskilfully or badly done. **bung'lingly** *adv*.

bunia see **bunnia**.

bunion /*bun'yən*/ *n* a lump or inflamed swelling on the first joint of the big toe. [Ety unknown; poss Ital *bugnone* a botch]

bunje, bunjee, bunjie, bunjy see **bungee**.

bunk¹ /*bungk*/ *n* a box or recess in a ship's cabin; a sleeping-berth anywhere; one of a pair of single beds one above the other (also **bunk bed**). ◆ *vi* to occupy a bunk; to sleep. [Cf ON *bunki*, Scand *bunke* heap]

■ **bunk'er** *n* a compartment for fuel on board a ship; the fuel oil carried by a ship for its own use; a large bin or chest, *esp* for coal; a sandpit or sandy gap in turf, *esp* as a hazard in a golf course; a window seat and chest (*Scot*); a turf seat (*Scot*); a slab beside a sink (*Scot*). ◆ *vt* to fuel; to play (a golf ball) into a bunker. ◆ *vi* to fuel. **bunk'ered** *adj* in a bunker; in difficulties.

❑ **bunk'house** *n* a building containing sleeping accommodation for labourers on a ranch, etc.

bunk² /bungk/ (*sl*) *n* the act of fleeing, running away (*esp* in the phrase *do a bunk*). ◆ *vi* to flee; (with *off*) to do a bunk, to play truant.

bunk³ see **bunkum**.

bunker¹ /bung'kər/ *n* an underground bomb-proof shelter. [Ger]
❑ **bunker buster** *n* (*inf*) a thermobaric bomb designed to penetrate thick layers of rock. **bunker mentality** *n* a belief that one is secure and that one's world will survive unchanged in spite of evidence to the contrary.

bunker² see under **bunk¹**.

bunko or **bunco** /bung'kō/ (*US*) *n* (*pl* **bunk'os** or **bunc'os**) a form of confidence trick in which the victim is swindled or taken somewhere and robbed. ◆ *vt* to rob or swindle in such a way. [Perh from Sp *banca* a kind of card game]
❑ **bunk'o-steerer** *n* a con man.

bunkum or (*esp US*) **buncombe** /bung'kəm/, also **bunk** /bungk/ *n* (*old inf*) bombastic speechmaking intended for the newspapers rather than to persuade the audience; humbug, claptrap. [From *Buncombe*, a county in North Carolina, whose representative is said to have gone on talking in Congress, explaining apologetically that he was 'only talking for Buncombe']

bunk-up /bung'kup/ (*inf*) *n* a push or hoist from below to help someone to climb up. [From **bunt¹** in its orig dialect sense, to push]

bunnia or **bunia** /bun'i-ə or bun'jə/ *n* a Hindu merchant. [Hindi]

bunny /bun'i/ *n* a young rabbit, *esp* a pet name for one (also **bunny rabbit**); a simpleton, a scapegoat (*Aust inf*). [Ety unknown; cf **bun³**]
❑ **bunn'y-boiler** *n* (*sl*) a woman who is likely to behave in a deranged and vindictive manner when spurned. **bunny girl** *n* (sometimes with *caps*) a nightclub hostess provocatively dressed in a brief, tight-fitting costume with a white fluffy tail, and wearing rabbit-like ears. **bunny hop** *n* a rocking jump from a squatting position, with both feet kicked backwards together. **bunny hug** *n* a 20c American dance. **bunn'y-hug** *vi*. **bunn'y-hugger** *n* (*sl, usu derog*) an animal lover.
■ **not a happy bunny** (*inf*) not pleased or contented.

bunodont /bū'nō-dont or -nə-/ *adj* having tuberculate molars (cf **lophodont**). [Gr *bounos* a rounded hill, and *odous, odontos* a tooth]

bunraku /boon-rä'koo/ *n* a Japanese form of puppet theatre in which the puppets, *usu* about 3ft (1m) high, are each manipulated by three men who remain visible throughout the performance. [Jap]

Bunsen burner or **Bunsen** (also without *cap*) /bun'sən or bŭn'sən (bûr'nər)/ *n* a gas-burner, used in laboratories, in which a good supply of air is caused to mingle with the gas before ignition, to produce a smokeless flame of low luminosity but great heating power. [RW Bunsen (1811–99), German chemist]

bunt¹ /bunt/ *vi* to push with the horns, butt; to block a ball with the bat, *usu* to allow a baserunner to advance (*baseball*; also *vt*). ◆ *n* a push; an attempt at bunting (*baseball*); the act of flying an aircraft in an inverted loop.
■ **bunt'ing** *n* the act of pushing; a boys' game, played with sticks and a small piece of wood; a strong timber, a stout prop.

bunt² /bunt/ *n* a disease of wheat; the fungus (genus *Tilletia*) that causes it. [Ety unknown]
■ **bunt'ed** *adj*. **bunt'y** *adj*.

bunt³ /bunt/ *n* the bagging part of a fishing-net, a sail, etc. ◆ *vi* (of a sail, etc) to belly. [Ety unknown]
❑ **bunt'line** *n* a rope passing from the foot-rope of a square sail to prevent bellying in furling.

buntal /bun'təl/ *n* the straw of the talipot palm. [Tagálog]

Bunter /boon'tər or bun-/ (*geol*) *n* the lowest division of the Trias. [From Ger *bunt* mottled]

bunter /bun'tər/ (*dialect*) *n* a female ragpicker; a low woman.

bunting¹ /bun'ting/ *n* a thin worsted fabric for ships' colours; flags; small strips of coloured cloth or paper hung from strings as decorations for a boat, street, etc. [Ety uncertain]

bunting² /bun'ting/ *n* any of the small finch-like birds of the subfamily Emberizinae (family Emberizidae, or perhaps Fringillidae). [Ety uncertain]

bunting³ see under **bunt¹**.

buntline see under **bunt³**.

bunya /bun'yə/ or **bunya-bunya** /bun'yə-bun'yə/ *n* an Australian tree (*Araucaria bidwillii*), the cones of which contain large edible seeds. [From an Aboriginal language]

bunyip /bun'yip/ *n* a fabulous monster of Australian Aboriginal legend; an impostor. [From an Aboriginal language]

buonamano /bwō-na-mä'nō/ or **bonamano** /bo'na-/ (*Ital*) *n* (*pl* **buonama'ni** or **bonama'ni** /-nē/) a tip or gratuity.

buona sera /bwō'na sā'ra/ (*Ital*) good evening.

buon giorno /bwōn jor'nō/ (*Ital*) good day.

buoy /boi/ (in N Am often *boo'ē* and in derivatives below *boo'y-*)/ *n* a floating secured mark, serving (by its shape, colour, light, sound, etc) as a guide or as a warning. ◆ *vt* to provide or mark with buoys or marks; to keep afloat, bear up, or sustain (*usu* with *up*); to raise, lift (the spirits, etc; *usu* with *up*). ◆ *vi* to rise. [Du *boei* buoy, fetter, through Romance forms (Norman Fr *boie*), from LL *boia* a collar of leather]
■ **buoy'age** *n* a series of buoys or floating beacons to mark the course for vessels; the provision, or system, of buoys. **buoy'ance** or (*rare*) **buoy'ancy** *n* the capacity for floating or causing to float lightly on water or in the air; loss of weight owing to immersion in a fluid; lightness of spirit, cheerfulness, resilience. **buoy'ant** *adj* tending to float or to buoy up; (of spirits, etc) light, cheerful and resilient; (of share prices, sales, profits, etc) tending to rise; (of a firm) with rising profits, etc. **buoy'antness** *n*.
❑ **buoyancy aid** *n* an inflated support for *esp* children learning to swim. **buoyant density** *n* the density of molecules, particles or viruses as determined by flotation in a suitable liquid.

BUPA /boo'pə or bū'pə/ *abbrev*: British United Provident Association, a private medical insurance organization.

Buphaga /bū'fä-gə/ *n* a small genus of African birds, closely related to the starlings, which feed on the larvae of gadflies, etc, parasitic on the backs of cattle, camels, etc (also **beefeater** and **oxpecker**). [Gr *bous* an ox, and *phagein* to eat]

bupkes, bupkis see **bubkes**.

buplever /bū-plev'ər/ *n* the plant hare's-ear (genus *Bupleurum*). [Fr *buplèvre*, from L *būpleurum*, from Gr *bous* ox, and *pleuron* rib]

buppy /bup'i/ (*inf*) *n* a black urban professional. [Cf **yuppie**]

Buprestis /bū-pres'tis/ *n* a genus of beetles of a large family, **Bupres'tidae**, those occurring in warmer countries having brilliant colour and metallic sheen, some of which are known as golden beetles. [Gr *bouprēstis* a kind of poisonous beetle, from *bous* ox, and *prēthein* to swell]
■ **bupres'tid** *n* and *adj*.

bupropion /bū-prō'pi-on/ *n* an antidepressant drug used in the treatment of nicotine addiction.

BUR *abbrev*: Myanmar (Burma; IVR).

bur see **burr¹,²**.

Burakumin /boo'rə-koo-min/ (*Jap*) *n pl* members of the lowest feudal caste in Japan, officially abolished in 1871 but in fact still regarded as untouchables, who perform the most menial tasks.

buran /boo-rän' or boo'rän/ *n* a violent blizzard blowing from the NE in Siberia and central Asia. [Russ]

burb /bûrb/ (*US inf*) *n* a short form of **suburb**.

Burberry® /bûr'bə-ri/ *n* a brand of trench coat or raincoat; a checked design *orig* used in the lining of Burberry coats. [From the manufacturer's name]

burble¹ /bûrb'l/ *n* a murmur; a rather incoherent stream of speech. ◆ *vt* and *vi* to murmur; to gurgle; to talk excitedly and rather incoherently (*inf*). [Prob onomatopoeic]
■ **burb'ler** *n*. **burb'ling** *n* separation of the flow of air from the upper surface of a moving aerofoil.
❑ **burble point** or **burbling point** *n* (*aerodynamics*) the angle of attack at which the sharp drop in the ratio of lift to drag (an effect of burbling too near the leading edge) first appears.

burble² /bûrb'l/ (*Scot*) *n* a tangle. ◆ *vt* to confuse. [Prob connected with OFr *barbouiller* to jumble]

burbot /bûr'bət/ *n* a freshwater fish, like the ling, with a longish barbel on its lower jaw. [Fr *bourbotte, barbotte*, from LL *borba* mud, or L *barba* a beard]

burd¹ /bûrd/ (*obs*) *n* a maiden; a lady. [OE *byrde* well-born, or perh *brȳd* bride), prob combined or confused with ON *byrthr*, OE *byrd* birth, offspring]

burd² /bûrd/ (*Scot*) *n* a bird; a young bird; a young animal of any kind; offspring, progeny; a term of endearment.
■ **burd'ie** *n* (*dimin*).
❑ **burd'-alane** or **bird'-alane** *n* the last remaining of a family. ◆ *adj* and *adv* (*William Morris* **bird'-alone**) quite alone.

burdash /bûr-dash'/ *n* a fringed sash worn by gentlemen in the time of Queen Anne and George I. [Origin unknown]

burden¹ /bûr'dn/ (*archaic* **burthen** /bûr'dhn/) *n* a load; a ship's carrying capacity (still often **burthen**); something grievous, oppressive, or difficult to bear; an obligation; any restriction, limitation or encumbrance affecting person or property (*Scots law*); a child in the womb (*obs*); a birth, confinement (*obs*); (in *pl*) a boat's floorboards. ◆ *vt* to load; to oppress; to encumber. [OE *byrthen*, from *beran* to bear]

■ **bur'denous** or **bur'densome** *adj* heavy; oppressive.
■ **burden of proof** the obligation to prove one's contention.

burden² /*bûr'dən*/ (*archaic* **burthen** /*bûr'dhən*/) *n* a bourdon or bass; the part of a song repeated at the end of every stanza, a refrain; the main theme of anything. [Fr *bourdon* a humming tone in music, from LL *burdō* a drone bee; confused with **burden¹**]

burden³ /*bûr'dən*/ *n* a pilgrim's staff. [See **bourdon²**]

burdock see under **burr¹**.

bureau /*bū'rō* or *bū-rō'*/ *n* (*pl* **bureaux** or **bureaus** /*-ōz*/) a writing table combined with a chest of drawers; a chest of drawers (*US*); a room or office where a writing table is used; a department or office for the transacting of business, such as collecting and supplying information; a government department. [Fr from OFr *burel* coarse russet cloth, from L *burrus* red]

bureaucracy /*bū-rok'rə-si*/ *n* a system of government or administration by officials, responsible only to their departmental chiefs; any system of administration in which matters are hindered by excessive adherence to minor rules and procedures; officials as a group. [**bureau**, and Gr *kratos* power]
■ **bur'eaucrat** *n* a government official; a bureaucratist. **bureaucrat'ic** *adj*. **bureaucrat'ically** *adv*. **bureau'cratist** *n* someone who practises or favours bureaucracy. **bureaucratizā'tion** or **-s-** *n*. **bureauc'ratize** or **-ise** *vt* to form into a bureaucracy; to make bureaucratic.

bureau de change /*bū-rō də shäzh'*/ (*Fr*) *n* an office where currency can be exchanged.

burette /*bū-ret'*/ *n* (also *US* **buret**) a graduated glass tube with a tap, for measuring liquids run off; a cruet for religious ceremonies. [Fr]

burg /*boorg* or *bûrg*/ *n* a fortress or a walled town (*hist*); a town (*US inf*). [W Gmc *burg*; OE *burh*; cf **burgh** and **borough**]

burgage /*bûr'gij*/ *n* a tenure in socage for a yearly rent; a tenure in Scotland in royal burghs under nominal service of watching. [LL *burgāgium*, from the root of **borough**, **burgh**]

burganet or **burgonet** /*bûr'gə-net*/ *n* a light 16c helmet with cheek-pieces. [Fr *bourguignotte*, literally, Burgundian]

burgee /*bûr'jē* or *bûr-jē'*/ *n* a triangular or swallowtailed flag or pennant; a kind of small coal for furnaces. [Origin uncertain]

burgeon or (*obs*) **bourgeon** /*bûr'jən*/ *vi* to produce sprouts or buds; to grow. [Fr *bourgeon* a bud, shoot]

burger /*bûr'gər*/ (*inf*) *n* short form of **hamburger**, **cheeseburger** (see under **cheese¹**), etc (also *adj*). ♦ *combining form* denoting (a bread roll containing) a fried or grilled cake of meat, etc made of, or accompanied by, the particular food mentioned, as in *beefburger*, *cheeseburger*.
□ **burger bun** *n* a bread roll for a hamburger, often topped with sesame seeds.

burgess /*bûr'jis*/ *n* a freeman or citizen of a borough or burgh (technically, cf **burgher**); a member of a privileged class in a town; a member of parliament for a borough (*hist*); an elected member of the American colonial assembly (*hist*); a borough magistrate or town councillor (*hist*). [OFr *burgeis*]
□ **burgess oath** see **Antiburgher**.

burgh /*bûr'ə*/ spelling of **borough**, used for Scottish burghs, otherwise archaic. [See **borough**]
■ **burghal** /*bûrg'l*/ *adj*. **burgher** /*bûrg'ər*/ *n* a freeman or citizen of a borough (used non-technically of British towns, in technical sense chiefly of continental towns, cf **burgess**); a townsman; (with *cap*) a Seceder who felt free to take the burgess oath (see **Antiburgher**) (*Scot*); a citizen of one of the S African Boer republics (*hist*); in Sri Lanka, a Eurasian of Dutch or Portuguese extraction, or a person of European race assimilated to the native population (*hist*).
□ **burgh court** *n* formerly in Scotland, an inferior court of summary jurisdiction presided over by a bailie. **burgh of barony** *n* a corporation under a feudal superior or baron, who sometimes nominated the magistrates. **burgh of regality** *n* a burgh of barony enfranchised by crown charter, with regal or exclusive criminal jurisdiction within its territory.
■ **parliamentary burgh** a burgh whose boundaries, as first fixed in 1832 for parliamentary representation, were adopted later for municipal purposes; a burgh which by itself or in combination elected a member of parliament. **police burgh** a burgh constituted by the sheriff for purposes of improvement and police. **royal burgh** a corporate body deriving its existence, constitution and rights from a royal charter, actual or presumed to have existed.

burghul /*bûr'gūl*/ *n* bulgur. [Pers]

burglar /*bûr'glər*/ *n* a person who enters a building as a trespasser (before 1969, by night) to commit a felony, eg to steal. ♦ *vi* and *vt* (*obs*) to perform such a crime. [Ety uncertain]

■ **burglarious** /*-lā'ri-əs*/ *adj*. **burglār'iously** *adv*. **burg'larize** or **-ise** *vt* (*N Am inf*). **burg'lary** *n*. **burgle** /*bûr'gl*/ *vi* (back-formation from **burglar**) to commit burglary. ♦ *vt* to enter as a burglar.
□ **burglar alarm** *n* an electronic alarm triggered by an intruder to a building, room, etc.
■ **aggravated burglary** burglary involving the use of weapons or explosives.

burgomaster /*bûr'gō-mä-stər*/ *n* the chief magistrate of an Austrian, Dutch, Flemish or German town. [Du *burgemeester*; Ger *Bürgermeister*, literally, borough-master]

burgonet see **burganet**.

burgoo /*bûr-goo'* or *bûr'goo*/ *n* a sailor's dish of boiled oatmeal with salt, butter and sugar; a stew or thick soup for American picnics. [Ety prob ult same as **bulgur**]

burgrave /*bûr'grāv*/ (*hist*) *n* the governor or hereditary ruler of a German town or castle. [Ger *Burggraf*]

burgundy /*bûr'gən-di*/ *n* (*usu* with *cap*) a French wine (red unless specified otherwise), made in *Burgundy*; a similar wine made elsewhere; the purplish-red or dark-red colour of red Burgundy.
□ **Burgundy mixture** *n* a fungicide composed of copper sulphate, sodium carbonate and water. **Burgundy pitch** *n* a resin properly prepared by melting and straining the exudation from Norway spruce (now obtained mainly elsewhere).

burhel same as **bharal**.

burial /*ber'i-əl* or *bar'*/ *n* the act of burying; a funeral; a tomb (*archaic*). [OE *byrgels* a tomb; see **bury**]
□ **burial ground** *n* a ground set apart for burials. **bur'ial-place** *n* a burial ground; the place where anyone is buried. **burial society** *n* an insurance society for providing the expenses of burial.

Buridan's ass /*bū'ri-danz as* or *äs*/ *n* in the sophism doubtfully attributed to the French 14c schoolman Jean *Buridan*, an ass dying of starvation through inability to choose between two equidistant and equally desirable sources of food.

burin /*bū'rin*/ *n* a kind of chisel of tempered steel, used in copper engraving; the distinctive style of an engraver; a palaeolithic flint tool. [Fr; from root of **bore¹**]
■ **bur'inist** *n* an engraver.

buriti /*boo-ri-tē'*/ *n* the miriti palm. [Tupí]

burk see **berk**.

burka, **burkha** or **burqa** /*bûr'kə*/ *n* a loose garment, with veiled eyeholes, covering the whole body, worn in public by some Muslim women. [Urdu *burga'*, from Ar]

burke /*bûrk*/ *vt* to murder, *esp* by smothering; to put an end to quietly, to silence, suppress; to evade. [From *Burke*, an Edinburgh Irishman (hanged 1829), who committed murder in order to sell the bodies of his victims for dissection]

Burkinabé /*bûr-kē-nə-bā'*/ *adj* of or relating to the republic of *Burkina Faso* in W Africa, or its inhabitants. ♦ *n* a native or citizen of Burkina Faso.

Burkitt lymphoma /*bûr'kit lim-fō'mə*/ or **Burkitt's lymphoma** /*bûr'kitz*/ *n* a malignant tumour of the immune system, chiefly affecting children in Africa and associated with Epstein-Barr virus. [Denis *Burkitt* (1911–93), British surgeon, who first described the condition in 1957]

burl¹ /*bûrl*/ *n* a small knot in thread or wool; a knot in wood. ♦ *vt* to pick knots, etc from (cloth) in finishing. [OFr *bourle* tuft of wool]
■ **bur'ler** *n*. **bur'ly** *adj*.
□ **bur'ling-iron** *n*. **bur'ling-machine** *n*.

burl² /*bûrl*/ (*Aust* and *NZ inf*) *n* an attempt, shot. [Prob Scot *birl*, *burl* a twist, turn]

burlap /*bûr'lap*/ *n* a coarse canvas of jute or hemp for wrappings, or a lighter material, eg of flax, for wall-coverings, etc, sometimes in *pl*. [Origin uncertain]

burlesque /*bûr-lesk'*/ *n* a ludicrous imitation; a piece of literature, of acting, or other performance that mocks its original by grotesque exaggeration or by combining the dignified with the low or the familiar; an entertainment combining often coarse jokes, striptease, songs and dancing (*N Am*); a playful or jocular composition (*music*). ♦ *adj* of the nature of burlesque; practising burlesque. ♦ *vt* to mock by burlesque; to make a burlesque of. [Ital *burlesco*; prob from LL *burra* a flock of wool, a trifle]

burletta /*bûr-let'ə*/ *n* a musical farce; a comic opera. [Ital; dimin of *burla* a jest]

burley¹ /*bûr'lē*/ *n* an American thin-leaved tobacco. [Prob from a personal name]

burley² see **berley**.

burly¹ /*bûr'li*/ *adj* big and sturdy. [ME *borlich*; perh the same as OHGer *burlīh* high, from *bor* a height]

■ **bur'liness** n.

burly[2] see under **burl**[1].

Burman /bûr'mən/ adj relating to Burma (since 1989, the Republic of Myanmar). ◆ n a person belonging to the majority ethnic group of Myanmar.
■ **Burmese** /bûr'mēz or -mēz'/ adj Burman. ◆ n the official language of Myanmar; (until 1989) a native or citizen of Burma (pl **Burmese**). ▫ **Burmese cat** n a breed of short-haired domestic cat, similar to the Siamese, typically dark brown in colour, with golden eyes. **Burmese glass** n a kind of unpolished semi-opaque coloured glass, popular in Victorian times.

burn[1] /bûrn/ vt (pat and pap **burnt** or **burned**) to consume or injure by fire or great heat; to produce an effect of heat on (as to bake pottery, produce charcoal, calcine lime, scorch food, wither grass); to brand; to oxidize; to make a copy of (a CD-ROM); to use (up), eg uranium, in a nuclear reactor (usu with up); to corrode; to sting; to make (a hole, etc) by fire or analogous means. ◆ vi to be burnt; to be on fire; to give out heat or light; to glow; to feel very hot; to sting; to be inflamed with passion. ◆ n a hurt or mark due to burning; a controlled fire to reduce vegetation, or the area so cleared (N Am, Aust, NZ); the firing of a rocket engine in order to produce thrust; tobacco, a smoke, a cigarette (sl); a very fast ride, etc on a motorcycle, in a speedboat, etc; pain felt in a muscle, experienced during demanding exercise. [In OE the transitive weak verb bærnan, bærnde, bærned has been confused with the intransitive strong verb beornan, byrnan, barn, bornen; cf Ger brennen to burn]
■ **burn'er** n a person or thing that burns; a fixture or part of a lamp, gas jet or gas cooker from which a flame comes. **burn'ing** n the act of consuming by fire; conflagration; inflammation; a quantity burned at one time; controlled expenditure of rocket propellant for course adjustment purposes. ◆ adj very hot; scorching; ardent; excessive. **burn'ingly** adv.
▫ **burn bag** n a bag or other receptacle used to hold classified documents that are to be destroyed after a certain period of time. **burn'-in** n a test of the reliability of computer hardware or software involving a period of extended use. **burning bush** n the emblem of the Church of Scotland and other Presbyterian churches, with the motto 'Nec tamen consumebatur', referring to the Covenanters overcoming the persecutions of the 17c (from Bible, Exodus 3.2); applied to various plants, such as dittany, whose volatile oil may catch fire in the air, some American species of spindle-tree with bright-red fruits, artillery-plant, etc. **burn'ing-glass** n a convex lens concentrating the sun's rays at its focus to produce fire or heat. **burn'ing-house** n a kiln. **burning issue** see **burning question** below. **burn'ing-mirror** n a concave mirror for producing fire or heat by concentrating the sun's rays. **burning mountain** n a volcano. **burn'ing-point** n the temperature at which a volatile oil in an open vessel will take fire from a match held close to its surface. **burning question** or **issue** n one keenly discussed. **burn-out** see **burn out** below. **burn rate** n (finance) the rate at which a new company spends its capital. **burnt almonds** n pl almonds in burnt sugar. **burnt cork** n charred cork used for blacking the face. **burnt-cork'** vt. **burnt cream** n crème brûlée. **burnt'-ear** n smut in oats, wheat, etc. **burnt'-the-wind** n (Scot) a blacksmith. **burnt ochre** see under **ochre**. **burnt-off'ering** n something offered and burned on an altar as a sacrifice (also facetious). **burnt sienna** see **sienna** under **Sienese**. **burnt umber** see under **umber**[1]. **burn'-up** n the using up of fuel in a nuclear reactor.
■ **burn a hole in one's pocket** said of money when one is eager to spend it. **burn blue** see under **blue**[1]. **burn daylight** (Shakesp) to waste time. **burn down** to burn to the ground. **burned out** ineffective, exhausted. **burned up** (US sl) angry. **burn in** to fix and make durable by intense heat; to imprint indelibly. **burn one's boats** or **bridges** to cut oneself off from all chance of retreat; to stake everything on success. **burn one's fingers** or **get one's fingers burnt** to suffer as a result of interfering, speculating, etc. **burn out** to destroy or drive out by burning; to burn until the fire dies down from want of fuel; to (cause to) break down or fail to work as a result of overheating; to (cause to) become ineffective through overwork, exhaustion, etc (**burn'-out** n). **burn the candle at both ends** see under **candle**. **burn the midnight oil** to study late into the night. **burn up** to consume completely by fire; to be burned completely; to increase in activity of burning; to make short or easy work of; to become or make angry (US sl). (**money**) **to burn** (money) in great abundance.

burn[2] /bûrn/ (now chiefly Scot) n a small stream or brook. [OE burna brook, spring; cf Du born, Ger Born]
▫ **burn'side** n the ground beside a burn.

burnet /bûr'nit/ adj (obs) dark brown. ◆ n a fine dark woollen cloth of the Middle Ages; the name of two closely related rosaceous plants, the great burnet (Sanguisorba officinalis or Poterium officinale), a meadow-plant, and common or salad burnet (Sanguisorba minor), both with close aggregates of brownish-purple flowers; the burnet moth. [OFr burnete, brunette; see **brunette**]

▫ **burnet moth** n a moth of the family Zygaenidae, esp of the genus Zygaena, with red-spotted or red-streaked forewings. **burnet rose** or **burnet-leaved rose** n a wild rose (Rosa spinosissima) with leaves like burnet, the Scotch rose. **burnet saxifrage** n a plant (Pimpinella saxifraga) related to anise, with burnet-like leaves.

burnettize or **-ise** /bûr'ni-tīz/ vt to treat with Burnett's fluid, a solution of zinc chloride, a preservative for timber, etc against dry rot and insects, patented by Sir William Burnett (1779–1861).

burnish /bûr'nish/ vt to polish; to make bright by rubbing. ◆ n polish; lustre. [Fr brunir, bruniss- to burnish, from brun brown]
■ **burn'isher** n. **burn'ishing** n. **burn'ishment** n.

burnous /bûr-noos'/ or **burnouse** /-nooz'/ n a hooded cape worn by Arabs. [Fr, from Ar burnus]

Burnsian /bûrn'zi-ən/ adj relating to Robert Burns (1759–96), the Scottish poet. ◆ n a student or admirer of Burns.
■ **Burns'ite** n a devotee of Burns.
▫ **Burns Night** n 25 January, celebrated by Scots as the anniversary of the birth of Burns, often involving a meal with haggis, whisky, verse and song (a **Burns Supper**).

burnt pat and pap of **burn**[1].

buroo /bə-roo'/ or **broo** /broo/ (Scot and Irish) n a Jobcentre. [**bureau**]
■ **on the buroo** or **broo** receiving Jobseeker's Allowance.

burp /bûrp/ vi (inf) to belch. ◆ vt to rub or pat the back of (a baby) after it has been fed, thought to help it to belch. ◆ n (inf) a belch. [Imit]
▫ **burp gun** n (US inf) a light submachine-gun.

burpee /bûr-pē' or bûr'pē/ n a gymnastic exercise combining a squat thrust and a star jump. [RH Burpee, its US inventor]

burqa see **burka**.

burr[1] or **bur** /bûr/ n the prickly seed-case or head of certain plants, which sticks to clothes or animals; any impediment or inconvenience; any adherent; any lump, ridge, etc, more or less sharp, an excrescence on a tree, or markings representing it in wood (as in burr-walnut); a knot in thread; a knob at the base of a deer's horn; the rough edge to a line made by an engraving tool, which, when the plate is inked, gives a further quality to the line; waste raw silk; the sweetbread or pancreas; club moss (Scot); the name for various tools and appliances, such as the triangular chisel for clearing the corners of mortises, etc; the blank driven out of a piece of sheet metal by a punch; burrstone; a partly vitrified brick. [Cognate with Dan borre a bur]
■ **burr'y** adj.
▫ **bur'dock** n a composite plant (Arctium lappa) with hooked involucral bracts and dock-like leaves; any species of the genus Xanthium. **bur-mar'igold** n any plant of the composite genus Bidens, with barbed pappus; a species of Xanthium. **bur'-reed** n a reedlike genus (Sparganium) of water plants with globular flower-heads. **burrstone** see **buhrstone**. **bur'-thistle** n spear-thistle. **bur'weed** n any of various burry plants such as burdock, bur-reed, cocklebur (genus Xanthium), etc.
■ **burr in the throat** something seeming to stick in the throat, producing a choking sensation.

burr[2] or **bur** /bûr/ n the rough sound of r pronounced in the throat, as by many Northumberland people; a continual humming sound as of a machine. ◆ vi to speak with a burr; to whisper hoarsely, to murmur. [Usu associated with **burr**[1] but perh imit]

burramundi /bu-rə-mun'di/ an obsolete variant of **barramundi**.

burra sahib /bur'ə sä'ib/ n in India, a title of respect for the head of a family, a superior officer, etc. [Hindi bara great, and **sahib**]

burrata /bū-rä'tə/ n an Italian cheese made from mozzarella and cream. [Ital, buttered]

burrawang /bur'ə-wang/ (Aust) n any of various cycad plants of the genus Macrozamia or Cycas, having edible nuts. [From Mount Budawang, New South Wales]

burrel[1] /bur'əl/ n a coarse russet cloth of medieval times. [See ety for **bureau**]

burrel[2], **burrell** or **burrhel** same as **bharal**.

burrito /bə-rē'tō/ n (pl **burri'tos**) a Mexican dish consisting of a flour tortilla, filled with meat, beans, chilli, etc and folded. [Mex Sp, a young donkey, from Sp burro a donkey, and dimin suffix]

burro /boo'rō/ n (pl **burr'os**) a donkey. [Sp]

burrow /bur'ō/ n a hole in the ground dug esp by certain animals for shelter or defence; a passage, hole or gallery dug or eaten through wood, stone, etc; a refuge. ◆ vi to make holes underground as rabbits do; to work one's way deeply under the surface; to live or hide in a concealed place; to delve. ◆ vt to make a burrow in; to make by burrowing. [Prob a variant of **borough**, from OE beorgan to protect]
▫ **burr'ow-duck** n the sheldrake or bergander. **burr'owing-owl** n a small long-legged diurnal American owl nesting in burrows.

burrowstown /bur'ə-stŭn/ or -stown/ (Scot) n a town that is a burgh. [**burgh**]

■ words derived from main entry word; ▫ compound words; ■ idioms and phrasal verbs

burrstone see **buhrstone**.

bursa /bûr'sə/ n (pl **bur'sae** /-sē/) (zool) a pouch or sac, esp one containing viscid lubricating fluid at points of friction. [LL bursa a purse, from Gr byrsa skin or leather]

■ **bur'sal** adj relating to a bursa. **bursic'ūlate** adj resembling a small pouch. **burs'iform** adj pouch-shaped. **bursī'tis** n inflammation of a bursa.

bursal see under **bursa** and **bursar**.

bursar /bûr'sər/ n a person who keeps the purse, a treasurer; in Scotland and New Zealand, a student or pupil maintained at a university or school by funds derived from endowment. [**bursa**]

■ **bur'sal** adj fiscal. **bursarial** /-sā'ri-əl/ adj. **bur'sarship** n the office of a bursar. **bur'sary** n the treasury of a college or monastery; the bursar's room in a college; in Scotland and New Zealand, a scholarship. **burse** /bûrs/ n a purse; a case for holding the corporal (chiefly RC); a scholarship (obs Scot); an obsolete form of **bourse**.

Bursch /boorsh/ n (pl **Bursch'en**) a student in a German university. [Ger Bursch a companion, student]

■ **Bursch'enism** n. **Bursch'enschaft** /-shäft/ n a students' association.

burse see under **bursar**.

Bursera /bûr'sə-rə/ n a tropical American genus of trees yielding elemi and timber, giving name to the family **Burserā'ceae**, related to the rue family. [Joachim Burser (1593–1649), German botanist]

■ **burserā'ceous** adj.

bursiculate, bursiform, bursitis see under **bursa**.

burst /bûrst/ vt (pat and pap **burst**, archaic, dialect and US **burst'ed** or **bust'ed**; obs pap **burst'en**) to break into pieces; to break open or cause to give way suddenly or by violence; to make or have (something) burst; to tear apart the perforated sheets of (continuous stationery). ◆ vi to fly open or into pieces, esp owing to a force from within; to give way suddenly; to break forth or away; to force a way (through, etc); to break suddenly into being, or into some condition, activity, or expression of feeling; to be full to the point of overflowing. ◆ n an act, occasion or result of bursting; a sudden outbreak; a hard gallop; a spurt; a drunken bout (obs inf); a measure of the strength of an envelope. ◆ adj ruptured. [OE berstan; Ger bersten; see also **bust²**]

■ **burst'er** n a person or thing that bursts; specif a machine that separates continuous stationery. ▫ **burst binding** n an unsewn bookbinding in which the gathered sections are perforated at the fold and glue is made to penetrate through the perforations. **burst'-up** n a complete break; disruption; commotion; collapse; failure.

burthen /bûr'dhn/ n and vt see **burden¹,²**.

Burton /bûr'tən/ n a drink. [A town in Staffordshire famous for its beer]

■ **gone for a Burton** drowned, dead (RAF sl); destroyed; lost; missing; no longer in existence.

burton /bûr'tən/ (naut) n a tackle of two or three blocks. [Ety unknown]

Burundian /bə-rŭn'di-ən/ adj of or relating to the Republic of Burundi in Central Africa, or its inhabitants. ◆ n a native or citizen of Burundi.

burweed see under **burr¹**.

bury /ber'i or bər'i/ vt (**bur'ying; bur'ied**) to hide in the ground; to cover, hide, put (something) deep inside something else; to consign (a dead body) to the grave, the sea, etc; to hide or blot out of remembrance; (in passive) to be deeply engrossed (in). ◆ n (dialect) a burrow. [OE byrgan to bury; Ger bergen to hide]

▫ **burying beetle** n a beetle (Necrophorus or a related genus) that buries small animals as food for its larvae. **burying ground** n a plot of ground set apart for burying the dead; a graveyard. **burying place** n.

■ **bury one's head in the sand** to refuse to face the facts. **bury the hatchet** see under **hatchet**.

bus (now rare **'bus**; obs **buss**) /bus/ n (pl **bus'es** or (less commonly) **buss'es**) a road vehicle with one (single-decker) or two (double-decker) decks for transporting a considerable number of passengers, usu on a regular or prearranged route; a car, aeroplane, etc (as a term of affection; sl); a number of conductors forming a circuit or route along which data may be transmitted (also **highway** or **trunk**; comput); the part of the payload of a space exploration vehicle (or a missile) which contains the atmospheric (re-)entry probes (or warheads). ◆ vt to transport by bus, sometimes specif in the sense of **busing** below. ◆ vi to go by bus; in a restaurant, etc, to clear dirty dishes from tables, replenish supplies of needed items, and otherwise assist the waiting staff (N Am). ◆ adj of or relating to a bus or buses. [Short form of **omnibus**]

■ **bus'ing** or (less commonly) **buss'ing** n (chiefly N Am) the transporting by bus of people from one district to another, esp children

to school, to achieve a more even racial, etc balance, for economic reasons, etc.

▫ **bus'bar** n an electric conductor connecting with a number of circuits (electronics, etc). **bus'boy** or **bus'girl** n (N Am) an assistant waiter or waitress, a person who buses. **bus conductor** n. **bus'-driver** n. **busgirl** see **busboy** above. **bus lane** n a traffic lane restricted to buses for all or part of the day. **bus'load** n the number of people a bus can carry. **bus'man** n the driver or conductor of a bus. **bus pass** n a pass entitling its holder to travel on services run by specified bus companies without (further) payment or at a reduced fare. **bus shelter** n an open-sided structure at a bus stop, giving some protection against the weather. **bus stop** n a halting-place for a bus, for passengers to board it or alight; the post or sign usu marking such a place.

■ **busman's holiday** a holiday spent in activities similar to one's work. **miss the bus** to lose an opportunity.

bus. abbrev : business.

BUSA abbrev : British Universities Sports Association.

busby /buz'bi/ n a fur hat with a bag hanging on its right side, worn esp by hussars; a bearskin hat (inf). [Prob Hung]

bush¹ /bŏŏsh/ n a woody plant between a tree and an undershrub in size; a shrub thick with branches; anything of bushy tuft-like shape, eg a bushy head of hair or the pubic hair; forest; wild uncultivated country covered with bushes, trees, etc; such country even though treeless; the wild; a bunch of ivy hung up as a tavern sign (obs); a tavern (obs). ◆ vi to grow thick or bushy. ◆ vt to set bushes round; to support with bushes; to cover (seeds) by means of the bush-harrow. [ME busk, busch, from ON buskr, from a Gmc root found in Ger Busch, LL boscus, Fr bois. Some uses are from the corresponding Du bosch]

■ **bushed** adj lost in or as in the bush (Aust and NZ); suffering mental disturbance as a result of living in isolation (Can); tired (inf). **bush'iness** n. **bush'y** adj full of or like bushes; thick and spreading. ◆ n (Aust and NZ inf) someone who lives in the bush.

▫ **bush'baby** n any of several nocturnal small African lemur-like primates, such as Galago senegalensis, also called **night-ape**. **bush'buck** n (also (Du) **boschbok** /bos'bok/ or (Afrik) **bosbok** /bos'bok/) a small S African antelope, or any other of the same genus (Tragelaphus). **bush'-cat** n the serval. **bush'craft** n practical knowledge of the bush and skill in its ways. **bush dog** n a small wild dog native to S American forests. **bush'fire** n (esp Aust and NZ) a fire in forest or scrub. **bush'-fly** n a small black Australian fly (Musca vetustissima or other species). **bush'-fruit** n a fruit growing on a bush, such as gooseberry or raspberry. **bush'-harrow** n a light harrow for covering grass-seeds, formed of a barred frame interwoven with bushes or branches. **bush'-house** n (Aust) a house or hut in the bush or in a garden. **bush jacket** see **bush shirt** below. **bush'land** n (Aust) the outback. **bush'-lawyer** n (Aust) any of several prickly climbing plants, esp of the genus Calamus; someone who pretends a knowledge of law. **bush'man** n a settler or traveller in the bush (Aust and NZ); (with cap) another name for **San**. **bush'manship** n bushcraft. **bush'master** n a venomous S American snake (Lachesis mutus). **bush'meat** n the meat of wild animals, esp apes, eaten as food. **bush pig** n a wild pig of S Africa and Madagascar (also called **red river hog**). **bush pilot** n an airline pilot operating over uninhabited country. **bush'ranger** n a lawless person, often an escaped criminal, who takes to the bush and lives by robbery (Aust); a backwoodsman; a rapacious person. **bush'-rope** n a liana. **bush shirt** or **bush jacket** n a cotton, etc garment with four patch pockets and a belt. **bush'-shrike** n any bird belonging to certain genera of an African subfamily of the shrikes, applied collectively to the subfamily as a whole; an ant thrush (Formicariidae family). **bush sickness** n (Aust and NZ) a disease of cattle, sheep and goats, caused by a mineral deficiency in pastures. **bush tea** n tea made from the leaves of various S African shrubs. **bush telegraph** n the rapid transmission of news among primitive communities by drum-beating, etc; gossip, rumour (facetious). **bush'tit** n a small long-tailed tit of W America, which builds a large hanging nest. **bush tucker** n (Aust) food available for eating in the bush, such as wild plants, animals and insects. **bush'veld** or **bosch'veld** /bos'/ n veld made up largely of woodland. **bush'walk** vi (Aust) to walk or hike through the bush as a leisure activity (also n). **bush'walker** n. **bush'walking** n. **bush'whack** vi (chiefly N Am) to range through the bush; to fight in guerrilla warfare; to travel through woods, esp by clearing a way to do so; to work in the bush, esp as an unskilled labourer felling timber (Aust and NZ). ◆ vt (N Am) to ambush. **bush'whacker** n a guerrilla fighter; a backwoodsman, country-dweller, often (derog) a country bumpkin or lout (N Am and Aust); a short heavy scythe for cutting bushes; a person who clears a way in the bush; a sniper. **bush'whacking** n the habits or practices of bushwhackers; the process of forcing a way for a boat by pulling at the bushes overhanging a stream. **bush'woman** n a woman living in the African or Australian bush.

■ **beat about the bush** to prevaricate, avoid coming to the point. **go bush** (*Aust inf*) to go off into the bush; to leave town or one's usual haunts; to abandon civilized life.

bush² /*bŭsh*/ *n* a cylindrical sleeve which forms a bearing surface or a guide for drilling. ◆ *vt* to provide with a bush. [MDu *busse*, from L *buxis* a box]
■ **bush'ing** *n* a bush; an insulator which enables a live conductor to pass through an earthed wall (*elec eng*).
❑ **bush'-metal** *n* hard brass, gunmetal, a composition of copper and tin, used for journals, bearings, etc.

bushel¹ /*bŭsh'əl*/ *n* a dry measure of 8 gallons, in UK no longer official, for grain, fruit, etc (**imperial bushel** 2219.36 cu in); a container for this quantity; a large amount or number (now *US inf*). [OFr *boissiel*, from root of **box¹**]
■ **hide one's light under a bushel** to keep quiet about or conceal one's talents or abilities.

bushel² /*bŭsh'əl*/ (*US*) *vt* and *vi* to mend or alter (eg men's clothes). [Cf Ger *bosseln*]
■ **bush'eller** *n*. **bush'elling** *n*.
❑ **bush'elman** or **bush'elwoman** *n*.

bushido /*boo'shē-dō*/ *n* a Japanese code of chivalry. [Jap *bushi* warrior, and *dō* doctrine]

business /*biz'nis*/ *n* employment; a trade, profession or occupation; a task or errand incumbent or undertaken; a matter requiring attention; dealings, commercial activity; a commercial or industrial operation; a commercial or industrial concern; the level of commercial activity; one's concerns or affairs; a matter or affair; a complex, difficult or awkward matter or affair; action as distinguished from dialogue (*theatre*); thing, used quite indefinitely, sort of thing (*inf*); /*biz'i-nis*/ (also written **busyness**) the state of being busy. [**busy**]
■ **bus'inesslike** *adj* methodical, systematic, practical; (of clothing, appearance, etc) severe.
❑ **business card** *n* a card carried by businesspeople, with their name and designation, and the name, address, telephone number and description, etc of their firm. **business class** *n* club class. **business cycle** *n* (*N Am*) trade cycle. **business end** *n* (*inf*) the end or part of something that actually functions or does the work (as in the *business end of a fork*). **business hours** *n pl* office hours. **bus'inessman**, **bus'inesswoman** or **bus'inessperson** *n* someone engaged in commercial or industrial business, *esp* as a manager. **business park** *n* an area, landscaped and provided with infrastructure, set aside for business use and intended to attract new industry. **business plan** *n* a detailed projection of the objectives, products, market, financing, etc of a proposed business venture. **business reply service** *n* a postal service allowing replies to correspondence to be sent at the expense of the business addressee. **business suit** *n* a formal suit appropriate for office wear. **businesswoman** see **businessman** above.
■ **do one's business** (*euphem*) to defecate. **do the business** to settle, make an end of; to do what is needed; to have sexual intercourse (*vulgar sl*); (with *for*) to ruin. **genteel business** (*theatre*) such parts as require good dressing. **get down to business** to set to work seriously. **go out of business** to cease trading, *esp* through bankruptcy. **in business** working, *esp* in commerce; able to proceed. **like nobody's business** (*inf*) keenly, energetically. **make it one's business** to undertake to accomplish something or see it done. **man of business** a law agent who conducts one's affairs. **mean business** to be in earnest. **mind one's own business** to confine oneself to one's own affairs. **place of business** a workplace. **send someone about his** or **her business** to dismiss someone unceremoniously. **the business** (*sl*) exactly what is required, the right person, etc for the job.

busk¹ /*busk*/ *vi* to cruise along a shore, beat about (*naut*); (with *for* or *after*) to seek; to play an instrument, sing, dance, display paintings, etc in the street or other public place for money. [Prob Sp *buscar* to seek]
■ **busk'er** *n* a street musician, actor or artist. **busk'ing** *n*.
■ **busk it** (*inf*) to improvise.

busk² /*busk*/ *vt* or *vi* to prepare; to dress. [ON *būa* to prepare, and *-sk*, contraction of *sik* oneself]

busk³ /*busk*/ *n* a piece of bone, wood or steel in the front of a corset; a corset. [Fr *busc*]
■ **busked** *adj*.

busket /*bus'kət*/ (*Spenser*) *n* a little bush. [See **bush¹**]

buskin /*bus'kin*/ *n* a high thick-soled boot worn in ancient times by actors in tragedy; a calf- or knee-length boot (*obs*); tragedy as a dramatic genre. [Ety uncertain; cf OFr *brousequin*; Du *brooksken*; Sp *borcegui*]
■ **busk'ined** *adj* wearing buskins; tragic.

busky /*bus'ki*/ (*Shakesp*) *adj* same as **bosky** (see under **bosk**).

buss¹ /*bus*/ *n* a rude or playful kiss, a smacker. ◆ *vt* to kiss, *esp* in a rude or playful manner. [Cf Ger dialect *buss*, Welsh and Gaelic *bus*, L *bāsium*]

buss² /*bus*/ *n* a small two-masted Dutch vessel, used in the herring and mackerel fisheries. [OFr *busse*, LL *bussa*; cf Ger *Büse*]

buss³ see **bus**.

bussu /*bŭs'oo*/ *n* a tropical American palm (genus *Manicaria*) with gigantic leaves and netted spathes that serve as cloth. [Port, from Tupí *bussú*]

bust¹ /*bust*/ *n* a sculpture representing the head and breast of a person; the upper front part of the human body, *esp* a woman's. [Fr *buste*, Ital and Sp *busto*]
■ **bust'ed** *adj* breasted; adorned with busts. **bust'y** *adj* (*inf*; of a woman) having a large bust.

bust² /*bust*/ (*inf*) *vt* and *vi* to break, shatter; to make or become bankrupt. ◆ *vi* (*pat* and *pap* **bust'ed** or **bust**) (*cards*, *darts*) to exceed the required score. ◆ *vt* (*N Am*) to arrest; to raid; to punch; to demote (*milit*). ◆ *n* a drinking bout, spree; a police raid (*sl*); a sudden collapse of the economy; a bad hand at cards; a punch (*N Am*). ◆ *adj* ruined, penniless; broken. [Orig a colloquial form of **burst**]
■ **bust'er** *n* something large; a frolic (*old sl*); a roisterer (*old sl*); a horse-breaker; a form of address to a man or boy; a strong south wind (*Aust*); someone or something that destroys or shatters (*esp* as *combining form*, as in *blockbuster*). **bust'ing** *n* (*esp* as *combining form*).
❑ **busted flush** see under **flush³**. **bust'-up** *n* a quarrel or disruption; a disturbance or brawl.
■ **bust a gut** or **one's butt** to work very hard to achieve something. **bust up** to part after a quarrel or disagreement; to break up (a meeting). **go bust** to become bankrupt; to exceed the required score (*darts*, *cards*).

bustard /*bus'tərd*/ *n* any bird of the genus *Otis*, *usu* ranked with cranes. [Fr *bistard*, from L *avis tarda* slow bird (a misnomer)]

busted see **burst**.

bustee /*bus'tē*/ *n* in India, a settlement or a collection of huts. [Hindi *bastī*]

bustier /*bŭ-styā'*/ (*Fr*) *n* a strapless long-line brassière or tight-fitting bodice.

bustle¹ /*bus'l*/ *vi* to busy oneself noisily or fussily (often with *about*); to be full of or busy with (with *with*). ◆ *vt* to hasten unceremoniously. ◆ *n* hurried activity; stir; tumult. [ME *bustelen*, of uncertain ety]
■ **bust'ler** *n*. **bust'ling** *adj* lively and busy.

bustle² /*bus'l*/ (*hist*) *n* a frame or pad for making a skirt stand out from the hips. [Origin uncertain]

busy /*biz'i*/ *adj* fully employed; active; diligent; meddling; fussily active; (of a telephone line or a room) engaged; (of a picture or design) unrestful because it has too much detail. ◆ *n* (*sl*) a detective. ◆ *vt* (**bus'ying**; **bus'ied**) to make busy; to occupy. [OE *bysig*]
■ **bus'ily** *adv*. **bus'yness** *n* the state of being busy (see **business**).
❑ **bus'ybody** *n* a person who meddles in others' affairs; a mirror at a window arranged to show the street below. ◆ *vi* to behave like a busybody. **busy Lizzie** *n* a popular fast-growing pot-plant of the *Impatiens* genus, *usu* with pink or white flowers. **busy signal** *n* (*N Am*) the engaged tone. **bus'ywork** *n* (*N Am*) work that occupies a person's time without producing much of value.

but¹ /*but*/ *prep* except; without (*obs*); in or towards the outer room of (*Scot*). ◆ *conj* on the other hand; in contrast; nevertheless; unless, if not (*archaic*); other than (that); without it being the case that; introducing emphasis, as in *nobody, but nobody, must go*; except that (merging in *prep*); that not (developing into a negative *relative pronoun*); than, sooner than (*archaic*). ◆ *adv* only, merely; however (*dialect*); in or to the outer room, outwards (*Scot*). ◆ *n* an objection; an outer room or kitchen of a house, *opp* to ben (*Scot*; also *adj*). ◆ *vt* (**butt'ing**; **butt'ed**) to put forward as an objection. [OE *be-ūtan*, *būtan* without, from *be* by, and *ūtan* out, near and yet outside]
■ **anything but** certainly not. **but and** (*obs*) and also. **but and ben** see under **ben²**. **but for** or **but that** were it not for, or that. **but if** (*obs*) unless.

but² /*but*/ *n* another spelling of **butt²,³,⁴**.

butadiene /*bū-tə-dī'ēn*/ *n* a hydrocarbon, C_4H_6, used in making synthetic rubber. [*butane*, *di-* and chem sfx *-ene*]

butane /*bū'tān*/ *n* a hydrocarbon of the alkane series, C_4H_{10}, widely used as a fuel (see **bottle gas** under **bottle¹**). [**butyl**]
■ **bu'tanol** /*-tə-nol*/ *n* the name of two of the isomers of butyl alcohol one of which exists in two enantiomeric forms.
❑ **butanoic acid** /*bū-tə-nō'ik*/ *n* butyric acid (qv).

■ words derived from main entry word; ❑ compound words; ■ idioms and phrasal verbs

Butazolidin® /bū-tə-zol'i-din/ n phenylbutazone (qv).

butch /bŭch/ adj tough; aggressively masculine in appearance or manner (sl). ◆ n a very short haircut for men or women; an aggressively tough man (sl); a noticeably masculine person, esp a lesbian or homosexual man (sl). [N Am boy's nickname]

butcher /bŭch'ər/ n a person whose business is to slaughter animals for food, or who deals in their meat; a person who delights in bloody deeds; a vendor of sweets, newspapers, etc on a railway train (US). ◆ vt to slaughter and prepare (animals) for sale as food; to put to a bloody death, kill cruelly; to spoil, botch. [OFr bochier, bouchier a person who kills he-goats, from boc a he-goat; cf **buck**[1]]
■ **butch'ering** or **butch'ing** n (back-formation) the act of killing for food, or cruelly. **butch'erly** adj butcher-like, cruel, murderous (formerly also adv). **butch'er's** (orig **butcher's hook**) n (Cockney rhyming sl) a look. **butch'ery** n the trade of a butcher; great or cruel slaughter; a slaughterhouse.
❑ **butch'erbird** n a shrike; a bird of the genus Cracticus which impales its prey on thorns (Aust). **butcher meat** or **butcher's meat** n the flesh of animals slaughtered by butchers, as distinguished from fish, fowls and game. **butcher's broom** n an evergreen shrub (Ruscus aculeatus) with phyllodes, formerly used by butchers for sweeping their blocks.

bute or **Bute** /būt/ (sl) n a shortened form of **Butazolidin**®.

Butea /bū'ti-ə/ n a genus of papilionaceous trees, including the dhak, yielding Bengal kino. [Named after Lord Bute (1713–92), prime minister and botanist]

but-end same as **butt-end** (see under **butt**[2]).

butene /bū'tēn/ n butylene.

buteo /bū'ti-ō/ (US) n (pl **bū'teos**) a buzzard. [L būteō, -ōnis]

Buteyko method /bū-tā'kō me'thəd/ n a technique of breathing exercises designed to alleviate asthma and other breathing disorders. [KP Buteyko (1923–2003), Ukrainian scientist who devised it]

butler /but'lər/ n a male servant in charge of liquors, plate, etc; an officer in a royal household. ◆ vi to act as butler (also (facetious) **butt'le**). [Norman Fr butuiller, from LL buticulārius. Cf **bottle**[1]]
■ **but'lerage** n the department of a domestic butler; duty on imported wine once paid to the king's butler (obs); the office of king's butler (obs). **but'lership** n. **but'lery** n the butler's pantry.
❑ **butler's pantry** n the pantry where the plate and glassware are kept.

butment same as **abutment** (see under **abut**).

butt[1] /but/ vt to strike with the head, as a goat, etc does. ◆ vi to strike with the head (also with at or against); to go or drive head first; to jut out. ◆ n a push or blow with the head. [OFr boter to push, strike]
■ **butt'er** n an animal that butts.
▨ **butt in** to interfere, thrust oneself into a conversation, etc. **butt out** (N Am and Aust) to refrain from interfering.

butt[2] /but/ n the thick and heavy end; the stump; a tree trunk; the part of a hide from or towards the rear of an animal; thick leather; the fag end of a cigar or cigarette; the buttocks (N Am inf); the wooden, etc handle or steadying shoulder part of a pistol or rifle; a remnant; a place where two edges meet; a butt-end. ◆ vi to abut; to meet end to end. [Ety uncertain; poss connected with **butt**[3] and **abut**]
❑ **butt'-dial** vi and vt (inf) to call (a telephone number) by accidentally pressing against the buttons of a phone in one's pocket (also n). **butted joint** n a joint formed between the squared ends of the two jointing pieces, which come together but do not overlap. **butt'-end** n the square end of a plank meeting another end to end. **butt'head** n (derog sl) a stupid person. **butt hinge** n a hinge formed from two butt-ends joined by a pin. **butt-ugly** adj (inf; chiefly US) extremely ugly. **butt welding** n welding the seam formed by joining two butt-ends.

butt[3] /but/ n a mark or mound for archery or shooting practice; a mound behind targets; someone who is made an object of ridicule; a hiding place for grouse-shooters. [Fr but goal]
❑ **butt'-shaft** n (Shakesp) an arrow.

butt[4] /but/ n a large cask of varying capacity; a wine butt properly = 126 gallons (approx 573 litres), a beer and sherry butt properly = 108 gallons (approx 491 litres). [Cf Fr botte, Sp bota, LL butta]

butt[5] /but/ n a flatfish of various kinds. [Poss connected with **butt**[2]; cf Swed butta turbot, Du bot, Ger Butt flounder; cf **halibut**, **turbot**]

butte /būt/ (N Am) n a conspicuous and isolated hill, cliff-sided, often flat-topped, in the western USA and Canada. [Fr]

butter[1] /but'ər/ n an edible fatty solid obtained from cream by churning; extended to various substances resembling or containing it; an old chemical name for certain oily chlorides (butter of antimony, of tin, etc); flattery (inf). ◆ vt to spread over with butter, mortar, or other soft substance; to flatter (usu with up; inf); to fail to catch, drop (archaic). [OE butere; Ger Butter; both from L būtȳrum, from Gr boutȳron, appar from bous ox, and tȳros cheese]
■ **butt'erine** /-ēn/ n a margarine made partly from milk. **butt'eriness** n. **butt'ery** adj like butter; smeared with butter or the like. ◆ n (Scot) a roll made with a buttery dough.
❑ **butt'er-and-eggs** n any of various plants with two-toned yellow flowers. **butt'er-bake** (Scot) or **butt'er-biscuit** n a cake like a biscuit but softer. **butt'erball** n a single portion of butter rolled into a ball; a bufflehead (US); a chubby, roly-poly person (chiefly US inf). **butter bean** n any of several varieties of lima bean. **butt'er-bird** n in Jamaica, the bobolink. **butter-biscuit** see **butter-bake** above. **butt'er-boat** n a container for melted butter at table. **butt'er-box** n a box for butter; an old nickname for a Dutchman. **butt'erbur** or **butt'erdock** n a plant related to coltsfoot with knobbed masses of flower-heads and great rhubarb-like leaves. **butter cloth** or **muslin** n a loose-woven cloth formerly used for wrapping butter. **butt'er-cooler** n a dish for keeping butter in water at table. **butter cream** n butter and sugar beaten together with flavouring and sometimes colouring and used to fill and top cakes, etc. **butt'ercup** n a crowfoot (genus Ranunculus), esp one of those species that have golden-yellow cup-shaped flowers. **butter dish** or **plate** n a dish or plate for holding butter at table. **butterdock** see **butterbur** above. **buttered eggs** n pl (archaic) scrambled eggs. **butt'erfat** n the fat contained in butter, chiefly glycerides of palmitic and oleic acids. **butt'erfingered** adj (inf). **butt'erfingers** n sing (inf) someone who lets a ball, etc they ought to catch slip through their fingers. **butt'erfish** n a name for various slimy fishes, esp the gunnel. **butt'erfly** n (pl **butt'erflies**) a general name for any of the daylight Lepidoptera, roughly distinguished from moths by their clubbed antennae; a frivolous, flighty person; butterfly stroke (often shortened to **fly**); (in pl) butterflies in the stomach. ◆ adj light, flighty, like a butterfly. **butt'erfly-bow** n a bow whose loops and ends are spread like a butterfly's wings. **butterfly bush** n buddleia. **butterfly clip** or **plaster** n a lightweight adhesive plaster, with broadened ends, used in place of a suture to draw together the edges of superficial wounds. **butterfly effect** n the theory that a small variation at the beginning of a process can lead to a huge variation at a later stage. **butterfly fish** n a blenny with an eye-spot on the dorsal fin; any fish of the family Chaetodontidae. **butterfly flower** n one adapted for pollination by butterflies. **butterfly kiss** n a caress consisting of fluttering the eyelashes against one's partner's skin. **butterfly knife** n a folding pocket knife with two rotating handles. **butterfly net** n a small-meshed conical net with a wide round open end on a hoop attached to a handle, used for catching butterflies. **butterfly nut** see **butterfly screw** below. **butterfly orchis** or **orchid** n any of various orchids with flowers resembling a butterfly. **butterfly plaster** see **butterfly clip** above. **butterfly screw** or **nut** n a screw or nut turned by winged finger-grips. **butterfly stroke** n (swimming) a stroke performed lying on one's front, the arms working simultaneously with an overarm action, and with an undulating movement of both legs together from the hips. **butterfly valve** n a disc-shaped valve in a carburettor, etc; a valve consisting of two hinged plates. **butterfly weed** n pleurisy-root. **butterhead lettuce** n a kind of soft-leaved yellow-hearted lettuce. **butter icing** n butter cream. **butter knife** n a blunt knife for taking butter from a butter dish. **butt'ermilk** n the liquid that remains after butter has been separated from cream by churning. **butter muslin** see **butter cloth** above. **butt'ernut** n the oily nut of the N American white walnut, the tree itself; its light-coloured close-grained wood; a brownish-grey; an edible nut of the souari (genus Caryocar) tree of Guiana (also called **souari-nut**). **butter oil** n a dairy product consisting almost entirely of milk fat. **butt'er-paper** n a translucent greaseproof paper suitable for wrapping butter. **butter pat** n a pat of butter; each of a pair of wooden bats for working butter into shape. **butter plate** see **butter dish** above. **butt'er-print** n a mould for shaping butter; a child (obs sl). **butt'erscotch** n a kind of hard toffee containing much butter; a flavouring made from or similar to this. **butt'er-tree** n any of various trees that yield a buttery substance, esp of the genera Bassia, Butyrospermum, Caryocar, Pentadesma. **butt'er-wife** or **butt'er-woman** n (obs) a woman who makes and sells butter. **butt'erwort** n any species of Pinguicula, a genus of insectivorous bog-plants (family Lentibulariaceae) with glistening sticky leaves. **butt'ery-fingered** adj butterfingered. **buttery fingers** n sing butterfingers.
■ **butterflies in the stomach** (inf) nervous tremors in the stomach. **butter up** (inf) to flatter. **look as if butter wouldn't melt in one's mouth** to look speciously innocent or well-behaved.

butter[2] see under **butt**[1].

butter-bump /but'ər-bump/ n the bittern. See **bittern**[1] and **bump**[2].

butterfly, **butterine**, etc see under **butter¹**.

buttery¹ /but'ə-ri/ n a storeroom for provisions, esp liquors; a room in esp an Oxford or Cambridge college where food and drink are supplied to students. [Fr bouteillerie, literally, place for bottles; cf **butler**, **bottle¹**]
□ **butt'ery-bar** n the ledge for holding tankards in the buttery. **butt'ery-hatch** n a half-door over which provisions are handed from the buttery.

buttery² see under **butter¹**.

buttle see **butler**.

buttock /but'ək/ n either side of the rump or protuberant part at the back of the body above the legs; a cut of meat from the buttock, eg silverside; a throw by use of the buttock (wrestling). ◆ vt to throw in this way. [Dimin of **butt²**]
□ **buttock planes** n pl sectional planes drawn longitudinally through a ship, used in calculating volumes, etc.

button /but'n/ n a knob or disc, used as a fastening, ornament or badge; a knob, eg that at the end of a foil, that for winding a watch, that to which a violin tailpiece is looped; a bud; the knob which is the beginning of a horn on a stag's head; a projection on the loom of an oar to keep it inside the gate; the head of an unexpanded mushroom (also **button mushroom**); a pimple; the push-button of an electric bell, a vending machine, etc; on a mouse or joystick, a small part pressed to cause it to function (comput); a small on-screen shape clicked on to select an option (comput); anything of little value; a person who acts as a decoy or accomplice (obs sl); (in pl) sheep's dung. ◆ adj like a button, used eg of small varieties of vegetables, blooms, etc of a compact, globular shape. ◆ vt to fasten by means of buttons; to close up tightly. ◆ vi to be capable of being fastened with buttons. [Fr bouton any small projection, from bouter to push]
■ **butt'ons** n sing a page in a hotel, etc (also **boy in buttons** (obs)). **butt'ony** adj set with buttons; like a button or buttons.
□ **button accordion** n an accordion played by means of buttons. **butt'on-back** adj (of chairs, etc) decorated with buttons pressed into the upholstery at regular intervals on the back and sometimes elsewhere. **butt'onball** see **buttonwood** below. **butt'onbush** n a N American shrub (genus Cephalanthus) of the madder family, with globular flower-heads. **button cell** or **button cell battery** n a small, flat, circular battery, used to power a watch, etc. **button chrysanthemum** n a kind of chrysanthemum with small round flowers. **butt'on-down** adj (of a shirt collar) with ends fastened by buttons to the shirt front. **butt'oned-down** adj (US inf) conservative, esp in dress or behaviour. **butt'oned-up** adj (inf) uncommunicative or repressed. **butt'onhole** n the slit through which a button is passed; a flower or flowers for wearing in the buttonhole of a lapel. ◆ vt to make buttonholes in; to sew with a stitch suitable to reinforce (esp cut) edges (**buttonhole stitch**); to detain in talk (orig **butt'onhold**). **butt'onholer** n a person or sewing-machine attachment that makes buttonholes. **butt'onhook** n a hook for pulling buttons through buttonholes in boots, gloves, etc. **butt'on-mould** n the wooden, plastic, etc base for leather- or cloth-covered buttons. **button mushroom** see under n above. **button quail** n any of several ground-living birds of the genus Turnix inhabiting warm grasslands of Australasia. **button scurvy** n yaws. **butt'on-through** adj (of a woman's dress or skirt) buttoning in front from top to bottom. **butt'onwood** n a small tropical Atlantic coast evergreen tree (Conocarpus erecta) of the myrobalan family; (also **butt'onball**) a plane-tree (US).
■ **as bright as a button** full of energy and enthusiasm. **buttoned up** (sl) successfully fixed up; safe in hand; ready for action; see also **buttoned-up** above. **button up** or **button your lip** (inf) be quiet. **have all one's buttons (on)** (inf) to be completely sane. **have one's finger on the button** to be poised for action. **in his buttons** a conjectural reading in Shakespeare's Merry Wives of Windsor where the quarto has betmes, probably a misprint for talons. **on the button** (inf) exactly right; precisely, exactly, punctually. **press the button** to set in motion some momentous action, esp the launching of nuclear weapons against an enemy target.

buttress /but'rəs/ n a projecting support built onto the outside of a wall; any support or prop; something that looks like a buttress, eg a projection from a hill. ◆ vt to prop or support with, or as if with, a buttress. [OFr bouterez, from bouter to push, bear against]
□ **butt'ress-root** n a root, often growing from the trunk, that helps to keep a tree upright. **butt'ress-thread** n an asymmetric screw thread with one face at right angles to and the other inclined to the shaft.

butty¹ /but'i/ (N Eng) n a sandwich, snack. [**butter¹** and **-y²**]

butty² /but'i/ (dialect) n a chum, comrade, workfellow, partner, esp in a coalmine (also **butt'yman**); someone who takes a contract for work in a coalmine (obs); a barge towed by another. [Appar dimin of dialect buttar a companion]
□ **butt'y-collier** n. **butt'y-gang** n.

butut /boo'toot/ n (pl **bu'tut** or **bu'tuts**) a Gambian monetary unit, $\frac{1}{100}$ of a dalasi.

butyl /bū'til/ or (US) -təl/ n a radical C_4H_9. [See **butter¹**, and Gr hylē matter]
■ **bū'tylene** (also **bū'tene**) n an olefine hydrocarbon (C_4H_8) in three isomers.
□ **butyl alcohol** n any of four isomeric alcohols of formula C_4H_9OH used as solvents, etc. **butyl rubber** n a synthetic rubber polymerized from isobutylene and isoprene.

butyric /bū-tir'ik/ adj relating to or derived from butter. [See **butter¹**]
■ **butyrā'ceous** adj buttery, containing butter. **bū'tyrate** n a salt of butyric acid.
□ **butyric acid** n a volatile fatty acid (C_3H_7COOH), one isomer of which gives rancid butter its smell.

buvette /bū-vet'/ (obs, Fr) n a small refreshment bar eg at a roadside or in a station.

buxom /buk'səm/ adj (of a woman) plump and comely; busty; lively, jolly; yielding, elastic (obs). [ME buhsum pliable, obedient, from OE būgan to bow, yield, and **-some¹**]
■ **bux'omness** n.

buy /bī/ vt (**buy'ing**; **bought** /böt/; archaic pap **bought'en**) to purchase for money; to bribe; to obtain in exchange for something; to redeem (theol); to accept, believe (sl). ◆ vi to be or act as a buyer. ◆ n something purchased. [OE bycgan, bohte, boht; Gothic bugjan]
■ **buy'able** adj and n. **buy'er** n a person who buys; a person employed to buy goods (eg for a store or company).
□ **buy'-back** n the optional or obligatory buying back by the seller of all or part of what was sold (commerce); the purchasing by a company of its own shares (finance). **buyers'** (or **buyer's**) **market** n one in which buyers control the price, because supply exceeds demand. **buy'-in** n the purchase of a company by an individual or group from outside the company (see also **buy in** below).
■ **a good buy** (inf) a wise purchase, a bargain. **buy and sell** (Shakesp) to traffic in. **buy in** to collect a stock (of) by buying; to buy shares; to buy into; to buy back for the owner at an auction when the reserve price is not reached (**buy'-in** n). **buy into** to pay for a share or interest in; to accept as valid, subscribe to (inf). **buy off** to buy exemption or release for; to get rid of by paying. **buy out** to dispossess or take over possession from by payment (**buy'out** n), specif the purchase of a company by its own staff or managers; to buy off. **buy over** to win over by payment; to bribe. **buy up** to purchase the whole available stock of. **have bought it** (sl) to have been killed.

buzz¹ /buz/ vi to make a noise like that of insects' wings; to murmur; to talk excitedly; to move quickly, bustle; of a place, to be busy and lively. ◆ vt to utter with a buzzing sound; to whisper or spread secretly; to transmit by Morse over a telephone wire by means of a key; to summon with a buzzer; to make a telephone call to (inf); to throw (sl); to fly very low over or very close to (inf); to interfere with in flight by flying very near to (aeronautics). ◆ n the noise of bees or flies in flight; a humming sound; a voiced hiss; a whispered report; a telephone call (inf); a pleasant or excited feeling, a kick (inf); enthusiasm (inf); a craze, fad (inf). [From the sound]
■ **buzz'er** n an apparatus that makes a buzzing sound; a person who buzzes; a whisperer or telltale (Shakesp). **buzz'ing** n and adj. **buzz'ingly** adv. **buzz'y** adj.
□ **buzz'bait** n (angling) an artificial bait with small blades that stir the water. **buzz bomb** n (inf) a flying bomb. **buzz'cut** n a style of haircut in which the hair is cut very short with electric clippers. **buzz'kill** n (chiefly US) a person or thing that destroys an enjoyable atmosphere. **buzz phrase** see **buzz word** below. **buzz saw** n (N Am) a circular saw. **buzz word** or **buzz'word**, **buzz phrase** or **buzz term** n (inf) a fashionable new term in the jargon of a particular subject, science, etc, its use by other individuals or groups conveying the impression of specialized knowledge and of being very up to date.
■ **buzz off** (sl) to go away.

buzz² /buz/ vt to drain (a bottle) to the last drop of wine. [Origin uncertain]

buzzard¹ /buz'ərd/ n a large bird of prey of the genus Buteo, despised by falconers; extended to some others, such as the honey buzzard, turkey-buzzard; a form of abuse for a person, sometimes euphemistic for **bastard**. [Fr busard]

buzzard² /buz'ərd/ n a blundering insect, such as a cockchafer or night-flying moth. [**buzz¹**]
□ **buzz'ard-clock** n (dialect) cockchafer.

BV *abbrev* : *Beata Virgo* (L), Blessed Virgin; *Bene vale* (L), farewell; *Besloten Vennootschap* (Du), limited company.

BVI *abbrev* : British Virgin Islands (IVR).

BVM *abbrev* : *Beata Virgo Maria* (L), Blessed Virgin Mary.

BVM&S *abbrev* : Bachelor of Veterinary Medicine and Surgery.

BW *abbrev* : Botswana (IVR); British Waterways (formerly British Waterways Board).

b/w or **B/W** *abbrev* : black and white.

bwana /bwä'nä or -nə/ (*obs E Afr*) *n* master; sir. [Swahili]

bwazi see **buaze**.

BWR *abbrev* : boiling-water reactor.

BWV *abbrev* : *Bach Werke Verzeichnis* (*Ger*), catalogue of Bach's works.

BY *abbrev* : Belarus (IVR).

by¹ /bī/ *prep* at the side of; near to; along a route passing through, via; past; (in oaths) in the presence of, or with the witness of; through (denoting the agent, cause, means, etc); to the extent of; in quantity measurable in terms of; in accordance with; in respect of; (of time) not after; during (day, night, etc); multiplied into, or combined with another dimension of; in succession to; (of horses, etc) sired by; besides (*Scot*); in comparison with (*Scot*). ♦ *conj* by the time that (*archaic* and *Scot*); than (*Scot*). ♦ *adv* near; aside; away; past; in reserve; to or at one's home. ♦ *n* and *adj* see **bye¹**. [OE *bī, bi, big* ; Ger *bei*, L *ambi*]
■ **by-** or **bye-** *pfx* near; aside; past; side, subsidiary; indirect; incidental.
◻ **by-and-by¹** *n* (*N Am*) the future, a future occasion. ♦ *adv* in succession (*Spenser*). **by'-blow** *n* a side blow; an illegitimate child (*archaic*). **by'catch** *n* fish that are inadvertently caught along with the desired catch, *esp* immature fish or fish of a protected species. **by'-corner** *n* an out-of-the-way place. **by'-drinking** *n* (*Shakesp*) drinking between meals. **by'-election** *n* a parliamentary election for a seat during the sitting of parliament. **by'-end** *n* a subsidiary aim. **by'-form** *n* a subsidiary form; a form varying from the usual one. **by'-going** *n* the action of passing by (*esp* in **in the by-going**, in passing). **by'gone** /-gon/ *adj* former, past. **by'gones** *n pl* past happenings or grievances; ornaments, household articles, etc of former times which are not fine enough, or not old enough, to be valued as antiques (also in *sing*). **by'-lane** *n* a side lane or passage out of the common road. **by'law** or **bye'-law** see separate entry. **by'line** *n* a line at the head of a newspaper or magazine article or photograph naming the author or photographer; the touchline (*football*). **by'-motive** *n* an unavowed motive. **by'-name** or **by'name** *n* a nickname; another name by which a person is known. **by'-ordinar** *adj* (*Scot*) extraordinary. **by'pass** *n* a road, route or passage for carrying traffic, fluids, electricity, etc round an obstruction, congested place, etc (**cardiopulmonary bypass** a method whereby (in cardiac surgery) circulation and oxygenation of blood are maintained artificially, bypassing the heart and lungs; **coronary bypass** a surgical operation to bypass a blocked coronary artery with a grafted blood vessel from eg the patient's leg). ♦ *vt* to supply with a bypass; to direct (eg fluid) along a bypass; to go round and beyond by a bypass; to ignore, leave out; to evade. **by'-passage** *n* a side passage. **by'-past** *adj* (*Shakesp*) past; gone by. **by'path** *n* a secluded or indirect path. **by'place** *n* a secluded place. **by'-play** *n* action subordinate to and apart from the main action, *esp* in a play. **by'-plot** *n* a subsidiary plot. **by'-product** *n* a product created incidentally in the process of making something else; an unintended side effect. **by'road** *n* a minor or side road. **by'room** *n* (*Shakesp*) a side or private room. **by'-speech** *n* (*obs*) an incidental speech, an aside. **by'stander** *n* someone who stands by or near one; an onlooker. **by'-street** *n* an obscure street. **by'-thing** *n* (*archaic*) a thing of minor importance. **by'-time** *n* (*archaic*) leisure time. **by'way** *n* a sideroad, a private, secluded or obscure way; an obscure or minor area of interest. **by'word** *n* a common saying, proverb; an object of scorn; someone or something noted for a specified characteristic. **by'-work** *n* (*obs*) work done in leisure time.
■ **by and by** at some future time; before long, presently; in the course of time; in succession, in order of succession (*obs*). **by and large** speaking generally; on the whole; whether close-hauled or before the wind (*naut*). **by oneself** alone; without assistance. **by the by** (or **bye**) or **by the way** in passing, incidentally. **cardiopulmonary bypass** and **coronary bypass** see **bypass** above. **let bygones be bygones** let past quarrels be ignored. **without** (**so much as**) **a by-your-leave** without (even) asking permission.

by² see **bye¹**.

by- see under **by¹**.

by-blow, **bycatch** see under **by¹**.

bycoket /bī'ko-kit/ *n* an ornamental cap with peaks at both front and back worn in the 15c. [OFr *bicoquet*, prob *bi-* (L *bis*) double, and *coque* a shell]

by-corner, **by-drinking** see under **by¹**.

bye¹ or **by** /bī/ *n* (*pl* **byes** or **bys**) anything of minor importance, a side issue, a thing not directly aimed at; (in games) the state of a player or team that has not drawn an opponent, and passes without contest to the next round; (in golf) the holes remaining after the match is decided, played as a subsidiary game (*obs*); (in cricket) a run made from a ball that passes the batsman but is not struck or touched by him, credited to the batsman's team but not his individual score; (in cockfighting) a battle not forming part of a main (see **main³**; *obs*). ♦ *adj* subsidiary; part; indirect.
■ **by the bye** see under **by¹**. [See **by¹**]

bye² /bī/ or **bye-bye** /bī'-bī' or bə-bī'/ informal forms of **goodbye**.

bye- see under **by¹**.

bye-byes /bī'bīz/ (*inf*) *n* (used to children) sleep, *esp* in **go to bye-byes**. [Prob **bye-bye**, perh with influence from **beddy-byes**]

bye-law see **bylaw**.

by-election see under **by¹**.

Byelorussian see **Belorussian**.

by-end...to...**bygones** see under **by¹**.

byke see **bike²**.

bylander see **bilander**.

by-lane see under **by¹**.

bylaw or **bye-law** /bī'lö/ *n* a law of a local authority or private corporation; a supplementary law or an inferred regulation. [The same as **byrlaw**, from ON *bȳjar-lög* ; Dan *by-lov* town-law; from ON *būa* to dwell. Cf **bower¹**]

byline see under **by¹**.

bylive (*Spenser*) same as **belive**.

by-motive, **by-name** see under **by¹**.

bynempt obsolete *pat* of **bename**.

BYO *abbrev* : bring your own, *esp* bring your own alcohol.

BYOB *abbrev* : bring your own bottle, beer or (*inf*) booze.

BYOD *abbrev* : bring your own device (to a place of work).

by-ordinar...to...**by-product** see under **by¹**.

byre /bīr/ (mainly *Scot*) *n* a cowhouse. [OE *bȳre*]
◻ **byre'man** or **byre'woman** *n* a farm-servant who looks after cows.

byrlady /bər-lā'di/ and **byrlakin** /bər-lā'kin/ (*archaic*) *interj* short forms of *By Our Lady* or *Ladykin*.

byrlaw /bir'lö/ (*archaic Scot and N Eng*) *n* local law, surviving longest in rural areas, and dealing with local customs and civil disputes (also **bourlaw** /boor'/). [See **bylaw**]
◻ **byr'law-man** (*Walter Scott* **bir'lieman**) *n* an arbiter, oddsman or umpire in such matters.

byrnie /bir'ni/ (*Scot hist*) *n* a mail-coat; a breastplate. [ON *brynja* ; OE *byrne*]

byroad see under **by¹**.

Byronic /bī-ron'ik/ *adj* possessing the characteristics of Lord *Byron* (1788–1824) or his poetry, overstrained in sentiment or passion, cynical and libertine; of a man, attractively dark, brooding and romantic.
■ **Byron'ically** *adv*. **By'ronism** *n*.

byroom, **by-speech** see under **by¹**.

byssus /bis'əs/ *n* a fine yellowish flax; linen made from it (the 'fine linen' of the Bible); the bundle of filaments by which some shellfish attach themselves. [L, from Gr *byssos* a fine flaxen substance]
■ **byssá'ceous** *adj* composed of a mass of fine threads; delicately filamentous. **byss'al** *adj* relating to a mollusc's byssus. **byss'ine** *adj* made of fine linen. **byssinōs'is** *n* a lung disease of textile workers. **byss'oid** *adj* byssaceous.

bystander, **by-street** see under **by¹**.

byte /bīt/ (*comput*) *n* a set of *usu* eight binary digits (bits) considered as a unit; the amount of storage space occupied by such a unit. [From **bit²** and **bite**]

by-thing, **by-time** see under **by¹**.

bytownite /bī'tow-nīt/ (*mineralogy*) *n* a plagioclase intermediate between anorthite and labradorite. [*Bytown*, former name of Ottawa, where it occurs]

byway see under **by¹**.

bywoner /bī'wō-nər or -vō-/ (S Afr) n an authorized squatter on another's farm; a landless poor white person. [Du *bijwonen* to be present]

byword, **by-work** see under **by**[1].

byzant /biz'ənt or bi-zant'/ same as **bezant**.

Byzantine /bi-zan'tīn, bī-zan'tīn, -tin or biz'ən-/ adj relating to *Byzantium* (later Constantinople, now Istanbul), the Byzantine Empire or Church; designating the variety of Greek spoken and written in the Byzantine Empire; rigidly hierarchic; intricate, tortuous. ◆n an inhabitant of Byzantium. [Gr *Byzantion*]
■ **Byzan'tinism** n the manifestation of Byzantine characteristics. **Byzan'tinist** n a person who studies, or is expert in, Byzantine history, affairs, etc.
❑ **Byzantine architecture** n. **Byzantine Church** n the Eastern or Greek Orthodox Church. **Byzantine Empire** n the Eastern or Greek Empire from 330AD to 1453.

BZ abbrev : Belize (not in official use; IVR).

■ words derived from main entry word; ❑ compound words; ■ idioms and phrasal verbs

Cc

C or **c** /sē/ n the third letter in the modern English alphabet as in the Roman, in origin a rounded form of the Greek *gamma* (Γ, γ), generally pronounced either as a voiceless velar stop, as in *cat*, or a voiceless sibilant, as in *city*; the first note of the diatonic scale of C major, the sound on which the system is founded (*music*); the key or scale having that note for its tonic (*music*); the designation of the C series of paper sizes (used for envelopes), ranging from C0 (917 × 1297mm) to C7/6 (81 × 162mm); in hexadecimal notation, 12 (decimal) or 1100 (binary); the third highest in a category or range; a high-level computer programming language; anything shaped like the letter C. □ **C1** n (*Brit*) (a member of) the social class or group categorized as supervisory and clerical. **C2** n (*Brit*) (a member of) the social class or group categorized as skilled or manual. **C3** *adj* in a poor state of physical fitness; inferior (*inf*) (see also **A1** under **A¹**); see also separate entry **c-cubed**. **C clef** n (*music*) a symbol, an ornamental form of the letter C, used to indicate middle C on the stave. **C'-horizon** n (*geol*) the layer of soil above the bedrock, consisting mainly of weathered rock. **C'-list** *adj* (*inf*) belonging to an insignificant or unadmired group (of celebrities, etc). **C'-lister** n. **c'-spring** see **cee-spring** under **cee**.

C or **C.** *abbrev* : Calorie, a kilocalorie; *esp* in place names on maps, Cape; Catholic; clubs (*cards*); cocaine (*sl*); Coloured (*S Afr*); Command Paper (series 1870–1899); Conservative; Corps; Cuba (IVR); the sum of $100 (*N Am sl*).

C *symbol* : carbon (*chem*); century (preceding numeral, eg C21, twenty-first century); common time, four crotchets in a bar (*music*); coulomb (SI unit); (as a Roman numeral) 100.

C *symbol* : compliance (*phys*); electrical capacitance.

C̄ *symbol* : (Roman numeral) 100000.

°C *symbol* : degree Celsius (SI unit); degree(s) Centigrade.

C- (*esp US*) *abbrev* : in designation of military aircraft, cargo transport.

c or **c.** *abbrev* : canine (*dentistry*); caput (L), chapter (*pl* **cc**); carat; caught (by) (*cricket*); cent(s); centi-; centimes; century (following numeral, eg 21c, twenty-first century); circa (L), about; cloudy (*meteorol*); cold (water); college; colt; constant (*maths*); contralto; cubic.

c (*maths* and *phys*) *symbol* : the speed of light.

¢ *symbol* : cent(s).

© *symbol* : copyright.

c/- (*Aust* and *NZ*) *symbol* : in addresses, care of.

CA *abbrev* : California (US state); Carer's Allowance; Central America; Chartered Accountant (Scotland and Canada); chief accountant; consular agent; Consumers' Association; County Alderman.

Ca (*chem*) *symbol* : calcium.

ca *abbrev* : cases; circa (L), about.

c/a (*banking* and *commerce*) *abbrev* : capital account; credit account; current account.

ca' or **caa'** /kö/ (*Scot*) *vt* and *vi* to call; to drive, urge on or propel; to knock or push (with *down, off, over*, etc). [**call¹**]
□ **ca'ing** or **caa'ing whale** n a pilot whale, formerly hunted by ca'ing or driving ashore.
■ **ca' canny** to go easy; to proceed warily; deliberately to restrict output or effort.

CAA *abbrev* : Civil Aviation Authority.

Caaba see **Kaaba**.

caatinga /kä-ting'gə/ n in Brazil, open, comparatively low forest, on white sandy soil derived from granite. [Tupí, white forest]

CAB *abbrev* : Citizens' Advice Bureau.

cab¹ /kab/ n a taxi-cab; a compartment for the driver or operator of a lorry, railway locomotive, crane, etc; a light, *usu* two-wheeled, horse-drawn carriage for public hire (*hist*). See also **hansom**. ◆ *vi* (*inf*, chiefly *US*) to take or drive a taxi-cab. [Shortened from **cabriolet**]
■ **cabb'y** or **cabb'ie** n a familiar *dimin* of **cab'-driver** a taxi driver, or of **cab'man** a person who drives a horse-drawn cab.
□ **cab'-rank** or **cab'-stand** n a place where cabs stand for hire. **cab'-rank principle** or **rule** n (*inf; law*) a rule requiring barristers to take the first case offered to them, regardless of their opinion of it. **cab'-runner** or **cab'-tout** n a person whose business it is to call cabs.

cab² /kab/ n an ancient Hebrew measure of capacity equal to *approx* 1.6 litres (about three pints). [Heb *qab*]

caba (*pl* **cabas**) US form of **cabas**.

cabal /kə-bal'/ n a small group or council united for some secret purpose, *esp* political intrigue; a secret plot or intrigue; a name in English history given to the King's inner group of advisors, *esp* five unpopular ministers (1667–73) of Charles II, whose initials happened to make up the word. ◆ *vi* (**caball'ing**; **caballed'**) to form such a group or council for a secret purpose; to intrigue. [Fr *cabale*; from Heb *qabbālāh*; see **cabbala**]
■ **caball'er** n.

cabala, etc see **cabbala**.

cabaletta /ka-bə-let'ə/ n (*pl* **cabalett'as** or **cabalett'e** /-ə/) a simple operatic song or instrumental melody in rondo form, characterized by a continuously repeated rhythm; *esp* in 19c Italian opera, the lively final section of an aria or duet. [Ital, *prob* from *coboletta*, dimin of *cobola* a couplet, stanza, from Old Provençal *cobla*, from L *copula*; perh influenced by Ital *cavallo* horse, from being thought to be rhythmically similar to a horse's canter]

caballero /kab-al-yā'rō/ n (*pl* **caballer'os**) a Spanish gentleman; *esp* in SW USA, a horseman. [Sp, from L *caballārius* horseman, from *caballus* horse]

caballine /kab'ə-līn/ *adj* relating or suited to a horse. [L *caballīnus*, from *caballus* a horse]

cabana /kə-bä'nə/ (*esp US*) n a small tentlike cabin, *esp* used as a changing hut on the beach or by a swimming-pool; a cabin or chalet. [Sp *cabaña*]

cabaret /kab'ə-rā/ n an entertainment, at a nightclub or restaurant, made up of performances by singers, dancers, comedians, etc; a nightclub or restaurant where such entertainment is provided (*orig Fr*; now chiefly *US*). [Fr, tavern; *prob* for *cabaneret*, from *cabane* a hut]

cabas /kab'ä/ n a woman's workbasket, shopping bag or handbag (see also **caba**). [Fr, flat basket]

cabbage¹ /kab'ij/ n a vegetable (*Brassica oleracea*) of the Cruciferae family, having several cultivated varieties with large green or dark-red leaves forming a central, rounded edible head; the edible leaf bud of certain palms; a brain-damaged or mentally subnormal person (*inf; offensive*); a dull, inactive person (*inf, derog*); banknotes or paper money (*N Am sl*). [Fr *caboche* head, poss from L *caput*]
■ **cabb'agy** *adj*.
□ **cabbage-butt'erfly** or **cabbage-white'** n a large white butterfly (genus *Pieris*) whose larvae feed on the leaves of cabbage and similar plants. **cabb'age-fly** see **cabbage-root fly** below. **cabb'age-lettuce** n a type of lettuce with a cabbage-like head. **cabb'age-moth** n a moth (*Mamestra brassicae*) whose larvae feed on cabbage and similar plants. **cabbage palm** n a cabbage tree; any of several palms having leaf buds that are eaten like cabbage, *esp Oreodoxa oleracea* of the West Indies, and including the **cabbage palmetto** (*Sabal palmetto*) of tropical America. **cabbage-root fly** n a fly (*Delia radicum*) whose maggots damage cabbage roots. **cabbage rose** n a rose with a rounded, cabbage-like form. **cabb'agetown** n (*Can*) a city slum (from an area in Toronto whose inhabitants were believed to exist on a diet of cabbage). **cabbage tree** n a New Zealand plant (*Cordyline australis*), with bushy heads of grass-shaped leaves. **cabbage-tree hat**

n (*Aust*) a broad-brimmed hat made from the leaves of the cabbage tree. **cabb'age-worm** *n* the larva of the cabbage-butterfly or of the cabbage-moth.

cabbage[2] /kab'ij/ (*archaic sl*) *vt* and *vi* to cheat, steal or purloin, *orig* of tailors who took small pieces of a customer's cloth as a perquisite. ◆ *n* cloth so appropriated. [Origin uncertain; perh from MFr *cabas* cheating, theft]

cabbala or **cabala** /kab'ə-lə or kə-bä'lə/ *n* (also **kabala**, **kabbala**, **kabbalah** or **qabalah**) a secret mystical tradition of Jewish rabbis, who read hidden meanings into the Old Testament and other texts; any secret, esoteric, occult or mystic doctrine or lore. [Med L, from Heb *qabbālāh* tradition, from *qibbēl* to receive]
  ■ **cabb'alism** or **cab'alism** *n* the science of the cabbala. **cabb'alist** or **cab'alist** *n* someone versed in the cabbala. **cabbalist'ic**, **cabbalist'ical**, **cabalist'ic** or **cabalist'ical** *adj* relating to the cabbala; having a hidden meaning.

cabbie, **cabby** see under **cab**[1].

caber /kā'bər/ *n* a heavy pole, generally the trimmed trunk of a tree, which is held upright and tossed or hurled by athletes at Highland games. [Gaelic *cabar*]

Cabernet /kab'ər-nā/ *n* either of two varieties of black grape (**Cabernet Franc** and **Cabernet Sauvignon**) used to produce dry red wine, *orig* grown in Bordeaux and now found in many other wine-producing regions. [Fr]

cabezon /kab'i-zon/ *n* a large food-fish (*Scorpaenichthys marmoratus*), found in shallow waters along the Pacific coast of N America. [Sp *cabeza* head, from L *caput*]

CABG (*surg*) *abbrev* : coronary artery bypass graft.

cabin /kab'in/ *n* a hut or small, simple dwelling-house, often constructed of wood; (in a ship) a room used for living accommodation or as an office; (on a small boat) a compartment used as a shelter by the crew and passengers; (in an airliner) the section of the aircraft for carrying passengers and luggage; a compartment for the driver or operator of a large commercial vehicle; a railway signal-box. ◆ *vt* to shut up in a cabin or in a cramped space; to hamper in action (*fig*). ◆ *vi* to live in a cabin. [Fr *cabane*, from LL *capanna*]
  ❑ **cabin altitude** *n* the nominal pressure maintained in the cabin of a pressurized aircraft. **cab'in-boy** *n* a boy who waits on the officers or cabin passengers of a ship. **cabin class** *n* the class of accommodation, *esp* on a passenger ship, between tourist and first class. **cabin crew** *n* the members of an aircraft crew who look after passengers. **cabin cruiser** *n* a power-driven boat with living accommodation on board. **cabin fever** *n* (chiefly *N Am*) a feeling of restlessness after remaining indoors during bad weather; *orig* a state of severe depression brought on by living for long periods in isolated places and in cramped conditions, eg in a small cabin during the long winter months. **cabin passenger** *n* formerly, a passenger entitled to superior accommodation; a passenger having cabin accommodation. **cabin ship** *n* a ship carrying only one class of passengers.

cabinet /kab'(i)-nit or -nət/ *n* a cupboard, or piece of furniture, with doors, shelves and drawers, for storing or displaying articles; the outer case housing a radio, television, etc; *orig* a private room, *esp* one in which a sovereign's advisors met for consultation; hence (*usu* with *cap*) the committee made up of a group of senior ministers who together formulate policy in the government of a country; in UK, a meeting of this group of ministers; in USA, the president's advisory council, consisting of heads of government departments; the bed or nest of a beast or bird (*Shakesp*). [Dimin of **cabin**; cf Fr *cabinet*]
  ■ **cab'inetry** *n* cabinets collectively; cabinetwork.
  ❑ **Cabinet Council** *n* an earlier name for the Cabinet. **cab'inet-edition** *n* one less in size and price than a library edition, but elegant enough in format to be suitable for display. **cab'inetmaker** *n* a craftsman skilled in making cabinets and other fine furniture. **cab'inetmaking** *n* the occupation or art of the cabinetmaker; the getting together of a new set of cabinet ministers. **cabinet minister** *n* a member of a cabinet. **cabinet photograph** *n* one of about 15 by 10cm (6 by 4 inches) in size. **cabinet picture** *n* a small detailed easel painting intended for close viewing. **cabinet pudding** *n* a steamed pudding containing dried fruit. **cab'inetwork** *n* (an example of) the fine craftsmanship of a cabinetmaker.

Cabiri /ka-bī'rī/ (or kä-bē'rē/ *n pl* a group of ancient deities, protectors of seafarers, whose cult spread from Lemnos, Samothrace and Imbros (also **Cabei'ri**). [Latinized from Gr *Kabeiroi*]
  ■ **Cabir'ian** or **Cabir'ic** *adj*.

cable /kā'bl/ *n* a strong rope or chain for hauling or tying anything, *esp* a ship's anchor; a cable-laid rope; a cable-length; a cable-stitch, or the pattern formed by a series of these; a line of submarine telegraph wires embedded in gutta-percha and encased in coiled strands of iron wire; a bundle of insulated wires encased in a sheath for transmitting electricity or electrical signals and *usu* laid underground; a cabled message or cablegram; cable television. ◆ *vt* and *vi* to provide with or fasten with a cable; to tie up; to telegraph or send by cable; to provide with cable television. [OFr, from LL *capulum* a halter, from L *capēre* to hold]
  ■ **ca'blecast** *n* a broadcast on cable television. **ca'blegram** *n* a telegram sent by cable. **cablet** /kā'blət/ *n* a cable or cable-laid rope with a circumference of less than 25cm (10 inches). **cā'bling** *n* a bead or moulding like a thick rope.
  ❑ **ca'ble-car** *n* a car suspended from a moving overhead cable, used as a method of transport up mountains, across valleys, etc; a car on a cable railway. **ca'ble-drilling** *n* rope-drilling with the drill attached to a steel cable. **ca'ble-laid** *adj* (of a rope) composed of three strands or ropes with a right-handed twist, twisted together in a left-handed direction. **ca'ble-length** or **ca'ble's-length** *n* a tenth of a nautical mile, *approx* 183 metres (200 yards) or 100 fathoms (in USA, *approx* 219 metres (720 feet) or 120 fathoms). **ca'ble-moulding** *n* a bead or moulding carved in imitation of a thick rope. **cable railway** see **cable tramway** below. **cable release** *n* (*image technol*) a device, a length of stiff wire cable in a flexible tube, for releasing a camera shutter. **cable-stayed bridge** *n* a type of suspension bridge in which the supporting cables are connected directly to the bridge deck from one or more towers. **ca'ble-stitch** *n* (a series of stitches producing) a pattern or design resembling a twisted rope. **cable television** *n* the transmission of television programmes by cable to individual subscribers. **cable tramway** or **cable railway** *n* one along which cars or carriages are drawn by a cable operated by a stationary motor. **ca'blevision** *n* cable television. **cā'bleway** *n* a structure for transport of material in cars suspended from a cable.

cabob same as **kebab**.

caboc /ka'bək/ *n* a double cream cheese rolled in oatmeal. [Ety as for **kebbock**]

caboceer /ka-bō-sēr'/ *n* a W African headman. [Port *cabeceira*, from *cabo*, from L *caput* head]

caboched or **caboshed** /kə-bosht'/ (*heraldry*) *adj* in full face with no neck showing. [Fr *caboché*, from L *caput* head]

cabochon /ka-bō-shɔ̄'/ *n* a precious stone polished but uncut, or cut **en** /ä/ **cabochon**, ie rounded on top and flat on the back, without facets (also *adj*). [Fr *caboche*, from L *caput* head]

caboodle /kə-boo'dl/ (*inf*) *n* a crowd or collection. [Origin unknown]
  ■ **the whole** (**kit and**) **caboodle** everything in a collection, group, etc.

caboose /kə-boos'/ *n* a ship's kitchen; a cooking stove on a ship's deck; a car, *usu* at the rear of a goods or construction train for the train crew or workmen (*N Am*); someone bringing up the rear (*US*); a mobile hut equipped with a stove (*N Am*). [Du *kabuis*; cf Ger *Kabuse*]

caboshed see **caboched**.

cabotage /kab'o-tij/ *n* the right of control, exercised by a particular country, over traffic within its own territory, *esp* over air traffic; coastal navigation and trading (*naut*). [Fr]

cabré /kä'brā/ *adj* rearing (*heraldry*); (of an aeroplane) flying upturned with tail down. [Fr *cabrer* to caper]

cabretta /kə-bret'ə/ *n* a soft leather made from the skins of a hairy S American sheep. [From Sp *cabra* a nanny goat]

cabrie /kab'rē/ *n* a pronghorn (also **cab'rit**). [Sp *cabrito* kid]

cabriole /kab'ri-ōl/ *n* a leap with one leg outstretched and the other struck against it (*ballet*); a curved furniture leg, often ending in an ornamental foot like an animal's paw (also **cabriole leg**). [Fr, from L *capra* a goat]
  ■ **cab'riolet** /-lā/ *n* a type of motor car with a folding top (short form **cab'rio**); a light horse-drawn carriage with two wheels and a folding hood; a small 18c armchair of curved design.

caca /kak'ə/ (*US sl*) *n* excrement; heroin. [Sp]

ca' canny see under **ca'**.

cacao /kə-kä'ō or kə-kā'ō/ *n* the tropical American tree *Theobroma cacao* or its edible seeds from which cocoa and chocolate are made. [Mex, from Nahuatl *cacahuatl* cacao tree]
  ❑ **cacao beans** same as **cocoa beans** (see under **cocoa**). **cacao butter** same as **cocoa butter** (see under **cocoa**).

cacciatore /kach-ə-tö'ri/ or **cacciatora** /-tö'rə/ (*cookery*) *adj* of meat, *esp* chicken or veal, cooked with tomatoes, mushrooms, onions and herbs. [Ital, hunter]

cachaça /kə-chas'ə/ *n* a white Brazilian rum made from sugarcane. [Port]

cachaemia /ka-kē'mi-ə/ (*archaic*) *n* an abnormal and chronic condition of the blood. [Gr *kakos* bad, and *haima* blood]
  ■ **cachae'mic** *adj*.

cachalot /kash'ə-lot or -lō/ *n* the sperm whale. [Fr]

CACHE *abbrev* : Council for Awards in Children's Care and Education.

cache /kash/ n a hiding-place for treasure, provisions, ammunition, etc; a collection of stores hidden away; a hoard. ◆ vt to hide; to store in a cache memory (comput). [Fr cacher to hide]
❑ **cache controller** n (comput) a hardware device which controls the transfer of data to and from the cache memory. **cache memory** n (comput) an extremely fast part of the main store. **cachepot** /kash'pō or -pot/ n an ornamental container used to hold and conceal a flowerpot. **cache-sexe** /kash-seks'/ n a piece of fabric, etc covering only the genitals.

cachet /kash'ā/ n a private seal, esp affixed to a letter or document; any distinctive stamp or distinguishing characteristic (fig), esp something showing or conferring prestige; a thin wafer-like case enclosing an unpleasant-tasting medicine; a design or mark stamped on mail to commemorate an event, or for advertising purposes. [MFr, from cacher to press]

cachexy /ka-kek'si/ or **cachexia** /ka-kek'si-ə/ (med) n a condition of profound physical weakness and wasting of the body associated with severe starvation or chronic disease, eg tuberculosis or cancer. [L, from Gr kachexiā, from kakos bad, and hexis condition, from the root of echein to have]
■ **cachec'tic** or **cachec'tical** adj.

cachinnate /kak'i-nāt/ (formal; esp literary) vi to laugh loudly. [L cachinnāre]
■ **cachinna'tion** n. **cachinn'atory** (or /kak'/) adj.

cacholong /kach'o-long/ n a variety of quartz or of opal, generally of a milky colour. [Fr, from Kalmuck]

cacholot same as **cachalot**.

cachou /ka-shoo'/ n a pill or lozenge, used to sweeten the breath; a variant of **catechu**. [Fr]

cachucha /ka-choo'chə/ n a lively Spanish solo dance in 3–4 time, with a rhythm like the bolero; music for this dance. [Sp]

cacique /ka-sēk'/ n (also **cazique'**) a West Indian or Native American chief; in Spain or Latin America, a local political boss; any of various tropical American blackbirds of the genus Cacicus, with conical bills. [Haitian]
■ **caciqu'ism** n esp in West Indies and Latin America, government by a cacique.

cack or **kack** /kak/ n faeces (vulgar sl); rubbish, nonsense (sl). [Dialect]
❑ **cack'-hand'ed** or **kack'-hand'ed** adj (inf) left-handed; clumsy. **cack'-hand'edly** adv. **cack'-hand'edness** n.

cackle /kak'l/ n a loud, squawking or clucking sound made by a hen or goose; noisy or raucous talk or laughter. ◆ vi to make such a sound; to chatter or laugh noisily or raucously. ◆ vt to utter in a cackling manner. [ME cakelen; cognate with MDu kākelen]
■ **cack'ler** n.
■ **cut the cackle** (inf) to stop the aimless chattering (and come to the point).

CACM abbrev : Central American Common Market.

caco- /ka-kō- or sometimes ka-ko-/ combining form denoting bad or incorrect. [Gr kakos bad]

cacodemon or **cacodaemon** /kak-ō-dē'mən/ n an evil spirit or devil; a nightmare (Shakesp). [Gr kakos bad, and daimōn spirit]

cacodoxy /kak'ō-dok-si/ n a bad doctrine or wrong opinion. [Gr kakos bad, and doxa an opinion]

cacodyl /kak'ō-dil/ n a colourless, poisonous, foul-smelling liquid, composed of arsenic, carbon and hydrogen. [Gr kakōdēs stinking, and hȳlē matter]
■ **cacodyl'ic** adj.

cacoepy /ka-kō'ə-pi/ n bad or wrong pronunciation. [Gr kakos bad, and epos word]

cacoethes /ka-kō-ē'thēz/ n a bad habit or itch; an uncontrollable urge or desire; an itch or intense longing. [Gr kakoēthēs, -es ill-disposed, from kakos bad, and ēthos habit]
❑ **cacoethes loquendi** /kak-ō-ē'thēz or ka-kō-āth'ās lō-kwen'dī or lo-kwen'dē/ n (L) a mania for talking, esp for giving speeches, literally an itch for speaking. **cacoethes scribendi** /skrī-ben'dī or skrē-ben'dē/ n a mania for writing or getting things into print, literally an itch for writing.

cacogastric /ka-kō-gas'trik/ adj of or relating to an upset stomach; dyspeptic. [Gr kakos bad, and gastēr the belly]

cacogenics /ka-kō-jen'iks/ n sing dysgenics. [Gr kakos bad, and genos race]

cacography /ka-kog'rə-fi/ n bad handwriting or spelling. [Gr kakos bad, and graphē writing]
■ **cacog'rapher** n. **cacographic** /-ō-graf'ik/ or **cacograph'ical** adj.

cacolet /kak'ō-lā/ n a double pannier; a military mule litter. [Fr, prob from Basque]

cacology /ka-kol'ə-ji/ n a bad choice of words or faulty pronunciation. [Gr kakos bad, and logos speech]

cacomistle or **cacomixl** /ka'kə-mi-səl/ or **cacomixl** /-mik-səl/ n a small carnivorous mammal (genus Bassariscus) related to the raccoon and found in SW USA and Central America (also **ringtail** or **ringtailed cat**). [Mex Sp, from Nahuatl tlaco half, and miztli cougar]

cacoon /ka-koon'/ n the large seed of a leguminous tropical climber (Entada scandens), used for making scent-bottles, snuff-boxes, etc; the purgative and emetic seed of a tropical American climber (Fevillea cordifolia). [Origin uncertain]

cacophony /ka-kof'ə-ni/ n a harsh or disagreeable sound; a discordant mixture of sounds; dissonance. [Gr kakos bad, and phōnē sound]
■ **cacoph'onous**, **cacophonic** /-ō-fon'ik/, **cacophon'ical** or **cacophonious** /-fō'ni-əs/ adj harsh-sounding.

cacotopia /kak-ō-tō'pi-ə/ n a state, imaginary or otherwise, in which everything is as bad as it can possibly be, opp to utopia. [Gr kakos bad, and topos a place]
■ **cacotō'pian** adj.

cacotrophy /ka-kot'rə-fi/ n bad or inadequate diet. [Gr kakos bad, and trophē nourishment]

cactus /kak'təs/ n (pl **cac'tī** or **cac'tuses**) a general name for any plant of the family **Cactā'ceae** (now divided into several genera) of desert regions of America, having thick fleshy stems that store water, and leaves reduced to spines or scales; (also **cactus dahlia**) a variety of double-flowered dahlia with quill-like petals. [L, from Gr kaktos cardoon, a prickly plant of S Europe]
■ **cactā'ceous** adj. **cac'tiform** adj.

cacumen /ka-kū'men/ n a top or point. [L cacūmen, -inis top, point, tip]
■ **cacu'minal** adj produced by turning the tip of the tongue up and back towards the hard palate (phonetics); retroflex (phonetics). **cacu'minous** adj with pointed or pyramidal top.

CAD or **Cad** (often /kad/) abbrev : computer-aided design (or draughting); compact audio disc.

cad /kad/ n an inferior assistant (obs); a person who runs errands (obs); a man who lacks the instincts of a gentleman or who behaves dishonourably (old or facetious). [Shortened from **cadet**; see also ety at **caddie**]
■ **cadd'ish** adj. **cadd'ishly** adv. **cadd'ishness** n.

cadastral /ka-das'trəl/ adj of, or as recorded in, a **cadastre** /ka-das'tər/, the official public register of the ownership, boundaries and value of landed property of a country for taxation purposes; applied also to a survey on a large scale. [Fr, from Ital catastro, from late Gr katastichon a register]

cadaver /kə-dav'ər or -dä'ver/ (surg and anat) n a human corpse, esp one used for organ transplant or dissection. [L cadāver a dead body, from cadere to fall (dead)]
■ **cadav'eric** adj. **cadav'erous** /-rəs/ adj corpse-like; sickly-looking; gaunt or haggard. **cadav'erousness** n.

Cadbury code /kad'bə-ri kōd/ n a set of principles regarding the composition and behaviour of boards of directors in the UK. [Sir Adrian Cadbury (born 1929), British businessman]

CADCAM /kad'kam/ abbrev : computer-aided design and (computer-aided) manufacture.

caddice see **caddis²**.

caddie or **caddy** /kad'i/ n someone who assists a golfer during a round, esp by carrying the clubs; an 18c messenger or errand porter in some large Scottish towns (also **cad'ie** or **cad'ee**). ◆ vi to act as a caddie; to carry clubs. [Ety as for **cadet**, through Scot use]
❑ **caddie car** or **cart** n a small motorized vehicle for transporting players and equipment around a golf course; a light, two-wheeled trolley for carrying a bag of golf clubs.

caddis¹ /kad'is/ n the larva of the caddis fly, which lives in water in a **cadd'is-case**, a silken sheath covered with fragments of wood, stone, shell, leaves, etc, open at both ends (also **cadd'is-worm**). [Origin obscure]
❑ **caddis fly** n any small mothlike insect of the order Trichoptera that lives near, and lays its eggs in, water.

caddis² or **caddice** /kad'is/ n worsted ribbon or braid (also (Shakesp) **cadd'yss**). [OFr cadaz, cadas tow]

Caddoan /kad'ō-ən/ n a family of Native American languages including Caddo, Pawnee and Arikara, formerly spoken in the Midwest.

caddy¹ /kad'i/ n a small box for holding tea; any storage container (N Am). [Malay kati, the weight of a small packet of tea]

caddy² see **caddie**.

caddyss see **caddis²**.

cade¹ /kād/ n a barrel or cask. [Fr, from L *cadus* a cask]

cade² /kād/ n a lamb or colt left by its mother and brought up by hand, a pet lamb (also adj). [Ety unknown]

cade³ /kād/ n a bushy Mediterranean juniper (*Juniper oxycedrus*) that yields **oil of cade**, used in the treatment of skin disorders. [Med L *catanus*]

-cade /-kād/ combining form denoting a procession or show, as in *motorcade*. [See **cavalcade**]

cadeau /ka-dō'/ (Fr) n (pl **cadeaux** /-ō/) a gift or present.

cadee see **caddie**.

cadelle /kə-del'/ n a small black beetle (*Tenebroides mauritanicus*) found worldwide, that lives on stored food, eg grain. [Fr, from Provençal *cadello*, from L *catellus* little dog]

cadence /kā'dəns/ n the fall in pitch of the voice, as at the end of a sentence; rise and fall of sound, modulation or intonation; rhythm; a succession of chords closing a musical phrase or at the end of a complete melody (*music*; see **imperfect**, **perfect**, **plagal**); falling, sinking (*Milton*). [Fr, from L *cadere* to fall]
■ **ca'denced** adj rhythmical. **ca'dency** n rhythm; the relative status of the branch of a family descended from a younger son (*heraldry*). **ca'dent** adj (*Shakesp*) falling. **cadential** /kə-den'shəl/ adj.

cadential see under **cadence** and **cadenza**.

cadenza /kä-dent'sa or kə-den'zə/ (*music*) n an outstanding virtuoso passage or flourish, sometimes improvised, given by a solo instrument or voice towards the end, or at some important stage, of a movement, concerto or aria. [Ital *cadenza*, from L *cadere* to fall]
■ **cadential** /kə-den'shəl/ adj.

cadet /kə- or ka-det'/ n a person undergoing training for the armed forces or the police; a pupil training in a cadet corps; in New Zealand, an apprentice or trainee gaining experience in sheep-farming; a younger son or a member of a **cadet branch** of a family, descended from a younger son. [Historically, a younger son or brother sent away to be trained for a commission in the army, from Fr *cadet*, from Gascon dialect *capdet*, from dimin of L *caput* the head]
■ **cadet'ship** n.
❑ **cadet corps** n an organized body undergoing basic military training, *esp* schoolboys.

cadge¹ /kaj/ vt and vi to scrounge (money, etc); to beg or go about begging. [Prob connected with **catch**]
■ **cadg'er** n a scrounger; *orig* a dealer who travelled around remote country areas, buying and selling farm produce; a hawker or pedlar.
■ **on the cadge** engaged in scrounging.

cadge² /kaj/ (*falconry*) n a padded wooden frame on which a number of hawks may be carried. [Prob **cage**; perh **cadge¹**]

cadgy /kaj'i/ (*NE Scot dialect*) adj (also **kidg'ie**) cheerful, friendly and hospitable; wanton. [Cf Dan *kaad* wanton, from ON *kātr* merry]

cadi or **kadi** /kä'di or kā'di/ n an Islamic judge. [Ar *qādī* a judge]

cadie see **caddie**.

CADMAT /kad'mat/ abbrev : computer-aided design, manufacture and test(ing).

Cadmean /kad-mē'ən/ adj relating to *Cadmus*, who, according to legend, introduced the **Cadmean letters**, sixteen simple letters that formed the original Greek alphabet.
❑ **Cadmean victory** n one very costly to both sides (from the story that Cadmus sowed a dragon's teeth from which sprang an army of soldiers who fought amongst themselves until only five were left).

cadmium /kad'mi-əm/ n a bluish-white metallic element (symbol **Cd**; atomic no 48) occurring in zinc ores, used in alloys, magnets, metal-plating and as a control in nuclear reactors. [Gr *kadmiā*, *kadmeiā* (gē) Cadmean (earth), calamine]
❑ **cadmium cell** n a photocell with a cadmium electrode. **cadmium yellow** n a vivid orange or yellow pigment of cadmium sulphide used in paints, etc.

cadrans /kad'rənz/ n an instrument by which a gem is adjusted while being cut. [Fr dialect *cadran* a quadrant]

cadre /käd'ər or kād'ər, also -rə, (Fr) kad'r'/ n a basic structure, *esp* the nucleus of a military unit, the commissioned and non-commissioned officers, etc, around whom the rank and file may be quickly grouped; any nucleus of key personnel; (*prob* from Fr through Russ) a group of activists in a revolutionary, *orig* Communist, party; a member of such a group. [Fr, from L *quadrum* square]

caduac /kad'ū-ak/ (*obs*) n a casualty or windfall. [Scot, from L *cadūcum*]

caduceus /ka-dū'si-əs/ (*classical myth*) n (pl **cadū'ceī**) the rod of Hermes (Mercury), messenger of the gods, generally represented as a wand surmounted with two wings and entwined by two serpents; a symbol resembling this rod, used as an emblem by the medical profession. [L, from Gr *kārȳkeion* a herald's wand, from *kēryx*, *-ykos* a herald]
■ **cadū'cean** adj.

caducibranchiate /ka-dū-si-brang'ki-āt/ (*biol*) adj (of amphibians) losing the gills on attaining maturity. [L *cadūcus* caducous, and *branchiae* gills]

caducous /ka-dū'kəs/ (*biol*) adj (of parts of a plant or animal) shed or falling at an early stage; easily detached. [L *cadūcus*, from *cadere* to fall]
■ **caducity** /ka-dū'si-ti/ n the quality of being perishable or transitory; senility.

CAE abbrev : (formerly in Australia) College of Advanced Education; computer-aided engineering (also **Cae**).

caecilian /sē-sil'i-ən/ n any wormlike, burrowing amphibian of the order Apoda (or Gymnophiona), having sightless eyes, and living in moist earth in tropical regions. [L *caecus* blind]

caecum or (*N Am*) **cecum** /sē'kəm/ (*biol*; *anat*) n (pl **cae'ca** or **cē'ca**) (in plants and animals) any blind diverticulum or pouch, *esp* one arising from the alimentary canal. [L, neuter of *caecus* blind]
■ **cae'cal** or **cē'cal** adj. **caecitis** or (*N Am*) **cecitis** /sē-sī'tis/ n inflammation of the caecum.

caeno- /sē-nō-/ or **caino-** /kī-nō-/ combining form denoting recent. [Gr *kainos* new]
■ **caenogen'esis** n (*zool*) the state where adaptations to the needs of the young stages develop early, and disappear in the adult stage.

Caenozoic /sē-nō-zō'ik/ same as **Cenozoic**.

caen-stone /kā'ən-stōn/ n a cream-coloured limestone from Caen /kä/ in France.

Caerns. abbrev : Caernarvonshire (formerly a county in Wales).

Caerphilly /kār-fil'i/ n a mild white cheese, *orig* made in *Caerphilly*, a town in S Wales.

caerule, caerulean see **cerulean**.

caesalpiniaceous /ses-al- or sē-zal-pi-ni-ā'shəs/ adj of, or belonging to, the **Caesalpiniā'ceae**, a family of tropical leguminous plants, including brazil-wood, cassia and dividivi. [Named after Andrea *Cesalpino* (1519–1603), Italian botanist]

Caesar /sē'zər/ n an absolute monarch, an autocrat, from the Roman dictator Gaius Julius *Caesar* (100–44BC); (also without *cap*) a Caesarean section (*inf*). [Perh from L *caedere* to cut, from the tradition that the first bearer of the cognomen *Caesar* was delivered in this way]
■ **Caesarean** or **Caesarian** /-ā'ri-ən/ adj relating to Julius Caesar or the Caesars; relating to (a) birth carried out by Caesarean section. ♦ n a Caesarean section; an adherent of Caesar, an imperialist. **Cae'sarism** n. **Cae'sarist** n. **Cae'sarship** n.
❑ **Caesarean section** or **operation** n delivery of a child by cutting through the walls of the abdomen. **caesaropapism** /sē-zə-rō-pā'pizm/ n (also with *cap*; LL *pāpa* pope) control of the church by a secular ruler or by the state. **Caesar salad** n a salad of lettuce, Parmesan cheese and croutons, served with a dressing of oil, lemon juice and garlic, and sometimes raw or half-cooked egg (reported to have been created in 1924 by *Caesar* Cardini, an Italian chef).

caese a variant reading for **sessa**.

caesious /sē'zi-əs/ adj bluish or greyish green. [L *caesius* bluish grey]

caesium or (*N Am*) **cesium** /sē'zi-əm/ n a silver-white soft alkaline metallic element (symbol **Cs**; atomic no 55) used in the form of compounds or alloys in photoelectric cells, etc. [Ety as for **caesious**]
❑ **caesium clock** n an atomic clock regulated by the natural resonance frequency of excited caesium atoms.

caespitose or (*N Am*) **cespitose** /sĕs'pi-tōs/ (*bot*) adj tufted, growing in tufts; turf-like. [L *caespes*, *-itis* turf]

caestus variant of **cestus²**, or, less often, **cestus¹**.

caesura or (*N Am*) **cesura** /si-zū'rə/ (*prosody*) n (pl **caesu'ras** or **caesu'rae** /-ī/) division of a metrical foot between two words; a pause or natural breathing space occurring anywhere in a line of verse (*usu* near the middle). [L *caesūra*, from *caedere*, *caesum* to cut off]
■ **caesū'ral** or (*N Am*) **cesū'ral** adj.

CAF (*US*) abbrev : cost and freight.

cafard /ka-fär'/ n depression, the blues. [Fr, literally, a cockroach, hypocrite]

café or **cafe** /kaf'ā, ka'fi or ka-fā'/ n a coffee house or a small, inexpensive restaurant; a bar-room (*N Am*). [Fr *café* coffee house]

■ words derived from main entry word; ❑ compound words; ■ idioms and phrasal verbs

❏ **café au lait** /ō lā/ *n* coffee made with milk; the light brown colour of this. **café bar** *n* a café serving coffee and alcohol. **café-chantant** /-shā-tā/ or **café-concert** /-kɔ̄-ser/ *n* a café providing musical entertainment. **café curtain** *n* a short straight curtain, *esp* for covering the lower part of a window. **café filtre** /fil-tr/ *n* strong black filtered coffee. **café noir** /nwär/ *n* black coffee (ie without milk). **café society** *n* fashionable society.

cafeteria /ka-fə-tē'ri-ə/ *n* a restaurant where customers serve themselves, or are served from, and *usu* pay at, a counter before sitting down to eat. [Cuban Sp, a tent in which coffee is sold]

cafetière /ka-fi-tyär'/ *n* a type of coffee-maker with a plunger to force the grounds to the bottom before pouring. [Fr]

caff /kaf/ *n* slang term for **café** or **cafeteria**.

caffeine or **caffein** /kaf'ēn/ *n* an alkaloid that occurs naturally in coffee, tea, cocoa, and cola nuts, acting as a mild stimulant to the nervous system. [Fr *caféine*; see **coffee**]
■ **caff'einated** *adj* containing caffeine (cf **decaffeinated** under **decaffeinate**). **caff'einism** or **caffeism** /kaf-ē'izm/ *n* an unhealthy condition caused by taking excessive amounts of caffeine; an addiction to caffeine.

caffè latte same as **latte**.

Caffre see **Kaffir** and **Kafir**.

cafila, **caffila** or **kafila** /kaf'i-lə or kä'fi-lə/ *n* a caravan, caravan train. [Ar *qāfilah*]

CAFOD /kä'fod or kaf'od/ *abbrev*: Catholic Agency for Overseas Development (formerly known as the Catholic Fund for Overseas Development).

caftan or **kaftan** /kaf'tən or kaf-tan'/ *n* a long-sleeved garment, reaching to the ankles and often tied with a sash, worn in Middle-Eastern countries; any loose shirt or dress with wide sleeves made in imitation of this. [Turk *qaftān*]

cage /kāj/ *n* a compartment or enclosure, *usu* made from bars and wires, for confining captive animals and birds; a prison; a frame with a platform or platforms used in hoisting in a vertical shaft, eg in a mine or lift; a framework that encloses, protects or supports; any structure resembling a cage in function; a structure of steel supports and netting to protect garden fruit and vegetables from birds; a squirrel's nest (*dialect*); a goal, consisting of a frame with a net attached, as in ice hockey; an enclosed area used for batting practice (*baseball*). ◆ *vt* (**cag'ing**; **caged**) to imprison in a cage. [Fr, from L *cavea* a hollow place]
■ **caged** *adj* confined. **cage'ling** *n* a bird that is or has been kept in a cage.
❏ **cage'-bird** *n* a bird of a kind habitually kept in a cage. **cage'-cup** *n* a kind of glass bowl of late Roman times, with a filigree-type glass decoration attached to the bowl by tiny struts (also **diatrē'tum**). **cage fighter** *n*. **cage fighting** *n* a form of ultimate fighting (qv under **ultimate**) in which the opponents fight inside a wire enclosure. **cage'work** *n* open-work like the bars of a cage.
■ **cage in** (*usu fig*) to imprison. **rattle someone's** (or **the**) **cage** (*inf*) to stir (someone) up, provoke (someone's) anger or irritation.

cagey or **cagy** /kā'ji/ (*inf*) *adj* not frank, secretive; artfully shy, wary, chary. [Origin unknown]
■ **cag'ily** *adv*. **cag'iness**, **cag'yness** or **cag'eyness** *n*.

cagot /kä'gō/ *n* (*hist*) a member of an outcast people living in the W Pyrenees, supposed to be the descendants of lepers. [Fr; origin unknown]

cagoul, **cagoule**, **kagool**, **kagoul** or **kagoule** /kə-gool'/ *n* a lightweight, hooded waterproof anorak, often knee-length. [Fr *cagoule* a monk's hood]

cagy see **cagey**.

cahier /ka-yā'/ (*Fr*) *n* a notebook; a report, *esp* of the proceedings of a meeting; in bookbinding, a section ready for binding.

cahoot /kə-hoot'/ *n* (*N Am*; *obs*) a company or partnership. [Ety uncertain]
■ **go cahoots** to go shares. **in cahoots** (*sl*) in collusion (with).

cahow /kə-how'/ *n* a rare Atlantic seabird, once thought to be extinct (also **Bermuda petrel**). [Imit of its call]

CAI *abbrev*: computer-aided (or -assisted) instruction.

caille /ka'y'/ (*Fr cookery*) *n* quail.

cailleach /kal'yəhh/ (*Scot*) *n* an old woman (also **caill'ach** or **caill'iach**). [Gaelic *cailleach*]

caimac /kī'mäk/ or **caimacam** same as **kaimakam**.

caiman see **cayman**.

Cain /kān/ *n* in the Bible, Adam's son, murderer of Abel (Genesis 4), hence (allusively) a murderer.
■ **Cain'ite** *n* a descendant of Cain; a member of a 2c sect of Gnostics who revered Cain and Judas.

❏ **Cain'-coloured** *adj* (*Shakesp*) of the traditional colour of Cain's beard and hair, red.
■ **raise Cain** to make a determined or angry fuss.

cain or **kain** /kān/ (*hist*) *n* in Scotland and Ireland, rent paid in kind, *esp* in produce from a tenanted farm; tribute. [Sc and Ir Gaelic *càin* rent, tax]
❏ **cain'-hen** *n* a hen given up as cain.
■ **pay** (**the**) **cain** to pay the penalty.

ca'ing whale see under **ca'**.

cainogenesis see **caenogenesis** under **caeno-**.

Cainozoic /kī-nō-zō'ik/ same as **Cenozoic**.

caipirinha /kī-pi-rē'nyə/ *n* a Brazilian cocktail made with cachaça, crushed lime and sugar. [Port, literally, little peasant girl]
■ **caipiroska** /-ros'kə/ *n* (pseudo-Russ) a variation on caipirinha made with vodka instead of cachaça.

caique or **caïque** /kä-ēk'/ *n* a light narrow boat as used on the Bosporus; the skiff of a galley. [Fr, from Turk *kaik* a boat]

caird /kärd/ (*Scot*) *n* an itinerant tramping tinker, a gypsy, a vagrant. [Sc and Ir Gaelic *ceard*]

Cairene /kī'rēn or kī-rēn'/ *adj* relating to Cairo. ◆ *n* a native or citizen of Cairo.

cairn /kärn/ *n* a heap of stones, *esp* one raised over a grave, or as a landmark on a mountain-top or path; a small variety of Scottish terrier (in full **cairn terrier**) *orig* bred for driving foxes from their earths among cairns. [Gaelic *càrn*]
■ **cairned** *adj* marked with cairns. **cairngorm'** or **cairngorm'-stone** *n* a semi-precious stone, a brown or yellow quartz found in the Cairngorm Mountains in Scotland.

caisson /kā'sən or kə-soon'/ *n* a tumbril or ammunition wagon; a strong case for keeping out the water while the foundations of a bridge are being built; an apparatus for lifting a vessel out of the water for repairs or inspection; the pontoon or floating gate used to close a dry-dock. [Fr, from *caisse* a case or chest. See **case¹**]
❏ **caisson disease** see **decompression sickness** under **decompress**.

caitiff /kā'tif/ *n* a mean despicable fellow. ◆ *adj* mean, base. [OFr *caitif* (Fr *chétif*), from L *captīvus* a captive, from *capere* to take]
■ **cai'tive** *n* (*Spenser*) captive, subject.

cajeput see **cajuput**.

cajole /kə-jōl'/ *vt* to coax (into); to cheat by flattery (into or out of). [Fr *cajoler* to chatter; ety doubtful]
■ **cajole'ment** *n* coaxing in order to delude; wheedling, flattery. **cajol'er** *n*. **cajol'ery** *n*.

Cajun /kā'jən/ *n* a descendant of the French-speaking Acadians deported from Canada to Louisiana in 1755; the language of the Cajuns. ◆ *adj* (sometimes without *cap*) of or relating to Cajun or the Cajuns; belonging to or characteristic of Cajun traditions (*esp* in reference to their lively syncopated music or spicy cookery). [Corruption of **Acadian**]

cajuput /kaj'ə-put/ *n* a pungent, volatile aromatic oil, distilled from leaves of an Indo-Malayan and Australian myrtaceous tree (*Melaleuca leucodendron*) used in the treatment of skin disorders (also **caj'eput**). [Malay]

cake /kāk/ *n* a breadlike composition enriched with additions such as sugar, eggs, spices, currants, peel, etc; a separately made mass of such composition; a piece of dough that is baked; a small loaf of fine bread; any flattened mass baked, as *oatcake*, or formed by pressure or drying, as of soap, clay, snow, blood; cattle cake; a madcap or fool (*archaic sl*). ◆ *vt* and *vi* to form into a cake or hard mass. [ON *kaka*]
■ **cāk'ing** *n* and *adj*. **cāk'y** or **cak'ey** *adj*.
❏ **cake hole** *n* (*sl*) mouth. **cake'walk** *n* a dance developed from a prancing movement once performed by black Americans in competition for a cake; something accomplished with supreme ease. ◆ *vi* to perform a cakewalk or execute similar movements; to accomplish with supreme ease. **caking coal** *n* a bituminous coal that fuses into a mass in burning.
■ **a piece of cake** (*inf*) something very easy to do. **cakes and ale** vaguely, all the good things of life. **go** or **sell like hot cakes** see under **hot¹**. **have one's cake and eat it** or **eat one's cake and have it** to have the advantage of both alternatives. **his cake is dough** his hope has failed. **take the cake** (*sl*) to carry off the honours; to be the ultimate in idiocy or intolerable behaviour (*ironic*); to top it all.

CAL (often /kal/) *abbrev*: computer-aided (or -assisted) learning.

Cal. *abbrev*: California (US state); (great or large) calorie, kilocalorie.

cal. *abbrev*: calendar; calibre; (small or gram-)calorie.

Calabar-bean /ka-lə-bär'bēn or kal'ə-/ n the dark-brown extremely poisonous seed of the tropical African climbing plant (*Physostigma venenosum*), a source of physostigmine.

calabash /kal'ə-bash/ n a gourd, or its shell used as a vessel, tobacco pipe, etc; the fruit of the calabash tree or its shell similarly used. [Fr *calebasse*, from Sp *calabaza*, from Pers *kharbuz* melon]
   □ **calabash nutmeg** n the fruit of a tropical anonaceous tree (*Monodora myristica*) whose seeds are used as nutmegs. **calabash tree** n a tropical American tree (*Crescentia cujete*) with large melonlike fruit.

calaboose /kal'ə-boos or ka-lə-boos'/ (*US sl*) n a prison. [Sp *calabozo*]

calabrese /ka-lə-brā'zā or -brē'zi/ n a variety of green sprouting broccoli. [Ital, Calabrian]

caladium /ka-lā'di-əm/ n (pl **cala'diums**) any tropical plant of the genus *Caladium*, of the family Araceae, the plants of which are grown for their attractive foliage. [Latinized from Malay *kelady*, a related plant]

calaloo or **callaloo** /kal-ə-loo'/ n the amaranth; a thick West Indian soup containing the leaves of this plant. [Prob from an African language]

calamanco /ka-lə-mang'kō/ n (pl **calamanc'os** or **calamanc'oes**) a satin-twilled woollen fabric, with a chequered or brocaded design woven into the warp; a garment made of this. [Du *kalamink*, Ger *Kalmank*, Fr *calmande*; origin unknown]

calamander /kal-ə-man'dər/ n a hard valuable wood of the ebony genus, brownish with black stripes, used in making furniture and imported from India and Sri Lanka. [Prob Sinhalese]

calamari /ka-lə-mä'rē/ (*Mediterranean cookery*) n pl squid. [Ital, pl of *calamaro*, squid; see ety for **calamary**]

calamary /kal'ə-mə-ri/ n any of various species of squid. [L *calamārius*, from *calamus*, from Gr *kalamos* pen, from the shape of their internal shell]

calamine /kal'ə-mīn, -min/ n zinc carbonate (smithsonite); in USA, a major ore of zinc (hemimorphite). [Fr, from LL *calamīna*, prob from L *cadmia*; see **cadmium**]
   □ **calamine lotion**, **ointment** or **powder** n a soothing lotion, ointment or powder for the skin, containing zinc carbonate mixed with ferric oxide.

calamint /kal'ə-mint/ n a genus (*Calamintha*) of labiate aromatic plants allied to mint and thyme. [Fr, from Gr *kalaminthē*]

calamite /kal'ə-mīt/ n a general name for an extinct family of treelike plants from Carboniferous times, thought to be related to horsetails. [L *calamus* a reed]

calamity /kə-lam'i-ti/ n a great misfortune; a disaster, *esp* a sudden one; affliction. [Fr *calamité*, from L *calamitās*, *-ātis*]
   ■ **calam'itous** *adj* disastrous, tragic or dreadful. **calam'itously** *adv*. **calam'itousness** n.

calamondin /ka-lə-mon'din/ n a small citrus tree (*Citrus mitis*), native to the Philippines; its acid-tasting orange-like fruit. [Tagálog *kalamunding*]

calamus /kal'ə-məs/ n (pl **cal'amī**) (with *cap*) a genus of palms whose stems make canes or rattans; the hollow shaft at the base of a bird's feather, a quill (*zool*); the reed pen used in ancient times; the traditional name of the sweet flag or its aromatic root. [L, from Gr *kalamos* reed, cane, pen]

calando /kä-län'dō/ (*music*) *adj* and *adv* gradually slowing with diminishing volume. [Ital, lowering, letting down]

calandria /ka-lan'dri-ə/ n a sealed vessel through which tubes pass, used in the core of certain types of nuclear reactor as a heat exchanger. [Sp, lark]

calanthe /ka-lan'thi/ n an orchid of the genus *Calanthe*, having tall spikes of long-lasting flowers. [Gr *kalos* beautiful, and *anthē* blossom]

Calanus /ka-lā'nəs or kal'ə-nəs/ n a genus of copepods, swimming in plankton, important as whale and fish food.

calash /kə-lash'/ n a light low-wheeled carriage with a folding top; a large hood with a framework of hoops fashionably worn by ladies in the 18c. [Fr *calèche*; of Slav origin]

calathea /kal-ə-thē'ə/ n a plant of the S American genus *Calathea*, many of which have variegated leaves, often grown as houseplants, eg the zebra plant. [L, from Gr *kalathos* basket]

calathus /kal'ə-thəs/ n (pl **cal'athi**) a symbol of fruitfulness in classical art, a fruit basket with a wide top carried on the head. [Gr *kalathos* basket]

calavance /kal'ə-vans/ n a name for certain varieties of pulse (also **car'avance**). [Sp *garbanzo* chickpea, said to be Basque *garbantzu*]

calcaneum /kal-kā'ni-əm/ or **calcaneus** /-ni-əs/ (*anat*) n (pl **calca'nea** or **calca'nei**) the heel-bone. [L *calcāneum* the heel, from *calx* the heel]
   ■ **calca'neal** or **calca'nean** *adj*.

calcar[1] /kal'kär/ n (pl **calcār'ia**) a spur-like projection, *esp* from the base of a petal (*bot*); a spur on a bird's leg (*zool*). [L, a spur, from *calx* the heel]
   ■ **cal'carate** *adj*. **calcarif'erous** *adj* (*bot* and *zool*) having a spur or spurs. **calcar'iform** *adj* spur-shaped. **cal'carine** *adj* spurlike.
   □ **calcar avis** /ā'vis/ n (*zool* and *anat*) the hippocampus minor in the brain (literally, bird's spur).

calcar[2] /kal'kär/ n an oven or furnace for calcining the materials of frit before melting; a furnace or oven for annealing. [L *calcāria* a lime-kiln]

calcareous /kal-kā'ri-əs/ *adj* chalky; limy; of, or containing, calcium carbonate. [L *calcārius*, from *calx* lime]
   □ **calcareous tufa** see **tufa**.

calceamentum /kal-si-ə-men'təm/ n a red silk embroidered sandal forming part of the insignia of the Holy Roman Empire. [L *calceāmentum* a shoe]

calced /kalst/ *adj* (*rare*) of Carmelites, wearing shoes, *opp* to *discalced*. [LL *calceus* a shoe]
   ■ **cal'ceate** *vt* to shoe. **cal'ceate** or **cal'ceated** *adj* shod. **cal'ceiform** or **cal'ceolate** *adj* (*bot*) slipper-shaped.

calcedonio /kal-che-don'i-ō/ n a type of Venetian coloured glass resembling natural stones like chalcedony. [Ital, chalcedony]

calcedony a variant form of **chalcedony**.

calceolaria /kal-si-ō-lā'ri-ə/ n any plant of the S American genus *Calceolaria*, the plants of which are largely cultivated for the beauty of their slipperlike flowers; slipperwort. [L *calceolus*, dimin of *calceus* a shoe]

calces see **calx**.

calci- /kal-si-/ or **calc-** /kals-/ *combining form* denoting calcium or limestone. [See **calcium**]

calcic see under **calcium**.

calcicole /kal'si-kōl/ n any plant that thrives on soil containing lime or chalk (also *adj*). [L *calx*, *calcis* lime, limestone, and *colere* to dwell]
   ■ **calcic'olous** *adj*.

calciferol /kal-sif'ə-rol/ n vitamin D[2]. [*calciferous* and *ergosterol*]

calciferous /kal-sif'ə-rəs/ *adj* containing lime; forming or producing salts of calcium. [L *calx*, *calcis* lime, limestone, and *ferre* to bear]
   □ **Calciferous Sandstone** n the oldest category of Carboniferous rocks in Scotland.

calcifuge /kal'si-fūj/ n any plant that will not tolerate limy or chalky soil (also *adj*). [L *calx*, *calcis* lime, limestone, and *fugere* to flee]
   ■ **calcifugous** /-sif'ū-gəs/ *adj*.

calcify /kal'si-fī/ *vt* and *vi* (**cal'cifying**; **cal'cified**) to convert or become converted into lime; to harden or become hard by the deposition of calcium salts or compounds, as in body tissue; to make or become rigid and inflexible (*fig*). [**calcium**]
   ■ **calcif'ic** *adj* calcifying or calcified. **calcificā'tion** n the process of calcifying or becoming calcified, a conversion into lime.

calcigerous /kal-sij'ə-rəs/ see under **calcium**.

calcimine see **Kalsomine**®.

calcine /kal'sin or kal'sīn/ *vt* to reduce (*esp* a metal ore or mineral) to a calx by heating; to subject to prolonged heating, *esp* so as to oxidize, or so as to drive out water and carbon dioxide. [Med L *calcināre*, from L *calx*, *calcis* lime]
   ■ **cal'cinable** *adj*. **calcinā'tion** n.

calcineurin /kal-si-nū'rin/ n an enzyme which plays a role in many brain functions, abnormal levels of which are associated with schizophrenia. [*calcium*, **neur-** with sfx *-in*]

calcite /kal'sīt/ n a mineral, calcium carbonate crystallized in the hexagonal system, the main constituent of limestone and many marbles (also **calcspar** /kalk'spär/).
   ■ **calcitic** /-sit'ik/ *adj*.

calcitonin /kal-si-tō'nin/ n a hormone, produced in the thyroid gland, which regulates the amount of calcium in the blood and inhibits loss of calcium from the bones of the skeleton. [*calcium* and *tone* with sfx *-in*]

calcium /kal'si-əm/ n a soft greyish-white metallic element (symbol *Ca*; atomic no 20) of the alkaline earth group, present in limestone, chalk and gypsum, and *usu* occurring in the form of one of its compounds. [L *calx*, *calcis* lime, limestone]
   ■ **cal'cic** *adj* containing calcium. **calcig'erous** *adj* containing lime.
   □ **calcium antagonist** or **blocker** n a drug preventing the influx of calcium ions into cardiac and smooth muscle, used in the treatment

of angina and high blood pressure. **calcium carbide** n a grey solid chemical compound, CaC_2, used in the production of acetylene. **calcium carbonate** n an insoluble chemical compound, $CaCO_3$, found naturally in limestone and chalk, and used in the production of lime and cement. **calcium chloride** n a white crystalline compound, $CaCl_2$, used as a de-icer and dehydrating agent. **calcium hydroxide** n a white powder made by adding water to lime and used in the production of plaster and cement, slaked lime. **calcium oxide** n a white chemical compound, CaO, used in producing other calcium compounds and in agriculture to reduce acidity in soil (also **calx**, **lime** or **quicklime**). **calcium phosphate** n a mineral salt essential in the formation of bones and teeth in animals, and for the healthy growth of plants. **calcium sulphate** n a white crystalline solid, $CaSO_4$, occurring naturally as gypsum, used to make plaster of Paris and paint.

calcrete /kal'krēt/ (geol) n a composite rock made up of sand and gravel cemented with calcium carbonate. [calci- and concrete]

calc-sinter /kalk'sin-tər/ n travertine. [Ger Kalksinter, from kalk lime, and sinter slag]

calcspar see **calcite**.

calc-tuff or **calc-tufa** same as **tuff** or **tufa**.

calculate /kal'kyŭ-lāt/ vt to count or reckon; to think out, esp mathematically; to think, intend, purpose or suppose (US). ◆ vi to make a calculation; to estimate. [L calculāre, -ātum to count using little stones, from calculus, dimin of calx a stone]
■ **cal'culable** adj. **cal'culably** adv. **cal'culāted** adj thought out; premeditated; reckoned; computed; fitted, likely, of such a nature as probably (to). **cal'culating** adj deliberately selfish and scheming; shrewd, circumspect; tending to think or plan ahead. **cal'culatingly** adv. **calculā'tion** n the art or process of calculating; an estimate; a forecast or projection. **calculā'tional** or **cal'culative** adj relating to calculation. **cal'culātor** n a person who or thing that calculates; an electronic device that performs arithmetical calculations; a book, set of tables, etc for obtaining arithmetical results.
□ **calculated risk** n a possibility of failure, the degree of which has been estimated and taken into account before a venture is undertaken. **calculating machine** n any machine for speedily obtaining arithmetical results, eg a pocket calculator, computer, etc.

calculus /kal'kyŭ-ləs/ n a system of computation or calculation used in higher branches of mathematics permitting the manipulation of continually varying quantities (pl **cal'culuses**); a stone-like concretion which forms in certain vessels or organs of the body, eg the kidney or gall bladder (pl **cal'culī**); the mixture of plaque and saliva that forms a hard brownish-yellow layer on the teeth, tartar. [For ety see **calculate**]
■ **cal'cular** adj relating to the mathematical calculus. **cal'culary**, **cal'culose** or **cal'culous** adj relating to or affected with stone or with gravel.
■ **calculus of finite differences** calculus concerned with changes in functions due to finite changes in variables, and which does not assume continuity. **differential calculus** a branch of calculus which enables calculation of the rate at which one quantity changes in relation to another, used to find velocities, slopes of curves, etc. **integral calculus** a branch of calculus concerned with finding integrals and applying them to find eg the areas enclosed by curves, the solution of differential equations, etc. **predicate calculus** a notation system by which the logical structure of simple propositions may be represented. **propositional calculus** a notation system in which symbols representing propositions and logical constants such as negation, conjunction and implication are used to indicate the logical relations between propositions.

caldarium /kal-dā'ri-əm or kal-dä'ri-ŭm/ n (pl **caldar'ia**) a hot room in Roman baths. [L]

caldera /käl-dā'rə/ (geol) n a large crater formed by the collapse of the central part of a volcano after eruption. [Sp, cauldron]

caldron same as **cauldron**.

Caledonian /ka-li-dō'ni-ən/ adj of or relating to ancient Caledonia, to the Highlands of Scotland, or to Scotland generally (esp poetic); relating to a mountain-forming movement of Silurian and Old Red Sandstone times, well developed in Scotland (geol). ◆ n (literary) a Scot. [L Calēdonia northern Britain]

calefaction /ka-li-fak'shən/ n the act of heating; the state of being heated. [L calefacere, from calēre to grow hot, and facere, factum to make]
■ **calefacient** /-fā'shənt/ adj warming. ◆ n anything that warms; a medicinal preparation that warms the area it is applied to. **calefac'tive** adj communicating heat. **calefac'tor** n a small stove. **calefac'tory** adj warming. ◆ n (hist) a room in which monks warmed themselves; a warming pan, or priest's pome or hand-warmer. **cal'efy** vt and vi to make or grow warm.

calembour /ka-lã-boor'/ (Fr) n a pun.

calendar /kal'ən-dər/ n the way in which the natural divisions of time are arranged with respect to each other for the purposes of civil life; an almanac or table of months, days, and seasons, or of facts about specific days, etc; a list of documents arranged chronologically with summaries of contents; a list of canonized saints, or of prisoners awaiting trial; a list of events, appointments, etc; any list or record. ◆ vt to place in a list or enter in a calendar; to analyse and index. [L calendārium an account book, from kalendae calends]
■ **cal'endarer** n. **cal'endarist** n. **calendariza'tion** or **-s-** n. **cal'endarize** or **-ise** vt in accounting, to divide (something, eg a budget) into equal units of time within a year (usu months). **calen'dric** or **calen'drical** adj of, relating to, or like a calendar in some way.
□ **cal'endar-line** n the dateline. **calendar month** see under **month**. **calendar year** see under **year**.
■ **perpetual calendar** see under **perpetual**.

calender¹ /kal'ən-dər/ n a machine with rollers for finishing or glazing the surface of cloth, paper, etc, using a combination of moisture, heat, and pressure. ◆ vt to press in a calender. [Fr calandre, from L cylindrus, from Gr kylindros roller]
■ **cal'endering** n. **cal'endrer** n. **cal'endry** n a place where calendering is done.

calender² /kal'ən-dər/ n a member of a mendicant order of wandering dervishes in Persia and Turkey. [Pers qalandar]

calendrer see under **calender¹**.

calendric, **calendrical** see under **calendar**.

calends or **kalends** /kal'əndz/ n pl the first day of each month in the ancient Roman calendar. [L kalendae, from calāre, from Gr kaleein to call (because the order of the days was proclaimed at the beginning of each month)]

calendula /ka-len'dū-lə/ n any plant of the genus Calendula, the marigold genus; a preparation of marigold flowers formerly used in plasters, etc, for the healing of wounds. [L kalendae calends (but the connection is obscure)]

calenture /kal'ən-chər/ (hist) n a tropical fever or delirium caused by heat; heatstroke. [Fr, from Sp calentura, from L calēns, -entis, from calēre to be hot]

calescence /ka-les'əns/ n increase in heat. [L calēscere, inchoative of calēre to be hot]

calf¹ /käf/ n (pl **calves** /kävz/ or (of calfskin) **calfs**) the young of any bovine animal, esp the cow; the young of the elephant, whale, and certain other mammals; calfskin leather; an iceberg that has broken off a glacier or larger iceberg; a stupid or loutish person (sl). [OE (Anglian) cælf (WSax cealf)]
■ **calve** /käv/ vt and vi to give birth to a calf; to detach (a glacier or iceberg).
□ **calf'-bound** adj bound in calfskin. **calf'-country** or **calf'-ground** n (Scot) the place where one spent one's youth. **calf'dozer** n a small bulldozer. **calf'lick** n a cowlick. **calf'-love** n immature or youthful amorous attachment or affection. **calf's'-foot** or **calves''-foot jelly** n a savoury jelly made from the gelatine produced by boiling the foot of a calf. **calf'skin** n the skin of the calf, making a fine leather suitable for bookbinding and shoes. **calf'-time** n youth.
■ **divinity calf** a dark-brown calf bookbinding with blind stamping, and without gilding, used on theological books. **golden calf** the image set up by Aaron and worshipped by the Israelites during the absence of Moses on Sinai (Bible); any false object of worship. **half'-calf** a bookbinding in which the back and corners are in calfskin. **in** or **with calf** (of cows) pregnant. **kill the fatted calf** to celebrate or welcome lavishly or extravagantly. **mottled calf** a light-coloured bookbinding, decorated by sprinkling drops of acid on its surface. **smooth calf** a binding in plain or undecorated calf leather. **tree calf** a bright brown calf bookbinding, stained by acids with a pattern resembling the trunk and branches of a tree.

calf² /käf/ n (pl **calves** /kävz/) the thick fleshy part at the back of the leg below the knee. [ON kálfi]
■ **calf'less** adj (archaic) having a thin leg.

caliature-wood /kal'i-ə-chər-wŭd/ n an old term for a tropical dyewood, perhaps red sanders (also **caliatour**, **calliature**, etc).

Caliban /kal'i-ban/ n a man of brutish or uncouth nature, from the character of that name in Shakespeare's Tempest.

calibre or (esp N Am) **caliber** /kal'i-bər/ n the diameter of a bullet or shell; the diameter of the bore of a gun or tube; character or capacity, degree of suitability or excellence (fig). [Fr calibre the bore of a gun, perh from L quā librā of what weight, or from Ar qālib a mould]
■ **cal'ibrate** vt to determine the diameter of a gun barrel or tube; to determine true values by comparison with an accurate standard; to mark or adjust gradations or positions on. **calibrā'tion** n the act of

calibrating; one of a series of marks or gradations that indicate values or positions. **cal'ibrātor** n. **cal'ibred** or **cal'ibered** adj.
❑ **calibrated airspeed** n (aeronautics) an airspeed value obtained from instruments and corrected for instrument error but not for altitude.

caliche /ka-lē'chä/ n sand containing Chile saltpetre; a crust of calcium carbonate that forms on the surface of the soil in arid regions. [Sp]

calicivirus /kə-lis'i-vī-rəs/ n any of a group of related viruses, many of which have cup-shaped surface depressions. [L calix, -icis cup, and virus]

calicle see under **calyx**.

calico /kal'i-kō/ n (pl **cal'icos** or **cal'icoes**) a cotton cloth first imported from Calicut in India; plain white unprinted cotton cloth, bleached or unbleached; coarse brightly-coloured printed cotton cloth (esp N Am); a spotted or piebald animal, esp a horse (N Am). ◆ adj made of calico; with a brightly-coloured design (N Am); spotted (N Am).
❑ **cal'ico-bush**, **cal'ico-flower** or **cal'ico-tree** n kalmia. **cal'ico-printing** n the process of printing coloured patterns on cloth, eg calico. **cal'ico-wood** n the snowdrop-tree.

calid /kal'id/ adj warm. [L calidus hot]
■ **calid'ity** n.

Calif. abbrev : California (US state).

calif see **caliph**.

Califont® /kal'i-font/ (NZ) n a gas-fuelled water-heater.

Californian /ka-li-för'nyən or -ni-ən/ adj of or relating to the region of California in SW USA and N Mexico (also n).
❑ **Californian bees** same as **ginger beer plant** (see under **ginger**). **California poppy** n an annual poppy-like plant (Eschscholtzia californica) of W America, having bright yellow or orange flowers.

californium /ka-li-för'ni-əm/ n an artificially produced radioactive transuranic element (symbol Cf; atomic no 98). [First produced at the University of California]

caligo /ka-lī'gō/ n (med) reduced vision, dimness of sight. [L cālīgō, -inis fog]
■ **caligino'ity** n. **caliginous** /kal-ij'i-nəs/ adj (archaic) dim, obscure, dark.

Caligulism /ka-lig'yoo-li-zm/ n an example of debauched or excessive behaviour, eg sexual depravity, extreme cruelty, etc. [From the Roman emperor Caligula, who often exhibited such behaviour]

calina /kal'i-nə/ n a dust storm or cloud that spreads over S Europe from the Sahara desert, causing heatwaves. [Sp, haze]

caliology /kal-i-ol'ə-ji/ n the science and study of birds' nests. [Gr kaliā, kaliā a nest, and logos discourse]

calipash /kal'i-pash/ n the edible flesh of a turtle close to the upper shell, a dull greenish fatty gelatinous substance. [Prob from W Ind words]
■ **cal'ipee** n the edible light-yellowish flesh from around the turtle's lower shell.

calipers see **callipers**.

caliph /kal'if or kā'lif/ n esp formerly (the title given to) a spiritual leader of Islam regarded as a successor of Mohammed (also **calif**, **kalif** or **khalif**). [Fr calife, from Ar khalīfah a successor]
■ **cal'iphal** adj. **cal'iphate** n the office, rank, government or empire of a caliph.

Calippic or **Callippic Period** /ka-lip'ik pēr'i-əd/ n the cycle discovered by the Athenian astronomer Kal(l)ippos (c.350BC) equalling four Metonic cycles less one day, or a period of seventy-six years, when the new moons fall on the same days of the year.

calisaya /ka-li-sā'(y)ə/ n a variety of Peruvian bark. [From a native name]

calisthenics see **callisthenics**.

caliver /kal'i-vər/ (Shakesp) n a kind of light musket. [Same as **calibre**]

calix /kā'liks or kal'iks/ n (pl **cal'ices** /-sēz/) a cup, chalice (cf **calyx**). [L calix a cup]

Calixtin[1] or **Calixtine** /ka-lik'stin/ n a member of the 15c Bohemian sect of Hussites, an Utraquist (also adj). [From their demanding the chalice (L calix) as well as the bread for the laity in communion]

Calixtin[2] or **Calixtine** /ka-lik'stin/ n a follower of the syncretist Lutheran divine, Georg Calixtus (1586–1656).

calk[1] see **caulk**.

calk[2] /kök/ n a pointed piece on a horseshoe to prevent slipping (also **calk'in**, **calk'er**, **caulk'er** or **cawk'er**). ◆ vt to provide with a calk. [OE calc shoe, from L calx a heel]

calk[3] or **calque** /kök, kalk/ vt to transfer (a design, etc) by rubbing the back with colouring matter and then tracing with a blunt point onto a surface placed beneath. ◆ n /kalk/ (usu **calque**) a loan-translation (see under **loan**[1]). [L calcāre to tread, from calx the heel]

calker, **calkin** see **calk**[2].

call[1] /köl/ vi to cry aloud, speak loudly, shout (often with out); of an animal or bird, to utter a cry or characteristic sound; to make a short visit (with on, for, at); to make a telephone call; to demand that a player show his hand after repeated raising of stakes (poker); to try to predict the result of tossing a coin; to make a bid (bridge). ◆ vt and vi (cards) to declare (trump suit, etc). ◆ vt to name; to summon or request to be present; to rouse from sleep or from bed; to designate or reckon; to select for a special office, eg to the Bar; to telephone; to read out the names in (a roll); to demand the repayment of (a debt, loan, redeemable bonds, etc); to give the order for (a strike); to make a call (sport); to demand the playing of (an exposed card) (poker); to apply (an offensive name) to (inf); to broadcast a commentary on (a race, etc) (Aust and NZ); to transfer control to (a subroutine) (comput). ◆ n a summons or invitation (to the witness box, the telephone, the stage or rehearsal, etc); a sense of vocation; a demand; an act of waking someone; a short visit; a signal by trumpet, bell, etc; a telephone connection or conversation, or a request for one; occasion, cause (inf); a declaration or undertaking, or the right to make it in turn (cards); a direction in square dancing; a decision on the status of a shot, articulated by an umpire or (esp tennis) a line judge (sport); a cry, esp of a bird; admission to the rank of barrister; an invitation to the pastorate of a congregation; (also **call option**) an option of buying within a certain time certain securities or commodities at a stipulated price (stock exchange); the money paid to secure such an option; one instalment of the payment for newly-issued securities. [OE ceallian and ON kalla]
■ **call'er** n. **call'ing** n vocation, an occupation or profession.
❑ **call alarm** n a small radio transmitter used, esp by elderly people living alone, to summon help in an emergency. **call'-at-large** n a form of pastoral call sometimes adopted by a presbytery where a congregation is not unanimous, in which the name of the person to be called is not inscribed beforehand, and the names cannot be adhibited by mandate. **call'-back** n a return telephone call; an act of recalling. **call'-barring** n (telecom) the ability to restrict outgoing telephone calls to certain numbers. **call'-bird** n a bird trained to lure others into snares by its call. **call'-box** n a public telephone-box. **call'-boy** n a boy who calls the actors when they are required on stage. **call centre** n a building where workers provide services to a company's customers by telephone. **Caller ID** n a facility which displays the telephone number of an incoming call. **call gapping** n a technique used to prevent congestion in telephone systems by limiting the number of calls that can pass through the network at any time. **call'-girl** n a prostitute who arranges appointments with clients by telephone. **call house** n a house of prostitution. **calling card** n a visiting card; anything that reveals the identity of a person (fig). **call'ing-crab** n the fiddler crab, which waves its larger claw when disturbed. **call'-loan** or **call'-money** n (finance) a loan or money called in for repayment or payable when demanded. **call'-note** n the note by which a bird or animal calls to its own kind. **call option** n (stock exchange) see n above. **call-out** see **call out** below. **call sign** or **call signal** n (communications) a combination of letters and numbers, identifying a particular ship, aircraft, transmitter, etc. **call'time** n time available for use in making calls on a mobile phone; the time used on a single phone call. **call'-up** n an act of calling up, esp conscription into the armed forces. **call waiting** n (telecom) the ability to accept an incoming telephone call routed by another number while holding a call on one's own number.
■ **call attention to** to point out. **call away** to divert the mind. **call back** to recall; to visit again; to telephone again. **call by** to visit briefly in passing. **call collect** (N Am) to make a reverse-charge telephone call. **call cousins** to claim kindred. **call down** to invoke; to rebuke, reprove sharply and angrily (esp US inf). **call for** to come for and take away with one; to ask loudly for; to demand; to require (**called'-for** required, necessary; **not called for** uncalled-for). **call forth** to evoke. **call in** to bring in from public use old currency notes, etc (banking); to demand repayment of (a debt, etc); to call to one's help (eg a doctor, the police); to withdraw from circulation; to withdraw (eg an application). **call in on** to visit briefly and informally. **call in** (or **into**) **question** to challenge, cast doubt on. **call off** to order to come away; to withdraw or back out; to cancel or abandon. **call of nature** (euphem) a need to urinate or defecate. **call on** or **upon** to invoke, appeal to; to make a short visit to. **call out** to challenge to fight, eg a duel; to summon to service, bring into operation; to instruct (members of a trade union) to come out on strike; to request or arrange a visit (eg of a repairman, service engineer; **call'-out** n and adj). **call over** to read aloud (a list). **call round** to visit informally. **call the shots** (orig US)

or **call the tune** to say what is to happen, to order, or to be in command. **call to account** see under **account**. **call to mind** to recollect, or cause to recollect. **call to order** to call upon (participants) to observe the rules of debate; (of a chairman) to announce that a formal meeting is starting. **call up** to summon eg to a tribunal, to *esp* military service, or to memory; to telephone; to display (information, data, etc on a computer screen). **have first call on** to have the right to use (something) in preference to anyone else. **it's your**, **his**, etc **call** it is up to you, him, etc to make a decision. **on call** available if required; ready to answer a summons. **pay a call** (*inf; euphem*) to go to the lavatory. **within call** within calling distance.

call² /köl/ (*Spenser*) *n* a caul or cap.

calla /kal'ə/ *n* a poisonous marsh plant (*Calla palustris*) of the family Araceae; (also **calla lily**) any African lily of the genus *Zantedeschia* having showy brightly-coloured flowers. [Origin doubtful]

Callanetics /ka-lə-net'iks/ *n pl* a method of exercises involving frequent repetition of small muscular movements, designed to improve muscle tone. [*Callan* Pinckney (1939–2012), its US inventor]

callant /kä'lənt/ or **callan** /kä'lən/ (*Scot*) *n* a lad or fellow. [Du *kalant*]

caller /kä'lər or kö'lər/ (*Scot*) *adj* (of fish, vegetables, etc) fresh; (of wind, water, etc) cool and refreshing. [Prob the same as **calver**]

callet /kal'it/ (*Shakesp*) *n* a scold, a woman of bad character, a prostitute. [Origin doubtful]

calliature see **caliature-wood**.

Callicarpa /ka-li-kär'pə/ *n* a genus of deciduous Japanese and Chinese shrubs and small trees, grown for their attractive berries and autumn foliage. [Gr *kalos* beautiful, and *karpos* fruit]

calligram or **calligramme** /kal'i-gram/ *n* a design using the letters of a word. [*calligraphy* and *-gram*]

calligraphy /ka- or kə-lig'rə-fi/ *n* fine handwriting or penmanship; artistic script produced with a brush; a line or lines in art suggesting this; loosely, a characteristic style of writing. [Gr *kallos* beauty, and *graphein* to write]
  ■ **callig'rapher** *n*. **calligraphic** /kal-i-graf'ik/ or **calligraph'ical** *adj*. **callig'raphist** *n*.

Calliope /kə-lī'ə-pi or ka'li-ōp/ *n* the Muse of epic poetry (*Gr myth*); (without *cap*) a keyboard musical instrument similar to an organ, with a set of whistles operated by steam or compressed air. [Gr *Kalliopē*]

callipers or (*esp N Am*) **calipers** /kal'i-pərz/ *n pl* or sometimes *n sing* compasses with legs suitable for measuring the inside or outside diameter of bodies (also **call'iper-compasses**); a calliper splint. [*calibre*]
  ■ **call'iper** *n* in papermaking, a measure of the thickness of a single sheet of paper, *usu* expressed in microns or millimetres. ◆ *vt* to measure with callipers.
  □ **calliper splint** *n* a metal splint fitted to the leg to provide support.

Callippic see **Calippic**.

callipygous /ka-li-pī'gəs or -pī'jəs/ *adj* having beautiful buttocks (also **callipygean** /-pij'i-ən/). [Gr *kallipȳgos* an epithet of Aphrodite, from *kallos* beauty, and *pȳgē* buttock]

Callistemon /kal-i-stē'mon/ *n* an Australian genus of the myrtle family, bottlebrush shrubs. [Gr *kallos* beauty, and *stēmōn* a thread (stamen)]

callisthenics or (*esp N Am*) **calisthenics** /ka-lis-then'iks/ *n pl* exercises designed to achieve gracefulness, fitness and strength. [Gr *kallos* beauty, and *sthenos* strength]
  ■ **callisthen'ic** or **calisthen'ic** *adj*.

Callitriche /ka-lit'ri-kē/ *n* the water-starwort genus, constituting the **Callitrichā'ceae**, a family of widely-distributed aquatic plants. [Gr *kallos* beauty, and *thrix, trichos* hair]

callop /kal'əp/ *n* a pale yellow or golden edible freshwater fish (*Plectroplites ambiguus*), found in Australia. [From an Aboriginal language]

callous /kal'əs/ *adj* (*esp* of the skin) hardened; unfeeling, unsympathetic, cruel. [L *callōsus*, from *callus* hard skin]
  ■ **callos'ity** *n* a thickening of the skin; callousness. **call'ously** *adv*. **call'ousness** *n* lack of feeling, brutality.

callow¹ /kal'ō/ *adj* unfledged, unbearded; inexperienced. [OE *calu*; Ger *kahl* bald]

callow² /kal'ō/ *adj* low-lying and liable to be submerged. ◆ *n* an alluvial flat. [Perh Ir *calad* a riverside meadow]

calluna /ka-loo'nə/ *n* a plant of the heather genus *Calluna*. [Gr *kallȳnein* to beautify, to sweep, from *kalos* beautiful]

callus /kal'əs/ *n* an area of thickened or hardened skin; new material by which fractured bones are consolidated (*pathol*); soft tissue that forms over a cut surface (*bot*). [L]

calm¹ /käm/ *adj* still or quiet; of the weather, not windy; (of a person or an action) serene, tranquil, assured; cool, impudent. ◆ *n* absence of wind (also in *pl*); a reading of 0 on the Beaufort scale, indicating a wind speed of less than 1mph (*meteorol*); repose; serenity of feelings or actions. ◆ *vt* and *vi* (also **calm down**) to make or become calm; to quiet. ◆ *vt* to becalm. [Fr *calme* (Ital *calma*), from LL *cauma*, from Gr *kauma* noonday heat, from *kaiein* to burn]
  ■ **calmant** or **calmative** (both /kal' or kä'/) *n* and *adj* (*med*) (a drug) having a calming effect. **calmed** /kämd/ *adj*. **calm'ly** *adv*. **calm'ness** *n*. **calm'y** *adj* (*Spenser*) characterized by calm.

calm², etc see **cam³**.

calm³ see **came²**.

calmodulin /kal-mod'yŭ-lin/ (*biochem*) *n* a protein found in plant and animal cells that is a receptor of calcium and affects many processes involving calcium within cells. [**calcium**, **modulate** and sfx *-in*]

Calmuck see **Kalmuck**.

calmy¹ see under **calm¹**.

calmy² see under **cam³**.

calo (*music*) *abbrev* : calando.

calomel /ka'lō-mel/ *n* mercurous chloride, used in medicine as a purgative. [Fr *calomel*, appar from Gr *kalos* beautiful and *melās* black]

calorie or **calory** /kal'ə-ri/ *n* the amount of heat needed to raise one gram of water 1° centigrade in temperature, *usu* from 14.5°C to 15.5°C (*small* or *gram-calorie*) (in 1950 it was recommended that this should be superseded as a unit of heat and internal energy by the *joule*); an *international table calorie* (cal$_{IT}$) = 4.1868 joules, a *thermo-chemical calorie* = 4.1840 joules; (sometimes with *cap*) the amount of heat needed to raise one kilogram of water 1° centigrade in temperature (*great*, *large*, or *kilogram-calorie*, *kilocalorie* ; = 1000 small calories) (used in expressing the heat- or energy-producing value of foods); the hundredth part of the heat required to raise a gram from 0° to 100° (*mean calorie*; equal to 4.1897 joules). [L *calor* heat]
  ■ **calorescence** /kal-ər-es'əns/ *n* (an ill-formed word meaning the opposite of what it should mean) the transmutation of heat rays into luminous rays. **caloric** /ka-lor'ik/ *adj* of or relating to heat or calories. ◆ *n* (*archaic*) the nature of heat as a subtle, self-repellent fluid, according to a principle, **caloric theory**, widely held up to c.1850. **caloric'ity** *n*. **calorif'ic** *adj* of, relating to, or causing heat; heating. **calorif'ically** *adv*. **calorifica'tion** *n*. **calor'ifīer** *n* an apparatus for heating water in a tank, the source of heat being a coil of heated pipes immersed in the water. **calorim'eter** *n* an instrument or apparatus for measuring heat capacities, latent heats, thermal constants, etc. **calorimet'ric** *adj*. **calorim'etry** *n*. **cal'orist** *n* a person who believes the caloric theory (see under **caloric** above).
  □ **Calor Gas®** *n* a type of gas for cooking, heating, etc, *usu* sold in large metal containers for use where there is no permanent supply of gas. **caloric test** *n* (*med*) a test (used to determine whether a patient with hearing loss has a diseased inner ear) in which the outer ear is flooded with water at temperatures above and below body temperature and the consequent effect on the inner ear is apparent in reflex flickering of the eye. **calorie conscious** *adj* being aware of the number of calories in food, *esp* in order to lose weight. **calorie controlled** *adj* of a diet in which consumption of calories is strictly controlled in order to lose weight. **calorie** (or **Calorie**) **counter** *n* a person who or device that counts calories, *esp* as part of a weight-reducing diet. **calorific value** *n* of a food or fuel, the number of heat units produced by complete combustion of unit mass.

calotte /ka-lot'/ *n* a plain skullcap as worn by Roman Catholic clergy. [Fr]

calotype /ka'lō-tīp/ *n* an early kind of photography (invented c.1834 by WH Fox Talbot) in which a positive was produced from a negative image laid down on paper treated with silver iodide. [Gr *kalos* beautiful and *typos* an image]
  ■ **cal'otȳpist** *n*.

caloyer /ka'lo-yər/ *n* a Greek Orthodox monk, *esp* of the order of St Basil. [Fr, from Ital, from Late Gr *kalogēros*, from Gr *kalos* beautiful, and *gēras* old age]

calp /kalp/ *n* in Ireland, a dark shaly limestone occurring in the middle of the Carboniferous Limestone.

calpa same as **kalpa**.

calpac, calpack see **kalpak**.

calque see **calk³**.

Caltech /kal'tek'/ *abbrev* : California Institute of Technology.

caltha /kal'thə/ *n* a plant of the *Caltha* genus of flowers to which the marsh marigold belongs. [L]

caltrop /kal'trop/ n (also **cal'trap** or **cal'throp**) an old military weapon, an iron ball with four spikes, so arranged that when it is laid on the ground one spike always stands upright, used to obstruct an enemy; a name for several plants with fruits so shaped, eg (esp in pl) water chestnut. [OE coltetræppe, calcatrippe, from L calx heel, and the root of **trap**[1]]

calumba /ka-lum'bə/ n the root of an E African plant (Jateorhiza columba) used as a tonic and aid to digestion. [Perh from Colombo in Sri Lanka]

calumet /kal'ū-met/ n the peace pipe of the Native Americans, a tobacco pipe smoked in token of peace. [Norman Fr calumet shepherd's pipe (Fr chalumet), from L calamus reed]

calumny /kal'əm-ni/ n false accusation or statement; slander, defamation. [L calumnia, prob connected with calvī to deceive]
■ **calumniate** /kə-lum'ni-āt/ vt to accuse falsely; to slander. ◆ vi to spread false or slanderous reports. **calumniā'tion** n. **calum'niātor** n. **calum'niātory** or **calum'nious** adj of the nature of calumny; slanderous. **calum'niously** adv.

calutron /kal' yŭ-tron/ n a mass spectrometer used in the separation of isotopes. [California University and **-tron**]

Calvados /kal'və-dos or -dos'/ n a brandy made from cider or apple-pulp, esp in the Calvados department of Normandy.

calvaria /kal-vā'ri-ə/ n the upper part of skull enclosing the brain in vertebrates. [L, skull]

Calvary /kal'və-ri/ n the name of the place near Jerusalem where Jesus was crucified; (sometimes without cap) a representation of Christ's crucifixion, or a series of scenes connected with it (Christianity); an experience of intense mental suffering. [LL calvāria skull, from calvus bald; also used to translate Aramaic gogulthō or gogolthā (Heb gulgōleth, Grecized as golgotha)]
❏ **Calvary cross** n (heraldry) a Latin cross mounted on three steps.

calve, calves see **calf**[1,2].

calver /kal'vər/ vt to prepare (salmon or other fish) when alive or freshly caught. [Cf **caller**]
■ **cal'vered** adj.

Calvinism /kal'vi-ni-zm/ n the Christian doctrines as interpreted by the French protestant theologian and religious reformer, John Calvin (1509–64) in his Institutions of the Christian Religion, and as adopted by the Reformed and Presbyterian Churches, esp the scriptures and the Holy Spirit as the sole authority and truth, predestination of particular election, the incapacity for true faith and repentance of the natural man, efficacious grace, and final perseverance (continuance of the saints in a state of grace until the final state of glory).
■ **Cal'vinist** n. **Calvinist'ic** or **Calvinist'ical** adj.

calvities /kal-vish'i-ēz/ (med) n baldness. [L calvitiēs, from calvus bald]

calx /kalks/ n (pl **calxes** /kalk'siz/ or **calces** /kal'sēz/) the substance of a metal ore or mineral that remains after it has been subjected to intense heat; see also **calcium oxide** under **calcium**. [L calx, calcis lime]

calycanthemyytoy**calyculus** see under **calyx**.

calypso /ka-lip'sō/ n (pl **calyp'sos**) a West Indian ballad, usu dealing with topical events, usu made up as the singer goes along and sung in syncopated rhythm to an accompaniment of simple percussion instruments. [Poss from 17c–18c W African kaiso ceremonial song]
■ **calypso'nian** n a writer or singer of calypsos.

calyptra /ka-lip'trə/ or **calyptera** /-lip'tər-ə/ (bot) n a hood or hoodlike structure, esp that covering the spore capsule of mosses and liverworts; a root cap. [Gr kalyptrā a veil]
■ **calyp'trate** adj capped or hooded. **calyp'trogen** n the layer of cells on the growing tip of a root giving rise to the root cap.

calyx /kā'liks or kal'iks/ n (pl **ca'lyxes** or **ca'lyces** /-sēz/) the outer covering of a flower, its modified leaves termed sepals that protect the developing flower (bot); any cup-like structure in the body, esp any of the cavities of the kidney. [Gr kalyx a covering, from kalyptein to cover]
■ **calycanthemy** /kal-ik-an'thi-mi/ n (Gr anthemon flower) the condition of having the calyx like a corolla. **calycanthus** /kal-ik-an'thəs/ n the Carolina allspice or strawberry shrub, a N American shrub of the **Calycantha'ceae** a family of plants in which there is a transition from sepals to petals. **Calyciflorae** /-is-i-flō'rē or -flō'/ n pl (L flōs, flōris flower) a subclass of dicotyledons with a corolla of distinct petals. **calyciform** /kal-is'i/ adj having the form of a calyx. **calyc'inal** or **calycine** /kal'i-sīn/ adj relating to or resembling a calyx. **cal'ycle**, **cal'icle** or **cal'ycule** n a whorl of bracts, epicalyx or involucre (bot); a cup-like structure, such as the cup of a coral (zool). **cal'ycled** adj having a calycle. **cal'ycoid** or **calycoi'deous** adj like a calyx. **calyculate** /kə-lik'ū-lāt/ adj having a calyculus. **calyculus** /-lik'ū-/ n a cup-like structure.

calzone /kal-tsō'ni/ n (pl **calzo'ni** or **calzo'nes**) a folded over pizza. [Ital]

CAM abbrev : Cameroon (IVR); complementary and alternative medicine; (often /kam/) computer-aided manufacturing (or manufacture).

cam[1] /kam/ (mech) n an irregular projection on a revolving shaft or rotating cylinder, shaped so as to transmit regular movement to another part, eg to open the cylinder valves of a car engine. [Du kam cam or comb; cf **comb, kame**]
❏ **cam follower** n a slider or roller that is in contact with a cam and transmits movement. **cam'shaft** or **cam'-wheel** n a shaft or wheel bearing a cam or cams.

cam[2] adj and adv see **kam**.

cam[3], **caum** or **calm** /käm or köm/ (Scot) n pale bluish-grey clay or soft slate; a slate pencil; pipeclay; limestone (obs). ◆ vt to whiten with camstone. [Origin unknown]
■ **calm'y** adj clayey.
❏ **cam'stone, caum'stone, calm'stone** or **cam'stane, caum'stane, calm'stane** n a white argillaceous stone used for whitening hearthstones and doorsteps.

-cam /-kam/ combining form forming nouns denoting photographic equipment, as in webcam. [**camera**]

Cama see **Kama**.

camaïeu /ka-ma-yə'/ n (pl **camaïeux** /-yə'/) orig a cameo; a painting in monochrome, or in simple colours not imitating nature; a style of printing pictures producing the effect of pencil-drawing; a literary work or play that is monotonous or lacks interest. [Fr; see **cameo**]

Camaldolite /ka-mal'dō-līt/ n a member of a religious order founded by St Romuald at Camaldoli early in the 11c (also adj).
■ **Camal'dolese** n and adj.

caman /kam'an/ n a shinty stick. [Gaelic]
■ **camanachd** /kam'an-ahh(k)/ n shinty.

camaraderie /kam-ə-rä'də-rē/ n good fellowship; the intimacy of comradeship. [Fr]

camarilla /ka-mə-ril'ə/ n a band of secret intriguers, esp against legitimate ministers at court; a cabal or coterie; orig a small room. [Sp, dimin of cámara a chamber]

camaron /ka-ma-rōn'/ or kam'ə-ron/ n a kind of freshwater crustacean similar to a crayfish (also (esp Aust) **maron**). [Sp camarón a shrimp, from L cam(m)arus a sea crab, from Gr kammaros]

camass, camas, camash or **quamash** /kam'as, -ash, kwom'ash or kwa-mash'/ n any of several N American plants of the genus Camassia of the family Hyacinthaceae, esp the variety found in NW USA having a sweet edible bulb; the bulb of this plant. [Chinook kámass]
❏ **cam'ass-rat** n a small gopher-like rodent that feeds on the bulbs of the camass.

Camb. abbrev : Cambridge; Cambridgeshire (also **Cambs.**).

Cambazola see **Cambozola**®.

camber /kam'bər/ n a slight convexity on an upper surface (as on a road, a beam, the deck of a ship, the wing section of an aeroplane, etc); a slight tilt given to each of a pair of wheels on the axle of a road vehicle; the arching curve of an aerofoil (aeronautics). ◆ vt to form a camber on or give a camber to. ◆ vi to arch slightly. [Fr cambre, from L camerāre to vault]
■ **cam'bering** n (geol) a type of rock-folding that forms rounded hills and valleys.

Camberwell beauty /kam'bər-wəl bū'ti/ n a large butterfly (Nymphalis antiopa) having deep maroon wings with a row of blue spots and an edging of cream, so called because first recorded in England in 1748 at Camberwell.

cambist /kam'bist/ n a person skilled in the science of financial exchange; a manual or listing of currency exchange rates. [Ital cambista, from L cambīre to exchange]
■ **cam'bism** or **cam'bistry** n.

cambium /kam'bi-əm/ (bot) n (pl **cam'biums** or **cam'bia**) a layer or cylinder of meristem in roots and stems, by whose differentiation into xylem and phloem lateral growth or girth is added. [LL, from L cambīre to change]
■ **cam'bial** adj. **cam'biform** adj.

Cambodian /kam-bō'di-ən/ adj of or relating to the Kingdom of Cambodia in SE Asia or its inhabitants. ◆ n another name for **Khmer**.

camboge obsolete form of **gamboge**.

Cambozola® or **Cambazola** /kam-bə-zō'lə/ n a type of German soft cheese with a hard skin like Camembert and blue mould like Gorgonzola. [Camembert, Gorgonzola]

cambrel same as **gambrel**.

Cambrian /kam'bri-ən/ adj relating to Cambria or Wales; Welsh; of or belonging to a period (well represented in Wales) of the Palaeozoic era, between 540 and 490 million years ago (geol). ◆ n an inhabitant of Cambria, or Wales; the Cambrian period. [Latinized from Welsh Cymry Welshmen, and Cymru Wales]

cambric /kam'brik/ or /kām'brik/ n a fine white linen, orig manufactured at Kamerijk (Cambrai) in French Flanders; a cotton imitation of this.
❑ **cambric tea** n a beverage made of hot water, milk, sugar and sometimes a small amount of tea.

Cambridge /kām'brij/ adj of or relating to Cambridge, an English university town. See also **Cantabrigian**.
❑ **Cambridge blue** n a light blue (see also **blue**¹). **Cambridge ring** n (comput) a computer network facility developed at Cambridge University, designed so that packets of data are entered and removed from frames which move continuously around the ring. **Cambridge roller** n a ring roller (qv under **ring**¹).

Cambs. see **Camb.**

camcorder /kam'kör-dər/ n a portable video camera and sound recorder combined in one unit.

came¹ /kām/ pat of **come**.

came² /kām/ or **calm** /kām/ n a lead rod for framing a pane in a leaded or stained-glass window. [Origin unknown]

camel /kam'əl/ n either of two large ruminant mammals of Asia and Africa, having a single hump on the back (**dromedary** or **Arabian camel**), or two humps (**Bactrian camel**), used as beasts of burden or for riding in desert regions because of their ability to survive for long periods without food and water; a watertight float attached to a vessel to increase its buoyancy; a humped type of early aeroplane, used in World War I; a light yellowish-brown colour. ◆ adj of the colour camel. [L camēlus, from Gr kamēlos, from Phoenician or Heb gāmāl]
■ **cameleer**' n someone who drives or rides a camel. **cam'elid** n an animal of the **Camel'idae**, the family of artiodactyls which includes camels and llamas (also adj). **cam'eline** n a material made from camel hair. ◆ adj of the nature of a camel. **cam'elish** adj like a camel, obstinate. **cam'eloid** adj of the camel family (also n). **cam'elry** n troops mounted on camels.
❑ **cam'elback** n an inferior grade of rubber, made from reclaimed or synthetic rubber, used for retreading tyres. **cam'el-backed** adj hump-backed. **cam'el-corps** n troops mounted on camels. **camel hair** or **camel's hair** n the hair of the camel, used for making a soft cloth; the hair of the squirrel's tail used for making artists' paintbrushes. **camel spider** n a member of the Solifugae order of spider-like arachnids of hot arid regions. **camel spin** n (ice skating) a type of spin in which one leg is extended horizontally behind the skater. **camel's thorn** n a papilionaceous manna-yielding desert plant (Alhagi maurorum) on which camels graze.

cameleon same as **chameleon**.

camellia /kə-mē'lyə or -li-ə, -mel'yə or mel'i-ə/ n any shrub of the Camellia genus of evergreen shrubs closely related to tea, native to E Asia, and grown for their beautiful rose-like flowers. [Named from Kamel, Latinized as Camellus, a Moravian Jesuit who collected plants in the Philippine Islands]

camelopard /ka-mel'ō- or kam'ə-lō-pärd/ n an obsolete term for the giraffe (also **cameleopard** /kam-ə-lep'ərd/). [L camēlopardus, from Gr kamēlopardalis from Gr kamēlos the camel, and pardalis the panther]
■ **Camelopardalis** /kə-mel-ə-pär'də-lis/ n a northern constellation close to Ursa Minor.

camelot¹ /kam'lot/ (Fr) n a hawker, pedlar; a newspaper vendor.

camelot² see **camlet**.

Camembert /kam'əm-ber or (Fr) kam-ā-ber/ n a soft rich cheese, orig made near Camembert, in Normandy.

cameo /kam'i-ō/ n (pl **cam'eos**) a gem with a figure (usu a head or bust in profile) carved in relief, esp one in which a differently coloured lower layer serves as a ground; a short literary piece; a small role in a play or film, often giving scope for character acting. ◆ adj miniature, small and perfect of its kind. [Ital cammeo, from LL cammaeus, of uncertain origin]
❑ **cam'eo-part** or **cam'eo-role** see cameo (n) above. **cam'eo-shell** n a helmet-shell. **cameo ware** n pottery with relief decoration on a ground of a different colour.

camera /kam'(ə-)rə/ n (pl **cam'eras**) the photographer's apparatus, for recording an image on a light-sensitive plate or film; the apparatus that receives the image of the scene and converts it into electrical impulses for transmission (TV); (pl **cam'erae** /-ē/) a judge's private chamber; a legislative chamber; a vaulted room; the papal treasury; a cavity or chamber, esp in mollusc shells (biol). [L camera, Gr kamarā vault]

■ **cam'eral** adj of or relating to a judge's or a legislative chamber. **cam'erated** adj chambered; vaulted. **camerā'tion** n.
❑ **camera lucida** /lū'sid-ə/ n (L, light chamber) a device by which the image of the object under a microscope is made to appear by reflection on a piece of paper so that it may be viewed and drawn simultaneously. **cam'eraman** n a person who operates a television or film camera. **camera obscura** /ob-skūr'ə/ n (L, dark chamber) a dark chamber in which an image of outside objects is projected on a screen. **camera phone** or **cam'phone** n a mobile phone incorporating a camera, enabling the transmission of digital images. **camera-ready copy** n (printing) finished text and/or illustrations ready for conversion to film from which printing plates will be made. **cam'era-shy** adj (inf) not liking or unwilling to be photographed. **camera tube** n the transducer device in a television or video camera that converts an optical image of a scene into electrical signals. **cam'erawork** n the process or technique of filming or taking photographs.
■ **in camera** in a judge's private room; in secret; in private. **on** (or **off**) **camera** (not) in the process of being filmed. **to camera** (of a person) facing or addressing a TV or film camera.

camerlengo /ka-mər-leng'gō/ or **camerlingo** /-ling'gō/ n (pl **camerleng'os** or **camerling'os**) a papal treasurer. [Ital; connected with **chamberlain**]

Cameronian /kam-ə-rō'ni-ən/ n a follower of the Covenanter Richard Cameron, a member of the Reformed Presbyterian Church, a body that refused to accept the Revolution settlement (most of whom united with the Free Church in 1876); a soldier of the Cameronian regiment (the 26th and 90th Foot, later First Battalion of Scottish Rifles, disbanded in 1968), formed from a body of Cameronians (1689). ◆ adj of or relating to Cameron or the Cameronians.

Cameroonian /ka-mə-roo'ni-ən/ adj of or relating to the Republic of Cameroon in W Africa, or its inhabitants. ◆ n a native or citizen of Cameroon.

camese see **camise**.

cami- /ka-mi-/ combining form denoting camisole.
■ **cam'iknickers** n pl a woman's undergarment combining a camisole and knickers; loose silky knickers for women. **cam'i-top** n.

camino real /kä-mē'nō rā-äl'/ (Sp) n a highway. [Literally, royal road]

camion /kam'i-ən/ n a heavy lorry or wagon. [Fr]

camis /kam'is/ or **camus** /kam'əs/ n (Spenser) a loose light robe. [Sp and Provençal camisa shirt, from L camisia]

camisade /kam'i-sad/ or **camisado** /-sä'dō/ n (pl **cam'isades** or **camisa'dos**) a night attack, probably because shirts were often put on over armour for identification. [Sp camisada shirts]

Camisard /kam'i-sär or -zär/ n an insurgent Huguenot of the Cévennes who fought against the French king's forces from 1685 to 1705, so called from the camise or blouse worn by the peasants.

camise or **camese** /ka-mēs'/ n a loose shirt or tunic, as worn by Arabs. [Ar qamīç, perh L camisia]

camisole /kam'i-sōl/ n a loose under-bodice with thin shoulder straps rather than sleeves; a sleeved jacket, a woman's loose negligée or jacket. [Fr]

camlet /kam'lit/ or **camelot** /kam'lot/ n a cloth perhaps orig of camel's hair, but now chiefly of wool and goat's hair; a strong waterproof cloth. [Fr, from LL camelotum, from L camēlus; or perh Ar khamlat nap]

camo /kam'ō/ n an informal short form of **camouflage**.

camogie /ka-mō'gē/ n in Ireland, a game, a form of hurling, played by women. [Anglicized from Ir Gaelic camògaìocht, from camòg a crooked stick]

camomile or **chamomile** /kam'ə-mīl/ n a name for several plants related to chrysanthemum, or their dried flowers, used medicinally for the stomach, as a tonic, etc, esp Anthemis nobilis (common camomile) and Matricaria chamomilla (wild camomile). [Fr camomille, from L chamomilla, from Gr chamaimēlon, literally, earth-apple, from the apple-like smell of its blossoms, from chamai on the ground, and mēlon an apple]
❑ **camomile** (or **chamomile**) **tea** n an infusion made with dried camomile flowers.

Camorra /ka-mor'ə/ n a Neapolitan secret society formed c.1820, similar to the Mafia; (without cap) any similar society or organization. [Ital]
■ **Camorr'ism** n. **Camorr'ist** or **Camorris'ta** n.

camote /ka-mō'tā/ n esp in West Indies, a yam or sweet potato. [Sp]

camouflage /kam'ə-fläzh or -fläj/ n any device or means for disguising or concealing, or for deceiving an adversary, esp by adopting the colour, texture, etc of natural surroundings or backgrounds; the use of such a device or means. ◆ *vt* and *vi* to deceive, counterfeit or disguise. [Fr *camoufler* (verb); see also **camouflet**]

■ **cam'oufleur** *n* (*Fr*) a person or animal skilled in the art of camouflage.

camouflet /kă-moo-flā'/ (*milit*) *n* a mine used to destroy an underground enemy gun emplacement. [Fr, a whiff of smoke intentionally blown in the face, an affront]

camp[1] /kamp/ *n* a place on which a tent or tents or the like are pitched; a collection of temporary dwellings, or their inhabitants collectively; temporary quarters of an army, tribe, travellers, holiday-makers, or others; an ancient fortified site; a permanent military station, depot or training school; a settlement that has grown up rapidly, eg a mining town; a place where prisoners of war are detained; military service or life; an area of pasture that has been fenced off (*S Afr*); a place where sheep or cattle assemble (*Aust* and *NZ*); a party or group supporting a certain set of beliefs or doctrine. ◆ *vi* to encamp, or pitch tents; to live in a tent or in temporary or makeshift accommodation (often with *out*, ie in the open); (of sheep or cattle) to gather in a group (*Aust* and *NZ*). ◆ *vt* to put in a camp; to fence off (pasture) (*S Afr*). [Fr *camp* camp, from L *campus* a plain]

■ **camp'er** *n* a person who camps; a motor vehicle purpose-built, or which can be converted, for use as temporary living accommodation (also **camper van**). **camp'ing** *n*.

❑ **camp'-bed, -chair** or **-stool** *n* a portable folding bed, chair or stool. **camp'craft** *n* knowledge and skills useful when camping outdoors. **camp'-drafting** *n* (*Aust*) a competition in which stockmen on horseback display their skill in drafting cattle. **camp van** see **camper** above. **camp'-fever** *n* typhus, typhoid, or other fever tending to occur in camps with poor sanitary conditions. **camp'fire** *n* the outdoor fire of an encampment; a reunion, lodge, or section, of certain organizations. **camp-foll'ower** *n* a civilian who follows behind an army or works in a military camp, providing services for the military personnel; a person associated with a (political, etc) group without actually being a member. **camp'ground** *n* (*N Am*) an area set aside for camping. **camp-meet'ing** *n* a religious gathering in the open air or in a temporary encampment. **camp oven** *n* (*Aust* and *NZ*) a metal box used for baking over a campfire. **camp-preach'er** *n* a person who preaches at camp-meetings. **camp'site** *n* ground suitable, or specially laid out, for camping; an individual location on a campground (*N Am*).

■ **break camp** to pack up tents, equipment, etc and leave a camp. **camp on** (*telecom*) to put (a telephone call) through to an engaged extension, to be connected automatically when the extension is free. **camp out** to live temporarily in a tent or in the open air; to stay temporarily in improvised accommodation. **go camping** to spend a holiday living in a tent or tents in the countryside. **pitch camp** to set up a tent, etc on a campsite.

camp[2] /kamp/ *adj* theatrical, affected, exaggerated; effeminately homosexual; characteristic of homosexuals. ◆ *n* absurd and vulgar extravagance in manner, deliberate (**high camp**) or without full awareness of the effect (also *vi*). [Ety unknown]

■ **camp'ery** *n*. **camp'ly** *adv*. **camp'ness** *n*. **camp'y** *adj*.

■ **camp it up** to show camp qualities ostentatiously. **camp up** to make exaggerated, etc.

camp[3] /kamp/ (*obs*) *n* conflict; an old form of the game of football. ◆ *vi* to fight, struggle. [OE *camp* battle; cf Ger *Kampf*]

■ **cam'ple** *vi* to wrangle.

campagna /käm-pän'yä/ (*Ital*) *n* once equivalent to **champaign**, now only a geographical proper name.

campaign /kam-pān'/ *n* a series of co-ordinated operations designed to achieve a military objective, in or at a certain time, and influenced by factors such as geography, position and strength of the enemy, etc; military service in the field; an organized series of activities aimed at achieving some goal or object, as in advertising or in politics, *esp* before an election or in order to influence policy. ◆ *vi* to serve in or conduct a campaign (*usu* with *for* or *against*). [Fr *campagne*, from L *campania*, from *campus* a field]

■ **campaign'er** *n* a person actively involved in a political or other campaign; one who has served in several campaigns, a veteran (also **old campaigner**).

campana /kam-pä'nə/ *n* a bell-shaped object, such as the core of a Corinthian capital; a flower, perhaps the pasqueflower. [LL, a bell]

campanero /kam-pa-nā'rō/ *n* (*pl* **campane'ros**) the S American bell-bird or arapunga, having snowy-white plumage and a call like the peal of a church bell. [Sp, bellman]

campaniform /kam-pan'i-förm/ (*biol*) *adj* bell-shaped. [LL *campana* a bell, and **-form**]

campanile /kam-pa-nē'lā/ *n* (*pl* **campani'les**, or sometimes (*Ital*) **campani'li** /-lē/) a bell tower, *esp* a tall one detached from a church. [Ital from *campana* a bell]

campanist /kam'pə-nist/ *n* a person with an expert knowledge of bells. [Ety as for **campana**]

campanology /kam-pə-nol'ə-ji/ *n* the study of bells; the art of bellringing. [LL *campana* a bell, and **-ology**]

■ **campanolog'ical** *adj*. **campanol'ogist** *n*.

campanula /kam-pan'yŭ-lə/ *n* (*pl* **campan'ūlas**) a plant of the *Campanula* genus (giving its name to a family **Campanulā'ceae**) commonly known as bellflowers or bells, the best-known being the harebell or Scottish bluebell. [New L, from LL *campana* a bell]

■ **campanūlā'ceous** *adj*. **campan'ūlar** *adj*.

Campanularia /kam-pan-ū-lār'i-ə/ *n* a common genus of Hydrozoa with simple or branched stems and polyps surrounded by bell-shaped sheaths. [Ety as for **campanula**]

campanulate /kam-pan'yŭ-lāt* or *-lət/ *adj* bell-shaped. [LL *campana* a bell]

Campari /kam-pä'ri/ *n* a bitter-tasting, bright-red Italian apéritif flavoured with herbs. [Name of manufacturers; trade name in USA]

Campbellite /kam'bə-līt/ *n* a member of the US sect known as Disciples of Christ, founded by Alexander *Campbell* (1788–1866).

campeachy wood /kam-pē'chi wŭd/ *n* logwood, first exported from Campeachy (*Campeche*, in SE Mexico).

campeador /kam-pi-ə-dör'/ *n* a champion, *esp* the Cid. [Sp]

campesino /kam-pə-sē'nō/ *n* (*pl* **campesin'os**) a Latin-American peasant farmer. [Sp, from *campo* country, field, from L *campus* field]

campestral /kam-pes'trəl/ *adj* of or relating to fields or open country (also **campes'trian**). [L *campester*, from *campus* field]

camphire /kam'fīr/ *n* an old name for camphor; henna (*Bible*). [**camphor**]

camphone see **camera phone** under **camera**.

camphor /kam'fər/ *n* a solid essential oil, derived from the camphor laurel (a species of cinnamon tree) of Taiwan, etc, or synthetically manufactured, having an aromatic smell and bitter taste, used as a liniment in medicine, as a plasticizer, and as an insect repellent; any similar compound of the terpene series. [Fr *camphre*, from LL *camphora*, from Ar *kāfūr*]

■ **camphane** /kam'fān/ *n* a saturated terpene hydrocarbon ($C_{10}H_{18}$), parent substance of the camphor group. **camphene** /kam'fēn* or *-fēn'/ *n* an unsaturated camphor-like terpene hydrocarbon ($C_{10}H_{16}$) used in insecticides. **camphine** /kam'fēn* or *-fīn/ *n* an old name for rectified oil of turpentine. **camphorā'ceous** *adj* like camphor. **cam'phorate** *vt* to impregnate or treat with camphor. **camphoric** /-for'ik/ *adj* of or relating to camphor.

❑ **camphorated oil** *n* a liniment containing camphor, used to relieve irritation of the skin.

campimetry /kam-pim'ə-tri/ *n* a technique for assessing the field of vision. [L *campus* field, and Gr *metron* a measure]

campion /kam'pi-ən/ *n* any plant of the genera *Lychnis* and *Silene* having *usu* pink or white star- or salver-shaped flowers with notched petals. [Origin obscure; poss from obs *campion* champion]

cample see under **camp**[3].

campo /kam'pō/ *n* (*pl* **cam'pos**) an area of open grassland in S America, *esp* in Brazil. [Sp, from L *campus* a field]

campodeid /kam-pō'dē-id/ *n* a primitive wingless insect of the order Diplura having an elongated body and mouth parts hidden in the head. [Gr *kampē* caterpillar, and *eidos* form]

■ **campodē'iform** *adj* of or resembling the **Campodē'idae**, like certain six-legged, hard-bodied active insect larvae.

camporee /kam-pə-rē'/ *n* a local meeting of Scouts. [**camp**[1] and (*jamb*)*oree*]

campo santo /kam'pō san'tō/ (*Ital*) *n* a cemetery, literally sacred field.

camp-sheathing /kamp'shē'dhing/, **camp-shedding** /-shed'ing/, **camp-sheeting** /-shē'ting/ or **camp-shot** /-shot/ *n* piles and boarding protecting a river bank, etc. [Origin unknown]

Camptonite /kamp'tə-nīt/ *n* an igneous rock, a lamprophyre composed essentially of plagioclase and hornblende. [*Campton* in New Hampshire]

campus /kam'pəs/ *n* (*pl* **cam'puses**) university or college grounds; a self-contained division of a university; a university or college, *esp* one in which all the buildings are on a single site; the academic world. [L, field]

Campus Martius /kam'pəs mär'shəs, kam'pŭs mär'ti-ŭs/ (*L*) *n* a grassy plain used by the ancient Romans for athletic games, military drill, etc. [Field of Mars]

---

campylobacter /kam'pi-lō-bak-tər/ n a bacterium that is a common cause of gastroenteritis in humans, and also of abortion in cattle and sheep. [Gr *kampylos* bent, and *bacterion* a little rod (from its shape)] ■ **campylobactēriō'sis** n infection with campylobacter.

campylotropous /kam-pi-lot'rə-pəs/ (*bot*) adj (of an ovule) curved over so that the micropyle and stalk are at approximately right angles and the stalk appears to be attached to the side. [Gr *kampylos* curved, and *tropē* turning]

CAMRA /kam'rə/ abbrev : Campaign for Real Ale.

camsho /kam'shō/, **camshoch** or **camsheugh** /kam'shuhh/ (*Scot*) adj crooked or deformed. [Cf **cam¹**, and OE *sceolh* awry]

camstairy, camsteerie or **camsteary** /kam-stār'i or -stēr'i/ (chiefly *Scot*) adj perverse, unruly, quarrelsome. [Ety dubious]

camstone or **camstane** see under **cam³**.

camus¹ /kam'əs/ adj flat-nosed. [Prob Fr *camus*]

camus² see **camis**.

camwood /kam'wŭd/ n the wood of a W African tree (*Baphia nitida*) used in making a red dye. [Perh from Afr name *kambi*]

Can. abbrev : Canada; Canadian; Canal; Canberra (*Aust*).

can¹ /kan/ vt (*3rd pers* **can**; *pat* **could**; *obs 2nd pers sing prt* **canst**; *participle* obsolete except **could** in Scots; *infinitive* obsolete except in Scots) to be able; to have sufficient power; to have skill in; to be a possibility; used for *gan* in ME and in Spenser. [OE *cunnan* to know (how to do a thing), to be able; present indicative *can*; Gothic *kunnan*, Ger *können* to be able. See **con³**, **ken¹**, **know**; also **cannot**, **can't**, **couth¹**] □ **can-do'** adj (*inf*) denoting a willing and positive attitude. ■ **can do** (*inf*) I (or we) can do it, it can be done. **no can do** (*inf*) I (or we) can't do it, it can't be done.

can² /kan/ n a tin, a container of tin-plate in which meat, fruit, etc are sealed up to preserve them; a container for holding or carrying liquids, generally of tinned iron, with a handle over the top; the amount that a can holds (see also **canful** below); a container for various things, such as ashes or rubbish (*N Am*); a drinking-mug; a chimney pot; a cylindrical container for storing film; a jacket in which a fuel rod is sealed in an atomic reactor; a depth charge (*naval sl*); (with *the*) jail (*sl*); a lavatory (*sl*); the buttocks (*N Am sl*); (in *pl*) headphones (*sl*). ◆ vt (**cann'ing**; **canned**) to put into tins in order to preserve; to store in containers; to stop, put an end to (*N Am sl*; see also **can it** below); to dismiss or sack from a job (*N Am sl*); to record (music, etc) in advance. [OE *canne*] ■ **can'ful** n (*pl* **can'fuls**) the amount that a can holds. **canned** adj packed in tins; (of music, etc) recorded in advance for reproduction on a sound track or video, prerecorded; drunk (*sl*). **cann'er** n a person whose job it is to put foodstuffs in cans. **cann'ery** n a place where provisions are tinned. □ **can'bank** n the equivalent of a bottle bank for cans. **can buoy** n a cylindrical navigational buoy, painted black, that marks the port, or left side, of a channel (cf **nun buoy**). **can'-opener** n a tin-opener. ■ **can it** (*sl*) stop talking about, doing, etc that. **can of worms** an unpredictable and potentially difficult situation or problem. **carry the can** (*sl*) to take the blame or responsibility. **in the can** (of a motion picture, piece of music, etc) having been satisfactorily recorded, completed, etc, and ready for release; (of radio or TV material) recorded and stored for future use.

can. abbrev : canon (*music*); canto (*music*); canton.

Canaanite /kā'nə-nīt/ n one of the people of the ancient land of *Canaan*, on the eastern coast of the Mediterranean Sea. ◆ adj of or relating to Canaan.

cañada /kan-yä'də/ n a small narrow canyon, *esp* in the western USA. [Sp]

Canadian /kə-nā'di-ən/ adj of or relating to *Canada*. ◆ n a native or citizen of Canada. □ **Canada balsam** n a transparent resin obtained from the balsam fir, used, when cured, as a mounting medium for microscopic specimens. **Canada Day** n a Canadian public holiday, the anniversary of the union of the provinces, 1 July 1867 (formerly called **Dominion Day**). **Canada goose** n a common wild goose (*Branta canadensis*) of N America. **Canada lily** n a N American lily (*Lilium canadense*), with small yellow or orange bell-shaped flowers. **Canada rice** see **zizania**. **Canada thistle** n a European thistle (*Cirsium arvense*), now common as a fast-spreading weed throughout the northern USA (also **creeping thistle**). **Canadian canoe** n a long narrow canoe, pointed at both ends, that is propelled by hand-held single-bladed paddles. **Canadian football** n a game resembling American football, but with twelve players per side and a longer field of play. **Canadian French** n French as spoken in Canada. **Canadian pondweed** or **waterweed** n a N American aquatic plant (*Anacharis* or *Elodea canadensis*),

introduced into Europe and commonly used in ponds as an oxygenator.

canaigre /kə-nā'gər or kə-nī'grē/ n a large Texan dock plant (*Rumex hymenosepalus*), whose root is used in tanning. [Mex Sp]

canaille /ka-näy', ka-nī' or kə-nāl'/ n the mob, the vulgar rabble, the masses. [Fr, from L *canis* a dog]

Canajan /kan'a-jan/ (*Can inf*) n Canadian English.

canakin see **cannikin**.

canal /kə-nal'/ n an artificial watercourse, *esp* for navigation; a duct or passage that contains fluids (*biol*); a groove; any of the indistinct channel-like markings apparent on the surface of Mars when viewed through a telescope (*astron*). [L *canālis* a water pipe] ■ **canalicular** /kan-ə-lik'ū-lər/ adj like or relating to a canaliculus. **canalic'ulate** or **canalic'ulated** adj channelled, grooved or having furrows. **canalic'ulus** n (*pl* **canalic'ulī**) (*biol* and *anat*) a small furrow or channel, eg one that occurs in bone. **canalization** or **-s-** /kan-əl-ī-zā'shən/ n the construction of canals; the formation of an artificial channel; conversion into a canal; direction into a fixed channel (*lit* and *fig*). **can'alize** or **-ise** vt to make a canal through; to convert into a canal; to direct into a fixed channel (*lit* and *fig*). □ **canal'-boat** n a boat for use on canals. **canal'-cell** n (*bot*) a cell in the neck of an archegonium.

canapé /ka'nə-pi or -pā/ n a small biscuit or piece of pastry or bread, etc, with a savoury filling or spread, *usu* served with drinks; a sofa; a method of bidding in contract bridge in which a player bids a weak suit first, then rebids in his or her strongest suit. [Fr]

canard /ka-när(d)'/ n a false rumour, a hoax; a second wing fitted near the nose of an aircraft, *esp* one smaller than the main wing and acting as the horizontal stabilizer; an aircraft with such a wing. ◆ adj denoting such a wing, aircraft configuration, etc. [Fr, literally duck]

Canarese see **Kanarese**.

canary /kə-nā'ri/ n a songbird (finch) found in the *Canary* Islands, bright yellow in domestic breeds; a bright yellow colour (also **canary yellow**); a light sweet wine from the Canary Islands; a lively dance said to have originated in the Canary Islands (often in *pl*); an informer (*sl*); a convict (*obs Aust sl*); a guinea or sovereign (*obs sl*). ◆ adj canary-coloured, bright yellow. ◆ vi to dance the canary; to prance about. □ **canā'ry-bird** n a canary; a jailbird or convict (*sl*); a mistress. **canā'ry-creeper** n a S American climbing plant (*Tropaeolum peregrinum* or *canariense*), cultivated for its rapid growth and bright yellow flowers. **canā'ry-grass** n a grass (*Phalaris canariensis*) whose seed (**canā'ry-seed**) is used as bird seed. **canā'ry-wood** n the timber of two species of *Persea* or *Laurus* of the Canary Islands, Azores and Madeira.

canasta /kə-nas'tə/ n a card game similar to rummy, played with two full packs of cards, in which up to six players amass points by declaring sets of cards of the same rank; a set of seven or more cards of the same rank in canasta (also **meld**). [Sp, basket]

canaster /kə-nas'tər/ n a roughly broken kind of tobacco (so called from the rush basket in which it was *orig* imported from Spanish America). [Sp *canastra*, *canasta*, from Gr *kanastron*]

canc. abbrev : cancellation; cancelled.

cancan /kan'kan/ n an uproarious dance of French origin, *usu* performed on stage by women of the chorus and *orig* considered very improper because of the high kicking and raising of skirts. [Fr *cancan* chatter, scandal, the cancan; usu referred to L *quamquam*, the pronunciation of which was long hotly disputed by French intellectuals; poss connected with OFr *caquehan* a noisy assembly]

cancel /kan'səl/ vt (**can'celling** or (*N Am*) **can'celing**; **can'celled** or (*N Am*) **can'celed**) to annul or suppress; to revoke or discontinue; to abolish or call off; to counterbalance, compensate for or offset; to cross out or delete; (often with *out*) to eliminate as balancing each other, eg equal quantities from opposite sides of an equation, common factors from numerator and denominator of a fraction; to mark or stamp (eg a postage stamp) to prevent reuse. ◆ vi (with *out*) to neutralize each other; to call off a planned event. ◆ n the process of correcting a serious error in a book, etc by removing a printed leaf or sheet; the part so cancelled, or (*usu*) the new one substituted; a natural note (*music*; *US*). [L *cancellāre* to cross out, *cancellī* latticework, dimin of *cancer* a lattice] ■ **can'cellate** or **can'cellated** adj marked with a lattice-like pattern, reticulate; porous or spongy (*anat*). **cancellā'tion** n cancelling; a thing cancelled, eg a theatre ticket; crosswise marking. **can'celler** n. **cancelli** /kan-sel'ī or kang-kel'ē/ n pl crosspieces forming a latticework or grating, as in the division between the choir and the body of a church; reticulations (*anat*). **can'cellous** adj (*anat*) of bone, etc, having a spongy or porous structure.

□ **can'celbot** *n* a computer program that identifies and deletes unwanted articles sent to an Internet newsgroup.

cancelier or **canceleer** /kan-si-lēr'/ (*Walter Scott*) *vi* (of a hawk) to turn on the wing before stooping (also *n*).

cancellarial /kan-sə-lā'ri-əl/ or **cancellarian** /-ri-ən/ *adj* relating to a chancellor. [L *cancellārius*; see **chancellor**]
  ■ **cancellā'riate** *n* chancellorship.

Cancer /kan'sər/ *n* the genus to which the edible crab belongs; the Crab, a constellation giving its name to, and formerly coinciding with, a sign of the zodiac (*astron*); the fourth sign of the zodiac, between Gemini and Leo (*astrol*); a person born between 22 June and 23 July, under the sign of Cancer (*astrol*). See also **tropic**. [L, crab]
  ■ **Cancer'ian** *n* and *adj* (relating to or characteristic of) a person born under the sign of Cancer.
  ■ **first point of Cancer** the limit of the sun's course northward during summer in the northern hemisphere.

cancer /kan'sər/ *n* loosely, any malignant new growth or tumour; properly, a carcinoma or disorderly growth of epithelial cells which invade adjacent tissue and are frequently spread by the lymphatics and blood vessels to other parts of the body; any corroding evil or evil influence (*fig*). [L, crab, poss from the crablike blood vessels that radiate from a cancerous tumour]
  ■ **can'cerate** *vi* to become cancerous. **cancerā'tion** *n*. **can'cerous** *adj* of, like or affected with cancer. **cancerphobia** or **cancerophobia** /-fō'bi-ə/ *n* excessive fear of contracting, or that one may have, cancer.
  □ **cancer root** *n* beech-drops. **cancer stick** *n* (*sl*) a cigarette.

cancionero /kän-thyō-nā'rō/ *n* (*pl* **cancione'ros**) a collection of songs or poems, a songbook. [Sp]

cancriform /kang'kri-förm/ *adj* crab-shaped; like cancer. [**cancer** and **-form**]

cancrine /kang'krīn/ *adj* crabwise; (of verses, etc) reading both ways, palindromic. [L *cancer* crab (from the false notion that a crab walks backwards)]

cancrizans /kang'kri-zanz/ (*music*) *adj* of a canon, having the imitating vocal part repeating the theme backwards (see also **crab canon** under **crab**[1]). [L *cancrizāre* to move backwards (as crabs were believed to)]

cancroid /kang'kroid/ *adj* crablike; cancer-like. ◆ *n* a type of slow-growing skin cancer. [**Cancer**, **cancer** and **-oid**]

c and b (*cricket*) *abbrev*: caught and bowled (by).

candela /kan-del'ə or -dē'lə/ *n* (*pl* **candel'as**) a base SI unit, the unit of luminous intensity (symbol **cd**), defined as the luminous intensity in a given direction of a source that emits monochromatic radiation of frequency 540×10^{12} hertz and that has a radiant intensity in that direction of $\frac{1}{683}$ watt per steradian. [L *candēla* candle]

candelabrum /kan-di-lä'brəm or -lä'/ *n* (*pl* **candela'bra** also used as a false singular with *pl* **candela'bras**) a branched and ornamented candlestick or lampstand. [L *candēlābrum*, from *candēla* candle]
  □ **candelabrum tree** *n* any of several African trees with branches arranged like a candelabrum.

candelilla /kän-dā-lē'lya/ *n* a Mexican wax-yielding spurge. [Sp, dimin of *candela* candle]

candescent /kan-des'ənt/, also (*archaic*) **candent** /kan'dənt/ *adj* glowing; white-hot. [L *candēre* to glow (inceptive *candēscere*)]
  ■ **candescence** /kan-des'əns/ *n* a white heat.

candf *abbrev*: cost and freight.

C and G *abbrev*: City and Guilds Institute.

candid /kan'did/ *adj* frank, ingenuous; unposed, unrehearsed, informal; free from prejudice, unbiased; fair, impartial; white (*obs*); shining, clear (*obs*). [L *candidus* white]
  ■ **can'didly** *adv*. **can'didness** *n*.
  □ **candid camera** *n* a camera used for taking unposed photographs or films of people (*usu* without their knowledge) engaged in the normal activities of their daily life; this style of photography.

candida /kan'di-də/ *n* a member of the genus *Candida* of parasitic, yeastlike imperfect fungi. [L *candida*, fem of *candidus* white]
  ■ **can'didal** *adj*. **candidiasis** /kan-di-dī'ə-sis/ *n* an infection of the skin or mucous membranes caused by a candida (*usu C. albicans*, which causes thrush).

candidate /kan'di-dāt or -dət/ *n* a person who seeks or is nominated for any office or honour or who applies for a job, promotion, etc; a person or thing apparently suitable for a particular end; an examinee. [L *candidātus* dressed in white (because in Ancient Rome, candidates for election wore white togas), from *candidus* white]
  ■ **can'didature, can'didateship** or **can'didacy** /-də-si/ *n*.

candie see **candy**[2].

candied see under **candy**[1].

candiru /kan-di-roo'/ *n* a tiny S American fish (*Vandellia cirrhosa*) which can swim into a body orifice, where it attaches itself by means of a spine and feeds on blood and body tissue. [Tupí *kandirú*]

candle /kan'dl/ *n* a block, *usu* a cylinder, of wax, tallow or the like surrounding a wick, burned to give light; something resembling this in appearance or function; a photometric unit; (also **new candle**) candela; (**international candle** or **standard candle**) a former unit of luminous intensity; a jet in a gas stove; a luminary (*literary*). ◆ *vt* to test (an egg) for freshness by holding up before a candle or other light. [OE *candel*, from L *candēla*, from *candēre* to glow]
  ■ **can'dler** *n*.
  □ **can'dleberry** *n* the wax myrtle or bayberry (*Myrica cerifera*), or its fruit. **candle bomb** *n* a small glass container filled with water, that explodes when placed in a candle flame. **can'dle-coal** same as **cannel**. **can'dle-dipping** *n* the method of making candles by dipping instead of moulding. **can'dle-doup** see under **doup**. **can'dle-end** *n* the end-piece of a burned-out candle. **can'dlefish** *n* see **eulachon**; a W American fish, *Anaplopoma fimbria*, cheek-armoured and spiny-finned, the *black candlefish*. **can'dle-holder** *n* a candlestick or candelabrum; a person who holds a candle to provide light for another while working or reading; hence someone who abets, connives or assists. **can'dlelight** *n* the light of a candle; illumination by candles; the time when candles are lighted, dusk. **can'dle-lighter** *n* a person whose job it is to light candles; a spill. **can'dlelit** *adj* lit by candles; done or performed by the light of candles. **can'dlenut** *n* the oil-yielding fruit of a species of a tropical tree (*Aleurites mollucana*) of the Pacific Islands. **can'dle-paring** *adj* miserly, stingy or parsimonious. **can'dle-power** *n* the illuminating power of a source of light; a former name for luminous intensity. **can'dle-snuffer** *n* a person or device that snuffs out candles (see **snuff**[2]; also *fig*). **can'dlestick** *n* a portable stand for a candle, *orig* a stick or piece of wood. **can'dle-tree** *n* a tropical American tree (*Parmientiera cerifera*) with candle-like pods. **can'dle-waster** *n* (*old sl*) someone who studies late. **can'dlewick** *n* a soft cotton tufted material used for bedspreads, etc; the wick of a candle. **can'dlewood** *n* the wood of various West Indian and Mexican resinous trees.
  ■ **burn the candle at both ends** to exhaust oneself by attempting to do too much, *usu* by going to bed late and getting up early for work. **do a candle** of a parachute, to fail to open out properly. **not fit to hold a candle to** (*derog*) not to be compared with; very inferior to. **sell by the candle** (*hist*) to offer for sale by auction as long as a small piece of candle burns, the successful bid being the one made just before it goes out. **the game is not worth the candle** the thing is not worth the effort or expense required.

Candlemas /kan'dl-məs/ *n* the church festival of the purification of the Virgin Mary, on 2 February, when candles are blessed; a quarter day in Scotland (now fixed as 28 February). [**candle** and **mass**]

candock /kan'dok/ *n* the yellow water lily. [**can**[2] and **dock**[3]]

Candomble or **Candomblé** /kän-dəm-blā'/ *n* a Brazilian religion combining African traditions with elements derived from Christianity. [Port *candomblé* ritual drum music; of Bantu origin]

candour or (*N Am*) **candor** /kan'dər/ *n* frankness and openness; sincerity; freedom from prejudice, impartiality; purity (*obs*); kindness (*obs*); whiteness (now *rare*). [Fr *candeur*, from L *candor* whiteness, from *candēre* to shine]

CANDU or **Candu** /kan'doo/ (*nuclear eng*) *n* a type of thermal nuclear power reactor using unenriched uranium oxide as fuel and heavy water as moderator, developed by and widely used in Canada. [*Ca*nada, *d*euterium and *u*ranium]

C and W *abbrev*: country-and-western (music).

candy[1] /kan'di/ *n* a sweet of sugar boiled and crystallized (also **su'gar-can'dy**); any form of confectionery (*N Am*; *pl* **can'dies**); any hard drug, eg cocaine (*sl*). ◆ *vt* to preserve or coat with sugar; to crystallize (sugar, etc); to encrust. ◆ *vi* to crystallize; to become encrusted. [Fr *candi*, from Ar *qandah* candy]
  ■ **can'died** *adj* encrusted or preserved with sugar; sugared, flattering (*obs*).
  □ **candy apple** *n* (*N Am*) a toffee apple. **can'dy-ass** *n* (*US sl*) a weak or feeble person. **can'dyfloss** or (*N Am*) **cotton candy** *n* a fluffy ball of spun sugar, coloured and flavoured, sold on the end of a stick; something insubstantial or ephemeral (also *adj*). **can'dyman** *n* (*N Am sl*) a drug pusher. **candy store** *n* (*N Am*) a sweet shop or confectioner's. **candy stripe** *n* a textile fabric pattern, consisting of narrow coloured stripes on a white background at intervals equal or nearly equal to the width of the stripe. **can'dy-striped** *adj* patterned in this way. **can'dy-striper** *n* (*N Am inf*) a female volunteer hospital nurse (from the red and white striped uniform).

---

candy[2] /kan'di/ n a S Indian weight, generally containing 20 maunds, *approx* 500 imperial pounds (also **can'die** or **kan'dy**). [Tamil]

candytuft /kan'di-tuft/ n a cruciferous plant of the genus *Iberis*, with flowers in tufts or corymbs, the outer petals larger than the inner. [From *Candia* Crete, where a species was found, and **tuft**]

cane /kān/ n the stem of one of the small palms (eg calamus or rattan) or the larger grasses (eg bamboo or sugarcane), or raspberry or the like; sugarcane; wicker, rattan, etc used to weave baskets or light furniture; a slender stick used as a support for plants, etc; a slender, flexible rod used for beating, *esp*, formerly, as a school punishment; a walking-stick. ◆ vt to beat with a cane; to defeat thoroughly (*inf*); to make or weave (eg chairs) with canes. [Fr *canne*, from L *canna*, from Gr *kannē* a reed]
■ **caned** adj (*inf*) intoxicated by drink or drugs. **can'er** n. **can'ing** n a thrashing with a cane; a severe beating or defeat (*inf*). **can'y** adj like, made of, or abounding in cane.
❑ **cane'-bottomed** adj (of a chair, etc) having a seat of interwoven cane strips. **cane'brake** n a thicket of canes, *esp* (in southern USA) of a giant reed. **cane'-chair** n a chair made of rattan. **cane'fruit** n fruit borne upon canes, such as raspberries and blackberries. **cane grass** n (*Aust*) any of several long-stemmed grasses growing in swamps and marshes. **cane'-mill** n a mill for crushing sugarcane. **cane piece** n (*W Indies*) a field of sugarcane, *esp* one belonging to a peasant farmer. **cane rat** n a tropical African rat of the genus *Thryonomys* that lives in swampy regions and is often a pest of sugar plantations. **cane sugar** n sucrose, *esp* that obtained from the sugar-cane. **cane'-toad** n (*Aust*) the large toad (*Bufo marinus*) introduced to Queensland, and now abundant in Australia. **cane'-trash** n refuse of sugar-cane used for fuel when boiling the juice.

caneh see **kaneh**.

canella /ka-nel'ə/ n any of the low aromatic trees of the genus *Canella*, of the family **Canellā'ceae** /-si-ē/, *esp C. winterana* of the West Indies which yields white cinnamon or **canella bark**; cinnamon (*obs*). [LL, dimin of *canna* reed]

canellini see **cannellini**.

canephor /kan'i-för, -för/ (*archit*) n a sculptured figure carrying a basket on the head (also **cane'phora**, **can'ephore** or **canephorus** /ka-nē'for-əs/). [Gr *kanēphoros* a basket bearer, as at the Panathenaic festival, from *kaneon* basket and *phoros* bearing]

canescent /ka-nes'ənt/ adj tending to or becoming white or grey; hoary. [L *cānēscēns*, from *cānēre*, from *cānus* hoary]
■ **canesc'ence** n.

Canes Venatici /kā'nēz və-nat'i-sī/ n a faint constellation in the northern hemisphere close to Ursa Major. [L, hunting dogs]

canfield /kan'fēld/ (*cards*) n a game adapted from patience in which money is gambled on the turn of each card. [RA *Canfield* (1855–1914), US gambler]

cang see **cangue**.

cangle /kang'gl/ (*Scot*) n noise or disturbance; a dispute. ◆ vi to argue or wrangle. [Cf Norw *kjangle* to quarrel]

cangue or **cang** /kang/ n formerly a Chinese portable pillory carried on the shoulders by petty offenders. [Fr *cangue*, from Port *cango* a yoke]

canicular /ka-nik'ū-lər/ adj relating to Sirius, the Dog Star (**Canic'ula**). [L *canīculāris*, adj, and *canīcula*, dimin of *canis* a dog]
❑ **canicular days** n pl the dog days. **canicular period** or **cycle** same as **Sothic period** or **cycle** (see under **Sothic**). **canicular year** same as **Sothic year** (see under **Sothic**).

canid /kan'id/ (*zool*) n a member of the genus *Canis*, or of the family **Can'idae** /-i-dē/, including dogs, wolves, foxes and jackals. [New L *Canidae*, from L *canis* dog]

canikin see **cannikin**.

canine /kā'nīn or kan'īn/ adj like or relating to the dog or related species. ◆ n any animal of the dog family; a canine tooth. [L *canīnus*, from *canis* a dog]
■ **caninity** /kə- or kā-nin'i-ti/ n.
❑ **canine appetite** n a huge appetite. **canine distemper** see **distemper**[1]. **canine letter** n R (from its growling sound). **canine tooth** n one of four sharp-pointed teeth between the incisors and the pre-molars.

Canis /kan'is/ n the dog genus, typical of the family **Canidae**. [L, dog]

Canis Major /kan'is mā'jər/ n (genitive (L) **Canis Majoris** /mə-jö'ris/) a constellation in the southern hemisphere containing Sirius, the Dog Star. [L, greater dog]

Canis Minor /kan'is mī'nər/ n (genitive (L) **Canis Minoris** /mi-nö'ris/) a constellation in the northern hemisphere near Gemini and Orion. [L, lesser dog]

canister /kan'i-stər/ n a box or case, *usu* of metal, for holding tea, shot, etc. [L *canistrum* a wicker basket; Gr *kanastron*, from *kannē* a reed]

■ **can'ister**, **can'isterize** or **-ise** vt to put into, pack in, a canister or canisters. **canisteriza'tion** or **-s-** n.
❑ **canister shot** n (*hist*) metal shot enclosed in an artillery projectile which explodes when fired, case-shot.

canker /kang'kər/ n an ulcer; ulceration; a fungal disease in trees and shrubs; inflammation in horses' feet; irritation and ulceration in dogs' and cats' ears; an abscess or ulcer in birds; anything that corrupts, consumes, irritates or decays; a cankerworm; a dog rose (*Shakesp*). ◆ vt to eat into, corrupt or destroy; to infect or pollute; to make sour and ill-conditioned. ◆ vi to grow corrupt; to decay. [L *cancer* a crab]
■ **cank'ered** adj malignant, soured, crabbed; corroded (*obs*); polluted (*obs*). **cank'eredly** adv. **cank'eredness** n. **cank'erous** adj corroding like a canker. **cank'ery** adj affected with canker; crabbed (*Scot*).
❑ **cank'erworm** n a larva that feeds on and destroys plants, *esp* fruit.

cann same as **con**[4].

canna[1] /kan'ə/ n a tropical or subtropical plant of the genus *Canna*, several species being cultivated for their showy asymmetrical reddish-orange flowers. [L, a reed]

canna[2] see **cannot**.

canna[3] /kan'ə/ or **cannach** /kan'əhh/ (*Scot*) n cotton grass. [Gaelic *canach*]

cannabis /kan'ə-bis/ n hemp, a plant of the *Cannabis* genus, *esp C. sativa* (common hemp) and *C. indica* (Indian hemp); a narcotic or mood-altering drug, variously known as hashish, bhang, marijuana, etc, obtained from the cannabis plant. [Gr *kannabis*; cf OE *hænep*]
■ **cann'abic** adj. **cann'abin** n a resin obtained from the dried leaves and flowers of the cannabis plant, containing the active principle of the drug (also **cannabis resin**). **cann'abinoid** n any of a number of substances found in cannabin, having narcotic or mood-altering properties. **cann'abinol** n a crystalline phenol obtained from cannabin.

cannae see **cannot**.

cannel /kan'əl/ n a bituminous coal that burns with a bright flame, used for making oils and gas (also **cann'el-coal** or **can'dle-coal**). [Prob form of **candle**]

cannellini or **canellini** /ka-nə-lē'nē/ n pl the white haricot beans used in French and Italian cooking (also **can(n)ellini beans**). [Ital]

cannelloni /ka-nə-lō'nē/ n pl hollow tubes of pasta, stuffed with cheese, meat, etc. [Ital *cannelloni*, augmentative of *cannello* small tube]

cannelure /kan'i-lyoor/ n a groove or a fluting; a groove round the cylindrical part of a bullet. [Fr]

cannibal /kan'i-bl/ n any eater of the flesh of its own species. ◆ adj relating to or practising cannibalism. [Sp *Canibal, Caribal* Carib]
■ **cann'ibalism** n the practice of eating one's own kind. **cannibalist'ic** adj. **cannibalist'ically** adv. **cannibaliza'tion** or **-s-** n. **cann'ibalize** or **-ise** vt to repair (a vehicle, aircraft, machine, etc) with parts taken from other vehicles, etc; to take (parts), or take parts from (vehicles, aircraft, machines), for such repairs. **cann'ibally** adv (*Shakesp*).

cannikin /kan'i-kin/ n a small can (also **can'akin** or **can'ikin**). [Dimin of **can**]

cannoli /kə-nō'li/ n pl a dessert of fried pastry tubes with a creamy filling containing ricotta. [Ital]

cannon /kan'ən/ n a great gun *usu* mounted on wheels (*hist*; pl **cann'ons** or **cann'on**); a rapid-firing, large-calibre gun fitted to an aeroplane, ship or helicopter gunship (pl **cann'ons** or **cann'on**); a heavy tube or drum, *esp* one able to rotate freely on a shaft; a cannon bone; a cannon bit; a stroke in which the cue ball hits both the red and the opponent's ball (also *esp N Am*) **carom**; *billiards*); a similar stroke in snooker and certain other games; the metal loop at the top of a bell. ◆ vi to cannonade; to make a cannon (*billiards* and *snooker*); to strike on the rebound; to collide (*usu* with into). ◆ vt to collide with. [Fr *canon*, augmentative, from L *canna* a reed]
■ **cannonade'** n an attack with heavy artillery. ◆ vt and vi to attack or batter continuously with heavy artillery. **cannoneer'** or **cannonier'** n a soldier who managed and fired a cannon (*hist*); an artilleryman. **cann'onry** n an attack or volley of heavy artillery fire; artillery.
❑ **cann'onball** n a ball to be shot from a cannon (*hist*); something resembling this in appearance, weight or force, eg a fast serve in tennis. ◆ vi to move rapidly with great force. **can'nonball-tree** n a S American tree (*Couroupita guianensis*) with a large woody fruit. **cannon bit** n a smooth round bit (of a bridle). **cannon bone** n a bone below the knee or hock in hoofed mammals, formed by the fusion of the persisting metacarpals or metatarsals; (in birds) the tarsometatarsus. **cannon fodder** n men in a (*usu*) large army, regarded merely as material to be expended in war. **cann'on-game** n a form of billiards in which, the table having no pockets, the game consists in making a series of cannons. **cann'on-metal** n gun-metal. **cann'on-proof** adj able to withstand cannon-shot.

cann'on-shot *n* a cannonball; the distance to which a cannon will throw a cannonball.

cannot /kan'ət/ *v* can not (contracted to **can't** /känt/, *Scot* **canna** /kan'ā or kan'ə/ or **cannae** /kan'ā/). [**can**[1] and **not**]

cannula or **canula** /kan'yū-lə/ (*surg*) *n* (*pl* **can**(**n**)'**ulae** /-ū-lē/ or **can**(**n**)'**ulas**) a narrow tube, *esp* one for removing fluid from bodily cavities, or the breathing tube inserted in the windpipe after tracheotomy. [*Dimin* of *canna* a reed]

■ **cann'ular** or **cann'ulate** *adj*. **cann'ulate** *vt* to insert a cannula into. **cannulā'tion** *n*.

canny /kan'i/ *adj* knowing; skilful; shrewd, *esp* in business; sparing in money matters; lucky or fortunate (*Scot*); gentle; innocent; good or nice (*Scot and N Eng*); sly or pawky. ◆ *adv* in a canny manner. [*Appar* connected with **can**[1]]

■ **cann'ily** *adv*. **cann'iness** *n*.
■ **ca' canny** see under **ca'**. **no' canny** preternatural; dangerous.

canoe /kə-noo'/ *n* a light, narrow, flat-bottomed boat, propelled by one or more paddles (*orig* made of a hollowed tree trunk, or of bark or skins). ◆ *vi* to paddle a canoe; to travel in a canoe. [Sp *canoa*, from Haitian *canoa*]

■ **canoe'ing** *n*. **canoe'ist** *n*.
■ **in the same canoe** (*NZ*) of, or belonging to, the same tribe. **paddle one's own canoe** see under **paddle**[2].

canola /kə-nō'lə/ *n* an oil derived from the seed of any of several varieties of the rape plant, used in cooking; any of the plants from which this oil is made. [*Can*adian *o*il *l*ow *a*cid]

canon[1] /kan'ən/ *n* a law or rule, *esp* in ecclesiastical matters; a generally accepted rule or principle, eg in morals; a standard or criterion; the books of the Bible accepted as the standard or rule of faith by the Jewish or Christian faiths; works forming any similar standard; a series of prayers in the Mass during which the Host is consecrated (*RC*); the recognized genuine works of any author; a type of vocal or instrumental musical composition in which the melody is repeated by one part following another in imitation; a list of the canonized saints; formerly a large size of type (*printing*). [OE *canon*, from L *canōn*, from Gr *kanōn* a straight rod, from *kannē* a reed]

■ **canonic** /kə-non'ik/ or **canon'ical** *adj* of the nature of, according to, or included in a canon; regular; orthodox or accepted; ecclesiastical. **canon'ically** *adv*. **canon'icals** *n pl* the official dress of the clergy, regulated by the church canons. **canonicity** /kan-ən-is'i-ti/ *n* the state of belonging to the canon. **can'onist** *n* a person learned in canon law. **canonist'ic** *adj*. **canonizā'tion** or **-s-** *n*. **can'onize** or **-ise** (also (*Shakesp*) /-non'/) *vt* to enrol in the canon or list of saints; to recognize as canonical.

□ **canonical hours** *n pl* set hours for prayer or the services prescribed for these times in the Roman Catholic Church, traditionally listed as matins, lauds, prime, terce, sext, none, vespers and compline); any time between 8am and 6pm, when marriages may take place in an English parish church (*C of E*). **canon law** *n* a digest of the formal decrees of councils, ecumenical, general and local, of diocesan and national synods, and of patriarchal decisions concerning religious doctrine and discipline. **canon lawyer** *n* a canonist.

■ **canon of the mass** that part of the mass that begins after the 'Sanctus' with the prayer 'Te igitur', and ends just before the 'Paternoster'.

canon[2] /kan'ən/ *n* a member of a body of clergymen serving a cathedral or other church and living under a rule; a clerical dignitary belonging *esp* to a cathedral, enjoying special emoluments, and obliged to reside there part of the year. [OE *canonic*, from L *canonicus*, from *canōn*; see **canon**[1]]

■ **can'oness** *n* a member of a community of women living under a religious rule but not under a vow; a woman holding a prebend or canonry, often living in the secular world. **canon'icate** *n* the rank or office of a canon. **can'onry** *n* the office or benefice of a canon; canons collectively; (often with *cap*) a building in which a canon resides.

□ **canon regular** *n* a member of either of two religious orders (Augustinian or Black Canons, and Premonstratensian or White Canons) who live in communities as monks but perform the duties of secular clergy. **canon residentiary** *n* a canon obliged to reside at a cathedral and take a share in the duty. **canon secular** *n* a canon who is not a canon regular.

■ **honorary canon** a person with the titular rank of canon in a cathedral, but without duties or emoluments. **minor canon** a person who conducts cathedral services but is not a member of the chapter.

cañon see **canyon**.

canoodle /kə-noo'dl/ (*inf*) *vi* to kiss and cuddle. [Origin obscure]

canophilist /kə-nof'i-list/ or **cynophilist** /si- or sī-/ (often *facetious*) *n* a lover of dogs. [L *canis* and Gr *kyon*, *kynos*, a dog, and Gr *phileein* to love]

■ **canophilia** /kan-ō-fil'i-ə/ or **cynophilia** /sin- or sīn-/ *n* love of dogs.

canophobia /ka-nō-fō'bi-ə/ or **cynophobia** /si- or sī-/ *n* morbid fear of dogs. [L *canis* and Gr *kyon*, *kynos* a dog, and Gr *phobos* fear]

Canopus /kə-nō'pəs/ *n* the brightest star in the southern constellation *Carina*; an ancient Egyptian vase with a carved top or stopper in the form of a human or animal head, for holding the entrails taken from a body during the embalming process (also **Canopic jar**, **vase** or **urn**). [L, from Gr *Kanōpos*, Menelaus's steersman who died at Canopus in Egypt, was transformed into the star Canopus, and identified with an Egyptian god worshipped in the form of a jar with a human head]

■ **Cano'pic** *adj*.

canopy /kan'ə-pi/ *n* a covering hung over a throne, bed, etc; a ceremonial covering held over the head; any overhanging covering, such as the sky; the topmost layer of branches and foliage in a forest; a rooflike projection over a niche, tomb, statue, stall, altar, etc; the transparent cover over the cockpit of an aircraft; the overhead fabric part of a parachute. ◆ *vt* (**can'opying**; **can'opied**) to cover with a canopy. [Fr *canapé*, from L *cōnōpium*, *cōnōpēum*, from Gr *kōnōpion* a couch with a mosquito curtain, from *kōnōps* a mosquito]

canorous /ka-nō'rəs or -nō'-, also kan'ō- or kan'ö-/ (*formal*) *adj* musical; singing; resonant. [L *canōrus*, from *canor* melody, from *canere* to sing]

■ **cano'rously** (or /kan'/) *adv*. **cano'rousness** (or /kan'/) *n*.

canst see **can**[1].

canstick /kan'stik/ (*Shakesp*) *n* a candlestick. [Contraction]

Cant. *abbrev* : Canterbury; Canticles.

cant[1] /kant/ *vi* to speak in a whining or wheedling manner; to use language whose meaning has evaporated from continued repetition; to use the specialized vocabulary or jargon of thieves, politicians, lawyers, etc; to talk in an affectedly solemn or hypocritical way. ◆ *n* a hypocritical, affected or perfunctory style of speech or thought; the vocabulary or language peculiar to a particular group or sect; odd or peculiar talk of any kind; slang; a common saying or stock phrase; affected use of religious phrases or moral sentiments. ◆ *adj* of or relating to cant. [L *cantāre*, frequentative of *canere* to sing]

■ **cant'er** *n* a person who cants, *esp* a beggar; a person who makes hypocritical or affected statements. **cant'ing** *adj* whining, pretending to piety. **cant'ingly** *adv*.

□ **canting arms** *n pl* (*heraldry*) a coat of arms in the form of a rebus, or a visual pun on the bearer's surname.

cant[2] /kant/ *n* an inclination from the vertical or horizontal plane; a toss or jerk which tilts or turns anything; a sloping or tilted position or face; one of the segments forming a side-piece in the head of a cask; a ship's timber lying obliquely to the line of the keel. ◆ *vt* and *vi* to turn on the edge or corner; to tilt or toss suddenly; to tilt or slope. —Also spelt **kant**. [Prob connected with Du *kant* ; Ger *Kante* corner]

■ **cant'ed** *adj* tilted, sloping. **cant'ing** *n* tilting.

□ **cant'-board** *n* a sloping board. **cant'dog** or **cant'hook** *n* (*forestry*) a metal hook on a long handle, for rolling logs. **canted deck** *n* (*aeronautics*) see **angled deck** under **angle**[1]. **cant'ing-coin** *n* a piece of wood to prevent casks rolling. **cant'ing-wheel** *n* a wheel with bevelled cogs. **cant'-rail** *n* a timber supporting the roof of a railway carriage.

cant[3] /kant/ *n* sale by auction. ◆ *vt* to sell by auction. [OFr *encant* auction; origin uncertain, cf LL *incantāre* to put up to auction]

cant[4] /kant/ (*Scot and N Eng*) *adj* brisk; lively; merry. [Cf LGer *kant*, and **canty**]

can't contraction of **cannot**.

Cantab. /kan'tab/ *abbrev* : *Cantabrigiensis* (L), of Cambridge.

cantabank /kan'tə-bangk/ *n* a strolling singer. [Ital *cantambanco*]

cantabile /kan-tä'bē-lā/ (*music*) *adj* and *adv* flowing and melodious, like singing (also *n*). [Ital, suitable for singing]

Cantabrigian /kan-tə-brij'i-ən/ *adj* of or relating to Cambridge or Cambridge University. ◆ *n* a member of staff, graduate or undergraduate of Cambridge University. [LL *Cantabrigia* Cambridge]

Cantal /kan'tal or kä'tal/ *n* a hard, full-fat French cheese made from cow's milk, from the *Cantal* department of the Auvergne.

cantala /kan'ta-lə/ *n* a coarse fibre used in making strong thread or twine, obtained from a tropical American plant (*Agave cantala*). [Origin unknown]

cantaloupe or **cantaloup** /kan'tə-loop/ *n* a small musk melon with a ribbed skin; in the USA, any of several varieties of cultivated melon. [Fr, from Ital *Cantalupo*, near Rome, where it was first grown in Europe]

cantankerous /kan-tang'kə-rəs/ *adj* irascible; contrary, quarrelsome or stubborn. [Perh ME *contek* strife]

■ **cantan'kerously** *adv*. **cantan'kerousness** *n*.

■ words derived from main entry word; □ compound words; ■ idioms and phrasal verbs

cantar same as **kantar**.

cantata /kan-tä'tə/ n orig the name applied to a sort of musical narrative by one person, accompanied by a single instrument; since the later introduction of an air, the modern concert aria; now also a choral work, a short oratorio or opera intended for concert performance only. [Ital, from L *cantāre*, frequentative of *canere* to sing]

■ **cantatrice** /kan-ta-trē'chä or kan'tə-trēs/ n a female singer.

cantate /kan-tä'tā or -tä'tē/ n Psalm 98, from its opening words in Latin, 'Cantate Domino'.

canteen /kan-tēn'/ n a flask for carrying liquids, used by soldiers, etc; a set of cooking utensils for soldiers, campers, etc; a box containing a set of knives, forks and spoons; a set of cutlery; a cafeteria or small shop for soldiers; a restaurant attached to an office, factory, etc; a public house (S Afr). [Fr *cantine*, from Ital *cantina* a cellar]

□ **canteen culture** n (inf) a system of behaviour said to exist in certain, *usu* male-dominated, organizations, promoting loyalty to the group and discriminating against outsiders.

■ **wet** or **dry canteen** one in which alcoholic drinks are, or are not, sold.

cante jondo or **cante hondo** /kän'tä hhon'dō/ (Sp) n an emotional and melancholy type of song sung *esp* by Andalusian gypsies. [Sp, intense song]

canter /kan'tər/ n an easy gallop. ◆ vi to move at an easy gallop. ◆ vt to make (a horse, etc) canter. [Orig *Canterbury-gallop*, from the easy pace at which the pilgrims rode to Canterbury]

canterbury /kan'tər-bə-ri/ n (pl **can'terburys** or **can'terburies**) a stand with divisions in it for holding books, music, etc.

□ **Canterbury bell** n orig the nettle-leaved bellflower, or throatwort; now applied to a cultivated biennial plant (*Campanula medium*) with large blue, white, or pink bell-like flowers; loosely applied to other large-flowered bellflowers. **Canterbury lamb** n frozen or chilled New Zealand lamb imported by the UK.

cantharis /kan'thə-ris/ n a blister beetle or Spanish fly (*Lytta vesicatoria*); (in pl **cantharides** /kan-thar'i-dēz/) a blistering agent and stimulant made from their dried bodies, formerly also used as an aphrodisiac. [L *cantharis*, from Gr *kantharis* (a blister beetle), pl *kantharides*]

■ **can'tharid** n a member of the family Cantharidae, the soldier beetles. **canthar'idal**, **cantharid'ian** or **cantharid'ic** adj. **canthar'idin** n the active compound secreted by blister beetles.

cantharus /kan'thə-rəs/ n (pl **can'tharī**) a large two-handled drinking cup; a laver in the atrium at the front of ancient churches. [L, from Gr *kantharos*]

canthaxanthin /kan-thə-zan'thin/ or **canthaxanthine** /kan'thə-zan'thēn/ (chem) n an orange dye, formerly widely used as a food additive in salmon and eggs to enhance colour, now banned in many countries because of its link with certain cancers.

canthus /kan'thəs/ n (pl **can'thī**) the angle where the upper and lower eyelids meet. [L, from Gr *kanthos*]

canticle /kan'ti-kl/ n a song; a non-metrical hymn, *esp* one used in a church service, such as the Magnificat; a canto (Spenser); a short canto; (in pl; *usu* with cap) the Song of Solomon (also **Canticle of Canticles**). [L *canticum*, dimin *canticulum*]

■ **can'ticum** n a canticle; a part-song in an ancient play.

cantico, **canticoy** see **kantikoy**.

cantilena /kan-ti-lē'nə/ n a ballad or light song; a vocal or instrumental melody; a canto fermo or melody for church use; a singing exercise or solfeggio. [L *cantilēna*]

cantilever /kan'ti-lēv-ər or -lēv'/ n a support or beam fixed at one end and free at the other; a large bracket for supporting cornices, balconies, and stairs. ◆ vt to construct (a support or beam) so that it is fixed at one end only. ◆ vi to project or support like a cantilever. [Perh **cant²**, and **lever**]

■ **can'tilevered** adj.

□ **cantilever bridge** n a bridge constructed of beams or cantilevers built into piers at each end of the span and connected together in the middle of the span.

cantillate /kan'ti-lāt/ vt and vi to chant or intone, *esp* Hebrew scriptures in the Jewish liturgical service. [L *cantillāre* to sing softly, from *cantāre* to sing]

■ **cantillā'tion** n. **can'tillatory** adj.

cantina /kan-tē'nə/ n a bar or saloon; a wine shop. [Sp and Ital]

cantion /kan'shən/ (Spenser) n a song. [L *cantiō, -ōnis*]

cantle /kan'tl/ n a corner, edge or slice of anything; the raised hind part of a saddle; the crown of the head (Scot). ◆ vt to cut or break a piece from; to divide. [**cant²**]

■ **cant'let** n a fragment.

canto /kan'tō/, also (Shakesp) **canton** /kan'ton/ n (pl **can'tos** or **can'tons**) a division of a long poem; the part in a piece of music that carries the melody; the highest part in a piece of choral music (also **can'tus**). [Ital *canto*, from L *cantus*, from *canere* to sing]

□ **canto fermo** /fûr'mō/ n plainsong, the unornamented melody used in the Western Church from the earliest times, to which later other parts in counterpoint were added.

canton¹ /kan'tən or kan-ton'/ n a division of territory, constituting in Switzerland a separate government, in France a subdivision of an arrondissement; a pilastered or quoined corner of a building (archit); (on a shield) an ordinary, ie a square occupying generally the dexter, sometimes the sinister, chief of the field (heraldry); a corner (obs); a division or space (obs). ◆ vt (**can'toning**; **can'toned**) to divide into cantons; /kən-toon'/ to allot quarters to (military personnel). [OFr *canton*; Ital *cantone* corner, district, from *canto* a corner; cf **cant²**]

■ **can'tonal** adj relating to or divided into cantons. **can'toned** adj ornamented at the corners with projecting pilasters (archit); placed amongst charges occupying the corners of a shield (heraldry). **cantoniza'tion** or **-s-** n. **can'tonize** or **-ise** vt to divide (a town, etc) into separate areas according to the religions, ethnic origins, etc of the inhabitants. **cantonment** /kən-toon'mənt/ n (milit) the temporary quarters, *esp* winter quarters, of troops taking part in manoeuvres or active operations; in British India, a permanent military town (hist).

canton² see **canto**.

Canton crepe /kan-ton' krāp/ n a fine crinkled silk or crepe, orig made in Canton in China.

Cantonese /kan-tə-nēz'/ adj belonging to or typical of Canton, (now *usu* Guangzhou) a city in S China; of a style of cooking originating there. ◆ n (pl **Cantonese'**) a native of Canton; the dialect of Canton.

cantor /kan'tör/ n the leader of the singing in a church, a precentor; in a synagogue, the person who chants the liturgy and leads the congregation in prayer (also **hazan**). [L, singer, from *canere* to sing]

■ **cantorial** /-tō'ri-əl or -tö'/ adj of or relating to a precentor or his position on the north side of a cathedral (cf **decanal**). **cantō'ris** adj denoting the north side of a church choir, where the cantor sits, *opp* to *decani*.

cantred /kan'tred/ or **cantref** /kan'trev/ (hist) n a division of a county, a hundred. [Welsh *cantref*, from *cant* hundred, and *tref* town]

cantrip /kan'trip/ (Scot) n a wilful piece of trickery or mischief; a witch's spell. [Ety unknown]

Cantuar. /kan'tū-är/ abbrev: *Cantuaria* (L), Canterbury (as the archiepiscopal see of the primate of the Church of England).

cantus /kan'təs/ n (pl **can'tus**) a melody or chant, *esp* in medieval ecclesiastical music; the highest part in a piece of choral music (also **can'to**). [L, song, from *canere* to sing]

□ **cantus firmus** /fûr'məs/ n (pl **cantus fir'mī**) canto fermo.

canty /kan'ti/ (Scot) adj cheerful, lively. [**cant⁴**; cf LGer *kantig*]

■ **can'tiness** n.

Canuck /kə-nuk'/ (inf; often derog) n a Canadian (N Am); a French-Canadian or the French-Canadian language (Can); a small Canadian horse or pony. ◆ adj relating to Canada or to Canadians. [Ety uncertain]

canula see **cannula**.

canvas /kan'vəs/ n a coarse cloth made of cotton, hemp or other material, used for sails, tents, etc, and for painting on; the sails of a vessel collectively (naut); a tent or tents; a piece of stretched canvas, painted or to be painted; the covered front or back of a racing-boat, as in a *canvas-length*, *win by a canvas* (rowing); open-weave material on which embroidery or tapestry is worked; the floor of a boxing or wrestling ring; the background against which events occur (lit and fig). ◆ vt (**can'vassing**; **can'vassed**) to cover or line with canvas. [OFr *canevas*, from L *cannabis*, from Gr *kannabis* hemp]

□ **can'vasback** n a N American duck (*Aythya valisineria*), with an ashy white back crossed by dark zigzag lines, closely related to the pochard. **can'vas-climber** n (Shakesp) a sailor. **can'vas-stretcher** n a wooden frame on which canvas is stretched for oil-painting. **can'vas-work** n embroidery on canvas, or on cloth over which canvas has been laid to guide the stitches.

■ **under canvas** having the sails unfurled, under sail; in a tent or tents.

canvass /kan'vəs/ vt to solicit votes, orders, contributions etc from; to scrutinize (votes, etc) in order to establish their validity (chiefly N Am); to toss in a canvas blanket (obs); hence, to criticize roughly; to examine; to discuss thoroughly. ◆ vi to solicit votes, etc (with for); to go from person to person seeking information. ◆ n close examination; a seeking or solicitation of votes, information, etc; a scrutiny of votes (chiefly N Am). [**canvas**]

■ **can'vasser** n.

cany see under **cane**.

canyon or **cañon** /kan'yən/ n a deep gorge or ravine. [Sp *cañón* a hollow, from root of **cannon**]
■ **can'yoning** n an adventure sport involving travelling by various methods along a river canyon.

canzone /kan-tsō'nā/ or **canzona** /kan-zō'nə/ n (pl **canzo'ni** /-nē/ or **canzo'nas**) a song or air resembling, but less elaborate than, a madrigal; an instrumental piece of similar character; a Provençal or Italian form of lyric poetry, consisting of a series of stanzas without a refrain. [Ital, a song, from L *cantiō, -ōnis*, from *canere* to sing]
■ **canzonet** /kan-zō-net'/ or **canzonetta** /kan-tsō-net'ə/ n (pl **canzonets'** or **canzonet'te** /-tä/) a dimin form of **canzone**.

caoutchouc /kow'chŭk/ n raw rubber, gum-elastic; the latex of rubber trees. [Fr, from Carib *cahuchu*]

CAP (sometimes /kap/) abbrev : Common Agricultural Policy (of the EU); computer-aided production.

cap[1] /kap/ n a flat brimless hat, usu with a peak; formerly, a woman's light head covering, usu worn indoors and made from lace, fine linen, etc; an official or symbolic headdress or one appropriated to a special class or use, academic, athletic, etc; an occasion of being selected for *esp* a national team, symbolized by a cap; a person so selected; the enamel which covers a tooth (*anat*); an artificial covering for a tooth, replacing the natural enamel; a caplike covering of any kind; the top of a toadstool; the uppermost or terminal part of anything; a percussion cap for a toy gun, etc; a collection of money taken at a fox hunt (*orig* in a cap) for hunt servants, charity, etc; (also **Dutch cap**) a contraceptive diaphragm. ◆ vt (**capp'ing**; **capped** /kapt/) to cover the end or top of; to touch with a cap in conferring a degree (chiefly *Scot* and *NZ*); to select as a member of a team; to outdo or surpass by following with something better, more significant, etc; to seal off and halt the flow from (an oil or gas well); to set a limit to (*esp* local authority budgets). ◆ vt and vi to salute by raising the cap. [OE *cæppe*, from LL *cappa* a cape or cope]
■ **cap'ful** n (pl **cap'fuls**). **capp'er** n. **capp'ing** n the action of the verb *cap*; a covering, eg a hard crust that forms on soil during dry weather; a graduation ceremony (*inf*).
□ **cap'-case** n (*obs*) a small travelling-case, a chest. **cap'-paper** n a kind of wrapping paper; a size of writing paper. **cap pistol** n a toy gun using a percussion cap. **cap rock** n a stratum of (*usu* impervious) rock overlying oil- or gas-bearing strata. **cap screw** n a bolt with a threaded shaft and cylindrical head with a hexagonal indentation for turning it. **cap sleeve** n a short sleeve, just covering the shoulder. **cap'stone** n a coping-stone; the top or finishing stone of a structure; a stone slab laid flat over the top of a cist (*archaeol*); the horizontal stone of a dolmen (*archaeol*); a flat stone acting as a cap, eg to a shaft or chimney.
■ **black cap** see under **black**. **cap and bells** the insignia of a professional jester. **cap and collar mortgage** one having a minimum (**collar**) and maximum (**cap**) rate of interest. **cap in hand** submissively; supplicatingly. **cap of liberty** the conical cap, *usu* made of red material, given to a Roman slave on enfranchisement, and adopted during the French revolution as an emblem of freedom, now the symbol of republicanism. **cap of maintenance** see under **maintain**. **cap verses** to quote verses in turn, according to rule. **college cap** a mortarboard or trencher cap. **set one's cap at** (of a woman) to set oneself to captivate (a man). **the cap fits** the allusion is felt to apply. **throw up one's cap** to make this gesture (*lit* or *fig*) in token of immoderate joy. **to cap it all** as a (frequently unpleasant) climax.

cap[2] /kap/ or **caup** /köp/ (*Scot*) n a wooden drinking bowl, with two handles. [OE *copp* a cup; or Scand *koppr*]

cap. (sometimes /kap/) abbrev : capacity; *capiat* (*L*), let him or her take; capital; capitalize; capital letter; *caput* (*L*), chapter.

capa /kä'pə/ n a Spanish cloak; fine Cuban tobacco for the outer layers of cigars. [Sp]

capable /kā'pə-bl/ adj having practical ability; able (often with *of*); qualified; comprehensive (*Shakesp*); having (*esp* legal) right, or (with *of*) right to (*obs*). [Fr, from LL *capābilis*, from L *capere* to hold, take]
■ **capabil'ity** n the quality or state of being capable; (usu in *pl*) a feature capable of being used or developed; ability for the action indicated, because provision and preparation have been made; manufacturing facilities, such as factories or plant. **cā'pableness** n. **cā'pably** adv.
■ **capable of** able to take in, contain, understand, etc (*archaic*); sufficiently able, good, well-made, etc to, or sufficiently bad, foolish, etc, to (followed by verbal noun or other action noun); susceptible of.

capacious see under **capacity**.

capacitance /kə-pas'i-təns/ n the property that allows a system to store an electric charge; the value of this expressed in farads. [**capacity**]

■ **capac'itor** n an electrical device capable of storing electric charge, *usu* consisting of conductors separated by an insulator.

capacity /kə-pas'i-ti/ or /-ə-ti/ n the power of holding, containing, absorbing or grasping; the maximum amount that may be contained, held, absorbed, etc; volume; an ability or talent; mental power; the position or function in which one does something; legal competence; maximum possible output or performance; formerly, capacitance (*electronics*); possession of industrial plant, technology, etc, with resulting ability to produce goods. ◆ adj attaining or containing the maximum number possible. [Fr *capacité*, from L *capāx, -ācis* able to receive, from *capere* to hold]
■ **capacious** /kə-pā'shəs/ adj able to hold much; roomy; wide; extensive. **capā'ciously** adv. **capā'ciousness** n. **capac'itate** vt to make legally competent; to make or render capable; to qualify; to cause (a sperm) to undergo changes while in the female reproductive tract enabling it to fertilize an egg. **capacitā'tion** n.
■ **capacity for heat** power of absorbing heat. **legal capacity** the power to alter one's rights or duties by the exercise of free will, or responsibility for one's acts. **to capacity** to the utmost capacity, the fullest extent possible.

cap-à-pie or **cap-a-pie** /kap-ə-pē'/ (*archaic* or *facetious*) adv (dressed) from head to foot, eg of a knight in armour. [OFr *cap a pie* (Mod Fr *de pied en cap*), from L *caput* head, *ad* to, and *pēs* foot]

caparison /kə-par'i-sən/ n an ornamented covering for a horse, *esp* a rich cloth laid over a warhorse; rich clothing and ornaments generally. ◆ vt to cover (a horse or other animal) with a caparison; to dress very richly. [Fr *caparaçon*, from Sp *caparazón*, augmentative of *capa* cap, cover, from LL *cappa* cape]
■ **capar'isoned** adj.

cape[1] /kāp/ n a covering for the shoulders attached as a tippet to a coat or cloak; a sleeveless cloak. [OFr *cape*, from LL *cappa*]
■ **cape'let** n a small cape.
□ **cape'work** n the skill or technique of a bullfighter in making the bull follow the cape.

cape[2] /kāp/ n a head or point of land jutting into the sea or a lake; (with cap) see **the Cape** below. ◆ vi (*naut*) to keep a course. [Fr *cap*, from L *caput* the head]
□ **Cape buffalo** see **buffalo**. **Cape cart** n (*S Afr*) a two-wheeled horse-drawn vehicle with a hood. **Cape Coloured** n (*hist*) a person of mixed race, in the former Cape Province of South Africa. **Cape doctor** n (*S Afr*) a strong south-east wind in the Cape, so named because it was believed to blow away germs. **Cape Dutch** n a former name for Afrikaans; an architectural style of the Cape, characterized by whitewashed, gabled, thatched-roof, single-storey houses. **Cape gooseberry** n the strawberry tomato (*Physalis peruviana*), a S American solanaceous plant with bladdery calyx, naturalized in S Africa; its edible, soft, yellow fruit. **Cape hyacinth** see **hyacinth**. **Cape jasmine** n a common variety of gardenia (*Gardenia jasminoides*). **Cape nightingale** n a frog. **Cape pigeon** n a species of petrel (*Daption capensis*), a common winter visitor to the Cape area of South Africa. **Cape primrose** n the streptocarpus plant. **Cape smoke** n (*S Afr sl*) South African brandy, dop. **Cape sparrow** see under **mossie**[2].
■ **the Cape** the Cape of Good Hope; Cape Province, Capetown and Cape Peninsula.

capecitabine /ka-pə-sīt'ə-bēn/ n a drug used in the treatment of advanced cancers.

capelet[1] see under **cape**[1].

capelet[2] see **capellet**.

capelin /kap'ə-lin/ or **caplin** /kap'lin/ n a small fish (*Mallotus villosus*) of the smelt family, abundant off Newfoundland, much used as bait. [Fr *capelan*]

capeline or **capelline** /kap'ə-lin/ n a small iron skullcap worn by archers; a light woollen hood for evening wear; a surgical bandage for the head. [Fr, from LL *capella*, from *capa* a cap]

Capella /ka-pel'ə/ n a first-magnitude star in the northern constellation Auriga. [L, literally she-goat]

capellet or **capelet** /kap'ə-lit/ (*vet*) n a cyst-like swelling on a horse's elbow, or on the back part of the hock. [Fr, from LL *capella*, from *capa* a cap]

capellmeister same as **kapellmeister**.

caper[1] /kā'pər/ n a thorny S European shrub (*Capparis spinosa*), with edible flower-buds (also **cap'er-bush**); a flower-bud of this shrub, pickled and used in cooking as a flavouring or garnish. [L *capparis*, from Gr *kapparis*]
□ **cā'per-sauce** n a sauce for boiled mutton, etc, made with capers. **cā'per-spurge** n a kind of spurge whose capsules are sometimes pickled. **cā'per-tea** n a black tea with a knotty curled leaf.

caper² /kā'pər/ vi to leap or skip like a goat; to dance playfully; to frolic. ♦ n a leap; a gambol; an escapade; any activity or pursuit (sl); an illegal or questionable act, a crime (sl). [L caper (masc), capra (fem) a goat]
■ **cā'perer** n.
■ **cut a caper** or **cut capers** to gambol; to attempt to attract attention by one's behaviour.

caper³ see **capercailzie**.

capercailzie or **capercaillie** /ka-pər-kā'lyi, -li or (non-standard) -lzi, also kā'pər-/ n a large European woodland grouse (Tetrao urogallus), the male of which has dark plumage and a fan-shaped tail (also **ca'per**). [Gaelic capull coille horse of the wood]

Capernaite /ka- or kə-pûr'ni-īt/ n an inhabitant of Capernaum in Galilee; (in Christian polemics) a believer in transubstantiation (Bible, John 6.35,51).
■ **Capernaitic** /-it'ik/ adj. **Capernait'ically** adv.

capeskin /kāp'skin/ n a type of soft leather made from the skins of long-haired sheep or lambs. [Cape of Good Hope]

capex /kap'eks'/ n short for **capital expenditure**.

capias /kā'pi-as or kap'i-/ (law) n a writ which authorizes the arrest of the person named in it. [L, you should seize, from capere to take]

capillaceous /ka-pi-lā'shəs/ adj hairlike; having numerous fine filaments. [L capillāceus resembling hair, from capillus hair]

capillaire /ka-pi-lār'/ n a syrup, an infusion of maidenhair fern flavoured with orange-flower water. [Fr]

capillary /kə-pil'ə-ri, sometimes kap'i-lə-ri/ adj relating to hair; hairlike; of very small bore; relating to capillary action. ♦ n a fine-bored tube; a minute thin-walled blood vessel that forms a network connecting arteries with veins (anat). [L capillus hair]
■ **capillarity** /-lar'i-ti/ n capillary quality; an obsolete term for capillary action. **capillitium** /kap-i-lish'i-əm/ n a mass of threads.
□ **capillary action** n the force that causes a liquid in contact with a solid to rise (as in a capillary tube), or to spread (as through blotting-paper), caused by surface tension. **capillary electrometer** n an electrolytic cell, consisting of a capillary tube joining two electrodes that contain mercury, used as a measuring device for small voltages. **capillary joint** n a plumbing joint in which the ends of two pipes are inserted into either end of a marginally wider piece of piping and soldered in. **capillary matting** n highly absorbent matting made of fine filaments, used in watering greenhouse, etc plants. **capillary tube** n a glass tube with a fine bore used in medicine, thermometers, etc.

capita see **caput**.

capital¹ /kap'i-təl/ n the chief or most important thing; the chief town or seat of government; a capital letter; the property and equipment and/or money used for carrying on a business; money invested or lent at interest; capitalists collectively, or their political and economic influence and interests; any advantage used as a means of gaining further advantages. ♦ adj main, principal, most important; excellent (inf); (of a letter) of the form or size which begins a sentence or name, upper-case; relating to the head; relating to capital; involving or punishable by the death penalty; placed at the head. ♦ interj excellent. [OFr capitel, from L capitālis, from caput the head]
■ **cap'italism** n the condition of possessing capital or wealth; the economic system which is driven by the profit-motive and depends on investment of private capital to provide the means of production, distribution and exchange. **cap'italist** n and adj (a person) owning capital, esp when invested for profit in business; (a person) advocating capitalism as an economic system. **capitalist'ic** adj. **capitalīzā'tion** or **-s-** n. **cap'italize** or **-ise** vt to provide with capital; to convert into capital or money; to turn to account; to print or write with capital letters or an initial capital letter. ♦ vi to turn to one's advantage, to profit from (with on). **cap'itally** adv chiefly; principally; excellently (inf); by capital punishment.
□ **capital account** n a financial statement showing the value of a company, calculated by deducting total liabilities from total assets to give a net value; an account of fixed assets (US). **capital assets** n pl fixed assets. **capital cross** n a Greek cross with terminations like Tuscan capitals. **capital expenditure** n spending on capital assets; expenditure from which benefits may be expected in the long term. **capital gains** n pl profits from the sale of bonds or other assets. **capital gains tax** n a tax levied on the profit made on the sale of assets. **capital goods** n pl goods to be used in production of other goods, not for sale to consumers. **capital-intens'ive** adj requiring a comparatively large amount of capital relative to the amount of labour involved. **capitalization issue** n an issue of shares given free by a company to its shareholders (in proportion to the size of their holdings) in order to capitalize reserves, a bonus issue. **capital levy** n a tax on capital or the profit derived from the sale of property, etc, as opposed to a tax on earned income. **capital maintenance** n (account) the

principle that profit is made only after preserving the value of the capital invested in the company. **capital murder** n a murder involving the death penalty. **capital offence** n a crime punishable by the death penalty. **capital punishment** n the death penalty. **capital ship** n a warship of the largest and most heavily armoured class in a fleet. **capital sin** n (obs) deadly sin. **capital sum** n a lump sum payable on an insurance policy. **capital territory** n the part of a country in which the capital city is situated. **capital transfer tax** n a tax payable on gifts of money or property over a certain value, made either during the lifetime of the giver or after his or her death, replaced in 1986 by inheritance tax.
■ **circulating** or **floating capital** (old) working capital. **fixed capital** (business) assets having a working life of more than one year, such as buildings, machines, tools, etc. **make capital** (**out**) **of** to turn to advantage. **working capital** (business) short-lived assets and liabilities, such as stocks, trade creditors, etc, which arise from day-to-day operations; long-term capital needed to finance the difference between current assets and current liabilities

capital² /kap'i-təl/ n the head or top part of a column, that supports the entablature (archit); a chapter of a book (rare). [L capitellum, dimin of caput head]

capitalism, etc see under **capital¹**.

capitan /kāp-i-tän' or kap'i-tan/ (hist) n the chief admiral of the Turkish fleet. [Sp capitán, and Ital capitano; see **captain**]
■ **capitan'o** n (pl capitan'os or capitan'i /-ē/) a head-man.

capitate /kap'i-tāt/ (bot and zool) adj having a head, knob or capitulum; shaped like a head. [L capitātus, from caput head]

capitation /ka-pi-tā'shən/ n a numbering of heads or individuals; a poll-tax; the levying of this. [L capitātus headed, and capitātiō, -ōnis poll-tax, from caput head]
□ **capitation allowance** or **grant** n an allowance or grant of so much a head. **capitation fee** n a payment made to a general practitioner for each patient on his or her list.

capitayn /ka-pi-tān'/ (Spenser) n a captain.

capitellum see **capitulum**.

Capitol /kap'i-tol or -təl/ n the temple of Jupiter at Rome, built on the Capitoline hill; the building where Congress or a state legislature meets (US). [L Capitōlium, from caput the head]
■ **capitō'lian** or **capit'oline** adj.

capitular¹ /kə-pit'yŭ-lər/ n a statute passed in a chapter or ecclesiastical court; a member of a chapter. ♦ adj relating or belonging to a chapter in a cathedral. [See ety for **chapter**]
■ **capit'ularly** adv. **capit'ulary** n a collection of ordinances of Charlemagne, etc; a heading. ♦ adj of a chapter.

capitular² see under **capitulum**.

capitulate¹ /kə-pit'ū-lāt or -yə-lāt/ vi to yield or surrender, esp on certain stated conditions; orig to draw up terms of agreement (obs). [LL capitulātus, pap of capitulāre to arrange under heads, from capitulum a chapter]
■ **capit'ulant** n a person who capitulates. **capitulā'tion** n. **capit'ulator** n. **capit'ulatory** adj.

capitulate² see under **capitulum**.

capitulum /kə-pit'yŭ-ləm/ n (pl capit'ula) a close head of sessile flowers, as in the Compositae family of daisies and related flowers (bot); the head or enlarged knob-like part at the end of a long bone, eg a rib (also **capitell'um**; pl **capitell'a**) (anat). [L, dimin of caput head]
■ **capit'ular** adj. **capit'ulate** adj.

capiz /kap'iz/ n the translucent shell of a bivalve mollusc (Placuna placenta) used in making jewellery, etc. [Tagálog]

caple or **capul** /kā'pl/ n (obs) a horse. [ME capel; cf ON kapall; Ir capall; LL caballus a horse]

caplet /kap'lət/ n a solid medicinal tablet with a hard coating (of a soluble material as used to make capsules), usu in an elongated oval form to ease swallowing. [capsule and tablet]

caplin see **capelin**.

capnomancy /kap'nō-man-si/ n divination by smoke. [Gr kapnos smoke, and manteiā divination]

capo¹ /kap'ō/ n (pl cap'os or capi) the head of a branch of the Mafia; by extension, the leader of any band or organization, criminal or otherwise. [Ital capo, from L caput head]

capo² /kap'ō/, in full **capotasto** /ka-pō-tas'tō/ or **capodastro** /ka-pō-das'trō/ n (pl cap'os, capotas'tos or capodas'tros) a movable bridge secured over the fingerboard and strings of a lute or guitar, to alter the pitch of all the strings together. [Ital capo tasto or dastro head stop]

capocchia /kä-pok'yə/ (Shakesp) n a fool (also **chipoch'ia** /kē-/). [Ital]

capodastro see **capo²**.

capoeira or **capuera** /kap-oo-ā'rə/ n a martial art and dance combination developed by African slaves in 19c Brazil. [Port]

capon /kā'pon/ n a castrated cock fattened for eating; a humorous name for certain fish, variously a herring, haddock or sole; a love letter (*Shakesp*). [OE *capun*; L *capō, -ōnis*, Gr *kapōn*, from *koptein* to cut]
■ **ca'ponize** or **-ise** vt to make (a cock) into a capon by castration.

caponata /kap-ə-nä'tə/ n a relish of aubergine, olives, onions and herbs in olive oil, *usu* served as an antipasto. [Ital]

caponier or **caponiere** /ka-pə-nēr'/ n a covered passage across the ditch around a fortified place. [Fr *caponnière*, Sp *caponera* capon-coop]

caporal /ka-po-räl'/ n a kind of strong, dark, shag tobacco. [Fr]

capot /kə-pot'/ (*cards*) n the winning of all the tricks by one player at the game of piquet, and scoring forty. ◆ vt (**capotting**; **capotted**) to score capot against. [Fr]

capotasto see **capo²**.

capote /kə-pōt'/ n a long, *usu* hooded, cloak or mantle. [Fr, dimin of *cape* a cloak; see **cape¹**]

capouch see **capuche**.

Cappagh-brown /kap'ä-brown/ n a brown bituminous earth pigment, stained with oxide of manganese and iron from *Cappagh* near Cork (also **Capp'ah-brown**).

capparidaceous /ka-pə-ri-dā'shəs/ adj of the **Capparidā'ceae** family of plants, related to the crucifers, and including the caper (genus *Capparis*). [See **caper¹**]

cappelletti /ka-pə-let'i/ n pl small hat-shaped pasta pieces, filled with meat or cheese. [Ital]

cappuccino /ka-pŭ-chē'nō/ n (pl **cappuccin'os** or **cappuccin'i** /-ē/) espresso coffee topped with steamed milk and milk froth, sometimes sprinkled with powdered or grated chocolate. [Ital, Capuchin, perh from the colour of a Capuchin's gown]

capreolate /kap'ri-ō-lāt/ (chiefly *bot*) adj having or resembling tendrils. [L *capreolus* a tendril]

capric /kap'rik/, **caproic** /kə-prō'ik/ and **caprylic** /kə-pril'ik/ adj applied to three fatty acids obtained from butter, etc, having a goat-like smell. [L *caper* a goat]
■ **cap'rate**, **cap'roate** and **cap'rylate** n salts respectively of these acids. **caprolactam** /kap-rō-lak'tam/ n a crystalline amide used in the production of nylon.

capriccio /kä-prē'cho or kə-prē'chi-ō/ (*music*) n (pl **capri'ccios** or **capricci** /-prē'chē/) a kind of free composition, not keeping to the rules of any particular form. [Ital, perh from L *caper*; see **caper²**]
■ **capriccioso** /-ō'sō/ adv (*music*) in a free style.

caprice /kə-prēs'/ n an unpredictable or unaccountable change of mind, opinion or behaviour; a whim; changeableness; a capriccio (*music*). [Fr *caprice* and Ital *capriccio*; perh from L *caper* (masc), *capra* (fem) a goat]
■ **capricious** /kə-prish'əs/ adj humorous (*Shakesp*); full of caprice; changeable. **capri'ciously** adv. **capri'ciousness** n.

Capricorn /kap'ri-körn/ n the Goat, a constellation giving its name to, and formerly coinciding with, a sign of the zodiac (also **Capricornus**; *astron*); the tenth sign of the zodiac, between Sagittarius and Aquarius (*astrol*); a person born between 23 December and 20 January, under the sign of Capricorn (*astrol*). See also under **tropic**. [L *capricornus*, from *caper* a goat, and *cornū* a horn]
■ **Capricorn'ian** n and adj (relating to or characteristic of) a person born under the sign of Capricorn.
■ **first point of Capricorn** the limit of the sun's course southward during winter in the northern hemisphere.

caprid /kap'rid/ (*zool*) n a member of the goat family (also *adj*). [L *caper*, a goat]
■ **Capridae** /kap'ri-dē/ n pl in former classifications, the family of Artiodactyla comprising sheep, goats, etc. **Cap'rinae** n pl in modern classification, the family which includes goats and ibex.

caprifig /kap'ri-fig/ n the goat-fig, a species of wild fig of Europe and Asia. [L *caprīcus* the wild fig, from *caper* a goat, and *fīcus* a fig]
■ **caprifica'tion** n a method of promoting the fertilization of cultivated edible figs (which are mainly dioecious) by hanging branches of caprifig flowers (which have both male and female flowers) on the edible fig trees so that the parasitic gall-wasps living on the female (or gall) flowers carry pollen to the flowers of the cultivated fig. **cap'rify** vt.

caprifole /kap'ri-fōl/ or (*Spenser*) **caprifoil** /-foil/ n an old name for honeysuckle. [L *caper* goat, and *folium* leaf]
■ **Caprifoliä'ceae** /-si-ē/ n pl the honeysuckle family or plants. **caprifoliä'ceous** adj.

capriform /kap'ri-förm/ adj goat-like. [L *caper* goat, and *fōrma* form]

caprify see under **caprifig**.

caprine /kap'rīn/ adj of or like a goat. [L *caprīnus*, from *caper* a goat]

capriole /kap'ri-ōl/ n a high leap made from bent knees (*ballet*); an upward leap without advancing, in which the horse has all four feet off the ground and kicks its back legs at the height of the jump (*dressage*). ◆ vi to perform a capriole; to caper. [OFr *capriole*, from Ital *capriola*, from L *caper* (masc), *capra* (fem) a goat]

Capri pants /kə-prē' pants/ n pl (sometimes without *cap*) women's tapering trousers ending above the ankle, with a short slit on the outside leg (also **Capris'**). [*Capri*, island in the Bay of Naples]

caproic, caprolactam, caprylic, etc see **capric**.

CAPS abbrev : Combined Actuarial Performance Services.

caps /kaps/ abbrev : capitals, capital letters (in printing and writing).

capsaicin see under **capsicum**.

Capsian /kap'si-ən/ n a Mesolithic culture (of the period 8c–3c BC) of N Africa, distinguished by its microlithic and geometrically-shaped tools. ◆ adj of, or characteristic of, this culture. [Latinized *Capsa* Gafsa, in Tunisia]

capsicum /kap'si-kəm/ n (pl **cap'sicums**) a tropical American shrubby plant of the genus *Capsicum*, of the family Solanaceae, yielding a fleshy, many-seeded fruit; the fruit of one species, eaten as a vegetable (also called **green** or **red pepper**); the dried seeds of other species, yielding paprika and cayenne pepper. [Perh L *capsa* a case]
■ **capsaicin** /kap-sā'i-sin/ n the hot-tasting principle of certain species of capsicum.

capsid¹ /kap'sid/ n the outer protein shell of a virus. [L *capsa* case]

capsid² /kap'sid/ n any of several small active bugs of the order Heteroptera, that feed on plants, a common pest of fruit and other crops. [Gr *kapsis* gulping, from *kaptein* to gulp down]

capsize /kap-sīz'/ vt to overturn (*esp* a boat). ◆ vi to be overturned. ◆ n an overturning. [Origin unknown]
■ **capsiz'able** adj. **capsiz'al** n.

capstan /kap'stən/ n an upright mechanical device turned by bars, levers or a motor, used for winding in heavy ropes or cables, *esp* on a ship; the revolving shaft which engages with and draws a tape through a tape-recorder, etc; (also **capstan lathe**) a lathe with a revolving turret holding several tools which can be used in succession. [Fr *cabestan*, *capestan*, from L *capere* to take, hold]
❏ **capstan table** n a round-topped, often revolving table.

capsule /kap'sūl/ n a dry seed-case which splits to release seeds (*bot*); the spore-bearing part of a moss (*bot*); a fibrous or membranous covering (*zool*); an envelope of protein or polysaccharides surrounding the cell walls of certain bacteria; a gelatine case for holding a dose of medicine; a small container; a metallic cap or covering, as on a wine cork; a spacecraft or aircraft, or a part of one, that houses the instruments and crew in a self-contained unit; a similar craft, to be used on or under water. [Fr, from L *capsula*, dimin of *capsa* a case, from *capere* to hold]
■ **cap'sular** adj in the form of, or resembling, a capsule; brief, condensed (also **cap'sule**). **cap'sulary** adj. **cap'sulate** adj made into or contained in a capsule. **cap'sulize** or **-ise** vt to condense; to enclose in a capsule.

Capt. abbrev : Captain (in titles).

captain /kap'tin/ n a head or chief officer; the commander of a ship; the commander of a company of troops (*obs*); in the navy, an officer of the rank below commodore and above commander; in the army (in USA also the Air Force), an officer of the rank below major and above lieutenant; the senior pilot of a civil aircraft; a senior police or fire officer (*N Am*); the overseer of a mine; the leader of a team or club; a person in charge of waiters and bellboys in a hotel (*N Am*); the head boy or head girl of a school. ◆ vt to lead as captain. [OFr *capitaine*, from LL *capitāneus* chief, from L *caput* head]
■ **cap'taincy** n the rank or commission of a captain; the period of office of a captain; the leadership of a captain. **cap'tainship** or (*obs*) **cap'tainry** n the rank or condition of a captain; skill in commanding.
❏ **captain-gen'eral** n the commander of an army. **captain's biscuit** n a fancy kind of hard biscuit. **captain's chair** n a wooden armchair with back and arms in one semicircular piece on vertical spindles.
■ **captain of industry** a leading industrial figure.

Captain Cooker /kap'tin kŭk'ər/ (*NZ*) n a wild pig. [Captain James Cook (1728–79), who is thought to have released pigs in the New Zealand bush]

captan /kap'tən/ n a type of agricultural fungicide produced from mercaptan. [From **mercaptan**]

■ words derived from main entry word; ❏ compound words; ■ idioms and phrasal verbs

CAPTCHA or **captcha** /kap'chə/ (comput) n a program to generate tests that humans can pass but computer programs cannot, such as the ability to recognize a distorted word, used to ensure that a response is not computer generated. [From Completely Automated Public Turing Test to tell Computers and Humans Apart]

caption /kap'shən/ n a heading, legend or accompanying wording of an article, chapter, illustration or sequence of a cinema film, etc; the act of taking (formal); an arrest (law); the formal title of an indictment or deposition which shows the authority under which it is executed or taken (Eng law); in Scotland, before 1837, a formal warrant to apprehend a debtor or other defaulting obligant, given in the Bill Chamber after letters of horning had been executed. ◆ vt to give a caption (heading, etc) to. [L captiō, -ōnis, from capere to take]

captious /kap'shəs/ adj ready to find esp trivial faults or take offence; carping; peevish. [L captiōsus, from captiō; see **caption**]
■ **cap'tiously** adv. **cap'tiousness** n.

captive /kap'tiv/ n a prisoner; a person or animal kept in confinement. ◆ adj confined; kept in bondage; of an animal, living its whole life in a zoo or other controlled habitat; restrained by a line (as a balloon); charmed or subdued by anything (fig); relating to captivity; that cannot refuse what is offered (as a captive audience, market, etc). ◆ vt /kap'tiv or (Spenser and Milton) kap-tiv'/ to make captive or to captivate. [L captīvus, from capere, captum to take]
■ **cap'tivance** or **cap'tivaunce** n (Spenser) captivity. **cap'tivate** vt to charm; to fascinate or engage the affections of. **cap'tivating** adj. **cap'tivatingly** adv. **captiva'tion** n. **captiv'ity** n the condition or period of being captive or imprisoned.
❏ **captive bolt** or **captive bolt pistol** n a gunlike device which fires a rod, used in slaughtering animals. **captive time** n time during which a person is not working but must be available at the place of work.

capture /kap'chər/ n the act of taking; the thing taken; an arrest; transference of a tributary to another river by erosion (geol); the acquisition by an atomic or nuclear system of an additional particle (phys). ◆ vt to take as a prize; to win control or possession of; to take by force; to succeed in representing (something intangible or elusive) in a fixed or permanent form; of an atomic or nuclear system, to acquire an additional particle (phys); (of a star or planet) to bring another body into orbit round it (astron); to transfer (data) into a computer. [L captura, captor, from capere, captum to take]
■ **cap'tor** or **cap'turer** n.

capuccio /kə-poot'chō/ (Spenser) n a hood. [Ital]

capuche or **capouch** /kə-poosh' or -pooch'/ n a hood or cowl, esp that worn by the Capuchins. [Ital cappuccio, from LL cappa]

Capuchin /kap'yŭ-chin or kap-oo-shēn'/ n a friar of a strict branch of the Franciscan order, which became a separate order in 1619, so called from the pointed hood worn; (without cap) a hooded cloak like a Capuchin's; (usu without cap) a hooded pigeon; (without cap) a capuchin monkey. [Fr, cowl, from LL cappa; see **cap¹**, **cape¹**]
❏ **capuchin cross** n a cross with each arm terminated by a ball. **capuchin monkey** n a S American monkey of the genus Cebus, with thick hair like a monk's cowl.

capuera see **capoeira**.

capul see **caple**.

caput /kap'ut or -ət/ n (pl **cap'ita**) the head (anat); a head; a bony protuberance (anat). [L]
❏ **caput mortuum** /mör'tū-əm/ n the residuum after distillation or chemical analysis, literally dead head; worthless residue.
■ **per caput** see **per capita** under **per²**.

capybara /ka-pi-bä'rə/ n the largest living rodent, a native of S America, resembling a large guinea-pig. [Port, from Tupí]

CAR abbrev : compound or compounded annual rate.

Car. abbrev : Carolus (L), Charles.

car /kär/ n a self-propelled wheeled vehicle designed to carry passengers (also **motor car**); a wheeled vehicle of a specified type (as jaunting car, tramcar, etc); a railway carriage, esp of a specified type (as dining-car, sleeping-car, etc); any railway carriage, wagon or truck (N Am); the part of a balloon, cable-car, or airship that carries passengers and load; a chariot or cart (poetic). [OFr carre, from LL carra, a Celtic word, seen in Ir carr, Breton karr]
❏ **car bomb** n an explosive device concealed beneath or inside a car, detonated by remote control or when the car engine is started. **car'-bomb** vt. **car'-bomber** n. **car boot sale** n a sale at which goods are sold direct from the boots of the owners' cars. **car'-coat** n a short coat designed for wearing in a car. **car'-crash TV** n (inf) distasteful or deplorable material broadcast on television that exercises a compulsion on the viewer comparable to the ghoulish fascination or schadenfreude often experienced by witnesses of road accidents. **car'fare** n (N Am) the fare on a bus, tram, etc. **car ferry** n a ferry-boat on which cars can be transported. **car'hop** n (N Am inf) a waiter or waitress at a drive-in restaurant. **car'jack** vt to hijack a road vehicle and its occupants. **car'jacker** n. **car'jacking** n. **car'load** n as much as a car will carry. **car'man** n (archaic) a man who drives a car or cart; a carter. **car park** n an open space or a building for parking cars. **car phone** or **car'phone** n a radio-operated telephone for use in a car. **car pool** n an arrangement by which several car owners take turns in giving lifts to each other; a number of cars owned by a business for use by employees. **car'-pool** vi. **car'-pooler** n. **car'port** n a covered parking space, esp a space under a roof projecting from a building. **car'-sick** adj affected with nausea by the movement of a car. **car'-sickness** n. **car'-wash** n a place specially equipped for the automatic washing of cars.

carabao /kä'rə-bä-o/ n the domesticated Asiatic buffalo. [Philippine Sp, from Visayan (a native language in the Philippines) karaba'aw]

carabid /kar'ə-bid/ n a beetle of the genus Carabus, of the ground-beetle family **Carabidae** /kə-rab'i-dē/. ◆ adj of, or characteristic of, the Carabidae. [Gr kārabos a kind of beetle]

carabine see **carbine**.

carabineer, **carabinier** see under **carbine**.

carabiner see **karabiner**.

carabinero /kar-ə-bi-nä'rō/ n (pl **carabine'ros**) a member of the Spanish Civil Guard; a member of the Chilean national police force.

carabiniere /kä-rä-bē-nyä'rä/ (Ital) n (pl **carabinie'ri** /-rē/) a member of the Italian national police force.

caracal /kar'ə-kal/ n the desert lynx of N Africa and S Asia, having long legs and black-tipped ears; its fur. [Fr, prob from Turk qara-qulaq black ear]

caracara /kä-rä-kä-rä' or kä-rä-kä'rä/ n a name for several American carrion-eating birds of prey. [Imit]

carack see **carrack**.

caracol or **caracole** /kar'ə-kol or -kōl/ n a half-turn or wheel (dressage); a spiral staircase. ◆ vi to turn half-round; to prance about. [Fr caracole, from Ital caracollo, from Sp caracol a spiral snail shell]

caract /kar'əkt/ (Shakesp) n a mark; a sign. [Appar Gr charaktos marked]

caracul see **karakul**.

carafe /kə-raf'/ n a water bottle or wine-flask for the table; the amount contained in a carafe. [Fr carafe, prob from Ar gharafa to draw water]

caragana /ka-rə-gä'nə or -gä'/ n any of a genus (Caragana) of hardy leguminous shrubs grown for their showy golden flowers. [Mod L, from Turk kharaghan the Siberian pea shrub]

caramba /kär-äm'bə/ (Sp) interj expressing admiration, annoyance or surprise.

carambola /ka-rəm-bō'lə/ n a small tropical tree (Averrhoa carambola) of the family Oxalidaceae; its acrid yellow pulpy fruit (also called **star fruit**). [Port]

carambole see **carom**.

caramel /kar'ə-mel/ n a dark-brown substance produced from sugar by loss of water on heating, used in colouring and flavouring food and drink; a chewy sweet made with sugar, butter, etc. ◆ adj made of or containing caramel; of the colour of caramel. ◆ vt and vi to turn into caramel. —Also (rare) **car'omel**. [Fr, from Sp caramelo]
■ **carameliza'tion** or **-s-** n. **car'amelize** or **-ise** vt and vi to change into caramel. ◆ vt to cook so as to become coated in caramel.

carangid /kə-rang'gid or -jid/ or **carangoid** /-goid/ n any spiny-finned marine fish of the genus Caranx, of the family **Carangidae** /kar-an'ji-dē/ which includes the scads, jacks, pilot fish, etc (also adj). [Origin obscure]

caranna /ka-ran'ə/ or **carauna** /-rö'nə/ n a resinous substance yielded by various S American burseraceous trees. [Sp caraña, from Tupí]

carap /kar'ap or kə-rap'/ n any tree of the genus Carapa, tropical trees of the mahogany family yielding **car'ap-nuts**, **car'ap-oil** or **car'ap-wood** (or **crab'-nuts**, **-oil** or **-wood**). [caraipi, the native Guiana name]

carapace /kar'ə-pās/ n the thick hard shell, made of bone or chitin, of the crab, tortoise, turtle, etc; a layer of heat-resistant tiles on a spacecraft; an inpenetrable outer shell, eg a reserved manner used as a protection against outside influences. [Fr, from Sp carapacho]
■ **carapa'cial** /-shl/ adj.

carat or **carrat** /kar'ət/ n a unit of weight (metric carat = 200mg) used for gems; (also (esp N Am) **karat**) a unit used in expressing the proportion of gold in an alloy, 24-carat gold being pure gold; worth; estimate (obs). [Fr, from Ar qīrāt, perh from Gr keration a carob-seed used as a weight]

carauna see **caranna**.

caravan /kar'ə-van or ka-rə-van'/ n a covered van; a house on wheels; a company travelling together for security, esp in crossing the desert; a company of people; a fleet with convoy. ◆ vi (**car'avaning** or **car'avanning**; **car'avaned** or **car'avanned**) to travel in a caravan. [Pers kārwān caravan, and kārwānsarāī from (sarāī inn)]
■ **caravaneer'** n the leader of a caravan. **caravan'er** or **caravann'er** n a caravaneer; someone who stays in a caravan, esp for holidays. **caravanette'** n a motorized mobile home. **car'avaning** or **car'avanning** n. **caravanserai** /-van'sə-rī/ n esp formerly in some Eastern countries, a kind of unfurnished inn or extensive enclosed courtyard where caravans stop (also **caravan'sarai** or (US) **caravan'sary**).
□ **caravan site** or **caravan park** n an open space laid out for caravans.

caravance see **calavance**.

caravel /kar'ə-vel/ n a light Mediterranean sailing-ship (also **car'vel**). [Fr caravelle, from Ital caravella; cf LL cārabus, Gr kārabos a light ship]

caraway or **carraway** /kar'ə-wā/ n an umbelliferous plant (Carum carvi) with aromatic fruits (**caraway seeds**) used as a tonic and condiment. [Prob Sp alcaravea (carvi), Ar karwiyā, from Gr karon]

carb /kärb/ (inf) n short for **carbohydrate**; short for **carburettor**.

carbachol /kär'bə-kol or -kōl/ n a synthetic drug formerly used in the treatment of urinary retention. [carbamic acid and choline]

carbamate /kär'bə-māt or kär-bam'āt/ n a salt or ester of carbamic acid, used esp as a pesticide. [**carbon**, **amide** and **-ate**]
■ **carbamide** /kär'bə-mīd, kär-bam'īd/ n urea. **car'baryl** /-bə-ril/ n a carbamate insecticide.
□ **carbam'ic acid** n an acid, NH$_2$COOH, which occurs only as its derivatives including its esters, the urethanes.

carbamazepine /kär-bə-mā'zi-pēn/ n an anticonvulsant and analgesic drug used in the treatment of epilepsy, etc. [carbon, amide and benzodiazepine]

carbanion /kär-ban'ī-ən/ (chem) n an ion carrying a negative electric charge at the carbon position.

carbaryl see under **carbamate**.

carbazole /kär'bə-zōl/ n a chemical compound derived from coal tar and used in making dyes.

carbene /kär'bēn/ (chem) n a neutral divalent free radical, such as methylene.

carbide /kär'bīd/ n a compound of carbon with another element, esp calcium carbide. [**carbon**]
□ **carbide tool** n (engineering) a cutting and forming tool made of tungsten carbide and used for hard materials or at high temperatures.

carbine /kär'bīn/ n a short light rifle (also (esp formerly) **car'abin** or **car'abine**). [Fr carabine]
■ **carbineer'**, **carabiner'**, **carbinier'** or **carabinier'** n a soldier armed with a carbine; a light cavalryman; a soldier of the 6th Dragoon Guards (from 1939, 3rd Carabineers).

carbo- /kär-bō-/, sometimes kär-bo-/ or before a vowel **carb-** /kärb-/ combining form denoting carbon.

carbocyclic /kär-bō-sī'klik or -sik'lik/ adj homocyclic. [**carbon** and **cyclic**]

carbofuran /kär-bō-fū'rən or -fū-ran'/ n a powerful root-crop carbamate insecticide, highly toxic to birds. [**carbo-** and **furan**]

carbohydrate /kär-bō-hī'drāt/ n a compound of carbon, hydrogen and oxygen, the last two being in the same proportion as in water; extended to similar compounds, the sugars and starches which form the main source of energy in food. [See **carbon** and **hydrate**]

carbolic /kär-bol'ik/ n (in full **carbolic acid**) phenol. [L carbō coal, and oleum oil]
□ **carbolic soap** n soap containing carbolic acid.

carbon /kär'bən/ n a non-metallic element (symbol **C**; atomic no 6), widely diffused, occurring uncombined as diamond, graphite and buckminsterfullerene; a piece of carbon (esp an electrode or a lamp-filament), or of carbon paper; a carbon copy; a carbonado diamond. ◆ adj of or relating to carbon. [Fr carbone, from L carbō, -ōnis coal, charcoal]
■ **carbonā'ceous** adj coaly; containing much carbon; like carbon. **car'bonate** n a salt of carbonic acid. ◆ vt to combine or impregnate with carbon dioxide; to carbonize. **carbonā'tion** n. **car'bonatite** n an intrusive carbonate rock. **carbonic** /-bon'ik/ adj of or relating to carbon. **carbonif'erous** adj producing carbon or coal; (with cap) of or belonging to a period of the Palaeozoic era, between 360 and 300 million years ago (geol; also n). **carbonizā'tion** or **-s-** n.

car'bonize or **-ise** vt to reduce to carbon; to char or coke; to cover with carbon. ◆ vi to become carbonized.
□ **carbon anhydride** same as **carbon dioxide** below. **carbon arc** n an arc between two carbon electrodes, used for high-intensity lighting. **carbon black** n a form of finely divided carbon produced by partial combustion of hydrocarbons, used in making inks and rubber. **carbon capture and storage** n the capture and storage of carbon dioxide emitted from eg power plants, in order to prevent it entering the atmosphere (abbrev **CCS**). **carbon copy** n a duplicate of writing or typed matter made by interleaving **carbon paper**, a paper coated with a pigment made of carbon or other material; any exact duplicate. **car'bon-cop'y** vt to copy exactly. **carbon credit** n a unit, representing part of a country's or organization's total allowance for the emission of carbon dioxide, which may be traded to another country or organization if the full allowance is not used. **carbon cycle** n the circulation and transfer of carbon between animals, plants and the atmosphere; the function of carbon in various nuclear reactions in stars. **carbon dating** n estimating the date of death of prehistoric organic material from the amount of carbon-14 still present in it. **carbon dioxide** n an oxide of carbon (CO$_2$), a colourless, odourless, incombustible gas, present in the atmosphere, which in solution in water forms carbonic acid (formerly called **carbon'ic-acid gas**). **carbon dioxide snow** n dry ice (see **ice**). **carbon disulphide** n (CS$_2$) a colourless, flammable liquid with an unpleasant smell, used in the manufacture of man-made fibres and solvents. **carbon fibres** n pl very fine filaments of carbon used in bundles, bound together by resins, to form strong lightweight materials. **carbon footprint** n the extent to which a person, community or organization is responsible for the emission of carbon dioxide into the atmosphere through use of fossil fuels. **car'bon-14** n a radioactive isotope of carbon, used eg as a tracer element in biological studies or in dating archaeological material. **carbonic acid** n (H$_2$CO$_3$) a weak acid. **carbonic anhydrase** n an enzyme in blood cells that catalyses the decomposition of carbonic acid into carbon dioxide and water. **carbon microphone** n a microphone in which variations in sound pressure produced in a diaphragm are detected in a current passing through carbon granules which register a decrease of contact resistance as the sound pressure increases. **carbon monoxide** n (CO) a colourless, odourless, very poisonous gas which burns with a blue flame to form carbon dioxide. **carbon-neut'ral** adj (of a human activity) creating no overall increase or decrease in the emission of carbon dioxide into the atmosphere. **carbon offsetting** n the reduction in the emission of carbon from a source to compensate for an emission made elsewhere. **carbon process** n (photog) a printing process using paper sensitized with potassium bichromate and coated with gelatine and a pigment. **carbon sink** n an area, rich in natural flora, that absorbs more carbon dioxide than it produces. **carbon steel** n steel containing carbon, with different properties according to the quantity of carbon used. **carbon tax** n a tax imposed on industry, and on the users of motor vehicles, to try to limit the amount of carbon being released into the atmosphere from the burning of fossil fuels. **carbon tetrachloride** n (CCl$_4$) a solvent made from chlorine and carbon disulphide (also **tetrachloromethane**). **carbon trading** n the trading of carbon credits (qv above). **car'bon-12** n an isotope of carbon with a mass of 12, used as a standard in determining relative atomic and molecular weight.

carbonado[1] /kär-bə-nā'dō/ n (pl **carbona'does** or **carbona'dos**) a piece of meat cut crossways for broiling on coals (obs); (also **carbonnade'** or **carbonade'**) a beef stew made with beer. ◆ vt to cut crossways for broiling (obs); to slash (obs). [Sp carbonada]

carbonado[2] /kär-bə-nā'dō/ n a black, opaque variety of diamond, used in industry for drilling, etc (also called **black diamond** or **black carbon**). [Port, carbonated]

carbonara /kär-bə-nä'rə/ n a pasta sauce made with eggs, bacon and cheese, sometimes enriched with cream. [Ital]

Carbonari /kär-bo-nä'rē/ n pl members of a secret society in Italy at the beginning of the 19c, founded to help forward a republican government. [Ital, literally charcoal burners]
■ **Carbonar'ism** n.

carbonyl /kär'bə-nil/ (chem) n the radical CO. [carbon, oxygen and Gr hȳlē matter]
■ **carbonylate** /kär-bon'i-lāt/ vt to introduce the carbonyl group into. **carbonylā'tion** n.

Carborundum® /kär-bə-run'dum/ n a silicon carbide, used as a substitute for corundum in grinding, etc. [**carbon** and **corundum**; a trademark in some countries]

carboxyhaemoglobin or (US) **carboxyhemoglobin** /kär-bok-si-hē-mə-glō'bin/ n a haemoglobin co-ordinated with carbon monoxide.

carboxyl /kär-bok'sil/ n the radical COOH. [**carbon**, **oxygen** and Gr hȳlē matter]
■ **carboxylic** /-bok-sil'ik/ adj.

■ words derived from main entry word; □ compound words; ■ idioms and phrasal verbs

carboy /kär'boi/ *n* a large glass or plastic bottle, with basketwork or other casing, used for containing or transporting dangerous chemicals. [Pers *qarābah*]

carbuncle /kär'bung-kl/ *n* a mythical self-luminous gem; a fiery-red precious stone (almandine or precious garnet); a large pimple *esp* on the face or neck; a local inflammation of the skin and subcutaneous tissues, caused by bacterial infection; an architectural monstrosity or eyesore. [L *carbunculus*, dimin of *carbō* a coal]
■ **car'buncled** *adj* set with the gem carbuncle; afflicted with carbuncles; having red inflamed spots. **carbun'cular** *adj* belonging to or like a carbuncle; red; inflamed; unsightly.

carburet /kär'bū-ret/ or /-ret'/ *n* (*obs*) a carbide. [Fr *carbure*, from L *carbō* coal]
■ **carbura'tion, carburetion** /-räsh'ən, -resh'ən/ or **carburīzā'tion** or **-s-** *n*. **carburet, car'burate** or **car'burize** or **-ise** *vt* to combine with carbon; to charge with carbon compounds. **car'buretted** (or /-ret'id/) *adj*. **car'burettor, carburett'er**, or *US* **car'buretor** or **car'bureter** (also /-ret'ər/) *n* an apparatus for charging a gas with carbon compounds, *esp* part of an internal-combustion engine in which air is mixed with volatile fuel in the desired proportion.
❑ **carburetted gas** *n* a mixed illuminant obtained by passing water gas over hot hydrocarbons. **carburetted hydrogen** *n* a compound of carbon and hydrogen such as marsh-gas or olefiant gas.

carby /kär'bi/ (*Aust inf*) *n* short for **carburettor**.

carcajou /kär'kə-joo or -zhuu/ *n* the glutton or wolverine. [Can Fr, prob from a Native Canadian word]

carcake /kär'kāk/ (*Scot*) *n* a kind of cake for Shrove Tuesday. [OE *caru* grief, and **cake**]

carcanet /kär'kə-net/ (*obs*) *n* a collar of jewels; a jewelled head-ornament. [Fr (and obs Eng) *carcan* an iron collar used for punishment, from LL *carcannum*, from Gmc]

carcase or **carcass** /kär'kəs/ *n* a dead body of an animal, *esp* one to be used as meat; a live human body (*disrespectful* or *facetious*); the framework of anything; a ruin; an incendiary shell; the body of a tyre as distinct from the tread. ◆ *vt* to put up the framework of; to make a carcase of. [OFr *carquois* (Fr *carcasse*) a skeleton]
❑ **carcase meat** or **carcass meat** *n* raw meat as prepared for the butcher's shop, not tinned.

carceral /kär'sə-rəl/ *adj* of or relating to prison or a prison. [L *carcerālis*, from *carcer* prison]

carcinogen, carcinogenic see under **carcinoma**.

carcinology /kär-si-nol'ə-ji/ *n* the study of crustaceans. [Gr *karkinos* a crab, and *logos* discourse]
■ **carcinological** /-ə-loj'i-kl/ *adj*. **carcinol'ogist** *n*.

carcinoma /kär-si-nō'mə/ *n* (*pl* **carcinō'mata** or **carcinō'mas**) a cancer. [Gr *karkinōma*, from *karkinos* crab]
■ **carcin'ogen** /-jen/ *n* a substance that encourages the growth of cancer. **carcinogen'esis** *n*. **carcinogen'ic** *adj*. **carcinogenic'ity** *n*. **carcinō'matous** *adj*. **carcinō'sis** or **carcinōmatō'sis** *n* spread of cancer in the body.

Card. *abbrev* : Cardinal.

card¹ /kärd/ *n* a small, *usu* rectangular piece of cardboard or stiff paper; one with figures or symbols for playing a game; one with a person's name and address, with a greeting, invitation, message, etc (*calling card, visiting card, Christmas card, birthday card*, etc); (in *pl*) an employee's work documents, held by an employer; a small piece of cardboard or plastic carrying information, showing membership or proof of identity, etc, either in print or on a magnetic strip (*identity card, membership card, credit card*, etc); a domino; the dial of a mariner's compass (also **compass card**); a map; a perforated plate used as a guide in weaving; a personal announcement in a newspaper or elsewhere (*N Am*); the programme of races at a race-meeting; a scorecard; a printed circuit board (*comput*); a punched card (*comput*); an expansion card (*comput*); a person, usually qualified in some way, as in *a knowing card* (*inf*); a comical or eccentric person; (in *pl*) a game played with cards. ◆ *vt* to return (a certain score) on a scorecard (*golf*); (of a referee in sport, *esp* football) to show a yellow or red card to a player to indicate a punishment for breaking the rules; to enter in a card index. [Fr *carte*, from L *c(h)arta*, from Gr *chartēs* paper; cf **carte²**]
❑ **card'-carrying** *adj* openly expressing membership of or support for a party or group; *orig* holding a membership card of a party, etc, *esp* the Communist party. **card'case** *n* *esp* formerly, a case for carrying visiting cards. **card'-castle** *n* a structure of playing cards built one upon the other in storeys; any flimsy or precarious structure. **card catalogue** *n* a card index. **card column** *n* (*comput*; *obs*) one of the eighty or ninety columns of a punched card with lines parallel to the short edge of the card (cf **card row**). **card file** *n* a card index. **card game** *n* any game played with playing-cards. **card'-holder** *n* someone who has a membership card; hence a member of a club,

organization, etc; someone who owns a credit or debit card. **card index** *n* one with entries on separate cards. **card'-in'dex** *vt*. **card mechanic** see under **mechanic**. **card'phone** *n* a public telephone from which calls are made using a pre-paid plastic card rather than money. **card'punch** *n* (*comput*; *obs*) a machine which perforates cards to record data. **card reader** *n* (*comput*; *obs*) a device which reads the data represented by holes on a punched card and converts them to a form suitable for storage or processing. **card row** *n* (*comput*; *obs*) one of the rows of a punched card with lines parallel to the long edge of the card (cf **card column**). **card'-sharp** or **card'-sharper** *n* a person who cheats at cards. **card swipe** *n* an electronic device that reads information on a credit or debit card when the card is passed through it. **card'-table** *n* a table for playing cards on. **card'-vote** *n* a voting system that gives each delegate's vote a value in proportion to the number he represents.
■ **a card up one's sleeve** an advantageous factor or argument kept in reserve. **cards in one's hands** everything under one's control. **cards on the table** one's resources and moves freely laid open. **cooling card** (*Shakesp*) anything that discourages, or dashes hopes. **get one's cards** to be dismissed from one's employment. **hold all the cards** to have control over all of the factors that may determine the outcome of a situation. **house of cards** a card-castle, cards built up into storeys; any flimsy or precarious structure, scheme, etc. **keep** or **play one's cards close to one's chest** to conceal one's full intentions. **knowing card** someone who is astute, sharp or wide awake. **leading card** a strong point in one's case. **make a card** to win a trick in a card game. **on the cards** not improbable; likely to happen. **play one's cards well** or **right** (or **badly**) to make (or not to make) the best of one's chances; to act (or not to act) in a way that will bring one benefit or advantage. **play one's strongest** or **trump card** to make use of one's greatest advantage. **show** (**all**) **one's cards** to expose one's secrets or designs, *esp* when giving an advantage to someone else by so doing. **speak by the card** to speak with precision and to the point. **sure card** someone who is wide awake. **the cards are stacked against** (**someone** or **something**) the circumstances, or facts, are ranged against (a person, an argument, etc). **throw up** (or **in**) **the cards** to give in; to admit defeat.

card² /kärd/ *n* an instrument for combing wool, flax, etc, before spinning. ◆ *vt* to comb (wool, etc); to mix, adulterate (*Shakesp*). [Fr *carde*, from L *carduus* a thistle]
■ **card'er** *n*. **card'ing** *n*.
❑ **carding wool** *n* short-stapled wool.

cardamine /kär-dam'i-nē/ *n* a plant of the genus of cress (*Cardamine*) including the cuckoo flower or lady's smock. [Gr *kardaminē*, from *kardamon* cress]

cardamom or **cardamum** /kär'də-məm/ *n* the seed capsules of several tropical plants of the ginger family, used as an aromatic spice (also **card'amon**). [L *cardamōmum*, from Gr *kardamōmon*]

cardan joint /kär'dan joint/ *n* a type of universal joint which can rotate out of alignment within its shaft. [Invented by Geronimo *Cardano* (1501–76), Italian mathematician]

cardboard /kärd'börd/ *n* a thin, stiff, finely-finished pasteboard; a rougher, thicker material made from paper pulp and used to make cartons or boxes. ◆ *adj* made of cardboard; flimsy, insubstantial; stiff. [**card¹** and **board**]
■ **card'boardy** *adj*.
❑ **cardboard city** *n* an area in which homeless people live or sleep, using cardboard boxes, etc, as shelter.

cardecu or **cardecue** /kär'di-kū/ (*obs*) *n* an old French silver coin. [Fr *quart d'écu* quarter of a crown]

cardi, cardie or **cardy** /kär'di/ (*inf*) *n* short for **cardigan**.

cardiac /kär'di-ak/ *adj* belonging to the heart or to the upper end of the stomach. ◆ *n* a cordial or heart stimulant; a person with cardiac disease. [L *cardiacus*, from Gr *kardiakos*, from *kardiā* heart, the upper end of the stomach]
■ **cardiacal** /-dī'ə-kl/ *adj* cardiac.
❑ **cardiac arrest** *n* stopping of the heartbeat. **cardiac failure** *n* heart failure. **cardiac massage** *n* rhythmic manual massage of the heart, either directly or by pressure on the chest wall, to restart or maintain blood circulation after heart failure. **cardiac muscle** *n* specialized muscle, able to contract and expand indefinitely, found only in the walls of the heart.

cardialgia /kär-di-al'ji-ə/ or **cardialgy** /kär'di-al-ji/ *n* discomfort or a burning pain at the upper orifice of the stomach, apparently at the heart; heartburn. [Gr *kardia* heart, and *algos* pain]

cardie see **cardi**.

cardigan /kär'di-gən/ *n* a knitted woollen jacket with buttons up the front, named after Lord *Cardigan* (1797–1868).
■ **car'diganed** *adj* wearing a cardigan.

cardinal /kär'di-nəl/ *adj* of fundamental importance, chief; relating to a hinge; on which a thing hinges; of a deep scarlet colour, like a cardinal's cassock or hat. ◆*n* (with *cap* in titles) one of the leading dignitaries of the church constituting the Sacred College at Rome, to whom pertains the right of electing a new pope (*RC*); a cardinal number; a short cloak, worn by ladies in the 17c and 18c; a cardinal-bird; a S European butterfly (*Pandoriana pandora*). [L *cardinālis*, from *cardō, cardinis* a hinge]

■ **car'dinalate** or **car'dinalship** *n* the office or dignity of cardinal; the cardinals collectively. **cardinalā'tial** or **cardinali'tial** *adj* relating to a cardinal or to the office of cardinal. **car'dinally** *adv* fundamentally.

❑ **cardinal beetle** *n* any of various large, red-coloured beetles of the family Pyrochroidae. **car'dinal-bird** or **cardinal grosbeak** *n* (also called (*US*) **redbird**) a large American seed-eating finch (*Richmondena cardinalis*), the male bright-red with a crest, the female brown. **car'dinal-bishop**, **car'dinal-priest**, **car'dinal-deacon** *n* the three orders of cardinal in the Sacred College. **cardinal flower** *n* a N American plant (*Lobelia cardinalis*) with bright scarlet lobed flowers. **cardinal number** *n* a number expressing quantity (1, 2, 3, etc) as distinct from an ordinal (first, second, third, etc). **cardinal point** *n* any of the four chief points of the compass, north, south, east, or west. **cardinal sin** *n* any of the seven deadly sins (see under **seven**); an inexcusable mistake or error of judgement (*inf*). **cardinal virtue** *n* one of the chief moral qualities, justice, prudence, temperance, fortitude, upon which the whole of human nature was supposed to hinge.

cardio /kär'di-ō/ *adj* and *n* cardiovascular (exercise).

cardio- /kär-di-ō-/ or before a vowel **cardi-** /kär-di-/ *combining form* denoting heart. [Gr *kardiā* heart]

■ **car'diogram** *n* a tracing obtained from a cardiograph. **car'diograph** *n* an instrument for recording movements of the heart. **cardiog'rapher** *n* a person who uses a cardiograph. **cardiog'raphy** *n*. **cardiological** /-loj'i-kl/ *adj*. **cardiol'ogist** *n*. **cardiology** /-ol'ə-ji/ *n* the science that deals with the structure, function and diseases of the heart. **cardiomeg'aly** *n* abnormal enlargement of the heart. **cardiomō'tor** *adj* relating to the action of the heart. **cardiomyop'athy** *n* myocardiopathy. **cardiopul'monary** *adj* relating to the heart and lungs (**cardiopulmonary resuscitation** mouth-to-mouth respiration and heart massage to revive a patient whose heart has stopped beating). **cardiorespir'atory** *adj* relating to the action of the heart and lungs. **cardiothoracic** /-thō-ras'ik/ *adj* relating to the heart and chest. **cardiotocograph** /-tok'ə-graf/ *n* (Gr *tokos* birth, offspring) a record of the heart rate of a fetus. **cardiotocography** /-tə-kog'rə-fi/ *n* the study and interpretation of cardiotocographs. **cardiovascular** /-vas'kū-/ *adj* relating to or involving the heart and blood vessels (**cardiovascular system** the circulatory system). **cardī'tis** *n* inflammation of the heart.

cardioid /kär'di-oid/ *adj* heart-shaped. ◆*n* a heart-shaped curve traced by a fixed point on the circumference of a circle rolling around another circle of equal radius. [Gr *kardiā* heart]

cardoon /kär-doon'/ *n* a Mediterranean plant (*Cynara cardunculus*) closely related to the true artichoke, its leafstalks and ribs eaten like celery. [Obs Fr *cardon*, from L *carduus* a thistle]

Cards. *abbrev* : Cardiganshire, a former county of Wales (now part of Dyfed).

carduus /kär'dū-əs/ (*Shakesp*) *n* a thistle. [L]

cardy see **cardi**.

CARE /kär/ *abbrev* : Co-operative for American Relief Everywhere.

care /kär/ *n* affliction; anxiety; heedfulness; heed; charge, oversight; residential or non-residential medical or social welfare services; an object of anxiety or watchfulness. ◆*vi* to be anxious; to be inclined; to be concerned; to mind; to have affection, fondness or regard for (with *for* or *about*); to provide for, look after, watch over (with *for*). [OE *caru*; Gothic *kara* sorrow; ON *kæra* to lament]

■ **care'ful** *adj* full of care; heedful; painstaking, thorough; anxious (*Bible*); grievous (*Spenser*); sorrowful (*Spenser*). **care'fully** *adv*. **care'fulness** *n*. **care'less** *adj* without care; heedless, unconcerned. **care'lessly** *adv*. **care'lessness** *n*. **car'er** *n* a person who cares; a person who takes responsibility for another, dependent, person. **car'ing** *adj* compassionate; concerned professionally with social, medical, etc welfare (as the *caring professions*, ie social workers, nurses, etc). **car'ingly** *adv*.

❑ **care assistant** *n* a person employed to look after children or old or disabled people in a home, hospital, etc. **care attendant** *n* a person employed by social services to care for physically or mentally handicapped people in day centres or residential homes. **care card** *n* a plastic card with an inbuilt memory chip used for storing an individual's medical records. **care'-crazed** *adj* (*Shakesp*) crazed or broken with care and solicitude. **care'free** *adj* free from anxiety, worry or responsibility. **care'giver** *n* (*US*) a carer. **care home** *n* a residential institution for young, elderly, or disabled

people. **care label** *n* a label on a garment giving washing, dry-cleaning, etc, instructions. **care'take** *vt* and *vi* to act as caretaker (for a property, etc). **care'taker** *n* someone put in charge of a place, *esp* a building. ◆*adj* exercising temporary supervision or control, as *caretaker government*. **care'ware** *n* (*comput sl*) computer software that is made available in exchange for making a donation of one's services, money, etc to a charity. **care'worker** *n* a person employed to help look after dependent people in their own homes. **care'worn** *adj* showing signs of stress, anxiety, etc.

■ **care and maintenance** the keeping of an industrial plant, shipyard, etc in sound condition at times when production has been discontinued so that it may be restarted immediately new orders are received. **care (and protection) order** an order by a magistrate placing a child in care. **care of** to be delivered to the custody of, or at the address of (*abbrev* **c/o**). **for all I** (or **you**, etc) **care** it is a matter of indifference to me (or you, etc). **have a care** to take care. **I**, etc **couldn't care less** I, etc do not care in the least. **in care** (of a child) in the guardianship of a local authority or other official organization; (of an elderly person) in an old people's home or geriatric ward. **in care of** (*US*) care of (see above). **take care** to be careful or cautious. **take care of** to look after with care; to make the necessary arrangements regarding (*inf*).

careen /kə-rēn'/ *vt* and *vi* to tilt or cause to tilt to one side. ◆*vt* (*naut*) to turn (a vessel) over on the side, *esp* for repairing or cleaning. ◆*n* an upturned position. [L *carīna* keel]

■ **careen'age** *n* a place where ships are careened; the cost of careening.

career /kə-rēr'/ or (*obs*) **cariere** /kar'/ (*Spenser*) *n* a rush; progress through life; one's profession or occupation; progress or advancement in one's profession or occupation. ◆*adj* having a career; dedicated to a career. ◆*vi* to gallop; to rush wildly; to move rapidly. [Obs Fr *carrière* a racecourse, from LL *carrāria* carriage-road, from *carrus* wagon]

■ **career'ism** *n*. **career'ist** *n* a person intent on his or her own advancement (also *adj*).

❑ **career break** *n* a period away from one's occupation or profession for study, childcare, etc. **career diplomat** *n* one who has risen through the profession, rather than a political appointee. **careers adviser** or **officer** *n* a person who advises schoolchildren, students, etc on their choice of career. **career woman** or **career girl** *n* a woman who follows a career.

carême or **Carême** /ka-rem'/ (*Fr*) *n* Lent.

caress /kə-res'/ *vt* to touch affectionately or lovingly; to fondle. ◆*n* a gentle, loving or affectionate touch. [Fr *caresser*, from Ital *carezza* an endearment, from L *cārus* dear]

■ **caress'ing** *n* and *adj*. **caress'ingly** *adv*. **caress'ive** *adj*.

caret /kar'ət/ *n* (in proofreading, etc) a mark, ⅄, to show where to insert something omitted. [L, literally there is missing]

carex /kā'reks/ *n* (*pl* **cā'rices** /-ris-ēz/) a plant of the genus of sedges *Carex*. [L]

Carey Street /kā'ri strēt/ (*euphem*) *n* the state of bankruptcy. [The street in London where the bankruptcy court was formerly situated]

carfax /kär'faks/ or **carfox** /-foks/ *n* a place where four roads meet, *esp* an intersection of main roads in the centre of a town. [L *quadrifurcus* four-forked]

carfuffle or **curfuffle**, also **kerfuffle** or **kefuffle** /kər-fuf'l/ (*orig Scot*) *n* commotion, agitation. ◆*vt* to disorder or agitate. [Gaelic pfx *car-*, and Scot *fuffle* to disorder]

cargo /kär'gō/ *n* (*pl* **car'goes**) the goods carried by a ship or aeroplane; any load to be carried. ◆*vt* to load, weigh down (with *with*). [Sp, from root of **car**]

❑ **cargo cult** *n* a type of religion in certain S Pacific islands based on the belief that ancestors or supernatural beings will return bringing products of modern civilization and thus make the islanders rich and independent; any setting of too high a value on material possessions. **cargo cultist** *n*. **cargo pants** or **trousers** *n pl* wide, baggy trousers with large pockets on the side of the thighs.

cargoose /kär'goos/ *n* (*pl* **car'geese**) the crested grebe. [ON *kjarr* copsewood, and **goose**]

cariacou /kar'i-ə-koo/ or **carjacou** /kär'jə-koo/ *n* any deer of the subgenus *Cariacus*, including the Virginian deer. [Tupí *cariacu*]

cariama /kä-ri-ä'mə/ *n* same as **seriema**.

Carib /kar'ib/ *n* a member of a race of Native Americans inhabiting parts of Central America and northern S America; their language. ◆*adj* of or relating to the Caribs or their language. [Sp *Caribe*]

■ **Car'iban** *adj*.

Caribbean /ka-ri-bē'ən/ or (*esp N Am*) kə-rib'i-ən/ *adj* of or relating to the Caribbean Sea and the islands of the West Indies, their inhabitants or their culture; of or relating to the Caribs or their language. ♦ *n* (with *the*) the Caribbean Sea and its islands; the Carib language.

Caribbee bark /ka-ri-bē' bärk/ *n* the bark of several West Indian rubiaceous trees of the genus *Exostema* used as a substitute for cinchona. [**Carib**]

caribe /ka-rē'bā/ *n* the S American piranha fish. [Sp, cannibal]

caribou /kar'i-boo or kar-i-boo'/ *n* (*pl* **car'ibou** or **car'ibous**) the N American reindeer. [Can Fr]

Carica /kar'i-kə/ *n* the papaw genus of plants of the family **Caricā'ceae**, related to the passion flowers. [L *Carica* (*fīcus*) a dried fig from Caria, an ancient region in Asia Minor]

caricature /kar'i-kə-tūr, -tūr', -chər or -choor'/ *n* a likeness or representation of anything so exaggerated or distorted as to appear ridiculous or comical (formerly **caricatū'ra**); an absurd or ludicrous imitation or version of something. ♦ *vt* to ridicule by representing an exaggerated or distorted likeness; to burlesque. [Ital *caricatura*, from *caricare* to load, from root of **car**]
■ **caricatūr'al** *adj*. **caricatūr'ist** *n*.

carices see **carex**.

CARICOM or **Caricom** /kar'i-kom/ *abbrev* : *Caribbean Community*, a Caribbean Common Market.

cariere an obsolete form of **career**.

caries /kā'rēz/ *n* decay, *esp* of teeth. [L *cariēs*]
■ **cariogenic** /-ri-ō-jen'ik/ *adj* tending to give rise to caries. **cā'rious** *adj* decayed.

CARIFTA /ka-rif'tə/ *abbrev* : *Caribbean Free Trade Association*.

carillon /kə-ril'yən or kar'il-yən/ *n* a set of bells for playing tunes; a mechanism for playing them; a melody played on them; an instrument or organ stop imitating a peal of bells. ♦ *vi* to play a carillon. [Fr, from LL *quadriliō, -ōnis* a quaternary, as formerly rung on four bells]
■ **carill'onneur** (also /-nûr'/) or **carill'onist** (also /kar'/) *n*.

carina /kə-rī'nə/ (*biol*) *n* (*pl* **cari'nae** /-ē/ or **cari'nas**) a keel-like ridge as in a bird's breastbone; the boat-shaped structure formed by the two lower petals in the pea family; (with *cap*) a constellation in the southern hemisphere containing the second brightest star, Canopus. [L *carīna* a keel]
■ **carinate** /kar'i-nāt/ or **car'inated** *adj* keeled.

carioca /ka-ri-ō'kə/ *n* a Brazilian dance or its tune, a maxixe or variety of it; (with *cap*) a native of Rio de Janeiro. [Port]

cariogenic see under **caries**.

cariole or **carriole** /kar'i-ōl/ *n* a small open carriage; a light cart. [Fr *carriole*, from root of **car**]

carious see under **caries**.

caritas /kar'i-tas or kä'ri-täs/ (L) *n* (Christian) charity.

carjacou see **cariacou**.

cark[1] /kärk/ (*archaic*) *n* care, anxiety or solicitude. ♦ *vt* to burden or harass. ♦ *vi* to be anxious. [Norman Fr *kark*(e), from LL *carcāre*, from *carricāre* to load; see also **charge**]
■ **cark'ing** *adj*.

cark[2] see **kark**.

carl /kärl/ *n* a husbandman (*obs*); a churl (*archaic*); a miser (*Scot*). [ON *karl* a man, a male; see **churl**]
■ **car'line** /-lin/ *n* (*Scot*) an old woman; a witch. **carl'ish** *adj* (*archaic*) churlish; clownish. **car'lot** *n* (*Shakesp, As You Like It*) a churl or peasant.
❑ **carl'-hemp** *n* the female plant of hemp (literally, male-hemp, as stronger than fimble, the true male).

Carley float /kär'li flōt/ *n* an emergency rubber raft. [HS *Carley*, its US inventor]

carline[1] /kär'lin/ *n* any plant of the genus *Carlina* closely related to the true thistles, *esp* the **carline thistle** (*C. vulgaris*). [From a legend that an angel showed the root to *Carolus*, ie Charlemagne, as a remedy for a plague]

carline[2], **carlish** see under **carl**.

carling /kär'ling/ (*naut*) *n* a strong beam used for supporting the deck in a ship, etc.

Carlist /kär'list/ *n* a supporter of the claims of the Spanish pretender Don *Carlos* de Borbón (1788–1855), second son of Charles IV, and his representatives (also *adj*).
■ **Car'lism** *n*.

carlock /kär'lok/ *n* Russian isinglass. [Russ *karluk*]

carlot see under **carl**.

Carlovingian see **Carolingian**.

Carlylese /kär-līl-ēz'/ *n* the vigorous, irregular phraseology and vocabulary of the essayist and historian Thomas *Carlyle* (1795–1881).
■ **Carlylesque'** or **Carlyl'ean** *adj*. **Car'lylism** (or /-līl'/) *n*.

carmagnole /kär-man-yōl'/ *n* a popular song and dance of the French Revolution; a kind of short jacket worn by revolutionaries at that time with a broad collar and lapels and several rows of buttons. [Prob from *Carmagnola* in Piedmont]

Carmelite /kär'mi-līt/ *n* a White Friar, or friar of the order of Our Lady of Mount *Carmel*, in Palestine (now Israel), which was founded there c.1156, becoming a mendicant order in 1247; a member of a contemplative order of nuns founded in 1452 (also *adj*); (without *cap*) a fine woollen fabric of beige or similar colour.

Carmenère /kär-mə-när'/ *n* a grape variety grown *esp* in Chile, used to produce red wine; a red wine produced from this grape. [Fr, from *carmin* crimson]

carminative /kär'mi-nə-tiv or -min'ə-/ *adj* expelling or relieving flatulence. ♦ *n* a medicine with that effect. [L *cārmināre* to card, comb out, from *cārmen* a card for wool]

carmine /kär'mīn or -min/ *n* the bright-red pigment obtained from the cochineal insect; its colour. ♦ *adj* of that colour. [Fr *carmin* or Sp *carmín*, from Sp *carmesí* crimson, from Ar *qirmazī* crimson, from same root as **crimson**]

carnage /kär'nij/ *n* extensive or indiscriminate slaughter, *esp* of people. [Fr, from Ital *carnaggio* carnage, from L *carō, carnis* flesh]

carnahuba see **carnauba**.

carnal /kär'nəl/ *adj* fleshly; sensual; unspiritual; bodily; sexual; murderous, flesh-eating (*Shakesp*). ♦ *vi* (*obs*) to act carnally. [L *carō, carnis* flesh]
■ **car'nalism** *n*. **car'nalist** *n* a sensualist. **carnality** /-nal'i-ti/ *n* the state of being carnal. **car'nalize** or **-ise** *vt* to sensualize. **car'nally** *adv*.
❑ **carnal knowledge** *n* (*law*) sexual intercourse. **carnal-mind'ed** *adj* worldly-minded.

carnallite /kär'nə-līt/ *n* a milk-white or pinkish hydrous chloride of potassium and magnesium. [Named after the mineralogist Rudolf Von *Carnall* (1804–74)]

carnaptious /kär-nap'shəs/ or **curnaptious** /kər-/ (*Scot* and *Irish*) *adj* bad-tempered, cantankerous. [Origin obscure]

carnaroli /kär-nə-rō'li/ *n* a round-grained rice, used in making risotto. [Ital]

carnassial /kär-nas'i-əl/ *adj* adapted for flesh-eating. ♦ *n* one of the teeth of carnivores specially adapted for tearing flesh, being the last premolar of the upper jaw and first molar of the lower jaw (also **carnassial tooth**). [Fr *carnassier* flesh-eating, from L *carō, carnis* flesh]

carnation /kär-nā'shən/ *n* a double-flowering cultivated variety of the clove pink, *Dianthus caryophyllus*; a colour ranging from light pink to deep crimson; a flesh colour in painting. ♦ *adj* of the colour carnation. [L *carnātiō, -ōnis* fleshiness]
■ **carnā'tioned** *adj* ruddy.

carnauba or **carnahuba** /kär-nö'bə or -now', also kär-nä-oo'bə/ *n* a Brazilian palm (*Copernicia cerifera*); the yellowish wax obtained from its leaves (also **Brazilian wax** or **carnauba wax**). [Port]

carnelian see **cornelian**[1].

carneous see **carnose**.

carnet /kär'nā/ *n* a customs or other permit; a book of tickets, vouchers, or coupons. [Fr]

carney see **carny**[1,2].

carnifex /kär'ni-feks/ (L) *n* an executioner.

carnify /kär'ni-fī/ (*pathol*) *vt* and *vi* (**car'nifying**; **car'nified**) of soft tissue, *esp* in the lungs, to alter and become like muscle, as a result of disease. [L *carō* flesh, and *facere* to make]
■ **carnifica'tion** *n*. **carnific'ial** *adj*.

carnival /kär'ni-vəl/ *n* a festive occasion, often with a procession, sideshows, etc; a feast observed by Roman Catholics just before the fast of Lent; riotous feasting, merriment or amusement; an entertainment similar to a fair. [Ital *carnevale*, from LL *carnelevārium*, appar from L *carnem levāre* to put away meat]
■ **carnivalesque'** *adj* characteristic of or appropriate to a carnival.

Carnivora /kär-niv'ə-rə/ *n pl* an order of flesh-eating mammals, including dogs, cats, bears, weasels, etc. [L *carō, carnis* flesh, and *vorāre* to devour]
■ **car'nivore** /-vör or -vör/ *n* an animal or plant that feeds on flesh; a mammal of the order Carnivora. **carniv'orous** *adj* flesh-eating. **carniv'orously** *adv*. **carniv'orousness** *n*.

carnose /kär'nōs/ or **carneous** /kär'ni-əs/ *adj* fleshy; of or like flesh. [See **carnal**]
■ **carnos'ity** *n* (*pathol*) a fleshy excrescence growing in and obstructing any part of the body.

Carnot cycle /kär'nō sī'kl/ n an ideal heat engine cycle of maximum thermal efficiency. [Nicolas *Carnot*, French physicist (1796–1832)]

carnotite /kär'nō-tīt/ n a yellow mineral (hydrated vanadate of uranium and potassium) important as a source of radium, vanadium and uranium. [Adolphe *Carnot* (died 1920), French mine inspector]

carny[1] or **carney** /kär'ni/ (dialect) vt and vi to coax, wheedle. ◆ n flattery; a flatterer. ◆ adj cunning, sly. [Origin unknown]

carny[2] or **carney** /kär'ni/ (N Am sl) n (pl **car'nies** or **car'neys**) a carnival; a person who works in a carnival.

carnyx /kär'niks/ n a long war trumpet used by the Celts. [Gr *karnyx*]

carob /kar'əb or -ob/ n the algarroba or locust-tree (*Ceratonia siliqua*), a caesalpiniaceous Mediterranean tree; its edible fruit (also called **St John's Bread**); a substitute for chocolate prepared from its fruit. [Fr *carobe*, from Ar *kharrūbah*; cf **algarroba**]

caroche /kä-rosh'/ (hist) n a stately carriage used on ceremonial occasions. [Fr, from Ital *caroccio*, *carro*, from L *carrus* car]

carol /kar'əl/ n a song of joy or praise; a Christmas song or hymn; a round dance or the song accompanying it (*archaic*); an enclosure for a study in a cloister, etc (also **carrel**). ◆ vi (**car'olling**; **car'olled**) to dance or sing a carol; to sing or warble. ◆ vt to praise or celebrate in song. [OFr *carole*; Ital *carola* orig a round dance, perh from L *chorus*, Gr *choros*, or L or Gr *choraulēs*, a flute player who accompanies a chorus]
■ **car'oller** n. **car'olling** n.

Carolina /ka-rə-lī'nə/ n either of two states (North and South) of the United States (also adj).
■ **Carolinian** /-lin'i-ən/ adj.
◻ **Carolina allspice** see **calycanthus** under **calyx**. **Carolina pink** n an American species of *Silene* (bladder campion); pinkroot (see under **pink**[1]).

Caroline /kar'ə-līn/ or **Carolean** /kar-ə-lē'ən/ adj of, belonging to, or characteristic of the British kings Charles I or II, or the periods of their reign (also **Carolin'ian**); of, belonging to, or characteristic of the reign of any other king named Charles. [L *Carolus* Charles]
◻ **Caroline minuscule** see under **Carolingian**.

Carolingian /kar-ə-lin'ji-ən/ or **Carlovingian** /kär-lō-vin'ji-ən/ adj relating to a dynasty of Frankish kings, so called from *Karl* (L *Carolus*) the Great or Charlemagne (742–814). ◆ n a member of this dynasty.
◻ **Carolingian** (or **Caroline**) **minuscule** n a style of handwriting developed in France at the time of Charlemagne.

carolus /kar'ə-ləs/ n (pl **car'oluses** or **car'oli** /-lī/) a gold coin of the time of Charles I; any gold coin of the reigns of various kings named Charles. [L *Carolus* Charles]

carom /kar'əm/ n short form of **carambole** /kar'əm-bōl/ a cannon in billiards; any rebound or ricochet (*US*). ◆ vi to make a carom. [Fr *carombole*, from Sp *carambola* the red ball in billiards]

caromel see **caramel**.

caron /ka'rən/ n another name (*esp* in typesetting) for the **hacek**. [Origin obscure]

carotene /kar'ə-tēn/ or **carotin** /-tin/ n any of a number of reddish-yellow pigments widely distributed in plants that are converted to vitamin A in the body. [L *carōta* carrot, and sfx -*ene*]
■ **carotenoid** or **carotinoid** /kar-ot'in-oid/ n any of a group of pigments including carotenes and xanthophylls, found in plant and some animal tissues.

carotid /kə-rot'id/ adj relating to the two great arteries that supply blood to the head and neck (also n). [Gr *karōtides* (pl), from *karos* sleep, so named because compression of them caused unconsciousness]

carouse /kə-rowz'/ vi to hold a drinking bout; to drink freely and noisily. ◆ n a drinking bout or party; a noisy revel. [OFr *carous*, Fr *carrousse*, from Ger *gar aus* quite out, ie empty the glass]
■ **carous'al** n a carouse; a feast. **carous'er** n. **carous'ingly** adv.

carousel or (N Am) **carrousel** /ka-rə-sel' or -zel'/ n a merry-go-round (N Am); a circular magazine for a slide projector that rotates as each slide is shown; a rotating conveyor, eg for luggage at an airport or air terminal; a tilting match or tournament, to which were added games, shows and allegorical representations (*hist*).
◻ **carousel fraud** n (inf) a type of fraud involving the claim of tax refunds for bogus transactions. [Fr *carrousel*]

carp[1] /kärp/ n an edible freshwater fish of the family Cyprinidae. [OFr *carpe*, from LL *carpa*; poss Gmc]

carp[2] /kärp/ vi to find fault (with *at*); to nag about trivialities. [Most prob Scand, ON *karpa* to boast, modified in meaning through likeness to L *carpere* to pluck, deride]
■ **carp'er** n. **carp'ing** n and adj cavilling; fault-finding. **carp'ingly** adv.

-carp /-kärp/ (bot) combining form denoting a fruit or fruiting body.

carpaccio /kär-pach'i-ō/ n an hors-d'œuvre of thin strips of raw meat or fish often eaten with a relish. [Vittore *Carpaccio* (c.1455–1522), Venetian painter, noted for his vivid red colours]

carpal see under **carpus**.

carpe diem /kär'pē dī'em or kär'pā dē'em/ (L) make the most of the present time, literally seize the day.

carpel /kär'pəl/ (bot) n the female organ of a flower, a modified leaf comprising ovary, stigma and style and forming, singly or with others, the gynoecium (qv). [Gr *karpos* fruit]
■ **car'pellary** adj. **car'pellate** adj (of a flower) female. ◆ n a flower containing carpels. **carpogō'nium** the female organ in red seaweeds, indirectly producing **car'pospores**. **carpolog'ical** adj. **carpo'logist** n. **carpo'logy** n the study of fruit and seeds. **carpoph'agous** adj (zool) fruit-eating. **carp'ophore** n a prolongation of a flower axis below or between the carpels; a spore-bearing structure in some fungi.

Carpentaria palm /kär-pən-tä'ri-ə päm/ n an ornamental palm tree growing around the Gulf of *Carpentaria* in N Australia.

carpenter /kär'pin-tər/ n a person skilled in woodwork as used in building houses, ships, etc. ◆ vi to do the work of a carpenter. ◆ vt to make by carpentry; to put together or construct. [OFr *carpentier*, from LL *carpentārius*, from *carpentum* a car, from root of **car**]
■ **car'pentry** n the trade or work of a carpenter.
◻ **car'penter-bee** or **-ant** n a bee or ant that excavates its nest in wood.

carpenteria /kär-pən-tē'ri-ə/ n an evergreen shrub of the hydrangea family, cultivated for its glossy foliage and yellow-centred white flowers. [From William *Carpenter* (1811–48), American botanist]

carpet /kär'pit/ n a woven, felted or tufted covering for floors, stairs, etc; a smooth, or thin, surface or covering; the surface of the ground (cricket); a prison sentence of three months (sl); odds of three to one (bookmakers' sl); 300 (salesmen's sl); a carpet-moth; a tablecloth (Shakesp). ◆ vt (**car'peting**; **car'peted**) to cover with or as if with a carpet; to reprimand. [OFr *carpite*, from LL *carpeta*, -*pita* coarse fabric made from rags pulled to pieces, from L *carpere* to pluck]
■ **car'peting** n material of which carpets are made; carpet, or carpets; a reprimand.
◻ **car'petbag** n a travelling bag made of carpeting. **car'petbagger** n (derog) a person who uses a place or organization with which he or she has no previous connection for political, financial or other ends; in the USA, an adventurer from the Northern states who sought a political career in the South after the end of the Civil War, whose only property qualification for office was his carpetbag of personal belongings. **carpetbag steak** n a beefsteak stuffed with oysters. **carpet beating** n the removal of dust from carpets by beating. **car'pet-bed** or **car'pet-bedding** n a system of horticulture in which plants are arranged in mosaic or geometrical designs. **carpet beetle** or (N Am) **carpet bug** n any of several beetles or their larvae which are harmful to carpets and fabrics. **carpet biter** n (inf) a person prone to violent fits of rage. **car'pet-bomb** vt. **car'pet-bombing** n systematic bombing of a whole area; the delivery of unsolicited mail, esp advertising matter. **car'pet-knight** n a knight dubbed at court by favour, not on account of his military exploits; hence a shirker, idler. **car'petmonger** n (Shakesp) an effeminate person. **carpet-moth** n any of the larger moths of the geometrid subfamily Larentiinae. **carpet plot** n (maths) the function of more than one variable represented as values on a graph, the shape of which resembles a flying carpet. **car'pet-rod** n one of the rods used to keep a stair carpet in its place. **carpet shark** n a shark of the genus *Orectolobus*, with a spotted back like a patterned carpet. **car'pet-slipper** n a slipper with an upper orig made of carpeting. **carpet snake** or **python** n a variegated python of Australia (*Morelia variegata*). **car'pet-sweeper** n an apparatus with a revolving brush and a dustpan, for sweeping carpets. **carpet tile** n one of a number of squares of carpeting which are laid together in such a way as to form an area of carpet.
■ **brush** or **sweep under the carpet** to hide from someone's notice, put out of one's mind (unpleasant problems or facts). **on the carpet** under discussion (jocular transl of Fr *sur le tapis*); up before someone in authority for reprimand; at or near ground level (RAF sl).

carphology /kär-fol'ə-ji/ (rare) n floccillation, fitful plucking movements as in delirium. [Gr *karphos* straw, and *logeiā* gathering]

carpogonium, carpology, carpophagous see under **carpel**.

carpus /kär'pəs/ (anat) n (pl **carpi** /kär'pī or -ē/) the wrist, or corresponding part of the forelimb. [Latinized from Gr *karpos* wrist]
■ **car'pal** adj relating to the carpus. ◆ n a bone of the carpus. **carpometacar'pus** n in birds, a bone of the wing formed by fusion of some of the carpals with the metacarpals.
◻ **carpal tunnel syndrome** n numbness and pain in the fingers caused by compression of the nerve as it passes through the **carpal tunnel** (between the bones of the wrist and the tendons).

carr /kär/ n (a copse, esp of willow, in) boggy ground. [ON *kjarr*]

carrack /kar'ək/ (*hist*) n a large Mediterranean galleon, used for transporting goods (also **car'ack**, **carr'act** or **carr'ect**). [OFr *carraque*, from LL *carraca*; ety dubious]

carrageen or **carragheen** /kar'ə-gēn/ n a purplish-red N Atlantic seaweed (*Chondrus crispus*) and a related species (*Gigartina mamillosa*), used for making soup and a kind of blancmange, and as an emulsifying and gelling agent (also called **Irish moss**). [Prob Ir *carraigín* little rock, from *carraig* rock]
■ **carragee'nan**, **carraghee'nin** or **carragee'nin** n a colloid prepared from red algae, used in food processing, pharmaceuticals, etc.

carrat same as **carat**.

carraway same as **caraway**.

carrect see **carrack**.

carrel or **carrell** /kar'əl/ n an enclosure for study in a cloister, a carol (*hist*); a desk or alcove in a library for private study. [See **carol**]

carriage /kar'ij/ n the act or cost of carrying; a four-wheeled horse-drawn vehicle for passengers; a railway passenger-coach; a wheeled support of a gun; the structures on which an aeroplane lands; a carrying part of a machine; the part of a typewriter that carries the paper; bearing, deportment; the loop of a sword-belt (*Shakesp*); behaviour (*archaic*); a burden (*Shakesp*); baggage (*Bible*). [See **carry**]
■ **carr'iageable** adj that may be conveyed or transported in carriages.
□ **carriage bolt** n a N American name for **coach bolt** (see under **coach**). **carriage clock** n a small portable clock, *usu* with a case with a handle on top. **carriage dog** n a coachdog; another name for **Dalmatian**. **carr'iage-drive** n a road for carriages through parks, etc. **carriage driving** n the competitive sport of driving a carriage and horse(s). **carriage-free'** adv without charge for transport. **carriage-for'ward** adv without prepayment of charges for carriage. **carriage horse** n a horse that draws a carriage. **carriage line** n another name for **coachline** (see under **coach**). **carriage-paid'** adv with prepayment of charges for carriage. **carriage return** n (*comput*) a control character that causes a device to return to a left-hand margin. **carriage trade** n trade from the wealthy. **carr'iageway** n a road, or part of a road, used by vehicles.
■ **carriage and pair** a carriage drawn by two horses.

carrick bend /kar'ik bend/ (*naut*) n a knot for joining two ropes, formed by looping and interlacing the ends together. [Perh connected with **carrack**, and the root of **bind**]

carrick bitt /kar'ik bit/ (*naut*) n one of two posts used to support a windlass. [See ety for **carrick bend**, and **bitt**]

carrier see under **carry**.

carriole see **cariole**.

carrion /kar'i-ən/ n the dead and rotting body or flesh of any animal; anything vile or rotten. ◆ adj relating to, or feeding on, putrid flesh. [Fr *charogne*, from LL *carōnia*, from L *carō*, *carnis* flesh]
□ **carrion beetle** n a beetle of the family Silphidae, which feeds on carrion. **carrion crow** n the common crow (*Corvus corone*); the black vulture (*US*). **carr'ion-flower** n a N American climbing plant (*Smilax herbacea*), with flowers that smell like putrid flesh; a S African asclepiad plant (genus *Stapelia*) with fleshy stem and stinking flowers.

carritch /kar'ich/ (*Scot*) n a catechism. [Fr *catéchèse*, taken to be a plural]

carriwitchet /kar-i-wich'it/ n a quip; a quibble. [Origin unknown]

Carroll diagram /ka'rəl dī-ə-gram/ (*maths*) n a diagram in which items are categorized as having, or not having, a given characteristic and grouped in subdivisions of a square (also called **Lewis Carroll's square**). [Lewis Carroll (1832–98), English writer and mathematician]

carrom ball /kar'əm böl/ (*cricket*) n a spinning delivery bowled by flicking the ball between the thumb and a bent middle finger. [Named after the Indian game of *carrom*]

carronade /kar-ə-nād'/ (*hist*) n a short naval cannon of large bore. [From *Carron*, a town in central Scotland at whose ironworks such guns were cast]

carron oil /kar'ən oil/ n a liniment *orig* of linseed oil and limewater. [Formerly used for burns at *Carron* (see **carronade**) ironworks]

carrot /kar'ət/ n a plant of the family Umbelliferae, having a tapering root of a reddish or yellowish colour; the root itself, which is edible and sweet; an incentive, enticement. [Fr *carotte*, from L *carōta*]
■ **carr'oty** adj carrot-coloured (*esp* of the hair).
□ **carrot fly** n an insect, *Chamaepsila rosae*, whose larvae are a serious pest of carrots.
■ **carrot and stick** incentive and punishment, as alternative methods of persuasion.

carrousel a N American spelling of **carousel**.

carry /kar'i/ vt (**carr'ying**; **carr'ied**) to convey; to bear; to lead or transport; to take by force or capture; to effect; to gain; to behave or conduct oneself; to pass or win, by a majority; to add to another column (*maths*); (of a newspaper, television or radio programme, etc) to publish or include (eg an item of news), or to publish or include as a regular feature; to do the work of, or perform in sport or entertainment well enough to cover up the deficiencies of (another); to keep (merchandise, etc) in stock; (of money) to be sufficient for; to maintain; to be sufficient to maintain; (of a ball) to travel (*sport*); to be pregnant with; to hold in saluting position (*milit*). ◆ vi (of a sound) to reach or be transmitted; (of a gun) to have (a specified) range; to be pregnant; to have drugs or an illegal weapon on one's person (*sl*). ◆ n the distance a ball travels from where it was struck to where it touches the ground, *esp* the distance that a golf ball needs to be hit in the air in order to reach a target; range; an act of carrying; the portage of a boat; land across which a boat has to be carried between one navigable stream or stretch and another (chiefly *N Am*); the position of 'carry arms' (*milit*); the sky, movement of clouds (*Scot*); the digit carried to the next digit position when the base number is exceeded (*comput*). [OFr *carier*, from LL *carricāre* to cart, from L *carrus* a car]
■ **carr'ier** n a person who or an organization that carries, *esp* for hire; anything that carries; an instrument for carrying; a passenger aircraft; a basket, framework, etc for carrying luggage, as on a bicycle; a person who or animal that transmits disease (without suffering from it) by carrying a particular gene or by harbouring germs, or a virus; a vehicle for communicating a signal in cases where the medium cannot convey the actual signal (as speech, etc, in radio transmission); (also **carrier wave**) a constant frequency in an amplitude-modulation transmission (*telecom*); non-active material mixed with, and chemically identical to, a radioactive substance (*nuclear phys*); a carrier pigeon; a carrier bag; an aircraft-carrier. **carr'ying** adj (of a voice) able to be heard a long way away.
□ **carrier bag** n a strong paper or plastic bag with handles, for carrying shopping, etc. **carrier gas** n a gas, eg helium, mixed with oxygen, used in providing an air supply to divers when at great depths. **carrier pigeon** n a pigeon with homing instincts, used for carrying messages; a pigeon of a fancy breed no longer so used. **carrier rocket** n a rocket used to carry, eg a satellite into orbit. **carr'ycot** n a small portable cot for a baby. **carrying capacity** n the number of people or weight of goods that a vehicle, etc can convey; the maximum number of people or animals that a given area of land can support (*ecology*). **carrying value** n (*account*) the value of an asset or liability in a company's books or balance sheet. **carr'y-on** n a fuss (also **carrying-on'** (*pl* **carryings-on'**)); a book published in the style of, and marketed in connection with, an established and lucrative writer; see also **carry on** below. **carr'y-out** n (chiefly *Scot*) a meal or (*esp* alcoholic) drink bought and taken away to be consumed elsewhere; a place supplying such food and drink. **carr'y-over** n something left over for future use; a sum or balance carried forward; a residue or remainder that exerts a significant influence. **carr'ytale** n (*Shakesp*) a tale-bearer. **carry trade** n (*finance*) a transaction in which funds are borrowed in a country that has low interest rates and invested in a country that has higher interest rates.
■ **carry all before one** to bear down all obstacles; to be very successful in a competition or endeavour. **carry away** to carry off; to deprive of self-control by exciting the feelings; to transport. **carry back** (*account*) to set (a loss) against the previous year's profit, in order to obtain a reduction of earlier taxation (**carr'y-back** n). **carry both ends of the log** (*Aust*) to do all the work that should be shared by two people. **carry forward** to transfer written or printed matter to the next page, or a subtotal to the next column of figures (**carr'y-forward** n). **carry into effect** to accomplish. **carry it** to behave, demean oneself; to gain the advantage, carry the day (also **carry it away**). **carry off** to cause the death of; to kidnap, abduct; to gain or to win, as a prize; to cause to pass muster, to make to pass by assurance or dissimulation. **carry on** to manage; to continue; to proceed; to complain or behave unrestrainedly; to flirt (*with*). **carry one's bat** see under **bat**[1]. **carry one's point** to overrule, or overcome by argument, objections to one's plan or view. **carry out** to accomplish; to carry out for burial (*old*). **carry over** to bring into the other (political, etc) party; to take (eg an account) to a new page; to postpone to the next occasion; to postpone payment of (an account) to the next accounting period. **carry the can** to accept responsibility for a misdemeanour or error. **carry the day** to be successful; to win the day. **carry through** to support through difficulties; to succeed in putting into effect, to accomplish. **carry too far** to continue beyond reasonable or acceptable limits. **carry up** to continue a building upward; to trace back. **carry weight** to possess authority; to have force.

carryall[1] /kar'i-öl/ n a light four-wheeled one-horse carriage; a type of motor vehicle with bench-seats facing sideways, for carrying several passengers (*N Am*). [**cariole**, changed by folk etymology]

carryall[2] or **carry-all** /kar'i-öl/ n (*N Am*) an overnight bag, a holdall.

carse /kärs/ (*Scot*) n an alluvial riverside plain. [Perh **carr**]

carsey same as **kazi**.

cart /kärt/ n a two- or four-wheeled vehicle without springs, used for farm purposes, or for conveying heavy loads; a light two-wheeled horse-drawn vehicle with springs; any small vehicle drawn by an animal, eg an ox or donkey, or pushed or pulled by hand. See also **dogcart** under **dog**[1], **mail-cart** under **mail**[1], **tax cart** under **tax**, etc. ◆ vt to convey in a cart; to carry, esp with difficulty or effort (often with *around*); to carry and display (a person) publicly in a cart as a punishment (hist). [Ety doubtful; OE cræt, or ON kartr]
■ **cart'age** n the act or cost of carting. **cart'er** n a person who drives a cart. **cart'ful** n (pl **cart'fuls**) as much as a cart will hold.
▫ **cart'-horse** n a horse suitable for drawing heavy loads. **cart'-house** n a shed for keeping carts. **cart'load** n as much as a cart can carry; a large quantity (inf). **cart'road**, **cart'-track** or **cart'way** n a road or way used by or suitable for carts. **cart's'-tail** n (hist) the rear of a cart, esp when used as a place of punishment. **cart'wheel** n the wheel of a cart; a sideways somersault with arms and legs extended. ◆ vi to make a sideways somersault. **cart'wright** n a carpenter who makes carts.
■ **cart off** (inf) to remove; to take away. **in the cart** (sl) in an awkward predicament; in trouble. **put the cart before the horse** to reverse the natural or sensible order of things. **village cart** an uncovered two-wheeled carriage for one horse, with a low body and one seat. **Whitechapel cart** or **chapel cart** a light two-wheeled spring-cart formerly used in delivering shop goods.

carta see **charta**.

carte[1] see **quart**[2].

carte[2] /kärt/ n a card, esp one of pasteboard; a bill of fare; a ticket; a playing card (Scot); a carte-de-visite. [Fr, from L c(h)arta; see **card**]
▫ **carte blanche** /-bläsh/ n (pl **cartes blanches**) a blank paper, esp one bearing a signature, to be filled up at the recipient's discretion; (in piquet) a hand containing no court cards; unlimited authority, freedom of action. **carte des vins** n wine list. **carte-de-visite** /-də-vē-zēt'/ n (pl **cartes-de-visite**) a visiting card; a small photographic portrait pasted on a card. **carte du jour** /dü zhoor/ n menu (of the day). **carte du pays** n lay of the land, literally map of the country.

carte blanche see under **carte**[2].

cartel /kär-tel'/ n a combination of independent firms or enterprises formed to control a market, eg by keeping up prices, monopolizing production, etc; a political alliance or bloc; a written challenge (obs); an agreement for exchange of prisoners (obs); a card with writing on it. [Fr, from L c(h)arta; see **card**]
■ **car'telism** n. **car'telist** n a member of a cartel; a supporter of cartels. **carteliza'tion** or **-s-** n. **car'telize** or **-ise** vt and vi.
▫ **cartel clock** n a hanging wallclock with the case usu of metal.

Cartesian /kär-tē'zi-ən or -zhyən/ adj relating to the French philosopher René *Descartes* (1596–1650), or his philosophy, or mathematical methods. ◆ n a follower of Descartes.
■ **Carte'sianism** n.
▫ **Cartesian co-ordinates** n pl (maths) co-ordinates in which the position of a point in a plane or in space is specified by its distances from two lines or three planes respectively.

carthamine /kär'thə-min/ n a dye obtained from safflower. [LL carthamus, from Ar qartum saffron]

Carthusian /kär-thū'zi-ən or -thoo'/ n a monk or (since 1229) a nun of an order founded by St Bruno in 1084, noted for its strictness; a scholar of the Charterhouse School, founded on the site of a Carthusian monastery in London, now in Godalming. ◆ adj of or relating to the order or the school. [L Cartusiānus, from Catorissium Chatrousse, a village in Dauphiné, near which their first monastery, La Grande Chartreuse, was founded]

cartilage /kär'ti-lij/ n gristle, a firm pearly white substance forming the embryonic skeleton of vertebrates (temporary cartilage) converted into bone in adults. [Fr, from L cartilāgō, -inis; cognate with crātis wickerwork, and Gr kartallos a basket]
■ **cartilaginous** /-laj'/ adj.
▫ **cartilaginous fishes** n pl fishes with a cartilaginous skeleton, including the sharks, rays and chimeras.

cartography /kär-tog'rə-fi/ n the skill or practice of making maps and charts. [L c(h)arta, from Gr chartēs a sheet of paper, and Gr graphein to write]
■ **car'togram** n a map presenting statistical information in diagrammatic form. **cartog'rapher** n. **cartographic** /-tō-graf'ik/ or **cartograph'ical** adj. **cartograph'ically** adv. **cartolog'ical** adj. **cartol'ogy** n the science of maps and charts.

cartomancy /kär'tō-man-si/ n divination or the telling of fortunes using playing cards. [LL carta a card, and Gr manteiā divination]
■ **car'tomancer** n.

carton /kär'tən/ n a container made of cardboard, waxed paper or plastic; a small white disc within the bull's-eye of a target; a shot that strikes it. ◆ vt to put into a carton. [Fr; see **cartoon**]
■ **car'tonage** or **car'tonnage** n pasteboard or cardboard; the outer covering of a mummy.

▫ **carton-pierre** /kär'tə-pyer/ n a kind of papier-mâché, imitating stone.

cartoon /kär-toon'/ n a comic or satirical drawing commenting on topical events or politics; a strip cartoon; a cinematograph film made by photographing a succession of drawings (also **animated cartoon**); a preparatory drawing on strong paper to be reproduced in fresco, tapestry, etc; any large sketch or design on paper. ◆ vt to make a cartoon or working design of; to caricature by a cartoon. [Fr carton or Ital cartone, augmentative of carta]
■ **cartoon'ish** adj exaggerated in design or colour like a strip or film cartoon. **cartoon'ist** n a person who draws or makes cartoons.

cartophily /kär-tof'i-li/ n the hobby of collecting cigarette cards. [L c(h)arta, from Gr chartēs a sheet of paper, and Gr philiā a liking]
■ **cartophile** /kär'tō-fīl/ or **cartoph'ilist** n. **cartophil'ic** adj.

cartouche, also **cartouch** /kär-toosh'/ n a scroll-like ornament or decorative border with rolled ends (archit); in hieroglyphics, an ancient Egyptian oval figure enclosing royal or divine names; an oval shield used for women or ecclesiastics (heraldry); in certain fireworks, a paper case containing combustible materials; a case for cartridges or mortar bullets (hist). [Fr, from Ital cartoccio, from L c(h)arta, from Gr chartēs paper]

cartridge /kär'trij/ n a case containing the charge for a gun (**blank cartridge** with powder only; **ball cartridge** with a bullet as well); a small container which can easily be inserted into and removed from a machine, holding eg film for a camera, ink for a pen or printer, a typewriter ribbon, part of the pick-up head of a record player; a type of cassette of magnetic tape; a small piece of hardware containing data, memory, fonts, etc (comput). [A corruption of **cartouche**]
▫ **car'tridge-belt** n a belt having pockets for cartridges. **cartridge clip** n a metal container holding cartridges for loading an automatic firearm. **car'tridge-pāper** n a light-coloured, strong paper for drawing or printing on, orig manufactured for making cartridges. **cartridge pen** n a pen with a removable container for ink which may be replaced when empty. **cartridge starter** n (aeronautics) a device for starting aero-engines in which a slow-burning cartridge is used to operate a piston or turbine unit geared to the engine shaft.

cartulary /kär'tyū-lə-ri/ n a register-book of a monastery, etc; the person who kept the records; the place where the register is kept. [LL chartulārium, from L chartula a document, from charta paper]

carucate /kar'ū-kāt/ n (hist) as much land as a team of oxen could plough in a season. [LL carrūcāta ploughland, from carrūca plough, from root of **car**]
■ **car'ucage** n a tax on the carucate, first imposed by Richard I in 1198.

caruncle /ka- or kə-rung'kl/ n a small fleshy outgrowth on the heads of certain birds, eg a cock's comb; an outgrowth near the micropyle on some seeds; any fleshy growth in or on the body. [Fr, from L caruncula]
■ **carun'cular**, **carun'culate** or **carun'culous** adj.

carvacrol /kär'və-krol/ (chem) n an isomer of and substitute for thymol, obtained from camphor by heating with iodine, present in origanum, etc. [Fr carvi caraway, and L acer sharp, with oleum oil]

carve /kärv/ vt (infinitive (Spenser) **carv'en**; pap **carved** or archaic **carv'en**) to cut (wood, stone, ivory, etc) into forms, patterns, etc; to make or shape by cutting; to cut up (meat) into slices or pieces; to apportion or distribute. ◆ vi to exercise the art or perform the act of carving; to make affected gestures or amorous advances (Shakesp). [OE ceorfan to cut; Du kerven; Ger kerben to notch]
■ **carv'en** adj carved. **carv'er** n a person who carves; a woodcarver; a sculptor; a carving knife (or fork); a tree used for carving (Spenser); a dining chair with arms. **carv'ery** n a type of buffet-service restaurant where the main course meat is served from the joint on request. **carv'ing** n the act or art of sculpture, esp in wood or ivory; a carved form, shape or figure; the act or art of cutting up meat at table; a technique used in skiing and snowboarding in which fast turns are made by turning the skis or board so that the edges cut into the snow, thus preventing skidding.
▫ **carving knife** n a large sharp knife for carving meat. **carving skis** n pl skis with wide tips and a narrow centre, suitable for carving.
■ **carve out** to cut out; to make or create by one's own efforts (fig). **carve up** (sl) to divide, esp booty; to injure a person, esp by slashing with a knife or razor (**carve'-up** n). **cut and carve** to refine.

carvel /kär'vəl/ n an old form of **caravel**.
▫ **car'vel-built** adj (of boats) built without overlap of planks (distinguished from **clinker-built**).

carvy /kär'vi/ (Scot) n caraway; a caraway seed, esp one coated with sugar. [Fr carvi; see **caraway**]

caryatid /ka-ri-ä'tid or -at'id/ n (pl **caryat'ids** or **caryat'ides** /-i-dēz/) a female figure used instead of a column to support an entablature. [Gr Karyātis a priestess of Artemis at Karyai (Caryae), pl Karyātides]
■ **caryat'ic**, **caryat'idal**, **caryatidē'an** or **caryatid'ic** adj.

Caryocar /kär'i-ō-kär/ n the butternut genus of plants, giving name to the family **Caryocarā'ceae** /-si-ē/. [Gr *karyon* nut, and *karā* head]

caryophyllaceous /kar-i-ō-fi-lā'shəs/ adj of or belonging to the **Caryophyllā'ceae**, a family of plants including the pink, carnation and sweet william. [*Caryophyllus*, early botanical name for clove pink, from Gr *karyophyllon* clove-tree (from similar smell)]

caryopsis /kar-i-op'sis/ n (pl **caryop'ses** /-sēz/ or **caryop'sides** /-si-dēz/) a dry indehiscent fruit in which the pericarp is united with the testa, characteristic of the grasses. [Gr *karyon* a nut, and *opsis* appearance]

caryopteris /ka-ri-op'tə-ris/ n any of several deciduous subshrubs of the genus *Caryopteris*, of the Verbenaceae, having small, blue flowers.

casa /kä'sa or -sə/ (*Ital* and *Sp*) n a house, mansion.

casaba or **cassaba** /kə-sä'bə/ n any of a group of cultivated melons with a hard yellow rind and sweet flesh (also called **winter melon**). [*Kasaba*, former name of Turgutlu, Turkey]

Casanova /ka-sə-nō'və/ n a man conspicuous for his amorous adventures, as was Giovanni Jacopo *Casanova* de Seingalt (1725–98).

casbah same as **kasbah**.

cascabel /kas'kə-bel/ n the part behind the base ring of a cannon. [Sp]

cascade /ka-skād'/ n a waterfall; a trimming of lace or other material in loose waves like a waterfall; apparatus connected in series, each piece operating the next one in turn or acting on the output of the preceding one; a way of arranging open windows on a desktop such that they overlap, with the title bar of each remaining visible (*comput*). ◆ vi to fall in cascades; to form a cascade. [Fr, from Ital *cascata*, from L *cadere* to fall]

cascadura /kas-kə-doo'rə/ n a type of catfish of the family Callichthyidae, having an armoured scaly skin. [Sp, from *casca* shell, and *dura* hard]

cascara /ka-skä'rə, -skä'rə or kas'kə-rə/ n a Californian buckthorn, *Rhamnus purshiana*, also known as the **cascara buckthorn**; the bark of the cascara, also known as **cascara sagrada** /sə-grä'də or -grä'/ (Sp, sacred) used as a tonic and laxative. [Sp *cáscara* bark]
■ **cascarill'a** n the aromatic bitter bark of a West Indian shrub, *Croton eluteria*, also known as **cascarilla bark**; the shrub itself.
❑ **cascara amarga** /ə-mär'gə/ n (Sp, bitter) the bitter bark of a tropical American tree of the family Simarubaceae, formerly used to treat syphilis and skin diseases.

caschrom /kas'krōm/ n a sort of spade with a bent handle, formerly used in the Scottish Highlands for tilling the ground (also **cas crom**). [Gaelic *cas* foot, handle, and *chrom* fem of *crom* bent, crooked]

casco /kas'kō/ n (pl **cas'cos**) a Philippine cargo barge. [Sp]

Case /kās/ abbrev : computer-aided software (or systems) engineering.

case[1] /kās/ n a covering, box or sheath containing something; the contents of such a box, etc, as in *a case of wine*; a set, eg of pistols; a facing for walls; the boards and back of a hardback book; a tray with many compartments in which a compositor keeps types of different sizes and styles (*printing*). ◆ vt to enclose in a case. [ONFr *casse* (Mod Fr *châsse* and *caisse*), from L *capsa*, from *capere* to take]
■ **cās'ing** n the act of putting on a case; an outside covering of any kind, as of boards, plaster, etc; a strong rigid pipe or tube lining a well, shaft, etc; the outer covering of a tyre; the outer deck of a submarine; cleaned animal intestines, or a substitute, used to case sausage meat, etc.
❑ **case'-bottle** n a bottle made to fit into a case with others, a bottle with a covering. **case'-bound** adj (of a book) with a hard cover. **cased glass** or **case glass** n a type of 19c glass consisting of one or more layers of coloured glass laid on clear glass and cut away to form various patterns. **case'-harden** vt to harden on the surface, as by carbonizing iron (*metallurgy*); to make callous or insensitive through previous experience. **case'-hardening** n. **case'-knife** n a large knife kept in a sheath. **case'maker** n a person who makes covers for books. **case'man** n a compositor. **case'-sensitive** or (**-insensitive**) adj of a computer program, etc, taking (no) account of whether a text character is upper-case or lower-case. **case'-shot** n canister shot, an artillery projectile for use at close quarters. **case'-worm** n a caddis-worm. **cas'inghead** n (*mining*) the part of the well that is above the surface and to which the pipelines and control valves are attached.

case[2] /kās/ n that which happens, an event or occurrence; state or condition; subject of question, investigation or inquiry; (an instance of) a person or animal having a disease; (records relating to) a person under medical treatment or being dealt with by a social worker, etc; an odd or humorous character, usually qualified in some way as in *he's a strange case* (*inf*); a legal statement of facts either in total or as presented by the defence or the prosecution; a lawsuit; a plausible contention, something to be said for a position or action, a point; (any of the specific types of) grammatical relation of a noun, pronoun, or (in some languages) adjective to another word in the sentence, and/or its variation in form to express that relation. ◆ vt (*sl*) to reconnoitre or examine, *usu* with a view to burglary. [OFr *cas*, from L *cāsus*, from *cadere* to fall]
❑ **case'book** n formerly, a book in which a doctor records the history of his cases; a book recording medical, legal, etc cases which are valuable as examples for reference. **case history** n a record of ancestry, environment, personal history, etc for use in diagnosis and treatment, or for some other purpose. **case law** n law established by judicial decisions made in previous cases. **case'-load** n the number of cases a doctor, social worker, etc has to deal with at a particular time. **case'mix** n a database system for storing information about medical patients, based on classification according to specific predetermined characteristics such as age, severity of illness, diagnosis, etc. **case'-study** n a study based on the analysis of one or more cases or case histories; (the gathering and organizing of information for) a case history. **case'work** n (*social work*) the study of individuals or of families, their environment and social history, often together with supervision and guidance. **case'worker** n.
■ **as the case may be** depending on or in accordance with the particular circumstances. **case in point** an example or illustration of what is under discussion. **in any case** anyway, however; whatever happens. **in case** in the event that; in order to make safe, make sure, etc. **in case to** in fit condition for. **in that case** since that is the situation. **make out one's case** to give reasons for one's statements or position. **on** (or **off**) **one's case** persistently (or no longer) harassing or carping at one. **put** (**the**) **case** to suppose an instance; to take for example. **the case** the fact, the reality.

casein /kā'sēn or -si-in/ n a protein obtained from milk, forming the basis of cheese. [From L *cāseus* cheese, and sfx *-in*]

casemate /kās'māt/ n any bombproof vaulted chamber or an armoured compartment, eg in a ship; *orig* a loopholed gallery, from which the garrison of a fort could fire upon an enemy who had obtained possession of the ditch. [Fr; derivation uncertain]
■ **case'mated** adj.

casement /kās'mənt/ n the case or frame of a window; a window that opens on vertical hinges (also **casement window**); a hollow moulding. [For **encasement** (Fr *enchassement*), or LL *casamentum* house-frame, or directly from **case**[1]]
■ **case'mented** adj having casements.
❑ **casement cloth** n a plain cotton fabric, suitable for casement curtains. **casement curtain** n a curtain hung from a window sash.

caseous /kā'si-əs/ adj cheeselike. [L *cāseus* cheese; see **casein**]
■ **cāsea'tion** n the formation of cheese through casein; degeneration of tissue into a cheeselike mass (*pathol*).

casern or **caserne** /kə-zûrn'/ (*hist*) n a barrack or billet for soldiers. [Fr, from Sp *caserna*]

casevac /kaz'i-vak/ (*milit*) n the transport of a casualty away from a theatre of combat. ◆ vt (**cas'evacing**; **cas'evaced**) to transport (a casualty) away from a theatre of combat. [From *casualty evacuation*, on the model of **medevac**]

cash[1] /kash/ n coins or paper money; available or ready money. ◆ adj using cash; paid by cash. ◆ vt to turn into or exchange for money. [A doublet of **case** a box, from OFr *casse* a box]
■ **cash'able** adj. **cashi'er** n a person who has charge of the receiving and paying of money. **cash'less** adj operated, paid for, conducted, performed, etc using credit cards or computer transfers, without the use of cash.
❑ **cash account** n (*bookkeeping*) an account which shows cash transactions. **cash-and-carr'y** adj of or denoting a business, method of trading, etc which involves *cash and carry* (see below). **cash'back** n a facility offered by some retailers, whereby a person paying for goods by debit card may also withdraw cash; a sum of money offered as an incentive to someone entering into a financial agreement, *esp* a mortgage. **cash'-book** n (*bookkeeping*) a book of account in which a record of all receipts and disbursements is kept. **cash'-box** n. **cash card** n a coded plastic card issued by a bank that allows the holder to obtain money from a bank account via a cash dispenser. **cash cow** n a well-established business or other enterprise that produces cash with a minimum of maintenance or management. **cash crop** n a crop intended for sale, not for consumption by the producer. **cash desk** n a table, etc with a till where money is taken for goods purchased. **cash dispenser** n a machine, *usu* in or outside a bank, which dispenses banknotes on the insertion of a coded plastic card (also **automatic teller machine**). **cash flow** n the movement of money in and out of a business. **cash'-keeper** n a treasurer. **cash limit** n a limit set on the total amount of money a company, institution, local authority, etc may spend. **cash machine** n a cash dispenser. **cash payment** n payment in ready money. **cash'point** n the place in a shop, supermarket, etc where money is taken for goods purchased; (**Cashpoint**®) an

automatic teller machine, a cash dispenser. **cash'-railway** *n* formerly, a mechanical device for interchange of cash between counter and cashdesk in a shop. **cash ratio** *n* the ratio of cash on hand to total deposits legally or customarily maintained by commercial banks. **cash register** *n* a till that automatically and visibly records the net amount put in. **cash'-strapped** *adj* (*inf*) short of money.

■ **cash and carry** sale for cash, with uplift and delivery of goods to be performed by the buyer; a *usu* large shop which trades in this way, often at wholesale prices. **cash down** with payment at the time of purchase. **cash in** to exchange for money; to seize an advantage. **cash in hand** payment for goods or labour in cash with no record being kept, *usu* as a way of avoiding tax, etc (**cash-in-hand'** *adj*); the total of cash balances held in a company's tills (*account*). **cash in on** to turn to one's advantage. **cash in** (**one's checks** or **chips**) to exchange counters for money on leaving a gaming-table or gambling-house; to die (*sl*). **cash on delivery** payment for goods to the person delivering them (**cash-on-deliv'ery** *adj*). **cash out** to convert one's assets into cash. **cash up** to count the total amount of money taken in a shop, department, etc, *usu* at the end of the day. **hard cash** see under **hard¹**. **out of cash, in cash** without, or with, money; out of, or in, pocket.

cash² /*kash*/ *n* a small Eastern coin. [Port *caixa*, from Sinhalese *kāsi* coin, from Tamil *kāsu*]

cashaw /*kə-shö'*/ *n* a kind of pumpkin (also **cushaw**; *US*); a West Indian mesquite. [Algonquian]

cashew /*kə-shoo'* or *kash'oo*/ *n* a spreading tropical American tree (*Anacardium occidentale*) with kidney-shaped nuts (**cashew nuts**) whose kernels (edible only when roasted) and fleshy stalks (**cashew apples**) are used as food. [Tupí *caju*; cf **acajou**]

cashier¹ /*kə-shēr'*/ *vt* to dismiss from a post *esp* in the armed forces, in disgrace; to discard or put away; to annul. [Du *casseren* (*kasseren*) to cashier, from Fr *casser*, from L *cassāre*, from *cassus* void, empty]

■ **cashier'er** *n*. **cashier'ing** or **cashier'ment** *n* dismissal; a punishment for army and naval officers, more severe than dismissal, in that it disqualifies from entry into public service in any capacity (abolished 1970).

cashier² see under **cash¹**.

cashmere /*kash'mēr*/ *n* (a fabric made from) fine soft *Kashmir* goats' hair; any (product made from) similar wool. ◆ *adj* made of cashmere.

casimere see **cassimere**.

casino /*kə-sē'nō*/ *n* (*pl* **casi'nos**) an establishment for gambling, *usu* with roulette and card and dice games; a card game in which players match cards in hand with others on the table (also **cassi'no**); formerly, a building with public dance halls, gaming tables, etc, or a room for public dancing. [Ital, dimin of L *casa* a house]

cask /*käsk*/ *n* a hollow round container for holding liquor, made of wooden staves bound with hoops; a quantity contained in such a vessel; a casque (*obs*); a lead case for transporting highly radioactive material, a flask (*nuclear eng*). ◆ *vt* to put in a cask. [Fr *casque*, from Sp *casco* skull, helmet, cask]

☐ **cask'-conditioned** *adj* (of beer) continuing to ferment and mature in the cask after brewing. **cask'stand** *n*.

casket /*käs'kit*/ *n* a little cask or case; a small case for holding jewels, etc; a coffin (*esp N Am*). [Ety uncertain]

Caslon /*kaz'lən*/ *n* a style of printing type designed by William *Caslon* (1692–1766); a typeface imitating this style.

caspase /*kas'pāz*/ *n* any of a group of enzymes that control apoptosis.

casque /*käsk*/ *n* a cover for the head (*obs* **cask**); a helmet; a helmet-like horny protuberance, as on the beak or head of some birds (*zool*). [A doublet of **cask**]

cassaba see **casaba**.

Cassandra /*kə-san'drə*/ (*Gr myth*) *n* a daughter of Priam, king of Troy, loved by Apollo, who gave her the gift of prophecy, but not of being believed; hence, anyone who expresses pessimistic views of the political or social future and is not listened to.

cassareep or **cassaripe** /*kas'ə-rēp*/ *n* the juice of the bitter cassava root, a potent antiseptic, made into syrup and used in sauces, *esp* in West Indian cookery. [From Tupí]

cassata /*ka-sä'tə*/ *n* an (*orig* Italian) ice-cream containing candied fruit and nuts. [Ital]

cassation /*ka-sā'shən*/ *n* annulment; in French law, the quashing of a decision of a court; hence **court of cassation** the supreme tribunal or higher court of appeal; an 18c instrumental suite similar to a serenade or divertimento (*music*). [LL *cassātiō, -ōnis*, from *cassāre* to bring to nought]

cassava /*kə-sä'və*/ *n* a tropical American plant of the *Manihot* genus whose roots yield a nourishing starch (also **manioc**, **tapioca** or **yucca**). [From a Taino (language of extinct W Ind tribe) name]

Cassegrain(ian) telescope /*kas-ə-grān'*(*i-ən*) *tel'i-skōp*/ *n* a type of reflecting telescope devised by, and named after, a 17c Frenchman, N *Cassegrain*.

casserole /*kas'ə-rōl*/ *n* a stew-pan; a covered pot in which food is both cooked and served; the dish of food or stew cooked in this way. ◆ *vt* to cook in a casserole. [Fr]

☐ **casserole cookery** *n* cooking in the dish in which the food is to be served.

cassette /*ka-set'*/ *n* a small casket; a light-tight container for an X-ray film, or one for film that facilitates loading in a camera, projector, microfilm-reader, etc; a plastic case containing a reel of magnetic tape, often with pre-recorded material on it. [Fr, dimin of *casse* case]

☐ **cassette deck** *n* the cassette player in a set of hi-fi units. **cassette recorder** or **player** *n* a machine which records onto or plays magnetic tape cassettes. **cassette single** or **cassing'le** *n* a pre-recorded tape cassette containing only one or two tunes.

cassia /*kas*(*h*)*'yə*/ *n* a coarser kind of cinnamon (**cass'ia-bark**); the tropical Asian tree (*Cinnamomum cassia*) that yields it; (often with *cap*) a genus of leguminous shrubs whose pods yield senna and the drug cassia fistula or purging cassia. [L *casia*, from Gr *kasiā* (also *kassiā*), from Heb *qetsī'āh*]

cassimere or **casimere** /*kas'i-mēr*/ *n* a twilled cloth of the finest wools (also **ker'seymere**). [Corruption of **cashmere**]

cassino see **casino**.

Cassiopeia /*kas-i-ō-pē'*(*y*)*ə*/ *n* a northern constellation named after the mother of Andromeda.

■ **cassiopē'ium** *n* a former name for **lutetium**.

cassis /*ka-sēs'*/ *n* a syrupy blackcurrant drink or flavouring. [Fr]

cassiterite /*ka-sit'ə-rīt*/ *n* a brown or black mineral, SnO_2, a dioxide of tin, found in alluvial deposits and acid igneous rocks (also called **tinstone**). [Gr *kassiteros* tin]

cassock /*kas'ək*/ *n* a long robe or outer coat worn by clergy and choristers; a shorter garment, *usu* of black silk, worn under the Geneva gown by Scottish ministers. [Fr *casaque*, from Ital *casacca*]

■ **cass'ocked** *adj*.

cassolette /*kas'ō-let*/ *n* a censer; a perfume-box with perforated lid. [Fr, from Sp *cazoleta*, from *cazo* a saucepan]

cassonade /*ka-so-nād'*/ *n* unrefined sugar. [Fr]

cassone /*kä-sō'nā*/ (*Ital*) *n* a large chest, elaborately carved and painted.

cassoulet /*ka-soo-lā'*/ (*Fr*) *n* a stew consisting of haricot beans, onions, herbs and various kinds of meat.

cassowary /*kas'ə-wə-ri*/ *n* any member of a genus (*Casuarius*) of flightless birds, found *esp* in New Guinea, closely related to the emu. [Malay *kasuārī* or *kasavārī*]

cassumunar /*ka-soo-mū'nər*/ *n* a SE Asian variety of ginger. [Origin unknown]

cast /*käst*/ *vt* (*pat* and *pap* **cast**) to throw or fling, *esp* violently; to throw (a fishing-line or net) into the water; to throw off, get rid of, drop or discard; (of animals) to shed or moult (hair, etc); to project or create (a shadow); to throw out or give out (light, heat, etc); to mould or shape (metal, plastic, etc, or artefacts from it); to appoint (an actor *for* a part, or *as* a character in a play, etc); to assign (the parts in a play, etc); to voice, express or create (doubts, etc); to reject, condemn, dismiss or decide against; to purpose, devise or consider (*archaic*); to calculate, compute or add up (now *rare*); to direct (a glance, thoughts, etc); to formulate, or to arrange in a suitable order or form; to register (a vote); to predict or calculate (a horoscope) (*astrol*); to direct hounds over ground where their quarry may have passed (*hunting*); (of animals) to give birth, *esp* prematurely; to make (printing plates) in stereotype or electrotype (*printing*); to dig and cut (peat) (*Scot*). ◆ *vi* to throw a fishing-line into the water; (of wood) to warp; (of sailing vessels) to veer; to look or seek; (of animals) to moult. ◆ *n* the act of casting; a throw of anything, eg the sounding-lead, a fishing-line, etc; the thing thrown, *esp* in angling; the distance thrown; a twist or squint, eg of the eye; a turn or sample performance; a good turn, eg a lift or conveyance in a vehicle (*Scot*); indigestible matter ejected by a bird, earthworm, etc; a throw or turn of fortune, a chance; a mould; a rigid casing, *usu* of plaster of Paris and, often, gauze, for holding a broken bone in place while it sets; form, manner, stamp or quality (*esp* of a person); an overall shade or tinge of colour; the assignment of the various parts of a play, etc to the several actors, etc; the company of actors playing roles in a given play, film, etc; a pair of hawks (*falconry*); a second swarm of bees leaving a hive after the first swarm. ◆ *adj* moulded; rejected, cast off; defeated at law; (of an animal) on its back and unable to get up. [ON *kasta* to throw]

■ **cast'ed** *adj* (*Shakesp*) cast off. **cast'ing** *n* the act of casting or moulding; that which is cast; a mould.

☐ **cast'away** *n* a person shipwrecked in a desolate or isolated place; an outcast. ◆ *adj* worthless, rejected. **casting couch** *n* (*facetious*)

■ words derived from main entry word; ☐ compound words; ■ idioms and phrasal verbs

a couch on which actresses are said to be seduced with the promise of a part in a film, play, etc. **casting director** *n* a person responsible for casting actors for all the parts in a film, TV production, play, etc. **cast'ing-net** *n* a type of net for fishing. **casting vote** *n* a chairman's deciding vote in case of deadlock. **cast'ing-weight** *n* the weight that makes the balance cast or turn when exactly poised. **cast iron** *n* an iron-carbon alloy distinguished from steel by its containing substantial amounts of cementite or graphite, meaning it is unsuitable for working and must be cast. **cast-i'ron** *adj* hard, rigid; very strong; unarguable, incontestable. **cast'-off** *adj* rejected, laid aside, given away, no longer wanted, etc. ◆ *n* anything, *esp* clothing, given or thrown away, no longer wanted, etc; the act or result of casting off manuscript or keyed copy. **cast-steel'** *n* steel that has been cast, not shaped by mechanical working.
■ **cast about** or **around** to look about, to search (for) literally or in one's mind; to turn, to go round (*Bible*). **cast a horoscope** or **nativity** to make an astrological calculation of someone's future or character. **cast anchor** to anchor a ship. **cast an eye** or **a glance** to look briefly and informally. **cast a spell (upon)** to utter or perform an enchantment or to put under an enchantment. **cast a vote** to record or make a vote. **cast away** to wreck; to waste. **cast back** to direct one's thoughts to the past. **cast down** to deject or depress mentally; to turn downward. **cast loose** to set loose or adrift. **cast lots** see under **lot**. **cast off** to reject; to release (hawks or hounds) in order to hunt or pick up a scent; to release (a boat) from its moorings; (in knitting, etc) to eliminate stitches by looping them together and removing them from the pins; to calculate the amount of printed matter that manuscript or keyed copy will make when typeset. **cast on** (in knitting, etc) to make stitches. **cast out** (*Scot*) to quarrel. **cast up** to throw up; to bring up or mention (a past error, wrongdoing, etc) as a reproach; to turn up, appear or emerge (*Scot*); to total a column of figures. **cast water** (*archaic*) to inspect or test urine in medical diagnosis. **the last cast** extremities.

-cast /-*kast*/ *combining form* forming nouns and verbs denoting a form of broadcasting, as in *newscast*, *webcast*. [**broadcast**]

Castalian /ka-stā'li-ən/ *adj* relating to *Castalia*, a fountain on Parnassus, sacred to Apollo and the Muses and thought to be a source of poetic inspiration.

Castanea /ka-stān'i-ə/ *n* the chestnut genus, of the beech family (Fagaceae). [Gr *kastanon* chestnut]
■ **castanospermine** /kas-tan-ō-spûr'mēn/ *n* (Gr *sperma* a seed) an alkaloid obtained from the seeds of the Moreton Bay chestnut. **Castanospermum** /-məm/ *n* an Australian papilionaceous tree, the Moreton Bay chestnut, so called from the taste of its nuts.

castanet /kas'tə-net or ka-stə-net'/ *n* either of a pair of hollow shell-shaped pieces of ivory or hard wood, bound by a band on the thumb, and struck by the finger to produce a clicking sound used as an accompaniment to Spanish dances and guitars. [Sp *castañeta*, from L *castanea* a chestnut]

caste /käst/ *n* a social class amongst Hindus in India; an exclusive or hereditary social class; a type of individual in some polymorphic social insects. [Port *casta* breed, race, from L *castus* pure, unmixed]
■ **caste'ism** *n*. **caste'less** *adj* having no caste.
❑ **caste'-mark** *n* a mark indicating a person's caste, worn on the forehead (also *fig*).
■ **lose caste** to descend in social rank.

castellan, **castellated** and **castellum** see under **castle**.

caster see **castor**[1].

castigate /kas'ti-gāt/ *vt* to punish or scold; to criticize severely; to emend (*obs*). [L *castīgāre*, -*ātum*, from *castus* pure]
■ **castiga'tion** *n*. **cas'tigator** *n*. **cas'tigatory** /-ə-tər-i/ *adj*.

Castilian /kas-til'yən/ *adj* of, or typical of, Castile. ◆ *n* a person born or living in Castile; the language of Castile, standard Spanish. [Sp *Castellano*]
❑ **Castile soap** *n* a hard soap made with olive oil and soda.

castle /käs'l/ *n* a fortified house or fortress; the residence of a prince or nobleman, or a large country mansion generally; in chess, a rook (*inf* or *childish*); a defensive tower borne on an elephant's back (*hist*); a large ship, *esp* of war (*hist*). ◆ *vt* to enclose or fortify with a castle. ◆ *vi* in chess, to move the king two squares along the row towards a rook and then place the rook on the square the king has passed over. [OE *castel*, from L *castellum*, dimin of *castrum* a fortified place]
■ **castellan** /kas'təl-an/ *n* the governor or keeper of a castle. **castellated** /kas'tel-āt-id/ *adj* having turrets and battlements like a castle; (of a nut, etc) having grooves or indentations. **castellā'tion** *n* provision of battlements; battlements. **castell'um** *n* a small Roman fort; a mile-castle. **cas'tled** *adj* provided with or having castles.
❑ **cas'tle-building** *n* the act of building castles in the air or forming visionary projects. **cas'tle-guard** *n* the guard for the defence of a castle. **castle nut** *n* a six-sided nut with six radial slots, two of

which line up with a hole in the bolt or screw, a split pin preventing turning.
■ **castles in the air** or **in Spain** imaginary or unrealistic plans, projects or hopes.

castock /kas'tək/ or **custock** /kus'tək/ (*Scot*) *n* a cabbage stock. [**kale** and **stock**[1]]

Castor /kas'tör or -tər/ *n* one of the Dioscuri, twin brother of Pollux, son of Leda, renowned for his skill in horse-taming (*Gr myth*); a bright star in the constellation Gemini (the Twins). [L, from Gr *Kastōr*]

castor[1] or **caster** /kä'stər/ *n* a small swivelling wheel attached to furniture and trolleys with its hub displaced away from the swivel axis, so that movement in any direction causes the wheel to follow this axis; a vessel with perforated top for sprinkling sugar, etc. [Ety as for **cast**]
❑ **castor action** or **caster action** *n* (*motoring*) the use of inclined swivel axes or kingpins to give the steerable front wheels a self-centring tendency after angular deflection. **castor sugar** or **caster sugar** *n* white granulated sugar crushed to form fine grains.

castor[2] /kä'stər/ *n* the beaver (genus *Castor*); castoreum; a hat of beaver or similar fur. [L *castŏr*, -*oris*, from Gr *kastōr*, -*oros* beaver]
■ **castoreum** /-tö'ri-əm or -tö'/ *n* the dried perineal sacs of the beaver, or a brown unctuous strong-smelling substance obtained from them, formerly used in medicine and perfumery. **cas'tory** *n* (*Spenser*) a red or pink colour obtained from castoreum.

castor[3] /kä'stər/ (*obs Aust sl*) *adj* good; excellent.

castor oil /kä'stər oil/ *n* a medicinal and lubricating oil obtained from the seeds of a tropical African euphorbiaceous plant, *Ricinus communis*, the **castor-oil plant** (or (*US*) **castor bean**). [Perh from use as substitute for **castoreum**]

castral /kas'trəl/ *adj* belonging to the camp. [L *castra*]

castrametation /kas-trə-me-tā'shən/ *n* the art of designing a camp. [L *castra* a camp and *mētārī*, -*ātus* to measure off, from *mēta* a boundary]

castrate /ka-strāt'/ *vt* to deprive of the power of generation; to remove the testicles from, to geld or emasculate; to render powerless, lacking in impact, etc. [L *castrāre*, -*ātum*]
■ **castrat'ed** *adj* gelded; rendered ineffective, expurgated. **castrā'tion** *n*. **castrato** /käs-trä'tō/ *n* (*pl* **castra'ti** /-tē/ or **castra'tos**) (Ital) a male singer castrated in boyhood so as to preserve a soprano or alto voice.

casual /kaz(h)'ū-əl or kazh'oo-əl/ *adj* accidental; unforeseen; occasional; off-hand; (of sexual relations) lacking in depth of feeling or commitment; negligent; careless; unceremonious, relaxed, free and easy; (of a worker) employed only according to demand, without permanent employment. ◆ *n* an occasional employee; (also with *cap*) a member of a gang of hooligans who frequent football matches and deliberately start fights, cause disturbances, etc. [L *cāsuālis*, from *cāsus*; see **case**[2]]
■ **cas'ualism** *n* the belief that chance governs all things; the employment of casual labour. **casualiza'tion** or **-s-** *n*. **cas'ualize** or **-ise** *vt* to render casual; to turn (regular workers) into casual workers. **cas'ually** *adv*. **cas'ualness** *n*. **cas'uals** *n pl* slip-on flat-heeled shoes; loose-fitting, comfortable and informal clothing.
❑ **casual clothes** *n pl* informal clothing. **casual labour** *n* (*usu* seasonal) workers without permanent employment. **casual labourer** *n* a worker employed for short periods as required. **casual ward** *n* (*hist*) a workhouse department providing temporary accommodation for labourers, paupers, etc.

casualty /kazh'ū-əl-ti or -oo-/ *n* a person injured or killed; an accident; a misfortune; a person lost to one side in a conflict by wounds, death, desertion, etc (*milit*); a thing damaged or destroyed; the casualty department of a hospital; an incidental charge or payment. [Ety as for **casual**]
❑ **casualty department** or **ward** *n* a hospital department or ward, in which accident and emergency patients are treated.
■ **casualties of superiority** in the feudal law of Scotland, payments to the superior in certain contingencies (eg death), ultimately redeemed or extinguished by the Act of 1914.

casuarina /kas-ū-ə-rī'nə/ *n* any tree of the genus *Casuarina*, including the she-oak and beefwood of Australia and S Asia, constituting a family **Casūarinā'ceae**. [Named from its resemblance to *cassowary* plumage]

casuist /kaz'ū-ist/ *n* a person who studies and resolves cases of conscience (*philos*); often, someone who argues plausibly but falsely in such cases. [Fr *casuiste*, from L *cāsus*; see **case**[2]]
■ **casūist'ic** or **casūist'ical** *adj*. **casūist'ically** *adv*. **cas'ūistry** *n* the science or doctrine of cases concerned with moral conscience (*philos*); the reasoning which enables a person to decide in a particular case between apparently conflicting duties; plausible but flawed reasoning.

casus belli /kā'səs be'lī or be'lē/ *n* something that causes, involves or justifies war. [L]

casus conscientiae /kā'səs kon-shi-en'shi-ē or kōn-skē-en'tē-ī/ *n* a case of conscience. [L]

casus foederis /kā'səs fē'də-ris or foi'de-ris/ *n* a case clearly coming within the provisions of a treaty. [L]

CAT /kat/ *abbrev* : College of Advanced Technology; computed (or computerized) axial tomography; computer-assisted (or computer-aided) training.
  ❏ **CAT scanner** or **CT scanner** *n* see separate entry.

cat[1] /kat/ *n* a carnivore of the genus *Felis, esp* the domesticated kind or any of the smaller wild species; a spiteful or malicious woman (*derog*); a piece of wood tapering at each end, struck with the **cat'-stick** in the game of tipcat; the game of tipcat; a cat-o'-nine-tails; a heavy tackle for raising the anchor to the cathead (*naut*); a movable penthouse to protect besiegers (*hist*); a double tripod with six legs; a showily dressed man (*old sl*); a man, chap (*sl*); a jazz fan (*sl*); a coward or timid animal (*Aust sl*); short for caterpillar (tractor). ◆ *vt* to lash with a cat-o'-nine-tails; to raise the anchor to the cathead (*naut*); to vomit. [OE *cat*; found also in Celtic, Slav, Ar, Finn, etc]
  ■ **cat'hood** *n* the state of being a cat or having the nature of a cat. **cat'kin** *n* a crowded spike or tuft of small unisexual flowers with reduced scalelike bracts, found on wind-pollinated plants such as willow, hazel, etc. **cat'like** *adj* like a cat; noiseless, stealthy. **cat'ling** *n* a surgical knife used in amputations; a little cat, a kitten (*archaic*); a catgut string (*Shakesp*). **catt'ery** *n* a place where cats are bred, or cared for in their owners' absence. **catt'ish** or **catt'y** *adj* like a cat; spiteful; backbiting. **catt'ishly** or **catt'ily** *adv*. **catt'ishness** or **catt'iness** *n*.
  ❏ **cat'amount** *n* any of various large wild cats, applied *esp* to the puma and the lynx. **catamoun'tain** or **cat o' mountain** *n* any of various large wild cats, applied *esp* to the leopard, panther or ocelot. ◆ *adj* ferocious, savage. **cat-and-dog'** *adj* constantly quarrelling. **cat-and-mouse'** *adj* used of harassing or toying with an opponent, victim, etc before finally killing, defeating or otherwise disposing of them; also of waiting and watching for the right moment to attack and dispose of one's opponent. **cat'bird** *n* an American bird of the thrush family with a mewing note; any Australian bowerbird having a catlike call. **cat'-burglar** *n* a burglar who performs nimble climbing feats or employs stealth and agility to gain access to premises. **cat'call** *n* formerly, a squeaking instrument used in theatres to express disapprobation; a shrill whistle or cry expressing disapproval or derision, *esp* at an artiste's performance. ◆ *vi* to make a catcall. ◆ *vt* to direct catcalls at. **cat-cracker** *n* see separate entry. **cat door** *n* a cat-flap. **cat'-eyed** *adj* having eyes like a cat; able to see in the dark. **cat'-fight** *n* (*inf*) an unseemly fight, *esp* one between women involving slapping and scratching. **cat'fish** *n* a fish with catlike whiskers near its mouth; the wolffish. **cat'flap** *n* a small door set in a larger door to allow a cat entry and exit. **cat'gut** *n* a kind of cord made from the intestines of sheep and other animals used for violin strings, surgical ligatures, etc; the violin or other stringed instrument (*old* or *facetious*); a coarse corded cloth. **cat'-hammed** *adj* with thin hams like a cat's. **cat'head** *n* (*naut*) one of two strong beams projecting from the bow of a ship through which passes the tackle by which the anchor is raised; a spider tool, a lathe accessory consisting of a turned sleeve with four or more radial screws at each end (*engineering*). **cat'hole** *n* (*naut*) one of two holes in the after part of a ship through which hawsers may pass for steadying the ship or for heaving astern. **cat'house** *n* a brothel (*esp N Am sl*); a place where cats are cared for. **cat'-lap** *n* any thin or unappetizing drink. **cat litter** *n* a granular absorbent material used to line a tray, on which a domestic cat may urinate and defecate indoors. **cat'mint, cat'nep** or **cat'nip** *n* a mint-like labiate plant (*Nepeta cataria*) attractive to cats. **cat'nap** *n* a brief sleep, *esp* without lying down. **cat o' mountain** see **catamountain** above. **cat-o'-nine'-tails** *n* a whip with nine knotted tails or lashes, once used in the army and navy. **cat's'-brains** *n* (*archaic*) a geological formation of sandstone veined with chalk. **cat's-cra'dle** *n* a pastime in which a string looped about the fingers and passed from player to player is transformed from one symmetrical pattern to another; an impenetrably intricate set of regulations, instructions, etc. **cat's'-ear** *n* any plant of the European genus *Hypochoeris* of the family Compositae, having yellow dandelion-like flowers. **cat's'-eye** *n* a name for various chatoyant minerals that resemble a cat's eye when polished, *esp* a greenish-yellow variety of chrysoberyl; (**Cat's-eye**®) a small reflector set in a frame fixed in a road surface to indicate traffic lanes. **cat's'-foot** *n* a European plant (*Antennaria dioica*) of the family Compositae, having woolly leaves and white flowers (also called **mountain-everlasting**); ground ivy. **cat'-silver** *n* a variety of silvery mica. **cat'skin** *n*. **cat's'-meat** *n* horse's flesh, or the like, sold for cats; any rather unappetizing food. **cat's'-paw** *n* a person who is used by another (from the fable of the monkey who used the paws of the cat to draw chestnuts out of the fire); a hitch in a rope providing two loops for a hook; a light breeze forming ripples on the water's surface (*naut*). **cat's'-tail** *n* a catkin;

timothy-grass; the reed-mace or bulrush. **cat'suit** *n* a type of one-piece trouser suit. **cat's-whisk'er** *n* (*radio*) a delicate wire brought into contact with a crystal to rectify the current in some forms of crystal detector and produce audibility. **cat'walk** *n* a narrow footway, eg on a bridge, above the stage in a theatre, or for the models in a fashion show. **cat'-witted** *adj* small-minded, conceited and spiteful. **cat'works** *n* (*mining*) the assemblage of motors and catheads providing power for secondary activities on drilling platforms, eg pipe-hoisting. **cat'worm** *n* a polychaete worm (*Nephthys hombergi*) frequently used as a fishing bait (also called **white worm**).
  ■ **bell the cat** see under **bell**[1]. **big cats** see **the big cats** below. **care killed the** (or **a**) **cat** worry killed the cat, even with its proverbial nine lives. **catted and fished** (of an anchor) raised to the cathead and secured to the ship's side. **Cheshire cat** /chesh'ər or chesh'ēr/ a cat renowned for grinning, like the Cheshire cat in Lewis Carroll's *Alice's Adventures in Wonderland*. **enough to make a cat laugh** ie even the least inclined. **in the catbird seat** (*N Am*) in an advantageous position. **Kilkenny cats** proverbial cats who fight until each destroys the other. **let the cat out of the bag** to disclose a secret. **like a cat on hot bricks** or **on a hot tin roof** (*inf*) uneasy, restive; very nervous. **like something the cat brought in** or **dragged in** bedraggled, slovenly in dress, scruffy, etc. **like the cat that's got the cream** extremely smug or pleased with oneself. **not have a cat in hell's chance** (*inf*) to have no chance at all. **play cat-and-mouse with** to deal with in a cat-and-mouse way. **put** (or **set**) **the cat among the pigeons** to stir up a great deal of trouble. **rain cats and dogs** (*inf*) to rain very heavily. **room to swing a cat** a minimum of space. **see which way the cat jumps** to see how things are going to turn out before committing oneself (also **wait for the cat to jump**). **the big cats** lions, tigers, leopards, etc. **the cat's got your tongue** you seem unexpectedly reluctant to speak. **the cat's pyjamas** or **the cat's whiskers** (*inf*) the very thing that is wanted, the ideal thing; anyone or anything considered to be the best or greatest. **turn** (**the**) **cat in** (**the**) **pan** to change sides with dexterity. **wait for the cat to jump** see **see which way the cat jumps** above. **whip the cat** see under **whip**.

cat[2] /kat/ *n* an old name for a coal and timber vessel on the NE coast of England. [Obscurely connected with **cat**[1]]
  ❏ **cat'boat** *n* a cat-rigged boat. **cat'-rigged** *adj* having one great fore-and-aft mainsail spread by a gaff at the head and a boom at the foot, for smooth water only.

cat[3] /kat/ *n* short for **catamaran** and **catalytic converter**.

cat. *abbrev* : catalogue; catechism.

catabasis /kə-tab'ə-sis/ *n* a downward movement; the decline of a disease in a population. [Gr *kata* down, and *basis* base]

catabolism or **katabolism** /kə-tab'ə-li-zm/ (*biol*) *n* destructive metabolism, the disruptive processes of chemical change in organisms, *opp* to anabolism. [Gr *katabolē*, from *kataballein* to throw down, from *kata* down, and *ballein* to throw]
  ■ **catabolic** /kat-ə-bol'ik/ *adj*. **catab'olite** *n* a product of catabolism.

catacaustic /ka-tə-kös'tik/ (*maths* and *phys*) *adj* relating to or denoting a caustic curve or caustic surface formed by reflection. ◆ *n* a catacaustic curve or surface. [Gr *kata* against, and **caustic**]

catachresis /ka-tə-krē'sis/ (*rhetoric*) *n* misapplication or incorrect usage of a word. [Gr *katachrēsis* misuse, from *chrēsis* use]
  ■ **catachrestic** /-kres'tik or -krēs'tik/ or **catachres'tical** *adj*. **catachres'tically** *adv*.

cataclasm /kat'ə-kla-zm/ *n* a disruption, a breaking down. [Gr *kataklasma*, from *kata* down, and *klaein* to break]
  ■ **cataclās'is** *n* (*geol*) deformation of rocks by crushing. **cataclas'mic** *adj* relating to or of the nature of a cataclasm. **cataclas'tic** *adj* (*geol*) (of rocks) mylonitic, or granular as a result of crushing.

cataclysm /kat'ə-kli-zm/ *n* a great flood or other major disaster; a debacle; a great revolution or change, *esp* one that affects an entire political or social system. [Gr *kataklysmos*, from *kata* downward, and *klyzein* to wash]
  ■ **cataclys'mic** *adj*. **cataclys'mically** *adv*.

catacomb /kat'ə-kōm or -koom/ *n* a subterranean excavation used as a burial-place, *esp* near Rome, where many of the early Christian victims of persecution were buried; any place built with crypt-like recesses for storing books, wine, etc. [Ital *catacomba*, from LL *Catacumbas*, perh in some way from Gr *kata* down, and *kymbē* a cup]
  ■ **catacumbal** /-kum'bl/ *adj*.

catacoustics /ka-tə-koo'stiks or (*esp formerly*) -kow'stiks/ *n sing* the area of the science of acoustics that deals with echoes or reflected sounds. [Gr *kata* back, and **acoustics**]

catacumbal see under **catacomb**.

catadioptric /kat-ə-dī-op'trik/ or **catadioptrical** /-kl/ *adj* relating to or employing both reflection and refraction, as in the construction of some long-focal-length photographic lenses. [See **catoptric** and **dioptric**]

■ words derived from main entry word; ❏ compound words; ■ idioms and phrasal verbs

catadromous /kə-tad′rə-məs/ adj (of fishes) descending periodically for spawning to the lower parts of a river or to the sea, opp to anadromous. [Gr kata down, and dromos a run]

catafalque /kat′ə-falk/ n a temporary tomb-like structure used in funeral ceremonies and processions (also **catafal′co** (pl **catafal′coes**)). [Fr, from Ital catafalco]

Cataian or **Catayan** /kə-tā′ən/ (Shakesp) n a Cathayan or Chinese, used as a vague term of reproach. [Cathay, poetical name for China]

Catalan /kat′ə-lan/ adj of or belonging to Catalonia; of or concerning Catalan. ◆ n a person born or living in Catalonia; the Romance language spoken esp in Catalonia, Andorra and the Balearic Islands.

catalase see under **catalysis**.

catalectic /ka-tə-lek′tik/ adj incomplete; lacking one syllable in the last foot (prosody). [Gr katalēktikos incomplete, from katalēgein to stop]
■ **catalex′is** n.

catalepsy /kat′ə-lep-si/ n a state where one is more or less completely incapacitated, with bodily rigidity, as in hypnotic trances and sometimes in schizophrenia; cataplexy in animals. [Gr katalēpsis seizure, catalepsy, from kata down, and lēpsis taking, seizure]
■ **catalep′tic** adj and n.

catalexis see under **catalectic**.

catallactic /ka-tə-lak′tik/ adj relating to exchange. [Gr katallaktēs a moneychanger]
■ **catallac′tically** adv. **catallac′tics** n sing political economy.

catalo same as **cattalo**.

catalogue /kat′ə-log/ or (N Am) **catalog** n a systematic list of names, books, pictures, etc; a list of university courses and descriptions, usu including a calendar (US). ◆ vt to put in a catalogue; to make a catalogue of. [Gr katalogos, from kata in order, and legein to reckon]
■ **cat′aloguer** or (N Am) **cat′aloger** n. **cat′aloguize** or **-ise** or (N Am) **cat′alogize** vt.

catalogue raisonné /ka-ta-log re-zo-nā′/ (Fr) n a classified descriptive catalogue.

catalpa /kə-tal′pə/ n a low bignoniaceous tree of the American and Japanese genus Catalpa with profuse fragrant blossoms and long cigar-like pendent pods. [Creek kutuhlpa]

catalysis /kə-tal′i-sis/ n the chemical influence of a substance which is not itself permanently changed. [Gr katalysis, from kata down, and lyein to loosen]
■ **cat′alase** n an enzyme that reduces hydrogen peroxide. **cat′alyse** or (N Am) **-yze** /-līz/ vt to subject to catalysis; to act as a catalyst for. **cat′alyser** or **-yzer** n a catalysing agent; a catalytic converter. **cat′alyst** n a catalysing agent; a catalytic converter; a person who causes or promotes change by their presence in a situation or their input into it (fig). **catalytic** /-lit′ik/ or **catalyt′ical** adj. **catalyt′ically** adv.
❑ **catalytic converter** n a device fitted to the exhaust of a motor vehicle which converts harmful impurities in the exhaust gases to carbon dioxide, nitrogen and water by oxidation. **catalytic cracker** see **cat-cracker**.

catamaran /kat-ə-mə-ran′/ or /kat′/ n orig a raft of logs lashed together; a boat, esp a sailing boat with two hulls; an old kind of fireship, long superseded; a bad-tempered woman (rare). [Tamil kattu-maram tied wood]

catamenia /ka-tə-mē′ni-ə/ (physiol) n pl the menstrual discharge or menses. [Neuter pl of Gr katamēnios monthly, from kata against, and mēn a month]
■ **catame′nial** adj.

catamite /kat′ə-mīt/ n a boy kept as a homosexual lover. [L catamītus, from Gr Ganymēdēs Ganymede]

catamount, **catamountain** see under **cat**[1].

catananche /ka-tə-nang′kē/ n any plant of the S European genus Catananche, some of which are grown for their blue and white flowers (also **cupid′s dart**). [Gr, a spell, from katanankazein to coerce]

catapan /kat′ə-pan/ n the governor of Calabria and Apulia for the Byzantine emperor. [According to the 19c French lexicographer Littré, from Gr katepanō tōn axiōmatōn one placed over the dignities]

cataphonics /ka-tə-fon′iks/ n sing catacoustics. [Gr kata back, and phōnē sound]
■ **cataphon′ic** adj.

cataphora /kə-taf′ə-rə/ n the use of a word that has the same reference as another word used later. [Gr kata down, and pherein to bear]
■ **cat′aphor** n a word used in this way. **cataphoric** /-for′ik/ adj. **cataphor′ically** adv.

cataphoresis /kat-ə-fə-rē′sis/ n electrophoresis; the introduction into the body of medicinal substances by means of an electric current. [Gr kata down, and phorēsis a carrying]

cataphract /kat′ə-frakt/ n a suit of mail; a soldier in full armour (old milit). [Gr kataphraktēs a coat of mail, from kata (intens), and phrassein to enclose, protect]
■ **cataphrac′tic** adj.

cataphyll /kat′ə-fil/ n a rudimentary or simplified leaf. [Gr kata down, and phyllon leaf]
■ **cataphyll′ary** adj.

cataplasm /kat′ə-pla-zm/ n a plaster or poultice. [Gr kataplasma]

cataplexy /kat′ə-plek-si/ n a condition of immobility induced by extreme emotion, eg shock (med); a physical state resembling death, adopted by some animals to discourage predators. [Gr kataplēxis amazement, from kata down, and plēssein to strike]
■ **cataplec′tic** adj.

catapult /kat′ə-pult/ n a small forked stick having an elastic string fixed to the two prongs, used for firing small stones; any similar device, eg for launching aeroplanes from an aircraft-carrier; (in ancient history) a war machine for throwing boulders, etc. ◆ vt and vi to shoot out from, or as if from, a catapult. [L catapulta, in the historical sense, from Gr katapeltēs]
■ **catapul′tic** adj. **catapultier** /-tēr′/ n.
❑ **catapult fruit** n a fruit that shoots out its seeds.

cataract /kat′ə-rakt/ n a waterfall; a waterspout, etc; an opaque condition of the lens of the eye, painless, unaccompanied by inflammation; the area rendered opaque, which is surgically removable; a portcullis (obs); a floodgate (Milton). [L cataracta, from Gr kataraktēs portcullis, waterfall]

catarrh /kə-tär′/ n a discharge of fluid resulting from the inflammation of a mucous membrane, esp of the nose; a cold in the head. [L catarrhus, from Gr katarrhous, from kata down, and rheein to flow]
■ **catarrh′al** or **catarrh′ous** adj.

catarrhine or **catarhine** /kat′ə-rīn/ adj of or relating to one of the two divisions of Primates, including all the Old World monkeys, having a narrow partition between the nostrils. ◆ n a catarrhine primate. [Gr katarris with hanging nose, from kata down, and rhīs, rhīnos nose]

catasta /kə-tas′tə/ n a block on which slaves were exposed for sale; a stage, scaffold or place for torture. [L]

catastasis /kə-tas′tə-sis/ n the part of a drama in which the action has reached its height. [Gr katastasis settlement]

catastrophe /kə-tas′trə-fi/ n a sudden disaster or misfortune; an unfortunate conclusion, outcome, etc; a final event; the climax of the action of the plot in a play or novel; a sudden and violent upheaval in some part of the surface of the earth (geol); in catastrophe theory (see below), a discontinuous change (maths); rear (Shakesp). [Gr kata down, and strophē a turning]
■ **catastrophic** /kat-ə-strof′ik/ adj. **catastroph′ically** adv. **catas′trophism** n the old theory of geological change by vast, unconnected catastrophes and new creations, opp to uniformitarianism. **catas′trophist** n.
❑ **catastrophe theory** n the branch of mathematics dealing with continuous changes in the input of a system which cause a discontinuous change (ie a catastrophe) in the output of the system.

catatonia /ka-tə-tō′ni-ə/ n a type of schizophrenia characterized by periodic states of rigidity or immobility (also **catatony** /kat-at′ə-ni/). [Gr kata down, and tonos stretching, straining, from teinein to stretch]
■ **catatonic** /-ton′/ adj and n.

catawba /kə-tö′bə/ n an American variety of grape (Vitis labrusca); a red wine made from it. [Catawba River in Carolina]

catbird, **catcall**, etc see under **cat**[1].

catch /kach/ vt (infinitive in Spenser sometimes **catch′en** or **ketch**; pat and pap **caught** /köt/, also obs dialect **catched** or **catcht**; pat in Spenser also **keight** /kīt/) to take hold of, esp of a thing in motion; to take hold of (the ball) after the batsman has hit it and before it touches the ground (cricket); to dismiss (a batsman) in this way; to hear (inf); to understand or comprehend; to seize (a person, etc) after pursuit; to trap or ensnare when hunting, fishing, etc; to entangle or fasten on (to); to come upon, to happen to see; to meet or contact (a person) (inf); to be in time for; to take (a train, bus, etc) as a means of transport; to strike, hit; to get (a disease) by infection or contagion; to attract (a person's attention, notice, etc); to succeed in reproducing (someone's qualities or likeness) by painting, photography or imitation; to take (fire). ◆ vi to be contagious; to be entangled or fastened; (of a fire, or of anything to be burned) to catch light. ◆ n seizure; an act of catching, esp the ball in cricket, etc; a clasp, or anything that fastens or holds; that which is caught; a person who is considered worth catching as a marriage partner; a sudden advantage taken; a concealed difficulty or disadvantage; in someone's voice, an indistinctness caused by strong emotion; a children's game in which a ball, etc is thrown and caught in turn; a round for three or more voices, often deriving comic effect from the interweaving of the words (*music*). [From OFr *cachier*, from LL *captiāre* from *captāre*, intens of *capere* to take; see **chase¹**]

■ **catch'able** *adj* capable of being caught. **catch'er** *n* a person or thing that catches; a fielder positioned behind the batter (*baseball*). **catch'iness** *n*. **catch'ing** *n* the action of the verb; a nervous or spasmodic twitching. ◆ *adj* infectious (*med* or *fig*); captivating, attractive. **catch'ment** *n* the act of collecting water; the water collected from a river, etc; a catchment area; the pupils collected from a school catchment area. **catch'y** *adj* attractive; deceptive; (of a tune, etc) readily taking hold in the mind, memorable; fitful.

❑ **catch'-all** *adj* covering or dealing with a number of instances, eventualities or problems, *esp* ones not covered or dealt with by other provisions. **catch-as-catch-can'** *n* a style of wrestling in which any hold is allowed. ◆ *adj* and *adv* (*esp N Am*) using any method that is available. **catch'-basin** or **catch'-pit** *n* a trap for dirt in a drain. **catch'-crop** *n* a secondary crop grown before, after, or at the same time as, and on the same piece of ground as, a main crop. **catch'-drain** *n* a drain on a hillside to catch the surface-water. **catch'fly** *n* a name for a species of campion (*Lychnis viscaria*) and several bladder campion (genus *Silene*) with sticky stems. **catching pen** *n* (*Aust* and *NZ*) a pen for holding sheep awaiting shearing. **catch'line** *n* a slogan, esp in advertising or politics. **catchment area** *n* the area from which a river or reservoir is fed (also **catchment basin**); the area from which the pupils for a school are drawn, or the locality served by some other public facility such as a library or a hospital. **Catchment board** *n* (*NZ*) a public body responsible for water supply from a catchment area. **catch'penny** *n* a worthless thing made only for profit (also *adj*). **catch'phrase** *n* a phrase that becomes popular and is much repeated; a slogan. **catch-pit** see **catch-basin** above. **catch points** *n pl* railway points which can derail a train to prevent it accidentally running onto a main line. **catch-the-ten'** *n* a card game in which the aim is to capture the ten of trumps. **Catch'-22** *adj* (title of novel by J Heller, 1961) denoting an absurd situation in which one can never win, being constantly balked by a clause, rule, etc which itself can alter to block any change in one's course of action, or being faced with a choice of courses of action, both or all of which would have undesirable consequences. ◆ *n* such a situation. **catch'weed** *n* goosegrass or cleavers. **catch'weight** *adj* (*wrestling*) denoting a contest in which weight is unrestricted. **catch'word** *n* the word at the head of the page in a dictionary or encyclopaedia; (in typed correspondence) the first word of a page given at the bottom of the preceding page; any word or phrase taken up and repeated, *esp* as the watchword or slogan of a political party; an actor's cue.

■ **catch at** to make a hasty attempt to catch. **catch cold (at)** to suffer a financial or other misfortune (as a result of making an unwise investment, etc). **catch fire** or **light** to become ignited; to become inspired by passion or enthusiasm. **catch hold of** to seize. **catch it** (*inf*) to get a scolding or reprimand. **catch me** or **him**, etc an emphatic colloquial phrase implying that there is not the remotest possibility of my or his, etc doing the thing mentioned. **catch on** to comprehend; to become fashionable, to catch the popular imagination. **catch one's breath** see under **breath**. **catch one's death** see under **death**. **catch out** to detect in error or deceit. **catch sight of** to get a glimpse of. **catch someone's drift** to follow and understand what someone is talking about. **catch up** to draw level (with) and sometimes overtake; to bring oneself up to date with. **catch up** or **away** to snatch or seize hastily. **caught up in** engrossed or involved in.

catchpole or **catchpoll** /kach'pōl/ (*hist*) *n* a constable, a sheriff's officer. [Through OFr from LL *cachepolus*, *chassipullus* someone who chases fowls; see **chase¹** and **pullet**]

catchup see **ketchup**.

cat-cracker /kat'kra-kər/ *n* (in full, **catalytic cracker**) an industrial plant in which the chemical cracking of crude petroleum is speeded up by the use of a catalyst.

■ **cat'-cracking** (in full, **catalytic cracking**) *n*.

cate /kāt/ (*archaic*) *n* (nearly always in *pl*) a viand; a dainty, a delicacy. [Aphetic; see **acates**; cf **cater¹**]

catechize or **-ise** /kat'i-kīz/ *vt* to instruct, *esp* in the Christian faith, by question and answer; to question as to belief; to examine systematically by questioning. [L *catēchismus*, formed from Gr *katēchizein*, *katēcheein* to din into the ears, from *kata* back, and *ēchē* a sound]

■ **catechetic** /-ket'ik/ or **catechet'ical** *adj* relating to catechism or oral instruction in the first principles, *esp* of Christianity. **catechet'ically** *adv*. **catechet'ics** *n sing* the art or practice of teaching by question and answer; that part of theology which deals with **catechesis** /-kē'sis/, or primary oral instruction, as that given to catechumens. **cat'echism** *n* any comprehensive system of teaching drawn up in form of question and answer; a set of questions; a

thorough examination by questions. **cat'echist** *n* a person who catechizes; a teacher of catechumens; an indigenous teacher in a mission church. **catechis'tic**, **catechis'tical** or **catechis'mal** *adj* relating to a catechist or catechism. **cat'echizer** or **-s-** *n*. **cat'echizing** or **-s-** *n*.

catechu /kat'i-choo or -shoo/ *n* a dark extract of Indian plants (acacia, betel nut, etc) which are rich in tannin. [Cf Malay *cachu*]

■ **cat'echin** /-kin/ *n* a soluble crystalline compound, a major constituent of catechu, used in tanning and dyeing. **cat'echol** /-kōl/ or **-chōl**/ *n* a white crystalline phenol-alcohol derived from catechu. **catechō'lamine** /-kō'lə-mēn or -chō'/ *n* any of several compounds (eg adrenaline and noradrenaline) that are derivatives of catechol.

catechumen /ka-ti-kū'mən/ *n* a person who is being taught the rudiments of Christianity; in the early Christian Church, a converted Jew or heathen undergoing instruction preparatory to baptism. [Gr *katēchoumenos* being taught, prp passive of *katēcheein* to teach; cf **catechize**]

■ **catechū'menate** *n*. **catechūmen'ical** *adj*. **catechūmen'ically** *adv*. **catechū'menism** or **catechū'menship** *n*.

category /kat'i-gə-ri, or -ə-/ *n* a class or order of things, people, etc possessing similar characteristics; (in *pl*) the highest classes under which objects of philosophy can be systematically arranged, understood as an attempt at a comprehensive classification of all that exists (*philos*); (in *pl*) in Kant's system, the root-notions of the understanding, the specific forms of the *a priori* or formal element in rational cognition (*quantity*, *quality*, *relation*, *modality*, etc) (*philos*). [Gr *katēgoriā* assertion, predication, accusation, from *katēgoros* an accuser, *kata* down, against, and *agorā* assembly]

■ **categorematic** /-gor-i-mat'ik/ *adj* capable of being used by itself as a term. **categorial** /ka-tə-gōr'i-əl or -gör'/ *adj* of or relating to a category. **categor'ially** *adv*. **categorical** or **categoric** /-gor'/ *adj* positive; absolute; unconditional; without exception. **categor'ically** *adv* absolutely; without qualification, unconditionally; expressly. **categor'icalness** *n* the quality of being absolute and unqualified. **cat'egorist** *n* a person who categorizes. **categoriza'tion** or **-s-** *n*. **cat'egorize** or **-ise** *vt* to place in a category or list; to class.

❑ **categorical imperative** *n* (*philos*) in the ethics of Kant, the absolute unconditional command of the moral law, irrespective of every ulterior end or aim, obliging people to act responsibly. **category killer** *n* (*commercial jargon*) a large retailer with the power to force its competitors out of business. **category mistake** *n* (*philos*) an error resulting from assigning to something a quality or action that is properly assigned to things of another category.

catelog an obsolete spelling of **catalogue**.

catena /kə-tē'nə/ *n* (*pl* **cate'nae** /-nē/ or **cate'nas**) a chain or connected series, as in **catena patrum**, a chronological series of extracts from the Fathers on any doctrine of theology; the differences in the moisture, acidity, etc of soil along a slope (*geog*). [L *catēna* chain]

■ **cat'enane** *n* (*chem*) a compound having molecules linked like a chain. **catenarian** /kat-i-nā'ri-ən/ *adj* of, or of the nature of, a chain or a catenary. **catē'nary** (or (*US*) /kat'/) *n* the curve formed by a flexible cord, hanging freely between two points of support, and acted on by no other force than gravity; the arrangement of pylons and cables through which electricity is supplied on some electrified railway lines. ◆ *adj* relating to, or like, a chain. **catenate** /kat'i-nāt/ *vt* to connect as in or by a chain. ◆ *adj* linked as in a chain. **catenā'tion** *n*. **cat'enoid** *n* the surface generated by rotating a catenary about its axis.

cater¹ /kā'tər/ *vi* to provide food, entertainment, etc (for); to provide the requirements of (a person, occasion, etc; with *to* or *for*). ◆ *vt* (*N Am*) to provide food, entertainments, etc for (an occasion). ◆ *n* (*obs*) an acater; a person who supplies provisions (sometimes *fig*). [Ult from L *captāre* to seize]

■ **cā'terer** *n*. **cā'teress** *n*. **cā'tering** *n*.

cater² /kā'tər/ *n* (*obs*) the four in dice. ◆ *vt* and *vi* (*dialect*) to move diagonally. ◆ *adj* and *adv* (*dialect*) diagonal(ly). [MFr *quatre* four, from L *quattuor*]

■ **catercor'ner** or **catercor'nered** *adj* (also **catty-cor'ner** or **catty-cor'nered**) diagonal (also *adv*).

cateran /kat'ə-rən/ (*esp literary*) *n* a Highland reiver or freebooter; a robber or brigand generally. [Old Gaelic *ceatharn*, *ceithern* a band of soldiers (Ir *ceithern* foot soldiers; see **kern²**)]

cater-cousin /kā'tər-kuz'n/ (*Shakesp*) *n* a person allied by familiarity, affection or sympathy, rather than kindred; an intimate friend. [More prob connected with **cater¹**, than *quatre* or *quarter*]

caterpillar /kat'ər-pi-lər/ *n* a butterfly or moth grub; extended to other insect larvae; an unproductive consumer (*archaic*); (**Caterpillar®**) a tractor or other (*esp* earthmoving) vehicle running on endless articulated tracks made up of a series of flat metal plates. [Prob OFr *chatepelose* hairy cat; see also **cat¹** and **pile¹**]

caterwaul /kat'ər-wöl/ n the shriek or cry emitted by a domestic cat, esp when in heat. ◆ vi to make such a noise; to make any discordant sound similar to this, esp loud and tuneless singing; to behave lasciviously (archaic); to quarrel like cats. [cat¹; the second part prob imitative]
■ **cat'erwauling** n.

cates see cate.

catfish and **catgut** see under cat¹.

Cath. abbrev : Catholic.

cath. abbrev : cathedral; cathode.

Cathaian see Cathayan.

Cathar /kath'ər/ n (pl Cath'ars or Cath'arī) a member of a medieval Manichaean sect, chiefly in S France and N Italy, the Albigensians. [Gr katharos pure]
■ **Cath'arism** n. **Cath'arist** n.

cathartic /ka-thär'tik/ or **cathartical** /-ti-kl/ adj cleansing, purifying; having the power or effect of cleansing the bowels (med); purgative; causing emotional or psychological catharsis. ◆ n a purgative medicine. [Gr kathartikos fit for cleansing, from katharos clean]
■ **cath'arize** or **-ise** vt to render absolutely clean; to purge. **cathar'sis** n (pl **cathar'ses** /-sēz/) purification; evacuation of the bowels; purification of the emotions, achieved, according to Aristotle, through the witnessing of theatrical tragedy; the purging of the effects of pent-up emotion and repressed thoughts, by bringing them to the surface of consciousness (psychol). **cathart'ically** adv.

Cathayan or **Cathaian** /ka-thā'ən/ n and adj Chinese. [See Cataian]
cathead see under cat¹.

cathectic see under cathexis.

cathedral /kə-thē'drəl/ n the principal church of a diocese, containing the bishop's throne. ◆ adj belonging to a seat of authority or a cathedral; having a cathedral. [L cathēdra, cathedra, from Gr kathedrā a seat]
■ **cathedra** /-thē'drə or -thed'rə/ n a bishop's throne; the episcopal dignity; see also **ex cathedra**. **cathedrat'ic** adj promulgated ex cathedra, authoritative.

Catherine pear /kath'(ə-)rin pār/ n a small and early variety of pear.

Catherine-wheel /kath'(ə-)rin-(h)wēl/ n a rotating firework; a rose window (archit); a wheel set round with teeth (heraldry); a sidewise somersault. [From St Catherine of Alexandria (4c), who survived torture on a wheel]

catheter /kath'i-tər/ n a tube for admitting or removing gases or liquids through channels of the body, esp for removing urine from the bladder. [Gr kathetos perpendicular, kathetēr a catheter, from kathienai to send down, from kata down, and hienai to send]
■ **cath'eterism** n the use of the catheter. **catheteriza'tion** or **-s-** n insertion of a catheter. **cath'eterize** or **-ise** vt. **cath'etus** n a straight line perpendicular to another straight line or surface.

cathetometer /ka-thi-tom'i-tər/ n an instrument for measuring vertical distances not exceeding a few decimetres (also called **reading telescope** or **reading microscope**). [Gr kathetos, perpendicular, and -meter]

cathexis /kə-thek'sis/ (psychol) n (pl **cathex'es** /-sēz/) a charge of mental energy attached to any particular idea or object. [Gr kathexis holding]
■ **cathec'tic** adj.

cathinone /kath'i-nōn/ n an alkaloid stimulant, C₉H₁₁NO, obtained from khat; a similar synthetic compound. [New L catha khat, and -one]

cathisma /kə-thiz'mə/ n in Greek use, a section of the psalter; a troparion or short hymn used as a response. [Gr, from kathizein to sit down]

cathode /kath'ōd/ n the electrode of an electrolytic cell at which positively charged ions are discharged into the exterior electric circuit; the negative terminal or electrode of a dry battery; in valves and tubes, the source of electrons. Cf anode. [Gr kathodos a going down, from kata down, and hodos a way]
■ **cath'odal** adj. **cathod'ic** adj. **cathod'ograph** n a photograph created using X-rays. **cathodog'rapher** n. **cathodog'raphy** n. **cathodoluminesc'ence** n luminescence caused by irradiation with cathode rays.
□ **cathode-ray oscillograph** n the complete equipment for registering transient waveforms on a photographic plate within the vacuum of a cathode-ray tube. **cathode rays** n pl streams of negatively charged particles (electrons) proceeding from the cathode of a vacuum tube. **cathode-ray tube** n a device in which a narrow beam of electrons, which can be deflected by magnetic and/or electrostatic fields, acts on a fluorescent screen or photographic surface, used in television sets, etc. **cathodic protection** n protection of a metal structure

underground or under water against electrolytic corrosion by making it the cathode in an electrolytic cell.

catholic /kath'(ə-)lik/ adj (with cap) belonging to the Christian Church before the great schism between East and West, or to any church claiming to be historically related to it, esp (after the schism) the Western Church, and (after the Reformation) the Church of Rome (Roman Catholic), but applied also eg to Anglicans; (with cap) relating to the Roman Catholics; liberal, opp to exclusive ; universal; general; embracing the whole body of Christians; orthodox, opp to heterodox and sectarian. ◆ n (with cap) an adherent of the Roman Catholic Church. [Gr katholikos universal, from kata throughout, and holos the whole]
■ **cathol'ically** or **cathol'icly** adv. **Cathol'icism** n the tenets of the Roman Catholic Church; (without cap) catholicity (rare). **catholicity** /-is'i-ti/ n universality; liberality or breadth of view; Catholicism (rare). **catholiciza'tion** or **-s-** n (also with cap). **cathol'icize** or **-ise** vt and vi (also with cap) to make or become Catholic. **cathol'icon** /-kon/ n a universal remedy, a panacea; (sometimes with cap) a comprehensive work, eg an encyclopaedic dictionary. **Cathol'icos** n (pl **Catholicō'ses** /-ēz/ or **Cathol'icoi** /-oi/) the Patriarch of Armenia.
□ **Catholic (and) Apostolic Church** n a body formed in England about 1835, having an elaborate, symbolic ritual and a complex ecclesiastical hierarchy, and emphasizing the existence in the present day of miracles and prophecy, and the imminent second coming of Christ. **catholic creditor** n (Scots law) a creditor whose debt is secured over two or more subjects belonging to the debtor, eg over two or more heritable estates. **Catholic emancipation** n the relief of the Roman Catholics from certain vexatious penal regulations and restrictions, granted in 1829. **catholic** or **general epistles** n pl certain epistles in the canon addressed to the Church universal or to a large and indefinite circle of readers. **Catholic King** n (hist) a title given to the king of Spain.
■ **German Catholics** a body that broke away from the Roman Catholic Church in Germany in 1844 on the occasion of the exhibition of the Holy Coat at Trier. **Old Catholics** a body that broke away from the Roman Catholic Church in Germany in opposition to the dogma of papal infallibility proclaimed by the Vatican Council in 1870.

Catiline /kat'i-līn/ (rare) n a daring and reckless conspirator. [After Sergius Catilina, who plotted to destroy the senate in Rome in 63BC]
■ **Catilinarian** /-li-nā'ri-ən/ adj.

cation or **kation** /kat'ī-ən/ n an ion that travels towards the cathode; a positively-charged ion. [Gr kata down, and ion, neuter, from prp of ienai to go]
■ **cation'ic** adj.

catkin, catling, catmint, catnep, catnip, etc see under cat¹.

Catonian /kə-tō'ni-ən/ adj resembling or relating to Cato, the Roman censor (234–149BC), or Cato Uticensis (95–46BC), both noted for gravity of manners; hence grave, severe, unbending.

catoptric /ka-top'trik/ adj relating to reflection. [Gr katoptron a mirror, from kata back, and the root of opsomai I shall see]
■ **catop'trics** n sing the branch of optics which is concerned with reflected light.

CAT scanner /kat skan'ər/ or **CT scanner** /sē-tē'/ n a computed (or computerized) axial tomography scanner, an X-ray machine that produces three-dimensional images built up from a sequential series of X-ray sections of (a part of) the body.
■ **CAT scan** or **CT scan** n an image produced by such a machine; an examination with such a machine.

CAT standard /kat stan'dərd/ n one of a number of government standards setting fair Charges, Access and Terms for financial products; a financial product that complies with these standards.

catsup see ketchup.

cattabu /kat'ə-bū/ n a cross between domestic cattle and zebu. [From cattle and zebu]

cattalo or **catalo** /kat'ə-lō/ n (pl **catt'alo(e)s** or **cat'alo(e)s**) a cross between the bison ('buffalo') and the domestic cow. [From cattle and buffalo]

cattle /kat'l/ n pl bovine mammals of the genus Bos, esp oxen, bulls and cows; domesticated mammals including oxen, etc and also horses, sheep, etc (archaic). [OFr catel, chatel, from LL captāle, L capitāle, from caput the head]
□ **cattle cake** n a concentrated, processed food for cattle, in the form of blocks or cakes. **catt'le-class** adj (inf) economy-class. **cattle grid, cattle guard** (N Am) or **cattle stop** (NZ) n a frame of spaced bars covering a trench or depression in a road where it passes through a fence, crossable by motor vehicles or pedestrians but not by hoofed animals. **catt'le-lifter** n a stealer of cattle. **catt'le-lifting** n. **catt'leman** n a person who tends cattle, or who rears them on a ranch. **cattle market** n (sl) a place, esp a nightclub, where sexual partners are acquired without romance, sentiment or dignity. **catt'le-plague** n a

term applied to certain diseases of domestic cattle, *esp* rinderpest or steppe murrain. **cattle prod** *n* a rod or goad, often capable of delivering low-voltage electric shocks, for driving cattle, etc. **cattle show** *n* an exhibition of cattle or other domestic animals in competition for prizes.

cattleya /kat-lē'ə/ *n* any Central and S American orchid of the genus *Cattleya*, grown for their large flowers. [New L, from William *Cattley* (died 1832), English botanist]

catty¹ /kat'i/ *n* a unit of measurement used in SE Asia and China, equal to about 1.3lb avoirdupois in SE Asia and Hong Kong, and about 1.1lb avoirdupois (500 grammes) in China (also **kat'i** or **katt'i**). [Malay *kati*]

catty² see under **cat¹**.

catty-corner see under **cater²**.

Caucasian /kö-kā'z(h)i-ən or -zhən/ *n* a person belonging to that one of the main ethnological divisions of mankind which is native to Europe, N Africa and western and central Asia; a member of the white race; a white person; a native of the *Caucasus* or the country around it; any of the languages forming the Caucasian family. ◆ *adj* of or relating to a Caucasian or Caucasians in any of the above senses; relating to the Caucasus or the country around it; of or relating to the languages spoken in the Caucasus which do not belong to the Indo-European, Semitic or Ural-Altaic groups (*linguistics*).

Caucasoid /kö'kə-zoid/ *adj* of or relating to the ethnic group of light-complexioned people indigenous to Europe, N Africa, SW Asia and the Indian subcontinent; Caucasian. ◆ *n* a member of this group.

cauchemar /kōsh-mär'/ (*Fr*) *n* a nightmare.

caucus /kö'kəs/ *n* a meeting or group of members of a political party formed to nominate candidates or delegates or to decide how to vote on any question in a legislative assembly, its decision binding on those who attend (*esp N Am*); the members of such a group; any small group which acts as a (semi-)autonomous body within a larger group or organization, *esp* (*derog*) one which is excessively influential. ◆ *vi* to hold a caucus; to control by means of a caucus. [Ety doubtful; perh John Smith's Algonquian word *Caw-cawaassough*, an adviser; perh a corruption of 'caulkers' meetings']

caudal /kö'dəl/ *adj* relating to the tail or tail end. [L *cauda* tail]
■ **cau'dad** *adj* (*esp zool* and *anat*) towards the tail. **cau'dally** *adv*. **cau'dāte** or **cau'dated** *adj* having a tail or tail-like appendage.
□ **caudal anaesthesia** *n* a form of epidural anaesthesia.

caudex /kö'deks/ (*bot*) *n* (*pl* **caud'icēs** /-i-sēz/ or **caud'exes**) the stem of a tree, *esp* of a palm or tree-fern. [L]
■ **caud'icle** *n* the stalk of the pollen-masses of certain orchids.

caudillo /kow-dē'lyō/ *n* (*pl* **caudil'los**) in Spanish-speaking countries, a military or political leader; the head of the state. [Sp]

caudle /kö'dl/ *n* a warm drink, sweetened and spiced, formerly given to the sick. ◆ *vt* to give a caudle to; to mix. [ONFr *caudel*, from L *calidus* hot]
□ **caudle cup** *n* a two-handled cup, *usu* of silver, with a bulbous or cylindrical body and *usu* a lid.
■ **hempen caudle** (*Shakesp*) the hangman's noose.

caudron /kö'drən/ a Spenserian form of **cauldron**.

cauf /köf/ (*dialect*) *n* (*pl* **cauves**) a basket for fish. [**corf**]

caught /köt/ *pat* and *pap* of **catch**.

cauk or **cawk** /kök/ *n* chalk (*dialect*); barytes in platy crystals. [A form of **chalk**]

cauker see under **caulk**.

caul /köl/ *n* a net or covering for the head (*hist*); the membrane covering the head of some infants at birth, being part of the inner membrane of the fetal sac; the great omentum. [OFr *cale* a little cap, prob Celtic; cf Ir *calla* a veil, hood]

cauld¹ /köld/ (*Scot*) *n* a dam in a stream, a weir. [Origin obscure]

cauld² /köld/ (*Scot*) *adj* and *n* cold.
■ **cauldrife** /köld'rif/ *adj* apt to feel chilly; chilling, lifeless, without vigour.

cauldron or **caldron** /köl'drən/ *n* a large kettle for boiling or heating liquids. [OFr *caudron*, from L *caldārium*, from *calidus* hot, from *calēre* to be hot]
□ **cauldron subsidence** *n* (*geol*) the subsidence of a cylindrical mass of the Earth's crust, bounded by a circular fault up which the lava has *usu* risen to fill the cauldron.

cauliflower /ko' or kö'li-flowr/ *n* a variety of cabbage (*Brassica oleracea botrytis*) with a white, closely-packed, flower-head, eaten as a vegetable. [Earlier *cole-florye*, *colie-florie*, from LL *cauliflōra*, from L *caulis* cabbage; see **cole** and **flower**]
□ **cauliflower cheese** *n* boiled or steamed cauliflower with a cheese sauce. **cauliflower ear** *n* an ear permanently swollen and misshapen by injury, *esp* from boxing.

caulis /kö'lis/ or (*L*) kow'lis/ *n* (*pl* **cau'les** /-lēz/ or -lās/) the stem of a plant; one of the main stems at the angles of the Corinthian capital (*archit*). [L *caulis* a stalk]
■ **caulesc'ent** *adj* (of plants) having a stem rising above the ground. **cau'licle** *n* (*bot*) a rudimentary stem. **caulic'olous** *adj* (*bot*) growing on a stem. **caulic'ūlāte** *adj*. **caulic'ūlus** *n* (*archit*) one of the slender stems springing from the *caules* or main stalks supporting the volutes in the Corinthian capital. **cauliflo'ry** *n* (*bot*) production of flowers on trunks, branches and old stems of woody plants, rather than near the ends of smaller twigs. **caul'iform** *adj* having the form of a stem. **caulig'enous** *adj* borne on the stem. **caul'inary** or **cau'line** *adj* belonging to or growing from a stem. **cau'lōme** *n* a plant's stem structure as a whole.

caulk or **calk** /kök/ *vt* to render (planks, etc of a boat) watertight by pressing oakum or another suitable material into the seams. ◆ *vi* (*naut sl*) to snooze. [OFr *cauquer* to press, from L *calcāre* to tread, from *calx* heel]
■ **caulk'er** *n* a person who caulks; a dram; a big lie (also **cauk'er**). **caulk'ing** *n*.
□ **caulk'ing-iron** *n* an instrument like a chisel used for pressing oakum (tarred rope) into the seams of ships.

caulker see under **caulk** and **calk²**.

caum, etc see **cam³**.

caup see **cap²**.

causa /kow'zə/ (*L*) *n* cause.
□ **causa causans** /kow'zanz/ *n* (*law*) the immediate cause; the cause giving rise to liability.
■ **causa sine qua non** /sī'nē kwä non or sin'e kwä nōn/ (*law*) an indispensable cause or condition allowing something, eg the causa causans, to be operative, but not itself a causa causans.

causalgia /kö-zal'ji-ə/ *n* a burning pain, *usu* caused by a peripheral nerve injury. [Gr *kaukos* heat, and **-algia**]

cause /köz/ *n* that which produces an effect; that by or through which anything happens; a motive; an inducement; a legal action between contending parties; sake, advantage; an ideal, principle or belief in the name of which people band together to do something; an accusation (*Shakesp*); a matter, affair in general (*Shakesp*). ◆ *vt* to produce; to bring about the existence of; to bring about the occurrence of; to give excuses for (*Spenser*; *infinitive* **caus'en**). ◆ *conj* (*dialect* or *inf*) because (*usu* **'cause**). [Fr, from L *causa*]
■ **caus'al** *adj* being the cause, that causes; relating to a cause or causes. **causal'ity** *n* the relationship between cause and effect; the principle that everything has a cause; the mechanics of the cause of something. **caus'ally** *adv*. **causā'tion** *n* the act of causing; the bringing about of an effect; causality. **causā'tional** *adj*. **causā'tionism** *n* the principle of universal causation. **causā'tionist** *n*. **caus'ative** *adj* causal; of the nature of, or expressing, causation. ◆ *n* (*grammar*) a form or class of verb expressing causation. **caus'atively** *adv*. **cause'less** *adj* without cause; without just cause. **cause'lessly** *adv*. **cause'lessness** *n*. **caus'er** *n*.
□ **cause list** *n* (*law*) a list of cases awaiting trial.
■ **cause of action** (*law*) actionable facts. **efficient cause** the means by which a thing took its present form. **final cause** see under **final**. **first cause** the original cause or creator of all, God. **formal cause** the essence or idea of a thing. **have** or **show cause** to have to give reasons for a certain line of action. **hour of cause** (*Scots law*; *hist*) hour or time of trial. **make common cause** (often with *with*) to unite for a common object. **material cause** that out of which a thing is framed. **natural causes** causes (of death) such as old age or disease, as opposed to violence or accident. **occasional causes** see under **occasion**. **secondary causes** causes derived from a primary or first cause. **show cause** (*Eng law*) to argue against the confirmation of a provisional order or judgement.

cause célèbre /kōz sā-le'br'/ (*Fr*) *n* (*pl* **causes célèbres** /kōz/) a very notable or famous trial; a notorious controversy or highly controversial person.

causerie /kö'zə-rē/ *n* a chat or gossip; a conversational paragraph about literature or art; a short and informal essay on any subject in a newspaper or magazine. [Fr]

causeway /köz'wā/ *n* a raised road or path through a marsh or across water; a pathway raised and paved with stone; a paved or cobblestoned road. [ME *causee*, from OFr *caucie*, from LL (*via*) *calciāta* a trodden way, from L *calx* heel]
■ **cause'wayed** *adj*.

causey /kö'zi/ *n* a causeway (*dialect*); a paved road or street, formerly of cobblestones (*Scot*).
■ **caus'eyed** *adj*.

caustic /kö'stik/ *adj* burning; corroding; relating to, or of the shape of, a caustic (*maths* and *phys*); (of remarks, etc) bitter, severe, cutting (*fig*).
◆ *n* a chemical substance that has a corroding or burning action; an envelope of light rays proceeding from a fixed point and reflected

(*catacaustic*) or refracted (*diacaustic*) by a curve (*maths*); a caustic curve or caustic surface (*phys*). [L *causticus*, from Gr *kaustikos*, from *kaiein* future, and *kausein* to burn]

■ **caus'tically** *adv.* **causticity** /-*tis'i-ti*/ *n* quality of being caustic. **caus'ticness** *n.*

❑ **caustic ammonia** *n* ammonia as a gas, or in solution. **caustic curve** *n* (*phys*) a curve in the shape of a caustic, the form of a plane section through a caustic surface. **caustic lime** *n* quicklime. **caustic potash** *n* potassium hydroxide. **caustic soda** *n* sodium hydroxide, used in making soap. **caustic surface** *n* (*phys*) a caustic-shaped surface, the envelope of rays of light reflected or refracted by a curved surface.

■ **common caustic** potash; also silver nitrate. **lunar caustic** silver nitrate in sticks for surgical use.

cautel /kö'tl/ *n* cunning, craft (*Shakesp*); insidious purpose (*Shakesp*); caution (*obs*); wariness (*obs*); a traditional caution or written direction about the proper manner of administering the sacraments (*obs*). [Fr *cautèle*, from L *cautēla*, from *cavēre*, *cautum* to guard against]

■ **cau'telous** *adj* cautious (*obs*); insidious (*Shakesp*); artful (*Shakesp*).

cauterize or **-ise** /kö'tə-rīz/ *vt* to burn or destroy with a caustic substance, a hot metal implement, etc, *esp* to destroy infected tissue in a wound; to sear (*fig*). [Fr *cautériser*, from LL *cautērizāre*, from Gr *kautēr* a hot iron, from *kaiein* to burn]

■ **cau'ter** or **cau'tery** *n* burning or destroying with caustics, a hot metal implement, etc; a burning, caustic substance, etc for burning or destroying tissue. **cau'terant** *n* a cauterizing substance. **cau'terism** *n.* **cauterīza'tion** or **-s-** *n.* **cauterīzing** or **-s-** *adj.*

caution /kö'shən/ *n* heedfulness, carefulness; a warning; a warning that what a person says may be used as evidence (*law*); a notice preventing an owner from disposing of his land without consulting the person who entered the notice; an alarming, amusing or astonishing person or thing (*inf*); (also /kā'/) security, surety, bail (*Scots law*). ◆ *vt* to warn to take care; to give (someone) a caution (*law*). [Fr, from L *cautiō*, *-ōnis*, from *cavēre* to beware]

■ **cau'tionary** *adj* containing caution or cautions; given as a pledge. **cau'tioner** *n* a person who cautions or advises; (also /kā'/) a surety (*Scots law*). **cautionry** /kā'/ *n* (*Scots law*) the act of giving security for another. **cautious** /kö'shəs/ *adj* possessing or using caution; watchful, heedful; prudent. **cau'tiously** *adv.* **cau'tiousness** *n.*

❑ **caution money** *n* money paid in advance as security for good conduct.

Cava /kā'və/ *n* a white sparkling wine, similar to champagne, produced mainly in the Penedès region of NE Spain. [Sp, from *cava* cellar]

cavalcade /kav-əl-kād' or kav'/ *n* a procession of people on horseback or in vehicles; a parade. ◆ *vi* to proceed in a cavalcade. [Fr, through Ital and LL, from L *caballus* a horse]

cavalier /ka-və-lēr'/ *n* a knight; (with *cap*) a Royalist in the English Civil War; a swaggering fellow; a gallant or gentleman in attendance upon a lady, as her escort or partner in a dance or the like; (in military fortification) a raised work so situated as to command the neighbouring country. ◆ *adj* like a cavalier; warlike; haughty, supercilious, devil-may-care, incautious. ◆ *vi* to act as cavalier to a lady. [Fr, from Ital *cavallo*; see **cavalcade**]

■ **cavalier'ish** *adj* like, or characteristic of, a cavalier. **cavalier'ism** *n.* **cavalier'ly** *adv* offhand; haughtily, with supercilious disregard or curtness. ◆ *adj* cavalierish.

❑ **Cavalier King Charles spaniel** see under **spaniel**.

cavaliere servente /kä-vä-lē-er'e ser-ven'te/ (*Ital*) *n* a gallant or lover of a married woman; a lady's man.

cavalla /kə-val'ə/ or **cavally** /kə-val'i/ *n* an American fish of the scad family, or any of several related carangoid fish. [Sp *caballa* and Port *cavalla* mackerel]

cavalry /kav'əl-ri/ *n* the part of an army made up of soldiers on horseback; (a troop of) mounted soldiers; the armoured section of a modern army. [Fr *cavallerie*, from Ital *cavalleria*, from L *caballārius* horseman, from *caballus* horse]

■ **cav'alryman** *n.*

❑ **cavalry twill** see under **twill**[1].

cavass see **kavass**.

cavatina /ka-vä-tē'nə or -və-/ (*music*) *n* a melody with no second part or da capo; loosely, a short operatic air of a smooth and melodious character, often part of a grand scena. [Ital]

cave[1] /kāv/ *n* a hollow in a rock, a cliff or underground; a small faction of seceders from a political party (from the Cave of Adullam in Bible, 1 Samuel 22.1–2); the ash-pit under the furnace in glassworks. ◆ *vt* to hollow out. ◆ *vi* to inhabit a cave. [Fr *cave*, from L *cavus* hollow]

■ **ca'ver** *n* a person who explores caves. **ca'ving** *n* the sport or pastime of cave-exploration.

❑ **cave'-bear** *n* (*Ursus spelaeus*) a bear of the Pleistocene epoch of which fossil remains have been found in caves. **cave'-dweller** *n* a person who lives in a cave, *esp* one of the Stone Age people of prehistoric times. **cave'-earth** *n* a fine deposit on cave floors. **cave'fish** *n* (*pl* **cave'fish** or **cave'fishes**) any of various small freshwater fishes of the Ambyopsidae family with reduced or absent eyes, living in subterranean waters in N America. **cave-in** see **cave in** below. **cave'man** *n* a cave-dweller; a modern male of primitive and chauvinistic attitudes and ways (*inf*).

■ **cave in** to slip, to subside, to collapse inwards (**cave'-in** *n*); to yield to outside pressure, to give way, to collapse (*fig*).

cave[2] /kav'i or kā'vi/ *interj* (*school sl*) beware. [L *cavē*, imperative sing of *cavēre* to take care]

■ **cave canem** /kā'vi, ka'vā, -wā, kā'nəm, ka'nem/ (L) beware of the dog, a frequent inscription on Roman thresholds. **keep cave** to keep watch.

caveat /kā'vi-at or kav'i-at/ *n* a notice or warning; a proviso; a formal warning, entered in the books of a court or public office, that no step be taken in a particular matter without notice to the person lodging the caveat. [L, 3rd person sing subjunctive of *cavēre* to take care]

■ **caveat actor** /kā'vi-at, ka've-at, -we-, ak'tör/ let the doer beware. **caveat emptor** /emp'tör/ let the buyer beware, it is the buyer's responsibility.

cavel /kāv'l/ (*Scot*) *n* a piece of wood, etc used in casting lots; a lot cast; fate, chance (*fig*). [Du *kavel*]

cavendish /kav'ən-dish/ *n* tobacco moistened and pressed into rectangular cakes. [Poss from the name of the orig manufacturer]

cavendo tutus /kā- or ka-ven'dō tū'təs, or kä-wen'dō too'tŭs/ (L) safe by taking heed.

cavern /kav'ərn/ *n* a large cave or a large underground chamber. ◆ *vt* to put in a cavern; to hollow out. [Fr *caverne*, from L *caverna*, from *cavus* hollow]

■ **cav'erned** *adj* made up of or full of caverns; inhabiting a cavern. **cav'ernous** *adj* like a cavern in size, huge and dark; containing or full of caverns. **cav'ernously** *adv.* **caver'nŭlous** *adj* full of little cavities, porous.

cavesson /kav'ə-sən/ *n* a noseband for a horse. [Fr *caveçon*, from Ital *cavezzone*, from L *capitia*, *capitium* a head-covering]

cavetto /ka-vet'ō/ (*archit*) *n* (*pl* **cavett'i** /-i/) a hollowed moulding whose curvature is the quarter of a circle, used chiefly in cornices. [Ital dimin of *cavo*, from L *cavus* hollow]

caviar or **caviare** /kav'i-är or ka-vi-är'/ *n* (also (*Shakesp*) **caviar'ie** and (*obs*) **cavier'**) salted roe of the sturgeon fish; something whose flavour is too fine for the common taste (*fig*). [Prob 16c Ital *caviale*, from Turk *khāvyār*]

cavicorn /kav'i-körn/ *adj* hollow-horned, as a ruminant is. ◆ *n* an animal of the **Cavicor'nia** or Bovidae. [L *cavus* hollow, and *cornū* a horn]

cavie or **keavie** /kāv'i/ (*Scot*) *n* a hen-coop or cage. [Cf Du *kevie*, Ger *Käfig*, from L *cavus*]

cavil /kav'il/ *vi* (**cav'illing**; **cav'illed**) to make petty, trifling objections (with *at* or *about*); to quibble. ◆ *n* a trifling objection. [OFr *caviller*, from L *cavillārī* to practise jesting]

■ **cavilla'tion** *n.* **cav'iller** *n.* **cav'illing** *n* and *adj.*

cavity /kav'i-ti/ *n* a hollow; a hollow space or hole; a decayed hollow in a tooth. [L *cavitās*, from *cavus* hollow]

■ **cav'itate** *vi* to form hollows. **cavita'tion** *n* the formation of cavities in a structure, or of gas bubbles in a liquid, or of a vacuum, or of a partial vacuum as between a body moving in a fluid and the fluid; a cavity. **cav'itied** *adj.*

❑ **cavity radiation** *n* (*phys*) the radiation emerging from a small hole leading from a constant temperature enclosure. **cavity wall** *n* a wall consisting of two layers with an air-space between (this space often later filled in with insulating material to provide energy-conserving **cavity-wall' insulation**).

cavolo nero /kav'ə-lō när'ō/ *n* a strong-flavoured Italian cabbage with dark green leaves (also **black cabbage**, **Tuscan kale**). [Ital, black cabbage]

cavo-rilievo /kä'vō-rē-lyā'vō/ *n* a kind of relief sculpture in which the highest surface is below the level of the original stone, which is left round the outlines of the design (see also **intaglio**). [Ital *cavo* hollow, and *rilievo* relief; see **cave**[1] and **relief**]

cavort /kə-vört'/ *vi* to frolic, bound about joyfully. [Perh corruption of **curvet**]

cavy /kā'vi/ *n* a member of the guinea-pig genus (*Cavia*) of rodents. [*Cabiai*, native name in French Guiana]

caw, also **kaw** /kö/ *vi* to cry as a crow. ◆ *n* the cry of a crow. [Imit]

■ **caw'ing** *n.*

cawk see **cauk**.

cawker see **calk**².

caxon /kak'sən/ (hist) n a kind of wig. [Origin obscure]

Caxton /kak'stən/ n a book printed by William *Caxton* (1422–91), the first English printer; a kind of printing-type in imitation of Caxton's.

cay /kā or kē/ n a low islet, the same as **key**³. [Sp *cayo*]

cayenne /kī or kā-en'/ n a very strong, pungent red pepper (**cayenne pepper**) made from several species of capsicum. [Usu referred to *Cayenne* in French Guiana; but prob from Tupí]
■ **cayenned**' adj seasoned with cayenne.

cayman or **caiman** /kā'mən/ n (pl **cay'mans** or **caimans**) any of the Central and S American crocodilian animals of the genus *Caiman* and related genera, similar to alligators. [Sp *caimán*, most prob Carib]

cayuse /kī-ūs'/ (N Am) n a small Native American pony; a small or poor horse. [Native American]

cazique a form of **cacique**.

CB abbrev : Citizens' Band (radio); Companion of the (Order of the) Bath; confined (or confinement) to barracks; County Borough.

Cb (chem) symbol : columbium.

cb abbrev : centre of buoyancy (of a boat, etc).

CBC abbrev : Canadian Broadcasting Corporation.

CBD (chiefly Aust and US) abbrev : Central Business District.

cbd abbrev : cash before delivery.

CBE abbrev : Commander of the (Order of the) British Empire.

CBer /sē-bē'ər/ n short for Citizens' Band radio user.

CBI abbrev : Confederation of British Industry.

CBIS abbrev : computer-based information system.

CBP (US) abbrev : Customs and Border Protection.

CBS abbrev : Columbia Broadcasting System.

CBSO abbrev : City of Birmingham Symphony Orchestra.

CBT abbrev : cognitive-behavioural therapy; computer-based training.

CC abbrev : closed-circuit (transmission); Competition Commission; confined to camp (milit); County Council or County Councillor; Cricket Club; Croquet Club.

cc abbrev : capita (L), chapters; carbon copy or copies; cubic centimetre(s).

CCC abbrev : County Cricket Club.

CCCP see **USSR**.

CCD abbrev : charge-coupled device.

CCF abbrev : Central Control Function; chronic heart failure (med); Combined Cadet Force.

CCJ abbrev : county court judgement.

CCLRC abbrev : Council for the Central Laboratory of the Research Councils (now replaced by the Science and Technology Facilities Council).

CCMI abbrev : Companion of the Chartered Management Institute.

CCR abbrev : critical compression ratio.

CCT abbrev : compulsory competitive tendering.

CCTV abbrev : closed-circuit television.

CCU abbrev : coronary care unit.

C-cubed or **C3** /sē-kūbd'/ abbrev : (milit; esp US) communications, command and control.

CD abbrev : Civil Defence; compact disc; contagious disease(s); controlled drug; *Corps Diplomatique* (Fr), Diplomatic Corps.

Cd abbrev : coefficient of drag; Command Paper (series 1900–1918).

Cd (chem) symbol : cadmium.

cd abbrev : cash discount.

cd symbol : candela (SI unit).

c/d (bookkeeping) abbrev : carried down.

CDC abbrev : Centers for Disease Control and Prevention, a US government agency.

CDI or **CD-i** abbrev : Compact Disc Interactive.

C. diff abbrev : Clostridium difficile.

CDMA abbrev : code division multiple access, a sophisticated digital transmission system used in devices such as mobile phones.

CDN abbrev : Canada (IVR).

Cdn abbrev : Canadian.

CDO abbrev : collateralized debt obligation, a financial instrument in which loans are packaged into tradeable commodities.

CD-R abbrev : compact disc recordable.

Cdr abbrev : Commander.

Cdre abbrev : Commodore.

CD-ROM /sē-dē-rom'/ (comput) abbrev : compact disc read-only memory, a system allowing access to, but not alteration of, information on a compact disc.

CD-RW abbrev : compact disc rewritable.

CDS abbrev : credit default swap.

CDT abbrev : craft, design, technology.

CDU abbrev : *Christlich Demokratische Union* (Ger), Christian Democratic Union.

CDV abbrev : canine distemper virus (vet); Civil Defence Volunteer(s).

CD video /sē'dē' vid'i-ō/ n synchronized sound and video pictures stored on a compact disc.

CE abbrev : Chancellor of the Exchequer; chemical or chief engineer; Church of England; civil engineer; Common Entrance; Common Era, used (instead of AD) in numbering the years of the current era; *Communauté européenne* (Fr), the mark showing that toys, electrical equipment, etc conform with EU safety standards; Council of Europe.

Ce (chem) symbol : cerium.

ceanothus /sē-ə-nō'thəs/ n any shrub of the American genus *Ceanothus*, of the family Rhamnaceae. [Gr *keanōthos* corn-thistle]

ceas a variant reading for **sessa**.

cease /sēs/ vt and vi to desist from; to stop; to end. ◆ n an end; cessation. [Fr *cesser*, from L *cessāre* to give over, from *cēdere* to yield]
■ **cease'less** adj without stop, continuous; incessant. **cease'lessly** adv. **ceas'ing** n.
❑ **cease'fire** n an order to cease firing; an agreed end of hostilities.

ceaze an obsolete spelling of **seize**.

cebadilla see **sabadilla**.

Cebus /sē'bəs/ n the generic name of the capuchin monkeys. [Gr *kēbos* a kind of monkey]
■ **Cebidae** /seb'i-dē/ n pl a family including all the New World monkeys except the marmosets.

ceca, cecal, cecum see **caecum**.

Cecidomyia /ses-i-do-mī'i-ə/ n a gall midge, a genus of flies destructive to vegetation. [Gr *kēkis, -idos* a gall, and *myia* a fly]

cecitis N American spelling of **caecitis**.

cecity /sē'si-ti/ n blindness. [L *caecus* blind]
■ **cecutiency** /si-kū'shyən-si/ n a tendency to blindness.

cecropia /si-krō'pi-ə/ n any tree of the tropical American genus *Cecropia*, some with hollow stems that give food and housing to a protective garrison of ants. [Named after the mythical Attic King *Cecrops* (Gr *Kekrōps*) represented as half-dragon, half-human]
■ **cecro'pin** n a peptide with antibacterial properties, orig obtained from the cecropia moth.
❑ **cecropia moth** n a large brightly-coloured American moth.

cecum N American spelling of **caecum**.

cecutiency see under **cecity**.

cedar /sē'dər/ n a large evergreen coniferous tree (*Cedrus*, including *Cedar of Lebanon*, *Atlantic cedar* and *deodar*) remarkable for the durability and fragrance of its wood; applied also to many more or less similar trees, as the Barbados cedar, properly a juniper, and the Bastard Barbados cedar, a tree of the genus *Cedrela*; the wood of these trees. ◆ adj made of cedar. [L *cedrus*, from Gr *kedros*]
■ **ce'dared** adj covered with cedars. **ce'darn** adj (poetic) of cedar. **ce'drine** adj belonging to the cedar tree.
❑ **ce'dar-bird** n an American waxwing. **ce'dar-nut** n the seed of the cembra pine. **ce'darwood** n (also adj).

cede /sēd/ vt to yield or give up to another person, country, etc; (of an insurer) to transfer all or part of the risk of a liability to a reinsurer. ◆ vi to give way, yield. [L *cēdere, cessum* to yield, to give up]

cedi /sed'i/ n (pl **ced'is**) the standard monetary unit of Ghana (100 pesewas).

cedilla /si-dil'ə/ n a mark, orig a subscript Z, placed under the letter c (thus ç), formerly used in Spanish to indicate that the letter had the sound of (Spanish) /z/ where that of /k/ would be expected, still used esp in French and Portuguese to indicate an /s-/ sound as before a, o, u, and in other languages used to denote other sounds, eg Turkish s /sh/ and ç /ch/. [Sp (Fr *cédille*, Ital *zediglia*), all diminutives from *zēta*, the Greek name of z; see **Z**]

cedrate /sē'drāt/ n citron. [Fr *cédrat*, from L *citrus*]

Cedrela /se-drē'lə/ n a tropical genus of Meliaceae, allied to mahogany. [Sp dimin of *cedro, cedra* cedar; see **cedar**]
■ **cedrelā'ceous** adj.

---

cedrine see under **cedar**.

cedula /sed'ū-lə/ n a S American promissory-note or mortgage-bond on lands. [Sp; cf **schedule**]

cee /sē/ n the third letter of the modern English alphabet (C or c); anything shaped like it.
❑ **cee-spring** or **c-spring** /sē'spring/ n a spring in the shape of a C to support the frame of a carriage.

Ceefax® /sē'faks/ n formerly, the teletext service of the British Broadcasting Corporation. [**see** and **facts**]

CEGB abbrev : Central Electricity Generating Board (now defunct).

CEHR abbrev : Commission for Equality and Human Rights.

ceiba /sī'bə/ n any of various tropical silk-cotton trees (genus Ceiba); kapok, silk cotton. [Arawak]

ceil /sēl/ vt to overlay the inner roof of (obs); to overlay or line; to provide with a ceiling. [Prob connected with Fr ciel, Ital cielo, LL caelum a canopy]
■ **ceiled** adj. **ceil'ing** n the inner roof of a room; the highest altitude at which an aircraft can fly; the height above the ground of the base of the cloud-layer; an upper limit; the planking forming the interior in the framework of a vessel (naut). **ceil'inged** adj having a ceiling. **ceilom'eter** n (meteorol) an instrument for measuring the cloud ceiling.
❑ **ceiling rose** see **rose¹**.

ceilidh /kā'li/ n esp in Scotland and Ireland, an informal evening with traditional music and dancing (also (Irish) **ceil'i**). [Gaelic, a visit]

ceinture /sē-tür'/ (Fr) n a girdle, belt.

cel see **Celluloid®**.

cel. abbrev : celebrated.

cel- see **coel-**.

celadon /sel'ə-don/ n a pale-green colour; a Chinese pottery glaze of the colour; the pottery so glazed. [Fr, perh after a character in Honoré D'Urfé's pastoral romance Astrée (1610–27)]

celandine /sel'ən-dīn/ n either of two plants (**greater celandine**, Chelidonium majus, and **lesser celandine**, Ranunculus ficaria) supposed to flower when the swallows came, and to perish when they went. [OFr celidoine, from Gr chelīdonion, from chelīdōn a swallow]

-cele /-sēl/ combining form denoting a tumour, swelling or hernia. [Gr kēlē]

celebrate /sel'i-brāt/ vt to mark by solemn ceremonies, as a festival or an event; to perform with proper rites and ceremonies, such as a mass, the Eucharist, marriage, etc; to publish the praises of; to make famous. ◆ vi to do something enjoyable because of a feeling of pleasure at some event, achievement, etc. [L celebrāre, -ātum, from celeber frequented]
■ **cel'ebrant** n a person who celebrates; the principal person officiating at a rite or ceremony. **cel'ebrated** adj distinguished; famous. **celebrā'tion** n the act of celebrating; any solemn or joyous ceremony. **cel'ebrātor** n. **cel'ebratory** adj. **celebrity** /si-leb'ri-ti/ n fame; notoriety; a person of distinction or fame (inf short form **celeb'**).

celecoxib /sel-i-kok'sib/ n a coxib used in the treatment of severe pain.

celerity /si-ler'i-ti/ n quickness, speed; rapidity of motion or thought. [Fr célérité, from L celeritās, from celer quick]

celery /sel'ə-ri/ n an umbelliferous plant (Apium graveolens) whose blanched leafstalks are eaten cooked or uncooked as a vegetable. [Fr céleri, from Gr selīnon parsley]
■ **celeriac** /si-ler'i-ak/ n a variety of celery with a swollen stem-base like a turnip.
❑ **celery pine** n a New Zealand evergreen tree (genus Phyllocladus) with celery-like shoots. **celery salt** n a seasoning of salt and ground celery seed.

celesta /si-les'tə/ or **celeste** /si-lest'/ n a keyboard instrument in which bell-like sounds are produced by hammers striking steel plates suspended over wooden resonators. [Fr céleste heavenly]

celeste /si-lest'/ adj sky-blue. ◆ n voix céleste; a kind of soft pedal on a piano. [Fr céleste]

celestial /si-lest'yəl/ adj heavenly, divine, sublime; living in heaven; of or in the visible heavens (esp astron); Chinese (old inf; usu humorously). ◆ n an inhabitant of heaven, a celestial being; a Chinese person (old inf). [Through Fr from L caelestis, from caelum heaven]
■ **celest'ially** adv.
❑ **Celestial Empire** n (hist) China, the Chinese Empire. **celestial equator** n (astron) a great circle in which the plane of the earth's equator cuts the celestial sphere. **celestial globe** n a model of the celestial sphere showing the relative positions of stars, etc. **celestial horizon** see **horizon**. **celestial latitude** see **latitude**. **celestial longitude** see **longitude**. **celestial mechanics** n sing (astron) the study of the motions of celestial objects in gravitational fields, esp, as by Newton, satellite and planetary motion in the solar system. **celestial navigation** n navigation by the stars, etc (also

astronavigation). **celestial poles** n pl (astron) the two points at which the earth's axis, extended indefinitely, cuts the celestial sphere. **celestial sphere** n (astron) an imaginary sphere of infinite radius, of which the observer is the centre, onto which stars and other celestial bodies are projected.

Celestine /sel'i-stīn or si-les'tin/ n a monk of an order founded in 1264 by Pietro da Morrone, afterwards Pope Celestine V.

celestite /sel'ə-stīt or sə-les'tīt/ or **celestine** /sel'ə-stin or -stīn/ n a sky-blue, red or white mineral, strontium sulphate, crystallized in the orthorhombic system, and occurring in rock salt and gypsum. [Through Ger, from L caelestis celestial]

celiac N American spelling of **coeliac**.

celibacy /sel'i-bə-si/ n the unmarried state, esp as adhered to under a religious vow; abstention from sexual relations. [L caelebs single]
■ **celibatā'rian** adj favouring or advocating celibacy. **cel'ibate** /-it/ adj living as a single person; abstaining from sexual relations. ◆ n a person who is unmarried, or bound by a vow not to marry.

cell¹ /sel/ n the unit, consisting of nucleus and cytoplasm and bounded by a membrane, of which plants and animals are composed, surrounded in the former by a non-living wall; the whole bacterium or yeast, the bacterial cell; a small room in a prison, monastery, etc; a vessel with electrodes and an electrolyte for electrolysis, or an apparatus for generating an electric current by chemical action, esp a dry battery; a unit group, esp of espionage personnel, political activists or terrorists; a small monastery or nunnery dependent on another; one compartment of a honeycomb; a hermit's one-roomed dwelling; the cavity containing pollen in an anther lobe (bot); one chamber in an ovary (bot); one of the spaces into which the wing of an insect is divided (zool); (a radio transmitter serving) one of the geographical areas into which Britain is divided for the coverage of cellular radio (qv below); a part of the atmosphere that behaves as a unit (meteorol); a cellphone (inf); a unit of homogenous reactivity in a nuclear reactor core; a unit or area of storage, eg the smallest unit capable of storing a single bit (comput); a location on a spreadsheet (comput). [OFr celle, from L cella, connected with celāre to cover]
■ **celled** adj having cells, cellular. **cellif'erous** adj having or producing cells. **cell'ūlar** adj consisting of, characterized by or containing cells or compartments; relating to or involving cells in the body; consisting of a number of separate rooms, as in cellular office ; composed of ordinary cells without vessels (as the lower cryptogams); porous; of open texture. **cellular'ity** n. **cell'ūlāted** adj. **cell'ule** n a little cell. **cellūlif'erous** adj having or producing little cells. **cellulite** n see separate entry. **cellūli'tis** n inflammation of the subcutaneous body tissue caused by pyogenic bacteria. **Celluloid®** n see separate entry. **cell'ulose** n and adj see separate entry.
❑ **cell cycle** n (biol) the series of processes undergone between one cell division and the next. **cell division** n (biol) the process in which cells each split into two new cells during growth or reproduction. **cell-free transcription** n (biol) in vitro transcription. **cell-free translation** n (biol) in vitro translation. **cell line** n (biol) a cell culture derived from a single cell and thus having a uniform genetic make-up. **cell membrane** n (biol) the surface membrane surrounding a cell. **cell'phone** or **cellular phone** n a portable telephone for use in a cellular radio system. **cellular immunity** or **cell-mediated immunity** n an acquired immunity in which T lymphocytes play a major part. **cellular radio** n a system of radio communication based on a network of roughly hexagonal geographical cells each served by a transmitter, the receiving equipment automatically tuning in to each in turn as it moves across the cells' borders. **cellular therapy** n intramuscular injection of humans with the fetal tissue of certain unborn animals to stimulate the regeneration of damaged cells and tissues (also called **live cell therapy**). **cell wall** n (biol) the nonliving covering or separating wall of a cell, esp the semi-rigid covering of a plant cell, containing cellulose, lignin, etc.

cell² see **Celluloid®**.

cella /sel'ə/ n (pl cell'ae /-ē/) the naos, or inner chamber of a classical temple. [L, shrine]

cellar¹ /sel'ər/ n any underground room or vault; a room for storing wine, beer, coal, etc, often below ground level; a stock of wine. ◆ vt to store in a cellar. [OFr celier, from L cellārium, from cella]
■ **cell'arage** n (a quantity of) cellar space; a charge for storing in cellars. **cell'arer** or **cell'arist** n a person who is in charge of the cellar; an officer in a monastery who looks after the provisions. **cell'aret** n a case, cupboard or drawer for holding bottles of wine, etc. **cell'arous** adj (Dickens) belonging to a cellar; excavated; sunken.
❑ **cell'ar-book** n a record of wines kept in a cellar. **cell'ar-flap** n a plate covering an entrance to a cellar. **cell'arman** n a person responsible for a cellar.

cellar² same as **saltcellar** (see under **salt¹**).

Cellnet® /sel'net/ n in UK, a system of mobile telecommunications using cellular radio.

cello /chel'ō/ n (pl **cell'os**) short for violoncello (sometimes written **'cello**).

■ **cell'ist** or **'cell'ist** n a violoncellist.

cellobiose /se-lō-bī'ōz or -ōs/ (biol) n a disaccharide, $C_{12}H_{22}O_{11}$, obtained by complete hydrolysis of cellulose (also **cell'ose**). [From cellulose, **bi-**, and **-ose**]

Cellophane® /sel'ə-fān/ n a tough, transparent, paperlike wrapping material made from viscose. [cellulose and Gr phainein to show]

cellose see **cellobiose**.

cellphone, **cellular** see under **cell**[1].

cellulase /sel'yū-lāz or -lās/ n an enzyme that can split cellulose into glucose, present in organisms in the guts of animals and in the leaf stalks of higher plants. [cellulose and **-ase**]

cellulite /sel'yū-līt/ n deposits of fat cells, not responsive to dieting or exercise, which give the skin a dimpled, pitted appearance. [Fr, from cellule a little cell]

Celluloid® /sel'yū-loid/ n (also without cap) a thermoplastic, made from nitrocellulose, camphor and alcohol, which is elastic, very strong and often transparent or translucent; (often shortened to **cel** or **cell**) a sheet of this material; cinematographic film generally; the world of film and cinema.

cellulose /sel'yə-lōz or -lōs, or -ū-/ n a carbohydrate forming the chief component of cell walls in plants and in wood (cotton-down, linen fibre and wood pulp being almost pure cellulose). ◆ adj containing cells. [Fr, from cellule a little cell]

■ **cellulosic** /-lōz'ik/ adj containing or derived from cellulose.
❏ **cellulose acetate** n a chemical compound obtained by the action of acetate and sulphuric acid on cellulose, used in the manufacture of textiles, varnish and photographic film. **cellulose nitrate** n a chemical compound obtained by the action of nitric acid on cellulose, used in the manufacture of textiles, explosives, plastics, etc.

celo- see **coel-**.

celom see **coelom**.

celosia /sə-lō'si-ə/ n any plant of the genus Celosia, including C. cristata, the cock's-comb. [Mod L, from Gr kēlos burnt]

celsitude /sel'si-tūd/ n loftiness. [L celsitūdō, from celsus lofty]

Celsius /sel'si-əs/ adj relating to the centigrade scale used in the thermometer constructed by Anders Celsius (1701–44), in which the freezing point of water is 0° and the boiling point is 100°.
■ **degree Celsius** a derived SI unit, the unit of Celsius temperature (symbol °**C**), equal to one kelvin.

Celt /kelt or selt/ also **Kelt**, etc /kelt/ n a Gaul (hist); extended to include members of other Celtic-speaking or recently Celtic-speaking peoples, esp the inhabitants of parts of Britain, Ireland and NW France. [L Celtae ; Gr Keltoi or Keltai]
■ **Celt'ic** adj relating to the Celts; of a branch of the Indo-European family of languages including Breton, Welsh, Cornish, Irish, Gaelic, Manx. ◆ n a Celt; the Celtic branch of languages. **Celt'icism** n a Celtic idiom or custom. **Celt'icist** n an expert or specialist in Celtic language and/or culture. **Celtomā'nia** n.
❏ **Celtic cross** n a Latin cross, carved in the style common to the Celts, Scandinavians and Northumbrian Angles and used conventionally for Christian memorials, etc, with a broad circle around the point of intersection of the crossbar and the upright, sometimes miscalled Runic cross. **Celtic fringe** n an offensive term applied to Wales, Ireland and the Highlands and Islands of Scotland, which have different cultural, social and political characteristics from the rest of the British Isles. **Celtic Sea** n the area of sea to the south of Ireland and west of Cornwall.
■ **P-Celtic** and **Q-Celtic** (relating to) respectively, those Celtic languages in which the sound /kw/ became /p/ and those in which it became /k/ (written c).

Celt. abbrev : Celtic.

celt /selt/ (archaeol) n a prehistoric axe-like implement with a bevelled edge. [From a supposed L word celtes a chisel]

Celtiberian /sel- or kel-ti-bē'ri-ən/ n an extinct language spoken by a Celtic people (the **Celtibē'ri**) in the Iberian peninsula in classical times.

cembalo /chem'bä-lō/ n (pl **cem'balos** or **cem'bali**) another name for the **harpsichord**; a musical instrument with strings struck by hammers, a dulcimer. [Ital; see **cymbal**]
■ **cem'balist** n a person who plays a cembalo; (also /sem'/) a person who plays the pianoforte in an orchestra (rare).

cembra /sem'brə/ n the Swiss stonepine (also **cembra pine**). [New L, from Ger dialect zember timber; cf Ger Zimmer room]

cement /si-ment'/, formerly sem'ənt/ n anything that makes two substances or objects stick together; a fine powder made of clay and calcined limestone, mixed with water and sand to make mortar or mixed with water, sand and aggregate to make concrete; mineral matter that binds together particles of sediment to form solid rock; a bond or union; glue or adhesive; material used for dental fixings; cementum. ◆ vt to unite or bond with cement; to join firmly. [OFr ciment, from L caementum chip of stone used to fill up in building a wall, short for caedimentum, from caedere to cut]
■ **cementation** /sem-ən-tā'shən/ n the act of cementing; the process of impregnating the surface of one substance with another by surrounding it with powder and heating, as in steel-making, case-hardening, turning glass into porcelain; precipitation; the process of injecting fluid cement mixture for strengthening purposes. **cemen'tatory** or **cementi'tious** adj having the quality of cementing or uniting firmly. **cemen'ter** n. **cemen'tite** n compound of iron and carbon (Fe₃C), found in cast iron, etc. **cemen'tum** n the bony outer covering of the root of a tooth.
❏ **cement'-copper** n copper obtained by precipitation. **cement gun** n an apparatus for spraying fine concrete or cement mortar. **cement mixer** n a machine with a revolving drum for mixing concrete. **cement'-stone** n a clayey limestone, suitable for making hydraulic cement. **cement'-water** n water containing copper salts, as in copper mines.

cemetery /sem'i-t(ə-)ri/ n a burial ground for the dead. [LL coemētērium, from Gr koimētērion sleeping-place]

cemitare Spenser's spelling of **scimitar**.

CEN abbrev : Comité Européen de Normalisation (Fr), European Committee for Standardization.

cen. abbrev : central; century.

cenacle /sen'ə-kl/ n a supper room or guest room, esp that in which the Last Supper was eaten by Christ and the apostles; a group with common interests; a literary coterie, or its meeting-place. [Fr cénacle, from L cēnāculum, from cēna supper]

cendré /sã-drā'/ (Fr) adj ash-blond.

-cene /-sēn/ combining form denoting a recent division of geological time in the Tertiary and Quaternary periods, eg Eocene, Pliocene. [Gr kainos new]

CENELEC abbrev : Comité Européen de Normalisation Electrotechnique (Fr), European Committee for Electrotechnical Standardization.

cenesthesis same as **coenaesthesis**.

CEng /sē-eng'/ abbrev : Chartered Engineer.

cenobite same as **coenobite**.

cenogenesis N American spelling of **caenogenesis**.

cenospecies /sē'nō-spē-shēz/ (biol) n all members of an ecospecies related to each other by the ability to interbreed or hybridize. [Gr koinos common, and **species**]

cenotaph /sen'ə-täf/ n an empty tomb; a sepulchral monument in honour of one or more people buried elsewhere. [Gr kenotaphion, from kenos empty, and taphos a tomb]

cenote /si-nō'ti/ n a deep, natural hole in the ground with a pool at the bottom of it, esp in the Yucatán peninsula, often used by the Mayas as a place of sacrifice. [Mex Sp, from Maya conot, tyonot]

Cenozoic /sē-nō-zō'ik/ (geol) adj of or belonging to the youngest era of the Phanerozoic eon, from 65 million years ago to the present day (also n). [Gr kainos new, and zōē life]

cens /sãs/ (French-Canadian law) n a nominal annual payment given to the owner of an estate or property in recognition of his or her title. [Fr L cēnsēre to estimate]

cense[1] /sens/ vt to burn incense in front of (an altar, etc). [**incense**[1]]

cense[2] /sens/ (obs) vt to think; to assess. ◆ n a public rate of tax; rank or condition. [L cēnsēre to estimate]

censer /sen'sər/ n a ceremonial container in which incense is burned. [OFr censier, encensier (Fr encensoir), from LL incēnsorium, from L incendere, incēnsum to burn]

censor /sen'sör or -sər/ n a magistrate who kept account of the property of Roman citizens, imposed taxes, and watched over their morals (hist); an official with similar functions elsewhere; any of various officials in certain universities; an official who examines books, papers, telegrams, letters, films, etc, with powers to delete material, or to forbid publication, delivery or showing; an unconscious inhibitive mechanism in the mind, that prevents what is painful to the conscious from emerging from the subconscious (psychol); a person who censures or blames. ◆ vt to subject to censorship or to censorial examination or condemnation. [L cēnsor, -ōris]
■ **censorial** /-ō'ri-əl, -ö'/ adj relating to a censor, or to the correction of public morals. **censo'rian** adj censorial. **censo'rious** adj expressing censure or blame; fault-finding. **censo'riously** adv. **censo'riousness** n. **cen'sorship** n the work of a censor, censoring; the office of censor; the time during which a censor holds office.

□ **censor morum** /sen'sər mör'əm or kăn'sor mŏ'rŭm/ n (L) censor of morals.

censure /sen'shər/ n an unfavourable opinion or judgement; blame; reproof. ◆ vt to form or give an unfavourable opinion or judgement of; to blame; to condemn as wrong; to sentence (Shakesp). [L cēnsūra, from cēnsēre to estimate]
■ **cen'surable** adj deserving censure; blamable. **cen'surableness** n. **cen'surably** adv.

census /sen'səs/ n an official enumeration of inhabitants with statistics relating to them; any official count. ◆ vt to carry out a census of. [L cēnsus, -ūs a register]
■ **cen'sual** /-sū-əl/ adj relating to or containing a census.

cent. abbrev : centigrade; central; centum (L), a hundred; century.

cent /sent/ n a hundredth part of various monetary units, esp of a dollar (pl **cents**); a hundredth part of a euro (pl **cent**); a coin worth one cent. [L centum a hundred]
■ **cent'age** n rate by the hundred. **cent'al** n a unit of weight equal to 100lb (45.3kg), formerly used for measuring grain.
■ **per cent** by the hundred (symbol **%**).

centare see **centiare**.

centas /sen'tas/ n (pl **cen'tas** or **cen'tai** /-tā/) a Lithuanian monetary unit, $\frac{1}{100}$ of a litas. [Lithuanian]

centaur /sen'tör/ n a mythical creature, half man and half horse. [Gr kentauros]
■ **centau'rian** adj.

centaurea /sen-tö'ri-ə or -tö-rē'ə/ n a plant of the genus Centaurea including knapweed, cornflower, etc. See also **centaury**.

Centaurus /sen-tö'rəs/ n a constellation in the southern hemisphere containing Alpha Centauri and Beta Centauri. [Gr kentauros centaur]

centaury /sen'tö-ri/ n a name applied to plants of the gentianaceous genera Erythraea and Chlora, and to the composite genus Centaurea. [According to Gr myth the centaur Chiron healed a wound with kentaurion, one of these plants]

centavo /sen-tä'vō/ n (pl **centa'vos**) a Spanish American coin and monetary unit, also formerly used in Portugal, one hundredth of the standard unit of currency. [Sp and Port]

centenary /sen-tē'nə-ri (also -ten'ə- or sen')/ n a hundred; a century or hundred years; a hundredth anniversary. ◆ adj relating to a hundred or to a centennial. [L centēnārius, from centēnī a hundred each, from centum]
■ **centenā'rian** n a person who is a hundred years old or more. ◆ adj at least a hundred years old; of or relating to a centenarian. **centenā'rianism** n. **centenier** /sen'tən-ēr/ n a centurion; in Jersey, an honorary part-time police officer with judicial powers.

centennial /sen-ten'yəl or -i-əl/ adj happening once in a hundred years; lasting a hundred years. ◆ n (N Am) a hundredth anniversary, a centenary. [L centum a hundred, and annus a year]

center¹ the N American spelling of **centre**.

center² /sen'tər/ (Shakesp) n a cincture, waistbelt.

centering see **centring**.

centesimal /sen-tes'i-məl/ adj hundredth; having divisions of a hundredth, as a centigrade thermometer has. [L centēsimus, from centum]
■ **centes'imally** adv.

centesimo /chen-tez'i-mō or sen-tes'i-mō/ n (pl **centes'imos** or **centes'imi** /-mē/) a coin and monetary unit of Uruguay and Panama, also formerly used in Italy, $\frac{1}{100}$ of the standard monetary unit. [Ital and Sp]

centesis /sen-tē'sis/ (surg) n and combining form (pl **centeses** /sen-tē'sēz/) a puncture, as in amniocentesis. [Gr kentēsis, from kentein to prick]

centi- /sen-ti-/ or **cent-** /sent-/ combining form denoting: in names of units, a hundredth part (10^{-2}); one hundred, as in centipede. [L centum a hundred]

centiare /sen'ti-är/ or **centare** /sen'tär/ n a unit of area, the hundredth part of an are, 1 sq m (1.196 sq yd). [L centum a hundred, and ārea area]

centigrade /sen'ti-grād/ adj of a scale, esp the Celsius temperature scale, having a hundred degrees between the freezing and boiling points of water. [L centum a hundred, and gradus a step, a degree]

centigram or **centigramme** /sen'ti-gram/ n the hundredth part of a gram. [Fr, from L centum a hundred, and **gram¹**]

centile /sen'tīl/ n same as **percentile** (see under **per cent**).

centilitre or (N Am) **centiliter** /sen'ti-lē-tər/ n the hundredth part of a litre, 10 cubic centimetres. [Fr, from L centum a hundred, and **litre**]

centillion /sen-til'yən/ n in UK and Germany, the hundredth power of a million, ie 1 followed by 600 zeros; in N America and France, the hundred-and-first power of a thousand, ie 1 followed by 303 zeros. [L centum a hundred, and the ending of **million**]
■ **centill'ionth** n.

centime /sä'tēm or sä-tēm'/ n a coin, formerly used in France, Belgium and Luxembourg, $\frac{1}{100}$ of a franc; any of several coins of various countries, one hundredth of the standard unit of currency. [Fr, from L centesimum a hundredth]

centimetre or (N Am) **centimeter** /sen'ti-mē-tər/ n a linear measure, the hundredth part of a metre. [Fr, from L centum a hundred, and **metre¹**]
■ **centimet'ric** adj having a wavelength of between one and ten centimetres.
□ **centimetre-gram-sec'ond** adj formerly applied to a system of scientific measurement with the centimetre, gram and second as units of length, mass and time (abbrev **CGS** or **cgs**).

centimo /sen'ti-mō or then'ti-mō/ n (pl **cen'timos**) a coin and monetary unit of Venezuela, Paraguay and Costa Rica, also formerly used in Spain, one hundredth of the standard unit of currency. [Sp]

centi Morgan /sen'ti mör'gen/ (genetics) n a measure of the distance between the loci of two genes on the same chromosome obtained from the crossover frequency and used in genetic mapping. [**centi-** and TH Morgan (1866–1945), US biologist]

centinel or **centinell** /sen'ti-nəl/ obsolete spellings of **sentinel**.
□ **centinel** (**private**) n a private soldier.

centipede /sen'ti-pēd/ n any myriapod of the class Chilopoda, carnivorous flattened animals with many segments, each bearing one pair of legs. [L centum a hundred, and pēs, pedis a foot]

centner /sent'nər/ n a unit of weight in Germany and Scandinavia equal to 50kg (110.23lb), or in Russia 100kg (220.46lb); a unit of weight equal to 100lb (45.3kg) (also called in USA **short hundredweight**). [Ger, from L centēnārius; cf **centenary**]

cento /sen'tō/ n (pl **cen'tos** or **cen'tones**) a poem manufactured by putting together lines or passages of one author or of several authors; a composition formed by joining bits and pieces from various authors; a string of commonplace phrases and quotations. [L centō, -ōnis, Gr kentrōn patchwork]
■ **cen'toist** or **cen'tonist** n. **cen'tonate** adj (bot) blotched, patchy.

centonel(l) Spenserian spellings of **sentinel**.

central, etc see under **centre**.

centre or (N Am) **center**, etc /sen'tər/ n the middle point of anything, esp a circle or sphere; the middle area of anything; a person or thing in the middle; a fixed point of reference; the point towards which all things move or are drawn; a nucleus or focal point; a resort; a stronghold; a meeting place; a place, institution, etc devoted to a specified activity; a part or area of the brain or nervous system that controls a specified action or function (physiol); a player in a central position (sport); one of the two players positioned in the middle of the three-quarter-back line (rugby); the player in the centre of the offensive line, who starts the play by passing the ball through his legs to a backfield player (American football); (a shot that hits) the ring around the bull's eye (archery); a political party, or its members, having moderate opinions; the point of a conic section through which all diameters pass (maths); a rod with a conical tip for supporting a workpiece in a lathe or other machine tool (machinery). ◆ vt (**cen'tring**, **cen'tred**) to place on or connect to a centre; to focus (one's thoughts). ◆ vi to be placed in the middle; to have a centre; to lie or move in relation to a centre (often with on or upon, round or around). ◆ adj relating to the political centre. [Fr, from L centrum, from Gr kentron a sharp point]
■ **cen'tral** adj belonging to, in, or near, the centre; principal, dominant, most important, essential. **cen'tralism** n the tendency or policy of administering by the sovereign or central government matters which would be otherwise under local management. **cen'tralist** n (also adj). **centrality** /-tral'i-ti/ n central position; dominance, the quality of being essential or principal. **centraliza'tion** or **-s-** n the act or process of moving or drawing towards a centre; centralism. **cen'tralize** or **-ise** vt and vi to move to, draw to, or concentrate at a centre. **cen'trally** adv. **cen'tred** adj positioned in the centre; mentally composed, emotionally stable, confident. **cen'treing** n see separate entry **centring**. **cen'tric** adj relating to, placed in, or containing the centre; (of plants) cylindrical and tapering, terete. ◆ combining form having a specified type of centre. **cen'trical** adj. **cen'trically** adv. **cen'tricalness** n. **centricity** /-tris'i-ti/ n. **cen'trism** n the practice of sticking to the middle ground in politics; the holding of moderate, non-extreme political opinions. **cen'trist** adj and n.
□ **central angle** n (maths) an angle bounded by two radii of a circle. **central bank** n a bank, usu state-owned or state-controlled, which carries out government financial policy, regulates the money supply, influences interest rates and acts as a link between the government and the banking system. **central conic** n a conic section that has a centre. **central dogma** n the principle that the transfer of genetic

information from DNA to the protein sequence is irreversible, ie it cannot flow from protein to DNA. **Central European Time** *n* one of the standard times used in Europe, being 1 hour ahead of Greenwich Mean Time (*abbrev* **CET**). **central fire** *n* a cartridge having the fulminate in the centre of the base (**cen'tre-fire** *adj*). **central force** *n* (*phys*) the force on a moving body that is always directed towards or from a fixed point, the centre of force. **central government** *n* the government controlling a whole country, as opposed to local government. **central heating** *n* a system of heating a building by water, steam or warm air conducted throughout the building from one point. **central locking** *n* in a motor vehicle, the automatic locking of all the doors as the driver's door is locked. **cen'trally-heated** *adj*. **central nervous system** *n* (*zool*) the main ganglia of the nervous system with their associated nerve cords, in vertebrates consisting of the brain and spinal cord. **Central Powers** *n pl* in and before the war of 1914–18, the German Empire and Austria-Hungary. **central processor** or **central processing unit** *n* the part of a computer which performs the logical and arithmetical operations on the data and which controls other units of the computer system (*abbrev* **CPU**). **central reservation** *n* a *usu* tarred or paved area in the centre of a motorway or major road acting as a division between traffic travelling in opposite directions. **Central Standard Time** or **Central Time** *n* one of the standard times used in N America, being 6 hours behind Greenwich Mean Time (*abbrev* **CST** or **CT**). **cen'tre-back** *n* (*football*) a player in the middle of the defence; the position of such a player. **centre bit** *n* a joiner's tool, turning on a centre, for boring circular holes in wood. **cen'treboard** *n* a retractable keel fitted to small racing yachts and dinghies. **centre-fire** see **central fire** above. **cen'trefold** or **centre spread** *n* the two facing centre pages of a newspaper, magazine, etc; an article, design or set of photographs printed on these; a photograph of a nude woman or man printed on these; (**centrefold**) a person who has appeared in such a photograph. **centre-for'ward** *n* (*football, hockey*, etc) the central player in the line of forwards; the position of this player. **centre-half'** *n* (*football, hockey*, etc) the central player in the line of halfbacks; the position of this player. **centre lathe** *n* (*engineering*) a machine tool for cutting metal in which the tool is held steady and the workpiece rotates. **cen'treline** *n* an often imaginary line that divides a body or shape into two equal halves. **cen'trepiece** *n* something placed at the centre, *esp* an ornament for the middle of a table, ceiling, etc; a central character or feature in a story, film, etc. **centre punch** *n* a tool, a steel bar with a conical point, used for marking the centre of holes to be drilled. **cen'tre-rail** *n* a rail between the ordinary rails on a railway track. **centre spread** see **centrefold** above. **centre stage** *adj* and *adv* in or to the centre of a theatre stage; at or to the position where (eg political, media, etc) attention is focused.
■ **central to** essential, most important for the understanding or working of. **centre of attraction** the point to which bodies tend by the force of gravity or the like. **centre of buoyancy** or **displacement** the centre of mass of liquid displaced by an immersed body. **centre of curvature** (of a curve) the centre of the circle which can be superimposed on it on the concave side. **centre of excellence** a focal point, *esp* a university (or one of its departments), for work at the highest level (in a particular subject). **centre of gravity** the single point at which the resultant gravitational forces of a body act. **centre of inertia** or **mass** (*phys*) the point in an assembly of mass particles where the entire mass of the assembly may be regarded as being concentrated. **centre of oscillation** the point in a pendulum such that, if all the matter were concentrated there, the pendulum would have the same period. **centre of percussion** the point where the direction of a blow meets the plane in which lie the centre of inertia and a possible axis of rotation such that the blow imparts a rotation without pressure on the axis. **centre of pressure** the point on a surface immersed in fluid at which the resultant pressure may be taken to act (*phys*); the point at which the resultant of aerodynamic forces intersects the chord line of an aerofoil. **centre of symmetry** a point in a figure such that any straight line through it meets the figure in two points at equal distances on either side.

centri- /*sen-tri-*/, **centr-** or **centro-** /*sen-tr(ō)-*/ *combining form* denoting centre.

centric, etc see under **centre**.

centrifugal /*sen-trif' yŭ-gəl* or *sen-tri-fū'gəl*, also *sen'* / *adj* tending to move away from a centre; conducting or carrying outwards from the centre, as in efferent nerves (*biol*); using, or produced by centrifugal force; proceeding in development from the apex towards the base (*bot*). [Ety as for **centre**, and L *fugere* to flee]
■ **centrif'ugalize** or **-ise** (or /*sen'*, *-fū'*/) *vt* to subject to centrifugal force. **centrif'ugally** *adv*. **centrifugation** /*-fū-gā'shən*/ or **centrifugence** /*-trif'ū-jəns*, *sen'* or *-fū'*/ *n* centrifugal tendency or force; (**centrifugation**) centrifuge separation. **cen'trifuge** /*-fūj*/ *n* a machine which, using rapid rotation, separates substances of different shapes or densities by centrifugal force; any rotating device used for

studying the effects of gravitational force and varying accelerations on humans and animals. ♦ *vt* to subject to such rotation.
❑ **centrifugal force** *n* the resistance of a revolving body, by virtue of its inertia, to an acceleration towards the centre, equal and opposite to centripetal force. **centrifugal machine** *n* a centrifuge. **centrifugal pump** *n* a pump that forces a liquid outwards using a rotating impeller. **centrifuge separation** *n* the technique of isotope separation applied to the enrichment of ^{235}U in uranium (sometimes called **centrifugation**).

centring or (*N Am*) **centering** /*sen't(ə-)ring*/ (*building*) *n* the framework upon which an arch or vault of stone, brick or iron is supported during its construction (also **cen'treing**).

centriole /*sen'trē-ōl*/ (*zool*) *n* a rodlike body (*usu* one of a pair) in animal cells that forms the centre of polymerization of the microtubules in certain thread-like structures, eg in sperm flagelli and the mitotic spindle. [New L *centriolum*, dimin of L *centrum*]

centripetal /*sen-trip'ə-təl* or *-tri-pē'təl*/ *adj* tending towards a centre; conducting or carrying towards the centre, as in afferent nerves (*biol*); proceeding in development from the base towards the apex (*bot*). [Ety as for **centre**, and L *petere* to seek]
■ **centrip'etalism** *n*. **centrip'etally** *adv*.
❑ **centripetal force** *n* a force acting on a revolving body, causing it to tend inward towards the centre, equal and opposite to centrifugal force.

centrist see under **centre**.

centrobaric /*sen-trō-bar'ik*/ *adj* relating to the centre of gravity. [Ety as for **centre**, and Gr *baros* weight]

centroclinal /*sen-trō-klī'nəl*/ (*geol*) *adj* dipping towards a centre from all directions. [Ety as for **centre**, and Gr *klīnein* to lean]

centrode /*sen'trōd*/ (*maths*) *n* a locus traced out by the successive positions of an instantaneous centre of pure rotation. [Ety as for **centre**, and Gr *hodos* a path]

centroid /*sen'troid*/ (*maths*) *n* the point where the medians of a triangle intersect; the centre of mass. [Ety as for **centre**, and Gr *eidos* form]
■ **centroid'al** *adj*.

centromere /*sen'trə-mēr*/ (*biol*) *n* the portion of a chromosome that attaches to the spindle during cell division. [Ety as for **centre**, and Gr *meros* part]

Centronics interface /*sen-tron'iks in'tər-fās*/ (*comput*) *n* a standard parallel interface for printers, etc.

centrosome /*sen'trə-sōm*/ (*biol*) *n* a minute, self-duplicating structure near the interphase nucleus, from which the fibres of the spindle radiate at mitosis. [Ety as for **centre**, and Gr *sōma* a body]

centrosphere /*sen'trə-sfēr*/ (*geol*) *n* the central part of the earth below the crust, the barysphere.

centrum /*sen'trəm*/ (*anat*) *n* (*pl* **cen'trums** or **cen'tra**) the main part of a vertebra. [L]

centry¹ /*sen'tri*/ *n* centre (*Shakesp*); centering (*obs*).

centry² an obsolete spelling of **sentry**.

centum /*sen'təm* or *ken'tŭm*/ *n* a hundred. [L *centum* a hundred]
❑ **centum languages** *n pl* the group of Indo-European languages in which an original palatal consonant appears as a guttural sound, as in L *centum* hundred in which the 'c' is sounded 'k' (cf **satem languages**). **centumvir** /*sen-tum'vir*/ *n* (*pl* **centum'virī**) (L *vir* a man) one of the Roman judges chosen annually for civil suits, *orig* 105 in number (three from each of the thirty-five tribes). **centum'virate** *n*.

centuple /*sen'tū-pl*/ *adj* hundredfold. ♦ *vt* to multiply or increase a hundred times. [L *centuplus* and *centuplex*, from *centum* hundred, and *plicāre* to fold]
■ **centū'plicate** *n* and *adj* (one) of a hundred like things or copies. ♦ *vt* to centuple. **centuplica'tion** *n*.

century /*sen'tyŭ-ri* or *sen'chə-ri*/ *n* a set or series of a hundred, *esp* of consecutive years (*usu* reckoned from the conventionally accepted date of Christ's birth), runs at cricket, or Roman soldiers. [L *centuria* a century, from *centum* a hundred]
■ **centū'rial** *adj*. **centuriā'tion** *n* division into hundreds. **centū'riātor** *n* one of a group of 16c Reformed divines of Magdeburg who compiled a church history in 13 volumes, each volume covering a century. **centū'rion** *n* in the ancient Roman army, an officer who had the command of a hundred men; a person who has scored or achieved a hundred in any way.
❑ **century plant** *n* an agave (*Agave americana*) of Mexico and southern USA which flowers only once in many years.

CEO *abbrev* : Chief Executive Officer.

ceòl mór /*kyol mōr* or *mör*/ same as **pibroch**. [Gaelic, great music]

ceorl /*chä'örl* or *kä'örl*/ *n* in England before the Norman Conquest, an ordinary freeman of the lowest rank. [OE *ceorl*; see **churl**]

■ words derived from main entry word; ❑ compound words; ■ idioms and phrasal verbs

cep /sep/ n a type of edible mushroom of the *Boletus* genus with a brown shiny cap and white underside. [Fr *cèpe*, from L *cippus* a stake]

cepaceous /si-pā'shəs/ (*bot*) *adj* smelling or tasting of onion or garlic. [From the species name of the onion, *Allium cepa*]

cépage /sā-päzh'/ (*Fr*) *n* the grape variety or combination of grape varieties used to make a particular wine.

cephal- or **cephalo-** /se-fəl- or se-fə-lō/ *combining form* denoting head. [Gr *kephalē* head]
■ **ceph'alad** *adj* (*zool* and *anat*) situated near, facing towards, or passing to the head. **cephalag'ra** *n* (Gr *agrā* a catching) gout in the head. **cephalal'gia** *n* (Gr *algos* pain; *med*) headache. **cephalal'gic** *adj*. **Cephalas'pis** *n* (Gr *aspis* shield) an Upper Silurian and Old Red Sandstone genus of extinct fishes or fish-like animals with a head-shield. **ceph'alate** *adj* having a head. **cephal'ic** *adj* of or belonging to the head (**cephalic index** the ratio of the breadth to the length of the skull expressed as a percentage; **cephalic presentation** the usual position of a child in the womb just before birth, head downwards). ◆ *n* a remedy for headache. **-cephalic** and **-cephalous** *adj combining form*. **ceph'alin** *n* (*biochem*) a compound of phosphorus found in the brain and nervous tissue (also **kephalin**). **cephalī'tis** *n* inflammation of the brain. **cephalizā'tion** or **-s-** *n* in animal evolution, the specialization of the anterior end or head as the site of the mouthparts, sensory organs and principal ganglia of the central nervous system. **cephalocele** /sef'əl-ə-sēl/ *n* (*med*) the protrusion of the membranes of the brain through a hole in the skull. **cephalochordate** /-ō-kör'dāt/ *n* (Gr *chordē* cord) a member of the subphylum *Cephalochordata*, of chordate fish-like animals (including the lancelets and amphioxus), having a persisting notochord projecting beyond the nerve cord to the end of the snout (also *adj*). **cephalom'etry** *n* (*med*) the measurement of the fetal head in the uterus, by ultrasound or radiology; the measurement of the head by x-ray, *esp* in orthodontics. **ceph'alopod** /-pod/ *n* (Gr *pous, podos* foot) a member of the **Cephalopoda** /-op'od-ə/, the highest class of molluscs, *usu* large, exclusively marine animals (including cuttlefish, squid, octopus, etc), with the foot modified into arms or tentacles surrounding the mouth. **cephalospō'rin** *n* any of a group of wide-spectrum antibiotics derived from the fungus *Cephalosporium*. **cephalōtho'rax** *n* the fused head and thorax in some arthropods. **cephalotomy** /kef-al-ot'ə-mi/ *n* (Gr *tomē* a cut) the dissection of the head. **ceph'alous** *adj* having a head.

Cepheus /sē'fē-əs or -fūs/ *n* a northern constellation named after Andromeda's father, a mythical king of Ethiopia. [Gr *Kēpheus*]
❑ **Cepheid variable** /sē'fi-id/ *n* (*astron*) any star of the same type as δ Cephei ('classical' cepheid) or of a similar short-period star of the 'cluster type', from whose rhythmically varying brightness its distance can be inferred, this characteristic being important for the determination of distance scale in the universe.

ceraceous see under **cere**.

ceramic /se-ram'ik/ *adj* relating to a ceramic or to ceramics; made of a ceramic. ◆ *n* any product that is first shaped and then hardened by means of heat, or the material from which it is formed (*esp* traditional potter's clay, but also a large range of modern materials of quite different composition); (in *pl*) articles made of ceramic material. [Gr *keramos* potter's earth]
■ **ceram'al** *n* a cermet. **ceram'ics** *n sing* the potter's art; the science or study of ceramic materials. **cer'amide** *n* any of a family of lipids, used in cosmetics. **ceram'ist** or **ceram'icist** *n* a person who makes a scientific study of clays and other ceramic materials, or who puts them to practical use. **ceramog'raphy** *n* the description or study of pottery. **cer'met** *n* a material made from a combination of ceramic particles and a *metal* matrix, used in aeronautics and engineering; a type of electronic resistor made of such material.
❑ **ceramic hob** *n* a type of cooking surface on an electric cooker, consisting of a flat ceramic plate with heating elements on the underside. **ceramic oxide** *n* a combination of an inorganic material with oxygen having superconducting qualities at high temperature.

cerargyrite /se-rär'jə-rīt/ *n* a mineral consisting of silver chloride in crystalline form, horn silver. [Gr *keras* horn, and *argyros* silver]

cerasin /ser'ə-sin/ *n* the insoluble portion of cherry-tree gum. [L *cerasus*, Gr *kerasos* the cherry tree]

cerastes /se-ras'tēz/ *n* (*pl* **ceras'tes**) any venomous viper of the genus *Cerastes*, *esp* the N African horned viper, with a horny process over each eye. [Gr *kerastēs*, from *keras* a horn]
■ **ceras'tium** *n* (*pl* **ceras'tiums**) any low ground-covering plant of the genus *Cerastium*, including the alpine mouse-ear chickweed, with horn-shaped capsules, and *Cerastium tomentosum*, snow-in-summer.

cerat- /se-rat-/ or **cerato-** /se-rə-tō-/ *combining form* denoting horn. [Gr *keras, -atos* horn]

cerate, cerated see under **cere**.

ceratitis same as **keratitis** (see under **keratin**).

ceratodus /se-rat'ō-dəs/ *n* (a fossil of) any extinct lungfish of the genus *Ceratodus*, of the Cretaceous and Triassic periods; the barramundi, an Australian lungfish, formerly included in the genus, but now classified *Neoceratodus*. [Gr *keras, -atos* horn, and *odous* tooth]

ceratoid /ser'ə-toid/ (*anat*) *adj* having the form or texture of a horn. [Gr *keratoeidēs*, from *keras* horn, and *eidos* form]

ceratopsian /se-rə-top'si-ən/ or **ceratopsid** /-top'sid/ *n* a member of a large group of bird-hipped, plant-eating dinosaurs of the late Cretaceous, having armoured neck-frills and horns or beaks, the best known example being *Triceratops* (also *adj*). [Gr *keras* horn, and *ops* face]

Ceratosaurus /se-rə-tō-sö'rəs/ *n* a flesh-eating dinosaur of the Jurassic period. [Gr *keras* horn, and *sauros* lizard]

Cerberus /sûr'bə-rəs/ *n* the monster that guarded the entrance to Hades, a dog with three heads (*myth*); a grim, dangerous and watchful guardian. [L, from Gr *Kerberos*]
■ **cerbē'rian** or more correctly **cerbē'rean** *adj*.
■ **a sop to Cerberus** see under **sop**.

cercal see under **cercus**.

cercaria /sər-kā'ri-ə/ (*zool*) *n* (*pl* **cercā'riae**) the final larval stage of many trematode worms. [Gr *kerkos* a tail]
■ **cercā'rian** *adj*.

cerclage /sûr-kläzh'/ (*obstetrics*) *n* any of several procedures in which the cervix of the womb is closed to prevent miscarriage. [Fr, encircling]

cercopid /sûr'kō-pid/ *n* any insect of the froghopper family (Cercopidae). [Gr *Kerkōpēs* a race of apelike thieves]

cercopithecid /sûr-kō-pith'ə-sid/ or **cercopithecoid** /-koid/ *n* any of several Old World long-tailed monkeys of the genus *Cercopithecus*, including the Diana monkey, vervet, and moustached monkey (also *adj*). [Gr *kerkos* tail, and *pithēkos* monkey]

cercus /sûr'kəs/ *n* (*pl* **cerci'** /-sē/) a tail-like appendage, *esp* a flexible sensory organ at the tip of the abdomen in certain arthropods. [Gr *kerkos* tail]
■ **cer'cal** *adj* relating to a tail.

cere /sēr/ *vt* to cover with wax; to wrap (a dead body) in cerecloth. ◆ *n* the bare waxlike patch at the base of the upper part of a bird's beak. [L *cēra* wax]
■ **cerā'ceous** *adj* waxy. **cēr'ate** *n* (*med*) a medicated paste or stiff ointment containing wax. **cēr'ated** *adj* (of a bird) having a cere. **cēr'eous** *adj* waxy. **cerif'erous** *adj* (*biol*) producing wax.
❑ **cere'cloth** or **cerement** /sēr'mənt/ *n* a cloth dipped in melted wax, formerly used to wrap a dead body in; any burial clothes.

cereal /sē'ri-əl/ *adj* of crops, etc, relating to edible grain. ◆ *n* a grain used as food, such as wheat, barley, oats, etc; a food prepared from such grain, *esp* any of the various breakfast foods. [L *cereālis* of grain or agriculture, from *Cerēs* Roman goddess of corn]
■ **cē'realist** *n* a specialist in cereals; a feeder on cereals.
❑ **cereal bar** *n* a rectangular biscuit containing cereal, eaten as a snack.

cerebellum /se-ri-bel'əm/ *n* (*pl* **cerebell'a** or **cerebell'ums**) the lower posterior part of the brain, whose function is to co-ordinate voluntary movements and maintain balance. [L, little brain, dimin of *cerebrum*]
■ **cerebell'ar**, **cerebell'ic** or **cerebell'ous** *adj*.

cerebrum /ser'i-brəm or sə-rē'brəm/ *n* (*pl* **cer'ebrums** or **cer'ebra**) the front and larger part of the brain; loosely, the whole brain. [L *cerebrum* the brain; prob cognate with Gr *karā* the head, and *krānion* the cranium]
■ **cer'ebral** (also /sə-rē'brəl/) *adj* relating to the brain or the cerebrum; intellectual, as opposed to practical; of consonant sounds, produced by inverting the tip of the tongue on the palate (*phonetics*). **cer'ebralism** *n* the theory that all mental operations originate in the brain. **cer'ebralist** *n*. **cer'ebrally** *adv*. **cer'ebrate** *vi* to think, to use the brain. **cerebrā'tion** *n* action of the brain, *esp* unconscious. **cer'ebric** (or /sər-eb'rik/) *adj* cerebral. **cereb'riform** *adj* brain-shaped. **cerebrī'tis** *n* inflammation of the cerebrum. **cer'ebroside** *n* any of various lipids found in nerve tissue. **cerebrōspin'al** *adj* relating to the brain and spinal cord together. **cerebrotonia** /-tō'ni-ə/ *n* (L *tonus* tone) the temperament associated with ectomorphic body type characterized by introversion and hypersensitivity. **cerebrōton'ic** *adj*. **cer'ebrōvas'cūlar** *adj* relating to the cerebrum and its blood vessels.
❑ **cerebral cortex** *n* the outer layers of the cerebral hemispheres associated with higher function of the nervous system. **cerebral death** see **brain death** under **brain**. **cerebral dominance** *n* the tendency of one side of the brain to dominate certain functions, eg the left side of the cerebrum produces right-handedness in the majority of people. **cerebral haemorrhage** *n* haemorrhage of a blood vessel or blood vessels in the brain, *esp* the rupture of an artery. **cerebral hemisphere**

n one of the two lateral halves of the cerebrum. **cerebral palsy** *n* a form of congenital paralysis marked by lack of muscular co-ordination, etc. **cerebrospinal fever** *n* meningitis. **cerebrospinal fluid** *n* the clear colourless fluid that surrounds the spinal cord and ventricles in the brain. **cerebrovascular accident** *n* a sudden interruption of the blood supply to the brain, as in a cerebral haemorrhage.

cerement, cereous see under **cere**.

ceremony /ser'i-mə-ni or ser'ə-mō-ni/ *n* a rite; a formal act, custom, convention, etc; such rites, acts, etc regarded collectively; pomp, formality, etc. [L *caerimōnia* sanctity]
■ **ceremonial** /-mō'ni-əl/ *adj* relating to or of the nature of ceremony or a ceremony. ♦ *n* an act that conforms with custom or convention; a set of formal rituals or actions; (a book containing) a prescribed order of service or ritual (*Christianity*). **ceremō'nialism** *n* adherence to formality or custom. **ceremō'nialist** *n*. **ceremō'nially** *adv*. **ceremō'nious** *adj* given to ceremony; scrupulously careful in observing formalities; precise, punctilious. **ceremō'niously** *adv*. **ceremō'niousness** *n*.
■ **master of ceremonies** the person who directs the form and order of the ceremonies to be observed on some public occasion, eg a banquet; a compère. **stand on ceremony** to be punctilious about formalities. **without ceremony** informally; without adhering to conventions, customs, etc.

Cerenkov radiation /che-ren'kof (*or* -ryen'kof) rā-di-ā'shən/ (*phys*) *n* the bluish light emitted by a beam of charged particles passing through a transparent medium at a speed greater than the speed of light through that medium. [PA *Cerenkov* (1904–90), Russian physicist]

Ceres /sē'rēz/ *n* the Roman name for the Greek Demeter, goddess of agriculture and corn; the largest asteroid (minor planet). [L *Cerēs*, *-eris*, prob from root of *creāre* to create]

ceresin *or* **ceresine** /ser'ə-sin *or* -sēn/ *n* a kind of hard, whitish wax prepared from ozokerite and used as a substitute for beeswax. [L *cera* wax]

cereus /sē'ri-əs/ *n* any of several species of columnar American cacti of the genus *Cereus*, having spiny stems with pronounced ribs, and including some species that grow to 9m (30ft) in height. [L *cēreus* waxen, wax-taper (from their stiff form)]

ceria, ceric see under **cerium**.

ceriferous see under **cere**.

Cerinthian /sə-rin'thi-ən/ *adj* relating to *Cerinthus*, one of the earliest heretics in the Christian Church, against whose crude Gnosticism the Gospel of John was written, according to Irenaeus.

ceriph see **serif**.

cerise /sə-rēz', *also* -rēs'/ *n* and *adj* (a) light and clear purplish red. [Fr, cherry]

cerium /sē'ri-əm/ *n* a metallic chemical element (symbol Ce; atomic no 58), one of the rare-earth metals. [Named from the asteroid *Ceres* discovered about the same time]
■ **cē'ria** *n* its oxide. **cē'ric** *or* **cē'rous** *adj* of or containing cerium. **cē'rite** *n* a mineral, its hydrous silicate.
❑ **cerium metals** *n pl* a group of rare-earth metals including cerium, lanthanum, neodymium, samarium, promethium and praseodymium.

cermet see under **ceramic**.

CERN /sûrn/ *abbrev* : *Conseil Européen pour la Recherche Nucléaire* (Fr), European Organization for Nuclear Research, now also known as the European Laboratory for Particle Physics.

cerne /sûrn/ (*Shakesp*) a shortened form of **concern**.

cernuous /sûr'nū-əs/ (*bot*) *adj* (of flowers and buds) nodding, bowing down, drooping. [L *cernuus* inclined forwards]

cero /sē'rō/ *n* a large marine fish (*Scomberomorus regalis*) found in the tropical W Atlantic. [L *serra* a saw]

cerograph /sē'rō-gräf/ *n* a writing on wax; an encaustic painting; printing by means of engraving on a plate spread with wax. [Gr *kēros* wax, and *graphein* to write]
■ **cērograph'ic** /-graf'ik/ *or* **cērograph'ical** *adj*. **cērograph'ist** /-rog'rə-fist/ *n*. **cērog'raphy** *n*.

ceromancy /sē'rō-man-si/ *n* divination by dropping melted wax in water. [Gr *kēros* wax, and *manteiā* divination]

ceroon a N American spelling of **seron**.

ceroplastic /sē-rō-plas'tik/ *adj* relating to wax modelling; modelled in wax. [Gr *kēros* wax, and *plastikos* plastic, from *plassein* to mould]
■ **ceroplas'tics** *n sing* the art of wax modelling.

cerotic acid /si-rot'ik as'id/ *n* a fatty acid ($C_{26}H_{52}O_2$) found in beeswax and certain fats. [Gr *kēros* wax]

cerotype /sē'rō-tīp/ (*printing*) *n* an engraving on a copper plate coated with wax used as a mould for preparing an electrotype printing plate. [Gr *kēros* wax, and **type**]

cerous see under **cerium**.

cerrado /se-rä'dō/ *n* an area of wooded savanna in S America. [Port, closed]

cerris /ser'is/ *n* the turkey oak (*Quercus cerris*). [L *cerreus*]
■ **cerr'ial** *adj*.

cert /sûrt/ (*inf*) *n* a certainty, sometimes in the phrase *dead cert*. [Short form]

cert. *or* **certif.** *abbrev* : certificate; certificated; certified; certify.

certain /sûr'tn/ *adj* sure, confident; not to be doubted, indisputable; resolved; fixed, decided, determined; reliable, dependable; regular; inevitable; named or specified but not known; some (indeterminate number or quantity of). [OFr, from L *certus*, from *cernere* to decide]
■ **cer'tainly** *adv* without doubt, undoubtedly; in a resolved, fixed, etc manner. ♦ *interj* yes, of course. **cer'tainty** *n* something certain (also in short form **cert**); the state of being sure. **cer'titude** *n* (a) certainty.
■ **a certain person** a person known but not specifically named, implying some degree of contempt. **a lady of a certain age** a woman who is no longer young. **for certain** assuredly, certainly. **in a certain condition** (*euphem*) pregnant. **make certain** see under **make**[1]. **moral certainty** see under **moral**.

CertEd *abbrev* : Certificate in Education.

certes /sûr'tiz/ (*archaic*) *adv* certainly; truly. [Fr]
■ **(by) my cer'tie** *or* **cer'ty** (*Scot*) assuredly.

certif. see **cert**.

certificate /sər-tif'i-kət *or sometimes* -kāt/ *n* a written declaration, official or formal, of some fact; a printed statement of qualification(s) or recognized professional status. ♦ *vt* to give a certificate to. [Fr *certificat*, from L *certificāre*, from *certus* certain, and *facere* to make]
■ **cer'tifiable** /-fī-ə-bl/ *adj* capable of being certified (*esp* as insane). **cer'tifiably** *adv*. **certif'icated** *adj* (of eg a teacher) holding a certificate of training and fitness. **certificā'tion** *n*. **certif'icātory** *n* a certificate (also *adj*). **cer'tifier** *n* a person who certifies. **cer'tify** *vt* to declare as true; to inform; to declare or confirm in writing; to declare (someone) insane; to refer by certiorari (*law*).
❑ **certificate of deposit** *n* a certificate issued by a bank representing a fixed-term interest-bearing deposit. **Certificate of Secondary Education** *n* a certificate in a particular subject at secondary level in England and Wales, replaced in 1988 by the General Certificate of Secondary Education. **certified accountant** *n* a member of the Chartered Association of Certified Accountants, authorized to audit company accounts. **certified check** *n* (*US*) a cheque on which a bank has guaranteed payment. **certified milk** *n* milk certified as yielded by tuberculin-tested herds, fulfilling required conditions as to bacterial content, etc. **certified public accountant** *n* in USA, an officially accredited professional accountant.

certiorari /sûr-shi-ō-rā'rī/ (*law*) *n* a writ to call up the records of a lower court for consideration in the High Court of Justice. [LL *certiōrārī* to be informed of, from *certior*, compar of *certus* certain]

certitude see under **certain**.

certy see under **certes**.

cerulean *or* **caerulean** /si-roo'li-ən/ *adj* sky-blue; dark-blue; sea-green. [L *caeruleus* dark blue or green]
■ **cerule** *or* (*Spenser*) **caerule** /sēr'ūl/ *adj* sky-blue. **cerū'lein** /-lē-in/ *n* a coal-tar dyestuff, producing fast olive greens. **cerū'leous** *adj*.

ceruloplasmin /si-roo-lō-plaz'min/ *n* a protein in the blood that facilitates the storage and transport of copper. [L *caeruleus* dark blue and **plasmin**]

cerumen /si-roo'min/ *n* the brownish-yellow secretion produced by glands in the outer ear, ear wax. [L *cēra* wax]
■ **ceru'minous** *adj*.

ceruse /sē'roos *or* si-roos'/ *n* white lead used as a pigment. [Fr, from L *cērussa*, connected with *cēra*, Gr *kēros* wax]
■ **cē'rusite** *or* **cē'russite** *n* naturally-occurring lead carbonate.

cervelat /ser've-lä/ *n* a kind of smoked sausage, made of pork. [Fr, from Ital *cervellata*]

cervid /sûr'vid/ *adj* and *n* (of or relating to) one of the true deer of the family Cervidae, in which all the members (except the water deer) have antlers in the male animal. [L *cervus* a stag, and **-id**[1]]

cervine /sûr'vīn/ *adj* relating to deer; resembling deer; fawn-coloured. [L *cervīnus*, from *cervus* a stag]

cervix /sûr'viks/ *n* (*pl* **cer'vixes** *or* **cer'vices** /-sēz/) a technical name for the (back of the) neck; a necklike narrowing of an organ, *esp* the lower part of the uterus. [L *cervīx, cervīcis* neck]

■ words derived from main entry word; ❑ compound words; ■ idioms and phrasal verbs

■ **cervical** /sûr′vi-kl, sər-vī′kl/ *adj.* **cervici′tis** *n* inflammation of the neck of the womb. **cervicog′raphy** *n* the photographing of the neck of the womb to identify early signs of cancer.
❑ **cervical screening** *n* the routine and regular examination of women to facilitate the early identification of cancer of the cervix. **cervical smear** *n* the collection of a sample of cells from the neck of the womb and the examination of these cells (**cervical cytology**) under a microscope, as an early test for cancer.

Cesarean a spelling (*esp N Am*) of **Caesarean** (see under **Caesar**).

cesarevi(t)ch, cesarewi(t)ch, cesarevna see under **tsar**.

cesium N American spelling of **caesium**.

cespitose see **caespitose**.

cess /ses/ (*obs*) *n* in UK, a tax, a local rate; in Ireland, the obligation by a local population to provide food, lodgings and supplies for the soldiers of the lord deputy. ◆ *vt* to impose (a tax) or billet (soldiers) in this way. [Shortened from **assess**]
■ **bad cess to** (*Anglo-Irish*) bad luck to. **out of all cess** (*Shakesp*) excessively; immoderately.

cessation /se-sā′shən/ *n* a ceasing or stopping; a rest; a pause. [L *cessātiō, -ōnis*. See **cease**]

cesse /ses/ (*Spenser*) *vi* same as **cease**.

cesser /ses′ər/ (*law*) *n* the cessation of a term or liability when an obligation is fulfilled. [Fr *cesser* to cease]

cession /sesh′ən/ *n* a yielding up, ceding. [L *cessiō* surrender]
■ **cess′ionary** *n* someone to whom an assignment (of eg property) has been legally made.
❑ **cessio** /ses′i-ō/ or /sesh′i-ō/ **bonō′rum** *n* (*Scots law*) a debtor's surrender of his estate to his creditors in return for a judicial protection from imprisonment in respect of his debt, from 1880 a summary process in small bankruptcies, finally abolished 1913.

cesspit /ses′pit/ or **cesspool** /-pool/ *n* a pit or pool for collecting sewage or filthy water. [Origin obscure]

c'est-à-dire /sā- or se-ta-dēr′/ (*Fr*) that is to say.

c'est la vie /sā or se la vē′/ (*Fr*) that's life.

cestode /ses′tōd/ *n* any parasitic worm of the subclass **Cestoda**, including the tapeworm or bladderworm. [Gr *kestos* a girdle, a strap, and *eidos* form]
■ **ces′toid** *n* a ribbon-like cestode (also *adj*). **cestoid′ean** *n* and *adj*.

cestos see **cestus**[1].

Cestracion /se-strā′si-on/ *n* a primitive type of shark represented by the Australian Port Jackson shark. [Perh Gr *kestrā* a kind of fish, or *kestros* sharp, and *akē* point]

cestui /se-tē′ or ses′twē/ (*esp law*) *n* he, that one, used in such phrases as **cestui que trust** /ki-trust/ a person entitled to the benefit of a trust, and **cestui que use** a person for whose benefit property is granted in trust to another. [OFr, dative of *cest* that]

cestus[1] or **cestos** /ses′təs/ *n* a girdle, *esp* that of Aphrodite (Venus) in classical mythology. [L, from Gr *kestos* girdle]

cestus[2] or **caestus** /ses′təs/ *n* an ancient Roman boxing glove loaded with metal. [L *caestus*]

cesura see **caesura**.

cesure /sē′zūr/ (*Spenser*) *n* a break; interruption. [**caesura**]

CET *abbrev*: Central European Time.

cetacean /si-tā′shi-ən/ or /-shən/ *n* and *adj* (a member) of the order Cetacea of aquatic mammals having streamlined fish-like form, including the toothed whales, or Odontoceti (sperm whales, bottle-noses, dolphins, etc) and the baleen whales, or Mystacoceti (right whale, hump-backs, rorquals). [Gr *kētos* a sea-monster]
■ **cetā′ceous** *adj.* **cete** /sēt/ *n* a whale or sea-monster. **cetol′ogy** *n* the study of whales.

cetane /sē′tān/ (*chem*) *n* a colourless liquid hydrocarbon found in petroleum, used in determining the cetane number of diesel fuel. [Gr *kētos* a sea-monster]
❑ **cetane number** or **cetane rating** *n* a measure of the ignition quality of diesel engine fuel.

cete[1] /sēt/ *n* a collective noun for a group of badgers. [Poss L *coetus*, assembly]

cete[2] see under **cetacean**.

ceteosaurus /sē-ti-ə-sö′rəs/ *n* a large Jurassic dinosaur. [Gr *kētos* a sea-monster and *sauros* a lizard]

ceterach /set′ə-rak/ *n* a member of the scale-fern genus *Ceterach*, including *C. officinarium*, the rusty-back fern. [Med L *ceterach*, from Ar *shītarakh*]

cetera desunt /set′ə-ra dē′sunt or kā′te-ra dā′sŭnt/ (*L*) the rest are missing.

ceteris paribus /set′ə-ris par′i-bus or kā′te-rēs pa′ri-bŭs/ (*L*) other things being equal.

cetology see under **cetacean**.

cet. par. *abbrev*: ceteris paribus.

cetrimide /set′ri-mīd/ *n* a quaternary ammonium compound used as a detergent and antiseptic. [*cetyl* tri*methyl* ammonium brom*ide*]

Cetti's warbler /chet′iz wör′blər/ *n* a small European songbird, *Cettia cetti*. [Francesco *Cetti*, 18c Italian zoologist]

Cetus /sēt′əs/ *n* the fourth largest constellation, lying above the celestial equator, near Pisces and Aquarius. [L *cetus* whale]

cetuximab /se-tuk′si-mab/ *n* a therapeutic antibody used to treat advanced cancer of the colon or rectum. [*ce* (arbitrary syllable), *tumour*, *xi* (denoting a chimaeric antibody), and *monoclonal antibody*]

cetyl /sē′til/ (*chem*) *n* the univalent radical $C_{16}H_{33}$. [Gr *kētos* a sea-monster, and *hȳle* matter]
❑ **cetyl alcohol** *n* a waxy crystalline solid used in detergents and pharmaceuticals, so-called because compounds of it occur in spermaceti (also called **hexadecan-1-ol**).

cetywall see **setwall**.

cevadilla see **sabadilla**.

cevapcici /che-vap-chi′chi/ *n pl* a Balkan dish of minced beef and pork, flavoured with mint and paprika and formed into small sausages. [Serbo-Croat, kebabs]

ceviche /sə-vē′chi/ (*Mex*, etc *cookery*) *n* raw fish marinated in lime juice and served as an hors d'œuvre. [Am Sp]

cevitamic acid /sē-vi-tam′ik as′id/ *n* ascorbic acid, vitamin C. [The letter *c* and *vitamin*]

Ceylon /si-lon′/ *n* the name (until 1972) of the island of Sri Lanka.
■ **Ceylonese** /se- or sē-lə-nēz′/ *adj* and *n*. **cey′lonite** or **cey′lanite** *n* see **pleonaste** under **pleonasm**.
❑ **Ceylon moss** *n* a red seaweed (*Gracilaria lichenoides*) of the E Indian Ocean. **Ceylon tea** *n* a high-quality variety of tea.

CF *abbrev*: Chaplain to the Forces; (also **cf** or **c and f**) cost and freight.

Cf (*chem*) *symbol*: californium.

cf *abbrev*: confer (L), compare.

c.f. (*sport*) *abbrev*: centre-forward.

c/f or **c.f.** (*bookkeeping*) *abbrev*: carried forward.

CFA *abbrev*: Colonies Françaises d'Afrique (*FR*), French African Colonies; Communauté financière africaine (*FR*), African Financial Community.
❑ **CFA franc** *n* the standard monetary unit of various (former) French territories in Africa (100 cents) (*abbrev* **CFAFr**).

CFC *abbrev*: chlorofluorocarbon.

CFD *abbrev*: computational fluid dynamics; contract for difference: an agreement to pay the difference between the current value of a share and its value at a specified future date (*finance*).

CFE *abbrev*: College of Further Education; Conventional Armed Forces in Europe (formerly the subject of arms reduction talks held between the USA, European nations and the Soviet bloc).

cfg *abbrev*: cubic feet of gas.

CFI, **cfi** or **cf and i** *abbrev*: cost, freight, (and) insurance.

CFO *abbrev*: Chief Financial Officer; Chief Fire Officer.

CFP *abbrev*: Colonies Françaises du Pacifique (*FR*), French Pacific Colonies; Common Fisheries Policy (of the EU); Comptoirs français du Pacifique (*FR*), French Pacific Banks.
❑ **CFP franc** *n* the standard monetary unit of various (former) French Pacific territories (*abbrev* **CFPFr**).

CFR *abbrev*: commercial fast reactor (in the nuclear industry).

CFS *abbrev*: chronic fatigue syndrome.

cft *abbrev*: cubic feet (or foot).

CG *abbrev*: captain-general; Captain of the Guard; coastguard; Coldstream Guards; commanding general; consul general; Croix de Guerre (*Fr*), war decoration.

cg *abbrev*: centigram(s) or centigramme(s); centre of gravity.

CGA (*comput*) *abbrev*: colour graphics adapter.

CGBR *abbrev*: central government borrowing requirement.

CGC *abbrev*: Conspicuous Gallantry Cross.

cge *abbrev*: carriage.
■ **cge fwd** carriage-forward. **cge pd** carriage-paid.

CGI *abbrev*: City and Guilds (of London) Institute (also **CGLI**); computer-generated imagery.

CGIAR *abbrev*: Consultative Group on International Agricultural Research, an intergovernmental agency.

CGM *abbrev* : Conspicuous Gallantry Medal (now replaced by the **CGC**).

CGPM *abbrev* : *Conférence Générale des Poids et Mesures* (*Fr*), General Conference on Weights and Measures.

CGS *abbrev* : centimetre-gram-second (also **cgs**); Chief of the General Staff.

CGT *abbrev* : capital gains tax (also **cgt**); *Confédération Générale du Travail* (*Fr*), General Confederation of Labour, the largest French trade union.

CH *abbrev* : Companion of Honour; Switzerland (from L *Confederatio Helvetica*; IVR).

Ch. *abbrev* : Champion; Chaplain; Chapter; Chief; China; Chinese; Christ; Chronicles (*Bible*); Church.

ch /*ch*/ (*SW Eng dialect*; *obs*) a short form of the first person singular pronoun **ich**, always fused with the verb, as **cham** I am, **chave** I have, **chill** I will. [ME *ich*, from OE *ic*]

ch. *abbrev* : chain (linear measure); chapter; chart; check (in chess); chestnut; child; children; chirurgeon (*archaic*), surgeon; choir; church.

c.h. *abbrev* : central heating; centre-half (*sport*); clearing house; clubhouse; court house; customs house.

cha /*chä*/ *n* tea; char. [Chin *chá*; see **char³**]

chabazite /*kab'ə-zīt*/ *n* a mineral of the zeolite group, a white or colourless hydrated silicate of aluminium and calcium, found in rhombohedral crystals. [From a misreading of Gr *chalazios* a kind of stone, from *chalaza* hailstone]

Chablis /*shab'lē*/ *n* a very dry white Burgundy wine made at *Chablis*, department of Yonne, in France.

chabouk /*chä'book*/ *n* a horse-whip. [Pers *chābuk*]

chace see **chase¹**.

cha-cha or **cha-cha-cha** /*chä'chä'(chä')*/ *n* a dance of Latin American origin, consisting of a series of short steps followed by a rhythmic hip-swaying shuffling movement; music for this dance. ◆ *vi* (**cha'-(cha'-)cha'ing**, **cha'-(cha'-)chaed'**) to perform this dance.

chack /*chak* or *chäk*/ *n* (*Scot*) a snack; a snapping shut or pinching, as by a door or window. ◆ *vt* to pinch or nip in such a way. [Imit]

chacma /*chak'mə*/ *n* a large baboon (*Papio ursinus*) of S and E Africa. [From Khoikhoi]

chaco same as **shako**.

chaconine /*shak'ə-nēn*/ *n* a toxic alkaloid found in potatoes, related to solanine and in high concentrations imparting a bitter taste.

chaconne /*sha-* or *shə-kon'*/ *n* an old Spanish dance *prob* originating in Mexico, with slow stately movement; its musical form, a series of variations on a ground bass, in triple time, appearing in vocal and instrumental music as well as in ballets. [Fr, from Sp *chacona*, from Basque *chucun* pretty]

chacun à son goût /*shak-œ̃ a sɔ̃ goo'*/ (*Fr*) each person to his own taste (also **à chacun son goût**).

Chad¹ /*chad*/ or **Chadic** /*chad'ik*/ *n* a branch of the Afro-Asiatic language spoken in West and Central Africa. [Lake *Chad*]
 ■ **Chad'ic** *adj*.

Chad² /*chad*/ *n* (*usu* **Mr Chad**) a character in facetious sketches *esp* of the 1940s, portrayed as a bald head peering over a wall, with a caption beginning 'Wot no?', in protest at wartime shortages, etc. [Origin uncertain]

chad¹ /*shad*/ *n* a kind of fish. [See **shad**]

chad² /*chad*/ (*comput*) *n* one of the little bits of paper or cardboard punched out of paper tape or cards. [Origin uncertain]

chadar, **chaddar**, **chaddor**, **chador**, **chuddah** or **chuddar** /*chud'ə(r)*/ *n* the large veil worn by Muslim and Hindu women, covering head and body; a cloth spread over a Muslim tomb. [Pers *chaddar*, Hindi *caddar* a square cloth]

chadarim see **cheder**.

Chadian /*chad'i-ən*/ *adj* of or relating to the Republic of *Chad* in N Africa, or its inhabitants. ◆ *n* a native or citizen of Chad.

chaebol /*chä'bol*/ *n* (*pl* **chae'bol** or **chae'bols**) a large business conglomerate in South Korea, *orig* one that was family-owned. [Korean *chae* wealth, and *bol* powerful family; from Middle Chin]

chaenomeles /*kē-nom'ə-lēz*/ *n* a shrub of the *Chaenomeles* genus of flowering shrubs, such as the japonica and flowering quince.

chaeta /*kē'tə*/ *n* (*pl* **chaetae** /*kē'tē*/) a chitinous bristle on the body of the earthworm and other invertebrates. [Gr *chaitē* hair, spine; cf **seta**]
 ■ **chaetif'erous** *adj* (*zool*) having bristles.

chaetodon /*kē'tō-don*/ *n* (Gr *odous, odontos* tooth) any fish of the tropical genus *Chaetodon* having slender teeth and making up the family **Chaetodon'tidae**.

chaetognath /*kē'tag-nath*/ *n* (Gr *gnathos* jaw) a coelomate, wormlike marine invertebrate, including the arrowworm, having bristles round

the mouth. **chaetopod** /*kē'tō-pod*/ *n* (Gr *pous, podos* foot) a worm (such as the earthworm, lobworm, sea-mouse, etc), that moves with the help of bristles.

chafe /*chāf*/ *vt* to heat, fret, irritate or wear by rubbing; to cause to fret or rage. ◆ *vi* to heat, irritate, etc, by rubbing; to fret or rage (with *against* or *at*). ◆ *n* irritation caused by rubbing. [Fr *chauffer*, from L *calefacere*, from *calēre* to be hot, and *facere* to make]
 ■ **chaf'er** *n* (*obs*) a chafing-dish, a saucepan.
 ❏ **chaf'ing-dish** *n* a vessel for heating by hot coals, etc; a dish for cooking on the table. **chaf'ing-gear** *n* mats, spun-yarn, battens, etc used on the rigging and spars of a ship to prevent damage by rubbing.

chafer /*chā'fər*/ *n* any of several kinds of beetle, *esp* of the Scarabaeidae, eg the cockchafer. [OE *cefer* ; Du *kever* ; Ger *Käfer*]

chaff /*chäf* or *chaf*/ *n* husks from corn that has been threshed or winnowed; chopped hay and straw used as animal feed or bedding; strips of metallic foil, bits of wire, etc, fired into or dropped through the air to deflect radar signals and so interfere with detection; rubbish, or worthless material; the dry bracts enclosing the flowers of some members of the daisy family; light banter, badinage. ◆ *vt* to tease; to banter with. [OE *ceaf* ; cf Du *kaf*]
 ■ **chaff'ing** *n* and *adj*. **chaff'ingly** *adv*. **chaff'y** *adj*.
 ❏ **chaff'-cutter** or **chaff'-engine** *n* a machine for cutting up straw or hay.

chaffer /*chaf'ər*/ *vi* to bargain; to haggle about price; to sell, exchange, or bandy (*obs*). ◆ *n* haggling, bargaining. [ME *chapfare* a bargain, from OE *cēap* price, and *faru* way]
 ■ **chaff'erer** *n* a haggler. **chaff'ery** *n* buying and selling; haggling (*obs*).

chaffinch /*chaf'inch* or *-insh*/ *n* a little songbird of the finch family, the male having a pinkish body and grey head with black-and-white markings. [**chaff** and **finch**]

chaffron see **chamfrain**.

chaft /*chaft* or *chäft*/ (*Scot*) *n* (*usu* in *pl*) the jaw; the cheek. [ON *kjaptr* ; cf Swed *kaft*, Dan *kieft*]

chagan /*kä-gän'*/ *n* an early form of **khan²**.

Chagas' disease /*shä'gəs di-zēz*/ *n* a tropical disease transmitted by the parasitic microorganism *Trypanosoma cruzi*, and characterized by high fever and inflammation and swelling of the heart muscles, spleen, liver, etc. [Carlos Chagas (1879–1934), Brazilian physician]

chagrin /*shag'rin*, also *shə-grēn'* or *-grin'*/ *n* a feeling of vexation, annoyance or embarrassment. ◆ *vt* to vex, annoy or embarrass. [Fr *chagrin* shagreen, rough skin, ill-humour]
 ■ **chagrined'** *adj*.

chai¹ or **chi** /*chī*/ *fem* of **chal**.

chai² /*chī*/ *n* a strong black tea infused with milk, sugar and spices; a general name for tea used *esp* in India. [Hindi, tea; cf **cha**]

chain /*chān*/ *n* a series of links or rings passing through one another, used to restrain, support, pull, etc, or in jewellery; a number of things connected in series; a linked series, eg of house-buyers and -sellers; a mountain range; a string of islands; something that binds; a connected course or train (of events); a measure of 100 links, or 66 feet (see **Gunter's chain** under **gunter**); a measure of 100 feet (see **engineer's chain** under **engine**); a series of shops, hotels, restaurants, etc under the same ownership or management; a number of atoms linked in succession (*chem*); a routine consisting of segments each of which uses the output of the preceding segment as input (*comput*); (in *pl*) fetters, bonds, confinement or restriction generally. ◆ *vt* to fasten (also **chain up** or **down**); to fetter; to restrain; to measure, with chain or tape (*surveying*). [OFr *chaeine*, from L *catēna*]
 ■ **chained** *adj* bound or fastened, as with a chain; fitted with a chain. **chain'less** *adj* without chains; unfettered; unrestricted. **chain'let** *n* a small chain.
 ❏ **chain armour** *n* chain mail. **chain bolt** *n* a large bolt used to secure the chainplates to the ship's side. **chain'brake** *n* a cut-off safety device on a chainsaw, activated automatically if the chainsaw kicks back. **chain'-breaker** *n* a method or device for resolving or avoiding the difficulties created by a chain of house-buyers and -sellers each awaiting action on the part of others earlier or later in the sequence. **chain bridge** *n* a bridge suspended on chains; a suspension bridge. **chain cable** *n* a cable made up of iron links. **chain drive** *n* transmission of power by chain-gear. **chain-driven** *adj*. **chain gang** *n* a gang of convicts wearing leg-irons, *esp* chained together on an outside working party. **chain'-gear** or **chain'-gearing** *n* gearing consisting of an endless chain and (generally) sprocket-wheels. **chain grate** *n* a device for stoking a (*usu* industrial) furnace in which fuel is drawn into the furnace by means of a rotating chain. **chain harrow** *n* a harrow made up of chainwork. **chain letter** *n* a letter soliciting (among other things) the sending, by the recipient, of similar letters with or without a limit to other people. **chain lightning** *n* forked or zigzag lightning; a strong or harsh-tasting whisky (*sl*).

■ words derived from main entry word; ❏ compound words; ■ idioms and phrasal verbs

chain'-link fence *n* an openwork fence made from interconnecting wire. **chain locker** *n* (*naut*) a compartment at the forward end of a ship for storing the anchor chain when the anchor is not in use. **chain mail** *n* armour of small connected metal links, much used in Europe in the 12c and 13c. **chain'man** *n* (*surveying*) an assistant to a surveyor who takes measurements with a chain. **chain moulding** *n* (*archit*) moulding in the form of a chain. **chain of command** *n* a series of military or civic functionaries, each taking orders from the one immediately senior to himself. **chain of office** *n* a heavy ornamental chain worn around the neck as a symbol of office. **chain pier** *n* a pier supported by chains like a chain bridge. **chain'plates** *n pl* (*naut*) iron plates bolted below the channels on a ship, to serve as attachments for the deadeyes, through which the standing rigging or shrouds and backstays are secured. **chain printer** *n* (*comput*) a type of line printer with the characters mounted on a metal or plastic chain, forming a continuous loop. **chain pump** *n* a pump consisting of an endless chain, *usu* with discs. **chain reaction** *n* a process in which each reaction is in turn the stimulus of a further reaction. **chain reactor** *n* a nuclear reactor. **chain rule** *n* an arithmetical rule, so called from the terms of the problem being stated as equations, and connected, as if by a chain, so as to obtain by one operation the same result as would be obtained by a number of different operations in simple proportion; the rule for solving problems by compound proportion. **chain'saw** *n* a power saw with cutting teeth linked in an endless chain. **chain'shot** *n* two bullets or half-bullets fastened together by a chain, used formerly to destroy ships' rigging. **chain'-smoke** *vt* and *vi* to smoke (cigarettes, etc) non-stop, often lighting each from the previous one. **chain'-smoker** *n*. **chain'stitch** *n* a stitch in knitting or sewing resembling the links of a chain. **chain store** *n* one of a series of shops, *esp* department stores, under the same ownership or management and located in different places. **chain'wheel** *n* a toothed wheel, as on a bicycle, which meshes with a chain to transmit motion. **chain'work** *n* work looped or linked like a chain; network.

chaîné /shen-āʹ/ (*ballet*) *n* a series of small fast turns, often with the arms extended, used to cross a floor or stage. [Fr]

chair /chār/ *n* a movable seat for one person, with a back, *usu* four legs, and sometimes arms; a sedan chair (*hist*); the seat or office of someone in authority, eg a judge, a bishop, or the person presiding over any meeting; a chairperson; *orig* the seat from which a professor delivered his or her lectures; a professorship; the instrument or the punishment of death by electrocution (*inf*; with *the*); a support for a railway rail securing it to a sleeper. ◆ *vt* to conduct (a meeting, etc) as chairperson; to carry publicly in triumph; to place in a seat of authority. [Fr *chaire*, from L, from Gr *kathedrā*]
▫ **chair'-bed** *n* a chair capable of being turned into a bed. **chair'borne** *adj* (*inf*) working at a desk. **chair'bound** *adj* unable to walk; confined to a wheelchair. **chair'days** *n pl* (*Shakesp*; *fig*) the evening of life. **chair'lift** *n* a set of seats suspended from cables used to carry skiers, etc uphill. **chair'man** *n* a person (male or female) who takes the chair, or presides at an assembly or meeting (also **chair'person**; *fem* **chair'woman**); a sedan-bearer (*hist*). **chair'manship** *n*. **chair'-organ** *n* a choir organ (perhaps because it sometimes formed the back of the organist's seat). **chairperson, chairwoman** see under **chairman** above.
▪ **in the chair** acting as the chairperson of a meeting. **take the chair** to preside over a meeting as chairperson.

chaise /shāz/ *n* a light open carriage for one or more persons; a travelling carriage (see **post-chaise** under **post³**); a chaise-longue. [Fr, a form of *chaire*; see **chair**]
▪ **chaise'less** *adj*.
▫ **chaise'-cart** *n* (*pl* **chaise'-carts**) a light cart for travelling about in. **chaise-longue** /shāzʹlög'/ *n* (*pl* **chaises'-longues'**) a couch with back at one end only and short armrest, designed for lying on.

chakra /chakʹrə/ *n* in Sikh culture, a disc-shaped knife used as a missile; a discus representing the sun, as in portrayals of Hindu gods; in yoga, one of the seven centres of spiritual power in the body. [Sans *cakra* wheel]

chal /chal/ (*obs*) *n* (also *fem* **chai** or **chi** /chī/) a person. [Romany]

chalan or **challan** /chulʹən/ (*Ind*) *n* a waybill; a pass; the sending up of an accused person before a magistrate; a form used when money due to a government department is paid, not to the department itself, but to the government Treasury. [Hindi *calan*]

chalaza /ka-lāʹzə/ *n* (*pl* **chala'zas** or **chala'zae** /-ē/) in a bird's egg, one of two spiral chords of albumen that hold the yolk sac in position (*zool*); the base of the ovule (*bot*). [Gr *chalaza* hail, lump]
▪ **chala'zal** *adj*.

chalazion /kə-lāʹzi-ən/ (*med*) *n* a round painless cyst or swelling in the eyelid resulting from the blocking of a gland (also **meibomian cyst**). [Gr *chalaza* lump]

chalazogamy /ka-la-zogʹə-mi/ (*bot*) *n* the entry of the pollen tube through the chalaza, *opp* to porogamy. [See **chalaza** and **-gamy**]

▪ **chalazogamic** /kəl-az-ō-gamʹik/ *adj*.

chalcanthite /kal-kanʹthīt/ *n* a blue mineral, $CuSO_4.5H_2O$, hydrated copper sulphate in crystalline form. [Gr *chalkos* copper, and *anthos* flower]

chalcedony /kal-sedʹə-ni or kalʹsi-dō-ni/ *n* a microcrystalline, white or bluish-white mineral composed of silica, *usu* of banded and translucent appearance and having a waxy lustre, a variety of quartz found in sedimentary rocks. [Gr *chalkēdōn*, poss from *Chalcedon*, in Asia Minor]
▪ **chalcedonic** /-si-donʹik/ *adj*. **chalced'onyx** (or /-on'/) *n* an agate of alternating white opaque and greyish translucent chalcedony.

chalcid /kalʹsid/ *n* any small parasitic insect of the family Chalcididae, that lay their eggs inside the bodies of other insects, or, as with the **chalcid wasp**, within the seeds of plants. [Gr *chalkos* copper, from the metallic colouring of their bodies]

Chalcidian /kal-sidʹi-ən/ *adj* relating to *Chalcis* in Euboea, or its people.
▫ **Chalcidian alphabet** *n* the alphabet used by Chalcidian settlers in S Italy and Sicily, from which the Latin alphabet developed.

chalco- /kal-kō-/ *combining form* relating to or containing copper.

chalcocite /kalʹkə-sīt/ *n* a greyish-black mineral, Cu_2S, sulphide of copper of orthorhombic crystalline structure. [Gr *chalkos* copper, and **-ite**]

chalcogen /kalʹkə-jn/ (*chem*) *n* an element from group VI(B) of the periodic table, namely sulphur, selenium or tellurium. [Gr *chalkos* copper, and **-gen¹**]
▪ **chalcogenide** /-kojʹə-nīd/ *n* a compound containing a chalcogen.

chalcography /kal-kogʹrə-fi/ *n* the art of engraving on copper or brass. [Gr *chalkos* copper, and *graphein* to write]
▪ **chalcog'rapher** or **chalcog'raphist** *n*. **chalcograph'ic** or **chalcograph'ical** *adj*.

Chalcolithic /kal-kō-lithʹik/ same as **Aeneolithic** (see under **aeneous**). [Gr *chalkos* copper, and *lithos* stone]

chalcopyrite /kal-kō-pīʹrīt/ *n* copper pyrites, $CuFeS_2$, a yellow double sulphide of copper and iron, the commonest ore of copper. [Gr *chalkos* copper, and **pyrite**]

Chaldaic /kal-dāʹik/ or **Chaldee** /kalʹdē/ *adj* relating to *Chaldaea*, an ancient region of S Babylonia. ◆ *n* the language of the Chaldaeans; an inhabitant of the ancient region of Chaldaea; a soothsayer (*rare*); a member of the Chaldaean church.
▪ **Chaldae'an** or **Chalde'an** /-dēʹən/ *adj* Chaldaic. ◆ *n* a native of Chaldaea. **Chal'daism** *n* a Chaldaic idiom.

chalder /chölʹdər/ *n* an old Scottish dry measure, containing 16 bolls. [Prob a form of **chaldron**]

chaldron /chölʹdrən/ *n* an old unit of capacity, equal to 36 heaped bushels (= $25\frac{1}{2}$cwt). [Fr *chaudron*; see **cauldron**]

chalet /shalʹā/ (the spelling **châlet** is wrong) *n* a summer hut used by Swiss herdsmen in the Alps; a wooden villa; a small house, *usu* of wood, built for use by holidaymakers, etc. [Fr]

chalice /chalʹis/ *n* a drinking cup or bowl; a (*usu* gold or silver) communion cup; a cup-shaped flower (*bot*). [OFr *chalice*, from L *calix, calicis*; cf Gr *kylix* a cup; **calyx** is a different word]
▪ **chal'iced** *adj* (*bot*) (of flowers) cup-like.

chalicothere /kalʹi-kō-thēr/ *n* a member of an extinct group of large perissodactyl animals of the Tertiary period, typically having a horse-like head and feet bearing three large claws. [New L, small stone beast, from Gr *chalix* pebble, and *thērion*, dimin of *thēr* beast]

chalk /chök/ *n* a white soft rock, composed of finely-grained calcium carbonate, chiefly minute fragments of fossil shells and organic remains; a substitute for this used for writing, etc; a piece of this; methamphetamine (*US sl*). ◆ *vt* to write, rub or mark with chalk; to fertilize (land) with chalk. ◆ *vi* of paint, to become chalky. [OE *cealc*, from L *calx* limestone]
▪ **chalk'iness** *n*. **chalk'like** *adj*. **chalk'y** *adj*.
▫ **chalk'board** *n* (*esp* N Am) a blackboard. **chalk'face** *n* (*inf*) the classroom, regarded as the scene of a teacher's exertions, *usu* in the phrase *at the chalkface*. **chalk'pit** *n* a pit from which chalk is quarried. **chalk'stone** *n* a stone or piece of chalk; one of the white concretions that form round the joints in chronic gout, a tophus. **chalk talk** *n* (N Am) an informal talk or lecture using explanatory notes and diagrams on a blackboard.
▪ **as like** (or **as different**) **as chalk and cheese** completely unalike. **by a long chalk** by a considerable distance or degree. **chalk and talk** the formal, traditional teaching method that relies on oral instruction and use of the blackboard. **chalking the door** (*hist*) in Scotland, a form of warning tenants to move out of burghal tenements; a method of giving tenants notice to quit. **chalk out** to trace out, as with chalk, to outline (a plan, etc). **chalk up** to make a special (*esp* mental) note of; to record (a score, etc); to charge or ascribe to (a person or to a

person's account, etc). **not know** (or **tell**) **chalk from cheese** (*usu derog*) to be incapable of seeing, or unable to distinguish between, important differences because of lack of knowledge or judgement. **the Chalk** (*geol*) the uppermost part of the Cretaceous system in England.

challah /hhal'ə/ *n* (*pl* **chal'lahs** or **chal'loth**) Jewish bread, *usu* in the form of a plaited loaf, eaten to celebrate the Sabbath. [Heb *hallāh*]

challan see **chalan**.

challenge /chal'inj/ *vt* to summon (someone) to settle a matter by fighting or by any kind of contest; to subject to stress, examination or test; to stimulate; to accuse; to object to; to dispute (a statement, judgement, etc); to administer a challenge to (*med*). ♦ *vi* (of a hunting dog or hound) to show that a scent has been picked up by emitting a howl or cry. ♦ *n* a summons to a contest of any kind; a calling into question of anyone or anything; an objection to a juror; the demand for identification and authority made by a sentry; an accusation or charge; a claim; a difficulty which stimulates interest or effort; a task, undertaking, etc to test one's powers and capabilities to the full; the administration to an immunized person or animal of a substance which causes allergic reaction or infection, in order to test the effectiveness of immunization (*med*). [OFr *chalenge* a dispute, claim, from L *calumnia* a false accusation, from *calvi* or *calvere* to deceive] ■ **chall'engeable** *adj* that may be challenged. **chall'enged** *adj* (*esp N Am*) handicapped or impaired, as in *physically challenged*. **chall'enger** *n* a person who challenges to a combat or contest of any kind; a claimant; a person who objects or calls someone or something into question. **chall'enging** *adj*. **chall'engingly** *adv*. ■ **challenge to the polls** (*law*) an objection to a person or persons selected to serve on a jury, or **challenge to the array**, to the whole body of jurors.

challis /chal'is, shal'is or shal'i/ or **challie** /shal'i/ *n* a soft glossless silk or lightweight fabric made of wool, cotton or synthetic fibres (also **shall'i**). [Origin uncertain]

chalone /kal'ōn or kā'lōn/ *n* one of a group of chemicals occurring in animal tissues, whose action inhibits the growth and differentiation of cells in the tissue. [Gr *chalaein* to relax] ■ **chalon'ic** *adj*.

chalumeau /shal-ū-mō' or shal-ŭ-mō'/ *n* (*pl* **chalumeaux** /-mōz'/) an early rustic reed instrument that developed into the clarinet; now applied to the lowest register of the clarinet. [Fr, from OFr *chalemel*, from LL *calamellus*, dimin of *calamus* a pipe, a reed]

chalutz /hä'lŭts/ *n* a member of the early group of immigrants to Israel that established and worked the first kibbutzim (agricultural settlements). [Heb *halutz* pioneer]

chalybean /ka-li-bē'ən or ka-lib'i-ən/ (*metallurgy*) *adj* tempered. [Gr *chalyps, chalybos* steel, or *Chalyps* one of the *Chalybes*, a nation in Pontus famous for steel-making] ■ **chalyb'eate** *adj* containing iron compounds. ♦ *n* a water or other liquid, *esp* a drug, containing iron salts. **cha'lybite** *n* siderite (see under **sidero-**).

Cham /cham/ *n* (*pl* **Cham** or **Chams**) a member of a people of central Vietnam and Cambodia; the language of this people. ♦ *adj* relating to the Cham or their language.

cham[1] /kam/ *n* an obsolete form of **khan**[2]; an autocrat.

cham[2] see **ch**.

chamade /shə-mäd'/ (*milit hist*) *n* a drum or trumpet call inviting an enemy to parley or surrender. [Fr]

chamaeleon see **chameleon**.

chamaephyte /kam'i-fīt/ (*bot*) *n* a woody or herbaceous plant that produces buds close to the ground. [Gr *chamai* on the ground, and **-phyte**]

Chamb. *abbrev* : Chamberlain.

chamber /chām'bər/ *n* a room; the place where an assembly meets; a house of a legislature, eg the French Chamber of Deputies; an assembly or body of people met for some purpose, such as a chamber of commerce; a hall of justice; a compartment, an enclosed space; a cavity; a chamberpot; a compartment in a gun where the bullet or cartridge is placed prior to firing; a small cannon (*archaic*); (in *pl*) a suite of rooms occupied separately, *esp* by lawyers; (in *pl*) a judge's room for hearing cases not taken into court. ♦ *vt* to put in a chamber; to confine. ♦ *vi* (*archaic*) to be wanton. [Fr *chambre*, from L *camera*, from Gr *kamarā* a vault, a room] ■ **cham'bered** *adj* confined; having rooms or space separated by a succession of walls; (of a shell) having partitions that form a chamber or chambers. **cham'berer** *n* a person who plots or intrigues (*archaic*); a gallant, a lover (*archaic*). **cham'bering** *n* (*Bible*) lewd or wanton behaviour. ❑ **chamber concert** *n* a concert of chamber music. **chamber council** *n* (*Shakesp*) a private or secret council. **chamber counsel** or **chamber counsellor** *n* a counsel who gives his advice privately, but does not plead in court. **chambered nautilus** *n* a pearly nautilus

(see **nautilus**). **cham'ber-lye** *n* (*archaic*) urine. **cham'bermaid** *n* a girl or woman employed to clean bedrooms in hotels, etc; formerly, and still in USA, a housemaid. **chamber music** *n* music, performed by a small group such as a quartet, suitable for a room rather than a theatre or a large hall. **chamber of commerce** *n* (sometimes with *caps*) a group of businesspeople working together to promote local trade. **chamber of trade** *n* (sometimes with *caps*) a national organization representing local chambers of commerce. **chamber orchestra** *n* a small orchestra for the performance of chamber music. **chamber organ** *n* a small organ suitable for a room. **cham'berpot** *n* a container for urine, etc, used in a bedroom (often called merely **chamber** or **pot**). **chamber practice** *n* the business of a chamber counsel. **cham'ber-stick** *n* a candlestick designed to be carried.

chamberlain /chām'bər-lin/ *n* an officer appointed by a monarch, nobleman or corporation, to perform domestic and ceremonial duties or to act as factor, steward or treasurer. [OFr *chambrelenc*; OHGer *chamerling*, from L *camera* a chamber, and **-ling**[1]] ■ **cham'berlainship** *n*. ■ **Lord Chamberlain** an officer of high standing in the royal household, having control over all the officers and servants 'above stairs', except those of the bedchamber, over the establishment attached to the Chapel Royal, and the physicians, surgeons and apothecaries of the household. **Lord Great Chamberlain** a hereditary officer who is in charge of the palace of Westminster and to whom on solemn occasions the keys of Westminster Hall and of the Court of Requests are delivered.

Chambertin /shã-ber-tẽ'/ *n* a dry red Burgundy from the vineyard of that name near Dijon.

chambranle /shã-brãl'/ (*archit*) *n* a decoration around the frame of a doorway, fireplace or other opening. [Fr]

chambray /shöm'brā/ *n* a fine cotton or linen fabric, with interwoven white and coloured threads. [Orig US; related to **cambric**]

chambré /shã-brā'/ (*Fr*) *adj* (of wine) at, or brought to, room temperature.

chameleon or **chamaeleon** /kə-mē'lyən or -li-ən/ *n* a small African lizard with a prehensile tail and tongue, eyes capable of independent movement and the ability to change colour to blend with its surroundings; an inconstant, changeable, or readily adaptable person (*fig*; also *adj*). [L *chamaeleōn*, from Gr *chamaileōn*, from *chamai* (cf L *humī*) on the ground (ie dwarf), and *leōn* a lion] ■ **chameleonic** /-i-on'ik/ and **chamel'eon-like** *adj*.

chamelot /cham' or kam'e-lot/ (*Spenser*) *n* same as **camlet**.

chametz or **chometz** /ha-mets' or hha'mets/ (*Judaism*) *n* leavened food, which may not be eaten during the Passover. [Heb *hames*]

chamfer /cham'fər/ *n* a bevel or slope made by paring off the edge or corner of a *usu* right-angled surface; a groove, channel or furrow. ♦ *vt* to cut or grind off bevel-wise (eg a corner); to channel or make furrows upon; to flute (eg a column). [Fr *chanfrein*, from OFr *chanfraindre*, appar from *chant fraindre*, from L *cantum frangere* to break the edge or side] ■ **cham'fered** *adj* bevelled; furrowed, grooved, wrinkled.

chamfrain /cham'frən/ *n* a piece of leather or plate of steel to protect the face of a horse in battle (also **cham'fron** or **chaf'fron**). [Fr *chanfrein*; origin unknown]

chamiso /shə-mē'sō/ or **chamise** /shə-mēz'/ *n* (*pl* **chami'sos** or **chamis'es**) a rosaceous shrub (*Adenostoma fasciculatum*) of California. [Am Sp *chamiza* cane] ■ **chamisal'** *n* a dense thicket of chamisos.

chamlet /cham' or kam'let/ *n* same as **camlet**.

chammy see **chamois**.

chamois /sham'wä or -oi/ *n* (*pl* **cham'ois**) a goat-like antelope (*Rupicapra rupicapra*) inhabiting high mountains in southern and central Europe; a pale greyish-brown colour; /sham'i/ a soft pliant leather *orig* made from the skin of this animal (also **chammy**, **shammy** or **chamois**, etc **leather**). [Fr, perh from Swiss Romanic; cf Ger *Gemse* a chamois]

chamomile see **camomile**.

champ[1] /champ/ *vi* to make a snapping or munching noise with the jaws while chewing. ♦ *vt* to bite or chew; to munch; to crush; to mash. ♦ *n* the act of champing; (*esp* in N Ireland) a dish made of potatoes, leeks and spring onions. [Poss onomatopoeic; connected with **jam**[2]] ■ **champ at the bit** (of a horse) to gnaw at the bit nervously or impatiently; to show signs of impatience while waiting for something to begin.

champ[2] /champ/ (*heraldry*) *n* field. [Fr]

champ[3] /champ/ (*sl*) *n* short form of **champion**.

champac see **champak**.

champagne /sham-pān'/ *n* a white sparkling wine, strictly from *Champagne* in France (sometimes coloured pink); the pale

yellowish-white colour of white champagne; loosely, a wine similar to that from Champagne. ♦ *adj* yellowish-white.
□ **Champagne Cocktail** *n* a cocktail containing champagne, brandy, sugar and Angostura bitters. **champagne socialist** *n* (*derog*) a person whose comfortable or extravagant standard of living belies his or her professed socialist politics.

champaign /*cham-* or *sham-pān*'/ *adj* level, open. ♦ *n* an expanse of open level country. [Doublet of **campaign**, from OFr *champaigne*, from L *campānia* a plain]

champak or **champac** /*chum'puk* or *cham'pak*/ *n* a tree of E India (*Michelia champaca*) of the magnolia family, with oppressively scented yellow flowers, regarded as sacred by Hindus. [Hindi]

champart /*shä-pär'*/ *n* the division of the produce of land, the right of the feudal lord. [Norman Fr, from L *campī pars* part of the field]

champers /*sham'pərz*/ (*inf*) *n* champagne.

champerty /*cham'pər-ti*/ (*law*) *n* a contract, unenforceable in law but not a criminal offence, in which an outside party agrees to finance a litigant's action in return for a share of the proceeds. [See **champart**] ■ **cham'pertous** *adj*.

champignon /*sham'pin-yɔ̃*/ *n* a mushroom or other edible fungus, *esp* the fairy-ring champignon (*Marasmius oreades*). [Fr]

champion /*cham'pi-ən*/ *n* someone who defends a cause; a successful combatant; a person who fights in single combat for himself or for another (*hist* or *archaic*); (in sports) a competitor who has excelled all others; anything, eg an animal or cultivated plant, that wins first place in a show; a hero. ♦ *adj* acting or ranking as champion, first; excellent (*inf*). ♦ *adv* (*dialect*) excellently. ♦ *vt* to challenge (*obs*); to defend; to support. [Fr, from LL *campiō, -ōnis*, from L *campus* a plain, a place for games]
■ **cham'pioness** *n* (*rare*). **cham'pionship** *n* the position of honour gained by being champion; a contest held to decide who is the champion; the act of championing a cause.

champlevé /*shä-lə-vā* or *sham'plə-vā*/ *n* a type of enamel work in which vitreous powders are laid in channels cut in a metal base (also *adj*). [Fr]

Champs Elysées /*shä-zā-lē-zā'*/ (*Fr*) Elysian Fields (Elysium); also a famous open space and avenue in Paris.

chana /*chä'nə*/ (*Ind cookery*) *n* the chickpea. [Hindi]

Chanc. *abbrev* : Chancellor; Chancery.

chance /*chäns*/ *n* that which happens or results fortuitously, or without assignable cause; fortune; an unexpected event; risk; opportunity; possibility of something happening; (sometimes in *pl*) probability; (in *pl*) misfortunes (*archaic*). ♦ *vt* to risk. ♦ *vi* to happen. ♦ *adj* happening by chance. ♦ *adv* perchance. [OFr *cheance*, from LL *cadentia*, from L *cadere* to fall]
■ **chance'ful** *adj* full of risk or danger (*archaic*); full of chance(s). **chance'less** *adj* without an opportunity. **chanc'er** *n* (*inf*) an unscrupulous person prepared to seize any opportunity to make money or for his or her own advancement, an opportunist. **chanc'ily** *adv*. **chanc'iness** *n*. **chanc'y** or **chanc'ey** *adj* risky; uncertain; lucky, safe (*Scot*).
□ **chance'-comer** *n* someone who arrives by chance or unexpectedly.
■ **by chance** accidentally. **chance in a million** the faintest possibility; an opportunity not to be missed (also **chance of a lifetime**). **chance it** or **chance one's arm** (or **luck**) (*inf*) to take a chance, often recklessly or with little hope of success. **chance upon** or **on** to find or come across by chance. **chance would be a fine thing** (*inf*) there is not much hope of it. **even chance** equal probability for or against. **how chance?** (*Shakesp*) how does it happen that? **no chance** or **not a chance** (*inf*) that will not happen or succeed. **on the off chance** in hope rather than expectation. **stand a good chance** to have a reasonable expectation. **take one's chance** to accept what happens; to risk an undertaking. **the chances are** it is probable or likely. **the main chance** the chief object or best opportunity (*esp* in the phrase **have an eye to the main chance** to be aware of opportunity for self-enrichment).

chancel /*chän'səl*/ *n* the eastern part of a church, *orig* separated from the nave by a screen of latticework to prevent general access to the altar, sanctuary and choir. [OFr, from L *cancellī* lattices]

chancellor /*chän'sə-lər*/ *n* a court secretary (*hist*); a chief minister; the president, or a judge, of a court of chancery or other court; the official who keeps the registers of an order of knighthood; the titular or (*US*) active head of a university; the foreman of a jury (*Scot*). [Fr *chancelier*, from LL *cancellārius* orig an officer that had charge of records, and stood near the *cancelli* (L), crossbars surrounding the judgement seat]
■ **chan'cellery** or **chan'cellory** *n* the position, department, residence, etc of a chancellor; the office attached to an embassy or consulate. **chan'cellorship** *n*.

■ **chancellor of a cathedral** an officer who had charge of the chapter library, custody of the common seal, superintendence of the choir practices, and headship of the cathedral schools. **chancellor of a diocese** an ecclesiastical judge uniting the functions of vicar-general and official principal, appointed to assist the bishop in questions of ecclesiastical law, and hold his courts for him. **Chancellor of the Duchy of Lancaster** a government minister employed on parliamentary work, nominally appointed as representative of the Queen as Duchess of Lancaster. **Chancellor of the Exchequer** the chief minister of finance in the British government. **Lord Chancellor** or **Lord High Chancellor** a senior member of the British government, historically holding the roles of Speaker of the House of Lords, head of the judiciary of England and Wales, and keeper of the Great Seal.

chance-medley /*chäns-med'li*/ *n* unintentional homicide, *usu* resulting from a sudden violent dispute, in which the killer is not entirely without blame (*law*); action with an element of chance. [OFr *chance medlée* mingled chance]

Chancery /*chän'sə-ri*/ *n* formerly, the highest court of justice next to the House of Lords, presided over by the Lord High Chancellor, now a division of the High Court of Justice; a court of public record generally; the office of a chancellor; (without *cap*) the political office in an embassy or legation (*Brit diplomacy*). [Fr *chancellerie*]
□ **Chancery Office** *n* in Scotland, an office in the General Register House at Edinburgh, managed by a director, in which all royal charters of novodamus, patents of dignities, gifts of offices, remissions, legitimations, presentations, commissions, and other writs appointed to pass the Great and Quarter Seals are recorded.
■ **in chancery** (of an estate, etc) in litigation; (of a wrestler's or boxer's head) held firmly under his adversary's arm (*sl*); hence, in an awkward or helpless predicament (*sl*).

chancre /*shang'kər*/ (*med*) *n* a hard nodular swelling, *esp* one that develops in the primary stage of syphilis. [Fr; a form of **canker**]
■ **chanc'roid** *n* a non-syphilitic sexually transmitted disease, caused by *Haemophilus ducreyi* and characterized by ulceration of the genital organs and enlarged lymph nodes in the groin (also called **soft chancre**). **chancroid'al** *adj*. **chanc'rous** *adj*.

chancy see under **chance**.

chandelier /*shan-di-lēr'*/ *n* an ornamental lighting fixture, suspended from the ceiling and often branched, for holding several lights. [Fr, from LL *candēlāria* a candlestick, from L *candēla* a candle]

chandelle /*shan-del'* or (*Fr*) *shä-del*/ *n* a sharp upward turn of an aircraft using momentum to achieve the maximum rate of climb. ♦ *vi* to perform this manoeuvre. [Fr, candle]

chandler /*chand'lər*/ *n* a maker of candles; a dealer in candles, oil, soap, etc; a dealer in a specified type of goods (as in *corn-chandler*, *ship-chandler*). [Fr, from LL *candēlārius* a candle-maker, from L *candēla* a candle]
■ **chand'lering** *n*. **chand'lerly** *adj*. **chand'lery** *n* the business of, premises of, or goods sold by a chandler.

Chandrasekhar limit /*chan-drə-sā'kər lim'it*/ (*astron*) *n* the upper limit of mass for a White Dwarf. [S *Chandrasekhar* (1910–95), Indian-American astrophysicist]

change /*chänj*/ *vt* to alter or make different; to give or receive for another or for an equivalent; to cause to move or to pass from one state to another; to exchange or replace. ♦ *vi* to undergo change; to change one's clothes; to transfer from (one bus, train, etc) to another. ♦ *n* the act of changing; alteration or variation of any kind; exchange (*archaic*); fickleness (*archaic*); a shift; variety; money given for money of a different kind, or in adjustment of a payment; coins of low value (*collectively*); satisfaction (*inf*); an exchange (now *usu* '**change**); any of the various orders in which a peal of bells can be rung. [Fr *changer*, from L *cambīre* to barter]
■ **changeabil'ity** or **change'ableness** *n* fickleness; the power of being changed. **change'able** *adj* subject or prone to change; fickle; inconstant; able to or capable of change; showing variation of colour. **change'ably** *adv*. **change'ful** *adj* full of change; changeable. **change'fully** *adv*. **change'fulness** *n*. **change'less** *adj* without change; constant. **change'lessly** *adv*. **change'lessness** *n*. **change'ling** *n* a surreptitious substitute; a child substituted for another, *esp* one supposed to be left by the fairies; hence, an undersized crabbed child; a half-witted person (*archaic*); a person apt to change (*archaic*). **chäng'er** *n* someone or something that changes the form of anything; a person employed in changing or discounting money (*obs*).
□ **change'-house** *n* (*Scot*) a small inn or alehouse. **change'over** *n* transition to a new system, position or condition; the act or process of passing over, exchanging or transferring from one to another. **change point** *n* (*surveying*) a staff station to which two sights are taken, a foresight and a backsight (also called **turning point**). **change-ringing** see **ring the changes** below. **change'-up** *n* (*baseball*) a slower pitch, thrown to deceive the batter. **chang'ing-piece** *n* (*Shakesp*) a fickle

person. **changing room** *n* a room or cubicle set aside for the use of people changing clothes.

■ **change colour** to blush or turn pale. **change down** (*motoring*) to change to a lower gear. **change face** (*surveying*) to rotate a theodolite telescope about its horizontal axis so as to change the sighting from left to right or vice versa. **change front** (*milit*) to change the direction of fire of (troops, artillery, etc); to alter one's opinion. **change gear** to select a higher or lower gear (*motoring*); to increase or decrease the pace of activity (*fig*). **change hands** to be transferred from one owner to another. **change of air** a different climate or environment (also *fig*). **change of heart** a change of attitude, viewpoint or opinion, often resulting in the reversal of a decision. **change of life** the time of a woman's life at which menstruation is about to cease, the menopause. **change of state** (*phys*) any change in the state of matter, eg from solid to liquid, liquid to gas, etc. **change oneself** (now only *Scot*) to change one's clothes. **change one's mind** to form a different opinion. **change one's tune** to change one's attitudes or opinions; to change one's manner of speaking. **change over** to change from one system, position, or attitude to another; to exchange or transfer. **change up** (*motoring*) to change to a higher gear. **get no change out of** (*inf*) to be unsuccessful in attempts to obtain concessions, information, co-operation, etc from (a person or organization). **put the change on** (*old* and *dialect*) to delude or trick. **ring the changes** to go through all the possible permutations in ringing a peal of bells (**change'-ringing** *n*); to perform a repeated action or actions in varying ways, order, etc. **small change** (*collectively*) coins of low value; a petty thing (*inf*). **the change** same as **change of life** above.

chank /*changk*/ or **chank-shell** /*changk'shel*/ *n* the shell of several species of *Turbinella*, gastropod molluscs of the East Indian seas, sliced into bangles and worn by Hindu women. [Hindi *chankh*; cf **conch**]

channel[1] /*chan'əl*/ *n* the bed of a stream of water; a strait or narrow sea; a navigable passage through a body of water; a passage for conveying a liquid; a groove or furrow; a gutter; means of passing or conveying; a spiritual medium (also **chann'el(l)er**); gravel, shingle (also **chann'er**; *Scot*); (in *pl*) means of communication; a one-way path for a signal; a physical path for data, eg between a central processing unit and a peripheral device (*comput*); a narrow range of frequencies, part of a frequency band, for the transmission of radio and television signals without interference from other channels; a television or radio organization broadcasting on a particular frequency. ◆ *vt* (**chann'elling**; **chann'elled**) to make a channel; to furrow; to convey (through); to direct (into a particular course; *lit* and *fig*); to act as a spiritual medium for. [OFr *chanel*, *canel*, from L *canālis* a canal]

■ **chann'elize** or **-ise** *vt* to create or provide a channel for; to direct or convey through a channel. **chann'elled** *adj*. **chann'el(l)er** *n*.
❑ **channel'-hop** *vi* (*inf*) to cross the English Channel, *usu* for shopping, and return on the same day; same as **channel-surf** below. **chann'el-hopper** *n*. **chann'el-hopping** *n*. **channel seam** *n* a seam on clothing outlined by stitching running along both sides. **channel seaming** *n*. **channel stone** or **channel stane** *n* (*Scot*) a curling-stone. **chann'el-surf** *vi* (*inf*) to switch rapidly between different television channels in a forlorn attempt to find anything of interest. **chann'el-surfer** *n*. **chann'el-surfing** *n*.
■ **channel of distribution** (*marketing*) the means by which a product reaches the consumer from the producer, eg through wholesalers, retailers, etc (also **distribution channel**). **the Channel** the English Channel.

channel[2] /*chan'l*/ (*naut*) *n* a flat piece of wood or iron projecting horizontally from a ship's side to spread the various shrouds (*fore*, *main*, and *mizzen* channels) and keep them clear of the bulwarks. [For *chain-wale*]

chanoyu /*chä'no-ū*/ *n* a Japanese tea ceremony. [Jap, hot water for tea]

chanson /*shä'sɔ̃*/ *n* a song. [Fr]
■ **chansonette** /*-son-et'*/ *n* a little song, a ditty. **chansonnier** /*-son'ē-ā*/ *n* a collection of songs, *esp* old French ones; a cabaret performer of, *esp* satirical, songs.
❑ **chanson de geste** /*də zhest*/ *n* an old French epic poem, *usu* celebrating the exploits of knights.

chant or (*rare*) **chaunt** /*chänt*/ *vt* to recite in a singing manner; to intone repetitiously or rhythmically; to sing; to celebrate in song. ◆ *n* song; melody; a kind of church music, in which prose is sung; a slogan spoken or sung in a repetitious or rhythmic manner. [Fr *chanter*, from L *cantāre*, from *canere* to sing]
■ **chant'er**, **chaunt'er** or **chant'or** *n* a singer; a precentor; (in bagpipes) the pipe with fingerholes, on which the melody is played. **chant'ress** or **chaunt'ress** *n*. **chant'ry** or **chaunt'ry** *n* an endowment, or chapel, for the chanting of masses. **chanty** *n* see **shanty**[2].

chantage /*shä-täzh'*/ *n* blackmail, *esp* the extortion of money so as not to make scandalous facts public. [Fr]

chanterelle[1] /*shan-* or *shä-tə-rel'*/ *n* the treble string of a musical instrument, such as a violin or lute. [Fr, from L *cantāre* to sing]

chanterelle[2] or **chantarelle** /*chan-tə-rel'*/ *n* a yellowish edible fungus (*Cantharellus cibarius*). [Fr, dimin from Gr *kantharos* cup]

chanteuse /*shan'tooz* or *-tooz*, also *shä-tøz*/ *n* a female nightclub singer. [Fr]

chantey see **shanty**[2].

chanticleer /*chan'ti-klēr* or *-klēr'*/ *n* a cock. [From the name of the cock in the old fable of *Reynard the Fox*, from OFr *chanter* to sing, and *cler* clear]

chantie see **shanty**[2].

Chantilly /*shan-ti'li* or *shä-tē-yē'*/ *n* a silk or linen ornamental lace, black or white, having a delicate floral or scrolled pattern (also **Chantilly lace**). ◆ *adj* (of cream) sweetened and whipped, and *usu* flavoured with vanilla; prepared or served with such cream. [From *Chantilly*, France, where the lace was first made]

chantor, **chantress**, **chantry** see under **chant**.

chanty[1] see **shanty**[2].

chanty[2] /*chan'ti*/ (*Scot sl*) *n* a chamberpot. [Origin unknown]

Chanukah or **Chanukkah** see **Hanukkah**.

chaos /*kā'os*/ *n* the state of matter before the universe was reduced to order; disorder; shapeless mass. [Gr]
■ **chaol'ogist** *n*. **chaol'ogy** *n* the study of chaos or of chaos theory. **chaot'ic** *adj* confused. **chaot'ically** *adv*.
❑ **chaos theory** *n* the theory that apparently random phenomena observed in various branches of science result from complex dynamic underlying principles.

chap[1] /*chap*/ *vi* to crack; to strike, of a clock, etc, or to knock at a door (*Scot*). ◆ *vt* to cause to crack or divide. ◆ *n* a crack; an open crack or split in the skin, caused by exposure to cold; a knock (*Scot*). [ME *chappen*; cognate with Du and Ger *kappen*]
■ **chap'less** *adj*. **chapped** *adj* cracked, of a heavy soil in dry weather, or of the skin in cold weather; cut short. **chapp'y** *adj*.
❑ **chap'stick** *n* a small stick of a substance for soothing chapped lips.

chap[2] /*chap*/ (*inf*) *n* a man or boy, a fellow. [OE *cēap* trade, *cēapman* trader; cf **cheap**, Ger *kaufen*, *Kaufmann*]
■ **chap'ess** or **chapp'ess** *n* (*facetious*) a woman or girl. **chapp'ie** *n* a familiar *dimin* of **chap**.
❑ **chap'book** *n* a book or pamphlet of popular stories, etc, such as was formerly hawked by chapmen or pedlars. **chap'man** *n* a person who buys or sells (*archaic*); an itinerant dealer; a pedlar.

chap[3] /*chap*/ *n* a chop or jaw; a cheek. [Cf **chop**[3]; from N Eng and Scot *chaft*, ON *kjaptr* jaw]
■ **chap'fallen** *adj* same as **chopfallen** (see under **chop**[3]). **chap'less** *adj* without a lower jaw.

chap. *abbrev* : chaplain; chapter.

chaparajos /*sha-pə-rä'ōs* or *chä-pä-rä'hhos*/ or **chaparejos** /*-rä'* or *-rē'*/ *n pl* cowboy's leather riding leggings (short form **chaps** or **shaps**). [Mex Sp]

chaparral /*sha-pə-ral'* or *chä-pä-räl'*/ *n* a thicket of dense tangled brushwood. [Sp, from *chaparro* dwarf evergreen oak, one of the plants growing there]
❑ **chaparral cock** *n* the roadrunner.

chapati or **chapatti** /*chə-pä'ti*/ (*Ind cookery*) *n* (*pl* **chapat(t)'i**, **chapat(t)'is** or **chapat(t)'ies**) a thin flat piece of unleavened bread. [Hindustani]

chapbook see under **chap**[2].

chape /*chāp*/ *n* the plate of metal at the point of a scabbard; the catch or hook by which the sheath of a weapon was attached to the belt; the metal spike of a buckle. [Fr, from LL *capa* a cap]
■ **chape'less** *adj*.

chapeau /*shä-põ'*/ *n* (*pl* **chapeaux**) a hat. [Fr]
❑ **chapeau-bras** /*-brä*/ *n* (*pl* **chapeaux-bras**) (*hist*) a compressible three-cornered hat designed to be carried under the arm.

chapel /*chap'əl*/ *n* a place of Christian worship inferior or subordinate to a regular church, or attached to a house or institution; an oratory in a mausoleum, etc; a cell of a church containing its own altar; a dissenters' place of worship, as of Nonconformists in England, Roman Catholics or Episcopalians in Scotland, etc; a chapel service; a body of musicians, such as a choir, an orchestra, or both, whether connected with a chapel or not; a newspaper or printing office, or an association or trade union of printing workers or journalists. ◆ *adj* Nonconformist. [OFr *capele*, from LL *cappella*, dimin of *cappa* a cloak or cope; orig from the cloak of St Martin]
■ **chap'elry** *n* the jurisdiction of a chapel.
❑ **chapel cart** see under **cart**. **chapel master** *n* (Ger *Kapellmeister*) a director of music. **chapel royal** *n* the oratory of a royal palace.

■ **chapel of ease** a chapel for worshippers living at some distance from the parish church. **father** or **mother of the chapel** the president of a printing office or chairperson of a printers' or journalists' association or trade union branch. **lady chapel** see under **lady**. **proprietary chapel** a chapel that is private property.

chapelle ardente /sha-pel är-dät'/ (Fr) n a chapel or chamber in which a corpse lies in state before burial, surrounded by lighted candles.

chaperon or **chaperone** /shap'ə-rōn/ n formerly, a kind of hood or cap; a person (esp an older woman) who accompanies a girl or young woman to social events for protection, restraint, or appearance's sake; someone who supervises a group of children or young people, eg on school outings, etc. ◆ vt to attend in such a capacity. [Fr, a large hood, from chape a hooded cloak, from LL cappa; see **cape**[1]]
■ **chap'eronage** n.

chapess see under **chap**[2].

chapiter /chap'i-tər/ (archit) n the head or capital of a column. [Fr chapitre, from L capitulum, dimin of caput the head]

chapka or **czapka** /chap'kə/ n a military cap of a shape adapted from the traditional Polish peasant cap, worn by lancer regiments (also **schapska** /shaps'kə/). [Pol czapka a cap]

chaplain /chap'lin/ n a Christian clergyman attached to an institution, establishment, organization or family. [OFr chapelain, from LL cappellānus, from cappella; see **chapel**]
■ **chap'laincy**, **chap'lainry** or **chap'lainship** n.

chaplet /chap'lit/ n a garland or wreath for the head; a circlet of gold, etc; a string of beads used in counting prayers, one-third of a rosary in length; the prayers counted on this string; anything forming a string or in the shape of a string of beads; a metal support of a cylindrical pipe. [OFr chapelet, from chape a headdress]
■ **chap'leted** adj.

Chaplinesque /chap-lin-esk'/ adj of or similar to the style of comedy of Charles Chaplin (1889–1977), a combination of anarchic humour and endearing pathos.

chapman see under **chap**[2].

chappal /chupəl or chapəl/ n a type of open sandal worn in India, having a single strap of leather attached to the sole between the first and second toes. [Hindi]

chappess, **chappie** see under **chap**[2].

chaprassi, **chaprassy** or **chuprassy** /chu-prä'si/ n an office messenger; a household attendant; an orderly. [Hindi chaprāsi badge-wearer, messenger, from chaprās a badge]

CHAPS or **Chaps** /chaps/ (banking) abbrev : clearing house automated payment system.

chaps /chaps or shaps/ n chaparajos. [Short form]

chapstick see under **chap**[1].

chaptalize or **-ise** /chap'tə-līz/ vt to add extra sugar to wine during its fermentation to increase its alcohol content, usu a prohibited or closely controlled practice. [JA Chaptal (1756–1832), French chemist]
■ **chaptalīzā'tion** or **-s-** n.

chapter /chap'tər/ n a main division of a book, or of any written work; a subject or category generally; a period in history, of a person's life, etc; a numbered division of the Acts of Parliament of a session; an assembly of the canons of a cathedral or collegiate church, or the members of a religious or military order (from the custom of reading a chapter of the rule or of the Bible); the members of any of these collectively; an organized branch of a society, club or fraternity; a Roman numeral on a clock or watch face; a chapiter (Spenser). ◆ vt to put or divide into chapters; to take to task. [OFr chapitre, from L capitulum, dimin of caput the head]
❑ **chapter eleven** n the chapter of the US Federal Bankruptcy Act that sets out conditions under which a company may declare a temporary state of bankruptcy (**chapter-elev'en bankruptcy**) with the intention of continuing as a going concern after it has been reorganized and its creditors have been paid. **chap'terhouse** n a building used for meetings of the chapter of a cathedral or church; the meeting place of a society or college fraternity (esp US).
■ **chapter and verse** exact reference to, or a complete specification of, the source or sources of one's information. **chapter of accidents** see under **accident**. **to the end of the chapter** throughout.

chaptrel /chap'trəl/ (archit) n the capital of a pillar which supports an arch. [Dimin of **chapiter**]

char[1] /chär/ vt (**charr'ing**; **charred**) to reduce (wood) to carbon. ◆ vt and vi to scorch. ◆ n a substance, eg charcoal, resulting from charring. [Origin obscure]
■ **charr'y** adj relating to charcoal.
❑ **char'broil** or **char'grill** vt to grill over charcoal. **char'broiled** or **char'grilled** adj.

char[2] /chär/ or **chare** /chār/ n an occasional piece of work, an odd job; (in pl) household work; a charwoman. ◆ vi (**charr'ing** or **chär'ing**; **charred** or **chāred**) to do odd jobs of work; to do house-cleaning. ◆ vt (Walter Scott) to do, accomplish. [OE cerran, cierran to turn; see also **jar**[3], **ajar**[1]]
❑ **char'woman** or **char'lady** n a woman employed to do rough cleaning.

char[3] /chär/ (sl) n tea. [Cockney spelling of **cha**]

char[4] or **charr** /chär/ n any fish of the genus Salvelinus, of the salmon family, found in mountain lakes and rivers. [Prob Celtic; cf Gaelic ceara red, blood-coloured]

char[5] /chär/ n (on the Indian subcontinent) a newly-formed island created by the deposition of silt in the channel of a large river, eg the Ganges.

chara[1] /kā'rə/ n any plant of the genus Chara, freshwater algae of a family and class, including the stoneworts, **Chärä'ceae** and **Charoph'yta**, having stems encrusted with calcareous matter and whorled branches. [L, some plant]

chara[2] /shar'ə/ n a charabanc. [Short form]

charabanc or **char-à-banc** /shar'ə-bang or -bä/ n formerly, a long open vehicle with rows of transverse seats; more recently, a tourist coach. [Fr char à bancs carriage with benches]

characid /ka-ras'id/ or **characin** /kar'ə-sin/ n any carnivorous freshwater fish of the family **Charac'idae**, usu small and brightly-coloured, including the piranha. [Gr charax a fish of some kind]
■ **char'acin** adj. **chara'cinoid** adj.

character /kar'ək-tər (Spenser, Shakesp, etc -ak')/ n the aggregate of peculiar qualities which constitutes personal or national individuality; moral qualities collectively; the reputation of possessing these; any essential or distinguishing feature; a quality; nature; personal appearance (obs); a letter, sign, figure, stamp or distinctive mark; a mark of any kind, a symbol in writing, etc; writing generally, handwriting; a secret cipher (obs); one of a set of symbols, eg letters of the alphabet, numbers, punctuation marks, that can be arranged in groups to represent data for processing (comput); the variant or abnormality in structure, appearance or function in any organism that is attributed to the presence of a specific gene or set of genes (genetics); a formal statement of the qualities of a person who has been in one's service or employment, a testimonial; position, rank or status, or a person who has filled it; a person, esp one noted for eccentricity or distinctive personality; a personality as created in a play or novel (Shakesp **char'act**) or appearing in history; a literary genre, consisting in a description in prose or verse of a human type, or of a place or object on that model, a dominant form of literature in the 17c under the influence of Theophrastus and the theory of humours; a person (sl). ◆ vt (archaic) to engrave, imprint or write; to represent, delineate or describe. [Fr caractère, from L charactēr, from Gr charaktēr, from charassein to cut, engrave]
■ **char'acterful** adj. **char'acterism** n a characteristic; a characterization. **characteris'tic** n that which marks or constitutes the character; the integral part of a logarithm (maths). **characteris'tic** or **characteris'tical** adj. **characteris'tically** adv. **characterīzā'tion** or **-s-** n. **char'acterize** or **-ise** vt to describe by distinctive qualities; to be a distinguishing mark or quality of. **char'acterless** adj without character or distinctive qualities. **char'acterlessness** n. **characterol'ogist** n. **characterol'ogy** n the science or study of the variety and development of character. **char'actery** (also (Shakesp) /-ak'/) n (archaic) writing; a system of symbols or letters used to express thoughts; the symbols so used.
❑ **character actor** n an actor who plays character parts. **character assassination** n the destruction of a person's reputation by slander, rumour, etc. **character code** n (comput) the particular binary code used to represent a character. **characteristic curve** n (image technol) a graph used to plot the relationship of the density of a photographic material and the logarithm of the exposure producing this density. **characteristic function** n (maths) of a set, a function that assigns the value 1 to all points in the set, but zero to those outside. **characteristic radiation** n (phys) the wavelength of radiation that characterizes the atom of a particular substance. **characteristic spectrum** n (phys) the ordered arrangement of the frequencies of radiation characteristic of the material giving rise to it. **characteristic X-rays** see under **X**. **character part** n a stage or film role portraying an unusual or eccentric personality type. **character recognition** n (comput) a process used to recognize individual printed or written characters. **character sketch** n a short description of the main traits in a person's character. **character witness** n a person who makes a statement or gives evidence providing details of eg an accused person's character and past behaviour to a court of law.
■ **in character** in harmony with the part assumed, appropriate; in keeping with the person's usual conduct or attitudes; dressed for the part. **out of character** not in character, unlike that which one would expect from the person concerned.

---

charade /shə-räd'/ or (N Am) usu -räd'/ n a type of riddle, the subject of which is a word proposed for solution from an enigmatical description of its component syllables and of the whole; an acted riddle in which the syllables and the whole are uttered or represented in successive scenes; a piece of ridiculous pretence or absurd behaviour. [Fr, perh from Provençal charrada chatter, or Sp charrada clownishness]

Charadrius /ka-rad'ri-əs/ n the plover genus, giving name to the family **Charad'riidae**. [Gr charadrios a bird, prob the thick knee]

charango /chə-rang'gō/ n (pl **charan'gos**) a small S American stringed instrument, with a soundbox made from an armadillo shell, that produces a sound similar to a mandolin.

charas /chä'rəs/ or **churrus** /chur'əs/ n the resinous exudation of hashish, a narcotic and intoxicant. [Hindustani]

charcoal /chär'kōl/ n charred wood, or fuel made by charring wood; the carbonaceous residue of wood or animal matter that has undergone combustion with exclusion of air; a stick of charcoal used for drawing; a drawing made in charcoal. ◆ adj and n (also **charcoal grey**) (of) a dark grey colour. ◆ vt to draw with or blacken with charcoal. [**char¹** and **coal**]
❑ **charcoal burner** n a person whose job is to burn wood to produce charcoal.

charcuterie /shär-kü-t(ə-)rē'/ n a pork butcher's shop or wares; a delicatessen, or the meats sold in it. [Fr]

chard /chärd/ n the edible leafstalk of a variety of white beet, Beta vulgaris cicla (also called **Swiss chard** or **leaf beet**). [L carduus thistle]

chardonnay /shär-do-nā'/ n a type of grape, orig from the Burgundy region of France but now grown in all the major wine-growing regions of the world, used in making dry white wine; the wine made from this grape. [Fr]

chare see char².

Charentais /sha-rä-tā'/ n a type of small, round greenish-yellow melon with sweetly-scented orange flesh. [Fr, from Charente, a department of France]

charet /char'et/ (Spenser) n same as **chariot**.

charge /chärj/ vt to exact or demand from, to ask as the price; to set down as a liability or debt against; to accuse; to deliver an official injunction, exhortation or exposition to; to advance in accusation (that); to give a task to, to order or command; to load, to put something into, to fill; to load heavily, to burden; to fill completely; to cause to accumulate electricity; to place a bearing upon (with with; heraldry); to attack at a rush. ◆ vi to make an attack; to accumulate electricity. ◆ n cost or price; a financial liability, a debt; an accusation (law); an attack or onset; care or custody; the person or thing in one's care or custody; a command; an order; that which is laid on; a load or burden; the load of powder, fuel, etc, for a gun, furnace, etc; an accumulation of electricity; a device borne on a shield (heraldry); a thrill, an agreeable sensation (esp drug sl); (in pl) expenses. [Fr charger, from LL carricāre to load, from L carrus a wagon; see **car**, **cargo**]
■ **charge'able** adj liable to be charged; open to accusation; blamable; burdensome (Bible). **charge'ableness** n. **charge'ably** adv. **charged** adj (phys) (of a capacitor, battery, conductor, etc) holding, storing or receiving electrical charge or energy. **charge'ful** adj (archaic) burdensome or expensive. **charge'less** adj. **char'ger** n a flat dish capable of holding a large joint of meat, a platter; a warhorse; a battery charger.
❑ **charge account** n an account in which goods obtained are entered to be paid for later. **charge'back** n a process by which the cost of a credit- or debit-card transaction is borne by the retailer rather than the cardholder, eg because it has sanctioned a fraudulent payment. **charge'-cap** vt. **charge'-capping** n the imposition, by central government, of an upper limit on the amount that may be levied by local government in respect of community charges on individuals. **charge card** n a card issued by a store, shop, etc which authorizes a customer to obtain goods on credit. **charge carrier** n the electron, hole, or ion that carries the charge in an electric current. **charge'-coupled device** n (comput) a semiconductor device which relies on the short-term storage of minority carriers in spatially defined depletion zones on its surface and where the stored charges can be moved over the surface by the application of control voltages. **charge density** n the electric charge per unit volume of a field or body, or per unit area of a surface. **charge(-discharge) machine** n (nuclear eng) a device for inserting or removing fuel without escape of radiation and often without reactor shutdown (also called **(re)fuelling machine**). **charge'-hand** or **charge'-man** n the leader of a group of workmen, but lower in rank than foreman. **charge'-house** n (Shakesp) a school. **charge nurse** n a nurse in charge of a ward in a hospital. **charge'sheet** n a police document listing details of an accused person and the charges against him or her.

■ **bring a charge** (law) to accuse (with against). **charge down** (rugby) to run towards (a kicked ball) and block it. **give in charge** to hand over to the police. **in charge** in control or authority, responsible (often with of). **lay to someone's charge** to accuse someone. **press** (or **prefer**) **charges** to make an official accusation of a crime. **take charge of** to assume the care or control of.

chargé-d'affaires /shär-zhä-da-fer'/ n (pl **chargés-d'affaires** /shär'zhä-/) a diplomatic agent of lesser rank, accredited to the department for foreign affairs and holding his or her credentials from the minister; the person in charge of a diplomatic mission in the absence of the ambassador (short form **chargé**). [Fr]

charily, chariness see under **chary**.

chariot /char'i-ət/ n a horse-drawn, two-wheeled vehicle used in ancient warfare or racing; a light four-wheeled carriage with back seats and box; any ceremonial vehicle or carriage. ◆ vt (archaic) to carry in a chariot. ◆ vi (archaic) to ride in a chariot. [Fr, dimin of char a car]
■ **charioteer'** n someone who drives a chariot. ◆ vt and vi (archaic) to drive or to ride in a chariot or similar vehicle.

Charis /kar'is, Gr hhä'ris/ n any one of the three **Charites** /-tēz, Gr -tes'/ the Graces (Aglaia, Euphrosyne and Thalia), Greek goddesses of all that imparts graciousness to life.

charisma /kə-riz'mə/ or **charism** /kar'i-zm/ n a personal quality or gift that enables an individual to impress and influence others; a similar quality felt to reside in an office or position; a spiritual power given by God. [Gr charis, -itos grace]
■ **charismat'ic** adj of, relating to, or having charisma or charism.
❑ **charismatic movement** n a non-denominational religious movement based on a belief in the divinely-inspired gifts of speaking in tongues, healing, prophecy, etc.

charity /char'i-ti/ n the disposition to think favourably of others, and do them good; the donation of goods, money, etc to those in need; alms or almsgiving; a usu non-profit-making foundation, institution or cause, caring for those in need of help, etc; universal love (Bible); (in pl; archaic) affections. [Fr charité, from L cāritās, -ātis, from cārus dear]
■ **char'itable** adj of or relating to, showing, inspired by charity; (of an institution, etc) having the status of, being in the nature of, a charity. **char'itableness** n. **char'itably** adv.
❑ **char'ity-boy** or **char'ity-girl** n a pupil in a **char'ity-school**, a school for the poor supported by endowments or gifts. **Charity Commission** n an organization that regulates charitable trusts in England and Wales. **charity shop** n a shop selling second-hand goods to raise money for charity.
■ **charity begins at home** help, support, etc should first be given to one's own family, countrymen, etc before others, usu an excuse for not helping others. **cold as charity** see under **cold**.

charivari /shä-ri-vär'i/ n a cacophonous mock serenade, orig to newly-weds, using kettles, pans, lids, etc; a cacophony of sound, din. —Also (N Am) **shivar'ee** or **chivar'ee** (also /shiv'/). [Fr, from LL caribaria a headache]

chark /chärk/ vt to burn (wood, etc) to charcoal. ◆ n charcoal, coke. [**charcoal**]

charka or **charkha** /chär'- or chûr'kə/ n a spinning wheel used in Indian households for spinning cotton. [Hindi]

charlady see under **char²**.

charlatan /shär'lə-tən/ n someone who pretends to have special knowledge or ability, esp one who claims to have medical knowledge; a quack; a fraud. [Fr, from Ital ciarlatano, from ciarlare to chatter; imit]
■ **charlatanic** /-tan'ik/ or **charlatan'ical** adj. **char'latanism** n. **char'latanry** n.

Charles's law /chärl'ziz lö/ (phys) n the principle (only approximately true) that all gases have the same coefficient of expansion at constant pressure (also called **Gay-Lussac's law**). [JAC Charles (1746–1823), French chemist who originated it]

Charles's Wain /chärl'ziz wān/ (old) n the seven bright stars that make up the Plough (Ursa Major). [OE Carles wægn, Carl being Charlemagne]

charleston /chärl'stən/ n a lively dance, popular esp in the 1920s, characterized by spasmodic kicking with the knees turned inwards. ◆ vi to dance the charleston. [Charleston in South Carolina]

Charlie¹ or **Charley** /chär'li/ (also without cap) n a credulous person; an inefficient, ineffectual person, a fool, often in the phrase a proper Charlie; (a member of) the Vietcong (US milit sl); a night-watchman (obs); the small triangular beard familiar in the portraits of Charles I; a small moustache, resembling that worn by Charlie Chaplin; a name for a fox. [From the name Charles]
❑ **charley horse** n (N Am sl) muscle strain as a result of strenuous exercise. **Char'ley-pitcher** n (sl) a thimblerigger.

Charlie[2] or **charlie** /chär'li/ n (in international radio communication) a code word for the letter c; cocaine (drug sl).

charlock /chär'lək/ n wild mustard (Sinapis arvensis), a common yellow-flowered cornfield weed. [OE cerlic]

charlotte /shär'lət/ n a kind of deep tart containing fruit and covered with sponge or bread. [From the name Charlotte]
□ **charlotte russe** /rüs/ n a dessert of custard or cream enclosed in a kind of sponge-cake.

charm[1] /chärm/ n power of fascination; attractiveness; (in pl) personal attractions; that which can please irresistibly; a spell; something thought to possess occult power, esp that brings good luck, such as an amulet, a metrical form of words, etc; a talisman, amulet, etc; a trinket, esp one worn on a bracelet; in particle physics, (the quantum number used to account for) the unusual properties and behaviour of certain elementary particles. ◆ vt to influence by a charm; to subdue by secret influence; to enchant; to delight; to allure. [Fr charme, from L carmen a song]
■ **charmed** adj bewitched; delighted; protected as by a special or magic charm; (in particle physics) having charm. **charm'er** n. **charm'ful** adj abounding in charms. **charm'ing** adj highly pleasing; delightful; fascinating. **charm'ingly** adv. **charm'less** adj devoid of charm. **charm'lessly** adv.
□ **charm school** n a fee-paying academy where young women are taught social graces.
■ **charm offensive** a method of trying to get what one wants by overwhelming with reasonableness, attractive offers, etc. **like a charm** having the desired result as if influenced by a magic spell, perfectly.

charm[2] same as **chirm**.

charmeuse /shär'mooz/ or -mûrz/ or (Fr) shar-møz/ n a soft satin material made orig of silk, but now also of synthetic fibres. [Orig a tradename]

charneco /chär'ni-kō/ (Shakesp) n (pl char'necos) a kind of sweet wine. [Prob from a village near Lisbon]

charnel /chär'nəl/ n a burial-place (obs); a charnel house. ◆ adj sepulchral; deathlike. [OFr charnel, from LL carnāle, from L carnālis, from carō, carnis flesh]
□ **charnel house** n a place where bodies or bones are deposited (also fig).

Charolais or **Charollais** /shar'ō-lā/ n a breed of beef cattle and, more recently, of sheep named after an old district of France (Charolais) of which Charolles was the capital.

Charon /kā'rən/ n the ferryman who rowed the spirits of the dead across the river Styx and Acheron in the lower world (Gr myth); a satellite of Pluto (astron). [Gr Charōn]

charoset, charoseth see **haroset, haroseth**.

charpie /shär'pē or -pē'/ n lint shredded down to form a soft material for dressing wounds. [OFr charpir, from L carpere to pluck]

charpoy /chär'poi/ n a lightweight Indian bedstead or cot, made up of webbing stretched on a four-legged frame. [Hindustani chārpāī, from Pers chahār-pāī four feet]

charqui /chär'kē/ n beef cut into long strips and dried in the sun, jerked beef. [Quechua]

charr same as **char**[4].

charreada /char-i-ä'də/ n a Mexican entertainment involving competitive riding and herding events. [Mex Sp]

chart /chärt/ n a marine or hydrographical map, showing part of a sea or other water, with the islands, contiguous coasts, soundings, currents, etc; an outline map, diagram, or a tabular statement giving information of any kind; (usu in pl) the lists of the ten, twenty, etc most popular records, ie those which have sold the most copies, each week. ◆ vt to map; to make a chart. ◆ vi (of a popular recording) to enter the pop charts. [OFr charte, from L c(h)arta a paper, from Gr chartēs]
■ **chart'ism** n. **chart'ist** n a person who makes and/or studies charts of past performances, esp of stocks and shares, with a view to forecasting future trends. **chart'less** adj not mapped, uncharted.
□ **chart'-buster** n. **chart'-busting** adj (inf) esp of recording artists or their music, very successful. **chart'house** or **chart'-room** n the room in a ship where charts are kept.
■ **off the charts** (inf) at or to a previously unknown level.

charta or **carta** /kär'tə/ n a charter. [L c(h)arta, from Gr chartēs a sheet of paper]
■ **chartā'ceous** adj papery.

charter /chär'tər/ n any formal writing in evidence of a grant, contract, or other transactions, conferring or confirming titles, rights or privileges; the formal deed by which a sovereign guarantees the rights and privileges of his or her subjects; a document creating a borough or other corporation; any instrument by which powers and privileges are conferred by the state on a body of persons for a special object; a set of principles that form the constitution of an organization; (an agreement or contract for) the let or hire of eg a ship or aircraft; a patent; a grant; an allowance. ◆ vt to establish by charter; to let or hire (eg a ship or aircraft) on contract. ◆ adj hired (as in charter plane); made in a hired aircraft (as in charter flight). [OFr chartre, from L cartula, c(h)arta, from Gr chartēs a sheet of paper]
■ **chart'ered** adj granted or protected by a charter; privileged; licensed; hired by contract. **chart'erer** n.
□ **chart'er-chest** n a box in which charters are preserved. **chartered accountant**, **engineer** or **surveyor**, etc n a person qualified under the regulations of the relevant institute or professional body which has a royal charter. **chartered company** n a trading company acting under a charter from the crown. **chart'er-hand'** n court hand. **Charter Mark** n in the UK, an award bestowed on organizations that achieve a high standard of service under the Citizen's Charter. **charter mayor** n the mayor of a borough at the time of its charter. **charter member** n an original member of an incorporation. **chart'erparty** n see separate entry.

Charterhouse /chär'tər-hows/ n a Carthusian monastery; the famous hospital and school instituted in London in 1611, on the site of a Carthusian monastery. [See **Carthusian**]

charterparty /chär'tər-pär-ti/ n (also **charter party**) the common written form in which a contract of affreightment is expressed, as in the hiring of the whole or part of a ship for the conveyance of goods; an individual or group chartering a ship or aircraft. [Fr charte partie, literally, a divided charter, as the practice was to divide it in two and give a half to each person, from L c(h)arta partīta ; see **charta**]

Chartism /chär'ti-zm/ n (the programme and principles of) a 19c reform movement in Great Britain that campaigned for the extension of political power to the working classes, whose aims as included in the People's Charter (1838) have since been achieved, except annual parliaments. [See **charter**]
■ **Chart'ist** n and adj.

chartism, chartist see under **chart**.

chartography /kär-tog'rə-fi/ same as **cartography**.

Chartreuse /shär-trœz'/ n a Carthusian monastery, esp the original one, La Grande Chartreuse near Grenoble in France; (sometimes without cap) a green or yellow liqueur, manufactured there by the monks from aromatic herbs, flowers and brandy; (without cap) a greenish-yellow colour. ◆ adj of this colour. [See **Carthusian**]

chartulary /kär'tū-lə-ri/ same as **cartulary**.

charwoman see under **char**[2].

chary /chā'ri/ adj cautious; wary (of doing, saying, giving, etc); careful (of) (archaic); fastidious, shy; precious (obs). [OE cearig, from cearu care]
■ **char'ily** adv. **char'iness** n.

Charybdis /kə-rib'dis/ (Gr myth) n a dangerous monster that dwelt under a fig tree on a rock opposite to Scylla (qv), and three times a day swallowed and threw up the waters of the sea, later identified with a current or a whirlpool on the Sicilian side of the Straits of Messina.
■ **Charyb'dian** adj.

chase[1] /chās/ vt (also (obs) **chace**) to pursue; to hunt; to seek; to drive away; to put to flight; to follow with a chaser or chasse. ◆ vi (inf) to hurry (about, around or after). ◆ n pursuit; a hunting; (with the) the sport of hunting; the object of a hunt, quarry; an unenclosed private game preserve; a steeplechase; the second impact of an unreturned ball, for which the player scored unless his opponent bettered it (and scored) by a similar impact nearer the end wall (real tennis). [OFr chacier, chasser, from L captāre, frequentative of capere to take]
■ **chas'er** n a pursuer; a hunter; a horse for steeplechasing; a drink of a different, usu complementary or contrasting, type, drunk immediately after another (inf); a woman over-assiduous in pursuit of men (old sl); an aeroplane for pursuing hostile aircraft (RAF sl); a chasse.
□ **chase'port** n the porthole at the bow or stern of a naval ship (through which a gun is fired during pursuit).
■ **beasts of chase** (archaic) properly the buck, doe, fox, marten and roe; wild animals that are hunted generally. **chase rainbows** see **rainbow-chaser** under **rain**[1]. **chase the dragon** (drug sl) to inhale the fumes of melting powdered heroin. **give chase** to set off in pursuit. **go and chase yourself** (inf) go away, clear out. **wild-goose chase** a chase hither and thither; any foolish or profitless pursuit of the unattainable.

chase[2] /chās/ vt to enchase, to decorate (metal) by engraving. [Short for **enchase**]
■ **chas'er** n a person who engraves metal; a tool for engraving metal or for cutting threads on screws. **chās'ing** n the art of engraving on the outside of raised metalwork; the art of cutting the threads of screws.

chase³ /chās/ n a case or frame for holding printing type making up a page; a groove; the part of a gun barrel that encloses the bore. [Fr *châsse* a setting, from L *capsa* a chest; see **case¹**]

Chasid, Chasidic, etc see **Hasid**.

chasm /kaz'əm/ n a yawning or gaping hollow; a gap or opening; a void space. [Gr *chasma*, from *chainein* to gape; cf **chaos**]
■ **chas'med** adj. **chasmic** /kaz'mik/ or **chas'mal** adj. **chas'my** adj.

chasmogamy /kaz-mog'ə-mi/ (*bot*) n the condition of having flowers that open, allowing cross-pollination. Cf **cleistogamy**. [Gr *chasma* a gape, and *gameein* to marry]
■ **chasmogamic** /-mō-gam'ik/ adj.

chasse /shas/ n a dram or liqueur taken after coffee (also **chasse-café'**). [Fr *chasser* to chase]

chassé /shas'ā/ n a gliding step in dancing. ◆ vi to make such a step. ◆ vt (*sl*) to dismiss. [Fr]
□ **chassé-croisé** /-krwä'zā/ n (pl **chassés-croisés**) a dance movement in which partners change places by means of a chassé.

chassepot /shas'pō/ n a breech-loading rifle used by the French Army between 1866 and 1874. [From AA *Chassepot*, who invented it]

chasseur /shas-œr'/ n a hunter or huntsman; a member of a body of French light infantry or cavalry; a liveried attendant, *esp* in hotels. ◆ adj (*cookery*) of or cooked in a sauce containing mushrooms, shallots, white wine and herbs. [Fr, from *chasser* to hunt; see **chase¹**]

Chassid, Chassidic, etc see **Hasid**.

chassis /shas'ē or -i/ n (pl **chassis** /shas'ēz or -iz/) the structural framework of a motor car to which the movable working parts and body may be attached; the framework of a radio, television, etc; an aeroplane's landing-carriage; a casemate gun carriage; a wooden frame or sash for eg a window (*obs*); a woman's body (*joc sl*). [Fr *chassis* frame]

chaste /chāst/ adj sexually virtuous; modest; decent and pure in taste and style; restrained. [OFr *chaste*, from L *castus* pure]
■ **chaste'ly** adv. **chasten** /chās'n/ vt to free from faults by punishing; hence, to discipline or punish; to purify or refine; to restrain, subdue, moderate, or temper. **chās'tened** adj purified; modest; tempered. **chās'tener** n. **chaste'ness** n. **chās'tenment** n. **chastīs'able** adj. **chastise** /chas-tīz'/ vt to inflict *esp* physical punishment upon for the purpose of correction; to subdue to a state of order or obedience; to refine, purify, correct (*obs*); to moderate, restrain (*archaic*). **chastisement** /chas'tiz-mənt/ n. **chastis'er** n. **chastity** /chas'ti-ti/ n sexual purity; virginity or celibacy; refinement of style; moderation.
□ **chaste tree** n a small European and Asian tree (*Vitex agnus-castus*) with upright panicles of violet-blue, fragrant flowers. **chastity belt** n a device said to have been worn by eg wives of absent crusaders, to prevent their having sexual intercourse; a device made in modern times according to its supposed design.

chasuble /chaz' or chas'ū-bl/ n a sleeveless vestment worn over the alb by the priest while celebrating Mass. [Fr, from LL *casubula*, from L *casula*, dimin of L *casa* a hut]

chat¹ /chat/ vi (**chatt'ing; chatt'ed**) to talk easily or familiarly. ◆ vt (often with *up*) to talk to informally and often flirtatiously in order to gain something, eg to cajole or seduce. ◆ n familiar, informal talk. [From **chatter**]
■ **chatt'ily** adv. **chatt'iness** n. **chatt'y** adj given or inclined to chat; of the nature of chat.
□ **chat'bot** n a robot that is able to produce intelligent language. **chat'-line** or **chat'line** n a telephone service in which callers contact each other through a monitored central switchboard, to engage in informal conversation (also *adj*). **chat room** n a virtual space on the Internet where any number of people can exchange messages, often about a specific topic. **chat show** n (*inf*) a radio or television programme in which invited personalities talk informally with their host (also **talk show**).

chat² /chat/ n any small songbird of a subfamily (Turdinae) of thrushes, including the stonechat and the whinchat; any of various Australian wrens. [Imit]

chat³ /chat/ (*dialect*) n a small potato of poor quality.

chat⁴ /chat/ (*obs sl* and *Aust* and *NZ inf*) n a louse. [Orig cant *chat(t)s* lice]
■ **chatt'y** adj lousy, flea-infested; dirty (*Aust* and *NZ inf*).

château /shä'tō/ n (pl **chât'eaux** /-tōz/) a castle or large country house, *esp* in France; a vineyard estate around a castle, house, etc, *esp* in Bordeaux (common in names of wines associated with specific estates, eg *Château Lafite, Château Margaux*). [Fr *château* (OFr *chastel*), from L *castellum*, dimin of *castrum* a fort]
■ **châtelain** /shat'ə-lĩ/ n a castellan, lord of the manor. **chât'elaine** /-len/ n a female keeper or mistress of a castle or a large household; formerly, an ornamental bunch of short chains bearing keys, scissors, etc, attached to a waistbelt and worn by women; a similar thing in miniature attached to a watch chain.

□ **château bottled** adj of wine, bottled on the estate in which it has been produced.
■ **châteaux en Espagne** /shä-tō-zä-nes-päny'/ (Fr) castles in Spain, castles in the air (qv).

Chateaubriand /shä-tō-brē-ã'/ (also without *cap*) n a thick steak cut from grilled fillet of beef, *usu* served with fried potatoes and mushrooms. [François René, Vicomte de *Chateaubriand* (1768–1848), French author and statesman]

chaton /shä-tõ'/ n the setting or stone of a finger-ring. [Fr]

chatoyant /sha-twä-yã' or sha-toi'ənt/ adj (eg of gems, birds' plumage, etc) with a changing lustre, iridescent, shimmering. [Fr]
■ **chatoyance** /shat-wä-yãs or shat-oi'əns/ or **chatoy'ancy** n.

chatta /chä'tə/ n an umbrella. [Hindi]

chattel /chat'l/ n (*law*) any kind of property which is not freehold, distinguished further into **chattels-real** and **chattels-personal**, the latter being personal moveables (furniture, etc), the former including leasehold interests. [OFr *chatel*, from LL *captāle*, from L *capitāle*, etc, property, goods]
□ **chattel house** n (in the West Indies) a movable wooden house. **chattel mortgage** n (*N Am*) a mortgage on moveable personal property.
■ **goods and chattels** all personal moveable possessions.

chatter /chat'ər/ vi to talk idly or rapidly; (of some birds and animals) to utter a rapid succession of short notes or sounds; (of the teeth when one shivers) to make a series of rapid clicking sounds. ◆ n a noise like that made by a magpie, or by the teeth striking together; idle talk. [From the sound]
■ **chatt'erer** n someone who or something that chatters; an idle or rapid talker; a name applied to two families of birds, the waxwings and the cotingas. **chatt'ering** n. **chatt'ery** adj.
□ **chatt'erbox** n (*inf*) someone who talks or chatters incessantly. **chattering classes** n pl (*derog*) the section of society, *usu* the educated or well-informed, who are in the habit of discussing and commenting on social, economic, political, etc issues.

chatty¹ see under **chat¹**.

chatty² or **chatti** /chat'i/ (*Anglo-Ind*) n an earthenware water pot. [Hindi *chāṭī*, from Dravidian]

chatty³ see under **chat⁴**.

Chaucerian /chō-sē'ri-ən/ adj like or relating to the writings of Geoffrey Chaucer (c.1345–1400). ◆ n a student, imitator or follower of Chaucer.
■ **Chau'cerism** n anything characteristic of Chaucer.

chaudfroid /shō-frwä'/ n a jellied sauce, or a dish, eg of chicken, including it. [Fr, literally, hot-cold]

chaud-mellé /shōd-mel'ā/ (*esp Scots law; obs*) n (pl **chauds-mell'és**) a fight arising in the heat of passion; the killing of a person in such a fight. [OFr *chaude-mellee* hot fight; see **mêlée**]

chaufe or **chauff** /chōf/ (*Spenser*) forms of **chafe**.

chauffer or **chaufer** /chō'fər/ n a small portable furnace or stove. [See **chafer** under **chafe**]

chauffeur /shō'fər or -fær'/ n a person employed to drive a motor car. ◆ vi and vt to drive or act as a chauffeur (for). [Fr, stoker]
■ **chauffeuse** /-fœz'/ n a female chauffeur (also *facetious* vi and vt).

chaulmoogra or **chaulmugra** /chōl-moo'grə/ n a name for various Asian trees of the family Flacourtiaceae, yielding **chaulmoogra oil**, used, *esp* formerly, in the treatment of leprosy. [Bengali]

chaumer /chō'mər/ (*Scot*) n formerly, a room or building in which male farm workers slept. [**chamber**]

chaunce old form of **chance**.

chaunge old form of **change**.

chaunt, chaunter, chauntress, chauntry see **chant**.

chausses /shōs or shō'zis/ n pl medieval closely-fitting breeches, hose generally; the protective pieces for the legs in armour. [OFr *chauces*, from L *calcia* hose]
■ **chaussure** /-ür'/ n (*old*) a general name for boots and shoes, footgear.

Chautauqua /shə-tök'wə or chō-/ n a village and lake in USA where summer educational meetings were instituted in the late 19c; (also without *cap*) a *usu* outdoor meeting of this type, with lectures, etc.
■ **Chautauquan** /shə-tök'wən/ adj relating to a system of instruction for adults by home reading and study under guidance, evolved from the *Chautauqua* (New York State) Literary and Scientific Circle, organized in 1878.

chauvinism /shō'vi-ni-zm/ n an exaggerated or fanatical pride in one's country, with a corresponding contempt for foreign nations; fanatical or extravagant attachment to any group, place, cause, etc. [From Nicolas *Chauvin*, an ardent veteran of Napoleon's, who figures in Cogniard's *La Cocarde Tricolore*]

■ words derived from main entry word; □ compound words; ■ idioms and phrasal verbs

■ **chau'vin** n. **chau'vinist** n and adj. **chauvinist'ic** adj. **chauvinist'ically** adv.

■ **male chauvinist (pig)** see under **male¹**.

chav /chav/ (derog sl) n someone who appears to have access to money but not necessarily to taste. [Prob from Romany chavi child]

■ **chavette'** n a female chav. **chavv'y** adj.

chave see **ch**.

chavender /chav'ən-dər/ n another name for the chub. [Cf **cheven**]

chavutti thirumal /chə-voo'ti ti'rŭ-məl/ (also with caps) n in traditional Indian medicine, therapeutic deep massage, performed by the feet. [Malayalam]

chaw¹ /chö/ (Spenser) n a jaw. [See **jaw¹**]

chaw² /chö/ vt to chew (tobacco; also dialect). ◆ n a quantity for chewing (esp of tobacco). [By-form of **chew**]
□ **chaw'bacon** n (derog) a country person, an uncouth rustic.

■ **chawed up** (dialect or old US sl) destroyed; defeated; crushed; reprimanded.

chawdron /chö'drən/ (Shakesp) n the entrails of an animal. [OFr chaudun]

chay¹ an informal form of **chaise**.

chay² /chī or chā/, **chaya** /chī'ə/ or **shaya** /shī'ə/ n an Indian plant (genus Oldenlandia) of the madder family whose root (**chay'root**) yields a red dye. [Cf Tamil saya]

chayote /chä-yō'tē or chī-ō'tē/ n a tropical American cucurbitaceous climbing plant (Sechium edule); its edible fruit eaten as a vegetable. — Also **chō'chō** (pl **cho'chos**). [Sp, from Nahuatl chayotli]

chazan see **hazan**.

ChB abbrev : Chirurgiae Baccalaureus (L), Bachelor of Surgery.

CHD abbrev : coronary heart disease.

ChE abbrev : Chemical Engineer.

che /chə/ (Shakesp) pronoun a SW English dialect form of I. [OE ic; cf **ch**]

cheap /chēp/ adj low in price or cost; charging low prices; of a low price in relation to the real or market value; easily obtained; obtained or gained using unworthy, low or contemptible means; of little value, or considered to be so; paltry; inferior; having low moral standards; vulgar. ◆ adv at a low price; in a vulgar manner. ◆ n (obs) bargain, buyer's advantage. [OE cēap price, a bargain, and ceapian to buy; ON kaupa, Ger kaufen to buy]

■ **cheap'en** vt to make cheap, to lower the price of; to lower the reputation of; to make vulgar or tawdry; to beat down the price of, to bargain; to ask the price of (archaic). **cheap'ener** n. **cheap'ie** or **cheap'y** n (inf) something which is low in price or cost (also adj). **cheap'ish** adj. **cheap'ly** adv. **cheap'ness** n. **cheap'o** adj (inf; usu derog) cheap, esp with connotations of inferiority or tawdriness (also n).

□ **cheap'-jack** (orig **cheap Jack** or **John**) n a travelling hawker who professes to give great bargains. ◆ adj inferior, of bad quality, worthless. **cheap labour** n labour paid at a poor rate. **cheap shot** n (inf) a blow administered to a person who is not in a position to defend against it; an unkind remark or action directed at a weak or disadvantaged person. **cheap'skate** n (inf) a miserly person.

■ **cheap and cheerful** inexpensive but practical or attractive. **cheap and nasty** offensively inferior and of low value. **cheap of** (Scot) having got off lightly with; served right. **dirt cheap** extremely or ridiculously cheap. **feel cheap** to have a sense of inferiority and humiliation, esp relating to one's moral standards. **on the cheap** cheap or cheaply.

cheat¹ /chēt/ n a person who cheats; a fraud; a deception; a computer program, piece of software or technique that allows a user, esp a game player, to carry out an unauthorized action; a card game in which deception is allowed; an escheat, a forfeit (obs); a piece of plunder, a stolen thing (obs); a thing in general, esp the gallows (criminal sl; see also **nubbing-cheat** under **nub³**). ◆ vt to deceive, defraud or impose upon. ◆ vi to be deceitful. [escheat]

■ **cheat'er** n a person who cheats; an officer who collected the fines and taxes to be paid into the Exchequer (hist); (in pl) spectacles (old N Am sl); (in pl) falsies (sl). **cheat'ery** n (inf) cheating. **cheat'ing** n and adj.

■ **cheat on** (inf) to deceive, esp to be unfaithful to (one's wife, husband, lover, etc). **put a cheat upon** to deceive. **tame cheater** (Shakesp) a decoy.

cheat² /chēt/ n another name for **chess³**. [Origin uncertain]
□ **cheat bread** n (obs) bread of a lower quality than manchet, made of a somewhat coarser wheat flour.

chechako, chechaqua, chechaquo see **cheechako**.

Chechen /chech'en or chə-chen'/ n a native or inhabitant of Chechnya in the Caucasus; their Caucasian language. ◆ adj of or relating to the Chechens or their language.

chéchia /shā'shyə/ n a cylindrical skullcap, worn by Arabs and adopted by French troops in Africa. [Fr, from Berber tashashit, pl tishushai skullcap]

check /chek/ vt to verify, often by comparison; to bring to a stop; to restrain or hinder; to rebuke; to punch (eg a ticket); to tick (N Am); to nip, pinch, crush, as by biting or shutting (also **chack**; Scot); to deposit or receive in exchange for a check; to send (baggage) on a passenger's ticket (N Am); in chess, to place in check; to mark with a pattern of crossing lines. ◆ vi to make investigations; to come to a stop; to forsake the quarry for some other bird (with at; falconry); to decline the option of opening the betting (poker). ◆ n a means of verification or testing, eg to evaluate the standard of something; anything that checks; a sudden stop, repulse or rebuff; in chess, a position when a player's king is exposed to attack and so must be protected or moved; in certain games, a stopping of an opposing player's forward progress; restraint; control; a rebuke, a reprimand (obs); a mark put against items in a list; a tick (N Am); an order to transfer money (usu written **cheque** except US); any token or ticket used as security, to indicate ownership, etc, a counterfoil; a ticket or token, given to show that a person has paid, eg for admission (see also **raincheck** under **rain¹**); a restaurant bill; a counter used in games at cards (hence **pass in one's checks** to die); a pattern of cross lines forming small squares, as in a chessboard; any fabric woven with such a pattern; a mechanism that holds a piano hammer after striking; a small crack in veneer, timber, etc. ◆ adj divided into small squares by crossing lines. [OFr eschec, eschac, originally in the chess sense, through Ar from Pers shāh king]

■ **check'able** adj. **checked** adj having a check pattern. **check'er** n someone who hinders, rebukes or scrutinizes; a cashier; a cloakroom attendant (N Am); (in pl; N Am) the game of draughts. **check'y** or **che'quy** adj (heraldry) chequered.

□ **check action** n piano action with checks. **check box** n (comput) a square on a screen on which the user can click the mouse to activate a particular feature. **check'book** n (N Am) a chequebook. **check'clerk** n a clerk who checks accounts, etc. **check digit** n (comput) a redundant bit in a stored word, used in a self-checking procedure such as a parity check. **checked square** n a square in a crossword that belongs to the solution of two clues. **check'erboard** n a checked board on which checkers or draughts is played. **check'-in** see **check in** below. **checking account** n (N Am) a current account. **check'-key** n a latch-key. **check'list** n a list for verification purposes; a comprehensive list; an inventory. **checkmate** n see separate entry. **check'-off** see **check off** below. **check'out** n the cash desk where goods bought in a supermarket, etc are paid for; the act of checking out (see below). **check'point** n a place where an official check of documents, etc is made. **check'rail** n an inner rail on a railway track that prevents a train from being derailed, esp when going round corners (also **guardrail**). **check'rein** n a bearing rein, a strap hindering a horse from lowering its head. **check'room** or **check'ing-room** n (N Am) a cloakroom, luggage room or room where goods are checked. **check'-string** n a string by which the occupant of a carriage may attract the driver's notice. **check'sum** n (comput) an error-detection system in which a figure signifying the number of bits is transmitted along with data so that the receiving device can verify the accuracy of the data received. **check'-tak'er** n someone who takes tickets. **check'-till** n a till that records sums received. **check'-up** n a testing scrutiny; a medical examination, esp one of a series of regular examinations. **check'weigher** or **checkweigh'man** n a colliery worker who, on behalf of the miners, checks the weight of coal sent up to the pit-mouth.

■ **check in** to record one's arrival at work; to register one's arrival at a hotel, airport, etc (**check'-in** n). **check off** to mark off on a list, usu with a tick, as having arrived, been completed, etc; to deduct (trade union dues) from a worker's pay before he or she receives it (N Am; **check'-off** n). **check out** to record one's departure from work; to depart, having paid one's bill, etc, from a hotel, etc; to investigate, examine or test; to look at or inspect (sl; **check'-out** or **check'out** n). **checks and balances** a system of competition and mutual restraint that curbs the potential of individuals to abuse power. **check up** to investigate; to examine and test (often with on). **hold** or **keep in check** to restrain, control or keep back.

checker see under **check**.

checkerberry /chek'ər-be-ri/ n the fruit of various American plants, esp the wintergreen (genus Gaultheria).

checklaton /chek-lat'ən/ n understood and explained by Spenser as gilded leather used for making embroidered jacks (also **schecklaton** or **shecklaton**). [ciclaton, perh by association with **latten**]

checkmate /chek'māt/ n in chess, a position where a player's king is under attack and can neither be protected nor move to escape, ending the game; a complete check, defeat or winning manoeuvre. ◆ *vt* in chess, to put (a player's king) in checkmate; to defeat or render incapable of counter-attack. ◆ *interj* in chess, a call made to indicate that one's opponent's king has been placed in checkmate. [OFr *eschec mat*, from Ar *shāh māt*(*a*) the king is dead]

checkoutytoy**checky** see under **check**.

Cheddar /*ched'ər*/ *n* a kind of hard cheese *orig* made at *Cheddar* in Somerset.
□ **Cheddar pink** *n* a species of pink (*Dianthus gratianopolitanus*) found on the limestone cliffs at Cheddar.

cheddite /*ched'īt*/ (*chem*) *n* a mixture of castor oil, ammonium perchlorate and a solvent, used as an explosive. [Fr *Chedde*, town in France where first manufactured]

cheder or **heder** /*hhed'er* or *hā'dər*/ (*Judaism*) *n* (*pl* **chadarim**, **hadarim** /*hhad-a-rīm'*/, **che'ders** or **he'ders**) religious instruction given outside normal school hours; an elementary religious school.

cheechako /*chē-chā'kō* or *-chə'*/ (*Can* and *Alaska*) *n* (*pl* **cheecha'kos** or **cheecha'koes**) a tenderfoot (also **checha'ko**, **cheechal'ko**, **checha'qua** or **checha'quo**). [Chinook Jargon, new-come]

chee-chee see **chi-chi**.

cheek /*chēk*/ *n* the side of the face below the eye, the fleshy lateral wall of the mouth; effrontery, impudence; a side-post of a door, window, etc; the cheek strap of a horse's bridle; the ring at the end of a bit; any of various things arranged in lateral or opposite pairs, such as one of the jaws of a vice; either of the buttocks (*inf*). ◆ *vt* (*inf*) to address insolently. [OE *cēce*, *cēace* cheek, jaw; cf Du *kaak*]
■ **cheek'ily** *adv*. **cheek'iness** *n*. **cheek'y** *adj* (*inf*) rude; saucy.
□ **cheek'bone** *n* the bone above the cheek. **cheek'piece** *n* the part of a helmet, bridle, etc that covers the cheek. **cheek'pouch** *n* a dilatation of the cheek, forming a bag, as in rodents, monkeys, etc, used for storing food. **cheek'tooth** *n* a molar tooth.
■ **cheek by jowl** side by side, in close proximity. **tongue in cheek** see under **tongue**. **turn the other cheek** see under **turn**.

cheep /*chēp*/ *vi* to chirp, as a young bird. ◆ *n* a sound of cheeping. [Imit]
■ **cheep'er** *n* a young bird, *esp* a young game bird or chicken.

cheer /*chēr*/ *n* a shout of approval or welcome; disposition, frame of mind (with *good*, etc); joy; face (*archaic*); kind treatment (*obs*); entertainment; fare, food. ◆ *vt* to applaud; to comfort; to encourage (often with *on*); to inspirit. ◆ *vi* to shout encouragement or applause; to take comfort (*obs*); to be of good cheer (*obs*). [OFr *chiere* face, from LL *cara* the face]
■ **cheer'er** *n*. **cheer'ful** *adj* in, of, resulting in, or accompanied by good spirits; pleasant, bright, lively. **cheer'fully** *adv*. **cheer'fulness** *n*. **cheer'ily** *adv*. **cheer'iness** *n*. **cheer'ing** *adj* bringing comfort. **cheerio'** *interj* goodbye!; good health! (used when drinking a toast). ◆ *n* (*pl* **cheerios'**) a bright informal goodbye; a kind of small frankfurter (*Aust* and *NZ*). **cheer'ishness** *n* (*obs*) cheeriness. **cheer'less** *adj* dreary, without comfort, gloomy. **cheer'lessly** *adv*. **cheer'lessness** *n*. **cheer'ly** *adj* (*archaic*) cheerful. ◆ *adv* (*archaic*) in a cheery manner; heartily. **cheers!** *interj* (*inf*) good health! (used when drinking a toast); thank you!; cheerio, goodbye! **cheer'y** *adj* cheerful; promoting or resulting in cheerfulness.
□ **cheer'leader** *n* (*esp N Am*) a person who directs organized cheering, as at team games.
■ **cheer up** (*inf*) to make or become more cheerful. **three cheers** see under **three**. **what cheer?** (*archaic*) how are you?

cheese[1] /*chēz*/ *n* a kind of food made from the curd of milk coagulated by rennet, separated from the whey, of a soft creamy consistency or pressed into a solid or semi-solid mass, traditionally and usually wheel-shaped; a solid mass of this; a flavoured kind of food, with the consistency of soft cheese, eg *lemon cheese*; anything of the shape of a whole cheese; the receptacle of a thistle-head; the cheese-shaped disc used in skittles. [OE *cēse*, *cȳse* curdled milk (cf Ger *Käse* cheese), from L *cāseus*]
■ **chees'iness** *n*. **chees'y** *adj* having the nature of cheese; (of a smile) broad (*inf*); having a popular appeal in spite of being artificial or inferior (*inf*).
□ **cheese'board** *n* a flat wooden board on which cheese is cut and served; a collection of cheeses served on such a board. **cheese'burger** *n* a hamburger with melted cheese on top of it. **cheese'cake** *n* a kind of cake having a base of pastry or biscuit crumbs, with a filling of cream cheese, sugar, eggs, flavouring, etc; women with sex appeal, *esp* when pictured erotically or pornographically in magazines, etc (*sl*; cf **beefcake**). **cheese'cloth** *n* a loose-woven light gauze used for wrapping cheeses; a stronger type of loosely-woven cotton cloth used for making shirts, etc. **cheese'cutter** *n* (*naut*) a movable keel that may be drawn up inside a boat; a square-peaked cap. **cheese'-head** *adj* (of bolts and screws) having a short thick cylindrical head. **cheese'hopper**

or **cheese skipper** *n* a small fly (*Piophila casei*) whose larvae feed on cheese and move by jumping. **cheese'mite** *n* a very small arachnid (*Tyroglyphus longior*) that breeds in cheese. **cheese'monger** *n* a dealer in cheese. **cheese'parer** *n* a mean or stingy person, a skinflint. **cheese'paring** *n orig* a paring of cheese rind; parsimony, stinginess. ◆ *adj* mean and parsimonious. **cheese plant** see **Swiss cheese plant** under **Swiss**. **cheese'press** *n* a machine or device in which curds for cheese are pressed. **cheese'-rennet** *n* the plant lady's bedstraw, said to have been used formerly as rennet in curdling milk. **cheese'steak** *n* (US) a long roll filled with grilled sliced beef and melted cheese. **cheese straw** *n* a long thin piece of pastry flavoured with cheese. **cheese'taster** *n* a long hollow tool for taking a sample from the inside of a cheese. **cheese'vat** *n* a vat or wooden case in which curds are separated or pressed in cheese making. **cheese'wire** *n* a thin wire used for cutting cheese. **cheese'wood** *n* (*Aust*) the yellow wood of various Australian trees of the genus *Pittosporum*. **cheese'wring** *n* another name for a cheesepress.
■ **green cheese** unripe or unmatured cheese. **hard cheese** (*inf*) hard luck. **make cheeses** (*archaic*) to whirl round and then sink down suddenly so as to make the skirt stand out like a cheese.

cheese[2] /*chēz*/ *n* the correct thing (*obs sl*); anything of excellent quality. [Prob Pers and Hindi *chīz* thing]
■ **big cheese** (*inf*) a person of importance, a boss.

cheese[3] /*chēz*/ (*sl*) *vi* to grovel.
■ **cheesed off** (also **cheesed**) fed up, disgusted, disgruntled. **cheese it** to stop it; to run away, clear off, make oneself scarce (*esp criminal sl*).

cheetah or **chetah** /*chē'tə*/ *n* a large animal of the cat family, found in Africa and SW Asia, the fastest land animal, having long legs, a spotted coat and claws that cannot be retracted. [Hindi *cītā*, from Sans *citraka*, *citrakāya* having a speckled body]

cheewink same as **chewink**.

chef /*shef*/ *n* a cook, *esp* a head cook (in full **chef de cuisine** /*də kwē-zēn*/ the head of a kitchen), *esp* in a hotel or restaurant; a medieval reliquary in the shape of a head. [Fr, head, chief; see **chief**]
□ **chef d'œuvre** /*shā-dœ-vr'*/ *n* (*pl* **chefs d'œuvre** /*shā-*/) a masterpiece.

cheiro- see **chiro-**.

cheka /*chā'kə*/ (also with *cap*) *n* the Russian secret police of 1917–22. [Russ *che ka*, names of the initial letters of the words for 'extraordinary commission']
■ **chek'ist** *n* a member of the cheka.

Chekhovian or **Chekovian** /*che-kō'vi-ən*/ *adj* relating to the Russian writer Anton *Chekhov* (1860–1904), or to (the style of) his stories and plays.

chela[1] /*kē'lə*/ *n* (*pl* **chē'lae** /*-ē*/) (*zool*) the prehensile claw of an arthropod such as the crab. [Latinized from Gr *chēlē* claw]
■ **chē'late** *n* (*chem*) a co-ordination compound (eg haemoglobin) in which a central metallic ion is attached to an organic molecule at two or more positions (also *adj*). ◆ *vi* (*chem*) to form a chelate. **chēlā'tion** *n*. **chēlā'tor** *n*. **chelif'erous** *adj* (*zool*) having a chela or chelae. **chē'liform** *adj* (*zool*) shaped like a chela or pincer. **chē'liped** *n* one of the pair of legs carrying the chelae in arthropods.
□ **chelation therapy** *n* the treatment of heavy metal (eg lead) poisoning or certain other diseases by a substance (**chelating agent**) which combines chemically with the toxic substances and renders them harmless.

chela[2] /*chā'lə*/ *n* a novice in Buddhism; a disciple of a religious teacher or leader. [Hindi *celā* servant, disciple]
■ **che'laship** *n*.

chelate, **chelation**, etc see under **chela**[1].

chelicera /*kē-lis'ə-rə*/ *n* (*pl* **chēlic'erae** /*-rē*/) one of a pair of biting appendages on the heads of arachnids. [Gr *chēlē* a crab's claw, and *keras* horn]
■ **chelic'eral** *adj*. **chelic'erate** *adj* and *n* (*zool*) (of or like) a member of the subphylum Chelicerata, including arachnids and the horsehoe crab.

cheliferous, **cheliped** see under **chela**[1].

Chellean /*shel'i-ən*/ (*old archaeol*) *adj* belonging to an early Palaeolithic culture, older than Acheulean. [*Chelles*, near Paris, where flints of this stage are found]

cheloid see **keloid**.

chelone /*kə-lō'nē*/ *n* any perennial N American plant of the genus *Chelone*, *esp* varieties cultivated for their lilac, pink or white flowers, the turtle-head. [Gr *chelōnē* tortoise]

chelonian /*ki-lō'ni-ən*/ *n* a reptile of the order Chelonia, with a horny shell and horny beak, including tortoises and turtles (also *adj*). [Gr *chelōnē* tortoise]

■ words derived from main entry word; □ compound words; ■ idioms and phrasal verbs

Chelsea /chel'sē/ n a district of London formerly noted as an artists' quarter.
□ **Chelsea boot** n an ankle boot with elasticated sides. **Chelsea bun** n a rolled bun filled with currants and raisins. **Chelsea clip** n a hooked attachment on a table, wall, etc, providing a secure place for one's personal belongings. **Chelsea pensioner** n an elderly, often disabled, ex-soldier, connected with the Chelsea Royal Hospital. **Chelsea tractor** n (sl) a four-wheel-drive vehicle used for driving around an urban environment. **Chelsea ware** n a variety of china made in the 18c.

cheluviation /kē-loo-vi-ā'shən/ (bot) n the leaching of iron and aluminium oxides from soils, esp those planted with conifers and heaths.

chem. abbrev : chemical; chemistry.

chem- /kem-/, **chemi-** /ke-mi-/ or **chemo-** /kē-mō- or ke-mō-/ combining form denoting chemicals or indicating the involvement of chemical reactions. [New L, from Late Gr chēmeiā (see **alchemy**)]
■ **chemiat'ric** adj iatrochemical, of medicine and physicians. **chemiluminesc'ence** n luminescence arising from chemical processes, eg that of the glow-worm. **chemiluminesc'ent** adj. **chemisorp'tion** n an irreversible adsorption in which the absorbed surface is chemically bonded to a substance. **chem'itype** n any chemical process for obtaining impressions from an engraving. **chem'itȳpy** n. **chemoattrac'tant** n a chemical which provokes a chemotactic movement of eg cells or bacteria towards its area of highest concentration. **chemoautotroph** /ke-mō-öt'ə-trof/ n (biol) any organism, eg bacteria, that produces energy by the oxidation of inorganic compounds, such as iron, ammonia and hydrogen sulphide. **chem'ōnasty** n (bot) plant movement provoked, but not orientated by a chemical stimulus. **chemopreven'tion** n the use of chemical compounds to prevent the development of cancers. **chemoprophylax'is** n the prevention of infectious disease by drugs. **chemōpsychiat'ric** adj. **chemōpsychī'atry** n treatment of mental illness by drugs. **chemōrecep'tive** adj. **chemoreceptiv'ity** n. **chemōrecep'tor** n a sensory nerve-ending that responds to a chemical stimulus. **chem'osphere** n (meteorol) the thermosphere. **chem'ōstat** n an apparatus for growing cultures of bacteria, fungi, tissue, etc. **chemōsyn'thesis** n (bot) the formation of organic molecules by some bacteria by means of energy derived from chemical reactions. **chemōtac'tic** adj relating to chemotaxis. **chemōtax'is** n movement of cells or a whole organism in a definite direction in response to chemical stimulus. **chemōtherapeu'tic** adj. **chemōtherapeu'tics** or more commonly **chemōther'apy** n sing treatment of infectious diseases or cancer by means of chemical compounds selectively directed against microorganisms or cancerous tissue (inf short form **chē'mō**). **chemōther'apist** n. **chemōtrop'ic** adj. **chemot'ropism** n (bot and zool) orientation by differential growth in response to chemical stimulus. **chem'trail** n a vapour trail believed to contain toxic chemicals. **chemur'gic** or **chemur'gical** adj. **chemurgy** /kem'ər-ji/ n a branch of applied chemistry concerned with the use of agricultural products, or other organic raw materials, for industry.

chemic, **chemical**, etc see under **chemistry**.

chemico- /ke-mi-kō-/ combining form signifying a combination with chemistry or chemicals.

chemin de fer /shə-mĕ də fer'/ (cards) n a variety of baccarat (inf short form **chemmy** /shem'i/). [Fr, railway]

chemise /shə-mēz'/ n a woman's shirt-like undergarment; a straight dress, a smock. [Fr chemise, from LL camisia a nightgown, surplice]
■ **chemisette'** n a kind of bodice worn by women; formerly, a piece of lace or muslin filling up the open front of a woman's dress.

chemistry /kem'i-stri/ n the physical science of the properties of elementary and compound substances, and the laws of their combination and action upon one another (also archaic **chymistry** /kim'is-tri/); loosely, the elements contained in or making up any complex structure or phenomenon; an indefinable or instinctual quality that causes an interaction between two people, as in sexual chemistry. [See ety for **alchemy**]
■ **chem'ic** adj alchemical (obs); iatrochemical (obs); chemical. ◆n an alchemist or a chemist (obs); bleaching powder (archaic). ◆vt (**chem'icking**; **chem'icked**) to treat with bleaching powder. **chem'ical** adj relating to chemistry; versed in or studying chemistry; alchemical (obs); iatrochemical (obs). ◆n a substance obtained by chemical means or used in chemical operations. **chem'ically** adv. **chem'ism** n (obs) chemical action. **chem'ist** n a person skilled in chemistry; a manufacturer of or dealer in chemicals and drugs; a pharmacist; an alchemist (obs).
□ **chemical abuse** n the act of taking, smoking or sniffing harmful drugs, chemical solvents, etc. **chemical affinity** n the tendency to combine with one another exhibited by many substances, or the force by which the substances constituting a compound are held together. **chemical closet** or **toilet** n a kind of toilet containing deodorizing and liquefying chemicals, used when running water is not

available. **chemical cosh** n (inf) a drug treatment that is administered in order to pacify the patient rather than for any medical benefit. **chemical dependency** n addiction to alcohol and/or drugs. **chemical engineer** n. **chemical engineering** n engineering applied to the design, construction and operational processes of (esp industrial) chemical plant and works. **chemical peel** n a cosmetic treatment in which chemicals are used to remove damaged cells from the skin surface. **chemical reaction** n a process in which the structure of a chemical is changed to form another substance which retains the nuclei of the original chemical or chemicals but with a different configuration or content of atoms, energy, etc. **chemical warfare** n warfare involving the use of irritating or asphyxiating gases, oil flames, etc. **chemical wood** n wood pulp broken down by the action of chemicals, used in the manufacture of synthetic fibres, paper, etc.

chemmy see **chemin de fer**.

chenar /chē-när'/ n the oriental plane tree (Platanus orientalis). [Pers chinār]

chenet /shə-ne'/ (Fr) n an andiron.

chenille /shə-nēl'/ n a thick, velvety cord or yarn of silk or wool resembling a woolly caterpillar; a velvet-like material used for table covers, etc and in the clothing industry. [Fr chenille hairy caterpillar, from L canicula a little dog, from canis a dog]

chenix see **choenix**.

chenopod /ken'ō-pod/ n any dicotyledonous flowering plant of the family **Chenopodiā'ceae** including leaf beet, sugar beet, beetroot, mangelwurzel, spinach and goosefoot. [Gr chēn goose, and pous, podos foot]
■ **chenopodiā'ceous** adj.

cheongsam /ch(i-)ong-sam'/ n a tight-fitting high-necked dress with slits at the sides, as worn traditionally by Chinese women. [Chin (Cantonese), long dress]

cheque or (US) **check** /chek/ n an order to a bank, etc to transfer money, usu to a named beneficiary; a counterfoil (obs). [See **check**]
□ **cheque account** n a bank or building society account against which cheques can be drawn. **cheque'book** or (US) **check'book** n a book of cheque forms. **chequebook diplomacy** n negotiations where financial considerations are the most important element. **chequebook journalism** n news, articles, etc based on information bought, usu at a high price. **cheque (guarantee) card** n a card issued by a bank to a client, guaranteeing payment of cheques up to a certain limit.
■ **blank cheque** a cheque signed by the drawer without having the amount indicated; concession of power without limit (fig). **crossed cheque** an ordinary cheque with two transverse lines drawn across it, which have the effect of making it payable only through a bank account.

chequer /chek'ər/ n a chessboard, also a chess piece (archaic); alternation of colours, as on a chessboard; one of the pieces used in Chinese chequers and draughts. ◆ vt to mark in squares of different colours; to variegate; to interrupt. [See **check**]
■ **cheq'uered** or **check'ered** adj variegated, like a chessboard; varying in character; eventful, with alternations of good and bad fortune, as in a chequered career. **cheq'uers** n sing the game of draughts; any of various similar games, such as Chinese chequers. **cheq'uerwise** adv.
□ **cheq'uerboard** n a draughtboard. **chequered flag** n the black-and-white flag shown to the winner and subsequent finishers in a motor race. **chequered skipper** n a rare British butterfly (Carterocephalus palaemon) having dark-brown wings with light gold markings resembling those on a chessboard. **cheq'uerwork** n any pattern having alternating squares of different colours.

chequy see under **check**.

cher or fem **chère** /sher/ (Fr) adj dear.

cheralite /cher'ə-līt/ n a radioactive mineral rich in thorium and uranium. [Chera, ancient name of Travancore, where discovered, and Gr lithos a stone]

cherchef't a Miltonic spelling of **kerchiefed**.

Cherenkov radiation a variant spelling of **Cerenkov radiation**.

cherimoya /che-ri-moi'ə/ or **cherimoyer** /-ər/ n a Peruvian fruit (Anona cherimolia) resembling the custard apple. [Quechua]

cherish /cher'ish/ vt to protect and treat with great care and affection; to treasure; to nurture, nurse; to entertain in the mind. [Fr chérir, chérissant, from cher dear, from L cārus]
■ **cher'ished** adj (of number plates) with a combination of letters and numbers specially chosen by the owner of the vehicle. **cher'ishment** n.

Cherkess /chər-kes'/ n (pl **Cherkess'es**) a Circassian; the Caucasian language of the Cherkesses. [Russ]

chermoula /chər-moo'lə/ n a marinade containing onion, coriander, and parsley, used in N African cookery. [Ar]

chernozem /chûr'nō-zem/ n a very fertile soil of sub-humid steppe, consisting of a dark topsoil over a lighter calcareous layer (also **tscher'nosem**). [Russ, black earth]

Cherokee /cher'ə-kē/ n (a member of) a tribe of Iroquoian Native Americans, now mainly living in Oklahoma; the Iroquoian language of the Cherokee. ◆ adj relating to the Cherokee or their language. □ **Cherokee rose** n an evergreen climbing rose (Rosa laevigata), native to China but now growing wild in the southern USA.

cheroot /shə-root'/ n a cigar cut square at either end. [Fr cheroute, representing the Tamil name shuruttu a roll]

cherry[1] /cher'i/ n a small fleshy fruit having a large hard stone; the tree (Cerasus, a subgenus of Prunus) that bears it; any tree bearing similar fruits; the wood of any of these trees; a bright-red colour, cherry-red; a new ball (cricket sl); virginity or the hymen (sl). ◆ adj like a cherry in colour, usu bright-red; ruddy. [OE ciris, from L cerasus, from Gr kerasos a cherry tree; it is said to have been introduced from Kerasous (Cerasus) in Pontus, by Lucullus, but was known in Europe long before his time] □ **cherry bean** n another name for the cowpea. **cherr'y-bob** n in children's games, two cherries joined by the stalks. **cherry bounce** n cherry brandy; brandy and sugar. **cherry brandy** n a liqueur made by steeping Morello cherries in brandy. **cherr'y-coal** n a soft shining coal. **cherry laurel** n a species of cherry with evergreen laurel-like leaves. **cherr'y-pepper** n a West Indian capsicum. **cherr'y-pick** vi (inf) to select a few exceptional specimens, esp in order to achieve a predetermined result; in insurance, to accept only the best risks, rejecting the poor ones. **cherry picker** n a type of crane consisting of a jointed or telescopic hydraulic arm ending in a platform which is raised to enable work or inspection to be carried out at heights; a person or organization that practises cherry-picking. **cherr'y-picking** n (inf) choosing the best people, insurance risks, etc. **cherry-pie**[1] n a pie made with cherries; the common garden heliotrope. **cherr'y-pit** n (obs) a game in which cherry-stones are thrown into a small hole. **cherry plum** n a plum that has a flavour similar to a cherry. **cherr'y-stone** n the hard endocarp of the cherry, the stone. **cherry tomato** n a small cherry-sized red or yellow tomato. ■ **a bowl of cherries** an extremely easy or enjoyable situation. **have (or take) two bites (or a second bite) at the cherry** (inf) to have (or take) a second chance or opportunity. **the cherry on the cake** the finishing touch to an already excellent situation.

cherry[2] /cher'i/ (Spenser) vt to cheer. [See **cherish**]

chersonese /kûr'sə-nēz or -nēs/ (esp poetic) n a peninsula. [Gr chersonēsos, from chersos land, dry land, and nēsos an island]

chert /chûrt/ (geol) n a siliceous rock of cryptocrystalline silica occurring as bands or concretions in sedimentary rock, eg limestone. [Ety doubtful] ■ **chert'y** adj.

cherub /cher'əb/ n (pl **cher'ubs**, **cher'ubim** /-ə or -ū-bim/ or **cher'ubims**) a winged being with human face, an attendant of God (Bible); an angelic being of the second order of celestial spirits, ranking above thrones and below seraphim; a sweet innocent-looking chubby-faced person, esp a child. [Heb k'rub, pl k'rubim] ■ **cherubic** /-oo'bik/, **cheru'bical** or **cherubim'ic** adj angelic. **cheru'bically** adv. **cher'ubin** n (Shakesp) a cherub.

cherup /cher'up/ same as **chirrup**.

chervil /chûr'vil/ n an umbelliferous plant (Anthriscus cerefolium) cultivated as an aromatic pot-herb; also other species of Anthriscus (common, wild and rough chervil); extended to sweet cicely (sweet chervil). [OE cerfille, from L caerefolium, from Gr chairephyllon, from chairein to enjoy, and phyllon a leaf]

chervonets /chər-vō'nets/ n a Russian gold coin worth ten roubles. [Russ]

Ches. abbrev : Cheshire.

Cheshire /chesh'ər or -ēr/ n a type of mild cheese, orig made in the county of Cheshire (also **Cheshire cheese**).

Cheshire cat see under **cat**[1].

Cheshvan see **Hesvan**.

chesil /chez'il/ n (also **chis'el**) gravel, shingle (obs); bran (dialect). [OE cisil]

chesnut see **chestnut**.

chess[1] /ches/ n a game of skill for two players, in which figures or men of different kinds are moved on a chequered board. [OFr esches (Fr échecs; Ital scacchi; Ger Schach, from Pers shāh a king] □ **chess'board** n the board on which chess is played; a chequered design. **chess'man** n any of the sixteen figures used by each player in a game of chess.

chess[2] /ches/ n one of the parallel planks forming the deck of a pontoon-bridge (usu in pl).

chess[3] /ches/ (US) n a type of grass found growing with wheat. [Ety unknown]

chessel /ches'l/ n a cheese mould. [**cheese**[1]]

chessylite /ches'i-līt/ n basic carbonate of copper, vivid blue in colour, azurite. [Chessy, near Lyon in France, where it occurs]

chest /chest/ n a large strong box; the part of the body between the neck and the abdomen, the non-technical name for the thorax; a treasury; a chestful. ◆ vt (esp in football) to hit or direct (the ball) with one's chest. [OE cyst, from L cista, from Gr kistē; Scot kist] ■ **chest'ed** adj having a chest; placed in a chest. **chest'ful** n enough to fill a chest. **chest'ily** adv. **chest'iness** n. **chest'y** adj of the quality of the chest voice; suggestive of disease of the chest (inf); having a large chest or bosom; self-important (sl). □ **chest freezer** n a long, low freezer which opens at the top. **chest'note** n in singing or speaking, a deep note. **chest protector** n a covering to keep the chest warm. **chest register**, **chest tone** or **chest voice** n the lowest register of the voice (cf **head voice**). ■ **chest of drawers** a piece of furniture consisting of a case in which a number of drawers slide. **chest of viols** (archaic) a set of viols (usu two trebles, two tenors, two basses) for ensemble playing. **get (something) off one's chest** (inf) to relieve oneself of anxiety, tension, etc about (a concern) by admitting, stating or declaring (it) openly.

chesterfield /ches'tər-fēld/ n a heavily padded sofa; formerly, a long overcoat. [Lord Chesterfield (1694–1773), English statesman and author]

chestnut (now rarely **chesnut**) /ches'nut/ n a tree of genus Castanea, esp the Spanish or sweet chestnut; its edible nut, encased (three together) in a prickly husk; its hard timber; the **horse chestnut** (Aesculus hippocastanum), its fruit, nut or timber; a chestnut horse; a horny knob on the inner surface of a horse's foreleg; a stale joke or cliché. ◆ adj of chestnut colour, reddish-brown. [OFr chastaigne, from L castanea, perh from Castana, in Thessaly] ■ **pull the chestnuts out of the fire** to take control and rescue someone or something from a difficult situation, esp one that seems hopeless.

Chesvan see **Hesvan**.

chetah see **cheetah**.

cheth /hheth or hhāth/ n the eighth letter of the Hebrew alphabet. [Heb]

chetnik /chet'nik/ n a Serbian resistance fighter involved in guerrilla warfare against Turkish rule in the 19c and against occupying forces in both World Wars. [Serb cetnik, from ceta a troop]

chetrum /chet'rəm/ n (pl **chet'rum** or **chet'rums**) a Bhutanese monetary unit, $\frac{1}{100}$ of an ngultrum. [Dzongkha]

cheval de bataille /shə-val də bă-tä'y'/ (Fr) n a favourite topic or subject, a hobby, literally warhorse.

cheval-de-frise /shə-val-də-frēz'/ n (pl **chevaux-de-frise** /shə-vō-/) a defensive structure of iron spikes set in wood, used esp to stop cavalry. [Fr cheval horse, de of, and Frise Friesland]

chevalet /shə-va'lā or she'/ (music) n the bridge of a stringed instrument. [Fr, dimin of cheval a horse]

cheval-glass /shə-val'gläs/ n a large glass or mirror supported on a frame and able to swivel (also **cheval mirror**). [Fr cheval horse, stand]

chevalier /she-və-lēr'/ n a cavalier; a knight; a gallant. [Fr, from LL caballārius, from L caballus a horse] □ **chevalier d'industrie** /shə-va-lyā dē-düs-trē/ n (Fr) an adventurer, a person who lives by his wits, literally a knight of industry.

chevelure /shev'(ə-)lür/ n a head of hair or arrangement of the hair; a periwig; the nebulous part of a comet (astron). [Fr, from L capillātūra, from capillus hair]

cheven /chev'ən/ n the chub (also **chev'in**). [Fr chevin, chevanne]

cheverel or **cheveril** /chev'ər-əl/ n a kid; soft, flexible kidskin leather. ◆ adj like kid leather, soft and pliable. [Fr chevreau, chevrette a kid, from chèvre; L capra a she-goat] ■ **chevrette** /shəv-ret'/ n a thin kind of goatskin. **chevron** or **cheveron** /shev'/ n (obs) a kid glove.

cheverye (Spenser) see **chiefery** under **chief**.

chevesaile /chev'ə-sāl/ n an ornamental collar of a coat. [OFr chevesaile, from chevece the neck]

chevet /shə-vā'/ (archit) n the eastern end of a Christian church comprising the apse and chapels. [Fr]

cheville /shə-vē'/ n the peg of a stringed instrument (music); a redundant word or expression used in a verse or sentence for purposes of metre or balance only. [Fr, peg, from L clāvicula, dimin of clāvis a key]

chevin see **cheven**.

Cheviot /chē'vi-ət or chev'i-ət/ n a hardy breed of short-woolled sheep reared on the *Cheviot* Hills; a cloth made from their wool.

chevisance /chev'i-zəns/ n (obs) achievement; resource; gain; money dealings; performance (*Spenser*); an unidentified flower. [Fr, from *chevir* to accomplish; *chef* the head, the end]

chèvre /she'vr'/ (Fr) n cheese made from goat's milk.

chevrette see under **cheverel**.

chevron[1] /shev'rən/ n a rafter; the representation, *usu* on a shield, of two rafters of a house meeting at the top (*heraldry*); a V-shaped band on the sleeve, a mark of non-commissioned rank or (in army and RAF, inverted) of long service and good conduct; a pattern consisting of a line of horizontal black-and-white V-shapes on a board (**chevron board**) used as a road sign to indicate a sharp bend. [Fr *chevron* rafter, from L *capreolus*, dimin of *caper* a goat]
■ **chev'roned** adj. **chev'rony** adj (heraldry).

chevron[2] see under **cheverel**.

chevrotain /shev'rō-tān or -tən/ n a member of the family Tragulidae, an Old World primitive group of tropical forest-dwelling small, deer-like animals intermediate in form between true deer and other ungulates such as pigs, and including the water chevrotain (*Hyemoschus aquaticus*) of C Africa, and three species of the genus *Tragulus* found in SE Asia. [Fr, dimin of *chèvre*, from L *capra* she-goat]

chevy see **chivvy**.

chew /choo/ vt to bruise and grind with the teeth; to masticate; to meditate, reflect. ◆ n the action of chewing; something that is chewed, *esp* a quid of tobacco. [OE *cēowan*; Ger *kauen*; cf **jaw**[1]]
■ **chew'able** adj. **chew'er** n. **chew'ie** n (*esp Aust sl*) chewing gum. **chew'iness** n. **chew'y** adj soft and sticky, able or requiring to be chewed, like toffee.
□ **chewing gum** n a preparation made from chicle gum, produced by the sapodilla plum tree, sweetened and flavoured, or a substitute for this.
■ **chew out** (inf) to tell off, reprimand. **chew the cud** (of cows, etc) to masticate for a second time food that has already been swallowed and partly digested in the first stomach; to ruminate in thought (also **chew over**). **chew the rag** or **chew the fat** (sl) to keep on arguing the point; to converse, gossip. **chew up** to destroy, damage or disfigure (something) by a biting or grinding action like chewing; to cause (someone) to be upset or nervous (inf).

chewet[1] /choo'it/ n a chough (obs); a chatterer (*Shakesp*). [Fr *chouette* chough (now owl)]

chewet[2] /choo'it/ (obs) n a pie or pudding of miscellaneous chopped meats.

Cheyenne /shī-an' or -en'/ n (a member of) a tribe of Native Americans now living in Montana and Oklahoma; the Algonquian language of this tribe. [Can Fr, from Dakota *Shahiyena* people who speak unintelligibly]

Cheyne-Stokes breathing /chān'stōks' brēdh'ing/ n abnormal respiration in which periods of deep and shallow breathing alternate. [John *Cheyne* (1777–1836), Scottish physician, and William *Stokes* (1804–78), Irish physician]

chez /shā/ (Fr) prep at the home or establishment of.

chg. abbrev : charge.

chi[1] /kī or hhē/ n the twenty-second letter (X or χ) of the Greek alphabet, representing an aspirated *k* sound; as numeral χ' = 600, ,χ = 600000; in inscriptions χ = 1000 (from Gr *chílioi* thousand). [Gr *chei*, *chī*]

chi[2], **ch'i** or **qi** /chē/ (*Chinese med*) n an individual person's life-force, the free flow of which within the body is believed to ensure physical and spiritual health. [Chin *qì* breath, energy]

chi[3] /chī/ same as **chai**[1].

chiack, also **chyack** /chī'ak/ (*Aust inf*) vt to tease, deride, jeer at (also n). [UK obs slang, to greet, salute]
■ **chī'acking** n.

Chian /kī'ən/ adj relating to *Chios*, an island in the Aegean Sea. ◆ n an inhabitant of Chios.

Chianti /kē-an'ti or -än', also (*Ital*) kyän'tē/ n a dry red (or white) wine of Tuscany. [*Chianti* Mountains]
■ **Chian'tishire** n (inf) a facetious name for a part of Tuscany regarded as having been colonized by affluent British residents and holidaymakers.

chiao /jow/ n (pl chiao) old spelling of **jiao**. [Chin *jiǎo*]

chiarezza /kya-ret'za/ (*music*) n purity, clarity, brightness. [Ital]

chiaroscuro /kyä-rō-skoo'rō/ (*esp art*) n (pl chiaroscu'ros) management or disposition of light and shade in a picture; a painting in black and white; the effect of light and shade or variety and contrast (also *fig*). [Ital, literally bright dark, from *chiaro* clear, and *oscuro* obscure, dark]

chiasma /kī-az'mə/ or **chiasm** /kī'azm/ n (pl chias'mas, chias'mata or chi'asms) the cross-shaped connection formed by the crossing over of chromatids during meiosis (biol); a decussation or intersection, *esp* that of the optic nerves (anat). [Gr *chiasma* a cross-shaped mark, *chiastos* laid crosswise, like the Greek letter X (*chi, chei*)]
■ **chias'mus** n (pl chias'mi) (rhetoric) contrast by parallelism in reverse order, as *Do not live to eat*, *but eat to live*. **chias'tic** adj. **chias'tolite** n (Gr *lithos* a stone; *mineralogy*) a variety of andalusite with black cruciform inclusions of carbonaceous matter.

chiaus /chows/ same as **chouse**.

Chibchan /chib'chən/ n a family of languages used by indigenous peoples of E Colombia and elsewhere in S America; a person who speaks any of these languages. ◆ adj relating to this family of languages.

chibol see **cibol**.

chibouk or **chibouque** /chi-bŭk'/ n a long straight-stemmed Turkish tobacco pipe. [Turk *chibūk*]

chic /shēk/ n style, elegance; artistic skill. ◆ adj having chic; smart, elegant and fashionable. [Fr]
■ **chic'ly** adv.

chica, **chicha** or **chico** /chē'kə/ n an orange-red dyestuff, used by native peoples in S America as a stain for the skin, and obtained by boiling the leaves of bignonia. [From a native name]

Chicago /shi-kä'gō/ n a form of contract bridge played in sets of four deals, not in rubbers. [The US city]

chicane /shi-kān'/ n a series of sharp bends on a motor-racing track; a trick or artifice; a bridge hand without trumps, for which a score above the line used to be allowed. ◆ vi (archaic) to use tricks and artifice. ◆ vt (archaic) to deceive. [Fr *chicane* sharp practice at law, from Late Gr *tzykanion* a game at mall, *tzykanizein* to play at mall, from Pers *tchugagan* a crooked mallet]
■ **chica'ner** n a person who chicanes; a quibbler. **chica'nery** n trickery or sharp practice, *esp* in legal proceedings; quibbling, deception. **chica'ning** n quibbling, deception.

chicano /chi-kä'nō or shi-/ (US, sometimes considered *derog*; also with cap) n (pl chica'nos) an American of Mexican descent (also adj). [Sp *mejicano* Mexican]
■ **chica'na** n (pl chica'nas) an American woman of Mexican descent (also adj).

chiccory see **chicory**.

chich /chich/ same as **chickpea**.

chicha[1] /chē'chə/ n a S American liquor fermented from maize or cane sugar, etc; a S American tree with edible nut-like seeds. [Am Sp]

chicha[2] see **chica**.

Chichewa /chi-chā'wə/ n a form of Nyanja spoken in Malawi.

chichi or **chi-chi** /shē'shē or chē'chē/ adj pretentious; fussy, precious, affected; stylish, chic, self-consciously fashionable. ◆ n something that is, or the quality of being, chichi; red tape; fuss. [Fr]

chi-chi, also **chee-chee** /chē'chē/ (derog) n formerly in British India, a Eurasian; affected or mincing Eurasian English. ◆ adj Eurasian; affected or mincing. [Perh Hindi *chī-chī* nasty, fie!, as characterizing the manner of their speech]

chick[1] /chik/ n the young of fowls, *esp* of the hen; a child, as a term of endearment; a girl or young woman (sl). [OE *cicen*; cf Du *kieken*, Ger *Küken*]
■ **chick'en** n the young of birds, *esp* of the domestic fowl; the flesh of a fowl (not always very young); a prairie chicken; a youthful person, *esp* a girl; a faint-hearted person (inf); a type of game, challenge or competition in which physically dangerous or forbidden activities are undertaken until one of the participants loses their nerve (inf). ◆ adj (inf) cowardly, frightened, scared. ◆ vi (inf) to show fear. **chick'ling** n a little chicken.
□ **chick'-a-biddy** or **chick'-a-diddle** n terms of endearment addressed to children. **chicken breast** n the breast of a chicken; the condition of being pigeon-breasted (qv under **pigeon**[1]). **chick'enfeed** n poultry food; small change or a trifling sum of money (inf); something of little value (inf). **chicken hawk** n (*esp US*) any hawk that preys on domestic chickens; a male homosexual who seeks out younger partners (sl). **chick'en-hazard** n a game at hazard for low stakes. **chick'en-hearted** or **chick'en-livered** adj timid, cowardly. **chick'enpox** n a contagious febrile disease, chiefly affecting children, not unlike a mild form of smallpox. **chicken run** n an enclosure for hens. **chicken wire** n wire netting having a small hexagonal mesh. **chick flick** n (derog inf) a film likely to appeal only to women. **chick lit** n (derog inf) a type of fiction with themes designed to appeal to young women. **chick'pea** see separate entry. **chick'weed** n any

plant of the genus *Stellaria*, esp *S. media*, one of the commonest of weeds, much relished by fowls and cage-birds; a similar related plant, **mouse-ear chickweed**, of the genus *Cerastium*. **chickweed wintergreen** see **wintergreen** under **winter**.
■ **chicken-and-egg situation** one in which it is impossible to tell which is the cause and which the effect. **chicken out** (*inf*; often with *of*) to desert, quit, through losing one's nerve or cowardice. **count one's chickens before they are hatched** to plan or act on the basis of expectations or future results without conclusive evidence that they will be fulfilled. **like a headless chicken** in a frantic, panic-stricken manner. **no (spring) chicken** (*derog* or *facetious*) no longer young. **the chickens have come home to roost** see under **roost**[1].

chick[2] /chik/ (*Anglo-Ind*) *n* a hanging door screen or sun blind of narrow strips of bamboo laced together or fastened loosely with string. [Hindi *ciq*]

chickadee /chik-ə-dē'/ *n* a N American songbird of the titmouse family (Paridae). [Imit, from its note]

chickaree /chik-ə-rē'/ *n* another name for the American red squirrel, *Tamiasciurus hudsonicus*. [Imit, from its cry]

Chickasaw /chik'ə-sö/ *n* (a member of) a tribe of Native Americans, now mainly living in Oklahoma; the Muskogean language of the Chickasaw. ◆ *adj* of or relating to the Chickasaw or their language.

chickling[1] /chik'ling/ *n* a species of pea (also **chickling vetch** *Lathyrus sativus*). [Earlier *chich*, *chichling*, from Fr *chiche*, from L *cicer* chickpea]

chickling[2] see under **chick**[1].

chickpea /chik'pē/ *n* a leguminous plant, *Cicer arietinum*; its edible pea-like seed. [Earlier *chick-pease*, with ety as **chickling**]

chicle /chik'l/ or /chik'li/ *n* the gum of the sapodilla tree, the main ingredient in chewing gum. [Sp, from Nahuatl]

chicly see under **chic**.

chico see **chica**.

chicory or **chiccory** /chik'ə-ri/ *n* a blue-flowered composite plant (*Cichorium intybus*); its carrot-like root (roasted and ground and used as a coffee substitute); its leaves used for salad. [Fr *chicorée*, from L *cichorēum*, from Gr *kichorion*]
■ **chic'on** /-ən/ *n* the shoot of the chicory plant, eaten like lettuce.

chide /chīd/ *vt* (**chid'ing**; **chid** or sometimes **chīd'ed** or **chode** (*archaic*); **chid** or **chidd'en** or sometimes **chīd'ed**) to scold, rebuke, reprove by words. ◆ *vi* to make a snarling, murmuring sound, as a dog or trumpet does. [OE *cīdan* (a weak verb)]
■ **chīd'er** *n* (*Shakesp*) a quarrelsome person. **chīd'ing** *n* scolding. **chīd'ingly** *adv*.

chidlings see **chitterling**.

chief /chēf/ *adj* head; principal, highest; first; outstanding, important (with *compar* **chief'er**, *superl* **chief'est**); intimate (*Scot*). ◆ *adv* chiefly. ◆ *n* a head or principal person; a leader; the principal part or top of anything; the greater part; the upper part of the field cut off by a horizontal line, generally occupying the upper third of the area of the shield (*heraldry*). [Fr *chef*, from L *caput* the head]
■ **chief'dom** or **chief'ship** *n* the state of being chief; sovereignty. **chief'ery** or **chief'ry** (*Spenser* **chev'erye**) *n* an Irish chieftaincy; the dues paid to a chief or the supreme lord; a chief's lands. **chief'ess** *n* a female chief. **chief'less** *adj* without a chief or leader. **chief'ling** *n*. **chief'ly** *adv* in the first place; principally; for the most part. **chief'tain** *n* (also *fem* **chief'tainess**) the head of a clan; a leader or commander. **chief'taincy** *n*. **chief'tainry** *n*. **chief'tainship** *n*.
❑ **chief-bar'on** *n* the President of the Court of Exchequer. **Chief Constable** *n* (in UK) an officer commanding the police force in an administrative area. **chief executive** *n* the senior director of a business organization. **chief justice** see under **justice**. **chief petty officer** *n* a non-commissioned officer in the navy above petty officer in rank. **chief technician** *n* a non-commissioned officer in the RAF below flight sergeant in rank.
■ **chief of staff** (*milit*) a senior staff officer; (with *cap*) the senior officer of each of the armed forces (in the USA of the army and air force). **in chief** borne in the upper part of the shield (*heraldry*); (of a tenure) held directly from the sovereign; most importantly (**-in-chief** *combining form* denoting at the head, first in rank, as in *commander-in-chief*).

chield /chēld/ (*Scot*) *n* a lad, a man (also **chiel**). [Appar a form of **child**]

chiffchaff /chif'chaf/ *n* a small European warbler, *Phylloscopus collybita*. [Imit of its call]

chiffon /shif'on or shē'fɔ̃/ *n* a thin fine clothing fabric of silk, nylon, etc; a light frothy mixture used to make soufflés, cakes, etc; (in *pl*) trimmings, or other adornments. [Fr, rag, adornment, from *chiffe* rag]
■ **chiffonier** or **chiffonnier** /shif-ən-ēr'/ *n* an ornamental cabinet; a chest of drawers.

chigger see **chigoe**.

chignon /shē'nyon or shē-nyɔ̃'/ *n* a knot or roll of hair worn at the back of the head and neck. [Fr, the nape of the neck (jointed like a chain), from *chaînon* link of a chain, from *chaîne* a chain]

chigoe /chig'ō/, **chigre** or **chigger** /chig'ər/ *n* (also **jigg'er**) a tropical American, African and Indian sand flea (*Tunga penetrans*), the pregnant female of which buries itself in the skin of its host, esp beneath the toenails; the parasitic larva of a harvest mite (genus *Trombicula*) of America, Europe and Asia, that burrows in the skin. [W Ind name; cf Carib *chigo*, and Wolof (W African language) *jiga* an insect]

chihuahua /chi-wä'wə/ *n* a breed of very small dog, orig from Mexico, weighing around 1kg (2lb), with big eyes and pointed ears. [*Chihuahua* in Mexico]

chik same as **chick**[2].

chikara[1] /chi-kä'rə/ *n* a four-horned Indian antelope; an Indian gazelle (also **chinka'ra**). [Hindi]

chikara[2] /chik'ə-rə/ *n* an Indian instrument of the violin class. [Hindi *cikārā*]

chikhor or **chikor** see **chukor**.

chi kung same as **qigong**.

chikungunya /chik-ən-gŭn'yə/ *n* a mosquito-borne virus which causes symptoms of fever, dehydration and severe joint pain. [Makonde (a Tanzanian language), literally 'that which bends up', referring to the contorted posture of its victims]

chilblain /chil'blān/ *n* a painful red swelling, esp on hands and feet, caused by constriction of small blood vessels in cold weather. [**chill**[1] and **blain**[1]]
■ **chil'blained** *adj*.

child /chīld/ *n* (*pl* **children** /chil'drən/; double *pl* from (*old* and *dialect*) **chil'der**) a very young person (up to the age of sixteen for the purpose of some acts of parliament, under fourteen in criminal law); a female infant (*dialect* and *archaic*); a son or daughter; a childish person; a person strongly influenced by, associated with, or a product of (another person, or group of people, an age or environment, etc); a disciple or adherent; (also **childe** or **chylde**) a youth of gentle birth, esp in ballads, etc (*archaic*); an offspring; a descendant; an inhabitant. ◆ *vt* and *vi* (*archaic*) to bring forth. [OE *cild*, pl *cild*, later *cildru*, *cildra*]
■ **child'ed** *adj* (*Shakesp*) possessed of a child. **child'hood** *n* the state of being a child; the time of being a child. **child'ing** *adj* (*Shakesp*) fruiting, teeming. **child'ish** *adj* of or like a child; silly; trifling. **child'ishly** *adv*. **child'ishness** *n* that which is suitable or natural to a child; puerility. **child'less** *adj* without children. **child'lessness** *n*. **child'like** *adj* like a child; becoming a child; docile; innocent. **child'ly** *adj* (*archaic*) natural or becoming to a child. **child'ness** *n* (*Shakesp*) the nature or character of a child.
❑ **child abuse** *n* any form of physical or mental cruelty to or neglect of a child by a parent or guardian. **child allowance** *n* child benefit (see below). **child'bearing** *n* the act or condition of carrying and giving birth to children. **child'-bearing** *adj*. **child'bed** *n* (*archaic*) the state or condition of a woman giving birth to a child. **childbed fever** *n* an old name for puerperal fever. **child benefit** *n* (*Brit* and *NZ*) an allowance granted by the government to parents for children. **child'birth** *n* the giving birth to a child; parturition. **child'care** *n* the provision of residential care by local authorities or other organizations for children whose parents are unable to care for them; the provision of part-time care for children while their parents are at work. **child'crowing** *n* a nervous affection with spasm of the muscles closing the glottis. **child endowment** *n* (*Aust*) child benefit. **child guidance** *n* professional counselling of disturbed or disruptive children. **child lock** *n* a device that prevents a child opening or tampering with something, such as a car door, video equipment, etc. **child'minder** *n* a person, usu untrained but often listed on an official register as being fit, who looks after other people's children. **child'proof** or **child'-resistant** *adj* not able to be damaged, opened, worked, etc by a child. **Children's Panel** *n* (in the Scottish legal system) a panel of people drawn from social services, the community and other relevant agencies that hear (in private) cases of child crime or child abuse that occur in a locality (in 1970 Children's Panels took over most of the functions of the juvenile courts). **child's play** *n* something very easy to do. **child'-study** *n* the psychology and physiology of children. **child support** *n* financial support provided by a parent no longer directly supporting his or her child. **Child Support Agency** *n* in Britain, a government agency established in 1993 with responsibility for determining levels of child support required from parents (*abbrev* **CSA**). **child welfare** *n* the health and wellbeing of young children as an object of systematic social work. **child-wife** *n* a very young wife.
■ **second childhood** the childishness of old age. **with child** (*archaic* or *literary*) pregnant.

Childermas /chil'dər-məs or -mas/ (archaic) n Holy Innocents' Day, a festival (28 December) to commemorate the slaying of the children by Herod. [OE cildra, genitive pl of cild child, and mæsse mass]

Chile /chil'i/ adj of or relating to Chile, a republic in S America. ■ **Chil'ean** or obs **Chil'ian** n and adj. ◻ **Chile** (or **Chilean**) **pine** n the monkey puzzle. **Chile saltpetre** n impure naturally-occurring sodium nitrate.

chile /chīl/ variant form of **child**.

chili[1] or **chile** /chil'i/ variant forms of **chilli**.

chili[2] /shil'ē/ n a hot dry wind of N Africa. [Berber]

chiliad /kil'i-ad or -əd/ n the number 1000; 1000 of anything; a period of 1000 years, a millennium. [Gr chīlias, -ados, from chīlioi 1000] ■ **chil'iagon** n a plane figure with 1000 angles. **chiliahē'dron** n a solid figure with 1000 plane faces. **chiliarch** /kil'i-ärk/ n a leader or commander of a thousand men. **chil'iarchy** n the position of chiliarch. **chil'iasm** n the doctrine that at some future time Christ will reign bodily upon the earth for 1000 years. **chil'iast** n a person who holds this belief; a person who believes in a coming happier time on earth. **chilias'tic** adj.

chill[1] /chil/ n coldness; a cold that causes shivering; an attack of shivering with chattering teeth, pale skin and a sensation of coldness, often preceding a fever (med); anything that disheartens or damps the spirits; a type of foundry mould that accelerates cooling. ◆ adj shivering with cold; slightly cold; unfriendly, aloof. ◆ vi to grow cold; (of a metal) to become hardened by cooling; to relax (inf). ◆ vt to make chill or cold; to cool; to preserve by cold; to injure with cold; to discourage or dishearten; to fill with dread; to cloud or bloom the surface of (by cold air); to harden (a metal) by cooling; to take the chill off (dialect). [OE cele, ciele cold; see **cold**, **cool**] ■ **chilled** adj made cold; hardened by chilling, as iron; preserved by cold, as beef. **chill'er** n. **chill'ily** adv. **chill'iness** n. **chill'ing** n and adj. **chill'ingly** adv. **chill'ness** n. **chill'y** adj cold; chilling; sensitive to cold; unfriendly, aloof. ◻ **chill cabinet** n a refrigerated cabinet for displaying perishable foods in shops, supermarkets, etc. **chilled meal** n a ready-prepared dish kept at a low temperature but not frozen, and sold from a chill cabinet. **chilled-out** adj (inf) having a relaxed mood or atmosphere. **chill factor** n the degree by which weather conditions, eg wind (as in wind-chill factor), increase the effect of low temperatures. **chill'-out** (inf) a period of relaxation. ◆ adj (esp of music) suitable for relaxation. **chilly bin** n (NZ) an insulated container for transporting food and drink packed in ice, eg for picnics, etc. ■ **chill out** (inf) to relax, eg after a period of hard work or strenuous exercise. **take a chill pill** (sl) to calm down. **take the chill off** to warm slightly; to make lukewarm.

chill[2] see **ch**.

chillada /chi-lä'də/ n in Mexican cookery, a spiced fried cake made from puréed vegetables and lentils, flavoured with green peppers.

chillax /chi-laks'/ (sl) vi to relax completely. [**chill**[1] and **relax**]

chilli, **chili** or **chile** /chil'i/ n (pl **chill(i)'is**, **chil(i)'ies** or **chil'es**) the pod of one of the varieties of capsicum, extremely pungent and stimulant, used in sauces, pickles, etc, and dried and ground to form cayenne pepper; chilli con carne (inf). [Nahuatl] ◻ **chilli con carne** /kon kär'nē/ n a spicy dish of minced meat, chillis or chilli powder, and often kidney beans, tomatoes, etc, originating in Mexico. **chilli dog** n (US) a hot-dog served with a topping of chilli sauce. **chilli powder** n a blend of spices, containing ground dried red chillis.

Chillingham cattle /chil'ing-əm kat'əl/ n pl an ancient breed of wild, white-coated cattle, bred on the Chillingham estate in Northumberland.

chillum /chil'um/ n the part of a hookah containing the tobacco and charcoal balls; a hookah itself; the act of smoking it. [Hindi chilam]

Chilognatha /kī-log'nä-thə/ n pl the order which contains the millipedes. [Gr cheilos lip, and gnathos jaw]

chilopod /kī'lə-pod or -lō-/ or **chilopodan** /kī-lop'ə-dən/ n a member of the order Chilopoda which contains the centipedes. [Gr cheilos lip, and pous, podos foot]

Chiltern Hundreds see under **hundred**.

chimaera older spelling of **chimera**.

chimb see **chime**[2].

chime[1] /chīm/ n a set of bells tuned in a scale; (often in pl) the ringing of such bells in succession; a definite sequence of bell-like notes sounded as by a clock; the harmonious sound of bells or other musical instruments; agreement of sound or of relation; harmony; rhyme; jingle. ◆ vi to sound a chime or in chime; to accord or agree; to jingle; to rhyme; to say words or recite in a rhythmic or mechanical manner. ◆ vt to strike, or cause to sound in chime; to indicate by chiming. [ME chimbe, perh from OFr cymbale, from L cymbalum a cymbal] ■ **chime in** (inf) to join in, in agreement.

chime[2] or **chimb** /chīm/ n (also **chine**) the rim formed by the ends of the staves of a cask; a hollowed or bevelled channel in the waterway of a ship's deck (naut). [Cognate with Du kim, Ger Kimme edge]

chimer /chim'ər/ or **chimere** /chi-mēr'/ n a long sleeveless tabard; the upper robe worn by a bishop. [OFr chamarre ; cf **cymar**; Sp zamarra, chamarra sheepskin]

chimera or **chimaera** /kī- or ki-mē'rə/ n (sometimes with cap) any idle or wild fancy; an organism (plant or animal) made up of two genetically distinct tissues (biol); a DNA molecule with sequences from more than one organism (biol); a fabled fire-spouting monster, with a lion's head, a serpent's tail, and a goat's body (Gr myth); a picture or representation of an animal having its parts made up of various animals. [L, from Gr chimaira a she-goat] ■ **chimeric** /-mer'ik/ or **chimer'ical** adj of the nature of a chimera; wild; fanciful; relating to an organism made up of, or created by combining, genetic material from two distinct species. **chimer'ically** adv. **chimer'id** n a fish of the genus Chimaera or related genera of the family **Chimaer'idae** /-i-dē/. **chimer'ism** n the state of being, or the process of creating, a genetic chimera.

chimere see **chimer**.

chiminea /chim-i-nā'ə/ n a free-standing fireplace for outdoor use. [Sp, chimney]

chimney /chim'ni/ n a passage for the escape of fumes, smoke or heated air from a fireplace, engine or furnace; a chimney stack; a glass tube surrounding a lamp flame; a volcanic vent; a steeply-inclined part of a lode or one that branches from the main lode (mining); a cleft in a rock-face just large enough for a mountaineer to enter and climb. —Also (dialect) **chim'ley** or **chum'ley**. ◆ vt (mountaineering) to climb (a narrow crevice) with one's back against one wall and feet against the other. [Fr cheminée, from L camīnus a furnace] ◻ **chim'neyboard** n a board blocking up a fireplace. **chim'neybreast** n the part of a wall that projects into a room and contains the fireplace and chimney. **chimney can** n a chimney pot. **chim'ney-corner** or **chim'ney-nook** (Scot **-nuik**) n in old chimneys, (a seat in) the space between the fire and the side wall of the fireplace; the fireside, commonly spoken of as the place for the aged and infirm. **chimney piece** n a shelf over the fireplace, a mantelpiece. **chimney pot** n a cylindrical pipe of earthenware or other material at the top of a chimney; a top-hat (in full **chimney-pot hat**). **chimney shaft** n the part of a chimney which rises above the roof, or a chimney standing isolated, such as a factory chimney. **chimney stack** n a group of chimneys or flues contained within a single unit; a chimney stalk. **chimney stalk** n a very tall chimney, usu serving a factory or power station. **chimney swallow** n the common swallow; a species of N American swift (also **chimney swift**). **chim'ney-sweep** or **chim'ney-sweeper** n a person who sweeps or cleans chimneys. **chimney top** n the top of a chimney.

chimo /chē'mō/ (Can) interj a word used as a greeting. [From Eskimo-Aleut]

Chimonanthus /kī-mō-nan'thəs/ n a genus of shrubs native to China, esp C. praecox, the winter-sweet, a deciduous species cultivated for its yellow spicy-scented flowers which appear in winter. [New L, from Gr cheimon winter, and anthos flower]

chimpanzee /chim-pan-zē'/ n (often shortened to **chimp**) an intelligent anthropoid ape (Pan troglodytes) inhabiting the tropical central African forests, usu living as part of a group of four to twenty individuals and considered to be the primate that most closely resembles man in intelligence and social behaviour. [W African dialect]

Chin. abbrev : China; Chinese.

chin /chin/ n the jutting part of the face below the mouth, the front of the lower jaw. ◆ vt to attack by striking on the chin (sl); to question or tackle aggressively or impertinently (sl); to pull oneself up so that one's chin reaches (a horizontal bar), as a gymnastics exercise. [OE cin ; Ger Kinn, Gr genys (jaw)] ■ **chin'less** adj having a receding chin; ineffectual and not very clever, esp applied to an upper-class person, as in chinless wonder (facetious). ◻ **chin'strap** n the strap on a helmet, etc that goes under the chin. **chin'-up** n a physical exercise in which the arms are used to lift the chin over a bar suspended above head height. **chin'wag** n and vi (sl) chat. ■ **keep one's chin up** to keep cheerful in a difficult situation (usu shortened to **chin up!** used as an encouragement). **take it on the chin** to face misfortune, defeat, criticism, etc courageously and without flinching.

china[1] /chī'nə/ n (orig **chi'naware**) articles of porcelain brought from China in the 16c; Chinese porcelain or esp any Western imitation or version of it; mate (from *china plate*; *Cockney rhyming sl*). ◆ *adj* made of china; (with *cap*) of, from, etc China. [Prob from the Ch'in dynasty, 3c BC]

■ **Chinee'** *n* (*archaic*; *inf*) a Chinese person. **Chinese** /chī-nēz'/ *n* a native or citizen of China (*pl* **Chinese'**); the language of China; a meal of Chinese food (*inf*); a Chinese restaurant (*inf*). ◆ *adj* (in names of commodities, sometimes without *cap*) of, concerning or relating, etc to China, its language or its people.

❑ **China aster** see under **aster**. **china bark** see **cinchona**. **chi'naberry** *n* a tropical Asian tree (*Melia azedarach*) of the family Meliaceae (also called **china tree**); its yellow, bead-like fruit; soapberry. **china clay** *n* kaolin, fine white clay used in making porcelain, etc. **China goose** *n* the Chinese goose. **China grass** *n* rami. **China ink** see under **ink**. **China jute** *n* a species of *Abutilon*. **Chi'naman** *n* a Chinese person (*derog*); (without *cap*) a ball bowled by a left-arm bowler that spins in the opposite direction to the bowler's usual delivery (*cricket*). **chi'naroot** *n* root-stock of *Smilax china*. **China rose** *n* any of several garden roses, *esp Rosa chinensis*, a shrub rose, ancestor of many cultivated varieties. **china stone** *n* partly kaolinized granite. **China tea** *n* a kind of tea grown in China and smoke-cured. **Chi'natown** *n* a Chinese quarter in a city or town. **china tree** see **chinaberry** above. **Chinese block** *n* the Chinese temple block. **Chinese boxes** *n pl* a set of boxes nesting one inside another, so that when one box is opened, yet another is found to be opened inside it. **Chinese broccoli** or **Chinese kale** *n* another name for gai lan. **Chinese burn** *n* the burning pain caused by gripping another person's lower arm with two hands and deliberately twisting the flesh in opposite directions. **Chinese cabbage** *n* either of two kinds of plant, *Brassica chinensis* or *Brassica pekinensis*, with edible leaves (also called **bok choy**, **pak choi**). **Chinese checkers** or **chequers** *n* a board game similar to draughts for two, four or six players. **Chinese Chippendale** *n* a style of Chippendale furniture in which Chinese motifs are used. **Chinese copy** *n* an exact copy, including all the defects in the original. **Chinese goose** *n* the largest living goose, *Anser* (or *Cygnopsis*) *cygnoides*, domesticated in E Asia. **Chinese gooseberry** *n* another name for kiwi fruit. **Chinese herbal medicine** *n* the use of combinations of various properties and attributes of herbs to restore balance of qi and nourish the constitution. **Chinese lantern** *n* a collapsible paper lantern. **Chinese lantern plant** same as **winter cherry** (see under **winter**). **Chinese layering** *n* air layering (qv). **Chinese leaves** *n pl* the edible leaves of Chinese cabbage. **Chinese paper** *n* a fine soft brownish paper-like material made from bamboo bark, used in making fine impressions of engravings; also the so-called rice paper. **Chinese pavilion** see under **pavilion**. **Chinese puzzle** *n* a very difficult puzzle or problem. **Chinese radish** *n* mooli (also **white radish**, **daikon**). **Chinese red** *n* a bright-red colour or pigment. **Chinese restaurant syndrome** *n* a short-lived illness with symptoms including chest pain, dizziness and flushing, attributed to the consumption of too much monosodium glutamate, common in Chinese food. **Chinese sugarcane** see under **sorghum**. **Chinese temple block** *n* a percussion instrument consisting of a hollow wooden block that is struck with a hammer. **Chinese wall** *n* (often in *pl*) the strict demarcation barrier which must exist between eg the corporate finance and investment advisory departments of a bank, etc in order to ensure that privileged information available to one department is not available to the other and so prevent conflicts of interest from arising. **Chinese water deer** *n* a small deer (*Hydropotes inermis*) of swampland in China and Korea, having tusks and no antlers. **Chinese whispers** *n sing* a game in which a message is passed in a whisper from one to another of a group of people, with the result that the final version is different from the original, often amazingly or humorously so. **Chinese white** *n* a zinc oxide pigment.

china² /kin'ə, kē'nə/ see **quina**.

Chinagraph® /chī'nə-gräf/ *n* a kind of pencil that writes on glass, porcelain, etc. [**china¹**, and Gr *graphein* to write]

chinampa /chi-nam'pə/ *n* a 'floating garden' or artificial island, as used in an Aztec method of agriculture in which areas of shallow lake bed were made cultivable by being built up with layers of twigs and earth. [Sp, from Nahuatl *chinamitl*]

chinar same as **chenar**.

chincapin see **chinkapin**.

chinch /chinch/ (*Southern US*) *n* the bedbug. [Sp *chinche*, from L *cimex*]

❑ **chinch bug** *n* a heteropterous insect (*Blissus leucopterus*), a serious pest of cereal crops in the USA.

chinchilla /chin-chil'ə/ *n* a small rodent of S America valued for its soft grey fur; the fur itself; (with *cap*) a breed of rabbits, or of cats, with soft grey fur. [Sp]

chin-chin /chin'chin'/ (*inf*) *interj* hello; goodbye; good health (as a toast). [Anglo-Chin, from Chin *qǐng qǐng*]

chincough /chin'kof/ (*dialect*) *n* whooping cough. [For *chink-cough*; cf Scot *kink-hoast*, Du *kinkhoest*; see **chink³** and **cough**]

chindit /chin'dit/ (also with *cap*) *n* a member of General Orde Wingate's Allied commando force in Burma (now Myanmar) during World War II. [Burmese *chinthey* a griffin, the force's badge]

chine¹ /chīn/ *n* a piece of the backbone and adjoining parts of an animal (*esp* of a pig) for cooking; the spine or backbone (*archaic*); anything resembling a backbone; the crest of a ridge; the extreme outside longitudinal member of the planing bottom of a flying-boat hull or a seaplane float, running parallel with the hull (*aeronautics*). ◆ *vt* to break the back of. [OFr *eschine*, prob from OHGer *scina* pin, thorn]

chine² /chīn/ *n* a ravine. [OE *cinu* a cleft]

chine³ see **chime²**.

chiné /shē-nā'/ *adj* (of fabric) mottled, with the pattern printed on the warp. [Fr, dyed in a (supposedly) Chinese way]

Chinee, **Chinese** see under **china¹**.

Chink /chingk/, **Chinkie** or **Chinky** /ching'ki/ (*inf* and *offensive*) *n* and *adj* Chinese. [*China*]

■ **chink'ie** or **chink'y** *n* a meal of Chinese food; a Chinese restaurant.

chink¹ /chingk/ *n* a cleft, a narrow opening; a narrow beam of light. ◆ *vi* to crack. ◆ *vt* to fill up cracks. [Appar formed upon ME *chine* a crack, from OE *cinu* a cleft]

■ **chink'y** *adj* full of chinks.

■ **chink in someone's armour** a significant weakness or vulnerable point in someone's personality.

chink² /chingk/ *n* a clinking sound, as of coins or glasses; money (in *Shakesp* **chinks**) (*sl*). ◆ *vi* to emit a sharp ringing sound. ◆ *vt* to cause (coins, glasses, etc) to make a sharp ringing by clinking together. [Imit]

chink³ /chingk/ (*Scot and N Eng* **kink** /kingk/) (*dialect*) *n* a gasp for breath. ◆ *vi* to gasp. [Cf Du *kinken* to cough; Ger *keichen* to gasp]

chinkapin, **chincapin** or **chinquapin** /ching'kə-pin/ *n* the dwarf chestnut of the USA. [Algonquian]

chinkara see **chikara¹**.

chinkerinchee, **chinks** see **chincherinchee**.

Chino- /chī-nō-/ *combining form* denoting of or relating to China. See also **Sino-**.

chino /shē'nō or chē'nō/ (*orig US*) *n* (*pl* **chi'nos**) a strong cloth of twilled cotton; (in *pl*) trousers made from this cloth. [Am, from Sp]

chinoiserie /shē-nwä-z(ə-)rē'/ (*Fr*) *n* (a decorative or fine art object in) a style of design or decoration that uses or copies Chinese motifs or methods.

Chinook /chi-nook'/ *n* (a member of) a tribe of Native Americans of the NW Pacific coast; their Penutian language; a pidgin language, consisting of words from French, English, Chinook, and other Native American tongues, formerly used by fur traders and settlers in NW USA (also **Chinook Jargon**); (without *cap*) a warm dry wind blowing down the eastern side of the Rocky Mountains, making winter grazing possible; also, a warm moist wind blowing onto the NW coast of the USA from the Pacific.

❑ **Chinook salmon** *n* the king salmon.

chinovnik /chi-nov'nik/ *n* a high official in the Russian civil service; a bureaucrat. [Russ, from *chin* rank]

chinquapin see **chinkapin**.

chintz /chints/ *n* a fabric cotton, sometimes glazed, *usu* printed in several colours on a white or light ground. [Orig *pl*, from Hindi *chīt* spotted cotton cloth]

■ **chintz'y** *adj* covered with, or like, chintz; (of decor) flowery, like chintz (often *derog*); cheap, tawdry; mean, miserly.

chionodoxa /kī-ə-nō-dok'sə/ *n* any plant of the genus *Chionodoxa*, commonly called glory-of-the-snow, having early-blooming star-shaped flowers. [Gr *chion* snow, and *doxa* glory]

chip /chip/ *vt* (**chipp'ing**; **chipped**) to strike with small sharp cutting blows; to strike or break small pieces off the surface of (also with *at*); to remove by chipping (often with *away* or *off*); to slice or pare; to cut as with an adze; to chaff, tease (*inf*). ◆ *vi* to become chipped; to play a chip shot. ◆ *n* an act of chipping; a piece chipped off, *esp* a flattish fragment; a small fragment of stone (also **chipp'ing**); a surface flaw or mark left when a small piece has been broken off; a thin slice or small piece of food, eg fruit; a potato-chip; a potato crisp (*N Am*); a thin strip of wood, used for making boxes, baskets, etc; a basket or container made in this way; a small, flat piece of wood, plastic, etc used to represent money in certain games; a popular name for an integrated circuit, derived from the method of manufacture in which each chip, containing the microcircuit, is made as part of a wafer (also called **microchip** or **silicon chip**); a piece of money (*sl*); a piece of dried dung of cow or bison; a hit or kick which sends a ball high into the air over a short distance (*sport*); a chip shot (*golf*); a key on a musical instrument (*archaic*). [ME *chippen*; MLGer, MDu *kippen* to hatch by chipping shell]

■ **chipp'er** *n* a device that makes chips; a chip shop (*Irish inf*). **chipp'ie** *n* (*NZ*) a potato crisp. **chipp'ing** *n*. **chipp'y** *adj* abounding in chips; dry as a chip; seedy from taking too much alcohol; touchy, quarrelsome, aggressive (*Can inf*); having a chip on one's shoulder (see below; *inf*). ◆ *n* (also **chipp'ie**) (a meal from) a chip shop (*inf*); see also **chips** and separate entry **chippy**[1]. **chips** *n* (*sl*) a carpenter (also **chipp'y**); a regimental pioneer sergeant, *usu* a carpenter; money. ◆ *n pl* (*inf*) fried potato-chips.

❑ **chip and PIN** *n* a system of payment using a credit or debit card with an integrated microchip, the card-holder entering a personal identification number to authorize the payment. **chip'-based** *adj* (*electronics*) (of parts or equipment) using, controlled by or incorporating microchips. **chip basket** *n* a fruit basket of interwoven chips; a metal basket in which potato-chips are placed for frying. **chip'board** *n* reconstructed wood made by consolidation of chips from woodland trimmings, workshop waste, etc, with added resin; a wastepaper cardboard used in box-making. **chip carving** *n* wood carving by removal of small splinters. **chip hat** *n* a hat of palm-leaf strips. **chip heater** *n* (*Aust* and *NZ*) a type of water-heater that is fuelled by burning chips of wood. **chip'set** *n* (*comput*) a group of chips that performs particular functions. **chip shop** *n* a restaurant selling takeaway meals of fish and chips, etc. **chip shot** *n* (*golf*) a shot, *usu* from close to the green, giving the ball a low trajectory so that it runs forward on pitching.

■ **chip in** to enter the game by putting chips on the table (*gambling*); to interpose; to pay part of the cost of something (*inf*). **chip off** (or *orig* **of**) **the old block** someone with the characteristics of (*usu* one of) their parents. **chip on one's shoulder** an aggressively defiant manner, as if daring anyone to knock it off; sensitivity or readiness to take offence, *usu* about a supposed fault or weakness in one's personality or background; bitterness, grievance. **have had one's chips** to have died; to have had and lost one's chance; to have been beaten. **when the chips are down** at a moment of crisis or critically important time.

chipmunk /*chip'mungk*/ or **chipmuck** /*-muk*/ *n* any mainly terrestrial squirrel (*Tamias* or *Eutamias*) of N America and parts of Asia, with dark stripes on the back and cheekpouches for storing and carrying food. [From Native American name]

chipochia see **capocchia**.

chipolata /*chip-ə-lä'tə*/ *n* a small sausage, used as a garnish, etc. [Fr, from Ital *cipolla* onion]

chipotle /*chi-pot'lā*/ *n* a dried and smoked jalapeño chilli pepper, used in Mexican cooking. [Mex Sp]

Chippendale /*chip'ən-dāl*/ *adj* applied to a style of furniture, made by, designed by, or after the style of Thomas *Chippendale*, an 18c English cabinetmaker; also applied to a style of bookplates.

chipper[1] /*chip'ər*/ (*inf*) *adj* briskly cheerful; well, fit. [Perh same word as Scot and N Eng dialect *kipper* lively]

chipper[2] see under **chip**.

Chippewa /*chip'ə-wä*/ *n* same as **Ojibwa**.

chipping sparrow /*chip'ing spar'ō*/ *n* a small N American sparrow (*Spizella passerina*) with a reddish-brown crown and white breast. [Imit of its cry]

chippy[1] /*chip'i*/ (*N Am*) *n* a flirtatious or promiscuous woman. [**chip**, variant of **cheep**]

chippy[2] see under **chip**.

chiquichiqui /*chē-kē-chē'kē*/ *n* a piassava palm (genus *Leopoldinia*). [Tupí]

chiragra /*kī-rag'rə*/ *n* gout in the hand. [Gr *cheiragrā*, from *cheir* hand, and *agrā* a catching]

■ **chirag'ric** or **chirag'rical** *adj*.

chirality /*kī-ral'i-ti*/ *n* the property of a chemical, *esp* a crystal, of existing in left-handed and right-handed structural forms; the handedness of such a chemical. [Gr *cheir* hand]

■ **chī'ral** *adj*.

chi-rho /*kī'rō'*/ (*Christianity*) *n* (also *cap*) a monogram of XP (*chī*, *rhō*, ch, r), the first letters of the Greek *Christos* (Christ).

chirimoya same as **cherimoya**.

chirk /*chûrk*/ *vi* to chirp or squeak; to grate (*Scot*). [OE *cearcian* to creak]

chirl /*chîrl* or *chûrl*/ (*Scot*) *vi* to emit a low sound; to warble. ◆ *n* a kind of musical warble. [Imit]

chirm /*chûrm*/ *vi* to cry out; to chirp. ◆ *n* noise, din, hum of voices; a flock of goldfinches (also **charm**). [OE *cirman* to cry out; cf Du *kermen*]

chiro- or **cheiro-**, etc /*kī-rō-* or *kī-ro-*/ *combining form* denoting hand. [Gr *cheir* hand]

■ **chirog'nomy** *n* (Gr *gnōmē* understanding) palmistry. **chi'rŏgraph** *n* (Gr *graphein* to write) a written or signed document. **chirog'rapher** *n* (*obs*) an official of the Court of Common Pleas. **chirŏgraph'ic** or **chirŏgraph'ical** *adj*. **chirog'raphist** *n* an expert in handwriting; a palmist (*Pope*). **chirog'raphy** *n* handwriting, penmanship; calligraphy. **chirol'ogist** *n*. **chirol'ogy** *n* the language of gesture; the study of the hand. **chi'rŏmancy** /*-man-si*/ *n* (Gr *manteiā* divination) fortune-telling by reading the hand. **chirŏmant'ic** or **chirŏmant'ical** *adj*. **chiron'omer** *n* (Gr *nomos* law) a gesticulator. **chirŏnom'ic** *adj*. **chironomid** /*kī-ron'ō-mid*/ *n* a member of a large genus of common midges (*Chironomus*) of the family **Chironomidae** /*kī-rō-nom'i-dē*/. **chiron'omy** *n* the art of gesticulation or of mime. **chirop'teran** *n* (Gr *pteron* wing) a member of the **Chirop'tera**, an order of mammals comprising the bats. **chiropteroph'ilous** *adj* (Gr *phileein* to love) (of flowers) pollinated by bats. **chirop'terous** *adj*. **Chirŏthē'rium** *n* (Gr *thērion* beast) a Triassic labyrinthodont animal with hand-like footprints.

Chiron /*kī'ron* or *-rən*/ *n* a body *orig* thought to be a minor planet with an orbit between Saturn and Uranus, but now reckoned to be a very large comet. [Named after a centaur in Gr mythology]

chiropodist /*ki-rop'ə-dist* (older *kī-*, also *shi-*)/ *n* a person who treats minor ailments of the feet, eg corns, verrucas. [Appar Gr *cheir* hand, and *pous*, *podos* foot; but *cheiropodēs* means having chapped feet]

■ **chiropŏ'dial** *adj*. **chirop'ody** *n*.

chiropractic /*kī-rə-prak'tik*/ *n* a method of treating disorders of the locomotor system, which relies upon the removal of abnormal nerve functioning by manipulation of the spinal column; a chiropractor. [Gr *cheir* hand, and *praktikos* concerned with action, from *prattein* to do]

■ **chīroprac'tor** *n* a person who practises chiropractic.

chirp /*chûrp*/ *n* the sharp thin sound of certain birds and insects. ◆ *vi* to make such a sound; to talk in a cheerful and lively fashion. ◆ *vt* to urge by chirping. [Imit]

■ **chirp'er** *n* a little bird. **chirp'ily** *adv*. **chirp'iness** *n*. **chirp'ing** *adj*. **chirp'y** *adj* lively; merry.

chirr or **chirre** /*chûr*/ *vi* to chirp like a cricket or grasshopper. ◆ *n* this sound. [Imit]

chirrup /*chir'əp*/ *vi* to chirp; to make a clucking sound with the mouth, as when urging on a horse; to cheer up. ◆ *n* the sound made when chirruping. [Lengthened form of **chirp**, associated with **cheer up**]

■ **chirr'upy** *adj* cheerful.

chirt /*chûrt*/ *n* a squeeze; a squirt. ◆ *vt* to squeeze; to squirt. [Connected with **chirr**]

chiru /*chi'*/ or *chē'roo*/ *n* (*pl* **chi'ru**) a species of Tibetan antelope (*Pantholops hodgsonii*) whose fine wool is used to make shahtooshes. [Tibetan]

chirurgeon /*kī-rûr'jən*/, **chirurgery** /*-jə-ri*/ and **chirurgical** /*-ji-kl*/ old forms of **surgeon**, **surgery** and **surgical**. [Fr *chirurgien*, from Gr *cheirourgos*, from *cheir* hand, and *ergon* a work]

■ **chirur'geonly** *adv* (*obs*) in a manner becoming a surgeon.

chisel[1] /*chiz'əl*/ *n* a hand tool consisting of a steel blade with the end bevelled to a cutting edge, used for shaping or working wood, stone or metal. ◆ *vt* (**chis'elling**; **chis'elled**) to cut, carve, etc with a chisel; to cheat (*sl*). [OFr *cisel*, from L *caedere* to cut]

■ **chis'elled** *adj* cut or shaped with a chisel; having sharp outlines, as if cut by a chisel (*fig*). **chis'eller** *n* a person who uses a chisel; a cheat or swindler (*sl*); a child (*Irish sl*). **chis'elling** *n*.

❑ **chisel tooth** *n* a rodent's chisel-shaped incisor.

chisel[2] /*chiz'əl*/ *n* see **chesil**.

Chislev same as **Kislev**.

chit[1] /*chit*/ or **chitty** /*chit'i*/ *n* a short informal letter or note; a bill which one signs and pays at a later date, *esp* in a club, service mess, etc; a voucher or receipt; an order or pass; a testimonial, *esp* a character reference given to a servant. [Anglo-Ind, from Hindi *citthī*]

chit[2] /*chit*/ *n* a child; a girl (*derog*). [*kit*, contraction of **kitten**]

■ **chitt'y** *adj*.

❑ **chitt'y-faced** *adj*.

chit[3] /*chit*/ (*dialect*) *n* a shoot. ◆ *vi* to sprout. ◆ *vt* to cause or encourage (seeds, *esp* seed potatoes) to sprout. [Perh OE *cīth* a shoot]

chital /*chē'təl*/ *n* the axis deer. [Hindi]

chitarrone /*kē-tə-rō'nā*/ *n* (*pl* **chitarro'ni**) a large lute-like instrument with a long double neck. [Ital]

chitchat /*chit'chat*/ *n* chatting or idle talk; prattle; gossip. ◆ *vi* to chat, gossip. [A reduplication of **chat**[1]]

chitin /*kī'tin*/ *n* the substance consisting of polysaccharide which forms most of the hard outer skeletons of arthropods and of the cell walls of fungi. [Fr *chitine*, from Gr *chitōn* a tunic]

■ **chī'tinous** or **chit'inoid** *adj*.

chitlings see **chitterling**.

chiton /kī'ton/ n the loose tunic worn in ancient Greece; any primitive marine mollusc of the genus *Chiton*, with an elongated body covered with a shell of movable plates. [Gr *chitōn* a tunic]

chitosan /kī'tō-zan or -san/ n an amino polysaccharide formed from chitin, claimed to aid weight loss. [**chitin**]

chittagong /chit'ə-gong/ n an Indian variety of domestic fowl. [*Chittagong* in Bangladesh]
□ **chittagong wood** n a cabinetmaker's wood, *usu* that of *Chickrassia tabularis* of the mahogany family.

chitter /chit'ər/ vi to shiver or (of the teeth) to chatter (*dialect*); to chirp or twitter (*N Am*). [Cf **chatter**]
■ **chitt'ering** n and adj.

chitterling /chit'ər-ling/ n (also in *pl*) the smaller intestines of a pig or other edible animal, prepared as a dish (also (*dialect*) **chid'lings** or **chit'lings**); a frill (*obs*). [Ety uncertain]

chiv /chiv or shiv/ (*sl*) n and vt knife (also **shiv**). [From older *chive* knife (thieves' slang) or perh Romany *chiv* blade]

chivalry /shiv'əl-ri (*orig* chiv')/ n the usages and qualifications of chevaliers or knights; bravery and courtesy; the system of knighthood in feudal times and its social code; a body of knights; noblemen, knights collectively. [Fr *chevalerie*, from *cheval*, from LL *caballus* a horse]
■ **chivalric** /-al'/ or **chiv'alrous** adj relating to chivalry; bold; gallant. **chiv'alrously** adv. **chiv'alrousness** n.

chivaree see **charivari**.

chive[1] /chīv/, also **cive** /sīv/ n a herb of the onion family, with tufts of hollow leaves (used in cooking) and clustered bulbs; a small bulb (*archaic*). [Fr *cive*, from L *cēpa* an onion]

chive[2] /chiv/ same as **chiv**.

chivvy, chivy /chi'vi/ or **chevy** /che'vi/ vt to harass, pester or urge; to hunt or chase. ◆ n (*obs*) a hunting cry, a pursuit or hunt. [Perh from the Border ballad of battle, *Chevy Chase*]

chiyogami /chi-yō-gä'mi/ n hand-printed patterned Japanese paper. [Jap]

chizz or **chiz** /chiz/ n (*school sl*) a cheat, swindle; a nuisance. ◆ vi to cheat. [**chisel**[1]]

Ch.J. abbrev : Chief Justice.

Chladni figures same as **sonorous figures** (see under **sonorous**). [After E *Chladni*, 19c German physicist]

chlamys /klam'is/ n (*pl* **chlam'yses** or **chlam'ydes** /-i-dēz/) a short cloak worn by men in ancient Greece; a purple cope. [Gr *chlamys*, pl *chlamydes*]
■ **chlam'ydate** adj (*zool*) (of molluscs) having a mantle. **chlamyd'eous** adj (*bot*) having a perianth. **chlamydia** /klə-mid'i-ə/ n (*pl* **chlamyd'iae** /-ī/ or **chlamyd'ias**) any micro-organisms of the genus *Chlamydia*, resembling viruses and bacteria, which cause various diseases in man and birds and abortion (**chlamydial abortion**) in animals; a sexually transmitted disease caused by *Chlamydia trachomatis*. **chlamyd'ial** adj. **chlamydomo'nas** n a member of the genus *Chlamydomonas* of (mainly freshwater) green algae. **chlam'ydospore** n a thick-walled spore of certain fungi.

chloanthite /klō-an'thīt/ n a valuable nickel ore, nickel arsenide occurring in the cubic system. [From Gr *chloanthēs* sprouting]

chloasma /klō-az'mə/ (*med*) n a condition in which the skin becomes marked by yellowish-brown patches, sometimes occurring during pregnancy or at the time of the menopause. [Gr *chloasma* greenness, yellowness, from *chloē* verdure]

chlor- /klör-/ or **chloro-** /klö-rō- or -rə-/ combining form denoting: chlorine; green. [Gr *chlōros* pale green]
■ **chlor'al** (or /-al'/) n a limpid, colourless, oily liquid (CCl$_3$CHO), of penetrating odour, formed when anhydrous alcohol is acted on by dry chlorine gas (also **trichloroeth'anal**); (loosely) **chloral hydrate**, a white crystalline substance used as a hypnotic and sedative. **chlo'ralism** n the habit, or the morbid effects, of using chloral hydrate. **chlo'ralose** n a hypnotic drug mainly used for anaesthetizing animals in laboratory experiments. **chloram'bucil** /-byū-sil/ n an oral drug used to treat some cancers, eg cancer of the ovary and leukaemia. **chlor'amine** n (*chem*) any of several compounds formed when chlorine reacts with an amine group, used as disinfectants. **chloramphen'icol** n an antibiotic drug used to treat serious infections such as typhoid and cerebrospinal meningitis, and (in the form of eye drops) for bacterial conjunctivitis. **chlorargyrite** /klör-är'ji-rīt/ n (Gr *argyros* silver) horn silver. **chlo'rate** n a salt of chloric acid used in defoliant weedkillers, etc. **chlor'dan** or **chlor'dane** /-dan or -dān/ n a highly poisonous liquid insecticide. **chlordiazepoxide** /-dī-az-i-poks'īd/ n a tranquilliser (C$_{16}$H$_{14}$ClN$_3$O) used to treat anxiety; a hydrochloride derivative of this. **chlorella** /klo-rel'ə/ n a member of the genus *Chlorella* of green freshwater algae. **chlorhexidine** /-heks'id-ēn/ n an antiseptic compound used in skin cleansers,

mouthwashes, etc. **chlo'ric** adj of, containing or derived from chlorine in its pentavalent form (**chloric acid** a monobasic acid (HClO$_3$), a vigorous oxidizing agent). **chlo'ridate** vt to chloridize. **chlo'ride** n a compound of chlorine with another element or radical; bleaching powder (**chloride of lime**), not a true chloride. **chlo'ridize** or **-ise** vt to convert into a chloride; to cover with chloride of silver (*photog*). **chlorim'eter** n same as **chlorometer** below. **chlorimet'ric** adj. **chlorim'etry** n. **chlor'inate** vt to treat or cause to combine with chlorine (as in sterilization of water, extraction of gold from ore). **chlorina'tion** n. **chlor'inator** n. **chlorine** /klō', klö'rēn/ n a yellowish-green halogen gaseous element (symbol **Cl**; atomic no 17) with a peculiar and suffocating odour, used in bleaching, disinfecting, and poison gas warfare (**chlorine water** an aqueous solution of chlorine). **chlorin'ity** n (*esp* in seawater) a measure of the amounts of chlorine, iodine, bromine and fluorine present. **chlo'rinize** or **-ise** vt to chlorinate. **chlo'rite** n a salt of chlorous acid combined with a metal or other chemical (*chem*); a general name for a group of minerals, hydrated silicates of magnesia, iron and alumina, typically dark green and rather soft, resembling mica but not elastic (**chlorite-schist'** a schistose rock composed of chlorite, *usu* with quartz, epidote, etc). **chlorit'ic** adj relating to, of the nature of, or containing, the mineral chlorite (**chloritic marl** a marl at the base of the English Chalk stained green with glauconite (not chlorite). **chloritīzā'tion** or **-s-** n (*geol*) the alteration of ferromagnesian minerals into chlorite or similar material. **chlorobrō'mide** n a compound of chlorine and bromine with a metal or organic radical; a photograph taken on paper coated with this. **chlorocru'orin** n a green respiratory pigment found in some Polychaeta. **chlo'rodyne** n a patent medicine of anodyne and hypnotic effect, containing chloroform. **chlorofluorocar'bon** n an alkane in which chlorine and fluorine atoms have been substituted for hydrogen atoms, used in aerosols, refrigerants, etc, some of which are thought to break down ozone in the earth's atmosphere (*abbrev* **CFC**). **chloroform** /klor'ō-förm/ n a limpid, mobile, colourless, volatile liquid (CHCl$_3$) with a characteristic odour and a strong sweetish taste, used as an anaesthetic, and as a solvent for oils, resins and various other substances (also **trichloromē'thane**). ◆ vt to administer chloroform to, in order to render unconscious. **chlor'oformer** or **chlor'oformist** n. **chlorom'eter** n an apparatus for measuring available chlorine in bleaching powder, etc. **chloromet'ric** adj. **chlorom'etry** n. **Chloromy'cetin**® (or /-mī-sēt'in/) n a brand name for the drug chloramphenicol. **Chlorophyceae** /-fis'i-ē/ n pl (Gr *phykos* seaweed) a class of green algae living predominantly in fresh water. **chlorophyll** or **chlorophyl** /klor'ə-fil or klō'rō-fil/ n (Gr *phyllon* leaf) the green pigment present in all plants and algae, involved in the process of photosynthesis. **chlorophyllous** /klör-of'i-ləs/ adj. **Chlorophyta** /-fī'tə/ n pl (Gr *phyton* plant) the green algae, from which all higher plants evolved. **chlo'roplast** n (Gr *plastos* moulded) a chlorophyll-bearing plastid in plants and algae. **chloroplast'al** adj. **chlor'oprene** n a colourless liquid derived from acetylene and hydrochloric acid and used in the production of neoprene. **chlo'roquin** or **chlor'oquine** n a drug used to suppress malaria and as an anti-rheumatic. **chlorō'sis** n formerly, a wasting disease (**green sickness**) typically affecting young women, characterized by anaemia, extreme lassitude and a greenish tinge of the skin, caused by deficiency of iron; blanching of the green parts of a plant in which production of chlorophyll has been affected by mineral deficiency, lack of light, etc (*bot*). **chlorothī'azide** n a synthetic drug (C$_7$H$_6$ClN$_3$O$_4$S$_2$), used in treating hypertension, heart failure, etc. **chlorot'ic** adj relating to or affected by chlorosis. **chlo'rous** adj of, containing or derived from chlorine in its trivalent form (**chlorous acid** a hypothetical acid (HClO$_2$), known in solution and by its salts). **chlorprō'mazine** n an antipsychotic drug used in the treatment of schizophrenia and mania. **chlorpyr'ifos** n a powerful organophosphate insecticide. **chlortetracyc'line** n a yellow antibiotic used to treat some bacterial infections.

chloracne /klō-rak'ni/ n a type of disfiguring skin disease resembling acne in appearance, caused by contact with or exposure to chlorinated hydrocarbons.

ChM abbrev : Chirurgiae Magister (L), Master of Surgery.

Chm abbrev : chairman (also **chmn.**); checkmate.

CHO abbrev : Confederation of Healing Organizations.

choano- /kō-ə-nō-/ or **choan-** /kō-ən-/ combining form denoting relating to a funnel. [Gr *choanē* funnel]
■ **choana** /kō'ə-nə/ n (*pl* **cho'anae**) (*zool*) a funnel-shaped aperture; (*usu* in *pl*) one of the internal nostrils which open into the roof of the mouth in air-breathing vertebrates. **cho'anocyte** n (*zool*) a cell in which the flagellum is surrounded by a sheath of protoplasm, found in sponges and stalked protozoa (also **collar cell**).

chobdar /chōb'där/ n in India, an usher. [Pers]

choc /chok/ and **choccy** /chok'i/ (*inf*) n and adj short forms of **chocolate**.

❏ **choc'-ice** or **choc'-bar** *n* a bar of ice cream with a chocolate covering.

chocaholic or **chocoholic** /cho-kə-hol'ik/ (*facetious*) *n* a person who has a craving for chocolate. [*chocolate*, and **-aholic** or **-oholic**]

chocho see **chayote**.

chock /chok/ *vt* to fasten or secure with or as if with a block or wedge. ◆ *n* a wedge to prevent movement; a log; a fair-lead with a top opening through which a line or rope can be run (*naut*). [See **choke**[1]] ▪ **chock'er** *adj* full up (*sl*; *orig Aust and NZ*); annoyed, fed up (*sl*). ❏ **chock'-a-block**, **chock-full'** or **choke-full'** *adj* quite full. **chock'stone** *n* (*mountaineering*) a stone jammed in a mountain crack, chimney or crevice. **chock'-tight** *adj* very tight.

chocko or **choco** /chok'ō/ (*old Aust sl*) *n* member of the Australian armed forces in World War II. [From *chocolate soldier*]

chocoholic see **chocaholic**.

chocolate /chok'(ə-)lət/ *n* a paste made of the ground roasted seeds of *Theobroma cacao* (cocoa), with sugar, cocoa butter, etc *usu* hardened into slabs; a sweet made of, or covered with, the paste; a beverage made by dissolving the paste (or a powder prepared from it) in hot water or milk. ◆ *adj* chocolate-coloured, dark reddish-brown; made of or flavoured with chocolate. [Sp *chocolate*; from Nahuatl *chocólatl* a mixture containing chocolate] ▪ **chocolatier'** *n* a person who makes, or a manufacturer of, chocolate sweets. **choc'olaty** or **choc'olatey** *adj*. ❏ **choc'olate-box** *adj* (*esp* of a picture or painting) pretty or charming in a stereotypical or sentimental manner.

Choctaw /chok'tö/ *n* a Native American of a tribe formerly chiefly in Mississippi; the tribe, or its language; (*without cap*) a skating movement, forward on the edge of one foot, then backward on the opposite edge of the other (cf **Mohawk**). [Choctaw *Chahta*]

chode /chōd/ an archaic *pat* of **chide**.

choenix or **chenix** /kē'niks/ *n* in ancient Greece, a dry measure equivalent to rather more than a quart. [Gr, Bible, Revelation 6.6]

Chogyal /chog'yäl/ *n* the traditional title of the ruler of Sikkim (a formerly independent state in the Himalayas, now part of India). [Tibetan, *righteous ruler*]

choice /chois/ *n* the act or power of choosing; the thing chosen; an alternative; a preference; the preferable or best part; variety from which to choose. ◆ *adj* worthy of being chosen; select; of superior quality; appropriate. [Fr *choix*, from *choisir*; cf **choose**] ▪ **choice'ful** *adj* (*archaic*) making many choices, fickle. **choice'ly** *adv* with discrimination or care. **choice'ness** *n* particular value; excellence; nicety. ❏ **choice'-drawn** *adj* (*Shakesp*) selected with care. ▪ **by, for** or **from choice** by preference. **Hobson's choice** the choice of the thing offered or nothing (from *Hobson*, a Cambridge horsekeeper, who let out the horse nearest the stable door, or none at all). **make choice of** to select. **take one's choice** to take what one wishes or prefers.

choir /kwīr/ *n* a chorus or band of singers, eg those belonging to a church; the part of a church appropriated to the singers; the part of a church, cathedral, etc in front of the altar, often separated from the nave by a rail or screen; a group of instruments of the same class playing together. ◆ *vi* (*Shakesp*) to sing in chorus. [Fr *chœur*, from L *chorus*, from Gr *choros*; see **chorus**] ❏ **choir'boy**, **choir'girl** or **choir'man** *n* a boy, girl or man who sings in a choir. **choir loft** *n* a gallery in a church, cathedral, etc used by the choir. **choir'master** *n* the director of a choir. **choir organ** *n* *orig* a small organ separate from, but played with, a 'great organ', now a section of a large organ played on the lowest manual and suitable for accompanying a choir. **choir school** *n* a school, *usu* maintained by a cathedral, to educate children who also sing in the choir. **choir'screen** *n* a screen of latticework, separating the choir from the nave. **choir'stalls** *n pl* fixed seats in the choir of a church, generally of carved wood. ▪ **preach to the choir** (*US*) to advocate a course of action to people who are already in favour of it.

Choisya /choi'zē-ə/ *n* the Mexican orange blossom genus.

choke[1] /chōk/ *vt* to stop or interfere with the breathing of (whether by compression, blocking, fumes, emotion, or otherwise); to injure or suppress by obstruction, overshadowing, or deprivation of air, etc; to constrict; to block; to clog; to obstruct. ◆ *vi* to be choked; to die (*sl*); to lose one's nerve when facing an important challenge. ◆ *n* a complete or partial stoppage of breath; the sound of choking; a constriction; a valve in a carburettor which reduces the air supply and thus enriches the petrol/air mixture; a choking coil. [*Ety* dubious] ▪ **choked** *adj* (*inf*) angry; disappointed; upset. **chōk'er** *n* something or someone that chokes; formerly, a large neck-cloth; a very high collar, *esp* as worn by the clergy; a close-fitting necklace or jewelled collar.

chokey or **choky** *n* see separate entry **choky**[1]. **chōk'y** *adj* tending to, or inclined to, choke. ❏ **choke'berry** *n* a small astringent fruit of various N American shrubs related to the apple. **choke'bore** *n* a gun-bore narrowed at the muzzle; a shotgun so bored. **choke chain** *n* a collar and lead for a dog consisting of a looped chain which tightens around the dog's neck when it pulls on the lead. **choke'cherry** *n* an astringent American cherry. **choke'coil** *n* a choking coil. **choke'damp** *n* carbon dioxide or other suffocating gas in mines. **choke-full** see **chock-full** under **chock**. **choke'hold** *n* a method of restraining someone by holding one's arm across his or her throat (also *fig*). **choke line** see **kill line** under **kill**[1]. **choke'-pear** *n* an astringent pear; anything that reduces one to silence. **choking coil** *n* a coil of thick wire of high impedance, used to limit the flow of alternating electric current. ▪ **choke back** or **choke down** to suppress (emotion) as if by a choking action. **choke off** to get rid of; to deter by force, to discourage. **choke up** to fill completely; to block up; (*usu* in passive) to overcome with emotion.

choke[2] /chōk/ *n* the inedible central part of a globe artichoke.

chokidar see under **choky**[1].

choko /chō'kō/ *n* (*pl* **cho'kos**) the fruit of a tropical vine (*Sechium edule*), similar to cucumber and eaten as a vegetable in the West Indies and Australia. [From a S American name]

chokra /chō'krə/ *n* a boy; a boy or young man employed as a servant in a household or regiment. [Anglo-Ind, from Hindi *chhokrā*] ▪ **chok'ri** *n* a girl; a young female servant.

choky[1] or **chokey** /chō'ki/ *n* a prison (*sl*); a toll-station; a lock-up; a chokidar. [Anglo-Ind, from Hindi *caukī*] ▪ **chokidar** or **chowkidar** /chō'* or *chow'ki-där/ *n* a watchman.

choky[2] see under **choke**[1].

chol- see **chole-**.

cholaemia or **cholemia** /ko-lē'mi-ə/ (*med*) *n* an accumulation of bile pigments in the blood. [Gr *cholē* bile, and *haima* blood] ▪ **cholae'mic** *adj*.

cholagogue /kol'ə-gog/ *n* a purgative causing evacuations of bile from the gall bladder into the duodenum. [Gr *cholē* bile, and *agōgos* leading] ▪ **cholagog'ic** /-gog'ik or -goj'ik/ *adj*.

cholangiography /ko-lan-ji-og'rə-fi/ *n* the examination by X-ray of bile ducts. [Gr *cholē* bile, and *angeion* case, vessel]

chole- /kol-* or *kō-li-* or *-lə-/ or **chol-** /kol-* or *kōl-/ *combining form* denoting bile or gall. [Gr *cholē* bile]

cholecalciferol /kō-li-kal-sif'ə-rol/ *n* vitamin D₃, a substance found in oily fish and liver, which regulates the balance of calcium and phosphate in the body.

cholecyst /kō'li-sist or kol'i-/ *n* the gall bladder. [Gr *cholē* bile, and *kystis* a bladder] ▪ **cholecystec'tomy** *n* a surgical operation to remove the gall bladder. **cholecystī'tis** *n* inflammation of the gall bladder. **cholecystog'raphy** *n* the examination of the gall bladder and common bile duct by X-ray. **cholecystokī'nin** *n* a hormone, secreted by duodenal cells, that stimulates the release of bile into the intestine and the secretion of pancreatic enzymes. **cholecystos'tomy** *n* (Gr *stoma* mouth) or **cholecystot'omy** (Gr *tomē* a cut) the surgical formation of an opening in the wall of the gall bladder.

cholelith /ko'lə-lith/ *n* a gallstone. [Gr *cholē* bile, and *lithos* stone] ▪ **cholelithiasis** /ko-lə-li-thī'ə-sis/ *n* the presence of stones in the gall bladder and bile ducts.

cholent /cho'lənt/ *n* (in Judaism) a stew, prepared on Friday and cooked slowly overnight for serving at lunch on the Sabbath, consisting of meat, beans, potatoes and dumplings. [Yiddish]

choler /kol'ər/ *n* anger, irascibility; yellow bile, one of the four bodily humours, an imbalance of which was thought to produce irritability (*archaic*); the bile (*obs*); biliousness (*obs*). [Gr *cholera*, from *cholē* bile, partly through Fr] ▪ **chol'eric** *adj* full of choler; passionate; angry, bad-tempered. **chol'erically** (also /-er'/) *adv*.

cholera /kol'ə-rə/ *n* an acute and frequently fatal infection of the small intestine, characterized by bilious vomiting and severe diarrhoea, acquired by ingesting food or water contaminated by the bacterium *Vibrio cholerae*. [Gr *cholera*, from *cholē* bile] ▪ **choleraic** /kol-ər-ā'ik/ *adj*. ❏ **cholera belt** *n* a waistband of eg flannel worn as a precaution against disease. ▪ **British cholera** an acute gastro-intestinal infection formerly common in summer.

choleric see under **choler**.

cholestasis /kō-lə-stā'sis/ n a condition in which stagnation of bile in the liver results in jaundice and/or liver disease. [Gr cholē bile, and stasis stoppage, stationariness]

cholesterol /kə-les'tə-rol/ n a sterol ($C_{27}H_{45}OH$), occurring in all body cells and involved in the transport of fats through the bloodstream to tissues throughout the body, and in the formation of bile salts and hormones. High levels of cholesterol in the blood are thought to increase the risk of arteriosclerosis (formerly called **choles'terin**). [Gr cholē bile, and stereos solid]
■ **cholester'ic** adj. **cholesterolae'mia** or **cholesterole'mia** n (med) the presence of comparatively high levels of cholesterol in the blood.

choli /chō'lē/ n a short, short-sleeved bodice as worn by Indian women under a sari. [Hindi colī; from Sans but prob of Dravidian origin]

choliamb /kō'li-amb/ (prosody) n a variety of iambic trimeter having a spondee for an iambus as the sixth foot. [Gr chōliambos, from chōlos lame, and iambos iambus]
■ **choliam'bic** n and adj.

cholic /kol'ik or kō'lik/ adj relating to bile. [Gr cholē bile]
❑ **cholic acid** n an acid ($C_{24}H_{40}O_5$) obtained from bile and used as an emulsifier.

choline /kō'lin, -lēn'/ n a compound found in bile, used in the synthesis of lecithin, etc, and in preventing accumulation of fat in the liver. [Gr cholē bile and **-ine¹**]

cholinergic /ko-li-nûr'jik/ adj (of nerve fibres) releasing acetylcholine; activated or transmitted by acetylcholine; (of an agent) having the same effect as acetylcholine. [From acetylcholine and Gr ergon work]

cholinesterase /ko-li-nes'tə-rāz/ n an enzyme which breaks down a choline ester into choline and an acid, esp acetylcholine into choline and acetic acid. [**choline**, **ester** and **-ase**]

cholla /chō'lyä or choi'ə/ n a spiny cactus of the genus Opuntia, growing in SW USA and Mexico. [Sp, skull]

choltry /chōl'tri/ n (also **choul'try**) a caravanserai; a shed used as a place of assembly. [From Malayalam]

chometz same as **chametz**.

chomp /chomp/ (inf) vt and vi to munch with noisy enjoyment. ◆ n the act or sound of munching thus. [Variant of **champ¹**]

Chomskyan or **Chomskian** /chom'ski-ən/ adj of or relating to the US linguist and political activist Noam Chomsky (born 1926), or to his linguistic or political theories.

chon /chōn/ n (pl **chou**) a Korean monetary unit, $\frac{1}{100}$ of a won.

chondro- /kon-drō-/ or **chondri-** /-dri-/ combining form of or relating to cartilage; granular. [Gr chondros a grain, grit, cartilage]
■ **chon'driosome** n an old name for a mitochondrion, a minute body generating ATP in the cytoplasm of a cell. **chondrit'ic** adj. **chondrī'tis** n (med) inflammation of a cartilage. **chon'droblast** n a cell that forms cartilage. **chondrocrān'ium** n a cartilaginous skull, as in embryos, fishes, etc. **chondrogen'esis** n chondrification. **chondroitin** /-droi'tin/ **sulphate** (or simply **chondroitin**) n a carbohydrate used as a dietary supplement to alleviate arthritic pain. **chondromalā'cia** n (med) softening of cartilage. **chondromato'sis** n (med) a condition in which benign tumours (**chondro'mas**) made up of cartilage cells form in the bones, esp of the hand. **chondroph'orine** n (zool) a member of the Chondrophora, a suborder of hydrozoans similar to medusae but with a different internal structure. **chondrostian** /kon-dros'ti-ən/ n (Gr osteon bone) a member of the Chondrostei, an order of bony fishes including the sturgeon, bichir and paddlefish.

chondrus /kon'drəs/ n (pl **chondrī**) a cartilage; a chondrule; (with cap) a genus of cartilaginous red seaweeds to which carrageen belongs. [Gr chondros a grain, grit, cartilage]
■ **chon'dral** adj. **chondre** /kon'dər/ n a chondrule. **chondrificā'tion** n formation of chondrin, or development of or change into cartilage. **chon'drify** vt and vi to change into cartilage. **chon'drin** n a firm, elastic, translucent, bluish-white gelatinous substance, the matrix of cartilage. **chon'drite** n a meteorite containing chondrules; a fossil resembling Chondrus. **chon'droid** adj like cartilage. **chon'drule** n a rounded granule found in meteorites and in deep-sea deposits.

choo-choo /choo'choo/ n a child's word for a railway train. [Imit]

choof /chŭf/ (esp Aust sl) vi and interj (usu with off) to go away.

chook /chŭk/ (inf, esp Aust and NZ) n a hen, chicken (also (Aust, NZ and Scot) **chook'ie**). [Imit]

choom /chŭm/ (obs Aust inf) n (often with cap) an Englishman.

choose /chooz/ vt (pat **chose** /chōz/; pap **chos'en**) to take or pick out in preference to another thing; to select; to will or determine; to think fit. ◆ vi to make a choice (between, from, etc). [OE cēosan, Du kiesen]
■ **choos'er** n. **choos'y** or **choos'ey** adj (inf) difficult to please, fastidious.
■ **cannot choose but** (archaic) can have no alternative but. **not much to choose between** each about equally good or bad. **pick and**

choose to select with care or at leisure. **the chosen few** (often facetious) a select or privileged group. **the chosen people** a name given to the Israelites in the Bible (1 Chronicles 16,13).

chop¹ /chop/ vt (**chopp'ing**; **chopped**) to cut with a sudden blow (away, down, off, etc); to cut into small pieces; to strike with a sharp blow (karate; also vi); to thrust or clap (archaic); to reduce greatly or abolish (inf). ◆ vi to hack; to come suddenly or accidentally (archaic); to thrust (archaic); to crack or fissure; to take a direction (meaning converging with **chop²**). ◆ n an act of chopping; chopped food; a piece cut off; a slice of mutton, lamb or pork, usu containing a rib; food (W Afr inf); a share (Aust and NZ sl); a crack; a sharp downward blow; (with the) dismissal (inf). [A form of **chap¹**]
■ **chopp'er** n a person or thing that chops; a cleaver; a helicopter (sl); the penis (sl); a type of motorcycle or bicycle with very high handlebars and a low saddle; a device for intermittently interrupting an electric current or beam of radiation; a submachine-gun (sl); (in pl) teeth (sl). **chopp'ily** adv. **chopp'iness** n. **chopp'ing** n and adj. **chopp'y** adj full of chops or cracks; (of the sea, etc) running in irregular waves, rough (also **chopp'ing**).
❑ **chop'-house** n esp formerly, a house where mutton-chops and beefsteaks are served; an eating-house. **chopp'ing-block** or **chopp'ing-board** n one on which material is to be chopped is placed. **chopp'ing-knife** n a knife for chopping or mincing meat.
■ **chop at** to aim a blow at. **chop in** to break in, interrupt. **chop up** to cut into small pieces. **for the chop** (inf) about to be dismissed or killed. **get the chop** (inf) to be dismissed from one's job, etc; to be killed. **not much chop** (Aust and NZ inf) not much good. **on the chopping block** in serious danger of being abolished or discarded.

chop² /chop/ vt and vi (**chopp'ing**; **chopped**) to buy and sell, barter, or exchange (Milton); to change direction (meaning converging with **chop¹**). ◆ n an exchange; a change. [Connection with **chop¹** and with **chap²** is not clear]
❑ **chop'logic** n false reasoning, illogicalness, sophistry; a person who chops logic.
■ **chop and change** to buy and sell; to change about. **chop logic** to argue contentiously or fallaciously. **chops and changes** vicissitudes.

chop³ /chop/ (inf) n the chap or jaw; (in pl) a person with fat cheeks; the mouth or jaws of anything, such as a cannon or a vice. ◆ vt (**chopp'ing**; **chopped**) to eat. ◆ vi to snap. [See **chap³**]
■ **chop'fallen** adj literally, having the chop or lower jaw fallen down; cast-down; dejected.
■ **lick one's chops** to wait eagerly or greedily.

chop⁴ /chop/ n in China and India, a seal; a brand; a sealed document. [Hindi chāp seal, impression]
■ **chop'house** n in China, a customs house.
■ **first chop** best quality. **no chop** no good.

chop-chop /chop-chop'/ adv promptly. ◆ interj hurry up! [Pidgin English, from Chin (Cantonese)]

chopin¹ /chop'in/ n an old French liquid measure containing nearly an English imperial pint; an old Scottish measure containing about an English quart. [OFr chopine, MDu schoppe; Scot chappin, Ger Schoppen a pint]

chopin² or **chopine** /cho-pēn' or chop'in/ n a high clog or patten introduced into England from Venice during the reign of Elizabeth I. [Sp chapin]

chopping /chop'ing/ adj stout, strapping, plump. [Perh **chop¹**; cf **thumping**]

chopsocky /chop-sok'i/ (sl, usu derog) n a genre of films featuring martial arts. [**chop¹**, and **sock²**; influenced by **chop suey**]

chopstick /chop'stik/ n (usu in pl) either of two small sticks used instead of a fork for eating, esp in Oriental countries. [**chop-chop**, and **stick¹**]

chop suey /chop-soo'i/ n a miscellaneous Chinese-style dish made up of chopped meat, bean sprouts, etc fried in sesame oil. [Chin (Cantonese), mixed bits]

choragus /ko-rā'gəs/ or **choregus** /-rē'gəs/ n (in ancient Greek drama) the organizer, sponsor or leader of a chorus; the leader of a choir or organizer of musical activities, festivals, etc. [Gr chorāgos, chorēgos, from choros chorus, and agein to lead]
■ **choragic** /-raj'/ or **choregic** /-rēj'ik/ adj.

choral, **chorale** see under **chorus**.

chord¹ /körd/ (music) n the simultaneous combination of notes of a different pitch. ◆ vt to provide (a melody) with chords. [From **accord**]
■ **chord'al** adj. **chord'ing** n the distribution of chords in a piece of harmony.
❑ **chord symbol** n any symbol used to indicate a chord in musical notation.
■ **common chord** a note combined with its third, perfect fifth and octave.

chord² /körd/ n a string of a musical instrument (*archaic and poetic*); a sensitive area of the emotions, feelings, etc (*fig*); a straight line joining any two points on a curve (*geom*); an old spelling of cord (see **spinal cord** under **spine** and **vocal cords** under **vocal**); the straight line joining the leading and the trailing edges of an aerofoil section (*aeronautics*); one of the principal members of a truss (*engineering*). [Gr *chordē* a string, intestine]
■ **chor'da** n (*pl* **chor'dae**) (*zool*) any stringlike structure in the body; the notochord. **chord'al** *adj*. **chordames'oderm** n (*anat* and *zool*) the layer of specialized cells in the middle of a developing embryo which forms the notochord and structures of the central nervous system. **chor'date** n a member of the **Chordāta**, a phylum of the animal kingdom, including the vertebrates and protochordates, animals possessing a notochord at some stage of their development (also *adj*). **chordophone** /kör'dō-fōn/ n (*music*) any instrument in which a string vibrates to produce a sound, including the zither, piano, lute, lyre and harp. **chordophonic** /-fon'ik/ *adj*. **chordotomy** n see under **cord**.
■ **strike a chord** to prompt a feeling of recognition, familiarity, empathy, etc. **touch the right chord** to elicit the appropriate emotional or sympathetic response.

chordee /kör'dē/ (*med*) n a condition, *usu* of infant boys, in which there is an abnormal downward curvature of the penis.

chore /chōr/ or /chör/ n a routine, *esp* household, task; an unpleasant or tedious task. [Form (orig US) of **char²**]

-chore /-kör/ (*bot*) combining form denoting a plant distributed by a specified means or agency, eg *zoochore*. [Gr *chōrein* to go, move]

chorea /ko-rē'ə/ n a nervous condition, characterized by irregular involuntary movements of the limbs or face, a feature of *Huntington's chorea* and *Sydenham's chorea*. [L, from Gr *choreiā* a dance]

choree /kō'rē/ or /kö'/ (*prosody*) n a trochee (also **chorē'us**). [Gr *choreios*]
■ **chorē'ic** *adj*.

choregus see **choragus**.

choreography /ko-rē-og'rə-fi/ n the art, or the notation, of dancing, *esp* ballet-dancing; the art of arranging or composing dances, *esp* ballets; the arrangement or composition of a ballet. [Gr *choros* dance, and **-graphy**]
■ **chor'eograph** vt to arrange or compose (a dance, dances, etc). ◆ vi to practise choreography. **choreog'rapher** or **chor'eograph** n. **choreograph'ic** *adj*. **choreograph'ically** *adv*. —Also **choreg'raphy**, **chor'egraph**, etc.

choreology /ko-rē-ol'ə-ji/ n the study of ballets and their history. [Gr *choros* dance, and **-ology**]
■ **choreol'ogist** n.

chorepiscopal /kö- or kō-ri-pis'kə-pəl/ *adj* relating to a local or suffragan bishop of the early church. [Gr *chōrā* place, country]

choria see **chorion**.

choriamb /kor'i-amb/ or **choriambus** /ko-ri-am'bəs/ (*prosody*) n a foot of four syllables, the first and last long, the others short. [Gr *choriambos*, from *choreios* a trochee, and *iambos* iambus]
■ **choriam'bic** *adj* and n.

choric, **chorine** see under **chorus**.

chorion /kō'ri-on or kör'i-on/ (*anat*) n (*pl* **cho'ria**) one of the two membranes that surround an embryo and which in mammals develops into the placenta as the embryo develops in the uterus. [Gr *chorion*]
■ **chorion'ic** or **cho'rial** *adj* of or relating to the chorion. **cho'roid** or **cho'rioid** *adj* of or resembling a chorion. ◆ n the vascular tunic of the eyeball, between the retina and the sclera (also **cho'rioid coat**). **choroidī'tis** n (*med*) inflammation of the choroid.
□ **choriocarcinō'ma** n a malignant tumour that develops from the placenta in the uterus. **chorionic gonadotrophin** n a hormone produced in mammals when an embryo begins to form in the uterus, its presence in the urine being an indication of pregnancy. **choroid plexus** n (*med*) a vascular membrane projecting into the ventricles of the brain and secreting cerebrospinal fluid.
■ **chorionic villus sampling** a method of diagnosing abnormalities in a fetus by removing a tiny sample of chorionic tissue from the edge of the placenta for laboratory analysis.

chorisis /kō'ri-sis or kör'i-/ (*bot*) n multiplication of parts, organs, etc by branching or splitting. [Gr *chōrisis* separation]
■ **chō'rism** n. **chōrizā'tion** or **-s-** n.

chorist, etc see under **chorus**.

chorizo /cho-rē'zō/ n (*pl* **choriz'os**) a dry, highly-seasoned sausage, made from pork. [Sp]

chorizont /kō'ri-zont/ or **chorizontist** /-zon'tist/ n a person who disputes identity of authorship, *esp* one who ascribes the *Iliad* and *Odyssey* to different authors. [Gr *chōrizōn, -ontos* separating]

chorography /kö- or kō- or kə-rog'rə-fi/ (*geog*) n the process or technique of mapping or describing particular districts or regions (cf **topography**). [Gr *chōrā* region, country, and **-graphy**]
■ **chorog'rapher** n. **chorographic** /-ro-graf'ik/ or **chorograph'ical** *adj*.

choroid see under **chorion**.

chorology /ko-rol'ə-ji/ n the science or study of the geographical distribution of anything. [Gr *chōrā* region, country, and **-logy**]
■ **cholog'ical** *adj*. **chorol'ogist** n.

choropleth map /kor'ə-pleth map/ n a map in which areas sharing similar geographical, climatic, etc features are represented by the same colour. [Gr *chōrā* region, country, and *plēthos* great number]

chortle /chört'l/ vi to chuckle; to utter a gurgling, gleeful laugh. ◆ n such a laughing noise. [Coined by Lewis Carroll in 1872]

chorus /kö' or kō'rəs/ n a band of singers and dancers; in Greek tragic drama, a group of people who, between the episodes, danced and chanted counsel and comment on the action; in later drama, a person who performs similar functions alone, including speaking the prologue; a company of singers, a choir; a composition which is sung by a chorus; the combination of voices in one simultaneous utterance; a refrain, in which the company or audience may join with the soloist or choir. ◆ vt (**cho'rusing**; **cho'rused**) to sing or say together. [L, from Gr *choros* dance; see also **choir**]
■ **chor'al** *adj* relating to or sung by a chorus or a choir. ◆ n /kö-räl'/ (often altered to **chorale'**) a simple harmonized composition with slow rhythm; a psalm or hymn tune; any part of the service sung by the whole choir (*RC*); a choir or chorus (*esp N Am*). **chor'ally** *adv* in the manner of a chorus; suitable for a choir. **choric** /kor'ik or kō'rik/ *adj*. **chorine** /kör'ēn or kör'/ n (*esp US sl*) a chorus girl. **chorist** /kor'ist, kō'rist/, **chor'alist**, **chor'ister** or (*obs*) **quirister** /kwir'is-tər/ n a member of a choir, *esp* a choirboy.
□ **choral prelude** n a composition, *usu* for the organ, in the manner of a chorale. **choral society** n a group meeting regularly to practise and perform choral music. **chorus girl** n a woman who dances and sings in a chorus on the stage. **chorus master** n the director of a choir or chorus.
■ **in chorus** in unison.

chose¹, **chosen** see **choose**.

chose² /shōz/ (*law*) n a thing; a piece of personal property, a chattel. [Fr, from L *causa* thing]
□ **chose jugée** /shōz zhü-zhā/ n something already decided and profitless to discuss, a settled matter.
■ **chose in action** a personal right of property which can only be claimed by a court action and not by taking physical possession.

chota /chō'tə/ (*Anglo-Ind*) *adj* small, little; younger, junior. [Hindi *chhotā*]
□ **chota hazri** /haz'ri or häz'ri/ n early light breakfast of tea, toast and *usu* fruit. **chota peg** n a small drink, *usu* whisky with soda or water.

chott same as **shott**.

chou /shoo/ n (*pl* **choux** /shoo/) a cabbage; an ornamental soft rosette; a cream bun; dear, pet (*inf*). [Fr]
□ **choux pastry** n very light, rich pastry made with flour, butter and eggs.

choucroute /shoo-kroot'/ n pickled cabbage. [Fr]

chough¹ /chuf/ n a passerine bird (*Pyrrhocorax pyrrhocorax*), of the crow family, inhabiting sea-cliffs and mountains and having glossy black plumage, red legs and a red down-curved bill (also called **red-legged crow**, **Cornish chough**); a related bird, the Alpine chough (*Pyrrhocorax graculus*), of Europe and Asia. [Perh imit of its cry]

chough² see **chuff²**.

choultry see **choltry**.

chounter see **chunter**.

chouse /chows/ n a cheat, a swindler; a person who is easily cheated, a dupe (*obs*); a trick or swindle. ◆ vt to cheat, swindle. [Prob from Turk *chaush* a messenger or envoy]

chout /chowt/ n in India, one-fourth part of the revenue, extorted by the Mahrattas as blackmail; hence, blackmail, extortion. [Hindi *chauth* the fourth part]

choux see **chou**.

chow /chow/ n food; (also with *cap*) a Chinese person (*Aust, NZ and archaic sl*). ◆ *adj* mixed, miscellaneous. [Pidgin Eng, food]
□ **chow'-chow** n a Chinese mixed condiment; a mixed fruit preserve; a breed of long-haired dog with a curly tail, originating in China (also **chow**).
■ **chow down** (*N Am inf*) to eat greedily.

chowder /chow'dər/ (*esp N Am*) n a stew or thick soup made of fish or clams with vegetables; a similar soup made with other main ingredients. [Fr *chaudière* a pot]

chowkidar see under **choky**[1].

chow mein /chow mān or mēn/ n fried noodles; a Chinese-style dish of seasoned shredded meat and vegetables, served with fried noodles. [Chin (Cantonese), fried noodles]

chowry or **chowri** /chow'ri/ n a hand-held device used for driving away flies. [Hindi caurī]

choy-root same as **chay**[2].

CHP abbrev : combined heat and power.

Chr. abbrev : Christ; Christian.

chrematist /krē'mə-tist/ n a political economist. [Gr chrēmatistēs a money-getter, from chrēma, -atos a thing, possession, money]
■ **chrematis'tic** adj relating to finance, moneymaking, or political economy. **chrematis'tics** n sing the science or study of wealth; political economy.

chrestomathy /kre-stom'ə-thi/ n an anthology of choice or literary passages, usu used by students in the learning of a foreign language. [Gr chrēstos useful, and mathein (aorist) to know]
■ **chrestomathic** /-tō-math'ik/ or **chrestomath'ical** adj.

chrism /kri'zm/ n consecrated or holy oil; a sacramental anointing, unction; confirmation; chrisom. [OFr chresme (Fr chrême), from Gr chrīsma, from chriein to anoint]
■ **chris'mal** adj relating to chrism. ◆ n a case for containing chrism; a pyx; a veil used in christening. **chris'matory** n a vessel for holding chrism. **chris'om** or **christ'om** n a white cloth or robe (also **chris'om-cloth** or **chris'om-robe**) put on a child newly anointed with chrism at its baptism; the child itself.
❑ **chrisom child** n (archaic) a child still wearing the chrisom-cloth; a child that died in its first month after baptism, buried in its chrisom-cloth; an innocent child.

Chrissie /kris'i/ (esp Aust sl) n Christmas.

Christ /krīst/ n the Anointed, a name given to Jesus of Nazareth; the Messiah. ◆ interj (sl) an expression of irritation, surprise, anger, etc. [OE Crīst, from Gr Christos, from chriein to anoint]
■ **christen** /kris'n/ vt to baptize in the name of Christ; to give a name to; to use for the first time (inf). **Christendom** /kris'n-dəm/ n that part of the world in which Christianity is the received religion; the whole body of Christians. **christener** /kris'n-ər/ n. **christening** /kris'ning/ n the ceremony of baptism. **Chrīst'hood** n the condition of being the Christ or Messiah. **Christian** /kris'chən/ n a believer in the religion based on the teachings of Christ, or one so classified; a follower of Christ; a person whose behaviour is considered becoming to a follower of Christ; often a vague term of approbation, a decent, respectable, kindly, charitably-minded person; a human being (inf). ◆ adj relating to Christ or His religion; in the spirit of Christ. **Christ'ianism** n. **Christianity** /kris-ti-an'i-ti/ n the religion based on the teachings of Christ; the spirit of this religion; Christendom. **Christianīzā'tion** or **-s-** n. **Christ'ianize** or **-ise** vt to make Christian; to convert to Christianity. **Christ'ianizer** or **-s-** n. **Christ'ianlike** adj. **Christ'ianly** adj and adv. **Christ'ianness** n. **Christ'ingle** /krist'ing-gəl/ n a Christmas symbol for children, usu consisting of an orange containing a candle, with fruit and nuts and red paper or ribbon, representing Christ as the light of the world, its creation and His passion. **Chrīst'less** adj. **Chrīst'like** adj. **Chrīst'liness** n. **Chrīst'ly** adj like Christ.
❑ **Christ-cross-row** or **criss-cross-row** /kris'kros-rō/ n (archaic and dialect) the alphabet, from hornbooks in which the alphabet was preceded by the figure of a cross (**Christ-cross** or **criss-cross**). **Christian Brothers** n pl (RC church) a lay order, founded in France in 1684, involved in the education of the young. **Christian era** n the era counted from the traditionally accepted date of the birth of Christ. **Christian name** n the name given at one's christening; the personal name as distinguished from the surname. **Christian Science** n a religion based on spiritual or divine healing with rejection of orthodox medicine, founded in 1879 by Mary Baker Eddy. **Christian Scientist** n. **Christian Socialism** n a mid-19c movement for applying Christian ethics to social reform; the principles of a pre-World War II Austrian Roman Catholic political party. **Christ's'-thorn** n any of several prickly shrubs, eg Paliurus spina-christi of the family Rhamnaceae, common in the Mediterranean region, or a kind of jujube tree (Zizyphus spina-christi), from which Christ's crown of thorns is thought to have been made.

Christadelphian /kri-stə-del'fi-ən/ n a member of a small religious sect, founded in the USA, which believes that only the righteous will achieve eternal life, the wicked and sinners will be utterly destroyed, and which bases its teaching and practice on literal interpretation of the Bible. [Gr Christos Christ, and adelphos brother]

Christiania /kris-ti-ä'ni-ə/, also **Christie** or **Christy** /kris'ti/ (skiing; also without cap) n a turn with skis parallel executed when descending at speed. [Former name of Oslo]

Christie see **Christiania**, **Christy**[2].

Christingle see under **Christ**.

Christmas /kris'məs/ n an annual festival, orig a mass, in celebration of the birth of Christ, held on 25 December (**Christmas Day**); the season at which it occurs; evergreens, esp holly, for Christmas decoration (archaic and dialect). ◆ adj of, for or relating to Christmas. [**Christ** and **mass**[2]]
■ **Christ'massy** or **Christ'masy** adj of or suitable for Christmas.
❑ **Christmas beetle** n any of various Australian scarab beetles. **Christmas box** n a box containing Christmas presents; a Christmas gift, often of money, to tradesmen, etc. **Christmas cactus** n a S American cactus with showy red flowers. **Christmas cake** n a rich fruitcake, usu iced, made for Christmas. **Christmas card** n a greeting card sent at Christmas. **Christmas daisy** n the aster. **Christmas disease** n a genetically acquired bleeding disorder similar to haemophilia, in which absence of a protein (factor IX) affects the proper coagulation of the blood. **Christmas eve** n 24 December. **Christmas pudding** n a rich, spicy fruit pudding, eaten at Christmas. **Christmas rose** or **flower** n an evergreen plant (Helleborus niger) that bears cup-shaped white flowers in winter or early spring. **Christmas stocking** n a stocking that children hang up on Christmas eve to be filled with presents by Santa Claus. **Christ'mas-tide** or **Christ'mas-time** n the season of Christmas. **Christmas tree** n a tree, usu fir, set up in a room or a public place at Christmas-time and decorated with lights, gifts, etc; an apparatus fitted to the outlet of an oilwell to control the flow of oil or gas.

Christocentric /kri-stō-sen'trik or -tə-/ adj (of theology, religion, etc) centring on Christ.

Christogram /kris'tə-gram or -tō-/ n a symbol representing Christ, esp the monogram chi-rho.

Christolatry /kri-stol'ə-tri/ n worship of Christ. [Gr Christos Christ, and latreiā worship]

Christology /kri-stol'ə-ji/ n that branch of theology which is concerned with the nature and person of Christ. [Gr Christos, and logos discourse]
■ **Christolog'ical** adj. **Christol'ogist** n.

christom /kriz'əm/ see **chrisom** under **chrism**.

christophany /kri-stof'ə-ni/ n an appearance of Christ to men. [Gr Christos, and phainesthai to appear]

christophene or **christophine** /kris'tə-fēn/ n another name for the **chayote**.

Christy[1] see **Christiania**.

Christy[2] or **Christie** /kris'ti/ (Can; also without cap) n a bowler hat. [An English manufacturer]

Christy minstrel /kris'ti min'strəl/ n one of a troupe of entertainers with blackened faces. [Instituted by George Christy, 19c US composer]

chroma /krō'mə/ n quality of colour; a hue; (in colour television) the colour component of a signal. [Gr chrōma, -atos colour]
■ **chromat'ic** adj relating to, or consisting of, colours; coloured; relating to notes in a melodic progression, which are raised or lowered by accidentals, without changing the key of the passage, and also to chords in which notes occur (music). **chromat'ically** adv. **chromat'icism** n (music) the state of being chromatic; the use of chromatic tones. **chromaticity** /-tis'-/ n the colour quality of light, one method of defining it being by its purity (saturation) and dominant wavelength. **chromat'ics** n sing the science of colours. **chrō'minance** n (TV) the difference between any colour and a reference colour of equal luminance.
❑ **chrō'makey** n (TV) a special effect in which a coloured background can be removed from a picture and a different background substituted. **chromatic aberration** n the blurring of an optical image, with colouring of the edges, caused by light of different wavelengths being focused at different distances. **chromatic adaption** n (bot) differences in amount or proportion of photosynthetic pigments in plants in response to the amount and colour of available light. **chromaticity co-ordinates** n pl (phys) numbers whose values are used to specify a colour. **chromaticity diagram** n (phys) a diagram on which the chromaticity of a colour is plotted. **chromatic scale** n (music) a scale proceeding by semitones.

chromate see under **chrome**.

chromatic, etc see under **chroma**.

chromato- /krō-ma-tə-/, **chromat-** /krō-mat-/ or **chromo-** /krō-mə-/ combining form denoting: colour; chromosome. [See **chroma**]
■ **chrō'matid** n one of the two thread-like structures formed by the longitudinal division of a chromosome. **chrō'matin** n a readily stained substance in the nucleus of a cell made up of DNA, RNA and proteins. **chrōmatograph'ic** adj. **chrōmatog'raphy** n methods of separating substances in a mixture which depend on selective adsorption, partition between non-mixing solvents, etc, using a

---

■ words derived from main entry word; ❑ compound words; ■ idioms and phrasal verbs

chrōmat'ograph, and which present the substances as a **chrōmat'ogram**, such as a series of visible bands in a vertical tube. **chrōmat'ophore** n (biol) a cell which contains pigment granules and may change its shape and colour due to nervous or hormonal stimulation. **chrōmatop'sia** n (Gr opsis sight) coloured vision. **chromatosphere** n see **chromosphere** below. **chrō'matype** or **chrō'motype** n a photographic process that uses chromium salts; a photograph in colours; a sheet printed in colour. **chrō'mō** n (pl chrō'mos) (inf) a chromolithograph. **chrō'mogen** n a substance that can be made into a dye; a coloured compound containing a chromatophore. **chrōmogen'ic** adj producing colour; of or relating to a chromogen. **chrō'mōgram** n a combination of photographs in different colours to give an image in natural colours. **chrōmōlith'ograph** n a lithograph printed in colours. **chrōmōlithog'rapher** n. **chrōmōlithog'raphic** adj. **chrōmōlithog'raphy** n. **chrō'momere** n (biol) one of the characteristic granules of compacted chromatin which appear on a chromosome during the early stages of meiosis. **chrō'mophil** or **chrōmophil'ic** adj (biol) staining heavily in certain microscopic techniques. **chrō'mophore** n the group of atoms in a chemical compound responsible for its colour. **chrōmophor'ic** adj. **chrō'mōplast** n (bot) a chromatophore. **chrō'mōscope** n an apparatus for combining coloured images. **chrōmosō'mal** adj of or relating to chromosomes (**chromosomal aberration** any visible abnormality in chromosome number or structure). **chrō'mōsome** n in eukaryotes, any of the deeply staining rod-like structures seen in the nucleus at cell division, made up of a continuous thread of DNA which with its associated protein is essential for the transmission of hereditary characteristics (**chromosome mapping** the assigning of genes to chromosomes and the determination of their exact position on the chromosome; **chromosome number** the number of chromosomes in a cell nucleus, constant for any given species). **chrō'mōsphere** n a layer of incandescent gas surrounding the sun through which the light of the photosphere passes (also **chrōmat'osphere**). **chrōmōspher'ic** adj. **chrōmōther'apy** n colour therapy using red, green and violet as three primary colours. **chromotype** n see **chromatype** above. **chrōmōtypog'raphy** n printing in colours. **chrōmōxy'lograph** n (Gr xylon wood) a picture printed in colours from wooden blocks. **chrōmōxylog'raphy** n.

chrome /krōm/ n chromium or a chromium compound (also adj). ♦ vt (in dyeing) to treat with a chromium solution; to plate with chromium. [See **chroma**]
■ **chrō'mate** n a salt of chromic acid. **chrō'mel** n an alloy of nickel and chromium, used in heating elements. **chrō'mene** n a chemical compound produced by certain plants that acts as an insecticide. **chrō'mic** adj relating to trivalent chromium. **chrō'mite** n a mineral, a double oxide of chromium and iron. **chrō'mium** n a metallic element (symbol **Cr**; atomic no 24) remarkable for the beautiful colour of its compounds. **chrō'mous** adj relating to divalent chromium.
❑ **chrome alum** n a violet-coloured crystalline substance, used as a mordant in dyeing. **chrome leather** n leather prepared by chrome tanning. **chrome plating** n electroplating with chromium. **chrome spinel** n picotite. **chrome steel** or **chromium steel** n an alloy steel containing chromium. **chrome tanning** n tanning with salts of chromium. **chrome tape** n magnetic tape coated with chrome dioxide. **chrome yellow** n a pigment of lead chromate. **chromic acid** n an acid of chromium (H_2CrO_4), of an orange-red colour, much used in dyeing and bleaching.

chromidium /krō-mid'i-əm/ n (pl chrōmid'ia) an algal cell in a lichen; a free fragment of chromatin. [See **chroma**]

chrominance see under **chroma**.

chromite, chromium see under **chrome**.

chromoytoy**chromotypography** see under **chromato-**.

chromous see under **chrome**.

chromoxylograph, etc see under **chromato-**.

Chron. (Bible) abbrev : (the Books of) Chronicles.

chron. abbrev : chronicle; chronological; chronology.

chron- /kron- or krən-/ or **chrono-** /krō-nō-, -nə- or kro-no-/ combining form denoting time. [Gr chronos time; adj chronikos]
■ **chrōn'axie** n (med) a time constant in the excitation of a nerve or muscle which equals the smallest time required to produce a response when the stimulus is double the minimum intensity required to produce a basic response. **chron'ic** adj lasting a long time; (of a disease) deep-seated or long continued, opp to acute (**chronic fatigue syndrome** a long-term post-viral syndrome with chronic fatigue and muscle pain on exercise); deplorable (sl); relating to time (obs). ♦ n a chronic invalid; a student who repeatedly fails in examinations (old sl). **chron'ical** adj chronic. **chron'ically** adv. **chronic'ity** n. **chronobiol'ogy** n the science of biological rhythms, esp where the properties of the rhythms are measured. **chron'ogram** n (Gr gramma letter) an inscription or phrase in which letters form

a date in Roman numerals. **chron'ograph** n (Gr graphein to write) a chronogram; an instrument for taking exact measurements of time, or for recording graphically the moment or duration of an event. **chronog'rapher** n a chronicler. **choronograph'ic** adj. **chronog'raphy** n chronology. **chronol'oger** or **chronolog'ic** or **chronolog'ical** adj (**chronological age** age in years, etc, as opposed eg to mental age). **chronolog'ically** adv. **chronol'ogist** n. **chronol'ogize** or **-ise** vt to arrange in chronological order or establish the order in time of (events, etc). **chronol'ogy** n (Gr logos discourse) the science of computing time; a scheme of time; order of time. **chronom'eter** n (Gr metron measure) an instrument for accurate measurement of time. **chronomet'ric** or **chronomet'rical** adj. **chronomet'rically** adv. **chronom'etry** n the art of measuring time accurately by means of instruments; measurement of time. **chrō'non** n (phys) a unit of time, ie that required for a photon to travel the diameter of an electron, 10^{-24} seconds. **chron'oscope** n (Gr skopeein to look) an instrument used for measuring extremely short intervals of time, esp in determining the velocity of projectiles. **chron'otron** n a device which measures very small time intervals by comparing the distance between electric pulses from different sources.

chronicle /kron'i-kl/ n a continuous record of events in order of time; a history; a story, account; (in pl; with cap) the name of two of the Old Testament books. ♦ vt to record as a chronicle. [Anglo-Fr cronicle, from L chronica, from Gr chronika annals]
■ **chron'icler** n a writer of a chronicle.
❑ **chronicle play** n a drama which depicts or portrays historical events or characters (also **history play**).

chronique scandaleuse /kro-nēk skã-da-løz'/ (Fr) n a story full of scandalous events or details; unsavoury gossip or tittle-tattle.

chrys- /kris-/ or **chryso-** /kri-sō- or -sə-/ combining form denoting gold. [Gr chrysos gold]
■ **chrys'alis** or **chrys'alid** n (pl chrysalides /kris-al'i-dēz/, chrys'alises or chrys'alids) (Gr chrysallis) orig a golden-coloured butterfly pupa; a pupa generally; a pupa case. **chrysan'themum** /kris- or kriz-/ (pl chrysan'themums) n (Gr anthemon flower) a plant of the Chrysanthemum genus of composite plants, eg the corn marigold and ox-eye daisy; any of several cultivated plants of the genus, with colourful double flower-heads (often shortened to **chrysanth'**). **chrysarō'bin** n (see **araroba**) a yellow crystalline mixture obtained from the wood of a S American tree, Andira araroba; a derivative of this used medicinally as a purgative and in the treatment of skin disease. **chryselephant'ine** adj (Gr elephantinos, from elephas, -antos ivory) (esp of ancient Greek sculpture) made of or overlaid with gold and ivory. **chrysober'yl** n a mineral, beryllium aluminate, of various shades of greenish-yellow or gold colour. **chrysocoll'a** n (Gr chrysokolla gold-solder, perh applied to this mineral, from kolla glue) a silicate of copper, bluish-green in colour. **chrysoc'racy** n (Gr krateein to rule) the rule of wealth, plutocracy. **chrys'olite** n (Gr lithos stone) olivine, esp yellow or green precious olivine; olivine used as a gemstone. **chrys'ophan** n (Gr phainesthai to appear) an old name for chrysarobin (**chrysophanic acid** an oxidation product of chrysarobin used against skin diseases). **chrysoph'ilite** n (Gr phileein to love) a lover of gold. **chrys'oprase** /-prāz/ n (Gr prason a leek) a green variety of chalcedony used as a gemstone. **chrys'otile** n (Gr tilos a shred) a fibrous variety of serpentine, a form of asbestos.

chs. abbrev : chapters.

chthonian /(k-)thō'ni-ən/ or **chthonic** /(k-)thon'ik/ adj relating to the earth or the underworld and the deities inhabiting it; ghostly. [Gr chthōn, chthonos the ground]

chub /chub/ n a small European river fish (Leuciscus cephalus) of the carp family; any of several N American fishes, eg the black bass. [Origin unknown]

Chubb® /chub/ n a type of lock which cannot be picked, invented by Charles Chubb (1772–1846), a locksmith in London (also **chubb'-lock**).

chubby /chub'i/ adj plump. [Perh from **chub**]
■ **chubb'ily** adv. **chubb'iness** n.

chuck¹ /chuk/ n the call of a hen; a clucking noise; (dimin chuck'ie) a chicken; (also **chuck'ie**) a term of endearment. ♦ vi to make the noise of a hen. [A variant of **cluck**]

chuck² /chuk/ vt to toss; to pitch; to abandon or dismiss; to stroke or tap lightly under the chin. ♦ n a gentle stroke or tap under the chin; a toss or throw, hence dismissal (inf); a pebble or small stone (more usu **chuck'ie**, **chuck'ie-stone** or Scot **chuck'ie-stane**); (in pl) a game with such stones (often called **chuck'ies**); any game of pitch-and-toss. [Fr choquer to jolt; allied to **shock¹**]
■ **chuck'er** n.
❑ **chucker-out'** n (inf) a person who expels undesirable people, eg from a public house, a meeting, etc, a bouncer. **chuck-far'thing** n formerly, a game in which a farthing was chucked into a hole. **chuck'hole** n (N Am) a pothole.

■ **chuck in** (*inf*) to give up; to abandon; to make a contribution to the cost of (*Aust*). **chuck it** (*inf*) to stop, give over; to rain (down) heavily. **chuck off** (*Aust* and *NZ sl*; *usu* with *at*) to abuse. **chuck out** (*inf*) to expel (a person); to throw away, get rid of. **chuck up** (*inf*) to give up; to give in; to vomit.

chuck³ /*chuk*/ *n* a lump or chunk; an instrument for holding an object so that it can be rotated, as on the mandrel of a lathe; food (*sl*); a cut of beef extending from the neck to the shoulder blade. [Origin uncertain; cf Ital *ciocco* a block, stump]
❑ **chuck wagon** *n* a wagon carrying food, cooking apparatus, etc, for cattle herders, etc.

chuck⁴ /*chuk*/ (*Can*) *n* any large body of water. See also **saltchuck** under **salt¹**. [Native American *chauk*]

chuck-full same as **chock-full** (see under **chock**).

chuckie see under **chuck¹,²**.

chuckle¹ /*chuk'l*/ *n* a quiet or suppressed laugh. ◆ *vt* to call, as a hen does her chickens. ◆ *vi* to laugh in a quiet or suppressed manner. [Cf **chuck¹**]
■ **chuck'ler** *n*. **chuck'ling** *n*.

chuckle² /*chuk'l*/ *adj* clumsy. [Prob **chock** a log]
❑ **chuck'le-head** *n* a stupid loutish person; a blockhead, dolt. **chuck'le-headed** *adj* stupid; awkward, clumsy.

chuckwalla /*chuk'wo-lə*/ *n* any of a genus (*Sauromalus*) of large, edible iguanas living in Mexico and the southern USA. [Mex Sp *chacahuala*, from a Native American language]

chuck-will's-widow /*chuk-wilz-wid'ō*/ *n* a large nightjar (*Caprimulgus carolinensis*) of the southern USA. [Imit of its call]

chuddah, chuddar variants of **chadar**.

chuddies /*chud'iz*/ (*sl*) *n pl* underpants. [Hindi]

chuddy /*chud'i*/ (*Aust* and *NZ inf*) *n* chewing gum.

chufa /*choo'fə*/ *n* a sedge (*Cyperus esculentus*), with edible nut-like tubers. [Sp]

chuff¹ /*chuf*/ or **chuff-chuff** /*chuf'chuf*/ *vi* to make a series of puffing sounds, as a steam locomotive does; to move while making such sounds. [Imit]

chuff² or **chough** /*chuf*/ (*dialect*) *n* a clown; a surly or boorish fellow. [ME *chuffe*, *choffe* a boor, of obscure origin]
■ **chuffed** *adj* disgruntled. **chuff'iness** *n* boorishness. **chuff'y** *adj* coarse and surly.

chuffed¹ /*chuft*/ (*inf*) *adj* very pleased. [Dialect *chuff* happy, chubby]

chuffed² see under **chuff²**.

chug /*chug*/ *n* a short, dull explosive noise, as of an internal-combustion engine; a quick or large swallow, *esp* of an alcoholic drink (*sl*). ◆ *vi* to make a chugging noise; (of a vehicle) to move while making such a noise. ◆ *vt* (*sl*) to drink in quick gulps. [Imit]
■ **chugg'ing** *adj*.

chugger /*chug'ər*/ (*sl*) *n* a charity worker who approaches people on the street in an attempt to solicit regular donations. [From *charity mugger*]

chukker or **chukka** /*chuk'ər* or *-ä*/ *n* a period of play, being one of the divisions in a game of polo. [Hindi *cakkar* a round]
❑ **chukka boot** *n* an ankle-length leather or rubber boot, like those worn for polo.

chukor /*chu-kör'*/, **chukar** /*-kär'*/, **chikhor** or **chikor** /*chi-kör'*/ *n* an Indian partridge (*Alectoris chukar* or *graeca*), having light plumage with black markings. [Hindi *cakor*]

chum¹ /*chum*/ *n orig* a person who shares a room or rooms with another; a friend or associate. ◆ *vi* to share a room; to be or become a chum. ◆ *vt* (**chumm'ing**; **chummed**) to assign as a chum (with *on*); to be or become a chum to; to accompany (*dialect*). [Perh a corruption of *chamber-fellow*]
■ **chumm'age** *n* the quartering of two or more persons in one room; a fee demanded from a new chum. **chumm'ily** *adv*. **chumm'iness** *n*. **chumm'y** *adj* sociable. ◆ *n* a chum.
■ **chum up with** to become friendly or intimate with.

chum² /*chum*/ *n* a type of salmon (*Oncorhynchus keta*), of the Pacific. [Chinook Jargon *tsum* spots]

chum³ /*chum*/ (*esp N Am*) *n* a groundbait of chopped fish, etc used by anglers. [Origin uncertain]

chumley see **chimney**.

chummy /*chum'i*/ *n* a chimney-sweep's boy (*old sl*); a criminal, *esp* a thief (*police sl*). See also **chum¹**. [**chimney**]

chump /*chump*/ *n* an end lump of wood, mutton, etc; a thick lump; a blockhead; the head. [Perh related to **chunk**]
■ **chump'ing** *n* (*N Eng dialect*) collecting wood for Guy Fawkes bonfires.
■ **off one's chump** (*sl*) out of one's mind, mad.

chunder /*chun'dər*/ (*Aust sl*) *vi* to vomit (also *n*).
■ **chun'derous** *adj* sick-making, nauseating.

chunk /*chungk*/ *n* a thick piece of anything, eg wood or bread. [Perh related to **chuck³**]
■ **chunk'ily** *adv*. **chunk'iness** *n*. **chunk'ing** *n* (*psychol*) the association of a number of items so that they are retained in the memory as a single entity. **chunk'y** *adj* in chunks; short and broad; (of sweaters, etc) thick and heavy.

Chunnel /*chun'l*/ (*inf*; also without *cap*) *n* the tunnel underneath the English Channel, connecting England and France. [*Channel* t*unnel*]

chunter /*chun'tər*/ (*inf*) *vi* (also (*obs* or *dialect*) **choun'ter**, **chun'der** or **chunn'er**; often with *on*) to mutter; to grumble; to chatter unceasingly and meaninglessly. [Imit]

chupati, chupatti same as **chapati, chapatti**.

chuppah or **huppah** /*hŭp'ə* or *hhŭp'ə*/ *n* the canopy under which a Jewish marriage ceremony is performed; the wedding ceremony. [Heb]

chuprassy /*chə-prä'si*/ see **chaprassi**.

church /*chûrch*/ *n* a building set apart for public worship, *esp* that of a parish, and *esp* that of an established or once established form of the Christian religion; a church service; the whole body of Christians; the Christian clergy; any particular sect or denomination of Christians; any body professing a common creed. ◆ *adj* of the church; ecclesiastical; belonging to the established church (*inf*). ◆ *vt* to perform a service in church with (eg a woman after childbirth, a newly-married couple, etc). [OE *cirice*, *circe*, from Gr *kȳriakon* belonging to the Lord, from *kȳrios* lord]
■ **churchian'ity** *n* devotion to the church rather than to Christ. **church'ing** *n*. **church'ism** *n* adherence to the form of principles of some church; ecclesiasticism. **church'less** *adj* not belonging to a church; without church approval or blessing. **church'ly** *adj* concerned with the church; ecclesiastical. **church'ward** or **church'wards** *adv*. **church'y** *adj* obtrusively devoted to the church; like or savouring of the church or church life.
❑ **church'-ale** *n* a church festival. **Church Army** *n* an organization of the Church of England, resembling the Salvation Army. **church'-bench** *n* (*Shakesp*) a seat in the porch of a church. **Church Commissioners** *n pl* a group of churchmen, government and legal representatives, who act as trustees in administering the property of the Church of England. **church court** *n* a court for deciding ecclesiastical causes; a kirk session; a presbytery, synod, or general assembly. **church'goer** *n* a person on the way to, or who regularly goes to, church. **church'going** *n* the act or habit of going to church. **church key** *n* (*US*) a pointed lever-like tool for making pouring- or drinking-holes in tin cans. **church'man** *n* a clergyman or ecclesiastic; a member or upholder of the established church. **church'manship** *n* the beliefs, practices, etc, of a clergyman or practising church member, *esp* high or low church attitudes to Anglican doctrine. **church militant** *n* the church on earth in its struggle against the powers of evil. **church mouse** *n* a mouse inhabiting a church, a proverbial example of poverty. **church officer** *n* a church attendant or beadle. **church-parade'** *n* a uniformed parade of a military or other body for the purpose of churchgoing. **church'people** *n pl*. **church'-rate** *n* an assessment for the sustentation of the fabric, etc of the parish church. **church school** *n* a school controlled or run by a church; an organization for religious education run by a church (*N Am*). **church service** *n* a religious service in a church; the form followed; a book containing it. **Church Slavonic** *n* the liturgical language used in the Orthodox Church in Russia, Serbia, etc. **church text** *n* a thin and tall form of black-letter Gothic print. **church triumphant** *n* the portion of the church which has overcome this world and entered into glory. **church'warden** *n* an elected lay officer who represents the interests of a parish or church; a long-stemmed clay pipe. **church'way** *n* the public way or road that leads to the church. **church'woman** *n* a female member or upholder of a church, *esp* the Anglican Church. **church'yard** *n* a burial ground round a church. **churchyard beetle** *n* a nocturnal ground beetle (*Blaps mucronata*) typically found in damp places such as cellars.

Churchillian /*chûr-chil'i-ən*/ *adj* of, in the manner of, or resembling (*esp* the rhetorical style or statesmanlike qualities of) Sir Winston Churchill (1874–1965), British prime minister.

churidars /*choo'ri-därz*/ *n pl* tight-fitting trousers as worn by Indian men and women. [Hindi]

churinga /*chŭ-ring'gə*/ *n* a sacred amulet of the Australian Aborigines. [From an Aboriginal language]

churl /*chûrl*/ *n* a rustic, an agricultural labourer (*hist*); an ill-bred, surly fellow. [OE *ceorl* a countryman; ON *karl*, Ger *Kerl* a man; Scot *carl*]
■ **churl'ish** *adj* rude; surly; ungracious. **churl'ishly** *adv*. **churl'ishness** *n*.

churn /*chûrn*/ *n* an apparatus used for making butter in which cream or whole milk is repeatedly stirred and turned until the fat is separated from the liquid; a large milk-can suggestive of an upright churn; anything that mixes, turns over or agitates. ◆ *vt* to agitate so as to obtain butter; to stir or agitate violently (often with *up*); to turn over persistently (eg ideas in the mind). ◆ *vi* to perform the act of churning; to move restlessly or in an agitated manner; (of brokers, financial advisers, etc) to encourage clients excessively to buy and sell investments, etc, thereby generating commissions; (of a government) to pay state benefits to a certain category of people from funds obtained by taxing others, eg those with higher incomes; (of consumers) to switch frequently between service providers in order to take advantage of the most favourable terms. [OE *cyrin*; ON *kirna* a churn, Du *karnen*, and Ger *kernen* to churn]

■ **churn'ing** *n* the act of making butter; the quantity of butter made at a churning; the practice of encouraging clients excessively to buy and sell investments, etc in order to generate commissions (*finance*).

❑ **churn'-drill** *n* a drill worked by hand, not struck with the hammer, a jumper. **churn'milk** *n* buttermilk. **churn'-staff** *n* the plunger which agitates the milk in an upright churn; the sun-spurge.

■ **churn out** to produce rapidly, continuously or mechanically, *esp* in large quantities.

churnalism /chŭr'nəl-izm/ (*inf*) *n* the writing of news reports based on existing reports and press releases rather than original investigation. [**churn** and **journalism** (see **journal**[1])]

churn-owl /chûrn'owl/ *n* a dialect name for the nightjar. [Appar **churr** and **owl**]

churr /chûr/ *n* a low trilling sound made by certain birds and insects. ◆ *vi* to make this sound. [Prob imit]

❑ **churr'-worm** *n* the mole cricket (qv under **mole**[1]).

churrigueresque /chŭ-ri-gə-resk'/ (*archit*) *adj* of an extravagant style of architecture and ornament of the baroque period in Spain and Spanish America. [José de *Churriguera* (1665–1725), Spanish architect]

churro /choo'rō/ *n* (*pl* **churr'os**) a stick of sweet fried dough, eaten as a snack. [Sp]

churrus see **charas**.

chuse /chooz/ an obsolete spelling of **choose**.

chut /chut/ *interj* an expression of impatience.

chute[1] or **shute**, also **shoot** /shoot/ *n* a waterfall, rapid; a passage or sloping trough for sending down goods, water, logs, coal, rubbish, etc; a slide in a park, etc; a narrow passage for controlling cattle. [Fr *chute* fall, combined with **shoot**]

chute[2] /shoot/ (*inf*) *n* short form of **parachute**.

■ **chut'ist** *n* a parachutist.

chutney /chut'ni/ *n* a condiment of mangoes, chillis, etc; an imitation made with various alternative ingredients, such as apples. [Hindi *catnī*]

chutzpah or **hutzpah** /hhŭt'spə/ *n* effrontery, brazenness, impudence. [Heb and Yiddish]

chyack see **chiack**.

chylde see **child**.

chyle /kīl/ (*med, zool*) *n* a white fluid, mainly lymph mixed with fats derived from food in the body, formed in the small intestine during digestion. [Gr *chȳlos* juice, from *cheein* to pour]

■ **chylā'ceous** *adj.* **chylif'erous** *adj* containing chyle. **chylifica'tion** *n* the production of chyle. **chyl'ify** *vt* to turn into or produce chyle. **chyl'omicron** *n* a tiny globule of fat, the form in which fat is carried in blood and chyle. **chylū'ria** *n* (Gr *ouron* urine) the presence of chyle in the urine.

chyme /kīm/ *n* the pulp to which food is reduced in the stomach before entering the small intestine. [Gr *chȳmos* chyme, juice, from *cheein* to pour]

■ **chymif'erous** *adj.* **chymifica'tion** *n* the act of being formed into chyme. **chym'ify** *vt* to form into chyme. **chymotryp'sin** *n* an enzyme produced in the pancreas, active in the hydrolysis of proteins during digestion. **chym'ous** *adj.*

chymistry see **chemistry**.

chymous see under **chyme**.

chynd /chīnd/ (*Spenser*) *adj* cut into chines.

chypre /shē'pr'/ *n* a perfume made from sandalwood, *orig* from Cyprus. [Fr, Cyprus]

chytrid /kit'rid/ or **chytrid fungus** /fung'gəs/ *n* any fungus belonging to the phylum *Chytridiomycota*, *esp* the fungus *Batrachochytrium dendrobatidis*, which is fatal to amphibians. [Gr *chytridion* little pot]

CI *abbrev*: Channel Islands; Côte d'Ivoire (IVR).

Ci *symbol*: curie.

CIA (*US*) *abbrev*: Central Intelligence Agency.

Cia. *abbrev*: *Compagnia* (Ital), *Compañía* (Sp), Company.

ciabatta /chə-bä'tə or -bat'ə/ *n* (*pl* **ciabatt'as** or **ciabatt'e** /-tā/) a type of Italian white bread made with olive oil and wheat flour, popular for its thick, soft centre. [Ital, slipper]

ciao /chä'ö or (*Eng*) *chow*/ *interj* an informal greeting used on meeting or parting. [Ital]

CIB *abbrev*: Chartered Institute of Bankers; Criminal Investigation Branch (of the police force) (*NZ*).

cibachrome /sē'bə-krōm/ (*photog*) *n* a type of colour print made directly from a colour transparency without first making a negative.

cibation /si-bā'shən/ (*obs*) *n* the seventh of the twelve processes employed by alchemists in the search for the philosopher's stone, 'feeding the matter'; taking food, feeding. [L *cibātiō, -ōnis* feeding]

cibol /sib'əl/ or **chibol** /chib'əl/ *n* a variety of onion (*Allium fistulosum*); a spring onion. [Fr *ciboule*, Sp *cebolla*, from LL *cēpola*, dimin of L *cēpa* an onion; see **sybo**]

ciborium /si-bō'ri-əm or -bö'/ *n* (*pl* **cibo'ria**) a vessel closely resembling a chalice, *usu* with an arched cover, in which the host is deposited (*Christianity*); a free-standing structure consisting of a canopy supported on four pillars over the high altar (*archit*). [L, a drinking cup, from Gr *kibōrion* the seed vessel of the Egyptian water lily]

CIC *abbrev*: Commander-in-Chief.

CICA *abbrev*: Criminal Injuries Compensation Authority.

cicada /si-kä'də or -kä'də/ or **cicala** /-kä'lə/ *n* (*pl* **cica'das, cica'dae** /-dē/, **cica'las** or **cica'le** /-lē/) a large homopterous insect of warm regions, having a broad body and large transparent wings, the male of which makes a loud chirping sound. [L *cicāda*; Ital *cicala*]

■ **cicadell'id** *n* any homopterous insect of the genus *Cicadella*, the leaf-hoppers, which feed by sucking plant tissue, some species being a serious pest of crops.

cicatrice /sik'ə-tris/or **cicatrix** /si-kā'triks or sik'ə-triks/ *n* (*pl* **cicatrī'cēs** or **cicatrixes**) a scar over a healed wound; a scar in the bark of a tree; the scar-like mark left where a leaf, etc has been attached; a mark, impression (*Shakesp*). [L *cicātrīx, -īcis* a scar]

■ **cicatricial** /sik-ə-trish'əl/ *adj.* **cicatric'ula, cicat'richule** or **cicat'ricle** *n* a white spot, the germinating point in the yolk of an egg; the hilum of grains (*bot*); a small scar. **cicatrīzā'tion** or **-s-** *n* the process of healing over to form a cicatrice. **cic'atrīze** or **-ise** *vt* to promote the formation of a cicatrice on; to scar. ◆ *vi* to heal.

CICB *abbrev*: Criminal Injuries Compensation Board (now replaced by **CICA**).

cicely /sis'ə-li/ *n* a name for several umbelliferous plants related to chervil, *esp Myrrhis odorata* (sweet cicely). [L and Gr *seseli*]

cicero /sis'ə-rō or (L) *kik-e-rō*/ *n* a measure of type between pica and English. [After the Roman orator *Cicero*]

■ **cicerone** /chich-ə-rō'ni, also *sis-ə-rō'ni*/ *n* (*pl* **cicerō'ni** /-nē/ or **cicerō'nes**) a person who shows and explains the curiosities of a place to visitors and sightseers; a guide. ◆ *vi* to act as cicerone.

Ciceronian /si-sə-rō'ni-ən/ *adj* relating to or in the style of the Roman orator *Cicero* (died 43BC); (of language) eloquent or rhythmical. ◆ *n* an imitator or admirer of the Latin diction and style of Cicero.

■ **Cicerō'nianism** *n* the character of Cicero's Latin style or an imitation of this in literature, etc. **Ciceronic** /-ron'ik/ *adj.*

cichlid /sik'lid/ *n* any teleost fish of the family **Cich'lidae**, which carries its young in its mouth, including the angelfish of the Amazon. [Gr *kichlē* a kind of wrasse]

■ **cich'loid** *adj.*

cichoraceous /si-kə-rā'shəs/ (*bot*) *adj* of or belonging to the Cichoraceae, a suborder of plants including the chicory, endive, dandelion, etc. [New L *cichorāceae*, from *cichorium* chicory, from Gr *kichorion*]

Cicindelidae /si-sin-dē'li-dē/ *n* a family of carnivorous beetles, the tiger beetles, that hunt their insect prey on the run. [L *cicindēla* glow-worm, from *candēla* a candle]

cicinnus /si-sin'əs/ *n* a cincinnus. [Latinized from Gr *kinkinnos* a ringlet]

cicisbeo /chē-chēz-bā'ö or chi-chiz-/ *n* (*pl* **cicisbe'i** /-ē/) *esp* formerly, a married woman's gallant or *cavaliere servente* in Italy; the acknowledged lover of a married woman. [Ital]

■ **cicisbē'ism** *n.*

ciclaton /sik'lə-tən/ or **ciclatoun** /-toon/ (*obs*) *n esp* in medieval times, cloth of gold or other rich material. [OFr *ciclaton*, from Ar, perh from the root of **scarlet**]

cicuta /si-kū'tə/ *n* a plant of the genus *Cicuta* of poisonous umbelliferous plants including water hemlock and cowbane. [L *cicūta* hemlock]

CID *abbrev*: Criminal Investigation Department (of the police force).

cid /sid or sēd/ n a chief, captain or hero; (with cap) the title given to the 11c Castilian champion Rodrigo (or Ruy) Diaz. [Sp, from Ar *sayyid* lord]

cidaris /sid'ə-ris/ n a Persian royal tiara; (with cap) a genus of sea urchins, mostly fossil. [Gr *kidaris*]

cide /sīd/ vt a proposed emendation for Shakespeare's 'side', as if aphetic for **decide**, to adjudge.

-cide /-sīd/ combining form denoting: (1) killing, murder; (2) killer, murderer. [L *caedere* to kill]
■ **-cidal** adj combining form.

cider or **cyder** /sī'dər/ n an alcoholic drink made from apples; an unfermented drink made from crushed apples (N Am). [Fr *cidre*, from L *sīcera*, from Gr *sikera* strong drink, from Heb *shēkār*]
■ **ci'derkin** n a type of weak cider. **cī'dery** adj.
❏ **ci'der-and** n a mixture of cider and spirits. **ci'der-cup** n a drink of sweetened cider, with other ingredients. **cider press** n an apparatus for pressing the juice from apples in cider-making.

ci-devant /sē-də-vã'/ (Fr) adj and adv before this, former, formerly. ◆ n a formerly important person.

CIE abbrev : Companion of the (Order of the) Indian Empire; (**CIÉ**) Córas Iompair Éireann (Irish), Transport Organization of Ireland.

Cie. abbrev : Compagnie (Fr), Company.

ciel, **cieling** variants of **ceil**, **ceiling**.

cierge see **cerge**.

cif abbrev : cost, insurance, freight.

cig, etc see **cigarette** under **cigar**.

cigar /si-gär'/ n a roll of tobacco leaves (usu with a tapered end) for smoking. [Sp *cigarro*]
■ **cigarette** /sig-ə-ret'/ n finely-cut tobacco rolled in thin paper (inf shortened forms **cig**, **cigg'ie** and **cigg'y**). **cigarillo** /sig-ə-ril'ō/ n (pl **cigarill'os**) a small cigar.
❏ **cigarette card** n a picture card formerly given away with a packet of cigarettes, valued by cartophilists. **cigarette case** or **cigar case** n a small case for carrying cigarettes or cigars. **cigarette end** or **cigarette butt** n the unsmoked remnant of a cigarette. **cigarette holder** or **cigar'-holder** n a holder with a mouthpiece for smoking a cigarette or cigar. **cigarette lighter** n a mechanical device which produces a flame for lighting cigarettes. **cigarette paper** n thin paper for making cigarettes. **cigar'-shaped** adj cylindrical with tapered ends. **cigar tree** n a species of *Catalpa* with long cigar-like pods.

ci-gît /sē-zhē'/ (Fr) here lies.

CIGS (Brit hist) abbrev : Chief of the Imperial General Staff.

ciguatera /sig-wə-tär'ə/ n a type of food poisoning caused by eating seafood containing natural ciguatoxins. [Sp *cigua* a type of small snail orig believed to cause the illness]
❏ **ciguatox'ic** adj. **ciguatox'in** n any of several toxic substances that occur naturally in some fish.

CII abbrev : Chartered Insurance Institute.

cilantro /si-lan'trō/ n coriander. [Sp]

cilice /sil'is/ n haircloth; an undergarment worn by penitents, orig made of haircloth, but now usu a band of pronged wire. [L, from Gr *kilikion* a cloth made of Cilician goat's hair]
■ **cilicious** /-ish'əs/ adj.

CILIP abbrev : Chartered Institute of Library and Information Professionals.

cilium /sil'i-əm/ (biol) n (pl **cil'ia**) one of the fine hair-like structures that are borne on the surface of a cell, that move liquid over its surface or act as locomotor organs in eg protozoans and flatworms. [L *cilium* eyelash]
■ **cil'iary** adj. **cil'iate** adj bearing a cilium or cilia; fringed with hairs; of or relating to Ciliata, a subclass of Protozoa, having cilia for locomotion. ◆ n a member of the subclass Ciliata. **cil'iolate** adj fringed with very short fine hairs. **Ciliophʹora** n pl (Gr *phoros* bearing) a subphylum of Protozoa, including the ciliates, that possess cilia at some time in the life cycle.
❏ **ciliary body** n (anat) the circular muscle ring attached by fibres to the lens of the eye, which by contracting can alter the shape of the lens to change its focus.

cill /sil/ (building) n a variant of **sill**, sometimes used in the trade.

CILT abbrev : Chartered Institute of Logistics and Transport.

CIM abbrev : Chartered Institute of Marketing; computer input on microfilm; computer integrated manufacture.

cimar see **cymar**.

cimbalom /sim'bə-ləm/ n a Hungarian form of the dulcimer. [Hung, from Ital *cembala* cymbal]

ciment fondu /si-mã fõ-doo'/ (building) n (also with caps) a type of rapid-hardening cement with a high aluminium content. [Fr, melted cement]

cimetidine /sī-met'i-dēn/ n a generic drug that reduces the secretion of hydrochloric acid in the stomach and thus promotes the healing of gastric and duodenal ulcers.

cimex /sī'meks/ n (pl **cimices** /sim'i-sēz/) any heteropterous insect such as the bed bug, of the genus *Cimex*, which gives name to the family **Cimicidae** /sī- or si-mis'i-dē/. [L, bug]

cimier /sē-myā'/ n the crest of a helmet. [Fr]

ciminite /sim'i-nīt/ n a rock intermediate between trachyte and andesite, containing olivine. [Monte *Cimini*, in Italy]

Cimmerian /si-mē'ri-ən/ adj relating to the Cimmerii, a tribe fabled to have lived in perpetual darkness; hence, extremely dark or gloomy.

cimolite /sim'ō-līt/ n a type of clay, or hydrous silicate of aluminium, similar to fuller's earth. [Gr *kimōliā*, prob from *Kimōlos* an island of the Cyclades]

C-in-C abbrev : Commander-in-Chief.

cinch /sinch/ n a saddle girth (US); a secure hold (inf); a certainty (inf); something easy (inf); a card game in which the five of trumps ranks highest. ◆ vi (esp N Am) to tighten the cinch; to tighten one's grip on (fig). ◆ vt to bind firmly, esp with a belt around the waist; to make sure of (inf); to pull (clothing) in tightly at the waist. [Sp *cincha*, from L *cingula*]
■ **cinch'ing** n distortion of magnetic tape caused by low winding tension resulting in slippage of the layers of tape on the spindles.

cinchona /sing-kō'nə/ n any rubiaceous tree of the *Cinchona* genus of trees, which yield the bark from which quinine and related by-products are obtained; the dried bark of these trees (also called **Peruvian bark**, **china bark**); a drug obtained from the bark. [Said to be so named from the Countess of *Chinchón*, who was cured of a fever by it in 1638]
■ **cinchonaceous** /-kən-ā'shəs/ or **cinchonic** /-kon'ik/ adj. **cinch'onine** n an alkaloid obtained from cinchona bark and used as a substitute for quinine. **cinchoninic** /-nin'ik/ adj. **cinch'onism** n a condition resulting from overdoses of cinchona or quinine. **cinchonīzā'tion** or **-s-** n. **cinch'onize** or **-ise** vt to treat with cinchona or quinine.

cincinnus /sin-sin'əs/ (bot) n a uniparous cymose inflorescence in which the plane of each daughter axis is at right angles, alternately to right and left, with that of its parent axis. [L, a curl]
■ **cincinn'ate** adj.

cincture /singk'chər/ n a girdle or belt; a moulding around the top or bottom of a column (archit). ◆ vt to gird, encompass, surround. [L *cinctūra*, from *cingere*, *cinctum* to gird]
■ **cinct** adj (rare) surrounded, encircled. **cinc'tured** adj having a cincture.

cinder /sin'dər/ n the refuse of burned coals; an ember; anything charred by fire; a scoriaceous fragment of lava; a strong stimulant such as whisky put in tea, soda-water, etc (old sl). ◆ vi and vt to turn to cinder(s). [OE *sinder* slag; cf Ger *Sinter*; not connected with Fr *cendre*]
■ **Cinderell'a** n a scullery-maid, a drudge; a despised and neglected person or thing; a person from poor or obscure origins who achieves success or fame (also adj). **cin'dery** adj.
❏ **cinder block** n (N Am) breeze block. **cinder cone** n a hill of loose volcanic materials. **Cinderella dance** n a dancing party ending at midnight. **cinder path** or **cinder track** n a path or racing-track laid with cinders.

cine or **ciné** /sin'i/ adj cinematographic.
❏ **cine camera** or **ciné camera** n a camera for taking moving photographs. **cine film** n film suitable for use in a cine camera. **cine projector** or **ciné projector** n. **ciné vérité** n cinéma vérité.

cine- or **ciné-** /si-ni-/ combining form denoting cinema or cinematograph.
■ **cineangiog'raphy** n the recording of the movement of blood in the blood vessels by photographing a series of X-ray images to create a moving picture. **cin'ebīol'ogy** or **cinébīol'ogy** n the study of biological phenomena by means of cinematographic records. **cinemicrog'raphy** n cinematographic recording of changes under the microscope. **cin'ephile** n a devotee of the cinema. **cin'eplex** n a multiple-cinema complex. **Cinerama**® /-ə-rä'mə/ n a method of film projection on a wide curved screen to give a three-dimensional effect (being the picture photographed with three **cineram'ic** cameras).

cinéaste, **cineaste** or **cineast** /sin'ē-ast/ n a person who takes an artistic interest in, or who makes, motion pictures. [Fr]

cinema /sin'i-mə or -mä/ n a building in which motion pictures are shown; (with the) motion pictures collectively, or as an art; material or method judged by its suitability for the cinema; a cinematograph. [**cinematograph**]

■ **cin'emathèque** or **cin'ematheque** /-tek/ n a small, intimate cinema; a film archive. **cinemat'ic** adj relating to, suitable for, or characteristic of, the cinema. **cinemat'ically** adv.
❑ **cin'ema-goer** n a person who goes (regularly) to the cinema. **cin'ema-organ** n an organ with showier effects than a church organ. **Cin'emaScope**® n a method of film projection on a wide screen using film that has photographed the image at twice the normal width. **cinéma vérité** n realism in films by portraying scenes that have the appearance of real life.

cinematograph /si-nə-mat'ə-gräf/ n (also (old) **kinemat'ograph**) apparatus for filming, printing and projecting a series of instantaneous photographs so as to give a moving representation of a scene, with or without reproduction of sound; an exhibition of such photographs. [Fr cinématographe, from Gr kīnēma, -atos motion, and graphein to write, represent]
■ **cinematog'rapher** n. **cinematograph'ic** or **cinematograph'ical** adj. **cinematograph'ically** adv. **cinematog'raphist** n a film-maker. **cinematog'raphy** n the art of making motion pictures; motion picture photography.

cineol or **cineole** /sin'i-ol or -ōl/ n eucalyptol, a camphor-smelling disinfectant liquid ($C_{10}H_{18}O$), obtained from several essential oils, such as eucalyptus, wormwood and cajuput. [From Artemisia cīna a species of wormwood, and L oleum oil]

cineplex, Cinerama® see under **cine-**.

cineraria[1] /si-nə-rā'ri-ə/ n a composite plant, a member of the genus Senecio, esp S. cruentus a brightly-flowered cultivated variety with ashy down on the leaves. [L cinerārius ashy, from cinis, cineris ash]

cineraria[2] see **cinerarium** under **cinerary**.

cinerary /sin'ə-rə-ri/ adj relating to ashes; for containing ashes of the dead. [L cinereus ashy, from cinis, cineris ash]
■ **cinerā'rium** n (pl **cinerā'ria**) a place for depositing the ashes of the dead after cremation. **cinerā'tion** n. **cinerā'tor** n the grey matter of the brain. **cinē'real** adj ashy; cinerary. **cinē'reous** adj ashy-grey; ashy. **cineri'tious** adj ashy-grey; relating to the grey matter of the brain.

cinerin /sin'ə-rin/ n either of two compounds derived from pyrethrum and used as insecticides. [L ciner, cineris ash, and chem sfx **-in**]

Cingalese see **Sinhalese**.

cingulum /sing'gū-ləm/ n (pl **cing'ula**) a girdle, as of a priest's alb; a girdle-like structure, such as the band round the base of the crown of a tooth. [L cingere to gird]
■ **cing'ulate** or **cing'ulated** adj.

cingulum Veneris /sing'gū-ləm ve'nə-ris or king'gū-lŭm we'ne-ris/ (L) the girdle of Venus.

cinnabar /sin'ə-bär/ n a mineral, sulphide of mercury, called vermilion when used as a pigment. ◆ adj vermilion-coloured. [Gr kinnabari, from Pers]
■ **cinnabaric** /-bär'ik/ adj. **cinn'abarine** /-bə-rēn/ adj.
❑ **cinnabar moth** n a large red European moth whose black-and-yellow caterpillars feed on ragwort.

cinnamon /sin'ə-mən/ n the spicy bark of a lauraceous tree of Sri Lanka; the tree; a light yellowish brown. [Gr kinnamōmon, later kinnamon, from Heb qinnāmōn]
■ **cinnamic** /-am'ik/ or **cinnamonic** /-ə-mon'ik/ adj obtained from, or consisting of, cinnamon.
❑ **cinnamic acid** n weak white organic acid found in cinnamon oil and used in perfumery. **cinnamon bear** n a cinnamon-coloured variety of the American black bear. **cinnamon stone** n a yellowish grossular garnet, hessonite.

cinnarizine /si-nar'i-zēn/ n a generic antihistamine drug used to relieve nausea and travel sickness, and, in higher doses, in the treatment of certain peripheral vascular diseases.

cinquain /sing'kān or -kān'/ n a poetic form consisting of five lines of two, four, six, eight and two syllables respectively. [Fr]

cinque /singk/ n the number five, as on dice. [Fr]
❑ **cinque'foil** n a common bearing representing a flower with five petals borne full-faced and without a stalk (heraldry); a similar figure formed by cusps in a circular window or the head of a pointed arch (archit); the plant Potentilla reptans (bot); the five-bladed clover (bot). **cinque'-pace** n (Shakesp also **sinke'-a-pace**) formerly, a lively dance, the pace or movement of which is characterized by five beats. **Cinque Ports** n pl the five ancient ports on the south coast of England lying opposite to France, orig Sandwich, Dover, Hythe, Romney and Hastings, and later including Winchelsea, Rye, and a number of subordinate ports. **cinque'-spotted** adj (Shakesp) having five spots.

cinquecento /ching-kwe-chen'tō/ n the 16th century, esp in reference to Italian art and architecture of the Renaissance period. [Ital, five hundred (mil-, one thousand, being understood)]

Cinzano® /chin-zä'nō/ n an Italian vermouth. [Manufacturers' name]

CIO see **AFL-CIO**.

CIOB abbrev : Chartered Institute of Building.

CIoJ abbrev : Chartered Institute of Journalists.

cion a spelling of **scion** still used in the USA.

CIP abbrev : cataloguing in publication.

CIPA abbrev : Chartered Institute of Patent Agents.

CIPD abbrev : Chartered Institute of Personnel and Development.

CIPFA abbrev : Chartered Institute of Public Finance and Accountancy.

cipher (sometimes **cypher**) /sī'fər/ n a secret code; an interweaving of the initials of a name; any person or thing of little value, a nonentity; any of the Arabic numerals; formerly, the character 0 (maths); in an organ, continuous sounding of a note not played, due to a mechanical defect. ◆ vi to work at arithmetic; of an organ, to sound a note continuously when it is not played. ◆ vt to write in cipher; to calculate; to decipher (Shakesp). [OFr cyfre, Fr chiffre, from Ar sifr zero, empty]
■ **cī'phering** n.
❑ **cipher key** n a key to a cipher or piece of secret writing.

CIPM abbrev : Comité International des Poids et Mesures (Fr), International Committee for Weights and Measures.

cipollino /chē-pol-lē'nō/ or **cipolin** /sip'ə-lin/ n (pl **cipolli'nos**) a marble with green and white bands in which calcite is interfoliated with mica or talc, the chief source of which is the island of Euboea. [Ital cipolla an onion]

cippus /sip'əs/ n (pl **cipp'ī**) the stocks; a monumental pillar (archit). [L cippus a post]

Cipro® /sī'prō/ n the brand name of a broad-spectrum antibiotic, **ciprofloxacin**, $C_{17}H_{18}FN_3O_3$, a synthetic quinolone.

cir. or **circ.** abbrev : circa, circiter or circum (L), about.

circa /sûr'kə/ prep and adv about, around. [L]

circadian /sûr-kā'di-ən/ adj relating to any biological cycle (eg of varying intensity of metabolic or physiological process, or of some feature of behaviour) which is repeated, usu approx every 24 hours (esp in circadian rhythm). [From L circa about, di(em) day, and **-an**]

Circaean or **Circean** /sûr-sē'ən/ adj relating to the beautiful sorceress Circe, who transformed the companions of Odysseus into swine by a magic beverage (Gr myth); infatuating and degrading. [L Circē, from Gr Kirkē]
■ **Circae'a** n the enchanter's nightshade genus.

circar same as **sircar**.

Circassian /sûr-kas(h)'yən/ adj belonging to Circassia, a region in the western Caucasus. ◆ n a native of Circassia, a Cherkess; the language of the Cherkesses; (without cap) a kind of light cashmere (also **circassienne'**).
❑ **Circassian circle** n a progressive dance in reel time.

circensian /sûr-sen'shi-ən/ adj relating to the Circus Maximus in Rome, where games were held (also (obs) **circen'sial**). [L circēnsis, from circus]

circinate /sûr'si-nāt/ adj ring-shaped; rolled inwards (bot). [L circināre, -ātum to make round]

Circinus /sûr'si-nəs/ n a small constellation in the southern hemisphere lying next to Centaurus. [L circinus a pair of compasses]

circiter /sûr'si-tər/ prep (formerly used with dates) about, around. [L]

circle /sûr'kl/ n a plane figure bounded by one line every point of which is equally distant from a fixed point called the centre; the circumference of the figure so defined; a circular object; a ring; a planet's orbit; a parallel of latitude; a series ending where it began; a figure in magic; a group of things in a circle; an area of seating in a theatre or cinema above the stalls, such as the dress circle or upper circle; a company surrounding or associating with the principal person; those of a certain class or group; an administrative unit. ◆ vt to move round; to encompass; to draw a circle around. ◆ vi (often with round or around) to move in a circle; to stand in a circle. [OE circul, from L circulus, dimin of circus; related to OE hring a ring]
■ **cir'cled** adj circular; encircled. **cir'cler** n. **cir'clet** n a little circle; a little circular band or hoop, esp a metal headband. **cir'cling** n and adj moving in a circle.
❑ **cir'cle-rider** n a person who rides in circles to round up cattle. **cir'cle-riding** n.
■ **come full circle** to return to the beginning; to regain or turn out to be in a former state. **dress circle** see under **dress. go round in circles** to get no results in spite of effort; not to get anywhere. **great** (or **small**) **circle** a circular section of a sphere whose centre is (or is not) the centre of the sphere. **reasoning in a circle** assuming what is to be proved as the basis of the argument. **run round in circles** to act in too frenzied a way to achieve anything useful.

circlip /sûr'klip/ (engineering) n a spring washer in the form of an incomplete circle, which fits into a groove and is used as a retaining ring.

circs /sûrks/ (sl) n pl a shortened form of **circumstances**.

circuit /sûr'kit/ n a journey round; a way round; a perimeter; a roundabout way; an area enclosed; the path, complete or partial, of an electric current; a round made in the exercise of a calling, esp in England (until 1972) by judges; the judges making the round; a district in which such a round is made, as by Methodist preachers, commercial travellers, etc; a group of theatres, cinemas, etc under common control, through which an entertainment circulates; the venues visited in turn and regularly by sports competitors, performers, etc; a series of exercises to be carried out consecutively and repeated; a motor-racing track; a diadem (Shakesp). ◆ vt to go round. [Fr, from L circuitus, from circuīre, from circum round, and īre to go]
■ **circuiteer**' n a judge who goes on a circuit. **circuitous** /-kū'i-təs/ adj indirect, roundabout. **circū'itously** adv. **circū'itousness** n. **circuitry** /sûr'kit-ri/ n the detailed plan of a circuit, as in radio or television, or its components. **circū'ity** n motion in a circle; an indirect or roundabout course.
◻ **circuit board** n a printed circuit board (qv under **print**). **circuit breaker** n a switch or other device for interrupting an electric circuit; anything which halts or interrupts a process temporarily. **circuit judge** n a judge in a county or crown court. **circuit rider** n (hist) a preacher who goes on a circuit. **circuit training** n a form of athletic training consisting of a repeated series of exercises.

circuitus verborum /sûr-kū'i-təs vûr-bō'rəm, -bō' or kir-kū'i-tŭs wer-bō'rŭm/ (L) a circumlocution.

circular /sûr'kyū-lər/ adj of or relating to a circle; in the form of a circle; round; ending in itself; recurring in a cycle; addressed to a circle of persons. ◆ n a letter or notice sent to a number of persons. [L circulāris]
■ **circularity** /-lar'i-ti/ n. **circularizā'tion** or **-s-** n. **cir'cularize** or **-ise** vt to make circular; to send circulars to. **cir'cularly** adv.
◻ **circular breathing** n a technique used in playing a wind instrument, in which a phrase is sustained by forcing air out of the mouth while breathing through the nose. **circular file** n (comput) a file in which each item has a pointer to the next, the last leading back to the first. **circular function** n any of the trigonometrical functions with argument in radians. **circular letter** n a letter of which copies are sent to several persons. **circular measure** n the reckoning of angles in radians. **circular note** n a former letter of bank credit addressed to foreign bankers for the use of a traveller, being a kind of bill personal to the bearer. **circular polarization** n (telecom) an electromagnetic wave for which either the electric or magnetic field vector describes a circle at the wave frequency, used in satellite communications. **circular saw** n a power-driven saw in the shape of a flat disc with a serrated edge. **circular velocity** n the horizontal velocity of a body required to keep it in orbit, at a given altitude, around a planet.

circulate /sûr'kū-lāt or -kyə-/ vt to cause to go round as in a circle; to spread. ◆ vi to move round; to be spread about; to repeat in definite order (of decimals). [L circulāre, -ātum]
■ **cir'culable** adj capable of being circulated. **cir'culating** n and adj. **circulā'tion** n the act of moving in a circle or in a closed path (as the blood); spreading or moving about; dissemination; the sale of a periodical; the money in use at any time in a country. **cir'culative** or **cir'culatory** adj circulating. **cir'culātor** n.
◻ **circulating capital** n (old) working capital. **circulating library** n a small library that moves around a group of schools, hospitals, etc; one from which books are circulated among subscribers. **circulatory system** n the system of blood and lymph vessels, including the heart.
■ **in** or **out of circulation** in or out of general use, activity, etc.

circum- /sûr'kəm-, sər-kum-/ combining form denoting around. [L circum]

circumambages /sûr-kəm-am-bā'jēz or -am'bi-jiz/ n sing and n pl roundabout methods of speech. [L circum around, and ambāgēs a winding]
■ **circumambā'gious** /-jəs/ adj roundabout in speech.

circumambient /sûr-kəm-am'bi-ənt/ adj going round about, encompassing. [L circum around, and ambīre to go round]
■ **circumam'bience** or **circumam'biency** n.

circumambulate /sûr-kəm-am'bū-lāt/ vi to walk round about. [L circum around, and ambulāre, -ātum to walk]
■ **circumambulā'tion** n. **circumam'bulatory** adj.

circumbendibus /sûr-kəm-ben'di-bəs/ n a roundabout way, method or expression. [Joc formation from L circum round, **bend**, and L ablative pl ending -ibus]

circumcentre /sûr'kəm-sen-tər/ n the centre of the circumscribed circle or sphere. [**circum-**]

circumcise /sûr'kəm-sīz/ vt to cut or cut off all or part of the foreskin of (a male) or all or part of the clitoris of (a female), often as a religious rite; to purify (fig). [L circumcīdere, -cīsum, from caedere to cut]
■ **cir'cumciser** n. **circumcision** /-sizh'n/ n the act of circumcising; the state of being circumcised; those who are circumcised, esp the

Jews (archaic); (with cap) a festival celebrated on 1 January in commemoration of the circumcision of Christ (RC church).

circumdenudation /sûr-kəm-den-ū-dā'shən/ (geol) n denudation or erosion of surroundings, leaving an isolated elevation. [**circum-**]

circumduct /sûr-kəm-dukt or -dukt'/ vt to lead around or about, to cause to revolve round an imaginary axis so as to describe a cone. [L circum round, and dūcere, ductum to lead]
■ **circumduce** /-dūs'/ vt (Scots law; obs) to declare to be at an end (the term for leading proof). **circumduc'tion** n. **circumduct'ory** adj.

circumference /sər-kum'fə-rəns/ n the boundary line, esp of a circle; compass; distance round. [L circum around, and ferre to carry]
■ **circumferential** /-en'shl/ adj. **circumferen'tially** adv. **circum'ferentor** /-en-tər/ n an instrument for measuring horizontal angles, consisting of a graduated circle, sights, and a magnetic needle; a graduated wheel for measuring the circumference of wheels.

circumflect /sûr-kəm-flekt'/ vt to bend round; to mark with a circumflex. [L circum around, and flectere, flexum to bend]
■ **cir'cumflex** n an accent (ˆ) orig denoting a rising and falling of the voice on a vowel or syllable (also adj). ◆ vt to bend round. **circumflexion** /-flek'shən/ n a bending round.

circumfluence /sər-kum'flū-əns/ n a flowing around; the engulfing of food by surrounding it (eg by protozoa, etc). [L circum around, and fluere to flow]
■ **circum'fluent** or **circum'fluous** adj.

circumforaneous /sûr-kəm-fo-rā'ni-əs/ or **circumforanean** /-ni-ən/ adj wandering about as from market to market, vagrant. [L circum around, and forum the forum, market-place]

circumfuse /sûr-kəm-fūz'/ vt to pour around or about. [L circum around, and fundere, fūsum to pour]
■ **circumfused'** adj. **circumfus'ile** adj molten; poured around or about. **circumfusion** /-fū'zhən/ n.

circumgyrate /sûr-kəm-jī-rāt' or -jī'rāt/ vi to whirl or roll round. [L circum around, and gyrāre, -ātum to turn]
■ **circumgyrā'tion** n. **circumgy'ratory** adj.

circumincession or **circuminsession** /sûr-kəm-in-sesh'ən/ (theol) n the reciprocity of existence in one another of the three persons of the Trinity. [L circum around, and incessus, pap of incēdere to go, proceed]

circumjacent /sûr-kəm-jā'sənt/ adj lying round; bordering on every side. [L circum around, and jacēns, -entis lying, from jacēre to lie]
■ **circumjā'cency** n.

circumlittoral /sûr-kəm-lit'ə-rəl/ adj adjacent to or bordering the shoreline. [L circum around, and littus, for lītus, -oris shore]

circumlocution /sûr-kəm-lō-kū'shən/ n expressing an idea in more words than are necessary; an instance of this; evasive talk. [L circum around, and loquī, locūtus to speak]
■ **circumlocūte'** vi to use circumlocution. **circumlocū'tional** or **circumlocū'tionary** adj. **circumlocū'tionist** n a person who uses circumlocution. **circumlocutory** /-lok'ū-tər-i/ adj.
◻ **Circumlocution Office** n in Dickens's Little Dorrit, a very dilatory government department.

circumlunar /sûr-kəm-loo'nər, -lū'/ adj situated or moving round the moon. [L circum around, and lūna the moon]

circummure /sûr-kəm-mūr'/ (Shakesp) vt to wall around. [L circum around, and mūrus a wall]

circumnavigate /sûr-kəm-nav'i-gāt/ vt to sail or fly right round. [**circum-**]
■ **circumnav'igable** adj. **circumnavigā'tion** n. **circumnav'igātor** n.

circumnutation /sûr-kəm-nū-tā'shən/ (bot) n rotation in a nodding position, as the helical path described by the growing point of a plant. [L circum around, and nūtāre, -ātum to nod]
■ **circumnū'tate** vi. **circumnū'tatory** adj.

circumpolar /sûr-kəm-pō'lər/ adj situated or ranging round the pole. [**circum-**]
◻ **circumpolar stars** n pl stars so near the pole of the heavens that (for places at the latitude in question) they never set but merely revolve round the pole.

circumpose /sûr-kəm-pōz'/ vt to place round. [L circumpōnere by analogy with impose, etc]
■ **circumposi'tion** n the act of placing round.

circumscissile /sûr-kəm-sis'il/ (bot) adj (of a seed vessel) opening by a circular transverse line. [L circum around, and scissilis cleavable]

circumscribe /sûr-kəm-skrīb'/ vt to draw a line round; to describe a curve or figure touching externally; to enclose within certain limits, to curtail, abridge. [L circum around, and scrībere, scrīptum to write]
■ **circumscrīb'able** adj. **circumscrīb'er** n a person who circumscribes. **circumscription** /-skrip'shən/ n limitation; the line that limits; the act of circumscribing; an inscription running round; a

defined district. **circumscrip'tive** *adj* marking the external form or outline.

circumsolar /sûr-kəm-sō'lar/ *adj* situated or moving round the sun. [L *circum* around, and *sōl* the sun]

circumspect /sûr'kəm-spekt/ *adj* looking round on all sides watchfully; cautious; prudent. [L *circum* around, and *specere, spicere, spectum* to look]
■ **circumspec'tion** *n* watchfulness; caution; examining. **circumspec'tive** *adj* looking around; wary. **cir'cumspectly** *adv*. **cir'cumspectness** *n*.

circumstance /sûr'kəm-stans or -stəns/ *n* the logical surroundings of an action; an attendant fact; an accident or event; ceremony; detail; (in *pl*) the state of one's affairs. ◆ *vt* to place in particular circumstances. [L *circum* around, and *stāns, stantis* standing, from *stāre* to stand]
■ **circumstantial** /-stan'shl/ *adj* relating to or dependent on circumstance; consisting of details; minute, tiny. **circumstantiality** /-stan-shi-al'i-ti/ *n* the quality of being circumstantial; minuteness in details; a detail. **circumstan'tially** *adv*. **circumstan'tials** *n pl* incidentals; details. **circumstan'tiate** *vt* to prove by circumstances; to describe exactly. **circumstantiā'tion** *n*.
❑ **circumstantial evidence** *n* evidence which is not positive nor direct, but which is gathered inferentially from the circumstances in the case.
■ **in good** (or **bad**) **circumstances** prosperous (or unprosperous). **in** or **under no circumstances** never. **in** or **under the circumstances** conditions being what they are. **not a circumstance to** (*old US inf*) nothing in comparison to.

circumterrestrial /sûr-kəm-te-res'tri-əl or -ti-/ *adj* situated or moving round the earth. [L *circum* around, and *terrestris*, from *terra* the earth]

circumvallate /sûr-kəm-val'āt/ *vt* to surround with a rampart. [L *circum* around, and *vallum* rampart]
■ **circumvallā'tion** *n* a surrounding with a wall; a wall or fortification surrounding a town or fort; engulfing of food by surrounding it (eg by protozoa) (*zool*).

circumvent /sûr-kəm-vent'/ *vt* to go round; to encompass; to surround so as to intercept or capture; to get round, or to outwit. [L *circum* around, and *venīre, ventum* to come]
■ **circumven'tion** *n*. **circumvent'ive** *adj* deceiving by artifices.

circumvolve /sûr-kəm-volv'/ *vt* to roll round. ◆ *vi* to revolve. [L *circum* around, and *volvere, volūtum* to roll]
■ **circumvolution** /-loo' or -lū'/ *n* a turning or rolling round; anything winding or sinuous.

circus /sûr'kəs/ *n* a circular or oval building for public entertainments (*ancient Rome*); a place, building or tent for entertainment by acrobats, clowns, performing animals, etc; a show of this kind or the company of performers (also *fig*); a group of houses arranged in the form of a circle; an open place at a street junction; a natural amphitheatre; a group of people who travel around putting on a display (such as a *flying circus*), often in the form of a competition (such as a *tennis circus*); a noisy entertainment or scene. [L *circus*, from Gr *kirkos*]
■ **cir'cussy** or **cir'cusy** *adj*.

ciré /sē'rā/ *n* (a fabric with) a highly glazed finish. [Fr pap of *cirer* to wax]

cire perdue /sēr per-dü'/ (*Fr*) *n* a method of casting in metal, the mould being formed round a wax model which is then melted away, literally lost wax.

cirl /sûrl/ or **cirl bunting** /bun'ting/ *n* a species of bunting (*Emberiza cirlus*). [Ital *cirlo*]

cirque /sûrk/ *n* a circus; a ring (*poetic*); a deep round hollow, a natural amphitheatre, formed by glaciation (*geog*). [Fr]

cirrate, **cirriform**, etc see under **cirrus**.

cirrhopod /sir'ə-pod/ and **Cirrhopoda** /si-ro'pə-də/ older forms of **cirripede** and **Cirripedia** (as if from Gr *kirrhos* tawny, and *pous, podos* foot).

cirrhosis /si-rō'sis/ *n* a wasting of the proper tissue of the liver, accompanied by abnormal growth of connective tissue. [Gr *kirrhos* tawny, from the colour of the liver so diseased]
■ **cirrhot'ic** *adj*.

cirripede /sir'i-pēd/ or **cirriped** /-ped/ *n* one of the **Cirripe'dia**, a subclass of marine Crustacea, including the barnacles (also, by confusion, **cirrh'ipede** and **Cirrhipe'dia**). [L *cirrus* a curl, and *pēs, pedis* foot]

cirrus /sir'əs/ *n* (*pl* **cirr'ī**) the highest form of clouds, consisting of curling fibrous shapes; a tendril (*bot*); any curled filament (*zool*). [L, a curl, tuft; the common misspellings cirrhus, etc are due to confusion with Gr *kirrhos* tawny]

■ **cirr'ate** or **cirr'iform** *adj* like a cirrus. **cirr'igrade** *adj* moving by cirri. **cirr'ose** *adj* with tendrils. **cirr'ous** *adj* having a cirrus.
❑ **cirr'o-cū'mulus** *n* (*pl* **cirr'o-cū'mūlī**) a cloud of small white flakes or ripples (also called **mackerel sky**). **cirro-stratus** /sir'ō-strā'təs/ *n* (*pl* **cirr'o-stra'tī**) a high thin sheet of haze-like cloud.

cirsoid /sûr'soid/ (*med*) *adj* of or resembling a dilated vein or varix. [Gr *kirsos* swollen vein]

CIS *abbrev*: cataloguing in source; Commonwealth of Independent States.

cis- /sis-/ *combining form* denoting on this side. [L *cis* on this side]
■ **cisalpine** /sis-alp'īn or -īn/ *adj* on this (ie the Roman) side of the Alps. **Cisatlan'tic** *adj*. **Cisleithan** /-lī't(h)ən/ *adj* on this side of the Leitha (which once in part separated Austria and Hungary). **cislu'nar** *adj* on this side of the moon, ie between the moon and the earth. **cismon'tane** *adj* on this side of the mountains, *opp* to *ultramontane*. **cispadane** /-pā'dān or sis'pa-dān/ *adj* (L *Padus* the river Po) on this (the Roman) side of the Po. **cispon'tine** *adj* on this side of the bridges, ie in London, north of the Thames.

cisco /sis'kō/ *n* (*pl* **cis'coes** or **cis'cos**) any of several salmonoid fish of the genus *Coregonus*, esp *C. artedi*, found in the Great Lakes of N America (also called **lake herring**). [Can Fr *cisco(ette)*, from Ojibwa *pemite-wiskawet* that which has oily flesh]

ciselure /sēz'loor/ *n* the art or operation of chasing; the chasing upon a piece of metalwork. [Fr]
■ **cis'eleur** /-lər/ *n* a chaser.

cislunar, cispadane see under **cis-**.

cisplatin /sis-plat'in/ *n* a generic anticancer drug, used *esp* in the treatment of cancer of the ovary and testis. [**cis-** and *platin*um]

cispontine see under **cis-**.

cissing /sis'ing/ (*building*) *n* the appearance of pinholes, tiny craters, etc in paintwork.

cissoid /sis'oid/ (*maths*) *n* a plane curve consisting of two infinite branches symmetrically placed with reference to the diameter of a circle, so that at one of its extremities they form a cusp, while the tangent to the circle at the other extremity is an asymptote. [Gr *kissoeidēs* ivy-like, from *kissos* ivy, and *eidos* form]

cissus /sis'əs/ *n* any climbing plant of the genus *Cissus*, including the kangaroo vine. [New L, from Gr *kissos* ivy]

cissy /sis'i/ (*sl*) *n* an effeminate man; a timid, nervous boy; a crybaby. ◆ *adj* effeminate or weak. [Partly from the name *Cecily*, partly from **sister**; cf **sis¹**]

cist /sist or kist/ *n* a tomb consisting of a stone chest covered with stone slabs (also **kist**; *archaeol*); (in ancient Greece and Rome) a wooden box for holding ritual utensils. [See **chest**]
■ **cist'ed** *adj* containing cists. **cist'ic** *adj* like a cist.

Cistercian /si-stûr'sh(i-)ən/ *n* a member of the order of monks established in 1098 in the forest of Cîteaux (*Cistercium*) in France, an offshoot of the Benedictines (also *adj*).

cistern /sis'tərn/ *n* an artificial reservoir or tank for holding water or other liquid; a natural underground reservoir. [L *cisterna*, from *cista* a chest]
■ **cistern'a** *n* (*pl* **cistern'ae**) (*anat*) a sac or space containing eg cerebrospinal or lymph fluid.

cistic see under **cist**.

cistron /sis'tron or -trən/ (*genetics*) *n* a section of a chromosome which controls a single function. [*cis*-*trans* test, one defining the unit of genetic function]

cistus /sis'təs/ *n* (*pl* **cis'tuses**) any plant of the rock rose genus (*Cistus*) of shrubby plants, giving name to the family **Cistāceae**, cultivated for the beauty of their flowers. [Gr *kistos* rock rose]
■ **cistaceous** /-ā'shəs/ *adj*.

cistvaen see **kistvaen**.

CIT *abbrev*: Chartered Institute of Transport (now known as **CILT**).

cit /sit/ (*archaic sl*) *n* a term of contempt for a townsman, not a gentleman. [**citizen**]
■ **cit'ess** *n* a townswoman. **cits** *n pl* (*US sl*) civilian clothes.

cit. *abbrev*: citation; citizen.

citadel /sit'ə-dəl/ *n* a fortress in or near a city; the place where the guns are kept in a warship; in the Salvation Army, the hall in which meetings are held. [Ital *cittadella*, dimin of *città* a city; see **city**]

cite /sīt/ *vt* to call or summon; to summon to appear in court; to quote; to name; to adduce as proof. [L *citāre, -ātum* to call, intens of *ciēre, cīre* to make to go]
■ **cit'able** or **cite'able** *adj* that can be cited. **cīt'al** *n* summons to appear. **citā'tion** /sīt- or sit-/ *n* an official summons to appear; a document containing the summons; the act of quoting; the passage or name quoted; mention in dispatches; official recognition of

achievement. **cit'atory** adj having to do with citation; addicted to citation. **cīt'er** n.

CITES /sī'tēz/ abbrev: Convention on International Trade in Endangered Species of Wild Fauna and Flora.

cithara /sith'ə-rə/ n an ancient Greek musical instrument differing from the lyre in its flat shallow sound chest. [L, from Gr kitharā; cf **guitar**, **zither**]

■ **cith'arist** n a player on it. **citharist'ic** adj. **cith'er**, **cith'ern** or **citt'ern** n an early modern metal-stringed musical instrument similar to the lute, played either with a plectrum or with the fingers; the Tyrolese zither.

citify see under **city**.

citigrade /sit'i-grād/ adj moving quickly, applied to the Lycosidae or wolf-spiders that run down their prey. [L citus quick, and gradus a step]

citizen /sit'i-zən/ n (also fem **cit'izeness**) an inhabitant of a city; a member of a state; a townsman; a freeman; a civilian (US). [ME citesein, from OFr citeain; see **city**]

■ **cit'izenize** or **-ise** vt to make a citizen of. **cit'izenry** n the general body of citizens. **cit'izenship** n the state of being, or of having rights and duties of, a citizen; conduct in relation to these duties.

❑ **Citizens' Advice Bureau** n an organization that offers free advice and information to the public. **citizen's arrest** n an arrest, legally allowable, made by a member of the public. **Citizens' Band** n a band of radio frequencies on which the public are permitted to broadcast personal messages, etc. **Citizens' Band radio** n (also **CB radio**). **Citizen's Charter** n a government document stating standards of service for public organizations.

cito /sī'/ or /ki'tō/ (L) adv quickly.

citole /sit'ōl/ or /si-tōl'/ n a medieval stringed instrument, probably an early form of the cither (qv under **cithara**).

citron /sit'rən/ n the fruit of the citron tree (qv below), resembling a lemon; its rind, candied and used as a decoration and flavouring for food. [L citrus, from which comes also Gr kitron a citron]

■ **cit'ral** n a terpene (C₁₀H₁₆O) found in oils of lemon, lime, etc, used in perfumery. **cit'range** /-rənj/ n a hybrid between citron and orange. **cit'rate** n a salt of citric acid. **cit'reous** adj citrine. **cit'ric** adj derived from the citron. **cit'riculture** n the cultivation of citrus fruits. **cit'rin** n the water-soluble vitamin P, found in citrus fruits, etc (also called **bioflavonoid**). **cit'rine** /-rin/ adj dark and greenish yellow, like a citron or lemon. ◆ n citrine colour; a rock crystal of this colour, false topaz. **citronell'a** n a S Asian grass (**citronella grass**, Cymbopogon nardus) yielding **citronella oil**, a yellow oil used in perfumery and in insect repellents. **citronell'al** n a colourless aldehyde with a lemon scent, present in citronella and other essential oils, used as a flavouring and in perfumery. **cit'rous** adj. **cit'rus** n a citron tree; (with cap) a genus of Rutaceae including the citron, lemon, orange, etc; any tree of the Citrus genus. **citruss'y** or **citrus'y** adj of, tasting or smelling of citrus fruit.

❑ **citric acid** n the acid to which lemon and lime juice owe their sourness, C₆H₈O₇. **citric acid cycle** n another name for **Krebs cycle**. **citron tree** n the tree that bears the citron fruit (Citrus medica), considered to be the ancestor of the lemon and lime. **citron wood** or **citrus wood** n the most costly furniture wood of the ancient Romans (perh sandarach); the wood of the citron tree. **citrus fruits** n pl citrons, lemons, limes, oranges, grapefruit, and their hybrids.

citrulline /si-trul'ēn or īn, also sit'rə-lēn/ n an amino acid formed as an intermediate in the production of urea. [L citrullus a type of watermelon (in which it is found), from citron]

cittern same as **cither** (see under **cithara**).

city /sit'i/ n a large town; an incorporated town that has or had a cathedral; a town on which the dignity has been conferred by tradition or grant; in various countries a municipality of higher rank, variously defined; the business centre or original area of a large town; (with the and often with cap) the centre of British financial affairs, most banks, etc, being in the City of London. [Fr cité a city, from L civitās, -ātis the state, from cīvis a citizen]

■ **citifica'tion** or **cityfica'tion** n. **cit'ified** or **cit'yfied** adj. **cit'ify** or **cit'yfy** vt to give the characteristics or attitudes of the city, or city culture, to (a person, etc).

❑ **city academy** n a secondary school in a disadvantaged urban area, funded by the state and by private sponsorship, and operating independently of its local authority. **city article** n in a newspaper, a financial or commercial article. **City Company** n a London corporation representing any of the medieval trade guilds. **city desk** n the desk or (fig) the department or field of work of a city editor. **city editor** n the financial editor of a newspaper; the editor in charge of local news, etc of a newspaper (US). **city farm** n an area established within an urban area in order that city children may learn something about farming, esp animal husbandry. **city fathers** n pl the magistrates; the town or city council. **city hall** n a town hall; (the

officials of) municipal government (N Am); city bureaucracy (N Am). **city man** n a man engaged in commercial or financial work in a city. **city manager** n a person appointed by an elected body to manage the administrative affairs of a city. **city mission** n a mission for evangelizing the poor classes in the large cities. **city planning** n (N Am) town planning. **cit'yscape** n a drawing, painting or picture of a city (modelled on landscape). **city slicker** n a city-dweller regarded as over-sophisticated and untrustworthy. **cit'y-state** n (also without hyphen) a sovereign state consisting of a city with a small surrounding territory. **city technology college** n a secondary school set up in an inner city district, funded by central government and (local) industry, specializing in teaching scientific and technological subjects.

■ **City and Guilds Institute** an examining body for technical and craft subjects, generally at a lower standard than degree level. **city of God**, **heavenly city**, etc the ideal of the Church of Christ in glory. **city of refuge** by Mosaic law, any of six cities on the River Jordan where the perpetrator of an accidental homicide might flee for refuge. **the Eternal City** Rome. **the Holy City** Jerusalem.

civ. abbrev: civil; civilian.

cive see **chive**[1].

civet /siv'it/ n a small catlike carnivore of the genus Viverra, of Africa and S Asia, that secretes a musky fluid from anal glands (also **civet cat**); the fur of this animal; a fatty yellowish musk obtained from this animal and used in perfumery. [Fr civette, from Ar zabād]

civic /siv'ik/ adj relating to a city or citizen. [L cīvicus, from cīvis citizen]

■ **civ'ically** adv. **civ'ics** n sing the science of citizenship; the study of government and its business (N Am).

❑ **civic centre** n a place in which the chief public buildings of a town are grouped. **civic crown** n an oak wreath awarded to a Roman soldier for saving a citizen's life in battle.

civil /siv'il/ adj relating to the community; polite (in any degree short of discourtesy); relating to ordinary life, not military; lay, secular, temporal, not ecclesiastical; relating to the individual citizen; relating to private relations amongst citizens, and such suits as arise out of these (cf **criminal**) (law); naturally good, as opposed to good through regeneration (theol). [L cīvīlis, from cīvis citizen]

■ **civil'ian** n and adj (a person) engaged in civil as distinguished from military and naval pursuits; (a professor or student) of civil law, as opposed to canon law. **civil'ianize** or **-ise** vt to convert from military to civilian use; to replace military personnel in (a factory, etc) by civilians. **civ'ilist** n (archaic) a person versed in civil law. **civil'ity** n politeness; (often in pl) an act of politeness; civilization (archaic); good breeding (obs). **civ'illy** adv. **civ'ism** n good citizenship; the state of being favourably inclined to French Revolution principles.

❑ **civil aviation** n non-military flying, esp commercial airlines and their operation. **civil commotion** n a term used in insurance policies denoting a state of civil unrest between riot and civil war. **civil day**, **year** or **time** n the day, year or time, as reckoned for ordinary purposes. **civil death** n (law) formerly, the loss of all civil and legal privileges. **civil defence** n a civilian service for the wartime protection of the civilian population against enemy attack. **civil disobedience** n refusal to obey laws and regulations, pay taxes, etc, used as non-violent means of forcing concessions from government. **civil engineer** n a person who plans and builds railways, roads, bridges, docks, etc, as opposed to a military engineer, or to a mechanical engineer. **civil engineering** n. **civil law** n the law laid down by a state regarding the rights of the inhabitants, esp that founded on Roman law (cf **criminal law**). **civil liberty** n (often in pl) personal freedom of thought, word, action, etc. **civil list** n formerly, a list of charges for civil government purposes; now a fixed annual sum provided by Parliament to meet the sovereign's expenses incurred as head of state (**civil list pensions** those granted by royal favour). **civil marriage** n a marriage performed by an official who is not a clergyman and involving a civil contract without religious ceremony and vows. **civil partnership** or **union** n an agreement between two people, usu of the same sex, giving them a legal status similar to that of a married couple. **civil rights** n pl (often with caps) the rights of a citizen to personal freedom, ie political, racial, legal, social, etc. **civil-rights'** adj. **civil servant** n a person who works in the **civil service**, the paid service of the state chiefly in public administration (other than military, naval, legislative and judicial). **civ'il-suited** adj (Milton) sombrely clad. **civil twilight** n (astron) the interval of time during which the sun is between the horizon and 6° below the horizon, morning and evening. **civil union** see **civil partnership** above. **civil war** n a war between citizens of the same state. **civil year** see under **year**.

civilize or **-ise** /siv'i-līz/ vt to reclaim from barbarism; to instruct in arts and refinements. [See **civil**]

■ **civilīz'able** or **-s-** adj. **civilizā'tion** or **-s-** n the state of being civilized; culture; cultural condition or complex; cities or populated areas as contrasted with uncultivated or sparsely populated parts. **civ'ilized** or **-s-** adj (having) advanced beyond the primitive savage

---

■ words derived from main entry word; ❑ compound words; ■ idioms and phrasal verbs

state; refined in interests and tastes; sophisticated, self-controlled and well-spoken. **civ'ilizer** or **-s-** n.

civvy /siv'i/ (inf) n and adj civilian; (in pl **civv'ies**) civilian clothes. ■ **civvy street** (inf) civilian life after a period of service in the armed forces, police, etc.

cizers an old spelling (Shakesp) of **scissors**.

CJ abbrev : Civil Justice.

CJD abbrev : Creutzfeldt-Jakob disease.

CL abbrev : Sri Lanka (formerly Ceylon; IVR).

Cl (chem) symbol : chlorine.

cl abbrev : centilitre.

CLA abbrev : conjugated linoleic acid.

clabber /klab'ər/ (esp Scot and Irish) n mud. [Ir clabar mud]

clabby-doo see **clappy-doo**.

clachan /klä'hhən or klahh'ən/ (Scot) n a small village. [Gaelic clachan, from clach stone]

clack /klak/ vi to make a noise as of a hard, flat thing flapping; to chatter; to cackle. ♦ n a noise of this kind; an instrument making it; the sound of chattering voices; the tongue (inf). [Prob imit]
■ **clack'er** n.
❑ **clack'box** n the box containing the clack valve of an engine. **clack'dish** n (archaic) a wooden dish carried by beggars, having a movable cover which they clacked to attract attention. **clack valve** n a valve consisting of a hinged flap or other device that falls back with a clacking noise.

Clactonian /klak-tō'ni-ən/ (archaeol) adj of or relating to a palaeolithic culture characterized by tools of flaked stone used as chopping and hewing implements (also n). [From Clacton-on-Sea, Essex, where the tools were first found]

clad /klad/ pat and pap of **clothe**. adj clothed, or covered. ♦ vt (**cladd'ing**; **clad** or **cladded**) to cover one material with another, eg one metal with another (as in a nuclear reactor), or brick or stonework with a different material (in building).
■ **cladd'er** n. **cladd'ing** n.

Claddagh ring /klad'ə ring/ n a ring, usu having the shape of two hands clasping a heart, traditionally given in Ireland as a token of affection. [Claddagh, village on the edge of Galway city]

clade /klād/ (biol) n a group of organisms that have evolved from a common ancestor. [Gr klados branch]
■ **clād'ism** n adherence to cladistic theories. **clād'ist** n. **cladist'ic** adj. **cladist'ics** n sing a taxonomic theory which classifies organisms according to the shared characteristics which distinguish one group from another. **cladogen'esis** n evolution of clades as if by branching from a common ancestor. **cladogenet'ic** adj. **clād'ogram** n a branching diagram showing the development of a clade.

cladode /klad'ōd/ (bot) n a branch or stem with the appearance and functions of a leaf. [Gr klados a shoot]

cladosporium /klad-ō-spō'ri-əm/ (bot) n a fungus affecting the leaves of plants, particularly those cultivated in greenhouses.

claes /klāz/ (Scot) n pl clothes.

clafoutis /klaf'ū-tē or -oo-/ n (pl **claf'outis**) a dessert of fresh fruit (orig cherries) topped with a thick batter and baked. [Fr, from OFr claufir to attach with nails]

clag /klag/ (dialect) vi (**clagg'ing**; **clagged**) to stick. ♦ vt to bedaub. ♦ n a sticky mass or clot of dirt, etc. [Prob Scand; Dan klag mud; cf **clay**]
■ **clagg'y** adj tenacious, sticky.

claim /klām/ vt to demand or assert as a right; to maintain or assert; to call for; to take (life). ♦ vi to make a claim (on one's insurance policy, etc). ♦ n a demand for something supposed due; an assertion that something is a fact; a right or ground for demanding; the thing claimed, esp a piece of land appropriated by a miner; (Spenser **clame**) a call, shout. [OFr claimer, from L clāmāre to call out]
■ **claim'able** adj that can be claimed. **claim'ant** n a person who makes a claim; a person who commences a lawsuit against another person. **claim'er** n.
❑ **claiming race** n (US) a race in which any horse having taken part in the race may be bought at a previously fixed price by anyone starting a horse at the meeting (cf **selling race**). **claim'-jumper** n a person who takes possession of another's mining claim. **claims assessor** n an assessor employed by an insurance company, usu in motor accident claims.
■ **jump a claim** to take possession of another's mining claim. **lay claim to** to assert a right to. **stake a claim** see under **stake**[1].

clairaudience /klā-rö'di-əns/ n the alleged power of hearing things beyond the range of the normal sense of hearing. [Fr clair, from L clārus clear, and **audience**]
■ **clairaud'ient** n and adj.

claircolle see **clearcole**.

clair de lune /klûr də loon'/ n a bluish colour, esp that of a certain kind of porcelain glaze; porcelain glazed in this way; a kind of shiny bluish glass. [Fr, moonlight]

clair-obscure or **clare-obscure** /klā-rəb-skūr'/ n chiaroscuro (qv). [Fr clair, from L clārus clear, and Fr obscur, from L obscūrus obscure]

clairschach /klär'shähh/ a variant spelling of **clarsach**.

clairvoyance /klār-voi'əns/ n the alleged power of discerning things beyond the normal range of sense or perception (also **clairvoy'ancy**). [Fr clair, from L clārus clear, and Fr voir, from L vidēre to see]
■ **clairvoy'ant** n and adj. **clairvoy'antly** adv.

clam[1] /klam/ n an edible shellfish of various kinds, esp the round clam or quahog (Venus mercenaria) and the long clam (Mya arenaria); a scallop or scallop-shell; a very reticent person (inf). ♦ vi (**clamm'ing**; **clammed**) to gather clams. [**clam**[2]]
❑ **clam'bake** n a baking of clams on hot stones, with layers of potatoes, fish, sweetcorn, etc, popular at picnic parties in USA; such a party; any informal party. **clam chowder** n chowder made with clams. **clam'-diggers** n pl a style of women's trousers reaching just below the knee. **clam'shell** n a cockpit canopy hinged at front and rear (aeronautics); a hinged part of the thrust reverser in a gas turbine; (an excavating machine with) a bucket with two hinged jaws (N Am). **clamshell phone** n a mobile phone consisting of two working parts joined by a hinge so that it can be folded and unfolded.
■ **clam up** (inf) to become silent.

clam[2] /klam/ n a gripping instrument. [OE clam fetter]

clam[3] /klam/ n noise produced by ringing two or more bells together (also vt and vi). [Prob onomatopoeic]

clamant /klam'ənt or klā'mənt/ adj calling aloud or earnestly. [L clāmāre to cry out]
■ **clam'ancy** n urgency. **clam'antly** adv.

clambe /klām/ (Spenser) pat of **climb**.

clamber /klam'bər/ vi and vt to climb with difficulty, grasping with hands and feet (often with up or over). ♦ n the act of clambering. [From the root of **climb**; cf Ger klammern, from klemmen to squeeze or hold tightly]

clame see **claim**.

clamjamphrie, **clamjamfry** /klam-jam'fri/ or **clanjamfray** /klan-/ (Scot) n rubbish; nonsense; rabble. [Derivation uncertain]

clammed, **clamming** see **clam**[1].

clammy /klam'i/ adj sticky; moist and adhesive; unpleasantly damp, and often warm. [Dialect clam dampness, from OE clæman to anoint]
■ **clamm'ily** adv. **clamm'iness** n.

clamour[1] or (N Am) **clamor** /klam'ər/ n a loud continuous outcry; uproar; any loud noise; persistent expression of dissatisfaction. ♦ vi to cry aloud in demand (often with for); to make a loud continuous outcry. [L clāmor, -ōris]
■ **clam'orous** adj noisy, boisterous. **clam'orously** adv. **clam'orousness** n. **clam'ourer** n.

clamour[2] /klam'ər/ (Shakesp) vt to silence, check the ringing of. [Perh connected with **clam**[3]]

clamp[1] /klamp/ n a piece of timber, iron, etc used to fasten things together or to strengthen any framework; any instrument for holding; a wheel clamp. ♦ vt to bind with a clamp; to grasp or press firmly; to put (on) authoritatively, impose; to fit a wheel clamp to (a car). [From a root seen in OE clam fetter; Du klamp a clamp; related to **clip**, **climb**]
■ **clamp'er** n someone or something that clamps.
■ **clamp down on** to suppress, or suppress the activities of, firmly (**clamp'down** n).

clamp[2] /klamp/ n a heavy tread. ♦ vi to tread heavily. [Prob imit]

clamp[3] /klamp/ n a stack, as of bricks for burning, peats, etc; a heap; a heap of root vegetables covered with earth or straw to protect it in cold weather. ♦ vt to put in clamps. [Prob Du klamp heap]

clamper /klam'pər/ (Scot) vt to botch up. [Origin unknown; prob connected with **clamp**[1]]

clan /klan/ n a tribe or collection of families subject to a single chieftain, commonly bearing the same surname, and supposed to have a common ancestor; a clique, sect; a collective name for a number of persons or things. [Gaelic clann offspring, tribe, from L planta a shoot]
■ **clann'ish** adj closely united and holding aloof from others, like the members of a clan. **clann'ishly** adv. **clann'ishness** n. **clan'ship** n association of families under a chieftain; feeling of loyalty to a clan.
❑ **clans'man**, **clans'woman** n a member of a clan.

clandestine /klan-des'tin or -tīn/ adj concealed or hidden; private; sly. [L clandestīnus, from clam secretly]
■ **clandes'tinely** adv. **clandes'tineness** or **clandestin'ity** n.

clang[1] /klang/ vi to produce a loud deep ringing sound. ♦ vt to cause to clang. ♦ n a ringing sound, like that made by striking large pieces of metal, or that of a trumpet; the sonorous cry of some birds, such as cranes or geese. [L *clangere* to sound; *clangor* noise of birds or wind instruments]

■ **clang'er** *n* a tactless or ill-timed remark or comment; a stupid mistake. **clang'ing** *n* and *adj*. **clangorous** /*klang'gər-əs*/ *adj*. **clang'orously** *adv*. **clang'our** or (*N Am*) **clang'or** *n* a clang; a loud ringing noise. ◆ *vi* to make a clangour.

❑ **clang'box** *n* a deflector fitted to a jet engine to divert gas flow for eg VTOL or STOL operation.

■ **drop a clanger** (*inf*) to say something tactless; to make a stupid blunder.

clang² see **klang**.

clanjamfray see **clamjamphrie**.

clank /*klangk*/ *n* a metallic sound, less prolonged than a clang, such as is made by chains hitting together. ◆ *vi* or *vt* to make or cause to make a clank. [Prob formed under the influence of **clink¹** and **clang¹**]

■ **clank'ing** *n*. **clank'ingly** *adv*.

clap¹ /*klap*/ *n* the noise made by the sudden striking together of two things, *esp* the hands; a slap; a pat (*Scot*); a sudden blow or stroke (*lit* or *fig*); a burst of sound, *esp* thunder. ◆ *vt* (**clapp'ing**; **clapped**) to strike together so as to make a noise; to applaud with the hands; to bang; to pat (*Scot*); to thrust or drive together suddenly; to fasten or close promptly; to put suddenly or throw (eg in prison). ◆ *vi* to strike the palms of the hands together; to strike or slam with a noise; to applaud; to come or go suddenly (*archaic*). [ON *klappa* to pat; Du and Ger *klappen*]

■ **clapp'er** *n* a person who claps; a thing that claps, eg the tongue of a bell; a device for shaking a mill hopper; an instrument for making a striking noise, such as a rattle; the tongue (*sl*). ◆ *vi* to make a noise like a clapper. ◆ *vt* to ring by pulling on a clapper. **clapp'ering** *n* and *adj*. **clapp'ing** *n* applause; the noise of striking.

❑ **clap'board** (or /*klab'ərd*/) *n* wood for barrel staves, wainscot (*archaic*); a thin board used in covering wooden houses (*esp N Am*). **clap'bread** *n* a kind of hard-baked oatmeal cake. **clap'dish** same as **clackdish** (see under **clack**). **clap'net** *n* a net made to clap together suddenly by pulling a string. **clapo'meter** *n* (*inf*) a device for gauging the level of audience appreciation in talent contests, etc by measuring the volume of noise generated by their applause. **clapped'-out'** *adj* (*inf*) tired, exhausted; worn-out, of no more use. **clapp'erboard** or **clapp'erboards** *n* a hinged board (or a set of hinged boards) clapped together in front of the camera before or after shooting a piece of film, to help synchronize sound and vision. **clapp'erboy** *n* the person who works the clapperboards. **clapp'erclaw** *vt* (*archaic*) to claw or scratch; to scold or abuse. **clapp'erclawer** *n*. **clap'-sill** *n* a lock-sill, the bottom part of the frame on which lock-gates shut. **clap'trap** *n* flashy but insincere or empty words; meaningless nonsense; *orig* a trick to gain applause (*archaic*). **claptrapp'ery** *n*.

■ **clap eyes on** to catch sight of, to see. **clap hands** to applaud with the hands; to make an agreement (*archaic*). **clap hold of** to seize roughly or firmly. **clap on** (*inf*) to put on (clothes) quickly. **clap up** (*archaic*) to conclude suddenly. **like the clappers** (*inf*) at top speed.

clap² /*klap*/ (*sl*) *n* (with *the*) gonorrhoea. ◆ *vt* (**clapp'ing**; **clapped**) to infect with gonorrhoea. [Cf Du *klapoor*]

clapper¹ /*klap'ər*/ *n* a simple bridge of slabs or planks laid across supports, *usu* piles of stone (also **clapper bridge**; *dialect*); a raised footpath (*dialect*); a rabbit hole (*obs*). [LL *claperium* heap of stones, rabbit hole]

clapper² see under **clap¹**.

claque /*klak*/ *n* a group of hired applauders; sycophantic supporters. [Fr, from *claquer* to clap]

■ **claqueur** /*kla-kûr'*/ *n* a member of a claque.

clarabella /*kla-rə-bel'ə*/ *n* an organ stop having a sweet, fluty tone. [L *clārus* clear, and *bellus* beautiful]

clarain /*klar'ān*/ (*mineralogy*) *n* lustrous, brightly-coloured bands in coal.

Clare /*klār*/ *n* a nun of a Franciscan order founded by St Clare in 1212 (also **Poor Clare**).

clarence /*klar'əns*/ *n* a four-wheeled carriage, having interior seating for two or more persons. [Named after the Duke of *Clarence* (William IV)]

Clarenceux or **Clarencieux** /*klar'ən-sū*/ (*heraldry*) *n* the second king-of-arms in England, so named from the Duke of *Clarence*, son of Edward III.

clarendon /*klar'ən-dən*/ (*printing*) *n* a form of condensed roman type having a heavy face.

clare-obscure see **clair-obscure**.

claret /*klar'ət*/ *n orig* applied to wines of a light-red colour, but now used in UK for the dark-red wines of Bordeaux; a dark red colour (also *adj*); blood (*old sl*). ◆ *vi* to drink claret. [Fr *clairet*, from *clair*, from L *clārus* clear]

❑ **claret cup** *n* a drink made up of iced claret, brandy, sugar, etc. **claret jug** *n* a fancy jug for holding claret.

clarichord /*klar'i-körd*/ *n* a clavichord. [As if from L *clārus* clear; see **clavichord**]

clarify /*klar'i-fī*/ *vt* (**clar'ifying**; **clar'ified**) to make clear or easily understood; to make (*esp* butter) clear or pure. ◆ *vi* to become clear. [L *clārus* clear, and *facere* to make]

■ **clarificā'tion** *n*. **clar'ifier** *n*.

clarinet /*kla-ri-net'*/ or /*klar'i-net*/ or (*archaic*) **clarionet** /*-ri-ə-net'*/ *n* a woodwind instrument in which the sound is produced by a single thin reed, the range of pitch being approximately that of the violin. [Fr, from L *clārus* clear]

■ **clarinett'ist** or **clarinet'ist** *n*.

■ **bass clarinet** one pitched an octave lower than the ordinary clarinet.

clarino /*kla-rē'nō*/ *n* (*pl* **clari'ni** or **clarin'os**) the highest register of the trumpet in baroque music; (also **clarion**) an organ stop imitating this; a trumpet, a clarion. ◆ *adj* relating to the trumpet's highest register. [Ital]

clarion /*klar'i-ən*/ *n* a kind of trumpet whose note is clear and shrill; the sound of a trumpet, or a sound resembling that of a trumpet; see also **clarino**. [Fr *clairon*, from *clair*, from L *clārus* clear]

❑ **clarion call** *n* (*fig*) a stirring summons (to duty, etc).

clarionet see **clarinet**.

clarity /*klar'i-ti*/ *n* clearness. [ME *clarte*, from L *clāritās*, *-ātis*]

clarkia /*klär'ki-ə*/ *n* any plant of the N American genus *Clarkia* (family Onagraceae), a favourite border plant. [Named in honour of William *Clark* (1770–1838), US explorer of the Pacific North-west]

claro /*klä'rō*/ *n* (*pl* **cla'ros** or **cla'roes**) a light-coloured mild cigar. [Sp, light, from L *clarus*]

clarsach /*klär'səhh*/ *n* the old Celtic harp strung with wire. [Gaelic *clàrsach* and Ir *clàirseach* a harp]

clart /*klärt*/ (*Scot* and *N Eng*) *n* (often in *pl*) mud; dirt. ◆ *vt* to dirty. [Origin unknown]

■ **clart'y** *adj* sticky and dirty.

clary /*klā'ri*/ *n* a labiate plant (*Salvia sclarea*) with pale-blue flowers and aromatic leaves, sometimes used as a culinary herb. [LL *sclarea*; origin unknown]

clash /*klash*/ *n* a loud noise, such as is caused by the striking together of sheets of metal; noisy opposition or contradiction; inconvenient coinciding of events; an outbreak of fighting; chatter, gossip (*Scot*). ◆ *vi* to dash noisily together; to meet in opposition; to act in a contrary direction; to disagree; (of events) to coincide disturbingly or inconveniently; (of colours) to jar visually when placed together; to gossip (*Scot*). ◆ *vt* to strike noisily against; to bang, slam (*dialect*). [Imit; cf Ger *Klatsch* and Swed *klatsch*]

■ **clash'er** *n*. **clash'ing** *n* a striking against; opposition, conflict, disagreement.

■ **clash'-ma-clā'vers** (modelled on **clishmaclaver**; *Scot*) idle chat, gossip.

clasp /*kläsp*/ *n* a fastening, eg for a piece of jewellery; a bar or insignia on a medal ribbon (*milit*); an embrace; a grasp. ◆ *vt* to fasten with a clasp; to enclose and hold in the hand or arms; to embrace. [ME *clapse*]

■ **clas'per** *n* that which clasps; the tendril of a plant; (*usu* in *pl*) a clasping organ (*zool*). **clasp'ing** *n*.

❑ **clasp knife** *n* a knife whose blade folds into the handle.

class /*kläs*/ *n* a rank or order of persons or things; high rank or social standing; the system or situation in any community in which there is division of people into different social ranks; a number of schoolchildren or students who are taught together, or are in the same year of school or of their course; a lesson or lecture; a group of students graduating together (in a certain year, eg *class of 1986*) (*orig N Am*); a scientific division or arrangement in biological classification; a division above an order; a grade (of merit in examination, accommodation in a ship or railway train, etc); a section of a Methodist congregation; style, quality (*inf*). ◆ *vt* to form into a class or classes; to arrange methodically. ◆ *vi* to take rank. ◆ *adj* (*sl*) of high class. [L *classis* a division of the Roman people]

■ **class'able** or **class'ible** *adj* capable of being classed. **classed** *adj*. **class'ily** *adv*. **class'iness** *n* (*inf*) the quality of being classy. **class'ism** *n* prejudice or discrimination on grounds of social class. **class'ist** *n* and *adj* (a person) motivated or influenced by classism. **class'less** *adj* having no class distinctions; not belonging to any social class; not confined to any particular category; relating to sports with events of this sort. **class'lessness** *n*. **classy** *adj* (*inf*) of or characteristic of high or upper class; stylish.

❑ **class action** (*US law*) in USA, an action taken by one or more persons on their own behalf and on that of all others adduced as having the same grievance. **class'-book** *n* a book used in class teaching. **class'-conscious** *adj* clearly or acutely conscious

clavis /klā'vis (L klā'wis)/ n (pl **clā'ves** /-vēz (L klā'wās)/) a key, hence a clue or aid for solving problems, interpreting a cipher, etc, a glossary. [L clāvis a key]
■ **claviger** /klav'i-jər/ n someone who keeps a key, a custodian. **clavig'erous** adj keeping keys.

clavulate see under **clave**[1].

claw /klö/ n the hooked nail of a bird, mammal or reptile, or the creature's foot with a number of such nails; the leg of a crab, insect, etc, or its pointed end or pincer; the narrow basal part of a petal (bot); anything shaped or used like a claw. ◆ vt to scratch, tear, scrape, seize (with or as if with a claw or claws); to flatter, fawn on (obs). ◆ vi (often with at) to make an arm movement with the fingers bent into the shape of a claw. [OE clawu; cognate with Ger Klaue and related to **cleave**[2]]
■ **clawed** adj having claws. **claw'less** adj.
❑ **claw'-and-ball'** adj (of furniture) having feet carved to represent an animal's claw holding a ball (also **ball'-and-claw'**). **claw'back** n an arrangement by which the financial benefit from allowances, etc is partially recouped by the government in extra taxation; extended to other situations where financial outlay is recovered by taxation or penalty. **clawed frog** or **toad** n an African or S American aquatic frog having claws on three hind toes. **claw'-foot** n (med) pes cavus, a deformity of the foot in which the toes are turned under and the arch is exaggerated. **claw hammer** n a hammer with one part of the head divided into two claws, for pulling out nails. **claw'-hamm'er-coat** n a facetious name for a dress coat.
■ **claw back** to recoup (money) by means of taxation, etc. **claw me and I'll claw thee** (obs) you scratch my back and I'll scratch yours. **claw off** (naut) (of sailing vessels) to move away from (a hazard) by beating.

clay /klā/ n earth in very fine particles, tenacious and impervious (agric); a tenacious ductile earthy material, hydrated aluminium silicates more or less impure (chem and mineralogy); a prepared hard surface of a tennis court; earth in general; the human body; a clay pigeon; (in full **clay pipe**) a tobacco pipe of baked clay. ◆ vt to purify (eg sugar) with clay. [OE clæg; cf Dan klæg and Ger Klei]
■ **clayed** adj clay-like. **clay'ey** adj made of clay; covered with clay; like clay. **clay'ish** adj of the nature of clay. **claymāt'ion** n (film) the animation of clay or Plasticine figures.
❑ **clay'-bank** adj (US) brownish yellow. ◆n (US) a horse of this colour. **clay'-brained** adj (Shakesp) stupid. **clay'-cold** adj cold as clay, lifeless. **clay court** n clay-covered tennis court. **clay eater** n a person addicted to chewing a fatty clay in Brazil and elsewhere. **clay'-ground** n ground consisting mainly of clay. **clay-ir'onstone** n a clayey chalybite. **clay'-marl** n a whitish chalky clay. **clay'-mill** n a mill for preparing clay. **clay mineral** n any of a group of water-soluble aluminium silicates that are the chief constituents of clay. **clay'pan** n a compacted layer of subsoil that retains water; a shallow depression in clay soil, holding water after rain (Aust). **clay pigeon** n (often shortened to **clay**) a saucer-shaped disc (usu made of pitch and powdered limestone) thrown from a spring-loaded trap and shot at as a substitute for various types of game bird. **clay'-pit** n a pit from which clay is dug. **clay road** n (NZ) an unmetalled road. **clay'-slate** n hard, fissile argillaceous rock.
■ **feet of clay** (fig) faults and weaknesses of character not at first apparent or suspected. **wet one's clay** to drink.

claymore /klā'mör or -mör/ n a large sword formerly used by the Scottish Highlanders; the old Celtic one-handed, two-edged longsword; now applied inaccurately to the basket-hilted sword of the officers of Highland regiments; (also **claymore mine**) a type of explosive mine. [Gaelic claidheamh mòr, from Gaelic and Ir claidheamh sword, and mòr great]

claytonia /klā-tō'ni-ə/ n a N American plant of the genus Claytonia, related to Lewisia, having succulent leaves and small cup-shaped flowers. [J Clayton (1693–1773), US botanist]

clean /klēn/ adj free from dirt, stain, or anything that contaminates; pure, fresh; guiltless; honest, uncorrupted; neat in execution, unerring; clear-cut, sharply defined; even; having nothing of an incriminating nature, such as a weapon, illegal drugs, etc on one's person (sl); (of a driving licence) without any endorsements for motoring offences; (of an athlete) clear of drugs when tested; (of humour) not offensive; (of a fight) fair; complete; without a catch (angling); free of radioactive fallout; of a design that causes little turbulent wake (aerodynamics); (of technology, energy, etc) designed not to harm the environment. ◆ adv quite, entirely; smoothly; without mishap. ◆ vt to make clean, or free from dirt, corruption, contamination, etc. ◆ n an act of cleaning; a lift of the weight to the shoulders, where it is held with arms bent (weightlifting; **clean and jerk** such a lift followed immediately by a jerk (qv). [OE clæne; Ger klein small]
■ **clean'er** n a person or thing that cleans. **clean'ing** n and adj (the act of) making clean. **cleanliness** /klen'li-nis or -nes/ n habitual cleanness

or purity. **cleanly** /klen'li/ adj clean in habits and person; pure; neat. ◆ adv /klēn'li/ in a clean manner. **cleanness** /klēn'nis or -nes/ n.
❑ **clean-cut'** adj neat, well-shaped or well-formed; uncluttered; without blemish or unnecessary ornament; with a neat, respectable appearance. **cleaning lady** or **cleaning woman** n a woman employed to clean a house, office, etc. **clean-limbed'** adj with shapely limbs; trim. **clean-liv'ing** adj morally upright; respectable. **clean'-out** n a thorough cleaning; a swindle. **clean room** n (in the manufacture of computer and precision components) an area in a factory, etc where rigorous standards of cleanliness are maintained; a special facility for handling material, destined for space activities, in a sterile and dust-free environment. **clean-shav'en** adj with all facial hair shaved off. **clean sheet** n a record with no blemishes; a situation in which no goals are conceded (sport). **clean'skin** n an unbranded animal (Aust; also **clear'skin**); a person with a clean police record (inf). **clean'-tim'bered** adj (Shakesp) well-proportioned. **clean'-up** n an act of thorough cleaning; the stamping out of an evil or illegal activity (see also **clean up** below).
■ **a clean slate** a fresh start. **a clean sweep** a complete change; the winning or gaining of all the prizes, votes, etc (usu with of). **clean as a whistle** very clean or cleanly; completely emptied. **clean bowled** (cricket) dismissed by a ball which hits the stumps without hitting the bat or pad. **clean out** to clean the inside of; to take away all someone's money from (someone) (inf). **clean up** to make clean; to free from vice, corruption, etc; to make (large profits) (**clean'-up** n and adj). **clean up one's act** (inf) to reform one's behaviour or bad practices. **come clean** (sl) to confess or divulge everything. **have clean hands** to have no connection with a crime or immoral act. **make a clean break** to sever a relationship, etc completely. **show a clean pair of heels** to run away. **take (someone) to the cleaners** (sl) to take all, or a great deal of, a person's money, etc; to beat or criticize (someone) severely.

cleanse /klenz/ vt to make clean or pure. [OE clænsian]
■ **cleans'able** adj. **cleans'er** n a person who, or that which, cleanses; cleansing-cream, lotion or the like. **cleans'ing** n cleaning, purification.
❑ **cleans'ing-cream** n a type of cream used to remove make-up or dirt from the face. **cleansing department** n the section of local administration that deals with the collecting and disposing of refuse and the cleaning of streets.

CLEAR /klēr/ abbrev: Campaign for Lead-free Air.

clear /klēr/ adj pure, bright, undimmed, unclouded, undulled; free from obstruction, difficulty, complication, contents, blame or accusation; disengaged; plain, obvious; distinct; without blemish, defect, drawback, or diminution; lucid; transparent; not coded; not blocked. ◆ adv in a clear manner; plainly; wholly; quite; out of the way (of). ◆ vt to make clear; to empty; to free from obscurity, obstruction or guilt; to free, acquit or vindicate; to leap, or pass by or over; to make as profit; to settle (eg a bill); to decode; to unscramble; to declare free from security, etc restrictions; to remove (data) from memory so that fresh data can be recorded (comput); to pass (a cheque, etc) through a clearing bank; to pass through (customs, etc). ◆ vi to become clear; to grow free, bright, transparent; to sail after satisfying all demands and obtaining permission. [Fr clair, from L clārus clear]
■ **clear'able** adj. **clear'age** n a piece of land cleared. **clear'ance** n the act of clearing; general removal or emptying; eviction from lands; removal of hindrances; intervening space; play between parts, as of a machine; a certificate that a ship has been cleared at the custom house; a declaration of freedom from restrictions. **clear'er** n someone who or something that clears; a clearing bank. **clear'ing** n the act of making clear; an area with no trees within a forest or woodland; the tract of land cleared of wood, etc for cultivation; the method by which bankers change cheques and drafts, and arrange the differences; the method or process by which the final remaining university and college places are allocated to hitherto unsuccessful applicants shortly before the courses start. **clear'ly** adv in a clear manner; distinctly; obviously. **clear'ness** n.
❑ **clearance cairn** n (archaeol) a heap of stones cleared from agricultural land, as distinct from a burial cairn. **clearance sale** n a sale of goods at reduced prices in order to make room for new stock. **clear-cut'** adj sharp in outline, definite; free from obscurity. **clear'-cutting** n the practice of cutting down all the trees in an area of forest. **clear-eyed'** adj clear-sighted, discerning. **clear felling** n the wholesale felling of all the trees in a particular area. **clear-head'ed** adj having a clear understanding. **clear-head'edly** adv. **clearing bank** n a bank that is a member of the London Bankers' Clearing House, through which it makes credit and cheque transfers to and from other banks. **clearing house** n an office where financial clearing business is done; a central source or pool of information, etc. **clear'ing-nut** n the seed of Strychnos potatorum used in India and SE Asia for clearing muddy water. **clearing sale** n (Aust) the sale of moveable property and stock from a farm or similar property, esp following the sale of the

---

■ words derived from main entry word; ❑ compound words; ■ idioms and phrasal verbs

land and buildings. **clear-obscure'** same as **chiaroscuro**. **clear-sight'ed** adj having clearness of sight; discerning. **clear-sight'edly** adv. **clear-sight'edness** n. **clear'skin** see **cleanskin** under **clean**. **clear'-starch'er** n a laundress. **clear-starch'ing** n the act of stiffening linen with clear starch. **clear'story** see **clerestory**. **clear'way** n a stretch of road on which motorists are not allowed to stop. **clear'wing** n a transparent-winged moth of the family Sesiidae, often resembling wasps.
 ■ **clear as a bell** see under **bell¹**. **clear away** to remove (crockery, uneaten food, etc) after a meal. **clear off** to get rid of, dispose of; to go away, esp in order to avoid something (inf). **clear one's throat** to give a slight cough. **clear out** to get rid of; to empty; to empty out, sort through, tidy up (eg a room or cupboard), throwing away unwanted material (**clear'-out** n); (of a ship) to clear and leave port; to take oneself off. **clear the air** to simplify the situation and relieve tension. **clear the decks** (fig) to clear away everything surplus, so as to prepare for action. **clear the way** to make the way open. **clear up** to make or to become clear; (of weather) to become fine after cloudiness, rain or snow; to explain (a mystery, misunderstanding, etc); to tidy up (**clear'-up** n); (of an ailment) to get better. **in the clear** free of suspicion; out of a difficulty; solvent.

clearcole /klēr'kōl/ n a priming coat consisting of size or glue with whiting (also **clere'cole** or **claircolle** /klār'/). [Fr claire colle clear glue]

cleat /klēt/ n a wedge; one of several pieces attached to the sole of a shoe for protection or grip; a piece of wood, etc nailed across anything to keep it in its place or give it an additional strength; a piece attached to parts of a ship for fastening ropes. ◆ vt to strengthen with a cleat; to fasten to or by a cleat. [From a supposed OE clēat; cf Du kloot; Dan klode; Ger Kloss]

cleavage see under **cleave¹**.

cleave¹ /klēv/ vt (prp **cleav'ing**; pat **clōve**, **cleaved** or **cleft**, (archaic) **clāve**; pap **clōv'en**, **cleaved** or **cleft**) to divide or to split; to separate with violence; to go or cut through; to pierce. ◆ vi to split apart; to crack. [OE clēofan, cognate with Ger klieben]
 ■ **cleav'able** adj capable of being cleft. **cleav'ableness** n. **cleav'age** n a split; a tendency to split, esp (in rocks and minerals) in certain directions; the series of mitotic divisions by which the fertilized ovum is transformed into a multicellular embryo (biol); the hollow between a woman's breasts, esp as shown by a low-cut dress. **cleav'er** n a person or thing that cleaves; a butcher's chopper. **cleav'ing** adj splitting. ◆ n a cleft.

cleave² /klēv/ vi (pat **cleaved** or (archaic) **clāve**; pap **cleaved**) to stick or adhere; to unite. [OE clifian; cognate with Ger kleben]
 ■ **cleav'ers** or **clivers** /kliv'ərz/ n goose-grass (Galium aparine) which cleaves to fur or clothes by its hooks. **cleav'ing** n the act of adhering (also adj).

cleché /klech'ā, klesh'ā/ (heraldry) adj voided or hollowed throughout, showing only a narrow border. [Fr]

cleck /klek/ (Scot) vt to hatch. [ON klekia; cf Dan klække to hatch]
 ■ **cleck'ing** n a brood.

cleek /klēk/ n a large hook (Scot); an old-fashioned narrow-faced iron-headed golf club, corresponding to a two-iron. ◆ vt (pat and pap **cleeked**, **cleek'it** or **claught** /klöhht/) to seize, to hook. ◆ vi (Scot) to go arm in arm; to link; to marry. [Scot and N Eng, perh related to **clutch**]

cleep see **clepe**.

cleeve see **cleve**.

clef /klef/ (music) n a character placed on the stave by which the absolute pitch of the following notes is fixed. [Fr clef key, from L clāvis; Gr kleis a key]

cleft¹ /kleft/ pat and pap of **cleave¹**.
 □ **cleft palate** see under **palate**.
 ■ **in a cleft stick** (fig) in a difficult situation; in a dilemma.

cleft² /kleft/ n (also (Bible) **clift**) an opening made by cleaving or splitting; a crack, fissure, or chink. ◆ adj split, divided. [Cf Ger Kluft, and Dan klyft a hole]

cleg /kleg/ n a gadfly, horse-fly. [ON kleggi]

cleidoic /klī-dō'ik/ (zool) adj (of a bird's or insect's egg) enclosed in a more or less impervious shell and thus isolated from the environment. [Gr kleidoun to lock up, from kleis, kleidos key]

cleistogamy or **clistogamy** /klī-stog'ə-mi/ (bot) n production of small flowers, often simplified and inconspicuous, which do not open, and in which self-pollination occurs. [Gr kleistos closed, and gamos marriage]
 ■ **cleistogamic** /-tə-gam'ik/ or **cleistog'amous** adj.

cleithral or **clithral** /klī'thrəl/ adj completely roofed over. [Gr kleithron a bar]

clem /klem/ vi and vt to starve. [Eng dialect clam; Ger klemmen to pinch]

clematis /klem'ə-tis/ or /klə-mā'tis/ n any ranunculaceous temperate climbing plant of the genus Clematis, cultivated for their colourful flowers, including traveller's joy. [L, from Gr klēmatis a plant, prob periwinkle, from klēma a twig]

clement /klem'ənt/ adj (esp of weather) mild; gentle; kind; merciful. [Fr, from L clēmēns, -entis]
 ■ **clem'ency** n the quality of being clement; mildness; readiness to forgive. **clem'ently** adv.

Clementine /klem'ən-tēn/ or /-tīn/ adj relating to any of the popes named Clement, esp Clement I or Clement V.

clementine /klem'ən-tēn/ or /-tīn/ n a type of orange, either a variety of tangerine or a hybrid of orange and tangerine. [Fr]

clenbuterol /klen-bū'tə-rol/ n a drug used in the treatment of asthma, sometimes used illegally to enhance sporting performance.

clench /klench/ or /klensh/ vt to close tightly; to grasp; to clinch. ◆ n the act of clenching; a tight grasp. [Same as **clinch**]
 □ **clench'-built** adj (of boats) clinker-built.

cleome /klē-ō'mē/ n any of a large genus (Cleome) of mostly tropical plants of the family Capparaceae, cultivated for their clusters of white or purplish flowers. [New L]

cleopatra /klē-ə-pat'rə/ n a yellow European butterfly (Gonepteryx cleopatra), with wings ranging from cream to orange-yellow. [New L, from Cleopatra, queen of Egypt (reigned 51–30BC)]

clepe or **cleep** /klēp/ (archaic) vt (pap **yclept** /i-klept'/, also **ycleped'** or (Milton) **ycleap'd** /i-klēp'id or i-klēpt'/) to call; to name. [OE clipian to call]

clepsydra /klep'si-drə/ n (pl **clep'sydras** or **clep'sydrae** /-rē/) an instrument for measuring time by the trickling of water, a water clock. [L, from Gr klepsydra, from kleptein to steal, and hydōr water]

cleptomania see **kleptomania**.

clerecole see **clearcole**.

clerestory or **clearstory** /klēr'stö-ri or -stō-/ (archit) n an upper storey or part with its own row of windows, esp the storey above the triforium in a church. [**clear** (prob in sense of lighted) and **storey**]

clergy /klûr'ji/ n the ministers of the Christian or other religion collectively, as holders of an allotted office, opp to laity; learning, education (archaic). [Fr clergé, from L clēricus, from Gr klērikos, from klēros a lot, a heritage, then the clergy]
 ■ **cler'gyable** or **cler'giable** adj entitled to or admitting of the benefit of clergy.
 □ **cler'gyman** n one of the clergy, a regularly ordained minister. **clergyman's knee** n inflammation of the bursa above the bony prominence below the knee caused by prolonged kneeling. **clergyman's sore throat** n chronic pharyngitis. **cler'gywoman** n a woman who is a minister of religion; a woman belonging to a clergyman's family (facetious).
 ■ **benefit of clergy** see under **benefit**. **black clergy** in Russia, all the regular or monastic, as distinct from the secular or parochial, clergy.

cleric /kler'ik/ n a clergyman. [LL clēricus a priest, clerk]
 ■ **cler'ical** adj belonging to the clergy; of, done by or relating to a clerk, office worker, or to general office work. **cler'icalism** n undue influence of the clergy, sacerdotalism. **cler'icalist** n. **cler'icals** n pl clerical garb. **cler'icate** n the position of a clergyman; clerical position. **clericity** /klər-is'i-ti/ n.
 □ **clerical collar** n the white collar worn by many Christian clergy, fastened behind the neck.

clerihew /kler'i-hū/ n a humorous poem that sums up the life and character of some notable person in two short couplets. [Started by E Clerihew Bentley in his Biography for Beginners (1905)]

clerisy /kler'i-si/ n scholars, educated people as a class. [Ger Klerisei, from LL clēricia]

clerk /klärk or (N Am) klûrk/ n a person employed to deal with correspondence, accounts, records, etc in an office; a record-keeper or account-keeper, esp for a law court or legislative body; a senior official in the House of Commons; a shop-assistant (N Am); a hotel receptionist (N Am); a lay minister (C of E); a clergyman or priest; a scholar (archaic). ◆ vi to act as clerk. [OE clerc a priest, from LL clēricus; see **clergy**]
 ■ **clerk'dom** n. **clerk'ess** n a female clerk. **clerk'ish** adj like a clerk. **clerk'like** adj scholarly. **clerk'ling** n a young clerk. **clerk'ly** adj (obs) scholarly. ◆ adv in a scholarly or learned manner. **clerk'ship** n.
 ■ **clerk of the course** (in horse- or motor-racing) an official in charge of administration. **clerk of the weather** an imaginary functionary facetiously supposed to govern the weather. **clerk of works** or **clerk of the works** a person who superintends building work or the maintenance of a building, etc. **Lord Clerk-Register** see under

register. **St Nicholas's clerks** (*archaic*) thieves. **town clerk** see under **town**.

cleromancy /kler'ə-man-si/ *n* divination by lot. [Gr *klēros* lot, and *manteiā* divination]

cleruch /kler'ook or -uk/ (*Gr hist*) *n* a citizen of Athens granted an allotment of land in foreign territory while retaining his Athenian citizenship. [Gr *klērouchos*, from *klēros*, allotment and *echein* to have]
■ **cler'uchy** or **cleruch'ia** *n*.

cleuch and **cleugh** /klooḥḥ/ Scots forms of **clough**.

cleve or **cleeve** /klēv/ (*dialect*) *n* a cliff; a hillside. [ME *cleof*, a variant of **cliff**[1]]

cleveite /klē'vīt or klā'və-īt/ (*mineralogy*) *n* a pitchblende in octahedral crystals containing helium, a variety of uraninite. [PT *Cleve* (1840–1905), Swedish chemist]

clever /klev'ər/ *adj* dexterous, deft; able; bright, intelligent; ingenious; skilful; good-natured (*US dialect*). [Orig dialect; poss connected with ME *clivers* claws]
■ **cleveral'ity** *n* (*Scot*). **clev'erish** *adj* somewhat clever. **clev'erly** *adv*. **clev'erness** *n*.
❏ **clev'er-clev'er** *adj* flaunting a superficial knowledgeableness; too clever. **clever clogs** or **clever dick** *n* (*sl*) a person who thinks himself or herself clever.

clevis /klev'is/ *n* a U-shaped piece of metal through which tackle may pass, fixed at the end of a beam. [Ety uncertain]

clew or **clue** /kloo/ *n* a ball of thread, or the thread in it (*archaic*); a thread that guides through a labyrinth; the lower corner of a sail (*naut*); one of the cords by which a hammock is suspended. ◆ *vt* to coil up into a clew or ball; to tie up to the yards (*usu* with *up*); to fix up (*fig*). [OE *cliwen*; cf Du *kluwen*; Ger *Knäuel*]
❏ **clew'-garnet** *n* (*naut*) a tackle for clewing up the smaller square sails for furling. **clew'-lines** *n pl* (*naut*) ropes attached to the clews on square sails by which they are clewed up for furling.
■ **clew down** (*naut*) to let down a sail by the lower edges. **clew up** to draw up the lower edges of a square sail ready for furling (*naut*); to tie up loose ends (*fig*).

clianthus /kli-an'thəs/ *n* any climbing shrub or subshrub of the genus *Clianthus*, of Australia and New Zealand, with red or white flowers, including the parrot's bill and glory pea. [L, from Gr *kleos* glory, and *anthos* flower]

cliché /klē'shā/ *n* a stereotyped phrase, or literary tag; something hackneyed as idea, plot, situation; an electrotype or stereotype plate (*printing*); the impression made by a die in any soft metal. [Fr]
■ **clichéd**, **cli'chéed** or **cli'ché'd** *adj* stereotyped, hackneyed.
❏ **cli'ché-ridden** *adj* filled with clichés.

click /klik/ *n* a short, sharp ticking sound; anything that makes such a sound, such as a latch for a gate; a clucking sound produced by sudden retraction of the tongue from the upper teeth, palate, or elsewhere, characteristic of certain S African native languages, represented, eg in Zulu, by C (dental), Q (retroflex), and X (lateral); an act of pressing and releasing one of the buttons on a mouse (*comput*). ◆ *vi* to make a light, sharp sound; to fit into place opportunely or successfully, *esp* to be naturally compatible, either socially or sexually, with another person (*inf*); to press and release one of the buttons on a mouse to select an option on the screen (*comput*). ◆ *vt* (*dialect*) to fasten the latch of (a gate). ◆ *adj* (*inf*) performed by, or relating to the use of, computers, as in *click fraud*. [Dimin of **clack**]
■ **click'able** *adj* (*comput*) able to be activated by clicking on a mouse. **click'er** *n* a person who or thing that clicks; the compositor who distributes the copy among a companionship of printers, makes up pages, etc; a person who cuts up leather for the uppers and soles of boots. **click'ing** *n* the action of the verb.
❏ **click'bait** *n* (*comput sl*) intriguing or sensational hyperlinks that encourage readers to click through to another website. **click beetle** any of various beetles of the family Elateridae, which can flip over with a clicking sound if on their back. **click'-clack** *n* a persistent clicking noise. **click'ety-click'** or **click'ety-clack** *n* a continuous, *usu* regular, clicking sound. **click fraud** the use of an automated process to click repeatedly on an online advertisement in order to gain undue revenue from the advertiser. **click'jacking** *n* (*comput sl*) the practice of diverting a computer user to an undesired website by means of a disguised hyperlink (from *hijack*). **clicks and mortar** *n* (*commercial jargon*) retailing that combines traditional outlets with the use of the Internet. **click'stream** *n* (*comput sl*) a path used in navigating cyberspace. **click'-through** *n* an instance of a visitor to a website clicking on an advertisement in order to visit the advertiser's website. **click'-track** *n* a series of regular beats played to musicians, *usu* through headphones, to help them to keep to the required tempo during a recording session.

clicket /klik'ət/ *n* a latch. ◆ *vi* to make a clicking sound. [OFr (and Fr) *cliquet*]

client /klī'ənt/ *n* a person who employs a lawyer or other professional adviser; a customer; a vassal, dependant or hanger-on; a program used to retrieve and process data from a server (*comput*); a computer running such a program (a **thin client** is very dependent on the processing power of the server, a **fat client** hardly at all). [L *cliēns*, *-entis* a dependant upon a *patrōnus* (protector)]
■ **cli'entage** *n* the whole number of one's clients; the client's relation to the patron. **cli'ental** /-ent'l/ *adj*. **clientèle** /klē-ã-tel' or **clientele** /klī'ən-tēl/ *n* a following; all the clients of a lawyer, shopkeeper, etc. **cli'entship** *n*.
❏ **client-centred therapy** *n* (*psychol*) a method of psychotherapy in which clients are encouraged to learn to resolve their own problems by developing their ability to interpret and take responsibility for their own actions. **cli'ent-ser'ver** *adj* (*comput*) denoting a system in which high-level functions are separated and distributed between a powerful central server and a number of client devices which request information from the server and receive the results of its processing. **client state** *n* a state which depends on another for protection, economic aid, etc.

cliff[1] /klif/ *n* a high steep rock face or, *esp* bordering the sea, side of a mountain. [OE *clif*; Du *clif*; ON *klif*]
■ **cliffed** or **cliff'y** *adj* having cliffs; craggy.
❏ **cliff'-face** *n* the sheer or steep front of a cliff. **cliff'hang** *vi*. **cliff'hanger** *n* a tense, exciting adventure or contest; an ending line of an episode of a serial, etc that leaves one in suspense; a serial, film, etc that keeps one in suspense. **cliff'hanging** *n* and *adj*.

cliff[2] /klif/ (*music*) *n* an old name for **clef**.

ciift[1] see **cleft**[2].

clift[2] /klift/ *n* same as **cliff**[1] (through the influence of **cleft**[2]).
■ **clift'ed** or **clift'y** *adj* broken into cliffs.

climacteric /klī-mak'tə-rik or klī-mak-ter'ik/ *n* a critical period in human life, in which some great bodily change takes place, *esp* the menopause, or the equivalent in men; any critical time. ◆ *adj* relating to such a period; critical. [Gr *klīmaktēr*, from *klīmax* a ladder]
■ **climacter'ical** *adj*.
❏ **climacteric phase** *n* (*bot*) (in certain fruits) the period when full growth has been achieved and an increased respiration rate promotes rapid ripening.
■ **the grand climacteric** (generally) the sixty-third year, supposed to be a critical period for men.

climactic, **climactical** see under **climax**.

climatal see under **climate**.

climate /klī'mit or -mət/ *n* the condition of a country or place with regard to temperature, moisture, etc (also *fig*); the character of something (*fig*); a region (*Shakesp*). ◆ *vi* (*Shakesp*) to remain in a certain place. [Fr *climat*, from L *clima*, from Gr *klima*, *-atos* slope, from *klīnein* to slope]
■ **cli'matal** *adj*. **clīmatic** /-mat'ik/ or **clīmat'ical** *adj*. **clīmat'ically** *adv*. **cli'matize** or **-ise** *vt* see **acclimatize**. **clīmatograph'ical** *adj*. **clīmatog'raphy** *n* a description of climates. **clīmatolog'ical** *adj*. **clīmatol'ogist** *n*. **clīmatol'ogy** *n* the science of climates, or an investigation of the causes on which the climate of a place depends. **cli'mature** *n* (*Shakesp*) a region.
❏ **climate control** *n* air-conditioning.
■ **climate of opinion** the critical atmosphere or complex of opinions prevalent at a particular time or in a particular place.

climatic, **climatical** see under **climate**.

climax /klī'maks/ *n* (of a story, play, piece of music, etc) the most interesting and important or exciting part; a culmination; sexual orgasm; the arranging of discourse in order of increasing strength (*rhetoric*); loosely, the last term of the rhetorical arrangement; the relatively stable culmination of a series of plant and animal communities developing in an area (also **climax community**). ◆ *vi* to ascend in a climax; to culminate (in); to experience sexual orgasm. ◆ *vt* to bring to a climax. [Gr *klīmax*, *-akos* a ladder, from *klīnein* to slope]
■ **climact'ic** or **climact'ical** *adj* relating to a climax. **climact'ically** *adv*.

climb /klīm/ *vi* or *vt* (*pat* and *pap* **climbed**) to ascend or mount by clutching with the hands and feet; to ascend with difficulty; to mount; (of plants) to ascend by clinging to other objects, by means of hooks, tendrils, twining stems, or otherwise; extended to similar downward movement (to *climb down*). ◆ *n* an act of climbing; an ascent. [OE *climban*; cf Ger *klimmen*; **clamber**, **cleave**[2]]
■ **climb'able** *adj*. **climb'er** *n* someone or something that climbs; a person who is intent upon his or her own social advancement; an old-fashioned name for a bird whose feet are mainly adapted for climbing; a climbing plant (*bot*). **climb'ing** *n* and *adj*.
❏ **climbing boy** *n* formerly, a small boy employed by a chimney-sweep to climb chimneys. **climb'ing-frame** *n* a wooden or metal structure on or through which children can climb. **climbing iron** *n*

---

a metal frame with a horizontal spike, worn strapped to the feet as an aid in climbing trees, telegraph poles, etc. **climbing perch** *n* a small edible freshwater fish native to Asia and Africa with a respiratory organ above the gills enabling it to breathe air and move over land. **climbing wall** *n* a wall, specially constructed with hand and foot holds for practising mountaineering and rock-climbing techniques.
■ **climb down** to become more humble; to abandon a firmly stated opinion or resolve, or an excessive or overweening demand, position or attitude (**climb'-down** *n*). **climb the walls** (*inf*) to be in a state of high anxiety.

clime /klīm/ (chiefly *poetic*) *n* a country, region, tract. [**climate**]

clinamen /klin-ā'mən/ *n* inclination. [L *clināmen*]

clinch /klinch or klīnsh/ *vt* to drive home (an argument); to settle or confirm; to fasten or rivet a nail by bending and beating down the point; to fasten (a rope) by means of a half hitch with the end turned back and secured (*naut*); to clench (*obs*). ◆ *vi* to grapple. ◆ *n* an act of clinching; an embrace (*inf*); a holding grapple (*boxing*); the fastening of a nail by beating it back; a half hitch with the end turned back and secured (*naut*); a pun; a punning retort. [Same as **clench**; causal form of **clink**⁴]
■ **clinch'er** *n* someone that clinches; a decisive argument.
❏ **clinch'er-built** *adj* clinker-built. **clinch'er-work** *n* the disposition of the side planks of a vessel, when the lower edge of one row overlaps the row next under it.

clindamycin /klin-də-mī'sin/ *n* an antibiotic drug used for serious infections that do not respond to other antibiotics.

cline /klīn/ (*biol*) *n* a gradation of differences of form, etc seen eg within one species over a specified area of the world. [See **clino-**]
■ **clī'nal** *adj*.

cling /kling/ *vi* (*pat* and *pap* **clung**) to stick close by adhesive surface or by clasp; to adhere in interest or affection; to hold to an opinion; (of wood) to shrink. ◆ *vt* (*archaic*) to attach; to shrivel. ◆ *n* adherence. [OE *clingan*]
■ **cling** or **cling'stone** *adj* (of peaches, etc) having the pulp adhering firmly to the stone, *opp* to *freestone*. **cling'er** *n*. **cling'iness** *n*. **cling'y** *adj* tending to cling; sticky.
❏ **cling'film** *n* a type of transparent plastic film used to wrap food, seal food containers, etc. **cling'fish** *n* any small marine bony fish of the family Gobiesocidae, having a sucking disc near the head for clinging to rocks, etc. **clingstone** see **cling** (*adj*) above. ◆ *n* a clingstone fruit.

clinic /klin'ik/, also **clinique** /kli-nēk'/ *n* a private hospital or nursing-home; an institution, or a department of one, or a group of doctors, for treating patients or for diagnosis or giving advice; any group meeting for instruction, often remedial, in a particular field; the instruction of medicine or surgery at the bedside of hospital patients; a session of such instruction; a person confined to bed by sickness (*archaic*). [Gr *klīnikos*, from *klīnē* a bed]
■ **clin'ical** *adj* hospital-like; denoting the branch of a subject concerned with treating disorders, as in *clinical psychology*; concerned with or based on observation; strictly objective; analytical; plain, functional in appearance. **clin'ically** *adv*. **clinician** /-ish'ən/ *n* a doctor, etc who works directly with patients; a doctor, etc who runs, or works in, a clinic.
❏ **clinical baptism** *n* baptism administered to persons on their sickbed. **clinical convert** *n* a person converted on his or her deathbed. **clinical death** *n* a state of the body in which the brain has entirely ceased to function, though artificial means can be used to maintain the action of the heart, lungs, etc. **clinical lecture** *n* one given to students at the bedside of the sick. **clinical medicine** or **surgery** *n* medicine or surgery as taught by clinics. **clinical thermometer** *n* a finely-calibrated thermometer in which the temperature taken continues to be indicated until reset by shaking. **clinical trial** *n* the study of existing data on or the obtaining of new data from human patients directly in order to test the efficacy of a treatment or a hypothesis related to the cause of a disease.

clink¹ /klingk/ *n* a ringing sound made by striking metal, glass, etc. ◆ *vt* to cause to make a short, soft, ringing sound. ◆ *vi* to make a short, soft, ringing sound; to go with a clink. [A form of **click** and **clank**]
■ **clink'er** *n* someone who or something that is popular, well-liked or exceedingly good (*sl*); something of poor quality, or a mistake or failure (chiefly *US*). **clink'ing** *adj* (*sl*) excellent.
❏ **clink'stone** *n* phonolite (from its metallic clink when struck).

clink² /klingk/ *n* (*sl*) prison. [Appar orig *Clink* prison in Southwark]

clink³ /klingk/ (*Spenser*) *n* said to mean a keyhole, or a latch. [Cf Du *klink* latch]

clink⁴ /klingk/ *vt* to clinch; to rivet. [Scot and N Eng form of **clinch**]
❏ **clink'er-built** *adj* (*esp* of ships' and boats' hulls) made of planks which overlap those below (as distinguished from carvel-built) and fastened with clinched nails.

clinker¹ /kling'kər/ *n* the incombustible residue of fused ash raked out of furnaces; furnace slag; the cindery crust of some lava flows; a hard brick (also **klink'er**). [Du *klinker* (the brick); **clink**¹]
❏ **clink'er-block** *n* a block for building made from ash from furnaces.

clinker² /kling'kər/ *n* a nail used as a protective stud in footwear, *esp* in climbing boots. [**clink**⁴]

clinker³ see under **clink**¹.

clino- /klī-nō-/ *combining form* signifying oblique, reclining. [Gr *klīnein* to lean and *klīnē* a bed]
■ **clī'nōaxis** *n* (*crystallog*) the clinodiagonal. **clīnōdiag'onal** *n* in a monoclinic crystal, that lateral axis which is not perpendicular to the vertical axis (also *adj*). **clinometer** /klīn- or klin-om'i-tər/ *n* any of various instruments for measuring slope, elevation, or inclination. **clinomet'ric** *adj*. **clinom'etry** *n*. **clīnōpin'acoid** or **clinopin'akoid** *n* a form consisting of two faces parallel to the clinoaxis and the vertical axis. **clīnōpyrox'ene** *n* a member of the pyroxene group of minerals, having a monoclinic crystal structure.

clinochlore /klī'nō-klör or -klör/ *n* a green mineral, a distinctly monoclinic variety of *chlorite*.

clinquant /kling'kənt/ *adj* tinselly; glittering with gold or tinsel. ◆ *n* tinsel; imitation gold leaf. [Fr, from Du *klinken* to clink]

clint /klint/ (*geol* and *dialect*) *n* (*usu* in *pl*) one of a series of limestone blocks or ridges divided by fissures or grikes; any exposed outcrop of flinty rock on a hillside or stream bed. [ME, cliff, connected with Swed, Dan and MLGer *klint* crag, cliff; cf ON *klettr* rock]

Clio¹ /klī'ō/ (*Gr myth*) *n* the Muse of history. [Gr *Kleiō* proclaimer]

Clio² /klī'ō/ *n* a genus of shell-less pteropods, 'whales' food'. [Gr *Kleiō*, a sea-nymph]

cliometrics /klī-ə-met'riks or klē-ō-/ *n sing* the application of statistical analysis of data in economic history. [**Clio**¹ and *econometrics*]
■ **cliomet'ric** *adj*. **cliometrician** /-tri'shən/ *n*.

clip¹ /klip/ *vt* (**clipp'ing**; **clipped** or **clipt**) to cut with shears; to cut off; to trim or cut off the hair, twigs, ends, edges, etc of; to cut out (a magazine article, etc); to excerpt a section from (a film, etc); to pare down; to reduce or curtail; to shorten (a speech sound); to abbreviate (a word) *esp* in speech, as 'sec' for 'second'; to punch a piece from (a ticket, etc); to cheat, overcharge (*inf*); to hit with a sharp blow. ◆ *vi* to go at a high speed, *esp* when this is sustained over a distance. ◆ *n* an act of clipping; the thing removed by clipping; the yield of wool from a number of sheep, goats, etc; a sharp, stinging blow; a high speed; a piece taken from a film for separate showing. [Prob from ON *klippa* to cut; Dan *klippe*]
■ **clipped** or (*archaic*) **clipt** *adj*. **clipp'er** *n* a person who clips; a clipping instrument; a swift mover, *specif* a fast sailing vessel; a showy spirited person or anything admired (*old sl*). **clipp'ie** *n* (*inf*) a woman bus or tram conductor. **clipp'ing** *n* the act of clipping, *esp* the edges of coins; a small piece clipped off, a shred or paring; a newspaper cutting; an act of obtaining money by deception or cheating. ◆ *adj* superb (*old sl*); fast in movement.
❏ **clip'art** *n* (*comput*) files containing graphics for use in documents or desktop publishing. **clip joint** *n* (*sl*) a place of entertainment, eg a night-club, where customers are overcharged or cheated. **clip show** *n* a television programme, one of a series, consisting largely of clips from previous episodes.
■ **clip coin** to pare the edges of coins. **clip (someone's) wings** (*fig*) to restrain or thwart (someone's) ambition; to cramp (someone's) freedom of action.

clip² /klip/ *vt* to encircle, hold firmly or embrace. ◆ *n* a device for gripping, clasping, fastening or holding things together; a piece of jewellery that clips onto clothing, etc; a container for ammunition which is clipped onto, and from which the bullets pass directly into, a pistol, rifle, etc. [OE *clyppan* to embrace; Ger *Kluppe* pincers]
❏ **clip'board** *n* a portable board with a spring clip for holding papers; a temporary store for text or graphics, used for the convenient transfer of data between documents or programs (*comput*). **clip'-fas'tener** *n* a name for a press-stud. **clip'-fed** *adj* (of firearms) loaded automatically from an ammunition clip. **clip'-hook** *n* a sister-hook. **clip'-on** *adj* fastening onto something or fastened by means of a clip. ◆ *n* a clip-on tie; (in *pl*) earrings that clip onto the ear-lobes; (in *pl*) sunglasses that clip onto ordinary spectacles.

clip-clop see **clop**.

clipe see **clype**.

clipt see **clip**¹.

clique /klēk/ *n* an exclusive group of people; a faction; a coterie (*usu derog*). [Fr, orig in sense of claque; prob connected with **click**]
■ **cliqu'ey**, **cliqu'y** or **cliqu'ish** *adj* relating to a clique; exclusive. **cliqu'iness** *n*. **cliqu'ishness** *n*. **cliqu'ism** *n* the tendency to form cliques.

clistogamy see **cleistogamy**.

C.Lit. *abbrev* : Companion of Literature (awarded by the Royal Society of Literature).

clit /klit/ (*vulgar sl*) *n* the clitoris. [Short form]

clitellum /kli or klī-tel'əm/ (*zool*) *n* (*pl* **clitell'a**) a saddle-like structure around the anterior part of some annelid worms, having glands which secrete mucus to form a sheath around a copulating pair and a cocoon around the eggs. [L *clītellae* packsaddle]
■ **clitell'ar** *adj*.

clithral same as **cleithral**.

clitic /klit'ik/ (*linguistics*) *adj* (of a word, eg French 'me', 'te', 'le') not capable of being pronounced with full word-stress, but dependent on, and pronounced as though part of, the preceding or following word (also *n*). [Back-formation from **proclitic, enclitic**]

clitoris /kli' or klī'tə-ris/ *n* a small elongated erectile structure at the front of the vulva in female mammals. [Gr *kleitoris*]
■ **clit'oral** *adj*. **clitoridec'tomy** *n* surgical removal of part or all of the clitoris, female circumcision.

clitter /klit'ər/ *vt* and *vi* to make, or cause to make, a shrill rattling noise. [Related to **clatter**]
❑ **clitt'er-clatt'er** *n* idle talk, chatter.

clivers same as **cleavers** (see under **cleave²**).

clivia /klī'vi-ə/ *n* any of the leek-like S African plants of the genus *Clivia*, with strap-shaped leaves and flower stems which produce many orange flowers in terminal umbels. [From Lady Charlotte *Clive* (1787–1866)]

Cllr. *abbrev* : Councillor.

Clo. *abbrev* : Close (in street names).

cloaca /klō-ā'kə/ (L -ä'ka) *n* (*pl* **cloacae** /klō-ā'sē or -ä'kī/) (in most vertebrates excluding higher mammals) the terminal part of the gut into which the urinary and reproductive ducts open forming a single posterior opening; a sewer, a privy; a sink of moral filth. [L *cloāca*, from *cluēre* to purge]
■ **clōā'cal** or **cloacinal** /klō-ə-sī'nl/ *adj*. **clōā'calin** or **clōā'caline** *adj*.

cloak or (*archaic*) **cloke** /klōk/ *n* a loose outer garment; a covering; that which conceals; a disguise, pretext. ◆ *vt* to clothe with a cloak; to cover; to conceal (*usu* with *with* or *in*). [OFr *cloke, cloque*, from LL *cloca* a bell, horseman's bell-shaped cape; see **clock¹**]
❑ **cloak and dagger** *adj* concerned with plot and intrigue, *esp* espionage. **cloak'-and-sword'** *adj* concerned with fighting, intrigue and romance. **cloak'-bag** *n* (*obs*) a portmanteau. **cloak'room** *n* a room for keeping coats and hats; a room in a public place, eg a theatre, in which outer garments and luggage may be temporarily deposited; a lavatory.

cloam /klōm/ (*dialect*) *adj* and *n* (made of) earthenware or clay. [OE *clām* mud]

clobber¹ /klob'ər/ (*sl*) *vt* to strike very hard; to attack, cause to suffer (*fig*); to defeat overwhelmingly. [Origin unknown]

clobber² /klob'ər/ (*sl*) *n* clothing, equipment. [Origin uncertain]

clobber³ /klob'ər/ *n* a paste used by shoemakers to hide the cracks in leather. ◆ *vt* to overpaint a piece of porcelain and enamelled decoration. [Origin uncertain]

clochard /klo-shär'/ (*Fr*) *n* a tramp.

cloche /klosh/ *n* a glass or plastic cover (*orig* bell-shaped) under which plants are forced or protected from frost, etc; a lady's close-fitting bell-shaped hat. [Fr, from LL *cloca, clocca* a bell]

clock¹ /klok/ *n* an instrument for measuring time, operated mechanically, electronically or by some other means, on which the hours, minutes, etc are indicated by means of pointers on a dial face, or displayed digitally; any device or instrument for recording, measuring, etc, either operated by similar means or which may be read like a clock; a speedometer or mileometer (*inf*); an electrical circuit that generates a regular stream of pulses, used eg to synchronize the operations in a computer; the downy seed-head of a dandelion; the face (*sl*). ◆ *vt* to time by a clock or stopwatch; to achieve (a certain officially attested time for a race); to record (a certain speed) on a speedometer (*sl*); to hit (*sl*); to observe, notice (*sl*); to turn back the mileometer of (a car, etc), so that it registers a lower figure than the actual mileage (**clock'ing** *n* this (illegal) practice). ◆ *vi* to register a time by a recording clock. [ME *clokke*, prob through OFr from LL *cloca, clocca* a bell; Mod Fr *cloche* bell, Du *klok* bell, clock, Ger *Glocke* bell]
■ **clock'er** *n* someone who clocks; a twenty-four-hour dealer in drugs (*sl*). **clock'wise** *adv* in the direction in which the hands of a clock move.
❑ **clock card** *n* a card on which the hours worked by an employee are recorded by a time clock. **clock'-golf** *n* a putting game on a green marked like a clock dial, in which the player putts from the position of each hour figure to a hole near the centre. **clock'maker** *n*. **clock radio** *n* an electronic apparatus combining the functions of alarm

clock and radio, *esp* for bedside use (also **alarm radio** or **radio alarm**). **clock speed** *n* (*comput*) the speed of a microprocessor's internal clock, controlling the rate at which it can make calculations, expressed in megahertz. **clock tower** *n* a *usu* square tower having a clock at the top with a face on each exterior wall. **clock-watcher, clock-watching** see **watch the clock** below. **clock'work** *n* the works or machinery of a clock; steady, regular machinery like that of a clock (see also **like clockwork** and **regular as clockwork** below). ◆ *adj* operated by clockwork.
■ **against the clock** making an effort to overcome shortage of time or achieve the shortest time. **beat the clock** to finish a job, task, etc before the time limit runs out. **clock in, out, on** or **off** to register time of coming or going, in or out, or on or off duty. **clock up** (*inf*) to reach or record (a certain speed, score, etc). **know what o'clock it is** to be wide awake, to know how things are. **like clockwork** as smoothly as if driven by clockwork. **o'clock** (for earlier **of the clock**) as reckoned or shown by the clock; in a direction corresponding to that which would be taken by the hour-hand of a horizontal clock relative to a person standing at the centre and facing twelve. **put back the clock** or **put the clock back** to return to earlier time and its conditions; to take a retrograde step. **put the clock** (or **clocks**) **back** or **forward** to alter the clocks to allow for the change from or to summer time. **regular as clockwork** always happening at the same time. **round the clock** for the whole of a twenty-four hour period. **watch the clock** to keep watch on the passage of time, eagerly waiting for one's work-time to finish and *usu* doing only the minimum amount of work required (**clock'-watcher** *n*; **clock'-watching** *n*).

clock² /klok/ *n* an ornament on the side of a stocking. [Ety uncertain]
■ **clocked** *adj* ornamented with such clocks.

clock³ /klok or klōk/ (*Scot* and *dialect*) *n* a beetle. [Origin unknown; cf Swed dialect *klocka* beetle, earwig]
■ **clock'er** *n* a large beetle.

clock⁴ /klok/ (*Scot*) *vi* to cluck; to brood or sit. ◆ *n* a brooding hen's cry; a cluck. [OE *cloccian*; Du *klokken*]
■ **clock'er** *n* a clocking hen.

clod /klod/ *n* a thick round mass or lump that sticks together, *esp* of earth or turf; a concreted mass; the ground; a bed of fireclay in a coalmine; the body of a man, as formed of clay; a stupid person; a cut of ox meat taken from the shoulder. ◆ *vt* (**clodd'ing; clodd'ed**) to pelt (*archaic*); to throw (*Scot*). ◆ *vi* (*archaic*) to throw clods. [A later form of **clot**]
■ **clodd'ish** *adj*. **clodd'ishly** *adv*. **clodd'ishness** *n*. **clodd'y** *adj* earthy. **clod'ly** *adv*.
❑ **clod'hopper** *n* a countryman; a peasant; a clumsy dolt; a heavy, clumsy shoe or boot (*sl*). **clod'hopping** *adj* boorish. **clod'pated** *adj*. **clod'poll, clod'pole** or **clod'pate** *n* a stupid fellow, a bumpkin.

cloff¹ /klof/ (*Scot*) *n* a cleft. [Cf ON *klof*]

cloff² /klof/ (*commerce*) *n* an allowance given on buying certain goods wholesale, of 2lb in every 3cwt, after tare and tret have been deducted. [Origin obscure]

clofibrate /klō-fib'rāt or -fī'brāt/ *n* a lipid-lowering drug formerly used to reduce high levels of fats and cholesterol in the blood.

clog /klog/ *n* a wooden shoe; a shoe with a wooden sole; a block or log of wood; a heavy block of wood fastened to a man or animal to restrict movement; anything hindering motion, an impediment; an obstruction. ◆ *vt* to choke up with an accumulation (often with *up*); to obstruct, impede; to fasten a clog to; to sole with wood. [Ety dubious]
■ **clogged** *adj* choked up, blocked; encumbered. **clogg'er** *n* a person who makes clogs. **clogg'iness** *n*. **clogg'y** *adj* lumpy, sticky.
❑ **clog'-al'manac** *n* an early form of almanac or calendar having characters notched on wood, horn, etc to indicate the weeks, months, festivals, etc. **clog box** *n* a Chinese temple block. **clog'dance** *n* a dance performed with clogs, the clatter keeping time to the music. **clog dancer** *n*. **clog dancing** *n*.
■ **pop one's clogs** (*euphem*) to die.

cloison /klwä-zõ or kloi'zn/ *n* a partition, dividing fillet or band. [Fr]
■ **cloisonnage** /klwäz-on-äzh'/ *n* cloisonné work or process. **cloisonné** /klwäz-on-ā, kloi-zon'ā or -ä'/ *adj* decorated with enamel which is inlaid in compartments formed by small fillets of metal. ◆ *n* enamelwork of this kind.

cloister /kloi'stər/ *n* a covered arcade forming part of a monastic or collegiate establishment; a place of religious retirement, a monastery or nunnery; an enclosed place; monastic life. ◆ *vt* to confine in a cloister; to confine within walls. [OFr *cloistre* (OE *clauster*), from L *claustrum*, from *claudere, clausum* to shut]
■ **clois'tered** *adj* dwelling in or enclosed by cloisters; sheltered from reality and the full experience of life. **clois'terer** *n* a person belonging to a cloister. **clois'tral** *adj* claustral, relating or confined to a cloister; secluded. **clois'tress** *n* (*Shakesp*) a nun.
❑ **clois'ter-garth** *n* the court or yard enclosed by a cloister.

cloke see **cloak**.

clomb /klōm/ (*archaic*) pat and pap of **climb**.

clomiphene /klom'i-fēn/ n a synthetic drug used to stimulate ovulation in apparently infertile women. [Coined from *chloramine* and **phene**]

clomipramine /klō-mip'rə-min/ n an antidepressant drug used to treat depression and obsessive-compulsive disorder.

clomp /klomp/ n a heavy tread or similar sound. ◆ vi to walk with a heavy tread. [Variant form of **clump**]

clonal, etc see under **clone**.

clonazepam /klō-naz'i-pam/ n a sedative drug used as an anticonvulsant in the prevention of epileptic fits.

clone /klōn/ n a group of two or more individuals with identical genetic make-up derived, by asexual reproduction, from a single common parent or ancestor, *orig* applied to plants but now applied much more widely, *esp* to an individual derived from an egg in which a diploid nucleus from an adult has been substituted for the original (*biol*); any of such individuals; a person or thing closely similar to another, a copy or replica (*inf*); a copy of a computer, software, etc that is compatible with the original. ◆ vt to reproduce as a clone; to produce a clone or clones of; to copy the number of (a stolen mobile phone) onto a microchip which is then used in a different phone, so that the owner of the original phone is billed for any calls. [Gr *klōn* shoot]
■ **clo'nal** adj. **clo'nally** adv.
❑ **clonal deletion** n (*biol*) the removal of potentially lethal clones specific for self-antigens, one of the main ways in which self-tolerance is achieved. **clonal selection** n (*biol*) in a young mammal, the method of immunoglobulin production ensuring that there is a large lymphocyte population with a wide variety of antigen-binding sites, so that when a foreign antigen binds to a lymphocyte it will stimulate the proliferation of a clone capable of binding and neutralizing the intruder.

clonic see under **clonus**.

clonk /klongk/ n the dull sound of something heavy falling onto a surface. ◆ vi to make such a sound. ◆ vt to hit. [Imit]

clonus /klō'nəs/ n a type of spasm in which a muscle undergoes a series of rapid contractions and relaxations, *usu* a sign of damage to nerve fibres in the motor cortex of the brain or a characteristic feature of grand mal epilepsy. [Latinized from Gr *klonos* tumult]
■ **clonic** /klon'ik/ adj. **clonicity** /-nis'-/ n.

cloop /kloop/ n the sound of drawing a cork from a bottle. [Imit]

cloot[1] /klüt, Scot klüt or klit/ n a division of a cloven hoof; loosely, a hoof. [Scot; ety uncertain]
■ **Cloot'ie** or **Cloots** n the Devil.

cloot[2] /klüt, klüt or klit/ (*Scot*) n a cloth. [**clout**]
❑ **clootie dumpling** n a suet pudding, containing currants, raisins, etc, steamed or boiled in a cloth.

clop /klop/ n the sound of a horse's hoof-tread against a hard surface. ◆ adv with a clop. ◆ vi to make or go with such a sound. —Also **clip'-clop'** and **clop'-clop'**. [Imit]

clopidogrel /klō-pid'ə-grel/ n a drug that prevents blood clotting, administered to patients undergoing heart surgery.

cloqué /klo-kā'/ n an embossed fabric (also *adj*). [Fr]

close[1] /klōs/ adj near, in time or place (often with *to* or *by*); shut up or shut tight with no opening; strictly confined; narrow; nearly equal or even; near the surface, short; tight in fit; compact; crowded, dense; stifling, unventilated, airless; intimate; stingy, miserly; (of money, finance, etc) difficult to obtain; private, restricted to a certain class or group; reserved; hidden or secluded; secret; thorough, detailed; rigorous, careful; (of a vowel) pronounced with slight opening, or with the tongue tense. ◆ adv in a close manner or position; tightly; nearly; densely; secretly. ◆ n an enclosed place; a small enclosed field; a small, quiet, *esp* dead-end road; a narrow passage off a street, *esp* leading to a tenement stairway or courtyard; the precinct of a cathedral. [Fr *clos* shut, from L *claudere*, *clausum* to close, shut up]
■ **close'ly** adv. **close'ness** n.
❑ **close-band'ed** adj closely united. **close'-barred** adj firmly closed. **close-bod'ied** adj fitting close to the body. **Close Brethren** n pl the Exclusive Brethren, a branch of the Plymouth Brethren whose members will not associate with (eg eat in company with) people outside their group. **close call** n a narrow escape. **close company** n a firm controlled by five, or fewer, people who own a majority of the shares. **close corporation** n a corporation which fills up its own vacancies, without outside interference. **close'-cropped** adj (of hair) cut very short; (of grass, etc) cut, or eaten by animals, down to the level of the ground. **close-coup'led** adj (of two parts) attached close together. **close encounter** n a direct personal confrontation with an extraterrestrial being (also *fig*). **close-fist'ed** or **close-hand'ed** adj penurious, covetous. **close'-fitting** adj (of clothes) designed to fit

tightly. **close'-grained** adj with the particles, fibres, etc close together, compact. **close harmony** n (*music*) harmony in which the notes of chords lie close together. **close'-hauled** adj (*naut*) (in trim for) sailing as near as possible towards where the wind is coming from. **close'head** n (*Scot*) the entrance to a close, or the gossips that congregate there. **close-in'** adj positioned or operating at a small distance. **close'-knit** adj (of communities, etc) closely connected, bound together. **close-lipped'** or **close-mouthed'** adj reticent, saying little. **close quarters** see **at close quarters** below. **close-range'** adj in, at or within a short distance. **close'-reefed** adj (*naut*) having all reefs taken in. **close-run'** adj (of a contest) fiercely contested, with a narrow margin of victory. **close season** or **closed season** n a time of the year when it is illegal to kill certain game or fish, *usu* the breeding season; a prohibited or inactive period. **close-set'** adj (of eyes) positioned close together. **close shave** or **close thing** n a close call. **close'-stool** n a chamberpot enclosed in a box or stool. **close tennis** n real tennis, distinguished from lawn tennis. **close'-tongued** adj (*archaic*) cautious in speaking, reticent. **close'-up** n a photograph or film taken near at hand and thus detailed and big in scale; a close scrutiny.
■ **at close quarters** (of fighting) hand-to-hand or at close range; in close proximity. **close at** or **to hand** easily accessible. **close on** almost, nearly. **close to the chest** without revealing one's intentions. **close to home** too near to one's own situation to be comfortable. **run someone close** to be very near someone in standard or achievement.

close[2] /klōz/ vt to complete, conclude; to end, terminate; to block, make impassable or impenetrable; to forbid access to; to place (a door, etc) so as to cover an opening, to shut; to put an end to discussion of; to cease operating or trading; to make close, draw or bring together, narrow; to unite; to approach or pass near to. ◆ vi to come to an end; to cease operating or trading; to come together; to unite; to narrow; to grapple; to agree (with); (of currency, a financial index, etc) to measure or be worth (a specified figure) at the end of the day's business (with *at*). ◆ n the manner or time of closing; a pause or stop; a cadence; the end; a junction, union; an encounter, a conflict (*Shakesp*). [Fr *clore*, *clos*, from L *claudere*, *clausum*]
■ **closed** adj shut; blocked; not open to traffic; with permanent sides and top; having a lid, cover, etc; exclusive, having few contacts outside itself, eg a *closed community*; not open to all, restricted; continuous and finishing where it began. **clos'er** n someone or something that concludes; any portion of a brick used to close up the bond next to the end brick of a course (*building*); a pitcher who specializes in defending a lead late in the game (*baseball*). **clos'ing** n enclosing; ending; coming together, agreement. **clos'ure** n the act of closing; something that closes or fastens; the end; the ending of a parliamentary debate by a member calling for a vote; a feeling of satisfaction or resignation when a particular episode has come to an end. ◆ vt to apply the closure to (a parliamentary debate).
❑ **closed book** n (*fig*) a mystery, something about which one knows or understands nothing; a subject or matter that has been concluded and which is no longer for consideration, discussion, etc. **closed-chain'** adj (*chem*) having a molecule in which the atoms are linked ringwise, like a chain with the ends united. **closed circuit** n an electrical circuit in which current flows when voltage is applied; a television system in which the transmission is restricted to a limited number of screens connected to the television camera by cables, etc (also **closed-circuit television**). **closed community** n (*ecology*) a plant community that is so dense that no new species can colonize. **closed couplet** n (*prosody*) two metrical lines whose grammatical structure and sense conclude at the end of the second line. **closed-door'** see **behind closed doors** below. **closed-end'** adj having fixed limits; (of an investment trust) offering shares up to a limited number. **closed-in'** adj claustrophobically enclosed. **closed-loop'** adj denoting a computer system in which performance is controlled by comparing output with an expected standard. **closedown** see **close down** below. **closed population** n (*biol*) a population in which there is no new gene input from outside and in which mutation is the only source of genetic variation. **closed scholarship** n a scholarship open only to those candidates able to fulfil certain criteria, such as attendance at a particular school, etc. **closed set** n (*maths*) a set in which the result of combining any two members of the set using a given operation always results in a member of the original set. **closed shop** n an establishment in which only members of a trade union, or of a particular trade union, will be employed; the principle or policy implied in such a regulation. **closed syllable** n (*phonetics*) one ending in a consonant. **closing date** n the date by which something must be submitted, completed, etc. **closing price** n the value of shares on the stockmarket when business stops for the day. **closing time** n the time at which business stops, *esp* in public houses.
■ **behind closed doors** in private, the public being excluded, as in court cases, committee meetings, etc (**closed-door'** adj). **close a bargain** to come to an agreement. **close down** to come to a standstill or stoppage of work; (*esp* in team games, eg football) to slow the pace

of a game and prevent the opposition from making any attacking manoeuvres; (of a television or radio station) to end a period of broadcasting; (of a business) to cease trading (**close'down** n). **close in** (of days) to contain a progressively shorter period of daylight, as between the autumnal equinox and the winter solstice. **close in upon** to surround and draw near to. **close on** to catch up with. **close one's eyes** (euphem) to die. **close one's eyes to** to ignore or disregard purposely. **close ranks** (of soldiers drawn up in line) to stand closer together in order to present a more solid front to the enemy; to unite, make a show of solidarity in order to protect a member or all the members of a group from attack. **close up** to cease operating; to draw together. **close with** to accede to; to grapple or engage in combat with. **with closed doors** same as **behind closed doors** (see above).

closet /kloz'it/ n a recess or cupboard off a room, esp in N America, a clothes cupboard or wardrobe; a small private room, formerly the private chamber of the sovereign; a privy; a horizontal band one-half the width of a bar (heraldry). ◆ adj secret, private. ◆ vt (**clos'eting**; **clos'eted**) to shut up in or as if in, or take into, a closet; to conceal. [OFr closet, dimin of clos an enclosure; see **close**]
□ **closet play** or **closet drama** n a play to be read rather than acted. **closet queen** n (sl) a male homosexual who does not openly admit his homosexuality. **closet strategist** n a mere theorist in strategy.
■ **be in the closet** (inf) to keep something secret (esp one's homosexuality). **come out of the closet** (inf) openly to admit a practice, tendency, habit, etc previously kept a close secret (esp one's homosexuality).

clostridium /klo-strid'i-əm/ n (pl **clostrid'ia**) any of several species of ovoid or spindle-shaped bacteria including those causing botulism and tetanus. [New L, from Gr klōstēr a spindle]
■ **clostrid'ial** adj.
□ **Clostridium difficile** /di-fi-sēl'/ n (L difficile difficult) a strain of clostridium that is resistant to many antibiotics (abbrev **C. difficile** or (inf) **C. diff**).

closure see under **close²**.

clot /klot/ n a mass of soft or fluid matter solidified, such as blood; a fool (inf). ◆ vt and vi (**clott'ing**; **clott'ed**) to form into clots. [OE clott, a clod of earth; cf Du klos block; Dan klods; Ger Klotz]
■ **clott'er** vt to coagulate. **clott'iness** n. **clott'ing** n coagulation. **clott'y** adj.
□ **clot'buster** n (inf) any drug used to dissolve blood clots. **clot'poll** n (Shakesp) a clodpoll, a blockhead. **clotted cream** n a famous Devonshire delicacy, thick cream made from scalded milk (also called **clouted cream**). **clotting factor** n any of a group of proteins in the blood essential in the process of blood clotting (also called **coagulation factor**).

clote /klōt/ n the burdock; extended to other plants with hooks or burs. [OE clāte]
□ **clotbur** /klot'bər/ or **clote'bur** n same as **cocklebur** (see under **cockle²**).

cloth /kloth or klöth/ n (pl **cloths** /kloths or klödhz/) woven material from which garments or coverings are made; a piece of this material for a particular use, such as a floorcloth or tablecloth; clothing (archaic); (with the) the clerical profession, the clergy; sails; a theatre curtain. [OE clāth cloth; Ger Kleid a garment]
□ **cloth cap** n a flat cap. **cloth-cap** adj symbolic of the working class. **cloth'-eared** adj (sl) deaf, usu because inattentive. **cloth'-ears** n sing (derog sl) a cloth-eared person. **cloth'-hall** n an exchange building or market for the cloth trade. **cloth head** n (derog sl) a stupid person. **cloth'-yard** n the yard by which cloth was measured, formerly 37in.
■ **cloth of gold** cloth woven of threads of gold and silk or wool. **cloth of state** a canopy. **cloth-yard shaft** an arrow a cloth-yard long.

clothe /klōdh/ vt (**clothing** /klō'dhing/; **clothed** /klōdhd/ or **clad**) to cover with a garment; to provide with clothes; to invest; to equip; to cover. [OE clāthian, from clāth cloth]
■ **clothes** /klōdhz or (inf) klōz/ n pl garments or articles of dress; blankets, sheets, etc, bedclothes. **clothier** /klō'dhi-ər/ n a person who makes or sells cloth or clothes. **clothing** /klō'dhing/ n clothes, garments; covering.
□ **clothes'-basket** n a large basket for holding and carrying clothes for washing. **clothes'-brush** n a brush for removing dirt, fluff, etc from clothes. **clothes'-conscious** adj concerned about one's clothes and appearance. **clothes'-horse** n a frame for hanging laundry on to air or to dry; a person, usu a woman, whose value is primarily perceived as a model for fashionable clothes (inf). **clothes'line** vt (in wrestling, etc) to strike (an opponent who is running past) across the face or in the windpipe with one's horizontally extended arm. **clothes'-line** n a rope or wire, etc for hanging washing on to dry. **clothes moth** n any of various tineid moths whose larvae feed on wool or fur. **clothes'-peg** n a wooden or plastic clip to hold washing on a clothes-line. **clothes'-pin** n a clothes-peg. **clothes'-pole** n a pole from which clothes-lines are hung; a clothes-prop. **clothes'-press** n a cupboard, often with drawers, for storing clothes; an apparatus for pressing clothes.

clothes'-prop n a movable notched pole for raising or supporting a clothes-line. **clothes'-screen** n a frame for hanging clothes on to dry. **clothes'-sense** n dress sense.
■ **clothed on** (or **upon**) **with** (archaic) having as a covering or adornment. **clothe in words** to express in words.

Clotho /klō'thō/ (Gr myth) n the Fate that holds the distaff from which Lachesis spins the thread of life. [Gr Klōthō]

cloture /klō'chər or (Fr) klō-tür'/ n closure; a method of ending a debate in a legislative assembly, usu by calling for an immediate vote (esp US). ◆ vt to end (a debate) this way. [Fr clôture; see **closure**]

clou /kloo/ n the main point of interest, the centre of attraction; a dominant idea. [Fr, nail]

cloud /klowd/ n a mass of fog, consisting of minute particles of water, often in a frozen state, floating in the atmosphere; anything unsubstantial (fig); a great number of things; anything that obscures as a cloud does; a dullness; a dark or dull spot; a great volume of dust or smoke; anything gloomy, overhanging or ominous; the Internet, regarded as a repository of software that can be accessed without having to be installed on a personal computer (comput sl). ◆ vt to overspread with clouds; to darken; to defame; to stain with dark spots or streaks; to dull. ◆ vi to become clouded or darkened (often with over). [OE clūd a hill, then a cloud; cf **clod**, **clot**]
■ **cloud'age** n. **cloud'ed** adj hidden by clouds; darkened, indistinct, dull (fig); variegated with spots. **cloud'ily** adv. **cloud'iness** n. **cloud'ing** n a cloudy appearance. ◆ adj growing dim. **cloud'less** adj unclouded, clear. **cloud'lessly** adv. **cloud'let** n a little cloud. **cloud'scape** n a view or picture of clouds. **cloud'y** adj darkened with, or consisting of, clouds; obscure; gloomy; stained with dark spots; (of liquid) lacking (proper or expected) clarity or limpidity.
□ **cloud base** n the undersurface of a cloud or clouds; the height of this above sea level. **cloud'berry** n a rosaceous plant of N America and N Europe, related to the bramble, usu found on high open moorland, with an orange-red sweet-flavoured berry. **cloud'-built** adj made of clouds, unsubstantial. **cloud'burst** n a sudden downpour of rain over a small area. **cloud'-capt** adj (Shakesp) capped with or touching the clouds. **cloud ceiling** n the height of the cloud base above the ground. **cloud chamber** n (phys) an apparatus in which the path of high-energy charged particles is made visible by means of droplets condensed on gas ions. **cloud'-compelling** adj driving or collecting the clouds, an epithet of Zeus. **cloud computing** n (comput) computing in which data and services are not held by the user but stored on the Internet for use when needed. **cloud-cuck'oo-land** or **cloud'land** or **cloud'town** n an imaginary situation or land, esp as the product of impractical or wishful thinking. **clouded leopard** n an arboreal cat (Neofelis nebulosa) smaller than a leopard. **clouded yellow** n any butterfly of the family Pieridae having yellowish wings and black margins. **cloud forest** n an area of high-altitude tropical forest characterized by permanent cloud cover. **cloud'-kissing** adj (Shakesp) touching the clouds. **cloud'-seeding** n the induction of rainfall by scattering particles, eg dry ice, silver iodide, on clouds from aircraft. **cloud'-topped** adj covered with or touching the clouds.
■ **in the clouds** out of touch with reality. **on cloud nine** (inf) extremely pleased or happy. **under a cloud** in trouble, disgrace or disfavour. **with one's head in the clouds** in a dreamy impractical way or state.

clough /kluf or klow/ (dialect) n a ravine; a valley. [OE would be clōh; Scot cleuch]

clour /kloor/ (Scot) n a knock; a swelling caused by a knock, a bruise. ◆ vt to knock; to raise a bump. [Origin doubtful]

clout /klowt/ n influence, power (inf); a blow or cuff; (in archery) the mark or target, usu in long-distance shooting; a shot that hits its mark; a piece of cloth, esp used for mending, a patch; a garment; a protective plate or nail. ◆ vt to hit with great force, to cuff; to cover with a cloth; to mend with a patch; to protect with a plate or with nails. [OE clūt; cf ON klūtr a kerchief; Dan klud rag]
■ **clout'ed** adj (Shakesp) heavy and patched or having nails in the soles, as shoes; covered with a clout. **clout'er** n. **clout'erly** adj clownish.
□ **clout'-nail** n a large-headed nail. **clout'-shoe** n a shoe with clout-nails.

clouted /klow'tid/ adj clotted. [See **clot**]

clove¹ /klōv/ n the flower-bud of the **clove'-tree** (Eugenia caryophyllus or Syzygium aromaticum), dried as a spice, and yielding an essential oil, **oil of cloves**, used in medicine to relieve abdominal pain or as a remedy for toothache; (in pl) a flavouring obtained from it. [Fr clou nail, from its shape, from L clāvus a nail]
□ **clove gillyflower** or **clove pink** n a variety of pink, smelling of cloves.

clove² /klōv/ n a division of a bulb, as in garlic. [OE clufu; cf **cleave¹**]

clove³ /klōv/ pat of **cleave¹**.

❑ **clove hitch** *n* a kind of hitch knot, used to connect a rope to another rope of greater thickness or to secure a rope to a post, etc. **clove'-hook** *n* a sister-hook.

clove[4] /klōv/ *n* an old weight (7, 8, or 10 pounds) for wool and cheese. [Fr *clou*, from L *clāvus* nail]

cloven /klō'vn/ *adj* split; divided. [Pap of **cleave**[1]]
❑ **cloven-foot'ed** or **cloven-hoofed'** *adj* having the hoof divided, as does the ox or sheep.
■ **the cloven hoof** applied to any indication of devilish agency or temptation, from the early representation of the Devil with cloven hoofs, probably from Pan, some of whose characteristics he shares.

clover /klō'vər/ *n* any papilionaceous plant of the genus *Trifolium*, with heads of small flowers and trifoliate leaves, affording rich pasturage. [OE *clāfre* (usu *clǣfre*); Du *klaver*; Dan *klöver*; Ger *Klee*]
■ **clov'ered** *adj* covered with clover. **clov'ery** *adj* abounding in clover. ❑ **clov'ergrass** *n* clover as pasturage. **clov'erleaf** *n* a traffic arrangement in which one road passes over the top of another and the roads connecting the two are in the pattern of a four-leafed clover; any interlinked arrangement of this shape. ◆ *adj* shaped like a four-leafed clover.
■ **live in clover** to live luxuriously or in abundance.

clow /klow/ *n* a Scots form of **clove**[1].
❑ **clow-gill'ieflower** *n*.

clowder /klow'dər/ (*rare*) *n* a collective name for a number of cats. [Variant of **clutter**]

clown /klown/ *n* a comic entertainer, *esp* in the circus, with colourful clothes and make-up; a person who behaves in a comical way; a stupid person (*inf*); a rude or clumsy person. ◆ *vi* to play the clown (often with *about* or *around*). [Perh from LGer, cf Fris *klönne*, *klünne*]
■ **clown'ery** *n* a clown's performance. **clown'ing** *n*. **clown'ish** *adj* of or like a clown; coarse and awkward; rustic. **clown'ishly** *adv*. **clown'ishness** *n*.
❑ **clown'fish** *n* any of various brightly coloured fish of the subfamily Amphiprioninae, whose markings resemble a clown's make-up.

cloxacillin /klok-sə-sil'in/ *n* a penicillin-type antibiotic used to treat infections by staphylococcal bacteria.

cloy /kloi/ *vt* to satiate to the point of disgust; to disgust, weary; to block up (*archaic*); to prick (a horse in shoeing) (*obs*); to gore (*Spenser*); to spike (a cannon) (*archaic*). ◆ *vi* to become distasteful from excess; to cause distaste, *esp* by being too sweet or rich. [Aphetized from *accloy*, from OFr *encloyer* (Fr *enclouer*), from LL *inclāvāre* to drive in a nail (see the archaic senses above), from *in* in, and *clāvus* a nail]
■ **cloyed** *adj*. **cloy'ing** *adj*. **cloy'ingly** *adv*. **cloy'less** *adj* (*Shakesp*) that cannot cloy. **cloy'ment** *n* (*Shakesp*) satiety, surfeit. **cloy'some** *adj* satiating.

cloye /kloi/ (*Shakesp*) *vt* (*appar*) to claw, stroke with the claw. [Perh **claw**]

clozapine /klō'zə-pēn, -pin or pīn/ *n* a neuroleptic drug used as a sedative and to treat schizophrenia. [**chloro-** and **benzodiazepine**]

cloze /klōz/ (*educ*) *adj* denoting a type of exercise in which the reader is required to supply words that have been deleted from a text, as a test of comprehension in reading (**cloze test**). [Formed from **closure**]

CLP *abbrev*: Constituency Labour Party.

CLR *abbrev*: computer language recorder.

CLT *abbrev*: computer language translator.

club /klub/ *n* a heavy tapering stick, knobby or thick at one end, used to strike with; a cudgel; an Indian club (qv); a bat used in certain games; an instrument for playing golf, with a metal or wooden head on the end of a thin metal shaft; a playing card with black trefoil pips; a combination, bunch; a clique, set; an association of persons for social, political, athletic or other ends; an association of persons who possess premises or facilities which all members may use; a clubhouse, or the premises occupied by a club; a nightclub. ◆ *vt* to beat with a club; to use a heavy object as a club; to throw into confusion (*milit*); to gather into a bunch; to combine. ◆ *vi* (*esp* with *together*) to join together for some common end; to combine together; to share in a common expense; to visit nightclubs. [ON and Swed *klubba*; same root as **clump**]
■ **clubbabil'ity** or **clubabil'ity** *n*. **clubb'able** or **club'able** *adj* sociable. **clubbed** *adj* enlarged at the end like a club. **clubb'er** *n* a person who frequents nightclubs. **clubb'ing** *n* beating; combination; a thickening, as of finger-ends, or of cabbage-stems attacked by insect larvae; the frequenting of nightclubs. **clubb'ish** *adj* given to clubs. **clubb'ism** *n* the club system. **clubb'ist** *n* a clubman. **clubb'y** *adj* characteristic of a club; sociable; exclusive, cliquey. **clubs** *n sing* see **clumps** under **clump**.
❑ **club class** *n* a class of seat on an aircraft between tourist class and first class. **club deal** *n* (*finance*) a takeover by a group of private equity companies working as a syndicate. **club'-face** *n* the face of a golf club. **club foot** *n* a deformed foot. **club-foot'ed** *adj*. **club'-haul** *vt*

(*naut*) to tack, *esp* in an emergency, by dropping the lee anchor and hauling in the anchor cable to bring the stern of the boat to windward. **club'head** *n* the head of a golf club. **club'-head'ed** *adj* having a thick head. **club'house** *n* a house for the accommodation of a club. **club'land** *n* the area around St James's in London, where many of the old-established clubs are; an area or region containing a large number of nightclubs or working-men's clubs. **club'-law** *n* government by violence. **club'-line** *n* (*printing*) a short line at the end of a paragraph, an orphan. **club'man** *n* a member of a club or clubs; a frequenter of clubs, a man-about-town. **club'manship** *n*. **club'master** *n* the manager of, or purveyor for, a club. **club moss** *n* any primitive plant of the family Lycopodiaceae, allied to the ferns, typically having small overlapping leaves and creeping stems. **club'room** *n* the room in which a club meets. **club'root** *n* a fungal disease which attacks the roots of plants of the Cruciferae. **club'rush** *n* any sedge of the genus *Scirpus*. **club sandwich** *n* a sandwich of three slices of bread or toast, containing two fillings. **club soda** *n* soda water. **club'woman** *n*.
■ **in the club** or **in the pudding club** (*sl*) pregnant. **join the club** (*inf*) we are all in the same position; me too. **on the club** (*old sl*) certified unfit to work.

cluck /kluk/ *n* the call of a hen to her chickens; any similar sound; (now also **dumb'-cluck**) a fool (*N Am*). ◆ *vi* to make such a sound. [Imit; cf Du *klokken*, Ger *glucken*, Dan *klukke*, and **clock**[4]]
■ **cluck'y** *adj* (*Aust sl*) obsessed with babies, broody.

cludgie /klud'ji/ (*Scot sl*) *n* a lavatory, *esp* a communal one. [Origin uncertain]

clue[1] /kloo/ *n* anything that points to the solution of a mystery or puzzle. ◆ *vt* to direct or indicate with a clue. [See **clew**]
■ **clue'less** *adj* (*inf*) ignorant, stupid; helpless. **clue'lessness** *n*. ❑ **clued-up'** *adj* (*inf*) (well-)informed.
■ **clue in** (*inf*) to inform. **not have a clue** to have no information; to have no idea at all; to be without the necessary skills to do something.

clue[2] see **clew**.

clumber /klum'bər/ *n* a kind of thickset spaniel, *orig* bred at *Clumber*, in Nottinghamshire.

clump /klump/ *n* a shapeless mass of anything; a cluster; a clot; a thick additional sole; a heavy tread; a blow. ◆ *vi* to walk heavily; to clot; to cluster. ◆ *vt* to put in a clump; to beat. [Prob Scand; Dan *klump* a lump. Cf Ger *Klump*, and **club**]
■ **clump'er** *n*. **clump'iness** *n*. **clump'ing** *adj* (*inf*) heavy and clumsy. **clumps** *n sing* a parlour game of question and answer (also called **clubs**). **clump'y** *adj* having many clumps; heavy.

clumsy /klum'zi/ *adj* badly made; unwieldy; awkward; ungainly; unskilfully executed; lacking manual dexterity or co-ordination. [ME *clumsen* to be stiff or benumbed]
■ **clum'sily** *adv*. **clum'siness** *n*.

clunch /klunch or klunsh/ *n* a tough clay. [Prob related to **clump**]

clung /klung/ *pat* and *pap* of **cling**.

Cluniac /kloo'ni-ak/ *n* a monk or nun of a branch of the Benedictine order originating at *Cluny* in France in 910AD (also *adj*).

clunk /klungk/ *n* a dull metallic noise; a thump; a dolt (*N Am*). ◆ *vi* to fall with a dull sound. ◆ *vt* (*dialect*) to gurgle while swallowing. [Imit]
■ **clunk'er** *n* (*inf*) an incompetent person; an unsatisfactory object, eg a useless old car. **clunk'y** *adj* making a clunking noise; awkward, clumsy (*inf*); badly written.

clupeid /kloo'pē-id/ *n* any fish of the family **Clupē'idae**, including the herring genus *Clupea*, typically having forked tails and slim, flattened bodies (also *adj*). [L *clupea* a kind of river fish]
■ **clu'peoid** *n* any fish of the suborder Clupeoidea, including herring, sardine and pilchard.

clusia /kloo's(h)i-ə/ *n* any plant of the American genus *Clusia*, evergreen climbing plants, shrubs and trees. [*Clusius*, Latinized name of Charles de L'Écluse (1526–1609), French botanist]

cluster /klus'tər/ *n* a number of things of the same kind growing or joined together; a bunch; a mass; a crowd; a statistically significant number of people within a sample, who have given characteristics; a number of sectors grouped together on a disk (*comput*); a group of computers joined together on a network. ◆ *vi* to grow in or gather into clusters. ◆ *vt* to collect into clusters; to cover with clusters. [OE *clyster*; LGer *kluster*; cf **clot**]
■ **clus'tered** *adj* grouped. **clus'tering** *adj*. **clus'tery** *adj*. ❑ **clus'ter-bean** *n* the guar (qv). **cluster bomb** *n* a bomb that opens on impact to throw out a number of small bombs. **clus'ter-cup** *n* an aecidium. **clustered column** *n* a pier which consists of several columns or shafts clustered together. **cluster fly** *n* a large dark-brown fly related to the bluebottle, that gathers in large numbers in attics, etc during autumn. **cluster graft** *n* (*surg*) an organ transplant in which the patient receives more than one organ. **cluster marketing** *n* advertising, etc aimed at people with specific characteristics. **cluster**

physics *n sing* the physics of very small numbers of atoms. **cluster pine** *n* the pinaster (*Pinus pinaster*), a pine with clustered cones.

clutch¹ /kluch/ *vt* to close the hand upon; to hold firmly; to seize or grasp. ◆ *vi* to make a snatching movement (with *at*). ◆ *n* a grasping hand (often in *pl*); a claw (*archaic*); a device by which two shafts or rotating members may be connected or disconnected either while at rest or in relative motion; the pedal of a motor vehicle which controls such a device; grasp; a snatching movement; (in *pl*) power, control. ◆ *adj* (*N Am*) relating to a critical situation. [OE *clyccan* to clench]
◻ **clutch bag** *n* a kind of handbag without strap or handle, carried in the hand or under the arm.
▪ **in the clutch** (*N Am*) in a critical situation.

clutch² /kluch/ *n* a brood of chickens; a sitting of eggs; (loosely) a number, group. ◆ *vt* to hatch. [Cf **cleck**]

clutter /klut'ər/ *n* a clotted or confused mass; a disorderly accumulation; confusion; stir (*dialect*); noise (*dialect*); irregular interference on radar screen from echoes, rain, buildings, etc. ◆ *vi* to crowd together; to go about in noisy confusion (*dialect*). ◆ *vt* to litter, clog with superfluous objects, material, etc (often with *up*). [From **clot**; influenced in meaning by **cluster** and **clatter**]

cly /klī/ (*old sl*) *vt* to seize, steal. [Prob related to **claw**; referred by some to Du *kleed* a garment, *to fake a cly* to take a garment]
◻ **cly'-faker** *n* a pickpocket. **cly'-faking** *n* pocket-picking.

Clydesdale /klīdz'dāl/ *adj* (of a breed of cart-horses) originating in *Clydesdale*, the area of Scotland through which the Clyde flows. ◆ *n* a Clydesdale horse.
▪ **Clyde'side** *adj* relating to *Clydeside*, the area along the Clyde estuary, or to shipbuilding, formerly its main industry. **Clyde'sider** *n* an inhabitant of Clydeside or a worker in its shipbuilding industry.

clype or **clipe** /klīp/ (*Scot*) *vi* to tell tales (also *n*). [ME *clepien* to call]

clypeus /klip'i-əs/ *n* (*pl* **clyp'ei** /-ī/) the shield-like plate on the heads of some insects. [L *clipeus* a round shield]
▪ **clyp'eal** *adj* of the clypeus. **clyp'eate** or **clyp'eiform** *adj* buckler-shaped.

clyster /klis'tər/ (*archaic*) *n* a liquid injected into the rectum, an enema. [Gr *klystēr* a clyster-pipe, from *klyzein* to wash out]
◻ **clys'ter-pipe** *n* a pipe or syringe for injecting a clyster.

CM *abbrev*: *Chirurgiae Magister* (*L*), Master of Surgery; Corresponding Member.

Cm *abbrev*: Command Paper (series 2 November 1986–date).

Cm (*chem*) *symbol*: curium.

cm *abbrev*: *carat métrique* (*Fr*), metric carat; *causa mortis* (*L*), by reason of death; centimetres.

Cmd *abbrev*: Command Paper (series 1919–56).

Cmdr. *abbrev*: Commander.

CMG *abbrev*: Companion of (the Order of) St Michael and St George.

CMH (*US*) *abbrev*: Congressional Medal of Honor.

CMHR *abbrev*: combustion modified highly resilient.

CMI *abbrev*: Chartered Management Institute; computer-managed instruction.

CML *abbrev*: computer-managed learning; Council of Mortgage Lenders.

Cmnd *abbrev*: Command Paper (series 1956–7 November 1986).

CMOS (*comput*) *abbrev*: complementary metal-oxide semiconductor.

CMS *abbrev*: Church Mission Society; content management system, a program used to manage digital content, such as on a website.

CMV *abbrev*: cytomegalovirus.

CN *abbrev*: Canadian National, a railway freight company.

Cn (*chem*) *symbol*: copernicium.

c/n or **cn** *abbrev*: credit note.

CNAA *abbrev*: Council for National Academic Awards (now defunct).

CnaG *abbrev*: Comunn na Gàidhlig, the national Scottish agency concerned with the development of Gaelic language and culture.

CNAR *abbrev*: compound net annual rate.

CND *abbrev*: Campaign for Nuclear Disarmament.

cnemial /(k)nē'mi-əl/ (*anat*) *adj* of or relating to the tibia or shin. [Gr *knēmē* tibia, leg]

Cnicus /(k)nī'kəs/ *n* a genus of thistles. [Gr *knikos*, *knēkos* safflower, thistle]

cnida /(k)nī'də/ *n* (*pl* **cnī'dae** /-dē/) a nematocyst. [New L, from Gr *knīdē* a nettle, a sea-anemone]
▪ **cnida'rian** *n* a member of the *Cnidaria*, a division of the Coelenterata characterized by cnidae (also *adj*). **cnī'doblast** *n* (*zool*) a stinging thread cell containing a nematocyst (also **nematoblast**).

CNN *abbrev*: Cable News Network; certified nursery nurse.

CNRS *abbrev*: *Centre National de la Recherche Scientifique* (*Fr*), National Centre for Scientific Research.

CNS *abbrev*: central nervous system.
◻ **CNS stimulant** *n* (*med*) a drug (eg caffeine, amphetamine) that increases mental alertness.

CO *abbrev*: Colombia (IVR); Colorado (US state); combined operations; Commanding Officer; Commonwealth Office; conscientious objector; Crown Office.

Co (*chem*) *symbol*: cobalt.

Co. *abbrev*: Company; County.

co- see **com-**.

c/o *abbrev*: care of.

coacervate /kō-as'ər-vāt (or -ûr')/ *vt* to heap; to cause to mass together. ◆ *adj* heaped together. ◆ *n* (also **coacerva'tion**) a reversible aggregation of particles of an emulsoid into liquid droplets before flocculation. [L *coacervāre*, *-ātum*, from *acervus* heap]

coach /kōch/ *n* a *usu* single-deck bus for long-distance travel or for tourists and sightseers; a railway carriage; a large, closed, four-wheeled carriage, *esp* one for state occasions or for conveyance of passengers; formerly, a private carriage; a ship's cabin near the stern; a private tutor; a professional trainer in athletics, football, etc. ◆ *vt* to carry in a coach (*archaic*); to tutor, instruct, prepare for an examination, sporting event, etc. ◆ *vi* to go by coach; to act as tutor; to study with a tutor. [Fr *coche*, from Hung *kocsi*, from *Kocs* in Hungary]
▪ **coach'able** *adj* (of a person) receptive to coaching; (of a skill) able to be passed on or improved by coaching. **coach'ee** or **coach'y** *n* (*inf*) a coachman. **coach'er** *n* a person who coaches; a coach-horse. **coach'ing** *n* travelling by coach; tutoring; instruction. **coach'y** *adj* relating to a coach. ◆ *n* see **coachee** above.
◻ **coach bolt** *n* a large mushroom-headed bolt used for securing wood to masonry. **coach box** *n* the driver's seat on a horse-drawn coach. **coach'builder** *n* a craftsman who builds the bodies of cars, lorries, railway carriages, etc. **coach'building** *n*. **coach'built** *adj* (of a vehicle body) built to individual specifications and constructed by coachbuilders. **coach'-class** *adj* (*N Am*) economy-class. **coach'dog** *n* a spotted dog, formerly kept as an attendant on carriages, a Dalmatian dog. **coach'-hire** *n* money paid for the use of a hired coach. **coach'-horn** *n* a post-horn. **coach'-horse** *n* a horse used for pulling a coach. **coach house** *n* a building in which a coach or carriage is kept. **coaching inn** *n* (*hist*) an inn standing on a route used by horse-drawn coaches, providing overnight rest for travellers and stabling for horses. **coach'line** *n* a decorative line along the body of a motor vehicle. **coach'load** *n* the number of people a coach can carry. **coach'man** *n* the driver of a coach; a servant employed to drive a private carriage. **coach'-office** *n* a coach booking office. **coach party** *n* a group of people travelling by coach. **coach road** *n* formerly, a road for coaches, *esp* one kept in reasonable repair for mail coaches. **coach screw** *n* a large square-headed screw. **coach'-stand** *n* a place where coaches stand for hire. **coach tour** *n* a holiday or outing on which people travel from place to place by coach. **coach'-way** *n*. **coach'-wheel** *n*. **coach'whip** *n* a coachman's whip; a kind of whip snake. **coach'whip-bird** *n* either of two Australian birds of the genus *Psophodes*, that utter a sound like the crack of a whip. **coach'wood** *n* an Australian tree (*Ceratopetalum apetalum*), yielding a light cross-grained wood used in furniture-making and (formerly) coachbuilding; this wood. **coach'work** *n* vehicle bodywork.

coact¹ /kō-akt'/ *vi* to act together.
▪ **coaction** /kō-ak'shən/ *n* joint action; mutual relations, *esp* between organisms in a community. **cōac'tive** *adj* acting together. **cōactiv'ity** *n*.

coact² /kō-akt'/ (*obs*) *vt* to compel. [L *cōgere*, *cōāctum* to compel]
▪ **coaction** /kō-ak'shən/ *n* compulsion. **coac'tive** *adj* compulsory.

coad. *abbrev*: coadjutor.

coadapted /kō-ə-dap'tid/ *adj* mutually adapted.
▪ **coadapta'tion** *n*.

coadjacent /kō-ə-jās'ənt/ *adj* contiguous.
▪ **coadja'cency** *n*.

coadjutant /kō-aj'ə-tənt/ *adj* mutually helping, co-operating. ◆ *n* a person who helps or co-operates with another. [L *adjūtor* a helper, from *ad* to, and *juvāre* to help]
▪ **coadj'utor** *n* a bishop appointed as assistant to a diocesan bishop; (also *fem* **coadj'utress** or **coadj'utrix**) an associate. **coadj'utorship** *n*.

coadunate /kō-ad'ū-nāt/ (*biol* and *phys*) *vt* to unite; to combine. ◆ *adj* combined. [L *adūnāre*, *-ātum* to unite, from *ad* to, and *unus* one]
▪ **coadūnā'tion** *n*. **coad'ūnātive** *adj*.

co-agent /kō-ā'jənt/ *n* a joint agent.
▪ **co-ā'gency** *n*.

coagulate /kō-ag'yə-lāt or -ū-/ *vt* to cause to curdle, clot, or form into a semisolid mass by a chemical reaction. ◆ *vi* to curdle, clot, or thicken into a semisolid mass. ◆ *n* a semisolid mass produced by this process. ◆ *adj* clotted (*rare*); curdled. [L *coāgulāre*, *-ātum*, from *agere* to drive]

■ **cōagūlabil'ity** *n*. **cōag'ūlable** *adj*. **cōag'ūlant** *n* a substance that causes or facilitates coagulation. **cōag'ūlāse** *n* any enzyme that causes coagulation of the blood. **cōagūlā'tion** *n*. **cōag'ūlātive** *adj*. **cōag'ulator** *n*. **cōag'ūlatory** *adj*. **cōag'ūlum** *n* (*pl* **cōag'ūla** /-ə/) a coagulated mass.

◻ **coagulation factor** same as **clotting factor** (see under **clot**).

coaita /*kō-ī-tä'* or *kō-ī'tə*/ *n* the red-faced spider monkey (*Ateles paniscus*), of S America. [Tupí]

coal /*kōl*/ *n* a firm, brittle, generally black combustible carbonaceous rock derived from vegetable matter; a piece of this rock; charcoal (*obs*); a piece of charcoal, *esp* glowing; a cinder; an ember. ◆ *vi* to take in coal. ◆ *vt* to supply with coal; to char. [OE *col*; cognate with ON *kol*, Ger *Kohle*]

■ **coal'er** *n* a ship or train which transports coal. **coal'y** *adj* of or like coal; covered with coal.

◻ **coal'ball** *n* a calcareous nodule found in coal. **coal'-bed** *n* a stratum of coal. **coal'-black** *adj* black as coal, very black. **coal'-box** *n* a box for holding coal; a shell that emits black smoke (*milit sl*). **coal'-brass** *n* iron pyrites found with coal. **coal bunker** *n* a box, recess or compartment for storing coal. **coal cellar** *n* a cellar or similar place for storing coal. **coal'-cutter** *n* a machine for undercutting a coal-bed. **coal dust** *n* coal in fine powder. **coal'face** *n* the exposed surface of coal in a mine (see also **at the coalface** below). **coal'field** *n* a district or area containing coal strata. **coal'-fired** *adj* burning or fuelled by coal. **coal'fish** *n* a dusky fish (*Pollachius virens*) of the cod family (also called **coley**, **saithe** or (*US*) **pollack**). **coal'-flap** or **coal'-plate** *n* a flap or plate covering the entrance from the pavement to a coal cellar. **coal gas** *n* the mixture of gases produced by the distillation of coal, used for lighting and heating. **coal heaver** *n* a person employed to carry or move coal. **coal hole** *n* a small coal cellar; a hole in the pavement for filling a coal cellar. **coal'house** *n* a covered-in place for keeping coal. **coaling station** *n* a port at which ships take on coal. **coal'man** *n* a man who sells and carries coal. **coal'master** *n* the owner or lessee of a coalfield. **Coal Measures** *n pl* (*geol*) the uppermost division of the Carboniferous. **coal merchant** *n* a dealer in coal. **coal'mine** or **coal'pit** *n* a mine or pit from which coal is dug. **coal'miner** *n*. **coal mouse** see **coal tit** below. **coal oil** *n* (*N Am*) rock oil, shale-oil, paraffin. **coal owner** *n* someone who owns a colliery. **coal plant** *n* a fossil plant of the Carboniferous strata. **coal'-porter** *n* a person who carries coal. **coal pot** *n* a cooking device consisting of an iron grid over a raised iron bowl containing charcoal. **Coal Sack** *n* (*astron*) a dark patch in the Milky Way. **coal scuttle** *n* a fireside container for holding coal. **coal tar** *n* a thick, black, opaque liquid formed when coal is distilled. **coal tit** or **cole tit** *n* a dark species of tit (*Parus ater*), with greyish plumage on its back and a black head marked with white patches at the nape (also **coal titmouse**, **cole titmouse** or **coal mouse**). **coal'-trimmer** *n* someone who stores or shifts coal on board vessels. **coal'-whipper** *n* someone who unloads coal on board vessels.

■ **at the coalface** (*fig*) employed in physical or practical work or directly involved with production, as opposed to administrative or managerial work; working in an exposed, difficult or dangerous situation. **blow the coals** to excite passion, foment strife. **carry coals to Newcastle** to take a thing where it is already most abundant. **haul** or **call over the coals** to reprimand, from the discipline applied to heretics. **heap coals of fire on someone's head** to excite someone's remorse and repentance by returning good for evil (from Bible, Romans 12.20).

coalesce /*kō-ə-les'*/ *vi* to grow together or unite into one whole; to fuse. [L *coalēscere*, from *alēscere* to grow up, increase]

■ **coalesc'ence** *n* growing into each other; fusion. **coalesc'ent** *adj*.

Coalite® /*kō'ə-līt*/ *n* a smokeless fuel produced by low-temperature carbonization of coal.

coalition /*kō-ə-lish'ən*/ *n* the act of merging into one mass or body; a combination or alliance short of union, *esp* of states or political parties for some specific purpose. [L *coalitiō*; see **coalesce**]

■ **cōali'tional** *adj*. **cōali'tioner** *n*. **cōali'tionism** *n*. **cōali'tionist** *n*.

■ **coalition government** government by a coalition of parties, sometimes called a national government.

coalize or **-ise** /*kō'ə-līz*/ *vt* and *vi* to bring or come into coalition. [Fr *coaliser*]

Coalport /*kōl'pōrt* or *-pört*/ *n* patterned porcelain ware made at *Coalport*, near Shrewsbury, during the 19c.

coaming /*kō'ming*/ (*naut*) *n* (*usu in pl*) a raised framework around the edges of the hatches of a ship to keep water out. [Origin unknown]

Coanda effect /*kō-an'də i-fekt'*/ *n* the tendency of liquid, when it encounters a curved surface, to run along it. [Henri Marie *Coanda* (1885–1972), French engineer]

coapt /*kō-apt'*/ *vt* to adjust. [L *coaptāre*, from *aptāre*, to fit]

■ **coaptā'tion** *n* adjustment; the reuniting of separated tissue or bone (*med*).

coarb, also **comarb** /*kō'ärb*/ (*hist*) *n* the head of a family in an Irish sept; an ecclesiastical successor. [Ir *comharba* successor]

coarctate /*kō-ärk'tāt*/ *adj* compressed; constricted, narrowed. ◆ *vi* (*esp* of the aorta) to become constricted; to narrow. [L *coar(c)tāre*, *-ātum*, from *ar(c)tāre* to draw together]

■ **cōarctā'tion** *n*.

coarse /*kōrs* or *körs*/ *adj* common, base, inferior; rough; rude; uncivil; harsh; gross; large in grain, fibre or mesh, etc; without refinement; roughly approximate. [From phrase 'in course', hence *ordinary*]

■ **coarse'ly** *adv*. **coars'en** *vt* and *vi* to make or become coarse. **coarse'ness** *n*. **coars'ish** *adj* somewhat coarse.

◻ **coarse fish** *n* freshwater fish other than those of the salmon family (cf **game fish**). **coarse fishing** *n*. **coarse'-grained** *adj* large in grain; coarse-natured; gross. **coarse metal** *n* impure cuprous sulphide obtained in the smelting process.

coast /*kōst*/ or (*obs*) **cost** or **coste** /*kōst*, (also, eg *Spenser*) *kost*/ *n* the border of land next to the sea; the seashore; (often with *cap*; with *the*) the Pacific coast of the USA (*N Am*); a side (*obs*); a limit or border (*obs*); a region (*obs*); direction (*obs*); footing, terms (*Spenser*); a hill suitable for tobogganing (*N Am*); an act or period of sliding down a slope. ◆ *vi* to sail along or near a coast; to travel downhill on a sledge, on a cycle without pedalling or in a motor car out of gear; to glide; to succeed or proceed with minimum effort; (also *obs* **cost**) to approach (*obs*). ◆ *vt* to sail by or near to. [OFr *coste* (Fr *côte*), from L *costa* rib, side]

■ **coast'al** *adj*. **coasteer'ing** *n* an adventure sport involving travelling along cliffs before jumping down from them into the sea. **coast'er** *n* a vessel engaged in coastal trade; a person or thing that coasts; a container or mat for a decanter or glasses on a table; in W Africa, a European resident; (*usu* with *cap*) in NZ, an inhabitant or native of the West Coast of South Island. **coast'ing** *adj* keeping near the coast; trading between ports in the same country. ◆ *n* the act of sailing, or of trading, along the coast; sliding downhill. **coast'ward** or **coast'wards** *adv* toward(s) the coast. **coast'wise** *adv* along or by the coast. ◆ *adj* carried on along the coast.

◻ **coast'guard** *n* an organization with responsibility for watching coastal waters to prevent smuggling and illegal fishing, to assist shipping, and for life-saving; a member of this organization. **coast'guardsman** *n* (chiefly *US*). **coast'land** *n* land along a coast. **coast'line** *n* the line or boundary of a coast; shoreline. **coastline effect** see **shore effect** under **shore**[1]. **coast-to-coast** *adj* covering the whole country, nationwide. **coast'-waiter** *n* (*hist*) a custom-house officer for coasting shipping.

■ **the coast is clear** there is no obstacle or danger in the way.

coat[1] /*kōt*/ *n* an outer garment with sleeves; an overcoat; the hair or wool of an animal; any covering; a membrane or layer, as of paint, etc; a coat of arms (see below); a skirt or petticoat (*dialect*). ◆ *vt* to clothe; to cover with a coat or layer. [OFr *cote* (Fr *cotte*), from LL *cottus*, *cotta* a tunic; the further ety is uncertain]

■ **coat'ee** *n* a short close-fitting coat. **coat'er** *n* a worker, machine, etc that applies a layer or covering. **coat'ing** *n* a covering, layer; cloth for coats. **coat'less** *adj* without a coat or a coat of arms.

◻ **coat'-armour** *n* a coat of arms, or heraldically embroidered garment worn over armour; armorial devices. **coat'-card** *n* a card bearing the representation of a coated figure, the king, queen or jack (now called *court card*). **coat'-dress** *n* a tailored dress with fastening from neckline to hem, *usu* worn without a coat or jacket (also **coat'-frock**). **coated lens** *n* a lens coated with a thin film of transparent material to reduce the reflection of light from its surface. **coat'hanger** *n* a curved piece of wood, etc, with a hook, by which clothes may be hung and kept in shape. **coat of arms** *n* the family insignia embroidered on the surcoat worn over the hauberk, or coat of mail; the heraldic bearings of a person, family or organization. **coat of mail** *n* a piece of armour for the upper part of the body, made of interlinked metal scales or rings. **coat-of-mail' shell** *n* a marine mollusc, the chiton. **coat'rack** or **coat'stand** *n* a rack or stand with pegs for hanging coats on. **coat'-style** *adj* of a shirt, buttoning all the way down the front. **coat tails** *n pl* the long back-pieces of a tail coat.

■ **on someone's coat tails** achieving one's position as a result of the promotion or advancement of a person to whom one has attached oneself, and not by one's own merit. **trail one's coat** (**tails**) (*orig Irish*) to be aggressive, pick a quarrel (**coat'-trailing** *n*). **turn one's coat** to change one's principles, or to turn from one party to another.

coat[2], **coate** Shakespearean forms of **quote**.

coati /*kō-ä'tē*, *-ti* or *kə-wä'tē*/ *n* a tropical American plantigrade carnivorous mammal of the genera *Nasua* and *Nasuella*, related to, but larger than, the raccoons (also **coati-mun'di** or **coati-mon'di**). [Tupí]

co-author /*kō-ö'thər*/ *n* a joint author. ◆ *vt* to be the co-author of.

coax¹ /kōks/ vt to persuade by fondling or flattery; to humour or soothe; to pet. [**cokes** a simpleton]
■ **coax** or **coax'er** n. **coax'ingly** adv.

coax² or **co-ax** /kō'aks/ n short for **coaxial cable**.

coaxial /kō-ak'si-əl/ adj having the same axis.
■ **coax'ially** adv.
❑ **coaxial cable** n a cable consisting of one or more **coaxial pairs**, each a central conductor within an outer tubular conductor.

cob¹ /kob/ n a short-legged strong horse; a male swan (also **cob'-swan**); a lump (esp of coal, ore or clay); a rounded object; a cobloaf; the axis of a head of maize, a corncob; a cobnut; an irregularly-shaped Spanish-American dollar of the 17c–19c (also **cob money**). [Perh connected with **cop²**]
■ **cobb'y** adj like a cob; stout, brisk, lively, arrogant (dialect).
❑ **cob'loaf** n a rounded, round-headed or misshapen loaf; an archaic expression of contempt. **cob'nut** n the nut of the European hazel; the European hazel; a children's game played with nuts. **cob pipe** n a tobacco pipe made from a corncob.
■ **have a cob on** (dialect) to be in a bad temper.

cob² /kob/ n (in parts of Britain and in New Zealand) a building material composed of clay and chopped straw; a building constructed of this material. [Origin unknown]
❑ **cob cottage** n. **cob wall** n.

cob³ /kob/ (dialect) n a wicker basket used by sowers. [Origin unknown]

cob⁴ /kob/ vt to strike; to thump on the buttocks. [Origin uncertain; perh onomatopoeic]

cob⁵ or **cobb** /kob/ (archaic) n a gull, esp the greater black-backed gull. [Cf Du kob gull]

cobalamin /kō-bal'ə-min or -bol'/ n a complex molecule containing cobalt that is a constituent of vitamin B₁₂. [cobalt and vitamin]

cobalt /kō'bolt/ n a metallic element (symbol Co; atomic no 27), having similarities to nickel; a blue pigment prepared from it (also **cō'balt-blue**). ♦ adj of this deep-blue colour. [Ger Kobalt, from Kobold a demon, a nickname given by the German miners, because they supposed it to be a mischievous and hurtful metal]
■ **cobalt'ic** adj. **cobaltif'erous** adj containing cobalt. **cō'baltite** n a mineral containing cobalt, arsenic, and sulphur (also **cobalt glance**).
❑ **cobalt bloom** n erythrite. **cobalt bomb** n a suggested bomb consisting of a hydrogen bomb encased in cobalt, with increased destructive qualities resulting from the cobalt-60 dust released. **cobalt-60** n a radioactive isotope of cobalt used as a source of gamma rays, eg in radiotherapy.

cobb see **cob⁵**.

cobber /kob'ər/ (Aust and NZ; inf) n mate, chum, buddy. [Perh from dialect cob to take a liking to]

cobble¹ /kob'l/ or **cobblestone** /-stōn/ n a rounded stone, esp formerly used in paving. ♦ vt to pave with cobblestones. [Ety dubious]

cobble² /kob'l/ vt to mend shoes; to patch up, assemble, put together, or mend hastily or with parts or materials from various sources (often with together or up). ♦ n see **coble**. [Origin unknown]
■ **cobb'ler** n a person who cobbles or mends shoes; an iced drink made up of wine or spirits, sugar, lemon, etc; a (usu fruit) pie with a thick crunchy topping; (in pl) nonsense (inf); (in pl) testicles (sl). **cobb'lery** n. **cobb'ling** n.
❑ **cobbler's pegs** n an Australian weed with peg-like bristles on the flower-heads. **cobbler's punch** n a hot drink made of beer, with the addition of spirit, sugar and spice.

cobble³ see **coble**.

Cobb salad /kob sal'əd/ n a salad dish including lettuce, bacon, chicken, tomato, and avocado. [Robert Cobb (died 1970), US restaurateur]

Cobdenism /kob'də-ni-zm/ n the policy of Richard Cobden (1804–65), the English 'Apostle of Free Trade'.
■ **Cob'denite** n a supporter of Cobdenism, esp a free-trader.

cobelligerent /kō-bi-lij'ə-rənt/ adj co-operating in warfare (also n).

cobia /kō'bi-ə/ n the sergeant fish. [Perh of W Ind origin]

coble or **cobble** /kōb'l or kob'l/ n a small flat-bottomed boat for use on rivers and estuaries (Scot); a single-masted sea-fishing boat with a flat bottom and square stern (NE Eng). [Cf Welsh ceubal a hollow trunk, a boat]

COBOL or **Cobol** /kō'bol/ n an internationally accepted computer programming language, for general commercial use, which uses statements in English. [Common business oriented language]

COBR or **COBRA** /kō'brə/ n a British government committee that is convened to co-ordinate action in cases of national emergency. [Cabinet Office Briefing Rooms, in which it meets]

cobra /kō'brə or kob'rə/ n any poisonous snake of the genus Naja, found in India and Africa, which dilates the skin of its neck so as to resemble a hood. [Port cobra (de capello) snake (of the hood)]
■ **cob'ric** adj. **cob'riform** adj like or related to the cobra.

coburg /kō'bûrg/ n a thin fabric of worsted with cotton or silk, twilled on one side; the name of various pieces of bakery and confectionery, including a type of round loaf and a type of sponge cake (also adj). [Coburg, in Germany]

cobweb /kob'web/ n a spider's web or net; any snare or device intended to entrap; anything flimsy or easily broken; anything that obscures. ♦ vt to cover with cobwebs. [Prob attercop-web; see **attercop** and **web**]
■ **cobwebb'ery** n. **cob'webby** adj.

cobza /kob'zə/ n a short-necked, ten-stringed, unfretted Romanian folk-instrument. [Romanian cobză]

coca /kō'kə/ n either of two Andean shrubs (Erythroxylon coca or E. truxinense) of the family Linaceae, whose leaves contain cocaine. [Sp, from Quechua]

Coca-Cola® /kō-kə-kō'lə/ n a carbonated soft drink first made in the USA (often shortened to **Coke**). ♦ adj denoting the spread of American culture to other parts of the world.

Cocagne, **Cocaigne** same as **Cockaigne**.

cocaine /kō'kān/ n an alkaloid obtained from coca-leaves or produced synthetically; an addictive narcotic used medicinally as a local anaesthetic (often shortened to **coke**; drug sl). [coca and **-ine¹**]
■ **cocain'ism** n a morbid condition induced by addiction to cocaine. **cocain'ist** n. **cocainizā'tion** or **-s-** n. **cocain'ize** or **-ise** vt to anaesthetize with cocaine.

coccid, etc see under **coccus**.

coccineous /kok-sin'i-əs/ (obs) adj bright-red. [L coccineus, from coccum cochineal]

cocco /kok'ō/ or **coco** /kō'kō/ n (pl **cocc'os** or **co'cos**) the taro or other edible araceous tuber.

coccolite /kok'ō-līt/ n a variety of pyroxene; a small rounded body found in chalk formations, consisting of microscopic plates secreted by extinct algal plankton (also **cocc'olith**). [Gr kokkos a berry, and lithos a stone]

coccus /kok'əs/ n (pl **cocci** /kok'sī/) a one-seeded portion of a dry fruit that breaks up at maturity (bot); a spherical bacterium (zool). [New L, from Gr kokkos a berry]
■ **coccal** /kok'əl/ adj. **coccid** /kok'sid/ n and adj (any insect) of the family **Coccidae** /kok'si-dē/, which includes the scale insects, or of the superfamily **Coccoidea**. **coccidioidomycosis** /-oi-dō-mī-kō'sis/ n (also **coccidiomyco'sis**) infection resulting from the inhalation of the spores of the fungus Coccidioides immitis, occurring either as an influenza-like respiratory illness, or as a severe, progressive disease affecting the skin, viscera, nervous system and lungs. **coccidiosis** /kok-sid-i-ōs'is/ n a contagious infection of birds and animals by coccidia. **coccidiostat** /kok-sid'i-ō-stat/ n an agent which builds up a resistance by the host to coccidia by retarding the latter's lifecycle, etc; any of various drugs used to prevent the development of coccidium-caused diseases, often added to feedstuffs or drinking water. **coccidium** /kok-sid'i-əm/ n (pl **coccid'ia**) a parasitic protozoan of the order **Eucoccid'ia**. **coccoid** /kok'oid/ adj. **Cocc'ulus** n a tropical genus of climbing plants (family Menispermaceae).
❑ **cocculus indicus** n the dried fruit of Anamirta cocculus (family Menispermaceae), narcotic and poisonous.

coccyx /kok'siks/ (anat) n (pl **coccyges** /kok-sī'jēz/) the terminal triangular bone of the vertebral column in man and certain apes, consisting of four tiny bones fused together. [Gr kokkyx, -ȳgos cuckoo, coccyx (its shape resembling a cuckoo's bill)]
■ **coccygeal** /kok-sij'i-əl/ or **coccyg'ian** adj.

coch /kōch/ (Spenser) n same as **coach**.

co-chair /kō'chār/ n a joint chairperson. ♦ vt to act as joint chairperson of (a meeting, etc).

Cochin /koch'in/ n a large feathery-legged domestic hen (also **Cochin-China** /-chī'nə/). [Orig from Cochin-China, now part of Vietnam]

cochineal /koch'i-nēl or -nēl'/ n a scarlet dyestuff consisting of the dried bodies of the female **cochineal insect**, used as a colouring for foodstuffs, etc; the insect itself (Dactylopius coccus), that feeds on cacti in Mexico, the West Indies, etc. [Sp cochinilla, dimin of L coccinus scarlet, from coccum (Gr kokkos) a berry, as the similar coccid insect was formerly supposed to be the berry or seed of an oak]

cochlea /kok'li-ə/ n (pl **coch'leae**) anything spiral-shaped, esp a snail-shell; the spiral cavity of the inner ear (anat). [L coc(h)lea a shell, screw, from Gr kochlias a snail]
■ **coch'lear** /-li-ər/ adj relating to the cochlea of the ear; spoon-shaped. **coch'lear** or **cochleār'e** n (L) a spoon. **Cochlear'ia** n pl the

scurvy-grass genus. **cochlear'iform** adj spoon-shaped. **coch'leāte** or **coch'leated** adj twisted spirally.

cock¹ /kok/ n a male bird, esp of the domestic fowl (also often as combining form, eg cockbird, cock-robin, cock-sparrow); a male crab, lobster or salmon; a weathercock; (sometimes as old cock) a familiar form of address to a man (sl); a strutting chief or leader (sl); anything set erect; a tap; part of the lock of a gun, held back by a spring, which, when released by the trigger, produces the discharge; the penis (vulgar sl); nonsense (inf). ◆ vt to set erect or upright (often with up); to set up the brim of; to draw back (eg the cock of a gun); to turn up or to one side; to tilt up (one's head, ears, etc) knowingly, inquiringly or scornfully. ◆ vi to strut; to swagger. [OE coc; ON kokkr]
■ **cocked** adj set erect; turned up or to one side; (of a gun) with the cock drawn back, ready to fire. **cock'er** n someone who follows cockfighting; a cocker spaniel (see below); a term of familiarity (sl). **cock'erel** n a young cock (see also **cockle⁵**). **cock'ily** adv. **cock'iness, cocks'iness** or **cox'iness** n. **cock'y, cocks'y** or **cox'y** adj self-important, bumptious; pert.
□ **cock-a-doodle-doo'** n (imit) the crow of a cock. ◆ vi to crow. **cock-a-hoop'** adj in exultant spirits; boastful. **cockaleekie** see cockieleekie below. **cockalō'rum** n a bumptious little person; a boys' jumping game. **cock'amamie** adj (US sl) ridiculous, incredible. **cock'-and-bull'** adj (of a story) fabricated and incredible. **cock'-broth** n the broth made from a boiled cock. **cockchafer** n see separate entry. **cock'-crow** n early morning, when cocks crow. **cocked hat** n an old-fashioned three-cornered hat; a small triangle on a navigational chart formed in taking account of three bearing measurements (naut). **cocker spaniel** n a small spaniel used to retrieve birds in game shooting. **cock'eye** n a squinting eye. **cockeye bob** or **cockeyed bob** n (Aust sl) a sudden thunderstorm; a cyclone. **cock'eyed** adj having a cockeye; off the straight, awry (inf); tipsy (inf); crazy, absurd (inf). **cock'fight** or **cock'fighting** n a fight or contest between gamecocks; a fight. **cockhorse'** n a child's imaginary or toy horse. ◆ adj prancing, proud. ◆ adv properly **a-cockhorse'** (ie on cockhorse) on horseback; exultingly. **cockieleek'ie** or **cockyleek'y** or **cock(-)a(-)leek'ie** n (Scot) soup made from a fowl and leeks. **cocking piece** n a piece of wood used to build a roof out over eaves (also **sprocket**). **cock'laird** n (Scot) the owner of a small farm, who farms it in person. **cock'loft** n a small room just under the roof. **cock'match** n a cockfight. **cock-of-the-rock'** n a S American bird of the family Cotingidae. **cock-pad(d)le** or **cock-paidle** see **paddle³**. **cock'pit** n a sheltered depression in the deck of a yacht or small ship; (in aircraft) a compartment in the fuselage, usu for the pilot or rarely for the passenger(s); the driver's seat in a racing car; a pit or enclosed space where gamecocks fought; a frequent battleground; part of a ship-of-war's lower regions used for the wounded in action. **cock's'-comb** or **cocks'comb** n the comb or crest on a cock's head; a jester's cap; a crest-like crystalline mineral aggregate (as in cockscomb pyrites); a name for various plants, esp Celosia cristata (family Amarantaceae), with a fasciated inflorescence like a cock's comb, also yellow rattle (genus Rhinanthus), and sainfoin; a coxcomb. **cocks'foot** n a Eurasian grass (Dactylis glomerata) with inflorescences like a cock's foot. **cock'-shoot** n (obs) a glade where woodcock were netted as they shot through. **cock'shot** n a cockshy. **cock'shut** n (archaic or dialect) twilight, prob referring to the time when poultry are shut up for the night. **cock'shy** n a throw at a target, orig a cock, for amusement; an object set up for this purpose; an object of criticism or ridicule. **cock-sparr'ow** n a male sparrow; a small, lively person. **cock'spur** n a spur on the leg of a gamecock; a type of catch used on casement windows; a hawthorn (Crataegus crusgalli) with long thorns and orange autumn foliage. **cockspur grass** n (Echinochloa crusgalli) an invasive grass of warmer, orig only tropical, climates. **cock'sucker** n (vulgar sl) a contemptible person who attempts to ingratiate himself with his superiors; a toady; a male homosexual. **cock'sure** adj irritatingly self-confident or self-assured. **cock'surely** adv. **cock'sureness** n. **cock'teaser** n (vulgar sl) a woman who deliberately provokes a man's sexual arousal, then refuses sexual intercourse. **cock-thropp'led** or **cock-thrapp'led** adj of a horse, bending the windpipe on bridling. **cock'throwing** n the old sport of throwing sticks at a cock. **cock'-up** adj turned up; rising above the tops of the other letters, superior (printing). ◆ n (inf) a muddle, mess, confusion. **cockyleeky** see **cockieleekie** above.
■ **cock a snook** see under **snook²**. **cock of the walk** a person who (thinks he or she) is the most important in a group. **cock up** (inf) to do or perform very badly. **go off at half cock** (inf) to begin too soon, when not properly prepared. **knock into a cocked hat** to give a profound beating, to defeat. **live like fighting cocks** to have every luxury.

cock² /kok/ n a small pile of hay, dung, etc. ◆ vt to pile or heap into cocks. [Cf ON kökkr a lump]
■ **cocked** adj heaped up in cocks.

cock³ /kok/ (Shakesp) n a cockboat.

cock⁴ /kok/ (obs) altered form of **god**.
■ **cock and pie** see under **pie⁴**.

cock-a-bondy /kok-ə-bon'di/ or (inf) kok-i-bun'di/ n a fly for angling. [Welsh coch a bon ddu red, with black stem]

cockabully /ko-kə-bŭ'li/ or kok'ə-bŭ-li/ n any of various small freshwater fish of New Zealand. [Maori kokopu]

cockade /ko-kād'/ n a rosette worn on the hat as a badge. [Fr cocarde, from coq cock]
■ **cockād'ed** adj.

Cockaigne or **Cockayne** /ko-kān'/ n (orig in medieval story) an imaginary country of luxury and delight. [Ety doubtful]

cock-a-leekie see **cockieleekie** under **cock¹**.

cockalorum, cockamamie see under **cock¹**.

cockapoo /ko-kə-poo'/ n a cross between a cocker spaniel and a poodle.

cockatoo /ko-kə-too'/ n any of a number of large crested parrots (genus Kakatoe) of the Australian region; a small farmer (also **cock'y**) (Aust and NZ); a lookout (Aust inf). [Malay kakatua]
■ **cockatiel** or **cockateel** /-tēl'/ n a small crested parrot of Australia.
□ **cocky's joy** n (Aust sl) golden syrup.
■ **cow cocky** (Aust and NZ) a dairy farmer.

cockatrice /kok'ə-trēs or -trīs or -tris/ n a fabulous monster, a serpent with the wings of a bird and the head of a cock; a cock-like monster with a dragon's tail (heraldry); a prostitute (obs); a mischievous or treacherous person (fig). [OFr cocatris]

Cockayne see **Cockaigne**.

cockboat /kok'bōt/ n (also **cockle boat**) any small frail boat; a ship's small boat. [Obs cokke a small boat, from OFr coque]

cockchafer /kok'chā-fər/ n a large European flying beetle (Melolontha melolontha), with reddish-brown wing-cases and fan-like antennae, the larvae of which are a serious pest of farm and garden crops (also called **May beetle, May bug**). [cock¹ and chafer]

Cocker /kok'ər/ n a standard of accuracy and orthodoxy, esp in the phrase according to Cocker. [Edward Cocker (1631–75), author of a popular arithmetic book]

cocker¹ /kok'ər/ vt to pamper; to fondle; to indulge. [Ety doubtful; cf Du kokelen, OFr conqueliner to dandle]

cocker², **cockerel** see under **cock¹**.

cockernony /ko-kər-non'i/ (obs Scot) n the gathering of hair in a fillet; a coiffure; a pad of false hair; a starched cap. [Origin obscure]

cocket /kok'it/ n the custom-house seal (hist); a custom-house certificate. [Origin doubtful]

cockeye(d), **cockhorse** see under **cock¹**.

cockieleekie see under **cock¹**.

cockle¹ /kok'l/ n a large bivalve mollusc (Cardium edule or other species) with thick, ribbed, heart-shaped, equal-valved shell; its shell; a bivalve shell generally. [Fr coquille, from Gr konchylion, from konchē a cockle]
■ **cock'led** adj shelled like a cockle. **cock'ling** n the act of gathering cockles.
□ **cockle hat** n a hat bearing a scallop shell, the badge of a pilgrim. **cockle'man** n a cockle-fisherman. **cock'leshell** n the shell of a cockle; a frail boat.
■ **cockles of the heart** one's inmost heart.

cockle² /kok'l/ n a cornfield weed, esp now the corncockle. [OE coccel]
□ **cock'lebur** n a composite weed of the genus Xanthium; a spiny bur of this plant (also called **clotebur**).

cockle³ /kok'l/ n a pucker. ◆ vi to pucker. ◆ vt to cause to pucker. [Perh Fr coquiller to blister, from coquille; see **cockle¹**]

cockle⁴ /kok'l/ n a furnace or stove. [Perh Du kachel]

cockle⁵ /kok'l/ n a young man (also **cock'erel**). [See **cock¹**]
□ **cock'le-brained** adj foolish.

cockney /kok'ni/ n (often with cap) a person born in London, strictly within hearing of Bow Bells; London dialect, esp of the East End; a young snapper fish (Aust). ◆ adj (often with cap) characteristic of a Cockney. [ME coken-ey cock's egg, hence, an oddity; or perh connected with Fr coquin a rogue, from L coquus a cook]
■ **cock'neydom** n the domain of Cockneys. **cockneyficā'tion** n. **cock'neyfy** or **cock'nify** vt to make Cockney. **cock'neyish** adj. **cock'neyism** n a Cockney idiom or characteristic.

cockroach /kok'rōch/ n an orthopterous insect, the so-called black beetle. [Sp cucaracha woodlouse, cockroach]

cockscomb, cocksfoot, etc see under **cock¹**.

cockswain see **coxswain**.

cocktail¹ /kok'tāl/ n a mixed drink containing spirits; an appetizer consisting of eg seafood with a sauce; any mixture of substances or elements. ◆ *adj* (of food items) suitable to be served with cocktails. [**cock**[1] and **tail**[1]]

□ **cocktail bar** or **lounge** *n* a bar or room in a hotel or restaurant where cocktails and other spirits are served. **cocktail dress** *n* a dress for semi-formal wear. **cocktail shaker** or **mixer** *n* a container for mixing cocktails. **cocktail stick** *n* a small wooden or plastic stick with pointed ends for holding a cherry, olive, small sausage, etc when eaten with drinks.

■ **fruit cocktail** a salad of finely-diced fruit.

cocktail[2] /kok'tāl/ *n* an animal, *esp* a racehorse, of mixed breeding; a person of low breeding who pretends to be a gentleman; a horse with a docked tail.

■ **cock'tailed** *adj* having the tail cocked or tilted up.

cocky[1] see under **cock**[1].

cocky[2] see **cockatoo**.

cockyleeky see **cockieleekie** under **cock**[1].

coco[1] /kō'kō/ *n* (*pl* **cō'cos**) a tropical seaside palm tree (*Cocos nucifera*) with curving stem (also **co'co-palm**, **coconut palm** or **co'co-tree**), which produces the coconut. [Port and Sp *coco* a grimace, grinning face; applied to the nut from the three marks at the end of it, which resemble a grotesque face]

□ **coco-de-mer** /-də-mer'/ *n* (*Fr*) a palm tree of the Seychelles (*Lodoicea maldivica*); its large two-lobed nut. **coco fibre** *n* coir used as a growing medium in horticulture. **co'conut** less correctly **co'coanut** or **co'kernut** *n* a large edible nut, yielding **coconut butter** (or **coconut oil**) and **coconut milk**. **coconut crab** *n* the robber crab (qv under **rob**[1]). **coconut ice** *n* a kind of sweet made of coconut and sugar. **coconut matting** *n* matting made from the husk of the coconut. **coconut shy** *n* a fairground throwing game with coconuts as targets or as prizes.

■ **double coconut** the nut of the coco de mer.

coco[2] see **cocco**.

cocoa /kō'kō/ *n* the seed of the cacao or chocolate tree; a powder made from the seeds; a drink made from the powder; a light brown colour. [**cacao**]

□ **cocoa beans** *n pl* the seeds, *esp* when dried and fermented. **cocoa butter** or **cocoa fat** *n* a fat obtained from the seeds and used in confectionery, soaps, etc. **cocoa nibs** *n pl* cocoa beans shelled and bruised.

■ **I should cocoa** (*rhyming sl*; often *ironic*) I should say so.

cocoanut see under **coco**[1].

cocoa-wood see **coco-wood**.

co-codamol /kō-kō'də-mol/ *n* an analgesic containing a combination of *codeine* and paracet*amol*.

COCOM or **CoCom** /kō'kom/ *abbrev*: Co-ordinating Committee for Multilateral Export Controls (now replaced by the Wassenaar Agreement).

coconscious /kō-kon'shəs/ *adj* aware of the same things, or aware of various things within the same consciousness; relating to the coconscious. ◆ *n* mental processes in a subsidiary stream, apart from the main stream of consciousness.

■ **cōcon'sciousness** *n*.

cocoon /ko-koon'/ *n* the silken sheath spun by many insect larvae in passing into the pupa stage and by spiders for their eggs; the capsule in which earthworms and leeches lay their eggs; a preservative covering for military and other equipment; a cosy, secure place or situation. ◆ *vt* to wrap or preserve carefully as in a cocoon. [Fr *cocon*, from *coque* a shell, from L *concha* a shell]

■ **cocoon'ery** *n* a place for keeping silkworms when feeding and spinning cocoons. **cocoon'ing** *n*.

cocopan /kō'kə-pan/ *n* (in S Africa) a wagon on a narrow-gauge railway serving a mine. [Altered from Zulu '*ngkumbana*]

cocoplum /kō'kō-plum/ *n* a West Indian rosaceous tree (*Chrysobalanus icaco*); its edible fruit. [Sp *icaco*, and **plum**]

cocotte /ko-kot'/ *n* a small fireproof dish, *usu* for an individual portion, a casserole; a loose woman, prostitute. [Fr, child's word for hen, from *coq* cock]

co-counselling /kō-kown'sə-ling/ *n* a form of self-help therapy in which two people act alternately as client and counsellor.

coco-wood or **cocoa-wood** /kō'kō-wŭd/ *n* the wood of a West Indian mimosaceous tree, *Inga vera*; kokrawood.

cocoyam /kō'kō-yam/ *n* either of two W African food plants of the arum family, having edible corms. [**coco**[1] and **yam**]

coction /kok'shən/ *n* boiling; cooking. [L *coquere*, *coctum* to boil, cook]

■ **coc'tile** *adj* baked; hardened by fire, as a brick.

coculture /kō-kul'chər/ *vt* to grow (two or more organisms) in the same growing medium or culture; to grow (an organism) on or in more than one organic medium.

cocuswood /kō'kəs-wŭd/ *n* the so-called Jamaica ebony (*Brya ebenus*).

Cod. *abbrev*: Codex.

cod[1] /kod/ or **codfish** /kod'fish/ *n* a food-fish (*Gadus morrhua*) of northern seas; any fish of the genus *Gadus* or the family Gadidae. [Ety dubious]

■ **codd'er** *n* a cod fisherman or his boat. **cod'ling** *n* a small cod. □ **cod'-fisher** *n*. **cod'-fishery** *n*. **cod'-fishing** *n*. **cod-liver oil** *n* a medicinal oil extracted from the fresh liver of the common cod or related fish.

cod[2] /kod/ (*obs*) *n* a bag; a pod; the male genitals. [OE *codd* a small bag]

■ **codd'ed** *adj* enclosed in a cod. **codd'ing** *adj* (*Shakesp*) lecherous. □ **cod'piece** *n* a pouch once worn by men in the front of tight hose or breeches.

cod[3] /kod/ (*Scot*) *n* a pillow or cushion. [ON *koddi* a pillow]

cod[4] /kod/ (*sl*) *n* a jest; a hoax. ◆ *adj* mock, sham; done, intended, etc as a joke or take-off. ◆ *vt* (**codd'ing**; **codd'ed**) to hoax; to poke fun at. [Ety dubious]

■ **codol'ogy** *n* impressive-sounding nonsense.

cod[5] /kod/ (*dialect*) *n* a fellow, chap; a codger. [See **codger**]

c.o.d. *abbrev*: cash (or collect) on delivery.

coda /kō'də/ *n* a passage forming the completion of a piece, rounding it off to a satisfactory conclusion (*music*); any similar passage or piece in a story, dance sequence, etc. [Ital, from L *cauda* a tail]

■ **codett'a** *n* (*music*) a short coda.

codder see under **cod**[1].

coddle /kod'l/ *vt* to pamper, mollycoddle; to cook (*esp* eggs) gently over hot water. ◆ *n* an effeminate person. [Ety dubious]

■ **codd'ler** *n*.

code /kōd/ *n* a system of words, letters or symbols which represent sentences or other words, to ensure economy or secrecy in transmission; a cipher; a set of rules and characters for converting one form of data to another (*comput*); the characters of the resulting representation of data (*comput*); the pattern of holes in a punched card or paper tape which represents a character or instructions; a collection or digest of laws; a system of rules and regulations (*specif* regarding education); established principles or standards (of art, moral conduct, etc); a volume; a system of signals. ◆ *vt* to codify; to express in code. [Fr *code*; see **codex**]

■ **co'der** *n* a person who writes something in code; a computer programmer. **codificā'tion** /kod- or kōd-/ *n*. **codifīer** /kod' or kōd'/ or **cōd'ist** *n* a person who codifies. **codify** /kod' or kōd'/ *vt* to put into the form of a code; to digest; to systematize. **cod'ing** *n* and *adj*. □ **code'book** *n* a book containing the words, symbols, etc of a code or codes. **code'-breaker** *n* a person who tries to interpret secret codes. **code'-breaking** *n*. **code'name** or **code'-number** *n* a name or number used for convenience, economy, secrecy, etc. **code'-named** *adj*. **code of conduct** or **code of practice** *n* an established method or set of rules for dealing with, behaving in, etc a particular situation. **code'-sharing** *n* a system by which two airlines independently sell seats on the same flight. **code'word** *n* a word with a secret meaning; a codename.

codec /kō'dek/ (*electronics*) *n* an apparatus for encoding and decoding signals. [*code* and *decode*]

codeclination /kō-dek-li-nā'shən/ *n* polar distance.

codeine /kō'dēn/ or /-di-ēn/ *n* an alkaloid, derived from morphine, used as an analgesic and antitussive. [Gr *kōdeia* poppy-head]

co-dependant or (*esp US*) **co-dependent** /kō-di-pen'dənt/ (*psychol*) *n* a person who seeks to fulfil his or her own emotional needs by caring for or controlling a dependant.

■ **co-depend'ency** *n*. **co-depend'ent** *adj*.

co-determination /kō-di-tûr-mi-nā'shən/ *n* a process of joint decision-making by employers and employees.

codex /kō'deks/ *n* (*pl* **codices** /kōd'i-sēz/) a code; a manuscript volume. [L *cōdex* or *caudex*, *-icis* the trunk of a tree, a set of tablets, a book]

■ **cōdicolog'ical** *adj*. **cōdicol'ogy** *n* the study of manuscript volumes.

codger /koj'ər/ (*inf*) *n* a man, a chap, *esp* if old and eccentric. [Prob a variant of **cadger**]

codicil /kod'i-sil/ or /kō'di-sil/ *n* a supplement to a will. [L *cōdicillus*, dimin of *cōdex*]

■ **codicill'ary** *adj*.

codicology see under **codex**.

codification, etc see under **code**.

codilla /kō-dil'ə/ n the coarsest part of hemp or flax. [Dimin of Ital *coda*, from L *cauda* a tail]

codille /kō-dil'/ n a situation in ombre when the challenger loses. [Fr]

codling[1] /kod'ling/ or **codlin** /kod'lin/ n a variety of elongated apple. [Ety uncertain]
❑ **codling moth** or **codlin moth** n a brownish-gold moth (*Cydia pomonella*), whose larvae are a common pest of apples, quinces, pears, etc.

codling[2] see under **cod**[1].

codology see under **cod**[4].

codomain /kō'də-mān/ (*maths*) n the set containing all the possible values of a particular function.

codominant /kō-dom'i-nənt/ adj (of a pair of alleles) expressing themselves equally in heterozygotes (*genetics*); (of two or more species) sharing domination of an area (*ecology*). [**co-** and **dominant**]

codon /kō'don/ (*biol*) n a triplet of three consecutive bases in DNA or in messenger RNA, which specifies a particular amino acid in protein synthesis. [**code** and **-on**]

codpiece see under **cod**[2].

co-driver /kō'drī-vər/ n one of two alternating drivers, *esp* in a race or rally.

codswallop or **cod's-wallop** /kodz'wo-ləp/ (*inf*) n nonsense, rubbish. [Thought to be from a bottle patented by Hiram Codd (19c), the fizzy drink it contained being ridiculed as 'Codd's wallop']

COE abbrev : Council of Europe.

COED abbrev : computer-operated electronic display.

coeducation /kō-e-dū-kā'shən/ or /-jə-/ n education of the sexes together.
■ **co'ed** n a girl or woman educated at a coeducational institution (chiefly N Am); a coeducational school. **co'ed** or **coeduca'tional** adj. **coeduca'tionally** adv.

coefficient /kō-i-fish'ənt/ n that which acts together with another thing; a numerical or literal expression for a factor of a quantity in an algebraic term (*maths*); a numerical constant used as a multiplier to a variable quantity, in calculating the magnitude of a physical property (*phys*).

coehorn or **cohorn** /kō'hörn/ (*milit hist*) n a small mortar for throwing grenades. [Baron van *Coehoorn* (1641–1704)]

coel- or **coelo-** (also N Am **cel-** or **celo-**) /sēl- or sē-lō-/ *combining form* denoting a cavity, or hollow part. [Gr *koilos* hollow]

coelacanth /sē'lə-kanth/ n any of a group of primitive crossopterygian fishes all of which were thought to be extinct until 1938, when a living specimen of the genus *Latimeria* was discovered off the coast of E Africa. [From Gr *koilos* hollow, and *akantha* spine]
■ **coelacan'thic** adj (*facetious*) ancient but worth preserving.

coelanaglyphic /sēl-a-nə-glif'ik/ (*sculpt*) adj in cavo-rilievo (hollow relief). [Gr *koilos* hollow, *ana* up, and *glyphein* to carve]

coelenterate /sə- or sē-len'tər-āt/ n any invertebrate of the phylum **Coelenterata** of many-celled animals, radially symmetrical, with a single body-cavity (the enteron) including the hydroids (Hydrozoa), jellyfish (Scyphozoa), sea anemones and corals (Actinozoa), and (in some classifications) the sea gooseberries (Ctenophora). ◆ adj of or relating to the coelenterates. [Gr *koilos* hollow, and *enteron* intestine]

coeliac or (*esp* N Am) **celiac** /sē'li-ak/ adj relating to the abdomen; relating to coeliacs, coeliac disease, etc. ◆ n a person suffering from coeliac disease. [Gr *koiliakos* from *koiliā* the belly]
❑ **coeliac disease** n a condition of the intestines in which a sensitivity to gluten prevents the proper absorption of nutrients (also called **gluten enteropathy**).

coelom, **coelome** or (*esp* N Am) **celom** /sē'lōm or -lom/ n the body-cavity, or space between the intestines and the body-wall in most animals. [Gr *koilōma*, *-atos* a cavity]
■ **Coelo'mata** n pl animals possessing a coelom. **coe'lomate** adj having a coelom. ◆ n a coelomate animal. **coelomat'ic** or **coelom'ic** adj.

coelostat /sē'lō-stat/ n an astronomical instrument consisting of a clock-driven mirror on an axis parallel to the earth's, so that light is reflected continuously from a celestial body such as the sun onto a telescope. [L *caelum* (misspelt *coelum*) sky, and Gr *statos* fixed]

coelurosaur /sē-lū'rə-sör/ n a bipedal carnivorous dinosaur of the Triassic and Cretaceous periods, thought to be the ancestor of archaeopteryx. [Gr *koilos* hollow, *ourā* tail, and *sauros* lizard]

coemption /kō-emp'shən/ n the buying up of the whole supply of a commodity; a form of marriage under the fiction of a mutual sale of the two parties (*Roman law*). [L *coemptiō*, *-ōnis*, from *emere* to buy]

coen- or **coeno-** (also (chiefly N Am) **cen-** or **ceno-**) /sēn- or sēnō-/ *combining form* signifying common. [Gr *koinos* common]

coenaesthesis or **cenesthesis** /sē-nēs-thē'sis or -nis-/, **coenaesthesia** or **cenesthesia** /-thē'zi-ə or -zyə/ (*psychol*) n general consciousness or awareness of one's body. [Gr *koinos* common, and *aisthēsis* perception]

coenenchyma /sē-neng'ki-mə/ (*bot*) n gelatinous material uniting the polyps of an anthozoan colony. [Gr *koinos* common, and *enchyma* infusion]

coeno- see **coen-**.

coenobite or **cenobite** /sē'nō-bīt or sen'ō-/ n a monk who lives in a community. [Gr *koinobion*, from *koinos* common, and *bios* life]
■ **coenobitic** /-bit'ik/ or **coenobit'ical** adj. **coen'obitism** n. **coenō'bium** n (pl **coenō'bia**) a religious community; a colony of unicellular organisms which grows only by enlargement of the cells (*biol*).

coenocyte /sē'nə-sīt/ (*biol*) n a multinucleate cell formed by nuclear division without cell division, as in fungi and striated muscle fibres. [**coeno-** and **-cyte**]
■ **coenocytic** /sit'ik/ adj.

coenosarc /sē'nō-särk/ (*biol*) n the common tissue uniting the polyps of a coral or other colonial organisms. [Gr *koinos* common, and *sarx* flesh]

coenospecies an alternative spelling of **cenospecies**.

coenosteum /si- or sē-nos'ti-əm/ (*biol*) n the calcareous skeleton of a coral colony. [Gr *koinos* common, and *osteon* bone]

coenurus /sē-nū'rəs/ n an encysted tapeworm larva consisting of a bladder from whose inner wall several heads develop. [New L, from Gr *koinos* common, and *oura* tail]

coenzyme /kō-en'zīm/ n a non-protein organic molecule (such as a vitamin) that bonds with a specific enzyme only while the biochemical reaction is being catalysed, being essential to, but unaffected by, the reaction.
❑ **coenzyme Q** see **ubiquinone**.

coequal /kō-ē'kwəl/ adj equal with another of the same rank or dignity. ◆ n one of the same rank.
■ **coëquality** /-i-kwol'/ n. **coë'qually** adv.

coerce /kō-ûrs'/ vt to restrain by force; to compel. [L *coercēre*, from *arcēre* to shut in]
■ **coer'cible** adj. **coer'cibly** adv. **coercim'eter** n an instrument for measuring coercive force. **coer'cion** n compulsion; restraint; government by force. **coer'cionist** n. **coer'cive** adj having power to coerce; compelling; tending to or intended to coerce. **coer'cively** adv. **coer'civeness** n. **coerciv'ity** n the coercive force needed to demagnetize a material that is fully magnetized.
❑ **coercive force** n the reverse magnetizing force required to bring the magnetization of a ferromagnetic material to zero.

coessential /kō-i-sen'shəl or -e-/ adj being of the same essence or nature.
■ **coessentiality** /-shi-al'i-ti/ n.

coetaneous /kō-i-tā'ni-əs/ adj of the same age; coeval. [L *aetās*, *aetātis* age]

coeternal /kō-i-tûr'nəl or kō-ē-/ adj equally eternal; jointly eternal.
■ **coeter'nally** adv. **coeter'nity** n.

coeval /kō-ē'vəl/ adj of the same age. ◆ n a person or thing of the same age; a contemporary. [L *coaevus*, from *aevum* age]
■ **coëval'ity** n. **coëv'ally** adv.

coevolution /kō-ē-va-loo'shən or -lū'/ n the process of adaptation in which the evolution of two (or more) organisms is dependent on, or is a response to, the interactions between them.
■ **coevolu'tionary** adj.

coexist /kō-ig-zist' or -eg-/ vi to exist at the same time or together; to exist together in peace, in spite of differences.
■ **coexist'ence** n. **coexist'ent** adj.
■ **peaceful coexistence** the condition of living side by side in mutual toleration.

coextend /kō-ek-stend' or -ik-/ vi to extend equally in space or time.
■ **coexten'sion** n. **coexten'sive** adj.

C of A abbrev : Certificate of Airworthiness.

cofactor /kō-fak'tər/ n a factor which occurs along with other factors in multiplication; a nonprotein organic molecule or a metallic ion that binds with an enzyme and is essential to the enzyme's activity (*biol*).

C of C abbrev : Chamber of Commerce.

C of E abbrev : Church of England; Council of Europe.

coff /kof/ (*Scot*) vt (pat and pap **coffed** or **coft**) to buy. [From pap of **cope**[4]]

coffee /kof'i/ n a powder made by roasting and grinding the seeds of a tree (*Coffea arabica*, *robusta*, etc) of the family Rubiaceae; a drink made from the powder; the brown colour of this drink when mixed with milk. [Turk *kahveh*, from Ar *qahwah* orig meaning wine]

◻ **coffee bag** *n* a small porous bag containing ground coffee beans, used to make coffee. **coffee bar** or **shop** *n* a small restaurant where coffee, tea, cakes, etc are served. **coffee bean** *n* the seed of the coffee tree. **coffee berry** *n* the fruit or the seed of the coffee tree. **coffee break** *n* a short break for coffee during the working day. **coffee bug** *n* the scale insect (*Saissetia coffeae*) destructive to the coffee tree. **coffee cup** *n* a cup for coffee, *usu* smaller than a teacup. **coffee disease** *n* a disease affecting the leaves of the coffee tree, caused by a rust fungus (*Hemileia vastatrix*). **coffee essence** *n* concentrated liquid coffee extract. **coffee grinder** *n* a coffee mill. **coffee grounds** *n pl* the sediment left after coffee has been infused. **coffee house** *n* an establishment where coffee and other refreshments are sold. **coff'ee-housing** *n* gossiping while a covert is drawn (*hunting*); talking during a game, *esp* in order to distract or mislead players (*cards*). **coffee klatsch** *n* (*US*) a coffee party. **coff'ee-maker** *n*. **coffee mill** *n* a machine for grinding coffee beans. **coffee morning** *n* a morning social gathering at which coffee is drunk. **coffee pot** *n* a pot in which coffee is prepared and served. **coffee room** *n* a room in a hotel where coffee and other refreshments are served; a public room. **coffee service** or **set** *n* a set of utensils for serving and drinking coffee. **coffee shop** see **coffee bar** above. **coffee stall** *n* a movable street stall selling coffee and other refreshments. **coffee table** *n* a small low table. **coffee-table book** *n* (*orig facetious*, sometimes *derog*) a large, expensive and profusely illustrated book of the kind one would set out on a coffee table for visitors to admire. **coffee tree** *n*.

■ **white** (or **black**) **coffee** coffee with (or without) milk.

coffer /kof'ər/ *n* a chest for holding money or treasure; an ornamental deep panel in a ceiling; a cofferdam. ◆ *vt* to hoard or store; to ornament with coffers. [OFr *cofre* a chest, from L *cophinus* a basket, from Gr *kophinos* a basket]

■ **coff'ered** *adj*.

◻ **coff'erdam** *n* a watertight structure that is pumped dry, allowing underwater foundations, etc to be built. **coff'er-fish** *n* any fish of the genus *Ostracion* that has a box-like bony covering enveloping its entire body (also called **box'-fish**, **trunkfish**).

coffin /kof'in/ *n* a box for a dead body; a thick-walled container, *usu* of lead, for transporting radioactive materials, a flask; the horny part of a horse's hoof. ◆ *vt* to place in a coffin. [OFr *cofin*, from L *cophinus*, from Gr *kophinos* a basket]

◻ **coffin bone** *n* a bone enclosed in a horse's hoof. **coff'in-dodger** *n* (*offensive sl*) an elderly person. **coffin nail** *n* (*sl*) a cigarette. **coffin ship** *n* a dangerously unsound ship.

■ **drive a nail in one's coffin** to do something tending to hasten death or ruin.

coffinite /kof'i-nīt/ *n* a uranium-yielding ore. [RC *Coffin*, a worker of the ore in Colorado]

coffle /kof'l/ *n* a gang, *esp* of slaves tied together. [Ar *qāfilah* a caravan]

coffret /kof'rət/ *n* a small coffer; a small presentation box. [Fr, dimin of *coffre* coffer]

C of I *abbrev* : Church of Ireland.

cofiring /kō-fī'ring/ *n* the generation of power using a combination of two fuels, eg coal and biomass.

C of S *abbrev* : Chief of Staff; Church of Scotland.

coft /koft/ (*Scot*) *pat* and *pap* of **coff**.

cog[1] /kog/ *n* a projection, eg on a toothed wheel; a cogwheel; an unimportant person in a large organization. ◆ *vt* (**cogg'ing**; **cogged**) to furnish with cogs; to stop (a wheel) by putting a block in front of it. [ME *cogge*; ety uncertain; cf Swed *kugge*]

◻ **cog railway** *n* a rack railway (qv under **rack**[1]). **cog'wheel** *n* a toothed wheel.

cog[2] /kog/ *vt* to cheat or deceive; to wheedle; to manipulate (dice) so that they may fall in a given way. ◆ *n* the act of cheating; deception. [Thieves' slang]

■ **cogg'er** *n*.

cog[3] /kog/ (*building*) *n* a tenon used in cogging. ◆ *vt* to join by means of cogs. [Poss **cog**[1]]

■ **cogg'ing** *n* a type of joint used to join two wooden beams, where the upper beam is bearing on the lower by cutting a tenon in the lower beam and a corresponding notch in the upper.

cog[4] /kog/ *n* formerly, a large merchant ship or warship; a small boat; a cockboat. [ME *cogge*, perh from OFr *cogue* a ship, or ON *kuggr* a merchant ship]

cog[5] see **coggie**.

cog[6] see **cogue**.

cog. *abbrev* : cognate.

COGB *abbrev* : Certified Official Government Business.

cogener /kō'ji-nər/ *n* a variant of **congener**.

cogent /kō'jənt/ *adj* (*esp* of an argument) powerful; convincing. [L *cōgēns*, *-entis*, prp of *cōgere*, from *coagere* to drive]

■ **co'gence** or **co'gency** *n* convincing power. **co'gently** *adv*.

coggie or **cogie** /kog'i or kō'gi/ (*Scot*) *n* a small wooden bowl (also **cog**). [Dimin of **cogue**]

coggle /kog'l/ *vi* to be unsteady, to wobble. ◆ *n* a cobblestone. [Origin uncertain]

■ **cogg'ly** *adv* (*Scot*) shaky.

cogitate /koj'i-tāt/ *vi* to turn a thing over in one's mind; to meditate; to ponder. [L *cōgitāre*, *-ātum* to think deeply, from *co-*, intens, and *agitāre* to put in motion]

■ **cog'itable** *adj* capable of being thought, conceivable. **cogitā'tion** *n* deep thought; meditation. **cog'itative** *adj* having the power of thinking; given to cogitating. **cog'itātor** *n*.

cogito, ergo sum /kō'gi-tō er'gō sŭm/ (*L*) I think, therefore I am (the basic tenet of Descartes' philosophy).

Cognac /kon'yak/ *n* a French brandy made near *Cognac*, in Charente.

cognate /kog'nāt/ *adj* of the same family, kind or nature; derived from the same ancestor, root or other original; related or allied. ◆ *n* someone related by blood (whether agnate or not) (*Roman law* and *general*); often, any relative on either side other than an agnate; a relative on one's mother's side (*Scots law*); a cognate word. [L *cognātus*, from *co-*, and (*g*)*nāscī* to be born]

■ **cog'nately** *adv*. **cog'nateness** *n*. **cognā'tion** *n*.

◻ **cognate object** *n* a noun related in origin or meaning to a normally intransitive verb, and used as its object, as in *sing a song*. **cognatic succession** *n* succession to the throne by the eldest child, irrespective of sex.

cognition /kog-nish'ən/ *n* the act or process of knowing, in the widest sense, including sensation, perception, etc, distinguished from emotion and conation; the knowledge resulting or acquired. [L *cognitiō*, *-ōnis*, from *cognōscere*, *cognitum*, from *co-*, and (*g*)*nōscere* to know]

■ **cognit'ional** *adj*. **cog'nitive** *adj* capable of, or relating to, cognition. **cog'nitively** *adv*. **cog'nitivism** *n* (*philos*) the belief that moral judgements state facts and therefore have true value (cf **emotivism** and **prescriptivism**). **cognitiv'ity** *n*. **cognizable** or **-s-** /kog'niz-ə-bl** (also *kon'iz-*)/ *adj* that may be known or understood; that may be judicially investigated. **cog'nizably** or **-s-** *adv*. **cog'nizance** or **-s-** (or /kon'iz-/) *n* knowledge or notice, judicial or private; observation; jurisdiction; that by which one is known, a badge. **cog'nizant** or **-s-** (or /kon'iz-/) *adj* having cognizance or knowledge of. **cognize'** or **-ise'** *vt* to become conscious of.

◻ **cognitive dissonance** *n* (*psychol*) the mental conflict resulting from incompatible cognitions. **cognitive enhancer** *n* (*med*) another term for **smart drug** (see under **smart**). **cognitive map** *n* (*psychol*) a mental map of one's physical environment. **cognitive science** *n* the study or science of cognition including aspects of psychology, philosophy, linguistics, semantics and artificial intelligence. **cognitive therapy** *n* (*psychol*) a method of psychotherapy in which the patient is encouraged to replace negative attitudes with positive ones, most often applied in the treatment of depression (also **cognitive-behavioural therapy**).

■ **take cognizance of** to recognize, take into consideration.

cognomen /kog-nō'mən/ *n* (*pl* **cognō'mens** or **cognō'mina**) *orig* the last of the three names of an ancient Roman indicating the house or family to which he belonged; a surname; an epithet or nickname. [L *cognōmen*, *-inis*, from *co-*, and (*g*)*nōmen* a name]

■ **cognominal** /-nom'/ *adj* like-named; relating to a cognomen. **cognom'inate** *vt* to name. **cognominā'tion** *n*.

cognosce /kog-nos'/ (*Scots law*) *vt* to examine; to give judgement upon; to declare to be an idiot. [L *cognōscere*, from *co-*, intens, and (*g*)*nōscere*, to know]

■ **cognosc'ible** *adj*.

cognoscente /ko-nyō-shen'tā/ *n* (*pl* **cognoscent'i** /-ē/) a person professing an expert knowledge, *esp* of works of art, music, literature, etc; a connoisseur. [Ital (modal *conoscente*), from L *cognōscere* to know]

cognovit /kog-nō'vit/ (*law*) *n* an acknowledgement by a defendant that the plaintiff's cause is just. [L *cognōvit actiōnem* (he) has acknowledged the action]

cogue or **cog** /kōg or kog/ (*esp Scot*) *n* a round wooden vessel, *usu* of staves and hoops. [Ety uncertain]

cohabit /kō-hab'it/ *vi* to live together as husband and wife, or as if husband and wife. [L *cohabitāre*, from *co-*, and *habitāre* to dwell]

■ **cohab'itant** *n* someone living with another or others. **cohabitā'tion** *n* living together; government by a head of state and a ruling party of opposing views. **cohabitee'** or **cohab'iter** *n* (*inf* short form **co'hab**).

coheir /kō-ār'/ *n* (also *fem* **coheir'ess**) a joint heir.

■ **coheritor** /kō-her'it-ər/ *n* a coheir.

cohen same as **kohen**.

cohere /kō-hēr'/ vi to stick together; to be consistent. ◆ vt to fit together in a consistent, orderly whole. [L cohaerēre, -haesum, from co-, and haerēre stick]
■ **cohē'rence** or **cohē'rency** n a tendency to cohere; a sticking together; consistency. **cohēr'ent** adj consistent or orderly in thought or speech; sticking together; connected; (of a system of units) such that one unit multiplied or divided by another gives a third unit in the system exactly; (of a beam of radiation) showing definite, not random, relationships between points in a cross-section. **cohēr'ently** adv. **cohēr'er** n formerly, an apparatus for detection of electric waves by reduced resistance of imperfect contact, as if by cohesion. **cohēsibil'ity** n. **cohēsible** /-hēz'-/ adj capable of cohesion. **cohē'sion** /-zhən/ n the act of sticking together; a form of attraction by which particles of bodies stick together; concrescence of like parts (bot); logical connection. **cohē'sive** /-siv or -ziv/ adj having the power of cohering; tending to unite into a mass. **cohē'sively** adv. **cohē'siveness** n.

coheritor see under **coheir**.

cohibit /kō-hib'it/ (rare) vt to restrain. [L cohibēre, from co-, and habēre to have, hold]
■ **cohibition** /-ish'ən/ n. **cohib'itive** adj.

coho or **cohoe** /kō'hō/ n (pl **co'hos** or **co'hoes**) a Pacific salmon, a species of Oncorhynchus. [Ety unknown]

cohobate /kō'hō-bāt/ (chem) vt to redistil (a liquid distillate), esp by pouring again and again over the matter from which it is distilled. [New L cohobāre]

cohog same as **quahog**.

cohorn see **coehorn**.

cohort /kō'hört/ n a tenth part of a Roman legion; any band of warriors; formerly, a division of plants between a class and an order or, according to some, between a suborder and a family; in the classification of higher animals, one of the divisions between subclass and order; a group of individuals; a group with a shared characteristic, esp being the same age (stats); (popularly) a companion or follower. [L cohors, -tis an enclosed place, a multitude enclosed, a company of soldiers]

cohortative /kō-hör'tə-tiv/ adj (archaic) encouraging. ◆ n (Heb grammar) a lengthened form of the imperfect. [L cohortārī, -ātus, from co-, intens, and hortārī to exhort]

cohosh /kō'hosh or kō-hosh'/ n any of several N American herbs, such as bugbane and baneberry, with medicinal properties. [Algonquian]

co-host /kō'hōst/ vt to act as joint host to or of. ◆ n a joint host.

cohune /kō-hoon'/ n a Central and S American palm (Attalea cohune) yielding **cohune nuts** and **cohune oil**. [From Am Sp]

cohyponym /kō-hī'pō-nim/ n a word which is one of two or more hyponyms of another word.

COI abbrev : Central Office of Information.

coif /koif/ n a covering for the head, esp the close-fitting cap of white lawn or silk originally worn by serjeants-at-law; a covering for the head worn by women; a hairstyle (inf). ◆ vt (**coiff'ing**; **coiffed**) to provide with a coif; to dress (the hair). [Fr coiffe, from LL cofia a cap]
■ **coiffeur** /kwä-fœr'/ or (fem) **coiffeuse** /-œz'/ n a hairdresser. **coiffure** /kwä-für'/ n a style of hairdressing; a headdress. ◆ vt to dress (the hair).

coign or **coigne** /koin/ n variant spellings of **quoin** or **coin**.
■ **coign of vantage** an advantageous position.

coil¹ /koil/ vt to wind in rings; to enclose in twists. ◆ vi to wind. ◆ n a coiled object; one of the rings into which anything is coiled; a wire wound spirally to conduct electricity; a contraceptive device consisting of a metal or plastic coil fitted in the uterus. [OFr coillir (Fr cueillir), from L colligere, from col- together, and legere to gather; cf **cull** and **collect**]

coil² /koil/ (archaic) n tumult; hubbub; noise; fuss. [Origin unknown]
■ **mortal coil** (Shakesp, Hamlet III.1.67) the toil and trouble of human life.

coin /koin/ n a piece of metal legally stamped and current as money; money; a cornerstone or quoin (archaic). ◆ vt to manufacture or make into (coins); to stamp; to invent, fabricate (esp a new word); to gain money by means of (archaic). [Fr coin a wedge (see **quoin**), also the die to stamp money, from L cuneus a wedge]
■ **coin'age** n the act of coining money; the currency; the pieces of metal coined; the invention, or fabrication, of something new, esp a word or phrase; what is invented. **coin'er** n a person who coins money; a maker of counterfeit coins; an inventor (of words, etc). **coin'ing** n minting; invention.
□ **coin box** n a telephone or other machine which one operates by putting coins in a slot. **coin'-operated**, **coin'op'** or **coin-in-the-slot'** adj (of a machine) operated by inserting a coin in a slot.

■ **coin a phrase** to use a new phrase or expression (usu ironic, ie to repeat a cliché). **coin money** or **coin it** to make a lot of money rapidly. **pay someone in his** or **her own coin** to give tit for tat; to give as good as one got. **the other side of the coin** the alternative or contrasting viewpoint, argument, etc.

coincide /kō-in-sīd'/ vi to occupy the same place or time; to agree; to correspond; to be identical. [L co-, and incidere, from in in, and cadere to fall]
■ **coincidence** /kō-in'si-dəns/ n the fact, event, or condition of coinciding; the occurrence of events simultaneously or consecutively in a striking manner but without any causal connection between them. **coin'cidency** n. **coin'cident** adj. **coincidental** /-dent'l/ adj. **coincident'ally** adv. **coin'cidently** adv.

coinhere /kō-in-hēr'/ vi to inhere together.
■ **coinhēr'ence** n.

coinheritor /kō-in-her'i-tər/ n a joint heir.
■ **coinher'itance** n.

coinstantaneous /kō-in-stən-tā'ni-əs/ adj exactly simultaneous.
■ **coinstantaneity** /-stan-tə-nē'i-ti/ or **coinstantā'neousness** n. **coinstantā'neously** adv.

coinsurance /kō'in-shoo-rəns or -shō-/ n insurance jointly with another, esp when the owner of the property to be insured bears part of the risk.

Cointreau® /kwē-trō or kwon' or kwän'/ n an orange-flavoured liqueur.

coir /koir/ n the strong fibre of coconut husk, used in making rope and matting; a growing medium for garden and pot plants made from this fibre. [From Tamil or Malayalam]

coistrel or **coistril** /kois'tril/ n a groom (obs); a knave (Shakesp). [See **custrel**]

coit or **quoit** /koit/ (Aust sl) n the buttocks, the backside.

coitus /kō'it-əs/ or **coition** /kō-ish'ən/ n sexual intercourse. [L coitiō, -ōnis, from co- together, and īre, itum to go]
■ **cō'ital** adj.
□ **coitus interruptus** n coitus intentionally interrupted by withdrawal of the penis from the vagina before semen is ejaculated. **coitus reservatus** n coitus in which ejaculation is avoided.

cojoin /kō-join'/ (Shakesp) vt same as **conjoin**.

cojones /kō-hō'nāz or -nez/ (sl, chiefly US) n pl testicles, balls; courage, spirit. [Sp]

coke¹ /kōk/ n a form of fuel obtained by the heating of coal in confined space whereby its more volatile constituents are driven off; the residue when any substance (eg petrol) is carbonized. ◆ vt and vi to make into, or become, coke. [Ety uncertain]
■ **cō'ky** adj like coke.
□ **coking coal** n bituminous coal good for coking.

coke² /kōk/ n cocaine (sl); (**Coke®**) Coca-Cola.
■ **coke'head** n (sl) a drug addict.
□ **coked-up'** adj (sl) intoxicated with cocaine.

cokernut see under **coco¹**.

COL abbrev : computer-orientated language.

Col. abbrev : Colonel; Colorado (US state); (the Letter to the) Colossians (Bible).

col /kol/ n a depression or pass in a mountain range, a defile (geog); a region between two anticyclones giving a similar figure when represented in contour (meteorol). [Fr, from L collum a neck]

col. abbrev : colour; column.

col- see **com-**.

COLA (chiefly US) abbrev : cost-of-living adjustment.

cola or **kola** /kō'lə/ n (with cap) a genus of W African trees (Cola acuminata, C. nitida) producing nuts used in drugs and for flavouring soft drinks; a soft drink so flavoured. [African name]

colander or **cullender** /kol'ən-dər or kul'/ n a perforated vessel used as a strainer in cookery. [L cōlāre to strain]

colatitude /kō-lat'i-tūd/ n the complement of the latitude. [**complement** and **latitude**]

Colbertine /kol'bər-tin or -tēn/ n a kind of lace. [Jean Baptiste Colbert (1619–83), Minister of Finance to Louis XIV, and a great patron of the arts]

colcannon /kol-kan'ən/ n an Irish dish, consisting of boiled cabbage and potatoes mashed with butter. [**cole** cabbage, and Ir ceannan white-headed]

colchicum /kol'ki-kəm/ n (pl **col'chicums** or **col'chica**) any plant of the genus Colchicum, meadow saffron or autumn crocus; its dried corm and seeds, used as a source of colchicine. [L, from Gr kolchikon meadow saffron, neuter of Kolchikos, relating to Kolchis, the sorceress Medea's country]

■ **col'chicine** /-chi- or -ki-sēn/ n an alkaloid obtained from meadow saffron and used in the treatment of gout.

colcothar /kol'kō-thär/ n a dark-red iron peroxide powder formed by calcining iron sulphate, used as a pigment and for polishing glass, etc. [Ar qolqotār]

cold /kōld/ adj giving or feeling a sensation that is felt to be the opposite of hot; chilly; low in temperature; without passion or zeal; spiritless; unfriendly; indifferent; reserved; dead; (of colours) suggesting cold rather than heat, as blue or grey; without application of heat; used of operations formerly requiring heat, eg cold-casting, -forging, -moulding and -welding; (in marketing, politics, etc) involving contacting people thought to be potential customers or supporters, without the contact having been prearranged or primed, and with no knowledge of the people's likely reactions or opinions, as in cold calling or cold canvassing. ◆ n a relative absence of heat; the feeling or sensation caused by the absence of heat; coldness; a spell of cold weather; a catarrhal inflammation of the mucous membrane of the respiratory organs, caused by a virus, usually accompanied by hoarseness and coughing; catarrh; chillness. ◆ adv without preparation or rehearsal. [OE (Anglian) cald (WSax ceald); Scot cauld, Ger kalt; cf cool, ON kala to freeze, L gelidus, from gelū frost]
■ **cold'ie** n (Aust sl) a cold can or bottle of beer. **cold'ish** adj somewhat cold. **cold'ly** adv. **cold'ness** n.
❑ **cold'blood** n and adj (of) a horse belonging to the heavy draught breeds (cf **warmblood**). **cold'-blooded** adj having a body temperature that varies with the temperature of the environment, as in fishes; (of persons) sensitive to cold (inf); (**cold-blood'ed**) lacking in feeling; (of persons or actions) hard-hearted. **cold-blood'edly** adv. **cold-blood'edness** n. **cold boot** n (comput) the rebooting of a machine by turning the power source off and on. **cold-boot** vt. **cold cathode** n (elec) an electrode from which electron emission results from high-potential gradient at the surface at normal temperatures. **cold chisel** n a strong and finely-tempered chisel for cutting cold metal; a tool used with a heavy hammer to cut or break stone, concrete, etc. **cold comfort** see under **comfort**. **cold cream** n a creamy ointment used to remove make-up or as a cooling or moisturizing dressing for the skin. ◆ vt (inf) to apply cold cream to. **cold cuts** n pl slices of cold cooked meat. **cold'-drawn** adj (of metal, wire, etc) drawn through a die without heating; (of vegetable oil) subjected to pressure without heat. **cold duck** n a drink made from equal parts of champagne and burgundy. **cold feet** n pl loss of nerve; cooling-off of courage or ardour. **cold fish** n a person who shows no emotion. **cold frame** n a structure, usu of wood and glass and without artificial heat, for protecting young plants. **cold front** n the surface of an advancing mass of cold air where it meets a retreating mass of warmer air. **cold fusion** n nuclear fusion without prior heating, ie effected at normal room temperature. **cold harbour** n a wayside travellers' shelter. **cold-heart'ed** adj lacking feeling; indifferent. **cold-heart'edly** adv. **cold-heart'edness** n. **cold'house** n a plant frame or greenhouse, without artificial heat. **cold light** n luminescence. **cold-mould'ed** adj. **cold moulding** n the moulding of articles using resins that polymerize chemically. **cold pack** n a wet pack prepared with cold water, to counteract fever, inflammation, etc. **cold pig** n (inf) an application of cold water to rouse a sleeper. **cold'-rolled** adj (of metal) rolled without heating. **cold rubber** n a hard-wearing synthetic rubber made at a temperature of 5°C (41°F). **cold'-short** adj brittle when cold; (of feelings) brittle, sensitive. **cold-should'er** vt to give the cold shoulder to (see below). **cold slaw** n coleslaw. **cold snap** n a sudden short spell of cold weather. **cold sore** n a blister or group of blisters on or near the mouth, caused by a viral infection (herpes simplex). **cold start** n the reloading of a computer program (comput); the starting of an engine at the ambient temperature. **cold steel** n cutting or stabbing weapons, as opposed to bullets. **cold storage** n storage and preservation of goods in refrigerating chambers; abeyance. **cold table** n a selection of cold meat and other food eaten in a formal setting. **cold turkey** n sudden withdrawal of narcotics; the symptoms experienced by a drug user on such withdrawal (also fig); the plain unvarnished truth. **cold war** n an intense, remorseless struggle for the upper hand by all means short of actual fighting, orig and esp as between the Communist and non-Communist powers after World War II. **cold water** n water at its natural temperature in ordinary conditions. **cold wave** n an artificial wave produced by a chemical solution (hairdressing); a sudden spell of cold weather over a large area. **cold'-weld** vt to force together (two like or unlike metals) so that normal oxide surface films are ruptured and adhesion occurs. **cold welding** n. **cold'-without** n brandy with cold water and no sugar. **cold'-work** vt to shape (metals) at or near atmospheric temperature by rolling, pressing, etc (**cold work** n).
■ **catch cold** to contract a cold; to make an unexpected loss. **cold as charity** a proverbial phrase expressing ironically great coldness or indifference. **cold dark matter** in cosmology, a material thought to be detectable in the microwave background of the universe whose existence may disprove the big-bang theory. **come in from the cold** to gain acceptance or recognition after a period of isolation or neglect. **give** or **show the cold shoulder** to show studied indifference; to give a rebuff. **go cold (on)** to lose enthusiasm for or interest in; to peter out or disappear; to fail to respond to. **in a cold sweat** (as if) sweating with fear. **in cold blood** with deliberate intent, not under the influence of passion. **in the cold light of day** see under **day**. **leave one cold** to fail to impress. **leave out in the cold** to neglect, ignore. **out cold** unconscious. **pour** or **throw cold water on** to discourage. **turn down cold** to refuse absolutely and immediately, allowing no discussion.

cole /kōl/ n a general name for plants of the cabbage family. [OE cawel; Ger Kohl, Scot kale; all from L cōlis, caulis a stem, esp of cabbage]
❑ **cole'-garth** n a cabbage garden. **cole'seed** n the seed of rape; rape. **cole'slaw** /-slö/ n (Du koolsla for kool salade cole salad) a salad consisting mainly of shredded cabbage with a dressing. **cole'wort** n cabbage, esp varieties with no heart.

colectomy see under **colon²**.

colemanite /kōl'mə-nīt/ (mineralogy) n hydrated calcium borate, crystallized in the monoclinic system, occurring as nodules in clay. [WT Coleman (1824–93), American mine owner]

coleopteran or **coleopteron** /ko-li-op'tə-rən/ n any insect of the order Coleop'tera, having hard or horny forewings which serve as wing-cases for the functional wings, the beetles. [Gr koleos a sheath, and pteron a wing]
■ **coleop'teral** or **coleop'terous** adj. **coleop'terist** n a person who studies and collects beetles.

coleoptile /ko-li-op'tīl/ (bot) n a protective sheath around the first leaves of cereals. [Gr koleos a sheath, and ptilon a feather]

coleor(r)hiza /kol-i-ō-rī'zə/ (bot) n (pl **coleōr(r)hī'zae** /-ē/) a protective layer on the radicle of some plants, eg grasses. [Gr koleos sheath, and rhiza root]

coleslaw see under **cole**.

cole tit, **cole titmouse** alternative spellings of **coal tit**, **coal titmouse** (see under **coal**).

coleus /kō'li-əs/ n (pl **cō'leuses**) any plant of the genus Coleus with variegated coloured leaves often used for indoor decoration. [Gr koleos a sheath]

colewort see under **cole**.

coley /kō'li/ n another name for the coalfish, an edible fish of the cod family.

colibri /kol'i-brē or ko-lē'/ n a type of hummingbird. [Sp colibri, Fr colibri, said to be the Carib name]

colic /kol'ik/ n severe spasmodic pain in the abdomen without diarrhoea, due to an obstruction of the intestine, intestinal infection or excessive intestinal gas. [colon²]
■ **col'icky** adj like, suffering from or causing colic.
❑ **col'icroot** n a N American bitter herb (Aletris farinosa); its root, formerly used to cure colic.

coliform¹ /kol'i-förm or kō'li-/ adj like a sieve. [L cōlium a strainer]

coliform² see under **colon²**.

colin /kol'in/ n the Virginian quail. [Ety uncertain; perh Sp]

coliseum or **colosseum** /ko-lə-sē'əm or -li-/ n a large building or stadium, used as a place of entertainment, named after the Flavian amphitheatre in Rome. [Med L, from L colossus (see **colossus**), from the huge statue of Nero near which the Flavian amphitheatre was built]

colitis see under **colon²**.

coll /kol/ (obs) vt to embrace, hug. [Fr col, from L collum the neck]
■ **coll'ing** n embracing.

coll. abbrev : colleague; collective; collector; college; colloquial.

collaborate /kə-lab'ə-rāt/ vi to work in association (with); to assist or co-operate (with an enemy, esp one occupying one's country). [L collabōrāre, -ātum, from labōrāre to work]
■ **collabora'tion** n. **collabora'tionism** n collaboration with an enemy. **collabora'tionist** n. **collab'orative** adj. **collab'oratively** adv. **collab'orātor** n.

collage /ko-läzh'/ n a picture made from scraps of paper and other odds and ends pasted up; any work or construction put together from assembled fragments. [Fr, pasting]
■ **collag'ist** n.

collagen /kol'ə-jən/ n a protein in fibrous connective tissue, readily turned into gelatin. [Gr kolla glue, and gen-, the root of gignesthai to become]
■ **coll'agenase** n one of a group of enzymes that break down collagen. **collagen'ic** or **collag'enous** adj.

collapse /kə-laps'/ n a falling away or breaking down; any sudden or complete breakdown or prostration. ◆ vi to cave in; to close or fold up; to break down; to go to ruin; to lose heart; to drop in a state of exhaustion or unconsciousness. ◆ *vt* to fold up or close. [L *collāpsus*, from *col-* together, and *lābī*, *lāpsus* to slide or fall]

■ **collap'sar** *n* (*astron*) a black hole. **collapsibil'ity** or **collapsabil'ity** *n*. **collaps'ible** or **collaps'able** *adj* (*esp* of furniture) capable of being folded or dismantled.

collar /*kol'ər*/ *n* something worn round the neck by a person, horse, dog, etc; the neck or (sometimes detachable) neckband of a garment; the part of an animal's skin or coat, or a bird's feathers, round the neck; a marking around an animal or bird's neck; a surrounding band; the junction of root and stem in a plant; a piece of meat rolled up and tied; a joint of bacon from the neck; an arrest (*sl*). ◆ *vt* to seize by the collar; to put a collar on; to seize or arrest (*sl*). [OFr *colier*, from L *collāre*, from *collum* the neck]

■ **coll'ared** *adj* having, or ornamented with, a collar; rolled up and bound with a string, as a piece of meat having the bones removed; captured. **collarette'** *n* a small collar for a garment. **coll'arless** *adj*.
❑ **collar beam** *n* a horizontal piece of timber connecting or bracing two opposite rafters, to prevent sagging. **coll'arbone** *n* the clavicle, a bone connecting the shoulder blade and breastbone. **collar cell** *n* a choanocyte. **collared dove** *n* a dove (*Streptopelia decaocto*) of Europe and Asia, with light grey plumage marked with a narrow black stripe around the back of the neck. **collar stud** *n* a stud for fastening a shirt collar. **coll'ar-work** *n* hard work by a draught horse pulling against the horse-collar; drudgery.
■ **have one's collar felt** (*sl*) to be arrested or apprehended by the police. **hot under the collar** in a state of agitation or anger.

coll'arco /*kol-är'kō*/ (*music*) *adj* and *adv* with the bow. [Ital]

collard /*kol'ərd*/ *n* colewort. [**colewort**]

collat. *abbrev* : collateral; collaterally.

collate /*kə* or *ko-lāt'*/ *vt* to bring together for comparison; to examine and compare, eg books, and *esp* old manuscripts; to place (sheets of a book or document) in order for binding or stapling, and to examine with respect to completeness and sequence of sheets, etc; to merge (two or more files, sets of records, etc); to place in or confer a benefice upon. [L *collātum*, used as supine of *conferre*, from pfx *col-*, and *lātum* (from *ferre* to bring)]

■ **colla'table** *adj*. **colla'tion** *n* the act of collating; a bringing together for examination and comparison; the presentation of a clergyman to a benefice; a description of a book as collated; a light meal taken on fast-days in monasteries; any light meal. **colla'tive** *adj* having the power of conferring; of livings where the bishop and patron are one and the same person. **colla'tor** *n* a person who collates or compares; a person who bestows or presents; a machine that merges sets of punched cards or separates cards from a set; a machine that puts copied or printed sheets into sequential sets.

collateral /*kə-lat'ə-rəl*/ *adj* side by side; running parallel or together; corresponding; subsidiary, additional; descended from the same ancestor, through a different line. ◆ *n* a collateral relation; a contemporary; a rival; an asset providing collateral security. [L *col-* and *latus*, *lateris* a side]

■ **collateralization** or **-s-** *n*. **collat'eralize** or **-ise** *vt* to treat (an asset) as collateral. **collat'eral'ity** *n*. **collat'erally** *adv*.
❑ **collateral damage** *n* (*milit euphem*) civilian casualties or damage to property, etc that was not a military target.
▨ **collateral security** *n* an additional and separate security for repayment of money borrowed.

colleague[1] /*kol'ēg*/ *n* a person associated with another in some employment. [Fr *collègue*, from L *collēga*, from *col-* and *legere* to choose]

■ **coll'eagueship** *n*.

colleague[2] /*ko-lēg'*/ (*obs*) *vi* (**colleaguing** /*kol-ēg'ing*/; **colleagued** /*kol-ēgd'*/) to ally; to conspire. [OFr *colliguer* to join in alliance, from L *colligāre* to bind together]

collect /*ko-* or *kə-lekt'*/ *vt* to assemble or bring together; to put (one's thoughts) in order; to receive payment of; to call for and remove; to collide with (*Aust* and *NZ inf*). ◆ *vi* to come together; to accumulate. ◆ *n* /*kol'*/ a short prayer, specific to the liturgies of the Western Church, consisting of one sentence, conveying one main petition. ◆ *adj* and *adv* /*-ekt'*/ (*N Am*; of a telephone call, telegram, etc) paid for by the recipient. [L *colligere*, *collēctum*, from *legere* to gather]

■ **collectabil'ity** *n*. **collect'able** or **collect'ible** *adj* of interest to a collector. ◆ *n* any item of interest to a collector; one of a set of toys or ornaments each purchasable separately but priced and marketed in such a way as to encourage the purchase of all or much of the range. **collectā'nea** *n pl* a collection of passages from various sources; a miscellany. **collect'ed** *adj* gathered together; (of a poet's or other writer's works) assembled in one volume, one set of volumes, etc; composed, cool. **collect'edly** *adv*. **collect'edness** *n* self-possession; coolness. **collect'ing** *n* and *adj*. **collec'tion** *n* the act of collecting; the gathering of contributions, *esp* of money; the money collected; money intended for collection in church; an accumulation; an assemblage; a

book of selections; a regular removal of rubbish for disposal, or letters from a postbox for delivering; composure; (in *pl*) an examination at the end of the term in certain colleges; the range of new fashion clothes shown by a couturier. **collect'ive** *adj* considered as forming one mass or sum; congregated; common; denoting a number or group (of people, animals, etc) (*grammar*). ◆ *n* a gathering, assemblage; a unit of organization in a collectivist system; loosely, a group of people who run a business, etc, for their mutual benefit, often with no specifically designated jobs. **collect'ively** *adv*. **collect'ivism** *n* the economic theory that industry should be carried on with a collective capital, a form of socialism; a system embodying this. **collect'ivist** *n* and *adj*. **collectivist'ic** *adj*. **collectiv'ity** *n*. **collectivizā'tion** or **-s-** *n*. **collect'ivize** or **-ise** *vt* to give a collectivist organization to. **collect'or** *n* something which or someone who collects; a person who seeks to acquire and set together examples or specimens, as of books, minerals, curiosities; any electrode that collects electrons that have already fulfilled their function, as in a screen grid; the outer section of a transistor which delivers a primary flow of charge carriers; in India, the chief official of a district, collecting revenue and acting as a magistrate. **collect'orate** or **collect'orship** *n*.
❑ **collecting box** *n* a box for specimens used by naturalists in the field; a box for receiving money contributions. **collective agreement** *n* one reached by collective bargaining. **collective bargaining** *n* negotiation on pay and conditions of service between one or more trade unions on one side and an employer or association of employers on the other. **collective farm** *n* a state-controlled farm consisting of a number of small-holdings operated on a co-operative basis. **collective fruit** *n* (*bot*) a multiple fruit, one derived from several flowers, eg fig, mulberry. **collective noun** *n* a singular noun referring to a group of people or things. **collective responsibility** *n* the convention that all decisions of a cabinet, committee, etc are presented and treated as being unanimous. **collective security** *n* general security among nations to be achieved through guarantee of each nation's security by all. **collective unconscious** *n* (*psychol*) the part of the unconscious mind that originates in ancestral experience. **collector's item** or **piece** *n* an object beautiful, valuable, interesting, etc enough to be sought for or included in a collection.
■ **collect on delivery** (*N Am*) cash on delivery.

colleen /*kol'ēn* or *ko-lēn'*/ *n* a girl, *specif* an Irish girl. [Ir *cailín*]

college /*kol'ij*/ *n* an institution for higher, professional or vocational education; a body or society that is a member of a university or is coextensive with a university; a literary, political or religious institution; an incorporation, company or society of persons joined together generally for a specific function, often having exclusive privileges; the premises housing a college; a prison (*sl*). [Fr *collège*, from L *collēgium*, from *col-* and *legere* to gather]

■ **coll'eger** *n* a member of a college; one of the foundationers at Eton College. **collegial** /*kə-lē'ji-əl*/ *adj* relating to a college or university, or to a collegium. **collē'gialism** *n* the theory that the church is a self-governing body independent of the state. **collegial'ity** *n* sharing by bishops in papal decision-making (*RC*); the process of making decisions, agreeing on actions, etc, shared by all the bishops of a church. **collē'gian** *n* a member or inhabitant of a college; a student; an inmate of a prison (*obs sl*). **collē'gianer** *n* a member of a college, a student. **collē'giate** *adj* relating to or resembling a college; (of a town, etc) containing a college; instituted like a college; corporate. ◆ *n* (*obs sl*) an inmate of a prison, etc.
❑ **college pudding** *n* a kind of steamed pudding containing dried fruit. **collegiate church** or **collegial church** *n* a church having a college or chapter, consisting of a dean or provost and canons, attached to it; in Scotland, a church occupied by two or more pastors of equal rank (also **collegiate charge** (*hist*)).
■ **College of Arms** or **Herald's College** a collegiate body incorporated in 1483, presided over by the Earl Marshal, and including Garter, principal King-of-arms, Clarenceux and Norroy, besides six heralds and four pursuivants. **college of cardinals** (*RC*) the whole body of cardinals, electors of and advisors to the Pope. **college of education** a college for training teachers. **College of Justice** in Scotland, the Court of Session, composed of judges, advocates, writers to the signet, and solicitors.

collegium /*ko-lē'ji-əm*/ *n* (*pl* **collē'gia** or **collē'giums**) college of cardinals; an administrative board, eg of a government department in the former USSR. [L *collēgium*; see **college**]
❑ **collegium musicum** /*ko-lē'i-əm mū'si-kəm* or *ko-lāg'i-ūm moo'si-kŭm*/ *n* a group of amateur musicians, often connected with a university.

col legno /*kol len'yō* or *kō lān'yō*/ (*music*) an instruction to string players to use the wood of the bow. [Ital, with the wood]

collembolan /*ko-lem'bə-lən* or *-bō-*/ *n* a member of the order Collembola of wingless insects (the springtails) whose abdomen has no more than six segments and typically having a springing organ (a furcula). [Gr *kolla* glue, and *embolos* a peg]

collenchyma /ko-leng'ki-mə/ (bot) n a type of plant tissue having thickened cellulose walls (particularly at the angles of the cell walls) acting to strengthen and support, esp in leaves and young stems. [Gr kolla glue, en in, and chyma that which is poured]
■ **collenchym'atous** adj.

Colles' fracture /kol'is frak'chər/ n a fracture of the radius near the wrist, with backward displacement of the hand. [Abraham Colles (1773–1843), Irish surgeon]

collet /kol'it/ n a circular flange or collar; the collar of a plant; the part of a ring or other piece of jewellery which contains the stone. [Fr, from L collum]
▫ **collet chuck** n a device having a circular flange or collar for holding work or a tool on a lathe.

colliculus /kə-lik'ū-ləs/ (zool) n (pl **collic'uli** /-ī or -ē/) a small prominence, as on the surface of the optic lobe of the brain. [New L]

collide /kə-līd'/ vi to dash together; to clash. ◆ vt to cause to collide. [L collīdere, collīsum, from col- and laedere to strike]
■ **colli'der** n (in particle physics) a type of accelerator which causes subatomic particles to collide or be smashed together using electromagnets. **collision** /-lizh'n/ n the state of being struck together; a violent impact, a crash; conflict; opposition; clashing.
▫ **collision course** n a course which, if persisted in, will result in a collision (lit and fig).
■ **elastic collision** a collision in which both kinetic energy and momentum are conserved (phys); a collision in which the bombarding particle does not excite or break up the struck nucleus, and is simply scattered, the process being termed **elastic scattering** (nuclear industry). **inelastic collision** a collision in which momentum, but not kinetic energy, is conserved (phys); a collision in which there is a change in the total energies of the particles involved, the resultant scattering being termed **inelastic scattering** (nuclear industry).

collie or **colly** /kol'i/ n a long-haired, intelligent breed of sheepdog, originating in Scotland. [Origin uncertain]

collier /kol'yər or -i-ər/ n a coalminer; a ship that carries coal; a sailor in such a ship; a charcoal burner or dealer in charcoal or coal (obs). [coal]
■ **coll'iery** n a coalmine.

collieshangie /ko-li-shang'i/ (Scot) n a noisy wrangling; an uproar; a disturbance. [Origin unknown]

colligate /kol'i-gāt/ vt to bind together. [L colligāre, -ātum, from col- and ligāre to bind]
■ **colliga'tion** n conjunction; bringing together under a general principle or conception. **coll'igative** adj (physical chem) depending on the concentration, not the nature, of the atoms and molecules in a substance.

collimate /kol'i-māt/ vt to make parallel; to adjust accurately the line of sight of (an optical instrument, such as a surveying telescope). [collīmāre, a wrong reading for L collīneāre to bring into line with, from col- together, and līnea a line]
■ **collima'tion** n. **coll'imātor** n a device for obtaining a beam of parallel rays of light or other radiation, or one for obtaining a beam of particles moving in parallel paths; a subsidiary telescope for collimating other instruments.

collinear /ko-lin'i-ər/ adj in the same straight line.
■ **collinear'ity** n.

Collins¹ /kol'inz/ n a cocktail made with a spirit, lemon or lime juice, sugar and soda water (also without cap, eg vodka collins, whiskey collins).
■ **Tom Collins** or **John Collins** this drink made with gin.

Collins² /kol'inz/ n a letter of thanks for hospitality. [From the notable example sent by Mr Collins in Jane Austen's Pride and Prejudice]

colliquate /kol'i-kwāt/ vt (obs) to melt; to fuse. [L col- together, and liquāre, -ātum to cause to melt]
■ **colliq'uable** or **colliq'uant** adj (obs) melting, wasting. **colliquā'tion** n the process of melting or wasting away. **colliq'uative** adj profuse in flow; wasting. **colliquesc'ence** n readiness to liquefy.

collision see under **collide**.

collocate /kol'ə-kāt/ vt to place together; to set; to arrange. ◆ vi (linguistics) (of a word) to be habitually placed with another word. [L collocāre, -ātum, from col- and locāre to place]
■ **colloca'tion** n the placing of something together with something else; the habitual placing together of one specific word with one or more other specific words (linguistics); the group of words so formed (linguistics).

collocutor, collocutory see under **colloquy**.

collodion /kə- or ko-lō'di-ən/ n a gluey solution of nitrated cotton (or cellulose nitrates) in alcohol and ether, used in surgery and photography. [Gr kollōdēs, from kolla glue, and eidos form, appearance]

collogue /kə-lōg'/ vi to converse confidentially; to conspire or intrigue (usu with with). ◆ vt (obs) to coax, flatter. [Prob from L colloquī to speak together]

colloid /kol'oid/ n a substance in a state in which, though apparently dissolved, it cannot pass through a membrane; a substance that readily assumes this state; a colloidal system. [Gr kolla glue, and eidos form]
■ **colloid'al** adj.
▫ **colloidal system** n a dispersed substance plus the material in which it is dispersed.

collop /kol'əp/ (dialect) n a slice of meat; any small thing or piece of something. [Origin obscure; cf Swed kalops stew of sliced beef]
■ **Collop Monday** the day before Shrove Tuesday, when collops-and-eggs were eaten. **minced collops** (Scot) minced meat.

colloquy /kol'ə-kwi/ n a speaking together; mutual discourse; conversation; an informal conference for discussion of theological matters. ◆ vi (rare) to converse. [L colloquium, from col- and loquī to speak]
■ **collocutor** /kol-ok'ū-tər/ n. **colloc'ūtory** adj. **colloque** /kol-ōk'/ vi to hold colloquy. **colloquial** /kə-lō'kwi-əl/ adj relating to or used in common conversation. **collō'quialism** n a form of expression used in familiar talk. **collō'quialist** n. **collō'quially** adv. **coll'oquist** n a speaker in a colloquy. **collō'quium** n (pl **collō'quia** or **collō'quiums**) a conference; a meeting for discussion; a seminar. **coll'oquize** or **-ise** vi to converse.

collotype /kol'ō-tīp or -ə-/ n a printing process using a hardened gelatine plate, used in book illustration and advertising; a print produced by this process. [Gr kolla glue, and **type**]
■ **collotypic** /-tip'ik/ adj.

colluctation /ko-luk-tā'shən/ (archaic) n strife; opposition. [L colluctārī, from col-, and luctārī to wrestle]

collude /kol-ūd'/ or -ood'/ vi to conspire, esp in a fraud. [L collūdere, collūsum, from col-, and lūdere to play]
■ **collud'er** n. **collu'sion** n the act of colluding; a secret agreement to deceive, eg one made between the opposing parties in a lawsuit; conspiracy. **collu'sive** adj relating to a collusion; conspiratorial. **collu'sively** adv.

colluvies /ko-lū'vi or ko-loo'vi-ēz/ n accumulated filth, a foul discharge; a rabble. [L colluviēs washings, from colluere to wash thoroughly]
■ **collu'vial** adj. **collū'vium** n (pl **collū'via** or **collū'viums**) rock fragments which accumulate at the foot of cliffs and steep slopes.

colly¹ /kol'i/ vt (archaic) to begrime or darken, as with coal dust. ◆ n soot, smut (archaic or dialect); (also **colly bird**) a blackbird (dialect). [See **coal**]

colly² see **collie**.

collyrium /ko-lir'i-əm/ n (pl **collyr'ia** or **collyr'iums**) eye lotion or ointment. [Latinized from Gr kollỹrion eye-salve, dimin of kollỹrā a roll of bread]

collywobbles /kol'i-wo-blz/ (facetious) n abdominal pain or disorder; nervous stomach, or a state of apprehensiveness generally. [Prob **colic** and **wobble**]

Colmar /kol'mär/ n a kind of fan fashionable in Queen Anne's time; a kind of pear. [Perh Colmar in Alsace]

Colo. abbrev: Colorado (US state).

coloboma /ko-lo-bō'mə or -lō-/ (med) n a congenital defect of the eye affecting the development of the lens, iris or retina. [New L, from Gr kolobos cut short]

colobus /kol'ō-bəs or -ə-/ n (pl **col'obi** /-bī/ or -bē/ or **col'obuses**) any arboreal African monkey of the genus Colobus, with black (or black-and-white) fur forming a crest down its back, a long tail and vestigial or absent thumbs. [Gr kolobos maimed]
■ **col'obid** adj.

Colocasia /ko-lō-kā'zi-ə or -si-ə/ (bot) n a genus of plants of the arum family including the taro (C. esculenta) grown for its edible tubers, and several varieties grown for their decorative foliage. [Gr kolokāsiā water-lily root]

colocynth /kol'ə-sinth/ n a cucurbitaceous plant of Europe and Asia, bearing bitter-tasting gourd-like fruits (Citrullus colocynthis); a purgative obtained from its dried fruit. [Gr kolokynthis]

colog /kō'log/ (maths) n a cologarithm. [Short form]

cologarithm /kō-log'ə-ri-dhəm or -thəm/ (maths) n the logarithm of the reciprocal of a number (short form **colog**).

cologne /kə-lōn'/ n a perfumed mixture of alcohol and essential oils, first made at Cologne in 1709 by Johann Farina (also called **Cologne water** or **eau de Cologne**).

■ words derived from main entry word; ▫ compound words; ■ idioms and phrasal verbs

Colombian /kə-lum'bi-ən or -lom'/ *adj* of or relating to *Colombia* in S America, or its inhabitants. ◆ *n* a native or inhabitant of Colombia.

colon[1] /kō'lən/ *n* the punctuation mark (:), used to indicate a distinct clause of a sentence, or to introduce a list, spoken or reported words, etc, or (in figures) to indicate ratio. [Gr *kōlon* a limb, member]

colon[2] /kō'lən/ *n* the large intestine from the caecum to the rectum; in insects, the wide posterior part of the hind-gut. [Gr *kolon* the large intestine]

■ **colec'tomy** /kə-/ *n* surgical removal of all or part of the colon. **coliform** /kol'i-förm/ *n* the coliform bacillus. **colitis** /kō- or ko-lī'tis/ or **colonī'tis** *n* inflammation of the colon. **colon'ic** *adj* of the colon. ◆ *n* a colonic irrigation. **colonos'copy** *n* examination of the inside of the colon using a **colon'oscope**, a flexible viewing instrument passed into the colon through the anus. **colorec'tal** *adj* relating to the colon and rectum. **colos'tomy** /kə-/ *n* a surgical procedure in which part of the colon is brought through an incision in the abdomen to form an artificial anus. **colot'omy** /kə-/ *n* cutting of or incision into the colon. □ **coliform bacillus** or **colon bacillus** *n* any of several bacilli living in the intestines of man and some animals. **colonic hydrotherapy** or **irrigation** *n* cleansing and detoxification of the colon by the injection into it of warm water, subsequently drained away with accompanying waste matter. **colostomy bag** *n* a bag for collecting waste products from the body, used by people who have undergone a colostomy.

colon[3] /kō-lōn'/ *n* (*pl* **cōlōns'** or **cōlōn'es**) the standard monetary unit of El Salvador and Costa Rica (100 centavos). [From Columbus (Sp *Colón*)]

colon[4] /kə-lon' or (*Fr*) ko-lɔ̄/ *n* a colonist, *esp* a colonial farmer, in Algeria. [Fr, see **colony**]

colonel /kûr'nəl/ *n* a senior army officer ranking between a lieutenant-colonel and a brigadier (*US* brigadier general); in USA, an officer of equivalent rank in the Marines or the Air Force; in some regiments, an honorary rank given *usu* to a distinguished former member of the regiment; in USA, an honorary title sometimes given to a person not connected with the armed forces; (loosely) a form of address to a lieutenant-colonel. [Older Fr and Sp *coronel*, from Ital *colonello*, the leader of a *colonna*, or column, from L *columna*; spelling assimilated to Mod Fr]

■ **col'onelcy** /-si/ *n* the office or rank of colonel. **col'onelling** *n* (*archaic*) (or /kor-ō-nel'ing/) playing the colonel. **col'onelship** *n* colonelcy; the quality of being a colonel. □ **Colonel Blimp** see **blimp**[1]. **colonel-comm'andant** *n* the honorary commander of a military corps. **colonel-in-chief'** (*pl* **colonels-in-chief'**) *n* an honorary colonel, in Britain generally a member of the Royal Family.

colonial, etc see under **colony**.

colonic see under **colon**[2].

colonnade /ko-lə-nād'/ *n* a range of columns placed at regular intervals and *usu* supporting an entablature; a similar row, as of trees. [Fr, from L *columna*]

■ **colonnād'ed** *adj*.

colony /kol'ə-ni/ *n* a name vaguely applied to a state's dependencies overseas or abroad (distinguished from a *dominion*); a military settlement planted in subject territory (*Roman hist*); a band of emigrants or their new home, connected with but without political ties to their city of origin (*Gr hist*); a body of people settled in a foreign country, or forming a separate ethnic, cultural or occupational group; the settlement so formed; the place they inhabit; a number of organisms, *esp* of one kind, living together as a community (*biol*); a coenobium; a group or company of Beaver Scouts. [L *colōnia*, from *colōnus* a husbandman, from *colere* to cultivate, inhabit]

■ **colonial** /kə-lō'ni-əl/ *adj* relating to, of the nature of, or dating from the time when a territory was, a colony. ◆ *n* an inhabitant, citizen or member of a colony, a colonist. **colō'nialism** *n* a trait of colonial life or speech; the colonial system (see below); the policy or practice of obtaining, or maintaining hold over, colonies, *esp* with the purpose of exploiting them. **colōn'ialist** *adj* and *n*. **colōn'ially** *adv*. **col'onist** *n* an inhabitant of a colony; a voter set up for election purposes (*US hist*); a weed of cultivated ground (*bot*). **colonīzā'tion** or **-s-** *n* the act or practice of colonizing; state of being colonized. **col'onize** or **-ise** *vt* to plant or establish a colony in; to form into a colony; to place voters in an area to decide a closely-fought election (*US*); (of plants, animals, etc) to spread into (a new habitat). ◆ *vi* to settle as colonists. **col'onizer** or **-s-** *n*. □ **colonial animals** *n pl* organisms consisting of numerous individuals in bodily union. **colonial experience man** *n* (*old Aust*) a jackaroo. **colonial goose** *n* (*old Aust* and *NZ*) a joint of mutton, boned, stuffed and roasted. **Colonial Office** *n* (*hist*) the government office dealing with the colonies. **colonial system** *n* the theory that the settlements abroad should be treated as proprietary domains exploited for the benefit of the mother country. **colony collapse disorder** *n* a serious and unexplained disease capable of bringing about the complete

destruction of bee colonies. **colony stimulating factors** *n pl* (*immunol*) substances which cause blood-forming stem cells to proliferate and differentiate into colonies of mature blood cells. ■ **the Colonies** formerly, the subject territories of the British Empire; the thirteen states that formed the United States of America at the Declaration of Independence in 1776.

colophon /kol'ə-fon or -fən/ *n* a publisher's imprint or emblem; formerly, an inscription at the end of a book or literary composition, often naming the author and scribe or printer, with place and date of execution, etc, as on a modern title page. [L *colophōn*, from Gr *kolophōn* summit, finishing touch]

colophony /ko-lof'ə-ni or kol'ə-fō-ni/ *n* rosin. [Gr *kolophōniā* (*rhētinē* gum) from *Kolophōn* (Colophon), in Asia Minor]

coloquintida /ko-lə-kwin'ti-də/ an alternative name for **colocynth**.

color N American spelling of **colour**.

Colorado beetle /ko-lə-rä'dō bē'tl/ *n* a yellow-and-black-striped beetle (*Leptinotarsa decemlineata*), a serious pest of potatoes, originating in the USA but now found in Europe and elsewhere. [*Colorado*, the US state]

colorant, coloration see under **colour**.

coloratura /kol-ə-rə-too'rə or -tū'/ (*music*) *n* embellished vocal passages including runs, trills, etc. ◆ *adj* florid, embellished. [Ital, colouring] □ **coloratura soprano** *n* a high and flexible soprano voice, capable of singing coloratura passages; a singer with such a voice.

colorectal see under **colon**[2].

colorific, etc see under **colour**.

Coloss. (*Bible*) *abbrev*: (the Letter to) the Colossians.

colossal /kə-los'əl or ko-/ *adj* like a colossus; gigantic; of the order of columns and pilasters that extend more than one storey (*archit*). ■ **coloss'ally** *adv*.

colosseum see **coliseum**.

colossus /ko- or kə-los'əs/ *n* (*pl* **coloss'i** /-sī/ or **coloss'uses**) a person or organization of gigantic power and influence; *orig* a gigantic statue, *esp* that of Apollo at (but not astride) the entrance of the harbour of Rhodes. [L, from Gr *kolossos*] ■ **coloss'us-wise** (*Shakesp*) astride.

colostomy see under **colon**[2].

colostrum /kə- or ko-los'trəm/ *n* a yellowish fluid produced from a mammal's nipples in the first few hours or days after giving birth, consisting mainly of lymphocytes and immunoglobins and preceding the production of milk. [L] ■ **colos'tric** or **colos'trous** *adj*.

colotomy see under **colon**[2].

colour also (*esp N Am*) **color** /kul'ər/ *n* a sensation of light induced in the eye by electromagnetic waves of a certain frequency, the colour being determined by the frequency; a property whereby bodies have different appearances to the eye through surface reflection or absorption of rays; hue, one of the constituents into which white light can be decomposed; appearance of blood in the face; race or race-mixture other than Caucasian; appearance; plausibility; reason, pretext; tint; shade; paint; vividness; timbre (*music*); variety; (in *sing* or *pl*; often with *cap*) a flag, ensign or standard; (in *pl*) a symbol of membership of a party, club, college, team, etc; (in particle physics) any of six varieties of a particular characteristic of quarks and antiquarks, used to define possible combinations of these particles in baryons and mesons. ◆ *vt* to put colour on; to stain; to paint; to set in a favourable light; to exaggerate; to disguise; to misrepresent, distort. ◆ *vi* to take on colour; to blush. [OFr *color*, from L *color*, *-ōris*; related to *cēlāre* to cover, to conceal]

■ **col'orant** or **col'ourant** *n* a substance used for colouring. **colorā'tion** or **colourā'tion** *n* colouring; mode of colouring; disposition of colours. **colorif'ic** /kol- or kul-/ *adj* producing colours. **colorim'eter** /kol- or kul-/ *n* an instrument for comparison of colours. **colorimet'ric** *adj*. **colorim'etry** *n*. **colourable** /kul'-/ *adj* capable of being coloured; plausible; feigned. **col'ourably** *adv*. **col'oured** *adj* having colour; having a specious appearance, deceitful (*obs*); (of the complexion) other than white; loosely, belonging to a dark-skinned race (often *derog*); (*usu* with *cap*) in South Africa, of mixed racial descent, partly Caucasian, partly of darker race; (also with *cap*) in South Africa, of one of the former official racial groups, neither white nor African; not of Caucasian race. ◆ *n* (*usu* with *cap*) in South Africa, a person of mixed racial descent; (also with *cap*) in South Africa, a member of one of the former official racial groups, one who is neither white nor African; (in *pl*) coloured items of clothing for washing, *opp* to *whites*. **col'ourer** *n*. **col'ourful** *adj* full of or having colour; vivid; (of language) full of swear-words. **col'ourfully** *adv*. **col'ourfulness** *n*. **col'ouring** *n* any substance used to give colour; the actual colours of anything, and their arrangement; manner of applying colours;

appearance, *esp* a person's hair and skin colour; tone. **col'ourist** *n* a person who colours or paints; a person who excels in colouring or painting with colour. **colourist'ic** *adj*. **colourīzā'tion** or **-s-** *n*. **col'ourize** or **-ise** *vt* to add colour to (a film made in black and white). **col'ourless** *adj* without colour; transparent; pale; neutral; lacking distinctive character. **col'ourlessly** *adv*. **col'oury** *adj* having much colour.

□ **colour bar** *n* social discrimination *esp* by whites against other races. **col'our-blind** *adj* unable to distinguish some colours from others; not discriminating between people on the basis of skin colour or race. **colour blindness** *n*. **colour code** *n* a system of identification, eg of electrical wires, by different colours. **col'our-code** *vt* to mark with different colours for identification. **colour contamination** *n* (*image technol*) a fault in colour reproduction caused by incomplete separation of primary colours. **colour contrast** *n* the perceived change in a colour when surrounded by another colour, used in psychology and tests for colour blindness. **colour correction** *n* in colour printing, compensation either by hand, by colour masking, or electronically, for inherent faults of the printing inks available. **coloured pencil** *n* one containing a coloured lead as distinct from graphite or blacklead. **col'ourfast** *adj* (of material, etc) with colours that are resistant to change when exposed to water, light or rubbing. **colour fastness** *n*. **colour film** *n* a film for producing colour photographs. **colour filter** *n* (*photog*) a transparent material, *usu* coloured glass or gelatin, used to modify the light transmitted through a camera's lens, by absorbing or transmitting selectively certain colours or wavelengths. **colour hearing** *n* the association of colours with sounds heard. **colour index** *n* the difference between the photographic and visual magnitudes of a star used to calculate its temperature (*astron*); a number representing the dark-coloured heavy silicates in an igneous rock (*geol*); a systematic arrangement of colours according to their hue, saturation and brightness or an index giving chemical compositions of dyes and pigments. **colour line** *n* a social and political separation between white and other races. **col'ourman** *n* a person who prepares or sells paints. **colour masking** *n* in photographic colour reproduction, the use of additional images to compensate for the deficiencies of the dyes forming the principal colour records. **colour music** *n* the art of displaying colours on a screen with effect analogous to music. **colour organ** *n* an instrument for doing this. **colour party** or **colour guard** *n* a military guard carrying a flag or colours. **colour phase** *n* any seasonal or abnormal variation in the coloration of an animal. **col'ourpoint** *n* a Persian cat that has been crossed to achieve the colouring of a Siamese. **colour reversal** *n* (*photog*) a process in which the negative image in the respective colour layers is reversed to give a positive transparency. **colour scheme** *n* a planned combination of colours in a design or interior decoration. **colour screen** *n* a colour filter. **col'our-sergeant** *n* a non-commissioned officer, *orig* responsible for guarding the Colours of a regiment. **colour subcarrier** *n* in colour television, a signal conveying the colour or chrominance information as a modulation, added to the monochrome video and synchronizing signals. **colour supplement** or **magazine** *n* an illustrated magazine printed in colour and published *usu* as a part of a weekly newspaper (also (*inf*) **col'our-sup, -supp** or **-mag**). ♦ *adj* of a style often pictured in such a magazine, ie expensive and rather exclusive. **colour temperature** *n* (*phys*) that temperature of a black body that radiates with the same dominant wavelengths as those apparent from a source being described or considered. **colour therapy** *n* the therapeutic use, both psychologically and physically, of coloured light and of appropriate colours generally. **colour threshold** *n* the luminance level below which colour differences are indiscernible. **col'ourwash** *n* a cheap form of distemper coating. ♦ *vt* to paint with this. **col'ourway** *n* one of several combinations of colours in which eg a patterned fabric is available. **colour wheel** *n* a disc having coloured segments showing the relationship between colours.

■ **colour a pipe** to cause a pipe, *esp* a meerschaum, to darken by smoking. **colour in** to fill in an area on a piece of paper, etc with colour. **colour up** to blush, flush. **false colours** a false pretence. **fear no colours** to fear no enemy. **give** or **lend colour** to give plausibility. **high colour** ruddiness of complexion. **join the colours** to enlist. **lose colour** to lose one's good looks; to become pale; to appear less probable (*fig*). **nail one's colours to the mast** to commit oneself to some party or plan of action. **off colour** faded; unwell; past one's best; slightly indecent. **one's true colours** as one really is, one's real character. **pair of colours** see under **pair**[1]. **primary colours** see under **primary**. **see the colour of a person's money** to be sure that a person has sufficient money to pay before agreeing to a transaction. **under colour of** under the pretext of. **with flying colours** with distinction or brilliance.

colporteur /kol-pŏr-tûr', -pŏr-/ or /kol'pŏr-tər/ *n* a pedlar, *esp* one selling religious tracts and books. [Fr *colporteur*, from *col*, from L *collum* the neck, and *porter*, from L *portāre* to carry]
■ **col'portāge** (or /-täzh'/) *n* the distribution of books by colporteurs.

colposcope /kol'pə-skōp/ *n* an instrument for examining the neck of the uterus, *esp* for early signs of cancer. [Gr *kolpos* the womb, and *skopeein* to see]
■ **colposcop'ical** *adj*. **colposcop'ically** *adv*. **colpos'copy** *n* examination using a colposcope.

Colt® /kōlt or kolt/ *n* a single-action revolver invented by Samuel Colt (1814–62); any pistol, revolver, etc bearing this tradename.

colt /kōlt or kolt/ *n* a young horse; an awkward, somewhat clumsy, person; an inexperienced youth; *esp* in sports and games, a young, inexperienced player; a rope's end used as an instrument of punishment (*naut*). ♦ *vi* (*archaic*) to frisk like a colt. ♦ *vt* to cheat (*archaic*); to give the rope's end, to beat. [OE *colt*; Swed *kult* a young boar, a stout boy]
■ **colt'ish** *adj* like a colt; frisky. **colt'ishly** *adv*. **colt'ishness** *n*.
□ **colts'foot** *n* (*pl* **colts'foot** or **colts'foots**) a composite plant (*Tussilago farfara*) with a shaggy stalk and large soft leaves. **colt's tooth** *n* one of a horse's first set of teeth; love of youthful pleasures (*Shakesp*); wantonness. **colt'wood** *n* (*Spenser*) a plant used by Glauce in her incantations (*Faerie Queene* III.2.49.8), said to be coltsfoot, which is not woody.

coltan /kol'tan/ *n* a dull metallic ore from which tantalum is derived. [Short for *columbite-tantalite*]

colter see **coulter**.

colubrid /kol'yŭ-brid/ *n* any snake of the family **Colū'bridae**, the largest family of snakes, of about 300 genera worldwide, being mostly non-venomous and including the grass snake, water snakes and whip snakes (also *adj*). [L *coluber* a snake]
□ **colūb'riad** *n* (*Cowper*) the epic of a snake. **colubriform** /-oo'- or -ū'-/ *adj* resembling the Colubridae. **col'ūbrine** *adj* of, relating to or resembling the Colubridae; snakelike.

colugo /ko-loo'gō/ *n* (*pl* **colu'gos**) the flying lemur (qv under **fly**). [Prob from Malaysian word]

Columba /kə-lum'bə/ *n* one of the southern constellations. [L *columba* dove]
■ **Colum'ban** *adj* relating to St *Columba* (521–597), the Irish apostle who founded a monastery at Iona and converted the northern Picts to Christianity.

columbarium, columbary see under **columbine**.

Columbian /kə-lum'bi-ən/ *adj* (*poetic*) of or relating to the United States, American. ♦ *n* (*printing*) a size of type between English and Great Primer, *approx* 16-point. [Christopher *Columbus*, discoverer of America]
■ **colum'bate** *n* niobate. **colum'bic** *adj* niobic. **columb'ite** *n* a mineral, niobate and tantalate of iron and manganese. **colum'bium** *n* the former name for **niobium**.
□ **Columbus Day** *n* 12 October, a holiday in the USA.

columbine /kol'əm-bīn/ *adj* of or like a dove; dove-coloured. ♦ *n* any plant of the ranunculaceous genus *Aquilegia*, with coloured sepals and spurred petals, giving the appearance of a bunch of pigeons; (with *cap*) in pantomime, the sweetheart of Harlequin. [L *columba* a dove]
■ **columbā'rium** *n* (*pl* **columbāria**) a dovecot; a niche for a sepulchral urn; a recess in a wall to receive the end of a rafter. **col'umbary** *n* a dovecot.

Columbus /kə-lum'bəs/ *n* the European Space Agency's programme ensuring a European contribution to the International Space Station.

column /kol'əm/ *n* an upright cylinder, used as support or adornment; any upright body or mass like a column; a body of troops forming a long, narrow procession; a vertical row of figures, etc; a vertical section of a page or of a table of information; a particular section in a newspaper, often habitually written by the same person; a bundle of nerve-fibres; the central part of an orchid. [L *columna*, related to *celsus* high; Gr *kolōnē* a hill; see **hill**]
■ **col'ūmel** *n* a small column. **colūmell'a** *n* (*pl* **columell'ae** /-lē/) (*biol*) the central axis of a spiral univalve; in lower vertebrates, the auditory ossicle connecting the tympanum with the inner ear (also **columella auris**); the central axis of the spore-case of mosses; the central axis of a fruit that remains after the carpels have split away. **colūmell'ar** *adj*. **columnal** /kə-lum'nl/ or **colum'nar** *adj* relating to columns; like a column; formed or arranged in columns. **columnar'ity** *n*. **columnated** /kol'əm-nāt-id or kə-lum'-/, **columned** /kol'əmd/ or **colum'niated** *adj* having columns. **columniation** /kə-lum-ni-ā'shən/ *n* the use or arrangement of columns. **columnist** /kol'əm-ist or -nist/ *n* a person who writes a regular column in a newspaper.
■ **column inch** the measure used in newspapers, etc, being an area one column wide by one inch deep.

colure /kō-lūr', kōl' or kol'yər/ *n* a great circle of the celestial sphere passing through the poles of the equator and either the solstitial or the equinoctial points. [Gr *kolouros*, from *kolos* docked, and *ourā* tail]

coly /kō'li/ n any of various S African arboreal birds of the genus *Colius*, having a long tail and crested head. [Gr *kolios* woodpecker]

colza /kol'zə/ n coleseed, yielding **colza oil**. [Du *koolzaad* cabbage-seed]

COM /kom/ abbrev : computer output on microfilm.

Com. abbrev : Commander; Commissioner; Committee; Commodore; Commonwealth; Communist.

com. abbrev : comedy; commerce; committee; common; commune.

com- /kom-/, **con-** /kon-/ or **co-** /ko- or kō-/, also, by assimilation, **col-** /kol-/ or **cor-** /kor-/ pfx denoting: together, with; similar; used as intensive as in *consolidate*, *constant*. [L *com*, old form of *cum* with]

COMA abbrev : Committee on Medical Aspects of Food and Nutrition Policy (now replaced by **SACN**).

coma¹ /kō'mə/ n a deeply unconscious state characterized by absence of response to external and internal stimuli, caused by an accumulation of poison in the brain tissue, head injury, cerebral haemorrhage, etc; stupor. [Gr *kōma, -atos*]
■ **com'atose** adj affected with coma; extremely drowsy or sleeping heavily (*facetious*).

coma² /kō'mə/ n (pl **com'ae** /-mē/) a tuft of hairs attached to the testa of a seed (*bot*); a crown of leaves on certain trees; the nebulous envelope of the head of a comet (*astron*); (the manifestation of) a defect in an optical system (eg in a telescope) in which the image of a point appears as a blurred pear-shaped patch (*optics*). [Gr *komē* the hair of the head]
■ **cō'mal, cō'mate, cō'mose** or **cō'mous** adj. **comat'ulid** n a feather star.
❑ **Coma Berenices** /ber-ə-nī'sēz/ n Berenice's Hair, a small northern constellation.

Comanche /ko-man'chē/ n (pl **Coman'che** or **Coman'ches**) (a member of) a Native American people now living in Oklahoma; the Uto-Aztecan language of this people. ◆ adj of or relating to the Comanche or their language.
■ **cōmanche'rō** n (pl **comanche'ros**) in the 19c, a person who traded with plains native peoples of south-western N America.

comarb see **coarb**.

comart /kō-märt'/ (*Shakesp*) n an agreement. [Perh **co-** and **mart¹**; or a misprint for *cou'nant* ie **covenant**]

comate see under **coma²**.

co-mate /kō'māt'/ (*Shakesp*) n a mate or companion.

comatose see under **coma¹**.

comb¹ /kōm/ n a toothed implement or part of a machine, for separating, arranging and cleaning hair, wool, flax, etc; anything of similar form; an act of combing; the fleshy crest on the head of some birds; the top or crest of a wave, of a roof, or of a hill; a regular structure made by bees for storing honey, a honeycomb. ◆ vt to separate, arrange or clean by means of a comb or as if with a comb; to search methodically and thoroughly. ◆ vi to break with a white foam, as the top of a wave does. [OE *camb*]
■ **combed** adj. **comb'er** n someone or something that combs wool, etc; a long foaming wave. **comb'ings** n pl hairs or wool fibres combed off. **comb'less** adj. **comb'wise** adv. **comb'y** adj.
❑ **comb jelly** n same as **ctenophore** (see under **ctene**). **comb'over** n a vain attempt to make the most of one's dwindling resources of hair (see also **comb over** below).
■ **comb out** to arrange (hair) by combing after rollers, etc have been removed; to remove (tangles, etc) from hair by combing; to search thoroughly for and remove (eg lice, men for military service; **comb'-out** n). **comb over** to comb long strands of hair from one side of the head over to the other to disguise a bald patch. **go over with a fine-tooth(ed) comb** to examine or search thoroughly.

comb², combe see **coomb¹,²**.

combat /kom or kum'bat (N Am usu kəm-bat')/ vi (**com'bating**; **com'bated**) to contend or struggle. ◆ vt to fight against, to oppose; to contest; to debate. ◆ n /kom' or kum'/ a struggle; a fight; fighting, military action. ◆ adj (esp US) of or relating to fighting troops, as opposed to eg base units. [Fr *combattre* to fight, from L pfx *com-* mutual, and *bātuere* to strike]
■ **com'batable** adj. **com'batant** adj disposed to combat; taking part in or liable to take part in military action. ◆ n a person who takes part in (a) combat. **com'bative** adj inclined to quarrel, aggressive. **com'bativeness** n.
❑ **combat fatigue** n same as **battle fatigue** (see under **battle¹**). **combat jacket** n a jacket (in the style of those) worn by soldiers when fighting, *usu* khaki with camouflage markings. **combat stress** n emotional and psychological stress experienced by members of the armed forces engaged in combat. **combat trousers** n pl a style of loose-fitting trousers with side pockets, as worn by soldiers in action (short form **combats**).

comber¹ /kom'bər/ n the gaper (a sea-perch); a species of wrasse.

comber² see under **comb¹**.

combine /kəm-bīn'/ vt to join together; to unite chemically (with) to form a new compound; to bind, restrict (*Shakesp*). ◆ vi to come into close union (with); to co-operate; to unite and form a new compound (*chem*). ◆ n /kom'bīn/ a syndicate, a trust, an association of trading companies; a combine harvester. [L *combīnāre* to join, from *com-* and *bīnī*, two and two]
■ **com'bi** n (*inf*, often used *attrib*) a device having more than one function. **combinabil'ity** n. **combīn'able** adj. **combinate** /kom'bin-āt/ adj combined; betrothed (*Shakesp*). **combinā'tion** n the act of combining; union, joining of individual things; chemical union, forming a new compound; a motorcycle with sidecar (also called **motorcycle combination**); a group of people united for a purpose; in mathematics, a possible set of a given number of things selected from a given number, irrespective of arrangement within the set (distinguished from a *permutation*); the series of letters or numbers that must be dialled to open a combination lock. **combinā'tional** adj. **combinā'tions** n pl (*inf* short form **coms** or **combs** /komz/) a warm undergarment covering the whole body with long sleeves and legs. **com'binātive** adj. **combinato'rial** adj (*maths*) concerned with arrangements, combinations and permutations. **combinator'ics** n sing (*maths*) the branch of mathematics concerned with the theory and function of combinations and permutations. **combin'atory** adj. **combīned'** adj. **combīn'ing** adj. **combo** /kom'bō/ n (pl **com'bos**) a small jazz- or dance band; any combination (*inf*); a white man who cohabits with an Aboriginal woman (*Aust*).
❑ **combination lock** n a lock used on safes, suitcases, etc, with numbered dials which must be turned in a special order a certain number of times, or to a certain number or numbers, to open it. **combination oven** n an oven that functions both as a microwave and as a conventional oven (*inf* short form **combi**). **combination room** n at Cambridge University, a common room. **combination therapy** n (*med*) treatment of a single form of cancer or other disease with more than one drug. **combined operations** n pl (*milit*) operations in which army, navy and air force work together. **combine harvester** n (*agric*) a combined harvesting and threshing machine. **combining form** n a linguistic element that is only used as part of a composite word.

comble /kɔ̃'-bl'/ (*Fr*) n the acme.

combo see under **combine**.

combretum /kom-brē'təm/ n a member of the genus *Combretum* (family **Combretā'ceae**), tropical and subtropical trees and shrubs noted for the beauty of their flowers. [L *combrētum* an unknown plant]
■ **Combretastat'in®** n a drug derived from the African bush willow tree, used as an experimental treatment for cancer.

combs see **combinations** under **combine**.

comburgess /kom-bûr'jis/ n a fellow burgess.

combust /kom-bust'/ vt and vi to burn up. ◆ adj in conjunction with the sun, or apparently very near it, so as to be obscured by its light, said of a planet when it is not more than $8\frac{1}{2}°$ from the sun. [L *combūrere, combūstum* to consume, from *com-*, intens, and *ūrere* to burn]
■ **combustibil'ity** n. **combust'ible** adj liable to catch fire and burn; excitable. ◆ n something that will catch fire and burn. **combust'ibleness** n the quality of being combustible. **combust'ion** /-yən/ n burning; the action of fire on combustible substances; oxidation or similar process with production of heat. **combust'ious** adj (*Shakesp*) combustible, inflammable; turbulent. **combust'ive** adj capable of catching fire. **combust'or** n the system in a jet engine or gas turbine in which combustion takes place; a combustion chamber.
❑ **combustion chamber** n in a boiler furnace, the space in which combustion of gaseous products from the fuel takes place; in an internal-combustion engine, the space above the piston in which combustion occurs (*motoring*).
■ **spontaneous combustion** burning caused by heat generated in the substance or body itself.

Comdr. abbrev : Commander.

Comdt. abbrev : Commandant.

come /kum/ vi (**com'ing**; **came** /kām/; **come**) to move toward the place that is the point of view of the speaker or writer, opp of *go*; to draw near; to arrive at a certain state or condition; to occupy a specific place in order, priority, etc; to issue, to happen, to turn out; to yield (*Shakesp*); to become; to amount (to); to reach; to begin to be in some condition; to achieve a sexual orgasm, to ejaculate (*sl*); to be had, got or gained; (only *3rd pers sing*; *esp* in *subjunctive*) when (a certain time) comes (as in *Come five o'clock, it will be dark outside*). ◆ vt (*inf*) to act the part of, assume the behaviour of, as in *Don't come the innocent with me*; (with *it*) to try to impress, assert one's authority over, etc. ◆ interj (or *imperative*) expressive of encouragement, protest or reproof (often in phrases *come come* or *come now*). ◆*n* (*vulgar sl*; also **cum**) ejaculated semen. [OE *cuman*; Ger *kommen*]

■ **com'er** (also *archaic* **comm'er**) *n* someone who comes or has come; a person who shows promise (*inf*). **com'ing** *n* arrival or approach; (*esp* with *cap*) the Advent, or the hoped-for return (also **Second Coming**) of Christ. ◆*interj* used as a response to a request or requirement; ready to attend to one's attention or presence. ◆*adj* future; of future importance; ready to make or meet advances (*archaic*).

❏ **come-and-go'** *n* passage to and fro. **come-at'-able** *adj* (*inf*) accessible. **come'back** *n* a return, *esp* to a former activity or good, popular, successful, etc state; a revival; a retort, rejoinder; cause or ability to complain; recrimination. **come'down** *n* a descent; a disappointment or deflation; a degradation. **come-hith'er** *n* an invitation to approach; allure. ◆*adj* (of a look, manner, etc) inviting (*esp* sexually), alluring. **come'-off** *n* a conclusion; an evasion of duty. **come'-on** *n* (*inf*) encouragement, *esp* sexual; persuasion. **come'-o'-will** *n* something that comes of its own accord; an illegitimate child (also **come'-by-chance**). **comeupp'ance** *n* (*inf*) deserved rebuke or punishment. **com'ings-in'** *n pl* income.

■ **all comers** everyone who arrives, volunteers, etc. **as/as they come** to the greatest extent possible. **as it comes** however it is made, in any way whatsoever. **come about** to happen; to turn to face the opposite way (*naut*). **come across** to find (a specific thing) *esp* during a general search; to make an impression; to give or supply (often with *with*); (of a woman) to be responsive to sexual advances (*sl*). **come again?** (*inf*) what did you say?; pardon? **come along** to progress; to arrive; (in *imperative*) hurry up. **come and go** to fluctuate; to have freedom of movement or action. **come apart** to fall to pieces. **come at** to reach; to attack; to approach. **come away** to leave; to become detached. **come back** to return to popularity, office, etc after being in a losing position, a period of obscurity, etc; to return to life; to become fashionable again; to return to memory; to retort (*esp N Am*). **come before** to appear in response to a summons by (a figure of authority) to be dealt with. **come between** to cause a rift between (two people, etc); to create a barrier or division between. **come by** to come near; to pass by; (as a command to sheepdogs) move to the left of the group of sheep being herded; to visit (*esp N Am*); to obtain or acquire; to come in. **come down** to descend; to be reduced, to decrease; to lose (*esp* financial) status; to emerge from the state induced by a hallucinogenic or addictive drug; to leave university, *esp* Oxford or Cambridge; (with *to*) to be a question of; to be an inheritance. **come down (up)on** to be severe with, to punish. **come down with** to become ill with or contract (a disease). **come for** to arrive in order to collect; to attack. **come forward** to identify or present oneself (as a volunteer, as a witness, etc). **come from** to originate from or in. **come high** or **low** to cost much or little. **come home** to return to one's house; to touch one's interest or feelings closely, to affect (with *to*); (of an anchor) to drag or slip through the ground (*naut*). **come in** to enter; to arrive; to receive (money, income, etc); to have a role or function; to become fashionable; to reply to a radio signal or call; (of the tide) to rise; to start an innings (*cricket*); to get within the opponent's guard (*fencing*). **come in for** to receive as, or as if as, one's share; to receive incidentally. **come in on** to become a partner, etc in (eg a business venture). **come into** to inherit; to be involved in; (of plants) to begin producing (flowers, leaves, etc). **come into one's own** to have the opportunity to demonstrate or practise one's special skills, aptitudes, etc. **come it strong** (*inf*) to do or say much, go to great lengths, exaggerate. **come of** to be a descendant of; to be the consequence of, arise or result from; to become of. **come of age** to reach full legal adult status. **come off** to come away; to become detached (from); to obtain a specified type of result (with *best*, *worst*, etc); to desist from; to prove successful; to have an orgasm (*vulgar sl*). **come off it!** (*inf*) don't be ridiculous! **come on** to advance; to thrive, succeed; to proceed; to begin; to appear; to give the impression of being (*inf*); often in *imperative* as a challenge or exhortation to attack, proceed, hurry, recover from low spirits, etc. **come on stream** (of oil-wells) to start regular production (also *fig*). **come on strong** (*inf*) to speak or act forcefully or aggressively. **come on to** (*inf*) to make sexual advances towards. **come out** to emerge; to appear; to result (well, etc); to be published or made available; to become known or evident; to be solved; to enter society; to be released or leave (prison, hospital, etc); to declare openly one's homosexuality (*sl*); (of photographs) to develop successfully; (of stains, marks, etc) to be removed; to erupt (in spots, a rash, etc); to stop work, strike; to declare oneself (against or in favour of). **come out with** to utter, to say; to exclaim. **come over** to befall; to change sides or allegiance; to come into the mind of; to make an impression (with *as*); suddenly to experience a certain feeling or mood (as in *come over faint*; *inf*). **come round** to come by a circuitous path; to visit; to happen in due course; to recur; to veer; to become favourable (in opinion, etc); to become amenable; to recover consciousness from a faint, etc. **come short** to fail. **come short of** to fail to attain. **come through** to survive; to succeed or complete successfully (an exam, test, etc); to arrive, having passed through a (*usu* administrative) process or system; to pass through. **come**

through for to be a source of help for. **come to** to obtain; to amount to; to be a question of; to proceed as far as; to recover consciousness; to stop (*naut*). **come to grief** to meet with disaster or failure. **come to oneself** to return to one's normal state of mind. **come to pass** (*esp Bible*) to happen. **come to rest** to halt. **come to stay** to become permanent. **come to that** in actual fact, that being the case. **come true** to be fulfilled, to happen. **come under** to be included under; to be subjected to (fire, attack, etc). **come undone** or **unfastened**, etc to become detached, loose, etc. **come up** to present itself in discussion, etc; to appear; to shine after cleaning or polishing. **come up against** to encounter (an obstacle, difficulty). **come up to** to reach (a specified point in space or time); to equal. **come upon** to attack; to affect; to hold answerable; to meet; to find. **come up with** to suggest. **come what may** whatever happens. **give someone the come-on** to invite or entice, *esp* sexually. **have it coming** (*inf*) to have no chance of avoiding, or to get, one's just deserts. **how come?** how does it happen that? **not know if one is coming or going** to be totally confused or disorientated. **to come** future. **up and coming** approaching; promising. **when it comes to** as far as, regarding.

Comecon /kom'i-kon/ *n* a Communist organization, the Council for Mutual *Econo*mic Aid, or Assistance, dissolved in 1991.

Comédie Française /ko-mā-dē frä-sez'/ (*Fr*) *n* the official name of Le Théâtre français, the French national theatre.

Comédie humaine /ko-mā-dē ü-men'/ (*Fr*) *n* the Human Comedy, the title of Balzac's series of novels, intended to form a complete picture of contemporary society.

comedo /kom'i-dō/ *n* (*pl* **com'edos** or **comedones** /-dō'nēz/) a blackhead, a black-tipped white mass often found in the blocked skin pores. [L *comedō*, *-ōnis* glutton, from *comedere* to eat up, from its wormlike appearance]

■ **comedogen'ic** *adj* causing blackheads.

comedy /kom'i-di/ *n* a dramatic work or production having a pleasant or humorous character; the literary genre consisting of such works; a story with a happy ending; an incident of a comic or humorous nature. [Fr *comédie*, from L *cōmoedia*, from Gr *kōmōidiā*, from *kōmos* revel, or *kōmē* village and *ōidē* song]

■ **comedian** /kə-mē'di-ən/ *n* a person who acts in or writes comedies; an entertainer who tells jokes, etc; an entertaining and amusing person (often *ironic*). **comē'dic** *adj* of or relating to comedy. **comedienne** /ko-me-di-en'/ or /ko-mē-/ *n* (*orig Fr*, and still often spelt **comédienne**) a female comic entertainer. **comédiett'a** *n* a short comic piece. ■ **comedy of manners** (a) satirical comedy dealing with the manners or fashions of a social class.

comely /kum'li/ *adj* (**come'lier**; **come'liest**) pleasing; graceful; handsome or pretty. ◆*adv* in a pleasing or graceful manner. [OE *cȳmlic* glorious, beautiful, from *cȳme* suitable, fine and *lic* like]
■ **come'liness** *n*.

comestible /ko-mes'ti-bl/ *adj* eatable. ◆*n* (*usu* in *pl*) food. [Fr, from L *comedere* to eat up]

comet /kom'it/ *n* a heavenly body with a (*usu*) elliptical orbit round the sun, having a main nucleus composed of rocky fragments held together with ice and surrounded by a cloud of dust and gas (the coma), which, when the comet nears the sun, may be driven away from the head of the comet to form a luminous tail. [Gr *kometēs* long-haired, from *komē* hair]

■ **com'etary** or **cometic** /-et'ik/ *adj*. **cometog'raphy** *n*. **cometol'ogy** *n*. ❏ **com'et-finder** *n* a telescope of low power used to search for comets.

comether /kə-medh'ər/ (*dialect*) *n* wheedling; charm. [*come hither*, a call to cows, etc]

comfit /kum'fit/ *n* a sweet; a sugar-coated seed or almond. [A doublet of **confect**; Fr *confit*, *confiture*]
■ **com'fiture** *n* (*obs*) conserve, preserved fruit.

comfort /kum'fərt/ or (*Spenser*) /kom-fort'/ *vt* to relieve from pain or distress; to soothe, cheer, console; to support or encourage. ◆*n* relief; something that gives ease, consolation, enjoyment, etc; freedom from annoyance; quiet enjoyment; ease, a degree of luxury; encouragement, support; a bed quilt (*US inf*). [OFr *conforter*, from L *con-* intensive, and *fortis* strong]

■ **com'fortable** *adj* imparting or enjoying comfort; easy (*fig*); confident in the (*esp* moral) correctness of a choice or decision; having enough money to live well. **com'fortableness** *n*. **com'fortably** *adv*. **com'forter** *n* a person who gives comfort; (with *cap*; with *the*) the Holy Ghost (*Bible*); a long narrow woollen scarf; a dummy teat; a bed quilt (*N Am*). **com'forting** *adj*. **com'fortingly** *adv*. **com'fortless** *adj*. **com'fortlessness** *n*. **com'fy** *adj* (*inf*) comfortable. ❏ **comfort food** *n* mood-enhancing food that meets the approval of one's taste buds but not of one's doctor. **comfort station** *n* (*N Am*) a (public) lavatory. **comfort woman** *n* (*hist*) a woman or girl forced into prostitution by Japanese armed forces in World War II. **comfort zone** *n* (*inf*) a place, either physical or psychological, where one feels at ease.

■ **cold comfort** little, if any, comfort.

comfrey /kum'fri/ *n* a boraginaceous plant of the genus *Symphytum*, having hairy leaves often used in herbal medicine. [OFr *confirie*]

comic /kom'ik/ *adj* relating to comedy; raising mirth or laughter; funny, humorous. ◆ *n* the quality or element that arouses mirth or laughter; a humorous entertainer on stage, in clubs, on TV, etc; an actor playing humorous parts; an amusing person (*inf*); a paper or magazine, *esp* for children, with illustrated stories, strip cartoons, etc (*orig* comic, later also serious, even horrific; also **comic book**). [Gr *kōmikos*, from *kōmos* revel]

■ **com'ical** *adj* funny, amusing. **comical'ity** or **com'icalness** *n*. **com'ically** *adv*.

□ **comic opera** see under **opera¹**. **comic relief** *n* relief from dramatic tension provided by humour or a comic episode. **comic strip** *n* a strip cartoon.

comice /kom'is/ *n* a variety of pear (also **comice pear**).

Cominform /kom'in-förm/ *n* the Communist Information Bureau (1947–56), which succeeded the Comintern.

■ **Com'informist** *n*.

COMINT /kom'int/ *abbrev*: Communications Intelligence, that branch of military intelligence concerned with monitoring and intercepting communications transmitted by the enemy (cf **ELINT**, **HUMINT**).

Comintern /kom'in-tûrn/ *n* the Communist International (1919–43), or Third International (see under **international**).

comique /kō-mēk'/ *n* a comic actor or singer. [See **comic**]

comitadji same as **komitaji**.

comitatus /ko-mi-tā'təs/ *n* a prince's escort or retinue; a county or shire. [L *comitātus, -ūs*, from *comes, -itis* companion, count]

■ **com'ital** *adj* relating to a count, earl, or county. **com'itative** *adj* (of a grammatical case) expressing accompaniment. ◆ *n* a comitative case.

comitia /ko-mish'i-ə or ko-mit'i-a/ *n pl* the assemblies of the Romans for electing magistrates, passing laws, etc. [L, from *com* together, and *īre, itum* to go]

□ **comitia centuriata** /sen-tū-ri-ā'tə or ken-tū-ri-ā'ta/ *n pl* the assembly of Roman people, voting by centuries. **comitia curiata** /kū-ri-ā'tə or koo-ri-ā'ta/ *n pl* that of the patricians, voting by curiae. **comitia tributa** /tri-bū'tə or tri-boo'ta/ *n pl* that of the people, voting by tribes.

comity /kom'i-ti/ *n* courteousness; civility. [L *cōmitās, -ātis*, from *cōmis* courteous]

■ **comity of nations** (L *comitas gentium*) the international courtesy between nations in which recognition is accorded to the laws and customs of each state by others; a group of nations adhering to this code of behaviour.

comm. *abbrev*: commander; commentary; communication.

comma /kom'ə/ *n* in punctuation, the sign (,) that marks the smallest division of a sentence; a phrase (*rhetoric*); the smallest interval, break or discontinuity; a comma butterfly; a name for various minute intervals, *esp* the difference between twelve perfect fifths and seven octaves (*music*). [L, from Gr *komma* a section of a sentence, from *koptein* to cut off]

□ **comma bacillus** *n* the micro-organism (*Vibrio comma*) that causes cholera. **comma butterfly** *n* a brown and orange nymphaline butterfly (*Polygonia calbum*), having wings with ragged outlines and with a white comma-shaped mark on the underside of the hind wing.

■ **inverted commas** a set of double or single superscript commas used to introduce and close a quotation, the introductory one(s) being inverted (''y'' or 'y').

command /kə-mänd'/ *vt* to order; to exercise supreme (*esp* military) authority over; to demand; to have within sight, range, influence or control. ◆ *vi* to have chief authority; to govern. ◆ *n* an order; authority; control; power to overlook, influence or use; the thing or people under one's authority; a military division under separate control; a group of high-ranking army officers; ability or understanding; a signal or message activating a mechanism or setting in motion a sequence of operations (*esp comput*); a command paper. [Fr *commander*, from LL *commandāre* (L *commendāre*), from L *mandāre* to entrust]

■ **commandant** /kom-ən-dant' or kom'/ *n* an officer who has the command of a place or of a body of troops. **commandant'ship** *n*. **commandeer'** *vt* to seize for military use; to take over for one's own use, without asking. **command'er** *n* a person who commands; an officer in the navy next in rank under a captain; a high-ranking police officer in charge of a district; a member of a higher class in an order of knighthood; a district administrator in religious military orders; the highest ranking officer in the Royal Society for the Prevention of Cruelty to Animals. **command'ership** *n*. **command'ery** *n* the district under a commander, *esp* in the religious military orders. **command'ing** *adj* dominating, impressive, authoritative; strategic.

command'ingly *adv.* **command'ment** *n* a command; a religious rule for living by, *esp* one of the Ten Commandments. **command'o** *n* (*pl* **command'os**) a unit of a special service brigade, *esp* the Royal Marine Corps (*milit*); a person serving in such a unit; an armed force of Boers (*S Afr hist*).

□ **command economy** *n* an economy in which all means of creating wealth and business activities are controlled by government rather than market forces. **commander-in-chief'** *n* (*pl* **commanders-in-chief**) the officer in supreme command of an army, or of the entire forces of the state. **command language** *n* (*comput*) the language used to communicate with the operating system. **command line** *n* (*comput*) a blank line on the screen to the right of a prompt where the user types a command. **command module** *n* the part of a spacecraft from which operations are directed. **command paper** *n* a government document, *orig* one presented to parliament by command of the monarch. **command performance** *n* a performance before royalty. **command post** *n* a military unit's (temporary) headquarters.

■ **at one's command** available for use. **commander of the faithful** a title of the caliphs. **go commando** (*orig US sl*) to forgo the use of underpants. **on commando** on military service in the field. **Ten Commandments** the ten commandments given by God to Moses on Mount Sinai, as described in the Old Testament Book of Exodus.

commeasure /kə-mezh'ər/ *vt* to equal in measure; to coincide with.

■ **commeas'urable** *adj* same as **commensurable**.

comme ci, comme ça /kom sē' kom sa'/ (*Fr*) so-so, neither good nor bad.

commedia dell'arte /ko-mā'dē-a de-lär'te/ (*Ital*) *n* Italian Renaissance comedy, mainly improvised and with stock characters.

comme il faut /kom ēl fō'/ (*Fr*) *adj* as it should be; proper; correct; approved by the fashionable world; genteel, well-bred.

Commelina /ko-mə-lī'nə/ *n* a tropical genus of monocotyledons, of the family **Commelinaceae** /-li-nā'si-ē/. [Johannes (1629–72) and Caspar (1667–1731) *Commelin*, Dutch botanists]

commemorate /kə-mem'ə-rāt/ *vt* to signify remembrance by a solemn or public act; to celebrate; to preserve the memory of. [L *commemorāre, -ātum* to remember, from *com-*, intens, and *memor* mindful]

■ **commem'orable** *adj.* **commemorā'tion** *n* preserving the memory of some person or thing, *esp* by a solemn ceremony; the specification of individual saints in the prayers for the dead; the great festival of the Oxford academic year, *usu* taking place on the third Wednesday after Trinity Sunday. **commem'orative** or **commem'oratory** *adj* tending or serving to commemorate. **commem'orator** *n*.

commence /kə-mens'/ *vi* and *vt* to begin; to originate. [OFr *com(m)encier*, from L *com-*, intens, and *initiāre* to begin, from *in* into, and *īre* to go]

■ **commence'ment** *n* the beginning; at certain universities, the act of taking a degree; the ceremony when degrees are conferred (*esp US*).

commend /kə-mend'/ *vt* to commit as a charge or responsibility; to recommend as worthy; to praise; to adorn, set off (*obs*). [L *commendāre*, from *com-*, intens, and *mandāre* to trust]

■ **commend'able** *adj* praiseworthy. **commend'ableness** *n*. **commend'ably** *adv.* **commend'am** *n* an ecclesiastical benefice held, or the tenure or grant of a benefice held, *in commendam*, in trust, ie theoretically temporarily, until a pastor was provided for it, but often for life and without duties. **commendation** /kom-ən-dā'shən/ *n* the act of commending; praise; a public award for praiseworthy action. **comm'endator** *n* a person who holds a benefice *in commendam*; a titular abbot, etc. **commend'atory** *adj* commending; containing praise or commendation; presenting to favourable notice or reception; held or holding *in commendam*.

■ **commend me to** (*archaic*) remember me kindly to; give me by preference.

commensal /kə-men'səl/ *adj* eating at the same table; living together in close association and with mutual benefit, *esp* an association of less intimate kind than that called symbiosis (*biol*). ◆ *n* a messmate; an organism living in partnership or association with another of a different species without affecting or benefiting it. [L *com-* together, and *mēnsa* a table]

■ **commen'salism** *n*. **commensal'ity** *n*. **commen'sally** *adv*.

commensurable /kə-men'shə-rə-bl or -sū-/ *adj* having a common measure (*maths*); capable of being measured exactly by the same unit (*maths*); well-proportioned. [L *com-* and *mēnsūra* a measure, from *mētīrī, mēnsus* to measure]

■ **commensurabil'ity** or **commen'surableness** *n*. **commen'surably** *adv*. **commen'surate** *adj* equal in measure or extent; in due proportion (with). **commen'surately** *adv*. **commen'surateness** *n*. **commensurā'tion** *n*.

comment /kom'ent or -ənt/ *n* a note conveying illustration or explanation; a remark, observation or criticism. ◆ *vi* (or /kəm-ent'/) to make critical or explanatory notes (on); to make remarks,

observations, etc; to annotate. ◆ vt to say in comment. [L commentārī to devise, contrive, from com- and mēns, mentis the mind]
■ **commentā'riat** n the group of people who act as commentators on political, social, etc matters. **comm'entary** n a comment; a remark; a series or book of comments or critical notes; a continuous description of a sport, event, etc broadcast on television or radio (also **running commentary**). **comm'entate** vi to give a running commentary. **commentā'tion** n annotation. **comm'entātor** n a person who comments; the writer of a critical commentary; a broadcaster of a running commentary. **commentatò'rial** (or /-tö'/) adj relating to the making of commentaries. **comm'enter** or **comm'entor** (or /-ment'/) n.
■ **no comment** (inf) I have nothing to say (usu to a newspaper or television reporter).

commer (archaic) see under **come**.

commerce /kom'ûrs/ n interchange of merchandise on a large scale between nations or individuals; trade or traffic; social dealings; sexual intercourse (archaic). ◆ vi /kəm-ûrs'/ (rare) to trade; to have communication (with). [Fr, from L commercium, from com- mutual, and merx, mercis merchandise]
■ **commer'cial** /-shl/ adj relating to commerce; mercantile; having profit as the main aim (sometimes implying disregard of quality); commercially viable; sponsored by an advertiser. ◆ n a commercially-sponsored advertisement on radio or TV; a commercial traveller; a commercial vehicle. **commercialese'** n business jargon. **commer'cialism** n commercial attitudes and aims; an expression that is characteristic of commercial language. **commer'cialist** n and adj. **commerciality** /-shi-al'i-ti/ n. **commercializā'tion** or **-s-** n. **commer'cialize** or **-ise** vt to make profit the main aim of; to turn (something) into a source of profit (often derog). **commer'cially** adv. ❑ **commercial art** n graphic art for commercial products or purposes, such as packaging, advertising, etc. **commercial bank** n a bank whose primary profitability comes from making short- to medium-term loans, often from deposits of other clients. **commercial break** n a short break in a radio or TV programme to allow commercials to be broadcast. **Commercial Court** n (in England and Wales) a court within the Queen's Bench Division that hears large commercial cases. **commercial paper** n short-term negotiable documents issued by companies and used regularly in the course of business. **commercial room** n a room in a hotel set apart for commercial travellers. **commercial traveller** n a travelling sales representative of a business concern. **commercial vehicle** n generally, a goods-carrying vehicle; by some, understood to include passenger-carrying vehicles such as buses.

commère /ko-mer'/ n fem of **compère**. [Fr, godmother; cf **cummer**]

commerge /kə-mûrj'/ vi to merge together.

commie or **commy** /kom'i/ (derog inf) n and adj short form of **communist**.

comminate /kom'i-nāt/ vt to threaten. [L comminārī, -ātum, from com-, intens, and minārī to threaten]
■ **comminā'tion** n (an instance of) threatening, denunciation; a recital of God's judgements against sinners, made on Ash Wednesday and at other times in the Church of England. **comm'inative** or **comm'inatory** adj threatening punishment.

commingle /kə-ming'gl/ vt and vi to mingle or mix together.
■ **comming'led** adj.

comminute /kom'i-nūt/ vt to reduce or break into minute particles or fragments; to pulverize. [L comminuere, -ūtum to break into pieces, from com-, intens, and minuere to make small, from root of minus less]
■ **comm'inuted** adj pulverized; broken into tiny pieces. **comminū'tion** n.
❑ **comminuted fracture** see under **fracture**.

Commiphora /ko-mif'ə-rə/ n a genus of plants of the family Burseraceae, natives of tropical Asia and Africa, yielding myrrh, bdellium and other resins. [Gr kommi gum, and phoreein to bear]

commis /ko'mē/ n an agent, deputy; an apprentice waiter, steward or chef. [Fr]

commiserate /kə-miz'ə-rāt/ vt and vi to feel or express sympathy or pity for (often with with). [L com- with, and miserārī to deplore, from miser wretched]
■ **commis'erable** adj (rare) requiring commiseration; pitiable. **commiserā'tion** n pity, sympathy. **commis'erative** adj feeling or expressing sympathetic sorrow. **commis'erator** n.

commissaire /ko-mi-sār'/ n (in cycle racing) a referee who observes a race from an open-topped vehicle. [Fr, commissioner]

commissar /kom'i-sär or ko-mi-sär'/ n a commissary (officer); (also **People's Commissar**) in the former Soviet Union, a head of a government department (after 1946 called **minister**); (also **political commissar**) in the former Soviet Union, a Communist Party official

responsible for political education, encouragement of party loyalty, etc, esp in military units. [LL commissārius, from committere, commissum]
■ **commissā'riat** n the department charged with the furnishing of provisions, eg for an army; the supply of provisions; the office of a commissary or of a commissar; a body of commissars.

commissary /kom'i-sə-ri/ n a store supplying equipment and provisions (US); (the supply of) provisions, commissariat (US); a restaurant or canteen, esp in a film studio (orig US); an officer who supplies provisions, etc to an army; an officer representing a bishop, and performing his duties in distant parts of the diocese (relig); a commissar; a person to whom any charge is committed; a deputy; the judge in a commissary court (Scots law). [Ety as for **commissar**]
■ **commissā'rial** adj relating to a commissary. **comm'issaryship** n.
❑ **commissary court** n a Scottish court, abolished in 1836, with jurisdiction in matters that had formerly belonged to the bishops' courts. **commissary general** n the head of the department for supplying provisions, etc to an army.

commission /kə-mish'ən/ n the act of committing; the state of being commissioned or committed; that which is committed; a document, etc conferring authority, or the authority itself, esp that of a military, naval, or air officer, or a justice of the peace; a percentage paid to an agent; a body of persons appointed to perform certain duties; an order for a piece of work, esp of art; (of a warship, etc) the state of being manned, equipped, and ready for service; (of an office) temporary or permanent delegation to a number of persons who act jointly. ◆ vt to give a commission to or for; to empower; to appoint; to put into service. ◆ vi to be put into service. [See **commit**]
■ **commissionaire** /-ār'/ n a uniformed doorkeeper or messenger; a member of a corps of former soldiers and sailors employed as doorkeepers, etc. **commiss'ioned** adj. **commiss'ioner** n a person who holds a commission to perform some business; a member of a commission; the representative of high authority in a district, etc. **commiss'ionership** n.
❑ **commission agent** or **commission merchant** n a person who transacts business for another for a commission. **commissioned officer** n one appointed by commission. **commissioner for** (or **of**) **oaths** n a solicitor authorized to authenticate oaths on statements, etc.
■ **High Commission** the embassy representing one country that is a member of the British Commonwealth in another such country. **High Commission Court** a court established in 1549 to investigate ecclesiastical cases, abolished as illegal in 1641. **High Commissioner** the chief representative in a High Commission. **in** (or **out of**) **commission** (of warships) prepared (or unprepared) for service; in (or not in) usable or working condition. **Lord High Commissioner** the representative of the Crown at the General Assembly of the Church of Scotland.

Commissr abbrev : Commissioner.

commissure /kom'i-sūr/ n a joint; a joining surface; a bundle of nerve fibres connecting two nerve centres, eg those crossing the midline of the central nervous system. [L commissūra a joining; see **commit**]
■ **commissū'ral** adj.

commit /kə-mit'/ vt (committ'ing; committ'ed) to give in charge or trust; to consign, send; to become guilty of, perpetrate; to involve (esp oneself); to pledge, promise. ◆ vi to make a commitment, esp to a personal relationship. [L committere, from com- with, and mittere to send]
■ **commit'ment** n the act of committing; an order for sending to prison; imprisonment; an obligation (to be) undertaken; declared attachment to a doctrine or cause. **committ'able** adj. **committ'al** n commitment; imprisonment; (the ceremony of) the placing of a coffin in a grave, crematorium furnace or the sea; a pledge, actual or implied. **committ'ed** adj having entered into a commitment; (of literature or the work of a writer or other artist) advocating certain beliefs (esp religious or political ideology) or with some fixed purpose (eg to effect social reform) (also **engagé**). **committ'er** n.
■ **commit oneself** to make a definite decision or judgement (on); to make a definite agreement. **commit to memory** to learn by heart, memorize.

committee /kə-mit'ē/ n a group selected from a more numerous body (or the whole body) to which some special business is committed; /kom-i-tē'/ a person to whom something is committed; formerly, a person entrusted with the care of an insane or mentally handicapped person (law). [ME, from committere to entrust]
■ **committ'eeman** or **committ'eewoman** n a member of a committee. **committ'eeship** n.
❑ **Committee of the Regions** n a consultative committee of the European Union, consisting of representatives from regional and local authorities and expressing the opinions of these groups on regional policy, environment and education. **committee stage** n the stage in the passage of a bill through parliament, between the second and third readings, when it is discussed in detail in committee.

■ words derived from main entry word; ❑ compound words; ■ idioms and phrasal verbs

■ **Committee of the whole House** the House of Commons or other legislative body, when it resolves itself into a committee with chairman, etc. **go into committee** to resolve itself into a committee. **in committee** participating in, during or subject to the deliberations of a committee.

commix /kə-miks'/ (*rare*) *vt* and *vi* to mix together.

■ **commix'tion** /-chən/ or **commix'ture** *n* the act of mixing together; the state of being mixed; the compound formed by mixing; the rite of putting a piece of the host into the chalice, emblematic of the reunion of body and soul at the resurrection; sexual intercourse (*obs*).

commn *abbrev* : commission.

commo /kom'ō/ (*Aust inf*) *n* (*pl* **comm'os**) a communist.

commode /kə-mōd'/ *n* a small sideboard; an ornamental chest of drawers; a chair containing a chamberpot; a large high headdress formerly worn by ladies. [Fr]

commodification /ko- or kə-mod-i-fi-kā'shən/ *n* making a commodity of something, commercialization of something not normally seen in commercial terms. [**commodity**]

■ **commod'ify** *vt*.

commodious /kə-mō'dyəs or -di-əs/ *adj* roomy, spacious; comfortable; suitable or convenient (*archaic*); serviceable (*archaic*). [L *commodus*, from *com-* together, and *modus* measure]

■ **commo'diously** *adv*. **commo'diousness** *n*.

commodity /ko- or kə-mod'i-ti/ *n* an article of trade; (in *pl*) goods, produce; a raw material; profit, expediency, advantage, convenience or privilege (*archaic*). [MFr *commodité*, from L *commoditās*, *-ātis* fitness, convenience]

■ **commoditiza'tion** or **-s-** *n*. **commod'itize** or **-ise** *vt* to make into a commodity; to commercialize.

❑ **commodity exchange** or **commodity market** *n* a market where raw materials, such as wool, sugar, etc, are traded.

commodo or **comodo** /ko-mō'dō or (*Ital*) kom'o-do/ (*music*) *adj* and *adv* with ease; relaxed. [Ital, comfortable]

commodore /kom'ə-dör or -dōr/ *n* an officer of a rank between an admiral and a captain; the senior captain in a fleet of merchant ships; the president of a yacht club; a commodore's ship. [Perh from Du *kommandeur*]

common /kom'ən/ *adj* belonging equally to more than one; mutual; public; general; usual; frequent; ordinary; easily got or obtained; of little value; vulgar; of low degree. ◆ *n* the commonalty (*Shakesp*); a tract of open land, used by all the inhabitants of a town, parish, etc; a right to take something from the land of another person (*law*); common sense (*sl*). ◆ *vi* to share (*Shakesp*); to board (*archaic*). [Fr *commun*, from L *commūnis*, prob from *com-* together, and *mūnis* serving, obliging]

■ **comm'onable** *adj* held in common, mutual; (of animals) that may be pastured on common land. **comm'onage** *n* the right of pasturing in common with others; the right of using anything in common; a common. **commonal'ity** *n* the state of being common to all; standardization; frequency, prevalence; (*esp Scot*) the common people. **comm'onalty** *n* the general body of ordinary people; the common people. **comm'oner** *n* a person who is not a noble; a member of the House of Commons; at Oxford University, a student who does not have a scholarship. **comm'oney** *n* an ordinary playing marble. **comm'oning** *n* the conversion of land to common. **comm'only** *adv* in a common manner; meanly, vulgarly; ordinarily; usually, frequently, often; generally; familiarly, intimately (*archaic*); publicly (*Bible*). **comm'onness** *n*. **comm'ons** *n pl* the common people, commonalty; (with *cap*) their representatives, ie the lower House of Parliament or **House of Commons**; common land, kept for the mutual benefit of ordinary people; food at a common table, *esp* at an Oxford college; the building or hall attached to a college serving as a dining room, recreation area, etc; food in general, rations.

❑ **common carrier** *n* a person or company that deals with the transporting of goods, messages, etc for which he or it is legally responsible. **common chord** *n* (*music*) a chord made up of three notes in a major or minor scale, ie the fundamental or generating note with its third and perfect fifth. **common cold** *n* a viral infection causing inflammation of the mucous membranes lining the nose and throat, resulting in a runny nose, headache, etc. **common debtor** *n* (*Scots law*) a debtor who is also owed money by a third party: the sum owed to him or her may be arrested (*qv*) and transferred directly to his or her creditor. **common denominator** see under **denominate**. **Common Entrance** *n* an entrance examination for public school, usually taken at the age of thirteen. **Common Era** *n* the Christian Era. **common forms** *n pl* the ordinary clauses which frequently occur in identical terms in writs and deeds. **common fraction** *n* a vulgar fraction. **common gender** *n* the gender of a noun or pronoun having one form for male and female, such as L *bōs* bull or cow, Eng *student*. **common ground** *n* a subject of mutual interest, argument,

agreement, etc. **comm'onhold** *n* a freehold held in common by a number of owners, who have joint responsibility for managing the property (eg a block of flats). **common law** *n* the law of England based on custom and precedent (cf **statute law** and **civil law**). **common-law marriage** *n* in England, any of various informal types of marriage ceremony given legal recognition until 1753, some of which, if performed abroad, are still legally valid; loosely, the bond between a man (**common-law husband**) and woman (**common-law wife**) living together as husband and wife but not legally married. **common logarithm** *n* a logarithm to the base ten. **common market** *n* an association of countries as a single economic unit with internal free trade and common external tariffs; (with *caps*) the European Economic Community (qv). **common measure** *n* a quantity that is a measure of several quantities (*maths*); common time (*music*); the usual form of a ballad stanza, a quatrain containing alternating four-stress and three-stress lines. **common metre** *n* a four-line hymn stanza with eight syllables in the first and third lines, six in the second and fourth. **common-mode failure** *n* (*nuclear eng*) the failure of two or more supposedly independent parts of a system (eg a reactor) from a common external cause or from interaction between the parts. **common noun** *n* (*grammar*) a name that can be applied to all the members of a class, *opp* to *proper noun*. **common-or-gar'den** *adj* ordinary. **comm'onplace** *n* a platitude, pointless remark; a common topic or subject (*obs*); a passage to be copied into a commonplace book. ◆ *adj* frequent, common, usual; lacking distinction; hackneyed, overused. ◆ *vt* to make notes of; to put in a commonplace book. ◆ *vi* to platitudinize. **commonplace book** *n* a book in which ideas, notes, memoranda, etc are jotted down. **comm'onplaceness** *n*. **common rail** *n* a type of diesel injection system. **comm'on-rid'ing** *n* in the Scottish Borders, the equivalent of beating the bounds. **common room** *n* (in schools, colleges, etc) a sitting room to which the students or teachers have common access. **common school** *n* (*US*) a public elementary school. **common seal** *n* the official seal of a corporate body. **common sense** *n* average understanding; good sense or practical wisdom. **commonsense'** or **commonsens'ical** *adj*. **common-shore'** see under **shore**[5]. **common stair** *n* an interior stair giving access to several independent flats or dwellings. **common stock** *n* (*US*) ordinary shares. **common time** *n* (*music*) rhythm with two, four, eight or sixteen beats to the bar.

■ **Book of Common Prayer** the liturgy of the Church of England. **common in the soil** (*law*) the ancient right to take stone, sand, gravel and minerals from common land. **common of pasture** (*law*) the ancient right to graze animals on common land. **Court of Common Bench** or **Common Pleas** one of the divisions of the High Court of Justice. **in common** together (*archaic*); together (with); shared or possessed equally. **make common cause with** to cast in one's lot with; to have the same interest and aims as. **philosophy of common sense** the school of philosophy that takes the universally admitted impressions of mankind as corresponding to the facts of things without any further scrutiny. **short commons** (*inf*) meagre rations. **the common** that which is common or usual. **the common good** the interest of the community at large; the property of a former Scottish royal burgh which is not raised by tax nor held by special act of parliament. **the common people** the people in general. **the common touch** the ability to empathize with ordinary people.

commonweal /kom'ən-wēl/ (*archaic*) *n* the common good, welfare of the community; commonwealth.

commonwealth /kom'ən-welth/ *n* the public or whole body of the people; a group of states united by a common interest or joint history, such as *the British Commonwealth*; a form of government in which the power rests with the people, *esp* that in England after the overthrow of Charles I; a state or dominion, *esp* applied to the Australian federation and certain states of America; the common good, welfare of the community (*archaic*). [See **wealth**]

❑ **Commonwealth Day** *n* the second Monday in March, formerly kept as a day of celebration in the British Commonwealth. **comm'onwealth'sman** or **comm'onwealthsman** *n* (*obs*) a (good) citizen; an adherent of Cromwell's Commonwealth.

commorant /kom'ə-rənt/ *n* and *adj* resident (*esp* at a university). [L *commorāns*, *-antis*, prp of *commorārī* to abide]

commorientes /kom-mor-i-en'tēz/ (*law*) *n pl* persons who die together on the same occasion, where it cannot be determined which died first, and death is assumed to have taken place in order of seniority by age. [L]

commot or **commote** /kum'ət/ (*hist*) *n* a subdivision of a cantred. [Med L *commotum*, from Welsh *cymwd*]

commotion /kə-mō'shən/ *n* a violent motion or moving; excited or tumultuous action, physical or mental; agitation; tumult, noise, disturbance. [See **commove**]

■ **commō'tional** *adj*.

commove /kə-moov'/ (*archaic*) *vt* to put in motion; to agitate; to disturb, excite. [L *com-*, intens, and *movēre*, *mōtum* to move]

comms /komz/ *abbrev* : communications.

communautaire /ko-moo-nō-tār'/, also **communitaire** /-ni-/ *adj* of, relating to or in a spirit or attitude in keeping with or appropriate to the aims and principles of the European Union (also *n*). [Fr, communitarian]

commune[1] /kom'ūn/ *n* a group of people living together, sharing possessions, income, etc, for the benefit of the group as a whole; in some communist countries, an agricultural community; a corporation; in France, etc, a small administrative district with some self-government and a mayor. [Fr *commune* ; see **common**]
■ **communal** /kom'ū-nl or kə-mū'/ *adj* relating to a commune or a community; owned in common, shared. **commū'nalism** *n*. **commū'nalist** *n* and *adj*. **communalist'ic** *adj*. **communalizā'tion** or **-s-** *n*. **commū'nalize** or **-ise** (or /kom'/) *vt* to make communal. **comm'ūnally** *adv*. **Comm'ūnard** (or /-ärd'/) *n* an adherent of the Paris *Commune* in 1871; (without *cap*) a communist; (without *cap*) a member of a commune.
■ **the Paris Commune** a revolt by Parisian workers, radicals and socialists in 1871 against the national government, with the aim that each city or district should be ruled independently by its own commune or local government.

commune[2] /kə-mūn' or kom'ūn/ *vi* to converse or talk together; to have intimate (*esp* spiritual) communication with (eg nature); to receive Holy Communion. ◆ *n* /kom'/ communication. [OFr *communer* to share]
■ **commūn'ing** *n* and *adj*.

commune bonum /ko-mū'nē bō'nəm or ko-moo'ne bon'ŭm/ (L) the good of all, common good.

communibus annis /ko-mū'ni-bəs an'ēs or ko-moo'ni-bŭs an'ēs/ (L) on the annual average.

communicate /kə-mū'ni-kāt/ *vt* to impart; to reveal, demonstrate; to bestow. ◆ *vi* to succeed in conveying one's meaning to others; to have something in common (with another person); to have communication, correspondence, verbal or written contact (with *with*); to have a means of communication; to partake of Holy Communion. [L *commūnicāre, -ātum*, from *commūnis* common]
■ **commūnicability** /-kə-bil'i-ti/ or **commū'nicableness** *n*. **commū'nicable** *adj* that may be communicated (*esp* of a disease). **commū'nicably** *adv*. **commū'nicant** *n* a person who partakes of Holy Communion; a person who communicates or informs. **commūnicā'tion** *n* (an act of) communicating; that which is communicated; (a piece of) correspondence; a means of communicating, a connecting passage or channel; (in *pl*) means of giving and receiving information, such as speech, telecommunications, the press, and cinema; a means of transporting, *esp* troops and supplies. **commū'nicative** *adj* inclined to communicate or give information; talkative; unreserved; relating to communication. **commū'nicatively** *adv*. **commū'nicativeness** *n*. **commū'nicātor** *n*. **commū'nicātory** *adj* imparting knowledge.
◻ **communicable disease** *n* any disease caused by a parasite or micro-organism that may be transferred from one person (or animal) to another. **communicating door** *n* a door which gives access from one room, office, etc to another. **communication cord** *n* a cord in the wall or ceiling of a railway train which can be pulled in an emergency to stop the train. **communications satellite** *n* an artificial satellite in orbit around the earth, used to relay radio, television and telephone signals. **communication** or **communications theory** *n* the theory of the transmitting of information, *esp* to, from, or between machines.

communi consensu /ko-mū'nī kon-sen'sū or ko-moo'nē kon-sen'soo/ (L) by common consent.

communion /kə-mū'nyən or -ni-ən/ *n* the act of communing; spiritual intercourse or contact; fellowship; the interchange of transactions; union of a number of people in a religious service; the body of people uniting in such a service; (**Holy Communion**) the Eucharist, the sacrament commemorating the Last Supper (*Christianity*). [L *commūniō, -ōnis*, from *commūnis* common]
◻ **communion card** *n* a card used *esp* in the Presbyterian church to invite to, or register attendance at, Holy Communion. **communion cloth, communion cup, communion table**, etc *n* those used at a service of Holy Communion. **communion rail** *n* the rail in front of the altar in some churches, at which the communicants kneel.
■ **Communion of Saints** the spiritual fellowship of all true Christian believers, the blessed dead and the faithful living, in Roman Catholic doctrine held to involve a mutual exchange of examples, prayers, merits and satisfactions. **take communion** to receive the bread and wine at a service of Holy Communion.

communiqué or **communique** /kə-mū'ni-kā/ *n* an official announcement or bulletin, *esp* one given to the press, radio or television. [Fr, related to **communicate**]

communism /kom'ū-ni-zm/ *n* a social theory according to which society should be classless, private property should be abolished, and land, factories, etc collectively owned and controlled; a system of government adhering to these principles; (often with *cap*) Marxian socialism as understood in Russia. [Fr *communisme*, from *commun* common]
■ **comm'ūnist** *n* a supporter of or believer in communism; (often with *cap*) a member of a Communist party. ◆ *adj* of or relating to communism; believing in or favouring communism. **commūnist'ic** *adj* believing in or favouring communism; of or favouring communal living and ownership. **comm'ūnize** or **-ise** *vt* to make common property; to make communist.

Community /kə-mū'ni-ti/ *n* a trade union formed in 2004 from ISTC and KFAT.

community /kə-mū'ni-ti/ *n* a body of people in the same locality; the public in general; people having common rights, etc; a body of people leading a common life, or under socialistic or similar organization; a group of people who have common interests, characteristics or culture; a monastic body; any group of plants growing together under natural conditions and forming a recognizable sort of vegetation; a common possession or enjoyment; agreement; communion; commonness (*archaic*). ◆ *adj* of, for or by a local community. [OFr *communité*, from L *commūnitās, -ātis*, from *commūnis* common]
■ **communitā'rian** *n* a member of a community; an advocate of living in communities. **communitā'rianism** *n* a political theory stressing the individual's role in the community.
◻ **community architect** *n* an architect employed to design buildings in consultation with the local community. **community card** *n* (*poker*) a card that can be used by any player to help form a hand. **community care** *n* (responsibility for) the provision of social and welfare services to eg sick or old people in their own homes by local organizations rather than large institutions such as hospitals or old people's homes. **community centre** *n* a place where members of a community may meet for social and other activities. **community charge** *n* a tax replacing the rating system, itself replaced by the council tax, levied to pay for local government services and facilities, poll tax. **community chest** *n* (*US*) a fund of voluntary contributions for local welfare. **community college** *n* a secondary school that also acts as an adult educational and recreational centre for an urban area (cf **village college**); a public junior college offering two-year courses to students (*N Am*). **community council** *n* a lay body elected to look after local interests. **community health** *n* preventive health services, including the surveillance of special groups (children, the elderly, etc) in their homes, at special clinics, etc. **community home** *n* the successor to the approved school (see under **approve**[1]). **community medicine** *n* the branch of medicine concerned with public health. **community nurse** *n* a nurse (eg a health visitor, district nurse or midwife) employed by a local health authority to visit patients in their own homes, staff various clinics, etc. **community physician** *n* a physician, appointed by the local health authority, with administrative responsibility for the medical and social welfare of an area (also **public health physician**). **community policing** *n* the provision of police officers in an area who are either from the area or are well-known to the residents. **community property** *n* property owned equally by each partner in a marriage. **community radio** *n* broadcasts made from stations independent of local radio, aimed at involving people in their own community, and serving specialist groups, eg ethnic minorities, jazz enthusiasts, etc. **community relations** *n pl* the relationships, interactions and conflicts existing between different ethnic, social, political or religious groups in an area; the process or work of reconciling or mediating with these groups. **community school** *n* a school that is open outside school hours for the use and recreation of the community. **community service** *n* unpaid work for the community, eg that done by minor criminals as an alternative to imprisonment under a **community-service order**. **community singing** *n* organized singing by a large gathering of people. **community spirit** *n* the sense of belonging to, and participating in, a (local) community. **community work** *n* a form of social work based on the needs of local communities. **community worker** *n*.

commute /kə-mūt'/ *vt* to substitute or exchange; to change or transform (into); to exchange (*esp* the death sentence) for a less severe punishment; to pay off (eg a debt being paid by instalments) early by a single payment, by a simpler or more convenient method, etc; to change (electric current) from alternating to direct or vice versa. ◆ *vi* to travel some distance regularly, *esp* daily to work. ◆ *n* a regular journey of some distance, *esp* between home and work. [L *commūtāre*, from *com-* with, and *mūtāre* to change]
■ **commūtabil'ity** *n*. **commūt'able** *adj* that may be commuted or exchanged. **commūtate** /kom'/ *vt* (*elec*) to commute. **commūtā'tion** *n* the act of commuting (a sentence, payment or current); change or exchange of one thing for another; the travelling done by a commuter (*N Am*). **commū'tative** (or /kom'ū-tā-tiv/) *adj* relating to exchange;

interchangeable; such that $x*y = y*x$, where $*$ denotes a binary operation (*maths*). **commū'tatively** *adv*. **comm'ūtātor** *n* an apparatus for reversing electric currents. **commūt'er** *n* a person who travels some distance daily between home and work.
□ **commutation ticket** *n* (*N Am*) a season ticket. **commuter belt** *n* an area within travelling distance of a large city or town, from which people commute to work.

commutual /kə-mū'chū-əl/ or -tyū-/ *adj* mutual, reciprocal.

comodo see **commodo**.

comorbid /kō-mör'bid/ (*med*) *adj* (of a disease or disorder) existing together with another. [L *con-* together, and *morbus* disease]
■ **comorbid'ity** *n*.

Comorian /kə-mö'ri-ən/ or **Comoran** /'ran/ *adj* of or relating to the republic of the *Comoros* in the Indian Ocean, or its inhabitants. ◆ *n* a native or citizen of the Comoros.

comose, **comous** see under **coma²**.

comp /komp/ (*inf*) *n* a compositor; an accompanist; a competition; a complimentary ticket, etc; a comprehensive school. ◆ *vi* to work as a compositor; to play an accompaniment; to enter competitions in newspapers, magazines, etc.
■ **com'per** *n* a person who regularly enters competitions.

comp. *abbrev*: comparative (also **compar.**); compare; compiler; composer; compound; compounded; comprehensive; comprising.

compact¹ /kom'pakt/ or kəm-pakt'/ *adj* closely placed or fitted together; tightly grouped, not spread out; (of a person) smallish; close; brief; denoting a quality newspaper printed in a smaller format than a broadsheet, typically measuring *approx* 30 × 40cm (about 12 × 16in); (of a car) medium-sized and economical (*N Am*); composed or made up of (with *of*). ◆ *n* /kom'/ a compacted body or structure, a combination (of elements); a small case containing face powder for carrying in the handbag (also **powder compact**); a quality newspaper printed in compact format; a compact car (*N Am*); a compact camera. ◆ *vt* /-pakt'/ to press closely together; to consolidate. [L *compāctus*, pap of *compingere*, from *com-* and *pangere* to fix]
■ **compact'ed** *adj*. **compact'edly** *adv*. **compact'edness** *n*. **compactificā'tion** *n* the act or process of making or becoming compact or tightly grouped together. **compact'ify** *vt*. **compac'tion** *n* the act of compacting, or state of being compacted; sediments compacted by pressure from above (*geol*); an area formed by dumping rock waste, etc, pressing it together by means of heavy machines, and causing or allowing grass to grow over the whole. **compact'ly** *adv*. **compact'ness** *n*. **compact'or** *n* a machine which crushes and compacts eg solid waste into the ground. **compac'ture** *n* (*Spenser*) close union or knitting together.
□ **compact camera** *n* a small 35mm camera, *usu* with automatic focusing and exposure and often with a zoom lens and automatic winding. **compact disc** or (*comput*) **disk** *n* a small disc from which digitally-recorded sound, graphics or text can be read by laser (*abbrev* **CD**). **compact disc player** *n* a machine that plays compact discs by means of a laser beam. **compact video disc** *n* an audiovisual disc that records and plays both pictures and sound (*abbrev* **CVD**).

compact² /kom'pakt/ *n* a mutual bargain or agreement; a league, treaty or union. ◆ *adj* /kom-pakt'/ united (eg in a league). [L *compactum*, from *compacīscī*, from *com-* with *pacīscī* to bargain]

compadre /kom-pä'drā/ *n* a male friend or companion. [Sp, godfather]

compages /kəm-pā'jēz/ *n* (*pl* **compa'ges**) a structure (also *obs* **compage'**). [L *compāgēs*, *compāgināre*, -*ātum*, from *com-* and root of *pangere* to fasten]
■ **compag'inate** *vt* to join, connect. **compagination** /-paj-i-nā'shən/ *n*.

compagnie anonyme /k3-pa-nyē a-no-nēm'/ (*Fr*) same as **société anonyme**.

compagnon de voyage /k3-pa-ny3 də vwa-yäzh'/ (*Fr*) *n* a travelling companion.

compander or **compandor** /kəm-pan'dər/ *n* a system of transmitting or reproducing sound by compressing and then re-expanding the volume-range so as to produce a clearer signal by reducing the contrast. [*compress*, *expand*, and -*er* or -*or*]
■ **compand'** *vt* to put (a signal) through the process of a compander.

companing (*Spenser*) see under **company**.

companion¹ /kəm-pan'yən/ *n* a person who keeps company or frequently associates with another, either voluntarily or as a profession; a member of an order of knighthood, *esp* in a lower grade; one of a pair or set of things; an often pocket-sized book on a particular subject (as in *angler's companion*). ◆ *vt* (*rare*) to accompany. ◆ *adj* of the nature of a companion; accompanying. [Fr *compagnon*, from LL *compānium* a mess, from L *com-* with, and *pānis* bread]

■ **compan'iable** *adj* (*obs*) sociable. **compan'ionable** *adj* fit to be a companion; agreeable. **compan'ionableness** *n*. **compan'ionably** *adv*. **compan'ionate** *adj* acting as or resembling a companion; suited to be a companion. **compan'ioned** *adj* having a companion. **compan'ionhood** *n*. **compan'ionless** *adj*. **compan'ionship** *n* the state of being a companion; company, fellowship; a body of companions.
□ **companionate marriage** *n* a form of marriage proposed in the 1920s with legalized birth control and divorce by mutual consent. **companion animal** *n* (in politically correct language) a pet. **compan'ion-in-arms** *n* a fellow soldier. **companion set** *n* a set of fireside implements on a stand. **companion star** *n* a star appearing to be close to another though not necessarily near it in space, eg the fainter component of a double star.
■ **Companion of Literature** an honour (instituted 1961) conferred by the Royal Society of Literature (*abbrev* **CLitt.**).

companion² /kəm-pan'yən/ (*naut*) *n* the skylight or window frame through which light passes to a lower deck or cabin; a companion ladder. [Cf Du *kompanje* ; OFr *compagne* ; Ital *compagna* storeroom]
□ **companion hatch** *n* the covering of an opening in a deck. **companion ladder** *n* the ladder or stair leading from the deck to a cabin or to the quarterdeck. **compan'ionway** *n* a staircase from the deck to a cabin.

company /kum'pə-ni/ *n* a person or people with whom one associates; any assembly of people, or of animals or birds; an association for trade, etc, recognized as a distinct legal entity; a society; a subdivision of a regiment; the crew of a ship; a group of actors working together; a unit of Guides; a collective noun for a flock of wigeon; the state of being a companion; friendship, companionship; social interaction. ◆ *adj* belonging to, relating to, or associated with, a commercial company. ◆ *vt* (*prp* **com'panying**; *Spenser* **com'paning**; *pat* and *pap* **com'panied**) (*archaic*) to accompany. ◆ *vi* (*rare*) to associate; to cohabit. [Fr *compagnie* ; same root as **companion¹**]
□ **company doctor** *n* an adviser, consultant or businessman who turns unprofitable or inefficient companies into profitable or efficient businesses (*inf*); a medical practitioner who works for a company and oversees the health of the staff. **company man** *n* an employee who puts loyalty to his company before his personal life, friends, etc. **company promoter** *n* a person who promotes or superintends the formation of joint-stock companies. **company secretary** *n* the chief administrative officer of a company, having certain duties and obligations, eg ensuring that company documentation is in order. **company sergeant-major** see under **sergeant**. **company union** *n* (*N Am*) an association of workers within a single company, unaffiliated to any wider trade union body, a staff association.
■ **bad company** unsuitable, *esp* criminal, companions or associates. **be good** (or **bad**) **company** to have (or lack) companionable qualities. **in company** in the presence of other people outside one's immediate family or intimate acquaintance. **in company with** together with, along with. **keep company** to associate (with *with*); to court. **know a man by his company** to assess a man's character by the quality of his friends. **part company** to separate, go different ways (*lit* or *fig*). **you are in good company** you are in the same situation as those around you.

compar. *abbrev*: comparative; comparison.

compare¹ /kəm-pār'/ *vt* to put (as if) side by side so as to ascertain how far things agree or disagree (often with *with*); to liken or represent as similar (with *to*); to give the degrees of comparison of (*grammar*). ◆ *vi* to make comparison; to relate (well, badly, etc) in comparison; to vie or compete (*archaic*). ◆ *n* (*obs*) compeer; comparison. [L *comparāre* to match, from *com-* and *parāre* to make or esteem equal, from *par* equal]
■ **comparabil'ity** *n*. **comparable** /kom'pər-ə-bl or kəm-par'ə-bl/ *adj*. **com'parableness** (or /kom-par'/) *n*. **com'parably** (or /kəm-par'/) *adv*. **compar'atist** *n* a person who conducts a comparative study. **comparative** /kəm-par'ə-tiv/ *adj* relating to or making comparison; estimated by comparing with something else; relative, not positive or absolute; (of adjectives and adverbs) expressing more or greater degree (*grammar*; also *n*). **compar'atively** *adv*. **compar'ator** *n* any device for comparing accurately, so as eg to detect deviations from a standard or to confirm identity. **comparison** /-par-i-sən/ *n* the act of comparing; the capacity of being compared; a comparative estimate; a simile or figure by which two things are compared; the inflection of an adjective or adverb to express different relative degrees of its quality (*grammar*).
□ **comparability study** *n* a comparison of wages, conditions, etc in different jobs, or the same job in different areas, *usu* in order to determine future levels of wages. **comparative linguistics** *n sing* the study of similarities and differences between languages and dialects. **comparative literature** *n* the study of the relationships and similarities between literatures of different nations and languages. **comparison microscope** *n* a microscope in which there are two objective lenses, so that images from each can be examined side by side.

■ **beyond** or **without compare** without any rival or equal. **compare notes** to share or exchange one's ideas (with someone else).

compare² /kəm-pār'/ (*archaic*) *vt* to get or provide. [L *comparāre*, from *com-*, intens, and *parāre* to prepare]

compartment /kəm-pärt'mənt/ *n* a partitioned-off or marked-off division of an enclosed space or area; a closed-off division of a railway carriage; a division of anything. [Fr *compartiment*, from L *com-*, intens, and *partīrī* to divide, from *pars, partis* a part]
■ **compart'** *vt* (*rare*) to divide into parts. **compartment'al** *adj*. **compartmentalizā'tion** or **-s-** *n*. **compartment'alize** or **-ise** *vt* to divide into categories or into units, *esp* units with little intercommunication. **compartment'ally** *adv*.
❑ **compartment syndrome** *n* (*med*) a painful muscle cramp due to obstruction of blood flow to a group of muscles compressed within a confined space after exercise or injury.

compass /kum'pəs/ *n* an instrument consisting of a magnetized needle, used to find directions; (in *pl*) a pair of jointed legs, for drawing circles, etc (also **pair of compasses**); a circuit or circle; limit; range of pitch of a voice or instrument; circumference; girth. ♦ *vt* to pass or go round; to surround or enclose; to grasp, comprehend; to bring about, accomplish, achieve or obtain; to contrive or plot (*obs*); to curve, bend (*Shakesp*). [Fr *compas* a circle, prob from LL *compassus*, from L *com-*, intens, and *passus* a step]
■ **com'passable** *adj* capable of being compassed. **com'passing** *n* (*obs*) contrivance, design. **com'past** *adj* (*archaic*) rounded.
❑ **compass card** *n* the circular card of a compass marked with directional points and degrees. **compass plane** *n* a plane, convex on the underside, for smoothing curved timber. **compass plant** *n* any plant (such as *Silphium laciniatum* and certain species of lettuce) that aligns its leaves north and south to avoid the midday sun. **compass rose** *n* the circular device showing the principal directions on a map or chart. **compass saw** *n* a narrow-bladed saw for cutting in curves. **compass signal** *n* a signal denoting a point in the compass. **compass timber** *n* curved timber, used for shipbuilding, etc. **compass window** *n* a semicircular bay window.
■ **box the compass** see under **box¹**.

compassion /kəm-pash'ən/ *n* a feeling of sorrow or pity for the suffering of another, *usu* with a desire to alleviate it. ♦ *vt* (*archaic*) to pity. [Fr, from LL *compassiō, -ōnis*, from *com-* with, and *patī, passus* to suffer]
■ **compass'ionable** *adj* pitiable. **compass'ionate** *adj* inclined to pity; merciful. **compass'ionately** *adv*. **compass'ionateness** *n*.
❑ **compassionate leave**, **discharge**, etc *n* leave, discharge, etc in exceptional circumstances for personal reasons. **compassion fatigue** *n* progressive disinclination to show charity or compassion, *usu* due to the sheer volume of deserving cases.

compast see under **compass**.

compatible /kəm-pat'i-bl/ *adj* consistent (with), congruous; capable of coexistence; admissible in combination; able to be transplanted into another's body without rejection (*med* and *biol*); able to form grafts, or capable of self-fertilization (*bot*); (of drugs) able to be used simultaneously without undesirable side-effects or interaction (*chem*); (of computer peripherals, machinery, etc) able to be used together without special modification; (of computers) able to use the same software; (of a television system) enabling colour transmissions to be received in black and white by monochrome sets; enabling stereophonic signals to be treated as monophonic by mono equipment (*old*). [Fr, from L *com-* with, and *patī* to suffer]
■ **compatibil'ity** or **compat'ibleness** *n*. **compat'ibly** *adv*.

compatriot /kəm-pā'tri-ət or -pa'-/ *n* a fellow countryman (also *adj*). [Fr *compatriote*, from L *compatriōta*; see **patriot**]
■ **compatriotic** /-ot'ik/ *adj*. **compa'triotism** *n*.

compear /kəm-pēr'/ (*Scots law*) *vi* to appear in court. [Fr *comparoir*, from L *compārēre*, from *com-*, intens, and *pārēre* to appear]
■ **compear'ance** *n*. **compear'ant** *n*.

compeer /kəm-pēr' or kom'pēr/ *n* a person who is the equal of another in rank, ability or status; a companion. ♦ *vt* /-pēr'/ (*archaic*) to equal. [L *compār*, from *com-*, intens, and *pār* equal]

compel /kəm-pel'/ *vt* (**compell'ing**; **compelled'**) to drive or urge on forcibly (to); to bring about or obtain by irresistible pressure; to force; to drive together (*archaic*). [L *com-*, intens, and *pellere, pulsum* to drive]
■ **compell'able** *adj*. **compell'er** *n*. **compell'ing** *adj* forcing attention or interest, irresistible; powerfully persuasive. **compell'ingly** *adv*.

compellation /kom-pə-lā'shən/ (*rare*) *n* an act or style of addressing someone; an appellation. [L *compellāre, -ātum* to address, frequentative of *compellere*]
■ **compellative** /kəm-pel'ə-tiv/ *n* compellation (also *adj*).

compendium /kəm-pen'di-əm/ *n* (*pl* **compen'diums** or **compen'dia**) (also (*old*) **com'pend**) a shortening or abridgement; a summary of a larger work or subject, containing the most important or useful extracts

or facts, an abstract; a collection of board games or puzzles in one box. [L *compendium* what is weighed together, or saved (opposed to *dispendium* what is weighed out or spent), from *com-* together, and *pendere* to weigh]
■ **compen'dious** *adj* short; concise but comprehensive. **compen'diously** *adv*. **compen'diousness** *n*.

compensate /kom'pən-sāt/ *vt* to make (*esp* financial) amends to, to recompense; to counterbalance. ♦ *vi* to make amends (for). [L *com-*, intens, and *pēnsāre*, frequentative of *pendere* to weigh]
■ **compen'sable** *adj* for which or for whom compensation can be obtained. **compensā'tion** /kom-/ *n* the act of compensating; amends, *esp* financial, for loss, injury, etc sustained; the neutralization of opposing forces (*phys*); payment, remuneration (*N Am*); process of compensating for sense of failure or inadequacy by concentrating on achievement or superiority, real or fancied, in some other sphere; the defence mechanism involved in this (*psychol*). **compensā'tional**, **com'pensātive** (or /kəm-pen'sə-tiv/) or **compen'satory** (also /sā'/) *adj* giving compensation. **com'pensātor** *n*.
❑ **compensation balance** or **pendulum** *n* a balance wheel or pendulum so constructed as to counteract the effect of the expansion and contraction of the metal under variation of temperature. **compensation neurosis** *n* (*psychol*) a set of physical and psychological symptoms affecting some victims of industrial, etc injury who have the prospect of receiving financial compensation for their injury, thought by some to be a genuine reaction to trauma and by others to be an attempt to profit from the initial injury. **compensation water** *n* the water passed downstream from a reservoir to supply users who, before the construction of the reservoir dam, took their water directly from the stream.

comper see under **comping**.

compère /kɔ̃-per' or kom'pār/ *n* a person who introduces and provides the links between items of an entertainment (also *fem* **commère**'). ♦ *vt* to act as compère to. [Fr, godfather]

compesce /kəm-pes'/ (*archaic Scot*) *vt* to restrain. [L *compēscere*]

compete /kəm-pēt'/ *vi* to seek or strive for something in rivalry with others; to contend for a prize. [L *competere* to strive together, from *com-* together, and *petere* to seek, strive after]
■ **competition** /kom-pi-tish'ən/ *n* the act of competing; rivalry in striving for the same goal; a match or trial of ability; a contest in which a winner is selected at random from among entrants satisfying the apposite criteria; those things or people with which or whom others are competing; in a community of plants or animals, the simultaneous demand for the same limited resource, eg light or water, by two or more organisms or species. **competitive** /kəm-pet'i-tiv/ *adj* relating to or characterized by competition; suitable to compete or relishing the challenge of competition; (of price) at a level likely to attract potential customers, being at least as cheap as or cheaper than competitors. **compet'itively** *adv*. **compet'itiveness** *n*. **compet'itor** *n* a person who competes; a rival or opponent.
❑ **Competition Commission** *n* an independent body set up to inquire into monopolies and unfair business practices. **competitive exclusion** *n* (*biol*) the dominance of one species over another in competition for the same limited resource.
■ **in competition** competing (with).

competent /kom'pi-tənt/ *adj* sufficiently good or skilful; fit; suitable; efficient; belonging as a right; (of a witness) legally qualified; legitimate. [L *competere* to come together, be convenient, from *com-* and *petere* to seek]
■ **com'petence** or **com'petency** *n* fitness; suitability; efficiency; capacity, ability; sufficiency; legal power or capacity. **com'petently** *adv*.

compile /kəm-pīl'/ *vt* to write or compose (a work, document, etc) by collecting the materials from other books or sources; to draw up or collect (a list, etc); (of a computer) to convert into machine code using a compiler; (in golf, etc) to put together (a score of). [Fr *compiler*, prob from L *compīlāre*, from *com-* together, and *pilāre* to plunder, or *pīlāre* to pound down; influenced by **pile¹**]
■ **compilā'tion** /-pil- or -pīl-/ *n* the act of compiling; the thing compiled, eg a literary work made by gathering the material from various authors, sources, etc or a collection of audio recordings. **com'pilātor** *n* a person who compiles. **compī'latory** *adj*. **compile'ment** *n* a compilation. **compī'ler** *n* a person who compiles; a program that translates each high-level-language instruction into several machine-code instructions to produce a new program that can be executed rapidly and independently (*comput*); cf **interpreter**).

compital /kom'pi-təl/ *adj* relating to crossroads, or to the intersection of leaf-veins; acutely intersecting. [L *compita* crossroads]

complacent /kəm-plā'sənt/ *adj* showing satisfaction, *esp* when self-satisfied, *usu* with insufficient regard to problems, dangers, etc; pleased; inclined to please, complaisant (*archaic*). [L *complacēre*, from *com-*, intens, and *placēre* to please]

■ words derived from main entry word; ❑ compound words; ■ idioms and phrasal verbs

■ **complā'cence** or **complā'cency** n (self-)satisfaction; pleasure; complaisance (archaic). **complā'cently** adv.

complain /kəm-plān'/ vi to express grief, pain, unfavourable opinion, grievance (at or about); to express a sense of injury or dissatisfaction; to make an accusation or charge; to make a mournful sound; to state that one has pain, an illness, etc (with of). ♦ vt to utter as a complaint. ♦ n (obs or poetic) complaint. [Fr complaindre, from LL complangere, from L com-, intens, and plangere to bewail]
■ **complain'ant** n a person who complains; a person who raises a suit, a plaintiff (law). **complain'er** n a complainant. **complain'ing** n and adj. **complain'ingly** adv. **complaint'** n an instance or the act of complaining; an expression of grief and dissatisfaction; finding fault; the thing complained about; a grievance; a disease or illness, an ailment.

complaisant /kəm-plā'zənt or kom'plā-zant, esp formerly -zant'/ adj wishing to please or tending to comply with the wishes of others; obliging. [Fr complaire, from L complacēre]
■ **complais'ance** (or /kom'ple-zans or -zans'/) n desire to please, esp in excess; an obliging manner or attitude. **complai'santly** adv.

complanate /kom'plə-nāt/ (esp bot) adj flattened. [L complānāre, -ātum to make flat]
■ **complanā'tion** n.

compleat see **complete**.

complect /kəm-plekt'/ (archaic) vt to embrace; to interweave. [L complectī to embrace, from com- and plectere to twine]
■ **complect'ed** adj interwoven.

complected see **complexioned** under **complexion**.

complement /kom'pli-mənt/ n that which completes or fills up; a number or quantity required to make something complete; that amount by which an angle or arc falls short of a right angle or quadrant; one of the parallelograms not intersected by the diagonal of a given parallelogram when it is divided into four parallelograms by straight lines through a point in the diagonal; that by which a logarithm falls short of 10; all members of a set not included in a given subset (maths); that which is added to certain verbs to make a complete predicate; that by which an interval falls short of an octave (music); either of a pair of colours which together give white; a group of proteins in blood plasma that combine with antibodies to destroy antigens (formerly called **alexin**; immunol); fullness (of the moon) (heraldry). ♦ vt /-ment' or kom'pli-mənt/ to be the complement of. [L complēmentum, from com-, intens, and plēre to fill]
■ **complement'al** adj completing. **complement'arily** adv. **complement'ariness** n. **complementar'ity** n a concept, first adopted in microphysics, which accepts the existence of superficially inconsistent views of an object or phenomenon, eg which accepts a dual aspect of light (consisting of particles, as shown by certain experiments, and of waves, as shown by others). **complement'ary** adj completing; together making up a whole, right angle, ten, an octave or white; (of medical treatment, therapies, etc) non-conventional. **complementā'tion** n the full or partial restoration of normal function when two chromosomes each with a different recessive mutant gene combine in one cell (genetics); a method of representing negative numbers in the binary system (comput).
❑ **complementary DNA** n synthetic DNA used in genetic engineering to produce gene clones. **complementary medicine** n treatments and therapies, often based on a holistic view of the patient, used in conjunction with, and typically not as alternatives to, conventional medicine. **complement fixation test** n a serological test that detects the presence of an antibody or antigen, used in the diagnosis of infection.

complete /kəm-plēt'/ adj (also (archaic) **compleat** /-plēt'/) free from deficiency; not lacking any part; perfect; finished; entire, whole; fully equipped; consummate, fully skilled; (in American football) denoting a pass that is successfully caught. ♦ vt to finish; to make perfect or entire; to accomplish; to throw (a pass) that is caught by a receiver (American football). ♦ vi to finish. [L complēre, -ētum to fill up, from com-, intens, and plēre to fill]
■ **complēt'able** adj. **complet'ed** adj. **complete'ly** adv. **complete'ness** n. **complet'er** n an aid to completing, as in crossword completer. **complē'tion** n the fact of completing; the state of being complete; fulfilment. **complet'ist** n a person who wants all of something (esp a collection of items). **complet'ive** adj. **complēt'ory** adj fulfilling; completing.

complex /kom'pleks/ adj composed of more than one, or of many parts; not simple or straightforward; intricate; difficult. ♦ n a complex whole; a group of (repressed and forgotten) ideas or impressions to which are ascribed abnormal mental conditions and abnormal bodily conditions due to mental causes (psychol); loosely applied to the mental condition itself; a complex chemical substance such as a co-ordination compound (qv); a collection of interrelated buildings, units, etc forming a whole, eg a sports complex. ♦ vt to complicate; to

combine into a complex. [L complex, from com- together, and root of plicāre to fold; see **complicate**]
■ **complex'edness**, **com'plexness** or **complex'ity** n the state of being complex; complication. **complexificā'tion** n. **complex'ify** vt and vi to make or become complex or complicated. **com'plexly** adv. **complex'us** n an aggregate of parts; a complicated system; a broad muscle of the back, passing from the spine to the head (anat).
❑ **complex number** n the sum of a real and an imaginary number. **complex sentence** n one consisting of a principal clause and one or more subordinate clauses.

complexion /kəm-plek'shən/ n colour or look of the skin, esp of the face; general character, aspect or nature (fig); general appearance, temperament or texture (obs). [Fr, from L complexiō, -ōnis a combination, physical structure of body, from com- together, and plectere to plait]
■ **complex'ional** adj relating to the complexion. **complex'ioned** adj (US also **complect'ed**) having a certain specified complexion. **complex'ionless** adj colourless; pale.

compliance /kəm-plī'əns/ n yielding; agreement, complaisance; assent; submission; under the deregulated stock market, self-policing by securities firms to ensure that the rules to prevent information passing between departments with potentially conflicting interests are being obeyed; correct application of accounting standards; the degree to which patients follow medical advice; the linear displacement produced by unit force in a vibrating system (phys); the capacity of different pieces of hardware or software to operate together (comput). [See **comply**]
■ **complī'able** adj disposed to comply. **complī'ancy** n compliance. **complī'ant** adj yielding; flexible, submissive; civil. **complī'antly** adv.
❑ **compliance officer** n a person, usu a lawyer, whose job it is to ensure compliance within a company or financial group.

complicate /kom'pli-kāt/ vt to make complex; to entangle. ♦ adj (bot) folded together. [L com- together, and plicāre, -ātum to fold]
■ **com'plicacy** /-kə-si/ n the quality or state of being complicated, complexity. **com'plicant** adj overlapping. **com'plicated** adj intricate, complex; difficult, confused. **com'plicatedly** adv. **complicā'tion** n a complexity; an intricate blending or entanglement; (usu in pl) further disease or illness starting during treatment of or recovery from an existing medical condition; something which causes or adds to difficulty or confusion. **com'plicative** adj tending to complicate.
❑ **complicated fracture** n a fracture where there is some other injury (eg a flesh wound not communicating with the fracture, a dislocation or a rupture of a large blood vessel).
■ **complication of diseases** a number of diseases present at the same time.

complice /kom'plis/ (obs) n an associate or accomplice. [Fr, from L complex allied]

complicity /kom-plis'i-ti/ n the state or condition of being an accomplice; complexity. [From **complice**]
■ **complic'it** adj being an accomplice; sharing guilt.

complied, **complier** see **comply**.

compliment /kom'pli-mənt/ n an expression of admiration or praise; (usu in pl) an expression of formal respect or civility. ♦ vt /-ment' or kom'pli-mənt/ to pay a compliment to; to express respect for; to praise; to flatter; to congratulate. ♦ vi to make compliments. [Fr compliment, from L complīmentum; see **comply**]
■ **compliment'al** adj expressing or implying compliment. **compliment'ary** adj conveying or expressing civility or praise; using compliments; given free. **compliment'er** n.
■ **backhanded** or **left-handed compliment** a compliment that is indirect, ambiguous or insincere. **compliments of the season** compliments appropriate to special times, esp Christmas, New Year, etc. **pay** or **present one's compliments** to give one's respects or greeting. **with compliments** free of charge.

compline or **complin** /kom'plin/ (RC) n (also cap) the last of the hours of the Divine Office, orig held at 9pm, also known as night prayer. [OFr complie (Mod complies), from L complēta (hōra)]

complish /kom'plish/ (archaic) vt to accomplish.

complot /kom'plot/ (archaic) n a conspiracy. ♦ vi (**complott'ing**; **complott'ed**) /kəm-plot'/ to plot together; to conspire. ♦ vt to plan. [Fr]

comply /kəm-plī'/ vi (**comply'ing**; **complied'**) to yield to the wishes of another; to agree or consent to (with with); to be ceremoniously complaisant or courteous (obs). [Ital complire to fulfil, to suit, to offer courtesies, from L complēre to fulfil; see **complete**]
■ **complī'er** n. **comply'ing** adj compliant, yielding, flexible.

compo¹ /kom'pō/ n (pl **com'pos**) a mortar of cement; a mixture of whiting, resin and glue for ornamenting walls and cornices; a bankrupt's composition. [Short form of **composition**]
❑ **compo ration** n (milit) a composite 'hard' ration for use in the field when no fresh food is available.

compo² /kom'pō/ n (pl **com'pos**) compensation for industrial injuries, paid out of a central fund (inf); (unemployment) compensation, redundancy pay (Aust sl). [Short form of **compensation**]

component /kəm-pō'nənt/ adj making up; forming one of the elements or parts. ◆ n one of the parts or elements of which anything is made up, or into which it may be broken down. [L compōnere to compose]
■ **compō'nency** n. **componental** /kom-pō-nent'l/ or **componential** /-nen'shəl/ adj.

compony or **componé** /kom-pō'ni/ (heraldry) adj consisting of a row of squares of alternate tinctures. [Origin doubtful]

comport¹ /kəm-pört' or -pōrt'/ vi to agree, suit (with with). ◆ vt to behave (reflexive); to bear (obs). [L comportāre, from com- with, and portāre to carry]
■ **comport'ment** n behaviour, manner, bearing (also (Spenser) **comport'ance**).

comport² /kom'pört/, **compote** /kom'pōt/ or **compotier** /kɔ̃-po-tyä' or kom-pō'/ n a dish, usu with a stemmed base, for serving desserts, fruit, etc. [See compot]

compose /kəm-pōz'/ vt to form by putting together or being together; to put in order or at rest; to settle or soothe; to design artistically; to set up for printing; to create (esp in literature and music). ◆ vi to write (esp) music; to set type. [Fr composer, from L com- with, and pausāre to cease, rest; confused and blended in meaning with words from pōnere, positum to place]
■ **composed'** adj settled; quiet; calm. **compōs'edly** adv. **compōs'edness** n. **compōs'er** n a writer or author, esp of music. **composi'tion** n the act or art of composing; the nature or proportion of the ingredients (of anything); a thing composed; a work of art, esp in music; an exercise in writing prose or verse; arrangement of parts; combination; an artificial mixture, esp one used as a substitute; mental or moral make-up; a compromise; a percentage accepted by a bankrupt's creditors in lieu of full payment; the compounding of vector quantities, such as velocities forces, into a single resultant; a picture or photograph formed from several images; the transition from a concept or assertion about individuals to one about the class to which they belong (philos). **composi'tional** adj. **composure** /kəm-pōzh'(y)ər/ n calmness; self-possession; tranquillity; composition; temperament, character (archaic).
◻ **composing room** n a room in a printing works in which type is set. **composing stick** n (printing) a box-like holder in which type is fitted before it is placed on the galley.

composite /kom'pə-zit or (formerly and N Am) -poz'it/ adj made up of distinct parts or elements; (esp with cap) blending Ionic and Corinthian styles (archit); belonging to the **Compositae** /kəm-poz'i-tē/, a large family of plants related to the campanulas but having small florets crowded together in heads on a common axis surrounded by bracts, the whole resembling and functioning as a single flower; (of a proposal, etc) combining points from several sources; capable of being factorized (maths). ◆ n a composite thing; something made up of distinct parts or diverse elements; a composite portrait (esp N Am); a plant of the Compositae; a material consisting of a matrix such as cement or plastic reinforced by fibres. ◆ vt /-zīt/ to create from diverse elements; to pool (proposals from various sources, eg local branches of a political party) so as to produce a list for discussion at a higher, esp national level. [L compositus, compostus, from com- together, and pōnere to place]
■ **com'positely** adv. **com'positeness** n. **compositive** /-poz'/ adj. **compos'itor** n a person who sets up type for printing. **compos'itous** adj (bot) composite.
◻ **composite carriage** n a railway carriage with compartments of different class. **composite cinematography** n cinematography involving blending images from two or more sources, eg live actors and painted settings. **composite class** n a primary school class made up of children from two or more age groups. **composite photograph** n a photograph printed by superimposing several negatives. **composite portrait** n a blend of several portraits. **composite resolution** n a resolution or proposal made up from several similar resolutions and incorporating all their main points. **composite school** n (Can) a school offering both academic and non- academic courses.
■ **composition of felony** compounding of felony. **metal composite** n a metal with steel wires or glass fibres incorporated in it.

compos mentis /kom'pos men'tis/ (L) adj of sound mind, sane.

compossible /kəm-pos'i-bl/ adj possible in coexistence with something else.
■ **compossibil'ity** n.

compost /kom'post/ or (obs) **composture** /kəm-pos'chər/ n a mixture; manure consisting of a mixture of decomposed organic substances. ◆ vt to treat with compost; to convert into compost. [OFr compost, from L compositum; see **composite**]

■ **com'poster** n an apparatus for converting garden waste into compost.
◻ **compost heap** n a pile of plant refuse, soil and often chemical fertilizer, which decomposes to form compost.

composure see under **compose**.

compot or **compote** /kom'pot or kom'pōt/ n fruit stewed in sugar or syrup; a dessert of stewed fruit; a savoury ragout, usu of game. [Fr compote ; cf **composite**]

compotation /kom-pō-tā'shən/ n an act of carousing in company. [L compōtātiō, -ōnis, from com- together, and pōtāre to drink]
■ **compotā'tionship** n. **com'potător** n a drinking companion. **compot'atory** adj.

compote, compotier see compot, comport².

compound¹ /kəm-pownd'/ vt to make up; to combine (chem); to settle or adjust by agreement; to agree for a consideration not to prosecute (a felony); to intensify, make worse or greater. ◆ vi to agree, or come to terms. ◆ adj /kom'/ mixed or composed of a number of parts; so united that the whole has properties of its own which are not necessarily those of its constituents, as in the case of a mixture (chem); not simple, dealing with numbers of various denominations of quantity, etc, as in compound addition, etc, or with processes more complex than the simple process, as in compound proportion. ◆ n a mass made up of a number of parts; a word made up of two or more words; a compound substance (chem); a compounded drug. [OFr compundre, from L compōnere, from com- together, and pōnere to place]
■ **compound'able** adj. **compound'er** n.
◻ **compound animals** same as **colonial animals** (see under **colony**). **compound engine** n a condensing engine in which the mechanical action of the steam is begun in one cylinder, and ended in a larger cylinder. **compound eye** n in insects, etc, an eye made up of many separate units. **compound fracture** see under **fracture**. **compound interest** n interest added to the principal at the end of each period (usu a year) to form a new principal for the next period, thus giving further interest on the interest to date. **compound interval** n (music) any interval plus an octave. **compound leaf** n a leaf divided into leaflets by divisions reaching the midrib. **compound number** n a quantity expressed in two or more different units, as in 3 feet 6 inches. **compound quantity** n (maths) a quantity consisting of more than one term, such as $a + b$. **compound ratio** n the product of ratios. **compound sentence** n (grammar) a sentence containing more than one principal clause. **compound time** n (music) time in which each bar is made up of two or more simple measures, each divided into three (see also **simple time** under **simple**).

compound² /kom'pownd/ n an enclosure round a house or factory (esp in India), or for housing labourers (in South Africa), prisoners or detainees. [Malay kampong, kampung enclosure]

comprador or **compradore** /kom-prə-dör' or -dōr'/ n (esp in China and the Far East) a native agent or intermediary through whom a foreign firm trades; an agent of a foreign power. [Port, buyer, from L com-, intens, and parāre to furnish]

comprehend /kom-prə-hend'/ vt to grasp with the mind, to understand; to comprise or include. [L comprehendere, -hēnsum, from com- and prehendēre to seize]
■ **comprehensibil'ity** or **comprehen'sibleness** n. **comprehen'sible** adj capable of being understood. **comprehen'sibly** adv. **comprehen'sion** n understanding; power of the mind to understand; an exercise for testing pupils' understanding of a text; the intension of a term or the sum of the qualities implied in the term, connotation (logic); the inclusion of Nonconformists within the Church of England. **comprehen'sive** adj having the quality or power of comprehending or containing much; including everything; complete. ◆ n a comprehensive school; a detailed layout or proof. **comprehen'sively** adv. **comprehen'siveness** n. **comprehensivīzā'tion** or **-s-** n the act of converting schools to comprehensives. **comprehen'sivize** or **-ise** vt.
◻ **comprehensive insurance** n a form of motor insurance providing cover for most risks, including accidental damage. **comprehensive school** n a secondary school, serving a particular area, that provides education for pupils of all levels of ability.

compress /kəm-pres'/ vt to press together; to force into a narrower space; to condense or concentrate; to embrace (archaic). ◆ n /kom'/ (surg) a pad used to apply pressure to any part of the body, eg to reduce swelling; a folded cloth applied to the skin. [L compressāre, from com- together, and pressāre, to press, from premere, pressum to press]
■ **compressed'** adj pressed together; compacted; laterally flattened or narrowed (biol). **compressibil'ity** n the property of being reduced in volume by pressure; the ratio of the amount of compression per unit volume to the compressing force applied; a shock-wave phenomenon causing increased drag, which asserts itself when an aircraft in flight

approaches the speed of sound, the hypothesis of the air as an incompressible fluid being no longer valid (*aerodynamics*). **compress'ible** *adj* that may be compressed. **compress'ibleness** *n*. **compression** /*kəm-presh'ən*/ *n* the act of compressing; the state of being compressed or condensed; flattening; deformation by pressure; the stroke that compresses the gases in an internal-combustion engine. **compress'ional** *adj*. **compress'ive** *adj* tending to compress. **compress'or** *n* anything that compresses or raises pressure, such as a device that compresses air or gas; a muscle that compresses certain parts. **compressure** /*-presh'ər*/ *n*.

❑ **compressed air** *n* air at more than atmospheric pressure. **compression-ignition engine** *n* an internal-combustion engine in which ignition of the liquid fuel injected into the cylinder is performed by the heat of compression of the air charge. **compression joint** *n* a joint between two pipes, the seal being created by tightening a threaded nut onto a metal ring. **compression ratio** *n* (in an internal-combustion engine) the ratio of the maximum to the minimum volume enclosed by the cylinder.

comprimario /*kom-prē-mä'ri-ō*/ *n* (*pl* **comprimar'ios**) (in opera or ballet) a role of secondary importance; a singer or dancer playing such a role. [Ital]

comprint /*kəm-print'*/ *vt* to share in printing of the former privilege shared with the Stationers' Company and the King's Printer by Oxford and Cambridge Universities.

comprise /*kəm-prīz'*/ *vt* to contain, include; to comprehend; to consist of (often, incorrectly, with *of*). [Fr *compris*, pap of *comprendre*, from L *comprehendere*; see **comprehend**]

■ **comprīs'able** *adj*. **comprīs'al** *n* the act, condition or fact of comprising.

compromise /*kom'prə-mīz*/ *n* partial waiving of theories or principles for the sake of settlement; anything of intermediate or mixed kind, neither one absolute nor another; a settlement of differences by concession on each side; arbitration (*archaic*). ◆ *vt* to settle by concession on each side; to involve or bring into question; to expose to risk of injury, suspicion, censure or scandal. ◆ *vi* to make a compromise. [Fr *compromis*, from L *comprōmittere*, *-missum*, from *com-* together, and *prōmittere* to promise]

■ **com'promiser** *n*.

comprovincial /*kom-prə-vin'shəl*/ *adj* belonging to the same province.

Compsognathus /*komp-sog'nə-thəs*/ *n* one of the smallest known dinosaurs, lizard-hipped, bipedal and carnivorous. [Gr *kompsos* elegant, and *gnathos* jaw]

compt, **compter**, **comptible** /*kownt, kown'tər, -tə-bl*/ obsolete forms of **count**[1], etc.

compte rendu /*kɔ̃t rā-dü'*/ (*Fr*) *n* (*pl* **comptes rendus** /*kɔ̃t rā-dü*/) an account rendered; an official report.

Comptometer® /*kom(p)-tom'ə-tər*/ *n* a machine that adds, subtracts, multiplies and divides.

comptroll, **comptroller** see **control**.

compulse /*kəm-puls'*/ *vt* (*obs*) to compel. [Ety as **compulsion**]

■ **compul'satory** or **compul'sative** *adj* (*Shakesp*) compulsory.

compulsion /*kəm-pul'shən*/ *n* the act of compelling; force; a strong irrational impulse. [L *compulsāre*, frequentative of *compellere*; see **compel**]

■ **compul'sionist** *n* a believer in compulsion. **compul'sitor** *n* (*Scots law*) a means of compelling. **compul'sive** *adj* with power to compel; relating to compulsion; (of a person) driven by, (of an action) caused by, a specific, constant and irresistible impulse; (loosely) irresistible, gripping, fascinating. **compul'sively** *adv*. **compul'sorily** *adv*. **compul'soriness** *n*. **compul'sory** *adj* obligatory; compelling. ◆ *n* an exercise comprising specified compulsory figures, movements or dances, eg in ice-skating.

❑ **compulsion neurosis** *n* a disorder in which the patient suffers from compulsions and/or obsessions, depression, etc. **compulsory purchase** *n* enforced purchase by a public authority of property needed for public purposes.

compunction /*kəm-pungk'shən*/ *n* remorse tinged with pity, regret; uneasiness of conscience (*obs*). [OFr, from L *compunctiō*, *-ōnis*, from *com-*, intens, and *pungere*, *punctum* to prick]

■ **compunc'tious** *adj* of the nature of compunction; feeling compunction. **compunc'tiously** *adv*.

compurgation /*kom-pûr-gā'shən*/ *n* (in Old English and other Germanic law) the clearing of the accused by the evidence of a number of witnesses swearing to his or her innocence; evidence in favour of the accused; vindication. [L *compūrgāre* to purify entirely, from *com-*, intens, and *pūrgāre* to purify; see **purge**]

■ **com'purgator** *n* a witness who testifies to the innocence or truthfulness of the accused. **compurgatō'rial** /*kom-*/ *adj*. **compur'gatory** *adj*.

compursion /*kəm-pûr'shən*/ (*Sterne*) *n* a pursing together.

compute /*kəm-pūt'*/ *vt* to calculate, *esp* with a computer; to estimate. [L *computāre*, from *com-* (intensive) and *putāre* to reckon]

■ **computabil'ity** *n*. **computable** /*kom'* or *-pūt'*/ *adj* calculable. **com'putant**, **com'putātor** or **com'putist** *n* a person who calculates. **computā'tion** *n* the act of computing; (a) calculation; an estimate; arithmetic. **computā'tional** *adj* involving calculation. **com'putative** (or /*-pūt'*/) *adj* of or relating to computation. **comput'er** *n* an electronic machine for carrying out complex calculations, dealing with numerical data or with stored items of other information, also used for controlling manufacturing processes, or co-ordinating parts of a large organization; a calculator; a person who computes. **comput'erate** *adj* computer literate. **computerese'** *n* (*facetious*) computer language; the jargon used by people who deal with computers. **computerizā'tion** or **-s-** *n*. **comput'erize** or **-ise** *vt* to bring computer(s) into use to control (a process, an operation, or a system of operations formerly done by manual or mechanical means); to process (data) by computer. **comput'ing** *n* the use of computers.

❑ **computational linguistics** *n sing* the application of computers to the analysis of language, *esp* artificial intelligence. **computed** (or **computerized**) **axial tomography scanner** *n* a machine which produces X-ray pictures of cross-sections of the body with the assistance of a computer (*abbrev* **CAT** or **CT scanner**). **computer-aided design** *n* the process of design using computer technology, eg the use of a computer terminal to manipulate, select and store data and as a draughting board (*abbrev* **CAD**). **computer-aided diagnosis** *n* (*med*) the use of computer technology to aid in the diagnosis of disease, such as imaging and scanning techniques, probability-based data systems and pattern recognition systems. **computer-aided learning** *n* a tutorial method using a computer to teach, question and assess a student. **computer-aided manufacturing** *n* a system of integrating various aspects of a manufacturing process using computers (*abbrev* **CAM**). **computer code** *n* another name for **machine code** (see under **machine**). **computer conferencing** *n* a facility whereby individuals at widely scattered locations can communicate interactively using interconnected computer terminals. **computer crime** or **fraud** *n* crime such as embezzlement committed through the manipulation of company finances, etc by computer. **computer dating** *n* the meetings arranged by an agency that matches seemingly compatible couples by using personal details held on computer. **computer-friend'ly** *adj* suitable for use with computers. **computer game** *n* a game that can be played on a personal computer, the player(s) attempting to manipulate moving images on the screen by operating certain keys, a control pad or joystick; a video game. **computer graphics** *n pl* diagrammatic or pictorial matter produced by computer, on a screen or in printed form. **computer language** *n* a system of alphabetical or numerical signs used for feeding information into a computer, a programming language. **computer literacy** *n*. **computer literate** *adj* competent, or fully versed, in the use of computers. **computer-read'able** *adj* able to be read and understood by computers. **computer science** *n* the sciences connected with computers, eg computer design, programming, data processing, etc. **computer scientist** *n*. **computer virus** see under **virus**.

Comr. *abbrev*: Commissioner.

comrade /*kom'rād, -rad* or *-rid*, also (*archaic*) *-rād'*/ *n* a close companion; an intimate associate or friend; a fellow soldier; in some socialist and communist circles used as a term of address, or prefixed to a name; a communist (*derog sl*). [Sp *camarada* a roomful, a roommate, from L *camera* a room, from Gr *kamarā*]

■ **com'radely** *adj* and *adv*. **com'radeship** *n*.

❑ **com'rade-in-arms** *n* (*pl* **com'rades-in-arms**) a fellow soldier.

coms /*komz*/ short for **combinations**.

Comsat® /*kom'sat*/ *n* a type of communications satellite.

Comsomol variant of **Komsomol**.

comstockery /*kom'sto-kə-ri* or *kum'*/ (*esp US*) *n* vigorous censorship or suppression of literary and artistic material considered to be salacious. [Anthony *Comstock* (1844–1915), American denunciator of the salacious in literature and art]

■ **com'stocker** *n*. **com'stockism** *n*.

Comté /*kɔ̃-tā*/ *n* a hard, full-fat cow's-milk cheese, made in the Franche-*Comté* region of E France.

Comtism /*komt'izm* or *kɔ̃t-ēzm*/ *n* the philosophical system of Auguste *Comte* (1798–1857), the founder of Positivism.

■ **Comt'ian** and **Comt'ist** *n* and *adj*.

Comus /*kō'məs*/ *n* a god of mirth and revelry, son of Bacchus and Circe (*Roman myth*); (without *cap*) a revel. [L, from Gr *kōmos* a revel, carousal]

Con. *abbrev*: Conformist; Conservative; Consul.

con[1] /*kon*/ (*sl*) *adj* short for **confidence**, as in **con game** or **con trick** a swindle. ◆ *vt* to swindle; to trick; to persuade by dishonest means. ◆ *n* a trick, swindle.

con

❑ **con artist**, **con'man** or **con'woman** *n* a swindler, *esp* one with a persuasive way of talking.

con² /kon/ *adv* and *n* a contraction of L *contrā* against, as in **pro and con** for and against.

con³ (Spenser **conne** or **kon**) /kon/ (*archaic*) *vt* (**conn'ing**; **conned**, Spenser **cond** /kond/) to know; to learn; to study carefully, scan, pore over; to commit to memory; to acknowledge (as in *to con thanks*); to teach or show. [Another form of **can**, OE *cunnan* to know; perh partly *cunnian* to seek to know, examine. (See **conner²**)]
■ **conn'er** *n*. **conn'ing** *n*.

con⁴ or **conn** /kun or kon/ (*naut*) *vt* to direct the steering of (also *vi*). ◆ *n* the act or station of conning. [Older forms **cond**, **condue**, etc, from Fr *conduire*, from L *condūcere*; see **conduct**]
■ **con'der** or **conner** /kun'ər or kon'ər/ *n* a person who directs steering; a lookout on land, who signals the movements of fish to fishermen. **conn'ing** *n*.
❑ **conn'ing-tower** *n* the pilot house of a warship or the raised structure on the hull of a submarine, acting as a bridge when the submarine is on the surface.

con⁵ /kon/ (*sl*) *n* a prisoner. [Short form of **convict**]

con⁶ /kon/ (*dialect*) *n* a knock. [Fr *cogner* to knock]

con. *abbrev* : conclusion; conservation; *contra* (*L*), against.

con- see **com-**.

conacre /kon'ā-kər/ *n* (also **corn'acre**) in Ireland, the custom of letting farmland in small portions for rent in money or labour; the farmland let in this way. ◆ *vt* to sublet in conacre. [**corn¹** and **acre**]
■ **con'acreism** *n*.

con amore /kon ə-mö're or -mö'/ *adj* and *adv* with love; heartily; with tenderness (*music*). [Ital]

conarium /kō-nā'ri-əm/ (*anat*) *n* (*pl* **conā'ria**) the pineal gland. [Gr *kōnarion* pineal gland, dimin of *kōnos* cone]
■ **conā'rial** *adj*.

conation, conative see under **conatus**.

conatus /kō-nā'təs/ *n* (*pl* **conā'tus**) an effort or striving; a natural impulse or tendency. [L *cōnātus, -ūs* effort]
■ **conā'tion** *n* the psychological processes, including desire, instinct and volition, that lead to purposeful action (cf **cognition**). **conative** /kon' or kōn'ə-tiv/ *adj*.

con brio /kon brē'ō/ (*music*) *adj* and *adv* with vivacity; forcefully. [Ital]

conc. *abbrev* : concentrated; concentration.

con calore /kon ka-lö're/ (*music*) *adj* and *adv* with warmth; passionately. [Ital]

concatenate /kon-kat'ə-nāt/ *vt* to link together as in a chain; to connect in a series. [L *con-* and *catēna* a chain]
■ **concatenā'tion** *n* a series of links united; a series of things depending on or resulting from each other; the act of linking together.

concause /kon'köz/ *n* a co-operating cause.

concave /kon'kāv or kon-kāv'/ *adj* curved inwards, *opp* to *convex*. ◆ *n* a hollow; an arch or vault. ◆ *vt* and *vi* to make or become hollow. [L *concavus*, from *con-*, intens, and *cavus* hollow; see **cave¹**]
■ **con'cavely** (or /-kāv'/) *adv*. **concavity** /kən-kav'i-ti/ *n* the quality of being concave; a hollow.
❑ **concā'vo-con'cave** or **doub'le-con'cave** *adj* (both also /-kon-kāv'/) concave on both sides. **concā'vo-con'vex** (or /-kon-veks'/) *adj* concave on one side, and convex on the other.

conceal /kən-sēl'/ *vt* to hide completely or carefully; to keep secret; to disguise; to keep from telling. [OFr *conceler*, from L *concēlāre*, from *con-*, intens, and *cēlāre* to hide]
■ **conceal'able** *adj*. **conceal'er** *n* someone or something that conceals; a cosmetic applied to the face to hide spots and other blemishes. **conceal'ment** *n* hiding; keeping secret; secrecy; disguise; a hiding place; a mystery (*archaic*).

concede /kən-sēd'/ *vt* to yield or give up; to admit, allow. ◆ *vi* to make a concession; to admit defeat. [L *concēdere, -cēssum*, from *con-* wholly, and *cēdere* to yield]
■ **conced'er** *n*.

concedo /kon-kā'dō/ (*logic*) *vt* (*1st pers sing*) I admit; I grant. [L; see **concede**]

conceit /kən-sēt'/ *n* overbearing self-esteem, vanity; a witty thought, *esp* far-fetched, affected or (over-)ingenious; a fanciful idea; thought (*obs*); understanding (*archaic*); a small ornament (*obs*). ◆ *vt* (*obs*) to conceive; to think or imagine. [From **conceive** on the analogy of **deceive, deceit**]
■ **conceit'ed** *adj* having a high opinion of oneself; egotistical, vain; clever, witty (*obs*); fantastical (*archaic*). **conceit'edly** *adv*. **conceit'edness** *n*. **conceit'ful** *adj* (Spenser) thoughtful. **conceit'less** *adj* (Shakesp) without conceit, stupid. **conceit'y** *adj* (*dialect*) characterized by conceit.

■ **out of conceit with** displeased with.

conceive /kən-sēv'/ *vt* to receive into or form in the womb; to form in the mind; to imagine or think; to understand; to grasp as a concept; to express. ◆ *vi* to become pregnant; to think. [OFr *concever*, from L *concipere, conceptum*, from *con-* together, and *capere* to take]
■ **conceivabil'ity** or **conceiv'ableness** *n*. **conceiv'able** *adj*. **conceiv'ably** *adv*.

concelebrate /kon-sel'ə-brāt/ *vt* (of two or more priests) to celebrate (mass) jointly. [L *con-* together, and **celebrate**]
■ **concel'ebrant** *n* a priest taking part in a concelebrated mass. **concelebrā'tion** *n*.

concent /kən-sent'/ or **concentus** /-sen'təs/ (*archaic*) *n* a harmony or concord of sounds or voices. [L *concentus*, pap of *concinere*, from *con-* together, and *canere* to sing]

concentrate /kon'sən-trāt, sometimes kən-sen'/ *vt* to direct (attention, etc) exclusively upon the matter in hand; to bring towards, or collect at, a common centre; to focus; to condense, to increase the quantity of in a unit of space. ◆ *vi* to direct one's thoughts or efforts towards one object; to move towards a common centre. ◆ *n* a product of concentration; something in concentrated form. ◆ *adj* concentrated. [A lengthened form of **concentre**]
■ **concentrā'tion** *n* the act of concentrating; the condensing of anything; the number of molecules or ions to a unit of volume; the directing of the mind on something, *esp* for a sustained period. **concen'trative** *adj* tending to concentrate. **concen'trativeness** *n*. **con'centrator** *n* an apparatus for concentrating solutions or for obtaining minerals from ores by physical means.
❑ **concentration camp** *n* a prison camp for people (*esp* civilians) whom the authorities wish to remove or segregate from society.

concentre or (*N Am*) **concenter** /kən-sen'tər/ *vi* (**concent'ring** or **concent'ering**; **concent'red** or **concent'ered**) to tend to or meet in a common centre; to be concentric. ◆ *vt* to bring or direct to a common centre or point. [Fr *concentrer*, from L *con-* and *centrum*, from Gr *kentron* point]
■ **concen'tric** or **concen'trical** *adj* having a common centre. **concen'trically** *adv*. **concentricity** /kon-sən-tris'i-ti/ *n*.

concept /kon'sept/ *n* a thing thought of, a general notion; an idea, invention; (used *attrib*) denoting something new or innovatory of its kind. [L *concipere, -ceptum* to conceive]
■ **conceptacle** /kon-sep'tə-kl/ *n* (*obs*) a receptacle; a reproductive cavity. **concep'tion** *n* the act of conceiving; the fertilization of an ovum; the formation, or power of forming in the mind, of a concept, plan, thought, etc; a concept; (often in negative expressions) a notion, thought, idea; a mere fancy (Shakesp); a plan. **Concep'tionist** *n* a nun of an order founded in Portugal in 1489 in honour of the Immaculate Conception. **concep'tious** *adj* (Shakesp) fruitful. **concep'tive** or **concep'tional** *adj* capable of conceiving. **concep'tual** *adj* relating to conception or concepts. **concep'tualism** *n* the doctrine in philosophy that universals exist only in the mind. **concep'tualist** *n*. **conceptualis'tic** *adj*. **conceptualizā'tion** or **-s-** *n*. **concep'tualize** or **-ise** *vt* to form a concept, idea, notion or mental picture of. ◆ *vi* to form concepts; to think abstractly. **concep'tually** *adv*. **concep'tus** /-təs/ *n* (*pl* **concep'tuses** or (incorrectly) **concep'tī** (the Classical L *pl* being *conceptūs*)) the products of conception; the developing fetus and surrounding tissue in the uterus.
❑ **concept album** *n* an album of recorded music in which each piece is linked to a common theme. **concept car** *n* a prototype car produced by a manufacturer to illustrate a general idea or genre of vehicle. **conceptual art** *n* a revolutionary type of art of the 1960s and 1970s, concentrating not so much on a completed image as on the means of producing an image or concept.

concern /kən-sûrn'/ *vt* to relate or belong to; to have to do with, deal with, have as subject matter; to affect or interest; to involve by interest, occupation or duty; to trouble, make anxious; to bother (oneself) with. ◆ *n* that which relates or belongs to one; affair; business; interest; regard; (an) anxiety; a business establishment; in Quaker terminology, a spiritual directive to act in a given matter. [L *concernere* to distinguish, (later) to have respect to, from *con-*, intens, and *cernere* to distinguish]
■ **concern'ancy** *n* (Shakesp) bearing, relevancy. **concerned'** *adj* interested; involved; taking an active interest in current social, etc problems; troubled, anxious. **concern'edly** *adv*. **concern'edness** *n*. **concern'ing** *prep* regarding; about. **concern'ment** *n* concern; a matter of importance (*archaic*).
■ **as concerns** with regard to. **have no concern with** to have nothing to do with.

concert /kon'sərt/ *n* a musical performance; union or agreement in any undertaking; harmony, *esp* musical. ◆ *vt* /kən-sûrt'/ to construct or devise together; to arrange, adjust. [Ital *concertare* to sing in concert, from L *con-* and *certāre* to strive]
■ **concertante** /kon-sər-tan'tē* (Ital *kon-cher-tän'te*)/*n* a symphonic composition in which two or more solo instruments or voices take the

principal parts alternately. ◆ *adj* providing an opportunity for brilliant virtuosity by an instrumentalist or singer. **concerted** /-*sûrt*'/ *adj* mutually planned or orchestrated; arranged in parts (*music*). **concertino** /*kon-chər-tē*'*nō*/ *n* (*pl* **concerti'nos**) a short concerto; solo instruments in a concerto grosso. **concertize** or **-ise** /*kon'sər-tīz*/ *vi* to give concerts. **concerto** /*kon-chûr*'*tō*/ *n* (*pl* **concer'tos** or **concer'ti**) a composition for solo instrument(s) and orchestra in sonata form; applied by earlier composers to various combinations and forms. ❑ **con'certgoer** *n* a habitual attender of concerts. **concert grand** *n* a grand piano suitable for concerts. **concert hall** *n*. **con'certmaster** *n* (*N Am* or as a translation of Ger *Konzertmeister*) the leader of an orchestra. **concerto grosso** *n* (*pl* **concerti grossi**) a musical work in which solo parts are played by a small group of instruments, *usu* alternating with strings or an orchestra; the main body of instruments in such a work. **concert overture** *n* a piece of music like an overture, but composed specially to be played at a concert. **concert party** *n* a small group of performers, entertainers, etc, often at a private function; a group of people working together to buy shares separately, in order to use them later as one holding (*stock exchange sl*). **concert pitch** *n* a standard of pitch that has varied considerably during musical history, but is now internationally standardized so that A above middle C has a frequency of 440 hertz (see **international** (**concert**) **pitch** under **international**, **French pitch** under **French**); a high state of readiness, tension, etc. ◼ **in concert** working or conspiring together; performing at a concert venue.

concertina /*kon-sər-tē*'*nə*/ *n* a (*usu* hexagonal) musical instrument consisting of a pair of bellows, the sounds produced (when the bellows are squeezed and the buttons pressed) by free vibrating reeds of metal, as in the accordion; anything of similar folded-up shape. ◆ *vi* and *vt* (**concerti'naing**; **concerti'naed**) to collapse or fold up like a concertina. [Ety as for **concert**, plus dimin sfx]

concession /*kən-sesh*'*ən*/ *n* the act of conceding; the thing conceded; a grant; in Canada, a piece of land granted by the government; the grant of such land; the right, granted under government licence, to drill for oil or gas in a particular area; (the right to conduct) a branch of one business within a branch or on the premises of a larger one; a reduced-price ticket (for the elderly, schoolchildren, the unwaged, etc). [See **concede**] ◼ **concessible** /-*ses*'/ *adj*. **concessionaire** or **concessionnaire**' *n* a holder of a concession, *esp* one granted by a business or government. **concess'ionary** *adj*. **concess'ionist** *n*. **concess'ive** *adj* implying concession. ❑ **concession road** *n* in Canada, a road running between concessions.

concetto /*kon-chet*'*tō*/ *n* (*pl* **concet'ti** /-*tē*/) an ingenious turn of expression; a flash of (*esp* affected or fanciful) wit; a conceit. [Ital, from L *conceptum* conceit] ◼ **concet'tism** *n* the use of concetti. **concet'tist** *n*.

conch /*kongk* or *konch* or *konsh*/ *n* (*pl* **conchs** /*kongks*/ or **conches** /*kon'chiz*/) the name for various marine molluscs and their shells; such a shell used as a trumpet; a poor white inhabitant of the Florida Keys, *esp* if of Bahamian origin (from their feeding on conchs); a concha; a shell-like device for kneading and mixing chocolate during manufacture. [L *concha*, from Gr *konchē* a cockle or mussel; connected with **chank**, and **cockle**[1]] ◼ **conch'a** /*kong'kə*/ *n* (*pl* **conchae** /*kong'kē* or *-chē*/) the semi-dome of an apse (*archit*); the apse itself; the outer ear, or its cavity; a small cigar tapered at each end. **conch'al** *adj*. **conch'ate** or **conch'iform** *adj* shaped like a shell, *esp* one valve of a bivalve shell. **conche** /*kongk* or *konch*/ *vt* to knead and mix (chocolate) during manufacture. **conchif'erous** *adj* having a shell; shell-like or with many shells. **conchiolin** /*kon-kī*'*ə-lin*/ *n* a fibrous protein substance that forms the basic structure of the shell of molluscs. **conchi'tis** *n* inflammation of the concha. **conch'oid** *n* (*geom*) a plane curve, $(x^2+y^2)(x-a)^2 = l^2x^2$, the locus of a point making with a fixed straight line a constant intercept on the ray of a pencil through a fixed point. **conchoid'al** *adj* relating to a conchoid; shell-like, applied to a fracture like that seen in glass (*mineralogy*). **conchological** *adj*. **conchol'ogist** *n*. **conchol'ogy** *n* the study of molluscs and their shells.

conchiglie /*kon-kē*'*lē-ə*/ *n pl* shell-shaped pasta. [Ital]

conchy or **conchie** /*kon'shi*/ (*derog sl*) *n* a *consci*entious objector; an over-conscientious person (*Aust*).

concierge /*kon-si-ārzh*' or (*Fr*) *kɔ̃-syerzh*'/ *n* a warden; a janitor; a hall porter (male or female). [Fr; ety unknown]

conciliar /*kən-sil*'*i-ər*/ *adj* of, from or relating to a council, *esp* an ecclesiastical council (also **concil'iary**). [L *concilium* council]

conciliate /*kən-sil*'*i-āt*/ *vt* to gain, or win over; to reconcile, bring together (*esp* opposing sides in an industrial dispute). ◆ *vi* to make

friends, having been hostile. [L *conciliāre*, *-ātum* from *concilium* council] ◼ **concil'iable** *adj* (*obs*). **concilia'tion** *n* the act or process of conciliating. **concil'iative** (or /-*ā-tiv*/) *adj*. **concil'iātor** *n*. **concil'iatorily** *adv*. **concil'iatoriness** *n*. **concil'iatory** *adj*.

concinnity /*kən-sin'i-ti*/ *n* harmony; congruity; elegance. [L *concinnus* well-adjusted] ◼ **concinn'ous** *adj* elegant; harmonious.

concipient /*kən-sip'i-ənt*/ *adj* conceiving. [L *concipiēns*, *-entis*, prp of *concipere* to conceive] ◼ **concip'iency** *n*.

concise /*kən-sīs*'/ *adj* cut short; brief but pertinent. ◆ *vt* (*Milton*) to mutilate. [L *concīsus*, pap of *concīdere*, from *con-*, intens, and *caedere* to cut] ◼ **concise'ly** *adv*. **concise'ness** *n* the quality of being concise; terseness. **concision** /-*sizh'ən*/ *n*.

conclamation /*kon-klə-mā'shən*/ (*formal*) *n* a shout of many together. [L *conclāmātiō*, *-ōnis*]

conclave /*kon'klāv*/ *n* the room in which cardinals meet to elect a pope; the body of cardinals; any secret assembly; a private room (*obs*). [L *conclāve* lockable room, from *con-* with, and *clāvis* a key] ◼ **con'clāvist** *n* an attendant on a cardinal in conclave.

conclude /*kən-klood*'/ *vt* to close; to end; to decide; to settle or arrange finally; to infer; to enclose (*archaic*); to restrain or debar (*obs*). ◆ *vi* to end; to form a final judgement; to state the remedy sought in a court action (*Scots law*). [L *conclūdere*, *conclūsum* from *con-*, intens, and *claudere* to shut] ◼ **conclud'ed** *adj* finished; settled. **conclud'ing** *adj* final, closing. **conclu'sion** /-*zhən*/ *n* the act of concluding; the end, close, or last part; inference, result, assumption; judgement; an experiment (*obs*); a problem, a riddle (*Shakesp*). **conclusive** /-*kloo'siv*/ or **conclu'sory** *adj* final; convincing. **conclus'ively** *adv*. **conclus'iveness** *n*. ◼ **in conclusion** finally. **jump to conclusions** see under **jump**[1]. **try conclusions** to experiment; to engage in a contest (with).

concoct /*kən-kokt*'/ *vt* to fabricate; to plan, devise; to make up or put together; to prepare or mature. [L *concoquere*, *concoctum* from *con-* together, and *coquere* to cook, to boil] ◼ **concoct'er** or **concoct'or** *n*. **concoc'tion** *n* the action of concocting; something fabricated or made up from separate parts, eg a story, a lie, a food dish or drink; preparation of a medical prescription, etc. **concoct'ive** *adj*.

concolor /*kon'ku-lər*/ (*esp biol*) *adj* of uniform colour (also **concol'orate** or **concol'orous**). [L, from *con-* together, and *color* colour]

concomitant /*kən-kom'i-tənt*/ *adj* accompanying; conjoined; occurring along with, because of, or in proportion to (something else). ◆ *n* someone who or something that necessarily accompanies. [L *con-*, intens, and *comitāns*, *-antis* prp of *comitārī* to accompany, from *comes* a companion] ◼ **concom'itance** or **concom'itancy** *n* the state of being concomitant; the doctrine that the body and blood of Christ are present in the Eucharist (*theol*). **concom'itantly** *adv*.

concord /*kon'körd* or *kong*'/ *n* the state of being of the same opinion or feeling; harmony; agreement; a treaty or pact; a combination of sounds satisfying to the ear, *opp* to discord. ◆ *vi* /*kən-körd*'/ to agree; to harmonize. [Fr *concorde*, from L *concordia*, from *concors* of the same heart, from *con-* and *cor*, *cordis* the heart] ◼ **concord'ance** *n* agreement; an index of the words or passages of a book or author; any similar physical characteristic found in both of a pair of twins. **concord'ant** *adj* harmonious, united. **concord'antly** *adv*. **concord'at** *n* a pact or agreement, eg between the Pope and a secular government. **concor'dial** *adj* harmonious.

concorporate /*kon-* or *kən-kör'pə-rāt*/ (*archaic*) *vt* to unite in one body. ◆ *adj* /-*ət*/ united in the body.

concours /*kɔ̃-koor*'/ (*Fr*) *n* a contest, competition; a competitive examination; a meeting. ❑ **concours d'élégance** /*dā-lā-gãs*/ a competition among cars in which marks are allotted for appearance, not speed.

concourse /*kon'körs*, *kong*' or *-kōrs*/ *n* a large hall; an open space, *esp* in a railway station, airport, etc for transit, meeting, etc; (an) assembly of people for some event; concurrence of an officer who has the legal right to grant it (*Scots law*). [Fr *concours*, from L *concursus*, from *con-* and *currere* to run]

concreate /*kon-krē-āt*'/ (*archaic*) *vt* to create with; to create at the same time.

concremation /*kon-kri-mā'shən* or *-krē-*/ *n* complete burning; cremation; burning together; suttee. [L *concremāre*, *-ātum*, from *con-*, intens, and *cremāre* to burn]

concrescence /kən-kres'əns/ (*biol* and *med*) *n* a coalescence or growing together of separate parts or organs. [L *concrēscentia*, from *con-* and *crēscere* to grow]
■ **concresc'ent** *adj*.

concrete /kon'krēt or kən-krēt'/ *adj* formed into one mass; real, actual, specific, not abstract, able to be experienced; /kon'/ made of concrete. ◆ *n* /kon'/ a mixture of sand, gravel, etc and cement, used in building; a solid mass formed by parts growing or sticking together. ◆ *vt* /-krēt'/ to form into a solid mass; /kon'/ to cover or fix with concrete. ◆ *vi* /-krēt'/ to harden. [L *concrētus*, from *con-* together, and *crēscere*, *crētum* to grow]
■ **concrēte'ly** (or /kon'/) *adv*. **concrēte'ness** (or /kon'/) *n*. **concrētion** /-krē'shən/ *n* a concreted mass; a nodule or lump formed within a rock by materials rearranging themselves about a centre (*geol*); a solid mass formed within an animal or plant body, whether by deposition or by accumulation of foreign matter (*biol* and *med*). **concrē'tionary** *adj*. **con'cretism** *n* regarding or representing abstract things as concrete. **con'cretist** *n* and *adj*. **concrēt'ive** *adj* having the power to concrete. **concretizā'tion** or **-s-** *n*. **con'cretize** or **-ise** *vt* to render concrete, realize.
□ **concrete art** *n* non-figurative art using geometrical forms and simple planes. **concrete jungle** *n* (*facetious*) an area of bleakly ugly (*esp* high-rise) buildings. **concrete mixer** *n* a machine with a large revolving drum for mixing concrete. **concrete music** same as **musique concrète**. **concrete poetry** *n* an art form which seeks to introduce a new element into poetry by means of visual effects such as special arrangements of the letters of the poem on the printed page. **concrete steel** *n* reinforced concrete.

concrew /kon-kroo'/ (*archaic*) *vi* to grow together. [Fr *concrû*, pap of *concroître*, from L *concrēscere*]

concubine /kong'kū-bīn/ *n* a woman who cohabits with a man without being married to him; a kept mistress; (in certain polygamous societies) a secondary wife. [Fr, from L *concubīna*, from *con-* together, and *cubāre* to lie down]
■ **concubinage** /kon-kū'bin-āj/ *n* the state of living together as husband and wife without being married to each other; being or having a concubine. **concū'binary** *adj*. **concū'bitancy** *n* a custom by which marriage between certain persons is obligatory. **concū'bitant** *n* a person subject to such an obligation (also *adj*).

concupiscence /kən-kū'pi-səns/ *n* a strong desire; sexual appetite, lust. [L *concupīscentia*, from *concupīscere*, from *con-*, intens, and *cupere* to desire]
■ **concū'piscent** *adj*. **concū'piscible** *adj*.

concupy /kon(g)'kū-pi/ (*Shakesp*) *n* short form of **concupiscence** (or perhaps of **concubine**).

concur /kən-kûr'/ *vi* (**concurr'ing**; **concurred'**) to agree; to assent; to coincide; to meet in one point; to run together. [L *concurrere*, from *con-* and *currere* to run]
■ **concurrence** /-kur'/ *n* agreement; assent; the meeting of lines in one point; coincidence. **concurr'ency** *n*. **concurr'ent** *adj* running, coming, acting or existing together or simultaneously; coinciding; accompanying; meeting in the same point. ◆ *n* a person who or thing that concurs; formerly, a person who accompanied a sheriff's officer as witness (*obs*). **concurr'ently** *adv*. **concurr'ing** *adj* agreeing.

concuss /kən-kus'/ *vt* to affect with concussion; to disturb; to shake. [L *concussus*, pap of *concutere*, from *con-* together, and *quatere* to shake]
■ **concussion** /-kush'/ *n* the state of being shaken or jarred; (a state of brief or partial unconsciousness resulting from) a violent blow to the head or neck causing a (*usu* temporary) disturbance in brain function; a violent shock caused by the sudden contact of two bodies. **concuss'ive** *adj* having the power or quality of concussion.

concyclic /kən-sī'klik or kən-sik'lik/ (*geom*) *adj* lying or situated on the circumference of the same circle. [L *con-* together, and Gr *kyklos* wheel]
■ **concy'clically** *adv*.

cond see **con³**.

condemn /kən-dem'/ *vt* to declare (a person, action, etc) to be wrong, immoral, reprehensible, etc; to judge unfavourably or blame; to sentence (to imprisonment or death); to demonstrate the guilt of; to force into or doom to some fate or unhappy condition; to pronounce unfit for use or consumption. [L *condemnāre*, from *con-*, intens, and *damnāre* to hurt]
■ **condemnable** /-dem'nə-bl/ *adj* that may be condemned. **condemnātion** /kon-dəm-nā'shən/ *n* the state of being condemned; the act of condemning. **condem'natory** *adj* expressing or implying condemnation. **condemned'** *adj* pronounced to be wrong, guilty or worthless; belonging or relating to one who is sentenced to

punishment by death (eg *condemned cell*); declared dangerous or unfit.

condense /kən-dens'/ *vt* to reduce to smaller extent or volume; to render more dense, intense or concentrated; to subject to condensation (*chem*). ◆ *vi* to become condensed. [L *condēnsāre*, from *con-*, intens, and *dēnsus* dense]
■ **condensabil'ity** *n*. **condens'able** *adj*. **condens'āte** *vt* and *vi* to condense. ◆ *n* /kon'dən-sāt/ a product of condensation; a hydrocarbon liquid, a light form of oil. **condensā'tion** /kon-/ *n* the act of condensing; water which, having vaporized, returns to its liquid state, eg on a cold window; the union of two or more molecules of the same or different compounds with the elimination of water, alcohol, or other simple substances (*chem*); (loosely) applied to almost any reaction in which a product of higher molecular weight than the original substance is obtained; anything that has been shortened, eg a concise version of a text. **condens'er** *n* an apparatus for reducing vapours to a liquid form; a mirror or lens for focusing light, eg in a microscope; a capacitor. **condens'ery** *n* a condensed-milk factory.
□ **condensation trail** *n* a vapour trail. **condensed milk** *n* milk reduced and thickened by evaporation, with added sugar. **condensed type** *n* printing type of narrow face.

conder see under **con⁴**.

condescend /kon-di-send'/ *vi* to act graciously to those one regards as inferior; to deign (to do something) (now *usu facetious*); to stoop to what is unworthy of one; to comply (*obs*); to agree, consent (*obs*). ◆ *vt* to concede or grant (*obs*); to specify (*esp* Scots *law*). [L *con-*, intens, and *dēscendere* to descend, from *dē* down from, and *scandere* to climb]
■ **condescend'ence** *n* condescension; an articulate statement annexed to a summons, setting down the allegations in fact upon which an action is founded (Scots *law*). **condescend'ing** *adj* gracious; offensively patronizing. **condescend'ingly** *adv*. **condescen'sion** *n*.
■ **condescend upon** to specify; to mention.

condiddle /kən-did'l/ (Walter Scott) *vt* to steal. [L *con-*, intens, and **diddle¹**]

condie see **cundy**.

condign /kən-dīn'/ *adj* (*usu* of punishment) well-deserved, fitting. [L *condīgnus*, from *con-*, intens, and *dīgnus* worthy]
■ **condign'ly** *adv*. **condign'ness** *n*.

condiment /kon'di-mənt/ *n* a seasoning, *esp* salt or pepper. ◆ *vt* to season. [L *condīmentum*, from *condīre* to preserve, to pickle]

condisciple /kon-di-sī'pl/ *n* a fellow disciple; a school-friend, classmate; a fellow student. [L *condiscipulus*, from *con-* together, and *discipulus* (see **disciple**)]

condition /kən-dish'ən/ *n* the state in which things exist, eg *the human condition*; a good or fit state; a particular quality of existence, good, bad, etc; rank (as in *a person of condition*; *archaic*); prerequisite, prior requirement; temper (*obs*); a term of a contract; (in *pl*) circumstances; that which must be true for a further statement to be true (*logic*); a clause in a will, etc which requires something to happen or be done before the part of the will to which it relates can take effect (*law*). ◆ *vi* (*rare*) to make or impose terms. ◆ *vt* to restrict, limit; to put into the required state; to prepare or train (a person or animal) for a certain activity or for certain conditions of living; to secure by training (a certain behavioural response to a stimulus which would not normally cause it; *psychol*). [L *condiciō* (wrongly *conditiō*), -*ōnis* an agreement, from *condicere*, from *con-* together, and *dīcere* to say]
■ **condi'tional** *adj* depending on conditions; expressing a condition or conditions. **conditional'ity** *n*. **condi'tionally** *adv*. **condi'tionate** *vt* (*obs*) to act as a condition. **condi'tioned** *adj* having a certain condition, state or quality; caused by psychological conditioning; subject to condition. **condi'tioner** *n* a person, substance or apparatus that brings something into a good or required condition. **condi'tioning** *n*.
□ **conditional discharge** *n* a court order whereby an offender is not sentenced for an offence unless he or she commits a further offence within a given period. **conditional probability** *n* (*stats*) the probability of one event occurring given that another has already occurred. **condition code** *n* (*comput*) one of a set of bits indicating the state of a logic or arithmetic operation. **conditioned reflex** or **response** *n* a reflex response to a stimulus which depends upon the former experience of the individual. **conditioning house** *n* an establishment in which the true weight, length, and condition of articles of trade and commerce are determined scientifically.
■ **in** or **out of condition** in good or bad condition; physically fit or unfit. **on no condition** absolutely not, not under any circumstances.

condo /kon'dō/ (*N Am inf*) *n* (*pl* **con'dōs**) short for **condominium**.

condole /kən-dōl'/ *vi* to grieve (with another person); to express sympathy in sorrow. [L *con-* with, and *dolēre* to grieve]

■ **condol'atory** *adj* expressing condolence. **condole'ment** *n*. **condol'ence** *n* (*usu* in *pl*) an expression of sympathy with another's sorrow. **condol'ent** *adj*.

con dolore /kon do-lō're or -lō're/ (*music*) *adj* and *adv* with grief, mournfully. [Ital]

condom /kon'dom or -dəm/ *n* a thin rubber sheath worn on the penis during sexual intercourse to prevent conception or infection. [Origin uncertain]

condominium /kon-də-min'i-əm/ *n* joint sovereignty; a country whose government is controlled by two or more other countries; a block of apartments in which each apartment is separately owned (*N Am*); such an apartment (*N Am*). [L *con-* together, and *dominium* lordship, ownership]

condone /kən-dōn'/ *vt* to forgive; to pass over without blame, overlook intentionally; to excuse. [L *con-*, intens, and *dōnāre* to give; see **donation**]

■ **condon'able** *adj*. **condonā'tion** /kon-/ *n* forgiveness; forgiveness granted by the injured party, often formerly a reason for refusing to grant a divorce on the grounds of adultery (*law*).

condor /kon'dör or -dər/ *n* either of two large American vultures, the Andean condor (*Vultur gryphus*) having black plumage and a wingspan up to 3.5m (11¼ft), and the nearly extinct Californian condor (*Gymnogyps californianus*), having grey-brown plumage and a slightly shorter wingspan. [Sp *cóndor*, from Quechua *cuntur*]

condottiere /kon-dot-tyā'rā/ *n* (*pl* **condottie'ri** /-rē/) a leader of a mercenary band of military adventurers, *esp* in the 13c to 16c. [Ital, from *condotto* way, from L *condūcere* to assemble, from *con-* together, and *dūcere* to lead]

conduce /kən-dūs'/ *vi* to help to bring about, lead to, or contribute towards (a result). [L *con-* together, and *dūcere* to lead]

■ **conduce'ment** *n* (*Milton*). **conduc'ible** *adj*. **conduc'ingly** *adv*. **conduc'ive** *adj* leading, contributing or tending; favourable to or helping towards something.

■ **conducive** to helping towards, promoting or encouraging.

conduct /kən-dukt'/ *vt* to lead or guide; to convey (water, blood, sap, etc); to direct; to manage (one's life, business affairs, etc); to behave (*esp* oneself); to carry, transmit, allow to pass (*elec*; also *n*); to beat time for and co-ordinate (an orchestra, piece of music, etc; also *vi*). ◆ *n* /kon'dukt/ the act or method of leading or managing; behaviour; guidance; management. [L *conductus*, from *condūcere*; see **conduce**]

■ **conduct'ance** *n* a conductor's power of conducting electricity, the reciprocal of the resistance. **conductibil'ity** *n*. **conduct'ible** *adj* capable of conducting heat, etc; capable of being conducted or transmitted. **conduc'tion** *n* the act or property of conducting or transmitting; transmission (of eg heat) by a conductor; the passage of a nerve impulse. **conduct'ive** *adj* having the quality or power of conducting or transmitting. **conduct'ively** *adv*. **conductiv'ity** *n* the power of transmitting heat, electricity, etc; the power of a specific substance to conduct electricity. **conduct'or** *n* the person or thing that conducts; a leader; a manager; a director of an orchestra or choir; a person sometimes in charge of taking fares on a bus, etc but not driving it (*fem* **conduc'tress**); a railway guard (*N Am*); anything that has the property of transmitting electricity, heat, etc. **conduct'orship** *n* the office of conductor. **conduct'us** *n* (*pl* **conduc'tī**) a style of metrical Latin song of the 12c and 13c (*usu* for no more than three voices), in which all the voice parts move together.

❑ **conduct disorder** *n* a persistent pattern of antisocial or aggressive behaviour, *usu* in children or adolescents, which may include vandalism, truancy, assault, substance abuse, etc. **conducted tour** *n* a tour (of places of interest, a workplace, factory, etc) led by a guide. **conductive education** *n* a system of teaching children (and sometimes adults) suffering from motor disorders (eg cerebral palsy) to achieve their maximum potential by guiding them to attain specific goals in their own way by providing a concentrated course of exercise and intellectual stimulation. **conductor rail** *n* a rail which transmits electricity to an electric train.

■ **safe-conduct** see under **safe**.

conduit /kon'dit or kun', also kon'dū-it or -dwit/ *n* a channel, pipe, tube or duct conveying water or other fluid, or covering electric wires, etc; a means of transmission or communication; a fountain for supplying the public with water (*rare*). [Fr *conduit*, from L *conductus*, from *condūcere* to lead]

conduplicate /kən-dū'pli-kət or -doo'-/ *adj* folded together lengthwise. [L *conduplicāre*, -ātus to double, from *con-* and *duplex* double]

condyle /kon'dil or -dīl/ (*anat*) *n* a rounded protuberance at the end of a bone for articulation with another bone, such as the ball in a ball-and-socket joint. [Gr *kondylos* knuckle]

■ **con'dylar** or **con'dyloid** *adj*. **condylō'ma** *n* (*pl* **condylō'mas** or **condylō'mata**) a raised warty growth on the skin, the mucous passages or around the genitals. **condylō'matous** *adj*.

cone /kōn/ *n* a solid figure bounded by a plane base in the shape of a circle or ellipse tapering to a fixed point (the vertex) (*geom*); anything shaped like a cone; the typical reproductive structure of the Coniferae, woody and more or less conical, with a mass of scale-like sporophylls set closely about an axis; a similar structure in other plants, eg horsetails; an ice-cream cornet, often including the ice cream; one of a series of plastic bollards, shaped like geometrical cones, placed round obstacles, etc in the road in order to divert traffic; one of the two types of light-sensitive cells in the retina of the eye; a volcanic hill; a fan of alluvium where a torrent is checked at the foot of a declivity or in a lake. ◆ *vt* to shape like a geometrical cone. ◆ *vi* to bear cones. [Gr *kōnos*]

■ **conic** /kon'ik/ *n* a conic section. ◆ *adj* (also **con'ical**) having the form of, or relating to, a cone. **con'ically** *adv*. **con'ics** *n sing* the geometry of the cone and its sections. **cō'niform** *adj* in the form or shape of a cone.

❑ **cone'flower** *n* any of several genera of showy plants of the family Compositae, *esp* Rudbeckia, Ratibida, and Echinacea. **cone shell** *n* a carnivorous mollusc of the family Conidae with large conical shells. **cone wheat** *n* a bearded variety of wheat. **conic** (or **conical**) **projection** *n* a map projection in which the earth is projected onto a cone with its apex over one of the poles. **conic section** *n* a curve made by the intersection of a cone by a plane.

■ **cone off** to close off (eg one carriageway of a motorway) with cones.

con espressione /kon es-pres-yō'ne/ (*music*) *adj* and *adv* with expression.

coney see **cony**.

conf /konf/ (*inf*; *comput*) *n* an online discussion. [Poss short for **conference**]

confabulate /kən-fab'ū-lāt/ *vi* to chat (*inf* **confab'**); to invent past experiences, either consciously or unconsciously, to compensate for loss of memory (*psychiatry*). [L *cōnfābulārī*, from *con-* and *fābulārī* to talk]

■ **confab'ūlar** *adj*. **confabūlā'tion** *n* a chat (*inf* **confab** /kon'/); the act or process of confabulating (*psychiatry*). **confab'ūlator** *n*. **confab'ūlatory** *adj*.

confarreation /kən-far-i-ā'shən/ *n* a Roman patrician mode of marriage, in which a spelt cake was offered up. [L *cōnfarreātiō*, from *con-* with, and *fār* spelt]

■ **confarr'eāte** *adj*.

confect /kən-fekt'/ *vt* to prepare by combining ingredients; to preserve. ◆ *n* /kon'fekt/ fruit, etc, prepared with sugar; a sweet; a comfit. [L *cōnficere*, *cōnfectum* to make up together, from *con-* and *facere* to make]

■ **confec'tion** *n* composition, compounding, mixing; a sweet substance mixed with a medicinal preparation to make it more palatable; a sweet; a light, frothy entertainment; an elaborate article of clothing for women's wear. **confec'tionary** *n* a place where confections are made or kept; a confection. ◆ *adj* relating to or of the nature of confections. **confec'tioner** *n* a person who makes or sells confectionery, sweet cakes or sweets; a sweet shop. **confec'tionery** *n* confectioners' work or art; sweets in general.

❑ **confectioner's sugar** *n* (*US*) icing sugar.

confederate /kən-fed'ə-rət/ *adj* leagued together; allied (*esp* with *cap*, of the seceding American states in the Civil War). ◆ *n* a person, etc united in a league; (with *cap*) a supporter of the seceding states in the American Civil War; an ally; an accomplice. ◆ *vi* and *vt* /-āt/ to league together or join in a league. [L *cōnfoederāre*, -ātum, from *con-* and *foedus*, *foederis* a league]

■ **confed'eracy** *n* a league or alliance; people or states united by a league; a conspiracy; (with *cap*) the league of eleven seceding states in the American Civil War (*US hist*). **confed'eral** *adj* belonging or relating to a confederation. **confederā'tion** *n* a league; an alliance, *esp* of princes, states, etc; an association of more or less autonomous states united permanently by a treaty. **confed'erative** *adj* of or belonging to a federation.

confer /kən-fûr'/ *vt* (**conferr'ing**; **conferred'**) to give or bestow (*esp* a privilege or honour); to compare (*obs*; now only in use in the abbreviation **cf**). ◆ *vi* to talk or consult together. [L *cōnferre*, from *con-* together, and *ferre* to bring]

■ **conferee'** /kon-/ *n* a person with whom one confers; a person on whom something is bestowed; a person taking part in a conference. **conference** /kon'/ *n* the act of conferring; an appointed meeting or series of meetings for instruction or discussion; (with *cap*) a kind of pear. **con'ferencing** *n* the practice of holding a conference in which the participants are linked by telephone, by telephone and video equipment, or by computer. **conferential** /kon-fər-en'shl/ *adj*. **confer'ment** or **conferr'al** *n* bestowal; a thing bestowed. **conferr'able** *adj*. **conferr'er** *n*.

❑ **conference call** *n* a telephone or computer communication in which three or more people can participate simultaneously.

■ **in conference** attending a meeting; engaged, busy.

conférence /kɔ̃-fā-rās'/ (Fr) n a lecture.
■ **conférencier** /-rā-syā/ n a lecturer.

conferva /kon-fûr'və/ n (pl **confer'vae** /-vē/ or **confer'vas**) any freshwater alga of the genus *Conferva* (class Heterocontae) forming slimy masses or tufts of unbranched filaments; loosely applied to any filamentous freshwater alga. [L *cōnferva* a kind of water plant]
■ **confer'void** adj resembling conferva.

confess /kən-fes'/ vt to acknowledge fully (*esp* something wrong); to own up to or admit; to make known (eg sins to a priest); (eg of a priest) to hear a confession from; to reveal, betray, or make manifest (*poetic*). ◆ vi to make confession (*esp* to a priest). [Fr *confesser*, from L *cōnfitērī, cōnfessus*, from *con-* (signifying completeness) and *fatērī* to confess, from *fārī* to speak]
■ **confess'ant** n a person who makes a confession of sins to a priest. **confessed'** or **confest'** adj admitted; avowed; declared; evident. **confess'edly** or **confest'ly** adv. **confession** /kən-fesh'ən/ n acknowledgement or admission of a crime or fault; the act of confessing; the thing confessed; a statement of religious belief; acknowledgement of sin to a priest (*auricular confession*); a religious body of common belief (*obs*). **confess'ional** n the seat or enclosed recess where a priest hears confessions; the institution of confession. ◆ adj relating to confession. **confess'ionalism** n. **confess'ionalist** n. **confess'ionary** adj of or belonging to confession. ◆ n a confessional. **confess'or** (or /kon'/) n a priest who hears confessions and grants absolution; a person who makes a confession; a person who makes a declaration *esp* of religious faith; a person who endures persecution but not death. **confess'oress** n. **confess'orship** n.
■ **confession of faith** a formal statement embodying the religious beliefs of a church or sect; a creed. **confess to** to admit, acknowledge. **stand confessed** (*formal* or *archaic*) to be revealed.

confetti /kən-fet'i or kon-fet'tē/ n pl small pieces of coloured paper flung at brides and bridegrooms; sweets or comfits (or plaster or paper imitations of them) flung in carnival in Italy. [Ital (sing *confetto*); see **comfit, confect**]

confide /kən-fīd'/ vi to trust wholly or have faith (with *in*); to impart secrets to someone as confidences (with *in*). ◆ vt to entrust; to tell with reliance upon secrecy. [L *cōnfīdere*, from *con-* (signifying completeness) and *fīdere* to trust]
■ **confidant** /kon-fi-dant'/ or (*fem*) **confidante** n a person confided in or entrusted with secrets, *esp* in love affairs; a close friend. **confidence** /kon'fi-dəns/ n firm trust or belief; faith; trust in secrecy; self-assurance, self-belief; assuredness, *esp* in the outcome of something; admission to knowledge of secrets or private affairs; a confidential communication. **con'fidency** n. **con'fident** adj trusting firmly; having full belief; (*esp* self-)assured; bold. ◆ n a confidential friend. **confidential** /-den'shl/ adj given in confidence; admitted to a person's confidence; private. **confidential'ity** n. **confiden'tially** adv. **con'fidently** adv. **confid'er** n. **confid'ing** adj trustful. **confīd'ingly** adv. **confid'ingness** n.
◻ **confidence interval** n (*stats*) an interval so constructed as to have a prescribed probability of containing the true value of an unknown parameter. **confidence trick** n a swindler's trick, whereby (*usu*) a person is induced to hand over money to the swindler for something they will never receive (often shortened to **con trick**; see **con¹**). **confidence trickster** n. **confident person** n (*Scots law*) a confidential person, partner, agent, etc.
■ **in confidence** secretly, as a secret. **in someone's confidence** trusted by the person in question with confidential matters.

configuration /kən-fi-gū-rā'shən or -gə-/ n external figure, shape or arrangement; outline; relative position or aspect, *esp* of planets; the spatial arrangement of atoms in a molecule (*chem*); Gestalt, the organized whole (*psychol*); the selection of components, eg modes, drivers, defaults, that make up a computer system. [L *cōnfigūrāre* to form]
■ **config'urate** vt to shape, arrange. **configurā'tional** adj. **config'ure** vt to configurate; to set up (a computer system).

confine /kon'fīn/ n a border, boundary or limit (generally in *pl*); /kən-fīn'/ confinement (*archaic*); a prison (*Shakesp*). ◆ vt /kən-fīn'/ to limit, enclose, bound; to imprison; to border (*obs*); to be adjacent to (*obs*). [L *cōnfīnis* bordering, from *con-* together, and *fīnis* the end]
■ **confin'able** adj. **confined'** adj limited; imprisoned; narrow, small. **confine'less** adj (*Shakesp*) without bound; unlimited. **confine'ment** n the state of being shut up; restraint; imprisonment; the time during which a woman is confined to bed during labour and immediately after giving birth; another name for **containment** (see under **contain**; *nuclear eng*). **confin'er** n. **confin'ing** adj bordering; limiting.
■ **be confined** to be limited; to be imprisoned; (of a woman) to go through the process of childbirth.

confirm /kən-fûrm'/ vt to strengthen; to fix or establish; to ratify; to repeat the assertion of (eg a statement, an order for goods) so as to make it more definite or certain; to verify, give proof of the truth or justification of; to assure; to put through a ceremony to admit to full religious communion. [OFr *confermer*, from L *cōnfirmāre*, from *con-*, intens, and *firmāre*, from *firmus* firm]
■ **confirm'able** adj. **con'firmand** n a candidate for religious confirmation. **confirmā'tion** n a making firm or sure; convincing proof; the rite by which people are admitted to full communion in many Christian churches; ratification by a competent court of the appointment of an executor, constituting his right to act (*Scots law*). **confirm'ative** adj tending to confirm. **con'firmator** n. **confirm'atory** adj giving additional strength to; confirming. **confirmed'** adj settled; inveterate, habitual, addicted. **confirmee'** n a person to whom a confirmation is made. **confirm'er** n. **confirm'ing** n. **confirm'or** n.

confiscate /kon'fi-skāt or (*obs*) kən-fis'/ vt to appropriate to or seize for the state, as a penalty; to take possession of (property) by authority. ◆ adj forfeited. [L *cōnfiscāre, -ātum*, from *con-* together, and *fiscus* a basket, purse, treasury]
■ **con'fiscable** (or /-fis'/) adj. **confiscā'tion** n the act of confiscating. **con'fiscātor** n a person who confiscates. **confiscatory** /kon'fis-kā-tər-i or kən-fis'kə-tər-i/ adj of the nature of confiscation.

confiserie /kɔ̃-fēz-ə-rē'/ (Fr) n a confectionery.
■ **confiseur** /kɔ̃-fēz-œr/ n a confectioner.

confit /kon'fit, kon'fē or kɔ̃-fē'/ n a dish made by cooking a duck, goose, etc in its own fat; /kon'fit/ an obsolete form of **comfit**. [Fr, preserved]

confiteor /kon-fit'i-ör/ (RC) n (often with *cap*) a form of prayer of public confession. [L *cōnfiteor* I confess]

confiture /kon'fi-tūr/ n (*obs*) same as **comfiture** (see under **comfit**).

confix /kən-fiks'/ (*esp Shakesp*) vt to fix firmly. [L *cōnfīgere, -fīxum*, from *con-*, intens, and *fīgere* to fix]

conflagrate /kon'flə-grāt/ vt and vi to burn up. [L *cōnflagrāre*, from *con-*, intens, and *flagrāre* to burn; see **flagrant**]
■ **conflāg'rant** adj (*archaic* or *formal*) burning. **conflagrā'tion** n a great burning or fire; a war or other major destructive disturbance.

conflate /kən-flāt'/ vt to fuse; to combine (eg two different versions of a text) into one. [L *cōnflāre, -ātum* to blow together, from *con-* and *flāre* to blow]
■ **conflā'tion** n.

conflict /kon'flikt/ n unfortunate coincidence or opposition; violent collision; (a) struggle, contest, war, etc; a mental or emotional struggle. ◆ vi /kən-flikt'/ to fight; to contend; to be in opposition; to clash, be unfortunately simultaneous. [L *cōnflīgere, -flīctum*, from *con-* together, and *flīgere* to strike]
■ **conflict'ed** adj (of a person) struggling to reconcile contradictory impulses. **conflict'ing** adj clashing; competing; contradictory. **conflic'tion** n (*rare*). **conflict'ive** adj tending to conflict.
◻ **conflict diamond** n (*usu* in *pl*) a blood diamond (qv under **blood**).
■ **in conflict** incompatible or irreconcilable (with).

confluence /kon'floo-əns/ n a flowing together; a meeting place, *esp* of rivers; a concourse; the act of meeting together. [L *cōnfluere*, from *con-* together, and *fluere, fluxum* to flow]
■ **con'fluent** adj flowing together; running into one; uniting. ◆ n a stream uniting and flowing with another. **con'fluently** adv. **con'flux** /-fluks/ n a flowing together.

confocal /kon-fō'kəl/ adj (of a microscope) in which an aperture in the illuminating system confines the illumination to a small spot on the specimen, and a corresponding aperture in the imaging system allows only light transmitted, reflected or emitted by that spot to contribute to the image. [**con-**]

conform /kən-förm'/ vt to make like or of the same form or type; to adapt. ◆ vi to be or become of the same form or type (often with *to*); to comply (with *to*); to obey (with *with*). ◆ adj and adv (*Scot*) in conformity. [L *cōnförmāre*, from *con-* and *förmāre*, from *förma* form]
■ **conformabil'ity** n the state of being conformable. **conform'able** adj corresponding in form or type; compliant, agreeable; (of rock layers, etc) as, or in the position in which, originally laid down (*geol*). **conform'ably** adv. **conform'al** adj (of a map) representing small areas in their true shape. **conformā'tion** n particular form, shape or structure; adaptation. **conformā'tional** adj. **conform'ator** n a device for measuring a rounded shape, *esp* the human head. **conform'er** n a conformist. **conform'ism** n. **conform'ist** n and adj (a person) tending to comply with social, etc norms; (a person) complying with the practices of the Established Church. **conform'ity** n similarity or adherence to the norm; compliance; consistency with a standard; conformability (*geol*); compliance with the practices of the Established Church.
◻ **conformal transformation** see under **transform**. **conformational analysis** n (*chem*) the study of the spatial arrangements of atoms in molecules, particularly in saturated organic molecules.
■ **in conformity with** in accordance with.

confound /kən-fownd'/ vt (*pap* (*Spenser*) **confound'**) to overthrow, defeat; to confuse, fail to distinguish between; to throw into disorder;

to defeat in argument (*obs*); to perplex; to astonish. [OFr *confondre*, from L *cōnfundere*, *-fūsum*, from *con-* together, and *fundere* to pour]
■ **confound'ed** *adj* confused; astonished; damned, blasted (a term of disapproval; *inf*). **confound'edly** *adv* (*inf*) hatefully, shamefully; cursedly. **confound'ingly** *adv* astonishingly.
■ **confound it**, **him**, **you**, etc an interjection expressing a mild curse.

confraternity /kon-frə-tûr'ni-ti/ *n* a brotherhood, *esp* a religious or charitable one; clan; brotherly friendship. [L *con-* and *frāter* brother]

confrère /kɔ̃-frer'/ *n* a colleague; a fellow member or associate. [Fr, from L *con-* together, and *frāter* a brother]
■ **confrérie** /kɔ̃-frā-rē/ *n* a brotherhood.

confront /kən-frunt'/ *vt* to come or be face to face with; to face in opposition; to bring face to face; to compare. [Fr *confronter*, from L *con-* together, and *frōns*, *frontis* forehead; see **front**]
■ **confronta'tion** /kon-/ or (*archaic*) **confront'ment** *n* the bringing of (*usu* opposing or hostile) people face to face; continued hostile attitude, with hostile acts or statements but without declaration of war. **confronta'tional** *adj* involving, causing, etc confrontation. **confronta'tionism** *n* the favouring of confrontation as a political means. **confronta'tionist** *n* and *adj*. **confronté** /kon-frunt'ā/ *adj* (*heraldry*) face to face.

Confucian /kən-fū'sh(y)ən/ *adj* of or belonging to (the doctrines of) *Confucius*, the Chinese philosopher (551–479BC). ◆ *n* a follower of Confucianism.
■ **Confu'cianism** *n*. **Confu'cianist** *n*.

con fuoco /kon foo-ök'ö or kon fwö'kö/ (*music*) *adj* and *adv* with fire. [Ital]

confuse /kən-fūz'/ *vt* to perplex; to throw into disorder; to fail to distinguish between; to cause to be embarrassed or flustered; to jumble or mix together so that things cannot be distinguished. ◆ *vi* to be confused. [See **confound**]
■ **confusabil'ity** or **confusibil'ity** *n*. **confu'sable** or **confu'sible** *adj* liable to be confused (also *n*). **confused'** *adj* perplexed; disordered. **confu'sedly** *adv* in a confused manner; disorderly. **confu'sedness** *n* the state of being confused; disorder. **confu'sing** *adj* causing confusion. **confu'singly** *adv*. **confu'sion** /-zhən/ *n* the state of being confused; disorder; overthrow, perdition (*archaic*); perplexity; embarrassment, shame; turmoil.

confute /kən-fūt'/ *vt* to prove to be false, disprove; to refute; to bring to naught or put an end to (*obs*). [L *cōnfūtāre* to silence]
■ **confut'able** *adj*. **confutā'tion** /kon-/ *n*. **confut'ative** *adj* tending to confute. **confute'ment** *n*.

Cong. *abbrev*: Congregation; Congregational; Congress; Congressional.

cong. (*pharm*) *abbrev*: *congius* (L), gallon.

conga /kong'gə/ *n* a Latin American dance in which dancers are linked in single file and move forward in a series of steps and side kicks; music for this dance; a conga drum. ◆ *vi* to dance the conga. [Am Sp, Congo]
❑ **conga drum** *n* a tall narrow drum beaten with the hands.

congé or **congee** /kɔ̃-zhā' or kon'ji/ *n* permission to depart; a dismissal; a discharge; leave, furlough (*milit*); a type of concave moulding (*archit*). ◆ *vi* to take leave. [Fr *congé*, from L *commeātus* leave of absence, from *com-* together, and *meāre* to go]
■ **congé d'élire** /dā-lēr/ permission to elect; the crown's formal permission to a dean and chapter to elect a certain person as bishop.

congee see **congé** and **conjee**.

congeal /kən-jēl'/ *vt* and *vi* to freeze; to change from fluid to solid, eg by cooling; to coagulate; to stiffen (also *fig*). [L *congelāre*, from *con-*, intens, and *gelū* frost]
■ **congeal'able** *adj*. **congeal'ableness** *n*. **congeal'ment** or **congelation** /kon-ji-lā'shən/ *n* the act or process of congealing; anything congealed.

congee see **congé** and **conjee**.

congener /kon'ji-nər/ *n* something of the same kind or nature, *esp* a plant or animal of the same genus; a secondary product in an alcoholic drink that helps to determine its flavour, colour and power to intoxicate. ◆ *adj* akin, of the same kind or nature. [L *con-* with, and *genus*, *generis* kind]
■ **congeneric** /-ner'ik/ or **congener'ical** *adj* of the same genus, origin or nature; of the congeners of an alcoholic beverage. **congener'ic** *n* a member of the same genus; in the manufacture of alcoholic beverages, a congener. **congenerous** /kən-jen'ar-əs/ *adj* of the same origin, nature or kind. **congenetic** /kon-ji-net'ik/ *adj* having a common origin.

congenial /kən-jē'ni-əl/ *adj* pleasant, friendly or agreeable; of the same spirit or tastes; kindred, sympathetic; to one's taste; suitable. [L *con* with, and *geniālis* (see **genial**¹)]
■ **congē'niality** /-al'i-ti/ *n*. **congē'nially** *adv*.

congenic /kən-jen'ik/ *adj* (of animal cells) bred so as to be genetically identical except for a single gene locus. [**con-** and **genic**]

congenital /kən-jen'i-təl/ *adj* (of diseases, defects or deformities) dating from birth, but not necessarily hereditary; complete or absolute, as if from birth (*esp* in the phase *congenital idiot*). [L *congenitus*, from *con-* together, and *gignere*, *genitum* to beget]
■ **congen'itally** *adv*.

conger¹ /kong'gər/ or **conger-eel** /kong-gər-ēl'/ *n* a large sea fish of the eel family (Congridae). [L, from Gr *gongros* sea eel]

conger² /kong'gər/ (*hist*) *n* a society of co-operating booksellers. [Origin uncertain]

congeries /kon-jē'ri-ēz or kon'jə-rēz/ *n* (*pl* **conger'ies**) a collection, mass or heap. [L *congeriēs*, from *con-* together, and *gerere*, *gestum* to bring]

congest /kən-jest'/ *vt* to bring together or heap up; to accumulate; to cause congestion in. ◆ *vi* to become overcrowded. [L *congerere*, *congestum*, from *con-* together, and *gerere*, *gestum* to bring]
■ **congest'ed** *adj* overcrowded; packed closely together; overcharged; clogged; affected with an accumulation of blood or mucus. **congest'ible** *adj*. **congestion** /-jes'chən/ *n* an overcrowded condition; an accumulation of blood, lymph or mucus in any part of the body; fullness. **congest'ive** *adj* indicating congestion or tending to become congested.
❑ **congestion charge** *n* a charge levied on vehicles entering a heavily congested part of a transport network.

congiary /kon'ji-ə-ri/ *n* in ancient Rome, a gift distributed amongst the people or soldiery, *orig* in corn, oil, etc, later in money. [L *congiārium*, from *congius* the ancient Roman gallon]

congius /kon'ji-əs/ (*pharm*) *n* (*pl* **con'gii** /-i-ī/) a unit of liquid measure equal to the imperial gallon. [L *congius* the ancient Roman gallon]

conglobe /kən-glōb'/ *vt* or *vi* to collect together into a globe or round mass. [L *con-* together, and *globāre*, *-ātum* from *globus* a ball, globe]
■ **conglobate** /kon'glō-bāt or kən-glō'bāt/ *adj* formed into a globe or ball. ◆ *vt* or *vi* to form into a globe or ball. **conglobā'tion** *n*. **conglobūlate** /-glob'/ *vi* to gather into a globule or small globe. **conglobūlā'tion** *n*.

conglomerate /kən-glom'ə-rət/ *adj* gathered into a mass; bunched; (of an industrial group) made up of companies with diverse interests; composed of pebbles cemented together (*geol*). ◆ *vt* and *vi* /-āt/ to gather into a ball. ◆ *n* /-it/ a conglomerate rock (*geol*); a miscellaneous mass or collection; an industrial group made up of companies which often have diverse and unrelated interests. [L *conglomerāre*, *-ātum*, from *con-* together, and *glomus*, *glomeris* a ball of thread]
■ **conglomeratic** /-at'ik/ *adj* (*geol*) of the nature of conglomerate. **conglomerā'tion** *n* the state of being conglomerated; a collection or jumble of things.

conglutinate /kən-gloo'ti-nāt/ *vt* to glue together; to heal by uniting or joining. ◆ *vi* to unite or grow together. [L *conglūtināre*, *-ātum* from *con-* together, and *glūten* glue]
■ **conglu'tinant** *adj*. **conglutinā'tion** *n* a joining by means of some sticky substance; the process of healing by joining or growing together. **conglu'tinātive** *adj* having power to conglutinate. **conglu'tinator** *n*.

congo see **congou**.

Congolese /kong-gō-lēz' or kong'/ or (now *rare*) **Congoese** /kong-gō-ēz'/ *adj* of or relating to the Republic of *Congo* or to the Democratic Republic of *Congo* in central Africa, or to their people or languages. ◆ *n* a native of either of these countries; any of the Bantu languages spoken in these countries.

Congo red /kong'gō red/ *n* a scarlet dyestuff used as a chemical indicator for acid solutions in the pH range 3–5, and as a biological stain.

congou /kong'goo/ *n* a kind of black tea from China (also **con'go**). [Chinese *gōng* time, and *fú* skill, referring to that expended in producing it]

congrats /kən-grats'/ (*inf*) *n pl* and *interj* congratulations.

congratulate /kən-grat'ū-lāt/ *vt* to express pleasure in sympathy with; to felicitate; to consider lucky or clever (*esp reflexive*). [L *congrātulārī*, *-ātus*, from *con-*, intens, and *grātulārī*, from *grātus* pleasing]
■ **congrat'ulable** *adj*. **congrat'ulant** *adj* expressing congratulation. ◆ *n* a congratulator. **congratulā'tion** *n*. **congrat'ulative** or **congrat'ulatory** (or /-lā'/) *adj* expressing congratulation. **congrat'ulator** *n*.

congree /kən-grē'/ (*archaic*) *vi* to agree; to accord. [L *con-* together, and Fr *gré* goodwill, from L *grātus* pleasing]

congreet /kən-grēt'/ (*archaic*) *vi* to greet one another. [L *con-* together, and **greet**¹]

congregate /kong'grə-gāt/ *vi* to flock together. ◆ *vt* to gather together; to assemble. ◆ *adj* (*Spenser*) congregated. [L *congregāre*, *-ātum*, from *con-* together, and *grex*, *gregis* a flock]

■ **con'gregant** n a member of a congregation (esp a Jewish one). **con'gregated** adj assembled; gathered together. **congregā'tion** n a body of people actually or habitually attending a particular church; a gathering or assembly of people or things; the act of congregating; a board charged with some department of administration in the Roman Catholic Church; a name given to certain religious orders without solemn vows; the body of Protestant Reformers in Scotland in the time of Mary Stuart; a name given to the children of Israel (Bible); an academic assembly. **congregā'tional** adj relating to a congregation; (with cap) relating to the Independent Church. **Congregā'tionalism** n a form of church government in which each congregation is independent in the management of its own affairs (also called **Independency**). **Congregā'tionalist** n.
❑ **Congregation for the Doctrine of the Faith** n the doctrinal court of the Roman Catholic Church.

congress /kong'gres/ n an assembly of delegates, specialists, ambassadors, etc for the discussion or settlement of problems, creating legislation, etc; (with cap) the federal legislature of the United States; the act of meeting together; sexual intercourse. ◆ vi to meet in congress. [L con- together, and gradi, gressus to step, to go]
■ **congressional** /kən-gresh'ən-l/ adj. **Con'gressman**, fem **Con'gresswoman** n a member of Congress, esp of the House of Representatives (also **Con'gressperson**).
❑ **Congressional Record** n (US) the official published record of the proceedings of Congress.

Congreve /kong'grēv/ n a rocket for use in war. [Perh invented by Sir William Congreve (1772–1828)]
❑ **Con'greve-match** n a kind of friction match.

congrue /kong-groo'/ vi (Shakesp) to agree. [L congruere to run together]
■ **con'gruence** or **con'gruency** n suitability or appropriateness; agreement; the quality of being congruent (geom). **con'gruent** adj suitable; agreeing or corresponding; congruous; identical in shape so that all parts correspond (geom); (of two numbers) having the same remainder when divided by a third number (maths). **con'gruently** adv. **congru'ity** n agreement between things; consistency; suitability. **con'gruous** adj suitable or appropriate; consistent. **con'gruously** adv. **con'gruousness** n.

conia see **coniine**.

conic, conical see under **cone**.

conidium /kō- or ko-nid'i-əm/ (bot) n (pl **conid'ia**) an asexual fungal spore produced exogenously from a hyphal tip, not in a sporangium. [Gr konis dust]
■ **conid'ial** adj. **conid'iophore** n (Gr phoros bearing) a hypha that produces conidia. **conid'iospore** n a conidium.

conifer /kon'i- or kō'ni-fər/ n any tree or shrub of the group Coniferae, including yews, pines, firs, etc, which typically bear cones. [L cōnus (Gr kōnos) a cone, and ferre to bear]
■ **conif'erous** adj cone-bearing; of the conifer family.

coniform see under **cone**.

coniine /kō'ni-ēn/ n a liquid, highly poisonous alkaloid (C₈H₁₇N) found in hemlock (also **cō'nia**, **cō'nine** or **cō'nin**). [From New L Conium, genus name of hemlock, from Gr kōneion]

conima /kon'i-mə/ n the fragrant resin of a tropical American burseraceous tree (genus Protium). [Carib name]

conine see **coniine**.

conirostral /kō-ni-ros'trəl/ (zool) adj (eg of most finches) having a strong conical beak. [L cōnus (Gr kōnos) cone, and rōstrālis, from rōstrum a beak]

conj. abbrev : conjunction; conjunctive.

conject /kən-jekt'/ vi (Shakesp; also as a modern back-formation) to conjecture. [L conjicere, conjectum to throw together, from con- and jacere to throw]

conjecture /kən-jek'chər/ n an opinion formed without proof; an opinion formed on slight or defective evidence or none at all; a guess. vi to guess. vt to make conjectures regarding; to conclude by conjecture. [From **conject**]
■ **conject'urable** adj. **conject'ural** adj involving conjecture; given to conjecture. **conject'urally** adv. **conject'urer** n.

conjee or **congee** /kon'jē/ (Anglo-Ind) n water in which rice has been boiled; rice or millet gruel. ◆ vt to starch with conjee. [Tamil kañji]

conjoin /kən-join'/ vt to join together; to combine. ◆ vi to unite. [Fr conjoindre, from L con- and jungere, junctum to join; see **join**]
■ **conjoined'** adj united; in conjunction. **conjoint'** adj joined together; united. **conjoint'ly** adv.
❑ **conjoined twins** n pl Siamese twins.

conjugal /kon'jŭ-gəl/ or /kən-joo'gəl/ adj relating to marriage. [L conjugālis, from conjux a husband or wife, from con- together, and jugum a yoke]
■ **conjugality** /-gal'i-ti/ n. **con'jugally** adv.
❑ **conjugal rights** n pl the right to have sexual relations with one's spouse.

conjugate /kon'jŭ-gāt/ vt to give the various inflections or parts of (a verb) (grammar); to unite (biochem). ◆ vi to undergo inflection (grammar); to unite (biochem). ◆ adj /-gət or -gāt/ joined; connected or coupled; occurring in pairs (bot); reciprocally related, as of two complex numbers, having their real parts equal and their imaginary parts equal but of opposite sign (maths); having the same root, cognate (grammar). ◆ n /-gət/ a word with the same root as another word; anything joined or connected with, or related to, something else. [L conjugāre, -ātum, from con- together, and jugāre, from jugum a yoke]
■ **con'jugant** n (biol) one of a pair of cells or individuals undergoing conjugation. **Conjuga'tae** /-tē'/ n pl a class of freshwater algae reproducing by conjugation of like gametes, including desmids, Spirogyra, etc. **con'jugated** adj conjugate; (of atoms, groups, bonds, or the compounds in which they occur) showing a special type of mutual influence, esp characterized by an arrangement of alternate single and double bonds between carbon atoms (chem). **con'jugating** n and adj. **conjuga'tion** n the set of all the inflectional forms of a verb, including tense, person, voice, aspect, etc (grammar); inflection in verbs (grammar); the act of joining; union; temporary or permanent union of two cells or individuals preparatory to the development of new individuals, esp the union of isogametes in some algae and fungi (biol); (in prokaryotes) the process by which genetic information is transferred from one bacterium to another (biol). **conjuga'tional** or **con'jugative** adj conjugate.
❑ **conjugate angle** n one of a pair of angles whose sum is 360°. **conjugate diameters** n pl two diameters in a conic section, such that each is parallel to the tangent at the extremity of the other. **conjugated protein** n a substance in which a protein is combined with a non-protein. **conjugate foci** n (phys) two points such that rays of light diverging from either of them are brought to a focus at the other. **conjugate mirrors** n pl mirrors set so that rays from the focus of one are reflected to that of the other.

conjunct /kən-junkt'/ or /kon'junkt/ adj conjoined; joint; of or relating to two adjacent degrees of a scale (music). ◆ n (grammar) an adverbial that joins two discourse units. [L conjunctiō, -ōnis from conjungere ; see **conjoin**]
■ **conjunc'tion** n connection, union; combination; simultaneous occurrence in space and time; a word that connects sentences, clauses and words (grammar); one of the aspects of the planets, when two bodies have the same celestial longitude or the same right ascension (formerly when they were in the same sign) (astrol). **conjunc'tional** adj. **conjunc'tionally** adv. **conjunctiva** /kon-jungkt-ī'va/ n (pl **conjuncti'vas** or **conjuncti'vae** /-ē/) the mucous membrane of the front of the eye, covering the external surface of the cornea and the inner side of the eyelid. **conjunctī'val** adj of the conjunctiva. **conjunc'tive** adj closely united; serving to join; connective (anat); being a conjunction or related to (the use of) conjunctions (grammar). ◆ n (grammar) a conjunction. **conjunc'tively** adv. **conjunc'tiveness** n. **conjunctivitis** /-iv-ī'tis/ n (med) inflammation of the conjunctiva. **conjunct'ly** adv conjointly; in union. **conjunc'ture** n a combination of circumstances, esp one leading to a crisis.
❑ **conjunctive mood** n (grammar) the subjunctive mood generally, or when used in a principal clause, or in the principal clause of a conditional sentence. **conjunct tetrachords** n pl (Gr music) tetrachords in which the highest note of the lower is the lowest note of the higher.
■ **in conjunction (with)** together (with).

conjure /kun'jər/ vi to practise magical tricks, esp for public entertainment; to make an invocation; to conspire (obs). ◆ vt (usu /kən-joor'/) to call on or summon by a sacred name or in a solemn manner; to implore earnestly; to compel (a spirit) by incantations; to call before the imagination (often with up); to render, effect, cause to be or become, by magic (often with out, away, etc). [Fr conjurer, from L conjūrāre to swear together, from con- and jūrāre to swear]
■ **conjurā'tion** n a magic trick or spell; the performing of magic tricks; a solemn appeal or entreaty, supplication (archaic). **con'jurator** n. **conjure'ment** n adjuration. **conjurer** or **conjuror** /kun' or kon'/ n a person who performs magic tricks by sleight-of-hand, etc. **con'juring** n the performing of magic tricks; the production of apparently miraculous effects by natural means. **con'jury** n magic.
■ **to conjure with** regarded as influential, powerful or important, esp in the phrase a name to conjure with.

conk¹ /kongk/ (sl) n the nose; the head; a blow on the head. ◆ vt to strike (a person) on the head.

conk² /kongk/ (sl) vi to get out of order, fail, break down (esp with out); to fall asleep, collapse from exhaustion, die (with out). [Origin uncertain]

■ words derived from main entry word; ❑ compound words; ■ idioms and phrasal verbs

conk[3] /kongk/ n the fructification of a fungal parasite on a tree (N Am); timber disease due to this parasite (N Am). [Prob **conch**]
■ **conk'er** n a horse chestnut (or formerly a snail shell) threaded on a string and used in the game of **conkers**, in which each player tries to break their opponent's by hitting it with their own; a horse chestnut. **conk'y** adj affected by the disease conk.

con moto /kon mō'tō/ (music) adj and adv with movement; briskly. [Ital]

Conn. abbrev : Connecticut (US state).

conn see **con**[4].

connascent /kə-nā'sənt/ adj born or produced at the same time. [L con- and nāscī, nātus to be born]
■ **connasc'ence** or **connasc'ency** n.

connate /kon'āt/ adj inborn; innate; allied; congenital (med); united in growth (biol). [Ety as for **connascent**]
■ **connā'tion** n (biol) union, esp of similar parts or organs.
❑ **connate water** n water which has been trapped in sediments since their deposition.

connatural /kə-nach'ə-rəl/ adj of the same or similar nature; congenital (med). [Ety as for **connascent**]
■ **connat'uralize** or **-ise** vt. **connat'urally** adv. **connat'uralness** or **connā'ture** n.

conne see **con**[3].

connect /kə-nekt'/ vt to tie, join, link or fasten together; to establish a relation between; to associate. ♦ vi to be or become joined; to be significant or meaningful (inf); to hit a target with a blow, a kick, etc (inf); to have or develop an understanding or rapport (N Am); (with up) to join a computer network (esp the Internet); to find a source of illicit drugs (sl). [L con- and nectere, nexum to tie]
■ **connect'able** or **connect'ible** adj. **connect'ed** adj joined; linked; coherent; related. **connect'edness** n. **connect'edly** adv. **connect'er** or **connect'or** n. **connection** or **connexion** /-ek'shən/ n the act of connecting; that which connects; a religious body or society held together by a set of shared beliefs; context; relation; intimacy; coherence; intercourse; the opportunity or time to change trains, buses, etc; a relative, esp a distant one, or one by marriage; (usu in pl) a friend or relative in a position of power or influence; (in pl) the owner and trainer of a racehorse and their associates; the supplying of narcotic drugs (sl); a supplier of such drugs, a dealer or pusher (sl). **connec'tional** or **connex'ional** adj. **connec'tionism** n the theory that connections between neurons govern behaviour and thought (psychol); (in artificial intelligence) the modelling of systems on networks made up of electronic neurons connected in a simplified model of the network of neurons in the brain. **connect'ive** adj (anat) binding together. ♦ n something that connects; a word that connects sentences and words (grammar). **connect'ively** adv. **connectiv'ity** n. **connex'ive** adj (obs).
❑ **connecting rod** n a rod attached to two parts of a machine to allow motion in one part to cause motion in the other part, esp such a rod connecting a piston to a crankshaft. **connective tissue** n any of several kinds of animal tissue fulfilling mechanical functions, consisting of an amorphous matrix embedded with specialized cells, and forming bone, cartilage, tendons, ligaments, and enfolding membranes.
■ **in connection with** concerning. **in this connection** with reference to this. **well-connect'ed** related to people of good social standing.

conner[1] /kun'ər/ n an inspector or tester. [OE cunnere, from cunnian to learn, seek to know]

conner[2] or **cunner** /kun'ər/ n a kind of wrasse, the goldsinny or corkwing; a related American fish. [Origin obscure]

conner[3] see under **con**[3,4].

connexion, connexive see under **connect**.

conning-tower see under **con**[4].

conniption /kə-nip'shən/ (N Am sl) n a fit of rage or hysteria (also **conniption fit**); a tantrum. [Perh Ger knipsen to snap, click]

connive /kə-nīv'/ vi to plot or conspire (often with with); to agree to take no notice of, and thus tacitly encourage (a crime, wrongdoing, etc) (often with at); to have a private understanding (often with with). [L connīvēre, cōnīvēre to wink]
■ **conniv'ance** or **conniv'ancy** n. **conniv'er** n.

connivent /kə-nī'vənt/ (biol) adj (of insect or plant parts) converging and touching, but not united or fused. [See **connive**]
■ **conniv'ence** or **conniv'ency** n.

connoisseur /ko-nə-sûr' or kon'ə-/ n a person with a well-informed knowledge and appreciation, esp of fine food and wine or of the arts. [Fr (now connaisseur), from connoître (connaître), from L cognōscere to know]
■ **connoisseur'ship** n the skill and knowledge of a connoisseur.

connote /ko-nōt'/ vt to signify or suggest (ideas, associations, etc) in addition to the direct meaning; to imply as inherent attribute(s); to include as or involve a condition. [L con- with, and notāre to mark]
■ **connotate** /kon'ō-tāt/ vt to connote. **connotā'tion** n the act of connoting; an idea, association or implication additional to the idea, object, etc denoted. **conn'otative** (or /-nō'tə-tiv/) or **connō'tive** adj.

connubial /kə-nū'bi-əl/ adj relating to marriage. [L con- and nūbere to marry]
■ **connubiality** /-al'i-ti/ n. **connū'bially** adv.

connumerate /kə-nū'mə-rāt/ vt to count together.
■ **connumerā'tion** n.

conodont /kon'ə-dont or kō-nə-/ n a microscopic phosphatic toothlike fossil, mainly from the Devonian period, derived from an unknown group of animals, but thought to be vertebrates (also adj). [Gr kōnos cone, and odous, odontos tooth]

conoid /kō'noid/ n anything like a cone in form; a solid generated by the revolution of a parabola, hyperbola or ellipse about its axis. ♦ adj cone-like. [Gr kōnos a cone, and eidos form]
■ **cōnoid'al, cōnoid'ic** or **cōnoid'ical** adj.

conquer /kong'kər/ vt to overcome or vanquish (also fig); to gain control of by force or with an effort (also fig). ♦ vi to be the victor. [OFr conquerre, from L conquīrere, conquaerere, from con-, intens, and quaerere to seek]
■ **con'querable** adj. **con'querableness** n. **con'queress** n (rare) a female conqueror. **con'quering** adj. **con'queringly** adv. **con'queror** n a person who conquers; a victor. **conquest** /kong'kwest/ n the act of conquering; that which is conquered or acquired by physical or moral force; the act of gaining the affections of another; the person whose affections have been gained; acquisition otherwise than by inheritance (old Scots law).
■ **the Conqueror** William I of England (L conquestor). **the Conquest** the acquisition of the throne of England by William, Duke of Normandy, in 1066.

conquistador /kong-kē-sta-dör' or kong-kē'sta-dör, also -kwis(')/ n (pl **conquis'tadors** or **conquistadores** /-dör'es or -dör'es/) a conqueror, esp applied to the Spanish conquerors of Mexico and parts of S America in the 16c. [Sp, from L conquīrere]

con-rod /kon'rod/ n short for **connecting rod**.

cons. abbrev : consecrated; conservative; consigned; consignment; consolidated; consonant; constable; constitution; constitutional; construction; consulting.

consanguine /kon-sang'gwin/ adj related by blood; of the same family or descent (also **consanguin'eous**). [L cōnsanguineus, from con- with, and sanguis or sanguīs blood]
■ **consanguin'ity** n relationship by blood as opposed to affinity or relationship by marriage; a close relationship or connection.

conscience /kon'shəns/ n the sense of moral correctness that governs or influences a person's actions or thoughts; scrupulousness, conscientiousness, diligence; inmost thought, consciousness (Shakesp). ♦ interj (Scot) an expression of surprise (also **my conscience**). [Fr, from L cōnscientia knowledge, from cōnscīre to know well, in one's own mind, from con-, intens, and scīre to know]
■ **con'scienceless** adj. **con'scient** adj aware; conscious. **conscientious** /-shi-en'shəs/ adj regulated by a regard to conscience; scrupulous; tending to take great care, show diligence, etc. **conscien'tiously** adv. **conscien'tiousness** n. **conscientizā'tion** or **-s-** n. **con'scientize** or **-ise** vt to make (someone) aware of (political, social rights, etc). **con'scionable** /-shən-ə-bl/ adj (obs) governed or regulated by conscience. **con'scionableness** n (obs). **con'scionably** adv (obs).
❑ **conscience clause** n a clause in a law, contract, etc which allows people with moral objections not to obey, be bound, etc. **conscience money** n money given to relieve the conscience, as compensation for wrongdoing. **con'science-proof** adj unvisited by any compunctions of conscience. **con'science-smitten** or **-stricken** adj stung by conscience, feeling guilty. **conscientious objector** n a person who objects on grounds of conscience, esp to military service.
■ **case of conscience** a question in casuistry. **crisis of conscience** a state of acute unease over a difficult moral decision. **freedom of conscience** the right to hold religious or other beliefs without persecution. **good** (or **bad**) **conscience** an approving (or reproving) conscience. **in all conscience** certainly; by all that is right and fair (inf). **make a matter of conscience** to have scruples about. **on one's conscience** causing feelings of guilt. **prisoner of conscience** a person imprisoned on account of his or her political beliefs. **speak one's conscience** (Shakesp) to speak frankly; to give one's opinion. **upon conscience** or **o' my conscience** (archaic) truly.

conscious /kon'shəs/ adj having the feeling or knowledge of something; aware; deliberate; having consciousness. ♦ n the conscious mind. ♦ combining form being very aware of and concerned about, as in *clothes-conscious*, *cost-conscious*. [L *cōnscius*, from *cōnscīre* to know; see **conscience**]

■ **con'sciously** *adv*. **con'sciousness** *n* the waking state of the mind; the knowledge which the mind has of anything that is actually being experienced; awareness; thought.

❑ **con'sciousness-raising** *n* development of awareness of one's identity and potential or of (*esp* public) awareness of social and political issues (also *adj*).

conscribe /kən-skrīb'/ *vt* to enlist by conscription. [L *cōnscrībere* to enrol, from *con* together, and *scrībere*, *scrīptum* to write]

■ **conscript** /kon'skript/ *adj* enrolled or registered, *esp* compulsorily. ◆ *n* someone enrolled and liable to serve compulsorily, *esp* in the armed forces. ◆ *vt* /kən-skript'/ to enlist compulsorily. **conscrip'tion** *n* a compulsory enrolment for service; the obtaining of recruits by compulsion. **conscrip'tional** *adj*. **conscrip'tionist** *n* and *adj*.

❑ **conscript fathers** *n pl* (L *patrēs cōnscrīptī*) the senators of ancient Rome; hence, any august legislators.

consecrate /kon'si-krāt/ *vt* to render holy or venerable; to set apart for a holy use; to hallow; to devote (time, energy, etc). ◆ *adj* consecrated; sanctified; devoted. [L *cōnsecrāre, -ātum* to make wholly sacred, from *con-*, intens, and *sacrāre* to set apart as sacred, from *sacer* sacred]

■ **con'secratedness** *n*. **consecrā'tion** *n* the act or process of rendering holy. **con'secrative** *adj*. **con'secrātor** *n*. **consecratory** /-krā'tər-i/ *adj* making sacred or holy.

consectary /kən-sek'tə-ri/ (*archaic*) *n* a deduction, conclusion or corollary. ◆ *adj* consequent; following logically or naturally (also **consectā'neous**). [L *cōnsectārī*, frequentative of *cōnsequī*; see **consecutive**]

consecutive /kən-sek'yə-tiv* or *-ū-/ *adj* following in regular order or one after another; expressing consequence (*grammar*); parallel (*music*). [L *cōnsequī*, from *con-*, intens, and *sequī*, *secūtus* to follow]

■ **consecution** /kon-si-kū'shən/ *n* a train of consequences or logical deductions; a series of things that follow one another; succession of parallel intervals in harmony (*music*). **consec'utively** *adv*. **consec'utiveness** *n*.

conseil /kɔ̃-sāy'/ (*Fr*) *n* advice; council.

❑ **conseil d'administration** *n* a board of directors. **conseil de famille** /də fa-mē-y'/ *n* a family consultation. **conseil d'état** /dā-ta/ *n* a council of state.

consenescence /kon-sə-nes'əns/ (*formal*) *n* general decay (also **consenesc'ency**). [L *con-*, intens, and *senēscere* to grow old]

consensus /kən-sen'səs/ *n* agreement of various parts; agreement in opinion; unanimity; (loosely) trend of opinion. [L *cōnsēnsus*, from *cōnsentīre* ; see **consent**]

■ **consen'sion** *n* mutual consent. **consen'sual** *adj* relating to consent; existing by or based only on consent (*law*); (of reflex actions) responding to stimulation in another part of the body (*med*). **consen'sually** *adv*.

❑ **consensual contract** *n* a contract drawn up and requiring only the consent of all parties. **consensus sequence** *n* a DNA sequence found with minor variations and similar function in widely divergent organisms.

consent /kən-sent'/ *vi* to agree; to give permission; to accede; to comply; to be of the same mind. ◆ *vt* to agree. ◆ *n* agreement; permission; accordance with or acceptance of the actions or opinions of another; concurrence; acquiescence. [L *cōnsentīre*, from *con-* and *sentīre* to feel, to think]

■ **consentaneous** /kon-sən-tā'ni-əs/ *adj* agreeable or accordant; consistent. **consentā'neously** *adv*. **consentā'neousness** or **consentaneity** /kon-sen-tə-nē'i-ti/ *n*. **consentience** /kən-sen'shəns/ *n* agreement. **consen'tient** *adj* agreeing. **consent'ingly** *adv*.

❑ **consenting adult** *n* an adult who consents to something, *esp* a sexual relationship.

■ **age of consent** the age at which a person is legally competent to give consent to certain acts, *esp* sexual intercourse. **be of consent** (*Shakesp*) to be accessory. **with one consent** unanimously.

consequence /kon'si-kwəns/ *n* that which follows or comes after as a result or inference; effect; importance; social standing; the relation of an effect to its cause (*logic*); consequentiality; (in *pl*) a game describing the meeting of a man and a woman and its consequences, each player writing a part of the story, without knowing what previous writers have written. ◆ *vi* (*archaic*) to draw inferences. [Fr, from L *cōnsequī*, from *con-*, intens, and *sequī* to follow]

■ **con'sequent** *adj* following, *esp* as a natural effect or deduction; flowing in the direction of the original slope of the land (distinguished from *subsequent* and *obsequent*; *geol*). ◆ *n* that which follows; the natural effect of a cause. **consequential** /-kwen'shl/ *adj* following as a result, *esp* an indirect result; significant, important; self-important. **consequen'tialism** *n* (*ethics*) the principle stating that the morality of an action is judged according to how good or bad its consequences

are. **consequen'tialist** *n*. **consequential'ity** *n*. **consequen'tially** *adv*. **con'sequently** *adv*.

■ **in consequence (of)** as a result (of). **of no consequence** trivial, unimportant. **take the consequences** to accept the (often unpleasant) results of one's actions.

conservative /kən-sûr'və-tiv/ *adj* tending to support the preservation of established views, customs, institutions, etc; opposed or averse to change; traditional; moderate; cautious; (with *cap*) belonging, or relating, to the Conservative Party. ◆ *n* a person opposed or averse to change; a traditionalist; (with *cap*) a person belonging to or supporting the political party which favours the preservation of existing institutions and seeks to promote free enterprise. [Ety as for **conserve**]

■ **conser'vatism** *n* opposition to innovation; (with *cap*) the policies and principles of the Conservative Party. **conser'vatively** *adv* traditionally; in a traditional way; moderately or cautiously. **conser'vativeness** *n* conventionality; moderation.

❑ **Conservative Party** *n* the British political party advocating support of established customs and institutions, free enterprise, and opposition to socialism; any of various similar parties in other countries.

conserve /kən-sûrv'/ *vt* to keep in a whole, safe or undamaged state; to retain; to preserve; to preserve in sugar (*obs*). ◆ *n* (also /kon'/) something preserved, eg fruits in sugar. [L *cōnservāre*, from *con-* and *servāre* to keep]

■ **conser'vable** *adj*. **conserv'ance** *n* (*rare*) conservation. **conser'vancy** *n* in the UK, a court or commission having authority to preserve a river, forest, port or area of countryside; the act of preserving, *esp* official care of a river, forest, etc; an area so preserved. **conser'vant** *adj*. **conservā'tion** /kon-/ *n* the act of conserving (*esp* old buildings, flora and fauna, the environment). **conservā'tional** *adj*. **conservā'tionist** *n* a person who is trained or actively interested in conservation, *esp* of the environment, its wildlife or natural resources. **conservatoire** /kɔ̃-ser-va-twär or kən-sûr-və-twär'/ or **conservatō'rium** *n* a school of music. **con'servātor** (or /kən-sûr'və-tər/) *n* (also *fem* **conservā'trix**) a person who preserves from injury or violation; an official with (*usu* administrative) responsibility for a conservancy; a guardian, custodian. **conser'vatorship** *n*. **conser'vatory** *n* a storehouse; a greenhouse or place in which exotic plants are kept; a similar glass structure, interconnecting with a house, used as a lounge; a school of music. ◆ *adj* (*rare*) preservative. **conser'ver** *n*.

❑ **conservation area** *n* an area designated as being of special architectural or historic interest, and therefore protected from any alterations which would destroy its character. **conservation law** *n* (*phys*) a law that states that in the interaction between particles, certain quantities, such as mass, energy, etc, remain constant.

■ **conservation of energy** (*phys*) the principle that the sum of the total amount of energy in a given isolated system is constant. **conservation of mass** (*phys*) the principle that the sum of the total amount of mass in a given isolated system is constant.

consider /kən-sid'ər/ *vt* to look at attentively or carefully; to think or deliberate on; to take into account; to attend to; to regard as; to think, hold the opinion (that); to reward (*obs*). ◆ *vi* to think seriously or carefully; to deliberate. [L *cōnsīderāre* perh orig a term of augury, and from *con-* and *sīdus*, *sīderis* star]

■ **consid'erable** *adj* large enough to be worthy of consideration, significant; worthy of respect or attention; of some importance; showing or having a high degree of (a quality, eg courage). **consid'erableness** *n*. **consid'erably** *adv*. **consid'erance** *n* (*archaic*) consideration. **consid'erate** /-ət/ *adj* thoughtful for the feelings and interests of others; considered, deliberate (*archaic*). **consid'erately** *adv*. **consid'erateness** *n* thoughtfulness for others. **considerā'tion** *n* careful thought; something considered; motive or reason; considerateness; importance; recompense, payment; the reason or basis of an agreement or contract; the thing given or done or abstained from by agreement with another, dependent on or in consequence of that other giving, doing or abstaining from something (*law*). **consid'erative** *adj* (*obs*) thoughtful; prudent; considerate. **consid'eratively** *adv* (*obs*). **consid'ered** *adj* carefully thought out, deliberate. **consid'ering** *prep* in view of. ◆ *conj* seeing that. ◆ *adv* everything considered. **consid'eringly** *adv* with consideration.

■ **all things considered** taking all circumstances into account. **in consideration of** because of; as payment for. **take into consideration** to allow for. **under consideration** being considered or dealt with.

consigliere /kon-sig-li-ā'ri/ *n* an adviser, *esp* a person advising a Mafia godfather. [Ital]

consign /kən-sīn'/ *vt* to entrust; to commit; to transmit; to transfer; to devote; to sign or seal (*obs*). [L *cōnsignāre* to attest]

■ **consign'able** *adj*. **consignation** /kon-sig-nā'shən/ *n*. **consignatory** /kən-sig'nə-tər-i/ *n* a cosignatory. **consigned'** *adj* given in trust. **consignee** /kon-sīn-ē'/ *n* a person to whom anything is consigned or entrusted. **consign'er** or **consign'or** n. **consign'ment** n a thing consigned; a set of things consigned together; the act of consigning.

consignify /kon-sig'ni-fī/ (formal) vt to mean when taken along with something else.
■ **consignifica'tion** n. **consignif'icative** adj.

consilience /kən-sil'i-əns/ n concurrence; coincidence. [L con-together, and salīre to leap]
■ **consil'ient** adj agreeing.

consimilar /kən-sim'i-lər/ adj like each other. [L cōnsimilis]
■ **consimilar'ity** n. **consimil'itude** n. **consimil'ity** n.

consist /kən-sist'/ vi to be composed or formed (of); to exist, lie or have its being (in); to be expressed or shown (by); to be compatible or consistent. [L cōnsistere, from con- together, and sistere to set, stand]
■ **consist'ence** or **consist'ency** degree of density or thickness; substance; agreement with something previously stated or shown; harmony, compatibility. **consist'ent** adj free from contradiction; fixed or steady; not fluid; agreeing together, harmonious, compatible; true to principles. **consist'ently** adv. **consistō'rial** adj. **consistō'rian** adj. **con'sistory** (or /-sist'-/) n an assembly or council (archaic); a spiritual or ecclesiastical court or governing body; an assembly of cardinals and the Pope (RC); the place where such a court or assembly meets.
■ **consist in** to inhere in (obs); to have as essence; to be composed of. **consist of** to be made up of.

consociate /kon-sō'shi-āt/ vt and vi to associate together or bring into association. [L cōnsociāre, -ātum, from con- and sociāre to associate, from socius a companion]
■ **consō'ciated** adj. **consociation** /-si-** or -shi-ā'shən/ n companionship; association; alliance, esp of churches; a federal council of Congregational churches; a subdivision of an association dominated by one particular species (bot). **consocia'tional** adj. **consocies** /-sō'shi-ēz/ n a community in nature with a single dominant species.

console[1] /kən-sōl'/ vt to give solace or comfort to; to cheer in distress. [L cōnsōlāri, from con-, intens, and sōlāri to comfort]
■ **consōl'able** adj. **consolate** /kon'səl-āt/ vt (Shakesp) to console. **consolā'tion** n solace; alleviation of misery; a comforting action or circumstance. **consolatory** /kən-sol'ə-tər-i or -sōl'/ adj comforting. ◆ n (Milton) a message of comfort. **consolā'trix** n (rare) a woman who consoles. **console'ment** n. **consol'er** n. **consōl'ingly** adv.
❏ **consolation match, prize, race,** etc n a match, prize, race, etc, for those participants who have been unsuccessful or have not won.

console[2] /kon'sōl/ n the frame enclosing the keyboards, stops, pedals, etc of an organ; a unit with dials, switches, etc, that is used to control an electrical, electronic or mechanical system; an ornamental device resembling a bracket, frequently in the form of the letter S, used to support cornices, or for placing busts, vases or figures on; a large radio or television set that stands, in a cabinet, on the floor; a cabinet for this or similar apparatus. [Fr, prob connected with **consolidate**]
❏ **console game** n a computer game in which the movement of figures in a virtual environment is governed by instructions made through a console. **console table** n a table supported against a wall by consoles or brackets.

consolidate /kən-sol'i-dāt/ vt to make solid; to form into a compact mass; to unite into one; to merge; to rearrange and strengthen (milit). ◆ vi to grow solid or firm; to unite. ◆ adj made firm or solid; united. [L cōnsolidāre, -ātum, from con-, intens, and solidus solid]
■ **consol'idated** adj. **consolidā'tion** n the act or process of consolidating; the process of aggregating the financial statements of a group of companies, or the working document in which this is done; (in industry) a programme of compulsory redundancies (euphem). **consol'idative** adj tending to consolidate; having the quality of healing. **consol'idator** n.
❏ **consolidated annuities** see **consols**. **consolidated fund** n a fund made up by uniting the yield of various taxes, etc to meet standing charges, eg interest on national debt, grants to royal family, etc. **consolidation acts** n pl acts of parliament which combine into one general statute several special enactments.

consols /kon'solz or kon-solz'/ n pl government securities without a maturity date. [Short for **consolidated annuities**]

consolute /kon'sə-loot/ adj (of liquids) mutually or equally soluble. [L consolūtus, from con- and solvere to dissolve]

consommé /kən-som'ā or (Fr) kɔ̃-so-mā'/ n a clear soup made from meat by slow boiling. [Fr, pap from L cōnsummāre, -ātum to consummate]

consonant /kon'sə-nənt/ n any speech sound other than a vowel; a letter of the alphabet representing such a sound. ◆ adj consistent (with); suitable; harmonious. [L cōnsonāns, -antis, prp of cōnsonāre to harmonize, from con- and sonāre to sound]
■ **con'sonance** n a state of agreement or accord; agreement or unison of sounds, harmony; a combination of musical notes which can sound together without the harshness produced by beats; concord.

con'sonancy n harmony. **consonantal** /-ant'l/ adj. **con'sonantly** adv. **con'sonous** adj harmonious.

con sordino /kon sör-dē'nō/ (music) adj (of an instrument) played with a mute. [Ital]

consort /kon'sört or -sərt (archaic, -sört')/ n a partner; a companion; a wife or husband, esp of a reigning monarch; an accompanying ship; a partnership or association (obs); agreement, accord (obs); formerly, a small group of instruments played or musicians playing together. ◆ vt /kən-sört'/ to accompany; to associate, combine or unite (with). ◆ vi to associate or keep company (with); to agree. [L cōnsors, -sortis, from con- and sors a lot]
■ **consort'ed** adj associated. **consort'er** n. **con'sortism** n symbiosis. **consortium** /kon-sör'ti-əm, -shəm or -shi-əm/ n (pl **consor'tia** or (esp N Am) **consor'tiums**) a combination of several banks, business concerns, or other bodies; fellowship; association; the association of fungus and alga in a lichen; in marriage, the right of a spouse to the company, affection and assistance of the other (law).
■ **in consort** in company; in harmony.

conspecific /kon-spə-sif'ik or -spi-/ (biol) adj of the same species. ◆ n a plant or animal of the same species. [L con- with, and **specific**; see **species**]

conspectus /kən-spek'təs/ n a comprehensive view or survey; a synopsis, summary. [L cōnspectus, from cōnspicere to look at; see **conspicuous**]
■ **conspectuity** /kon-spek-tū'i-ti/ n (Shakesp) sight.

conspicuous /kən-spik'ū-əs/ adj catching the eye; noticeable; prominent or attracting attention. [L cōnspicuus, from cōnspicere, from con-, intens, and specere to look]
■ **conspicū'ity** /kon-/ or **conspic'uousness** n. **conspic'uously** adv. ❏ **conspicuous consumption** n extravagant, ostentatious spending on luxury goods in order to impress other people.

conspire /kən-spīr'/ vi to plot or scheme together; to devise; to act together to one end. ◆ vt to plan, devise. [L cōnspīrāre, from con- together, and spīrāre to breathe]
■ **conspir'acist** n a person who supports a conspiracy theory. **conspiracy** /-spir'ə-si/ n the act of conspiring; a banding together for a (often secret, usu unlawful) purpose; a plot; joint action, concurrence. **conspīr'ant** adj conspiring. **conspirā'tion** n conspiracy. **conspir'ator** n a person who conspires. **conspiratō'rial** adj. **conspiratō'rially** adv. **conspir'atress** n a female conspirator. **conspīr'er** n conspirator. **conspīr'ingly** adv.
❏ **conspiracy theory** n a belief that unexplained misfortune is invariably caused by the deliberate action of powerful agencies.
■ **conspiracy of silence** an agreement, esp between a group of people, not to talk about a particular matter in order to prevent others from obtaining information.

con spirito /kon spir'i-tō or spēr'ē-tō/ (esp music) adj and adv with spirit. [Ital]

conspue /kən-spū'/ vt to spit upon; to despise. [L conspuēre, from con-, intens, and spuēre to spit]

conspurcation /kon-spûr-kā'shən/ (obs) n defilement. [L cōnspurcāre, -ātum to defile]

const. abbrev : constant; constitution.

constable /kon' or kun'stə-bl/ n a policeman or policewoman of the lowest rank; applied to various other peace officers; the warden or keeper of a royal castle or fort; a military or administrative officer in an area or district or high-ranking officer of the royal household (medieval hist). [OFr conestable (Fr connétable), from L comes stabulī count or companion of the stable]
■ **con'stableship** n. **con'stablewick** n (hist) the district of a constable. **constabulary** /kən-stab'ū-lər-i/ n an organized body of constables; a police force. ◆ adj of or relating to constables, or peace officers.
■ **Constable of France** chief of the household under the old French kings, then commander-in-chief of the army, judge in questions of chivalry, tournaments and martial displays. **High Constable** one of two constables formerly appointed in every hundred or franchise, to raise the military levy, and with responsibility for maintenance of the peace. **Lord High Constable of England** an officer of the Crown, formerly a judge in the court of chivalry. **Lord High Constable of Scotland** a similar officer (now a mere hereditary title). **petty constable** a parish constable who was under the High Constable. **special constable** a person sworn in by the justices to preserve the peace, or to execute warrants in special circumstances.

constant /kon'stənt/ adj fixed; unchangeable; firm; continual; faithful. ◆ n a quantity (or parameter) which remains the same while the variables may change (maths); an unchanging situation or circumstance. [L cōnstāns, -stantis, from cōnstāre to stand firm, from con-, intens, and stāre to stand]

■ **con'stancy** n fixedness; unchangeableness; steadfastness; stability; faithfulness; perseverance (*Shakesp*); certainty (*Shakesp*). **con'stantly** adv.

constantan /kon'stən-tan/ n an alloy of about 40% nickel and 60% copper, having a high and constant resistance to flow of electricity or heat. [**constant**]

Constantia /kən-stan'shi-ə/ n a sweet wine produced around *Constantia*, near Cape Town.

constantia et virtute /kon-stan'shi-ə et vŭr-tū'tē (or kon-stan'ti-ä et vir-too'te or wir-)/ (L) by constancy and virtue.

Constantinian /kon-stən-tin'yən or -i-ən/ adj relating to Constantine I (c.274–337AD), the first Christian Roman emperor (306–337AD).

Constantinopolitan /kon-stan-ti-nō-pol'i-tən/ adj of or relating to *Constantinople* (now Istanbul).

constate /kən-stāt'/ vt (*Gallicism*) to assert. [Fr *constater*, from L *constat* it is certain]
  ■ **constatation** /kon-stə-tā'shən/ n a statement, assertion; ascertaining, verification. **constative** /kon'stə-tiv, -stā'tiv/ adj (*philos*) (of a statement) that can be true or false; that implies assertion rather than performance, eg *It is raining*. ◆n such a statement, *opp* to *performative*.

constellate /kon'stə-lāt or kən-stel'āt/ vt to cluster; to compel or affect by stellar influence. ◆vi to cluster together. [L *cōnstellātus* studded with stars, from *con-* and *stellāre*, from *stella* a star]
  ■ **constellā'tion** n stars which form a group as seen from the earth; a group or gathering of famous or brilliant people; any group of people, ideas, factors in a situation, etc, related in some way; a particular disposition of the planets, supposed to influence the course of human life or character (*astrol*). **constell'atory** adj.

conster see **construe**.

consternate /kon'stər-nāt/ vt to fill with dismay or confusion. [L *cōnsternāre*, *-ātum*, from *con-* wholly, and *sternere* to strew]
  ■ **consternā'tion** n dismay or anxiety, often causing confusion or lack of understanding.

constipate /kon'sti-pāt/ vt to cause an irregular and insufficient evacuation of the bowels of; to deprive of vigour or useful action (*fig*); to stop up or close (*obs*). [L *cōnstīpāre*, *-ātum* to press together, from *con-* and *stīpāre* to pack]
  ■ **con'stipated** adj. **constipā'tion** n.

constitute /kon'sti-tūt/ vt to form or make up; to establish or found; to set up; to appoint. [L *cōnstituere*, *cōnstitūtum*, from *con-*, intens, and *statuere* to make to stand, to place]
  ■ **constituency** /kən-stit'ū-ən-si/ n the whole body of voters, or a district or population, represented by a member of parliament, etc; a set of people supporting, patronizing, or forming a power-base for, a business organization, pressure group, etc. **constit'uent** adj constituting or forming; essential; component; electing; constitution or law-making. ◆n an essential part; one of those who elect a representative, *esp* to parliament; an inhabitant of the constituency of a member of parliament, etc. **constitū'tion** /kon-/ n a system of laws and customs established by the sovereign power of a state for its own guidance; an established form of government; the act of constituting; the way in which something is formed or made up; the natural condition of body or mind; a set of rules or guidelines by which an organization is governed; molecular structure, taking into account not only the kinds and numbers of atoms but the way in which they are linked (*chem*). **constitū'tional** adj conforming to the constitution or frame of government; existing subject to fixed laws; inherent in the natural make-up or structure of a person or thing. ◆n a walk for the benefit of one's health. **constitū'tionalism** n adherence to the principles of the constitution. **constitū'tionalist** or **constitū'tionist** n a person who favours or studies a constitution or the constitution. **constitūtional'ity** n. **constitū'tionalize** or **-ise** vt to make constitutional. **constitū'tionally** adv. **con'stitutive** adj that constitutes or establishes; having power to constitute; essential; component. **con'stitutively** adv. **con'stitutor** n someone or something that constitutes; a person who makes a constitution.
  ❑ **constitutional monarchy** n a monarchy in which the power of the sovereign is defined and limited by the constitution. **constitutive enzyme** n an enzyme that is formed under all conditions of growth.

constr. abbrev : construction.

constrain /kən-strān'/ vt to force, compel; to confine, limit; to restrict by a condition; to cause constraint to. [OFr *constraindre*, from L *cōnstringere*, from *con-* and *stringere* to press]
  ■ **constrain'able** adj. **constrained'** adj forced, compelled; lacking ease and spontaneity of manner, unnatural; embarrassed. **constrain'edly** adv. **constraint'** n compulsion; confinement; repression of one's feelings; embarrassment; a restricting condition.

constrict /kən-strikt'/ vt to press together; to contract; to cramp; to limit. [L *cōnstringere*, *-strictum*]

■ **constrict'ed** adj narrowed; cramped; narrowed in places (*bot*). **constric'tion** n the process of narrowing or pressing together; contraction; tightness; something constricted; (in a chromosome) a narrow, localized region, normally found at the centromere and elsewhere including the nucleolar-organizing region. **constrict'ive** adj. **constrict'or** n something that constricts or draws together; a muscle that compresses an organ or hollow structure; a snake that crushes its prey in its coils.

constringe /kən-strinj'/ (*rare*) vt to draw together; to cause to contract or shrink. ◆vi to contract or shrink. [L *cōnstringere*]
  ■ **constrin'gency** n. **constrin'gent** adj having the quality of contracting.

construct /kon-strukt'/ vt to build up; to make; to put together the parts of or from parts; to compose; to compile; to put in grammatical relation. ◆adj constructed. ◆n /kon'strukt/ a thing constructed, *esp* in the mind; an image or object of thought constructed from a number of sense-impressions or images (*psychol*). [L *cōnstruere*, *-structum*, from *con-* and *struere* to build]
  ■ **construct'able** or **construct'ible** adj. **construct'er** or **construct'or** n. **construc'tion** n the act or process of constructing; anything constructed; a building; the syntactic relations of words in a sentence (*grammar*); a word or group of words; interpretation; meaning. **construc'tional** adj relating to construction; used for structures; making use of structures. **construc'tionally** adv. **construc'tionist** n (*US law*) a person, *esp* a judge, who interprets constitutional law in a particular way. **construct'ive** adj capable of, tending towards, or concerned with, constructing; representing positive advice, *opp* to *destructive*; (of facts) inferred (*law*). **construct'ively** adv. **construct'iveness** n. **construct'ivism** n a non-representational style of art, *esp* sculpture and architecture, using man-made industrial materials and processes such as twisting and welding; a simplified, non-realistic style in stage sets, using steps, platforms, etc (also **construc'tionism**). **construct'ivist** n. **construc'tivism** n.
  ❑ **constructive dismissal** n action by an employer which leaves an employee no alternative but to resign. **construct state** n in Semitic languages, the state of a noun depending on another noun, where in Indo-European languages the other would be in the genitive case, eg *House of God*, house being in the construct state.
  ■ **bear a construction** to allow of a particular interpretation.

construe /kon-stroo/ old form **conster** /kon'stər/ vt to interpret; to infer; to construct grammatically; to analyse the grammatical structure of (*esp* a classical Greek or Latin text), preparatory to translating; to translate word for word, *esp* aloud (*old*). ◆vi to be capable of or permit grammatical analysis. ◆n /kon'stroo/ (*rare*) an act of construing; something construed, a piece of translation. [L *cōnstruere*, *constructum* to pile together]
  ■ **construabil'ity** n. **constru'able** adj. **construer** /kon'* or *-stroo'/ n.

constuprate /kon'stū-prāt/ (*obs*) vt to ravish. [L *cōnstuprāre*, from *con-*, intens, and *stuprum* defilement, disgrace]
  ■ **constuprā'tion** n.

consubsist /kon-sub-sist'/ vi to subsist together.

consubstantial /kon-sub-stan'shəl/ adj of the same substance, nature or essence, *esp* (*theol*) of the Trinity. [L *consubstāntiālis*, from *con-* with, and *substantia* substance]
  ■ **consubstan'tialism** n the doctrine of consubstantiation. **consubstan'tialist** n a person who believes in consubstantiation. **consubstantiality** /-shi-al'i-ti/ n. **consubstan'tially** adv. **consubstan'tiate** /-shi-āt/ vt and vi to unite in one common substance or nature, *esp* (*theol*) bread and wine and the body of Christ (also adj). **consubstantiā'tion** n the doctrine of the actual, substantial presence of the body and blood of Christ coexisting in and with the bread and wine used at the Lord's Supper (cf **transubstantiation**). **consubstantiā'tionist** n.

consuetude /kon'swi-tūd/ n (a) custom; familiarity. [L *cōnsuētūdō*, *-inis* custom]
  ■ **consuetū'dinary** adj customary. ◆n an unwritten law established by usage, derived by immemorial custom from antiquity; a ritual of customary devotions.

consul /kon'səl/ n an agent for a foreign government appointed to attend to the interests of its citizens and commerce; one of the two chief magistrates in the Roman republic; one of the three heads of the French republic, 1799–1804. [L *cōnsul*]
  ■ **con'sulage** n (*hist*) duty paid to a consul for protection of goods. **con'sular** /-sū-lər/ adj relating to a consul. ◆n a person of consular rank. **con'sulate** /-sūl- or -səl-/ n the office, residence, jurisdiction, government or time of a consul or consuls. **con'sulship** n the office, or term of office, of a consul.
  ❑ **consul general** n (pl **consuls general**) a consul of the first rank.

consult /kən-sult'/ vt to ask advice of; to look up for information or advice; to consider (wishes, feelings, etc of others); to discuss. ◆vi to consider jointly (with *with*); to give or take advice. ◆n /kən-sult'/ or *kon'sult*/ consultation; council; a meeting for conspiracy or intrigue (*hist*). [L *cōnsultāre*, intensive of *cōnsulere* to consult]

■ **consult'ancy** *n* an agency which provides professional advice; the post or work of a consultant. **consultant** /*kən-sult'ənt*/ *n* a person who gives professional advice or takes part in consultation; the most senior grade of doctor in a given speciality in a hospital; a person who seeks advice or information. **consultā'tion** /*kon-səl-* or *-sul-*/ *n* deliberation, or a meeting for deliberation, *esp* of physicians or lawyers. **consult'ative** *adj* of or relating to consultation, *esp* of bodies without vote on the final decision. **consult'atory** *adj* of the nature of consultation. **consultee'** *n* a person consulted. **consult'er** *n* a person who consults. **consult'ing** *adj* (of a physician, lawyer, etc) prepared to give professional advice to others in the same field. **consult'ive** *adj*. **consult'or** *n*. **consult'ory** *adj*.

❑ **consulting room** *n* the room in which a doctor sees a patient.

consulta /*kon-sool'tä*/ (*Ital* and *Sp*) *n* a meeting of council.

consume /*kən-sūm'* or *-soom'*/ *vt* to use up; to eat; to devour; to overcome completely; to waste or spend; to destroy by wasting, fire, evaporation, etc; to exhaust. ◆ *vi* to waste away. [L *cōnsūmere*, *-sūmptum* to destroy, from *con-* (signifying completeness) and *sūmere* to take]

■ **consum'able** *n* and *adj* (something) that can be consumed. **consum'edly** *adv* (*archaic*) exceedingly. **consum'er** *n* a person who consumes; a person who uses an article produced, *opp* to *producer*. **consum'erism** *n* (the promotion of) the protection of the interests of buyers of goods and services against defective or dangerous goods, etc; excessive devotion to the buying of material goods; the theory that steady growth in the consumption of goods is necessary for a sound economy. **consum'erist** *n* and *adj*. **consum'ing** *n* and *adj* wasting or destroying; engrossing. **consum'ingly** *adv*.

❑ **consumer durables** *n pl* consumer goods designed to last a relatively long time, such as televisions, washing machines, cars, etc. **consumer goods** *n pl* goods in a finished state for sale to and use of consumers. **consumer research** *n* the study of the needs and preferences of consumers. **consumer society** *n* a society in which consumers' acquisition of goods and use of services is a key economic factor. **consumer terrorism** *n* the deliberate contamination by harmful substances of certain food products, *usu* in order to blackmail the producers or retailers of the products. **consumer terrorist** *n*.

consummate /*kon'sə-māt* or *-sū-*/ *vt* to raise to the highest point; to perfect or finish; to make (marriage) legally complete by sexual intercourse. ◆ *adj* /*kən-sum'āt* or *-ət* or *kon'sū-*/ complete, supreme or perfect of its kind; skilled or competent. [L *cōnsummāre*, *-ātum* to perfect, from *con-*, intens, and *summus* highest, perfect, *summa* a sum]

■ **consumm'ately** *adv* perfectly; with accomplishment. **consummā'tion** *n* the act of completing; perfection; the act of sexual intercourse which makes a marriage legally valid. **consumm'ative** *adj*. **con'summātor** *n*. **consumm'atory** *adj*.

consumption /*kən-sum(p)'shən*/ *n* the act or process of consuming or using up; the quantity consumed; wasting of the body; an earlier name for pulmonary tuberculosis. [See **consume**]

■ **consumpt** /*kon'sum(p)t* or *kən-sum(p)t'*/ *n* (*Scot*) consumption. **consump'tive** *adj* wasting away; relating to, inclined to or suffering from the disease consumption; relating to the using up of something, *esp* resources. ◆ *n* a person who suffers from consumption. **consump'tively** *adv*. **consump'tiveness** or **consumptiv'ity** /*kon-*/ *n*.

cont. *abbrev* : continued.

contabescent /*kon-tə-bes'ənt*/ *adj* wasting away, atrophied; failing to produce pollen (*bot*). [L *contābēscēns*, *-entis*, from *contābēscere* to waste away]

■ **contabesc'ence** *n*.

contact /*kon'takt*/ *n* touch; meeting; association; means or occasion of communication; a person one can call upon for assistance, information, introductions, etc in a business or other organization; a person who has been exposed to contagion; meeting in a point without intersection (*maths*); a coming close together such as to allow passage of electric current or communication of disease; a place or part where electric current may be allowed to pass; a contact lens. ◆ *adj* involving contact; caused or made active by contact. ◆ *vt* and *vi* (also /*kon-takt'*/) to bring or to come into contact; to get in touch with, or establish a connection with. [L *contingere*, *contactum* to touch, from *con-* wholly, and *tangere* to touch]

■ **contact'able** *adj* able to be contacted. **contactee'** *n* a person who claims to have received communications from extraterrestrial beings. **con'tactless** *adj* denoting a payment system in which credits stored on a smart card (qv) are deducted without the card being passed through a card reader. **con'tactor** *n* a device for repeatedly making and breaking an electric circuit. **contact'ual** *adj* relating to contact.

❑ **contact centre** *n* a building where workers provide services to a company's customers by telephone, computer, etc. **contact flight** *n*

navigation of an aircraft by ground observation alone. **contact lens** *n* a lens, *usu* of thin plastic material, worn in direct contact with the eyeball, instead of spectacles, to correct defects of vision. **contact man** *n* (*inf*) an intermediary in transactions, *esp* shady ones. **contact metamorphism** *n* (*geol*) alteration of rocks in the neighbourhood of igneous materials. **contact poison** *n* a poison which can penetrate the skin, and which can act without being swallowed or inhaled. **contact print** *n* (*photog*) a print made by putting a negative or positive transparency in direct contact with a sensitized paper or film and exposing to light. **con'tact-print** *vt*. **contact process** *n* the process of large-scale manufacture of sulphuric acid by the oxidation of sulphur dioxide to sulphur trioxide in the presence of a catalyst. **contact sport** *n* a sport involving much physical contact between players. **contact tracing** *n* a system used by health workers and certain clinics, to control the spread of a disease, eg sexually transmitted disease, by finding as many individuals who have had contact with a patient as possible.

contadino /*kon-tä-dē'nō*/ *n* (*pl* **contadi'ni** /*-nē*/) an Italian peasant. [*Ital*]

■ **contadi'na** /*-nä*/ *n* (*pl* **contadi'ne** /*-nā*/ or **contadi'nas**) an Italian peasant woman.

contagion /*kən-tā'jən*/ *n* transmission of a disease by direct contact with an infected person or object; a disease or poison transmitted in this way; the means of transmission; the transmission of an emotional state, eg excitement; a harmful influence. [L *contāgiō*, *-ōnis*, from *con-* and *tangere* to touch]

■ **contā'gionist** *n* (*obs*) a person who believes in the contagiousness of certain diseases. **contā'gious** *adj* (of disease) communicable by ordinary social contact (cf **infectious**); carrying disease or other contagion; noxious (*obs*); spreading easily (*fig*; *inf*). **contā'giously** *adv*. **contā'giousness** *n*. **contā'gium** *n* contagion; contagious matter.

❑ **contagious abortion** see **brucellosis**.

contain /*kən-tān'*/ *vt* to have within, enclose; to comprise, include; to restrain; to keep fixed; to hold back; to keep in check; to retain (*archaic*); to be divisible by (a number) with no remainder (*maths*). [OFr *contenir*, from L *continēre*, from *con-* and *tenēre* to hold]

■ **contain'able** *adj*. **contain'er** *n* something that contains goods, etc for storage; a large box-like receptacle of standard shape and size in which goods are enclosed for transport on a lorry, train or ship; a vessel for holding gas. **containerizā'tion** or **-s-** *n*. **contain'erize** or **-ise** *vt* to put (freight) into standard sealed containers; to use such containers for (eg a transport operation); to convert so as to handle containers. **contain'ment** *n* the act of containing; the act or policy of preventing the spread beyond certain limits of a power or influence regarded as hostile, by means other than war; the successful result of this; (also **confinement**) in fusion, the use of shaped magnetic fields or of inertial confinement to contain a plasma (*nuclear eng*).

❑ **container crane** *n* a very large bridge-type quayside crane for handling large containers. **container port** *n* a port equipped for handling containers. **container ship** *n* a ship designed for the most efficient stowing and transport of containers. **container terminal** *n* a port, railway station, etc, or part of one, set aside and equipped for handling containers. **containment building** *n* a structure enclosing a nuclear reactor, designed to withstand high pressure and temperatures and to contain the escape of radiation.

contaminate /*kon-tam'i-nāt*/ *vt* to pollute, eg by radioactivity; to infect; to defile by touching or mixing with; to corrupt. ◆ *adj* contaminated. [L *contāmināre*, *-ātum*, from *contāmen* (for *contagmen*) pollution; see **contact**]

■ **contam'inable** *adj*. **contam'inant** *n*. **contaminā'tion** *n* pollution; adulteration; corruption; defilement. **contam'inative** *adj*. **contam'inator** *n*.

contango /*kən-tang'gō*/ (*stock exchange*) *n* (*pl* **contang'os**) a percentage paid by the buyer to the seller of stock for keeping back its delivery to the next settling-day, continuation, *opp* to **backwardation**. ◆ *vt* to agree to pay a contango on (shares). [Arbitrarily from **continue**]

❑ **contang'o-day** *n* that on which contangos are fixed (also **continuation-day**).

cont. bon. mor. *abbrev* : *contra bonos mores* (L), contrary to good manners.

contd. *abbrev* : continued.

conte /*kɔ̃t*/ *n* a short story (as a literary genre). [Fr]

conté /*kɔ̃-tā'* or *kon'tā*/ *n* (sometimes with *cap*) a hard crayon, *usu* black, brown, or red, made of graphite and clay. [NJ *Conté*, 18c Fr chemist]

conteck /*kon'tek*/ (*archaic*) *n* strife. [OFr *contek*, prob connected with *contekier* to touch]

contemn /*kən-tem'*/ *vt* (*Spenser pap* **contempt'**) to despise. [L *contemnere*, *-temptum* to value little, from *con-*, intens, and *temnere* to slight]

contemper ... continue

■ **contem′ner** or **contem′nor** /-ər or -nər/ n a person who contemns; a person who has been found guilty of contempt of court. **contem′nible** adj.

contemper /kən-tem′pər/ vt to blend together, to qualify by mixture; to adapt. [L contemperāre]
■ **contemperā′tion** n (obs). **contem′perature** n.

contemplate /kon′təm-plāt, older kən-tem′plāt/ vt to consider or look at attentively; to meditate on or study; to intend. ◆ vi to think seriously; to meditate (on or upon). [L contemplārī, -ātus to mark out carefully a templum or place for auguries, from con- (signifying completeness) and templum]
■ **contemp′lable** adj. **contem′plant** n. **contemplā′tion** n meditation; a meditative condition of mind; attentive viewing or consideration; matter for thought; purpose. **contemp′latist** n. **con′templātive** (or /kən-tem′plə-/) adj given to contemplation. ◆ n a person leading a life of religious contemplation. **con′templatively** (or /-tem′/) adv. **con′templativeness** (or /-tem′/) n. **con′templātor** n a person who contemplates; a student (rare).
■ **contemplative life** (theol and philos) life devoted to meditation (cf **active life**). **in contemplation of** in the expectation of; bearing in mind as a possibility.

contemporaneous /kən-tem-pə-rā′nyəs or -nē-əs/ adj living, happening or being at the same time; belonging approximately to the same relative place in the succession, not necessarily strictly synchronous (geol). [L con- and tempus, -oris time]
■ **contemporā′nean** n and adj contemporary. **contemporaneity** /-ə-nē′i-ti/ n. **contemporā′neously** adv. **contemporā′neousness** n. **contemporar′ily** adv. **contem′porariness** n. **contem′porary** adj belonging to the same time (with); of the same age; (loosely) present-day, esp up-to-date, fashionable, etc; of a style of house decoration and furnishing popular in the 1950s. ◆ n a person who lives at the same time as another; a person of approximately the same age as another; a newspaper or magazine of the same time. **contem′porize** or **-ise** vt to make contemporary.

contempt /kən-tempt′/ n scorn; disgrace; disregard of the rule of law, or an offence against the dignity of a court, etc, as in contempt of court, contempt of Parliament. [**contemn**]
■ **contemptibil′ity** or **contempt′ibleness** n. **contempt′ible** (or (Spenser) /kon′/) adj despicable; paltry. **contempt′ibly** adv. **contempt′ūous** adj haughty, scornful. **contempt′ūously** adv. **contempt′uousness** n.
■ **beneath contempt** utterly despicable. **hold in contempt** to despise.

contend /kən-tend′/ vi to strive; to struggle in emulation or in opposition; to dispute or debate (with against, for, with or about). ◆ vt to maintain in dispute (that). [L contendere, -tentum, from con- and tendere to stretch]
■ **contend′ent** (rare) or **contend′er** n a person who contends. **contend′ing** n and adj striving. **conten′tion** n strife; debate; a point argued. **conten′tious** adj in, or relating to, dispute; controversial; quarrelsome; tending to engage in disputes. **conten′tiously** adv. **conten′tiousness** n.

contenement /kən-ten′i-mənt/ (obs) n property necessary to maintain one's station. [L con-, intens, and tenement]

content¹ /kon′tent/ n that which is contained; capacity; the substance; (in pl) the things contained; (in pl) the list of chapters, sections, etc in a book. [See **contain**]
□ **content word** n a word which has a meaning independent of its context, opp to function word.

content² /kən-tent′/ adj satisfied; quietly happy. ◆ n peace of mind; satisfaction. ◆ interj I am content or agreed, the formula of assent in the House of Lords. ◆ vt to make content. [Fr, from L contentus contained, hence, satisfied, from con- and tenēre to hold]
■ **contentā′tion** n (obs). **content′ed** adj content. **content′edly** adv. **content′edness** or **content′ment** n. **content′less** adj without content; discontented.

contention, contentious see under **contend**.

conterminous /kən-tûr′mi-nəs/ or now usually **coterminous** /kō-tûr′mi-nəs/ adj adjacent, meeting along a common boundary; meeting end to end; coincident; coextensive in range. [L conterminus neighbouring, from con- and terminus a boundary]
■ **conter′minal** or **coter′minal** adj adjacent; end to end. **conter′minant, conter′minate, coter′minant** or **coter′minate** adj adjacent. **conter′minously** or **coter′minously** adv.

contessa /kon-tes′ə/ n (pl contess′as) an Italian countess.

contest /kən-test′/ vt to call in question or make the subject of dispute; to strive to gain. ◆ vi to contend. ◆ n /kon′/ a struggle for victory; a competition; strife; a debate, dispute, argument. [Fr contester, from L contestārī to call to witness, from con-, intens, and testārī to be a witness, from testis a witness]
■ **contestabil′ity** n the power to challenge a monopoly. **contest′able** adj. **contest′ant** n a person who takes part in a contest. **contestā′tion**

n the act of contesting; contest, strife; emulation. **contest′ed** adj. **contest′er** n. **contest′ing** adj. **contest′ingly** adv.
□ **contested election** n one in which there are more candidates than are to be elected; one whose validity is disputed (US).

context /kon′tekst/ n the parts of a piece of writing or speech which precede and follow a particular word or passage and may fix, or help to fix, its true meaning; associated surroundings, setting. [L contextus, contexere, from con- and texere, textum to weave]
■ **context′ual** adj. **contextūaliza′tion** or **-s-** n. **context′ūalize** or **-ise** vt to place in context; to study (words, etc) in their context. **context′ūally** adv. **context′ure** n the process or manner of weaving together; structure; fabric.
■ **in** (or **out of**) **context** with (or without) consideration of surrounding circumstances, etc.

conticent /kon′ti-sənt/ (Thackeray) adj silent. [L conticēns, -entis, from con-, intens, and tacēre to be silent]

contignation /kon-tig-nā′shən/ (archaic) n joining together of timber; framework boarding. [L contignātiō, -ōnis, from contignāre, from con- and tignum beam]

contiguous /kən-tig′ū-əs/ adj touching, adjoining; near; next (to) in space or time. [L contiguus, from contingere to touch on all sides, from con- wholly, and tangere to touch]
■ **contigū′ity** n. **contig′uously** adv. **contig′uousness** n.

continent /kon′ti-nənt/ n a vast landmass not broken up by seas; one of the great divisions of the land surface of the globe; the mainland portion of one of these; (usu with cap) the mainland of Europe, as opposed to the British Isles; sum and substance (archaic); solid earth (obs); the main or whole body of anything (obs). ◆ adj restraining within due bounds, or absolutely abstaining from, the indulgence of pleasure, esp sexual; able to control the movements of one's bladder and bowels; temperate; virtuous. [L continēns, -entis, from continēre to contain, from con- and tenēre to hold]
■ **con′tinence** or **con′tinency** n self-restraint or abstinence; chastity; ability to control one's bladder and bowels. **continental** /-ent′l/ adj of, characteristic of, or of the nature of, a continent, esp the mainland of Europe, the colonies of N America at the period of the War of Independence, or the main landmass of the United States. ◆ n a native or inhabitant of a continent, esp the mainland of Europe; an American soldier of the War of Independence; a currency note of the Continental Congress. **continent′alism** n anything peculiar to the usage of a continent, esp Europe. **continent′alist** n. **continental′ity** n the extent to which a climate is influenced by location in the interior of a large land mass. **con′tinently** adv in a continent manner.
□ **continental breakfast** n a light breakfast of rolls and coffee (cf **English breakfast**). **continental climate** n the climate characteristic of the interior of a continent, with hot summers, cold winters, and little rainfall. **Continental Congress** n an assembly of delegates of the American colonies, before the United States constitution was in force. **continental crust** n the part of the earth's crust lying underneath the large landmasses. **continental day** n a school day that begins early in the morning and ends shortly after midday. **continental divide** n a range of mountains forming the watershed of a continent. **continental drift** n (geol) the theory of the slow drifting apart of land masses, as eg in the theory of the formation of world continents from one original land mass, now supported by the theory of **plate tectonics** (see under **plate**). **continental plate** n a plate (qv) of the lithosphere. **continental quilt** n a duvet. **continental shelf** n a gently sloping zone, under relatively shallow seas, offshore from a continent or island. **Continental System** n Napoleon's plan for excluding Britain from all commercial connection with Europe.

contingent /kən-tin′jənt/ adj dependent on something else; (usu with on or upon) liable but not certain to happen; accidental. ◆ n an event liable but not certain to occur; a share, quota or group, esp of soldiers. [L contingēns, -entis, from con- mutually, and tangere to touch]
■ **contin′gence** n contact; contingency (obs). **contin′gency** n the quality or state of being contingent; a possible future event; a chance happening or concurrence of events; something dependent on such an event (also adj); chance; uncertainty; an incidental; close connection; contact (obs). **contin′gently** adv.
□ **contingency plans** n pl plans or arrangements made in case a particular situation should arise. **contingency table** n (stats) a table of figures used to examine the correlation between two variables.

continue /kən-tin′ū/ vt to draw out or prolong; to extend; to maintain; to go on with; to resume; to adjourn (law); to be a prolongation of. ◆ vi to remain in the same place or state; to last or endure; to persevere; to resume. [L continuāre, from continuus joined, connected, from continēre to hold together]
■ **contin′uable** adj. **contin′ual** adj constantly happening or done; repeated; unceasing; persistent. **contin′ually** adv. **contin′uance** n duration; uninterrupted succession; stay; adjournment (law). **contin′uant** adj continuing; capable of continuing. ◆ n (phonetics) a consonant sound which is produced on an uninterrupted flow of

breath (also *adj*). **contin'uāte** *adj* closely united (*obs*); unbroken (*Shakesp*). **continuā'tion** *n* going on; persistence; constant succession; extension; resumption; a further instalment. **contin'uative** *adj* continuing. ◆ *n* a continuative word or phrase, such as *so* or *yes*. **contin'uator** *n* a person who continues; a person who keeps up a series or succession. **contin'ued** *adj* uninterrupted; unceasing; sustained; extended; resumed; in instalments. **contin'uedly** *adv*. **contin'uedness** *n*. **contin'uer** *n* someone who or something that continues; a person who has the power of persevering. **continū'ity** *n* the state of being continuous or consistent; uninterrupted connection; a complete scenario of a cinema film; the person who writes it (in full **continuity writer**); the ordering or arrangement of film or television shots and scenes, or of parts of a radio broadcast, in a correct or consistent way. **continuo** /kon-tin'ū-ō (Ital -tēn'wō)/ *n* (*pl* **contin'uos**) thorough bass; the bass part as written for a keyboard instrument, with or without an accompaniment; the instruments playing this part. **contin'uous** *adj* extending without interruption in space or time; denoting a continuing action or state, in English *usu* expressed by *be* with the present participle, eg *is working* as distinct from *works* (*grammar*). **contin'uously** *adv*. **contin'uousness** *n*. **contin'ūum** *n* (*pl* **contin'uums** or **contin'ua**) that which is continuous; that which must be regarded as continuous and the same and which can be described only relatively.
❏ **continuation class** *n* (*old*) a class for continuing the education of those who have left school. **continuā'tion-day** same as **contango-day** (see under **contango**). **continuing education** *n* part-time courses of study for adult students. **continuity announcer** *n* (*radio, TV*) a person who supervises the continuity of a sequence of programmes, by linking programmes, filling gaps with interlude material, etc. **continuity girl** or **man** *n* a person employed on the set of a cinema film to ensure continuity, *esp* in matters of costume, make-up, props, etc, between different shots. **continuous assessment** *n* the assessment of the progress of a pupil or student by intermittent checks, eg class tests, essays, etc, throughout the year. **continuous creation** *n* the notion of creation as going on always, not as a single act at one particular time (*philos*); the steady-state theory of cosmology (*astron*). **continuous spectrum** *n* (*phys*) an emission spectrum which shows continuous non-discrete changes of intensity with wavelength or particle energy. **continuous stationery** *n* (*comput*) stationery consisting of a long sheet of paper with regular perforations, *usu* folded fanwise and fed through a printer. **continuous wave** *n* (*phys*) an electromagnetic wave of constant frequency and amplitude.
■ **space-time continuum** see under **space**.

conto /kon'tō/ *n* (*pl* **con'tos**) a former Portuguese and Brazilian monetary unit worth 1000 of the standard unit. [Port, million (reis), from L *computus* a sum]

contorno /kon-tör'nō/ *n* (*pl* **contor'nos**) contour or outline. [Ital *contorno* circuit, contour]
■ **contor'niate** *n* a coin or medal with a deep groove round the disc. ◆ *adj* having this.

contort /kən-tört'/ *vt* to twist or turn violently; to writhe. [L *con-*, intens, and *torquēre, tortum* to twist]
■ **contort'ed** *adj* twisted; twisted, as some flower-buds when each floral leaf overlaps its neighbour always on the same side round the circle; much and irregularly plicated (*geol*). **contor'tion** *n* a violent twisting; deformation. **contor'tional** or **contor'tionate** *adj*. **contor'tionist** *n*. **contor'tionist** *n* an entertainer who is able to twist his or her body into contorted postures; a person who twists words and phrases. **contort'ive** *adj*.

contour /kon'toor/ *n* outline, shape or surface; general character or aspect; artistic quality of outline; a contour line; a point, line or surface at, along or on which some property or characteristic is constant, or its representation in a map or diagram. ◆ *adj* having, showing or based on contours; contoured. ◆ *vt* to mark with contour lines; to follow the contour lines of. [Fr *contour* (Ital *contorno*), from Ital *contornare*, to surround, outline, from L *con-* and *tornāre* to turn in a lathe, from *tornus* (Gr *tornos*) a lathe]
■ **con'toured** *adj* (of chairs, etc) shaped to fit the lines of the human body.
❏ **contour cultivation**, **farming** or **ploughing** *n* the ploughing (and planting) of sloping land along the contour lines to counter erosion. **contour feathers** *n pl* feathers lying along a bird's body providing insulation and streamlining. **contour line** *n* an imaginary line on the ground whose points are all at the same height above sea-level, or the intersection of the ground surface by a level surface of constant elevation; a representation of such a line on a map. **contour map** *n* a map in which the configuration of land is shown by contour lines.

contra /kon'trə/ *adv* and *prep* against. ◆ *n* an argument against; the opposing side.
❏ **contra account** *n* (*bookkeeping*) an account in which items are held in suspense pending settlement or definitive classification.

contra- /kon-tra- or -trə-/ *pfx* denoting: against; contrary; pitched below (*music*). [L *contrā*]

contraband /kon'trə-band/ *adj* forbidden by law to be imported or exported; illegally imported or exported, smuggled; prohibited. ◆ *n* illegal trade; smuggled or prohibited goods; (in the American Civil War) a refugee slave. [Sp *contrabanda*, from Ital *contrabbando*, from L *contrā*, and LL *bandum* ban]
■ **con'trabandism** *n* trading in contraband goods. **con'trabandist** *n* a smuggler.
■ **contraband of war** commodities not to be supplied by neutral to belligerent powers.

contrabass /kon'trə-bās/ *n* the double bass. ◆ *adj* applied to other instruments taking a similar part (also **contrabasso**, **contrabbasso** /-bäs'ō/ and (*rare*) **coun'terbase**). [Ital *contra(b)basso*, from pfx *contra-* (indicating an octave lower), and *basso* bass]

contrabassoon /kon-trə-ba-soon' or -bə-/ *n* a metal or wooden instrument, like a bassoon but sounding an octave lower, the double bassoon. [*contra-* (see **contrabass** above) and **bassoon**]

contra bonos mores /kon'tra bō'nōs mō'rēz or bo' or -rās/ (*L*) contrary to good manners or morals (*inf* short form **cont. bon. mor.**).

contraception /kon-trə-sep'shən/ *n* the prevention of unwanted pregnancy. [L *contrā* against, and **conception**]
■ **contracep'tive** *n* a drug, device or other means of contraception (also *adj*).

contract /kon- or kən-trakt'/ *vt* to draw together; to lessen; to shorten; to effect by agreement; to come into, become the subject of; to incur; to catch (a disease); to bargain for; to betroth. ◆ *vi* to shrink; to become less; to become shorter; to make a contract (*with* or *for*). ◆ *n* /kon'trakt/ an agreement on fixed terms; a bond; a betrothal; the written statement representing an agreement; contract bridge; a final bid in contract bridge; an undertaking; an undertaking or agreement to kill a particular person, *esp* for an agreed sum of money (*criminal sl*). [L *contractus*, from *con-* together, and *trahere, tractum* to draw]
■ **contractabil'ity** *n*. **contract'able** /kən-/ *adj* (*esp* of a disease or habit) able to be contracted. **contract'ed** *adj* drawn together; shortened; narrow; mean; engaged to be married. **contract'edly** *adv*. **contract'edness** *n*. **contractibil'ity** *n*. **contract'ible** *adj* capable of being contracted or shortened. **contract'ile** *adj* tending or having power to contract or to draw in. **contractil'ity** /kon-/ *n*. **contrac'tion** /kən-/ *n* the act of contracting; a decrease in length, size or volume; a word shortened in speech or spelling; a symbol for shortening or a shortened form of (part of) a word (*palaeog*); a tightening of the muscles or muscle fibres, *esp* one of the regular spasms of the uterine muscles or fibres involved in the process of giving birth. **contrac'tional** or **contrac'tionary** *adj* having the effect of contracting. **contract'ive** *adj* tending to contract. **contract'or** *n* a person who, or company that, engages to execute work or provide supplies at a stated rate; one of the parties to a bargain or agreement; something that contracts, *esp* a muscle. **contract'ūal** *adj*. **contrac'tually** *adv*. **contrac'tural** *adj* relating to contracture (*med*); contractual (*non-standard*). **contract'ure** *n* persistent muscular contraction; a deformity or shortening of a part of the body due to shrinkage of the tissue in the muscles, skin, etc; tapering of a column (*archit*).
❏ **contract bridge** *n* the standard modern form of the game of bridge, developed from auction bridge, in which only tricks that are bid for count towards winning a game.
■ **contract in** to agree to participate on certain conditions. **contract out** to decide not to participate in a pension scheme, etc; to withdraw from an obligation, agreement, etc; to arrange that certain conditions shall not apply; to offer (work previously carried out by in-house staff, in a school, hospital, etc) to private contractors.

contracyclical /kon-trə-sī'kli-kl or -sik'li-/ *adj* (of an economic policy) offsetting fluctuation cycles in the economy by reducing taxes during a recession and raising them during a boom. [L *contrā* against, and **cyclical** (see **cycle**)]

contradance or **contredance** /kon'trə-däns/ *n* a country dance, *esp* a French version of the English country dance.

contradict /kon-trə-dikt'/ *vt* to deny what is affirmed by; to assert the contrary of; to deny; to be contrary to in character. [L *contrādīcere, -dictum*, from *contrā-* against, and *dīcere* to say]
■ **contradict'able** *adj*. **contradic'tion** *n* the act of contradicting; a statement asserting the contrary; denial; inconsistency. **contradic'tious** *adj* prone to contradiction. **contradic'tiously** *adv*. **contradict'ive** *adj* contradicting or tending to contradict. **contradict'ively** *adv*. **contradict'or** *n*. **contradict'orily** *adv*. **contradict'oriness** *n* the quality of being contradictory. **contradict'ory** *adj* affirming the contrary; inconsistent. ◆ *n* a word, principle, etc that contradicts another; either of two propositions such that both cannot be true, or both cannot be false (*logic*).
■ **contradiction in terms** a group of words containing a contradiction.

contradistinguish /kon-trə-di-sting'gwish/ vt to distinguish by contrasting different qualities or conditions. [**contra-**]
■ **contradistinc'tion** n. **contradistinc'tive** adj.

contrafagotto /kon-trə-fə-got'tō/ n (pl **contrafagot'tos**) the contrabassoon. [Ital contra- (indicating an octave lower), and fagotto bassoon]

contraflow /kon'trə-flō/ n a system of traffic regulation on motorways, when one carriageway is closed and the other is arranged for two-way traffic. [**contra-**]

contragestion /kon-trə-jes'chən/ n a form of birth control that is effective after fertilization of the ovum has taken place. [**contraception** and **gestation**]
■ **contrages'tive** adj and n.

contrahent /kon'trə-hənt/ (hist) adj entering into a contract. ◆ n a contracting party. [L contrahēns, -entis, from contrahere to contract]

contrail /kon'trāl/ n short form of **condensation trail** (see under **condense**).

contraindicate /kon-trə-in'di-kāt/ vt to point to (a particular treatment or procedure) as unsuitable or unwise (med); to show or give as reason for not being, doing or having, etc; to forbid.
■ **contrain'dicant** n. **con'traindicā'tion** n any factor in a patient's condition which indicates that surgery, drug therapy, inoculation, etc would involve a greater than normal degree of risk and is therefore unwise to pursue. **contraindic'ative** adj.

contrair /kən-trār'/ an obsolete dialect form of **contrary**.

contra ius gentium /kon'trə yoos jen'shəm or kon'trä yoos gen'ti-ŭm/ (L) against the law of nations.

contralateral /kon-trə-lat'ə-rəl/ (esp med) adj on the opposite side, esp of the body; affecting the opposite side of the body. [**contra-**]

contralto /kən-tral'tō or -träl'/ n (pl **contral'ti** /-tē/ or **contral'tos**) the lowest musical voice in women; a singer with such a voice; a part for such a voice. ◆ adj of or suitable for a contralto. [Ital, from contra- and **alto¹**]

contra mundum /kon'trə mun'dum or kon'trä mŭn'dŭm/ (L) against the world.

contranatant /kon-trə-nā'tənt/ adj swimming upstream. [L contrā, and natāns, -antis, prp of natāre to swim]

contra pacem /kon'trə pā'sem or pä'chem, or kon'trä pä'kem/ (L) against the peace.

contraplex /kon'trə-pleks/ (telegraphy) adj having messages passing opposite ways at the same time. [L contrā against, and sfx -plex, as in **complex**]

contraposition /kon-trə-pə-zish'ən/ n opposition, contrast; an immediate inference, which consists in denying the original subject of the contradictory of the original predicate (logic).
■ **contrapos'itive** adj and n.

contrapposto /kon-trə-pos'tō/ (art) n (pl **contrappo'stos**) a pose of the human body with hips, shoulders and head in different planes. [Ital]

contraprop /kon'trə-prop/ contraction of **contrarotating propeller**.

contraption /kən-trap'shən/ n a contrivance. [Perh contrivance adaption]

contrapuntal, contrapuntist see under **counterpoint¹**.

contrarotating propeller /kon-trə-rō-tā'ting prə-pel'ər/ n one of a pair of propellers rotating in opposite directions (also **contrapropell'er**).

contrary /kon'trə-ri/ adj opposite; contradictory; (usu /kən-trā'ri/) perverse. ◆ n an extreme opposite; a proposition so related to another that both cannot be true though both may be false (logic). ◆ vt and vi to oppose; to contradict; to annoy. [L contrārius, from contrā against]
■ **contrarian** /kən-trā'ri-ən/ n and adj (a person) taking a contrary view (esp in politics and journalism). **contrariety** /-rī'i-ti/ n opposition; inconsistency; the relationship between two contraries (logic). **contrarily** /kon' or -trā'/ adv. **contrariness** /kon' or -trā'/ n. **contrarious** /kən-trā'ri-əs/ adj (archaic) showing contrariety, **contra'riously** adv (archaic) contrarily. **con'trariwise** or /-trā' or -tra'/) adv in the contrary way; on the other side; on the other hand. ❑ **contrary motion** n (music) movement of parts in opposite directions, one up, another down.
■ **on the contrary** quite the opposite, not at all. **to the contrary** to the opposite effect.

contrast /kən-träst'/ vi to stand in opposition. ◆ vt to set in opposition to, in order to show difference. ◆ n /kon'träst/ opposition or unlikeness in things compared; a contrasting person or thing; the (degree of) difference in tone between the light and dark parts of a photograph or a television picture. [Fr contraster from L contrā opposite to, and stāre to stand]

■ **contrast'ive** adj. **contrast'y** adj (photog) (of prints or negatives) showing a high degree of contrast.
❑ **contrast medium** n a suitable substance, eg barium sulphate, used in diagnostic radiology in order to give contrast.

contrasuggestible /kon-trə-sə-jes'ti-bl/ (psychol) adj responding to suggestion by believing or doing the opposite. [**contra-**]

contrat /k3-tra'/ (Fr) n a contract; an agreement.
❑ **contrat aléatoire** /ä-lā-ä-twär/ n (Fr law) a conditional contract. **contrat de vente** /də vät/ n a contract of sale; social contract.

contrate /kon'trāt/ adj (of wheels, esp in watchmaking) having cogs parallel to the axis. [L contrā opposite]
❑ **con'trate-wheel** n a crown-wheel (qv).

contra-tenor /kon-trə-ten'ər/ same as **countertenor** (see under **counter-**).

contraterrene /kon-trə-ter'ēn/ adj opposite in character to earthy or terrestrial. [**contra-**]

contravallation /kon-trə-va-lā'shən/ n a fortification built by besiegers about the place besieged. [L contrā against, and vallāre, -atum to fortify]

contravene /kon-trə-vēn'/ vt to oppose; to infringe. [L contrā, against, and venīre, ventum to come]
■ **contraven'er** n. **contraven'tion** n.

contrayerva /kon-trə-yûr'və/ n a tropical American plant of the mulberry family, once believed to be an antidote to poisons; a Jamaican birthwort of similar reputation. [Sp (now contrahierba), from L contrā against, and herba a herb]

contrecoup /k3-tr'-koo'/ n an injury, esp to the brain within the skull, resulting from a blow on the side opposite to it (med); a kiss (billiards). [Fr, counterblow]

contredance see **contradance**.

contre-jour /k3-tr'-zhoor'/ (photog) n the technique of taking photographs with the light source in front of the camera lens. [Fr contre against, and jour day, daylight]

contretemps /k3-tr'-tä'/ n (pl **contretemps** /-täz/) something happening inopportunely or at the wrong time, anything embarrassing or vexatious, a hitch; a minor disagreement. [Fr contre (L contrā) against, and temps (L tempus) time]

contrib. abbrev : contribution; contributor.

contribute /kən-trib'ūt or kon'tri-būt/ vt to give along with others; to give for a common purpose; to add towards a common result, to a fund, etc; to write and send for publication with others. ◆ vi to give or bear a part; to be a contributor. [L con- and tribuere, -ūtum to give]
■ **contrib'utable** adj payable; subject to contribution. **contribū'tion** /kon-/ n the act of contributing; something contributed; a levy or charge imposed upon a number of people; anything given for a common purpose or done towards a common end; a written composition supplied to a periodical, etc. **contrib'utive** adj giving a share; helping. **contrib'utor** n a person who contributes; a person who sends written articles for publication. **contrib'utory** or (obs) **contrib'utary** adj given or giving to a common purpose or fund; having partial responsibility; (of a pension scheme) to which the employee makes a contribution as well as the employer. ◆ n a person or thing that contributes; a director or member of a company who is liable to contribute to the assets if the company is wound up.
❑ **contributory negligence** n failure to take adequate precautions against an accident, etc, resulting in partial legal responsibility for injury, damage, etc.

contrist /kən-trist'/ (obs) vt to sadden. [Fr contrister, from L contristāre, from con-, intens, and tristis sad]
■ **contristā'tion** n.

contrite /kon'trīt or kən-trīt'/ adj full of guilt and remorse for a wrongdoing or sin; wholly penitent; (of an action) showing a sense of guilt or sin. [L contrītus, from conterere, from con- wholly, and terere to bruise]
■ **con'tritely** (or /-trīt'/) adv. **con'triteness** (or /-trīt'/) n. **contrition** /kon-trish'ən/ n remorse; deep sorrow for past sin and resolve to avoid future sin (Christianity).

contriturate /kən-trit'ū-rāt/ (rare) vt to pulverize. [con-, intens, and **triturate**]

contrive¹ /kən-trīv'/ vt to plan; to invent; to bring about or effect; to manage or arrange; to plot; to conceive, understand (archaic). [OFr controver, from con-, intens, and trover to find]
■ **contriv'able** adj that may be contrived. **contriv'ance** n an invention; the act of contriving; a deceitful plan. **contrived'** adj laboured, artificially intricate. **contrive'ment** n an act of contriving; the thing contrived; invention; design; artifice. **contriv'er** n a schemer, a manager.

contrive² /kən-trīv'/ (Shakesp) vt to spend, as time. [L conterere, contrītum (perf contrīvī) to wear out]

control /kən-trōl'/ n restraint; authority; command; regulation; a check; a means of operating, regulating, directing or testing; a station for doing so; a scientific experiment performed without variables to provide a standard of comparison for other experiments (also **control experiment**); a subject or group of subjects (**control group**) providing such a standard of comparison; a number or letter printed on a sheet of postage stamps as an indication of authenticity (also **control mark**); a disembodied spirit or other agency supposed to direct a spiritualistic medium; a lever ('joystick') or wheel to move ailerons and elevator, and so control the movements of aircraft (also **control column, lever** or **stick**); an aerofoil that controls the movements of an aircraft, such as rudder, elevator or stabilizer (also **control surface**); a control key (comput); a secret service agent who supervises other agents. ◆ adj relating to control. ◆ vt (**controll'ing; controlled'**) to check; to restrain; to govern; to command or operate. —Formerly **comptroll'**, **countrol'**, **controul'**. [Fr contrôle, from contre-rôle a duplicate register, from L contrā against, and rotulus a roll]
■ **contrōllabil'ity** n. **controll'able** adj capable of or subject to control. **controll'ably** adv. **controll'er** n a person who supervises financial affairs or examines financial accounts (also **comptroll'er**); an official authorized to control some activity or department; a person who controls or regulates; an apparatus for regulating, eg the speed of an electric car. **controll'ership** n. **control'ment** n the act or power of controlling; the state of being controlled; control.
❏ **control account** n (bookkeeping) an account recording debit and credit totals of other accounts, used for cross-checking purposes and the preparation of financial statements. **control character** n (comput) a keyboard character which is not printed but which starts or controls an operation or device. **control engineering** n the study of the way in which complex systems respond to their controls. **control event** n (finance) a share transaction between companies that gives one of them a controlling interest. **control freak** n (inf) someone who is extremely or obsessively reluctant to share power or responsibility with others. **control key** n (comput) a key on a computer keyboard which when used in conjunction with standard keys will perform a variety of functions, eg editing. **controlled airspace** n clearly defined areas in which an aircraft may fly only if it is under radio instructions from air-traffic control. **controlled drug** n any of certain drugs (incl morphine, cocaine, heroin, etc) to the manufacture, prescribing, etc of which stringent regulations apply (**Controlled Drugs Act** the act under which these drugs are scheduled). **controlling interest** n number of shares sufficient to ensure control over the running of a company. **control panel** or **board** n a panel or board containing dials, switches and gauges for operating and monitoring electrical or other apparatus. **control register** n (comput) one which stores a single control instruction in the control unit of a central processor. **control rod** n (nuclear eng) a neutron absorbing rod moved in and out of a reactor core to vary reactivity. **control room** n a room in which control instruments are placed, eg in a broadcasting station. **control total** n (comput) a method of checking that data in a group of records has not been altered in error by comparing totals of certain items before and after processing. **control tower** n a building at an airport from which take-off and landing instructions are given. **control unit** n (comput) the part of a central processor which interprets instructions and controls the execution of a program.

contrôlé /kɔ̃-trō-lā'/ (Fr) adj registered; hallmarked.

controversy /kon'trə-vûr-si or kon-trov'ər-si/ n a debate; contention; dispute; a war of opinions, in books, pamphlets, etc. [From **controvert**]
■ **con'troverse** n (archaic) dispute. **controver'sial** /-shəl/ adj relating to controversy; arousing controversy. **controver'sialist** n a person given to controversy. **controver'sially** adv.

controvert /kon'trə-vûrt/ vt to oppose; to argue against; to dispute. [L contrā against, and vertere to turn]
■ **controvert'ible** adj. **controvert'ibly** adv. **con'trovertist** (or /-vûrt'ist/) n.

contubernal /kən-tū'bər-nəl/ or (archaic) **contubernyal** /kon-tū-būr'ni-əl/ adj living together (in the same tent); relating to companionship. [L contubernālis (noun), from cum with, together, and taberna hut, tavern]

contumacious /kon-tū-mā'shəs/ adj opposing lawful authority with contempt; obstinate; stubborn. [L contumāx, -ācis insolent, from con-, intens, and tumere to swell, or temnere to despise]
■ **contumā'ciously** adv. **contumā'ciousness** n. **contumacity** /-mas'i-ti/ or **con'tumacy** /-məs-i/ n obstinate disobedience or resistance; refusal to comply with the orders of a court of law.

contumely /kon'tūm-li (or kon'tū-mi-li)/ n scornful insolence; a scornful insult. [L contumēlia, prob from the same source as contumāx]
■ **contumē'lious** adj haughtily insolent. **contumē'liously** adv. **contumē'liousness** n.

contuse /kən-tūz'/ vt to bruise (the body); to crush. [L contundere, contūsum, from con-, intens, and tundere to bruise]
■ **contund** /kən-tund'/ vt (archaic) to bruise or pound. **contusion** /-tū'zhən/ n the act of bruising; the state of being bruised; a bruise. **contū'sive** adj tending to bruise.

conundrum /kə-nun'drəm/ n a riddle, esp one whose answer is a play on words; any puzzling question. [Origin unknown]

conurbation /ko-nûr-bā'shən/ n a dense cluster of neighbouring towns considered as a single unit in some respects, eg industrial, economic, administrative. [L con- together, and urbs city]
■ **conur'ban** adj. **conurbia** /kən-ûr'bi-ə/ n conurbations considered as a class.

conure /kon'ūr/ n one of several small S American parrots of the genus Aratinga and related genera. [Gr kōnos cone, and ourā tail]

conus /kō'nəs/ (anat) n (pl **cō'ni** /-nē/) any of several cone-shaped structures in the body, including the **conus arteriosus**, the upper front part of the right ventricle of the heart. [L, cone]

convalesce /kon-və-les'/ vi to regain health, esp by resting. [L con-, intens, and valēscere, from valēre to be strong]
■ **convalesc'ence** or (rare) **convalesc'ency** n (the period of) gradual recovery of health and strength. **convalesc'ent** adj gradually recovering health; promoting or encouraging convalescence. ◆ n a person recovering health.

Convallaria /kon-və-lā'ri-ə/ n the lily-of-the-valley, a genus of Liliaceae. [L convallis a sheltered valley]

convection /kən-vek'shən/ n a transmission, esp that of heat or electricity through liquids or gases by means of currents; vertical movement, esp upwards, of air or atmospheric conditions (meteorol). [L convectiō, -ōnis bringing together, from con- and vehere to carry]
■ **convect'** vt (back-formation) to transfer (heat) by convection. ◆ vi to undergo convection. **convec'tional** adj. **convec'tive** adj. **convec'tor** n an apparatus for heating by convection.

convenable see under **convenance**, **convene** and **convenient**.

convenance /kɔ̃-və-nãs or kon'və-nãns/ n what is suitable or proper; (in pl) the conventional usages or social proprieties, etiquette. [Fr]
■ **convenab'le** /-äbl/, or kon'/ adj conforming to the convenances.

convene /kən-vēn'/ vi to come together; to assemble. ◆ vt to call together; to summon before a court, etc. [Fr convenir, from L convenīre, from con- together, and venīre to come]
■ **convēn'able** adj. **convēn'er** or **convēn'or** n a person who convenes a meeting; a person who chairs a committee.

convenient /kən-vē'nyənt or -ni-ənt/ adj suitable, fitting in with one's plans; handy. [L convenīre]
■ **convenable** /kon'vən-ə-bəl/ adj (obs) fitting. **convēn'ience** n suitability; an advantage; any means or device for promoting (esp domestic) ease or comfort; a lavatory or water closet, esp (**public convenience**) a building containing several for use by the public. **convēn'iency** n (rare) convenience. **convēn'iently** adv.
❏ **convenience food** n food (partly) prepared before sale so as to be ready, or almost ready, for the table. **convenience store** n (N Am) a small grocery shop, often part of a chain, that stays open after normal hours and is conveniently situated in a local area.
■ **at one's (earliest) convenience** (on the first occasion or at the earliest time) when it is suitable or opportune.

convent[1] /kon'vənt/ n a closed community of people, usu women, devoted to a religious life; the house in which they live, a monastery or (now usu) nunnery; (in full **convent school**) a school where teaching is carried out by nuns. [Through Fr from L convenīre, conventum to come together]
■ **convent'ual** adj belonging to a convent. ◆ n a monk or nun; (with cap) a member of one of the two divisions of the Franciscans, following a mitigated rule, the other division being the Observants.

convent[2] /kən-vent'/ (Spenser, Shakesp) vt to convene, summon, cite. ◆ vi (archaic) to be suitable. [L convenīre, conventum, from con- and venīre to come]

conventicle /kən-vent'i-kl (earlier kon'vənt-)/ n a secret, illegal or forbidden religious meeting, applied esp to those of English dissenters and to the Scottish Presbyterians in the persecutions under Charles II and James II; any private, clandestine or irregular meeting or the place where it is held. ◆ vi to hold such a meeting. [L conventiculum a secret meeting of monks]
■ **conven'ticler** n.

convention /kən-ven'shən/ n an assembly, esp of representatives or delegates for some common object; any extraordinary assembly called upon any special occasion; a parliament not summoned by the sovereign (hist); an assembly for framing or revising a constitution; the act of convening; fashion; established usage; any temporary treaty; an agreement; a meeting of political party delegates for nominating a candidate for the presidency or other purpose (US); in card games, a mode of play in accordance with a prearranged code of signals, not determined by the principles of the game. [L *conventiō, -ōnis*; see **convene**]

■ **conven'tional** *adj* customary; growing out of tacit agreement or custom; bound or influenced by convention; formed or adopted by convention; (of medical treatments, therapies, etc) mainstream, not alternative; not spontaneous; stylized; arbitrary; (of weapons, warfare, energy sources) not nuclear. **conven'tionalism** *n* adherence to, or advocacy of, that which is established conventionally, such as a mode of speech, etc; something conventional. **conven'tionalist** *n* a person who adheres to a convention, or is influenced by conventionalism. **conventional'ity** *n* the state of being conventional; something which is established by use or custom. **conven'tionalize** or **-ise** *vt* to make conventional; to delineate according to a convention rather than nature. **conven'tionally** *adv*. **conven'tionary** *adj* acting under contract. **conventioneer'** *n* (*N Am*) a person attending a convention. **conven'tioner** or **conven'tionist** *n*.

converge /kən-vûrj'/ *vi* to tend towards or meet in one point, value, quality, etc; (of animals) to undergo convergence. [L *con-* and *vergere* to bend, to incline]

■ **conver'gence** *n* the act or point of converging (also **conver'gency**); the moving inwards of the eyes in focusing on a near object (*physiol*); the property of having a limit, for infinite series, sequences, products, etc (*maths*); the independent development, in animals not related evolutionarily, of similar features or characteristics; the movement towards a state of parity in the economies of the several countries of the EU; the accumulation of air over a particular region, giving rise to upward air currents (*meteorol*). **conver'gent** *adj* converging; due to or characterized by convergence. **conver'ging** *adj* meeting or tending to meet in a point; coming nearer together (also *fig*).

❏ **convergence zone** *n* (*geol*) an area where tectonic plates collide causing earth tremors, volcanic eruptions, etc. **convergent thinking** *n* (*psychol*) the examination of ideas by deductive thinking, *usu* following a set of rules or logical steps.

conversazione /kon-vər-sat-si-ō'ni/ *n* (*pl* **conversazio'nes** or **conversaziō'ni** /-nē/) a meeting for conversation, particularly on learned subjects. [Ital]

converse¹ /kən-vûrs'/ *vi* to talk (with or about); to commune spiritually (with); to associate familiarly with; (*obs*). ♦ *n* /kon'vûrs/ conversation; spiritual communing. [Fr *converser*, from L *conversārī* to turn about, go about, associate, dwell, from *con-*, intens, and *versāre* to keep turning, from *vertere* to turn]

■ **convers'able** *adj* disposed to converse; sociable. **convers'ably** *adv*. **convers'ance** or **convers'ancy** (also /kon'/) *n* the state of being conversant; familiarity. **convers'ant** (also /kon'/) *adj* acquainted by study; familiar. **conversā'tion** *n* talk; an instance of communication by talking. **conversā'tional** *adj*. **conversā'tionalist** or **conversā'tionist** *n* a person who enjoys or excels in conversation. **conversā'tionally** *adv*. **conversā'tionism** *n* (*rare*) a colloquialism. **conver'sative** *adj* (*obs*) ready to talk. **convers'er** *n*.

❏ **conversation piece** *n* an object that arouses comment by its novelty; a painting of a number of people in their usual environment, engaged in their usual pastimes, etc; a play, etc, in which the dialogue is as important as, or more important than, the action. **conversation stopper** *n* a comment that allows no appropriate response, *usu* because it is shocking, embarrassing or obtuse.

converse², **conversion** see under **convert**.

convert /kən-vûrt'/ *vt* to change or turn from one thing, condition, opinion, party or religion to another; to cause to acquire faith in a particular religion; to change by a spiritual experience; to change into the converse; to alter into something else (eg iron into steel, a try into a goal, a large house into several flats, a merchant ship into a cruiser); to apply to a particular purpose; to exchange for an equivalent; to turn about (*obs*). ♦ *vi* to undergo conversion; to be convertible (from one form into another); to switch (religious or political) allegiance. ♦ *n* /kon'vûrt/ a person who is converted, *esp* to a particular religious faith. [L *convertere, conversum*, from *con-* and *vertere* to turn]

■ **con'verse** (or /-vûrs'/) *adj* reversed in order or relation. ♦ *n* (only /kon'/) that which is the opposite of another; a proposition in which the subject and predicate have changed places (*logic*); a proposition in which that which is given and that which is to be proved in another proposition are interchanged (*maths*). **converse'ly** *adv*. **conver'sion** *n* a change from one condition, use, opinion, party, religion or spiritual state to another; something (*esp* a building) adapted for a different purpose; the expression of repressed emotions as physical symptoms (*psychiatry*); the act of constructing a proposition in accordance with the rules of direct inference, in which the terms of another proposition are interchanged (*logic*); unauthorized dealing with another's property (*law*); a score made after a try by kicking the ball over the crossbar (*rugby*); an additional score after a touchdown, worth one or two points (*American football*). **con'vertend** *n* (*logic*) the proposition to be converted. **convert'er** *n* someone or something

that converts; a vessel in which materials are changed from one condition to another (*esp* iron into steel); an apparatus for making a change in electric current (also **conver'tor**); a device which converts data from one form into another (*comput*); a reactor which converts fertile material into fissionable material. **convertibil'ity** *n*. **convert'ible** *adj* that may be converted; (of currency) that may be freely converted into other currencies, or into gold (or dollars) at a fixed price. ♦ *n* anything convertible; a car with a folding top. **convert'ibly** *adv*. **convertiplane** /kən-vûr'tə-plān/ *n* an earlier name for a vertical take-off and landing aircraft. **con'vertite** *n* (*archaic*) a convert; a reformed prostitute.

❏ **conversion course** *n* a course of study designed to facilitate the change from one subject to another. **conversion disorder** *n* (*psychol*) a form of neurosis in which a person represses painful emotions and unconsciously converts them into physical symptoms, particularly when the bodily site symbolizes the repressed idea.

■ **convertible-term insurance** a life insurance policy providing cover for a given period but which may be converted to eg a whole-life policy at some time during this period at favourable terms.

convex /kon'veks, also kon-veks'/ *adj* rising into a round form on the outside, the reverse of concave; (of a polygon) having no interior angle greater than 180°. ♦ *n* a convex figure, surface, body or part. [L *convexus* vaulted, from *convehere*, from *con-* and *vehere* to carry]

■ **convexed'** *adj* made convex. **convex'edly** *adv*. **convex'ity** *n* roundness of form on the outside; a convex part or figure. **con'vexly** (or /-veks'/) *adv*. **con'vexness** (or /-veks'/) *n*.

❏ **convexo-con'cave** (or /-kāv'/) *adj* convex on one side, and concave on the other. **convexo-con'vex** (or /-veks'/) *adj* convex on both sides.

convey /kən-vā'/ *vt* to carry; to transmit; to impart; to steal; to communicate (ideas, etc); to make over in law. [OFr *conveier*, from L *con-* and *via* a way]

■ **convey'able** *adj*. **convey'al** *n*. **convey'ance** *n* the act or means of conveying; trickery; a vehicle of any kind; the act of transferring property (*law*); the document that transfers it. **convey'ancer** *n* a person who prepares deeds for the transference of property. **convey'ancing** *n*. **convey'er** or **convey'or** *n* a person or thing that conveys in any sense; a mechanism for continuous transport of materials, packages, goods in process of manufacture, etc (also **conveyor belt**).

convicinity /kon-vi-sin'i-ti/ (*rare*) *n* a neighbourhood.

convict /kən-vikt'/ *vt* to prove guilty; to pronounce guilty. ♦ *n* /kon'vikt/ a person convicted or found guilty of crime; a person serving a prison sentence. [Ety as for **convince**]

■ **convic'tion** *n* the state of being convinced; strong belief; the act of convincing; an act or an instance of proving guilty; the condition of being consciously convicted of sin (*theol*). **con'victism** *n* (*hist*) the system of establishing penal settlements for convicted prisoners. **convict'ive** *adj* able to convince or convict.

■ **carry conviction** to be convincing.

convince /kən-vins'/ *vt* to persuade by evidence; to satisfy as to truth or error; to overcome, get the better of (*archaic*). [L *convincere*, from *con-* (signifying completeness) and *vincere*, *victum* to conquer]

■ **convince'ment** *n* (*obs*). **convinc'er** *n*. **convinc'ible** *adj*. **convinc'ing** *adj* producing conviction; certain, positive, beyond doubt; (of a victory, etc) by a large or significant margin. **convinc'ingly** *adv*.

convivial /kən-viv'i-əl/ *adj* social; jovial; feasting or drinking in company; relating to a feast. [L *convīvium* a living together, a feast, from *con-* together, and *vīvere* to live]

■ **convive** /-vīv'/ *vi* (*archaic*) to feast together. ♦ *n* /kɔ̃-vēv, kon'vīv/ (*archaic*) a companion at table. **conviv'ialist** *n*. **convivial'ity** *n*. **conviv'ially** *adv*.

convo /kon'vō/ (*Aust inf*) *n* (a) conversation.

convoke /kən-vōk'/ *vt* to call together; to assemble (also **convocate** /kon'vō-kāt/). [L *convocāre*, from *con-* together, and *vocāre, -ātum* to call]

■ **convocā'tion** *n* the act of convoking; a synod of clergy, *esp* those of the provinces of Canterbury and York (*C of E*); a large (*esp* formal) assembly, eg of the members of a university court. **convocā'tional** *adj*. **convocā'tionist** *n*.

convolve /kən-volv'/ *vt* to roll together, or one part on another. [L *con-* together, and *volvere, -volūtum* to roll]

■ **convolute** /kon'və-loot, -lūt/ *adj* rolled together, or one part on another; coiled laterally with one edge inside, one outside (*bot*); (of a flower-bud) contorted (*bot*); (of a gastropod shell) having the inner whorls concealed or overlapped by the outer (*zool*). **convolut'ed** *adj* (of argument, style of speech or writing) intricate, tortuous, difficult to understand; unclear; convolute, rolled together. **convolut'edly** *adv*. **convolution** /-loo'-, -lū'/ *n* a twist or coil; a fold or sinuosity, *esp* of the brain surface; a complication. **convolu'tional** *adj*.

convolvulus /kən-vol'vū-ləs/ n (pl **convol'vuluses**) any of a large number of twining or trailing plants of the genus *Convolvulus*, including bindweed. [L *convolvere* ; see ety for **convolve**]
■ **convolvūlā'ceous** adj belonging or relating to the **Convolvulaceae** /kən-vol-vū-lā'si-ē/, a family of plants with trumpet-shaped flowers and twirling or trailing stems.

convoy /kon-voi', also kon'voi/ vt to accompany (vehicles, *esp* ships) for protection; to escort. ◆ n /kon'/ the act of convoying; a ship or ships of war guarding a fleet of merchant-vessels; the ships protected in this way; an escort; any group of vehicles, *esp* lorries, travelling together; a supply of stores, etc under escort. [Fr *convoyer* ; see **convey**]

convulse /kən-vuls'/ vt to agitate violently; to affect by spasms (also *fig*). [L *con-*, intens, and *vellere*, *vulsum* to pluck, to pull]
■ **convuls'ant** n and adj (an agent, *esp* a drug) causing convulsions. **convul'sible** adj subject to convulsion. **convul'sion** n any violent involuntary contraction of the voluntary muscles of the body; any violent disturbance; (in *pl*) fits of uncontrollable laughter (*inf*). **convul'sional** or **convul'sionary** adj relating to convulsions. **convul'sionary** n a person who has convulsions, *esp* one of a fanatical sect of Jansenists in 18c France. **convul'sionist** n a religious convulsionary; a believer in the importance of convulsions in geological history, *opp* to *uniformitarian*. **convuls'ive** adj causing or affected with convulsions; spasmodic. **convuls'ively** adv. **convuls'iveness** n.

cony or **coney** /kō'ni/ or (historically accurate) kun'i/ n a rabbit; rabbit-skin; a pika; a hyrax (*Bible*); a term of endearment for a woman (*obs*); a dupe or fool (*obs*). [Prob through OFr *conil*, from L *cunīculus* a rabbit]
❑ **co'ny-burrow** n a rabbit-burrow. **co'ny-catch** vt (*Shakesp*) to cheat. **co'ny-catcher** n (*obs*) a cheat. **co'ny-wool** n rabbits' fur.

COO *abbrev* : Chief Operating Officer.

coo[1] /koo/ vi (**coo'ing**, **cooed** /kood/) to make a sound like a dove; (of lovers) to speak fondly. ◆ vt to murmur softly or ingratiatingly; to effect as by cooing. ◆ n the sound made by doves. [Imit]
■ **coo'ing** n and adj. **coo'ingly** adv.

coo[2] /koo/ (*sl*) interj expressive of surprise.

cooee or **cooey** /koo'ē/ n a call to attract attention, *orig* a signal used in the Australian bush. ◆ vi to utter the call. ◆ interj attracting attention. [From an Aboriginal language]
■ **within cooee** (*Aust* and *NZ inf*) nearby, within calling distance.

coof, also **cuif** /koof or kif/ (*Scot*) n a lout; a fool. [Origin obscure]

cook[1] /kŭk/ vt to prepare (food) by heating; to subject to great heat; to manipulate for any purpose, or falsify (accounts, etc); to concoct (a story, excuse, etc) (often with *up*); to ruin, tire out (*sl*); to spoil or ruin; to prepare (*esp* an illegal drug) by heating (*sl*). ◆ vi to practise cookery; to undergo cooking; (of, *esp* jazz, musicians) to play skilfully generating excitement (*sl*). ◆ n a person who undertakes or is skilled in cooking. [OE *cōc* a cook (cf Ger *Koch*), from L *coquus*]
■ **cook'able** adj. **cook'er** n a stove, special vessel, or other apparatus for cooking; a variety (eg of apple) suitable for cooking. **cook'ery** n the art or practice of cooking food; a place for cooking (*N Am*); a camp kitchen (*Can*).
❑ **cook'-chill** adj (of foods and meals) cooked, then packaged and stored in a refrigerated state, requiring reheating before serving. ◆ n the process of preparing food in this way. **cooked breakfast** n a breakfast which comprises or includes cooked food such as grilled or fried bacon, eggs, sausages, etc. **cooker hood** n a canopy over a cooker, containing filters, for the extraction of steam and smells. **cook'ery-book** or **cook'book** n a book of recipes for cooking dishes. **cook-gen'eral** or **cook-house'maid** n a domestic servant combining the functions of cook and general servant or housemaid. **cook'house** n a building or room for cooking in; a military dining hall. **cooking apple** n an apple specially suitable for cooking. **cook'ing-range** n a stove adapted for cooking several things at once. **cook'maid** n a maid who cooks or assists a cook. **cook off** n (*N Am*) a cooking competition. **cook'out** n (*N Am*) a barbecue party. **cook'room** n a room in which food is cooked. **cook shop** n a shop that sells cookery equipment; an eating-house (*US*). **cook'top** n (*N Am*) a hob set into a work surface. **cook'ware** n pans, dishes, etc used for cooking.
■ **cook someone's goose** (*inf*) to spoil someone's plans; to make someone's downfall inevitable. **cook the books** (*inf*) to falsify accounts, etc. **what's cooking?** (*sl*) what is being planned?

cook[2] /kŭk/ vi to make the sound of the cuckoo.

cook[3] or **kook** /kŭk/ (*Scot*) vi to dart in and out of sight; to peep. [Origin obscure]

cookie /kŭk'i/ n a plain bun (*Scot*); (also **cook'y**) a small sweet biscuit or cake (*N Am*); a person, *esp* in the phrase *a tough cookie* ; a small piece of persistent code that is downloaded to a hard drive when a website is accessed, allowing the computer to be identified on subsequent visits (*comput*). [Du *koekje* a cake]

❑ **cook'ie-cutter** n (*N Am*) a template with a sharp edge used for cutting biscuit dough into shapes. ◆ adj (*N Am inf*) having no distinctive features, as if produced from a template. **cook'ie-pusher** n (*US sl*) an effeminate man or a sycophantic person, *esp* a man. **cook'ie-shine** n (*old joc*) a tea-party.
■ **that's how** (or **that's the way**) **the cookie crumbles** (*inf*) that's what the situation is; that's the way things usually happen.

Cook's tour /kŭks toor/ (*inf*) n a rapid but extensive tour; a wide-ranging superficial inspection. [Thomas *Cook* (1808–92), English travel agent]

cool /kool/ adj slightly cold; free from excitement; calm, imperturbable; disinterested, unenthusiastic; indifferent; impudent; unemotional and relaxed; (of jazz music) restrained, economical and relaxed; excellent, admirable (*inf*); acceptable (*inf*); (of large amounts, *esp* of money) all of, not less than, as in *a cool million* (*inf*). ◆ vt to make cool; to allay or moderate (eg heat, excitement, passion, etc). ◆ vi (often with *down*) to grow cool; to lose radioactivity. ◆ n that which is cool; coolness, imperturbability, self-possession, sangfroid. [OE *cōl*; cf Ger *kühl*]
■ **cool'ant** n a cooling agent; a fluid used to cool the edge of a cutting tool (*engineering*); a fluid used as the cooling medium in an engine (*engineering*); the gas or liquid circulated through a reactor core to carry the heat generated in it to boilers or heat exchangers. **cool'er** n anything that cools; a vessel in which something is cooled; a cool box or bag; a spritzer with additional fruit juice; jail, *esp* a military jail (*sl*); a refrigerator (*N Am*). **cool'ish** adj somewhat cool. **cool'ly** adv in a cool manner; with composure; indifferently; impudently. **cool'ness** n moderate cold; indifference; diminution of friendship; lack of zeal; lack of agitation; self-possession. **coolth** n (*dialect*) coolness. **cool'y** adj (*Spenser*) cool.
❑ **cool box** or **bag** n an insulated box or bag, used to keep food, etc cool. **cool change** n (*Aust*) a change in wind direction resulting in cooler weather. **cool'headed** adj not easily excited; capable of acting with composure. **cool'house** n a greenhouse kept at a cool temperature. **cool'hunter** n (*inf*) a person who studies and advises on probable trends in fashion. **cooling card** n (*Shakesp*) anything that discourages, or dashes hopes. **cooling-off** see **cool off** below. **cooling-off period** n the time, *usu* a period of five to seven days, in which a consumer has the right to serve notice of cancellation of a credit, insurance, etc agreement. **cooling tower** n a large structure in which water heated in an industrial process is cooled for re-use. **cool'-tankard** n an old name for a cooler with spices and borage; a local name for borage.
■ **cool it** (*sl*; often *imperative*) to calm down, act in a relaxed fashion. **cool off** to become less angry and more amenable to reason (**cooling-off'** n and adj); to grow less passionate (**cool'ing-off'** n and adj). **cool one's heels** to be kept waiting. **keep one's cool** (*inf*) to remain calm, keep one's head. **lose one's cool** (*inf*) to become flustered. **play it cool** to act in a deliberately controlled and calm manner.

coolabah, **coolibah** or **coolibar** /koo'lə-bä(r)/ or *-li-*/ n any of several species of Australian eucalyptus tree, *esp Eucalyptus microtheca*. [From an Aboriginal language]

coolamon /koo'lə-mon/ (*Aust*) n a shallow vessel made of wood or bark used by Australian aborigines to hold water, etc. [From an Aboriginal language]

Cooley's anaemia /koo'liz ə-nē'mi-ə/ n a former name for **thalassaemia** (see under **thalassian**). [TB *Cooley* (1871–1945), US paediatrician]

Coolgardie safe /kool-gär'di sāf/ n a cupboard with fabric walls which are soaked with water, used, *esp* in the Australian outback, to keep food cool. [From *Coolgardie* in W Australia]

coolie or **cooly** /kool'i/ (*hist*) n an Indian or Chinese labourer who emigrated under contract to a foreign country; a hired native labourer in India and China (*offensive*); in South Africa, an Indian (*offensive*). [Prob *Kolī*, a tribe of W India; or Tamil *kūli* hire]
❑ **coolie hat** n a type of conical straw sunhat with a wide circular brim, as formerly worn by coolies.

coolly, **coolth**, etc see under **cool**.

coom[1] /koom/ n soot; coal dust; dust or grime of various kinds. ◆ vt to begrime. [Appar Scot and N Eng form of **culm**[2]]
■ **coom'y** adj.

coom[2] /koom/ (*Scot*) n the wooden centering on which a bridge is built; anything arched or vaulted. [Origin obscure]
■ **coom'ceiled** adj said of an attic room with the inside ceiling sloping from the wall.

Coomassie Blue® /koo-mas'i bloo/ (*biochem*) n a dye used as a stain to locate proteins separated by electrophoresis.

coomb[1], **coombe**, **comb** or **combe** /koom/ n a short deep valley; a hollow in a hillside. [OE *cumb* a hollow]

coomb² or **comb** /koom/ n an old measure of capacity = 4 bushels. [OE *cumb* a measure]

Coombs test /koomz test/ n a test to detect rhesus antibodies on the surface of red blood cells, used in the diagnosis of haemolytic anaemia. [RRA *Coombs* (1921–2006), British immunologist]

coon /koon/ n the raccoon (*inf*); a sly thief; a black person (*offensive*). [**raccoon**]
□ **coon'hound** or **coon'dog** n a hound (*usu* a crossbred bloodhound), or dog used to hunt raccoon. **coon'skin** n the pelt of a raccoon. **coon'-song** n (*offensive*) a black American song.

cooncan /koon'kan/ n a card game for two players in which they try to form sequences. [Sp *con quién* with whom]

coontie or **coonty** /koon'ti/ n an American plant (*Zamia floridana*) related to the cycads, from whose roots a starch similar to arrowroot is obtained. [Seminole *kunti*]

coop /koop/ n a box or cage for poultry or small animals; a confined, narrow place, *esp* a prison cell; a wicker basket. ◆ vt (often with *up*) to confine in a coop or elsewhere. [Perh from an unknown OE *cūpe*, related to *cȳpe* cask; cf L *cūpa* cask]

co-op /kō'op/ or /kō-op'/ (*inf*) n short for **co-operative society** or **co-operative store**.

cooper¹ /koo'pər/ n a person skilled in making barrels, casks, etc; a mixture of stout and porter. ◆ vt to make or repair (tubs, etc); to prepare, patch up. ◆ vi to work as a cooper. [Also LGer, from LL *cūpārius*, from *cūpa* cask; cf **coop**]
■ **coop'erage** n the work or workshop of a cooper; the sum paid for a cooper's work. **coop'ering** n. **coop'ery** n the business of a cooper.

cooper² /kō'pər/ see **coper¹**.

co-operate or **cooperate**, etc /kō-op'ə-rāt/ vi to work together.
■ **co-op'erant** adj working together. **co-operā'tion** n joint operation; assistance; willingness to help; combination in co-operative societies; an interaction between two species which is of mutual benefit but on which neither is dependent (*ecology*). **co-op'erative** adj. ◆ n an organization in which there is collective ownership or control of the means of production and distribution, such as *workers' co-operative, farming co-operative*, etc. **co-op'eratively** adv. **co-op'erativeness** n. **co-op'erātor** n.
□ **co-operating grace** n (*theol*) the Roman Catholic, Arminian and Socinian doctrine that the human will co-operates with the divine in the matter of saving grace. **co-operative society** n a commercial enterprise from which the profits are passed on to workers and customers. **co-operative store** n the shop of a co-operative society.

Cooper pairs /koo'pər pārz/ (*phys*) n pl pairs of weakly-bound electrons found in a superconducting material below its transition temperature. [LN *Cooper* (born 1930), US physicist]

Cooper's hawk /koo'pərz hök/ n a small N American hawk (*Accipiter cooperii*). [W *Cooper* (died 1864), US ornithologist]

co-opt or **coopt** /kō-opt'/ vt to elect into any body by the votes of its members. [L *cooptāre, -ātum*, from *co-* together, and *optāre* to choose]
■ **co-optā'tion** or **co-op'tion** n. **co-op'tative** or **co-op'tive** adj.

co-ordinal or **coordinal** /kō-ör'di-nəl/ (*biol*) adj (of plants and animals) of or belonging to the same order.

co-ordinate (also **coor-** in all words) /kō-ör'di-nāt/ vt to place or classify in the same order or rank; to adjust the relations or movements of; to combine or integrate harmoniously (also *vi*); to harmonize (also *vi*); to match; to combine by means of a co-ordinate bond (*chem*). ◆ n an element of the same order as another; each of a system of two or more magnitudes used to define the position of a point, line or surface by reference to a fixed system of lines, points, etc; (in *pl*) outer garments in harmonizing colour, material and pattern. ◆ adj of the same order or rank; relating to or involving co-ordination or co-ordinates.
■ **co-or'dinance** n a joint ordinance. **co-or'dinately** adv. **co-or'dinateness** n the quality of being matched or harmonized. **co-ordinā'tion** n ordered action together; balanced or skilful movement. **co-or'dinative** adj co-ordinating; co-ordinated, indicating co-ordination. **co-ord'inator** n.
□ **co-ordinate geometry** n geometry by the use of co-ordinates, analytical geometry. **co-ordinating conjunction** n (*grammar*) a conjunction linking clauses of equal status. **co-ordination compound** n (*chem*) a compound in which the atoms or groups are united by **co-ordinate bonds**, secondary valences supplementary to the principal valences (eg addition compounds), *esp* (**co-ordination complex compound**) one in which there is a central atom or ion.

coosen and **coosin** obsolete spellings of **cousin** and **cozen**.

cooser see **cusser**.

coost /kŏst/ a Scottish form of **cast** (*pat*).

coot¹ /koot/ n a short-tailed waterfowl, with black plumage, a white bill and an area of bare white skin (the frontal shield) on the forehead (hence the phrase **bald as a coot**); a foolish or silly person (*inf*). [ME *cote*; cf Du *koet*]

coot², **cootikin** see **cuit**.

cootie /koo'ti/ (*N Am* and *NZ sl*) n a head or body louse. [From Polynesian *kuty* parasite]

COP (*NZ*) abbrev: Certificate of Proficiency (a pass in a subject at university).

cop¹ /kop/ (*sl*) vt to capture; to catch; to acquire, get, obtain. ◆ n a policeman; a capture or arrest, as in the phrase *a fair cop*; a catch (*esp* in the phrase **not much cop** of little value, not worth much). [Perh Fr *caper* to seize, from L *capere, captum* to take; cf Du *kapen* to steal]
■ **copp'er** n a policeman.
□ **cop'shop** n a police station.
■ **cop a plea** (*criminal sl*) to plead guilty to a lesser charge in order to speed the judicial process and/or avoid a heavier sentence. **cop it** to suffer a punishment. **cop it sweet** (*Aust sl*) to accept punishment without complaint. **cop off** (**with**) (*sl*) to have a romantic or sexual encounter (with). **cop out** to avoid or evade responsibility for, to refuse to participate in (**cop'-out** n).

cop² /kop/, also **coppin** /kop'in/ n a conical ball of thread on a spindle; a top or head of anything. [OE *cop, copp*]
■ **copped** adj rising to a cop or head.

copacetic, **copasetic** or **kopasetic** /kō-pə-set'ik/ (*US inf*) adj sound, satisfactory; excellent. ◆ interj all clear. [Origin obscure]

copaiba /kō-pī'bə or -pā'/ or **copaiva** /-və/ n a transparent resin obtained from S American caesalpiniaceous trees of the genus *Copaifera*, used in medicine and in varnishes; a tree of the genus *Copaifera*. [Sp and Port, from Tupí]

copal /kō'pəl/ n a hard aromatic resin obtained from many tropical trees, and used to make varnishes and lacquers. [Sp, from Nahuatl *copalli* resin]

coparcener /kō-pär'sə-nər/ (*law*) n a joint heir to a property or an estate (also **parcener**).
■ **copar'cenery** or **copar'cenary** n joint ownership of property, *esp* by inheritance (also *adj*).

copartner /kō-pärt'nər/ n a joint partner.
■ **copart'nership** or (*old*) **copart'nery** n.

copataine /kop'ə-tān/ (*rare*) adj high-crowned like a sugar-loaf. [Ety obscure]

copatriot a form of **compatriot**.

Copaxone® /kō-pak'sōn/ n a synthetic protein, simulating myelin, used in treating multiple sclerosis.

co-payment /kō-pā'mənt/ n a payment, eg for medical services, made by the holder of an insurance policy, in addition to a payment from the insurer; a method of insurance that involves such payments.

COPD (*med*) abbrev: chronic obstructive pulmonary disease (emphysema).

cope¹ /kōp/ vi (*esp* with *with*) to contend; to deal (with) successfully. ◆ vt to encounter, meet (*archaic*); to match (*Shakesp*). [Fr *couper*, from L *colaphus* (Gr *kolaphos*) a blow with the fist]
□ **copes'-mate** or **cope'mate** n (*obs*) a companion; an accomplice; a partner; an adversary; a paramour.

cope² /kōp/ n a semicircular, sleeveless, hooded vestment worn over the alb or surplice by priests at certain Christian ceremonies; a covering shaped like a cope. ◆ vt to cover as with a cope. [ME *cape*, from hypothetical OE *cāpe*, from LL *cāpa*; cf **cap¹**]
■ **cop'ing** n the covering course of masonry of a wall.
□ **cope'stone** or **cop'ing-stone** n a stone that tops or forms part of the coping of a wall.

cope³ /kōp/ vt to cut (a piece of moulding) so that it fits over another piece. [Fr *couper* to cut]
□ **cop'ing-saw** n a narrow saw blade held under tension in a wide, U-shaped metal frame, used for cutting curves.

cope⁴ /kōp/ (*dialect*) vt and vi to barter or exchange. [Cf Du *koopen*]
■ **cōp'er** n a dealer, *esp* in horses.

cope⁵ /kōp/ (*obs*) vt to tie or sew up the mouth of (a ferret). [Origin obscure; cf **uncape**, **uncope**]

copeck same as **kopeck**.

copepod /kō'pi-pod/ n any minute planktonic or parasitic crustacean of the subclass **Copepoda** /kō-pep'əd-ə/, an important source of food for eg pelagic fish such as the herring. [Gr *kōpē* handle, oar, and *pous, podos* foot]

coper¹ or **cooper** /kō'pər/ n a ship used clandestinely to supply alcohol to deep-sea fishermen. ◆ vi to supply alcohol in such a way. [Du *kooper*, from *koopen* to trade (cf **cope⁴**); cf Ger *kaufen* to buy; OE *cēapan*]

coper² see under **cope⁴**.

Copernican /kō- or kə-pûr'ni-kən/ adj relating to Copernicus, the famous Polish astronomer (1473–1543), or to his system, in which it was demonstrated that the earth revolves about the sun.

■ **copernicium** /kō-pər-nis'i-əm/ n an artificially produced radioactive transuranic metallic element (symbol Cn; atomic no 112).

copia verborum /kō'pi-ə vûr-bō'rəm or kō'pi-a ver-bō'rŭm, also wer-/ (L) plenty of words, fluency, prolixity.

copier see under **copy**.

co-pilot or **copilot** /kō'pī-lət/ n a second pilot in an aircraft. ◆ vt to be the second pilot of (an aircraft).

coping see under **cope²**.

copious /kō'pi-əs/ adj plentiful; overflowing; abounding. [L cōpiōsus, from cōpia plenty, from co-, intens, and ops, opis wealth]
■ **co'piously** adv. **co'piousness** n.

copita /ko-pē'tə/ n a tulip-shaped sherry glass. [Sp]

coplanar /kō-plā'nər/ adj on the same plane.
■ **coplanarity** /kō-plān-ar'i-ti/ n.

co-polymer or **copolymer** /kō-pol'i-mər/ n a substance polymerized along with another, the result being a chemical compound, not a mixture.
■ **co-polymerizā'tion** or **-s-** n. **co-pol'ymerize** or **-ise** vt.

co-portion /kō-pōr'shən or -pör'/ (rare) n a share.

copper¹ /kop'ər/ n a reddish moderately hard metallic element (symbol **Cu**; atomic no 29), perhaps the first metal used by man, and used as an electrical conductor and in alloys; a coin, made orig of copper or bronze; a copper vessel; a boiler (orig of copper) for laundry, etc; the reddish-brown colour of copper; any of several kinds of copper-coloured butterfly, eg the small copper, Lycaena phlaeas.
◆ adj made of copper; of the colour of copper. ◆ vt to cover with copper. [OE copor, from LL cuper, from L cuprum a form of cyprium (aes) Cyprian (brass), because found in Cyprus]
■ **copp'ering** n the act of sheathing with copper; a covering of copper. **copp'erish** adj somewhat like copper. **copp'ery** adj like copper.
❑ **Copper Age** n a stage in culture in some regions leading up to the Bronze Age, characterized by the use of copper unmixed with tin. **copper-beech** n a variety of the common beech with purplish, copper-coloured leaves. **copper-bott'om** vt to cover the bottom of (a ship) with copper. **copper-bott'omed** adj (of a ship) having the bottom covered with copper as protection; sound, safe, reliable, esp financially. **copper-cap'tain** n one who appropriates the title of captain without any right to it. **copp'er-faced** adj faced with copper, as type. **copp'er-fasten** vt to fasten with copper bolts; to make (an agreement) binding. **copp'er-glance** n redruthite, cuprous sulphide, chalcocite. **copp'erhead** n a venomous reddish-brown snake of the eastern USA, similar to the rattlesnake; a similar Australian snake; a Northern sympathizer with the South in the Civil War (US hist). **copper-nick'el** n niccolite, a copper-red mineral, arsenide of nickel. **copper nose** n a red nose. **copp'erplate** n a plate of polished copper on which something has been engraved; an impression taken from such a plate; a fine handwriting based on the style used in copperplate engravings. **copper pyrites** n pl a yellow double sulphide of copper and iron, chalcopyrite. **copp'erskin** n (archaic) a Native American. **copp'ersmith** n a smith who works in copper. **copper sulphate** n a salt of copper (CuSO₄), used in solution as a fungicide. **copp'erwork** n work in copper; (also **copp'erworks** n sing) a place where copper is worked or manufactured. **copp'erworm** n the ship-worm.
■ **hot coppers** (old sl) a parched tongue and throat after a bout of drinking.

copper² see under **cop¹**.

copperas /kop'ə-rəs/ n a name formerly applied to copper and other sulphates, now only to ferrous sulphate (see **melanterite**). [Fr couperose (Ital coparosa), perh from L cuprī rosa rose of copper, or aqua cuprōsa copper water]

coppice /kop'is/ or **copse** /kops/ n a dense thicket of trees and bushes, esp one used for periodical cutting of twigs and branches; a thicket of sprouting branches growing from cut stumps. ◆ vt to cut back (trees, bushes, etc) to form a coppice; to cover with coppice. ◆ vi to form a coppice. [OFr copeiz wood, newly cut, from LL colpāre to cut]
■ **copp'icing** n. **cop'sy** adj.
❑ **copse'wood** n.

coppin see **cop²**.

copple /kop'l/ (obs) n a bird's crest. [Appar from **cop²**]
❑ **copp'le-crown** n. **copp'le-crowned** adj.

copple-stone an obsolete form of **cobblestone** (see **cobble¹**).

copra /kop'rə/ n the dried kernel of the coconut, yielding coconut oil. [Port, from Malayalam]

co-presence or **copresence** /kō-prez'əns/ n presence together.
■ **copres'ent** adj.

copro- or **copr-** /ko-pr(ō)-/ combining form denoting dung, faeces, obscenity. [Gr kopros dung]
■ **coprolāl'ia** n (Gr lalia talk; psychiatry) obsessive or repetitive use of obscene language, eg as a characteristic of Tourette's syndrome. **coprolāl'iac** adj. **coprolite** /kop'rə-līt/ n (Gr lithos stone; geol) a phosphatic pellet thought to be the fossilized faeces of fish, reptiles and birds; any similar phosphatic concretion of indeterminate origin. **cop'rolith** n (med) a mass of hard (sometimes calcified) faeces in the colon or rectum, due to chronic constipation. **coprolitic** /-lit'ik/ adj containing or made of coprolites; like, or relating to, coprolites. **coprol'ogy** n the use of obscenity in speech, literature and art. **coproph'agan** n (Gr phagein to eat) a dung-beetle. **coprophag'ic** /-aj'ik/ adj. **coproph'agist** /-jist/ n a dung-eater. **coproph'agous** /-gəs/ adj. **coproph'agy** /-ji/ n. **coprophil'ia** n (Gr philiā love) an abnormal interest in, or preoccupation with, faeces. **coproph'ilous** adj abnormally interested in faeces or dung; (of plants, etc) growing on or in dung. **copros'terol** n a compound formed from cholesterol in the intestine. **coprozō'ic** adj (of animals) living in dung.

coprocessor /kō-prō'se-sər or kō'/ (comput) n a microprocessor that supplements the functions of a main processor, eg for performing arithmetical functions.

coprosma /kə-proz'mə/ n any Australian evergreen shrub or small tree of the genus Coprosma with glossy, leathery leaves and egg-shaped white or orange berries. [New L, from Gr kopros dung, and osmē smell]

copse, copsewood, copsy see **coppice**.

Copt /kopt/ n a Christian descendant of the ancient Egyptians. [Gr Aigyptios Egyptian]
■ **Copt'ic** adj of or relating to the Copts or their language. ◆ n the language of the Copts.

copter /kop'tər/ (inf) n short for **helicopter**.

copula /kop'ū-lə/ n (pl **cop'ulas** or **cop'ulae** /-ē/) that which joins together; a bond or tie; the word joining the subject and predicate (logic or linguistics). [L cōpula, from co- and apere to join]
■ **cop'ular** adj. **cop'ulate** vi to have sexual intercourse (with). ◆ vt (obs) to unite. **copulā'tion** n. **cop'ulātive** adj uniting; of or relating to copulation; indicating combination, not alternative or adversative relation. ◆ n (grammar) a conjunction that indicates combination. **cop'ulātively** adv. **cop'ulatory** adj.

copy /kop'i/ n an imitation; a transcript; a reproduction; that which is imitated or reproduced; a single specimen of a book, magazine, newspaper, etc; matter (eg a newspaper article) for printing; something newsworthy. ◆ vt (**cop'ying**; **cop'ied**) to write, paint, etc in the manner of; to imitate closely; to transcribe; to reproduce or duplicate; to provide a copy of (eg a letter) for (someone); to move (data) without alteration from one part of a storage device to another part or device (comput). ◆ vi to make a copy of another's work and pass it off as one's own. [Fr copie, from L cōpia plenty; in LL a transcript]
■ **cop'ier** n someone or something that copies; an imitator. **cop'yism** n servile or plagiaristic copying. **cop'yist** n a person whose job is to copy documents; an imitator.
❑ **cop'ybook** n a writing or drawing book of models printed for imitation; a collection of copies of documents. ◆ adj conventional, commonplace; (of an example, operation, etc) perfect, or carried out flawlessly. **cop'ycat** n (inf) a term applied in resentful derision to an imitator. ◆ adj imitated; done in imitation. ◆ vt and vi to imitate. **cop'y-edit** vt to prepare (newspaper copy, etc) for printing by correcting errors, etc. **cop'y-editing** n. **cop'y-editor** n. **cop'yhold** n (Eng law) formerly, a type of estate or right of holding land, according to the custom of a manor, by copy of the roll originally made by the steward of the lord's court. **cop'yholder** n formerly, a holder of land by copyhold; an assistant who reads copy to a proofreader; a device that holds copy for a compositor; a piece of equipment which holds copy upright for a computer keyboard operator. **copying ink** n ink suitable for copying by impression. **copying(-ink) pencil** n an ink-pencil. **copying press** n a machine for copying manuscripts by pressure. **cop'yleft** n a method of licensing intellectual property that allows users to modify and redistribute the work without restriction. ◆ adj published under such an arrangement. ◆ vt to publish (intellectual property) under such an arrangement. **cop'yread** vt (US) to subedit. **cop'yreader** n. **cop'yreading** n. **cop'yright** n the sole right to reproduce a literary, dramatic, musical or artistic work, or to perform, translate, film or record such a work (in the UK, for artistic works, books, etc, the term is the author's lifetime and seventy years after his or her death). ◆ adj protected by copyright. ◆ vt to secure the copyright of. **cop'yrightable** adj. **copyright library** n one of six libraries in the British Isles entitled to receive a free copy of every book published in the UK. **copy taster** n a person who selects items for publication or broadcast from the range of material submitted by reporters, etc. **cop'y-typing** n. **copy typist** n a typist who copies written, printed, etc

matter, not working from shorthand or recorded sound. **cop'ywriter** *n* a writer of copy (*esp* advertisements) for the press. **cop'ywriting** *n*. ■ **a copy of verses** a set of verses, *esp* a college exercise. **copy in** to provide a copy of (eg an email) for (someone).

coq au vin /kok-ō-vě'/ (*Fr*) *n* a dish of chicken cooked in red wine, with onions, herbs and garlic. [Fr, cock in wine]

coquelicot /kok'li-kō/ *n* another name for the poppy (*esp literary*); a brilliant red, the colour of the red poppy. [Fr, poppy]

coquet or **coquette** /ko- or kō-ket'/ *vi* (**coquett'ing**; **coquett'ed**) to flirt; to dally. ◆ *vt* (*obs*) to flirt with. [Fr *coqueter*, from *coquet*, dimin of *coq* a cock]
■ **cō'quetry** /-kit-ri/ *n* the act of coquetting; the attempt to attract admiration, without serious affection; deceit in love; any cleverly created prettiness. **coquette'** *n* a woman who flirts (also *adj*); a S American hummingbird of the genus *Lophornis*. **coquett'ish** *adj* practising coquetry; befitting a coquette. **coquett'ishly** *adv*. **coquett'ishness** *n*.

coquilla /kō-kil'yə/ *n* the nut of the piassava palm (*Attalea funifera*), whose mottled, dark-brown endosperm is used by button-makers and turners. [Sp; dimin of *coca* shell]

coquille /ko-kē'/ *n* (often in *pl*) a scallop or other seafood served in a scallop shell; a dish or pastry case in the shape of a scallop or shell; a pat, eg of butter; a basket-hilt of a sword in the shape of a shell (*fencing*). [Fr, from L *conchȳlium*, from Gr *konchylion* a cockle or mussel]

coquimbite /kō-kim'bīt/ *n* a yellowish hydrous sulphate of iron found in certain volcanic rocks. [From *Coquimbo* in Chile where it was originally found]

coquina /ko-kē'nə/ *n* a clastic limestone made up of cemented shell debris. [Sp, shell-fish]

coquito /kō-kē'tō/ *n* (*pl* **coqui'tos**) a Chilean palm (*Jubaea spectabilis*) having edible nuts. [Sp; dimin of *coco* coco-palm]

Cor. *abbrev* : (the Letters to the) Corinthians (*Bible*); Coroner.

cor¹ /kör/ (*inf*) *interj* an expression of surprise. [Corruption of *God*]
■ **cor blimey** a form of **gorblimey**.

cor² /kör/ *n* a Hebrew measure, the homer, 10 ephahs or baths (roughly 11 bushels). [Heb *kōr* round vessel]

cor. *abbrev* : corner; cornet.

cor- see **com-**.

coraciiform /ko-rə-sī'i-förm/ (*zool*) *adj* of, belonging to or related to the *Coraciiformes*, an order of birds including the kingfishers, hornbills, bee-eaters and rollers.

coracle /kor'ə-kl/ *n* a small oval rowing boat made by stretching hides over a wickerwork frame, *esp* in Wales and Ireland. [Connected with Welsh *corwg* anything round; cf Gaelic *curach* (see **currach**)]

coracoid /kor'ə-koid/ *adj* shaped like a crow's beak. ◆ *n* (*anat*) a paired ventral bone in the breast-girdle, forming, with the scapula, the articulation for the forelimb; in mammals, except monotremes, reduced to a **coracoid process** fused to the scapula. [Gr *korax*, *korakos* a crow, and *eidos* form]

co-radicate or **coradicate** /kō-rad'i-kāt/ (*philology*) *adj* of the same root. [**co-** and **radicate** (see **radical**)]

coraggio /ko-rad'jō/ *interj* courage. [Ital]

CORAL /kor'əl/ (*comput*) *n* a computer programming language used in a real-time system.

coral /kor'əl/ *n* a rocklike substance of various colours deposited on the bottom of the sea, formed from the skeletons, mostly calcareous, of certain invertebrates of the classes Anthozoa and Hydrozoa; the invertebrates themselves; a young child's toy of coral or other material for biting on while teething; (in *pl*) a necklace of coral; a deep orange-pink colour; cooked seafood having this colour. ◆ *adj* made of or like coral, *esp* red coral of a deep orange-pink. [L *corallum*, from Gr *korallion*]
■ **corallā'ceous** *adj* like, or having the qualities of, coral. **Corallian** /-al'-/ *n* (*geol*) a Jurassic stratum overlying the Oxfordian, including the Coral Rag and Coralline Oolite (also called **Lusitanian**). **corallif'erous** *adj* containing coral. **coralliform** /-al'-/ *adj* having the form of coral. **corallig'enous** *adj* producing coral. **cor'alline** *adj* of, like or containing coral. ◆ *n* a red alga with a delicate pinkish or purplish colour; a coral-like substance or animal. **cor'allite** *n* the cup of a simple coral or of one polyp; a fossil coral. **cor'alloid** or **coralloid'al** *adj* in the form of coral; resembling coral. **corallum** /-al'-/ *n* (*pl* **corall'a**) the skeleton of a coral colony.
❑ **coral berry** *n* an American shrub of the snowberry genus, or its red berry. **coral fern** *n* a type of Australian fern with fronds shaped like branching coral. **cor'al-fish** *n* any of several kinds of coloured, spiny-finned fish which inhabit coral reefs. **coral flower** *n* any flowering plant of the N American genus *Heuchera*, of the family Saxifragaceae, typically having heart-shaped evergreen leaves and bell-shaped

flowers on slender stems. **coral island** *n* an island formed from coral. **Coralline Crag** *n* (*geol*) a division of the English Pliocene, shelly sands and clays with fossil polyzoa. **Coralline Oolite** *n* a massive limestone underlying the Coral Rag. **Coral Rag** *n* a coarse limestone rock formed chiefly of coral in the Corallian formation. **coral reef** *n* a reef or bank formed by the growth and deposit of coral. **cor'al-rock** *n* a limestone composed of coral. **cor'alroot** *n* a species of *Cardamine* with knobbed root stock; an orchid of the genus *Corallorhiza* with branching coral-like roots. **coral snake** *n* a venomous American elapid snake of the genus *Micrurus* and related genera; any of various brightly-coloured snakes of Africa and Asia. **coral spot** *n* a fungus (*Nectria cinnabarina*) that *usu* lives on dead twigs but may become parasitic if it enters living shoots, killing branches and occasionally whole trees. **coral tree** *n* a tree or shrub of the tropical genus *Erythrina*, with red coral-like flowers. **cor'alwort** *n* coralroot, in either sense.

coram /kō'ram/ (*L*) *prep* before; in the presence of.
■ **coram domino rege** /kō'ram dom'i-nō rē'jē or rā'ge/ before our lord the king. **coram nobis** /nō'bis or -bēs/ before us (ie the monarch), in our presence. **coram paribus** /par'i-bəs or pär'i-bŭs/ before equals or one's peers. **coram populo** /pop'ū-lō or -ŭ-/ in the presence of the people; publicly.

coranach same as **coronach**.

cor anglais /kör ä'glä or ong'glä/ *n* (*pl* **cors anglais** /körz or kör/) an oboe set a fifth lower than the ordinary oboe (also called (*Ital*) **corno inglese** /kör'nō ing-glā'sä/ (*pl* **corni inglesi** /kör'nē in-glā'sē/)). [Fr, English horn, though it is probably not English]

coranto /kō- or ko-ran'tō/ *n* (*pl* **coran'tos** or **coran'toes**) a rapid and lively dance, the courante; the music for it, in triple time. [Fr *courante* (literally) running, from L *currere* to run (Ital *coranta*, from Fr)]

corban /kör'bən/ (*Bible*) *n* anything devoted to God in fulfilment of a vow. [Heb *qorbān* an offering, sacrifice]

corbe /körb/ (*Spenser*) see **corbel**, **courb**.

corbeau /kör-bō'/ *n* a blackish-green colour. [Fr, crow, raven]

corbeil /kör'bəl or -bā'/ *n* a basket filled with earth, set up as a defensive missile (*fortif*); a carved representation of a basket (*archit*). [Fr *corbeille*, from L *corbicula*, dimin of *corbis* a basket]
■ **corbeille'** *n* a basket of flowers.

corbel /kör'bəl/ (*archit*) *n* a projection from the face of a wall, supporting a weight (*Spenser* **corbe**); a bracket. ◆ *vt* (**cor'belling**; **cor'belled**) to lay (stone, etc) so it forms a corbel. [OFr *corbel*, from LL *corvellus*, dimin of *corvus* a raven]
■ **cor'belled** or (*N Am*) **cor'beled** *adj*. **cor'belling** or (*N Am*) **cor'beling** *n*.
❑ **corbel step** *n* a corbie step. **corbel table** *n* a row of corbels and the parapet or cornice they support.
■ **corbel out** or **corbel off** to (cause to) project on corbels.

Corbett /kör'bət/ *n* a Scottish mountain of between 2500 and 2999 feet that has a reascent of 500 feet on all sides (cf **Munro**). [After JR Corbett (1876–1949), who compiled the first list of these]

corbicula /kör-bik'ū-lə/ *n* (*pl* **corbic'ulae** /-lē/) the pollen basket of bees, consisting of the dilated posterior tibia with its fringe of long hairs. [L dimin of *corbis* a basket]
■ **corbic'ulate** *adj*.

corbie /kör'bi/ (*Scot*) *n* a raven; a crow. [OFr *corbin*, from L *corvus* a crow]
❑ **corbie gable** *n* a stepped gable. **corbie messenger** *n* a messenger who returns too late, or not at all. **cor'bie-steps** *n pl* the small stonework steps on the slopes of a gable, crow-steps.

corcass /kör'kəs/ *n* in Ireland, a salt-marsh, or land susceptible to flooding by a river. [Ir *corcach*]

Corchorus /kör'kə-rəs/ *n* the jute genus. [Gr *korchoros* the name of a plant]

cord /körd/ *n* a small rope or thick string; a part of the body resembling a cord (eg *spinal cord*, *umbilical cord*); a measure of cut wood (128 cu ft), *orig* determined by use of a cord or string; a raised rib on cloth; ribbed cloth, *esp* corduroy (also *adj*); (in *pl*) corduroy trousers; a string crossing the back of a book in binding; a flex for an electrical apparatus. ◆ *vt* to supply with a cord; to bind with a cord. [Fr *corde*, from L *chorda*; see **chord**]
■ **cord'age** *n* a quantity of cords or ropes, such as the rigging of a ship, etc; a quantity of wood measured in cords. **cordec'tomy** *n* surgical removal of a vocal cord. **cord'ed** *adj* fastened with cords; wound about with cords (*heraldry*); ribbed; (of wood) piled in cords. **cord'ing** *n* the act of binding; cordage. **cord'ite** *n* a cordlike smokeless explosive. **cord'less** *adj* (of an electrical device) operating without a flex; battery-powered. **cordocentē'sis** *n* (*med*) the removal of a sample of fetal blood from the umbilical vein by inserting a hollow needle through the wall of the pregnant woman's abdomen.

---

cordot'omy *n* the surgical division of bundles of nerve fibres in the spinal cord to relieve severe or persistent pain (also **chordot'omy**).
□ **cord grass** *n* a grass of the genus *Spartina* which is found in muddy salt-marshes and is used for making ropes. **cord'wood** *n* wood cut up and stacked in cords.

Cordaites /kör-dā-ī'tēz/ *n* a Palaeozoic genus of fossil plants of the family **Cordaitā'ceae**, gymnosperms nearer the conifers than the cycads. [AKJ *Corda* (1809–49), Bohemian botanist]

cordate /kör'dāt/ *adj* heart-shaped; having the base indented next to the petiole (*bot*). [L *cordātus* (in modern sense), from L *cor, cordis* the heart]
■ **cord'iform** *adj* heart-shaped.

Cordelier /kör-də-lēr'/ *n* a Franciscan friar, from the knotted cord worn as a girdle; (in *pl*) a club in the French Revolution which met in an old Cordelier convent. [OFr *cordele*, dimin of *corde* a rope]

cordial /kör'di-əl/ *adj* friendly; hearty; sincere; affectionate; reviving the heart or spirits. ◆ *n* a soft drink with a fruit base, *usu* diluted before being drunk; a medicine or drink for refreshing the spirits; anything which revives or comforts the heart; a liqueur (*N Am*). [Fr, from L *cor, cordis* the heart]
■ **cordiality** /-al'i-ti/ *n*. **cor'dialize** or **-ise** *vi* to become cordial, to fraternize. **cor'dially** *adv*. **cor'dialness** *n*.

cordierite /kör'di-ə-rīt/ *n* the mineral iolite or dichroite. [PLA *Cordier* (1777–1861), French mineralogist]

cordiform see under **cordate**.

cordillera /kör-dil-yā'rə/ *n* a chain of mountains, *esp* the chain including the Andes and the Rocky Mountains. [Sp, from Old Sp *cordilla*, from L *chorda* cord, from Gr *chordē*]

cordiner /kör'di-nər/ see under **cordovan**.

cordite see under **cord**.

córdoba /kor'dō-bə or -bä/ *n* the standard monetary unit of Nicaragua (100 centavos). [Named after Francisco Fernandez de *Córdoba* (died about 1518)]

cordon /kör'don or -dən/ *n* a cord or ribbon bestowed as a badge of honour; a line of police, soldiers, etc, or a system of road-blocks, encircling an area so as to prevent or control passage into or out of it; a row of stones along the line of a rampart (*fortif*); a single-stemmed fruit tree. ◆ *vt* (often with *off*) to close (off) an area with a cordon of men, ring of barriers, etc. [Fr]
■ **sanitary cordon** (*rare*) a cordon sanitaire.

cordon bleu /kor-dɔ̃ blö'/ (*Fr*) *n* formerly, the blue ribbon worn by the knights of the Holy Ghost; hence, a person of distinction, *esp* a cook of the highest excellence, *specif* one who has attended Le Cordon Bleu®, a famous school of cookery founded in Paris in 1895. ◆ *adj* (of a cook or cookery) of a very high standard; in cooking, denoting a method of preparation in which a thin slice of meat is rolled around a filling of cheese and ham and then fried in breadcrumbs, as in *chicken cordon bleu*.

cordon sanitaire /kor-dɔ̃ sa-nē-ter'/ (*Fr*) *n* a line of sentries posted to restrict passage into and out of an area and so keep contagious disease within that area; neutral states keeping hostile states apart; a barrier (*lit* or *fig*) isolating a state, etc considered dangerous.

cordotomy see under **cord**.

cordovan /kör'də-van or -vən/ or (*archaic*) **cordwain** /körd'wān/ *n* goatskin leather, *orig* from Cordova (*Córdoba*) in Spain.
■ **cord'wainer** or **cord'iner** or (*archaic*) a worker in cordovan or cordwain; a shoemaker. **cord'wainery** *n* (*archaic*).

cords /kördz/ (*inf*) *n pl* corduroy trousers. [Short form]

corduroy /kör'də-roi or -roi'/ *n* a ribbed cotton pile fabric; (in *pl*) corduroy trousers (*inf* short form **cords**). ◆ *adj* made of corduroy. [Perh Fr *corde du roi* king's cord, although the term is not used in French; perh *cord* and **duroy**]
□ **corduroy road** *n* a track laid transversely with tree trunks.

cordwain, cordwainer see **cordovan**.

cordyline /kör-di-lī'nē/ *n* any tropical or subtropical palmlike shrub or tree of the genus *Cordyline*, frequently cultivated for their handsome multicoloured foliage, and including the New Zealand cabbage tree and the good-luck plant or ti tree. [Gr *kordylē* club]

CORE /kör/ (*US*) *abbrev*: Congress of Racial Equality.

core[1] /kör or kōr/ *n* in an apple, pear, etc, the central casing containing the seeds; the innermost or most essential part of something (also *adj*); the central part of the earth (*geol*); a cylindrical sample of rock, soil, etc extracted by driving a hollow-core drill into strata; the lump of stone or flint remaining after flakes have been struck off it (*archaeol*); the part of a nuclear reactor containing the fissile material; (also **magnetic core**) a small ferromagnetic ring which, either charged or uncharged by electric current, can thus assume two states corresponding to the binary digits 0 and 1 (*comput*); a solid mass of specially prepared sand or loam placed in a mould to provide a hole or cavity in metal casting; a computer memory made up of a series of three rings (also **core store**, **core memory**). ◆ *vt* to take out the core of (an apple, etc). [Poss L *cor* the heart, or Fr *cor* horn, corn (on the foot), or *corps* body]
■ **cored** *adj* having the core removed; cast by means of a core; having a core. **core'less** *adj* without a core; pithless; hollow. **cor'er** *n* a device for removing the core of an apple, etc.
□ **core curriculum** see under **curriculum**. **core dump** *n* (*comput*) the transfer of the contents of main memory to disk, *usu* made when debugging. **core store** or **core memory** *n* (*comput*) see **core** (*n*) above. **core temperature** *n* (*biol*) the temperature towards the middle of an organism which is unaffected by the outside temperature. **core times** see **flexitime** under **flexi-**.

core[2] /kör or kōr/ *n* a company, gang or shift. [**corps**]

coreferential /kō-re-fə-ren'shəl/ *adj* (*philos*) (of more than one linguistic expression) designating the same individual or class.

coregent /kō-rē'jənt/ *n* a joint regent.

Coregonus /kö- or ko-ri-gō'nəs/ *n* whitefish, a genus of herring-like fishes of the salmon family, pollan, vendace, etc. [Gr *korē* pupil of the eye, and *gōniā* angle]
■ **corego'nine** (or /-nin/) *adj*.

corelation, corelative /kō-/ same as **correlation** and **correlative** (see under **correlate**).

coreligionist /kō-rə-lij'ə-nist/ *n* a follower of the same religion as another.

corella /kə-rel'ə/ *n* an Australian long-billed cockatoo. [From an Aboriginal language]

coreopsis /ko-ri-op'sis/ *n* any annual or perennial composite plant of the genus *Coreopsis*, mostly native to America, some species of which are cultivated for their showy flowers. [Gr *koris* a bug, and *opsis* appearance, from the shape of the seed]

corespondent /kō-ri-spon'dənt/ (*law*) *n* a man or woman cited in divorce cases as having committed adultery with the wife or husband who is the *respondent*.
□ **corespondent shoes** *n pl* two-coloured shoes for men, generally black or brown and white.

corey see **cory**.

corf /körf/ *n* (*pl* **corves** /körvz/) a coalminer's basket, now *usu* a trolley or wagon; a cage for fish or lobsters. [Du, from L *corbis* basket]
□ **corf'house** *n* (*Scot*) a salmon-curing house.

Corfam® /kör'fam/ *n* a synthetic, porous material used as a substitute for leather, *esp* in shoes.

Corfiot or **Corfiote** /kör'fi-ət/ *n* a native or citizen of Corfu. ◆ *adj* of or relating to Corfu.

CORGI /kör'gi/ *abbrev*: Council for Registered Gas Installers.

corgi /kör'gi/ *n* (*pl* **cor'gis**) a Welsh breed of dog, having a fox-like head and short legs. [Welsh *corr* dwarf, and *ci* dog]

coriaceous see under **corium**.

coriander /ko-ri-an'dər/ *n* a European umbelliferous plant (*Coriandrum sativum*), whose leaves and seeds are used as a flavouring in food. [Fr *coriandre*, from L *coriandrum*, from Gr *koriannon*]
□ **coriander seed** *n*.

Corinthian /ko-rin'thi-ən/ *adj* of Corinth (Gr *Korinthos*) in Greece; of an ornate style of Greek architecture, with acanthus capitals; (of literary style) over-embellished or over-brilliant; (often without *cap*; of sport, sportsmen, etc) amateur; profligate, dissolute. ◆ *n* a native or inhabitant of Corinth; an amateur sportsman; a dissolute man of fashion.
■ **Cor'inth** *n* (*obs*) a brothel. **corinth'ianize** or **-ise** *vi* (*archaic*) to be licentious.
□ **Corinthian brass** or **bronze** *n* an alloy made in Corinth, much valued in ancient times.

Coriolis effect /ko-ri-ō'lis i-fekt'/ (*phys*) *n* the deflection (to the right in the northern, left in the southern, hemisphere) and acceleration of bodies, etc moving relative to the earth's surface, caused by the earth's rotation. [First studied by GB *Coriolis* (1792–1843), French civil engineer]

corium /kō'ri-əm or kō'/ *n* the true skin, under the epidermis (also **dermis**; *anat*); leather armour (*ancient hist*). [L *corium*, from Gr *chorion* skin, leather]
■ **coria'ceous** or **co'rious** *adj* (*esp* of plant structures) having a leathery appearance.

corival, corivalry, corivalship /kō-/ same as **corrival**, etc.

cork /körk/ *n* the outer bark of the cork tree, a species of oak found in S Europe, N Africa, etc; a stopper, eg for a wine bottle, made of cork; any stopper; a tissue of close-fitting, thick-walled cells, almost airtight and watertight, forming bark or covering the surfaces of wounds (*bot*); a piece of cork; a fisherman's float made of cork. ◆ *adj* made of cork. ◆ *vt* to stop with a cork; to stop up; to bottle up or repress (with *up*; *fig*); to blacken (*esp* the face) with burnt cork. [Perh from Sp *alcorque* cork slipper, which may be from L *quercus* oak, with the Arabic article *al*; Sp has also *corche, corcha, corcho*, perh from L *cortex* bark, rind] ■ **cork'age** *n* a charge made in a restaurant, etc for serving wine not bought on the premises. **corked** *adj* stopped as by a cork; (of wine) tainted as if by the cork, generally in fact by a fungus which develops on the cork; blackened by burnt cork; drunk (*old sl*). **cork'er** *n* a person or thing that is an excellent example of its kind (*sl*); a person or device that inserts corks. **cork'iness** *n*. **cork'ing** *adj* (*sl*) surpassing; excellent; tremendous. **cork'y** *adj* of or resembling cork; (of wine) corked (*N Am*). ▫ **cork'board** *n* a thin composite board made of cork and resin, used as flooring and as insulation. **cork'borer** *n* an instrument for boring holes in corks to receive glass tubes in chemical apparatus. **cork cambium** *n* phellogen. **cork'-cutter** *n* a person employed in cutting corks for bottles, etc; an instrument used for this. **cork'-heeled** *adj* (of shoes, etc) having cork heels; wanton (*obs*). **cork mat** *n* a mat made of pieces of cork with rubber and linseed oil. **cork oak** *n* a S European species of oak (*Quercus suber*) from which cork is obtained for commercial use in Spain and Portugal. **cork'screw** *n* a device, *usu* consisting of a piece of metal in the shape of a screw, for drawing corks from bottles. ◆ *adj* like a corkscrew in shape. ◆ *vi* to move in a spiral manner. ◆ *vt* to pull out with difficulty (eg a cork); to obtain information from by force or cunning. **cork-sole'** *n* an inner shoe-sole made of cork. **cork'-tipped** *adj* (of a cigarette) having a filter of cork. **cork'tree** *n* the cork oak; a name applied to various trees with corky bark or very light wood. **corkwing wrasse** *n* a small reddish-brown or greenish wrasse (*Crenilabrus melops*) found in N European waters. **cork'wood** *n* very light wood; a name applied to many trees with light wood, eg balsa, alligator apple.

corking-pin /kör'king-pin/ *n* a pin of the largest size. [Perhaps from *caulking pin* (see **caulk**)]

corkir or **korkir** /kör'kər/ (*Scot*) *n* a lichen used for dyeing (red or purple). [Gaelic *corcur*, from L *purpura* purple]

corm /körm/ *n* a modified underground stem (without scale leaves, as in a bulb), the storage structure of the crocus, meadow saffron, etc. [Gr *kormos* the lopped trunk of a tree] ■ **corm'el** *n* a small corm produced from the base of a larger one. **corm'ophyte** /-fīt/ *n* a plant differentiated into leaf, stem and root. **cormophytic** /-fit'/ *adj*. **corm'ous** *adj* producing corms. **corm'us** *n* the differentiated body of a cormophyte; the whole body of a compound animal.

cormidium /kör-mid'i-əm/ *n* an aggregation of polyps in a colonial marine hydrozoan.

cormorant /kör'mə-rənt/ *n* a member of a genus (*Phalacrocorax*) of shiny black webfooted seabirds, related to the pelicans, that feeds on large quantities of fish and breeds in colonies on rocks and cliffs; a glutton. [Fr *cormoran*, from L *corvus marīnus* sea crow]

Corn. *abbrev* : Cornish; Cornwall.

corn[1] /körn/ *n* collectively, seeds of cereal plants, or the plants themselves, *esp* (in England) wheat, (in Scotland and Ireland) oats, (in N America) maize; a grain, a hard particle; a kernel or small hard seed; something old-fashioned or hackneyed. ◆ *adj* of, for, relating to, made from, growing among, or feeding upon, corn; granular. ◆ *vt* to make granular (*archaic*); to preserve with salt or brine; to give corn to (eg a horse) (*dialect*); to intoxicate (*old sl*). ◆ *vi* to form seed. [OE *corn*; Gothic *kaurn*; related to L *grānum*] ■ **corned** *adj* salted. **corn'ily** *adv*. **corn'iness** *n*. **corn'y** *adj* (*inf*) of, like or abounding in corn; old-fashioned; uninteresting from frequent use; dull; over-sentimental. ▫ **cornacre** see **conacre**. **corn'-baby** see under **kirn**[1]. **corn'ball** *n* (*US*) a sweetened ball of popcorn; an unsophisticated person; something trite, banal or sentimental. ◆ *adj* unsophisticated; banal or sentimental. **corn'-beef** or **corned beef** *n* preserved salted beef. **corn bin** *n* a bin for storing corn. **corn'borer** *n* a European moth (*Ostrinia nubilalis*) whose larvae have become a pest of maize in America. **corn'brake** *n* a maize plantation. **cornbran'dy** *n* spirits made from grain; whisky. **corn'brash** *n* (*geol*) a clayey limestone whose presence in soil affords good growth for cereal crops. **corn'bread** (or **corn'-cake**) *n* (*US* and *W Indies*) bread (or cake) made of maize meal. **corn bunting** *n* a common brown bunting (*Miliaria calandra*) of Europe and Asia. **corn'-chandler** *n* a retailer of grain. **corn'-chandlery** *n*. **corn circle** see **crop circle** under **crop**. **corn'cob** *n* the woody core of a maize ear. **corncob pipe** *n* a tobacco pipe with the bowl made of a maize cob. **corn'cockle** *n* a tall-growing cornfield weed (*Agrostemma githago*) with reddish-purple flowers, similar to the campion. **corn'-cracker** *n* (*US*) a poor white; a Kentuckian. **corn'crake** *n* a type of rail (*Crex crex*), of elusive habit and with a characteristic rasping cry, commonly nesting in hayfields. **corn'crib** *n*

(chiefly *N Am*) a ventilated building for storing maize. **corn'-dealer, corn'-factor** or **corn'-merchant** *n* a merchant who buys and sells corn. **corn dodger** *n* (*US*) a cake, small loaf or dumpling made of maize. **corn dog** *n* (*US*) a sausage covered in batter, served on a stick. **corn-dollie** see under **kirn**[1]. **corn earworm** *n* the larva of a noctuid moth (*Heliothis zea*) that feeds on corn ears and other crops. **corn exchange** *n* a building where trade in corn is (or was) carried on. **corn'-fed** *adj* fed on corn; well-fed. **corn'field** *n* a field in which corn is growing. **corn'flag** *n* another name for a gladiolus. **corn'flake** *n* a crazy or silly person (*US sl*); (in *pl*) toasted flakes of maize, eaten *esp* as a breakfast cereal. **corn'flour** *n* finely ground maize, rice, or other grain, used *esp* for thickening sauces. **corn'flower** *n* a beautiful blue-flowered cornfield weed of the Compositae (*Centaurea cyanus*). **corn'fly** *n* the gout-fly. **corn'husk** *n* (*N Am*) the outer covering of an ear of maize. **corn'husker** *n* a person or machine that removes cornhusks. **corn'husking** *n*. **corning house** *n* formerly, a place where gunpowder was granulated. **corn'-kist** *n* (*Scot*) a grain chest. **corn'-kister** *n* a farm worker's song of his or her life and work. **corn'land** *n* ground suitable for growing grain. **corn law** *n* a law regulating trade in grain, *esp* (in *pl*; with *caps*) laws that restricted importation to Britain by a duty, repealed in 1846. **corn'loft** *n* a granary. **corn'-maiden** see under **kirn**[1]. **corn marigold** *n* a yellow cornfield chrysanthemum (*Chrysanthemum segetum*). **corn'meal** *n* meal made from corn or maize flour. **corn'mill** *n* a flour mill. **corn'-miller** *n*. **corn'moth** *n* a moth (*Tinea granella*) of the clothes moth genus, whose larvae feed on grain. **corn oil** *n* oil extracted from maize, used in cooking, etc. **corn'pipe** *n* a musical instrument made of a stalk of an oat or other cereal. **corn pit** *n* (*US*) part of an exchange where business is done in maize. **corn pone** *n* (*US*) maize-bread, often baked or fried; a maize loaf. **corn'-pone** *adj* unsophisticated. **corn popper** *n* a pan or grating for popping corn. **corn poppy** *n* the field poppy. **corn rent** *n* rent paid in corn, not money. **corn rig** *n* (*Scot*) a ridge or strip on which oats are grown. **corn'row** *n* a hairstyle, *esp* Afro-Caribbean, in which the hair is arranged in tightly braided flat rows. **corn'-salad** *n* a plant of the genus *Valerianella*, *esp V. locusta* the common corn-salad, sometimes used as salads and formerly called lamb's lettuce. **corn shuck** *n* (*N Am*) the husk enclosing a maize ear. **corn shucker** *n* (*N Am*) a person or machine that removes corn shucks. **corn'-shucking** *n* (*N Am*) the removal of corn shucks. **corn silk** *n* (*N Am*) the silky tuft at the tip of an ear of maize, formerly used as a diuretic. **corn snake** *n* a harmless snake (*Coluber guttatus*) of the southern USA. **corn snow** *n* (*N Am*) granular snow. **corn spirit** *n* (*folklore*) a god or spirit concerned in the growth of corn. **corn spurrey** *n* a common weed of cornfields (*Spergula arvensis*), with small white five-petalled flowers. **corn'stalk** *n* a stalk of corn; a tall thin person, *esp* one born in New South Wales (*Aust*). **corn'starch** *n* (*N Am*) cornflour. **corn'stone** *n* a silicious limestone, favourable for cereal growing. **corn thrips** *n* a minute flying insect of the order Thysanoptera, that sucks the sap of grain. **corn van** *n* an instrument for winnowing corn. **corn weevil** *n* a small weevil (*Calandra granaria*), destructive in granaries. **corn whisky** *n* an American whisky made from maize. **corn'worm** *n* a corn weevil; a corn moth larva. ■ **corn in Egypt** abundance (Bible, Genesis 42.2). **corn on the cob** a cob of maize with grains still attached, cooked whole and eaten as a vegetable.

corn[2] /körn/ *n* a small hard growth chiefly on the toe or foot, resulting from thickening of the cuticle, caused by pressure or friction. [L *cornū* a horn] ■ **corn'eous** *adj* horny. **corn'icle** or **cornic'ulum** *n* a little horn; a hornlike process, *esp* one of the wax-secreting tubes of a greenfly. **cornic'ulate** *adj* horned; horn-shaped. **cornif'erous** *adj* containing hornstone. **cornif'ic** *adj* producing or forming horn or horns. **cornifica'tion** *n*. **corn'iform** *adj* shaped like a horn. **cornigerous** /kör-nij'ər-əs/ *adj* horned. **cor'nū** /kör'noo/ *n* (*pl* **cor'nūa**) (*anat*) a horn, hornlike part or process. **cor'nūal** *adj* hornlike. **corn'y** *adj* of or relating to horns or corns; having corns; horny. ▫ **corn'-cure** *n* a remedy for corns. **corn'-cutter** *n* a person who cuts corns. **corniferous limestone** *n* a coral limestone with chert nodules in the Devonian of N America. **corn plaster** *n* a remedial plaster for corns. ■ **tread on someone's corns** to hurt someone's feelings.

cornaceous see under **cornel**.

cornage /kör'nij/ (*hist*) *n* a feudal service or rent fixed according to number of horned cattle, horngeld. [OFr, from L *cornū* horn]

cornea /kör'ni-ə/ *n* the transparent horny membrane that forms the front covering of the eye. [L *cornea* (*tēla*) horny (tissue)] ■ **cor'neal** *adj*. ▫ **corneal graft** *n* a surgical operation in which healthy corneal tissue is grafted onto a patient's eye to replace diseased or damaged tissue. **corneal lens** *n* a contact lens covering the transparent part of the eye.

---

cornel /kör'nəl/ n any tree of the genus *Cornus*, particularly the cornelian cherry or cornelian tree, a small tree (*Cornus mas*) of central and S Europe. [LL *cornolium*, from L *cornus* cornel]
■ **cornā'ceous** adj of or belonging to the **Cornāceae**, a family of trees and shrubs including the dogwood, cornel and spotted laurel. **cornē'lian** n the fruit of the cornel tree; the tree itself.
❑ **cornelian cherry** n.

cornelian[1] /kör-nē'li-ən/ or **carnelian** /kär-/ n a fine kind of quartz, generally translucent red. [Fr *cornaline*, from L *cornū* a horn, or *cornum* cornelian cherry, from its appearance; confused with *carō, carnis* flesh]

cornelian[2] see under **cornel**.

cornemuse /kör'ni-mūz/ n a French bagpipe. [Fr]

corneous see under **corn**[2].

corner /kör'nər/ n the point where two lines or several planes meet; an angular projection or recess; a secret or confined place; an awkward or embarrassing position; a point in a rubber at whist (*obs*); a free shot, taken from the corner of the field, given to the opposite side when a player in eg football or hockey plays the ball over his own goal line; an operation by which the whole of a stock or commodity is bought up so that the buyers may resell at their own price. ◆ vt to supply with corners; to put in a corner; to put in a fix or difficulty; to form a corner against; to get control of (a market for a particular commodity) by forming a corner. ◆ vi to turn a corner. [OFr *corniere*, from L *cornū* horn]
■ **corn'ered** adj having corners; put in a difficult position. **corn'erwise** or **corn'erways** adv with the corner in front; diagonally. ❑ **corn'erback** n (*American football*) a defensive back, *usu* covering an opposing wide receiver. **corn'er-boy** n (*Irish*) a loafer, a street-corner layabout. **corn'er-man** n a person who assists a boxer between rounds by treating cuts, giving advice, etc; a street-corner layabout; the man at the end of the row in a black-and-white-minstrel performance (*obs*). **corn'erstone** n a stone that unites the two walls of a building at a corner; the principal stone, *esp* the corner of the foundation of a building; something of prime importance. **corner teeth** n pl the lateral incisors of a horse.
■ **cut corners** see under **cut**. **fight** or **stand one's** (**own**) **corner** to defend strongly, maintain, one's (own) position, stand, argument, etc. **in someone's corner** supportive of someone. (**just**) **round the corner** close at hand; soon to be attained, reached, etc. **turn the corner** to go round the corner; to get past a difficulty or danger; to begin to pick up.

cornet[1] /kör'nit/ (*N Am* also -*net'*)/ n a three-valved brass instrument, more tapering than the trumpet; an organ stop of various kinds; an old woodwind instrument (*usu* **cornett**); a cornet-player; any funnel-shaped object, eg a piece of gold for assaying, an ice-cream-filled wafer cone, or a cream-filled pastry. [Fr *cornet*, dimin of *corne*, from L *cornū* horn]
■ **cor'netist** or **cornett'ist** n a cornet-player. **cornettino** /-tē'nō/ n (pl **cornetti'ni** /-nē/) a woodwind instrument of the cornet family with a range a fourth above that of the cornet (also **small cornet**). **cornett'o** n (pl **cornett'i** /-ē/) a woodwind cornet. **cornō'pean** n a brass cornet. ❑ **cornet-à-piston(s)** /kor-nā-ä-pēs-tɔ̃/ n (Fr) a brass cornet.

cornet[2] /kör'nit/ n an old form of lady's headdress, with side lappets; a lappet of this; a cavalry standard (*obs*); up to 1871, a cavalry officer, later a sub-lieutenant; a standard-bearer at a common-riding. [Fr *cornette*, ult from L *cornū* horn]
■ **cor'netcy** n the commission or rank of cornet.

cornet[3] see **coronet**.

cornett, etc see **cornet**[1].

cornice /kör'nis/ n a projecting moulding along the top of a building, window, etc; a plaster moulding at the junction between a ceiling and walls; a picture moulding; an overhanging crest of snow on the edge of a mountain ridge, etc; the uppermost member of the entablature, surmounting the frieze (*classical archit*). ◆ vt to provide with a cornice. [Fr, from Ital, poss from Gr *korōnis* a curved line, cf L *corōna*]
■ **cor'niced** adj.
❑ **cor'nice-hook**, **cor'nice-pole** or **cor'nice-rail** n a hook, pole or rail for hanging pictures, curtains, etc. **cornice ring** n a ring or moulding on a cannon next below the muzzle-ring.

corniche /kor-nēsh'/ (Fr) n a coast road built along a cliff-face; in Egypt, a boulevard along a bank of the Nile.

cornichon /kör'ni-shon or kor-ni-shɔ̃'/ n a small pickled gherkin. [Fr, gherkin]

cornicle, **corniculate**, **corniferous**, **cornigerous**, etc see under **corn**[2].

Cornish /kör'nish/ adj relating to Cornwall. ◆ n the Celtic language of Cornwall, dead since the later 18c.
❑ **Cornish clay** n china clay. **Cornish pasty** n a pasty with meat and vegetables.

corno /kör'nō/ n (pl **cor'ni** /-nē/) the French horn. [Ital, from L *cornū* a horn]
■ **corn'ist** n a horn-player.
❑ **corno di bassetto** /ba-set'ō/ n the basset horn; an organ stop. **corno inglese** see **cor anglais**.

cornopean see under **cornet**[1].

cornu, **cornual** see under **corn**[2].

cornucopia /kör-nū-kō'pi-ə/ n the horn of plenty, according to one fable, the horn of the goat that suckled Jupiter, placed among the stars as an emblem of plenty (*Gr myth*); an ornamental vase in the shape of a horn overflowing with fruits; an abundant source of supply. [L *cornū cōpiae*, from *cornū* horn, and *cōpia* plenty]
■ **cornucō'pian** adj.

cornute /kör-nūt'/ vt (*obs*) to cuckold. ◆ adj (also **cornut'ed**) horned; hornlike; cuckolded (*obs*). [L *cornūtus* horned, from *cornū* horn]
■ **cornūt'o** (or /-noo'/) n (pl **cornut'os**) (*Ital*; *obs*) a cuckold.

corny see under **corn**[1,2].

corocore /kor'ō-kör or -kör/ n a Malay form of boat (also **cor'ocorō** (pl **cor'ocoros**)). [Malay *kurakura*]

corody see **corrody**.

corol. abbrev : corollary.

corolla /ko-ro'lə or -rō'/ (*bot*) n the inner circle or whorl of petals in a flower. [L *corolla*, dimin of *corōna* a crown]
■ **corollā'ceous** adj. **Corollíflorae** /-i-flō'rē/ n pl (L *flōs, flōris* flower) in some classifications the Gamopetalae or Sympetalae. **corolliflo'ral** adj. **corolliflo'rous** adj. **coroll'iform** adj. **coroll'ine** (or /kor'/) adj.

corollary /kə-ro'lə-ri or kor'ə-lə-ri/ n an easy inference; a natural consequence or result. ◆ adj consequent; supplementary. [L *corollārium* a garland, money for a garland, a tip, from *corolla*]

coromandel /kor-ə-man'dəl or -rō-/ (sometimes with *cap*) n or adj (also **Coromandel wood**) calamander; (also **coromandel ebony**) a wood of the same genus (*Diospyros*) as calamander; the colour colcothar. [*Coromandel* Coast in SE India]
❑ **Coromandel screen** n a Chinese folding lacquered screen. **Coromandel work** n lacquer work in which an incised design is filled with colour or with gold.

corona /kə- or ko-rō'nə/ n (pl **corō'nas** or **corō'nae** /-ē/) a crown or crown-like structure; the large, flat, projecting member of a cornice crowning the entablature (*archit*); the trumpet of a daffodil, etc, composed of ligules of the perianth leaves (*bot*); a coloured ring round the sun or moon, distinguished from a halo by having a red outerpart; one of the sun's envelopes, outside the chromosphere, observable during total eclipse (*astron*); a similar atmospheric envelope of a star (*astron*); the glowing region produced by ionization of the air surrounding a high-voltage conductor (*phys*); a round pendent chandelier, as hung from the roof of a church (also **corona lucis** /lū'sis or loo'kis/); a long cigar with straight sides and a blunt end. [L *corōna* a crown]
■ **coronagraph** or **coronograph** /-ōn'ə-gräf/ n a special telescope used to observe prominences and the corona around the edge of the sun. **cor'onal** /-ə-nl/ n a circlet, small crown or garland for the head. ◆ adj /-ō'nəl/ relating to a crown, a corona, or to the top of the head; like a crown; cacuminal (*phonetics*). **coronary** adj see separate entry. **cor'onāte** or **cor'onāted** adj crowned; (of shells) having a row of projections round the apex. **coronā'tion** n the ceremony of crowning. **corō'nium** n the name given to a hypothetical element in the solar corona assumed to explain spectral lines now known to be due to iron and nickel atoms that have lost a large number of electrons.
❑ **coronal suture** n the serrated line across the skull separating the frontal bone from the parietal bones. **coronavirus** n any of a family of viruses that have proteins protruding from the surface in a crown-like structure.

coronach /kor'ə-nähh or -nəhh/ n a dirge. [Said to be a Gaelic word *corranach* (cf Ir *corányach*, from *comh-* with, together, and *rànach* a cry)]

coronagraph, **coronal** see under **corona**.

coronary /kor'ə-nə-ri/ adj relating to the region around an organ, *esp* the heart (*anat*); coronal. ◆ n a coronary thrombosis. [**corona**]
❑ **coronary artery** n one of the branching arteries supplying blood to the heart-wall from the aorta. **coronary artery bypass** n a surgical procedure to restore adequate oxygen supply to the heart muscle by attaching lengths of vein taken from eg the leg to the aorta and bypassing blocked coronary arteries (also **coronary bypass graft**). **coronary care unit** n a hospital ward in which patients are treated after a heart attack (*abbrev* **CCU**). **coronary thrombosis** n a stoppage in a branch of a coronary artery by a clot of blood, which causes part of the heart muscle to die (see also **myocardial infarction** under **myo-**).

coronate see under **corona**.

---

fāte; fär; mē; fûr; mīne; mōte; för; mūte; pŭt; dhen (then); el'ə-mənt (element) ● For other sounds see detailed chart of pronunciation

coronation[1] (*Spenser*) an archaic variant of **carnation**.

coronation[2] see under **corona**.

coroner /*kor'ə-nər*/ *n orig* the guardian of the pleas of the Crown; now an official (*usu* a medical practitioner or lawyer) who presides at an inquest and enquires into the causes of accidental or suspicious deaths; in the Isle of Man, the principal officer of a sheading. [OFr *corouner*, from L *corōna* crown]
■ **cor'onership** *n*.

coronet /*kor'ə-nit*/ *n* a small crown worn by the nobility; an ornamental headdress; a ring of bone at the bottom of a deer's antler; the part of a horse's pastern just above the coffin (also **cor'net**). [OFr *coronete*, dimin of *corone* crown, from L *corōna*]
■ **cor'oneted** *adj*.

coronis /*ko-rō'nis*/ *n* in Greek, a sign (') marking a crasis, as κᾄν = καὶ ἄν. [Gr *korōnis* a curved line]

coronium, coronograph see under **corona**.

coronoid /*kor'ə-noid* or *ko-rō'noid*/ (*anat*) *adj* like a crow's bill, as in the *coronoid process* of the lower jaw or the upper end of the ulna. [Gr *korōnē* a crow, and *eidos* form, shape]

co-routine /*kō'roo-tēn*/ *n* a procedure in a computer program that can pass control to any other procedure, or suspend itself and continue later.

corozo /*ko-rō'sō*/ *n* (*pl* **corō'zos**) a S American short-stemmed palm (genus *Phytelephas*) whose seed (**corozo nut**) gives vegetable ivory; the cohune palm. [Sp, from a S American language]

corp. *abbrev*: corporal; corporation.

corpora see **corpus**.

corporal[1] /*kör'pə-rəl*/ *n* a non-commissioned officer ranking below a sergeant; in the navy, a petty officer under a master-at-arms; the leader of a gang of miners, etc. [Fr *caporal*, from Ital *caporale*, from *capo* the head, from L *caput* the head]
■ **cor'poralship** *n*.

corporal[2] /*kör'pə-rəl*/ *adj* belonging or relating to the body; having a body; material; not spiritual. ◆ *n* in Catholic and episcopal churches, the cloth on which the bread and wine of the Eucharist are laid out and with which the remains are covered (also **corporas** /*-ras*/; *obs*). [L *corpus*, *corporis* the body]
■ **corporality** /*-al'i-ti*/ *n*. **cor'porally** *adv*.
□ **corporal punishment** *n* punishment inflicted on the body, eg flogging.

corporate /*kör'p(ə-)rət*/ *adj* legally united into a body so as to act as an individual; belonging or relating to a corporation; united. ◆ *n* a corporate body. [L *corpus*, *corporis* the body]
■ **cor'porately** *adv*. **cor'porateness** *n*. **corpora'tion** *n* a succession or collection of people authorized by law to act as one individual and regarded as having a separate existence from the people who are its members; a town council; a company (*N Am*); a belly, *esp* a pot-belly (*inf*). **cor'poratism** or **cor'porativism** *n* (the policy of) control of a country's economy through the combined power of the trade unions, large businesses, etc. **cor'poratist** or **cor'porativist** *n* and *adj*. **cor'porative** *adj*. **cor'porator** *n* (*rare*) a member of a corporation.
□ **corporate advertising** *n* promotion of a company or group of companies as distinct from a particular product. **corporate bond** *n* a long-term fixed-interest bond offered by a corporation. **corporate governance** *n* the system by which a company is controlled and its management supervised. **corporate hospitality** *n* the entertainment by business companies of potential clients, *esp* by wining and dining them at prestigious sporting events. **corporate raider** *n* a company or individual who seeks to gain control of a business by acquiring a large proportion of its stock. **corporate state** *n* a system of government by corporations representing employers and employed, its purpose being to increase national production and obviate party politics. **corporate venturing** *n* the provision of venture capital by a company to another with the intention of obtaining inside information relating to the borrower or in order to gain control of that company at some future date. **corporation aggregate** *n* a corporation consisting of several persons. **corporation sole** *n* a corporation which consists of one person and his or her successors. **corporation tax** *n* a tax levied on the profits of companies.

corporeal /*kör-pö'ri-əl* or *-pö'-*/ *adj* having a body or substance; material; not spiritual. [L *corporeus* bodily, from *corpus* the body]
■ **corpö'realism** *n* materialism. **corpö'realist** *n*. **corpöreality** /*-al'i-ti*/ *n*. **corpö'realize** or **-ise** *vi* and *vt*. **corpö'really** *adv*.

corporeity /*kör-pə-rē'i-ti*/ *n* the fact or quality of having a body; corporeality. [L *corpus* the body]
■ **corporifica'tion** *n* the act of corporifying. **corpor'ify** *vt* to embody; to solidify.

corposant /*kör'pə-zant*/ *n* St Elmo's fire, an electrical discharge forming a glow about a masthead, etc. [Port *corpo santo*, from L *corpus sanctum* holy body]

corps /*kör* or *kōr*/ *n* (*pl* **corps** /*kōrz* or *körz*/) a division of an army forming a tactical unit; a branch or department of an army; an organized body; a set of people working more or less together. [Fr, from L *corpus* body]
□ **corps de ballet** /*kor də ba-le*/ *n* the company of ballet-dancers at a theatre. **corps d'élite** /*kor dā-lēt*/ *n* a small number of people picked out as being the best in any group. **corps diplomatique** /*dē-plō-ma-tēk*/ *n* the whole diplomatic staff at a particular capital.

corpse /*körps* or (*archaic*) *körs*/ *n* a dead, *usu* human body. ◆ *vi* (*theatre sl*) (of an actor on stage) to forget one's lines, etc, to be incapable of speaking one's lines because of a sudden attack of hysterical laughter. ◆ *vt* (*theatre sl*) to cause (an actor) to corpse. [ME *corps*, earlier *cors*, from OFr *cors*, from L *corpus* the body]
□ **corpse candle** *n* a light seen hovering over a grave, an omen of death. **corpse'-gate** *n* a lichgate.

cor pulmonale /*kör pül-mə-nä'lē*/ *n* enlargement and failure of the right ventricle of the heart as a result of lung disease. [L, lung-like heart]

corpus /*kör'pəs*/ *n* (*pl* **cor'pora** /*-pə-rə*/) any mass of body tissue that may be distinguished from its surroundings; a body of literature, writings, etc; a body of written and/or spoken language used as the basis for linguistic research; the main part of anything. [L *corpus* the body]
■ **cor'pulence** or **cor'pulency** *n* fleshiness of body; excessive fatness. **cor'pulent** *adj*. **cor'pulently** *adv*. **cor'puscle** /*-pus-l*/ (sometimes /*-pus'l*/) *n* a cell or other minute body suspended in fluid, *esp* a red or white cell in the blood; a minute particle (also **corpus'cule**). **corpus'cular** *adj*. **corpuscūlā'rian** *adj*. ◆ *n* a person who holds the corpuscular theory. **corpuscular'ity** *n*.
□ **corpus callosum** /*kə-los'əm*/ *n* (*pl* **corpora callosa**) (L *callosus* callous, hard-skinned) (in humans and higher mammals) a broad band of nerve fibre between the two cerebral hemispheres. **corpus cavernosum** /*ka-vər-nō'səm*/ *n* (*pl* **corpora cavernosa**) (L *cavernosus* cavernous, hollow) a section of erectile tissue in the penis or clitoris. **Corpus Christi** /*kris'tē* or *-tī*/ *n* the festival in honour of the Eucharist, held on the Thursday after the festival of the Trinity. **corpus delicti** /*di-lik'tī* or *de-lik'tē*/ *n* (*law*) the substance or fundamental facts of the crime or offence, eg in a murder trial, that somebody is actually dead and has been murdered. **corpus iuris** /*yoo'ris*/ *n* a body of law, eg of a country or jurisdiction. **corpus luteum** /*loo'ti-əm*/ *n* (*pl* **corpora lutea**) (L *luteus* yellow) a mass of yellow glandular tissue that develops in a Graafian follicle after the eruption of an ovum and secretes progesterone to prepare the uterus for implantation. **corpus spongiosum** /*spun-ji'ŏ'zəm*/ *n* (*pl* **corpora spongiosa**) (New L *spongiosus* spongy) the blood sinus which together with the corpus cavernosum forms the erectile tissue in the penis. **corpus striatum** /*strī-ā'təm*/ *n* (*pl* **corpora striata**) (L *striātus* furrowed) the section of the basal ganglia in the cerebral hemispheres of the brain that consists of the claudate and lentiform nuclei. **corpus vile** /*vī'lē* or *vē'lē* also *wē-*/ *n* (*pl* **corpora vilia**) (L *vilis* worthless) a person or thing considered so expendable as to be a fit object for experimentation, regardless of the consequences.
■ **corpuscular theory of light** Newton's theory that light consists of a stream of material particles, applied in quantum theory. **Corpus Juris Canonici** /*joo'ris ka-non'i-sī* or *ū'ris ka-non'i-kē*/ the body of the canon law. **Corpus Juris Civilis** /*si-vī'lis, kē-vē'* or *-wē'*/ the body of the civil law.

corr. *abbrev*: correspond; corrupted; corruption.

corrade /*ko-* or *kə-rād'*/ (*geol*) *vt* to wear away (land) through the action of loose solid material, eg pebbles in a stream or windborne sand. [L *corrādere* to scrape together, from *con-* together, and *rādere*, *rāsum* to scratch]
■ **corrasion** /*-rā'zhən*/ *n*.

corral /*ka-* or *ko-ral'*, also *-räl'*/ *n* a pen for cattle; an enclosure to drive hunted animals into; a defensive ring of wagons. ◆ *vt* (**corrall'ing**; **corralled'**) to pen; to form into a corral. [Sp]

correct /*kə-* or *ko-rekt'*/ *vt* to make right or supposedly right; to remove or mark faults or supposed faults from or in; to do this and evaluate; to set (a person) right; to punish; to counterbalance; to bring into a normal state; to reduce to a standard. ◆ *adj* right; according to standard; free from faults. [L *corrigere*, *corrēctum*, from *cor-*, intens, and *regere* to rule]
■ **correct'able** or **correct'ible** *adj*. **correc'tion** *n* emendation or would-be emendation; amendment; reduction; compensation; quantity to be added to bring to a standard or balance an error; bodily punishment; a period of reversal or counteraction during a strong market trend (*US finance*). **correc'tional** *adj*. **correc'tioner** *n* (*Shakesp*) a person who administers correction. **correct'itude** *n* correctness of conduct or behaviour. **correct'ive** *adj* of the nature of or by way of correction; tending to correct; correcting. ◆ *n* that which corrects; any agent or drug that modifies the action of another substance (also **corrigent**). **correct'ively** *adv*. **correct'ly** *adv*.

correct'ness *n.* **correct'or** *n* someone who or something that corrects; a director or governor; a proofreader. **correct'ory** *adj* corrective.

❏ **correction fluid** or **correcting fluid** *n* a white or coloured liquid used to cover an error in writing or typing and written or typed over when dry. **corrective training** *n* reformative imprisonment for persistent offenders of 21 and over for periods from 2 to 4 years.

■ **I stand corrected** I acknowledge my mistake. **under correction** subject to correction, often used as a formal expression of deference to a superior authority.

corregidor /ko-rehh'i-dōr/ *n* the chief magistrate of a Spanish town. [Sp, corrector]

correlate /kor'i-lāt/ *vi* to be related to one another. ♦ *vt* to bring into relation with each other; to establish relation or correspondence between. ♦ *n* either of two things so related that the one implies the other or is complementary to it; an analogue (*rare*). ♦ *adj* (*rare*) correlated. [L *cor-* with, and **relate**]

■ **correla'table** *adj*. **correla'tion** *n* the state or act of correlating; mutual relation, *esp* of phenomena regularly occurring together; interdependence, or the degree of it. **correla'tional** *adj*. **correlative** /-el'ə-tiv/ *adj* mutually linked; (of words) used as an interrelated pair, although not necessarily together, eg *either* and *or* (*grammar*). ♦ *n* a person or thing correspondingly related to another person or thing; a correlative word (*grammar*). **correl'atively** *adv*. **correl'ativeness** or **correlativ'ity** *n*.

❏ **correlation coefficient** *n* (*stats*) a dimensionless quantity between – 1 and 1 measuring the degree of linear association between two variables.

correligionist /kor-ə-lij'ə-nist/ same as **coreligionist**.

correption /kə-rep'shən/ (*obs*) *n* shortening in pronunciation; a reproof. [L *correptiō*, *-ōnis*, from *cor-*, intens, and *rapere* to seize]

corres. *abbrev* : corresponding.

correspond /ko-ri-spond'/ *vi* to answer, suit, agree (with *to* or *with*); to communicate, *esp* by letter. [L *cor-* with, and *respondēre* to answer]

■ **correspond'ence** or (*archaic*) **correspond'ency** *n* relation or agreement, part to part, or one to one; communication by letter; friendly communication (*archaic*); a body of letters; suitability; harmony. **correspond'ent** *adj* answering; agreeing; suitable. ♦ *n* a person with whom communication is kept up by letters; a person who contributes letters, or is employed to send special reports (eg *foreign correspondent*, *war correspondent*) to a newspaper, radio station, etc; a person or firm that regularly does business for another elsewhere. **correspond'ently** *adv*. **correspond'ing** *adj* similar, comparable, matching; suiting; carrying on correspondence by letters; correspondent; answering. **correspond'ingly** *adv*. **correspon'sive** *adj* corresponding; answering.

❏ **correspondence course**, **school**, etc *n* one conducted by postal correspondence. **correspondence principle** *n* (*phys*) the principle stating that the predictions of quantum and classical mechanics must correspond in the limit of very large quantum numbers. **corresponding member** *n* a member living at a distance who communicates with a society without taking part in its administration.

■ **doctrine of correspondences** the theory of Swedenborg that there is a spiritual antitype corresponding to every natural object and that Scripture contains the key to these correspondences.

corrida or **corrida de toros** /kō-rē'dhä (dā tō'rōs)/ (*Sp*) *n* a bullfight.

corridor /kor'i-dōr/ *n* a passageway or gallery communicating with separate rooms or dwellings in a building or compartments in a railway train; a strip of territory or airspace by which a country has access to a particular place, eg a port, or providing access through another's land for a particular purpose; (in *pl*) places outside the administrative centre where unofficial news circulates and gossip is carried on (*politics*). [Fr, from Ital *corridore*, from Ital *correre* to run, from L *currere*]

❏ **corr'idor-carriage** or **corr'idor-train** *n* a railway carriage or train in which one can pass along from one compartment to another. **corridor work** *n* (*inf*) discussion behind the scenes at a meeting.

■ **corridors of power** (*fig*) the higher reaches of government administration.

corrie /kor'i/ *n* a semicircular hollow on a hillside (*Scot*); (also **cirque** or **cwm**) a bowl-shaped recess on a mountainside formed by a glacier (*geol*). [Gaelic *coire* a cauldron]

corrie-fisted /ko'ri-fis-təd/ (*Scot*) *adj* left-handed. [From Gaelic *cearr* left(-handed)]

corrigendum /ko-ri-jen'dəm/ *n* (*pl* **corrigen'da**) something which requires correction; (in *pl*) corrections to be made in a book. [L, gerundive of *corrigere* to correct]

corrigent /kor'i-jənt/ *adj* corrective. ♦ *n* something with corrective properties or function, *esp* a drug to reduce or counteract undesirable effects of others in a formula. [L *corrigere* to correct; see **correct**]

■ **corrigibil'ity** *n*. **corr'igible** *adj* that may be corrected; open to correction.

corrival /ko- or kə-rī'vəl/ (*rare*) *n* a rival; a competitor; an equal. ♦ *adj* contending; emulous. ♦ *vt* (**corrī'valling**; **corrī'valled**) to rival. ♦ *vi* to vie. [L *con-* with, and **rival**]

■ **corrī'valry** *n*. **corrī'valship** *n*.

corroborate /kə-rob'ə-rāt/ *vt* to confirm; to make more certain. ♦ *adj* (*archaic*) confirmed. [L *cor-*, intens, and *rōborāre*, *-ātum* to make strong; see **robust**]

■ **corrob'orable** *adj*. **corrob'orant** *adj*. **corroborā'tion** *n* confirmation. **corrob'orative** *adj* tending to confirm. ♦ *n* that which corroborates. **corrob'orātor** *n*. **corrob'oratory** *adj* corroborative.

corroboree /kə-rob'ə-rē/ *n* a ceremonial dance of Australian Aborigines; a song for such a dance; a festive gathering. ♦ *vi* to hold a corroboree. [From an Aboriginal language]

corrode /kə-rōd'/ *vt* to eat away by degrees, *esp* chemically; to rust. ♦ *vi* to be eaten away. [L *cor-*, intens, and *rōdere*, *rōsum* to gnaw]

■ **corrōd'ent** *adj* having the power of corroding. ♦ *n* that which corrodes. **Corrodentia** /ko-rə-den'shyə/ *n pl* the Psocoptera, or booklice, etc. **corrōsibil'ity** *n*. **corrōs'ible** *adj* (also **corrōd'ible**). **corrosion** /-rō'zhən/ *n* the act or process of eating, wearing, or wasting away; a corroded part. **corrōs'ive** *adj* having the quality of eating away. ♦ *n* that which has the power of corroding. **corrōs'ively** *adv*. **corrōs'iveness** *n*.

❏ **corrosive sublimate** *n* mercuric chloride.

corrody or **corody** /kor'ō-di or -o-/ *n* an allowance; a pension; *orig* the right of the lord to claim free lodging from the vassal. [OFr *conrei*, *conroi*]

corrugate /kor'ə- or kor'ū-gāt/ *vt* to wrinkle or draw into folds. [L *cor-* (intensive) and *rūgāre*, *-ātum* to wrinkle, from *rūga* a wrinkle]

■ **corrugā'tion** *n* the act of wrinkling or state of being wrinkled; a wrinkle. **corr'ugator** *n* (*anat*) a muscle that creates wrinkles when contracted.

❏ **corrugated iron** *n* sheet iron bent by rollers into ridges for strength. **corrugated paper** *n* a multi-layered paper with the top layer ridged, used as wrapping material.

corrupt /kə-rupt'/ *vt* to taint, destroy the purity of; to pervert; to debase; to spoil; to bribe; to introduce errors into (a computer program or data). ♦ *vi* to rot, go bad; to lose purity, spoil. ♦ *adj* defiled; depraved; dishonest, venal; of the nature of, or involving, bribery; bribed; not genuine or pure; rotten, putrid; debased or made very faulty in transcription; (of a computer program or data in store) containing errors arising eg from a fault in the hardware or software. [L *cor-*, intens, and *rumpere*, *ruptum* to break]

■ **corrupt'er** or **corrupt'or** *n*. **corruptibil'ity** *n*. **corrupt'ible** *adj* liable to be corrupted. **corrupt'ibleness** *n*. **corrupt'ibly** *adv*. **corrup'tion** *n* the quality of being corrupt; a corrupt action; bribery; dishonesty; rottenness; impurity. **corrup'tionist** *n* a person who defends or who practises corruption. **corrupt'ive** *adj* having the quality of corrupting. **corrupt'ly** *adv*. **corrupt'ness** *n*.

■ **corruption of blood** the former inability of a disgraced or convicted person to inherit or transmit lands, titles or dignities.

corsac /kör'sak/ *n* an Asian fox, *Vulpes corsac*. [From Turk]

corsage /kör-säzh'/ *n* a small bouquet to be worn on the bodice or waist of a woman's dress or elsewhere; the bodice or waist of a woman's dress. [OFr, bodice from *cors*, from L *corpus* the body]

corsair /kör'sār/ (*hist*) *n* a privateer (*esp* of the Barbary coast); a privateering ship; a pirate. [Fr *corsaire* one who courses or ranges, from L *cursus* a running, from *currere* to run]

corse /körs/ *n* a poetic form of **corpse**.

corslet, **corselette** see **corslet**.

corset /kör'sit/ *n* a close-fitting stiff inner bodice; stays; a stiff belt coming down over the hips; the controls imposed by the Bank of England to restrict banks' capacity to lend money, eg by limiting the amount of new interest-bearing deposits a bank can accept (*inf*). ♦ *vt* to supply with a corset. [Dimin of OFr *cors*, from L *corpus* the body]

■ **corsetier** /kor-sə-tyā, also *-tēr'*/ or (*fem*) **corsetière** /kor-sə-tyer, also *-tēr'*/ *n* a maker or seller of corsets. **cor'setry** *n* corsets; the making or selling of corsets.

corsive /kör'siv/ (*obs*) *n* and *adj* same as **corrosive** (see under **corrode**).

corslet or **corselet** /kör'slit/ *n* a cuirass, a protective body-covering of leather, or steel, etc; (also **corselette'**) a modified corset, or combined belt and brassière. [Fr *corselet*, dimin of OFr *cors*, from L *corpus* the body]

■ **cors'leted** *adj*.

corsned /körs'ned/ (*hist*) *n* a piece of bread or cheese, swallowed in trial by ordeal and believed to prove guilt if it stuck in the throat.

[OE *corsnǣd*, from *gecor* (cf *coren*, pap of *cēosan* to choose) and *snǣd*, a piece, from *snīdan* to cut]

corso /kör'sō/ *n* (*pl* **cor'sos**) a race, run, course; a race of riderless horses; a procession of carriages; a street where these are held; an avenue, a wide street, a broad thoroughfare. [Ital]

Cortaderia /kör-tə-dē'ri-ə/ *n* a genus of tall-stemmed S American grasses with large thick panicles. [Am Sp *cortadera* a plant with sharp-edged leaves]

cortège /kör-tezh'/ *n* a train of attendants, a retinue; a procession, *esp* a funeral procession. [Fr, from Ital *corte* court]

Cortes /kor'tes/ *n* the parliament of Spain and of Portugal. [Sp and Port pl of *corte* a court]

cortex /kör'teks/ *n* (*pl* **cortices** /kör'ti-sēz/ or sometimes **cor'texes**) the bark or skin of a plant between the epidermis and the vascular bundles (*bot*); the outer layer of certain organs, *esp* of the brain (*cerebral cortex*) (*zool*). [L *cortex*, *corticis* bark]
■ **cor'tical** *adj* relating to the cortex; external. **cor'ticāte** or **cor'ticāted** *adj* provided with bark. **corticā'tion** *n*. **corti'colous** *adj* (*biol*) growing or living on the bark of trees, etc. **corticosteroid** /kör-tik-ō-stē'roid or ster'/ or **cor'ticoid** *n* any steroid hormone, eg cortisone, synthesized by the adrenal cortex; a group of drugs derived from or similar to naturally produced corticosteroid hormones. **corticosterone** /kör-ti-kos'tə-rōn/ *n* a glucocorticoid secreted by the adrenal cortex. **corticotrophin** /kör-tik-ō'trof-in/ *n* adrenocorticotrophin (ACTH).

cortile /kör-tē'lā/ *n* (*pl* **cortili** /-lē/) an enclosed, *usu* roofless, courtyard within a building. [Ital]

cortisol /kör'ti-sol/ *n* hydrocortisone. [*cortisone*, and L *ol(eum)* oil]

cortisone /kör'ti-zōn or -sōn/ *n* 'compound E', a naturally-occurring corticosteroid isolated from the adrenal cortex, or prepared from ox bile, etc, used as an anti-inflammatory agent and in the treatment of Addison's disease.

Corti's organ same as **organ of Corti** (see under **organ**).

corundum /kə-run'dəm/ *n* a mineral consisting of alumina, second in hardness only to the diamond (varieties include sapphire, ruby, emery). [Tamil *kurundam*]

coruscate /kor'ə-skāt/ *vi* to sparkle; to throw off flashes of light. [L *coruscāre*, *-ātum* to vibrate, glitter]
■ **coruscant** /-rus'/ *adj* flashing. **cor'uscating** *adj* flashing; sparkling (*esp fig*, of wit). **coruscā'tion** *n* a glittering; a sudden flash of light.

corvée /kör-vā'/ *n* the obligation to perform unpaid labour (such as the maintenance of roads) for the sovereign or feudal lord (*hist*); a fatigue duty or party (*milit*); extra duty (*fig*). [Fr, from LL *corrogāta*, from L *corrogāre*, from *cor-* together, and *rogāre* to ask]

corves see **corf**.

corvet same as **curvet**.

corvette /kör-vet'/ *n* an escort vessel specially designed for protecting convoys against submarine attack; formerly, a flush-decked vessel, with one tier of guns. [Fr, from Sp *corbeta*, from L *corbīta* a slow-sailing ship, from *corbis* a basket]

corvus /kör'vəs/ *n* (with *cap*) a southern constellation; a grappling-hook in ancient Roman naval warfare; a hooked ram for destroying walls. [L *corvus* a raven]
■ **cor'vid** *n* (*zool*) a member of the crow genus *Corvus*, of the family **Corvidae** /-vi-dē/ and subfamily **Corvinae** /-vī'nē/. **cor'vine** /-vīn/ *adj*.

cory or **corey** /kö'ri/ (*vulgar sl*) *n* the penis. [Romany *kori* thorn]

corybant /kor'i-bant/ *n* (*pl* **cor'ybants** or **corybant'es** /-tēz/) a priest of Cybele, whose rites were accompanied with noisy music and wild dances (*ancient Greece*); a reveller. [Gr *korybās*, *korybantos*]
■ **coryban'tic** *adj* wildly excited. **cor'ybantism** *n*.

corydalis /ko-rid'ə-lis/ *n* any perennial plant of the genus *Corydalis* of the Papaveraceae, of Europe and Asia, having fern-like foliage and tubular flowers. [Gr *korydallis* crested lark, from a supposed resemblance of the flower]
■ **cor'ydaline** (or /-rid'/) *n* an alkaloid ($C_{22}H_{27}O_4N$) obtained from the root of *Corydalis lutea*.

Corydon /kor'i-don or -dən/ (*poetic*) *n* a generic proper name for a rustic. [L, from Gr *Korydōn*, a shepherd's name in Theocritus and Virgil]

corylopsis /ko-ri-lop'sis/ *n* any deciduous flowering shrub or small tree of the genus *Corylopsis*, of China and Japan, typically having racemes of yellow flowers appearing before the leaves in spring. [New L, from **corylus** and Gr *opsis* appearance]

corylus /kor'i-ləs/ *n* a deciduous nut-bearing tree of the genus *Corylus* including *C. avellana*, the European hazel, and *C. maxima*, the filbert. [L]

corymb /kor'imb/ (*bot*) *n* a flattish-topped raceme. [L *corymbus*, from Gr *korymbos* a cluster]
■ **cor'ymbose** (or /-imb'/) *adj*.

Corynebacterium /kor-ə-nē-bak-tē'ri-əm/ *n* a genus of rodlike bacteria including *C. diphtheriae* that occurs in three forms and is the causative organism of diphtheria. [New L, from Gr *korynē* club, and **bacterium**]

Corypha /kor'i-fə/ *n* the talipot genus of gigantic tropical Asian palms. [Gr *koryphē* top]

coryphaeus /kor-i-fē'əs/ *n* (*pl* **coryphaei** /-fē'ī/) the chief or leader, *esp* the leader or speaker of a Greek chorus (also (*archaic*) **coryphe** /kor'if/). [L, from Gr *koryphaios*, from *koryphē* the head]
■ **coryphee** /kor-ē-fā'/ *n* (Fr *coryphée*) *orig* a male dancer (*n* is *masc* in Fr); now, one of a group between soloists and corps de ballet, a leading ballet-dancer (also **cor'yphe**).

coryphene /kor'i-fēn/ *n* a fish of the genus *Coryphaena*, called the dolphin or dorado. [Gr *koryphaina*]

coryza /ko-rī'zə/ *n* a cold in the head; nasal catarrh as a result of a cold in the head or hay fever. [L, from Gr *koryza*]

CoS *abbrev*: Chief of Staff.

cos¹ /kos/ *n* a crisp, long-leaved lettuce (also **cos lettuce**). [Introduced from the Aegean island of Cos (Gr *Kōs*)]

cos² see **cosine**.

'cos /koz or kəz/ (*inf*) *adv* and *conj* because.

Cosa Nostra /kō'zə nos'trə/ *n* the Mafia organization, *esp* in the USA. [Ital, our thing]

coscinomancy /kos'i-nō-man-si/ *n* an ancient mode of divination by a sieve and pair of shears. [Gr *koskinon* a sieve, and *manteiā* divination]

cosecant /kō-sek'ənt or -sē'kənt/ *n* one of the six trigonometrical functions of an angle, the reciprocal of the sine (*abbrev* **cosec** /kō'sek/).

cosech /kō-sek'/ *abbrev*: hyperbolic *cosec*ant (see **hyperbolic functions** under **hyper-**).

coseismal /kō-sīz'məl/ *adj* experiencing an earthquake shock simultaneously (also **coseis'mic**). [L *co-* together, and Gr *seismos* earthquake]

cosentient /kō-sen'sh(i-)ənt/ *adj* perceiving or aware at the same time.

coset /kō'set/ (*maths*) *n* a set which when added to another set results in a larger set.

cosh /kosh or kos'äch/ *abbrev*: hyperbolic *cosine* (see **hyperbolic functions** under **hyper-**).

cosh¹ /kosh/ (*sl*) *n* a bludgeon, truncheon, lead-pipe, piece of flexible tubing filled with metal, or the like, used as a weapon (also *vt*). [Prob Romany, from *koshter* a stick]
❏ **cosh boy** a thug, a mugger.

cosh² /kosh/ (*Scot*) *adj* cosy, snug. [Orig unknown]

cosher¹ /kosh'ər/ (*dialect*) *vt* to pamper, to coddle. ◆ *vi* to chat in a friendly way.

cosher² same as **kosher**.

coshery /kosh'ə-ri/ *n* the ancient right of an Irish chief to quarter himself and his retainers on his tenantry (also **cosh'ering**). [Ir *coisir* a feast]
■ **cosh'er** *vi* to live on dependants. **cosh'erer** *n*.

COSHH *abbrev*: Control of Substances Hazardous to Health.

cosier see **cozier**.

così fan tutte /kō-sē' fan too'tā/ (*Ital*) that is what all women do; all women are like that.

cosignatory /kō-sig'nə-tə-ri/ *adj* uniting with others in signing. ◆ *n* a person who does so.
■ **cosignif'icative** *adj* (*rare*) having the same signification.

cosine /kō'sīn/ *n* one of the six trigonometrical functions of an angle, the ratio in a right-angled triangle of the adjacent side to the hypotenuse (*abbrev* **cos** /kos/).

COSLA /koz'lə/ *abbrev*: Convention of Scottish Local Authorities.

cosmea /koz'mi-ə/ *n* a plant of the genus *Cosmos*.

cosmeceutical /koz-mə-sū'ti-kəl or -soo-/ *n* (in *pl*) products which overlap the cosmetics and drugs industries. [*cosmetics* and *pharmaceutical*]

cosmetic /koz-met'ik/ *adj* purporting to improve beauty, *esp* that of the complexion; correcting defects of the face, etc, or making good particular deficiencies (eg *cosmetic surgery*); involving or producing an apparent or superficial concession, improvement, etc without any real substance to it. ◆ *n* (*usu* in *pl*) a preparation for the improvement of beauty, etc. [Gr *kosmētikos*, from *kosmeein* to adorn, from *kosmos* order]
■ **cosmē'sis** *n* cosmetic surgery or treatment. **cosmet'ical** *adj*. **cosmet'ically** *adv*. **cosmetic'ian** *n* a person who produces,

sells, or is skilled in the use of, cosmetics (sometimes *fig*). **cosmet'icism** *n*. **cosmet'icize** or **-ise** *vt* to give cosmetic treatment to. **cosmetol'ogist** *n*. **cosmetol'ogy** *n* the art or profession of applying cosmetics or hairdressing, or of carrying out plastic surgery. ❑ **cosmetic surgery** *n* a surgical operation carried out to improve a patient's appearance rather than to cure disease or improve function.

cosmic, etc see under **cosmos¹**.

cosmism /*koz'mi-zm*/ *n* the notion of the cosmos as a self-existing whole. [Gr *kosmos* universe, world]
■ **cos'mist** *n* a secularist.

cosmochemistry /*koz-mə-kem'i-stri*/ *n* the study of the chemical composition of stars, planets, etc.
■ **cosmochem'ical** *adj*.

cosmocrat /*koz'mə-krat*/ *n* (*rare*) a ruler of the world. [**cosmos¹** and **-crat**]
■ **cosmocrat'ic** *adj*.

cosmodrome /*koz'mə-drōm*/ *n* a launching-site for spacecraft, *esp* in the former Soviet Union. [Russ *kosmodrom*]

cosmogony /*koz-mog'ə-ni*/ *n* a theory or myth of the origin of the universe, *esp* of the stars, nebulae, etc (also **cosmogeny** /*-moj'*/). [Gr *kosmogonia*, from *kosmos* order, the universe, and root of *gignesthai* to be born]
■ **cosmogon'ic** or **cosmogon'ical** *adj* relating to cosmogony. **cosmog'onist** *n* a person who speculates on the origin of the universe.

cosmography /*koz-mog'rə-fi*/ *n* the science of the constitution of the universe; a description of the world or universe. [Gr *kosmographia*, from *kosmos* the universe, and *graphein* to write]
■ **cosmog'rapher** *n*. **cosmograph'ic** or **cosmograph'ical** *adj*.

cosmolatry /*koz-mol'ə-tri*/ (*rare*) *n* the worship of the world. [Gr *kosmos* world, and *latreiā* worship]

cosmology /*koz-mol'ə-ji*/ *n* the science of the universe as a whole; a treatise on the structure and parts of the system of creation. [Gr *kosmos* order, the universe, and *logos* discourse]
■ **cosmological** /*-loj'*/ *adj*. **cosmol'ogist** *n*.
❑ **cosmological argument** *n* (*philos*) one of the arguments purporting to prove the existence of God, claiming that everything in nature is contingent, and that there therefore exists a first cause, God. **cosmological constant** *n* a constant introduced by Einstein into his General Relativity equations to produce a solution in which the universe would be static, abandoned by him when the universe was later shown to be expanding, but still retained in various theoretical cosmological models with a value close to or equal to zero. **cosmological principle** *n* according to the cosmology of general relativity, the principle that, at a given time, the universe would look the same to observers in other nebulae as it looks to us.

cosmonaut /*koz'mə-nöt*/ *n* an astronaut, *specif* a Russian astronaut. [Russ *kosmonaut*, from Gr *kosmos* the universe, and *nautēs* a sailor]
■ **cosmonau'tics** *n sing*.

cosmoplastic /*koz-mə-plas'tik* or *-plä'stik*/ *adj* moulding or forming the universe; world-forming. [Gr *kosmos* the universe, world, and *plassein* to form]

cosmopolis /*koz-mop'ə-lis*/ *n* an international city. [Gr *kosmos* world, and *polis* city]

cosmopolitan /*koz-mə-pol'i-tən*/ *n* a citizen of the world; someone free from local or national prejudices; a communist sympathetic towards or tolerant of non-communism in other countries; (with *cap*) a cocktail containing vodka, an orange liqueur, lime juice and cranberry juice. ◆ *adj* belonging to, representative of, etc, all parts of the world; unprejudiced; sophisticated, worldly. [Gr *kosmopolitēs*, from *kosmos* the world, and *politēs* a citizen, from *polis* a city]
■ **cosmopol'itanism** *n*. **cosmopolite** /*koz-mop'ə-līt*/ *n* and *adj* (a) cosmopolitan. **cosmopol'itic** or **cosmopolit'ical** *adj*. **cosmopol'itics** *n sing* world politics. **cosmop'olitism** (or /*-pol'*/) *n*.

cosmorama /*koz-mə-rä'mə*/ *n* a view, or a series of views, of different parts of the world, using mirrors, lenses, etc. [Gr *kosmos* world, and *horāma* a spectacle]
■ **cosmoramic** /*-ram'*/ *adj*.

cosmos¹ /*koz'mos*/ *n* the world or universe as an orderly or systematic whole, *opp* to *chaos*; a complex or orderly system. [Gr *kosmos* order, world, universe]
■ **cos'mic** *adj* relating to the cosmos; universal; orderly; large or significant (*inf*). **cos'mical** *adj* cosmic; happening at sunrise (*astron*); rising with the sun (*astron*). **cos'mically** *adv*. **cosmogenic** /*-jen'ik*/ *adj* of an isotope, capable of being produced by the interaction of cosmic rays with the atmosphere or the surface of the Earth. **cosmothet'ic** or **cosmothet'ical** *adj* assuming an external world.

❑ **cosmic abundance** *n* the relative proportion of each atomic element found in the universe. **cosmic background radiation** see **microwave background** under **microwave**. **cosmic constant** same as **cosmological constant** (see under **cosmology**). **cosmic dust** *n* fine particles occurring in interstellar space. **cosmic radiation** *n* radiation consisting of cosmic rays. **cosmic rays** *n pl* highly penetrating rays from interstellar space, consisting of protons, electrons, positrons, etc. **cosmic string** *n* (*astron*) any of the massive hypothetical filaments of matter predicted to be an important component of the very early universe (see also **string theory** under **string**).

cosmos² /*koz'mos*/ *n* any composite flowering plant of the American genus *Cosmos*, related to the dahlia. [Gr *kosmos* ornament]

cosmosphere /*koz'mə-sfēr*/ *n* an apparatus for showing the position of the earth at any given time with reference to the fixed stars.

cosmotheism /*koz-mō-thē'i-zm*/ *n* the belief that identifies God with the cosmos; pantheism. [Gr *kosmos* world and **theism**]

cosmotron see **accelerator** under **accelerate**.

cosphered /*kō-sfērd'*/ (*archaic*) *adj* being in the same sphere.

cosplay /*kos'plā* or *koz'*/ (*inf*) *n* the practice of dressing as a fictional character to attend social events. [*costume play*]

cosponsor /*kō-spon'sər*/ *vt* to sponsor jointly. ◆ *n* a joint sponsor.

coss /*kos*/ *n* a measure of distance in India, averaging about $1\frac{3}{4}$ miles. [Hindi *kōs*, from Sans *krosà* a call]

Cossack /*kos'ak*/ *n* a member of a free peasant people in SE Russia, formerly holding by military tenure and serving as cavalry under the tsar. ◆ *adj* of, or characteristic of, the Cossacks. [Turk *quzzāq* adventurer, guerilla]
❑ **Cossack boots** *n pl* Russian boots. **Cossack hat** *n* a brimless hat of fur or similar material. **Cossack post** *n* a small group of mounted troops on outpost duty.

cosset /*kos'it*/ *n* a hand-reared lamb; a pet. ◆ *vt* to fondle; to pamper. [Perh OE *cot-sǣta*, *cot-setla* cot-dweller]

cossie /*koz'i*/ (*inf*) *n* a swimming costume.

cost¹ /*kost*/ *vt* (*pat* and *pap* **cost'ed**) or *vi* (*pat* and *pap* **cost**) to be obtainable at a price of; to involve an expenditure of; to require to be outlaid or suffered or lost. ◆ *vt* to estimate the cost of production of. ◆ *n* what is or would have to be outlaid, suffered or lost to obtain anything; (in *pl*) the expenses of a lawsuit. [OFr *couster* (Fr *coûter*), from L *cōnstāre* to stand at]
■ **costing** *n* an estimation of the cost of something. **cost'liness** *n*. **cost'ly** *adj* bought or sold at a high price; valuable.
❑ **cost'-account** *vt*. **cost'-accountant** *n* a person who analyses and classifies elements of cost, eg material, labour, etc, or who devises systems of doing this. **cost'-accounting** *n*. **cost centre** *n* a department, process or piece of equipment for which costs can be worked out as part of the costing process in business. **cost-effec'tive** or **cost-effi'cient** *adj* giving adequate return for outlay. **cost-effec'tiveness** or **cost efficiency** *n*. **cost-free'** *adj* free of charge (also *adv*). **cost plus** *n* a work contract where payment is based on the actual production cost plus an agreed percentage of that cost as profit. **cost-plus'** *adj*. **cost price** *n* the price the dealer pays for goods bought. **cost push** *n* (*econ*) inflation due to rising production costs (also **cost-push inflation**).
■ **at all costs** or **at any cost** no matter what the cost or consequences may be (also *old*) **cost what may**). **cost-benefit analysis** (or **assessment**) the comparison of the cost of a particular course of action with the benefits (to be) derived from it. **cost of living** the total cost of goods ordinarily required in order to live up to one's usual standard. **cost of living index** an official number showing the cost of living at a certain date compared with that at another date taken as a standard. **cost someone dear** (or **dearly**) to prove very costly or detrimental to someone. **count the cost** to assess the risks of an action before attempting it; to comprehend fully the unfortunate consequences of an action. **prime cost** the price of production, without regard to profit or overhead expenses. **to one's cost** with some loss or disadvantage.

cost² or **coste** /*kost*/ *n* a Spenserian form of **coast**. ◆ *vt* and *vi* (*Shakesp, Spenser*) to approach. [**coast**]

costa /*kos'tə*/ *n* (*pl* **cos'tae** /*-ē*/) a rib; a rib-like structure, vein, ridge; the fore-edge of an insect's wing; the nervure next to it. [L *costa* a rib]
■ **cos'tal** *adj* of or near the ribs, the costa, or the side of the body. ◆ *n* the costal nervure. **costalgia** /*-al'ji-ə*/ *n* pain around the chest due to damage to a rib or a nerve running beneath the ribs. **cos'tāte** or **costā'ted** *adj* having or resembling ribs.

co-star /*kō'stär*/ *n* a cinema, etc star appearing with other stars. ◆ *vi* (**co'-starring; co'-starred**) (with *with*) to appear with other stars. ◆ *vt* (of a production) to feature as fellow stars.

costard /kos'tərd/ n a large variety of cooking apple; the human head (archaic sl). [Perh L costa a rib]
  ❏ **cos'tardmonger** /kos'tər-mung-gər/ same as **costermonger**.

Costa Rican /kos-tə rē'kən/ adj of or relating to the Republic of Costa Rica in Central America, or its inhabitants. ◆ n a native or citizen of Costa Rica.

costate, costated see under **costa**.

coste see **cost²**.

costean /ko-stēn'/ vi to dig down to bedrock in prospecting. [Said to be from Cornish cothas dropped, and stean tin]
  ■ **costean'ing** n.
  ❏ **costean'-pit** n.

costermonger /kos'tər-mung-gər/ or **coster** /kos'tər/ n a seller of fruit and other wares from a barrow. [Orig costardmonger, from **costard** and **monger**]

costive /kos'tiv/ adj constipated; stingy. [Fr constipé; see **constipate**]
  ■ **cos'tively** adv. **cos'tiveness** n.

costmary /kost'mār-i/ n a composite plant of S Europe (Chrysanthemum balsamita), grown for its fragrant leaves and used as a seasoning and to flavour ale. [L costum, from Gr kostos costus, and Maria the Virgin Mary]

costrel /kos'trəl/ (obs or dialect) n an eared bottle or small flask, to be hung at the waist. [OFr costerel]

costume /kos'tūm or (N Am) -toom/ n a manner of dressing; dress, clothing; a woman's outer dress as a unit; fancy dress; (a piece of) clothing for a particular purpose, as in swimming-costume. ◆ vt /kos-tūm' or (N Am) -toom'/ to dress. [Fr, from Ital costume, from L cōnsuētūdō, -inis custom]
  ■ **costumed'** adj. **costum'er** or **costum'ier** n a person who makes or deals in costumes.
  ❏ **costume drama, piece** or **play** n one in which the actors wear the costumes of an earlier era. **costume jewellery** n decorative jewellery made of paste and base metals rather than precious stones and gold or silver.

costus /kos'təs/ n an aromatic root wrongly assigned to the genus Costus, really a composite of Kashmir, Saussurea hypoleuca (also **cos'tus arab'icus** or **cos'tus-root**). [Latinized from Gr kostos]

cosy or (N Am) **cozy** /kō'zi/ (orig Scot) adj snug; comfortable; intimate. ◆ n a covering used for a teapot, to keep the tea warm (also **tea'-cosy**); a similar covering for a boiled egg. ◆ vt (inf) to comfort or make comfortable. [Ety unknown]
  ■ **cō'sily** adv. **cō'siness** n.
  ■ **cosy along** (inf) to reassure, often with falsehoods. **cosy up** (inf, esp US; with to or with) to try to gain someone's favour or friendship; to snuggle up.

Cot see **Malbec**.

cot¹, also **cott** /kot/ n a small bed, esp one with high sides for a young child; a swinging bed of canvas (for officers, the sick, etc) (naut); a camp-bed (N Am); a hospital bed; a light bedstead; a portable bed. [Anglo-Ind, from Hindi khāt]
  ❏ **cot case** n a person who is drunk and incapable (esp Aust); a person who is too ill to get out of bed (chiefly NZ). **cot death** n the sudden, unexplained death, often happening at night, of an apparently healthy baby (also called **sudden infant death syndrome**).

cot² /kot/ (archaic and poetic) n a small dwelling, a cottage. [OE cot; cf ON and Du kot]
  ■ **cott'ed** adj lined with cots.
  ❏ **cot'-folk** n pl (Scot) cottars. **cot'-house** n (Scot) a house occupied by a cottar. **cot'land** n land belonging to a cottage. **cot'quean** n (obs) a scolding woman; a man who busies himself with women's affairs such as housework. **cot'town** n (Scot) a group of cot-houses.

cot³ (Spenser **cott**) /kot/ n a small boat. [Ir]

cot⁴ see **cotangent**.

cot⁵ see **cote¹**.

cotangent /kō-tan'jənt/ n one of the six trigonometrical functions of an angle, the reciprocal of the tangent (abbrev **cot** /kot/).

cote¹ /kōt/ or **cot** /kot/ n a place of shelter for animals (as in dovecote or dovecot, sheep-cote). [OE cote; cf **cot²**]

cote² /kōt/ (archaic) vt to pass by; to outstrip (as one dog another). [Poss connected with **coast**]

cote³ a Shakespearean form of **quote**.

coteau /kot'ō/ (N Am) n (pl **cot'eaux** /-tō or -tōz/) a hilly upland area, rising ground; an upland or ridge between two valleys (esp Can). [Fr, a sloping hillside, from OFr costel, dimin of coste slope]

cote-hardie /kōt'här'di/ n a medieval close-fitting tight-sleeved body garment. [OFr]

côtelette /kōt-let'/ (Fr) n a cutlet, a chop.
  ❏ **côtelette de filet** n a loin chop.

coteline /kot-lēn'/ n a kind of muslin, corded or ribbed. [Fr côte a rib, from L costa]

cotemporaneous, etc /kō-/ same as **contemporaneous**, etc.

cotenant /kō-ten'ənt/ n a joint tenant.
  ■ **coten'ancy** n.

coterie /kō'tə-ri/ n a social, literary, or other exclusive circle. [Fr; orig a number of peasants holding land jointly from a lord, from LL cota a cot]

coterminous, etc see **conterminous**.

coth /koth/ abbrev : hyperbolic cotangent (see **hyperbolic functions** under **hyper-**).

cothurnus /kō-thûr'nəs/ or **cothurn** /kō'thûrn or -thûrn'/ n (pl **cothur'nī** or **cothurns**) the buskin worn in ancient Greek tragedy. [Latinized from Gr kothornos]

coticular /kō-tik'ū-lər/ (obs) adj relating to whetstones. [L cōticula, dimin of cos, cotis whetstone]

cotidal /kō-tī'dəl/ adj having high tide occurring at the same time.

cotillion /ko-til'yən/ or **cotillon** /ko-tē'yŏ/ n a type of lively dance with varied steps; a formal (esp a coming-out) ball (N Am). [Fr cotillon petticoat, from cotte a coat, from LL cotta a tunic; see **coat**]

cotinga /kō-ting'gə/ n any brightly-plumaged passerine bird of the tropical American genus Cotinga, or the family **Cotingidae** /-tin'ji-dē/. [Of Tupí origin]

cotinine /kot'ə-nēn/ n a nicotine metabolite, an indicator of nicotine intake. [Poss from **nicotine** and **-ine²**]

cotise or **cottise** /kot'is/ (heraldry) n an ordinary, one quarter of a bend in breadth. ◆ vt to border with cotises, barrulets, etc. [Fr cotice; origin obscure]

cotoneaster /kō- or ko-tō-ni-as'tər/ n any shrub or small tree of the genus Cotoneaster, related to hawthorn. [L cotōnea quince]

co-trimoxazole /kō-trī-mok'sə-zōl/ (med) n an antibiotic, a mixture of trimethoprim and sulphamethoxazole, used to treat urinary tract infections and pneumocystis carinii pneumonia.

Cotswold /kots'wōld or -wəld/ n a breed of sheep. [Cotswold Hills, SW England]

cott see **cot¹,³**.

cotta /kot'ə/ n a short surplice. [LL cotta]

cottabus /kot'ə-bəs/ n in ancient Greece, an amusement among young men, involving throwing wine into a vessel, success at which supposedly indicated fortune in love. [L, from Gr kottabos]

cottage /kot'ij/ n a small dwelling-house; a country residence; a summer residence (N Am); a one-storey house, a bungalow (Aust); a public lavatory used by homosexuals for soliciting (sl). [LL cottagium, from OE cot; see **cot²**]
  ■ **cott'aged** adj covered with cottages. **cott'ager** n a person who lives in a cottage, esp a rural labourer; a person holidaying in a cottage (US). **cott'agey** adj cottage-like. **cott'aging** n (sl) soliciting by male homosexuals in public lavatories.
  ❏ **cottage cheese** n soft white loose cheese made from skim-milk curds. **cottage hospital** n a small, rural hospital without resident doctors. **cottage industry** n one in which the work is done wholly or largely by people in their own homes, esp one on a relatively small scale. **cottage loaf** n a loaf shaped as a smaller lump on the top of a bigger one. **cottage orné** n (Fr /ko-täzh or-nā/) an ornately-designed small country house built in rustic style. **cottage piano** n a small upright piano. **cottage pie** n shepherd's pie, esp when made with beef.

cottar or **cotter** /kot'ər/ n one of a class of medieval villeins; a peasant occupying a cot or cottage for which he has to give labour (Scot). [cot²]

cotter /kot'ər/ n a pin or wedge for fastening and tightening. [Origin obscure]
  ❏ **cott'er-pin** n a pin for keeping a cotter in place.

cottid, cottoid see **cottus**.

cottier /kot'i-ər/ n a cottar; an Irish tenant holding land as the highest bidder. [Fr cotier; see **cot²**]
  ■ **cott'ierism** n the cottier system of land tenure.

cottise see **cotise**.

cotton /kot'n/ n a soft substance like fine wool, the long hairs covering the seeds of the cotton plant; the plant itself, individually or collectively; yarn or cloth made of cotton; cotton wool (N Am). ◆ adj made of cotton. ◆ vi to agree, to become friendly or attached. [Fr coton, from Ar qutun]
  ■ **cottonade'** n an inferior cotton cloth. **cottonoc'racy** n the cotton planting or cotton manufacturing interests. **cott'ony** adj like cotton; soft; downy.

  ■ words derived from main entry word; ❏ compound words; ■ idioms and phrasal verbs

cotton belt *n* (sometimes with *caps*) the region in SE USA in which much cotton is produced. **cotton boll** *n* the pod of the cotton plant. **cotton bud** *n* a small stick with a piece of cotton wool on the end(s), used for cleaning small body orifices, etc. **cotton bush** *n* (*Aust*) any of various downy-leaved shrubs used to feed cattle, etc. **cotton cake** *n* cakes or pellets of compressed cottonseed, used as an animal feed. **cotton candy** *n* (*N Am*) candyfloss. **cotton gin** *n* a machine for separating the seeds from the fibre of cotton. **cotton grass** *n* a genus (*Eriophorum*) of sedges with long, silky or cottony hairs about the ripened ovary. **cotton mill** *n* a factory where cotton is spun or woven. **cott'onmouth** *n* the venomous water mocassin snake (from the white inside of its mouth). **cott'on-picking** *adj* (*US sl*; sometimes *facetious*) used as a relatively mild intensifier. **cotton plant** *n* one of various species of *Gossypium* (family Malvaceae), yielding cotton. **cotton press** *n* a press for compressing cotton into bales. **cotton sedge** *n* (*Can*) cotton grass. **cott'onseed** *n* the seed of the cotton plant, yielding a valuable oil. **cotton spinner** *n* a person who spins cotton, or employs those who do. **cotton stainer** *n* any of a genus (*Dysdercus*) of small red hemipterous insects that puncture cotton bolls and stain the fibres. **cott'ontail** *n* any of several species of rabbits of the genus *Sylvilagus*, the ordinary rabbit of the USA. **cotton thistle** *n* a strong thistle (*Onopordum acanthium*) covered with a cottony down. **cotton tree** *n* the American cottonwood; an Indian tree *Bombax malabaricum*; an Australian hibiscus. **cotton waste** *n* refuse from cotton mills, used for cleaning machinery, etc. **cott'onweed** *n* cudweed, a cottony seaside composite plant (*Diotis maritima*). **cott'onwood** *n* any one of several American species of poplar. **cotton wool** *n* cotton in its raw or woolly state; loose cotton pressed in a sheet as an absorbent or protective agent, for stuffing, etc; a protected, cushioned or cosseted state; padding, waffle. **cott'onworm** *n* the caterpillar of an owlet moth (*Aletia xylina*), destructive to American cotton crops. **cottony-cushion scale** *n* a small scale insect (*Icerya purchasi*), a serious pest of citrus trees. ■ **cotton on** (*sl*) (sometimes with *to*) to catch on, understand. **cotton on to** (*sl*) to take to.

cottus /kot'əs/ or **cottid** /kot'id/ *n* any fish of the genus *Cottus* or family **Cottidae** /-i-dē/ including the bullhead and father-lasher. [Gr *kottos* a fish, perh the bullhead] ■ **cott'oid** *adj*.

cotwal see **kotwal**.

cotyle /kot'i-lē/ *n* (*pl* **cot'ylae** /-lē/ or **cot'ylēs**) an ancient Greek drinking cup; a cup-like cavity (*zool*). [Gr *kotylē*] ■ **cotyl'iform** *adj* (*bot*) disc-shaped with raised rim. **cot'yloid** *adj* cup-shaped.

cotyledon /ko-ti-lē'dən/ *n* a seed leaf (*bot*); a convex subdivision of the mature placenta, each division containing a major blood vessel (*zool*); a plant of the S African genus *Cotyledon*. [Gr *kotylēdōn*, from *kotylē* a cup] ■ **cotylē'donary** *adj*. **cotylē'donous** *adj* relating to or having cotyledons.

coucal /koo'käl or -kəl/ *n* any member of a genus (*Centropus*) of common ground-dwelling birds in Africa, India and Australia, the lark-heeled cuckoos. [Imit]

couch[1] /kowch/ *n* a kind of sofa with half back and one raised end; any sofa; any place for rest or sleep; a bed, *esp* for daytime use, eg one on which a doctor's or psychiatrist's patient lies for examination; the lair of a wild beast (*poetic*). ◆ *vt* to express (ideas, etc) in language of a particular kind; to lay down; to lower, place in a horizontal position; to depress or remove (a cataract in the eye) (*surg*). ◆ *vi* to lie down for the purpose of sleep, concealment, etc. [Fr *coucher* to lay down, from L *collocāre* to place, from *col-* together, and *locus* a place] ■ **couch'ant** *adj* (*heraldry*) lying down with head up. **couch'ing** *n* embroidery in which the surface is covered with threads and these are secured by stitches forming a pattern. ❑ **couch potato** *n* (*sl*) a person whose leisure time is spent sitting shiftlessly in front of the television or video. **couch'surfing** *n* (*inf*) the practice of spending the night at friends' houses when one is homeless. ■ **couch a spear** to fix it in its rest at the side of the armour.

couch[2] or **couch grass** /kowch' or kooch' (gräs)/ *n* a grass related to wheat, a troublesome weed owing to its creeping rootstocks. [A variant of **quitch**[1]]

couchee /koo-shā'/ *n* an evening reception (also (formerly) **couchée** or **couché**). [Fr *couché* a reception before going to bed; see **couch**[1]]

couchette /koo-shet'/ *n* a sleeping-berth on a continental train or a cross-channel boat, convertible from and into ordinary seating. [Fr]

cou-cou /koo'koo/ *n* a West Indian dish of boiled corn meal with okra. [Origin uncertain]

coudé /koo-dā'/ (*astron*) *adj* (of a reflecting telescope) in which one or more plane mirrors reflect the light down the polar axis. [Fr, bent like an elbow]

Couéism /koo'ā-i-zm/ *n* psychotherapy by auto-suggestion. [Emile Coué (1857–1926), its expounder] ■ **Cou'éist** *n*.

cougar /koo'gər/ or **couguar** /-gwär/ *n* a puma; (*chiefly US sl*) a woman who chooses a male lover significantly younger than herself. [Fr *couguar*, from Port *cucuarana*, adapted from a Tupí-Guaraní name]

cough /kof/ *vi* to expel air with a sudden opening of the glottis and a characteristic harsh sound; to confess to a crime or give information (*sl*). ◆ *vt* to expel by coughing. ◆ *n* the act or the sound of coughing; an ailment of which coughing is a symptom; (with *the*) equine flu. [ME *coughen*; cf Du *kuchen*, Ger *keuchen*, *keichen* to gasp] ■ **cough'er** *n*. **cough'ing** *n*. ❑ **cough drop** *n* a cough lozenge; a person of spicy character. **cough lozenge** *n* a medicated lozenge to relieve a cough. **cough mixture** *n* a liquid medicine to relieve a cough. ■ **cough down** to silence (a speaker) by coughing. **cough up** (*sl*) to pay out, hand over, under compulsion.

could /kŏod/ *pat* of **can**[1]. [ME *coude*, *couth*, from OE *cūthe* for *cunthe* was able; *l* is inserted from the influence of *would* and *should*] ■ **could be** (*inf*) perhaps, maybe.

couldn't contraction of **could not**.

coulée /koo-lā'/ *n* a lava-flow; a rocky ravine (*N Am*). [Fr *couler* to flow]

couleur de rose /koo-lœr də rōz'/ (*Fr*) *adj* rose-coloured; seen or presented in a way that exaggerates attractiveness. ◆ *n* false attractiveness.

coulibiac /koo-li-byäk' or -byak'/ or **koulibiaca** /-byä'kə or -byak'a/ *n* a Russian pie of flaked fish mixed with semolina. [Russ]

coulis /koo-lē'/ (*Fr*) *n* a thin purée of fish, fowl, fruit or vegetables.

coulisse /koo-lēs'/ *n* a piece of grooved wood, eg the slides in which the side-scenes of a theatre run; hence (in *pl*) the wings (*theatre*); (sometimes with *cap*) the part of the Paris Bourse where unofficial securities are traded. [Fr *couler* to glide, to flow, from L *cōlāre* to strain]

couloir /kool-wär'/ *n* a gully, *esp* an Alpine gully. [Fr, passage]

coulomb /koo-lom' or -lōm'/ *n* a derived SI unit, the unit of electric charge (static or as a current) (symbol **C**), equal to the charge which is transported when a current of one ampere flows for one second. [CA de *Coulomb* (1736–1806), French physicist] ■ **coulom'eter** *n* a voltameter (also **coulomb'meter**). **coulomet'ric** *adj*. **coulom'etry** *n* (chemical analysis by) the measuring of the number of coulombs used in electrolysis.

Coulommiers /koo-lom-yā'/ *n* a white, soft cheese, fresh or cured, made near *Coulommiers* in central France.

coulter or (*esp N Am*) **colter** /kōl'tər or (*Scot*) koo'tər/ *n* the iron cutter in front of a ploughshare. [OE *culter*, from L *culter* knife]

coumarin or **cumarin** /koo'mə-rin/ *n* a crystalline compound ($C_9H_6O_2$) obtained from Tonka beans, woodruff, melilot, etc, used medicinally to prevent coagulation of the blood. [Tupí *cumarú* Tonka bean] ■ **coumaric** /-mar'-/ or **coumaril'ic** *adj*.

coumarone /koo'mə-rōn/ *n* a colourless liquid, C_8H_6O, derived from coal tar and used in the production of synthetic resins. [**coumarin** and **-one**]

council /kown'sl or -sil/ *n* an assembly called together for deliberation, advice, administration or legislation; the people making up such an assembly; the body directing the affairs of a town, county, parish, etc; an assembly of clergy to regulate doctrine or discipline; a governing body in a university; a committee that arranges the business of a society. ◆ *adj* of, relating to or provided by a council. [Fr *concile*, from L *concilium*] ■ **coun'cillor** or (*N Am*) **coun'cilor** *n* a member of a council. **coun'cillorship** or (*N Am*) **coun'cilorship** *n*. **coun'cilman** *n* (*esp US*) a member of a municipal council. **councilman'ic** *adj*. ❑ **coun'cil-board** *n* the board or table round which a council meets for deliberation; the council itself. **council chamber** *n* the room where a council is held. **council estate** *n* an area set apart for council houses. **council house** *n* a house built, owned and rented out by a municipal council; a building in which a council meets. **council school** *n* a school governed by a town or county council. **council tax** *n* a local government tax based on and banded according to property values, with each household deemed to have two residents (with discount for people living alone), a replacement for the poll tax or community charge.

■ **Council of Europe** a consultative body of European states, at first (1949) thought of as the parliament of a future European federation. **Council of Ministers** in the EU, the decision-making body comprising ministers of the member countries. **Council** or **House of States** the upper house of the Indian parliament. **council of war** a conference of military officers called to consult with the commander (also *fig*). **ecumenical council** one of the seven general councils convened by the undivided Catholic Church between 325 and 787AD. **European Council** the body comprising the French head of state and the prime ministers of the other EU countries. **general council** a council convened by an invitation to all the bishops of the church. **in council** in the council chamber; in consultation. **legislative council** a council to assist a governor, with power to make laws.

counsel /kown'sl/ *n* advice; consultation; deliberation; a person who gives counsel, a barrister or advocate. ◆ *vt* (**coun'selling**; **coun'selled**) to advise; to warn. [Fr *conseil*, from L *consilium* advice, from *consulere* to consult]
■ **couns'ellable** *adj* that may be counselled. **coun'selling** *n* (a service consisting of) helping people to adjust to or deal with personal problems, etc by enabling them to discover for themselves the solution to the problems while receiving sympathetic attention from a counsellor; (sometimes) the giving of advice on miscellaneous problems. **coun'sellor** or (*N Am*) **coun'selor** *n* a person who counsels; a person involved in counselling; a barrister (now chiefly *US*); a senior diplomatic officer. **coun'sellorship** or (*US*) **coun'selorship** *n*.
□ **coun'sel-keeper** *n* (*Shakesp*) one who can keep counsel or a secret. **coun'sel-keeping** *adj*.
■ **counsel of perfection** a commendation of something beyond the binding minimum, something not absolutely imperative, but commended as the means of reaching greater 'perfection'; an impractical ideal. **keep counsel** to keep a secret. **Queen's Counsel** or **King's Counsel** a barrister or advocate appointed by letters patent (the office is honorary, but gives the right of precedence in all the courts) (*abbrev* **QC** or **KC**).

count¹ or (*obs*) **compt** /kownt/ *vt* to number, sum up; to name the numerals up to; to take into account, reckon as significant or to be recognized; to reckon, esteem, consider. ◆ *vi* to number; to be numbered; to be of account; to be recognized in reckoning; to have a certain value; to reckon; to name the numerals in order. ◆ *n* the act of numbering; reckoning; the number counted; a number indicating size of yarn; the counting (by a referee) of the seconds in which a boxer or wrestler may rise and resume fighting (also **count'-out**); esteem, consideration, account; a particular charge in an indictment (*law*). [OFr *cunter* (Fr *compter*), from L *computāre*]
■ **count'able** (*obs* **compt'able** or **compt'ible**) *adj* capable of being counted; to be counted; accountable; (of a noun) count. **count'ed** *adj* accounted, reckoned. **count'er** *n* a person or thing that counts; that which indicates a number; a disc or similar thing, used in calculations or (*games*) as a substitute for a coin or a marker of one's position on a board; the name of certain prisons (officially **compt'er**; *obs*); see also separate entry. **count'less** *adj* that cannot be counted; innumerable.
□ **count'back** *n* a method for determining the winner of a sporting event when two competitors have an equal final score by taking into account their performance throughout the competition; any of various similar techniques for determining an outcome by taking account of existing data. **count'down** *n* a descending count or counted check to a moment of happening regarded as zero, as in the firing of a rocket (see also **count down** below). **count'er-caster** *n* (*Shakesp*) an arithmetician, reckoner. **counting frame** *n* a frame having rows of movable beads, used for elementary counting, an abacus. **counting house** or **counting room** *n* formerly, a room in which a merchant, etc kept his accounts and transacted business. **count'line** *adj* and *n* (of) a confectionery bar made as an individual line (eg a filled or chocolate-covered combination bar) as distinct from moulded chocolate. **count noun** *n* a noun which, since it denotes an entity of which there can be one or more than one, is able to form a plural. **count-out** see *n* above. **count wheel** *n* a wheel with notched edge controlling the stroke of a clock in sounding the hours.
■ **count down** to count in descending order to zero (see also **countdown** above). **count in** (or **out**) to include (or exclude) from an activity. **count on** to rely on, depend on. **count out** of a meeting (*esp* of the House of Commons) to bring to an end by pointing out that a quorum is not present; (in children's games) to eliminate (players) by counting while repeating a rhyme (**counting-out rhyme**); to judge a boxer, wrestler, etc defeated by counting the maximum allowable seconds in which to resume. **keep count** to keep an accurate numerical record (of). **lose count** to fail to keep count (of). **out for the count** unable to rise and resume the fight during the count (*boxing*); in general, unconscious, or asleep.

count² /kownt/ *n* in continental Europe, a noble equal in rank to an earl; an imperial official (*Roman hist*). [OFr *conte*, from L *comes*, *comitis* a companion, from *con-* with, and *īre* to go]

■ **count'ess** *n* a lady of the same rank as a count or earl; the wife or widow of a count or earl; a size of roofing slate, 508 × 254mm (20 × 10in). **count'ship** *n* a count's prestige or domain (also used as a title).

countenance /kown'tə-nəns/ *n* the face; the expression of the face; favour, approbation; acquiescence, sanction; appearance (*obs*); demeanour shown towards a person (*obs*). ◆ *vt* to favour, approve or sanction; to make a show of (*Spenser*). [OFr *contenance*, from L *continentia* restraint, demeanour, from *continēre* to contain]
■ **coun'tenancer** *n*.
■ **change countenance** to change the expression of the face. **give countenance to** to support (a proposal, etc). **in countenance** unabashed. **out of countenance** abashed.

counter¹ /kown'tər/ *adv* the opposite way; in opposition. ◆ *adj* contrary; opposing; opposite. ◆ *n* that which is counter or opposite; the voice part set in immediate contrast with the melody (*music*); a parry in which one foil follows the other in a small circle (*fencing*); the inside area of typeface that does not print, eg the centre of an O (*printing*); the part of a horse's breast between the shoulders and under the neck; the part of a ship's stern from the lower moulding to the waterline (*naut*). ◆ *vt* to contradict; to meet or answer by a stroke or move; to strike while receiving or parrying a blow (*boxing*). [Partly aphetic for **encounter**, partly directly from Anglo-Fr *countre*, OFr (Fr) *contre*, from L *contrā* against]
■ **run counter to** to move in the opposite direction (to); to act or happen in a way contrary (to instructions, expectations, etc).

counter² /kown'tər/ *n* a table with a raised surface over which money is counted, goods are laid, food is served, etc; see also under **count¹**. [From **count¹**]
□ **coun'ter-jumper** or **coun'ter-skipper** *n* contemptuous names for a shopkeeper or shop assistant. **coun'terman** *n* (*archaic*) someone who serves at a counter.
■ **over-the-counter** of goods, *esp* drugs, legally sold directly to the customer; involving trading in shares not on the official Stock Exchange list. **under-the-counter** hidden from customers' sight; reserved for the favoured customer; sold, or procured, illegally or secretly.

counter- /kown-tər-/ *combining form* signifying against. [Anglo-Fr *countre*, OFr *contre*, from L *contrā* against]
■ **coun'ter-agent** *n* anything which counteracts. **coun'ter-approach** *n* a structure thrown up outside a besieged place to command or check the approaches of the enemy. **coun'ter-attack** *n* an attack in response to an attack (also *vt* and *vi*). **counter-attrac'tion** *n* attraction in an opposite direction; a rival show. **counter-attract'ive** *adj*. **counterbal'ance** *vt* to balance by weight on the opposite side; to act against with equal weight, power or influence. ◆ *n* /kown'/ an equal weight, power or agency working in opposition. **counterbase** *n* see **contrabass**. **coun'ter-batt'ery** *n* (*milit*) a battery erected to oppose another. **coun'terbid** *n* a bid made in opposition to another bid. **coun'terbidder** *n*. **coun'terblast** *n* a defiant pronouncement or denunciation. **coun'terblow** *n* a return blow. **coun'terbluff** *n* actions or words intended as a bluff, made in opposition to someone else's bluff. **coun'terbond** *n* a bond to protect a person who has given bond for another from contingent loss. **coun'terbore** *n* a straight-sided widening of the end of a bored hole; a drill for making this. ◆ *vt* to form a counterbore in. **coun'terbrace** *vt* (*naut*) to brace or fasten (the head-yards and after-yards) in opposite ways. ◆ *n* the lee-brace of the foretopsail-yard. **coun'terbuff** *n* a stroke that stops motion or causes a recoil; a return blow; a rebuff. ◆ *vt* to rebuff. **coun'ter-cast** *n* (*Spenser*) a contrary cast, counter-plot, trick. **coun'terchange** *n* a balanced contrast in a picture, etc between eg light on a dark background and dark on a light background; exchange (*Shakesp*); reciprocation (*Shakesp*). ◆ *vt* to chequer, eg with contrasting colours. **coun'terchanged** *adj* (*heraldry*) having the tinctures reversed or interchanged. **coun'tercharge** *n* a charge brought forward in opposition to another charge (also *vi*). **coun'tercharm** *vt* to destroy or dissolve the effects of (another charm). ◆ *n* that which destroys the effects of another charm. **countercheck'** *vt* to check by opposing, separate or additional means; to rebuke. ◆ *n* /kown'/ a check in opposition or addition to another; a restraint; a rebuke. **coun'terclaim** *n* (*esp law*) a claim brought forward as a partial or complete set-off against another claim (also *vi*). **counter-clock'wise** *adv* and *adj* in a direction contrary to that of the hands of a clock. **countercondi'tioning** *n* (*psychol*) the conditioning of a response that is opposite to a response previously acquired or learned. **coun'terculture** *n* a way of life deliberately different from that which is normal or expected. **coun'ter-current** *n* a current flowing in an opposite direction. **coun'ter-drain** *n* a drain alongside a canal, etc, to carry off water oozing out. **coun'terdraw** *vt* to trace on oiled paper or other transparent material. **counter-esp'ionage** *n* espionage directed against the enemy's spy system or action taken to counter it in one's own country. **counter-ev'idence** *n* evidence that is brought forward in opposition to other evidence. **counterexam'ple** *n* an example cited

as part of an argument against a statement, hypothesis, etc. **counterexten′sion** *n* (in orthopaedics) the traction of part of a limb with the remainder held in a static position. **counterfact′ual** *adj* and *n* (*philos*) (denoting) a condition that has not been fulfilled or is not likely to be fulfilled, but would have a certain consequence if it were. **coun′ter-fleury** /-*floo′*ri or -*flū′*ri/ **-flō′ry** or **-flow′ered** *adj* (*heraldry*) with flowers placed the contrary way. **coun′terfoil** *n* the part of a bank cheque, postal order, ticket, etc retained by the giver as a record of the transaction (see **foil²**). **coun′ter-force** *n* an opposing force. **coun′terfort** *n* a buttress or arch supporting a retaining wall. **coun′ter-gauge** *n* an adjustable scribing gauge for marking the measurements of a mortise on a piece to be tenoned. **coun′ter-glow** *n* gegenschein. **coun′ter-guard** *n* (*fortif*) an outwork consisting of two lines of rampart running parallel to the faces of the bastion, to guard the bastion from being breached. **coun′ter-influence** *n* an opposing influence. **counter-insur′gency** *n* action taken against insurgents (also *adj*). **counter-intell′igence** *n* activities, such as censorship, camouflage, use of codes, etc, aimed at preventing an enemy from obtaining information, or the organization that carries these out. **counterintu′itive** *adj* not what would be intuitively expected; apparently improbable. **counterintu′itively** *adv*. **counter-irr′itant** *n* (*esp med*) an irritant used to relieve another irritation or discomfort. **counter-irrita′tion** *n*. **coun′terlight** *n* (*art*) a light opposite to any object, disturbing the effect of its light. **coun′termarch** *vi* and *vt* to march or cause to march back or in a direction opposite to a former one. ♦ *n* a marching back or in a direction opposite to a former one; a manoeuvre by which a body of men change front, and still retain the same men in the front rank (*milit*). **coun′termark** *n* an additional mark put on a bale of goods belonging to several merchants, so that it may not be opened except in the presence of all the owners; a mark put on standard metal by the London Goldsmiths′ Company in addition to the artificer′s; an artificial cavity made in the teeth of horses to disguise their age. **coun′termeasure** *n* an action intended to counteract the effect of another action or happening. **countermine′** *vt* to make an excavation in opposition to; to oppose by means of a countermine; to frustrate by secret working (*fig*). ♦ *n* an excavation made to counteract or destroy excavations made by the enemy (*fortif*); any means of counteraction (*fig*). **coun′termotion** *n* an opposite motion. **coun′termove** or **coun′termovement** *n* a contrary move or movement. **coun′termure** *n* a wall-facing; a supplementary wall; a wall raised by besiegers against a wall (*fortif*). ♦ *vt* /-*mūr*/ to defend with a countermure. **coun′teroffensive** *n* a counter-attack; an attack by the defenders. **coun′teroffer** *n* a response made by a seller to a buyer′s bid, *usu* lowering the price *orig* asked for, in an attempt to clinch a bargain. **coun′ter-opening** *n* an aperture or vent on the opposite side, or in a different place. **coun′terpace** *n* a step in opposition to another; a contrary measure. **coun′ter-paled** *adj* (*heraldry*) divided equally, as an escutcheon, first palewise, then by a line fesse-wise, with tinctures counterchanged. **coun′ter-parole** *n* a word in addition to the password. **counter-pass′ant** *adj* (*heraldry*) passing each other going in opposite directions. **coun′terplea** *n* a replication to a plea or request. **counterplead′** *vt* to plead the contrary of. **coun′ter-plot** *vt* to plot against in order to frustrate another plot. ♦ *n* a plot or stratagem opposed to another plot. **coun′terpoise** (*obs* **coun′terpeise** /-*pēz*/) *vt* to poise, balance or weigh against or on the opposite side; to act in opposition to with equal effect. ♦ *n* an equally heavy weight in the other scale (also *fig*); a state of equilibrium. **coun′ter-poison** *n* a poison used as the antidote of another. **coun′ter-pressure** *n* opposing pressure. **counterproduc′tive** *adj* acting against productivity, efficiency or usefulness; having the opposite effect to that intended. **counterproduc′tiveness** *n*. **coun′terproof** *n* an inverted impression obtained from a newly printed proof of an engraving, by laying it, while the ink is still wet, upon plain paper, and passing it through the press. **coun′ter-proposal** *n* one which proposes an alternative to a proposal already made. **coun′ter-punch** *vt* to return a punch or blow (also *fig*). ♦ *n* a return blow. **Counter-Reforma′tion** *n* (*hist*) a reform movement within the Roman Catholic Church, following and counteracting the Reformation. **counter-revolu′tion** *n* a subsequent revolution counteracting the effect of a previous one. **counter-revolu′tionary** *n* and *adj* (a person) opposing a particular revolution or opposed to revolutions. **coun′ter-roll** *n* (*law*; *obs*) a copy of the rolls relating to appeals, inquests, etc, serving as a check on another′s roll. **coun′ter-round** *n* (*milit*; *obs*) a body of officers to inspect patrols. **counter-sa′lient** *adj* (*heraldry*) salient in opposite directions. **coun′terscarp** *n* (*fortif*) the side of the ditch nearest to the besiegers and opposite to the scarp. **counterseal′** *vt* (*Shakesp*) to seal with an extra seal for further security. **counter-secur′ity** *n* (*finance*) security given to someone who has become surety for another. **coun′ter-sense** *n* an interpretation contrary to the real sense. **coun′tershading** *n* (in animals) dark and light areas of colour on the body serving to camouflage or protect. **coun′tershaft** *n* an intermediate shaft driven by the main shaft. **countersign′** *vt* to sign on the opposite side of a document, etc; to sign in addition to the signature of a superior or principal signatory, to attest the authenticity

of a document. ♦ *n* /*kown′*/ a military private sign or word, which must be given in order to pass a sentry; a counter-signature. **coun′ter-signal** *n* a signal used in reply to another. **counter-sig′nature** *n* a name countersigned to a document. **coun′tersink** *vt* (*pap* and *adj* **coun′tersunk**) to enlarge the upper part of (a hole), eg for the head of a screw; to set the head or top of (eg a nail, screw, etc) on a level with, or below, the surface of the surrounding material. ♦ *n* a tool for doing this; the enlargement made to the hole. **coun′terspy** *n*. **coun′terspying** *n* counter-espionage. **coun′terstain** *vt* (*microscopy*) to apply additional dye to a specimen to produce a contrasting background. **coun′ter-stand** *n* opposition, resistance. **coun′ter-statement** *n* a statement in opposition to another statement. **coun′terstroke** *n* a stroke in return. **coun′ter-subject** *n* (*music*) a second theme by the first voice (*esp* in a fugue) when accompanying the second voice performing the main subject. **coun′tersue** *vt* and *vi* to sue a person by whom one is being sued. **coun′ter-tally** *n* a tally serving as a check for another. **coun′tertenor** *n* the highest alto male voice (so called because a contrast to tenor). **counterterr′orism** *n* action taken to counter the activities of terrorists. **coun′ter-time** *n* resistance, opposition; the resistance of a horse that interrupts his cadence and the measure of his manège. **coun′ter-trading** *n* trading by barter. **coun′ter-turn** *n* a turn in a play different from what was expected. **coun′ter-view** *n* an opposing view; a posture in which two people face each other; opposition; contrast. **counter-vote′** *vt* to vote in opposition to. **counter-weigh′** *vt* to weigh against, counterbalance. **coun′ter-weight** *n* weight in an opposite scale; a counterbalancing influence or force. **coun′ter-wheel** *vi* to wheel in an opposite direction. **coun′ter-work** *n* a work intended to oppose another. **counterwork′** *vt* to work in opposition to. **coun′ter-wrought** *adj*.

counteract /*kown-tə-rakt′*/ *vt* to act counter or in opposition to; to neutralize. [**counter-**]
  ■ **counterac′tion** *n*. **counterac′tive** *adj*. **counteract′ively** *adv*.

counterfeit /*kown′tər-fît* or -*fēt*/ *vt* to imitate; to copy without authority; to forge. ♦ *n* something false or copied, or that pretends to be true and original. ♦ *adj* (also *Spenser* **coun′terfect**) pretended; made in imitation; forged; false. [OFr *contrefet*, from *contrefaire* to imitate, from L *contrā* against, and *facere* to do]
  ■ **coun′terfeisance** /-*fē-zəns*/ (or *archaic* **coun′terfēsaunce**) *n* an act of counterfeiting; forgery. **coun′terfeiter** *n* a person who counterfeits. **coun′terfeitly** *adv* in a counterfeit manner; falsely.

countermand /*kown-tər-mänd′*/ *vt* to give a command in opposition to one already given; to revoke. ♦ *n* /*kownt′*/ a revocation to a former order. [OFr *contremander*, from L *contrā* against, and *mandāre* to order]
  ■ **countermand′able** *adj*.

counterpane /*kown′tər-pān*/ or (*obs*) **counterpoint** /-*point*/ *n* a covering for a bed, a bedspread. [OFr *contrepoint*, from *coultepointe*, from L *culcita puncta* a stitched pillow; see **quilt**]

counterpart /*kown′tər-pärt*/ *n* the part that answers to, fits into or completes another part, having the qualities which the other lacks; a corresponding or equivalent person or thing; a duplicate, a close or exact copy. [**counter-**]

counterpoint¹ /*kown′tər-point*/ *n* the art of combining melodies (*music*); a melody added to another (*music*); an opposite point. ♦ *vt* to write in counterpoint; to set in contrast for effect. [Fr *contrepoint* and Ital *contrappunto*, from L *contrā* against, and *punctum* a point, from the pricks, points or notes placed against those of the melody; also in some senses **counter-** and **point**]
  ■ **contrapuntal** /*kon-tra-punt′əl*/ *adj*. **contrapunt′ally** *adv*. **contrapunt′ist** *n* a composer skilled in counterpoint.

counterpoint² see **counterpane**.

countervail /*kown′tər-vāl*/ *vt* to be of value or service against; to act against with equal effect; to be of equal value to; to compensate. [OFr *contrevaloir*, from *contre* (from L *contrā* against), and *valoir* to be of avail (from L *valēre* to be strong)]
  ■ **countervail′able** *adj*.
  □ **countervailing duty** *n* extra import duty imposed to prevent dumping or to counter subsidies in the exporting country.

countrol see **control**.

country /*kun′tri*/ *n* a region; a state; a nation; rural districts as distinct from town; the land of one′s birth or citizenship; the district hunted by a pack of foxhounds; the rock surrounding a mineral lode (also **coun′try-rock**); country music. ♦ *adj* belonging to the country; rural; rustic. [OFr *contrée*, from LL *contrāta*, *contrāda*, an extension of L *contrā* placed against]
  ■ **coun′trified** or **coun′tryfied** *adj* like or suitable for the country in style; like a person from the country in style, dress or manner. **countrywide** *adj* and *adv* all over the country.
  □ **country-and-west′ern** *n* a popularized form of music deriving from the rural folk music of the United States (also *adj*). **coun′try-box** *n* a small country house. **country club** *n* a club in a rural area which has

facilities for sport, leisure and social activities. **country code** *n* a code of behaviour to be followed by people using the countryside, *esp* for recreational purposes. **country cousin** *n* a relative from the country, unaccustomed to town sights or manners. **country dance** *n* a dance as practised by country people; a type of dance in which either an indefinite number of couples in a circle or two lines, or groups of fixed numbers of couples in two lines, can take part, tracing a precise and sometimes complex pattern of movements. **country dancing** *n*. **coun'try-folk** *n pl* fellow countrymen; rural people. **country gentleman** *n* a landed proprietor who resides on his estate in the country. **country house** or **country seat** *n* the residence and estate of a country gentleman. **coun'tryman** *n* a man who lives in the country; a man belonging to the same country, fellow countryman. **country mile** *n* (*inf*) a very long distance. **country music** *n* the folk music of the rural areas of the United States; country-and-western music; both of these taken together. **country party** *n* the political party opposed to the court (*hist*); a political party supporting the interests of farmers. **country rock** *n* electrically amplified music which combines the styles of rock and roll and country-and-western music. **country-rock** see under **country** above. **coun'tryside** *n* rural districts in general; a district or part of the country. **country town** *n* a small town in a rural district. **coun'trywoman** *n* a woman who lives in the country; a woman of the same country.
■ **go to the country** (*politics*) to appeal to the voters of the country by calling a general election.

county[1] /kown'ti/ *n* a portion of a country separated for administrative, parliamentary or other purposes, a shire; the territory or dominion of a count (*hist*). ◆ *adj* of a, or the, county; of a county family. [**count**[2]]
❑ **county borough** see **borough**. **county council** *n* a council for managing the public affairs of a county. **county councillor** *n*. **county court** *n* the highest court of law within a county. **county cricket** *n* cricket played in matches between clubs representing counties. **county family** *n* a family of nobility or gentry (**coun'ty-people**) with estates and a seat in the county. **county hall** *n* the administrative centre of a county. **county palatine** see under **palatine**[1]. **County school** *n* a school provided and maintained by a local education authority. **county seat** *n* (*US*) the seat of county government. **county town** *n* the town in which the public business of the county is transacted.

county[2] /kown'ti/ (*obs*) *n* a count. [Prob Anglo-Fr *counte*]

coup[1] /koo/ *n* a blow, stroke; a sudden action or motion; a clever and successful stroke in a board or card game; a masterstroke, clever and successful stratagem; the act of putting a ball in a pocket without having hit another ball (*billiards*); a coup d'état. [Fr, from LL *colpus*, from L *colaphus*, from Gr *kolaphos* a blow]
❑ **coup de bonheur** /də bon-œr/ *n* a stroke of luck; a lucky hit or shot. **coup d'éclat** /dā-klä/ *n* a bold stroke. **coup de foudre** /də foo-dr'/ *n* a sudden and astonishing happening, a thunderclap; love at first sight. **coup de grâce** /də gräs/ *n* a finishing blow to put out of pain; a deathblow; a finishing stroke generally. **coup de main** /də mẽ/ *n* a sudden vigorous attack. **coup de maître** /də metr'/ *n* a masterstroke. **coup de poing** /də pwẽ/ *n* a blow or punch with the fist; a typical Old Stone Age axe, a roughly pointed piece of stone held in the hand. **coup d'essai** /de-sā/ *n* an experimental work; a first attempt. **coup d'état** /dā-tä/ *n* a violent or subversive action resulting in a change of government or state policy. **coup de théâtre** /də tā-ätr'/ *n* a sudden and sensational turn eg in a play, a theatrical effect; a theatrical success. **coup d'oeil** /dœ-i/ *n* a general view at a glance.

coup[2] /kowp/ (*Scot*) *vt* to exchange or barter. [ON *kaupa* to buy]
■ **coup'er** *n* a dealer.

coup[3] or **cowp** /kowp/ (*Scot*) *vt* and *vi* to overturn; to tip up. ◆ *n* an upset; a tip for rubbish. [OFr *colp* blow]

coupe[1] /koop/ (*Fr*) *n* a dessert, *usu* made with ice cream and often fruit, served in a glass bowl; a glass container for serving such a dessert, *usu* with a shallow bowl and a short stem.

coupe[2] /koop/ (*N Am*) *n* a coupé (motor-car).

coupé /koo-pā/ *n* a two-door motor car with a roof sloping towards the back; a four-wheeled carriage with interior seating for two and a separate seat for the driver; an end compartment of a railway carriage with seats on one side only; the front part of a French stagecoach (*hist*); (in dancing) a salute to a partner, while swinging one foot (also **coupee** /koo-pē'/). ◆ *adj* (*heraldry*) (of the head or limb of an animal) cut off evenly (also **couped** /koopt/). [Fr pap of *couper* to cut]

couple /kup'l/ *n* two of a kind joined together, or connected; two, a pair; two people considered as partners, *esp* a man and woman; that which joins two things together; a pair of equal forces acting on the same body in opposite and parallel directions (*phys*). ◆ *vt* to join together. ◆ *vi* to form a sexual relationship. [OFr *cople*, from L *cōpula*]

■ **coup'ledom** *n*. **coup'lement** *n* union; a couple. **coup'ler** *n* someone who or something that couples or unites; an organ mechanism by which stops of one manual can be played from another or from the pedals; an acoustic coupler (qv). **coup'let** *n* a pair, couple; a twin; two successive lines of verse (*esp*) that rhyme with each other. **coup'ling** *n* that which connects; an appliance for transmitting motion in machinery, or for connecting vehicles, as in a railway train; the part of the body of a quadruped lying between the forequarters and hindquarters.
❑ **coup'ling-box** *n* the box or ring of metal connecting the contiguous ends of two lengths of shafts.
■ **well-coupled** of a horse, well-formed at the part where the back joins the rump. **a couple of** (loosely) two or three; a few.

coupon /koo'pon, -pən, -pɔ̃ or -pong/ *n* a billet, check, or other slip of paper cut off from its counterpart; a separate ticket or part of a ticket; a voucher certifying that payments will be made, services performed, goods sold, etc; a piece cut from an advertisement entitling one to some privilege; a party leader's recommendation of an electoral candidate; a printed betting form on which to enter forecasts of sports results. [Fr *couper* to cut off]

coupure /koo-pūr'/ *n* a cutting, incision; an entrenchment made by the besieged behind a breach (*fortif*); the deletion of passages in a play, piece of music, etc. [Fr *couper* to cut]

cour and **coure** obsolete forms of **cover** and **cower**.

courage /kur'ij/ *n* the quality that enables people to meet danger without giving way to fear; bravery; spirit. ◆ *interj* take courage. [OFr *corage* (Fr *courage*), from L *cor* the heart]
■ **cour'ageful** *adj*. **courageous** /kə-rā'jəs/ *adj* full of courage; brave. **coura'geously** *adv*. **coura'geousness** *n*.
■ **Dutch courage** artificial courage induced by drinking alcohol. **pluck up courage** or **take one's courage in both hands** to nerve oneself; to gather boldness. **take courage** to be fearless and optimistic in a difficult situation. **the courage of one's convictions** courage to act up to, or consistently with, one's opinions or principles.

courant /koo-rant'/ *adj* (*heraldry*) in a running position. [Fr, prp of *courir* to run; see **current**]
■ **courante** or **courant** /kū-ränt'/ *n* an old dance with a kind of gliding step, a coranto; music for it; /kū-rant'/ a newspaper (now in titles only).

courb or **curb** /koorb or kûrb/ (*archaic*) *vi* to bend or stoop in order to supplicate. ◆ *adj* bent (also *obs* **corbe**). [Fr *courber*, from L *curvāre* to bend]

courbaril /koor'bə-ril/ *n* the West Indian locust-tree, *Hymenaea courbaril*; its resin, gum anime. [Fr from Carib]

courbette /kūr-bet'/ *n* the French form of **curvet**.

courd an obsolete form of **covered**.

coureur de bois /kū-rœr də bwa'/ (*Can hist*) *n* a French-Canadian woodsman who traded furs with the Native Canadian tribes. [Can Fr, literally, woods runner]

courgette /koor-zhet'/ *n* a type of small marrow (also called **zucchini**). [Fr *courge* gourd, pumpkin]

courier /kūr'i-ər/ *n* a messenger, *esp* one employed to deliver special or urgent messages or items; a state or diplomatic messenger; an official guide and organizer who travels with tourists; a title of certain newspapers. ◆ *vt* to send by courier. [Fr, from L *currere* to run]

courlan /kūr'lən/ *n* any bird of the American genus *Aramus*, related to the rails, *esp* the limpkin. [Fr, from a S American name]

course /körs or kōrs/ *n* the path in which anyone or anything moves; the ground over which a race is run, golf is played, etc; a channel for water; the direction pursued; a voyage; a race; regular progress from point to point; a habitual method of procedure; a prescribed series, sequence, process or treatment, eg of lectures, training, education, pills, etc; each of the successive divisions of a meal, ie soup, fish, etc; a range of bricks or stones on the same level in building; (in the lute, etc) one of two or more strings tuned in unison or in octaves (*music*); the series of positions of a bell in the changing order in which a set of bells is struck (*bellringing*); one of the sails bent to a ship's lower yards (*main course* mainsail, *fore course* foresail, and *mizzen course* crossjack; *naut*); (in *pl*) the menses. ◆ *vt* to run, chase or hunt after; to use in coursing. ◆ *vi* to run; to move with speed, as in a race or hunt. [Fr *cours*, from L *cursus*, from *currere*, *cursum* to run]
■ **cours'er** *n* a runner; a swift horse; a person who courses or hunts; a swift running bird (genus *Cursorius*). **cours'ing** *n* hunting of *esp* hares with greyhounds or lurchers, by sight rather than by scent.
❑ **course'book** *n* a textbook intended for a particular course of study. **course'ware** *n* computing software designed to be used in educational courses. **course'work** *n* work that goes to make up an educational course. **cours'ing-joint** *n* a joint between two courses of masonry.

■ words derived from main entry word; ❑ compound words; ■ idioms and phrasal verbs

■ **in course** in regular order; of course (*archaic*). **in due course** eventually; at a suitable later time. **in the course of** during; in the process of; undergoing (something). **in the course of time** eventually; with the passing of time. **of course** by natural consequence; indisputably; it must be remembered (often used to introduce a comment on a preceding statement). **off course** deviating from the correct route; astray. **on course** following the correct route; on schedule. **run** (or **take**) **its** (or **their**) **course** to proceed or develop freely and naturally, *usu* to a point of completion or cessation. **stay the course** see under **stay**[1]. **the course of nature**, or **the normal**, etc **course of events** the usual way in which things happen or proceed.

court /kört or kōrt/ *n* an enclosed space, such as one surrounded by houses; a piece of ground or floor on which certain games are played; a division marked off by lines on such a place; the palace of a sovereign; the body of persons who form the sovereign's suite or council; an assembly of courtiers; a hall of justice (*law*); the judges and officials who preside there; any body of persons assembled to decide causes; a sitting of such a body; a court shoe. ◆ *vt* to pay attentions to, to woo; to solicit; to seek. [OFr *cort* (Fr *cour*), from LL *cortis* a courtyard, from L *cors, cohors, cohortis* an enclosure; related to Gr *chortos* an enclosed place, L *hortus* a garden (see **yard**[2])] ■ **court'ier** *n* someone in attendance at a court or palace; someone who courts or flatters. **court'ierism** *n* the behaviour or practices of a courtier. **court'ierlike** *adj* and *adv*. **court'ierly** *adv*. **court'ing** *n* wooing; attendance at court (*Spenser*). **court'let** *n* a petty court. **court'like** *adj* courtly; polite. **court'liness** *n*. **court'ling** *n* a hanger-on at court. **court'ly** *adj* (**court'lier**; **court'liest**) having manners like those of, or befitting, a court; politely stately; fair and flattering. **court'ship** *n* the act or process of wooing a woman in order to persuade her to become one's wife; the period of time over which this is carried out; courtly behaviour. ◻ **court-bar'on** *n* (*hist*) the assembly of freehold tenants of a manor under a lord. **court card** see **coat-card** under **coat**[1]. **court circular** *n* a daily report in certain newspapers of the appointments, activities, etc of the sovereign and/or other members of a royal family. **court'craft** *n* the courtier's art, intrigue. **court cupboard** *n* (*hist*) a movable cupboard or sideboard on which plate was displayed. **court'-day** *n* a day on which a judicial court sits. **court dress** *n* the special formal costume worn on state or ceremonious occasions. **court'-dresser** *n* (*obs*) a flatterer. **court fool** *n* a fool or jester, formerly kept at court for amusement. **court guide** *n* (*hist*) a guide to, or a directory of, the names and residences of the nobility in a town. **court hand** *n* a modification of the Norman handwriting, as distinguished from the modern or Italian handwriting, in use in the English lawcourts from the 16c to the reign of George II. **court'house** *n* a building where the lawcourts are held. **court'-leet** *n* (*hist*) a court of record held in a manor before the lord or his steward. **courtly love** *n* a conception and tradition of love, originating in late medieval European literature, in which the knight sublimates his love for his lady in submission, service and devotion. **court martial** *n* (*pl* **courts martial** or (*inf*) **court mar'tials**) a court held by officers of the army, navy or air force for the trial of offences against service laws (one improvised in time of war round an upturned drum for summary judgement was a **drumhead court martial**). **court-mar'tial** *vt* (**court-mar'tialling**; **court-mar'tialled**) to try before a court martial. **court order** *n* a direction or command of a justiciary court. **court plaster** *n* sticking-plaster made of silk, originally applied as patches on the face by ladies at court. **court'-roll** *n* the record of land holdings, etc of a manorial court. **court'room** *n* a room in a courthouse in which lawsuits and criminal cases are heard. **court shoe** *n* a low-cut ladies' shoe without straps or laces. **court sword** *n* a light sword worn as part of court dress. **court tennis** *n* the game of real tennis, distinguished from lawn tennis. **court'yard** *n* a court or enclosed ground attached to a building, *usu* a large house. ■ **court holy water** (*obs*) empty compliments; flattery. **Court of Appeal, Arches, Exchequer**, etc see under **appeal, arch**[1], **exchequer**, etc. **court of first instance** a lawcourt in which proceedings are first heard. **go** (or **take someone**) **to court** to institute legal proceedings against someone. **hold court** to preside over admiring followers, etc. **laugh someone out of court** see under **laugh**. **out of court** without a trial in a lawcourt; without claim to be considered. **pay court to** to woo or flatter. **put** (or **rule**) **out of court** to prevent a case from being heard; to dismiss emphatically (*fig*). **the ball's in your court** see under **ball**[1].

court-bouillon /koor boo-yõ'/ *n* (*pl* **courts-bouillons**) a seasoned stock made with water, vegetables and wine or vinegar, in which fish is boiled. [Fr *court* short, from L *curtus*, and **bouillon**]

Courtelle® /kŭr-tel' or kör-/ *n* a synthetic acrylic wool-like fibre.

courteous /kûr'tyəs or kör'tyəs/ *adj* polite, considerate or respectful in manner and action; obliging. [OFr *corteis, cortois*; see **court**] ■ **court'eously** *adv*. **court'eousness** *n*. **courtesy** /kûrt'ə-si or kört'/ *n* courteous behaviour; an act of civility or respect; a curtsy (*obs*); (until 1964) the life interest of the surviving husband in his wife's

heritable property (Scots law). ◆ *vi* (**court'esying; court'esied**) to make a curtsy.
◻ **courtesy light** *n* a small light in a motor vehicle, *usu* operated by the opening and closing of the doors. **courtesy title** *n* a title really invalid, but allowed by the usage of society, as for children of peers. ■ **(by) courtesy of** with the permission of; by the favour of. **remember your courtesy** (*obs*) please put on your hat. **strain courtesy** see under **strain**[1].

courtesan or **courtezan** /kör'ti-zan, kûr'- or -zan'/ *n* a mistress or prostitute, *esp* of a man of status or wealth. [Fr *courtisane*, from Ital *cortigiana*, orig a woman of the court]

couscous, kouskous /kŭs'kŭs or koos'koos/ or **couscousou** /-soo'/ *n* hard wheat semolina; a N African dish of steamed couscous with meat, vegetables, etc. [Fr, from Ar *kuskus*, from *kaskasa* to pound; see **cuscus**[2]]

cousin /kuz'n/ *n* the son or daughter of an uncle or aunt; formerly, a kinsman generally; a term used by a sovereign in addressing another, or to one of his own nobles; a person belonging to a group related by common ancestry, interests, etc; something kindred or related to another. [Fr, from L *consōbrīnus*, from *con-* (signifying connection), and *sobrīnus*, applied to the children of sisters, from the root of *soror* a sister] ■ **cous'inage** *n*. **cous'inhood** *n*. **cous'inly** *adj* like, or having the relation of, a cousin. **cous'inry** *n* cousins collectively. **cous'inship** *n*. ◻ **cousin-ger'man** *n* (*pl* **cousins-german**) a first cousin; something closely related. **Cousin Jack** *n* a native of Cornwall. ■ **cross cousin** the son or daughter of one's father's sister or mother's brother. **first cousin** the child of one's aunt or uncle, a full cousin. **first cousin once removed** the son or daughter of a cousin-german, sometimes loosely called *second cousin*. **forty-second cousin** vaguely, a distant relative. **second cousin** the child of one's parent's first cousin; loosely, a first cousin once removed.

couter /koo'tər/ (*sl*) *n* a sovereign (coin). [Said to be from Romany *cuta* a gold piece]

couth[1] /kooth/ (*obs*) *pat* and *pap* of **can** could; knew; known; did. [OE *pat cūthe, pap cūth*]

couth[2] /kooth/ *adj* good-mannered, refined, sophisticated. [Back-formation from **uncouth**]

couthie or **couthy** /koo'thi/ (*Scot*) *adj* friendly, kindly; comfortable; snug. [Prob OE *cūth* known]

coutil or **coutille** /koo-til'/ *n* a strong cotton fabric used in mattresses, etc. [Fr *coutil*]

couture /koo-tür or (*N Am*) -toor'/ *n* dressmaking or dress designing. [Fr] ■ **couturier** /koo-tür'yā or (*N Am*) -tŭr-/ or *fem* **couturière** /-yer'/ *n* a dressmaker or dress designer.

couvade /koo-väd'/ *n* a custom among certain peoples in many parts of the world for the father to take to his bed at the birth of a child, and submit to certain restrictions of food, etc; loosely, the symptoms occasionally experienced by an expectant father, eg stomach pains. [OFr *couvade*, from *couver* to hatch, from L *cubāre* to lie down]

couvert /koo-ver'/ (*Fr*) *n* a cover (at table).

COV *abbrev* : covariance (*stats*); crossover value (*genetics*).

covalency /kō-vā'lən-si/ *n* the union of two or more atoms by the sharing of one or more pairs of electrons (cf **electrovalency**). [L *co-* together, and **valency**] ■ **cova'lent** *adj*. **cova'lently** *adv*. ◻ **covalent bond** *n* a chemical bond involving the sharing of a pair of electrons by two atoms.

covariance /kō-vā'ri-əns/ *n* the property of varying concomitantly (*maths*); the mean value of the products of the deviations of two or more variates from the respective mean values of these variates (*stats*). ■ **covār'iant** *n* and *adj*. **covār'y** *vi*.

cove[1] /kōv/ *n* a small inlet of the sea; a bay; a cavern or rocky recess; a curved junction of wall and ceiling (*archit*); the moulding covering the junction of wall and ceiling (also **cō'ving**). ◆ *vt* to form or provide with an architectural cove. [OE *cofa* a room; ON *kofi*, Ger *Koben*] ■ **coved** *adj* formed with an arch. **cove'let** *n* a small cove.

cove[2] /kōv/ (*Aust inf* or *old Brit sl*) *n* a man, a chap. [Origin obscure]

covellite /kō-vel'īt or kō'və-līt/ *n* a blue mineral, cupric sulphide. [N Covelli (1790–1829), Italian mineralogist]

coven /kuv'in or -ən/ *n* a gathering of witches; a gang of thirteen witches. [See **covin**]

covenant /kuv'ə-nənt/ *n* a mutual agreement; the writing containing the agreement; an engagement entered into between God and a person or a people, a dispensation, testament. ◆ *vi* to enter into an agreement. ◆ *vt* to agree to; to stipulate. [OFr, from L *con-* together, and *venīre* to come]

■ **covenantal** /-*nant*'/ *adj*. **cov'enanted** *adj* agreed to by covenant; bound by covenant; holding a position under a covenant or contract. **covenantee'** *n* the person to whom a covenant is made. **cov'enanter** *n* (*usu* in Scotland /*kuv-ə-nant*'*ər*/) a person who signed or adhered to the *Scottish National Covenant* of 1638 (the *Solemn League and Covenant* of 1643 was in effect an international treaty between Scotland and England for securing civil and religious liberty). **cov'enantor** *n* that party to a covenant who subjects himself or herself to a penalty if it is broken.

■ **covenant of grace** or **redemption** (*theol*) that by which life is freely offered to sinners on condition of faith in Christ. **covenant of works** that made with Adam as federal representative of the human race on condition of obedience.

covent /*kov*'*ənt* or *kuv*'*ənt*/ (*archaic*) *n* a variant of **convent**[1].

Coventry /*kov*' or *kuv*'*ən-tri*/ *n* a city in the W Midlands of England. ❑ **Coventry blue** *n* a blue thread once made there.

■ **send to Coventry** to ostracize, *esp* to refuse to talk to.

cover /*kuv*'*ər*/ *vt* to put or spread something on, over or about; to come or be on, over or about; to hide; to clothe; to protect; to screen; to brood or sit on; to suffice for; to provide for or against; to comprise; to traverse; to extend; to take as field of operations; to play a higher card upon; to put down (a stake of equal value) in betting; (*esp* of a stallion) to copulate with; to protect with a weapon by being within range for returning fire against any attacker; (of a journalist) to report on (a news story); to record a new version of (a song). ◆ *vi* to take over the duties of another temporarily (see also **cover for** below); to lay a table for a meal (*obs*); to put one's hat on. ◆ *n* that which covers or is intended to cover; a bedcover; a lid; the binding of a book; the jacket of a book; an envelope, *esp* one with a stamp and postmark, as in *first-day cover*; undergrowth or thicket concealing game, etc; a pretext or disguise; an apparently genuine identity, job, etc used as a front, *esp* by spies; the protection provided by an insurance policy; the funds available to cover liabilities; a confederate; a table setting for one person (hence *cover charge* below); a cover version; a cover point. ◆ *adj* intended to conceal the true nature or identity of a person, organization, etc. [Fr *couvrir* (Ital *coprire*), from L *cooperīre* from *co-* and *operīre* to cover]

■ **cov'erable** *adj*. **cov'erage** *n* the area or (*fig*) amount covered or included; the group or section of the community reached by an advertising medium; the (extent of) reporting of a topic, event, etc on television, in the press, etc; insurance cover. **cov'ered** *adj* having a cover; sheltered; concealed; roofed over; with a hat on. **cov'ering** *n*. ❑ **cov'erall** *n* a boiler suit (*US*; often in *pl*); a one-piece garment for babies, covering arms, legs and body. ◆ *adj* covering or including everything. **cover charge** *n* a charge per person made by a restaurant, in addition to charge for food. **cover crop** *n* a subsidiary crop grown partly to protect the soil. **cover drive** *n* (*cricket*) a drive past cover point. **covered wagon** *n* a large wagon with a bonnet-shaped canvas hood, *esp* that used by pioneers to the American West; used as a symbol of pioneering spirit. **covered way** or **covert way** *n* (*fortif*) a path outside the ditch of a fort, sunk below the crest of the glacis to provide protection. **cover girl** *n* a girl pictured on a magazine cover. **cover glass** *n* (*microscopy*) a coverslip. **covering letter** *n* a letter to explain documents enclosed with it. **cover mount** *n* a promotional gift attached to the cover of a book, magazine, etc. **cover note** *n* (*insurance*) a note certifying that the holder has a current insurance policy; a note issued to an insured person certifying that the latter has insurance coverage while their policy is being prepared. **cover point** *n* a fielding position on the offside, between point and extra cover, or a player in this position (*cricket*); (in lacrosse) (the position of) one of the defending players. **cover price** *n* (of magazines, etc) the price printed on the outside cover. **cov'erslip** *n* a loose cover for a duvet; a thin slip of glass used for covering a specimen under a microscope (*microscopy*). **cov'er-slut** *n* (*hist*) an outer garment worn to cover rags or dirty clothes. **covert coat** *n* (*hist*) a short light overcoat. **covert coating** *n* cloth for this. **covert way** see **covered way** above. **cover-up** see **cover up** below. **cover version** *n* a recording of a song, etc which has been recorded by someone else, *usu* very similar to the original.

■ **cover for** to act in the place of (someone who is absent, etc); to conceal the mistake or misdemeanour of (someone). **cover in** to fill in; to complete the covering of, *esp* of a roof of a building. **cover into** to transfer into. **cover one's back** to take action to protect oneself from danger. **cover shorts** to buy in such stocks as have been sold short, in order to meet one's engagements, etc. **cover the buckle** to execute a certain difficult step in dancing. **cover up** to cover completely; to conceal, withhold information (*inf*; **cov'er-up** *n*). **from cover to cover** from beginning to end of a book. **under cover** in secret; protected by shelter. **under cover of** hidden by, using as concealment. **under plain cover** in a plain envelope. **under separate cover** in a separate envelope or package.

coverlet /*kuv*'*ər-lit*/ *n* a bedcover (also **cov'erlid**). [Fr *couvrir* to cover, and *lit* (from L *lectum*) a bed]

covers /*kō*'*vûrs*/ *abbrev* : coversed sine.

coversed sine /*kō*'*vûrsd sīn*/ *n* one of six trigonometrical functions of an angle equal to one minus the sine of a specified angle.

covert /*kō*'*vərt* or *kuv*'*ərt*/ *adj* (also /*kō*'*vûrt*/) concealed; secret. ◆ *n* a feather covering the quill-bases of wings and tail of a bird; a shelter; cover for game. [ME, covered, from OFr pap of *covrir* to cover]

■ **cov'ertly** *adv* in a secret, stealthy or concealed manner. **cov'erture** *n* covering, shelter; disguise; the status of a married woman considered as being under the protection of her husband (*law*). ❑ **covert coat**, **covert coating**, etc see under **cover**.

covet /*kuv*'*it*/ *vt* to desire or wish for eagerly; to wish for (something belonging to another). ◆ *vi* (*archaic*) to desire (with *for*). [OFr *coveit(i)er* (Fr *convoiter*), from L *cupiditās*, -*ātis*, from *cupere* to desire]

■ **cov'etable** *adj*. **cov'eted** *adj*. **cov'etingly** *adv*. **cov'etise** *n* (*obs*) covetousness; ardent desire. **cov'etiveness** *n* (*obs*; *phrenology*) acquisitiveness. **cov'etous** *adj* inordinately desirous; avaricious. **cov'etously** *adv*. **cov'etousness** *n*.

covey[1] /*kuv*'*i*/ *n* a brood or hatch of partridges; a small flock of game birds; a small party or set of people. [OFr *covée*, from L *cubāre* to lie down]

covey[2] dimin of **cove**[2].

covin or **covyne** /*kō*'*vin*, *kuv*'*in*/ *n* an agreement (*archaic*); a conspiracy, *esp* (*law*) one between two or more people to act to the injury of another; a coven. [OFr *covin*, from LL *convenium*, from *con-* together, and *venīre* to come]

■ **covinous** /*kuv*'/ *adj* (*archaic*) fraudulent. ❑ **cov'in-tree** *n* a tree in front of a Scottish mansion at which guests were met and farewells were made.

coving /*kō*'*ving*/ (*archit*) *n* a quadrant moulding covering the joint between wall and ceiling; the projection of upper storeys over lower; the vertical sides connecting the jambs with the breast of a fireplace. [See **cove**[1]]

covyne see **covin**.

cow[1] /*kow*/ *n* (*pl* **cows**, (*old*) **kine** /*kīn*/ and (still in Scot) **kye** /*kī*/) the female of the bovine animals; the female of certain other animals, such as the elk, elephant, whale, etc; an ugly, ungainly, slovenly or objectionable woman (*offensive sl*); an objectionable or rather despicable person or thing (*Aust sl*); a trying situation or occurrence (*usu a fair cow*) (*Aust sl*). [OE *cū*, *pl cȳ*; Ger *Kuh*; Sans *go* a bull, cow]

■ **cow'ish** *adj* like a cow; cowardly (*Shakesp*).

❑ **cow'bane** *n* the water hemlock (*Cicuta virosa* or other species), often fatal to cattle. **cow'bell** *n* a bell for a cow's neck; a similar bell, with the clapper removed, used as a percussion instrument. **cow'berry** *n* the red whortleberry (*Vaccinium vitis-idaea*). **cow'bird** or **cow blackbird** *n* an American bird (genus *Molothrus*) of the family Icteridae, that accompanies cattle, and drops its eggs into other birds' nests. **cow'boy** *n* a man who has the charge of cattle on a ranch (*N Am*); any rather rough male character in stories, etc of the old American West, such as a gunfighter or a man involved in fighting Indians; a rodeo performer (*N Am*); a young inexperienced lorry-driver, or anyone who drives an unsafe or overloaded lorry (*sl*); a person who behaves recklessly or irresponsibly (*sl*); a derogatory term for an often inadequately qualified or slapdash person providing inferior services or shoddy workmanship for a quick profit (*inf*). ◆ *adj* relating to or appropriate for cowboys; (of a business, tradesman, etc) providing slapdash and inferior work (*inf*). **cowboy boots** *n pl* high-heeled boots, *usu* with ornamental stitching, etc, worn by, or reminiscent of styles worn by, cowboys and ranchers. **cow'-calf** *n* a female calf. **cow'catcher** *n* (*N Am*) an apparatus on the front of a railway engine to throw off obstacles. **cow'-chervil**, **cow'-parsley** or **cow'-weed** *n* wild chervil. **cow cocky** see under **cockatoo**. **cow college** *n* (*US sl*) a college in a remote rural area. **cow'-dung** *n* cattle excrement. **cow'feeder** *n* a dairyman; a device for dispensing feed to cattle. **cow'fish** *n* a coffer-fish or trunk-fish (with cowlike head); a manatee; any small cetacean. **cow'girl** *n* a young woman who dresses like and does the work of a cowboy. **cow'grass** *n* perennial red clover; zigzag clover. **cow'hand** *n* a person who has charge of or assists with cattle. **cow'heel** *n* the foot of an ox which can be stewed to a jelly. **cow'herb** *n* a European flowering plant (*Saponaria vaccaria*), related to the carnation. **cow'herd** *n* a person who herds cows; see also separate entry **cowheard**. **cow'hide** *n* the hide of a cow; the hide of a cow made into leather; a coarse whip made of twisted strips of cowhide. ◆ *vt* to whip with a cowhide. **cow'house** *n* a building in which cows are stalled, a byre. **cow'-leech** *n* (*obs*) a cow-doctor. **cow'lick** *n* a tuft of turned-up hair on the forehead (also **cow's lick**). **cow'man** *n* a man who tends cows; a man who owns a cattle ranch (*US*). **cow-parsley** see **cow-chervil** above. **cow parsnip** *n* an umbelliferous plant, hogweed (*Heracleum sphondylium*) used as fodder. **cow'pat** *n* a roundish lump of cow-dung. **cow'pea** *n* a leguminous plant (*Vigna sinensis*) indigenous to Asia but cultivated in other parts of the world and used like French beans. **cow'-pilot** *n* a West Indian demoiselle fish, said to accompany the cowfish. **cow'-plant** *n* an asclepiadaceous plant of Sri Lanka (*Gymnema lactiferum*) with a milky juice. **cow'poke** *n* (*US inf*) a cowboy. **cow'pox** *n* an infection similar to smallpox caused by the *Vaccinia* virus, and *usu* affecting cows (the cowpox virus was found to confer immunity to smallpox and was used in the vaccination programme to eradicate smallpox). **cow'puncher** *n* (*US inf*) a cowboy; a herder of cows. **cow's arse** *n* (*vulgar sl*) a mess, botched job, etc. **cow shark** *n* any primitive shark of the family Hexanchidae, having six or seven gill slits. **cow'shed** see **cowhouse**. **cow's lick** see **cowlick** above. **cow'tree** *n* a S American tree (*Brosimum galactodendron*) of the family Moraceae, that produces a nourishing fluid resembling milk. **cow-weed** see **cow-chervil** above. **cow'-wheat** *n* a yellow-flowered scrophulariaceous plant (genus *Melampyrum*), with seeds somewhat like grains of wheat.

■ **till the cows come home** for a long time of unforeseeable duration.

cow² /kow/ *vt* to subdue the spirit of; to keep under. [Perh from ON *kūga*; Dan *kue* to subdue]

■ **cowed** *adj* abjectly depressed or intimidated.

cow³ or **kow** /kow/ (*Scot*) *n* a branch, bunch of twigs, besom. [Poss OFr *coe*, from L *cauda* tail]

cow⁴ /kow/ (*Dickens*) *n* a chimney-cowl. [Variant of **cowl¹**]

cowage see **cowhage**.

cowal /kow'əl/ (*Aust*) *n* a shallow lake or swamp. [From an Aboriginal language]

cowan /kow'ən/ (*Scot*) *n* a dry-stone-dyker; a mason who never served an apprenticeship; someone who tries to enter a Freemasons' lodge, or the like, surreptitiously. [Origin doubtful]

coward /kow'ərd/ *n* a reprehensibly faint-hearted person; a person who lacks courage; someone who brutally takes advantage of the weak. ◆ *vt* to make cowardly. ◆ *adj* cowardly; with tail between legs (*heraldry*). [OFr *couard* (Ital *codardo*), from L *cauda* a tail]

■ **cow'ardice** /-is/ *n* lack of courage; timidity; brutal conduct towards the weak or undefended. **cow'ardliness** *n*. **cow'ardly** *adj* having the character of a coward; characteristic of or to be expected of a coward. ◆ *adv* like a coward; with cowardice. **cow'ardry** (*obs*; Spenser **cow'ardree**) or **cow'ardship** (*Shakesp*) *n*.

cowdie-gum, **cowdie-pine** same as **kauri gum**, **kauri-pine** (see **kauri**).

cower /kow'ər/ *vi* to crouch or cringe in fear. [Cf ON *kūra*, Dan *kure* to lie quiet]

■ **cow'eringly** *adv*.

■ **cower away** to shrink back in fear.

Cow Gum® /kow gum/ *n* a rubber solution used as an easily removable quick-drying adhesive.

cowhage, **cowage** or **cowitch** /kow'ij* or *-ich/ *n* a tropical leguminous climbing plant (genus *Mucuna*); the stinging hairs on its pod, used as a vermifuge; its pods. [Hindi *kavāch*]

cowheard, **cowherd** Spenserian spellings of **coward**.

cowitch see **cowhage**.

cowl¹ /kowl/ *n* a large loose hood, *esp* of a kind worn by a monk; a hooded monk's habit; a cover, *usu* revolving, fitted over a chimney to improve ventilation; the part of a motor vehicle to which the windscreen and instrument panel are fixed; a cowling. ◆ *vt* to cover like a cowl. [OE *cugele*; ON *kofl*; related to L *cucullus* hood]

■ **cowled** *adj* wearing a cowl. **cowl'ing** *n* the metal casing round an aeroplane engine.

❏ **cowl'-necked** *adj* (of a dress, sweater, etc) having a collar which lies in loose folds over the neck and shoulders as a monk's cowl does.

cowl² /kōl, kool or kowl/ (*dialect or archaic*) *n* a tub or large vessel for liquids. [OE *cūfel* or OFr *cuvele*, both from L *cūpella* dimin of *cūpa* a cask]

❏ **cowl'-staff** *n* (*Shakesp*) a pole on which a basket or vessel is slung.

co-worker /kō-wûr'kər/ *n* an associate, colleague; someone who works with one on a project, etc.

cowp see **coup³**.

Cowper's glands /kow'pərz glandz* or *koo-/ *n pl* a pair of glands near the prostate in mammals which under sexual stimulation secrete mucus which forms part of the seminal fluid (also called **bulbourethral glands**). [William *Cowper* (1666–1709), English anatomist]

cowrie or **cowry** /kow'ri/ *n* a gastropod mollusc (genus *Cypraea* and related genera), the shells of which are used in certain primitive societies as money or invested with magical properties; a shell of the mollusc. [Hindi *kaurī*]

cowrie-pine same as **kauri**.

co-write /kō'rīt/ *vt* to write with another or others.

■ **co'-writer** *n*.

cowslip /kow'slip/ *n* a species of primrose (*Primula veris*), with fragrant yellow flowers arranged in umbels, common in pastures; the marsh-marigold (*US*). [OE *cūslyppe*, from *cū* cow, and *slyppe* slime, ie cow-dung]

■ **cow'slip'd** *adj* (*poetic*) covered with cowslips.

cox /koks/ a short form of **coxswain**.

coxa /kok'sə/ *n* (*pl* **cox'ae** /-ē/) the hip bone; the proximal joint of an arthropod's leg. [L]

■ **cox'al** *adj*. **coxal'gia** /-ji-ə/ *n* pain in the hip or disease of the hip joint.

coxcomb /koks'kōm/ *n* a foolishly vain or conceited man; a strip of red cloth notched like a cock's comb, which professional fools used to wear; the head (*obs*). [**cock's-comb**]

■ **coxcombic** /-kōm' or *-kom'/*, **coxcomb'ical** or **coxcom'ical** *adj* foppish; vain. **coxcombical'ity** *n*. **coxcomb'ically** *adv*. **cox'combry** *n* the behaviour of a coxcomb.

coxib /kok'sib/ *n* any of a group of non-steroidal anti-inflammatory drugs used in the treatment of arthritis. [cyclo-oxygenase-2 inhibitor]

coxiness see under **cock¹**.

Coxsackie virus /kŭk-sä'kē vī'rəs/ *n* (sometimes without *cap*) any of a group of RNA-containing viruses that occur in the human intestinal tract and cause various diseases, including meningitis and inflammation of muscle, brain and heart tissue. [*Coxsackie*, New York state, where the virus was first discovered]

Cox's orange pippin /kok'siz o'rinj pip'in/ *n* a sweet-tasting variety of apple with a brownish-green skin tinged with orange when ripe (in *pl* often shortened to **Coxes** /kok'səz/). [R *Cox*, 19c English horticulturalist]

coxswain or **cockswain** /kok'sn* or *kok'swān/ *n* the helmsman of a lifeboat; (*usu* shortened to **cox**) the person who steers certain racing boats (*rowing*); a petty officer in charge of a boat and crew. ◆ *vt* and *vi* to act as coxswain (for). [Obs *cock* a boat (cf **cockboat**) and **swain**]

■ **coxed** *adj* having a cox. **cox'less** *adj* without a cox.

coxy see under **cock¹**.

Coy (*milit*) *abbrev*: Company.

coy /koi/ *adj* bashful, modest; affectedly shy; evasive. ◆ *vt* to caress (*Shakesp*); to disdain (*Shakesp*); to affect coyness (with it) (*archaic*). [Fr *coi*, from L *quiētus* quiet]

■ **coy'ish** *adj*. **coy'ishly** *adv*. **coy'ishness** *n*. **coy'ly** *adv*. **coy'ness** *n*.

coyote /koi'ōt, or *-ō'ti*, or *kī-ōt* or *kī'ō-ti/ *n* (*pl* **coyo'tes** or **coyo'te**) a prairie-wolf, a small wolf of N America; a person who imports or exploits illegal immigrants, *esp* from Mexico (*US sl*). [Mex *coyotl*]

coyotillo /kō-yō-tē'lyō/ *n* a thorny shrub (*Karwinskia humboldtiana*) of Mexico and the USA, related to the buckthorn, and bearing berries that can cause paralysis. [Mex Sp, literally, little coyote]

coypu /koi'poo, *-poo'* or *-pū/ *n* (*pl* **coy'pus** or **coy'pu**) a large S American aquatic rodent (*Myopotamus* or *Myocastor coypus*) now found wild in Europe, the source of nutria fur. [Native name]

coystrel, **coystril** same as **coistrel**.

coz /kuz/ (*archaic*) *n* a contraction of **cousin**.

coze /kōz/ *vi* to chat (also *n*). [Fr *causer*]

cozen /kuz'n/ *vt* to cheat or trick. [Perh Fr *cousiner* to claim kindred; see **cousin**]

■ **coz'enage** *n* deceit. **coz'ener** *n*.

cozier or **cosier** /kō'zi-ər/ (*Shakesp*) *n* a cobbler. [OFr *cousere* tailor, from L *cōnsuere* to sew together]

cozy US spelling of **cosy**.

CP *abbrev*: Command Post; Common Prayer; Communist Party.

cp *abbrev*: candle-power; chemically pure.

cp. *abbrev*: compare.

CPA *abbrev*: certified public accountant (in the USA).

CPAG *abbrev*: Child Poverty Action Group.

CPAP *abbrev*: continuous positive airway pressure, the pumping of pressurized air through a mask as a treatment for sleep apnoea.

CPD *abbrev*: continuing professional development.

Cpd *abbrev*: compound.

CPG *abbrev*: Coronary Prevention Group.

CPGB *abbrev*: Communist Party of Great Britain.

CPI *abbrev*: consumer price index, a method of demonstrating the inflation rate.

---

cpi (*comput*) *abbrev* : characters per inch.

Cpl *abbrev* : Corporal.

CP/M (*comput*) *abbrev* : Control Program for Microcomputers, an obsolete operating system.

cpm (*comput*) *abbrev* : characters per minute.

CPO *abbrev* : Chief Petty Officer; Compulsory Purchase Order; Crime Prevention Officer.

cpp *abbrev* : current purchasing power.

CPR *abbrev* : Canadian Pacific Railway; cardiopulmonary resuscitation (*med*).

CPRE *abbrev* : Campaign to Protect Rural England.

CPRS *abbrev* : Central Policy Review Staff, a former body (1971–83) reviewing and reporting on British Government strategy, also known as the **Government Think-Tank**.

CPS *abbrev* : carrier pre-selection, a mechanism for routing telephone calls through an alternative operator without entering an additional dialling code (*telecom*); Crown Prosecution Service.

cps *abbrev* : characters per second (*comput*); cycles per second (*phys*).

CPSM *abbrev* : Council for Professions Supplementary to Medicine (now replaced by **HPC**).

CPU (*comput*) *abbrev* : central processing unit.

CPVE *abbrev* : Certificate of Pre-vocational Education, introduced in 1986 for over-16s completing a one-year preparatory course for further vocational training.

CQ (*radio*) *symbol* : transmitted by an amateur operator to establish communication with any other amateur operator.

CR *abbrev* : Community of the Resurrection; Costa Rica (IVR).

Cr *abbrev* : Councillor.

Cr (*chem*) *symbol* : chromium.

cr (*comput*) *abbrev* : carriage return.

cr. *abbrev* : credit; creditor; crown.

crab[1] /*krab*/ *n* any of the marine decapod crustaceans, having a wide, flat carapace in which the abdomen is folded under the cephalothorax; its flesh as food; (with *cap* and *the*) Cancer; a portable winch; a crab-louse; (in *pl*) infestation by crab-lice (*inf*). ◆ *vi* (**crabb'ing**; **crabbed**) to drift or move sideways; to fish for crabs; to fly (an aircraft) slightly sideways into a crosswind. [OE *crabba*; Ger *Krebs*]

■ **crabb'er** *n* a crab fisherman. **crabb'y** *adj* crablike. **crab'like** *adj*. **crab'wise** *adj* and *adv* with sideways motion like a crab's.

❑ **crab canon** *n* (*music*) a canon in which the notes of the theme are repeated in reverse order. **crab'-eater** *n* a sergeant fish; an antarctic seal. **crab'-faced** *adj* having a peevish expression. **crab grass** *n* any of several weedy annual grasses of the genus *Digitaria* which take root freely in lawns and gardens. **crab'-louse** *n* a crab-shaped parasitic louse (*Pthirus pubis*) infesting the hair of the pubis, etc in humans. **Crab Nebula** *n* the expanding cloud of gas in the constellation of Taurus, being the remains of a supernova observed in 1054AD. **crab's'-eyes** or **crab'-stones** *n pl* prayer-beads, the scarlet and black seeds of the Indian liquorice tree (*Abrus precatorius*); a limy concretion in the crayfish's stomach. **crab'-sī'dle** *vi* to go sideways like a crab. **crab stick** *n* a stick-shaped piece of processed fish, coloured and flavoured to resemble crab meat. **crab'-yaws** *n pl* yaws on the soles and palms.

■ **catch a crab** (*rowing*) to sink the oar too deeply (or not enough) in the water and fall back in consequence.

crab[2] /*krab*/ *n* a wild apple (tree or fruit); a sour-tempered person. [Ety uncertain]

❑ **crab'-apple** *n*. **crab'stick** *n* a walking-stick or cudgel made of crab-apple wood. **crab tree** *n*.

crab[3] /*krab*/ *vt* (of hawks) to claw; to decry, criticize; to obstruct, wreck or frustrate. ◆ *n* dejection; fault-finding. [**crab**[1]]

crabbed /*krab'id*/ *adj* ill-natured, perverse or irascible; (of handwriting) cramped or difficult to decipher. [**crab**[1] conflated in meaning with **crab**[2]]

■ **crabb'edly** *adv*. **crabb'edness** *n*. **crabb'ily** *adv*. **crabb'iness** *n*. **crabb'y** *adj* (**crabb'ier**; **crabb'iest**) bad-tempered, ill-natured.

crabbit /*krab'it*/ (*inf*) *adj* bad-tempered, irritable (*Scot* and *Irish*); cunning, smart (*Irish*).

crabby see under **crab**[1], **crabbed**.

crab-nut, -oil, -wood see carap.

crack /*krak*/ *vt* and *vi* to (cause eg a whip to) make a sharp sudden sound; to split; to break partially or suddenly; to fracture, the parts remaining in contact; to (cause to) give way under strain, torture, etc; (of petroleum, etc) to break into simpler molecules. ◆ *vi* (of the voice) to change tone or register suddenly; to chat, gossip (*Scot* and *US*); to talk incessantly, to boast (with *on*; *inf*). ◆ *vt* to break open (a safe, etc); to solve the mystery of (a code, etc); to utter in jest; to hit with a

resounding noise. ◆ *n* a sudden sharp splitting sound; a partial fracture; a narrow opening; a flaw; a sharp resounding blow; a friendly chat (*Scot* and *Irish*); (also **craic** /*krak*/; with *the*) the latest news, gossip (*Irish*); (also **craic**) fun, enjoyable activity and conversation, often in a pub (*Irish*); an expert; a quip, gibe; a try (*sl*); the vagina (*vulgar sl*); a highly addictive form of cocaine mixed with other substances (*usu* baking powder) and sold and used in small pellet-like pieces (*sl*). ◆ *adj* (*inf*) excellent, first-rate; expert. [OE *cracian* to crack; cf Du *kraken*, Gaelic *crac*]

■ **cracked** *adj* split; damaged; (of a voice) harsh; crazy (*inf*). **crack'er** *n* a person or thing that cracks; a thin crisp unsweetened biscuit; a colourful tubular package that comes apart with a bang, when the ends are pulled, to reveal a small gift, motto, etc; a small, noisy firework; the apparatus used in cracking petroleum; something exceptionally good or fine of its type (*inf*); someone who illegally breaks into a computer system; a poor white (*US sl*). **crack'ers** *adj* (*inf*) crazy; unbalanced. **crack'ing** *adj* (*inf*) (of speed, etc) very fast; very good.

❑ **crack baby** *n* a baby born to a mother addicted to the drug crack that has suffered physical damage as a result of being exposed to the drug while in the womb, or is itself addicted. **crack'brain** *n* a crazy person. **crack'brained** *adj*. **crackdown** see **crack down on** below. **cracked wheat** *n* wheat coarsely ground, boiled and then dried for use as a cereal food, bulgur. **crack'er-barrel** *adj* (*US*) rural, rustic, of homely philosophy. **crack'erjack** or **crack'ajack** *n* a person or thing of highest excellence (also *adj*). **crack'-halter**, **crack'-hemp** or **crack'-rope** *n* (*obs*) someone likely to or deserving to be hanged. **crack'head** *n* (*sl*) a person who uses, or is addicted to, the drug crack. **crack house** *n* a place where the drug crack is made and consumed. **crack'jaw** *adj* hard to pronounce. **crack'pot** *n* a crazy person (also *adj*). **cracks'man** *n* a burglar. **crack'-tryst** *n* (*obs*) someone who breaks an engagement. **crack willow** *n* a species of commonly grown willow, *Salix fragilis*, with branches and twigs that snap off easily, found widely in Europe and now the USA. **crackup** see **crack up** below.

■ **at the crack of dawn** at daybreak; very early in the morning. **crack a bottle, can**, etc to open or drink a bottle, can, etc. **crack a crib** (*criminal sl*) to break into a building. **crack a joke** to utter a joke with some effect. **crack a smile** (*inf*) to allow oneself to smile. **crack credit** to destroy one's credit. **crack down on** to take firm action against (**crack'down** *n*). **crack it** (*inf*) to succeed, *esp* in the seduction of a woman. **crack on** (*inf*) to proceed or go forward quickly. **crack the whip** to assert authority suddenly or forcibly. **crack up** to praise; to fail suddenly, to go to pieces; to suffer a mental breakdown; to distress considerably; to (cause to) burst into laughter (*inf*) (**crack'up** *n*). **fair crack of the whip** a fair opportunity. **get cracking** to get moving quickly.

crackle /*krak'l*/ *vi* to make a slight but sustained cracking noise as a wood fire does; to rustle loudly. ◆ *n* a slight crackling or loud rustling; a kind of porcelain with the glaze purposely cracked in the kiln as a form of decoration (also **crack'leware**); paper money, banknotes, money in general (*sl*). [Frequentative of **crack**]

■ **crack'ling** *n* the rind of roast pork; (in *pl*) the part of suet made up of skin without tallow; women as objects of desire (*offensive sl*). **crack'ly** *adj* producing a crackling or rustling noise; brittle, crisp.

cracknel /*krak'nəl*/ *n* a light, brittle biscuit; a hard nutty filling for confectionery; (in *pl*) crisply fried pieces of fat pork (*N Am*). [ME *krakenelle*, perh from OFr *craquelin*]

Cracovian /*kra-kō'vi-ən*/ *adj* of or relating to Cracow in Poland.

■ **cracovienne** /*-en'*/ *n* (also **krakowiak** /*kra-kō'vi-ak*/) a lively Polish dance; music for it in 2–4 time. **cracowe** /*krak'ow*/ *n* a long-toed boot fashionable under Richard II.

-cracy /*-krə-si*/ *combining form* used to indicate rule, government (by a particular group, etc) as in *democracy*, *mobocracy*. [Gr *-kratia*, from *kratos* power]

■ **-crat** /*-krat*/ *combining form* a person supporting, or partaking in, government (by a particular group, etc). **-cratic** or **-cratical** *adj combining form*.

cradle /*krā'dl*/ *n* a small bed for a baby, *usu* suspended or on rockers; (with *the*) infancy; the place of origin or nurture of a particular person or thing; a stand, rest or holder for supporting something; a suspended platform or trolley which can be raised and lowered and from which work can be carried out on the side of a ship, building, etc; a framework, *esp* one for keeping bedclothes from pressing on a patient, or one under a ship for launching; a rocking-box for gold-washing; an engraver's knife used with a rocking motion; a wooden pronged attachment for a scythe, for combining the operations of cutting and gathering. ◆ *adj* having been so since infancy, as in *cradle Catholic*. ◆ *vt* to lay or rock in a cradle; to hold and rock lovingly; to wash (soil containing gold) into a rocking-box; to nurture. ◆ *vt* and *vi* (in lacrosse) to keep (the ball) in the net of one's stick while running, by means of a rocking action. [OE *cradol*; ety obscure]

■ words derived from main entry word; ❑ compound words; ■ idioms and phrasal verbs

■ **cra'dling** n (*archit*) a wooden or iron framework within a ceiling. ❑ **cradle cap** n a form of seborrhoeic dermatitis common in babies, in which patches of scaly skin form on the scalp. **cra'dle-scythe** n a broad scythe used in a cradle framework for cutting grain. **cra'dle-snatcher** n (*usu derog*) someone who chooses as a lover or marriage partner someone much younger than himself or herself (also **baby-snatcher**). **cra'dle-snatching** n. **cra'dle-song** n a lullaby. **cra'dlewalk** n (*obs*) an avenue arched over with trees. ■ **from the cradle to the grave** throughout one's life.

craft /kräft/ n art; creative artistic activity involving construction, carving, weaving, sewing, etc as opposed to drawing (also **craft'work**); a skilled trade; the members of a trade collectively; an occupation; cunning; dexterity; a ship or ships of any kind (*orig small*); an air vehicle or a space vehicle. ◆ vt to make or construct, *esp* with careful skill. [OE *cræft*; Ger *Kraft* power]
■ **craft'ily** adv. **craft'iness** n. **craft'less** adj free from craft; unskilled in any craft. **craf'ty** adj (**craf'tier**; **craf'tiest**) having skill (*archaic*); cunning; wily. ❑ **craft brother** n a person engaged in the same trade as another. **craft guild** n an association of people engaged in the same trade. **craft shop** n a shop in which materials and tools for creative activities such as embroidery, basketry, model-making, etc are sold. **crafts'man** n a person engaged in a craft. **crafts'manship** or **craft'manship** n. **crafts'person** n (*pl* **crafts'people**). **crafts'woman** n. **craft union** n a trade union whose membership is restricted to people in a single trade. **craft'work** see **craft** (n) above. ■ **arty-crafty** see under **art**[1].

crag[1] /krag/ n a rough steep rock or point, a cliff; a shelly deposit mixed with sand, found in the Pliocene of East Anglia (*geol*). [Appar connected with Gaelic *creag, carraig*]
■ **cragg'ed** adj craggy. **cragg'edness** or **cragg'iness** n. **cragg'y** adj (**cragg'ier**; **cragg'iest**) full of crags or broken rocks; rough; rugged. ❑ **crag-and-tail** n (*geol*) a hill-form with steep declivity at one end and a gentle slope at the other. **crag'fast** adj (*mountaineering*) unable to move from a position on a crag. **crags'man** n a person skilled in rock climbing.

crag[2] /krag/ n the neck; the throat. [Cf Du *kraag*, Ger *Kragen* the neck]

craic see **crack** (n).

craig /krāg/ n Scots form of **crag**[1] and **crag**[2].
❑ **craig'fluke** n the witch (*Pleuronectes cynoglossus*), a flat fish.

crake[1] /krāk/ (*dialect*) n a crow, raven; a corncrake; a croak; the cry of the corncrake. ◆ vi to utter a crake. [Cf **corncrake, croak**]
❑ **crake'berry** n crowberry.

crake[2] /krāk/ (*dialect and Spenser*) n, vt and vi (to) boast. [**crack**]

cram /kram/ vt (**cramm'ing**; **crammed**) to press closely together; to stuff; to fill to superfluity; to overfeed; to feed with a view to fattening; to make believe false or exaggerated tales (*old sl*); to teach, or learn, hastily for a certain occasion (such as an examination or a lawsuit). ◆ vi to eat greedily; to prepare for an examination, etc by hasty and intensive learning. ◆ n a crush; a lie (*old sl*); information that has been crammed (*obs*); the system of cramming. [OE *crammian*; ON *kremja* to squeeze; Dan *kramme* to crumple]
■ **cramfull'** adj. **cramm'able** adj. **crammed** adj. **cramm'er** n a person or machine that crams poultry; someone who, or an establishment that, crams pupils or a subject.

crambo /kram'bō/ n (*pl* **cram'boes**) a game in which one player gives a word to which another finds a rhyme; rhyme. [Prob from L *crambē repetīta* cabbage served up again]
❑ **cram'boclink** or **crambo-jin'gle** n (*Burns*) rhyming doggerel.

crame /krām/ (*Scot*) n a booth for selling goods. [From Du or LGer]

cramoisy or **cramesy** /kram'ə-zi/ or -*oi-zi*/ (*archaic*) adj crimson. ◆ n crimson cloth. [See **crimson**]

cramp /kramp/ n an involuntary and painful contraction of a voluntary muscle or group of muscles; (*in pl*) acute abdominal pain; restraint; a cramp-iron; a device with a movable part that can be screwed tight so as to press things together. ◆ adj (*old*) (used of handwriting) hard to make out; cramped; narrow. ◆ vt to affect with spasms; to confine; to hamper; to fasten with a cramp-iron. [OFr *crampe*; cf Du *kramp*, Ger *Krampf*]
■ **cramped** adj (of handwriting) small and closely written; compressed; restricted, without enough room, confined. **cramp'et** or **cramp'it** n a scabbard-chape; a cramp-iron; a crampon. **cramp'ing** adj restricting, confining. **cramp'on** n a grappling-iron; a spiked attachment for boots for climbing mountains or telegraph poles or walking on ice. **cramp'y** adj affected or diseased with cramp; producing cramp. ❑ **cramp ball** n a hard spherical black fungus, *Daldinia concentrica*, formerly thought to ward off cramp. **cramp'bark** n (*US*) the guelder rose, or its medicinal bark. **cramp'-bone** n the patella of the sheep, an old charm for cramp. **cramp'-fish** n the electric ray or torpedo. **cramp'-iron** n a piece of metal bent at both ends for binding things

together. **cramp'-ring** n a ring formerly blessed by the sovereign on Good Friday against cramp and falling sickness.
■ **cramp someone's style** to restrict someone's movements or actions. **writer's cramp** a common disease affecting those in the habit of constant writing, the muscles refusing to respond only when an attempt to write is made (also called **scrivener's palsy**).

crampon see under **cramp**.

cran /kran/ n a measure of capacity for herrings just landed in port, equal to $37\frac{1}{2}$ gallons. [Prob from Gaelic *crann* a measure]
■ **coup the cran** (*Scot*) to upset, or be upset, (eg of plans).

cranachan /kran'ə-hhən/ n a Scottish dessert containing oatmeal, honey, raspberries, cream and *usu* whisky. [Gaelic]

cranage see under **crane**[1].

cranberry /kran'bə-ri/ n the red acid berry of a small evergreen shrub (*Vaccinium oxycoccos*) growing in peaty bogs and marshy grounds, or the larger berry of an American species (*V. macrocarpum*), both made into jellies, sauces, etc; extended loosely to other species of the genus; the shrub itself. [For *craneberry*; a late word; origin obscure; cf Ger *Kranbeere* or *Kranichbeere*]
❑ **cranberry bush** or **cranberry tree** n (*US*) the guelder rose.

cranch /kranch/ n and vt same as **crunch**.

crane[1] /krān/ n any bird of the Gruidae, large wading birds with long legs, neck and bill; a machine for raising heavy weights, *usu* having a rotating boom from the end of which the lifting gear is hung; a travelling platform for a film camera; a bent pipe for drawing liquor out of a cask. ◆ vt to raise with a crane. ◆ vi and vt to stretch out the neck, *usu* in order to see better. [OE *cran*; Ger *Kranich*, Welsh *garan*]
■ **cran'age** n the use of a crane; the price paid for the use of it. ❑ **crane'fly** n a fly (genus *Tipula*) with very long legs, the daddy-long-legs. **crane'-necked** adj. **cranes'bill** or **crane's'-bill** n any wild species of the *Geranium* genus, from the beaked fruit.

crane[2] same as **cranium**.

craniopharyngioma /krā-ni-ō-far-in-jō'mə/ n a tumour of the pituitary gland, which if untreated may cause permanent brain damage. [**cranium**, *pharyngi-* from Gr *pharynx, pharyngos* pharynx, throat, and **-oma** tumour]

cranium /krā'ni-əm/ n (*pl* **crā'niums** or **crā'nia**) the skull; the bones enclosing the brain. [LL *crānium*, from Gr *krānion* the skull]
■ **crā'nial** adj. **crā'nially** adv. **Crā'niā'ta** n pl (*zool*) the main division of the Chordata, which has a cranium. **crā'niate** adj /-ət or -āt/ having a cranium. ◆ n and adj (a) vertebrate. **crāniec'tomy** n (Gr *ektomē* cutting out) the surgical removal of a piece of the skull. **crāniog'nomy** n (Gr *gnōmē* knowledge) cranial physiognomy. **crāniolog'ical** adj. **crāniol'ogist** n. **crāniol'ogy** n the study of skulls; phrenology. **crāniom'eter** n an instrument for measuring the skull. **crāniom'etry** n. **crānios'copist** n a phrenologist. **crānios'copy** n phrenology. **crāniot'omy** n (Gr *tomē* a cut) the act of compressing the skull of a fetus in obstructed deliveries (*obstetrics*); incision into or removal of part of the skull, *esp* for the purpose of neurosurgery. ❑ **cranial index** n the breadth of a skull as a percentage of the length. **cranial nerve** n any of the ten to twelve paired nerves that have their origin in the brain. **crāniosac'ral therapy** n an alternative therapy involving gentle manipulation of the bones and membranes of the skull, in order to treat a wide range of physical and psychological disorders (*abbrev* **CST**).

crank[1] /krangk/ n an arm on a shaft for communicating motion to or from the shaft (*machinery*); a handle on this principle for starting a motor (also **crank'handle** or **starting handle**); a person of eccentric or faddy habits and tastes (*derog*); an irascible person (*N Am*); a whim. ◆ vi to turn (with) a crank (often with *up*). ◆ vt to turn (a shaft) using a crank; to start (a motor) with a crank. [OE *cranc*; cf Ger *krank* ill]
■ **crank'ily** adv. **crank'iness** n. **crank'y** adj (**crank'ier**; **crank'iest**) eccentric, faddy and full of whims (*derog*); crabbed, ill-tempered (*N Am*); shaky, unsteady (*inf*). ❑ **crank'case** n a box-like casing for the crankshaft and connecting rods of some types of reciprocating-engine. **crank pin** n the pin fitted into the arm of a crank and to which a connecting rod is attached. **crank'shaft** n the main shaft of an engine or other machine, which carries a crank or cranks for the attachment of connecting rods. ■ **crank up** to increase the intensity of, eg volume of sound.

crank[2] /krangk/ (*drug sl*) n any amphetamine drug. [From motoring image]
■ **crank up** to inject narcotics.

crank[3] /krangk/ or **crank-sided** /krangk-sī'did/ (*naut*) adj liable to capsize. [Ety uncertain]
■ **crank'ness** n liability to capsize.

crankle /krang'kl/ *n* a turn, winding, or wrinkle; an angular protuberance. ◆ *vt* and *vi* to bend; to twist. [Frequentative of **crank¹**]

crannog /kran'og/ (*archaeol*) *n* a lake dwelling in Scotland and Ireland, typically a tiny island artificially enlarged and fortified. [Gaelic *crann* a tree]

cranny /kran'i/ *n* a fissure; a chink; a secret place. ◆ *vi* to enter crannies. [Fr *cran* a notch]
■ **crann'ied** *adj* having crannies or fissures.

cranreuch /krän'ruhh/ (*Scot*) *n* hoarfrost. [Origin obscure; poss from Gaelic]

crants /krants/ (*Shakesp*) *n* the garland carried before the bier of a maiden and hung over her grave. [Ger *Kranz* a wreath, a garland]

crap¹ /krap/ (*vulgar sl*) *n* excrement; rubbish, dirt; worthless nonsense; unpleasant or petty behaviour. ◆ *vi* (**crapp'ing**; **crapped**) to defecate. ◆ *vt* to fear (something) (also **crap it**). [ME *crappe* chaff, from MDu *krappe*, prob from *krappen* to tear off]
■ **crapp'er** *n* (*sl*, chiefly *US*) a toilet; a room containing a toilet. **crapp'y** *adj*.
■ **crap out** to give up, opt out, chicken out.

crap² /krap/ *n* Scots form of **crop**. ◆ *vt* to crop; to cram or stuff.
❑ **crappit-head** or **crappit-heid** /krap'it-hēd/ *n* a haddock's head stuffed with a mixture of oatmeal, suet, onions and pepper.

crap³ see under **craps**.

crape /krāp/ *n* a thin crinkled silk or other fabric formerly *usu* dyed black and used for mourning clothes; a band of this for putting round a mourner's hat or arm. ◆ *adj* made of crape. [OFr *crespe* (Fr *crépe*), from L *crispus* crisp; see also **crêpe**]
■ **crāp'y** *adj*.
❑ **crape'hanger** or **crepe'hanger** *n* (*inf*) a pessimist. **crape'hanging** or **crepe'hanging** *n*. **crape** (or **crepe**) **myrtle** *n* an ornamental shrub, *Lagerstroemia indica*, with pinkish crinkled crapelike flowers.

craple /krap'l/ (*Spenser*) *n* same as **grapple**.

crappie /krap'i/ *n* any of a genus (*Pomoxis*) of small N American sunfishes. [Can Fr *crapet*]

craps /kraps/ *n sing* a gambling game in which a player rolls two dice (also **crap**). [**crab¹**, lowest throw at hazard]
■ **crap** *n* a losing throw in craps.
❑ **crap'shoot** *n* (*N Am*) a game of craps; a matter of chance. **crap'shooter** *n*.
■ **crap out** (*US*) to make a losing throw in craps; to fail. **shoot craps** to play craps.

crapulence /krap'ū-ləns/ *n* sickness caused by excessive drinking; intemperance. [Fr *crapule*, from L *crāpula* intoxication]
■ **crap'ulent** or **crap'ulous** *adj*. **crapulos'ity** *n*.

craquelure /krak'ə-lūr or -loor/ *n* the fine cracking that occurs in the varnish or pigment of old paintings; this effect or pattern. [Fr]

crare or **crayer** /krār/ *n* a trading vessel. [OFr *craier*]

crases see **crasis**.

crash¹ /krash/ *n* a noise as of things breaking or being crushed by falling; the shock of two bodies meeting; a collision between vehicles, etc; the failure of a commercial undertaking; economic collapse; a fall or rush to destruction; the complete breakdown of a computer system or program; the disagreeable after-effects of a high (*drug sl*). ◆ *adj* planned to meet an emergency quickly; involving suddenness, speed or short-term intensive effort. ◆ *vt* and *vi* to dash or fall to pieces with a loud noise; to move with a harsh noise; to collide or cause to collide with another vehicle, etc; to fall or cause (an aircraft) to fall violently to earth or into the sea, *usu* with extensive damage; to gatecrash (*inf*); to break down or cause (a computer system or program) to break down completely. ◆ *vi* to come to grief, fail disastrously; to suffer the unpleasant after-effects of a high (*drug sl*); to crash out (*sl*). [Imit]
■ **crash'ing** *adj* (*inf*) extreme, overwhelming, *esp* in *a crashing bore*. **crash'worthiness** *n* the ability of a product to withstand a crash. **crash'worthy** *adj*.
❑ **crash barrier** *n* a protective barrier, *usu* of steel, placed eg along the edge of a road or the central reservation of a motorway. **crash course** *n* a short-lasting but intensive programme of instruction. **crash dive** *n* a sudden dive of a submarine; a sudden dive of an aircraft, resulting in a crash. **crash'-dive'** *vi* and *vt*. **crash'-helmet** *n* a padded safety headdress for motorcyclists, racing motorists, etc. **crash'-land'** *vi* and *vt* in an emergency, to land (an aircraft) abruptly, with resultant damage. **crash'-land'ing** *n*. **crash'-mat** *n* a thick mattress used by athletes and gymnasts to absorb the impact of landing after a jump, etc. **crash'-matting** *n*. **crash'pad** *n* padding inside a motor vehicle to protect the occupants in case of accident; a place providing temporary accommodation (*sl*). **crash'-proof** *adj* designed to withstand a crash. **crash recorder** see **flight recorder** under **flight¹**. **crash team** *n* a medical team specially trained and equipped to deal quickly with a patient suffering a cardiac arrest. **crash'-test** *vt* to test (a new product) to establish its breaking point by subjecting it to heat, pressure, impact, etc. ◆ *n* such a test.
■ **crash and burn** (*inf*) to fail disastrously. **crash out** (*sl*) to fall asleep; to become unconscious.

crash² /krash/ *n* a coarse strong linen. [Perh from Russ *krashenina* coloured linen]

crasis /krā'sis/ (*grammar*) *n* (*pl* **crā'sēs** /-sēz/) the mingling or contraction of two vowels into one long vowel, or into a diphthong. [Gr *krāsis* mixture]

crass /kras/ *adj* coarse, boorish; grossly stupid, tactless or insensitive. [L *crassus*]
■ **crassament'um** *n* the thick part of coagulated blood; the clot. **crass'itude** *n* coarseness; stupidity, tactlessness or insensitivity. **crass'ly** *adv*. **crass'ness** *n*.

crassulaceous /kras-ū-lā'shəs/ (*bot*) *adj* of, belonging to, or relating to the **Crassūlā'ceae**, a family of succulent plants including the stonecrops and house leeks. [From the genus name *Crassula* stonecrop, from L *crassus* thick]
❑ **crassulacean acid metabolism** *n* a method of photosynthesis in desert and succulent plants, in which carbon dioxide is taken in at night and stored to be used during the day (*abbrev* **CAM**).

-crat, **-cratic**, **-cratical** see under **-cracy**.

cratch /krach/ (*dialect* and *archaic*) *n* a crib to hold hay for cattle, a manger. [Fr *crèche* manger; from a Gmc root, whence also **crib**]
■ **cratch'es** *n pl* a swelling on a horse's pastern, under the fetlock.

crate /krāt/ *n* a strong metal, plastic, wooden or wickerwork case with partitions, for carrying breakable or perishable goods; a packing case; the contents of a crate; a decrepit aeroplane or car (*inf*). ◆ *vt* to pack in a crate. [L *crātis* a hurdle]
■ **crate'ful** *n* (*pl* **crate'fuls**).

crater /krā'tər/ *n* the bowl-like mouth of a volcano; a hole in the ground where a meteorite has fallen, or a shell, mine or bomb exploded; a circular rimmed depression in the surface of the moon; a cavity formed in the carbon of an electric arc; (*usu* **krat'er**) a large two-handled bowl for mixing wine in (*archaeol*); (with *cap*) a small faint constellation in the southern hemisphere. ◆ *vt* to form craters in. [L, from Gr *krātēr* a mixing bowl]
■ **crateriform** /krat-er'i-förm or krāt'er-i-förm/ *adj* cup-shaped. **crat'erlike** *adj*. **crat'erous** *adj*.
❑ **crater lake** *n* a lake formed in the crater of an extinct volcano.

crathur see **cratur**.

craton /krā'ton/ (*geol*) *n* any of the comparatively rigid and immobile areas in the earth's crust. [Gr *kratos* strength]
■ **craton'ic** /krə-ton'ik/ *adj*.

cratur /krā'tər/ or **crathur** /krāth'/ (*Irish* and *Scot*) *n* a creature.
■ **the cratur** whisky.

craunch /krönch/ a dialect form of **crunch**.

cravat /krə-vat'/ *n* a formal neckerchief worn, *esp* by men, as an alternative to a tie. ◆ *vt* (**cravatt'ing**; **cravatt'ed**) to dress in a cravat. [Fr *cravate*, from *Cravates*, 17c Croatian mercenaries who wore a scarf in battle]

crave /krāv/ *vt* to ask for earnestly, to beg; to require; to long or yearn for. ◆ *vi* to long (with *for* or *after*). ◆ *n* a longing; a claim (*Scots law*). [OE *crafian* to crave; ON *krefja*]
■ **crav'er** *n* someone who craves; a beggar. **crav'ing** *n* a longing or great desire.

craven /krā'vn/ *adj* cowardly; spiritless. ◆ *n* a coward; a spiritless person. ◆ *vt* (*Shakesp*) to render spiritless. [ME *cravant*, perh from L *crepāre* crack]
■ **crav'enly** *adv*. **crav'enness** *n*.

craw /krö/ *n* the crop, throat or first stomach of fowls; the crop of insects; the stomach of animals generally. [ME *crawe*; not found in OE; cf Du *kraag* neck]
■ **stick in one's craw** see **stick in one's throat** under **stick²**.

crawfish /krö'fish/ (*esp N Am*) *n* a crayfish. ◆ *vi* to retreat or back out, *esp* from a position in which one is being challenged.

crawl¹ /kröl/ *vi* to move slowly with the body on or close to the ground; to move on hands and knees; to creep; to move slowly or stealthily; to behave abjectly or obsequiously; to be, or feel as if, covered with crawling things (with *with*); to swim using the crawl stroke. ◆ *n* the act of crawling; a slow pace; a swimming stroke in which the arms are held in front of the body and rotated from the shoulder alternately and the feet kicked up and down. [ME, perh from ON *krafla* creep]
■ **crawl'er** *n* someone who or something that crawls; an abject, obsequious or sycophantic person; a sluggish or slow person; a creeping thing; a heavy slow-moving vehicle, *esp* one that moves on caterpillar tracks; a baby's overall, a romper suit; a computer program

---

■ words derived from main entry word; ❑ compound words; ■ idioms and phrasal verbs

that extracts information from sites on the World Wide Web in order to create entries for a search engine's index. **crawl'ing** n. ◆ adj creeping; lousy, verminous. **crawl'ingly** adv. **crawl'y** adj (**crawl'ier**; **crawl'iest**) (inf) with, or like the feeling of, something crawling over one; creepy.

❑ **crawler lane** n an extra lane for the use of slow-moving vehicles on an uphill stretch of a road. **crawling peg** n (econ) a system of stabilizing prices or exchange rates by allowing a limited amount of rise or fall at predetermined intervals. **crawl'space** n a shallow area below a floor or above a ceiling, giving access to pipes and ducts.

crawl² /kröl/ n a pen for keeping fish or lobsters. [From Afrik *kraal* a pen]

crayer see **crare**.

crayfish /krā'fish/ or (esp N Am) **crawfish** /krö'fish/ n a large edible freshwater decapod crustacean; the Norway lobster; the spiny lobster. [ME *crevice*, from OFr *crevice* (Fr *écrevisse* a crayfish), from OHGer *krebiz* a crab]

crayon /krā'ən/ or *-on*/ n a pencil made of chalk, wax or pipe-clay, variously coloured, used for drawing; a drawing done with crayons. ◆ vt and vi to draw or colour with a crayon. [Fr *crayon*, from *craie* chalk, from L *crēta* chalk]

craze /krāz/ vt or vi to become or to cause (the mind) to become deranged; to weaken; to impair; to develop or cause (pottery, metal, etc) to develop a series of fine cracks; to shatter or break (archaic). ◆ n a fashion or fad; a crack or flaw; a series of fine cracks; a small structural defect in plastic; insanity. [Scand; cf Swed *krasa*, Dan *krase* to crackle; also Fr *écraser* to crush]

■ **crazed** adj. **crāz'ily** adv. **crāz'iness** n. **crāz'y** adj (**crāz'ier**; **crāz'iest**) demented, deranged; ridiculous, stupid; exuberantly wild in behaviour (inf); extravagantly enthusiastic or passionate (about) (inf); impractical; (of paving, etc) composed of flat, irregular pieces; rickety (old). ◆ n (pl **cra'zies**) (inf) a crazy person.

❑ **crazing mill** n a mill for crushing tin-ore. **crazy ant** n a long-legged tropical ant that moves erratically when disturbed and is a major environmental pest. **crazy bone** n (N Am) the funny bone. **crazy golf** n a form of putting in which balls have to be hit past, through, over, etc obstacles such as humps, tunnels, bends, etc to reach the hole. **crazy paving** n paving composed of irregularly shaped slabs of stone or concrete, used for ornamental effect on terraces, garden paths, etc. **crazy quilt** n a patchwork quilt made up haphazardly of irregular pieces of material sewn together.

■ **like crazy** fast and furiously.

CRC (printing) abbrev: camera-ready copy.

CRE abbrev: Commission for Racial Equality (now replaced by Commission for Equality and Human Rights).

creagh or **creach** /krehh/ (Scot) n a foray; booty. [Gaelic *creach*]

creak /krēk/ vi to make a sharp grating or squeaking sound, as of an unoiled hinge or sagging floorboard. ◆ n such a grating noise. [From the sound, like *crake* and *croak*]

■ **creak'ily** adv. **creak'iness** n. **creak'ingly** adv. **creak'y** adj (**creak'ier**; **creak'iest**) squeaky; tending to creak; badly made or performed (fig).

cream /krēm/ n the oily substance that rises to the surface of milk, yielding butter when churned; the colour of this substance, yellowish white; the best part of anything; the pick of a group of things or people; a food largely made of cream or like cream in consistency or appearance, as *ice cream*; any other substance having the appearance or consistency of cream, as *cold-cream* for skin. ◆ vt to take off the cream from (milk), to skim; to select (the best) from a group, etc (with *off*); to beat or mix to the consistency of thick cream (eg a mixture of sugar and butter in cake-making); to treat with cream; to thrash or defeat soundly (inf). ◆ vi to form cream; to gather like cream. ◆ adj of the colour of cream, yellowish-white; prepared with cream; (of sherry) sweet. [OFr *cresme, creme*, from LL *cramum* of Celtic origin, infl by ecclesiastical *chrisma* unction]

■ **cream'er** n a vessel or device for separating cream from milk; a small jug for cream (esp N Am); a substitute for milk, in powder form, for use in coffee, etc. **cream'ery** n an establishment where butter and cheese are made from the milk supplied by a number of producers; a shop selling milk, butter, etc. **cream'ily** adv. **cream'iness** n. **cream'y** adj (**cream'ier**; **cream'iest**) full of cream, or like cream in appearance, consistency, etc; forming or gathering like cream.

❑ **cream bun** or **cream cake** n a kind of bun or cake filled with cream or a substitute for cream. **cream cheese** n soft white cheese. **cream'-coloured** adj of the colour of cream, yellowish-white. **cream cracker** n a crisp, unsweetened type of biscuit, often eaten with cheese. **cream horn** n a horn-shaped pastry filled with cream, etc. **cream jug** n a small jug for serving milk or cream. **cream'laid** adj (of paper) cream or white in colour with a laid watermark. **cream'-nut** n another name for the Brazil nut. **cream of tartar** n a white crystalline compound made by purifying argol, potassium hydrogen tartrate. **cream of tartar tree** n

another name for the baobab; an Australian tree of the same genus, *Adansonia gregorii*. **cream puff** n a confection of puff pastry filled with cream; (esp used of men) an ineffectual person (esp N Am); a male homosexual (derog sl). **cream'-slice** n a wooden blade for skimming cream from milk. **cream soda** n (esp N Am) a vanilla-flavoured fizzy drink. **cream tea** n a meal consisting of tea and scones filled with cream and jam. **cream'ware** n a type of earthenware first produced in the 18c, having a cream-coloured glaze. **cream'wove** adj (of wove paper) cream or white in colour.

■ **cream of chicken**, **mushroom**, etc **soup** chicken, mushroom, etc soup made with milk or cream.

creance /krē'əns/ (falconry) n the cord which secures the hawk in training. [Fr *créance*]

creant /krē'ənt/ adj creating; formative. [L *creāns, -antis*, prp of *creāre*; see **create**]

crease¹ /krēs/ n a mark made by folding, pressing or crumpling; such a mark pressed centrally and longitudinally into a trouser-leg; a wrinkle or line on the face; any of the lines that regulate the positions of batsman and bowler at the wicket in cricket (see also **bowling crease**, **popping crease** and **return crease** below); (in ice-hockey and lacrosse) a marked area round the goal. ◆ vt to make a crease or creases in; to graze with a bullet, sometimes used as a method of temporarily disabling rather than killing (an animal). ◆ vi to become creased. ◆ vt and vi (inf) to double up with laughter (often with *up*). [Origin uncertain]

■ **creas'er** n. **creas'y** adj full of creases; liable or tending to crease. ❑ **crease'-resistant** or **crease'-resisting** adj (of a fabric) not becoming creased in normal wear.

■ **bowling crease** (cricket) a line marked perpendicularly across the pitch at the level of the wicket, from astride which the bowler must bowl. **popping crease** (cricket) a line marked perpendicularly across the pitch four feet in front of the bowling crease, at which the batsman plays and behind which he or she must have a foot or bat in order not to be run out or stumped. **return crease** (cricket) a line marked at right angles to the bowling crease and popping crease on either side of the wicket, inside which the bowler must bowl the ball.

crease² see **kris**.

creasote see **creosote**.

create /krē-āt'/ vt to bring into being or form out of nothing; to bring into being by force of imagination; to make, produce or form; to design; to invest with a new form, office or character; to institute; to be the first actor to play (a certain role). ◆ vi (sl) to make a fuss. [L *creāre, -ātum* to create, *creātūra* a thing created]

■ **creāt'able** adj. **creation** /krē-ā'shən/ n the act of creating; (with *cap* and *the*) God's act of creating the universe (*Christianity*); that which is created; the world, the universe; a specially designed, elaborate, or particularly striking, garment, eg a hat. **creā'tional** adj. **creā'tionism** n the theory that the universe has its origin in the specific acts of creation by God recorded in the Book of Genesis, opp to *evolutionism*; the theory that God immediately creates a soul for every human being born, opp to *traducianism*. **creā'tionist** n and adj. **creā'tive** adj having power to create; creating; showing or relating to imagination or originality; (esp of accounting or accountancy) characterized by an imaginative re-interpretation or dubious manipulation of established rules of procedure, for personal benefit or ease of operation (euphem). ◆ n a person who works in a creative role, esp in the advertising industry. **creā'tively** adv. **creā'tiveness** n. **creativity** /krē-ə-tiv'/ n the state or quality of being creative; the ability to create. **creā'tor** n someone who creates; a maker; (with *cap* and *the*) the Supreme being, God. **creā'torship** n. **creā'trix** or **creā'tress** n (rare) a female creator. **creatural** /krē'chər-əl/ or **crea'turely** adj relating to a creature or thing created. **creature** /krē'chər/ n an animate being, esp an animal; a human being, in this sense often used in contempt or compassion; something created, whether animate or inanimate; a person completely under one's control, a dependant, instrument, or puppet; (usu with *the*) alcoholic drink (inf). **crea'tureship** n.

❑ **creation science** n creationism treated as a scientific viewpoint or theory. **creative accounting** or **creative accountancy** see **creative** above. **creative therapy** n the use of art, dance, music, etc to assist human development and social interaction, eg during recovery from illness. **creature comforts** n pl material comforts such as food, drink, a place to sleep, etc; alcohol, esp whisky. **creature of habit** n an animal with fixed behavioural patterns; a person of unchanging routines.

■ **the Creator** see **creator** above.

creatic /krē-at'ik/ adj relating to flesh. [See **creatine**]

creatine or **creatin** /krē'ə-tin or *-tēn*/ n a nitrogenous compound ($C_4H_9N_3O_2$), found in the striped (voluntary) muscle of vertebrates. [Gr *kreas, kreatos* flesh]

■ **crē'atinine** /-nin or *-nēn*/ n dehydrated creatine ($C_4H_7N_3O$) found in urine and muscles.

---

fāte; fär; mē; fûr; mīne; mōte; för; mūte; pŭt; dhen (then); *el'ə-mənt* (element) • For other sounds see detailed chart of pronunciation

❑ **creatine phosphate** n the phosphate ester of creatine, capable of converting ADP to ATP, and used as a short-term source of energy during bursts of muscular activity.

creative, creator, creature see under **create**.

crèche /kresh/ n a nursery for either brief or daylong care of young children; (sometimes with cap) a model representing the scene of Christ's nativity. [Fr crèche manger]

cred /kred/ (sl) n short for **credibility**, esp in the phrase street cred.

credal see under **creed**.

credence /krē'dəns/ n belief; trust; precautionary tasting of food before serving, eg to a king, etc (obs); a sideboard; the small table beside the altar on which the bread and wine are placed before being consecrated (also **credence table**); a shelf over a piscina (also **credence shelf**). [LL crēdentia trust, from L crēdere to believe]

■ **credendum** /kri-den'dəm/ n (pl **creden'da**) a thing to be believed, an act of faith. **crē'dent** adj (obs) credible, believable; credulous, believing. **credential** /kri-den'shl/ adj recommending for credit or confidence. **creden'tialism** n undue favouring of paper qualifications over experience and other qualities. **creden'tials** n pl evidence of competence, taken as one's entitlement to authority, etc; letters of introduction, certificates, etc entitling one to trust or confidence. **credenza** /kri-den'zə/ or (Ital) krä-dent'sa/ n a credence table or shelf; a sideboard; a bookcase, esp if without legs.

credible /kred'i-bl/ adj capable of being believed; seemingly worthy of belief or of confidence; reliable; (of a nuclear weapon) in whose use and effectiveness one can believe. [L crēdibilis believable, from crēdere to believe]

■ **credibil'ity** /kred-/ n the quality of deserving belief or confidence; the amount of confidence placed in one on the basis of one's record, knowledge or proven abilities, eg in a particular social group or environment. **cred'ibleness** n. **cred'ibly** adv.

❑ **credibility gap** n (politics, etc) the discrepancy between what is claimed or stated and what actually is, or seems likely to be, the case.

credit /kred'it/ n esteem; reputation or honour; distinction; good character; acknowledgement or recognition of something contributed or achieved; belief or trust; time allowed for payment; an entry in the right-hand column of an account making acknowledgement of a payment or an obligation to pay in the future (bookkeeping); the side of an account on which such entries are made (bookkeeping); a sum placed at a person's disposal in a bank, up to which they may draw; certified completion of a course of study counting towards a final pass; a distinction awarded for performance on a course; (in pl) credit titles; (in pl) a list of acknowledgements in a book, etc. ◆ vt to believe; to trust; to sell or lend to on condition that payment is made within a specified period; to enter on the credit side of an account; to ascribe to (with to or with); to mention in the credit titles. [OFr crédit, from L crēditum loan, from crēdere to believe]

■ **creditabil'ity** n. **cred'itable** adj trustworthy; bringing credit or honour; praiseworthy. **cred'itableness** n. **cred'itably** adv. **cred'itor** n a person (or business) to whom a debt is due. **cred'itworthiness** n entitlement to credit as judged from earning capacity, promptness in debt-paying, etc. **cred'itworthy** adj.

❑ **credit account** n a facility with a store or supplier enabling customers to purchase goods on credit. **credit balance** n the value of a liability or equity account (bookkeeping); an amount standing to someone's benefit, eg in a bank account. **credit card** n a card obtainable from a credit card company which, in places where the card is recognized, enables the holder to have purchases, services, etc debited to an account kept by the company; a similar card issued by other organizations or by certain banks. **credit crunch** n (inf) a sudden and drastic reduction in the availability of credit. **credit default swap** n (finance) a contract insuring against the risk of non-payment of a bond (abbrev **CDS**). **credit insurance** n insurance against bad debts, taken out when a business sells on credit. **credit limit** n the maximum amount of credit extended to an individual or business. **credit line** n an acknowledgement of authorship in a newspaper, film, etc; an agreement to borrow up to a certain amount. **credit note** n a document issued by a retailer, esp a shop or store, to a customer who has returned goods, which can be used to obtain other goods to the same value; an amendment to an invoice (account). **credit rating** n (an assessment of) the level of a person's or business's creditworthiness. **credit-reference agency** n an organization that specializes in providing credit ratings. **credit scoring** n the calculation of a person's credit rating by adding up points awarded according to the person's age, marital status, occupation, address, etc; a similar process used to calculate the creditworthiness of a business organization. **credit squeeze** n a method of controlling the money supply in an economy by imposing restrictions on the amount of credit available to individuals and businesses, used by governments as a counter-inflationary instrument. **credit standing** n the reputation of a person or organization for meeting financial obligations. **credit titles** (or, more usually, **cred'its**) n pl acknowledgements of the work of

contributors shown at the beginning or end of a film, television programme, etc. **credit transfer** n a method of settling a debt by transferring cash from an account at a bank or post office to the creditor's account. **credit union** n a non-profit-making co-operative savings association which makes loans to its members at low interest.

■ **be a credit to someone**, etc to achieve success, perform or act in praiseworthy manner as proof of time, trouble, etc well-invested in one by someone, etc. **give credit for** to acknowledge as having (a quality, certain level of competence, etc).

credo /krā'dō or krē-/ n (pl **crē'dos**) a belief or set of beliefs; (with cap) the Apostles' Creed or the Nicene Creed, or a musical setting of either of these for church services. [L, I believe]

credulity /kri-dū'li-ti/ n disposition to believe without sufficient evidence. [L crēdulus over-trustful, from crēdere to believe]

■ **credulous** /kred'-/ adj apt to believe without sufficient evidence; unsuspecting. **cred'ulously** adv. **cred'ulousness** n.

Cree /krē/ n (pl **Cree** or **Crees**) a member of a Native American tribe living in Montana and parts of Canada; the Algonquian language of this people, or its syllabic writing system. ◆ adj of the Cree or their language. [Short for Can Fr Christianaux, from Algonquian kiristino, kinistino]

cree /krē/ vt and vi (of grain) to soften by boiling or soaking. [Fr crever to burst]

Creed /krēd/ n a form of teleprinter. [Frederick George Creed (1871–1957), its Canadian inventor]

creed /krēd/ n a summary of articles of religious belief; any system of belief or set of principles. [OE crēda, from L crēdō I believe]

■ **creed'al** or **cred'al** adj.
■ **the Creed** the Apostles' Creed or the Nicene Creed.

Creek /krēk/ n (pl **Creek** or **Creeks**) a member of any of the tribes of Native Americans of Florida, Alabama and Georgia (now mainly in Oklahoma), who formed the **Creek Confederacy**; the Muskogean language of the Creek. ◆ adj of or relating to the Creek or their language. [Prob peak a river]

creek /krēk/ n a small inlet or bay, or the tidal estuary of a river; a small river or brook (N Am, Aust and NZ). [Prob Scand, ON kriki a nook; cf Du kreek a bay; Fr crique]

■ **creek'y** adj full of creeks; winding.
■ **up the creek** or (vulgar) **up shit creek** (**without a paddle**) (sl) in dire difficulties (without the means or ability to save oneself).

creel /krēl/ n a basket, esp a fish basket; a lobster trap; a rack on a spinning frame for holding bobbins. [Origin obscure]

creep /krēp/ vi (pat and pap **crept**) to move with the belly on or near the ground; to move or advance slowly or stealthily; to slip or encroach very gradually; to develop insidiously; to grow along the ground or on supports, as a vine does; to fawn or cringe; (of the skin or flesh) to have a shrinking sensation, as a concomitant of horror, etc; to shudder; to drag with a creeper (naut); to undergo creep (metallurgy). ◆ vt (Milton, etc) to creep on. ◆ n the act or process of creeping; a slow slipping or yielding to stress; crystallization or rise of a precipitate on the side of a vessel above the surface of a liquid; gradual alteration of shape under stress (metallurgy); a narrow passage; an enclosure in which young farm animals may feed, with an approach too narrow to admit the mother; a cringing, unassertive or otherwise unpleasant person (sl). [OE crēopan; Du kruipen]

■ **creep'er** n someone or something that creeps; a creeping plant, eg the Virginia creeper; a small bird that runs up trees, a tree creeper (N Am); a kind of grapnel used for dragging the seabed, etc (naut); an endless chain or conveyor; a crêpe-soled, or other soft-soled, shoe (inf); a wheeled board on which one may lie and move about while working under a vehicle; a ball that stays low after bouncing (cricket). **creep'ered** adj covered with a creeper. **creep'ie** n a low stool; a stool of repentance. **creep'ily** adv. **creep'iness** n. **creep'ing** adj. **creep'ingly** adv. **creep'y** adj (**creep'ier**; **creep'iest**) mysterious, rather eerie or chilling.

❑ **creep'-hole** n a hiding hole; a subterfuge. **creeping bent grass** n a common European pasture grass, Agrostris palustris. **creeping eruption** n an irritating skin condition caused by the larvae of certain flies or nematodes which burrow through the skin tissue leaving thin red lines (also **larva migrans**). **creeping Jenny** n moneywort, a creeping plant of the primrose family (Lysimachia nummularia). **creeping Jesus** n (derog sl) a cringingly sanctimonious person. **creeping thistle** n Canada thistle (qv). **creep'mouse** adj (archaic) silent and shrinking. **creepy-crawl'y** n (inf) a creeping insect (also adj).

■ **the creeps** (inf) a feeling of horror or revulsion.

creese see **kris**.

creesh /krēsh/ (Scot) vt to grease. ◆ n grease. [OFr craisse, from L crassus fat]

■ **creesh'y** adj.

crem /krem/ (*inf*) *n* a crematorium.

crémaillère /krä-mī-yer'/ *n* a zigzag line of fortification; a rack railway. [Fr, pot-hook]

cremains /kri-mānz'/ (*inf*) *n pl* the ashes of a cremated person. [Contraction of *cremated remains*]

cremaster /kri-mas'tər/ *n* a muscle of the spermatic cord; a hook-like projection on the pupae of butterflies and moths from which the pupa is suspended. [Gr *kremastēr* suspender, from *kremannynai* to hang]

cremate /krē- or kri-māt'/ *vt* to burn (*esp* a dead body). [L *cremāre*, *-ātum* to burn]

■ **crema'tion** *n*. **crema'tionist** *n*. **cremat'or** *n* a person who undertakes cremations; a furnace for cremation; an incinerator. **crematorial** /krem-ə-tō'ri-əl or -tö'/ *adj*. **cremato'rium** *n* (*pl* **cremato'ria** or **cremato'riums**) a place for cremating dead bodies. **crem'atory** /-ə-tər-i/ *n* a crematorium. ◆ *adj* relating to cremation.

creme /krēm/ *n* a form of **cream**, used *specif* for skin creams, frequently used in proprietary names.

crème or **crême** /krem/ (*Fr*) *n* cream, applied to various creamy substances.

❏ **crème anglaise** /ã'glāz or ong'glāz/ *n* a light pouring custard made from egg yolks, sugar, milk and vanilla. **crème brûlée** /brü-lā'/ *n* a dish of egg yolks, cream and vanilla topped with caramelized sugar. **crème caramel** /kar-a-mel/ *n* an egg custard baked in a dish lined with caramel. **crème de cacao** /kə-kä'ō or -kä'ō/ *n* a chocolate-flavoured liqueur. **crème de menthe** /də mãt/ *n* a green peppermint-flavoured liqueur. **crème fraîche** /fresh/ *n* cream thickened with a culture of bacteria.

■ **crème de la crème** /də la krem/ cream of the cream, the very best.

cremocarp /krem'ō-kärp/ (*bot*) *n* the characteristic fruit of the Umbelliferae, composed of two one-seeded halves which split apart and dangle from the top of the axis. [Gr *kremannynai* to hang, and *karpos* fruit]

Cremona /kri-mō'nə/ *n* the name applied to any of the superior violins or stringed instruments made at *Cremona* in Italy (16c–18c), including those made by Stradivari.

cremona /kri-mō'nə/ and **cremorne** /kri-mör'nə/ non-standard forms of **cromorna**.

cremor /krē'mör/ *n* thick juice. [L]

cremosin or **cremsin** /krem'zin/ *adj* obsolete forms of **crimson**.

crenate /krē'nāt, kren'āt or kren-āt'/ or **crenated** /-id/ (*bot*) *adj* (of plant leaves) having a notched or scalloped edge. [New L *crēnātus*, from an inferred L *crēna* a notch]

■ **crē'na** *n* a notch or tooth. **crēnā'tion** *n* a crenated formation; the process of shrinkage and formation of scalloped edges on red blood cells in a hypertonic solution. **crenature** /krē' or kren'/ *n*. **cren'ulate** or **cren'ulated** *adj* finely or irregularly notched or serrated. **crenulā'tion** *n*.

crenel or **crenelle** /kren'əl/ (*archit*) *n* an indentation in a parapet, a crenellation. ◆ *vt* to indent with crenels. [OFr *crenel*, from inferred L *crēna* a notch]

■ **cren'ellate** or (*US*) **cren'elate** /kren'i-lāt/ *vt* to provide with battlements. **cren'ellate** or **cren'ellated** *adj* having or forming battlements; indented. **crenellā'tion** *n*. **cren'elled** *adj*.

crenulate see under **crenate**.

creodont /krē'ō-dont/ *n* any member of a group of primitive fossil carnivores, appearing in Eocene times. [Gr *kreas* flesh, and *odous*, *odontos* tooth]

creole /krē'ōl or krē-ōl'/ *n* (*usu* with *cap*) strictly, applied in the former Spanish, French and Portuguese colonies of America, Africa and the West Indies to natives of pure European blood, as opposed to immigrants born in Europe or to coloured natives; (*usu* with *cap*) a native, but not aboriginal or indigenous; (*usu* with *cap*) loosely, a native of mixed blood, *esp* a West Indian of mixed Spanish or French and black African blood; (*usu* with *cap*) applied to the native French or Spanish settlers in Louisiana (*US*); (*usu* with *cap*) a colonial patois (French, Spanish, etc); (also **creolized** or **creolised language**) a language formerly a pidgin which has developed and become the accepted language of a region, *esp* in the West Indies. ◆ *adj* (sometimes with *cap*) relating to a Creole or creole; of a type of West Indian cookery, *usu* including rice, okra, peppers and spices or strong seasoning. [Fr *créole*, from Sp *criollo*, dimin of *criado* nursling, from *criar*, literally, to create, hence to bring up, nurse, from L *creāre*]

■ **creo'lian** *n* and *adj* an earlier form of **creole**. **crē'olist** *n* a person who studies creole languages. **crēōlizā'tion** or **-s-** *n* the development of a pidgin into a creole.

creophagous /krē-of'ə-gəs/ *adj* flesh-eating, carnivorous. [Gr *kreas* flesh, and *phagein* to eat]

creosol /krē'ə-sol/ *n* one of the active consituents of creosote, an oily insoluble liquid with a characteristic smoky aroma.

creosote or **creasote** /krē'ə-sōt/ *n* an oily liquid obtained by destructive distillation of wood tar, used as an antiseptic; a somewhat similar liquid obtained from coal tar, used to preserve wood (also **creosote oil** or **coal-tar creosote**). ◆ *vt* to treat with creosote. [Gr *kreas* flesh, *sōtēr* saviour, from *sōzein* to save]

❏ **creosote plant** *n* an American bush (*Larrea mexicana*) that has an odour of creosote and forms dense scrub.

crepance /krē'pəns/ *n* a wound on a horse's hind ankle joint, caused by the shoe of the other hind-foot. [L *crepāre* to break]

crêpe or **crepe** /krāp or krep/ *n* any of several finely wrinkled fabrics similar to crape (qv); rubber rolled in thin crinkly sheets (**crêpe rubber**); (*usu* **crêpe**) a thin pancake. [See **crape**]

■ **crep'erie** *n* a restaurant or eating establishment that specializes in pancakes with various fillings. **cre'piness** *n*. **crep'oline** *n* a light crape-like dress material. **crep'on** *n* a thick crape-like fabric made of silk or nylon. **crêp'y**, **crep'y** or **crep'ey** *adj* (*esp* of skin) wrinkled, crêpe-like, crape-like.

❏ **crêpe-de-chine** /də shēn/ *n* (also **crepe-**) a crape-like fabric, *orig* of silk. **crêpe'hanger**, **crepe myrtle** see under **crape**. **crêpe paper** *n* thin crinkled paper. **crêpe sole** *n*. **crêpe'-soled** *adj* (of shoes) having a sole of crêpe rubber. **crêpe suzette** /sü-zet'/ *n* (*pl* **crêpes suzettes**) a thin pancake in a hot orange- or lemon-flavoured sauce, *usu* flambéed.

crepitate /krep'i-tāt/ *vi* to crackle, snap; to rattle; (of beetles) to discharge an offensive fluid. [L *crepitāre*, *-ātum*, frequentative of *crepāre* to crack, rattle]

■ **crep'itant** *adj* crackling. **crepitā'tion** *n* the act of crepitating; crackling; a soft crackling sound detected through a stethoscope, and *usu* resulting from inflammation due to pneumonia or other disease. **crep'itātive** *adj*.

crepitus /krep'i-təs/ (*med*) *n* the grating sound produced when an arthritic joint is moved or when a fractured bone is disturbed; crepitation. [L, a creaking or rattling]

crepoline, **crepon** see under **crêpe**.

crept /krept/ *pat* and *pap* of **creep**.

crepuscular /kri-pus'kū-lər/, also **crepusculous** /-ləs/ *adj* of or relating to twilight; dim, dark; (of certain animals) active, or appearing, at twilight. [L *crepusculum* twilight]

■ **crepuscule** /krep'əs-kūl, or -ūs'/ or **crepuscle** /krep'əs-l or -us'/ *n* twilight.

Cres. *abbrev* : Crescent (in street names).

cresc. (*music*) *abbrev* : crescendo.

crescendo /kri- or kre-shen'dō/ (*music*) *adj* and *adv* gradually increasing in loudness. ◆ *n* (*pl* **crescen'dos**) an increase of loudness; a passage of increasing loudness; a high point, a climax (*fig*). ◆ *vi* to reach a crescendo. [Ital, increasing]

crescent /kres'ənt or krez'/ *n* (more *usu* **the crescent moon**) the waxing moon; a curved shape like the moon in its first or last quarter; the Turkish (*orig* Byzantine) standard or emblem; the Turkish power; (a symbol of) the Islamic faith; a curved street or terrace; a crescent-shaped roll or bun, a croissant. ◆ *adj* shaped like the waxing moon; increasing, growing (*formal*). [L *crēscere* to grow, prp *crēscēns*, *-entis*]

■ **cresc'entade** *n* a religious war for Islam. **cresc'ented** or **crescentic** /-ent'ik/ *adj* formed like a crescent. **cresc'ive** *adj* (*formal*) increasing.

crescograph /kres'kə-gräf/ *n* a sensitive instrument capable of measuring and recording the rate of growth of plants. [L *crēscere* to grow, and **-graph**]

cresol /krē'sol/ *n* any of three isomeric compounds with the formula $C_6H_4(CH_3)OH$ found in tar and creosote, resembling phenol, used as an antiseptic and disinfectant and in making plastics, explosives and dyestuffs (also called **cresylic acid**).

cress /kres/ *n* a name for many pungent-leaved cruciferous plants of various genera often used as a culinary garnish and in salads, eg *Lepidium* (garden cress), *Rorippa* (watercress), *Arabis* (rock cress); extended to other plants of similar character, such as Indian cress (*Tropaeolum*). [OE *cresse*, *cerse* ; cf Du *kers*, Ger *Kresse*]

cresset /kres'it/ (*hist*) *n* an iron basket in which oil or pitch could be burned to provide light, *usu* placed on the top of a pole; a torch generally. [OFr *cresset*, *crasset* (Fr *creuset*), from ODu *kruysel* a hanging lamp]

CREST /krest/ (*finance*) *n* a computerized system of share management.

crest /krest/ *n* the comb or tuft on the head of a cock or other bird; a long narrow ridge forming the summit of anything, as a roof-ridge or the top of a hill or wave; the mane of a horse, etc; a ridge along the surface of a bone (*anat*); a plume of feathers or other ornament on the top of a helmet; an accessory figure *orig* surmounting the helmet in a coat of arms, also used separately as a device on personal effects (*heraldry*). ◆ *vi* to culminate, reach a high point. ◆ *vt* to surmount (a hill or wave). [OFr *creste* (Fr *crête*), from L *crista*]

■ **crest'ed** *adj* having a crest; having an elevated appendage like a crest (*bot*). **crest'ing** *n* an ornamental ridge along the top of a roof, wall, etc. **crest'less** *adj* without a crest; not of high birth.

❑ **crested tit** *n* a European tit (*Lophophanes cristatus*) which has a speckled black-and-white crest. **crest'fallen** *adj* dejected or cast-down.

■ **on** (or **riding**) **the crest of a wave** enjoying a run of success.

creston /*kre-ston*/ (*geol*) *n* an outcrop. [Sp]

cresylic /*krə-sil'ik*/ (*chem*) *adj* of cresol or creosote. [From *cresol* with sfx *-yl* and sfx *-ic*]
❑ **cresylic acid** *n* cresol.

cretaceous /*kri-tā'shəs*/ *adj* composed of or like chalk; (with *cap*) of or belonging to a period of the Mesozoic era, between 145 and 65 million years ago (*geol*; also *n*). [L *crētāceus*, from *crēta* chalk]

Cretan /*krē'tən*/ or **Cretic** /*krē'tik*/ *adj* belonging to Crete. ◆ *n* a native or inhabitant of Crete. [Gr *krētikos*, from *Krētē* Crete]
■ **crē'tic** *n* (*prosody*) a metrical foot consisting of one short syllable between two long. **crē'tism** *n* a lie.

cretin /*kret'in* or *krēt'in*/ *n* an idiot; a child suffering from a congenital deficiency of thyroxine (thyroid hormone) which, if untreated, can lead to mental retardation and incomplete physical development; a person affected by these conditions as a result of such a deficiency. [Fr *crétin*, from L *christiānus* human creature]
■ **cret'inism** *n*. **cret'inize** or **-ise** *vt*. **cret'inoid** *adj* and *n*. **cret'inous** *adj*.

cretonne /*krə-ton'* or *kret'on*/ *n* a strong printed cotton fabric used for curtains or for covering furniture. [Fr, prob from *Creton* in Normandy]

creutzer same as **kreutzer**.

Creutzfeldt-Jakob disease /*kroits'felt yak'ob di-zēz'*/ *n* a degenerative condition of the brain thought to be caused by infection with a brain protein, called a prion, and characterized by diminishing muscle co-ordination, deterioration of the intellect and often blindness and loss of speech, one form of which (**variant** or **new variant Creutzfeldt-Jakob disease**) is thought to be associated with exposure to bovine spongiform encephalopathy from infected beef products (*abbrev* **CJD**). [HG *Creutzfeldt* (1885–1964), and AM *Jakob* (1884–1931), German psychiatrists]

crevasse /*kri-vas'*/ *n* a crack or split, *esp* applied to a cleft in a glacier; a fissure in a river embankment (*US*). ◆ *vt* (*US*) to make a fissure in (a dyke, etc). [Fr; cf **crevice**]

crève-cœur /*krev-kœr'*/ (Fr) *n* heartbreak.

crevette /*krə-vet'*/ (Fr) *n* a shrimp or prawn.

crevice /*krev'is*/ *n* a narrow crack or split, *esp* in a rock. [OFr *crevace*, from L *crepāre* to creak, break]

crew[1] /*kroo*/ *n* (Milton *crue*) a gang; a ship's company; the oarsmen or oarswomen and cox, where appropriate) of a racing boat; a group or team of people with individual duties in charge of a bus, train or aeroplane. ◆ *vi* to act as a crew member on a ship, etc (*esp* with *for*). [OFr *creue* increase, from *croistre* to grow]
❑ **crew bus** *n* a commercial vehicle with seating for several people, used *esp* for transporting workmen to and from their place of work. **crew cab** *n* a four-wheel-drive vehicle with a spacious cabin at the front and a rear like that of a flatbed lorry. **crew cut** *n* a style of haircut in which the hair is cut so close to the head that it stands upright. **crew'man** *n* a member of the crew of a boat, aircraft, etc. **crew neck** *n* a round, close-fitting style of neck on a jersey. **crew'-necked** *adj*.

crew[2] /*kroo*/ *pat* of **crow**.

crewe /*kroo*/ (archaic) *n* a pot. [OFr *crue*]

crewel /*kroo'əl*/ *n* a fine worsted yarn used for embroidery and tapestry; embroidery or tapestry work in which crewels are used. ◆ *vt* to work in crewel. [Orig a monosyllable, *crule*, *crewle*; ety uncertain]
■ **crew'elist** *n*. **crew'ellery** *n*. **crew'elwork** *n*.

crewels, **cruells** or **cruels** /*kroo'əlz*/ (archaic Scot) *n pl* the king's evil, scrofula. [Fr *écrouelles*]

cria /*krē'ə*/ *n* the offspring of a llama or related animal. [Sp]

criant /*krī'ənt* or *krē-ä'*/ *adj* garish, discordantly coloured. [Fr]

crib /*krib*/ *n* a child's bed, *usu* with slatted sides, a cot (*esp* N Am); a manger or container for animal fodder; a representation, *esp* a model, of the scene around the manger that served as a bed for the newborn Christ; a stall for oxen; a home, *esp* one's own (*sl*); a rudimentary dwelling; a beach or holiday cottage (*NZ*); a small confined space; a brothel (*sl*); a container for grain; a wickerwork basket; a timber framework for a dam, a pier foundation, a mine-shaft lining, etc (also **crib'work**); a pilfering, or the thing pilfered; an act of stealing, or something stolen, from another's work, a plagiarism; a key or baldly literal translation, used as an aid by students, etc; the discarded cards at cribbage, used by the dealer in scoring; cribbage (*inf*); a light meal (*Aust* and *NZ*). ◆ *vt* (**crib'bing**; **cribbed**) to put in a crib; to confine; to steal (another's work), to plagiarize. [OE *crib*; Ger *Krippe*]
■ **cribb'er** *n*.
❑ **crib'-biting** *n* (in horses) a harmful habit of seizing the edge of the crib or manger in the teeth, often accompanied by the swallowing of air (wind-sucking). **crib death** *n* (*N Am*) cot death. **crib'work** see **crib** (*n*) above.

cribbage /*krib'ij*/ *n* a card game in which each player discards a certain number of cards for the *crib*, and scores by holding certain combinations and by bringing the sum of the values of cards played to certain numbers. [*crib* discarded cards; see under **crib**]
❑ **cribb'age-board** *n* a scoring board for cribbage, with holes for pegs.

cribble /*krib'l*/ *n* a coarse screen or sieve used for sand, gravel or corn; coarse flour or meal (*obs*). ◆ *vt* to sift or riddle (*obs*); (in engraving) to produce a dotted or punctured effect. [L *crībrum*, dimin *crībellum* a sieve]
■ **cribb'led** *adj*. **cribell'ar** *adj*. **cribell'um** *n* (*pl* **cribell'a**) a sieve-like spinning-organ of certain spiders. **criblé** /*krē-blā'*/ *adj* (Fr; engraving) punctured like a sieve, dotted. **crib'rate** (or /*krīb'*/), **crib'rose** or **crib'rous** *adj* perforated like a sieve. **cribrā'tion** *n* sifting. **crib'riform** *adj* (*anat* and *bot*) perforated, sieve-like.

cribellar, **criblé**, **cribrate**, etc see under **cribble**.

cricetid /*krī-sē'tid*/ *n* a member of the **Crice'tidae**, a family of rodents including the hamsters. [New L, from Slav name for hamster]

crick[1] /*krik*/ *n* a spasm or cramp of the muscles, *esp* of the neck. ◆ *vt* to produce or cause a crick in. [Prob imit]

crick[2] /*krik*/ (*N Am* dialect) *n* a creek.

cricket[1] /*krik'it*/ *n* an outdoor game played by two teams of eleven players on a large field with two wickets (22 yards apart) near the centre, in which batsmen from one team attempt to defend the wickets and score the maximum number of runs (by hitting a hard leather ball) without being bowled, caught, run out or otherwise dismissed by members of the opposing team. ◆ *vi* to play cricket. [Fr *criquet* goalpost]
■ **crick'eter** *n*. **crick'eting** *n* and *adj*.
■ **not cricket** (*inf*) not fair and sporting.

cricket[2] /*krik'it*/ *n* a jumping insect of the family Gryllidae, related to the grasshopper and locust, the male of which makes a chirping sound by rubbing its forewings together. [OFr *criquet*; cf Du and LGer *krekel*]

cricket[3] /*krik'it*/ (now dialect) *n* a low stool. [Ety unknown]
❑ **cricket table** *n* a small low table with a circular foldable top on a triangular base.

crickey, **cricky** see **crikey**.

cricoid /*krī'koid*/ (*anat*) *adj* ring-shaped. ◆ *n* a ring-shaped cartilage forming the wall of the larynx. [Gr *krikoeides*, from *krikos* a ring, and *eidos* form]

cri de cœur /*krē də kœr'*/ (Fr) *n* (*pl* **cris de cœur** /*krē*/) a cry from the heart, a heartfelt, passionate entreaty, complaint or reproach.

cri du chat (**syndrome**) /*krē dü shä' (sin'drōm)*/ *n* a rare, often fatal, congenital condition, so called because underdevelopment of the larynx results in a catlike cry, and caused by the absence of a particular chromosome in all the body cells. [Fr]

cried, **crier**, **cries** see **cry**.

crikey /*krī'ki*/, **cricky** or **crickey** /*krik'i*/ (*sl*) *interj* a mild oath or expression of surprise. [Euphemism for **Christ**]

crim /*krim*/ (*inf*) *n* short for **criminal**.

Crimbo /*krim'bō*/ (*inf*) *n* Christmas.

crim. con. (law) *abbrev*: criminal conversation.

crime /*krīm*/ *n* a violation of law, *esp* if serious; an act punishable by law; such acts collectively or in the abstract; an act of serious moral wrongdoing; sin; something deplorable (*inf*). ◆ *vt* (*milit*) to charge or convict of an infraction of regulations. [Fr, from L *crīmen*, *-inis*]
■ **crime'ful** *adj* criminal. **crime'less** *adj* without crime, innocent.
criminal /*krim'*/ *adj* relating to crime; guilty of crime; violating the law; deplorable (*inf*). ◆ *n* a person who is guilty of crime. **criminalēse'** *n* criminals' slang. **crim'inalist** *n* a person versed in criminal law. **criminal'ity** *n* the condition of being a criminal; guiltiness. **criminalīzā'tion** or **-s-** *n*. **crim'inalize** or **-ise** *vt* to declare someone or something criminal; to make illegal. **crim'inally** *adv*. **crim'inate** *vt* to accuse. **criminā'tion** *n* the act of criminating; accusation. **crim'inative** or **crim'inatory** *adj* involving crimination. **criminogen'ic** *adj* causing crime. **criminolog'ical** *adj*. **criminol'ogist**

n. **criminol'ogy** *n* the science and study of crime and criminals.
crim'inous *adj* criminal, chiefly in the ecclesiastical phrase *a criminous clerk.* **crim'inousness** *n.*

□ **crime prevention** *n* measures taken to deter or prevent criminal acts, *esp* those safeguards advocated by a police **crime prevention officer** to prevent theft, burglary, etc. **crime sheet** *n* (*milit*) a record of offences against regulations. **crime wave** a sharp rise in the level of criminal activity (see **wave**). **criminal conversation** *n* (*law*) adultery; formerly, an action in which a husband could claim damages against the adulterer (*abbrev* **crim. con.**). **criminal court** *n* a court in which those accused of criminal offences are tried, *opp* to *civil court.* **criminal law** *n* the body of law dealing with criminal offences, offenders and punishment. **criminal lawyer** *n.*

crimen /krī'men/ or /krē'men/ (L) *n* (*pl* **cri'mina**) a crime.

□ **crimen falsi** /fal'sī, fal'sē/ *n* the crime (or charge) of perjury. **crimen laesae majestatis** /lē'sē maj-əs-tā'tis/ or /lī'sī ma-yes-tä'tis/ *n* high treason.

crime passionnel /krēm pa-syo-nel'/ (*Fr*) *n* a crime committed from (sexual) passion.

criminal, criminate, etc see under **crime.**

crimine or **crimini** /krim'i-ni/ (*archaic*) *interj* an ejaculation of surprise or impatience. [Perh from *Christ*; see **crikey**]

criminogenic, criminology, etc, **criminous,** etc see under **crime.**

crimmer see **krimmer.**

crimp /krimp/ *vt* to press into folds, flutes or ridges; to put tight waves or curls into (the hair) with curling tongs; to bend (eg metal) into shape; to thwart or hinder (*N Am*). ◆ *n* a curl or wave; a bend or crease; a hindering factor (*N Am*). [OE *gecrympan* to curl; cf **cramp**, and Du *krimpen* to shrink]

■ **crimp'er** *n* a person who or device that crimps or corrugates; a hairdresser (*sl*). **crimp'le** *vt* to curl, wrinkle or crumple. **crimp'y** *adj* (**crimp'ier; crimp'iest**).

□ **crimp'ing-iron** *n* a metal tonglike device used for crimping hair, fabric, etc. **crimp'ing-machine** *n* a machine for forming crimps.

Crimplene® /krim'plēn/ *n* (a crease-resistant, synthetic fabric made from) a thick polyester yarn.

crimson /krim'zn/ *n* a deep red colour, tinged with blue; red in general. ◆ *adj* deep red. ◆ *vt* to dye crimson; ◆ *vi* to become crimson; to blush. [ME *crimosin*, from OFr *cramoisin*; from Ar *qirmizī* scarlet, from *qirmiz* kermes, from which it is made]

crinal /krī'nəl/ *adj* of or belonging to the hair. [L *crīnis* the hair]

■ **crīn'ate** or **crīn'ated** *adj* having hair. **crīnicul'tural** *adj* relating to the culture or growth of the hair. **crīnig'erous** *adj* hairy. **crī'nose** *adj* hairy.

crine /krīn/ (*Scot*) *vi* to shrink or shrivel. [Gaelic *crion* dry]

cringe /krinj/ *vi* to stoop in a servile manner; to cower in fear; to behave timidly or obsequiously; to fawn or to flatter with servility; (loosely) to wince or flinch. ◆ *n* a servile obeisance. [Related to OE *crincan, cringan* to shrink; cf **crank**[1]]

■ **cringe'ling** or **crin'ger** *n* a person who cringes. **crin'ging** *n* and *adj.* **crin'gingly** *adv* in an obsequious manner.

□ **cringe'-making** or **cringe'worthy** *adj* (*inf*) acutely embarrassing, sickening, excruciating, of poor quality.

cringle /kring'gl/ *n* a small piece of rope worked into the bolt rope of a sail, and containing a metal ring or thimble. [LGer *Kringel* little ring]

crinicultural, crinigerous see under **crinal.**

crinite[1] /krī'nīt/ *adj* hairy; having or resembling a tuft of hair (*bot*). [See **crinal**]

crinite[2] /krī'nīt/ *n* an encrinite or fossil crinoid. [See **crinoid**]

crinkle /kring'kl/ *vt* to twist, wrinkle, crimp. ◆ *vi* to wrinkle up, curl. ◆ *n* a wrinkle; a virus disease of strawberry plants, transmitted by aphids; (also **crink'ly**) paper money, money in general (*sl*). [Related to OE *crincan*; see **cringe**]

■ **crink'ly** *adj* (**crink'lier; crink'liest**) wrinkly. ◆ *n* (*sl*) an old person. □ **crinkle-crank'le** *n* (*dialect*) (something) winding or zigzag.

crinoid /krin'oid or krī'noid/ *n* a primitive echinoderm of the class **Crinoid'ea**, with cup-shaped body and branching arms, including the feather star, sea lily and numerous fossil forms (also *adj*). [Gr *krinoeides* like a lily]

■ **crinoid'al** *adj* shaped like a lily. **crinoid'ean** *adj* and *n.*

crinoline /krin'ə-lin, -lēn/ *n orig* a stiff fabric of horsehair and flax used to stiffen or line women's skirts; a hooped petticoat or skirt made to project all round by means of steel wire; a netting round ships as a guard against torpedoes. [Fr, from *crin*, from L *crinis* hair, and *lin*, from L *linum* flax]

■ **crinolette'** *n* a small crinoline causing the dress to project behind only. **crin'olined** *adj.*

crinose see under **crinal.**

crinum /krī'nəm/ *n* any of various plants of the Amaryllis family, characterized by luxuriant clusters of lily-like flowers. [Gr *krinon* a lily]

criollo /krē-ōl'ō/ *n* (*pl* **crioll'os**) a Latin American native of European, *esp* Spanish, blood; any of several S American breeds of animal; the name given to a fine variety of cocoa. [Sp, native, indigenous; see **creole**]

criosphinx /krī'ō-sfingks/ *n* a ram-headed sphinx. [Gr *krīos* a ram, and *sphinx* a sphinx]

cripes /krīps/ (*sl*) *interj* an expression of surprise or worry. [Euphemism for **Christ**]

cripple /krip'l/ *n* a lame or disabled person (now *offensive*); a person damaged, disabled or deficient in some way, as in *emotional cripple* ; a bracket attached to a ladder on the ridge of a roof to support scaffold boards. ◆ *adj* (now *offensive*) lame. ◆ *vt* to make lame, to disable; to impair, undermine or curtail with disastrous effect. [OE *crypel*; connected with **creep**]

■ **cripp'led** *adj.* **cripple'dom** *n.* **cripp'ler** *n.* **cripp'ling** *n* a prop set up as a support against the side of a building.

□ **cripp'leware** *n* (*comput sl*) software that has been partly disabled to provide a limited demonstration of its use.

crise /krēz/ *n* (*pl* **crises** /krēz/) a peak of emotional distress, an emotional crisis. [Fr]

■ **crise de conscience** /də-kō-syäs/ a crisis of conscience, a moral dilemma. **crise de foi** /də-fwä/ an attack of doubt, distrust or disillusionment. **crise de nerfs** /də-ner/ an attack of nerves, hysterics.

crisis /krī'sis/ *n* (*pl* **crises** /krī'sēz/) a crucial or decisive moment; a turning point, eg in a disease; a time of difficulty or distress; an emergency. [Gr *krisis* a decision, judgement, from *krīnein* to decide]

□ **crisis management** *n* action taken to limit damage and establish the most profitable strategy in a difficult situation.

crisp /krisp/ *adj* curling closely; so dry as to break or crumble easily, brittle; (of pastry) short; (of weather) fresh and bracing, *esp* when frosty; (of fabric) clean, starched; (of hair) springy; firm, the opposite of limp or flabby; (of wording) neat, terse, well-turned; (of manner) firm, decisive, authoritative. ◆ *vt* and *vi* to make or become crisp. ◆ *n* (*usu* in *pl*) a thin slice of potato fried until crisp, a potato-crisp; any piece of food fried or roasted until crisp. [OE, from L *crispus* curled, wrinkled]

■ **crisp'ate** *adj* (*bot* and *zool*) having a wavy edge. **crispa'tion** *n* the state of being curled; a ripple or slight wave, as on the surface of water; a creeping or rippling sensation caused by a slight muscle contraction. **crisp'ature** *n* a curling. **crisp'er** *n* anything that crisps; a compartment in a refrigerator in which to keep lettuce, etc fresh. **crisp'iness** *n.* **crisp'ly** *adv.* **crisp'ness** *n.* **crisp'y** *adj* (**crisp'ier; crisp'iest**).

□ **crisp'bread** *n* a brittle, unsweetened type of biscuit of rye or wheat, *usu* eaten as a substitute for bread.

■ **burn to a crisp** to burn until charred and brittle.

crispin /kris'pin/ *n* a poetic name for a shoemaker, from *Crispin* of Soissons, the patron saint of shoemakers, martyred 25 October 287.

criss-cross or **crisscross** /kris'kros/ *n* a network of crossing lines; the Latin cross at the beginning of the alphabet on a hornbook (see **criss-cross-row** under **Christ**); a mark formed by two lines in the form of a cross, as the signature of a person unable to write his or her name; a game of noughts and crosses (*esp N Am*). ◆ *adj* and *adv* crosswise; consisting of a network of crossed lines. ◆ *vt* and *vi* to cross repeatedly. [From *christ-cross*]

crissum /kris'əm/ *n* (*pl* **criss'a**) the area surrounding a bird's cloaca, including the under-tail feathers. [L *crissāre* to move the thighs sensuously]

crista /kris'tə/ *n* (*pl* **cris'tae** /-ē/) a crest; a ridge or fold resembling a crest, eg the infolding of the inner membrane of a mitochondrion (*biol*). [L].

■ **crist'ate** *adj* crested. **crist'iform** *adj.*

cristobalite /kri-stō'bə-līt/ *n* one of the principal forms of silica, produced from quartz at high temperatures, occurring in volcanic rocks, slags, etc. [Cerro San *Cristóbal* in Mexico, where it was discovered]

crit /krit/ (*inf*) *n* short for **criticism.**

crit. *abbrev* : critical.

criterion /krī-tē'ri-ən/ *n* (*pl* **crite'ria**) a means or standard of judging; a test; a rule, standard or canon. [Gr *kritērion*, from *kritēs* a judge]

□ **crite'rion-referenced** *adj* (of an examination or assessment) judging examinees on the basis of their demonstrated mastery of certain skills and abilities (rather than by comparison with the achievements of their peers; cf **norm-referenced**). **criterion referencing** *n.*

criterium /krī-tē'ri-əm/ n a cycling race consisting of a series of laps over public roads. [Fr *critérium* test, criterion; see **criterion**]

crith /krith/ (*phys*) n a unit of mass, that of 1 litre of hydrogen at standard temperature and pressure, ie 89.88mg. [Gr *krīthē* barleycorn, a small weight]

crithidial /kri-thid'i-əl/ (*zool*) adj of, relating to or resembling the flagellate genus *Crithidia*, particularly applied to a stage in the life cycle of certain trypanosomes.

crithomancy /krith'ō-man-si/ n divination by strewing meal over sacrificial animals. [Gr *krīthē* barley, and *manteiā* divination]

critic /krit'ik/ n someone who assesses the quality of something, a judge; a professional reviewer of literature, art, drama or music; a person skilled in textual studies and the ascertainment of the original words where readings differ; a fault-finder. [Gr *kritikos*, from *krīnein* to judge]

■ **crit'ical** adj at or relating to a turning point, transition or crisis; decisive, crucial; (loosely) seriously ill; relating to criticism; rigorously discriminating; finding fault; of a condition in which a chain reaction is self-sustaining (*phys*). **crit'ically** adv. **crit'icalness** or **critical'ity** n. **crit'icaster** n a petty critic (see **-aster**). **crit'icism** n the art of judging, *esp* in literature or the fine arts; a critical judgement or observation. **criticizable** or **-s-** /-sīz'-/ adj. **crit'icize** or **-ise** vt to analyse and pass judgement on; to find fault with, to censure. **crit'icizer** or **-s-** n.
□ **critical angle** n the smallest possible angle of incidence at which a light ray is totally reflected. **critical apparatus** same as **apparatus criticus** (see **apparatus**). **critical coupling** n (*elec eng*) the coupling giving maximum energy transfer between two circuits or systems tuned to the same frequency. **critical damping** n (*phys*) the minimum amount of damping that results in an oscillatory electric circuit or mechanical system sufficient to prevent free oscillation. **criticality accident** n (*nuclear eng*) the accidental attainment of a critical mass of fissile material by eg the drying out of a solution containing uranium-235. **critical mass** n (*nuclear eng*) the minimum amount of fissile material needed to sustain a chain reaction. **critical path analysis** n the working out with the aid of a computer the sequence of operations that must be followed in order to complete a complex piece of work in the minimum time. **critical philosophy** n that of Kant which is based on a critical examination of the foundations of knowledge. **critical point** or **critical state** n the point when a substance is between its gaseous and liquid states. **critical temperature** n that temperature above which a gas cannot be liquefied by pressure alone.
■ **higher criticism** scholarly investigation into general questions surrounding the Bible, such as authorship and date. **lower criticism** scholarly investigation concerning specific textual passages in the Bible.

critique /kri-tēk'/ n (the art of) criticism; a critical estimate of a work of literature, art, etc; a critical dissertation or review. ◆ vt to discuss or analyse critically. [Fr, from Gr *kritikē* (*technē*) the art of criticism]

critter or **crittur** /krit'ər/ (*dialect and inf*; now *esp US*) n a creature; an animal.

crivens or **crivvens** /kriv'ənz/ (*Scot sl*) interj an exclamation expressing amazement or dismay. [Perh from *Christ* combined with *heavens*]

CRO abbrev: Criminal Records Office.

croak /krōk/ vi (of eg a frog or raven) to utter a low hoarse sound; to speak similarly hoarsely; to grumble or talk dismally; to die (*sl*). ◆ vt to utter (words) hoarsely; to kill (*esp N Am sl*). ◆ n the sound or a sound similar to that made by a frog or raven. [Imit]
■ **croak'er** n an animal or bird that croaks; a grumbler; any of several types of tropical seafish of the Sciaenidae family that emit croaking noises. **croak'ily** adv. **croak'ing** n. **croak'y** adj (**croak'ier**; **croak'iest**).

Croat /krō'at/ n a native or inhabitant of Croatia, in the former Yugoslavia; the language of Croatia. ◆ adj of or relating to the Croats or their language. [Serbo-Croat *Hrvat*]
■ **Croatian** /-ā'shən/ adj belonging to Croatia or its people. ◆ n a Croat; the Croat language.

croc /krok/ (*inf*) n short for **crocodile**.

croceate, croceous see under **crocus**[1].

crocein /krō'si-in/ n one of a group of red and yellow artificial dyes. [L *croceus* yellow]

croche /krōch/ n a knob at the top of a deer's horn. [Fr]

crochet /krō'shā/ n decorative work consisting of intertwined loops, executed in wool or thread with a small hook. ◆ vi and vt (**crocheting** /krō'shā-ing/; **crocheted** /krō'shād/) to work in crochet. [Fr *crochet*, from *croche*, *croc* a hook]
■ **cro'cheter** n. **cro'cheting** n the action of crochet. ◆ n crochetwork.

crocidolite /krō-sid'ə-līt/ n a fibrous mineral consisting mainly of silicate of iron and sodium, called *blue asbestos*; in S Africa also a golden alteration product or pseudomorph of this mineral, consisting largely of quartz. [From Gr *krokis, -idos* nap of cloth, and *lithos* stone]

crock[1] /krok/ n a pot or jar; a potsherd; short form of **crock of shit** (see below). [OE *croc*; Ger *Krug*; perh of Celtic origin, as in Welsh *crochan* a pot, Gaelic *crogan* a pitcher]
■ **crocked** adj (*N Am sl*) drunk. **crock'ery** n all types of domestic pottery.
▦ **crock of shit** (*vulgar sl*; chiefly *N Am*) something considered worthless or nonsense.

crock[2] /krok/ (*inf*) n a broken down or decrepit person or thing. ◆ vi to break down (often with *up*). ◆ vt to disable. [Cf Norw and Swed *krake* a poor beast]

crock[3] /krok/ (*dialect*) n dirt, smut. ◆ vt to fill or cover with dirt or smut. [Origin doubtful]

crockery see under **crock**[1].

crocket /krok'it/ (*archit*) n an ornament on the sloping sides of a pediment, pinnacle, etc, *usu* like curled leaves or flowers. [See **croquet**]

crocodile /krok'ə-dīl/ n a large long-tailed tropical reptile of the genus *Crocodilus* (order Crocodilia), with powerful tapering jaws and a thick skin covered with bony plates; sometimes extended to the order Loricata including alligators and gavials; leather from crocodile skin; a double file of school pupils taking a walk. [L *crocodīlus*, from Gr *krokodeilos* a lizard]
■ **crocodilian** /-dil'/ adj and n.
□ **crocodile bird** n an African bird (*Pluvianus aegyptius*) said to pick the crocodile's teeth or take leeches from its throat. **crocodile clip** n a clip for making electrical connections, with serrated jaws that interlock. **crocodile tears** n pl hypocritical grief, from the old story that crocodiles (which have large lachrymal glands) shed tears over the hard necessity of killing animals for food.

crocoite see under **crocus**[1].

crocosmia /krə-koz'mi-ə/ n any iridaceous plant with the genus *Crocosmia*, including montbretia, typically bearing orange or yellow flowers in late summer. [Gr *krokos* crocus, and *osmē* smell]

crocus[1] /krō'kəs/ n (pl **cro'cuses**) a bulbous iridaceous plant with brilliant yellow, purple or white flowers. [L *crocus*, from Gr *krokos*; prob of Eastern origin; cf Heb *karkom* and Ar *kurkum* saffron]
■ **croceate** /krō'si-āt/ (*obs*) or **croceous** /krō'shi-əs/ adj saffron-coloured. **crocoite** /krō'kō-īt/ or **crocoisite** /krō'-* or *-kō'-/ n a bright-red mineral, lead chromate.

crocus[2] /krō'kəs/ (*sl*) n a quack doctor.

Croesus /krē'səs/ n a very rich man. [*Croesus*, king of Lydia, of fabulous wealth]

croft /kroft/ n a small piece of arable land, in Scotland *esp* adjoining a dwelling; a small farm. ◆ vi to expose cloth to the elements in the course of bleaching it. [OE *croft*; perh cognate with Du *kroft* hillock]
■ **croft'er** n someone who runs or farms a croft. **croft'ing** n.

Crohn's disease /krōnz di-zēz'/ n a chronic medical condition involving severe inflammation of the gastrointestinal tract, particularly the ileum, and causing scarring and thickening of the bowel wall. [B *Crohn* (1884–1983), US physician]

croissant /krwä'sã/ n a crescent-shaped bread-roll made with a large quantity of butter and having a flaky consistency. [Fr]

croix de guerre /krwä də ger'/ (Fr) n a military decoration for bravery in action.

cromack same as **crummock**.

Cro-Magnon /krō-mag'nən or krō-man'yõ/ adj relating to an early type of *Homo sapiens*, long-skulled but short-faced, of late Palaeolithic times. [From *Cro-Magnon*, in Dordogne, where the first skulls of this type were found]

crombec /krom'bek/ n an African warbler of the genus *Sylvietta*, having colourful plumage. [Du *krom* crooked, and *bek* beak]

Crombie® /krom'bi/ n a woollen cloth manufactured in Aberdeen, used for overcoats, etc; a garment made from such cloth.

crome or **cromb** /krōm or kroom/ (*dialect*) n a hook or crook. ◆ vt to draw with a crome. [Cf Du *kram*]

cromlech /krom'lehh or -lek/ n a prehistoric stone circle; formerly applied to a dolmen. [Welsh *cromlech*, from *crom* curved, circular, and *llech* stone]

cromorna or **cromorne** /krō-mörn' or -mör'nə/ n a krummhorn; a krummhorn stop. [Fr *cromorne*, from Ger *Krummhorn*]

■ words derived from main entry word; □ compound words; ▦ idioms and phrasal verbs

Cromwellian /krom-wel'i-ən/ adj of or relating to Oliver *Cromwell*, Puritan and Lord Protector of the Commonwealth (1653–8). ◆ *n* a supporter of Cromwell; a settler in Ireland in the settlement of 1652; a chair of plain design with leather seat and back, said to have been popularized by the Puritans.

cron /kron/ (*comput*) *n* a command used to schedule a job that is executed periodically or at a specified time (also *adj*). [From **chronological**]

crone /krōn/ *n* an old woman (*derog*); an old ewe. [Perh OFr *carogne* carrion, hag, directly or through Du]

cronet /krō'net/ (*obs*) *n* the hair growing over the top of a horse's hoof. [**coronet**]

cronk /krongk/ (*Aust inf*) *adj* ill; of poor quality; fraudulent. [From **crank¹**]

Cronut /krō'nut/ (*US*) *n* a sweet pastry that combines the qualities of a croissant and a donut.

crony /krō'ni/ *n* an intimate companion. [Said to be orig university slang, from Gr *chronios* long-continued, perennial]
■ **crō'nyism** *n* (*inf*) the appointment of friends to well-paid or influential posts regardless of their fitness for these posts.

croodle¹ /krōō'dl/ (*Scot*) *vi* to cower down, snuggle. [Origin unknown]

croodle² /krōō'dl* or *krŭd'l/ (*Scot*) *vi* to murmur like a dove. [Imit]

crook /krŭk/ *n* a bend, or something bent; a staff bent at the end, as a shepherd's or bishop's; a professional swindler, thief or criminal in general; a curved tube used to lower the pitch of a wind instrument; a curved tube carrying the mouthpiece of a bassoon; a gibbet (*obs*). ◆ *adj* (*Aust* and *NZ inf*) ill; unfair; wrong, dubious; not working properly; inferior; nasty, unpleasant. ◆ *vt* and *vi* to bend or form into a hook. [Prob ON *krōkr* hook; cf Swed *krok*, Dan *krog*]
■ **crooked** /krŭk'id/ *adj* bent like a crook; containing an angle or series of angles; twisted, contorted; not straight, tipped at an angle; dishonest or illegal (*inf*); (often /krŭkt/) angry with (with *on*) (*Aust* and *NZ*). **crook'edly** *adv*. **crook'edness** *n*.
❑ **crook'back** *n* (*Shakesp*) a hunchback. **crook'backed** *adj*.
■ **a crook in one's lot** any trial in one's experience. **go crook** (*Aust inf*) to lose one's temper. **go crook on** or **at** (*Aust* and *NZ inf*) to upbraid, rebuke.

Crookes glass /krŭks gläs/ *n* a type of glass that inhibits the passage of ultraviolet light, used in sunglasses, etc. [Sir William *Crookes* (1832–1919), British scientist]

Crookes tube /krŭks tūb/ (*phys*) *n* a sealed, evacuated tube in which stratification in electric discharges can be observed. [Ety as for **Crookes glass**]

croon /krōōn* or (*Scot*) *krün/ *vi* to sing or hum in an undertone. ◆ *vt* and *vi* to sing softly in a sentimentally contemplative manner. ◆ *n* an instance of crooning. [Cf Du *kreunen* to groan]
■ **croon'er** *n*. **croon'ing** *n*.

croove see **cruive**.

crop /krop/ *n* the total quantity produced, cut or harvested; the total growth or produce; a cultivated plant, collectively; a number, quantity (of products, ideas, etc) produced or appearing at a time, a supply; a season's yield; an end cut off; an act or mode of cutting; a style of cutting or wearing short hair; a hunting whip with loop instead of lash; the craw, a dilatation of a bird's oesophagus; a similar structure in another animal; a complete tanned hide of an animal; a finial (*archit*); an outcrop. ◆ *vt* (**cropp'ing**; **cropped**) to cut off the top, ends, margins or loose parts of; to cut short; to mow, reap or gather; (*esp* of grazing animals) to bite off in eating; to raise crops on; to cut the hair of. ◆ *vi* to yield a crop; to come to the surface (with *up* or *out*); hence, to come (up) casually, as in conversation. [OE *crop* the top shoot of a plant, the crop of a bird; Du *crop* a bird's crop]
■ **crop'ful** *n* (*pl* **crop'fuls**) as much as a bird's crop can hold. **cropfull'** *adj* satiated, filled to repletion. **cropp'er** *n* someone or something that crops; a plant that yields a crop; a person who raises a crop in exchange for a share of it (also **share cropper**); a kind of pigeon noted for its large crop; a small platen printing machine; a fall (*inf*); a failure (*inf*). **cropp'ing** *n* the act of cutting off; the raising of crops; an outcrop (*geol*). **cropp'y** *n* one of the Irish rebels of 1798 who cut their hair short, like the French Revolutionists.
❑ **crop'bound** *adj* (of birds) suffering from impaction of the crop. **crop circle** *n* a swirled or flattened circle in a field of arable crop, orig thought to be a natural phenomenon caused by particular meteorological conditions on an undulating landscape but in most instances now proved to be man-made as a hoax (also called **corn circle**). **crop'duster** *n* an aircraft that sprays crops from the air with fungicides or insecticides; the pilot of such an aircraft. **crop'-dusting** *n*. **crop'-ear** *n* (*obs*) a person, horse, dog, etc with cropped ears. **crop'-eared** *adj* (of a person, horse, dog, etc) having the ears cropped; (of a Puritan) having hair cropped to show the ears (used by Cavaliers

as gibe). **crop'land** *n* land used for growing crops. **crop'-marks** *n pl* (*archaeol*) variations in the depth or colour of a crop growing in a field, which, viewed from the air, can show the presence of a structure beneath the soil. **crop rotation** *n* the growing of different crops in sequence on the same piece of land over a number of years in order to minimize depletion of the soil. **crop'sick** *adj* sick of a surfeit. **crop top** *n* a garment for the upper body, cut short to reveal the wearer's stomach.
■ **come a cropper** (*inf*) to have a fall, perhaps from the phrase *neck and crop*.

croquante /krok-āt'/ (*cookery*) *n* a crisp pie or tart; a crisp cake containing almonds. [Fr]

croque-monsieur /krok-mə-syø'/ (*Fr*) *n* a type of toasted sandwich filled with ham and cheese.

croquet /krō'kā/ *n* a game, played on a lawn, in which wooden balls are driven by means of long-handled mallets through a series of hoops; an act of croqueting. ◆ *vt* to drive away by striking another ball in contact. [Northern Fr *croquet*, a dialect form of *crochet*, dimin of *croc*, *croche* a crook]

croquette /krō-ket'/ *n* a ball or cylindrical cake, usu of minced and seasoned meat, fish or potato, coated in breadcrumbs and fried. [Fr, from *croquer* to crunch]

croquis /kro-kē'/ (*Fr*) *n* an outline or rough sketch.

crore /krōr* or *krör/ (*Anglo-Ind*) *n* (*esp* of rupees) ten million, or one hundred lakhs. [Hindi *karo*]

crosier or **crozier** /krō'z(h)yər/ *n* the pastoral staff or crook of a bishop or abbot; an archbishop's cross (*non-standard*); the coiled growing tip of a young plant, *esp* a fern. [ME *crose* or *croce*, from LL *crocia* a crook]
■ **cro'siered** *adj*.

cross /kros/ *n* a gibbet on which the Romans exposed criminals, typically consisting of two pieces of timber, one placed transversely to the other; (with *cap*) the particular one on which Christ suffered; (with *cap*) the symbol of the Christian religion, or of the crusades; a representation of Christ's cross; any object, figure or mark formed by two parts or lines transverse to each other, with or without elaboration; such a mark used instead of a signature by an illiterate person; such a mark used to symbolize a kiss in a letter, etc, or as an indicator of location, intersection or error; a staff surmounted by a cross; a monument not always in the form of a cross, where proclamations are made, etc; a place in a town or village where such a monument stands or stood; a cross-shaped pendant or medal; the transverse part of an anchor, or the like; a surveyor's cross-staff; a crossing or crossway; anything that crosses or thwarts; adversity or affliction in general, or a burden or cause of suffering, as in *bear one's cross*; mixing of breeds, hybridization; a hybrid; something intermediate in character between two other things; unfairness or dishonest practices, *esp* in sport where a contestant corruptly allows himself or herself to be beaten; a game or race lost by collusion or which has been rigged; the obverse of a coin, formerly often stamped with a cross (*obs*); hence, a coin (*archaic*); a transverse pass, *esp* into the area in front of the opposing team's goal (*football*, etc); a punch delivered from the side (*boxing*). ◆ *adj* lying across or crosswise; transverse; oblique; adverse; interchanged; peevish; angry, displeased (with); hybrid; dishonest; balancing, neutralizing. ◆ *adv* and *prep* across. ◆ *vt* (*pat* and *pap* **crossed**, sometimes **crost**) to mark with a cross; to make the sign of the cross over; to set something, or draw a line, across; to set in position across the mast (*naut*); to place crosswise; to cancel by drawing cross lines; to pass from one side to the other of; to pass transversely, *esp* in the direction of the opposing team's goal (*football*); to extend across; to interbreed; to draw two lines across (a cheque), thereby restricting it to payment through a bank; to obstruct; to thwart; to annoy; to confront (*archaic*); to bestride. ◆ *vi* to lie or pass across; to meet and pass; (of two reciprocal letters) to be in the postal system simultaneously, each having been posted before the other is received; (of telephone lines) to connect and interfere with each other causing callers on one line to hear conversations on another; to interbreed. [OE *cros*, from ON *kross*, from L *crux, crucis*]
■ **crossed** *adj*. **cross'er** *n*. **cross'ing** *n* the act of making the sign of the cross; the act of going across; a place where a roadway, etc, may be crossed; an intersection, *esp* of transepts and nave in a church; an act of thwarting; crossbreeding. **cross'ish** *adj*. **cross'let** *n* a small cross. **cross'ly** *adv*. **cross'ness** *n*. **cross'wise** or **cross'ways** *adv* and *adj* across; in the form of a cross (*archaic*).
❑ **cross action** *n* (*law*) an action brought by the defender against the pursuer. **cross aisle** *n* (*obs*) a transept. **cross-and-pile** (or **-or-**) *n* (*archaic*) heads or tails; a toss-up. **cross'-armed** *adj* having the arms crossed. **cross assembler** *n* (*comput*) an assembler that runs on one computer, producing a machine code for a different computer. **cross'band** *n*. **crossband'ed** *adj* (of a handrail) having the grain of the veneer run across that of the rail. **cross'banding** *n*. **cross'bar** *n* a horizontal bar, eg on a man's bicycle or across a pair of goal posts; a

kind of lever. **cross'barred** *adj*. **crossbar switch** *n* (*electronics*) a switch having multiple vertical and horizontal paths, with electromagnetically operated contacts for connecting any vertical path with any horizontal one. **crossbar switching** *n* using a crossbar switch system. **cross'beam** *n* a large beam stretching across a building and serving to hold its sides together. **cross'bearer** *n* a person who carries a cross in a procession. **cross bedding** (*geol*) another term for **false bedding** (see under **false**). **cross'bench** *n* a bench laid crosswise; a bench on which independent or neutral members of the House of Commons or the House of Lords sit. ◆ *adj* independent; impartial. **cross'bencher** *n*. **cross bill** *n* a bill brought by the defendant in a Chancery suit against the plaintiff. **cross'bill** *n* a finch of the genus *Loxia* with mandibles crossing near the points. **cross'birth** *n* a birth in which the child lies transversely in the uterus. **cross'bite** *vt* (*archaic*) to bite in return; to cheat in return; to outwit; to entrap. **cross'bones** *n sing* a figure of two thigh bones laid across each other, forming with the skull a conventional emblem of death or piracy. **cross'-border** *adj* concerning or involving several neighbouring countries. **cross'bow** *n* a weapon for shooting bolts, formed of a bow placed crosswise on a stock. **cross'bower** or **cross'bowman** *n*. **cross'bred** *adj*. **cross'breed** *n* a breed produced by crossing two distinct breeds; the offspring of such a cross. ◆ *vt* to cross two distinct breeds. **cross'breeding** *n*. **cross'buck** *n* (*N Am*) a cross-shaped sign placed at a level crossing to warn motorists. **cross bun** see **hot cross bun** under **hot**[1]. **cross-butt'ock** *n* a throw in which the hip is used to unbalance one's opponent in wrestling. **cross'check** *vt* and *vi* to test the accuracy of eg a statement or piece of information by consulting various other sources of information; (in ice hockey) to check (one's opponent) illegally by hitting his upper body or stick. ◆ *n* an instance of crosschecking. **cross'claim** *n* a claim made by the defendant against the plaintiff. **cross-claim'** *vt* and *vi*. **cross colour** *n* spurious colour flashes in a colour-television receiver caused by misinterpretation of high-frequency luminance detail as colour information. **cross compiler** *n* (*comput*) a compiler that runs on one computer, producing a machine code for a different computer. **cross-corr'elate** *vt*. **cross-correlā'tion** *n* comparison of one set of data against another set. **cross correspondence** *n* (*psychic research*) fitting together of communications separately unintelligible to give an intelligible whole. **cross'-coun'try** *adj* and *adv* through fields, woods, over hills, etc, rather than by road, *esp* (of running, skiing, etc) over a long distance. ◆ *n* a cross-country competition. **cross'-court** *adj* of a shot in tennis, travelling diagonally from one side of the court to the other. **cross cousin** see under **cousin**. **cross-cross'let** *n* a cross with a smaller cross at each of its ends. **cross-cul'tural** *adj* relating to the differences between cultures; bridging the gap between cultures. **cross'-current** *n* (in the air, sea, or a river) a current flowing across the main current. **cross-curric'ular** *adj* of an educational approach that draws from a variety of disciplines and viewpoints. **cross'cut** *n* a transverse cut or course; a short way across from one point to another. ◆ *adj* cutting transversely or across the grain. ◆ *vt* /-*kut*'/ to cut across; to carry out crosscutting. **crosscut saw** *n* a large saw worked by two men, one at each end, for cutting timber across the grain. **cross'cutting** *n* (*film* and *TV*) cutting and fitting together film sequences so that in the finished picture the action moves from one scene to another and back again, thus increasing dramatic tension. **cross'-dāting** *n* (*archaeol*) a method of dating one site, level, etc by comparison with others. **cross-divi'sion** *n* division into groups or classes that overlap. **cross-dress'** *vi*. **cross-dress'er** *n*. **cross-dress'ing** *n* transvestism, the wearing of clothes normally associated with the opposite sex. **crossed line** *n* a telephone line connected in error to a different line or circuit. **cross-examinā'tion** *n*. **cross-exam'ine** *vt* to question minutely, or with a view to checking evidence already given; to subject to examination by the other side, *esp* by the prosecution or defence in a court of law. **cross-exam'iner** *n*. **cross'-eye** *n* a squint in which the eye turns inwards towards the nose. **cross-eyed'** *adj* squinting; having a cross-eye. **cross'-fade** *vt* (*TV* and *radio*) to cause (a sound source or picture) to fade away while gradually introducing another (also *vi*). **cross'fall** *n* the transverse inclination on a road. **cross'-fertilizā'tion** or **-s-** *n* the fertilization of a plant by pollen from another; fruitful interaction of ideas from eg different cultures. **cross-fer'tilize** or **-ise** *vt*. **cross'field** *adj* (*football*) (of a pass, etc) *usu* long and sideways in direction. **cross'fire** *n* (*milit*) the crossing of lines of fire from two or more points (also *fig*). **cross'fish** *n* another name for the common starfish (*Asterias rubens*). **cross-gar'net** *n* a T-shaped hinge, used *esp* to attach a door to a door frame. **cross-gar'tered** *adj* (*Shakesp*) wearing the garters crossed on the leg. **cross'-grained** *adj* having the grain or fibres crossed or intertwined; perverse; contrary; intractable. ◆ *adv* across the grain; perversely. **cross-grained'ness** *n*. **cross guard** *n* the bar, at right angles to the blade, forming the hilt-guard of a sword. **cross hairs** *n pl* two fine lines crossing at right angles at the centre of the lens of an optical instrument, used for focusing. **cross'-hatch** *vt* and *vi*. **cross'-hatching** *n* (in drawing, etc) shading by intersecting sets of parallel lines. **cross'head** *n* a beam across the head of something, *esp* the bar

at the end of the piston-rod of an engine; a screw having an indented cross in its head; a subsection heading within the body of a text (*printing*). **cross-in'dex** *n* a cross-reference referring the reader to other material. ◆ *vi* to cross-refer to related material. ◆ *vt* to list under another heading as a cross-reference. **cross-infect'** *vt*. **cross-infec'tion** *n* infection of an already ill or injured person with another illness unrelated to his or her own complaint, liable to occur eg in hospitals where a variety of diseases are being treated; infection from one species to another. **crossing over** *n* (*biol*) an exchange of segments of homologous chromosomes during meiosis whereby linked genes become recombined. **cross'ing-sweeper** *n* (*hist*) a person employed to sweep a street crossing. **cross'ing-warden** *n* a person appointed to conduct children across a busy street. **cross'jack** *n* (*naut*) a square sail set on the mizzenmast. **cross'-kick** *n* a crossfield kick. **cross-lat'eral** *n* and *adj* (a person) affected with cross-laterality. **cross-lateral'ity** *n* a mixture of physical one-sidedness, eg the combination of a dominant left eye with a dominant right hand. **cross'-leaved** *adj* having leaves in four rows, set crosswise. **cross'-legged** *adj* sitting on the ground having the ankles and legs crossed (also *adv*). **cross'light** *n* a light whose direction makes an angle with that of another light, and which illuminates additional parts or regions. **cross'-lighted** *adj*. **cross'-link** *vt* and *vi*. **cross'-linking** *n* (*chem*) the formation of side bonds between different chains in a polymer. **cross-magnet'ic** *adj* diamagnetic. **cross-marketing** see **cross-selling** below. **cross'-match** *vt* to test (blood samples from a donor and a recipient) for compatibility by checking that agglutination does not occur when red cells from each are put into the other's serum. **cross'-matching** *n*. **cross'over** *n* a road passing over the top of another; another term for **crossing over** (see above; *biol*); a place or point at which a crossing or transfer is made. ◆ *adj* (of a musician, singer, etc) popular with or appealing to a wider audience beyond the category of music with which first associated; having, incorporating or combining two or more styles, functions, methods, etc. **crossover network** *n* (*acoustics*) a frequency selective network which divides an audio signal into two or more frequency ranges in a loudspeaker, etc. **crossover vote** *n*. **crossover voter** *n* (*US politics*) a person registered with one political party who votes for another in a primary. **cross'-party** *adj* covering or drawn from all political parties. **cross'patch** an ill-natured person (see **patch**[2]). **cross'piece** *n* a piece of material of any kind crossing another; a timber over the windlass, with pins for belaying the running rigging (*naut*). **cross-plat'form** *adj* (*comput*) compatible with different types of computers or software. **cross-ply tyre** *n* a tyre in which the plies of fabric in the carcass are wrapped so as to cross each other diagonally. **cross-poll'inate** *vt*. **cross-pollinā'tion** *n* transfer of pollen from the anther of one flower to the stigma of another (cf **self-pollination**). **cross-pur'pose** *n* a contrary purpose; (in *pl*) a game in which answers to questions are transferred to other questions; (in *pl*) confusion in conversation or action by misunderstanding. **cross-quar'ters** *n sing* an ornament of tracery like the four petals of a cruciform flower; a quatrefoil. **cross-ques'tion** *vt* to cross-examine. ◆ *n* a question asked during a cross-examination. **cross-ra'tio** *n* of four points in a range, or rays in a pencil, the quotient of the positions ratios of two with respect to the other two. **cross-refer'** *vt* to refer or direct (a reader, etc) to another place, entry, passage, title, etc. ◆ *vi* to make a cross-reference. **cross-ref'erence** *n* a reference in a book to another entry, passage or title; any similar reference, eg in a filing system, directing the user to another place or position for further information. ◆ *vt* and *vi* to cross-refer. **cross'-rib** *n* an arch supporting a vault. **cross'road** *n* a road crossing the principal road, a bypath; a road joining main roads; (often in *pl*) a place where roads cross; (in *pl*) a stage at which an important decision has to be made. **cross'roads** *adj*. **cross'-row** same as **Christ-cross-row** (see under **Christ**). **cross-ruff'** *n* (*cards*) (*esp* in whist and bridge) a situation in which tricks are won by alternate trumping, with each of the partners leading a suit that the other lacks. **cross sea** *n* a sea that sets at an angle to the direction of the wind. **cross'-section** *n* a transverse section; a comprehensive representation; the probability, measured in barns, that a particular interaction will take place between atomic particles, which depends on their energy and nature and is zero when no reaction can take place (*phys*). ◆ *vt* to make a cross-section of. **cross-sec'tional** *adj*. **cross-sell'ing** or **cross-mark'eting** *n* the selling of services in addition to the services normally associated with a particular business or organization, eg the selling of insurance by banks, building societies, etc to existing customers. **cross'-sill** *n* a railway sleeper. **cross'-slide** *n* the sliding part of a lathe or planing machine which carries the tool at right angles to the bed of the lathe. **cross-spring'er** *n* a rib following the line of the groin in a groined vault. **cross'-staff** *n* a surveying instrument consisting of a staff surmounted with a frame carrying two pairs of sights at right angles. **cross'-stitch** *n* a stitch in the form of a cross; needlework made up of such stitches. ◆ *vt* to embroider with such stitches. **cross'-stone** *n* (*obs*) chiastolite; staurolite; harmotome. **cross'-talk** *n* interference caused by the energy from one telephone conversation invading another by electrostatic or electromagnetic coupling; backchat; repartee. **cross'tie** *n* a supporting tie placed transversely; a railway sleeper. **cross-tīn'ing** *n* (*agric*) a method of harrowing crosswise. **cross'town** *adj* and *adv* (*N Am*) extending over, or crossing, a town, as in *crosstown bus*. **cross'-training** *n* fitness training alternating between exercises involving gymnasium equipment and aerobic exercises in the same session. **cross'tree** *n* a piece of timber or metal placed across the upper end of a ship's mast. **cross-vault'ing** *n* vaulting formed by the intersection of simple vaults. **cross'walk** *n* (*N Am*) a pedestrian crossing. **cross'way** *n* a way that crosses another or links others. **cross'wind** *n* a wind blowing across the path of eg an aeroplane. **cross'word** or **crossword puzzle** *n* a type of puzzle invented in America in 1913, in which a square with blank spaces is to be filled with letters which, read across or down, will give words corresponding to clues given. **cross'wort** *n* a bedstraw with leaves set crosswise.

■ **at cross purposes** having a contrary understanding of the situation. **cross a bridge when one comes to it** see under **bridge**[1]. **cross as two sticks** particularly perverse and disagreeable. **cross one's fingers** or **keep one's fingers crossed** to place one finger across another in the hope of ensuring good luck. **cross one's heart (and hope to die)** to emphasize that one is being truthful by making the sign of a cross over one's heart. **cross someone's lips** to be uttered by someone. **cross someone's mind** to flash across someone's mind. **cross someone's palm** to put a coin in someone's hand, as a payment. **cross someone's path** to come in someone's way, to meet someone; to thwart someone. **cross swords** to enter into a dispute (with). **on the cross** diagonally; dishonestly (*sl*).

crossandra /kro-sän'drə/ *n* any evergreen shrub of the genus *Crossandra*, cultivated for their pink, yellow or red flowers. [New L, from Gr *krossos* fringed, and *andros* genitive of *anēr* male (signifying anther)]

crosse /kros/ *n* the stick with which the game of lacrosse is played, having at its top end a network of leather thongs enclosed in a triangular frame. [Fr]

crossette /kro-set'/ (*archit*) *n* a small projecting part of an impost stone at the extremity of an arch; a shoulder in an archstone fitting into the stone next to it. [Fr]

crossopterygian /kros-op-tə-rij'(i-)ən/ *n* a member of a subclass (**Crossopteryg'ii**) of mostly extinct bony fishes, thought to be the ancestors of amphibians, having paired fins with the axis fringed with rays, and including the coelacanth (also *adj*). [New L *crossopterygii*, from Gr *krossoi* tassels, fringe, and *pteryx, -gos* fin]

crost see **cross**.

crostini /kro-stē'ni/ *n* small pieces of toasted or fried bread with a savoury topping. [Ital, pl of *crostino*, dimin of *crosta* a crust]

crotal[1] /krŏ'təl/ *n* a crotalum; a small spherical bell. [Gr *krotalon* a rattle, castanet]
■ **crotalaria** /krot- or krŏt-ə-lā'ri-ə/ *n* any plant of the genus *Crotalaria*, including the American rattleboxes (from their inflated pods). **Crotalidae** /-tal'i-dē/ *n pl* the rattlesnake family. **crotaline** /krot'ə-līn/ *adj* like a rattlesnake. **crot'alism** *n* poisoning by crotalaria. **crotalum** /krot'ə-ləm/ *n* (*pl* **crot'ala**) a clapper or castanet used in ancient religious rites. **Crotalus** /krot'-/ *n* the rattlesnake genus.

crotal[2] or **crottle** /krot'l/ *n* a lichen (of various kinds) used for dyeing. [Gaelic *crotal*]

crotch /kroch/ *n* a fork, as of a tree; the bifurcation of the human body; the corresponding area in eg a pair of trousers; the human genital area. [Ety obscure]
■ **crotched** *adj*.
❏ **crotch rocket** *n* (*inf*) a particularly powerful motorcycle.

crotchet /kroch'it/ *n* a note in music, equal to half a minim, ♩; a crooked or perverse fancy; a whim, or ingenious notion; a small hook (*obs*). [Fr *crochet* dimin of *croche* a hook; see **crochet**]
■ **crotch'eted** or **crotch'ety** *adj* having crotchets or peculiarities; whimsical; short-tempered. **crotch'etiness** *n*.

croton /krŏ'tən/ *n* any plant of the *Croton* genus of tropical plants of the family Euphorbiaceae or of the related genus *Codiaeum*. [Gr *krotōn* a sheep-tick, which the seed resembles]
❏ **croton oil** *n* a powerful purgative obtained from the seeds of *Croton tiglium*.

Croton bug /krŏ'tən bug/ *n* the German cockroach. [From the *Croton* river, which supplies water to the city of New York]

crottle see **crotal**[2].

crouch /krowch/ *vi* to squat or lie close to the ground; to bend low with legs doubled; to cringe; to fawn. ♦ *vt* to bend. ♦ *n* act or position of crouching. [Poss connected with **crook**]

Crouched-friars see **Crutched-friars** under **crutch**.

crouch-ware /krowch'wär/ *n* an old salt-glazed stoneware made at Burslem. [Origin unknown]

croup[1] /kroop/ *n* inflammation and consequent narrowing of the larynx and trachea in children, associated with difficulty in breathing and a peculiar ringing cough; a burr. ♦ *vi* to croak or speak hoarsely. [From the sound made]
■ **croup'iness** *n*. **croup'ous** *adj*. **croup'y** *adj*.

croup[2] or **croupe** /kroop/ *n* the rump of a horse; the place behind the saddle. ♦ *vi* (*dialect*) to squat on one's haunches. [Fr *croupe* a protuberance; related to **crop**]
■ **croup'on** *n* (*obs*) the croup; the human buttocks.

croupade /kroo-pād'/ (*dressage*) *n* a leap in which the horse draws up its hind-legs toward the belly. [Fr]

croupe see **croup**[2].

crouper /kroo'pər/ *n* an obsolete form of **crupper**.

croupier /kroo'pi-ər/ or -pi-ā/ *n* a person who officiates at a gaming-table, dealing the cards, collecting the stakes and paying the winners. [Fr, one who rides on the croup]

croupon see **croup**[2].

croupous, **croupy** see under **croup**[1].

crouse /kroos/ (*Scot*) *adj* lively, confident, brisk. ♦ *adv* boldly, pertly. [ME *crūs*; cf LGer *krûs* gay, Ger *kraus*, Du *kroes* crisp, cross]
■ **crouse'ly** *adv*.

croustade /kroo-städ'/ *n* a case of fried bread or pastry for serving game, etc. [Fr]

crout /krowt/ *n* same as **sauerkraut**.

croûte /kroot/ *n* a thick slice of fried or toasted bread for serving entrées. [Fr *croûte* crust]
■ **croûton** /-tŏ or -ton'/ *n* a small cube of fried or toasted bread, as used in soups and salads.
■ **en croûte** (*cookery*) wrapped in pastry and baked.

Crow /krō/ *n* (*pl* **Crow** or **Crows**) a member of a Native American people living in the upper basins of the Yellowstone and Bighorn rivers; the Siouan language of this people. ♦ *adj* of or relating to the Crow or their language. [Literal translation of Siouan *apsáaloke* crow people]

crow /krō/ *n* any of several large black birds of the genus *Corvus*, esp *C. corone* (the so-called carrion crow); extended to other birds of this genus, esp the rook; the defiant or triumphant cry of a cock; an infant's inarticulate cry of joy; an ugly old woman (*sl*); short for crowbar. ♦ *vi* (*pat* **crew** /kroo/ or **crowed**; *pap* **crowed** or **crown** /krōn/) to croak; to utter a crow; to boast, swagger, triumph (often with *over*). [OE *crāwe* a crow, *crāwan* to crow]
❏ **crow'bar** *n* a heavy iron bar *usu* bent and flattened at one end, used as a lever. **crow'berry** *n* a low creeping moorland shrub (genus *Empetrum*) producing small black berries. **crow boot** *n* a boot made of leather and fur, as worn by the Inuit. **crow'-flower** *n* applied to various plants, in Shakesp perhaps crowfoot. **crow'foot** *n* (*pl* **crow'foots**) a buttercup, sometimes extended to other plants. **crow'-keeper** *n* (*Shakesp*) a scarecrow. **crow'-quill** *n* a pen made of the quill of a crow, etc, for fine writing or etching. **crow's'-bill** or **crow'-bill** *n* (*surg*) a kind of forceps for extracting bullets, etc, from wounds. **crow's'-foot** *n* one of the wrinkles spreading out from the corners of the eyes, formed as the skin ages (*pl* **crow's'-feet**); a caltrop (*obs milit*). **crow'-shrike** *n* a piping crow (see under **pipe**[1]). **crow's'-nest** *n* (*naut*) an elevated platform near the top of a ship's mast for a man on lookout. **crow'-steps** *n pl* step-like stonework on a gable. **crow'-toe** *n* applied to various plants, in Milton probably crowfoot.
■ **as the crow flies** in a straight line. **draw the crow** (*Aust*) to draw the short straw, come off worst in an allocation. **eat (boiled) crow** to be forced to do something very disagreeable, humiliate oneself. **have a crow to pluck with** to have something to settle with someone. **stone the crows** (*esp Aust sl*) an expression of amazement, horror, etc.

crowd[1] /krowd/ *n* a number of people or things closely pressed together, without order; the rabble; multitude; a social set. ♦ *vt* to gather into a lump or crowd; to fill by pressing or driving together; to compress; to thrust, put pressure on. ♦ *vi* to press on; to press together in numbers; to swarm. [OE *crūdan* to press]
■ **crowd'ed** *adj*. **crowd'edness** *n*.
❏ **crowd'funding** *n* the raising of funding from a large number of people who each make a small contribution. **crowd'-pleaser** *n* a product, etc that has popular appeal. **crowd'-puller** *n* a person, event, etc attracting a large audience. **crowd'source** *vt*. **crowd'sourcer** *n*. **crowd'-sourcing** *n* attempting to solve a problem, improve a system, etc by obtaining suggestions from eg members of the public, typically using the Internet as a medium. **crowd surf** *vi* (of a performer at a rock concert) to dive from the stage into the crowd in order to be held up and moved around supported by the audience's hands.
■ **crowd out** to overwhelm so as to force out; to fill completely. **crowd sail** to hoist as many sails as possible for speed.

crowd² /krowd/ (*obs* or *dialect*) *n* the crwth. [See **crwth**]
■ **crowd'er** *n* a fiddler.

crowdie /krow'di/ (*Scot*) *n* a mixture of meal and water, brose; a soft curd cheese made from soured milk. [Ety unknown; perh in part from **crud**]

crown¹ /krown/ *n* a circular head ornament, *esp* as a mark of honour; the diadem or state-cap of royalty;·kingship; (*usu* with *cap*) the sovereign; governing power in a monarchy; honour; the top of anything, eg a head, hat, tree, arch; a type of spire or lantern, formed by converging flying buttresses (*archit*); a stag's surroyals; the visible part of a tooth; a substitute for this, made of gold or synthetic material, etc, fitted over a broken or decayed tooth; (in gem-cutting) the upper of the two conical surfaces of a brilliant; the junction of root and stem of a plant; a short rootstock; a clasping metal cap for a bottle; chief ornament; completion or consummation; a coin originally stamped with a crown, *esp* a 5-shilling piece; used to translate various coin names, such as krone; the old French écu; a British size of paper before metrication (or a US size of paper 15 × 19in), originally watermarked with a crown. ◆ *vt* to cover or invest with a crown; to cap; to invest with royal dignity; to fill with foaming alcoholic liquid; in draughts, to convert into a king or crowned man by the placing of another draught on the top on reaching the crown-head; to adorn; to dignify; to complete happily; to hit on the head (*sl*). ◆ *vi* (of a baby's head) to pass through the vaginal opening (*obstetrics*). [OFr *corone*, from L *corōna*; cf Gr *koronos* curved]
■ **crowned** *adj*. **crown'er** *n* a shaped paper label attached to a product, eg a bottle, printed with advertising or promotional material; a coroner (*obs*). **crown'et** *n* a coronet. **crown'ing** *n* coronation; the final stage of labour, when the top of the child's head passes through the vaginal opening (*obstetrics*). ◆ *adj* highest; greatest. **crown'less** *adj*. **crown'let** *n* a small crown.
❏ **crown agent** *n* the solicitor appointed to be in charge of the Crown Office in Scotland; (with *caps*) one of a British body of business agents operating internationally, appointed by the Overseas Development Administration. **crown and anchor** *n* a game played with dice marked with crowns and anchors. **crown antler** *n* the uppermost tine of an antler. **Crown attorney** *n* (*Can*) a lawyer who acts for the Crown in criminal cases. **crown'-bark** *n* a kind of cinchona bark. **crown cap** *n* a lined metal cap for a bottle. **crown colony** *n* a colony administered directly by the home government. **crown cork** *n* a crown cap. **crown courts** *n pl* the system of courts in England and Wales that administer criminal jurisdiction. **Crown Derby** *n* a late-18c porcelain made at Derby, marked with a crown. **crowned head** *n* a monarch. **crown gall** *n* a disease of plants, *esp* fruit trees, caused by a bacterium (*Agrobacterium tumefaciens*), forming tumours along roots and shoots. **crown glass** *n* alkali-lime glass; window glass formed in circular plates or discs. **crown graft** *n* (*hortic*) insertion of scions between bark and wood. **crown green** *n* a bowling green with the centre higher than the edges. **crown'-head** *n* (in draughts) the back row of squares, where a piece is crowned. **crown imperial** *n* a garden plant, a species of fritillary having bell-shaped orange flowers. **crown jewels** *n pl* the jewels, including the regalia, worn by the sovereign on state occasions; the male genitalia (*euphem*); any group of things regarded as the most valuable items in a collection. **crown land** *n* land belonging to the crown or sovereign; land under control of the state in some countries and colonies of the Commonwealth. **crown lawyer** *n* a lawyer who acts for the crown in criminal cases. **crown living** *n* a church financially supported by the crown. **crown octavo** *n* an octavo 5 × 7½in. **Crown Office** *n* the administrative office of the Queen's Bench Division of the High Court; the office in which the great seal is affixed; the headquarters of the administration of criminal justice in Scotland. **crown of thorns** *n* a starfish that preys on living coral; a thorny Madagascan shrub (*Euphorbia splendens*) with red flowers and slender thorns. **crown piece** *n* a five-shilling piece. **crown'-post** *n* a king-post in a roof. **crown prince** *n* the heir apparent to the crown. **crown princess** *n* the female heir to a throne; the wife of a crown prince. **Crown Prosecution Service** *n* the independent prosecuting body in England and Wales which decides whether cases brought by the police should be tried in the courts. **Crown prosecutor** *n* (*Can*) a Crown attorney. **crown roast** *n* roast ribs of lamb or pork arranged in a circle like a crown. **crown rot** *n* a disease affecting rhubarb, caused by a soil-borne bacterium (*Erwinia rhapontici*). **crown saw** *n* a saw consisting of a rotating cylinder with cutting teeth. **crown vetch** *n* a trailing plant (*Coronilla varia*), of the pea family with pink or purple flowers. **crown'-wheel** *n* (*horology*) a wheel with teeth set at right angles to its plane. **crown witness** *n* a witness for the crown in a criminal prosecution instituted by it. **crown'work** *n* the manufacture and fitting of artificial crowns for teeth; such an artificial crown or crowns; an outwork composed of a bastion between two curtains, with demi-bastions at the extremes (*fortif*).
■ **crown of the causeway** the middle of the street. **to crown it all** as the culminating event (in a series of unfortunate events).

crown² see **crow**.

croze /krōz/ *n* the groove in the staves of a cask in which the edge of the head is set; a tool for setting this groove. [Perh OFr *croz* (Fr *creux*) groove]

crozier see **crosier**.

CRT *abbrev* : cathode-ray tube; composite rate tax.

cru /krü/ (*Fr*) *n* a vineyard or group of vineyards; a vintage.

crubeen /kroo-bēn'/ or /kroo'bēn/ *n* a pig's trotter, as food. [Ir *crúibín*, dimin of *crúb* hoof]

cruces see **crux**.

crucial /kroo'shəl/ *adj* testing or decisive; essential, very important; very good (*sl*); crosslike; of the nature of a crux. [**crux**]
■ **cru'cially** *adv*.

crucian or **crusian** /kroo'shən/ *n* a colourful carp, commonly kept as an aquarium fish. [LG *karusse* (Ger *Karausche*), from L *coracīnus*, from Gr *korakīnos*, a black perch-like fish, from *korax* raven]

cruciate /kroo'shi-āt/ *adj* cross-shaped; arranged like a cross. [L *crux*, *crucis* a cross]
❏ **cruciate ligament** *n* either of two ligaments (**anterior cruciate ligament** and **posterior cruciate ligament**) that cross each other in the knee, connecting the femur and the tibia.

crucible /kroo'si-bl/ *n* an earthen pot for melting ores, metals, etc; a severe test or trial (*fig*). [LL *crucibulum*]

crucifer /kroo'si-fər/ *n* a crossbearer in a procession; a member of the Cruciferae. [L *crux*, *crucis* a cross, and *ferre* to bear]
■ **Crucif'erae** *n pl* (*bot*) a family of archichlamydeous dicotyledons, with cross-shaped flowers, including cabbage, turnip, cress, wallflower. **crucif'erous** *adj* bearing or marked with a cross; with four petals placed crosswise; of the Cruciferae.

cruciform /kroo'si-förm/ *adj* cross-shaped. ◆ *n* something shaped like a cross. [L *crux*, *crucis* a cross, and **-form**]

crucify /kroo'si-fī/ *vt* (**cru'cifying**; **cru'cified**) to expose or put to death on a cross; to fasten to a wheel or the like, as a military field punishment; to subdue completely; to mortify; to torment; to treat harshly or cruelly; to hold up to scorn or ridicule. [OFr *crucifier*, from L *crucifīgere*, *crucifīxum*, from *crux* cross, and *fīgere* to fix]
■ **cru'cifier** *n* someone who crucifies. **cru'cifix** *n* a figure or picture of Christ fixed to the cross; a gymnastic exercise in which the weight of the body is supported while both arms are extended horizontally. **crucifixion** /-fik'shən/ *n* execution by crucifying; (with *cap* and *the*) the crucifying of Christ, or a representation of this.

cruciverbal /kroo-si-vûr'bəl/ (*usu facetious*) *adj* of or relating to (the compiling and solving of) crosswords. [L *crux* cross, and *verbum* a word]
■ **cruciver'balism** *n*. **cruciver'balist** *n* a crossword addict.

cruck /kruk/ *n* one of a pair of curved timbers supporting a roof. [Cf **crook**]

crud /krud/ or /krüd/ (*sl*) *n* anything dirty, filthy, disgusting or worthless; excrement or anything similar to it; a gluey half-melted snow (*skiing sl*); radioactive waste; a contemptible person. ◆ *vt* and *vi* to (cause to) be encrusted with or blocked with dirt, filth, etc (*usu* with *up*). [**curd**]
■ **crudd'le** *vt* and *vi* (*Spenser*) to curdle. **crudd'y** *adj* (*sl*) dirty, unpleasant, worthless; contemptible.

crude /krood/ *adj* raw, unprepared; not reduced to order or form; unfinished; undigested; immature; unrefined; coarse, vulgar, rude; inartistic. ◆ *n* crude oil. [L *crūdus* raw]
■ **crude'ly** *adv*. **crude'ness** *n*. **crud'ity** *n* rawness; unripeness; that which is crude. **crud'y** *adj* (*Shakesp*) crude, raw.
❏ **crude oil** *n* petroleum in its unrefined state.

crudités /krü-dē-tā'/ (*Fr*) *n pl* raw fruit and vegetables served as an hors d'œuvre.

crue a Miltonic spelling of **crew¹**.

cruel /kroo'əl/ *adj* (**cruell'er**; **cruell'est**) disposed to inflict pain, or deriving pleasure from the suffering of others; devoid of pity, merciless, savage; severe. [Fr *cruel*, from L *crūdēlis*]
■ **cru'elly** *adv*. **cru'elness** *n* (*obs*). **cru'elty** *n*.
❏ **cruelty-free'** *adj* (of a product, *esp* a pharmaceutical product) manufactured by a process that does not involve testing on animals.

cruels, **cruells** same as **crewels**.

cruet /kroo'it/ *n* a small jar or bottle for sauces and condiments for the table; a vessel for wine, oil, or water for religious ceremonies. [Anglo-Fr, dimin of OFr *cruye* jar, from root of **crock¹**]
❏ **cru'et-stand** *n* a stand or frame for holding cruets.

cruise /krooz/ *vi* to sail to and fro; (of a vehicle, aircraft, etc) to progress smoothly at a speed economical in fuel, etc; to wander about seeking something (with *about*, etc; *inf*); to go round public places looking for a sexual partner (*sl*; also *vt*). ◆ *n* a sailing to and fro; a wandering voyage in search of an enemy or for the protection of vessels or for pleasure or health; a land journey of similar character. [Du *kruisen* to cross]

■ **cruis'er** *n* someone or something that cruises; a speedy warship, specially for cruising; a privateer; a large cruising yacht; a cruiserweight boxer.

❑ **cruise control** *n* (in certain cars) an electronic device which controls cruising speed on motorways. **cruise missile** *n* a low-flying computer-controlled subsonic missile. **cruis'erweight** see **heavyweight** under **heavy. cruise'way** *n* a canal for exclusively recreational use. **cruise'wear** *n* clothing suitable for a leisure cruise.

cruisie see **crusie.**

cruive, cruve or **croove** /kroov, also krøv or kriv/ (*Scot*) *n* a pen or sty; a wattled fish-trap used in a river or estuary. [Scot, from *crue* sheepfold, of Celtic origin]

cruller /krul'ər/ (*N Am*) *n* a type of sweet cake fried in fat (also **krull'er**). [Cf Du *krullen* to curl]

crumb /krum/ *n* a small bit or morsel of dry food, *esp* bread; a small particle of anything; the soft part of bread; a worthless or contemptible person (*sl*). ♦ *vt* to break into crumbs; to put crumbs in or on; to remove crumbs from. ♦ *vi* to crumble. [OE *cruma*; Du *kruim*; Ger *Krume*; **crimp**]

■ **crumb'y** *adj* (**crumb'ier; crumb'iest**) in crumbs; soft. **crum'miness** *n*. **crum'my** *adj* (**crum'mier; crum'miest**) crumby; covered in lice (*sl*); not good, worthless, inferior, unpleasant, out of sorts, etc (*inf*). ♦ *n* (*N Am*) a truck for carrying loggers to work.

❑ **crumb'-brush** *n* a brush for sweeping crumbs off the table. **crumb'cloth** *n* a cloth laid under a table to keep crumbs from the carpet. **crumb'-tray** *n* a tray onto which crumbs are brushed from the table or one on which crumbs collect at the base of a toaster.

crumble /krum'bl/ *vt* to break into crumbs. ♦ *vi* to fall into small pieces; to decay. ♦ *n* a crumb; that which crumbles easily; a sweet dish consisting of a layer of stewed fruit covered with a crumbled mixture of flour, butter and sugar. [Orig dimin of **crumb**; Du *kruimelen*; Ger *krümeln*]

■ **crum'blies** *n pl* (*sl*) very old people. **crum'bliness** *n*. **crum'bly** *adj*.

crumbs /krumz/ (*orig school sl*) *interj* expressing surprise, dismay, etc. [Euphemism for *Christ*]

crumen /kroo'mən/ *n* a deer's tear-pit. [L *crumēna* a purse]
■ **cru'menal** *n* (*Spenser*) a purse.

crumhorn see **krummhorn.**

crummock or **crummack** /krum'ək/ *n* a crook, a stick with a curved head. [Gaelic *cromag* hook, crook]

crummy[1] /krum'i/ (*Scot*) *n* a cow with a crumpled horn. [Scot *crum* to bend; cf MLGer *krummen*]

crummy[2] see under **crumb.**

crump[1] /krump/ (*milit sl*) *n* (the sound of) an exploding bomb, etc. ♦ *vi* to make such a sound. [Imit]

crump[2] /krump/ *adj* (*Scot*) crisp, friable. [Imit; cf **crimp**]
■ **crump'y** *adj* (*dialect*) crisp.

crumpet /krum'pit/ *n* a pancake made of batter, variously small and thick or large and thin in different parts of the UK; a small thick yeast cake with holes on the top, *usu* eaten hot with butter, sometimes called a muffin; the head (*sl*); a woman, or women collectively, as sexual objects, now also used of a man or men (*sl*). [Ety uncertain]

crumple /krum'pəl/ *vt* to crush into irregular wrinkles; to wrinkle; to cause to collapse. ♦ *vi* to wrinkle; to collapse. ♦ *n* a crease or wrinkle. [**crump**[2]]
■ **crump'led** *adj*. **crump'ling** *n*. **crump'ly** *adj*.
❑ **crumple zones** *n pl* the front and rear portions of a motor car designed to crumple and absorb the impact in a collision while the passenger area remains intact.

crunch /krunch/ *vt* to crush with harsh noise, with the teeth, under foot, or otherwise; to chew anything hard, and so make a noise; to process large quantities of (data, numbers, etc). ♦ *vi* to make such a noise; to chew with, or bite into with, such a noise; to walk, or move, with such a noise. ♦ *n* the act or sound of crunching; (with *the*) the real testing or critical moment, trial of strength, time or cause of difficulty, etc (*inf*); a crisis, emergency (*inf*); a sit-up. [Altered form of *craunch*; prob influenced by **munch**]
■ **crunch'er** *n* (*inf*) a testing or critical moment; someone or something that processes large quantities of data, figures, etc. **crunch'ily** *adv*. **crunch'iness** *n*. **crunch'y** *adj* (**crunch'ier; crunch'iest**).
■ **number-cruncher** and **number-crunching** see under **number.**

crunk or **krunk** /krungk/ *adj* (*US sl*; also **crunked** or **krunked**) in a state of excitement or exhilaration; intoxicated. ♦ *n* a type of hip-hop music; the uninhibited style of dancing done to this. [Perh from *cranked up*]

crunkle /krung'kl/ *vi* to crumple. [Cf **crinkle**]

cruor /kroo'ör/ (*med*) *n* (*pl* **cruores** /krŭ-ör'ēz/) a mass of coagulated blood; a blood clot. [L]

crupper /krup'ər/ *n* a strap of leather fastened to the saddle and passing under the horse's tail to keep the saddle in its place; the hind part of a horse. [OFr *cropiere*, from *crope* the croup]

crus /krus/ (*anat*) *n* (*pl* **crura** /kroo'rə/) the leg, *esp* from the knee to the foot; any leg-like structure. [L]
■ **crural** /kroo'rəl/ *adj* belonging to or like a leg.

crusade /kroo-sād'/ *n* any one of many medieval military expeditions under the banner of the cross to recover the Holy Land from the Muslims; any daring or romantic undertaking; concerted action to further a cause. ♦ *vi* to go on a crusade. [Fr *croisade*, from Provençal *crozada*, from *croz*, from L *crux* a cross]
■ **crusad'er** *n* someone engaged in a crusade.

crusado /kroo-sä'dō/ *n* (*pl* **crusā'dos**) an old Portuguese coin, so called because the reverse side was marked with a cross. [Port *cruzado*]

cruse /krooz/, also *kroos/ *n* an earthenware pot; a small cup or bottle. [Cf ON *krūs*; Ger *Krause*]

cruset /kroo'sit/ *n* a goldsmith's crucible. [Cf Fr *creuset*, MDu *kruysel*, MLGer *krusel*]

crush /krush/ *vt* to press or squeeze so as to squash, deform or break; to break into tiny fragments; to beat down or overwhelm; to subdue; to ruin. ♦ *vi* to become broken or crumpled under pressure; to have a crush or be infatuated with (with *on*). ♦ *n* a violent squeezing; a close crowd of persons or things; a drink made from fruit pulp or fruit juice; a narrowing passage into which cattle, etc are driven; an infatuation (with *on*), or its object (*sl*). [OFr *croissir*; perh cognate with MHGer *krosen* to crunch]
■ **crush'able** *adj*. **crushed** *adj*. **crush'er** *n* someone who or something that crushes or subdues; a policeman (*sl*). **crush'ing** *adj*. **crush'ingly** *adv*.
❑ **crush bar** *n* a bar in a theatre for selling drinks in the intervals of a play, etc. **crush barrier** *n* a barrier erected to restrain a crowd and prevent crushing. **crushed strawberry** *n* the pinky colour of strawberries that have been crushed (also *adj*). **crush hat** *n* a collapsible opera hat. **crush room** *n* a room where an audience may promenade during the intervals of the entertainment. **crush syndrome** *n* a medical condition in which traumatic damage to a large amount of body muscle impairs the functioning of the kidneys and may lead to kidney failure.
■ **crush a cup** to empty a cup; to quaff.

crusian see **crucian.**

crusie, crusy or **cruisie** /kroo'zi/ (*Scot*) *n* an open iron lamp used with a rush wick. [From **cruset**]

crust /krust/ *n* the hard rind or outside coating of anything; the outer part of bread; a dried-up scrap of bread; the covering of a pie, etc; ice on top of soft snow (*skiing*); the solid exterior of the earth, consisting mainly of sedimentary rocks resting on ancient igneous rocks; the dry scaly covering on a skin lesion; a layer of sediment on the side of the bottle in some wines and ports; a livelihood (*sl*); the head, *usu* in the phrase *off one's crust*; impertinence (*old sl*). ♦ *vt* to cover with a crust or hard case. ♦ *vi* to gather into a hard crust. [L *crusta* rind]
■ **crust'al** *adj* relating to a crust, *esp* the earth's. **crust'ate** or **crustāt'ed** *adj* covered with a crust. **crustā'tion** *n* an adherent crust. **crust'ily** *adv*. **crust'iness** *n*. **crust'less** *adj*. **crust'ose** *adj* (*biol*) having a crust-like appearance. **crust'y** *adj* (**crust'ier; crust'iest**) of the nature of or having a crust, as port or other wine; having a hard or harsh exterior; hard; snappy; surly. ♦ *n* a person who appears fashionably unkempt, often with matted hair or dreadlocks, as part of an alternative lifestyle.

crusta /krus'ta/ *n* (*pl* **crus'tae** /-tē/) a piece prepared for inlaying; a hard coating; a cocktail served in a glass, its rim encrusted in sugar (*pl* **crus'tas**). [L]

crustacean /kru-stā'sh(y)ən or -shi-ən/ *n* a member of a large class (**Crustā'cea**) of arthropod animals with hard shells, almost all aquatic, including crabs, lobsters, shrimps, sandhoppers, woodlice, water-fleas, barnacles, etc (also *adj*). [L *crusta* shell]
■ **crustā'ceous** *adj* having a crust or a shell.

crusy see **crusie.**

crutch /kruch/ *n* a staff with a crosspiece at the head to place under the arm of a lame person; any support of similar form; a bifurcation, crotch; a small figure inserted to show the number to be carried (*maths*). ♦ *vt* to support; to prop; to clip wool from the hindquarters of (a sheep) (*Aust*). ♦ *vi* to go on crutches. [OE *crycc*]
■ **crutched** *adj* marked by the sign of, or wearing, a Cross.
❑ **Crutch'ed-friars** or **Crouch'ed-friars** *n pl* an order of mendicant friars so called from the cross which they wore.

cruve see **cruive**.

crux /kruks/ n (pl **crux'es** or **cruces** /kroo'sēz/) a cross; something that creates difficulty or perplexity, a puzzle; that on which a decision turns; the essential point, eg in a problem; (with cap) the Southern Cross (astron). [L crux, crucis a cross]
□ **crux ansata** /an-sä'ta, or krŭks an-sä'ta/ n a T-shaped cross with a loop at the top, the ankh. **crux criticorum** /krit-i-kö'rəm or -rŭm/ n a puzzle for the critics. **crux decussata** /dē-kus-ä'tə or dā-kŭs-ä'ta/ n an X-shaped cross, such as the cross of St Andrew or St Patrick. **crux medicorum** /me-di-kö'rəm or -rŭm/ n a puzzle for the doctors.

cruzado /kroo-zä'dō/ n (pl **cruzados** or **cruzadoes**) a former unit of currency in Brazil, replaced by the cruzeiro.

cruzeiro /kroo-zā'rō/ n (pl **cruzei'ros**) a former unit of currency in Brazil, replaced by the real. [Port cruz cross]

crwth /krooth/ n the crowd, an old Welsh stringed instrument, four of its six strings played with a bow, two plucked by the thumb. [Welsh crwth a hollow protuberance, a fiddle; Gaelic, Ir cruit]

cry /krī/ vi (**cry'ing**; **cried**) to utter a shrill loud sound, esp one of pain or grief; to lament; to weep; to bawl; to call (Scot). ◆ vt to utter loudly; to exclaim; to proclaim or make public; to offer for sale by crying out; to call (Scot); to proclaim the banns of marriage of (Scot). ◆ n (pl **cries**) any loud sound, esp of grief or pain; a call or shout; a fit of weeping; a pack of hounds, hence of people; a particular sound uttered by an animal; bawling; lamentation; prayer; clamour; report or rumour; a general utterance; a watchword, battle-cry, or slogan; a street call of wares for sale or services offered. [Fr crier, from L quirītāre to scream]
■ **crī'er** n someone who cries, esp an official maker of proclamations. **cry'ing** n the act of calling loudly; weeping. ◆ adj calling loudly; claiming notice and immediate action or redress, as in a crying need; distressing, heartbreaking, lamentable, as in a crying shame.
□ **cry'baby** n someone who cries too easily or frequently, like a baby. ■ **a far cry** a great distance; a very different matter. **cry against** to protest against. **cry down** to decry, disparage. **cry for the moon** to want or beg for something unattainable. **crying in the wilderness** voicing opinions or making suggestions that are not (likely to be) heeded. **cry off** to withdraw from an agreement; to back out. **cry on** (Scot) to call upon. **cry one's eyes** (or **heart**) **out** to weep copiously or bitterly. **cry out** to give a shout or shriek, eg of alarm, pain, etc. **cry out for** to be in urgent or obvious need of. **cry out to be** (**done, used,** etc) to be someone or something that very much ought to be (done, used, etc). **cry over spilt milk** to waste time in bemoaning what is irreparable. **cry quits** to declare a thing even. **cry up** to praise. **cry you mercy** (obs) I beg your pardon. **for crying out loud** (sl) an expression of frustration, impatience, etc. **great cry and little wool** much ado about nothing. **hue and cry** see under **hue²**. **in full cry** in full pursuit, orig used of dogs in hunt. **out of cry** (obs) beyond measure; beyond dispute. **within cry of** within hearing distance.

crymotherapy see **cryotherapy** under **cryo-**.

cryo- /krī'ō- or krī-o-/ combining form denoting frost, ice, ice-cold. [Gr kryos frost]
■ **cryoablā'tion** n a cosmetic procedure in which extremely cold temperatures are used to remove skin blemishes. **cryobiolog'ical** adj. **cryobiol'ogist** n. **cryobiol'ogy** n the study of the effects of extreme cold on living organisms. **cryoc'onite** n (Gr konis dust) dust found on the surface of polar ice. **cry'ogen** /-jən/ n (Gr root of gignesthai to become) a substance used for obtaining low temperatures, a freezing mixture. **cryogen'ic** adj relating to the science of cryogenics, or to work done, apparatus used, or substances kept, at low temperatures. **cryogen'ically** adv. **cryogen'ics** n sing the branch of physics concerned with phenomena at very low temperatures. **cryogeny** /-oj'ə-ni/ n refrigeration; cryogenics. **cryoglobulin** /-glob'ū-lin/ n (med) an immunoglobulin formed in the blood in certain diseases which forms obstructions in small blood vessels when the extremities are subjected to low temperatures. **cry'olite** n (Gr lithos a stone) an icestone or Greenland spar, sodium aluminium fluoride, earliest source of aluminium. **cryom'eter** n (Gr metron measure) a thermometer for low temperatures. **cryomet'ric** adj. **cryon'ic** adj. **cryon'ics** n sing the practice of preserving human corpses by freezing them, with the idea that advances in science may enable them to be revived at some future time (also **cryonic suspension**). **cryophil'ic** adj (Gr phileein to love; biol) able to thrive at low temperatures. **cryoph'orus** n (Gr pherein to bear) an instrument for showing the decrease of temperature in water by evaporation. **cryophys'ics** n sing low temperature physics. **cryoprecip'itate** n a precipitate, eg from blood plasma, produced by freezing and thawing under controlled conditions. **cryopreservā'tion** n the preservation of living cells (eg blood, human eggs and sperm) by freezing; cryonics. **cryopreserve'** vt. **cry'oprobe** n a fine instrument with a cooled tip used in cryosurgery. **cry'oscope** n an instrument for determining freezing points. **cryoscop'ic** adj. **cryos'copy** n the study of the effect of dissolved substances on the freezing points of solvents. **cry'ostat** n an

apparatus for achieving or demonstrating cooling by evaporation; any apparatus for maintaining a low temperature. **cryosur'geon** n a surgeon specializing in cryosurgery. **cryosur'gery** n surgery using instruments at very low temperatures to cut and destroy tissue. **cryother'apy** or **crymother'apy** /krī-mō-/ n medical treatment using extreme cold. **cry'otron** n a tiny form of electronic switch operating in a bath of liquid helium a few degrees above absolute zero.

crypt /kript/ n an underground cell or chapel; a small cavity, a tubular gland (zool). [L crypta, from Gr kryptē, from kryptein to hide; cf **grot²**]
■ **cryp'tal** adj relating to, or of the nature of, a crypt.

crypt- /kript-/ or **crypto-** /krip-tō- or -to-/ combining form denoting hidden. [Gr kryptos hidden]
■ **cryptadia** /krip-tā'di-ə/ n pl (Gr) things to be kept secret. **cryptaesthesia** or (N Am) **cryptesthesia** /kript-ēs-thē'zyə or -zhə/ (Gr aisthēsis perception) supranormal perception, eg clairvoyance. **cryptaesthet'ic** adj. **cryptanal'ysis** n the art of deciphering codes, etc. **cryptan'alyst** n. **cryptanalyt'ic** adj. **cryptobi'ont** n an organism that undergoes cryptobiosis. **cryptobiō'sis** n a temporary suspension of metabolic activity in hostile environments, which can be reversed when conditions improve. **cryptobiotic** /-bī-ot'ik/ adj. **crypto-Chris'tian** n. **cryp'tochrome** n a light-sensitive pigment, a photoreceptor protein, thought to control the circadian rhythm. **cryptococcō'sis** n a rare infection caused by the yeastlike fungus Cryptococcus neoformans, which, if inhaled, may cause meningitis and growths in the lungs. **crypto-comm'unist** n. **cryptocryst'alline** adj with crystalline structure visible only under the microscope. **cryp'togam** n any member of the **Cryptogamia** /krip-tō-gā'mi-ə/, a former class of flowerless plants (including mosses, ferns, etc) that reproduce by means of spores rather than seeds. **cryptogā'mian** adj. **cryptogamic** /-gam'ik/ adj. **cryptog'amist** n. **cryptog'amous** adj. **cryptog'amy** n. **cryptogen'ic** adj (of diseases) of unknown or obscure cause. **cryp'togram** or **cryp'tograph** n anything written in cipher. **cryptog'rapher** or **cryp'tographist** n. **cryptograph'ic** adj. **cryptograph'ically** adv. **cryptog'raphy** n the study of writing and deciphering codes. **cryptolog'ical** adj. **cryptol'ogist** n. **cryptol'ogy** n secret language; the scientific study of codes. **cryptomē'ria** n the Japanese cedar, Cryptomeria japonica. **cryptomnesia** /-mnē'zi-ə or -zhə/ n latent or subconscious memory. **cryptomnēs'ic** adj. **crypton** n see **krypton**. **cryp'tonym** n (Gr onyma name) a secret name. **crypton'ymous** adj. **cryptor'chid** n a male human or animal in whom one or both testes fail to descend into the scrotum. **cryptor'chidism** n. **cryptosporidiō'sis** n an infection affecting humans and domestic animals, caused by the protozoan **cryptosporid'ium** (pl **-id'ia**), and characterized by diarrhoea, fever and stomach pains. **cryptozō'ic** adj (Gr zōē life) (of animals) living concealed in dark places; (with cap) denoting Precambrian time when rocks contained little or no trace of living organisms (geol). **cryptozool'ogy** n the study and attempted discovery of creatures, such as the Loch Ness monster, that are generally regarded as mythical.

cryptic /krip'tik/ adj hidden; secret; unseen; mysteriously obscure. [LL crypticus from Gr kryptikos, from kryptos hidden]
■ **cryp'tical** adj. **cryp'tically** adv.
□ **cryptic coloration** n (zool) protective resemblance to some part of the environment by countershading or mimicry (eg of leaves or twigs).

crypto /krip'to/ n (pl **cryp'tos**) a person who is secretly a member of a party, sect, organization, etc, eg a crypto-communist. [**crypt-**]

crystal /kris'tl/ n rock-crystal, a clear quartz, like ice; a body, generally solid, whose atoms are arranged in a definite pattern, outwardly expressed by geometrical form with plane faces; a crystalline element, of piezoelectric or semiconductor material, functioning as eg a transducer, oscillator, etc in an electronic device; a globe of rock-crystal or the like in which one may see visions (also **crystal ball**); anything bright and clear; a superior glass of various kinds; cut glass; a watchglass; cocaine or amphetamine (drug sl). ◆ adj composed of or like crystal. [OFr cristal, from L crystallum, from Gr krystallos ice, from kryos frost]
■ **crys'talline** /-īn, -in or in poetry also -tal'/ adj like crystal or a crystal; composed of crystal, crystals, or parts of crystals; having the structure of a crystal. ◆ n a crystalline substance. **crystallin'ity** n. **crys'tallite** n a small, imperfectly formed or incipient crystal; a minute body in glassy igneous rocks. **crystalli'tis** n inflammation of the crystalline lens. **crystallī'zable** or **-s-** adj. **crystallīzā'tion** or **-s-** n. **crys'tallize** or **-ise** vt and vi to form into crystals; to make or become definite or concrete; (esp of fruit) to coat with sugar crystals. **crystallogen'esis** n origination of crystals. **crystallogenet'ic** adj. **crystallog'rapher** n. **crystallograph'ic** adj. **crystallograph'ically** adv. **crystallog'raphy** n the science of the structure of crystals, including proteins and other biological molecules. **crys'talloid** n a substance in a state in which it dissolves to form a true solution

which will pass through a membrane; a minute crystalline particle of protein (*bot*). ◆ *adj* like a crystal; of the nature of a crystalloid. **crys'tallomancy** *n* (Gr *manteiā* divination) divination by transparent bodies.

❑ **crys'tal-gazer** *n*. **crys'tal-gazing** *n* gazing in a crystal or the like to obtain visual images, whether in divination or to objectify hidden contents of the mind. **crystal healing** *n* crystal therapy. **crystalline heaven** or **sphere** *n* in ancient astronomy, a sphere between the fixed stars and the *primum mobile*, assumed to explain precession of the equinoxes. **crystalline lens** *n* the transparent refractive body of the eye. **crystal meth** *n* (*inf*) the drug methamphetamine in its crystalline state. **crystal rectifier** *n* a rectifier that depends on differential conduction in doped semiconductor crystals. **crystal set** *n* a simple early type of wireless receiving apparatus having a crystal detector. **crystal therapy** *n* the use of crystal energies or vibrations to treat physical or emotional problems. **crystal violet** *n* an antiseptic dye, hexamethylpararosaniline hydrochloride (also **gentian violet**).

■ **crystal clear** very or completely clear.

CS *abbrev*: chartered surveyor; Christian Science; Civil Service; Clerk to the Signet; Court of Session. See also **CS gas**.

Cs (*chem*) *symbol*: caesium.

c/s *abbrev*: cycles per second (hertz).

CSA *abbrev*: Child Support Agency; Confederate States of America (*hist*).

csárdás /*chär'däsh*/ *n* a Hungarian dance, or its music, in two movements, one slow and one fast (also (*non-standard*) **czar'das**). [Hung]

CSC *abbrev*: Civil Service Commission.

CSCE *abbrev*: Conference on Security and Co-operation in Europe (now known as **OSCE**).

CSE *abbrev*: Certificate of Secondary Education; Combined Services Entertainment, an organization providing entertainment for the armed forces.

C-section /*sē'sek-shən*/ *n* a short form of **Caesarean section** (see under **Caesar**).

CSEU *abbrev*: Confederation of Shipbuilding and Engineering Unions.

CSF *abbrev*: cerebrospinal fluid.

CS gas /*sē'es gas*/ *n* an irritant gas that affects vision and respiration, synthesized in 1928 by *Corson* and *Stoughton* and used in riot control.

CSI *abbrev*: crime scene investigator, or investigation.

CSIRO *abbrev*: Commonwealth Scientific and Industrial Research Organization.

CSM *abbrev*: Committee on Safety of Medicines; Company Sergeant-Major.

CSO *abbrev*: community-service order.

CSP *abbrev*: Chartered Society of Physiotherapy.

c-spring see **cee-spring** under **cee**.

CSR *abbrev*: corporate social responsibility.

CSS *abbrev*: Cascading Style Sheets, a computer language used to describe the basic design characteristics of a document written in a mark-up language.

CST *abbrev*: Central Standard Time; Council for Science and Technology; craniosacral therapy.

CSTD *abbrev*: Commission on Science and Technology for Development.

CSV *abbrev*: community-service volunteer.

CSYS (*Scot*) *abbrev*: Certificate of Sixth Year Studies (now replaced by **Advanced Higher** (see under **advance**)).

CT *abbrev*: Central Time; computed (or computerized) tomography (see under **compute**); Connecticut (US state).

Ct *abbrev*: Court (in addresses, etc).

ct *abbrev*: carat; cent; court.

CTBI *abbrev*: Churches Together in Britain and Ireland.

CTC *abbrev*: city technology college; Cyclists' Touring Club.

CTCC *abbrev*: Central Transport Consultative Committee (now replaced by **RPC**).

ctene /*tēn*/ *n* a comb-like swimming organ in the Ctenophora. [Gr *kteis, ktenos* comb]

■ **ctenid'ium** /*ten-*/ *n* (*pl* **ctenid'ia** /*-i-ə*/) a comb-like respiratory gill of molluscs. **cteniform** /*tēn'* or *ten'*/ or **cten'oid** *adj* comb-shaped. **ctenoph'oran** *n* a member of the **Ctenoph'ora**, a class of coelenterates which are transparent, free-swimming marine organisms resembling jellyfishes, and which move by means of meridionally-placed comb-like plates (also *adj*). **cten'ophore** *n* any member of the Ctenophora.

Ctesiphon arch /*tes'i-fon ärch*/ (*archit*) *n* an arch of inverted catenary shape, such as the great ruined arch at Ctesiphon, on the Tigris south-east of Baghdad.

CTF *abbrev*: Child Trust Fund, a long-term savings account for children.

CTOL *abbrev*: conventional take-off and landing.

Ctrl key (*comput*) short for **control key**.

CTS *abbrev*: carpal tunnel syndrome.

CTT *abbrev*: capital transfer tax.

C2C *abbrev*: consumer-to-consumer.

CU *abbrev*: Christian Union.

Cu (*chem*) *symbol*: copper. [L *cuprum*]

Cu. or **cub.** *abbrev*: cubic.

cuadrilla /*kwä-drē'(l)yə*/ *n* the attendants of a matador. [Sp, gang, troop]

cub¹ /*kub*/ *n* the young of certain carnivorous animals, such as foxes, bears, etc; a whelp; a rude or cheeky young boy or girl; (in full **Cub Scout**) a member of the junior section of the Scout Association; a beginner, novice, apprentice; a young or inexperienced person, *esp* a newspaper reporter. ◆ *vt* and *vi* (**cubb'ing; cubbed**) to give birth to (cubs); to hunt (fox-cubs). [Origin unknown]

■ **cubb'ing** *n* cub-hunting. **cubb'ish** *adj* like a cub; awkward or ill-mannered. **cub'hood** *n*. **cub'less** *adj*.

❑ **cub'-hunting** *n* hunting of young foxes.

cub² /*kub*/ *n* a cattle-pen; a chest. [Prob from LGer]

■ **cubb'y** *n* (also **cubb'y-hole**) a snug enclosed place; a small compartment in a desk, cabinet, etc.

cub. see **Cu.**

Cuban /*kū'bən*/ *adj* of or relating to *Cuba*, an island republic in the Caribbean, or to its people. ◆ *n* a native of Cuba.

❑ **Cuba libre** /*lē'bra*/ *n* a long drink of rum and lime juice. **Cuban heel** *n* (on footwear) a heel of medium height, straight at the front and slightly tapered at the back.

cubby-hole see under **cub²**.

cube /*kūb*/ *n* a solid body having six equal square faces, a solid square; anything with this shape; the third power of a quantity (*maths*). ◆ *vt* to raise to the third power (*maths*); to cut into cubes; to calculate the amount or contents of in cubic units. [Fr, from L *cubus*, from Gr *kybos* a die]

■ **cūb'age** or **cū'bature** *n* the act or process of finding the solid or cubic content of a body; the result thus found. **cū'bic** *adj* (also **cū'bical**) relating to a cube; solid, three-dimensional; isometric (*crystallog*); (**cubic**) of or involving the third power or degree (*maths*); (of volume) equal to that contained in a cube of specified dimensions. ◆ *n* (*maths*) a cubic equation. **cū'bically** *adv*. **cū'bicalness** *n*. **cū'biform** *adj*. **cū'bism** *n* a modern movement in painting, which seeks to represent several aspects of an object seen from different viewpoints arbitrarily grouped in one composition, making use of cubes and other solid geometrical figures. **cū'bist** *n* and *adj*. **cūbist'ic** *adj*. **cūbist'ically** *adv*. **cū'boid** *n* (*maths*) a solid with six rectangular faces, the opposite faces being of equal size. ◆ *adj* (also **cū'boidal**) resembling a cube in shape; relating to the cuboid bone.

❑ **cube root** *n* (*maths*) the quantity of which the given quantity is the cube. **cuboid bone** *n* (*anat*) (in the foot) the outer bone of the tarsus connected to the heel bone and the fourth and fifth metatarsal bones.

cubeb /*kū'beb*/ *n* the dried berry of *Piper cubeba*, an Indonesian climbing pepper shrub, formerly used as a drug to treat infections of the urinary tract. [Fr *cubèbe*, from Ar *kabābah*]

cubic see under **cube**.

cubica /*kū'bi-kə*/ *n* a fine worsted fabric used for linings. [Sp *cubica*]

cubicle /*kū'bi-kl*/ *n* a small compartment used for dressing and undressing as at a clinic, swimming pool, etc; a bedroom; part of a dormitory or other large room which is partitioned off; a cell. [L *cubiculum* bedroom, from *cubāre* to lie down]

cubic zirconia see under **zircon**.

cubism, etc see under **cube**.

cubit /*kū'bit*/, also **cubitus** /*-bi-təs*/ *n* an old measure, the length of the arm from the elbow to the tip of the middle finger, from 18 to 22in (*approx* 46 to 56cm). [L *cubitum* the elbow; cf L *cubāre* to lie down]

■ **cū'bital** *adj* of the length of a cubit; relating to the elbow or forearm.

cuboid, etc see under **cube**.

cucking stool /*kuk'ing stool*/ (*hist*) *n* a stool in which quarrelsome women, dishonest traders and other miscreants were placed, *usu* before their own door, to be pelted and jeered at by the mob. [Mentioned in the Domesday Book as in use in Chester, and called *cathedra stercoris*; from an obs word *cuck*, to defecate; cf ON *kūka*]

---

fāte; fär; mē; fûr; mīne; mōte; för; mūte; pūt; dhen (then); *el'ə-mənt* (element) • For other sounds see detailed chart of pronunciation

cuckold /kuk'əld/ n a man whose wife has proved unfaithful. ◆ vt to make a cuckold (of). [OFr cucuault, from cucu cuckoo]

■ **cuck'oldize** or **-ise** vt to make a cuckold. **cuck'oldly** adj (Shakesp). **cuck'oldom** or **cuck'oldry** n the state of a cuckold; the act of making a cuckold.

❑ **cuck'old-maker** n.

cuckoo /kŏŏk'ōō/ n a bird (Cuculus canorus) that cries cuckoo, noted for depositing its eggs in the nests of other birds who then rear the chicks as their own; any bird of this or related genera; the call of the cuckoo; a silly or slightly mad person. ◆ adj (inf) silly or slightly mad. [Imit; cf Fr coucou, Ger Kuckuck, L cucūlus, Gr kokkyx, -ȳgos]

❑ **cuckoo bee** n any of several species of bee which lay their eggs in the nest of a different species of bee, sometimes killing the queen. **cuck'oo-bud** n (Shakesp) the name of a plant. **cuckoo clock** n a clock in which a mechanical bird pops out of a door, making the sound of a cuckoo to announce the hours. **cuckoo flower** n a plant (Cardamine pratensis) commonly found in damp pastures in Europe and America, with divided leaves and small lilac or white flowers, lady's smock; another name for ragged robin. **cuckoo fly** n a gold-wasp, so named from laying its eggs in the nests or larvae of other insects. **cuckoo pint** (orig **cuckoo pintle**) /-pint or -pīnt/ n a European plant (Arum maculatum) with a cylindrical purple flower-stalk (spadix) enclosed within a yellowish modified leaf (spathe), and poisonous red berries (also called **lords and ladies**). **cuckoo shrike** n an Old World tropical songbird of the family Campephagidae, somewhat similar to a cuckoo when in flight. **cuckoo-spit** or **cuckoo-spittle** n a froth secreted by froth-flies or frog-hoppers on plants, surrounding and protecting the larvae and pupae.

cucullate /kū'ku-lāt or -ku'/ or **cuculated** /-lā-tid/ adj hooded; shaped like a hood. [L cucullatus, from cucullus a hood]

cucumber /kū'kum-bər or -kəm-/ n a climbing plant (Cucumis sativus) of the Cucurbitaceae, with bristly lobed leaves and tendrils; its long cylindrical fruit, used as a salad vegetable and pickle; a cucumber tree (US). [L cucumis, -eris]

■ **cūcūm'iform** adj.

❑ **cucumber tree** n the bilimbi tree; a species of magnolia whose fruit resembles a cucumber (US).

■ **cool as a cucumber** calm, imperturbable.

cucurbit /kū-kûr'bit/ n a chemical vessel used in distillation, orig shaped like a gourd; a cucurbitaceous plant. [L cucurbita a gourd]

■ **cucur'bital** or **cucurbita'ceous** adj relating to the **Cucurbita'ceae**, a family of sympetalous dicotyledons, including gourd, marrow, melon, etc; gourd-like.

cud /kud/ n food brought back from the first stomach of a ruminating animal to be chewed again. [OE cwidu]

❑ **cud'weed** n a woolly composite plant of the genus Gnaphalium, or a related plant.

■ **chew the cud** (inf) to meditate, to reflect.

cudbear /kud'bār/ n a purple or reddish dyestuff obtained from various lichens. [Dr Cuthbert Gordon, 18c Scottish chemist]

cuddeehih see **cuddy²**.

cudden or **cuddin** see **cuddy⁴**.

cuddie see **cuddy³,⁴**.

cuddle /kud'l/ vt to hug; to embrace; to fondle. ◆ vi to lie close and snug together. ◆ n a close embrace. [Origin unknown]

■ **cuddle'lesome** or **cudd'ly** adj pleasant to cuddle, being eg attractively plump, soft, etc; suggestive of, conducive to, cuddling.

cuddy¹ /kud'i/ n a small cabin or cookroom, in the forepart of a boat or lighter; in large vessels, the officers' cabin under the poop-deck. [Origin uncertain; cf Fr cahute; Du kajuit; Ger Kajüte]

cuddy² /kud'i/ (hist) n the right of a lord to entertainment from his tenant (also (Spenser) **cudd'eehih**); rent. [Ir cuid oidhche, from cuid a share, and oidche night]

cuddy³ or **cuddie** /kud'i/ (Scot and dialect) n a donkey; a horse; a stupid person. [Perh Cuthbert]

cuddy⁴ or **cuddie** /kud'i/ (Scot) n a young coalfish (also **cudd'en** or **cudd'in**). [Gaelic cudainn, cudaig]

cudgel /kuj'l/ n a heavy staff; a club. ◆ vt (**cudg'elling**; **cudg'elled**) to beat with a cudgel. [OE cycgel]

■ **cudg'eller** n. **cudg'elling** n.

❑ **cud'gel-play** n. **cudg'el-proof** adj.

■ **cudgel one's brains** to think hard. **take up the cudgels** to join in defence or support, esp energetically or forcefully.

cue¹ /kū/ n the last words of an actor's speech serving as a signal to the next speaker to begin; any word or action that serves as a signal to begin a speech, action, operation, etc; a stimulus that produces a response (psychol); the part one has to play (archaic). ◆ vt (**cue'ing** or **cū'ing**; **cued**) to give a cue to; to insert (eg a film sequence, sound effect, etc) into a script. [According to some from Fr queue tail (see next word); in 17c written Q, and derived from L quando when, ie when the actor was to begin]

❑ **cue bid** n (bridge) a bid in a suit other than the intended trump suit, made to describe a feature of one's hand to one's partner.

■ **cue someone in** (orig US sl) to inform (someone). **on cue** just at the right moment. **take one's cue from** to follow someone's advice or example.

cue² /kū/ n a twist of hair at the back of the head; a rod used in playing snooker, billiards, etc. ◆ vt (**cue'ing** or **cū'ing**; **cued**) to form a cue in (hair); to hit (a ball) with a cue (also vi). [Fr queue, from L cauda a tail]

■ **cue'ist** n a snooker- or billiard-player.

❑ **cue ball** n the ball struck by the cue in snooker, billiards, etc. **cue'man** n (inf) a snooker player.

cue³ /kū/ n the seventeenth letter of the modern English alphabet (Q or q).

cuerpo see **en cuerpo**.

cuesta /kwes'ta/ n (esp in SW USA) a hill ridge having a steep scarp on one side and a gradual slope on the other, caused by denudation of gently dipping hard rock strata. [Sp]

cuff¹ /kuf/ n the end of the sleeve near the wrist; a covering for the wrist; a handcuff; a turned-up fold at the bottom of a trouser leg (N Am). ◆ vt (police sl) to put handcuffs on. [Prob cognate with **coif**]

❑ **cuff link** n either of a pair of usu decorative fasteners, orig consisting of two buttons linked together, now usu one button-like object attached to a pivoting bar, used for fastening a shirt cuff.

■ **off the cuff** unofficially and offhand; improvised. **on the cuff** (US) on tick; on the house.

cuff² /kuf/ n a light blow with the open hand. ◆ vt to strike with the open hand; to beat (inf). [Origin obscure; cf Swed kuffa to knock]

cuff³ /kuf/ n a Scottish form of **scuff²**, **scruff¹**.

cuffin /kuf'in/ n a man. [Criminal slang]

■ **queer cuffin** a justice of the peace; a churl.

cuffle /kuf'l/ (obs) vi to scuffle.

cuffo /kuf'ō/ (old US sl) adv without any admission charge. [Prob derived from **on the cuff** (see under **cuff¹**)]

cuffuffle /kər-fuf'l/ (inf) n same as **carfuffle**.

Cufic same as **Kufic**.

cui bono? /kī or kwē bō'nō, or koo'ē bo'nō/ (L) for whose benefit or advantage is it?; who is the gainer?

cuif same as **coof**.

cui malo? /kī or kwē mä'lō, or koo'ē mal'ō/ (L) whom will it harm?

cuique suum /kwē'kwə soo'əm, also -kwā/ (L) to each his own.

cuirass /kwi-ras' or kū'/ n a defensive breastplate and backplate fastened together; a breastplate alone. ◆ vt to equip or cover with a cuirass. [Fr cuirasse, from cuir leather, from L corium skin, leather]

■ **cuirassier** /-ēr'/ n a cavalry soldier wearing a cuirass.

cuir-bouilli /kwēr-boo'yē/ n leather boiled or soaked in hot water and moulded, orig used for armour (also **cuir-bou'illy**). [Fr, boiled leather]

Cuisenaire rods /kwē-zə-nār' rodz/ n pl a set of small wooden rods, of significant related sizes and colours, used in teaching arithmetic. [Georges Cuisenaire, 20c Belgian educationalist]

cuish see **cuisse**.

cuisine /kwi- or kwē-zēn'/ n the art or style of cooking; the dishes cooked; a kitchen or cooking department. [Fr, from L coquīna, from coquere to cook]

■ **cuisin'ier** /-yā/ n a cook.

❑ **cuisine bourgeoise** n plain cooking. **cuisine minceur** /mē-sœr'/ n a style of cooking characterized by imaginative use of light, simple ingredients.

■ **nouvelle cuisine** /noo-vel'/ a style of simple French cooking excluding rich creamy sauces, etc in favour of fresh vegetables and light sauces.

cuisse /kwis/ or **cuish** /kwish/ (Shakesp **cush** /kush/) n thigh armour. [Fr cuisse, from L coxa hip]

❑ **cuisse-madame** /-däm'/ n a jargonelle pear.

cuisser see **cusser**.

cuit, **cute** or **coot** /køt, küt or kit/ (Scot) n the ankle. [Cf Du koot, Flem keute]

■ **cuit'ikin**, **cut'ikin** or **coot'ikin** n a gaiter.

cuit à point /kwē-tä pwē'/ (Fr) done to a turn.

cuiter /küt'ər/ (Scot) vt to wheedle; to indulge, pamper.

cuittle /küt'l/ (Scot) vt to coax; to cajole; to curry (favour). [Origin obscure]

culch or **cultch** /kulch/ (S Eng) n rubbish; the flooring of an oyster-bed; oyster-spawn. [Origin doubtful]

---

culchie /kul'chi/ (*Irish derog inf*) *n* a rustic; a country labourer. [Origin unknown]

Culdee /kul'dē/ *n* one of a fraternity of monks living in Scotland from the 8c in groups of cells. [OIr *cēle dē*, servant or companion of God, Latinized into *Culdei* (pl) as if *cultōrēs Deī*]

cul-de-four /kü(l)-də-foor'/ (*Fr kü*) (*archit*) *n* a low vault shaped like a quarter sphere; a demicupola. [Fr *cul* bottom, *de* of, and *four* furnace]

cul-de-lampe /kül-də-lãp'/ *n* an ornamental design used in filling up blank spaces in a book. [Fr *cul* bottom, *de* of, and *lampe* lamp]

cul-de-sac /kül'də-sak or kul'/ *n* a street, etc closed at one end; a blind alley; a route that leads nowhere (*fig*). [Fr *cul* bottom, *de* of, and *sac* sack]

culet /kū'lit/ *n* the flat back or base of a brilliant-cut gemstone; armour protecting the hips and buttocks. [OFr *culet*, dimin of *cul* bottom]

culex /kū'leks/ *n* (*pl* **culices** /kū'li-sēz/) an insect of the genus *Culex*, of the mosquito family **Culic'idae**, including the common European mosquito *C. pipiens*. [L *culex*, *-icis*]
■ **cu'licid** *n*. **culiciform** /-lis'/ *adj*. **cu'licine** *n* and *adj*.

culinary /kul'i-nə-ri/ *adj* relating to the kitchen or to cookery; used in the kitchen. [L *culīnārius*, from *culīna* a kitchen]
■ **cul'inarily** *adv*.

cull¹ /kul/ *vt* to gather; to select; to pick out and destroy (individuals, eg seal, deer), as inferior or superfluous members of a group. ◆*n* an act of culling; an unsuitable or superfluous animal eliminated from a flock or herd. [Fr *cueillir* to gather, from L *colligere*, from *col-* together, and *legere* to gather]
■ **cull'er** *n*. **cull'ing** *n*.

cull² see under **cully**.

cullender see **colander**.

Cullen skink /kul'ən skingk/ *n* a thick soup of smoked fish, potato and milk, *orig* made at *Cullen* in NE Scotland.

cullet /kul'it/ *n* waste glass, melted up again with new material. [Fr *collet*, from L *collum* neck]

cullion /kul'yən/ (*archaic*) *n* a mean or base person; a wretch, rascal. [Fr *couillon* testicle, poltroon (Ital *coglione*), from L *cōleus* a leather bag, from Gr *koleos* sheath]
■ **cull'ionly** *adj* mean, base.

cullis¹ /kul'is/ (now *rare*) *n* a strong broth. [OFr *coleis*, from L *cōlāre* to strain]

cullis² /kul'is/ *n* a roof gutter or groove. [Fr *coulisse*]

cully /kul'i/ *n* a dupe (*archaic*); a pal, mate, a man generally (*sl*; *rare*). ◆ *vt* (**cull'ying**; **cull'ied**) (*archaic*) to deceive or cheat. [Prob a contraction of **cullion**]
■ **cull** *n* (*archaic*) a dupe. **cull'yism** *n* (*archaic*) the state of being a cully.

culm¹ /kulm/ *n* a stem of grass or sedge. ◆ *vi* to form a culm. [L *culmus* a stalk]
■ **culmif'erous** *adj* having a culm.

culm² /kulm/ *n* coal dust; anthracite dust; anthracite (*dialect*). [Origin unknown; cf **coom¹**]
■ **culmif'erous** *adj* producing culm.
◻ **Culm** or **Culm Measures** *n pl* a Lower Carboniferous formation of Europe and SW England, with grits, sandstones, shales, etc.

culmen /kul'men/ *n* (*pl* **cul'mina**) the highest point; the top ridge of a bird's bill. [L; see **culminate**]

culmiferous see under **culm¹,²**.

culminate /kul'mi-nāt/ *vi* to reach the highest point (with *in*); to be on, or come to, the meridian, and thus the highest (or lowest) point of altitude (*astron*). ◆ *vt* to bring to the highest point. [LL *culmināre*, *-ātum*, from *culmen* or *columen*, *-inis* a summit]
■ **cul'minant** *adj* at its highest point. **culmina'tion** *n* the act of culminating; the top; the highest point; transit of a body across the meridian (*astron*).

culottes /kū- or kū-lot(s)'/ *n pl* a divided skirt (also (*sing*) **culotte**). [Fr *culotte* breeches]

culpable /kul'pə-bl/ *adj* meriting or deserving blame or condemnation; guilty, criminal (*archaic*). [L *culpa* a fault]
■ **culpabil'ity** or **cul'pableness** *n* blameworthiness. **cul'pably** *adv*. **cul'patory** *adj* expressive of blame.
◻ **culpable homicide** *n* (*Scots law*) manslaughter.

culpa lata /kul'pə lät'ə or kül'pa lä'ta/ (*L*) *n* gross negligence.

culpa levis /kul'pə lē'vis or kül'pa lev'is or le'wis/ (*L*) *n* a fault of little importance; excusable neglect.

culprit /kul'prit/ *n* a person at fault; a criminal; a prisoner who has pleaded not guilty to a charge and is awaiting trial (*Eng law*). [From the fusion in legal phraseology of *cul-* (*culpable*, *culpābilis*), and *prit*, *prist* (OFr *prest*) ready]

cult /kult/ *n* a system of religious belief; a sect; an unorthodox or false religion; a great, often excessive, admiration for a person or idea; the person or idea giving rise to such admiration; (with *of*) a fad. ◆ *adj* applied to objects associated with pagan worship; relating to, or giving rise to, a cult, extremely fashionable. [L *cultus*, from *colere* to worship]
■ **cult'ic** *adj* relating to or characteristic of a religious cult. **cult'ish** or **cult'y** *adj* fashionable. **cult'ism** *n* adherence to a cult. **cult'ist** *n*.

cultch same as **culch**.

culter /kul'tər/ *n* an obsolete form of **coulter**. [L, knife]
■ **cul'trate**, **cultrā'ted** or **cul'triform** *adj* knife-shaped.

cultigen /kul'ti-jən/ *n* a cultivated type of plant of uncertain origin. [See **cultivate**, and Gr root of *gignesthai* to become]

cultivar see under **cultivate**.

cultivate /kul'ti-vāt/ *vt* to fill or produce by tillage; to prepare for crops; to devote attention to; to seek actively to gain or foster (an association, friendship, etc); to civilize or refine. [LL *cultivāre*, *-ātum*, from L *colere* to till, to worship]
■ **cul'tivable** or **cultivāt'able** *adj* capable of being cultivated. **cultivar** /kul'ti-vär/ *n* a cultivated variety of plant that is distinct, uniform and stable in character, selected for a particular attribute or combination of attributes. **cultivā'tion** *n* the art or practice of cultivating; civilization; refinement. **cul'tivātor** *n* a person who cultivates; an agricultural implement, a grubber.

cultrate, cultriform see under **culter**.

culture /kul'chər/ *n* cultivation; the result of cultivation; the state of being cultivated; refinement in manners, thought, taste, etc; loosely, the arts; a type of civilization; the attitudes and values which inform a society; a crop of micro-organisms, eg bacteria, grown in a solid or liquid medium in a laboratory. ◆ *vt* to cultivate; to grow (living organisms or cells) in a culture medium. [L *cultūra*, from *colere*]
■ **cul'turable** *adj*. **cul'tural** *adj*. **cul'turally** *adv*. **cul'tured** *adj* cultivated; well-educated, *esp* in the arts and humanities; refined. **cul'tureless** *adj*. **cul'turist** *n* a devotee of culture; a person who grows cultures in a laboratory.
◻ **cultural anthropology** *n* social anthropology. **cultural cringe** *n* (*esp Aust*) a subservient attitude (*usu* of a nation) to what are regarded as the superior cultures of others. **culturai** or **culture lag** *n* a slower rate of cultural change in one part of a society compared with the whole, or in one society compared with others. **cultural** or **culture shock** *n* disorientation caused by a change from one environment, culture, ideology, etc to another that is radically different or alien. **cultured pearl** *n* a pearl grown round a small foreign body deliberately introduced into an oyster's shell. **culture medium** *n* a nutritive substance on which laboratory cultures can be grown, eg gelatin, agar, etc. **culture vulture** *n* (*inf*) someone who has an avid interest in the arts.

cultus /kul'təs/ *n* a religious ritual; a cult. [L]

culver /kul'vər/ *n* a dove, a pigeon; a wood pigeon. [OE *culfre*]
◻ **cul'ver-key** *n* (often in *pl*) the cowslip; (in *pl*) ash-keys. **cul'vertailed** *adj* dove-tailed.

culverin /kul'və-rin/ *n* an early form of handgun; later a type of cannon with a long barrel of relatively narrow bore, used in the 16c and 17c. [Fr *coulevrine*, from *couleuvre* snake, from L *colubrīnus* snake-like, from *coluber* snake]
■ **culverineer'** *n*.

Culver's physic /kul'vərz fiz'ik/ or **root** /root/ *n* the dried rhizome of a N American plant related to the speedwell (*Veronicastrum virginicum*), formerly used medicinally. [Dr *Culver*, 18c US physician]

culvert /kul'vərt/ *n* an arched construction or channel enclosing a drain or watercourse beneath a road, railway, etc. [Perh from Fr *couler* to flow, from L *colāre*]

culvertage /kul'vər-tij/ (*hist*) *n* degradation of a vassal to the position of a serf. [OFr *culvert* a serf]

cum¹ /kum/ *prep* combined with; with the addition of (as *cum-dividend*, of shares, including the right to the next dividend); used as a combining form to indicate dual function, nature, etc, as in *kitchen-cum-dining-room*. [L]

cum² see **come**.

cumarin see **coumarin**.

Cumb. *abbrev*: Cumbria.

cumbent /kum'bənt/ *adj* lying down; reclining. [L *cumbēns*, *-entis*, prp of *cumbere* to lie down]

cumber /kum'bər/ *vt* to trouble or hinder with something useless; to get in the way of; to occupy obstructively. ◆ *n* an encumbrance;

cumbering. [Appar OFr *combrer* to hinder, from LL *cumbrus* a heap, from L *cumulus* a heap]

■ **cum'bered** *adj* hampered; obstructed. **cum'berer** *n*. **cum'berless** *adj* unencumbered. **cum'berment** *n*. **cum'bersome** *adj* unwieldy, awkward, unmanageable. **cum'brance** *n* an encumbrance; hindrance, burden. **cum'brous** *adj* hindering; obstructing; unwieldy. **cum'brously** *adv*. **cum'brousness** *n*.

□ **cum'ber-ground** *n* (*Bible*) a useless thing.

cumec /kū'mek/ (*engineering*) *n* short for cubic metre per second, a unit for measuring volumetric rate of flow.

cum grano salis /kum grā'nō sā'lis or kŭm grä'nō sal'is/ (*L*) with a grain of salt.

cumin or **cummin** /kum'in or kū'min/ *n* an umbelliferous plant (*Cuminum cyminum*) of the Mediterranean region, with seeds like caraway, used for flavouring and valuable as carminatives. [OE *cymen*, from L *cumīnum*, from Gr *kymīnon*, cognate with Heb *kammon*]

cum laude /kum lö'dē or kŭm low'de/ (*L*) with distinction (used on a diploma to denote special merit or the lowest grade of honours). See also **magna cum laude, summa cum laude**.

cummer /kum'ər/ or **kimmer** /kim'ər/ (*Scot*) *n* a godmother (*obs*); a gossip; a woman; a girl. [Fr *commère*, from L *con-* with, and *māter* mother]

cummerbund /kum'ər-bund/ *n* a waistband, a sash. [Hindi *kamarband* a loinband]

cummin see **cumin**.

cummingtonite /kum'ing-tə-nīt/ *n* a mineral of the amphibole group, hydrated magnesium iron silicate, occurring in metamorphic rocks. [*Cummington*, town in the USA where it was first found]

cum multis aliis /kum mul'tis ā'lē-is or kŭm mŭl'tēs a'lē-ēs/ (*L*) with many other things.

cum notis variorum /kum nō'tis vā-ri-ō'rəm (or -ö') or kŭm no'tēs va-ri-ö'rŭm (or -ö')/ (*L*) with notes of various (critics or commentators).

cum privilegio /kum pri-vi-lē'ji-ō or kŭm prē-vi-lā'gi-ō or -wi-/ (*L*) with privilege.

cumquat same as **kumquat**.

cum-savvy /kum-sav'i/ (*sl*) *n* know-how.

cumshaw /kum'shö/ *n* a gift, a tip, gratuity. [Pidgin Eng, from Chin *gǎnxiè* grateful thanks]

cumulate /kū'myə-lāt/ *vt* and *vi* to heap together, combine; to accumulate. ◆ *adj* /-lət/ heaped together (also **cum'ulated**). [L *cumulāre, -ātum*, from *cumulus* a heap]

■ **cumula'tion** *n* accumulation. **cum'ulative** *adj* increasing by successive additions. **cum'ulatively** *adv*. **cum'ulativeness** *n*.

□ **cumulative action** *n* (*med*) (of a drug) toxic effects produced when repeated doses are taken and the body has had insufficient time to break down or excrete each dose. **cumulative distribution function** *n* (*stats*) a function, f(x), which gives the probability that a related random variable, y, is less than or equal to the argument of the function, x. **cumulative dose** *n* (*radiol*) the integrated radiation dose resulting from repeated exposure. **cumulative vote** *n* a system by which a voter may distribute a number of votes at will among the candidates, giving more than one to a candidate if he or she chooses.

cumulus /kū'myə-ləs/ *n* (*pl* **cū'mulī**) a kind of cloud consisting of rounded heaps with a darker horizontal base; a heap. [L *cumulus* a heap]

■ **cū'muliform** *adj*. **cū'mulose** *adj*.

□ **cū'mulocirr'us** *n* (*pl* **cū'mulocirr'i** /-ī/) a delicate cirrus-like cumulus cloud. **cū'mulonim'bus** *n* (*pl* **cū'mulonim'bi**) /-bī/ a cumulus cloud of great height, often discharging showers or characteristic of thunderstorms. **cū'mulostra'tus** /-strā' or strä' / *n* (*pl* **cū'mulostra'ta** /-tə/) a cumulus cloud with an extended base.

cunabula /kū-nab'ū-lə/ *n pl* a cradle; incunabula. [L *cūnābula*]

cunctator /kungk-tā'tər/ *n* someone who delays or procrastinates. [L *cunctātor*, from *cunctārī* to delay, hesitate]

■ **cuncta'tion** *n* delay, procrastination. **cuncta'tious, cunc'tative** or **cunc'tatory** *adj* inclined to delay or procrastinate.

cundy, also **condie** /kun'di or kon'di/ (*Scot*) *n* a covered drain; a tunnel or passage. [Altered form of **conduit**]

cuneal /kū'ni-əl/ or **cuneate** /kū'ni-āt/ *adj* wedge-shaped. [L *cuneus* a wedge]

■ **cuneat'ic** *adj* cuneiform. **cuneiform** /kū-nē'i-förm or kū'ni-(-i)-förm/ *adj* wedge-shaped, *usu* applied to the old Hittite, Babylonian, Assyrian and Persian writing, of which the characters were impressed by the wedge-shaped facets of a stylus. ◆ *n* cuneiform writing.

□ **cuneiform bones** *n pl* (*anat*) (in the foot) three small bones of the tarsus.

cunette /kū-net'/ (*fortif*) *n* a trench sunk along the middle of a dry ditch or moat, serving as a drain, a cuvette. [Fr, from Ital *cunetta*, aphetic from *lacunetta* a small lagoon or ditch]

cunjevoi /kun'ji-voi/ (*Aust*) *n* a sea squirt; a large-leaved araceous plant (*Alocasia macrorrhiza*) with edible rhizomes. [From an Aboriginal language]

cunner see **conner**[2].

cunnilingus /ku-ni-ling'gəs/ or **cunnilinctus** /-lingk'təs/ *n* oral stimulation of the female genitalia. [L *cunnus* vulva, and *lingere* to lick]

cunning /kun'ing/ *adj* knowing, clever; skilful, ingenious; artful; crafty; dainty or quaintly pleasing (*N Am*). ◆ *n* knowledge, cleverness; skill, ingenuity; the faculty of using stratagem to accomplish a purpose; craftiness; artifice. [OE *cunnan* to know]

■ **cunn'ingly** *adv*. **cunn'ingness** *n* the quality of being cunning; artfulness, slyness.

cunt /kunt/ (*taboo sl*) *n* the female genitalia, *esp* the vagina; a woman regarded as a sexual object; an unpleasant, contemptible person of either sex. [ME *cunte*; ety dubious]

CUP *abbrev*: Cambridge University Press.

cup /kup/ *n* a drinking vessel, roughly hemispherical, *usu* with one handle; a hollow; a cup-shaped structure (*biol*); either of the two cup-shaped supports for the breasts in a brassière; a cupful; a dry or liquid measure used in cooking, equal to *approx* half a pint (a little over one quarter of a litre); the liquid, etc contained in a cup; a mixed beverage made with wine (as in *claret cup*); an ornamental vessel offered as a prize; a competition with such a vessel as a prize; the plastic or metal casing that lines a hole (*golf*); the hole itself; the chalice, or the consecrated wine, at the Eucharist; that which one receives or undergoes in life, one's lot in life. ◆ *vt* (**cupp'ing; cupped**) to form (one's hands) into the shape of a cup; to hold in one's cupped hands; to lodge in or as if in a cup; to draw blood to the surface of the skin by means of cupping-glasses in order to facilitate bloodletting or to relieve chest infection, etc (*med*); to make drunk (*obs*). ◆ *vi* to become cup-shaped. [OE *cuppe*, from L *cūpa, cuppa* a tub]

■ **cup'ful** *n* (*pl* **cup'fuls**) as much as fills a cup. **cup'pa** (*inf*) a cup of tea. **cupp'er** *n* a cupbearer; a person professionally engaged in cupping. **cupp'ing** *n* (*med*) (*esp* formerly) the application of cups from which the air is removed in order to draw blood to the surface of the skin.

□ **cup'-and-ball** *n* a ball-and-socket joint; the game of catching a tethered ball in a cup on the end of a stick. **cup'-and-ring** (**mark**) *n* (*archaeol*) a cup mark surrounded by one or more incised rings, carved on stones. **cup'bearer** *n* a person who attends at a feast to fill and hand out wine cups. **cup'cake** *n* a small round cake baked in a foil or paper case; an attractive woman (*N Am sl*); a mad or eccentric person (*N Am sl*); a term of endearment (*N Am*). **cup coral** *n* a simple cup-shaped coral. **cup final** *n* (*sport*) the final and deciding match in a competition for a cup. **cup fungus** *n* any fungus of the order Pezizales. **cup'gall** *n* a cup-shaped gall in oak-leaves. **cup'head** *n* a hemispherical (or nearly so) bolthead or rivet head. **cup lichen** or **cup moss** *n* any lichen with cup-shaped structures. **cup'man** *n* a convivial companion. **cup mark** *n* a cup-shaped hollow made by prehistoric man on rocks, standing-stones, etc. **cupp'ing-glass** *n* a glass vessel used in cupping. **cup'-tie** *n* (*sport*) one of a series of games to determine the winners of a cup. **cup'-tied** *adj* (of a player) unable to play in a cup-tie because of injury or other disallowance; (of a team) involved in a cup-tie and therefore unable to play in other games.

■ **in one's cups** under the influence of alcohol, drunk. **one's cup of tea** see under **tea**. **there's many a slip 'twixt the cup and the lip** the success of a venture should not be assumed and the possibility of failure or disaster should be recognized.

cupboard /kub'ərd/ *n* an item of furniture or a recess fitted with a door, used for storage. ◆ *vt* to store.

□ **cupboard faith** *n* a show of faith for material end. **cup'board-love** *n* hypocritical show of affection for material gain.

■ **cry cupboard** to cry for food.

cupel /kū'pəl/ *n* a small vessel used by goldsmiths in assaying precious metals; the movable hearth of a reverberatory furnace for refining. ◆ *vt* (**cū'pelling** or *N Am* **cūpeling; cū'pelled** or *N Am* **cū'peled**) to assay in a cupel. [L *cūpella*, dimin of *cūpa*; see **cup**]

■ **cūpellā'tion** *n* a method of refining precious metal in which impure metal is melted in a cupel and impurities are oxidized or run off.

Cupid /kū'pid/ *n* the Roman god of sexual love, identified with Greek Eros; (*without cap*) a winged figure of a young boy often carrying a bow and arrow representing love (*art*, etc); (*without cap*) a kind of jam-tart (*US*). [L *Cupīdo, -inis*, from *cupere* to desire]

■ **cūpid'inous** *adj* full of desire, *esp* amorous. **cūpid'ity** *n* covetousness.

■ **Cupid's bow** an archery bow in the shape of a double curve; the human lips shaped (either naturally or by lipstick) like this. **cupid's dart** a herbaceous plant (*Catananche caerulea*) of the family Compositae, with blue and white flowers.

cupola /kū'pə-lə/ *n* a spherical vault, or concave ceiling, on the top of a building; the internal part of a dome; a dome; a lantern on the top of a dome; any dome-shaped structure, eg at the end of the cochlea (*anat*); an armoured dome or turret to protect a gun; a furnace used in iron-foundries. ◆ *vt* to furnish with a cupola. [Ital, from L *cūpula*, dimin of *cūpa* a cask]
■ **cū'pola'd** or **cū'polaed** *adj.* **cū'polar** *adj.* **cū'polated** *adj.*

cuppa see under **cup**.

cuprammonium /kū-prä-mō'ni-əm/ *n* a solution of cupric hydroxide in ammonia. [L *cuprum* copper, and **ammonium**]
□ **cuprammonium rayon** *n* artificial silk made by dissolving cellulose in cuprammonium.

cupreous /kū'pri-əs/ *adj* of, containing, or like copper. [L *cupreus*, from *cuprum*; see **copper**]
■ **cu'prate** *n* any of several compounds containing modified oxides of copper, which act as superconductors. **cū'pric** *adj* of or containing bivalent copper. **cūprif'erous** *adj* yielding copper. **cū'prite** *n* red copper ore, ruby copper, cuprous oxide (Cu₂O). **cū'prous** *adj* of or containing univalent copper.
□ **cū'pronick'el** *n* an alloy of copper and nickel.

Cupressus /kū-pres'əs/ *n* the cypress genus. [L]

cuprictyoy**cuprous** see under **cupreous**.

cupule /kū'pūl/ *n* a small cup in a liverwort containing gemmae (*bot*); a cup-shaped structure on the fruit of some trees, eg oak, beech, chestnut. [L *cūpula*, dimin of *cūpa* tub]
■ **cū'pular** or **cū'pulate** *adj* cup-like; relating to a cupule. **Cūpūlif'erae** /-ə-rē'/ *n pl* in some classifications a family including beech, oak, chestnut, with or without birch, hazel, and hornbeam. **cūpūlif'erous** *adj* of the Cupuliferae; bearing cupules.

cur /kûr/ *n* a worthless dog, of low breed; someone deserving contempt, a scoundrel. [ME *curre*; cf ON *kurra* to grumble]
■ **curr'ish** *adj.* **curr'ishly** *adv.* **curr'ishness** *n*.

cur. or **curt.** *abbrev* : current (ie this month).

curaçao /koo-rä-sä'ō/ or **curaçoa** /kū'rə-sō or kū-ra-sō'/ *n* a liqueur flavoured with bitter orange peel. [*Curaçao*, island in the W Indies, where it was first made]

curacy see under **curate¹**.

curare or **curari** /kū- or kū-rä'ri/ *n* a paralysing poison extracted from the bark of S American trees (eg *Strychnos* or *Chondodendron*), *orig* used by S Americans to coat the tips of arrows, later used as a muscle relaxant, eg to control muscle spasm in tetanus, and in surgery (also **cura'ra**). [Port from Carib *kurari*]
■ **cura'rine** *n* a highly poisonous alkaloid derivative, used in surgery in the form of tubocurarine, as a muscle relaxant. **cu'rarize** or **-ise** *vt*.

curassow /kū'rə-sō or kū-rä'sō/ *n* any of a number of pheasant- or turkey-like arboreal S American birds. [From the island of *Curaçao*]

curat /kū'rət/ (*obs*) *n* a cuirass. [See **cuirass**]

curate¹ /kū'rit/ *n* a clergyman in the Church of England, assisting a rector or vicar; someone who has the cure of souls (*archaic*); in Ireland, an assistant barman. [LL *cūrātus*, L *cūra* care]
■ **cur'acy** /-ə-si/ or **cur'ateship** *n* the office, employment or benefice of a curate.
□ **curate's egg** *n* anything of which some parts are excellent and some parts are bad.

curate² /kū-rāt'/ *vt* to act as a curator for (eg an exhibition or museum); to organize look after. [Back-formation from **curator**]

curative see under **cure¹**.

curator /kū-rā'tər or (in Scots law) kū'rə-tər/ *n* (also *fem* **cūrā'trix**) a person who has the charge of anything; a superintendent, *esp* of a museum; a person appointed by law as guardian; a member of a board for electing university professors and the like. [L *cūrātor*]
■ **curatorial** /-ə-tō'ri-əl/ *adj.* **cūrā'torship** *n*.

curatory see **curative** under **cure¹**.

curb¹ /kûrb/ *n* a chain or strap attached to the bit for restraining a horse; the bit itself; another spelling for **kerb** (chiefly *N Am*); a raised edge or border; a check or restraint; a disease of horses, marked by hard swellings on the leg; the swelling itself. ◆ *vt* to furnish with or guide by a curb; to restrain or check. [Fr *courbe*, from L *curvus* bent]
■ **curb'able** *adj.* **curb'less** *adj.*
□ **curb'-roof** *n* a mansard-roof. **curb'side** *n* a N American spelling of **kerbside**. **curb'stone** *n* a N American spelling of **kerbstone**.

curb² see **courb**.

curch /kûrch/ *n* a covering for the head, a kerchief. [See **kerchief**]

curculio /kûr-kū'li-ō/ *n* (*pl* **curcu'lios**) any member of the **Curcūlion'idae**, a family of weevils, many of which are serious pests of stored foodstuffs and fruit crops, *esp* the **plum curculio** of N America. [L, rice or grain weevil]

curcuma /kûr-kū'mə/ *n* any plant of the genus *Curcuma*, especially *C. longa* yielding turmeric. [Ar *kurkum* saffron]
■ **cur'cumine** or **cur'cumin** *n* the saffron-yellow colouring matter of turmeric, used *esp* in food colouring.

curd /kûrd/ *n* milk thickened or coagulated by acid; the cheese part of milk, as distinguished from the whey; any substance of similar consistency; (in soap-making) the granular soap that rises in the lye upon salting; the fatty matter between the flakes of salmon flesh; the flowering head of cauliflower, broccoli, etc. ◆ *vt* and *vi* to curdle. [Prob Celtic; Gaelic *gruth*, Ir *cruth*]
■ **curd'iness** *n.* **curd'le** *vt* and *vi* to turn into curd; to coagulate; to thicken. **curd'ler** *n.* **curd'y** *adj* like or full of curd.
□ **curd cheese** *n* a mild white cheese made from skimmed milk curds.

cure¹ /kūr/ *n* that which heals; a remedy, or course of remedial treatment; a means of improving a situation; a course or method of preserving or arresting decomposition; the total quantity cured; treatment by which a product is finished or made ready for use; care of the sick; an act of healing; care of souls or spiritual charge. ◆ *vt* to heal or make better; to eliminate (an illness, harmful habit, etc); to preserve by drying, salting, etc; to finish by means of chemical change, eg to vulcanize (a rubber), or to use heat or chemicals in the last stage of preparing (a thermosetting plastic). ◆ *vi* to undergo a process or course of curing. [OFr *cure*, from L *cūra* care]
■ **cūrabil'ity** *n.* **cūr'able** *adj.* **cūr'ableness** *n.* **cūr'ative** *adj* tending to cure (also **cūr'atory**). ◆ *n* a substance that cures. **cūr'atively** *adv.* **cūre'less** *adj* that cannot be cured. **cūr'er** *n*.
□ **cūre'-all** *n* a panacea.

cure² /kūr/ (*sl*) *n* an odd or queer person. [Ety dubious]

curé /kū'rā/ *n* a parish priest in France. [Fr; see **curate¹**]

curettage /kū-ret'ij or kū-ri-täzh'/ (*surg*) *n* the scraping of a body cavity or internal surface of an organ, *usu* to remove diseased tissue or a sample of tissue for diagnostic purposes. [Fr *curer* to clean, clear]
■ **curette'** or (*US*) **curet'** *n* the spoon-shaped instrument used in curettage. ◆ *vt* to scrape with a curette. **curette'ment** *n* curettage.

curfew /kûr'fū/ *n* a regulation obliging people to be indoors within certain hours; the ringing of a bell at a certain hour as a traditional custom, or the bell itself; the time of curfew; in feudal times, the ringing of a bell as a signal to put out all fires and lights. [OFr *covrefeu*; *couvrir* to cover, *feu* fire, from L *focus*]

curfuffle see **carfuffle**.

curia /kū'ri-ə/ *n* the court of the papal see; one of the ten divisions of a Roman tribe; a building in which the senate met; a provincial senate. [L *cūria* a division of a Roman tribe, a senate, a court]
■ **cū'rial** *adj.* **cū'rialism** *n.* **cū'rialist** *n.* **cūrialist'ic** *adj.*
□ **Curia Regis** see **aula**.
■ **curia advisari vult** (*law*) the court wishes to be advised, or consider (*abbrev* **cur. adv. vult** or **c.a.v.**).

curie /kū-rē' or kū'rē/ *n orig* the quantity of radon in radioactive equilibrium with a gram of radium; a former unit of radioactivity, defined as 3.7×10^{10} disintegrations per second (becquerels), or the quantity of a radioactive substance which undergoes this number of disintegrations. [Marie and Pierre *Curie*, discoverers of radium]
■ **curium** /kū'/ *n* an artificially produced radioactive transuranic element (symbol **Cm**; atomic no 96).
□ **curiether'apy** *n* a former name for the treatment of disease by radium.

curiet /kū'ri-et/ (*obs*) *n* a cuirass. [See **cuirass**]

curio /kū'ri-ō/ *n* (*pl* **cū'rios**) any article of bric-à-brac, or anything considered rare and curious. [For **curiosity**]

curiosa /kū-ri-ō'sə/ *n pl* strange or unusual objects, *specif* books, manuscripts, etc that are pornographic or erotic. [New L, from same root as **curious**]

curious /kū'ri-əs/ *adj* anxious to learn; inquisitive; skilfully made; singular; rare, unusual; odd, strange. [Fr *curieux*, from L *cūriōsus*, from *cūra*]
■ **curiosity** /-os'i-ti/ *n* the state or quality of being curious; inquisitiveness; that which is curious; anything rare or unusual. **cū'riously** *adv.* **cū'riousness** *n*.
□ **curious arts** *n pl* (*Bible*) magical practices.

curium see under **curie**.

curl /kûrl/ vt to twist into ringlets; to coil; to cause to move in a curve; to ripple. ◆ vi to grow in or shrink into ringlets; to move in curves; to writhe; to ripple; to eddy; to play at the game of curling. ◆ n a ringlet of hair, or something resembling it; a wave, bending or twist; an eddy; a plant disease in which leaves curl; a curled condition. [ME *crull*; Du *krullen*, Dan *krolle* to curl]

■ **curled** adj. **curl'er** n someone or something that curls; a player at the game of curling. **curl'iness** n. **curl'ing** n a game played on ice, *esp* common in Scotland, in which two teams slide a series of heavy smooth stones with the aim of reaching a target circle and/or dislodging the opposing team's stone(s) already in the circle. **curl'y** adj (**curl'ier**; **curl'iest**) having curls; full of curls; (of a problem) difficult to solve (*Aust* and *NZ inf*). □ **curled'-pate** adj (*Shakesp*) having curled hair. **curling irons** n pl another name for curling tongs. **curling pond** n a pond on which curling is played. **curl'ing-stone** n a heavy smooth stone with a handle, used in the game of curling. **curling tongs** n pl an instrument consisting of a heated rod (round which hair is wound) and a hinged plastic or metal grip, used for curling the hair. **curl'paper** n a strip of paper round which the hair is twisted to give it curl. **curl'y-greens** n pl kale. **curl'y-headed** adj.

■ **curl one's lips** to sneer. **curl up** (*inf*) to be embarrassed. **out of curl** lacking energy, limp.

curlew /kûr'loo or -lū/ n a wading bird (*Numenius arquata*) of the woodcock family, inhabiting moorland, the shoreline and other damp areas, with a long curved bill and long legs, and a plaintive whistling cry; any related bird of the genus *Numenius*. [OFr *corlieu*; prob from its cry]

□ **cur'lew-berry** n another name for crowberry.

■ **stone curlew** see under **stone**.

curlicue /kûr'lə-kū/ n a fancy twist or curl, *esp* in handwriting. [**curly** and **cue**[1]]

curliewurlie /kûr'li-wûr'li/ (*Scot*) adj and n (of) a twisted or curled object or ornament.

curmudgeon /kər-muj'ən/ n an avaricious, ill-natured churlish person; a miser. [Origin unknown]

■ **curmud'geonly** adj and adv.

curn /kûrn/ (*Scot*) n a grain; a particle; a small quantity, a little. [**corn**]

■ **curn'y** or **curn'ey** adj granular, coarse-grained.

curnaptious see **carnaptious**.

curpel /kûr'pl/ n a Scots form of **crupper**.

curr /kûr/ (*dialect*) vi to make a purring sound. [Imit]

currach or **curragh** /kur'ə(hh)/ n a boat of similar construction to a coracle. [Ir *curach*]

currajong see **kurrajong**.

currant /kur'ənt/ n a small black raisin or dried seedless grape; extended to several species of Ribes (*black, red, white, flowering currant*), and to various other plants, and their fruits. [**Corinth** (currants orig known as *raisins of Corinth*)]

■ **curr'anty** adj full of currants.

□ **currant bread** n a sweetened bread containing (grape) currants. **currant bun** or **currant loaf** n a dark spiced cake full of currants. **currant cake** n a cake with currants in it. **curr'ant-jelly** n a jelly made from red or black currants. **curr'ant-wine** n.

currawong /kur'ə-wong/ n any of several Australian crow-like birds of the genus *Strepera*, with a distinctive, resounding call. [From an Aboriginal language]

current /kur' or kur'ənt/ adj belonging to the period of time now passing; up-to-date; present; generally or widely received; passing from person to person. ◆ n a running or flowing; a stream; a portion of water or air moving in a certain direction; a flow of electricity; course. [L *currēns, -entis*, from prp of *currere* to run]

■ **curr'ency** n that which circulates, *esp* the money of a country; circulation; general acceptance or prevalence; up-to-dateness; native-born Australians collectively, as opposed to immigrants (*old Aust sl*). **curr'ently** adv. **curr'entness** n.

□ **currency note** n a treasury note (qv under **treasure**). **current account** n a bank account on which one is *usu* not paid interest and from which money may be withdrawn by cheque. **current affairs** n pl important political, financial, and social events currently happening. **current assets** n pl (*finance*) short term assets generated by operations, likely to convert to cash within one year. **current bedding** n (*geol*) false bedding. **current coil** n (*elec eng*) a coil connected in series with a circuit and therefore carrying the main current. **curr'ent-cost** adj (*account*) of a system that values assets at the current cost of replacement (cf **historic cost** under **history**). **current density** n (*phys*) the ratio between the electric current flowing in a conductor and the cross-sectional area of the conductor. **current liabilities** n pl (*finance*) liabilities due to be paid to creditors within a year.

■ **pass current** to be received as genuine.

currente calamo /ku-ren'tē (or kū-ren'te) ka'la-mō/ (*L*) with a running pen, offhand.

curricle /kur'i-kl/ n a two-wheeled open chaise, drawn by two horses abreast. [L *curriculum* course, race, racing chariot, from *currere* to run]

curriculum /kə-rik'ū-ləm/ n (pl **curric'ula** or **curric'ulums**) a course, *esp* the course of study at a school, college, university, etc. [L; see **curricle**]

■ **curric'ular** adj of or relating to a curriculum or to courses of study.

□ **curriculum vitae** /kə-rik'ūl-əm vē'tī, vī'tē or koor-ik'ŭ-lŭm vē'tī or wē'tī/ n (pl **curric'ula vi'tae**) (a biographical summary of) the course of someone's life, *esp* details of education and achievements in chronological order requested by or supplied to potential employers (*abbrev* **cv** or **CV**).

■ **core curriculum** the subjects that a pupil or student is obliged to study while at school. **National Curriculum** see under **nation**[1].

currie see **curry**[3].

curried, **currier** see **curry**[2].

currish, **currishly**, etc see under **cur**.

curry[1] /kur'i/ n a dish of meat, eggs or vegetables cooked and seasoned with hot or aromatic spices, eg turmeric, chillis, cumin, coriander, etc. ◆ vt to make a curry of by seasoning with mixed spices or adding curry sauce. [Tamil *kari* sauce]

□ **curr'y-leaf** n a rutaceous Indian tree (*Murraya koenigii*) whose leaves are an ingredient in curry powder. **curry powder** n ground mixed spices, including turmeric, cumin, chillis, fenugreek, cloves, coriander, etc. **curr'ywurst** n a German snack of sliced sausage in a curry sauce.

curry[2] /kur'i/ vt (**curr'ying**; **curr'ied**) to dress or treat (leather); to rub down and groom (eg a horse) with a currycomb; to beat; to scratch. [OFr *correier* (Fr *corroyer*), *conrei* outfit, from L *con*- with, and the root seen in **array**]

■ **curr'ier** n a person who curries or dresses tanned leather. **curr'ying** n.

□ **curr'ycomb** n a plastic or rubber brush used for currying horses; a comb with metal teeth used to remove hair caught in such a brush.

■ **curry favour** (earlier *curry favell* to curry the chestnut horse) to seek to ingratiate oneself.

curry[3], **currie** obsolete forms of **quarry**[2].

cursal see under **cursus**.

curse /kûrs/ vt to invoke or wish evil upon; to blaspheme; to afflict with; to damn; to excommunicate. ◆ vi to utter abuse; to swear. ◆ n an invocation or wishing of evil or harm; evil invoked on another person; the excommunication sentence; an imprecation; any great evil; (with *the*) menstruation, a menstrual period (*inf*). [OE *cursian*, from *curs* a curse; ety doubtful; not connected with **cross**]

■ **curs'ed** adj under or deserving a curse; hateful. **curs'edly** adv. **curs'edness** n. **curs'er** n. **curs'ing** n. **curst** adj cursed; ill-tempered (*archaic*). **curst'ness** n the state of being curst; peevishness; perverseness.

■ **curse of Scotland** (*cards*) the nine of diamonds (origin uncertain; a number of theories have been put forward).

curselarie, **cursenary** see **cursorary** under **cursor**.

cursitor /kûr'si-tər/ (*obs*) n a clerk or officer in the Court of Chancery who made out original writs *de cursu*, ie of ordinary course; a vagrant. [LL *cursitor*]

cursive /kûr'siv/ adj (of handwriting) written with a running hand; flowing; (of a typeface) designed to imitate handwriting. ◆ n cursive writing. [LL *cursīvus*, from L *currere* to run]

■ **cur'sively** adv.

cursor /kûr'sər/ n one of several (*usu* flashing) devices appearing on a VDU screen used to indicate position, eg of the next input character, of a correction, etc; a sliding part of a measuring instrument. [L *cursor*, pl *cursōrēs* a runner, from *currere*, *cursum* to run]

■ **cur'sorary** (*Shakesp*; other readings **cur'senary**, **cur'selarie**; *prob* intended for **cursitory**) adj (*obs*) cursory. **cursores** /-sō'rēz, -sō'/ n pl in old classifications, running birds, variously limited. **curso'rial** adj (of an animal or bird or part of its anatomy) adapted for running. **cur'sorily** /-sər-/ adv. **cur'soriness** n. **cur'sory** adj superficial; hasty; running quickly over.

curst see under **curse**.

cursus /kûr'səs/ n an elongated prehistoric earthwork found only in Britain, consisting of parallel banks with ditches outside. [L, a course]

■ **cur'sal** adj.

curt /kûrt/ adj short; concise; discourteously brief or summary. [L *curtus* shortened]

■ **curt'ly** adv. **curt'ness** n.

curt. see **cur.**

curtail /kûr- or kər-tāl'/ vt to cut short; to cut off a part of; to abridge. [Old spelling *curtal*, OFr *courtault*, from L *curtus* shortened]

■ **curtail'er** *n.* **curtail'ment** *n.*

❑ **cur'tail-step** *n* a round-ended step at the bottom of a flight.

curtain /kûr'tən/ *n* hanging drapery at a window, around a bed, etc; the part of a rampart between two bastions (*fortif*); a curtain wall; (in a theatre) a screen of cloth or metal concealing the stage, or restricting the spread of fire; the fall of the curtain, close of a scene or act (*theatre*); a protective barrier in general, as the fire of many guns directed along a certain line to prevent the passage of an enemy (also called **cur'tain-fire**). ◆ *vt* to enclose or furnish with curtains; (with *off*) to separate with, or as if with, a curtain. [OFr *cortine*, from LL *cortīna*; prob L *cōrs*, *cōrtis* a court]

❑ **curtain call** *n* a summons to a performer or performers from the audience to reappear to receive further applause after the curtain has been lowered at the end of a performance. **curtain lecture** *n* a lecture or reproof given in private, *esp* in bed by a wife to her husband. **cur'tain-raiser** *n* a short play preceding the main performance; an event which precedes a more important event. **cur'tain-sider** *n* a lorry or truck having fabric sides. **curtain speech** *n* a speech made in front of a theatre curtain. **curtain up** *n* (*theatre*) the beginning of a performance. **curtain wall** *n* a wall that is not load-bearing, eg does not support a roof. **curtain walling** *n* pre-fabricated large framed sections of lightweight, *usu* predecorated, material used in building.

■ **bamboo curtain** see under **bamboo**. **be curtains (for)** (*sl*) to be the end or death (of). **behind the curtain** away from public view. **draw the curtain** to draw it aside, so as to show what is behind, or to draw it in front of anything so as to hide it. **iron curtain** see under **iron**.

curtal /kûr'təl/ (*obs*) *n* a horse or other animal with a docked tail; anything docked or cut short, eg a kind of bassoon, cannon, etc. ◆ *adj* docked or shortened. [See **curtail**]

❑ **curtal friar** *n* (*Walter Scott*) a friar with a short frock.

curtalax, curtalaxe /kûr'tə-laks/ or **curtaxe** /kûr'taks/ (*archaic*) *n* a short, broad sword, a cutlass. [A corruption of the earlier forms *coutelas*, *curtelas*. See **cutlass**]

curtana /kûr-tä'nə/ or /-tā'nə/ *n* a sword without a point, symbolic of mercy, carried at coronations. [L *curtus* short]

curtate /kûr'tāt/ *adj* shortened or reduced, *usu* applied to the distance of a planet from the sun or earth projected on the plane of the ecliptic. [See **curt**]

■ **curtā'tion** *n.*

curtaxe see **curtalax**.

curtesy /kûr'tə-si/ (*law*; now *rare*) *n* the right of a widower to a life estate in the land of his late wife.

curtilage /kûr'ti-lij/ *n* a court, garden, field or area of land attached and belonging to a house, etc. [OFr *courtillage*; see **court**]

curtsy or **curtsey** /kûrt'si/ *n* a formal indication of respect (by women) made by bending the knees with one leg behind the other. ◆ *vi* to make or 'drop' a curtsy. [See **courtesy**]

curule /kū'rool/ *adj* of high authority, as a higher Roman magistrate who was entitled to a **curule chair**, one like a camp-stool with curved legs. [L *curūlis*, from *currus* a chariot]

curvaceous, curvate, etc see under **curve**.

curve /kûrv/ *n* a line that is not straight; a line (including a straight line) answering to an equation; a graph; the curved line on a graph representing the rise and fall of measurable data, eg birth rate; a curved surface; anything bent; an arch; (in *pl*) the rounded contours of a woman's body (*inf*). ◆ *vt* to bend; to form into a curve. ◆ *vi* to bend; to move in a curve. [L *curvus* crooked]

■ **curvaceous** or **curvacious** /kûr-vā'shəs/ *adj* (*inf*) (of a woman) having shapely curves. **cur'vāte** or **curvā'ted** *adj* curved or bent in a regular form. **curvā'tion** *n.* **cur'vative** /-və-tiv/ *adj.* **cur'vature** /-və-chər/ *n* a curving or bending; the continual bending, or the amount of bending, from a straight line; the reciprocal of the radius at any point. **curved** *adj.* **curve'some** *adj* curvaceous. **curvicau'date** *adj* having a crooked tail. **curvicos'tate** *adj* having curved ribs. **curvifō'liate** *adj* having curved leaves. **cur'viform** *adj.* **curvilin'eal** or **curvilin'ear** *adj* bounded by curved lines. **curvilin'eally** *adv.* **curvilinear'ity** *n.* **curv'iness** *n.* **cur'ving** *adj.* **curviros'tral** *adj* (of a bird) with the bill curved downward. **cur'vital** *adj* of or relating to curvature. **cur'vity** *n* the state of being curved. **curv'y** *adj* (**curv'ier**; **curv'iest**).

❑ **curve'ball** *n* a slower pitch with an arcing trajectory (*baseball*); something that is unexpected or contains a hidden trick (*fig*).

curvet /kûr'vet/ or /kər-vet'/ *n* a light leap of a horse in which the forelegs are raised together, followed by the hindlegs with a spring before the forelegs touch the ground (*dressage*); a leap, frolic. ◆ *vi* /kər-vet'/ or /kûr'vet/ (**curvett'ing** or **cur'veting**; **curvett'ed** or **cur'veted**) to leap in curvets; to frisk. [Ital *corvetta*, dimin of *corvo*, from L *curvus*]

curvicaudate, curvifoliate, curvilineal, etc see under **curve**.

cuscus¹ /kus'kus/ or /kŭs'kŭs/ *n* an arboreal phalanger of the Malay Archipelago, having thick fur, a long tail and large eyes. [Native name in the Moluccas]

cuscus² /kus'kus/ *n* the grain of the African millet (see also **couscous**).

cuscus³ /kus'kus/ *n* the fragrant fibrous root of an Indian grass (*Andropogon squarrosus*), used for making fans, etc. [Pers *khas khas*]

cusec /kū'sek/ (*engineering*) *n* short for *cubic feet per second*, a unit for measuring volumetric rate of flow.

cush see **cuisse** and **cushion**.

cushat /kush'ət/ (*Scot*) *n* the ringdove or wood pigeon. [OE *cūscute*, perh from its note, and *scēotan* to shoot]

cushaw /kə-shö'*, kush'ö/ see **cashaw**.

Cushing's syndrome /kŭsh'ingz sin'drōm/ *n* a condition characterized by obesity, raised blood pressure, metabolic disorders, osteoporosis, etc, caused by excess amounts of corticosteroid hormones in the body due to an adenoma of the pituitary gland (**Cushing's disease**), or a malignant tumour elsewhere. [Described by HW *Cushing* (1869–1939), American surgeon]

cushion /kush'ən/ *n* a case of material, plastic, etc filled with some soft, elastic stuff, eg feathers or foam rubber, for resting on; a pillow; a pad; an engraver's pad; the pillow used in making bone-lace; the cap of a pier (*archit*); the padded lining of the inner side of a snooker or billiard table (*inf* **cush**); a body of steam remaining in the cylinder of a steam-engine, acting as a buffer to the piston; any body of air or steam acting as a protection against shock; anything that serves to deaden a blow, act as a protection against harm, unpleasant effects, etc. ◆ *vt* to seat on, or provide with, a cushion or cushions; to serve as a cushion for or against; to suppress (complaints) by ignoring. [OFr *coissin*, from L *coxīnum*, *coxa* hip, or perh L *culcita* mattress, cushion]

■ **cush'ioned** *adj* furnished with a cushion, padded; protected, shielded from anything unpleasant; having cushion-tyres. **cush'ionet** *n* a little cushion. **cush'iony** *adj* like a cushion, soft.

❑ **cush'ion-plant** *n* a plant of cushion-like form reducing transpiration. **cushion star** *n* the starlet. **cush'ion-tyre** or (*N Am*) **-tire** *n* a cycle tyre of rubber tubing, with rubber stuffing.

Cushite or **Kushite** /kush'īt/, also **Cushitic** or **Kushitic** /kū-shit'ik/ *n* a group of languages of E Africa, eg Ethiopia, Somalia, Sudan; a (member of a) race speaking any of these languages. ◆ *adj* of or relating to the languages or the race. [*Cush*, an ancient kingdom in the Nile valley, and **-ite**]

cushty /kŭsh'tē/ (*sl*) *adj* highly satisfactory, excellent (also *interj*). [Perh related to **cushy**]

cushy /kush'i/ (*sl*) *adj* (**cush'ier; cush'iest**) easy and comfortable; not dangerous. [Perh Hindi *khush* pleasant, *khushī* happiness]

■ **cush'iness** *n.*

cusk /kusk/ (*N Am*) *n* the torsk.

cusp /kusp/ *n* a point; the point or horn of the moon, etc; a toothlike meeting of two branches of a curve, sudden change of direction; a toothlike ornament common in Gothic tracery (*archit*); a cone-shaped prominence on a tooth, *esp* a molar or premolar; one of the folds of membrane forming a valve in the heart or in a vein; a division between signs of the zodiac (*astrol*). [L *cuspis*, *-idis* a point]

■ **cus'pate** *adj.* **cusped** *adj.* **cus'pid** *n* a tooth with a single point, a canine tooth (also *adj*). **cus'pidal** *adj.* **cus'pidate** or **cus'pidated** *adj* (*biol*) having a rigid point or ending in a point.

Cusparia bark /kə-spar'i-ə bärk/ *n* Angostura (qv).

cuspidor or **cuspidore** /kus'pi-dör/ or /-dōr/ (*N Am*) *n* a spittoon. [Port, from L *conspuere* to spit upon]

cuspy /kus'pi/ (*comput sl*) *adj* (of a computer program) well-written and easy to use. [commonly *used system program*, and **-y¹**]

cuss /kus/ (*sl*) *n* a curse; a person or animal, *esp* if stubborn. ◆ *vt* and *vi* to curse. [**curse**; prob sometimes associated with **customer**]

■ **cussed** /kus'id/ *adj* cursed; obstinate. **cuss'edly** *adv.* **cuss'edness** *n* contrariness.

❑ **cuss'word** *n* (*esp N Am*) a swearword.

cusser, cuisser or **cooser** /kus'ər, koo'sər or küs'ər/ (*Scot*) *n* a stallion. [**courser**]

custard /kus'tərd/ *n* a baked mixture of milk, eggs, etc, sweetened or seasoned (now *usu* **egg custard**); a cooked mixture of similar appearance, thickened with cornflour. [Earlier *custade*, a corruption of *crustade* a pie with a crust; see **crust**]

❑ **custard apple** *n* the fruit of a West Indian tree (*Anona reticulata*) with edible pulp of the appearance and consistency of custard. **custard coffin** *n* (*Shakesp*) paste or crust covered with custard. **custard pie** *n* (*comedy*) slapstick, applied *esp* to early US films in which comedians threw **custard pies** (pies containing custard) at each other. **custard powder** *n* a flavoured preparation containing cornflour, etc for using with milk and sugar to make custard. **custard tart** *n* a pastry containing custard.

custock see **castock**.

custody /kus'tə-di/ *n* guardianship of a minor, awarded by a court of law; care; security; a watching or guarding; the condition of being held by the police. [L *custōdia* guard, from *custōs*, *-ōdis* a keeper]
■ **custo'dial** *adj*. **custō'dian, custō'dier** or **cus'tode** *n* a person who has care, *esp* of some public building. **custō'dianship** *n*.

custom /kus'təm/ *n* what one is accustomed to doing; usage; frequent repetition of the same act; regular trade or business; any of the distinctive practices and conventions of a people or locality; an unwritten law dating back to time immemorial; a tax on goods; (in *pl*) duties on imports and exports; (in *pl*) the collecting authorities; (in *pl*) the place at a port, airport, etc where baggage is inspected for taxable or illegal goods. ◆ *adj* (*esp N Am*) made to order or individual specification. [OFr *custume*, *costume*, from L *cōnsuētūdō*, *-inis*, from *cōnsuēscere* to accustom]
■ **cus'tomable** *adj* (*archaic*) customary; common; dutiable. **cus'tomarily** *adv*. **cus'tomariness** *n*. **cus'tomary** *adj* according to use and habit; usual; holding or held by custom; copyhold. ◆ *n* (also **customary** /kus'tūm-ər-i/) a body or book of the customs of a manor, etc or the ritual of a religious community. **cus'tomed** *adj* accustomed; usual. **cus'tomer** *n* a person who usually frequents a certain place of business; a buyer; a person, usually qualified in some way as in a *tricky customer* (*inf*). **cus'tomizable** or **-s-** *adj*. **customīzā'tion** or **-s-** *n*. **cus'tomize** or **-ise** *vt* to make in such a way as to suit specified individual requirements. **cus'tomized** or **-s-** *adj*.
❑ **cus'tom-built** or **cus'tom-made** *adj* built or made to a customer's order or specification. **customs house** or (*esp N Am*) **custom house** *n* the place, *esp* at a port, where customs or duties on exports and imports are collected. **cus'tom-shrunk** *adj* (*Shakesp*) having fewer customers than formerly. **customs union** *n* a group of states having free trade between themselves, and a common tariff policy toward non-member states.

custos /kus'tas/ *n* (*pl* **custō'des** /-dēz/) a guardian, custodian or keeper; a superior in the Franciscan order. [L]
❑ **custos rotulorum** /ro-tū-lō'rəm or kū'stōs ro-tū-lō'rŭm/ *n* (*L*) keeper of the rolls.

custrel /kus'trəl/ (*hist*) *n* an attendant on a knight; a knave. [OFr *coustillier*, from *coustille* dagger; cf **coistrel**]

custumary see **customary** under **custom**.

cusum /kū'sum/ *n* a statistical technique that attempts to identify individuals by their characteristic use of language. [Contraction of *cumulative sum* analysis]

cut /kut/ *vt* (**cutt'ing**; **cut**) to penetrate with a sharp edge, make an incision in; to cleave or pass through; to divide; to carve, hew, trim or make or fashion by cutting; to sever; to reap; to excise; to intersect, cross; to divide (a pack of cards) by lifting the upper portion at random; to expose (a card or suit) in this way; (in tennis, etc) to strike obliquely, imparting spin to; (in golf) to hit (the ball) in such a way that it intentionally moves from left to right in the air (for a right-handed player); to reduce, lessen or abridge; to wound, hurt or affect deeply; to shorten; to interrupt or break; to switch off (an engine, lights, etc); to break off acquaintance with; to pass intentionally without greeting; to renounce, give up; to stay away from; to castrate; to perform or execute (eg a caper); to make (a sound recording, eg a disc); to grow (teeth) through the gums (see also **cut one's teeth (on)** below); to mix another substance with (an illegal drug) to increase weight and volume (*sl*); to dilute or adulterate. ◆ *vi* to make an incision; to intersect; to strike obliquely; to be cut; to dash, go quickly; to run away, to be off (*sl*); (in film-making) to cease photographing; (of a film) to change rapidly to another scene. ◆ *n* a cleaving or dividing; an excavation for a road, railway, etc; a canal; a cross-passage; a stroke or blow; (in tennis, etc) a downward stroke, implying spin; (in golf) a shot in which the ball intentionally moves from left to right in the air (for a right-handed player); (in cricket) an attacking stroke to the offside played with a horizontal bat; the spin imparted to the ball; a reduction or diminution; a stoppage, as in *power cut*; an act of unkindness; the result of fashioning by cutting, carving, etc (eg clothes, hair, gemstones); the act, or outcome, of cutting a pack of cards; an incision or wound; an excision; a piece cut off; total quantity cut; a varying unit of length for cloth and yarn; an engraved block or the picture from it; manner of cutting, or fashion; the reduction of the field in a golf tournament after a set number of rounds, only those players with the better scores qualifying to play in the final round(s); an individual product obtained during the distillation of petroleum; a working horse (*archaic*); a rake-off or share (*sl*); a record, extract of a sound recording, etc (*sl*); (in films) the action of cutting or its result. ◆ *adj* (*sl*) (of a drug) adulterated or diluted. [Origin unknown]

■ **cutt'er** *n* a person or thing that cuts; a cut-throat (*obs*); a tailor who measures and cuts out the cloth; a small vessel with one mast, a mainsail, a forestay-sail, and a jib set to bowsprit-end; any sloop of narrow beam and deep draught; a powerful motor-launch (as used by coastguard and navy) which may be armed; (in quarrying) a joint parallel to the dip of the rocks; a small whisky bottle holding half a mutchkin, shaped for carrying in the hip pocket (*Scot*); a medium-sized pig carcase, from which joints and fillets are taken. **cutt'ing** *n* a dividing or lopping off; an incision; a piece cut from a newspaper; a piece of a plant cut off for propagation; an open excavation for a road, railway, etc; editing of a film or recording. ◆ *adj* (of a remark, etc) intended to be cruel or hurtful; (of wind) cold and penetrating. **cutt'ingly** *adv*.
❑ **cut-and-thrust** see **cut and thrust** below. **cut'away** *n* a coat with the skirt cut away in a curve in front; an angled edge on a door; a model or picture showing the interior workings of something, with the overlying parts removed; (in films or television) a shot of action that is related to, or happening simultaneously to, the central events. ◆ *adj* having parts cut away. **cut'back** *n* a going back in a plot to earlier happenings; a reduction or decrease, *esp* in expenditure, workforce, production, etc. **cut'-down** *adj* (*used attrib*) reduced. **cut flowers** *n pl* flowers cut from their plants for display in vases, etc. **cut glass** *n* flint glass shaped by cutting or grinding. **cut'glass** *adj* made of cut glass; (of an accent) upper-class, refined. **cut'-in** *n* the act of cutting in; (in films) a shot edited into another shot. **cut'-leaved** *adj* (*bot*) having leaves deeply cut. **cut'line** *n* (*US*) a caption. **cut'-off** *n* that which cuts off or shortens, eg a straighter road, a shorter channel cut across a bend of a river; a bend thus cut off; a device for shutting off steam, water, light, electricity, supply of cartridges in a magazine rifle, etc; the point at which something ceases to operate or apply (also *adj*); (in *pl*) shorts made by cutting off the legs of jeans just above the knee (*inf*). **cut'-out** *n* the act of cutting out; something which has been cut out; a safety device, eg for breaking an electric circuit. **cut-over** *adj* (*US*) (of land) having had its timber removed. **cut-price** *adj* at a reduced rate. **cut'purse** *n* (*hist*) a person who stole by slitting purses worn at the belt; a pickpocket. **cut-rate** *adj* (*esp N Am*) cut-price. **cut'-throat** *n* an assassin; a ruffian; a modification of bridge, etc for three players, each playing alone; an open razor. ◆ *adj* murderous; (of competition) extremely tough, relentless; (of card games) for three players. **cutting edge** *n* a part or area (of an organization, branch of study, etc) that breaks new ground, effects change and development, etc (**cutting-edge'** *adj*). **cutting grass** *n* a cane rat. **cutting list** *n* (*building*) a list giving dimensions of timber required for any given work. **cutting room** *n* (*cinematog*) a place where film is cut and edited. **cut'-up** *n* (*orig US*) a person who makes jokes or plays tricks; a literary collage, composed of cut-up and rearranged passages of prose or verse (also *adj*). **cut'water** *n* the forepart of a ship's prow; the angular edge of a bridge pier. **cut'work** *n* openwork embroidery or appliqué (also *adj*). **cut'worm** *n* a caterpillar, *esp* of the moth genus *Agrotis*, that feeds on the stems of young plants near ground level.
■ **a cut above** something distinctly better (than). **cut across** to go or extend beyond the limits of; to take a shorter route across. **cut a dash** or **figure** to have a striking appearance. **cut a deal** (*chiefly N Am*) to make a deal. **cut along** (*inf*) to leave, go away quickly. **cut and come again** abundant supply, from the notion of cutting a slice, and returning at will for another. **cut and cover** a method of constructing a tunnel by making an open cutting, arching it over, and covering in. **cut and dry** or **cut and dried** ready made; fixed beforehand, decided in advance. **cut and paste** (in the design of page layouts for newspapers, magazines, etc) a method of arranging areas of text, illustrations, etc by cutting and sticking down with paste; (in word processing, DTP, etc) a technique for moving blocks of text, etc. **cut and run** to be off or escape quickly. **cut and thrust** (in fencing) the use of the edges and the point of the weapon; swift, shrewd and cleverly-calculated action or reaction, argument, etc (**cut-and-thrust'** *adj*). **cut back** to prune close to the stem; to revert to a previous scene; to reduce (expenditure, etc). **cut both ways** (of a decision, action, situation, etc) to have or result in both advantages and disadvantages. **cut corners** to turn corners by the quickest way, not keeping close to the edge of the road; to do something (eg a piece of work) with the minimum of effort and expenditure and therefore often imperfectly. **cut dead** to refuse to recognize or acknowledge (another person). **cut down** to bring down by cutting; to reduce, curtail; to maim or kill. **cut down to size** to cause (a person) to feel less important or to be less conceited. **cut from the same cloth** very similar in nature. **cut in** to interpose; (of an electrical device) to begin working automatically; to deprive someone of a dancing partner; to intercept on the telephone; to manoeuvre into a line of traffic in front of an overtaken vehicle, etc, *esp* without adequate warning or indication; to come into a game by cutting a card; to give a share. **cut it** (*sl*) to succeed or manage. **cut it fine** to take risks by leaving insufficient margin for error. **cut it out** (*inf*) to make an end of it, leave off. **cut it too fat** to overdo a thing. **cut loose** to break free from constraints. **cut no ice** see under **ice**. **cut off** to sever; to isolate; to put to an end prematurely; to intercept; to stop;

(of an electrical device) to stop working, *usu* automatically, *esp* as a safety measure; to disinherit. **cut off with a shilling** to bequeath only a shilling; to disinherit. **cut one's coat according to one's cloth** to adapt oneself to (*esp* financial) circumstances. **cut one's losses** to have done with an unprofitable venture. **cut one's stick** to take one's departure. **cut one's teeth (on)** (*inf*) to gain experience (by means of); to practise (on). **cut out** to shape; to contrive; to debar; to block (light, etc); to supplant; to separate from a herd; to pass out of a game on cutting a card; to pass out of a line of traffic in order to overtake; to capture and carry off (a ship) as from a harbour, etc, by getting between her and the shore; (of an engine) suddenly to stop functioning. **cut out for** naturally fitted for. **cut short** to abridge; to make short by cutting; to silence by interruption. **cut teeth** to have teeth grow through the gums, as an infant. **cut to the chase** to get to the point. **cut up** to cut into pieces; to criticize severely; to turn out (well or ill) when divided into parts; (in *passive*) to be deeply distressed; to make jokes, play tricks or behave in a boisterous manner (*N Am*); to drive recklessly in front of (another vehicle) causing danger to it (*sl*). **cut up rough** to take something amiss, become difficult or angry. **draw cuts** (*archaic*) to cast lots. **make the cut** (*golf*) to qualify for the final round(s) of a tournament. **miss the cut** (*golf*) to fail to qualify for the final round(s) of a tournament. **short cut** see under **short**.

cutaneous see under **cutis**.

cutch[1] /kuch/ *n* catechu. [Malay *kachu*]

cutch[2] or **kutch** /kuch/ *n* a set of tough paper or vellum sheets used by gold-beaters. [Appar from Fr *çaucher*, from L *calcāre* to tread]

cutcha /kuchʹə/ *adj* of dried mud; makeshift. [Hindi *kaccā* raw]

cutcherry, **cutchery** same as **kachahri**.

cute[1] /kūt/ *adj* daintily or quaintly pleasing; clever, astute; sexually attractive (chiefly *N Am*). [**acute**]
■ **cuteʹly** *adv*. **cuteʹness** *n*. **cuteʹsy** *adj* (*esp US*) sentimentally or affectedly cute, twee. **cūʹtie** or **cūʹtey** *n* a smart girl; something cute. □ **cūʹtie-pie** *n* (*sl*) someone cute or sweet, a poppet.

cute[2] see **cuit**.

Cuthbert /kuthʹbərt/ *n* the apostle of Northumbria (c.635–687); a derisive name given to someone suspected of evading military service, and hence to any shirker.
■ **(St) Cuthbert's beads** perforated joints of encrinites found on Holy Island. **(St) Cuthbert's duck** the eider duck.

cuticle /kūʹti-kl/ *n* the outermost or thin skin; the dead skin at the edge of finger- and toenails; the waxy or corky layer on the epidermis of plants (*bot*); the protective outer layer of many invertebrates, eg insects (*zool*). [L *cutīcula*, dimin of *cutis* skin]
■ **cūtic'ular** *adj*.

cutikin same as **cuitikin** (see under **cuit**).

cutis /kūʹtis/ *n* the dermis; the true skin, as distinguished from the cuticle (*anat* and *zool*). [L]
■ **cūtān'eous** *adj* belonging to or relating to the skin. **cūʹtin** *n* (*bot*) a waxy material forming plant cuticle. **cūtinizāʹtion** or **-s-** *n*. **cūʹtinize** or **-ise** *vt* and *vi*.

cutlass /kutʹləs/ *n* a short, broad sword, with one cutting edge, formerly used in the navy. [Fr *coutelas*, augmentative from L *cultellus*, dimin of *culter* a ploughshare, a knife]
□ **cutlass fish** *n* the hair-tail.

cutler /kutʹlər/ *n* a person who makes or sells cutlery. [Fr *coutelier*, from OFr *coutel*, from L *culter* knife]
■ **cutʹlery** *n* implements for eating food; edged or cutting instruments in general; the business of a cutler.

cutlet /kutʹlit/ *n* a piece of rib and the meat belonging to it, *esp* of mutton, veal, etc; other food made up in the shape of a cutlet. [Fr *côtelette*, dimin of *côte*, from L *costa* a rib]

cuttle[1] /kutʹl/ *n* a cephalopod mollusc (genus *Sepia*), able to eject a black, inky liquid (also **cuttʹlefish**); extended to other cephalopods. [OE *cudele*]
□ **cuttʹle-bone** or **cuttlefish bone** *n* the internal shell of the cuttlefish, used for making tooth-powder, for polishing the softer metals and for cage-birds to sharpen their beaks on.

cuttle[2] /kutʹl/ *n* a knife (*obs*); a bully (*archaic*). [Perh L *cultellum* knife; perh also for **cut-throat**, **cutpurse** or **cuttlefish**]

cutto or **cuttoe** /kutʹō/ *n* (*pl* **cuttʹoes**) a large knife. [Fr *couteau*]

cutty /kutʹi/ (*Scot*) *adj* short, curtailed. ◆ *n* a short clay pipe; a short, dumpy girl; applied to a woman, a term of reprobation, serious or playful; a mischievous or teasing girl or woman. [**cut**]
□ **cuttʹy-sark** *n* a short shift, or its wearer. **cuttʹy-stool** *n* the stool of repentance in old Scottish church discipline.

CUV *abbrev* : crossover utility vehicle.

cuvée /kü-vāʹ or koo-vāʹ/ *n* (the contents of) a vat of blended wine of uniform quality. [Fr]

cuvette /koo- or kü-vetʹ/ *n* a shallow vessel or dish for holding liquids, eg in a laboratory; a cunette (*fortif*). [Fr, dimin of OFr *cuve* a cask, vat, from L *cupa*]

cuz /kuz/ an obsolete spelling of **coz**.

CV *abbrev* : *chevaux* (Fr), as in **2CV** *deux chevaux* two horsepower (car); Cross of Valour (*Aust* and *Can*); curriculum vitae.

cv *abbrev* : cultivar; curriculum vitae; *cursus vitae* (L), course or progress of life.

cva *abbrev* : cerebrovascular accident.

CVCP *abbrev* : Committee of Vice-Chancellors and Principals of Universities of the United Kingdom (now known as Universities UK).

CVD *abbrev* : compact video disc.

CVO *abbrev* : Commander of the (Royal) Victorian Order.

CVS *abbrev* : chorionic villus sampling.

CVT *abbrev* : continuously variable transmission.

CW *abbrev* : chemical warfare.

CWC *abbrev* : Chemical Weapons Convention.

CWD *abbrev* : chronic wasting disease, a progressive and fatal prion disease, similar to BSE, affecting deer and elk.

cwm /koom/ *n* the Welsh name for a valley or glen; a cirque or corrie (*geol*). [Welsh (cf **coomb**[1]), and Fr *combe*]

CWO or **cwo** *abbrev* : cash with order.

cwt *abbrev* : hundredweight(s). [c for L *centum* a hundred, and *wt* for *weight*]

CWU *abbrev* : Communication Workers Union.

CY *abbrev* : Cyprus (IVR).

cyan /sīʹan/ *n* a greenish blue; blue ink used as a primary colour in printing. ◆ *adj* of a greenish blue colour. [Gr *kyanos* blue]

cyan- or **cyano-** /sīʹan- or sīʹa-nō-/ *combining form* denoting blue or dark blue; indicating cyanide or cyanogen. [Gr *kyanos* blue]
■ **cyan'amide** *n* the amide of cyanogen, a white crystalline substance ($NCNH_2$); loosely, applied to **calcium cyanamide** (NCNCa), a fertilizer. **cyanate** /sīʹan-āt/ *n* a salt of cyanic acid. **cyan'ic** *adj* of or belonging to cyanogen (**cyanic acid** an acid composed of cyanogen, oxygen and hydrogen (HCNO)). **cy'anide** *n* a direct compound of cyanogen with a metal; a poisonous salt of hydrocyanic acid, *esp* potassium cyanide or sodium cyanide. ◆ *vt* to treat with a cyanide. **cy'aniding** *n* extraction of gold or silver from ore by means of potassium cyanide. **cy'anin** *n* a plant pigment, blue in cornflower, but red in the rose because of its reaction with acids. **cy'anine** *n* any of a group of dyes used as sensitizers in photography. **cyanite** *n* see **kyanite**. **cy'anize** or **-ise** *vt* to turn into cyanide. **cyanoacet'ylene** *n* (*chem*) a large and complex organic molecule found in space. **cyanoac'rylate** *n* any of several strong, fast-setting adhesives derived from acrylic acid. **cyanobacté'rium** *n* a blue-green alga. **cyanocobal'amin** *n* (*cobalt* and vit*amin*) vitamin B_{12}, which has a large and complicated molecule, in one form including a cyanide group, in all forms including a cobalt atom. **cyan'ogen** /-jen/ *n* a compound of carbon and nitrogen $(CN)_2$ forming a colourless poisonous gas with an almond-like odour, an essential ingredient of Prussian blue. **cyanogen'esis** *n* (*bot*) the production of hydrogen cyanide by certain plants as a reaction to cell damage or invasion by disease. **cyanogen'ic** *adj*. **cyanohydrin** /-hīʹdrin/ *n* an organic compound containing a cyanide group and a hydroxyl group bound to the same carbon atom. **cyanom'eter** *n* an instrument for measuring the blueness of the sky or ocean. **cyan'ophyte** *n* a blue-green alga. **cy'anosed** *adj* (*inf*). **cyanō'sis** *n* bluish discoloration of the skin resulting from lack of oxygen in the blood. **cyanot'ic** *adj*. **cyan'otype** *n* blueprint. **cyan'ūret** *n* (*obs*) a cyanide.

Cyanophyta /sī-ən-ō-fīʹta/ *n pl* the blue-green algae, a division of bacteria, growing in water and on damp earth, rocks or bark. [See **cyan**]

cyathus /sīʹa-thəs/ *n* the ancient Greek or Roman filling or measuring cup; a measure equal to about $\frac{1}{2}$ pint. [L, from Gr *kyathos* a wine cup, a measure]
■ **Cyath'ea** *n* a genus of tree-ferns, often with cup-shaped indusium, giving name to the family **Cyatheá'ceae**. **cy'athiform** *adj* cup-shaped. **cyath'ium** *n* (*pl* **cyath'ia**) the characteristic inflorescence of the spurges. **Cyathophyll'um** *n*.

Cybele /sibʹi-lē/ *n* a flora, treatise on the plants of a region. [L *Cybelē*, from Gr *Kybelē* the mother goddess]

cyber- /sīʹbər-/ *combining form* denoting computers or computer networks, *esp* the Internet. [From **cybernetics**]

cyberbully /sī'bər-bŭl-i/ n a person who uses online communication to distress or persecute others. [**cyber-** and **bully¹**]

cybercafé /sī'bər-kaf-ā or -ka-fi/ n a place where the public can obtain access to computer networks, esp the Internet, for a charge. [**cyber-** and **café**]

cybercrime /sī'bər-krīm/ n the use of computers to perpetrate criminal acts. [**cyber-** and **crime**]

■ **cy'berbullying** n.

Cyber Monday /sī'bər mun'dā/ (chiefly US) n the Monday after Thanksgiving, considered as a peak day for online shopping. [**cyber-**]

cybernate /sī'bər-nāt/ vt to control (a manufacturing process, etc) by means of a computer. [**cyber-** and -ate, suffix forming a verb]
■ **cy'bernated** adj. **cyberna'tion** n.

cybernaut /sī'bər-nöt/ (inf) n a person who uses the Internet. [**cyber-** and Gr nautēs a sailor]

cybernetics /sī-bər-net'iks/ n sing the comparative study of communication processes and automatic control systems in mechanical or electronic systems (such as in computers) and biological systems (such as the nervous system). [Gr kybernētēs a steersman]
■ **cybernet'ic** adj. **cybernet'icist** /-sist/ n.

cyberpet /sī'bər-pet/ n an electronic device that simulates the behaviour and requirements of a pet (also **virtual pet**). [**cyber-** and **pet¹**]

cyberphobia /sī-bər-fō'bi-ə/ n an intense or irrational fear of computers. [**cyber-** and **phobia**]
■ **cy'berphobe** n. **cyberphō'bic** adj.

cyberpunk /sī'bər-pungk/ n a genre of science fiction featuring a bleak and wretched society controlled by computer networks in which the hero is usu a gifted young computer hacker who uses his or her skills to rebel against the system; a writer or devotee of this genre. [**cyber-** and **punk¹**]

cybersecurity /sī-bər-si-kūr'i-ti/ n the protection of computers and networks against unauthorized access and sabotage. [**cyber-** and **security**]

cybersex /sī'bər-seks/ n sexual activity or information available through computer networks. [**cyber-** and **sex**]

cyberslacking /sī'bər-slak-ing/ (inf) n the use of computers for recreational purposes when one is supposed to be working. [**cyber-** and **slack¹**]

cyberspace /sī'bər-spās/ n the three-dimensional environment, or space, of virtual reality, generated by computer; the notional space in which electronic communication takes place over computer networks. [**cyber-** and **space¹**]

cyberspeak /sī'bər-spēk/ (inf) n the jargon of Internet users. [**cyber-** and **speak** (combining form)]

cybersquatting /sī'bər-skwot-ing/ (inf) n the registering of an Internet domain name, usu one of a company or a famous person, with the intention of selling it on at a profit. [**cyber-** and **squatting**]
■ **cy'bersquatter** n.

cyberstalking /sī'bər-stö-king/ n the use of the Internet, email, etc to harass or abuse another person. [**cyber-** and **stalking** (under **stalk²**)]

cyberterrorist /sī'bər-ter-ə-rist/ n a person who attempts to cause disruption through the use of computers, eg by spreading a computer virus. [**cyber-** and **terrorist**]
■ **cyberterr'orism** n.

cyborg /sī'börg/ n a robot made of biological and machine components. [**cyber-** and organism]

cybrid /sī'brid/ (biol) n a cell, plant, etc possessing the nuclear genome of one plant with at least some part of the chloroplastal or mitochondrial genome of the other, as opposed to a hybrid in which some parts of both parental nuclear genomes are present. [cell and hybrid]

cycad /sī'kad/ n any member of an order of primitive gymnospermous plants, related to conifers but superficially resembling ferns and palms. [Formed from supposed Gr kykas, a misreading of koīkas, accusative pl of koīx doum-palm]
■ **cycadā'ceous** adj.

cycl- see **cyclo-**.

cyclamate /sik'lə-māt or sī'klə-/ n any of a number of very sweet substances derived from petrochemicals, formerly used as sweetening agents in food, soft drinks, etc.

cyclamen /sik'lə-mən/ n a plant of the S European Cyclamen genus, related to the primulas, with nodding flowers and bent-back outer petals; a strong bright pink colour, characteristic of this plant (also adj). [Gr kyklamīnos]

cyclandelate /sī-klan'də-lāt/ n a drug whose effect is to dilate the veins, etc, formerly used to improve circulation.

Cyclanthaceae /sī-klan-thā'si-ē/ n pl a tropical S American family of plants related to the screw-pines, with a spadix sometimes resembling a pile of discs. [Gr kyklos wheel, and anthos flower]
■ **cyclanthā'ceous** adj.

cycle /sī'kl/ n a period of time in which events happen in a certain order, and which constantly repeats itself; a recurring series of changes; an age; an imaginary circle or orbit in the heavens; a series of poems, romances, etc centring in a figure or event (also **cy'clus**); a group of songs with related subjects; a bicycle or tricycle; a cycle ride; a complete series of changes in a periodically varying quantity, eg an alternating current, during one period; a sequence of computer operations which continues until a criterion for stoppage is reached, or the time of this. ◆ vt to cause to pass through a cycle of operations or events; to transport or accompany on a cycle. ◆ vi to move in cycles; to ride on a cycle. [Gr kyklos circle]
■ **cy'cler** n (N Am) a cyclist. **cy'clic** or **cy'clical** adj relating to or containing a cycle; recurring in cycles; arranged in a ring or rings. **cyclical'ity** n. **cy'clically** adv. **cy'clicism** n. **cyclic'ity** n. **cy'cling** n. **cy'clist** n a person who rides on a cycle. **cy'cloid** n a figure like a circle; a curve traced by a point on the circumference of a circle which rolls along a straight line; a person of cyclothymic temperament, or one suffering from a cyclic type of manic-depressive psychosis (psychol). ◆ adj nearly circular; (of fish) having scales with evenly curved border; cyclothymic; characterized by mood swings (psychol). **cycloid'al** adj. **cycloid'ian** n a fish with cycloid scales. **cyclō'sis** n (pl **cyclō'ses** /-sēz/) circulation.
❑ **cycle lane** n a section of road marked off for the use of cyclists only. **cy'clepath** or **cy'cleway** n a track or path, often running alongside a road, constructed and reserved for cyclists. **cyclic AMP** (in full **cyclic adenosine monophosphate**) n (biol) a compound which regulates processes within cells by its effects on enzymes. **cyclic compound** n a closed-chain or ring compound in which the ring consists of carbon atoms only (carbocyclic compound) or of carbon atoms linked with one or more other atoms (heterocyclic compound). **cyclic group** n (maths) a group on which every element can be expressed as a power of a single element. **cy'cling shorts** n pl close-fitting shorts designed for cyclists, made of lightweight synthetic material.
■ **cycle per second** see under **hertz**.

cyclin /sī'klin/ n any of a class of proteins that help to control progression in the cell cycle. [**cycle** and -**in** (1)]

cyclizine /sī'klə-zēn/ n an antihistamine drug used to relieve travel and postoperative sickness, etc.

cyclo /sī'klō/ (inf) n (pl **cy'clos**) a trishaw. [**cycle**]

cyclo- or **cycl-** /sī-kl(ō)-/ combining form denoting: cycle; ring; circle; cyclic compound; the ciliary body (anat). [Gr kyklos circle]
■ **cy'clo-cross** n a pedal-cycle race over rough country in which bicycles have to be carried over natural obstacles.

cycloalkane /sī-klō-al'kān/ n a saturated hydrocarbon containing a ring of carbon atoms joined by single bonds. [**cyclo-**]

cyclobarbitone /sī-klō-bär'bi-tōn/ n a barbiturate drug formerly prescribed as a hypnotic and sedative. [**cyclo-**]

cyclodextrin /sī-klō-dek'strin/ n any of several water-soluble carbohydrates with hydrophobic interiors, used to provide capsules for drugs. [**cyclo-** and **dextrin**]

cyclodialysis /sī-klō-dī-al'i-sis/ (surg) n an operation to reduce pressure in the eye in glaucoma patients, in which part of the ciliary body is separated from the sclera. [**cyclo-**]

cyclograph /sī'klō-gräf or sī'klə-/ n an instrument for describing arcs of circles without compasses, an arcograph; a camera that can reproduce the whole surface of a cylindrical object as a single photograph. [**cyclo-**]
■ **cyclograph'ic** adj.

cyclohexane /sī-klə-hek'sān/ n a highly flammable ring chemical, C_6H_{12}, with a pungent odour, used in making synthetic fibres, as a paint solvent, etc. [**cyclo-**]

cycloid see under **cycle**.

cyclolith /sī'klō-lith/ n a peristalith or stone circle. [**cyclo-** and Gr lithos a stone]

cyclometer /sī-klom'i-tər/ n a device for recording the revolutions of a wheel. [**cyclo-**]

cyclone /sī'klōn/ n a system of winds blowing spirally inwards towards a centre of low barometric pressure; loosely a windstorm; a separating apparatus, a kind of centrifuge. [Gr kyklōn, contracted prp of kykloein to whirl round]
■ **cyclon'ic** adj. **cyclon'ically** adv.

■ words derived from main entry word; ❑ compound words; ■ idioms and phrasal verbs

cyclonite see **RDX**.

cycloparaffin /sī-klō-par'ə-fin/ n cycloalkane.

cyclopean, cyclopian, etc see under **Cyclops**.

cyclopedia or **cyclopaedia** /sī-klə-pē'di-ə/ n a short form of **encyclopedia**.
■ **cyclope'dic** or **cyclopae'dic** adj.

cyclopentolate /sī-klə-pen'tə-lāt/ n a drug used in eye drops to dilate the pupil and also to treat inflammatory disorders of the eye.

cyclophosphamide /sī-klō-fos'fə-mīd/ n a potent alkylating drug which interferes with DNA synthesis and is used in the treatment of leukaemia and lymphoma, and for immunosuppression. [**cyclo-**, phosphorus and **amide**]

cycloplegia /sī-klə-plē'j(i-)ə/ (pathol) n paralysis of the ciliary muscle in the eye, which impedes the adjustment of the lens. [**cyclo-**]

cyclopropane /sī-klə-prō'pān/ n a three membered ring hydrocarbon, C_3H_6, a general anaesthetic. [**cyclo-**]

Cyclops /sī'klops/ n one of a fabled race of giants who lived chiefly in Sicily, with one eye in the middle of the forehead (pl **Cy'clops, Cyclō'pes,** or **Cy'clopses**); (without cap) a one-eyed monster (pl **cyclō'pes**); a genus of minute freshwater copepods with an eye in front; (without cap) a member of the genus (pl **cy'clops**). [Gr kyklōps, pl kyklōpes, from kyklos a circle, and ōps an eye]
■ **cyclopē'an, cyclō'pian** or **cyclop'ic** adj relating to or like the Cyclopes; giant-like; vast; relating to a prehistoric Greek style of masonry with immense stones of irregular form.

cyclorama /sī-klə-rä'mə/ n a circular panorama; a curved background in stage and cinematograph sets, used to give impression of sky distance, and for lighting effects. [**cyclo-** and Gr horāma view]
■ **cycloram'ic** adj.

cycloserine /sī-klō-sēr'in/ n an antibiotic used against tuberculosis and other infections. [**cyclo-** and serine an amino acid]

cyclospermous /sī-klō-spûr'məs/ (bot) adj with the embryo bent round the endosperm. [**cyclo-** and Gr sperma seed]

cyclosporin A /sī-klō-spör'in ā/ n an immunosuppressant drug used following transplant surgery to reduce the risk of tissue rejection. [**cyclo-** and Gr spora seed]

cyclostome /sī'klə-stōm/ n a member of the **Cyclostomata** /-stō'mə-tə/, a class of animals with fixed open mouth, including the lampreys. [**cyclo-** and Gr stoma mouth]
■ **cyclostomous** /-klos'to-məs/ adj.

cyclostyle /sī'klō-stīl/ n a device for creating multiple copies of a written document by use of a pen with a small puncturing wheel (also vt). [**cyclo-**]

cyclothymia /sī-klə-thī'mi-ə/ n a temperament inclined to marked alternation of mood, from elation to misery, usu indicative of a personality disorder. [**cyclo-** and Gr thymos spirit]
■ **cy'clothyme** n a person with such a temperament. **cyclothy'mic** adj.

cyclotron /sī'klə-tron/ n a type of particle accelerator (see **accelerator** under **accelerate**) for accelerating the heavier atomic particles (such as protons), used in the treatment of cancer. [**cyclo-** and **-tron** (3)]

cyder same as **cider**.

cyesis /sī-ē'sis/ n (pl **cyē'ses** /-sēz/) pregnancy. [Gr kyēsis]

cygnet /sig'nit/ n a young swan. [Dimin from L cygnus, directly or through Fr cygne, which seems to be a reshaping of cisne, from LL cicinus, L cycnus, from Gr kyknos a swan]

Cygnus /sig'nəs/ (astron) n a large northern constellation, the Swan, lying between Pegasus and Draco. [L cygnus swan]

cylinder /sil'in-dər/ n a solid figure of uniform cross-section generated by a straight line remaining parallel to a fixed axis and moving round a closed curve, ordinarily in a circle perpendicular to the axis (giving a right circular cylinder); a roller-shaped object; a cylindrical part, solid or hollow, such as a rotating part of a printing press, the tubular chamber in which a piston works (mech); all the tracks on the same radius on a disk (comput). [Gr kylindros roller, from kylindein to roll]
■ **cylindrā'ceous** adj somewhat cylindrical. **cylin'dric** or **cylin'drical** adj. **cylin'drically** adv. **cylindricity** /-dris'i-ti/ n. **cylin'driform** adj in the form of a cylinder. **cylin'drite** n a mineral of cylindrical habit, compound of tin, lead, antimony and sulphur. **cyl'indroid** n a body like a cylinder (also adj).
❑ **cylinder block** n a casing in which the cylinders of an internal-combustion engine are contained. **cylinder head** n the closed end of the cylinder of an internal-combustion engine. **cylinder lock** n a type of lock comprising a movable cylinder which can be rotated inside a fixed cylinder only when the correct key is inserted. **cylinder seal** n a stone engraved in intaglio, used in the ancient East for rolling an impression on clay tablets. **cylindrical grinding** n (engineering) the operation of accurately finishing cylindrical work by a high-speed abrasive wheel.
■ **firing** (or **working**, etc) **on all cylinders** working at full strength or perfectly; in good working order.

cylix /sil'iks or sī'liks/ (ancient Greece) n (pl **cyl'ices** /-sēz/) a shallow two-handled stemmed drinking cup (also **kyl'ix**). [Gr kylix, -ikos]

Cym. abbrev : Cymric.

cyma /sī'mə/ (archit) n (pl **cy'mas** or **cy'mae** /-mē/) an ogee moulding of the cornice (**cyma recta** concave above, convex below; **cyma reversa** convex above, concave below). [Gr kyma a billow]
■ **cymat'ics** n sing the therapeutic use of high frequency sound waves. **cymā'tium** n a cyma. **cy'mograph** n (non-standard **cy'magraph**) an instrument for tracing the outline of mouldings (see also **kymograph**).

cymar or **cimar** /si-mär'/ n a loose coat of various styles, formerly worn by women; an undergarment, a shift; a chimer. [Fr simarre, of comparable meanings, from Sp zamarra sheepskin; cf **chimer**]

cymbal /sim'bəl/ n a hollow brass plate-like musical instrument, beaten with a stick, etc or against another of a pair. [L cymbalum, from Gr kymbalon, from kymbē flat-bottomed boat]
■ **cym'balist** n a cymbal-player. **cym'balo** n (pl **cym'baloes** or **cym'balos**) the dulcimer.

cymbidium /sim-bid'i-əm/ n (pl **cymbid'iums** or **cymbid'ia**) any orchid of the genus Cymbidium, with large, colourful, long-lasting flowers. [New L Cymbidium, from L cymba a boat]

cymbiform /sim'bi-förm/ adj boat-shaped. [Gr kymbe flat-bottomed boat, and **-form**]

cyme /sīm/ (bot) n a young shoot; any sympodial inflorescence, the main shoot ending in a flower, the subsequent flowers growing on successive lateral branches. [L cyma, cīma, from Gr kȳma a sprout]
■ **cym'oid** adj. **cym'ose** adj. **cym'ous** adj.

cymograph see under **cyma**.

cymoid see under **cyme**.

cymophane /sī'mō-fān/ (mineralogy) n cat's-eye, a variety of chrysoberyl with wavy opalescence. [Gr kȳma wave, and phainein to show]
■ **cymophanous** /-mof'ə-nəs/ adj opalescent.

cymose, cymous see under **cyme**.

cymotrichous /sī-mot'ri-kəs/ (anthrop) adj wavy-haired. [Gr kȳma wave, and thrix (genitive trichos) hair]
■ **cymot'richy** n.

Cymric /kim'rik, kum' or sim'/ adj Welsh. ✦ n the Welsh language. [Welsh Cymru Wales]
■ **Cym'ry** n the Welsh nation.

cyn- see **cyno-**.

cynanche /si-nang'kē/ n disease of the throat, esp quinsy. [Gr kyōn, kynos a dog, and anchein to throttle]

cynegetic /si-nē-jet'ik/ adj relating to hunting. [Gr kynēgetēs huntsman, from kyōn, kynos dog, and hēgetēs leader]

cynghanedd /kəng-han'edh/ n a system of sound correspondences used in Welsh verse, esp alliteration and rhyme within a line. [Welsh, from cym with, and canu to sing]

cynic /sin'ik/ n someone who takes a pessimistic view of human motives and actions; (with cap) one of a sect of philosophers founded by Antisthenes of Athens (born c.444BC), characterized by an ostentatious contempt for riches, arts, science and amusements (so called from their morose manners). ✦ adj cynical; disinclined to recognize or believe in goodness or selflessness; literally dog-like; surly, snarling. [Gr kynikos dog-like, from kyōn, kynos dog, or perh from Kynosarges, the gymnasium where Antisthenes taught]
■ **cyn'ical** adj cynic; expressing or showing self-serving disregard for accepted morality or conventions. **cyn'ically** adv. **cyn'icalness** n. **cyn'icism** /-i-sizm/ n surliness; contempt for and suspicion of human nature; heartlessness, misanthropy; a cynical remark.

Cynips /sin'ips or sī'nips/ n a genus of gall-wasps, giving name to the family **Cynip'idae**. [Origin doubtful]

cyno- or **cyn-** /sī-nō- or si-nō- or sīn- or sin-/ combining form denoting dog or dogs. [Gr kyon, kynos dog]

Cynocephalus /sin-ō- or sī-nō-sef'ə-ləs/ n the flying lemur (qv); the dog-faced baboon; a dog-headed man. [Gr *kyon, kynos* dog, and *kephale* head]

cynomolgus /si-nə-mol'gəs/ n (pl **cynomol'gī**) a type of macaque. [Gr *Kynamolgoi* a Libyan tribe, lit. 'dog-milkers']

cynophilia, cynophilist, cynophobia see **canophilist** and **canophobia**.

cynosure /sin'o- or sī'nō-shoor or -zhoor/ n the dog's tail, or Lesser Bear (*Ursa Minor*), the constellation containing the North Star; the North Star itself; hence, anything that strongly attracts attention or admiration; something that acts as a guide. [Gr *kyōn, kynos* a dog, and *ourā* a tail]

cyperaceous /si- or sī-pə-rā'shəs/ adj of, belonging to, or resembling the **Cyperā'ceae**, a family of grasslike plants including the sedges, certain rushes and papyrus. [From Gr *kypeiros* sedge]

cypermethrin /sī-pər-meth'rin/ n a pyrethroid used as a pesticide.

cypher see **cipher**.

cy pres /sē prā/ (*law*) n the principle of applying the money donated to a charity, etc to some object as near as possible to the one specified by the donor or testator, when that itself is impracticable (also *adv* and *adj*). [OFr, so near]

cypress[1] /sī'prəs or -pris/ n a coniferous tree (genus *Cupressus*), whose branches used to be carried at funerals; hence, a symbol of death; extended to various other trees, *esp* in America to the swamp-growing deciduous conifer *Taxodium distichum*. [OFr *ciprès* (Fr *cyprès*), from L *cupressus* from Gr *kyparissos*]
□ **cypress knee** n a hollow upgrowth from the root of the swamp-cypress, an organ of respiration. **cypress swamp** n. **cypress vine** n a tropical American climbing plant (*Quamoclit pennata*), frequently cultivated for its scarlet or orange tubular flowers.

cypress[2], also **cyprus** /sī'prəs or -pris/ (*obs*) n a thin transparent black fabric like crape. ♦ adj made of cypress. [Prob from the island of *Cyprus*]

Cyprian /sip'ri-ən/ adj of the island of *Cyprus* in the NE Mediterranean; lewd, licentious (Cyprus being the place where Aphrodite was worshipped). ♦ n a Cypriot; (also without *cap*) a lewd woman.
■ **Cyp'riot** or **Cyp'riote** n a native of Cyprus; the Greek dialect spoken in Cyprus. ♦ adj of Cyprus, its people or their dialect of Greek.
□ **Cypro-Mino'an** n an undeciphered Bronze Age script of Cyprus (also adj).

cyprid see under **cypris**.

cyprinid /si-prī'nid or sip'ri-nid/ n a member of the carp family (**Cyprinidae** /si-prin'i-dē/) of freshwater fishes, including the common carp (*Cyprinus carpio*), goldfish, bream and many other related species, typically having pharyngeal teeth and a single dorsal fin (also adj). [L, from Gr *kyprīnos* a kind of carp]
■ **Cyprine** /sip'rīn/ adj. **Cyprin'odont** n (Gr *odous, odontous* tooth) any of several *esp* marine types of soft-finned tropical or subtropical carp-like fishes with toothed jaws, including guppies and swordtails (also adj). **cyp'rinoid** /-rin-oid/ adj of, related to, or resembling the carp (also n).

Cypriot, Cypriote see under **Cyprian**.

cypripedium /si-pri-pē'di-əm/ n (pl **cypripē'dia**) any orchid of the genera *Cypripedium* or *Paphiopedalum*, eg lady's slipper. [Gr *Kypris* Aphrodite, and *podion* a little foot, modified by L *pēs* foot]

cypris /sip'ris/ n (pl **cyp'rides** /-dēz/) a bivalve crustacean of the genus *Cypris* of freshwater ostracods. [Gr *Kypris* Aphrodite]
■ **cyp'rid** n any member of the genus; a cypris.

cyproheptadine /sī-prō-hep'tə-dēn/ n a powerful antihistamine drug used to treat allergies.

Cypro-Minoan see under **Cyprian**.

cyprus see **cypress**[2].

cypsela /sip'sə-lə/ (*bot*) n (pl **cyp'selae** /-lē/) the fruit of members of the daisy family, consisting of two carpels fused together and surrounded by a calyx sheath. [New L, from Gr *kypselē* a hollow vessel]

Cyrenaic /sī-ri-nā'ik/ adj relating to *Cyrēnē*, or to the hedonism of its philosopher Aristippus.

Cyrillic /si-ril'lik/ adj relating to the alphabet attributed to St Cyril (9c), distinguished from the other Slavonic alphabet, the Glagolitic.

cyst /sist/ n a sac or bag-like structure, whether normal or containing diseased matter (*anat* or *pathol*); a membrane enclosing an organism (such as a protozoan or parasitic worm) in a dormant stage of its life cycle, or such an organism (*biol*). [LL *cystis*, from Gr *kystis* a bladder]
■ **cystec'tomy** n surgical removal of the bladder; surgical removal of an abnormal cyst. **cyst'ic** or **cyst'iform** adj of or relating to a cyst; having or enclosed within a cyst; of or relating to the gall bladder or urinary bladder. **cysticercō'sis** /-ser-/ n (disease caused by) infestation of the body tissues by cysticerci. **cysticer'cus** /-ser'kəs/ n (pl **cysticerci** /-ser'sī/) (Gr *kerkos* tail) the larval stage of certain tapeworms in which invagination of the neck and scolex forms a fluid-filled cyst, bladderworm. **cyst'id** or **cystid'ean** n a cystoid. **cysti'tis** n inflammation of the inner lining of the bladder. **cyst'ocarp** n (Gr *karpos* fruit) the fructification in red seaweeds. **cys'tocele** n (Gr *kēlē* tumour) hernia of the bladder. **cyst'oid** n any echinoderm of the extinct class **Cystoid'ea**, globular or bladder-like animals enclosed in calcareous plates, stalked or sessile. **cyst'olith** n (Gr *lithos* stone) a stalked limy concretion in some plant cells. **cystolithī'asis** n the presence of calculi (stones) in the bladder. **cyst'oscope** n (Gr *skopeein* to view) an instrument inserted up the urethra for examining the inside of the bladder. **cystoscopic** /-skop'ik/ adj. **cystos'copy** n. **cystos'tomy** n the surgical operation of creating an artificial opening from the bladder to the abdomen. **cystot'omy** n (Gr *tomē* a cut) surgical incision into the bladder.
□ **cystic fibrosis** /fī-brō'sis/ n a hereditary disease of the exocrine glands, present from birth or appearing in infancy or childhood, characterized by secretion of sticky mucus, a tendency to chronic lung infections and an inability to absorb nutrients from food.

cystine /sis'tēn or -tin/ n the dimer, $C_6H_{12}O_4N_2S_2$, resulting from oxidation of the amino acid cysteine, that forms a disulphide bridge in proteins, eg keratin. [**cyst** and **-ine**[1]]
■ **cysteine** /sis'ti-ēn or -in/ n an amino acid, $C_3H_7O_2NS$, that oxidizes to form cystine. **cystinō'sis** n a defect of the metabolism present from birth which leads to abnormal accumulations of cystine in the kidneys, blood, etc. **cystinū'ria** n a condition in which excessive levels of the amino acid cystine are present in the urine, leading to formation of cystine stones in the kidney.

cytase /sī'tās or -tāz/ n an enzyme that breaks down cellulose.

cyte /sīt/ n (*biol; rare*) a cell. [Gr *kytos*, vessel, hollow]

-cyte /-sīt/ (*biol*) *combining form* denoting cell. [Gr *kytos* vessel, hollow]

Cytherean /si-thə-rē'ən/ adj relating to Aphrodite. [L *Cytherēa*, from Gr *Kythereia* Cytherean (goddess), Aphrodite, worshipped in the island of *Kythēra*]

cytisus /sit'i-səs/ n (pl **cyt'isī**) any leguminous plant of the broom genus *Cytisus*. [Gr *kytisos* a kind of medick, laburnum]
■ **cyt'isine** n a poisonous alkaloid found in laburnum.

cyto- /sī-to-/ or **cyt-** /sīt-/ *combining form* denoting cell. [Gr *kytos* vessel, hollow]
■ **cytidine** /sī'ti-dēn/ n a nucleoside formed from cytosine and ribose. **cytochem'istry** n the study of chemical compounds and their actions in living cells. **cyt'ochrome** n any of a group of substances in living cells, of great importance in cell oxidation. **cyt'ode** n a protoplasm body without nucleus. **cytodiagnos'is** n medical diagnosis following the close examination of the cells of the body tissues or fluids, eg the smear test for cervical cancer. **cytodifferentiā'tion** n the process of specialization, in cell development. **cytogen'esis** n cell formation. **cytogenet'ic** adj. **cytogenet'ically** adv. **cytogenet'icist** n. **cytogenet'ics** n sing the science linking the study of genetics with cytology, *esp* the structure, function and origin of chromosomes. **cyt'oid** adj cell-like. **cyt'okine** n (*immunol*) a protein chemical messenger that assists the immune system in combating infection and has a role in cell division; a drug based on this protein, used in the treatment of cancer, etc. **cytokinē'sis** n the division of the cytoplasm of a cell during mitosis. **cytokīn'in** n (Gr *kineein* to move) any of numerous substances which regulate plant growth by inducing cell division. **cytolog'ical** adj. **cytolog'ically** adv. **cytol'ogist** n. **cytol'ogy** n (*biol*) the study of the structure and function of individual cells, *esp* used for the detection of abnormal cells. **cytol'ysis** n (Gr *lysis* loosening) the dissolution of cells, *esp* by breakdown of their outer membrane. **cytolytic** /-lit'ik/ adj. **cy'tomegalovī'rus** n any of a group of viruses containing DNA of the herpes family, which cause cells which they infect to enlarge and may cause an illness similar to glandular fever, or (if transmitted by a pregnant woman to her unborn child) brain damage or malformations in newborn babies (*abbrev* **CMV**). **cytom'eter** n any of various devices for counting cells. **cytomet'ric** adj. **cytom'etry** n. **cyt'on** n the body of a nerve-cell. **cytopathol'ogy** n the study of cells in illness. **cytopē'nia** n (Gr *penia* poverty) deficiency of one or more types of blood cell. **cytophotom'eter** n an instrument for measuring the light allowed through a cell. **cytophotom'etry** n the examination of a cell by measuring the light allowed through it following staining.

cyt'oplasm *n* (Gr *plasma* form, body) the protoplasm of a cell surrounding the nucleus. **cytoplas'mic** *adj*. **cy'tosine** *n* one of the nitrogen-containing bases forming nucleotides in deoxyribonucleic acids. **cytoskel'etal** *adj*. **cytoskel'eton** *n* the internal fibrous structure within cytoplasm, determining the shape of a cell, and influencing its movement. **cy'tosol** *n* the soluble component of the cytoplasm. **cy'tosome** *n* the part of a cell outside the nucleus. **cytotox'ic** *adj* and *n* (denoting) a substance which damages or kills cells, *esp* a drug used to treat cancer. **cytotoxic'ity** *n*. **cytotox'in** *n* a cytotoxic substance.

CZ *abbrev*: Czech Republic (IVR).

czapka see **chapka**.

czar, czardom, czarevich, czarevna, czarina, etc see **tsar**, etc.

czardas a non-standard spelling of **csárdás**.

Czech /*chek*/ *n* a member of a westerly branch of the Slavs including the Bohemians and the Moravians; an inhabitant of the Czech Republic; formerly, a Czechoslovak; the language of the Czechs, Bohemian, closely related to Polish. ◆ *adj* of or relating to the Czechs or their language. [Polish]
■ **Czech'ic** *adj* (rare). **Czechoslo'vak** *n* a native or citizen of the former country of *Czechoslovakia*; a member of the Slavic people including the Czechs and the Slovaks. ◆ *adj* (also **Czechoslovak'ian**) of or relating to Czechoslovakia or to the Czechs and the Slovaks.

Dd

D or **d** /dē/ n the fourth letter in the modern English alphabet analagous to the fourth letters in the Phoenician, Hebrew, Greek and Roman alphabets (from the last of which it was immediately derived), its sound a voiced alveolar stop; the second note of the diatonic scale of C major (*music*); the key or scale having that note for its tonic (*music*); in hexadecimal notation, 13 (decimal) or 1101 (binary); the fourth highest in a category or range; anything shaped like the letter D, such as the semicircular marking on a snooker or billiard table.

◻ **D'-ring** n a metal ring or clip in the shape of a capital D, used in various kinds of harness or as trimming on garments.

D or **D.** abbrev : Democrat or Democratic (*US*); Department; *Deus* (*L*), God; Deutsch (catalogue of Schubert's works); Germany (ie *Deutschland*; IVR); diamonds (*cards*); dimension; dinar; Director; *Dominus* (*L*), Lord; Dutch.

◻ **D-day** /dē'dā/ n (D for unnamed day) the opening day (6 June 1944) of the Allied invasion of Europe in World War II; any critical day of action. **D'-mark** n Deutschmark (see mark[2]).

■ **3-D** three-dimensional (see **dimension**).

D symbol : (as a Roman numeral) 500; deuterium (*chem*).

D symbol : electric flux (displacement).

D̄ symbol : (Roman numeral) 500 000.

d or **d.** abbrev : date; daughter; day; dead; deci-; degree; *dele* (*L*), delete; *denarius* or *denarii* (*L*), a penny or pence (before 1971); departs; depth; deserted; diameter; died; duke.

d (*phys*) symbol : density.

'd /d/ short form of **had**[1], **would** or **did**; see also **'dst**.

DA abbrev : dinar; Diploma in Anaesthetics; Diploma of Art; District Attorney (*US*); duck's arse (hairstyle).

D/A (*comput*) abbrev : digital-to-analogue.

da[1] /dä/ n dialect form of **dad**[1].

da[2] or **dah** /dä/ n a heavy Burmese knife. [Burmese *da*]

da abbrev : deca-.

DAAG abbrev : Deputy Assistant Adjutant-General.

daal see **dal** (n).

DAB abbrev : digital audio broadcasting.

dab[1] /dab/ vt (**dabb'ing**; **dabbed**) to touch or press gently with something soft or moist; to peck; to smear; to dress (the face of stone) using a steel point. ◆ n a gentle touch or wipe with something soft or moist; a small amount of anything soft or moist; (*usu* in *pl*) a fingerprint (*sl*); a species (*Limanda limanda*) of flatfish of the family Pleuronectidae; applied to other (*esp* small) flatfish. [Cf MDu and early Mod Du *dabben* to pinch; Ger *Tappe* a pat; confused with **daub** and **tap**[1]]

■ **dabb'er** n a pad for dabbing ink on blocks or plates. **dabb'ity** n (*Scot*) a cheap pottery figure sold at fairgrounds, etc; a small picture on paper that is transferred onto a child's hand by moistening.

◻ **dab'chick** n the little grebe (*Podiceps ruficollis*).

dab[2] /dab/ n an expert person (also *adj*). [Origin unknown]

■ **dab'ster** n (*inf*).

▦ **a dab hand at** an expert at.

dabble /dab'l/ vt to shake about in liquid; to spatter with moisture. ◆ vi to play in liquid with hands or feet; (of ducks) to feed by moving the bill around below the water; to do anything in a trifling or small way. ◆ n the act of dabbling. [Frequentative of **dab**[1]]

■ **dabb'ler** n. **dabb'ling** n and adj. **dabb'lingly** adv.

dabchick see under **dab**[1].

Daboecia see **St Dabeoc's heath** under **saint**.

dabster see under **dab**[2].

da capo /dä kä'pō/ (*music*) an indication that the performer must return to the beginning of the piece (*abbrev* **DC**). [Ital, from the head]

■ **da capo al fine** /äl fïn'ā/ an indication that the performer must return to the beginning of the piece and conclude at the double bar

marked *Fine*. **da capo al segno** /äl sän'yō/ an indication that the performer must return to the beginning of the piece and conclude at the sign *$*:.

d'accord /da-kör'/ (*Fr*) interj and adv agreed; in tune.

dace /dās/, **dare** /där/ or **dart** /därt/ n a small river fish (*Leuciscus leuciscus*) of the carp family and chub genus. [ME *darce*, from OFr *dars*, from LL *dardus* a dart or javelin, of Gmc origin; from its quickness]

dacha or **datcha** /dä'chə/ n a country house or cottage in Russia. [Russ, orig gift (esp from a ruler)]

dachshund /däks'hŭnt, daks'hŭnd, -hŭnt/ n a breed of dog of German origin with a long body and very short legs. [Ger *Dachs* badger, and *Hund* dog]

dacite /dā'sīt/ n a fine-grained eruptive rock composed of quartz and plagioclase, with mica, etc. [From *Dacia*, a Roman province]

dacker /dak'ər/, **daker** or **daiker** /dā'kər/ (*Scot*) vi to lounge, saunter; to potter. [Origin unknown]

dacoit or **dakoit** /də-koit'/ n one of a gang of robbers in India and Burma (now Myanmar). [Hindi *dākait, dakait* a robber]

■ **dacoit'y, dakoit'i** or **dacoit'age** n robbery by a gang, brigandage.

Dacron® /dak'ron or dāk'ron/ n US tradename for **Terylene**®.

dactyl /dak'til/ n a digit (*zool*); a foot of three syllables, one long followed by two short, like the joints of a finger (*classical prosody*); in English, etc, a foot of three syllables, the first accented. [Gr *daktylos* a finger]

■ **dac'tylar** or **dactyl'ic** adj. **dactyl'ically** adv. **dactyliog'raphy** or **dactyliol'ogy** n the study or lore of rings or engraved gems. **dactyl'iomancy** n divination by means of a ring. **dac'tylist** n a writer of dactylic verse. **dactyl'ogram** (or /dak'/) n a fingerprint. **dactylog'raphy** n the study of fingerprints; dactylology. **dactylol'ogy** n the art of talking with the fingers using sign language. **dactylos'copy** n identification by or classification of fingerprints.

Dactylis /dak'til-is/ n the cocksfoot grass genus.

dad[1] /dad/ or **daddy** /dad'i/ (*childish* and *inf*) n father; used familiarly in addressing any older man. [History uncertain]

◻ **dad dancing** n (*inf*) dancing with an embarrassing disregard for rhythm and fashion, considered characteristic of middle-aged men. **dadd'y-long'-legs** n the cranefly; a harvestman (*N Am*).

▦ **the daddy of them all** (*inf*) the biggest, best, etc.

dad[2] /dad/ or **daud** /död/ (*dialect*) vt (**dadd'ing**; **dadd'ed**) to throw against something; to dash, thump. ◆ n a lump; a blow, thump. [Derivation unknown]

Dada /dä'dä/ or **Dadaism** /dä'dä-i-zm/ n a short-lived (from 1916 to c.1920) movement in art and literature which sought to abandon all form and throw off all tradition. [Fr, *dada* hobby-horse, a name said to have been arbitrarily chosen by the German writer Hugo Ball]

■ **Da'daist** n. **Dadais'tic** adj.

daddle[1] /dad'l/ (*dialect*) vi to walk in an unsteady manner, like a child or very old person; to totter. [Perh connected with **dawdle**]

daddle[2] /dad'l/ (*dialect*) n the hand. [Origin uncertain]

daddy see **dad**[1].

dado /dā'dō/ n (pl **dā'dos** or **dā'does**) the cubic block forming the body of a pedestal (*classical archit*); a deep border of wood along the lower part of the walls of a room, often merely represented by wallpaper or painting, etc. ◆ vt (**dā'doing**; **dā'doed**) to fit with a dado. [Ital; see **die**[2]]

dae /dā/ (*Scot*) vt and vi a form of **do**.

daedal or **dedal** /dē'dəl/ adj formed with art; displaying artistic or inventive skill; intricate, varied. [From L *Daedalus*, Gr *Daidalos*, the mythical artist who constructed the Cretan labyrinth and made wings for his son Icarus and himself]

■ **Daedalian** or **Dedalian** /di-dā'li-ən/ adj of, relating to, or resembling the work of Daedalus (Gr myth); (without cap) daedal. **daedal'ic** adj.

daemon /dē'mən/ or **daimon** /dī'mōn/ n a spirit holding a middle place between gods and men, such as the daemon or good genius of Socrates; an evil spirit, devil. [L daemōn, -onis, from Gr daimōn, -onos a spirit, a genius, and later a devil; see **demon**]
■ **daemonic** or **daimonic** /-mon'ik/ adj supernatural; of power or intelligence more than human; inspired.

dae-nettle see **day-nettle**.

daff[1] n (inf) short for **daffodil**.

daff[2] /daf/ (archaic) vi to make sport, to play the fool. [Origin doubtful]
■ **daff'ing** n foolery, gaiety.

daff[3] /daf/ (Shakesp) vt to put off; to turn aside, dismiss, put by. [A variant of **doff**]

daffodil /daf'ə-dil/, often inf **daff** /daf/ or **daffy** /daf'i/ n a yellow-flowered narcissus (also (poetic) **daffadowndilly** /daf'ə-down-dil'i/ or **daffodill'y**). ◆ adj pale yellow. [ME affodille, from OFr asphodile, from Gr asphodelos asphodel; the d is unexplained]

daffy[1] n (inf) short for **daffodil**.

daffy[2] /daf'i/ (inf) adj daft, crazy. [**daff**[2]]

daffy[3] /daf'i/ n an 'elixir of health' invented by a certain Thomas Daffy (died 1680).

daft /däft/ (inf) adj silly; weak-minded; insane; unreasonably merry; very fond (of) or enthusiastic (about). [ME dafte mild, meek. See **deft**]
■ **daft'ie** n a daft person. **daft'ly** adv. **daft'ness** n.
□ **daft days** n pl (Scot) the period of festivity and leisure at Christmas and New Year; the carefree days of one's youth.

daftar /daf'tär/ (Ind) n an office, esp a military orderly room; a bundle of documents. [Hindi]

DAG abbrev : Deputy Adjutant-General.

dag[1] /dag/ n a tag, scallop or lacination (obs); a dirt-clotted tuft of wool on a sheep (also **dag'lock** or (in pl) **dagg'ings**); a scruffy, untidy, slovenly person (Aust inf); a person, esp an adolescent, who is or feels socially awkward or graceless (Aust inf). ◆ vt (**dagg'ing**; **dagged**) to cut into dags; to bedraggle (obs); to cut off a sheep's dags. [Origin uncertain]
■ **dagg'y** adj (Aust and NZ inf) scruffy, dishevelled; unfashionable.

dag[2] /dag/ (Aust inf) n a person who is rather eccentric or comically entertaining (see also **dag**[1]). [UK dialect dag a dare]

dag[3] /dag/ n a heavy pistol of the 15c and 16c. [Origin uncertain]

dagaba see **dagoba**.

dagga /dag'ə or duhh'ə/ n Indian hemp (called **true dagga**); an African labiate plant Leonotis leonurus or other species (**Cape** or **red dagga**) smoked as a narcotic, called the love-drug. [Khoikhoi dachab]

dagger /dag'ər/ n a knife or short sword for stabbing at close quarters; a mark of reference (†), an obelus (printing). [ME dagger; cf Fr dague]
□ **dagg'erboard** n (naut) a light, narrow, completely removable centreboard.
■ **at daggers drawn** in a state of hostility. **double dagger** a mark of reference (‡), a diesis (printing). **look daggers** to look in a hostile manner.

daggings see **dag**[1].

daggle /dag'l/ vt and vi to wet or grow wet by dragging or sprinkling. [Frequentative of **dag**[1]]
□ **dagg'le-tail** n a draggle-tail.

daggy see under **dag**[1].

daglock see **dag**[1].

dago /dā'gō/ (offensive) n (pl **dā'goes** or **dā'gos**) a man of Spanish, Portuguese or Italian origin. [Prob Sp Diego, from L Jacōbus James]

dagoba or **dagaba** /dā'gə-bä/ n in Sri Lanka, a dome-shaped memorial shrine (for Buddhist relics), a tope. [Sinhalese dāgaba]

Dagon /dā'gən/ or -gon/ (Bible) n the national god of the Philistines, half-man, half-fish. [Heb dāgōn, from dāg fish]

daguerreotype /də-ger'ō-tīp/ n a method of photography by mercury vapour development of silver iodide exposed on a copper plate; a photograph taken by this method; a faithful representation (obs). ◆ vt to photograph by that process. [Fr, from Louis Daguerre (1789–1851), its French inventor]
■ **daguerr'ean** adj. **daguerre'otyper** or **daguerre'otypist** n. **daguerre'otypy** n the art of daguerreotyping.

dagwood /dag'wŭd/ same as **dogwood** (see under **dog**[1]).

dah[1] /dä/ n a word representing the dash in the spoken form of Morse code. See also **dit**[4].

dah[2] see **da**[2].

dahabiyah, **dahabiyeh**, **dahabieh** or **dahabeeah** /dä-hä-bē'(y)ä, -ə/ n a Nile sailing boat. [Ar dhahabīyah golden]

dahl see **dal** (n).

dahlia /dāl'yə, in US däl'yə/ n any perennial garden plant of the Mexican genus Dahlia, with large brightly-coloured flowers and tuberous roots. [From Anders Dahl (1751–89), Swedish botanist]

daidle /dā'dl/ (Scot) vi to waddle; to stagger; to idle about; to trifle; to potter. [**daddle**[1]]
■ **daid'ling** adj feeble; dawdling.

daidzein /dād'zēn/ n an oestrogen extracted from the root of the kudzu plant, thought to have therapeutic properties.

daiker[1] /dā'kər/ (obs Scot) vi to decorate. [Perh Fr décorer]

daiker[2] see **dacker**.

daiko see **taiko**.

daikon /dī'kon/ n a long white Japanese root vegetable of the radish family, similar to a mooli. [Jap]

Dáil /doil/ or **Dáil Eireann** /ā'rən/ n the lower house of the legislature of the Republic of Ireland. [Ir, assembly (of Ireland)]

daily /dā'li/ adj coming, done or happening every day or every weekday; constant; lasting for one day. ◆ adv every day or every weekday; constantly, regularly. ◆ n a daily paper; a non-resident servant, esp a cleaning woman; (in pl) film rushes. [**day**]
□ **daily bread** n one's living, livelihood. **daily double** n (horse-racing) a single bet on the winners of two races on the same day. **daily dozen** n (old inf) physical exercises done regularly, usu every morning.

daimen /dem'ən, dā'mən/ (Scot) adj occasional. [Origin obscure]

daimio /dī'myō, -mi-ō/ n (pl **dai'mios**) a Japanese territorial noble under the old feudal system. [Jap]

daimon see **daemon**.

daine /dān/ (Shakesp) same as **deign**.

dainty /dān'ti/ adj pleasant to the taste, choice; delicate; tasteful; genteel; fastidious; choicely or fastidiously neat; elegant (Spenser). ◆ n that which is dainty, a delicacy, esp a small cake. [ME deintee anything worthy or costly, from OFr daintié worthiness, from L dignitās, -ātis, from dignus worthy]
■ **daint** or **daynt** adj (Spenser) dainty. **dain'tily** adv. **dain'tiness** n.

daiquiri /dī'kə-ri/ or **daquiri** /dak'ə-ri/ n a cocktail containing rum and lime juice. [Daiquiri, Cuban place name]

dairy /dā'ri/ n a place where milk is kept, and butter and cheese made; a shop where milk and other dairy produce is sold; a company which processes or supplies milk or milk products; food containing milk or milk products; a small grocery store serving a local community (NZ). [ME deye, from OE dǣge a dairymaid; orig a kneader of dough; see **dough**]
■ **dai'rying** n.
□ **dairy cattle** n pl cattle reared mainly for the production of milk (cf **beef cattle**). **dairy cream** n cream made from milk, not artificial substitutes. **dairy farm** n. **dai'rymaid** n. **dai'ryman** n. **dai'rywoman** n. **dairy products** n pl milk and its derivatives, butter, cheese, etc. **dayr'house** n (Spenser) a dairy.

dais /dās, dā'is/ n a raised floor at the upper end of a dining-hall where the high table stands; a raised floor, usu with a seat or throne and perhaps a canopy; the canopy over an altar, etc; a platform for the use of speakers, etc. [OFr deis, from LL discus a table, from L discus a quoit, from Gr diskos a disc]

daisy /dā'zi/ n a composite wild or garden plant (Bellis perennis), whose flowers have a yellow disc and white rays; extended to other plants such as the ox-eye daisy, which is a chrysanthemum; a general term of admiration, often ironical (old US sl). [OE dæges éage day's eye]
■ **dai'sied** adj covered with daisies.
□ **daisy chain** n a string of daisies each threaded through the stem of the next; a group of dealers who buy and sell a commodity among themselves in order to inflate the price to outside buyers (commerce). **dai'sy-chain** vt to inflate (prices) by means of a daisy chain; to form a sequence of (electronic devices). **dai'sy-cutter** n (inf) a fast-going horse that does not lift its feet high (archaic); (in cricket) a ball bowled along the ground or that keeps low on pitching; a powerful bomb designed to explode close to the ground, destroying anything within a wide radius. **dai'sy-wheel** n a flat, horizontal, wheel-shaped device in a typewriter or printer with printing characters at the end of the spokes.
■ **fresh as a daisy** bright and vigorous, with strength and spirits unimpaired. **New Zealand daisy bush** a half-hardy shrub of the genus Olearia, with daisy-like flowers. **pushing up the daisies** (sl) dead (and buried).

dak /däk/ or **dawk** /dök/ n in India, the mail-post; hence mail, a letter, a parcel, etc; a method of travelling like that of the mail (orig by relays of bearers or horses). [Hindi dāk a relay of men]
□ **dak bungalow** n a house for travellers in India. **dak runner** n a runner or horseman who carried mail.

daker see **dacker**.

Dakin's solution /dā'kinz sǝ-, so-loo'shǝn or -ū'shǝn/ (chem) n a dilute solution of sodium hypochlorite and boric acid, used as an antiseptic. [From Henry Dakin (1880–1952), British chemist]

dakoit see **dacoit**.

Dakota /dǝ-kō'tǝ/ n (pl **Dakō'ta** or **Dakō'tas**) a member of a Siouan people living in the northern Mississippi valley and the surrounding plains; (also **Sioux**) the Siouan language of this people. ◆ adj of the Dakota or their language. [Dakota, allies]

daks /daks/ (Aust inf) n pl trousers. [Orig a trademark]

dal, daal, dahl or **dhal** /däl/ n (also spelt **dholl**) the pigeon pea, a pea-like plant (Cajanus indicus) cultivated in India and the tropics; pulse; a purée of pulse. [Hindi dal to split]

dal abbrev : decalitre(s).

Dalai Lama /dä'lī lä'mǝ/ n the head of the Tibetan Buddhist hierarchy. [Mongolian dalai ocean, and Tibetan lama high-priest]

dalasi /dǝ-las'ē/ n (pl **dalas'i** or **dalas'is**) the standard monetary unit of The Gambia (100 butut).

dale[1] /däl/ n the low ground between hills; the valley through which a river flows. [OE dæl, reinforced by ON dalr; cf Swed dal; Ger Tal]
□ **dales'man** n specif a man of the dales of Yorkshire.

dale[2] /dä'le/ (Sp) interj expressing agreement or encouragement. [Literally, give it!]

Dalek /dä'lek/ n a mobile mechanical creature with a harsh staccato voice. [Created for the BBC television series Dr Who]

daleth /dä'leth/ n the fourth letter of the Hebrew alphabet. [Heb]

dali /dä'li/ n a tropical American tree related to nutmeg, yielding staves, etc, and wax seeds. [Native name]

Dalila, Dalilah see **Delilah**.

Dalit /dä'lit/ n a member of the former untouchable class in India. [Hindi]

dalle /däl/ n a slab or tile, esp decorative; (in pl) a rapid where a river runs in a gorge between steep rocks (US). [Fr]

dallop see **dollop**.

dally /dal'i/ vi (**dall'ying**; **dall'ied**) to waste time by idleness or trifling; to dawdle, delay; to play (with); to have an amorous relationship (with); to exchange caresses (archaic). [OFr dalier to chat]
■ **dall'iance** n dallying, toying or trifling; an amorous relationship; mutual exchange of embraces (archaic); delay. **dall'ier** n a trifler.

dalmahoy /däl'mǝ-hoi, -hoi'/ (hist) n a bushy bobwig worn in the 18c. [Said to be named from a wearer]

Dalmatian /dal-mā'shǝn/ adj belonging to Dalmatia (in Croatia). ◆ n a native or inhabitant of Dalmatia; a large, short-haired breed of dog, white with dark spots (also adj).

dalmatic /dal-mat'ik/ n a loose-fitting, wide-sleeved ecclesiastical vestment, worn esp by deacons in the Roman Catholic Church, also sometimes by bishops. [LL dalmatica a robe worn by persons of rank, on the pattern of a dress worn in Dalmatia]

Dalradian /dal-rā'di-ǝn/ (geol) adj applied to a series of Precambrian rocks well represented in the Scottish Highlands (also n). [From the ancient kingdom of Dalriada]

dal segno /däl sān'yō/ (music) an indication that the performer must return to the sign 𝄋 (abbrev **DS**). [Ital, from the sign]

dalt or **dault** /dölt/ (Scot) n a foster-child. [Gaelic dalta]

dalton /döl'tǝn/ n another name for **atomic mass unit** (see under **atom**). [John Dalton (1766–1844), English chemist and physicist]
■ **Daltō'nian** adj. **Dal'tonism** n (also without cap) colour blindness; inability to distinguish red from green.
□ **Dalton's law** see under **law**[1].

Daltonism[1], **daltonism** see under **dalton**.

Daltonism[2] /döl'tǝ-ni-zm/ n a school method (the **Dalton plan**) by which each pupil pursues separately in his or her own way a course divided into monthly instalments, and designed to suit each individual. [First tried in 1920 at Dalton, Massachusetts]

DALY abbrev : disability-adjusted life year, a unit used to assess the loss of economic output in a society due to illness, mortality, etc.

dam[1] /dam/ n an embankment to restrain water; the water so confined; a millstream (Scot); a restraint (fig). ◆ vt (**damm'ing**; **dammed**) to keep back by a bank; to restrain (eg tears or an emotion) (fig). [Gmc; Du dam, Ger Damm, etc]

dam[2] /dam/ n a mother, usu of cattle, horses, etc. [A form of **dame**[1]]

dam[3] /däm/ n an obsolete Indian copper coin, one fortieth of a rupee. [Hindi dām]

dam[4] /dam/ (obs Scot) n a draughtsman. [Fr dame lady]
■ **dams** n sing the game of draughts.
□ **dam'board** or **dam'brod** n a draughtboard.

dam[5] /dam/ (inf) a form of **damn** or **damned**.
□ **dam'fool'** adj stupid, ridiculous. **damme** /dam'(m)ē/ interj damn me. **damm'it** interj damn it.
■ **as near as dammit** see under **near**.

dam abbrev : decametre(s).

damage /dam'ij/ n hurt, injury, loss; the value of what is lost; cost (inf); (in pl) the financial reparation due for loss or injury sustained by one person through the fault or negligence of another (law). ◆ vt to harm, cause injury to. ◆ vi to be injured or harmed. [OFr damage (Fr dommage), from L damnum loss]
■ **damageabil'ity** n. **dam'ageable** adj. **dam'aging** adj harmful, injurious. **dam'agingly** adv.
□ **damage control** or **limitation** n action carried out to minimize the harmful effects of an incident. **damage feasant** /fez'ǝnt/ adj doing damage (of beasts trespassing).
■ **direct** or **general damages** damages awarded for the immediate consequences of a hurt as distinct from **indirect** or **special damages** turning on the remoter consequences. **what's the damage?** (inf) how much do I owe? what is the cost?

daman /dam'an/ n the Syrian hyrax, the cony of the Bible. [Ar]

damar /dam'ǝr/ same as **dammar**.

damascene /dam'ǝ-sēn, dam-ǝ-sēn'/, also **damasceene**, **damaskeen, damaskin** or **damasquin** /-kēn/ n a Damascus or damascened sword; inlay of metal (esp gold) or other materials on steel, etc; the structure or surface appearance of Damascus steel; a damson or damson plum; (with cap) a native or inhabitant of Damascus. ◆ vt to decorate (esp steel) by inlaying or encrusting; to ornament with the watered or wavy appearance of Damascus steel, or in imitation of it. [From Damascus, famous for its steel and (see **damask**) silk work]
■ **damascen'ing** n inlaying upon steel; the production of watered appearance on steel.
□ **Damascene conversion** n a sudden and dramatic conversion to a cause, such as that experienced by St Paul on the road to Damascus (Bible, Acts 9). **Damascus blade** n a sword made from Damascus steel. **Damascus steel** n a hard steel, repeatedly folded and hammered, giving a wavy surface pattern.

damask /dam'ǝsk/ n material, originally of silk, now usually of linen, also of cotton or wool, woven with a pattern; Damascus steel or its surface appearance; the red colour of a damask rose. ◆ vt to weave patterns into (cloth); to damascene. ◆ adj red, like a damask rose. [From Damascus (see **damascene**)]
■ **dam'assin** n damask with flowered patterns in gold or silver thread.
□ **damask plum** n a damson. **damask rose** n a fragrant pink or red variety of rose. **dam'ask-steel** n Damascus steel.

damboard, dambrod see under **dam**[4].

dame[1] /dām/ n the mistress of a house, a matron (now usu joc or patronizing); a mother (obs); a woman (sl); the comic vulgar old woman of the pantomime, usu played by a male actor; a noble lady; (the title of) a lady of the same rank as a knight; a baronet's or knight's wife or widow (as a formal title prefixed to the lady's name) (obs); a name given to members of certain orders of nuns, esp Benedictine. [Fr dame, from L domina a lady]
□ **dame'-school** n (hist) a school for young children, usu kept by a woman. **dame's'-vī'olet** n a cruciferous plant (Hesperis matronalis) formerly cultivated in pots by ladies for its sweet scent at night.

dame[2] /dam/ (Fr) n a woman, lady.
□ **dame d'honneur** /don-œr/ n a maid of honour. **dames de la halle** /dǝ la al/ n pl market women.

damfool see under **dam**[5].

dammar or **dammer** /dam'ǝr/ n a hard resin used for making varnish, obtained from various conifers. [Malay damar]

damme, dammit see under **dam**[5].

damn /dam/ vt to censure; to sentence to eternal punishment; to doom; to condemn as worthless; to prove guilty; to curse or swear at. ◆ vi to utter curses. ◆ n an interjection expressing annoyance, disgust or impatience (inf); something of little value (inf); a curse. ◆ adj or adv as an intensifier. [Fr damner, from L damnāre to condemn, from damnum loss]
■ **damnable** /dam'nǝ-bl/ adj deserving or tending to damnation; hateful; pernicious. **dam'nableness** or **damnabil'ity** n. **dam'nably** adv. **damnation** /-nā'shǝn/ n condemnation; the punishment of the impenitent in the future state (theol); eternal punishment. ◆ interj expressing displeasure. **dam'natory** /-nǝ-tǝr-i/ adj consigning to damnation. **damned** /damd/ or (poetic) dam'nid/ adj sentenced to

everlasting punishment (**the damned** /damd/ those so sentenced); hateful; thorough, complete; used to express surprise (as in *I'll be damned!*; *inf*). ◆ *adv* (*inf*) very, exceedingly. **damned'est** *adj* (*inf*) most remarkable or puzzling, *esp* in *the damnedest thing*. **damnification** /dam-ni-fi-kā'shən/ *n* infliction of injury or loss. **dam'nify** *vt* to cause loss to. **damning** /dam'ing or -ning/ *adj* exposing to condemnation.

■ **damn all** (*inf*) nothing at all. **damn with faint praise** to condemn in effect by expressing too cool approval. **do one's damnedest** /damd'əst/ (*inf*) to do one's very best. **not give a damn** (*inf*) to be completely unconcerned. **not worth a damn** (*inf*) of no value. **the damned** see **damned** above.

Damoclean /dam-ō-klē'ən/ *adj* like *Damoclēs*, flatterer of Dionysius of Syracuse, taught the insecurity of happiness by being made to sit through a feast with a sword suspended over his head by a single hair; hence, carrying the threat of imminent calamity.

damoisel, damosel or **damozel** /dam'ō-zel/ *n* same as **damsel**.

damp /damp/ *n* vapour, mist; moisture; moist air; (in mines, etc) any gas other than air; lowness of spirits (*archaic*); a gloom; discouragement. ◆ *vt* to wet slightly; to discourage; to check; to make dull; to slow down the rate of burning (of a fire) (often with *down*; see also **damp down** below); to diminish the amplitude of (*phys*). ◆ *adj* moist; foggy; unenthusiastic (*inf*). [ME *dampen*; related to Du *damp*, and Ger *Dampf* vapour]

■ **damp'en** *vt* and *vi* to make or become damp or moist; to stifle (*fig*). **damp'er** *n* someone who or something that damps; a depressive influence; a door or shutter for shutting off or regulating a draught; a device for diminishing the amplitude of vibrations (*phys*); a mute (*music*); (in a piano or harpsichord, etc) the pad that silences a note after it has been played; a kind of unleavened bread (*orig Aust*); a cake of this. **damp'ing** *n* reduction in vibration through the dissipation of energy (*phys*); diminution in sharpness of resonance through the introduction of resistance (*electronics*). **damp'ish** *adj*. **damp'ishness** *n*. **damp'ly** *adv*. **damp'ness** *n*. **damp'y** *adj* (*archaic* and *poetic*) damp.

□ **damp'-course** *n* a layer of moisture-proof material in a masonry wall. **damp'ing-off'** *n* a disease of seedlings caused by *Pythium* or other fungus in an excess of moisture. **damp'-proof** *adj* impervious to moisture. ◆ *vt* to make (eg a wall) damp-proof. **damp-proof course** *n* a damp-course. **damp squib** *n* something that fails to go off with the expected bang (*lit* and *fig*).

■ **damp down** to close down a furnace, etc (**damp'ing-down** *n*). **put a damper on** to inhibit or subdue.

damsel /dam'zəl/ *n* (*archaic* or *poetic*) a young girl or unmarried woman. [OFr *dameisele* (Fr *demoiselle*), from LL *domicella*, dimin of L *domina* lady]

□ **dam'selfish** *n* a small brightly-coloured tropical fish of the family Pomacentridae. **dam'selfly** *n* an insect of the order Odonata, resembling the dragonfly.

damson /dam'zən/ *n* a rather small, oval, dark-purple plum, or the tree producing it. [Shortened from *Damascene*, from *Damascus*]

□ **damson cheese** *n* a thick damson jam.

Dan /dan/ *n* a title of honour equivalent to Master or Sir formerly applied (*eg*) to monks, and by the poets to great poets, etc. [OFr *dan* (Sp *don*; Port *dom*), from L *dominus* lord]

Dan. *abbrev* : (the Book of) Daniel (*Bible*); Danish.

dan¹ /dan/ *n* (in Japanese combative sports) a level of proficiency (*usu* 1st rising to 10th); a person who has gained such a level. [Jap]

dan² /dan/ *n* a small sea marker-buoy (also **dan buoy**). [Origin obscure]

dan³ /dan/ (*dialect*) *n* a box for carrying coal; a tub.

dance /däns/ *vi* to move rhythmically, *esp* to music; to spring. ◆ *vt* to cause to dance or jump; to perform or execute (as a dance). ◆ *n* a sequence of steps or rhythmic movements, *usu* to music; the tune to which dancing is performed; the musical form of a dance tune; a meeting for dancing; a series of dance-like movements performed by birds, etc, eg as a mating display. [OFr *danser*, from Gmc; OHGer *dansōn* to draw along]

■ **dance'able** *adj*. **danc'er** *n*. **danc'ing** *n*. **danc'y** or **danc'ey** *adj* (*esp* of electronic music) suitable for dancing to.

□ **dance band** *n*. **dance drug** *n* any of various stimulant drugs taken *esp* by people dancing in clubs, at raves, parties, etc. **dance floor** or **dance'floor** *n* an uncarpeted area for dancing in a club, bar, etc. **dance'hall** *n* a form of reggae, originating in the 1980s, characterized by the use of electronic sounds and bawdy lyrics (also **bashment**). **dance hall** *n* a public hall providing facilities for dancing. **dance music** *n* music specially composed or arranged for accompanying dancing. **dance of death** *n* a series of allegorical paintings symbolizing the universal power of death, which is represented as a skeleton. **dance tune** *n*. **danc'ing-girl** *n* a woman who entertains in a club, etc by dancing. **danc'ing-master** *n*.

■ **dance a bear** (*obs*) to exhibit a performing bear. **dance attendance** to wait assiduously (on). **dance to someone's tune** to conform to someone's wishes. **dance upon nothing** to be hanged. **lead someone a (merry) dance** to keep someone involved unnecessarily in a series of perplexities and vexations. **merry dancers** (*dialect*) the aurora borealis.

dancercise /dän'sər-sīz/ *n* exercises combining elements of aerobics with dance movements. [*dance* and *exercise*]

dancette /dän-set'/ *n* a zigzag or indented line or figure (*heraldry*); the chevron or zigzag moulding common in Romanesque architecture. [OFr *dent*, *dant* tooth, notch, from L *dēns*, *dentis*]

■ **dancetté, dancettee** or **dancetty** /dän'set-i or -set'/ *adj* deeply indented.

D and C (*med*) *abbrev* : dilatation and curettage (a diagnostic and/or curative procedure frequently used in obstetrics and gynaecology, involving dilatation of the cervix, and curettage, or cleaning out, of the uterus).

D and D *abbrev* : drunk and disorderly.

dandelion /dan'di-lī-ən/ *n* a common yellow-flowered composite plant (*Taraxacum officinale*) with jagged-toothed leaves. [Fr *dent de lion* lion-tooth]

dander¹ /dan'dər/ *n* a form of **dandruff**; anger; passion.

■ **get someone's** (or **one's**) **dander up** or **raise someone's** (or **one's**) **dander** to make or become angry.

dander² /dan'dər/, **daunder** /dön'dər/, **dauner** or **dawner** /dö'nər/ (*Scot* and *N Eng dialect*) *vi* to stroll, saunter. ◆ *n* a stroll, saunter. [Origin unknown]

dander³ /dan'dər/ (*Scot*) *n* furnace cinders. [Origin unknown]

Dandie Dinmont /dan'di din'mənt/ *n* a short-legged rough-coated terrier of Scottish Border breed, of pepper or mustard colour. [From *Dandie Dinmont* in Scott's *Guy Mannering*, whose Peppers and Mustards are represented as the origin of the breed]

dandify, etc see under **dandy¹**.

dandiprat or **dandyprat** /dan'di-prat/ (*obs*) *n* a silver three-halfpenny piece; an insignificant person; a little boy. [Origin unknown]

dandle /dan'dl/ *vt* to play with; to fondle (a young child), toss it in the arms or dance it lightly on one's knee. [Origin unknown]

■ **dand'ler** *n*.

dandruff or (*rare*) **dandriff** /dan'drəf/ *n* a scaly scurf on the skin under the hair. [Origin unknown]

dandy¹ /dan'di/ *n* a foppish, silly fellow; a man who pays great attention to his dress; a dandy-cock; a dandy-roll. ◆ *adj* (*inf*) smart, fine, a word of general commendation. [Origin unknown; orig Scot; poss a person spoiled by too much dandling]

■ **dandī'acal** or **dand'ified** *adj* inclined to be a dandy. **dan'dify** *vt* to dress up. **dan'dily** *adv*. **dan'dyish** *adj*. **dan'dyism** *n*.

□ **dan'dy-brush** *n* a stiff-bristled brush for grooming a horse. **dan'dy-cart** *n* (*hist*) a light spring-cart. **dan'dy-cock** or (*fem*) **dan'dy-hen** *n* (*dialect*) a bantam. **dan'dy-horse** *n* an early bicycle without pedals, driven by kicking the ground. **dan'dy-roll** *n* a wire-gauze cylinder that impresses the ribs and watermark on paper.

dandy² /dan'di/ *n* a sloop-like vessel with jigger-mast abaft. [Perh from **dandy¹**]

□ **dan'dy-rigged** *adj*.

dandy-fever see **dengue**.

dandyfunk see **dunderfunk**.

dandyprat see **dandiprat**.

Dane /dān/ *n* a native or citizen of Denmark in N Europe; a Scandinavian invader of Britain in the 9–11c; a very large dog (Great Dane); a Dalmatian dog (lesser Dane). [Dan *Daner* (pl); OE *Dene*]

■ **Danish** /dān'ish/ *adj* belonging to Denmark. ◆ *n* the language of the Danes (also **Dan'isk** (*Spenser*)); a Danish pastry.

□ **Danish blue** *n* a blue-veined, strongly-flavoured cheese. **Danish pastry** *n* a flaky confection of sweetened dough, containing a filling such as custard, fruit or nuts, and often iced.

danegeld /dān'geld/ or **danegelt** /-gelt/ *n* a tax imposed in the 10c to buy off the Danes or to defend the country against them (*hist*); payment or concessions made to avoid trouble. [OE *Dene* Danes, and *geld* payment]

dane-hole /dān'hōl/ same as **dene-hole**.

Danelaw or **Danelagh** /dān'lö/ (*hist*) *n* that part of England, NE of Watling Street, occupied (9–11c) by the Danes; (without *cap*) the Danish law which prevailed there. [OE *Dena lagu* Danes' law]

dang¹ /dang/ (*euphem*) a form of **damn**.

dang² see **ding²**.

danger /dān'jər/ *n* peril, hazard or risk; insecurity; power (*obs*). ◆ *vt* (*archaic*; *Shakesp*) to endanger. [OFr *dangier* absolute power (of a feudal lord), hence power to hurt, from LL *dominium* feudal authority, from L *dominus* a lord]

■ **dan'gerous** *adj* full of danger (also (*Shakesp*) *adv*); unsafe; insecure; arrogant, stand-offish (*obs*). **dan'gerously** *adv*. **dan'gerousness** *n*.

❑ **danger line** *n* the boundary between safety and danger. **danger man** *n* a man seen as being a particular source of threat or trouble. **danger money** *n* extra money paid for doing a more than usually perilous job. **danger point** *n* the place where safety gives way to danger.

■ **in danger of** liable to; on the point of. **on the danger list** (in a hospital, etc) categorized as being dangerously ill (also *fig*).

dangle /*dang'gl*/ *vi* to hang loosely or with a swinging motion. ◆ *vt* to cause to dangle; to show as an encouragement or enticement. [Cf Dan *dangle*, from ON *dingla*]

■ **dang'ler** *n* (*archaic*) a person who dangles about after others, *esp* women. **dang'ling** *n* and *adj*. **dang'ly** *adj*.

❑ **dangling participle** *n* (*grammar*) a misrelated participle.

Daniel /*dan'yəl*/ *n* a wise judge (in phrases such as *a second Daniel* and *a Daniel come to judgement* (both in Shakespeare's *Merchant of Venice*)). [From Daniel in the Bible, Apocryphal Book of Susanna]

Daniell cell /*dan'yəl sel*/ (*chem; hist*) *n* a type of primary cell with zinc and copper electrodes. [From John *Daniell* (1790–1845), British scientist]

danio /*dā'ni-ō*/ *n* (*pl* **da'nios**) any of several brightly-coloured tropical freshwater fish. [Origin obscure]

Danish see under **Dane**.

Danite /*dan'īt*/ *n* a member of a secret society amongst the early Mormons. [*Dan*; cf Bible, Genesis 49.16–17]

dank /*dangk*/ *adj* unpleasantly moist, wet. ◆ *n* (*obs*; *Milton*) a wet place. [Origin uncertain]

■ **dank'ish** *adj*. **dank'ness** *n*.

danke schön /*dang'kə shœn*/ (*Ger*) many thanks.

dannebrog /*dan'e-brog*/ *n* the Danish national flag; the second of the Danish orders instituted by King Valdemar in 1219. [Dan]

DA-Notice /*dē-ā'nō-tis*/ *abbrev* : Defence Advisory Notice, a notice officially sent to newspapers, etc, asking them not to publish certain information on the grounds of national security.

danse macabre /*däs ma-kä'br'*/ (*Fr*) *n* the dance of death (qv).

danseur /*dä-sœr'*/ *n* a male ballet-dancer. [Fr]

■ **danseuse** /*dä-sœz*/ *n* a female dancer; a female ballet-dancer.

❑ **danseur noble** /*nobl'*/ *n* (*pl* **danseurs nobles** /*dä-sœr nobl'*/) a principal male ballet-dancer.

Dansker /*dan'skər*/ (*Shakesp*) *n* a Dane.

dant and **danton** earlier forms of **daunt** and **daunton**.

Dantean /*dan'ti-ən*/ or **Dantesque** /*dan-tesk'*/ *adj* like (the work of) the Italian poet *Dante* Alighieri (1265–1321); sublime; austere.

■ **Dan'tist** *n* a Dante scholar. **Dantoph'ilist** *n* a lover of Dante.

danthonia /*dan-thō'ni-ə*/ *n* a tufted grass native to Australia and New Zealand. [E *Danthoine*, 19c French botanist]

DAP *abbrev* : digital audio player; distributed array processor (*comput*).

dap¹ /*dap*/ *vi* (**dapp'ing**; **dapped**) to bounce; to dip gently into water; to fish with a fly bounced gently on the surface. ◆ *n* a bait so used; a bounce. [Origin obscure]

■ **dapp'er** *n*.

dap² /*dap*/ (*dialect*) *n* a gym shoe, plimsoll. [Prob **dap**¹]

daphne /*daf'ni*/ *n* any plant of the *Daphne* genus (family Thymelaeaceae) of poisonous shrubs, *incl* mezereon and spurge laurel. [Gr *daphnē* sweet bay]

Daphnia /*daf'ni-ə*/ *n* a genus of water flea. [Gr *Daphnē*]

■ **daph'nid** /*-nid*/ *n* any member of the genus.

dapper¹ /*dap'ər*/ *adj* quick; little and active; neat; spruce. [Du *dapper* brave; cf Ger *tapfer* quick, brave]

■ **dapp'erling** *n* (*archaic*) a dapper little fellow. **dapp'erly** *adv*. **dapp'erness** *n*.

dapper² see under **dap**¹.

dapple /*dap'l*/ *adj* marked with spots or splotches; mottled. ◆ *vt* to variegate with splotches of colour or shade. [Origin unknown]

■ **dapp'led** *adj*.

❑ **dapp'le-bay'** *adj* and *n* (an animal, *esp* a horse) of bay colour, variegated with dapples. **dapp'le-grey'** *adj* and *n* (an animal, *esp* a horse) of a pale grey colour with darker spots.

dapsone /*dap'sōn*/ *n* a drug widely used in the treatment of leprosy, dermatitis, etc. [*d*iaminodi*p*henyl*s*ulph*one*]

daquiri see **daiquiri**.

DAR *abbrev* : National Society Daughters of the American Revolution, a patriotic women's organization dating from 1890 (also **NSDAR**).

daraf /*dar'af*/ (*elec*) *n* a unit of elastance, the reciprocal of capacitance in farads. [*Farad* backwards]

darbies /*där'biz* or *-bēz*/ (*sl*) *n pl* handcuffs. [Appar from the personal name *Darby*]

Darby and Joan /*där'bi-ənd-jōn'*/ *n* a devoted elderly married couple. [Poss from characters in an 18c song]

❑ **Darby and Joan Club** *n* a social club for elderly people.

Darbyite /*där'bi-īt*/ *n* a member of the Plymouth Brethren, more particularly of the Exclusive branch of the sect. [From their principal founder, JN *Darby* (1800–82)]

darcy /*där'si*/ (*geol*) *n* (*pl* **dar'cys** or **dar'cies**) a unit used to express the permeability coefficient of a rock, for example in calculating the flow of oil, gas or water. [From HPG *Darcy* (1803–58), French engineer]

Dard /*därd*/ *n* a person belonging to any of the peoples who speak Dardic languages.

■ **Dard'ic** *adj* and *n* (of or relating to) a particular Indo-European language group spoken in parts of N India, Pakistan and Afghanistan.

Dardan /*där'dən*/ or **Dardanian** /*där-dā'ni-ən*/ same as **Trojan**.

dare¹ /*dār*/ *vi* (3rd pers sing **dares**; *pat* and *pap* **dared**) and *vt* (3rd pers sing **dare(s)**, before infinitive often **dare**; *pat* **dared** or **durst** (now *rare*, used *esp* in subjunctive sense); *pap* **dared**) to be bold enough (to); to venture. ◆ *vt* to challenge; to defy; to face. ■ *n* an act of daring or a challenge to perform it; boldness (*obs*; *Shakesp*). [OE *durran* (preterite-present verb), prt *dearr*, preterite *dorste*; Gothic *daursan*; related to Gr *tharseein*]

■ **dare'ful** *adj* (*obs*; *Shakesp*) full of daring, adventurous. **dar'ing** *adj* bold; courageous; fearless; shocking. ◆ *n* boldness. **dar'ingly** *adv*.

❑ **dare'-devil** *n* a rash, daring person. ◆ *adj* unreasonably rash and reckless. **dare'-dev'ilry** *n*. **dar'ing-do** same as **derring-do**. **dar'ing-hard'y** *adj* (*Shakesp*) foolhardy.

■ **how dare you!** exclamation expressing anger or outrage at another's action. **I dare say** or **I daresay** I suppose.

dare² /*dār*/ (*obs*) *vi* to lurk, crouch, shrink, be dismayed, doze, be fascinated, stare. ◆ *vt* (*obs* or *dialect*; *Spenser* and *Shakesp*) to daze; to frighten. ◆ *n* a contrivance with mirrors such as was once used to fascinate larks. [OE *darian* to lurk, be hidden]

dare³ /*dār*/ same as **dace**.

darg /*därg*/ (*Scot* and *N Eng dialect*) *n* a day's work; a task. [Contraction from *dawerk*, *day-wark* day-work]

darga or **dargah** /*dûr'gä*/ *n* (a structure over) a place where a Muslim holy person was cremated or buried. [Hindi *dargāh*]

dargle /*där'gl*/ (*Walter Scott*) *n* a dell. [Prob from the *Dargle* in County Wicklow, mistaken by Scott for a common noun]

dari see **durra**.

daric /*dar'ik*/ *n* an old gold or silver Persian coin named after *Darius* I of Persia.

dariole /*dar'ē-ōl* or *dar'yōl*/ *n* a shell of pastry, etc, or small round mould; a dish comprising such a shell and its filling; one prepared in such a mould. [Fr]

Darjeeling /*där-jē'ling*/ *n* a high-quality variety of tea produced around *Darjeeling* (now Darjiling) in NE India.

dark /*därk*/ *adj* without light; black, or rather blackish; (of hair and skin colouring) not of a fair or light hue; gloomy; (of a theatre) closed; difficult to understand; unenlightened; secret; sinister. ◆ *n* absence of light; nightfall; a state of ignorance; a dark colour. ◆ *adv* (*Shakesp*) in a state of dark. [OE *deorc*]

■ **dark'en** *vt* to make dark or darker; to sully. ◆ *vi* to grow dark or darker. **dark'ey**, **dark'ie** *n* see **darky** below. **dark'ish** *adj*. **dark'le** *vi* (*literary*) to grow dark (a back-formation from *darkling*). **dark'ling** *adv* and *adj* dark; in the dark. **dark'lings** *adv* (*poetic*) in the dark. **dark'ly** *adv*. **dark'ness** *n*. **dark'some** *adj* dark; gloomy (*poetic*). **dark'y** *n* an old, now offensive, name for a black person (also **dark'ie** or **dark'ey**); a dark lantern (also **dark'ey**; *sl*).

❑ **dark adaptation** *n* the automatic adjustment of the eye to enable it to continue to see in reduced light. **dark'-adapt'ed** *adj*. **Dark Ages** *n pl* the period of European history from the 5c to the 9c or 12c (or 15c), once considered to be a time of intellectual darkness. **Dark Continent** *n* (*old*) Africa. **dark current** *n* (*image technol* and *phys*) residual current in a photoelectric cell, video camera tube, etc, when there is no incident illumination. **dark energy** *n* a hypothetical form of energy believed to be responsible for the continuous expansion of the universe. **darkfield microscope** *n* an ultramicroscope. **dark glasses** *n pl* sunglasses. **dark-ground illumination** *n* (*biol*) a method for the microscopic examination of living material by scattered light, specimens appearing luminous against a dark background (cf **brightfield illumination**). **dark horse** *n* (in racing) a horse whose capabilities are not known; a person whose abilities or motives are not known; a candidate not brought forward until the last moment (*esp US*).

dark'-house n (*Shakesp*) a mad-house. **dark lantern** n a lantern whose light can be covered. **darkling beetle** n any dark-coloured beetle of the Tenebrionidae. **dark'mans** n (*criminal sl*) night. **dark matter** n undetectable but influential matter, possibly in the form of neutrinos, making up a large proportion of the mass of the universe. **dark meat** n the darker meat from the legs, etc of poultry (cf **white meat**). **dark'net** n (*comput*) a private network of computer users within which file sharing (qv under **file¹**) takes place. **dark reaction** n the second phase of photosynthesis, which needs no light. **dark'room** n a room for developing and printing photographs free from such light as would affect photographic plates. **dark star** n a star that emits no visible light, and can be detected only by its radiowaves, gravitational effect, etc. **dark web** n deep web (qv under **deep**).

■ **darken someone's door** (often with *neg*, often implying unwelcomeness) to appear as a visitor. **in the dark** ignorant, unaware. **keep dark** to be silent or secret. **keep it dark** to conceal something. **prince of darkness** Satan.

darling /där'ling/ n a dearly-loved person (often as a form of address); a favourite; a kind, lovable person. ◆ *adj* beloved; sweet; delightful (*inf*). [OE *dēorling*; see **dear¹**]

Darlingtonia /där-ling-tō'ni-ə/ n a Californian pitcher plant of the Sarracenia family. [Named after William *Darlington* (1782–1863), American botanist]

darmstadtium /därm-stat'i-əm/ n an artificially produced radioactive transuranic element (symbol **Ds**; atomic no 110), formerly called **ununnilium**. [*Darmstadt*, Germany, where it was discovered]

darn¹ /därn/ vt to mend by interwoven stitches; to embroider or sew with the stitches used in mending holes. ◆ n a darned place. [Etymology uncertain]

■ **darn'er** n a person who darns; a darning-needle. **darn'ing** n. ❑ **darning egg** or **darning mushroom** n a smooth curved object, *usu* wooden, to support material being darned. **darn'ing-needle** n.

darn² /därn/, **darned** /färnd/ and **darnedest** /färn'dəst/ forms of **damn**, **damned** and **damnedest**.

darnel /där'nəl/ n a species of rye-grass; *perh* the tares of the Bible. [Poss connected with OFr *darne* stupid, from its supposed narcotic properties]

darraign, **darraigne**, **darrain**, **darraine**, **darrayn** or **deraign** /də-rān'/ (*obs*) vt to vindicate; to justify; to prove; to claim; to challenge; to decide; to set in battle array, or to do (battle) (*Spenser* and *Shakesp*). [OFr *derainier*, *desraisnier* to plead, vindicate, from LL *dē-*, *disratiōnāre*, from L *dē-* or *dis-*, and *ratiō* reason; cf **arraign**]

darre /där/ (*Spenser*) same as **dare¹**.

darred /färd/ pap of **dare²**.

darshan /där'shən/ (*Hinduism*) n a blessing conferred by seeing or touching a great or holy person. [Hindi]

dart¹ /färt/ n a pointed weapon or toy for throwing with the hand; anything that pierces; a tapering fold sewn on the reverse of material in order to shape it; (in *pl*, treated as *sing*) a game in which darts are thrown at a board; a sudden forward movement; a plan, scheme (*Aust inf*); in some snails, a calcareous needle supposed to be used as a sexual stimulus; a cutworm moth with a dart-like mark on the forewing (in full **dart'-moth**). ◆ vt to hurl suddenly; to send or shoot out. ◆ vi to move, start or shoot out rapidly (*frequentative* **dar'tle**). [OFr *dart*; cf OE *daroth*]

■ **dar'ter** n a person who or thing which darts; a freshwater diving bird (genus *Anhinga*) related to cormorants; a medium-sized dragonfly of the genus *Sympetrum*; an archerfish; applied also to various small American fishes of the perch family. **dart'ing** adj. **dart'ingly** adv. ❑ **dart'board** n the target used in the game of darts. **dart'-sac** n the gland that secretes the dart in snails.

■ **Old Dart** see under **old**.

dart² see **dace**.

dartle see **dart¹**.

dartre /där'tər/ (*med*) n herpes, or some herpes-like skin disease. [Fr] ■ **dar'trous** adj.

Darwinism /där'wi-ni-zm/ n the theory of the origin of species propounded by Charles *Darwin* (1809–82). ■ **Darwin'ian** or **Dar'winist** adj and n.

darzi /där'zē, dûr'zē/ n an Indian tailor. [Hindi *darzī*]

dash¹ /dash/ vt to throw, thrust or drive violently; to break by throwing together; to bespatter; to blotch; to frustrate; to confound; to modify by dilution or mixing. ◆ vi to rush; to smash (against). ◆ n a violent striking; a rush; a sprint (*athletics*; *esp* N Am); a violent onset; a blow; a splash; a splash of colour; a stroke of the pen or similar mark; a mark (—) at a break in a sentence or elsewhere; a euphemism for damn (sometimes represented by this sign); a mark (▼ or ▲) above or beneath a note indicating that it is to be played staccato (*music*); an acute accent used in algebra and in lettering of diagrams as a

discriminating mark; a long element in the Morse code; verve; ostentation; a small quantity of added ingredient; a dashboard in a motor vehicle. ◆ *interj* expressing irritation or annoyance. [ME *daschen*, *dassen* to rush, or strike with violence; cf Dan *daske* to slap]

■ **dash'er** n someone who dashes; someone who makes a great show (*inf*); a plunger in a churn. **dash'ing** adj spirited; showy; stylish. **dash'ingly** adv.

❑ **dash'board** n the instrument panel of a motor vehicle or small aircraft; a board, screen or partition in front of a driver on a horse-vehicle, to keep off splashes of mud. **dash'pot** n a device for damping vibration by a piston moving in a cylinder containing liquid. **dash'-wheel** n a washing machine in the form of a partitioned drum.

■ **dash off** to throw off or produce hastily; to knock out by striking against something.

dash² /dash/ n a gift accompanying a commercial transaction; a gratuity; a bribe. [Port *das* will you give?]

dasheen /da-shēn'/ n the taro. [Poss Fr *de Chine* of China]

das heisst /das hīst'/ (*Ger*) that is (*abbrev* **d.h.**).

dashi /dash'i/ n a clear stock, *usu* flavoured with kelp, used in Japanese cookery. [Jap]

dashiki or **dasheki** /da-shē'ki/ n a type of colourful loose shirt worn in Africa, and also in the USA. [W African]

dassie /das'i/ (*S Afr*) n the hyrax. [Du *dasje*, dimin of *das* badger; Afrik *dassie*]

dastard /das'tərd/ n (*archaic*) a cowardly fellow; (*loosely*) someone who does a brutal act without giving their victim a chance. ◆ *adj* (*archaic*) shrinking from danger; cowardly. [Prob connected with **dazed**]

■ **das'tardliness** n. **das'tardly** adj despicable; cowardly (also *adv*). **das'tardness** or **das'tardy** n.

dasyphyllous /das-i-fil'əs/ (*bot*) adj having crowded, thick, or woolly leaves. [Gr *dasys* thick, bushy, hairy, and *phyllon* leaf]

Dasypus /das'i-pŭs/ or *-pəs/ n a genus of armadillos. [Gr *dasypous* a hare, from *dasys* hairy, and *pous*, *podos* foot]

■ **das'ypod** n any member of the genus. **Dasypod'idae** n pl the armadillo family.

dasyure /das'i-ūr/ n any marsupial of the flesh-eating genus *Dasyurus* (called native cat) or the subfamily Dasyurinae (Tasmanian devil, etc). [Gr *dasys* shaggy, and *ourá* tail]

DAT, **Dat** or **dat** /dat/ see **digital audiotape** under **digit**.

dat. abbrev: dative.

data /dä'tə/ or (in US and technical Eng) /dä'tə/ n pl (sing **da'tum**) or n sing facts given (quantities, values, names, etc) from which other information may be inferred; such facts, in the form of numbers or characters, which can be input to a computer. [L *data* things given, pap neuter pl of *dare* to give]

■ **da'tagram** n (*comput*) a communication channel that uses information routed through a packet-switching network. **datamā'tion** n shortened term for **automatic data processing** (see under **automatic**).

❑ **da'tabank** n (*comput*) a body of information (a collection of databases or large files of data) stored in a computer, which can process it, and from which particular pieces of information can be retrieved when required. **da'tabase** n (*comput*) an organized collection of files of information that has been systematically recorded, and may form the basis of a data-processing system. **da'tabus** or **data highway** n (*comput*) a path for transferring data. **data capture** see **direct data capture** below. **da'tacasting** n a form of broadcasting that enables the rapid dissemination of large amounts of data to a large number of users. **data communications** n sing the sending of computer-encoded data by means of telecommunications (short form **da'tacomms**). **data compression** n (*comput*) altering the form of data to reduce its storage space. **data encryption standard** n (*comput*) an automatic method of data encryption designed by IBM and adopted as a standard. **data flow** n (*comput*) an approach to the organization of complex algorithms and machines, in which operations are triggered by the arrival of data. **da'taglove** n (*comput*) an electronically wired glove-like device that transmits the wearer's movements to a virtual reality monitor. **data logger** see **logger** under **log¹**. **data mining** n (*comput*) the automated analysis of large stores of data using techniques such as pattern recognition. **data processing** see under **process¹**. **data protection** n (*comput*) safeguards to protect the integrity, privacy and security of data. **data room** n a secure site (either in the real world or on the Internet) where confidential information concerning a proposed financial transaction may be viewed. **data set** n (*comput*) a file. **data warehouse** n (*comput*) a database that brings together large amounts of data from a variety of sources in a structure that allows the efficient retrieval and analysis of the data.

■ **direct data capture** or **data capture** (*comput*) the putting of information, *esp* concerning (cash) sales, into a form that can be fed directly into a computer.

datacomms /dā'tə-komz/ n datacommunications (see under **data**). [Short form]

datal[1] see under **date**[1].

datal[2] see **daytale** under **day**.

datamation see under **data**.

datary /dā'tə-ri/ n an officer of the papal court charged with registering and dating bulls, etc, and with duties relating to the granting of indults and graces; his office (also **data'ria**). [LL *datārius*, from L *dare* to give]

dataveillance /dā-tə-vā'ləns or dä-/ n the monitoring of individuals through data records created by their use of credit cards, the Internet, mobile phones, etc. [From *data* sur*veillance*]

datcha see **dacha**.

date[1] /dāt/ n a statement of time, or time and place, of writing, sending or executing (on a letter, book, document, etc); a particular day of the month; the time of an event; duration, or end, of existence (*archaic*); term of life; death-day, doom (with pun on *debt*; *Spenser*); an appointment or engagement (*inf*); a person one goes out on a date with. ◆ *vt* to affix a date to; to ascertain the date of; to suggest the date of; to make an appointment with (*inf*); to go out with (a (potential) romantic or sexual partner), *esp* regularly (*inf*). ◆ *vi* to have begun (at a specified time); to be typical of a particular time; to become old-fashioned; to go out with a (potential) romantic or sexual partner, *esp* regularly (*inf*). [OFr *date*, from L *datum* given]
■ **dāt'able** or **dāt'eable** *adj*. **dāt'al** *adj*. **dat'ed** *adj* old-fashioned, out of date. **date'less** *adj* without date or fixed limit; unlikely to become old-fashioned; free from engagements. **dāt'er** n. **dāt'ing** n and *adj*.
❑ **date coding** n marking in code on the container a date after which food should not be used. **date line** n short for International Date Line (qv). **date'line** n a line giving the date and location (as on a newspaper). **date night** n an evening on which a couple with children arrange to go out together without them. **date rape** n rape committed by a person with whom the victim has gone out on a date. **date'-stamp** n a device for stamping the date on documents, etc; the impression made by this. ◆ *vt* to mark with a date-stamp. **dating agency** n an agency that aims to introduce clients seeking personal relationships.
■ **out of date** see under **out**. **to date** until now. **up to date** aware of and following modern trends; having the latest knowledge and information, etc; adapted or corrected to the present time; modern.

date[2] /dāt/ n the fruit of the date palm. [Fr *datte*, from L *dactylus*, from Gr *daktylos* a finger, a date]
❑ **date palm** or **tree** n a palm (*Phoenix dactylifera*) of N Africa. **date plum** n the persimmon. **date'-shell** n the date-shaped shell of *Lithodomus*, or the animal itself, of the mussel family, a borer in limestone rocks. **date'-sugar** n.

DATEC *abbrev*: data and telecommunications.

Datel® /dā'tel/ n a facility provided by British Telecom for the transfer of data between computers, via a central computer where it is processed and available for retrieval on demand. [*data* and *tele*communications]

Datin see **Datuk**.

dative /dā'tiv/ *adj* given or appointed (by a court) (*Scots law*); that may be disposed of or given (*Eng law*); expressing an indirect object (*grammar*). ◆ n the dative case; a word in the dative. [L *datīvus*, from *dare* to give]
■ **dātī'val** *adj*.

datolite /dat'ə-līt/ n a hydrated silicate of boron and calcium. [Gr *dateesthai* to divide, and *lithos* stone]

Datuk /da-tŭk'/ or (*fem*) **Datin** /da-tēn'/ n a member of a senior chivalric order in Malaysia. [Malay *datu* chief]

datum /dā'təm/ singular of **data**. [L *datum* given, from *dare* to give]
❑ **datum line**, **level** or **plane** n the horizontal baseline from which heights and depths are measured. **datum point** n a reference point against which measurements and comparisons can be made.

datura /də-tū'rə/ n any plant of the thorn apple genus *Datura*, of the family Solanaceae, with strongly narcotic properties; the poison derived from these plants. [Hindi *dhatūrā*]
■ **datu'rine** n atropine, or a mixture of atropine with other alkaloids.

dau. *abbrev*: daughter.

daub /döb/ *vt* to smear; to paint crudely. ◆ n a crude painting. [OFr *dauber* to plaster, from L *dealbāre* to whitewash; see **dealbate**]
■ **daub'er** n. **daub'ery** (or *Shakesp* **dawb'ry**) n a daubing, or crudely artful device, false pretence. **daub'ing** n. **daub'y** *adj* sticky.
■ **wattle and daub** see under **wattle**[1].

daube /dōb/ (*Fr*) n a meat stew.

daud, dawd or **dod** /död/ (*Scot*) *vt* to knock, thump. ◆ n a lump; a large piece. [**dad**[2]]

daughter /dö'tər/ n a female in relation to her parent; a female descendant; woman (generally). ◆ *adj* proceeding or formed, as from a parent; (of a cell) formed by division (*biol*); derived from a nuclide, formed by the radioactive decay of another (*phys*). [OE *dohtor*; Scot *dochter*, Ger *Tochter*, Gr *thygatēr*]
■ **daugh'terliness** n. **daugh'terling** n a little daughter. **daugh'terly** *adj* like or becoming a daughter.
❑ **daughter board** n (*comput*) a printed circuit board, or similar, which plugs into a motherboard. **daugh'ter-in-law** n (*pl* **daugh'ters-in-law**) a son's wife; formerly, a step-daughter.

dault see **dalt**.

daunder, dauner see **dander**[2].

daunt /dönt/ *vt* to frighten; to discourage; to subdue. [OFr *danter* (Fr *dompter*), from L *domitāre*, from *domāre* to tame]
■ **daunt'er** n. **daunt'ing** *adj*. **daunt'less** *adj* not to be daunted, resolute, bold. **daunt'lessly** *adv*. **daunt'lessness** n. **daun'ton** *vt* (*Scot*) to subdue; to dare (*obs*).

dauphin /dō-fɛ̃ or dö'fin/ n (in France, from 1349 to 1830) the eldest son of the king. [OFr *daulphin* (Fr *dauphin*), from *Delphinus*, family name of the lords of the Viennois; hence dolphins in their crest, and name Dauphiné for their province (ceded to the king, 1349)]
■ **dauphine** /dō-fēn or dö-fēn'/ or **dau'phiness** n the wife of a dauphin.

dauphinoise /dō-fēn-wäz'/ *adj* (of vegetables, *esp* potatoes) sliced thinly and baked in cream. ◆ n a dish prepared in this way. [*Dauphiné*, former province of SE France]

daur /dör/ (*Scot*) a form of **dare**[1].

daut or **dawt** /döt/ (*Scot*) *vt* to pet. [Origin unknown]
■ **daut'ie** or **dawt'ie** n a pet or darling.

daven /dä'vən/ (*Judaism*) *vi* to pray, to recite the prayers of the liturgies; to lead prayers. [Yiddish *davnen*]

davenport /dav'n-pört, -pört/ n a small ornamental writing desk (also **dev'onport**); a large sofa. [Origin uncertain; perh from the maker or a person who ordered such a writing desk]

davenport-trick /dav'n-pört-trik, -pört-/ n an artifice by which a person wound round and tied with ropes can break free. [From two impostors who practised it in mid-19c]

davidia /da-vid'i-ə/ n a shrub or small tree (*Davidia involucrata*), a native to China, with heart-shaped leaves and conspicuous white bracts.

Davis apparatus /dā'vis ap-ər-ā'təs/ n a device making possible escape from a crippled submarine, invented by Sir Robert *Davis* (1890–1965).

davit /dav'it, dā'vit/ n one of a pair of devices for hoisting and lowering, eg (on a ship) for lowering a boat. [Appar from the name *David*]

Davy /dā'vi/ or **Davy lamp** n the safety lamp used in coalmines, invented by Sir Humphry *Davy* (1778–1829).

Davy Jones /dā'vi jōnz/ n a sailor's familiar name for the (malignant) spirit of the sea, the Devil. [Origin unknown]
❑ **Davy Jones's locker** n the sea, as the grave of men drowned at sea.

daw[1] /dö/ (*obs*) *vi* to dawn. [OE *dagian*, from *dæg* day]

daw[2] /dö/ n a bird of the crow family, *esp* a jackdaw; a simpleton (*archaic*). [ME *dawe*]
■ **daw'ish** *adj*.
❑ **daw'cock** n (*archaic*) a cock jackdaw; a simpleton.

dawbry (*Shakesp*) see under **daub**.

dawd see **daud**.

dawdle /dö'dl/ *vi* to waste time by trifling; to act or move slowly. [Cf **daddle**[1]]
■ **daw'dler** n. **daw'dlingly** *adv*.

dawk see **dak**.

dawn /dön/ *vi* to become day; to begin to grow light; to begin to appear. ◆ n (also **dawn'ing**) daybreak; beginning. [Appears first as *dawning*, prob from ON; cf Swed and Dan *dagning*]
❑ **dawn chorus** n the singing of birds at dawn. **dawn cypress** or **redwood** n a conifer, abundant as a fossil, found growing in China in the 1940s and since planted widely. **dawn'-man** n Eoanthropus (qv). **dawn raid** n a stock market operation in which a large proportion of a company's shares are suddenly bought, often in anticipation of a takeover bid.
■ **dawn on** to begin to become evident to or be understood by.

dawner see **dander**[2].

dawt, dawtie see **daut**.

DAX /daks/ n an indicator of the relative prices of leading stocks and shares on the Frankfurt Stock Exchange. [*Deutscher Aktienindex*]

■ words derived from main entry word; ❑ compound words; ■ idioms and phrasal verbs

day /dā/ *n* the time from sunrise to sunset; twenty-four hours, from midnight to midnight (formerly by some reckoned from sunrise, or sunset, or (by astronomers) from noon); the time the earth takes to make a revolution on its axis, this being the *sidereal* day (between two transits of the first point of Aries, or approximately of the same star), distinguished from the *apparent solar* day (between two transits of the sun), and the *mean solar* day (between two transits of the mean, or imaginary uniformly moving, sun); morning and afternoon, as opposed to evening and night; the hours devoted to work (*working day*); a day set apart for a purpose, such as for receiving visitors; lifetime; time of existence, vogue or influence; a time; daylight; the space between mullions of a window; ground surface over a mine. [OE *dæg*; Ger *Tag*; not L *diēs*]

■ **days** *adv* (*inf*) during the day, each day.

❑ **day bed** *n* a kind of couch or sofa; a hospital bed for a day-patient; a bed for resting on during the day. **day'-blind'ness** *n* a defect of vision in which objects are best seen by a dim light, hemeralopia. **day'-board'er** *n* a pupil who attends but does not sleep at a boarding school. **day'boat** *n* a small pleasure boat with no sleeping accommodation. **day book** *n* (*bookkeeping*) a book for entering the transactions of each day; a book of original entry. **day'-boy** or **-girl** see **day-scholar** below. **day'break** *n* dawn. **day care** *n* daytime supervision and help given by trained nursing and other staff to a group of pre-school children, or elderly or disabled people. **day care centre** or **day centre** *n* a centre which provides social amenities and/or supervision for elderly or disabled people, vagrants, alcoholics, petty offenders, etc. **day'-coal** *n* the upper stratum of coal. **day'dream** *n* a pleasant fantasy or reverie (also *vi*). **day'dreamer** *n*. **day'flower** *n* a tropical plant of the *Commelina* genus with fast-wilting blue flowers. **day'-fly** *n* a mayfly. **day hospital** *n* a hospital where patients receive treatment or therapy during the day and return home or to another hospital at night. **day'-lā'bour** *n* labour paid by the day. **day'-lā'bourer** *n*. **day'-length** *n* (*bot*) the number of hours of daylight in a day, a trigger for flowering in some plants. **day'-level** *n* (*mining*) a level driven from the surface. **day'light** *n* the light of day; a clear space. **daylight lamp** *n* (*phys*) a lamp which emits light of wavelengths similar to those of ordinary daylight. **daylight robbery** see under **rob**[1]. **day'light-sav'ing** *n* increasing the amount of daylight available for work or play, by advancing the clock, *usu* by one hour. **Daylight Saving Time** *n* the time adopted for daylight-saving purposes. **day lily** *n* a plant (genus *Hemerocallis*) whose blossoms last only for a day. **day'long** *adj* during the whole day. **day'mark** *n* an unlighted sea-mark. **day name** *n* (*W Afr*) a personal name given to indicate the day of the week on which the person was born. **day-neutral plant** *n* (*bot*) a plant in which flowering is not sensitive to day-length. **day nursery** *n* a place where young children are cared for while their parents work. **day of action** *n* a day designated by an organization for industrial action, demonstrations, etc in support of a cause. **Day of Atonement** *n* Yom Kippur. **day off** *n* a day's holiday. **Day of Judgement** *n* the day of God's final judgement on mankind. **day'-old** *adj* one day old. **day one** *n* the first day; the very beginning. **day out** *n* a day spent away from home for pleasure, as a holiday, etc; a servant's free day (*archaic*). **day'pack** *n* (*US*) a daysack. **day'-patient** *n* a hospital patient who attends for treatment (eg minor surgery) and goes home the same day. **day release** *n* a system by which workers are freed from employment during the day so as to attend an educational course. **day-release'** *adj*. **day return** *n* a *usu* reduced rail or bus fare for a journey to a place and back on the same day; a ticket for this type of journey. **day room** *n* a room used as a communal living room in a school, hospital or hostel, etc. **day'sack** *n* a small rucksack for use on short walks or hikes. **day'sailor** or **day'sailer** *n* a dayboat powered by sail. **day'-scholar** *n* a pupil who attends a boarding school during the school-hours, but lives at home (also **day'-boy** or **day'-girl**). **day school** *n* a school held during the day, as opposed both to a night school and to a boarding school. **day shift** *n* a group of workers that takes its turn during the day; the daytime period of work. **day'-sight** *n* night-blindness. **days'man** *n* (*archaic*) a person who appoints a day to hear a cause; an umpire. **Days of Awe** *n pl* High Holidays (qv under **high**[1]). **days of grace** *n pl* three days allowed for payment of bills, etc beyond the day named. **day'spring** *n* (*literary*) dawn. **day'star** *n* the morning star; the sun (*poetic*). **day surgery** *n* minor surgery that is carried out in hospital on a patient who goes home the same day. **day'tale** /-tāl/ or -*tal*/ or **dā'tal** /-*tal*/ *n* (*old*) reckoning by the day, *esp* of work or wages. **day'taler** or **dā'taller** /-*tal-ar*/ *n* a day-labourer. **day'time** *n* the time of daylight; day as opposed to evening and night. ◆ *adj* happening during the day. **day'-to-day'** *adj* daily, routine; short-term. **day trader** *n* a person who buys and sells securities on the same day with a view to making quick profits from price movements. **day trading** *n*. **day trip** *n* a trip made to somewhere and back within one day. **day'-tripper** *n*. **day'wear** *n* clothes intended for wearing during the day or informally. **day'-wea'ried** *adj* (*Shakesp*) wearied with the work of the day. **day'-work** *n*.

■ **all in a** (or **the**) **day's work** a normal or acceptable part of one's job or of what one is doing. **at the end of the day** (*inf*) when all is said and done. **back in the day** (*inf*) at some earlier time. **call it a day** to announce a decision to cease. **day about** on alternate days. **day by day** daily. **day in, day out** for an indefinite succession of days. **from day to day** concerned only with the present. **have had its** (or **one's**) **day** to have become worn-out or useless. **in the cold light of day** in full and impartial knowledge of the facts. **in this day and age** at the present time. **knock** or **beat the** (**living**) **daylights out of** (*inf*) to beat severely. **make someone's day** to make the day memorable for someone. **one day** or **one of these days** at some indefinite time in the (near) future. **scare the** (**living**) **daylights out of** (*inf*) to terrify. **see daylight** to arrive at some comprehension, illumination or prospect of a solution. **that will be the day** (*inf*) that is very unlikely. **the day** the time spoken of or expected; today (*Scot*). **the day after the fair** too late. **the other day** not long ago. **the time of day** the hour of the clock; a greeting. **those were the days** those times were the best. **win the day** to gain the victory.

Dayak see **Dyak**.

dayan /da-yan'/ *n* a senior rabbi or judge in a Jewish religious court. [Heb *dayyān*, from *dān* to judge]

dayes-man (*Spenser*) same as **daysman** (see under **day**).

dayglo or **Day-Glo**, /dā'glō/ *adj* of a luminously brilliant green, yellow, pink or orange. [*Day-glo*® a brand of paint]

day-nettle, also **dae-nettle** /dā'net'l/ *n* a dead-nettle; (in Scotland and N England) the hemp-nettle; a suppurating swelling on the finger. [Perh for **dead-nettle**; but cf ON (*akr*)*dai* hemp-nettle]

daynt (*Spenser*) see under **dainty**.

dayr'house (*Spenser*) see under **dairy**.

day-woman (*Shakesp*) same as **dey**[1].

daze /dāz/ *vt* to stun, to stupefy; to confuse, to bewilder. ◆ *n* (a state of) bewilderment; mica (*archaic*). [ON *dasa-sk* (reflexive) to be breathless]

■ **dazed** /dāzd/ *adj*. **dazedly** /dāz'id-li/ *adv*. **da'zer** *n*.

■ **in a daze** stunned.

dazzle /daz'l/ *vt* to daze or overpower with strong light; to amaze by brilliancy, beauty or cleverness. ◆ *vi* to be dazzled. ◆ *n* dazzlement. [Frequentative of **daze**]

■ **dazz'lement** *n* the act of dazzling; that which dazzles. **dazz'ler** *n*. **dazz'ling** *n* and *adj*. **dazz'lingly** *adv*.

❑ **dazz'le-paint'ing** *n* fantastic painting for camouflage.

Db (*chem*) *symbol*: dubnium.

dB *abbrev*: decibel(s).

dBA *symbol*: acoustic decibel.

DBE *abbrev*: Dame (Commander of the Order) of the British Empire.

dbl *abbrev*: double.

DBMS *abbrev*: database management system.

DBS *abbrev*: direct broadcast (or broadcasting) by satellite; direct broadcast (or broadcasting) satellite.

DC *abbrev*: da capo (*Ital*; *music*), return to the beginning; Detective Constable; direct current (also **dc**; *elec*); District Commissioner; District of Columbia (US federal district); Doctor of Chiropractic.

DCA *abbrev*: (until 2007) Department for Constitutional Affairs.

DCB *abbrev*: Dame Commander of the (Order of the) Bath.

DCC *abbrev*: digital compact cassette (see under **digit**).

DCF *abbrev*: discounted cash flow.

DCh *abbrev*: *Doctor Chirurgiae* (*L*), Doctor of Surgery.

DCI *abbrev*: Detective Chief Inspector.

DCL *abbrev*: Doctor of Civil Law.

DCLG *abbrev*: Department for Communities and Local Government.

DCM *abbrev*: Distinguished Conduct Medal (now replaced by the **CGC**); District Court Martial.

DCMG *abbrev*: Dame Commander of (the Order of) St Michael and St George.

DCMS *abbrev*: Department for Culture, Media and Sport.

DCS *abbrev*: Deputy Clerk of Session.

DCSF *abbrev*: (until 2010) Department for Children, Schools and Families.

DCVO *abbrev*: Dame Commander of the (Royal) Victorian Order.

DD *abbrev*: *Deo dedit* (*L*), gave to God; designated driver; direct debit (also **dd** or **d/d**); *Divinitatis Doctor* (*L*), Doctor of Divinity; *dono dedit* (*L*), gave as a gift (or **dd**).

D/D or **dd** *abbrev*: days after date; day's date.

dd or **d/d** see **DD** and **D/D**.

D-day see under **D** (*abbrev*).

DDD *abbrev* : *dat, dicat, dedicat* (*L*), gives, devotes and dedicates; *dono dedit dedicavit* (*L*), gave and dedicated as a gift.

DDE *abbrev* : dichlorophenyldichloroethylene, a chemical produced by the breakdown of DDT; dynamic data exchange, a system for immediately updating similar data in two or more applications (*comput*).

DDR *abbrev* : (until October 1990) *Deutsche Demokratische Republik* (*Ger*), German Democratic Republic (East Germany).

DDS *abbrev* : digital data storage; Doctor of Dental Surgery.

DDT see **dichlorodiphenyltrichloroethane** under **dichlor-**.

DE *abbrev* : Delaware (US state); Department of Employment.

de- /dē-, di-/ *pfx* (1) meaning down from, away; (2) indicating a reversal of process, or deprivation; (3) used intensively. [L, or Fr, from L]

DEA *abbrev* : Department of Economic Affairs; Drug Enforcement Administration (*US*).

deaccession /dē-ak-sesh'ən/ *vt* to remove (a book or work of art) from the holdings of a library, museum, etc in order to sell it (also *n*). [**de-** (2)]

deacon /dē'kən/ *n* in Episcopal churches, a member of the order of clergy under priests; (in some Presbyterian churches) an officer, man or woman, distinct from the elders, who attends to the secular affairs of the church; (in Congregational and some other churches) an officer who advises the pastor, distributes the bread and wine at communion, and dispenses charity; (in Scotland) the master of an incorporated company; an adept (*Scot*); the skin of a very young calf. See also **diaconate**. [L *diāconus*, from Gr *diākonos* a servant]

■ **dea'coness** *n* a female servant of the Christian society in the time of the apostles; (in a convent) a nun who has the care of the altar; a member of an order of women in some Protestant churches whose duties are pastoral, educational, social and evangelical. **dea'conhood** *n*. **dea'conry** *n*. **dea'conship** *n*.

■ **permanent deacon** an officer in the Roman Catholic Church, minimally below a priest.

deacquisition /dē-ak-wi-zish'ən/ *vt* to deaccession (also *n*). [**de-** (2)]

deactivate /dē-ak'ti-vāt/ *vt* to diminish or remove the activity of. [**de-** (2)]

■ **deactiva'tion** *n*.

dead /ded/ *adj* no longer alive; inanimate; deathlike; (of a ball) at rest, out of play; out of use; obsolete; inactive; no longer alight; cold and cheerless; dull; numb; insensitive; unproductive; as good as dead; inelastic; without vegetation; utter, complete, absolute (*sl*); unerring. ◆ *vt* (*obs*) to deaden, dull; to benumb. ◆ *vi* (*obs*) to lose vitality; to become numb. ◆ *adv* in a dead manner; absolutely; utterly; directly; exactly (*inf*); extremely, *esp* as *intensive* eg *dead easy, dead slow*. ◆ *n* the time of greatest stillness, coldness, etc, eg *the dead of night, of winter*. [OE *dēad*; Gothic *dauths*, Ger *tot*, from root of **die**[1]]

■ **dead'en** *vt* to make dead; to deprive partly of vigour, sensibility or sensation; to blunt; to lessen; to make soundproof. **dead'ener** *n*. **dead'ening** *n* and *adj*. **dead'er** *n* (*inf*) a corpse. **dead'liness** *n*. **dead'ly** *adj* causing death; fatal; implacable; very great (*inf*). ◆ *adv* in a manner resembling death; extremely (*inf*). **dead'ness** *n*.

❑ **dead air** *n* an unintentional and undesirable period of silence during a radio broadcast. **dead'-alive** or **dead'-and-alive** *adj* dull, inactive. **dead-ball line** *n* (*rugby*) a line marked out behind the goal-line at each end of the pitch, beyond which the ball is out of play. **dead'beat** *n* (*inf*) a down-and-out; a lazy person; one who does not pay debts (*US*). **dead-beat** *adj* (*inf*) quite overcome, exhausted. **dead-beat escapement** *n* a clock escapement in which there is no recoil to the escape wheel. **dead'-bolt** or **-lock** *n* one moved by turning the key or knob without intervention of a spring. **dead'-born** *adj* stillborn. **dead'-cart** *n* a cart for collecting the bodies of those who died of a pestilence. **dead-cat bounce** *n* (*stock exchange sl*) a temporary recovery of share prices following a sharp fall, not indicative of a true upturn but merely caused by some reinvestment by speculators who had already sold shares. **dead centre** *n* in a reciprocating engine or pump, either of the positions, at top and bottom of a piston stroke, at which the crank and connecting rod are in line and there is no actual turning effect (*usu* **top** or **bottom dead centre**); a non-rotating centre in the tailstock of a lathe. **dead cert** *n* (*sl*) something absolutely certain, eg a certain winner in a horse race. **dead'-clothes** *n pl* clothes to bury the dead in. **dead'-col'ouring** *n* the first broad outlines of a picture. **dead'-deal** *n* a board for measuring and lifting a corpse. **dead'-do'ing** *adj* (*Spenser*) putting to death, destructive. **dead drop** same as **dead-letter box** below. **dead duck** *n* (*inf*) a plan, idea or person, etc that has no chance of success or survival. **dead end** *n* a pipe, passage,

etc closed at one end; a blind alley (*lit* and *fig*). **dead-end'** *adj* leading nowhere (*lit* and *fig*). **dead'eye** *n* a round, flattish wooden block with a rope or iron band passing around it, and pierced with three holes for a lanyard (*naut*); an unerring marksman. **dead'-fall** *n* a trap with a weight that falls when its support is removed. **dead'-fin'ish** *n* (*Aust*) a thicket or a thicket-forming shrub of the mimosa family (genus *Albizia* or *Acacia*); a complete standstill or vanquishment. **dead'-fire** *n* an appearance of fire taken as an omen of death. **dead'-freight** *n* money paid for the empty space in a ship by a person who engages to freight her, but fails to make out a full cargo. **dead'-ground** *n* (*milit*) ground that cannot be covered by fire. **dead hand** *n* a persisting oppressive influence; mortmain. **dead'-head** or **dead'head** *n* a person who enjoys privileges without paying, eg a seat in a theatre, etc; an ineffective, unproductive person; a sprue (see **sprue**[1]). ◆ *vt* to remove the withered heads of (flowers), in order to encourage further growth. **dead heat** *n* a heat or race in which two or more competitors are equal; the result of this, a tie. **dead-heat'** *vi*. **dead'house** *n* a mortuary. **dead language** *n* one no longer spoken. **dead'-lett'er** *n* a letter undelivered and unclaimed at the post-office; a law or ordinance made but not enforced. **dead-letter box** or **drop** *n* a place where secret messages, etc may be left for later collection. **dead'-lift** or **-pull** *n* a lift or pull made without help or leverage, etc; hence an effort under discouraging conditions. **dead'lights** *n pl* storm-shutters for a cabin window; thick windows in a ship's side or deck. **dead'line** *n* closing date, last possible time; *orig* a line in a military prison, on going beyond which a prisoner was liable to be shot. **dead load** *n* the weight of a structure, vehicle, etc itself without any burden. **dead'lock** *n* the case when matters have become so complicated that all is at a complete standstill; see also **dead-bolt** above. ◆ *vi* and *vt* to reach or bring to a standstill because of difficulties, etc. **dead loss** *n* a complete loss; a useless ally or endeavour (*fig*). **dead'-lev'el** *n* a stretch of land without any rising ground; sameness. **deadly nightshade** *n* belladonna. **deadly sin** *n* a mortal sin (see under **seven**). **dead man's handle** *n* a device, eg on an electric train, which allows current to pass only so long as there is pressure on it. **dead man's pedal** *n* a foot-operated safety device on the same principle, used *esp* on diesel trains. **dead march** *n* a piece of solemn music played at funeral processions, *esp* of soldiers. **dead'-meat** *n* the flesh of animals ready for the market. **dead men** *n pl* (*inf*) empty bottles after a party or drinking bout. **dead-men's bells** *n* the foxglove. **dead men's fingers** *n pl* a type of soft coral, a very common actinozoan coelenterate (*Alcyonium digitatum*); the poisonous parts of a crab or other edible shellfish (*inf*). **dead'-nettle** *n* any species of *Lamium*, labiate plants superficially like nettles but stingless. **dead-on'** *adj* (*inf*) accurate, spot-on (see also **dead on** below). **dead'pan** *n* an expressionless face; a person having or assuming such a face. ◆ *adj* expressionless; emotionless; completely serious or mock serious. ◆ *adv* in a deadpan manner. **dead'-pay** *n* continued pay dishonestly drawn for men who are actually dead. **dead point** *n* another (eg *engineering*) name for **dead centre** above. **dead'-reck'oning** *n* an estimation of a ship's or aircraft's place simply by the logbook. **dead ringer** *n* (*sl*) a person who, or a thing that, looks exactly like someone or something else. **dead'-rope** *n* a rope not running in any block. **Dead Sea apple** or **fruit** *n* another name for **apple of Sodom** (see under **apple**). **dead'-set'** *n* a complete standstill, as of a gun dog pointing at game; a determined and prolonged onslaught, *esp* with a view to captivation. ◆ *adj* absolutely determined. **dead shot** *n* an unerring marksman. **dead's part** *n* (*Scots law*) the part of a person's moveable property which may be bequeathed by will, and which is not due to spouse and children. **dead spit** *n* (*inf*) an exact likeness. **dead'stock** *n* farm equipment. **dead'stroke** *adj* without recoil. **dead tree edition** *n* (*comput sl*) a paper version of material also available electronically. **dead'-wall** *n* a wall unbroken by windows or other openings. **dead'-wa'ter** *n* still water; eddy water closing in behind a ship's stern. **dead'-weight** *n* unrelieved weight; heavy and oppressive burden; difference in a ship's displacement loaded and light. **dead white European male** *n* (*inf*) any of the writers, philosophers, etc traditionally studied and seen by some as representing an excessively Eurocentric and masculine view of culture. **dead'-wind** *n* calm (in the vortex of a storm); headwind (*obs*). **dead wood** or **dead'-wood** *n* pieces of timber laid on the upper side of the keel at either end; useless material or personnel. **dead'-work** *n* work, itself unprofitable, but necessary as a preliminary.

■ **be dead meat** (*inf*) to be in very serious trouble. **dead against** see **dead set against** below. **dead as a dodo, as a doornail, as a herring** or **as mutton** absolutely dead. **dead drunk** helplessly drunk. **dead from the neck up** (*inf*) impenetrably stupid. **dead in the water** (of a ship) without the power to move; unable to make progress or succeed (*fig*). **dead men's shoes** succession to someone who dies. **dead on** (used of time, musical notes, etc) exact or exactly. **dead set** see under **set**. **dead set against** or **dead against** utterly opposed to.

dead to the world (*inf*) very soundly asleep; unconscious. **I**, etc **wouldn't be seen dead** (*inf*) I, etc would make sure never to be seen. **leave for dead** to abandon, presuming dead; to surpass spectacularly (*inf*). **over my dead body** (*inf*) when I am beyond caring, and not until then. **put the dead wood on** (*sl*) to gain a great advantage over. **the dead** those who are dead.

deaf /def/ *adj* with no, or with impaired, hearing; not willing to hear; inattentive; hollow, with no kernel (now *dialect*). [OE *dēaf*; Du *doof*, Ger *taub*]
■ **deaf'en** *vt* to make deaf; to stun (with noise); to render impervious to sound. **deaf'ening** *n* stuffing put into floors, partition walls, etc to prevent sounds from passing through. ◆ *adj* making deaf (with noise); very loud. **deaf'ly** *adv.* **deaf'ness** *n.*
▫ **deaf aid** *n* a hearing aid. **deaf alphabet** *n* digital and manual signs used to express letters (and words and phrases) visually (also **deaf-and-dumb alphabet**, a name now deprecated). **deaf language** *n* sign language used by the deaf (also **deaf-and-dumb language**, a name now deprecated). **deaf'-mute'** *n* and *adj* (a person who is) both deaf and dumb (considered *offensive* by some deaf people). **deaf'-mut'ism** *n.*
■ **deaf as a post** absolutely deaf. **turn a deaf ear (to)** to pretend not to have heard; to ignore.

deal[1] /dēl/ *n* a portion; an indefinite quantity; a large quantity; the act of distributing cards; a business transaction (*esp* a favourable one); treatment. ◆ *vt* (pat and pap **dealt** /delt/) to divide, to distribute; to throw about; to deliver; to peddle (illegal drugs) (*inf*). ◆ *vi* to transact business (in); to act; to distribute cards; to peddle illegal drugs (*inf*). [OE *dǣlan*, from *dǣl* a part; Ger *teilen*, from *Teil* a part or division; cf **dole**[1]]
■ **deal'er** *n* a person who deals (cards) or whose turn it is to deal, or who has dealt the hand in play; a trader; a person who peddles illegal drugs (*inf*). **deal'ership** *n* the state of being a dealer; the authority to sell products or services as an appointed dealer; dealers as a group. **deal'ing** *n* (often in *pl*) manner of acting towards others; business transactions.
▫ **deal'breaker** *n* a factor that is or threatens to be a bar to the successful completion of a transaction. **dealer brand** *n* a retailer's own brand label.
■ **deal with** to have to do with, to treat of; to take action in regard to.

deal[2] /dēl/ *n* a fir or pine board of a standard size; soft wood. ◆ *adj* made of deal. [MLGer *dele*; cf OE *thel*, *thille*, and Mod **thill**[1]]
▫ **deal'fish** *n* a ribbonfish (genus *Trachypterus*).

dealbate /dē-al'bāt/ *adj* whitened. [L *dealbāre*, *-ātum* to whitewash, from pfx *de-* in sense of over a surface, and *albus* white]
■ **dealbā'tion** *n.*

de-alcoholize or **-ise** /dē-al'ko-ho-līz/ *vt* to reduce the amount of alcohol in (wine, beer, etc).

dealt see **deal**[1].

deambulatory /dē-am'bū-lə-tər-i/ *n* a place for walking about in; a passage or aisle round the choir and apse of a church. [L *deambulāre*, *-ātum* to walk about]

deaminate /dē-am'i-nāt/ *vt* to remove an amino group from (a chemical compound). [**de-** (2)]
■ **deaminā'tion** *n.*

dean[1] /dēn/ *n* a dignitary in cathedral and collegiate churches who presides over the canons; a rural dean; the chief cardinal-bishop of the College of Cardinals; the president of a faculty in a college or of the *Faculty of Advocates*; a resident fellow of a college who has administrative and disciplinary functions; the senior member of a corps or body; the chief chaplain of the Chapel Royal; the chief judge of the Court of Arches; the president of a trade-guild. [OFr *deien* (Fr *doyen*), from LL *decānus* or Gr *dekānos* a chief of ten, from L *decem* or Gr *deka* ten]
■ **dean'ery** *n* the office of a dean; a group of parishes presided over by a dean; a dean's house. **dean'ship** *n* the office or rank of a dean.
▫ **Dean of Arches** *n* dean of the Court of Arches (see under **arch**[1]). **Dean of Faculty** *n* president of the *Faculty of Advocates* in Scotland. **Dean of Guild** *n* formerly, a municipal functionary in Scotland who had authority over building and altering of houses.
■ **rural dean** a clergyman who, under the bishop, has the special care and inspection of the clergy in certain parishes.

dean[2] or **dene** /dēn/ *n* a small valley. [OE *denu* a valley; cf **den**[1]]

deaner /dē'nər/ (*old sl*) *n* a shilling. [Prob L *denārius*]

dear[1] /dēr/ *adj* high in price; costly; characterized by high prices; scarce; highly valued; beloved; a conventional form of address used in letter-writing; earnest (*Shakesp*). ◆ *n* a person who is dear or beloved; a kind, lovable person; an affectionate term of address (also **dear'ie** or **dear'y**). ◆ *adv* at a high price; dearly. ◆ *interj* indicating surprise, pity, or other emotion. [OE *dēore*, *dȳre*; cognate with Ger *teuer*]

■ **dear'est** *adj* most dear. ◆ *n* an affectionate term of address. **dear'ling** *n* and *adj* (*Spenser*) darling. **dear'ly** *adv* affectionately; earnestly; at great cost. **dear'ness** *n.*
▫ **dear'bought** *adj* (*poetic*) precious. **Dear John letter** *n* (*inf*; *orig US*) a letter from a woman to her husband or boyfriend ending their relationship.
■ **dear knows** an expression of ignorance. **dear me** or **dearie** (or **deary**) **me** an expression of dismay, etc. **oh dear!** an expression of surprise, sorrow, pity or dismay.

dear[2], **deare** or **deere** /dēr/ (*Spenser*; *Shakesp*; *Milton*) *adj* grievous (also *adv*). [OE *dēor*]

deare see **dere**.

dearn, dearnful, dearnly see **dern**[2], etc.

dearth /dûrth/ *n* scarcity; want; famine; barrenness; dearness, high price (*obs*). [**dear**[1]]

dearticulate /dē-är-tik'ū-lāt/ *vt* to disjoint. [**de-** (2)]

deasil, also **deasoil**, **deiseal**, **deisheal** or **deasiul** /dē'zl, des'l, desh'l, dē'shl/ (*Scot*) *n* sunwise motion, *opp* to *withershins*. ◆ *adv* sunwise. [Gaelic *deiseil*]

deaspirate /dē-as'pi-rāt/ *vt* to remove the aspirate from. [**de-** (2)]
■ **deaspirā'tion** *n.*

death /deth/ *n* the state of being dead; extinction or cessation of life; manner of dying; mortality; a deadly plague; the cause of death; the end or destruction of something; a thing considered as fearsome or painful, etc as death; spiritual lifelessness; the killing of the animal in hunting. [OE *dēath*; Ger *Tod*; see **dead** and **die**[1]]
■ **death'ful** *adj* deadly, destructive; mortal; deathlike. **death'less** *adj* never dying; everlasting. **death'lessness** *n.* **death'like** *adj* deadly; like death. **death'liness** *n.* **death'ly** *adj* deadly; deathlike. **death'ward** or **death'wards** *adv.* **death'y** *adj.*
▫ **death adder** *n* a poisonous Australian elapid snake (*Acanthophis antarcticus*). **death'-ag'ony** *n* the struggle often preceding death. **death angel** *n* death cap. **death'bed** *n* the bed on which a person dies; the last illness; see also **on one's deathbed** below. **deathbed repentance** *n* repentance for one's faults, sins, etc when it is too late to reform one's life. **death'-bell** *n* the passing bell. **death'blow** *n* a blow that causes death; an action that brings about the end (*fig*). **death cap** or **cup** *n* a very poisonous toadstool (*Amanita phalloides*) often mistaken for an edible mushroom. **death cell** *n* a prison cell for condemned prisoners awaiting execution. **death certificate** *n* a legal certificate on which a doctor states the fact and *usu* the cause of a person's death. **death'-damp** *n* a cold sweat preceding death. **death'-dealing** *adj* fatal, likely to cause death. **death duty** *n* (often in *pl*) duty paid on inheritance of property (now replaced by **inheritance tax** (see under **inherit**)). **death'-fire** *n* a light supposed to presage death. **death futures** *n pl* the life insurance policies of people who are terminally ill, bought for a lump sum by an investor who receives the proceeds of the policy on the death of the insured. **death house** *n* (*US inf*) death row. **death knell** *n* the ringing of a bell to announce a death; something that announces the end of one's hopes, ambitions, etc (*fig*). **death'-marked** *adj* marked for or by death, destined to die. **death mask** *n* a plaster cast taken from the face after death. **death'match** *n* (*inf*) in computer games, a mode of play in which players deliberately attempt to eliminate one another. **death metal** *n* a particularly loud and fast style of heavy metal music, *usu* characterized by a preoccupation with death, the vocabulary and imagery of horror films and the occult. **death penalty** *n* the legal taking of a person's life as punishment for crime. **death'-prac'tised** *adj* (*Shakesp*) threatened with death by malicious arts. **death rate** *n* the proportion of deaths to the population. **death rattle** *n* a rattling in the throat that sometimes precedes death. **death ray** *n* an imaginary ray able to kill. **death roll** *n* (*obs*) a death toll. **death row** *n* (*US*) the part of a prison where prisoners who have been sentenced to death are confined. **death's'-head** *n* the skull of a human skeleton, or a figure of it; a memorial ring bearing such a figure. **death's-head moth** *n* a hawk moth with pale markings on the back of the thorax somewhat like a skull. **death slide** *n* another name for a zipwire. **deaths'man** *n* (*Shakesp*) an executioner. **death'-song** *n* a song sung before dying. **death squad** *n* an unofficial terrorist group who murder those whose views or activities they disapprove of, often operating with the tacit or covert support of the government of the country. **death star** *n* a small thin star-shaped metal plate with sharpened points, used as a missile. **death'-stroke** *n* a death blow. **death throe** *n* the dying agony. **death'-token** *n* (*Shakesp*) a sign or token of impending death, a plague-spot. **death toll** *n* a list of the dead, eg after an accident or a natural disaster. **death'trap** *n* an unsafe structure, vehicle or place that exposes one to great danger of death. **death warrant** *n* an order from the authorities for the execution of a criminal. **death'watch** *n* a vigil, a watch kept beside a dying person; a deathwatch beetle. **deathwatch beetle** *n* a beetle that makes a ticking noise, found *esp* in house timbers (genus *Xestobium*). **death wish** *n* (*psychol*) a wish, conscious

or unconscious, for death for oneself or another. **death'-wound** *n* a wound that causes death.

■ **at death's door** very near to death. **catch one's death** (**of cold**) (*inf*) to catch a very bad cold. **death on** fatal to, fond of, good at. **do** or **put to death** to kill; to cause to be killed. **gates** or **jaws of death** the point of death. **in at the death** having caught up with a hunted animal before the dogs have killed it; present at the finish, crux, climax, etc of anything (*fig*). **like death warmed up** or **over** (*inf*) very unwell. **like grim death** tenaciously. **on one's deathbed** about to die. **sign one's own death warrant** to do something that makes one's downfall inevitable. **to death** (until) dead; to a state of exhaustion; to a point of overuse. **to the death** to the very end.

deattribute /dē-ə-trib'ūt/ *vt* to withdraw the attribution of (a work of art or literature, etc) to a particular artist, writer, etc. [**de-** (2)]

deave or **deeve** /dēv/ (*Scot* and *dialect*) *vt* to deafen; to worry (*esp* with noise); to bother; to break. [See **deaf**]

deaw and **deawy** or **deawie** (*Spenser*) same as **dew**¹ and **dewy**.

deb /deb/ *n* an informal form of **debutante**.

debacle or **débâcle** /di-bak'l or dā-bä'kl/ *n* a complete failure, break-up or collapse; a breaking up of ice on a river; a sudden flood of water leaving its path strewed with debris (*geol*); a stampede. [Fr *débâcle*; *dé-*, *des-*, and *bâcler* to bar, from L *baculus* a stick]

debag /di-bag'/ (*inf*) *vt* to remove the trousers of, as a prank or punishment. [**de-** (2) and **bags**]
■ **debagg'ing** *n*.

debar /di-bär'/ *vt* (**debarr'ing**; **debarred'**) to bar out; to exclude; to hinder. [**de-** (3)]
■ **debar'ment** *n*.

debark¹ /di-bärk'/ *vt* or *vi* to disembark. [Fr *débarquer*, from *des* (from L *dis-*) away, and Fr *barque* a ship]
■ **dēbarka'tion** or **dēbarcā'tion** *n*.

debark² /dē-bärk'/ *vt* to strip the bark from. [**de-** (2)]

debarrass /di-bar'əs/ (*archaic*) *vt* to disembarrass, disentangle, free. [Fr *débarrasser*; *dé-*, *des-*, and *barre* a bar]

debase /di-bās'/ *vt* to lower; to make poor (of quality) or of less value; to adulterate. [**de-** (1)]
■ **debased'** *adj* degraded; reversed (*heraldry*). **debās'edness** *n*. **debāse'ment** *n* degradation. **debās'er** *n*. **debās'ing** *adj*. **debās'ingly** *adv*.

debate /di-bāt'/ *n* argument; a formal discussion, *esp* in parliament or some other forum; fight, strife (*obs*). ◆ *vt* to contend for in argument; to argue about; to fight for (*archaic*). ◆ *vi* to deliberate; to consider; to join in debate; to fight, contend (*obs*). [OFr *debatre*, from L *dē*, and *batuere* to beat]
■ **debāt'able** or **debate'able** *adj* liable to be disputed; open to argument; contentious. **debate'ful** *adj* (*obs*; *Spenser*) quarrelsome. **debate'ment** *n* (*obs*; *Spenser* and *Shakesp*) controversy. **debāt'er** *n*. **debāt'ingly** *adv*.
❑ **Debatable** (or **Debateable**) **Land** *n* a tract of border land between the rivers Esk and Sark, formerly claimed by both England and Scotland.

debauch /di-böch'/ *vt* to lead away from duty or allegiance; to corrupt with lewdness; to seduce; to vitiate. ◆ *vi* to overindulge. ◆ *n* a fit or period of intemperance or lewdness. [OFr *desbaucher* (Fr *débaucher*) to corrupt, from *des-* (L *dis-*) and *baucher* to hew]
■ **debauched'** *adj* corrupt; profligate. **debauch'edly** *adv*. **debauch'edness** *n*. **debauchee** /di-böch-ē'* or *-bösh-ē'/ *n* a libertine. **debauch'er** *n*. **debauch'ery** *n* excessive intemperance; habitual lewdness. **debauch'ment** *n*.

debby see under **debut**.

debel /di-bel'/ (*obs*; *Milton*) *vt* (**debell'ing**; **debelled'**) to conquer in war. [L *dēbellāre*, from *dē* down, and *bellāre* to war, from *bellum* war]

debenture /di-ben'chər/ *n* a written acknowledgement of a debt; a security issued by a company for money borrowed on the company's property, having a fixed rate of interest and *usu* fixed redemption rates; a certificate entitling an exporter of imported goods to a repayment of the duty paid on their importation. [L *dēbentur* there are due (the first word of the receipt), 3rd pers pl passive of *dēbēre* to owe]
■ **debent'ured** *adj* (of goods) entitled to drawback or debenture.

debilitate /di-bil'i-tāt/ *vt* to make weak; to impair the strength of. [L *dēbilitāre*, *-ātum*, from *dēbilis* weak, from *dē*, and *habilis* able. See **ability**]
■ **debile** /deb'il or dē'bīl/ *adj* (*archaic*) weak, feeble. **debil'itating** *adj*. **debilitā'tion** *n*. **debil'itative** *adj*. **debil'ity** *n* weakness and languor; a weak action of the bodily functions.

debit /deb'it/ *n* a debt or something due; a sum removed from a bank account; an entry on the left-hand column of an account, recording an asset (*bookkeeping*); the side of an account on which such entries are made (*bookkeeping*). ◆ *vt* to charge with debt; to deduct from a bank

account; to enter on the debit side of an account. [L *dēbitum* what is due, from *dēbēre* to owe]
■ **deb'itor** *n* (*obs*; *Shakesp*) a debtor.
❑ **debit card** *n* a card used by a purchaser by means of which money is directly transferred from his or her bank account to the retailer's. **debit note** *n* a document advising an account holder that his or her account has been debited with the amount shown.

de-blur /dē-blûr'/ *vt* (**de-blurr'ing**; **de-blurred'**) to make (blurred photographs) sharp, *esp* with the aid of computers. [**de-** (2)]

debonair or **debonnaire** /deb-ə-nār'/ *adj* of good appearance and manners; elegant; courteous; carefree. [Fr *de* of, *bon* good, and the old word *aire* (masc) manner, origin; Mod Fr *débonnaire*]
■ **debonair'ly** *adv*. **debonair'ness** *n*.

debosh /di-bosh'/ an old form of **debauch**.

deboss /di-bos'/ *vt* to impress (a design, symbol, character, etc) into, *opp* to **emboss**. [**de-** (2) and **boss**²]

debouch /di-bowch', di-boosh'/ *vi* to issue or emerge, to march or flow out from a narrow pass or confined place. [Fr *déboucher*, from *de* from, and *bouche* mouth, from L *bucca* cheek]
■ **débouché** /dā-boo-shā'/ *n* an outlet. **debouch'ment** *n* an act or place of debouching. **debouchure** /di-boo-shūr'/ *n* the mouth of a river or strait.

Debrett /di-bret'/ or **Debrett's Peerage** /pēr'əj/ *n* a peerage edited and published from 1784 until his death by John Field *Debrett*, still in publication and the model for all exclusive lists.

débridement /dā-brēd-mä' (*Fr*), dā-brēd'mənt or dī-/ (*med*) *n* the removal of foreign matter or dead or infected tissue from a wound. [Fr, literally unbridling]
■ **débride'** *vt* to clean or treat (a wound) by débridement; to remove (dead tissue, etc) by débridement.

debrief /dē-brēf'/ *vt* to gather information from (soldiers, spies, etc) at the end of a mission or activity. [**de-** (2)]
■ **debrief'ing** *n*.

debris or **débris** /deb'rē, də-brē', dā'-brē/ *n* wreckage; ruins; rubbish; a mass of rocky fragments. [Fr, from *briser*, related to **bruise**]

debruised /di-broozd'/ (*heraldry*) *adj* surmounted or partly covered by one of the ordinaries. [OFr *debruisier*, from *de-* apart, and *bruiser* to break]

debt /det/ *n* an amount owed by one person to another; what one becomes liable to do or suffer; a state of obligation or indebtedness; a duty; a sin (*Bible*). [OFr *dette*, from L *dēbitum*, *dēbēre* to owe]
■ **deb'ted** *adj* (*Shakesp*) indebted, obliged. **debtee'** *n* a creditor. **debt'or** *n* a person who or country, body, etc that owes a debt.
❑ **debt bondage** *n* a system (often amounting to virtual slavery) whereby a person is obliged to work for a moneylender in an attempt to pay off debt. **debt overhang** *n* (*econ*) a situation which arises when a government or company faces such a level of debt that it is not expected to be able to repay it in the future, resulting in decreased spending on infrastructure and lower levels of investment. **debt swap** *n* a financial transaction in which debt liabilities are exchanged with the aim of profiting from differing rates. **debt of honour** *n* a debt not recognized by law, but binding in honour (*esp* a gambling or betting debt). **debt of nature** *n* death.
■ **bad debt** a debt of which there is no prospect of payment. **floating debt** miscellaneous public debt, like exchequer and treasury bills, as opposed to **funded debt**, that which has been converted into perpetual annuities like consols in Britain. **in someone's debt** under an obligation (not necessarily pecuniary) to someone. **national debt** see under **nation**¹.

debug /dē-bug'/ *vt* to remove concealed listening devices from; to find faults or errors in and remove them from (*esp* a machine or a computer program); to remove insects from (*inf*). [L *dē* from, and **bug**¹]
■ **debugg'er** *n* a computer program designed to find and remove faults or errors.

debunk /dē-bungk'/ (*inf*) *vt* to clear of bunk or humbug; to remove the whitewash from (a reputation); to show up (eg a theory) as false. [**de-** (2)]
■ **debunk'er** *n*.

debur /dē-bûr'/ *vt* to remove rough edges from (a metal object, piece of wood, etc). [**de-** (2)]

debus /dē-bus'/ *vt* and *vi* (**debuss'ing**; **debussed'**) to unload from or get out of a bus or other vehicle. [**de-** (1)]

debut or **début** /dā-bū' or dā'bū/ *n* a beginning or first attempt; a first appearance before the public, or in society. ◆ *vi* to start, make a first appearance. [Fr *début* a first stroke, from *débuter*, from *de* from, and *but* aim, mark]
■ **debb'y** *adj* (*inf*) of or like a deb (see below) or debs. **debutant** /deb'ū-tənt/ or **débutant** /dā-bū-tä/ *n* a male performer who makes

his first appearance. **debutante** /deb'ū-tənt/ or **débutante** /dā-bü-tät/ n a young woman making her first appearance in society (shortened to inf **deb** or **debb'y**); a female performer making her first appearance.

Debye /də-bī'/ or **Debye unit** /ū'nit/ n a unit of electric dipole moment. [PJW Debye (1884–1966), Dutch physicist]

DEC abbrev : Disasters Emergency Committee.

Dec. abbrev : December.

dec. abbrev : deceased; declaration (also **dec**); declension (also **decl.**).

deca- /dek-ə-/ combining form in names of units, denoting ten times (10¹). [Gr deka]

decachord /dek'ə-körd/ n an old ten-stringed musical instrument. [Gr dekachordos, from deka ten, and chordē a string]

decade /dek'ād, di-kād', dek'əd/ or (obs) **decad** /-ad/ n a series of ten years; any group or series of ten. [Gr dekas, -ados, from deka ten]
■ **dec'adal** adj.

decadence /dek'ə-dəns/ or **decadency** /-i/ n state of decay; a decline from a superior state, standard or time; applied to a school in late 19c French literature, the symbolists, and their like. [Fr décadence, from LL dēcadentia, from L dē down, and cadere to fall]
■ **dec'adent** adj decaying, declining; lacking in moral and physical vigour; symbolist (see above). ♦ n a degenerate person; a symbolist (see above). **dec'adently** adv.

decaffeinate /dē-kaf'i-nāt/ vt to extract (most of) the caffeine from (coffee, tea, cola, etc). [**de-** (2)]
■ **de'caf** or **de'caff** n (inf) decaffeinated coffee. **decaff'einated** adj.

decagon /dek'ə-gon/ n a plane figure of ten angles and sides. [Gr deka ten, and gōniā an angle]
■ **decagonal** /-ag'ən-əl/ adj.

decagramme or **decagram** /dek'ə-gram/ n a weight of ten grammes. [Fr décagramme, from Gr deka ten, and **gramme**]

Decagynia /dek-ə-jin'i-ə/ (bot) n pl (in the Linnaean system) a class of plants with ten pistils. [Gr deka ten, and gynē a woman]
■ **decagyn'ian** or **decagynous** /-aj'/ adj.

decahedron /dek-ə-hē'drən/ n a solid figure having ten faces. [Gr deka ten, and hedrā a seat]
■ **decahē'dral** adj.

decal /dē'kal, dek'al/ n a transfer (picture or design). [Short form of decalcomania]

decalcify /dē-kal'si-fī/ vt to deprive of calcium. [**de-** (2)]
■ **decalcifica'tion** n.

decalcomania /dē-kal'ko-mā-ni-ə/ n the art or process of transferring a design from specially prepared paper onto another surface; a design transferred in this way. [Fr décalcomanie, from décalquer to trace, copy]

decalescence /dē-kəl-es'əns/ n the behaviour of iron or steel which in heating from red to white reaches a point where it seems to go back for a little (cf **recalescence**). [L dē down, and calēscere to grow hot]

decalitre /dek'ə-lē-tər/ n ten litres, 2.20 imperial gallons, 2.64 US gallons. [Fr décalitre, from Gr deka ten, and lītrā a pound]

decalogue /dek'ə-log/ n the ten commandments (see under **command**). [Gr deka ten, and logos a discourse]
■ **decalogist** /dē-kal'ə-jist/ n someone who writes or preaches about the decalogue.

Decameron /di-kam'ə-ron, -rən/ n Boccaccio's book of a hundred tales, supposed to be told in ten days. [Gr deka ten, and hēmerā a day]
■ **decameron'ic** adj.

decamerous /di-kam'ər-əs/ adj having the parts in tens. [Gr deka ten, and meros part]

decametre /dek'ə-mē-tər/ n ten metres. [Fr décamètre, from Gr deka ten, and metron a measure]

decamp /di-kamp'/ vi to make off, esp secretly; to break camp. [Fr décamper]
■ **decamp'ment** n.

decanal /de-kā'nəl/ adj relating to a dean or deanery; decani. [LL decānus, -ī]
■ **decān'ī** adj denoting the south side of a church choir where the dean sits, opp to cantoris.

Decandria /de-kan'dri-ə/ (bot) n pl (in the Linnaean system) a class of plants with ten stamens. [Gr deka ten, and anēr, andros a man, male]
■ **decan'drian** adj. **decan'drous** adj with ten stamens.

decane /dek'ān/ (chem) n a hydrocarbon ($C_{10}H_{22}$), tenth of the alkane series. [Gr deka ten]

decani see under **decanal**.

decant /di-kant'/ vt to pour off, leaving sediment; to pour from one vessel into another; to move (people) to another area, etc. [Fr décanter (Ital decantare), from L dē from, and canthus beak of a vessel, from Gr kanthos corner of the eye]
■ **decantā'tion** /dē-/ n.

decantate /dē-kan'tāt/ (obs) vt and vi to chant or say repeatedly. [L dēcantāre, from pfx dē-, and cantāre, intensive of canere to sing]

decanter /di-kan'tər/ n an ornamental stoppered bottle for holding decanted liquor. [**decant**]

decapitalization or **-s-** /di-kap-it-əl-ī-zā'shən/ n loss or draining away of capital in industry. [**de-** (2)]
■ **decap'italize** or **-ise** vt.

decapitate /di-kap'i-tāt/ vt to behead. [LL dēcapitāre, from L dē from, and caput, capitis the head]
■ **decapitā'tion** n.

Decapoda /di-kap'ə-də/ n pl an order of higher crustaceans with ten feet (including pincers), ie crabs, lobsters, shrimps, prawns, etc; an order of cephalopods with ten arms. [Gr deka ten, and pous, podos a foot]
■ **dec'apod** n a member of either of these orders (also adj). **decap'odal, decap'odan** or **decap'odous** adj.

decapsulate /dē-kap'sū-lāt/ (surg) vt to remove the capsule from (a body part). [**de-** (2)]

decarbonize or **-ise** /dē-kär'bə-nīz/ vt (also **decar'burize** or **-ise**; **decar'bonate**) to remove carbon or carbon dioxide from. [**de-** (2)]
■ **decarb'** vt an earlier form of **decoke**. **decarbonā'tion** n. **decarbonīzā'tion** or **-s-** n. **decarburīzā'tion** or **-s-** n.

decarboxylase /dē-kär-bok'si-lāz/ (bot) n an enzyme that catalyses the removal of carbon dioxide from its substrate (**decarboxylā'tion**). [**de-** (2), **carboxyl** and **-ase**]

decare /dek'är, dek-är'/ n 1000 square metres, 10 ares. [Gr deka ten, and **are²**]

decastere /dek'ə-stēr/ n ten steres. [Gr deka ten, and **stere**]

decastich /dek'ə-stik/ n (pl **dec'astichs**) a poem of ten lines. [Gr deka ten, and stichos a row, a verse]

decastyle /dek'ə-stīl/ (archit) n a portico with ten columns in front (also adj). [Gr deka ten, and stȳlos a column]

decasyllable /dek-ə-sil'ə-bl/ n a verse line or a word of ten syllables. [Gr deka ten, and syllabē a syllable; see **syllable**]
■ **decasyllabic** /-ab'ik/ adj.

decathlon /dek-ath'lon/ n a two-day contest of ten track-and-field events held at the modern Olympic Games since 1912. [Gr deka ten, and athlon a contest]
■ **decath'lete** n.

decaudate /dē-kö'dāt/ vt to cut off the tail of. [L dē from, and cauda tail]

decay /di-kā'/ vi to fall away from a state of health or excellence; to waste away; to decompose, rot; (of eg magnetism, radioactivity) to decrease in strength as the source of energy is removed. ♦ vt to cause to waste away; to impair. ♦ n a falling into a worse or less perfect state; a wearing away; rotting; bad or rotten matter (eg in a tooth); loss of fortune; ruin, downfall (obs); disintegration of a radioactive substance. [OFr decair, from L dē from, and cadere to fall]
■ **decayed'** adj rotten; reduced in circumstances, impoverished.
❑ **decay heat** n (nuclear eng) the heat produced by the radioactive decay of fission products formed in a nuclear reactor.

DECC abbrev : Department of Energy and Climate Change.

Decca® /dek'ə/ n the **Decca Navigator System**, consisting of a series of chains of long-wave radio transmitting stations, each chain formed of a master station and three slaves, providing a navigator or pilot with meter readings that have to be interpreted by special charts, or, alternatively, with a direct picture of the aircraft's track on a **Decca Flight Log**.

deccie /dek'i/ (sl) n an ornament or decoration; interior decoration; (also with cap) an interior-decoration enthusiast or interior designer. [Short form]

decease /di-sēs'/ n death. ♦ vi to die. [OFr deces (Fr décès), from L dēcessus departure, death, from dē away, and cēdere, cēssum to go]
■ **deceased'** adj dead; lately dead.
■ **the deceased** the dead person or people in question.

decedent /di-sē'dənt/ n (US law) a deceased person. [L dēcēdēns, -entis, prp of dēcēdere to depart, from dē away, and cēdere to go]

deceit /di-sēt'/ n the act of deceiving; anything intended to mislead another; fraud; falseness. [OFr deceite, from L dēcipere, dēceptum to deceive]

■ **deceit'ful** *adj* full of deceit; disposed or tending to deceive; insincere. **deceit'fully** *adv*. **deceit'fulness** *n*.

deceive /di-sēv'/ *vt* to mislead or cause to err; to cheat; to disappoint (*archaic*). [Fr *décevoir*, from L *dēcipere*, *dēceptum* to deceive]
■ **deceivabil'ity** or **deceiv'ableness** *n*. **deceiv'able** *adj* that may be deceived; exposed to imposture. **deceiv'ably** *adv*. **deceiv'er** *n*.

decelerate /dē-sel'ə-rāt/ *vt* and *vi* to retard, slow down. [L *dē* down, and *celer* swift]
■ **decelerā'tion** *n*. **decel'erator** *n*. **decelerom'eter** *n* an instrument for measuring deceleration.

December /di-sem'bər/ *n* the twelfth month of the year. [L *December*, from *decem* ten; in the original Roman calendar, December was the tenth month of a ten-month year]
■ **Decem'berish** or (*obs*) **Decem'berly** *adj* wintry, cold. **Decem'brist** *n* one of those who took part in the Russian conspiracy to overthrow the tsar in December 1825.

decemvir /di-sem'vər/ *n* (*pl* **decem'virs** or **decem'virī** (L) /dek'em-wi-rē or -vi-rī/) a member of a body of ten men; *esp* of those who drew up the Laws of the Twelve Tables at Rome (451–450BC). [L *decem* ten, and *vir* a man]
■ **decem'viral** *adj*. **decem'virāte** *n* a body of ten men in office; the term of office of decemvirs.

decency see under **decent**.

decennary /di-sen'ər-i/ *n* a period of ten years (also **decenn'ium**). [L *decem* ten, and *annus* a year]
■ **decenn'ial** *adj* consisting of, or happening every, ten years.

decennoval /di-sen'ō-vəl/ (*obs*) *adj* relating to the number 19. [L *decemnovalis*, from *decem* ten, and *novem* nine]

decent /dē'sənt/ *adj* becoming; seemly; proper; modest; moderate; fairly good; passable; showing tolerant or kindly moderation (*inf*); nice, pleasant (*inf*); sufficiently clothed to be seen by another person (*inf*). [L *decēns, -entis*, prp of *decēre* to be becoming]
■ **dē'cency** *n* conformity to accepted moral and ethical standards; fairness; (in *pl*) the conventions of respectable behaviour. **dē'cently** *adv*.

decentralize or **-ise** /dē-sen'trə-līz/ *vt* to withdraw from the centre; to transform by transferring functions from a central government, organization, authority or head to smaller local centres. [**de-** (2)]
■ **decentralizā'tion** or **-s-** *n*.

deception /di-sep'shən/ *n* an act of deceiving; the state of being deceived; a means of deceiving or misleading; a trick; an illusion. [OFr, from LL *dēceptiō, -ōnis*, from *dēcipere* to deceive]
■ **deceptibil'ity** *n*. **decept'ible** *adj* capable of being deceived. **decep'tious** *adj* (*Shakesp*) deceitful. **decep'tive** *adj* tending to deceive; misleading. **decep'tively** *adv*. **decep'tiveness** *n*. **decep'tory** *adj* tending to deceive.
□ **deceptive cadence** *n* (*music*) same as **interrupted cadence** (see under **interrupt**).

decerebrate /dē-ser'ə-brāt/ *vt* to deprive of the cerebrum (also **decer'ebrize** or **-ise**). [**de-** (2)]
■ **decerebrā'tion** *n*.

decern /di-sûrn'/ (*Scots law*) *vt* and *vi* to judge; to decree; to pass judgement. [OFr *decerner*, from L *dēcernere*, from *dē*, and *cernere* to distinguish]

decession /di-sesh'ən/ (*rare*) *n* departure. [See **decease**]

déchéance /dā-shā-äs'/ (Fr) *n* forfeiture.

dechristianize or **-ise** /dē-kris'tyə-nīz/ *vt* to turn from Christianity. [**de-** (2)]
■ **dechristianizā'tion** or **-s-** *n*.

deci- /des-i-/ *combining form* in names of units, denoting a tenth part (10^{-1}). [L *decimus* tenth]

deciare /des'i-är/ *n* the tenth part of an are. [Fr, from L *deci-* (in *decimus*), and **are**[2]]

decibel /des'i-bel/ *n* a term used to express a relationship between two currents, power levels or voltages, or to express a level of sound (the tenth part of a bel (qv), and more commonly used). [L *deci-*, and **bel**[1]]

decide /di-sīd'/ *vt* to determine; to end; to settle; to resolve. ◆ *vi* to make up one's mind. [OFr *decider*, from L *dēcīdere*, from *dē* away, and *caedere* to cut]
■ **decid'able** *adj* capable of being decided. **decid'ed** *adj* determined; clear, unmistakable; resolute. **decid'edly** *adv*. **decid'er** *n* someone who, or that which, decides; an action, etc that proves decisive, such as the winning goal in a match (*inf*).

deciduous /di-sid'ū-əs/ *adj* liable to be shed at a certain period; transitory, not permanent; shedding all the leaves together, *opp* to *evergreen* (*bot*); shedding wings (as some insects do). [L *dēciduus*, from *dēcidere*, from *dē* from, and *cadere* to fall]

decid'ua *n* (*pl* **decid'uas** or **deciduae** /di-sid'ū-ē/) (*med* and *zool*) a membrane of the uterus discharged after parturition. **decid'ual** *adj*. **decid'uāte** *adj*. **decid'uousness** *n*.

decigram or **decigramme** /des'i-gram/ *n* a tenth of a gram(me).

decile /des'īl/ (*stats*) *n* any of the ten equal groups into which the items in a frequency distribution can be divided; any of the nine values that divide the items in a frequency distribution into ten equal groups. [L *decem* ten]

decilitre or (*N Am*) **deciliter** /des'i-lē-tər/ *n* a tenth part of a litre.

decillion /di-sil'yən/ *n* a thousand raised to the eleventh power (10^{33}); (*esp* formerly, in Britain) a million raised to the tenth power (10^{60}). ◆ *adj* being a decillion in number. [Fr, from L *decem* ten and **million**]
■ **decill'ionth** *adj* and *n*.

decimal /des'i-məl/ *adj* numbered or proceeding by tens. ◆ *n* a decimal fraction. [L *decima* (*pars*) a tenth (part)]
■ **dec'imalism** *n* use or advocacy of a decimal system. **dec'imalist** *n*. **decimalizā'tion** or **-s-** *n*. **dec'imalize** or **-ise** *vt* to convert to a decimal system, *esp* the metric system. **dec'imally** *adv*.
□ **decimal classification** see **Dewey decimal system**. **decimal currency** *n* one in which the basic unit is divided into ten (or a multiple of ten) parts. **decimal fraction** *n* a fraction expressed by continuing ordinary decimal notation into negative powers of ten, a point being placed after the unit figure. **decimal notation** *n* a system of writing numbers based on ten and powers of ten, our ordinary system. **decimal places** *n pl* the number of figures written after the point (**decimal point**) which separates the unit and the decimal fraction. **decimal system** *n* a system in which each unit is ten times the next below it, *esp* the metric system of weights and measures. **decimal tab** *n* a facility of most word processors and some computers that arranges a column of numbers so that the decimal points are aligned.

decimate /des'i-māt/ *vt* to take or destroy the tenth part of; to punish by killing every tenth man; (loosely) to reduce very heavily. [L *decimāre, -ātum*, from *decimus* tenth, from *decem* ten]
■ **decimā'tion** *n*. **dec'imātor** *n*.

décime /dā-sēm'/ (*hist*) *n* a former unit of currency in France, $\frac{1}{10}$ of a franc. [Fr, from L *decima* (*pars*) tenth (part)]

decimetre or (*N Am*) **decimeter** /des'i-mē-tər/ *n* a tenth of a metre.

decinormal /des-i-nör'məl/ (*chem*) *adj* of one-tenth of normal concentration. [L *decimus* tenth, and **normal**]

decipher /di-sī'fər/ *vt* to uncipher; to read or transliterate or interpret from secret, unknown, or difficult writing; to make out; to detect (*obs*; *Shakesp*); to reveal (*obs*; *Shakesp*); to show forth (*obs*). [**de-** (2)]
■ **decipherabil'ity** *n*. **decī'pherable** *adj* capable of being deciphered. **decī'pherer** *n*. **decī'pherment** *n*.

decision /di-sizh'ən/ *n* the act or product of deciding; settlement; judgement; the quality of being decided in character. [See **decide**]
■ **decisive** /-sīs'iv/ *adj* having the power of deciding; showing decision; final; positive. **decī'sively** *adv*. **decī'siveness** *n*. **decī'sory** *adj* decisive.
□ **decision support system** *n* (*comput*) a system that assists in decision-making by using one or more computers and programs to provide and organize data. **decision table** *n* (*logic* and *comput*) a table comprising four sections showing a number of conditions and actions to be taken if these are or are not met, indicating the action to be taken under any condition or set of conditions. **decision theory** *n* the study of strategies for making decisions in conditions of uncertainty.

decistere /des'i-stēr/ *n* a tenth of a stere.

decitizenize or **-ise** /dē-sit'i-zə-nīz/ *vt* to deprive of citizenship. [**de-** (2)]

decivilize or **-ise** /dē-siv'i-līz/ *vt* to reduce from a civilized to a more savage state. [**de-** (2)]

deck /dek/ *n* a horizontal platform extending from one side of a vessel to the other, thereby joining the sides together, and forming both a floor and a covering (*naut*); a floor, platform, or tier as in a bus, bridge, etc; a covering (*obs*); the ground (*inf*); the platform of a skateboard; a pile of things laid flat; a pack of cards (*US*); the part of a pack used in a particular game, or the undealt part; the platform supporting the turntable of a record player; that part of a tape recorder or computer in which the magnetic tapes are placed, and the mechanism for running them; a set of punched cards (*comput*); a packet of heroin or other narcotic drug (*sl*). ◆ *vt* to cover; to clothe; to adorn; to provide with a deck (see also **deck over** below); to pile up on a platform; to knock to the ground (*inf*). [Verbal meanings from Du *dekken* to cover: cf **thatch**; Ger *decken*; L *tegere*; noun meanings from MDu *dec* roof, covering]
■ **decked** /dekt/ *adj* adorned, decorated. **deck'er** *n* the person or thing that decks; a person who adorns. ◆ *combining form* denoting a

---

■ words derived from main entry word; □ compound words; ■ idioms and phrasal verbs

vessel, vehicle or other structure that has a deck or decks, as in *three-decker*. **deck'ing** *n* adornment; a platform; material used to make a platform.

❑ **deck'-bridge** *n* a bridge whose upper stringer carries the roadway. **deck'-cargo** *n* cargo stowed on the deck of a vessel. **deck'chair** *n* a chair, *usu* folding and made of canvas and wood, such as passengers sit or lie on deck in. **deck game** *n* a game played on a ship's deck. **deck'hand** *n* a person employed on deck; an ordinary sailor. **deck'house** *n* a house, room, or box on deck. **deck'-load** *n* a deck-cargo. **deck officer** *n* a ship's officer dealing with navigation, cargo, etc, rather than engineering. **deck'-passage** *n* a passage securing only the right of being on deck, without cabin accommodation. **deck passenger** *n*. **deck quoits** *n sing* quoits as played on a ship's deck, with rope rings. **deck shoe** *n* a shoe with a rubber sole designed for wearing while boating; a casual shoe in a similar style. **deck tennis** *n* lawn tennis modified for playing on board ship.

■ **clear the decks** to tidy up, remove encumbrances, *esp* in preparation for action (*orig* naval action, now often *fig*). **deck out** to adorn, decorate. **deck over** to complete building the upper deck of (a vessel); to construct a roof over (eg a railway station) and build up upon that surface. **hit the deck** (*sl*) to lie, fall or be pushed down quickly (*esp* for safety); to get out of bed. **pedestrian deck** a safe pathway for pedestrians.

deckle /dek'l/ *n* (in paper-making) a contrivance for fixing width of sheet; a deckle-edge. [Ger *Deckel* lid]

■ **deckled** /dek'ld/ *adj* deckle-edged.

❑ **deck'le-edge** *n* the raw or ragged edge of handmade paper or an imitation of it. **deck'le-edged** *adj* having a rough uncut edge.

decko see **dekko**.

decl. see **dec.**

declaim /di-klām'/ *vi* to make a set or rhetorical speech; to harangue; to recite. ◆ *vt* to utter, repeat or recite declamatorily. [L *dēclāmāre*, from *de-* (intensive) and *clāmāre* to cry out]

■ **declaim'ant** *n*. **declaim'er** *n*. **declaim'ing** *n* and *adj*. **declamation** /dek-lə-mā'shən/ *n* act of declaiming; a set speech in public; display in speaking. **declamatorily** /di-klam'ə-tə-ri-li/ *adv*. **declam'atory** *adj* of the nature of declamation; appealing to the passions; noisy and rhetorical.

declare /di-klār'/ *vt* to make known; to announce; to assert; to make a full statement of (eg goods at customs); to expose and claim a score for (*bezique*, etc); to bid (a suit which becomes the trump suit) (*bridge*). ◆ *vi* to make a statement; to announce one's decision or sympathies; to show cards in order to score; to end an innings voluntarily before ten wickets have fallen (*cricket*). [L *dēclārāre*, *-ātum*, from pfx *dē-* wholly, and *clārus* clear (partly through Fr *déclarer*)]

■ **declar'able** *adj* capable of being declared, exhibited, or proved. **declar'ant** *n* a person who makes a declaration. **declaration** /dek-lə-rā'shən/ *n* the act of declaring; that which is declared; a written affirmation; a formal announcement (eg of war); an official announcement of entry for a race, etc; in the criminal law of Scotland, the statement made by the prisoner before the magistrate; in common law, the pleading in which the plaintiff in an action at law sets forth his or her case against the defendant. **declarative** /di-klar'ə-tiv/ *adj* making a statement or declaration; declaratory. **declar'atively** *adv*. **declar'ator** *n* a form of action in the Court of Session, with the view of having a fact judicially ascertained and declared. **declar'atorily** *adv*. **declar'atory** *adj* explanatory; declarative. **declāred'** *adj* avowed, stated. **declā'redly** *adv* avowedly. **declar'er** *n* a person who declares. ❑ **declaratory act** *n* an act intended to explain an obscure or disputed law.

■ **declare an interest** (of a member of parliament, etc) formally to make known that he or she has (financial) connections with an organization with which (parliamentary) discussions are concerned. **declare off** to renounce; to withdraw; to cancel. (**well**) **I declare!** an interjection expressing surprise.

declass /dē-kläs'/ *vt* to remove or degrade from one's class. [Fr *déclasser*]

■ **déclassé**, *fem* **déclassée** /dā-klä-sā/ *adj* (*Fr*) having lost caste or social standing.

declassify /dē-klas'i-fī/ *vt* to take off the security list; to remove from a classification. [**de-** (2)]

■ **declassificā'tion** *n*.

declension /di-klen'shən/ *n* a falling-off; decay; descent; a system of cases and case-endings (*grammar*); a class of words similarly declined; a statement in order of the cases of a word. [See **decline**]

■ **declen'sional** *adj*.

De Clerambault('s) syndrome /də kler'əm-bō(z) sin'drōm/ *n* see **erotomania** under **Eros**. [G *de Clerambault* (1872–1934), French physician]

decline /di-klīn'/ *vi* to fail or decay, eg in health or fortune; to stoop or condescend; to draw to an end; to bend or turn away; to deviate; to refuse; to bend or slope down. ◆ *vt* to give the various cases of (*grammar*); to bend down; to turn away from; to refuse; to avoid. ◆ *n* a falling-off; deviation; decay; a period of gradual deterioration; a gradual sinking of the bodily faculties, consumption (*archaic*); a downward slope. [L *dēclīnāre* to bend away, from *dē* down, away from, and *clīnāre* to bend (partly through Fr *décliner*)]

■ **declīn'able** *adj* (*grammar*) having different inflections according to the case. **declī'nal** *adj* bending downwards. **declinant** /dek'lin-ant/ *adj* (*heraldry*) having the tail hanging down. **dec'linate** *adj* (*bot*) curving downwards. **declinā'tion** *n* act of declining (*US*); a sloping or bending downwards; deviation; the angular distance of a heavenly body from the celestial equator (*astron*). **dec'līnātor** *n* an instrument determining declination. **declīn'atory** *adj* containing a declination or refusal. **declīn'ature** *n* act of declining or refusing; a plea declining the jurisdiction of a judge (*law*). **declinom'eter** *n* an instrument for measuring declination in various senses, *esp* the **declination of the compass** or **magnetic declination** (ie the deviation of the magnetic needle from the true north), or the declination or dip of a compass needle (see **dip of the needle** under **dip**).

■ **on the decline** in the process of becoming less, deteriorating.

declivity /di-kliv'i-ti/ *n* a place that slopes downwards, *opp* to *acclivity*; inclination downwards. [Fr *déclivité*, from L *dēclīvitās*, *-ātis*, from *dē* downward, and *clīvus* sloping, related to *clīnāre*]

■ **decliv'itous** *adj*. **declī'vous** *adj* (*rare*).

declutter /dē-klut'ər/ *vi* and *vt* to remove superfluous objects (from). [**de-** (2)]

declutch /dē-kluch'/ *vi* to release the clutch (of a motor vehicle). [**de-** (2)]

Deco or **deco** /dek'ō/ *adj* relating to or in the style of art deco (*qv* under **art¹**).

decoct /di-kokt'/ *vt* to prepare by boiling; to extract the substance of by boiling; to boil; to devise. [L *dēcoquere*, *dēcoctum*, from *dē* down, and *coquere* to cook]

■ **decoc'tible** *adj*. **decoc'tion** *n* an extract of anything got by boiling. **decoc'tive** *adj*. **decoc'ture** *n* a substance prepared by decoction.

decode /dē-kōd'/ *vt* to translate from a code. ◆ *vt* and *vi* to convert from sound or writing to meaning, or from a foreign language to one's own language (*linguistics*); to convert (computer data) into human-readable form; to convert (coded information) into analogue information (*electronics*). ◆ *n* /dē'kōd/ a decoded message. [**de-** (2)]

■ **decō'der** *n*.

decoherer /dē-kō-hē'rər/ (*old elec*) *n* a device for bringing a coherer back to its former condition after it has been affected by an electric wave. [**de-** (2)]

decoke /dē-kōk'/ and earlier **decarb** /dē-kärb'/ (*inf*) *vt* to decarbonize (an internal combustion engine). [**de-** (2)]

decollate¹ /dē-kol'āt/ *vt* (*archaic*) to behead. [L *dēcollāre*, from *dē* from, and *collum* the neck]

■ **decoll'ated** *adj* rounded off, as the apex of a shell. **decollā'tion** *n* the act of beheading; a picture of a decapitation; *esp* of the head of St John the Baptist on a platter; the festival of the Baptist, 29 August. **decoll'ator** *n*.

decollate² /dē-kə-lāt'/ *vt* and *vi* to separate continuous stationery into separate sheets or forms. [**de-** (2)]

■ **decollā'tion** *n*. **decollā'tor** *n*.

décolleté /dā-kol-tā'/ *adj* wearing a low-cut dress; (of clothes) low-cut. [Fr, pap of *décolleter* to bare the neck and shoulders, from *collet* collar. Cf **decollate¹**]

■ **décolletage** /dā-kol-täzh'/ *n* a low-cut neckline; a dress with this; the exposure of the neck and shoulders in such a dress.

decolonize or **-ise** /dē-kol'ə-nīz/ *vt* to release from being a colony, grant independence to. [**de-** (2)]

■ **decolonizā'tion** or **-s-** *n*.

decolour or **decolor** /dē-kul'ər/ *vt* to deprive of colour (also **decol'o(u)rize** or **-ise**) [L *dēcolōrāre*, from *dē* from, and *color* colour]

■ **decol'orant** *n* and *adj* (a substance) that bleaches or removes colour. **decol'orate** *vt* to deprive of colour. ◆ *adj* without colour. **decolorā'tion** *n* removal or absence of colour. **decolo(u)rizā'tion** or **-s-** *n*.

decommission /dē-kə-mish'ən/ *vt* to take (a warship, atomic reactor, etc) out of commission or operation. [**de-** (2)]

■ **decommiss'ioner** *n*. **decommiss'ioning** *n*.

decompensation /dē-kom-pən-sā'shən/ *n* the failure of an organ to cope with increasing demands made on it owing to disease (*med*); the failure of one's psychological defences to cope with increasing stress, resulting in further mental disturbance (*psychiatry*). [**de-** (1)]

decomplex /dē'kom-pleks/ adj repeatedly compound. [**de-** (3)]

decompose /dē-kom-pōz'/ vt to separate the component parts of; to resolve into elements; to break down, rot. ◆ vi to decay, rot; to break down into elements or components. [Fr décomposer, from pfx dé- (L dis-) apart, and composer; see **compose**]
■ **decompōsabil'ity** n. **decompōs'able** adj. **decompōs'er** n.

decomposition[1] /di-kom-pə-zish'ən/ n act or state of decomposing; decay. [Fr pfx dé- (L dis-) apart, and **composition**; accidentally associated in meaning with **decompose**]
■ **decompound** /dē-kəm-pownd'/ vt to decompose, decay. **decompound'able** adj.

decomposition[2] /dē-kom-pə-zish'ən/ n the compounding of things already compound. [**de-** (3)]
■ **decomp'osite** (or /-oz'/) adj doubly or further compounded. **decompound** /-kəm-pownd'/ vt to compound again, or further. ◆ adj /dē'/ compounded more than once; having leaflets themselves composed of separate parts (bot).

decompound see **decomposition**[1,2]

decompress /dē-kəm-pres'/ vt to release from pressure; to decrease the pressure on; to expand (compressed computer data) to its original size. [**de-** (2)]
■ **decompression** /-presh'ən/ n the act or process of releasing from pressure; the gradual release of air pressure on persons (such as divers, construction workers, etc) on returning to normal atmospheric conditions; any operation to relieve excessive pressure (surg); the expansion to its original size of compressed computer data. **decompress'ive** adj. **decompress'or** n.
❑ **decompression chamber** n a chamber in which excessive pressure can be reduced gradually to atmospheric pressure, or in which a person can be subjected gradually to decreased atmospheric pressure. **decompression sickness** n bends, a painful and sometimes fatal disorder affecting divers, etc who are too suddenly subjected to decreased air pressure, caused by the formation of nitrogen bubbles in the body as nitrogen comes rapidly out of solution from the blood and other body fluids.

decondition /dē-kən-dish'ən/ vt to eradicate a conditioned response in (a person or animal). [**de-** (2)]

decongest /dē-kən-jest'/ vt to relieve or end the congestion of. [**de-** (2)]
■ **deconges'tant** n (med) an agent that relieves congestion (also adj). **decongest'ion** /-yən/ n. **deconges'tive** adj.

deconsecrate /dē-kon'si-krāt/ vt to deprive of the character given by consecration; to secularize. [**de-** (2)]
■ **deconsecrā'tion** n.

deconstruction /dē-kən-struk'shən/ n a method of critical analysis applied esp to literary texts, which, questioning the ability of language to represent reality adequately, asserts that no text can have a fixed and stable meaning, and that readers must eradicate all philosophical or other assumptions when approaching a text. [**de-** (2) and **construct**]
■ **deconstruct'** vt to subject to deconstruction; to break (an idea or situation) down into its component parts. **deconstruc'tionist** n and adj.

decontaminate /dē-kən-tam'i-nāt/ vt to free from contamination. [**de-** (2)]
■ **decontam'inant** n. **decontaminā'tion** n. **decontam'inative** adj. **decontam'inātor** n.

decontextualize or **-ise** /dē-kon-teks'tū-ə-līz/ vt to remove from context; to study (words, etc) out of their context. [**de-** (2)]
■ **decontextualizā'tion** or **-s-** n.

decontrol /dē-kən-trōl'/ vt to remove (esp official) control from. ◆ n removal of control. [**de-** (2)]

décor or **decor** /dā'kör/ n scenery and stage embellishments; ornament; the general decorative effect (colour scheme, furnishings, etc) of a room. [Fr, decoration]

decorate /dek'ə-rāt/ vt to ornament, to beautify; to paint, put wallpaper on (a house, etc); to honour with a badge or medal. [L decorāre, -ātum, from decus what is becoming, from decēre to be becoming]
■ **dec'orated** adj. **decorā'tion** n ornament; the applied paint and wallpaper in eg a house; the badge of an order; a medal; (in pl) flags, bunting, paper chains, etc put out or hung at a time of celebration. **dec'orative** /-rə-tiv/ adj ornamental. **dec'oratively** adv. **dec'orativeness** n. **dec'orātor** n a person who decorates, esp houses.
❑ **Decorated style** n (archit) a style of Gothic architecture, elaborate and richly decorated, which prevailed until near the end of the 14c. **Decoration Day** see **Memorial Day** under **memory**. **decorative arts** n pl applied arts (such as ceramics or textiles) that produce functional as well as ornamental objects.

decorous /dek'ə-rəs or (old) -k'ō, -k'ö/ adj becoming; suitable; proper; decent. [L decōrus becoming; L decēre to be becoming]
■ **dec'orously** adv. **dec'orousness** n. **decō'rum** n that which is in keeping, congruous; that which is becoming in outward appearance; propriety of conduct; decency.

decorticate /dē-kör'ti-kāt/ vt to remove the bark, husk or peel of; to remove the cortex of (med). ◆ adj having lost the cortex or its function. [L dēcorticāre, -ātum, from dē from, and cortex bark]
■ **decorticā'tion** n.

decoupage or **découpage** /dā-koo-päzh'/ n the craft (originating in the 18c) of applying decorative paper cut-outs to eg wood surfaces; a picture produced in this way. [Fr découper to cut out]

decouple /dē-kup'l/ vt to reduce or prevent unwanted distortion or oscillation within (a circuit or circuits) (electronics); to separate from, end the connection with. [**de-** (2)]
■ **decoup'ling** n.

decoy /di-koi'/ vt to allure; to entrap; to lure into a trap. ◆ n /dē'koi/ anything intended to lure into a snare (lit and fig); a person, etc employed to lure others into a snare; an apparatus of hoops and network for trapping wild ducks (sometimes **duck'-coy**). [Perh Du de the, or L pfx dē down, and Du kooi, from L cavea a cage; or poss Du eendekooi a duck-trap]
❑ **de'coy-duck** n a wild duck tamed and trained to entice others into a trap; a person employed to lure others into a snare (fig).

decrease /di-krēs'/ vi to become less. ◆ vt to make less. ◆ n /dē'krēs/ a growing less; loss. [OFr decrois a decrease, from L dēcrēscere, from dē from, and crēscere to grow]
■ **decreas'ing** n and adj. **decreas'ingly** adv.

decree /di-krē'/ n an order by someone in authority; an edict or law; a judicial decision; a predetermined purpose (theol). ◆ vt (**decree'ing**; **decreed'**) to declare or determine by sentence in law; to appoint. ◆ vi to make a decree. [OFr decret and L dēcrētālis, from L dēcrētum, from dēcernere to decide]
■ **decree'able** adj capable of being decreed. **decreet'** n (Scots law; archaic) a court judgement. **decrē'tal** (or (Spenser) /dek'/) adj relating to a decree or decretal. ◆ n a decree, esp a papal edict; a book containing decrees; (specif in pl; often with cap) the second part of the canon law, the decrees of various popes determining points of ecclesiastical law. **decrē'tist** n in medieval universities, a student of the decretals, a student of law. **decrē'tive** adj. **decrē'tory** adj relating to a decree, judicial; having the force of a decree.
❑ **decree absolute** n a final decree; (in a divorce) that which makes the former partners free to marry again. **decree nisi** /nī'sī/ n (L nisi unless) a provisional decree which will be made absolute in due time unless cause is shown to the contrary (granted esp in divorce cases).

decrement /dek'ri-mənt/ n the act or state of decreasing; the quantity lost by decrease; the decrease in value of a variable (maths); the ratio of each amplitude to the previous one in an oscillator (phys). ◆ vt to decrease the value of by a given amount; (in computer programming) to subtract 1 from (the value in a storage location). [L dēcrēmentum]

decrepit /di-krep'it/ adj worn out by the infirmities of old age; in the last stage of decay. [L dēcrepitus noiseless, very old, from dē from, and crepitus a noise]
■ **decrep'itness** or **decrep'itude** n the state of being decrepit or worn out with age.

decrepitate /di-krep'i-tāt/ (phys) vi to crackle (like salts when heated). ◆ vt to roast so as to cause a continual crackling, to calcine. [L dē- (intensive) and crēpitāre to rattle much, frequentative of crepāre]
■ **decrepitā'tion** n.

decresc. (music) abbrev : decrescendo.

decrescendo /dā-kre-shen'dō/ (music) n, adj and adv (pl **decrescen'dos**) (a) becoming quieter; diminuendo. [Ital, decreasing]

decrescent /di-kres'ənt/ adj becoming gradually less. [L dē and crēscere]

decretal, etc see under **decree**.

decrew /di-kroo'/ (Spenser) vi to decrease. [OFr decru, pap of decroistre. See **decrease**]

decriminalize or **-ise** /dē-krim'i-nə-līz/ vt to make (a practice, etc) no longer a criminal offence in law. [**de-** (2)]
■ **decriminalizā'tion** or **-s-** n.

decrown /dē-krown'/ vt to discrown. [**de-** (2)]

decrustation /dē-kru-stā'shən/ n removal of a crust. [**de-** (2)]

decry /di-krī'/ vt (**decry'ing**; **decried'**) to cry down; to condemn; to criticize as worthless; to blame. [Fr dé-, des- (L dis-), and crier to cry; see **cry**]
■ **decrī'al** n. **decrī'er** n.

decrypt /dē-kript'/ vt to decode. [**de-** (2) and **crypt-**]
■ **decryp'tion** n.

DECT abbrev : Digital Enhanced Cordless Telecommunications, a standard for mobile telephone services.

dectet /dek-tet'/ n a group of ten (musicians, lines of verse, etc); a composition for ten musicians. [L *decem* ten, and **quartet**, **quintet**, etc]

decubitus /di-kū'bi-təs/ (*med*) n posture in bed. [L *dē* from, and *cubitus* bed, couch]
❑ **decubitus ulcer** n a bedsore.

decuman /dek'ū-mən/ adj principal, large (of waves, etc); connected with the principal gate of a Roman camp (near which the 10th cohort of the legion was stationed). ◆ n a great wave, as every tenth wave was supposed to be. [L *decumānus*, from *decem* ten]

decumbent /di-kum'bənt/ adj lying down; reclining on the ground; lying flat but having a rising tip (*bot*). [L *dēcumbēns, -entis*, from *dē* down, and *-cumbere* (in compounds only) to lie]
■ **decum'bence** or **decum'bency** n the act or posture of lying down. **decum'bently** adv. **decum'biture** n the time when a sick person takes to bed.

decuple /dek'ū-pl/ adj tenfold. ◆ n a number repeated ten times. ◆ vt to make tenfold, multiply by ten. [Fr *décuple*, from L *decuplus*]

decurion /di-kū'ri-ən/ (*hist*) n in the ancient Roman army, an officer who had the command of ten soldiers; any overseer of ten; a councillor. [L]
■ **decu'ria** or **decury** /dek'ū-ri/ n a company of ten (or more). **decu'rionate** n.

decurrent /di-kur'ənt/ adj running or extending downwards (*obs*); continued down the stem (*bot*). [L *dēcurrēns, -entis*, from *dē* down, and *currere, cursum* to run]
■ **decurr'ency** n. **decurr'ently** adv. **decursion** /-kûr'-/ n a running down (*obs*); a military manoeuvre or parade (*hist*). **decur'sive** adj. **decur'sively** adv.

decurve /di-kûrv'/ (*biol*) vi to curve downwards. [**de-** (1)]
■ **decurva'tion** n. **decurved'** adj.

decury see under **decurion**.

decus et tutamen /dek'əs et tūt'ə-men/ (*L*) an ornament and a protection (inscription on the milled edge of British one-pound coins and earlier on a coin of Charles II, at John Evelyn's suggestion). [From Virgil, *Aeneid* V.262]

decussate /di-kus'āt/ vt to divide in the form of an X. ◆ vi to cross in such a form; to cross, intersect, as lines, etc. [L *decussāre, -ātum*, from *decussis* a coin of ten *asses* (*decem asses*) marked with X, symbol of ten]
■ **decuss'ate** or **decuss'ated** adj crossed; arranged in pairs which cross each other, like some leaves (*bot*). **decuss'ately** adv. **decussā'tion** /dek-/ n.

DEd. /dē-ed'/ abbrev : Doctor of Education.

dedal, **Dedalian** see **daedal**.

dedans /də-dā'/ n an open gallery at the end of the service side of a court in real tennis; spectators at a court tennis match collectively. [Fr]

dedicate /ded'i-kāt/ vt to set apart and consecrate to some sacred purpose; to devote wholly or chiefly; to inscribe or give orally in tribute (to anyone); to inaugurate or open (*US*). ◆ adj (*obs*; *Shakesp*) devoted; dedicated. [L *dēdicāre, -ātum*, from *dē* down, and *dicāre* to declare]
■ **ded'icant** n a person who dedicates. **ded'icated** adj consecrated; giving one's whole interest and work to a particular cause or belief; single-minded, determined; manufactured or set aside for a specific purpose (eg a *dedicated calculator*), or made to work in conjunction with another specific piece of equipment (eg a *dedicated flash gun*). **dedicatee** /ded-i-kə-tē'/ n a person to whom a thing is dedicated. **dedica'tion** n the act of dedicating; the state of being dedicated; an address or tribute to a patron, mentor, etc prefixed to a book. **dedica'tional**, **dedicatorial** /-kə-tō'ri-əl or -tö'/, **ded'icatory** /-kə- or -kā-/ or **ded'icative** adj. **ded'icātor** n.
■ **Feast of Dedication** another name for **Hanukkah**.

dedifferentiation /dē-dif-ər-en-shi-ā'shən/ (*biol* and *med*) n a change by which specialized tissue with several cell types reverts to a generalized and simpler form. [**de-** (2)]

dedimus /ded'i-məs/ (*law*; *hist*) n a writ commissioning a person who is not a judge to act as a judge. [From the opening, L *dedimus* (*potestātem*) we have given (power), from *dare* to give]

dedramatize or **-ise** /dē-dra'mə-tīz/ vt to play down the importance of, lessen or keep low the tension or friction caused by. [**de-** (2)]

deduce /di-dūs'/ vt to derive, work out logically (that); to infer from what precedes or from premises, clues, remarks, etc. [L *dēdūcere, dēductum*, from *dē* from, and *dūcere* to lead]
■ **deduce'ment** n what is deduced. **deducibil'ity** or **deduc'ibleness** n the quality of being deducible. **deduc'ible** adj that may be deduced or inferred. **deduct** /-dukt'/ vt to take away; to subtract; to reduce, weaken (*obs*; *Spenser*); to separate (*obs*); to deduce (*obs*). **deductibil'ity** n. **deduct'ible** adj. **deduc'tion** n the act of deducing;

that which is deduced; the inference of a particular truth from a general truth previously known, as distinguished from *induction*, leading from particular truths to a general truth; the act of deducting; the thing or amount deducted; abatement. **deduct'ive** adj (of thought or reasoning) concerned with deduction from premises or accepted principles. **deduct'ively** adv.
❑ **deducted spaces** n pl the spaces on a ship that are required to be used for the running of the ship rather than for carrying cargo.

dee¹ /dē/ vi Scots form of **die¹**.

dee² /dē/ n the fourth letter of the modern English alphabet (D or d). ◆ n, vt and interj (*euphem*) a substitute for **damn**.

deed¹ /dēd/ n something done; an act; an exploit, *esp* heroic; a legal transaction, *esp* involving the transfer of property; the documentary evidence of it, signed, sealed and delivered. ◆ vt (*N Am*) to transfer (property). [OE *dǣd*, from *dōn* to do; Ger *Tat*]
■ **deed'ful** adj (*Tennyson*) marked by deeds or exploits. **deed'ily** adv. **deed'less** adj (*Shakesp*, etc) not having performed deeds. **deed'y** adj (*dialect*) industrious, active.
❑ **deed of covenant** n a legal agreement in which a person promises to pay a fixed sum (to another person or organization) for an agreed period of time, enabling the payer to deduct tax from the total payment. **deed poll** n a deed executed by one party, *esp* one by which a person changes his or her name, originally having the edge *polled* or cut even, not indented.
■ **deed of saying** (*Shakesp*) performance of what has been said or promised. **in deed** in reality.

deed² /dēd/ a Scottish form of **indeed**; also of **died** and **dead**.

deejay /dē'jā or -jā'/ (*inf*) n a phonetic representation of the initials **DJ**, standing for **disc jockey** (see under **disc**). ◆ vi to act as a deejay.

deek /dēk/ (chiefly *Scot*) interj look at, see. [Romany *dik* to look, see]

deem /dēm/ vt or vi (pat and pap **deemed** (*Spenser* **dempt**)) to judge; to think; to believe. ◆ n (*obs*; *Shakesp*) opinion. [OE *dēman* to form a judgement, from *dōm* judgement; see **doom**]
■ **deem'ster** n a judge (now only in the Isle of Man). **dempster** /dem'stər/ n a judge (*obs*); formerly in Scotland an officer who repeated the sentence after the judge (also **doom'ster**).

de-emphasize or **-ise** /dē-em'fə-sīz/ vt to take the emphasis away from, treat or consider as of little or less importance. [**de-** (2)]

deen /dēn/ (*Spenser*) for **din**.

de-energize or **-ise** /dē-en'ər-jīz/ vt to disconnect (an electrical circuit) from its source of power; to remove energy from. ◆ vi to lose energy. [**de-** (2)]

deep /dēp/ adj extending or placed far down or far from the outside; great in extent from top to bottom; penetrating a (relatively) long way; greatly recessed; very distant; greatly involved; engrossed (in); difficult to understand; very secret; wise and perceptive; profoundly versed; cunning; very still; profound; intense; excessive; heartfelt; sunk low; low in pitch; (of a road) encumbered with mud, sand or ruts; in the outfield, not close to the wickets (*cricket*); well behind one's fellow players (*football*). ◆ adv in a deep manner; at or to a great depth; far (in time); intensely, profoundly. ◆ n that which is deep; the sea (*poetic*); a deep place; the middle, deepest, or most intense part; anything profound or incomprehensible. [OE *dēop*; Ger *tief*; cf **dip**, **dive**]
■ **deep'en** vt to make deeper in any sense; to increase. ◆ vi to become deeper. **deep'ie** n (*old inf*) a three-dimensional cinematograph film. **deep'ly** adv. **deep'most** adj deepest. **deep'ness** n (see also **depth**). ❑ **deep'-browed** adj of high intellectual powers. **deep clean** n an exceptionally thorough cleaning process. **deep-clean** vt. **deep'-discount** adj (of financial securities) sold at a discount, earning low interest, and providing merely capital gain. **deep down** adv fundamentally, if not in appearance. **deep drawing** n (*engineering*) a process of shaping metal that involves considerable plastic distortion. **deep'-draw'ing** adj (of ships) requiring considerable depth to float in. **deep'-drawn** adj. **deep'-dyed** adj thoroughgoing, extreme (in a bad sense). **deep'felt** adj. **deep'-fet** adj (*Shakesp*) fetched from a depth. **deep'-freeze'** n storage of foodstuffs, or other perishable substances, at very low temperature; the appliance in which such goods are stored. ◆ vt to freeze or store in a deep-freeze. **deep'-fry'** vt to fry (food) completely submerged in fat or oil. **deep kiss** n a French kiss, a kiss using the tongue. **deep kissing** n. **deep'-laid** adj secretly plotted or devised. **deep linking** n the creation of a hyperlink to a specific page within a website, rather than to the homepage of that site. **deep litter** n a method of keeping hens in a hen house with a deep layer of peat material on the floor. **deep'-mouthed** adj (*archaic*) with a deep voice. **deep'-read** adj extremely well-versed. **deep-rooted** adj having deep roots (*bot*); not superficial, ingrained (*fig*). **deep'-sea** adj relating to the deeper parts of the sea. **deep'-seat'ed** adj not superficial, ingrained. **deep'-set** adj (*esp* of eyes) set deeply (into the face). **deep'-sink'er** n (*Aust*) a drinking vessel of the largest size. **deep-six'** vt (*N Am inf*) to get rid of, destroy, eliminate (from a slang term for the

depth of the grave or six fathoms under water). **Deep South** *n* a region of the USA, roughly Georgia, Alabama, Mississippi and Louisiana. **deep space** *n* the area of space beyond the moon's orbit. **deep structure** *n* (*linguistics*) the underlying grammatical concepts and relationships of words in a sentence from which its surface structure (*qv*) derives. **deep therapy** *n* the treatment of disease by deep X-rays or gamma rays. **deep throat** *n* (*inf*) a highly confidential informant. **deep'-toned'** *adj* having a deep tone or timbre. **deep'-vein thrombosis** *n* the formation of a blood clot in a deep vein, often caused by restricted movement in people travelling on long-distance flights with insufficient legroom (*abbrev* **DVT**). **deepwa'terman** *n* (*pl* **deepwa'termen**) a sea-going ship. **deep web** *n* that part of the World Wide Web which is not indexed by search engines.

■ **go in**, **dive in** or **be thrown in at the deep end** to plunge, or be plunged, straight into an activity, job, etc with little or no experience or preparation. **go off the deep end** to express strong feelings without restraint; to lose one's temper completely. **in deep water** in difficulties. **two deep**, **three deep**, etc in two, three, etc layers or rows.

deer /*dēr*/ *n* (*pl* **deer**) any animal of the Cervidae, a family of even-toed hoofed animals characterized by the possession of antlers by the males at least, *incl* red deer, reindeer, etc; any kind of animal (as in *small deer*; *obs*). [OE *dēor*; Ger *Tier*, Du *dier*; ON *dyr*]

■ **deer'let** *n* a chevrotain.

❑ **deer'berry** *n* the huckleberry (genus *Gaylussacia*); the fruit of a gaultheria; that of *Vaccinium stamineum*, an inedible American whortleberry. **deer fence** *n* a very high fence that deer should not be able to jump over. **deer fly** *n* a bloodsucking fly that attacks deer and can transmit diseases such as tularaemia to humans. **deer forest** *n* a wild tract of land (not necessarily woodland) reserved for deer. **deer'grass** *n* a cyperaceous tufted sedge that grows in bogs. **deer'-hair** *n* a small species of clubrush. **deer horn** or **deer'-horn** *n* a deer's antler or its material; a freshwater mussel (*US*). **deer'hound** *n* a large rough-coated greyhound. **deer lick** *n* a spot of salt ground to which deer come to lick the earth. **deer mouse** *n* an American mouse, *Peromyscus maniculatus* (so called from its agility). **deer'-neck** *n* a thin ill-shaped neck (of horses). **deer'-park** *n*. **deer'skin** *n* skin of the deer, or the leather made from it. **deer'stalker** *n* a person who stalks deer; a kind of hat with peaks at the front and back and flaps at the side that can cover the ears. **deer'stalking** *n*.

deere see **dear**².

de-escalate /*dē-es'kə-lāt*/ *vt* and *vi* to reduce or decline in scale or intensity. [**de-** (2)]

■ **de-escala'tion** *n*.

deet or **DEET** /*dēt*/ *n* a colourless compound used as an insect repellent. [Prob from its chemical name *d*iethyl *t*oluamide]

deev /*dēv*/ same as **div**³.

deeve see **deave**.

def /*def*/ (*sl*) *adj* excellent, brilliant (*orig* in hip-hop culture). [Appar from *def*initive or *def*initely]

def. *abbrev* : defendant; definition.

deface /*di-fās'*/ *vt* to destroy or mar the face or external appearance of, to disfigure; to obliterate; to put out of countenance (*obs*); to defame (*obs*). [OFr *desfacer*, from L *dis*- away, and *faciēs* face]

■ **deface'ment** *n* the act of defacing; injury to form or appearance; that which defaces. **defa'cer** *n*. **defa'cingly** *adv*.

de facto /*dē* or *dā fak'tō*/ (*L*) *adj* actual, if not rightful or legally recognized (eg *the de facto ruler*). ◆ *adv* in fact, actually. ◆ *n* (*Aust*) a de facto husband or wife.

defaecate same as **defecate**.

defalcate /*dē'*, *de'fal-kāt*, *di-fal'kāt* or (*rare*) *-föl'*/ *vt* (*obs*) to deduct a part of. ◆ *vi* to embezzle money held on trust. [LL *dēfalcāre*, *-ātum* to cut away, from L *dē* from, and *falcāre* to cut, from *falx*, *falcis* a sickle]

■ **defalca'tion** *n* a diminution; a defection; a misappropriation of funds entrusted to someone; the amount misappropriated. **de'falcator** *n* someone guilty of defalcation.

defame /*di-fām'*/ *vt* to take away or destroy the good fame or reputation of; to say malicious things about; to speak evil of; to charge falsely (*archaic*). ◆ *n* (*obs*; *Spenser*) infamy. [OFr *diffamer*, from L *diffāmāre*, from *dis*- away, and *fāma* report]

■ **defamation** /*def-ə-mā'shən*/ *n* the act of defaming; calumny; slander or libel. **defamatorily** /*di-fam'ə-tər-i-li*/ *adv*. **defam'atory** *adj* containing defamation; injurious to reputation; calumnious. **defa'ming** *n* and *adj*.

defast or **defaste** Spenserian spellings of **defaced** (*pap* of **deface**).

defat /*dē-fat'*/ *vt* (**defatt'ing**; **defatt'ed**) to remove fat or fats from. [**de-** (2)]

default /*di-fölt'*/ *n* a fault, failing or failure; defect; neglect to do what duty or law requires; failure to fulfil a financial obligation; the value of a variable used, or pre-set course of action taken, by a computer system when no specific instruction is given by the user or keyer to override it (also *adj*); fault or offence (*archaic*). ◆ *vi* to fail through neglect of duty; to fail to appear in court when called upon; to fail to fulfil a financial obligation (with *on* or *in*). [OFr *defaute* (noun) and *default* (3rd sing of *defaillir*), from L pfx *dē-* and *fallere*; see **fault**]

■ **default'er** *n* a person who fails to appear in court, or to account for money entrusted to his or her care, or to settle an ordinary debt or debt of honour; a military offender.

■ **by default** because of a failure to do something. **in default of** in the absence of; for lack of. **judgement by default** judgement given against a person because he or she fails to plead or make an appearance in court.

defeasance /*di-fē'zəns*/ *n* undoing, defeat (*obs*); a rendering null or void (*law*); a condition whose fulfilment renders a deed void (*law*). [OFr *defesance*, from *desfaire*; see **defeat**]

■ **defeas'anced** *adj* liable to be forfeited. **defeasibil'ity** *n*. **defeas'ible** *adj* that may be annulled. **defeas'ibleness** *n*.

■ **deed of defeasance** (*Eng law*; *hist*) an instrument which defeated the operation of some other deed or estate.

defeat /*di-fēt'*/ *vt* to win a victory over; to get the better of; to frustrate; to ruin, undo (*obs*; *Shakesp*); to annul (*law*); to disfigure (*obs*; *Shakesp*). ◆ *n* a frustration of plans; ruin; overthrow, eg of an army in battle; loss of a game, race, etc; annulment (*law*). [OFr *defait*, from *desfaire* to undo, from L *dis*- (negative) and *facere* to do]

■ **defeat'ism** *n* readiness or inclination to accept, welcome or help to bring on, defeat. **defeat'ist** *n* and *adj*. **defeat'ure** *n* (*obs*) undoing (*Spenser*); defeat; disfigurement (from **feature**; *Shakesp*). ◆ *vt* (*archaic*) to disfigure.

defecate /*def'i-kāt*/ *vi* to void excrement. ◆ *vt* to clear of dregs or impurities; to purify from extraneous matter. [L *dēfaecāre*, *-ātum* to cleanse, from *dē* from, and *faex*, *faecis* dregs]

■ **defeca'tion** *n*. **def'ecator** *n*.

defect /*dē'fekt*, *di-fekt'*/ *n* a deficiency; a lack; an imperfection; a blemish; a fault; an imperfection in a crystal lattice which may be caused by the presence of a minute amount of a different element in a perfect lattice (*crystallog*). ◆ *vi* /*di-fekt'*/ to desert one's country or a cause, transferring one's allegiance (to another). [L *dēficere*, *dēfectum* to fail, from *dē* down, and *facere* to do]

■ **defectibil'ity** *n*. **defect'ible** *adj* liable to imperfection; deficient. **defec'tion** *n* (an act of) desertion; a failure to carry out a duty; (an act of) revolt. **defec'tionist** *n*. **defect'ive** *adj* having defects; lacking in some necessary quality; imperfect; faulty; insufficient; incomplete in inflections or forms (*grammar*); mentally handicapped (*offensive*). ◆ *n* (*offensive*) a person who is mentally handicapped. **defect'ively** *adv*. **defect'iveness** *n*. **defect'or** *n* a person who deserts or betrays his or her country, etc.

❑ **defective equation** *n* (*maths*) an equation derived from another, but with fewer roots than the original. **defective virus** *n* (*biol*) a virus that is unable to replicate without a helper (qv).

■ **the defects of one's qualities** virtues carried to excess, the faults apt to accompany or flow from good qualities.

defence /*di-fens'*/ or *N Am* **defense** /*dē'fens*/ *n* (an act of) defending; capability or means of resisting an attack; protection; a protective piece of armour; vindication, justification (for an action, etc); a defendant's plea or argument (*law*); the defending party in legal proceedings; the members of a (football, hockey, etc) team whose role is to prevent the other team from scoring. [L *dēfendere*, *dēfēnsum* to ward off]

■ **defenced'** *adj* fortified. **defence'less** *adj*. **defence'lessly** *adv*. **defence'lessness** *n*. **defend** /*di-fend'*/ *vt* to keep off anything hurtful from; to guard or protect; to maintain against attack; to prohibit, forbid (*obs*); to ward off; to resist (eg a claim) (*law*); to act as a lawyer for (a defending party); to contest. ◆ *vi* (*sport*) to have, and act on, the responsibility for preventing scoring. **defend'able** *adj* that may be defended. **defend'ant** *n* a defender; a person accused or sued (*law*). **defend'ed** *adj* guarded; protected; maintained against attack; forbidden (*obs*; *Milton*). **defend'er** *n* a person who defends; a player who defends the goal, etc; the holder of a championship, etc who seeks to maintain his or her title; a person who accepts a challenge (*obs*); a person sued or accused (*Scots law*); (in *pl*; with *cap*) an Irish Roman Catholic society formed at the end of the 18c in opposition to the Peep-o'-day Boys and the Orangemen (*hist*). **Defend'erism** *n* (*esp hist*) the policies of the Defenders. **defen'sative** *n* (*obs*) a protection. **defensibil'ity** *n*. **defens'ible** *adj* capable of being defended. **defens'ibly** *adv*. **defens'ive** *adj* defending; cautious, attempting to justify one's actions; in a state or posture of defence. ◆ *n* that which defends; posture of defence. **defens'ively** *adv*. **defens'iveness** *n*.

❑ **defence'man** or (*esp N Am*) **defense'man** *n* (in ice-hockey and lacrosse) a player (other than the goalkeeper) who defends the goal. **defence mechanism** *n* an unconscious mental process by which an individual excludes ideas or experiences painful or unacceptable to

him or her (*psychiatry*); a response by the body, an organism, etc in reaction to harmful organisms, predators, etc.
■ **defender of the faith** a title held by the sovereigns of England since Henry VIII, on whom it was conferred in 1521 for his book against Luther. **stand** or **be on the defensive** to be in the position of defending oneself, not attacking.

defenestration /dē-fen-i-strā'shən/ (*formal* or *joc*) *n* (an act of) flinging someone out of a window. [L *dē* from, and *fenestra* window]

defense, etc see **defence**.

defer[1] /di-fûr'/ *vt* (**deferr'ing**; **deferred'**) to put off to another time; to delay. [L *differre*, from *dis-* asunder, and *ferre* to bear, carry; cf **differ**]
■ **defer'able** or **deferr'able** *adj*. **defer'ment** *n*. **deferr'al** *n*. **deferr'er** *n* a procrastinator.
❑ **deferred annuity** see under **annuity**. **deferred credit** *n* (*bookkeeping*) an item on a balance sheet denoting a value that will flow into a future period's profit and loss account instead of the current one. **deferred pay** *n* an allowance paid to soldiers on their discharge, or to their relations on their death; a government servant's pension. **deferred payment** *n* payment by instalments. **deferred sentence** *n* a legal sentence that is delayed until such time as the criminal's conduct can be examined. **deferred shares** *n pl* shares not entitling the holder to a full share of profits, and sometimes to none at all, until the expiration of a specified time or the occurrence of some event. **deferred taxation** *n* (*bookkeeping*) an item on a balance sheet denoting a difference between the amount of taxation actually paid and that shown as deducted in the profit and loss account.

defer[2] /di-fûr'/ *vi* (**deferr'ing**; **deferred'**) to yield (to the wishes or opinions of another person, or to authority). ◆ *vt* to submit to or lay before somebody. [L *dēferre*, from *dē* down and *ferre* to bear]
■ **deference** /def'ər-əns/ *n* a deferring or yielding in judgement or opinion; respectful compliance or acknowledgement; submission. **def'erent** *adj* bearing away, carrying off; deferential. ◆ *n* a deferent duct, *opp* to *afferent* (*anat*); in the Ptolemaic system of astronomy, any of the large eccentric circles which with the smaller epicycles were used to account for the apparent movements of the moon and the planets round the earth. **deferential** /-en'shl/ *adj* showing deference. **deferen'tially** *adv*.

defervescence /dē-fər-ves'əns/, also **defervescency** /ən-si/ *n* abatement of heat; coolness; decrease of feverish symptoms (*med*). [L *dēfervēscere* to cease boiling, from *dē* down, and *fervēscere*, from *fervēre* to boil]

defeudalize or **-ise** /dē-fū'də-līz/ *vt* to deprive of feudal character. [**de-** (2)]

deffly /def'li/ (*Spenser*) for **deftly**.

defiance /di-fī'əns/ *n* the act of defying; a challenge to combat; aggressiveness; brave or bold contempt of opposition. [**defy**]
■ **defi'ant** *adj* full of defiance, insolently bold. **defi'antly** *adv*. **defi'antness** *n* (*rare*).
■ **bid defiance to** to defy.

defibrillation /de-fib-ril-ā'shən or -fīb-/ (*med*) *n* the application of an electric current to the heart to restore the normal rhythm after fibrillation has occurred. [**de-** (2)]
■ **defib'rillator** (or /-fīb'/) *n* (*med*) a machine that applies an electric current to the chest or heart to stop irregular contractions, or fibrillation, of the heart.

defibrinate /dē-fī'bri-nāt/ *vt* to deprive of fibrin (also **defī'brinize** or **-ise**). [**de-** (2), and **fibrin**]
■ **defibrina'tion** *n*.

deficient /di-fish'ənt/ *adj* lacking (in); less than complete; defective; mentally handicapped (*offensive*). ◆ *n* (*offensive*) a person who is mentally handicapped. [L *dēficere*; see **defect**]
■ **defic'iency** (sometimes **defic'ience**) *n* defect; shortage; the amount which is lacking for completeness; the amount by which a non-profit-making organization's annual income falls short of the annual expenditure (*bookkeeping*). **defic'iently** *adv*. **defic'ientness** *n*.
❑ **deficiency disease** *n* a disease due to lack of necessary substances (*esp* vitamins) in the diet, such as rickets, scurvy, beri-beri, pellagra.

deficit /def'i-sit or -fis'/ *n* shortfall, *esp* of revenue, as compared with expenditure; the amount of a shortfall. [Fr *déficit*, from L *dēficit*, 3rd pers sing present indicative of *dēficere* to lack]
❑ **deficit financing** *n* an economic policy in which a government deliberately spends more than its revenue to stimulate the economy and funds this by borrowing. **deficit spending** *n* spending by a government of more than it gains in revenue, funded by borrowing.

de fide /dē fī'dē or dā fē'de/ (*L*) (of a teaching) in which belief is obligatory.

defied, **defier**, etc see **defy**.

defilade see under **defile**[1].

defile[1] /di-fīl'/ *vi* to march off in single file, or file by file. ◆ *n* /dē'fīl or di-fīl'/ a long narrow pass or way, in which troops can march only in

file, or with a narrow front; a gorge. [Fr *défiler*, from L *dis-*, and *fīlum* a thread]
■ **defilade** /def-i-lād'/ *vt* (*mil*) to plan a fortification so as to protect it or those in it from raking crossfire (also *n*). **defile'ment** *n* act of defilading.

defile[2] /di-fīl'/ *vt* to make foul or filthy; to pollute or corrupt; to violate. [L *dē*, and OE *fȳlan*, from *fūl* foul; confused with OFr *defouler* to trample, violate]
■ **defile'ment** *n* (an act of) defiling; foulness. **defil'er** *n*.

defilement see **defile**[1,2].

defiliation /dē-fil-i-ā'shən/ (*Lamb*) *n* depriving a parent of their child. [L *dē* from, and *filius* a son]

define /di-fīn'/ *vt* to fix or describe the meaning of; to determine with precision; to describe accurately; to decide; to fix the bounds or limits of; to make clear or sharp in outline or shape; to bring to an end (*obs*). [L *dēfīnīre*, *-ītum* to set bounds to, from *dē*, and *fīnis* a limit]
■ **definabil'ity** *n*. **defin'able** *adj*. **defin'ably** *adv*. **define'ment** *n* (*rare*; *Shakesp*) description. **defin'er** *n*. **definite** /def'i-nit/ *adj* defined; having distinct limits; fixed; certain, sure; exact; clear; sympodial or cymose (*bot*); referring to a particular person or thing (*grammar*; see also **article**). **def'initely** *adv* in a definite manner; determinately; yes indeed (*inf*). **def'initeness** *n*. **defini'tion** *n* a defining; a description of a thing according to its properties; an explanation of the exact meaning (of a word, term or phrase); sharpness of outline, visual clarity. **defini'tional** *adj*. **definitive** /di-fin'i-tiv/ *adj* defining or limiting; positive; final; most authoritative, expert or complete; (of a postage stamp) standard, not commemorative. ◆ *n* an adjective used to limit the extent of meaning of a noun, eg *this*, *that* (*grammar*); a definitive postage stamp. **defin'itively** *adv*. **defin'itiveness** *n*. **defin'itude** *n*.
❑ **definitive host** *n* (*zool*) an organism on which a parasite becomes sexually mature.
■ **by definition** intrinsically; by its very nature.

definiendum /di-fin-i-en'dəm/ *n* (*pl* **definien'da**) a word or phrase that is, or that is to be, defined, as in a dictionary (cf **definiens**). [L, neuter gerundive of *dēfīnīre* to define]

definiens /di-fin'i-ənz/ *n* (*pl* **definien'tia**) the word or words used as a definition, as in a dictionary (cf **definiendum**). [L, prp of *dēfīnīre*; see **define**]

deflagrate /def'lə-grāt/ *vi* and *vt* to burn suddenly, generally with flame and crackling noise. [L *dēflagrāre*, from *dē* down, and *flagrāre* to burn]
■ **deflagrabil'ity** *n*. **deflag'rable** *adj* which deflagrates; deflagrating readily. **deflagra'tion** *n*. **def'lagrātor** *n* apparatus for deflagration.
❑ **def'lagrating-spoon** *n* a cup with a long vertical shank for handling chemicals that deflagrate.

deflate /dē-flāt'/ *vt* and *vi* to collapse or cause to collapse due to emptying of gas; (of one's hopes, ego, etc) to reduce in extent due to disappointment, criticism, etc; (of an economy) to cause deflation in or suffer from deflation. [L *dē* from, and *flāre* to blow]
■ **deflā'ter** or **deflā'tor** *n*. **deflā'tion** *n* the act or process of deflating; the state of being deflated; a financial condition in which there is a decrease in the amount of money available relative to its buying power, *opp* to *inflation* (*econ*); removal of loose soil material by the wind. **deflā'tionary** *adj*. **deflā'tionist** *n* someone who favours deflation of currency (also *adj*).

deflect /di-flekt'/ *vi* and *vt* to turn aside; to swerve or deviate from a correct line or proper course. [L *dē* from, down, and *flectere*, *flexum* to bend, turn]
■ **deflect'ed** *adj* (*bot*) bent abruptly downwards. **deflec'tion** or **deflex'ion** *n* (L *dēflexiō*) (an act of) bending or turning away; deviation. **deflec'tional** or **deflex'ional** *adj*. **deflec'tive** *adj* causing deflection. **deflec'tor** *n* a device for deflecting a flame, electric arc, etc. **deflex'** *vt* (*zool* and *bot*) to bend down. **deflexed'** *adj*. **deflex'ure** *n* deviation.

deflorate /dē-flō'rāt or -flö'/ *adj* (*bot*) past flowering; (of an anther) having shed its pollen. ◆ *vt* (*rare*) to deflower. [L *dēflōrāre*; see **deflower**]
■ **deflora'tion** *n* the act of deflowering.

deflower /di-flowr'/ *vt* to strip of flowers; to deprive of grace and beauty, or of virginity; to rape (*euphem*). [OFr *desflorer*, from LL *dēflōrāre* to strip flowers off, from L *dē* from, and *flōs*, *flōris* a flower]
■ **deflower'er** *n*.

defluent /def'loo-ənt/ *adj* running down, decurrent. [L *dēfluere*, from *dē* down, and *fluere*, *fluxum* to flow]
■ **defluxion** /di-fluk'shən/ *n* (*obs*) a downflow; a disease supposedly due to a flow of humour; a discharge of fluid in the body.

defoaming agent /dē-fō'ming ā'jənt/ (*chem*) *n* a substance added to a boiling liquid to prevent or diminish foaming.

defocus /dē-fō'kəs/ vt and vi to (cause to) go out of focus. [**de-** (2)]

defoliate /di-fō'li-āt/ vt to strip of leaves. [LL dēfoliāre, -ātum, from dē off, and folium a leaf]
■ **defo'liant** n a chemical preparation used to remove leaves. **defōl'iate** or **defōl'iated** adj. **defolia'tion** n the falling off of leaves; the time of shedding leaves. **defō'liātor** n.

deforce /di-fōrs'/ or -fōrs'/ vt to keep out of possession by force (law); to resist (an officer of the law in the execution of his or her duty) (Scots law). [Anglo-Fr deforcer, from de- (L dis-); see **force¹**]
■ **deforce'ment** n. **deforc'iant** n someone who deforces.
□ **deforciā'tion** n (obs) a legal distress.

deforest /dē-for'ist/ vt to remove forests from. [**de-** (2)]
■ **deforestā'tion** n.

deform /di-fōrm'/ vt to alter or injure the form of; to disfigure; to change the shape of without breaking into pieces. ◆ vi to become altered in shape without breaking into pieces. ◆ adj (archaic; Milton, etc) hideous, unshapely. [L dēfōrmis ugly, from dē from, and fōrma beauty]
■ **deformabil'ity** n. **deform'able** adj. **dēforma'tion** n. **deformed'** adj misshapen, disfigured, etc. **deform'edly** adv. **deformed'ness** n. **deform'er** n. **deform'ity** n the state of being deformed; lack of proper shape; ugliness; disfigurement; anything that destroys beauty; an ugly feature or characteristic.

defoul /di-fowl'/ (obs) vt to make foul, defile. [OE fūl foul, with de- from confusion with OFr defouler to trample; cf **defile²**]

DEFRA or **Defra** abbrev: Department for Environment, Food and Rural Affairs.

defragment /dē-frag-ment'/ or (inf) **defrag** /dē-frag'/ (comput) vt to move parts of files or complete files on a hard disk so that each occupies consecutive sectors without blanks between them, thus reducing the time for retrieving data. [**de-** (2) and **fragment**, verb]
■ **defragg'er** n. **defragg'ing** n.

defraud /di-fröd'/ vt to deprive by fraud (of); to cheat or deceive. [L dēfraudāre, from dē from, and fraus, fraudis fraud]
■ **defraudā'tion** n. **defraud'er** n. **defraud'ment** n.

defray /di-frā'/ vt (**defray'ing**; **defrayed'**) to pay, settle; to satisfy, appease (Spenser). [OFr desfrayer, from des- (L dis-) and frais expenses]
■ **defray'able** adj. **defray'al** or **defray'ment** n. **defray'er** n.

defreeze /dē-frēz'/ vt to thaw out, defrost (esp frozen foods). [**de-** (2)]

defriend /dē-frend'/ vt (also **unfriend**) to remove someone from one's list of friends on a social networking website; to no longer be friends with someone (facetious). [**de-** (2)]

defrock same as **unfrock** (see under **un-**).

defrost /dē-frost'/ vt to remove frost or ice from; to thaw out. ◆ vi to become free of frost or ice. [**de-** (2)]
■ **defrost'er** n a device for defrosting esp a windscreen.

deft /deft/ adj handy, clever, dexterous, esp in movement. [ME defte, dafte simple, meek; OE gedæfte meek, from dæftan, gedæftan to prepare, make fit; the stem appears in gedafen fit]
■ **deft'ly** adv. **deft'ness** n.

defunct /di-fungkt'/ adj having finished the course of life, dead; finished, no longer working or in use (fig). ◆ n a dead person. [L dēfungī, dēfunctus to finish, from dē (intensive) and fungī to perform]
■ **defunc'tion** n (Shakesp) death. **defunc'tive** adj relating to the dead.

defund /dē-fund'/ vt to deprive of funding. [**de-** (2)]

defuse¹ or (esp US) **defuze** /dē-fūz'/ vt to remove the fuse of (a bomb, etc), so making it harmless; to lessen the tension or danger in.

defuse² /di-fūz'/ (Shakesp) vt to disorder. [For **diffuse¹**]
■ **defus'd'** adj.

defy /di-fī'/ vt (**defy'ing**; **defied'**) to brave, dare; to flout, or to resist (eg authority, convention, an order, a person); to challenge (archaic); to discard, dislike (obs). ◆ n (Dryden) a defiance. [OFr defier, from LL diffīdāre to renounce faith or allegiance, from L dis- asunder, and fīdēre to trust, from fidēs faith]
■ **defi'er** n.

deg. abbrev: degree or degrees.

dégagé /dā-gä-zhā'/ (Fr) adj unembarrassed, unconstrained, easy; uninvolved. [Pap of Fr dégager to disentangle]

degarnish /dē-gär'nish/ same as **disgarnish**.

degas /dē-gas'/ vt to remove gas from; to eject or emit in the form of a gas. [**de-** (2)]

degauss /dē-gows'/ or -gōs'/ vt to protect against magnetic mines by equipment for neutralizing a ship's magnetic field; to remove the magnetic field from (esp a television tube). [**de-** (2) and **gauss**]

degender /di-jen'dər/ (obs; Spenser) vi to degenerate. [Fr dégénérer, influenced by **gender²**]

degenerate /di-jen'ə-rit/ adj having neglected the high qualities of mankind, become base, immoral, etc; of two or more quantum states, having the same energy (phys). ◆ n a person who is degenerate. ◆ vi /-āt/ to decline from a more moral, desirable, etc state; to grow worse in quality or standard. ◆ vt (Milton) to cause to degenerate. [L dēgenerāre, -ātum to depart from its kind, from dē from, down, and genus, generis kind]
■ **degen'eracy** n the act or process of becoming degenerate; the state of being degenerate. **degen'erately** adv. **degen'erateness** n. **degen'erating** adj. **degenerā'tion** n the act or process of degenerating; the breakdown, death or decay of cells, nerve fibres, etc; an evolutionary change from a complex structural form to a simpler one. **degenerā'tionist** n someone who believes that the tendency of human beings is not to improve, but to degenerate. **degen'erative** adj tending or causing to degenerate. **degen'erous** adj (obs).
□ **degenerative joint disease** same as **osteoarthritis** (see under **osteo-**).

deglamorize or **-ise** /dē-glam'ə-rīz/ vt to make less attractive or romantic. [**de-** (2)]

deglaze /dē-glāz'/ vt to remove cooking deposits from (a meat roasting pan) with liquid which is then used as the base for a sauce or gravy. [**de-** (2)]

deglutinate /di-gloo'ti-nāt/ vt to separate (things glued together); to remove gluten from. [L dēglūtināre, -ātum, from dē from, and glūtināre, from glūten glue]
■ **deglutinā'tion** n.

deglutition /dē-gloo-tish'ən/ (physiol) n the act or power of swallowing. [L dē down, and glūtīre to swallow; see **glut**]
■ **deglu'titive** adj. **deglu'titory** adj.

dégoût /dā-goo'/ (Fr) n distaste.

degrade /di-grād'/ vt to lower in grade or rank; to deprive of office or dignity; to lower in character, value or position, or in complexity; to disgrace; to wear down, erode (geol); to decompose (chem). ◆ vi (chem) to decompose. [OFr degrader, from L dē down, and gradus a step. See **grade**]
■ **degrād'able** adj able to decompose chemically or biologically. **degradation** /deg-rə-dā'shən/ n becoming degraded; disgrace; degeneration; abortive structural development; a lowering in dignity; decomposition (chem); wearing down, erosion. **degrād'ed** adj reduced in rank; base, degenerate, declined in quality or standard; low; placed on steps (heraldry). **degrād'ing** adj morally debasing; humiliating; disgraceful.

degras /deg'räs/ n a fat obtained from sheepskins. [Fr dégras, from dégraisser to degrease]

degrease /dē-grēs'/ vt to strip, or cleanse of, grease. [**de-** (2)]
■ **degreas'ant** n a substance that removes grease.

degree /di-grē'/ n a gradation on a scale, or that which it measures; a unit of temperature; a grade or step (archaic); one of a series of advances or steps; relative position; rank; extent; amount; a mark of distinction conferred by universities and some colleges, either earned by examination or research or granted as a mark of honour; the 360th part of a revolution or circle; 60 geographical miles; nearness (of relationship); comparative amount (of severity, etc); one of the three stages (positive, comparative and superlative) in the comparison of an adjective or adverb; the highest sum of exponents in any term (maths); the number of points in which a curve may be met by a straight line (geom). [Fr degré, from L dē down, and gradus a step]
□ **degree day** n a unit used in measuring the heating requirements in a building, ie a fall of one degree of heat in one day; a day on which a university, college, etc formally awards academic degrees. **degree of freedom** n (phys) any one of the independent variables defining the state of a system (eg temperature, pressure, concentration); a capability of variation (eg a system having two variables, one of which is dependent on the other, has two degrees of freedom). **degree of dissociation** n (chem) the fraction of the total number of molecules that are dissociated.
■ **by degrees** by small amounts, gradually. **first**, **second** and **third degree burn** (med) the three categories of seriousness of a burn, third degree being most serious. **first**, **second** and **third degree murder** (N Am) the three categories of criminality of (and therefore severity of punishment for) a murder, first degree being most serious. **forbidden degrees** the degrees of blood relationship within which marriage is not allowed. **Songs of degrees** or **Songs of ascents** Psalms 120–134, either because sung by the Jews returning from captivity, or by the Jews coming up annually to attend the feasts at Jerusalem. **third degree** a method of extracting a confession by bullying and/or torture; any ruthless interrogation. **to a degree** to a certain extent; to a great extent, to extremes.

■ words derived from main entry word; □ compound words; ■ idioms and phrasal verbs

degression /di-gresh'ən/ n a gradual decrease, *esp* on tax rates. [L *dēgredī*, *dēgressus* to descend]
- **degressive** /di-gres'iv/ adj.

dégringoler /dā-gr̃e-go-lā'/ (*Fr*) vi to descend rapidly or steeply; to decline, fail.
- **dégringolade** /-go-läd/ n a sudden descent; a quick deterioration.
- vi to make a rapid descent.

degu /dā'goo/ n a small S American rodent (*Octodon degus*). [Prob from a native language of S America]

degum /dē-gum'/ vt to free from gum. [**de-** (2)]

degust /dē-gust'/ (*rare*) vt to taste, to relish. ◆ vi to have a relishing taste. [L *dē* down, and *gustāre* to taste]
- **degust'āte** vt to degust. **degustā'tion** n the act of tasting. **degust'atory** adj.

dehisce /di-his'/ vi to gape, burst open (*bot*, etc). [L *dehīscere*, from *dē*, (intensive) and *hīscere*, inceptive of *hiāre* to gape]
- **dehisc'ence** n. **dehisc'ent** adj.

dehorn /dē-hörn'/ vt to remove the horns from; to prune (a tree). [**de-** (2)]
- **dehorn'er** n.

dehort /di-hört'/ vt to dissuade. [L *dehortārī*, from *dē* off, and *hortārī* to exhort]
- **dehortā'tion** /dē-/ n dissuasion. **dehor'tative** or **dehor'tatory** adj dissuasive. **dehort'er** n.

dehumanize or **-ise** /dē-hū'mə-nīz/ vt to deprive of specifically human qualities, render inhuman. [L *dē* from, down, and **humanize**]

dehumidify /dē-hū-mid'i-fī/ vt (**dehumid'ifying**; **dehumid'ified**) to rid of moisture, dry. [**de-** (2)]
- **dehumidificā'tion** n. **dehumid'ifier** n.

dehydrate /dē-hī'drāt, dē'-/ vt to remove water from chemically; to remove moisture from, dry; to deprive of strength, interest, etc (*fig*). ◆ vi to lose water. [L *dē* from, and Gr *hydōr* water]
- **dehydrā'tion** n loss or withdrawal of moisture; excessive loss of water from the tissues of the body (*med*); the removal of water from oil or gas. **dehy'drātor** or **dehy'drater** n.

dehydrogenase /dē-hī'drō-jə-nāz/ n an enzyme that promotes the removal of hydrogen atoms from a molecule. [**de-** (2)]

dehydrogenate /dē-hī'drō-jə-nāt/ vt to remove hydrogen from (a compound). [**de-** (2)]

dehypnotize or **-ise** /dē-hip'nə-tīz/ vt to bring out of a hypnotic trance. [**de-** (2)]
- **dehypnotizā'tion** or **-s-** n.

de-ice /dē-īs'/ vt to dislodge ice from (aircraft surfaces, windscreens, etc), or to treat them so as to prevent its formation. [**de-** (2)]
- **dē-īc'er** n any means of doing this, whether a fluid, a paste, or a mechanical or pneumatic device.

deicide /dē'i-sīd/ n the killing or killer of a god. [L *deus* a god, and *caedere* to kill]
- **deicī'dal** adj.

deictic see under **deixis**.

deid /dēd/ Scots form of **dead** or **death**.
- ☐ **deid'-thraw** n death throe.

deify /dē'i-fī, dā'i-fī/ vt (**dē'ifying**; **dē'ified**) to exalt to the rank of a god; to worship as a deity; to make godlike. [Fr *déifier*, from L *deificāre*, from *deus* a god, and *facere* to make]
- **dēif'ic** or **deif'ical** adj making, or treating as if, godlike or divine. **deificā'tion** n the act of deifying; a deified embodiment. **dē'ifier** n. **dē'iform** adj formed or appearing like a god.

deign /dān/ vi to condescend, stoop (to doing something). ◆ vt to condescend to give or (*obs*; *Shakesp*) take. [Fr *daigner*, from L *dignārī* to think worthy, from *dignus* worthy]

dei gratia /dē'ī grā'shi-ə or dā'ē grä'ti-a/ (L) by the grace of God.

deil /dēl/ n Scots form of **devil**.

deindustrialize or **-ise** /dē-in-dus'tri-ə-līz/ vt to disperse or reduce the industrial organization and potential of (a nation, area, etc). [**de-** (2)]
- **deindustrializā'tion** or **-s-** n.

deino-, **Deinoceras**, **Deinornis**, **deinosaur**, **deinothere** see **dino-**.

deinstitutionalize or **-ise** /dē-in-sti-tū'shə-nə-līz/ vt to release from confinement in an institution. [**de-** (2)]
- **deinstitutionalizā'tion** or **-s-** n.

de integro /dē in'ti-grō or dā in-teg'rō/ (L) anew.

deionize or **-ise** /dē-ī'ə-nīz/ vt to remove ions from, *esp* from water as a process of purification. [**de-** (2)]
- **deionizā'tion** or **-s-** n.

deiparous /dē-ip'ə-rəs/ adj bearing a god (used of the Virgin Mary). [L *deus* a god, and *parere* to bring forth]

deiseal or **deisheal** same as **deasil**.

deist /dē'ist, dā'ist/ n a person who believes in the existence of God, but not in a divinely revealed religion. [L *deus* a god]
- **de'ism** n. **deist'ic** or **deist'ical** adj. **deist'ically** adv.

deity /dē'i-ti, dā'i-ty/ n godhood; divinity; godhead; a god or goddess; (with *cap* and with *the*) the Supreme Being. [Fr *déité*, from LL *deitās*, from L *deus* a god; Sans *deva*]

deixis /dīk'sis/ (*grammar*) n the use of words relating to the time and place of utterance, eg personal pronouns, demonstrative adverbs, adjectives and pronouns. [Gr *deiknynai* to show]
- **deictic** /dīk'tik/ adj designating words relating to the time and place of utterance (also n); proving directly (*logic*). **deic'tically** adv.

déjà vu /dā-zhä vü'/ n in any of the arts, unoriginal material, old stuff; an illusion of having experienced before something that is really being experienced for the first time, a form of the memory disorder paramnesia (*psychol*). [Fr, already seen]

deject /di-jekt'/ vt to depress the spirits of. ◆ adj (*archaic*; *Shakesp*) cast down. [L *dējicere*, *-jectum*, from *dē* down, and *jacere* to cast]
- **deject'ed** adj cast down; dispirited. **deject'edly** adv. **deject'edness** n. **dejec'tion** n lowness of spirits; (often in *pl*) faecal discharge (also **dejec'ta**; *med*); defecation. **dejec'tory** adj promoting evacuations of the bowel.

dejeune /di-joon'/ (*archaic*) n breakfast or lunch (see **disjune** and **déjeuner**).

déjeuner /dā-zhœ-nā'/ (*Fr*) n breakfast or lunch.
- **déjeuner à la fourchette** /a la foor-shet/ meat (literally, fork) breakfast, early lunch. **petit déjeuner** /pə-tē/ (literally, little breakfast) coffee and rolls on rising.

de jure /dē jū'rē, dā zhoo're/ (L) by right; rightful.

Dekabrist /dek'ə-brist/ n a Decembrist. [Russ *Dekabr'* December]

dekalogy /di-kal'ə-ji/ n a group of ten novels. [Gr *deka* ten, and *logos* discourse, by analogy with **trilogy**]

deke /dēk/ (*N Am*) vt (often with *out*) to deceive (an opponent), *esp* in ice hockey, with a deceptive movement; to deceive (somebody) (*inf*). ◆ n a deceptive movement. [Shortening of **decoy**]

dekko or **decko** /dek'ō/ (*sl*) n (pl **dekk'os** or **deck'os**) a look. ◆ vi to look. [Hindi *dekho*, imperative of *dekhnā* to see]
- **have** or **take a dekko** to have a (quick) look.

Del. *abbrev* : Delaware (US state).

del /del/ n another name for **nabla**.

del. *abbrev* : delegate; *delineavit* (L), (he or she) drew it.

delaine /di-lān'/ n an untwilled light dress material, originally of wool. [Fr *mousseline de laine* wool muslin]

delaminate /di-lam'i-nāt/ vi to split into layers. [L *dēlamināre*, from *dē* from, and *lāmina* a layer]
- **delaminā'tion** n.

delapse /di-laps'/ (*obs*) vi to sink down. [L *dē* down, and *lābī*, *lapsus* to slip]
- **delap'sion** n.

délassement /dā-las-mã'/ (*Fr*) n relaxation.

delate[1] /di-lāt'/ vt to pass on (*archaic*); to publish (*obs*); to charge with a crime (*archaic*). [L *dēlātum*, used as supine of *dēferre* to bring a report against, to inform on, from *dē-* (intensive) and *ferre*, *lātum* to bear]
- **delā'tion** n. **delā'tor** n.

delate[2] a Shakespearean form of **dilate**.

delay[1] /di-lā'/ vt (**delay'ing**; **delay'ed**) to put off to another time; to defer; to hinder or retard (eg an engine's timing). ◆ vi to pause, linger, or put off time. ◆ n a putting off or deferring; the (amount of) time during which something is put off; a pause; a hindrance; a device by which the operation of a mechanism can be timed to take place after an interval. [OFr *delaier*]
- **delay'er** n. **delay'ingly** adv.
- ☐ **delayed action** n the operation of a switch, detonation of explosives, etc some time after the mechanism has been set. **delayed drop** n (*aeronautics*) a parachute descent in which the parachutist deliberately delays pulling the ripcord. **delayed neutron** n (*phys*) a neutron emitted with an apparent delay during fission which arises from the breakdown of fission products, not the primary fission (cf **prompt neutron** under **prompt**). **delay line** n (*elec*) a device for delaying the transmission of an electrical signal.

delay[2] /di-lā'/ (*Spenser*, etc) vt to temper, dilute, weaken. [Fr *délayer* to dilute, from L *dēliquāre* to clarify or *dis-*, and *ligāre* to bind]

delayering /dē-lā'ə-ring/ n the reduction of the number of levels in the hierarchy of an organization. [**de-** (2)]

del credere /del krād'ə-ri/ adj applied to an agent who becomes surety for the solvency of persons to whom he or she sells. [Ital del of the, and credere to believe, trust]

dele /dē'li/ interj delete, efface, a direction in proofreading to remove a letter or word, indicated by δ or other sign. ◆ n such a direction or sign. [L dēlē, imperative of dēlēre to delete; or for dēlēātur subjunctive passive; dēlenda, neuter pl of gerundive]
■ **deleble** or **delible** /del'/ adj that can be deleted. **delen'da** n pl things to be deleted.

delectable /di-lek'tə-bl/ (or Spenser and Shakesp, del')/ adj delightful; very pleasing. [Fr, from L dēlectābilis, from dēlectāre to delight]
■ **delect'ableness** or **delectabil'ity** n. **delect'ably** adv. **delecta'tion** /dē-/ n delight, enjoyment.

delegate /del'i-gāt or del'ə-/ vt to send as a legate or representative; to entrust or commit (to a subordinate). ◆ n /-gət/ a person who is delegated; a deputy or representative; a person elected to Congress to represent a territory (eg Guam or American Samoa) as distinguished from the representatives of the States (US). ◆ adj delegated, deputed. [L dē away, and lēgāre, -ātum to send as ambassador]
■ **del'egable** adj. **del'egacy** n the act or system of delegating; a delegate's appointment or authority; a body of delegates; (in some universities) an elected standing committee; a department of a university. **delega'tion** n a delegating; the act or process of giving tasks to staff with authority to carry them out, whilst retaining the overall responsibility (business); a deputation; a body of delegates (US); a body of delegates that was appointed every ten years by each of the two portions of the Dual Monarchy to negotiate a treaty between the Austrian Empire and the Kingdom of Hungary (hist).
□ **delegated legislation** n rules and orders with the force of law made by the executive under statutory authority.

delenda see under **dele**.

delete /di-lēt'/ vt to blot out; to erase, take out (something written or printed), cancel; to destroy. ◆ n the delete key on a computer keyboard (abbrev **del**). [L dēlēre, dēlētum to blot out]
■ **delē'tion** n. **delē'tive** adj. **delē'tory** adj.
□ **delete key** n a key on a computer keyboard used to delete a character or other object. **deletion mutation** n (biol) a mutation in which a base or bases are lost from the DNA.

deleterious /del-i-tē'ri-əs/ adj harmful or destructive; poisonous. [Gr dēlētērios hurtful, from dēleesthai to hurt]
■ **deletē'riously** adv. **deletē'riousness** n.

deleverage /dē-lev'ər-ij/ (finance) vi and vt to reduce the amount of a business's debt. [**de-** (2)]
■ **delev'eraging** n.

delf¹ or **delph** /delf/ or **delft** /delft/ n (in full **Delft'ware**) a kind of earthenware originally made at Delft, Holland.

delf² or **delph** /delf/ n (pl **delfs, delphs** or **delves**) a drain, ditch, excavation; a charge representing a square sod (heraldry). [OE delf; delfan to dig]

Delhi belly /del'i bel'i/ (inf) n diarrhoea, esp as suffered by people visiting India and other developing countries. [Delhi in N India]

deli short form of **delicatessen**.

Delian /dē'li-ən/ adj relating to Dēlos, in the Aegean Sea, by tradition birthplace of Apollo and Artemis.

delibate /del'i-bāt/ (obs) vt to sip. [L dēlībāre, from dē from, and lībāre to take, taste]
■ **deliba'tion** n.

deliberate /di-lib'ə-rāt/ vt to consider, think about carefully. ◆ vi to consider the reasons for and against anything; to reflect; to consider; to take counsel; to debate. ◆ adj /-it/ well considered; not impulsive; intentional; (of movement) slow and careful; considering carefully; slow in determining; cautious. [L dēlīberāre, -ātum, from dē- (intensive) and lībrāre to weigh, from lībra a balance]
■ **delib'erately** adv in a deliberate manner; (loosely) quietly, without fuss or haste. **delib'erateness** n. **delibera'tion** n the act of deliberating; mature reflection; calmness; coolness. **delib'erative** adj proceeding or acting by deliberation. **delib'eratively** adv. **delib'erativeness** n. **delib'erātor** n.

delible see under **dele**.

delicate /del'i-kit/ adj gently pleasing to the senses, esp the taste; not strong; dainty; discriminating or perceptive; fastidious; of a fine, slight texture or constitution; tender; not robust (esp in health); (of a colour) pale; requiring careful handling (lit and fig); refined in manners; not immodest; gentle, polite; luxurious. ◆ n a luxurious or fastidious person (obs); a luxury (obs); a delicacy (archaic). [L dēlicātus, prob connected with dēliciae allurements, luxury, from dēlicere, from dē (intensive) and lacere to entice]
■ **del'icacy** /-kə-si/ n the state or quality of being delicate; refinement; nicety; tenderness, weakness (esp of health); luxuriousness; anything delicate or dainty, esp to eat; a special culinary luxury. **del'icately** adv. **del'icateness** n.

delicatessen /del-i-kə-tes'n/ n a place which sells high-quality, often foreign or unusual prepared foods, esp cooked meats and cheeses (inf short form **del'i**). [Ger pl of Fr dēlicatesse delicacy]

delicious /di-lish'əs/ adj pleasing to the senses, esp taste; giving exquisite pleasure. [L dēliciōsus, from dēliciae or dēlicium delight]
■ **delice** /di-lēs'/ or (Spenser) del'is/ n (obs) delight; a delight; a delicacy. **deli'ciously** adv in a delicious manner; luxuriously (Bible). **deli'ciousness** n.
■ **flower delice** see **fleur-de-lis**.

delict /di-likt'/ (law, esp Scots law) n a civil wrong; the branch of Scots law dealing with liability for unjustifiable harm or loss (corresponding to tort in English law). [L dēlictum an offence; see **delinquent**]

deligation /del-i-gā'shən/ (surg) n a binding up, ligature. [L dēligāre, to bind up, from dē (intensive) and ligāre to bind]

delight /di-līt'/ vt to please highly. ◆ vi to have or take great pleasure (with in); to please greatly. ◆ n a high degree of pleasure; extreme satisfaction; that which gives great pleasure. [OFr deliter, from L dēlectāre, intensive of dēlicere; cf **delicate** and **delicious**; spelling influenced by confusion with **light**]
■ **delight'ed** adj greatly pleased; delightful (Shakesp); capable of delight (Shakesp). **delight'edly** adv. **delight'edness** n. **delight'ful** adj causing or full of delight. **delight'fully** adv. **delight'fulness** n. **delight'less** adj giving no delight. **delight'some** adj (archaic) delightful.

Delilah /di-lī'lə/, also (Milton) **Dalilah** or **Dalila** /dal'i-lə/ n the Philistine woman who tricked Samson (Bible, Judges 16); a courtesan; a temptress; an alluring object.

delimit /di-lim'it/ or **delimitate** /di-lim'i-tāt/ vt to determine or mark the limit or limits of. [L dēlīmitāre, from dē (intensive) and līmitāre; see **limit**]
■ **delimita'tion** n. **delim'itative** adj. **delim'iter** n (comput) a character that marks the beginning or end of a piece of data.

delineate /di-lin'i-āt/ vt to mark out with, or as if with, lines; to represent by a sketch or picture; to draw; to describe. [L dēlīneāre, -ātum, from dē down, and līnea a line]
■ **delin'eable** adj. **delinea'tion** n the act of delineating; a sketch, representation or description. **delin'eative** adj. **delin'eātor** n.

delineavit /di-lin-i-ā'vit or -ā'wit/ (L) (he or she) drew (this), sometimes added to the signature of the artist or draughtsman on a drawing.

delinquent /di-ling'kwənt/ adj failing in duty; of or concerning a bad debt or debtor. ◆ n a person who fails in his or her duty, esp to pay a debt; an offender, esp a young criminal; a person lacking in moral and social sense, without showing impairment of intellect. [L dēlinquēns, -entis, prp of dēlinquere, from dē- (intensive) and linquere, lictum to leave]
■ **delin'quency** n failure in or omission of duty, esp financial; a fault; crime, the state of being delinquent. **delin'quently** adv.

deliquesce /del-i-kwes'/ vi to dissolve and become liquid by absorbing moisture, as certain salts, etc do. [L dēliquēscere, from dē- (intensive) and liquēscere to become fluid, from liquēre to be fluid]
■ **deliquesc'ence** n. **deliquesc'ent** adj liquefying in the air; (of the veins of a leaf) breaking up into branches (bot).

deliquium /di-lik'wi-əm/ n a swoon (obs); eclipse (archaic); melting away (Carlyle). [Really two different words, partly confused: (1) L dēliquium, from dēlinquere to leave, fail; (2) L dēliquium, from dēliquāre to melt]

delirious /di-lir'i-əs/ adj mentally confused, esp through fever or other illness; lightheaded; insane; tremendously pleased, happy or excited (inf). [L dēlīrus crazy, from dēlīrāre, literally, to turn aside, from dē from, and līra a furrow; tremēns the prp of tremere to tremble]
■ **delirā'tion** /del-/ n madness, aberration. **delir'iant** adj. **delirifacient** /di-lir-i-fā'shənt/ adj producing delirium. ◆ n that which produces delirium. **delir'iously** adv. **delir'iousness** n. **delir'ium** n (pl **delir'iums** or **delir'ia**) the state of being delirious, esp through fever; wild excitement, happiness or wild enthusiasm.
□ **delirium tremens** /trē'menz or tre'/ n a delirious disorder of the brain produced by over-absorption of alcohol, often marked by convulsions, trembling and hallucination (inf abbrev **DTs**).

delish /di-lish'/ adj informal shortening of **delicious**.

delitescent /del-i-tes'ənt/ (med) adj latent. [L dēlitēscēns, -entis, prp of dēlitēscere, from dē from, and latēscere, from latēre to lie hidden]
■ **delitesc'ence** n.

deliver /di-liv'ər/ vt to liberate or set free (from restraint or danger); to rescue (from evil or fear); to give up; to hand over, distribute or convey to the addressee; to communicate, pronounce (a speech, message, etc); to unleash, throw (a blow, a ball, etc); to supply as expected or promised; to discharge (eg water); to assist (a mother) at the birth (of). ◆ vi (inf) to keep a promise, fulfil an undertaking. ◆ adj (obs) nimble. [Fr dēlivrer, from L dē from, and līberāre to set free, from līber free]

■ **deliverabil'ity** n. **deliv'erable** adj. **deliv'erance** n liberation; release; parturition, giving birth (obs); the utterance of a judgement or authoritative opinion. **deliv'erer** n. **deliv'erly** adv (obs). **deliv'ery** n the act of delivering; the thing delivered; a giving up; the act or manner of speaking in public, of discharging a shot, or water, of bowling a cricket ball, etc; the voluntary transfer of possessions from one person to another in a contract for the sale of goods (law); withdrawal of a pattern from a mould; a distribution; the route or a round of distribution; (the manner of) an act of giving birth.

❏ **deliv'ery-man** n a man who goes round delivering goods. **delivery note** n a document sent with goods to the customer, detailing the goods and signed on receipt as evidence of their delivery. **deliv'ery-pipe** or **-tube** n one that delivers water, etc at the place where it is required. **deliv'ery-van** n a tradesman's van for delivering goods at customers' premises.

■ **be delivered of** (archaic) to give birth to. **deliver the goods** (inf) to carry out what is required or promised. **general delivery** the delivery of letters at a post office to the persons to whom they are addressed, opp to house-to-house delivery. **jail** or **gaol delivery** see under **jail**.

Del key /del kē/ (comput) short for **delete key**.

dell[1] /del/ n a deep hollow or small valley, usu covered with trees; a hole (obs; Spenser). [OE dell; cf **dale**]

dell[2] /del/ (archaic sl) n a young girl; a trull, a prostitute.

Della-Cruscan /del-ə-krus'kən, del-la-kroos'kən/ (hist) n a member of the old Florentine Accademia della Crusca (Ital, literally academy of the bran, as sifters of the language 1582), or of a group of sentimental poetasters crushed by Gifford's Baviad and Maeviad (1794 and 1796). ◆ adj of or relating to the Della-Cruscans.

Della-Robbia /del-la-rob'bya/ n a term applied to enamelled terracotta, after a 15c Florentine sculptor, Luca della Robbia, who is said to have perfected the art of producing it.

delouse /dē-lows'/ vt to free from lice, or (fig) from landmines, etc. [**de-** (2)]

delph see **delf**[1,2].

Delphic /del'fik/ or **Delphian** /-fi-ən/ adj relating to Delphi, a town of ancient Greece, or to its famous oracle; (also without cap) like an oracle, esp if ambiguous or difficult to interpret. [Gr Delphikos from Delphi]

■ **del'phically** adv.

delphin /del'fin/ adj relating to the dauphin (qv) of France, or to an edition of the Latin classics prepared for his use, 64 volumes, 1674–1730.

Delphinidae /del-fin'i-dē/ n pl a family of cetaceans, incl dolphins, grampuses, etc. [L delphinus, from Gr delphīs, -īnos a dolphin]

■ **del'phinoid** adj.

delphinium /del-fin'i-əm/ n (pl **delphin'iums** or **delphin'ia**) any plant of the Delphinium genus of Ranunculaceae, comprising the larkspurs and stavesacre. [Latinized from Gr delphīnion larkspur, dimin of delphīs dolphin (from the appearance of the flowers)]

delphinoid see under **Delphinidae**.

Delphinus /del-fī'nəs/ (astron) n the Dolphin, a northern constellation between Pegasus and Aquila. [L]

delt /delt/ (inf) n short for **deltoid muscle**.

Delta or **delta** /del'tə/ n (in international radio communication) a code word for the letter d.

delta /del'tə/ n the fourth letter (Δ or δ) of the Greek alphabet, equivalent to d; an alluvial deposit at the mouth of a stream or river, Δ-shaped in the case of the Nile, where the flow splits into several channels; as an ancient Greek numeral δ' = 4, ͵δ = 4000; in classification, the fourth or one of the fourth grade, the grade below gamma. [Gr, from Heb daleth a tent-door]

■ **delta'ic** adj relating to a delta. **del'toid** adj of the form of the Greek Δ; triangular. ◆ n a deltoid muscle.

❏ **delta ray** n a stream of low-energy electrons. **delta rhythm** or **wave** n one of the waves recorded on an electroencephalogram indicating the low-frequency brain activity of a sleeping person. **delta wing** adj and n (a jet aeroplane) with triangular wings. **deltoid muscle** n the large triangular muscle of the shoulder.

deltiology /del-ti-ol'ə-ji/ n the study and collection of picture postcards. [Gr deltion small writing tablet]

■ **deltiol'ogist** n.

delubrum /di-lū'brəm, -loo'/ n a temple, shrine, sanctuary; a church having a font; a font. [L dēlūbrum]

deluce see **fleur-de-lis**.

delude /di-lood', di-lūd'/ vt to deceive or cause to accept what is false as true; to play with (someone) so as to frustrate them or their hopes (obs); to elude (obs). [L dēlūdere to play false, from dē down, and lūdere, lūsum to play]

■ **delud'able** adj. **delud'ed** adj holding or acting under false beliefs. **delud'er** n.

deluge /del'ūj/ n a great overflow of water; a flood, esp the original biblical flood of Noah; an overwhelming flow or quantity (fig). ◆ vt to inundate; to overwhelm with, or as if with, water. [Fr deluge, from L dīluvium, from dīluere, from dis- away, and luere to wash]

delundung /del'ən-dung/ n the weasel cat of Java and Malacca, a small carnivore related to the civet. [Javanese]

delusion /di-loo'zhən, di-lū'zhən/ n the act of deluding; the state of being deluded; a hallucination; a false belief (esp psychol); error. [See **delude**]

■ **delu'sional** adj relating to or afflicted with delusions. **delu'sionist** n. **delu'sive** /-siv/ or **delu'sory** adj apt or tending to delude; deceptive. **delu'sively** adv. **delu'siveness** n.

delustrant /dē-lus'trənt/ (textiles) n dense inorganic material added to a man-made fibre that allows a range of fibres with different lustres and opacities to be obtained. [**de-** (2) and lustrant, from **lustre**[1]]

de luxe /di lūks', luks', də lūks'/ adj sumptuous, luxurious; having refinements or superior qualities. [Fr, of luxury]

delve /delv/ vt and chiefly vi (with in or into) to dig (esp with a spade or the hands); to search or rummage deep (with in); to make deep research (fig); (of a path, road, etc) to dip, slope suddenly. ◆ n (archaic; Spenser) a hollow, hole, depression, a cave. [OE delfan to dig; connected with **dale**, **delf**[2], **dell**[1]]

■ **delv'er** n.

delves see **delf**[2].

dem. or **Dem.** abbrev : democrat(ic).

demagnetize or **-ise** /dē-mag'ni-tīz/ vt to deprive of magnetic properties. [**de-** (2)]

■ **demagnetizā'tion** or **-s-** n. **demag'netizer** or **-s-** n.

demagogue /dem'ə-gog/ n a popular orator who appeals to the baser emotions of his or her audience; a leader of the people. [Gr dēmagōgos, from dēmos people, and agōgos leading, from agein to lead]

■ **demagogic** or **demagogical** /-gog'-, -goj'-/ adj. **demagogism** or **demagoguism** /dem'ə-gog-izm/ n. **dem'agoguery** /-gog-/ n. **dem'agogy** /-goj-/ n.

demain see **demesne**.

demaine see **demean**[2].

demand /di-mänd'/ vt to claim; to ask for peremptorily or authoritatively; to require, insist upon; to ask (a question) (obs). ◆ n the asking for what is due; peremptory asking for something, insistence upon something; a claim; desire shown by consumers; the amount of any article, commodity, etc that consumers will buy; inquiry. [Fr demander, from LL dēmandāre to demand, from L dē- (intensive) and mandāre to put into one's charge]

■ **demand'able** adj that may be demanded. **demand'ant** n someone who demands; a plaintiff (law). **demand'er** n. **demand'ing** adj requiring much attention, effort, etc.

❏ **demand curve** n (econ) a graph showing the quantity of a product that consumers will buy at different prices. **demand deposit** n a sum of money that can be withdrawn without notice from an account. **demand-driven, -led** adj (in marketing) determined by demand in the market. **demand feeding** n the practice of feeding a baby when it wants food, rather than at set times. **demand forecasting** n (in marketing) finding out what the demand for a product, etc will be at various selling prices so as to discover at which price the greatest profit will be made. **demand pull** n (econ) the availability of money regarded as a cause of inflation.

■ **in (great) demand** much sought after, desired. **on demand** whenever required.

demanning /dē-man'ing/ n the deliberate reduction of the number of employees in a particular industry, etc. [**de-** (2)]

■ **deman'** vt (**demann'ing**; **demanned'**).

demantoid /di-man'toid/ n a green variety of garnet. [Ger Demant, a poetic form of Diamant diamond]

demarcation or **demarkation** /dē-mär-kā'shən/ n the act of marking off or setting boundaries; separation; a fixed limit; in trade unionism, the strict separation of the area of work of one craft or trade from that of another. [Sp demarcación, from de from, and marcar to mark. See **mark**[1]]

■ **dē'marcate** (or /di-märk'/) vt (also **demark'**) to mark off or limit; to separate.

❏ **demarcation dispute** n a disagreement between trade unions in a particular factory or industry about which union's members are responsible for performing a particular task.

démarche /dā-märsh'/ (Fr) n a step, measure or initiative (esp diplomatic).

dematerialize or **-ise** /dē-mə-tē′ri-ə-līz or -tē′ryə/ vt and vi to become, or cause to become, invisible, to vanish, cease to exist. ◆ vt to deprive of material qualities or character. ◆ vi to become immaterial, lose material form or character. [**de-** (2)]
■ **dematerializā′tion** or **-s-** n.

demayne see **demean**[2].

deme /dēm/ n a subdivision of ancient Attica and of modern Greece, a township; a local population of interbreeding organisms (biol). [Gr dēmos people]

demean[1] /di-mēn′/ vt to lower in status, reputation, or (often reflexive) dignity. [Prob on the analogy of debase, from **de-** (1) and **mean**]

demean[2] /di-mēn′/ vt to bear, behave or conduct (reflexive); to treat (Spenser, etc); to ill-treat (Spenser, etc; obs Scot). ◆ n (Spenser **demaine**′, **demayne**′ or **demeane**′) air, bearing; treatment. [OFr demener, from de- (intensive) and mener to lead, from L mināre to drive, orig from mināri to threaten]
■ **demeanour** or (N Am) **demean′or** /di-mēn′ər/ (Spenser **demeasnure**) n behaviour; manner towards another.

dement /di-ment′/ (rare) vt to drive crazy, cause to become insane. ◆ vi to deteriorate mentally, esp in old age. ◆ adj (archaic) insane, demented. ◆ n (archaic) a demented person. [L dēmēns, dēmentis out of one's mind, from dē from, and mēns the mind]
■ **dement′āte** vt (archaic) to dement. **dement′ed** adj out of one's mind; insane; crazy (inf); suffering from dementia. **dement′edly** adv. **dement′edness** n. **dementia** /di-men′shi-ə/ n (psychol) any form of insanity characterized by the failure or loss of mental powers; the organic deterioration of intelligence, memory, and orientation, often (**senile dementia**) in advancing age.
❑ **dementia praecox** or **precox** /prē′koks/ n an older name for schizophrenia.

démenti /dā-mä-tē′/ n a contradiction, denial. [Fr démentir to give the lie to]

dementia see under **dement**.

demerara /dem-ə-rä′rə, -rä′/ n a type of brown sugar in large crystals; a type of dark rum. [Demerara in Guyana]

demerge[1] /dē-mûrj′/ vi (of companies, etc) to undergo a reversal of a merger, to become separate again. [**de-** (2)]
■ **demer′ger** n.

demerge[2] /dē-mûrj′/ (obs) vt to immerse, plunge. [L dē down, and mergere to plunge]

demerit /dē- or di-mer′it/ n a fault or defect esp in a person; a mark given for a fault or offence, esp in schools or the army, etc (N Am); lack of merit; desert, merit (obs). [L dēmerērī, dēmeritum to deserve fully, later understood as to deserve ill, from dē- fully, and merēri to deserve]
■ **demeritor′ious** adj.

demerse /də-mûrs′/ vt (obs) to immerse. [L dē down, and mergere, mersum to plunge]
■ **demer′sal** adj subaqueous, living underwater; found on or near the bottom. **demersed**′ adj (bot) growing under water. **demer′sion** n.

demesne /di-mān′, -mēn′/ or **demain** /di-mān′/ n a manor-house with lands adjacent to it not let out to tenants; any estate in land. [Forms of **domain**]

Demeter /di-mē′tər/ (Gr myth) n the Greek goddess of agriculture and corn, identified by the Romans with Ceres. [Gr]

demi- /dem-i-/ combining form denoting half or half-sized. [Fr demi, from L dīmidium, from di- apart, and medius the middle]
■ **dem′i-bast′ion** n (fortif) a kind of half-bastion, consisting of one face and one flank. **dem′i-cann′on** n (Shakesp; hist) an old kind of gun which threw a ball weighing from 30 to 36lb. **demi-caractère** /də-mē-kar-ək-tār/ n (Fr, half-character) in ballet, a character dance that uses the classical technique (also adj). **dem′i-cul′verin** n (hist) an old kind of cannon which threw a shot of 9 or 10lb. **demi-de′ify** vt to treat as a demigod; to go halfway towards deifying. **dem′i-dev′il** n a half-devil. **dem′i-dis′tance** n (fortif) the distance between the outward polygons and the flank. **dem′i-dī′tone** n (music) a minor third. **dem′igod** or **dem′igoddess** n a half-god; a person whose nature is partly divine, esp a hero fabled to be, or idolized as, the offspring of a god and a mortal. **dem′i-gorge** n (fortif) the part of the polygon remaining after the flank is raised, going from the curtain to the angle of the polygon. **dem′i-lance** n (hist) a short, light spear of the 16c; a soldier armed with such a weapon. **dem′ilune** /-loon/ n (fortif) a half-moon; an old name for **ravelin**. **demi-mondaine** /-en′/ n a woman member of the demi-monde (also adj). **demi-monde** /dem′i-mond, də-mē-mŏd/ n a class of women in an unrespectable social position, the kept mistresses of society men; the shady section of a profession or group. **demi-pension** /də-mē-pä-syɔ̃/ n (Fr, boarding house) the provision of bed, breakfast and one other meal, in hotels, etc, half board. **demipique** /dem′i-pēk/ adj (of an 18c war-saddle)

having a lower peak than usual (also n). **dem′irep** n (for demi-reputable; old) a person, esp a woman, of dubious reputation. **demirep′dom** n. **demisemiquaver** /dem-i-sem′i-kwā-vər/ n (music) a note equal in time to half of a semiquaver. **dem′i-volt** or **-volte** n a half-turn of a horse, the forelegs being raised in the air. **dem′i-wolf** n (Shakesp) a half-wolf, the offspring of a dog and a wolf.

demic see under **demos**.

demi-cannon...to...**demi-ditone** see under **demi-**.

demies see **demy**.

demigod...to...**demi-gorge** see under **demi-**.

demigration /dem-i-grā′shən/ n change of abode. [L dēmigrāre, -ātum depart, from dē from, and migrāre to remove]

demijohn /dem′i-jon/ n a glass bottle with a full body and narrow neck often with handles and enclosed in wickerwork. [Fr dame-jeanne Dame Jane, analogous to **bellarmine**, **greybeard**; not from the town Damaghan]

demi-jour /də-mē-zhoor′/ (Fr) n half-light, twilight, subdued light.

demi-lance see under **demi-**.

demilitarize or **-ise** /dē-mil′i-tə-rīz/ vt to release from military control, remove forces from. [**de-** (2)]
■ **demilitarizā′tion** or **-s-** n.
❑ **demilitarized zone** n a region from which military forces are excluded; a layer at the perimeter of a secure computer network which permits outgoing traffic but denies access from external networks (abbrev **DMZ**).

demilune...to...**demi-monde** see under **demi-**.

demineralize or **-ise** /dē-min′ə-rə-līz/ vt to remove salts from (water or the body). [**de-** (2)]
■ **demineralizā′tion** or **-s-** n.

demi-pension...to...**demirep** see under **demi-**.

demise /di-mīz′/ n a transferring by lease; death (euphem or formal), as of a sovereign or a distinguished person; end, failure; a transfer of the crown or of an estate to a successor. ◆ vt to give to a successor; to bequeath by will; to transfer by lease. [OFr demise, pap of desmettre to lay down, from L dis- aside, and mittere, missum to send]
■ **demī′sable** adj.

demi-sec /dem-i-sek′/ adj (of wine) medium-dry. [Fr]

demisemiquaver see under **demi-**.

demiss /di-mis′/ (rare) adj humble. [L dēmittere, -missum, from dē down, and mittere to send]
■ **demission** /di-mish′ən/ n lowering; degradation; depression; relinquishment; resignation. **demiss′ive** adj (obs) humble. **demiss′ly** adv (obs).

demist /dē-mist′/ vt to clear (eg a car windscreen) of condensation (also vi). [**de-** (2)]
■ **demist′er** n a mechanical device which does this, usu by blowing hot air.

demit[1] /di-mit′/ vt (**demitt′ing**; **demitt′ed**) to send down; to lower. [See **demiss**]

demit[2] /di-mit′/ (esp Scot) vt (**demitt′ing**; **demitt′ed**) to dismiss (archaic); to relinquish; to resign. [Fr démettre, from L dimittere, from dis- apart, and mittere to send]

demitasse /dem′i-tas/ n (the quantity contained by) a small cup of, or for, (esp black) coffee. [Fr, half-cup]

demiurge /dem′i-ûrj/, also **demiurgus** /-ûr′gəs/ n the maker of the world; among the Gnostics, the creator of the world and humankind, subordinate to God the supreme. [Gr dēmiourgos, from dēmos the people, and ergon a work]
■ **demiur′geous** /-jəs/, **demiur′gic** /-jik/ or **demiur′gical** adj. **demiur′gically** adv.

demi-volt, **demi-wolf** see under **demi-**.

demo /dem′ō/ (inf) n (pl **dem′os**) short for **demonstration**, esp in the sense of a public expression of feeling; a musical recording made to demonstrate the quality of an unsigned performer; a version of eg computer software released for trial purposes.

demobilize or **-ise** /di-mō′bi-līz/ vt to take out of action; to disband; to discharge from the army (inf). [**de-** (2)]
■ **demob** /dē-mob′/ n and vt (**demobb′ing**; **demobbed**′) informal shortening of **demobilization** and **demobilize**. **demobilizā′tion** or **-s-** n.
■ **demob happy** carefree in anticipation of being relieved of one's responsibilities.

democracy /di-mok′rə-si/ n (also formerly (Milton) **democ′raty**) a form of government in which the supreme power is vested in the people collectively, and is administered by them or by officers appointed by them; the common people; a state of society characterized by recognition of equality of rights and privileges for all people; political, social or legal equality; (*usu* with *cap*) the Democratic party (*archaic*; *US*). [Fr *démocratie*, from Gr *dēmokratiā*, from *dēmos* the people, and *kratos* strength]

■ **democrat** /dem'ō-krat/ *n* a person who adheres to or promotes democracy as a principle; (sometimes with *cap*) a member of the Democratic party in the United States, the party generally inclining to look to marginally left of centre; a member of any British, Irish, German, etc political party with *Democratic* in its title (*inf*); (also **democrat wagon**) a light four-wheeled cart with several seats (*US hist*). **democrat'ic** or **democrat'ical** *adj* relating to democracy; insisting on, advocating or upholding equal rights and privileges for all. **democrat'ically** *adv*. **democratifi'able** *adj* capable of being made democratic. **democ'ratist** *n* a democrat. **democratīzā'tion** or **-s-** *n*. **democratize** or **-ise** /di-mok'-/ *vt* to render democratic.

démodé /dā-mö-dā'/ (Fr) *adj* out of fashion.

demoded /dē-mō'did/ *adj* (*derog*) no longer in fashion. [**de-** (2)]

demodulate /dē-mod'ū-lāt/ (*radio*) *vt* to perform demodulation on (a wave). [**de-** (2)]

■ **demodulā'tion** *n* the inverse of modulation, a process by which an output wave is obtained that has the characteristics of the original modulating wave. **demod'ulator** *n*.

Demogorgon /dē-mō-gör'gən/ *n* a mysterious infernal deity first mentioned about 450AD. [Appar Gr *daimōn* deity, and *gorgō* Gorgon, from *gorgos* terrible]

demography /dē-mog'rə-fi/ *n* the study of population, *esp* with reference to size, density and distribution. [Gr *dēmos* the people, and *graphein* to write]

■ **demog'rapher** *n*. **demographic** /dem-ə-graf'ik/ *adj* of or relating to demography. ◆ *n* an analysis of the structure of a population; a section of a population whose members share a common characteristic. **demograph'ics** *n sing* data relating to the structure of a population. ❑ **demographic time bomb** *n* a decline in the birth rate leading eventually to the workforce being unable to give adequate support to the elderly.

demoiselle /dəm-wä-zel'/ *n* a young lady (*archaic* or *facetious*); a graceful variety of crane (*Anthropoides virgo*); a dragonfly; a fish of the genus *Pomacentrus* or its family (related to the wrasses); a tiger-shark. [Fr; see **damsel**]

demolish /di-mol'ish/ *vt* to ruin, lay waste; to destroy, put an end to, cause to collapse; to eat up greedily (*humorous*). [Fr *démolir*, from L *dēmōlīrī* to throw down, from *dē* down, and *mōlīrī* to build, from *mōlēs* a heap]

■ **demol'isher** *n*. **demol'ishments** *n pl*. **demoli'tion** /dem-ō-/ *n* the act of pulling down; ruin. **demoli'tionist** *n*.
❑ **demolition derby** *n* (*N Am*) a type of motor race in which cars are deliberately crashed into one another, the winner being the last car still running.

demology /dē-mol'ə-ji/ *n* demography; the theory of the origin and nature of communities. [Gr *dēmos* people, and *logos* a discourse]

demon /dē'mən/ *n* (also *fem* **dē'moness**) an evil spirit, a devil; sometimes (like **daemon**) a friendly spirit or good genius; an evil or wicked person (*fig*); a person of great energy or enthusiasm or skill (*fig*). ◆ *adj* of, relating to or like a demon. [L *daemōn*, from Gr *daimōn* a spirit, genius; in New Testament and Late Greek, a devil; see **daemon**]

■ **demoniac** /di-mōn'i-ak/ *adj*. ◆ *n* a person possessed by a demon or evil spirit. **demoniacal** /dē-mə-nī'ə-kl/ *adj* relating to or like demons or evil spirits; influenced by demons. **demonī'acally** *adv*. **demonī'acism** /-ə-sizm/ *n* the state of being a demoniac. **demō'nian** *adj* (*Milton*). **demō'nianism** *n* possession by a demon. **demonic** /dē-mon'ik/ *adj* demoniac. **dē'monism** *n* a belief in or worship of demons. **dē'monist** *n*. **dēmonizā'tion** or **-s-** *n*. **dē'monize** or **-ise** *vt* to stigmatize as evil; to convert into a demon; to control or possess by a demon. **dēmonoc'racy** *n* the power of demons. **dēmonol'ater** *n*. **dēmonol'atry** *n* the worship of demons. **dēmonolog'ic** or **dēmonolog'ical** *adj*. **dēmonol'ogist** *n*. **dēmonol'ogy** *n* an account of, or the study of, demons and their ways. **dēmonomā'nia** *n* a form of mania in which the subject believes himself or herself to be possessed by devils. **dē'monry** *n* demoniacal influence.

demon. see **demonstr.**

demonetize or **-ise** /dē-mun'i-tīz, -mon'-/ *vt* to abandon as a monetary standard; to remove from currency as money. [**de-** (2)]

■ **demonetīzā'tion** or **-s-** *n*.

demonstr. *abbrev* : demonstrative (also **demon.** or **demons.**).

demonstrate /dem'ən-strāt/ *vt* to make apparent; to give proof of; to prove with certainty; to teach, expound, explain or exhibit by practical means. ◆ *vi* to take part in a public protest; to exhibit one's feelings; to

act as demonstrator. [L *dēmōnstrāre*, *-ātum*, from *dē-* (intensive) and *mōnstrāre* to show]

■ **demonstrabil'ity** *n*. **demon'strable** (or /dem'ən-/) *adj* that may be demonstrated. **demon'strableness** *n*. **dem'onstrably** (or /di-mon'/) *adv*. **demonstrā'tion** *n* a pointing out, indication; proof beyond doubt; expression of the feelings by outward signs; a public expression of feelings (*esp* of protest), as by a mass-meeting, a procession, etc; show; a movement to exhibit military intention, or to deceive an enemy; a practical lesson, explanation or exhibition. **demon'strative** *adj* pointing out (eg a *demonstrative adjective*); making evident; proving with certainty; of the nature of proof; given to showing one's feelings openly. **demon'stratively** *adv*. **demon'strativeness** *n*. **dem'onstrātor** *n* a person who proves beyond doubt; a teacher or assistant who helps students with practical work; a person who goes about exhibiting the uses and merits of a product; a person who takes part in a public protest demonstration; a vehicle or other piece of merchandise used for demonstration to customers. **demon'stratory** *adj* demonstrative.

demoralize or **-ise** /dē-mor'ə-līz/ *vt* to corrupt morally; to lower the morale of, to deprive of spirit and confidence; to throw into confusion. [**de-** (2)]

■ **demoralīzā'tion** or **-s-** *n* the act of demoralizing; corruption or subversion of morals. **demoralīz'ing** or **-s-** *adj*.

demos /dē'mos/ *n* (*esp derog*) the people. [Gr *dēmos*]

■ **dem'ic** *adj* (*rare*) of the people. **demot'ic** *adj* relating to the people; popular; relating to the common spoken form of a language, as opposed to the literary form. ◆ *n* colloquial language; (with *cap*) a simplified kind of writing distinguished from the hieratic, or priestly, and from hieroglyphics (*ancient Egypt*). **demot'icist** or **demot'ist** *n* a person who studies demotic script.

Demosthenic /de-mos-then'ik/ *adj* of or like the Athenian orator *Dēmosthenēs*; oratorical; eloquent.

demote /dē-mōt'/ *vt* to reduce in rank. [On the analogy of **promote**; **de-** (2)]

■ **demō'tion** *n*.

demotic see under **demos**.

demotivate /dē-mō'ti-vāt/ *vt* to cause a loss of motivation in (someone, etc). [**de-** (2)]

■ **demotivā'tion** *n*.

demount /dē-mownt'/ *vt* to take down from a support, place of display, etc; to take (eg a building) to pieces in such a way that it can be reassembled. [**de-** (2) and **mount¹** to set in position]

■ **demount'able** *adj*.

dempster see **deemster** under **deem**.

dempt /demt/ (*Spenser*) *pap* and *pat* of **deem**.

demulcent /di-mul'sənt/ *adj* soothing. ◆ *n* a medicine that soothes irritation. [L *dēmulcēns*, *-entis*, from *dē* down, and *mulcēre* to stroke, to soothe]

demulsify /dē-mul'si-fī/ *vt* (**demul'sifying**; **demul'sified**) to separate from an emulsion; to make resistant to emulsification. [**de-** (2) and **emulsify**]

■ **demulsificā'tion** *n*. **demul'sifier** *n*.

demur /di-mûr'/ *vi* (**demurr'ing**; **demurred'**) to object, balk, dissent; to hesitate because of uncertainty or before difficulty (*archaic*). ◆ *vt* (*obs*; Milton) to hesitate about. ◆ *n* an act of demurring, objection; a pause, hesitation (*archaic*); a stop (*obs*). [Fr *demeurer*, from L *dēmorārī* to loiter, linger, from *de-* (intensive) and *morārī* to delay, from *mora* delay]

■ **demurr'able** *adj*. **demurr'age** *n* undue delay or detention of a cargo ship, railway wagon, etc, and thus in the completion of a contract; compensation for such detention; a charge made by the Bank of England for exchanging notes or gold for bullion. **demurr'al** *n* (*rare*) demur. **demurr'er** *n* a person who demurs; an objection (*law*); a plea in law that, even if the opponent's facts are as they say, they still do not support his or her case (*law*).

demure /di-mūr'/ *adj* sober; staid (in dress or manners); modest, chaste; affectedly modest; making a show of gravity. ◆ *vi* (*obs*; Shakesp) appar, to look demurely. [OFr *meur* (Fr *múr*), from L *matūrus* ripe; prefix unexplained]

■ **demure'ly** *adv*. **demure'ness** *n*.

demutualize or **-ise** /dē-mū'tū-ə-līz/ *vi* (*finance*) (of a mutual institution) to become a public company. [**de-** (2)]

■ **demutualizā'tion** or **-s-** *n*.

demy /dem'i or di-mī'/ *n* (pl **demies'**) before metrication, a size of printing and writing paper approximating to A2; a writing paper, 52.5 by 40cm (21 by 16in; *US*); a holder of certain scholarships in Magdalen College, Oxford, *orig* allowed half the commons (the allowance of food and drink) assigned to a fellow. [Fr *demi*, from L *dīmidium* half, from *dis-* apart, and *medius* the middle]

■ **demy'ship** *n*.

---

demyelinate /dē-mī'ə-li-nāt/ (*med*) *vt* to destroy the myelin of (nerve fibres). [**de-** (2)]
- **demyelinā'tion** *n*.

demystify /dē-mis'ti-fī/ *vt* to clear of mystification, to make no longer mysterious or obscure. [**de-** (2)]
- **demystificā'tion** *n*.

demythologize or **-ise** /dē-mi-thol'ə-jīz/ *vt* to remove mythology from (*esp* the Bible) in order to arrive at the basic meaning. [**de-** (2)]
- **demythologizā'tion** or **-s-** *n*.

den¹ /den/ *n* the hollow lair of a wild animal; a pit or cave; a haunt of vice or misery; a private domestic room or office for work or pleasure (*inf*); a Cub Scout group (*US*); a narrow valley, a dean (*Scot*). ◆ *vi* to retire to a den. [OE *denn* a cave, lair; related to *denu* a valley]
- ❏ **den mother** *n* (*US*) an adult female leader of a Cub Scout group; any adult female protective figure in general.

den² /den/ (*obs*) *n* used for **good-e'en** or **good-even** (see **good-den** under **good**).

denar see **dinar**.

denary /dē'nər-i/ *adj* containing or having as a basis the number ten; ten. ◆ *n* the number ten; a group of ten. [L *dēnārius*, from *dēnī* ten by ten, from *decem* ten]
- **denarius** /di-nā'ri-əs/ *n* (*pl* **dena'rii** /-ri-ī/) the chief Roman silver coin under the Republic, divided into ten asses (about 8d); translated *penny* in the New Testament, hence the use of d for penny (before the introduction of decimal coinage).

denationalize or **-ise** /dē-nash'ə-nə-līz/ *vt* to deprive of national rights or character; to return from state to private ownership, to privatize. [**de-** (2)]
- **denationalizā'tion** or **-s-** *n*.

denaturalize or **-ise** /dē-nach'ə-rə-līz/ *vt* to make unnatural; to deprive of naturalization as a citizen. [**de-** (2)]
- **denaturalizā'tion** or **-s-** *n*.

denature /dē-nā'chər/, also **denaturize** or **-ise** /dē-nā'chər-īz/ *vt* to change the nature or properties of (eg a protein by heat or other treatment); to render (alcohol, etc) unfit for human consumption; to add (non-radioactive material) to radioactive material, in order to prevent its being used in an atomic bomb (*nuclear industry*). [**de-** (2)]
- **denā'turant** *n* a substance used to denature another.

denay /di-nā'/ obsolete form of **deny** and **denial**.

denazify /dē-nā'tsi-fī/ *vt* to free from Nazi influence and ideology. [**de-** (2)]
- **denazificā'tion** *n*.

dench /dench/ (*sl*) *adj* excellent. [Dame Judi *Dench* (born 1934), British actress]

dendro- or **dendr-** /den'dr(ə) or den'dr(ō)/ *combining form* denoting tree. [Gr *dendron* tree]
- **dendrachate** /den'drə-kāt/ *n* (Gr *achātēs* agate) arborescent agate. **den'driform** *adj* treelike. **den'drimer** /-drəm-/ *n* (*chem*) a polymer that has a tree-like branched molecular structure. **den'drite** *n* (Gr *dendrītēs* of a tree) a treelike crystalline aggregate or skeleton crystal; a dendron. **dendrit'ic** or **dendrit'ical** *adj* treelike, arborescent; marked with branching figures like plants. **dendro'bium** *n* (Gr *bios* life) any plant of the large genus *Dendrobium* of epiphytic orchids, chiefly of tropical Asia. **Dendrocal'amus** *n* (Gr *kalamos* cane) a genus of bamboos. **dendrochronolog'ical** *adj*. **dendrochronol'ogist** *n*. **dendrochronology** /den-drō-kron-ol'ə-ji/ *n* the fixing of dates in the past by comparative study of the annual growth rings in timber and in ancient trees. **dendroclimatol'ogist** *n*. **dendroclimatol'ogy** *n* the study of growth rings in trees as evidence of climatic change. **den'droglyph** /-glif/ *n* (Gr *glyphē* carving) an ancient carving on a tree. **den'drogram** *n* a diagram with branches indicating the relationships of items in a classification. **den'droid** or **den'droidal** *adj* treelike. **dendrol'atry** *n* (Gr *latreiā* worship) the worship of trees. **dendrolog'ical** or **dendrol'ogous** *adj*. **dendrol'ogist** *n*. **dendrol'ogy** *n* a treatise on trees; the natural history of trees. **dendrom'eter** *n* an instrument for measuring trees. **den'dron** *n* a branching projection of a nerve cell. **den'drophis** *n* (Gr *ophis* snake) a snake of the genus *Dendrophis*, tree snakes found in India and Australia.
- ❏ **dendritic cell** *n* a cell with branching processes, *esp* a type of antigen-presenting cell.

dene¹ /dēn/ *n* a small valley. [See **dean²**]

dene² /dēn/ (*dialect*) *n* a sandy tract, a dune. [Ety doubtful]

Deneb /den'eb/ *n* the brightest star in the constellation Cygnus. [Ar *dhanab* tail]
- **Deneb'ola** *n* (Ar *al-asad* of the lion) a star at the tail of the constellation Leo.

denegation /den-i-gā'shən/ *n* a denial. [L *dēnegāre*, *-ātum* to deny, from *dē-* (intensive) and *negāre* to deny]

dene-hole /dēn'hōl/ *n* a prehistoric artificial chamber in the chalk, in Kent, Essex, etc, perhaps a flint-mine or a storehouse. [Perh from **dene¹**, or OE *Dene* Danes, from popular association; and **hole¹**]

denervated /den'ər-vā-tid/ (*med*) *adj* deprived of nerve supply. [**de-** (2) and **nervate**]

denet /dē-net'/ *vt* (**denett'ing**; **denett'ed**) formerly, to market (a book) without the constraints of the Net Book Agreement, allowing retailers to determine their own price. [**de-** (2)]

DEng. /dē-eng'/ *abbrev* : Doctor of Engineering.

dengue /deng'gā/ *n* an acute tropical epidemic fever, seldom fatal (also called **breakbone fever** or **dan'dy-fever**). [Appar Swahili *dinga*]

DENI *abbrev* : Department of Education Northern Ireland.

deniable, **denial**, etc see under **deny**.

denier¹ /den'i-ər/ *n* a unit of silk, rayon and nylon yarn weight; (*usu* /də-nēr/) an old small French silver coin (*obs*; *Shakesp*); also later, a copper coin of the value of ½ sou, hence a very trifling sum. [Fr, from L *dēnārius* silver coin]

denier² see under **deny**.

denigrate /den'i-grāt/ *vt* to blacken (*esp* a reputation). ◆ *adj* blackened. [L *dē-* (intensive) and *nigrāre* to blacken, from *niger* black]
- **denigrā'tion** *n*. **den'igrātor** *n*.

denim /den'im/ *n* coloured twilled cotton fabric for jeans, overalls, etc; (*in pl*) a garment (*esp* a pair of jeans) made of denim. [Fr *de* of, and *Nîmes*, town in S France]

denitrate /dē-nī'trāt/ *vt* to free from nitric acid or other nitrogen compounds. [**de-** (2)]
- **dēnītrā'tion** or **dēnītrificā'tion** *n* removal of nitrogen or its compounds. **dēnī'trificātor** *n*. **dēnī'trify** *vt*.

denizen /den'i-zn/ *n* an inhabitant (human, animal or plant); a person admitted to the rights of a citizen (of a given place); a wild plant, probably foreign, that keeps its footing when it has been introduced; a naturalized foreign word or expression. ◆ *adj* being or having the rights of a denizen. ◆ *vt* to make a denizen; to provide with occupants. ◆ *vi* to inhabit. [OFr *deinzein*, from *deinz*, *dens* (Fr *dans*) within, from L *dē intus* from within]
- **denizā'tion** *n* act of making a person a citizen. **den'izenship** *n*.

dennet /den'it/ *n* a light type of gig popular during the early 19c. [Prob a surname]

denominal /di-nom'i-nəl/ *adj* (of a word) formed from a noun. [*de-* from, and **nominal**]

denominate /di-nom'i-nāt/ *vt* to give a name to; to call. [L *dē-* (intensive) and *nōmināre* to name, from *nōmen* name]
- **denom'inable** *adj*. **denominā'tion** *n* the act of naming; a name or title; a class or group, *esp* of units in weights, money, etc; (of coins, etc) an allotted value; a collection (of individual plants, etc) called by the same name; a religious sect. **denominā'tional** *adj* belonging to a denomination or sect. **denominā'tionalism** *n* a denominational or class spirit or policy; devotion to the interests of a sect. **denominā'tionalist** *n*. **denominā'tionally** *adv*. **denom'inative** *adj* giving or having a title. **denom'inatively** *adv*. **denom'inātor** *n* the person who, or that which, gives a name (*archaic*); the lower number in a vulgar fraction, which names the parts into which the whole number is divided (*maths*).
- ◾ **common denominator** a number that is a multiple of each of the denominators of a set of fractions, *esp* the least; something that makes comparison, communication, agreement, etc between things or people possible.

de nos jours /də nō zhoor'/ (*Fr*) of our times.

denote /di-nōt'/ *vt* to note or mark off (a limit, border, etc); to indicate by a sign; to signify or mean; to indicate the objects comprehended in a class (*logic*). [Fr *dénoter*, from L *dēnotāre*, *-ātum*, from *dē* (intensive) and *notāre* to mark]
- **deno'table** *adj*. **dē'notate** *vt* (*obs*) to denote. **dēnotā'tion** *n* (*logic*) that which a word denotes, in contradistinction to that which it connotes. **deno'tative** (or /dē'/) *adj*. **deno'tatively** (or /dē'/) *adv*. **denōte'ment** *n* (*Shakesp*) a sign or indication.

dénouement or **denouement** /dā-noo-mä'/ *n* the unravelling of a plot or story; the issue, event or outcome. [Fr *dénouement* or *dénoûment*, from *dénouer*, OFr *desnoer* to untie, from L *dis-*, and *nodāre* to tie, from *nodus* a knot]

denounce /di-nowns'/ *vt* to inform against or accuse publicly; to condemn (*esp* an argument or theory); to inveigh against; to proclaim as imminent (*obs*); to notify formally termination of (treaties, etc); to announce (*obs*); to give formal notice of a claim for mining rights covering (*US*; through *Sp*). [Fr *dénoncer*, from L *dēnuntiāre*, from *dē-* (intensive) and *nuntiāre* to announce]
- **denounce'ment** *n* denunciation. **denounc'er** *n*.

de novo /dē nō'vō or dā nō'wō/ (*L*) anew, again from the beginning.

◾ words derived from main entry word; ❏ compound words; ◾ idioms and phrasal verbs

dense /dens/ adj thick, closely-spaced, compact; extremely stupid (inf). [L dénsus thick, dense]
■ **dense'ly** adv. **dense'ness** n. **dens'ifīer** n. **dens'ify** vt to increase the density of (wood, etc) by compression. **densim'eter** n an instrument for measuring the relative density or the closeness of grain of a substance. **densimet'ric** adj. **densim'etry** n. **densitom'eter** n an instrument for measuring the optical transmission or reflecting properties of a material, in particular the optical density of photographic images. **densitomet'ric** adj. **densitom'etry** n. **dens'ity** n the quality or degree of being thick, closely-spaced or compact; the proportion of a mass to its bulk or volume; the quantity of matter per unit of bulk; the extent to which data can be packed onto a magnetic disk (comput).
❑ **dense-media process** n (mining) a method of separation in which dispersion of a heavy mineral in water separates lighter (floating) ore from heavier (sinking) ore. **density gradient centrifugation** n (biol) the separation of cells, cell components or complex molecules on the basis of their density differences by centrifuging them to their density equilibrium positions in gradients established in appropriate solutions.

dent¹ /dent/ n a hollow in a surface, caused by a blow; a negative effect, esp a reduction in an amount of money. ◆ vt to make a hollow in; to do injury to (someone's pride, etc). —See also **dint**, **dunt¹**. [Confused with **dent²**]

dent² /dent/ (obs) n a notch. ◆ vt to notch. [Fr, tooth; see ety for **dental**; also infl by **indent**]

dent. abbrev : dental; dentist; dentistry.

dental /den'təl/ adj relating to or concerned with the teeth or dentistry; produced by the aid of the teeth. ◆ n (phonetics) a sound pronounced by applying the tongue to the teeth or (loosely) the gums. [L déns, dentis a tooth; dimin denticulus]
■ **dent'ary** adj (zool) belonging to dentition; bearing teeth. ◆ n a bone of the lower jaw of some vertebrates usu bearing teeth. **dent'ate** or **dent'ated** adj toothed; notched; having a tooth-shaped pattern. **dentā'tion** n condition of being dentate; a toothlike projection. **dent'ex** n a strongly toothed voracious fish related to perch, found in the Mediterranean. **dent'icle** n a small toothlike structure; a dentil. **dentic'ulāte** or **dentic'ulāted** adj notched; having dentils. **denticulā'tion** n. **dent'iform** adj having the shape of a tooth or of teeth. **dent'ifrice** /-fris/ n (L fricāre to rub) a substance used in rubbing or cleaning the teeth, toothpaste or toothpowder. **dentigerous** /-ij'-/ adj bearing teeth. **dentilin'gual** (L lingua tongue) formed between the teeth and the tongue, as th in thin and this. ◆ n a consonant sound so formed. **dent'ine** /-ēn/ or **den'tin** n the hard, calcareous substance of which teeth are mainly composed. **dentiros'tral** adj (L róstrum a beak) with notched bill. **dent'ist** n a person qualified to treat diseases and malformations of, and injuries to, teeth. **dent'istry** n the art or work of a dentist. **dent'ition** n the cutting or growing of teeth; the shape, number, and typical arrangement of the teeth in a given species. **dent'oid** adj (Gr eidos form) formed or shaped like a tooth. **dent'ure** n (in pl) a set of (esp artificial) teeth.
❑ **dental dam** n a thin rectangular sheet of latex used to isolate a tooth or teeth from the rest of the mouth during dental treatment, or as barrier protection during oral sex. **dental floss** see under **floss**. **dental formula** n a formula showing the number and distribution of the different kinds of teeth in an animal's jaws. **dental hygiene** n the (study, practice, of advice on, etc) maintenance of healthy teeth and gums, as by careful cleaning, scaling, etc. **dental hygienist** n a person trained and qualified in dental hygiene. **dental surgeon** n a dentist. **dental technician** n a person skilled in making and repairing artificial teeth.

dentalium /den-tā'li-əm/ n (pl **dentā'liums** or **dentā'lia**) any mollusc or shell of the genus Dentalium of scaphopod molluscs whose shells resemble an elephant's tusk. [New L, from LL dentālis dental, from L dens, dentis a tooth]

dentaria /den-tā'ri-ə/ n any plant of the genus Dentaria, incl the cruciferous toothwort. [New L, from L dens, dentis a tooth]

dentary, **dentate**, etc see under **dental**.

dentel see **dentil**.

dentelle /den-tel', dā-tel/ n lace, lacework; an ornamental pattern or border resembling lace and featuring toothed outlines, used in decorating book covers. [Fr, literally little tooth, from OFr dentele, dimin of dent tooth]

dentex, **denticle**, **denticulate**, **dentifrice**, etc see under **dental**.

dentil /den'til/ (archit) n one of a series of square blocks or projections as in the bed-moulding of a cornice of columns, a denticle (also **dent'el**). [Fr dentille, obs fem dimin of dent tooth]

dentine, **dentist**, etc, **dentoid**, **denture** see under **dental**.

denuclearize or **-ise** /dē-nū'klē-ə-rīz/ vt to remove nuclear weapons from (a country, state, etc). [de- (2)]
■ **denuclearizā'tion** or **-s-** n.

denude /di-nūd'/ vt to make nude or naked; to strip (esp an area of land; also rarely **denud'ate**). ◆ vi to divest oneself of a title, etc. [L dēnūdāre, from dē- (intensive) and nūdāre, -ātum to make naked]
■ **denudation** /den-ū-dā'shən/ n a making nude or bare; the wearing away of rocks whereby the underlying rocks are laid bare (geol).

denumerable /di-nū'mə-rə-bl/ (maths) adj able to be put in a one-to-one correspondence with the positive integers. [de- (3)]
■ **denu'merably** adv.

denunciate /di-nun'si-āt or -shi-āt/ vt to denounce. [L dēnunciāre or dēnuntiāre ; see **denounce**]
■ **denunciā'tion** n any formal declaration; the act of denouncing; a threat. **denun'ciātor** n a person who denounces. **denun'ciatory** adj containing a denunciation; threatening.

Denver boot /den'vər boot/ (US sl) n a wheel clamp. [From Denver, USA, its original place of use]

deny /di-nī'/ vt (deny'ing; denied') to gainsay or declare not to be true; to reject; to refuse; to refuse to admit; to refuse a visitor (access to); to disown. [Fr dénier, from L dēnegāre, from dē- (intensive) and negāre to say no]
■ **deniabil'ity** n. **denī'able** adj. **denī'ably** adv. **denī'al** n the act of denying; refusal; rejection. **denī'alist** n a person who rejects a widely accepted truth. **denī'er** n. **denī'ingly** adv.
■ **denial of service** (comput) the inundation of a website by a large number of user sessions (often automatically generated) which consume bandwidth and deny access to legitimate users (abbrev **DOS**). **deny oneself** to refuse to allow oneself pleasure (in); to exercise self-denial. **in denial** (psychol) subconsciously refusing to come to terms with a painful truth, emotion, etc.

Deo /dē'ō, dā'ō/ (L) to, for or with God.
■ **Deo favente** /fə-ven'tē or -wen'tā/ with God's favour. **Deo gratias** /grā'shi-əs or grä'ti-äs/ thanks to God. **Deo Optimo Maximo** /op'ti-mō mak'si-mō/ to God, the best, the greatest (the motto of the Benedictines) (abbrev **DOM**). **Deo volente** /vo-len'tē or wo-len'tā/ God willing (abbrev **DV**).

deobstruent /dē-ob'strū-ənt/ (med) adj removing obstructions (also n). [L dē away; see **obstruct**]

deoch-an-doruis /dohh-ən-dor'is/ n a stirrup cup, a parting drink (also **doch-an-doris**, **doch-an-dorach** /-əhh/ or **deuch-an-doris**). [Gaelic deoch drink, an the, and doruis, genitive of dorus door]

deodand /dē'ō-dand/ n (in old English law) a personal chattel that had been the immediate accidental cause of the death of a human being, forfeited to the crown for pious uses. [L deō to God, and dandum that must be given, from dare to give]

deodar /dē'ō-där/ n a cedar tree (Cedrus deodara) of the Himalayas, much praised by Indian poets; its hard, sweet-smelling wood. [Sans deva-dāru divine tree]

deodate /dē'ō-dāt/ (obs) n a gift to God; extended to mean a gift from God. [L deō to God (ā Deō by God), and datum given, pap of dare to give]

deodorize or **-ise** /dē-ō'də-rīz/ vt to take the (usu unpleasant) odour or smell from; to make inoffensive by euphemism, evasion, etc (fig). [de- (2)]
■ **deō'dorant**, also **deō'dorizer** or **-s-** n a substance that destroys or conceals unpleasant smells. **deōdorizā'tion** or **-s-** n.

deontology /dē-on-tol'ə-ji/ n the study of duty, ethics. [Gr deon, -ontos neuter prp of deein to be necessary, to behove, and logos discourse]
■ **deon'tic** adj. **deon'tics** n sing deontology. **deontological** /-tə-loj'-/ adj. **deontol'ogist** n.

deoppilate /dē-op'i-lāt/ (obs; med) vt to free from obstruction. [de- (2)]
■ **deoppilā'tion** n. **deopp'ilative** adj.

deoxidate /dē-ok'si-dāt/ or **deoxidize** or **-ise** /-dīz/ vt (chem) to remove oxygen from, or reduce. [de- (2)]
■ **deoxidā'tion** (also **deoxidīzā'tion** or **-s-**) n. **deox'idīzer** or **-s-** n a substance that deoxidizes. **deoxy-** or **desoxy-** pfx containing less oxygen. **deoxygenate** /dē-oks'ij-ən-āt/ vt to remove oxygen from (also **deox'ygenize** or **-ise**).
❑ **deoxyribonuclease** /dē-oks-i-rī-bō-nū'klē-āz/ n see **DNase** under **DNA**. **deoxyribonucleic acid** /-nū-klā'ik/ n a long simple molecule consisting of a sugar-phosphate backbone and four different nitrogenous bases, which in its double-stranded form comprises the genetic material of most organisms and organelles, the strands forming a double-helix and running in opposite directions with the bases projecting towards each other like the rungs of a ladder so that thymidine always pairs with adenine and cytosine with guanine (abbrev **DNA**).

Dep. or **dep.** abbrev : department; deputy.

dep. abbrev : depart or departs; departure; deposed; deposit.

depaint /di-pānt'/ (Spenser) vt to paint; to depict. [Fr dépeindre, from L dépingere ; see **depict**]

depart /di-pärt'/ vi to go away; to quit or leave; to deviate; to die (euphem); to separate from one another (obs). ◆ vt (obs) to separate, divide. ◆ n (obs; Shakesp and Spenser) departure, parting. [Fr départir, from L dis- apart, and partīre (partīrī) to part, to divide]

■ **depart'er** n. **depart'ing** n. **depart'ure** n act of departing; a going away from a place; deviation (from a normal course of action, etc); the distance in nautical miles travelled by a ship due east or west; a death (euphem); (in pl) the part of an airport or terminal where departing passengers report.

❑ **departure lounge** see under **lounge**.

■ **a new departure** a change of purpose, method or activity, a new course procedure. **depart this life** (obs) to die. **the departed** (euphem) a person (or people) who has (or have) died.

département /dā-pär-tə-mä'/ n any of the regional government divisions into which France is split. [Fr]

department /di-pärt'mənt/ n a part; a special or allotted function, sphere of activity, duty or expertise; a section of an administration, university, office or other organization, headed by a manager responsible for a specific area of work; a section of a large shop or store, selling a particular type of goods; a division of a country, esp a département of France. [Fr département, from départir (see **depart**)]

■ **departmental** /dē-pärt-ment'l/ adj. **department'alism** n too strict division of work among departments with little intercommunication. **departmentaliza** or **-s-** n. **department'alize** or **-ise** vt to form into separate departments; to deal with (a large amount of work, etc) by allotting a specific share to different departments. **department'ally** adv.

❑ **department store** n (orig US) a large shop selling a great variety of goods in different departments.

depasture /di-päs'chər/ vt to eat bare; to put to pasture; to afford pasture for. ◆ vi to graze. [**de-** (2)]

depauperize or **-ise** /di-pö'pə-rīz/ vt to remove from the state of pauper. [**de-** (2) and (3)]

■ **depau'perate** vt to impoverish. ◆ adj impoverished.

dépêche /dā-pesh'/ (Fr) n dispatch, message.

depeinct /di-pänt'/ (Spenser) vt to paint. [**depaint**]

depend /di-pend'/ vi to be sustained by or connected with anything; to be pending; to rely (on); to rest (on); to hang down (rare). [Fr dépendre, from L dēpendēre, from dē from, and pendēre to hang]

■ **dependabil'ity** n. **depend'able** adj that may be relied on; reliable. **depend'ably** adv. **depend'ant** (also **depend'ent**) n a person who depends on another for support (esp financial); a hanger-on. **depend'ence** n (rarely **depend'ance**) state of being dependent; reliance, trust; that on which one depends; a quarrel or duel pending (archaic). **depend'ency** n that which depends; connected consistency (Shakesp); a foreign territory dependent on a country, a kind of subordinate colony without self-government; dependence (esp excessive); submissiveness (Shakesp). **depend'ent** (also **depend'ant**) adj depending, relying, contingent, relative. **depend'ing** adj still undetermined; awaiting settlement (obs). **depend'ingly** adv.

❑ **dependency culture** n a type of society that relies upon, and (in a derog sense) expects, state benefits and support to maintain it. **dependent clause** n a subordinate clause.

■ **depending on** or **dependent on** according as.

depersonalize or **-ise** /dē-pûr'sə-nə-līz/ vt to take away the characteristics or personality of; to make impersonal, dehumanize. [**de-** (2)]

■ **dépersonaliza'tion** or **-s-** n.

dephlegmate /di-fleg'māt/ (old chem) vt to free from water; to concentrate, rectify. [**de-** (2)]

■ **dephlegma'tion** /dē-/ n. **dephlegma'tor** n.

dephlogisticate /dē-flo-jis'ti-kāt/ (old chem) vt to deprive of phlogiston. [**de-** (2)]

❑ **dephlogisticated air** n Joseph Priestley's name for oxygen, which he discovered in 1774.

dephosphorize or **-ise** /dē-fos'fə-rīz/ vt to remove phosphorus from, esp as part of a steel-making process. [**de-** (2)]

■ **dephosphoriza'tion** or **-s-** n.

depict /di-pikt'/ vt to paint or draw; to make a likeness of; to describe, esp minutely. [L dēpingere, dēpictum, from dē- (intensive) and pingere to paint]

■ **depict'er** or **depict'or** n. **depic'tion** n. **depict'ive** adj.

depicture /di-pik'chər/ (archaic) vt to picture; to paint; to represent. ◆ n depicting, representation. [**de-** (3) and **picture** (verb)]

depigment /dē-pig'mənt/ vt to take away or reduce the pigmentation in. [**de-** (2)]

■ **depigmenta'tion** n. **depig'mented** adj.

depilate /dep'i-lāt/ vt to remove the hair from. [L dēpilāre, -ātum, from dē out, and pilus hair]

■ **depila'tion** n the removal or loss of hair. **dep'ilator** n. **depilatory** /di-pil'ə-tər-i/ n an application for removing superfluous hairs. ◆ adj possessing this ability.

deplane /dē-plān'/ (N Am) vi to disembark from an aeroplane. [**de-** (2) and **plane¹**]

deplete /di-plēt'/ vt to empty, reduce, exhaust, use up. [L dēplēre, dēplētum to empty, from dē- (negative) and plēre to fill]

■ **deple'table** adj. **deple'tion** n the act of emptying or exhausting; the reduction in total value of a natural resource (eg oil, coal) as more of it is extracted and used or sold; the act of relieving congestion or plethora (med). **deple'tive** adj. **deple'tory** adj.

❑ **depleted uranium** n (chem) a sample of uranium having less than its natural content of ²³⁵U. **depletion layer** n (electronics) in semiconductor materials, the area where mobile electrons do not neutralize the combined charge of the donors and acceptors, barrier layer.

deplore /di-plör', -plör'/ vt to feel or express deep grief for; to express strong disapproval or disgust at; to give up as hopeless (obs). [L dēplōrāre, from dē- (intensive) and plōrāre to weep]

■ **deplor'able** adj lamentable, causing great regret; sad; hopelessly bad. **deplor'ableness** or **deplorabil'ity** n. **deplor'ably** adv. **deplora'tion** /dep- or dēp-/ n lamentation. **deplor'ingly** adv.

deploy /di-ploi'/ vt to unfold; to open out or extend; to spread out and place strategically (any forces); to bring into use. ◆ vi to open; (of a body of troops) to extend from column into line, to take up strategic positions. ◆ n deployment. [Fr déployer, from L dis- apart, and plicāre to fold]

■ **deploy'ment** n the act of deploying.

deplume /di-ploom'/ vt to strip of plumes or feathers. [**de-** (2)]

■ **depluma'tion** /dē-/ n.

depolarize or **-ise** /dē-pō'lə-rīz/ (phys) vt to deprive of polarity. [**de-** (2)]

■ **depolariza'tion** or **-s-** n.

depoliticize or **-ise** /dē-po-lit'i-sīz/ vt to remove the political nature or awareness from. [**de-** (2)]

depolymerize or **-ise** /dē-pol'i-mə-rīz/ vt to break a large molecule into simpler ones that have the same basic formula. ◆ vi to decompose in this way. [**de-** (2)]

■ **depolymeriza'tion** or **-s-** n.

depone /di-pōn'/ vt (mainly Scots law) to lay down; to deposit; to testify upon oath. [L dēpōnere; prp dēpōnēns, -entis, from dē down, and pōnere to place, lay]

■ **depo'nent** adj (grammar) having a passive form but active meaning, as if having laid aside the passive (really middle or reflexive) meaning. ◆ n a deponent verb (grammar); a person who makes a deposition, esp under oath, or whose written testimony is used as evidence in a court of justice.

Depo-Provera® /de-pō-prō-vā'rə/ n an injectable contraceptive for women, used esp in developing countries.

depopulate /dē-pop'ū-lāt/ vt to rid of people, remove (much of) the population from; to overrun and lay waste (obs). ◆ vi to become devoid of people. ◆ adj devoid of people. [L dēpopulārī, -ātus, from dē- (intensive) and populārī to swarm over, to spread over a country, said of hostile people (L populus), hence to ravage, to destroy; later understood as to deprive of people]

■ **depopula'tion** n the act of depopulating; havoc; destruction. **depop'ulator** n.

deport¹ /di-, dē-pört', -pört'/ vt to transport, to exile; to expel (eg as an undesirable alien or foreigner). [Fr déporter, from L dēportāre, from dē- away, and portāre, -ātum to carry]

■ **deporta'tion** /dē-/ n. **deportee'** /dē-/ n.

deport² /di-pört', -pört'/ vt to behave (reflexive). [OFr deporter, from L dē- (intensive) and portāre to carry]

■ **deport'ment** n behaviour; physical bearing, stance, gait; manners.

depose /di-pōz'/ vt to remove from a high office or post; to degrade; to set down; to remove; to attest; to examine or put upon oath (Shakesp). ◆ vi to give testimony; to swear (obs; Shakesp). [Fr déposer, from L dē from, and pausāre to pause, (later) to place]

■ **depos'able** adj. **depos'al** n. **depos'er** n.

deposit /di-poz'it/ vt to put or set down; to place; to lay; to lay up, set aside for later use; to entrust (esp money); to lodge as a pledge, give (esp money) as security; to lay down as a coating, bed, vein, etc (geol). ◆ n that which is deposited or put down; a sum of money paid to secure an article, service, etc, the remainder of the cost being paid later; an accumulation by sedimentation, precipitation, sublimation, or other natural means (geol); something entrusted to another's care, esp a sum of money put in a bank; a pledge; a bailment where one entrusts goods to another to be kept without recompense (in Scots law, **deposita'tion**); the state of being deposited. [L dēpositum placed, from dēpōnere, from dē down, and pōnere to place]

■ **depos'itary** n a person with whom anything is left for safekeeping; a guardian (also **depos'itory**). **depos'itive** adj. **depos'itor** n. **depos'itory** n a place where anything is deposited for safekeeping (also **depos'itary**).

❑ **deposit account** n a bank account usu used for savings, in which money is lodged to gain interest, and for which cheques are not used. **deposit money** n (econ) deposits in bank current accounts, the largest part of the money supply. **depos'it-receipt** n a receipt for money deposited in a bank, etc.

deposition /dē-pə- or dep-ə-zish'ən/ n the act of deposing; the act of deponing; declaration, written sworn testimony, to be used as a substitute for the production of the witness in open court; removal; the act or process of depositing; what is deposited, sediment. [**deposit**; blended with root of **depose**]

■ **deposi'tional** adj.

depot /dep'ō, di-pō', dā'pō or də'pō/ n a place of deposit; a storehouse; a military station where stores are kept and recruits trained; the headquarters of a regiment; the portion of a regiment left at home; a bus or railway station (N Am); a place where buses or tramcars are kept. [Fr dépôt, from L dēpōnere, -positum to put down, to place]

deprave /di-prāv'/ vt to make morally bad or worse; to corrupt; to represent as bad (obs). [L dēprāvāre, from dē- (intensive) and prāvus bad]

■ **depravation** /dep-rə-vā'shən/ n act of depraving; state of being depraved; depravity. **deprāved'** adj morally corrupt. **deprāv'edly** adv. **deprāv'edness** n. **deprāve'ment** n (archaic) vitiation. **deprāv'ingly** adv. **depravity** /di-prav'i-ti/ n a vitiated or corrupt state of moral character; extreme wickedness; corruption; an immoral act; the hereditary tendency of human beings towards sin (theol); original sin (theol).

deprecate /dep'ri-kāt/ vt to regret deeply; to argue or protest against; to express disapproval of; to disparage, belittle; to try to ward off by prayer (archaic); to desire earnestly the prevention or removal of; to invoke or beseech with a view to the averting or withholding of evil (archaic). [L dēprecāri, -ātus to pray away or against, from dē away, and precāri to pray]

■ **dep'recable** adj to be deprecated. **dep'recating** adj expressing contempt, disapproval, disparagement. **depreca'tion** n act of deprecating, earnest prayer, esp a special petition against some evil, in litanies. **dep'recatingly** adv. **dep'recative** adj. **dep'recātor** n. **dep'recātorily** adv. **dep'recātory** adj.

depreciate /di-prē'shi-āt/ vt to lower the worth of; to undervalue, to be contemptuous of the value of; to disparage. ◆ vi to fall in value. [L dēpretiāre, -ātum, from dē down, and pretium price]

■ **deprē'ciatingly** adv. **depreciation** /-s(h)i-ā'shən/ n the falling of value; the amount charged in any one year to a profit and loss account to reflect the consumption of long-lived assets (account); disparagement, ridicule. **deprē'ciative** or **deprē'ciatory** adj tending to depreciate or lower. **deprē'ciātor** n.

depredate /dep'ri-dāt/ vt to plunder or prey upon; to rob; to lay waste; to devour. [L dēpraedārī, -ātus, from dē- (intensive) and praedārī, from praeda plunder]

■ **depredā'tion** n the act of plundering; state of being depredated; (usu in pl) hardship, damage. **dep'redātor** n. **depredatory** /di-pred'ət-ə-ri/ adj.

deprehend /dep-ri-hend'/ (obs) vt to catch, seize; to apprehend; to detect. [L dēpraehendere, from dē- aside, and praehendere to take]

depress /di-pres'/ vt to press down; to let down; to lower; to cause to sink; to humble, to make subject; to dispirit, deject or cast a gloom over. [L dēprimere, -pressum, from dē down, and premere to press]

■ **depress'ant** n anything that lowers activity or spirits; a sedative; a chemical that causes a mineral to sink in flotation (mining). ◆ adj (esp of drugs) lowering activity or spirits. **depressed'** adj pressed down; lowered; flattened or slightly hollowed; humbled; dejected; dispirited; suffering from clinical depression (med); (of a market, trade, etc) reduced, not flourishing. **depress'ible** adj. **depress'ing** adj able or tending to depress, esp in spirits. **depress'ingly** adv. **depression** /di-presh'ən/ n a falling in or sinking; a lowering (eg of vital functions, or of vitality); a region of low barometric pressure, a cyclone; a hollow; a state of deep dejection and a pervasive feeling of helplessness, together with apathy and loss of self-esteem, causing retardation of thought and body functions (med); a condition of reduced trade activity and prosperity; (with the and cap) the period of worldwide economic depression from 1929 to 1934. **depress'ive** adj tending to depress; (of a person) suffering from periods of depression (med). ◆ n (med) a person suffering from periods of depression. **depress'or** n an oppressor; something that lowers activity; a muscle that draws down; a surgical instrument for pressing down.

❑ **depressed area** n a region suffering from reduced trade, and often consequently one of specially heavy unemployment, poor housing, etc.

depressurize or **-ise** /dē-presh'ə-rīz/ vt to reduce the air pressure in (eg an aircraft cabin) esp suddenly. [**de-** (2)]

■ **depressurizā'tion** or **-s-** n.

deprive /di-prīv'/ vt to dispossess; to keep from enjoyment (of); to degrade (esp a clergyman) from office (archaic); to bereave (archaic). [LL dēprīvāre to degrade, from L dē from, and prīvāre to deprive]

■ **depriv'able** adj. **depriv'al** or **deprivā'tion** /dep-ri- or dē-prī-/ n the act of depriving; the state of being deprived; degradation from office (archaic); loss; bereavement (archaic). **depriv'ative** adj. **deprived'** adj having been dispossessed (of); suffering from hardship, esp the lack of good educational, social, medical, etc facilities. **deprive'ment** n.

de profundis /dē prə-fun'dis, dā pro-fŭn'dēs/ (L) out of the depths (from Psalm 130).

deprogram /dē-prō'gram/ vt to remove a program from (a computer); (usu **deprō'gramme**) to prevail upon (a person) to reject obsessive beliefs, fears, etc. [**de-** (2)]

depside /dep'sīd/ (chem) n a product formed by the condensation of the carboxyl group of one molecule with the phenol group of a second, functioning in plant cells. [Gr depsein to knead]

Dept. or **dept.** abbrev : department (also **Dept** or **dept**); deputy.

depth /depth/ n deepness; the measure of deepness down or inwards; a deep place; intensity (of eg feeling); the innermost or most intense part, as in depth of winter; difficulty of understanding, obscurity; extent of wisdom and penetration of mental powers. [Not in OE; possibly ON dȳpth; or formed from **deep** on analogy of **length**, etc]

■ **depth'less** adj having no depth; bottomless.

❑ **depth bomb** or **charge** n a powerful bomb that explodes under water (dropped over or near submarines). **depth psychologist** n. **depth psychology** n the psychology of the unconscious mind. **depth sounder** n an echo-sounder.

■ **depth of field** the distance between the nearer and farther planes in an area photographed, seen through a microscope, etc, over which the image is in reasonably sharp focus. **depth of focus** the distance between a camera lens and the film at which the image will be clear. **in depth** extending far inwards; (of defence) consisting of several successive lines; extensive(ly) and thorough(ly) (**in'-depth'** adj see under **in¹**). **out of one's depth** in water where one cannot touch bottom with one's head above the surface, or too deep for one's safety; in a situation, etc beyond one's understanding. **the depths** the lowest pitch of humiliation and misery.

depurate /dep'ū-rāt, di-pū'rāt/ vi to purify. [LL dēpūrāre, -ātum to purify, from L dē- (intensive) and pūrāre to purify, from pūrus pure]

■ **dep'urant** adj and n. **depurā'tion** n. **depurative** /dep'ū-rā-tiv or di-pūr'ə-tiv/ n and adj. **dep'urātor** n. **depu'ratory** adj.

depute /di-pūt'/ vt to appoint or send as a substitute or agent; to send with a special commission; to give (one's authority) to someone else. ◆ combining form /dep'ūt/ in Scotland, appointed deputy (as in sheriff-depute, often simply the depute). [L dēputāre to prune, (later) to select]

■ **deputation** /dep-ū-tā'shən/ n the act of deputing; the person or persons deputed or appointed to transact business for another; a representative body of people sent to state a case in a dispute; the privilege of shooting game, or a document granting it, formerly given by the lord of a manor, nominally as to a gamekeeper. **dep'utize** or **-ise** vt to appoint as deputy. ◆ vi to act as deputy. **dep'uty** n a person deputed or appointed to act for another, esp (US) for a sheriff; a delegate or representative, or substitute; a legislator, member of a chamber of deputies; a person who attends to safety arrangements in a coalmine.

dequeue /dē-kū'/ (comput) vt to remove (a data-processing task) from a list of tasks awaiting processing in a buffer. [**de-** (2)]

der. abbrev : derivation; derivative; derived.

deracialize or **-ise** /dē-rā'shə-līz, -shyə-/ vt to divest of racial character. [**de-** (2) and **racial**]

deracinate /dē-ras'i-nāt/ vt to root up (lit and fig). [Fr déraciner, from L dē from, and LL rādicīna, dimin of L rādix a root]

■ **deracinā'tion** n. **déraciné** /dā-ras-ē-nā/ adj (Fr) uprooted (lit and fig).

deraign see **darraign**.

derail /di-rāl'/ (lit and fig) vt to cause to leave the rails. ◆ vi to go off the rails. [**de-** (2)]

■ **derail'er** n. **derail'ment** n.

dérailleur /dā-ra-yœr'/ or **dérailleur gear** /gēr/ n a variable bicycle gear depending on a mechanism by means of which the chain can be transferred from one sprocket wheel to another of different size. [Fr dérailler to derail]

derange /di-rānj'/ vt to put out of place or order; to disorder, put into confusion; to make insane. [Fr déranger, from dé- (L dis-) asunder, and ranger to rank]

■ **deranged'** *adj* disordered; insane. **derange'ment** *n* disorder, disarray; insanity; obsolete psychiatric term for psychosis.

derate /dē-rāt'/ *vt* to relieve (wholly or partially) from paying local rates; to reduce the maximum capacity ratings of (a piece of electrical equipment) to allow for deterioration, etc. [**de-** (2)]
■ **derat'ing** *n*.

deration /dē-ra'shən/ *vt* to free from rationing. [**de-** (2)]

deray /di-rā'/ (*obs*) *vt* to derange. ◆ *vi* to go wild. ◆ *n* tumult, disorder. [OFr *desreer*, from *des-* (negative) and *rei*, *roi* order; see **array**]

Derby /där'bi/ *n* a kind of porcelain made at *Derby*; (with *the*) a horse-race held annually on Epsom Downs (from Derby stakes, instituted by Earl of *Derby*, 1780); any of several horse-races modelled on this, such as the one at Churchill Downs, Kentucky; (often without *cap*) any race attracting much interest, or a keen sporting contest, *esp* one between neighbouring teams; a firm pale type of cheese *orig* made in Derbyshire; /dûr'bi/ (*US*; often without *cap*) a bowler hat; (sometimes without *cap*) a strong type of boot.
◻ **Derbyshire neck** *n* a form of goitre. **Derbyshire spar** *n* fluorite.

der-doing /dûr'doo'ing/ (*Spenser*) *adj* doing daring deeds. [See **derring-do**]

dere or **deare** /dēr/ (*obs*) *vt* to injure. ◆ *n* (*Spenser*) injury. [OE *derian*]

derecognize or **-ise** /dē-rek'əg-nīz/ *vt* to withdraw recognition from (*esp* a trade union). [**de-** (2)]
■ **derecogni'tion** *n*.

deregister /dē-rej'i-stər/ *vt* to remove from a register. [**de-** (2)]
■ **deregistra'tion** *n*.

de règle /də reg'l'/ (*Fr*) according to rule.

deregulate /dē-reg'ū-lāt/ *vt* to free from regulations or controls. [**de-** (2)]
■ **deregula'tion** *n*.

derelict /der'i-likt/ *adj* forsaken; abandoned, falling in ruins; neglectful of duty (chiefly *N Am*). ◆ *n* anything (*esp* a ship) forsaken or abandoned; a person abandoned by society, a down-and-out. [L *dērelinquere*, *-lictum*, from *dē* (intensive), *re-* behind, and *linquere* to leave]
■ **derelic'tion** *n* act of forsaking (*esp* duty), unfaithfulness or remissness; state of being abandoned; land gained from the water by a change of waterline.

dereligionize or **-ise** /dē-ri-lij'ə-nīz/ *vt* to make irreligious. [**de-** (2)]

derepress /dē-ri-pres'/ *vt* to activate (a gene) by suppressing its repressor. [de- (2)]
■ **derepress'ion** *n*.

derequisition /dē-rek-wi-zi'shən/ *vt* to return (something that has been used for a military purpose) to civilian use. [**de-** (2)]

derestrict /dē-ri-strikt'/ *vt* to free from restriction (*esp* a road from a speed limit). [**de-** (2)]
■ **derestric'tion** *n*.

derham see **dirham**.

deride /di-rīd'/ *vt* to laugh at; to mock. [L *dērīdēre*, *-rīsum*, from *dē* (intensive) and *rīdēre* to laugh]
■ **derid'er** *n*. **derid'ingly** *adv*. **derisible** /-riz'/ *adj*. **derision** /di-rizh'ən/ *n* act of deriding; mockery; a laughing stock. **derisive** /di-rīs'iv* or -riz'/ *adj* scoffing, mocking. **deris'ively** (or /-riz'/) *adv*. **deris'iveness** (or /-riz'/) *n*. **deris'ory** *adj* scoffing; ridiculous, *esp* ridiculously inadequate.

derig /dē-rig'/ (*theatre*, etc) *vt* to dismantle and remove (equipment, *esp* sound and lighting gear). [**de-** (2)]

de rigueur /də rē-gœr'/ (*Fr*) required by strict etiquette, or by fashion, etc.

derision, derisive, etc, **derisory** see under **deride**.

deriv. *abbrev* : derivation; derivative; derived.

derive /di-rīv'/ *vt* to conduct, draw, take, obtain, proceed or receive (from a source or origin); to infer; to trace to or from an origin; to bring down (upon oneself; *obs*; *Shakesp*). ◆ *vi* to descend, issue or originate. [Fr *dériver*, from L *dērīvāre*, from *dē* down, from, and *rīvus* a river]
■ **deriv'able** *adj*. **deriv'ably** *adv*. **derivate** /der'i-vāt/ *adj* derived. ◆ *n* a derivative. **deriva'tion** *n* act of deriving; a drawing off; the tracing of a word to its root; source, origin; that which is derived; descent or evolution; a sequence of statements showing how a certain result must follow from other statements already accepted, as in a mathematical formula, logical progression, etc. **deriva'tional** *adj*. **deriva'tionist** *n*. **derivative** /di-riv'ə-tiv/ *adj* derived or taken from something else; (sometimes *derog*) not radical or original, unoriginal. ◆ *n* that which is derived; a word formed from another word, *esp* by prefixation or suffixation; a product derived from one already produced; a differential coefficient (*maths*); any financial instrument (eg a futures contract or option) giving rights or obligations to an underlying asset or liability (*stock exchange*). **deriv'atively** *adv*.

◻ **derived demand** *n* (*econ*, *marketing*, etc) a demand that exists only as a result of another demand. **derived unit** *n* a unit of measurement derived from the fundamental units of a system.

derm /dûrm/, **derma** /dûr'mə/ or **dermis** /-mis/ *n* the true skin, below the outer layer. [Gr *derma*, *-atos* the skin]
■ **dermabra'sion** *n* a cosmetic operation in which the facial skin is scrubbed, peeled away and allowed to heal. **der'mal**, **dermat'ic** or **der'mic** *adj* relating to the skin; consisting of skin. **Dermap'tera** *n pl* an order of insects with forewings, when present, in the form of firm elytra, the earwigs. **dermatī'tis** *n* (*med*) inflammation of the skin. **dermat'ogen** *n* (*bot*) the layer from which epidermis is formed at the growing-point. **dermatoglyph'ics** *n pl* (Gr *glyphein* to carve) patterns of lines on the skin, *esp* the skin on the undersurfaces of the hands and feet; (as *sing*) the science of the study of skin patterns. **dermatograph'ia** *n* (*med*) a type of urticaria in which the physical allergy causes stroking or scratching, etc to raise a red weal on the skin. **dermatograph'ic** *adj*. **dermatog'raphy** *n* anatomical description of the skin (also **dermog'raphy**). **der'matoid** *adj* of the form of skin; skin-like. **dermatolog'ical** *adj*. **dermatol'ogist** *n*. **dermatol'ogy** *n* the branch of science that concerns itself with the skin. **derm'atome** *n* (Gr *tomos* a slice, section, from *temnein* to cut) a surgical instrument for cutting layers of skin, *esp* for grafting; the part of an embryonic somite, or skin segment, that produces the dermis; the area of skin supplied with nerves from a single spinal root. **dermatomyosi'tis** *n* a disease characterized by inflammation of the skin and muscles, and wasting of the muscles. **der'matophyte** *n* a parasitic fungus of the skin. **dermatophytic** /-fit'ik/ *adj*. **dermatoplas'tic** *adj*. **dermatoplas'ty** *n* (Gr *plassein* to mould) a plastic operation on the skin, *esp* grafting. **dermatō'sis** *n* (*pl* **dermatō'ses** /-sēz/) any skin disease. **dermes'tid** *n* a beetle of the **Dermestidae** family, many of which attack hides, wool, carpets, etc. **der'moid** *n* a cyst of similar cell structure to that of skin, *usu* congenital or occurring in the ovary. **Dermop'tera** *n pl* an order of mammals, the flying lemurs, sometimes included in Insectivora.

dern¹ see **durn**.

dern² or **dearn** /dûrn/ (*archaic* and *dialect*) *adj* secret; hidden; dreadful (*Shakesp*). ◆ *n* secrecy; hiding. [OE *dyrne*, *derne* secret]
■ **dern'ful** or **dearn'ful** *adj* solitary; mournful. **dern'ly** or **dearn'ly** *adv* secretly; sorrowfully; grievously.

dernier /der-nyā'/ (*Fr*) *adj* last.
◻ **dernier cri** /krē/ *n* the last word (literally, cry), the latest fashion. **dernier ressort** /res-sör/ *n* a last resort.

derogate /der'ō-gāt/ *vi* and *vt* to lessen by taking away; to detract. ◆ *adj* (*Shakesp*) degenerate. [L *dērogāre*, *-ātum* to repeal part of a law, from *dē* down, from, and *rogāre* to propose a law]
■ **der'ogately** *adv* (*Shakesp*) in a derogatory manner. **deroga'tion** *n* a taking from; detraction; depreciation; the allowed breaking of a rule. **derog'ative** *adj*. **derog'atively** *adv*. **derogatorily** /di-rog'ə-tər-i-li/ *adv*. **derog'atoriness** *n*. **derog'atory** *adj* detracting; injurious; insulting, adversely critical.

derrick /der'ik/ *n* an arrangement for hoisting materials, by a boom hung from a central post; a framework or tower over a borehole or the like. ◆ *vt* to luff (the jib of a crane). [From *Derrick*, a 17c hangman]

derrière /der-yer, der'i-er/ (*Fr*) *n* the behind, buttocks.

derring-do or **derring do** or **doe** /der'ing-doo/ (*pseudo-archaic*) *n* daring action. [Spenser mistook Lydgate's *dorryng do*, ie daring (to) do (misprinted *derrynge do*) for a noun]
◻ **derr'ing-do'er** *n*.

derringer /der'in-jər/ *n* a short American pistol. [After its inventor, US gunsmith Henry *Derringer* (1786–1868)]

derris /der'is/ *n* any plant of the tropical genus *Derris*, related to peas and beans, whose roots yield an insecticide powder. [Gr *derris* a leather coat]

derry /der'i/ (*sl*, *esp Aust*) *n* a feeling of dislike or resentment, *esp* in the phrase *have a derry on* (someone). [Prob from old refrain *derry down*]

der Tag /dār tähh, täk/ (*Ger*) the day when the struggle begins (*orig*, in Germany, the day when a career of conquest by Germany was to begin).

derth /dûrth/ (*Spenser*) *n* same as **dearth**.

derv /dûrv/ *n* diesel engine fuel oil. [From *d*iesel *e*ngined *r*oad *v*ehicle]

dervish /dûr'vish/ *n* (sometimes with *cap*) a member of one of numerous Muslim fraternities, professing poverty and leading an austere life. [Turkish *dervīsh*, from Pers *darvish* a dervish, literally a poor man]

desacralization or **-s-** /dē-sak-rə-lī-zā'shən or -sā'krə-/ *n* the removal of sacred character, operation, tradition, etc; secularization. [**de-** (2), **sacral**, **-ize** and **-tion**]
■ **desa'cralize** or **-ise** *vt*.

désagrément /dāz-ag-rā-mä'/ (*Fr*) *n* something disagreeable.

desalinate /dē-sal'i-nāt/, also **desalinize** or **-ise** /-nīz/ vt to remove salt from (esp sea water). [**de-** (2)]
■ **desalinā'tion** n. **desal'inātor** n. **desalinizā'tion** or **-s-** n.

desalt /dē-sölt'/ vt to remove salt from. [**de-** (2)]
■ **desalt'ing** n.

desaturation /dē-sat-ū-rā'shən/ (phys) see **saturation** under **saturate**.

descale /dē-skāl'/ vt to remove scales from (esp fish); to scrape away an encrustation from. [**de-** (2)]

descant /des'kant/ n an accompaniment above and harmonizing with the main melody (music); counterpoint (obs; music); a discourse or disquisition under several heads. ◆ adj (of a musical instrument) having a higher register and pitch than most others of the same family. ◆ vi (also /-kant'/) to sing a descant; to discourse at length (obs); to comment (obs). [ONFr descant, from L dis- apart, and cantus a song]

descend /di-send'/ vi to climb down; to pass from a higher to a lower place or condition; (with to) to stoop to what is unworthy of one; to move from general to particular topics, details, etc; to make an invasion; to be derived (from); (of the testes) to move from the abdominal cavity into the scrotum. ◆ vt to move down upon; to traverse downwards. [Fr descendre, from L dēscendere, from dē down, and scandere to climb]
■ **descend'ant** n a person who descends, ie offspring from an ancestor; the point on the ecliptic opposite the ascendant (astrol). **descend'ed** adj derived by descent. **descend'ent** adj going down; proceeding from an ancestor. **descend'er** n (printing) the part of a letter such as j or p that comes below the line on which x sits. **descend'ible** (also **descend'able**) adj that may descend or be descended; capable of transmission by inheritance, heritable. **descend'ing** n (Shakesp) lineage. **descen'sion** n. **descen'sional** adj. **descent'** n an act of descending; transmission by succession, inheritance; motion or progress downwards; slope; a raid or invasion; derivation from an ancestor; a generation, a degree in genealogy; descendants collectively.
■ **descent from the cross** a picture representing Christ being taken down from the cross.

descendeur /di-sen'dər/ n a metal device tightened or loosened on a rope by a climber to control speed of descent. [Fr]

deschool /dē-skool'/ vt and vi to free (children) from the restrictions of traditional classroom learning and a set curriculum, and educate them in a less formal way, esp at home. [**de-** (2)]
■ **deschool'er** n. **deschool'ing** n.

descramble /dē-skram'bl/ vt to unscramble, decipher. [**de-** (2)]

describe /di-skrīb'/ vt to trace out or delineate; to give an account of, recount the physical appearance or details of. [L dēscrībere, from dē down, and scrībere, scrīptum to write]
■ **describ'able** adj. **describ'er** n. **description** /di-skrip'shən/ n the act of describing; an account of anything in words; (loosely) sort, class or kind. **descrip'tive** adj containing description. **descrip'tively** adv. **descrip'tiveness** n. **descrip'tivism** n the use of, or belief in, descriptive linguistics (see below); a theory of ethics by which only empirical statements are acceptable. **descrip'tor** n (comput) a file name describing a subject in a storage system; a keyword or a heading.
□ **descriptive geometry** n the study of three-dimensional figures when projected onto a two-dimensional surface. **descriptive linguistics** n sing the study of the description of a language structure as it occurred individually at a particular time, ie with no reference to its history, any other language, etc.

descrive /di-skrīv'/ (obs) vt to describe. [OFr descrivre, from L dēscrībere]

descry /di-skrī'/ vt (**descry'ing**; **descried'**) to reveal (obs; Spenser); to discover by looking; to espy. ◆ n (obs) discovery; a thing discovered (Shakesp). [Appar two words: OFr descrire for descrivre, from L dēscrībere, and OFr descrier, decryer to proclaim, announce, from des-, de-, and crier to cry; cf **describe**, **decry**]

desecrate /des'i-krāt/ vt to make no longer consecrated; to profane, damage (something sacred). [Coined on the analogy of **consecrate**, with L dē from (L dēsecrāre meant to consecrate)]
■ **des'ecrater** or **des'ecrator** n. **desecrā'tion** n act of desecrating; profanation, damage (of anything sacred).

deseed /dē-sēd'/ vt to remove the seeds from. [**de-** (2)]
■ **deseed'ed** adj.

desegregate /dē-seg'ri-gāt/ vt to abolish racial segregation in. [**de-** (2)]
■ **desegregā'tion** n. **desegregā'tionist** n and adj.

deselect /dē-sə-lekt'/ vt (of a political party at constituency or ward level) not to select (the candidate who is already an MP or councillor) as a candidate for re-election; (of a selection panel or other body) not to reselect (eg an athlete) for a place on a team, to represent a country, county or the like. [**de-** (2)]
■ **deselec'tion** n.

desensitize or **-ise** /dē-sen'si-tīz/ vt and vi to make or become less sensitive. [**de-** (2)]
■ **desensitizā'tion** or **-s-** n. **desen'sitizer** or **-s-** n.

deserpidine /di-zûrp'i-din, -dēn/ n a synthetic sedative drug of which the natural base is Rauwolfia serpentina.

desert¹ /di-zûrt'/ vt to leave; to forsake. ◆ vi to run away; to leave a service, eg the army, without permission. [L dēserere, dēsertum, from dē- (negative) and serere to bind]
■ **desert'ed** adj empty or abandoned. **desert'er** n someone who deserts from or quits any of the armed forces without permission. **deser'tion** n an act of deserting; the state of being deserted; wilful abandonment of a legal or moral obligation.
■ **desert the diet** see under **diet²**.

desert² /dez'ərt/ n a desolate or barren tract, usu with little or no water; a waste; a place of solitude. ◆ adj deserted; desolate; uninhabited; uncultivated. [OFr desert, from L dēsertum, from dēserere to desert, unbind]
■ **desertificā'tion**, **desertizā'tion** or **-s-** n the deterioration or reversion of land to desert conditions, owing to over-grazing, erosion, etc.
□ **desert boots** n pl laced suede ankle boots with rubber soles. **desert island** n an uninhabited and remote tropical island. **desert pavement** n an underlying bed of gravel that remains after the finer material in a desert soil has been blown away. **desert pea** (usu Sturt's desert pea) n a showy Australian glory-pea (genus Clianthus) with a predominantly scarlet flower. **desert rat** n a jerboa, hence (from the divisional sign of a jerboa) a soldier of the British 7th Armoured Division with service in N Africa in 1941–42. **desert varnish** n a dark surface coating of oxides formed on exposed rock in deserts.

desert³ /di-zûrt'/ n anything that is deserved; claim to reward; merit. [OFr, pap of deservir; see **deserve**]
■ **desert'less** adj (rare) without merit.
■ **get one's just deserts** to meet a deservedly unpleasant fate.

deserve /di-zûrv'/ vt to be entitled to by merit; to warrant, be worthy of. ◆ vi to be worthy of reward. [OFr deservir, from L dēservīre, from dē (intensive) and servīre to serve]
■ **deserved'** adj. **deserv'edly** adv. **deserv'edness** n. **deserv'er** n. **deserv'ing** adj worthy. **deserv'ingly** adv according to what is deserved; justly. **deserv'ingness** n.

desex /dē-seks'/ vt to desexualize. [**de-** (2)]

desexualize or **-ise** /dē-sek'sū-ə-līz/ vt to deprive of sexual character or quality. [**de-** (2)]
■ **desexualizā'tion** or **-s-** n.

déshabillé /dā-zā-bē-yā/, also **dishabille** /dis-ə-bēl'/ n careless attention to one's dress, appearance, etc; a state of undress; a light casual garment. [Fr, pap of déshabiller to undress, from des- (L dis-) apart, and habiller to dress]

desi /dez'i/ (Ind and Pak) adj authentically Asian. [Hindi, from Sans deśa country]

desiccate /des'i-kāt/ vt to dry (up); to preserve by drying. ◆ vi to grow dry. [L dēsiccāre, -ātum to dry up, from dē- (intensive) and siccus dry]
■ **des'iccant** or **desiccative** /di-sik'ə-tiv/ adj drying; having the power of drying. ◆ n a drying agent. **des'iccated** adj dried; lacking in vitality, passion or interest. **desiccā'tion** n the act or process of drying up; the state of being dried up. **des'iccātor** n apparatus for drying.

desiderate /di-zid'ə-rāt/ (archaic) vt to long for or earnestly desire; to want or miss. [L dēsīderāre, -ātum to long for; dēsīderium longing. A doublet of **desire**]
■ **desiderā'tion** n the act of desiderating; the thing desiderated. **desid'erative** adj implying desire (as in desiderative verb). **desiderā'tum** (or /-ä'-/) n (pl **desidera'ta**) something desired or much wanted. **desiderium** /des-i-dē'ri-əm/ n longing; grief for what is lost.

design /di-zīn'/ vt to draw; to plan and execute artistically; to form a plan of; to contrive, invent; to intend; to set apart or destine; to indicate (Shakesp, Spenser, etc; obs). ◆ n a drawing or sketch; a plan in outline; a plan or scheme formed in the mind; arrangement of form and appearance; a plot; intention. [Fr désigner, from L dēsignāre, -ātum, from dē- off, and signum a mark]
■ **design'able** adj. **designedly** /di-zīn'id-li/ adv by design; intentionally. **design'er** n a person who provides designs or patterns; a draughtsman; a plotter; someone who designs sets for plays, operas, films, etc. ◆ adj of or relating to a designer; designed by (and bearing the name of) a known fashion designer; designed, created to follow the fashionable trend or image (loosely; slightly derog); custom-made, for a specific purpose or effect. **design'ful** adj full of design. **design'ing** adj artful; scheming; working secretly for self-interest. ◆ n the art of making designs or patterns. **design'ingly** adv. **design'less** adj. **design'ment** n (obs) the design or sketch of a work; intention, purpose, enterprise (Shakesp), etc.
□ **design engineer** n a designer in engineering. **designer baby** n (inf) a child in whose conception genetic engineering techniques are

used in order to assure specific genetic characteristics. **designer drug** *n* a drug manufactured so as to produce the same (*esp* hallucinogenic or narcotic) effects as one already existing (*esp* one restricted or illegal), by modifying the contents; a drug designed for a specific purpose.

■ **argument from design** the argument for the existence of God from evidence of design in creation. **by design** intentionally. **have designs on** to have plans to appropriate.

designate /*dez*'*ig-nāt*/ *vt* to mark out so as to make known; to show, indicate; to name; to be a name or label for; to appoint or nominate. ◆ *adj* nominated to but not yet in possession of an office (used after the noun, as in *chairman designate*). [L *designātus*, pap of *designare* to designate; see **design**]

■ **designā'tion** *n* a showing or pointing out; a name; a title; a style of address descriptive of occupation, standing, etc; the line typed after the signature in the complimentary close of a formal or business letter; nomination to office. **des'ignative** *adj*. **des'ignātor** *n*. **designā'tory** *adj*.

❑ **designated driver** *n* a person who attends a social event having decided in advance not to drink alcohol so as to be able to drive others home.

desilver /*dē-sil*'*vər*/ *vt* to remove silver from (also **desil'verize** or **-ise**). [**de-** (2)]

■ **desilverizā'tion** or **-s-** *n*.

desine (*Spenser*) same as **design**.

desinent /*des*'*i-nənt*/ or **desinential** /*des-i-nen*'*shəl*/ (*obs* or *archaic*) *adj* terminal. [L *dēsinēns, -entis*, prp of *dēsinere* to leave off, from *dē* from, and *sinere* to allow]

■ **des'inence** *n* ending.

desipient /*di-sip*'*i-ənt*/ *adj* playing the fool; trifling. [L *dēsipiēns, -entis*, prp of *dēsipere*, from *dē-* (negative) and *sapere* to be wise]

■ **desip'ience** *n*.

desire /*di-zīr*'/ *vt* to long for; to wish for; to ask; to regret the loss of (*archaic; Bible*). ◆ *vi* to be in a state of desire. ◆ *n* an earnest longing or wish; a prayer or request; the object desired; lust. [Fr *désirer*, from L *dēsīderāre*]

■ **desīrabil'ity** *n*. **desīr'able** *adj* worthy of desire or approval; to be approved of; pleasing; agreeable; sexually attractive. ◆ *n* a desirable person or thing. **desir'ableness** *n*. **desir'ably** *adv*. **desire'less** *adj*. **desīr'er** *n*. **desīr'ous** *adj* (*usu* with *of*) full of desire; wishful, wanting; eager; desirable (*obs*). **desir'ously** *adv*. **desir'ousness** *n*.

desist /*di-zist*'/ or **-sist**'/ *vi* to leave off, stop (doing something). [L *dēsistere*, from *dē-* away from, and *sistere* to cause to stand]

■ **desist'ance** or **desist'ence** *n*.

desk /*desk*/ *n* a sloping or flat table for writing or reading, often fitted with drawers, etc; a similar flat table for a computer; a receptacle for writing materials with a top that can be used as a writing surface when closed; a pulpit or lectern; a counter in a public place for information, registration, etc; a department of a newspaper office, eg *the sports desk*; a music stand; in an orchestra, *esp* among strings, (players in) a seating position determined by rank (eg *the first desk*). [ME *deske*, from L *discus*, from Gr *diskos*; see **dish**[1] and **disc**]

■ **desk'ing** *n* desks collectively.

❑ **desk'bound** or **desk'-bound** *adj* confined to a desk (eg of someone doing paperwork and administration rather than active or practical work); (of equipment, eg a computer) not portable. **desk clerk** *n* (*N Am*) a receptionist in a hotel. **desk editor** *n* a person who prepares a manuscript for typesetting, corrects proofs, etc. **desk jockey** *n* (*derog*) a clerical worker. **desk'top** (*comput*) *adj* (of a computer, etc) designed for use on a desk. ◆ *n* the main work area in a WIMP environment; a desktop computer. **desktop publishing** *n* (a system for) the performance of the typesetting, design, layout, illustration, etc of a document or publication on a desktop computer. **desk'-work** *n* work done at a desk, eg by a clerk or author.

■ **hot desking** see under **hot**.

deskill /*dē-skil*'/ *vt* to remove the element of human skill from (a job, process, operation, etc) through automation, computerization, etc. [**de-** (2)]

■ **deskill'ing** *n*.

desman /*des*'*mən*/ *n* a Russian aquatic insectivore with long snout and musk glands; a related Pyrenean species. [Swed *desman* musk]

desmid /*dez*'*mid*/ *n* (*bot*) one of a group of microscopic algae, unicellular or strung in chains. [Gr *desmos* a chain, fetter, *desmē* a bundle, and *eidos* form]

■ **desmine** /*dez*'*mēn* or *-min*/ *n* the mineral stilbite occurring in bundles. **desmōd'ium** *n* (*pl* **desmo'diums**) a plant of the telegraph-plant genus *Desmodium*. **desmodrom'ic** *adj* (Gr *dromos* running; *mech*) denoting a system, used in some motorcycle and racing car engines, that employs eg cams, rockers, etc to ensure that the opening and closing of valves, when the vehicle is at high speed, is fully controlled. **desmosō'mal** *adj*. **des'mosome** *n* (*biol*) a small

thickened patch on the membranes of adjacent cells which strongly bind them together, eg in the skin.

desmoid /*dez*'*moid*/ (*zool*) *adj* resembling a fascia or a ligament. ◆ *n* a firm swelling composed of scar tissue. [Ety as for **desmid**, and **-oid**]

Desmond /*dez*'*mənd*/ (*sl*) *n* a lower-second class honours degree. [Pun on the name of *Desmond Tutu*, South African archbishop, and 2:2, the common name for this class of degree]

désobligeante /*dā-zo-blē-zhãt*'/ *n* a carriage for one. [Fr, unaccommodating]

désœuvré /*dā-zœ-vrā*'/ (*Fr*) *adj* unoccupied; at a loose end.

desolate /*des*'*ə-lət*/ *adj* comfortless; dreary; forlorn; lonely; totally lacking in inhabitants; laid waste. ◆ *vt* /-*lāt*/ to make lonely or forlorn; to make extremely sad; to deprive of inhabitants; to lay waste. [L *dēsōlāre, -ātum*, from *dē-* (intensive) and *sōlāre* to make alone, from *sōlus* alone]

■ **des'olately** *adv*. **des'olateness** *n*. **des'olāter** or **des'olātor** *n*. **desolā'tion** *n* waste; destruction; a place desolated; misery, wretchedness. **des'olatory** *adj*.

desorb see under **desorption**.

désorienté /*dā-zo-rē-ā-tā*' or *-ryā-*/ (*Fr*) *adj* having lost one's bearings, confused.

desorption /*dē-sörp*'*shən*/ (*chem*) *n* release from an adsorbed state. [**de-** (2)]

■ **desorb'** *vt*.

desoxy- see **deoxy-** under **deoxidate**.

despair /*di-spār*'/ *vi* to be without hope (of). ◆ *n* hopelessness; anything that causes despair. [OFr *desperer*, from L *dēspērāre, -ātum*, from *dē-* (negative) and *spērāre* to hope]

■ **despair'ful** *adj* (*archaic; Spenser*). **despair'ing** *adj* apt to despair; full of despair. **despair'ingly** *adv*.

despatch see **dispatch**.

desperado /*des-pər-ä*'*dō* or *-ā*'*dō*/ *n* (*pl* **despera'dos** or **despera'does**) a desperate person, reckless of danger; a wild ruffian; an outlaw. [Old Sp (Mod *desesperado*), from L *dēspērātus*]

desperate /*des*'*pə-rit*/ *adj* in a state of despair; hopeless; beyond hope; despairingly reckless; (loosely) furious; extremely bad; extremely anxious or eager (for, to do, etc) (*inf*). [See **despair**]

■ **des'perately** *adv*. **des'perateness** *n*. **desperā'tion** *n* a state of despair; despairing; disregard of danger; fury; recklessness.

despicable /*dis-pik*'*ə-bl* or *des*'*pi-kə-*/ *adj* deserving to be despised; contemptible; worthless. [See **despise**]

■ **despicabil'ity** or **despic'ableness** (or /*des*'*pik-*/) *n*. **despic'ably** (or /*des*'/) *adv*.

despight /*di-spīt*'/ an old spelling of **despite**.

despise /*di-spīz*'/ *vt* to look down upon with contempt, scorn, hate. [OFr *despire* (*despis-*), from L *dēspicere*, from *dē* down, and *specere* to look]

■ **despīs'able** *adj*. **despīs'al** *n* contempt. **despīs'edness** *n* (*Milton*). **despīs'er** *n*.

despite /*di-spīt*'/ *prep* in spite of; notwithstanding. ◆ *n* (*obs*) a looking down with contempt; violent malice or hatred. [OFr *despit* (Mod *dépit*), from L *dēspectus*, from *dēspicere* ; see **despise**]

■ **despite'ful** *adj* (*archaic*) contemptuous. **despite'fully** *adv* (*archaic*). **despite'fulness** *n* (*archaic*). **despiteous** /*dis-pit'i-əs*/ *adj* (*archaic; Spenser*, etc).

despoil /*di-spoil*'/ *vt* to plunder completely; to strip; to bereave; to rob. [OFr *despoiller* (Mod *dépouiller* ; see **despoliation**)]

■ **despoil'er** *n*. **despoil'ment** *n*.

despoliation /*di-spō-li-ā*'*shən*/ *n* despoiling. [L *dēspoliāre*, from *dē-* (intensive) and *spolium* spoil]

despond /*di-spond*'/ *vi* to be lacking in hope, to be dejected. ◆ *n* (*Bunyan*) despondency. [L *dēspondēre* to promise, to devote, to resign, to despond, from *dē* away, and *spondēre* to promise]

■ **despond'ence** or **despond'ency** *n* lack of hope, dejection. **despond'ent** *adj*. **despond'ently** *adv*. **despond'ing** *n* and *adj*. **despond'ingly** *adv*.

despot /*des*'*pot* or *-pət*/ *n* someone invested with absolute power; a tyrant. [OFr *despot*, from Gr *despotēs* a master]

■ **des'potat** or **des'potate** *n* a territory governed by a despot. **despotic** /*dis-pot'ik*/ or **despot'ical** *adj* relating to or like a despot; having absolute power; tyrannical. **despot'ically** *adv*. **despot'icalness** *n*. **des'potism** *n* absolute power; a state governed by a despot. **despotoc'racy** *n* government by a despot.

despumate /*di-spū*'*māt* or *des*'*pū-māt*/ *vi* to throw off impurities in foam or scum. ◆ *vt* to skim. [L *dēspūmāre, -ātum*, from *dē-* off, and *spūma* foam]

■ **despumā'tion** *n*.

■ words derived from main entry word; ❑ compound words; ■ idioms and phrasal verbs

desquamate /des'kwə-māt/ vi (esp of the skin affected by disease) to scale off. [L dēsquāmāre, -ātum, from dē- off, and squāma a scale]
■ **desquamā'tion** n a scaling off; the separation of the cuticle or skin in scales. **desquamative** /di-skwam'ə-tiv/ adj. **desquam'atory** adj.

des res /dez rez/ (inf; facetious, or property jargon) n a desirable residence. [From abbrev used in small ads, brochures, etc]

desse /des/ (Spenser) n a desk. [dais]

dessert /di-zûrt'/ n a final course of a meal, pudding or other sweet item; fruit, sweetmeats, etc served at the end of a meal. [OFr dessert, from desservir to clear the table, from des- (L dis-) away, and servir to serve, from L servīre]
□ **dessert'-serv'ice** n the dishes used for dessert. **dessert'spoon** n a spoon used for eating desserts, smaller than a tablespoon and larger than a teaspoon. **dessert'spoonful** n (pl **dessert'spoonfuls**). **dessert wine** n a sweet wine usu drunk with or after dessert.

dessiatine, **dessyatine** or **desyatin** /des'yə-tēn/ n a Russian measure of land, 2.7 English acres (about 1.1 hectares). [Russ desyatīna a measure of land, a tenth; desyat' ten]

destabilize or **-ise** /dē-stā'bi-līz/ vt to make unstable or less stable (lit and fig). [de- (2)]
■ **destābilīzā'tion** or **-s-** n. **destā'bilizer** or **-s-** n.

de-Stalinize or **-ise** /dē-stā'li-nīz/ vt to remove the influence of Joseph Stalin from (Russian politics, etc).
■ **de-Stalinīzā'tion** or **-s-** n.

destemper see distemper².

De Stijl /də stīl/ n an (orig Dutch) artistic movement of the 1920s, embracing neoplasticism and Dada, and having an influence on contemporary architecture and design. [Du, the style (the title of the movement's magazine)]

destine /des'tin/ or (obs) **destinate** /-āt/ vt (often by fate) to ordain or appoint to a certain use or state; to intend; to fix; to doom. [Fr destiner, from L dēstināre, from dē- (intensive) and root of stāre to stand]
■ **destinā'tion** n the place to which one is going; the purpose or end to which anything is destined or appointed; end; purpose; design; fate; (the nomination of) the series of heirs to whom property, etc is to pass (Scots law). **des'tiny** n the purpose or end to which any person or thing is appointed; unavoidable fate; necessity.

destitute /des'ti-tūt/ adj in utter poverty; entirely lacking in (with of); left alone, forsaken (obs). ◆ vt (obs) to forsake; to deprive. [L dēstituere, -ūtum, from dē- away, and statuere to place]
■ **destitu'tion** n the state of being destitute; poverty; deprivation of office.

de-stress /dē-stres'/ vi to relax or become calm after a period of psychological stress or hard work. [de- (2)]
■ **de-stress'ing** n.

destrier /des'tri-ər, de-strēr'/ (archaic) n a warhorse. [Fr, from L dextrārius led by the (squire's) right hand]

destroy /di-stroi'/ vt (destroy'ing; destroyed') to demolish, pull down; to overturn; to defeat or kill; to ruin; to put an end to. [OFr destruire (Fr détruire), from L dēstruere, dēstructum, from dē- down, and struere to build]
■ **destroy'able** adj. **destroy'er** n a person or thing that destroys; a small, fast-moving warship.
□ **destroying angel** n Amanita phalloides or A. virosa, two poisonous toadstools, whitish in colour, with a volva at the base of the stalk.

destruction /di-struk'shən/ n the act or process of destroying; overthrow; physical or moral ruin; death; a cause of destruction. [L dēstruere, -structum; see destroy]
■ **destruct'** vt to destroy a rocket or missile in flight (also vi). **destructibil'ity** or **destruc'tibleness** n. **destruc'tible** adj capable of being or liable to be destroyed. **destruc'tional** adj. **destruc'tionist** n a person engaged in destruction; a person who believes in the final annihilation of the damned. **destruc'tive** adj causing or concerned with destruction; (of eg criticism) unhelpfully negative, opp to constructive; mischievous. ◆ n a destroying agent. **destruc'tively** adv. **destruc'tiveness** n. **destruc'tivist** n a representative of destructive principles. **destructiv'ity** /dē-/ n. **destruc'tor** /di-/ n a destroyer; a furnace for burning up refuse.
□ **destructive distillation** n (chem) the decomposition of solid substances by heating, and the subsequent collection of the volatile substances produced.

desuetude /di-sū'i-tūd, des'wi-tūd/ (formal) n disuse; discontinuance. [L dēsuētūdō, from dēsuētum, dēsuēscere, from dē (negative) and suēscere to become used]

desulphur /dē-sul'fər/ vt to remove sulphur from (also **desul'phurāte** or **desul'phurize** or **-ise**). [de- (2)]
■ **desulphurā'tion** n. **desulphurizā'tion** or **-s-** n. **desul'phurizer** or **-s-** n.

desultory /des'əl-tər-i/ adj jumping from one thing to another; without rational or logical connection; rambling; hasty; loose; random. [L dēsultōrius, from dēsultor a vaulter, dēsilīre, -sultum to leap, from dē from, and salīre to jump]
■ **des'ultorily** adv. **des'ultoriness** n.

desyatin see dessiatine.

desyne (Spenser) same as design.

Det. abbrev : Detective.

detach /di-tach'/ vt to unfasten; to take away or separate; to withdraw; to send off on special service (milit). ◆ vi to separate. [Fr détacher, from OFr pfx des- (L dis-) apart, and root of attach]
■ **detachabil'ity** n. **detach'able** adj. **detached'** adj unconnected; separate; impartial; aloof; free from care, passion, ambition and worldly bonds. **detach'edly** adv. **detach'edness** n. **detach'ment** n the state of being detached; the act of detaching; that which is detached, eg a unit of troops from the main body.
□ **detached retina** n a retina that has separated from the eyeball, causing loss of vision.

detail /di-tāl' or dē'tāl/ vt to relate minutely; to enumerate; to set apart for a particular service. ◆ vi to give details about anything. ◆ n /dē'tāl or (esp N Am) di-tāl'/ a small or unimportant part; an area of a painting, photograph, map, etc considered separately and often enlarged; an item; a particular account; inclusion of all particulars; too much attention to relatively unimportant particulars; a small body set apart for special duty (chiefly milit). [Fr détailler, from de- (intensive) and tailler to cut]
■ **detailed'** adj giving full particulars; exhaustive; showing many small elements clearly.
□ **detail drawing** n (building) large-scale working drawing (usu of a part only) giving information that does not appear on small-scale drawings of the whole construction.
■ **go into detail** to study, discuss, etc a matter deeply, considering the particulars. **in detail** circumstantially, point by point; piecemeal.

detain /di-tān'/ vt to hold back; to withhold; to delay; to stop; to keep; to keep in custody. ◆ n (Spenser) detention. [OFr detenir, from L dētinēre; see detent]
■ **detain'able** adj. **detainee'** n a person kept in custody. **detain'er** n a person who detains; the holding of what belongs to another (law); a warrant to a sheriff to keep in custody a person already in confinement. **detain'ment** n detention.

detangle /dē-tang'gl/vt to remove knots or tangles from. [de- (2)]
■ **detang'ler** n a cosmetic product for detangling hair.

detect /di-tekt'/ vt to discover; to discern; to find out (esp something elusive or secret); to uncover, expose (obs); to accuse (obs; Shakesp). [L dētegere, -tēctum, from dē- (negative), and tegere to cover]
■ **detect'able** or **detect'ible** adj. **detec'tion** n the discovery of something hidden or not easily observed; the state of being found out. **detect'ive** adj employed in or concerned with detection. ◆ n a policeman, usu not in uniform, or other person (**private detective**) who investigates cases of crime or watches the behaviour of suspected persons. **detect'ivist** n a writer of detective fiction. **detect'ophone** n a secret telephone for eavesdropping. **detec'tor** n someone who detects; an apparatus for detecting something, eg smoke, tampering with a lock, pressure of electric currents, electric waves, etc.
□ **detective story** n one in which clues to the detection of a criminal are set forth and unravelled.

detent /di-tent'/ n anything that checks motion; a catch, esp for regulating the striking of a clock. [L dētinēre, dētentum, from dē from, and tenēre to hold]

détente /dā-tãt'/ (Fr) n relaxation of strained relations (esp between countries).

detention /di-ten'shən/ n the act of detaining; the state of being detained; confinement, or restriction of liberty, esp of a political prisoner or any offender; punishment by being made to stay in school after classes have ended; delay. [L dētinēre, dētentum, from dē from, and tenēre to hold]
□ **detention centre** n a place of temporary confinement for illegal immigrants, young offenders, etc.

détenu /dā-tə-nü'/ (Fr) n (also fem **détenue**) a prisoner, esp a political prisoner in India.

deter /di-tûr'/ vt (deterr'ing; deterred') to frighten (from); to hinder or prevent. [L dēterrēre, from dē from, and terrēre to frighten]
■ **deter'ment** n. **deterrence** /di-ter'əns/ n. **deterrent** /di-ter'ənt/ adj serving to deter. ◆ n anything that deters; specif a nuclear weapon.

deterge /di-tûrj'/ vt (rare) to wipe off; to cleanse (eg a wound). [L dētergēre, dētersum, from dē off, and tergēre to wipe]
■ **deterg'ence** or **deterg'ency** n. **deterg'ent** n (also (rare) **deters'ive**) that which cleanses; a cleansing agent, such as an abrasive, a solvent or mixture of solvents, and certain water-soluble oils, esp

(commonly) a soapless cleanser. ◆ *adj* (also **deters'ive**) cleansing; purging.

deteriorate /di-tē'ri-ə-rāt/ *vi* to grow worse. ◆ *vt* to make worse. [L *dēteriōrāre, -ātum* to make worse, from *dēterior* worse, from *dē* down]
■ **detēriora'tion** *n* the act of making worse; the process of growing worse. **detēriora'tionist** *n* a believer in deteriorism. **detē'riorātive** *adj*. **detē'riorism** *n* the doctrine that the world grows worse. **detēriority** /-or'i-ti/ *n* (*obs*) worseness.

determine /di-tûr'min/ *vt* to put terms or bounds to; to limit; to fix or settle; to define; to decide; to resolve; to cause to resolve; to put an end to (*law*). ◆ *vi* to come to a decision; to come to an end (*law*); to cease to exist (*Shakesp*); to take part in a dispute, *esp* in completing the degree of bachelor of arts (*obs*). [L *dētermināre, -ātum*, from *dē* (intensive), and *terminus* a boundary]
■ **determinabil'ity** *n*. **deter'minable** *adj* capable of being determined, decided or finished. **deter'minableness** *n*. **deter'minably** *adv*. **deter'minacy** /-ə-si/ *n*. **deter'minant** *adj* serving to determine. ◆ *n* that which serves to determine; the sum of all the products obtained by taking one from each row and column of a square block of quantities, each product being reckoned positive or negative according as an even or an odd number of transpositions reduces it to the order of the rows (or of the columns), used for the solution of equations and other purposes (*maths*); a hypothetical unit in the germ plasm determining the course of development of a cell (*bot*); the mutual recognition sites on an antibody and antigen (*immunol*); a determining candidate for the BA degree (*obs*). **deter'mināte** *adj* determined or limited; fixed; decisive; cymose, having the main stem and branches ending in flowers (*bot*). ◆ *vt* (*obs; Shakesp*) to determine. **deter'minately** *adv*. **deter'minateness** *n*. **determinā'tion** *n* the act of determining; the condition of being determined; that which is determined or resolved on; end (*law*); judicial decision (*law*); direction to a certain end; resolution; fixedness of purpose; decision of character. **deter'minātive** *adj* that determines, limits or defines. ◆ *n* (in hieroglyphics) an additional sign attached to a word as a guide to its meaning. **deter'mined** *adj* ascertained; fixed; firm in purpose; resolute. **deter'minedly** *adv*. **deter'minedness** *n*. **deter'miner** *n* someone who, or that which, determines; a determinant (*bot*); a limiting adjective or modifying word such as *any, each, that, my*, etc (*grammar*). **deter'minism** *n* (*philos*) the doctrine that all things, including the will, are determined by causes (the converse of *free will*); necessitarianism. **deter'minist** *n*. **determinis'tic** *adj*.

deterrent see under **deter**.

detersion /di-tûr'shən/ *n* the act of cleansing. [See **deterge**]
■ **deter'sive** *adj* and *n* detergent.

detest /di-test'/ *vt* to hate intensely. [Fr, from L *dētestāri*, from *dē* (intensive) and *testārī* to call to witness, execrate, from *testis* a witness]
■ **detestabil'ity** or **detest'ableness** *n*. **detest'able** (also (*Spenser* and *Shakesp*) /dē'/) *adj* worthy of being detested; extremely hateful; abominable. **detest'ably** *adv*. **detestation** /dē-tes-tā'shən/ *n* (an object of) extreme hatred.

dethrone /di-thrōn'/ *vt* to remove from a throne; to remove from a position of authority or eminence. [**de-** (2)]
■ **dethrone'ment** *n*. **dethrōn'er** *n*. **dethrōn'ing** *n*.

detinue /det'in-ū/ (*law*) *n* wrongful detention of property. [OFr *detenue*, fem pap of *detenir*; see **detain**]

detonate /det'ə-nāt or dē'tō-nāt/ *vt* and *vi* to explode or cause to explode rapidly and loudly; in an internal-combustion engine, to explode by spontaneous combustion with a hammering sound (pinking or knock). [L *dētonāre, -ātum*, from *dē* down, and *tonāre* to thunder]
■ **detonā'tion** *n* an explosion with report; in an internal-combustion engine, premature combustion of part of the mixture, causing knocking or pinking. **det'onātor** *n* a substance that detonates; a substance or contrivance whose explosion initiates that of another explosive; a fog signal.

detort /di-tört'/ *vt* (*obs*) to distort; to untwist; to twist the other way. [L *dētorquēre, dētortum*; *dē* away (also negative) and *torquēre* to twist]
■ **detor'sion** or (*obs*) **detor'tion** *n* (*biol*).

detour /dē', dā'toor/ *n* a deviation; a circuitous way. ◆ *vt* and *vi* to go or cause to go on a detour. [Fr *dé-* (L *dis-*) asunder, and *tour* turning]

detox /dē-toks'/ (*inf*) *vt* and *vi* short form of **detoxify**. ◆ *n* /dē'toks/ short form of **detoxification**; a detoxification centre (also **detox tank**).

detoxify /dē-tok'si-fī/ or **detoxicate** /-i-kāt/ *vt* (**detox'ifying** or **detox'icating**; **detox'ified** or **detox'icated**) to rid of poison or the effects of it. ◆ *vi* to abstain from unhealthy substances in order to clear the system of poisons. [**de-** (2)]
■ **detox'icant** *n* a substance that detoxifies (also *adj*). **detoxificā'tion** or **detoxicā'tion** *n*.

□ **detoxification centre** *n* a centre for the treatment of alcoholism or drug addiction.

DETR *abbrev* : (until 2001) Department of the Environment, Transport, and the Regions.

detract /di-trakt'/ *vt* to take away, abate; to distract; to defame (*obs*). ◆ *vi* (with *from*) to take away from; to reduce in degree; to diminish. [L *dētrahere*, from *dē* from, and *trahere, tractum* to draw]
■ **detract'ing** *n* and *adj*. **detract'ingly** *adv*. **detrac'tion** *n* depreciation; slander. **detract'ive** or **detract'ory** *adj* tending to detract; derogatory. **detract'ively** *adv*. **detract'or** *n* (also *fem* **detract'ress**) a belittler or disparager.

detrain /dē-trān'/ *vt* to set down out of a railway train. ◆ *vi* to alight from a train. [**de-** (2)]
■ **detrain'ment** *n*.

détraqué /dā-trä-kā'/, *fem* **détraquée** *n* a person who is deranged. [Fr, upset, out of order]

detribalize or **-ise** /dē-trī'bə-līz/ *vt* to cause to lose tribal customs, characteristics, etc, *usu* in favour of an urban way of life. [**de-** (2)]
■ **detribalīzā'tion** or **-s-** *n*.

detriment /det'ri-mənt/ *n* diminution; damage; loss; a thing that causes diminution, damage or loss. [L *dētrīmentum*, from *dē* off, and *terere, trītum* to rub]
■ **detrimental** /-ment'l/ *adj* causing damage or loss. ◆ *n* (*archaic sl*) a suitor who is undesirable; someone whose presence lessens the chances of a good match. **detriment'ally** *adv*.

detritus /di-trī'təs/ *n* a mass of substance gradually worn off solid bodies; an aggregate of loosened fragments, *esp* of rock; accumulated debris; decaying organic material such as decomposing plants. [L *dētrītus* worn, from *dē* off, and *terere, trītum* to rub]
■ **detrī'tal** *adj*. **detrition** /di-trish'ən/ *n* wearing away. **detrī'tivore** *n* an animal that feeds on decaying organic material.

de trop /də trō'/ (*Fr*) *adj* (used after the noun) superfluous; in the way.

detrude /di-trood'/ *vt* to thrust down. [L *dētrūdere*, from *dē* down, and *trūdere* to thrust]
■ **detru'sion** *n*. **detru'sor** *n* a muscle in the wall of the bladder that contracts when the bladder is full.

detruncate /di-trung'kāt/ *vt* to cut short; to lop; to mutilate. [L *dētruncāre, -ātum*, from *dē* off, and *truncāre*, to lop]
■ **detruncā'tion** /dē-/ *n*.

detumescence /dē-tū-mes'əns/ *n* diminution of swelling, *opp* to **intumescence**. [**de-** (2)]
■ **detumesc'ent** *adj*.

detune /dē-tūn'/ *vt* to alter the oscillations of (violin strings, an electronic circuit, etc); to reduce the performance and efficiency of (a motor-car engine). [**de-** (2)]

deuce[1] /dūs or (*N Am*) *doos*/ *n* the two in cards and dice; a situation ('forty all') from which one side must gain two successive points to win the game (*tennis*); anything with a value of two (*US sl*). [Fr *deux* two, from L *duōs* accusative of *duo* two]
□ **deuce'-ace** *n* a throw of two dice turning up deuce and ace; bad luck. **deuce court** *n* the right side of a tennis court, from which the serve is made and received at even-numbered points.

deuce[2] /dūs/ *n* (in exclamatory phrases) the devil. [Prob from *the deuce* (see **deuce**[1]), the lowest throw at dice]
■ **deuced** /dū'sid or dūst/ *adj* (as an intensifier) damned, absolute, etc. ◆ *adv* (also **deuc'edly**) confoundedly; extremely.

deuch-an-doris see **deoch-an-doruis**.

deuddarn /dī'dhärn/ *n* a Welsh dresser or sideboard in two stages. [Welsh]

deus /dē'əs, dā'ŭs/ (*L*) *n* (pl **di** /dī/ or **dē**/ or **dei** /dā'ī/) god.
■ **Deus avertat** /a-vûr'tat, ä-wer'tat/ God forbid. **Deus det** /det/ God grant. **deus ex machina** /eks mak'in-a, sometimes mə-shē'nə/ *orig*, a god brought on the stage by a mechanical device; a contrived and inartistic solution of a difficulty in a plot. **Deus vobiscum** /vō-bis'kəm, wō-bēs'kŭm/ God be with you. **Deus vult** /vult or wŭlt/ God wills it (the Crusaders' cry).

Deut. (*Bible*) *abbrev* : (the Book of) Deuteronomy.

deuter- /dū-tər-/ or **deutero-** /dū-tə-rō-/ *combining form* denoting second or secondary. [Gr *deuteros* second]
■ **deuterag'onist** *n* the second actor in a Greek drama. **deu'teranope** *n* a person suffering from deuteranopia. **deuteranō'pia** *n* (Gr *ops* eye) a type of colour blindness in which red and green are confused, blue and yellow only being distinguished. **deuteranop'ic** *adj*. **deu'terate** *vt* to add deuterium to, or to replace hydrogen by deuterium in (molecules). **deuterā'tion** *n*. **deu'teride** *n* a hydrogen compound containing another element. **deuterium** /-tē'ri-əm/ *n* heavy hydrogen, an isotope of hydrogen of double mass (**deuterium oxide** heavy water). **deuterocanon'ical** *adj* (Gr *kanōn* rule) relating to a second canon of inferior authority, ie the Old Testament Apocrypha and the

New Testament Antilegomena. **deuterog'amist** *n* a person who allows or practises deuterogamy. **deuterog'amy** *n* (Gr *gamos* marriage) second marriage, *esp* of the clergy, after the death of the first wife. **deu'teron** *n* the nucleus of heavy hydrogen, of mass 2, carrying unit positive charge. **Deuteronom'ic** or **Deuteronom'ical** *adj*. **Deuteron'omist** *n* the author of the Book of Deuteronomy or part of it. **Deuteronomy** /-on'ə-mi or *dū'*/ *n* (Gr *nomos* law) the fifth book of the Pentateuch, containing a repetition of the decalogue and laws given in Exodus. **deu'toplasm** *n* same as **deutoplasm**. **deuteroscop'ic** *adj*. **deuteros'copy** *n* (Gr *skopiā* a look-out) a second view or meaning (*obs*); second sight.

deuton /*dū'ton*/ (*obs*) older form of **deuteron**.

deutoplasm /*dū'tō-plazm*/ (*biol*) *n* the food material, such as yolk or fat, within an egg or cell. [Fr *deutoplasme*]
■ **deutoplas'mic** *adj*.

Deutschmark /*doich'märk*/ or **Deutsche Mark** /*doi'chə märk*/ a former unit of currency of Germany, replaced by the euro. [Ger]

Deutzia /*dūt'si-ə* or *doit'si-ə*/ *n* a genus of saxifragaceous plants with panicles of white flowers, introduced from China and Japan. [Johann van der *Deutz*, 18c Dutch patron of botany]

Deuxième Bureau /*dœ-zyem bü-rō'*/ (Fr) *n* the French Department of Military Intelligence.

deva /*dā'vä*/ (*Hinduism* and *Buddhism*) *n* a god; a good spirit. [Sans *deva* a shining one, a god]

devall /*di-völ'*/ *vi* to sink, decline (*obs*); to cease (*Scot*). ◆ *n* (*Scot*) a stop. [Fr *dévaler*, from L *dē-* down, and *vallis* a valley]

devalue /*dē-val'ū*/ *vt* and *vi* to reduce in value. [**de-** (2)]
■ **devalorizā'tion** or **-s-** *n* devaluation. **deval'orize** or **-ise** *vt*. **deval'uate** *vt*. **devaluā'tion** *n* (*econ*) reducing the value internationally of a country's money, by lowering the exchange rate; reducing the accounting value of an asset to reflect a decline in economic value.

devanagari /*dā-və-nä'gə-ri*/ *n* (sometimes with *cap*) the script in which Sanskrit and Hindi are *usu* written and printed (the official script for Hindi); used also for other Indian languages. [Sans *devanāgari* town-script of the gods; see **nagari**]

devastate /*dev'ə-stāt*/ *vt* to lay waste; to plunder; to overwhelm with shock or grief. [L *dēvastāre, -ātum,* from *dē-* (intensive) and *vastāre* to lay waste]
■ **dev'astating** *adj* ravaging; overpoweringly effective (*inf*). **dev'astatingly** *adv*. **devastā'tion** *n* the act of devastating; the state of being devastated; havoc; waste of property by an executor. **dev'astātive** *adj*. **dev'astātor** *n*. **dēvastā'vit** *n* (L, has wasted) a writ lying against an executor for devastation; the offence of devastation.

devein /*dē-vān'*/ *vt* to remove the main vein from (the meat of a prawn or shrimp). [**de-** (2)]

devel see **devvel**.

develop (earlier also **develope**) /*di-vel'əp*/ *vt* (**devel'oping**; **devel'oped**) to bring out what is latent or potential in; to bring to a more advanced or more highly organized state; to work out the potentialities of; to elaborate; to cause to grow or advance; to evolve; to contract (a disease); to make more available; to exploit the natural resources of (a region); to build on or prepare (land) for building on; in chess, to bring into a position useful in attack; to disclose; to express in expanded form (*maths*); to unroll into a plane surface (*geom*); to render visible (the image on a negative) by the use of chemicals (*photog*); to free from integuments or that which envelops; to unroll (*obs*); to lay open by degrees (*obs*). ◆ *vi* to open out; to evolve; to advance through successive stages to a higher, more complex, or more fully grown state. [Fr *développer*, opposed to *envelopper*, of obscure origin]
■ **devel'opable** *adj*. **devel'oped** *adj*. **devel'oper** *n* a person who develops, *esp* property; a reagent for developing photographs; an apparatus for developing muscles. **develop'ment** *n* the act or process of developing; the state of being developed; a gradual unfolding or growth; evolution; (an area containing) a number of buildings constructed at the same time; the expression of a function in the form of a series (*maths*); elaboration of a theme, or that part of a movement in which this occurs (*music*); a new situation that emerges. **development'al** *adj* relating to development. **development'ally** *adv*.
❑ **developing country** *n* a country that is relatively poor and dependent on agriculture but which is becoming more industrialized. **development aid** *n* money and other assistance given by rich industrial nations to developing countries. **developmental psychology** *n* the psychology of mental development from birth to maturity. **development area** *n* a region of heavy unemployment where new industry is given official encouragement. **development studies** *n sing* a branch of knowledge concerned with economic, social and political change in developing countries.

développé /*dā-ve-lə-pā'*/ *n* a movement in ballet in which a dancer draws up one leg to the knee of the other then fully extends it. [Fr]

devest /*di-vest'*/ *vt* to undress (*Shakesp*); to alienate (*law*); to take off; to strip. [A form of **divest**]

Devi /*dā'vē*/ *n* in India, used as a title for a married woman (following her name). [Sans, goddess]

deviate /*dē'vi-āt*/ *vi* to go from the way; to turn aside from a certain course; to diverge or differ, from a standard, mean value, etc; to err; to step outside one's fundamental contractual duty (*law*). ◆ *vt* to cause to diverge. ◆ *n* /*dē'vi-ət*/ (*psychol*) a person who deviates much from the norm, *esp* sexually; a deviant. [L *dēviāre, -ātum,* from *dē* from, and *via* a way]
■ **dē'viance** or **dē'viancy** *n*. **dē'viant** *n* someone who deviates from the norm, *esp* sexually (also *adj*). **dēviā'tion** *n*. **dēviā'tionism** *n*. **dēviā'tionist** *n* a person (*orig* a communist) whose doctrine deviates from the strictly orthodox. **dē'viātor** *n*. **dēviā'tory** *adj*.
■ **deviation of the compass** departure of the mariner's compass from the magnetic meridian, owing to the ship's magnetism or other local causes. **standard deviation** (*maths*) the square root of the variance of a number of observations.

device /*di-vīs'*/ *n* that which is devised or designed; a contrivance; a plan or scheme; one of a number of physical parts of a system, eg a computer system (as *input device, storage device*); a bomb or its detonator; power of devising; an emblem (*heraldry*); a motto; a conceit (*obs*); a masque (*obs*). [OFr *devise*; see **devise**]
■ **device'ful** *adj* (*Spenser*; now *rare*) full of devices.
❑ **device driver** *n* (*comput*) a piece of software that controls the functioning of a printer, scanner, etc.
■ **leave someone to his** or **her own devices** to leave someone alone, not distracting or interfering with them.

devil /*dev'l* or *-il*/ *n* an evil spirit; (with *cap*) the supreme spirit of evil; a wicked person; a reckless, lively person; (*usu* pitying) a fellow; an animal, thing, problem, difficult, etc to deal with; someone who excels or exceeds in anything; a printer's devil; a drudge (*esp law* or *literary*); a firework; a grilled or highly seasoned dish; a dust storm; fighting spirit; a plumber's portable furnace; a machine of various kinds, *esp* for tearing; used as a mild oath, an expression of impatience, irritation, etc, or a strong negative. ◆ *vt* (**dev'illing** or (*N Am*) **dev'iling**; **dev'illed** or (*N Am*) **dev'iled**) to season highly and broil; to worry or pester (*N Am*). ◆ *vi* to perform another person's drudgery; to do very menial work. [OE *dēofol, dēoful,* from L *diabolus,* from Gr *diabolos,* from *diaballein* to throw across, to slander, from *dia* across, and *ballein* to throw; cf Ger *Teufel,* Fr *diable,* Ital *diavolo,* Sp *diablo*]
■ **dev'ildom** *n*. **dev'iless** *n*. **dev'ilet, dev'iling** or **dev'ling** *n* a young devil; a swift (*dialect*). **dev'ilish** *adj* fiendish, malignant; very bad. ◆ *adv* often /*dev'lish*/ (*inf*) very, exceedingly. **dev'ilishly** *adv*. **dev'ilishness** *n*. **dev'ilism** *n*. **dev'ilkin** *n*. **dev'illed** *adj*. **dev'ilment** *n* frolicsome mischief. **dev'ilry** *n*. **dev'ilship** *n*. **dev'iltry** *n* (*US*).
❑ **dev'il-crab** *n* the velvet-crab. **dev'ilfish** *n* the fishing-frog or angler; the giant ray of the United States; the octopus. **dev'il-in-a-bush** *n* a garden flower, love-in-a-mist. **dev'il-may-care'** *adj* reckless, audacious. **dev'il-on-the-neck** *n* an old instrument of torture. **dev'il-on-two-sticks** *n* an older name for diabolo. **devil's advocate** *n* advocatus diaboli, the Promoter of the Faith, an advocate at the papal court whose duty it is to propose objections against a canonization (*RC*); a person who states the case against a proposal, course of action, etc, *usu* for the sake of argument. **dev'il's-bit** *n* a species of scabious (*Succisa pratensis*) with rootstock as if bitten off. **devil's bones** *n pl* dice. **devil's books** *n pl* playing-cards. **devil's coach-horse** *n* a large dark-coloured beetle (*Staphylinus olens*) that turns up its tail when threatened. **devil's darning-needle** *n* (*inf*) a dragonfly or damselfly. **devil's dozen** *n* thirteen. **devil's dung** *n* asafoetida. **devil's dust** *n* shoddy made by a machine called the **devil**. **devil's food cake** *n* (chiefly *N Am*) a kind of chocolate cake. **devils on horseback** *n pl* prunes wrapped in bacon, grilled, and served on toast. **devil's own** *n* a name given to the 88th Regiment in the Peninsular War, also to the Inns of Court Volunteers. **devil's picture books** *n pl* (also in *sing*) same as **devil's books** above. **devil's snuff-box** *n* a puffball. **devil's tattoo** see under **tattoo²**. **dev'il-worship** *n* the worship of the Devil, or of devils; Satanism; the Yezidi religion. **dev'il-worshipper** *n*.
■ **between the devil and the deep (blue) sea** in a desperate dilemma; faced with alternatives that are equally undesirable. **devil a bit, a one** or **a thing**, etc not at all, not one, etc. **devil of a mess** a very bad mess. **devil take the hindmost** take care of yourself and never mind about others. **go to the devil** to become ruined; an interjection expressing angry dismissal or defiance. **like the devil** very hard or fast. **play the devil** to make havoc (with). **printer's devil** the youngest apprentice in a printing office; a printer's errand-boy. **raise hell** or **raise the devil** see under **raise¹**. **talk of the devil** here comes the person we were talking of. **the devil and all** much fuss; turmoil. **the devil to pay** serious trouble (as a consequence of an action, etc).

devious /dē'vi-əs/ adj tortuous of mind; scheming; deceitful; orig remote, out of the way (archaic); roundabout, winding; erring; insincere. [L dēvius; see **deviate**]
■ **de'viously** adv. **de'viousness** n.

devise /di-vīz'/ vt to imagine; to compose; to scheme, think out; to contrive; to bequeath (law); to suppose, guess (Spenser); to purpose (Spenser); to meditate (obs); to describe (obs); to depict (obs). ◆ vi (obs) to consider; to talk; to scheme. ◆ n (law) the act of bequeathing; a will; property bequeathed by will. [OFr deviser, devise, from LL dīvīsa a division of goods, a mark, a device, from L dīvidere, dīvīsum to divide]
■ **devīs'able** adj. **devīs'al** n. **devisee** /dev-ī-zē'/ n (law) a person to whom property is bequeathed. **devī'ser** n a person who contrives. **devīs'or** n (law) a person who bequeaths.
■ **devisal of arms** formerly synonymous with grant of arms, now used by the English College of Arms where the petitioner is an American corporate body and therefore ineligible for a grant of arms.

devitalize or **-ise** /dē-vī'tə-līz/ vt to deprive of vitality or life-giving qualities. [**de-** (2)]
■ **devitalīzā'tion** or **-s-** n.

devitrify /dē-vit'ri-fī/ vt (**devit'rifying**; **devit'rified**) to change from glassy to minutely crystalline. [**de-** (2)]
■ **devitrification** /-fi-kā'/ n.

devling see **devilet** under **devil**.

devocalize or **-ise** /dē-vō'kə-līz/ or **devoice** /dē-vois'/ vt to make voiceless. [**de-** (2)]

devoid /di-void'/ adj (with of) destitute, free; empty. [OFr desvoidier, from des- (L dis- away), and voider, from L viduāre, from viduus deprived]

devoir /dev'wär (historically dev'ər)/ n (often in pl) what is due, duty (archaic); service (obs); a courtesy; an act of civility. [Fr, from L dēbēre to owe]

devolution /dē-və- or dev-ə-loo'shən, -lū'/ n a passing from one person to another; a handing over of powers; a modified home rule, the delegation of certain powers to regional governments by a central government. [See **devolve**]
■ **devolu'tionary** adj. **devolu'tionist** n.

devolve /di-volv'/ vt to pass on; to hand down; to deliver over, esp powers to regional governments by a central government. ◆ vi to roll down (archaic); to fall or pass over in succession (with on). [L dēvolvere, -volūtum, from dē down, and volvere to roll]
■ **devolve'ment** n.

Devonian /di-vō'ni-ən/ adj belonging to or characteristic of the county of Devon in SW England; of or belonging to a period of the Palaeozoic era, between 415 and 360 million years ago, and esp to the marine rocks of this period, commonly found in Devon (the continental type being the Old Red Sandstone; geol). ◆ n a native of Devon; the Devonian period (geol).
❑ **Devon minnow** or **Devon** n an angler's lure that imitates a swimming minnow. **Devonshire cream** n clotted cream.

devonport /dev'n-pōrt, -pört/ same as **davenport**.

dévoré /dē-vō'rā/ adj (of velvet or satin) having a design etched with acid. ◆ n a dévoré fabric; an item of clothing made of such a fabric. [Fr, eaten]

dévot /dā-vō'/, fem **dévote** /dā-vōt'/ (Fr) n a devotee.

devote /di-vōt'/ vt to give up (oneself or something) wholly (to); to set apart or dedicate by a vow or solemn act; to doom (obs). ◆ adj (Shakesp and archaic) devoted. [L dēvovēre, dēvōtum, from dē away, and vovēre to vow]
■ **devōt'ed** adj given up (to), as by a vow; strongly attached (to); zealous; doomed (obs). **devōt'edly** adv. **devōt'edness** n. **devotee** /dev-ə-tē' or dev'/ n a person wholly or superstitiously devoted, esp to religion; a votary; someone strongly and consistently interested in something (with of). **devōte'ment** n (Shakesp and archaic). **devō'tion** n the act of devoting; the state of being devoted; consecration; giving up of the mind to the worship of God; piety; prayer; strong affection or attachment; ardour; faithful service; (in pl) prayers; religious offerings (obs); alms (obs). **devō'tional** adj. **devō'tionalist** n. **devotional'ity** n. **devō'tionally** adv. **devō'tionalness** n. **devō'tionist** n.

devour /di-vowr'/ vt to swallow greedily; to eat up; to consume or waste with violence or wantonness; to take in eagerly by the senses or mind. [OFr devorer, from L dēvorāre, from dē (intensive) and vorāre to swallow]
■ **devour'er** n. **devour'ing** adj. **devour'ingly** adv. **devour'ment** n.

devout /di-vowt'/ adj given up to religious thoughts and exercises; pious; solemn; earnest. [OFr devot, from L dēvōtus; see **devote**]
■ **devout'ly** adv. **devout'ness** n.

devvel or **devel** /dev'l/ (Scot) n a hard blow. ◆ vt (**devv'elling** or **dev'eling**; **devv'elled** or **dev'elled**) to hit hard; to stun with a blow. [Ety dubious]

DEW /dū or doo/abbrev: distant early warning.
❑ **DEW line** n a system of radar stations in the Arctic regions of N America intended to detect attack by missiles or aircraft (now replaced by **NWS**).

dew¹ /dū/ n moisture deposited from the air on cooling, esp at night, in minute specks upon the surface of objects; a similar deposit or exudation of other kinds; early freshness. ◆ vt (poetic) to moisten (as) with dew. [OE dēaw; cf ON dögg, Ger Tau dew]
■ **dew'ily** adv. **dew'iness** n. **dew'y** adj.
❑ **dew'berry** n a kind of bramble or blackberry (Rubus caesius; in America, other species) having a bluish, dew-like bloom on the fruit. **dew'-bow** n a rainbow-like appearance seen on a dewy surface. **dew'claw** n a rudimentary inner toe, esp on a dog's leg. **dew'drop** n a drop of dew; a drip, a drop of mucus on the end of the nose (inf). **dew'fall** n the deposition, or time of deposition, of dew. **dew'point** n the temperature at which a given sample of moist air becomes saturated and forms dew. **dew'-pond** n a hollow once thought to be supplied with water by mist. **dew'-retting** n the process of rotting away the gummy part of hemp or flax by exposure on the grass to dew and rain. **dew worm** n the common earthworm. **dew'y-eyed** adj (often ironic) fresh, innocent.
■ **mountain dew** (inf) whisky.

dew² /dū/ n an obsolete spelling of **due**.
■ **dew'full** adj (Spenser) due.

Dewali same as **Diwali**.

dewan or **diwan** /dē-wän'/ n in India, a financial minister; a state prime minister; the native steward of a business house. [Pers dīwān; see **divan**]
■ **dewani** or **dewanny** /dē-wä'nē/ n the office of dewan.

Dewar flask /dū'ər fläsk/ n (sometimes without cap; also **dew'ar**) a type of vacuum flask. [From Sir James Dewar (1842–1923), its inventor]

dewater /dē-wö'tər/ vt to drain or pump water from (eg coal). [**de-** (2)]
■ **dewat'ering** n partial or complete drainage by eg thickening, sedimentation or filtering to facilitate shipment or drying of a product.

Dewey decimal system /dū'i des'i-məl sis'tim/ or **Dewey decimal classification** /klas'i-fi-kā'shən/ n a system of library classification, based on the division of books into numbered classes, with further subdivision shown by numbers following a decimal point (also **decimal classification**). [Invented by Melvil Dewey (1851–1931), US librarian]

dewitt /di-wit'/ vt to lynch. [From the fate of Jan and Cornelius De Witt in Holland in 1672]

dewlap /dū'lap/ n the pendulous skin under the throat of cattle, dogs, etc; the fleshy wattle of the turkey. [Prob **dew¹** and OE læppa a loose hanging piece]
■ **dew'lapped** or **dew'lapt** adj.

deworm /dē-wûrm'/ vt to rid (an animal) of worms. [**de-** (2)]
■ **deworm'er** n.

dex /deks/ (sl) n short form of Dexedrine®; a pill containing this.

dexamethasone /dek-sə-meth'ə-sōn/ n a synthetic steroid drug used esp to treat inflammation. [**deca-**, **hexa-**, methyl and cortisone]

dexamfetamine or **dexamphetamine** see **dextroamphetamine** under **dextro-**.

Dexedrine® /dek'sə-drēn/ n dextroamphetamine.

dexiotropic /dek-si-ō-trop'ik/ adj turning to the right. [Gr dexios right, and tropos turning]

dexter¹ /deks'tər/ adj on the right-hand side; right; of that side of the shield on the right-hand side of the bearer, the spectator's left (heraldry); so sometimes in description of a picture, to avoid ambiguity. [L, right]
■ **dex'terwise** adv.

dexter² /deks'tər/ n a small breed of Kerry cattle. [Prob breeder's name]

dexterity /dek-ster'i-ti/ n skill of manipulation, or generally; adroitness; right-handedness (rare). [L dexter right]
■ **dex'terous** or **dex'trous** adj adroit; subtle; skilful; orig right-handed. **dex'terously** or **dex'trously** adv. **dex'terousness** or **dex'trousness** n.

dextral /deks'trəl/ adj right; turning to the right; of the right-hand side of the body; of flatfish, lying right-side-up; (of a spiral shell) turning in the normal manner, ie anticlockwise from the top. [Med L dextrālis, from dextra right hand]
■ **dextral'ity** n right-handedness. **dex'trally** adv.

dextran /deks'tran/ n a carbohydrate formed in sugar solutions by a bacterium (*Leuconostoc mesenteroides*), a substitute for blood plasma in transfusion. [**dextro-**]

dextrin /deks'trin/ or **dextrine** /-trēn/ n British gum, a gummy mixture obtained from starch by heating or otherwise, used as a thickener in foods and in adhesives.

dextro- /dek-strō-/ *combining form* denoting to, or towards, the right. [L *dexter*; Gr *dexios*, Sans *dakṣiṇa* on the right, on the south]
■ **dextroamphet'amine**, **dexamfet'amine** or **dexamphet'amine** n the dextrorotatory isomer of amphetamine, used as a stimulant. **dextrocar'dia** n (Gr *kardiā* heart) a condition in which the heart lies in the right side of the chest, not the left. **dextrocar'diac** n a person who has this condition. **dextrogyrate** /-jī'/ or **dex'trogyre** /-jīr/ adj causing to turn to the right hand. **dextrorota'tion** n. **dextroro'tatory** adj rotating to the right (clockwise), *esp* rotating thus the plane of polarization of light.

dextrorse /dek-strörs'/ or dek'/ (biol) adj rising helically and turning to the left, ie crossing an outside observer's field of view from left to right upwards (like a screw); formerly used in the contrary sense (sinistrorse). [L *dextrorsus* towards the right, from *dexter*, and *vertere* to turn]

dextrose /deks'trōs, -trōz/ n glucose.

dextro tempore /deks'trō tem'pər-ē, -por-e/ (L) at a lucky moment.

dextrous see under **dexterity**.

dey[1] /dā/ (obs or dialect) n a dairymaid (also **dey'-woman**). [See **dairy**]

dey[2] /dā/ n the pasha or governor of Algiers before the French conquest. [Turk *dāi*, orig a maternal uncle, a familiar title of the chief of the janizaries]

DF abbrev : Defender of the Faith; direction finder.

DFC abbrev : Distinguished Flying Cross.

DfE abbrev : Department for Education.

DfES abbrev : (until 2007) Department for Education and Skills.

DFID abbrev : Department for International Development.

DFM abbrev : Distinguished Flying Medal.

DfT abbrev : Department for Transport.

dft abbrev : defendant; draft.

DG abbrev : *Dei gratia* (L), by the grace of God; Director-General.

dg abbrev : decigram(s).

DGFT abbrev : Director General of Fair Trading.

DGRC abbrev : Director General of Research Councils.

DH abbrev : Department of Health.

d.h. abbrev : *das heisst* (Ger), that is.

DHA abbrev : docosahexaenoic acid, a fatty acid found in fish oils.

dhak /däk/ n an Indian tree of the genus *Butea*. [Hindi *dhāk*]

dhal same as **dal** (n).

dhansak /dän'säk/ (Ind cookery) adj denoting a dish of meat or vegetables cooked with lentils. [Gujarati]

dharma /där'mə, dûr'/ n virtue or righteousness arising from observance of social and moral law (*Hinduism*); truth as laid down in the Buddhist scriptures; the law. [Sans]

dharmsala /dûrm-sä'lä/ n a building having a religious or charitable purpose, as a free or cheap lodging for travellers (also **dharmshala**). [Hindi *dharmsālā*, from Sans *dharma*, and *śālā* hall]

dharna /dûr'nä/ n the practice of calling attention, *esp* to injustice, by sitting or standing in a place (where one will be noticed, *esp* sitting and fasting at the door of an offender). [Hindi]

dhimmi /dim'i/ n a non-Muslim subject of a state ruled by Islamic law. [Ar]
■ **dhimm'itude** n.

Dhivehi /di-vā'hi/ n the official language of the Maldives, related to Sinhalese.

dhobi /dō'bi/ (hist) n an Indian washerman. [Hindi *dhobī*]
❏ **dhobi itch** n a tropical allergic dermatitis.

dhol /döl/ n a large cylindrical drum, often with two heads, used in Indian music. [Hindi]

dhole /döl/ n the Indian wild dog. [Supposed to be from an Indian language]

dholl same as **dal** (n).

dhooly same as **doolie**.

dhoti /dō'ti/ or **dhooti** /doo'ti/ n the Hindu loincloth; a cotton fabric used for this. [Hindi *dhotī*]

dhow or **dow** /dow/ n an Arab lateen-sailed vessel of the Indian Ocean. [Origin unknown; cf Ar *dāw*, Marathi *dāw*]

DHS abbrev : Department of Homeland Security (in the USA).

DHSC abbrev : Directorate of Health and Social Care.

DHSS abbrev : (until 1989) Department of Health and Social Security.

dhurra see **durra**.

dhurrie same as **durrie**.

DI abbrev : Defence Intelligence; Detective Inspector; diabetes insipidus; donor insemination (see under **donation**).

di a plural of **deus**.

di- /dī-/ pfx denoting two, twice or double (see also **dis-**). [Gr *dis* twice]

DIA abbrev : Defense Intelligence Agency (in the USA).

dia. abbrev : diameter.

dia- /dī-ə- or -ə-/ pfx denoting: through; across; during; composed of. [Gr]

diabase /dī'ə-bās/ n formerly, diorite; an altered dolerite or basalt. [Appar orig a faulty derivative of Gr *di-* double, and *basis* base; associated with *diabasis*, transition]
■ **diabā'sic** adj.

diabetes /dī-ə-bē'tēz/ n any of several diseases, marked by an excessive discharge of urine, notably **diabetes insipidus** a disease caused by a disorder of the pituitary gland leading to malfunction of the kidney, and **diabetes mellitus** (L, honied) caused by insulin deficiency or, rarely, an excess of insulin, with excess of sugar in the blood and urine. [Gr *diabētēs* a siphon, from *dia* through, and *bainein* to go]
■ **diabetic** /-bēt'/ or *-bet'*/ or less commonly **diabet'ical** adj relating to, or suffering from, diabetes; for the use of diabetics. **diabet'ic** n a person suffering from diabetes. **diabetol'ogist** n a doctor specializing in the study and treatment of diabetes and the care of diabetics.

diable /dē-ä'bl' or dē-ab'l'/ n an unglazed earthenware casserole with a handle and a wide base tapering up to a narrow neck. [Fr]

diablerie or **diablery** /dē-äb'lə-rē/ n magic; the black art; sorcery; mischief. [Fr *diable*; see **devil**]

diabolic /dī-ə-bol'ik/ adj of the Devil; satanic; like a devil; extremely cruel. [Gr *diabolikos*, from *diabolos*; see **devil**]
■ **diabol'ical** adj (inf) very shocking, annoying or difficult; outrageous; very bad, unpleasant; (as an intensifier) complete or absolute. **diabol'ically** adv. **diab'olism** n devil-worship; devilry. **diab'olist** n a person knowledgeable on diabolism. **diabolize** or **-ise** /-ab'ə-līz/ vt to make devilish. **diabol'ogy** or **diabolol'ogy** n the doctrine of devils; devil-lore.

diabolo /di-ab'ol-ō or dī-/ n a game in which a two-headed top is spun, tossed, and caught on a string attached to two sticks, held one in each hand; (pl **diab'olos**) the top used in this game. [Gr *diaballō* I throw over, toss, or from *diabolos* devil; see also **devil**]

diacatholicon /dī-ə-kə-thol'i-kon/ (obs) n a purgative electuary, the drug being mixed with honey or syrup; a panacea. [Gr *dia katholikon* of universal (ingredients)]

diacaustic /dī-ə-kös'tik/ (maths and phys) adj relating to or denoting a caustic curve or caustic surface formed by refraction. ◆ n a curve so formed. [**dia-** and **caustic** (in mathematical sense)]

diacetylmorphine see **diamorphine**.

diachronic /dī-ə-kron'ik/ or **diachronical** /dī-ə-kron'ik-əl/ adj of the study of a subject (esp a language) through its historical development, opp to synchronic. [**dia-** and Gr *chronos* time]
■ **diachron'ically** adv. **diachronism** /dī-ak'/ n. **diachronist'ic** or **diach'ronous** adj. **diach'rony** n.

diachylon /dī-ak'i-lon/ or **diachylum** /dī-ak'i-ləm/ n formerly a plaster of plant juices; now lead-plaster. [Gr *dia chȳlōn* through (ie composed of) juices, or *diachȳlon* (neuter) juicy]

diacid /dī-as'id/ (chem) adj having two replaceable hydrogen atoms; capable of replacing two hydrogen atoms of an acid. [**di-**]

diacodion /dī-ə-kō'di-on/ or **diacodium** /dī-ə-kō'di-əm/ (obs) n a syrup of poppies. [L, from Gr *dia kōdeiōn* composed of poppy-heads, from *kōdeia* a poppy-head]

diaconate /dī-ak'ə-nāt/ n the office or period of service of a deacon; the body of deacons. [See **deacon**]
■ **diāc'onal** adj relating to a deacon.

diaconicon /dī-ə-kon'i-kən/ n a sacristy for sacred vessels, in a Greek church, on the south side of the bema or sanctuary. [Gr *diākonikon*]

diacoustic /dī-ə-koo'stik, old-fashioned -kow'/ adj relating to the refraction of sound. [**dia-**, and **acoustic**]
■ **diacoust'ics** n sing the branch of physics that deals with refracted sounds.

diacritic /dī-ə-krit'ik/ or **diacritical** /-əl/ adj distinguishing, a term used of marks (eg accents, cedillas, etc) attached to letters to indicate modified sound, value, etc. [Gr *diakritikos*, from *dia* between, and *kritikos*; see **critic**]
■ **diacrit'ic** n such a mark.

diact /dī'akt/ (*zool*) *adj* two-rayed. [**di-** and Gr *aktīs*, *aktīnos* ray]
■ **diactinal** /-ak'- or -tī'-/ or **diact'ine** *adj*.

diactinic /dī-ak-tin'ik/ (*phys*, *optics*, etc) *adj* capable of transmitting actinic rays. [**dia-**, and Gr *aktīs*, *aktīnos* ray]

diadelphous /dī-ə-del'fəs/ (*bot*) *adj* (of stamens) united by the filaments in two bundles; having stamens so joined. [**di-**, and Gr *adelphos* brother]
■ **Diadel'phia** *n pl* (in the Linnaean classification) a class with stamens so joined.

diadem /dī'ə-dem/ *n* a crown, a jewelled headband, or the like; an arch of a crown; regal power; a crowning glory. [OFr *diademe*, from L *diadēma*, from Gr *diadēma*, from *dia* round, and *deein* to bind]
■ **di'ademed** *adj* wearing a diadem.
❑ **diadem spider** *n* the common garden spider (from its markings).

diadochi /dī-ad'o-kī/ *n pl* the generals who became monarchs of the various kingdoms (Syria, Egypt, etc) into which the empire of Alexander the Great split after his death (323BC). [Gr *diadochos* succeeding, a successor; *diadechesthai* to succeed]

diadrom /dī'ə-drom/ *n* a course or passing; a vibration. ◆ *adj* (of leaf nerves) radiating fanwise. [Gr *dia* across, and *dromos* a run]

diaeresis or **dieresis** /dī-ēr'i-sis or -er'-/ *n* (pl **diaer'eses** or **dier'eses** /-ēz/) a mark (¨) placed over a vowel, *esp* the second of two adjacent ones to show that it is to be pronounced separately, as in *naïf* ; a pause or break where the end of the word coincides with the end of a foot (*prosody*). [Gr *diairesis* separation, from *dia* apart, and *haireein* to take]

diagenesis /dī-ə-jen'i-sis/ *n* the conversion of sediment into rock (*geol*); reconstitution of crystals to form a new product (*chem*). [**dia-** and **genesis**]
■ **diagenetic** /-ji-net'ik/ *adj*.

diageotropic /dī-ə-jē-ō-trop'ik/ (*bot*) *adj* taking a position perpendicular to the direction of gravity. [**dia-**]
■ **diageotrop'ically** *adv*. **diageotropism** /-ot'rə-pizm/ *n*.

diaglyph /dī'ə-glif/ *n* an intaglio. [Gr *dia* through, and *glyphein* to carve]

diagnosis /dī-əg-nō'sis/ *n* (pl **diagnō'ses** /-sēz/) the identification of a disease or other problem by means of its symptoms (also *fig*); a formal determining description, *esp* of a plant. [Gr, from *dia* between, and *gnōsis* knowing]
■ **diagnosabil'ity** *n*. **dī'agnosable** (or /-nō'-/) *adj*. **dī'agnose** (or /-nōz'*, or (*esp N Am*) -nōs or -nōs'/) *vt* to identify (a disease or other problem) from symptoms. **diagnos'tic** *adj* of, or useful in, diagnosis; distinguishing; differentiating. ◆ *n* that by which anything is known; a symptom; a diagnostic program or routine (*comput*). **diagnosti'cian** /-nos-tish'ən/ *n* a person skilled in diagnosis. **diagnos'tics** *n sing* diagnosis as a branch of medicine.
❑ **diagnostic characters** *n pl* (*zool*) characteristics by which one genus, species, family or group can be differentiated from another. **diagnostic program** or **routine** *n* a program or routine used in most computers as an aid in the debugging of programs and systems.

diagometer /dī-ə-gom'i-tər/ *n* a form of electroscope for ascertaining electric conductivity. [Gr *diagein* to conduct, and *metron* a measure]

diagonal /dī-ag'ə-nəl/ *adj* through the corners, or joining two vertices that are not adjacent, of a polygon; (of a plane) passing through two edges (not adjacent) of a polyhedron; slantwise. ◆ *n* a straight line or plane so drawn. [L *diagōnālis*, from Gr *diagōnios*, from *dia* through, and *gōniā* a corner]
■ **diag'onally** *adv*.
❑ **diagonal scale** *n* a scale for laying down small fractions of the unit of measurement, by lengthwise parallel lines intersected by two sets of parallel lines, crosswise and oblique.

diagram /dī'ə-gram/ *n* a figure or plan intended to explain rather than represent actual appearance; an outline figure or scheme; a curve symbolizing a set of facts; a record traced by an automatic indicator. ◆ *vt* (**di'agramming** or (*N Am*) **di'agraming**; **di'agrammed** or (*N Am*) **di'agramed**) to represent in diagrammatic form. [Gr *diagramma*, from *dia* round, and *graphein* to write]
■ **diagrammatic** /-grə-mat'ik/ *adj*. **diagrammat'ically** *adv*.

diagraph /dī'ə-gräf/ *n* an instrument for copying, enlarging or projecting drawings. [Gr *dia* round, and *graphein* to write]
■ **diagraphic** /-graf'ik/ *adj*.

diagrid /dī'ə-grid/ (*engineering*) *n* a structure of diagonally intersecting beams, used for support. [*diagonal grid*]

diaheliotropic /dī-ə-hē-li-ō-trop'ik/ (*bot*) *adj* turning transversely to the light. [**dia-**]
■ **diaheliotropism** /-ot'rə-pizm/ *n*.

diakinesis /dī-ə-kī-nē'sis or -ki-/ *n* in meiosis, the final stage of prophase, during which pairs of homologous chromosomes almost completely separate. [**dia-** and **kinesis**]

dial /dī'əl/ *n* the face of a watch or clock; a graduated plate on which a movable index shows the value of some quantity measured, or can be set to make an adjustment (such as the temperature control of an oven, etc or the tuning device on a radio); the numbered plate on an older type of telephone, and the movable disc fitted on top; a miner's compass with sights for surveying; a face (*sl*); an instrument for showing the time of day by the sun's shadow (as in *sundial*); a timepiece (*obs*). ◆ *vt* (**di'alling** or (*N Am*) **di'aling**; **di'alled** or (*N Am*) **di'aled**) to use a telephone dial or keypad to select (a telephone number); to measure or indicate or get into communication with by dial. ◆ *vi* to use a telephone dial or keypad. [LL *diālis* daily, from L *diēs* a day]
■ **dial-a-** *combining form* (also without *hyphens*) denoting goods and services available by telephone, as in *dial-a-ride*. **di'alist** *n* a maker of dials; someone skilled in dialling. **di'aller** *n* one who dials; a person who surveys by dial. **di'alling** *n* the art of constructing sundials; the science that explains the measuring of time by the sundial; surveying by dial.
❑ **dialling code** *n* a group of numbers dialled to obtain the desired exchange in an automatic dialling system. **dialling tone** or (*N Am*) **dial tone** *n* the continuous sound heard on picking up a telephone receiver which indicates that the equipment is functioning and ready to accept an input telephone number. **di'al-plate** *n* the plate to which the pillars of a watch are fixed. **di'al-up** *adj* (*comput*; of a connection) using a modem to connect to another computer or to the Internet.

dial. *abbrev* : dialect.

dialect /dī'ə-lekt/ *n* a variety or form of a language peculiar to a district or class, *esp* but not necessarily other than a literary or standard form; a peculiar manner of speaking; any of two or more variant forms of a particular computer language. [Through Fr and L from Gr *dialektos* speech, manner of speech, peculiarity of speech, from *dia* between, and *legein* to speak]
■ **dialect'al** *adj*. **dialect'ally** *adv*. **dialect'icism** *n*. **dialectolog'ical** *adj*. **dialectol'ogist** *n*. **dialectol'ogy** *n* the study of dialect(s).

dialectic /dī-ə-lek'tik/ *adj* (also **dialec'tical**) relating to discourse or to dialectics; logical. ◆ *n* (also **dialec'tics**) the art of discussing, *esp* a debate that seeks to resolve the conflict between two opposing theories, rather than disprove any one of them; that branch of logic that teaches the rules and modes of reasoning. [Gr *dialektikos*]
■ **dialec'tically** *adv*. **dialecti'cian** *n* a person skilled in dialectics, a logician.
❑ **dialectical materialism** see under **material**.

diallage¹ /dī-al'ə-jē/ (*rhetoric*) *n* a figure of speech by which arguments, after having been considered from various points of view, are all brought to bear upon one point. [Gr *diallagē*; see **diallage²**]

diallage² /dī'ə-lāj/ *n* a mineral, a brown, grey or green form of augite with play of colour. [Gr *diallagē* change, from *dia* between, and *allassein* to change, from *allos* other]
■ **diallagic** /-aj'ik/ or **diallagoid** /-al'ə-goid/ *adj*.

dialogite /dī-al'ə-jīt/ *n* a rose-red manganese carbonate. [Gr *dialogē* selection, doubt]

dialogue or (*N Am* sometimes) **dialog** /dī'ə-log/ *n* conversation between two or more people, *esp* of a formal or imaginary nature; the lines spoken by characters in plays, films, novels, etc; an exchange of views in the hope of ultimately reaching agreement. ◆ *vi* (*esp N Am*) to take part in a dialogue, converse (often with *with*). ◆ *vt* (*obs*; *Shakesp*) to put into dialogue form. [Fr, from L *dialogus*, from Gr *dialogos* a conversation, from *dialegesthai* to discourse]
■ **dialog'ic** /-loj'-/ *adj*. **dial'ogist** *n* a writer or speaker of dialogues. **dialogist'ic** or **dialogist'ical** *adj*. **dialogize** or **-ise** /dī-al'ə-jīz/ *vi* to discourse in dialogue.
❑ **dialog(ue) box** *n* (*comput*) in a WIMP environment, a window that seeks a response and/or gives information.

dialypetalous /dī-ə-li-pet'ə-ləs/ (*bot*) *adj* having the petals separate, polypetalous. [Gr *dialyein* to separate, from *dia* asunder, *lyein* to loose, and *petalon* a leaf]

dialysis /dī-al'i-sis/ (*chem*) *n* (pl **dial'yses** /-sēz/) the separation of substances by diffusion through a membranous septum or partition; dissolution; separation; removal of impurities from the blood by a kidney machine (qv) (*med*); diaeresis (*grammar*). [Gr *dialysis*, from *dia* asunder, and *lyein* to loose]
■ **dialysable** or (*N Am*) **-z-** /dī-ə-līz'ə-bl/ *adj*. **dialyse** or (*N Am*) **-yze** /dī'ə-līz/ *vt* to separate by dialysis. ◆ *vi* to use a kidney machine. **di'alyser** or (*N Am*) **-z-** *n*. **dialytic** /-lit'ik/ *adj*.

diam. *abbrev* : diameter.

diamagnetic /dī-ə-mag-net'ik/ *adj* applied to any substance of which a rod suspended between the poles of a magnet arranges itself across the lines of force, *opp* to *paramagnetic*. [**dia-**]

■ **diamag'net** *n* a diamagnetic substance. **diamagnet'ically** *adv.* **diamag'netism** *n* the form of magnetic action possessed by diamagnetic bodies; the branch of magnetism that deals with diamagnetic phenomena.

diamanté /*dē-a-mä-tā, dī-ə-man'ti* or *dī-ə-mon'tā*/ *n* a decoration, eg on a dress, consisting of glittering particles; a fabric so decorated. ◆ *adj* decorated with diamanté. [Fr *diamant* diamond]

■ **diamantine** /*dī-ə-man'tīn*/ *adj* of, or resembling, diamonds.

diamantiferous /*dī-ə-man-tif'ər-əs*/ *adj* yielding diamonds. [Fr *diamantifère*]

diameter /*dī-am'i-tər*/ *n* the measure through or across; a straight line passing through the centre of a circle or other figure, terminated at both ends by the circumference; in the parabola, a straight line parallel to the axis extending from the curve to infinity. [Through Fr and L from Gr *diametros*, from *dia* through, across, and *metron* a measure]

■ **diam'etral** or **diametric** /*dī-ə-met'rik*/, also **diamet'rical** *adj* in the direction of a diameter; relating to the diameter; as of opposite ends of a diameter (as in *diametrical opposition*). **diam'etrally** *adv* in a diametral manner. **diamet'rically** *adv* along a diameter; as at the ends of a diameter.

■ **tactical diameter** the perpendicular distance between a ship's courses before and after turning 180°.

diamine /*dī'ə-mēn*/ *n* a chemical compound containing two amino groups. [**di-** and **amine**]

diamond /*dī'ə-mənd*/ *n* a highly prized gemstone, and the hardest of all minerals, consisting of carbon crystallized in the cubic system; a rhombus; a card of a suit distinguished by pips of that form; a baseball field, or the part between bases; one of the smallest kinds of English printing type (about 4½-point). ◆ *adj* resembling, made of or marked with diamonds; lozenge-shaped, rhombic. [ME *diamaunt*, from OFr *diamant*, from LL *diamas, -antis*, from Gr *adamas, -antos*; see **adamant**]

■ **dī'amonded** *adj* furnished with diamonds. **dīamondif'erous** *adj* yielding diamonds.

❑ **diamond anniversary** *n* a sixtieth anniversary. **di'amondback** *n* a N American terrapin with diamond-shaped markings on its shell; a N American rattlesnake (*Crotalus adamanteus*) with diamond-shaped markings. **diamondback moth** *n* a small moth with diamond-shaped markings on its (folded) wings. **di'amond-beetle** *n* a beautiful sparkling S American weevil. **diamond bird** *n* any of several small insectivorous Australian songbirds; a pardalote. **di'amond-cut** *adj* cut in facets like a diamond. **diamond dove** *n* a small Australian dove (*Geopelia cuneata*) with white markings on the wings, often kept in cage or aviary. **di'amond-drill** *n* a borer whose bit is set with bort. **di'amond-dust** or **-powder** *n* the powder made by the friction of diamonds on one another in the course of polishing. **di'amond-field** *n* a region that yields diamonds. **di'amond-hitch** *n* a mode of fastening a rope for heavy burdens. **diamond jubilee** *n* a sixtieth anniversary (of marriage, **diamond wedding**). **diamond python** or **snake** *n* a python with diamond-shaped markings. **di'amond-wheel** *n* a wheel covered with diamond-dust and oil for polishing diamonds, etc.

■ **black diamonds** (*fig*) coal. **diamond cut diamond** an encounter between two very sharp people. **rough diamond** an uncut diamond; (also (*N Am*) **diamond in the rough**) a person possibly of great worth, but of rough appearance and unpolished manners.

Diamond-Blackfan anaemia /*dī'ə-mənd-blak'fan a-nē'mi-ə*/ *n* a rare form of anaemia in which the bone marrow fails to produce red blood cells. [LK *Diamond* (1902–1999) and KD *Blackfan* (1883–1941), US paediatricians]

diamorphine /*dī-ə-mör'fēn*/ *n* a short form of **diacetylmor'phine** /*dī-as'ə-til-*/ an acetyl derivative of morphine, commonly known as heroin.

diamyl /*dī-am'il*/ (*chem*) *adj* having two amyl groups. [**di-**]

Diana /*dī-an'ə*/ *n* (also **Dī'an**) the Roman goddess of light, the moon goddess, representative of chastity and hunting, identified with the Greek Artemis (*myth*); a huntress. [L *Diāna*]

❑ **Diana monkey** *n* a large long-tailed W African monkey (*Cercopithecus diana*) with a white crescent on the forehead. **Diana's tree** *n* tree of silver (see under **tree**).

■ **Diana of the Ephesians** a goddess of fertility worshipped at Ephesus.

diandrous /*dī-an'drəs*/ *adj* having, or allowing, two husbands or male mates (at a time); (of a flower or flowering plant) having two stamens or antheridia. [Gr *dis* twice, and *anēr, andros* a man, male]

■ **Dian'dria** *n pl* (in Linnaeus's classification) a class of plants with two stamens. **dian'dry** *n* the practice or condition of being diandrous.

Diane *abbrev* : Direct Information Access Network for Europe.

Dianetics® /*dī-ə-net'iks*/ *n sing* a system developed by the American writer L Ron Hubbard, with the aim of relieving psychosomatic illness by removing unwanted images from the mind. [Gr *dia* through, and *nous* mind]

dianodal /*dī-ə-nō'dəl*/ (*maths*) *adj* passing through a node. [**dia-**]

dianoetic /*dī-ə-nō-et'ik*/ *adj* capable of or relating to thought. [Gr *dianoētikos*, from *dia* through, and *noeein* to think]

dianthus /*dī-an'thəs*/ *n* any plant or flower of the *Dianthus* genus of herbaceous flowers to which carnations and pinks belong. [Poss Gr *Dios anthos* Zeus's flower; or *dianthēs* flowering in succession]

diapason /*dī-ə-pā'zən, -sən*/ (*music*) *n* (also (*Spenser; poetic*) **dī'apase**) a full volume of various sounds in concord; the whole range or compass of tones; a standard of pitch; a whole octave (*obs*); a bass part (*obs*); harmony (*obs*); a foundation-stop of an organ (**open** or **stopped diapason**) extending through its whole range. [Gr *dia pasōn chordōn symphōniā* concord through all the notes]

diapause /*dī'ə-pöz*/ *n* (in insects and the embryos of some animals) a period of suspended animation and growth. [Gr *diapausis* pause, from *diapauein* to pause, from *dia* between, and *pauein* to stop]

diapedesis /*dī-ə-pi-dē'sis*/ (*physiol*) *n* the migration of white blood corpuscles through the walls of the blood vessels without apparent rupture. [Gr *dia* through, and *pēdēsis* leaping]

■ **diapedetic** /*-det'ik*/ *adj.*

diapente /*dī-ə-pen'ti*/ *n* the interval of a fifth (*music*); a medicine of five ingredients. [Gr *dia* through, and *pente* five]

diaper or **dī'per**/ *n* (*esp N Am*) a baby's nappy; linen or cotton cloth with a square or diamond pattern, used chiefly for table linen and towels; the pattern itself; a pattern for ornamentation, woven, not coloured, in textiles; a floral or geometric pattern in low relief in architecture, often repeated over a considerable surface; paving in a chequered pattern. ◆ *vt* to variegate with figures, as in diaper; to put a nappy on (*N Am*). [OFr *diaspre, diapre*, from LL *diasprus*, from Byzantine Gr *diaspros* from *dia* through, and *aspros* white]

■ **dī'apering** *n.*

diaphanous /*dī-af'ə-nəs*/ *adj* transparent; translucent; pellucid; clear; light, delicate. [Gr *diaphanēs*, from *dia* through, and *phainein* to show, shine]

■ **diaphaneity** /*dī-ə-fə-nē'i-ti*/ *n.* **dīaphanom'eter** *n* an instrument for measuring the transparency of the air. **dīaph'anously** *adv.* **dīaph'anousness** *n.*

diaphone /*dī'ə-fōn*/ *n* a siren-like fog signal; a bass reed-organ stop made louder by vibrating material; all the variants of a phoneme. [Gr *dia* across, and *phōnē* voice]

diaphoresis /*dī-ə-fo-rē'sis* or *-fə-*/ (*med*) *n* sweat, *esp* artificially induced. [Gr *diaphorēsis* sweating, from *dia* through, and *pherein* to carry]

■ **diaphoretic** /*-et'ik*/ *adj* promoting sweating. ◆ *n* a sudorific, a diaphoretic substance.

diaphototropic /*dī-ə-fō-tō-trop'ik*/ (*bot*) *adj* diaheliotropic, turning transversely to the light. [**dia-**]

■ **diaphototrōp'ism** *n.* **diaphototropy** /*-tot'rə-pi*/ *n.*

diaphragm /*dī'ə-fram, -frəm*/ *n* a thin partition or dividing membrane; the midriff, the muscular structure separating the chest from the abdomen (*anat*); a metal plate with an adjustable central hole, for controlling the amount of light admitted in optical instruments; a strengthening or stiffening plate (*engineering*); (in a telephone, etc) a thin vibrating disc that converts electrical signals into sound waves and vice versa; a contraceptive device, a thin rubber or plastic cap placed over the neck of the uterus. [Gr *diaphragma* partition, midriff, from *dia* across, and *phragma* a fence]

■ **diaphragmal** /*-frag'*/ *adj.* **diaphragmatic** /*-frag-mat'*/ *adj.* **diaphragmati'tis** /*-frag-*/ *n* inflammation of the diaphragm.

❑ **diaphragm pump** *n* a pump that has a flexible membrane instead of a piston.

diaphysis /*dī-af'i-sis*/ *n* (pl **diaph'yses** /*-sēz*/) an abnormal elongation of the axis (*bot*); the shaft of a long bone (*anat*). [Gr *diaphysis* a separation, from *dia* through, and *phyesthai* to grow]

diapir /*dī'ə-pēr*/ (*geol*) *n* an anticlinal fold in which the overlying rock has been pierced by material from beneath. [Gr *diapeirainein* to pierce]

■ **diapir'ic** *adj.* **diapir'ism** *n* the upward movement of material through denser rocks to form diapirs.

diapophysis /*dī-ə-pof'i-sis*/ (*anat*) *n* (pl **diapoph'ysēs** /*-sēz*/) a dorsal transverse process of a vertebra. [Gr *dia* apart, and *apophysis* offshoot]

■ **diapophysial** /*dī-ap-ō-fiz'i-əl*/ *adj.*

diapositive /*dī-ə-poz'i-tiv*/ *n* a transparent photographic positive; a slide. [**dia-**]

diapyesis /*dī-ə-pī-ē'sis*/ (*pathol*) *n* suppuration. [Gr *diapyēsis*, from *dia* through, and *pyon* pus]

■ **diapyetic** /*-et'ik*/ *adj* producing suppuration. ◆ *n* a medicine having this property.

diarch /*dī'ärk*/ (*bot*) *adj* having two xylem strands. [Gr *di-* twice, and *archē* origin]

---

diarchy /dī'är-ki/ *n* a form of government in which two people, states, or bodies are jointly vested with supreme power (also (*non-standard*) **dī'narchy, du'archy** and **dy'archy**). [Gr *di-* twice, and *archein* to rule]
■ **diarch'al** or **diarch'ic** *adj*.

diarize see under **diary**.

diarrhoea or (*N Am*) **diarrhea** /dī-ə-rē'ə/ *n* a persistent purging or looseness of the bowels, evacuation of liquid faeces; an excessive flow of anything (*fig*; *inf*). [Gr *diarroia*, from *dia* through, and *rhoiā* a flow]
■ **diarrhoe'al** or **diarrhoe'ic** or (*N Am*) **diarrhē'al** or **diarrhē'ic** *adj*.

diarthrosis /dī-är-thrō'sis/ (*anat*) *n* articulation admitting free movement, as eg the shoulder joint. [Gr *diarthrōsis* jointing, from *dia* through, and *arthron* joint]

diary /dī'ə-ri/ *n* a daily record; a book for making daily records, noting engagements, etc. [L *diārium*, from *diēs* day]
■ **diarial** /dī-ā'ri-əl/ or **diā'rian** *adj*. **dī'arist** *n* a person who keeps a diary. **diarize** or **-ise** /dī'e-riz/ *vt* to enter in a diary. ◆ *vi* to keep a diary.

diascia /dī-as'i-ə/ *n* a plant of the genus *Diascia*, native to southern Africa, cultivated for its colourful, *usu* pink flowers. [Gr *diaskeein* to adorn]

diascope /dī'ə-skōp/ *n* an optical projector used for showing transparencies on a screen; a slide projector. [**dia-**, and Gr *skopeein* to view]

diascordium /dī-ə-skör'di-əm/ (*obs*) *n* a medicine made from water-germander, etc. [Medical L, from Gr *dia skordiōn* composed of *skordion* (perhaps water-germander)]

Diasone® /dī'ə-sōn/ *n* a proprietary name for a sulphonamide (a derivative of *diaminodiphenylsulphone*) used against leprosy.

Diaspora /dī-as'po-rə/ *n* the dispersed Jews after the Babylonian captivity, also used in the apostolic age for the Jews living outside of Palestine and now for Jews outside Israel; (*without cap*) a similar dispersion or migration of other peoples or communities. ◆ *adj* of or relating to the Diaspora or a diaspora. [Gr *diasporā* dispersion, from *dia* through, and *speirein* to scatter]

diaspore /dī'ə-spōr, -spör/ *n* a mineral, aluminium hydroxide, AlO(OH); a disseminule (*bot*). [Gr *diasporā* scattering, from its decrepitation]

diastaltic /dī-ə-stal'tik/ (*Gr music*) *adj* (of intervals) extended; (of style) bold. [Gr *diastaltikos* expanding]

diastase /dī'ə-stās/ (*biol*) *n* another name for amylase (qv under **amyl**). [Gr *diastasis* division, from *dia* apart, and *stasis* setting]
■ **diastā'sic** or **diastatic** /-stat'ik/ *adj*.

diastasis /dī-as'tə-sis/ (*surg*) *n* separation of bones without fracture. [See **diastase**]

diastema /dī-ə-stē'mə/ (*zool* and *anat*) *n* (*pl* **diastē'mata**) a natural space between two consecutive teeth, or series of teeth. [Gr *diastēma*, *-atos* interval]
■ **diastemat'ic** *adj*.

diaster /dī-as'tər/ (*biol*) *n* in cell division, a late stage in which the daughter chromosomes are situated in two groups near the poles of the spindle, ready to form the daughter nuclei. [Gr *di-* twice, and *astēr* a star]

diastereoisomer /dī-ə-stē-ri-ō-ī'sō-mər/ (*chem*) *n* a stereoisomer that is not an enantiomorph. [**dia-**]
■ **diastereoisomeric** /-me'rik/ *adj*. **diastereoisom'erism** *n*.

diastole /dī-as'tə-lē/ *n* dilatation of the heart and arteries, *opp* to *systole* (*physiol*); the lengthening of a short syllable, as before a pause. [Gr *diastolē*, from *dia* asunder, and *stellein* to place]
■ **diastolic** /dī-ə-stol'ik/ *adj*.

diastrophism /dī-as'trō-fi-zm/ (*geol*) *n* processes of deformation of the earth's crust. [Gr *diastrophē* distortion, from *dia* aside, and *strophē* a turning]
■ **diastrophic** /dī-ə-strof'ik/ *adj*.

diastyle /dī'ə-stīl/ (*archit*) *adj* with columns about three diameters apart. ◆ *n* a building or colonnade so proportioned. [Gr *diastylos*, from *dia* apart, and *stylos* column]

diatessaron /dī-ə-tes'ə-ron, -rən/ *n* an arrangement of the four Gospels as a single narrative, *esp* the earliest, that of Tatian (*prob* 110–180AD); the interval of a fourth (*music*); a medicine of four ingredients. [Gr *dia tessarōn* through, or composed of, four]

diathermic /dī-ə-thûr'mik/ *adj* permeable by or able to conduct radiant heat (also **diather'mal, diather'manous** and **diather'mous**). [Gr *dia* through, and *thermē* heat]
■ **diather'macy, diather'mancy** or **diathermanē'ity** *n* permeability by or conductibility of radiant heat. **di'athermy** *n* heating of internal parts of the body by electric currents.

diathesis /dī-ath'i-sis/ *n* a particular condition or habit of body, *esp* one predisposing to certain diseases (*med*); a habit of mind. [Gr *diathesis*, from *dia* asunder, and *tithenai* to place]
■ **diathetic** /-ə-thet'ik/ *adj*.

diatom /dī'ə-təm/ *n* one of a class of microscopic unicellular algae with flinty shells in two halves, fitting like box and lid. [Gr *diatomos* cut through, from *dia* through, and *temnein* to cut]
■ **diatomā'ceous** *adj*. **dī'atomist** *n* a person who studies diatoms. **diatomite** /dī-at'əm-īt/ or /dī'ət-/ *n* diatomaceous earth or kieselguhr, a powdery siliceous deposit of diatom frustules.
❑ **diatom ooze** *n* a deep-sea deposit of diatom frustules.

diatomic /dī-ə-tom'ik/ *adj* consisting of two atoms; having two replaceable atoms or groups; bivalent. [**di-** and **atom**]

diatonic /dī-ə-ton'ik/ *adj* proceeding by the tones and intervals of the natural scale in Western music. [Gr *diatonikos*, from *dia* through, and *tonos* tone]
■ **diaton'ically** *adv*. **diaton'icism** /-is-izm/ *n*.

diatretum see **cage-cup** under **cage**.

diatribe /dī'ə-trīb/ *n* an abusive or bitter harangue; a continued discourse or disputation (*archaic*). [Gr *diatribē* a spending of time, from *dia* through, and *tribein* to rub, wear away]
■ **dī'atribist** *n*.

diatropism /dī-at'rō-pi-zm/ *n* (of plants or parts of plants) orientation at right angles to the direction of a stimulus. [Gr *dia* across, and *tropos* turning]
■ **diatropic** /dī-ə-trop'ik/ *adj*.

diaxon /dī-aks'on/ *adj* (*zool*) having two axes or two axis-cylinder processes. ◆ *n* (*anat*) a bipolar nerve cell. [Gr *di-* twice, and *axōn* an axis]

diazepam /dī-az'i-pam/ or /-az'ə-/ *n* a tranquillizing drug that relieves tension and acts as a muscle relaxant. [**di-**, *azo-* and *epoxide*]

diazeuxis /dī-ə-zūk'sis/ (*Gr music*) *n* the separation of two tetrachords by a whole tone. [Gr *diazeuxis* disjunction, from *dia* apart, and *zeuxis* yoking]
■ **diazeuc'tic** *adj*.

diazinon /dī-az'in-on/ *n* a powerful insecticide. [**di-** and **azine**]

diazo /dī-az'ō/ *adj* (of compounds) containing two nitrogen atoms and a hydrocarbon radical; (of a photocopying process) using a diazo compound decomposed by exposure to light. ◆ *n* (*pl* **diaz'os** or **diaz'oes**) a copy made by the diazo method. [**di-** and **azo-**]
❑ **diazonium** /dī-ə-zō'ni-əm/ **salts** *n pl* a group of diazo compounds used in the manufacture of certain dyes.

dib[1] /dib/ *vi* (**dibb'ing; dibbed**) to dip; to fish by letting the bait bob up and down on the surface of the water. [Prob a form of **dab**]

dib[2] /dib/ *n* one of the small bones of a sheep's leg; (in *pl*) a children's game, played by throwing up such small bones or stones (**dib'-stones**), etc from the palm and catching them on the back of the hand (also **jacks**, or in Scots **chuckie-stanes** or **chucks**); (in *pl*) money (also **dibbs**; *sl*). [Ety uncertain]
■ **dibs on** (*US*) a claim to.

dibasic /dī-bā'sik/ *adj* capable of reacting with two equivalents of an acid; (of acids) having two replaceable hydrogen atoms. [**di-**]

dibber see **dibble**.

dibble /dib'l/ *n* a pointed tool used for making holes for seeds or plants (also **dibb'er**). ◆ *vt* to plant with a dibble. ◆ *vi* to make holes; to dip the bait lightly in and out of the water (*angling*). [Prob connected with **dab**[1]]
■ **dibb'ler** *n* someone who, or that which, dibbles; a dibble; a small carnivorous Australian marsupial (*Antechinus apicalis*) with long snout and short hairy tail.

dibranchiate /dī-brang'ki-āt/ (*zool*) *adj* having two gills. [Gr *di-* twice, and *branchia* gills]
■ **Dibran'chia** or **Dibranchiā'ta** *n pl* the two-gilled subclass of cephalopods.

dibromo- /dī-brō-mō-/ *combining form* signifying having two atoms of bromine, *esp* replacing hydrogen.

dibutyl /dī-bū'til/ (*chem*) *adj* having two butyl groups.
❑ **dibutyl phthalate** /thal'āt/ *n* the dibutyl ester of phthalic acid, used to keep off insects.

DIC *abbrev*: Diploma of the Imperial College.

dicacity /di-kas'i-ti/ (*archaic*) *n* raillery, banter. [L *dicāx* sarcastic]
■ **dicacious** /di-kā'shəs/ *adj*.

dicarpellary /dī-kär'pə-lər-i/ or /-pel'/ (*bot*) *adj* of or with two carpels. [**di-**]

dicast or **dikast** /dik'ast/ (*Gr hist*) *n* one of the 6000 Athenians annually chosen to act as judges. [Gr *dikastēs*, from *dikē* justice]
■ **dicas'tery** *n* the court at which the dicasts gave judgement. **dicas'tic** *adj*.

dice[1] /dīs/ n (pl **dice**) (also **die**) a small cube with faces numbered or otherwise distinguished, thrown in games of chance, etc; a small cubical piece; a game of chance. ◆ vi to play with dice; to take great risks. ◆ vt to cut into dice; to chequer. [Orig pl of **die**[2]]
■ **diced** adj ornamented with a chequered pattern; cut into dice. **dīc'er** n. **dīc'ey** adj (inf) risky; tricky; uncertain in result. **dīc'ing** n a chequered pattern; dice-playing.
❑ **dice'-box** n a box from which dice are thrown. **dice'-coal** n a coal that breaks into cubical blocks. **dice'-play** n. **dice'-player** n.
■ **dice with death** to take great risks. **no dice** no answer, or a negative answer; no success.

dice[2] /dīs/ vt (Aust inf) to reject, abandon. [Perh from **dice**[1]]

dicentra /dī-sen'trə/ n any plant of the genus Dicentra, incl bleeding heart (D. spectabilis), with the two outer petals broadly pouched (also (orig a misprint) **dielytra** /dī-el'i-trə/). [Gr di- double, and kentron a point, spur]

dicephalous /dī-sef'ə-ləs/ adj two-headed. [Gr dikephalos, from di-double, and kephalē a head]

dich /dich/ (Shakesp) supposed to be for do it, may it do.

dichasium /dī-kā'zi-əm/ (bot) n (pl **dichā'sia**) a cymose inflorescence in which each axis in turn produces a pair of nearly equal branches. [Gr dichāsis division, halving]
■ **dichā'sial** adj.

dichlamydeous /dī-klə-mid'i-əs/ (bot) adj having both a calyx and a corolla. [Gr di- double, and chlamys, -ydos mantle]

dichlor- or **dichloro-** /dī-klōr(-ō)-, -klör-/ combining form signifying having two atoms of chlorine, esp replacing hydrogen.
■ **dīchlō'rodiphēn'yltrichlō'roēth'ane** n known as **DDT**, a white powder orig used to kill lice and thus prevent the spread of typhus, effective also against other insects, but having long-term disadvantages. **dichlor'vos** n a pesticide used in fish farming to reduce sea lice.

dichloralphenazone /dī-klōr-əl-phen'ə-zōn, -klör-/ n a drug formerly used as a hypnotic and sedative. [**di-**, **chloral** (**hydrate**), and phenazone, an antipyretic drug]

dichogamy /dik- or dī-kog'ə-mi/ (bot) n an arrangement for preventing the self-fertilization of hermaphrodite flowers, the stamens and stigmas ripening at different times. [Gr dicha in two, and gamos marriage]
■ **dichog'amous** adj.

dichord /dī'körd/ n an ancient two-stringed lute. [Gr dichordos]

dichotic /dī-kot'ik/ adj involving the simultaneous stimulation of each ear by different sounds. [Gr dicha in two, and **otic**]

dichotomy /dī- or dī-kot'ə-mi/ n a division into two strongly contrasted groups, classes, opinions, etc; (loosely) a problem, situation, etc in which there is a clear split or difference of opinion, a variance, discrepancy or divergence; repeated branching (bot). [Gr dichotomiā, from dicha in two, and tomē a cut, from temnein to cut]
■ **dichot'omic** adj. **dichot'omist** n. **dichot'omize** or **-ise** vt and vi. **dichot'omous** adj. **dichot'omously** adv.
❑ **dichotomous question** n a question in a questionnaire that requires a simple answer of 'Yes' or 'No'.

dichroism /dī'krō-i-zm/ n the property of showing different colours exhibited by doubly refracting crystals when viewed in different directions by transmitted light. [Gr dichroos two-coloured, from di-twice, and chroā colour]
■ **dichrō'ic** or **dichrōit'ic** adj. **dī'chrōīte** n a strongly dichroic mineral, iolite or cordierite. **dī'chrōoscope** or **dī'chrōscope** n an instrument for testing the dichroism of crystals. **dichrōoscop'ic** or **dichrōscop'ic** adj.

dichromate /dī-krō'māt/ n a salt of **dichro'mic acid** ($H_2Cr_2O_7$) containing two chromium atoms (also called **bichromate**). [**di-** and **chromate**]

dichromatic /dī-krō-mat'ik/ adj having two colours, esp in different individuals of the same species; able to see two colours and two only, as in red-green colour-blind persons who see only blue and yellow. ◆ n a person of dichromatic vision, a dichromat. [Gr di- twice, and chrōma, -atos colour]
■ **dī'chromat** or **dī'chrōmate** n a person who can distinguish two colours only. **dichrō'matism** n. **dichrō'mic** adj dichroic; dichromatic. **dichrō'mism** n.

dichromic see under **dichromatic**.

dicht or **dight** /diht/ (Scot) vt to wipe. ◆ n a wipe. [**dight**]

dick[1] /dik/ (sl) n a man, a fellow (sometimes with cap; now usu derog); a detective; the penis (vulgar sl); an idiot, a fool, someone despised (vulgar sl). [Dick, for Richard]
❑ **dick'head** n (vulgar sl) an idiot; a fool; someone despised.
■ **clever Dick** a know-all.

dick[2] /dik/ (old sl) n fine words (used for **dictionary**); also used for **declaration**, as in to take one's dick, and probably in up to dick, meaning excellent (up to declared value).

dickcissel /dik-sis'l/ n the black-throated bunting, an American migratory bird. [Imit of call]

dickens /dik'ənz/ n the deuce, the devil, as in what the dickens or play the dickens. [Appar Dickon Richard, as a substitute for **devil**]

Dickensian /di-ken'zi-ən/ adj relating to or associated with Charles Dickens (1812–70), the novelist; relating to conditions, esp squalid social or working conditions, like those described in his novels. ◆ n an admirer or student of Dickens.

dicker[1] /dik'ər/ (N Am) n haggling or bargaining; petty trade by barter, etc. ◆ vi to haggle; to hesitate or dither. [Prob the obs dicker used for the number ten, esp for counting hides or skins, from L decuria]

dicker[2] /dik'ər/ (sl) n (in Ireland) someone who makes observations and passes information to a paramilitary organization. [dick (slang) to look, peer]
■ **dick'ing** n.

dickey[1], **dicky** or **dickie** /dik'i/ n a false shirt front; (also **dickey bow**) a bow tie; a leather apron for a gig, etc; the driver's seat in a carriage; a seat for servants at the back of a carriage; a folding seat at the back of a motor car. [Perh from dick, a dialect Eng word for a leather apron; perh Du dek a cover]

dickey[2,3] see **dicky**[1,2].

dickie see **dickey**[1].

dicking see under **dicker**[2].

Dickin medal /dik'in med'əl/ n a British award for animal heroism in wartime, instituted in 1943. [Maria Elisabeth Dickin, founder of the People's Dispensary for Sick Animals, which makes the awards]

Dicksonia /dik-sōn'i-ə/ n a tropical and southern genus of ferns, mainly tree-ferns. [James Dickson (died 1822), botanist]

dickty see **dicty**.

dicky[1] or **dickey** /dik'i/ (inf) adj shaky; not in good condition. [Poss from Tom and Dick, Cockney rhyming slang for sick]

dicky[2] or **dickey** /dik'i/ n (E Anglia) an ass. [Dick, for Richard]
❑ **dick'y-bird** n a small bird (childish); a word (esp in not a dicky-bird; rhyming sl).

dicky[3] see **dickey**[1].

diclinous /dī'kli-nəs or -klī'-/ (bot) adj having the stamens and pistils in separate flowers, whether on the same or on different plants. [Gr di-twice, double, and klīnē a bed]
■ **dī'clinism** n.

diclofenac /dī-klō'fə-nak/ n an anti-inflammatory and analgesic drug.

Diconal® /dī'kə-nəl/ n a painkilling opioid drug.

dicotyledon /dī-kot-i-lē'dən/ (bot) n (often shortened to **dī'cot**) a plant of the **Dīcotylē'donēs** /-ēz/ or **Dīcot'ylae** /-i-lē/, one of the two great divisions of Angiospermae, having embryos with two seed-leaves or cotyledons, leaves commonly net-veined, the parts of the flowers in twos, fives, or multiples of these, and the vascular bundles in the axes usually containing cambium. [Gr di- twice, and **cotyledon**]
■ **dicotylē'donous** adj.

dicrotic /dī-krot'ik/ adj (of the pulse) having two beats to one beat of the heart (also **dī'crotous**). [Gr di- twice, double, and krotos beat]
■ **dī'crotism** n.

dict see under **dictate**.

dict. abbrev : dictation; dictator; dictionary.

dicta see **dictum**.

Dictaphone® /dik'tə-fōn/ n a small tape-recorder for dictating letters, etc. [L dictāre to dictate, and Gr phōnē sound]

dicta probantia /dik'tə prō-ban'shi-ə or dik'ta prō-ban'ti-a/ (L) n pl proof texts.

dictate /dik-tāt' or formerly dik'tāt/ vt to say or read for another to write; to lay down with authority; to command. ◆ vi to give orders; to behave dictatorially. ◆ n /dik'tāt/ an order, rule, direction. [L dictāre, -ātum, frequentative of dīcere to say]
■ **dict** (obs) n a saying. ◆ vt to dictate. **dictā'tion** n the act, art or practice of dictating; speaking or reading of words for a pupil, secretary, etc to write; the words dictated; overbearing command. **dictā'tor** n a person invested with absolute authority, orig an extraordinary Roman magistrate; someone who, or that which, dictates. **dictatorial** /dik-tə-tö'ri-əl or -tö'-/ adj like a dictator; absolute; overbearing. **dictatō'rially** adv. **dictā'torship** n. **dic'tatory** adj. **dictā'tress** or **dictā'trix** n a female dictator. **dictā'ture** n.

diction /dik'shən/ n manner of speaking or expressing; choice of words; style; enunciation; a saying or speaking (obs). [L dictio, -ōnis, from dicere, dictum to say]

dictionary /dik'shə-nə-ri/ *n* a book containing the words of a language alphabetically arranged, with their meanings, etymology, etc; a lexicon; an additional program that will check text for spelling errors against a dictionary contained on the disk (*comput*); a work containing information on any area of knowledge, alphabetically arranged. [LL *dictiōnārium*; see **diction**]
◻ **dictionary attack** *n* an attempt to gain access to a computer system by submitting every known word as a password.

Dictograph® /dik'tō-gräf/ *n* an instrument for transmitting speech from room to room, with or without the speaker's knowledge, *usu* by means of a small concealed microphone. [L *dictum* thing said, and Gr *graphein* to write]

dictum /dik'təm/ *n* (*pl* **dic'ta**) something said; a saying; a popular maxim; an authoritative saying. [L]

dicty or **dickty** /dik'ti/ (*US sl*) *adj* proud, snobbish; high-class; excellent. [Origin unknown]

dictyogen /dik'ti-ō-jen/ (*obs*; *bot*) *n* a monocotyledon with net-veined leaves. [Gr *diktyon* a net, and *gennaein* to produce]

Dictyoptera /dik-ti-op'tə-rə/ *n* an order of insects with flattened body, long legs and two pairs of wings, including the cockroaches and mantises. [Gr *diktyon* a net, and **-ptera**]
■ **dictyop'teran** *adj* and *n*.

dicyclic /dī-sī'klik/ or *-sik'lik/* (*bot*) *adj* having two whorls or rings. [Gr *di-* twice, double, and *kyklos* wheel]

dicynodont /dī-sin'ō-dont/ *n* an extinct tusked reptile, showing affinities with mammals. [Gr *di-* twice, *kyōn, kynos* dog, and *odous, odontos* tooth]

did /did/ *pat* of **do**.

didactic /di-dak'tik, dī-/ or **didactical** /-ti-kəl/ *adj* designed or intended to teach; instructive (sometimes pedantically or dictatorially so); preceptive. [Gr *didaktikos*, from *didaskein* to teach; related to L *docēre, discere*]
■ **didac'tically** *adv.* **didac'ticism** /-sizm/ *n.* **didac'tics** *n sing* the art or science of teaching.

didactyl /dī-dak'til/ *adj* two-fingered, two-toed, or two-clawed (also *n*). [Gr *di-* twice, and *daktylos* finger, toe]
■ **didac'tylous** *adj.*

didakai, didakei see **diddicoy**.

didapper /dī'dap-ər/ *n* the dabchick or little grebe; someone who disappears and bobs up again. [**dive** and **dapper**, a variant of **dipper**; cf OE *dūfedoppa* pelican]

didascalic /di-da-skal'ik/ *adj* didactic. [Gr *didaskalikos*, from *didaskalos* teacher]

didder /did'ər/ (*dialect*) *vi* to shake. [See **dither**]

diddicoy, didicoy or **didicoi** /did'i-koi/, **didakai** or **didakei** /did'ə-kī/ *n* (*dialect*) an itinerant tinker or scrap dealer, not a true gypsy. [Romany]

diddle¹ /did'l/ *vt* to cajole, swindle, falsify; to waste time, to dawdle (*N Am*); to have sexual intercourse with (*N Am vulgar sl*). [Origin uncertain]
■ **didd'ler** *n.*

diddle² /did'l/ (*Scot*) *vt* and *vi* to make mouth music, sing without words (often dance tunes). [Onomatopoeic]
■ **didd'ler** *n.*

diddly-squat /did-li-skwot'/ (*N Am inf*) *n* nothing at all. [Prob *doodle* excrement, and *squat* to defecate]

diddy¹ /did'i/ (*inf*) *adj* small; tiny.

diddy² /did'i/ (*dialect*) *n* a female breast, a nipple or teat; a stupid or contemptible person (*inf*). [Perh from **tit**³ or from Ir *dide* a teat]

didelphic /dī-del'fik/ (*zool*) *adj* having or relating to a double womb. [Gr *di-* double, and *delphys* womb]
■ **Didel'phia** *n pl* the marsupials. **didel'phian, didel'phine** or **didel'phous** *adj.* **didel'phid** *n* an animal of the **Didel'phidae** /-ē/ or, less commonly, **Didelphyidae** /-fī'i-dē/, the opossum family. **Didel'phis** /-fis/ (less commonly **Didel'phys**) *n* an American genus of opossums.

didgeridoo /di-jə-ri-doo'/ *n* an Australian Aboriginal musical instrument, consisting of a very long tube producing a low-pitched resonant sound. [From an Aboriginal language]

didicoi, didicoy see **diddicoy**.

dido /dī'dō/ (*US inf*) *n* (*pl* **dī'does** or **dī'dos**) an antic, caper; a frivolous or mischievous act. [Origin unknown]
■ **act dido** to play the fool. **cut up didoes** to behave in an extravagant way.

didrachma /dī-drak'mə/ or **didrachm** /dī'dram/ *n* a double drachma. [Gr *di-* double, and **drachma**]

didst /didst/ (*archaic*) *2nd sing pat* of **did**.

Didunculus /di-dung'kū-lus/ *n* a genus of birds, the tooth-billed pigeon of Samoa. [Dimin of *Didus*, zoological name of the dodo, from its similar bill]

didymium /di-* or *dī-dim'i-əm/ *n* a supposed element discovered in 1841, later resolved into neodymium and praseodymium. [Gr *didymos* twin, from its constant association with *lanthanum*]

didymous /did'i-məs/ (*biol*) *adj* twin; twinned; growing in pairs; composed of two parts slightly connected. [Gr *didymos* twin]

Didynamia /di-di-nā'mi-ə/ *n pl* a class of plants in the Linnaean system with two long stamens and two short. [Gr *di-* double, and *dynamis* strength]
■ **didynā'mian** or **didyn'amous** *adj.*

die¹ /dī/ *vi* (or *vt* with object death) (**dy'ing**; **died** /dīd/) to lose life; to perish; to wither; (of an engine) to stop working; to languish, suffer, long, or be very eager (for), *esp* in *be dying for* (*inf*); to be overcome by the effects (of); to merge. See also **dying**. [Prob from a lost OE (Anglian) *dēgan*; but commonly referred to a Scand root seen in ON *deyja, döyja*; related to MHGer *touwen*, whence Ger *Tod*. The OE word in use was *steorfan* (see **starve**)]
◻ **die'-away** *adj* languishing, fading. **die'hard** *n* an irreconcilable conservative; a resolute, obstinate or dauntless person. ◆ *adj* irreconcilably conservative; resolute, obstinate.
■ **die away** to disappear by degrees, become gradually inaudible. **die back** (*bot*) to die by degrees from the tip backwards (**die'back** *n*). **die down** to subside; (of plants) to die above ground, leaving only roots or rootstocks. **die game** to keep up one's spirit to the last. **die hard** to struggle hard against death, to be long in dying; to be difficult to suppress, eradicate, or persuade. **die off** to die quickly or in large numbers. **die out** to become extinct, to disappear. **die the death** (*theatre sl*) to arouse no response from one's audience. **never say die** never give up. **to die for** (*inf*) highly desirable or alluring.

die² /dī/ *n* (*pl* **dies**) a stamp for impressing coins, etc; a cubical part of a pedestal; applied to various tools for shaping things by stamping or cutting; (*pl* **dice**) same as **dice**¹. [OFr *de*, *pl* *dez* (Provençal *dat*, Ital *dado*), from LL *dadus* = L *datus* given or cast]
◻ **die'-cast** *vt* to shape (metal or plastic) by casting in a metal mould. **die'-casting** *n.* **die'-sink'er** *n.* **die'-sink'ing** *n* the engraving of dies for embossing, etc. **die'-stock** *n* a contrivance for holding the dies used in screw-cutting. **die'-work** *n* ornamentation of a metal surface by impressions with a die.
■ **straight as a die** (ie a gaming dice) completely honest. **the die is cast** an irrevocable step has been taken; there is no turning back now.

dieb /dēb/ *n* a jackal of N Africa. [Ar *dhīb*]

Die Brücke /dē brük'ə/ *n* a group of expressionist painters formed in Dresden in 1905. [Ger, the bridge]

died see **die**¹.

diedral see **dihedral**.

dièdre /dē-ed'r'/ *n* a rock angle, or re-entrant corner, *usu* with a crack in it. [Fr]

dieffenbachia /dē-fən-bak'i-ə/ *n* any plant of the tropical American araceous genus *Dieffenbachia*, including the dumb-cane. [E *Dieffenbach* (died 1855), German botanist]

diegesis /dī-ē-jē'sis/ (*rhetoric*) *n* (in an oration) the narration of the facts. [Gr *diēgēsis*]
■ **diegetic** /-jet'ik/ *adj.*

dieldrin /dēl'drin/ *n* a crystalline organochlorine compound used as a contact insecticide. [O *Diels* (1876–1954), German chemist, and **aldrin**]

dielectric /dī-i-lek'trik/ *adj* non-conducting; transmitting electric effects without conducting. ◆ *n* a substance, solid, liquid or gas, capable of supporting an electric stress, and hence an insulator. [Gr *dia* through, and **electric**]
◻ **dielectric constant** *n* relative permittivity (see under **permit**). **dielectric heating** *n* the heating of a non-conducting substance as a result of loss of power in a dielectric.

dielytra /dī-el'i-trə/ (also with *cap*) *n* a non-standard name for **dicentra**. [As if Gr *di-* double, and *elytron* cover]

diencephalon /dī-en-sef'ə-lon, -kef'/ (*zool* and *anat*) *n* the posterior part of the forebrain in vertebrates, connecting the cerebral hemispheres with the midbrain. [**dia-**]
■ **diencephal'ic** *adj.*

diene /dī'ēn/ (*chem*) *n* an organic compound containing two double bonds between carbon atoms. [**di-**, and *-ene* as in **alkene, benzene**, etc]

dieresis see **diaeresis**.

dies¹ /dī'ēz, dē'ās/ (L) *n* (*pl* **di'es**) day.
◻ **dies fasti** /fas'tī or fäs'tē/ or **dies profesti** /pro-fes'tī or -tē/ *n pl* days on which judgement could be pronounced and on which courts could be held in ancient Rome. **dies faustus** /fös'təs or fows'tŭs/ *n* a

lucky day. **dies festi** /fes'tī or -tē/ or **dies feriae** /fer'i-ē or -ī/ n pl days of actual festival. **dies infaustus** /in-fös'təs or in-fows'tŭs/ n an unlucky day. **dies irae** / īr'ē or ēr'ī/ n the day of wrath; the day of judgement (from a Latin hymn); the hymn itself, used in the Mass for the dead. **dies nefasti** /ni-fas'tī or ne-fäs'tē/ n pl days on which a judgement could not be pronounced and on which assemblies of the people could not be held in ancient Rome. **dies non** /non or nōn/ n a day on which judges do not sit, or one on which normal business is not transacted.

dies² see **die²**.

diesel /dē'zl/ n a diesel engine; a locomotive, train, etc driven by a diesel engine; diesel oil. [Rudolph *Diesel* (1858–1913), German engineer]
- ■ **dieselizā'tion** or **-s-** n. **dies'elize** or **-ise** vt and vi to equip, or be equipped with, a diesel engine, locomotive or train.
- ▫ **dies'el-elec'tric** adj using power obtained from a diesel-operated electric generator. **diesel engine** n a compression-ignition engine in which the oil fuel is introduced into the heated compressed-air charge as a jet of liquid under high pressure. **dies'el-hydraul'ic** adj using power transmitted by means of one or more mechanisms (torque converters) filled with oil. **diesel oil** n heavy fuel oil used in diesel engines.

diesis /dī'i-sis/ n (pl **dī'eses** /-sēz/) a tiny difference in pitch, the difference between the sum of four minor thirds and an octave (**great diesis**) or three major thirds and an octave (**enharmonic diesis**) (*music*); the double dagger (‡), used to indicate a reference (*printing*). [Gr *diesis* a quarter-tone]

diestrus see **dioestrus**.

diet¹ /dī'ət/ n mode of living, *usu* now only with especial reference to food; a planned or prescribed selection of food, *esp* one designed for weight loss or the control of some disorder; the food habitually consumed by a person or animal; allowance of provisions (*obs*). ◆ adj and combining form (of food and, *esp*, soft drinks, often with brand name) having less sugar or fat than the standard version. ◆ vt to prescribe a diet for or put on a diet; to keep fasting; to supply with food (*archaic*). ◆ vi to take food according to rule, *esp* in order to lose weight; to feed (*archaic*). [Fr *diète*, from LL *diaeta*, from Gr *diaita* mode of living, diet]
- ■ **dīetā'rian** n (*rare*) a person who observes prescribed rules for diet. **dī'etary** adj relating to diet or the rules of diet. ◆ n a course of diet; allowance of food, *esp* in large institutions. **dī'eter** n someone who is on a diet; someone who regulates diet (*Shakesp*). **dīetet'ic** or **dietet'ical** adj relating to diet; for use in a medical diet. **dīetet'ically** adv. **dīetet'ics** n sing the study of, or rules for regulating, diet. **dī'etist**, **dīetitian** or **dīetician** /-ish'ən/ n an authority on diet.
- ▫ **dietary fibre** n fibrous substances in fruits, vegetables and cereals which keep bowel movements regular and are thus thought to help prevent certain diseases (also called **roughage**). **diet drink** n a drink containing few or no calories; a medically prescribed drink (*obs*). **diet sheet** n a list of permitted foods (and the quantities recommended) for a person on a diet.

diet² /dī'ət/ n a national, federal, or provincial assembly, council, or parliament, *esp* (*usu* with *cap*) the national legislature of Japan; a conference; the proceedings under a criminal libel '(*Scots law*); a clerical or ecclesiastical function in Scotland, such as a *diet of worship*. [OFr *diete*, from LL *diēta*, from Gr *diaita*; or according to Littré, from L *diēs* a (set) day, with which usage cf Ger *Tag* day, *Reichstag*]
- ■ **dī'etine** n a minor or local diet.
- ■ **desert the diet** (*Scots law*) to abandon criminal proceedings under a particular libel.

diethyl /dī-ē'thīl/ (*chem*) adj having two ethyl groups. [**di-**]
- ■ **diethylamine** /-ə-mēn'/ n a liquid resembling ethylamine, derived from ammonia, with ethyl groups replacing two hydrogen atoms.
- ▫ **diethyl ether** n ether. **diethylstilboest'rol** or (*US*) **diethylstilbest'rol** n stilboestrol.

Dieu /dyø/ (*Fr*) n God.
- ■ **Dieu avec nous** /a-vek noo/ God with us. **Dieu défend le droit** /dā-fɔ̃ lə drwä/ God defends the right. **Dieu et mon droit** /ā mɔ̃ drwä/ God and my right. **Dieu vous garde** /vŭ gärd/ God keep you.

DIF (*comput*) abbrev : data interchange format, a standard for moving files between different programs.

diff. abbrev : difference; different.

diffarreation /di-far-i-ā'shən/ (*hist*) n a divorce from an ancient Roman marriage by *confarreation*. [L *dif-* (*dis-*) asunder]

differ /dif'ər/ vi to be unlike, distinct or various (used by itself, or followed by *from*); to disagree (with *with* or sometimes *from*); to fall out, dispute (with). ◆ n (*Scot*) a difference of opinion. [L *differre*, from *dif-* .(for *dis-*) apart, and *ferre* to bear]
- ■ **diff'erence** or (*archaic*) **diff'erency** n dissimilarity; the quality distinguishing one thing from another; a contention or quarrel; the

point in dispute; the excess of one quantity or number over another; differentia; a distinguishing mark; a modification to distinguish the arms of a branch from those of the main line (*heraldry*); discrimination. ◆ vt (*rare*) to make or perceive a difference between or in. **diff'erent** adj distinct; separate; unlike; not the same (with *from*, also with *to* and (*esp US*) than); out of the ordinary (*inf*); novel. **differentia** /-en'shi-ə/ n (pl **differen'tiae** /-ē/) (L; *logic*) that property which distinguishes a species from others. **differentiabil'ity** n. **differen'tiable** adj able to be differentiated. **differen'tial** /-shəl/ adj constituting or relating to a difference or differentia; discriminating; relating to infinitesimal differences (*maths*). ◆ n an infinitesimal difference (*maths*); a differential gear; a price difference; the difference between rates of pay set for each category of employees within an industry; the difference in rates of pay between different industries. **differen'tially** adv. **differentiate** /-en'shi-āt/ vt to make different, cause to develop difference(s); to classify as different; to constitute a difference between; to obtain the differential coefficient of (*maths*). ◆ vi to become different by specialization; to distinguish (*from* or *between*). **differentiā'tion** n the act of distinguishing; description of a thing by giving its differentia (*logic*); exact definition; a change by which what was generalized or homogeneous became specialized or heterogeneous; the act or process of differentiating, or determining the ratio of the rates of change of two quantities, one of which is a function of the other (*maths*). **differen'tiātor** n someone who or that which differentiates. **diff'erently** adv.
- ▫ **difference tone** or **differential tone** n a tone heard when two tones are sounded together, its frequency the difference of their frequencies. **differential calculus** see under **calculus**. **differential coefficient** n (*maths*) the ratio of the rate of change of a function to that of its independent variable. **differential equation** n (*maths*) one involving total or partial differential coefficients. **differential gear** n a gear enabling one driving wheel of a vehicle to move faster than another, eg when cornering. **differential motion** n a mechanical movement in which the velocity of a driven part is equal to the difference of the velocities of two parts connected to it. **differential pricing** n pricing in which the same product is supplied to different markets at different prices according to their tolerance. **differential thermometer** n a thermometer for measuring difference of temperature. **differential tone** see **difference tone** above. **differently abled** adj (*euphem*) disabled.
- ■ **agree to differ** to agree to accept amicably a difference of opinion without further argument. **difference of opinion** a matter about which two or more people or groups disagree. **make a** (or **no**) **difference** to have (no) effect. **with a difference** with something special; in a special way.

difficile /di-fis'il, dif'-sil/ (*archaic* or reintroduced) adj difficult. [OFr and Fr *difficile* ; see **difficult**]

difficult /dif'i-kəlt/ adj not easy; hard to do; requiring labour and pains; hard to please; not easily persuaded; unmanageable; hard to resolve or extricate oneself from; potentially embarrassing, etc. [The adj was formed from *difficulty*, from Fr *difficulté*, from L *difficultās*, *-ātis*, from *difficilis*, from *dif-* (*dis-*) (negative), and *facilis* easy]
- ■ **diff'icultly** adv (mainly *chem*; eg *difficultly soluble*). **diff'iculty** n the quality or fact of being difficult; a difficult situation; laboriousness; an obstacle; an objection; that which cannot be easily understood or believed; (*usu* in *pl*) embarrassment of affairs, *esp* financial trouble; a quarrel.
- ■ **make difficulties** to be hard to please; to make objections.

diffident /dif'i-dənt/ adj lacking in self-confidence; excessively shy or modest; distrusting (*obs*). [L *diffīdēns*, *-entis*, prp of *diffīdere* to distrust, from *dif-* (*dis-*) (negative), and *fīdere* to trust, from *fidēs* faith]
- ■ **diff'idence** n. **diff'idently** adv.

diffluent /dif'lŭ-ənt/ adj readily flowing away; fluid; deliquescent. [L *dis-* apart, and *fluēns*, *-entis*, prp of *fluere* to flow]

difform /di-förm'/ (*obs*) adj unlike; irregular in form. [L *dis-* apart, and *förma* form]
- ■ **difform'ity** n.

diffract /di-frakt'/ vt to break up; to subject to diffraction. [L *diffringere*, *diffrāctum*, from *dis-* asunder, and *frangere* to break]
- ■ **diffrac'tion** n the spreading of light or other rays passing through a narrow opening or by the edge of an opaque body or reflected by a grating, etc, with interference phenomena, coloured and other. **diffrac'tive** adj. **diffractom'eter** n an instrument used in the examination of the crystal structure of matter by means of diffraction of X-rays, or of the atomic structure of matter by means of diffraction of electrons or neutrons. **diffrangibil'ity** /-franj-/ n. **diffrang'ible** adj capable of being diffracted.

diffuse¹ /di-fūz'/ vt to pour out all round; to send out in all directions; to scatter; to circulate; to publish. ◆ vi to spread. [L *diffundere*, *diffūsum*, from *dif-* (*dis-*) asunder, and *fundere* to pour out]
- ■ **diffused'** adj spread widely; loose. **diffus'edly** adv. **diffus'edness** n. **diffus'er** n someone or something that diffuses; an attachment

for a light fitting that prevents glare; a duct that, as it widens out, reduces the speed of an airflow or fluid; an attachment for a hairdryer that spreads the applied heat. **diffusibil'ity** n. **diffus'ible** adj. **diffu'sion** n a spreading or scattering abroad; extension; distribution; the movement of molecules and ions in a fluid from areas of high to areas of low concentration; spread of cultural elements from one region or community to another (anthrop). **diffu'sionism** n (anthrop) the theory that diffusion is mainly responsible for cultural similarities. **diffu'sionist** n. **diffu'sive** /-siv/ adj extending; spreading widely. **diffu'sively** adv. **diffu'siveness** or **diffusiv'ity** n.
❑ **diffused lighting** n lighting that is transmitted or reflected in all directions and, being evenly distributed, produces no glare. **diffusion line** n a range of clothing produced by a fashion designer for a high-street store, to be sold at relatively affordable prices. **diffusion plant** n (nuclear eng) a plant used for isotope separation by gaseous or thermal diffusion. **diffusion tube** n an instrument for determining the rate of diffusion for different gases.

diffuse² /di-fūs'/ adj diffused; widely spread; wordy; not concise. [Root as for **diffuse¹**]
■ **diffuse'ly** adv. **diffuse'ness** n.

DIG /dig/ abbrev : Disablement Income Group.

dig /dig/ vt (**digg'ing**; **dug** or (archaic; Bible) **digged**) to excavate; to turn up with a spade or otherwise; to get or put by digging; to poke or thrust; to taunt (inf); to understand or approve (old sl); to take note of (old sl). ◆ vi to use a spade; to seek (for) by digging (lit and fig); to burrow; to mine; to lodge (inf); to study hard (N Am sl). ◆ n an act or course of digging; an archaeological excavating expedition; an excavation made by archaeologists; a poke; a taunt (inf); a hard-working student (N Am sl). [Prob OFr diguer to dig; of Gmc origin]
■ **digg'able** adj. **digg'er** n a person or animal that digs; a miner, esp a gold-miner; an Australian or New Zealand soldier (Aust and NZ inf); an informal Australian term of address; a machine for digging. **digg'ings** n pl places where mining is carried on, esp for gold; digs (dated inf). **digs** n pl (inf) accommodation; lodgings.
❑ **digger wasp** n any of various kinds of burrowing wasp. **digging stick** n a primitive tool, a pointed stick, sometimes weighted, for digging the ground.
■ **dig a pit for** (fig) to set a trap for. **dig in** to cover over by digging; to work hard; to take up a defensive position (lit or fig); to begin eating (inf). **dig oneself in** to entrench oneself; to establish oneself in a position. **dig one's heels in** to refuse to be moved or persuaded. **dig out** to decamp (US sl); to unearth (lit or fig). **dig up** to remove from the ground by digging; to excavate; to obtain by seeking (inf); to produce, esp reluctantly (inf).

digamma /dī-gam'ə/ n vau, the obsolete sixth letter (Ϝ, Ϝ, later ϛ) of the Greek alphabet with the sound of our w; as a numeral, ϛ' = 6, ‚ϛ = 6000. See **episemon**. [Gr di- twice, and gamma, from its form like one capital Γ over another]

digamy /dig'ə-mi/ n a second marriage (after death of partner or divorce). [Gr di- twice, and gamos marriage]
■ **dig'amist** n. **dig'amous** adj.

digastric /dī-gas'trik/ (anat) adj double-bellied, or fleshy at each end, as is one of the muscles of the lower jaw. [Gr di- double, and gastēr the belly]

digerati /dij-ə-rä'tē/ (inf) n pl the body of people with expertise in or knowledge of computers and the Internet. [From **digital**; modelled on **literati**]

digest¹ /di-jest'** or **dī-/ vt to dissolve in the stomach; to soften by heat and moisture (chem); to distribute and arrange; to prepare or classify in the mind; to think over, to take in gradually, the meaning and implications of; to endure (eg an insult) without protest (old). ◆ vi to be dissolved in the stomach; to be softened by heat and moisture. [L dīgerere, dīgestum to carry asunder or dissolve, from dī- (dis-) asunder, and gerere to bear]
■ **digest'edly** adv (obs) in neat order. **digest'er** n someone who digests; a closed vessel in which by heat and pressure strong extracts are made from animal and vegetable substances. **digestibil'ity** n. **digest'ible** adj that may be digested. **digestif** /dē-zhes-tēf'/ n (Fr) a drink taken as a digestive. **digestion** /di-jest'yən/ n the dissolving of the food in the stomach; orderly arrangement; mental assimilation; exposing to slow heat, etc (chem). **digest'ive** adj relating to digestion; promoting digestion. ◆ n something that promotes digestion; (also **digestive biscuit**) a round, semi-sweet biscuit, the basic ingredient of which is wholemeal flour. **digest'ively** adv.
❑ **digestive tract** n the alimentary canal.

digest² /dī'jest/ n a body of laws collected and arranged, esp the Justinian code of civil laws; a synopsis; an abstract; a periodical abstract of news or current literature. [L dīgesta, neuter pl of dīgestus, pap of dīgerere to carry apart, to arrange]

dight /dīt/ vt to adorn (archaic); to equip (archaic); /dihht/ another spelling of **dicht**. ◆ adj disposed; adorned. [OE dihtan to arrange, prescribe, from L dictāre to dictate (whence Ger dichten to write poetry)]

Digibox® /dij'i-boks/n a brand of set-top box (qv under **set**) for receiving digital satellite television. [digital box]

digicam /dij'i-kam/ n a digital camera.

digipack /dij'i-pak/ n a storage case for a CD or DVD, with a paperboard outer binding. [digital package]

digit /dij'it/ n a finger or toe; a finger's breadth as a unit of measurement (1.9cm or $\frac{3}{4}$in); a figure, esp one used in arithmetic to represent a number; any one of the Arabic numerals from 0 to 9; the twelfth part of the diameter of the sun or moon (astron). [L digitus finger, toe]
■ **dig'ital** adj relating to the fingers, or to arithmetical digits; showing numerical information by a set of digits to be read off, instead of by a pointer on a dial, etc (as in digital clock, digital thermometer); (of electronic circuits) responding to and producing signals that at any given time are at any one of a number of possible discrete levels, generally either one of two levels; (of continuous data, eg sound signals) separated into discrete units to facilitate transmission, processing, etc, or of the transmission, etc of sound, etc, in this form. ◆ n a finger (joc); a key of a piano, etc. **digitalin** /dij-i-tā'lin or dij'it-ə-lin/ n a glucoside or mixture of glucosides obtained from digitalis leaves, used as a heart stimulant. **digitā'lis** n any plant of the foxglove genus Digitalis; dried foxglove leaves once used as a drug. **dig'italization** or **-s-** n. **dig'italize** or **-ise** vt and vi to give digitalis to (a patient) for the treatment of certain heart conditions; digitize. **dig'itate** or **dig'itated** adj (of leaves) consisting of several finger-like sections. **dig'itately** adv. **digitā'tion** n finger-like arrangement; a finger-like division. **dig'itiform** adj formed like fingers. **dig'itigrade** adj walking on the toes. ◆ n an animal that walks on its toes. **digitizā'tion** or **-s-** n. **dig'itize** or **-ise** vt to put (data) into digital form, eg for use in a digital computer. **dig'itizer** or **-s-** n (comput) a device that converts analogue signals to digital codes (also **analogue-to-digital** or **A/D converter**); a device that converts pictures captured by a video camera into digital form for computer input (also **video digitizer**). **digitō'rium** n a pianist's dumb keyboard for finger exercises.
❑ **digital audio player** n a device for storing and playing audio data that has been recorded in a digital file format (abbrev **DAP**). **digital audiotape** n a magnetic audiotape on which sound has been recorded digitally; this form of recorded sound, affording greater clarity and compactness, and less distortion than conventional recording (abbrev **DAT**, **Dat** or **dat**). **digital camera** n a camera in which images are captured by a charge-coupled device rather than film and stored on a memory card readable by a computer, which can be used to view, manipulate and print the images. **digital clock** or **watch** n a clock or watch, without a conventional face, on which the time is indicated directly by numbers. **digital compact cassette** n a digital audiotape, in standard cassette format, that is played via a fixed-head tape recorder; this form of recorded sound (abbrev **DCC**). **digital computer** n an electronic calculating machine using arithmetical digits, generally binary or decimal notation. **digital immigrant** n (comput sl) a person who has learnt to use computers as an adult, opp to digital native. **digital native** n (comput sl) a person who has learnt to use computers as a child, opp to digital immigrant. **digital pen** same as **stylus pen** (see under **stylus**). **digital plotter** n (comput) a device that plots graphs from data specifying co-ordinates, rather than from data specifying increments to the current position (cf **incremental plotter**). **digital radio** n a form of radio broadcasting in which the sounds are compressed into and transmitted in digital form. **digital recording** n a digital means of storing and transmitting information electronically, eg in sound recording where frequency and amplitude features of the sound wave are measured, expressed and stored in digital form (as on compact disc or digital audiotape). **digital signature** same as **electronic signature** (see under **electronic**). **digital socks** n pl socks with individual toe-coverings similar to the fingers of gloves. **digital television** n a form of television broadcasting in which the signal is transmitted in digital form and decoded by a special receiver. **digital transmission** n (comput) the sending of computer data from one location to another by using a modem to convert the data into electronic impulses which can be sent along telecommunications lines to a distant point, where a modem converts the impulses back to the original form of the data. **digital wallet** n a portable device that facilitates the transfer of funds between accounts to pay for goods and services. **digital watch** see **digital clock** above. **digitizing board**, **pad**, **table** or **tablet** n a device consisting of a flat surface on which diagrams may be drawn with a special stylus, the co-ordinates of the position of the stylus at any given point on the diagram being digitized for storage, etc.

digladiate /di-glad'i-āt/ vi (obs) to fight with swords; to fence; to wrangle. [L dīgladiārī to contend fiercely, from dis- this way and that, and gladius sword]
■ **digladia'tion** n. **diglad'iātor** n.

diglossia /dī-glos'i-ə/ (linguistics) n the existence in a community of both a colloquial and a formal or literary form of a language. [Gr diglōssos bilingual]

diglot /dī'glot/ adj able to speak two languages, bilingual; using or written in two languages. ◆ n a person who speaks two languages; a book written in two languages. [Gr diglōttos, from di- double, and glōtta tongue]

diglyph /dī'glif/ (archit) n an ornament consisting of a double groove. [Gr di- double, and glyphē carving]

dignify /dig'ni-fī/ vt (**dig'nifying; dig'nified**) to invest with honour; to exalt; to lend an air of dignity to (as in dignify with the name of). [LL dīgnificāre, from dīgnus worthy, and facere to make]
■ **significa'tion** n. **dig'nified** adj marked or consistent with dignity; exalted; noble; grave; ranking as a dignitary.

dignity /dig'ni-ti/ n the state of being dignified; elevation of mind or character; grandeur of bearing or appearance; elevation in rank, place, etc; calmness and self-control; degree of excellence; preferment; high office; a dignitary. [Fr dignité, from L dīgnitās, -ātis, from dīgnus worthy]
■ **dig'nitary** n someone in a high position or rank, esp in the church.
■ **beneath one's dignity** degrading, at least in one's own estimation. **stand on one's dignity** to assume a manner that asserts a claim to be treated with respect.

digonal /dig'ə-nl/ (maths, etc) adj (of symmetry about an axis) such that a half-turn (180°) gives the same figure. [Gr di- twice, and gōniā angle]

digoneutic /dig-ə-nū'tik/ (zool) adj breeding twice a year. [Gr di- twice, and goneus a parent]

digoxin /dī-jok'sin/ n a glycoside obtained from the foxglove and used as a heart stimulant. [Contracted form of digitoxin, from **digitalis** and **toxin**]

digraph /dī'gräf/ n two letters expressing a single sound, such as ph in digraph. [Gr di- twice, and graphē a mark, a character, from graphein to write]

digress /dī- or di-gres'/ vi to depart from the main subject; to introduce irrelevant matter. [L dīgredī, digressus, from dī- (dis-) aside, and gradī to step]
■ **digression** /-gresh'ən/ n a departure from the main point; a part of a discourse not about the main subject. **digress'ional** or **digress'ive** adj of the nature of a digression; departing from the main subject. **digress'ively** adv. **digress'iveness** n.

digs see under **dig**.

Digynia /dī-jin'i-ə/ n pl in various Linnaean classes of plants, an order with two styles or a deeply cleft style. [Gr di- twice, and gynē a woman]
■ **digyn'ian** adj. **digynous** /dij' or dīj'i-nəs/ adj digynian; with two styles or two carpels.

DIH abbrev : Diploma in Industrial Health.

dihedral /dī-hē'drəl/, sometimes **diedral** /dī-ē'drəl/ (maths, etc) adj bounded by two planes, or two plane faces. ◆ n a dihedral angle. [Gr di- twice, and hedrā a seat]
■ **dihē'dron** n the limiting case of a double pyramid when the vertices coincide.
❏ **dihedral angle** n the angle made by the wing of an aeroplane with the horizontal axis.

dihybrid /dī-hī'brid/ (biol) n a cross between parents that differ in two independently heritable characters (also adj). [Gr di- double, twice, and **hybrid**]

dihydric /dī-hī'drik/ (chem) adj having two hydroxyl groups. [**di-**]

dijudicate /dī-joo'di-kāt/ vt and vi to judge; to decide. [L dī- (dis-) asunder, and jūdicāre to judge]
■ **dijudica'tion** n.

dika /dī'kə, dē'kə/ n a West Indian tree of the Simarubaceae (Irvingia gabonensis), the so-called wild mango. [From a W Afr name]
❏ **di'ka-bread** n a compressed mass of dika and other seeds, smelling like chocolate. **di'ka-butter** or **-oil** n a fat expressed from its seeds.

dikast see **dicast**.

dik-dik /dik'dik/ n a name for several very small E African antelopes, of the genus Madoqua. [Said to be a name in Ethiopia]

dike¹, diker see **dyke¹**.

dike², dikey see **dyke²**.

dikkop /dik'əp/ (S Afr) n the stone curlew. [Afrik dik thick, and kop head]

diktat /dik-tät'/ n a harsh settlement forced on the defeated or powerless; an order or statement allowing no opposition. [Ger, something dictated]

dil. abbrev : dilute.

dilacerate /di-las'ər-āt/ vt to rend or tear asunder. [L dī- asunder, and **lacerate**]
■ **dilacerā'tion** n.

dilapidate /di-lap'i-dāt/ vt to pull down stone by stone; to waste; to allow to go to ruin. [L dīlapidāre, from dī- asunder, and lapis, lapidis a stone]
■ **dilap'idated** adj in ruin; in a state of disrepair. **dilapidā'tion** n the state of ruin; (in pl) damage done to a building during tenancy (law); impairing of church property during an incumbency (relig); (in pl) money paid at the end of an incumbency by the incumbent or his or her heirs for the purpose of putting the parsonage, etc in good repair (relig). **dilap'idātor** n.

dilate /dī'lāt or dī-lāt', di-lāt'/ vt to spread out in all directions; to expand; to enlarge; to set forth at full length (Shakesp, etc). ◆ vi to widen; to swell out; to expand; to speak at length. [L dīlātāre to spread out, from dī- (dis-) apart, and lātus wide]
■ **dilātabil'ity** n. **dilāt'able** adj that may be dilated or expanded. **dilat'ancy** n (chem) the property shown by some colloidal systems of thickening or solidifying under pressure or impact. **dilāt'ant** adj tending to dilate; showing dilatancy. **dilatation** /-lə-tā'shən/ or (irregularly formed) **dilā'tion** n expansion; a transformation that produces a figure similar to, but not congruent with, the original (maths). **dil'atātor** n an instrument or a muscle that expands. **dilāt'ed** adj expanded and flattened. **dilāt'ive** adj. **dilā'tor** n a dilatator; someone who dilates (also **dilāt'er**).
■ **dilatation and curettage** see **D and C**.

dilatory /dil'ə-tə-ri/ adj slow; given to procrastination; loitering; tending to delay. [L dīlātōrius, from differre, dilātum to postpone]
■ **dil'atorily** adv. **dil'atoriness** n.

dildo /dil'dō/ n (pl **dil'dos** or **dil'does**) an object serving as an erect penis substitute, esp used as a sex toy (also **dil'doe**); a word used in refrains of songs (obs); a weak or effeminate man (obs); a cylindrical curl; a West Indian spiny cactus (Lemaireocereus hystrix). [Origin uncertain]
❏ **dil'do-glass** n a cylindrical glass.

dilemma /di-, dī-lem'ə/ n a position where each of two alternative courses (or of all the feasible courses) is eminently undesirable; (loosely) a predicament, problem; a form of argument in which the maintainer of a certain proposition is committed to accept one of two propositions each of which contradicts his or her original contention (the argument was called a 'horned syllogism', and the victim compared to a man certain to be impaled on one or other of the horns of an infuriated bull, hence the **horns of a dilemma**; logic). [L, from Gr dilēmma, from di- twice, double and lēmma an assumption, from lambanein to take]
■ **dilemmat'ic** adj.
■ **on the horns of a dilemma** in a dilemma (see comments above).

dilettante /dil-e-tan'ti or dil'e-tant/ n (pl **dilettan'ti** /-tē/) a person who loves the fine arts but in a superficial way and without serious purpose (the amateur usually practises them); a dabbler in art, science or literature. ◆ adj of or relating to a dilettante. [Ital, prp of dilettare, from L dēlectāre to delight]
■ **dilettan'tish** adj. **dilettan'tism** or **dilettan'teism** n.

diligent /dil'i-jənt/ adj steady and earnest in application; industrious. [Fr, from dīligēns, -entis, prp of L dīligere to choose]
■ **dil'igence** n steady application; industriousness; a warrant to produce witnesses, books, etc, or a process by which persons or goods are attached (Scots law); (also pronounced /dē-lē-zhãs/) a French or continental stagecoach (also **dill'y**; hist). **dil'igently** adv.

dill¹ /dil/ n an umbelliferous annual Eurasian herb related to parsnip, the fruits or 'seeds' of which are used in condiments and as a carminative. [OE dile ; Ger Dill, Swed dill]
❏ **dill pickle** n pickled cucumber flavoured with dill. **dill'-wat'er** n a medicinal drink prepared from the seeds.

dill² /dil/ (Aust and NZ inf) n a fool. [Prob **dilly²**]

dilli see **dilly bag**.

dilling /dil'ing/ n a darling (obs); the youngest child (obs); the weakling of a litter (dialect). [Origin doubtful]

dilly¹ /dil'i/ (inf) n an excellent or very pleasing person or thing (also adj). [Perh contraction of **delightful**]

dilly² /dil'i/ (Aust and NZ inf) adj foolish, silly. [Prob **daft** and **silly**]

dilly³ see **diligence** under **diligent**, and **dilly bag**.

dilly bag /dil'i bag/ n (also **dill'i** or **dill'y**) an Australian Aboriginal bag, made of woven grass or fibre; a small bag. [Aboriginal word dilli, and **bag**]

dilly-dally /dil'i-dal'i/ (inf) vi to loiter or trifle. [Reduplication of **dally**; cf **shilly-shally**]

dilscoop /dil'skoop/ (cricket) n an attacking shot that lifts the ball over the wicketkeeper's head. [Tillakaratne Dilshan (born 1976), Sri Lankan cricketer, and **scoop**]

dilucidate /di-lū'si-dāt, di-loo'/ (obs) vt to elucidate. [L dīlūcidāre, -ātum]
■ **dilucidā'tion** n.

dilute /dī- or di-lūt', di-loot'/ vt to make thinner or more liquid; to diminish the concentration of, by mixing, esp with water; to make less strong, powerful or forceful; (of labour) to increase the proportion of unskilled to skilled in. ◆ vi to become mixed. ◆ adj /di-, dī-lūt', -loot' or dī'/ diminished in concentration by mixing. [L diluere, dīlūtum, from dī- away, and luere to wash]
■ **diluent** /dil'ū-ənt/ adj diluting. ◆ n that which dilutes. **dilut'able** adj able or intended to be diluted. ◆ n a drink such as a fruit squash that is diluted before being drunk. **dilut'ee** n an unskilled worker introduced into a skilled occupation. **dilute'ness** n. **dilut'er** or **dilut'or** n someone who or something that dilutes. **dilu'tion** n. **dilu'tionary** adj tending to dilute.

diluvium /di-lū'vi-əm, di-loo'/ n (also **dilu'vion**) an inundation or flood; a loose glacial deposit of sand, gravel, etc; a deposit of sand, gravel, etc made by extraordinary currents of water (geol; obs). [L dīluvium a deluge, from dīluere to wash away]
■ **dilu'vial** adj relating to a flood, esp that told of in the Bible, in the time of Noah; caused by a deluge; composed of diluvium. **dilu'vialism** n. **dilu'vialist** n someone who explains geological phenomena by Noah's flood, told of in the Bible. **dilu'vian** adj diluvial.

dim /dim/ adj (**dimm'er**; **dimm'est**) not bright or distinct; obscure; not seeing clearly; mentally dull, stupid (inf); not hopeful. ◆ vt (**dimm'ing**; **dimmed**) to make dark; to dip (headlights) (N Am); to obscure. ◆ vi to become dim. [OE dimm; related to ON dimmr dark, and Ger Dämmerung twilight]
■ **dim'ly** adv. **dimm'er** (switch) n a device for regulating the supply of light. **dimm'ish** adj somewhat dim. **dim'ness** n.
□ **dim'wit** n (inf) a stupid person. **dim-witt'ed** adj. **dim-witt'edness** n.
■ **a dim view** (inf) an unfavourable view. **dim out** to reduce the lighting (of) gradually (**dim'-out'** n).

dim. abbrev : dimension; diminuendo (also **dimin.**; music); diminutive (also **dimin.**).

di majorum gentium /dī mə-jō'rəm or -jö' jen'sh(y)əm or dē ma-yō'rŭm gen'ti-ŭm/ (L) the divinities of superior rank, ie the twelve greater gods of classical mythology.

dimble /dim'bl/ (dialect) n a dell, a dingle.

dime /dīm/ n one tenth of an American and Canadian dollar, equal to ten cents; a coin of this value; a small sum of money. [Fr, orig disme, from L decima (pars) a tenth (part)]
□ **dime bag** n (US inf) an amount of an illegal drug sold for a fixed price. **dime museum** n a cheap show. **dime novel** n a cheap novel, usu sensational. **dime store** n (old US) a shop selling cheap goods (orig costing not more than a dime).
■ **a dime a dozen** cheap, commonplace.

dimension /dī- or di-men'shən/ n measure in length, breadth or thickness (the three dimensions of space); scope, extent (also fig); size; the sum of the indices in a term (maths); a factor or aspect; a concept, development in range or quality, etc. ◆ vt to give the dimensions of; to make to specified dimensions. [Fr, from L dīmēnsiō, -ōnis, from dīmētīrī, dīmēnsus, from dī (dis-) apart, and mētīrī to measure]
■ **dimen'sional** adj concerning dimension. ◆ combining form of so many dimensions, as in three-dimensional. **dimen'sioned** adj. **dimen'sionless** adj.
□ **dimension work** n masonry in stones of specified size.
■ **fourth dimension** an additional dimension attributed to space; (in relativity theory, etc) time. **new dimension** a fresh aspect. **third dimension** depth, thickness; a rounding out, completeness, given by added information, detail, etc (fig).

dimer /dī'mər/ (chem) n a compound whose molecule has twice as many atoms as another compound of the same empirical formula (the monomer). [**di-**, and mono**mer**]
■ **dīmeric** /-mer'ik/ adj. **dīmerizā'tion** or **-s-** n. **dī'merize** or **-ise** vt.

dimercaprol /dī-mər-kap'rol/ n a colourless liquid used as an antidote to poisoning by heavy metals such as arsenic or mercury. [**di-**, **mercaptan** and **-ol**[1]]

dimerous /dim'ə-rəs/ adj consisting of two parts; with two members in each whorl (bot); having two-jointed tarsi (zool). [Gr di- double, twice, and meros a part]
■ **dimeric** /dī-mer'ik/ adj bilaterally symmetrical; dimerous. **dimerism** /dim'ər-izm/ n.

dimeter /dim'i-tər/ (prosody) adj containing two measures. ◆ n a verse of two measures. [L, from Gr dimetros, from di- twice, and metron a measure]

dimethyl /dī-mē'thil/ n ethane. ◆ adj containing two methyl radicals in combination. [**di-**]
■ **dimeth'oate** n a crystalline compound used as an insecticide. **dimeth'ylamine** /-ə-mēn/ n a gas derived from ammonia with two methyl groups replacing two hydrogen atoms. **dimethylan'iline** n an oily liquid, aniline heated with methyl alcohol and hydrochloric acid, from which dyes are obtained.
□ **dimethyl sulphoxide** n a colourless odourless liquid used as a solvent and in medicines to enable them to penetrate the skin (abbrev **DMSO**).

dimetric /dī-met'rik/ (crystallog) adj tetragonal. [**di-** and **metric** relating to distance]

dimidiate /di-mid'i-āt/ adj divided into halves; having a shape that appears as if halved; having only one side developed (biol); split on one side (bot). ◆ vt (heraldry) to represent the half of. [L dīmidiāre, -ātum to halve, from dīmidius half, from dis- apart, and medius the middle]
■ **dimidiā'tion** n.

dimin. see **dim.** (abbrev).

diminish /di-min'ish/ vt to make less; to take a part from; to degrade or belittle. ◆ vi to grow or appear less; to subside. [Coined from (archaic) **minish**, in imitation of L dīminuere to break in pieces, from dī- (from dis-) apart, and minuere to make less, which in LL replaced the earlier dēminuere to lessen, from dē from, and minuere]
■ **dimin'ishable** adj. **dimin'ished** adj made smaller; lessened; humbled; a semitone lower than perfect or minor (music). **dimin'ishing** n and adj. **dimin'ishingly** adv. **dimin'ishment** n.
□ **diminished responsibility** n limitation in law of criminal responsibility on the grounds of mental weakness or abnormality, not merely of actual insanity. **diminishing glass** n a lens or combination of lenses that makes objects appear smaller.
■ **law of diminishing returns** the fact that there is a point beyond which any additional amount of work, expenditure, taxation, etc results in progressively smaller output, profits, yields, etc.

diminuendo /di-min-ū-en'dō/ (music) adj and adv letting the sound die away. ◆ n (pl **diminuen'does** or **diminuen'dos**) a decrease in loudness; a passage of decreasing loudness. [Ital, from LL dīminuendus, for L dēminuendus, gerundive of dēminuere to lessen (see **diminish**)]

diminution /dim-i-nū'shən/ n a lessening; decrease. [**diminish**]
■ **dimin'utive** adj of a diminished size; very small; contracted. ◆ n a word formed from another to express a little one of the kind (grammar); a suffix used to form diminutives (grammar); a shortened form of a name (eg Rob for Robert); one of the smaller ordinaries, of the same shape as one of the larger ones (heraldry). **dimin'utively** adv. **dimin'utiveness** n.

dimissory /dim'i-sə-ri, di- or dī-mis'ə-ri/ adj sending away or giving leave to depart to another jurisdiction. [L dīmissōrius, from dīmittere, dīmissum, from dis- apart, and mittere to send]

dimity /dim'i-ti/ n a stout white cotton, striped or figured in the loom by weaving with two threads. [Gr dimitos, from di- twice, and mitos a thread]

DIMM (comput) abbrev : Dual In-line Memory Module, a plug-in board able to carry large amounts of memory chips.

dimmer, dimming see **dim**.

dimorphism /dī-mör'fi-zm/ n the occurrence of two forms in the same species (biol); the property of crystallizing in two forms (chem). [Gr di- twice, and morphē form]
■ **dī'morph** n either of the two forms of a dimorphous species or substance. **dimor'phic** or **dimor'phous** adj.

dimple /dim'pl/ n a small hollow, esp on a person's cheek or chin; a shallow depression in a surface; a depression or bubble in glass. ◆ vi to form dimples; to smile, showing dimples. ◆ vt to cause dimples to appear in. [Appar cognate with Ger Tümpel pool]
■ **dim'pled** adj. **dim'plement** n (rare). **dim'ply** adj.

dim sum /dim sum/ n a selection of Chinese foods, often eaten as an appetizer, usu including steamed or fried dumplings with various fillings. [Chin (Cantonese)]

dimwit see under **dim**.

dimyarian /dim-i- or dī-mī-ā'ri-ən/ (zool) adj having two adductor muscles. [Gr di- twice, and mȳs, myos muscle]

DIN /din/ n a unit of measurement of the speed of photographic film; a standard system of plugs and sockets used to connect domestic audio and video equipment. [Abbrev Ger Deutsche Industrie Norm, German Industry Standard]

■ words derived from main entry word; □ compound words; ■ idioms and phrasal verbs

din /din/ n a loud continued jarring noise. ◆ vt (**dinn'ing**; **dinned**) to assail (the ears) with noise; to annoy with clamour; to obtrude noisily and persistently. ◆ vi to make a continued loud noise. [OE dynn, dyne ; cf ON dynr, Dan dön noise]

■ **din'ful** adj.

■ **din into** (inf) to instil (knowledge) into (a person) by forceful repetition.

dinanderie /de̅-nä̅-də-re̅'/ n (also with cap) domestic decorative brassware, originally that made at Dinant in Belgium; extended to Indian and Levantine brassware. [Fr]

Dinantian /di-nan'shi-ən/ (geol) adj Lower Carboniferous (also n). [Dinant in Belgium]

dinar /de̅-när'/ n the standard monetary unit of Bosnia-Herzegovina, Macedonia (usu in the form **denar**), Yugoslavia and several Arab countries; an ancient Arab gold coin of 65 grains' weight. [L de̅na̅rius]

dinarchy see diarchy.

dindle see dinnle.

dine /di̅n/ vi to take dinner. ◆ vt to provide with a dinner. ◆ n (obs) dinner, dinner-time. [OFr disner (Fr dîner) prob from L dis- expressing undoing, and je̅ju̅nus fasting (cf **disjune**); according to others, from L de̅- (intensive), and ce̅na a meal]

■ **din'er** n a person who dines; a dining-car on a train; a small, inexpensive restaurant (esp N Am). **dinette'** n an alcove or other part of a room or kitchen set apart for meals.

❑ **din'er-out** n a person who dines out, esp on a regular basis. **din'ing-car** n a railway carriage in which meals are served. **din'ing-hall** n. **dining room** n. **dining table** n.

■ **dine off** or **on** to have as one's dinner. **dine out** to dine somewhere other than at home. **dine out on** to be invited to dinner, or (loosely) to enjoy social success, on the strength of (one's possession of eg interesting information). **dine with Duke Humphrey** (hist) to go without a meal, loiter about Duke Humphrey's Walk in Old St Paul's.

DIng abbrev : Doctor Ingeniariae (L), Doctor of Engineering.

ding¹ /ding/ vi to ring; to sound; to keep sounding. ◆ vt to reiterate to a wearisome degree. [Imit, but partly confused with **ding²**]

❑ **ding'-a-ling** n the sound of a bell ringing; a stupid or eccentric person (inf). **ding'-dong'** n the sound of bells ringing; monotony; sameness; an argument or fight (inf). ◆ adj and adv like a bell ringing; hammer-and-tongs; keenly contested with rapid alternations of success. ◆ vt and vi to ring; to nag.

ding² /ding/ vt (pat **dinged**, **dang** or **dung**; pap **dinged** or **dung**) (all senses archaic or dialect) to dash; to beat; to thump; to knock; to surpass (Scot). ◆ vi to beat (Scot); to dash (obs). [ME dingen, dyngen ; cf ON dengja, Swed dänga to bang]

■ **ding'er** n (sl) anything superlative of its kind; a home run (baseball). ■ **ding doun** /doon/ (Scot) to knock or throw down.

Ding an sich /ding an zihh' or -ziç' / (Ger ; philos) n the thing-in-itself, the noumenon.

dingbat /ding'bat/ n something whose name one has forgotten, or does not want to use (US inf); a text-embellishing symbol, such as ◊ or ₣; a foolish or eccentric person (inf); a tramp; money (US sl). [Perh **ding²** and **bat¹**]

■ **ding'bats** adj (Aust and NZ inf) daft, crazy.
■ **the dingbats** (Aust and NZ inf) delirium tremens.

dinge¹ /dinj/ (US offensive sl) n a black person. ◆ adj of or relating to black people.

dinge² see under dingy¹.

dinges /ding'əs/ n (S Afr inf) an indefinite name for any person or thing whose name one cannot or will not remember (also (esp US) **ding'us**). [Du, from Afrik ding thing; cf Eng **thingummy** and **thingumbob**]

dinghy or (esp formerly) **dingy** or **dingey** /ding'gi/ n a small open boat, propelled by oars, sails or an outboard motor; an inflatable boat, esp one kept for use in emergencies. [Hindi dinghi̅ a small boat]

dingle /ding'gl/ n a wooded hollow; a dell. [Origin uncertain]

dingle-dangle /ding'gl-dang'gl/ adv swinging to and fro. [Reduplication of **dangle**]

dingo /ding'go̅/ n (pl **ding'oes**) the tawny-coloured wild dog of Australia; a cheat or coward (Aust sl). [Name in obs Aboriginal dialect]

dingus see dinges.

dingy¹ /din'ji/ adj dim or dark; shabby and dirty-looking; dull; soiled. [Origin obscure]

■ **dinge** n dinginess. ◆ vt to make dingy. **din'giness** n.

dingy² see dinghy.

dinitro- /di̅-ni̅-tro̅-/ combining form denoting (a chemical) having two nitro-groups (NO_2), esp replacing hydrogen.

■ **dinitroben'zene** n $C_6H_4(NO_2)_2$, corresponding to benzene, C_6H_6.

dinitrogen /di̅-ni̅'trə-jən/ adj denoting a chemical compound containing two nitrogen atoms. [**di-**]

❑ **dinitrogen tetroxide** n a colourless or pale yellow liquid (N_2O_4) used as an oxidant in rocket fuel.

dink¹ /dingk/ adj (Scot) neat, trim. ◆ vt and vi (Scot) to dress neatly; to adorn.

■ **dink'y** adj (inf) neat; dainty; trivial, insignificant (N Am).

dink² /dingk/ (sport ; orig US) n an act of sending the ball over a short distance in a gentle arc. ◆ vt and vi to send (the ball) in a gentle arc. [Imit]

dink³ /dingk/ see dinky¹.

dinkum /ding'kəm/, also **dinky-di** or **-die** /ding'ki-di̅/ (Aust and NZ inf) adj real, genuine; square, honest. ◆ adv genuinely; honestly. [Eng dialect dinkum a fair share of work]

■ **fair dinkum** an emphatic form of dinkum.

Dinky® /ding'ki/ n any of a range of small toy model vehicles (also adj).

dinky¹ /ding'ki/(inf) n (pl **dink'ies**) double- (or dual-) income no kids, an acronym applied to a member of a young, childless couple both earning a high salary and enjoying an affluent lifestyle (also **dink**). ◆ adj of or relating to a dinky.

dinky² see under dink¹.

dinmont /din'mənt/ n a Border name for a male sheep between the first and second shearing. [Origin obscure]

dinna /din'ə/ or **dinnae** /din'ā/ a Scottish form of do not.

dinner /din'ər/ n the chief meal of the day, at midday or (usu) in the evening; a formal meal or public banquet, often in celebration of a person or event. ◆ vi to dine. ◆ vt to provide with dinner. [OFr disner (properly) breakfast; see **dine**]

■ **dinn'erless** adj.

❑ **dinn'er-dance** n a dance following a formal dinner. **dinn'er-gown** n a less formal evening dress. **dinner hour** n. **dinner jacket** n a (usu black) jacket without tails, worn by men on formal occasions. **dinner lady** n a woman who cooks and/or serves meals in a school canteen. **dinn'er-pail** n (US) a vessel in which a workman carries his dinner. **dinner party** n a party at which dinner is served. **dinner plate** n. **dinner service** or **dinner set** n a complete set of plates and dishes for a company at dinner. **dinner table** n. **dinner theatre** n (N Am) an entertainment including a meal and a theatrical show; a place providing this. **dinn'er-time** n. **dinn'er-wagon** n orig a shelved trolley for a dining room; a sideboard in two tiers, for holding dishes, etc.

dinnle /din'l/, also **dindle** /-dl/ (Scot) vi to tingle; to shake, vibrate. ◆ vt to cause to tingle, shake or vibrate. ◆ n a thrill, vibration, tremor, tingling. [Prob imitative]

dino- or (archaic) **deino-** /di̅-no̅-/ combining form denoting huge, terrible. [Gr deinos terrible]

■ **Dinoceras** /-nos'ə-ras/ n (Gr keras horn) a large Eocene fossil stump-footed ungulate of Wyoming, also known as **Uintatherium**, named from three pairs of protuberances on the skull. **dinoma'nia** n public interest in dinosaurs. **Dinornis** /di̅-nör'nis/ n (Gr ornis a bird) a genus of moas, including the biggest. **dinosaur** or (archaic) **deinosaur** /di̅'nə-sör/ n (Gr sauros a lizard) any extinct (Mesozoic) reptile of the order **Dinosaur'ia** from two to eighty feet in length (inf short form **di'no**); a chance survivor of a type characteristic of a bygone era (fig). **dinosaur'ian** adj (fig). **dinosaur'ic** adj (fig). **dinothere** or **deinothere** /di̅n'ə-the̅r/, **dinotherium** or **deinotherium** /-the̅'ri-əm/ n (Gr the̅rion a beast) any extinct elephantine mammal of the genus Deinotherium with downward-curving tusks. **dinoturba'tion** n (geol) the effects of dinosaurs trampling on the formation of sedimentary rock.

dinoflagellate /di̅-no̅-flaj'ə-lāt/ n a unicellular organism, a plant-like flagellate with two flagella. [Gr di̅nos whirl, and **flagellate**]

Dinornis, dinosaur, etc see under **dino-**.

dint /dint/ n a hollow made by a blow; force (as in by dint of); a blow or stroke (archaic). ◆ vt (archaic) to make a dint in. [OE dynt a blow; cf **dunt¹**; ON dyntr]

diocese /di̅'ə-sis or -se̅s/ n the circuit or extent of a bishop's jurisdiction. [Through Fr and L from Gr dioike̅sis, from dioikeein to keep house, from di-, for dia- (signifying completeness) and oikeein to keep house, from oikos a house]

■ **diocesan** /di̅-os'i-sn or -zn/ adj relating to a diocese. ◆ n a bishop in relation to his diocese; one of the clergy in the diocese.

diode /di̅'o̅d/ (electronics) n a semiconductor device that allows current to flow in only one direction around a circuit (also **semiconductor diode**); the earliest and simplest type of valve, an electron tube with heated cathode and anode. [Gr di- twice, and hodos way]

Diodon /di̅'ə-don/ n a genus of globe fishes with all the teeth in each jaw consolidated. [Gr dis- twice, double, and odous, odontos a tooth]

dioecious /dī-ē'shəs/ (biol) adj having the sexes in separate individuals; not hermaphrodite; having male and female flowers on different plants. ■ **Dioe'cia** /dī-ē'shə/ n pl a class in the Linnaean system, dioecious plants. **dioe'cism** /dī-ē'sizm/ n.

dioestrus or (N Am) **diestrus** /dī-ēs'trəs/ n a sexually quiescent period following ovulation, in the oestrous cycle in mammals.

Diogenic /dī-ə-jen'ik/ adj relating to the Cynic philosopher *Diogenēs* (c.412–323BC); cynical.

diol /dī'ol/ n an alcohol with two hydroxyl groups in the molecule. [**di-** and **-ol**[1]]

Dionaea /dī-ə-nē'ə/ n the Venus flytrap (*Dionaea muscipula*), an American droseraceous insectivorous plant. [L, from Gr *Diōnaiā* Aphrodite, from her mother *Diōnē*]

Dionysia /dī-ə-niz'i-ə/ or -nis'/ (Gr hist) n pl dramatic and orgiastic festivals in honour of *Dionȳsos* (Bacchus), Greek god of wine. ■ **Dionys'iac** adj Bacchic. **Dionys'ian** adj relating to *Dionȳsos* or to *Dionȳsios* (Dionysius of Syracuse, the Areopagite, Exiguus, or any other of the name).

Diophantine /dī-ə-fan'tīn/ adj relating to the Alexandrian mathematician *Diophantos* (c.275AD). ❑ **Diophantine analysis** n (maths) the part of algebra concerned with finding particular rational values for general expressions under a surd form. **Diophantine equation** n (maths) one for which only integral or rational solutions are required.

Diophysite see **Diphysite**.

diopside /dī-op'sīd/ (mineralogy) n a strongly birefringent monoclinic calcium-magnesium pyroxene. [Gr *di-* double, and *opsis* a view]

dioptase /dī-op'tās/ (mineralogy) n an emerald-green acid copper silicate. [Gr *dia* through, and *optazein* to see; from its internal glitter]

dioptric /dī-op'trik/ or **dioptrical** /-kəl/ adj relating to dioptrics or a diopter; transparent (as in *dioptric beehive*). [Gr *dioptrā* a levelling instrument, *dioptron* a spyglass, from *dia* through, and the root of *opsesthai*, used as future of *horaein* to see] ■ **diop'ter** n an ancient form of theodolite; the index-arm of a graduated circle; a dioptre (esp US). **diop'trate** adj (zool) having the compound eye divided transversely. **diop'tre** n a unit of measurement of the power of a lens, the reciprocal of the focal distances in metres, negative for a divergent lens. **diop'trics** n sing the part of optics that deals with refraction.

diorama /dī-ə-rä'mə/ n an exhibition of translucent pictures seen through an opening with lighting effects; a miniature three-dimensional scene with figures; a display of eg a stuffed animal in a naturalistic setting in a museum, etc; a miniature film or television set. [Gr *dia* through, and *horāma* a sight] ■ **dioram'ic** adj.

diorism /dī'ə-ri-zm/ n distinction, definition. [Gr *diorizein* to divide, from *dia* through, and *horos* a boundary] ■ **dioris'tic** or **dioris'tical** adj. **dioris'tically** adv.

diorite /dī'ə-rīt/ n a crystalline granular igneous rock composed of plagioclase and hornblende. [Gr *diorizein* to distinguish, from *dia* through, and *horos* a boundary] ■ **diorit'ic** adj.

diorthosis /dī-ör-thō'sis/ n the reduction of a dislocation (surg); the correction of a deformity; a critical revision of a text. [Gr *dia* through, and *orthos* straight] ■ **diorthot'ic** adj.

Dioscorea /dī-o-skō'ri-ə/ or -kö'/ n the yam genus, of the monocotyledonous family **Dioscoreā'ceae**. [From the 1c AD Greek physician *Dioskoridēs*] ■ **dioscoreā'ceous** adj.

Dioscuri /dī-os-kū'rī/ (Gr myth) n pl Castor and Pollux together, as sons of *Zeus*. [Gr *Dios*, genitive of *Zeus*, and *koros* (Ionian *kouros*) a son, a lad]

diosgenin /dī-os'jən-in/ n a crystalline substance obtained from the Mexican yam (genus *Dioscorea*), used in the preparation of steroid hormones.

diota /dī-ō'tə/ n a two-handled ancient vase. [Gr *diōtos* two-handled, from *di-* twice, and *ous*, *ōtos* ear]

Diothelism, Diothelite see **Ditheletism**.

dioxan /dī-ok'sən/ or **dioxane** /-sān/ (chem) n a colourless, flammable, toxic liquid, $C_4H_8O_2$ used as a solvent for waxes, resins, etc (also called **1,4-dioxycyclohex'ane**).

dioxide /dī-ok'sīd/ n an oxide with two atoms of oxygen in the molecule. [**di-** and **oxide**]

dioxin /dī-ok'sin/ n any of a family of toxic, lipophilic and persistent chlorinated aromatic hydrocarbons, several of which are found as trace compounds in the food chain; one of the most toxic of this group (**2,3,7,8-tetrachlorodibenzodioxin**), a contaminant of Agent Orange.

Dip. abbrev: Diploma, as in eg **Dip. Ed.** Diploma in Education, **Dip. Tech.** Diploma in Technology, **Dip. SW** Diploma in Social Work.

dip /dip/ vt (**dipp'ing**; **dipped**) to immerse for a time; to lower; to lower and raise again (eg a flag); to cause (headlights) to shine below the eye level of oncoming motorists; to baptize by immersion; to lift by dipping (usu with up); to dye, clean or coat by dipping; to immerse (fruit, wood, etc) in a preservative solution; to immerse (esp sheep) in a chemical solution to prevent or clear infestation by insects, etc; to moisten, suffuse (Milton); to involve in money difficulties (inf); to mortgage; to pawn. ◆ vi to plunge and emerge; to go down briefly then up again; to sink; to reach down into something; to enter slightly; to fish by lowering the bait slightly into the water, then bobbing it gently on the surface; to look cursorily; to incline downwards; to steal by picking pockets (sl); to practise snuff-dipping (qv under **snuff**[1]). ◆ n the act of dipping; a hollow; a sag; that which is taken by dipping; an inclination downwards; a sloping; (of the headlights of a car, etc) the state of being dipped; the angle a stratum of rock makes with a horizontal plane (geol); the angle between the horizontal and the earth's magnetic field; magnetic dip; a bath; a short swim; a liquid (such as a chemical solution or a dye) in which anything is dipped (such as sheep, garments, etc); a creamy mixture into which food may be dipped before being eaten; a candle made by dipping a wick in tallow; a pickpocket (sl); a stupid or foolish person (N Am sl). [OE *dyppan*, causal of *dȳpan* to plunge in, from *dēop* deep; cf Dan *dyppe*; Ger *taufen* to immerse] ■ **dipp'er** n someone who or that which dips; a ladle; a bucket or scoop of a dredge or excavator; a device for directing motor car headlights upwards or downwards (also **dipswitch**); a dipping bird (genus *Cinclus*), the water ouzel; the dabchick (US); (with cap) the Plough (astron); a pickpocket (sl); a nickname for a Baptist, esp a Dunker. **dipp'ing** n the action of the verb; snuff-dipping. ❑ **dip'-circle** or **dipp'ing-needle** n an instrument for determining magnetic dip. **dip'-net** n a long-handled net for dipping up fish. **dip'-pipe** n a pipe with submerged outlet, esp in gasworks. **dip'-sec'tor** n an instrument for determining the dip of the visible horizon. **dip'-slope** n (geol) a slope of ground coinciding with the dip of the rocks. **dip'stick** n a rod for measuring depth of liquid in a sump, etc; a stupid or foolish person (sl; derog). **dip'switch** see **dipper** above. **dip'-trap** n a bend in a pipe containing liquid to cut off gases. ■ **dip in** to take a share. **dip into** to put one's hand into to remove something; to take or use (eg money from a fund); to read cursorily in. **dip of the horizon** the angle of the visible horizon below the level of the eye. **dip of the needle** the angle a balanced magnetic needle makes with the horizontal plane. **dip snuff** to practise snuff-dipping (qv under **snuff**[1]).

dipchick /dip'chik/ same as **dabchick** (see under **dab**[1]).

di penates /dī pə-nä'tēz or dē pe-nä'tās/ (L) n pl household gods.

dipeptide /dī-pep'tīd/ (chem) n a peptide formed by the combination of two amino acids. [**di-** and **peptide** (see **pepsin**)]

dipetalous /dī-pet'ə-ləs/ adj having two petals. [Gr *di-* twice, and *petalon* a leaf]

diphenyl /dī-fē'nil/ n a hydrocarbon, $C_6H_5C_6H_5$, consisting of two phenyl groups, used as a fungicide and in dye manufacture, etc (also **biphe'nyl** and **phenylben'zēne**). ◆ adj having two phenyl groups, esp replacing hydrogen. [**di-**] ■ **diphen'ylamine** n a toxic crystalline compound used in the manufacture of dyes, rocket propellants and insecticides.

diphone /dī'fōn/ n a shorthand sign representing a diphthongal sound. [Gr *di-* twice, and *phōnē* sound]

diphtheria /dif-thē'ri-ə/ n an infectious throat disease in which the air-passages become covered with a leathery membrane. [Fr *diphthérie*, *diphthérite* (now *diphtérie*), from Gr *diphtherā* leather] ■ **diphtheric** /-ther'ik/ or **diphtheritic** /-thər-it'ik/ adj. **diphtherī'tis** n diphtheria. **diph'theroid** adj.

diphthong /dif'thong or dip'thong/ n two vowel sounds pronounced as one syllable (as in *out* or *loin*); (loosely) a digraph; the ligature æ or œ. [OFr *di(p)tongue* (Fr *diphtongue*), from L *dip(h)thongus*, from Gr *diphthongos*, from *di-* twice, and *phthongos* sound, vowel, reconstructed to more closely resemble the Greek] ■ **diphthongal** /-thong'gəl/ or **diphthongic** /-thong'gik/ adj. **diphthong'ally** adv. **diphthongizā'tion** or **-s-** n. **diph'thongize** or **-ise** /-gīz/ vt.

diphycercal /dif-i-sûr'kəl/ (zool) adj (of fishes, etc) having the tail symmetrical about the vertebral column, which runs horizontally, with the fin being equally developed above and below it. [Gr *diphyēs* of double nature, twofold, and *kerkos* a tail]

diphyletic /dif-i- or dī-fī-let'ik/ (biol) adj of dual origin; descended from two distinct ancestral groups. [Gr di- double, and phȳletikos relating to a tribesman, from phȳlē a tribe]

diphyodont /dif'i-ō-dont/ (zool) adj having two sets of teeth (milk and permanent). ◆ n a mammal with these. [Gr diphyēs of double nature, and odous, odontos a tooth]

Diphysite /dif'i-zīt or -sīt/ (also without cap) n a believer in the existence of two natures in Christ, a divine and a human, opp to Monophysite (also **Dyoph'ysite**, or less correctly **Dioph'ysite**). [Gr di- double, and physis nature]
■ **Diph'ysitism** /-it-izm/ n.

dipl- /dipl-/ or **diplo-** /dip-lō-/ combining form signifying double. [Gr diploos double]
■ **diploblas'tic** adj (Gr blastos bud; zool) (of invertebrates) deriving from only two layers of embryonic cell tissue, ectoderm and endoderm. **diplococcus** /dip-lə-kok'əs/ n (bacteriol) a coccus that divides by fission, the two resulting individuals remaining paired. **diplod'ocus** n (Gr dokos beam, bar, from its appearance) any gigantic, quadrupedal, herbivorous dinosaur, with very long neck and tail, of the genus Diplodocus, belonging to the sauropod group, remains of which have been found in the Jurassic rocks of the Rocky Mountains. **dip'logen** n (from **hydrogen**) a former name for deuterium or heavy hydrogen. **diplogen'esis** n (Gr genesis generation) doubling of parts normally single. **dip'loid** adj (Gr eidos form; biol) possessing two sets of chromosomes, one set coming from each parent, opp to haploid. **diploid'y** n. **dip'lon** n an alternative name for deuteron, the nucleus of heavy hydrogen. **dip'lont** n (Gr on, ontos, prp of einai to be; biol) an organism in which only the zygote is diploid, meiosis occurring at its germination and the vegetative cells being haploid, opp to haplont. **diplon'tic** adj. **diplō'pia** n (Gr ōps eye) double vision. **dip'lopod** n (Gr pous, podos foot) any myriapod of the class **Diplopō'da** (millipedes) bearing two pairs of legs on each segment. **diplostē'monous** adj (Gr stēmōn a thread; bot) having two whorls of stamens, the outer alternating with the petals, the inner with the outer. **dip'lotene** n (Gr tainia band; biol) the fourth stage of the prophase of meiosis, in which the chromosomes clearly double. **diplozō'on** n (pl diplozo'a) (Gr zōion an animal) a flatworm of the genus Diplozoon that lives fused together in pairs parasitically upon the gills of minnows, etc.

diplegia /dī-plē'ji-ə/ (med) n bilateral paralysis of similar parts of the body. [di- and Gr plēgē a blow]

dipleidoscope /di-plī'də-skōp/ n an instrument for ascertaining the moment of meridian passage by observing the coincidence of two images. [Gr diploos double, eidos appearance, and skopeein to view]

diplex /dī'pleks/ (telecom) adj relating to the transmission of two simultaneous messages over one wire in the same direction. [duplex, with substitution of Gr di- double]

diplo- see dipl-.

Diplock court /dip'lok kört/ n in Northern Ireland, a court of law that sits without a jury. [Lord Diplock, under whom such courts were introduced in 1972]

diplodocus see under dipl-.

diploe /dip'lō-ē/ (anat) n the spongy tissue between the hard inner and outer tables of the skull. [Gr diploē doubling, fold]

diplogen, diplogenesis, diploid see under dipl-.

diploma /di-plō'mə/ n a document conferring some honour or privilege, such as a university degree, etc. ◆ vt to confer a diploma upon. [L, from Gr diplōma a letter folded double, from diploos double]
■ **diplomate** /dip'lə-māt/ n someone who holds a diploma. ◆ vt (obs) to confer a diploma on.

diplomacy /di-plō'mə-si or -plom'ə-/ n the art of negotiation, esp in relations between states; tact in management of people concerned in any affair. [Fr diplomatie (pronounced -sie), from diplomate, diplomatique, ult from L (see **diploma**)]
■ **diplomat** /dip'lə-mat/ n a person employed or skilled in diplomacy. **diplomatese** /-ēz'/ n (inf) the jargon or obscure language used by diplomats. **diplomat'ic** adj relating to diplomacy (also **diplomat'ical**); tactful and skilful in negotiation or in dealing with people (also **diplomat'ical**); (of a document) copied exactly from an original. ◆ n a minister at a foreign court; diplomatics. **diplomat'ically** adv. **diplomat'ics** n sing the science of deciphering ancient writings, such as charters, etc; palaeography. **diplo'matist** n a diplomat. **diplo'matize** or **-ise** vi and vt to practise, or bring about by, diplomacy. **diplomatol'ogy** n the study or science of diplomatics, charters, decrees, etc.
◻ **diplomatic bag** or (US) **pouch** n a bag used for sending documents, etc to and from embassies, free of customs control; the contents of such a bag. **diplomatic corps** n the whole body of foreign diplomats resident in any capital. **diplomatic immunity** n immunity from local laws and taxation enjoyed by diplomats abroad. **diplomatic relations** n pl formal relations between states marked by the presence of diplomats in each other's country. **diplomatic service** n the government department that deals with diplomatic relations with other states.

diplomate see under **diploma**.

diplon...to...**diplozoon** see under **dipl-**.

Dipnoi /dip'nō-ī/ n pl an order of fishes, the lungfishes. [Gr di- double, and pnoē breath]
■ **dip'nōan** adj and n. **dip'nōous** adj having both lungs and gills.

Dipodidae /dī-pod'i-dē/ n pl the jerboa family of rodents. [Gr dipous two-footed, from di- twice and pous, podos a foot]

dipody /dip'ə-di/ (prosody) n a double foot. [Gr di- double, and pous, podos a foot]

dipolar /dī-pō'lər/ adj having two poles. [di-]
■ **di'pole** n two equal and opposite electric charges or magnetic poles of opposite sign set a small distance apart; a body or system containing either of these; a type of radio or television aerial.
◻ **dipole moment** n the product of the distance between the two ends of a dipole and their charges.

dipper see under **dip**.

dippy /dip'i/ (inf) adj crazy; insane. [Origin obscure]

diprionidian /dī-prī-ə-nid'i-ən/ (palaeontol) adj serrated on both sides (of graptolites). [Gr di- twice, and prīōn a saw]

diprotodont /dī-prō'tō-dont/ (palaeontol) n any marsupial of the **Diprotodont'ia**, the suborder (in some classifications) including kangaroos, wombats, etc, with one pair of incisors in the lower jaw. [Gr di- twice, prōtos, first, and odous, odontos tooth]
■ **dīprō'todon** n any animal of the extinct genus Diprotodon, the largest known marsupials. **diprotodon'tid** n an animal of the **Diprotodon'tidae** /-ē/, an extinct family of marsupials including the genus Diprotodon.

Dipsacus /dip'sə-kəs/ n the teasel genus, giving name to the **Dipsacā'ceae** related to the valerian and madder families. [Gr dipsakos teasel, from dipsa thirst, because the leaf-axils hold water]

dipsas /dip'sas/ n (pl dip'sades /-dēz/) a snake whose bite was believed to cause intense thirst; (with cap) a genus of non-venomous snakes. [Gr dipsas, from dipsa thirst]

dipsomania /dip-sō-mā'ni-ə/ n an intermittent pathological craving for alcohol. [Gr dipsa thirst, and maniā madness]
■ **dipsomā'niac** n a person who suffers from dipsomania (inf **dip'sō** (pl **dip'sōs**)).

DIP switch /dip swich/ (comput) n one of a bank of switches used to set options on a device, eg a printer; see also **dipswitch** under **dip**. [dual inline package, and **switch**]

Diptera /dip'tə-rə/ n the genus of two-winged insects or flies; (without cap) any insect of the genus. [Gr dipteros two-winged, from di- twice, and pteron a wing]
■ **dip'teral** adj two-winged; with double peristyle (archit). **dip'teran** n a dipterous insect. **dip'terist** n a person who studies flies. **dip'teros** n (archit) a building with double peristyle or colonnade. **dip'terous** adj with two wings or winglike expansions.

dipterocarp /dip'tə-rō-kärp/ n any tree of the genus Dipterocarpus or its family **Dipterocarpā'ceae** (chiefly Indian), in which some of the sepals enlarge as wings for the fruit. [Gr di- double, pteron wing, and karpos, fruit]
■ **dipterocarpā'ceous** or **dipterocarp'ous** adj.

diptych /dip'tik/ n a pair of pictures, esp with a religious theme, painted on hinged wooden panels; a double-folding wooden writing tablet; a register of bishops, saints, etc read aloud during the Eucharist. [Gr diptychos, from di- twice, and ptychē a tablet, a fold]

dipyridamole /dī-pi-rid'ə-mōl/ n a vasodilatory drug used to treat angina pectoris and prevent blood clotting. [di-, pyrimidine, piperidine, amino, and **-ol**[1]]

diquat /dī'kwot/ n a synthetic compound used as a herbicide. [di- and quaternary, part of its formula]

Dir. abbrev : Director.

Dirac's constant /dē'raks kon'stənt/ (phys) n a constant (ħ) used to express the behaviour of electron waves in a way consistent with special relativity, equal to Planck's constant divided by 2π. [Paul Dirac (1902–84), British physicist]

diram /dē'räm/ n (pl di'ram or di'rams) a monetary unit in Tajikistan, $\frac{1}{100}$ of a somoni.

dirdum, dirdam or **durdum** /dir'dəm or dûr'/ (Scot) n uproar; a scolding, punishment; blame. [Origin obscure]

dire /dīr/ adj dreadful; extremely calamitous; urgent; portentous. [L dīrus]
■ **dire'ful** adj (poetic). **dire'fully** adv. **dire'fulness** n. **dire'ness** n.
□ **dire wolf** n Canis dirus, a large extinct wolf of the Pleistocene epoch.

direct /di- or dī-rekt', dī'rekt/ adj straight; straightforward; by the shortest way; forward, not backward or oblique; at right angles; immediate; without intervening agency or interposed stages; (of a dye) fixing itself without a mordant; in the line of descent; outspoken; sincere; unambiguous; unsophisticated in manner. ◆n (music) an indication of the first note or chord of next page or line. ◆adv straight; by the shortest way; without deviation, intervening agency or interposed stages. ◆vt to keep or lay straight; to point or aim; to point out the proper course to; to guide; to order; to address, mark with the name and residence of a person; to plan and superintend the production of (a film or play). ◆vi to act as director of a film, play, etc; to direct letters, etc. [L dīrigere, dīrēctum, from dī-, apart, and regere, to rule]
■ **direc'tion** n aim at a certain point; the line or course in which anything moves or on which any point lies; guidance; command; a sense of purpose or goal; (in pl) instructions; the body of persons who guide or manage a matter; the address, or written name and residence of a person; the work of the director of a film, play, etc. **direc'tional** adj relating to direction in space; relating to or leading trends in fashion. **directional'ity** n. **direc'tionless** adj not moving, looking, etc in any particular direction; aimless. **direct'ive** adj having the power or a tendency to direct. ◆n a general instruction; a law passed by the European Union, addressed to member states, requiring the national Parliament to make changes to their law so as to effect the directive. **directiv'ity** n the property of being directional. **direct'ly** adv in a direct manner; without intermediary; immediately (in time and otherwise). ◆conj (often with that; inf) as soon as. **direct'ness** n. **direct'or** n (also fem **direct'ress** or **direc'trix**) a person who directs; a person who directs the shooting of a cinema film, etc; a manager or governor; a member of a board conducting the affairs of a company; a counsellor; a father confessor or spiritual guide; part of a machine or instrument that guides the motion; in automatic trunk dialling, the apparatus that obtains a channel through exchange junctions to the required exchange; a device that continuously calculates the position of a moving target and supplies firing data. **direct'orate** n the office of director; a body of directors; (with cap) the French Directory or Directoire. **directorial** /-tō' or -tö' adj. **direc'torship** n. **direct'ory** n a body of directions; a guide; a book with the names, telephone numbers and residences of the inhabitants of a place; a similar reference book compiled for a specific purpose, eg fax users, members of one profession or trade; a named grouping of files on a disk, controlled by an operating system (comput); a body of directors; (with cap) the Directoire, or French Republican government of 1795–99. ◆adj containing directions; guiding. **direct'rix** n (pl **directrices** /-trī'sēz/) see **director** above; a line serving to describe a conic section, which is the locus of a point whose distances from focus and directrix have a constant ratio (geom).
□ **direct access** n (comput) the ability to access data in a storage and retrieval system directly without having to scan any part of the storage file first (also **random access**). **direct action** n coercive methods of attaining industrial or political ends as opposed to pacific, parliamentary or political action. **direct broadcast satellite** n (telecom) a high-power geostationary communications satellite from which television programmes are beamed directly to the viewer, rather than being redistributed by cable or other means. **direct cost** n (account) one that can be measured and identified as being incurred on a specific job, contract or process. **direct current** n an electric current flowing in one direction only. **direct debit** n an arrangement by which a creditor can claim payment direct from the payer's bank account, and the payee can vary the amount paid. **direct discourse** see **direct speech** below. **direct drilling** n the ploughing and sowing of a field in one operation. **directed-energy weapon** n a weapon whose destructive force consists of beams of light, electromagnetic pulses, subatomic particles or the like. **direct-grant school** n (until 1979) a fee-paying school that received a state grant on condition that it took a specified number of non-fee-paying pupils. **direct injection** n a system of fuel injection in an internal-combustion engine where a carburettor is not used but fuel is injected directly into the cylinder. **directional aerial** n one that can receive or transmit radio waves in one direction only. **directional drilling** n (oil) a method of drilling in which the well is not drilled vertically, a technique, used esp in offshore drilling, where a number of wells may be drilled from a single platform. **directional microphone** n a microphone in which the response depends on the direction of the sound waves. **direc'tion-finder** n a radio receiver that determines the direction of arrival of incoming waves, used esp in navigation. **direc'tion-indicator** n an aerial navigation device in which needles of actual

and desired course overlap when the aircraft is on its true course. **direct labour** n labour employed directly, not through a contractor. **direct mail** n (marketing) the sending of promotional material to named potential customers by means of the postal service. **direct mail advertising** n (marketing). **direct mailshot** n (marketing) a single mailing in a campaign for a particular product or service, etc. **direct marketing** or **selling** n selling of products or services by manufacturers or producers directly to consumers without using a retail outlet. **direct method** n a method of teaching a foreign language through speaking it, without translation, and without formal instruction in grammar. **direct motion** n (music) progression of parts in the same direction (also called **similar motion**). **direct object** n a word or group of words denoting that upon which the action of a transitive verb is directed. **director circle** n the locus of the intersection of a pair of tangents to a conic at right angles to each other. **direct'or-gen'eral** n a chief administrator of a usu non-commercial organization. **director of public prosecutions** see under **prosecute**. **director's chair** n a light folding chair with seat and back of canvas or similar material and armrests. **director's cut** n the version of a cinema film preferred by its director as opposed to one edited by another, often incorporating scenes omitted from the commercially released version. **directory enquiries** n sing a telephone service in which a customer will be told the relevant telephone number from the directory for any name and address specified to the operator. **direct selling** see **direct marketing** above. **direct speech** or (US) **direct discourse** n speech reported as spoken, in the very words of the speaker (L ōrātiō rēcta). **direct tax** n one levied directly from individuals or organizations, rather than on goods or services.

Directoire /dē-rek-twär'/ (hist) n the French Directorate of 1795–99. ◆adj after the fashion in dress or furniture prevailing at that time; (of knickers) knee-length, with elastic at waist and knee. [Fr; see **direct**]

directress, directrix see **director** under **direct**.

diremption /dī-remp'shən/ n separation into two, disjunction. [L diremptiō, -ōnis, from dirimere, diremptus to separate; cf **diriment**]
■ **dīrempt'** vt.

dirge /dûrj/ n a funeral song or hymn; a slow and mournful piece of music. [Contracted from dīrige (imperative of L dīrigere to direct), the first word of an antiphon sung in the office for the dead, from the words from the Vulgate, Psalm 5, 8]

dirham /dûr-ham', də-ram', dē'ram/, sometimes **dirhem** /dûr-hem'/ n (also **derham'**) the standard monetary unit of Morocco (100 centimes) and the United Arab Emirates (100 fils); a coin equal to this in value; a coin used in several N African and Middle-Eastern countries, with varying value; (usu **dirhem**) an oriental unit of weight, orig two-thirds of an Attic drachma. [Ar, Pers, and Turk forms of the Greek drachmē a drachma or dram]

dirige /dir'i-ji/ (obs) n a dirge.

dirigible /dir'i-ji-bl, di-rij'i-bl/ adj that can be directed. ◆n a navigable balloon or airship. [See **direct**]
■ **dir'igent** adj directing.

dirigisme /dē-rē-zhē'zm'/ n control by the State in economic and social spheres (also **dirigism'**). [Fr, from Ital dirigismo]
■ **dirigiste** /-ēst'/ adj.

diriment /dir'i-mənt/ adj nullifying. [L dirimere]

dirk[1] /dûrk/ n a Highland dagger; a dagger worn as a sidearm by midshipmen and naval cadets (hist). ◆vt to stab with a dirk. [Orig Scot, in form durk; ety uncertain, but cf Du, Dan, Swed dolk dagger; Ir duirc is probably from the English word]

dirk[2] or **dirke** /dûrk/ adj, adv and vt (Spenser, etc) for **dark**, **darkly** or **darken**.

dirl /dûrl/ (Scot) vi and vt to (cause to) thrill, vibrate. ◆n vibration; a tingling as after a blow. [**drill**[1] and **thrill**]

dirndl /dûrn'dl/ n an Alpine peasant woman's dress with close-fitting bodice and full skirt; an imitation of this, esp a full skirt with a tight, often elasticated, waistband. [Ger dialect, dimin of dirne girl]

dirt /dûrt/ n any filthy substance, such as dung, mud, etc; foreign matter adhering to anything; loose earth; a mixture of earth, gravel and cinders, used as a surface for racetracks, etc; rubbish; obscenity; a worthless or despised person or thing; spiteful gossip. ◆vt to make dirty. [ME drit, prob ON drit excrement; cf OE gedrītan to defecate]
■ **dirt'ily** adv. **dirt'iness** n. **dirt'y** adj marked with dirt; soiled; foul, filthy; (of a colour) not bright or clear; stormy; obscene; unclean in thought or conversation; despicable; showing anger or reproof; mean; sordid; dishonest, treacherous; unsportingly rough. ◆vt (**dirt'ying**) **dirt'ied**) to soil with dirt; to sully. ◆adv in a dirty manner; (as an intensifier) enormous.
□ **dirt'bag** n (sl) a contemptible person. **dirt'-bed** n a quarryman's term for a layer representing an old soil, esp in the Purbeck group. **dirt bike** n a motorcycle designed for riding on dirt tracks. **dirt'-eating** n a

practice of eating clay as among various primitive peoples; a morbid impulse to eat dirt. **dirt farmer** *n* (*US*) a person who farms his or her own land, *esp* without hired help. **dirt'-pie** *n* mud moulded by children in play. **dirt'-poor** *adj* utterly poor, destitute. **dirt road** *n* (*Aust, N Am* and *NZ*) a soft road, unpaved and unmacadamized. **dirt'-rott'en** *adj* (*Shakesp*) wholly decayed. **dirt track** *n* a rough unsurfaced track; a motorcycle racing-track, with earthy or cinder surface. **dirty bomb** *n* one that produces a large amount of radioactive contamination. **dirty dog** *n* (*inf*) a dishonest or contemptible person. **dirty linen** *n* (*inf*) personal problems or grievances (*esp* in the phrase **wash one's dirty linen in public** to discuss private matters publicly). **dirty look** *n* (*inf*) a look of anger, disapproval or reproof. **dirty money** *n* money earned by immoral or illegal means; (in dock labour) extra pay for unloading offensive cargo; extra pay for any unpleasant, dirty, etc task. **dirty old man** *n* (*inf*) a man whose sexual aspirations and actions are considered appropriate only to a younger man. **dirty trick** *n* a dishonest or despicable act; a political intrigue, *esp* in the phrase *dirty-tricks campaign* or *operation*. **dirty war** *n* a conflict in which international conventions regarding the humane treatment of prisoners, civilians, etc are ignored. **dirty weekend** *n* (*inf*) a weekend containing much sexual activity, *esp* away from home and with someone other than one's usual partner. **dirty word** *n* an obscene word; a word for something (such as a feeling, principle, or belief) that is regarded with disfavour at the present time. **dirty work** *n* work that dirties the hands or clothes; dishonourable practices, *esp* undertaken on behalf of another person; foul play.

■ **dirt cheap** see under **cheap**. **dish the dirt** (*inf*) to distribute spiteful gossip, deal out malicious stories (about a person). **do the dirty on** to play a low trick on, cheat. **eat dirt** to acquiesce submissively in a humiliation. **throw dirt** to besmirch a reputation.

Dis /*dis* or *dēs*/ *n* a name for the god Pluto, hence, the infernal world. [L *Dīs*, cognate with *deus, dīvus* god]

dis see **diss**[1].

dis. *abbrev* : discontinued.

dis- /*dis-*/ or **di-** /*di-*/ *pfx* (1) meaning in two, asunder, apart; (2) meaning 'not' or a reversal; (3) indicating a removal or deprivation; (4) used intensively. [L *dis-, dī-*]

disa /*dī'sə, dī'zə*/ *n* an orchid of the *Disa* genus of African orchids with dark green leaves, or of certain other genera. [Origin unknown]

disable /*dis-ā'bl*/ *vt* to deprive of power; to weaken; to cripple or incapacitate; to disqualify legally; to depreciate, disparage, undervalue (*Shakesp*). [**dis-** (2)]
■ **disabil'ity** *n* lack of power; lack of legal power or qualification; a disqualification; a difficulty, *esp* physical. **disa'bled** *adj* having physical or mental disabilities; designed or intended for people with physical disabilities. **disa'blement** *n*. **disa'blism** *n* discrimination against, stereotyping of, or offensive behaviour towards anyone on the grounds of physical or mental disability. **disa'blist** *n* and *adj*.

disabuse /*dis-ə-būz'*/ *vt* to undeceive or set right. [**dis-** (2)]

disaccharide /*dī-sak'ə-rīd*/ *n* a sugar that hydrolyses into two molecules of simple sugars. [**di-**]

disaccommodate /*dis-ə-kom'ə-dāt*/ *vt* to put to inconvenience. [**dis-** (2)]
■ **disaccommodā'tion** *n*.

disaccord /*dis-ə-körd'*/ *vi* to refuse to accord; to be at discord; not to agree. ◆ *n* lack of agreement; discord. [**dis-** (2)]
■ **disaccord'ant** *adj*.

disaccustom /*dis-ə-kus'təm*/ *vt* to make to be lost through disuse. [**dis-** (2)]

disacknowledge /*dis-ək-nol'ij*/ *vt* to refuse to acknowledge, disown. [**dis-** (2)]

disadorn /*dis-ə-dörn'*/ (*obs* and *rare*) *vt* to deprive of ornaments. [**dis-** (2)]

disadvance /*dis-əd-väns'*/ (*obs*) *vt* to cause to retreat; to draw back, cease to put forward (*Spenser*). [**dis-** (2)]

disadvantage /*dis-əd-vän'tij*/ *n* unfavourable circumstance or condition; loss; damage. ◆ *vt* to put (someone) at a disadvantage. [**dis-** (2)]
■ **disadvan'tageable** *adj* (*obs*). **disadvan'taged** *adj* deprived of the resources and privileges (*usu* social) enjoyed by the majority of people; in unfavourable conditions relative to other (specified) people. **disadvantageous** /*dis-ad-vənt-ā'jəs*/ *adj* involving or bringing disadvantage; unfavourable. **disadvantā'geously** *adv*. **disadvantā'geousness** *n*.

disadventurous /*dis-əd-ven'chə-rəs*/ (*obs*) *adj* unfortunate. [**dis-** (2)]
■ **disadven'ture** or **disaven'ture** *n* (*Spenser*, etc) a mishap. **disaven'trous** *adj* (*Spenser*) unfortunate.

disaffect /*dis-ə-fekt'*/ *vt* to take away the affection of; to make discontented or unfriendly. [**dis-** (3)]

■ **disaffect'ed** *adj* ill-disposed or alienated; tending to break away. **disaffect'edly** *adv*. **disaffect'edness** *n*. **disaffec'tion** *n* the state of being disaffected; lack of affection or friendliness; alienation; ill-will; political discontent or disloyalty. **disaffec'tionate** *adj*.

disaffiliate /*dis-ə-fil'i-āt*/ *vt* and *vi* to end an affiliation (to); to separate oneself (from). [**dis-** (2)]
■ **disaffiliā'tion** *n*.

disaffirm /*dis-ə-fûrm'*/ *vt* to contradict; to repudiate or reverse (*law*). [**dis-** (2)]
■ **disaffirm'ance** or **disaffirmā'tion** /*dis-a-*/ *n*.

disafforest /*dis-ə-for'ist*/ *vt* to bring out of the operation of forest laws; to take away the legal status of a forest from; to clear of forest, deforest. [L *dis-* reversal, and LL *afforestāre* to make into a forest. See **forest**]
■ **disafforestā'tion** *n*. **disaffor'estment** *n*.

disaggregate /*dis-ag'ri-gāt* or *-rə-*/ *vt* to separate (something) into its component parts. [**dis-** (1)]
■ **disaggregā'tion** *n*.

disagree /*dis-ə-grē'*/ *vi* to differ or be at variance; to disaccord; to dissent; to quarrel; to be opposed; to prove unsuitable or a source of annoyance (eg of food upsetting the stomach). [**dis-** (2)]
■ **disagreeabil'ity** *n*. **disagree'able** *adj* not amicable; unpleasant; offensive. **disagree'ableness** *n*. **disagree'ables** *n pl* annoyances. **disagree'ably** *adv*. **disagree'ment** *n* lack of agreement; difference; unsuitableness; dispute.

disallow /*dis-ə-low'*/ *vt* not to allow; to refuse to sanction; to deny the authority, validity or truth of; to reject, to forbid; to dispraise (*obs*). ◆ *vi* (*obs*) to disapprove. [**dis-** (2)]
■ **disallow'able** *adj*. **disallow'ance** *n*.

disally /*dis-ə-lī'*/ *vt* to break the alliance of; to separate or sunder (*Milton*). [**dis-** (2) and (1)]

di salto /*dē säl'tō*/ (*Ital*) at a leap.

disambiguate /*dis-am-big'ū-āt*/ *vt* to take away the ambiguity from; to make unambiguous. [**dis-** (3)]
■ **disambigua'tion** *n*.

disamenity /*dis-ə-mē'ni-ti, -men'*/ *n* a lack of amenity; a disadvantage or drawback (eg of a property or district). [**dis-** (3)]

disanalogy /*dis-a-nal'ə-ji*/ *n* a non-correspondence; an aspect or feature in which something is not analogous to something else. [**dis-** (2)]
■ **disanal'ogous** /*-gəs*/ *adj*.

disanchor /*dis-ang'kər*/ *vt* to free from the anchor. ◆ *vi* to weigh anchor. [**dis-** (3)]

disanimate /*dis-an'i-māt*/ *vt* to deprive of spirit or animation; to deject (*Shakesp*, etc). [**dis-** (3)]

disannex /*dis-ə-neks'*/ *vt* to disjoin. [**dis-** (1)]

disannul /*dis-ə-nul'*/ *vt* to annul completely. [**dis-** (4)]
■ **disannull'er** *n*. **disannul'ment** or **disannull'ing** *n*.

disanoint /*dis-ə-noint'*/ *vt* to undo the anointing or consecration of. [**dis-** (2)]

disapparel /*dis-ə-par'əl*/ *vt* to disrobe. [**dis-** (2)]

disappear /*dis-ə-pēr'*/ *vi* to vanish from sight; to become lost; to leave or take flight without explanation or warning; to cease to exist, be felt or be known. ◆ *vt* to cause (someone) to vanish, be no longer around, *esp* by imprisoning or killing them *usu* for political reasons. [**dis-** (3)]
■ **disappear'ance** *n*.

disapply /*dis-ə-plī'*/ *vt* to render (a law) inapplicable. [**dis-** (2)]
■ **disapplicā'tion** *n*.

disappoint /*dis-ə-point'*/ *vt* to frustrate the hopes or expectations of; to prevent the fulfilment of; to deprive of what is appointed (*obs*). ◆ *vi* to cause disappointment. [OFr *desapointer*, from *des-* (L *dis-*) away, and *apointer* to appoint. See **appoint**]
■ **disappoint'ed** *adj* saddened by the frustration of hopes, etc; balked; frustrated; unequipped or ill-equipped (*obs*; *Shakesp*). **disappoint'ing** *adj* causing disappointment; unsatisfactory, of a less than adequate or expected standard. **disappoint'ingly** *adv*. **disappoint'ment** *n* the defeat of one's hopes or expectations; frustration; the vexation accompanying failure; a source of disappointment.

disapprobation /*dis-a-prō-bā'shən* or *-pro-*/ *n* disapproval. [**dis-** (2)]
■ **disapp'robātive** or **disapp'robātory** *adj*.

disappropriate /*dis-ə-prō'pri-āt*/ *vt* to take away from the condition of being appropriated. ◆ *adj* /*-it*/ deprived of appropriation. [**dis-** (3)]

disapprove /*dis-ə-proov'*/ *vt* and *vi* to give or have an unfavourable opinion (of); to reject. [**dis-** (2)]
■ **disapprov'al** *n*. **disapprov'ing** *adj*. **disapprov'ingly** *adv*.

disarm /*dis-ärm'*/ *vt* to deprive of arms; to strip of armour; to render defenceless; to deprive of the power to hurt; to conciliate or placate (*fig*); to deprive of suspicion or hostility; to reduce to a peace footing. ◆ *vi* to disband troops, reduce national armaments. [**dis-** (3)]

■ **disarm'ament** *n* the reduction of national armaments; the act of disarming or the state of being disarmed. **disarm'er** *n* someone who or something that disarms; a person in favour of reducing national armaments. **disarm'ing** *adj* charming; tending to placate.

disarrange /dis-ə-rānj'/ *vt* to undo the arrangement of; to disorder; to derange. [**dis-** (2)]

■ **disarrange'ment** *n*.

disarray /dis-ə-rā'/ *vt* to break the array of; to throw into disorder; to strip of array or dress (*archaic*). ◆ *n* lack of array or order; untidiness; undress (*archaic*). [**dis-** (2) and (3)]

disarticulate /dis-är-tik'ū-lāt/ *vt* to separate the joints of. ◆ *vi* to separate at a joint. [**dis-** (1)]

■ **disarticula'tion** *n*.

disassemble /dis-ə-sem'bl/ *vt* to take apart. [**dis-** (1)]

■ **disassem'bler** *n* (*comput*) a program that translates from machine code to an assembly language. **disassem'bly** *n*.

disassimilate /dis-ə-sim'i-lāt/ *vt* to subject to catabolism. [**dis-** (2)]

■ **disassimila'tion** *n*. **disassim'ilative** *adj*.

disassociate /dis-ə-sō'shi-āt/ *vt* (with *from*) to disconnect; to dissociate. [**dis-** (2)]

■ **disassocia'tion** *n*.

disaster /di-zäs'tər/ *n* an adverse or unfortunate event; a great and sudden misfortune; a calamity. [OFr *desastre*, from *des-* (L *dis-*) with evil sense, and *astre* a star, destiny, from L *astrum*, Gr *astron* star]

■ **disas'trous** *adj* calamitous, ruinous; gloomy, foreboding disaster. **disas'trously** *adv*.

❑ **disaster area** *n* an area in which there has been a disaster (eg flood or explosion), requiring special official aid; (loosely) any place where a misfortune has happened; anything that is untidy, ugly, disadvantageous, etc (*inf*). **disaster movie** *n* a film that has as its main theme or focus of action a disaster or catastrophe.

disattire /dis-ə-tīr'/ (*Spenser*) *vt* to undress. [**dis-** (2)]

disattribution /dis-at-ri-bū'shən/ *n* the act of adjudging a work of art, etc to be no longer the product of a particular artist, etc; an instance of this. [**dis-** (2)]

disattune /dis-ə-tūn'/ *vt* to put out of harmony. [**dis-** (2)]

disauthorize or **-ise** /dis-ö'thə-rīz/ *vt* to deprive of authority. [**dis-** (3)]

disavaunce (*Spenser*) same as **disadvance**.

disaventrous, disaventure see under **disadventurous**.

disavouch /dis-ə-vowch'/ (*obs*) *vt* to disavow. [**dis-** (2)]

disavow /dis-ə-vow'/ *vt* to disclaim knowledge of, or connection with; to disown; to deny. [OFr *desavouer*, from *des-* (L *dis-*) away, and *avouer* to avow. See **avow**]

■ **disavow'al** *n*.

disband /dis-band'/ *vt* to disperse, break up (a group, unit, etc). ◆ *vi* to break up. [OFr *desbander* to unbind, from *des-* (L *dis-*) reversal, and *bander* to tie]

■ **disband'ment** *n*.

disbar /dis-bär'/ (*law*) *vt* to expel from the bar. [**dis-** (3)]

■ **disbar'ment** *n*.

disbark¹ /dis-bärk'/ (*obs*) *vt* and *vi* to land from a ship; to disembark. [OFr *desbarquer*, from *des-* (L *dis-*) reversal, and *barque* bark]

disbark² /dis-bärk'/ *vt* to strip of bark, to bark. [**dis-** (3)]

disbelieve /dis-bi-lēv'/ or *-bə-/ *vt* to believe to be false; to refuse or be unable to believe. ◆ *vi* to have no faith (in). [**dis-** (2)]

■ **disbelief'** *n*. **disbeliev'er** *n*.

disbench /dis-bench', -bensh'/ *vt* to drive from a bench or seat (*Shakesp*); to deprive of the status of a member of a governing body in the Inns of Court. [**dis-** (3)]

disbenefit /dis-ben'i-fit/ *n* a drawback, disadvantage, loss, inconvenience, etc; absence or loss of a benefit. [**dis-** (2) and (3)]

disbodied /dis-bod'id or *-bod'ēd/ *adj* disembodied. [**dis-** (3)]

disbosom /dis-bŭz'əm/ *vt* to make known, reveal. [**dis-** (1)]

disbowel /dis-bow'əl/ (*fig*) *vt* (**disbow'elling**; **disbow'elled**) to disembowel. [**dis-** (3)]

disbranch /dis-bränch', -bränsh'/ *vt* to remove branches from; to sever. [**dis-** (3)]

disbud /dis-bud'/ *vt* to remove buds from. [**dis-** (3)]

disburden /dis-bûr'dən/ or **disburthen** /dis-bûr'dhən/ *vt* to rid of a burden; to free; to unload, discharge. [**dis-** (3)]

disburse /dis-bûrs'/ *vt* to pay out. [OFr *desbourser*, from *des-* (L *dis-*) apart, and *bourse* a purse]

■ **disburs'al** or **disburse'ment** *n* a paying out; that which is paid. **disburs'er** *n*.

disc or (*esp N Am*) **disk** /disk/ *n* any flat thin circular body or structure; a gramophone record; (usu as **disk**) a magnetic disc or a disk file (see entry at **disk**; *comput*); a compact disc; a videodisc; a quoit thrown by ancient Greek athletes; a circular figure, such as that presented by the sun, moon and planets; the enlarged torus of a flower; the inner part of a capitulum in composite plants; a layer of fibrocartilage between vertebrae, the slipping of which (**slipped disc**) causes pressure on spinal nerves and hence pain. ◆ *vt* and *vi* to work with a disc harrow. [Gr *diskos*]

■ **disc'al** *adj* relating to, or of the nature of, a disc. **discec'tomy** *n* surgical removal of a part of a vertebral disc. **discog'rapher** *n*. **discog'raphy** *n* collection or description, etc, of musical recordings; the history or description of musical recording; a list of recordings by one composer or performer. **disc'oid** or **discoid'al** *adj* in the form of a disc; (of a capitulum) without ray-flowers (*bot*). **disc'ophile** /-ō-fīl/ *n* someone who makes a study of and collects musical recordings.

❑ **disc brake** *n* a brake in which the friction is obtained by pads hydraulically forced against a disc on the wheel. **disc camera** *n* an obsolete camera in which the images are made on a disc instead of a roll of film. **disc flower** or **floret** *n* one of the tubular inner flowers of a capitulum, *opp* to ray-flower. **disc harrow** or **disc plough** *n* a harrow or plough in which the soil is cut by inclined discs. **disc jockey** *n* a person who introduces and plays recordings (*esp* of popular music) on a radio or television programme, in a club, etc. **disc parking** *n* a system according to which the motorist is responsible for affixing to his or her car special disc(s) showing the time of arrival and the time when permitted parking ends, there being no charge during the permitted period. **disc player** *n* a machine for playing audio or video material recorded on a disc. **disc wheel** *n* a wheel on a motor vehicle, etc in which the hub and rim are connected by a solid piece of metal rather than by spokes.

disc. *abbrev* : discount; discoverer.

discage /dis-kāj'/ *vt* to free from a cage. [**dis-** (2)]

discalced /dis-kalst'/ *adj* without shoes, barefooted or wearing only sandals, as a branch of the Carmelite order of friars and nuns noted for their austerity. [L *discalceātus*, from *dis-* (negative), and *calceāre*, *-ātum* to shoe, from *calceus* a shoe, from *calx* the heel]

■ **discal'ceate** *n* and *adj*.

discant /dis'kant/ same as **descant**.

discapacitate /dis-kə-pas'i-tāt/ *vt* to incapacitate. [**dis-** (2)]

discard /dis-kärd'/ *vt* and *vi* to reject; to get rid of as unwanted; to cast off; to throw (a card) away, as not needed or not allowed by the game; (in whist, etc) to throw away (a card of another suit) when one cannot follow suit and cannot or will not trump; to discharge. ◆ *n* (also /dis'/) the act of discarding; the card or cards thrown out of the hand; discharge, dismissal, abandonment; a cast-off, anything discarded. [**dis-** (3)]

■ **discard'able** *adj*. **discard'ment** *n*.

■ **throw into the discard** (*US*) to throw on the scrap-heap.

discarnate /dis-kär'nit, -nāt/ *adj* disembodied; separated from its or the body. [**dis-** (1), and L *carō*, *carnis* flesh]

discase /dis-kās'/ (*Shakesp*, etc) *vt* to remove a case or covering from, to undress. [**dis-** (3)]

discept /di-sept'/ *vi* to dispute, debate. [L *disceptāre*, *-ātum* to contend, from *dis-*, and *captāre*]

■ **disceptā'tion** *n* (*archaic*). **disceptā'tious** *adj* (*obs*). **discepta'tor** *n* (*obs*). **disceptātō'rial** *adj* (*obs*).

discern /di-sûrn'/ *vt* to make out; to distinguish by the eye or understanding; to judge (*obs*; a blunder for **decern**). [L *discernere*, from *dis-* thoroughly, and *cernere* to sift, perceive]

■ **discern'er** *n*. **discern'ible** *adj*. **discern'ibly** *adv*. **discern'ing** *adj* discriminating; showing acute judgement. **discern'ment** *n* the power or faculty of discriminating; acuteness.

discerp /di-sûrp'/ *vt* (*rare*) to separate. [L *discerpere* to tear in pieces, from *dis-* apart, and *carpere* to pluck]

■ **discerpibil'ity** *n* capability of being disunited. **discerp'ible** (*obs*) or **discerp'tible** *adj*. **discerp'tion** *n* (*rare*). **discerp'tive** *adj* (*rare*).

discharge /dis-chärj'/ *vt* to free from or relieve of a charge of any kind (burden, explosive, electricity, liability, accusation, etc); to set free; to acquit; to dismiss from employment; to release from hospital after treatment; to fire (eg a gun); to take the superincumbent weight from; to set down or send forth; to eject; to pour out; to emit or let out; to perform (eg a task or duty); to pay; to give account for; to distribute (as weight); to forbid (*obs*). ◆ *vi* to unload; to become released from a charged state; to allow escape of contents; to flow away or out. ◆ *n* (usu /dis'chärj/) the act of discharging; release from a charge of any kind; unloading; liberation; acquittal; dismissal; release from hospital after treatment; release of electricity; outflow; rate of flow; emission; release of tension; payment; performance; that which is discharged. [OFr *descharger*, from *des-* apart, and *charger*; see **charge**]

discharge'able *adj.* **discharg'er** *n* someone who discharges; an apparatus for discharging (*esp* electricity, eg a spark gap or discharging tongs); an apparatus for firing an explosive.
□ **discharge lamp** *n* a lamp in which light is created by a discharge tube. **discharge tube** *n* a tube in which an electric discharge takes place in a vacuum or in a gas at low pressure. **discharging arch** *n* an arch built in a wall to protect a space beneath from the weight above. **discharging tongs** *n pl* metal tongs used for discharging condensers.

dischuffed /dis-chuft'/ (*inf*) *adj* displeased; disappointed. [**dis-** (2)]

dischurch /dis-chûrch'/ (*obs*) *vt* to deprive of church rank or privileges. [**dis-** (3)]

discide /di-sīd'/ (*obs*; *Spenser*, etc) *vt* to cut asunder, to divide. [L *dis-* asunder, and *caedere* to cut]

discinct /di-singkt'/ *adj* ungirded. [L *discingere*, *-cinctum* to ungird]

disciple /di-sī'pl/ *n* a person who professes to receive instruction from another; a person who follows or believes in the doctrine of another; a follower, esp one of the twelve apostles of Christ. ♦ *vt* (*Spenser*, etc) to teach. [Fr, from L *discipulus*, from *discere* to learn; related to *docēre* to teach]
■ **discī'pleship** *n.*
□ **Disciples of Christ** *n pl* a sect that seeks a restoration of New Testament Christianity, by some called Campbellites.

discipline /dis'i-plin/ *n* training designed to engender self-control and an ordered way of life; the state of self-control achieved by such training; instruction; a branch of learning, or field of study; a branch of sport; an event in a sports meeting; subjection to control; order; severe training; mortification; punishment; an instrument of penance or punishment. ♦ *vt* to subject to discipline; to train; to educate; to bring under control; to chastise. [L *disciplīna*, from *discipulus*]
■ **disc'iplinable** *adj.* **disc'iplinal** (or /-plī'/) *adj.* **disc'iplinant** *n* a person who accepts the rule of a discipline, *esp* one of an order of Spanish flagellants. **disciplinā'rian** *n* a person who enforces strict discipline. ♦ *adj* disciplinary; advocating or practising strict discipline. **disciplinā'rium** *n* a scourge for penitential flogging. **disc'iplinary** *adj* relating to or of the nature of discipline. **disc'ipliner** *n* a person who disciplines.
■ **First** and **Second Book of Discipline** two documents (1560 and 1578) embodying the constitution and order of procedure of the Church of Scotland from the period of the Reformation.

discission /di-sish'ən/ *n* an incision into a tumour or cataract. [L *dīscissiō*, *-ōnis*, from *dīscindere*, *-scissum*, from *dī-* apart, and *scindere* to cut]

disclaim /dis-klām'/ *vt* to renounce all claim to; to refuse to acknowledge or be responsible for; to repudiate; to reject; to cry out against the claim of. ♦ *vi* to make a disclaimer; to declaim, cry out (*obs*). [OFr *disclaimer*, from L *dis-* apart, and *clāmāre* to cry out]
■ **disclaim'er** *n* a denial, disavowal or renunciation; a statement refusing to accept responsibility. **disclamā'tion** /-kləm-/ *n* a disavowal.

disclose /dis-klōz'/ *vt* (pap (*Spenser*) **disclōst**) to bring to light; to reveal; to unclose; to open; to lay open; to hatch (*Shakesp*); to transform and give vent to (*Spenser*). ♦ *n* a disclosure; emergence from the egg (*Shakesp*). [OFr *desclos*, from L *dis-* apart, and *claudere*, *clausum* to shut]
■ **disclō'sure** /-zhər/ *n* the act of disclosing; a bringing to light or revealing; that which is disclosed or revealed.
□ **disclosing tablet** *n* a tablet which, when chewed, reveals by means of a coloured dye any areas of plaque to be removed from the teeth.

disco /dis'kō/ (*inf*) *n* (*pl* **dis'cos**) a club or party where music for dancing is provided by records, *usu* played by a disc jockey; the equipment and records used to provide this. ♦ *adj* suitable or specially produced for discos, such as *disco dancing*, *disco music*. ♦ *vi* (**dis'coing**; **dis'coed**) (*inf*) to go to a disco; to dance to disco music. [Short form of **discotheque**]
■ **dis'coer** *n* someone who frequents discos.
□ **disco biscuit** *n* (*sl*) a tablet of the drug ecstasy.

discobolus /dis-kob'ə-ləs/ *n* a disc-thrower (*ancient hist*); the name of a famous lost statue ascribed to Myron, of which copies exist. [L, from Gr *diskobolos*, from *diskos* a quoit and *ballein* to throw]

discodermolide /dis-kō-dûr'mə-līd/ *n* a drug used in experimental treatments for cancer. [*Discodermia dissoluta*, name of a sponge from which it is derived]

discography, **discoid**, etc see under **disc**.

discolour or (*N Am*) **discolor** /dis-kul'ər/ *vt* to take away colour from; to change or to spoil the natural colour of; to alter the appearance of; to mark with other colours, to stain; to dirty, disfigure. ♦ *vi* to become discoloured. [OFr *descolorer*, from L *dis-* apart, and *colōrāre*, from *color* colour]

discolorā'tion or **discolourā'tion** *n* the act of discolouring; the state of being discoloured; stain. **discol'oured** *adj* stained, etc; many-coloured (*Spenser*).

discombobulate /dis-kəm-bob'oo-lāt, -ū-lāt/ or **discomboberate** /-bob'ər-āt/ (*esp N Am sl*) *vt* to disconcert, upset. [Origin obscure]

Discomedusae /dis-kō-me-dū'sē/ *n pl* an order of jellyfishes with flattened umbrella. [Gr *diskos* disc, and **medusa**]
■ **discomedu'san** *n* and *adj.*

discomfit /dis-kum'fit/ *vt* (**discom'fiting**; **discom'fited**) to disconcert or balk; to defeat or rout. ♦ *n* (*Milton*) defeat. [OFr *desconfit*, pap of *desconfire*, from L *dis-* (negative), and *conficere* to prepare, from *con-* (intensive), and *facere* to make]
■ **discom'fiture** *n.*

discomfort /dis-kum'fərt/ *n* lack of comfort; uneasiness; slight pain. ♦ *vt* to deprive of comfort; to make uneasy. [OFr *desconforter*, from *des-* (privative), and *conforter* to comfort; see **comfort**]
■ **discom'fortable** *adj* uncomfortable; causing discomfort (*obs*).

discommend /dis-kə-mend'/ *vt* to blame; to dispraise. [**dis-** (2)]
■ **discommend'able** *adj* worthy of blame. **discommend'ableness** *n.* **discommendation** /dis-ko-mən-dā'shən/ *n.*

discommission /dis-kə-mish'ən/ (*Milton*) *vt* to deprive of a commission. [**dis-** (3)]

discommode /dis-kə-mōd'/ *vt* to inconvenience. [**dis-** (2), and obsolete verb *commode* to suit]
■ **discommō'dious** *adj.* **discommō'diously** *adv.* **discommodity** /-mod'/ *n* inconvenience.

discommon /dis-kom'ən/ *vt* to deprive of the right of common (qv under **right¹**), or (at Oxford and Cambridge) of dealing with undergraduates. [**dis-** (3), and **common** (noun)]

discommunity /dis-kə-mū'ni-ti/ (*rare*) *n* lack of community. [**dis-** (2)]

discompose /dis-kəm-pōz'/ *vt* to deprive of composure; to disturb or agitate; to disarrange or disorder. [**dis-** (2)]
■ **discompō'sure** /-zhər or -zhyər/ *n.*

Discomycetes /dis-kō-mī-sē'tēz/ (*bot*) *n pl* a group of fungi (*Ascomycetes*) with open apothecia. [Gr *diskos* disc, and *mykētes*, pl of *mykēs* a fungus]
■ **dis'comycete** *n.* **discomycē'tous** *adj.*

disconcert /dis-kən-sûrt'/ *vt* to throw into confusion; to disturb; to frustrate; to defeat; to put out of countenance, to embarrass. ♦ *n* /dis-kon'sərt/ disunion. [Obs Fr *disconcerter*, from *des-* (L *dis-*) apart, and *concerter* to concert]
■ **disconcert'ing** *adj.* **disconcer'tion** *n* confusion. **disconcert'ment** *n.*

disconfirm /dis-kən-fûrm'/ *vt* to show that a statement, hypothesis, etc is not or may not be true. [**dis-** (2)]
■ **disconfirmā'tion** *n.*

disconformable /dis-kən-för'mə-bl/ *adj* not similar or consistent; (of strata) with their original relative positions disturbed (*geol*); not conformable. [**dis-** (2)]
■ **disconform'ity** *n* lack of conformity; unconformity (*geol*).

disconnect /dis-kə-nekt'/ *vt* and *vi* to separate or disjoin (from); to break the connection, *esp* electrical (between); to stop the supply of electricity, gas, telephone services, etc (to). ♦ *n* a separation; a lack of unity. [**dis-** (1)]
■ **disconnect'ed** *adj* separated; (eg of a discourse) loosely united. **disconnect'edly** *adv.* **disconnec'tion** or **disconnex'ion** *n.*

disconsent /dis-kən-sent'/ (*obs*) *vi* to differ or dissent. [**dis-** (2)]

disconsolate /dis-kon'sə-lit/ *adj* beyond consolation or comfort; very sad or disappointed. [L *dis-* (negative), and *consōlārī*, *consōlātus* to console]
■ **discon'solately** *adv.* **discon'solateness** *n.* **disconsolā'tion** *n.*

discontent /dis-kən-tent'/ *n* lack of contentment; dissatisfaction; a discontented person (*Shakesp*). ♦ *adj* not content; dissatisfied. ♦ *vt* to deprive of contentment; to stir up to ill-will. [**dis-** (2), (3)]
■ **discontent'ed** *adj* not content; dissatisfied. **discontent'edly** *adv.* **discontent'edness** *n.* **discontent'ful** *adj.* **discontent'ing** *adj* not contenting or satisfying; discontented (*Shakesp*). **discontent'ment** *n.*

discontiguous /dis-kon-tig'ū-əs/ *adj* not contiguous, not in contact. [**dis-** (2)]
■ **discontigu'ity** *n.*

discontinue /dis-kən-tin'ū/ *vt* to cease to continue; to put an end to; to leave off; to stop; to end the production of. ♦ *vi* to cease; to be separated (*obs*). [OFr *discontinuer*, from L *dis-* reversal, and *continuāre* to continue]
■ **discontin'uance** or **discontinuā'tion** *n* a breaking off or ceasing. **discontinu'ity** /-kon-/ *n.* **discontin'uous** *adj* not continuous; broken off; separated; interrupted by intervening spaces. **discontin'uously** *adv.*

discophile see under **disc**.

Discophora /dis-kof'ə-rə/ n pl the order of jellyfishes known as Discomedusae. [Gr diskos disc, and phoros carrying]
■ **discoph'oran** n and adj. **discoph'orous** adj.

discord /dis'körd/ n disagreement, strife, opp to concord; difference or contrariety of qualities; a combination of inharmonious sounds; uproarious noise; a dissonance, esp unprepared. ◆ vi /dis-körd'/ to disagree. [OFr descord, from L discordia, from dis- apart, and cor, cordis the heart]
■ **discord'ance** or **discord'ancy** n. **discord'ant** adj without concord or agreement; inconsistent; contradictory; harsh; jarring. **discord'antly** adv. **discord'ful** adj (Spenser).
■ **apple of discord** see under **apple**.

discorporate /dis-kör'pər-it/ adj disembodied. [**dis-** (2)]

discotheque or **discothèque** /dis'kə-tek/ n an older or more formal form of **disco**. [Fr discothèque, a record-library, from Gr diskos disc, and thēkē case, library]

discounsel /dis-kown'səl/ (Spenser, etc) vt to dissuade. [OFr desconseillier, from des- apart, and conseillier to counsel]

discount /dis'kownt/ n a deduction made for prompt payment of an account, or according to some other negotiated agreement; the rate or percentage of the deduction granted; a deduction made for interest in advancing money on a bill; the amount by which the price of a share or stock unit is below the par value. ◆ vt /dis-kownt'/ to disregard, or reject as unimportant; to reduce the effect of (eg an extravagant statement, a fabulous story or an event foreseen); to sell at a reduced price; to allow as discount; to allow discount on; to pay (rarely to receive) beforehand the present worth of a bill of exchange; to calculate the present value of future cash flows by deducting interest for the period between the present and the moment when the cash flow is expected to take place (finance); to ignore. ◆ vi to practise discounting. [OFr descompter, from des- (L dis-) away, and compter to count]
■ **discount'able** adj. **discount'er** n.
❑ **dis'count-broker** n a person who cashes notes or bills of exchange at a discount. **discount house** n a company trading in bills of exchange, etc; (also **discount store**) a shop where goods are sold at less than the usual retail price. **discount market** n the part of the financial market that trades in discounted bills of exchange. **discount rate** n the rate at which a discount is granted; the rate at which banks can borrow funds using bills as security; (in USA and Canada) minimum lending rate.
■ **at a discount** for less than the usual price; below par; not sought after; superfluous; depreciated in value. **discounted cash flow** (account) the present value of future estimated cash flows.

discountenance /dis-kown'tə-nəns/ vt to put out of countenance; to abash; to refuse approval of or support to; to discourage. ◆ n cold treatment; disapprobation. [OFr descontenancer, from des- reversal, and contenance countenance]

discourage /dis-kur'ij/ vt to take away the courage of; to dishearten; to oppose, prevent, or seek to prevent by showing disfavour. [OFr descourager. See **courage**]
■ **discour'agement** n act of discouraging; that which discourages; dejection. **discour'aging** adj disheartening, depressing. **discour'agingly** adv.

discoure /dis-kowr'/ (Spenser) vt to discover.

discourse /dis-körs', -körs' or dis'/ n speech or language generally; conversation; the reasoning faculty (obs or archaic); a treatise; a speech; a sermon; (apparently) process of combat (Spenser). ◆ vi to talk or converse; to reason; to treat formally (with on). ◆ vt to utter or give forth. [Fr discours, from L discursus, from dis- away, and currere to run]
■ **discours'al** adj. **discours'er** n (Shakesp). **discours'ive** adj (obs).
❑ **discourse analysis** n (linguistics) the study of continuous stretches of language to discover their structure and the features that bind sentences in a sequence.

discourteous /dis-kûr'tyəs, -kör' or -kör'/ adj (also (Spenser) **discourt'eise**) lacking in courtesy; uncivil. [**dis-** (2)]
■ **discourt'eously** adv. **discourt'eousness** n. **discourt'esy** n discourteousness; a discourteous remark or act.

discover /dis-kuv'ər/ vt (also (Spenser, etc) **discoure'** and **discure'**) to find or find out, esp for the first time; to uncover (obs); to lay open or expose (archaic); to exhibit (rare); to reveal (rare); to make known (archaic); to espy. [OFr descouvrir, from des- (L dis-) away, and couvrir to cover; see **cover**]
■ **discov'erable** adj. **discov'erer** n a person who makes a discovery, esp of something never before known; an informer (obs); a scout (Shakesp). **discov'ery** n the act of finding out; the thing discovered; gaining knowledge of the unknown; the unravelling of a plot; exploration or reconnaissance (as in **voyage of discovery** voyage of exploration).

❑ **discovered check** n in chess, a check produced by moving a piece to leave a second piece attacking the opponent's king. **discovery well** n an exploratory oil well that proves to yield a commercially viable amount of oil.

discovert /dis-kuv'ərt/ (law) adj (of a spinster or widow) not under the bonds of matrimony. [Literally, uncovered, unprotected; OFr descovert; see **discover** and **cover**]
■ **discov'erture** n.

discredit /dis-kred'it/ n lack of credit; bad credit; ill-repute; disgrace; a person or thing bringing ill-repute or disgrace. ◆ vt to refuse to believe in; to deprive of credibility; to deprive of credit; to disgrace. [**dis-** (2) and (3)]
■ **discred'itable** adj bringing discredit; disgraceful. **discred'itably** adv.

discreet /dis-krēt'/ adj careful in one's actions and choice of words, esp able to keep secrets; tactful; prudent; modest; unpretentious; discrete, separate, detached (archaic). [OFr discret, from L discrētus, from discernere to separate, to perceive; see **discern** and **discrete**]
■ **discreet'ly** adv. **discreet'ness** n.

discrepancy /dis-krep'ən-si/ n disagreement, variance of facts or sentiments. [L discrepāns, -antis different, from dis- apart, and crepāns, prp of crepāre to sound]
■ **discrep'ance** (or /dis'/) n. **discrep'ant** (or /dis'/) adj contrary, disagreeing.

discrete /dis-krēt'/ adj separate; discontinuous; consisting of distinct parts; referring to distinct objects; abstract, opp to concrete. [L discrētus; cf **discreet**]
■ **discrete'ly** adv. **discrete'ness** n. **discret'ive** adj separating; disjunctive. **discret'ively** adv.

discretion /dis-kresh'ən/ n quality of being discreet; prudence; liberty to act at pleasure. [OFr discrecion, from L discrētiō, -ōnis, from discernere, -crētum]
■ **discre'tional** or **discre'tionary** adj left to discretion; unrestricted. **discre'tionally** or **discre'tionarily** adv.
❑ **discretionary income** n the amount of income remaining from a person's salary or wages after all regular fixed expenditure on necessary items has been met.
■ **age of discretion** the age at which a person is considered to be mature enough to take responsibility for his or her own actions, etc (also **years of discretion**). **at discretion** according to one's own judgement or pleasure. **be at someone's discretion** to be completely under someone's power or control. **surrender at discretion** to surrender unconditionally, ie to another's discretion.

discriminate /dis-krim'i-nāt/ vt to note the difference of or between; to distinguish; to select from others. ◆ vi to make or note differences or distinctions; to distinguish (between); (with in favour of or against) to treat differently, esp because of one's feelings or prejudices about a person's sex, race, religion, etc. ◆ n (maths) a special function of the roots of an equation, expressible in terms of the coefficients, zero value of the function showing that at least two of the roots are equal. ◆ adj /-nit/ discriminated; discriminating. [L discrimināre, -ātum, from discrīmen that which separates; cf discernere to discern]
■ **discrim'inable** adj able to be discriminated. **discrim'inant** adj discriminating. **discrim'inately** adv. **discrim'inating** adj noting distinctions; gifted with judgement and penetration. **discrim'inatingly** adv. **discriminā'tion** n the act or process of discriminating; judgement; good taste; the selection of a signal having a particular characteristic (frequency, amplitude, etc) by the elimination of all the other input signals (telecom). **discrim'inative** adj that marks a difference; characteristic; observing distinctions. **discrim'inatively** adv. **discrim'inātor** n someone who or something that discriminates; a device that affects the routing and/or determines the fee units for a call originating at a satellite exchange (telecom); a circuit that converts a frequency or phase modulation into amplitude modulation for subsequent demodulation (telecom); a circuit that rejects pulses below a certain amplitude level and shapes the remainder to standard amplitude and profile (telecom). **discrim'inatory** adj biased, unfair, revealing prejudice; discriminative; making fine distinctions.
■ **positive discrimination** discrimination in favour of those who were formerly discriminated against, esp in the provision of social and educational facilities and employment opportunities.

discrown /dis-krown'/ vt to deprive of a crown. [**dis-** (3)]

disculpate /dis-kul'pāt/ vt to free from blame. [**dis-** (3)]

discumber /dis-kum'bər/ (archaic) vt to disencumber. [**dis-** (2)]

discure see **discover**.

discursive /dis-kûr'siv/ adj running from one thing to another; (of writing or speaking style) proceeding from one subject to another with no formal plan, given to digression, roving, desultory; proceeding regularly from premises to conclusion, intellectual or rational, rather than intuitive (*philos*). [See **discourse**]

■ **discur'sion** *n* (*rare*) desultory talk; act of reasoning. **discur'sist** *n* (*obs*) a disputer. **discur'sively** *adv*. **discur'siveness** *n*. **discur'sory** *adj* discursive. **discur'sus** *n* (*LL*) discourse, reasoned treatment.

discus /dis'kəs/ *n* a disc, a flat circular image or object; a heavy wooden disc, thickening towards the centre, thrown for distance in athletic contests, *orig* in ancient Greece; (also **discus throw**) such a contest; (*usu* with *cap*) a popular freshwater aquarium fish, a brightly-coloured disc-shaped S American cichlid. [L, from Gr *diskos*]

discuss /dis-kus'/ *vt* to examine in detail in speech or writing; to talk or argue about in conversation; to debate; to sift; to consume (eg a bottle of wine; *facetious*); to throw off (*obs*; *Spenser*); to dispel; to settle, decide (*obs*); to declare, make known (*obs*; *Shakesp*). [L *discutere*, *discussum*, from *dis-* apart, and *quatere* to shake]

■ **discuss'able** or **discuss'ible** *adj*. **discuss'ant** *n* one who discusses. **discuss'er** *n*. **discussion** /dis-kush'ən/ *n* debate, argument or conversation; a detailed treatment in speech or writing; the dispersion of a tumour (*surg*). **discuss'ive** or **discutient** /-kū'shi-ənt/ *adj* (*med*) able or tending to discuss or disperse tumours. **discu'tient** *n* a medicine with this property.

disdain /dis-dān'/ *vt* to think unworthy; to scorn. ♦ *n* a feeling of contempt, generally tinged with superiority; haughtiness. [OFr *desdaigner* with substitution of *des-* (L *dis-*) for L *dē* in L *dēdīgnārī*, from *dīgnus* worthy]

■ **disdained'** *adj* (*Shakesp*) disdainful. **disdain'ful** *adj* feeling or showing disdain. **disdain'fully** *adv*. **disdain'fulness** *n*.

disease /di-zēz'/ *n* an unhealthy state of body or mind; a disorder, illness or ailment with distinctive symptoms, caused eg by infection; unhealthiness, or a specific ailment, in plants; a social evil (*fig*); uneasiness (in this sense often written **dis-ease** and pronounced /dis'ēz'/; *archaic*). ♦ *vt* (*Spenser*, etc) to make uneasy. [OFr *desaise*, from *des-* (L *dis-* not), and *aise* ease; see **ease**]

■ **diseased'** *adj* affected with disease. **diseas'edness** *n*. **disease'ful** *adj* (*obs*).

diseconomy /dis-ə-kon'ə-mi/ *n* (an instance of) something that is economically wasteful or unprofitable. [**dis-** (2)]

disedge /dis-ej'/ (*Shakesp*, etc) *vt* to deprive of the edge; to blunt; to dull. [**dis-** (3)]

disembark /dis-im-bärk'/ *vi* to leave a ship; to land. ♦ *vt* to set ashore; to take out of a ship. [OFr *desembarquer*, from *des-* (L *dis-* removal), and *embarquer*. See **embark**]

■ **disembarkā'tion** /dis-em- or dis-im-/ or **disembark'ment** *n*.

disembarrass /dis-im-bar'əs/ *vt* to free from an embarrassment, burden or complication (with *of*). [**dis-** (2)]

■ **disembarr'assment** *n*.

disembellish /dis-im-bel'ish/ *vt* to deprive of embellishment. [**dis-** (2)]

disembitter /dis-im-bit'ər/ *vt* to free from bitterness. [**dis-** (2)]

disembody /dis-im-bod'i/ *vt* to remove or free (a spirit) from the body; to discharge from military embodiment. [**dis-** (3)]

■ **disembod'ied** *adj* separated from the body; emanating from no visible physical source. **disembod'iment** *n*.

disembogue /dis-im-bōg'/ *vt* (*usu* reflexive) and *vi* to discharge at the mouth, as a stream (with *into*). [Sp *desembocar*, from *des-* (L *dis-*) apart, and *embocar* to enter the mouth, from *en* (L *in*) into, and *boca* (L *bucca*) cheek, mouth]

■ **disembogue'ment** *n*.

disembosom /dis-im-būz'əm/ *vt* to separate from the bosom; to disburden. [**dis-** (1)]

disembowel /dis-im-bow'əl/ *vt* to take out the bowels of; to tear out the inside of. [**dis-** (3)]

■ **disembow'elment** *n*.

disembrangle /dis-im-brang'gl/ (*obs*) *vt* to free from dispute. [**dis-** (2)]

disembroil /dis-im-broil'/ *vt* to free from broil or confusion. [**dis-** (2)]

disemburden /dis-im-bûr'dən/ *vt* to disburden. [**dis-** (3)]

disemploy /dis-im-ploi'/ (*rare*) *vt* to remove from employment. [**dis-** (2)]

■ **disemployed'** *adj*. **disemploy'ment** *n*.

disempower /dis-im-pow'ər/ *vt* to deprive of a power or function. [**dis-** (3)]

disenable /dis-in-ā'bl/ *vt* to make unable; to disable; to deprive of power (*obs*). [**dis-** (2)]

disenchain /dis-in-chān'/ *vt* to free from restraint. [**dis-** (2)]

disenchant /dis-in-chänt'/ *vt* to free from enchantment, to disillusion. [**dis-** (2)]

■ **disenchant'ed** *adj*. **disenchant'er**, *fem* **disenchant'ress** *n*. **disenchant'ment** *n*.

disenclose or **disinclose** /dis-in-klōz'/ *vt* to free from the condition of being enclosed; to dispark. [**dis-** (2)]

disencumber /dis-in-kum'bər/ *vt* to free from an encumbrance; to disburden. [**dis-** (2)]

■ **disencum'brance** *n*.

disendow /dis-in-dow'/ *vt* to take away the endowments of (*esp* of an established church). [**dis-** (3)]

■ **disendowed'** *adj*. **disendow'ment** *n*.

disenfranchise /dis-in-fran'chīz, -shīz/ *vt* to deprive of a franchise, or of rights and privileges, *esp* that of voting for a member of parliament. [**dis-** (2)]

■ **disenfran'chisement** *n*.

disengage /dis-in-gāj'/ *vt* to separate or free from being engaged; to separate; to set free; to release; to withdraw from combat. ♦ *vi* to come loose; to break off from a fight. [OFr *desengager*, from *des-* (L *dis-* negative) and *engager* to engage]

■ **disengaged'** *adj* not engaged; detached; unoccupied, at liberty. **disengag'edness** *n*. **disengage'ment** *n* a separating, releasing; a mutual withdrawal from a position.

disennoble *dis-i(n)-nō'bl/ *vt* to deprive of title, or of what ennobles; to degrade. [**dis-** (2)]

disenrol /dis-in-rōl'/ *vt* to remove from a roll. [**dis-** (2)]

disenshroud /dis-in-shrowd'/ *vt* to divest of a shroud, to unveil. [**dis-** (3)]

disenslave /dis-in-slāv'/ *vt* to free from bondage. [**dis-** (2)]

disentail /dis-in-tāl'/ *vt* to break the entail of (an estate) (*law*); to divest (*obs*). ♦ *n* the act of disentailing. [**dis-** (2)]

■ **disentail'ment** *n*.

disentangle /dis-in-tang'gl/ *vt* to free from entanglement or disorder; to remove tangles from; to unravel; to disengage or set free. [**dis-** (2)]

■ **disentang'lement** *n*.

disenthral or **disenthrall** /dis-in-thröl'/ *vt* to free from enthralment. [**dis-** (2)]

■ **disenthrall'ment** or **disenthral'ment** *n*.

disenthrone /dis-in-thrōn'/ (*Milton*, etc) *vt* to dethrone. [**dis-** (2)]

disentitle /dis-in-tī'tl/ *vt* to deprive of title or right. [**dis-** (2)]

disentomb /dis-in-toom'/ *vt* to take out from a tomb. [**dis-** (2)]

disentrail or **disentrayle** /dis-in-trāl'/ (*Spenser*) *vt* to let forth as if from the entrails. [**dis-** (3)]

disentrain /dis-in-trān'/ *vt* to set down from a train. ♦ *vi* to alight from a train. [**dis-** (3)]

■ **disentrain'ment** *n*.

disentrance /dis-in-träns'/ *vt* to awaken from a trance or entrancement; to arouse from a reverie. [**dis-** (2)]

■ **disentrance'ment** *n*.

disentrayle see **disentrail**.

disentwine /dis-in-twīn'/ or *-en-/ *vt* to untwine. [**dis-** (2)]

disenvelop /dis-in-vel'əp/ *vt* to free from that in which a thing is enveloped; to unfold. [**dis-** (2)]

disenviron /dis-in-vī'rən/ *vt* to deprive of environment. [**dis-** (3)]

disepalous /dī-sep'ə-ləs/ (*bot*) *adj* having two sepals. [**di-** and **sepal**]

disequilibrium /dis-ek-wi-lib'ri-əm/ *n* (*pl* **disequilib'ria**) lack of balance, *esp* in economic affairs. [**dis-** (2)]

■ **disequil'ibrate** *vt* to cause a disequilibrium in.

disespouse /dis-i-spowz'/ (*Milton*) *vt* to separate after espousal or betrothal. [**dis-** (1)]

disestablish /dis-i-stab'lish/ *vt* to undo the establishment of; to deprive (a church) of established status. [**dis-** (2)]

■ **disestab'lishment** *n*.

disesteem /dis-i-stēm'/ *n* lack of esteem; disregard. ♦ *vt* to disapprove; to dislike. [**dis-** (2)]

■ **disestimā'tion** /-es-tim-/ *n*.

diseur /dē-zœr'/ or *fem* **diseuse** /dē-zœz'/ (*Fr*) *n* a reciter or entertainer.

disfame /dis-fām'/ (*rare*) *n* evil reputation. [**dis-** (2)]

disfavour or (*N Am*) **disfavor** /dis-fā'vər/ *n* the state of being out of favour or disapproved of; hostility, disapproval or dislike; a disobliging act. ♦ *vt* to be hostile to; to disapprove; to oppose. [**dis-** (2)]

■ **disfā'vourer** *n*.

disfeature /dis-fē'chər/ *vt* to deprive of a feature; to deface. [**dis-** (3)]

disfellowship /dis-fel'ō-ship/ *n* lack of or exclusion from fellowship. ♦ *vt* to excommunicate. [**dis-** (2)]

disfigure /dis-fig'ər/ *vt* to spoil the appearance of, to blemish or mar; to deface; to deform or distort. [OFr *desfigurer*, from L *dis-* (negative), and *figūrāre* to figure]

■ **disfigurā'tion** or **disfig'urement** *n*.

disflesh /dis-flesh'/ (archaic and poetic) vt to deprive of flesh, to disembody. [**dis-** (3)]

disfluency /dis-floo'ən-si/ n a lack of fluency in speech, with hesitations, repetitions, stammering, etc. [**dis-** (2)]
■ **disflu'ent** adj.

disforest /dis-for'ist/ vt to strip of trees, to deforest; to disafforest (law). [**dis-** (2)]

disform /dis-förm'/ vt to alter the form of. [**dis-** (2)]

disfranchise /dis-fran'chīz, -shīz/ (rare) vt to disenfranchise; to deprive of suffrage. [**dis-** (2)]
■ **disfran'chisement** n.

disfrock /dis-frok'/ vt to unfrock, deprive of clerical garb or character. [**dis-** (3)]

disfurnish /dis-fûr'nish/ (Shakesp and literary) vt to strip, render destitute. [**dis-** (2)]
■ **disfur'nishment** n.

disgarnish /dis-gär'nish/ vt to despoil. [**dis-** (3)]

disgarrison /dis-gar'i-sn/ vt to deprive of a garrison. [**dis-** (3)]

disgavel /dis-gav'l/ (law) vt to relieve from the tenure of gavelkind. [**dis-** (3)]

disgest /dis-jest'/ or -jēst'/ and **disgestion** /-yən/ obsolete or dialect forms of **digest¹** and **digestion**.

disglorify /dis-glö'ri-fī, -glö'/ (Milton) vt to deprive of glory. [**dis-** (3)]

disgodded /dis-god'id/ adj deprived of divinity. [**dis-** (2)]

disgorge /dis-görj'/ vt to discharge from the throat; to vomit; to discharge in great volume or with violence; to give up, esp reluctantly; to remove sediment from (champagne) after fermentation in the bottle. [OFr desgorger, from des away, and gorge throat. See **gorge**]
■ **disgorge'ment** n.

disgospelling /dis-gos'pə-ling/ (Milton) adj withholding the gospel, stopping the channel of the gospel. [**dis-** (3)]

disgown /dis-gown'/ vt or vi to strip of a gown; to deprive of or to renounce orders or a degree. [**dis-** (3)]

disgrace /dis-grās'/ n the state of being out of favour or of being dishonoured; a cause of shame, someone or something shameful; disrepute or dishonour; disfigurement; ugliness; defect of grace. ◆ vt to put out of favour; to bring disgrace or shame upon. [Fr disgrâce, from L dis- not, and grātia favour, grace]
■ **disgrace'ful** adj bringing disgrace; causing shame; dishonourable. **disgrace'fully** adv. **disgrace'fulness** n. **disgra'cer** n. **disgracious** /-grā'shəs/ adj (obs; Shakesp, etc) ungracious, unpleasing.
■ **in disgrace** out of favour; shamed.

disgrade /dis-grād'/ (archaic) vt to deprive of rank or status. [OFr desgrader, with substitution of des- (L dis-) for L dē in LL dēgradāre, from gradus a step]
■ **disgradation** /-grə-dā'shən/ n.

disgregation /dis-gri-gā'shən/ n separation; scattering. [L disgregātiō, -ōnis, from dis- apart, and grex, gregis flock]

disgruntle /dis-grun'tl/ (inf) vt to disappoint or displease. [**dis-** (4) and **gruntle**, frequentative of **grunt**]
■ **disgrun'tled** adj out of humour, discontented, sulky. **disgrun'tlement** n.

disguise /dis-gīz'/ vt to change the appearance or character of; to conceal the identity of, eg by dress intended to deceive, or by a counterfeit manner and appearance; to mask or hide (facts or feelings); to conceal the true nature of; to misrepresent; to intoxicate, usu in the phrase disguised in liquor (archaic and sl). ◆ n dress intended to disguise the wearer; a false appearance; a misleading representation; change of behaviour in intoxication (archaic and sl). [OFr desguiser, from des- (L dis- reversal), and guise manner; see **guise**]
■ **disguis'able** adj. **disguised'** adj. **disguis'edly** adv. **disguis'edness** n. **disguise'less** adj. **disguise'ment** n. **disguis'er** n. **disguis'ing** n.

disgust /dis-gust'/ n loathing, distaste, extreme disapproval, or annoyance; (formerly, eg in Milton, Johnson, Jane Austen) distaste, disfavour, displeasure. ◆ vt to cause disgust in. [OFr desgouster, from des- (L dis-) and gouster, from L gustāre to taste]
■ **disgust'ed** adj. **disgust'edly** adv. **disgust'edness** n. **disgust'ful** adj. **disgust'fully** adv. **disgust'fulness** n. **disgust'ing** adj. **disgust'ingly** adv. **disgust'ingness** n.
■ **in disgust** with or because of a feeling of disgust.

dish¹ /dish/ n a vessel, esp one that is flat, or shallow, or not circular, for holding or serving food during a meal; a dishful; the food in a dish; (in pl) the plates, cutlery, etc used in a meal and now to be washed; a cup (of tea, coffee, etc) (archaic); food prepared in a particular way for a meal; a hollow; concavity of form, as in a wheel or a chair-back; (also **dish aerial**) a microwave aerial in the form of a parabolic reflector used for radar or radio telescopes and for satellite broadcast reception; a good-looking or attractive person (inf). ◆ vt to put in a dish, for serving during a meal; to make concave; to outwit, circumvent (inf); to ruin (inf); to distribute spiteful gossip (N Am inf). [OE disc a plate, a dish, a table, from L discus, from Gr diskos; cf **disc**, **desk** and Ger Tisch table]
■ **dished** adj having a concavity; (of a pair of wheels on a car, etc) sloping in towards each other at the top; completely frustrated (inf). **dish'ful** n. **dish'ing** n putting in a dish; a hollow, a concavity. ◆ adj hollow like a dish. **dish'y** adj (inf) good-looking, attractive.
□ **dish aerial** see n above. **dish'cloth** or (archaic or dialect) **dish'-clout** n a cloth for washing, drying or wiping dishes. **dish'-cover** n a cover for a dish to keep it hot. **dish'-faced** adj having a round, flat face, or (in animals) a concavity in the face. **dish'rag** n a dishcloth. **dish'towel** n (esp N Am) a cloth for drying dishes, a tea towel. **dish'washer** n a machine that washes and dries dishes, cutlery, etc; a person employed to wash dishes. **dish'water** n water in which dishes have been washed; a liquid deficient in strength or cleanliness.
■ **dish out** to serve out; to share (food) among several people; to give, give out (inf; usu disparagingly; esp with it, of rough treatment, punishment, etc). **dish the dirt** see under **dirt**. **dish up** to serve up (food or other matter for consumption). **do the dishes** (inf) to wash the dishes, cutlery, etc used in a meal.

dish² /dish/ (printing) vt to distribute (type).

dishabilitate /dis-(h)ə-bil'i-tāt/ vt to disqualify; to attaint. [**dis-** (2)]
■ **dishabilitā'tion** n.

dishabille see **déshabillé**.

dishabit /dis-hab'it/ (Shakesp) vt to drive from a habitation. [OFr deshabiter, from L dis- (privative), and habitāre to inhabit]

dishable /dis-hā'bl/ an obsolete form (Spenser, etc) of **disable**.

dishallow /dis-hal'ō/ vt to desecrate. [**dis-** (2)]

disharmony /dis-här'mə-ni/ n lack of harmony; discord; disagreement, dissent; incongruity. [**dis-** (2)]
■ **disharmonic** /-mon'/ adj out of harmony; discordant; incongruous; dysharmonic. **disharmonious** /-mō'/ adj. **disharmō'niously** adv. **dishar'monize** or **-ise** vt and vi to put out of, or be out of, harmony.

dishdasha /dish'dash-ə/ or **dishdash** /dish'dash/n a long one-piece garment worn by men in some Arab countries. [Colloquial Ar]

dishearten /dis-här'tn/ vt to deprive of courage or spirits; to discourage or demoralize; to depress. [**dis-** (2)]
■ **disheart'ened** adj. **disheart'ening** adj. **disheart'eningly** adv.

dishelm /dis-helm'/ vt to divest of a helmet. [**dis-** (3)]

disherit /dis-her'it/ (Spenser, etc) vt to disinherit. [OFr desheriter, from L dis- (negative), and LL hērēditāre to inherit, from L hērēs heir]
■ **disher'ison** /-zən/ n. **disher'itor** n.

dishevel /di-shev'l/ vt (dishev'elling; dishev'elled) to ruffle (hair) or disarrange (clothing); to cause to hang loose. ◆ vi to spread in disorder. [OFr discheveler, from LL discapillāre to tear out or disorder the hair, from L dis- in different directions, and capillus the hair]
■ **dishev'elled** adj (of a person) untidy or bedraggled in appearance; (of hair) hanging loose, or merely untidy. **dishev'elment** n.

dishome /dis-hōm'/ vt to deprive of a home. [**dis-** (3)]

dishonest /dis-on'ist/ adj not honest; lacking integrity; disposed to cheat; insincere; unchaste (obs; Shakesp). [OFr deshoneste, from des- (L dis-; negative) and honeste (L honestus) honest]
■ **dishon'estly** adv. **dishon'esty** n.

dishonour or (N Am) **dishonor** /dis-on'ər/ n lack of respect or honour; disgrace; shame; something that brings discredit; an affront; reproach; failure of a debtor to make good a promise to pay. ◆ vt to deprive of honour; to disgrace; to cause shame to; to seduce; to degrade; to refuse the payment of (eg a cheque). [OFr deshonneur, from des- (L dis-; negative), and honneur, (from L honor) honour]
■ **dishon'orary** adj causing dishonour. **dishon'ourable** or (N Am) **dishon'orable** adj not in accordance with a sense of honour; disgraceful. **dishon'ourableness** or (N Am) **dishon'orableness** n. **dishon'ourably** or (N Am) **dishon'orably** adv. **dishon'ourer** or (N Am) **dishon'orer** n.
□ **dishonorable discharge** n dismissal from the US armed forces for serious misconduct (such as theft or desertion). **dishonorably discharged** adj.

dishorn /dis-hörn'/ vt to deprive of horns. [**dis-** (3)]

dishorse /dis-hörs'/ vt to unhorse. [**dis-** (3)]

dishouse /dis-howz'/ vt to deprive of house or housing; to turn out of doors; to clear of houses. [**dis-** (3)]

dishumour /dis-(h)ū'mər/ (obs) n ill-humour. ◆ vt to put out of humour. [**dis-** (2)]

dishy see under **dish¹**.

disillude /dis-i-lood', -lūd'/ vt to free from illusion. [**dis-** (3)]

■ words derived from main entry word; □ compound words; ■ idioms and phrasal verbs

disilluminate /dis-i-loo'mi-nāt, -lū'/ (rare) vt to destroy the light of, to darken. [**dis-** (2)]

disillusion /dis-i-loo'zhən, -lū'/ n a freeing from illusion; state of being disillusioned. ◆ vt to destroy the illusions of, to disenchant; to disabuse. [**dis-** (3)]
■ **disillu'sionary** adj. **disillu'sioned** adj disenchanted, disabused of an illusion; often, bereft of comfortable beliefs whether they were false or true. **disillu'sionize** or **-ise** vt. **disillu'sionment** n. **disillu'sive** /-siv/ adj.

disimagine /dis-i-maj'in/ vt to banish from the imagination; to imagine not to be. [**dis-** (3) and (2)]

disimmure /dis-i-mūr'/ vt to release from walls; to liberate. [**dis-** (2)]

disimpassioned /dis-im-pash'ənd/ adj free from the influence of passion, tranquil. [**dis-** (2)]

disimprison /dis-im-priz'n/ vt to free from prison or restraint. [**dis-** (2)]
■ **disimpris'onment** n.

disimprove /dis-im-proov'/ vt to render worse. ◆ vi to grow worse. [**dis-** (2)]

disincarcerate /dis-in-kär'sə-rāt/ vt to free from prison. [**dis-** (2)]
■ **disincarcerā'tion** n.

disincentive /dis-in-sen'tiv/ n a discouragement to effort; a deterrent. ◆ adj acting as a discouragement or deterrent. [**dis-** (2)]

disinclination /dis-in-kli-nā'shən/ n lack of inclination; unwillingness. [**dis-** (2)]
■ **disincline** /-klīn'/ vt to render unwilling, reluctant or averse. **disinclined'** adj not inclined; averse.

disinclose see **disenclose**.

disincorporate /dis-in-kör'pə-rāt/ vt to deprive of corporate rights. [**dis-** (2)]
■ **disincorporā'tion** n.

disindividualize or **-ise** /dis-in-di-vid'ū-ə-līz or -vij'oo-/ vt to deprive of individuality. [**dis-** (2)]

disindustrialize or **-ise** /dis-in-dus'tri-ə-līz/ vt to deprive of industry, reduce the amount of industry in. [**dis-** (2)]
■ **disindustrializā'tion** or **-s-** n.

disinfect /dis-in-fekt'/ vt to rid of disease-causing bacteria, etc by cleaning, esp with a chemical. [**dis-** (2)]
■ **disinfec'tant** n a chemical, etc that destroys bacteria (also adj). **disinfec'tion** n. **disinfec'tor** n.

disinfest /dis-in-fest'/ vt to rid (a place or animal, etc) of vermin. [**dis-** (2)]
■ **disinfestā'tion** n.

disinflation /dis-in-flā'shən/ (econ) n return to the normal condition after inflation; deflation which reduces or stops inflation. [**dis-** (2)]
■ **disinflā'tionary** adj.

disinformation /dis-in-fər-mā'shən/ n deliberate leakage of misleading information. [**dis-** (2)]

disingenuous /dis-in-jen'ū-əs/ adj not ingenuous; not frank or open; merely posing as being frank or open; crafty, devious. [**dis-** (2)]
■ **disingenu'ity** n (rare). **disingen'uously** adv. **disingen'uousness** n.

disinherit /dis-in-her'it/ vt to cut off from hereditary rights; to deprive of an inheritance. [**dis-** (3)]
■ **disinher'ison** /-zən/ n act of disinheriting. **disinher'itance** n.

disinhibit /dis-in-hib'it/ vt to remove restraints on (used esp of drugs affecting behaviour). [**dis-** (2)]
■ **disinhibition** /-hi-bish'ən/ n. **disinhib'itory** adj.

disinhume /dis-in-hūm'/ vt to take out of the earth, to disinter. [**dis-** (2)]

disintegrate /dis-in'ti-grāt/ vt and vi to separate into parts; to break up; to crumble. [**dis-** (1)]
■ **disin'tegrable** adj. **disintegrā'tion** n the act or state of disintegrating; a process in which a nucleus ejects one or more particles, esp in spontaneous radioactive decay (nucleonics). **disin'tegrative** adj. **disin'tegrātor** n a machine for crushing or pulverizing.

disinter /dis-in-tûr'/ vt (**disinterr'ing; disinterred'**) to remove from a grave or from the earth; to dig up or bring to light; to bring out of obscurity. [**dis-** (2)]
■ **disinter'ment** n.

disinterest /dis-in't(ə)-rest, -rəst, -rist/ n disadvantage (rare); impartiality, freedom from prejudice; lack of interest, unconcern. ◆ vt to free from interest. [**dis-** (2)]
■ **disin'terested** adj not influenced by private feelings or considerations; not deriving personal advantage; impartial; unselfish; generous; (revived from obsolescence) uninterested. **disin'terestedly** adv. **disin'terestedness** n. **disin'teresting** adj (obs) uninteresting.

disintermediation /dis-in-tər-mē-di-ā'shən/ (finance) n direct investment in unit trusts, funds, etc without the mediation of banks or brokers; the elimination of intermediaries such as banks or brokers in financial transactions. [**dis-** (3)]
■ **disintermē'diāte** vt.

disinthral same as **disenthral**.

disintricate /dis-in'tri-kāt/ vt to free from intricacy. [**dis-** (2)]

disinure /dis-i-nūr'/ (obs; Milton) vt to render unfamiliar. [**dis-** (2)]

disinvent /dis-in-vent'/ vt to undo the invention of. [**dis-** (2)]

disinvest¹ /dis-in-vest'/ vi and vt to remove investment (from) or cease investment (in; with in). [**dis-** (2)]
■ **disinvest'ment** n.

disinvest² /dis-in-vest'/ vt to divest. [**dis-** (2)]
■ **disinvest'iture** n the action of disinvesting.

disinvigorate /dis-in-vig'ə-rāt/ (rare) vt to weaken. [**dis-** (2)]

disinvite /dis-in-vīt'/ vt to withdraw an invitation to. [**dis-** (2)]

disinvolve /dis-in-volv'/ vt to unfold; to disentangle. [**dis-** (2)]

disject /dis-jekt'/ vt to dismember; to scatter. [L disjicere, -jectum, from dis- apart, and jacere to throw]
■ **disjec'tion** n.

disjecta membra /dis-yek'tə mem'brə/ (L) fragments of literary work. [Literally 'scattered limbs', from Ovid, Metamorphoses III.724]

disjoin /dis-join'/ vt to separate after having been joined; to form a disjunction of. ◆ vi to separate, disconnect. [OFr desjoindre, from L disjungere, from dis- apart, and jungere to join]
■ **disjoin'ing** adj disjunctive.

disjoint /dis-joint'/ vt and vi to disconnect or come apart at the joints; to dislocate or disunite; to break the natural order or relations of; to make incoherent. [OFr desjoinct, from desjoindre to disjoin]
■ **disjoint'ed** adj (of discourse, narrative, etc) incoherent; lacking connection or continuity; separated at the joints; badly assorted. **disjoint'edly** adv. **disjoint'edness** n.

disjunct /dis-jungkt', also dis'jungkt/ adj disjoined; having deep constrictions between the different sections of the body (zool); (of tetrachords) having the highest note of the lower and the lowest of the upper a tone or semitone apart (Gr music). ◆ n (logic) one of the propositions in a disjunction; a disjunctive proposition. [OFr desjoinct, desjoindre to disjoin]
■ **disjunc'tion** n the act of disjoining; disunion; separation; the separation during meiosis of the two members of a pair of homologous chromosomes (biol); a compound statement comprising propositions connected by an element denoting 'or', an **inclusive disjunction** being true when at least one proposition is true, an **exclusive disjunction** being true when at least one but no more than one of the propositions is true (logic). **disjunct'ive** adj disjoining; tending to separate; not continuous, interrupted; (of conjunctions) indicating an alternative or opposition (grammar); relating to, containing, forming or being part of a disjunction (logic). ◆ n a disjunctive word or element. **disjunct'ively** adv. **disjunct'or** n a device for breaking an electric circuit; a weak place where separation between conidia occurs (bot). **disjunct'ure** n disjunction.

disjune /dis-joon'/ (Scot; archaic) n breakfast. [OFr desjun, from L dis-expressing undoing, and jējūnus fasting]

disk /disk/ n a variant spelling (esp N Am) of **disc**; a magnetic disc used for backing up and storing information and programs (comput). [Variant of **disc**]
■ **diskette'** n (comput) a small magnetic floppy disk. **disk'less** adj. ☐ **disk capacity** n (comput) the amount of storage space on a disk. **disk drive** n a computer peripheral with a head that records data on, and retrieves data from disks. **disk file** or **store** n (comput) a random access device consisting of disks coated with magnetizable material, on which data is stored in tracks. **disk operating system** n software that manages the storage and retrieval of information on disk on personal computers (abbrev **DOS**). **disk pack** n (comput) a set of magnetic disks, called platters, fitted on a common spindle.

disleaf /dis-lēf'/ vt to deprive of leaves (also **disleave'**). [**dis-** (2)]

disleal /dis-lē'l/ (Spenser) adj disloyal, dishonourable. [See **disloyal**]

disleave see **disleaf**.

dislike /dis-līk'/ vt to have an aversion to, to find unpleasant or disagreeable; to disapprove of; to be displeased with; to displease (obs). ◆ n /dis-līk'/, sometimes dis'/ disinclination; aversion; distaste; disapproval; something disliked. [**dis-** (2) and **like²**; the genuine Eng word is **mislike**]
■ **dislike'able** or **dislīk'able** adj. **dislike'ful** adj. **dislik'en** vt (Shakesp) to make unlike. **dislike'ness** n (obs) unlikeness.

dislimb /dis-lim'/ vt to tear the limbs from; to dismember. [**dis-** (1)]

dislimn /dis-lim'/ (Shakesp) vt to efface. [**dis-** (3)]

dislink /dis-lingk'/ vt to unlink, to separate. [**dis-** (2)]

disload /dis-lōd'/ vt to unload, to disburden. [**dis-** (3)]

dislocate /dis'lō-kāt/ vt to displace (a bone) from its joint, to put out of joint; to disrupt, disorganize or disturb. [LL dislocāre, -ātum, from L dis- apart, and locāre to place]
- **dis'locatedly** adv. **dislocā'tion** n a dislocated joint; displacement; disorganization; derangement (of; traffic, plans, etc); a displacement in the lattice structure of a crystal; a fault (geol).

dislodge /dis-loj'/ vt to prise, knock or force out of position; to drive from a lodgement or place of rest; to drive from a place of hiding or of defence. ◆ vi to go away. [OFr desloger, from des- (L dis-) apart, and loger to lodge]
- **dislodge'ment** or **dislodg'ment** n.

disloign /dis-loin'/ (Spenser) vt to put far apart or at a distance, to remove. [OFr desloignier, from des- (L dis-) apart, and loignier to remove]

disloyal /dis-loi'əl/ adj not loyal; unfaithful. [OFr desloyal, from des- (L dis- negative), and loyal, leial, from L lēgālis legal]
- **disloy'ally** adv. **disloy'alty** n.

dislustre /dis-lus'tər/ (archaic or poetic) vt to deprive of lustre. ◆ vi to lose lustre. [**dis-** (3)]

dismal /diz'məl/ adj gloomy; dreary; sorrowful; lugubrious; depressing; of a very poor standard (inf). ◆ n unlucky days (obs); (with cap, usu in pl) a swamp (old US dialect); a dismal person; (in pl) the dumps; (in pl) mournings (obs). [OFr dismal, from L diēs malī evil or unlucky days]
- **dismality** /-mal'i-ti/ n. **dis'mally** adv. **dis'malness** n.
- ☐ **dismal day** n (Spenser) a day of ill omen. **dismal Jimmy** n (inf) a confirmed pessimist.
- ■ **the dismal science** economics, according to Carlyle.

disman /dis-man'/ vt to deprive (a country or ship) of men; to unman; to deprive of human character (of the body by death) (obs). [**dis-** (3)]

dismantle /dis-man'tl/ vt to take to bits, pull down; to demolish; to undo the structure of (an organization, etc) in consequence of a decision to terminate it; to strip; to deprive of furniture, fittings, etc, so as to render useless; to raze the fortifications of. [OFr desmanteller, from des- (L dis-) away, and mantele, from mantel a mantle]
- ■ **disman'tlement** n. **disman'tler** n.

dismask /dis-mäsk'/ vt to strip a mask from; to remove a disguise from; to uncover. [OFr desmasquer, from des- (L dis-; negative) and masquer to mask]

dismast /dis-mäst'/ vt to topple or remove a mast or masts from (a ship). [**dis-** (3)]
- ■ **dismast'ment** n.

dismay /dis-, diz-mā'/ vt to appal or alarm; to discourage; to distress (Spenser). ◆ vi (Shakesp, etc) to be daunted. ◆ n sadness arising from deep disappointment or discouragement; alarm or consternation; the loss of strength and courage through fear; a discouraging onslaught (Spenser). [Appar through OFr, from L dis- (negative) and OHGer magan (Ger mögen; OE magan) to have might or power; see **may**¹]
- ■ **dismay'edness** n. **dismay'ful** adj. **dismay'fully** adv (Spenser). **dismay'ing** adj.

dismayd /dis-mād'/ (Spenser) adj apparently, misshapen, deformed, mismade. [**dis-** (2)]

dismayl /dis-māl'/ (obs) vt to deprive of mail (armour); to break mail from (Spenser). [OFr desmailler, from des- (L dis-; privative), and maille mail]

disme /dīm/ (Shakesp, etc) n a tenth or tithe. [OFr; see **dime**]

dismember /dis-mem'bər/ vt to cut up or tear (a body) limb from limb; to separate a limb from; to disjoint; to tear to pieces; to divide up, break up; to carve the meat of (certain birds, eg herons, cranes) before serving (obs). [OFr desmembrer, from des- (L dis-) apart, and membre a member (L membrum)]
- ■ **dismem'bered** adj (heraldry) without limbs or with limbs detached. **dismem'berment** n.

dismiss /dis-mis'/ vt to send away or allow to go; to dispatch; to discard, dispose of (a suggestion, etc); to remove from office or discharge from employment, to sack, to terminate the contract of employment of; to reject, to put out of court (a case or claim), to discharge (law); to end the innings of (a batsman or a team) (cricket). ◆ vi imperative (as a military command) fall out. [**dis-** (3), and L mittere, missum to send; L dimissus]
- ■ **dismiss'al** or (esp formerly) **dismission** /-mish'ən/ n. **dismiss'ible** adj. **dismiss'ive** adj disrespectful, inconsiderate; showing no willingness to consider something. **dismiss'ory** adj.
- ■ **dismissal with disgrace** dismissal from the British armed forces for serious misconduct, as ruled by a court martial.

dismoded /dis-mō'did/ adj out of fashion. [**dis-** (2) and **mode**]

dismount /dis-mownt'/ vi to come down; to get down from a horse or a bicycle, etc. ◆ vt to throw or bring down from any elevated place; to remove from a stand, framework, setting, carriage or the like. [OFr desmonter, from des- (L dis-; negative) and monter to mount]

dismutation /dis-mū-tā'shən/ (biochem) n simultaneous oxidation and reduction. [**dis-** (2)]

disnatured /dis-nā'chərd/ adj unnatural, devoid of natural affection. [**dis-** (2)]
- ■ **disnaturalize** or **-ise** /-nat' or -nach'/ vt to make alien or unnatural.

disnest /dis-nest'/ vt to dislodge from a nest; to clear (of nestlings). [**dis-** (3)]

Disneyesque /diz-ni-esk'/ adj in the style of the characters, etc appearing in the cartoon films of (the studio founded by) Walt Disney (1901–66), American cartoonist and film producer; fantastical, whimsical, unreal.
- ■ **Dis'neyficātion** n. **Dis'neyfy** vt (**Dis'neyfying**; **Dis'neyfied**) to present or process the history of, or facts concerning (a site, etc) by means of video films or other visual aids, esp simplistically for the convenience of the tourist, instead of encouraging exposure to the actual environment.

disobedient /dis-ō-bē'dyənt or -di-ənt/ adj neglecting or refusing to obey. [**dis-** (2)]
- ■ **disobed'ience** n. **disobed'iently** adv.

disobey /dis-ō-bā', dis-ə-bā' or dis'/ vt and vi to neglect or refuse to obey. [OFr desobeir, from des- (L dis-; negative) and obeir to obey]

disoblige /dis-ō-blīj', -ə-blīj'/ vt to refuse or fail to oblige or grant a favour to; to disregard the wishes of; to offend or injure thereby; to inconvenience (inf); to relieve from an obligation (obs). [**dis-** (2)]
- ■ **disobligation** /dis-ob-li-gā'shən/ n freedom from obligation; act of disobliging. **disoblig'atory** /-ə-tə-ri/ adj releasing from obligation. **disobligement** /-blīj'/ n. **disoblīg'ing** adj not obliging; not careful to attend to the wishes of others; unaccommodating; unkind. **disoblīg'ingly** adv. **disoblīg'ingness** n.

disomy /dī-sō'mi/ n a condition in which a particular chromosome is present twice in each cell of the body. [**di-** and **-some**]
- ■ **diso'mic** adj.

disoperation /dis-op-ə-rā'shən/ (ecology) n a mutually harmful relationship between two organisms in a community. [**dis-** (2)]

disorbed /dis-örbd'/ (archaic and poetic) adj (of a star) thrown from its sphere (Shakesp); (of a ruler) deprived of the orb of sovereignty. [**dis-** (3)]

disorder /dis-ör'dər/ n lack of order; confusion; disturbance among the public, breach of the peace, crowd violence, rioting, etc; a malfunction of the body, an ailment or illness. ◆ vt to throw out of order; to disarrange, to reduce to confusion; to disturb the balance of (the mind, etc); to disturb the health of, to produce disease in. [OFr desordre, from des- (L dis-; negative) and ordre order]
- ■ **disor'dered** adj confused, deranged. **disor'derliness** n. **disor'derly** adj out of order; untidy; in a state of confusion; irregular; lawless, unruly; causing a disturbance of the peace (law); defying the restraints of decency. ◆ adv confusedly; in a lawless manner. ◆ n a disorderly person.
- ☐ **disorderly conduct** n (law) any of several minor infringements of the law likely to cause a breach of the peace. **disorderly house** n a brothel or gambling establishment, in either of which disorderly behaviour might be expected.

disordinate /dis-ör'di-nit/ adj not in order (rare); disorderly (rare); inordinate (Milton). [**dis-** (2)]
- ■ **disor'dinately** adv.

disorganize or **-ise** /dis-ör'gə-nīz/ vt to disarrange or disrupt; to disturb the system or structure of; to destroy the organic structure of. [**dis-** (2)]
- ■ **disorganic** /-gan'/ adj. **disorganizā'tion** or **-s-** n. **disor'ganized** or **-s-** adj disordered; unsystematic, muddled.

disorient /dis-ö'ri-ənt, -ö'/ or **disorientate** /-ən-tāt/ vt to confuse as to direction, cause (someone) to lose their bearings; to throw out of one's reckoning; (literally) to turn from the east. [**dis-** (2)]
- ■ **disorientā'tion** n.

disown /dis-ōn'/ vt to refuse to own or acknowledge as belonging to oneself; to deny any connection with; to repudiate, cast off. [**dis-** (2)]
- ■ **disown'er** n. **disown'ment** n.

dispace /dis-pās'/ (Spenser) vi and vt (reflexive) to range about. [Perh L di- apart, and spatiārī to walk about or from **dis-** (1) and **pace**¹]

disparage /dis-par'ij/ vt to talk slightingly of, to belittle; to match in marriage with an inferior; to lower in rank or estimation (obs); to dishonour by comparison with what is inferior (obs); to dishearten (Spenser). ◆ n /dis'/ (obs; Spenser) an unequal match. [OFr desparager, from des- (L dis-; negative) and parage; see **parage**]
- ■ **dispar'agement** n. **dispar'ager** n. **dispar'aging** adj showing contempt or disapproval. **dispar'agingly** adv.

■ words derived from main entry word; ☐ compound words; ■ idioms and phrasal verbs

disparate /dis'pə-rit, -rāt/ adj unequal; essentially unalike, and therefore incapable of being compared. ◆ n (in pl) things too unalike to be compared. [L disparātus, from dis- not, and parāre make ready; influenced by dispar unequal]
■ **dis'parately** adv. **dis'parateness** n.

disparity /dis-par'i-ti/ n inequality; unlikeness so great as to render comparison difficult and union unsuitable. [L dispar unequal, from dis- (negative) and par equal]

dispark /dis-pärk'/ vt to throw open, deprive of the character of a park; to remove from a park. [**dis-** (2) and (3)]

dispart /dis-pärt'/ vt to part asunder (obs); to divide, to separate (archaic). ◆ vi (archaic) to separate. ◆ n the difference between the thickness of metal at the breech and the mouth of a gun. [**dis-** (1)]

dispassion /dis-pash'ən/ n freedom from passion; a calm state of mind. [**dis-** (2)]
■ **dispass'ionate** /dis-pash'ə-nət/ adj free from passion; not affected by personal feelings; calm, cool; unprejudiced, fair, impartial. **dispass'ionately** adv. **dispass'ionateness** n.

dispatch or **despatch** /dis-pach'/ vt to send off (mail, or a person to do a task, etc); to send away hastily; to send out of the world; to kill or put to death; to dispose of; to perform or deal with speedily. ◆ vi (Shakesp, etc) to make haste. ◆ n a sending away in haste; dismissal; rapid performance of a task, etc; haste, promptitude; death, eg by execution or murder; the sending away of mail, a messenger, etc; that which is dispatched, such as a message, esp telegraphic; (in pl) state-papers or other official papers (diplomatic or military, etc). [Ital dispacciare or Sp despachar, from L dis- apart, and some LL word from the root of pangere, pactum to fasten; not connected with Fr dépécher]
■ **dispatch'er** n. **dispatch'ful** adj (Milton, etc) swift.
❑ **dispatch'-boat** n a vessel for carrying dispatches. **Dispatch Box** n a box in the House of Commons near which ministers stand when addressing Parliament. **dispatch box** or **case** n a box or case for holding dispatches or valuable papers. **dispatch rider** n a carrier of dispatches, on horseback or now esp motorcycle.
■ **mentioned in dispatches** as a distinction, commended in official military dispatches for bravery, etc. **with dispatch** (archaic) quickly; without delay.

dispathy an obsolete misspelling of **dyspathy**.

dispauperize or **-ise** /dis-pö'pə-rīz/ vt to free from pauperism or from paupers. [**dis-** (2)]
■ **dispau'per** vt to declare no longer a pauper.

dispeace /dis-pēs'/ n lack of peace; dissension. [**dis-** (2)]

dispel /dis-pel'/ vt (**dispell'ing**; **dispelled'**) to drive away and scatter; to cause to disappear. ◆ vi to scatter or melt away. [L dispellere, from dis- away, and pellere to drive]

dispence /dis-pens'/ (Spenser, etc) same as **dispense**.

dispend /dis-pend'/ (obs) vt to expend, pay out. [OFr despendre, from L dis- out, and pendere to weigh]

dispensary see under **dispense**.

dispense /dis-pens'/ vt to deal out or distribute; to administer (justice, etc); to make up (medicine, etc) for distributing or administering. ◆ vi (Spenser) to make amends; to compound. ◆ n expense; expenditure; supplies; dispensation (Milton). [Fr dispenser, from L dis-, and pēnsāre to weigh]
■ **dispensabil'ity** n. **dispens'able** adj able to be dispensed with, expendable, inessential; able to be dispensed; pardonable (archaic). **dispens'ableness** n. **dispens'ably** adv. **dispens'ary** n a place where medicines, etc are dispensed and medical care given (esp formerly, gratis; now eg in a hospital or school). **dispensation** /dis-pən-sā'shən/ n the act of dispensing or dealing out; administration (of justice, etc); the regulation or ordering of events by God, Providence or nature; a religious or political system specific to a community or period; licence or permission to neglect a rule, esp of church law in the Roman Catholic Church; ground of exemption. **dispensā'tional** adj. **dispens'ative** adj granting dispensation. **dispens'atively** adv. **dis'pensātor** n a dispenser; a distributor; an administrator. **dispens'atorily** adv. **dispens'atory** adj granting dispensation. ◆ n a book containing medical prescriptions. **dispensed'** adj. **dispens'er** n a person who dispenses, esp a pharmacist who dispenses medicines; a container, or machine that gives out (a commodity) in prearranged quantities.
❑ **dispensing optician** n one who fits and sells spectacles and contact lenses but is not qualified to prescribe them.
■ **dispense with** to permit the lack of; to disregard, forgo or waive; to do without.

dispeople /dis-pē'pl/ vt to empty of inhabitants. [**dis-** (2)]

dispermous /dī-spûr'məs/ (bot) adj having or yielding two seeds. [di- and Gr sperma seed]

disperse /dis-pûrs'/ vt to scatter in all directions; to spread; to diffuse; to drive asunder; to cause to vanish, to dissipate; to suspend (particles) in a medium so as to form a colloid (phys); to break up (white light) into the colours of the spectrum (phys). ◆ vi to separate; to spread widely; to vanish. [L dīspergere, dīspersum, from dī- asunder, apart, and spargere to scatter]
■ **dispers'al** n dispersion; distribution; the spread of a species to new areas. **dispers'ant** n a substance causing dispersion. **dispers'edly** adv. **dispers'edness** n. **dispers'er** n. **dispersion** /dis-pûr'shən/ n a scattering, or state or process of being scattered; the removal of inflammation (med); the dependence of wave velocity in a given medium on the frequency of wave motion, which enables a prism to form a spectrum (phys); the range of deviation of values of a variable from the average (stats); the state of a finely divided colloid; a substance in that state; the diaspora. **dispers'ive** adj tending or serving to disperse. **dispers'oid** n a substance in a state of dispersion (also **disperse phase**).
❑ **dispersal prison** n a prison designed to accommodate a certain number of particularly dangerous or high-risk prisoners in addition to other categories of detainees.

dispirit /di-spir'it/ vt to dishearten; to discourage. [**dis-** (2)]
■ **dispir'ited** adj dejected, discouraged; feeble, spiritless. **dispir'itedly** adv. **dispir'itedness** n. **dispir'iting** adj disheartening. **dispir'itingly** adv. **dispir'itment** n.

dispiteous /dis-pit'i-əs/ (obs) adj despiteous, contemptuous, malicious; pitiless. [See **despite**; influenced by **piteous**]
■ **dispit'eously** adv. **dispit'eousness** n.

displace /dis-plās'/ vt to put out of place; to disarrange; to remove from a state, office or post; to supplant, replace or supersede; to substitute something for. [OFr desplacer, from des- (L dis-; negative) and place place]
■ **displace'able** adj. **displace'ment** n a putting or being out of place; a supplanting or superseding; the difference between the position of a body at a given time and that occupied at first; the quantity of water displaced by a ship afloat or an immersed body; the disguising of emotional feelings by unconscious transference from one object to another (psychol).
❑ **displaced person** n a person forced from his or her country by war, revolution, persecution or oppression, a refugee or stateless person. **displacement activity** n an activity that is (often unconsciously) substituted for another, possibly more destructive or threatening, one. **displacement ton** see under **ton**[1].

displant /dis-plänt'/ vt to remove from a fixed position; to drive from an abode. [OFr desplanter, from L dis- (negative) and plantāre to plant]
■ **displantā'tion** n.

display /dis-plā'/ vt to unfold or spread out; to exhibit; to set out ostentatiously; to present (advertising copy, etc) in an eye-catching way (printing). ◆ n a displaying or unfolding; an exhibition or demonstration; presentation of advertising copy, etc so as to attract attention, through appropriate deployment of typefaces, use of space, illustrations, etc; ostentatious show; an animal's or bird's behaviour when courting, threatening intruders, etc, in which the crest is raised, feathers spread, etc; a visual display unit; the information visible on an electronic screen. [OFr despleier, from des- (L dis-; negative) and plier, ploier, from L plicāre to fold; doublet **deploy**; see **ply**[1]]
■ **displayed'** adj unfolded; spread; printed in prominent letters; erect, with wings expanded, as a bird (heraldry). **display'er** n.
❑ **display cabinet** or **case** n a piece of furniture, partly or wholly of glass, in which items are displayed.

disple /dis'pl/ (Spenser, etc) vt to discipline, chastise. [Apparently from **discipline**]

displease /dis-plēz'/ vt to offend; to annoy, irritate; to be disagreeable to. ◆ vi to cause aversion or be displeasing. [OFr desplaisir, from des- (L dis-) reversal, and plaisir to please]
■ **displeasance** /dis-plez'əns/ n (Spenser, etc) displeasure. **displeas'ant** adj (obs). **displeased'** adj vexed, annoyed. **displeas'edly** adv. **displeas'edness** n. **displeas'ing** adj causing displeasure; disagreeable; giving offence. **displeas'ingly** adv. **displeas'ingness** n. **displeasure** /dis-plezh'ər/ n the condition of being displeased; anger, annoyance; a cause of irritation. ◆ vt (archaic) to displease, offend.

displenish /dis-plen'ish/ (Scot) vt to deprive (eg a farm) of plenishing or furniture, implements, etc; to sell the plenishing of. [**dis-** (3)]
■ **displen'ishment** n.

displode /dis-plōd'/ (Milton) vt to discharge, to explode. ◆ vi to explode. [L displōdere, from dis- apart, and plaudere to beat]
■ **displō'sion** /-plō'zhən/ n.

displume /dis-ploom'/ vt to deprive of plumes or feathers. [**dis-** (3)]

dispondee /dī-spon'dē/ (prosody) n a double spondee. [Gr dispondeios, from di- twice, and spondeios spondee]
■ **dispondā'ic** adj.

dispone /dis-pōn'/ vt to set in order, dispose (archaic); to make over to another (Scots law); to convey legally. [L dispōnere to arrange]
■ **disponee'** n the person to whom anything is disponed. **dispon'er** n.

disponge see **dispunge**.

disport /dis-pört' or -pört'/ (literary) vt (usu reflexive) to divert or amuse (oneself). ◆ vi to play about, frolic or gambol. [OFr (se) desporter to carry (oneself) away from one's work, to amuse (oneself), from des- (L dis-), and porter, from L portāre to carry; see **sport**]
■ **disport'ment** n.

disposable, disposal see under **dispose**.

dispose /dis-pōz'/ vt to arrange or settle; to distribute; to place in order, or arrange in position; to apply to a particular purpose; to make over by sale, gift, etc; to bestow; to incline (with to or towards). ◆ vi to settle things; to ordain what is to be; to make a disposition. See also **dispose of** below. ◆ n disposal, management; behaviour, disposition. [Fr disposer, from dis- (L dis-) apart, and poser to place, from L pausāre to pause, (late) to place]
■ **disposabil'ity** n. **dispōs'able** adj able to be disposed of; intended to be thrown away or destroyed after use; (of assets, etc) available for one's use. ◆ n a product intended for disposal after use. **dispōs'ableness** n. **dispōs'al** n the act of disposing or of dealing with something; the act or process of getting rid of something; the act of bestowing, transferring or assigning property, etc; arrangement, disposition, deployment; management; right of bestowing; availability for use, control, service, etc. **disposed'** adj inclined; liable, having a tendency (with to); (used after well, ill or kindly, etc) having friendly or unfriendly, etc feelings (with to or towards). **dispōs'edly** adv (rare) in good order; with measured steps. **dispōs'er** n. **dispōs'ing** n and adj. **dispōs'ingly** adv. **disposure** /-pō'zhər/ n disposal, arrangement; disposition.
❑ **disposable income** n a person's gross income less any compulsory deductions, the income available for spending, saving, investing, etc.
■ **at one's disposal** at one's service, available for one's use; under one's management or control, to deploy as one wishes. **dispose of** to deal with, esp finally and decisively; to sell, transfer, part with or give away; to get rid of or throw away; to prove (an adversary, argument or claim) wrong; to consume (food, etc), esp in haste; to kill.

disposition /dis-pə-zish'ən/ n an arrangement, deployment or distribution; the act of or a plan for dealing with affairs etc, bestowing or assigning property, etc; a natural tendency or inclination; temperament or personality; ministration (Bible); a giving over to another, conveyance or assignment (often disposition and settlement); a deed for the disposal of a person's property at their death (Scots law); a deed transferring the ownership of heritable property (Scots law). [Fr, from L, from dis- apart, and pōnere, positum to place]
■ **disposi'tional** adj. **disposi'tioned** adj. **dispositive** /-poz'i-tiv/ adj. **dispos'itively** adv. **dispos'itor** n (astrol) a planet that disposes or controls another.

dispossess /dis-pə-zes'/ vt to deprive of property, land, etc. [dis- (2)]
■ **dispossessed'** adj deprived of possessions, property, etc; deprived of one's home, country or rights; deprived of hopes, expectations, etc. **dispossession** /dis-pə-zesh'ən/ n. **dispossess'or** n.

dispost¹ /dis-pōst'/ vt to displace from a post. [dis- (2)]

dispost² /dis-pōst'/ (Spenser) for **disposed** (see under **dispose**).

disposure see under **dispose**.

disprad (Spenser) see **dispread**.

dispraise /dis-prāz'/ n the expression of an unfavourable opinion; blame; reproach. ◆ vt to blame; to censure. [OFr despreisier, from des- (L dis-) reversal, and preisier to praise]
■ **disprais'er** n. **disprais'ingly** adv.

dispread /di-spred'/ vt to spread in different ways. ◆ vi to spread out; to expand. —Spenser has the forms **dispred**; 3rd pers pl **dispredden**; pa p **disprad**. [dis- (1)]

disprinced /dis-prinst'/ (Tennyson) adj deprived of the appearance of a prince. [dis- (3)]

disprison /dis-priz'n/ (poetic) vt to set free. [dis- (2)]

disprivacied /dis-priv'ə-sid, -sēd/ (poetic) adj deprived of privacy. [dis- (3)]

disprivilege /dis-priv'i-lij/ vt to deprive of a privilege. [dis- (3)]

disprize /dis-prīz'/ (archaic) vt to set a low price upon; to undervalue. [dis- (2)]

disprofess /dis-prə-fes'/ vt to cease to profess, renounce. [dis- (3)]

disprofit /dis-prof'it/ (archaic) n loss, damage. [dis- (2)]

disproof /dis-proof'/ n the disproving of something; evidence or argumentation that disproves something, refutation. [dis- (2)]

disproove /dis-proov'/ (Spenser) vt to disapprove of. [dis- (2)]

disproperty /dis-prop'ər-ti/ (Shakesp) vt to deprive one of possession of. [dis- (3)]

disproportion /dis-prə-pör'shən, -pör'/ n lack of appropriate proportion; lack of balance, symmetry or equality. ◆ vt to make unsuitable in form or size, etc. [dis- (2)]
■ **dispropor'tionable** adj (archaic). **dispropor'tionableness** n. **dispropor'tionably** adv. **dispropor'tional** adj. **dispropor'tionally** adv. **dispropor'tionate** adj out of proportion; not of the appropriate size or amount (usu too large or too much) in relation to something. **dispropor'tionately** adv. **dispropor'tionateness** n. **disproportionā'tion** n (chem) a reaction in which a substance is both oxidized and reduced, resulting in two different products.

dispropriate /dis-prō'pri-āt/ (obs) vt to disappropriate. [dis- (3)]

disprove /dis-proov'/ vt (pap **disproved'** or **disproven** /-prōv' or -proov'/) to prove to be false or wrong; to disapprove (archaic). [OFr desprover; see **prove**]
■ **disprov'able** adj. **disprov'al** n.

disprovide /dis-prə-vīd'/ (archaic) vt to leave or render unprovided. [dis- (2)]

dispunge (Shakesp) or **disponge** /dis-punj'/ vt to sprinkle or discharge as if from a sponge. [dis- (1)]

dispurse /dis-pûrs'/ (Shakesp) vt to disburse. [dis- (1)]

dispurvey /dis-pər-vā'/ (archaic) vt to deprive of provisions. [dis- (3)]
■ **dispurvey'ance** n (Spenser).

dispute /dis-pūt'/ vt to argue about; to contend for; to oppose by argument; to call in question. ◆ vi to argue or debate (with about or over). ◆ n a contest with words; an argument; a debate; a quarrel. [OFr desputer, from L disputāre, from dis- apart, and putāre to think]
■ **disputabil'ity** n. **dis'putableness** n. **dis'putable** (also /-pūt'/) adj that may be called in question; of doubtful certainty. **dis'putably** adv. **dis'putant** n a contestant in a debate, or party in an argument. ◆ adj engaged in debate or argument. **disputā'tion** n a contest in argument; an exercise in debate. **disputā'tious** or **disput'ative** adj inclined to dispute, cavil, or controvert. **disputā'tiously** or **disput'atively** adv. **disputā'tiousness** or **disput'ativeness** n. **disput'er** n.
■ **beyond, past** or **without dispute** indubitably, certainly. **in dispute** being debated or contested.

disqualify /dis-kwol'i-fī/ vt to render or declare unsuitable, unfit or unable to do a particular thing; to debar. [dis- (3)]
■ **disqualifi'able** adj. **disqualificā'tion** n state of being disqualified; anything that disqualifies or incapacitates. **disqual'ifier** n.

disquiet /dis-kwī'ət/ n lack of quiet; uneasiness, restlessness; anxiety. ◆ adj (archaic) unquiet, uneasy, restless. ◆ vt (also **disquī'eten**) to render unquiet; to make uneasy or anxious; to disturb or upset. [dis- (2)]
■ **disquī'etful** adj. **disquī'eting** adj. **disquī'etingly** adv. **disquī'etive** adj. **disquī'etly** adv (Shakesp). **disquī'etness** n. **disquī'etous** adj. **disquī'etude** n a feeling of anxiety or unease.

disquisition /dis-kwi-zish'ən/ n a carefully or minutely argued examination of a topic; an essay. [L disquīsītiō, -ōnis, from disquīrere, from dis- (intensive) and quaerere, quaesītum to seek]
■ **disquisi'tional, disquisi'tionary, disquis'itory,** or **disquis'itive** adj relating to or of the nature of a disquisition.

disrank /dis-rangk'/ vt to reduce to a lower rank; to throw into confusion (obs). [dis- (2)]

disrate /dis-rāt'/ (naut) vt to reduce (eg a petty officer) to a lower rating or rank. [dis- (3)]

disregard /dis-ri-gärd'/ vt to pay no attention to; to ignore; to dismiss as unworthy of attention. ◆ n lack of attention; neglect; lack of respect. [dis- (2)]
■ **disregard'ful** adj. **disregard'fully** adv.

disrelish /dis-rel'ish/ vt not to relish; to dislike the taste of; to dislike. ◆ n distaste; dislike; disgust. [dis- (2)]
■ **disrel'ishing** adj offensive.

disremember /dis-ri-mem'bər/ (dialect or US inf) vt not to remember, to forget. [dis- (2)]

disrepair /dis-ri-pār'/ n a worn-out or dilapidated condition; an unsatisfactory working condition; the state of needing to be repaired. [dis- (2)]

disrepute /dis-ri-pūt'/ n (also (old) **disreputation** /dis-rep-ū-tā'shən/) bad repute; discredit. [dis- (2)]
■ **disrep'utable** adj unreliable or untrustworthy; disgraceful; not respectable; disordered and shabby, dingy, not presentable. **disrep'utableness** or (rare) **disreputabil'ity** n. **disrep'utably** adv.

disrespect /dis-ri-spekt'/ n lack of respect; discourtesy; incivility. ◆ vt not to respect. [dis- (2)]
■ **disrespect'able** adj (rare) not respectable. **disrespect'ful** adj showing disrespect; irreverent; uncivil. **disrespect'fully** adv. **disrespect'fulness** n.

disrobe /dis-rōb'/ (esp literary) vt and vi to undress; to take off robes.
◆ vt to remove the covering or concealment from. [**dis-** (2) and (3)]

disroot /dis-root'/ vt to uproot. [**dis-** (3)]

disrupt /dis-rupt'/ vt and vi to interrupt (growth, progress, etc); to upset
or throw into disorder or confusion; to split or burst. [L disruptus,
dīruptus, from dīrumpere, from dis- apart, asunder, and rumpere to
break]
■ **disrupt'er** or **disrupt'or** n. **disrup'tion** n interruption, disturbance
or upheaval; (with cap and the) in Scottish ecclesiastical history, the
separation of the Free Church from the Established Church for the sake
of spiritual independence (1843). **disrup'tive** adj having an upsetting
or unsettling effect; obstreperous, unruly. **disrupt'ively** adv.

diss¹ or **dis** /dis/ (sl) vt to treat with disrespect or contempt. [Appar
abbrev of **disrespect**]

diss² /dis/ n an Algerian reedy grass (Ampelodesma tenax), used for
cordage, etc. [Ar dīs]

diss. abbrev: dissertation.

dissatisfactory /dis-sa-tis-fak'tə-ri/ adj causing dissatisfaction. [**dis-**
(2)]
■ **dissatisfac'toriness** n.

dissatisfy /dis-sat'is-fī/ vt to fail to satisfy; to disappoint; to make
discontented; to displease. [**dis-** (2)]
■ **dissatisfac'tion** n. **dissat'isfied** adj discontented; not pleased.

dissaving /dis-sā'ving/ (econ) n the spending of savings made in the
past to finance an excess of spending over disposable income, thus
diminishing accumulated assets. [**dis-** (2)]

disseat /dis-sēt'/ vt to unseat. [**dis-** (2) and (3)]

dissect /di-sekt'/ or /dī-/ vt to cut apart, to cut into small pieces; to cut (a
dead animal or a plant, etc) into parts for the purpose of minute
examination; to divide and examine; to analyse or criticize minutely.
[L dissecāre, dissectum, from dis- apart, and secāre to cut]
■ **dissect'ed** adj deeply cut into narrow segments (bot); cut up by
valleys (geol). **dissect'ible** adj. **dissect'ing** n. **dissec'tion** n the act
or the art of cutting in pieces a plant or animal in order to ascertain the
structure of its parts; anatomy. **dissect'ive** adj tending to dissect.
dissect'or n.
□ **dissected map** or **picture** n a map or picture on a board cut up so
as to form a puzzle. **dissecting microscope** n a form of microscope
that allows dissection of the object under examination. **dissecting
table** n a table on which anatomical dissection is practised.

disseise or **disseize** /dis-sēz'/ (law) vt to deprive of seisen or
possession of an estate of freehold; to dispossess wrongfully. [**dis-** (3)]
■ **disseis'in** or **disseiz'in** n wrongful dispossession. **disseis'or** or
disseiz'or n.

disselboom /dis'əl-boom/ (S Afr) n the single shaft of an ox-wagon or
other cart or wagon. [Du dissel shaft, and boom beam]

dissemble /di-sem'bl/ vt to disguise or mask (one's true feelings or
character); to feign (obs). ◆ vi to pretend; to assume a false
appearance; to play the hypocrite; to dissimulate. [L dissimulāre, from
dissimilis unlike, from dis- (negative), and similis like; perh remodelled
on resemble]
■ **dissem'blance** n (rare) lack of resemblance; the act of dissembling.
dissem'bler n. **dissem'bling** n and adj. **dissem'blingly** adv.

dissembly /dis-em'bli/ n the breaking up of an assembly; a
Dogberryism for assembly (Shakesp). [**dis-** (1)]

disseminate /di-sem'i-nāt/ vt to circulate widely; to sow or scatter
abroad; to propagate; to diffuse. ◆ adj scattered. [L dissēmināre, -ātum,
from dis- apart, and sēmināre to sow, from sēmen, sēminis a seed]
■ **dissemina'tion** n. **dissem'inative** adj. **dissem'inator** n.
dissem'inule n (bot) any part or organ of a plant that serves for
dissemination.
□ **disseminated sclerosis** n an older name for **multiple sclerosis**
(see under **multiple**).

dissensus /di-sen'səs/ n a widespread disagreement. [**dis-** (2) and
consensus]

dissent /di-sent'/ vi not to assent; to think differently; to disagree in
opinion; to differ (with from); to break away from an established
church and adopt new religious beliefs or practices. ◆ n the act of
dissenting; difference of opinion; a protest by a minority; a differing or
separation from an established church. [L dissentīre, dissēnsum, from
dis- apart, and sentīre to think]
■ **dissen'sion** n disagreement in opinion; discord; strife. **dissent'er** n
someone who disagrees; (with cap) someone, esp a Protestant, who
refuses to conform to the established church, a nonconformist.
dissent'erish adj. **dissent'erism** n. **dissen'tient** /-shənt/ adj
declaring dissent; disagreeing. ◆ n a person who disagrees; a person
who declares his or her dissent. **dissent'ing** adj. **dissent'ingly** adv.
dissen'tious /-shəs/ adj (Shakesp, etc, now rare) disposed to discord,
contentious.

dissepiment /di-sep'i-mənt/ n a partition in an ovary (bot); a partition
partly cutting off the bottom of a coral cup (zool). [L dissaepīmentum
a partition, from L dissaepīre, from dis- apart, and saepīre to hedge in,
to fence]
■ **dissepimental** /-ment'l/ adj.

dissertate /dis'ər-tāt/ vi (rare) to discourse (also (archaic) **dissert'**).
[L dissertāre, intensive of disserere to discuss, from dis-, and serere to
put together]
■ **disserta'tion** n a formal discourse; a treatise, a written thesis, usu
based on the author's research, often a requirement for an academic
qualification. **disserta'tional** adj. **diss'ertative** adj. **diss'ertator** n.

disserve /dis-sûrv'/ vt (archaic) to do a bad turn to; to clear (a table).
[OFr desservir, from L dis- (negative), and servīre to serve]
■ **disserv'ice** n injury, sometimes done in an attempt to help;
mischief; a bad turn. **disserv'iceable** adj.

dissever /di-sev'ər/ vt and vi to sever; to part in two; to separate; to
disunite. [OFr dessevrer, from L dis- apart, and sēparāre to separate]
■ **dissev'erance, disseverā'tion** or **dissev'erment** n a dissevering or
parting. **dissev'ered** adj disunited.

disshaeathe /dis-shēdh'/ (rare) vt to unsheathe. [**dis-** (2)]

disshiver /dis-shiv'ər/ vt (Spenser) and vi to shiver in pieces. [**dis-** (1)]

dissident /dis'i-dənt/ adj dissenting. ◆ n a dissenter, esp one who
disagrees with the aims and procedures of the government.
[L dissidēns, -entis, prp of dissidēre, from dis- apart, and sedēre to sit]
■ **diss'idence** n disagreement.

dissight /di(s)-sīt'/ (archaic) n an unsightly object. [**dis-** (2)]

dissilient /di(s)-sil'yənt/ adj springing apart; bursting open with force
(bot). [L dissiliēns, -entis, from dis- apart, and salīre to leap]
■ **dissil'ience** n.

dissimilar /di-sim'i-lər/ adj not similar; unlike, different. [**dis-** (2)]
■ **dissimilarity** /-ar'-/ n unlikeness. **dissim'ilarly** adv.

dissimilate /di-sim'i-lāt/ vi and vt (esp of speech sounds) to become or
make dissimilar. [**dis-** (2)]
■ **dissimila'tion** n the process of becoming or of rendering dissimilar;
catabolism.

dissimile /di-sim'i-li/ n the opposite of a simile, a comparison by
contrast. [**dis-** (2)]

dissimilitude /dis-(s)i-mil'i-tūd/ n the quality of being unalike,
dissimilarity. [**dis-** (2)]

dissimulate /dis-(s)im'ū-lāt/ vt to pretend the contrary of; to conceal or
disguise (one's real feelings, etc), to dissemble. ◆ vi to practise
dissimulation, play the hypocrite. [L dissimulāre, -ātum to dissimulate,
from dis- (negative), and similis like]
■ **dissimula'tion** n the act of dissembling; a hiding under a false
appearance; false pretension; hypocrisy. **dissim'ulative** adj.
dissim'ulator n.

dissipate /dis'i-pāt/ vt to scatter or disperse; to squander; to waste; to
dispel. ◆ vi to separate or disperse and disappear; to waste away; to be
dissolute in conduct; to indulge in trivial amusements. [L dissipāre,
-ātum, from dis- apart, and (archaic) supāre to throw]
■ **diss'ipable** adj that may be dissipated. **diss'ipated** adj dissolute,
esp addicted to drinking. **diss'ipatedly** adv. **dissipa'tion** n
intemperate, extravagant or dissolute living; the process of dissipating
or being dissipated; the wasteful spending of something. **diss'ipative**
adj tending to dissipate or disperse; connected with the dissipation of
energy.
□ **dissipation trail** n (meteorol) a lane of clear atmosphere formed by
the passage of an aircraft through a cloud.
■ **dissipation of energy** (phys) degradation of energy, or progressive
loss of availability of a portion for doing work at each transformation.

dissociate /di-sō'shi-āt, -si-/ vt to separate; to treat or regard as
separate and distinct; (reflexive) to distance (oneself), declare (oneself)
to be unconnected with something (with from). ◆ vi and vt to subject
to or undergo dissociation. ◆ adj separated. [L dissociāre, -ātum, from
dis- apart, and sociāre to associate]
■ **dissōciabil'ity** /-shə-/ n. **dissō'ciable** adj not sociable; ill
associated; incongruous; capable of being dissociated.
dissō'ciableness n. **dissō'ciably** adv. **dissō'cial** adj (archaic) not
social. **dissociality** /-sō-shi-al'-/ n. **dissō'cialize** or **-ise** vt to make
unsocial. **dissocia'tion** /-sō-shi- or -sō-si-/ n the act of dissociating; the
process or state of being dissociated; separation into simpler
constituents, esp a reversible separation caused by heat, or separation
into ions (chem); the splitting off from consciousness of certain ideas
and their accompanying emotions leading to fragmentation of the
personality into independent identities, as in cases of split or multiple
personality (psychol); breaking of associations. **dissō'ciative** adj
(chem) tending to dissociate.

dissoluble /dis-(s)ol'ū-bl/ adj capable of being dissolved, soluble.
[L dissolūbilis, from dissolvere to dissolve]
■ **dissolubil'ity** n. **dissol'ubleness** n.

dissolute /dis'ə-loot or -lūt/ adj loose, esp in morals, debauched. ◆ n a dissolute person. [L dissolūtus lax, from dissolvere to loosen]
■ **diss'olutely** adv. **diss'oluteness** n. **diss'olutive** adj.

dissolution /dis-ə-lō'shən or -lū'shən/ n break-up, disintegration into parts; decay and death; the annulment or ending of a partnership or relationship; the dispersal of an assembly, as of Parliament before an election; loosening; melting; dissoluteness or dissolute behaviour (archaic). [L dissolūtiō, -ōnis a breaking up, from dissolvere]
■ **dissolu'tionism** n. **dissolu'tionist** n.

dissolve /di-zolv'/ vt and vi to (cause to) go into solution; to (cause to) become liquid, to melt; to separate or break up and disperse; to terminate or dismiss (an assembly, such as Parliament) or be terminated or dismissed. ◆ vt to annul or terminate (eg a partnership or marriage); to resolve (eg doubts or riddles; archaic). ◆ vi to collapse or subside emotionally, eg into tears; to break up; to waste away; to fade away; to fade out one scene gradually while replacing it with another (also n; film and TV). [L dissolvere, dissolūtum, from dis-, and solvere, -ūtum to loose]
■ **dissolvabil'ity** n. **dissolv'able** adj capable of being dissolved. **dissolv'ableness** n. **dissolv'ent** n (rare) a solvent. ◆ adj having power to dissolve or disperse. **dissolv'ing** n and adj.

dissonant /dis'ə-nənt/ adj (of sounds, esp musical) discordant, inharmonious; jarring, clashing, incompatible, conflicting, contradictory or incongruous. [L dissonāns, -antis, from dis- apart, and sonāre to sound]
■ **diss'onance** n disagreement of sound; lack of harmony; discord; disagreement; specif (a chord or interval containing) a combination of musical sounds that calls for resolution or produces beats (also **diss'onancy**). **diss'onantly** adv.

dissuade /di-swād'/ vt to deter, esp through advice or argument, to persuade not to do something (with from); to give advice against (obs); to seek to divert by advice (obs). [L dissuādēre, from dis- apart, and suādēre, suāsum to advise]
■ **dissua'der** n. **dissua'sion** /-zhən/ n. **dissua'sive** /-siv/ adj tending to dissuade. ◆ n that which tends to dissuade. **dissua'sively** adv. **dissua'sory** n and adj (rare).

dissunder /dis-sun'dər/ (archaic) vt to sunder. [dis- (4)]

dissyllable a variant of **disyllable**.

dissymmetry /dis-sim'i-tri/ n lack of symmetry; enantiomorphy (the symmetry of right and left hand, or of object and mirror image). [dis- (2)]
■ **dissymmetric** or **dissymmetrical** /-et'/ adj. **dissymmet'rically** adv.

dist. abbrev : distance; distilled; distinguish; district.

distaff /dis'täf/ n the stick that holds the bunch of flax, tow or wool in spinning; women's work (literary). [OE distæf, from the root found in LGer diesse the bunch of flax on the staff; and stæf staff; see **dizen**]
❑ **distaff side** n the female part, line, side, or branch of a family or descent, the male equivalent being the spear side.

distain /di-stān'/ (archaic) vt to stain; to sully. [OFr desteindre to take away the colour of, from L dis- (negative), and tingere to colour]

distal /dis'təl/ adj (biol) farthest from the point of attachment, opp to proximal (anat and zool); farthest from the centre, opp to mesial (dentistry). [Formed from **distance** on the analogy of central]
■ **dis'tally** adv.

distance /dis'təns/ n the gap or interval between two points in space or time; the extent of such a gap or interval; remoteness or separation in space or time; a remote place, region or time; the remotest part of one's field of vision, or the equivalent part in a picture; progress, headway; degree of remoteness; opposition; standoffishness or aloofness of manner; the scheduled duration of a boxing match, etc; in horse-racing, a point 240 yards back from the winning post (Brit), or a final stretch of the course (US), which a horse, in heat-races, must reach by the time the winner has covered the whole course, in order to run in the final heat. ◆ adj (athletics) (of races) over a long or medium distance; (of athletes) competing in long-distance or middle-distance races. ◆ vt to place at a distance; to hold (oneself) aloof (with from); to leave at a distance behind. [See **distant**]
■ **dis'tanceless** adj not allowing a distant view (of hazy weather); having no indications of distance (of pictures).
❑ **distance education** or **teaching** n the provision of educational courses, eg by television, correspondence course or electronic media, for students unable to attend in person the educational institution concerned. **distance learning** n the following of such educational courses.
■ **go the distance** to complete what one has started (inf); to endure to the end of a (boxing, etc) bout. **keep someone at a distance** to treat someone with aloofness. **keep one's distance** to abstain from familiarity (with); to keep aloof (from). **middle distance** the part of a scene between the foreground and the furthest part.

distant /dis'tənt/ adj at a certain distance; at a great distance; remote, in time, place, resemblance or connection; indistinct; reserved or aloof in manner. [Fr, from L dīstāns, -antis, from dī- apart, and stāns, stantis, prp of stāre to stand]
■ **dis'tantly** adv. **dis'tantness** n.
❑ **distant healing** n a form of spiritual healing (also called **absent healing**). **dis'tant-signal** n on a railway, a signal farther from the destination than the home-signal.

distaste /dis-tāst'/ n disrelish (for); repugnance or dislike (for); an unpleasant experience (obs); an offence (obs). ◆ vt to dislike (archaic); to offend (obs); to spoil the taste of (obs; Shakesp). ◆ vi (obs; Shakesp) to be distasteful. [dis- (2)]
■ **distaste'ful** adj unpalatable; unpleasant; disagreeable; full of or indicating distaste (obs; Shakesp). **distaste'fully** adv. **distaste'fulness** n.

distemper¹ /dis-tem'pər/ n a morbid or disorderly state of body or mind (archaic); any of several infectious diseases affecting animals, esp a viral illness (**canine distemper**) of dogs, foxes, ferrets and mink; ill-humour (archaic). ◆ vt (archaic) to derange the temper; to disorder or disease. [OFr destemprer to derange, from L dis- apart, and temperāre to govern, regulate]
■ **distemp'erate** adj not temperate, immoderate; diseased. **distemp'erature** n (archaic) lack of proper temperature; intemperateness, disturbance; uneasiness of mind; indisposition. **distem'pered** adj disordered; intemperate, ill-humoured, put out of sorts.

distemper² /dis-tem'pər/ or (obs) **destemper** /des-/ n a mode of painting in size, waterglass, or other watery medium giving body to the pigment; paint of this kind for indoor walls, stage scenery, etc; tempera. ◆ vt to paint in distemper. [L dis- (reversal), and temperāre to regulate, mix in proportion; cf **distemper¹**]

distend /dis-tend'/ vt to stretch forth or apart; to stretch in three dimensions; to swell; to exaggerate. ◆ vi to swell up, expand, inflate (as though as a result of increasing internal pressure). [L distendere, from dis- apart, and tendere, tēnsum or tentum to stretch]
■ **distensibil'ity** n capacity for distension. **disten'sible** adj that may be stretched. **disten'sile** /-sīl/ adj distensible; able to cause distension. **disten'sion** n an act of distending or stretching; the state of being stretched; breadth (sometimes **disten'tion**; rare). **disten'sive** adj capable of stretching or of being stretched. **distent'** adj (Spenser) extended; distended, swollen.

disthene /dis'thēn/ n kyanite, so called from its difference in hardness when scratched in different directions. [Gr di- twice, and sthenos strength]

disthrone /dis-thrōn'/ vt to dethrone (also (Spenser) **disthrōn'ize**). [dis- (2) and (3)]

distich /dis'tik/ n (pl **distichs** /-tiks/) (prosody) two lines or verses, complete in themselves; a couplet. ◆ adj having two rows. [Gr distichos, from di- twice, and stichos a line]
■ **dis'tichal** adj. **dis'tichous** adj in or having two rows; (esp of parts of a plant) arranged in or having two opposite vertical rows.

distil or (N Am) **distill** /di-stil'/ vi (**distill'ing**; **distilled'**) to fall in drops; to flow gently; to evaporate and condense again; to use a still. ◆ vt to let fall or cause to fall in drops; to convert from liquid into vapour by heat, and then to condense again; to extract as an essence or concentrate by evaporation and condensation; to accumulate or amass little by little in pure form (fig); to reduce to essentials by sorting and sifting (fig). [OFr distiller, with substitution of prefix, from L dēstillāre, -ātum, from dē down, and stillāre to drop, from stilla a drop]
■ **distill'able** adj. **dis'tilland** n that which is to be, or is being, distilled. **dis'tillate** n the product of distillation. **distillā'tion** n the process of distilling or its product. **distill'atory** adj of or for distilling. **distill'er** n. **distill'ery** n a place where distilling, esp of alcoholic spirits, is carried on. **distill'ing** n. **distil'ment** n (Shakesp) that which is distilled.
❑ **distilled water** n water purified by distillation.
■ **destructive distillation** the collection of volatile matters released when a substance is destroyed by heat in a closed vessel (as coal is when making gas). **fractional distillation** the separation by distilling of liquids having different boiling points, the heat being gradually increased and the receiver changed. **vacuum distillation** distillation under reduced pressure (effecting a lowering of the boiling point).

distinct /dis-tingkt'/ adj separate; different; well-defined; clear; definite, unmistakable; distinguished, differentiated (obs; Milton, etc); marked, variegated (poetic; Spenser, Milton). [L dīstinctus separate]
■ **distinct'ly** adv clearly; definitely, unmistakably. **distinct'ness** n. **distincture** /-tingk'chər or -tyər/ n distinctness.

distinction /dis-tingk'shən/ n separation or division; discrimination; a distinguishing mark or character; distinctness (obs); difference; a mark or honorific recognition of excellence; an honour; discriminating favour; noticeable eminence; outstanding merit; impressive and meritorious individuality. [L *dīstinctio*, *-ōnis* separation, distinction]

distinctive /dis-tingk'tiv/ *adj* marking out as different, distinguishing; characteristic, readily recognizable, serving to identify. ◆ *n* a distinctive feature. [*dīstinct*, stem of pap of L *dīstinguere*, and sfx *-ive*]
■ **distinct'ively** *adv*. **distinct'iveness** *n*.

distincture see under **distinct**.

distingué, *fem* **distinguée** /dē-stē-gā'/ (*Fr*) *adj* distinguished; striking.

distinguish /dis-ting'gwish/ *vt* to mark off, set apart, differentiate (often with *from*); to recognize by characteristic qualities; to make out, identify; to make distinctions in or concerning (*obs*); to bring by drawing distinctions; to separate by a mark of honour; to make eminent or known; to conduct (oneself) noticeably well; to hold to be not directly comparable (*Scots law*). ◆ *vi* to make or show distinctions or differences, to recognize a difference (often with *between*). [L *dīstinguere*, *dīstinctum*, from *dī-* apart, and *stinguere* originally to prick, and *-ish*, in imitation of Fr verbs in *-ir*]
■ **disting'uishable** *adj* capable of being distinguished. **disting'uishably** *adv*. **disting'uished** *adj* illustrious, eminent; dignified in appearance or manner; remarkable (with *for*). **disting'uisher** *n*. **disting'uishing** *adj* peculiar, serving to identify. **disting'uishment** *n* (*Shakesp*, etc) distinction.
❑ **Distinguished Conduct Medal**, **Distinguished Flying Cross**, **Distinguished Service Medal**, **Distinguished Service Order** *n* military decorations awarded for distinguished conduct in action.

distort /dis-tört'/ *vt* to twist or pull awry, spoil the natural shape of, deform; to misrepresent (statements or facts, etc); to pervert, warp; to alter or make indistinct (a signal or sound) in transmission or reproduction (*radio* and *telecom*). [L *dis-* apart, and *torquēre*, *tortum* to twist]
■ **distort'ed** *adj*. **distort'edness** *n*. **distortion** /-tör'shən/ *n* the process of distorting or of being distorted; deformation; misrepresentation; change of waveform in course of transmission resulting in loss of clarity (*radio* and *telecom*); crookedness; warping, perversion. **distort'ional** *adj*. **distort'ive** *adj* causing distortion.

distract /dis-trakt'/ *vt* to draw the attention of (someone) away from something; to divert someone or someone's attention in another or several other directions; to confuse; to harass; to render crazy; to madden; to divert, amuse, entertain. ◆ *adj* (*archaic*) distracted; (also (*Shakesp*) /dis'/) separate. [L *distrahere*, *-tractum*, from *dis-* apart, and *trahere* to draw]
■ **distract'ed** *adj* confused, bewildered; harassed; crazy, mad, maddened. **distract'edly** *adv*. **distract'edness** *n*. **distractibil'ity** *n*. **distract'ible** *adj*. **distract'ing** *adj*. **distract'ingly** *adv*. **distrac'tion** *n* the state of being distracted; that which distracts; perplexity; agitation; madness; a diversion, amusement; recreation, relaxation. **distract'ive** *adj* causing perplexity. **distract'ively** *adv*. **distract'or** *n*.

distrail same as **dissipation trail** (see under **dissipate**).

distrain /di-strān'/ (*law*) *vt* to seize (*esp* goods for debt, *esp* for non-payment of rent or rates); to pull apart, burst (*Spenser*). ◆ *vi* to seize the goods of a debtor. [OFr *destraindre*, from L *dī-* apart, and *stringere* to draw tight]
■ **distrain'able** *adj*. **distrainee'** *n* a person whose property has been distrained. **distrain'er** or **distrain'or** *n*. **distrain'ment** *n*. **distraint'** *n* seizure of goods.

distrait /dē-stre'/, *fem* **distraite** /dē-stret'/ (*Fr*) *adj* absent-minded.

distraught /dis-tröt'/ *adj* distracted; frantic, eg with grief or worry; mad; perplexed; drawn aside or apart (*Spenser*). [Modified form of **distract** (adj), modified by association with words like **caught** and **taught**[1]]

distress /dis-tres'/ *n* extreme pain or suffering, *esp* mental or emotional; that which causes suffering; calamity; misfortune; acute poverty; exhaustion; peril; difficulty; compulsion (*archaic*); act of distraining goods (*law*); the goods seized; (in a structure) a sign of weakness arising from stress. ◆ *vt* to afflict with (*esp* mental or emotional) pain or suffering; to harass; to grieve; to reduce financially, impoverish; to impart an antique appearance to (furniture, leather, etc), age artificially, by knocking, scraping, etc; to distrain (*law*). [OFr *destresse*, from L *dīstringere* ; see **distrain**]
■ **distressed'** *adj* suffering mentally or physically; impoverished; (of furniture, leather, denim, etc) artificially aged. **distress'er** *n*. **distress'ful** *adj*. **distress'fully** *adv*. **distress'fulness** *n*. **distress'ing** *adj*. **distress'ingly** *adv*.
❑ **distressed area** *n* a region of unusually severe unemployment. **distress signal** *n* a radio signal or flare put out by a ship, etc in distress.
■ **in distress** (of a ship or aircraft) in danger, needing help.

distribute /dis-trib'ūt/ or *dis'tri-būt* / *vt* to divide amongst several; to deal out or allot; to classify; to disperse about a space; to spread out; to separate (type) and put back in compartments (*printing*); to use (a term) with full extension, including every individual to which it is applicable (*logic*). [L *distribuere*, from *dis-* apart, and *tribuere*, *tribūtum* to allot]
■ **distrib'uend** *n* that which is to be distributed. **distrib'utable** *adj* that may be divided. **distrib'utary** *adj* distributing. ◆ *n* a branch of a distributing system; an off-flow from a river that does not return to it (eg in a delta). **distributee'** *n* (*US law*) a person who shares in the estate of a deceased person. **distributer** *n* see **distributor** below. **distribu'tion** *n* the act or process of distributing; dispersal; the business activity of transferring goods from the producer to the consumer, *incl* packaging, transport and warehousing; division; range; allotment; classification; the application of a general term to all the objects denoted by it (*logic*); the manner in which the products of industry are shared among the people (*econ*); the range of values of a variable presented in terms of frequency (*stats*). **distribu'tional** *adj*. **distrib'utive** *adj* that distributes, separates or divides; giving to each his own; referring individually to all members of a group, as the words *each*, *every*, *either*, *neither* (*grammar*); (of a general term) applying to all objects denoted by it (*logic*); such that $a.(x+y+z+...) = a.x+a.y+a.z+...$ (*maths*). ◆ *n* (*grammar*) a distributive word, like *each* or *every*, that indicates the several individuals of a number taken separately. **distrib'utively** *adv*. **distrib'utiveness** *n*. **distrib'utor** or **distrib'uter** *n* someone who or something that distributes; an agent, or middleman, between the manufacturer and the retailer or customer, a wholesaler, a retailer; a device in a petrol engine whereby a high-tension current is transmitted in correct sequence to the sparking plugs.
❑ **distributed logic** *n* (*comput*) a system that allows the performance of central processing unit operations by a number of remote terminals rather than by the central unit. **distributed processing** *n* (*comput*) the use of an array processor to allow any machine instruction to operate on a number of data locations simultaneously. **distributed system** *n* (*comput*) a system of computers connected by a network with each major function of the system being assigned to a different computer. **distribution coefficient** *n* (*chem*) same as **partition coefficient** (see under **partition**).
■ **geographical distribution** see under **geography**.

district /dis'trikt/ *n* a portion of territory defined for political, judicial, educational, or other purposes (such as a registration district, a militia district, the District of Columbia); generally, an area, locality or region; (in local government) an administrative subdivision of a Scottish region or of an English or Welsh county; a constituency (*US*); a subdivision of a division (*Ind*). ◆ *vt* to divide into districts. [Fr, from LL *dīstrictus* jurisdiction, from *dīstringere* ; see **distrain**]
❑ **district attorney** *n* (*US*) a public prosecutor for a district. **district council** *n* in British local government, the council elected to govern a district. **district court** *n* the federal court for a district in the USA; the lowest grade of Scottish criminal court. **district heating** *n* the distribution of heat from a central source to buildings in the surrounding area. **district judge** *n* (in England and Wales) a judicial officer for each county court and magistrates' court empowered to try certain cases, and to supervise certain stages of others (before 1991 called **registrar** and **district registrar**). **district nurse** *n* a nurse appointed to attend to patients in their own homes. **district visitor** *n* a church worker who visits parishioners in a district.

distringas /di-string'gas/ *n* formerly, a writ directing a sheriff or other officer to distrain. [Second pers sing present subjunctive of L *dīstringere* ; see **distrain**]

distrouble /dis-trub'l/ (*obs*) *vt* to trouble greatly, to perplex, to disturb. [L *dis-* (intensive), and **trouble**]

distrust /dis-trust'/ *n* lack of trust; lack of faith or confidence; doubt. ◆ *vt* to have no trust in; to disbelieve; to doubt. [**dis-** (2) and (3)]
■ **distrust'er** *n*. **distrust'ful** *adj* full of distrust; apt to distrust others; suspicious; to be distrusted (*rare*). **distrust'fully** *adv*. **distrust'fulness** *n*. **distrust'less** *adj*.

distune /dis-tūn'/ (*archaic*) *vt* to put out of tune. [**dis-** (3)]

disturb /dis-tûrb'/ *vt* to interrupt; to inconvenience; to throw into confusion; to agitate; to upset. ◆ *n* disturbance. [OFr *destourber*, from L *disturbāre*, from *dis-* apart, and *turbāre* to agitate, from *turba* a crowd]
■ **disturb'ance** *n* interruption; a commotion or fracas; derangement; agitation; interference, molestation (*law*); perplexity. **disturb'ant** *adj* and *n* disturbing. **disturb'ative** *adj*. **disturbed'** *adj* worried; confused, *esp* emotionally; maladjusted. **disturb'er** *n*. **disturb'ing** *adj*. **disturb'ingly** *adv*.

distyle /dis'tīl, dī'stīl/ (*archit*) *n* a portico with two columns. [Gr *di-* twice, and *stylos* column]

disulfiram /dī-sul-fē'rəm/ *n* a drug used to treat chronic alcoholism, acting by inducing nausea, etc if alcohol is taken. [*disulf*ide (variant of *disulphide*) and th*iram*]

disulphate /dī-sul'fāt/ *n* a pyrosulphate; formerly, an acid sulphate. [**di-**]

■ **disul'phide** *n* a sulphide containing two atoms of sulphur to the molecule (also (*obs*) **disul'phuret**). **disulphu'ric** *adj* pyrosulphuric.

disunion /dis-ū'nyən/ *n* lack of union, dissension, disagreement; breaking up of union or concord; separation, estrangement. [**dis-** (2) and (1)]
■ **disun'ionist** *n* someone who favours dissolution of a union. **disunite'** *vt* to separate from union, detach, divide; to sever or sunder; to estrange, drive apart. ◆ *vi* to fall apart; to part, separate. **disu'nity** *n* lack of unity, dissension.

disuse /dis-ūs' or dis'ūs/ *n* the state of being out of use, no longer used, observed or practised; neglect, desuetude. ◆ *vt* /dis-ūz'/ to cease to use or practise; to leave out of use. [**dis-** (2) and (3)]
■ **disusage** /dis-ūz'ij/ *n* gradual cessation of use or custom. **disused'** *adj* no longer used, observed or practised.
❑ **disuse atrophy** *n* (*med*) the wasting away of a part as a result of diminution or cessation of functional activity.

disutility /dis-ū-til'i-ti/ *n* an inconvenience, drawback, disadvantage. [**dis-** (2)]

disvalue /dis-val'ū/ (*rare*) *vt* to disparage. [**dis-** (3)]

disvouch /dis-vowch'/ (*Shakesp*) *vt* to disavow. [**dis-** (3)]

disworship /dis-wûr'ship/ (*Milton*) *n* dishonour, disgrace. [**dis-** (2)]

disyllable or **dissyllable** /di-sil'ə-bl/ *n* a word of two syllables. [Through Fr *dissyllabe*, *dissilabe*, and L from Gr *di-* twice, and *syllabē* a syllable; with *l* as in **syllable**]
■ **disyllabic** /-ab'ik/ *adj*. **disyllabifica'tion** *n*. **disyllab'ify** *vt* to make into two syllables. **disyll'abism** *n* the character of having two syllables.

disyoke /dis-yōk'/ (*Tennyson*) *vt* to free from the yoke. [**dis-** (3)]

dit[1] or **ditt** /dit/ (*archaic*) *n* a poem; the words of a song. [Appar formed by Spenser from **dite**[1] influenced by **ditty**]

dit[2] /dit/ (now *Scot*) *vt* (pat and pap **ditt'ed** or **ditt'it**; *pap* also **dit**) to stop, block. [OE *dyttan* to shut]

dit[3] /dē/ (*Fr*) *adj* named; reputed.

dit[4] /dit/ *n* a word representing the dot in the spoken form of Morse code. See also **dah**[1].

dita /dē'ta/ *n* an apocynaceous tree (*Alstonia scholaris*), of India and the Philippines, with tonic bark. [Tagálog or Visayan]

ditch /dich/ *n* a trench dug in the ground for drainage or irrigation, or to serve to mark a boundary; any long narrow depression carrying water; the border of a bowling green; the sea (*sl*). ◆ *vi* to make, repair or clean a ditch or ditches; (of an aircraft or pilot) to come down in the sea (*inf*). ◆ *vt* to dig a ditch in or around; to drain by ditches; to throw, or drive, into a ditch; to crash (a vehicle) deliberately; to abandon, or get rid of (*sl*); to escape from or leave (a person) in the lurch (*sl*); to derail (*US*); to bring (an aircraft) down in the sea (*inf*). [OE *dīc*, whence also **dyke**; see notes at **dyke**[1]]
■ **ditch'er** *n* a person or machine that makes, cleans or repairs ditches.
❑ **ditch'-dog** *n* (*Shakesp*) a dead dog rotting in a ditch. **ditch'water** *n* stagnant foul water such as is found in ditches, proverbially dull.

dite[1] /dīt/ (*obs*) *n* writing; a composition. ◆ *vt* to compose, indite; to dictate; to indict. [OFr *dit* a saying, from *ditier*, *diter* to write, from L *dictum* an utterance, from *dictāre*, frequentative of *dīcere* to say]

dite[2] /dīt/ (*Spenser*) *vt* same as **dight** (*archaic*).

dithecal /dī-thē'kl/ (*bot*) *adj* having two thecae or sheaths (also **dīthē'cous**). [**di-**]

ditheism /dī'thē-i-zm/ *n* the doctrine of the existence of two supreme gods. [Gr *di-* twice, and *theos* a god]
■ **dī'theist** *n*. **dītheist'ic** or **ditheist'ical** *adj*.

Ditheletism /dī-thel'ə-ti-zm/ *n* the doctrine that Christ on earth had two wills, human and divine, *opp* to *Monotheletism* (also **Dī'thelism**, **Dīoth'elism**, **Dȳoth'elism**, **Dȳothel'etism** or **Dīthel'itism**). [Gr *di-* twice (or *dyo* two), and *thelētēs* a willer, from *thelein* to will]
■ **Dī'thelēte** *n* a believer in the doctrine of Ditheletism (also **Dīoth'elēte**, **Dīoth'elite**, **Dȳoth'elēte** or **Dȳoth'elite**). **Dīthelet'ic** or **Dīthelet'ical** (also **Dīothelet'ic(al)**, **Dȳothelet'ic(al)**, **Dȳothelit'ic(al)**) *adj*. —All words also without *cap*.

dither /didh'ər/ or (*dialect*) **didder** /did'ər/ *vi* to waver, vacillate; to agitate (chiefly *US*); to tremble, shiver, quake. ◆ *vt* to perturb, confuse. ◆ *n* a state of irresolution; a trembling condition; a quaking fit; tremulous excitement; perturbation. [Probably imit]
■ **dith'erer** *n*. **dith'ery** *adj*.
■ **all of a dither** nervous, agitated.

dithionate /dī-thī'ə-nāt/ *n* a salt of **dithionic** /-on'ik/ **acid**, otherwise hyposulphuric acid ($H_2S_2O_6$). [Gr *di-* twice, and *theion* sulphur]

dithyramb /dith'i-ram(b)/ *n* in ancient Greece, a wild impassioned choral hymn sung in honour of Bacchus; a poem or piece of writing in wildly rapturous or bombastic vein. [Gr *dīthyrambos*]
■ **dithyram'bic** *adj* of or like a dithyramb; rapturous; wild and boisterous. **dithyram'bically** *adv*. **dithyram'bist** *n*.

ditokous /dit'o-kəs/ (*zool*) *adj* producing two at a birth or in a clutch. [Gr *di-* twice, and *tokos* birth]

ditone /dī'tōn/ *n* in ancient Greek music, an interval of two major tones. [**di-**]

ditriglyph /dī-trī'glif/ (*archit*) *n* a space for two triglyphs in the entablature between columns. [**di-**]
■ **ditriglyph'ic** *adj*.

ditrochee /dī-trō'kē/ (*prosody*) *n* a trochaic dipody. [**di-**]
■ **dītroche'an** *adj*.

ditsy or **ditzy** /dit'si/ (*US inf*) *adj* amiably eccentric, scatterbrained; precious, affected.

ditt see **dit**[1].

dittander /di-tan'dər/ *n* a pepperwort (*Lepidium latifolium*), a pungent cruciferous plant; dittany. [A form of **dittany**]

dittany /dit'ə-ni/ *n* an aromatic rutaceous plant (*Dictamnus albus*), secreting much volatile oil. [OFr *dictame*, from L *dictamnus*, from Gr *diktamnos*; prob from Mt *Diktē* in Crete]

dittay /dit'ā/ (*obs Scots law*) *n* an indictment, charge. [OFr *ditte'*, from L *dictātum*; cf **ditty** and **dictate**]

dittit see **dit**[2].

ditto /dit'ō/ (in writing abbreviated to **do**, or replaced by ditto marks (qv below)) *n* (*pl* **ditt'os**) that which has been said; the same thing. ◆ *adv* as before, or aforesaid; in the same manner, likewise; (as assenting rejoinder) same here. ◆ *vt* (**ditt'oing**; **ditt'oed**) to duplicate, echo. [Ital *ditto*, from L *dictum* said, pap of *dīcere* to say]
■ **ditt'os** *n pl* a suit of clothes of the same colour throughout.
❑ **ditto marks** *n pl* a sign " written immediately below a word, etc to show that it is to be understood as repeated.

dittography /di-tog'rə-fi/ *n* unintentional repetition of letters or words by a scribe or printer in copying a manuscript. [Gr *dittos* double, and *graphein* to write]

dittology /di-tol'ə-ji/ *n* a double reading or interpretation. [Gr *dittologiā*, from *dittos* double, and *legein* to speak]

ditty /dit'i/ *n* a simple song; a little poem to be sung. ◆ *vt* to set to music. [OFr *ditie*, from L *dictātum*, neuter perfect participle (passive) of *dictāre* to dictate]

ditty bag /dit'i bag/ *n* a sailor's bag for personal belongings (also **ditty box**). [Origin unknown]

ditz /dits/ (*US inf*) *n* an eccentric or scatterbrained person. [Back-formation from **ditzy**]

ditzy see **ditsy**.

diuretic /dī-ū-ret'ik/ (*med*) *adj* increasing the flow of urine. ◆ *n* a medicine or other substance that increases the flow of urine. [Gr *diourētikos*, from *dia* through, and *ouron* urine]
■ **diurē'sis** *n* increased or excessive excretion of urine.

diurnal /dī-ûr'nəl/ *adj* daily; relating to or performed in or lasting a day; (of animals) at rest during the night and active during the day; (of flowers) open during the day; belonging to the daytime. ◆ *n* a service-book containing the day hours, except matins (a night-office; *relig*); a diary, journal (*archaic*). [L *diurnālis*, from *diēs* a day; see **journal**[1]]
■ **diur'nalist** *n* (*archaic*) a journalist. **diur'nally** *adv*.

DIUS *abbrev*: (until 2009) Department for Innovation, Universities and Skills.

diuturnal /dī-ū-tûr'nəl/ *adj* lasting long. [L *diūturnus*, from *diū* long]
■ **diutur'nity** *n*.

Div. *abbrev*: Division.

div[1] /div/ *n* short for **dividend**.

div[2] /div/ (*Scot and N Eng*; in *present indicative* only) *vt* a form of **do** (as an auxiliary verb).
■ **divna** /div'nə/ do not.

div[3] /dēv/ *n* an evil spirit of Persian mythology. [Pers *dīv*]

div[4] see **divvy**[2].

div. *abbrev*: divide; divine; division; divorce or divorced.

diva /dē'vä/ *n* a great female singer, *esp* an operatic prima donna; a temperamental demanding person, *esp* a woman (*inf*). [Ital, from L *dīva*, fem of *dīvus* divine]

divagate /dī'və-gāt/ (*literary*) *vi* to wander about; to digress. [L *dīvagārī* to wander]
■ **divagā'tion** *n*.

divalent /dī-vā'lənt/ or /div'ə-lənt/ *n* a chemical element or atom capable of uniting with two atoms of hydrogen or their equivalent. ◆ *adj* having two combining equivalents. [Gr *di-* twice, and L *valēre* to be worth]
■ **diva'lency** *n*.

Divali see **Diwali**.

divan /di-van'/ *n* a couch without back or sides; a bed without headboard or footboard (also **divan'-bed**'); (*esp* formerly) a smoking-room; (in some Muslim countries) a council chamber, court of justice or council of state, or a counting house; any council or assembly (*poetic*); an (*orig Pers*) name for a collection of poems; a dewan. [Ar and Pers *dīwān* a long seat]

divaricate /dī-var'i-kāt/ (*biol*) *vi* to part into two branches, to fork; to diverge. ◆ *vt* to divide into two branches. ◆ *adj* widely divergent, spreading apart. [L *dīvaricāre*, *-ātum*, from *dis-* apart, and *varicāre* to spread the legs, from *varus* bent apart]
■ **divaricā'tion** *n*.

dive /dīv/ *vi* (pat **dived** or (*N Am*) **dove** /dōv/) to plunge headfirst into or down through water or down through the air; (of a submarine) to submerge; (of an aircraft) to descend steeply, nose-first; to go headlong into a recess, forest, etc, or suddenly investigate the interior of a container, etc (with *into*); to plunge or go deeply into any matter; to involve oneself wholeheartedly (with *into*); to pretend to have been tripped by an opposing player in the hope of being awarded a foul (*football*). ◆ *vt* to plunge, dip. ◆ *n* a plunge; a swoop; a headlong descent; a refuge; a resort, generally disreputable, often underground, eg a bar (*sl*); a subway; a faked knockout (*boxing*); an instance of pretending to have been tripped by an opposing player (*football*). [OE *dȳfan*, *dūfan*, from ON *dȳfa*]
■ **div'er** *n* a person who dives or can dive; a person who dives for pearls; a person who works in a diving suit or from a diving bell beneath water; any member of a genus (*Gavia*) of duck-like diving birds; (loosely; *esp* formerly) any of various diving birds such as the auk, grebe, penguin, etc; a pickpocket (*sl*). **div'ing** *n* and *adj*.
□ **dive'-bomb** *vt* and *vi* to attack with, or as if with, a dive-bomber; to discharge bombs while diving. **dive'-bomber** *n* an aeroplane that discharges a bomb while in a steep dive. **dive'-bombing** *n*. **dive-dapp'er** *n* (*Shakesp*) a didapper, dabchick, little grebe. **diving beetle** *n* a predatory water beetle of the *Dytiscus* genus which traps air beneath its wing cases for breathing under water. **diving bell** *n* a hollow vessel or chamber, originally bell-shaped, open at the bottom and supplied with air by a tube from above, in which one may descend into and work under water. **diving board** *n* a board for diving from. **diving suit** or (formerly) **dress** *n* a watertight costume for a diver, with special provision for receiving air, etc.

divellent /dī-vel'ənt/ *adj* drawing apart. [L *dī-* apart, and *vellere*, *vellicāre* to pluck]
■ **divell'icate** *vt* to pull in pieces; to pluck apart.

diver see under **dive**.

diverge /di- or dī-vûrj'/ *vi* to incline or turn apart; to tend from a common point in different directions; to vary from the standard; to deviate, differ; (of a mathematical series) to increase indefinitely. ◆ *vt* to deflect, cause to diverge. [L *dī-* apart, and *vergere* to incline]
■ **diverge'ment** *n*. **diverg'ence** or **diverg'ency** *n* the act or amount of diverging; the condition of being divergent; the flow of air away from a particular region, *usu* associated with fine weather (*meteorol*); (of an infinite series, etc) the property of having no limit (*maths*); the turning outwards of the eyes in focusing on a distant object (*physiol*); initiation of a chain reaction in which more neutrons are released than are absorbed and lost (*nucleonics*). **diverg'ent** *adj* diverging; (of thought or thinking) following unconventional routes, so as to produce a variety of solutions in problem-solving (*psychol*). **diverg'ently** *adv*. **diverg'ing** *adj*. **diverg'ingly** *adv*.
□ **divergent thinking** *n* (*behaviourism*) thinking that is productive and original, involving the creation of a variety of ideas or solutions that tend to go beyond conventional categories, *opp* to *convergent thinking*. **diverging lens** *n* a concave or other lens that causes light rays to spread out.

divers /dī'vərz/ (*archaic* and *literary*) *adj* sundry; several; more than one; same as **diverse** (*Bible*). ◆ *adv* (*Milton*) in different directions. [L *dīversus* turned different ways, contrary, different]
■ **dī'versly** *adv*.

diverse /dī'vərs or dī-vûrs'/ *adj* various, assorted; multiform; different; distinct; distracting (*Spenser*). ◆ *vi* (*Spenser*) to turn aside. [L *dīversus* different, various]
■ **di'versely** or **diverse'ly** *adv*. **diversifi'able** *adj*. **diversificā'tion** *n*. **diver'sified** *adj*. **divers'ify** *vt* to give variety to, vary, variegate or

modify; to make (investments) in securities of different types so as to lessen risk of loss; to engage in production of a variety of (manufactures, crops), or in a variety of operations, so as to expand or lessen risk of failure or loss; to differentiate (*obs*). ◆ *vi* to become more diverse or varied. **diver'sion** *n* the act of diverting or turning aside; something that diverts; amusement, recreation; something done to turn the attention of an opponent; an official detour to avoid (part of) a road that is temporarily closed. **diver'sionary** *adj* of the nature of a diversion, designed to distract the attention of an opponent. **diver'sionist** *n* a deviationist. **diver'sity** *n* state of being diverse; difference; dissimilarity; variety.

divert /di-vûrt', dī-/ *vt* to turn aside (also (*archaic*) *vi*); to change the direction of; to distract from business or study; to amuse. ◆ *n* (*Scot*) an amusing person or thing. [Fr, from L *dīvertere*, *dīversum*, from *dī-* aside, and *vertere* to turn]
■ **divertibil'ity** *n*. **divert'ible** *adj*. **divert'ing** *adj* tending to divert; amusing, entertaining. **divert'ingly** *adv*. **divertisement** /di-vûrt'iz-mənt/ *n* a diversion; a divertimento. **divert'ive** *adj* tending to divert.

diverticulum /dī-vər-tik'ū-ləm/ (*anat*) *n* (*pl* **divertic'ula**) a sac or pouch formed eg by herniation in the wall of a tubular organ, *esp* the intestines. [L *dīverticulum* a byway, retreat]
■ **divertic'ular**, **divertic'ulate**, or **divertic'ulated** *adj*. **diverticulī'tis** *n* inflammation of one or more diverticula. **diverticulō'sis** *n* the presence of several diverticula in the intestines.

divertimento /di-vûr-ti-men'tō/ (*music*) *n* (*pl* **divertimen'ti** /-tē/) an entertaining piece of music, *esp* a suite for orchestra or chamber ensemble. [Ital]

divertissement /dē-ver-tēs-mã'/ (*Fr*) *n* a short entertainment, eg a ballet interlude, between the acts of a play, or between plays; generally, a diversion or entertainment.

Dives /dī'vēz/ *n* the rich man at whose gate Lazarus lay (Bible, Luke 16.19); a rich and luxurious person. [L *dīves* rich (man), understood as a proper name]

divest /dī-vest'/ *vt* to remove clothes from, strip (with *of*); to strip or deprive (with *of*); to disencumber or free (oneself) (with *of*). [OFr *desvestir*, with change of prefix (*dis-* for *dē-*) from L *dēvestīre*, from *dē* away from, and *vestīre* to clothe, from *vestis* a garment]
■ **divest'ible** *adj*. **divest'iture**, **divest'ment** or **divest'ure** *n*.

divi see **divvy**[1].

divide /di-vīd'/ *vt* to split up, or mark off, into parts, actually or in imagination; to separate, part; to distinguish, set apart; to classify; to share, distribute; to allot; to deal out; to ascertain how many times a quantity is contained in (*maths*); to perform with division or floridly (*music*); to be a boundary or a subject of difference between; to keep apart; to set at variance, cause disagreement between; to cause to vote for and against a motion; to sever. ◆ *vi* to separate; to fall apart; to branch; to vote for and against a motion; to be capable of or be susceptible to division; to be contained a specified number of times in another number (with *into*). ◆ *n* the act of dividing (*inf*); an area of high land between two water systems, a watershed (*esp N Am*); something that divides or separates, a gap or split. [L *dīvidere*, *dīvīsum*, from *dis-* apart, and the root *vid* to separate]
■ **divīd'able** (or /div'id-/) *adj* divisible; divided (*Shakesp*). **divīd'ant** *adj* (*Shakesp*) distinguishable, separable. **divīd'edly** *adv*. **divīd'er** *n* someone who or something that divides; a screen or partition (also **room'-divider**); a soup-ladle (*Scot*); (in *pl*) a kind of compasses for measuring. **divīd'ing** *adj* separating. ◆ *n* separation. **divīd'ual** *adj* divisible; separable (*Milton*); shared in common with others (*Milton*). **divīd'uous** *adj* divided, special, accidental.
□ **divided highway** *n* (*N Am*) a dual carriageway. **divided skirt** *n* wide-legged knee-length trousers for women, having the appearance of a skirt, culottes. **divīd'ing-en'gine** *n* an instrument for marking accurate subdivisions or graduating scales.

dividend /div'i-dend/ *n* a number that is to be divided by another; the share of a sum divided that falls to each individual, by way of interest or otherwise; the sum payable to creditors of an insolvent estate (*law*). [L *dīvidendum* to be divided, from *dīvidere*]
□ **dividend stripping** *n* a method of evading tax on dividends by a contrived arrangement between a company liable to tax and another in a position to claim repayment of tax. **dividend warrant** *n* a certificate entitling to payment of dividend.
■ **declare a dividend** to announce the amount per share a trading concern is prepared to pay its shareholders.

divider see under **divide**.

dividivi /div'i-div-i/ *n* the curved pods of a small tropical American tree (*Caesalpinia coriaria*), used for tanning and dyeing; the tree itself. [Carib name]

dividual, **dividuous** see under **divide**.

divine /di-vīn'/ adj belonging to or proceeding from a god; holy; excellent in the highest degree; wonderful, splendid (inf); prescient, having forebodings (Milton). ◆ n a person skilled in divine things; a minister of the gospel; a theologian. ◆ vt to foresee or foretell as if divinely inspired; to guess or make out; to prognosticate; to make divine (Spenser); to search for (underground water, etc), esp with a divining rod. ◆ vi to profess or practise divination; to have forebodings. [OFr devin soothsayer, and L dīvīnus, from dīvus, deus a god]
■ **divinā'tion** n the art or practice of divining; seeking to know the future or hidden things by supernatural means; instinctive prevision; prediction; conjecture. **div'inātor** (archaic) or **divīn'er** n (also fem **divīn'eress**) a person who divines or professes divination; a conjecturer. **divinatō'rial** or **divīn'atory** adj relating to divination, conjectural. **divīne'ly** adv. **divīne'ness** n. **diviner**, **divineress** n see **divinator** above. **divin'ify** or **div'inize** or **-ise** vt to treat as divine.
❑ **Divine Office** n (RC) prayers or services held daily at fixed hours, now also called the **Liturgy of the Hours**. **divine right** n the concept that monarchs rule by the authority of God rather than by consent of the people; any authority supposed to be unquestionable (inf). **divining rod** n a rod, usu of hazel, used by those professing to discover water or metals underground.

diving see under **dive**.

divinify see under **divine**.

divinity /di-vin'i-ti/ n godhead; the nature or essence of a god; a celestial being; a god; the science of divine things; theology. [OFr devinite, from L dīvīnitās, -tātis; see **divine**]
❑ **divinity hall** n (Scot) a theological college or department.

divinize see under **divine**.

divisible /di-viz'i-bl/ adj capable of being divided or separated; capable of being divided without remainder (maths). [L dīvīsibilis, from dīvīdere to divide]
■ **divisibil'ity** or **divis'ibleness** n. **divis'ibly** adv.

divisim /di-vī'zim, dē-wē'sim/ (L) adv separately.

division /di-vizh'ən/ n the act of dividing; the state of being divided; that which divides; a partition; a barrier; a portion or section; one of a set of graded classes or groups; one of the parts of a territorial or business, etc unit, divided for administrative, etc purposes; in India, a part of a province under a commissioner, divided into districts; an army unit (usu half an army corps) containing almost all branches of the service; separation; the taking of a vote; difference in opinion, etc; disunion; the process of finding how many times one quantity is contained in another (maths); a taxonomic grouping, the equivalent of a phylum (bot); a group of organ pipes played from one keyboard; a florid passage or performance in which many short notes may be regarded as taking the place of a long note (music; archaic). [L dīvīsiō, -ōnis, from dīvīdere to divide]
■ **divisional** /-vizh'/ adj relating to or marking a division or separation (also **divis'ionary**); relating to or belonging to a part of a larger unit. **divisionaliza'tion** or **-s-** n. **divis'ionalize** or **-ise** vt. **divis'ionism** n (often with cap; art) pointillism. **divis'ionist** n.
❑ **Divisional Court** n (in England and Wales) a court attached to a division of the High Court which hears appeals from that division. **division bell** n a bell rung in the House of Commons to signal an imminent vote. **division lobby** see **lobby**.
■ **division of labour** n the assigning of different functions to different agents. **fallacy of division** (logic) the fallacy of assuming that the part or individual partakes of the characteristic of the whole or group.

divisive /di-vī'siv/ adj forming division or separation; tending to divide or separate; tending to create dissension. [LL dīvīsīvus, from dīvīdere to divide]
■ **divī'sively** adv. **divī'siveness** n.

divisor /di-vī'zer/ (maths) n the number that divides the dividend; a number that divides another without remainder, a factor. [L dīvīsor, from dīvīdere to divide]

divorce /di-vörs', -vörs'/ n the legal dissolution of a marriage or the decree that dissolves it; complete separation or severance (fig). ◆ vt to dissolve the marriage of; to give or obtain a divorce (to a couple or one's spouse, or from one's spouse); to separate, sever. ◆ vi to obtain a divorce; to separate by divorce. [Fr, from L dīvortium, from dīvortere, another form of dīvertere (of a woman) to leave one's husband]
■ **divorce'able** adj. **divorcee'** n a divorced person (also (Fr) **divorcé** masc and **divorcée** fem /di-vör'sā/). **divorce'ment** n (Bible) divorce. **divor'cer** n. **divor'cive** adj having power to divorce.

divot /div'ət/ n a thin sod, cut for roofing, etc (Scot); a small piece of turf dug up by the head of a golf club during a stroke, or by a horse's hoof. [Origin unknown]
■ **feal and divot** (Scots law) a right of cutting sods.

divulge /di- or dī-vulj'/ vt to make public; to reveal, disclose; orig to spread abroad among the vulgar or the people. [L dīvulgāre, from dī- abroad, and vulgāre to publish, from vulgus the common people]
■ **divul'gate** /-gāt/ vt (archaic) to publish. **dīvulgā'tion**, **divul'gence** or **divulge'ment** n.

divulsion /di- or dī-vul'shən/ n act of pulling or rending apart or away. [L dīvulsiō, -ōnis, from dī-, and vellere, vulsum to pull]
■ **divul'sive** adj tending to pull apart.

divvy¹ or **divi** /div'i/ (sl) n a dividend; a share. ◆ vt (**divv'ying**; **div'ying**; **divv'ied** or **div'ied**) (often with up) to divide (spoils, etc), share out. [Short form of **divide** and **dividend**]

divvy² /div'i/, also **div** /div/ (inf) n a stupid person; a fool. ◆ adj stupid, foolish.

Diwali /di-wä'lē/ n the Hindu or Sikh festival of light held in October or November (also **Dewali** or **Divali**). [Hindi dīvālī]

diwan same as **dewan**.

dixi /dēk'sē/ (L) I have spoken.

dixie or **dixy** /dik'si/ n a military cooking-pail or camp-kettle. [Perh Hindi degcī, from Pers degcha, dimin of dīg large metallic cooking utensil]

Dixieland /dik'si-land/ n an early style of jazz in New Orleans, played by small combinations of instruments. [Dixie name given to Southern states of the USA]

DIY /dē-ī-wī'/ abbrev : do-it-yourself (see under **do¹**).

diya /dē'a/ n a small oil lamp, usu of terracotta, used in Hindu worship, esp at Diwali. [Hindi]

dizain /di-zān'/ (prosody) n a ten-line stanza or poem. [Fr dix ten, from L decem ten]

dizen /dī'zn or diz'n/ (obs) vt to dress or charge (a distaff) with flax; to dress up, dress gaudily. [From the root seen in **distaff**]

dizygotic /dī-zī-got'ik/ or **dizygous** /dī-zī'gəs/ (biol) adj developed from two zygotes or fertilized eggs. [Gr di- twice, and **zygote**]
❑ **dizygotic twins** n pl fraternal twins, ie twins that have developed from two zygotes.

dizzard /diz'ərd/ (obs) n a blockhead. [Perh ME and OFr disour story-teller]

dizzy /diz'i/ adj giddy; confused, bewildered; (of a height) so elevated as to cause giddiness in anyone looking down (often fig); (generally) giddy-making, confusing, bewildering; silly (inf); extreme (inf). ◆ vt (**dizz'ying**; **dizz'ied**) to make dizzy; to confuse. [OE dysig foolish; cf Dan dösig drowsy; cf also **doze**]
■ **dizz'ily** adv. **dizz'iness** n. **dizz'ying** adj making one dizzy. **dizz'yingly** adv.

DJ /dē'-jā/ n a deejay, disc jockey; someone who makes music by mixing samples of recordings; a dinner jacket (inf). ◆ vi to act as a deejay. [Abbrev]

djebel see **jebel**.

djellaba or **djellabah** /jə-lä'bə or jel'ə-bə/ n a cloak with a hood and wide sleeves (also **jellab'a** or **jelab'**). See also **gallabea(h)**. [Ar jallabah, jallāb]

djembe /jem'bā/ n a W African drum played with the hand. [Mandingo]

djibbah /jib'ä/ same as **jubbah**.

Djiboutian /ji-boo'ti-ən/ adj of or relating to the Republic of Djibouti in NE Africa, or its inhabitants. ◆ n a native or citizen of Djibouti.

djinn, **djinni** see **jinn**.

DK abbrev : Denmark (IVR); double knitting.

dk abbrev : dark; deck; dock.

DL abbrev : Deputy Lieutenant.

D/L abbrev : demand loan.

dl abbrev : decilitre(s).

DLA abbrev : disability living allowance.

DLit or **DLitt** /dē-lit'/ abbrev : Doctor Litterarum or Litteraturae (L), Doctor of Letters or Doctor of Literature.

DLL (comput) abbrev : dynamic link library.

DLO abbrev : dead-letter office.

dlr abbrev : dealer.

dlvy abbrev : delivery.

DM abbrev : Deutschmark or Deutsche Mark; diabetes mellitus.

dm abbrev : decimetre(s).

DMA (comput) abbrev : direct memory access.

D-mark or **D-Mark** abbrev : Deutschmark or Deutsche Mark.

■ words derived from main entry word; ❑ compound words; ■ idioms and phrasal verbs

DMD (*med*) *abbrev*: Duchenne muscular dystrophy.

DMO *abbrev*: District Medical Officer.

DMS *abbrev*: database management system.

DM's or **DMs** (*inf*) *abbrev*: Doc Martens®.

DMSO *abbrev*: dimethyl sulphoxide.

DMus *abbrev*: Doctor of Music.

DMZ *abbrev*: demilitarized zone.

DNA /dē-en-ā'/ *n* deoxyribonucleic acid (qv under **deoxidate**).
■ **DNase'** *n* deoxyribonuclease, an enzyme that promotes the hydrolysis of DNA into smaller molecules.
◻ **DNA library** *n* (*biol*) a mixture of cloned DNA sequences derived from a single source and containing all or most of the sequences from that source. **DNA profiling** or **fingerprinting** *n* genetic fingerprinting (see under **genetic**). **DNA virus** *n* a virus in which genetic information is contained in DNA rather than RNA.

DNB *abbrev*: Dictionary of National Biography (a reference work containing the biographies of significant people in British history).

D-Notice a former name for **DA-Notice**.

DNR *abbrev*: (in medical notes) do not resuscitate.

Dnr *abbrev*: dinar (unit of currency).

DNS (*comput*) *abbrev*: domain name system.

Do. *abbrev*: dominee.

do[1] /doo or dǝ/ *vt* (2nd sing (*archaic*) **do'est** or **dost** /dust/, 3rd sing **does** /duz/, also (*archaic*) **do'eth** or **doth** /duth/; *pat* **did**; *prp* **do'ing**; *pap* **done** /dun/; in *Spenser*, *infinitive* **doen**, **done**, and **donne**, 3rd pl *pat* **doen**) to accomplish, complete; to finish; to exhaust; to work at; to perform work upon; to put in some condition, eg to clean, to tidy; to render; to confer; to bestow; to provide; to perform; (of a vehicle) to (have the power to) travel at a (maximum) speed of; to beat up, thrash, assault (*inf*); to prepare, set in order, arrange; to cook; to cheat, or overreach (*inf*); to prosecute (*inf*); to raid, rob (*sl*); to treat; to make the round of, see the sights of (*inf*); to spend (a period of time) in prison; to take or use (a drug) (*sl*); to mimic, impersonate; to have sexual intercourse with (*sl*); to put, place (*obs*); to cause (*obs*). ◆ *vi* to act, be active; to behave; to fare; to thrive; to suffice; to be just good enough; to serve (with *for*); to arrange, devise or effect in respect of something or someone (with *with*). —*Do* serves as a substitute for a verb that has just been used. It is used as an auxiliary verb (where there is no other auxiliary) with an infinitive in negative, interrogative, emphatic, and rhetorically inverted sentences, in some dialects merely periphrastically, and in verse sometimes to gain a syllable or postpone the accent; but these uses are limited with the verbs *have* and *do*. ◆ *n* (*pl* **do's** or **dos**) activity (*obs*); a party, feast or celebration; a hairdo (*inf*); a swindle, hoax (*sl*); what one has to do (*obs*); fuss (*archaic*). [OE *dōn*, *dyde*, *gedōn*; Du *doen*, Ger *tun*; connected with Gr *tithenai* to put, place]
■ **do'able** *adj* (*inf*) able to be done. **do'er** *n* a person who does, or habitually does, anything; an agent; a busy, active or energetic person; a person who prefers taking action, or practical steps, to contemplation and discussion; a healthy farm animal (*NZ*); a horse in respect of its appetite, as in *a good doer* (*horse-racing*). **do'ing** *adj* active (as in *up and doing*). ◆ *n* (*inf*) a scolding; thrashing; severe treatment; the agency or handiwork of someone seen as instrumental in something; (in *pl*) activities, behaviour; (in *pl*) working parts or pieces of equipment; (in *pl*) fancy dishes or adjuncts; (in *pl*) what's-its-name. **done** *vt* and *vi* (*Spenser*) *infinitive* of **do**. ◆ *adj pap* of **do**; utterly exhausted (now *usu* **done in**); finished, completed; cooked to a degree suitable for eating; (of behaviour, etc) socially acceptable. ◆ *interj* (used in clinching a bargain, etc) agreed. **done'ness** *n* (*cookery*) the state of being, or degree to which something is, cooked.
◻ **do'-all** *n* a factotum. **do'-good'er** *n* a slighting name for someone who tries to benefit others by social reforms, etc, implying that his or her efforts are unwelcome, self-righteous or ineffectual. **do'-good'ery** *n* (*derog*). **do'-good'ing** *n* and *adj*. **do'-good'ism** *n* (*derog*). **do-it-yourself'** *adj* designed to be built or constructed, etc by an amateur rather than by someone specially trained (also *n*). **do-it-yourself'er** *n*. **do'-naught**, **do'-nought** or **do'-noth'ing** *n* a lazy or idle person; a fainéant (see **donnot**). **do'-noth'ingism** *n*. **do'-noth'ingness** *n*.
■ **all done** completely finished, used up. **be done** to be at an end; to have done or finished (*Scot*). **be** or **have done with** to finish with, end contact or dealings with. **do away with** to abolish, destroy. **do brown** see under **brown**. **do by** to act towards. **do down** to belittle; to put down, subdue (*obs*); to cheat, get the better of (*inf*). **do for** to suit; to provide for; to ruin; to kill (*inf*); to do domestic work for (*inf*). **do in** (*inf*) to deceive; to get the better of; to exhaust; to ruin; to murder. **do or die** to make a final desperate attempt to do or achieve something, no matter what the cost or consequences (**do'-or-die'** *adj*). **do out** (*inf*) to clean (a room, etc) thoroughly. **do out of** (*inf*) to deprive of by

cheating. **do over** to do again, repeat (*N Am*); to cover over, eg with paint; to rob (*sl*); to beat up (*sl*). **do's and don'ts** advice or rules for action, *esp* in particular circumstances. **do someone proud** (*inf*) to make someone feel flattered; to treat lavishly. **do something**, etc **for** to improve, enhance. **do to death** to murder; to repeat too often. **do up** to fasten up; to put up, make tidy, arrange, tie up; to redecorate; to apply cosmetics to; to dress, array oneself becomingly; to fatigue utterly. **do well** to be justified; to be wise or sensible to take a particular step; to prosper. **do with** to make use of; to benefit from; to meddle with; to get on with. **do without** not to be dependent on, to dispense with. **have done** to desist; to stop it; to have no more dealings. **have to do with** to have any sort of connection with. **have you done?** (*inf*) are you finished? **how do you do?** a conventional phrase used as a greeting. **I**, etc **can't be doing with** I, etc can't abide, have no patience with. **make do** see under **make**[1]. **nothing doing** no. **that's done it** (*inf*) it is completed; an interjection expressing dismay that something is spoiled or ruined. **to do with** concerning. **what are you**, etc **doing with** (**something**)? why have you, etc got (something)? **what's to do?** what is the matter?

do[2] see **doh**[1].

do[3] see **ditto**.

DOA *abbrev*: date of availability; dead on arrival.

doab /dō'äb/ *n* a tongue of land between two rivers (*esp* the Ganges and Jumna). [Pers *dōāb* two waters]

doable see under **do**[1].

doat, etc see **dote**.

dob /dob/ (*Aust* and *NZ inf*) *vt* (**dobb'ing**; **dobbed**) (*usu* with *in*) to inform on or betray. [Brit dialect *dob* to put down]
■ **dobb'er** *n*.
◻ **dobb'er-in** *n*.

dob *abbrev*: date of birth.

dobbin /dob'in/ *n* a workhorse. [An altered dimin of *Robert*, traditionally used as a name for a horse]

dobby or **dobbie** /dob'i/ *n* an attachment to a loom for weaving small figures; a dotard; a benevolent creature who may secretly help with domestic work (*folklore*). [Perh from *Robert*]

dobchick /dob'chik/ same as **dabchick** (see under **dab**[1]).

Doberman /dō'bǝr-mǝn/ or **Doberman pinscher** /pin'shǝr/ *n* a breed of terrier, large and muscular with a smooth black-and-tan coat, and long forelegs (also **Dobermann** (**pinscher**)). [*Dobermann*, the first breeder, and Ger *Pinscher* a type of terrier]

dobhash /dō'bash/ *n* an interpreter. [Hindi *dōbāshī*, *dūbhāshiya*, from *dō*, *dū* two, and *bhāshā* language]

dobra /dob'rǝ/ *n* the standard monetary unit of São Tomé and Príncipe (100 centavos). [From Port *dóbra* doubloon]

Dobro® /dō'brō/ *n* an acoustic steel guitar with metallic resonator, of a type *usu* laid flat on the knee to play, particularly associated with country music and producing a wavering sound.

Dobson unit /dob'sǝn ū-nit/ *n* a unit of measurement of the ozone layer, expressed in terms of its hypothetical thickness at sea-level pressure, 100 Dobson units representing a thickness of one millimetre. [GMB *Dobson* (1889–1976), English meteorologist]

DOC *abbrev*: Denominazione di Origine Controllata (*Ital*), the Italian equivalent of appellation contrôlée (qv); District Officer Commanding.

doc /dok/ *n* a familiar contraction of **doctor**.

docent /dō'sǝnt, dō-sent'/ (*US*) *n* a teacher or lecturer at a college or university; a voluntary guide at a museum, art gallery, etc. [From Ger, see **privat-dozent**]

Docetism /dō-sē'ti-zm/ *n* a 2c heresy, that Christ's body was only a semblance, or else of ethereal substance. [Gr *dokēsis* a phantom, semblance, from *dokeein* to seem]
■ **Do'cēte** or **Docē'tist** *n* (*pl* **Docē'tae** /-tē/ or **Docē'tists**) a holder of this belief. **Docetic** /-set'-/ or **-set'-**/ or **Docetist'ic** *adj*.

DOCG *abbrev*: Denominazione di Origine Controllata Garantita (*Ital*), a designation of wines, guaranteeing origin, quality, strength, etc.

doch-an-doris, **doch-an-dorach** see **deoch-an-doruis**.

dochmius /dok'mi-ǝs/ *n* (*prosody*) a foot of five syllables, typically with first and fourth short, the rest long. [L, from Gr *dochmios*]
■ **doch'miac** or **dochmī'acal** *adj*.

docht see **dow**[2].

docile /dō'sīl/ or (*US*) *dos'il*/ *adj* easy to teach or train; willing to learn; easily managed, obedient, compliant. [Fr, from L *docilis*, from *docēre* to teach]
■ **docibil'ity** *n*. **do'cible** *adj* (*obs*). **doc'ibleness** or **docil'ity** /-sil'-/ *n*.

docimasy /dos'i-mǝ-si/ *n* scrutiny; application of tests; assaying; examination of drugs. [Gr *dokimasiā* examination, from *dokimazein* to test]

■ **docimastic** /-*mas'tik*/ *adj*. **docimol'ogy** *n* the art of assaying.

dock¹ /*dok*/ *n* (often used in *pl*) an artificial basin for the reception of vessels and cargo; the waterway between two wharves or two piers; a wharf or pier; in a railway station, the place of arrival and departure of a train; in the theatre, a space for storing scenery. ◆ *vt* to place in a dock; to bring into dock; to equip with docks; to join (spacecraft) together in space; to embed in sand or ooze (*obs*; *Shakesp*). ◆ *vi* to enter a dock; to join together in space. [Origin obscure; cf ODu *dokke*]

■ **dock'age** *n* accommodation in docks for ships; dock-dues. **dock'er** *n* a dockside labourer whose job is to load and unload ships. **dock'ing** *n*. **dockizā'tion** or **-s-** *n*. **dock'ize** or **-ise** *vt* to convert into docks.
□ **dock'-dues** *n pl* payments for use of a dock. **dock'-la'bourer** *n* a docker. **dock'land** *n* a district round about docks. **dock'-master** *n* the person superintending a dock. **dock'side** *n* the area alongside a dock. **dock'-warrant** *n* a warehouse receipt. **dock'yard** *n* a naval establishment with docks, building-slips, stores, etc.
■ **dry dock** see under **dry**. **in (the) dock** (*facetious*) (of a vehicle) undergoing repairs and so unavailable for use; (of a person) in hospital.

dock² /*dok*/ *vt* to cut short; to curtail; to cut off the whole or part of (an animal's tail); to cut the tail off (an animal); to clip; to reduce (someone's pay), or deduct (a certain amount) from it. ◆ *n* the part of a tail left after clipping; the rump (*Scot*). [ME *dok*, prob from ON *dokkr* stumpy tail]

dock³ /*dok*/ *n* a polygonaceous weed (genus *Rumex*) with large leaves and a long root. [OE *docce*]
■ **dock'en** *n* (*Scot*, *perh orig pl*) a dock.
□ **dock'-cress** *n* the nipplewort.

dock⁴ /*dok*/ *n* the enclosure for the accused in a court of law. [Flem *dok* cage, hatch, sty]
■ **in the dock** on trial in a court of law; under attack, facing criticism (with *for*).

docken see under **dock³**.

docket, also (*obs*) **docquet** /*dok'it*/ *n* a summary of the contents of a document, etc; a bill or ticket affixed to anything indicating its contents; a label; a list or register of cases in court, or of legal judgements, or (*US*) business to be transacted; an official permit to buy; a custom-house certificate of payment. ◆ *vt* (**dock'eting**; **dock'eted**) to make a summary of the contents of a document, etc; to enter in a book; to mark the contents of papers on the back; to fix a label to; to categorize. [Perh a dimin of **dock²** to curtail]

Doc Martens® /*dok mär'tənz*/ *n pl* a make of lace-up leather boots or shoes with light thick resilient soles.

doctor /*dok'tər*/ *n* a licensed medical practitioner; a dentist (*N Am*); a veterinary surgeon (*N Am*); a mender or repairer of something; a name for various contrivances for removing defects or superfluities in manufacture; a person who has received a doctorate from a university (or the Archbishop of Canterbury), the most senior academic degree in any subject (*orig* implying competency to teach); a learned man, *esp* a teacher (*archaic*); one of a small number of *esp* revered early ecclesiastical writers (also **Doctor of the Church**); a cleric especially skilled in theology or ecclesiastical law; a ship's cook or camp-cook (*sl*); in some warm countries, a cool sea breeze conducive to health; material used to sophisticate, refine, adjust, etc something; brown sherry (*old sl*); a counterfeit coin (*old sl*); (in *pl*) loaded dice (*old sl*); a fish, the sea surgeon; a type of angler's fly. ◆ *vt* to treat, as a doctor does; to patch up, repair; to sophisticate, tamper with, falsify; to address as doctor; to confer a doctor's degree upon; to spay, castrate (*inf*). ◆ *vi* to practise medicine. [L, a teacher, from *docēre* to teach]
■ **doc'toral** *adj* relating to the academic degree of doctor. **doc'torand** *n* a candidate for the doctorate. **doc'torate** *vt* to confer the degree of doctor upon. ◆ *n* the academic degree of doctor. **doc'toress** or **doc'tress** *n* (*facetious*) a female doctor; a doctor's wife. **doctorial** /-*tō'ri-əl* or -*tö'ri-əl*/ *adj* appropriate to a doctor, showing a doctor's skill or concern. **doc'torly** *adj*. **doc'torship** *n*.
□ **doc'tor-fish** *n* a sea surgeon. **Doctors' Commons** *n pl* before the establishment of the Divorce Court and Probate Court in 1857, the college of the doctors of civil law in London, incorporated by royal charter in 1768. **doctor's stuff** *n* medicine.
■ **go for the doctor** (*Aust inf*) to make an all-out effort, give one's all. **what the doctor ordered** (*inf*) the very thing that's needed.

doctrinaire /*dok-tri-när'*/ *adj* theoretical; preoccupied with theory, inclined to carry principles to logical but unworkable extremes; impractical; dogmatic. ◆ *n* an unpractical theorist, disposed to carry principles to logical but unworkable extremes; in France, in 1815–30, one of a school who desired constitutional government. [Fr, from LL *doctrīnārius*]
■ **doctrinair'ism** or **doctrinā'rianism** *n* blind adhesion to one-sided principles. **doctrinā'rian** *n* and *adj* doctrinaire.

doctrine /*dok'trin*/ *n* a body of religious, political, etc teaching; a guiding principle, belief or precept; teaching (*archaic*). [L *doctrīna*, from *docēre* to teach]
■ **doctrinal** /*dok-trī'nl* or *dok'tri-nl*/ *adj*. **doctri'nally** (or /*dok'*/) *adv*.

docu /*dok'ū*/ (*inf*) *n* a documentary film.

docudrama /*dok'ū-drä-mə*/ *n* a play or film reproducing real events and characters. [*documentary drama*]

document /*dok'ū-mənt*/ *n* a paper, *esp* of an official character, affording information, proof or evidence of anything; a file of text produced and held on a computer, *esp* a word processor; evidence, proof (*archaic*); instruction (*Spenser*, etc); warning (*obs*). ◆ *vt* (also /-*ment'*/) to furnish (eg a ship) with documents; to record; to support or prove by documents or evidence. [Fr, from L *documentum*, from *docēre* to teach]
■ **documental** /-*ment'*/ *adj* documentary. **document'alist** *n* a specialist in documentation; a person who collects and classifies documents. **documentar'ily** *adv*. **documen'tarist** *n* a person who makes documentaries. **documentarizā'tion** or **-s-** *n*. **document'arize** or **-ise** *vt* and *vi* to present in, or make documentaries. **document'ary** *adj* relating to or found in documents; (of films, TV programmes, etc) aiming at presenting reality, presenting facts not fiction. ◆ *n* a film or a radio or TV programme about real people or events, without fictional colouring or professional actors. **documentā'tion** *n* preparation, setting forth, or use of documentary evidence and authorities; documents or other material provided in support, amplification or authentication; instruction (*archaic*); (in fiction) realistic reproduction of records, real or supposed; the written information on the structure and operation of hardware or software (*comput*).
□ **document reader** *n* (*comput*) an optical character reader that converts printed characters into digital code for a computer.

docusoap /*dok'ū-sōp*/ *n* a television series that follows the lives of real people over a period of time. [*documentary soap* opera]

DoD (*US*) *abbrev* : Department of Defense.

dod¹ /*dod*/ (*obs* or *dialect*) *vt* (**dodd'ing**; **dodd'ed**) to cut the hair of; to poll; to pollard; to clip. ◆ *n* (*Scot*) a rounded hilltop, *esp* a shoulder of a greater hill. [ME *dodden*]
■ **dodd'ed** *adj* polled; hornless; pollard. **dodd'y** *n* (*Scot*) a hornless cow.

dod² /*dod*/ (*Scot*) *n* a slight fit of ill-humour; (in *pl*; often with *the*) the sulks. [Gaelic *dod* peevishness]
■ **dodd'y** *adj*.

dod³ /*dod*/ *n* an old or archaic euphemistic form of **God**, used in oaths.

dod⁴ see **daud**.

doddard see **doddered**.

dodder¹ /*dod'ər*/ *vi* to shake, to tremble, to totter or progress unsteadily, as a result of age; to potter; to ramble in talk; to be decrepit in mind or body. [Perh connected with **doddered**]
■ **dodd'erer** *n* (*derog*) a feeble, senile person. **dodd'ering** *adj* (*derog*) decrepit in body and feeble in mind, senile. **dodd'ery** *adj* unsteady with age.

dodder² /*dod'ər*/ *n* a leafless, twining, pale parasitic plant (genus *Cuscuta*) of or related to the family Convolvulaceae. [ME *doder*; cf Ger *Dotter*]

doddered or (*obs*) **doddard** /*dod'ərd*/ *adj* perhaps *orig* pollard; decayed with loss of branches. [Cf **dod¹**]

doddipoll see **doddypoll**.

doddle /*dod'l*/ (*inf*) *n* something very easily accomplished. [Poss from **dawdle**]

doddy see **dod¹,²**.

dodeca- /*dō-dek-ə-*/ *combining form* denoting twelve. [Gr *dōdeka* twelve]
■ **dodec'agon** *n* (Gr *gōniā* an angle) a plane figure with twelve angles and sides. **Dodecagyn'ia** /-*jin'i-ə*/ *n pl* (Gr *gynē* a woman, a female) in some classes of the Linnaean classification, an order of plants with twelve styles. **dodecagyn'ian** or **dodecag'ynous** /-*aj'i-nəs*/ *adj*. **dodecahē'dral** *adj*. **dodecahedron** /-*hē'dron*/ *n* (Gr *hedrā* a seat) a solid figure, having twelve faces (equal pentagons in a *regular* dodecahedron, rhombs in a *rhombic* dodecahedron). **Dodecan'dria** *n pl* (Gr *anēr*, *andros* a man, male) a Linnaean class of plants, having twelve stamens. **dodecan'drous** *adj*. **dodecaphon'ic** *adj* (Gr *phōnē* voice; *music*) twelve-tone. **dodecaph'onism** *n* twelve-tone music. **dodecaph'onist** *n* a composer or admirer of twelve-tone music. **dodecaph'ony** *n* see **dodecaphonism** above. **dodecastyle** /*dō'dek-ə-stīl* or *dō-dek'ə-stīl*/ *adj* (Gr *stỹlos* a pillar; *archit*) having twelve columns in front. ◆ *n* a portico so built. **dodecasyllab'ic** *adj*. **dodecasyll'able** *n* (*prosody*) a line of twelve syllables.

dodge /*doj*/ *vi* to start aside or shift about, to move out of the way of a blow, etc; to evade or use mean tricks; to shuffle or quibble; (in change-ringing) to make two bells change order in the sequence (*bellringing*). ◆ *vt* to evade (a blow, etc) by a sudden shift of place or position; to evade by astuteness or deceit. ◆ *n* an evasion; a trick, ruse, stratagem; a quibble; an instance of dodging (*bellringing*). [Origin obscure]

■ **dodg'er** *n* a person who dodges, a shirker; a clever trickster; a screen on a ship's bridge for shelter in rough weather; food, *esp* bread (*dialect* and *Aust inf*); an advertising leaflet (*US*). **dodg'ery** *n* trickery. **dodg'ing** *n* (*image technol*) manipulation of the light projected through a negative by an enlarger to lighten or darken selected parts of the resultant print. **dodg'y** *adj* artful, tricky; difficult to do or carry out; risky, tricky; uncertain, unstable, unreliable; dishonest; dishonestly obtained.

❑ **dodge'ball** *n* a children's game in which players try to hit one another with a large ball.

■ **dodge the column** (*sl*) to evade one's duties.

Dodgems® /*doj'əmz*/ *n* a fairground amusement in which drivers of small electric cars within an enclosure try to bump others without being bumped.

■ **Dodg'em**® *n* one of these cars.

dodkin /*dod'kin*/ *n* a doit (also **doit'kin**). [**doit**]

dodman /*dod'mən*/ (*dialect*) *n* a snail. [Origin unknown]

dodo /*dō'dō*/ *n* (*pl* **do'does** or **do'dos**) a clumsy flightless bird, about the size of a turkey (native of Mauritius) which became extinct about the end of the 17c; an old-fashioned or stupid person (*inf*). [Port *doudo* silly]

Dodonaean /*dō-dō-nē'ən*/ *adj* relating to *Dodona* in Epirus, or its oracle sacred to Zeus, situated in a grove of oaks (also **Dodō'nian**).

DOE *abbrev* : Department of Energy (*US*); formerly, Department of the Environment.

Doe /*dō*/ see **John Doe** under **John**.

doe /*dō*/ *n* the female of the smaller deer such as the fallow deer or roe deer; extended to the female of antelope, kangaroo, rabbit, hare, and some other animals. [OE *dā*; Dan *daa*, deer]

❑ **doe'-eyed** *adj* having large, dark eyes like those of a deer. **doe'skin** *n* the skin of a female fallow deer; a smooth, close-woven, woollen cloth.

doek /*dook*/ (*S Afr*) *n* a square cloth for tying round the head, worn by African women. [Afrik, cloth]

doen, **doer**, **does** see **do**[1].

doesn't /*duz'ənt* or *duz'nt*/ contracted form of **does not**.

doest, **doeth** see **do**[1].

doff /*dof*/ *vt* to take off, remove (a piece of one's clothing); to put off; to lift (one's hat) in greeting someone. [**do**[1] and **off**]

■ **doff'er** *n* part of a carding machine that strips the cotton from the cylinder when carded; a person who removes full bobbins from a machine.

DOG *abbrev* : Directory of Opportunities for Graduates.

dog[1] /*dog*/ *n* a wild or domestic animal of the genus (*Canis*) that includes the wolf and fox; the domestic species, diversified into a large number of breeds; a male of this and other species; a mean scoundrel; a term of contempt for a man or boy; generally, a man (eg a *jolly dog*); either of the two constellations, the Greater and the Lesser Dog (Canis Major and Minor); an andiron; a hook for holding logs; a gripping appliance of various kinds; a cock, eg of a gun; a dogfish; a prairie dog; heavy ostentation (*sl*); (in *pl*) greyhound races (*inf*); (in *pl*) the feet (*inf*); a failure, something less than satisfactory (*N Am inf*); a traitor or informer (*Aust*); a boring or unattractive woman (*offensive sl*). ◆ *adj* and as combining form of dogs; male, *opp* to *bitch*; spurious, base, inferior (as in *dog Latin*). ◆ *adv esp as combining form* utterly. ◆ *vt* (**dogg'ing**; **dogged**) to follow like a dog; to track and watch constantly; to worry, plague, infest; to hunt with dogs; to fasten with a dog. [Late OE *docga*; cf Du *dog* a mastiff, and Ger *Dogge*]

■ **dogg'ed** *adj* dog-like; stubbornly persevering or determined; sullen; pertinacious. ◆ *adv* (*sl*) very. **dogg'edly** *adv*. **dogg'edness** *n*. **dogg'er** *n* someone who dogs. **dogg'ery** *n* doggish ways or doings; dogs collectively; rabble; a drinking resort (*US*). **dogg'ess** *n* (*facetious*) a bitch. **dogg'iness** *n*. **dogg'ing** *n* shooting with dogs; following like a dog; the pastime of visiting isolated public places, *usu* at night, to engage in, or observe people engaging in, sexual activity, eg in parked cars (*sl*). **dogg'ish** *adj* dog-like; characteristic of dogs; churlish; brutal. **dogg'ishly** *adv*. **dogg'ishness** *n*. **dogg'y** *adj* fond of dogs; of, for or characteristic of, a dog or dogs; dashing, beauish. ◆ *n* (also **dogg'ie**) diminutive form of **dog**. **dog'ship** *n* the quality or personality of a dog.

❑ **dog'-ape** *n* a baboon (from the shape of its head). **dog'bane** or **dog's'bane** *n* a plant (genus *Apocynum*) said to be poisonous to dogs. **dog'-bee** *n* (*obs*) a drone. **dog'-belt** *n* a broad belt put round the waist for hauling. **dog'berry** *n* the fruit of the wild cornel or dogwood; extended to many other plants and their fruits; (with *cap*) a pompous, muddle-headed person (from the character in

Shakespeare's play *Much Ado About Nothing*). **Dog'berrydom** *n*. **Dog'berryism** *n* an utterance worthy of Dogberry, ie wordy consequential blundering and malapropism. **dog biscuit** *n* a hard kind of biscuit for feeding dogs. **dog'bolt** *n* *orig* a kind of arrow; a contemptible person (*obs*). **dog'cart** *n* a two-wheeled horse-vehicle with seats back to back, *orig* used to carry sporting dogs. **dog'-cheap** *adj* extremely cheap. **dog collar** *n* a collar for a dog; a clerical collar fastened behind; a woman's stiff collar or neck ornament. **dog'-crab** *n* a very small crab. **dog'-dai'sy** *n* the common daisy; the ox-eye daisy. **dog days** *n pl* the period when the Dogstar rises and sets with the sun (*usu* reckoned 3 July to 11 August) and which is erroneously supposed to be the time when dogs are specially liable to hydrophobia; a period of inactivity. **dog'-ear** *n* a dog's-ear; a fold at the corner of a page in a book. **dog'-eared** *adj* (of pages of a book) turned down like the ears of a dog; hence, shabby and scruffy. **dog eat dog** *n* a ruthless pursuit of one's own interests, savage self-concern. **dog'-eat-dog'** *adj*. **dog'-end** *n* (*sl*) a cigarette end. **dog'-faced** *adj*. **dog'-fancier** *n* a breeder or seller of dogs. **dog fennel** see **dog's-fennel** below. **dog'fight** *n* a fight between dogs; any confused fight or mêlée; a fight between fighter aircraft, *esp* at close quarters. **dog'fighting** *n*. **dog'fish** *n* a small shark of various kinds. **dog'fox** *n* a male fox. **dog'-grass** or **dog'-wheat** *n* couch grass or a related species. **dog'gy-bag** *n* a bag used by diners to carry home leftover food from a restaurant (supposedly for their pets). **dog'gy-paddle** or **dog'-paddle** *n* a simple swimming stroke with alternate arm movements, similar to the swimming action of a dog (also *vi*). **dog handler** *n* a policeman, etc in charge of a specially trained dog. **dog'-head** *n* the hammer of a gunlock. **dog'-hip** or **-hep** *n* (*dialect*) the hip or fruit of the dog rose. **dog'hole** *n* a hole fit only for a dog; a wretched dwelling. **dog'house** *n* a dog-kennel (*esp US*); a state of disgrace (*fig*). **dog'-kennel** *n*. **dog Latin** *n* spurious or sham Latin. **dog'-leech** *n* (*obs*) a person who treated diseases of dogs. **dog'leg** *n* a sharp bend, like that in a dog's hindleg; something bent in that way, eg a golf hole with a bent fairway. ◆ *adj* (also **dog'legged**) bent like a dog's hind leg; (of stairs) having successive flights running opposite ways without a well hole; (of a fence) made of poles laid on cross-shaped supports. ◆ *vi* to become, or be bent like a dog's leg. ◆ *vt* to make such a bend in. **dog letter** *n* the letter *r* (from its growling sound). **dog-paddle** see **doggy-paddle** above. **dog'-pars'ley** *n* fool's parsley. **dog'-per'iwinkle** *n* a species of *Nucella* (also **dog'-winkle**). **dog'pile** *n* (*N Am inf*) a heap of bodies formed by people jumping on top of each other in an act of celebration. **dog racing** *n* greyhound racing. **dog rose** *n* a species of wild rose (*Rosa canina*). **dog's age** *n* (*inf*) a long time. **dog'-salmon** *n* keta and humpback, Pacific species of salmon. **dog's'-body** *n* (*orig naut sl*) pease pudding; a dish of biscuit, water and sugar; a junior naval (or other) officer; (*usu* **dogs'body**) a general drudge; someone who does menial, monotonous work for others. **dog's breakfast** or **dog's dinner** *n* (*inf*) anything very untidy or badly done. **dog's chance** *n* a bare chance; no chance. **dog's disease** *n* (*Aust inf*) any minor ailment, eg influenza. **dog's'-ear** *n* a fold at the corner of a page in a book. ◆ *vt* to fold at the corner. **dog's'-fenn'el** *n* mayweed. **dog'shores** *n pl* pieces of timber used to shore up a vessel before launching. **dog'-sick** *adj* thoroughly sick, sick as a dog. **dog'skin** *n* leather made of or in imitation of dog's skin (also *adj*). **dog'sled** (*esp N Am*) or **dog sledge** *n* a sledge pulled by a team of dogs. **dog'sleep** *n* a light sleep, very easily broken. **dog sleigh** *n* a dogsled. **dog's life** *n* a wretched, miserable life. **dog's'-meat** *n* scraps and refuse sold as food for dogs. **dog's'-mer'cury** *n* a euphorbiaceous European plant (*Mercurialis perennis*). **dog's'-nose** *n* gin and beer, or similar mixture. **dog'-soldier** *n* (*milit sl*) a soldier who acts as a last line of defence (*orig* a Native American who staked himself to the ground to signal his unwillingness to retreat). **dog's'-tail grass** *n* a common British pasture grass (genus *Cynosurus*). **Dog'star** *n* Sirius, in the constellation of the Great Dog, the brightest star in the heavens, giving name to the dog days. **dog's'-tongue** *n* hound's-tongue, a plant of the borage family. **dog's'-tooth** *n* a broken-check pattern used extensively in the weaving of tweeds. **dog's-tooth grass** *n* a seaside sand-binding grass (genus *Cynodon*). **dog's-tooth violet** see **dogtooth violet** below. **dog tag** *n* a metal identity disc for a dog or (*inf*) for a soldier. **dog'-tick** *n*. **dog'-tired** or (*Shakesp*) **dog'-wea'ry** *adj* completely worn-out. **dog'tooth** *n* a moulding in later Norman architecture, consisting of a series of ornamental square pyramids; a canine tooth. **dog'tooth-spar'** *n* calcite crystals like canine teeth. **dogtooth violet** or **dog's-tooth violet** *n* any plant of the genus *Erythronium*. **dog'town** *n* a prairie dog community. **dog'-trick** *n* a low trick. **dog'trot** *n* a gentle trot like a dog's; a jogtrot. **dog'vane** *n* (*naut*) a small vane to show direction of wind. **dog violet** *n* a scentless wild violet, *esp Viola canina*. **dog'watch** *n* (*naut*) on shipboard, a watch 4–6pm or 6–8pm, consisting of two hours only, instead of four. **dog-weary** see **dog-tired** above. **dog-wheat** see **dog-grass** above. **dog'-whelk** *n* a gastropod of the genus *Nassarius*, like a small whelk. **dog whistle** *n* a high-frequency whistle, inaudible to the human ear, used in dog training; (*esp* in political speeches) a message whose significance is understood by only a few people. **dog-winkle** see **dog-periwinkle** above.

dog'wood *n* the wild cornel (*Cornus* (or *Swida*) *sanguinea*), a small tree with white flowers and purple berries, the shoots and leaves turning red in autumn; extended to many other shrubs and trees.
■ **dog in the manger** a person who has no use for something but will not let others enjoy it. **dogs of war** (*fig*) troops, aggressors, mercenaries, warlike people (from Shakespeare, *Julius Caesar* III.1.274). **go to the dogs** to deteriorate markedly; to be ruined. **hot dog** a roll containing a hot sausage. **like a dog's dinner** (*inf*) very smart, dressed up flamboyantly, overdressed. **not to lead the life of a dog** to lead a life so wretched that even a dog would not be content with it. **put on the dog** (*US*) to put on airs, behave showily. **the dog's bollocks** (*vulgar sl*) someone or something particularly excellent. **throw**, **give** or **send to the dogs** to throw away or abandon.

dog² /dog/ (*obs*) *n* used in oaths for **God**.
■ **doggone** /dog-gon'/ *interj* (*US*) expressing vexation, from **dog on** (**it**), God damn (it) (**doggone'** or **doggoned'** *adj* and *adv*).

doge /dōj/ or /dō'jā/ *n* formerly the title of the chief magistrate in republican Venice and Genoa. [Ital (Venetian dialect) for *duce* duke, from L *dux* a leader]
■ **dogaressa** /dō-gä-res'a/ *n* a doge's wife. **dogate** /dō'gāt/ *n*. **dogeate** /dō'jāt/ *n*.
□ **doge'ship** *n*.

dogged, etc see **dog¹**.

dogger¹ /dog'ər/ *n* a two-masted Dutch fishing-vessel. [Du]
□ **dogg'erman** *n*.

dogger² /dog'ər/ (*geol*) *n* a concretion, *esp* of ironstone; a sandy ironstone or ferruginous sandstone; (with *cap*) part of the Middle Jurassic (also *adj*). [Origin uncertain; a northern word]

dogger³ see under **dog¹**.

doggerel /dog'ə-rəl/, also **doggrel** /dog'rəl/ *n* irregular verses in burlesque poetry, so named in contempt; poor quality comic or trivial verse; nonsense. ◆ *adj* irregular in rhythm, mean. [Origin unknown]

doggery...to...**doggishness** see under **dog¹**.

doggo /dog'ō/ (*inf*) *adv* remaining quiet and hidden until it is safe, appropriate, etc to emerge, *esp* in the phrase *to lie doggo*. [Poss from **dog¹**]

doggy see under **dog¹**.

dogie or **dogy** /dō'gi/ (*US*) *n* a motherless calf. [Origin obscure]

dogma /dog'mə/ *n* a settled opinion; a principle or belief, or code of belief, principles or doctrines; a doctrine laid down with authority. [Gr *dogma*, -*atos* an opinion, from *dokeein* to think, seem]
■ **dogmatic** /-mat'ik/ or **dogmat'ical** *adj* relating to a dogma; asserting a thing as if it were a dogma; asserting positively; overbearing. **dogmat'ically** *adv*. **dogmat'ics** *n sing* (*theol*) the statement of Christian doctrines, systematic theology. **dog'matism** *n* dogmatic or positive assertion of opinion. **dog'matist** *n* a person who makes positive assertions. **dog'matize** or **-ise** /-mə-tīz/ *vi* to state one's opinion dogmatically or arrogantly. **dog'matizer** or **-s-** *n*. **dogmatol'ogy** *n* the science of dogma. **dog'matory** *adj*.

dogy see **dogie**.

DoH *abbrev* : Department of Health.

doh or **do** /dō/ (*music*) *n* (*pl* **dohs**, **dos** or **do's**) the first note of the scale in sol-fa notation. [Perh L *Dominus* (Lord), *do* replacing the syllable *ut* used by the Italian originator; see **Aretinian**]
■ **up to high doh** (*inf*) in a state of great excitement or agitation.

d'oh /dō, du/ *interj* suggesting stupidity or a foolish action. [Imit]

dohyo /dō'yō/ *n* (in sumo wrestling) the ring or marked area in which the wrestlers compete. [Jap]

DOI *abbrev* : digital object identifier, a registration code given to a document published in electronic format.

doilt /doilt/ (*Scot*) *adj* crazy, foolish (also **doiled**). [Origin obscure]

doily, also **doyley** or **doyly** /doi'li/ *n* a small lace or lacy paper, etc ornamented napkin, often laid on or under dishes; *orig* an old kind of woollen fabric (*obs*). [From *Doily* or *Doyley*, a famous haberdasher]

do-in /dō'in/ *n* a form of self-applied acupressure massage, originating in China, used preventatively and therapeutically. [Jap, way of energy]

doing see **do¹**.

doit /doit/ *n* (also **doit'kin**) a small obsolete Dutch coin; a thing of little or no value. [Du *duit*]

doited or **doitit** /doit'id, -it/ (*Scot*) *adj* in dotage, senile. [Origin obscure]

dojo /dō'jō/ *n* (*pl* **do'jos**) a place where judo or karate, etc are taught or practised. [Jap]

dol. *abbrev* : dolce (*music*); dollar.

dolabriform /dō-lab'ri-förm/ *adj* like a hatchet or cleaver. [L *dolābra* a cleaver, and *förma* form]

Dolby® /dol'bi/ *n* an electronic system that reduces the amount of extraneous noise on recorded or broadcast sound. [R *Dolby* (1933–2013), its inventor]

dolce /dol'chā/ *adj* and *adv* sweet or sweetly (*esp* of music). ◆ *n* a soft-toned organ stop. [Ital, from L *dulcis*]
■ **dolcemente** /-men'tā/ *adv* (*music*) softly and sweetly.
■ **dolce far niente** /fär nē-en'tā/ (*Ital*) literally, sweet doing-nothing, pleasant idleness. **dolce vita** /vē'ta/ (Ital, sweet life) a life of wealth, pleasure and self-indulgence.

dolcelatte /dol'chā-lat'ā/ *n* a soft Italian cheese with blue veins. [Ital *dolce latte* sweet milk]

doldrums /dol'drəmz/ *n pl* those parts of the ocean near the equator where calms and baffling winds prevail (*naut*); a state of inactivity or stagnation; low spirits. [Prob connected with obsolete *dold* stupid, or *dol*, dull]

dole¹ /dōl/ *n* a dealing out; something given in charity (*old*); a payment made by the state to unemployed people (*inf*); a share (*archaic*); a small portion. ◆ *vt* (*usu* with *out*) to deal out in small portions. [OE *dāl*; related to **deal¹**]
□ **dole'-bludger** *n* (*Aust* and *NZ sl*) one who evades work and lives off state benefits.
■ **on the dole** (*inf*) living on unemployment or other benefit.

dole² /dōl/, also (*obs*) **dool** or **doole** /dool/ *n* pain or grief (*archaic* and *dialect*); heaviness at heart (*archaic* and *poetic*). [OFr *doel* (Fr *deuil*) grief, from L *dolēre* to feel pain]
■ **dole'ful** *adj* full of dole or grief; melancholy. **dole'fully** *adv*. **dole'fulness** *n*. **do'lent** *adj* (*obs*). **dole'some** *adj* dismal. **dole'somely** *adv*.

dole³ /dōl/ *n* guile (*obs*); criminal intention (*Scots law*). [L *dolus*, from Gr *dolos* guile]

dolerite /dol'ə-rit/ (*geol*) *n* a basic igneous rock like basalt in composition but coarser grained. [Fr *dolérite*, from Gr *doleros* deceptive]
■ **dolerit'ic** *adj*.

dolia see **dolium**.

doli capax /dol'i kap'aks/ (*law*) *adj* considered to be capable (*esp* because old enough) of intending to commit a crime. [L, literally, capable of evil]

dolicho- /dol-i-kō-/ *combining form* denoting long. [Gr *dolichos* long]
■ **dolichocephal** /-sef'əl/ *n* a long-headed person. **dolichocephalic** /-sif-al'ik/ *adj* (Gr *kephalē* the head) long-headed, ie having a breadth of skull (from side to side) less than 75 (or 78) per cent of the length (front to back), *opp* to **brachycephalic** (also **dolichoceph'alous**). **dolichoceph'aly** or **dolichoceph'alism** *n*. **Dolichos** /dol'i-kos/ *n* (Gr, long, also a podded plant) a genus of long-podded leguminous plants allied to the haricot; (without *cap*) any plant of the genus. **Dolichosaurus** /-sō'rəs/ *n* (Gr *sauros* lizard) the typical genus of **Dolichosau'ria**, a group of Cretaceous fossil reptiles. **Dolichotis** /-kō'tis/ *n* (Gr *ous*, *ōtos* the ear) a genus of long-eared S American rodents, comprising the mara or Patagonian hare.

dolichurus /dol-i-kū'rəs/ (*prosody*) *n* a dactylic hexameter with a redundant syllable at the end. [Gr *dolichouros* long-tailed]

doli incapax /dol'i in-kap'aks/ (*law*) *adj* considered to be incapable (*esp* because too young) of intending to commit a crime. [L, literally, incapable of evil]

dolina /dō-lē'nə/ or **doline** /dō-lēn'/ (*geol*) *n* a swallow hole. [Russ *dolina* valley, plain]

dolium /dō'li-əm/ *n* (*pl* **do'lia**) an ancient Roman earthenware jar for wine, oil or grain, etc. [L *dōlium*]

doll¹ /dol/ *n* a puppet; a toy in the form of a human being, *esp* a baby; an over-dressed and rather silly woman; a young woman, *esp* an attractive one (*sl*); an affectionate term of address (*inf*); the smallest or pet pig in a litter. ◆ *vi* and *vt* to dress (often with *up*) in a showy way. [Prob from *Dolly*, familiar dimin of *Dorothy*]
■ **doll'dom** *n*. **doll'hood** *n*. **doll'iness** *n*. **doll'ish** *adj*. **doll'ishness** *n*. **doll'y** *n* (*dimin* of **doll**) an attractive young girl (also **dolly girl** or **dolly bird**); formerly, a dolly-mop (qv below); a slow, easy catch (*cricket*); a slow-moving target that is easily hit.
□ **doll's house** or (*US*) **doll'house** *n*. **dolly mixture** *n* a mixture of small brightly-coloured sweets; one of these sweets. **doll'y-mop** *n* (*old sl*) a slut; a prostitute. **doll'y-shop** *n* (*hist*) a marine store (a low pawnshop) often having a black doll as sign.

doll² /dol/ (*horse-racing*) *n* a hurdle used as a barrier on a racecourse to exclude certain areas from use by riders.
■ **doll off** or **doll out** to mark off by means of dolls.

dollar /dol'ər/ *n* the standard monetary unit of many countries (100 cents), *incl* the USA, Canada, Australia, New Zealand, Hong Kong, etc; a thaler; five shillings (*old sl*). [Ger *T(h)aler* (LGer *daler*), short for

---

■ words derived from main entry word; □ compound words; ■ idioms and phrasal verbs

Joachimsthaler because first coined at the silver-mines in Joachimsthal (Joachim's dale) in Bohemia]

■ **doll'ared** *adj.* **dollariza'tion** or **-s-** *n* the alignment or replacement of a country's currency with that of the USA. **doll'arize** or **-ise** *vt* and *vi.* **doll'arless** *adj.* **dollaroc'racy** *n.* **doll'arship** *n.*

❑ **dollar area** *n* those countries as a whole whose currencies are linked to the US dollar. **doll'arbird** *n* an Asian and Australian roller with coin-like patches on its wings. **dollar diplomacy** *n* diplomacy dictated by financial interests; diplomacy that employs financial weapons to increase political power. **dollar gap** *n* the excess of imports from a dollar country over exports to it, necessitating settlement by dollar exchange or in gold.

dollop /dol'əp/, also (*obs*) **dallop** /dal'/ *n* a lump, a small shapeless mass; a tuft of grass or weeds (*obs*); a rank patch in a field (*obs*). ◆ *vt* to add or serve out in a small mass. [Prob connected with Norw dialect *dolp* a lump]

dolly[1] see under **doll**[1].

dolly[2] /dol'i/ *n* a trolley, truck or platform on wheels or rollers; an implement used to wash ore (*mining*); a wooden shaft attached to a disc with projecting arms, used for beating and stirring clothes in a washing-tub (*old*); a tool for holding the head of a rivet. ◆ *vt* to operate upon, yield or obtain with a dolly; to wheel or roll with a dolly; to beat with a hammer. [Prob from *Dolly*, the familiar form of *Dorothy*]

■ **doll'ied** *adj.* **doll'ier** *n.*

❑ **dolly camera** *n* a camera moving on a dolly. **dolly shot** *n* a shot taken with a dolly camera. **dolly switch** *n* a switch (for an electric light, etc) consisting of a pivotal lever pushed up and down vertically. **dolly tub** *n* a tub for washing clothes or ores with a dolly.

dolly[3] /dol'i/ *n* a complimentary offering of flowers, sweetmeats, etc on a tray. [Anglo-Ind, from Hindi *dālī*]

Dolly Varden /dol'i var'dən/ *n* a large hat for women, one side bent downwards, abundantly trimmed with flowers; a flowered muslin dress for women, with pointed bodice and tucked-up skirt; a large American fish of the char genus. [Named from a character in Dickens's novel *Barnaby Rudge*]

dolma /dol'mə/ *n* (pl **dol'mas** or **dolmades** /-mä'des/) a vine or cabbage leaf with a savoury stuffing. [Turk]

dolman /dol'mən/ *n* a Turkish robe with slight sleeves and open in front; a hussar's jacket, worn like a cloak, with one or both sleeves hanging loose; a woman's mantle. [Turk *dōlāmān*]

❑ **dolman sleeve** *n* a kind of sleeve which tapers from a very wide armhole to a tight wrist.

dolmen /dol'mən/ *n* a stone table; a prehistoric structure, possibly a tomb, of erect unhewn stones, supporting a flattish stone. [Fr *dolmen*; usually explained as derived from Breton *dol*, *taol* table, and *men* stone; but *tolmēn* in Cornish meant hole of stone]

dolomite /dol'ə-mīt/ *n* a mineral, double carbonate of calcium and magnesium; a rock composed of that mineral, magnesian limestone. [D Guy de *Dolomieu* (1750–1801), French geologist]

■ **dolomitic** /-mit'ik/ *adj.* **dol'omitīzātion** or **-s-** *n.* **dol'omitize** or **-ise** *vt* to convert into dolomite.

dolour or (N Am) **dolor** /dol'ər, dōl'ər or (*hist*) dul'ər/ (*poetic*) *n* pain; grief; anguish. [OFr, from L *dolēre* to grieve]

■ **dolorif'erous** or **dolori'fic** *adj* causing or conveying dolour, pain or grief. **dolorō'sō** *adv* (Ital; *music*) in a soft and sorrowful manner. **dol'orous** *adj* full of pain or grief; doleful. **dol'orously** *adv.* **dol'orousness** *n.*

dolphin /dol'fin/ *n* any of a group of small toothed whales belonging to the family Delphinidae, about 2.5–3m (8–10ft) long, with a beak-like snout; sometimes used loosely in the USA to include the porpoise; either of two fish of the genus *Coryphaena* about 1.5m (5ft) in length, *esp C. hippurus*, noted for the brilliancy of its colours when dying (also **dol'phinfish**); (with *cap*) a northern constellation (see **Delphinus**); a buoy or pile for mooring; a structure of piles used to protect a harbour entrance, etc. [OFr *daulphin*, from L *delphinus*, from Gr *delphīs*, *-phīnos*]

■ **dolphinarium** /-ā'ri-əm/ *n* (pl **dolphinā'riums** or **dolphinā'ria** /-ə/) an aquarium for dolphins. **dol'phinet** *n* (*Spenser*) a female dolphin.

❑ **dol'phinfish** see above. **dol'phin-fly** *n* a black aphis, destructive to beanplants.

dols *abbrev* : dollars.

dolt /dōlt/ *n* a dull or stupid fellow. [For *dulled*; see **dull**]

■ **dolt'ish** *adj* dull; stupid. **dolt'ishly** *adv.* **dolt'ishness** *n.*

DOM *abbrev* : *Deo optimo maximo* (L), see **Deo**; dirty old man; Dominican Republic (IVR); *Dominus omnium magister* (L), God the master of all.

Dom /dom/ *n* the Portuguese form of *Don* (see **don**[1]); also a title given to certain Catholic dignitaries and members of some monastic orders, *esp* the Benedictine. [L *dominus* lord]

Dom *abbrev* : Dominical; Dominican; Dominion; *Dominus* (L), Lord.

dom. *abbrev* : domestic.

-dom /-dom or -dəm/ *sfx* forming nouns, denoting: dominion, power, state or condition; a group of people (with a specified characteristic, eg *officialdom*). [OE *dōm* judgement; Ger *-tum*]

domain /dō-mān'/ *n* what one is master of or has dominion over; an estate or territory that is owned or governed by a person, a family or a ruler; ownership; a public park or recreation area (*Aust* and *NZ*); the scope or range of any subject or sphere of knowledge; an aggregate to which a variable belongs (*maths*); a small region in a ferromagnetic substance within which magnetism is uniform. [Fr *domaine*, from L *dominicum*, from *dominus* a master]

■ **domain'al** or **domā'nial** *adj.*

❑ **domain name** *n* (*comput*) the distinctive name of a specific computer network or service used as part of an Internet address. **domain name system** *n* (*comput*) the means by which a domain name is identified and translated into an Internet protocol address.

domal /dō'məl/ *adj* of or relating to a house, or dome. [L *domus* a house]

domatium /do-mā'sh(y)əm/ (*bot*) *n* (pl **domā'tia**) a plant structure that harbours mites or other symbiotic organisms. [Latinized form of Gr *dōmation*, dimin of *dōma* house]

Domdaniel /dom-dan'yəl/ (*literary*) *n* a hall under the sea inhabited by a sorcerer and his disciples (*Southey*); an infernal cave, den of iniquity generally (*Carlyle*). [Fr, from Gr *dōma Daniēl* house of Daniel; from Chavis and Cazotte's French continuation of the *Arabian Nights*]

dome[1] /dōm/ *n* a structure, *usu* hemispherical, raised above a large building; a large cupola; a cathedral (*obs*); a building, *esp* a great or stately building (*poetic*); anything approaching the form of a hemispherical vault, eg a head, the cover of a reverberatory furnace, the steam chamber on a locomotive boiler or a clip-fastener that fits into a hold; a pair of crystal faces parallel to a lateral axis, meeting in a rooflike edge (*crystallog*). ◆ *vt* to cover with a dome; to make into the shape of a dome. ◆ *vi* to become dome-shaped. [L *domus* a house; Fr *dôme*, Ital *duoma*, Ger *Dom*]

■ **domed** or **domical** /dōm' or dom'/ *adj* having a dome. **dōm'y** *adj.*

dome[2] (*Spenser*) same as **doom**.

Domesday book or **Doomsday book** /doomz'dā book/ *n* a book compiled by order of William the Conqueror, containing a survey of all the lands in England, their value, owners, etc, so called from its authority in judgement (OE *dōm*) on the matters contained in it.

domestic /dō-, də-mes'tik/ *adj* belonging or relating to the home or family; remaining much at home, enjoying or accustomed to being at home; private; tame; not foreign. ◆ *n* a servant in the house; a row between people living in the same house, *usu* a couple (*inf*); (in *pl*) articles of home manufacture, *esp* homemade cotton cloths; any product not imported. [L *domesticus*, from *domus* a house]

■ **domes'ticable** *adj* capable of being domesticated. **domes'tical** *adj* (*archaic*). **domes'tically** *adv.* **domes'ticate** *vt* to make domestic or familiar; to tame. **domes'ticated** *adj* adapted to or content with home life and activities; tamed. **domesticā'tion** *n.* **domes'ticātor** *n.* **domesticity** /dō- or do-mis-tis'i-ti/ *n* domestic or domesticated state; home life; (in *pl*) home conditions and arrangements. **domesticize** or **-ise** *vt* domesticate.

❑ **domestic architecture** *n* the architecture of mansions, dwelling-houses, cottages, etc. **domestic economy** *n* the principles of running a household efficiently. **domestic science** *n* the household skills of cooking, sewing, etc; the older term for home economics (qv).

domestique /dom-es-tēk'/ *n* a member of a professional cycling team whose role is to help the team leader. [Fr, domestic servant]

domett /dom'ət or -it/ *n* a plain cloth with cotton warp and woollen weft. [Perh a proper name]

domical see under **dome**[1].

domicile /dom'i-sīl, -sil/ or **domicil** /dom'i-sil/ *n* a dwelling-place, abode; a person's legally recognized place of residence. [Fr, from L *domicilium*, from *domus* a house]

■ **dom'icile** /-sīl/ *vt* to establish in a fixed residence. **dom'iciled** *adj.* **domiciliary** /-sil'/ *adj* of or relating to the domicile; dealing with or available to people in their own homes. **domiciliāte** /-sil'/ *vt* to establish in a permanent residence. **domiciliā'tion** *n.*

❑ **domiciliary visit** *n* an authorized visit to a private house for the purpose of searching it; a visit made by a doctor, etc to a patient's or client's home.

dominant /dom'i-nənt/ *adj* prevailing; predominant; having or tending to seek a commanding position; of an ancestral character, appearing in the first generation of crossbred offspring to the exclusion of the alternative character in the other parent, which may yet be transmitted to later generations (*genetics*). ◆ *n* the fifth above the tonic (*music*); a dominant gene or the character determined by it (*genetics*); one of the prevailing species in a plant or animal community. [L *domināns, -antis,* prp of *domināri* to be master]

■ **dom'inance** or **dom'inancy** *n* ascendancy; the state of being dominant. **dom'inantly** *adv*.

dominate /dom'i-nāt/ *vt* to be lord over; to have command or influence over, to govern; to prevail over; to tower over; to command a view of; to be the controlling position of; to be predominant in; to project one's personality, influence, etc strongly over. ♦ *vi* to be in a position of power or command. ♦ *n* the Roman Empire in its later more avowedly absolute form. [L *domināri, -ātus* to be master, from *dominus* a master, from *domāre* to tame]

■ **domina'tion** *n* government; absolute authority; tyranny; (in *pl*) a class of angelic spirits, the dominions. **dom'inative** *adj* governing; arbitrary (*rare*). **dom'inātor** *n* a ruler or governor (*Shakesp*); a ruling influence. **dom'inātrix** *n* a female dominator, *esp* one taking a sadistic role in sadomasochistic sexual activity.

dominee /doo'mi-ni/ (*S Afr*) *n* a minister of the Dutch Reformed Church or any other Afrikaner church. [See **dominie**]

domineer /dom-i-nēr'/ *vi* (often with *over*) to rule imperiously; to command arrogantly; to be overbearing. [Prob through Du from OFr *dominer,* from L *domināri*]

■ **domineer'ing** *adj* overbearing, authoritarian.

dominical /do-min'i-kl/ *adj* belonging to the Lord (as the Lord's Prayer or the Lord's Day). [LL *dominicālis,* from L *dominicus,* from *dominus* lord, master]

❑ **dominical letter** *n* one of the first seven letters of the alphabet, used in calendars to mark the Sundays throughout the year.

Dominican[1] /do-min'i-kən/ *adj* belonging to St *Dominic* or to the Dominicans. ♦ *n* a friar of the order of St Dominic (founded in 1215), the *Fratres Predicatores,* or *Black Friars* (from their black mantle).

Dominican[2] /do-min'i-kən/ *adj* of or relating to the *Dominican* Republic in the West Indies. ♦ *n* a native or inhabitant of the Dominican Republic.

Dominican[3] /do-mi-nē'kən/ *adj* of or relating to the island of *Dominica* in the West Indies. ♦ *n* a native or inhabitant of Dominica.

dominie /dom'i-ni/ *n* a schoolmaster, a tutor (*esp Scot*); a clergyman (*US dialect*). [L *domine,* vocative of *dominus* master]

dominion /də-min'yən/ *n* lordship; sovereignty; rule, power or authority; a domain or territory with one ruler, owner or government; a completely self-governing colony, not subordinate to but freely associated with the mother country; control; (in *pl*) a class of angelic spirits (Bible, Colossians 1.16). [LL *dominiō, -ōnis,* from *dominus* master]

❑ **Dominion Day** *n* until 1983, the name of Canada Day (*qv*).

dominium /də-min'i-əm/ *n* ownership of property. [L, lordship, ownership]

domino /dom'i-nō/ *n* (*pl* **dom'inoes** or **dom'inos**) a cape with a hood worn by a master or by a priest; a long cloak of black silk with a hood, used at masked balls, or its wearer; a mask covering the upper half of the face; one of the oblong pieces with which the game of **dom'inoes** /-nōz/ is played, *usu* twenty-eight in number, divided into two compartments, each of which is a blank or marked with from one to six spots; a card game played in a similar way; the end; a mistake in performance (*music; inf*). ♦ *adj* involving a series of multiple transplant operations on different patients (*surg*); denoting antenatal and postnatal care, together with a hospital delivery supervised by one's own midwife (*obstetrics*). [Appar Sp *dominó, dómino,* in some way connected with L *dominus* master]

❑ **domino theory** *n* the theory that one event sets off a series of similar events, thus exhibiting the **domino effect,** the fall of one domino standing on end causing the whole row to fall in turn.

domoic acid /də-mō'ik as'id/ *n* a poisonous amino acid found in marine algae. [Jap dialect *domoi* name of the seaweed in which the substance occurs]

DOMS *abbrev* : Diploma in Ophthalmic Medicine and Surgery.

domy see under **dome**[1].

don[1] /don/ *n* (with *cap*) a Spanish title, corresponding to English Sir and Mr, formerly applied only to noblemen, now to all classes (*fem* **Doña** /dōn'ya,* Italian form **Don'na**); a Spanish nobleman, a Spaniard; a fellow of a college or university; any member of the teaching staff of a college or university; an expert (*Aust* and *NZ*); a swell, adept (*inf*); a Mafia boss (*US inf*). [Sp, from L *dominus*]

■ **dona** or **donah** /dō'nə/ *n* a sweetheart (corruption of **Doña** or **Donna**). **donn'ish** *adj* relating to or acting like a college don. **donn'ishness** *n*. **donn'ism** *n* self-importance. **don'ship** *n* the rank or status of a don.

❑ **Don Juan** /hwän/ or /joo'ən/ *n* a legendary Spanish licentious nobleman, subject of plays, poems and operas in several European languages; an attractive libertine and profligate.

don[2] /don/ *vt* (**donn'ing; donned**) to do or put on; to assume. [**do** and **on**]

Doña see **don**[1].

dona, donah see under **don**[1].

dona nobis /dō'nä nō'bis/ *n* the last section of the Roman Catholic mass. [From the opening words, *Dona nobis pacem* Give us peace.

Donat or **Donet** /dō'nat/ (*obs*) *n* a grammar, a primer. [OFr *donat,* from Aelius *Dōnātus,* author about 358AD of a long-famous Latin grammar]

donation /dō-nā'shən/ *n* an act of giving; that which is given, a gift of money or goods; the act by which a person freely transfers his or her title to anything to another (*law*). [Fr, from L *dōnāre, -ātum,* from *dōnum* a gift, from *dare* to give]

■ **do'nary** *n* a thing given to a sacred use. **do'natary** *n* (*Scots law; hist*) a person to whom lands escheated to the crown were made over. **dōnate'** *vt* (a back-formation from **donation**) to give as gift; to contribute, *esp* to charity. **do'native** (or /don'/) *n* a gift; a gratuity; a benefice presented by the founder or patron without reference to the bishop. ♦ *adj* vested or vesting by donation. **dōna'tor** *n* a person who makes a gift, a donor. **do'natory** (or /don'/) *n* a recipient. **dōnee'** *n* the person to whom a gift is made. **dō'ning** *n* (*inf*; back-formation from **donor** below) the act of donating (eg blood). **dō'nor** *n* a giver; a benefactor; a person who (or animal that) provides blood, semen, or tissue or organs for use in transplant surgery; an impurity in semiconductor material which increases the conductivity by contributing electrons (*electronics*).

❑ **donor card** *n* a card carried by a person willing to have (sometimes specified) parts of his or her body used in transplant surgery in the event of his or her death. **donor insemination** *n* artificial insemination using semen from a donor.

Donatist /dō'nə- or don'ə-tist/ *n* a member of an African Christian sect of the 4c and 5c, who protested against any diminution of the extreme reverence paid to martyrs, treated the lapsed severely, and rebaptized converts from the Catholic Church. [From *Dōnātus,* one of their leaders]

■ **dōn'atism** *n*. **dōnatis'tic** or **donatis'tical** *adj*.

donder /don'ə/ (*S Afr sl*) *vt* to beat up, thrash. ♦ *n* a scoundrel, rogue. [Afrik, to thrash, from Du *donderen* to swear, bully]

done see **do**[1].

donee see under **donation**.

donepezil /dō-nep'ə-zil/ *n* a cholinesterase inhibitor used in the treatment of Alzheimer's disease.

doner kebab see **kebab**.

Donet see **Donat**.

dong[1] /dong/ *n* a deep ringing sound, such as that of a large bell; a heavy punch, thump (*Aust* and *NZ*). ♦ *vi* (of a bell) to make a deep ringing sound. ♦ *vt* (*Aust* and *NZ*) to punch or thump. [Imit]

dong[2] /dong/ (*vulgar sl; orig* and chiefly *US*) *n* the penis.

dong[3] /dong/ *n* the standard monetary unit of Vietnam (100 xu).

donga /dong'gə/ (*orig S Afr*) *n* a gully made by soil erosion. [Zulu, a bank, side of a gully]

dongle /dong'gl/ *n* a device plugged into a computer to allow an authorized application to run (*comput*); a device used in the illegal cloning of mobile phones. [Arbitrary coinage]

doning see under **donation**.

donjon /dun'jən/ *n* a strong central tower in ancient castles, to which the garrison retreated when hard pressed. [A doublet of **dungeon**]

donkey /dong'ki/ *n* (*pl* **don'keys**) an ass; a stupid person; a person used by drug dealers to carry drugs being smuggled through customs (*sl*). [Still regarded as slang in 1823; perh a double dimin of *dun,* from its colour; or from *Duncan*]

❑ **donkey derby** *n* one or more races by contestants on donkeys, eg at a fête. **don'key-en'gine** *n* a small auxiliary engine. **donkey jacket** *n* a strong jacket, with shoulders of leather or (*usu*) a substitute, and patch pockets. **don'key-man** /-man/ *n* a man in charge of a donkey; /-mən/ in the merchant navy, (formerly) a man in charge of a donkey-engine, (now) a petty officer or senior rating in a ship's engine-room. **don'key-pump** *n* an extra steam pump. **donkey vote** *n* (*Aust*) in a preferential system of voting, a vote accepting the order of candidates on the ballot paper; such votes collectively. **don'key-work** *n* drudgery.

■ **argue** or **talk the hindlegs** (or **-leg**) **off a donkey** to argue or talk persistently and therefore *usu* persuasively. **donkey's years** a long time (a pun on *ears*).

Donna see **don**[1].

donnard, donnart see **donnered**.

donnat see **donnot**.

donne see **do**[1].

donné or **donnée** /don'ā/ n (pl **donn'és** or **donn'ées** /-ā(z)/) a datum; basic assumption(s), as eg a given situation, on which a work of literature is founded; the main fact or condition determining the character and timing of an action. [Fr]

donned, **donning** see **don²**.

donnered, **donnerd**, **donnert**, **donnard** or **donnart** /don'ərd, -ərt/ (Scot) adj stupid; dull-witted.

Donnerwetter /don'ər-vet-ər/ (Ger) n thunderstorm (used as an interjection of annoyance, etc).

donnish, **donnism** see under **don¹**.

donnot or **donnat** /don'ət/ (Yorks) n a good-for-nothing; an idler. [Appar partly do-naught (**do¹**), and partly dow-nought (**dow²**)]

Donnybrook or **donnybrook** /don'i-brŏŏk/ n a riotous assembly, a rowdy brawl. [From the fair at Donnybrook, Dublin]

donor see donation.

donship see under **don¹**.

donsie /don'si/ (Scot) adj unlucky, perverse (obs); neat, trim (obs); sickly; stupid. [Origin unknown]

don't /dōnt/ v a contraction of **do not**. ◆ n something one must not do. □ **don't-know'** n (the answer given by) someone whose mind is not made up with regard to some, esp political, issue.

donut see **doughnut** under **dough**.

donzel /don'zəl/ (obs) n a squire, aspirant to knighthood. [Ital donzello, from LL domnicellus, dimin of L dominus lord]

doo /dŏŏ/ (Scot) n a dove. □ **doocot** or **dooket** /dŏŏk'ət/ n a dovecote.

doob /dŏŏb/ n dog's-tooth grass. [Hindi dūb]

doobrey or **doobrie** /dŏŏ'bri/ n a thing whose name is unknown or temporarily forgotten, a thingamy. [Orig military slang; origin unknown]

dooce /dŏŏs/ (inf) vt to dismiss (an employee) as a result of unguarded remarks published on the World Wide Web. [Coined by Heather Armstrong (born 1975), US website designer who was dismissed as a result of comments made on her website dooce.com]

doodah /dŏŏ'dä/ or (esp US) **doodad** /dŏŏ'dad/ (inf) n a small ornament or trinket; a piece of decoration; a gadget; thingamy. [Both coined from **do¹**]
■ **all of a doodah** very agitated.

doodle¹ /dŏŏ'dl/ vi to scrawl or scribble meaninglessly or aimlessly. ◆ n something doodled.
■ **dood'ler** n.

doodle² /dŏŏ'dl/ (Scot) vt to dandle.

doodle³ /dŏŏ'dl/ (Scot) vt to drone or play, as a bagpipe. [Ger dudeln]

doodlebug /dŏŏ'dl-bug/ n the larva of an antlion or other insect (used in divination in America; US); any instrument, scientific or unscientific, used by prospectors to indicate the presence of minerals; the V-1, a flying bomb (World War II sl).

doo-doo /dŏŏ'dŏŏ/ (inf; esp childish) n excrement, faeces.
■ **in deep doo-doo** in serious trouble.

doofer /dŏŏ'fər/ (sl) n a thing whose name one does not know or cannot recall, a thingamy. [Thought to be based on the phrase (it will) do for (now)]

doofus /dŏŏ'fəs/ (US inf) n a stupid person.

doohickey /dŏŏ'hiki/ (US inf) n a gadget, esp one whose name escapes one. [doodad and hickey]

dook¹ /dŭk/ (Scot) n a plug of wood driven into a wall to hold a nail, etc; a bung. [Unknown]

dook² /dŭk/ (Scot) vt and vi to duck; to bathe. ◆ n an act of plunging, dipping or bobbing; a bathe; an inclined adit at a mine. [**duck²**]

dook³ see **duke**.

dooket see doocot under **doo**.

dool¹, **doole** see **dole²** and **dule**.

dool² /dŏŏl/ or **dule** (Scot) /dül/ n a boundary mark; a goal. [Cf Du doel, LGer dole, Fris dôl, dôle]
■ **hail the dules** to score a goal.

doolally /dŏŏ-lal'i/ (sl) adj mentally unbalanced; crazy. [Deolali, a town near Mumbai]

doolie /dŏŏ'li/ n a litter or palanquin. [Hindi dolī]

doom /dŏŏm/ n destiny, fate; ruin; catastrophe; death; judgement or condemnation; final judgement; a picture of the Last Judgement. ◆ vt (**doom'ing**; **doomed**) to condemn to destiny or catastrophe; to pronounce judgement on; to sentence. [OE dōm judgement]
■ **doomed** adj under sentence; fated; destined to inevitable death, failure or ruin. **doom'ful** adj (Spenser, etc) dispensing judgement.

dooms adv (Scot) very, exceedingly. **doom'ster** n a judge (archaic); a dempster; a pessimist (inf); a doomwatcher (inf). **doom'y** adj (inf) pessimistic; depressed; depressing.
□ **doom'-laden** adj forecasting or redolent of disaster. **doom'-merchant** n (inf) a pessimist; someone continually expecting, and forecasting, disaster. **doom'sayer** n. **doom'saying** n. **dooms'day** n the day of doom, the last judgement; a day of reckoning. **Doomsday book** see Domesday book. **doomsday clock** n a notional clock indicating the imminence of catastrophe in terms of minutes left before midnight. **dooms'man** n (archaic) someone who pronounces doom or sentence, a judge; a pessimist (inf). **doom'watch** n pessimism about the contemporary situation and about the future, esp of the environment; observation of the environment to prevent its destruction by pollution, over-population, etc; a generally pessimistic view of the future. ◆ vi to make pessimistic observations. **doom'watcher** n. **doom'watching** n.
■ **crack of doom** the last trump. **till doomsday** forever.

doom-palm see **doum-palm**.

doona /dŏŏ'nə/ (Aust) n a duvet. [Orig a trademark]

door /dōr or dör/ n the usual entrance into a house, room or passage; a solid sheet (of door, metal, glass, etc) hung so that it permits access through or closes up an entrance; a house, etc (as in three doors away); a means of approach or access. [OE duru (fem) and dor (neuter); cf Ger Tür, Tor, Gr thyrā, L forīs, Sans dvār a door]
□ **door'bell** n. **door'case** n the frame that encloses a door. **door'cheek** n (Scot) a side post of a door. **door'frame** n a doorcase. **door'keeper** n. **door'knob** n. **door'knock** n (Aust) a fund-raising appeal in which agents go from door to door soliciting donations (also adj and vi). **door'knocker** n a knocker on a door; a person who doorknocks (Aust). **door'man** n a man, often uniformed, who monitors entrance to a hotel, restaurant, etc and assists guests and customers. **door'mat** n a mat for wiping shoes on, or for some other purpose at a door; an uncomplaining person whom others treat inconsiderately (inf). **door'nail** n a stud for a door, proverbially dead. **door'-plate** n a plate on or at a door with the householder's name on it. **door'post** n the jamb or side-piece of a door. **door'-sill** n the threshold of a doorway. **doors'-man** or **doors'man** n a porter, doorkeeper. **door'-stead** n a doorway. **door'step** n a step at a door; a thick slice of bread (inf). ◆ vi (**door'stepping**; **door'stepped**) to go from door to door round an area, eg canvassing in an election. ◆ vt (esp of journalists) to pester (someone), by waiting on his or her doorstep. **door'stepper** n. **door'stepping** n. **doorstep selling** n going from house to house to (try to) sell goods or services. **door'stone** n. **door'stop** n a wedge or heavy object to prevent a door swinging shut; a knob fixed to floor or wall to prevent a door opening too far; any thick, heavy object (fig). **door'-to-door'** adj calling at each house in an area in order to sell, canvass, etc; between specific points of departure and arrival (also adv). **door'way** n an opening where there is or might be a door. **door'-yard** n (US) a yard about the door of a house.
■ **close** (or **open**) **the door to** to make impossible (or possible). **lay at someone's door** to blame someone for. **leave the door open** to preserve a situation in which something remains possible. **next door (to)** in the next house; near or bordering upon; very nearly (fig). **on one's doorstep** close to one's house, etc. **out of doors** see under **out**. **show someone the door** to turn someone out of the house.

doorn /doorn/ (S Afr) n thorn. [Du doorn thorn]
□ **doornboom** /doorn'boom/ n (Du boom tree) a S African acacia.

doosra /dŏŏs'rə/ (cricket) n a leg break bowled with an apparent off-break action by a right-arm bowler. [Hindi and Urdu, literally, the other one]

doo-wop /dŏŏ'wop/ (music) n vocalizing in harmony in the style of rhythm-and-blues, orig developed in the USA during the 1950s.

doozy /dŏŏ'zi/ (N Am inf) n something exceptionally good or fine of its type.

dop¹ /dop/ n a copper cup in which a gem is fastened for cutting or polishing; Cape brandy made from grape-skins (S Afr); a tot (eg of wine; S Afr); a drink container (having the capacity of about one third of a bottle); an empty shell (of a nut); a cartridge-case (usu **dopp'ie**). [Du dop shell, husk]

dop² /dop/ (obs) vt and vi (**dopp'ing**; **dopped**) to dip; to dap. ◆ n a curtsy; a bob. [OE dop- (in compounds); connected with **dip**]
■ **dopp'er** n a didapper; a rod for dapping. **dopp'ing** n a flock of sheldrake.

dopa /dō'pə/ n a naturally-occurring amino acid, a form of which, L-dopa, is used in the treatment of Parkinson's disease. [From dioxyphenylalanine, a former name for the compound]

dopamine /dō'pə-mēn/ n a chemical found in brain tissue that acts as a neurotransmitter, necessary for the normal functioning of the brain. [dopa and amine]
■ **dopaminer'gic** adj (of a neuron) releasing dopamine.

dopatta or **dupatta** /dō-put'ə/ n a silk or muslin shawl or headscarf. [Hindi]

dope /dōp/ n a drug, esp one illegally administered to an athlete, a racehorse, or taken by an addict; marijuana (inf); opium (old); drug-taking; confidential or fraudulent information in advance (inf); information in general (inf); anything supplied to dull, blind or blunt the conscience or insight; a fool (inf); a thick liquid, semi-liquid, or pasty material (US); an absorbent; lubricating grease; aeroplane varnish; a substance added to improve the efficiency or modify the properties of anything. ◆ vt to give or apply dope to; to drug; to add impurities to (a semiconductor) to modify or improve its properties (electronics). ◆ vi to take dope. ◆ adj (sl) excellent. [Du doop a dipping, sauce; doopen to dip]
■ **dōp'ant** n (electronics) a substance used in doping. **dōp'er** n someone who applies, administers, deals in, or takes dope. **dope'y** or **dōp'y** adj narcotic; stupefied (inf); stupid (inf). **dōp'ily** adv. **dōp'iness** n. **dōp'ing** n drugging; the addition of known impurities to a semiconductor, to achieve the desired properties in diodes and transistors (electronics).
❑ **dope'-fiend** n (inf) a drug addict.

dopiaza /dō-pi-az'ə/ adj (in Indian cookery) denoting a dish of meat cooked with onions, as in lamb dopiaza. [Hindi, from do two and pyāz onion]

doppelgänger /dop'l-geng'ər/ or **doppelganger** /-gang'/ n a ghostly double of a human person, an apparition; a wraith. [Ger, literally, double-goer]

Dopper /dop'ər/ n a Baptist or Anabaptist; a member of a strict and conservative denomination, an offshoot of the Dutch Reformed Church in South Africa. [Du dooper, from doopen to dip]

doppie see **dop¹**.

doppio movimento /dop'pi-ō mo-vē-men'tō/ (Ital; music) double speed.

Doppler('s) principle /dop'lər(z) prin'si-pl/ n the law of change of wave frequency (**Doppler effect** or **shift**) when a source of vibrations is moving towards or from the observer, explaining the fall of pitch of a railway whistle when the engine passes, and enabling astronomers to measure the radial velocity of stars by the displacement of known lines of the spectrum. [From Christian Doppler (1803–53), Austrian physicist, who announced it in 1842]

dopplerite /dop'lə-rīt/ n a black elastic substance (calcium salts of humus acids) found in peat beds. [Named after Christian Doppler; see ety for **Doppler('s) principle**]

dopy see under **dope**.

Dor. abbrev : Doric.

dor² or **dorr** /dör/ n a kind of dung-beetle, also called **dor'-beetle** and **dor'-fly**; a cockchafer (in USA called **dor'-bug**); a drone (obs). [OE dora a humble-bee]
❑ **dor'hawk** n the nightjar.

Dora /dö'rä or dö'/ (inf; hist) n the Defence of the Realm Act (1914) which imposed wartime restrictions.

dorado /də-rä'dō/ n (pl **dora'dos**) the coryphene, a large edible marine fish, so called from its iridescent gold/blue colour when dying; the so-called golden salmon, a S American river fish (genus Salminus) of the Characinidae; (with cap) a small southern constellation, the Swordfish. [Sp, from dorar to gild, from L deaurāre, -ātum; see **dory¹**, and **El Dorado**]

Doras /dö'ras or dö'/ n a S American genus of Siluridae, bony-plated river fish with spines, with the habit of walking overland when drought threatens. [Gr dory spear]
■ **do'rad** n any member of the genus, or of the group to which it belongs.

Dorcas /dör'kəs/ n in the Bible (Acts 9.36), the name of a woman famous for good works, hence **Dorcas society** a ladies' society for making and providing clothes for the poor. [Gr dorkas, literal translation of Aramaic Tabitha, meaning gazelle]

doree see **dory¹**.

Dorian /dö'ri-ən or dö'/ adj belonging to Doris in Greece or to the Dorians; Doric. ◆ n a native of Doris; a member of one of the main divisions of the ancient Greeks who arrived about 1100BC and made their home in Doris, SE Peloponnese, Crete, Rhodes, etc. [L Dōrius, from Gr Dōrios, from Dōris]
❑ **Dorian mode** n a mode of ancient Greek music consisting of two tetrachords with a semitone between the two lowest notes in each, the tetrachords separated by a whole tone (as efga or bcde, but reckoned downwards by the Greeks), traditionally of a stirring, solemn, simple and martial quality; an authentic mode of old church music, extending from d to d with d as its final.

Doric /dor'ik/ adj belonging to Doris in Greece, or the Dorians, or their dialect; denoting one of the Greek orders of architecture, distinguished by its simplicity and massive strength. ◆ n an Ancient Greek dialect; any dialect thought to resemble it, esp that of NE Scotland. [L Dōricus, from Gr Dōrikos, from Dōris]
■ **Doricism** /dor'i-sizm/ n a peculiarity of the Doric dialect. **Dō'rism** n Doricism; a Dorian characteristic. **dör'ize** or **-ise** vt and vi to render or become like the Dorians, in language, manners, etc.

Doris /dö'ris or dö'/ n a genus of nudibranchiate gastropods, shell-less molluscs with a plumy tuft of gills on the back, giving name to the family **Dorid'idae**. [Gr Dōris a sea-goddess]
■ **do'ridoid** n and adj.

dork /dörk/ (sl) n an idiot, an object of contempt; a socially inept person; the penis (US).
■ **dork'ish** adj. **dork'y** adj.

Dorking /dör'king/ n a square-bodied breed of poultry, variously coloured, and with five claws on each foot. [Named after Dorking in Surrey]

dorlach /dör'lahh/ (Scot) n a bundle, a truss; a sheaf; a valise. [Gaelic]

dorm /dörm/ (inf) n short for **dormitory**.

dormant /dör'mənt/ adj sleeping; hibernating; (of seeds, etc) alive but not active or growing; (of volcanoes) inactive but not extinct; torpid, lethargic; resting; not used, in abeyance (as a title); in a sleeping posture (heraldry). ◆ n a crossbeam; a joist. [OFr dormant, prp of dormir, from L dormīre to sleep]
■ **dor'mancy** n.

dormer /dör'mər/ n a dormer window; a dormitory or bedroom (obs). [OFr dormeor, from L dormītōrium, from dormīre to sleep]
❑ **dormer window** n a small window with a gable, projecting from a sloping roof (orig a dormitory window).

dormie see **dormy**.

dormient /dör'mi-ənt/ (archaic) adj sleeping; dormant. [L dormiēns, -entis, prp of dormīre to sleep]

dormition /dör-mish'ən/ n falling asleep; death. [Fr, from L dormīre to sleep]
■ **dor'mitive** n and adj soporific.

dormitory /dör'mi-tə-ri/ n a large sleeping-room with many beds, whether in separate cubicles or not; a resting place; a college hostel (US); a small town or a suburb (also **dormitory town** or **suburb**), the majority of whose residents work elsewhere. [L dormītōrium, from dormīre to sleep]
❑ **dor'mitory-car** n (US) a railway sleeping-carriage.

Dormobile® /dör'mə-bēl/ n a type of van equipped for living and sleeping in.

dormouse /dör'mows/ n (pl **dor'mice**) any member of a family of rodents related to mice but somewhat squirrel-like in form and habit. [Perh connected with L dōrmīre to sleep (from their hibernation) and prob **mouse**]

dormy or **dormie** /dör'mi/ adj (in golf) as many holes ahead as there are still to play. [Perh connected with L dormīre to sleep; the player who is dormy cannot lose even by going to sleep]

dornick /dör'nik/ n a kind of stout figured linen, originally made at Doornik or Tournai in Belgium.

doronicum /dər-on'i-kəm/ n a composite plant of the genus Doronicum, having yellow, daisy-like flower-heads. [L, from Ar dorunaj]

Dorothy bag /dor'ə-thi bag/ n a type of ladies' handbag closed by draw-strings at the top and hung from the wrist.

dorp /dörp/ n a Dutch or S African village or small town; a town considered as provincial and backward (inf; derog). [Du and Afrik dorp; OE thorp]

dorr see **dor²**.

Dors. abbrev : Dorset.

dorsal /dör'sl/ adj relating or belonging to the back. ◆ n a dorsal fin; a dorsal vertebra; a dossal. [L dorsum the back]
■ **dor'sally** adv. **dorse** n the back of a book or writing; a dossal; the back. **dor'sel** n a dossal. **dor'ser** n a dosser. **dorsibranchiate** /-brangk'/ adj having gills on the back. **dorsif'erous** adj having sori on the back (bot); carrying young on the back (zool). **dor'sifixed** adj (bot; of an anther) attached by the whole length of the back to the filament. **dor'siflex** adj bent towards the back. **dorsiflex'ion** n a bending backwards; a bending of the back, a bow. **dor'sigrade** adj walking on the back of the toes. **dorsiven'tral** adj possessing two sides distinguishable as upper or ventral and lower or dorsal (eg as a leaf). **dorsiventral'ity** n. **dorsolat'eral** adj of or relating to both dorsal and lateral surfaces. **dorsolum'bar** adj of or relating to the dorsal and lumbar vertebrae, or the area of the body that they occupy. **dorsoven'tral** adj flat, and possessing dorsal and ventral surfaces; dorsiventral. **dor'sum** n (pl **dor'sa**) the back.
❑ **dorsal suture** n the seam at the midrib of a carpel.
■ **send to dorse** (obs sl) to throw on the back.

■ words derived from main entry word; ❑ compound words; ■ idioms and phrasal verbs

dorse¹ /dörs/ n a small cod. [Low Ger *dorsch*]

dorse², **dorsel**, **dorser** see under **dorsal**.

dort /dört/ (*Scot*) *vi* to sulk. [Origin unknown]
■ **dorts** n pl sulks. **dor'ty** adj pettish; delicate.

dorter or **dortour** /dör'tər/ (*archaic*) n a dormitory, *esp* monastic. [OFr *dortour*, from L *dormītōrium*; see under **dormer** and **dormitory**]

dory¹ /dö'ri, dö'/ n a golden-yellow sea fish (*Zeus faber*) (also called **John Dory** and **doree**). [Fr *dorée*, from *dorer* to gild, from L *deaurāre* to gild, from *dē-*, in the sense of over, and *aurum* gold]

dory² /dö'ri or dö'/ (*esp US*) n a small boat, with flat bottom, sharp bow and stern, especially suited for surf-riding. [Perh from a Central American language]

DOS /dos/ (*comput*) *abbrev* : denial of service; disk operating system (see **disk**).

dos or **do's** see **do¹**.

dos-à-dos /dō-zä-dö'/ adv (*archaic*) back to back. ◆ n a sofa constructed for sitting so; /dō-sē-dö'/ a square-dance figure in which dancers pass each other back to back (also **dosi-do'** (pl **dosi-dos'**)). [Fr]

dose /dōs, in Scotland commonly dōz/ n the quantity of medicine, electric current, X-rays, etc, administered at one time; a portion, *esp* a measured portion, of something given or added; anything disagreeable or medicinal to be taken; a bout, *esp* of an illness or something unpleasant; an infection with a sexually transmitted disease, *esp* gonorrhoea (*sl*). ◆ *vt* to order or give in doses; to give doses to. [Fr, from Gr *dosis* a giving, from *didonai* to give]
■ **dōs'age** n the practice, act or method of dosing; the regulation of dose; the addition of an ingredient; the proper size of dose. **dōsim'eter** n an instrument for measuring radiation, a small ionization chamber with a scale on which can be read the dose that has caused it partially to discharge (also **dose'-meter**). **dōsim'etry** n. **dōsiol'ogy** or **dosol'ogy** n the science of doses.
❑ **dose equivalent** n a quantity of absorbed radiation dosage, measured in sieverts or formerly in rems, being the value of the absorbed dose (qv below) adjusted to take account of the different effects different types of radiation have on the human body, etc.
■ **absorbed dose** the amount of radiation absorbed by a body, etc, measured in grays or (*esp* formerly) rads.

doseh /dö'se/ n a religious ceremony at Cairo (abolished 1884), during the festival of the Prophet's birth, when the sheikh of the Sa'di dervishes rode on horseback over the prostrate bodies of his followers. [Ar *dawsah* treading]

dosh /dosh/ (*sl*) n money. [Poss *dollars* and ca*sh*]

dosi-do see **dos-à-dos**.

doss /dos/ (*sl*) n a bed, sleeping-place (*esp* in a dosshouse); a sleep; a task very easily accomplished. ◆ *vi* to sleep; to go to bed; (with *around*) to lead an idle or aimless existence. [Perh from *doss*, a dialectal Eng name for a hassock; or perh **dorse** (see under **dorsal**)]
■ **doss'er** n a person who lodges in a dosshouse, or wherever they can, a vagrant.
❑ **doss'house** n a very cheap lodging-house.
■ **doss down** to go to bed in a dosshouse, or in a makeshift bed elsewhere.

dossal or **dossel** /dos'əl/ n a cloth hanging for the back of an altar, sides of a church chancel, etc. [LL *dossāle*, *dorsāle*, from L *dorsum* back]

dosser¹, **dosshouse** see under **doss**.

dosser² /dos'ər/ (*hist*) n a rich hanging or tapestry for the walls of a hall or of a chancel; a pannier. [OFr *dossier*, from *dos*, from L *dorsum* back]

dossier /dos'i-ā, do-syā', dos'i-ər/ (*orig law*) n a set of documents relating to a person, event or case; a brief. [Fr, from *dos*, from L *dorsum* back]

dossil /dos'il/ n a plug, spigot; a cloth roll for wiping ink from an engraved plate in printing; a pledget or wad of lint for dressing a wound (*surg*). [OFr *dosil*, from LL *ducillus* a spigot]

dost see **do¹**.

dot¹ /dot/ n a very small spot, a speck or mark; (in writing and printing) such a mark used as a full stop or point, one of a series used to indicate an omission, used to form the letters *i* and *j* or used as a diacritic; the symbol representing the short element in the written representation of Morse code; the symbol for the decimal point (*maths*); the symbol indicating multiplication or logical conjunction (*logic, maths*); the symbol used after a note or rest to indicate that its length is increased by half its value (*music*); the symbol used above or below a note to indicate that it should be played staccato (*music*); anything like a dot, a very small object; a very small amount. ◆ *vt* (**dott'ing; dott'ed**) to mark with a dot or dots; to scatter with objects;

to jot; to hit (*sl*); to place or stand, etc at irregular and relatively widely spaced intervals. ◆ *vi* to form dots; to limp. [OE has *dott* head of a boil; Du *dot* tuft, knot]
■ **dott'ed** adj composed of dots; marked with a dot or dots. **dott'iness** n. **dott'y** adj feeble-minded, eccentric (*inf*); (with *about*) crazy about, extremely fond of (*inf*); composed of or covered with dots; unsteady (*inf*).
❑ **dot ball** n (*cricket*) a ball from which no runs are scored (conventionally recorded on a scorecard with a dot). **dot matrix** n (*comput*) a method of printing using a rectangular matrix consisting of lines of pins, a selection of which is used to make each letter shape (hence **dot matrix printer**). **dotted line** n a line composed of dots or dashes that (on printed forms, etc) one is instructed to sign on or tear along, etc. **dotted note** or **rest** n (*music*) one whose length is increased by one half by a dot placed after it. **dotted rhythm** n one characterized by the use of dotted notes.
■ **dot and carry** (*maths*) to set down the units and carry over the tens to the next column. **dot one's i's and cross one's t's** to pay great attention to detail. **dotted around** or **over**, etc here and there. **on the dot (of)** exactly (at) (a given time). **the year dot** (*inf*) the very beginning of time.

dot² /dot/ n a marriage portion. [Fr, from L *dōs, dōtis*]
■ **dot'al** adj relating to dowry or to dower. **dōtā'tion** n the bestowing of a dowry; an endowment.

dotcom or **dot-com** /dot-kom'/ adj (of business) relating to or conducted on the Internet; (of a company) trading through the Internet or in products relating especially to electronic communications. ◆ n a dotcom company. [Pronunciation of *.com*, often part of the Internet address of companies trading through it]
■ **dotcomm'er** n a person who conducts business on the Internet.

dote or **doat** /dōt/ *vi* to be weakly affectionate; to show excessive love (with *upon* or *on*); to be stupid or foolish (*archaic*); (of timber) to decay. [Cf Old Du *doten* to be silly; Fr *radoter* to rave, is from the same root]
■ **dot'age** n a doting; the weakness and childishness of old age; excessive fondness. **dōt'ant** n (*Shakesp*) a dotard. **dōt'ard** n someone who dotes; someone showing the weakness of old age, or excessive fondness. **dōt'ed** adj (*obs*) stupid. **dōt'er** or **doat'er** n someone who dotes. **dōt'ing** or **doat'ing** adj and n. **dot'ingly** adv. **dōt'ish** adj silly. **dōt'y** adj (*dialect*) decaying (of timber).
❑ **dot'ing-piece** or **doat'ing-piece** n someone who is doted on.

doth see **do¹**.

dot matrix, **dotted** see under **dot¹**.

DOTS *abbrev* : Directly Observed Therapy, Short-course, a closely supervised drug treatment for tuberculosis.

dotterel or **dottrel** /dot'(ə-)rəl/ n a kind of plover, named from its apparent stupidity in allowing itself to be approached and caught; a stupid fellow, a dupe. [**dote**]

dottiness, **dotting** see **dot¹**.

dottipoll see **doddypoll**.

dottle¹ /dot'l/ n a plug, *esp* of tobacco left at the bottom of a pipe. [**dot¹**]

dottle² /dot'l/ (*Scot*) n a fool, a silly person, a dotard. ◆ adj (also **dott'led**) foolish, crazy; in dotage. [**dote**]

dottrel see **dotterel**.

dotty see under **dot¹**.

doty see under **dote**.

douane /doo-än' or dwän/ n a custom house. [Fr, from Ar *dīwān*; cf **divan** and **diwan**]
■ **douanier** /dwä-nyä'/ n a custom-house officer.

douar /doo'är/ see **duar**.

Douay Bible /doo'ā (among Catholics often dow'ǐ) bī'bl/ n an English Roman Catholic translation of the Bible, the New Testament in the Rhemish version (qv), the Old Testament done in 1609–10 at *Douai* in N France.

double /dub'l/ adj twofold; twice as much; of about twice the weight, size, quality or strength; two of a sort together; in pairs; paired; for two people; having two interpretations, ambiguous; acting two parts, insincere, hypocritical, deceitful; folded once; duple, having two beats in a bar (*music*); sounding an octave lower (*music*); having stamens in the form of petals, or having ligulate in place of tubular florets (*bot*). ◆ *adv* to twice the extent; twice over; two together; deceitfully. ◆ *vt* to multiply by two; to make twofold; to make twice as much or as many; to be the double of; (in acting) to play (two parts) in the one production; to be a substitute for or counterpart of; (in bridge) to raise the scores at stake in (a hand); to duplicate in unison or in another octave above or below (*music*); to line (*heraldry*); to fold; to clench (one's fist(s)); to pass (*esp* sail) round or by; to cause (a ball) to rebound (*snooker*, etc); in chess, to place two pawns or two rooks of the same colour on the same file, one behind the other. ◆ *vi* to increase to twice the quantity; to turn sharply back on one's course; to go or move at twice the usual speed; to act as substitute; to perform two functions, to serve in two capacities; to understudy (*usu* with *for*; *theatre*); (in acting) to play two different parts in the same piece; to (be able to) play one or more musical instruments in addition to one's usual one (*music*); (in bridge) to make a double (bid); (of a ball) to rebound from a cushion (*snooker*, etc). ◆ *n* a quantity twice as much; a double measure of spirits (*inf*); the score of twice the normal amount as a reward for hitting the narrow outer ring of a dartboard; a hit on this (*darts*); a stroke causing the ball one hits to rebound against a cushion and into the opposite pocket (*snooker*, etc); a combination of two things of the same kind (such as a binary star); (in *pl*) a game with two players on each side (*tennis*, etc); a double fault, two faults in succession (*tennis*); a bid that increases declarer's score for the hand if the contract is made and increases the penalty if the contract is defeated (*bridge*); a win or a defeat in two events on the same programme, in the same championship or series, or against the same opponent; a combined bet on two races, stake and winnings from the first being bet on the second; a Guernsey copper coin, ⅛th of a penny; a duplicate; an actor's substitute; a quick pace, at twice the speed of a normal march; one's wraith or apparition; an exact counterpart; a turning upon one's course; a trick; a feast on which the antiphon is said both before and after the psalms (*relig*); a size of roofing slate, 330×152mm (13×6in). [OFr *doble*, from L *duplus* double, from *duo* two, and the root seen in Eng **fold**[1], Gr *haploos*]

■ **doub'leness** *n* the state of being double; duplicity. **doub'ler** *n* someone who or something that doubles. **doub'leton** *n* (the possession of) two cards of a suit in a hand. **doub'ling** *n* the act of making double; a turning back in running; a trick; a plait or fold; mantling (*heraldry*). ◆ *adj* shifting, manoeuvring. **doub'ly** *adv*.

❑ **double act** *n* (*theatre*) a variety act for two people to perform; the two entertainers. **doub'le-act'ing** *adj* applying power in two directions; producing a double result. **double agent** *n* an agent secretly acting simultaneously for two opposing powers. **double-axe'** *n* a religious symbol of Minoan Crete and the Aegean, a double-headed axe, associated with the mother-goddess and her son (Zeus). **double axel** *n* (*ice skating*) an axel incorporating two and a half turns. **double-bank'** *vt* and *vi* to double-park; to ride two at a time on a bicycle or horse, etc (*Aust* and *NZ*). **doub'le-banked'** *adj* having two men at each oar, or having two tiers of oars one above the other, as in ancient galleys; double-parked. **doub'le-banking** *n* double-parking. **double bar** *n* a double vertical line or a single heavy vertical one marking the end of a movement or piece of music or one of its important divisions. **doub'le-barr'elled** or (*N Am*) **doub'le-barr'eled** *adj* having two barrels; (of a surname) hyphenated; (of a compliment) ambiguous. **double bass** *n* the largest and lowest-pitched instrument of the violin family, playing an octave below the cello. **double bassoon** see under **bassoon**. **double bed** *n* a bed wide enough for two people. **double bill** see under **bill**[1]. **double bind** *n* (*psychiatry*) a situation in which conflicting cues are given so that any choice of behaviour will be considered wrong; a dilemma. **doub'le-bit'ing** *adj* cutting on either side. **doub'le-blind'** *adj* denoting a comparative experiment or trial, etc in which the identities of the control group are known neither to the subjects nor to the experimenters. **double bluff** *n* an action or statement meant to seem to be a bluff, but in fact genuine. **double boiler** *n* (*N Am*) a double saucepan. **double bond** *n* (*chem*) a covalent bond involving the sharing of two pairs of electrons. **doub'le-book'** *vt* to accept two reservations for (the same room, seat or time, etc). **doub'le-bott'om** or **double-bottom lorry** *n* an articulated lorry pulling a second trailer (also **drawbar outfit**). **doub'le-breast'ed** *adj* (of a coat, etc) having two fronts, one overlapping the other. **double bridle** *n* a bridle with two sets of reins. **doub'le-bubb'le** *n* (*prison sl*) one hundred per cent interest. **doub'le-charge'** *vt* to load with double measure; to charge twice for (an item, service, etc). **doub'le-check'** *vt* and *vi* to check a second time (also *n*). **double chin** *n* a chin with a fold of flesh beneath it. **doub'le-chinn'ed** *adj*. **doub'le-click** *vi* (*comput*) to click the button of a mouse two times in rapid succession to select an option, start a program, etc. **double coconut** *n* the coco-de-mer. **double concerto** *n* a concerto for two solo instruments. **double cream** *n* a cream with a higher fat content than single cream. **doub'le-cross** *n* a betrayal or deceiving of someone for whom one was supposed to be betraying or deceiving someone else. ◆ *vt* /-*kros*/ to betray by double-cross. **doub'le-cross'er** *n*. **double dagger** see under **dagger**. **doub'le-deal'er** *n* a deceitful person. **doub'le-deal'ing** *n* duplicity, deceit (also *adj*). **doub'le-decked** *adj* having two decks or layers. **doub'le-deck'er** *n* a double-decked ship; a bus, tram-car, etc in two storeys or tiers; a sandwich having three pieces of bread and two layers of filling; a novel or film, etc in two separate parts; anything consisting of two layers (*inf*). **doub'le-declutch'** *vi* (*motoring*) to change into a different gear by first changing to neutral, increasing the engine speed, then engaging the chosen gear, disengaging the clutch at both stages. **doub'le-decomposi'tion** *n* a chemical action in which two compounds exchange some of their

constituents. **doub'le-dens'ity** *adj* (*comput*) (of a disk) capable of recording double the normal number of bytes. **double digging** *n* the practice in gardening of digging trenches two spade-lengths deep and replacing the lower level of soil in one trench with the upper level of another. **doub'le-dig'it** *adj* double-figure. **double dip** or **double-dip** *n* and *adj* (denoting) a twofold action or occurrence (*inf*); (denoting) a recession in which a brief period of growth is followed by another decline (*econ*). ◆ *vi* to carry out an action once and then again; to derive an income, *usu* illicitly, from two different sources simultaneously (*US*). **double disapproval** *n* an arrangement by which airlines are free to set the level of fares for a route unless the governments at both ends of the route raise objections to the rate set. **double door** or **doors** *n* a door consisting of two parts hung on opposite posts. **double-dotted note** or **rest** *n* (*music*) one whose length is increased by three-quarters, marked by two dots placed after it. **double-dotted rhythm** *n* one characterized by double-dotted notes. **double Dutch** see under **Dutch**. **doub'le-dyed** *adj* twice-dyed; deeply imbued; inveterate, confirmed. **double eagle** *n* (*US*) a gold coin worth \$20; a heraldic representation of an eagle with two heads, as in the old arms of Russia and Austria. **doub'le-edged'** *adj* having two edges; cutting or working both ways. **doub'le-end'er** *n* anything having two ends alike; a crosscut sawing machine with two adjustable circular saws for sawing both ends of timber. **double entendre** *n* see separate entry. **doub'le-en'try** *n* (*bookkeeping*) a method of recording accounts by which each transaction is entered twice, showing both the financing for a business and what values the business owns. **double exposure** *n* (*photog*) the accidental or deliberate superimposition of one image on another. **doub'le-eyed** *adj* doubly keen of sight. **doub'le-faced** *adj* hypocritical, false; (of fabric, etc) finished so that either side may be used as the right side. **doub'le-fa'cedness** /-*sid*-/ *n*. **double fault** *n* (*tennis*, etc) two faults served in succession, causing the loss of a point. **doub'le-fault'** *vi*. **double feature** *n* a cinema programme involving two full-length films. **doub'le-fig'ure** *adj*. **double figures** *n pl* a score or total, etc of any number equal to or greater than 10 but less than 100. **double first** *n* a university degree with first-class honours in two different subjects; a person who has such a degree. **double flat** *n* (*music*) a note already flat flattened again by a semitone; a sign (♭♭) indicating this. **doub'le-flow'ered** *adj* (of a plant) having double flowers. **doub'le-formed'** *adj* having, or combining, two forms. **doub'le-fount'ed** *adj* having two sources. **doub'le-front'ed** *adj* (of a house) having main-room windows on both sides of the front door. **doub'le-gild** *vt* to gild with double coatings of gold; to gloss over. **doub'le-glazed'** *adj*. **doub'le-glaz'ing** *n* a double layer of glass in a window with an air-space between the layers to act as insulation; the provision of this. **double Gloucester** or **double Gloster** /*glos'tər*/ *n* a Gloucestershire cheese of extra richness. **doub'le-hand'ed** *adj* having two hands; two-handled. **doub'le-head'ed** *adj* having two heads. **double-head'er** *n* a coin with a head on each side (*inf*; *esp Aust*); two games played on the same day (*sport*; *N Am*); two television programmes or other items of the same kind in succession; a train pulled by two locomotives coupled together. **doub'le-heart'ed** *adj* treacherous. **double helix** *n* the DNA molecule, two spirals coiled round an axis. **doub'le-hung** *adj* (of a window) having top and bottom sashes each balanced by sash-cord and weights, so as to be capable of vertical movement in its own groove. **double indemnity** *n* (*US*) a payment of twice the face value of a life insurance policy because the insured has died in an accident. **double jeopardy** *n* second trial for the same offence. **doub'le-joint'ed** *adj* having loose joints admitting some degree of movement backwards. **double knit** *n* a fabric knitted on two sets of needles, producing a double thickness joined by interlocking stitches. **doub'le-knit** *adj*. **double knitting** *n* a knitting yarn of medium thickness. **doub'le-lived'** *adj* having two lives. **doub'le-locked'** *adj* locked with two locks or bolts; locked by two turns of the key, as in some locks and many novels. **double majority** *n* (in the voting system of the European Union) a majority both in terms of the number of member states and in terms of the proportion of the EU's population represented, required before the Council can take any decision. **doub'le-manned'** *adj* supplied with twice the complement of men. **doub'le-mean'ing** *adj* ambiguous (also *n*). **doub'le-mind'ed** *adj* lacking determination, wavering. **doub'le-mind'edness** *n*. **doub'le-mouthed'** *adj* speaking with contradictory voices. **doub'le-na'tured** *adj* having a twofold nature. **double negation** *n* the principle that the negation of a negation of a proposition means the same as the proposition. **double negative** *n* a construction consisting of two negatives, *esp* when only one is logically required. **double obelisk** *n* (*printing*) a double dagger (see above). **double-page spread** or **double spread** *n* the two facing pages of a publication, as used for an advertisement or illustration, etc across both pages. **doub'le-park'** *vt* and *vi* to park (a car, etc) alongside vehicles already parked at the kerb. **double play** *n* (*baseball*) a play putting out two runners. **double pneumonia** *n* pneumonia of both lungs. **doub'le-quick'** *adj* and *adv* at a pace approaching a run; very fast. ◆ *n* the double-quick pace. **double reed** *n* a reed in a woodwind instrument which is composed of two halves vibrating against each

other. **double refraction** see under **refract**. **double rollover** n a second consecutive rollover in a lottery, etc. **double salt** n a salt whose crystals dissolve to give two different salts in solution. **double saucepan** n a pair of saucepans, the top one fitting closely into the lower one, and heated by boiling water in the lower one. **doub'le-shade'** vt (Milton) to double the darkness of. **doub'le-sharp'** n (music) a note already sharp sharpened again by a semitone; a sign (𝄪) indicating this. **doub'le-shott'ed** adj (of cannon) with double charge. **doub'le-shuff'le** n a scraping movement made twice with each foot; a dance of such steps; a trick. **doub'le-space'** vt and vi to type with a space of one line between each typed line. **double spacing** n. **doub'lespeak** n double-talk. **double spread** see **double-page spread** above. **double standard** n a principle, etc applied in such a way as to allow different standards of behaviour to different people, groups, etc; (in pl) the practice of advocating (for others) certain moral, etc standards not followed by oneself; bimetallism. **double star** n (astron) a binary star; two unrelated stars appearing close together when seen through a telescope. **doub'le-stopp'ing** n (music) simultaneous playing on two (stopped) strings of an instrument at once. **doub'le-sto'rey** adj (of a building) having two floors or tiers. **doub'le-stout'** n extra strong stout or porter. **double take** n an inattentive initial look followed by a second look impelled by surprise or admiration; delayed reaction. **doub'le-talk** n talk that sounds relevant but means nothing; ambiguous, deceptive talk. **doub'lethink** n the faculty of simultaneously harbouring two conflicting beliefs (coined by George Orwell in his novel Nineteen Eighty-Four). **double-threaded screw** n (engineering) a screw having two threads, whose pitch is half the lead (also **two-start thread**). **double time** n payment to a worker at twice the usual rate; a time twice as fast as the previous time (music); a slow running pace, a regulation running pace keeping in step as a troop; a fast marching pace (US). **double-tongue'** vi (music) to produce a staccato sound by rapid articulation when playing fast passages on a wind instrument (**double-tongu'ing** n). **doub'le-tongued'** adj having two tongues or a cleft tongue; self-contradictory; deceitful. **double top** n (darts) a score of double twenty. **double vision** n seeing two images of the same object, because of lack of co-ordination between the two eyes. **double-u** or **double-you** /dub'l-ū/ n the twenty-third letter of the modern English alphabet (W or w). **double wedding** n a wedding involving two couples. **double whammy** see **whammy** under **wham**. **double witching (hour)** n (stock exchange) the final hour of certain periods of trading, when two kinds of future and option contracts expire and the market is exposed to volatility (cf **triple witching (hour)** under **triple**). **double zero option** see **zero-zero option** under **zero**. **doubling time** n (nuclear eng) the time required for the neutron flux in a reactor to double; in a breeder reactor, the time required for the amount of fissile material to double.
■ **at the double** very quickly. **bent double** folded; doubled up, bending forward; stooping. **double back** to go back in the direction one has just come, but usu not by the same route. **double or quits** (in gambling) the alternative, left to chance, of doubling or cancelling payment (**double'-or-quits'** adj). **double up** to fold double; to clench (one's fists); to bend over (as with laughter or pain); to come at the double; to share with another; to join together, couple.

double entendre /doo-blã-tã'dr'/ n (the use of) a word or phrase with two meanings, one usually more or less indecent. [Fr of 17c, superseded now by (mot) à double entente]

doublet /dub'lit/ n a close-fitting garment for the upper part of the body with hose, the typical masculine dress during the 14–17c; a thing that is repeated or duplicated; one of a pair, esp one of two words orig the same but varying in spelling and meaning, eg balm, balsam. [OFr, dimin of double]

doubloon /dub-loon'/ n an obsolete Spanish gold coin, originally worth 2 pistoles. [Sp doblón, augmentative of doble double; see **double**]

doublure /də-blür'/ n a lining, esp of leather, inside the cover of a book. [Fr, lining]

doubly see under **double**.

doubt /dowt/ vi to be undecided in opinion; to be apprehensive (obs). ♦ vt to be uncertain about; to question; to hesitate or scruple; to incline to believe only with fear or hesitation; to distrust; to incline to think (esp Scot); to suspect (archaic; also reflexive); to cause to doubt or fear (obs). ♦ n uncertainty of opinion; a suspicion; fear (obs); a thing doubtful or questioned (obs); danger (obs; Spenser). [OFr douter, from L dubitāre, related to dubius doubtful, moving in two (duo) directions]
■ **doubt'able** adj. **doubt'ed** adj questioned; feared, redoubted (Spenser). **doubt'er** n. **doubt'ful** adj feeling or full of doubt; undetermined; subject to doubt; not clear; insecure; suspicious; not confident; not likely or not certain to participate, co-operate, etc. ♦ n a doubtful person or thing. **doubt'fully** adv. **doubt'fulness** n. **doubt'ing** n and adj. **doubt'ingly** adv. **doubt'less** adj free from doubt or (obs; Shakesp, etc) fear. ♦ adv without doubt; certainly; no doubt (often only allowing for the possibility). **doubt'lessly** adv.

❑ **doubting Thomas** n a doubter or sceptic; someone who needs proof before believing something (from the doubting of Thomas, in Bible, John 20.25).
■ **beyond doubt** or **beyond a shadow of doubt** certain or certainly. **in doubt** not certain, undecided. **no doubt** surely. **without (a) doubt** certainly.

douc /dook/ n a variegated monkey of SE Asia. [Fr, from Cochin name]

douce /doos/ adj sweet (obs); sober, peaceable, sedate (Scot). [Fr doux, douce mild, from L dulcis sweet]
■ **douce'ly** adv. **douce'ness** n. **doucet** or **dowset** /doo'sit or dow'/ n (obs) a sweet dish; (in pl) a deer's testicles. **douceur** /doo-sûr'/ n sweetness of manner (obs); a compliment (archaic); a conciliatory present, bribe or tip.

doucepere see under **douzepers**.

douche /doosh/ n a jet of water directed upon or into the body from a pipe, etc; an apparatus for producing such a jet. ♦ vt and vi to use a douche (on). [Fr, from Ital doccia a water pipe, from L dūcere to lead]
❑ **douche bag** n a bag holding water for a douche; a contemptible person (sl).

doucine /doo-sēn'/ (archit) n a cyma recta. [Fr]

dough /dō/ n a mass of flour or meal moistened and kneaded, but not baked; money (sl). [OE dāh dough; Ger Teig, ON deig dough; cf **duff¹**]
■ **dough'iness** n. **dough'y** adj like dough; soft; (of complexion) pallid, pasty.
❑ **dough'-baked** adj half-baked, defective in intelligence. **dough'ball** n a boiled flour dumpling. **dough'boy** n a doughball; an American infantryman (milit sl). **dough'faced** adj over-persuadable, specif of Northern politicians sympathetic towards the Southern cause before the American Civil War. **dough'-kneaded** adj (Milton) soft. **dough'nut** or (esp US) **donut** n a ring or ball of sweetened dough fried in fat; any object shaped like a ring; an accelerating tube in the form of a toroid (nucleonics); a toroidal assembly of enriched fissile material for increasing locally the neutron intensity in a reactor for experimental purposes, a tokamak (also **toroid**; nucleonics); a pile of annular laminations in toroidal shape for magnetic testing or a loading coil in toroidal shape on transmission lines, permitting exact balance in addition to inductance (elec eng). ♦ vi to practise doughnutting. **dough'nutting** n the surrounding of a speaker in parliament by other members to give an impression, esp to television viewers, of a packed house.

dought see **dow²**.

doughty /dow'ti/ adj able, strong; brave. [OE dyhtig (later dohtig) valiant, from dugan to be strong; Ger tüchtig able]
■ **dough'tily** adv. **dough'tiness** n.

Douglas fir /dug'ləs fûr/ n a tall W American coniferous timber tree (Pseudotsuga douglasii). [David Douglas (1798–1834), the Scottish botanist who introduced it to Britain]

Doukhobor see **Dukhobor**.

doula /doo'lə/ n a woman whose job is to provide emotional and physical, but not medical, care to a woman in labour and to the parents and child after birth. [Gr doulē slave girl]

douleia, doulocracy see **dulia**.

douma see **duma**.

doum-palm /dowm'päm, doom'päm/ n an African palm (genus Hyphaene), with a branched stem, and a fruit with the taste of gingerbread (also **doom'-** or **dum'-palm**). [Ar daum, dūm]

doup /dowp/ (Scot) n the bottom section of an eggshell; the buttocks; the bottom or end of anything. [Cf ON daup a hollow]
■ **can'dle-doup** a candle-end.

dour /door or dow'ər/ adj obstinate, determined; sullen; grim. [Appar L dūrus hard]
■ **dour'ly** adv. **dour'ness** n.

doura see **durra**.

dourine /doo-rēn', doo'rēn/ n a contagious disease of horses due to a trypanosome. [Fr dourin]

douroucouli or **durukuli** /doo-rū-koo'lē/ n a night-ape, any monkey of the S American genus Aotus. [S American name]

douse¹ or **dowse** /dows/ vt to plunge into water. ♦ vi to fall suddenly into water. [Cf Swed dunsa fall heavily; prob from sound; cf **souse**]

douse² or **dowse** /dows/ vt to put out, extinguish (esp in the sl **douse the glim** to put out the light). [Perh connected with **dout¹** or with **douse³**]
■ **dous'er** n a shutter for cutting off light in a cinema projector.

douse³ or **dowse** /dows/ vt to strike or lower (a sail); to strike (obs). ♦ n a heavy blow. [Prob related to Old Du dossen to beat]

dout¹ /dowt/ vt to put out, extinguish. [do and out]
■ **dout'er** n.

dout² see **dowt**.

douzepers /doo'zə-pär/ (archaic) n pl the twelve peers of Charlemagne, or a similar group. [OFr douze pers twelve peers]
■ **dou'zeper** or **dou'cepere** n (Spenser) a champion, great knight or noble.

dove¹ /duv/ n a pigeon (often in combination, as eg ringdove, turtle-dove) and used esp of the smaller species; an old word of endearment; an emblem of innocence and gentleness, also of the Holy Spirit (Bible, Matthew 3.17); in politics and industrial relations, etc, a person who seeks peace and conciliation rather than confrontation or war, opp to hawk; (with cap) the constellation Columba; a tablet of the drug Ecstasy (often with a figure of a dove stamped on it, sl). ◆ vt to treat as a dove. [OE dūfe, found only in the compound dūfe-doppa a diving bird; Ger Taube].
■ **dove'ishness** n. **dove'let** n a small dove. **dove'like** adj like a dove; innocent. **dov'ish** or **dove'ish** adj dovelike; seeking peace and conciliation rather than confrontation or war.
❑ **dove'-colour** n dove grey. **dove'cot** or **dove'cote** n a small building or structure in which pigeons breed; a pigeon-house. **dove'-drawn** adj (Shakesp) drawn by doves. **dove'-eyed** adj meek-eyed. **dove grey** n a greyish, bluish, pinkish colour. **dove'-house** n a dovecot. **dove's'-foot** n a name for some species of cranesbill (Geranium dissectum, Geranium molle, etc). **dove'tail** n a tenon shaped like a dove's spread tail, for fastening boards; a joint of alternate tenons and mortises of that shape. ◆ vt and vi to fit by one or more dovetails; to fit or join together neatly (often with into or with). **dove'tailing** n. **dovetail saw** n a small tenon saw.
■ **flutter the dovecots** to disturb commonplace, conventional people, as the eagle would a dovecot (see Shakespeare, Coriolanus V.6.115).

dove² /dōv/ (Scot) vi to be half asleep or stupefied. [OE dofian to be stupid]
■ **dō'ver** vi (Scot) to snooze, doze. ◆ vt to stun. ◆ n a snooze; a swoon; half-consciousness. **dō'vie** adj (Scot) stupid.

dove³ /dōv/ N American pat of **dive**.

dovecot, doveish see under **dove¹**.

dovekie /duv'ki/ n the little auk or rotch; the black guillemot. [Dimin of **dove¹**]

dover see under **dove²**.

Dover sole same as **sole²**.

Dover's powder /dō'vərz pow'dər/ n a sudorific compounded of ipecacuanha root, opium and potassium sulphate (or, in the USA, lactose). [First prescribed by Dr Thomas Dover (1660–1742)]

dovetail, dovish see under **dove¹**.

dow¹ see **dhow**.

dow² /dow/ (obs and Scot) vi (3rd pers sing **dow** or **dows**; pat **docht**, **dought** /dohht/ or **dowed**) to be good for a purpose; to avail; to be able. [OE dugan]
■ **downa** /dow'nə/ cannot; cannot be bothered. **downa-do** powerlessness.

dowable see under **dower**.

dowager /dow'ə-jər/ n a widow with a dower or jointure; a title given to a widow to distinguish her from the wife of her husband's heir (also adj); an elderly woman of imposing appearance. [OFr douagere, from LL dōtārium dower, from L dōtāre to endow]
❑ **dowager's hump** n (inf) a prominent curvature of the spine below the base of the neck that can develop due to osteoporosis.

dowar see **duar**.

dowd /dowd/ or **dowdy** /dowd'i/ n a woman who wears dull-looking, clumsy, ill-shaped clothes. [Origin unknown]
■ **dowd'ily** adv. **dowd'iness** n. **dowd'y** adj (of clothes) dull, ill-shaped and unfashionable; (of a woman) habitually wearing such clothes. **dowd'yish** adj. **dowd'yism** n.

dowed see **dow²**.

dowel /dow'əl/ n a pin for fastening things together by fitting into a hole in each. ◆ vt to fasten by means of dowels. [Prob related to Ger Döbel, Dübel a plug]
■ **dow'elling** n long, thin, usu wooden rods of circular section.
❑ **dow'el-joint** n. **dow'el-pin** n. **dow'el-rod** n.

dower /dow'ər/ n a jointure; a dowry; an endowment. ◆ vt to give a dowry to; to endow. [OFr douaire, from LL dōtārium, from L dōtāre to endow]
■ **dow'able** adj that may be endowed. **dow'erless** adj.
❑ **dower house** n the house set apart for the widow, usu on her late husband's estate.

dowf /dowf/ (Scot) adj dull, heavy, spiritless. [Prob ON daufr deaf]
■ **dowf'ness** n.

dowie /dow'i/ (Scot) adj dull, low-spirited, sad; dismal. [Prob OE dol dull]

dowitcher /dow'i-chər/ n a name given to two species of sand piper (Limnodromus griseus and Limnodromus scolopaceus; family Scolopacidae), found in arctic and subarctic N America. [From Iroquoian]

Dow-Jones average or **index** /dow'jōnz' av'ə-rij or in'deks/ n an indicator of the relative prices of stocks and shares on the New York Stock Exchange, based on the average price of a certain agreed list of securities. [Charles H Dow (1851–1902), and Edward D Jones (1856–1920), American economists]

dowl or **dowle** /dowl/ (obs or dialect; Shakesp) n a portion of down in a feather; a piece of fluff. [Origin obscure]

dowlas /dow'ləs/ n a coarse linen cloth. [From Daoulas or Doulas, near Brest, in Brittany]

dowlne a Shakespearean spelling of **down²**. [By confusion with **dowl**]
■ **dowl'ney** adj (Shakesp) downy.

down¹ /down/ adv (passing into adj in predicative use) to a lower position, level or state; away from a centre (capital, city, university, etc); southwards; to leeward; in a low or lowered position or state; below; on or to the ground; downstairs; under the surface; from earlier to later times; to a further stage in a series; from greater to less (in size, grain, activity, intensity, etc); to a standstill, exhaustion or conclusion; to a final state of defeat, subjection, silence, etc; in a fallen state; in adversity; at a disadvantage; ill; behindhand; in writing or record, in black and white; in flood; on the spot, immediately in cash; in readiness to pounce; in a state of alert awareness and understanding; in watchful opposition or hostility (with on, upon); broken, not operational (comput). —Also used elliptically, passing into an interjection or verb by omission of go, come or put, etc, often followed by with. ◆ adj going, reaching, directed towards or having a lower position or level; depressed; low; broken, not operational (comput). ◆ prep in a descent along, through or by; to or in a lower position on or in; along in the direction of the current; along. ◆ n a descent; a low place; a reverse of fortune, a time of comparative bad luck; an act of throwing or putting down; a tendency to treat one harshly; a feeling of dislike; one of four consecutive periods of play, during which a team must score or advance the ball 10 yards in order to retain possession (American football). ◆ vt to knock, throw, shoot or put down; to put down, overthrow; to depress; to swallow. ◆ interj ordering (esp a dog) to go or stay down; (with with) expressing a wish for the downfall of someone or something. [ME a-down, adun, from OE of dūne from the hill (dative case of dūn hill; see **down³** and **adown**)]
■ **down'er** n (sl) a depressant drug; a state of depression; any depressing experience, etc; a downward trend; a feeling of prejudice or dislike, antipathy. **down'ward** /-wərd/ or **down'wards** /-wərdz/ adv from higher to lower; from source to outlet; from more ancient to modern; in the lower part. **down'ward** adj. **down'wardly** adv. **down'wardness** n a sinking tendency; a state of being low.
❑ **down'-and-dirt'y** adj (US inf) basic; brutal. **down'-and-out'** adj at the end of one's resources; destitute and rejected by, or rejecting, society. **down'-and-out'** n. **down'-and-out'er** n. **down'-at-heel'** adj having the back of the shoe trodden down; generally shabby. **down'beat** n a downward movement of the conductor's baton; an accented beat. ◆ adj (inf) relaxed, unworried; unemphatic; depressed; gloomy; depressing. **down'bow** n (music) a movement of the bow over the strings beginning at the nut end. **down'burst** same as **microburst**. **down'cast** adj dejected; looking down. ◆ n a current of air into a mine; a shaft carrying it (**down'cast-shaft**); a downward throw; a downthrow. **down'-come** n a fall, ruin; a heavy pour of rain. **down'-draught** n a current of air downwards. **down'-east'er** n (US) someone living down east from the speaker, a New Englander, and esp an inhabitant of Maine. **down'fall** n fall, failure, humiliation; ruin; a heavy fall of rain. **down'fallen** adj ruined. **down'flow** n a running or flowing down; something that runs or flows down. **down'force** n aerodynamically caused downward force in a car, etc which eg improves its road holding. **down'-going** adj. **down-go'ing** (or /down'-/) n. **down'grade** n a downward slope or course. ◆ adj and adv downhill. ◆ vt to reduce in status, etc; to belittle, underrate. **down'-gyved** adj (Shakesp) hanging down like fetters. **down'haul** n a rope by which a jib, etc is hauled down when set. **downheart'ed** adj dejected. **down'hill** adj descending, sloping (also n). **downhill'** adv. **down'hole** adj of the drills, measuring instruments, and equipment used down a borehole (mining); applied to equipment that is used within the well (oil). **down'-home** adj (US inf) characteristic of the Southern states of the USA; characteristic of the country or country-dwellers; homemade; friendly. **down'lighter** n a downward-directed light-fitting, attached to or recessed in the ceiling. **down'-line** n the line of a railway leading from the capital, or other important centre, to

the provinces. **down'link** *n* a connection in a telecommunications system between a space vehicle or satellite and the earth (also *vt*). **download'** *vt* and *vi* (*comput*) to transfer (data or programs, *esp* on the Internet) from another computer to one's own; to broadcast programmes of material for specialist groups (eg doctors) outside normal broadcasting hours (often to be recorded on videotape for viewing later). ◆ *n* /*down'*/ an act or the process of downloading; something downloaded. **download'able** *adj*. **down'looked** *adj* (*Dryden*) downcast, gloomy. **down'-ly'ing** *n* (*dialect*) time of retiring to rest; a woman's confinement during childbirth. **downmar'ket** *adj* of (buying, selling or using) goods and services of relatively low price, quality or prestige (also *adv*). **down'most** *adv* and *adj* superlative of *down*. **down payment** *n* a deposit on an article, service, etc. **down'pipe** *n* a drainpipe that takes rainwater from the gutter of a roof. **down'play** *vt* to play down. **down'pour** *n* a heavy fall of rain, etc. **down'right** *adv* in plain terms; utterly. ◆ *adj* plain-spoken; brusque; utter, out-and-out (as in *downright madness*); thorough; perpendicular (*obs*). **down'rightness** *n*. **downriv'er** *adv* with the current. ◆ *adj* further down the river. **down'rush** *n* a rushing down (as of gas, hot air, etc). **down'scale** *vt* and *vi* (*US*) to reduce in scale. ◆ *adj* downmarket. **down'-sett'ing** *n* a setting down, a snub. **down'shift** *vi* to select a lower gear in a vehicle; to choose a less affluent lifestyle in order to enhance one's life in non-material ways, *esp* in having more leisure time. **down'shifter** *n*. **down'shifting** *n*. **down'side** *n* the adverse or disadvantageous aspect of a situation (also *adj*); (the risk of) a drop in share prices (*finance*). **down'-sitt'ing** *n* sitting down, time of rest (Psalm 139.2); a sitting, session (*Scot*); a settlement, establishment (*esp* by marriage; *Scot*). **down'size** *vt* to reduce in size (*esp* a workforce by redundancy); to design or make a smaller model of (a car, etc). ◆ *vi* to sell one's home and move to a smaller property. **down'sizer** *n*. **down'sizing** *n*. **down'spout** *n* (*N Am*) a downpipe, drainpipe. **down'stage** *adv* towards the footlights (also *adj*). **down'stair** or **down'stairs** *adj*. **downstairs'** *adv* in or towards a lower storey; belowstairs, in the servants' quarters. ◆ *n* a lower storey, *usu* the ground floor. **down'state'** *adj* and *adv* (*US*) in or to a southerly or rural part of a state. ◆ *n* a downstate area. **downstream'** *adv* with the current. ◆ *adj* /*down'*/ further down the stream; going with the current; in the hydrocarbons industry, denoting any stage subsequent to oil production, eg refining, the production of oil derivatives, etc (sometimes with *of*); in any process or activity, denoting a subsequent stage. **down'stroke** *n* a downward line made by the pen in writing. **down'swing** *n* a downward trend in volume of trade, etc; the part of the swing where the club is moving down towards the ball (*golf*). **down'-the-line** *adj* (of a ballet-dancer) inconspicuously placed, unimportant; thorough, unwavering (*US*). **down'throw** *n* an act of throwing down, or state of being thrown down; the amount of vertical displacement of the relatively lowered strata at a fault (*geol*). **down'time** *n* a period when work is halted, due to equipment failure, lack of materials, bad weather, etc. **down'-to-earth'** *adj* sensible; practical; realistic; plain-speaking. **down'town** *adj* and *adv* in or towards the lower part or (*esp N Am*) the business and shopping centre of the town. ◆ *n* this part of a town. **down'-train** *n* a railway train that leaves from the chief terminus. **down'trend** *n* a downward trend. **down'-trod** or **down'trodden** *adj* trampled on; tyrannized over. **down'turn** *n* a downward trend, decline. **down'turned** *adj* folded or turned down. **down'wash** *n* the downward current of air disturbed by an aerofoil. **down'wind'** *adj* and *adv* in the direction in which the wind is blowing; in or to a position (relative to someone or something) in this direction (often with *of*).

■ **down east** (*US*) in or into Maine and adjoining parts of New England. **down in the mouth** in low spirits. **down on one's luck** in unfortunate circumstances. **down south** (*US*) in the Southern states. **down to** (*sl*) the fault or responsibility of. **down tools** to stop work, strike. **down to the ground** (*inf*) completely. **down town** in or towards the centre of a town. **down under** in or to Australia and New Zealand. **down with** put down (*imperative*); swallow (*imperative*); an interjection expressing a wish to depose, get rid of or abolish; in tune with, in sympathy with (*inf*). **go down** (often with *with*) to be received (well or badly) (by); (often with *with*) to be acceptable (to); (with *with*) to contract (an illness). **go downhill** to deteriorate (in health, prosperity or morality). **go downstream** to begin operating the downstream stages of oil exploitation. **up and down** alternately well and ill; to and fro.

down² /*down*/ *n* soft feathers; a soft covering of fluffy hair. [ON *dūnn*; Ger *Daune*, LGer *dune*]
■ **downed** *adj* filled or covered with down. **Down'ie®** *n* a duvet. **down'iness** *n*. **down'y** *adj* covered with or made of down; like down; knowing (*sl*).
❑ **down'-bed** *n*. **down'-quilt** *n*. **downy mildew** *n* a plant disease causing downy patches to appear on leaves.
■ **the downy** (*old sl*) bed.

down³ /*down*/ *n* a bank of sand thrown up by the sea (same as **dune**); a treeless upland; (in *pl*) an undulating upland tract of pasture-land, *esp* in SE England (**the Downs**); the roadstead off E Kent. [OE *dūn* a hill, from Celtic *dun*]
■ **down'land** *n*.

downa, downa-do see under **dow²**.

Downie® see under **down²**.

Downing Street /*dow'ning strēt*/ *n* the street in London where the Prime Minister's official residence is, as well as the Foreign and Commonwealth Office; the British government.

downs see **down³**.

Down's syndrome /*downz sin'drōm*/ *n* a congenital disease caused by chromosomal abnormality, in which there is mental deficiency and a broadening and flattening of the features (formerly known as **Mongolism**). [John LH *Down* (1828–96), English physician]

downy see **down²**.

dowp same as **doup**.

dowry /*dow'ri*/ *n* the property that a woman brings to her husband at marriage, sometimes used for dower; sometimes a gift given to or for a wife at marriage; a natural endowment. [See **dower**]

dows see **dow²**.

dowse¹ /*dowz*/ *vi* to look for water with a divining rod; to use an indicator (eg a pendulum or a rule) to diagnose disease and often select a remedy. [Origin unknown]
■ **dows'er** *n* a person who divines water.
❑ **dowsing rod** *n* a divining rod.

dowse² /*dows*/ *vt* and *vi* see under **douse¹,²,³**.

dowset see under **douce**.

dowt or **dout** /*dowt*/ (*Scot*) *n* a cigarette end. [From **dout¹**]

doxapram /*dok'sə-pram*/ *n* a drug used as a respiratory stimulant.

doxastic /*dok-sas'tik*/ (*philos*) *adj* of or relating to belief. ◆ *n* the branch of logic concerned with belief. [Gr *doxastikos* conjectural]

doxology /*dok-sol'ə-ji*/ (*Christianity*) *n* a hymn or liturgical formula ascribing glory to God. [Gr *doxa* opinion, reputation, glory, and *logos* discourse]
■ **doxolog'ical** *adj*.

doxorubicin /*dok-sō-roo'bi-sin*/ *n* a bacterial antibiotic used to treat various forms of cancer. [**deoxy-**, L *rubus* red, and **-in** (3)]

doxy¹ /*dok'si*/ (*sl*; *archaic*) *n* a mistress (*Shakesp*, etc); a woman of loose character. [Origin unknown]

doxy² /*dok'si*/ (*inf*, *esp facetious*) *n* an opinion ('Orthodoxy', said Warburton, 'is my doxy – heterodoxy is another man's doxy'). [Gr *doxa* opinion]

doxycycline /*dok-si-sī'klēn*/ *n* a broad-spectrum antibiotic of the tetracycline group. [Contracted from *deoxytetracycline*]

doyen /*doi'ən* or *dwä-yã'*/ or (*fem*) **doyenne** /*doi-en'* or *dwä-yen'*/ *n* the most senior and most respected member (of an academy, diplomatic corps, class, profession, etc); a dean. [Fr, from L *decānus*]

doyley, doyly see **doily**.

doz. (sometimes /*duz*/) *abbrev*: dozen.

doze /*dōz*/ *vi* to sleep lightly, or to be half-asleep; (with *off*) to fall into a light sleep; to be in a dull or stupefied state. ◆ *vt* to spend in drowsiness (with *away*). ◆ *n* a short light sleep. [Cf ON *dūsa*, Dan *döse*]
■ **dozed** *adj* drowsy. **dō'zen** *vt* (*Scot*) to stupefy. ◆ *vi* to become stupefied. **dō'zer** *n*. **dō'ziness** *n*. **dō'zing** *n*. **dō'zy** *adj* drowsy; not alert, stupid (*inf*); beginning to decay.

dozen¹ /*duz'n*/ *n* (*pl* **doz'en** when preceded by a numeral, otherwise **doz'ens**) a set of twelve; also used, *esp* in *pl*, for a less exact number. [OFr *dozeine*, from L *duodecim* (*duo* two, and *decem* ten), and neuter *pl* ending *-ēna* (cf Sp *docena*)]
■ **doz'enth** *adj* and *n*.
■ **baker's, devil's** or **long dozen** thirteen. **daily dozen** see under **daily**. **half'-a-doz'en** six; approximately six. **round dozen** a full dozen.

dozen² see under **doze**.

dozer /*dō'zər*/ informal for **bulldozer** (see under **bulldoze**) or **calfdozer** (see under **calf¹**).

DP *abbrev*: data processing; displaced person.

DPH *abbrev*: Diploma in Public Health.

DPh. or **DPhil.** *abbrev*: Doctor of Philosophy.

dpi (*comput*) *abbrev*: dots per inch.

DPM *abbrev*: Diploma in Psychological Medicine.

DPP *abbrev*: Director of Public Prosecutions.

DPRK *abbrev*: Democratic People's Republic of Korea (North Korea).

DPT *abbrev*: diphtheria, pertussis and tetanus (vaccine).

dpt *abbrev* : department; dioptre.

DR *abbrev* : dry riser.

Dr *abbrev* : debtor; Doctor; Driver; Drummer.

Dr. *abbrev* : drachma; Drive (in street names).

dr. *abbrev* : drachma; dram; drawer.

drab[1] /drab/ *n* thick, strong, grey cloth; a grey or dull-brown colour, *perh* from the muddy colour of undyed wool; uninteresting unvaried dullness. ◆ *adj* of the colour of drab; dull and monotonous. [Perh Fr *drap* cloth, from LL *drappus*, prob Gmc; see **drape**]
■ **drabb'et** *n* a coarse linen fabric used for smock-frocks (also **drabette**'). **drab'ly** *adv*. **drab'ness** *n*.

drab[2] /drab/ (*obs*) *n* a sluttish woman; a whore. ◆ *vi* to associate with drabs. [Poss Gaelic *drabag*; Ir *drabog* slut; or LGer *drabbe* dirt]
■ **drabb'er** someone who associates with drabs. **drabb'iness** *n*. **drabb'ish** or **drabb'y** *adj* sluttish.

drabble /drab'l/ *vt* to besmear, bedraggle. [LGer *drabbeln* to wade about]
■ **drabb'ler** or **drab'ler** *n* an additional piece of canvas, laced to the bottom of the bonnet of a sail, to give it greater depth. **drabb'ling** *n* a manner of fishing for barbels with a rod and long line passed through a piece of lead.

Dracaena /drə-sē'nə/ *n* the dragon tree genus. [LL *dracaena* a she-dragon, from Gr *drakaina*, feminine of *drakōn* dragon]

drachm /dram/ *n* a drachma; a dram.

drachma /drak'mə/ *n* (pl **drach'mas**, **drach'mae** /-mē/, or **drach'mai** /-mī/) in ancient Greece, a weight and a silver coin of different values; a former unit of currency in modern Greece, replaced by the euro. [Gr *drachmē*, from *drassesthai* to grasp with the hand]

Draco /drā'kō/ *n* the Dragon, a northern constellation; a dragon lizard. [L *dracō*, *-ōnis*, and Gr *drakōn*, *-ontos* a dragon or snake, dimins L *dracunculus*, Gr *drakontion*, prob from the root of Gr *derkesthai* to look]
■ **dracone** or (*US*) **Dracone**® /drā'kōn, sometimes *dra-kō'ni/ *n* a large sausage-shaped, bag-like container for transporting liquids, towed on the surface of the sea, etc. **draconian** /drək-, drak-ō-ni-ən/ or **draconic** /-on'ik/ *adj* of or of the nature of a dragon. **draconites** /drak-ə-nī'tēz/ *n* a precious stone fabled to come from a dragon's brain. **dracontiasis** /drak-ən-tī'ə-sis/ *n* guinea worm disease. **Dracontium** /drə-kon'shi-əm/ *n* a S American araceous genus formerly of medical repute. **dracunculus** /drə-kungk'ū-ləs/ *n* (with *cap*) the green dragon genus of Araceae; the dragonet; the guinea worm.

Draconian /drə- or drā-kō'ni-ən/, **Draconic** /-kon'ik/ or **Dracontic** /-kon'tik/ (also without *cap*) *adj* extremely severe, like the laws of *Draco*, archon at Athens 621BC.
■ **Draconism** /drak'ən-izm/ *n*.

drad /drad/ (*Spenser*) *pat* and *pap* of **dread**. *adj* dread.

draff /dräf/ *n* dregs; the refuse of malt after brewing. [Prob related to Du *draf*, Ger *Treber*, *Träber*]
■ **draff'ish** or **draff'y** *adj* worthless.

draft /dräft/ *n* anything drawn; the selecting of a smaller body (of people, animals or things) from a larger; the body so selected (*esp milit*); a member of it; conscription (*US*); an order eg to a bank for the payment of money; a demand (upon resources, credulity, patience, etc); a plan; a preliminary sketch, or version of a piece of writing; a draught (in various senses; occasional and *US*). ◆ *vt* to draw an outline of; to draw up in preliminary form; to draw off; to detach. [**draught**]
■ **draftee'** *n* a conscript. **draft'er** or **draught'er** *n* a person who drafts; a draught horse. **draftiness** *n* see **draught**. **drafty** *adj* see **draught**.
□ **draft'-bar** *n* a drawbar. **draft'-dodger** *n* (*US inf*) a person who avoids conscription. **draft'-dodging** *n*. **draft horse**, **draft ox**, **drafts**, **drafts'man**, **drafts'manship** see under **draught**.

drag /drag/ *vt* (**dragg'ing**; **dragged**) to draw by force; to draw slowly; to move (an icon, file, etc) across the screen by using a mouse with its key kept depressed (*comput*); to pull roughly and violently; to trail; to explore with a dragnet or hook; to apply a drag to. ◆ *vi* to hang so as to trail on the ground; to be forcibly drawn along; to move slowly and heavily; to lag; to give the feeling of being unduly slow or tedious. ◆ *n* anything dragged; an act of dragging; a dragging effect; the component of the aerodynamic force on a body travelling through a fluid (*esp* a vehicle travelling through air) that lies along the longitudinal axis; a net or hook for dragging along to catch things under water; a device on a reel that puts pressure on the line to prevent it breaking (*angling*); a heavy harrow; a device for guiding wood to the saw; a car, lorry or wagon (*sl*); a mail-coach; a long open carriage, with transverse or side seats; a brake, *esp* an iron shoe that drags on the ground; any obstacle

to progress; a tedious, dreary occupation or experience (*inf*); influence, pull (*US sl*); a trail of scent left by an animal, or a trail of broken undergrowth caused by an animal dragging off its prey; an artificial scent dragged on the ground for foxhounds to follow; a short 'draw' on a cigarette (*inf*); a retarded motion of the cue ball imparted by striking somewhat under the centre (*snooker*, etc); (the wearing of) transvestite clothing, now *usu* women's clothing worn by a man, or a form of entertainment involving this (*inf*; also *adj*); a homosexuals' party (*sl*). [Scot and N Eng from OE *dragan* or ON *draga*]
■ **dragg'ing** *n* a technique in interior decoration, in which a brush is pulled through freshly-applied paint to give an irregular decorative effect. **dragg'y** *adj* (*inf*) boring, tedious. **drag'ster** *n* a car for drag-racing.
□ **drag'-bar** *n* a drawbar. **drag'-chain** *n* a chain used as drag to a wheel; a chain for coupling railway vehicles. **drag'hound** *n* a foxhound trained to follow a drag. **drag hunt** *n*. **drag lift** *n* a ski lift that pulls people wearing skis up a slope. **drag'line** *n* an excavating machine, crane-like in appearance, moving on articulated tracks (or **walking dragline**, on 'legs' having steel plates as 'feet'), and drawing towards itself a bucket suspended from a long jib. **drag'-man** *n* a fisherman who uses a dragnet. **drag'net** *n* a net to be dragged along the bottom of water or the ground; a systematic police search for a wanted person. **drag'-parachute** *n* a small parachute attached to the rear of an aircraft, which opens on landing to assist deceleration. **drag queen** *n* a professional female impersonator. **drag race** *n* a motor car or motorcycle contest in acceleration, with standing start and over a quarter-mile course. **drag'-racing** *n*. **drag'-shot** *n* a shot that imparts drag to a snooker or billiard ball. **drags'man** *n* the driver of a drag or coach.
■ **drag and drop** (*comput*) to move an icon, file, etc across the screen using a mouse and release it in a different place (**drag'-and-drop'** *adj*). **drag by** to pass slowly. **drag on** to continue slowly and tediously. **drag one's feet** or **heels** to hang back deliberately in doing something (**foot'-dragging** *n*). **drag out** to prolong unnecessarily or tediously. **drag out of** to get (information, etc) from (someone) with difficulty, sometimes by force. **drag up** (*inf*) to mention or quote (a story, etc, *esp* defamatory) inappropriately or unnecessarily; to bring up (a child) badly; to wear transvestite clothing, *usu* of a man wearing women's clothing. **main drag** (*inf*, chiefly *US*) the main street of a town.

dragée /drä'zhā or dra-zhā'/ *n* a sweet enclosing a drug, or a nut or fruit, etc; a medicated sweet; a chocolate drop; a small silvered ball for decorating a cake. [Fr]

draggle /drag'l/ *vt* or *vi* to make or become wet and dirty, as if by dragging along the ground; to trail. [Frequentative of **drag**, and a doublet of **drawl**]
□ **dragg'le-tail** *n* a slut. **dragg'le-tailed** *adj*.

draggy see under **drag**.

dragoman /drag'ō-mən/ *n* (pl **drag'omans**) an interpreter or guide in Eastern countries. [Fr, from Ar *tarjumān*, from *tarjama* to interpret]

dragon /drag'ən/ *n* a fabulous winged scaly-armoured fire-breathing monster, often a guardian of treasure, ravaging a country when its hoard is rifled; a fierce, intimidating or watchful woman; a paper kite; a dragon lizard; applied to various plants, *esp Dracunculus* (green dragon), and *Dracontium*; (with *cap*) a northern constellation (*Draco*); (also with *cap*) a racing yacht of the International Dragon class, 8.88m (29.2 feet) long. [Fr, from L *dracō*, *-ōnis*, from Gr *drakōn*, *-ontos*, perh from root *drak*, as in *edrakon*, aorist of *derkesthai* to see clearly]
■ **drag'oness** *n* a she-dragon. **drag'onet** *n* a little dragon; a brightly coloured fish of the genus *Callionymus*. **drag'onish** *adj*. **drag'onism** *n* unremitting watchfulness. **drag'onize** or **-ise** *vt* to turn into a dragon; to watch like a dragon. **drag'onlike** *adj*. **dragonné** /drag-o-nā'/ *adj* (*heraldry*) like a dragon in the rear part.
□ **dragon arum** *n* a European aroid plant (genus *Dracunculus*); dragonroot (*US*). **dragon boat** *n* a Chinese boat decorated to resemble a dragon and used in traditional races. **drag'on-fish** *n* a dragonet; a fish of the genus *Pegasus*. **drag'onfly** *n* a predaceous long-bodied often brilliantly-coloured insect of the order *Odonata*. **dragon fruit** *n* same as **pitahaya**. **drag'onhead** or **drag'on's-head** *n* a labiate garden plant (genus *Dracocephalum*; from the shape of the corolla). **dragon lizard** *n* a small tree-dwelling East Indian lizard (genus *Draco*) with parachute of ribs and skin; a S American lizard (genus *Thorictis*); a monitor, *esp* a species (*Varanus komodoensis*) found in Komodo (in Indonesia), reaching 3 metres (10 feet) in length. **drag'onroot** *n* (*US*) an araceous plant (genus *Arisaema*) or its tuberous root, used in medicine. **dragon's blood** *n* a red resinous exudation from the dragon tree and many other trees, used for colouring varnishes, etc. **drag'on-stand'ard** *n* a standard in, or bearing, the form of a dragon. **dragon's teeth** *n pl* concrete anti-tank obstacles. **dragon tree** *n* a great tree of the Canary Islands (*Dracaena draco*), remarkable for its resin (a variety of dragon's blood), its growth

---

■ words derived from main entry word; □ compound words; ■ idioms and phrasal verbs

in thickness like a dicotyledon, and the great age it attains; any of various other trees of the genus *Dracaena*.

■ **chase the dragon** (*sl*) to smoke heroin by heating it and inhaling the fumes. **to sow dragon's teeth** to stir up trouble, cause contention.

dragonnade /drag-ə-nād'/ *n* the persecution of French Protestants under Louis XIV by means of dragoons (*hist*); any persecution by military means (*usu* in *pl*). [Fr, from *dragon* dragoon]

dragoon /drə-goon'/ *n* a heavy cavalryman, as opposed to hussars and lancers, a term surviving in the names of certain regiments; an old fire-spitting musket; a mounted infantryman armed with it (*obs*). ◆ *vt* to compel by military bullying; to compel by force. [Fr *dragon* dragon, dragoon]
□ **dragoon'-bird** *n* the umbrella bird.

dragsman, **dragster** see under **drag**.

drail /drāl/ *n* the iron bow of a plough from which the traces draw; a piece of lead round the shank of the hook in fishing. ◆ *vi* to draggle. [Prob a combination of **draggle** and **trail**]

drain /drān/ *vt* to draw off by degrees; to filter; to draw off water, sewage or other liquid from; to provide a means of drainage, to install a drain; to make dry; to drink dry; to exhaust. ◆ *vi* to flow off gradually; to lose liquid gradually (eg by trickling or dripping); to discharge. ◆ *n* a watercourse; a channel allowing liquid to drain; a tube used to draw off fluid from a wound or cavity (*med*); a ditch; a sewer; a drink (*sl*); expenditure that exhausts or diminishes. [OE *drēahnian*]
■ **drain'able** *adj.* **drain'age** *n* an act, process, method or means of draining; means of discharging water; the system of drains in a town. **drain'er** *n* a device on which articles are placed to drain.
□ **drainage basin** *n* the area of land that drains into one river. **drain'age-tube** *n* a tube for discharge of pus, etc. **draining board** (or *US* **drain'board**) *n* a sloping surface beside a sink, where dishes, etc are placed to drain when washed. **drain'pipe** *n* a pipe to carry away waste water or rainwater; (in *pl*; *inf*; also **drainpipe trousers**) very narrow trousers. **drain'-tile** *n.* **drain'-trap** *n* a contrivance for preventing the escape of foul air from drains, while admitting water to them.
■ **down the drain** (*inf*) gone for good; wasted.

draisine or **draisene** /drā-zēn'/ (*hist*) *n* dandy-horse. [Invented in early 19c by Baron *Drais*, of Mannheim]

drake¹ /drāk/ *n* the male of the duck; a flat stone thrown so as to skip along the surface of water in playing *ducks and drakes* (also **drake'stone**). [Ety obscure; cf provincial Ger *draak*; OHGer *antrahho*, Ger *Enterich*, the first element usually explained as *eend*, *end*, *anut* duck]

drake² /drāk/ *n* a dragon (*archaic*); a fiery meteor (*obs*); a beaked galley, or Viking ship of war (*hist*); an angler's name for species of *Ephemera*. [OE *draca* dragon, from L *dracō*]

Dralon® /drā'lon/ *n* a type of acrylic fibre.

DRAM /dram/ (*comput*) *abbrev*: dynamic random access memory (*pl* **DRAMs**).

dram¹ /dram/ *n* a contraction of **drachm**; $\frac{1}{16}$th of an ounce avoirdupois; formerly (still *US*) apothecaries' measure of $\frac{1}{8}$th of an ounce; a small drink of alcohol, *esp* whisky; a tipple. ◆ *vi* to drink a dram. ◆ *vt* to give a dram to. [Through Fr and L, from Gr *drachmē*; see **drachma**]
□ **dram'-drink'er** *n.* **dram'-shop** *n* a bar.

dram² /dram/ *n* (*pl* **dram**) the standard monetary unit of Armenia (100 luma). [Armenian, ult from Gr *drachmē* (see **drachma**)]

drama /drā'mə/ *n* a story showing life and action, intended for representation by actors; a composition intended to be represented on the stage, radio or film, etc; the total range of dramatic literature; theatrical entertainment; a dramatic situation, or series of absorbing, exciting, tense or tragic, etc events. [L, from Gr *drāma*, *drāmatos*, from *drāein* to do]
■ **dramat'ic** /drə-mat'ik/ *adj* belonging to or of drama; appropriate to or in the form of drama; with the force and vividness of a drama; impressive or important because of speed, size, suddenness, etc. **dramat'ical** *adj* (*old*) dramatic. **dramat'ically** *adv.* **dramat'icism** *n.* **dramat'ics** *n* (*usu sing*) the acting, production and study of plays; a show of excessive, exaggerated emotion (*inf*). **dram'atist** *n* a writer of plays. **dramatiz'able** or **-s-** /dram-/ *adj.* **dramatiza'tion** or **-s-** *n* the act of dramatizing; the dramatized version of a novel or story. **dram'atize** or **-ise** *vt* to compose in or turn into the form of a drama or play; to exaggerate the importance of or emotional nature of.
□ **drama documentary** see **faction²**. **drama therapy** *n* a form of psychological therapy in which patients are encouraged to act out responses to situations and use role playing in order to address problems. **dramatic irony** *n* a situation, etc in a play, the irony of which is clear to the audience but not to the characters. **dramatic**

monologue *n* a literary work in the form of the speech of a single character. **dram'atis perso'nae** /-e or -ī/ *n* the characters of a drama or play.

dramaturgy /dram'ə-tûr-ji/ *n* the principles of dramatic composition; theatrical art. [Through Fr from Gr *drāmatourgiā*, *drāmatourgos* playwright, from *drāma*, and *ergon* a work]
■ **dram'aturg** *n* (from Ger) a member of a theatrical company who selects the repertoire and may assist in the arranging and production of the plays, compiling notes for the programme, etc. **dram'aturge** or **dram'aturgist** *n* a playwright. **dramatur'gic** or **dramatur'gical** *adj.*

Drambuie® /dram-boo'i, -bū'i/ *n* a Scotch whisky liqueur. [**dram¹**, and Gaelic *buidhe* yellow, golden, or agreeable, pleasant]

dramedy /drä'mi-di/ *n* a TV or film drama with comic elements. [*drama comedy*]

dramma giocoso /dram'ma jō-kō'sō/ *n* (Ital, comic drama) comic opera.
□ **dramma per musica** /per moo'zē-ka/ *n* (Ital, drama through music) an *esp* 17 and 18c term for opera, or for the musical drama that was its forerunner.

drammock /dram'ək/ *n* meal and water mixed raw (also **dramm'ach**). [Cf Gaelic *drama(i)g* a foul mixture]

Drang nach Osten /drang nahh os'tən/ *n* (Ger, *hist*) eastward thrust, the policy of German expansionists.

drank /drangk/ *pat* of **drink**.

drant or **draunt** /dränt, drönt/ (*dialect*) *vi* and *vt* to drawl, to drone. ◆ *n* a droning tone.

drap /drap/ *n* and *v* Scots form of **drop**.
■ **drapp'ie** or **drapp'y** *n* (*Scot*) a little drop, *esp* of spirits.

drap-de-Berry /drä-də-be-rē'/ (*obs*) *n* a woollen cloth made in Berry, in France (also *adj*). [Fr, Berry cloth]

drape /drāp/ *vt* to cover as with cloth; to hang cloth in folds about; (also *reflexive*) to put (oneself or a limb) in a casual and graceful pose. ◆ *n* a hanging or curtain (*N Am* and *theatre*); (in *pl*) a drape suit. [OFr *draper* to weave, drape, *drapier* draper, from *drap* cloth, prob Gmc; see **drab¹**]
■ **draped** *adj.* **drāp'er** *n* a dealer in cloth, textiles and clothing. **drāp'eried** *adj* draped. **drāp'ery** *n* (*pl* **drāp'eries**) a draper's goods, business or shop; hangings; the representation of clothes and hanging folds of cloth (*art*). ◆ *vt* to drape. **drapet** /drap'it/ *n* (*Spenser*) a cloth covering. **drapier** /drāp'i-ər/ *n* (*obs*) a draper.
□ **drape suit** *n* a man's suit with narrow trousers and a **drape coat** or **jacket**, a very long jacket (*esp* with velvet collar and cuffs), particularly popular during the 1950s.

drappie, **drappy** see under **drap**.

drastic /dras'tik/ *adj* forcible, powerful in action; violent; unsparing; great and quick or sudden; dramatic; bad, unpleasant; extreme. ◆ *n* (*med*) a severe purgative. [Gr *drastikos*, from *drāein*, to act, to do]
■ **dras'tically** *adv.*

drat /drat/ *interj* used to express vexation, (sometimes with an object). [Aphetic from *God rot*]
■ **dratt'ed** *adj.*

dratchell /drach'l/ (*dialect*) *n* a slut.

draught /dräft/ *n* the act of drawing or pulling; a pull; attraction; the thing or quantity drawn; readiness for drawing from the cask; the act of drinking; the quantity drunk in one breath; a dose of liquor or medicine; the outline of a picture, or a preliminary sketch or plan (*usu* **draft**); that which is taken in a net by drawing; a chosen detachment of men (*usu* **draft**); a current of air; the depth to which a ship sinks in the water; a move in a game (*obs*); a thick disc used in the game of draughts (also **draughts'man**); (in *pl*) a game played by two people moving draughtmen alternately on a chequered board; draught beer; a cesspool or privy (*Shakesp*, etc). ◆ *adj* served by being pumped directly from a cask, on draught. ◆ *vt* to sketch out or make a preliminary plan of or attempt at (also **draft**); occasionally for **draft** in sense of draw off or set apart from a larger body. [OE *draht*, from *dragan* to draw; see **drag** and **draw**]
■ **draughter** *n* see **draft**. **draught'iness** or (*N Am*) **draf'tiness** *n.* **draught'y** or (*N Am*) **draf'ty** *adj* full of draughts or currents of air.
□ **draught animal**, **horse**, **ox**, etc *n* one used for drawing heavy loads. **draught'-bar** see **drawbar** under **draw**. **draught'board** *n* a chessboard used for playing draughts. **draught'-en'gine** *n* the engine over the shaft of a coalpit. **draught'-hooks** *n pl* large iron hooks fixed on the cheeks of a cannon-carriage. **draught'-house** *n* (*Bible*, etc) a sink or privy. **draught'man** *n* a piece used for playing draughts. **draught'-net** *n* a dragnet. **draught'-proof** *adj* sealed, filled, etc to prevent draughts (also *vt*). **draught'-proofing** *n.* **draught'-screen** *n* a screen for warding off a current of air. **draughts'man** *n* a piece used in playing draughts; someone skilled or employed in drawing,

esp technical drawing; someone who draughts or draws up documents (in this sense usually **draftsman**). **draughts'manship** *n.* **draughts'person** *n.* **draughts'woman** *n.*

■ **feel the draught** (*fig*) to be unpleasantly conscious of difficult conditions, *esp* being short of money. **on draught** (of liquor) sold from the cask.

draunt see **drant**.

drave /drāv/ old *pat* of **drive**.

Dravidian /drə-vid'i-ən/ *adj* belonging to a dark, wavy-haired race of S India; belonging to a group of languages in S India, *incl* Tamil, Malayalam, Kannada, Telugu, etc. ◆ *n* a member of this race; the Dravidian group of languages. [Sans *Drāviḍa* an ancient province of S India]

draw /drö/ *vt* (*pat* **drew** /drōō/; *pap* **drawn**) to pull; to drag; to pull along; to bring forcibly towards or after one; to pull into position; to pull back; to pull back the string of; to pull together or away; to take (eg a raffle ticket) at random from a number; to entice, attract; to coax into giving information; to encourage to talk freely (*usu* **draw out**); to inhale; to take out; to unsheathe; to withdraw; to cause to flow out; to evoke or bring out by some artifice; to extract by pulling; to extract the essence of; to eviscerate; to pull through a small hole, as in making wire; to deduce; to lengthen; to extend to the full length; to force to appear (eg to force a badger from its hole); to receive or take from a source or store; to demand by a draft; to get by lot; to trace; to construct in linear form; to make a picture of by drawing lines; to describe; to put into shape, to frame; to write out (eg a cheque); to require as depth of water for floating; to finish without winning or losing; to deflect the ball with the inside edge of the bat (*cricket*); to hit (the ball) intentionally in such a way that it moves from right to left in the air (if right-handed) or from left to right (if left-handed) (*golf*); to deliver (a bowl) so that it moves in a curve to the point aimed for (*bowls*); to deliver gently (*curling*); to force one's opponents to play (all their cards of a suit, *esp* trumps) by continually leading cards of that suit (*bridge*, etc); to hit (the cue ball) so that it recoils after striking another ball (*snooker*, etc); in a foundry, etc, to remove (a pattern) from a mould. ◆ *vi* to pull; to practise drawing; to move; to make one's way, go; to resort; to approach; to make a draught; (of a flue, etc) to have a good current of air; to act as drawer; to draw a card, a sword or lots; to infuse; to end a game without winning or losing; to move in a curve to the point aimed for (*bowls*). ◆ *n* the act of drawing; assignment by lot of prizes, opponents in a game, etc; anything drawn; a drawn or undecided game; an attraction; a drawer (of a chest of drawers; *US*); a running play that is disguised to look like a passing play (*American football*). [OE *dragan*; cf **drag**]

■ **draw'able** *adj.* **drawee'** *n* the business or person on whom a bill of exchange is drawn; the bank on which a cheque is drawn. **draw'er** *n* a person or thing that draws; the person who signs a cheque or bill of exchange; someone who draws beer or fetches liquor in a tavern; /drör/ a thing drawn out, such as the sliding box in a **chest of drawers**; (in *pl*) a close-fitting undergarment for the lower part of the body and the legs. **draw'ing** *n* the art of representing objects or forms by lines drawn, shading, etc; a picture in lines; the act of assigning by lot; the act of pulling, etc. **draw'ings** *n pl* any monies or other assets taken by the owner of a business, or paid by the business on the owner's behalf. **drawn** *adj* pulled together; closed; neither won nor lost; unsheathed; eviscerated; strained, tense; etiolated (*bot*); pulled out, lengthened, as in *cold drawn* (*engineering*).

□ **draw'back** *n* a disadvantage; a receiving back of some part of the duty on goods on their exportation. **draw'bar** *n* a sliding bar; a bar used in coupling railway vehicles (also **drag'-bar** and **draught'-bar**). **drawbar outfit** *n* a lorry, whether or not articulated, with a trailer. **draw'-boy** *n orig* the boy who pulled the cords of the harness in figure-weaving; a mechanical device for this purpose. **draw'bridge** *n* a bridge that can be drawn up or let down as required; bridge played by two people, with two dummy hands, not exposed. **draw'down** *n* a reduction, diminution; the withdrawing of funds up to a specified limit, *esp* (**income drawdown**) the withdrawal of money from one's pension fund (*finance*). **draw'-gear** *n* the apparatus by which railway-cars are coupled. **draw hoe** *n* a hoe designed for pulling soil towards one, having a flat blade at about right angles to the handle. **drawing board** *n* a board, or a tilting surface attached to a desk, to which paper can be attached for drawing on; the planning stage of a project, etc (*fig*). **draw'ing-frame** *n* a machine in which carded wool, cotton or the like is drawn out fine. **draw'ing-knife** *n* a knife with a handle at each end, used by a cooper for shaving hoops by drawing it towards him. **draw'ing-master** *n.* **drawing paper** *n.* **draw'ing-pen** *n.* **draw'ing-pencil** *n.* **drawing pin** *n* a short broad-headed pin for fastening paper to a drawing board, etc. **drawing room** *n* in engineering, a room where plans and patterns are drawn; see also separate entry. **draw'ing-table** *n* (also **draw-leaf table, draw-table** and **draw-top table**) a table that can be extended in length by drawing out sliding leaves. **draw'-net** same as **dragnet** (see under **drag**). **drawn'-thread' work** or **drawn work** *n*

ornamental needlework done by pulling out some of the threads of a fabric. **draw'-plate** *n* a plate supporting dies for drawing wire or tubing. **draw'-sheet** *n* (in nursing) a sheet that can be drawn out from under a patient. **draw'-string** or **draw'string** *n* a string or cord, etc, in a casing in or threaded through material, by which the material may be drawn or gathered up. ◆ *adj* having or closed by such a string. **draw-table**, **draw-top table** see **drawing-table** above. **draw'-tube** *n* a tube sliding within another, as in a form of telescope. **draw'-well** *n* a well from which water is drawn up by a bucket and apparatus.

■ **at daggers drawn** openly hostile. **draw a bead on** see under **bead**. **draw a blank** literally, to get a lottery ticket that wins no prize; to get no result. **draw a cover** (or **covert**) to send the hounds into a cover to frighten out a fox. **draw attention to** see under **attention**. **draw back** to recoil; to withdraw. **draw blank** to draw a cover, but find no fox. **draw down** (*US*) to remove (troops) from a place where they have been stationed. **draw, hang and quarter** see under **hang**. **draw in** to reduce, contract; to become shorter; (of nights) to begin earlier with the change of season. **draw it fine** to be too precise. **draw it mild** (*inf*) to refrain from exaggeration. **draw near** to approach. **draw off** to cause to flow from a barrel, etc; to withdraw. **draw on** to approach; to pull on. **draw on** or **upon** to make a draught upon; to make a demand upon (eg one's credulity, patience or resources); to draw one's weapon against. **draw on one's imagination** to make imaginative or lying statements. **draw on one's memory** to try to remember; to make use of what one remembers. **draw out** to leave the place (of an army, etc); to lengthen; to entice into talk and self-expression. **draw rein** to slacken speed, to stop. **draw someone's attention** to see under **attention**. **draw stumps** to end play in cricket by removing the wickets. **draw the cloth, board** or **table** (*archaic*) to clear up after a meal. **draw the line** to fix a limit; to find finally and positively unacceptable. **draw the long bow** see under **bow²**. **draw the teeth of** to make harmless. **draw to a head** to mature. **draw up** to form in regular order; to compose, put into shape; to stop. **in drawing** correctly drawn. **out of drawing** inaccurately drawn, or drawn in violation of the principles of drawing. **out of the top drawer** of top grade, *esp* socially.

drawing room¹ /drö'ing rōōm, also *room*/ *n* a room to which the company withdraws after dinner, a formal sitting room; formerly, a reception of company at court; a private compartment of a railway parlour car (*US*). ◆ *adj* suitable for the drawing room. [Orig **withdrawing-room**]

drawing room² see under **draw**.

drawl /dröl/ *vi* to speak in a slow lengthened tone; to dawdle (*obs*). ◆ *vt* to say in a slow and sleepy manner. ◆ *n* a slow, lengthened utterance. [Connected with **draw**]

■ **drawl'er** *n.* **drawl'ingly** *adv.* **drawl'ingness** *n.*

drawn see **draw**.

dray¹ /drā/ *n* a low strong cart for heavy goods; a timber sledge; that which is dragged or drawn. [Cf OE *dræge* dragnet, from *dragan* to draw; see **drag** and **draw**]

■ **dray'age** *n.*
□ **dray'-horse** *n.* **dray'man** *n.* **dray'-plough** *n.*

dray² see **drey**.

drazel /drā'zl/ (*dialect*) *n* a slut. [Origin unknown]

DRC *abbrev*: Democratic Republic of Congo.

dread /dred/ *n* great fear; awe; an object of fear or awe; fury (*Spenser*); (in *pl*; *inf*) dreadlocks. ◆ *adj* dreaded; inspiring great fear or awe. ◆ *vt* to fear greatly; to reverence; to feel great apprehension towards or dismay about; to cause to fear, to frighten (*obs*). [ME *dreden*, from OE *ondrǣdan* to fear; ON *ondrēda*, OHGer *intratan* to be afraid]

■ **dread'ed** *adj* (now *usu* facetiously; with *the*) fearsome, terrifying. **dread'er** *n.* **dread'ful** *adj orig* full of dread; producing great fear or awe; terrible; very bad, unpleasant (*inf*). **dread'fully** *adv* in a dreadful way; very (much) (*inf*). **dread'fulness** *n.* **dread'less** *adj* without dread or fear. ◆ *adv* (*Spenser*, etc) doubtless. **dread'lessly** *adv.* **dread'lessness** *n.* **dread'ly** *adv.*

□ **dread'locked** *adj.* **dread'locks** or **dread locks** *n pl* the long tightly curled or plaited hairstyle adopted by Rastafarians. **dread'nought** or **dread'naught** *n* someone who dreads nothing; a thick woollen cloth or garment made of it for wear in inclement weather; a powerful type of battleship or battle-cruiser (dating from 1905–6).

■ **penny dreadful** a cheap sensational serial or book, etc.

dream¹ /drēm/ *n* a train of thoughts and images experienced during sleep, a vision; something only imaginary; a distant hope or ideal, probably unattainable; a state of mental abstraction; an extremely pleasant person or thing (*inf*). ◆ *vi* (*pat* and *pap* **dreamed** or **dreamt** /dremt/) to experience dreams during sleep; to think idly (with *of*); to think (of) as possible, contemplate as imaginably possible; to be lost in abstraction. ◆ *vt* to see or imagine in, or as in, a dream. ◆ *adj* ideal. [ME *dream*, *drēm*; perh the same word as **dream²**]

■ **dream'er** *n*. **dream'ery** *n* a place favourable to dreams; dreamlike fancies. **dream'ful** *adj* (*Tennyson*) dreamy. **dream'ily** *adv*. **dream'iness** *n*. **dream'ing** *n* and *adj*. **dream'ingly** *adv*. **dream'less** *adj*. **dream'lessly** *adv*. **dream'lessness** *n*. **dream'y** *adj* full of dreams; given to dreaming; appropriate to dreams; dreamlike; lovely (*inf*).

❑ **dream'boat** *n* (*inf*) a wonderful, attractive and desirable person. **dream'catcher** *n* an ornament consisting of a small net mounted on a decorated hoop, based on Native American originals which are believed to bring good dreams. **dream'land** *n* the land of dreams, reverie, or imagination. **dream'scape** *n* a picture or scene with an appearance of strangeness or unreality redolent of a dream. **dream team** *n* (*inf*) the perfect combination of people for a particular task. **dream ticket** *n* (*orig US*; *esp* a pair of candidates considered) the ideal or optimum electoral ticket. **dream'time** *n* in the mythology of Australian Aborigines, the time when the earth and patterns of life on earth took shape. **dream'while** *n* the duration of a dream. **dream'-world** *n* a world of illusions.

■ **dream on** see **in your dreams** below. **dream up** to plan in the mind, often unrealistically. **go like a dream** to work or progress, etc very well. **in your dreams** (*inf*; as a retort expressing scepticism) that is highly unlikely (also **dream on**).

dream² /drēm/ (*obs*) *n* joy; mirth; minstrelsy; music; sound. [OE *drēam* joy, mirth]

❑ **dream'hole** *n* a hole in the wall of a steeple, tower, etc for admitting light.

dreary /drē'ri/ *adj* gloomy; cheerless; dull and tedious. [OE *drēorig* mournful, bloody, from *drēor* gore]

■ **drear** *adj* (*literary*) dreary. **dreare** or **drere** *n* (*Spenser*) dreariness; gloom; mishap. **drear'ihead**, **drear'iment**, **drear'iness**, **drear'ing** (all *Spenser*) or **drear'ihood** *n*. **drear'ily** *adv*. **drear'isome** *adj* desolate, forlorn.

dreck /drek/ (*sl*) *n* rubbish, trash. [Yiddish *drek*, Ger *Dreck* dirt, filth, dung]

■ **dreck'y** *adj*.

dredge¹ /drej/ *n* a bag-net for dragging along the bottom to collect oysters, biological specimens, mud, etc; a machine for deepening a harbour, canal, river, etc, for excavating under water or on land, or for raising alluvial deposits and washing them for minerals, by means of buckets on an endless chain, pumps, grabs, or other devices. ◆ *vt* and *vi* to gather, explore or deepen with a dredge. [Connected with **drag** and **draw**]

■ **dredg'er** *n* someone who dredges; a machine for dredging; a boat, ship or raft equipped for dredging.

■ **dredge up** (*inf*) to mention or recall something (best) forgotten.

dredge² /drej/ *vt* to sprinkle. [OFr *dragie* sugar-plum, from Gr *tragēmata* dessert]

■ **dredg'er** *n* (also **dredge'-box** or **dredg'ing-box**) a container with a perforated lid for dredging.

dree /drē/ (*Scot*) *vt* to endure, bear. [OE *drēogan* to suffer, accomplish]

■ **dree one's weird** to undergo one's destiny.

dreg /dreg/ *n* a trace, a small quantity. [ON *dregg*]

dregs /dregz/ *n pl* impurities in liquid that fall to the bottom, the grounds; dross; the most worthless part of anything. [ON *dregg*]

■ **dregg'iness** *n*. **dregg'y** *adj* containing dregs; muddy; foul.

dreich /drēhh/ (*Scot*) *adj* long drawn out; tedious; dreary; (of weather) dismal. [See **dree**]

dreidel /drā'dl/ *n* in Jewish culture, a small spinning top used in games. [Yiddish]

drek same as **dreck**.

drench /drench, drensh/ *vt* to fill with drink or liquid; to wet thoroughly; to soak; to force a drench upon (an animal); to drown (*obs*). ◆ *vi* (*obs*) to drown. ◆ *n* a draught; a dose of liquid medicine forced down the throat (of an animal). [OE *drencan* to cause to drink (*drincan* to drink), *drenc* drink, drowning; Ger *tränken* to soak; see **drink**]

■ **drench'er** *n*.

drent /drent/ (*Spenser*) obsolete *pap* of **drench** (to drown).

drepanium /dri-pā'ni-əm/ (*bot*) *n* a cymose inflorescence in which each daughter axis is on the same side of its parent axis, and all in one plane. [Latinized from Gr *drepanion*, dimin of *drepanon* a reaping-hook]

drere, **drerihead**, etc Spenserian forms of **drear**, etc.

Dresden china, or **Dresden porcelain** or **ware** /drez'dən/ *n* fine decorated china made in Saxony (Royal Saxon porcelain factory established at Meissen, 1710).

dress /dres/ *vt* (*pat* and *pap* **dressed**, sometimes (*now obs*) **drest**) to clothe; to apply suitable materials to; to straighten; to flatten; to smooth; to erect; to set in order; to prepare, arrange; to adorn; to finish or trim; to draw (a fowl); to gut and trim (a fish, etc); to add seasoning to (food); to manure; to treat; to tend; to tie (a fly) (*angling*); to treat with severity; to chide; to thrash. ◆ *vi* to put on clothes; to put on finer, more elaborate, or more formal clothes; to come into line. ◆ *n* the covering or ornament of the body; a woman's one-piece skirted garment; style of clothing; ceremonial or formal clothing. ◆ *adj* relating to (formal) evening dress. [OFr *dresser* to prepare, from an inferred LL *dīrectiāre* to straighten; see **direct**]

■ **dress'er** *n* a person who dresses; a medical student who dresses wounds; a lady's maid; a person who assists an actor to dress (*theatre*); a tool or machine for dressing; a table on which meat is dressed or prepared for use; a kitchen sideboard, *esp* with a high back and shelves; a chest of drawers or dressing-table (*N Am*). **dress'ing** *n* dress or clothes; the action of someone who dresses; material applied to a wound; material applied to goods, eg a coat of preservative; matter used to give stiffness and gloss to cloth; sauce or (*US*) stuffing, etc, used in preparing a dish for the table, etc; manure or the like applied to land; an ornamental moulding; a thrashing. **dress'y** *adj* fond of dress; showy; formal or elegant; indicating care in dressing.

❑ **dress circle** *n* part of a theatre (*usu* the first gallery), *orig* intended for people in evening dress. **dress coat** *n* a man's fine black coat with narrow or cutaway skirts, worn in full dress (see below). **dressed day** *n* formerly, the second day of a three days' visit. **dress form** *n* a dressmaker's (*usu* adjustable) model. **dress'-goods** *n pl* fabrics for making women's and children's gowns, frocks, etc. **dress'guard** *n* (*archaic*) an arrangement of strings to protect the rider's dress from contact with a bicycle wheel. **dress'-improver** *n* (*obs*) a bustle. **dress'ing-case** *n* a case for toiletry requisites. **dress'ing-down** *n* a severe scolding; a thrashing. **dress'ing-gown** *n* a loose garment worn before or whilst dressing, or in déshabillé, etc. **dress'ing-jacket** or (*obs*) **dress'ing-sack** *n* a jacket worn by women in dressing. **dress'ing-room** *n*. **dressing station** *n* a place where wounded are collected and tended by members of a field ambulance. **dress'ing-table** *n*. **dress'-length** *n* enough (fabric) to make a dress. **dress'maker** *n* a person who makes clothes; a person who makes clothes for women and children as a living (**dress'make** *vi inf* back-formation). **dress'making** *n* the art or process of making clothes. **dress parade** *n* a military parade in dress uniform. **dress'-reform** *n* a late 19c movement seeking to make dress more practical. **dress'-rehears'al** *n* a full rehearsal in costume with everything as for the performance (also *fig*). **dress sense** *n* sense of style in dress, knowledge of what suits one. **dress'-shield** *n* a device to protect the armpit of a dress, etc against sweat. **dress shirt**, **dress suit**, **dress tie**, etc *n* those for formal evening dress. **dress uniform** *n* a formal, ceremonial uniform.

■ **dress down** to handle with severity; to reprimand severely; to thrash; to dress deliberately informally. **dress up** to dress elaborately; to dress for a part; to masquerade; to treat so as to make appear better or more interesting, etc than it really is. **evening dress** or **full dress** the costume prescribed by fashion for evening receptions, dinners, balls, etc. **get dressed** to put one's clothes on.

dressage /dres'äzh/ *n* training of a horse in deportment and response to controls; this equestrian discipline practised in competition; the manoeuvres practised. [Fr]

drest /drest/ (*obs*) *pat* and *pap* of **dress**.

drevill /drev'il/ (*Spenser*) *n* a foul person. [Cf MDu *drevel* scullion]

drew /droo/ *pat* of **draw**.

drey or **dray** /drā/ *n* a squirrel's nest. [Ety dubious]

drib /drib/ *vi* (**dribb'ing**; **dribbed**; *obs*) to trickle; to go little by little. ◆ *vt* (*obs*) to let trickle; to take a little, filch; to lead gradually; to shoot (an arrow) short or wide. ◆ *n* a drop; a trickle; a small quantity. [Related to **drip**]

■ **dribb'er** *n* (*obs*). **dribb'let** or **drib'let** *n* a drop; a trickle; a small quantity.

■ **dribs and drabs** small quantities at a time.

dribble /drib'l/ *vi* to fall in small drops; to drop quickly; to trickle; to slaver, like a child or an idiot. ◆ *vt* to let fall in drops; to give out in small portions; to drib (*archery*; *Shakesp*). ◆ *vt* and *vi* (*football*, *hockey*, etc) to move (the ball) forward little by little, keeping it under close control. ◆ *n* an instance of dribbling; a small amount, a trickle. [Frequentative of **drib**]

■ **dribb'ler** *n*. **dribb'ly** *adj*.

drice /drīs/ *n* frozen carbon dioxide in the form of granules. [**dry** and **ice**]

dricksie see **druxy**.

dried, **drier**, **dries**, **driest** see **dry**.

drift /drift/ n a heap of matter (eg snow) driven together; floating materials driven by water; a driving; a drove (archaic); a driving shower; a streaming movement; the direction in which a thing is driven; a slow current caused by the wind; leeway; passive travel with the current, wind, etc; abandonment to external influences; tendency; a cattle-track, drove road; a group of animals driven or herded; a pin or bar driven into a hole, eg to enlarge it (also **drift'pin**); a drift net; a set of nets; the object aimed at; the meaning or implication of words used; loose superficial deposits, esp glacial or fluvioglacial (geol); a horizontal or oblique excavation or passage (mining); a ford (S Afr; from Du). ◆ vt to drive; to carry by drift; to cause or allow to drift; to pierce or tunnel. ◆ vi to be floated along; to be driven into heaps; to leave things to circumstances; to wander around, or live, without any definite aim. [ME; ON drift snowdrift; root as **drive**]

■ **drift'age** n that which is drifted; the amount of deviation from a ship's course due to leeway. **drift'er** n someone or something that drifts; an aimless shiftless person; a fisherman or a fishing-boat that uses a drift net. **drift'less** adj without drift. **drift'y** adj full of or forming drifts.

□ **drift'-anchor** n an anchor for keeping the ship's head to the wind. **drift'-bolt** n a steel bolt used to drive out other bolts. **drift ice** n floating masses of ice drifting before the wind. **drift'-land** n an old tribute paid for the privilege of driving cattle through a manor. **drift'-mining** n gold-mining by means of drifts in the gravel and detritus of old river beds; coalmining by means of drifts. **drift net** n a net that is allowed to drift with the tide. **drift'pin** see **drift** (n) above. **drift'-sail** n a sail immersed in the water, used for lessening the drift of a vessel during a storm. **drift transistor** n (radio) one in which resistivity increases continuously between emitter and collector junctions, improving high-frequency performance. **drift tube** n (electronics) a tube-shaped electrode in which electrons pass without significant change in velocity, while the accelerating radio frequency voltage changes. **drift'-way** n a road over which cattle are driven; drift (mining). **drift'-weed** n gulf-weed; tangle; seaweed thrown up on the beach. **drift'wood** n wood drifted by water.

drill[1] /dril/ vt to bore, pierce; to make with a drill; to pierce with a bullet or bullets (sl); to exercise (soldiers, pupils, etc) by repeated practice; to sow in rows. ◆ n an instrument for boring stone, metal, teeth, or other hard substances; a large boring instrument used in mining, etc; a type of shellfish that bores into the shells of oysters; a training exercise, or a session of it; a drill-master; a ridge with seed or growing plants on it (esp vegetables such as turnips, potatoes, etc); the plants in such a row; the machine for sowing the seed; correct procedure or routine (inf). [Prob borrowed from Du drillen to bore; dril, drille a borer; cf **thrill**]

■ **drill'er** n.

□ **drill'-barrow** n a grain-drill driven by hand. **drill bit** n a removable cutting and boring head in a drill. **drill'-harrow** n a harrow for working between drills. **drill'hole** n a hole bored in the ground eg for rock samples. **drill'-husbandry** n the method of sowing seed in drills or rows. **drilling machine**, **drilling lathe** or **drill'-press** n a machine for boring with a drill or drills. **drilling mud** n a mixture of clays, water, density-increasing agents and sometimes thixotropic agents pumped down through the drilling pipe and used to cool, lubricate and flush debris from the drilling assembly, providing the hydrostatic pressure to contain the oil and gas when this is reached. **drilling pipe** n the tube that connects the drilling platform to the drill bit and imparts rotary motion to the latter. **drilling platform** n a floating or fixed offshore structure supporting a drilling rig. **drilling rig** or **drill rig** n the complete apparatus and structure required for drilling an oil well. **drill'-master** n a person who teaches drill, or who trains in anything, esp in a mechanical manner. **drill'-plough** n a plough for sowing grain in drills. **drill-press** see **drilling machine** above. **drill rig** see **drilling rig** above. **drill'-sergeant** n a sergeant who drills soldiers. **drill'ship** n a free-floating ship-shaped drilling platform. **drill string** n a pipe made of metal tubes that forms the bore of a drillhole, esp for oil or gas.

■ **drill down** (comput) to navigate from a higher to a lower level of a hierarchically structured database.

drill[2] /dril/ n a stout twilled linen or cotton cloth (also **drill'ing**). [Ger Drillich ticking, from L trilix three-threaded; trēs, tria three, and līcium thread]

drill[3] /dril/ n a W African baboon, smaller than the mandrill. [Perh a W Afr word]

drilling see **drill**[1,2].

drily see under **dry**.

D-ring see under **D** (n).

drink /dringk/ vt (prp **drink'ing**; pat **drank**, archaic **drunk**; pap **drunk**) to swallow (a liquid); to empty (a glass, bowl, etc) by swallowing the contents; to absorb; to take in through the senses; to smoke (tobacco; obs). ◆ vi to swallow a liquid; to drink alcohol; to drink alcohol to excess. ◆ n an act of drinking; a quantity drunk; something to be drunk; a beverage; intoxicating liquor, alcohol; a monetary inducement or reward, bribe (sl). —See also **drunk**. [OE drincan; Ger trinken]

■ **drink'able** adj. **drink'ableness** n. **drink'er** n a person who drinks; a tippler. **drink'ing** n the act or habit of drinking. ◆ adj fit to drink; for drinking.

□ **drink-drive'** adj relating to drink-driving. ◆ vi to drive under the influence of alcohol. **drink-dri'ver** n someone who drives a vehicle after having drunk alcohol, esp more than the legally permitted amount. **drink-dri'ving** n and adj. **drink'-hail** interj an Early Middle English reply to a pledge in drinking (waes hail (later **wassail**), be healthy, or lucky, was answered with drinc hail drink healthy or lucky, hail being ON adj heill, not OE hāl). **drinking bout** n. **drinking fountain** n. **drink'ing-horn** n. **drinking-up time** n in a public house, the few minutes allowed after official closing time for customers to finish their last drinks before leaving. **drink'-money** n a gratuity, ostensibly given to buy liquor for drinking to the health of the giver. **drink'-offering** n an offering of wine, oil, blood, etc to a god.

■ **drink in** to absorb (rain, etc), as dry land does; to take in eagerly (something seen, said, etc). **drink off** to quaff wholly and at a gulp. **drink oneself drunk** to drink until one is drunk. **drink (someone** or **the others**, etc) **under the table** to continue drinking and remain (comparatively) sober after others have completely collapsed. **drink to**, **drink to the health of** or **drink the health of** to drink wine, etc, with good wishes for the health, prosperity, etc of, to toast. **drink up** to empty by drinking; to finish drinking. **in drink** (while) intoxicated. **strong drink** alcoholic liquor. **the drink** (inf) the sea.

drip /drip/ vi (**dripp'ing**; **dripped**) to fall in drops; to let fall drops. ◆ vt to let fall in drops. ◆ n a falling in drops; that which falls in drops; the projecting edge of a roof or sill, etc; a device for passing a fluid slowly and continuously, esp into a vein of the body (also **drip-feed**); the material so passed; a weak, pathetic person (inf); drivel, esp sentimental (sl). [OE dryppan, from drēopan]

■ **dripp'ing** n that which falls in drops, esp fat from meat during roasting. **dripp'y** adj (inf) silly, inane.

□ **drip-dry'** adj (of a material or garment) requiring little or no ironing when allowed to dry by dripping. ◆ vi and vt to dry or become dry in this way. **drip'-feed** n a drip (see above). ◆ vt to treat (a patient, etc) with a drip. **drip irrigation** n a system of irrigation in which water is supplied through pipes to the roots of a crop. **dripp'ing-pan** n a pan for receiving the dripping from roasting meat. **dripping roast** n a source of easy and continuous profits. **drip'stone** n a projecting moulding over a doorway, etc, serving to throw off the rain. **drip'-tip** n (bot) a prolonged leaf-tip, serving to shed rain.

■ **dripping wet** extremely wet. **right of drip** a right in law to let the drip from one's roof fall on another's land.

drisheen /dri-shēn'/ n a type of Irish sausage made with sheep's blood. [Ir drisín]

drive /drīv/ vt (prp **drīv'ing**; pat **drōve** or archaic **drāve**, and Spenser **drive** /driv/; pap **driv'en**) to urge along; to hurry on; to control or guide the movements or operations of; to convey or carry in a vehicle; to urge or force in or through; to push briskly; to provide motive power to; to urge (a point of argument); to carry through (eg a bargain); to impel; to compel; to send away with force, eg a ball, esp (golf) to play from the tee or with a driver, (cricket) to hit strongly in front of the wicket, and (tennis) to return forcibly underarm; to chase; to excavate (eg a tunnel); to sort out (feathers) in a current of air. ◆ vi to control an engine, vehicle or draught animal, etc; to press forward with violence; to be forced along (like a ship before the wind); to be driven; to go in a motor vehicle or carriage; to aim or tend towards a point (with at); to strike with a sword or the fist, etc (with at). ◆ n an excursion in a vehicle; a road for driving on, esp the approach to a house within its own grounds; (with cap) used in street names generally; a driving stroke (sport); impulse; impulsive force; power of getting things done; a motivational concept used to describe changes in responsiveness to a consistent external stimulus (behaviourism); the chasing of game towards the shooters, or the sport so obtained, or the ground over which the game is driven; pushing sales by reducing prices; an organized campaign to attain any end; a meeting in order to play certain games, eg whist; apparatus for driving; a disk drive (comput). [OE drīfan to drive; Ger treiben to push]

■ **drivabil'ity** or **driveabil'ity** n. **driv'able** or **drive'able** adj. **driv'en** adj (inf) ambitious or highly motivated. **driv'er** n a person or thing that drives, in all senses; a golf club with a metal or wooden head used to hit the ball from the tee; a factor that facilitates the success of a strategy (commercial jargon). **driv'erless** adj running or able to run, without a driver. **driv'ing** n the act of driving. ◆ adj (of rain, etc) heavy and windblown; motivating; directing.

❑ **drive'-by** *adj* (*inf*, chiefly *N Am*) denoting a crime, *esp* a shooting, committed from a moving vehicle (also *n*). **drive'-in** *n* a refreshment stop, store, cinema, etc where patrons are catered for while still remaining in their motor cars (also *adj*). **driver ant** *n* an army ant. **driver's license** *n* (*US*) driving licence. **drive shaft** *n* driving shaft. **drive'through** *n* (chiefly *N Am*) a shop, restaurant or bank designed so that customers can be served without leaving their cars. **drive time** *n* the time taken to complete a journey by road; the time of day when many people are travelling to or from work, *esp* when considered as part of a broadcasting schedule. **drive'train** *n* the parts of a vehicle that are involved in causing it to move, including the engine, gears, wheels, etc. **drive'way** *n* a carriage-drive; a drive, *esp* connecting a house or other premises with the public road. **driv'ing-band** *n* the band or strap that communicates motion from one machine, or part of a machine, to another. **driv'ing-box** *n* a box on which a driver sits. **driving force** *n* the person or thing that causes something to happen. **driv'ing-gear** *n* apparatus by which power is transmitted from shaft to shaft. **driving licence** *n* an official licence to drive a motor vehicle. **driv'ing-mirror** *n* a small mirror in which a driver can see what is behind his or her vehicle. **driving range** *n* a place for golfers to practise driving the ball. **driving seat** *n* the seat in a vehicle in which the driver sits; a position of control. **driving shaft** *n* a shaft from a driving wheel communicating motion to machinery. **driving test** *n* a test of ability to drive safely, *esp* an official and obligatory test. **driving wheel** *n* a main wheel that communicates motion to other wheels; one of the main wheels in a locomotive.

■ **drive a coach and horses through** (*inf*) to demolish (an argument, etc) by demonstrating the obvious faults in it; to brush aside, ignore completely. **drive home** to force (eg a nail) completely in; to make completely understood or accepted. **let drive** to aim a blow.

drivel /*driv'l*/ *vi* (**driv'elling**; **driv'elled**) to dribble, slaver like an infant; to speak like an idiot; to be foolish. ◆ *n* slaver; nonsense. [ME *drevelen*, *dravelen*; OE *dreflian*]

■ **driv'eller** *n*.

driven see **drive**.

drizzle /*driz'l*/ *vi* to rain in fine drops. ◆ *vt* to shed in fine drops; to pour (a liquid) in drops (over) (*cookery*); to cover in fine drops or in mist. ◆ *n* a small, light rain. [Frequentative of ME *dresen*, from OE *drēosan* to fall; Gothic *driusan*]

■ **drizz'ly** *adj*.

DRM *abbrev* : digital rights management.

droger or **drogher** /*drō'gər*/ *n* a West Indian coasting vessel, with long masts and lateen sails. [Du, orig a vessel on which fish were dried, from *droogen* to dry]

drogue /*drōg*/ *n* the drag of boards, attached to the end of a harpoon-line, checking the progress of a running whale; a conical canvas sleeve open at both ends, used as one form of sea-anchor, or to check the way of an aircraft, etc; (also **drogue parachute**) a parachute used to reduce speed of a falling object, eg one fired from a descending space capsule; a funnel device on the end of the hose of a tanker aircraft; a windsock; an air target of similar shape. [Origin obscure]
❑ **drogue bomb** *n* an improvised terrorist bomb, made with a grenade or plastic explosive, using a plastic bag or similar as a drogue to stabilize it when thrown.

droguet /*dro-gā'*/ *n* a ribbed woollen dress fabric, a variety of rep. [Fr; cf **drugget**]

droich /*drōhh*/ (*Scot*) *n* a dwarf. [Gaelic *troich* or *droich*; orig from OE (see **dwarf**)]
■ **droich'y** *adj* dwarfish.

droil /*droil*/ (*obs*) *vi* to drudge. [Perh Du *druilen* to loiter]

droit /*drwä*/ or (before a vowel) *drwät*, also (*Eng*) *droit*/ *n* right, legal claim. [Fr]
❑ **droit administratif** /*ad-mēn-ē-stra-tēf'*/ *n* in France, administrative law. **droit au travail** /*ō tra-vä-y'*/ *n* right to work. **droit des gens** /*dā zhã*/ *n* international law. **droit de suite** /*də swēt*/ *n* a royalty for visual artists on the resale of their works. **droit du seigneur** /*dü se-nyœr*/ *n* same as **jus primae noctis** (see under **jus¹**).

drôle /*drōl*/ *n* a rogue or knave. ◆ *adj* amusing; odd. [Fr]

droll /*drōl*/ *adj* odd; amusing; laughable. ◆ *n* someone who excites mirth; a jester. ◆ *vi* to practise drollery; to jest. [Fr *drôle*, prob from Du *drollig* odd, from *trold* a hobgoblin; cf Ger *Droll* a short thick person]
■ **droll'ery** *n* drollness; waggery; a comic show, picture or story; a jest; a puppet show. **droll'ing** *n*. **droll'ish** *adj* rather droll. **droll'ness** *n*. **drolly** /*drōl'li*/ *adv*.

drome /*drōm*/ (*inf*) *n* an aerodrome.

dromedary /*drum'i-də-ri*, *drom'*, *-ə-*/ *n* (also (*Spenser*) **drom'edare**) a thoroughbred camel; a one-humped Arabian camel. [OFr *dromedaire*, from LL *dromedārius*, from Gr *dromas*, *dromados* running, from *dromos* a course, run]

dromond /*drom'*/ or *drum'ənd*/ *n* a swift medieval ship of war (also **drom'on**). [OFr, from LL *dromō*, *-ōnis*, from Byzantine Gr *dromōn*, from *dromos* a running, and *dramein* (aorist) to run]

dromophobia /*drom-ō-fō'bi-ə*/ *n* a morbid fear of crossing streets. [Gr *dromos* public walk, and *phobos* fear]

dromos /*drom'os*/ *n* (*pl* **drom'oi**) a Greek racecourse; an entrance-passage or avenue, as to a subterranean tomb, etc (*archaeol*). [Gr]
■ **drom'ic** or **drom'ical** *adj* relating to a racecourse; basilican.

drone /*drōn*/ *n* the male of the honey-bee; someone who lives on the labour of others, like the drone bee; a lazy, idle person; a deep humming sound; a bass-pipe of a bagpipe; its note; a pedal bass; the burden of a song; a monotonous speaker or speech; an aircraft piloted by remote control. ◆ *vi* to emit a monotonous humming sound; (with *on*) to talk at length in a monotonous or expressionless way. ◆ *vt* to say in such a tone. [OE *drān* bee, but the quantity of the *a* is doubtful, and relations obscure: perh from Old Saxon]
■ **drōn'ingly** *adv*. **drōn'ish** *adj* like a drone; lazy, idle. **dron'ishly** *adv*. **drōn'ishness** *n*. **drōn'y** *adj*.
❑ **drone fly** *n* a hoverfly. **drone'-pipe** *n* a pipe producing a droning sound.

drongo /*drong'gō*/ *n* (*pl* **drong'oes** or **drong'os**) any member of the family Dicruridae, glossy-black fork-tailed insect-catching birds of the Old World tropics (also **drong'o-shrike**); a stupid person, a no-hoper (*Aust sl*). [From Malagasy]
❑ **drong'o-cuck'oo** *n* a cuckoo that resembles a drongo.

droob /*droob*/ (*Aust inf*) *n* an ineffectual or contemptible person. [Prob from US slang *droop* a drip]

droog /*droog*/ *n* a gang-member, *specif* a violent hooligan of the type portrayed by Anthony Burgess in his novel *A Clockwork Orange* (1962). [Coined by Burgess after Russ *drug* a friend]
■ **droog'ish** *adj* (of dress, behaviour, etc) reminiscent of a droog.

drook, **drookit** see **drouk**.

drool /*drool*/ *vi* to slaver; to drivel; to show effusive or lascivious pleasure (with *over*). ◆ *n* drivel. [**drivel**]
■ **drool'worthy** *adj* (*sl*) wonderful, delightful.

droome /*droom*/ (*Spenser*) *n* another form of **drum¹**.

droop /*droop*/ *vi* to hang down; to grow weak or faint; to decline. ◆ *vt* to let hang down. ◆ *n* a drooping position. [ON *drūpa* to droop; see **drop**]
■ **droop'ily** *adv*. **droop'iness** *n*. **droop'ing** *adj*. **droop'ingly** *adv*. **droop'y** *adj*.
❑ **droop nose** (*inf* **droop snoot**) *n* (*aeronautics*) a cockpit section hinged onto the main fuselage to provide downward visibility at low speeds.

drop /*drop*/ *n* a small rounded blob of liquid that hangs or falls at one time; a very small quantity of liquid; anything hanging like a drop; a pendant; a small round sweet; a curtain dropped between acts (also **drop'-cur'tain**; *theatre*); (in *pl*) a medicine taken or applied in drops; a fall; a vertical descent or difference of level; the distance by which something falls or may fall; a lowering; a landing by parachute; an instance of dropping anything; an act of repositioning a golf ball from an unplayable position by letting it fall from one's outstretched arm; an unpleasant surprise; a trap in the gallows scaffold, the fall of which allows the person being executed to drop; a device for lowering goods into a ship's hold. ◆ *combining form* used of something that drops or that causes something to drop or that is used in or for dropping. ◆ *vi* (**dropp'ing**; **dropped**) to fall in drops; to let drops fall; to fall suddenly, steeply or sheer; to let oneself fall gently; to sink; to lapse; to diminish; to subside into a condition, come gradually to be; to come casually or accidentally; to move slowly with the tide. ◆ *vt* to let fall in drops; to let fall; to let go, relinquish, abandon, part with; to omit; to lower; to lay; (of an animal) to give birth to; to spot, bespatter, sprinkle; to say casually; to write and send (a note) in an offhand or informal manner; to set down, part with; to cause to fall; to hole, etc (a ball); to score (a goal) with a drop kick; to set down from a vehicle or a ship; to cease to associate with; to lose (a sum of money or a game as part of a contest); to take one more (shot, stroke) than par (*golf*); to cause to fall; to bring down by a shot. [OE *dropa* a drop, *dropian*, *droppian* to drop; Du *drop*, Ger *Tropfe*]
■ **drop'let** *n* a little drop. **dropp'er** *n* someone or something that drops; a tube or contrivance for making liquid come out in drops; a shoot that grows downwards from a bulb and develops a new bulb (*hortic*); a dog, eg a setter, that drops to earth on sighting game; an artificial fly attached to the leader (also **drop'fly**; *angling*). **dropp'ing** *n* that which is dropped; (*usu* in *pl*) dung, excrement. **dropp'le** *n* (*rare*) a trickle. **drop'wise** *adv* by drops.
❑ **drop'-dead** *adj* (*sl*) stunning, sensational, breathtaking (also *adv*). **drop'-down** *adj* denoting a menu on a computer screen that can be accessed by clicking on a button on the toolbar. **drop'-drill'** *n* an apparatus for dropping seed and manure into the soil simultaneously. **drop'-forging** *n* the process of shaping metal parts

by forging between two dies, one fixed to the hammer and the other to the anvil of a steam or mechanical hammer (**drop'-forge** *n* and *vt*). **drop goal** *n* (*rugby*) a goal secured by a drop kick. **drop'-hamm'er** or **drop'-press** *n* a swaging, stamping or forging machine. **drop handlebars** *n pl* bicycle handlebars that curve downwards. **drop'head coupé** *n* a car whose top can be opened. **drop'-in** *adj* see drop in below. **drop kick** *n* a kick made when the ball rebounds from the ground after dropping from the hand (*rugby*); a kick made by both feet while jumping in the air (*wrestling*). **drop'-kick** *vt*. **drop'-leaf** *adj* (of a desk or table) with a hinged leaf (or leaves) which can be raised or dropped to horizontal position, but lies vertical when not in use. **drop'-lett'er** *n* (*old US*) a letter left at a post office merely for local delivery. **drop lock** or **drop'lock loan** *n* (*finance*) a bank loan for which interest rates vary with the market, but if the long-term interest rates fall to a specified level it is converted to a fixed-rate long-term bond. **drop'-net** *n* a net suspended from a boom, to be suddenly dropped on a passing shoal of fish. **drop'-off** see drop off below. **drop'out** *n* a drop kick taken following the defender's touchdown (*rugby*); a person who has withdrawn from an academic course or from conventional society; a patch that fails to record data on a magnetic tape (*comput*); failure to reproduce sound from an audio tape or disk due to mechanical interference. **dropp'ing-well** *n* (*fig* in Tennyson) a well supplied by water falling in drops from above. **drop'-ripe** *adj* so ripe as to be ready to drop from the tree. **drop'-scene** *n* a drop-curtain (see under **drop** (*n*) above). **drop scone** or **dropped scone** *n* a small thick pancake, a Scotch pancake. **drop serene** *n* (*Milton*) an old medical name for (a type of blindness) amaurosis, literally translated from L *gutta serēna*. **drop'-shot** *n* (*tennis*, etc) a ball made to drop close to the net immediately after clearing it. **drop'stone** *n* a stalactitic calcite. **drop tank** *n* (*aeronautics*) a tank, *esp* for fuel, that can be dropped during flight. **drop test** *n* (*engineering*) a test of reliability done by dropping the item or component to be tested. **drop'wort** *n* a species of *Spiraea* (*S. filipendula*) with bead-like root tubercles. **drop zone** *n* an area where troops or supplies are to be landed by parachute.

■ **a drop in the bucket** or **ocean** an infinitesimally small quantity. **at the drop of a hat** immediately; on the smallest provocation. **drop a brick** see under **brick**. **drop a curtsy** to curtsy. **drop astern** (*naut*) to get left more and more behind. **drop away** to depart, disappear. **drop dead** to die suddenly; an interjection expressing refusal, dismissal, defiance, etc. **drop down** to sail, move or row down a coast, or down a river to the sea. **drop in** (also **drop by**) to come, fall or set, etc in, or to arrive or visit casually, informally, unintentionally, or one by one (**drop'-in** *n* and *adj*). **drop-in centre** a day centre run by a charity or the social services for casual callers. **drop off** to fall asleep; to become less, to diminish; to depart, disappear; (**drop'-off** *n* a decline; a delivery of goods). **drop on** or **drop down on** to single out for reproof or an unpleasant task. **drop out** to disappear from one's place; (of sound) to disappear (during a transmission, etc); to make a drop kick (*rugby*); to withdraw, *esp* from an academic course or from conventional life in society (**drop'out** *n* and *adj*). **dropping fire** unremitting irregular discharge of small arms. **drop someone a line** (*inf*) to write someone a letter. **for the drop** (*inf*) about to be relegated; about to be hanged. **get the drop on one** (*US*) to be ready to shoot first; hence to have at a disadvantage. **let drop** to disclose inadvertently, or seemingly so. **Prince Rupert's drops** or **Rupert's drops** drops of glass that have fallen in a melted state into cold water, and have assumed a tadpole-like shape, the whole falling to dust with a loud report if the point of the tail is nipped off.

dropsy /drop'si/ *n* a condition characterized by unnatural accumulation of watery fluid in any part of the body (now *usu* called **oedema**). [Aphetic for **hydropsy**]
■ **drop'sical** or **drop'sied** *adj* (*Shakesp*, etc) affected with dropsy.

drosera /dros'ə-rə/ *n* any plant of the sundew genus of **Droserā'ceae**, a family of insectivorous plants. [Feminine of Gr *droseros* dewy, from *drosos* dew]
■ **droserā'ceous** *adj*.

droshky /drosh'ki/ or **drosky** /dros'ki/ *n* a low four-wheeled open carriage used in Russia; a German four-wheeled cab. [Russ *drozhki*]

drosometer /dro-som'i-tər/ (*meteorol*) *n* an instrument for measuring dew. [Gr *drosos* dew, and *metron* measure]

drosophila /dro-sof'i-lə/ *n* any fly of the *Drosophila* genus of small yellow flies, fruit flies, which breed in fermenting fruit juices and are used in genetic experiments. [Gr *drosos* dew, moisture, and *phileein* to love]

dross /dros/ *n* the scum of melting metals; waste matter; small or waste coal; refuse; anything worthless; rust; lucre. [OE *drōs*]
■ **dross'iness** *n*. **dross'y** *adj* like dross; impure; worthless.

drostdy /dros'dā/ (*S Afr*) *n* formerly, the house and office of a landdrost. [Afrik, from Du *drost* bailiff, sheriff; cf Ger *Drost*, *Drostei*]

drought /drowt/ or **drouth** /drowth or (*Scot*) *drooth*/ *n* dryness; a shortage of rain or of water; a condition of atmosphere favourable to drying; thirst. [OE *drūgath* dryness, from *drūgian* to dry]
■ **drought'iness** or **drouth'iness** *n*. **drought'y** or **drouth'y** *adj* very dry; lacking rain; thirsty.

drouk or **drook** /drook/ (*Scot*) *vt* to drench. [Origin obscure; cf ON *drukna* to be drowned; Dan *drukne*]
■ **drouk'ing** or **drook'ing** *n*. **drouk'it** or **drook'it** *adj*.

drouth, etc see **drought**.

drove /drōv/ *pat of* **drive**. *n* a number of cattle, or other animals, driven or herded together; a crowd or horde, eg of people, moving along together; a broad-edged chisel for dressing stone; a drove road (*esp E Anglia*). [OE *drāf*, *drīfan* to drive]
■ **drov'er** *n* a person whose occupation is to drive cattle; a fishing-boat, drifter (*Spenser*, etc). **drov'ing** *n* the occupation of a drover; the action of herding cattle, etc.
□ **drove road** *n* an old generally grassy track used or once used by droves of cattle.

drow¹ /drow/ *n* (*Shetland* and *Orkney*) a form of **troll¹**.

drow² /drow/ (*Scot*) *n* a drizzling mist; a squall. [Origin obscure]

drown /drown/ *vi* to die of suffocation in liquid. ◆ *vt* to kill by suffocation in liquid; to submerge; to flood; to extinguish; to make indistinguishable or imperceptible. [ME *drounen*; origin obscure; the word used in OE was *druncnian*]
■ **drownd'ed** *adj* (*Spenser*; now *non-standard*) drowned. **drown'er** *n*. **drown'ing** *n* and *adj*.
□ **drowned valley** *n* a river valley that has been drowned by a rise of sea level relative to the land, due either to actual depression of the land or to a rise in sea level.
■ **drown someone out** (*inf*) to make someone inaudible by making a louder noise.

drowse /drowz/ *vi* to doze, sleep lightly. ◆ *vt* to make heavy with sleep, cause to doze; to stupefy; to pass in a half-sleeping state. ◆ *n* a half-sleeping state. [Appar OE *drūsian* to be sluggish; but not known between OE times and the 16c]
■ **drows'ihead** or **drows'ihed** *n* (*Spenser*) drowsiness, sleepiness. **drows'ily** *adv*. **drows'iness** *n*. **drows'y** *adj* sleepy; heavy; dull; inducing sleep.

DRS (*cricket*) *abbrev*: decision review system.

drub /drub/ *vt* (**drubb'ing**; **drubbed**) to beat or thrash. [Ar *daraba* to beat, bastinado, from *darb* a beating, has been suggested]
■ **drubb'ing** *n* a cudgelling; (in games) a thorough defeat.

drucken /druk'ən/ (*Scot*) *adj* drunken, used also as a *pap* of **drink**. [ON *drukkinn*, pap of *drekka* to drink]
■ **druck'enness** *n*.

drudge /druj/ *vi* to do dull, laborious or lowly work. ◆ *n* someone who does heavy monotonous work; a slave; a menial servant; dull taskwork. [Ety unknown; perh from root of OE *drēogan* to perform, undergo]
■ **drudg'er** *n*. **drudg'ery** or **drudg'ism** *n* the work of a drudge; uninteresting toil; hard or humble labour. **drudg'ingly** *adv*.

drug¹ /drug/ *n* any substance used in the composition of medicine to cure, diagnose or prevent disease; a narcotic substance, *esp* an addictive one; a poisonous or stupefying substance; something one is intoxicated by or craves for (*fig*); an article that cannot be sold, generally owing to overproduction. ◆ *vt* (**drugg'ing**; **drugged**) to mix or season with drugs; to administer a drug to; to dose to excess; to poison or stupefy with drugs. ◆ *vi* to administer drugs or medicines; to take drugs, *esp* narcotics, habitually. [OFr *drogue*, of uncertain origin]
■ **drugg'er** *n* a druggist (*obs*); someone who drugs. **drugg'ie** *n* (*inf*) a drug addict. **drugg'ist** *n* a person who deals in drugs; a pharmacist (*N Am*). **drugg'y** *adj*.
□ **drug abuse** *n* the taking of illegal drugs, *esp* narcotics, for non-medical purposes. **drug addict** or **drug fiend** *n* a habitual, addicted taker of (*esp* non-medicinal) drugs. **drug baron** *n* someone who runs an organization dealing in illegal drugs. **drug pusher** *n* a pusher, someone who peddles drugs illegally. **drug resistance** *n* the medical condition in which tissues become resistant after treatment with drugs, commonly found with many anti-tumour treatments. **drug'-runner** *n* someone who smuggles drugs. **drug'-running** *n*. **drug squad** *n* a police department concerned with enforcing anti-drugs laws. **drug'store** *n* (mainly *N Am*) a chemist's shop (usually selling a variety of goods, including refreshments).

drug² /drug/ (*obs*; *Shakesp*) *n* a form of **drudge**.

drugget /drug'it/ *n* a woven and felted coarse woollen fabric; a protective covering, made of such fabric, for a floor or carpet. [OFr *droguet*]

druid /droo'id/ *n* (also *fem* **dru'idess**; also with *cap*) a priest among the ancient Celts of Britain, Gaul and Germany; an Eisteddfod official;

---

a member of a benefit society founded in 1781. [L pl *druidae*, from a Celtic stem *druid-*, whence OIr *drai*, Ir and Gaelic *draoi* magician]
- **druid'ic** or **druid'ical** *adj*. **dru'idism** *n* the doctrines that the druids taught; the ceremonies they practised.
- □ **druidical circle** *n* a fanciful 18c name for a stone circle (not made by the druids).

drum[1] /*drum*/ *n* a percussion instrument, a skin stretched on a frame; anything shaped like a drum; the tympanum of the ear; the upright part of a cupola (*archit*); a cylinder, *esp* a revolving cylinder; a magnetic drum (*comput*; see under **magnet**); a cylindrical barrel; a bundle or swag (*Aust*); a house (*sl*); a large and tumultuous evening party (said to be so called because rival hostesses vied with each other in drumming up crowds of guests; *obs*); a drumfish. *vi* (**drumm'ing**; **drummed**) to beat a drum; to beat rhythmically; to solicit orders (*US*). *vt* to expel to the sound of a drum or drums (with *out*; *esp milit*; also *fig*); to summon, call together (with *up*); to impress or stress by repetition (with *into*). [From a Gmc root found in Du *trom*, Ger *Trommel* a drum; prob imit]
- **drumm'er** *n* a person who drums; a commercial traveller (*esp US*); a swagman (*Aust*); an Australian fish of shallow coastal waters (family Kyphosidae).
- □ **drum and bass** *n* a type of fast rhythmic popular music characterized by low bass lines and complex percussion. **drum'beat** *n*. **drum'-belly** see **hoove**[1]. **drum brake** *n* a type of brake in which two shoes grip the inside of the brake drum. **drum'fire** *n* massed artillery fire with a rolling sound. **drum'fish** *n* any fish of the Sciaenidae. **drum'head** *n* the head or skin of a drum; the top part of a capstan; (also **drumhead cabbage**) a type of flat-headed cabbage. *adj* (*milit*) improvised in the field (see also **court martial** under **court**). **drum kit** *n* a set of drums, cymbals, etc used in jazz or rock music. **drum machine** *n* a synthesizer for simulating the sound of various percussion instruments. **drum'-ma'jor** *n* the marching leader of a military band. **drum majorette** *n* a girl who heads a marching band, *usu* twirling a baton, in a parade, etc; a majorette. **drum roll** *n* a quick series of beats on a drum. **drum'stick** *n* the stick with which a drum is beaten; the tibia of a dressed fowl. **drum table** *n* a round, deep-topped table on a central leg, *usu* with drawers.
- **beat** or **bang the drum** to indulge in publicity.

drum[2] /*drum*/ *n* a ridge, drumlin (in many place names). [Scot and Ir Gaelic *druim* back]
- **drum'lin** *n* (*geol*) a usually oval ridge formed under the ice-sheet of the Glacial Period (also **drum**).

drumble /*drum'bl*/ (*Shakesp*; now *dialect*) *vi* to be sluggish.
- **drum'bledor** *n* a dumbledore.

drumlin see under **drum**[2].

drumly /*drum'li*/ (*Scot*) *adj* turbid, muddy; gloomy.

drummer see under **drum**[1].

drummock /*drum'ək*/ same as **drammock**.

Drummond light /*drum'ənd līt*/ *n* the limelight or oxyhydrogen light invented by Captain T *Drummond* (1797–1840).

drunk /*drungk*/ *pap* and old-fashioned *pat* of **drink**. *adj* intoxicated with alcohol (also *fig*); saturated. *n* a drunk person; a drunken bout (*inf*).
- **drunk'ard** *n* a person who frequently drinks to excess; a habitual drinker.
- □ **drunk-dri'ver** *n* (*US*) a drink-driver. **drunk-dri'ving** *n*. **drunk'en** *adj* given to excessive drinking; worthless, besotted; resulting from intoxication; (sometimes) drunk. **drunk'enly** *adv*. **drunk'enness** *n* intoxication; habitual intoxication.

drupe /*droop*/ *n* any fleshy fruit with a stone. [L *drūpa*, from Gr *dryppā* an olive]
- **drupa'ceous** *adj* producing or relating to drupes or stone fruits. **drup'el** or **drupe'let** *n* a little drupe, forming part of a fruit, as in the raspberry.

Druse, **Druze** or **Druz** /*drooz*/ *n* (one of) a people inhabiting chiefly a mountainous district in the south of Syria, whose religion contains elements found in the Koran, the Bible, Gnosticism, etc (also *adj*). [Perh from *Darazi* an early exponent of the religion]
- **Drus'ian** *adj*.

druse /*drooz*/ *n* a rock cavity lined with crystals (by geologists *usu* called a **drusy cavity**), a geode. [Ger *Druse*, from Czech *druza* a piece of crystallized ore]
- **dru'sen** *n pl* (*ophthalmol*) accumulations of extracellular material on the retina and optical disc. **dru'sy** *adj* rough with or composed of minute crystals; miarolitic.

druthers /*drudh'ərz*/ (*US inf*) *n* choice, preference. [Contraction of I'*d rather* do]

Druz, **Druze** see **Druse**.

DRV *abbrev*: dietary reference values.

dry /*drī*/ *adj* (**drī'er**; **drī'est**) without water or liquid, contained or adhering; free from or deficient in moisture, sap or rain; thirsty; out of water; failing to yield water, or milk, or other liquid; (of a fruit) not fleshy; not green; (of eg toast) unbuttered; not drawing blood; (of wines, etc) free from sweetness and fruity flavour; (of beer) brewed by a method that removes the bitter taste, aftertaste and smell of traditional beer; legally forbidding the liquor trade (*inf*); enforcing or subjected to prohibition; uninteresting; frigid, precise, formal; (of humour) quiet, restrained, uttered in a matter-of-fact way, as if not intended to be humorous; (of manner) distantly unsympathetic; (of a cough) not producing catarrh; (of natural gas) containing only small amounts of liquid constituents. *vt* (**dry'ing**; **dried**) to free from or empty of water or moisture (often with *off*). *vi* to become dry (often with *off*); to evaporate entirely. *n* (*pl* **dries**) a prohibitionist; a person who favours strict adherence to hardline right-wing Conservative policies (*Brit politics*). [OE *drȳge*; cf Du *droog*, Ger *trocken*]
- **drī'er** or **dry'er** *n* someone who or something that dries; a machine for extracting moisture from cloth, grain, etc; a drying agent for oils, paint, etc. **drī'ly** or **dry'ly** *adv* in a dry manner. **dry'ing** *n* and *adj*. **dry'ish** *adj*. **dry'ness** *n*.
- □ **Dry'asdust** *n* a character in the prefatory matter of some of Scott's novels; a dull, pedantic, learned person (also *adj*). **dry battery** *n* (*elec*) a battery composed of dry-cells. **dry'beat** *vt* (*obs*; *Shakesp*, etc) to drub, but without shedding blood. **dry'-bi'ble** *n* a disease of horned cattle in which the third stomach, or bible, is very dry. **dry blowing** *n* the use of a current of air to separate particles of mineral (*esp* gold) from the material in which it is found. **dry bob** *n* at Eton, a boy who plays cricket during the summer term (cf **wet bob**). **dry'-cell** *n* (*elec*) an electric cell in which the electrolyte is not a liquid but a paste. **dry'-clean** *vt* to clean (clothes, etc) using eg a petroleum-based solvent rather than water. **dry'-cleaner** *n*. **dry'-cleaning** *n*. **dry construction** *n* (*building*) the use of timber or plasterboard for partitions, lining of walls and ceilings, to eliminate the traditional use of plaster and the consequent drying-out period (also **dry lining**). **dry'-cupping** *n* (*old med*) application of cups without previous scarification. **dry'-cure** *vt* to cure by drying. **dry distillation** *n* destructive distillation (qv under **destruction**). **dry dock** *n* a dock from which the water can be pumped, in order to effect repairs to the underside of a ship. **dry'-dock** *vt* to put in a dry dock. **dry'-eyed** *adj* tearless. **dry farming** *n* a system of tillage in dry countries, surface soil being kept constantly loose, so as to retain scanty rains and reduce evaporation. **dry'-fist** *n* (*obs*) a niggard. **dry-fist'ed** *adj* and *adv* (*obs*) taking payment for gains and owing for losses. **dry'-fly** *adj* (of fishing) without sinking the fly in the water. **dry'-foot** *adv* (*Shakesp*) by scent of the foot alone. **dry goods** *n pl* drapery and the like distinguished from groceries, etc. **dry hole** *n* a well that does not yield commercially viable quantities of oil or gas; an unsuccessful project (*fig*). **dry ice**, **dry-iced** see under **ice**. **drying oils** *n pl* vegetable or animal oils that harden by oxidation when exposed to air. **drying-up cloth** *n* a cloth or towel for drying dishes, a dishtowel. **dry land** *n* land as opposed to sea. **dry light** *n* (*archaic*) an undeceptive light; an unprejudiced view. **dry lining** see **dry construction** above. **dry Mass** or **dry service** *n* *Missa sicca*, a rite in which there is neither consecration nor communion. **dry measure** *n* a system of measure by bulk, used for grain, etc (see eg **bushel**[1], **peck**[2], **pint**). **dry monsoon** see under **monsoon**. **dry'mouth** *n* xerostomia. **dry'-nurse** *n* a nurse who does not suckle (also *vt*). **dry'-plate** *n* a sensitized photographic plate, with which a picture may be made without the preliminary use of a bath. **dry'-point** *n* a sharp needle by which fine lines are drawn in copperplate engraving; a plate or impression produced with it. **dry riser** *n* a vertical pipe with an outside access through which water can be pumped from the street to the individual floors of a building in the event of a fire. **dry'-roast** *vt* to roast without oil or fat. **dry'-roasted** *adj*. **dry rot** *n* a decay of timber caused by *Merulius lacrymans* and other fungi which reduce it ultimately to a dry brittle mass; any of various fungal diseases of plants, bulbs, fruits, etc; a concealed decay or degeneration (*fig*). **dry run** *n* a practice exercise (*milit*); a rehearsal, test. **dry'-salt** *vt* to cure (meat) by salting and drying. **dry'salter** *n* a dealer in gums, dyes, etc, or (*obs*) in salted or dry meats, pickles, etc. **dry'saltery** *n*. **dry service** see **dry Mass** above. **dry'-shod** *adj* and *adv* without wetting the shoes or feet. **dry ski** *n* an adaptation of a ski with which one can practise skiing on a dry surface. **dry skiing** *n*. **dry steam** *n* steam unmixed with liquid drops. **dry'-stone** *adj* built of stone without mortar, as some walls. **dry'-stove** *n* a kind of hot-house with dry heat. **dry'suit** *n* a close-fitting air- and watertight synthetic suit for wearing in *esp* cold water, that retains warmth by a layer of air, and allows clothing to be worn underneath it. **dry'-transfer lettering** *n* lettering on the back of a plastic sheet that can be rubbed down onto paper, etc. **dry'wall** *n* (*US*) plasterboard. **dry'-wall'er** *n* a person who builds walls without mortar. **dry'-wash** *n* the bed of an intermittent stream.

■ **cut and dried** or **cut and dry** see under **cut**. **dry out** (*inf*) to take or give a course of treatment to cure oneself or another person of alcoholism. **dry up** to dry thoroughly or completely; to cease to produce liquid (water, milk, etc); (of an actor, etc) to forget one's lines or part (*inf*); to stop talking (*sl*). **go dry** to adopt liquor prohibition. **high and dry** see under **high**[1]. **the dry** (sometimes with *cap*; *Aust inf*) the dry season in central and N Australia.

dryad /drī'ad, -əd/ (*Gr myth*) *n* (pl **dry'ads** or **dry'adēs**) a wood nymph; a forest-tree. [Gr *dryas, -ados*, from *drȳs* oak tree]

DS *abbrev*: dal segno (*music*); Detective Sergeant; disseminated sclerosis; Doctor of Surgery; document signed; dual screen.

Ds (*chem*) *symbol*: darmstadtium.

DSA *abbrev*: Driving Standards Agency.

DSC *abbrev*: Distinguished Service Cross.

DSc. *abbrev*: *Doctor Scientiae* (*L*), Doctor of Science.

DSL *abbrev*: Digital Subscriber Line, a fast Internet connection over an analogue phone line.

DSM *abbrev*: Distinguished Service Medal.

DSO *abbrev*: (Companion of the) Distinguished Service Order.

dso, dsobo, dsomo see **zho**.

dsp *abbrev*: *decessit sine prole* (*L*), died without issue.

DSS *abbrev*: (from 1989 to 2001) Department of Social Security; Director of Social Services.

DSSS *abbrev*: direct-sequence spread spectrum, a technique for reducing interference in radio broadcasting.

DST *abbrev*: Daylight Saving Time.

'dst /dst/ a shortened form of **hadst, wouldst**, etc.

DT *abbrev*: data transmission.

DTh. or **DTheol.** *abbrev*: *Doctor Theologiae* (*L*), Doctor of Theology.

DTI *abbrev*: (until 2007) Department of Trade and Industry.

DTLR *abbrev*: Department for Transport, Local Government and the Regions (now replaced by **DfT** and **ODPM**).

DTP *abbrev*: desktop publishing.

DTs or **dt's** (*inf*) *abbrev*: delirium tremens (see under **delirious**).

DTT *abbrev*: digital terrestrial television.

DU *abbrev*: depleted uranium.

Du. *abbrev*: Dutch.

duad see under **dual**.

dual /doo' or dū'əl/ *adj* twofold; consisting of two; expressing or representing two things (*grammar*). ◆ *vt* (**du'alling; du'alled**) to make (a road) into dual carriageway. [L *duālis*, from *duo* two]
■ **du'ad** *n* a dyad; a pair (*rare*). **du'alin** *n* an explosive mixture of sawdust, saltpetre and nitroglycerine. **du'alism** *n* (*philos*) the view that seeks to explain the world by the assumption of two radically independent and absolute elements, eg (1) the doctrine of the entire separation of spirit and matter, *opp* to *idealism* and *materialism*, and (2) the doctrine of two distinct principles of good and evil, or of two divine beings of these characters. **du'alist** *n* a believer in dualism. **dualis'tic** *adj* consisting of two; relating to dualism. **dualis'tically** *adv*. **duality** /dū-al'i-ti/ *n* doubleness; state of being double. **du'ally** *adv*. **du'archy** *n* a non-standard form of **diarchy**.
❑ **du'al band** *adj* denoting a mobile phone that is capable of operating on two frequency bands. **dual carriageway** *n* a road consisting of two separated parts, each for use of traffic in one direction only. **dual control** *n* joint control or jurisdiction. **du'al-control** *adj* able to be operated by either or both of two persons. **du'al-density** *adj* (*comput*) same as **double-density** (see under **double**). **dual monarchy** *n* two (more or less) independent states with one and the same monarch; (*specif*) Austria-Hungary (before 1918). **dual nationality** *n* the state or fact of being a citizen of two countries. **dual personality** *n* a condition in which the same individual shows at different times two very different characters. **du'al-priced** *adj* (*stock exchange*) of trading, in which buyers and sellers deal at different prices. **dual pricing** *n* differential pricing. **du'al-pur'pose** *adj* serving or intended to serve two purposes; (of cattle) bred to produce meat and milk. **dual school** *n* one for both boys and girls.

duan /doo'än or doo'an/ *n* a division of a poem, a canto. [Gaelic]

duar /doo'är/ *n* a circular Arab encampment or tent village (also **douar** or **dowar**). [Ar *dūār*]

duarchy see under **dual**.

duathlon /dū-ath'lon/ *n* a long-distance race involving running and cycling stages. [L *duo* (or Gr *dyo*) two, and Gr *athlon* a contest]
■ **duath'lete** *n*.

dub[1] /dub/ *vt* (**dubb'ing; dubbed**) to confer knighthood upon (from the ceremony of striking the shoulders with the flat of a sword); to confer any name or dignity upon; to smooth with an adze; to trim; to cut the comb and wattles from; to rub a softening and waterproof mixture into (leather); to dress (a fly) for fishing. [OE *dubbian* to dub knight]
■ **dubb'ing** *n* the accolade; (also **dubb'in**) a preparation of grease for softening leather.

dub[2] /dub/ *vt* to give (a film) a new soundtrack, eg one in a different language; to add sound effects or music; to transfer (recorded music, etc) to a new disc or tape; to combine so as to make one record (music, etc from more than one source, eg a live performance and a recording). ◆ *n* a type of reggae music with bass and drums prominent. [Short form of **double**]
❑ **dub poet** *n*. **dub poetry** *n* a style of poetry, of West Indian origin, performed spontaneously in reggae rhythm to dubbed or recorded music. **dub'step** *n* a type of electronic popular dance music developed from dub and drum and bass.

dub[3] /dub/ (*dialect*; *esp Scot*) *n* a pool of foul water; a puddle; (in *pl*) mud. [Cf LGer *dobbe*]

dubbin, dubbing see **dub**[1].

dubious /doo' or dū'bi-əs/ *adj* doubtful, causing or having doubt; uncertain; of uncertain result or outcome; arousing suspicion or disapproval; hesitating (about). [L *dubius*]
■ **dubiety** /-bī'i-ti/ *n* doubt. **dubios'ity** or **du'biousness** *n*. **du'biously** *adv*.

dubitate /doo' or dū'bi-tāt/ (*formal*) *vi* to doubt, hesitate. [L *dubitāre*, *-ātum*]
■ **du'bitable** *adj*. **du'bitably** *adv*. **du'bitancy** *n* (*obs*). **dubitā'tion** *n*. **du'bitative** *adj*. **du'bitatively** *adv*.

dubnium /dub'ni-əm/ *n* an artificially produced radioactive transuranic element (symbol **Db**; atomic no 105), formerly called **unnilpentium**, **joliotium** and **hahnium**; a former name for **rutherfordium** (see under **rutherford**). [First produced in *Dubna*, Russia]

Dubonnet /doo-bon'ā, dū-/ *n* a type of sweet red wine flavoured with quinine, drunk as an apéritif. [Named after a family of French wine merchants]

ducal /dū'kəl/ *adj* relating to a duke. [Fr, from LL *ducālis*, from L *dux* leader]
■ **du'cally** *adv*.

ducat /duk'ət/ (*hist*) *n* a gold or silver coin of varying values, formerly much used in Europe. [OFr *ducat*, from Ital *ducato*, from LL *ducātus* a duchy]
■ **ducatoon'** *n* an old silver coin in Venice and elsewhere.

ducdame /dook'də-mi, dūk-dä'mi/ (*Shakesp, As You Like It*) *interj* perhaps a meaningless refrain; explained as L *duc ad mē* bring to me, as Welsh *dewch 'da mi* come with me, and as Romany *dukrā'mē* I tell fortunes, etc.

duce /doo'chä/ *n* the title assumed by the Italian dictator Mussolini. [Ital, leader, from L *dux*]

Duchenne muscular dystrophy /dū-shen' mus'kū-lər dis'trə-fi/ *n* (short form **Duchenne**) a common and severe form of muscular dystrophy, which strikes children (*esp* boys) under 10 years old. [Guillaume *Duchenne* (1806–75), French physician]

duchess, duchesse see under **duchy**.

duchy /duch'i/ *n* the territory of a duke, a dukedom. [OFr *duché*, from LL *ducātus*; Fr *duchesse*, from LL *ducissa*]
■ **duch'ess** *n* the wife or widow of a duke; a woman of the same rank as a duke in her own right; a size of roofing slate 610 × 305mm (24 × 12in). **duchesse** /duch'es or dū-shes'/ *n* (Fr, duchess) a table cover or centrepiece (also **duchesse cover**).
❑ **duchesse lace** *n* Flemish pillow lace with designs in cord outline. **duchesse potatoes** *n pl* piped shapes of mashed potato, butter, milk and egg yolk baked until light brown. **duchesse set** *n* a set of covers for a dressing-table. **duchy court** *n* the court of a duchy.

duck[1] /duk/ *n* any bird of the family Anatidae, the prominent features of which are short webbed feet, with a small hind-toe not reaching the ground, netted scales in front of the lower leg, and a long flattened bill; the female duck as distinguished from the male *drake*; (originally *duck's egg* for zero (0), on a scoresheet) no runs (*cricket*); a darling (used loosely as a term of address; *inf*); (*usu* **lame duck**) a defaulter, bankrupt; an oscillating shape used in wave-power technology (also **nodding duck**). [OE *dūce* (or perh *duce*) a duck; cf **duck**[2]]
■ **duck'ing** *n* duck-hunting. **duck'ling** *n* a young duck. **ducks** or **duck'y** *n* (*inf*) a term of endearment. **duck'y** *adj*.
❑ **duck'-ant** *n* a Jamaican termite nesting in trees. **duck'bill** *n* a platypus. **duck'-billed** *adj* having a bill like a duck. **duck'-board** *n* a board with slats nailed across it, used for walking in excavations, etc, on swampy ground, or as steps in repair work on roofs. **duck-coy** see

decoy. **duck'-egg blue** *n* a light greenish-blue colour. **duck'-footed** *adj.* **duck'-hawk** *n* a moorbuzzard or marsh-harrier; a peregrine falcon (*US*). **duck'-legged** *adj* short-legged. **duck'mole** *n* the duckbill. **duck'-pond** *n.* **duck's arse** (or *N Am* **ass**) *n* (*sl*) a man's hairstyle in which the hair is swept back to a point on the neck resembling a duck's tail, worn *esp* by Teddy boys (*abbrev* **DA**). **duck's'-foot** *n* lady's-mantle. **duck'-shot** *n* shot for shooting wild duck. **duck'shove** *vi* (*Aust* and *NZ*; *inf*) to jump a queue (*orig* of taxi-drivers); to cheat; to steal; to avoid responsibilities. **duck'shover** *n* (*Aust* and *NZ*, *inf*). **duck's'-meat** *n* duckweed. **duck soup** *n* (*US sl*) something very easy, a cinch; someone easy to handle, a pushover. **duck'-tail** *n* a white Teddy boy in South Africa. **duck'weed** *n* any plant of the family Lemnaceae, monocotyledons, most of which consist of a small flat green floating plate, from which one or more roots dangle.
 ■ **Bombay duck** a small Indian fish, the bummalo, dried and eaten as a relish. **break one's duck** to make one's first run (*cricket*); to enjoy a first success after several failures. **lame duck** a defaulter; a bankrupt; anything disabled; an inefficient or helpless person or organization. **like a dying duck** languishing. **make** or **play ducks and drakes** to make flat stones skip on the surface of water; to use recklessly; to squander, waste (with *of* or *with*). **sitting duck** an easy target, helpless victim. **wild duck** the mallard, *esp* the henbird.

duck² /duk/ *vt* to dip for a moment in water; to avoid (*inf*). ◆ *vi* to dip or dive; to lower the head suddenly; to cringe, yield. ◆ *n* a quick plunge, dip; a quick lowering of the head or body. [ME *douken* from an assumed OE *dūcan* to duck, dive; Ger *tauchen*, Du *duiken*]
 ■ **duck'er** *n* someone who ducks; a diving bird. **duck'ing** *n.*
 □ **duck hook** *n* (*golf*) a badly mishit shot that veers sharply and low to the left (for a right-handed player) as soon as it is hit. **duck'ing-pond** *n.* **duck'ing-stool** *n* (*hist*) a stool or chair in which adjudged offenders were tied and ducked in the water.
 ■ **duck and dive** to use one's wits to avoid or accomplish something. **duck out of** to shirk, avoid (responsibilities, etc).

duck³ /duk/ *n* a kind of coarse cotton or linen, etc cloth for small sails, sacking, etc; (in *pl*) garments made of duck. [Du *doek* linen cloth; Ger *Tuch*]

duck⁴ /duk/ *n* a kind of amphibious military transport vehicle or landing craft. [From manufacturers' code initials, DUKW]

ducking see **duck¹,²**.

Duckworth-Lewis method /duk'wərth-loo'is meth'əd/ *n* a method for determining the winner of a limited-over cricket match when the number of overs faced by each side is unequal due to rain, etc. [Frank *Duckworth* (born 1939) and Tony *Lewis* (born 1942), English statisticians]

duct /dukt/ *n* a tube conveying fluids in animal bodies or plants; a pipe for an electric cable; a hole, pipe or channel for carrying a fluid; an air-passage. ◆ *vt* to carry along, or as if along, a duct. [L *ductus*, from *dūcere* to lead]
 ■ **duct'ing** *n.* **duct'less** *adj.*
 □ **ducted fan** see **turbofan** under **turbo-**. **ductless glands** *n pl* (*anat*) masses of glandular tissue that lack ducts and discharge their products directly into the blood. **duct tape** *n* a strong adhesive water-resistant tape used *esp* for repairs to pipes.

ductile /duk'tīl, -til/ *adj* yielding; capable of being drawn out into threads; easily led. [Fr, from L *ductilis*, from *dūcere* to lead]
 ■ **ductility** /-til'it-i/ or **duc'tileness** *n* the capacity of being drawn out without breaking.

dud¹ /dud/ (*inf*) *n* a bomb or projectile that fails to go off; a dishonoured cheque; a counterfeit; any useless or ineffective person or thing; a failure. ◆ *adj* useless or ineffective; (of a cheque) dishonoured.

dud² /dud/ (*inf*) *n* (in *pl*) poor or ragged clothes, tatters; (in *pl*) clothes. [There is a ME *dudde* birrus, a cloak; cf ON *duthi* swaddling-clothes]
 ■ **dudd'ery** *n* (*dialect*) a shop where old clothes are sold; rags collectively. **dudd'ie** or **dudd'y** *adj* (*Scot*) ragged.
 □ **duddie weans** /wānz/ *n pl* (*Burns*) ragged children; (with *caps*) a Scottish literary society.

dudder /dud'ər/ (*dialect*) *n* confusion. [Cf **dither**]

duddery, duddie, duddy see under **dud²**.

dude /dūd, dood/ (*orig US sl*) *n* a fop or dandy; a man from the city holidaying out West; a man (also used as an informal term of address); a stylish or admirable man. [Origin uncertain; perh from **dud²**]
 ■ **du'dish** *adj.* **du'dism** *n.*
 □ **dude ranch** *n* a ranch run as a holiday resort or for training in ranching.
 ■ **dude up** to dress up flashily.

dudeen /doo-dēn', -dhēn'/ *n* a short clay tobacco pipe (also **dudheen'**). [Ir *dúidín*, dimin of *dúd* pipe]

dudgeon¹ /duj'ən/ *n* resentment; offended indignation, *esp* as in *in high dudgeon*. [Origin unknown]

dudgeon² /duj'ən/ *n* the haft of a dagger; a small dagger (*archaic*). [Anglo-Fr *digeon* knife-handle]

dudheen see **dudeen**.

dudish, dudism see under **dude**.

duds see **dud²**.

due¹ /doo' or dū/ *adj* owed; that ought to be paid or done to another; proper; appointed, under engagement (to be ready, arrive, etc). ◆ *adv* exactly, directly. ◆ *n* something that is owed; what one has a right to or has earned; fee, toll, charge or tribute; (in *pl*) subscription to a club or society. [OFr *deü*, pap of *devoir*, from L *debēre* to owe]
 ■ **due'ful** or **dew'full** *adj* (*Spenser*) proper, fit. **duly** *adv* see separate entry.
 □ **due date** *n* the date by which a payment must be paid; the date on which a payment falls due; the approximate date on which a pregnant woman is expected to give birth.
 ■ **due diligence** the steps expected to be taken by a prudent person before doing something. **due process (of law)** (subjection to) fair and established legal proceedings. **due to** caused by; owing to, because of (a use still deprecated by some, but now almost standard); (of horses) pregnant by. **give someone his** (or **her**) **due** to be fair to someone. **give the devil his due** to acknowledge some commendable quality, etc in someone otherwise disapproved of. **in due course** in the ordinary way when the time comes. **pay one's dues** (*inf*) to work hard and suffer hardship before achieving success.

due² /dū/ (*Shakesp*) *vt* to endue.

duel /doo' or dū'əl/ *n* a prearranged fight between two people under fixed conditions and generally on an affair of honour; single combat to decide a quarrel; any fight or struggle between two parties. ◆ *vi* (**du'elling; du'elled**) to fight in a duel. [Ital *duello*, from L *duellum*, the original form of *bellum*, from *duo* two]
 ■ **du'eller** *n.* **du'elling** *n.* **du'ellist** *n.* **duello** /doo-el'ō/ *n* (*pl* **duell'os**) a duel (*obs*); duelling; the laws that regulate duelling. **du'elsome** *adj* given to duelling.

duende /dwen'de/ (*Sp*) *n* (*pl* **duen'des**) literally, a ghost, goblin, demon; inspiration, magnetism, ardour.

duenna /dū-en'ə/ *n* a lady who acts the part of governess in Spain; a lady who watches over or chaperons a younger lady. [Sp *dueña*, a form of *doña* mistress, from L *domina*, feminine of *dominus* lord]

duet or **duett** /dū-et'/ *n* (*pl* **duets', duetts'**) a composition in music for two performers; the performance of this; the performers of this; any action involving two parties. ◆ *vi* (**duett'ing; duett'ed**) to perform a duet. [Ital *duetto*, dimin of *duo*, from *due* two, from L *duo*]
 ■ **duettino** /-tē'nō/ *n* (*pl* **duettin'os**) a simple duet. **duett'ist** /dū-/ *n.*

duetto /doo-et'tō/ (*Ital*) *n* (*pl* **duett'os** or **duett'i** /-ē/) a duet.

duff¹ /duf/ *n* dough; a stiff flour pudding boiled in a bag; decaying vegetable matter, fallen leaves; coal dust. [A form of **dough**]
 ■ **up the duff** (*sl*) pregnant.

duff² /duf/ (*inf*) *adj* no good; broken, not working. [Prob **duff³**]

duff³ /duf/ *vt* to bungle; to mishit (a shot), *esp* by hitting the ground behind the ball (*golf*). [Back-formation from **duffer¹**]

duff⁴ /duf/ (*sl*) *vt* to make to look new; to alter brands on (stolen cattle); to steal cattle. [Perh a back-formation from **duffer²**]
 □ **duff'ing-up** or **duff'ing-over** *n* (also **duff'ing**) a beating.
 ■ **duff up** or **duff over** to beat up.

duff⁵ /duf/ (*sl*) *n* the buttocks, rump. [Perh **duff¹**]

duffel or **duffle** /duf'l/ *n* a thick, coarse woollen cloth, with a thick nap; sporting or camping kit (*US*). [Du, from *Duffel* a town near Antwerp]
 □ **duffel bag** *n* a canvas bag, cylindrical in shape, *orig* used for a sailor's kit. **duffel coat** *n* a jacket or coat, *usu* hooded, made of duffel.

duffer¹ /duf'ər/ *n* an unskilful or worthless person (*inf*); a fogey, a useless old fellow (*inf*); a counterfeit coin; an unproductive mine. [Origin unknown]
 ■ **duff'erdom** or **duff'erism** *n.*

duffer² /duf'ər/ *n* a peddler of sham jewellery, etc; someone who fakes up sham articles or duffs cattle. [Origin unknown: thieves' slang]

duffle see **duffel**.

dug¹ /dug/ *pat* and *pap* of **dig**.
 □ **dug'out** *n* a boat made by hollowing out the trunk of a tree; a rough dwelling or shelter dug out of a slope or bank or in a trench; a (*usu* sunken) shelter or covered bench area beside a sports pitch in which players, etc wait when not in the game; a superannuated person brought back to employment (*sl*).

dug² /dug/ n a nipple or udder of a cow or similar animal; a woman's breast. [Cf Swed dægga, Dan dægge to suckle]

dug³ /dug/ n a Scots form of **dog¹**.

dugite /doo'gīt/ n a venomous Australian snake, *Pseudonaja affinis*. [Aboriginal]

dugong /doo'gong/ n a herbivorous marine mammal of the order Sirenia, up to 3m long, with flipper-like forelimbs (the supposed original of the mermaid). [Malay *dūyong*]

duh /du/ interj suggesting stupidity or a statement of the obvious. [Imit]

DUI (US) abbrev : driving under the influence (of alcohol or drugs).

duiker or **duyker** /dī'kər, dā'kər/ n a small S African antelope; /dī'kər/ a cormorant (S Afr). [Du, diver (from plunging into the bush, or into the sea)]

duke /dūk/ n a sovereign prince of a small state; a nobleman of the highest order; a chief (obs; Bible); /dook/ the fist (also **dook**, sl). ◆ vt (with it) to play the duke; to fight or hit with the fists (often *duke it out*; US sl). [OFr duc, from L dux, ducis a leader, from dūcere to lead]
■ **duke'dom** n the title, rank or lands of a duke. **duke'ling** n a petty duke. **duk'ery** n a duke's territory or seat. **duke'ship** n.
■ **the Dukeries** a group of ducal seats in Nottinghamshire.

Dukhobor or **Doukhobor** /doo'hhō-bör, doo'kō-bör/ n (pl **D(o)u'khobors** or **Dukhobort'sy**) a member of a Russian sect who trust to an inner light, reject the doctrine of the Trinity, and refuse military service, many of them settled in Canada since 1899. [Russ *Dukhoborets*, from *dukh* spirit, and *borets* fighter, from *boroty'* to fight]

dukkah /duk'ə/ n a mixture of ground nuts with herbs and spices, used in Middle Eastern cookery. [Ar]

dukkeripen /dŭk-ə-rip'ən/ n fortune-telling. [Romany *drukeriben*]

dulcamara /dul-kə-mā'rə, -mā'rə/ n the plant bittersweet. [L *dulcis* sweet, and *amāra* (feminine) bitter]

dulce de leche /dŭl'sā də lech'ā/ n an Argentine dessert made by caramelizing sugar in milk. [Sp, literally, milk confection]

dulce et decorum est pro patria mori /dŭl'chā et dā-kö'rŭm est prō pat'ri-a mö'ri/ (L) it is sweet and glorious to die for one's country. [Horace, *Odes* III.2.13]

dulcet /dul'sit/ adj sweet; melodious, harmonious. [L *dulcis* sweet]
■ **dul'cian** /dul'si-ən/ n (obs or hist) a small bassoon. **dulciana** /dul-si-ā'nə/ n an open diapason organ stop of pleasing tone and small scale. **dulcifica'tion** n. **dulcif'luous** adj flowing sweetly. **dul'cify** vt (rare) to make sweet. **dulcil'oquy** n a soft manner of speaking. **dul'cite**, **dul'citol** or **dul'cose** /-kōs/ n a saccharine substance derived from various plants (in its crude form, *Madagascar manna*). **Dul'citone**® n a keyboard instrument in which graduated tuning forks are struck by hammers. **dul'citude** n sweetness.
❑ **dulcified spirit** n a compound of alcohol with mineral acid.

dulcimer /dul'si-mər/ n a musical instrument like a flat box with a sounding-board and wires stretched across bridges, played with hand-held hammers; a Jewish musical instrument, probably a bagpipe. [Sp *dulcemele*, from L *dulce melos* a sweet song, from *dulcis* sweet, and Gr *melos* a song]

Dulcinea /dul-si-nē'ə, -sin'i-ə/ (literary) n a sweetheart. [From *Dulcinea* del Toboso, the name given by Don Quixote to the mistress of his imagination]

dulcite, Dulcitone®, **dulcose**, etc see under **dulcet**.

dule¹ /dŭl/ (Scot) n woe (also **dool** or (obs) **doole**). [See **dole²**]
❑ **dule'-tree** n the gallows.

dule² see **dool²**.

dulia or **douleia** /dū- or doo-lī'ə/ (RC) n the inferior veneration accorded to saints and angels (as opposed to **hyperdulia**, that accorded to the Virgin Mary, and **latria**, that accorded to God alone). [Gr *douleiā* servitude, *doulōsis* enslavement, from *doulos* a slave]
■ **douloc'racy** or **dulo'cracy** n government by slaves. **dulō'sis** n enslavement, practised by certain ants upon other kinds. **dulot'ic** adj.

dull /dul/ adj slow to learn or to understand; lacking sharpness in hearing (or other sense); insensible; without life or spirit; uninteresting; slow-moving; drowsy; sleepy; sad; downcast; cheerless; lacking brightness or clearness; cloudy; dim; muffled; obtuse; blunt. ◆ vt to make dull or stupid; to blunt; to damp; to cloud. ◆ vi to become dull. [Related to OE *dol* foolish, and *dwellan* to err; Du *dol*, Ger *toll* mad]
■ **dull'ard** n a dull and stupid person; a dunce. **dull'ish** adj. **dull'ness** or **dul'ness** n the state or quality of being dull. **dull'y** adj (poetic) somewhat dull. **dully** /dul'li/ adv.
❑ **dull'-brained** adj (Shakesp). **dull'-browed** adj. **dull'-eyed** adj (Shakesp). **dull'-sighted** adj. **dull'-witted** adj.

dulocracy, dulosis, dulotic see under **dulia**.

dulse /duls/ n an edible red seaweed, *esp Rhodymenia palmata*. [Gaelic *duileasg*, possibly from *duille* a leaf, and *uisge* water]

duly /dū'li/ adv properly; fitly; at the proper time. [See **due¹**]

duma or **douma** /doo'mə/ n an elected council, *esp* the Russian parliament before and since the Communist era. [Russ *duma*, of Gmc origin; cf **doom**]
■ **dum'aist** n a duma member.

dumb /dum/ adj without the power of speech; silent; soundless; stupid (inf, orig US after Ger or Du). ◆ vt (Shakesp) to render dumb. [OE *dumb*; Ger *dumm* stupid, Du *dom*]
■ **dumb'ly** adv in silence; mutely. **dumb'ness** n. **dumm'erer** n (old sl) a dumb person, *esp* a rogue who feigns dumbness.
❑ **dumb'-ass** n (US sl) a stupid person (also adj). **dumb'-bell** n a double-headed weight swung in the hands to develop the muscles; any object or figure of the same shape; a stupid person (US). **dumb blonde** n (in films, etc) the stock character of a blonde-haired beauty of limited intelligence. **dumb'-cane** n a tropical American araceous plant (*Dieffenbachia seguine*) whose juice contains crystals of calcium oxalate which cause swelling of the tongue. **dumb'-cluck** n a fool (orig US; same as **cluck**). **dumbfound'** or **dumfound'** vt to strike dumb; to confuse greatly; to astonish. **dumbfound'er** or **dumfound'er** vt to dumbfound. **dumbing-down** see **dumb down** below. **dumb piano** n a soundless keyboard for piano practice. **dumb'show** n gesture without words; pantomime. **dumb'struck** adj silent with astonishment. **dumb terminal** n (comput) an input or output terminal that has no independent processing capability. **dumb waiter** n a movable platform used for conveying food, dishes, etc at meals; a stand with revolving top for holding dessert, etc; a small lift for food and dishes.
■ **dumb down** (usu derog) to present information in a less sophisticated form in order to appeal to a larger number of people (**dumb'ing-down'** n). **strike dumb** to silence with astonishment.

dumbledore /dum'bl-dör, -dör/ (dialect) n the bumblebee; the brown cockchafer.

dumbo /dum'bō/ (inf) n a dimwit. [**dumb**]

dumdum /dum'dum/ n a soft-nosed expanding bullet, first made at *Dum Dum* near Calcutta.
❑ **dumdum fever** n kala-azar.

dum-dum /dum'dum/ (inf) n a stupid person. [A doubling of **dumb**]

dumfound, dumfounder see under **dumb**.

dumka /doom'kə/ (music) n (pl **dumky** /-kē/) a lament; a slow movement or piece; a piece alternating between lively and sorrowful moods. [Czech]

dummerer see under **dumb**.

dummy /dum'i/ n a sham or counterfeit article taking the place of a real one; a block, lay-figure or mannequin; a dumb person; a stupid person (US inf); a sample, eg an unprinted model of a book; a rubber teat for pacifying an infant; an exposed hand of cards; the imaginary player of such a game or hand; a feint of passing or playing the ball (rugby, etc). ◆ vt and vi (**dumm'ying**; **dumm'ied**) to sell a dummy (to; see below). ◆ adj silent; sham, feigned. [**dumb**]
■ **dumm'iness** n.
❑ **dummy run** n an experimental run; a try-out or testing.
■ **sell a** or **the dummy** (to) (rugby, etc) to deceive an opponent by a feint of passing or playing the ball (also fig).

dumortierite /dū-mör'ti-ə-rīt/ n a blue, greenish-blue, pink or violet semi-precious gemstone, aluminium borosilicate. [From the French palaeontologist Eugène *Dumortier* (1802–76), who discovered it]

dumose /dū'mōs/ (bot; rare) adj bushy (also **du'mous**). [L *dūmus* a thorn-bush]
■ **dumos'ity** n.

dump¹ /dump/ vt to set down heavily or with a thump; to unload; to land and sell at prices below cost of production in the exporting country, or (according to some) in the importing country (econ); to tip (esp rubbish); to get rid of; to end a romantic relationship with (inf); to transfer data held in computer memory to a printer or disk (comput). ◆ n a thud; a place for the discharge of loads, or for rubbish; a deposit; a store (milit); a dirty, dilapidated place (inf); a printout or other copy of data held in computer memory; the act of defecating (inf). [Cf Dan *dumpe*, Norw *dumpa* to fall plump]
■ **dumpee'** n (inf) someone who is abandoned by the other partner in a relationship. **dump'er** n someone who or something that dumps; a dumper truck; (in surfing) a wave that crashes suddenly downwards with great force, causing surfers to fall. **dump'ster** n (chiefly N Am) a large skip or container for refuse and building rubbish.
❑ **dump'bin** n (in a shop) a display stand or container, eg for bargain items. **dumper truck** or **dump truck** n a lorry that can be emptied by

---

■ words derived from main entry word; ❑ compound words; ■ idioms and phrasal verbs

raising the front of the carrier to allow the contents to slide out the back (also **dump'er**).

■ **dump on** (*US sl*) to do down, belittle; to take advantage of.

dump² /*dump*/ *n* dullness or gloominess of mind, ill-humour, low spirits (now only used in the *pl* **dumps**); an obsolete slow dance or dance tune in 4–4 time; a melancholy strain (*obs*; *Shakesp*, etc); any tune (*obs*). [Prob related to ODu *domp* mist; or Ger *dumpf* gloomy]

■ **dump'ish** *adj* depressed in spirits. **dump'ishly** *adv*. **dump'ishness** *n*.

dump³ /*dump*/ *n* a deep hole in a river bed, a pool. [Prob Norw *dump* pit]

dump⁴ /*dump*/ *n* a short thick person or thing; a marble; a counter; a small coin; (in *pl*) money (*sl*). [Perh a back-formation from **dumpy**]

dum-palm see **doum-palm**.

dumper see under **dump¹**.

dumpish, etc see under **dump²**.

dumple see under **dumpy**.

dumpling /*dum'pling*/ *n* a kind of thick pudding or mass of paste; a dumpling-shaped person or animal; a silly person. [Origin obscure]

dumps see **dump²**.

dumpy /*dum'pi*/ *adj* short and thick. ◆ *n* a dumpy person or animal, *esp* one of a breed of very short-legged fowls; a short umbrella. [First found in 18c; perh from **dumpling**]

■ **dump'iness** *n*.

❑ **dump'y-lev'el** *n* a surveyor's level with rigid connection of the telescope to the vertical spindle.

dum spiro, spero /*dŭm spē'rō, spā'rō*/ (*L*) while I breathe, I hope.

dum vivimus, vivamus /*dŭm vē'vi-mŭs, vē-vä'mŭs* or *wē'wi-mŭs, wē-wä'mŭs*/ (*L*) let us live while we are alive.

dun¹ /*dun*/ *adj* greyish brown; mouse-coloured; dingy; dusky. ◆ *n* a dun colour; a horse of dun colour. ◆ *vt* (**dunn'ing**; **dunned**) (*New England*) to cure and brown (eg cod). ◆ *vi* to become dun-coloured. [OE *dun*, prob not Celtic]

■ **dunn'ing** *n*. **dunn'ish** *adj* somewhat dun.

❑ **dun'-bird** *n* the pochard, *esp* the female. **dun'-cow** *n* a ray with a skin of shagreen. **dun'-div'er** *n* the goosander, *esp* the female or young male. **dun'-fish** *n* codfish cured by dunning.

dun² /*dun*/ *vt* (**dunn'ing**; **dunned**) to importune for payment; to plague, pester, harass. ◆ *n* someone who duns; a demand for payment. [Perh related to **din**]

dun³ /*dun*/ *n* a hill; a fortified mound. [Celtic; in many place names; adopted in OE as *dūn*; see **down³**]

dunce /*duns*/ *n* a slow learner; a stupid person. [*Duns* Scotus (died 1308), the Subtle Doctor, leader of the schoolmen, from him called *Dunses*, who opposed classical studies on the revival of learning, hence any opposer of learning, a blockhead]

■ **dunce'dom** *n* the class of dunces. **dun'cery** *n* stupidity. **Dun'ciad** *n* Pope's epic of dunces.

❑ **dunce's cap** *n* a tall conical hat, formerly worn at school to indicate stupidity.

dunch or **dunsh** /*dunsh*/ (*Scot*) *vt* to jog, nudge, bump; to butt. ◆ *n* a jog or push. [Ety doubtful]

Dundee cake /*dun'dē kāk*/ *n* a rich fruitcake topped with almonds, traditionally eaten at Christmas. [Orig made in *Dundee*, Scotland]

dunder /*dun'dər*/ *n* lees, dregs of sugarcane juice. [Sp *redundar* to overflow]

dunderfunk /*dun'dər-fungk*/ (*naut*) *n* ship biscuit, soaked in water, mixed with fat and molasses, and baked in a pan (also **dan'dyfunk**).

dunderhead /*dun'dər-hed*/ *n* a stupid person (also **dun'derpate**). [Origin uncertain]

■ **dun'derheaded** *adj*. **dun'derheadedness** *n*. **dun'derheadism** *n*.

Dundonian /*dun-dō'ni-ən*/ *n* and *adj* (a person) belonging to, coming from or born in Dundee, Scotland.

Dundreary /*dun-drē'ri*/ *adj* like Lord *Dundreary*, in Tom Taylor's *Our American Cousin* (presented as a lisping and brainless dandy, wearing long sidewhiskers).

dune /*dūn*/ *n* a low hill of sand, *esp* on the seashore. [Fr, from ODu *duna*; cf **down³**]

❑ **dune'-buggy** *n* (*orig US*) a beach buggy, a *usu* small car with large tyres, used for driving on beaches.

Dunelm. *abbrev*: *Dunelmensis* (*L*), of Durham.

dung¹ /*dung*/ *n* excrement; manure; a tailor or other worker submitting to low rates of pay, *opp* to **flint** (*obs sl*). ◆ *vt* to manure with dung. ◆ *vi* to void excrement. [OE *dung*; cf Dan *dynge* a heap; Ger *Dung*]

■ **dung'y** *adj*.

❑ **dung'-bee'tle** *n* the dor-beetle; a scarabaeid beetle generally. **dung'-cart** *n*. **dung'-fly** *n* any of a number of small two-winged flies (family Scatophagidae) that breed on dung or decaying vegetable matter. **dung'-fork** *n* a fork used for moving stable manure. **dung'heap** or **dung'hill** *n* a heap of dung; any squalid situation or place. **dung'-hunt'er** *n* a skua. **dung'mere** *n* a manure-pit.

dung² see **ding²**.

dungaree /*dung-gə-rē'* or *dung'gə-rē*/ *n* a coarse Indian calico; (in *pl*) work overalls made of it, *esp* loose trousers with a bib front and shoulder straps; (in *pl*) a similar garment for casual wear. [Hindi *dūgrī*]

dungeon /*dun'jən*/ *n* orig the principal tower of a castle; a close, dark prison; a cell underground. ◆ *vt* to confine in a dungeon. [OFr *donjon*, from LL *domniō, -ōnis*, from L *dominus* a lord]

■ **dun'geoner** *n* a gaoler.

duniewassal, **dunniewassal** or **duniwassal** /*doo-ni-wos'l*/ *n* a Highland gentleman of inferior rank. [Gaelic *duine* man, and *uasal* of gentle birth]

dunite /*dun'īt*/ *n* crystalline rock composed almost entirely of olivine. [*Dun* Mountain, near Nelson, in New Zealand]

duniwassal see **duniewassal**.

dunk /*dungk*/ *vt* and *vi* to dip (a biscuit, etc that one is eating) in one's tea or other beverage; to jump up and push (the ball) down through the basket (*basketball*). ◆ *n* an act of dunking. [Ger *tunken* to dip; cf **Dunker**]

■ **dunk'er** *n*.

Dunker /*dung'kər*/ or **Dunkard** /*-kərd*/ *n* a member of a sect of German-American Baptists who practise triple immersion (also **Tunk'er**). [Ger, dipper]

Dunkirk /*dun-kûrk'* or *dun'*/ *n* a successful military evacuation by sea against odds, as by the British in 1940 at *Dunkirk*; a complete abandonment of one's position; a rapid or desperate withdrawal.

dunlin /*dun'lin*/ *n* (*pl* **dunlins** or (*collectively*) **dunlin**) the red-backed sandpiper (*Calidris alpina*) a gregarious shorebird, also known as the **ox-bird**. [Dimin of **dun¹**]

Dunlop /*dun-lop'*/ *n* a cheese made of unskimmed milk. [From *Dunlop* in Ayrshire]

dunnage /*dun'ij*/ *n* loose wood of any kind laid in the bottom of the hold to keep the cargo out of the bilge-water, or wedged between parts of the cargo to keep them steady; sailor's baggage. [Ety unknown]

dunnakin /*dun'ə-kin*/ *n* a lavatory, often an outside lavatory. [Perh from **dung¹**]

dunnart /*dun'ärt*/ *n* a marsupial mouse of Australia and Papua New Guinea (genus *Sminthopsis*). [From an Aboriginal language]

dunniewassal see **duniewassal**.

dunnite /*dun'īt*/ *n* a kind of explosive based on ammonium picrate. [From its inventor, the US army officer, Col BW *Dunn* (1860–1936)]

dunno /*də-nō'*/ informal contraction of (**I**) **don't know**.

dunnock /*dun'ək*/ *n* the hedge sparrow. [Dimin of **dun¹**]

dunny¹ /*dun'i*/ (*dialect*) *adj* deaf; stupid. [Origin obscure]

dunny² /*dun'i*/ (*inf* or *dialect*) *n* a lavatory, often an outside lavatory (*esp Aust* and *NZ*).

dunny³ /*dun'i*/ (*Scot*) *n* a basement or cellar (of a tenement building, etc). [Perh from **dungeon**]

dunsh see **dunch**.

Dunstable /*dun'stə-bl*/ *n* a kind of straw-plait, first made at *Dunstable* in Bedfordshire; a straw hat, etc.

❑ **Dunstable road** or **highway** *n* anything plain and direct.

dunt¹ /*dunt*/ (*Scot*) *n* a thump; the wound or mark made by a thump. ◆ *vt* to thump, beat. [See **dint**]

dunt² /*dunt*/ (*dialect*) *n* the disease gid or sturdy in sheep, etc. [Origin obscure]

dunt³ /*dunt*/ *vt* (of ceramics) to crack in the oven because of too rapid cooling. [Origin obscure]

duo /*doo'ō, dū'ō*/ *n* (*pl* **du'os**) a duet; two persons, etc, associated in some way (eg a pair of musicians or variety artists). [Ital, from L *duo* two]

duodecennial /*dū-ō-di-sen'yəl*/ *adj* occurring every twelve years. [L *duodecim* twelve, and *annus* year]

duodecimal /*dū-ō-des'i-məl*/ *adj* computed by twelves; twelfth. [L *duodecim* twelve, from *duo* two, and *decem* ten]

■ **duodec'imals** *n pl* a method of calculating the area of a rectangle when the length and breadth are stated in feet and inches.

❑ **duodecimal system** *n* a system of numbers in which each denomination is twelve times the next, instead of ten times, as in ordinary (decimal) arithmetic; the name given to the division of unity into twelve equal parts.

duodecimo /dū-ō-des'i-mō/ adj (printing and publishing) formed of sheets folded so as to make twelve leaves. ◆ n (pl **duodecimos**) a book of such sheets, usu written **12mo**; an interval of a twelfth (music). [L in duodecimō, in twelfth (ablative of duodecimus twelfth) from duo two, and decem ten]

duodenary /dū-ō-dē'nə-ri/ adj relating to twelve, twelvefold. [L duodēnārius]

duodenum /dū-ō-dē'nəm/ (anat and zool) n (pl **duodē'na**) the first portion of the small intestine (so called because it is about twelve fingers'-breadth in length). [Formed from L duodēnī twelve each]
■ **duodē'nal** adj. **duodēnec'tomy** n excision of the duodenum. **duodēnī'tis** n inflammation of the duodenum.

duologue /dū'ō-log/ n a dialogue between two actors; a play for two actors. [Irregularly formed from L duo (or Gr dyo) two, and Gr logos discourse]

duomo /dwō'mō/ n (pl **duo'mos** or **duo'mi** /-ē/) (an Italian) cathedral. [Ital. See **dome¹**]

duopoly /dū-op'ə-li/ n a situation in which two companies, etc are the only suppliers in a particular market. [L duo (or Gr dyo) two, and monopoly]

duotone /dū'ō-tōn/ n and adj (a drawing, print, etc) done in two tones or colours. [L duo two, and **tone¹**]

DUP abbrev : Democratic Unionist Party (a Protestant loyalist party of Northern Ireland).

dup /dup/ (Shakesp) vt (**dupp'ing**; **dupped**) to undo, open. [**do up**; cf **don²** and **doff**]

dup. abbrev : duplicate.

dupatta see **dopatta**.

dupe /dūp/ n someone who is cheated. ◆ vt to deceive; to trick. [Fr dupe; of uncertain origin]
■ **dupabil'ity** n. **du'pable** adj. **du'per** n. **du'pery** n the art of deceiving others.

dupion /dū'pi-ən, -on/ n a double cocoon, made by two silkworms spinning together; a kind of coarse silk made from these cocoons. [Fr doupion, from Ital doppione double]

duple /dū'pl/ adj double, twofold; having two beats in the bar (music). [L duplus double; cf **double**]
■ **du'plet** n a like throw of two dice; a pair of electrons forming a single bond between two atoms; a group of two notes occupying the time of three (music).

duplex /doo'- or dū'pleks/ adj twofold, double; having some part doubled; allowing communication and transmission in both directions simultaneously (comput, telegraphy, etc). ◆ n a duplex apartment or house; a facility of a communications system enabling simultaneous transmission and reception (telecom). [L duplex, -icis]
■ **du'plexer** n (telecom and radar) a system allowing the use of the same aerial for transmission and reception.
❑ **duplex apartment** n a flat on two floors; a building on two floors, consisting of a flat on each (Can). **duplex house** n (N Am) a house, divided either horizontally or vertically, providing accommodation for two families.

duplicate /doo'- or dū'pli-kit/ adj double; twofold; like, equivalent or alternative. ◆ n another (esp subsidiary or spare) thing of the same kind; a copy or transcript; the condition of being in two copies. ◆ vt /-kāt/ to double; to copy; to repeat; to fold. [L duplicāre, -ātum, from duo two, and plicāre to fold]
■ **duplicand'** n (Scots law) double feu-duty, due on certain occasions. **duplicā'tion** n. **du'plicative** adj. **du'plicātor** n a copying machine. **du'plicāture** n a doubling; anything doubled; the fold of a membrane. **duply'** n a second reply in Scots law. ◆ vt to say in duply.
❑ **duplicate bridge** n a form of competition bridge in which each pair or four plays the same set of hands as all other pairs or fours. **duplicate ratio** n ratio of the squares of the quantities.
■ **duplication of the cube** the problem, eagerly discussed by the early Greek geometers, of constructing a cube equal to twice a given cube, impossible by use of straight line and circle only, but soluble by means of other curves. **in duplicate** in two copies, or original accompanied by a copy.

duplicity /doo'- or dū-plis'i-ti/ n doubleness, esp in conduct or intention; insincerity; double-dealing. [L duplex, -icis double]
■ **duplic'itous** adj.

duply see under **duplicate**.

dupondius /dū-pon'di-əs/ (hist) n (pl **dupon'dii**) an ancient Roman coin. [L]

duppy /dup'i/ n a ghost. [W Ind word]

Dupuytren's contracture /dū-pwē'trenz kən-trak'chər/ (pathol) n a condition in which one or more fingers (or, more rarely, toes) are caused to be bent towards the palm of the hand (or sole of the foot) by the contraction of a fibrous chord in the palmar (or plantar) tissue (also **Dupuytren's contraction**). [Baron Guillaume Dupuytren (1777–1835), French surgeon]

Dur. abbrev : Durham.

dura¹ see **durra**.

dura² /dū'rə/ n short for **dura mater**.

durable /dū'rə-bl/ adj able to last or endure; hardy; permanent. ◆ n something that will endure, esp (pl) goods that do not need replacing frequently. [L dūrāre to harden, endure, last]
■ **durabil'ity** or **dur'ableness** n. **dur'abiy** adv. **dur'ance** n continuance (obs); durability (obs); a durable cloth (obs); imprisonment (archaic). **dur'ant** n a strong cloth in imitation of buff-leather. **dur'ative** adj (grammar) indicating continuous action.

Duralumin® /dū-ral'ū-min/ n (also without cap; also **dur'al** or **duralumin'ium**) a strong, light, aluminium alloy containing copper. [L dūrus hard, and aluminium]

dura mater /dū'rə mā'tər or doo'ra mä'ter/ (anat and zool) n the exterior membrane of the brain and spinal column distinguished from the other two, the arachnoid and the pia mater. [L dūra māter hard mother, a translation of the Arabic name]

duramen /dū-rā'mən/ (bot) n heartwood. [L dūrāmen hardness, from dūrus hard]

durance, **durant** see under **durable**.

durante bene placito /dū-ran'tē ben'ē plas'i-tō or doo-ran'te ben'e plak'i-tō/ (LL) during good pleasure.

durante vita /dū-ran'tē vī'tə, vē'tə or doo-ran'te wē'tä/ (LL) during life.

duration /dū-rā'shən/ n continuance in time; time indefinitely; power of continuance; length of time. [Ety as for **durable**]
■ **durā'tional** adj.
■ **for the duration** (inf) as long as the war (or the situation under discussion) continues.

durative see under **durable**.

durbar /dûr'bär or dûr-bär'/ n an audience chamber; a reception or levee; an Indian court (hist); the body of officials at an Indian court. [Pers darbār a prince's court, literally a door of admittance]

durchkomponiert or **durchkomponirt** /dûrhh-kom-po-nērt'/ adj having the music specially adapted to each stanza. [Ger, literally, through-composed]

Durchlaucht /dûrhh-lowhht'/ (Ger) n Serene Highness.

Durchmusterung /dûrhh-mūs'tə-rûng/ (Ger, examination, scrutiny) n a star-catalogue.

durdum same as **dirdum**.

dure /dūr/ (obs) vi to endure, last or continue. [Fr durer, from L dūrāre, from dūrus hard]
■ **dure'ful** adj (Spenser) enduring, lasting.

duress or **duresse** /dū-res' or dū'res/ n constraint, force; imprisonment; coercion illegally exercised to force a person to perform some act; compulsion, pressure. [OFr duresse, from L dūritia, from dūrus hard]

Durga /door'gə/ n a Hindu goddess of victory. [Sans]

durgan /dûr'gən/ (dialect) n a dwarf, any undersized creature. [Related to **dwarf**]
■ **dur'gy** /-gi or -ji/ adj.

Durham /dur'əm/ n one of a particular breed of shorthorned cattle. [From the English county]

durian /doo'ri-ən or dū'/ n (also **du'rion**) a tall Indian and Malayan bombaccaceous fruit tree (Durio zibethinus), with leaves like a cherry's; its large fruit, with hard rind and foul-smelling but pleasant-tasting pulp. [Malay dūrī thorn]

duricrust /dūr'i-krust/ n a hard crust formed at the surface of soil from minerals deposited by evaporating water. [L dūrus hard, and **crust**]

during /dū'ring/ prep throughout the time of; in the course of. [Orig prp of **dure**]

durmast /dûr'mäst/ n a European oak bearing sessile acorns, with leaves downy below, noted for its tough wood (Quercus petraea or sessiliflora). [Origin unknown: perh a blunder for dun mast]

durn /dûrn/ (dialect) n a doorpost (also **dern**). [Prob Norse]

duro /doo'rō/ n (pl **dur'os**) a Spanish peso. [Sp (peso) duro hard (peso)]

duroy /doo-roi'/ (obs) n a type of coarse woollen fabric. [Orig uncertain]

durra /dūr'ə/ n Indian millet, a grass (Sorghum vulgare) related to sugarcane, much cultivated for grain in Asia and Africa, or other species of the genus (also **dou'ra**, **dhu'rra**, **du'ra** and **dari** /dur'i/). [Ar *dhurah*]

durrie /dur'i/ *n* an Indian cotton carpet fabric with fringes, used for curtains, covers, etc. [Hindi *darī*]

durst /dûrst/ *pat* of **dare**[1], to venture. [OE *dorste*, *pat* of *durran* to dare]

durukuli see **douroucouli**.

durum /dū'rəm/ or **durum wheat** /hwēt or wēt/ *n* a kind of spring wheat (*Triticum durum*), grown *esp* in Russia, N Africa and N America, whose flour is used in making pasta. [L *trīticum dūrum* hard wheat]

dush /dush/ (*Scot*) *vt* to strike heavily against; to throw down. ◆ *n* a heavy impact.

dusk /dusk/ *n* twilight; partial darkness; darkness of colour. ◆ *adj* darkish; of a dark colour. ◆ *vt* and *vi* to make or become dusky; to dim. [Appar connected with OE *dox* dark]

■ **dusk'en** *vt* and *vi* to make or grow dark. **dusk'ily** *adv*. **dusk'iness** *n*. **dusk'ish** *adj*. **dusk'ishly** *adv*. **dusk'ishness** *n*. **dusk'ly** *adv*. **dusk'ness** *n*. **dusk'y** *adj* partially dark or obscure; dark-coloured; dark-skinned; sad; gloomy.

dust /dust/ *n* fine particles of solid matter, *esp* earth, powdery matter or dirt; a cloud of this; the earth; the grave; the dead human body, remains; a debased or shabby condition; (with *the*) pneumoconiosis (*mining sl*); gold dust, hence money; turmoil (*sl*); a disturbance, a brawl (*inf*). ◆ *vt* to free from dust (also *vi*); to trash, beat (*inf*); to pass or leave in a trail of dust (*US inf*); to sprinkle; to cover lightly with a powdered substance (also *vi*). [OE *dūst*; cf Ger *Dunst* vapour]

■ **dust'er** *n* someone or something that dusts; a cloth or brush for removing dust; a sprinkler; a dustcoat (*US*). **dust'ily** *adv*. **dust'iness** *n*. **dust'less** *adj*. **dust'y** *adj* covered or sprinkled with dust; old-fashioned; dull; lifeless; like dust; contemptible, bad, as in the phrases *not so dusty* and *a dusty answer* (*sl*).

❑ **dust bag** *n* a cloth or paper sack intended to hold the material sucked up by a vacuum cleaner. **dust'-ball** *n* a ball of grain-dust, etc, in a horse's intestine. **dust'-bath** *n* the action of birds in rubbing dust into their feathers, probably to get rid of parasites. **dust'bin** *n* a receptacle for household rubbish; a repository for anything unwanted, unimportant, etc (*fig*). **dust bowl** *n* a drought area subject to dust storms (**Dust Bowl** the region of the USA along the western edge of the Great Plains). **dust'-brand** *n* smut. **dust'-brush** *n* a light brush for removing dust. **dust bunny** *n* (*N Am inf*) a ball of dust and fluff. **dust'cart** *n* a cart for taking away household rubbish. **dust'coat** *n* an overall; a light overcoat. **dust cover** *n* the jacket of a book; a dustsheet. **dust devil** or **dust storm** *n* a small storm in which a whirling column of dust or sand travels across a dry country. **dust explosion** *n* an explosion resulting from the ignition of small concentrations of flammable dust (eg coal dust or flour) in the air. **dust'-hole** *n* (*obs*) dustbin. **dusting powder** *n* fine powder, *esp* talcum powder. **dust jacket** *n* the jacket or dust cover of a book. **dust'man** *n* a person employed to remove household rubbish. **dust'pan** *n* a pan or shovel for removing dust swept from the floor. **dust'proof** *adj* impervious or inaccessible to dust. **dust'sheet** *n* a cloth for protecting furniture from dust. **dust'-shot** *n* the smallest size of shot. **dust storm** see **dust devil** above. **dust'-up** *n* (*inf*) a quarrel, a brawl. **dusty answer** *n* (*fig*) an unsatisfying, unfruitful, or sordid response. **dust'y-foot** see **piepowder**. **dust'y-mill'er** *n* the auricula, from the white dust on its leaves and flowers.

■ **bite the dust** see under **bite**. **dust someone's jacket** to give someone a beating. **kick up** or **raise a dust** see under **kick**. **throw dust in someone's eyes** (*fig*) to deceive someone.

Dutch /duch/ *adj* relating to the Netherlands, its people or language; German, Teutonic (*obs*, except *rare* or *old US*); heavy, clumsy, as in *Dutch-built*. ◆ *n* the language of the Netherlands; German (**High** and **Low Dutch**, *Hoch* and *Nieder* or *Platt Deutsch*, High and Low German; *obs* and *US*); (as *pl*) the people of the Netherlands; Germans (*obs* and *US*). [Ger *deutsch*, (literally) belonging to the people, from OHGer *diutisc*; cf OE *thēod*, Gothic *thiuda* nation; see **Teutonic**]

❑ **Dutch auction** see under **auction**. **Dutch bargain** *n* a one-sided bargain. **Dutch barn** *n* a storage barn consisting of a roof on a steel framework. **Dutch cap** see under **cap**[1]. **Dutch carpet** *n* a mixed material of cotton and wool for floor coverings. **Dutch cheese** *n* a small round cheese made in Europe from skimmed milk. **Dutch clinker** *n* a hard yellow brick for paving, etc. **Dutch clock** *n* a clock of wood and wire with brass wheels, made in the Black Forest. **Dutch clover** *n* white clover. **Dutch comfort** *n* 'Thank God it's no worse'. **Dutch concert** *n* a concert in which singers sing their various songs simultaneously, or each person sings a verse of any song of their choosing between bursts of some familiar chorus. **Dutch courage** see under **courage**. **Dutch doll** *n* a wooden doll with jointed legs. **Dutch drops** *n pl* a once popular medicine, composed of oil of turpentine, tincture of guaiacum, etc. **Dutch elm disease** *n* a fungal, *usu* fatal, disease of elm trees (in fact of Asian origin), spread by bark-

beetles, causing a gradual withering. **Dutch gold**, **leaf** or **metal** *n* a copper-zinc alloy, a substitute for gold leaf. **Dutch hoe** *n* a hoe with blade attached as in a spade. **Dutch liquid** *n* ethylene dichloride ($C_2H_4Cl_2$), an anaesthetic discovered by Dutch chemists. **Dutch lunch** or **Dutch supper** *n* one at which each person brings or pays for their own share. **Dutch'man**, *fem* **Dutch'woman** *n* a native or citizen of the Netherlands; an Afrikaner (*S Afr*; *derog*); a German or Teuton (*US*). **Dutchman's breeches** *n pl* dicentra. **Dutchman's pipe** *n* a species of *Aristolochia*. **Dutch oven** *n* a heavy covered cooking pot used by burying in coals; a heavy stewpot or casserole; a tin for roasting before an open fire. **Dutch pink** see **pink**[5]. **Dutch rush** *n* a horsetail (*Equisetum hyemale*) with much silica in its stem, used for polishing. **Dutch tiles** see under **tile**. **Dutch treat** *n* an occasion (eg a meal or an entertainment) when each person pays for himself or herself. **Dutch uncle** *n* someone who criticizes or reprimands one unsparingly. **Dutch wife** *n* an open frame of rattan or cane used in the East Indies, to rest the limbs upon in bed; a bolster used for the same purpose.

■ **double Dutch** any unknown or unintelligible language; a skipping game using two ropes. **go Dutch** (*inf*) to pay each for himself or herself. **High Dutch** see **Dutch** (*n*) above; formerly, Dutch as spoken in the Netherlands as opposed to South African Dutch; double Dutch (*obs*). **I'm a Dutchman** an expression used ironically to show disbelief and rejection of an earlier statement. **Pennsylvania Dutch** the mixed German dialect of the descendants of German settlers in Pennsylvania. **talk like a Dutch uncle** to utter a rebuke.

dutch /duch/ (*Cockney sl*) *n* a wife. [Perh short for *Duchess of Fife*, rhyming slang for *wife*]

duty /dū'ti/ *n* that which is due; what one is bound by any (*esp* moral) obligation to do; one's proper business; service; attendance; supervision of pupils out of school hours; performance of function or service; the work done by a machine under given conditions, or for a specified amount of energy supplied; the amount of water needed to irrigate an area for a particular crop; respect, deference; tax on goods, etc. [Anglo-Fr *dueté*; see **due**[1]]

■ **du'teous** *adj* devoted to one's duty; obedient. **du'teously** *adv*. **du'teousness** *n*. **du'tiable** *adj* subject to custom duty. **du'tied** *adj* subjected to duties and customs. **du'tiful** *adj* attentive to duty; respectful; expressive of a sense of duty. **du'tifully** *adv*. **du'tifulness** *n*.

❑ **du'ty-bound'** *adj* obliged by one's feeling of duty; honour-bound. **du'ty-free'** *adj* free from tax or duty. ◆ *n* (*inf*) a shop, *usu* at an airport or on board a ship, where duty-free articles are on sale; an article on sale at such a shop. **duty officer** *n* the officer on duty at any particular time. **du'ty-paid'** *adj* on which duty has been paid.

■ **do duty for** to serve as, to act as substitute for. **on** or **off duty** performing (or not performing) one's duties, or liable (or not liable) to be called upon to do so, during a specified period of time.

duumvir /doo-, dū-um'vir, -vər/ *n* (*pl* **duum'virs** or **duum'viri** /-ī, doo-oom-wir'ē/) one of two men associated in the same office or post. [L *duumvirī*, for *duovirī*, from *duo* two, and *vir* a man]

■ **duum'viral** *adj*. **duum'virate** *n* an association of two men in one office or post; a government by duumvirs.

duvet /doo'vā or (*Fr*) dū-vā'/ *n* (*pl* **du'vets**) a quilt stuffed with eiderdown, swan's-down or man-made fibres, used on a bed in place of blankets, etc; a quilted coat or jacket. [Fr]

❑ **duvet day** *n* (*inf*) a day's absence from work arranged at short notice between an employee devoid of inspiration for a plausible excuse and an employer who has heard them all before.

duvetyn /dū'və-tēn or duv'tin/ *n* a soft fabric with a nap, made of cotton, wool, silk or rayon, and often used for women's clothes (also **duvetyne** or **duvetine**). [Fr *duvetine*, from *duvet* down]

dux /duks/ *n* a leader; the top academic prize-winner in a school or class (*esp Scot*). [L, a leader]

duxelles /duk-sel', dook-, -selz'/ *n* a seasoning made from chopped mushrooms, onions or shallots, and parsley. [The Marquis d'*Uxelles*, 17c French nobleman]

duyker see **duiker**.

DV *abbrev* : Deo volente (*L*), God willing.

Dv. *abbrev* : Drive (in street names).

dvandva /dvän'dvä/ (*grammar*) *n* a compound word, each element equal in status (eg *tragicomedy*, *bitter-sweet*). [Sans *dvaṁdva* a pair]

DVD *abbrev* : digital versatile disc; digital video disc.

DVLA *abbrev* : Driver and Vehicle Licensing Agency.

DVLC *abbrev* : Driver and Vehicle Licensing Centre.

Dvorak keyboard /dvör'zhak kē'bōrd, -bôrd/ (comput) n a typewriter, etc keyboard laid out so as to minimize finger movement. [After its US inventor August Dvorak (1894–1975)]

dvornik /dvor'nēk, dvör'/ n a Russian concierge or porter. [Russ, caretaker, from dvor yard, court]

DVR abbrev : digital video recorder.

DVT abbrev : deep-vein thrombosis.

dwaal /dwäl/ (S Afr) n a state of inattention or confusion. [Afrik]

dwale /dwāl/ n deadly nightshade (bot); a stupefying drink (obs); a black colour (heraldry). [ON dvöl, dvali delay, sleep]

dwam or **dwalm** /dwäm/ or **dwaum** /dwöm/ (Scot) n a swoon (obs); a sudden sickness; a dream, state of inattention. ◆ vi to swoon (obs); to fail in health. [OE dwolma confusion]

dwang /dwang/ (Scot and NZ) n a piece of timber used to reinforce joists, etc, a strut. [Du, force, a constraint, from dwingen to force]

dwarf /dwörf/ n (pl **dwarfs** or (rare) **dwarves**) an abnormally small person, esp (in general but non-technical usage) a person with abnormally short limbs but normal body and head; a small manlike being, esp a metalworker (folklore); an animal or plant much below the ordinary height; anything very small of its kind; a small star of high density and low luminosity (**white dwarf**, **red dwarf**, **brown dwarf**, etc according to strength of light emitted). ◆ adj dwarfed; dwarfish; very small. ◆ vt to hinder from growing; to make to appear small. ◆ vi to become dwarfed. [OE dweorg; Du dwerg, ON dverg, Ger Zwerg]
■ **dwarfed** adj. **dwarf'ish** adj like a dwarf; very small; despicable. **dwarf'ishly** adv. **dwarf'ishness** n. **dwarf'ism** n condition of being a dwarf.
❑ **dwarfed tree** n bonsai. **dwarf planet** n (astron) a body in orbit round the sun, more developed than an asteroid but lacking the gravitational pull of a planet.

dweeb /dwēb/ (US derog sl) n a fool, nerd.

dwell /dwel/ vi (**dwell'ing**; **dwelt** or **dwelled**) to abide or reside (formal or archaic); to remain; to rest attention (on); to continue long (in; obs). ◆ vt (Milton) to inhabit; to cause to dwell. ◆ n a pause or hesitation in the working of a machine (engineering); a part of a cam shaped so as to allow a pause in operation at any point in its cycle (engineering). [OE dwellan to go astray, delay, tarry]
■ **dwell'er** n. **dwell'ing** n (formal or archaic) the place where one dwells; a house; habitation; continuance.
❑ **dwell'ing-house** n a house used as a dwelling, in distinction from a place of business or other building. **dwell'ing-place** n a place of residence.

DWEM abbrev : dead white European male (see under **dead**).

DWI abbrev : driving while intoxicated.

dwile /dwīl/ n a floorcloth or mop. [Cf Du dweil a mop]

dwindle /dwin'dl/ vi to grow less; to waste away; to grow feeble; to become degenerate. ◆ vt to lessen. ◆ n decline. [Dimin of dwine]
■ **dwin'dlement** n.

dwine /dwīn/ vi to pine; to waste away (Scot). [OE dwīnan to fade; cf ON dvīna, Dan tvine to pine away]

DWP abbrev : Department for Work and Pensions.

dwt abbrev : dead-weight tonnage.

DY abbrev : Benin (formerly Dahomey; IVR).

Dy (chem) symbol : dysprosium.

dyad /dī'ad/ n a pair of units treated as one; a bivalent atom, radical, or element (chem). [Gr dyas, -ados, from dyo two]
■ **dyad'ic** adj.

Dyak or **Dayak** /dī'ak/ n a member of any of the indigenous, generally non-Muslim tribes of the interior of Borneo; their languages and dialects. [Malay dayak up-country]

dyarchy /dī'är-ki/ n non-standard spelling of **diarchy**.

dybbuk /dib'ək/ (Jewish folklore) n an evil spirit, or the soul of a dead person, that enters the body of a living person and controls his or her actions. [Heb dibbūq]

dye¹ /dī/ vt (**dye'ing**; **dyed**) to stain; to give a new colour to. ◆ n colour produced by dyeing; tinge; stain; a colouring liquid. [OE dēagian to dye, from dēag, dēah colour]
■ **dy'able** or **dye'able** adj. **dyed** adj. **dye'ing** n. **dy'er** n a person whose trade is to dye cloth, etc. **dyester** /dī'stər/ n (Scot) a dyer.
❑ **dye'-house** n a building in which dyeing is done. **dyeline** /dī'līn/ adj and n diazo (qv). **dy'er's-green'weed** or **dy'er's-broom** n a papilionaceous shrub (Genista tinctoria), a source of yellow colouring matter. **dy'er's-rock'et**, **-weld** or **-yell'owweed** n a plant (Reseda luteola), related to mignonette, yielding a yellow dye. **dy'er's-weed** n

a name for various plants that yield dyes (woad, weld, dyer's-greenweed, etc). **dye'stuff** n a substance used in dyeing. **dye'wood** n any wood from which material is obtained for dyeing. **dye'-work** or **-works** n an establishment for dyeing.
■ **dye in the wool** to dye (the wool) before spinning, to give a more permanent result (**dyed-in-the-wool** adj (fig) (too) fixed in one's opinions or attitudes).

dye² /dī/ (Spenser) n same as **die²**.

dying /dī'ing/ prp of **die¹**. adj destined for death; mortal; declining; occurring immediately before death, eg dying words; relating to death; last, final. ◆ n death. [See **die¹**]
■ **dy'ingly** adv. **dy'ingness** n.
❑ **dying declaration** n (law) declaration made by a dying person who does not survive through the trial of the accused. **dying shift** n (mining) the night shift.

dyke¹ or **dike** /dīk/ n a trench, or the earth dug out and thrown up; a ditch; a mound raised to prevent flooding; in Scotland, a wall (**dry'-stane dyke** a wall without mortar; **fail'-dyke** a wall of turf), sometimes even a thorn-hedge; an igneous mass injected into a fissure in rocks, sometimes weathered out into wall-like forms (geol); a lavatory (old sl). ◆ vt to provide with a dyke. ◆ vi to make a dyke. [OE dīc, whence also **ditch**, this and related words in the Germanic languages denoting both a trench dug out and the mound of earth so formed; cf Ger Teich a pond, Deich (orig LGer) an embankment, Du dijk a bank, dam, Dan dige a bank, dam, Swed dike a ditch, trench]
■ **dyk'er** or **dīk'er** n a person who makes dykes.
❑ **dyke'-louper** n (Scot) an animal that jumps the fence, etc around its pasture; an immoral person (fig). **dyke swarm** n (geol) a series of dykes of the same age, usu trending in a constant direction over a wide area.

dyke² or **dike** /dīk/ (offensive sl) n a lesbian. [Origin unknown]
■ **dyk'ey** or **dīk'ey** adj.

dyn abbrev : dynamo; dynamometer; dyne.

dynamic /dī-nam'ik or di-/ adj relating to force; relating to dynamics; relating to the effects of forces in nature; relating to activity or things in movement; relating to dynamism; causal; forceful, very energetic. ◆ n a moving force; any driving force instrumental in growth or change (esp social); pattern of growth or change. [Gr dynamikos, from dynamis power, from dynasthai to be able]
■ **dynam'ical** adj. **dynam'ically** adv. **dynam'icist** n a person who studies dynamics. **dynam'ics** n sing the science of matter and motion, mechanics, sometimes restricted to kinetics; movement, change or the forces causing these; (often as pl) (signs indicating) varying levels of loudness (music). **dyn'amism** n a theory that explains the phenomena of the universe by immanent energy; operation of force; dynamic quality; quality of restless energy; quality of suggesting forceful movement (art, etc). **dyn'amist** n. **dynamis'tic** adj. **dyn'amize** or **-ise** vt to make dynamic.
❑ **dynamic link library** n (comput) a collection of computer programs for common functions which can be called and relinquished by an application whenever needed, often called a **DLL** after the file name extension used. **dynamic memory** n (comput) memory that needs to be periodically refreshed, read and rewritten about every 2ms. **dynamic range** n the range of volumes of sound in a single piece of music; the range of intensity of sound that can be reproduced by an electronic sound system. **dynamic routing** n (comput) a process for selecting the most appropriate path for a data packet to travel across a network.

dynamite /dī'nə-mīt/ (formerly also din')/ n an explosive consisting of absorbent matter, such as porous silica, saturated with nitroglycerine; something highly dangerous to deal with; someone or something excellent or thrilling (sl). ◆ vt to blow up with dynamite (also fig). [Gr dynamis power]
■ **dyn'amiter** or **dyn'amitard** /-mit-ärd/ n (archaic) a user of dynamite, esp for political purposes.

dynamo /dī'nə-mō/ n (pl **dyn'amos**) contraction for **dynamo-electric machine**, a machine for generating electric currents by means of the relative movement of conductors and magnets; a highly energetic person (inf). [Gr dynamis power]
■ **dynamogen'esis** or **dynamog'eny** n production of increased nervous activity. **dynamograph** /-am'/ n a recording dynamometer. **dynamom'eter** n an instrument for measuring force, or (brake horse-)power. **dynamomet'ric** or **dynamomet'rical** adj. **dynamom'etry** n. **dyn'amotor** n an electrical machine with two armature windings, one acting as a motor and the other as a generator, and a single magnetic field, for converting direct current into alternating current. **dyn'atron** n (electronics) a four-electrode thermionic valve used to generate continuous oscillation.
❑ **dyn'amo-elec'tric** or **dyn'amo-elec'trical** adj.
■ **human dynamo** a person of exceptional energy.

---

dynast /din'ast, -ast, also (US) dī'-/ n a ruler. [Fr dynastie, or LL dynastīa, from Gr dynasteia power, dominion, from dynasthai to be able]
■ **dynas'tic** or **dynas'tical** adj relating to a dynasty. **dynast'ically** adv. **dyn'asty** /-əs-ti/ n a succession of monarchs of the same family, or of members of any powerful family or connected group.

dynatron see under **dynamo**.

dyne /dīn/ n the CGS unit of force, equal to 10^{-5} newtons. [Gr dynamis force]
■ **dyn'ode** n (electronics) an intermediate electrode (between the cathode and final anode) that causes amplification by secondary emission of electrons.

Dyophysite same as **Diphysite**.

Dyothelete, Dyotheletism, Dyothelism see **Ditheletism**.

dys- /dis-/ pfx signifying ill, bad or abnormal. [Gr]

dysaesthesia /dis-əs-thē'si-ə, -zhi-ə, -zhə or -ēs-/ (med) n impaired sensation, partial insensibility. [**dys-** and Gr aisthēsis sensation, from aisthanesthai to feel]
■ **dysaesthetic** /-thet'ik/ adj.

dysarthria /dis-är'thri-ə/ (med) n impaired ability to articulate speech resulting from damage to the central or peripheral nervous system. [**dys-** and Gr arthron a joint]

dyscalculia /dis-kal-kū'li-ə/ same as **acalculia**.

dyschroa /dis'krō-ə/ (med) n discoloration of the skin from disease (also **dyschroia** /-kroi'ə/). [**dys-** and Gr chroa, chroiā complexion]

dyscrasia /dis-krā'si-ə, -zhi-ə, -zhə/ (obs pathol) n a disordered condition of the body attributed originally to unsuitable mixing of the body fluids or humours. [**dys-** and Gr krāsis a mixing]

dyscrasite /dis'kra-sīt/ n a mineral composed of silver and antimony. [**dys-** and Gr krāsis mixture]

dysentery /dis'ən-tə-ri, -tri/ (med) n a term formerly applied to any condition in which inflammation of the colon was associated with the frequent passage of bloody stools; now confined to amoebic dysentery, the result of infection with the Entamoeba histolytica, and to bacillary dysentery, due to infection with Bacterium dysenteriae. [Gr dysenterīa, from dys- amiss, and enteron intestine]
■ **dysenteric** /-ter'ik/ adj.

dysfunction /dis-fungk'shən or dis-fung'shən/ n impairment or abnormality of the functioning of an organ. [**dys-**]
■ **dysfunc'tional** adj failing to function properly; failing to maintain normal social relationships. **dysfunctional'ity** n.

dysgenic /dis-jen'ik/ (zool) adj unfavourable to racial improvement. [**dys-** and the root of Gr gennaein to beget]
■ **dysgen'ics** n sing the study of race degeneration; cacogenics.

dysgraphia /dis-graf'i-ə/ n inability to write, due to brain damage or other cause. [**dys-** and Gr graphein to write]
■ **dysgraph'ic** adj.

dysharmonic /dis-här-mon'ik/ adj unbalanced, lacking in harmony of proportion. [**dys-**]

dyskinesia /dis-kin-ē'zi-ə, -zhi-ə, -zhə/ (pathol) n lack of control over bodily movements; impaired performance of voluntary movements. [**dys-** and Gr kīnēsis movement]

dyslexia /dis-lek'si-ə/ n word blindness, great difficulty in learning to read or spell, unrelated to intellectual competence and of unknown cause. [**dys-** and Gr lexis word]
■ **dyslec'tic** or **dyslex'ic** adj and n.

dyslogistic /dis-lə-jis'tik/ adj conveying censure, opprobrious. [**dys-** and Gr logos discourse]
■ **dyslogis'tically** adv. **dys'logy** n dispraise.

dysmelia /dis-mēl'i-ə, -mel', -yə/ n the condition in which one or more limbs are misshapen or incomplete. [**dys-** and Gr melos limb]
■ **dysmel'ic** adj.

dysmenorrhoea or (esp US) **dysmenorrhea** /dis-men-ō-rē'ə/ (med) n difficult or painful menstruation. [**dys-**, and Gr mēn month, and rhoiā flow]
■ **dysmenorrhoe'al** or **dysmenorrhe'al** adj. **dysmenorrhoe'ic** or **dysmenorrhe'ic** adj.

dysmorphia /dis-mör'fi-ə/ n any psychological condition involving a distorted perception of one's own body, esp (**body dysmorphic disorder**) an obsessive preoccupation with a perceived defect in one's appearance. [**dys-** and Gr morphē form]
■ **dysmor'phic** adj. **dysmorphophō'bia** n abnormal fear of any personal physical deformity.

dysodyle, dysodile or **dysodil** /dis'ō-dīl, -dil/ n a yellow or greyish laminated bituminous mineral (often found with lignite) that burns

vividly, with an odour of asafoetida. [Gr dysōdēs stinking, from dys-ill, ozein to smell, and hýlē matter]

Dyson® /dī'sn/ n a brand of bagless vacuum cleaner. [Sir James Dyson (born 1947), English inventor]

dyspareunia /dis-pä-roo'ni-ə/ n painful or difficult coitus. [**dys-**, and Gr para beside, and eunē a bed]

dyspathy /dis'pə-thi/ n antipathy, dislike. [**dys-** and Gr pathos feeling]
■ **dyspathet'ic** adj.

dyspepsia /dis-pep'si-ə/ (med) n indigestion (also **dyspep'sy**). [Gr dyspepsiā, from dys- ill, and pepsis digestion, from peptein to digest]
■ **dyspep'tic** n a person afflicted with dyspepsia. **dyspep'tic** or **dyspep'tical** adj afflicted with, relating to, or arising from indigestion; gloomy, bad-tempered. **dyspep'tically** adv.

dysphagia /dis-fā'ji-ə/ (pathol) n difficulty in swallowing (also **dys'phagy** /-fə-ji/). [**dys-** and Gr phagein (aorist) to eat]
■ **dysphagic** /-faj'ik/ adj.

dysphasia /dis-fā'zi-ə, -zhi-ə, -zhə/ n difficulty in expressing or understanding thought in spoken or written words, caused by brain damage. [**dys-** and Gr phasis speech]

dysphemism /dis'fə-mi-zm/ n the replacing of a mild or inoffensive word or phrase by an offensive one; the offensive word or phrase substituted. [From **dys-** and **euphemism**]
■ **dysphemis'tic** adj.

dysphonia /dis-fō'ni-ə/ n difficulty in producing sounds. [**dys-** and Gr phōnē sound]
■ **dysphon'ic** adj.

dysphoria /dis-fō'ri-ə, -fō'/ n impatience under affliction; morbid restlessness; uneasiness; absence of feeling of wellbeing. [Gr dysphoriā affliction, pain, from dys- ill, and the root of pherein to bear]
■ **dysphor'ic** adj.

dysplasia /dis-plā'zi-ə/ (pathol) n abnormal development or growth of a cell, tissue, organ, etc. [**dys-** and Gr plāsis moulding]
■ **dysplas'tic** adj.

dyspnoea or (esp US) **dyspnea** /disp-nē'ə/ n difficult or laboured breathing. [Gr dyspnoia, from dys- ill, and pnoē breathing]
■ **dyspnoe'al** or **dyspne'al** adj. **dyspnoe'ic** or **dyspne'ic** adj.

dyspraxia /dis-prak'si-ə/ (pathol) n an impaired ability to co-ordinate and perform certain deliberate actions. [**dys-** and Gr prāxis doing]
■ **dysprax'ic** adj.

dysprosium /dis-prō'zi-əm/ n a metallic element of the rare earths (symbol Dy; atomic no 66). [Gr dysprositos difficult to reach, from dys- ill, difficult, pros to, and ienai to go]

dysrhythmia /dis-ridh'mi-ə/ n abnormal or defective rhythm. [**dys-** and Gr rhythmos rhythm]

dystectic /dis-tek'tik/ adj not easily fused. [Gr dystēktos, from dys- ill, and tēkein to melt]

dysteleology /dis-tē-li-ol'ə-ji or -tel-i-/ n the doctrine of purposelessness, or denial of final causes; the study of functionless rudimentary organs in animals and plants. [**dys-** (in a negative sense)]
■ **dysteleological** /-i-ə-loj'i-kl/ adj. **dysteleol'ogist** n.

dysthesia /dis-thē'zi-ə, -thē'zhə or -thē'si-ə/ n a morbid habit of body, resulting in general discomfort and impatience. [Gr dysthesiā, from dys- ill, and thesis position]
■ **dysthetic** /-thet'ik/ adj.

dysthymia /dis-thī'mi-ə/ (psychiatry) n abnormal anxiety and despondency. [**dys-** and Gr thymiā despair]
■ **dysthým'iac** n a person who suffers from dysthymia. **dysthým'ic** adj.

dystocia /dis-tō'shi-ə/ (med) n abnormal or difficult labour or childbirth. [**dys-** and Gr tokos birth]

dystonia /dis-tō'ni-ə/ (med) n a disorder of muscle tone, causing muscle spasm. [**dys-** and Gr tonos tension]
■ **dystonic** /-ton'ik/ adj.

dystopia /dis-tō'pi-ə/ n a place thought of as the opposite to utopia, ie where everything is as bad as possible. [From **dys-** and **Utopia**]
■ **dysto'pian** adj.

dystrophy /dis'trə-fi/ or **dystrophia** /-trō'fi-ə/ (biol) n impaired or imperfect nutrition; any of several disorders in which there is wasting of muscle tissue, etc. [**dys-** and Gr trophē nourishment]
■ **dystrophic** /-tro'fik/ adj (of a lake) over-acidic and lacking sufficient nutrients. **dys'trophin** n a protein essential to normal muscle function, found to be lacking in muscular dystrophy sufferers.
■ **muscular dystrophy** see under **muscle[1]**.

dysuria /dis-ū'ri-ə/ (med) n difficulty or pain in passing urine (also **dys'ury**). [Gr dysouriā, from dys- ill, and ouron urine]
■ **dysu'ric** adj.

Dytiscus /dī- or dī-tis'kəs/ n a genus of carnivorous water-beetles, *incl* a common large British species, *D. marginalis* (also **Dyticus** /dit'/). [Gr *dytikos* diving, from *dyein* to dive]
■ **dytiscid** /dī- or dī-tis'id/ adj and n.

dyvour /dī'vər/ (*obs Scot*) n a bankrupt person. [Perh from Fr *devoir* to owe]
■ **dyv'oury** n bankruptcy.

DZ abbrev : Algeria (from the Arabic name *al-Djazā'ir* ; IVR).

dz. abbrev : dozen.

dzeren /dzē'rən/ n a Central Asian antelope. [Mongolian]

dzho, **dzo** see **zho**.

dziggetai /dzig'ə-tī/ n a Central Asian wild ass (*Equus hemionus*), rather like a mule. [Mongolian *tchikhitei*]

Dzongkha /zong'kə/ n the official language of Bhutan. [Tibetan, language of the fortress]

Ee

Eras Designed by Albert Boton and Albert Hollenstein in 1969. France.

E or **e** /ē/ n the fifth letter in the modern English alphabet as in the Roman, with various sounds, as in me, get, *E*ngland, her, prey, and often mute, commonly indicating a preceding long vowel or diphthong: cf not, note ; bit, bite ; the third note of the diatonic scale of C major (*music*); the key or scale having that note for its tonic (*music*); in hexadecimal notation, 14 (decimal) or 1110 (binary); in advertising and marketing, a person who has no regular income or who is dependent on state benefit; a tablet of the drug Ecstasy (*inf*); anything shaped like the letter E.

E *abbrev* : Earl; earth; East; Eastern; Ecstasy, the drug (*inf*) ; (also **e**) electronic, *esp* as over the Internet, as in *e*mail, *e*-trading, *e*-economy ; English; European (as in *E* number); exa-; Spain (ie *España* ; IVR).
- **e-cigarette** or **e-cig** n see separate entry.
□ **e-banking** n see separate entry. **e-book** n see separate entry. **e-business** n see separate entry. **e-card** n see separate entry. **E. coli** see **Escherichia coli** under **Escherichia**. **e-commerce** n see separate entry. **e-economy** n see separate entry. **E'-fit®** n a form of identikit, the image being composed on screen and adjustable by fine degrees. **e-journal** n see separate entry. **E-layer** or **E-region** see **Kennelly-Heaviside layer**. **e-learning** n see separate entry. **email** or **e-mail** n see separate entry. **e-nose** n see separate entry. **E number** n an identification code required by EU law for food additives such as colourings and preservatives, consisting of the letter E followed by a number. **e-ticket** n see separate entry. **e-waste** n see separate entry.

E *symbol* : (as a medieval Roman numeral) 250; electric field strength; electromotive force; energy.

Ē *symbol* : (medieval Roman numeral) 250000.

e *symbol* : the base of the natural system of logarithms (see **Napierian**) (*maths*); the eccentricity of a conic section (*maths*); an electron (*chem*).

EA *abbrev* : Environment Agency.

ea /ē'ə or ē/ (*dialect*) n a river; running water; a drainage channel in the Fens, sometimes **eau**, as if taken from French. [OE ēa ; related to L *aqua* water]

ea. *abbrev* : each.

each /ēch/ adj and pronoun every one separately considered. ◆ adv to, for, from or by each one. [OE ǣlc, from ā ever, and gelīc alike]
- **each'where** adv (*obs*) everywhere.
- **each other** a compound reciprocal pronoun, one another, sometimes restricted in application to two. **each way** in betting, for a win and for a place (**each'-way** adj).

eadish obsolete form of **eddish**.

eager[1] /ē'gər/ adj longing to do or (with *for*) obtain; excited by desire; earnest (*obs*); keen, severe; (Shakesp **aygre**) sour, acid, bitter (*obs*). [OFr aigre, from L ācer, ācris sharp]
- **ea'gerly** adv. **ea'gerness** n.
□ **eager beaver** n (*inf*) an enthusiast; a zealous person; a person who is too eager for work.

eager[2] same as **eagre**.

eagle /ē'gl/ n a name given to many large birds of prey of the family Falconidae; a figure of an eagle, used eg as a national emblem; a military standard carrying the figure of an eagle; a lectern in the form of an eagle; the badge of certain orders, such as the Prussian **black** (1701) and **red** (1705) **eagle**, the Polish, afterwards Russian, **white eagle** (1705); a gold coin of the United States, formerly worth ten dollars and now available in denominations of 5, 10, 25 and 50 dollars; a colonel's shoulder insignia (*US*); a score of two strokes less than par on a hole at golf (also *vi* and vt). [OFr aigle, from L *aquila*]
- **ea'glet** n a young or small eagle.
□ **eagle eye** n exceptionally good eyesight; the ability to notice small details. **ea'gle-eyed** or **ea'gle-sighted** adj sharp-eyed; discerning. **ea'gle-flighted** adj flying high. **ea'gle-hawk** n a name applied to several eagles of comparatively small size. **ea'gle-owl** n any of a number of large horned owls of the genus *Bubo*. **ea'gle-ray** n a large

stingray. **ea'gle-stone** n a hard-encrusted nodule of argillaceous oxide of iron. **ea'gle-winged** adj having an eagle's wings.

eaglewood /ē'gl-wŭd/ n a genus (*Aquilaria*) of the daphne family, large spreading trees of E India, whose heartwood contains a resinous substance fragrant when burnt. [From the accidental resemblance of its name in some Eastern languages to **eagle**, L *aquila* ; cf **agalloch** and **agila**]

eagre /ā'gər or ē'gər/ n a bore or sudden rise of the tide in a river. [Origin doubtful; hardly from OE ēgor flood]

EAK *abbrev* : (East Africa) Kenya (IVR).

ealdorman obsolete form of **alderman**.

eale /prob ēl/ (Shakesp, Hamlet I.4.36) n various conjectures, generally supposed to be for **evil** but perhaps a misprint.

EAN *abbrev* : European Article Number, used for allocating barcodes.

ean /ēn/ (Shakesp) vt and vi to give birth (to). [OE ēanian]
- **ean'ling** n a young lamb.

-ean see **-ian**.

eaon *abbrev* : except as otherwise noted.

EAP *abbrev* : English for academic purposes.

EAR *abbrev* : European Agency for Reconstruction.

ear[1] /ēr/ n the organ of hearing, or just the external part; the sense or power of hearing; the faculty of distinguishing sounds *esp* of a different pitch; attention; anything projecting or shaped like an ear, such as the auricle of a leaf, the lug of a vessel or a projecting part for support, attachment, etc. [OE ēare ; cf Ger Ohr and L *auris*]
- **eared** adj having ears or external ears. **ear'ful** n (*inf*) rough or scolding words, a reprimand; as much talk or gossip as one's ears can stand. **ear'ing** n (*naut*) one of a number of small ropes for fastening the upper corner of a sail to the yard. **ear'less** adj without ears, or external ears.
□ **ear'ache** n an ache or pain in the ear. **ear'bash** vi (Aust *inf*) to talk incessantly. ◆ vt to nag or scold. **ear'basher** n. **ear'bashing** n a lengthy scolding. **ear'bob** n an earring. **ear'-bone** n. **ear'bud** n (*usu* in *pl*) an audio receiver that fits into the outer ear, used for listening to a portable radio, digital audio player, etc. **ear'-bussing** (Shakesp) another reading **ear'-kissing**) adj whispered. **ear'-cap** n (*archaic*) an earflap. **ear'-catching** adj (of a tune, etc) readily taking hold in the mind. **ear defenders** n pl plugs or muffs for insertion into, or fitting over, the ears to reduce noise reception. **ear'drop** n a pendant earring; (in *pl*) a medicine taken in the form of drops put into the outer ear. **ear'drum** n the tympanic membrane, a thin partition between the outer ear and the organs of the middle ear, which vibrates as sound waves strike it; the cavity of the middle ear, tympanum. **ear'flap** n one of two coverings for the ears, attached to a cap, to protect them from cold or injury; a small flap of skin forming the outer ear of some animals. **ear'-hole** n the opening in the ear; a person's ear (*inf*). **ear'lap** n the tip of the ear; an earflap. **ear'lobe** n the soft lower part of the outer ear. **ear'lock** n a curl near the ear worn by Elizabethan dandies. **ear'mark** n a distinctive mark; an owner's mark on an animal's ear. ◆ vt to set aside or intend for a particular purpose; to put an earmark on. **ear'muffs** n pl a pair of ear coverings, joined by a band across the head, worn to protect the ears from cold or noise. **ear'phone** n a headphone. **ear'pick** n an instrument for clearing the ear. **ear'piece** n the part of a telephone, etc that is placed next to the ear; a square box for advertisement, etc printed at the top of a newspaper page; the part of a pair of glasses that fits over and round the ear. **ear'-piercing** adj shrill, screaming. ◆ n the piercing of the lobe of the ear in order to insert earrings. **ear'plug** n a plug of soft material inserted into the outer ear to keep out sound, water, etc. **earring** /ēr'ing/ n a piece of jewellery hung from or fixed on or in the ear. **ear'-shell** n any shell of the family Haliotidae. **ear'shot** n the distance within which a sound can be heard. **ear'-splitting** adj ear-piercing. **ear'-trumpet** n a trumpet-shaped tube formerly used as a hearing aid. **ear'wax** n a waxy substance secreted by the glands of the ear. **ear'wig**

---

fāte; fär; mē; fûr; mīne; mōte; fŏr; mūte; pŭt; dhen (then); el'ə-mənt (element) • For other sounds see detailed chart of pronunciation n (OE *ēarwicga*, from *ēare* ear, and *wicga* insect or beetle) any dermapterous insect of the family Forficulidae, once supposed to creep into the ear; a flatterer. ◆ *vt* to eavesdrop (*sl*); to gain the ear of (*archaic*); to bias (*archaic*); to pester with continual demands (*archaic*). **ear'wigging** *n* (*inf*) a scolding. **ear'wiggy** *adj*. **ear'-witness** *n* a witness that can testify from his or her own hearing. **ear'worm** *n* (*inf*) an irresistibly catchy piece of music.

■ **about one's ears** said of something falling around one (eg a building or missiles) (also *fig*). **a thick ear** (*inf*) a blow on the ear, by way of chastisement. **a word in someone's ear** a private word with someone. **be all ears** to give every attention. **fall on deaf ears** (of a remark, request, etc) to be ignored. **give ear** to attend (to). **go in (at) one ear and out (at) the other** to make no permanent impression. **have itching ears** to want to hear news (Bible, 2 Timothy 4.3). **have** or **keep one's ear to the ground** to keep oneself well-informed about what is going on around one. **have someone's ear** to be sure of someone's favourable attention. **lend an ear** to listen (to). **make a pig's ear of** see **pig**[1]. **make someone's ears burn** to discuss someone in his or her absence. **out on one's ear** (*inf*) dismissed swiftly and without politeness. **pin back one's ears** to listen attentively. **pin back someone's ears** to reprimand, rebuke. **play by ear** to play on a musical instrument without the help of written music. **play it by ear** to deal with a situation as it develops without advance planning. **set by the ears** to set violently against each other. **tickle the ear of** to gratify, pander to the taste of or flatter. **turn a deaf ear** to refuse to listen (to). **up to one's ears** in deeply involved in. **walls have ears** someone may be listening. **wet behind the ears** (*inf*) naïve, immature.

ear[2] /ēr/ *n* the part of a cereal plant containing the seeds. ◆ *vi* to produce ears. [OE *ēar*; Ger *Ähre*]
■ **eared** *adj* (of a plant) having ears.
❑ **ear'-cockle** *n* a disease of wheat caused by a threadworm (genus *Tylenchus*).

ear[3] /ēr/ (*obs*) *vt* to plough or till. [OE *erian*; cf L *arāre* and Gr *aroein*]
■ **ear'ing** *n* (*obs*) ploughing.

earcon /ēr'kon/ (*comput*) *n* an audio signal given by a computer, eg indicating what task it is performing, as distinct from an *icon*, or visual signal. [Artificial coinage, from *ear* and *icon*]

eard, eard-hunger see **yird**.

earl /ûrl/ *n* a British nobleman ranking below a marquess and above a viscount (*fem* **countess**). [OE *eorl* a warrior or hero, a Danish underking, later a nobleman equivalent to a count; cf ON *jarl*]
■ **earl'dom** *n* the lands or rank and title of an earl.
❑ **Earl Grey** *n* a blend of various fragrant oriental teas flavoured with bergamot. **Earl Marshal** *n* an English officer of state, president of the Heralds' College (Scottish form **Earl Marischal**).

early /ûr'li/ *adv* (**ear'lier**; **ear'liest**) before the appointed time; near the beginning (of a time, period or series); soon; in good time; beforehand. ◆ *adj* ready, advanced, awake or on the spot in good time; belonging to or happening in the first part of a time, period or series; belonging to or happening in the first stages of development; beforehand; happening in the remote past or near future; (of temperatures, figures, etc) low. ◆ *n* (*usu* in *pl*) an early potato (*hortic*); (in *pl*) early shifts (*inf*). [OE *ǣrlīce* (adv), from *ǣr* before]
■ **ear'lierize** or **-ise** *vt* to do at a date earlier than that arranged. **ear'liness** *n*.
❑ **early bird** *n* the proverbial catcher of the (early) worm; an early riser; a person who arrives early; (with *caps*) a name given to a type of communications satellite. **early blight** see **potato blight** under **potato**. **early-clos'ing** *adj*. **early day motion** *n* a parliamentary motion for consideration on a day when business finishes early, ie (as such days rarely exist) merely to draw attention to a matter. **early door** *n* an entrance to a theatre or hall open before the ordinary door at a higher price (see also **early doors** below). **Early English** see under **English**. **early music** *n* Classical European music up to about 1700, *esp* when performed in authentic style. **early-Victor'ian** *adj* belonging to or characteristic of the early part of Queen Victoria's reign. **early-warn'ing** *adj* (also as two words) belonging to or part of an early warning system. **early warning system** *n* a system of advance warning or notice, *esp* of nuclear attack. **early wood** *n* (*bot*) the wood formed in the first part of a growth layer during the spring, typically with larger cells and thinner cell walls than the *late wood*.
■ **at the earliest** not before (a specified time or date). **earlier on** previously. **early and late** at all times. **early doors** (*sl*) at an early stage in the proceedings. **early on** before much time has elapsed. **have an early night** (*inf*) to go to bed earlier than usual. (**it's**) **early days** (*inf*) (it's) too soon to know, have a result, etc. **keep early hours** to rise and go to bed early.

earn[1] /ûrn/ *vt* to gain by labour; to acquire; to deserve; to bring to someone. [OE *earnian* to earn; cf OHGer *aran* harvest; Ger *Ernte*]
■ **earn'er** *n* a person who earns; something (*esp* illegal or slightly shady) that brings a good income or profit (*inf*). **earn'ings** *n pl* what

one has earned; money saved; the profits from a venture; income from investments.
■ **earn out** to make enough money from sales to recover costs or make a profit.

earn[2] /ûrn/ (*dialect*) *vt* and *vi* (of milk) to curdle (also **yearn**). [OE *iernan* = *rinnan* to run, and *ærnan* = *rennan* to cause to run; *gerinnan*, and causative *gerennan* to curdle]
■ **earn'ing** *n* rennet (also **yearning**).

earn[3] /ûrn/ (Spenser, Shakesp) *vi* see **yearn**[1].

earnest[1] /ûr'nist/ *adj* intent; sincere in intention; serious, *esp* over-serious, in disposition; determined or wholehearted; fervent or impassioned. ◆ *n* used in the expression **in earnest** (see below). [OE *eornost* seriousness; Ger *Ernst*]
■ **ear'nestly** *adv*. **ear'nestness** *n*.
■ **in all earnestness** most sincerely; urgently. **in earnest** serious or seriously, not joking; in a determined or unequivocal way; in reality.

earnest[2] /ûr'nist/ *n* payment given to confirm a contract (also **ear'nest-money** or **ear'nest-penny**); a pledge; a sign or foretaste of what is to come; first-fruits. [ME *ernes*, from OFr *erres* pledges, from Gr *arrabon* pledge, from Heb *'ērābōn*]

EAROM (*comput*) *abbrev*: electronically alterable read-only memory.

earst obsolete form of **erst**.

earth /ûrth/ *n* the third planet in order from the sun (often with *cap*); the material on the surface of the globe; soil, a mixture of disintegrated rock and organic material, in which plants are rooted; dry land as opposed to sea; the land and sea as opposed to the sky; the world; the inhabitants of the world; dirt; dead matter; the human body; a burrow, *esp* of a badger or fox; an electrical connection with the earth, *usu* by a wire soldered to a metal plate sunk in moist earth; an old name for certain oxides of metals (see **alkaline earth** under **alkali**, **rare earth** under **rare**[1]). ◆ *vt* to connect to earth electrically; to bury, inter (*obs*); to hide or make hide in the earth or in a hole; to clog, cover, smear or partially cover with earth (often with *up*). ◆ *vi* (*poetic* or *rhetoric*) to burrow; to hide. [OE *eorthe*; cf Du *aarde* and Ger *Erde*]
■ **earth'en** *adj* made of earth or clay; earthly. **earth'ily** *adv* in an earthy manner. **earth'iness** *n*. **earth'liness** *n*. **earth'ling** *n* a person living on the earth; a worldly-minded person. **earth'ly** *adj* belonging to the earth; vile; worldly; conceivably possible on earth. ◆ *n* (*inf*) chance (for *earthly chance*). **earth'ward** *adv* (also **earth'wards**) towards the earth. ◆ *adj* moving towards the earth. **earth'y** *adj* consisting of, relating to or resembling earth; inhabiting the earth; gross; unrefined.
❑ **earth'-bag** *n* a sack of earth used in fortifications. **earth'-bath** *n* a bath of earth or mud. **earth'-board** *n* the board of a plough or other implement that turns over the earth. **earth'born** *adj* born from or on the earth. **earth'bound** *adj* confined to the earth; heading towards the earth; lacking imagination. **earth'-bred** *adj* bred from earth; mean, grovelling. **earth-chest'nut** same as **earth-nut** below. **earth'-closet** *n* a lavatory in which the excreta are covered with earth. **earth'-created** *adj* made of earth. **earth'enware** *n* crockery; coarse pottery. **earth'fall** *n* a landslide. **earth'fast** *adj* fixed in the earth. **earth'-fed** *adj* contented with earthly things. **earth'flax** *n* asbestos. **earth'-hog** *n* the aardvark. **earth'-house** *n* an underground stone-lined gallery associated with the Iron Age, which may have functioned as a storehouse or dwelling, a souterrain, also called **Picts' house**. **earth'-hunger** *n* passion for acquiring land. **earthing tyres** *n pl* aircraft tyres that discharge static electricity on grounding. **earth-light** see **earth-shine** below. **earth'ly-mind'ed** *adj* having the mind intent on earthly things. **earth'ly-mind'edness** *n*. **earth'man** or **earth'woman** *n esp* in science fiction, a person who lives on the planet earth. **earth mother** *n* the earth personified as a goddess; a woman, typically fertile and of generous proportions, who seems to symbolize motherhood. **earth'-motherly** *adj*. **earth'-movement** *n* (*geol*) elevation, subsidence or folding of the earth's crust. **earth'mover** *n* any piece of machinery designed to move earth, eg a bulldozer. **earth'moving** *adj*. **earth'-nut** *n* the edible root-tuber of *Conopodium flexuosum*, a woodland umbelliferous plant; the plant itself (also **arnut**, **pig-nut**, **earth-chestnut**); the peanut (genus *Arachis*). **earth observation** *n* (*space*) observation of the earth from satellites by remote sensing techniques. **earth'-pea** *n* the peanut. **earth'-pillar** *n* (*geol*) a column of soft material protected from erosion by an overlying stone. **earth'-plate** *n* a buried plate of metal forming the earth connection of a telegraph-wire, lightning conductor, etc. **earth'quake** *n* a quaking or shaking of the earth; a heaving of the ground; a disruptive event, upheaval (*fig*). **earth'quaked** *adj* shaken or destroyed by an earthquake. **earth'quaking** *adj*. **earth science** *n* any of the sciences dealing with the earth, eg geography or geology. **earth'shaking** or **earth'shattering** *adj* of great importance or consequence. **earth'shakingly** or **earth'shatteringly** *adv*. **earth'-shine** or **earth'-light** *n* the faint light visible on the part of the moon not illuminated by the sun. **earth sign** *n* any of the three signs of the zodiac (Taurus, Virgo and Capricorn) believed to have an affinity with earth.

earth'-smoke *n* (*bot*) fumitory. **earth'-star** *n* a fungus (genus *Geaster*) related to the puffballs that opens out into a starlike form. **earth'-table** *n* (*building*) a course of stone or brick just above the ground. **earth'-tone** *n* a colour like that of the earth, eg a brown or green. **earth tremor** *n* a slight earthquake. **earth'wax** *n* ozokerite. **earth'wolf** *n* the aardwolf. **earthwoman** see **earthman** above. **earth'work** *n* a fortification of earth; an embankment; the act or process of excavation and embanking. **earth'worm** *n* the common worm; a mean person, a poor creature.

■ **cost the earth** (*inf*) to be very expensive. **down** or **back to earth** back to reality (**down-to-earth** *adj* see under **down**¹). **go to earth** to search for or take refuge in a hole or hiding-place (also *fig*). **green earth** see **green**¹. **on earth** used for emphasis in phrases such as *how on earth*, *why on earth*, etc; absolutely, without exception, as in *best on earth*. **run to earth** to search out or find; to go to earth (*lit* and *fig*). **the Earthshaker** (*Gr myth*) Poseidon, the god of earthquakes.

EASDAQ *abbrev*: European Association of Securities Dealers Automated Quotation System, a quotation system for European shares (now known as NASDAQ Europe).

ease /ēz/ *n* freedom from pain or disturbance; rest from work; quiet, peace; freedom from difficulty; naturalness; unconstrained manner; wealth. ◆ *vt* to free from pain, trouble or anxiety; to make comfortable; to relieve; to loosen or relax; to make less difficult; to calm; to move gently; to manoeuvre little by little. ◆ *vi* to become less acute or severe (often with *off* or *up*); to move very gradually; (of the price of shares, etc) to fall slightly. [OFr *aise*; cognate with Ital *agio*, Provençal *ais* and Port *azo*; ult from L *adjacēns*, see **adjacent**]

■ **ease'ful** *adj* ease-giving; quiet, fit for rest. **ease'less** *adj*. **ease'ment** *n* a right attaching to a piece of land entitling its owner to exercise some right over adjacent land owned by another person (*law*); relief, easing (*rare*); assistance (*obs*); support (*obs*); gratification (*obs*). **eas'er** *n*.

❏ **ease'-giving** *adj*.

■ **at ease** free from anxiety; in a comfortably relaxed frame of mind or physical attitude; (of soldiers) standing with feet apart, not at attention. **chapel of ease** see under **chapel**. **ease off** to slacken gradually; to make or become less intense. **ease oneself** (*archaic*; *euphem*) to urinate or defecate. **ill at ease** anxious; embarrassed or uneasy; uncomfortable. **stand at ease** (*milit*) a command to soldiers, etc to stop standing at attention, to stand with feet apart. **take one's ease** to make oneself comfortable.

easel /ē'zl/ *n* a frame for supporting a blackboard, a picture during painting, etc. [Du *ezel* or Ger *Esel* an ass]

easily, **easiness** see under **easy**.

easle or **aizle** /ā'zl/ (*Burns*) *n* hot ashes. [OE *ysle*]

eassel or **eassil** /ē'sl/ (*Scot*) *adv* eastward; easterly. [**east**]

■ **eass'elgate** or **eass'elward** *adv*.

east /ēst/ *n* the part of the sky where the sun rises at the equinoxes; one of the four cardinal points of the compass; (often with *cap* and *the*) the east part of the Earth or of a region, country or town; (with *cap* and *the*) the countries between the Balkans and China (see also **Near East** under **near**, **Middle East** under **middle** and **Far East** under **far**); (with *cap* and *the*) in mid-to-late 20c politics, the countries, chiefly of the eastern hemisphere, under communist rule; (with *cap* and *the*) the eastern part of the USA, used relatively and vaguely, but *usu* the part to the east of the Allegheny Mountains, or to the east of the Mississippi River and to the north of Maryland; (*usu* with *cap*) in bridge, the player or position occupying the place designated 'east' on the table; the east wind (*poetic*). ◆ *adj* situated towards the east; forming the part that is towards the east; (of wind) blowing from the east. ◆ *adv* towards the east. ◆ *vi* (*archaic*) to move or turn east. [OE *ēast*; related to Gr *ēōs* the dawn]

■ **east'erliness** *n*. **east'erling** *n* a native of the east; a trader from the shores of the Baltic (*hist*). **east'erly** *adj* situated in the east; towards the east; (*esp* of the wind) coming from the east. ◆ *adv* on the east; towards the east; from the east. ◆ *n* an east wind. **east'ern** or (*obs* except in place names) **east'er** *adj* situated in the east or further to the east; coming from the east; towards the east; connected with the east; living in the east; (with *cap*) of, from or relating to the East. ◆ *n* an easterner. **east'erner** *n* (sometimes with *cap*) a native or inhabitant of the east, *esp* of the USA. **east'ernism** *n* a form of expression or characteristic peculiar to the east. **east'ernize** or **-ise** *vt* to give an eastern character to. **east'ernmost**, **east'most** or (*obs*) **east'ermost** *adj* situated furthest east. **east'ing** *n* the course taken to the eastward; the distance eastward from a given meridian. **east'ling** or **east'lin** *adj* (*Scot*) easterly. **east'lings** or **east'lins** *adv* (*Scot*) eastward. **east'ward** *adv* towards the east (also *adj* and *n*). **east'wardly** *adv* and *adj*. **east'wards** *adv* eastward.

❏ **east'about** *adv* towards the east. **east'bound** *adj* travelling in an eastward direction. **east'-by-north** *n* the direction midway between east and east-north-east. **east'-by-south** *n* the direction midway between east and east-south-east. **East Coast fever** *n* (also called

African coast fever) a protozoan cattle disease resembling redwater, transmitted by ticks. **East End** *n* the eastern part of London or another town. **East-end'er** *n*. **Eastern bloc** *n* (*hist*) the Communist countries of E Europe. **Eastern Church** or **Eastern Orthodox Church** *n* the churches which follow the ancient rite of the East and accept the first seven councils, rejecting papal supremacy, as distinguished from the Western Church (also **Orthodox Church**, **Greek Church**, **Greek Orthodox Church**, **Orthodox Eastern Church**). **Eastern European Time** *n* one of the standard times used in Europe, being 2 hours ahead of Greenwich Mean Time (*abbrev* **EET**). **eastern hemisphere** *n* (also with *caps*) the hemisphere of the world containing Europe, Asia, Africa and Australia. **Eastern Standard Time** or **Eastern Time** *n* one of the standard times used in N America, being 5 hours behind Greenwich Mean Time (*abbrev* **EST** or **ET**). **East-Ind'iaman** *n* (*hist*) a ship used in the East Indian trade. **East Indian**, **East Indies** see under **Indian**. **east'land** *n* the east (also *adj*). **east'-north-east** *n* the direction midway between east and north-east (also *adj* and *adv*). **East Side** *n* the eastern part of the city of New York. **east'-south-east** *n* the direction midway between east and south-east (also *adj* and *adv*).

■ **about east** (*obs US sl*) correctly.

Easter /ē'stər/ *n* a Christian festival commemorating the resurrection of Christ, held on the Sunday after the first full moon following the spring equinox (21 March); the period during which the festival takes place, thought of as running from Good Friday to Easter Monday. [OE *ēastre*; Ger *Ostern*; Bede derives the word from *Eostre* (variant of *Eastre*), a goddess whose festival was held at the spring equinox]

❏ **Easter cactus** *n* a S American cactus having coral-coloured flowers. **Easter Day** *n* the day of the Easter festival, also **Easter Sunday**. **Easter dues** or **offerings** *n pl* customary sums of money paid to the priest by his congregation at Easter. **Easter egg** *n* a painted, decorated, stained or artificial egg, now *esp* made of chocolate, given as a present at Easter; an undocumented sequence of code in a computer program activated by a specific set of keystrokes, intended as a joke or often to identify the authors (*comput*). **Easter lily** *n* any of several white-flowered lilies. **Easter Monday** *n* the day after Easter Day, observed as a public holiday. **East'ertide** or **East'ertime** *n* the days around Easter; the fifty days from Easter to Whitsuntide (*relig*).

easy /ē'zi/ *adj* not difficult; at ease; free from pain; tranquil; unconstrained; giving ease; convenient; yielding; not straitened (in circumstances); not tight; not strict; in plentiful supply; (of the stock market) not showing unusually great activity. ◆ *adv* (*esp inf*) in an easy state or manner. ◆ *interj* a command to lower, to go gently, to stop rowing, etc. [Ety as for **ease**]

■ **eas'ily** *adv*. **eas'iness** *n*.

❏ **eas'y-care** *adj* (*esp* of materials) easy to look after, clean, etc. **easy chair** *n* a comfortable armchair. **eas'y-goer** *n*. **easy-go'ing** *adj* placid; indolent. **easy listening** *n* a category of modern popular music comprising pleasant but undemanding songs and tunes. **easy-list'ening** *adj*. **easy meat**, **game** or **mark** *n* a person or thing that is easy to beat, fool, persuade, hit, destroy, etc. **easy money** *n* money made without much exertion or difficulty; money that can be borrowed at a low rate of interest (*finance*). **eas'y-ō'sy** *adj* (*inf*) easy-going; without strong feelings, indifferent. **eas'y-peas'y** *adj* (*inf*) extremely easy. **easy street** *n* (*inf*) a situation of comfort or affluence. **easy terms** *n pl* a phrase used in describing a hire-purchase agreement to imply or emphasize that the payments will not be a burden to the customer. **easy touch** see under **touch**.

■ **be easy** to be quite willing to fall in with any arrangement (*inf*); to be ready and willing for sexual experiences (*sl*). **easy does it** take your time, do (it) slowly or carefully. **easy on the eye**, **ear**, etc (*inf*) pleasant to look at, listen to, etc. **easy over** (*inf*, *esp US*) (of an egg) fried on both sides. **go easy on** to be lenient with; to use sparingly. **honours easy** honours evenly divided (at cards, etc). **stand easy** (*milit*) a command to stand in a still more relaxed position. **take it easy** to avoid exertion; to be in no hurry.

EAT *abbrev*: (East Africa) Tanzania (IVR); Employment Appeals Tribunal.

eat /ēt/ *vt* (**eat'ing**; **ate** /et/ or /āt/; **eaten** /ē'tən/ or *obs* **eat** /et/) to take into the body by the mouth as food; to bite, chew or swallow; to include or tolerate in one's diet; to consume (often with *up*); to corrode or destroy (often with *away*); to upset, irritate or worry (*inf*). ◆ *vi* to take food; to take a meal, eg at a stated time; to make inroads, make a hole or gnaw (with *into* or *through*); to be eatable, to taste. ◆ *n* (*archaic* in *sing*, *inf* in *pl*) food. [OE *etan*; cf Ger *essen*, ON *eta*, L *edere* and Gr *edein*]

■ **eat'able** *adj* edible or fit to be eaten. ◆ *n* (*inf*; *esp* in *pl*) anything used as food. **eat'age** *n* grass or fodder for horses, etc; the right to eat. **eat'er** *n* someone who or something which eats or corrodes; a variety of fruit, vegetable, etc suitable for eating uncooked. **eat'ery** *n* (*inf*, *esp* N Am) a restaurant (also **eat'erie**). **eat'ing** *n* and *adj*.

❑ **eating apple**, etc *n* one suitable for eating uncooked. **eat'ing-house** *n* a restaurant. **eating irons** *n pl* (*sl*) knife, fork and spoon.
■ **eat away** to destroy gradually; to gnaw. **eat crow**, **dirt** or **humble pie** see under **crow**, **dirt**, **humbles**. **eat in** of acid, to corrode, etch, etc (a metal); to eat at home. **eating out of one's hand** completely under one's control. **eat into** of acid, to corrode, etc; to consume, use up or make inroads into. **eat off** to clear (a crop) by setting cattle to eat it. **eat one's hat** to be very surprised (if something turns out contrary to one's expectations). **eat one's head off** (*esp* of an animal) to cost more for food than one is worth. **eat one's heart out** to pine away, brooding over misfortune. **eat one's terms** (*law*) to study for the bar, with allusion to the number of times in a term that a student must dine in the hall of an Inn of Court. **eat one's words** to take back what one has said. **eat out** to have a meal away from home, *usu* in a restaurant; to eat everything edible in (a place); to encroach upon. **eat the air** (*Shakesp*) to be deluded with hopes. **eat up** to finish one's food; to devour entirely; to consume or absorb; (*esp in passive*) to obsess or preoccupy wholly. **what's eating you?** (*inf*) what is worrying or irritating you?

eatche /ēch/ (*Walter Scott*) *n* a Scots form of **adze**.

eath, **eathe** or **ethe** /ēth or eth/ (*Spenser*, etc) *adj* easy. ◆ *adv* easily. [OE *ēathe* easy or easily]
■ **eath'ly** *adv*.

EAU *abbrev* : (East Africa) Uganda (IVR).

eau[1] /ō/ *n* the French word for water, used in English in various combinations.
❑ **eau de Cologne** /də kə-lōn/ see **cologne**. **eau de Javel(le)** see **Javel(le) water**. **eau de Nil** /də nēl/ *n* a pale-green colour, Nile green. **eau des creoles** /dā krā-ol'/ *n* a fine Martinique liqueur, made by distilling the flowers of the mammee-apple with alcohol. **eau de toilette** /də twä-let'/ *n* same as **toilet water** (see under **toilet**). **eau de vie** /də vē/ *n* brandy.

eau[2] see **ea**.

eaves /ēvz/ *n pl* (*orig sing*) the projecting edge of the roof; anything projecting. [OE *efes* the clipped edge of thatch; cf Icel *ups*]
❑ **eaves'drip** or **eaves'drop** *n* the water that falls from the eaves of a house; the place where the drops fall; (**eavesdrop**) an act of eavesdropping. **eaves'drop** *vi* (**eaves'dropping**; **eaves'dropped**) to try to overhear other people's private conversations; *orig* to stand under the eaves or near the windows of a house to listen. ◆ *vt* to listen secretly to (a private conversation). **eaves'dropper** *n* someone who listens in this way; someone who tries to overhear private conversations. **eaves'dropping** *n*.

EAZ *abbrev* : (East Africa) Zanzibar (IVR)

EB *abbrev* : epidermolysis bullosa (see under **epidermis**); Epstein-Barr (virus).

e-banking /ē'bang-king/ *n* banking carried out through electronic communications.

ébauche /ā-bōsh'/ (*Fr*) *n* a rough draft or sketch.

ebb /eb/ *n* the going back or lowering of the tide; a decline. ◆ *vi* to flow back; to sink; to decline (often with *away*). ◆ *adj* (*obs* or *dialect*; *Walter Scott*) shallow. [OE *ebba*]
■ **ebb'less** *adj*.
❑ **ebb'-tide** *n* the ebbing tide.
■ **at a low ebb** (*fig*) in a low or weak state. **on the ebb** (*fig*) in decline; failing.

EBCDIC /eb'si-dik/ (*comput*) *abbrev* : extended binary-coded decimal interchange code, a code used on some IBM computers.

EBD *abbrev* : emotional and behavioural difficulties (or disorder).

ebenezer /eb-ə-nē'zər/ *n* a memorial stone set up by Samuel after the victory of Mizpeh (Bible, 1 Samuel 7.12); a name sometimes applied to a chapel or religious meeting-house. [Heb *eben-hā-ezer* stone of help]

ébéniste /ā-bā-nēst'/ (*Fr*) *n* a cabinetmaker.

Ebionite /ē'bi-ə-nīt/ *n* a member of a group of early Christians who believed they were bound by the Mosaic law and denied the apostolate of Paul and the miraculous birth of Jesus. [Heb *ebyōn* poor]
■ **ebionitic** /-it'ik/ *adj*. **e'bionītism** or **e'bionism** *n*. **e'bionize** or **-ise** *vt*.

EBITDA or **ebitda** /eb'it-dä/ *abbrev* : earnings before interest, tax, depreciation and amortization.

Eblis /eb'lis/ or **Iblis** /ib'lis/ *n* a Muslim name for the Devil. [Ar *Iblīs*]

E-boat /ē'bōt/ *n* a fast German motor torpedo-boat. [*enemy boat* or Ger *Eilboot*, from *Eile* speed]

Ebola virus /ē-bō'lə vī'rəs/ *n* a viral disease occurring in Africa, producing symptoms similar to, but with a much higher mortality rate than, green monkey disease (qv under **green**[1]). [From the *Ebola* river in the Democratic Republic of Congo, where an outbreak occurred in 1976]

Ebonics /i-bon'iks/ *n sing* a variety of English spoken by many African-Americans. [**ebony** and **phonic**]

ebony /eb'ə-ni/ (*rare*, *esp poetic*, **ebon** /eb'ən/) *n* a kind of wood produced by various species of the *Diospyros* tree (family **Ebenā'ceae**) almost as heavy and hard as stone, usually black and capable of being finely polished; a tree producing it; a very dark brownish-black colour; a black person (*old US derog*), now black people in general, their concerns and sensibilities. ◆ *adj* made of ebony; black as ebony. [L (*h*)*ebenus*, from Gr *ebenos*; cf Heb *hobnīm*, pl of *hobni* or *obni*, from *eben* a stone]
■ **eb'onist** *n* a worker in ebony. **eb'onite** *n* black vulcanized rubber, vulcanite. **eb'onize** or **-ise** *vt* and *vi* to make or become like ebony.

e-book or **ebook** /ē'bŏŏk/ *n* a publication in electronic form that can be stored and read on a computer (in full, **electronic book**).

Ebor. /ē'bör or e'bör/ *abbrev* : *Eboracum* (L), York; *Eboracensis* (L), of York.

éboulement /ā-bool-mä'/ *n* the falling in of the wall of a fortification; a landslide or landslip. [Fr]

ebracteate /ē-brak'ti-āt/ (*bot*) *adj* without bracts. [L *ē-* without or from, and *bractea* a thin plate]
■ **ebract'eolate** *adj* without bracteoles.

EBRD *abbrev* : European Bank for Reconstruction and Development.

ebriate /ē'bri-āt/ or **ebriated** /-id/ *adj* intoxicated. [L *ēbriāre*, *-ātum* to make drunk]
■ **ebriety** /ē-brī'i-ti/ *n* drunkenness. **e'briōse** *adj* drunk. **ebrios'ity** *n*.

ébrillade /ā-brē-(l)yäd'/ *n* the sudden jerking of a horse's rein when it refuses to turn. [Fr]

EBU *abbrev* : European Broadcasting Union.

ebullient /i-bul'yənt/ *adj* enthusiastic or exuberant; agitated; boiling up or over. [L *ēbulliēns*, *-entis*, prp of *ēbullīre* to bubble out, from *ē* out, and *bullīre* to boil]
■ **ebull'ience** or **ebull'iency** *n* cheerful enthusiasm; a boiling over. **ebull'iently** *adv*. **ebull'ioscope** *n* a device for determining the boiling points of liquids. **ebullioscop'ic** or **ebullioscop'ical** *adj*. **ebullioscop'ically** *adv*. **ebullios'copy** *n*. **ebullition** /eb-ə-lish'ən/ *n* the act of boiling; agitation; an outbreak.

eburnean /e-bûr'ni-ən/ *adj* of or like ivory (also **ebur'neous**). [L *eburneus*, from *ebur* ivory]
■ **eburnā'tion** /ēb- or eb-/ *n* (*med*) an abnormal change of bone by which it becomes very hard and dense. **eburnificā'tion** *n* the art of making like ivory.

e-business /ē-biz'nis/ *n* a business that carries out its operations through the Internet.

EBV *abbrev* : Epstein-Barr virus.

EC *abbrev* : East Caribbean; East Central; Ecuador (IVR); Established Church; European Commission; European Community; executive committee.

ECA same as **UNECA**.

ecad /ek'ad/ (*bot*) *n* a species with distinctive forms dependent on the environment rather than on genotypic differences. [Gr *oikos* home, and **-ad**[1]]

e-card /ē'kärd/ *n* a pictorial greeting, message, invitation, etc sent via email.

ecardinate /ē-kär'di-nāt/ *adj* hingeless. [L *ē-* without, and *cardō*, *-inis* hinge]
■ **Ecard'inēs** *n pl* (*zool*) a class of brachiopods without hinge or arm skeleton.

écarté[1] /ā-kär-tā'/ *n* in ballet, a position in which the arm and leg are extended to the side. [Fr, spread or separated]

écarté[2] /ā-kär-tā/ *n* a game in which cards may be discarded for others. [Fr, discarded, from *é-* (from L *ex* out of, from), and *carte* a card]

ecaudate /ē-kö'dāt/ *adj* tailless. [L *ē-* without, and *cauda* tail]

ECB *abbrev* : England and Wales Cricket Board; European Central Bank.

ecblastesis /ek-bla-stē'sis/ (*bot*) *n* proliferation of a floral axis. [Gr *ekblastēsis* budding forth, from *ek* out of, and *blastos* a sprout]

ecbole /ek'bo-lē/ *n* a digression (*rhetoric*); in ancient music, the raising or sharpening of a tone. [Gr *ekbolē* throwing out, from *ek* out of, and *ballein* to throw]
■ **ecbol'ic** *adj* (*med*) inducing contractions of the uterus leading to childbirth or abortion. ◆ *n* a drug having this effect.

eccaleobion /e-kal-i-ō-bī'on/ (*hist*) *n* a kind of incubator. [Gr *ekkaleō bion* I call forth life]

ecce /ek'si, ek'ā, ek'e or ech'ā/ (*L*) *interj* behold.

■ **ecce homo** /hō'mō or hom'ō/ behold the man (Bible, John 19.5); a portrayal of Christ crowned with thorns (*art*). **ecce signum** /sig'nəm or *-nŭm*/ behold the sign or proof.

eccentric /ek-sen'trik/ *adj* (of behaviour, etc) odd or unconventional; unusual, departing from the norm; not positioned centrally; with the axis to one side, not at the centre; (of superimposed circles) not concentric, not having the same centre; (of an orbit) not circular. ◆ *n* an eccentric person; a circle not having the same centre as another; a device for taking an alternating rectilinear motion from a revolving shaft (*mech*). [Gr *ek* out of, and *kentron* centre]

■ **eccen'trical** *adj* (*archaic*). **eccen'trically** *adv*. **eccentricity** /-sən-tris'/ *n* the condition of being eccentric; peculiarity of behaviour; oddness; in a conic section, the constant ratio of the distance of a point on the curve from the focus to its distance from the directrix (*usu* represented by *e*; *geom*); deviation from a circular orbit, etc; a measure of the extent of such deviation.

ecchymosis /ek-i-mō'sis/ (*med*) *n* discoloration caused by bleeding under the skin. [Gr *ekchӯmōsis*, from *ek* out of, and *chӯmos* juice]

■ **ecch'ymosed** *adj*. **ecchymot'ic** *adj*.

Eccl. or **Eccles.** (*Bible*) *abbrev* : the Book of Ecclesiastes.

eccl. or **eccles.** *abbrev* : ecclesiastical.

Eccles cake /ek'lz kāk/ *n* a small cake or bun filled with raisins, currants, etc. [*Eccles* in Greater Manchester]

ecclesia /i-klē'zi-ə/ *n* a popular assembly, *esp* of ancient Athens, where the people exercised full sovereignty and every male citizen above twenty years could vote; applied by the Septuagint commentators to the Jewish commonwealth, and from them to the Christian Church. [LL, from Gr *ekklēsia* an assembly called out of the world, the church, from *ek* out of, and *kaleein* to call]

■ **ecclē'sial** *adj*. **ecclē'siarch** /-ärk/ *n* (*archaic*) a ruler of the church. **ecclē'siast** *n* 'the preacher', the name given to the author of Ecclesiastes; an ecclesiastic. **Ecclesias'tes** *n* one of the books of the Old Testament, traditionally supposed to have been written by Solomon. **ecclesias'tic** *n* (*formal*) a person consecrated to the church, such as a priest or a clergyman. **ecclesias'tic** or **ecclesias'tical** *adj* relating to the church or to the clergy. **ecclesias'tically** *adv*. **ecclesias'ticism** /-sizm/ *n* excessive regard for ecclesiastical rules and observances; the principles constituting organized Christianity. **Ecclesias'ticus** *n* one of the books of the Apocrypha. **ecclesiol'ater** *n*. **ecclesiol'atry** *n* (Gr *latreiā* worship) excessive reverence for ecclesiastical traditions. **ecclesiolog'ical** *adj*. **ecclesiol'ogist** *n*. **ecclesiol'ogy** *n* the study of ecclesiastical traditions and of church architecture and decoration; the study or knowledge of the church.

❏ **ecclesiastical year** see under **year**.

Ecclus. (*Bible*) *abbrev* : (the Apocryphal Book of) Ecclesiasticus.

ecco /ek'kō/ (*Ital*) *interj* here is; there; look there.

eccoprotic /ek-ō-prot'ik/ *adj* laxative, mildly cathartic. ◆ *n* a laxative. [Gr *ekkoprōtikos*, from *ek* out of, and *kopros* dung]

eccrine /ek'rīn/ *adj* of a gland, *esp* the sweat glands, secreting externally. [Gr *ek* out of, and *krīnein* to separate, secrete]

■ **eccrinology** /ek-ri-nol'ə-ji/ *n* the branch of physiology relating to the secretions of the eccrine glands.

eccrisis /ek'ri-sis/ *n* expulsion of waste or abnormal matter. [Gr *ekkrisis* secretion, from *ek* out, and *krisis* separation]

■ **eccrit'ic** *n* a medicine having this effect.

ecdysis /ek'di-sis/ (*zool*) *n* the act of casting off the old skin (in reptiles) or the exoskeleton (in insects and crustaceans). [Gr *ekdysis*, from *ek* out of, and *dyein* to put on]

■ **ecdysiast** /-diz'/ *n* (*facetious*) a striptease performer. **ec'dysone** /ek-dī'sōn/ *n* a hormone that controls ecdysis in insects and crustaceans.

ECE same as **UNECE**.

ECG *abbrev* : electrocardiogram or electrocardiograph.

ECGD *abbrev* : Export Credits Guarantee Department, a UK government department.

ech see **eche**.

échappé /ā-sha-pā'/ (*ballet*) *n* a double leap from two feet, starting in fifth position, landing in second or fourth, and finishing in fifth. [Fr, pap of *échapper*, to escape]

eche /ēch/ (*Shakesp*) *vt* (also **ech**, **eech**, **ich**) to eke out; to augment. [OE *ēcan* ; related to L *augēre* to increase; see **eke**[1]]

echelon /esh'ə-lon or (Fr) āsh-lõ'/ *n* a particular level in the hierarchy of an organization; the group of people at any one of these levels; an arrangement of troops, ships, planes, etc as if in steps. ◆ *vt* to arrange in an echelon. ◆ *vi* to form an echelon. [Fr *échelon*, from *échelle* ladder, stair; see **scale**[2]]

echeveria /ek- or ech-ə-vē'ri-ə/ *n* a plant of the genus *Echeveria* of succulent plants of the family Crassulaceae. [Named after A. *Echeveri*, 19c Mexican botanical artist]

echidna /e-kid'nə/ *n* a member of the genus *Tachyglossus* of Australian toothless, spiny, egg-laying, burrowing monotremes (also called **spiny anteater**). [Gr *echidna* viper]

■ **echid'nine** *n* snake-poison.

echinus /e-kī'nəs/ *n* a sea-urchin; the convex projecting moulding (an eccentric curve in Greek examples) supporting the abacus of the Doric capital (*archit*). [Gr *echīnos* a hedgehog]

■ **echinacea** /ek-i-nā'si-ə/ *n* a N American composite plant of the genus *Echinacea* ; a herbal remedy prepared from it, thought to boost the immune system. **echinate** /ek'in-āt/ or **echinated** /-id/ *adj* prickly like a hedgehog; bristly. **Echīnocac'tus** *n* a large genus of ribbed, generally very spiny, cacti. **echīnococcō'sis** *n* hydatid disease. **echīnococc'us** *n* the bladderworm stage (parasitic in cow, sheep, pig and man) of the dog tapeworm. **echī'noderm** *n* (*zool*) any one of the **Echīnoder'ma** or **Echīnoder'mata**, a phylum of radially symmetrical marine invertebrates, with a hard body-wall strengthened by calcareous plates, and usually moving by tube-feet, including starfishes, sea-urchins, brittlestars, sea-cucumbers and sea-lilies. **echinoder'mal** *adj*. **echinoder'matous** *adj*. **echī'noid** *adj* like a sea-urchin. ◆ *n* a sea-urchin. **Echīnoid'ea** *n pl* the sea-urchins, a class of Echinoderma. **Echīn'ops** *n* (*bot*) a genus of Compositae found in S Europe, the globe thistle, with flowers in globular clusters.

echium /ek'i-əm/ *n* any plant of the viper's bugloss genus *Echium*. [Gr *echis* viper]

Echiura /ek-i-ū'rə/ *n pl* a phylum of marine invertebrates, the spoonworms. [Gr *echis* viper, and *oura* tail]

■ **echiū'ran** or **echiū'roid** *n* and *adj*.

Echo or **echo** /ek'ō/ *n* (in international radio communication) a code word for the letter *e*.

echo /ek'ō/ *n* (pl **echoes** /ek'ōz/) the sending back or reflection of sound or other waves; the repetition of sound by reflection; a reflected sound; a soft-toned organ stop forming a part of some large organs; a device in verse in which a line ends with a word which recalls the sound of the last word of the preceding line; response; (in *pl*) reverberations or repercussions; repetition; imitation; an imitator; something that reminds one of something else; a memory evoked; the signal emitted by an object being scanned by radar; the visual signal from such an object, appearing on screen; in card games, play of a higher card followed by a lower to indicate what cards one holds; in musical recording, an electronic reverberating effect. ◆ *vi* (**ech'oing**; **ech'oed** /-ōd/) to reflect sound; to be sounded back; to resound; to be full of echoes (*usu* with *with*); to play a card as an echo. ◆ *vt* to send back (sound or other waves); to send back the sound of; to repeat; to imitate; to follow slavishly. [L, from Gr *ēchō* a sound]

■ **ech'oer** *n*. **ech'oey** *adj*. **ech'ogram** *n* the record produced in echo-sounding. **echō'ic** *adj* of the nature of an echo; onomatopoeic (*philology*). **echō'ically** *adv*. **ech'oism** *n* the formation of imitative words. **ech'oist** *n* a person who repeats like an echo. **ech'oize** or **-ise** *vi*. **ech'oless** *adj* giving no echo; unresponsive.

❏ **echocar'diogram** *n* the record produced by **echocardiog'raphy**, the investigation by means of ultrasound of certain internal parts of the heart and the ways in which they move in order to detect disease *esp* of the heart valves. **echocar'diograph** *n*. **echocardiograph'ic** *adj*. **echoenceph'alogram** *n* (*med*) the record produced by **echoencephalog'raphy**, the investigation of brain tissues by means of ultrasound waves beamed through the head. **ech'ograph** *n* an echo-sounder. **echolalia** /ek-ō-lā'li-ə/ *n* (Gr *laliā* talk) senseless or compulsive repetition of words heard, occurring in forms of mental illness. **echoprax'ia** or **echoprax'is** *n* (Gr *praxis* doing) in mental illness, the imitation of postures or movements of those around one. **echo chamber** *n* a room in which sound can be echoed for recording or radio effects or when measuring acoustics. **echo location** *n* determining the position of objects by means of supersonic vibrations echoed from them, as a bat does. **ech'o-sounder** *n* the device used in echo-sounding. **ech'o-sounding** *n* a method of measuring the depth of water, locating shoals of fish, etc, by noting the time taken for an echo to return from the bottom, the shoal, etc. **ech'ovirus** or **ECHO virus** *n* any of a group of viruses which can cause respiratory and intestinal diseases and meningitis (enteric cytopathogenic *h*uman *o*rphan virus).

■ **cheer to the echo** to applaud heartily.

ECHR *abbrev* : European Convention on Human Rights.

echt /ehht/ (*Ger*) *adj* genuine, authentic. ◆ *adv* genuinely, authentically.

e-cigarette /ē'sig-ə-ret/ or **e-cig** /ē'sig/ *n* a battery-powered device that generates a vapour containing nicotine that is inhaled by the user (in full, **electronic cigarette**).

---

fāte; fär; mē; fûr; mīne; mōte; för; mūte; pŭt; dhen (then); *el'ə-mənt* (element) ◆ For other sounds see detailed chart of pronunciation

ECLAC *abbrev* : Economic Commission for Latin America and the Caribbean.

éclair /*ā-kler*', -*klār*' or *i*-/ *n* a cake, long in shape but short in duration, with cream filling and *usu* chocolate icing. [Fr *éclair* lightning]

éclaircissement /*ā-kler-sē-smä*'/ *n* the act of clearing up a misunderstanding; explanation. [Fr *éclaircir*, from L *ex* out, and *clārus* clear]
■ **come to an éclaircissement** to come to an understanding; to explain conduct that seemed equivocal.

eclampsia /*i-klamp*'*si-ə*/, also **eclampsy** /-*si*/ (*pathol*) *n* a condition resembling epilepsy; now only applied to acute toxaemia with convulsive fits in the last three months of pregnancy. [Gr *eklampsis*, from *eklampein* to flash forth, to burst forth violently (eg of a fever), from *ek* out of, and *lampein* to shine]
■ **eclamp'tic** *adj*.

éclat /*ā-klä*'/ *n* a striking effect; showy splendour; distinction; applause. [Fr *éclat*, from OFr *esclater* to break, to shine]

eclectic /*e-klek*'*tik* or *i*-/ *adj* selecting or borrowing from a variety of styles, systems, theories, etc; characterized by such selection or borrowing; choosing the best out of everything; broad, as opposed to exclusive. ◆ *n* someone who selects opinions from different systems *esp* in philosophy. [Gr *eklektikos*, from *ek* from, and *legein* to choose]
■ **eclec'tically** *adv*. **eclec'ticism** /-*sizm*/ *n* the practice of an eclectic; the doctrine of the **eclec'tics**, a name applied to certain Greek thinkers in the 2c and 1c BC, and later to Leibniz and Cousin.

eclipse /*i-klips*'/ *n* the total or partial disappearance of a heavenly body by the interposition of another between it and the spectator, or by passing into its shadow (it can be *total*, *partial* or *annular* (qv)); an overshadowing; loss of brilliancy; darkness; loss of fame or importance. ◆ *vt* to hide completely or partially; to darken; to overshadow, cut out or surpass. [OFr, from L *eclipsis*, from Gr *ekleipsis* failure, from *ek* out of, and *leipein* to leave]
■ **eclip'tic** *n* (*astron*) the great circle in which the plane containing the centres of the earth and sun cuts the celestial sphere; the apparent path of the sun's annual motion among the fixed stars; a great circle in which that plane cuts the earth's surface at any moment. ◆ *adj* characteristic of or belonging to an eclipse or the ecliptic.
❑ **eclipse plumage** *n* dull plumage apparent in certain usually brightly-coloured birds at the end of the breeding season.

eclogite or **eklogite** /*ek*'*lə-jīt*/ *n* a crystalline rock composed of red garnet and green omphacite or smaragdite. [Gr *eklogē* selection (from the unusual minerals that compose it), from *ek* out of, and *legein* to choose]

eclogue /*ek*'*log*/ *n* a short pastoral poem. [From *Eclogae*, the title given to a collection of such poems by Virgil, from Gr *eklogē* a selection, from *ek* out of, and *legein* to choose]

eclosion /*i-klō*'*zhən*/ *n* emergence, *esp* of an insect from a pupal case or a larva from an egg. [Fr *éclosion*, from L *ex*-, and *claudere* to shut]
■ **eclose**' *vi*.

ECM *abbrev* : electronic countermeasures.

ECO *abbrev* : English Chamber Orchestra.

eco- /*ēk*-, *ek-ō*- or *ek-ə*-/ *combining form* denoting ecology or concern for the environment. The form is currently very productive, and is found also as an *adj* form **ē'co**; only a selection of the commoner derivatives is given:
■ **ec'ocide** *n* the destruction of the aspects of the environment which enable it to support life. **ec'oclimate** *n* a local climate regarded as an ecological factor. **ec'ofreak** or **ec'onut** *n* (*derog sl*) a person concerned with the state and protection of the environment, an environmentalist. **ecofriend'ly** *adj* ecologically acceptable; in harmony with, or not threatening to, the environment. **e'co-label** *n* a label used by manufacturers of products claiming to be environmentally acceptable, specifying to the consumer their ecological credentials; a label certifying that certain ecological standards have been reached. **e'co-labelling** *n*. **e'comap** *n* a diagrammatic representation of a person's or family's interactions with other individuals and groups in the community. **ecophō'bia** *n* fear of one's home surroundings. **ec'ospecies** *n* a group of ecotypes. **ec'osphere** *n* the parts of the universe or *esp* the earth in which life is possible. **ec'osystem** *n* a unit consisting of a community of organisms and their environment. **ecoterr'orism** *n* acts of violence carried out in order to prevent or protest against destruction of the environment. **ecoterr'orist** *n*. **ec'otone** *n* (Gr *tonos* tension) an area marking the boundary between two distinct types of environment. **eco-tour'ism** *n* small-scale, carefully managed development of the natural environment for the holiday market. **eco-tour'ist** *n*. **ecotox'ic** *adj* poisonous to plants or animals, deleterious to the environment. **ecotoxicolog'ical** *adj*. **ecotoxicol'ogist** *n*. **ecotoxicol'ogy** *n* the study of the destructive effect of waste materials, etc on the environment. **ec'otype** *n* a group of organisms which have adapted to a particular

environment and so have become different from other groups within the species. **e'co-village** *n* a small-scale, environmentally friendly settlement designed for sustainable living. **ec'owarrior** (or /-*wor*'/) *n* a person who is willing to take direct, and often illegal, action on environmental issues.

ecod /*i-kod*'/ (*archaic*) *interj* same as **egad**.

Ecofin /*ek*'*ō-fin*/ *n* a legislative council of the *eco*nomic and *fin*ance ministers of all the EU member countries.

E. coli *abbrev* : Escherichia coli.

ecology /*ē-kol*'*ə-ji*, *e*- or *i*-/ *n* the scientific study of plants, animals, or peoples and institutions, in relation to environment (also **oecol'ogy**). [Gr *oikos* house, and *logos* discourse]
■ **ecologic** /-*ko-loj*'*ik*/ or **ecolog'ical** *adj* relating to or concerned with ecology; using, concerned with or relating to methods, processes, etc beneficial to the natural environment. **ecolog'ically** *adv*. **ecol'ogist** *n*. —Also **oecologic**, etc.
❑ **ecological efficiency** *n* the ratios between the amount of energy flow at different points along a food chain. **ecological footprint** *n* a measurement of the demands on the earth's resources made by a person, country, etc in relation to the planet's ability to regenerate those resources. **ecological niche** *n* the position or status of an organism within its community or ecosystem. **ecological succession** see **succession** under **succeed**.

e-commerce /*ē-kom*'*ûrs*/ *n* the use of electronic communications to buy and sell goods and services (in full, **electronic commerce**).

econ. *abbrev* : economic; economical; economics; economy.

economy /*ē-kon*'*ə-mi*, *i*- or *e*-/ *n* the administration of the material resources of an individual, community or country; the state of these resources; a frugal and judicious expenditure of money; thrift; (*usu* in *pl*) an instance of economizing, a saving; the management of a household (*archaic*); a religious system specific to a community or period, as *the Christian economy*; the efficient use of something, eg speech, effort, etc; making one's presentation of doctrine, etc suit the needs or not offend the prejudices of one's hearers (*theol*); an organized system; regular operations, eg of nature. ◆ *adj* of or relating to a cheaper class of air or sea travel; (of goods) of a size larger than standard and costing proportionately less. [L *oeconomia*, from Gr *oikonomiā*, from *oikos* a house, and *nomos* a law]
■ **economet'ric** or **economet'rical** *adj*. **econometrician** /-*mə-trish*'*ən*/ *n*. **economet'rics** *n sing* statistical analysis of economic data and their interrelations. **economet'rist** *n*. **economic** /*ē-kə-nom*'*ik* or *ek-ə-*/ *adj* relating or referring to economy or to economics; relating to industry or business, eg *economic geography, history*, etc, from the utilitarian viewpoint; operated at or capable of yielding a profit; cheap (*inf*); economical. **econom'ical** *adj* conducive to thrift; frugal; careful; economic. **econom'ically** *adv*. **econom'ics** *n sing* or *n pl* financial position and management; financial or economic aspects; the science of household management (*obs*; but see **home economics** under **home**). ◆ *n sing* the study of the production, distribution and consumption of money, goods and services. **econ'omism** *n* a belief, sometimes too great, that economic causes and theories are of primary importance. **econ'omist** *n* a person who studies or is an expert on economics; an economizer. **economizā'tion** or **-s-** *n* the act of economizing. **econ'omize** or **-ise** *vi* to manage with economy; to spend money carefully; to cut down on spending or waste; to save. ◆ *vt* to use prudently; to spend frugally. **econ'omizer** or **-s-** *n* a person who is economical; a device for saving heat, fuel, etc.
❑ **economic determinism** *n* the belief that all cultural, political, social, etc activity stems from economic considerations. **economic migrant** or **refugee** *n* someone who leaves his or her country because of poverty rather than religious or political considerations. **economic rent** *n* (*econ*) a payment in excess of the minimum required to keep a factor of production (qv) in its current use. **economic zone** *n* the coastal sea-area which a country claims as its own territory (for fishing, mining, etc). **econ'omy-class** *adj* relating to the cheapest and least luxurious type of seating in an aircraft. **economy-class syndrome** *n* an informal name for **deep-vein thrombosis** (see under **deep**). **economy of scale** *n* (*econ*) a reduction in unit cost that occurs as more of a commodity is produced.
■ **economical with the truth** causing deception or misunderstanding by revealing only a selection of available information.

e contra /*ē* (or *ā*) *kon*'*tra*/ (*LL*) contrariwise, conversely.

e contrario /*ē kon-trä*'*ri-ō* or *ā kon-trä*'*ri-ō*/ (*LL*) on the contrary.

e converso /*ē kon-vûr*'*sō* or *ā kon-ver*' (or -*wer*')/ (*LL*) conversely, by logical conversion.

écorché /*ā-kör-shā*'/ *n* a figure in which the muscles are represented stripped of the skin, for the purposes of artistic study. [Pap of Fr *écorcher* to flay]

ECOSOC *abbrev* : United Nations Economic and Social Council.

écossaise /ā-ko-sez'/ n orig a dance or dance tune in 3–4 or 2–4 time, believed to be of Scottish origin; later, a lively country dance or its music in 2–4 time. [Fr, fem of *écossais* Scottish]
■ **douche écossaise** the alternation of hot and cold douches.

ecostate /ē-kos'tāt/ adj ribless. [L *ē* from, and *costa* rib]

ECOWAS abbrev : Economic Community of West African States.

ecphonesis /ek-fō-nē'sis/ n (pl **ecphonē'ses**) exclamation (*rhetoric*); in the Greek Church, the part of the service spoken in an audible tone. [Gr *ekphōnēsis*, from *ek* out, and *phōnē* voice]

ecphractic /ek-frak'tik/ (*obs med*) adj serving to remove obstructions. ◆ n a drug with such properties. [Gr *ekphraktikos*, from *ek* from, and *phrassein* to enclose]

ecphrasis same as **ekphrasis**.

écraseur /ā-kra-zœr'/ n a surgical instrument in the form of a wire or chain loop which cuts as it tightens. [Fr *écraser* to crush]

écritoire /ā-krē-twär'/ (Fr) n the modern form of **escritoire**.

ecru /e-, ā-kroo' or -krü'/ n unbleached linen; its off-white or light greyish-brown colour. ◆ adj of this colour. [Fr *écru*, from L *ex-* (intens) and *crūdus* raw]

ECS abbrev : European Communications Satellite.

ECSC abbrev : European Coal and Steel Community.

ecstasy /ek'stə-si/ n a state of exalted pleasure or happiness, rapture; a state of temporary mental alienation and altered or diminished consciousness; excessive joy; enthusiasm or any exalted feeling; (often with *cap*) an informal name for methylene-dioxymethamphetamine, a drug taken for its stimulant and hallucinogenic properties (often shortened to **E**). ◆ vt to fill with joy. [Gr *ekstasis*, from *ek* from, and the root of *histanai* to make stand]
■ **ec'stasied** adj enraptured. **ec'stasis** n ecstasy. **ec'stasize** or **-ise** vt and vi. **ecstat'ic** adj causing ecstasy; amounting to ecstasy; rapturous. ◆ n a person (often) in a state of ecstasy; a user of the drug Ecstasy; something spoken in a state of ecstasy. **ecstat'ically** adv.

ECT abbrev : electroconvulsive therapy.

ectasis /ek'tə-sis/ n (pl **ectases** /-tā'sēz/) the lengthening of a short syllable; abnormal stretching (*med*). [Gr *ektasis* stretching]

ecthlipsis /ek-thlip'sis/ n (pl **ecthlip'ses** /-sēz/) the suppression of a sound, *esp* of a syllable ending in *m* in verse before a vowel. [Gr *ekthlīpsis*, from *ek* from, and *thlībein* to rub or squeeze]

ecthyma /ek-thī'mə/ n an eruption of the skin forming large pustules. [Gr *ekthȳma* a pustule]

ecto- /ek-tō- or ek-tə-/ combining form (often interchanging with **exo-**) denoting outside, opp to **endo-** and **ento-**. [Gr *ektos* outside]
■ **ec'toblast** n (Gr *blastos* a shoot or bud; *biol*) the outer layer of cells in a gastrula, the epiblast. **ectoblas'tic** adj. **ec'tocrine** n an organic substance released in minute amounts by an organism into the environment, which exerts an effect on its own and other species' form, development or behaviour. **ec'toderm** n (Gr *derma* skin; *biol*) the outer layer of cells forming the wall of a gastrula; the tissues directly derived from this layer (also **ex'oderm**). **ectoderm'al** or **ectoderm'ic** adj. **ectoen'zyme** n an exoenzyme. **ectogen'esis** n (Gr *genesis* generation; *biol*) development outside the body; variation in response to outside conditions. **ectogenet'ic** adj produced by or characteristic of ectogenesis. **ectogen'ic** adj of external origin; ectogenous. **ectogenous** /ek-toj'ə-nəs/ adj (*biol*) capable of living independently, or outside the body of the host (as some parasites). **ectog'eny** n the effect of pollen on the tissues of a plant. **ec'tomorph** n (Gr *morphē* form) a person of light and delicate build, thought to accompany a type of personality characterized by alertness, inhibition and intellectual activity; cf **endomorph** and **mesomorph**. **ectomorph'ic** adj. **ec'tomorphy** n. **ectopar'asite** n an external parasite. **ectoparasit'ic** adj. **ec'tophyte** n (Gr *phyton* a plant; *bot*) a vegetable ectoparasite. **ectophytic** /-fit'ik/ adj. **ec'toplasm** n (Gr *plasma* something moulded) the outer layer of cytoplasm of a cell (*biol*); a substance believed by some spiritualists to emanate from the body of a medium. **ectoplas'mic** adj. **ectoplas'tic** adj. **Ectoproc'ta** same as **Polyzoa** (see under **poly-**). **ec'tosarc** n (Gr *sarx, sarkos* flesh; *zool*) ectoplasm. **ec'totherm** n a cold-blooded animal. **ectotherm'ic** adj. **ectotherm'y** n. **ectotroph'ic** adj (Gr *trophē* food; *bot*) of a mycorrhiza, having its hyphae mainly on the outside of the root that it feeds. **ectozo'an** n and adj. **ectozo'ic** adj. **ectozo'on** n (pl **ectozo'a**) (Gr *zōion* animal) an animal ectoparasite.

ectopia /ek-tō'pi-ə/ or **ectopy** /ek'to-pi/ (*pathol*) n abnormal displacement of parts; a condition in which the fetus is outside the womb. [Gr *ek* from, and *topos* place]
■ **ectop'ic** adj in an abnormal position.
❑ **ectopic pregnancy** n the development of a fetus outside the uterus, *esp* in a Fallopian tube.

ectoplasm...to...**ectozoon** see under **ecto-**.

ectropion /ek-trō'pi-on/ or **ectropium** /-əm/ n the turning out of the margin of the eyelid, so that the red inner surface is exposed. [Gr *ek* out of, and *trepein* to turn]
■ **ectrop'ic** adj.

ectype /ek'tīp/ n a reproduction or copy. [Gr *ek* from, and *typos* a stamp]
■ **ectypal** /ek'ti-pəl/ adj. **ectypog'raphy** n.

ECU, Ecu or **ecu** /ā'kū or ek'ū/ n short for **European currency unit**, a former unit of currency whose rate was based on a range of European currencies within the EMS, seen as the notional single European currency before the adoption of the euro.

ECU abbrev : European Customs Union.

écu /ā-kū' or ā-kū'/ n a French silver coin, *usu* considered as equivalent to the English crown; a French gold coin weighing about 60 grains, etc (both *hist*); more recently, a common name for the five-franc piece. [Fr, from L *scutum* a shield]

Ecuadorian /ek-wə-dö'ri-ən/ adj of or relating to the Republic of *Ecuador* in S America, or its inhabitants. ◆ n a native or citizen of Ecuador.

écuelle /ā-kwel' or ā-kü-el'/ n a two-handled soup bowl. [Fr, from L *scutella* drinking bowl]

ECUK abbrev : Engineering Council UK.

ecumenic /ē-kū- or ek-ū-men'ik/ or **ecumenical** /-əl/ adj (also **oecumen'ic, oecumen'ical**) general, universal or belonging to the entire Christian Church; of or relating to the ecumenical movement. [L *oecumenicus*, from Gr *oikoumenikos*, from *oikoumenē* (*gē*) inhabited (world)]
■ **ecumen'icalism, ecumen'icism** /-is-izm/ or **ecumen'ism** (or /i-kū'mə-nizm/) n the doctrines and practice of the Christian ecumenical movement (also *fig*). **ecumen'ically** adv. **ecumen'ics** n sing the study of ecumenical awareness and the ecumenical movement in the Christian church. —Also **oecumenicalism**, etc.
❑ **ecumenical movement** n a movement within the Christian church towards unity on all fundamental issues of belief, worship, etc.

écurie /ā-kü-rē'/ n a team of motor-racing cars under individual or joint ownership. [Fr, a stable]

ECUSA or **Ecusa** /i-koo'sə/ abbrev : Episcopal Church of the United States of America.

eczema /ek'si-mə or ig-zē'mə/ n a skin disease in which red blisters form on the skin, usually causing an itching or burning sensation. [Gr *ekzeein*, from *ek* out of, and *zeein* to boil]
■ **eczematous** /-sem', -zem'ət-əs or -zēm'/ adj.

Ed. abbrev : editor.

ed. abbrev : edited; edition; editor; educated; education.

edacious /i-, ē- or e-dā'shəs/ (*literary* or *facetious*) adj devoted to eating; gluttonous. [L *edāx, edācis*, from *edere* to eat]
■ **edā'ciously** adv. **edā'ciousness** n. **edacity** /i-das'i-ti/ n.

Edam /ē'dam/ n a type of mild Dutch cheese shaped into globes with a red outer skin. [After *Edam* near Amsterdam]

edamame /ed-ə-mä'mē/ n any of various types of soy bean that are harvested when green and eaten as a vegetable. [Jap]

edaphic /i-daf'ik/ (*bot* or *ecology*) adj relating to the soil. [Gr *edaphos* ground]
■ **edaphology** /ed-ə-fol'ə-ji/ n.
❑ **edaphic factor** n any property of the soil, physical or chemical, that influences plants growing on that soil.

EdB abbrev : Bachelor of Education.

EDC abbrev : ethylene dichloride; European Defence Community (until 1954, replaced by Western European Union).

EdD abbrev : Doctor of Education.

Edda /ed'ə/ n the name of two Scandinavian books, the *Elder Edda*, a collection of ancient mythological and heroic songs (9c–11c or earlier), and the *Younger* or *Prose Edda*, by Snorri Sturluson (c.1230), mythological stories, poetics and prosody. [ON, appar related to *ōdr* mad, and *ōthr* spirit, mind or poetry; cf **wood²**, Ger *Wut* fury, and L *vātēs* poet or seer]
■ **Eddā'ic** or **Edd'ic** adj.

eddish /ed'ish/ (*dialect*) n pasturage, or the eatable growth of grass after mowing. [Dubiously referred to OE *edisc* a park]

eddoes /ed'ōz/ n pl (sing **edd'o**) the tubers of various plants *esp* taro (genus *Colocasia*). [From a W African word]

eddy /ed'i/ n a current running back against the main stream, so causing a circular motion in the water; a similarly whirling motion of smoke, mist or wind; a whirlpool; a whirlwind. ◆ vi (**edd'ying**; **edd'ied**) to move round and round. [Cf ON *itha*; prob connected with OE pfx *ed-* back]
❑ **eddy current** n an electric current caused by varying electromotive forces which are due to varying magnetic fields, and causing heating

in motors, transformers, etc (also **Foucault current**). **eddy vortex** *n* a column of air spinning inward and upward, sometimes forming in conditions of atmospheric temperature contrast.

edelweiss /ā'dəl-vīs or ā'dl-/ *n* a small white composite plant (*Leontopodium alpinum*) with woolly heads, found in damp places on the Alps. [Ger *edel* noble, and *weiss* white]

edema, edematose, edematous see **oedema**.

Eden /ē'dən/ *n* the garden in which Adam and Eve lived before the Fall (*Bible*); a paradise. [Heb *ēden* delight or pleasure]
■ **Edenic** /-den'/ *adj*.

edentate /ē-den'tāt/ *adj* without teeth; lacking front teeth. ♦ *n* a member of the **Edentā'ta**, a New World order of mammals having no front teeth or no teeth at all, such as sloths, anteaters, armadillos, and formerly certain Old World edentate animals such as the pangolins. [L *ēdentātus* toothless, from *ē* out of, and *dēns, dentis* a tooth]
■ **eden'tal** *adj* of the edentates. **eden'tulous** *adj* toothless.

Edexcel /ed-ik-sel'/ *n* a UK examining body that administers school, higher and further education qualifications.

EDF *abbrev*: European Development Fund.

edge /ej/ *n* the border of anything; a rim; the brink; the intersection of the faces of a solid figure; a ridge or crest; the cutting side of an instrument; something that wounds or cuts; keenness; incisiveness or trenchancy; sharpness of mind or appetite; bitterness; irritability; advantage (*inf*). ♦ *vt* to put an edge or border on or round; to border, form or be a border for; to egg or urge on (*archaic*); to move or push gradually, *esp* sideways or edgeways; to trim the edge of; to sharpen; to give a sharp quality to; to strike with the edge of the bat (*cricket*). ♦ *vi* to move sideways; to move gradually. [OE *ecg*; cf Ger *Ecke*, and L *aciēs*]
■ **edged** *adj* having an edge or edges. ♦ *combining form* denoting having an edge or edges of the stated kind or number, as in *sharp-edged, double-edged*. **edge'less** *adj* without an edge; blunt. **edg'er** *n* someone or something that edges; a garden tool for trimming the edge of a lawn. **edge'ways** or **edge'wise** *adv* with edge foremost or uppermost; in the direction of the edge; sideways. **edg'ily** *adv*. **edg'iness** *n* angularity or over-sharpness of outline; the state of being on edge. **edg'ing** *n* any border eg round a garment, flower-bed, etc; (a strip of) material, eg lace, for using as a trimming around the edge; the act of making an edge. ♦ *adj* used for making an edge. **edg'y** *adj* with edges; sharp or hard in outline; irritable, on edge; emotionally intense. □ **edge coal** *n* a steeply dipping coal seam. **edge effect** *n* (*image technol*) see **border effect** under **border**. **edge rail** *n* a rail of a form in which the carriage-wheels roll on its edges, being held there by flanges. **edge tool** or **edged tool** *n* a tool with a sharp edge. ■ **edge in a word** or **get a word in edgeways** to get a word in with difficulty. **edge out** to remove or get rid of gradually; to defeat by a small margin. **go** or **be over the edge** (*inf*) to go or have gone beyond what can be endured; to have or have had a nervous breakdown. **have the** or **an edge on, over** or **against** to have the advantage, or an advantage, over; to be better than. **inside** or **outside edge** a skating movement on the inner or outer edge of the skate; a deflection from the inner or outer extremity of the bat (*cricket*). **on edge** in a state of expectant irritability; nervous or tense with anticipation. **on the edge of one's seat** in a state of eager anticipation. **play with edge tools** to deal carelessly with dangerous matters. **set on edge** to excite. **set someone's teeth on edge** to set up a disagreeable sensation in the teeth and mouth, as sour fruit does; to cause to wince, irritate acutely; formerly, to make eager or stimulate desire. **take the edge off** to make less unpleasant or difficult; to weaken or diminish.

edgebone same as **aitchbone**.

edh see **eth**.

EDI (*comput*) *abbrev*: electronic data interchange.

edible /ed'i-bl/ *adj* able to be eaten. ♦ *n* an item of food (chiefly in *pl*). [L *edibilis*, from *edere* to eat]
■ **edibil'ity** or **ed'ibleness** *n* fitness to be eaten.

edict /ē'dikt/ *n* something proclaimed by authority; an order issued by a sovereign or government. [L *ēdictum*, from *ē* out of, and *dīcere, dictum* to say]
■ **edict'al** *adj*. **edict'ally** *adv*.

edifice /ed'i-fis/ *n* a building; a large building or house; a large and complex organization. [Fr *édifice*, from L *aedificium*, from *aedificāre*; see **edify**]
■ **edificial** /-fish'l/ *adj* structural.

edify /ed'i-fī/ *vt* (**ed'ifying; ed'ified**) to improve the mind of; to strengthen spiritually towards faith and holiness; to build up the faith of; to build (*archaic*); to establish (*obs*); to furnish with buildings (*Spenser*). [L *aedificāre*, from *aedēs* a temple or house, and *facere* to make]

■ **edifica'tion** *n* instruction; progress in knowledge or in goodness. **edif'icatory** (or /ed'/) *adj* giving edification. **ed'ifier** *n* a person who edifies. **ed'ifying** *adj* instructive; improving. **ed'ifyingly** *adv*.

edile same as **aedile**.

Edin. *abbrev*: Edinburgh.

edit /ed'it/ *vt* to prepare (a writer's work or works) for publication; to correct and improve (a piece of text, etc) ready for publication; to reword; to supervise the publication of; to be the editor of (a newspaper or periodical); to compile (a reference work); to garble or cook up; to revise; to censor or bowdlerize; to make up the final version of a film, video, etc by selection, rearrangement, etc of material filmed previously; to prepare for broadcasting; to prepare (data) for processing by a computer. ♦ *n* an act or instance of editing. [L *ēdere, ēditum*, from *ē* from, and *dare* to give]
■ **ed'itable** *adj* (of computer software, etc) that can be edited by the user. **edi'tion** *n* one of the different forms in which a book is published; the form given to a text by its editor; the number of copies of a book printed at a time, or at different times without alteration; the publication of a book (*obs*); a number of identical articles, eg copies of a work of art, issued at one time; reproduction. **ed'itor** *n* a person who edits books, etc; a person in charge of a newspaper, periodical, etc or a section of it; a person in charge of a radio or TV programme made up of different items; a person who makes up the final version of a film, etc. **edito'rial** *adj* of or relating to editors or editing. ♦ *n* an article in a newspaper written by an editor or leader writer. **edito'rialist** *n*. **editorializa'tion** or **-s-** *n*. **edito'rialize** or **-ise** *vi* to introduce personal opinions or bias into reporting; to expound one's views in an editorial or in the style of one. **edito'rially** *adv*. **ed'itorship** *n*. **ed'itress** *n* (*old*) a female editor.
■ **edit out** to remove (a piece of film, tape, etc) during editing.

edit. *abbrev*: edited; edition; editor.

édition de luxe /ā-dē-syɔ̃ də lüks'/ (*Fr*) *n* a de luxe edition of a book.

editio princeps /i-dish'i-ō prin'seps or ā-dit'i-ō prin'keps/ (*L*) *n* the original edition, *esp* of a work until then known only in manuscript.

editor, etc see under **edit**.

Edomite /ē'də-mīt/ *n* one of the people of the ancient kingdom of *Edom*, south of the Dead Sea.

EDO RAM (*comput*) *abbrev*: extended data out random access memory.

EDP *abbrev*: electronic data processing.

edriophthalmic /ed-ri-of-thal'mik/ *adj* (of crustaceans) with stalkless eyes (also **edriophthal'mian** or **edriophthal'mous**). [Gr *hedrion*, dimin of *hedrā* seat, and *ophthalmos* eye]

EDS (*hist*) *abbrev*: English Dialect Society.

EDTA *abbrev*: ethylene diamine tetra-acetic acid, a chelating agent used in chelation therapy.

educate /ed'ū-kāt/ *vt* to bring up and instruct; to provide school instruction for; to teach; to train. [L *ēducāre, -ātum* to rear, from *ēdūcere*, from *ē* from, and *dūcere* to lead]
■ **educabil'ity** *n*. **ed'ucable** *adj*. **educātabil'ity** *n*. **ed'ucātable** *adj*. **ed'ucated** *adj* having had a (good) education; cultivated, knowledgeable, refined in judgement or taste; (of a guess) authoritative, based by experience, to be accorded credence. **educā'tion** *n* bringing up or training, eg of a child; instruction, *esp* at a school or university; strengthening of the powers of body or mind; culture. **educā'tional** *adj*. **educā'tionalist** or **educā'tionist** *n* a person skilled in methods of educating or teaching; a person who promotes education. **educā'tionally** *adv*. **ed'ucātive** *adj* of or relating to education; producing education. **ed'ucātor** *n*. **educatory** /ed'* or -kā'tə-ri/ *adj*.

educe /i- or ē-dūs'/ (*formal*) *vt* to draw out; to extract; to make appear, to elicit; to develop; to infer. [L *ēdūcere, ēductum*, from *ē* from, and *dūcere* to lead]
■ **educe'ment** *n*. **educ'ible** *adj*. **educt** /ē'dukt/ *n* that which is educed. **eduction** /ē-duk'shən/ *n* the act of educing; the exhaust of an engine. **educ'tor** *n* someone who or something which educes.

edulcorate /i-dul'kə-rāt/ *vt* to sweeten (*obs*); to free from soluble particles by washing. [L *ē-* (intens), and *dulcōrāre* to sweeten, from *dulcis* sweet]
■ **edul'corant** *adj*. **edulcorā'tion** *n*. **edul'corātive** *adj*. **edul'corātor** *n*.

Eduskunta /ā-dŭs-kŭn'tä/ *n* the single-chamber Finnish parliament, elected every four years. [Finn]

edutainment /ed-ū-tān'mənt/ *n* the presentation of educational material as entertainment, *esp* in the form of television programmes or computer software. See also **infotainment** under **info**. [**education** and **entertainment**]

Edwardian /ed-wörd'i-ən (*archaic* and *US* also -wärd')/ *adj* belonging to or characteristic of the reign of (any) King *Edward*, *esp* Edward VII;

(of a motor-car) built in the period 1905 to 1918, between veteran and vintage cars. ♦ *n* a person of the Edwardian period.
■ **Edwardiana** /-ä'nə/ *n pl* furniture, ornamentation, artefacts, etc of the Edwardian period. **Edward'ianism** *n*.

EE *abbrev* : early English; (also **ee**) errors excepted.

ee /ē/ *n* (*pl* **een**) Scots form of **eye**[1].

-ee /-ē/ *sfx* signifying the person affected by some action, eg *evacuee*, *interviewee* ; a person in a particular situation, eg *absentee* ; a person performing some action, eg *attendee*, *standee* (*esp US*); a relatively small form of something, eg *bootee*. [Fr pap sfx *-é* or *-ée*, from L *-ātus*, *-āta*]

EEA *abbrev* : European Economic Area; European Environment Agency.

EEC *abbrev* : European Economic Community.

eech see **eche**.

e-economy /ē'i-kon-ə-mi/ *n* economic activity carried out through the Internet.

EED *abbrev* : electro-explosive device.

EEF *abbrev* : Engineering Employers' Federation.

EEG *abbrev* : electroencephalogram or encephalograph.

eejit /ē'jit/ (*Scot* and *Irish*) *n* an idiot. [Colloquial pronunciation of **idiot**]

eek /ēk/ *interj* denoting fright, used conventionally in children's comics, etc. [Representative of a shriek or squeal]

eel /ēl/ *n* any fish of the Anguillidae, Muraenidae or other family of Apodes, fishes with long smooth cylindrical or ribbon-shaped bodies, without pelvic fins and almost or totally scaleless; extended to various other fishes of similar form, such as the **sand eel** (or launce), and the **electric eel**; extended also to some eel-like threadworms (also **eel'worm**); a devious or evasive person, a slippery character. [OE *ǣl*; Ger *Aal*, and Du *aal*]
■ **eel'-like** *adj*. **eel'y** *adj*.
❑ **eel'-basket** *n* a basket for catching eels. **eel'fare** *n* (OE *faran* to travel) a migratory passage of young eels; a brood of young eels; a young eel. **eel'grass** or **eel'wrack** *n* grasswrack (genus *Zostera*), a grasslike flowering plant growing in seawater. **eel'pout** /-powt/ *n* (OE *ǣlepūte*) the burbot; the viviparous blenny. **eel'-set** *n* a net placed across a river to catch eels. **eel'-spear** *n* an instrument with broad prongs for catching eels. **eel'worm** *n* a nematode.
■ **salt eel** (*obs*) a rope's end.

een see **ee**.

e'en /ēn/ a poetic contraction of **even**[1,2].

eensy /ēn'zi/ (*inf*) *adj* very small. [Shortened from *teensy-weensy* (see teeny)]

EEPROM (*comput*) *abbrev* : electronically erasable programmable read-only memory.

e'er /ār/ a contraction of **ever**.

eerie or **eery** /ē'ri/ *adj* strangely frightening; weird; affected with fear, timorous (*dialect*). [Scot; ME *arh*, *eri*, from OE *ǣrg* (*earg*) timid]
■ **ee'rily** *adv*. **ee'riness** *n*.

EET *abbrev* : Eastern European Time.

EETS *abbrev* : Early English Text Society.

eeven, **eevn**, **eev'n** or **eevning** old spellings (*Milton*) of **even**[1,2] (*n*, *adj* and *adv*) and **evening**.

EEZ *abbrev* : exclusive economic zone.

ef /ef/ *n* the sixth letter of the modern English alphabet (F or f).

EFA *abbrev* : essential fatty acid; European fighter aircraft.

eff /ef/ euphemistic for **fuck**, *esp* in *effing* (*adj*) and *eff off*.
■ **effing and blinding** swearing.

effable /ef'ə-bl/ (*archaic*) *adj* capable of being expressed. [Fr, from L *effārī*, from *ex* out, and *fārī* to speak]

efface /i- or e-fās'/ *vt* to destroy the surface of; to rub out or erase; to obliterate, wear away. [Fr *effacer*, from L *ex* out, and *faciēs* face]
■ **efface'able** *adj*. **efface'ment** *n*. **effa'cer** *n*.
■ **efface oneself** to avoid notice.

effect /i-fekt'/ *n* the result of an action; the impression produced; the meaning conveyed; operation, a working state; reality; (in *pl*) goods or property; (in *pl*) sound and lighting devices contributing to the illusion of the place and circumstance in which the action is happening (*theatre, film*, etc). ♦ *vt* to produce; to accomplish or bring about. [OFr, from L *effectus*, from *ex* out, and *facere* to make]
■ **effec'ter** *n*. **effec'tible** *adj* that may be effected. **effec'tive** *adj* having power to effect; causing something; successful in producing a result or effect; powerful; serviceable; actual; in force. ♦ *n* a soldier or body of soldiers ready for service. **effec'tively** *adv*. **effec'tiveness** *n*. **effectiv'ity** *n*. **effect'less** *adj* without effect, useless. **effec'tor** *n* and *adj* (*biol*) (an organ or substance) that produces a response

to stimulus. **effec'tual** *adj* successful in producing the desired effect; valid; decisive (*Shakesp*). **effectual'ity** *n*. **effec'tually** *adv*. **effec'tualness** *n*. **effec'tuate** *vt* to accomplish. **effectuā'tion** *n*.
❑ **effective rate** *n* (also **sterling effective rate**) the percentage deviation of sterling from its Smithsonian parity (qv) against an average of selected foreign currencies, weighted according to their UK trade importance. **effectual calling** *n* (*theol*) the invitation to come to Christ received by the elect.
■ **come**, etc or **put**, etc **into effect** to become or make operative. **for effect** so as to make a telling impression. **general effect** the effect produced by a picture, etc as a whole. **give effect to** to carry out, perform. **in effect** in truth, really; substantially; in operation or operative. **leave no effects** to die without property to bequeath. **take effect** to begin to operate; to come into force. **to that effect** with the previously indicated meaning. **to the effect that** with the meaning or result that.

effeir[1] or **effere** /e-fēr'/ (*Scot*) *n* affair; appearance, show, array. [**affair**]

effeir[2] or **effere** /e-fēr'/ (*obs*) *vi* to appertain; to suit. [OFr *afferir*, from L *ad* to, and *ferrīre* to strike]

effeminate /i-fem'i-nət/ *adj* womanish; unmanly; weak; soft; voluptuous; feminine (*Shakesp*). ♦ *n* an effeminate person. ♦ *vt* and *vi* /-āt/ (*archaic*; also **effem'inize** or **-ise**) to make or become womanish; to weaken or unman. [L *effēmināre*, *-ātum* to make womanish, from *ex* out, and *fēmina* a woman]
■ **effem'inacy** /-ə-si/ *n* unmanly softness or weakness; indulgence in unmanly pleasures. **effem'inately** *adv*. **effem'inateness** *n*.

effendi /e-fen'di/ *n* in Turkey, a former title for civil officials, abolished in 1934 and now used orally with the force of *Mr* ; generally, in the E Mediterranean, a title of respect for educated or high-ranking people. [Turk; from Gr *authentēs* an absolute master]

effere see **effeir**[1,2].

efferent /ef'ə-rənt/ *adj* conveying outward or away, as in (*zool*) **efferent nerve**, a nerve carrying impulses away from the central nervous system. [L *ē* from, and *ferēns*, *-entis*, prp of *ferre* to carry]
■ **eff'erence** *n*.

effervesce /ef-ər-ves'/ *vi* to boil up; to bubble and hiss; to fizz or froth up; to behave or talk vivaciously. [L *effervēscere*, from *ex-* (intens), and *fervēre* to boil]
■ **effervesc'ence** or **effervesc'ency** *n*. **effervesc'ent** *adj* boiling or bubbling from the release of gas; lively, vivacious or exuberant. **effervesc'ible** *adj*. **effervesc'ingly** *adv*.

effete /i- or e-fēt'/ *adj* exhausted; degenerate, decadent; no longer capable of effective action; no longer able to reproduce. [L *effētus* weakened by having given birth, from *ex* out, and *fētus* the act of giving birth]
■ **effete'ly** *adv*. **effete'ness** *n*.

efficacious /ef-i-kā'shəs/ *adj* able to produce the result intended. [L *efficāx*, *-ācis*, from *efficere* ; see **efficient**]
■ **effica'ciously** *adv*. **effica'ciousness**, **efficacity** /-kas'i-ti/ or **eff'icacy** /-kə-si/ *n* the power of producing an effect; effectiveness.

efficient /i-fish'ənt/ *adj* capable of doing what may be required; effective; competent or proficient; working with speed and economy. ♦ *combining form* economical in the use or consumption of a particular resource, as in *energy-efficient*. ♦ *n* (*archaic*) the person or thing that effects. [Fr, from L *efficiēns*, *-entis*, prp of *efficere*, from *ex* out, and *facere* to make]
■ **effi'cience** *n* (*archaic*) efficient action or power. **effi'ciency** *n* the power to produce the result intended; the quality of being efficient; the ratio of a machine's output of energy to its input; (also **efficiency apartment**) a small flat (*US*). **effi'ciently** *adv*.
❑ **efficiency bar** *n* a point on a salary scale beyond which the award of increments depends on increased efficiency by the recipient.

effierce /e-fērs'/ (*Spenser*) *vt* to make fierce.

effigurate /e-fig'u-rāt/ *adj* having a definite shape. [L *ef-*, from *ex-* (intens), and **figurate**]
■ **effigurā'tion** *n* an axial outgrowth in a flower.

effigy /ef'i-ji/ or (*archaic*) **effigies** /e-fij'i-ēz/ *n* (*pl* **effigies** /ef'i-jiz or (*archaic*) ef-ij'i-ēz/) a likeness or figure of a person; the head or impression on a coin. [L *effigiēs*, from *effingere*, from *ex-* (intens), and *fingere* to form]
■ **burn** or **hang in effigy** to burn or hang a figure of a person, as an expression of hatred or disapproval.

effleurage /ef-lœ-räzh'/ *n* a stroking movement in massage (also *vi* and *vt*). [Fr, glancing or grazing]

effloresce /ef-lo-res'/ *vi* to blossom forth; to become covered with a powdery crust (*chem*); to form a powdery crust. [L *efflōrēscere*, from *ex* out, and *flōrēscere* to blossom, from *flōs*, *flōris* a flower]
■ **effloresc'ence** *n* the production of flowers; the time of flowering; a redness of the skin; a powdery surface crust; the formation of such a

crust; the giving up of the water of crystallization to the atmosphere. **effloresc'ent** *adj*.

effluent /ef'lū-ənt/ *adj* flowing out. ◆ *n* liquid industrial waste; outflow from sewage during purification; a stream that flows out of another stream or lake. [L *effluēns, -entis* prp of *effluere*, from *ex* out, and *fluere* to flow]
■ **eff'luence** *n* a flowing out; emanation.

effluvium /e-floo'vi-əm/ *n* (pl **efflu'via**) disagreeable vapours rising from decaying matter; minute particles that flow out from bodies; a generally unpleasant smell or exhalation. [LL, from L *effluere*]
■ **efflu'vial** *adj*.

efflux /ef'luks/ *n* the act of flowing out; something that flows out. [L *effluere*, from *ex* out, and *fluere, fluxum* to flow]
■ **effluxion** /e-fluk'shən/ *n* an efflux; the running out of time before a fixed deadline (*law*).

efforce /e-förs'/ (*obs*) *vt* to compel; to force; to force open; to use violence towards; to put forward with force. [Fr *efforcer*, from LL *exfortiāre*, from *ex* out, and *fortis* strong]

effort /ef'ərt/ *n* exertion of body or mind; an attempt; (a) struggle; a piece of work produced by way of attempt; anything done or produced (*inf*). [Fr, from L *ex* out, and *fortis* strong]
■ **eff'ortful** *adj* done with effort, laboured. **eff'ortfully** *adv*. **eff'ortless** *adj* making no effort, passive; easy, showing no sign of effort. **eff'ortlessly** *adv*. **eff'ortlessness** *n*.

effray, effraide obsolete forms of **affray** and **afraid**.

effrontery /i- or e-frun'tə-ri/ *n* shamelessness; impudence or impudent audacity; insolence. [Fr *effronterie*, from L *effrōns, effrontis*, from *ex* out, without, and *frōns, frontis* forehead]

effulge /i- or e-fulj'/ *vi* (**effulg'ing**; **effulged'**) to shine out; to beam. [L *effulgēre* to shine out, from *ex* out, and *fulgēre* to shine]
■ **efful'gence** *n* great brilliance or brightness; a flood of light. **efful'gent** *adj* giving off a brilliant light; shining; radiant; splendid. **efful'gently** *adv*.

effuse /i- or e-fūz'/ *vt* to pour out; to spread out; to pour forth (eg words); to shed (eg blood); to spread; to let loose (*poetic*). ◆ *vi* to flow out. ◆ *n* /e-fūs'/ (*Shakesp*) effusion or shedding. ◆ *adj* /i- or e-fūs'/ poured out; loosely spreading (*bot*); (of shells) with the lips separated by a groove. [L *effundere, effūsum*, from *ex* out, and *fundere* to pour]
■ **effusiometer** /e-fūz-i-om'i-tər/ *n* a device for comparing molecular weights of gases by observing the relative time taken to stream out through a small hole. **effusion** /i- or e-fū'zhən/ *n* pouring or streaming out; emission; shedding (eg of blood); an abnormal outpouring of fluid into the tissues or cavities of the body (*med*); an unrestrained outpouring of words, *esp* expressing warmth or enthusiasm; a literary outpouring, *esp* in poetic form (often *derog*); effusiveness; the act of pouring, or process of being poured, out; something poured over or shed. **effusive** /i- or e-fū'ziv/ *adj* poured out abundantly; poured out at the surface in a state of fusion, volcanic (*geol*); expressing emotion in an over-demonstrative manner; gushing. **effus'ively** *adv*. **effus'iveness** *n*.

Efik /ef'ik/ *n* (a member of) a people of SE Nigeria; the language of this people. ◆ *adj* of or relating to the Efiks or their language.

EFL *abbrev* : English as a foreign language.

eflornithine /e-flör'ni-thēn/ *n* a drug, an enzyme inhibitor used to slow hair growth, and also used in the treatment of sleeping sickness.

EFSA *abbrev* : European Food Safety Authority.

EFT (*comput*) *abbrev* : electronic funds transfer.

eft[1] /eft/ *n* a newt; a lizard (*obs*). [OE *efeta*; see **newt**]

eft[2] /eft/ (*obs*) *adv* afterwards; again; forthwith; moreover. [OE *æft* or *eft* after or again; see **aft**]
■ **eftsoons** /eft-soonz'/ *adv* (*obs*) soon afterwards or forthwith.

EFTA or sometimes **Efta** /ef'tə/ *abbrev* : European Free Trade Association.

eftest /ef'tist/ (*Warwickshire* and *Worcestershire*; *Shakesp*) *adj superl* readiest; most convenient.

EFTPOS or **Eftpos** /eft'pos/ (*comput*) *abbrev* : electronic funds transfer at point of sale.

EFTS (*comput*) *abbrev* : electronic funds transfer system.

eftsoons see under **eft**[2].

EG *abbrev* : equivalent grade.

eg or **ex gr** *abbrev* : *exempli gratia* (L), for example.

EGA (*comput*) *abbrev* : enhanced graphics adapter.

egad /i-gad'/ (*archaic*) *interj* a mild oath. [Perh orig *ah God*]

egal /ē'gəl/ *adj* (*Shakesp*) equal. [OFr *egal*, from L *aequālis*, from *aequus* equal]

egalitā'rian /i-gal-/ *adj* and *n* equalitarian; (a person) upholding the principle of equality among people. **egalitā'rianism** *n*. **egality** /ē- or i-gal'/ *n* equality. **ē'gally** *adv* (*Shakesp*).

égarement /ā-gar-mã'/ (*Fr*) *n* confusion, bewilderment.

egence /ē'jəns/ or **egency** /-si/ *n* need. [L *egēre* to be in need]

eger /ē'gər/ *n* same as **eagre**.

Egeria /e-jē'ri-ə or e-/ *n* a female adviser. [L *Egeria* or *Aegeria*, the nymph who instructed Numa Pompilius, king of Rome 715–673BC]

egest /i-jest' or ē-/ *vt* to discharge; to expel from the body in any way. [L *ēgerere, ēgestum*, from *ē* out, and *gerere* to carry]
■ **egest'a** *n pl* things thrown out; excreta; waste materials removed from the body. **egestion** /e-jest'yən/ *n*. **egest'ive** *adj*.

egg[1] /eg/ *n* an oval, round, etc object laid by the female of birds, reptiles, fish, insects and certain other animals from which the young is hatched, *esp* that laid by a hen and eaten as food; an ovum or female gamete (also **egg cell**); a zygote, the fertilized ovum, or the organism growing within it; anything shaped like a hen's egg; a bomb or mine (*sl*). ◆ *vt* to add egg to, *usu* in cooking; to throw eggs at (*inf*). [ON *egg*; cf OE *æg*, Ger *Ei*, perh L *ōvum*, Gr *ōon*]
■ **egg'er** *n* a person who collects wildfowl's eggs; any moth of the family Lasiocampidae, whose cocoons are egg-shaped (also **egg'ar**). **egg'ery** *n* (*archaic*) a place where eggs are laid. **egg'ler** *n* (*archaic*) a dealer in eggs. **egg'less** *adj*. **egg'y** *adj* tasting or smelling of or marked or covered with eggs; abounding in eggs; having just laid or about to lay an egg.
□ **egg'-and-anch'or**, **egg'-and-dart'**, **egg'-and-tongue'** *n* (*archit*) ornaments *esp* found on cornice mouldings, in the form of eggs alternating with anchors, darts or tongues. **egg-and-spoon race** *n* a race in which each competitor carries an egg in a spoon. **egg apparatus** *n* (*bot*) the egg and the synergidae in the embryo-sac of an angiosperm. **egg'-apple** *n* the eggfruit. **egg beater** *n* an egg whisk; a helicopter (*esp N Am inf*). **egg'-binding** *n* inability to expel an egg. **egg'-bird** *n* the sooty tern. **egg'-bound** *adj* in the state of being unable to expel eggs. **egg box** *n* a protective partitioned container for holding *usu* six eggs. **egg'-box** *adj* used of a type of building which looks like a simple square box or a number of these put together. **egg capsule**, **case** or **purse** *n* a protective covering in which the eggs of some animals are enclosed. **egg'-cōsy** *n* a cover for keeping a boiled egg hot. **egg cream** *n* a beverage made of chocolate syrup, milk and soda water. **egg'cup** *n* a small cup for holding a boiled egg (still in its shell). **egg custard** see under **custard**. **egg dance** *n* a dance performed blindfold among eggs. **egg'-flip** *n* a drink made of ale, wine, spirits or milk, with eggs, sugar, spice, etc. **egg'fruit** *n* the fruit of the eggplant. **egg glass** *n* an egg timer. **egg'head** *n* (*inf*) an intellectual. **egg'mass** *n* (*inf*) intellectuals as a group (also *adj*). **egg'nog** *n* a drink of eggs and hot beer, spirits, etc. **egg'plant** *n* (*esp US*) the aubergine. **egg plum** *n* a yellowish egg-shaped plum. **egg powder** *n* a powder of dried eggs, or a substitute. **egg purse** see **egg capsule** above. **eggs Benedict** /ben'i-dikt/ *n sing* a slice of ham and a poached egg placed on a slice of toast and covered with hollandaise sauce. **egg'shell** *n* the hard calcareous covering of a bird's egg; a smooth gastropod shell; a very thin kind of porcelain. ◆ *adj* thin and delicate; (of paint, etc) having only a slight gloss. **egg slice** *n* a utensil for lifting fried eggs out of a pan. **egg spoon** *n* a small spoon used for eating boiled eggs from the shell. **egg timer** *n* a small sand-glass for timing the boiling of eggs. **egg tooth** *n* a hard point on the beak by which an unhatched bird or reptile breaks the eggshell. **egg'wash** *n* a thin mixture of egg and milk (or water) used as a glaze for pastry. **egg whisk** *n* a utensil for beating raw eggs.
■ **a bad egg** (*inf*) a worthless person. **good egg** (*inf*) a fine person; an exclamation of approval. **have** or **put all one's eggs in(to) one basket** (*inf*) to risk all on one enterprise. **have, get** or **be left with egg on one's face** (*inf*) to be left looking foolish. **lay an egg** (*sl, chiefly US*) (of a joke, comedian, theatrical performance, etc) to fail, flop. **take eggs for money** to be put off with mere promises of payment. **teach your grandmother to suck eggs** to presume to teach someone older and wiser than oneself; to teach someone something that he or she knows already. **walk** (or **tread**) **on eggs** (or **eggshells**) to go warily, to steer one's way carefully in a delicate situation.

egg[2] /eg/ *vt* (with *on*) to incite, urge on. [ON *eggja*, from *egg* an edge; cognate with OE *ecg*; see **edge**]

eggar, egger, eggery, eggler, eggy see under **egg**[1].

egis same as **aegis**.

eglandular /ē-glan'dū-lər/ *adj* having no glands. [L *ē-* without, and *glandula* gland]
■ **eglan'dulose** *adj*.

eglantine /eg'lən-tīn or -tin/ *n* a fragrant species of wild rose, the sweetbrier; perhaps the honeysuckle (*Milton*). [Fr, from OFr *aiglent*, as if from a L adj *aculentus* prickly, from *acus* a needle, and sfx *-lentus*]

eglatere /eg-lə-tēr'/ (*archaic*) *n* the eglantine.

■ words derived from main entry word; □ compound words; ■ idioms and phrasal verbs

EGM *abbrev* : extraordinary general meeting.

egma /eg'mə/ *n* Costard's attempt at *enigma* in Shakespeare's *Love's Labours Lost*.

ego /ē'gō or eg'ō/ *n* the 'I' or self, that which is conscious and thinks; an image of oneself; self-confidence; egotism. [L *ego*, *egō*, and Gr *egō* I]
■ **egocen'tric** *adj* self-centred; regarding or regarded from the point of view of the ego. ◆ *n* an egocentric person. **egocen'trically** *adv*. **egocentri'city** *n*. **egocen'trism** *n*. **e'gōism** *n* the doctrine that we have proof of nothing but our own existence (*philos*); the theory of self-interest as the principle of morality (*ethics*); over-concern for one's own wellbeing; selfishness; self-centredness; egotism. **e'gōist** *n* a person who holds the doctrine of egoism; a person who thinks and speaks too much of himself or herself or of things as they affect himself or herself; an egotist. **egōist'ic** or **egōist'ical** *adj* relating to or displaying egoism. **egōis'tically** *adv*. **egō'ity** *n* the essential element of the ego. **e'goless** *adj*. **egomā'nia** *n* abnormal egotism. **egomā'niac** *n*. **egomanī'acal** *adj*. **e'gotheism** (or /-thē'/) *n* the deification of self; identification of oneself with God. **e'gotism** *n* a frequent use of the pronoun I; thinking or speaking too much of oneself; the fact of having a very high opinion of oneself. **e'gotist** *n* an egotistic person. **egotis'tic** or **egotis'tical** *adj* showing egotism; self-important; conceited. **egotist'ically** *adv*. **e'gotize** or **-ise** *vi* to talk a lot about oneself.
❑ **ego ideal** *n* (*psychol*) one's personal standards, ideals, ambitions, etc acquired as one recognizes parental and other social standards, formed into a composite of characteristics to which one would like to conform; one's idealized picture of oneself. **e'go-surfing** *n* the activity of searching for one's own name on the Internet. **e'go-trip** *n* (*sl*) an action or experience which inflates one's good opinion of oneself. **e'go-tripper** *n*.
■ **massage someone's ego** (*facetious*) to flatter someone, rub someone up the right way.

egregious /i-grē'jəs/ *adj* outrageous; notorious; prominent, distinguished (*archaic*). [L *ēgregius* standing out from the herd, from *ē* out of, and *grex, gregis* a herd]
■ **egrē'giously** *adv*. **egrē'giousness** *n*.

egress /ē'gres/ *n* the act of going out; departure; the way out; the power or right to depart. ◆ *vi* /ē-gres'/ to depart. [L *ēgredī, ēgressus*, from *ē* out of, and *gradī* to go]
■ **egression** /i- or ē-gresh'ən/ *n* the act of going out; departure. **egress'ive** *adj* (*phonetics*) (of speech sounds) pronounced with exhalation of breath. ◆ *n* an egressive speech sound.

egret /ē'gret/ *n* a white heron of several species; an aigrette. [See **aigrette**]

EGU *abbrev* : English Golf Union.

egurgitate /ē-gûr'ji-tāt/ (*rare*) *vt* to vomit; to cast forth. [L *ēgurgitāre, -ātum*, from *ē* out of, and *gurges, -itis* a whirlpool]

Egyptian /i- or ē-jip'shən/ *adj* belonging to *Egypt* in NE Africa; the Afro-Asiatic language of ancient Egypt; (of type) antique (*printing*). ◆ *n* a native or citizen of Egypt; a gypsy (*archaic*).
■ **Egyptīnizā'tion** or **-s-** *n*. **Egyp'tianize** or **-ise** *vt*. **Egyptolog'ical** *adj*. **Egyptol'ogist** *n*. **Egyptol'ogy** *n* the study of the language, culture and history of ancient Egypt.
❑ **Egyptian darkness** *n* darkness like that of Exodus 10.22 in the Bible.

eh /ā/ *interj* expressing inquiry, failure to hear or slight surprise. ◆ *vi* to say 'Eh'.

EHF *abbrev* : extremely high frequency.

EHO *abbrev* : Environmental Health Officer.

ehrlichiosis /ār-lik-ē-ō'sis/ *n* a tick-borne disease caused by several bacterial species in the genus *Ehrlichia*.

EI *abbrev* : East Indian; East Indies.

EIA *abbrev* : environmental impact assessment.

EIB *abbrev* : European Investment Bank.

Eid al-Adha /ēd al-ad'ha/ *n* a Muslim festival celebrating Abraham's willingness to sacrifice his son (also **Id al-Adha**). [Ar '*Id al-Adha* Feast of Sacrifice]

Eid al-Fitr /ēd al-fē'tər/ *n* a Muslim festival celebrated on the first day after Ramadan (also **Id al-Fitr**). [Ar '*Id al-Fitr* Feast of Breaking Fast]

EIDE (*comput*) *abbrev* : Enhanced Integrated Drive Electronics.

eident /ī'dənt/ (*Scot*) *adj* busy, diligent. [ME *ithen*, from ON *ithinn* diligent]

eider /ī'dər/ *n* the **eider duck**, a northern sea-duck whose fine down is used to make bedcovers. [Prob through Swed from ON *æthar*, genitive of *æthr* an eider duck]
❑ **ei'derdown** *n* the soft down of the eider duck; a bedcover, *usu* quilted.

eidetic /ī-det'ik/ (*psychol*) *adj* (of a mental image) extraordinarily clear and vivid, as though actually visible; (of a person or memory) reproducing, or able to reproduce, a vividly clear visual image of what has been seen previously. ◆ *n* a person with this ability. [Gr *eidētikos* belonging to an image, from *eidos* form]
■ **eidet'ically** *adv*.

eidograph /ī'dō-gräf/ *n* an instrument used for copying drawings. [Gr *eidos* form, and *graphein* to write]

eidolon /ī-dō'lon/ *n* (*pl* **eidō'la**) an image; a phantom or apparition; a confusing reflection or reflected image; an ideal or idealized person or thing. [Gr; see **idol**]

EIF *abbrev* : European Investment Fund.

eigen- /ī-gən-/ *combining form* denoting proper, own. [Ger]
■ **ei'gen-frequency** *n* (*phys*) one of the frequencies with which a particular system may vibrate. **ei'genfunction** *n* a solution of a wave function that satisfies a set of boundary conditions. **ei'gentone** *n* (*phys*) a tone characteristic of a particular vibrating system. **ei'genvalue** *n* (*maths* and *phys*) any of the possible values for a parameter of an equation for which the solutions will be compatible with the boundary conditions. **ei'genvector** *n* (*maths* and *phys*) a vector that when transformed by a matrix retains its direction but not necessarily its length.

eight /āt/ *n* the cardinal number next above seven; a symbol representing that number (8, viii, etc); a set of eight things or people (syllables, leaves, rowers, etc); an eight-oar boat; (in *pl*) a race for eight-oar boats; a score of eight points, strokes, tricks, etc; an article of a size denoted by 8; a playing card with eight pips; an eight-cylinder engine or car; the eighth hour after midnight or midday; the age of eight years. ◆ *adj* of the number eight; eight years old. [OE (Anglian) *æhta* (WSax *eahta*); Ger *acht*, L *octō*, Gr *oktō*]
■ **eight'fold** *adj* and *adv* in eight divisions; eight times as much. ◆ *adv* by eight times as much. **eighth** /ātth/ *adj* last of eight; next after the seventh; equal to one of eight equal parts. ◆ *n* an eighth part; a person or thing in eighth position; an octave (*music*); an eighth of an ounce (*drug sl*). **eighthly** /ātth'li/ *adv* in the eighth place. **eight'some** *n* a group of eight; eight together; a Scottish reel for eight dancers (also **eightsome reel**). **eight'vo** *n* (*pl* **eight'vos**) and *adj* same as **octavo**.
❑ **eight'-day** *adj* lasting or running for eight days. **eight'foil** *n* (*heraldry*) an eight-leaved flower. **eight'-foot** *adj* eight feet in measure (also *adv*); having the pitch of an open organ-pipe eight feet long, or having that pitch for the lowest note (*music*). **eighth note** *n* (*music*; chiefly *N Am*) a quaver. **eight'-hour** *adj* consisting of eight hours or eight working hours. **eight'-oar** *adj* manned by eight rowers. ◆ *n* an eight-oar boat. **eight'pence** *n* the value of eight pennies. **eight'penny** *adj* costing eightpence. **eight'score** *n* and *adj* eight times twenty. **eights'man** *n* one of a crew or team of eight. **eight'-square** *adj* regularly octagonal.
■ **an eight days** a week. **behind the eight ball** (*inf*) in a difficult situation (from the black ball in the game of pool, marked with the number eight, which must not be potted until the end of the game). **figure of eight** a figure shaped like an 8 made in skating, etc. **one over the eight** (*inf*) one (alcoholic) drink too many. **piece of eight** an old Spanish coin worth eight reals.

eighteen /ā-tēn' or ā'tēn/ *n* and adj eight and ten; (**18**) a certificate designating a film passed as suitable only for people of eighteen years and over. [OE (Mercian) *æhtatēne* (WSax *eahtatīene*); see **eight** and **ten**]
■ **eighteen'mo** *adj* and *n* (*pl* **eighteen'mos**) octodecimo. **eigh'teenth** (or /-tēnth'/) *adj* last of eighteen; next after the seventeenth; equal to one of eighteen equal parts. ◆ *n* an eighteenth part; a person or thing in eighteenth position. **eighteenth'ly** *adv*.
❑ **eigh'teen-hole** *adj* (of a golf course) having eighteen holes. **eigh'teen-pence** *n*. **eigh'teen-penny** *adj*. **eighteen-penny piece** *n* an obsolete English coin.

eighty /ā'ti/ *n* and adj eight times ten. [OE *æhtatig* (WSax *eahtatig* or *hundeahtatig*)]
■ **eight'ies** *n pl* the numbers eighty to eighty-nine; the years so numbered in life or any century; a range of temperatures from eighty to just less than ninety degrees. **eigh'tieth** *adj* last of eighty; next after the seventy-ninth; equal to one of eighty equal parts. ◆ *n* an eightieth part; a person or thing in eightieth position.

eigne /ān/ (*archaic*) *adj* first-born. [Fr *aîné*]

EIIR see **ER**.

eik /ēk/ Scots form of **eke**[1].

eikon same as **icon**.

eild[1] same as **eld**.

eild[2] /ēld/ (*Scot*) *adj* not bearing young; not yielding milk. [See **yeld**]

eilding see **eldin**.

eine /īn/ or /ēn/ (*obs*) *n pl* eyes. [See **ee, een**]

einkorn /īn'körn/ *n* a one-seeded wheat (*Triticum monococcum*) native to SW Asia and grown in arid regions. [Ger *ein* one, and *Korn* grain]

Einsteinian /īn-stī'ni-ən/ *adj* of or relating to Albert *Einstein*, physicist and mathematician (1879–1955) or his theories, *esp* that of relativity. ■ **einstein'ium** *n* an artificially produced radioactive transuranic metallic element (symbol **Es**; atomic no 99).

eirack /ē'rək/ (*Scot*) *n* a young hen. [Gaelic *eireag*]

eirenicon or **irenicon** /ī-rē'ni-kon/ *n* a proposition or scheme for peace; a peace-making message; the deacon's litany at the beginning of the Greek liturgy, from its opening petitions for peace. [A partly Latinized spelling of Gr *eirēnikon*, neuter of *eirēnikos* peaceful or peaceable, from *eirēnē* peace] ■ **eirē'nic** *adj* same as **irenic**.

EIS *abbrev* : Educational Institute of Scotland, a trade union for teachers; Enterprise Investment Scheme.

EISA (*comput*) *abbrev* : Extended Industry Standard Architecture, an obsolete bus system developed from ISA.

eisel or **eisell** /ā'səl or ī'səl/ (*obs*) *n* vinegar. [OFr *aisil*, *aissil*, from LL dimin of L *acētum* vinegar]

Eisen und Blut see **Blut und Eisen** under **Blut**.

eisteddfod /ī-sted'fəd or ī-stedh'vod, also (*US*) ā-/ *n* (pl **eistedd'fods** or **eisteddfodau** /-vo-dī/) *orig* a competitive congress of Welsh bards and musicians, now any of several gatherings in Wales for competitions in music, poetry, drama, etc, *esp* (with *cap*) the Royal National Eisteddfod. [Welsh, (literally) session, from *eistedd* to sit] ■ **eisteddfod'ic** *adj*.

eiswein /īs'vīn/ *n* a sweet dessert wine made from grapes which have been frozen while still on the vine. [Ger, ice wine]

either /ī'dhər or ē'dhər/ *adj* the one or the other; one of two; each of two, the one and the other. ♦ *pronoun* the one or the other. ♦ *conj* correlative to *or* ; or (*Bible*). ♦ *adv* (used in conjunction with a negative) also, likewise (not), as in *He isn't hungry and she isn't either* ; (after a negative) moreover, besides, as in *She's a golfer, and not a bad one, either*. [OE *ǣgther*, contraction of *ǣghwæther*, from *ā* aye, pfx *ge*-, and *hwæther* whether; see also **each**] ■ **either way** in both or two cases.

ejaculate /i-jak'ū-lāt/ *vi* to emit semen; to make a sudden emotional utterance. ♦ *vt* to utter with suddenness, to exclaim; to eject. ♦ *n* /-lət/ semen. [L *ē* from, and *jaculārī*, *-ātus*, from *jacere* to throw] ■ **ejaculā'tion** *n* emission of semen; ejection or emission; a sudden exclamation or cry; an unpremeditated emotional prayer or remark. **ejac'ūlative** (or /-lā-/) *adj*. **ejac'ūlātor** *n*. **ejac'ūlatory** (or /-lā-/) *adj*.

eject /i- or ē-jekt'/ *vt* to throw out; to dismiss; to turn out; to expel. ♦ *vi* to make oneself be ejected as from an aircraft or spacecraft. ♦ *n* /ē'jekt/ a mental state other than one's own, a thing thrown out of one's own consciousness, as distinguished from *object*, a thing presented in one's consciousness. [L *ējectāre*, frequentative of *ējicere*, *ējectum*, from *ē* from, and *jacere* to throw] ■ **eject'a** or **ejectament'a** *n pl* matter thrown out, *esp* by volcanoes. **ejec'tion** *n* discharge; expulsion; the state of being ejected; vomiting; something that is ejected. **ejec'tive** *adj* of or relating to ejection; (of a type of consonant in some languages) pronounced on an airstream created by raising the closed glottis (*phonetics*). ♦ *n* an ejective consonant. **ejec'tively** *adv*. **eject'ment** *n* expulsion; dispossession; an action for the recovery of the possession of land (*law*). **eject'or** *n* a person who ejects or dispossesses another of his or her land; any mechanical device for ejecting or discharging. ❑ **ejector seat** or (*US*) **ejection seat** *n* a seat in an aircraft, etc that can be shot clear with its occupant in an emergency.

e-journal /ē'jûr-nəl/ *n* a journal in electronic form that can be stored and read on a computer.

ejusd. *abbrev* : *ejusdem* (L), of the same.

ejusdem generis /ē-jus'dəm jen'ə-ris or ā-ūs'dem gen'e-ris/ *abbrev* : (L) of the same kind.

eka- /ā-kə- or ē-kə-/ *pfx* formerly prefixed to the name of an element to give a provisional name for the hypothetical undiscovered element that should follow in the periodic table. [Sans *eka* one]

ek dum /ek dum/ *adv* at once. [Hindi *ek dam*]

eke[1] (*Scot* **eik**) /ēk/ *vt* (now only with *out*) to add to or increase; to lengthen; to supplement or make up to the required measure; to manage with difficulty to make (a living, etc). ♦ *n* (*Scot*) an addition or supplement. [OE *ēcan* (WSax *īecan*); cf **eche**; L *augēre* ; Gr *auxanein*]

eke[2] /ēk/ (*archaic*) *adv* in addition; likewise. [OE *ēac*; Ger *auch*, perh from root of **eke**[1]]

ekistics /e-kis'tiks/ *n sing* the science or study of human settlements. [From Mod Gr coinage *oikistikē*, from Gr *oikistikos* of or relating to settlement, from *oikizein* to settle or colonize, from *oikos* a house] ■ **ekis'tic** *adj*. **ekistician** /-tish'ən/ *n*.

ekka /ek'ə/ *n* a small one-horse carriage. [Hindi, from *ekkā* one, from Sans *eka*]

eklogite see **eclogite**.

ekphrasis /ek'frə-sis/ *n* a description of a work of art, possibly imaginary, produced as a rhetorical exercise. [Gr, description]

ekuele /ā-kwā'lā/ or **ekpwele** /ek-pwā'lā/ *n* (pl **ekue'le** or **ekpwe'les** or **ekue'le**) a former unit of currency in Equatorial Guinea. [Native name]

el[1] /el/ (*US inf*) *n* an elevated railroad.

el[2] /el/ *n* the twelfth letter of the modern English alphabet (L or l); a wing giving a building the shape of the letter L (*US*).

e-la /ē'lä'/ *n* the highest note in old church music, E, the fourth space in the treble, sung to the syllable *la* in the highest hexachord; the highest pitch of anything. ❑ **e-la-mi** /ē'lä'mē'/ *n* E, the third space in the bass ('in bass') or the first line in the treble ('in alt'), sung to *la* in the first and fourth hexachords respectively, and *mi* in the second and fifth.

elaborate /i-lab'ə-rāt/ *vt* to produce by labour; to work out in detail; to build up from raw or comparatively simple materials; to add detail to; to convert (eg food) into complex substances (*physiol*). ♦ *vi* (with *on* or *upon*) to add detail, more information, etc to a bare account; to become elaborate. ♦ *adj* /i-lab'ər-ət/ done with fullness and exactness; highly detailed; complicated; wrought with labour. [L *ēlabōrāre*, *-ātum*, from *ē* from, and *labōrāre*, from *labor* labour] ■ **elab'orately** *adv*. **elab'orateness** *n*. **elabora'tion** *n* the act or process of elaborating; a refinement, detail or complication added; the process by which substances are built up in the bodies of animals or plants. **elab'orative** (or /-rā-/) *adj*. **elab'orātor** *n* someone who elaborates. **elab'oratory** *n* (*obs*) a laboratory.

Elaeagnus /el-i-ag'nəs/ *n* the oleaster genus, giving name to the family **Elaeagnā'ceae**. [Gr *elaiagnos* goat willow]

Elaeis /e-lē'is/ *n* the oil palm genus. [Gr *elaion* olive oil]

elaeolite /e-lē'ō-līt/ *n* a greasy-looking nepheline. [Gr *elaion* olive oil, and *lithos* stone]

El Al /el al/ the Israeli airline, (literally) towards the sky.

élan /ā-län' or ā-lā'/ *n* vigour and style; impetuosity. [Fr] ❑ **élan vital** /ā-lā vē-tal/ *n* (Bergson) the creative force responsible for the growth and evolution of organisms.

elance /i-läns' or -lans'/ *vt* to throw as a lance. [Fr *élancer*]

eland /ē'lənd/ *n* a S African antelope, resembling the elk in having a protuberance on the larynx. [Du, from Ger *Elend* (now *Elen*), from Lithuanian *élnis* elk]

elanet /el'ə-net/ *n* a kite of the genus *Elanus*. [Gr *elanos* a kite]

elaphine /el'ə-fīn/ *adj* like or belonging to a red deer. [Gr *elaphos* stag]

Elaps /ē'laps/ *n* an American genus of snakes, also called **Micrurus**, the coral snake; sometimes applied to a S African genus, also called **Homorelaps**, the garter-snake. [A form of **ellops**] ■ **el'apid** *n* any member of the *Elaps* genus (also *adj*).

elapse /i-laps'/ *vi* (of time, or units of time) to pass silently; *orig* to slip or glide away. ♦ *n* passing. [L *ēlāpsus*, *ēlābī*, from *ē* from, and *lābī*, *lāpsus* to slide]

elasmobranch /i-laz'mō-brangk or -las'/ *n* any member of the **Elasmobranch'iī**, a class of fishes including sharks and skates which have a cartilaginous skeleton and plate-like gills. [Gr *elasmos* a beaten-metal plate, and *branchia* gills]

elastic /i-las'tik or -läs'/ *adj* having a tendency or the ability to recover the original form or size after stretching, compression or deformation; springy or resilient; able to recover quickly a former state or condition, eg after a shock (*fig*); stretchy; flexible; capable of stretching to include a large number or amount (*lit* and *fig*); made of elastic; (of the demand for a product) highly sensitive to fluctuations in price. ♦ *n* a string or ribbon woven with rubber strands. [Late Gr *elastikos*, from *elaunein* to drive] ■ **elas'tance** *n* (*phys*) the reciprocal of the capacity of a condenser, from its electromechanical analogy with a spring. **elas'tane** *n* a synthetic fibre used in the manufacture of *esp* underwear, hosiery, etc for its ability to recover its original form after stretching. **elas'tase** *n* an enzyme found in the pancreatic juice that decomposes elastin. **elas'tically** *adv*. **elas'ticate** *vt* to make elastic. **elas'ticated** *adj*. **elasticity** /el- or el-əs-tis'i-ti/ *n* power of returning to its original form or size after stretching, compression or deformation; springiness, flexibility, resilience or stretchiness; power to recover from shock, depression, etc, or financial restraint; the extent to which the demand for a product is sensitive to fluctuations in price. **elas'ticize** or **-ise** /-ti-sīz/ *vt* to make elastic. **elas'ticness** *n*. **elas'tin** *n* a protein, the chief constituent of elastic tissue. **elas'tomer** *n* any rubber-like substance. **elastomeric** /-mer'-/ *adj*. ❑ **elastic band** *n* a narrow strip of rubber formed into a loop for holding objects together, etc (also called **rubber band**). **elastic collision** or **scattering** see under **collide**. **elastic limit** *n* the greatest stress a material can be subjected to without permanent deformation. **elastic tissue** *n* tissue having fibres with elastic quality, occurring *esp* in ligaments and tendons.

Elastoplast® /i-las'tō-plăst or -plast/ *n* a band of sticking plaster.

elate /i-lāt'/ *vt* to raise the spirits of, cheer or exhilarate, fill with optimism; to make exultant, proud or euphoric; to raise or exalt (*obs*). ◆ *adj* (*rare*) lifted up; puffed up with success; exalted. [L *ēlātus*, used as pap of *efferre*, from *ē* from, and *lātus* carried]
■ **elāt'ed** *adj*. **elāt'edly** *adv*. **elāt'edness** *n*. **elā'tion** *n* exaltation, high spirits or euphoria; pride resulting from success. **ē'lative** *adj* (*grammar*) (of a noun case) expressing place 'from which', as eg in Finnish. ◆ *n* the elative case.

elater /el'ə-tər/ *n* an elastic filament aiding spore-dispersal in certain fungi, in liverworts and in horse-tails (*bot*); a skipjack beetle. [Gr *elatēr* driver, from *elaunein* to drive]
■ **elaterite** /i-lat'ər-īt/ *n* elastic bitumen, a rubber-like mineral resin. **elatē'rium** *n* a substance contained in the juice of the fruit of the squirting cucumber, producing the purgative **elat'erin**.

elbow /el'bō/ *n* the joint where the arm bends; the corresponding joint in vertebrates; the part of a sleeve which covers the elbow; any sharp turn or bend, eg in a road. ◆ *vt* to push with the elbow, to jostle. [OE *elnboga*; see **ell**[1] and **bow**[1] noun and vt]
❏ **el'bow-chair** *n* an armchair. **el'bow-grease** *n* (*facetious*) vigorous rubbing; hard work. **elbow macaroni** *n* macaroni cut longer than usual, and with a pronounced bend. **el'bow-room** *n* room to extend the elbows; enough space for moving or acting; freedom and scope.
■ **at one's elbow** close at hand, ready for use. **bend**, **crook** or **lift the elbow** to drink alcohol, *esp* to excess. **elbow out** to remove or get rid of. **give** (or **get**) **the elbow** (*inf*) to dismiss (or be dismissed). **out at (the) elbow** or **the elbows** worn-out, or wearing worn-out clothes, *orig* worn at the elbows. **up to the elbows** completely engrossed or involved.

elchi, **eltchi** or **elchee** /el'chē or -chi/ *n* an ambassador. [Turk *īlchī*]

eld /eld/ (*archaic*) *n* age; old age or senility; former times or antiquity. [OE *eldo*]

elder[1] /el'dər/ *adj* older; having lived a longer time; prior in origin. ◆ *n* an older person; an ancestor; *esp* in some tribal societies, a person advanced to the office of adviser or administrator on account of age; one of a class of office-bearers in some Protestant churches (*presbyter* of the New Testament). [OE *eldra* (WSax *ieldra*, *yldra*) compar, and *eldesta* (WSax *ieldesta*) superl of *ald* (WSax *eald*) old]
■ **eld'erliness** *n*. **eld'erly** *adj* rather old; bordering on old age. ◆ *n* (with *the*) elderly people. **eld'ership** *n* the state of being older; the office of an elder. **eld'est** *adj* oldest. ◆ *n* the oldest of three or more.
❏ **elder abuse** *n* any form of physical or mental cruelty to or neglect of an older person. **Elder brethren** *n pl* the governing members of the Corporation of Trinity House. **elder care** *n* (*US*) the provision of residential or home-based care for older people who are unable to care for themselves. **elder** or **eldest hand** *n* in card-playing, the player on the dealer's left, who leads. **elders' hours** *n pl* respectable hours, formerly understood to mean not after 10pm. **elder statesman** *n* a retired statesman consulted by the government; any administrator of age and experience; (in *pl*; with *caps*) a reactionary group of retired statesmen who exercised a power behind the throne in Japan in the early 20c.

elder[2] /el'dər/ *n* a shrub or tree (genus *Sambucus*) of the Caprifoliaceae, related to honeysuckle, with pinnate leaves, small flowers (with a wheel-shaped corolla) and three-seeded fruits. [OE *ellærn*]
❏ **eld'erberry** *n* the acidulous purple-black drupaceous fruit of the elder. **elderberry wine** *n* a wine made from elderberries. **eld'erflower** *n* the flower of the elder. **elderflower water** *n* a distilled water made from these flowers. **eld'er-gun** *n* a popgun made from a length of elder by removing the pith.

eldin /el'din/ or **elding** /el'ding/ (*Scot and N Eng*), also (*Scot*) **eilding** /ēl'ding/ *n* fuel. [ON *elding*, from *eldr* fire]

ELDO *abbrev*: European Launcher Development Organization (now **ESA**).

El Dorado or **Eldorado** /el-də-rä'dō/ *n* the golden land or city imagined by the Spanish conquerors of America; any place where wealth is easily acquired. [Sp *el* the, and *dorado*, pap of *dorar* to gild, from 'the gilded man', the king of the legendary city of Manoa who smeared himself with gold-dust; afterwards transferred to the city itself]

eldritch /el'(d)rich/ (*Scot*) *adj* unearthly or supernatural; uncanny. [Perh connected with **elf**]

e-learning /ē'lûr-ning/ *n* (the provision of) learning by electronic means, eg the Internet.

Eleatic /el-i-at'ik/ *adj* belonging to *Elea*, an ancient Greek colony in S Italy, or to the school of philosophers connected with it, including Xenophanes, Parmenides and Zeno. ◆ *n* a philosopher belonging to this school.

elec. or **elect.** *abbrev*: electric; electricity.

elecampane /el-i-kam-pān'/ *n* a composite plant (*Inula helenium*) formerly much cultivated for its medicinal root; a sweet flavoured with an extract from the root. [L *enula* or *inula campāna* field or Campanian inula]

elect /i-lekt'/ *vt* to choose in preference to other options; to select for any office or purpose; to select by vote. ◆ *adj* chosen; taken by preference from among others; chosen for an office but not yet in it (almost always after the noun); in Christian doctrine, chosen by God for salvation (*theol*). ◆ *n* (with *the*) those chosen or set apart, *esp* by God for salvation. [L *ēligere*, *ēlectum*, from *ē* from, and *legere* to choose]
■ **electabil'ity** *n*. **elect'able** *adj*. **elec'ted** *adj*. **elec'tion** /-shən/ *n* the act of electing or choosing; the public choice of a person for office, *usu* by the votes of a constituent body; free will; the exercise of God's sovereign will in the predetermination of certain persons to salvation (*theol*); those elected in this way (*Bible*). **electioneer'** *vi* to work to secure the election of a candidate. ◆ *n* someone who takes part in this activity. **electioneer'er** *n*. **electioneer'ing** *n* and *adj*. **elect'ive** *adj* relating to, concerning, dependent on, or exerting the power of choice; optional; of medical procedures, undertaken at the decision of the patient, as in *elective surgery*. ◆ *n* an optional subject of study (*N Am*); an elective placement with a hospital, or to study abroad, etc (*med*). **elect'ively** *adv*. **electiv'ity** /ē- or e-/ *n*. **elect'or** (also *fem* **elect'ress** or **elect'oress**) a person who elects; a person who has a vote at an election; in the USA, a member of the electoral college; (*usu* with *cap*) the title formerly belonging to those princes and archbishops of the Holy Roman Empire who had the right to elect the Emperor. **elect'oral** or **electō'rial** /ē- or e-/ *adj* relating to elections or to electors; consisting of electors. **elect'orally** or **electō'rially** *adv*. **elect'orate** *n* the body of electors; the dignity or the territory of an elector. **elect'orship** *n*.
❏ **electoral college** *n* in the USA, the body of people who elect the President and Vice-President, themselves elected by popular vote; any body of electors with a similar function. **electoral roll** or **register** *n* the list of people in a particular area who are eligible to vote in local and general elections. **electoral vote** *n* (*US*) the vote of the members of the electoral college.

Electra complex /i-lek'trə kom'pleks/ (*psychol*) *n* a strong attachment of a daughter to her father, accompanied by hostility to her mother. [From the Greek story of *Electra*, who helped to avenge her mother's murder of her father]

electret /i-lek'trit/ (*elec*) *n* a permanently polarized (piece of) dielectric material. [*electricity* and *magnet*]

electric /i-lek'trik/ *adj* relating to electricity; charged with or capable of being charged with electricity; producing or produced by, conveying, operated by or making use of electricity; thrilling (*fig*); full of tension and expectation, as though charged with electricity; producing a sudden startling effect. ◆ *n* a non-conductor of electricity, such as amber, glass, etc, capable of being electrified by friction; an electric vehicle, machine, etc; the household electricity supply (*inf*); (in *pl*) electrical appliances; (in *pl*) wiring (*inf*). [L *ēlectrum* amber (in which electricity was first observed), from Gr *ēlektron*]
■ **elec'trical** *adj* electric. **elec'trically** *adv*. **elec'tricals** *n pl* electrical equipment; shares in electricity companies (*finance*). **electrician** /el-ik-trish'ən/ *n* someone who studies or is trained in the science of electricity; someone who makes, installs or repairs electrical equipment. **electricity** /el-ik-tris'i-ti/ *n* the manifestation of a form of energy associated with separation or movement of charged particles, such as electrons and protons; the science that deals with this; the supply of this energy to a household, etc; an electric charge or current; the magnetic power of amber and other substances when rubbed; an imaginary fluid supposed to explain this and related phenomena; a feeling of excitement. **electrīzā'tion** or **-s-** *n*. **elec'trize** or **-ise** *vt* to electrify.
❏ **electrical engineer** *n* a specialist in the practical applications of electricity as a branch of engineering. **electrical engineering** *n*. **electric arc** *n* a luminous space between electrodes when a current passes across. **electric battery** *n* a group of cells connected in series or in parallel for generating an electric current by chemical action. **electric blanket** *n* a blanket incorporating an electric element, used for warming a bed. **electric blue** *n* a vividly bright blue colour. **electric calamine** *n* the mineral hemimorphite, which becomes positively electrified at one end and negatively at the other when its temperature rises, and vice versa as it cools. **electric chair** *n* in the USA, the seat on which a condemned criminal is put to death by electrocution; (with *the*) execution by electrocution in this manner. **electric eel** *n* a cyprinoid fish, *Electrophorus electricus*, of S America, shaped like an eel and able to give powerful electric shocks by means of an electric organ in its long tail. **electric eye** *n* a photo-electric cell;

a miniature cathode-ray tube. **electric fence** *n* an electrically-charged wire fence. **electric field** *n* a region in which attracting or repelling forces are exerted on any electric charge present. **electric fire**, **heater** or **radiator** *n* a device using an electric current, for heating a room. **electric furnace** *n* a device for getting very high temperatures by means of an electric current. **electric guitar** *n* a guitar with an electrical amplifying device. **electric hare** *n* a dummy animal worked by electricity for racing greyhounds to chase. **electric motor** *n* any device for converting electrical energy into mechanical energy. **electric organ** *n* an organ in which the sound is produced by electrical devices instead of wind (*music*); in certain fishes, a structure that generates, stores and discharges electricity (*zool*). **electric piano** *n* one in which the sounds are produced electrically. **electric ray** *n* any fish of the genus *Torpedo*. **electric seal** *n* dyed rabbit or hare skin. **electric shock** *n* a convulsion caused by the passage of an electric current through the body. **electric storm** *n* a violent disturbance in the electric condition of the atmosphere.

electrify /i-lek'tri-fī/ *vt* (**elec'trifying**; **elec'trified**) to introduce electricity into, to charge with electricity; to adapt (something) to run on electricity; to excite suddenly; to astonish. [**electro-** and L *facere* to make]
■ **elec'trifïable** *adj*. **electrificā'tion** *n*. **elec'trifier** /-fī-ər/ *n*. **elec'trifying** *adj*. **elec'trifyingly** *adv*.

electro /i-lek'trō/ (*inf*) *n* (*pl* **elec'tros**) short for **electroplate** and **electrotype**.

electro- /i-lek-trō- or el-ik-tro-/ *combining form* denoting electric, electricity or electrolytic. [Gr *ēlektro*, combining form of *ēlektron* (see **electron**)]
■ **electroacous'tics** *n sing* the technology of converting acoustic energy into electrical energy and vice versa. **electroacous'tic** *adj*. **electro-ac'upuncture** *n* an acupuncture technique in which electrical currents, of frequencies and amplitudes varied according to the effects required, are passed between pairs of inserted acupuncture needles. **electroanal'ysis** *n* separation by electrolysis. **electroanalyt'ical** *adj*. **electrobiol'ogist** *n*. **electrobiol'ogy** *n* the science of the electrical phenomena in living organisms; an old name for hypnotism. **electrocar'diogram** *n* a photographic record of the electrical variations that occur during contraction of the muscle of the heart. **electrocar'diograph** *n* a galvanometer used for making such records. **electrocardiograph'ic** *adj*. **electrocardiog'raphy** *n* the study of electric currents produced during muscular activity of the heart. **electrocement'** *n* cement made in an electric furnace by adding lime to molten slag. **electrochem'ic** or **electrochem'ical** *adj*. **electrochem'ically** *adv*. **electrochem'ist** *n*. **electrochem'istry** *n* the study of the relation between electricity and chemical change. **elec'troclash** *n* a style of early 21c electronic dance music influenced by punk rock and performance art. **electroconvuls'ive** *adj* relating to treatment using electric shocks, as in *electroconvulsive therapy*. **elec'troculture** *n* the cultivation of plants under the stimulus of electricity. **elec'trocute** *vt* to inflict a death penalty by means of electrocution; to kill by electricity. **electrocū'tion** *n*. **elec'trōde** *n* (Gr *hodos* way) a conductor by which a current of electricity enters or leaves an electrolytic cell, gas-discharge tube or thermionic valve. **electrodeposi'tion** *n* deposition of a layer of metal by electrolysis. **electrodynam'ic** *adj*. **electrodynam'ics** *n sing* the study of electricity in motion, or of the interaction between different currents, or between currents and magnets. **electrodynamom'eter** *n* an instrument for measuring electric currents by the attraction or repulsion between current-bearing coils. **electroenceph'alogram** /-sef'- or -kef'-/ *n* a record made by an **electroenceph'alograph**, an instrument for recording small electrical impulses produced by the brain. **electroencephalog'raphy** *n*. **electroextrac'tion** or **electrowinn'ing** *n* the recovery of a metal from its salts by passing an electric current through a solution. **elec'trofish** *vi* to fish using an electric current that stuns fish before they are caught. **elec'trofishing** *n*. **elec'troforming** *n* (*electronics*) electrodeposition of copper on stainless steel formers to obtain complex waveguide components. **elec'trogen** *n* a molecule which emits electrons when it is illuminated. **electrogen'esis** *n* the production of electricity, *esp* in living cells, etc. **electrogen'ic** *adj* producing electricity; of or capable of electrogenesis. **electrogild'ing** *n* electroplating with gold. **elec'trograph** *n* a recording electrometer. **electrog'raphy** *n*. **electrohydraul'ic** *adj* using or worked by water and electricity (**electrohydraulic forming** shaping a piece of metal with a die by means of a shock wave in water set up by discharge of energy between immersed electrodes). **electrokinet'ic** *adj*. **electrokinet'ics** *n sing* the branch of science that deals with the motion of bodies under the influence of an electric field. **electrolier** /-lēr'/ *n* an electric-light fixture resembling a chandelier. **electrol'ogy** *n* the science of electricity; electrotherapy. **electroluminesc'ence** *n* luminescence produced by the application of an electric field to a dielectric phosphor. **electroluminesc'ent** *adj*. **electrolyse** *vt*, etc see separate entry. **electromag'net** *n* a piece of soft iron, etc, made magnetic by a current of electricity passing through a coil of wire

wound round it. **electromagnet'ic** *adj* (*phys*) of or relating to an electromagnet or electromagnetism (**electromagnetic interaction** an interaction between charged elementary particles intermediate in strength between *strong* and *weak interactions*, completed in about 10^{-18}s; **electromagnetic spectrum** the range of wavelengths of electromagnetic radiation. **electromagnetic theory** JC Maxwell's theory explaining light in terms of electromagnetic waves; **electromagnetic unit** any unit, such as the abampere or abvolt, in a centimetre-gram-second system of units based on the magnetic forces exerted by electric currents; **electromagnetic wave** a travelling disturbance in space produced by the acceleration of an electric charge, comprising an electric field and a magnetic field at right angles to each other, both moving at the same velocity in a direction normal to the plane of the two fields). **electromagnet'ically** *adv*. **electromag'netism** *n* magnetic forces produced by electricity; the relation between, and properties of, electric and magnetic force; the branch of science dealing with this subject. **electromechan'ical** *adj* of or relating to any mechanical process or device involving the use of electricity; of or relating to electromechanics. **electromechan'ically** *adv*. **electromechan'ics** *n sing* the mechanics of the electric circuit. **elec'tromer** *n* a substance showing electromerism. **electromer'ic** *adj*. **electrom'erism** *n* (*chem*) a form of tautomerism caused by a redistribution of electrons among the atoms of a molecule or group. **electrometallur'gical** *adj*. **electromet'allurgist** (or /-al'-/) *n*. **electromet'allurgy** (or /-al'-/) *n* the industrial working of metals by means of electricity. **electrom'eter** *n* an instrument for measuring difference of electric potential. **electromet'ric** or **electromet'rical** *adj*. **electromet'rically** *adv*. **electrom'etry** *n* the science of electrical measurements. **electromō'tive** *adj* of or relating to the motion of electricity or the laws governing it (**electromotive force** difference of potential or the force generated by an electromagnetic wave, being the force of an electric current (also called **electromō'tance**)). **electromō'tor** *n* a device for applying electricity as a motive power. **electromy'ogram** *n* a record made by an electromyograph. **electromy'ograph** *n* an instrument for recording voltages produced by muscular contraction. **electromyograph'ic** *adj*. **electromyograph'ically** *adv*. **electromyog'raphy** *n* the study of electric currents set up in muscles by their functioning. **electroneg'ative** *adj* carrying a negative charge; tending to form negative ions. **electronegativ'ity** *n* an electronegative state; the power of eg an atom to attract electrons. **electronystagmog'raphy** *n* (see **nystagmus**) the recording of eye movement by electronic means in medical diagnosis. **electro-op'tic** or **electro-op'tical** *adj* (**electro-optical effect** see Kerr effect). **electro-op'tics** *n sing* the study of the effects that an electric field has on light crossing it. **electro-osmō'sis** *n* movement of liquid under an applied electric field through a fine tube or membrane. **electro-osmot'ic** *adj*. **elec'trophile** *n* an electrophilic substance. **electrophil'ic** *adj* having or involving an affinity for electrons (ie for negative charge), electron-seeking. **electrophorē'sis** *n* (Gr *phoreein* to bear) the motion of charged particles through a fluid or gel under the influence of an electric field. **electrophoretic** /-et'ik/ *adj* of or relating to electrophoresis. **electrophoret'ically** *adv*. **electroph'orus** *n* an instrument for obtaining static electricity by means of induction. **electrophotograph'ic** *adj*. **electrophotog'raphy** *n* photography by means of electric rather than chemical processes, as in xerography. **electrophysiolog'ical** *adj*. **electrophysiolog'ically** *adv*. **electrophysiol'ogist** *n*. **electrophysiol'ogy** *n* the study of electric phenomena of living organisms. **elec'troplate** *vt* to plate or cover, *esp* with silver, by electrolysis. ◆ *n* electroplated articles. **elec'troplated** *adj*. **elec'troplater** *n*. **elec'troplating** *n*. **electropō'lar** *adj* having, as an electrical conductor, one end or surface positive and the other negative. **elec'tro-pop** *n* another name for **technopop** (see under **techno-**). **electropos'itive** *adj* carrying a positive charge; tending to form positive ions. **electrorheolog'ical** *adj* (*phys*) of a fluid, having a form that changes depending on the strength of the electric field present. **elec'troscope** *n* an instrument for detecting the presence of electricity in a body and the nature of it. **electroscop'ic** *adj*. **elec'troshock** *n* an electric shock. **elec'trosmog** or **electronic smog** *n* electromagnetic fields emitted by computers, mobile phones, etc, believed by some to be harmful to health. **elec'trosonde** *n* a sonde for measuring atmospheric electricity. **elec'trospinning** *n* a technique for transforming a polymer solution into nanoscale fibres by using an electrostatic force. **electrostat'ic** *adj* of or relating to electricity at rest (**electrostatic unit** any unit, such as the statampere and statvolt, in a centimetre-gram-second system of units based on the forces of repulsion existing between static electric charges). **electrostat'ically** *adv*. **electrostat'ics** *n sing* the branch of science concerned with electricity at rest. **electrotech'nic** or **electrotech'nical** *adj*. **electrotech'nics** *n sing* (also **electrotechnol'ogy**) electric technology. **electrotherapeu'tic** or **electrotherapeu'tical** *adj*. **electrotherapeu'tics** *n sing* (also **electrother'apy**) the branch of medicine in which electrotherapy is used. **electrother'apist** *n*. **electrother'apy** *n* the use of electrical currents or impulses to treat disease, ease pain, accelerate healing, restore muscle function, etc. **electrotherm'al** or **electrotherm'ic** adj of or relating to electricity and heat, or heat obtained electrically. **electrotherm'ics** n sing. **electrotherm'y** n. **elec'trotint** n a printing block produced by drawing with varnish on a metal plate, and depositing metal electrically on the parts not covered. **electroton'ic** adj. **electrot'onus** n the state of a nerve subjected to a steady discharge of electricity. **elec'trotype** vt to make a copy of something by electrolytically coating a mould with copper. ◆ n a printing plate made by this process; a facsimile of a coin made by this process. **elec'trotyper** n a person who makes electrotypes. **electrotȳp'ic** adj. **elec'trotypist** n. **elec'trotȳpy** n. **electrova'lency** or **electrova'lence** n union within a chemical compound achieved by transfer of electrons, the resulting ions being held together by electrostatic attraction (cf **covalency**). **electrova'lent** adj. **electroweak'** adj of or relating to a theory unifying electromagnetic and weak interactions between particles. **electrowinning** n see **electroextraction** above.

electrolyse or **electrolyze** /i-lek'trə-līz/ vt to break down by electrolysis; to subject to electrolysis. [electro- and Gr lysis loosing] ■ **elec'trolyser** n. **electrolysis** /-trol'i-sis/ n decomposition by electric current, with migration of ions shown by changes at the electrodes; the removal of hair by applying an electrically-charged needle to the follicle. **elec'trolyte** /-līt/ n a substance able to be broken down by electrolysis. **electrolytic** /-lit'ik/ or **electrolyt'ical** adj. **electrolyt'ically** adv.

electron /i-lek'tron/ n a minute particle charged with electricity, or a unit charge having inertia, normally forming part of an atom but capable of isolation as in cathode rays; a natural alloy of gold and silver used in ancient times (also Latinized as **elec'trum**). [Gr ēlektron amber] ❑ **electron beam** n a stream of electrons, esp in a cathode-ray tube. **electron camera** n any device that converts an optical image into a corresponding electric current directly by electronic means. **electron capture** n the capture of an electron by the nucleus of its own atom, the change of a proton into a neutron decreasing by one the atomic number of the atom. **electron diffraction** n the diffraction of a beam of electrons by crystal, used in the study of crystal structures. **electron gun** n the arrangement of electrodes in a cathode-ray tube which produces the electron beam. **electron lens** n a device for focusing an electron beam. **electron micrograph** n a photograph obtained by substituting a photographic plate for the fluorescent viewing screen of an electron microscope. **electron microscope** n a microscope that makes use of a beam of electrons instead of light. **electron optics** n sing the study of the effects of electric and magnetic fields on the direction of beams of electrons. **electron pair** n two valence electrons shared by adjacent nuclei, so forming a bond. **electron probe** n an X-ray device that bombards the specimen under examination with a very narrow beam of electrons, allowing non-destructive analysis. **electron ring accelerator** n an accelerator in which an intense ring of circulating electrons, being accelerated, can carry along and accelerate protons or stripped ions. **electron shell** n a group of electrons surrounding a nucleus of an atom and having adjacent energy levels. **electron telescope** n an optical instrument with electronic image converter used with a normal telescope. **electron tube** n an electronic device in which the electron conduction is in a vacuum or gas inside a gas-tight enclosure, eg a thermionic valve. **elec'tronvolt** n a unit of energy equal to that acquired by an electron when accelerated by a potential of one volt.

electronegative, **electronegativity** see under **electro-**.

electronic /el-ik-tron'ik or i-lek-, also ē-lek-/ adj of or relating to electronics or electrons; worked or produced by devices made according to the principles of electronics; concerned with or working with such devices; carried out using a computer or computer network (as in electronic banking). [Ety as for **electron**] ■ **electron'ica** n pl (inf) electronic products and data collectively. ◆ n sing electronic music. **electron'ically** adv. **electron'ics** n sing the science and technology of the conduction of electricity in a vacuum, a gas or a semiconductor. ◆ n pl the electronic parts of a machine or system. ❑ **electronic book** n see **e-book**. **electronic brain** n any electronic computer. **electronic cigarette** n see **e-cigarette**. **electronic commerce** n see **e-commerce**. **electronic countermeasures** n pl (milit) the use of electronic systems and reflectors to impair the effectiveness of enemy guidance, surveillance or navigational equipment. **electronic data processing** n (comput) the storage and manipulation of electronic data. **electronic flash** n an extremely intense and brief flash for high-speed photography produced by passing an electric charge through a gas-filled tube; the device for producing it. **electronic funds transfer (system)** n a method whereby financial credits and debits are transferred electronically (between banks and shops, etc) by computer network (**electronic funds transfer at point of sale** signifying such a system in operation at a shop checkout, etc, enabling payment by debit or credit card rather than by cash). **electronic ink** n (in an e-reader)

the charged black particles that are used to form the type for reading. **electronic mail** see **email**. **electronic mailbox** n a section of a central computer's memory reserved for a particular individual, into which messages can be directed. **electronic music** n music made by arranging electronically produced sounds either directly from a keyboard, etc, or previously recorded on tape (cf **musique concrète**). **electronic nose** see **e-nose**. **electronic organ** n (music) an organ in which the sound is produced electronically. **electronic piano** n a kind of synthesizer. **electronic point of sale** n (at shop checkouts) a computerized till system in which a cash till with a barcode reader is directly linked to a stock control system (abbrev **EPOS**). **electronic publishing** n the publishing of information such as text and graphics in machine-readable forms. **electronic signature** n (comput) a file that confirms the identity of a computer user to another user of a network (also **e-signature**). **electronic tagging** n a monitoring system allowing the supervision of an offender outside prison by means of an **electronic tag** (eg a bracelet or anklet fitted with a transmitter) which maintains regular signals to a central computer. **electronic ticket** n see **e-ticket**. **electronic waste** n see **e-waste**.

electronystagmography...to...**electrowinning** see under **electro-**.

electrum see **electron**.

electuary /i-lek'tū-ə-ri/ n a medicine mixed with honey or syrup. [LL ēlectuārium, perh from Gr ekleikton from ekleichein to lick up]

eleemosynary /el(-i)-ē-moz'i-nər-i or -mos'/ adj relating to charity or almsgiving; dependent on charity; of the nature of alms. [Gr eleēmosynē alms, from eleos pity; see **alms**]

elegant /el'i-gənt/ adj pleasing to good or discerning taste; very careful or ornate in dress; graceful in form and movement; refined and luxurious; (of style) polished; (of apparatus or work in science or mathematics) simple and effective; excellent (inf). [Fr, from L ēlegāns, -antis, from ē from, and root of legere to choose] ■ **el'egance** or **el'egancy** n the state or quality of being elegant; the finest propriety of manners (archaic); refinement; an exemplification of elegance. **el'egantly** adv.

elegit /i-lē'jit or ā-lā'git/ (law) n a writ of execution, abolished in England in 1956, whereby a debtor's property and lands could be delivered to the plaintiff until the debt was satisfied by profits, rents, etc. [L, he has chosen, from eligere to choose]

elegy /el'i-ji/ n a song of mourning; a funeral song (archaic); a poem of serious, pensive, or reflective mood; a poem written in elegiac metre. [L elegia, from Gr elegeiā from elegos a lament] ■ **elegī'ac** adj belonging to elegy; mournful; used in elegies, esp applied to classical verse in couplets of hexameter and pentameter lines (**elegiac couplets**), or to English verse in two stanzas of four iambic pentameters rhyming abab (**elegiac stanzas**). ◆ n (often in pl) elegiac verse. **elegī'acal** adj. **elegi'acally** adv. **elegiast** /e-lē'ji-ast/ (Goldsmith) or **el'egist** n a writer of elegies. **el'egize** or **-ise** vi to write elegiacally. ◆ vt to write an elegy on.

element /el'ə-mənt/ n a first principle; one of the essential parts of anything; an ingredient; a small amount; the proper medium, habitat or sphere of any thing or being; any one of the four substances, fire, air, earth and water, supposed by the ancients to be the foundation of everything (in China a fifth, wood, was included); (in pl) the rudiments of learning; (usu in pl) the bread and wine used in the Eucharist; a substance that cannot be resolved by chemical means into simpler substances (chem); a member or unit of a structure; a resistance wire in an electric heater, cooker, etc; an electrode; a determining fact or condition in a problem; the sky (archaic); a celestial sphere; (in pl) the weather or the powers of nature. [L elementum, pl elementa, first principle(s)] ■ **elemental** /-ment'l/ adj of or concerned with the elements; belonging to, produced by or inhabiting the elements. ◆ n an elemental spirit; a nature spirit; a disembodied spirit. **element'alism** n the worship of elemental spirits; the theory which resolves the divinities of antiquity into the elemental powers. **element'ally** adv. **elementar'ily** adv. **element'ariness** n. **element'ary** adj of a single element; primary or fundamental; rudimentary; simple; uncompounded; of or relating to the elements; dealing with first principles. ❑ **elemental spirits** n pl beings in medieval belief who presided over the four elements, living in and ruling them. **elementary particle** n any of three subatomic particles, electron, quark and gauge boson, so called because they are held to be indivisible. **elementary school** n a school in which the first years of formal education are given, obs in the UK since 1944, but still current in N America. ■ **elements of an orbit** (maths) the data mathematically necessary to determine it. **in one's element** in the surroundings most natural or pleasing to one.

elemi /el'i-mi/ n a fragrant resinous substance obtained from various tropical trees, esp a species of Canarium, used esp in varnishes and inks. [Perh Ar]

elenchus /i-leng'kəs/ (*logic*) *n* (pl **elench'ī**) refutation; a sophism. [L, from Gr *elenchos*, from *elenchein* to refute]
■ **elench** /i-lengk'/ *n* (*obs*). **elenc'tic** *adj* relating to argument, cross-examining or refuting.

elephant /el'i-fənt/ *n* a mammal (genus *Elephas*) of the order Proboscidea, the largest living land mammal, with a very thick skin, a trunk, and ivory tusks, found in two surviving species, the **African elephant** which has larger ears and a flatter head than the **Indian** or **Asian elephant**, and in several extinct species; a size of paper before metrication. [Remodelled after L from ME *olifaunt*, from OFr *olifant*, or poss OE *olfend* camel, from L *elephantus*, *elephās*, from Gr *elephās*, *-antos*]
■ **elephantī'asis** *n* (Gr *elephantiāsis*) a disease chiefly of tropical climates, causing excessive growth of the skin and connective tissue usually of the legs and scrotum. **elephant'ine** *adj* of or relating to an elephant; like an elephant; very large or ungainly; (of memory) capacious and reliable. **elephant'oid** *adj* elephant-like.
❑ **elephant cord** *n* thick, wide-ribbed corduroy. **elephant folio** *n* a folio of the largest size. **elephant grass** *n* a kind of reed-mace, *Typha elephantum*. **elephant gun** *n* a large-calibre rifle designed for killing elephants or other large animals. **elephant seal** *n* the largest of the seals, the male measuring about 6m (20 feet) in length. **el'ephant's-ears** or **-ear** *n* any of various begonias or varieties of ornamental arum with heart-shaped leaves; applied also to other large-leaved plants such as bergenias and species of *Colocasia*. **el'ephant's-foot** *n* a plant (*Testudinaria elephantipes*), whose root-stock resembles an elephant's foot, eaten by the Khoikhoi; a tropical composite plant, *Elephantopus* (from the shape of its radical leaves). **elephant shrew** *n* any member of the African family Macroscelididae, long-nosed, long-legged Insectivora.
■ **pink elephants** hallucinations caused by over-indulgence in alcohol. **white elephant** anything that gives more trouble than it is worth (a (so-called) white elephant being an honourable but onerous gift from the kings of Siam to a courtier they wished to ruin); an unwanted possession, often given away to a jumble sale; something which proves to be useless.

Eleusinian /el-ū-sin'i-ən/ *adj* relating to the town of *Eleusis* in Attica in ancient Greece.
❑ **eleusinian mysteries** *n pl* the religious festivities of Demeter celebrated there.

eleutherian /el-ū-thē'ri-ən/ *adj* freedom-giving. [Gr *eleutheros* free]
■ **eleu'therarch** /-thər-ärk/ *n* (Gr *archos* chief; *Shelley*) the chief of an invented secret society of **eleu'therī**. **eleutherococ'cus** *n* a creeping shrub found in Siberia, from which a drug is prepared that apparently increases stamina and concentration (also **Siberian ginseng**). **eleutherodac'tyl** *adj* (Gr *daktylos* toe) (of birds) having the hind toe free. **eleutheroma'nia** *n* a manic desire for freedom. **eleutheropho'bia** *n* fear of freedom. **eleutheropho'bic** *n* and *adj*.

elevate /el'i-vāt or el'ə-/ *vt* to raise to a higher position; to raise in mind and feelings; to exhilarate. ♦ *adj* (*archaic* or *poetic*) elevated. [L *ēlevāre*, *-ātum*, from *ē* from, and *levāre* to raise, from *levis* light; see **light²**]
■ **el'evated** *adj* raised; lofty; exhilarated; slightly drunk (*inf*). ♦ *n* (*US*) an elevated railroad. **el'evating** *adj*. **elevā'tion** *n* the act of elevating or raising, or the state of being elevated or raised; exaltation; an elevated place; a rising ground; height; the external flat side or face of a building, or a mathematically accurate drawing of it (*archit*); angular height above the horizon; an angle made by a line with the plane of the horizon; a leap with apparent suspension in the air (*ballet*); in the Eucharist, the lifting up (of the Host) in view of the people. **eleva'tional** *adj*. **el'evātor** *n* a person or thing that lifts up; a lift or machine for raising grain, etc, to a higher floor or level; a lift (*N Am*); a storehouse for grain; a muscle raising a part of the body; a movable control surface or surfaces at the tail of an aeroplane by which it is made to climb or dive. **el'evatory** *adj* able or tending to raise. **elevon** /el'ə-vən/ *n* a wing flap on delta wing or tailless aircraft acting both as an *elevator* and as an *aileron*.
❑ **elevated railroad** *n* (*US*) a raised railway over a roadway (*abbrev* **el** or **L**).

eleven /i-lev'n/ *n* the cardinal number next above ten; a symbol representing that number (11, xi, etc); a set of eleven things or people (such as a football or cricket team); a score of eleven points, strokes, tricks, etc; an article of a size denoted by 11; the eleventh hour after midnight or midday; the age of eleven years. ♦ *adj* of the number eleven; eleven years old. [OE *en(d)le(o)fan*; cf Gothic *ainlif*; perh (ten and) *one* left, from the root of L *linquere*, Gr *leipein* to leave]
■ **elev'enses** or **elev'ens** *n pl* (sometimes *sing*; *inf*) an eleven o'clock snack; morning coffee or other refreshment. **elev'enth** *adj* next after the tenth; equal to one of eleven equal parts. ♦ *n* an eleventh part; an octave and a fourth (*music*). **elev'enthly** *adv*.
❑ **eleven-plus** or **eleven-plus examination** *n* formerly, a school examination taken by pupils about the age of eleven to decide to which type of secondary education (academic, non-academic or technical) they were to proceed; this or any similar system of selection, still operated by a few local education authorities in England. **eleventh hour** *n* the very last moment, referring to the Bible, Matthew 20.6,9. **elev'enth-hour** *adj*.

elevon see under **elevate**.

ELF *abbrev*: extremely (or extra) low frequency.

elf /elf/ *n* (pl **elves** /elvz/) in European folklore, a supernatural being, generally of human form but diminutive size, sometimes more malignant than a fairy; a fairy; a dwarf; a mischievous or fairy-like being, *esp* a child. ♦ *vt* (*Shakesp*) to entangle (hair). [OE *ælf*; cf ON *álfr* and Swed *elf*]
■ **elf'hood** *n*. **elf'in** *adj* small, with delicate frame; small, mischievous and charming; relating to a good-natured elf. ♦ *n* a little elf; a child; a small N American butterfly. **elf'ish**, **elv'an**, **elv'en** or **elv'ish** *adj* elf-like or mischievous; tricky; distraught; self-willed.
❑ **elf'-arrow** or **elf'-bolt** *n* an elf-shot. **elf'-child** *n* a changeling, or a child supposed to have been left by elves in the place of one stolen by them. **elf cup** *n* any of several cup-shaped fungi. **elf'land** *n* the land of the elves or fairies. **elf'locks** *n pl* (*Shakesp*) locks of hair tangled together, supposedly by elves. **elf'-shoot** *vt* to shoot with an elf-arrow, bewitch. **elf'-shot** *n* a prehistoric flint or stone arrowhead, supposed to be used by elves; sickness attributed to it. ♦ *adj* shot with an elf-arrow; bewitched.

eliad see œillade.

Elian /ē'li-ən/ *adj* of or like the work of Charles Lamb, who wrote under the name of *Elia*. ♦ *n* a devotee or imitator of Lamb.

elicit /i-, ē- or e-lis'it/ *vt* to draw forth; to evoke. [L *ēlicere*, *ēlicitum*]
■ **elicitā'tion** *n*. **elic'itor** *n*.

elide /ē- or i-līd'/ *vt* to cut off (*esp* a syllable in verse); to suppress or abridge; to rebut (*archaic*). [L *ēlīdere*, *ēlīsum*, from *ē* from, and *laedere* to strike]
■ **elision** /i-lizh'ən/ *n* the suppression of a vowel or syllable; an omission.

Elien. *abbrev*: *Eliensis* (L), of (the diocese of) Ely.

eligible /el'i-ji-bl/ *adj* fit or worthy to be chosen; legally qualified for election or appointment; having a right to something or to do something; desirable. ♦ *n* (*inf*) an eligible person or thing. [Fr, from L *ēligere*; see **elect**]
■ **eligibil'ity** *n*. **el'igibly** *adv*.

eliminate /i-, ē- or e-lim'i-nāt/ *vt* to remove, cancel or get rid of; to expel (waste matter); to kill or murder (*sl*); to thrust out (*archaic*). [L *ēlīmināre*, *-ātum*, from *ē* from, and *līmen*, *-inis* a threshold]
■ **elim'inable** *adj*. **elim'inant** *adj* (*med*) causing elimination of waste or abnormal matter. ♦ *n* an eliminating agent. **eliminā'tion** *n*. **elim'inative** *adj*. **elim'inātor** *n* one who or that which eliminates; *esp* a device for substituting an electric main for a battery in a wireless receiving set. **elim'inatory** *adj*.

ELINT /el'int/ *abbrev*: Electronic *Int*elligence, the branch of military intelligence concerned with monitoring and recording electronic output (cf **COMINT**, **HUMINT**).

ELISA /i-lī'zə/ (*immunol*) *abbrev*: enzyme-linked immunosorbent assay, a laboratory technique, often used diagnostically, that detects the presence of specific antigens or antibodies by binding them to an enzyme.

elision see under **elide**.

élite or **elite** /i-, e- or ā-lēt'/ *n* a chosen or select part or group, the pick or best of anything (in this sense, sometimes used as *pl*); a size of typewriter type allowing twelve letters to the inch. ♦ *adj* of, characteristic of or relating to the élite. [Fr *élite*, from L *ēlecta* (*pars*) chosen (part); see **elect**]
■ **élit'ism** or **elit'ism** *n* (belief in) government by an élite; consciousness of belonging to an élite; the favouring or creation of an élite. **élit'ist** or **elit'ist** *adj* favouring, creating, etc an élite (also *n*).

elixir /i-, ē- or e-lik'sər/ *n* a liquid chemical preparation once supposed to have the power of indefinitely prolonging life (**elixir of life**) or of transmuting metals; the quintessence of anything; a substance which invigorates; a clear, syrupy, alcoholic or flavoured solution masking the taste of an unpalatable medicine; a panacea; a nostrum; a strong tincture; a compound tincture. [LL, from Ar *al-iksīr* the philosopher's stone, from *al-* the, and *iksīr*, prob from Late Gr *xērion* a desiccative powder for wounds, from Gr *xēros* dry]

Elizabethan /i- or e-liz-ə-bē'thən/ *adj* relating to or associated with a Queen *Elizabeth* or her reign, *esp* to the first Queen Elizabeth (1533–1603) or her reign (1558–1603), applied to dress, manners, literature, etc. ♦ *n* a person, *esp* a poet or dramatist, of that age.
■ **Elizabēth'anism** *n*.
❑ **Elizabethan architecture** *n* the mixed style that sprang up on the decline of Gothic, marked by Tudor bow windows and turrets decorated with classic cornices and pilasters, long galleries, enormous

---

■ words derived from main entry word; ❑ compound words; ■ idioms and phrasal verbs

square windows, large apartments, plaster ceilings divided into compartments, etc.

elk /elk/ n (pl **elk** or **elks**) a deer of N Europe and Asia, identical or closely related to the moose of N America, the largest of all living deer; the wapiti (N Am). [Poss OE elh (WSax eolh)]
❑ **elkhorn fern** n a fern of the genus Platycerium, tropical epiphytic ferns with a large leaf like an elk's horn. **elk'hound** n a large strong Norwegian spitz breed of dog with a thick coat and curled tail.
■ **Irish elk** a giant deer now extinct, known from the remains found in the Pleistocene, esp in Ireland.

ell¹ /el/ n a varying measure of length originally taken from the arm; a cloth measure equal to 1¼yd (obs). [OE eln; Du el, Ger Elle, L ulna, Gr ōlenē elbow]
❑ **ell'wand** n a measuring rod.
■ **give him an inch and he'll take an ell** a concession will encourage the taking of liberties.

ell² /el/ same as **el¹**.

ellagic /e-laj'ik/ adj relating to gallnuts, applied to an acid, $C_{14}H_6O_8$. [Fr galle gall, spelt backwards]

ellipse /i- or e-lips'/ (geom) n a figure produced by the section of one branch of a right circular cone by a plane passing obliquely and failing to meet the other branch. [L ellipsis, from Gr elleipsis from elleipein to fall short, from en in, and leipein to leave]
■ **ellip'sis** n (pl **ellip'sēs**) a figure of syntax by which a word or words are left out and merely implied (grammar); the mark (...) indicating ellipsis (printing). **ellip'sograph** n an instrument for drawing ellipses. **ellip'soid** n (geom) a surface of which every plane section is an ellipse or a circle; a solid object of this shape. **ellipsoi'dal** adj. **ellip'tic** or **ellip'tical** adj of or relating to an ellipse; oval; having a part understood; concise or comprehensive; obscure or dubious; (loosely) circumlocutory; rather narrow, slightly acute at each end and broadest in the middle (bot); of or relating to ellipsis. **ellip'tically** adv. **ellipticity** /el-ip-tis'i-ti/ n deviation from the form of a circle or sphere; the difference between the equatorial and polar diameters of the earth.
❑ **elliptic geometry** or **space** n Riemannian geometry or space.

ellops /el'ops/ (obs) n a kind of snake (Milton); a kind of sturgeon (also **el'ops**); a sea-serpent (Goldsmith). [Gr ellops, also elops, elaps perh mute, perh scaly, also an unknown fish and an unknown snake; cf **Elaps, elops**]

elm /elm/ n a tree (genus Ulmus) with serrated leaves unequal at the base and small flowers in clusters appearing before the leaves; its timber (also called **elm'wood**). ◆ adj of elm. [OE elm; Ger Ulme, L ulmus]
■ **elm'en** adj (obs) made of elm. **elm'y** adj full of or covered with elms.

El Niño /el nē'nyō/ n a periodic large-scale warming of the surface of the E Pacific Ocean, esp off the coast of Peru and Ecuador, associated with extreme meteorological phenomena in the Pacific region. [Sp, the child, short for El Niño de Navidad the Christ Child, denoting a warm current observed at Christmas]

Elo /ē'lō/ adj denoting a scale on which the ability of chess-players is assessed, devised by Arpad Elo (1903–92), US professor of physics.
❑ **Elo rating** n. **Elo scale** n.

elocution /el-ə-kū'shən/ n the art of effective speaking, esp public speaking, in terms of enunciation and delivery; eloquence (obs). [L ēlocūtiō, -ōnis, from ēloquī, -cūtus, from ē from, and loquī to speak]
■ **el'ocute** vi (often facetious) to declaim. **elocū'tionary** adj. **elocū'tionist** n a person trained or expert in or practising elocution; a teacher of elocution; a reciter. **eloc'ūtory** adj (rare).

Elodea /e-lō'di-ə/ (bot) n an American genus of Hydrocharitaceae, to which the Canadian waterweed belongs (also called **Helodea**, **Anacharis** and **Phyllotria**). [Gr helōdēs marshy or marsh-dwelling, from helos marsh, and eidos form]

éloge /ā-lōzh'/, **elogium** /ē-lō'ji-əm/ (obs), or **elogy** /el'ə-ji/ (obs) n a funeral oration; a panegyric. [Fr éloge and its source L ēlogium a short statement or an inscription on a tomb, perh confused with eulogy]
■ **el'ogist** n someone who delivers an éloge.

Elohim /e-lō'him/ n a Hebrew name for God. [Heb pl of Eloah, explained as a plural of intensity]
■ **Elō'hist** n the writer or writers of the passages of the Old Testament in which the Hebrew name Elohim (for God) is used instead of Yahweh (Jehovah). **Elohist'ic** adj relating to these passages.

eloin or **eloign** /e-loin'/ (archaic) vt to convey to a distance; to separate and remove. [OFr esloignier (Fr éloigner), from LL ēlongāre; see **elongate**]
■ **eloin'er** or **eloign'er** n. **eloin'ment** or **eloign'ment** n.

elongate /ē'long-gāt or i-long'gāt/ vt to make longer; to extend. ◆ vi to grow longer. [LL ēlongāre, -ātum, from ē from, and longus long]

e'longate or **e'longated** adj long and narrow. **elongā'tion** n the act of lengthening out; distance (obs); the angular distance of a moon or planet from the sun.

elope /e- or i-lōp'/ vi to run away secretly, esp with a lover (usu to get married); to run away or bolt. [Cf ODu ontlōpen, Ger entlaufen to run away]
■ **elope'ment** n. **elō'per** n.

elops /el'ops/ n see **ellops**; (with cap) a genus of fish (family Elopidae) related to the tarpon. [See ety of **ellops**]

eloquent /el'ə-kwənt/ adj having eloquence; persuasive; strongly expressive. [L ēloquēns, -entis, prp of ēloquī to utter]
■ **el'oquence** n the power, art or practice of expressing strong emotion in correct, appropriate, expressive and fluent language; the art of such language; persuasive speech. **el'oquently** adv.

elpee /el-pē'/ (inf) n a long-playing record, a phonetic representation of LP.

Elsan® /el'san/ n a type of portable lavatory in which chemicals are used to kill bacteria and destroy smell. [E L Jackson, the manufacturer, and sanitation]

else /els/ adj (or adv) other (in addition or instead). ◆ adv otherwise; besides; except that mentioned. [OE elles otherwise, orig genitive of el other; cf OHGer alles or elles, L alius, Gr allos other]
■ **elsewhere'** adv in or to another place. **elsewhith'er** adv. **else'wise** adv in a different manner; otherwise.

elsin /el'sin/ or **elshin** /el'shin/ (Scot) n an awl. [From ODu elssene (Mod els); cf **awl**]

ELT abbrev : English language teaching (to non-English speakers).

elt /elt/ (dialect) n a young sow. [Cf **yelt** and **gilt²**]

eltchi see **elchi**.

eluant, eluate see under **elution**.

elucidate /ē-, i-lū'si-dāt or -loo'/ vt to make lucid or clear; to throw light upon; to illustrate. [LL ēlūcidāre, -ātum, from ē- (intens), and lūcidus clear]
■ **elucidā'tion** n. **elu'cidative** or **elu'cidatory** adj making clear; explanatory. **elu'cidator** n.

elucubration an obsolete form of **lucubration**. [L ē- (intens)]

elude /ē-, i-lūd' or -lood'/ vt to escape in a clever or cunning way; to baffle; (of a fact, etc) to fail to be discovered, remembered, etc. [L ēlūdere, ēlūsum, from ē from, and lūdere to play]
■ **elu'der** n. **elu'dible** adj. **elu'sion** /-zhən/ n the act of eluding; evasion. **elu'sive** /-ziv or -siv/ adj practising elusion; difficult to find, catch, understand or remember; deceptive. **elu'sively** adv. **elu'siveness** n. **elu'soriness** n. **elu'sory** adj tending to elude or cheat; evasive; deceitful.

Elul /el'əl or -ūl/ n the 12th month of the Jewish civil year, and 6th of the ecclesiastical. [Heb, from ālal to reap]

elution /ē- or i-loo'shən, or -lū'/ (chem) n purification or separation by washing with a solvent. [L ēlūtiō, -ōnis washing, from ēluere, ēlūtum, from ē from, and luere to wash]
■ **el'uant** or **el'uent** n a liquid used for elution. **el'uate** n liquid obtained by eluting. **elute'** vt. **elu'tor** n a vessel for elution.

elutriate /ē-, i-loo'tri-āt or -lū'/ vt to separate by washing into coarser and finer portions. [L ēlutriāre, -ātum to wash out, from ēluere, from ē from, and luere to wash]
■ **elutriā'tion** n. **elu'triātor** n an apparatus for elutriating.

eluvium /i-, ē-loo'vi-əm or -lū'/ n an accumulation of rock debris formed on the spot or moved by wind only, such as loess. [Formed on the analogy of **alluvium** and **diluvium**; L ē from, and luere to wash]
■ **elu'vial** adj.

ELV abbrev : expendable launch vehicle (see under **expend**).

elvan¹ /el'vən/ n a granular crystalline dyke rock, composed of quartz and orthoclase (also **elv'anite**). [Cornish miners' name; prob Cornish elven spark]

elvan², elven, elves, elvish see **elf**.

elver /el'vər/ n a young eel. [**eelfare** (see **eel**)]

Elysium /ē-, i- or e-liz(h)'i-əm/ n the abode of the blessed dead (Gr myth); any delightful place or state. [L, from Gr elysion (pedion), the Elysian (plain)]
■ **Elys'ian** adj.
❑ **Elysian fields** n pl Elysium.

elytrum /el'i-trəm/ or **elytron** /el'i-tron/ n (pl **el'ytra**) a beetle's forewing modified to form a case for the hindwing; a dorsal plate in certain worms. [Latinized from Gr elytron a sheath]
■ **el'ytral** adj. **elyt'riform** adj. **elytrigerous** /-trij'ər-əs/ adj.

Elzevir /el'zi-vər or -vər/ adj published by the Elzevirs, a celebrated family of printers of Amsterdam, Leyden and other places in Holland, whose small neat editions were chiefly published between

1592 and 1681; of or relating to the type used in their 12mo and 16mo editions of the Latin classics. ◆ *n* a special form of printing type.

em /em/ *n* the thirteenth letter of the modern English alphabet (M or m); a unit of measurement (equal to the width of the lower-case letter 'm' in 12-point) used in spacing material and in estimating dimensions of pages (*printing*).
❑ **em dash** or **em rule** *n* (*printing*) a dash that is one em long, used as a punctuation mark.

em- /em-/ *pfx* a form of **en-** used before *b*, *m* or *p*.

'em /əm/ (*inf*) *pronoun* them; to them. [Orig the unstressed form of *hem*, dative and accusative pl of **he** (OE *him*, *heom* dative pl), but now used informally as if an abbreviation of **them**]

EMA *abbrev* : Engineers' and Managers' Association (now known as Prospect); European Monetary Agreement (abolished in 1972).

emaciate /i-mā'shi-āt or -si-/ *vt* to make extremely thin; to deprive of flesh; to waste. ◆ *vi* to become extremely thin; to waste away. [L *ēmaciāre*, *-ātum*, from *ē-* (intens), and *maciāre* to make lean, from *maciēs* leanness]
■ **emā'ciate** or **ema'ciated** *adj*. **emāciā'tion** *n* the condition of becoming emaciated or extremely thin; thinness.

email or **e-mail** /ē'māl/ *n* (in full **electronic mail**) the sending and receiving of written messages by electronic means; a message sent in this way. ◆ *vt* to send email to; to send by email.
■ **e'mailer** *n*. **e'mailing** *n*.

emalangeni see **lilangeni**.

emanate /em'ə-nāt/ *vi* to flow out of or from anything; to proceed from some source; to arise. [L *ēmānāre*, *-ātum*, from *ē* out from, and *mānāre* to flow]
■ **em'anant** *adj* flowing out. **emanā'tion** *n* a flowing out from a source, such as the universe considered as issuing from the essence of God; the *generation* of the Son and the *procession* of the Spirit, as distinct from the origination of created beings (*theol*); that which issues or proceeds from a source; a radioactive gas given off by radium, thorium and actinium (also called **radon**). **em'anatist** *n* (*theol*) someone who believes in emanation. **em'anative**, **em'anatory** or **emanā'tional** *adj*.

emancipate /e- or i-man'si-pāt/ *vt* to set free from legal, social or political restraint or bondage. [L *ēmancipāre*, *-ātum*, from *ē* away from, and *mancipāre* to transfer property, from *manceps*, *-cipis* someone who gets property, from *manus* the hand, and *capere* to take]
■ **emancipā'tion** *n* the act of setting free from bondage or restraint of any kind; the state of being set free. **emancipā'tionist** *n* an advocate of the emancipation of slaves. **eman'cipātor** *n*. **emancipa'tory** *adj*. **eman'cipist** *n* (*hist*) a convict who has served his time of punishment in a penal colony.

emarginate /ē-mär'ji-nāt/ *vt* to take away the margin of. ◆ *adj* depressed and notched instead of pointed at the tip, such as a leaf (*bot*); having all the edges of the primitive form crossed by a face (*mineralogy*); having the margin broken by a notch or segment of a circle (*zool*). [L *ēmargināre*, *-ātum*, from *ē* out, and *margināre* to provide with a margin, from *margō* a margin]
■ **emarginā'tion** *n*.

emasculate /i- or ē-mas'kū-lāt/ *vt* to deprive of male characteristics; to castrate; to deprive of masculine vigour; to make effeminate; to lessen or take away the power, force or effectiveness of (*fig*). ◆ *adj* emasculated. [LL *ēmasculāre*, *-ātum*, from *ē* from, and *masculus*, dimin of *mās* a male]
■ **emasculā'tion** *n*. **emas'culātor** *n*. **emas'culatory** /-lə-tər-i/ *adj*.

embace see **embase**.

embail /im- or em-bāl'/ (*obs*) *vt* (pap *Spenser* **embayld'**) to encircle; to hoop in. [**em-** (from **en-** (1a))]

embale /im- or em-bāl'/ *vt* to make up, eg into a bale; to bind up; to enclose. [Fr *emballer*, from *em-* (L *in*) in, and *balle* a bale]

emball /em-böl'/ *vt* to ensphere. [**em-** (from **en-** (1a))]
■ **emball'ing** *n* (*Shakesp*) the receiving of the ball (of sovereignty).

embalm /im- or em-bäm'/ *vt* to preserve (*esp* a dead body) from decay by treatment with chemicals or drugs; to preserve with fragrance; to preserve unchanged but lifeless; to impregnate with balm or perfume. [Fr *embaumer*, from *em-* in, and *baume* ; see **balm**]
■ **embalm'er** *n*. **embalm'ing** or **embalm'ment** *n*.

embank /im- or em-bangk'/ *vt* to enclose or defend with a bank or dyke. [**em-** (from **en-** (1a))]
■ **embank'er** *n*. **embank'ment** *n* the act of embanking; a bank or mound made to keep water within certain limits; a mound constructed so as to carry a road or railway over a low-lying place; a slope of grass, earth, etc rising from either side of a road or railway.

embar, also (*obs*) **imbar** /im- or em-bär'/ *vt* (**embarr'ing**; **embarred'**) (*archaic*) to shut in; to hinder or stop; to put under embargo. [**em-** (from **en-** (1a))]
■ **embarr'ing** *n*.

embarcation same as **embarkation** (see under **embark**).

embargo /em-bär'gō/ *n* (pl **embar'goes**) a stoppage of trade for a short time by authority; a prohibition or ban; a temporary order from the Admiralty to prevent the arrival or departure of ships (*hist*). ◆ *vt* (**embar'gōing**; **embar'goed** /-gōd/) to impose an embargo on; to seize for the state (*archaic*). [Sp, from *embargar* to impede or restrain, from Sp pfx *em-* in, and LL (and Sp) *barra* a bar]
■ **embarque'ment** *n* (*Shakesp*) a placing under embargo.

embark /im- or em-bärk'/ *vt* to put on board a ship or an aircraft; to engage or invest in any affair. ◆ *vi* to go on board a ship or an aircraft; to engage in or begin (with (*up*)*on* or *in*). [Fr *embarquer*, from *em-* in, and *barque* bark]
■ **embarkā'tion** /em-/ *n* a putting or going on board; anything which is embarked; a vessel (*obs*). **embarked'** *adj*. **embark'ing** *adj*. **embark'ment** *n*.

embarquement see under **embargo**.

embarras /ã-ba-ra'/ (*Fr*) *n* an embarrassment.
■ **embarras de** or **du choix** /də (dü) shwa/ a perplexing number of things to choose from, (literally) embarrassment in choice. **embarras de** or **des richesses** /də (dā) rē-shes/ a perplexing or disconcerting profusion of wealth or abundance of any kind.

embarrass /im- or em-bar'əs/ *vt* to cause to feel self-conscious, ashamed or awkward; to perplex; to involve in difficulty, *esp* in money matters; to encumber. ◆ *vi* to become self-conscious, ashamed or awkward. [Fr *embarrasser*, from *em-* in, and *barre*, LL *barra* bar]
■ **embarr'assed** *adj* self-conscious, ashamed or awkward; perplexed; constrained. **embarr'assedly** *adv*. **embarr'assing** *adj*. **embarr'assingly** *adv*. **embarr'assment** *n* the state of feeling embarrassed; something which makes one feel embarrassed; difficulties in money matters; a perplexing amount (see **embarras de choix**, etc).

embase or (*Spenser*) **embace**, also **imbase** /im-bās'/ *vt* (pat and pap **embased'** or (*Spenser*) **embaste'**) to lower; to bring down; to degrade; to debase. [**em-** (from **en-** (1b)) and **base**, or Fr *bas* low]
■ **embased'** *adj*. **embase'ment** *n*.

embassy /em'bə-si/ *n* an ambassador's residence or offices; an ambassador and his or her staff; the charge or function of an ambassador; the person or body of persons sent on an undertaking; an important or official mission. [See **ambassador**]
■ **em'bassade** *n* (*Shakesp*) an embassy. ◆ *adv* /-bas'/ (*Spenser*) on an embassy. **embassador** /-bas'/ *n* (*obs*) an ambassador. **em'bassage** *n* embassy; the sending or business of an embassy.

embaste see **embase**.

embathe or **imbathe** /im-bādh'/ (*archaic*) *vt* to bathe; to immerse; to bedew. [**em-** (from **en-** (1c))]

embattle[1] /im-bat'l/ *vt* to arrange in readiness for battle; to arm (*Spenser*). [OFr *embataillier*, from *em-* in, and *bataille* battle]
■ **embatt'led** *adj* arranged for battle; involved in battle (*esp fig*); troubled by problems or difficulties.

embattle[2] /im-bat'l/ *vt* to equip with battlements. [**em-** (from **en-** (1c)) and OFr *bataillier* to embattle; see **battlement**]
■ **embatt'led** *adj* having battlements; having an outline like a battlement (*heraldry*). **embatt'lement** *n* battlement.

embay[1] /im-bā'/ *vt* to enclose in a bay; to force into a bay; to land-lock. [**em-** (from **en-** (1a))]
■ **embay'ment** *n* a bay.

embay[2] /em-bā'/ (*Spenser*) *vt* to bathe, steep or imbue. [Fr *em-* in, and appar *baigner* ; see **bagnio**]

embayld see **embail**.

embed or sometimes **imbed** /im-bed'/ *vt* to place, set or plant firmly in a mass of matter (also *fig*); to lay, as in a bed; to enclose deeply or snugly; to place (a journalist) within a military unit to facilitate the reporting of a conflict; to insert information (an **embedded object**) from one document into another (*comput*). ◆ *n* /em'bed/ a journalist who is given an official placement within a military unit (also **embedded reporter**). [**em-** (from **en-** (1a))]
■ **embedd'ing** *n* (*biol*) the technique in which specimens are embedded in a supporting medium, such as paraffin wax or epoxy resin, in preparation for sectioning with a microtome and viewing with a microscope. **embed'ment** *n* the act of embedding; the state of being embedded.

embellish /im-bel'ish/ *vt* to make beautiful with ornaments; to decorate; to make graceful; to illustrate pictorially (eg a book); to add interesting and possibly untruthful details to (an account,

narrative, etc). [Fr *embellir*, *embellissant*, from *em-* in, and *bel* (*beau*) beautiful]
■ **embell'isher** *n*. **embell'ishingly** *adv*. **embell'ishment** *n* the act of embellishing or adorning; a decoration; ornament; a detail, possibly untrue, added to a story to make it more interesting.

ember /em'bər/ *n* a piece of live coal or wood; (the following definitions chiefly in *pl*) red-hot ashes; the smouldering remains of a fire, or (*fig*) of love, passion, etc. [OE *æmerge* ; ON *eimyrja*]

Ember-days /em'bər-dāz/ *n pl* the three Fast-days (Wednesday, Friday and Saturday) in each quarter, following the first Sunday in Lent, Whitsunday, Holy Cross Day (14 September), and St Lucia's Day (13 December). [OE *ymbryne* a circuit, from *ymb* round (cf Ger *um*, L *ambi-*), and *ryne* a running, from *rinnan* to run]
❑ **Em'ber-week** *n* the week in which they occur.

ember-goose /em'bər-goos/ *n* the great northern diver. [Norw *emmer* ; Ger *Imber*]

embezzle /im-bez'l/ *vt* to appropriate (money or property that has been entrusted to one) fraudulently; to impair (*obs*). [Anglo-Fr *embesiler* to make away with; perh influenced by **imbecile**]
■ **embezz'lement** *n* fraudulent appropriation of money or property entrusted to one. **embezz'ler** *n*.

embitter, also (*archaic*) **imbitter** /im-bit'ər/ *vt* to make bitter or more bitter; to make more bitterly hostile. [**em-** (from **en-** (1b))]
■ **embitt'ered** *adj* soured; having been made misanthropical, cynical or disappointed. **embitt'erer** *n*. **embitt'ering** *n* and *adj*. **embitt'erment** *n*.

emblaze[1] /im-blāz'/ *vt* to light up; to set on fire. [**em-** (from **en-** (1b))]

emblaze[2] /im-blāz'/ *vt* to describe or depict heraldically; to celebrate; to adorn heraldically. [**em-** (from **en-** (1c))]

emblazon /em- or im-blā'zn/ *vt* to adorn with figures (*heraldry*); to depict heraldically; to display in a conspicuous or striking way; to celebrate, glorify or praise. [**em-** (from **en-** (1c))]
■ **emblā'zoner** *n*. **emblā'zonment** *n* an emblazoning. **emblā'zonry** *n* the art of emblazoning or adorning; devices on shields.

emblem /em'bləm/ *n* a symbolic device or badge; a picture representing to the mind something different from itself; a type or symbol; an inlaid ornament (*Milton*). ◆ *vt* (*archaic*) to symbolize. [L, from Gr *emblēma, -atos* a thing inserted, from *en* in, and the root of *ballein* to throw]
■ **emblema** /em-blē'mə/ *n* (*pl* **emblē'mata**) an inlaid ornament. **emblemat'ic** or **emblemat'ical** *adj* relating to or containing emblems; symbolical; representing (with *of*). **emblemat'ically** *adv*. **emblem'atist** *n* a user or inventor of emblems. **emblematize** or **-ise** /-blem'ə-tīz/, **em'blemize** or **-ise** *vt* to represent by an emblem.

emblements /em'bli-mənts/ (*law*) *n pl* crops raised by the labour of the cultivator of land (but not tree-fruits or grass) or the profits arising from these. [OFr *emblaer* to sow with corn, from LL *imbladāre*, from *in* in, and *bladum* wheat]

emblic /em'blik/ *n* (also **emblic myrobalan** /mī-rob'ə-lən or mi-/) an East Indian tree (*Phyllanthus emblica*) of the family Euphorbiaceae; its fruit, used for tanning. [Ar *amlaj*, from Pers *amleh*]

embloom /im-bloom'/ *vt* to cover with bloom. [**em-** (from **en-** (1a))]

emblossom /im-blos'əm/ *vt* to cover with blossom. [**em-** (from **en-** (1a))]

embody, also (*archaic*) **imbody** /im-bod'i/ *vt* (**embod'ying**; **embod'ied**) to form into a body; to make tangible or material; to express (in words, in tangible form, etc); to typify or personify; to make part of a body, to incorporate; to organize. ◆ *vi* to unite in a body or mass; to become corporeal, carnal or sensual. [**em-** (from **en-** (1a))]
■ **embod'ied** *adj*. **embod'iment** *n* the act of embodying; the state of being embodied; that in which something is embodied; the tangible expression of an idea, quality or feeling.

embog /im-bog'/ *vt* to bog. [**em-** (from **en-** (1c))]

embogue /im-bōg'/ *vi* to disembogue.

emboil /em- or im-boil'/ (*obs*) *vi* (*Spenser*) to burn with anger. ◆ *vt* to make burn with anger; to irritate. [**em-** (from **en-** (1c))]

emboîtement /ã-bwät-mã'/ *n* encasement. [Fr]
❑ **emboîtement theory** *n* the abandoned theory of earlier embryologists that the egg contained the germs of all future descendants, box within box.

embolden /im-bōl'dn/ *vt* to make bold or courageous; to give the necessary courage for some action; to set in bold type (*printing*). [**em-** (from **en-** (1b))]
■ **embold'ener** *n*.

embolism /em'bo-li-zm or -bə-/ *n* the presence of one or more obstructing clots, etc in the blood vessels (*med*); an intercalation of days in the calendar to correct error; an intercalated prayer for deliverance from evil coming after the Lord's Prayer. [Late Gr *embolismos* intercalation, from Gr *embolos* a stopper, *embolē* insertion, ramming, from *emballein* to throw in]
■ **embolec'tomy** *n* a surgical removal of an embolus. **embolic** /-bol'/ *adj* relating to an embolus or to an emboly. **embolis'mal** *adj*. **embolis'mic** *adj*. **emboliza'tion** or **-s-** *n* the formation of an embolus. **em'bolize** or **-ise** *vt*. **em'bolus** *n* a clot obstructing a blood vessel. **em'boly** *n* an invagination.
❑ **embolismic year** see under **year**.

embonpoint /ã-bõ-pwẽ'/ *adj* stout, plump or full in figure. ◆ *n* stoutness or plumpness. [Fr, from *en bon point* in good form]

emborder /im- or em-bör'dər/ *vt* (also (*Milton*) **imbord'er**) to set as a border; to border. [**em-** (from **en-** (1c))]

emboscata /em-bo-skä'tə or -skä'tə/ *n* (*non-standard*) an ambush. [Erroneous form of Ital *imboscata* or Sp *emboscada*]

embosom or **imbosom** /im-būz'əm/ *vt* to take into or clasp to the bosom; to receive into the affections; to implant in the bosom or mind; to enclose or surround protectively. [**em-** (from **en-** (1a))]

emboss[1] /im-bos'/ *vt* to raise in relief; to ornament with raised work; to cover with bosses; to raise bosses on. [**em-** (from **en-** (1a))]
■ **embossed'** *adj* raised or standing out in relief; formed or covered with bosses; having a protuberance in the centre (*bot*). **emboss'er** *n*. **emboss'ment** *n* a prominence like a boss; raised work.

emboss[2], also **imboss** /im-bos'/ or **imbosk** /-bosk'/ (*obs*) *vi* (pap **embossed'**, *Milton* **embost'**) to go into the depths of a wood. ◆ *vt* to drive to extremity; to make foam at the mouth. [OFr *embosquer*, from *em-* (L *in* in), and *bosc* a wood; see **ambush**]

emboss[3] /em-bos'/ (*Spenser*) *vt* to clothe; to wrap; to enclose. [Origin obscure]

embouchure /ã-boo-shür'/ *n* the mouth of a river; the mouthpiece of a wind instrument; the positioning of the lips and tongue when playing a wind instrument. [Fr, from *emboucher* to put to the mouth or discharge, from *en* in, and *bouche* a mouth]

embound /em-bownd'/ (*Shakesp*) *vt* to enclose. [**em-** (from **en-** (1a))]

embourgeoise /im-boor'zhwäz or ã-boor-zhwaz'/ *vt* (**embourgeoising**; **embourgeoised**) to cause to become bourgeois or middle-class. [Fr *embourgeoiser* ; see **bourgeois**[1]]
■ **embourgeoisement** /im-boor'zhwäz-mənt or ã-boor-zhwaz-mã/ *n*.

embow /em-bow' or em-bō'/ (*archaic*) *vt* to bend; to arch or vault; to ensphere. [**em-** (from **en-** (1a))]
■ **embowed'** *adj* bent.

embowel /im-bow'əl/ *vt* (**embow'elling**; **embow'elled**) to remove the entrails from, disembowel; to enclose (*obs*); to enclose in, or (*Spenser*) to thrust into, the bowels (*obs*). [**em-** (from **en-** (1a))]
■ **embow'elment** *n*.

embower or **imbower** /im-bow'ər/ *vt* to place in a bower; to shelter, eg with trees. ◆ *vi* to take or give shelter. [**em-** (from **en-** (1a))]
■ **embow'erment** *n*.

embox /im-boks'/ *vt* to set in a box. [**em-** (from **en-** (1a))]

embrace[1] /im-brās'/ *vt* (**embrac'ing**; **embraced'**) to take in the arms; to clasp affectionately to the bosom; to take eagerly or willingly; to comprise, include; to admit, adopt or receive. ◆ *vi* to join in an embrace. ◆ *n* an act of embracing; a loving hug; (in *pl*) sexual intercourse (*archaic*). [OFr *embracer* (Fr *embrasser*), from L *in* in or into, and *brā(c)chium* an arm; see **brace**]
■ **embrace'able** *adj*. **embrace'ment** *n*. **embrac'er** *n*. **embrac'ing** *adj*. **embrac'ingly** *adv*. **embrac'ingness** *n*. **embrac'ive** *adj*.

embrace[2] /em-brās'/ (*Spenser*) *vt* to brace, fasten or bind. [**em-** (from **en-** (1a))]

embracer, **embraceor** or **embrasor** /em-brā'sər/ (*law*) *n* a person who seeks to influence jurors by corrupt means to deliver a partial verdict. [OFr *embraceor*, from *embraser* to set on fire]
■ **embrac'ery** *n* the offence of an embracer.

embraid /em-brād'/ (*Spenser*) *vt* to braid. [**em-** (from **en-** (1c))]

embranchment /im-bränch'mənt or -sh-/ *n* a branching off, such as an arm of a river, a spur of a mountain, etc. [Fr *embranchement*]

embrangle or **imbrangle** /im-brang'gl/ (*archaic*) *vt* to confuse or perplex. [**em-** (from **en-** (1a))]
■ **embran'glement** *n*.

embrasor see **embracer**.

embrasure[1], also **embrazure** /im-brā'zhər/ (*archit*) *n* a recess of a door or window which splays out on the inside; the slant of such a recess; an opening in a wall for cannon to fire through. [Fr, from OFr *embraser* to slope the sides of a window, from *em-* (from L *in*), and *braser* to skew]

embrasure[2] /em-brā'syər/ (*Shakesp*) *n* embrace. [**em-** (from **en-** (1a))]

embrave /em-brāv'/ *vt* to make showy, to decorate (*Spenser*); to inspire with bravery. [**em-** (from **en-** (1b))]

embread /em-brēd'/ (*Spenser*) *vt* to embraid. [**em-** (from **en-** (1c))]

embreathe /em-brēdh'/ (*archaic*) *vt* to breathe into; to breathe in. [**em-** (from **en-** (1a))]

embrewe (*Spenser*) see **imbrue**.

embrittle /im-brit'əl/ (*archaic*) *vt* and *vi* to make or become brittle. [**em-** (from **en-** (1b))]
■ **embrit'tlement** *n*.

embrocate /em'brō-kāt/ *vt* to moisten and rub eg with a lotion. [LL *embrocāre, -ātum*, from Gr *embrochē* a lotion, from *embrechein* to soak or embrocate, from *en-* in or into, and *brechein* to wet]
■ **embrōcā'tion** *n* the act of embrocating; the lotion used.

embroglio see **imbroglio**.

embroider /em- or *im-broi'dər*/ *vt* to ornament with designs in needlework; to add ornament or fictitious detail to. [ME *embrouderie*, from OFr *embroder*; confused with or influenced by OE *bregdan* to weave or braid]
■ **embroid'erer** *n*. **embroid'ery** *n* the art of producing ornamental designs in needlework on textile fabrics, etc; ornamental needlework; articles decorated with this work; variegation or diversity; artificial or elaborate ornamentation; embellishment; exaggeration or invented detail.

embroil /im-broil'/ *vt* to involve in a dispute or in perplexity (with); to entangle; to distract; to throw into confusion. [Fr *embrouiller*, from pfx *em-*, and *brouiller* to break out]
■ **embroil'ment** *n* a state of perplexity or confusion; disturbance.

embrown or **imbrown** /im-brown'/ *vt* to make brown; to darken or obscure. [**em-** (from **en-** (1b))]
■ **embrown'ing** *adj*.

embrue see **imbrue**.

embrute see **imbrute**.

embryo /em'bri-ō/, also (*archaic*) **embryon** /em'bri-on/ *n* (*pl* **em'bryos** or **em'bryons**) a young animal or plant in its earliest stages of development; the beginning of anything. ◆ *adj* embryonic. [LL, from Gr *embryon*, from *en* in, and *bryein* to swell]
■ **embryogen'ic** *adj*. **embryogen'esis** or **embryogeny** /-oj'i-ni/ *n* the formation and development of the embryo. **em'bryoid** *n* (*bot*) an embryo-like structure produced in tissue culture. **embryolog'ic** or **embryolog'ical** *adj*. **embryolog'ically** *adv*. **embryol'ogist** *n*. **embryol'ogy** *n* the science of the formation and development of embryos. **em'bryonal** *adj* embryonic. **em'bryonate** or **em'bryonated** *adj* (*obs*) (of minerals, etc) embedded in other material. **embryon'ic** or **embryot'ic** *adj* of or relating to an embryo; in an early stage of development; rudimentary. **embryon'ically** or **embryot'ically** *adv*. **em'bryophyta** *n pl* (*bot*) a major division of the plants, including the mosses and vascular plants. **embryot'omy** *n* (Gr *tomē* a cut) the division of a fetus to effect removal. **embryulcia** /-ul'shi-ä/ *n* (Gr *holkē* dragging) forcible extraction of a fetus.
❑ **em'bryo-sac** *n* the megaspore of a flowering plant, one of the cells of the nucellus. **embryo transfer** *n* surgical transfer of the young embryo into the uterus, a technique used in the treatment of infertility (*abbrev* **ET**).

embus /im-bus'/ *vt* (**embuss'ing**; **embussed'**) to put (*esp* troops) onto a bus. ◆ *vi* to board a bus. [**em-** (from **en-** (1a))]

embusqué /ä-büs-kā'/ (*Fr*) *adj* in ambush. ◆ *n* a slacker or shirker; a person who evades military service.

embusy /em-biz'i/ (*Spenser*) *vt* to occupy or make busy. [**em-** (from **en-** (1b))]

emcee /em-sē'/ (*inf*) *n* a master of ceremonies, a phonetic representation of the abbrev **MC**. ◆ *vi* and *vt* to act as a master of ceremonies (for).

eme /ēm/ (*obs*) *n* an uncle. [OE *ēam*; Du *oom*]

EMEA *abbrev*: European Medicines Evaluation Agency.

emeer see **emir**.

emend /ē-mend'/ *vt* to make alterations in with a view to improving (a text); to remove faults or blemishes from (now *rare*). [L *ēmendāre, -ātum*, from *ē* from, and *mendum* a fault]
■ **ēmend'able** *adj* that may be emended. **ēmend'als** *n pl* (*law*; *obs*) funds set apart for repairs, in the accounts of the Inner Temple. **ē'mendate** *vt* to correct errors. **ēmenda'tion** *n* the removal of an error or fault; correction. **ē'mendātor** *n* a person who corrects errors in writings; a person who corrects or improves. **ēmen'datory** *adj* mending or contributing to correction.

emerald /em'ə-rəld/ (*Spenser* **emeraude**) *n* a gemstone, a beautiful velvety green variety of beryl; (also **emerald green**) its colour. ◆ *adj* made of emerald; of the colour of emerald. [OFr *esmeralde*, from L *smaragdus*, from Gr *smaragdos*]
❑ **em'erald-copper** *n* dioptase. **em'erald-cut** *n* in gemstones, a multifaceted flat-topped rectangular cut (also *adj*). **Emerald Isle** *n*

Ireland, from its greenness. **emerald moth** *n* any of various bright-green moths. **emerald type** *n* (*printing*) a small size of type.

emerge /i- or ē-mûrj'/ *vi* to rise out of anything; to issue or come out; to reappear after being concealed; to come into view; to become known or apparent; to come into being in the course of evolution; to crop up. [L *ēmergere, ēmersum*, from *ē* out of, and *mergere* to plunge]
■ **emer'gence** *n* the act of emerging; a sudden or first appearance; an emergency (*obs*); an outgrowth from a plant, derived from epidermal and cortical tissues, which does not contain vascular tissue or develop into a stem or leaf (*bot*); the appearance above ground of germinating seedlings, as in *pre-emergence* and *post-emergence* (*bot*); in insects, the appearance of the imago from the cocoon, pupa-case or pupal integument. **emer'gency** *n* an unexpected occurrence, requiring immediate action; a patient needing immediate medical treatment; pressing necessity; emergence (*obs*); a substitute in reserve. ◆ *adj* of, relating to or used in an emergency. **emer'gent** *adj* emerging; suddenly appearing; arising unexpectedly; urgent; coming into being in the course of evolution; (of a state) having recently become independent. **emer'gently** *adv*. **emer'ging** *adj* developing; becoming important. **emerse** /ē-mûrs'/ or **emersed** /-mûrst'/ *adj* (*bot*) (eg of leaves) rising above the surface of water. **emer'sion** /-shən/ *n* the act of emerging; the reappearance of a heavenly body after eclipse or occultation (*astron*).
❑ **emergency exit** *n* an exit to be used only in an emergency, eg fire. **emergency room** *n* (*N Am*) the department in a hospital that deals with accidents and emergencies. **emergency services** *n pl* the police, fire and ambulance services collectively. **emerging market** *n* a developing country that recognizes and is adopting the benefits of capital funding and investment.
■ **state of emergency** a situation in which a government suspends the normal constitution in order to deal with an emergency such as a natural disaster or civil disorder.

emeritus /i- or ē-mer'i-təs/ *adj* (often following a noun) honourably discharged from the performance of public duty, *esp* denoting a retired professor. ◆ *n* (*pl* **emer'itī**) a person who has been honourably discharged from public duties. [L *ēmeritus* having served one's time, from *ēmerērī* to earn, from *ē-* (signifying completeness) and *merērī* to deserve]

emerse, **emersion** see under **emerge**.

emery /em'ə-ri/ *n* a very hard mineral, a variety of corundum, used as powder for polishing, etc. ◆ *vt* to rub or coat with emery. [OFr *esmeril, emeril*, from LL *smericulum*, from Gr *smēris, smỹris*]
❑ **emery bag** *n* a bag of emery powder for cleaning and sharpening needles. **emery board** *n* a small flat strip of wood or card coated with emery powder, used for filing the fingernails. **emery cloth** or **paper** *n* cloth or paper covered with emery powder for polishing. **emery powder** *n* ground emery. **emery wheel** *n* a wheel coated with emery for polishing.

emetic /i-met'ik/ (*med*) *adj* causing vomiting. ◆ *n* a medicine that causes vomiting. [Gr *emetikos*, from *emeein* to vomit]
■ **emesis** /em'i-sis/ *n* vomiting. **emet'ical** *adj*. **emet'ically** *adv*. **em'etin** or **em'etine** *n* the alkaloid forming the active constituent of the ipecacuanha root, violently emetic. **emetophō'bia** *n* a pathological fear of vomiting.

emeu see **emu**.

émeute /ā-mœt', sometimes *i-mūt'*/ *n* a popular rising or uproar. [Fr]

EMF *abbrev*: electromagnetic field; electromotive force (also **emf**).

EMG *abbrev*: electromyogram or electromyograph.

EMI *abbrev*: electromagnetic interference (also **emi**); Electrical and Musical Industries; European Monetary Institute, now replaced by **ECB**.

emicate /em'i-kāt/ *vi* to sparkle. [L *ēmicāre, -ātum*]
■ **em'icant** *adj* sparkling; flashing. **emicā'tion** *n*.

emiction /i-mik'shən/ *n* the discharging of urine. [L *ēmingere, ēmictum*, from *ē* from, and *mingere* to urinate]
■ **emic'tory** *adj* promoting the flow of urine.

emigrate /em'i-grāt/ *vi* and *vt* to move from one country or state and settle permanently in another. [L *ēmīgrāre, ēmigrāre, -ātum*, from *ē* from, and *migrāre* to remove]
■ **em'igrant** *adj* belonging or related to emigrants; emigrating or having emigrated. ◆ *n* someone who emigrates or has emigrated. **emigrā'tion** *n*. **emigrā'tional** *adj*. **emigrā'tionist** *n* an advocate or promoter of emigration. **em'igrātory** *adj*. **émigré** /ā-mē-grā'/ *n* an (*esp* political) emigrant; *orig* a royalist who fled from France during the Revolution.

éminence grise /ā-mē-näs grēz'/ (*Fr*) *n* someone exercising power in the background, as did Cardinal Richelieu's private secretary and alter ego Père Joseph, nicknamed l'*Éminence Grise* ('the Grey Eminence').

eminent /em'i-nənt/ adj distinguished; famous and admired; exalted in rank or office; rising above others; conspicuous. [L ēminēns, -entis, prp of ēminēre, from ē from, and minēre to project]
■ **em'inence** n a part eminent or rising above the rest; a rising piece of ground; a ridge or knob; height; distinction; a title given in 1631 to cardinals, previously styled Most Illustrious; advantage or upper hand (Shakesp). **em'inency** n. **eminen'tial** /-shəl/ adj (obs). **em'inently** adv in an eminent manner; very; obviously.
❑ **eminent domain** n the right by which the supreme authority in a state may appropriate an individual's property for public use.

emir /ā-mēr', sometimes ē'mər/ n a title given in Islamic countries to all independent rulers, and also (perh improperly) to all the supposed descendants of Mohammed through his daughter Fatima (also **ameer**, **amir** /a-mēr', ə-/ or **emeer**). [Ar amīr ruler]
■ **emir'ate** (or /em'i-rit/) n the office, jurisdiction, or state of an emir. **Emira'ti** adj of or relating to federation of the United Arab Emirates in the Arabian Peninsula, or its inhabitants. ◆ n a native or citizen of the United Arab Emirates.

Emi-Scanner® /em'i-skan-ər/ n a machine which produces computer-assisted X-ray pictures of the head or body. [EMI]

emit /i- or ē-mit'/ vt (**emitt'ing**; **emitt'ed**) to send out; to throw or give out; to issue; to utter (a declaration). [L ēmittere, ēmissum, from ē out of, and mittere to send]
■ **emissary** /em'is-ər-i/ n someone sent out on a mission, esp on behalf of a government or state; an agent sent out on a secret mission; a spy; an underground outlet, esp of a lake. ◆ adj sent out; outgoing. **emiss'ile** adj able to be pushed out or forward. **emission** /-mish'ən/ n the act of emitting; that which is issued at one time; the discharge of semen or other fluid from the body; the release of electrons from parent atoms on absorption of energy above the average electron energy (phys). **emiss'ive** adj emitting or sending out. **emissiv'ity** /ē-/ n the ratio of emissive power of a surface at a given temperature to that of a black body at the same temperature and with the same surroundings. **emitt'er** n in a transistor, the region from which charge carriers are injected into the base.
❑ **emission current** n (electronics) the total electron flow from an emitting source. **emission spectrum** n the wavelength distribution of electromagnetic radiation emitted by a self-luminous source. **emission theory** n the corpuscular theory of light (qv under **corpus**).

emma /em'ə/ n formerly, a signaller's name for the letter m.

Emmanuel or **Immanuel** /i-man'ū-əl or -el/ (Bible) the symbolic name of the child announced by Isaiah (Bible, Isaiah 7.14) and applied to Jesus as the Messiah in Matthew 1.23. [Gr Emmanouēl, from Heb 'Immānūēl, from 'im with, ānū us, and ēl God]

emmarble /i-mär'bl/ vt to turn to marble; to represent in marble; to adorn with marble. [**em-** (from **en-** (1b))]

emmenagogue /e-mē'nə-gog or -me'/ n a drug or substance intended to restore or to bring on menstruation (also adj). [Gr emmēna menstruation, (from mēn a month) and agōgos drawing forth]
■ **emmenagogic** /-goj'ik/ adj. **emmenol'ogy** n the study of menstruation.

Emmental or **Emmenthal** /em'ən-täl/, also **Emmentaler** or **Emmenthaler** /-ər/ n a hard Swiss cheese, similar to Gruyère, made in the Emmental or Emme valley.

emmer /em'ər/ n a species of wheat, Triticum dicoccum. [Ger dialect]

emmesh see **enmesh**.

emmet /em'it/ (archaic and dialect) n an ant; in Cornwall, a tourist. [OE æmete]

emmetropia /em-e-trō'pi-ə/ n the normal condition of the refractive media of the eye. [Gr en in, metron measure, and ops the eye]
■ **emm'etrope** n an emmetropic person. **emmetropic** /-trop'ik/ adj having normal vision.

emmew, **immew** /i-mū'/ or **enmew** /in-mū'/ vt to confine; in Shakespeare, appar for **enew**. [**em-** (from **en-** (1a))]

emmove /e-moov'/ (Spenser) vt to move or excite (also **enmove**).

Emmy /em'i/ n (pl **Emm'ys** or **Emm'ies**) a television trophy, corresponding to the cinema Oscar, awarded annually by the American Academy of Television Arts and Sciences. [Origin uncertain]

emo /ē'mō/ n a type of guitar-based popular music featuring brooding and introspective lyrics (also adj). [Shortening of emotional hardcore]

emoji /i-mō'ji/ n (pl **emo'jis** or **emo'ji**) a standardized image with a specific meaning, used in electronic communication. [Jap, picture letter]

emollient /i-mol'yənt/ adj softening; making supple; advocating a calmer, more peaceful attitude. ◆ n (med) a softening application such as a poultice, fomentation, etc. [L ēmollīre, ēmollītum, from ē (intens), and mollīre to soften, from mollis soft]

■ **emollesc'ence** n incipient fusion. **emoll'iate** vt to soften; to make effeminate. **emolli'tion** n the act of softening or relaxing.

emolument /i-mol'ū-mənt/ n (often in pl) profit arising from employment, such as salary or fees; advantage (obs). [L ēmolimentum, prob from ēmolere to grind out, from ē- and molere to grind, rather than from ēmōlīrī to work out, from mōlīrī to toil]
■ **emolumen'tal** adj. **emolumen'tary** adj.

emong, **emonges**, **emongest**, **emongst** obs forms of **among**, **amongst**.

emoticon /i-mō'ti-kon/ n (comput) a combination of characters used to express a personal feeling (such as pleasure or anger) in email, etc. [**emotion** and **icon**]

emotion /i-mō'shən/ n a moving of the feelings; agitation of mind; any of various phenomena of the mind, such as anger, joy, fear or sorrow, associated also with physical symptoms; feeling as distinguished from cognition and will (philos). [L ēmōtiō, -ōnis, from ēmovēre, -mōtum to stir up]
■ **emote** /i-mōt'/ vi to show or express exaggerated emotion. **emō'ter** n. **emō'tionable** adj. **emō'tional** adj. **emō'tionalism** n a tendency to emotional excitement (also **emotional'ity**); the habit of working on the emotions; the indulgence of superficial emotion. **emō'tionalist** n. **emō'tionalistic** adj. **emotionalize** or **-ise** vt. **emō'tionally** adv. **emō'tionless** adj. **emo'tionlessly** adv. **emō'tive** /-tiv/ adj of or relating to the emotions; emotional; tending to arouse emotion. **emō'tively** adv. **emō'tiveness** n. **emō'tivism** n (ethics) the theory that moral statements express the emotions of the speaker rather than an objective accepted truth. **emō'tivist** n. **emōtiv'ity** n. **emove** /i-moov'/ vt (archaic) to affect with emotion.
❑ **emotional intelligence** n the ability to perceive and assess the emotions of oneself and others.

Emp. abbrev : Emperor; Empire; Empress.

empacket /im-pak'it/ (Walter Scott) vt to pack up. [**em-** (from **en-** (1c))]

empaestic /em-pē'stik/ adj relating to the art of embossing; stamped or inlaid. [Gr empaiein to emboss]

empaire (Spenser) see **impair¹**.

empale /em-pāl'/ see **impale**.

empanada /em-pə-nä'də/ n in Spanish and Latin American cookery, a light pasty with a usu savoury filling. [Sp, from empanar to roll in pastry]

empanel, also **impanel** or **impannel** /im-pan'əl/ vt (**empan'elling**; **empan'elled**) to enter (the names of a prospective jury) on a list; to select (a jury) from such a list. [**em-** (from **en-** (1a))]
■ **empan'elment** n.

empanoply /im-pan'o-pli/ vt to clothe in full armour. [**em-** (from **en-** (1a))]

emparadise (Milton) see **imparadise**.

empare (Spenser) see **impair¹**.

emparl, **emparlaunce** see under **imparl**.

empart (Spenser) see **impart**.

empassionate, **empassioned** (Spenser) see **impassion**.

empathy /em'pə-thi/ n the power of entering into another's personality and imaginatively experiencing his or her experiences; the power of entering into the feeling or spirit of something (esp a work of art) and so appreciating it fully. [Gr en in, and pathos feeling]
■ **empathet'ic** adj. **empathet'ically** adv. **empath'ic** adj. **empath'ically** adv. **em'pathize** or **-ise** vi.

empatron /em-pā'trən/ (Shakesp) vt to patronize. [**em-** (from **en-** (1c))]

empayre (Spenser) see **impair¹**.

empeach (Spenser) see **impeach**.

empennage /em-pen'ij or ã-pe-näzh'/ n an aeroplane's tail unit, including elevator, rudder and fin. [Fr, the feathering of an arrow, from L penna feather or wing]

empeople /im-pē'pl/ (obs) vt to fill with people; to form into a people or community. [**em-** (from **en-** (1a))]

emperce see **empierce**.

emperish /im-per'ish/ (Spenser, etc) vt to impair. [Perh (irreg) from Fr empirer; cf **impair¹**]

emperor /em'pə-rər/ n (also fem **em'press**) the head of an empire; a high title of sovereignty; before metrication, a paper size (48 × 72in). [OFr emperere, from L imperātor a commander (fem imperātrix), from imperāre to command]
■ **em'perize** or **-ise** vt (obs) to play the emperor. **em'perorship** n. **em'pery** n (esp poetic) empire or power.
❑ **emperor moth** n the second largest British moth, with a wingspan of about three inches. **emperor penguin** n the largest of the penguins.

Empfindung /em-pfin'dŏong/ (Ger) n sensation or feeling.

emphasis /em'fə-sis/ n (pl **em'phases** /-sēz/) forcible or impressive expression; an insistent or vigorous way of attributing importance or enforcing attention; stress; accent; prominence; the use of language to imply more than is said (obs). [Gr emphasis image, outward appearance, significance or implied meaning, from en in, and phainein to show]

■ **em'phasize** or **-ise** vt to make emphatic; to lay stress on. **emphat'ic** /im- or em-fat'ik/ adj (also (rare) **emphat'ical**) expressed or expressing with emphasis; stressed forcibly; impressive; strongly marked; of some Arabic consonants, pronounced with dental articulation and accompanying pharyngeal constriction (linguistics). ◆ n (linguistics) an emphatic consonant. **emphat'ically** adv. **emphat'icalness** n.

emphlysis /em'fli-sis/ n (pl **em'phlyses**) a vesicular eruption. [Gr en in, and phlysis eruption, from phlȳein to bubble or break out]

emphractic /em-frak'tik/ adj blocking the pores of the skin. ◆ n a substance with this property. [Gr emphraktikos obstructive, from en in, and phrassein to stop]

emphysema /em-fi-sē'mə/ (med) n an unnatural distension of a part of the body with air; distension of the lung, with breathing difficulties, etc. [Gr emphȳsēma, from emphȳsaein to inflate]

■ **emphysē'matous** adj. **emphysē'mic** n someone suffering from emphysema.

emphyteusis /em-fi-tū'sis/ n in Roman law, a perpetual right to use a piece of land, for which a yearly sum was paid to the proprietor. [Gr, from emphyteuein to implant]

■ **emphyteu'tic** adj.

empiecement /em-pē'smənt/ n an insertion in a garment. [Fr empiècement]

empierce or **emperce** /em-pērs'/ (Spenser) vt to pierce. [**em-** (from **en-** (1c))]

empight /em-pīt'/ (Spenser) adj fixed. [**pitch**[1]]

empire /em'pīr/ n a dominion or group of states, peoples, nations, etc under the same sovereign power (esp an emperor) and spread over an extended area; supreme control or dominion; the government or office of an emperor; the time of the duration of an empire; a large industrial organization embracing many firms; that part of an organization, etc under the management of a particular person or group; a country whose sovereign owes no allegiance to another (hist). ◆ adj (usu with cap, esp of dress or furniture) relating to or in the style of the first French Empire (1804–14). [Fr, from L imperium]

❑ **em'pire-builder** n. **em'pire-building** n the practice or policy of increasing one's power or authority (also adj). **Empire Day** n formerly, a public holiday celebrated on or near 24 May (Queen Victoria's birthday). **Empire gown** n a gown with low neckline and high waist such as was worn during the first French Empire. **em'pire-line** adj in the style of an Empire gown.

empiric /em-pir'ik/, formerly em' / adj empirical. ◆ n a person who makes trials or experiments; someone whose knowledge is obtained from experience only; a quack. [Fr, from L empīricus, from Gr empeirikos, from en in, and peira a trial]

■ **empir'ical** adj depending on trial or experiment; known or knowing only by experience. **empir'ically** adv. **empir'icism** /-sizm/ n the system which accepts only knowledge based on direct experience (philos); the practice of empirical methods; the dependence of a physician on experience alone without a regular medical education; the practice of medicine without a regular education; quackery. **empir'icist** /-sist/ n someone who practises empiricism (also adj). **empiricūt'ic** (Shakesp **emperick qutique**) adj (modelled on therapeutic; obs) empirical.

❑ **empirical formula** n (chem) a formula showing in simplest form the ratio of atoms in a molecule, giving no structural information.

emplacement /im-plā'smənt/ n the act of placing; a gun-platform (milit). [Fr emplacement]

■ **emplace'** vt (back-formation) to put in or provide with an emplacement.

emplane /im-plān'/ or **enplane** /in-/ vt to put or take on an aeroplane. ◆ vi to board an aeroplane. [**em-** (from **en-** (1a)) and **plane**[1]]

emplaster /em-plä'stər/ (obs) n and v plaster. [OFr emplastre(r), from L emplastrum]

■ **emplastic** /-plas'/ adj glutinous; adhesive. ◆ n a medicine that blocks the pores. **emplas'tron** (Gr) or **emplas'trum** (L) n a medicated plaster.

empleach see **impleach**.

emplecton /em-plek'ton/ (archaic) n ashlar masonry filled up with rubble (also **emplec'tum**). [Gr emplekton, from en in, and plekein to weave]

emplonge (Spenser) see **implunge**.

employ /im-ploi'/ vt to give work to; to use as a means or agent; to occupy the time or attention of. ◆ n employment. [Fr employer, from

L implicāre to enfold, from in in, and plicāre to fold; cf **imply** and **implicate**]

■ **employabil'ity** n. **employ'able** adj fit or able to be employed. **employed'** adj having employment, in a job. **employ'ee** (or /em-ploi-ē'/) n a person employed. **employ'er** n. **employ'ment** n the act of employing; occupation; something which engages or occupies.

❑ **employment agency** n an agency which finds work for the unemployed and employees for vacant positions. **employment office** n a job centre. **Employment Service** n a former government agency for helping unemployed people find work (now replaced by Jobcentre Plus).

emplume /im-ploom'/ (archaic or poetic) vt to provide with a plume. [**em-** (from **en-** (1a))]

empoison /em- or im-poi'zn/ (archaic) vt to put poison into; to poison (obs); to embitter or corrupt. [**em-** (from **en-** (1a))]

■ **empoi'soned** adj. **empoi'sonment** n.

empolder see **impolder**.

emporium /em-pö'ri-əm/ n (pl **empö'ria** or **empö'riums**) a commercial or trading centre or mart; a large shop that sells a wide variety of goods. [L, from Gr emporion a trading station, from emporos a wayfarer or trader, from en in, and poros a way]

empoverish obsolete form of **impoverish**.

empower /im-pow'ər/ vt to authorize. [**em-** (from **en-** (1a))]

■ **empow'erment** n the giving to individuals of power to take decisions in matters relating to themselves, esp (in an organization) in relation to self-development.

empress see **emperor**.

empressement /ã-pres-mä'/ (Fr) n demonstrative warmth of manner. ■ **empressé** /-pres-ā/ adj (Fr) eager or enthusiastic.

emprise /em-prīz'/ (archaic) n an enterprise; a dangerous undertaking. [OFr emprise, from pap fem of emprendre, from L in in, and praehendere to take]

emption /emp'shən/ n the act of buying, purchase. [L emptiō, -ōnis, from emere to buy]

■ **emp'tional** adj.

empty /emp'ti/ adj having nothing inside; unoccupied; unfurnished; without effect; unsatisfactory; lacking substance; meaningless; empty-headed; hungry (inf); devoid (of; Shakesp with in). ◆ vt (**emp'tying; emp'tied**) to make empty; to deprive of contents; to remove from a receptacle. ◆ vi to become empty; to discharge. ◆ n (pl **emp'ties**) an empty container, esp a bottle or glass. [OE ǣmetig, from ǣmetta leisure or rest; the p is excrescent]

■ **emp'tier** n. **emp'tily** adv. **emp'tiness** n the state of being empty; lack of substance; unsatisfactoriness; inanity. **emp'tying** n.

❑ **empty-hand'ed** adj bringing or taking away nothing or no gift. **empty-head'ed** adj frivolous. **empty-nest'er** n (inf) a parent whose children have left the parental home.

emptysis /emp'ti-sis/ n spitting, esp of blood. [Gr emptysis spitting, from en in, and ptyein to spit]

empurple /em- or im-pûr'pl/ vt to dye or tinge purple. [**em-** (from **en-** (1b))]

Empusa /em-pū'zə/ n a goblin or spectre sent by Hecate (Gr myth; also without cap; also **empuse'**); a genus of fungi parasitic upon houseflies and other insects. [Gr Empousa]

empyema /em-pī-ē'mə or -pi-/ n a collection of pus in any cavity, esp the pleura. [Gr empyēma, empyēsis, from en in, and pyon pus]

■ **empye'mic** adj. **empyesis** /-ē'sis/ n an eruption on the skin containing pus.

empyreal /em-pi-rē'əl/ or (Milton, Pope) /em-pir'i-əl/ adj formed of pure fire or light; of or relating to the highest and purest region of heaven; sublime. [Gr empyros fiery, from en in, and pȳr fire]

■ **empyre'an** adj empyreal. ◆ n the highest heaven, where the pure element of fire was supposed to subsist; the heavens.

empyreuma /em-pi-rū'mə/ n (pl **empyreu'mata**) the smell and taste that occur when vegetable or animal substances are burned. [Gr empȳreuma, -atos embers, from en in, and pȳr fire]

■ **empyreumat'ic** or **empyreumat'ical** adj. **empyreu'matize** or **-ise** vt.

EMS abbrev : Emergency Medical Service; Enhanced Messaging (or Message) Service (for mobile phones); European Monetary System; expanded memory system (comput).

EMU abbrev : Economic and Monetary Union or European Monetary Union; electric multiple unit (also **emu**); electromagnetic unit (also **emu**).

emu or **emeu** /ē'mū/ n a flightless, fast-running Australian bird, Dromaius novaehollandiae, the largest living bird after the ostrich. [Port ema an ostrich]

❑ **emu wren** n a small Australian bird (genus Stipiturus) with tail feathers structurally similar to those of the emu.

emulate /em'ū-lāt/ vt to try to equal or surpass (esp a person or thing that one admires); to rival successfully; (loosely) to imitate; (of a computer or program) to reproduce the action or function of (a different computer or program). ◆ adj (Shakesp) ambitious, eager to rival. [L aemulārī, -ātus, from aemulus emulous] ■ **emulā'tion** n the act of emulating or attempting to equal or excel; rivalry; competition; contest; jealous rivalry (obs). **em'ulātive** adj inclined to emulation, rivalry or competition. **em'ulātor** n someone or something that emulates; a computer program that imitates the internal design of a microprocessor-based device. **em'ulātress** n (obs). **em'ule** vt (Southey) to emulate. **em'ulous** adj eager to emulate; keen to achieve or obtain the same success or excellence as someone else; engaged in competition or rivalry. **em'ulously** adv. **em'ulousness** n.

emulge /i-mulj'/ (archaic) vt to milk or drain out. [See emulsion] ■ **emul'gence** n. **emul'gent** adj (med) acting as a drain for.

emulsion /i-mul'shən/ n a colloidal suspension of one liquid in another; a light-sensitive coating on photographic plates; a liquid mixture containing globules of fat (such as milk), or of resinous or bituminous material; emulsion paint. ◆ vt (inf) to apply emulsion paint to something. [L ēmulgēre, ēmulsum to milk out, from ē from, and mulgēre to milk] ■ **emulsifi'able** adj. **emulsificā'tion** n. **emul'sifīer** n a chemical which forms or preserves an emulsion, esp one used as a food additive to prevent the constituents of processed foods separating out; an apparatus for preparing emulsions. **emul'sify** vt and vi. **emul'sin** n an enzyme obtained from bitter almonds. **emul'sionize** or **-ise** vt. **emul'sive** adj. **emul'soid** n an easily dispersed colloid, giving a suspension readily formed again after coagulation. **emul'sor** n an emulsifying apparatus. ◻ **emulsifying agent** n a substance whose presence in small quantities stabilizes an emulsion. **emulsion paint** n a water-thinnable paint made from a pigmented emulsion of a resin in water.

emure /i-mūr'/ (Shakesp) vt and n a variant of **immure**. [**em-** (from en- (1a))]

emys /em'is/ n (pl **em'ydēs**) any member of a genus (Emys) of freshwater and marsh terrapins. [Gr emys, -ydos]

EN abbrev : Enrolled Nurse.

en /en/ n the fourteenth letter of the modern English alphabet (N or n); a unit of measurement equal to half an em (printing). ■ **enn'age** n (printing) the length of a piece of type measured in ens. ◻ **en dash** or **en rule** n (printing) a dash that is one en long, used as a punctuation mark.

en- /en- or in-/ pfx (1) in words derived from L through Fr (a) used to form verbs with the sense from, into, upon; (b) used to form verbs with the sense cause to be; (c) used intensively or almost meaninglessly; (2) in words derived from Gr used to form verbs with the sense of in.

enable /in-ā'bl/ vt to make able; to give power, strength or authority to; to make possible. [**en-** (1b)] ■ **enab'lement** n. **enab'ler** n. **enab'ling** adj. ◻ **enabling act, bill** or **resolution** n one giving or proposing to give power to act.

enact /in-akt'/ vt to perform; to act the part of; to establish by law. ◆ n (Shakesp) an enactment. [**en-** (1b) and **act**] ■ **enact'able** adj. **enact'ing** adj. **enac'tion** /-shən/ or **enact'ment** n the passing of a bill into law; that which is enacted; a law. **enact'ive** adj. **enact'or** n a person who practises or performs anything; a person who forms decrees or establishes laws. **enac'ture** n (Shakesp) fulfilment.

enallage /en-al'ə-jē/ (grammar) n the exchange of one case, mood, tense, etc, for another. [Gr enallagē, from en in, and allassein to change]

enamel /in-am'əl/ n vitrified coating fired onto a metal or other surface; any glossy enamel-like surface or coating, esp that of the teeth; a work of art in enamel; a paint giving an enamel-like finish. ◆ vt (enam'elling; enam'elled) to coat with or paint in enamel; to form a glossy surface on, like enamel; see smelt[1] and melt[1]. [OFr enameler, from en in, and esmail enamel; see smelt[1] and melt[1]] ■ **enam'eller** or **enam'ellist** n. **enam'elling** n.

en ami /ã-na-mē'/ (Fr) as a friend.

enamour or (US) **enamor** /in-am'ər/ vt to inspire with love; to charm. [OFr enamourer, from pfx en-, and amour, from L amor, -ōris love] ■ **enamorado** /en-äm-ō-rä'dō/ n (pl **enamorad'os**) (obs; Sp) a lover. **enam'oured** adj. **enam'ouring** adj. ◻ **enamoured of** in love with; keen on.

enanthema /en-ən-thē'mə/ (med) n an ulcer on a mucous membrane. [Gr en in, and anthē blossom]

enantiodromia /en-an-ti-ō-drō'mi-ə/ n the process by which something becomes or is superseded by its opposite, esp the adopting of values, beliefs, etc opposite to those previously held; the interaction of such opposing values, beliefs, etc. [Gr, from enantios opposite, and dromos running] ■ **enantiōdrom'iacal** (or /-drō-mī'ə-kl/) adj. **enantiōdrō'mic** adj.

enantiomer /en-an'ti-ō-mər/ n an enantiomorph. [Gr enantios opposite, and meros part] ■ **enantiomer'ic** adj. **enantiomer'ically** adv.

enantiomorph /en-an'ti-ō-mörf/ (chem) n a shape or object (such as a crystal or molecule) exactly the same as another except that right and left are interchanged, each being a mirror image of the other. [Gr enantios opposite, and morphē shape] ■ **enantiomorph'ic** adj. **enantiomorph'ism** n. **enantiomorph'ous** adj. **enantiomorph'y** n.

enantiopathy /en-an-ti-op'ə-thi/ n allopathy. [Gr enantios opposite, and pathos suffering]

enantiosis /en-an-ti-ō'sis/ (rhetoric) n the expression of an idea by negation of its contrary (litotes), or by substitution of the contrary (antiphrasis, irony). [Gr enantiōsis contradiction]

enantiostyly /en-an-ti-ō-stī'li/ (bot) n a dimorphous condition in which the style projects at one side or the other in different flowers. [Gr enantios opposite, and stỹlos a column] ■ **enantiostý'lous** adj.

enantiotropy /en-an-ti-ot'rə-pi/ (physical chem) n the existence in a substance of two crystal forms, one stable above, the other below, a transition temperature. [Gr enantios opposite, and tropos turn, habit] ■ **enantiōtrop'ic** adj.

enarch see **inarch**.

enarched /en-ärcht'/ (heraldry) adj arched; like an arch. [**en-** (1b)]

enargite /en'är-gīt or -jīt/ (mineralogy) n a dark-grey crystalline copper arsenic sulphide, a minor ore of copper. [Gr enargēs clear]

enarm /en-ärm'/ vt to arm (obs); to lard (obs). [**en-** (1b)] ■ **enarmed'** adj (heraldry) having horns, hoofs, etc of a different colour from the body.

enarration /ē-nə-rā'shən/ (archaic) n exposition; detailed narration. [L ēnarrātiō, -ōnis, from ē- out, and narrāre to relate]

en arrière /ã-na-ryer'/ (Fr) behind or in the rear.

enarthrosis /en-är-thrō'sis/ (anat) n a ball-and-socket joint. [Gr enarthrōsis, from en in, and arthron a joint] ■ **enarthrō'dial** adj.

enate /ē'nāt/ (biol) adj growing out. [L ē- from, and nātus born] ■ **enā'tion** n an outgrowth.

en attendant /ã-na-tã-dã'/ (Fr) in the meantime or while waiting.

enaunter /en-ön'tər or en-än'tər/ (obs) conj lest by chance. [Contraction of in a(d)venture]

en avant /ã-na-vã'/ (Fr) forward.

en badinant /ã ba-dē-nã'/ (Fr) roguishly or humorously.

en beau /ã bō'/ (Fr) in a flattering style, eg of a person shown in a portrait.

en bloc /ã blok'/ (Fr) as one unit or wholesale.

en brochette /ã bro-shet'/ (Fr) (of food) on a skewer.

en brosse /ã bros'/ (Fr) (of hair) cut short and standing up stiffly. [Fr, like a brush]

enc. abbrev : enclosed; enclosure.

en caballo /ān kä-bä'lyo/ (Sp) on horseback.

en cabochon see **cabochon**.

encaenia /en-sē'ni-ə/ n (sometimes with cap) the annual commemoration of founders and benefactors at Oxford University, held in June. [L, from Gr enkainia (pl) a feast of dedication, from en in, and kainos new]

encage or (obs) **incage** /in-kāj'/ vt to shut up in a cage. [**en-** (1a)]

encalm /in-käm'/ (obs) vt to becalm. [**en-** (1b)]

encamp /in-kamp'/ vt to form into a camp; to provide with a camp. ◆ vi to pitch tents; to make or stay in a camp. [**en-** (1b)] ■ **encamp'ment** n the act of encamping; the place where a camper or company is encamped; a camp.

encanthis /en-kan'this/ (med) n a small tumour of the inner angle of the eye. [Gr enkanthis, from en in, and kanthos a canthus]

encapsidate /in-kap'si-dāt/ (biochem) vt to place the protein coat on the nucleic acid core of a virus. [**en-** (1a)] ■ **encapsidā'tion** n.

encapsulate /in-kap'sū-lāt/ vt to enclose in or as if in a capsule; to capture the essence of, to describe succinctly but sufficiently. [**en-** (1a)] ■ **encapsulā'tion** n.

encarnalize or **-ise** /in-kär'nə-līz/ vt to embody; to make carnal or sensual. [**en-** (1b)]

encarpus /en-kär'pəs/ *n* a festoon of fruit ornamenting a frieze. [Gr *enkarpa* (neuter pl), from *en* in, and *karpos* fruit]

encase or **incase** /in-kās'/ *vt* to enclose in or as if in a case; to surround or cover; to line. [en- (1a)]
■ **encase'ment** or **incase'ment** *n* the act of encasing; an enclosing substance; a covering; a lining.

encash /in-kash'/ *vt* to convert into cash. [en- (1b)]
■ **encash'able** *adj*. **encash'ment** *n*.

encaustic /en-kö'stik/ *adj* having the colours burned in; of or relating to encaustic. ◆ *n* an ancient method of painting in melted wax; a piece of pottery or other article decorated in this way. [Gr *enkaustikos*, from *enkaiein* to burn in, from *en* in, and *kaiein* to burn]
❑ **encaustic tile** *n* a decorative glazed and fired tile, having patterns of different coloured clays inlaid in it and burnt into it.

en cavalier /ã ka-va-lyā'/ (*Fr*) in a cavalier manner; astride (a horse) as opposed to side-saddle.

encave /en-kāv'/ or **incave** /in-kāv'/ (*Shakesp*) *vt* to hide. [Fr *encaver* to put in a cellar, from *en* in, and *cave* cellar]

enceinte[1] /ã-sẽt'/ (*fortif*) *n* an enclosure, generally the whole area of a fortified place. [Fr, from *enceindre* to surround, from L *in* in, and *cingere, cinctum* to gird]

enceinte[2] /ã-sẽt'/ *adj* pregnant, expecting a child. [Fr, from L *incincta* girt about or ungirt]

Encephalartos /en-sef-ə-lär'tos/ *n* a genus of S African cycads. [Gr *enkephalos* within the head, or palm-cabbage, and *artos* bread]

encephalon /en-sef'ə-lon or -kef'/ (*anat* and *zool*) *n* (pl **enceph'ala**) the brain. [Gr *enkephalos*, from *en* in, and *kephalē* head]
■ **encephalic** /-al'ik/ *adj* belonging to the head or brain. **encephalin** or **encephaline** /-sef'ə-lin/ *n* a rarer spelling of **enkephalin**. **encephalit'ic** *adj* relating to encephalitis. **encephalī'tis** *n* inflammation of the brain. **encephaliza'tion** or **-s-** *n* increased development of the brain in the course of the evolution of an organism. **enceph'alocele** /-əl-ō-sēl/ *n* (Gr *kēlē* tumour) a protrusion of a portion of the brain through the skull, where the bones are incomplete in infancy. **enceph'alogram** or **enceph'alograph** *n* an X-ray photograph of the brain. **encephalograph'ic** *adj*. **encephalog'raphy** *n* radiography of the brain, its cavities having been filled with air or dye injected into the space around the spinal cord. **enceph'aloid** *adj* resembling the matter of the brain. **encephalomyelit'is** *n* inflammation of the brain and spinal cord. **encephalop'athy** *n* a degenerative brain disease. **encephalot'omy** *n* (Gr *tomē* a cut) dissection of the brain. **enceph'alous** *adj* cephalous.
❑ **encephalitis lethargica** /-ji-kə/ *n* an acute disease marked by profound physical and mental lethargy (popularly called **sleepy sickness** or erroneously **sleeping sickness**).

enchafe /en-chāf'/ (*obs*) *vt* to make warm; to irritate. [Earlier *enchaufe* or *eschaufe*, from OFr *eschauffer*, from *es-* (L *ex*), and *chauffer*; see **chafe**]

enchain /in-chān'/ *vt* to put in chains; to hold fast (*fig*); to link together (*obs*). [Fr *enchaîner*, from *en* in, and *chaîne* chain, from L *catēna*]
■ **enchain'ment** *n* the act of enchaining; the state of being enchained.

enchant /in-chänt'/ *vt* to charm; to delight utterly; to cast a spell upon; to compel by enchantment; to act on by songs or rhymed formulas of sorcery. [Fr *enchanter*, from L *incantāre* to sing a magic formula over, from *in* on, and *cantāre* to sing]
■ **enchant'ed** *adj* under the power of enchantment; beguiled or captivated; delighted; possessed by witches or spirits. **enchant'edly** *adv*. **enchant'er** *n* (also *fem* **enchant'ress**) a person who enchants; a sorcerer or magician; a person who charms or delights. **enchant'ing** *adj*. **enchant'ingly** *adv* with the force of enchantment; in a charming or delightful manner. **enchant'ment** *n* the act of enchanting; the use of magic arts; an enchanted state; something that enchants.
❑ **enchanter's nightshade** *n* a plant, *Circaea lutetiana*, that grows in shady places, the name transferred apparently from another plant (perhaps mandrake or swallow-wort) for no obvious reason.

encharge /in-chärj'/ *vt* to enjoin (*obs*); to entrust (*archaic*). [OFr *encharger*; see **charge**]

encharm /in-chärm'/ (*obs*) *vt* to cast a spell on; to charm. [en- (1c)]

enchase /in-chās'/ *vt* to fix in a border or setting; to insert or let in; to set with jewels; to engrave or chase; to adorn with raised or embossed work; to enshrine (*obs*); to enclose (*obs*); to enshrine in verse (*obs*); *prob* to fewter or sheathe (*Spenser*). ◆ *n* (*Spenser*) enchasing. [Fr *enchâsser*, from *en* in, and *châsse* shrine, setting, from L *capsa* a case; see **case**[1] and **chase**[3]; **chase**[2] is a contraction]
■ **enchased'** *adj*.

encheason /en-chē'zn/ (*Spenser*) *n* a reason, cause or occasion. [OFr *encheson*, from *encheoir* to fall in; influenced by L *occāsiō, -ōnis* occasion]

encheer /in-chēr'/ (*archaic*) *vt* to cheer or comfort. [en- (1c)]

enchilada /en-chi-lä'də/ *n* a Mexican dish consisting of a rolled stuffed tortilla cooked with a chilli-flavoured sauce. [Am Sp, from Sp *enchilar* to season with chilli]
■ **the big enchilada** (*N Am inf*) a very important person or thing. **the whole enchilada** (*N Am inf*) everything.

enchiridion or **encheiridion** /en(g)-kī-rid'i-on/ *n* a handbook or a manual. [Gr *encheiridion*, from *en* in, and *cheir* hand]

enchondroma /en-kon-drō'mə/ (*pathol*) *n* (pl **enchondro'mas** or **enchondro'mata** /-tə/) an abnormal cartilaginous growth. [Gr *en* in, and *chondros* cartilage]

enchorial /en-kö'ri-əl/ or **enchoric** /-kor'ik/ *adj* belonging to or used in a country (*rare*); used by the people, *esp* (in ancient Egypt, of a writing system) demotic. [Gr *enchōrios*, from *en* in, and *chōrā* a place or country]

encierro /en-thyer'ō/ (*Sp*) *n* (pl **encier'ros**) in Spanish towns, an event in which bulls are driven through the streets to the bullring. [Literally, enclosure]

encincture /in-singk'chər/ *vt* to girdle. ◆ *n* a girdling; an enclosure. [en- (1b)]

encipher /in-sī'fər/ *vt* to put into cipher. [en- (1a)]
■ **enci'pherment** *n*.

encircle /in-sûr'kl/ *vt* to enclose in a circle; to go round (something). [en- (1a)]
■ **encir'clement** *n*. **encirc'ling** *adj*.

encl. *abbrev*: enclosed; enclosure.

en clair /ã kler'/ (*Fr*) not in cipher, uncoded.

enclasp /in-kläsp'/ *vt* to clasp. [en- (1c)]

enclave /en'klāv, also en-klāv' or ã-klāv'/ *n* a piece of territory entirely enclosed within foreign territory; an enclosure; a distinct racial or cultural group isolated within a country. ◆ *vt* to surround. [Fr, from LL *inclāvāre*, from L *in* in, and *clāvis* a key]

enclitic /en-klit'ik/ *adj* (of a word, *esp* a particle) without accent or stress, behaving as if not a separate word or, in ancient Greek, transferring its accent to the preceding word (*grammar*); inclined. ◆ *n* (*grammar*) a word or particle which always follows another word and which is enclitic to it. [Gr *enklitikos*, from *en* in, and *klīnein* to lean]
■ **enclisis** /eng'klis-is/ *n*. **enclit'ically** *adv*.

encloister /in-kloi'stər/ (*obs*) *vt* to shut in. [en- (1a)]

enclose or **inclose** /in-klōz'/ *vt* to close or shut in; to confine; to surround; to put within, *esp* of something sent within a letter or within its envelope; to seclude; to fence (*esp* waste land). [en- (1a) and **close**[2]]
■ **enclos'er** or **inclos'er** *n*. **enclosure** or **inclosure** /-klō'zhər/ *n* the act of enclosing; the state of being enclosed; that which is enclosed, *esp* in a letter; a space fenced off; an enclosed space at a sporting event reserved for certain spectators; that which encloses; a barrier; the division of common land into privately-owned plots (*hist*); the framing of a window.
❑ **enclosed order** *n* a Christian religious order leading an entirely contemplative life, not going out into the world to work.

enclothe /in-klōdh'/ *vt* to clothe. [en- (1a)]

encloud /in-klowd'/ *vt* to cover with clouds. [en- (1a)]

encode /in- or en-kōd'/ *vt* to encipher; to record in a form other than plain written or printed text; to convert an idea or message into words, or translate (something) into a foreign language (*linguistics*); (of a codon) to specify the genetic code required to produce a particular amino acid or protein (*biol*). [en- (1a)]
■ **encō'der** *n*.

encoignure /ã-kwa-nür'/ or *-nūr'/ *n* a piece of furniture, *esp* ornamental, eg a cupboard or cabinet, made to fit into a corner. [Fr, from *encoigner* to fit into a corner, from *en* in, and *coin* a corner]

encolour /in-kul'ər/ *vt* to colour or tinge. [en- (1b)]

encolpion /en-kol'pi-on/ *n* a reliquary, cross, etc worn on the breast (also **encol'pium**). [Gr, from *en* in or on, and *kolpos* bosom]

encolure /en(g)-ko-lūr'/ (*Browning*) *n* a horse's mane. [Fr, horse's neck]

encomienda /ān-kō-mē-ān'da/ (*Sp*) *n* a commander's district in colonial times.
■ **encomendero** /ān-kō-mān-dā'rō/ *n* (pl **encomender'os**) (*Sp*) the commander of such a district.

encomium /en-kō'mi-əm/, also **encomion** /-on/ *n* (pl **encō'miums** or **encō'mia**) high commendation; a eulogy. [L, from Gr *enkōmion* a song of praise, from *en* in, and *kōmos* festivity]
■ **encō'miast** *n* a person who delivers or writes encomiums; a praiser. **encomias'tic** or **encomias'tical** *adj* bestowing praise. **encomias'tically** *adv*.

encompass /in(g)-kum'pəs/ *vt* to surround or enclose; to include or embrace; to go round (*obs*); to bring about. [en- (1a)]
■ **encom'passment** *n*.

■ words derived from main entry word; ❑ compound words; ■ idioms and phrasal verbs

encopresis /en-kō-prē′sis/ (med) n involuntary defecation. [Gr en in, and copros dung]

encore /ä- or ong-kör′/ interj calling for repetition of a performance or an additional item. ◆ n a call of encore; an item given in response to such a call. ◆ vt to call encore to. ◆ vi to perform an encore. [Fr, again or still]

encounter /in(g)- or en(g)-kown′tər/ vt to meet or come upon, esp unexpectedly; to meet in a contest; to oppose or confront. ◆ n an unexpected or chance meeting; an interview; a fight or battle; a contentious meeting; a manner of meeting or accosting (Shakesp); an encounter group meeting. [OFr encontrer, from L in in, and contrā against]

❑ **encounter group** n a group which meets with a view to establishing greater self-awareness and greater understanding of others by indulging in unrestrained verbal and physical confrontation and contact.

encourage /in(g)- or en(g)-kur′ij/ vt to put courage in; to inspire with spirit or hope; to incite or spur on; to give patronage to; to cherish or sustain. [OFr encoragier (Fr encourager), from pfx en-, and corage courage]

■ **encour′agement** n the act of encouraging; something that encourages. **encour′ager** n. **encour′aging** n and adj. **encour′agingly** adv.

encradle /en-krā′dl/ (Spenser) vt to lay in a cradle. [en- (1a)]

encraty /en′krə-ti/ n self-control. [Gr enkrateia self-control, from en in, and kratos strength]

■ **En′cratism** n the doctrine of the Encratites. **En′cratite** n one of a heretical sect in the early church who abstained from marriage, and from meat and wine.

encrease obsolete form of **increase**.

encrimson /en-krim′zn/ vt to tinge with a crimson colour. [en- (1b)]

■ **encrim′soned** adj.

encrinite /en(g)′kri-nīt/ n a fossil crinoid; a crinoid. [Gr en in, and krinon a lily]

■ **en′crinal** adj. **encrin′ic** adj. **encrini′tal** adj. **encrinitic** /-it′ik/ adj.

encroach /in(g)-krōch′/ vi to extend esp gradually or stealthily into the territory, sphere, etc, of others; to seize on the rights of others; to intrude beyond boundaries. [OFr encrochier to seize, from en- and croc a hook]

■ **encroach′er** n. **encroach′ingly** adv. **encroach′ment** n an act of encroaching; something that is taken by encroaching.

en croupe /ä kroop′/ (Fr) on the crupper, on a pillion.

en croûte see under **croûte**.

encrust or **incrust** /en(g)- or in(g)-krust′/ vt to cover with a crust or hard coating; to form a crust on the surface of. ◆ vi to form a crust. [L incrustāre, -ātum, from in on, and crusta crust]

■ **encrustā′tion** /en-/ or **incrustā′tion** /in-/ n the act of encrusting; a crust or layer of anything; an inlaying of marble, mosaic, etc. **encrust′ment** n.

encryption /en(g)- or in(g)-krip′shən/ n the putting of messages or information into code. [See **crypt-**]

■ **encrypt′** vt. **encrypt′ed** adj.

en cuerpo /än kwär′pō/ (Sp) adv (also **in cuerpo** and **in querpo**) in close-fitting dress; without a cloak or coat; in undress, eg in one's shirtsleeves; sometimes used erroneously for stark naked, the Spanish for which is en cueros.

encumber or **incumber** /in-kum′bər/ vt to impede the motion of; to hamper; to embarrass; to burden; to load, eg with debts, etc. [OFr encombrer, from en-, and combrer (see **cumber**)]

■ **encum′berment** n the act of encumbering; the state of being encumbered. **encum′brance** n something which encumbers or hinders; a legal claim on an estate; someone dependent on another, esp a child. **encum′brancer** n.

encurtain /in-kûr′tin/ vt to curtain or veil. [en- (1a)]

ency., encyc. or **encycl.** abbrev : encyclopedia; encyclopedic.

encyclical /en-sik′li-kl/ adj (also **encyc′lic**) sent round to many persons or places. ◆ n a letter addressed by the Pope to all his bishops. [Gr enkyklios, from en in, and kyklos a circle]

encyclopedia or **encyclopaedia** /en-sī-klō-pē′di-ə/ n a work containing information on every branch, or on a particular branch, of knowledge, generally alphabetically arranged; (with cap) that by Diderot, D'Alembert and others; orig the circle of human knowledge. [False Gr enkyklopaideiā, a wrong reading for enkyklios paideiā general education (opposed to professional or special education), from enkyklios circular, recurring, everyday, from en in, and kyklos circle, and paideiā education, from pais, paidos a child]

■ **encyclope′dian** adj embracing the whole circle of learning. **encyclope′dic** or **encyclope′dical** adj of or relating to an encyclopedia; comprehensive; full of information. **encyclope′dism** n comprehensive knowledge; the rationalistic attitude of the French Encyclopedists. **encyclope′dist** n the compiler or someone who assists in the compilation of an encyclopedia; (also **Encyclopédiste**) a writer for the French Encyclopédie (1751–65).

encyst /en-sist′/ (biol) vt or vi to enclose or become enclosed in a cyst or vesicle. [en- (1a)]

■ **encystā′tion** n. **encyst′ed** adj. **encyst′ment** n.

end /end/ n the last point or portion; termination or close; death; consequence; an object aimed at; a fragment or odd piece; half a unit length of cloth; a warp thread; a waxed thread ending in a bristle (**shoemaker's end**); one of the two sides of a field, court, pitch, etc defended by a team, player, etc (sport); part of a game played from one end (of the bowling green, archery-ground, etc); a player positioned at the extremity of the line of scrimmage (American football); the part of an undertaking for which one is responsible; an outer district; a region; a cottage room (Scot). ◆ vt to bring to an end; to destroy. ◆ vi to come to an end; to cease; to be at the end. [OE ende; cf Ger Ende, Dan ende, Gothic andeis; Sans anta]

■ **end′ed** adj brought to an end; having ends. **end′ing** n a termination; a conclusion; death; extremity; something that is at the end; the final syllable or portion of a word, esp an inflection (grammar). ◆ adj concluding; finishing; completing; dying. **end′less** adj having or seeming to have no end; returning upon itself; everlasting; incessant; objectless. **end′lessly** adv. **end′lessness** n. **end′long** (Scot **end′lang**) adv from end to end (archaic); continuously (archaic); straight on (archaic). ◆ prep (obs) along. ◆ adj (rare) set on end. **end′most** adj farthest. **end′ways** or **end′wise** adv on end; with the end forward.

❑ **end′-all** n something that ends everything (see also **be-all and end-all** under **be**). **end′game** n the final stage of a game of chess or certain other games; a person's manner of playing the endgame. **end′gate** n (N Am) a tailboard. **endless chain** n a chain whose ends are joined. **endless gearing**, **screw** or **worm** n an arrangement for producing slow motion in machinery, consisting of a screw whose thread gears into a wheel with skew teeth. **end man** n the man at the end of a row of performers, etc. **end′note** n an explanatory note at the end of a chapter or volume. **end-of-the-pier′** adj impudent, frivolous and bawdy (in the style of variety shows traditionally performed at seaside piers). **end′-on** adv and adj in the direction in which the end points. **end organ** n a specialized sensory or motor structure at a nerve-end. **end′paper** n a paper at the beginning or end of a book, pasted to the binding and leaving an additional flyleaf. **end′play** vt (bridge) to place (an opponent) in a situation where no lead can be made which does not cost a trick (also n). **end′-product** n the final product of a series of operations. **end′-reader** n one who peeps at the end of a novel to see the outcome. **end result** n the final result or outcome. **end run** n (US) in American football, an attempt to run wide of the end of a defensive line rather than try to break through it; an act of circumventing a problem rather than confronting it. **end′ship** n (obs) a village. **end′-stopped** adj (poetry) having a pause at the end of each line (of verse). **end use** n the final use to which anything, esp a manufactured article, is put. **end′-user** n the person, company, etc who will be the recipient of a product being sold; (usu **end-user certificate**) in international trade, documentation naming the end-user of a product being sold, required eg in the exporting of arms. **end′zone** n (American football) one of the areas at either end of the field of play into which the offensive team attempts to take the ball.

■ **all ends up** completely; convincingly. **at a loose end** or **at loose ends** with nothing to do; in a state of uncertainty or confusion as to one's course of action. **at an end** terminated; discontinued; exhausted. **at one's wit's end** see under **wit**[1]. **at the end of one's tether** see under **tether**. **be the end of** to cause the death of (often an inf exaggeration). **end for end** with the position of the ends reversed. **end it all** to commit suicide. **end of story** see under **story**[1]. **end up** to arrive or find oneself eventually or finally; to finish (with with or by); to become in the end. **get hold of the wrong end of the stick** to misunderstand. **get** or **have one's end away** (sl) to have sexual intercourse. **in the end** after all; at last. **keep one's end up** to maintain one's part, position, appearance, etc; to be content to keep one's wicket standing without trying to score (cricket). **loose end** (often in pl) an unfinished, unsettled or unexplained matter. **make (both) ends meet** to live within one's income (both ends meaning both ends of the year). **no end** (inf) very much. **no end of** (inf) a great deal of. **on end** erect; at a stretch. **the end** the last straw; the limit. **the end of the road** (or **line**) the point beyond which one can no longer continue or survive.

end- see **endo-**.

endamage /in-dam′ij/ vt to damage. [en- (1b)]

■ **endam′agement** n damage, injury or loss.

endamoeba see **entamoeba**.

endanger /in-dān′jər/ vt to put in danger; to expose to loss or injury.

■ **endan'gerer** n. **endan'germent** n hazard, peril.
❑ **endangered species** n a species of animal that is in danger of extinction.

endarch /en'därk/ (bot) adj having the protoxylem on the inner edge. [Gr endō within, and archē origin]

endart or **indart** /in-därt'/ (Shakesp) vt to dart in. [en- (1a)]

endear /in-dēr'/ vt to make dear or more dear; to bind in gratitude (Shakesp). [en- (1b)]
■ **endeared'** adj beloved. **endear'ing** adj making dear; arousing or increasing affection; expressing love (archaic). **endear'ingly** adv. **endear'ingness** n. **endear'ment** n the act of endearing; the state of being endeared; something that excites or increases affection; a caress or a spoken or written expression of love.

endeavour or (US) **endeavor** /in-dev'ər/ vi to strive; to attempt. ◆ n an exertion of power towards some object; an attempt or trial. [From such phrases as to put oneself in devoir (Fr se mettre en devoir) to do what one can or make it one's duty, from Fr en in, and devoir duty]
■ **endeav'ourment** n (Spenser) endeavour.
■ **do one's endeavour** (archaic) to do one's utmost.

endecagon a non-standard form of **hendecagon**.

endeictic /en-dīk'tik/ adj showing, exhibiting or demonstrating. [Gr endeiktikos]
■ **endeix'is** n an indication.

endemic /en-dem'ik/ adj prevalent or regularly found among a people or in a district; confined to a particular area (biol). ◆ n an endemic disease or plant. [Gr endēmios, from en in, and dēmos a people or a district]
■ **endemial** /-dē'mi-al/ or **endem'ical** adj. **endem'ically** adv. **endemicity** /-is'i-ti/ or **en'demism** n the state of being endemic. **endemiol'ogy** /-dem- or -dēm-/ n the scientific study of endemic diseases.

endenizen /en-den'i-zn/ vt to naturalize, to make a denizen. [en- (1b)]

endermic /en-dûr'mik/ or **endermical** /-mi-kl/ adj through or applied directly to the skin (also **endermat'ic**). [Gr en in, derma skin]
■ **en'deron** n the corium, derma or true skin.

endew /en-dū'/ (obs) vt same as **endue**; to endow (Spenser).

endiron same as **andiron**.

endite obsolete form of **indict** or **indite**.

endive /en'div or -dīv/ n a salad plant (Cichorium endivia), related to chicory, with crisp, succulent, curly or broad leaves; (loosely) chicory (esp US). [Fr, from L intubus]

endlang, endlong see under **end**.

endo- /en-dō- or en-do-/ or before a vowel **end-** /end-/ combining form (often interchanging with **ento-**) inside or within, opp to ecto- and exo-. [Gr endon or endō within]
■ **endarterec'tomy** n surgical removal of material obstructing blood flow in an artery. **endarteri'tis** n inflammation of the inner lining of an artery. **endergonic** /en-dûr-gon'ik/ adj (Gr ergon work) of a biochemical reaction, requiring the absorption of energy. **en'doblast** n (Gr blastos a shoot or bud) the inner cell-layer of a gastrula, the hypoblast. **endocar'diac** or **endocar'dial** adj (Gr kardiā heart) within the heart. **endocarditic** /-dit'ik/ adj. **endocardi'tis** n inflammation of the endocardium, esp over the valves. **endocar'dium** n the lining membrane of the heart. **en'docarp** n (Gr karpos fruit; bot) a differentiated innermost layer of the pericarp, usu hard, such as a plum stone. **endocar'pic** adj. **endochylous** /en-dok'i-ləs/ adj (Gr chȳlos juice; bot) having internal water-storing cells. **endocri'nal** adj. **en'docrine** (or /-krin/) adj (Gr krīneín to separate; physiol) secreting internally; applied esp to certain glands that pour secretions into the blood (also n). **endocrinic** /-krin'ik/ adj. **endocrinolog'ical** adj. **endocrinol'ogist** n. **endocrinol'ogy** n the science of the internal secretory glands. **endocritic** /-krit'ik/ adj endocrine. **endocytō'sis** n (biol) the absorption into a cell of particles too large to diffuse through the cell wall. **endocytot'ic** adj. **en'doderm** n (Gr derma skin) the inner layer of cells in a gastrula; the tissues derived from that layer. **endoderm'al** or **endoderm'ic** adj. **endoderm'is** n a close-set sheath, one cell thick, enclosing the central cylinder in plants. **endodont'ics** n sing (Gr odous, odontos tooth) the branch of dentistry concerned with disorders of the tooth pulp. **en'dodyne** adj same as **autodyne**. **endogamic** /-gam'ik/ or **endogamous** /-dog'ə-məs/ adj. **endogamy** /en-dog'əm-i/ n (Gr gamos marriage) the custom forbidding marriage outside one's own group; inbreeding; pollination between two flowers on the same plant; the union of female gametes. **en'dogen** /-jen/ n (Gr genēs born; obs) any plant, including the monocotyledons, regarded as growing from within. **endogen'ic** adj relating to the processes of change within the earth. **endogenous** /en-doj'i-nəs/ adj increasing by internal growth; formed within; (of depression) with no external cause. **endog'enously** adv. **endog'eny** n. **en'dolymph** n the fluid within the membranous labyrinth of the ear. **endomēt'rial** adj. **endomētriō'sis** n (a condition caused by) the presence of active endometrial tissue where it should not be, esp when affecting other organs of the pelvic cavity. **endometrī'tis** n (Gr mētra womb) inflammation of the endometrium. **endomēt'rium** n the mucous membrane lining the cavity of the uterus. **endomitos'is** n (bot) the process in which the chromosomes divide without cell division, giving double the original number of chromosomes in the cell. **endomix'is** n (Gr mixis mingling) in Protozoa, a nuclear reorganization without conjugation. **en'domorph** n (Gr morphē form) a mineral enclosed within another mineral, the latter being termed a perimorph; a person of generally heavy or rounded body build, thought to accompany a type of personality characterized by placidity, lack of anxiety or tension, and the pursuit of pleasure (cf **ectomorph** and **mesomorph**). **endomorph'ic** adj. **endomorph'y** n. **endonuc'lease** n an enzyme that cuts a polynucleotide chain internally. **endopar'asite** n a parasite living inside the body of its host. **endoparasitic** /-sit'ik/ adj. **endophagous** /en-dof'ə-gəs/ adj. **endoph'agy** /-ə-ji/ n (Gr phagein to eat) cannibalism within the family or tribe; eating away from within. **endophyllous** /-fil'əs/ adj (Gr phyllon a leaf; bot) being or formed within a sheathing leaf; living inside a leaf. **endophyte** /en'dō-fīt/ n (Gr phyton a plant; bot) a plant living within another, whether parasitically or not. **endophytic** /-fit'ik/ adj. **en'doplasm** n (biol) the inner portion of the cytoplasm of a cell. **endoplas'mic** or **endoplas'tic** adj (**endoplasmic reticulum** a series of flattened membranous tubules and cisternae in the cytoplasm of eukaryotic cells, either with decorating ribosomes (**rough endoplasmic reticulum**) or without them (**smooth endoplasmic reticulum**), the site of synthesis of lipids and some proteins). **endopleura** /-ploo'rə/ n (Gr pleurā a side; bot) the inner seed coat. **endopodite** /en-dop'ə-dīt/ n (Gr pous, podos a foot) the inner branch of a crustacean's leg. **endora'diosonde** n (med) a miniature battery-powered transmitter designed to be swallowed by the patient to send out information about a bodily function such as digestion. **endorhizal** /-rī'zl/ adj (Gr rhiza root; bot) having the radicle of the embryo enclosed within a sheath, as in monocotyledons; monocotyledonous. **en'dosarc** n (Gr sarx, sarkos flesh) endoplasm. **en'doscope** n (Gr skopeein to look) an instrument for viewing the cavities of internal organs. **endoscopic** /-skop'ik/ adj. **endoscop'ically** adv. **endos'copist** n. **endoscopy** /en-dos'kə-pi/ n any technique for viewing internal organs, such as by fibre-optic apparatus. **endoskel'etal** adj. **endoskel'eton** n the internal skeleton or framework of the body. **endosmom'eter** n an instrument for measuring endosmotic action. **endosmomet'ric** adj. **endosmō'sis** n osmosis inwards, ie towards the solution (also **en'dosmose** /-mōs/). **endosmot'ic** adj relating to or of the nature of endosmosis. **endosmot'ically** adv. **en'dosperm** n (Gr sperma seed) (in a seed) nutritive tissue formed from the embryo-sac. **endosper'mic** adj. **en'dospore** n (Gr sporos seed; bot) the innermost layer of a spore-wall; a spore formed within a mother cell; a very resistant thick-walled spore formed within a bacterial cell. **Endostat'in**® n an angiogenesis-inhibiting drug, used in experimental treatments to inhibit the growth of cancerous tumours. **endos'teal** adj (Gr osteon bone) within a bone. **endos'teum** n (anat) the internal periosteum. **endosym'biont** n an organism living within the body of its symbiotic host. **endosymbiō'sis** n a symbiotic relationship in which one organism lives inside the body of another. **endosymbiot'ic** adj. **endothē'lial** adj. **endothē'lium** n (pl endothē'lia) (biol) the layer of cell tissue on the internal surfaces of blood vessels, lymphatics, etc. **en'dotherm** n an animal that is able to generate heat internally. **endotherm'ic** adj (Gr thermē heat) accompanied by, characterized by, or formed with absorption of heat; warm-blooded (zool). **endotherm'y** n. **en'dotoxin** n (biol) a toxin which forms part of the cell wall of a micro-organism and which is released when the cell breaks down. **endotroph'ic** adj (Gr trophē food) of a mycorrhiza, occurring mainly within the root of the plant it feeds. **endozō'ic** adj (bot) entozoic, having seeds dispersed by animals that swallow them. **endozō'on** n (pl endozō'a) (Gr zōion animal) an entozoon.

endorphin /en-dör'fin/ n any of a group of opiate-like substances produced by the brain and the pituitary gland with pain-killing and other properties similar to morphine. [endo- and morphine]

endorse¹ or **indorse** /in-dörs'/ vt to write (esp one's signature, a note of contents, a record of an offence) on the back of; to assign by writing on the back of; to give one's sanction to; to express approbation of; to do so as a form of advertising, usu in return for money; to lay on the back to load (archaic). [endoss changed under the influence of LL indorsāre, from in on, and dorsum the back]
■ **endors'able** adj. **endorsee'** /-en-/ n the person to whom a bill, etc is assigned by endorsement. **endorse'ment** n the act of endorsing; that which is written on the back; a sanction; a record of a motoring offence on a driving licence; an additional clause on a policy altering the coverage in some way (insurance). **endors'er** or **endors'or** n.
■ **endorse out** (S Afr) to order (a person) to leave a place because he or she lacks official permission to be there.

endorse² /en-dörs'/ (heraldry) n a vertical band or stripe on a shield, one-fourth or one-eighth of the width of a pale. [Origin obscure]

■ **endorsed'** *adj* (of a pale) with an endorse on each side of it; (of wings) thrown back.

endosarc...to...**endospore** see under **endo-**.

endoss /en-dos'/ (*obs*) *vt* to endorse; to inscribe (*Spenser*). [ME *endosse*, from OFr *endosser*]

Endostatin®...to...**endotrophic** see under **endo-**.

endow /in-dow'/ *vt* to settle a permanent provision on; to provide permanent means of support for; to enrich with any gift or faculty; to present; *orig* to give a dowry or marriage portion to. [Fr *en* (from L *in*), and *douer* to endow, from L *dōtāre*, from *dōs*, *dōtis* a dowry]
■ **endowed'** *adj* having (a gift, ability, etc) (with *with*). **endow'er** *n*. **endow'ment** *n* the act of endowing; something that is settled on any person or institution; a quality, aptitude or skill bestowed on anyone. ❑ **endowment assurance** or **insurance** *n* a form of insurance providing for the payment of a certain sum at a certain date or at death if earlier. **endowment mortgage** *n* a form of mortgage in which the capital sum is repaid by the eventual proceeds from endowment assurance.

endozoon, etc see under **endo-**.

endrin /en'drin/ *n* an organic pesticide, isomeric with dieldrin. [endo- and dieldrin]

endue or **indue** (*Spenser*, etc **endew** or **indew**) /in-dū'/ *vt* to supply or provide with; to put on (eg clothes); to invest with; to clothe; to take into the stomach, like a hawk (*obs*); to digest (*obs*); to take in or digest mentally (*Spenser*); to bring to (*Shakesp*). [OFr *enduire*, from L *indūcere*, from *in* into, and *dūcere* to lead, influenced by *induere* to put on]

endungeon /in-dun'jən/ *vt* to shut up in a dungeon or similar confinement. [en- (1a)]

endure /in-dūr'/ *vt* to tolerate, bear or put up with without giving in or up; to harden (*Spenser*); to remain firm under. ◆ *vi* to continue to exist; to remain firm; to last. [OFr *endurer*, from L *indūrāre*, from *in* in, and *dūrus* hard]
■ **endur'able** *adj* that can be endured or borne; lasting. **endur'ableness** *n*. **endur'ably** *adv*. **endur'ance** *n* the state or power of or capacity for enduring, bearing or surviving; patient suffering; patience; continuance; duration (*obs*); lasting quality; maximum performance under given conditions; captivity (*obs*). **endur'er** *n*. **endur'ing** *adj* lasting. **endur'ingly** *adv*.

enduro /in-dū'rō/ *n* a long-distance race testing the endurance of motor vehicles rather than their speed. [**endurance**]

endways, **endwise** see under **end**.

ENE *abbrev* : east-north-east.

ene same as **e'en**.

en effet /ã-ne-fe'/ (*Fr*) in effect; in fact.

enema /en'i-mə/ *n* (*pl* **en'emas** or **enem'ata**) a fluid injected into the rectum; the process of injecting such a fluid, eg to clean out the rectum or to introduce medication. [Gr *enema*, *-atos*, from *enienai* to send in, from *en* in, and *hienai* to send]

enemy[1] /en'i-mi/ *n* a person who hates or dislikes, or who is hated or disliked; a foe; a hostile nation or force; something which is harmful to or which acts against (*fig*). ◆ *adj* hostile. [OFr *enemi* (Fr *ennemi*), from L *inimīcus*, from *in-* (negative), and *amīcus* a friend]
■ **enemy at the door** or **gate** (*usu fig*) a person, force, event, etc that is a present or increasing threat. **how goes the enemy?** (*inf*) what time is it? **the Enemy** or **the Old Enemy** the Devil. **the last enemy** death.

enemy[2] a dialect form of **anemone**.

Eneolithic /ē-ni-ō-lith'ik/ same as **Aeneolithic** (see under **aeneous**).

energetic...to...**energizer** see under **energy**.

energumen /en-ər-gū'mən/ (*obs*) *n* a person who is possessed; a demoniac. [LL *energūmenus*, from Gr *energoumenos*, from *energeein*, from *en* in, and *ergon* work]

energy /en'ər-ji/ *n* the power required for doing work, for action, etc; the power exerted in working, etc; intensity; vigorous activity; vigour; forcefulness; a source or supply of power, eg electrical or mechanical; the capacity of a material body or of radiation to do work (*phys*). [Gr *energeia*, from *en* in, and *ergon* work]
■ **energet'ic**, also **energet'ical** *adj* having, requiring or showing energy; active; forcible; effective. **energet'ically** *adv*. **energet'ics** *n sing* the science of the general laws of energy; the production and use of energy, eg in animals. ◆ *n pl* the properties of something in terms of energy. **ener'gic** /in-ûr'jik/ *adj* exhibiting energy. **ener'gid** *n* a protoplasmic unit; the nucleus and active cytoplasm of a cell. **en'ergize** or **-ise** *vt* to give strength or active force to; to stimulate to activity; to supply with, eg electrical, energy. ◆ *vi* to release energy, *esp* by acting vigorously; to act with force. **en'ergizer** or **-s-** *n* a person or thing that energizes.

❑ **energetic herbalism** *n* a system that combines the diagnostic principles of traditional Chinese medicine with the therapeutic use of herbs. **energy drink** *n* a soft drink containing stimulants such as caffeine and sugar, marketed as imparting energy to the consumer. **energy gap** *n* the amount by which energy requirements exceed the energy supply. **energy level** *n* (*phys*) one of the fixed amounts of energy that an electron can possess at any given time. **energy-mass equation** same as **mass-energy equation** (see **mass-energy equivalence** under **mass**[1]).
■ **conservation of energy** see under **conserve**.

enervate /en'ər-vāt, still sometimes *i-nûr'*/ *vt* to weaken by depriving of nerve, strength, courage or vitality. ◆ *adj* weakened; spiritless. [L *ēnervāre*, *-ātum*, from *ē* out of, and *nervus* a nerve]
■ **en'ervating** or **en'ervative** *adj*. **enerva'tion** *n*. **enerve'** *vt* (*obs*) to enervate.

enew /e-nū'/ (*falconry*) *vt* to drive or (*reflexive*) plunge into water. [OFr *enewer*, from *en* in, and OFr *ewe* (Fr *eau*) water]

enface /in-fās'/ *vt* to stamp or print on the face of a document, bill, etc. [en- (1a)]
■ **enface'ment** *n*.

en face /ã fas'/ (*Fr*) in front; opposite; straight in the face; facing forward.

en famille /ã fa-mē'-y'/ (*Fr*) (literally) amongst the family; as at a family gathering; at home; without ceremony.

enfant /ã-fã'/ (*Fr*) *n* a child.
❑ **enfant de la maison** /də la me-zɔ̃/ *n* a child of the house, someone who feels quite at home. **enfant de son siècle** /də sɔ̃ sye-kl'/ *n* a person who reflects the spirit of his or her time, (literally) a child of his or her century. **enfant gâté** /gä-tā/ *n* a spoilt child or person (*fem* **gâtée**). **enfants perdus** /ã-fã per-dü/ *n pl* forlorn hope or shock troops, (literally) lost children. **enfant terrible** /te-rē-bl'/ *n* a precocious child whose behaviour causes embarrassment to other (*esp* older) people; a person whose behaviour, etc is indiscreet, embarrassing or (loosely) unconventional. **enfant trouvé** /troo-vā/ *n* a foundling.

enfeeble /in-fē'bl/ *vt* to make feeble; to weaken. [en- (1b)]
■ **enfee'blement** *n* weakening; weakness.

enfelon /en-fel'ən/ (*Spenser*) *vt* to make fierce. [en- (1b)]

enfeoff /in-fef', or en-fēf'/ *vt* to give a fief to; to invest with a possession in fee; to give up as a fief; to surrender. [OFr *enfeffer*, from *en-*, and *fief* (see **fief** and **feoff**)]
■ **enfeoff'ment** *n* the act of enfeoffing; the deed which invests someone with the fee of an estate.

enfested /en-fes'tid/ (*Spenser*) *adj* embittered. [Perh for **infest** hostile, or **enfestered**]

enfestered /en-fes'tərd/ *adj* festered. [en- (1b)]

en fête /ã fet'/ (*Fr*) in festivity or in festive mood; keeping, dressed for, etc a holiday.

enfetter /en-fet'ər/ (*Shakesp*) *vt* to bind in fetters. [en- (1c)]

enfevered /en-fē'vərd/ *adj* affected with or showing signs of fever. [en- (1c)]

enfierce /en-fērs'/ (*Spenser*) *vt* to make fierce. [en- (1b)]

enfilade /en-fi-lād'/ *n* a number of things arranged as if threaded on a string; a discharge of firearms that sweeps a line or position from end to end (*milit*); a series of rooms with the doors in line affording a continuous passage; a vista; a situation or a body open from end to end. ◆ *vt* to discharge or be in position to discharge firearms along the whole length of a line. [Fr *enfiler*, from *en* (L *in*), and *fil*, from L *fīlum* a thread; see **file**[1]]
■ **enfiled** /en-fīld'/ *adj* (*heraldry*) thrust through like a sword.

enfire /en-fīr'/ (*Spenser*) *vt* to set on fire or inflame.

enfix see **infix**.

enflame obsolete form of **inflame**.

enflesh /en- or in-flesh'/ *vt* to turn into flesh. [en- (1b)]
■ **enflesh'ment** *n*.

enfleurage /ã-flœ-räzh'/ *n* a method of extracting essential oils by saturating flowers in a layer of purified fat. [Fr, literally, saturation with flowers]

enflower /in-flow'ər/ *vt* to cover with flowers. [en- (1a)]

enfold or **infold** /in-fōld'/ *vt* to wrap up; to embrace or enclose; to encompass. [en- (1a)]
■ **enfold'ment** *n* the act of enfolding; something that enfolds.

enforce /in-fôrs'/ *vt* to gain by force; to impose by force; to give force to; to emphasize or reinforce; to put in force; to give effect to; to urge; to impress; to drive; to compel; to apply force to. ◆ *vi* (*Spenser*) to strive. [OFr *enforcer*, from *en* (L *in*), and *force*]
■ **enforceabil'ity** *n*. **enforce'able** *adj*. **enfor'cedly** *adv* by violence, not by choice. **enforce'ment** *n* the act of enforcing; compulsion; a

giving effect to; something that enforces. **enforc'er** *n* someone who or something which enforces; a member of a gang, etc who uses strong-arm tactics to enforce the power of the gang or its leaders (*sl*, *orig US*). ◻ **enforcement notice** *n* (*law*) an order served on someone who has breached town-planning regulations. **enforcement officer** *n*. **enforcement work** *n*.

enforest /*in-for'ǝst*/ *vt* to turn into forest. [**en-** (1b)]

enform (*Spenser*) an obsolete form of **inform**[1].

enfouldered /*en-fōl'dǝrd*/ (*Spenser*) *adj* charged with or like lightning. [**en-** (1c) and OFr *fouldre* (Fr *foudre*), from L *fulgur* lightning]

enframe /*in-frām'*/ *vt* to put in a frame. [**en-** (1a)]

enfranchise /*in-fran'chīz* or -*shīz*/ *vt* to set free; to give a franchise or political privileges to. [OFr *enfranchir*, from *en*, and *franc* free; see **franchise**]
∎ **enfran'chisement** /-*chiz-* or -*shiz-*/ *n* the act of enfranchising; liberation; admission to civil or political privileges.

enfree /*en-frē'*/ or **enfreedom** /*en-frē'dǝm*/ (*Shakesp*) *vt* to set free; to give freedom to. [**en-** (1b)]

enfreeze /*en-frēz'*/ *vt* (pap (*Spenser*) **enfrös'en**) to freeze; to turn to ice. [**en-** (1c)]

ENG *abbrev* : electronic news gathering.

EN(G) *abbrev* : Enrolled Nurse (General), formerly a State Enrolled Nurse.

Eng. *abbrev* : England; English.

eng /*eng*/ (*phonetics*) *n* the symbol *F*, representing the sound of English *ng* (see also **agma**). [From the sound]

eng. *abbrev* : engineer; engineering; engraver; engraving.

engage /*in*(*g*)- or *en*(*g*)-*gāj'*/ *vt* to bind by a promise; to secure for service, ensure the services of; to enlist; to win over or attract; to betroth; to book or reserve; to hold or occupy; to begin an action against (*milit*); to fasten (*archit*); to interlock; to entangle (*archaic*); to render liable (*obs*); to pledge (*obs*). ◆ *vi* to promise; to become bound; to take part; to become occupied or involved; to begin an action (*milit*); to interlock. [Fr *engager*, from *en gage* in pledge; see **gage**[1]]
∎ **engaged'** *adj* pledged; promised, *esp* in marriage; greatly interested; taken or booked; occupied; partly built or sunk into, or so appearing (*archit*); geared together or interlocked; (of literature or a writer) committed (cf **engagé**). **engage'ment** *n* the act of engaging; the state of being engaged; something that engages or binds; betrothal; promise; appointment; employment; a fight or battle; commitment (cf **engagé**). **engāg'er** *n* someone who engages in any sense; (with *cap*) an adherent of the *Engagement* of 1647, a secret treaty between Charles I and the Scottish Commissioners (*hist*). **engāg'ing** *adj* charming, winning or attractive. **engāg'ingly** *adv*. **engāg'ingness** *n*. ◻ **engaged tone** or **engaged signal** *n* a repeated long note that informs a telephone caller that the dialled number is engaged. **engagement ring** *n* a ring given *esp* by the man to the woman as a token of their engagement to marry.
∎ **engage for** (*archaic*) to answer for.

engagé /*ā-ga-zhā'*/ *adj* committed to a point of view or to social or political action. [Fr]
∎ **engagement** /*ā-gazh-mā* (sometimes *in-gāj'mǝnt*)/ *n* the state of being committed to a point of view or action.

engaol /*en-jāl'*/ (*Shakesp*) *vt* to put in gaol. [**en-** (1a)]

en garçon /*ā gar-sõ'*/ (*Fr*) like a bachelor; in bachelor style.

en garde /*ā gärd'*/ (*fencing*) a warning to assume a defensive position in readiness for an attack. [Fr]

engarland /*in-gär'lǝnd*/ *vt* to put a garland round. [**en-** (1a)]

engarrison /*in-gar'i-sn*/ *vt* to establish as a garrison. [**en-** (1b)]

engender /*in-jen'dǝr*/ *vt* to beget, generate or start the development of; to bear; to breed; to sow the seeds of; to cause to exist; to produce. ◆ *vi* to be caused or produced. [Fr *engendrer*, from L *ingenerāre*, from *in*, and *generāre* to generate]
∎ **engen'derer** *n*. **engen'derment** *n*. **engen'drure** or **engen'dure** *n* (*archaic*) the act of engendering; generation.

Enghalskrug /*eng'hals-krŭk* or -*krook*/ (*Ger*) *n* a type of beer jug. [Ger *eng* narrow, *Hals* neck, and *Krug* jug]

engild /*en-gild'*/ (*Shakesp*) *vt* to gild. [**en-** (1c)]

engine /*en'jin*/ *n* a piece of machinery, *esp* a complex one in which power is applied to do work; a locomotive; a military machine; anything used to effect a purpose; a source of power (*fig*); a software system underlying a class of computer programs; a device, contrivance or trick (*obs*); a snare (*obs*); an instrument of torture (*obs*); a person used as a tool (*archaic*); (see also **ingine**) ability, ingenuity, genius or turn of mind (*obs*). ◆ *vt* to equip with an engine or engines; to contrive (*obs*). [OFr *engin*, from L *ingenium* skill; see **ingenious**]
∎ **en'gined** *adj* having (a certain type, number, etc of) engines. **engineer'** *n* someone who designs or makes, or puts to practical use,

engines or machinery of any type, including electrical; someone who designs or constructs public works, such as roads, railways, sewers, bridges, harbours, canals, etc; someone who constructs or manages military fortifications, etc (*hist*), or engines (*obs*); a soldier trained for construction work, such as digging trenches, road-making, etc; an officer who is responsible for a ship's engines; an engine-driver (*esp US*); someone who does public work requiring little skill (*US*; *facetious*); someone who plots (*obs*) or who contrives to bring about (with *of*). ◆ *vi* to act as engineer. ◆ *vt* to arrange or contrive; to manoeuvre or guide; to produce by engineering. **engineer'ing** *n* the art or profession of an engineer; extended to apply to certain techniques or processes not connected with the work of engineers, such as *protein engineering*. **en'gineless** *adj*. **en'giner** *n* (*Shakesp*) engineer. **enginery** /*en'jin-ri*/ *n* the art of managing engines; engines collectively; machinery.
◻ **en'gine-driver** *n* a person who controls an engine, *esp* a railway locomotive. **engineer's chain** *n* a chain 50 or 100 feet long, made up of one-foot (0.3m) links; a unit of length of 100 feet (30.48m). **en'gine-fitter** *n* a person who fits together the parts of an engine. **en'gine-man** *n* a person who drives an engine. **en'gine-room** *n* the room in a ship, industrial plant, etc where the engines are; the source of strength or power (*fig*). **en'gine-turned** *adj*. **en'gine-turning** *n* a kind of ornament made by a rose engine, such as on the backs of watches, etc.

engird /*in-gûrd'*/ *vt* (pap and pat **engirt'**) to gird round; to encircle. [**en-** (1a)]
∎ **engir'dle** *vt*.

englacial /*in-glā'syǝl*, -*si-ǝl* or -*shǝl*/ *adj* occurring or situated in a glacier.
∎ **engla'cially** *adv*.

English /*ing'glish*/ *adj* belonging to *England* or its inhabitants; (loosely, and deprecated by the Scots, Welsh and Northern Irish) British; of or relating to the English language. ◆ *n* the English people (as *pl*); a Germanic language spoken in the British Isles, USA, most parts of the Commonwealth, etc; 14-point type (*printing*); side (*N Am*; *snooker*, etc). ◆ *vt* to translate into English (*archaic* or *rare*); to make English or anglicize; to influence with English characteristics, customs, etc; to impart side to (*N Am*; *snooker*, etc). [OE *Englisc*, from *Engle* Angles]
∎ **Eng'lander** *n* (*facetious*, as though a mistaken transl of eg Ger *Engländer*) an Englishman. **Eng'lified** *adj* like the English of England in speech or ways; affecting an English manner of speaking (*Scot*). **Eng'lisher** *n* a translator into English; an Englishman (*Scot*). **Eng'lishism** *n* (*US*; *rare*) an expression or idiom originating in or found only in the English of England or Britain; a custom or practice peculiar to England; great admiration or enthusiasm for England and its customs, etc. **Eng'lishness** *n*. **Eng'lishry** *n* the fact of being English; in Ireland, the population of English descent.
◻ **English bond** *n* a bricklayer's bond of alternate courses of headers and stretchers (cf **Flemish bond**). **English breakfast** *n* a cooked breakfast, *usu* including bacon, eggs and tomatoes (cf **continental breakfast**). **English disease** *n* the British disease. **English flute** *n* the recorder. **English horn** *n* the cor anglais. **Eng'lishman** or **Eng'lishwoman** *n* a native or naturalized inhabitant of England. **English mustard** *n* a hot, bright-yellow kind of mustard (the condiment). **English rose** *n* an English girl with a fair complexion and regarded as classically beautiful. **English sickness** same as **English disease** above. **English sweat** *n* (*old*) the sweating sickness (qv under **sweat**).
∎ **Basic English** see under **base**[1]. **Early English** often used vaguely, eg for early Middle English or for Middle and early Modern English; the form of Gothic architecture in which the pointed arch was first employed in Britain, succeeding the *Norman* towards the end of the 12c and merging into the *Decorated* at the end of the 13c (**Early-English** *adj*). **in plain English** in clear, simple language. **little Englander** a 19c British opponent of British imperialism and empire-building; a late-20c or early-21c British supporter of the view that Britain should retain its individual national identity rather than become part of a more integrated Europe. **little Englanderism** or **Englandism**. **Middle English** the English used in Britain from about 1100 or 1150AD until about 1500. **Modern English** the English used in Britain from about 1500 onwards. **Old English** a kind of black-letter typeface (*printing*); the English language up to about 1100 or 1150AD (formerly, and still popularly, called **Anglo-Saxon**). **Young England** see under **young**.

englobe /*in-glōb'*/ *vt* to enclose in or as if in a globe; to form into a globe. [**en-** (1a,b)]

engloom /*in-gloom'*/ *vt* to make gloomy. [**en-** (1b)]

englut /*in-glut'*/ *vt* (**englutt'ing**; **englutt'ed**) to glut or fill; to swallow. [**en-** (1c)]

engobe /*en-gōb'*/ *n* a slip applied to ceramics before the glaze, eg to mask their natural colour. [Fr]

∎ words derived from main entry word; ◻ compound words; ∎ idioms and phrasal verbs

engore /in-gör'/ vt to gore (Spenser); to pierce (obs); to wound (obs); to make gory. [**en-** (1c)]

engorge /in-görj'/ vt to glut, congest or cause to swell; to devour (Spenser). ◆ vi (Milton) to feed voraciously. [**en-** (1c)]
■ **engorged'** adj congested or excessively full of blood, etc. **engorge'ment** n the act of swallowing greedily; congestion eg with blood (med).

engouement or **engoûment** /ã-goo-mã'/ n excessive fondness; infatuation. [Fr]

engouled /en-goold'/ (heraldry) adj of bends, crosses, etc, having ends that enter the mouths of animals. [Fr engoulée, from en in, and OFr goule (Fr gueule) a beast's mouth]

engrace /in-grās'/ vt to put grace into. [**en-** (1a)]

engraff an obsolete form of **engraft**.

engraft or (obs) **ingraft** /in-gräft'/ vt to graft; to insert; to join on (to something already existing); to fix deeply; to cuckold (obs). [**en-** (1a)]
■ **engraftã'tion** /en-/ n the act of engrafting. **engraft'ment** n engrafting; the thing engrafted; a scion.

engrail /in-grāl'/ vt to border with little semicircular indents (heraldry); to make rough (archaic). ◆ vi to form an edging or border; to run in indented lines. [OFr engresler (Fr engrêler), from gresle slender, from L gracilis]
■ **engrail'ment** n the ring of dots round the edge of a medal; indentation in curved lines (heraldry).

engrain, etc see **ingrain**.

engram /en'gram/, sometimes **engramma** /en-gram'ə/ (psychol) n a permanent impression made by a stimulus or experience; a stimulus impression supposed to be inheritable; a memory trace. [Ger Engramm, from Gr en in, and gramma that which is written]
■ **engrammat'ic** adj.

en grande tenue /ã grãd tə-nü'/ (Fr) in full dress.

en grand seigneur /ã grã se-nyœr'/ (Fr) like a great lord.

engrasp /en-gräsp'/ (Spenser) vt to grasp. [**en-** (1c)]

engrave[1] /en- or in-grāv'/ vt (pap **engraved'** or **engrāv'en**) to cut or carve on wood, steel, etc; to cut into; to impress deeply; to form or represent by engraving. [**en-** (1a) and **grave**[1]]
■ **engrāv'er** n. **engrāv'ery** n (obs) the art of the engraver. **engrāv'ing** n the act or art of cutting or incising designs on metal, wood, etc esp in order to print impressions from them (in metal, the lines to be printed are sunk or incised; in wood, they appear in relief, the wood between them being cut away); an impression taken from an engraved plate; a print; a piece of stone, etc decorated with carving.

engrave[2] /in-grāv'/ (obs) vt to deposit in the grave. [**en-** (1a)]

engrenage /ã-grə-näzh'/ (Fr) n gearing (also fig); a series of events, decisions, etc, each of which leads inevitably to further ones; the taking of such decisions as moves towards some goal, thus avoiding the necessity of discussing the desirability of the goal itself.

engrieve /en-grēv'/ (Spenser) vt to grieve. [**en-** (1c)]

engroove or **ingroove** /in-groov'/ vt to cut a groove or furrow in; to fit into a groove. [**en-** (1a)]

engross /in-grōs'/ vt to absorb the attention, interest or powers of completely; to buy up wholesale or completely; to monopolize; to take wholly to oneself; to copy in large writing or in distinct characters; to write in legal form; to prepare a legal or official document; to name in a list or document (obs); to make thick (Spenser); to fatten (Shakesp). [Fr en gros, from L in in, and grossus large; see **gross**]
■ **engrossed'** adj. **engross'er** n. **engross'ing** adj absorbing; monopolizing. **engross'ment** n buying up wholesale; something (eg a document) which has been engrossed; a fair copy.
■ **engrossing a deed** writing it out in full form for signature.

enguard /en-gärd'/ (Shakesp) vt to guard or defend. [**en-** (1c)]

engulf or **ingulf** /in-gulf'/, also (obs) **engulph** or **ingulph** vt to swallow up completely; to cause to be swallowed up; to overwhelm. [**en-** (1a)]
■ **engulf'ment** n.

engyscope /en'ji-skōp/ (obs) n a microscope, esp a kind of reflecting microscope. [Gr engys near, and skopeein to view]

enhalo /in-hā'lō/ vt to surround with a halo. [**en-** (1a)]

enhance /en-, in-häns'/ vt to raise in value or quality; to heighten; to intensify; to add to or increase; to make more important; to improve. ◆ vi to increase; to rise in value; to lift (obs). [Anglo-Fr enhauncer, prob from OFr enhaucer, from L in, and altus high; cf **hance**]
■ **enhance'ment** n. **enhanc'er** n something that enhances; a DNA sequence that can stimulate transcription of a gene while being at a distance from it (biol). **enhanc'ive** adj.
❑ **enhanced interrogation** n (US; euphem) interrogation using severe coercive techniques. **enhanced radiation weapon** n a neutron bomb.

enharmonic /en-här-mon'ik/ or **enharmonical** /-i-kl/ adj relating to music constructed on a scale containing intervals of less than a semitone; of a scale of music current among the Greeks in which an interval of $2\frac{1}{2}$ tones was divided into two quarter tones and a major third; of a minute pitch difference eg between F sharp and G flat, not identifiable in a scale of equal temperament. [Gr enharmonikos, from en in, and harmoniā harmony]
■ **enharmon'ically** adv.
❑ **enharmonic modulation** n for instruments of equal temperament, change of notation without change of tone.

enhearse see **inhearse**.

enhearten /in-här'tn/ vt to encourage; to cheer. [**en-** (1b)]

enhunger /en-hung'gər/ vt to make hungry. [**en-** (1b)]

enhydros /en-hī'dros/ (mineralogy) n a chalcedony nodule with water or other liquid in a cavity. [Gr enydros containing water, from en in, and hydōr water]
■ **enhy'drite** n a mineral with fluid inclusions. **enhydrit'ic** or **enhy'drous** adj.

enhypostasia /en-hī-pō-stā'zi-ə/ (theol) n substantial or personal existence; personality not existing independently but by union with another, as the human nature of Christ was said to be dependent on his divine nature. [Gr en in, and hypostasis (see **hypostasis**)]
■ **enhypostatic** /-stat'ik/ adj. **enhypostatize** or **-ise** /-pos'tə-tīz/ vt.

eniac /en'i-ak/ n an early American electronic computer. [electronic numerical integrator and calculator]

enigma /in-ig'mə/ n a statement with a hidden meaning to be guessed; anything very obscure; a mysterious person or situation; a riddle; (with cap) a cipher used by Germany during World War II. [L aenigma, from Gr ainigma, from ainissesthai to speak darkly, from ainos a fable]
■ **enigmat'ic** or **enigmat'ical** /en-/ adj relating to, containing or resembling an enigma; obscure; puzzling; open to more than one interpretation. **enigmat'ically** adv. **enig'matist** n a person who makes up or deals in riddles; a person who expresses himself or herself in riddles. **enig'matize** or **-ise** vt to express enigmatically or symbolically. **enigmatog'raphy** n the composition of enigmas.

enisle or **inisle** /en- or in-īl'/ vt to put on or make into an island; to isolate. [**en-** (1a, b)]

enjambment or **enjambement** /in-jam(b)'mənt or ã-zhãb-mã'/ n in verse, the continuation of the sense without a pause beyond the end of the line. [Fr enjambement, from enjamber to stride, encroach, from en in, and jambe leg]
■ **enjamb** /in-jam'/ vt and vi.

enjoin /en- or in-join'/ vt to impose (a command, etc) on; to order or direct, esp with authority or urgency; to forbid or prohibit by injunction (law). [Fr enjoindre, from L injungere, from in in, and jungere to join]
■ **enjoin'er** n. **enjoin'ment** n.

enjoy /en- or in-joi'/ vt to take pleasure or delight in; to feel or perceive with pleasure; to possess or use with satisfaction or delight; to have the use or benefit of; (usu of a man) to have sexual intercourse with (archaic). [OFr enjoier to give joy to, from en (L in), and joie joy; or OFr enjoir to enjoy, from en, and joir, from L gaudēre to rejoice]
■ **enjoyabil'ity** n. **enjoy'able** adj capable of being enjoyed; giving pleasure, delightful. **enjoy'ableness** n. **enjoy'ably** adv. **enjoy'er** n. **enjoy'ment** n the state, act or condition of enjoying; the satisfactory possession or use of anything; pleasure; happiness.
■ **enjoy oneself** to have a pleasant time.

enkephalin or **enkephaline** /en-kef'ə-lin/ n a chemical found in small quantities in the brain, which relieves pain and can be produced synthetically. [Gr en in, and kephalē head]

enkernel /en- or in-kûr'nl/ vt to enclose in a kernel. [**en-** (1a)]

enkindle /en- or in-kin'dl/ vt to kindle or set on fire; to inflame; to excite or rouse. [**en-** (1c)]
■ **enkin'dled** adj.

enlace, also **inlace** /in-lās'/ vt to encircle as though with laces; to embrace; to entwine; to entangle; to cover with a network or with lace; to interlace. [**en-** (1c)]
■ **enlace'ment** n.

en l'air /ã ler'/ (Fr) in the air; being discussed or expected; without reality.

enlard /in-lärd'/ (Shakesp) vt to grease or baste. [**en-** (1a)]

enlarge /en- or in-lärj'/ or (Spenser) **enlargen** /-lär'jən/ vt to increase in size or quantity; to expand; to amplify; to make wider; to reproduce on a larger scale, esp of a photograph; to set free. ◆ vi to grow large or larger; to speak or write expansively (with on or upon); to expatiate. [OFr enlarger, from en (L in), and large large]
■ **enlarged'** adj. **enlar'gedly** adv. **enlar'gedness** n. **enlarge'ment** n the act of enlarging; the state of being enlarged; increase; extension; diffuseness of speech or writing; a photograph reproduced on a larger

scale; the act of setting free; release. **enlarg'er** *n* an apparatus with a lens for enlarging photographs.

enlevement /in-lēv'mənt/ *n* (obs, esp Scots law) the abduction of a woman or child (also (Fr) **enlèvement** /ā-lev-mā/).
■ **enlevé** /ā-lə-vā/ adj (Fr) carried away or kidnapped.

enlight /en- or in-līt'/ (archaic) vt to shed light on; to light up or kindle. [OE inlīhtan, from in in, and līhtan to light; or independently formed later]
■ **enlight'en** vt to impart knowledge or information to; to make aware or uplift by knowledge or religion; to free from prejudice and superstition; to lighten or shed light on (archaic); to give light to (archaic); to make clear to the mind (obs). **enlight'ener** *n*. **enlight'ening** adj. **enlight'enment** *n* the act of enlightening; the state of being enlightened; (usu with cap) the spirit of the French philosophers of the 18c, with a belief in reason and human progress and a questioning of tradition and authority.

enlink /in-lingk'/ vt to connect closely. [en- (1c)]

enlist /in-list'/ vt to enrol; to engage as a soldier, etc; to obtain the support and help of, for a cause or undertaking. ◆ vi (with in) to engage in public service, esp as a soldier; to support a cause with enthusiasm. [en- (1a)]
■ **enlist'er** *n*. **enlist'ment** *n* the act of enlisting; the state of being enlisted.
□ **enlisted man** *n* (US) a member of the armed forces below the rank of warrant officer, other than a cadet or midshipman (also **enlisted person**; fem **enlisted woman**).

enliven /in-lī'vn/ vt to put life into; to excite or make active; to make cheerful or bright; to animate. [en- (1b)]
■ **enlīv'ener** *n*. **enlīv'enment** *n*.

enlock /in-lok'/ vt to lock up; to enclose. [en- (1a)]

enlumine /en-loo'min or -lū'/ (Spenser) vt same as **illumine**.

en masse /ā mas'/ (Fr) in a body; all together.

enmesh or **inmesh** /in-mesh'/, **emmesh** or **immesh** /em-(m)esh', im-(m)esh'/ vt to catch in or as if in a mesh or net; to entangle. [en- (1a)]
■ **enmesh'ment** or **inmesh'ment** *n*.

enmew see **emmew**.

en militaire /ā mē-lē-ter'/ (Fr) as a military man.

enmity /en'mi-ti/ *n* the quality of being an enemy; unfriendliness; ill-will; hostility. [OFr enemistié, from L inimīcus; see **enemy**¹]

enmossed /in-most'/ adj covered with moss. [en- (1a)]

enmove /en-moov'/ (Spenser) vt same as **emmove**.

ennage see under **en**.

ennea- /en-i-ə-/ combining form denoting nine. [Gr ennea nine]
■ **ennead** /en'i-ad/ *n* (Gr enneas, -ados) the number nine; a set of nine things. **enneadic** adj. **enn'eagon** /-ə-gon/ *n* (Gr gōniā angle) a polygon with nine angles, a nonagon. **enneagonal** /-ag'ən-l/ adj. **enn'eagram** *n* (Gr gramma a letter) a nine-sided diagram, now often taken to represent the nine supposed different types of personality. **enneahē'dral** adj. **enneahē'dron** *n* a solid figure with nine faces. **Ennean'dria** *n pl* (Gr anēr, andros man or male) the ninth Linnaean class of plants, with nine stamens. **ennean'drian** adj. **ennean'drous** adj. **enn'eastyle** adj (Gr stȳlos column) having nine columns.

ennoble /i-nō'bl/ vt to make noble; to elevate or distinguish; to raise to the ranks of the nobility. [Fr ennoblir, from Fr en (L in), and **noble**]
■ **ennō'blement** *n* the act of making noble; conferment of the rank of noble. **enno'bling** adj.

ennui /ā-nwē', on'wē or on-wē'/ *n* a feeling of weariness or languor; boredom; the occasion of these feelings. ◆ vt (**ennuying**; **ennuied'** or **ennuyed'**) (found mostly as pap) to weary; to bore. [Fr, distress, from OFr anoi, from L in odiō, as in odiō habeō I hold in hatred, ie I am tired of; see **annoy**]
■ **ennuyé** /-yā/ adj (Fr) bored.

ENO abbrev: English National Opera.

enodal /ē-nō'dl/ adj without nodes.

enoki /ə-nok'ē/ *n* a thin white edible mushroom with a very small cap, native to Japan. [Jap]

enomoty /e-nom'o-ti/ (ancient Greece) *n* a band of sworn soldiers, esp the smallest subdivision of the Spartan army. [Gr enōmotiā, from en in, and omnynai to swear]

enormous /i-nör'məs/ or (obs) **enorm** /i-nörm'/ adj immense; huge; abounding, exceeding the normal esp in a bad sense (archaic); outrageous (archaic); atrocious (archaic); of considerable amount or extent (inf); exceedingly good (inf). [L ēnormis, from ē out of, and norma rule]
■ **enor'mity** *n* a great crime; great wickedness; outrage; immenseness or vastness; iniquity; abnormality (obs). **enor'mously** adv. **enor'mousness** *n*.

e-nose /ē'nōz/ *n* an electronic device which detects the presence of specified compounds, used in the food, defence and health industries (in full **electronic nose**).

enosis /en'ō-sis or en-ō'sis/ *n* (pl **enoses**) union, the aim and rallying-cry of the Greek Cypriot movement for union with Greece. [Gr (ancient and Mod) henosis, from heis, henos one]

enough /i-nuf'/ adj as much as needed to satisfy a requirement, lack, demand, etc; sufficient; satisfying. ◆ adv sufficiently; quite; fairly; tolerably; used in phrases which stress or admit the state of something, eg oddly enough, fair enough. ◆ *n* sufficience; as much as satisfies a desire or want; a sufficient degree or extent. [OE genōh (nominative, neuter accusative and adv for earlier genōg); Gothic ganōhs; Ger genug; ON gnōgr]
■ **enough is enough** the current state of affairs can no longer be tolerated. **enough said** there is no need to speak further.

enounce /i- or ē-nowns'/ vt to enunciate; to proclaim; to utter or articulate. [Fr énoncer, from L ēnuntiāre]

enow¹ /i-now'/ (archaic) adj and adv enough; formerly used as plural of enough. [OE genōge, with -g preserved in inflected forms; cf **enough**]

enow² /ē-noo'/ adv (Scot and dialect) a moment ago; presently. [Prob **even now**]

ENP abbrev : electronic number plate.

en pantoufles /ā pā-too'-fl'/ unconstrained, at one's ease. [Fr, in slippers]

en papillote /ā pa-pē-yot'/ (of food) cooked and served in an envelope of oiled paper or foil. [Fr papillote buttered or oiled paper for cooking in]

en passant /ā pa-sā'/ (Fr) in passing; by the way; in chess, applied to the taking of a pawn that has just moved two squares as if it had moved only one.

en pension /ā pā-syõ'/ (Fr) at a fixed rate for board and lodging.

enplane see **emplane**.

en plein air /ā ple-ner'/ (Fr) in the open air.

en plein jour /ā plẽ zhoor'/ (Fr) in broad daylight.

en poste /ā post'/ (Fr) of a diplomat, resident at a place in an official capacity.

en primeur /ā prē-mœr'/ (of tasting, buying or investing in wine) when the wine is new. [Fr en in, and primeur (of wine) youth or newness]

en prince /ā prēs'/ (Fr) in princely style.

en principe /ā prē-sēp'/ (Fr) in principle.

enprint /en'print/ *n* an enlarged photographic print, esp 5 × 3½in (approx 12.7cm × 9cm). ['Envelope-size print' and 'enlarged print' have both been suggested as origins]

en prise /ā prēz'/ (Fr) in chess, (of a piece) exposed to capture.

en pure perte /ā pür pert'/ (Fr) to mere loss or to no purpose.

enqueue /en-kū'/ (comput) vt to add (a data-processing task) to a list of tasks awaiting processing in a buffer. [en- (1a)]

en queue /ā kø'/ (Fr) like a tail; in a string or line; (of hair) tied at the nape of the neck, in a ponytail.

enquire see **inquire**.

enrace /en-rās'/ (Spenser) vt to implant. [en- (1a)]

enrage /in-rāj'/ vt to make extremely angry. [OFr enrager, from en (L in), and rage rage]
■ **enraged'** adj very angry; furious. **enrage'ment** *n* the act of enraging; the state of being enraged; rapture (Spenser).

enragé /ā-rä-zhā'/ (Fr; hist) *n* any of a group of revolutionaries during the French Revolution in favour of proto-socialist economic reform rather than political reform as a means of alleviating the distress of the populace. [Fr, violently angry or crazy]

enranckle /in-rang'kl/ (Spenser) vt to enrage. [en- (1b)]

enrange /en-rānj'/ or **enraunge** /en-rönj'/ (Spenser) vt to arrange; to rove over. [en- (1c)]

enrank /en-rangk'/ (Shakesp) vt to place in order. [en- (1a)]

en rappel /ā ra-pel'/ (Fr; mountaineering) using a rope which is easily pulled free after descent. [Fr, from rappel recall]

en rapport /ā ra-pör'/ (Fr) in direct relation; in close touch or harmony.

enrapture /in-rap'chər/ vt to put in rapture or ecstasy; to transport with pleasure or delight. [en- (1a)]
■ **enrap'tured** or **enrapt'** adj in ecstasy.

enraunge see **enrange**.

enravish /en-rav'ish/ vt to enrapture. [en- (1c)]

enregiment /in-rej'(i)-mənt/ vt to form into a regiment. [en- (1b)]

enregister /in-rej′i-stər/ vt to register; to enrol; to record; to put on record as ratified. [**en-** (1c)]

en règle /ã reg′l′/ (Fr) in due order; according to regulations.

en retraite /ã rə-tret′/ (Fr) in retirement; on half pay.

en revanche /ã rə-väsh′/ (Fr) in return or requital.

enrheum /en-room′/ (obs) vt to give a cold to or cause to catch a cold. [OFr enrheumer, from en (see **en-** (1b)), and Gr rheuma (see **rheum**)]
■ **enrheumed**′ adj (archaic).

enrich /in-rich′/ vt to make rich; to fertilize; to decorate; to enhance or improve; to increase the proportion of some valuable substance in; to increase the proportion of one or more particular isotopes in a mixture of the isotopes of an element, eg to raise the proportion of uranium-235 above that for natural uranium in reactor fuel (phys). ◆ vi (rare) to become richer. [**en-** (1b)]
■ **enrich**′**ment** n the act of enriching; something that enriches; ornamentation.

enridged /en-rij′id/ (Shakesp) adj formed into ridges. [**en-** (1b)]

enring /en- or in-ring′/ vt to encircle; to put a ring on. [**en-** (1a)]

enriven /en-riv′n/ (Spenser) adj torn. [**en-** (1c)]

enrobe /in-rōb′/ (formal) vt to dress, clothe, or invest. [**en-** (1c)]

enrol or (archaic or N Am) **enroll** /in-rōl′/ vt (**enroll**′**ing**; **enrolled**′) to insert in a roll, list or register; to enter in a list as a pupil, member, etc; to enlist; to record; to put in writing; to form into a roll (Spenser); to enwrap (Spenser). ◆ vi to enrol oneself. [OFr enroller (Fr enrôler), from en, and rolle roll]
■ **enrollee**′ n. **enroll**′**er** n. **enrol**′**ment** or **enroll**′**ment** n the act of enrolling; that in which anything is enrolled; a register.

enroot /in-root′/ vt to fix by the root; to implant firmly; to entangle (Shakesp). [**en-** (1c)]

enrough /in-ruf′/ (archaic) vt to make rough. [**en-** (1b)]

enround /en-rownd′/ (Shakesp) vt to surround. [**en-** (1a)]

en route /ã root′/ adv on the road, on the way. ◆ interj let′s go, march. [Fr]
■ **en route** for on the way towards.

ENS abbrev : European Nuclear Society.

Ens. abbrev : Ensign.

ens /enz/ (philos) n (pl **entia** /en′shi-ə/) being or existence; an entity, as opposed to an attribute. [LL ēns, prp of L esse to be]
❑ **ens per accidens** /enz pər ak′si-dɑnz or per a-ki-däns′/ n (in Aristotelian philosophy) that which exists only as an accident of a substance (an **ens per se** /sē or sā/). **ens rationis** /rā-shi-ō′nis or ra-ti-ō′/ n an entity of reason, existing purely in the mind opposed to **ens reale** /rē-ä′lē or re-ä′le/ which exists actually or potentially outside the mind.

ENSA /en′sə/ abbrev : Entertainments National Service Association, which provided entertainment for the armed forces during and after World War II (now replaced by **CSE**).

ensample /en-säm′pl/ (archaic) n example. ◆ vt to give an example of. [OFr essample ; see **example**]

ensanguine /in-sang′gwin/ vt to stain or cover with blood. [Fr pfx en- in, and L sanguis, -inis blood]
■ **ensan**′**guinated** or (esp facetious) **ensan**′**guined** adj bloody.

ensate /en′sāt/ (bot) adj sword-shaped. [L ēnsis sword]

enschedule /en-shed′ūl/ (Shakesp) vt to insert in a schedule. [**en-** (1a)]

ensconce /in-skons′/ vt to settle comfortably; to hide safely; to cover or protect with a sconce or earthwork (obs). [**en-** (1a)]

enseal /en-sēl′/ (archaic) vt to put one′s seal to; to seal up. [**en-** (1c)]

enseam[1] /en-sēm′/ vt to mark as if with a seam. [**en-** (1c), and **seam**[2]]

enseam[2] /en-sēm′/ vt to grease (obs); to defile (Shakesp); to free from superfluous fat (obs). [**en-** (1c), and **seam**[1]]

enseam[3] /en-sēm′/ (obs) vt to contain; to introduce to company. [Origin obscure; cf ME in same or in seme, OE ætsomne or tosomne together, ON semja to put together]

ensear /en-sēr′/ (Shakesp) vt to dry up. [**en-** (1b), and **sear**[1]]

ensemble /on-som′bl or ã-sã′bl′/ n a group of musicians playing together (music); the performance of such a group; the combined effect of the performance; all parts of a thing taken together; an outfit consisting of several (matching) garments; a group of supporting dancers, a corps de ballet; a set of a very large number of systems, all dynamically identical to a system under statistical consideration, but differing in the initial condition (phys). ◆ adj of or relating to an ensemble. [Fr ensemble together, from L in in, and simul at the same time]
■ **tout ensemble** /too-tä-/ general appearance or effect.

ensepulchre /en-sep′əl-kər/ vt to put in a sepulchre. [**en-** (1a)]

ensew (Spenser) same as **ensue**.

ensheath, **ensheathe** or **insheathe** /in-shēdh′/ vt to enclose in or as if in a sheath. [**en-** (1a)]
■ **ensheath**′**ment** n.

enshell same as **inshell**.

enshelter /en-shel′tər/ (Shakesp) vt to put in shelter. [**en-** (1a)]

enshield[1] /en-shēld′/ vt to shield or protect. [**en-** (1c)]

enshield[2] /in-shēld′/ (Shakesp) adj probably a variant of **enshelled** or **inshelled**.

enshrine /en-shrīn′/ vt to enclose in or as if in a shrine; to consider sacred, to cherish. [**en-** (1a)]
■ **enshrine**′**ment** n.

enshroud /en-shrowd′/ vt to cover up; to cover with a shroud; to cover, hide or envelop as if with a shroud. [**en-** (1a)]

ensiform /en′si-förm/ (bot and med) adj sword-shaped. [L ēnsis a sword, and fōrma form]
❑ **ensiform cartilage** same as **xiphoid cartilage** (see **xiphoid** under **xiph-**).

ensign /en′sin or -sīn/ n a sign or flag distinguishing a nation or a regiment (see also under **blue**[1], **red**[1] and **white**); a soldier who carries the Colours; orig a badge, sign or mark; until 1871, the officer of lowest commissioned rank in the British infantry; an officer of lowest commissioned rank in the US Navy. ◆ vt /-sīn′/ (heraldry) to mark with a badge or sign placed above. [OFr enseigne, from L īnsignia, pl of īnsigne a distinctive mark, from in on, and signum a mark]
■ **en**′**signcy** or **en**′**signship** n (hist) the rank or commission of an ensign in the army.

ensilage /en′si-lij or in-sī′lij/ n the process of making silage; silage. [Fr, from Sp en in, and silo, from L sīrus, from Gr siros, sīros or seiros pit for corn]
■ **ensile** /en-sīl′ or en′sīl/ or **en**′**silage** vt to store in pits or silos.

ensky /en-skī′/ (Shakesp) vt to place in the sky. [**en-** (1a)]

enslave /in-slāv′/ vt to make a slave or slaves of; to subject to a dominating influence. [**en-** (1b)]
■ **enslaved**′ adj. **enslave**′**ment** n the act of enslaving; the state of being enslaved; slavery; captivity. **enslav**′**er** n.

ensnare /in-snār′/ vt to catch in or as if in a snare; to entrap; to entangle. [**en-** (1a)]
■ **ensnare**′**ment** n.

ensnarl /en-snärl′/ vt to cause to become caught up in problems, difficulties or delays; to entangle (Spenser). [**en-** (1a)]

ensorcell /en-sör′səl or -sör′/ (archaic and poetic) vt to bewitch. [OFr ensorceler, from en, and sorcier a sorcerer]
■ **ensor**′**cellment** n.

ensoul or **insoul** /in-sōl′/ vt to join with the soul; to animate as a soul; to bestow a soul on. [**en-** (1b)]
■ **ensoul**′**ment** or **insoul**′**ment** n.

en spectacle /ã spek-tak′l′/ (Fr) as a spectacle.

ensphere or **insphere** /in-sfēr′/ vt (pap (Milton) **insphear'd**) to enclose or place in or as if in a sphere; to give a spherical form to. [**en-** (1a)]

enstamp /in-stamp′/ vt to mark as with a stamp. [**en-** (1c)]

enstatite /en′stə-tīt/ n a rock-forming mineral, an orthorhombic pyroxene, magnesium silicate. [Gr enstatēs adversary, from its refractory character]

ensteep /en-stēp′/ (Shakesp) vt to steep; to place under water. [**en-** (1c)]

enstructured /en-struk′chərd/ adj incorporated into or made part of the structure of something. [**en-** (1a) and **structure**]

enstyle /in-stīl′/ (archaic) vt to style or call. [**en-** (1c)]

ensue /in- or en-sū′/ vi (**ensū**′**ing**; **ensūed**′) to follow or come after; to result (with from). ◆ vt (Bible; archaic) to follow after. [OFr ensuir (Fr ensuivre), from L in after, and LL sequere, from L sequī to follow]

en suite /ã swēt′/ adv forming a unit or a set; in succession or a connected series; with an en suite bathroom. ◆ adj (of a bathroom) connecting directly with a bedroom. ◆ n an en suite bathroom. [Fr, in sequence or in succession]

ensure /in-shoor′/ vt to make sure; to make safe; to betroth (obs); to insure (obs). [See **insure**]
■ **ensur**′**er** n.

enswathe /in-swädh′/ vt to wrap in (also **inswathe**′). [**en-** (1c)]
■ **enswathe**′**ment** n.

ensweep /in-swēp′/ (archaic) vt to sweep over. [**en-** (1c)]

ENT (med) abbrev : ear, nose and throat, a specialized field of medicine.

ent., **entom.** or **entomol.** abbrev : entomology.

ent- see **ento-**.

entablature /en-tab'lə-chər/ n in classical architecture, the part which surmounts the columns and rests upon the capitals; any similar structure, such as an engine framework upon columns. [Ital *intavolatura*, from *in* in, and *tavola*, from L *tabula* a table]

entablement /in-tā'bl-mənt/ n a platform above the dado on a pedestal, on which a statue rests; an entablature. [Fr]

entail[1] /in-tāl'/ vt to bring on or result in as an inevitable consequence; to settle on a series of heirs for (an estate), so that the immediate possessor may not dispose of it (*law*). ◆ n the settlement of an entailed estate; an estate entailed; the transmission or rule of descent of an estate. [**en-** (1a) and **tail**[2]]
■ **entail'er** n. **entail'ment** n the act of entailing; the state of being entailed.

entail[2] or **entayle** /en-tāl'/ (*obs*) vt and vi to carve. ◆ n cut or fashion. [OFr *entailler*, from LL *intaleāre*, from *in* into, and *taleāre* to cut]

entame /en-tām'/ (*Shakesp*) vt to tame. [**en-** (1a)]

entamoeba /en-tə-mē'bə/ n any amoeba of the genus *Entamoeba*, one species of which causes amoebic dysentery in humans (also **endamoe'ba**). [**ento-** or **endo-** and **amoeba**]

entangle /in-tang'gl/ vt to twist into a tangle, or so as not to be easily separated; to involve in complications or in an embarrassing or compromising situation; to perplex or confuse; to ensnare. [**en-** (1c)]
■ **entang'lement** n a confused state; perplexity or confusion; a tangled obstacle; a tangle; the condition of being entangled; an entangling situation or involvement.

entasis /en'tə-sis/ (*archit*) n the slightly swelling outline of the shaft of a column or similar structure, used to counteract the illusion of concavity that an absolutely straight column would produce. [Gr *entasis*, from *en* in, and *tasis* a stretch]

entayle see **entail**[2].

entelechy /en-tel'ə-ki/ (*philos*) n actuality; distinctness of realized existence; a vital principle supposed by vitalists to direct processes in an organism towards realization of a certain end. [Gr *entelecheia*, from *en* in, *telos* perfection or end, and *echein* to have]

entellus /en-tel'əs/ n the hanuman monkey of India. [Appar from *Entellus*, the old Sicilian in Virgil's *Aeneid*, from its old-mannish appearance]

entender or **intender** /in-ten'dər/ (*obs*) vt to make tender; to weaken. [**en-** (1b)]

entente /ã-tãt'/ n an understanding; a friendly agreement or relationship between states, eg the **entente cordiale** /kör-dē-äl'/ between Britain and France (1904); those who are collectively party to such an agreement. [Fr]

enter /en'tər/ vi to go or come in; to penetrate; to come onto the stage; to take possession; to become a member; to put down one's name (as a competitor, candidate, etc); to join in or become a party or participator. ◆ vt to come or go into; to penetrate; to join or engage in; to begin; to put into; to enrol or record; to admit; to inscribe or have inscribed; to register (a vessel leaving a port, a horse for a race, a pupil for a school, etc); to insert a record of; to send (an instruction, etc) to a processor for it to be implemented (*comput*); to initiate; to become a member of; to take possession of; to obtain right of pre-emption to by recording one's name in a land office, etc (*US*). ◆ n (*Shakesp*) ingoing. [Fr *entrer*, from L *intrāre* to go into, related to *inter* between]
■ **en'terable** adj. **en'terer** n. **en'tering** n and adj.
❑ **enter key** n (*comput*) a key that terminates a line of text or executes a command (also **return key**).
■ **enter a protest** to write it in an official document; therefore simply, to protest. **enter into** to become concerned or involved in; to be interested in; to participate actively or heartily in; to understand sympathetically; to take up the discussion of; to be part of. **enter on** or **upon** to begin; to engage in.

enter-[1] /en-tər-/ or **entero-** /en-tə-rō-/ combining form denoting intestine. [Gr *enteron* gut]
■ **en'teral** adj relating to, within, or by way of the intestine. **en'terate** adj having an alimentary canal. **enterec'tomy** n (Gr *ektomē* a cutting out) surgical removal of part of the bowel. **enteric** /en-ter'ik/ adj relating to the intestines; possessing an alimentary canal (**enter'ic-coated** (of a medicinal capsule) coated in a substance that prevents it from releasing its contents until it has reached the intestines). ◆ n short form of **enteric fever**, typhoid fever, an infectious disease caused by a bacillus, characterized by fever, a red rash, enlargement of the spleen and ulceration of the intestines. **enterī'tis** n inflammation of the intestines, *esp* the small intestine. **en'terocele** /-sēl/ n (Gr *kēlē* tumour) a hernia containing intestine. **enterocentesis** /-sen-tē'sis/ n (Gr *kentēsis* pricking) operative puncturing of the intestine. **enterococcus** /-kok'əs/ n (pl **enterococci** /-kok'sī or -kok'i/) (Gr *kokkos* a grain) a bacterium that lives in the digestive tracts of humans and helps to break down waste substances. **en'terocyte** /-sīt/ n (Gr *kytos* vessel) a

cell of the intestinal wall. **en'terolith** n (Gr *lithos* stone) a concretion of organic matter with lime, bismuth or magnesium salts formed in the intestine. **Enteromor'pha** n (Gr *morphē* form) a genus of green seaweeds of tubular form. **en'teron** n (pl **en'tera**) in coelenterates (animals with only one body-cavity), the body-cavity itself; in higher animals, the gut or alimentary canal. **enteropathy** /-op'ə-thi/ n (Gr *pathos* suffering) an intestinal disorder. **enteropneust** /en'tər-op-nūst/ n (Gr *pneein* to breathe) any animal of the **Enteropneus'ta** (literally, gut-breathers) the Hemichordata or a division of them including Balanaglossus. **enteropneust'al** adj. **enteroptōs'is** n downward displacement of the intestines. **enteros'tomy** n (Gr *stoma* mouth) surgical formation of an opening in the intestine. **enterot'omy** n incision of the intestinal wall. **enterotox'in** n an intestinal toxin which causes food poisoning. **enterovī'rus** n any of several viruses occurring in and infecting the intestine.

enter-[2] form of **inter-**, *orig* through Fr *entre* between, etc.

enterchaunge /en-tər-chönj'/ an obsolete form of **interchange**.

enterdeale (*Spenser*) see **interdeal**.

entero- see **enter-**[1].

enterprise /en'tər-prīz/ n an undertaking or new project, *esp* when bold or dangerous; readiness, initiative and daring in undertaking; a business concern. ◆ vt (*archaic*) to undertake. [OFr *entreprise*, pap of *entreprendre*, from *entre* between (L *inter*), and *prendre*, from L *praehendere* to seize]
■ **en'terpriser** n an adventurer (*archaic*); an entrepreneur. **en'terprising** adj bold and imaginative in undertaking; adventurous; full of initiative. **en'terprisingly** adv.
❑ **enterprise culture** n a culture based on an economic policy that encourages commercial initiative and audacious, imaginative planning. **enterprise zone** n any of a number of sites in depressed areas in which industrial and commercial renewal is encouraged by the government by means of financial and other incentives.

entertain /en-tər-tān'/ vt to hold the attention or thoughts of; to hold the attention of in a pleasant or diverting manner; to amuse; to give pleasure or amusement to by means of a performance, show, etc; to provide food or drink as refreshment for; to give lodging or hospitality to; to treat hospitably; to receive and take into consideration; to keep or hold in the mind; to maintain or keep up (*obs*); to take on (as a servant, etc) (*obs*); to treat (*obs*); to receive (*obs*); to meet or experience (*Spenser*). ◆ n (*Spenser*; *Shakesp*) entertainment. [Fr *entretenir*, from L *inter* among, and *tenēre* to hold]
■ **entertain'er** n a person who entertains in any sense; a person who gives performances professionally, eg a singer or comedian. **entertain'ing** adj giving entertainment; amusing. ◆ n entertainment. **entertain'ingly** adv. **entertain'ment** n the act of entertaining; something that entertains or amuses; amusement; a performance or show intended to give pleasure; the reception of and provision for guests; hospitality at table; the provisions of the table (*archaic*); a banquet (*archaic*).

entertake /en-tər-tāk'/ (*Spenser*) vt to receive.

entertissued see **intertissued**.

entêté or (*fem*) **entêtée** /ã-te-tā'/ (*Fr*) adj infatuated; opinionated.

enthalpy /en-thal'pi or en'thəl-pi/ (*phys*) n the heat content of a substance per unit mass, defined as $H = U + PV$ (U = internal energy, P = pressure, and V = volume). [Gr *enthalpein* to warm in]

enthetic /en-thet'ik/ adj (of diseases, etc) introduced from outside the body. [Gr *enthetikos*, from *entithenai* to put in]

enthral or (*esp US*) **enthrall** /in-thröl'/ vt (**enthrall'ing**; **enthralled'**) (also (*obs*) **inthrall'** or **inthral'**) to hold spellbound; to bring into bondage or slavery; to hold in bondage or slavery. [**en-** (1a)]
■ **enthral'dom** n (*archaic*) the condition of being enthralled. **enthrall'ing** adj. **enthral'ment** or (*esp US*) **enthrall'ment** n the act of enthralling; slavery.

enthrone /in-thrōn'/ vt to place on a throne; to exalt to the seat of royalty; to install as bishop; to exalt. [**en-** (1a)]
■ **enthrōne'ment** n the act of enthroning or of being enthroned (also **enthroniza'tion** or **-s-**). **enthrō'nize** or **-ise** (or /en'/) vt to enthrone (eg a bishop); to exalt.

enthusiasm /in-, en-thū'zi-azm or -thoo'/ n intense and lively interest; passionate zeal; possession by a god, inspiration or religious exaltation (*obs*); religious extravagance (*obs*). [Gr *enthousiasmos* a god-inspired zeal, from *enthousiazein* to be inspired by a god, from *en* in, and *theos* a god]
■ **enthuse'** vt and vi (back-formation) to make, be, become, or appear enthusiastic. **enthu'siast** n a person filled with enthusiasm; a person deeply interested in a particular subject. **enthusias'tic** or (*archaic*) **enthusias'tical** adj filled with enthusiasm; zealous; ardent. **enthusias'tically** adv.

enthymeme /en'thi-mēm/ n an argument of probability only (*rhetoric*); a syllogism in which one premise is suppressed (*logic*). [Gr

enthȳmḗma a consideration, from *enthȳmeesthai* to consider, from *en* in, and *thȳmos* the mind]
■ **enthymemat'ical** *adj*.

entia see **ens**.

entice /in-tīs'/ *vt* to attract by exciting hope or desire; to tempt; to lead astray. [OFr *enticier* to provoke; prob related to L *titiō* a firebrand]
■ **entice'able** *adj*. **entice'ment** *n* the act of enticing; something which entices or tempts; allurement. **entic'er** *n*. **entic'ing** *n* and *adj*. **entīc'ingly** *adv*.

entire /in-tīr'/ *adj* whole; complete; unmingled; intact; unimpaired; untired (*Spenser*); not castrated (*esp* of a horse); with untoothed and unlobed margin (*bot*); inner or inward (*Spenser*); genuine (*archaic*). ◆ *adv* (*archaic*) within; sincerely. ◆ *n* the whole (*rare*); completeness (*rare*); a stallion; a stamped, used or unused, envelope (*philately*); porter or stout as delivered from the brewery. [OFr *entier*, from L *integer* whole, from *in-* not, and root of *tangere* to touch; in some senses showing confusion with **interior**]
■ **entire'ly** *adv*. **entire'ness** or **entī'rety** *n* completeness; the whole.
■ **in its entirety** in its completeness; (considered, taken, etc) as a whole.

entitle /en-tī'tl/ *vt* to give a title to; to style; to give a right or claim to. [OFr *entiteler*, from LL *intitulāre*, from *in* in, and *titulus* title]
■ **entī'tlement** *n* something to which one has a right or claim.

entity /en'ti-ti/ *n* being or existence; something that exists independently; the basic essential nature of something; an abstraction or archetypal conception. [LL *entitās*, *-ātis*, from *ēns* (see **ens**)]
■ **en'titative** *adj*.

ento- /en-tō- or en-to-/ or **ent-** /ent-/ *combining form* (often interchanging with **endo-**) denoting inside, *opp* to **ecto-** and **exo-**. [Gr *entos* within]
■ **en'toblast** *n* (Gr *blastos* shoot or bud) endoderm; a cell nucleolus. **en'toderm** *n* endoderm. **entophytal** /-fī'tl/ *adj*. **en'tophyte** /-fīt/ *n* (Gr *phyton* plant) an endophyte. **entophytic** /-fīt'ik/ or **entophytous** /en-tof'i-tas or en-tō-fī'tas/ *adj*. **entoplas'tral** *adj*. **entoplas'tron** *n* the unpaired plate behind the epiplastra in a turtle's plastron. **en'toproct** *n* a member of the **Entoproc'ta**, a phylum of marine invertebrates living mainly in coastal waters. **entopt'ic** *adj* (Gr *ōps*, *ōpos* eye) within the eyeball; relating to the visibility to the eye of objects within itself. **entop'tics** *n sing* the study of such appearances. **ento'tic** *adj* (Gr *ous*, *ōtos* ear) of the interior of the ear. **entozō'al** *adj*. **entozō'ic** *adj*. **entozō'on** *n* (*pl* **entozō'a**) (Gr *zōion* an animal) an animal living parasitically within the body of its host.

entoil /in-toil'/ *vt* to entangle or ensnare. [en- (1a)]
■ **entoil'ment** *n*.

entom. see **ent**.

entomb /in-toom'/ *vt* to place in a tomb; to bury. [OFr *entoumber*, from *en* in, and *tombe* a tomb]
■ **entomb'ment** *n* burial.

entomic /en-tom'ik/ *adj* relating to insects. [Gr *entoma* insects, from *entomos* cut up, from *en* in, and *tomē* a cut]
■ **entomolog'ical** /-loj'/ *adj*. **entomolog'ically** *adv*. **entomol'ogist** *n* a scientist who specializes in entomology. **entomol'ogize** or **-ise** *vi*. **entomol'ogy** /-ə-ji/ *n* the science of insects. **entomoph'agist** /-ə-jist/ *n*. **entomoph'agous** /-ə-gəs/ *adj* (Gr *phagein* to eat) insectivorous, insect-eating. **entomoph'agy** /-ə-ji/ *n* the practice of eating insects. **entomoph'ilous** *adj* (Gr *phileein* to love) specially adapted for pollination by insects. **entomoph'ily** *n* pollination by insects; adaptation to pollination by insects.

entomol. see **ent**.

Entomostraca /en-tō-mos'trə-kə/ *n pl* a general name for the lower orders of Crustacea, ie Phyllopods, Ostracods, Copepods and Cirripedes. [Gr *entomos* cut up, from *en* in, *tomē* a cut, and *ostrakon* a shell]
■ **entomos'tracan** *n* and *adj*. **entomos'tracous** *adj*.

entophyte, etc see under **ento-**.

entopic /en-top'ik/ *adj* developed, etc, in the normal place. [Gr *en* in, and *topos* place]

entoplastron...to...**entotic** see under **ento-**.

entourage /ä-too-räzh'/ *n* a group of followers or attendants. [Fr, from *entourer* to surround, from *en* in, and *tour* a circuit]

en tout cas /ä̃ too kä'/ *n* a parasol that can be used as an umbrella; (**En-Tout-Cas®**) a hard tennis court that can be used in all weathers. [Fr, in any case]

entozoon, etc see under **ento-**.

entr'acte /ä-trakt'/ *n* the interval between acts in a play; a piece of music or other performance between acts. [Fr, from *entre* between, and *acte* act]

entrail /en-trāl'/ (*Spenser*) *vt* to interlace or entwine. ◆ *n* twisting or entanglement. [OFr *entreillier*, from *en* in, and *treille* trelliswork]

entrails /en'trālz/ (*Spenser* **entralles** /en'trölz/) *n pl* (*sing* (*rare*)) **entrail** (*Spenser* **entrall** /en-tröl'/)) the internal organs of an animal or person; the bowels; the inside of anything; the seat of the emotions (*obs*). [OFr *entraille*, from LL *intrālia*, from *inter* within]

en train /ä̃ trẽ'/ (*Fr*) in progress.

entrain¹ /in-trān'/ *vt* to put (*esp* troops) on a railway train. ◆ *vi* to get on a train; to take a train. [en- (1a)]
■ **entrain'ment** *n*.

entrain² /in-trān'/ *vt* to transport one substance, eg small liquid particles, in another, eg a vapour (*phys*); to suspend bubbles or particles in a moving fluid (*phys*); to draw after (*archaic*); to cause to synchronize with (*biol*). [Fr *entraîner*]
■ **entrain'ment** *n*.

entrain³ /ä̃-trẽ'/ (*Fr*) *n* liveliness or spirit.
■ **entraînement** /ä̃-tren-mä̃/ *n* enthusiasm.

entrall(es) see **entrails**.

entrammel /in-tram'l/ *vt* to trammel or fetter. [en- (1c)]

entrance¹ /en'trəns/ *n* a place of entering; a door; an act of entering; a coming onto the stage; the power or right to enter; the beginning (*archaic*). [Fr *entrer*, from L *intrāre* to enter]
■ **en'trant** *n* someone who or something which enters.
❑ **entrance fee** *n* the money paid on entering a society, club, etc.

entrance² /in- or en-träns'/ *vt* to fill with enthusiastic or rapturous delight; to put into a trance. [en- (1a)]
■ **entrance'ment** *n* a state of trance or of great or excessive joy. **entranc'ing** *adj* charming, delightful. **entranc'ingly** *adv*.

entrant see under **entrance¹**.

entrap /in-trap'/ *vt* to catch in or as if in a trap; to ensnare; to entangle. [OFr *entraper*, from *en* in, and *trappe* a trap]
■ **entrap'ment** *n* the act of entrapping; the state of being entrapped; the act of luring a person into the commission of a crime so that he or she may be arrested and prosecuted (*law*). **entrapp'er** *n*.

en travesti /ä̃ tra-ve-stē'/ (*Fr*) (*esp* of a female dancer, singer or actress) wearing the clothes of the opposite sex.

entreasure /in-trezh'ər/ (*archaic*) *vt* to store in or as if in a treasury. [en- (1a)]

entreat, also (*Spenser*) **intreat** /in-trēt'/ *vt* to ask earnestly; to beseech; to beg for; to induce (*obs*); to treat, deal with or behave towards (*obs*); to occupy oneself with (*Spenser*); to pass or spend (time) (*Shakesp*). ◆ *vi* to beseech or ask. [OFr *entraiter*, from *en*, and *traiter* to treat]
■ **entreat'able** *adj* (*obs*). **intreat'full** *adj* (*Spenser*). **entreat'ing** *adj*. **entreat'ingly** *adv*. **entreat'ive** *adj* (*obs*). **entreat'ment** *n* the act of entreating; treatment (*obs*); perhaps discourse, verbal communication, or favours as objects of entreaty (*Shakesp*). **entreat'y** *n* the act of entreating; a desperate or earnest request; earnest prayer.

entrechat /ä-tr'-shä'/ (*ballet*) *n* a leap during which a dancer beats his or her heels together. [Fr, from Ital *intrecciata* plaited or complicated (caper)]

entrecôte /ä-tr'kōt/ *n* a steak cut from between two ribs (also *adj*). [Fr]

entrée /ä̃' or on'trā/ *n* a dish served between the chief courses of a formal dinner, ie between fish and roast meat, also (*esp N Am*) a main course, and (*esp Aust*) a starter; entry, freedom of access, admittance; introduction or means of access; an introduction or prelude (*music*); the act of entering, a formal entrance, or music for it. [Fr]
❑ **entrée dish** *n* a dish, usually silver, with a cover, suitable for an entrée.

entremets /ä̃'trə-mā or -me/ *n* a light dish served between the chief courses of a meal, formerly **entremes** or **entremesse**. [OFr *entremes*, from *entre* between, and *mes* (Fr *mets*) dish]

entrench or **intrench** /in-trench' or -trensh'/ *vt* to dig a trench around; to fortify with a ditch and parapet; to establish in a strong position (*esp milit*); to establish or fix firmly because of an unwillingness to change or in such a way that change is difficult or impossible; to cut into or wound (*Spenser*). ◆ *vi* to encroach. [en- (1c)]
■ **entrench'ment** or **intrench'ment** *n* a defensive earthwork of trenches and parapets; any protection; an encroachment (*obs*).
❑ **entrenched provisions** *n pl* in the constitution of a country, provisions specially safeguarded by being made subject to amendment or repeal only by exceptional procedure.

entre nous /ä̃-tr' noo'/ (*Fr*) between ourselves.

entrepot or **entrepôt** /ä̃'trə-pō/ *n* a port through which exports and imports pass, *esp* one from which imports are re-exported without duty being charged on them; a storehouse; a bonded warehouse. [Fr]

entrepreneur /ä̃-trə-prə-nœr'/ *n* a person who undertakes an enterprise *esp* a commercial one, often at personal financial risk; the managing proprietor of a firm who supplies the capital, bears the risks of production and is the controller of day-to-day management and

marketing; a contractor or employer; an organizer of musical or other entertainments. [Fr]
■ **entrepreneur'ial** /-nær'i-əl, -nū' or -noo'/ adj. **entrepreneur'ialism** n. **entrepreneur'ially** adv. **entrepreneur'ism** n. **entrepreneur'ship** n. **entrepreneuse** /-næz'/ n a female entrepreneur.

entresol /en'tər-sol/ or /ä'tr'sol/ n a low storey between two main storeys of a building, generally between the ground floor and the first floor. [Fr, from entre between, and sol the ground]

entrez /ä-trā'/ (Fr) interj come in.

entrism, etc see **entryism** under **entry**.

entrold, another reading **introld** /in-trōld'/ (Spenser; appar a pap of unknown meaning) enrolled, in the sense of encircled, has been conjectured.

entropion /en-trō'pi-on/ or **entropium** /-əm/ n inversion of the edge of the eyelid. [Gr en in, and tropē turning]

entropy /en'trə-pi/ (phys) n a measure of unavailable energy, energy still existing but lost for the purpose of doing work because it exists as the internal motion of molecules; a measure of the disorder of a system; a measure of heat content, regarded as increased in a reversible change by the ratio of heat taken in to absolute temperature. [Gr en in, and tropē turning, intended to represent 'transformation content']
■ **entro'pic** adj. **entro'pically** adv.

entrust or **intrust** /in-trust'/ vt to give in trust; to commit as a trust; to give responsibility to trustingly. [**en-** (1c)]
■ **entrust'ment** n.

entry /en'tri/ n the act of entering in any sense; the right to enter; a coming onto the stage; the coming in of an instrument or performer; entrance; a narrow lane between houses (dialect); a lobby or vestibule; a hostel (obs); the act of recording in writing; the thing so written; a person, etc entered for a competition; a list of competitors; a young hound, or hounds collectively, old enough to begin training; a card with which to win a trick in order to take the lead (bridge, etc); a taking possession (law). [Fr entrée, from entrer, from L intrāre to go into]
■ **en'tryism** or **en'trism** n the practice of joining esp a political body in sufficient numbers to influence its policy. **en'tryist** or **en'trist** n and adj.
❑ **entry corridor** n (space flight) same as **re-entry corridor** (see under **re-enter**). **entry fee** n an entrance fee. **entry form** n an application form for a competition. **en'try-level** adj (of a job) suitable for someone with no previous experience who is seeking to make a career in that industry (also fig). **entry portal** n (radiol) an area through which a beam of radiation enters the body. **entry value** n (account) the cost of acquiring an asset or liability. **entry wound** n a wound occurring where a bullet, etc enters the body.
■ **port of entry** see **port**[1].

Entryphone® /en'tri-fōn/ n an intercom system at the entrance to eg a block of flats, allowing communication between individual occupiers and visitors and usually incorporating a means of opening the main door.

Ent. Sta. Hall abbrev : Entered at Stationers' Hall, until 1924 a book registration requirement for copyright purposes.

entwine, also **intwine** /en- or in-twīn'/ vt to interlace; to weave together. [**en-** (1c)]
■ **entwine'ment** n.

entwist /in-twist'/ vt to twist round (also **intwist'**). [**en-** (1c)]

enucleate /i- or ē-nū'kli-āt/ vt to extract (eg a tumour, eyeball or swelling) (surg); to deprive of a kernel or nucleus; to explain. ◆ adj without a nucleus. [L ēnucleāre, from ē from, and nucleus a kernel]
■ **enucleā'tion** n.

enumerate /i-nū'mə-rāt/ vt to count the number of; to give a list of, one by one. [L ē from, and numerāre, -ātum to number]
■ **enū'merable** adj. **enūmera'tion** n the act of numbering; a detailed account; a summing-up (rhetoric). **enū'merative** adj. **enū'merātor** n someone who or something that enumerates; a person who collects and deals with population census figures, voters' lists, etc.

enunciate /i-nun'si-āt or i-nun'shi-āt/ vt to state formally; to pronounce distinctly; to utter. [L ēnuntiāre, -ātum, from ē from, and nuntiāre to tell, from nuntius a messenger]
■ **enun'ciable** /-si- or -shi-/ adj capable of being enunciated. **enunciation** /i-nun-si-ā'shən/ n the act of enunciating; the manner of speaking or pronouncing; a distinct statement or declaration; the words in which a proposition is expressed. **enun'ciative** /-si-ā-, -syā-, -sh(y)ā- or -shə-/ or **enun'ciatory** adj containing enunciation or utterance; declarative. **enun'ciātor** n someone who or something that enunciates.

enure, etc see **inure**[1].

enuresis /en-ū-rē'sis/ (med) n involuntary urination, esp while asleep. [Gr en in, and ourēsis urination]
■ **enūret'ic** adj and n.

enurn same as **inurn**.

envassal /en-vas'əl/ (obs) vt to make a vassal. [**en-** (1c)]

envault /en-völt'/ (obs) vt to enclose in a vault. [**en-** (1a)]

enveigle see **inveigle**.

envelop /en- or in-vel'əp/ vt to cover by wrapping; to surround entirely; to hide. [OFr enveloper ; origin obscure]
■ **envelope** /en'vəl-ōp/ n something which envelops, wraps or covers; a cover for a letter (in this sense sometimes pronounced /on'/ or /ä'/ in imitation of French); one of the coverings of a flower, the calyx or corolla (bot); the gasbag of a balloon or airship; the locus of ultimate intersections of a series of curves (maths); the outer containing vessel of a discharge tube (electronics); the curve connecting the peaks of successive cycles of a modulated carrier wave (telecom). **envel'oped** adj (heraldry) entwined, eg with serpents or laurels. **envel'opment** n a complete wrapping or covering.
❑ **envelope stuffer** n a person who puts printed material into envelopes, eg for a charity; an item of promotional material enclosed with a letter, invoice, statement, etc (marketing). **envelope stuffing** n. ■ **on the back of an envelope** (inf) said of a calculation that is performed quickly and without scrupulous regard to accuracy. **push the envelope** (inf) to try to achieve more than seems possible.

envenom /in-ven'əm/ vt to put venom into; to poison; to taint with bitterness or malice. [OFr envenimer, from en in, and venim venom]
■ **enven'omate** vt (of an animal) to poison by biting or stinging. **envenomā'tion** n. **enven'omed** adj.

en ventre sa mère /ä vä-tr' sa mer'/ (law) in his or her mother's womb. [Fr]

en vérité /ä vā-rē-tā'/ (Fr) in truth.

envermeil /en-vûr'mil/ (Milton) vt to dye red or give a red colour to. [OFr envermeiller, from en in, and vermeil red or vermilion]

Env. Ext. abbrev : Envoy Extraordinary.

en ville /ä vēl'/ (Fr) in town; not at home.

environ /in-vī'rən/ vt to surround; to encircle. [Fr environner, from environ around, from virer to turn round; cf **veer**[1]]
■ **environs** /in-vī'rənz or en'vi-/ n pl the places that environ; the outskirts of a town or city; neighbourhood.

environment /in- or en-vī'rən-mənt/ n surroundings; external conditions influencing development or growth of people, animals or plants; living or working conditions; a program, set of programs or an operating system that allows a particular application to be employed (comput). [Ety as for **environ**]
■ **environics** /en-vī-ron'iks/ n sing the study of methods of influencing behaviour by controlling environmental factors. **environment'al** adj. **environment'alism** n concern about the environment and its preservation from the effects of pollution, etc; the belief that environment rather than heredity is the main influence on a person's behaviour and development (psychol). **environment'alist** n a person who is concerned with the protection of the environment, esp from pollution; a person who advocates environmentalism (psychol). ◆ adj of or relating to environmentalists. **environment'ally** adv.
❑ **environmental audit** n an investigation of the extent to which an organization's activities pollute the environment. **environmental health officer** n an official whose duty is to enforce regulations regarding matters which might affect the health of the general public, eg hygiene in food-handling shops, maintenance of a clean water supply, waste disposal, etc (abbrev **EHO**; formerly called **public health inspector, sanitary inspector**). **environmentally friendly** or **envir'onment-friendly** adj designed to benefit, or at least not to harm, the environment. **environmentally sensitive area** n an area recognized by the government as having a landscape, wildlife or historic feature of national importance (abbrev **ESA**). **environmental pathway** n a route by which a radionuclide in the environment can reach man. **Environmental Protection Agency** n (US) a federal agency responsible for the protection of the environment and pollution control (abbrev **EPA**).

envisage /in-viz'ij/ vt to consider or contemplate; to picture in one's mind; to visualize; to see, suggest or expect as a possible or likely future target, result, etc; to face (archaic). [Fr envisager, from en in, and visage the face, in relation to the archaic sense]
■ **envis'agement** n.

envision /in-vizh'ən/ vt to see as if in a vision; to visualize; to envisage. [**en-** (1c)]

envoy[1] /en'voi/ n a messenger, esp one sent to transact business with a foreign government; a diplomatic minister of the second class (also called **envoy extraordinary**). [Fr envoyé, from pap of envoyer to send]
■ **en'voyship** n.

envoy[2] or **envoi** /en'voi/ n the concluding part of a poem or a book; the author's final words, esp the short stanza concluding a poem written in certain archaic metrical forms. [OFr envoye, from envoiier to send, from en voie on the way, from L in on, and via a way]

envy /en'vi/ n a feeling of discontent at the good looks, qualities, fortune, etc, of another; an object or person contemplated with grudging or envious feelings; ill-will or hostility (obs). ◆ vt (formerly /in-vī'/) (**en'vying**; **en'vied**) to feel envy towards or on account of; to wish to have or to covet (someone's property, good fortune, skills, etc); to grudge (obs); to feel vexation at (obs); to desire with emulation or rivalry. [Fr envie, from L invidia, from invidēre to look askance at, to envy, from in on, and vidēre to look]
■ **en'viable** adj that is to be envied; causing envy. **en'viableness** n. **en'viably** adv. **en'vier** n someone who envies. **en'vious** adj feeling or showing envy; directed by envy; enviable (Spenser). **en'viously** adv. **en'viousness** n. **en'vying** n (Bible) jealousy or ill-will.

enwall or **inwall** /in-wöl'/ vt to enclose within a wall. [en- (1a)]

enwheel /en-(h)wēl'/ (Shakesp) vt to encircle. [en- (1a)]

enwind or **inwind** /in-wīnd'/ vt to wind about or enwrap. [en- (1a)]

enwomb /en-woom'/ vt to make pregnant (Spenser); to conceive or have in the womb (Shakesp); to contain. [en- (1a)]

enwrap or **inwrap** /in-rap'/ vt to cover by wrapping; to enfold; to engross. [en- (1a)]
■ **enwrap'ment** n. **enwrapp'ing** adj and n.

enwreathe or **inwreathe** /in-rēdh'/ vt to wreathe; to envelop; to encircle with or as if with a wreath. [en- (1a)]

enzalutamide /en-zə-loo'tə-mīd/ n a drug that acts against androgen, used in treating prostate cancer.

Enzed /en-zed'/ (Aust and NZ inf) n New Zealand; (also **Enzedd'er**) a New Zealander. [The abbrev **NZ** phonetically represented]

enzian /ent'si-ən/ n a type of schnapps flavoured with gentian roots, drunk in the Tyrol. [Ger Enzian gentian]

enzone /in-zōn'/ vt to engirdle; to enclose with or as if with a zone or belt. [en- (1a)]

enzootic /en-zō-ot'ik/ adj of animal diseases, prevalent in a particular district or at a particular season. ◆ n a disease of this kind. [Gr en in, and zōion animal, in imitation of endemic]

enzyme /en'zīm/ n any one of a large class of protein substances produced by living cells which, usu in the presence of other substances eg coenzymes, act as catalysts in biochemical reactions. [Gr en in, and zȳmē leaven]
■ **enzymat'ic** or **enzym'ic** adj. **enzymolog'ical** adj. **enzymol'ogist** n. **enzymol'ogy** n the scientific study of enzymes.

E O /ē'ō'/ n a mid-18c gambling game, depending on a ball falling into slots marked either E or O.

eo abbrev : ex officio.

eoan /ē-ō'ən/ adj of or relating to dawn. [L, from Gr ēōs dawn]

Eoanthropus /ē-ō-an-thrō'pəs/ n what was thought to be an early form of man, represented by parts of a skull found at Piltdown, Sussex in 1912, but in 1953 exposed as a hoax when the jawbone was shown to be an ape's. [Gr ēōs dawn, and anthrōpos man]

EOC abbrev : Equal Opportunities Commission.

Eocene /ē'ō-sēn/ (geol) adj of or belonging to an epoch of the Tertiary period, between 55 and 34 million years ago (also n). [Gr ēōs daybreak, and kainos new, from the very small proportion of living species of molluscs among its fossils; cf **Miocene** and **Pliocene**]

eod abbrev : every other day.

eohippus /ē-ō-hip'əs/ n the oldest known horselike animal, an Eocene fossil. [Gr ēōs dawn, and hippos horse]

eo ipso /ē'ō or e'ō ip'sō/ (L) by that very fact.

EOKA /ā-ō'kə/ abbrev : Ethnikē Organōsis Kypriākou Agōnos (Gr), the National Organization of the Cypriot Struggle, a secret Greek Cypriot organization which fought for the union of Cyprus with Greece.

Eolian, Eolic same as **Aeolian, Aeolic**.

éolienne /ē-ō-li-en' or ā-o-lyen'/ n dress material of fine silk and wool. [Fr]

eolipile same as **aeolipile**.

eolith /ē'ō-lith/ n a very early roughly-broken stone implement, or one naturally formed but assumed to have been used by man. [Gr ēōs dawn, and lithos stone]
■ **eolith'ic** or **Eolith'ic** adj belonging to the early part of the Stone Age, when crude stone implements were first used by man.

eon see **aeon**.

eonism /ē'ə-ni-zm/ n (psychiatry) adoption by a male of female dress and manner. [Chevalier d'Eon, French diplomat (died 1810) who chose female dress as a disguise]

eo nomine /ē'ō nom'i-nē or e'ō nom'i-ne/ (L) by that name, on that claim.

eorl an obsolete form of **earl**.

eosin /ē'ō-sin/ n the potassium salt ($C_{20}H_6Br_4O_5K_2$) of tetrabromofluorescein, a red dye. [Gr ēōs dawn]
■ **eosin'ophil** adj (Gr philos loving) readily staining with eosin. ◆ n a type of white blood cell, so called because it is easily stained by eosin. **eosinophil'ia** n the condition of staining readily with eosin; the condition in which there is an abnormally large number of eosinophils in the blood. **eosinophil'ic** or **eosinoph'ilous** adj eosinophil; relating to eosinophils or eosinophilia.

EOT abbrev : end of tape (comput); end of transmission (telecom).

eothen /ē-ō'then/ (archaic) adv from the east, the name given by Alexander Kinglake to his book of travel in the East (1844). [Gr ēōthen (literally) from morn, at earliest dawn]

Eozoon /ē-ō-zō'on/ n what was thought to be a fossil organism in the Archaean system of Canada, which would have been the oldest known living thing, or the banded arrangement of calcite and serpentine at that time supposed to be its remains. [Gr ēōs dawn, and zōion an animal]
■ **Eozō'ic** adj.

EP /ē-pē'/ n an extended-play record.

EP abbrev : electroplated; European Parliament; extreme pressure (used in the grading of lubricants).

Ep. see **Epis**.

e.p. abbrev : en passant (in chess).

ep- see **epi-**.

EPA abbrev : eicosapentaenoic acid, a fatty acid found in fish oils; Environmental Protection Agency (US); European Productivity Agency.

epacris /e-pak'ris or ep'ə-kris/ n a plant of the chiefly Australian genus Epacris of heath-like plants, giving name to the family **Epacrida'ceae**, closely related to the heaths. [Gr epi upon, and akris a summit]
■ **epac'rid** (or /ep'/) n any member of the genus, or the family.

epact /ē'pakt/ n the moon's age at the beginning of the year; the excess of the calendar month or solar year over the lunar. [Fr épacte, from Gr epaktos brought on, from epi on, and agein to bring]

epaenetic /ep-ə-net'ik/ or **epainetic** /ep-ī-net'ik/ (archaic) adj eulogistic. [Gr epainetikos, from epainein to praise]

epagoge /ep-ə-gō'gē or -jē/ (logic) n induction. [Gr epagōgē, from epi on, and agōgē leading]
■ **epagog'ic** adj.

epagomenai /ep-ə-gom'ə-nəl/ adj (esp of days) intercalary, or inserted between others. [Gr epagomenos, from epi upon or in, and agein to bring]

epainetic see **epaenetic**.

epanadiplosis /ep-a-nə-di-plō'sis/ (rhetoric) n (pl **epanadiplō'sēs**) a figure by which a sentence begins and ends with the same word, eg 'Rejoice in the Lord alway, and again I say, rejoice'. [Gr]

epanalepsis /ep-a-nə-lep'sis/ (rhetoric) n (pl **epanalep'sēs**) repetition or resumption with the same words. [Gr]

epanaphora /ep-ə-naf'o-rə/ same as **anaphora**.

epanodos /e-pan'o-dos/ (rhetoric) n recapitulation of the chief points in a discourse. [Gr]

epanorthosis /ep-a-nör-thō'sis/ (rhetoric) n (pl **epanorthō'sēs**) the retracting of a statement in order to correct or intensify it, eg 'For Britain's guid! for her destruction!'. [Gr]

eparch /ep'ärk/ n the governor of a modern Greek province; a metropolitan (relig). [Gr eparchos, from epi upon, and archē dominion]
■ **ep'archate** or **ep'archy** n the province, territory or diocese of an eparch.

épatant /ā-pa-tä'/ (Fr) adj wonderful or marvellous; startling or shocking.

epaule /e-pöl'/ n (milit) the shoulder of a bastion. [Fr épaule shoulder, from L spatula]
■ **epaule'ment** n a side-work of a battery or earthwork to protect it from flanking fire (milit); a particular position of a dancer's shoulders, one forward, one back (ballet).

epaulette or (esp US) **epaulet** /ep'ə-let/ n an ornament on the shoulder of a military or naval officer's uniform (now disused in the British Army) or of civilian clothing; a shoulder-piece. [Fr épaulette, from épaule the shoulder]

epaxial /ep-ak'si-əl/ (zool) adj above the axis. [Gr epi on or over, and **axis**[1]]

epedaphic /ep-ə-daf'ik/ adj relating to atmospheric conditions. [Gr epi above, and edaphos ground]

épée /ā'pā/ n a sharp-pointed, narrow-bladed sword without a cutting edge, used for duelling and, with a button on the point, for fencing. [Fr]
■ **é'péeist** n.

epeira /ep-īr'ə/ n the common garden spider or any other spider of the former genus Epeira (now divided into several genera). [Perh Gr epi on, and eirein to string]
■ **epeir'id** n a spider of the former family Epeiridae, containing this genus.

epeirogenesis /ep-ī-rō-jen'i-sis/ or **epeirogeny** /-roj'i-ni/ (geol) n the building of continents by movement of the earth's crust. [Gr ēpeiros mainland, and genesis formation]
■ **epeirogen'ic** or **epeirogenetic** /-jin-et'ik/ adj.
❑ **epeirogenic earth movements** n pl continent-building movements, such as gentle uplift or depression, involving the coastal plain and the recently submerged continental shelf of the great land areas.

epencephalon /ep-en-sef'ə-lon or -kef'/ n the cerebellum. [Gr epi on, and enkephalon brain]
■ **epencephalic** /-si-fal'ik or -ki-/ adj.

ependyma /e-pen'di-mə/ (anat) n a layer of cells lining the brain and the central canal of the spinal cord. [Gr, from ependyein to put on over]
■ **epen'dymal** adj.

epenthesis /e-pen'thə-sis/ n (pl **epentheses**) the insertion of a sound within a word. [Gr]
■ **epenthetic** /-thet'ik/ adj.

epeolatry /ep-i-ol'ə-tri/ n worship of words. [Gr epos word, and latreiā worship]

éperdu (fem **éperdue**) /ā-per-dü'/ (Fr) adj distracted.
❑ **éperdument amoureux** (fem **amoureuse**) /ā-per-dü'mā a-moo-rə' (-rəz')/ adj desperately in love.

epergne /i-pûrn'/ n a branched ornamental centrepiece for a table. [Fr épargne (literally) saving, as used in phrases taille or gravure d'épargne metal or etching with parts left in relief]

epexegesis /ep-ek-si-jē'sis/ n (pl **epexegeses**) the addition of words to make the sense clearer. [Gr epexēgēsis, from epi in addition, and exēgeesthai to explain]
■ **epexeget'ic** /-jet'ik/ or **epexeget'ical** adj. **epexeget'ically** adv.

EPG abbrev : Eminent Persons' Group.

Eph. (Bible) abbrev : (the Letter to the) Ephesians.

epha or **ephah** /ē'fə/ n a Hebrew measure for dry goods. [Heb; prob of Egypt origin]

ephebe /e-fēb'/, **ephebus** or **ephebos** /-bəs/ n (pl **ephebes'** or **ephē'bī**) in ancient Greece, a young male citizen from 18 to 20 years of age. [L ephēbus, from Gr ephēbos, from epi upon, and hēbē early manhood]
■ **ephēb'ic** adj of or belonging to an ephebe; relating to the adult period in the life history of an individual (biol). **ephēbophilia** /-fil'/ n sexual desire for youths or adolescents.

ephedra /ef'e-drə, ef-ē'drə/ or /ef-ed'rə/ n a plant of the sea-grape genus (Ephedra) of jointed, nearly leafless desert plants. [Gr ephedrā horsetail]
■ **eph'edrine** (or /ef-ed'rin/) n an alkaloid obtained from ephedra or produced synthetically, used in treating hay fever, asthma, etc.

ephelis /e-fē'lis/ (med) n (pl **ephelides** /e-fel'i-dēz or -fēl'/) a freckle; a coloured patch on the skin. [L, from Gr]

ephemera /ef-em'ə-rə or -ēm'/ n (pl **ephem'eras** or **ephem'erae**) an insect of the mayfly genus Ephemera, whose adult life is very short; something which lasts a short time (but see also ephemeron below). [Gr ephēmeros living a day, from epi for, and hēmerā a day]
■ **ephem'eral** adj existing only for a day; short-lived; fleeting. ◆ n anything very short-lived. **ephemeral'ity** n. **ephem'erally** adv. **ephem'eralness** n. **ephem'erid** n an insect of the mayfly family **Ephemer'idae** /-mer'i-dē/ (order **Ephemerop'tera**). **ephemerid'ian** adj. **ephem'eris** n (pl **ephemerides** /ef-e-mer'i-dēz/) an astronomical almanac tabulating the daily positions of the sun, moon, planets and certain stars, etc; an individual table showing this; an account of daily transactions (archaic); a journal (archaic). **ephem'erist** n someone who studies the daily motions of the planets; a student or collector of ephemera. **ephem'eron** n (pl **ephem'era**) an insect that lives only for a day; (usu in pl) an object of limited worth or usefulness, having no lasting value; anything ephemeral. **ephem'erous** adj.
❑ **ephemeris time** n time measured by orbital movement of earth, moon and planets, differing from mean solar time in that it allows for irregularities due to variations in rate of rotation of the earth, an **ephemeris second** being a fixed fraction of the solar year 1900.

Ephesian /ef-ē'zi-ən or -ē'zhən/ adj of or relating to Ephesus, an ancient Greek city in modern Turkey. ◆ n an inhabitant of Ephesus; a jolly companion (Shakesp).

ephialtes /ef-i-al'tēz/ (archaic) n (pl **ephial'tes**) an incubus; a nightmare. [Gr ephialtēs]

ephod /ef'od/ n a kind of linen surplice worn by the Jewish priests (Bible); a surplice, generally. [Heb ēphōd, from āphad to put on]

ephor /ef'ör or ef'ər/ n in ancient Doric Greece, esp Sparta, a class of powerful senior magistrates elected annually. [Gr epi upon, and root of horaein to see]
■ **eph'oralty** n. **eph'orate** n.

epi- /ep-i-/ or before a vowel or h **ep-** /ep-/ pfx above, over, upon or on, as in epidermis; in addition or after, as in epiphenomenon and epirrhema. [Gr epi on or over]

epibenthos /ep-i-ben'thos/ n the organisms living on the floor of a sea or lake. [Gr epi upon, and benthos depth]
■ **epiben'thic** adj.

epiblast /ep'i-bläst/ n the outer germinal layer of an embryo. [Gr epi upon, and blastos a germ or shoot]
■ **epiblast'ic** adj.

epic /ep'ik/ adj applied to a long narrative poem that relates heroic events in an elevated style; characteristic of an epic poem; impressive; large-scale. ◆ n an epic poem; epic poetry as a genre; a story comparable to that of an epic poem, esp a long adventure novel or film; an epic poet (obs). [Gr epikos, from epos a word]
■ **ep'ical** adj. **ep'ically** adv. **ep'icism** n. **ep'icist** n.
❑ **epic dialect** n the dialect of Greek used by Homer. **epic theatre** n the theatre of **epic drama**, episodic drama with alienation (qv), narrative passages, etc.

epicalyx /ep-i-kā'liks or -kal'iks/ (bot) n an apparent accessory calyx outside the true calyx, composed of bracts or of fused stipules of sepals. [Gr epi on, and **calyx**]

epicanthus /ep-i-kan'thəs/ n a fold of skin over the inner canthus of the eye, characteristic of the Mongolian race. [Gr epi on, and **canthus**]
■ **epican'thic** adj.

epicardium /ep-i-kär'di-əm/ (anat) n (pl **epicar'dia**) the inner surface of the pericardium. [Gr epi upon, and kardiā heart]
■ **epicar'dial** adj.

epicarp /ep'i-kärp/ (bot) n the outermost layer of the pericarp or fruit. [Gr epi upon, and karpos fruit]

epicede /ep'i-sēd/ or **epicedium** /ep-i-sē'di-əm or -dī'/ n (pl **ep'icedes** or **epicē'dia** (or /-dī'/)) a funeral ode. [L epicēdīum, from Gr epikēdeion, from epi upon, and kēdos care]
■ **epicē'dial** or **epicē'dian** adj elegiac.

epicene /ep'i-sēn/ adj common to both sexes; having characteristics of both sexes or neither sex; effeminate; of common gender (grammar); sometimes restricted to those words that have one grammatical gender though used for both sexes. ◆ n an epicene person or animal; an epicene word. [Gr epi upon, and koinos common]

epicentre or (US) **epicenter** /ep'i-sen-tər/ n the point on the earth's surface directly over the point of origin of an earthquake (also fig). [Gr epi upon or over, and kentron a point]
■ **epicen'tral** adj.

epicheirema /ep-i-kī-rē'mə/ (logic) n a syllogism confirmed in its major or minor premise, or both, by an incidental proposition. [Gr epicheirēma an attempt or an attempted proof short of demonstrating, from epi upon, and cheir hand]

épicier /ā-pē-syā'/ (Fr) n a grocer.

epicism, epicist see under **epic**.

epiclesis /ep-i-klē'sis/ n (pl **epiclēsēs**) in the Eastern Church, an invocation of the Holy Spirit at the consecration of the elements. [Gr epiklēsis invocation, from epikalein to summon]

epicondyle /ep-i-kon'dīl or -dil/ (anat) n the upper or proximal part of the condyle of the humerus or femur. [**epi-**]
■ **epicon'dylar** adj. **epicondylitis** /-dil-ī'tis/ n inflammation of an epicondyle; inflammation of the tissues beside the epicondyle of the humerus.

epicontinental /ep-i-kon-ti-nen'tl/ adj denoting a shallow sea that forms over a continental shelf. [**epi-**]

epicormic /ep-i-kör'mik/ adj denoting shoots that grow from buds below the bark on the trunk or branch of a tree. [Gr epi on, and kormos tree trunk]

epicotyl /ep-i-kot'il/ (bot) n the stem of an embryo plant or seedling between the cotyledons and the next leaf. [Gr epi over, and **cotyledon**]

■ words derived from main entry word; ❑ compound words; ■ idioms and phrasal verbs

epicritic /ep-i-krit'ik/ *adj* (of certain sensory nerve fibres in the skin) able to discriminate accurately between small degrees of sensation. [Gr *epikritikos* determining, from *epi* on, and *krīnein* to judge]

epicure /ep'i-kūr/ *n* a person of refined and fastidious taste, *esp* in food, wine, etc; an Epicurean (*obs*); a person devoted to sensual enjoyment (*obs*). [L *Epicūrus*, from Gr *Epikouros*]
■ **Epicurē'an** *adj* of or relating to *Epicurus* (341–270BC), the Greek philosopher, who taught that the real world is a chance composition of atoms or particles and that pleasure controlled by social convention (misrepresented by opponents as brutish sensuality) is the greatest good; (without *cap*) devoted to luxury, *esp* refined luxury. ◆ *n* a follower of Epicurus; (without *cap*) a hedonist or epicure. **Epicurē'anism** *n* the doctrines of Epicurus; devotion to these doctrines; epicurism. **ep'icurism** *n* pursuit of pleasure; fastidiousness in luxury; also /ep-i-kūr'izm/ (*archaic*) Epicureanism. **ep'icurize** or **-ise** *vi* (*archaic*) to act as an epicure; to profess the philosophy of Epicurus.

epicuticle /ep-i-kū'ti-kl/ (*biol*) *n* the waxy outermost layer of an insect's cuticle. [**epi-**]
■ **epicūtic'ular** *adj*.

epicycle /ep'i-sī-kl/ *n esp* in Ptolemaic astronomy, a circle whose centre is carried round the circumference of another circle; the circle on whose circumference is the point which describes an epicycloid. [Gr *epi* upon, and *kyklos* a circle]
■ **epicy'clic** *adj*. **epicy'cloid** *n* the curve described by a point on the circumference of a circle rolling round the outside of the circumference of another circle. **epicycloi'dal** *adj*.
❑ **epicyclic gear** *n* a system of gears consisting of one or more wheels travelling round the outside or inside of another wheel whose axis is fixed.

epideictic /ep-i-dīk'tik/ or **epideictical** /-əl/ *adj* done for show or display. [Gr *epi* upon, and *deiknynai* to show]

epidemic /ep-i-dem'ik/ *adj* affecting a community at a certain time; prevalent. ◆ *n* an outbreak of disease that affects great numbers; any widespread outbreak. [Gr *epidēmos* general, from *epi* among, and *dēmos* the people]
■ **epidem'ical** *adj*. **epidem'ically** *adv*. **epidemic'ity** *n*. **epidēmiolog'ical** *adj* relating to epidemiology. **epidēmiol'ogist** *n*. **epidēmiol'ogy** *n* the study of the distribution, effects and causes of diseases in populations, and the means by which they may be treated or prevented.

epidendrum /ep-i-den'drəm/ *n* an orchid of the large genus *Epidendrum* of American orchids, mainly growing on other plants (also **epiden'drone**). [Gr *epi* upon, and *dendron* tree]

epidermis /ep-i-dûr'mis/ *n* cuticle or scarf-skin, forming an external protective covering for the true skin or corium (*zool*); an outer sheath of close-set cells, *usu* one deep (*bot*). [Gr *epidermis*, from *epi* upon, and *derma* skin]
■ **epider'mal**, **epider'mic** or **epider'moid** *adj*. **Epidermophyton** /-mof'i-tən/ *n* (Gr *phyton* a plant) a genus of parasitic ascomycete fungi or dermatophytes, a cause of athlete's foot.
❑ **epidermolysis bullosa** /-mol'i-sis bŭ-lō'sə/ *n* (Gr *lysis* loosening, New L *bulla* blister) a mutilating and incapacitating hereditary skin disease in which the skin on slight contact readily becomes covered with blisters (*abbrev* **EB**).

epidiascope /ep-i-dī'ə-skōp/ *n* an optical device for projecting images of objects whether opaque or transparent. [Gr *epi* upon, *dia* through, and *skopeein* to look at]

epididymis /ep-i-did'i-mis/ (*anat*) *n* (pl **epidid'ymides** /-mi-dēz or -dī-dim'/) a mass of sperm-carrying tubes at the back of the testis. [Gr, from *epi* on, and *didymos* a testicle or a twin]
■ **epidid'ymal** *adj*.

epidiorite /ep-i-dī'ə-rīt/ (*geol*) *n* a dioritic or gabbroitic rock more or less metamorphosed, the pyroxene being changed to amphibole. [Gr *epi* after, and **diorite**]

epidote /ep'i-dōt/ (*geol*) *n* a greenish mineral, silicate of calcium, aluminium, and iron. [Gr *epididonai* to give in addition or superadd, from the great length of the base of the crystal]
■ **epidosite** /ep-id'ə-sīt/ *n* a rock composed of epidote and quartz. **epidotic** /-dot'/ *adj*. **epidotizā'tion** or **-s-** *n*. **epid'otized** or **-s-** *adj* changed into epidote.

epidural /ep-i-dū'rəl/ *adj* situated on, or administered outside, the dura mater. ◆ *n* short for **epidural anaesthetic**, the epidural injection of an anaesthetic, *esp* in childbirth. [Gr *epi* upon, and *dura* mater]
❑ **epidural anaesthesia** *n* loss of painful sensation in the lower part of the body produced by injecting an anaesthetic into the lowest portion of the spinal canal.

epifauna /ep-i-fö'nə/ *n* the class of animals that inhabit submerged ground and river and seabeds. [**epi-** and **fauna**]
■ **epifau'nal** *adj*.

epifocal /ep-i-fō'kl/ *adj* epicentral.

epigaeal or **epigeal** /ep-i-jē'əl/, **epigaeous** or **epigeous** /-əs/, **epigaean** or **epigean** /-ən/ *adj* growing or living close to the ground; with cotyledons above ground. [Gr *epigaios* or *epigeios*, from *epi* on, and *gaia* or *gē* earth]

epigamic /ep-i-gam'ik/ *adj* attractive to the opposite sex. [Gr *epigamos* marriageable, from *epi* upon, and *gamos* marriage]

epigastrium /ep-i-gas'tri-əm/ (*anat*) *n* the part of the abdomen extending from the sternum towards the navel, the pit of the stomach. [Gr *epi* upon, and *gastēr* the stomach]
■ **epigas'tric** *adj*.

epigeal, etc see **epigaeal**.

epigene /ep'i-jēn/ (*geol*) *adj* acting or taking place at the earth's surface. [Fr *épigène*, from Gr *epigenēs* born after]

epigenesis /ep-i-jen'i-sis/ *n* the theory, now universally accepted, that the development of an embryo consists of the gradual production and organization of parts (as opposed to the theory of preformation, which supposed that the future animal or plant was already present complete, although in miniature, in the germ). [Gr *epi* upon or after, and *genesis* formation]
■ **epigen'esist** *n* and *adj*. **epigenet'ic** *adj* relating to epigenesis; (of minerals) formed subsequently to the enclosing rock. **epigenet'ically** *adv*. **epigenet'icist** *n*. **epigenet'ics** *n sing* the science which studies the causes at work in development.

epiglottis /ep-i-glot'is/ *n* a cartilaginous flap over the glottis. [Gr *epiglōttis*, from *epi* over, and *glōttis* glottis]
■ **epiglott'al** *adj*. **epiglott'ic** *adj*.

epigon /ep'i-gon/ or **epigone** /ep'i-gōn/ *n* (pl **ep'igons**, **ep'igones** /-gōnz/ or (often with *cap*) **epig'onī**) one of a later generation; (*usu* in *pl*) a son or successor; an inferior follower or imitator; (in *pl*) descendants (*esp* of the Seven against Thebes), or successors (*esp* of Alexander the Great); (in *pl*) undistinguished descendants, followers or imitators of the great. [Gr *epi* after, and *gonē* birth]

epigram /ep'i-gram/ *n* any concise and pointed or sarcastic saying; a short poem expressing an ingenious thought with point, usually satirical. [Through Fr and L, from Gr *epigramma*, from *epi* upon, and *gramma* a writing, from *graphein* to write]
■ **epigrammatic** /-grəm-at'ik/ or **epigrammat'ical** *adj* relating to or dealing in epigrams; like an epigram; concise and pointed. **epigrammat'ically** *adv*. **epigramm'atist** *n* someone who writes epigrams. **epigramm'atize** or **-ise** *vt* to make an epigram on.

epigraph /ep'i-gräf/ *n* an inscription, *esp* on a building; a citation or motto at the beginning of a book or section of a book. ◆ *vt* to provide with an epigraph. [Gr *epigraphē*, from *epi* upon, and *graphein* to write]
■ **epigrapher** /ep-ig'rə-fər/ or **epig'raphist** *n* someone who studies inscriptions. **epigraphic** /-graf'ik/ or **epigraph'ical** *adj*. **epigraph'ically** *adv*. **epig'raphy** *n*.

epigynous /e-pij'i-nəs/ (*bot*) *adj* growing upon the top of the ovary; having calyx, corolla and stamens inserted on the top of an inferior ovary. [Gr *epi* upon, and *gynē* woman or female]
■ **epig'yny** *n*.

epilate /ep'i-lāt/ *vt* to remove (hair) by any method. [Fr *épiler*, from L *ex* from, and *pilus* hair]
■ **epilā'tion** *n*. **ep'ilator** *n*.

epilepsy /ep'i-lep-si/ *n* a chronic functional disease of the nervous system, characterized by recurring attacks of sudden unconsciousness or impairment of consciousness, commonly accompanied by convulsive seizures. [Gr *epilēpsiā*, from *epi* upon, and root of *lambanein* to seize]
■ **epilep'tic** *n* someone who suffers from epilepsy. ◆ *adj* (also **epilep'tical**) of or relating to epilepsy.

epilimnion /ep-i-lim'ni-ən/ *n* (pl **epilim'nia**) the upper, warm layer of water in a lake. [Gr *epi* upon, and *limnion*, dimin of *limnē* a lake]

epilithic /ep-i-lith'ik/ *adj* (of plants) growing on the surface of rock. [Gr *epi* upon, and *lithos* stone]

epilobium /ep-i-lō'bi-əm/ *n* a willowherb, a plant of the genus *Epilobium*. [Gr *epi* upon, and *lobos* a pod, from the position of the petals]

epilogue or (*US*) also **epilog** /ep'i-log/ *n* the concluding section of a book, etc; a short poem or speech at the end of a play; the actor giving the epilogue; a radio or TV programme (*usu* religious) formerly broadcast as the last item of the day. [Fr, from L *epilogus*, from Gr *epilogos* conclusion, from *epi* upon, and *legein* to speak]
■ **epilogic** /-loj'ik/ or **epilogistic** /-jis'/ *adj*. **epil'ogist** *n*. **epilogize** or **-ise** /ep-il'ə-jīz or ep'/, **epiloguize** or **-ise** /-gīz/ *vi* to speak or write an epilogue.

epimeletic /ep-i-me-let'ik/ (*animal behaviour*) *adj* of a type of social behaviour in which the young are cared for by the parents or other individuals of the same species, eg worker bees. [Gr *epimelētikos* able to take charge, from *epimelētēs* a governor]

epimer /*ep'i-mər*/ *n* an isomeric compound, differing from its corresponding isomer only in the relative positions of an attached hydrogen and hydroxyl. [**epi-** and iso*mer*]
■ **epimeric** /*-mer'ik*/ *adj* having the characteristics or relationship of epimers. **epimerism** /*ep-im'*/ *n*. **epimerize** or **-ise** /*ep-im'*/ *vt*.

epimysium /*ep-i-miz'i-əm*/ (*anat*) *n* the covering of connective tissue that encloses a muscle. [Gr *epi* upon, and *mys* muscle]

epinasty /*ep'i-nas-ti*/ (*bot*) *n* the down-curving of an organ, caused by a more active growth on its upper side, *opp* to **hyponasty**. [Gr *epi* upon, and *nastos* pressed close]
■ **epinas'tic** *adj*. **epinas'tically** *adv*.

epinephrine /*ep-i-nef'rin* or *-rēn*/ or **epinephrin** /*-rin*/ (*esp N Am*) *n* adrenaline. [Gr *epi* upon, and *nephros* kidney]

epineural /*ep-i-nū'rəl*/ (*zool*) *adj* in Echinodermata, lying above the radial nerve; in vertebrates, lying above or arising from the neural arch of a vertebra. [Gr *epi* upon, and **neural**]

epinikion /*ep-i-nik'i-ən*/ or **epinicion** /*ep-i-nis(h)'i-ən*/ *n* in ancient Greece, a song of victory; an ode in honour of a victor or winner. [Gr *epinīkion*, from *epi* on or after, and *nīkē* victory]
■ **epinik'ian** or **epinic'ian** *adj*.

epinosic /*ep-i-nos'ik*/ *adj* unhealthy; unwholesome. [Gr *epi-*, and *nosos* disease]

EpiPen® /*ep'i-pen*/ *n* an injection device designed for self-administration of epinephrine (adrenaline) in medical emergencies such as anaphylactic shock.

epipetalous /*ep-i-pet'ə-ləs*/ (*bot*) *adj* inserted or growing on a petal or petals. [**epi-**]

Epiphany /*e-pif'ə-ni*/ *n* a church festival celebrated on 6 January in commemoration of the manifestation of Christ to the Wise Men of the East (or in the Eastern Church in commemoration of Christ's baptism and first miracle at Cana) (*abbrev* **Epiph.**); (the following senses *usu* without *cap*) the manifestation of a god; a *usu* sudden revelation or insight into the nature, essence or meaning of something. [Gr *epiphaneia* appearance, from *epi* to, and *phainein* to show]
■ **epiphanic** /*-fan'*/ *adj*.

epiphenomenon /*ep-i-fi-nom'in-ən*/ *n* (*pl* **epiphenom'ena**) an accompanying phenomenon, a fortuitous, less important or irrelevant by-product; something appearing after; a secondary symptom of a disease (*pathol*). [Gr *epi* after, and *phainomenon* neuter prp passive of *phainein* to show]
■ **epiphenom'enal** *adj*. **epiphenom'enalism** *n* interpretation of mind as an epiphenomenon upon the physical. **epiphenom'enalist** *n* and *adj*.

epiphonema /*ep-i-fō-nē'mə*/ (*rhetoric*) *n* an exclamation; a phrase or reflection added as a finishing touch. [Gr, from *epiphōneein* to exclaim, add in conclusion]

epiphragm /*ep'i-fram*/ *n* the disc with which certain molluscs close the aperture of their shell. [Gr *epiphragma* covering, from *epiphrassein* to obstruct]

epiphyllous /*ep-i-fil'əs*/ (*bot*) *adj* growing upon a leaf, *esp* on its upper surface. [Gr *epi* upon, and *phyllon* a leaf]

epiphysis /*e-pif'i-sis*/ *n* (*pl* **epiph'ysēs**) any portion of a bone having its own centre of ossification; the pineal gland (*epiphysis cerebri*); an ossicle of Aristotle's lantern in a sea-urchin; an upgrowth around the hilum of a seed. [Gr, excrescence]
■ **epiphyseal** /*-fiz'i-əl*/ *adj*.

epiphyte /*ep'i-fīt*/ *n* a plant growing on another plant without being parasitic; a vegetable parasite on the surface of an animal (*pathol*). [Gr *epi* upon, and *phyton* a plant]
■ **epiphyt'al**, **epiphytic** /*-fit'ik*/ or **epiphyt'ical** *adj*. **ep'iphytism** (or /*-fīt'*/) *n* the condition of being epiphytic; a similar relation among animals.

epiplastron /*ep-i-plä'stron*/ *n* (*pl* **epiplas'tra**) either of the two anterior lateral plates in the plastron of a turtle. [Gr *epi* upon, and **plastron**]
■ **epiplas'tral** *adj*.

epiploon /*e-pip'lō-on*/ (*anat*) *n* the great omentum. [Gr *epiploon*, from *epipleein* to float on]
■ **epiplō'ic** *adj*.

epipolism /*e-pip'o-li-zm*/ *n* fluorescence. [Gr *epipolē* surface]
■ **epipol'ic** *adj*.

epirrhema /*ep-i-rē'mə*/ *n* in Greek comedy, the address of the Coryphaeus to the audience after the parabasis. [Gr, from *epi* on or after, and *rhēma* word]
■ **epirrhemat'ic** *adj*.

Epis. *abbrev*: Episcopal (also **Episc.**); Epistle (also **Ep.**; *Bible*).

episcopacy /*e-pis'kə-pə-si*/ *n* church government by bishops; the office of a bishop; a bishop's period of office; the bishops, as a class. [Gr *episkopos* an overseer]
■ **epis'copal** *adj* governed by bishops; belonging to or vested in bishops. **episcopā'lian** *adj* relating to bishops or to an episcopal church; relating to or advocating government by bishops. ◆ *n* an adherent of episcopacy; a person who belongs to an episcopal (*esp* Anglican) church. **episcopā'lianism** or **epis'copalism** *n* episcopalian government and doctrine. **epis'copally** *adv*. **epis'copant** *n* (*Milton*) a holder of a bishopric. **epis'copate** *n* a bishopric; the office of a bishop; a bishop's period of office; the order of bishops. ◆ *vi* (*Milton*) to act as a bishop. **epis'copize** or **-ise** *vt* to make a bishop of; to make episcopalian. ◆ *vi* to play the bishop (also *vt* with *it*). **epis'copy** *n* (*Milton*) survey or superintendence.

episcope /*ep'i-skōp*/ *n* an optical device for projecting images of opaque objects. [Gr *epi* on or over, and *skopeein* to look]

episemon /*ep-i-sē'mon*/ *n* a badge or characteristic device; one of three obsolete Greek letters used as numerals: or ς, vau, or digamma (6); Ϟ, koppa (90); and Ϡ, san, sampi (900). [Gr *episēmon* a badge, from *epi* on, and *sēma* a sign]
■ **episēmat'ic** *adj* (*zool*) serving for recognition, distinguishing.

episepalous /*ep-i-sep'ə-ləs*/ (*bot*) *adj* growing or inserted upon a sepal or sepals. [**epi-**]

episiotomy /*ep-iz-i-ot'ə-mi*/ (*med*) *n* an incision made in the perineum to facilitate the delivery of a baby. [Gr *epision* pubic region, and **-tomy**]

episode /*ep'i-sōd*/ *n* a story introduced into a narrative or poem to give variety; an interesting or distinctive incident or occurrence; an occurrence, *esp* when one of a series of similar occurrences; a passage giving relief from the principal subject (*music*); an incident or period detachable from a novel, play, etc; a part of a radio or television serial which is broadcast at one time. [Gr *epeisodion*, from *epi* upon, and *eisodos* a coming in]
■ **ep'isōdal**, **episō'dial**, **episodic** /*-sod'*/ or **episod'ical** *adj* relating to or contained in an episode; brought in as a digression; having many episodes; (only **episodic** or **episodical**) sporadic, occurring at intervals. **episod'ically** *adv* by way of episode; incidentally.

episome /*ep'i-sōm*/ *n* a genetically active particle found *esp* in bacteria, able to exist and multiply either independently or integrated in a chromosome. [**epi-** and **-some²**]

epispastic /*ep-i-spas'tik*/ (*med*) *adj* blistering. ◆ *n* a blistering agent. [Gr *epispastikos*, from *epi* upon, and *spaein* to draw]

episperm /*ep'i-spûrm*/ (*bot*) *n* the outer seed coat. [Gr *epi* upon, and *sperma* seed]

epispore /*ep'i-spōr*/ (*bot*) *n* the outermost layer of a spore-wall. [**epi-**]

epistasis /*i-pis'tə-sis*/ *n* (*pl* **epistasēs**) the suppression by a gene of another non-allelomorphic gene; the arrest of a discharge or secretion; a scum which forms on the surface of a liquid, *esp* urine. [Gr, stopping, from *epi* on, and *stasis* stoppage]
■ **epistatic** /*ep-i-stat'ik*/ *adj*.

epistaxis /*ep-i-stak'sis*/ (*med*) *n* bleeding from the nose. [Gr *epistazein* to shed in drops]

epistemology /*ep-i-stə-mol'ə-ji*/ *n* the theory of knowledge. [Gr *epistēmē* knowledge, and *logos* discourse]
■ **epistē'mic** *adj* relating to knowledge, epistemology or epistemics. **epistē'mically** *adv*. **epistē'mics** *n sing* the scientific study of knowledge, its acquisition and its communication. **epistemological** /*-ə-loj'*/ *adj*. **epistemolog'ically** *adv*. **epistemol'ogist** *n*.

episternum /*ep-i-stûr'nəm*/ (*anat*) *n* the interclavicle; the epiplastron; the presternum of mammals.
■ **epister'nal** *adj*.

epistilbite /*ep-i-stil'bīt*/ (*mineralogy*) *n* a zeolite closely related to stilbite. [Gr *epi* on, after or in addition to, and **stilbite**]

epistle /*i-pis'l*/ *n* something written and sent to someone, a letter; (often with *cap*) *esp* a letter to an individual or church from an apostle, such as the Epistles of Paul in the Bible; (often with *cap*) the extract from one of the apostolical epistles read as part of the communion service; a verse composition in letter form. ◆ *vt* (*Milton*) to preface. [OFr, from L *epistola*, from Gr *epistolē*, from *epi* on the occasion of, and *stellein* to send]
■ **epistler** *n* see **epistoler** below. **epistolā'rian** *n* a letter-writer. **epistolā'rian**, **epis'tolary**, **epis'tolatory**, **epistolic** /*-is-tol'ik*/ or **epistol'ical** *adj* relating to or consisting of epistles or letters; suitable in or for an epistle; contained in letters. **epis'tolary** *n* a book containing the Epistles, used for readings in church. **epistoler** /*i-pist'ə-lər*/ or **epistler** /*-pis'* or *-pist'*/ *n* the reader of the Epistle in church; a letter-writer. **epis'tolet** *n* a short letter. **epis'tolist** *n* a writer of letters. **epis'tolize** or **-ise** *vi* to write a letter. **epistolog'raphy** *n* letter-writing. ◻ **epistle side** *n* in a church, the south side of the altar, *opp* to *gospel side*.

---

epistrophe /e-pis'trə-fē/ n the ending of successive clauses with the same word (rhetoric); a refrain in music. [Gr epistrophē a return, from epi upon, and strephein to turn]

epistyle /ep'i-stīl/ (archit) n an architrave. [Gr epi upon, and stȳlos a pillar]

epitaph /ep'i-täf/ n a tombstone inscription; a composition in the form of a tombstone inscription. ◆ vt to compose an epitaph upon. [Gr epitaphion, from epi upon, and taphos a tomb]
■ **epitapher** /ep'i-täf-ər/ or **ep'itaphist** n a composer of epitaphs. **epitaph'ian** or **epitaph'ic** adj.

epitasis /e-pit'ə-sis/ n (pl **epit'asēs**) the main action of a Greek drama leading to the catastrophe, opp to protasis. [Gr, from epi on, and tasis a stretching]

epitaxy /ep'i-tak-si/ (crystallog) n the growth of a thin layer of crystals on another crystal so that they have the same structure. [Gr epi on, and taxis arrangement]
■ **epitax'ial** adj. **epitax'ially** adv.

epithalamium /ep-i-thə-lā'mi-əm/ or **epithalamion** /-on/ n (pl **epithalā'miums** or **epithalā'mia**) a song or poem in celebration of a marriage. [L epithalamium, Gr epithalamion, from epi upon, and thalamos a bride-chamber]
■ **epithalam'ic** /ep-i-thə-la'mik/ adj.

epithelium /ep-i-thē'li-əm/ (anat) n (pl **epithē'lia**) the cell tissue that covers the outer surface of the body and the mucous membranes connected with it, and also the closed cavities of the body. [New L, from Gr epi upon, and thēlē nipple]
■ **epithē'lial** adj. **epithēliō'ma** n (pl epithelio'mas or epithelio'mata /-mə-tə/) carcinoma of the skin. **epithēliō'matous** adj.

epithem /ep'i-them/, also **epithema** /ep-i-thē'mə or ep-ith'i-mə/ n (pl **ep'ithems** or **epithe'mata**) a soft external application (med); a group of cells exuding water in some leaves (bot). [Gr epithema, epithēma, -atos, from epi on, and tithenai to place]

epithermal /ep-i-thûr'məl/ adj having energy just above the energy of thermal agitation. [**epi-**]

epithesis /e-pith'i-sis/ n the addition of one or more letters to a word, a paragoge. [Gr, setting on]

epithet /ep'i-thet/ n an adjective or adjectival phrase expressing some quality of the person or thing to which it is applied; a descriptive term; a term, expression (Shakesp). ◆ vt to term. [Gr epitheton, neuter of epithetos added, from epi on, and tithenai to place]
■ **epithet'ic** or **epithet'ical** adj relating to an epithet; having or using many epithets. **epithet'ically** adv. **epith'eton** (Shakesp **apath'aton**) n an epithet.

epithymetic /ep-i-thi-met'ik/ adj relating to or concerned with desire. [Gr epi upon, and thȳmos the soul]

epitome /i-pit'ə-mē/ n a typical example; a personification; an abridgement or short summary of anything, eg a book; a short or concentrated expression of something. [Gr epi upon, and tomē a cut]
■ **epitomic** /ep-i-tom'ik/ or **epitom'ical** adj. **epit'omist** n an epitomizer. **epitomizā'tion** or **-s-** n. **epit'omize** or **-ise** vt to make an epitome of; to shorten; to condense; to typify; to personify. **epit'omizer** or **-s-** n someone who abridges.
▪ **in epitome** on a small scale.

epitonic /ep-i-ton'ik/ adj overstrained. [Gr epitonos, from epi upon, and teinein to stretch]

epitope see **antigenic determinant** under **antigen**.

epitrachelion /ep-i-tra-kē'li-ən/ n an Orthodox priest's or bishop's stole. [Gr, on the neck, from epi upon, and trachēlos neck]

epitrite /ep'i-trīt/ (prosody) n a foot made up of three long syllables and one short. [Gr epitritos, from epi in addition to, and tritos third]

epitrochoid /ep-i-trō'koid/ n a curve like an epicycloid but generated by any point on a radius. [Gr epi on, and trochos wheel]

epizeuxis /ep-i-zūk'sis/ (rhetoric) n the immediate repetition of a word for emphasis. [Gr, joining on]

epizoon /ep-i-zō'on/ n (pl **epizō'a**) an animal that lives on the surface of another animal, whether parasitically or commensally. [Gr epi upon, and zōion an animal]
■ **epizō'an** adj and n. **epizō'ic** adj living on an animal; having seeds dispersed by animals. **epizoite** /-zō'īt/ n. **epizootic** /ep-i-zō-ot'ik/ adj relating to epizoa; affecting animals as an epidemic affects humans; containing fossil remains, as subsequent to the appearance of life (geol; obs). ◆ n an epizootic disease. **epizoöt'ics** n sing the science or study of epidemic animal diseases.

e pluribus unum /ē ploo'ri-bəs ū'nəm or ā ploo'ri-bŭs oo'nŭm/ (L) one out of many (the motto of the United States).

EPNS abbrev : electroplated nickel silver; English Place-Name Society.

EPO abbrev : erythropoietin; European Patent Office.

EPOCH abbrev : End Physical Punishment of Children.

epoch /ē'pok, ē'pohh or ep'ok/ or (archaic) **epocha** /-ə/ n a point of time fixed or made remarkable by some great event from which dates are reckoned; the particular time, used as a point of reference, at which the data had the values in question (astron); a planet's heliocentric longitude at the epoch (astron); a precise date; a time from which a new state of things dates; an age (geological, historical, etc). [Gr epochē, from epechein to stop, take up a position, from epi upon, and echein to hold]
■ **epochal** /ep'ok-l/ adj.
❏ **ep'och-mā king** adj important enough to be considered as beginning a new age. **ep'och-marking** adj. **epoch of osculation** n (astron) see **osculating orbit** under **osculant**.

epode /ep'ōd/ n a kind of lyric poem invented by the Greek poet Archilochus, in which a longer verse is followed by a shorter one; the last part of a lyric ode, sung after the strophe and antistrophe. [Gr epōidos, from epi on, and ōidē an ode]
■ **epodic** /-od'ik/ adj.

eponychium /ep-o-nik'i-əm/ (anat) n a narrow band of cuticle over the base of a nail. [Gr epi on, and onyx, onychos nail]

eponym /ep'ə-nim/ n a person, real or mythical, from whose name another name, esp a place name, is derived; the name so derived; a hero invented to account for the name of a place or people; a character who gives a play, etc its title; a distinguishing title. [Gr epōnymos eponymous, from epi upon, to, and onyma, onoma a name]
■ **eponym'ic** or **eponymous** /i-pon'i-məs/ adj.

epopee /ep'o-pē/ or **epopoeia** /ep-o-pē'yə/ n epic poetry; an epic poem. [Gr epopoiiā, from epos a word, an epic poem, and poieein to make]

epopt /ep'opt/ n in Ancient Greece, someone initiated into the Eleusinian mysteries. [Gr epoptēs, from epi upon, and root op- to see]

EPOS /ē'pos/ abbrev : electronic point of sale.

epos /ep'os/ n (pl **ep'oses**) the elementary stage of epic poetry; an epic poem; a series of events of the kind that form the subject of epic poetry. [Gr epos a word]

epoxy /e-pok'si/ adj containing oxygen bound to two other atoms, often carbon, which are already attached in some way. ◆ n an epoxy resin. ◆ vt (**epox'ying**; **epox'ied**) to glue using epoxy resin.
■ **epox'ide** n an epoxy compound.
❏ **epoxy** (or **epoxide**) **resins** n pl synthetic polymers used as structural plastics, surface coatings, adhesives and for encapsulating and embedding electronic components.

EPP abbrev : European People's Party.

épris /ā-prē'/ or fem **éprise** /-prēz'/ (Fr) adj captivated or smitten.

EPROM /ē'prom/ (comput) abbrev : erasable programmable read-only memory (see under **erase**).

éprouvette /ā-proo-vet'/ n a device for testing the strength of gunpowder. [Fr éprouver to try]

EPS abbrev : earnings per share (also **eps**); encapsulated PostScript (comput); expanded polystyrene.

epsilon /ep'si-lon or ep-sī'lən/ n the fifth letter (Ε or ε) of the Greek alphabet, short e; as a numeral ε' = 5 and ,ε = 5000. [Gr e psīlon bare or mere e]

epsomite /ep'sə-mīt/ n a mineral, hydrated magnesium sulphate ($MgSO_4.7H_2O$). [Orig obtained from Epsom in Surrey]
❏ **Epsom salts** n (sing or pl) a preparation derived from epsomite, used as a purgative medicine, and also in dyeing, etc.

EPSRC abbrev : Engineering and Physical Sciences Research Council.

Epstein-Barr virus /ep-stīn-bär' vī'rəs/ n a virus which causes glandular fever, thought also to be associated with various human cancers. [MA Epstein and YM Barr, British virologists, who first isolated it in 1964]

EPT abbrev : Environmental Protection Technology.

épuisé or fem **épuisée** /ā-pwē-zā'/ (Fr) adj worn-out.

epulis /e-pū'lis/ (pathol) n a tumour of the gums, either benign or malignant, and growing from the periosteum of the jaw. [Gr epi upon, and oulon gum]

epulotic /ep-ū-lot'ik/ (med) adj forming a scar over a wound. ◆ n a substance which encourages the forming of scar-tissue. [Gr epoulōtikos, from epi upon, and oulē a scar]

epurate /ep'ū-rāt/ vt to purify. [Fr épurer]
■ **epura'tion** or **épura'tion** n purification or purging, esp in reference to the denazification process in France after World War II.

epyllion /e-pil'i-ən/ n a poem with some resemblance to an epic but shorter. [Gr, dimin of epos word]

Epyornis a spelling of **Aepyornis**.

eq abbrev : equal; equation; equivalent.

---

fāte; fär; mē; fûr; mīne; mōte; för; mūte; pŭt; dhen (then); el'ə-mənt (element) ◆ For other sounds see detailed chart of pronunciation

equable /ek'wə-bl/ *adj* even or uniform; smooth; without wide variations or extremes; even-tempered. [L *aequābilis*, from *aequāre*, from *aequus* equal]
■ **equabil'ity** or **e'quableness** *n*. **e'quably** *adv*.

equal /ē'kwəl/ *adj* identical in quantity; of the same value; having the same status; adequate; in correct proportion; fit; equable; uniform; equitable; evenly balanced; just; equally developed on each side (*bot*). ◆ *n* one of the same age, rank, etc; equality (*Spenser*). ◆ *vt* (**e'qualling**; **e'qualled**) to be or make equal to; to be as good as; to match; to reach the same level as (*bot*). [L *aequālis* equal, and *aequāre*, -*ātum* to make equal, from *aequus* equal]
■ **equalitār'ian** /-kwol-/ *adj* of or relating to the equality of mankind. ◆ *n* a person who believes in or supports the political and social equality of mankind. **equalitā'rianism** *n*. **equality** /ē-kwol'i-ti/ *n* the condition of being equal; sameness; evenness. **equalizā'tion** or **-s-** *n* the act of making equal; the state of being equalized. **e'qualize** or **-ise** *vt* to make equal or uniform; to equal (*obs*). ◆ *vi* to become equal; to make one's score equal to one's opponent's. **equalī'zer** or **-s-** *n* a person or thing that equalizes; a goal, etc that levels the score; see also **graphic equalizer** under **graph**. **equally** /ē'kwə-li/ *adv*. **e'qualness** *n* equality, equability. **ē'quant** *n* in Ptolemy's astronomical system, a point on the line on which the earth and the centre of a given planet's deferent stand, or a circle centred on such a point, used to reconcile observed planetary motions with the hypothesis of uniform planetary velocity. ◆ *adj* of or relating to such a point or circle; of the geometric form taken by a crystal in which its diameter is equal or nearly equal in all directions (*crystallog*). **equāt'able** *adj*. **equate'** *vt* to reduce to an average or to a common standard of comparison; to state as equal; to regard as equal. ◆ *vi* to be or be regarded, treated, etc as equal. **equā'tion** /i-kwā'zhən or i-kwā'shən/ *n* the act of making equal; the state of being equal; a statement of the equality of two quantities; reduction to a common standard; correction to compensate for an error, irregularity or discrepancy; the quantity added for this purpose; a formula expressing a chemical action and the proportions of the substances involved. **equā'tional** *adj*. **equā'tive** *adj* (*grammar*) denoting identity or equivalence.
❏ **equal opportunities** *n pl* in employment, etc, the avoidance of any discrimination between applicants, etc on the grounds of sex, race, etc, monitored by the government-appointed **Equal Opportunities Commission**. **equal** or **equals sign** *n* the symbol =, which indicates that two (numerical) values are equal. **equal temperament** see under **temperament**. **equation of time** *n* (*astron*) mean solar time minus apparent solar time, or the right ascension of the true sun minus that of the mean sun.
■ **equal to** having the necessary ability for. **equal to the occasion** or able to cope with an emergency. **personal equation** a correction to be applied to the reading of an instrument on account of the observer's tendency to read too high, too low, etc; any tendency to error or prejudice due to personal characteristics for which allowance must be made.

equanimity /ek-wə-nim'i-ti or ē-/ *n* evenness of mind or temper. [L *aequanimitās*, from *aequus* equal, and *animus* the mind]
■ **equanimous** /i-kwan'i-məs/ *adj*. **equan'imously** *adv*.

equant, **equate**, **equation** see under **equal**.

Equatoguinean /ek-wə-tō-gin'i-ən/ *adj* of or relating to the Republic of *Equatorial Guinea* in W Africa, or its inhabitants. ◆ *n* a native or citizen of Equatorial Guinea.

equator /i-kwā'tər/ *n* an imaginary great circle passing round the middle of the Earth and equidistant from the north and south poles; the imaginary great circle in which the plane of the earth's equator intersects the celestial sphere (so called because day and night are equal when the sun reaches it); the middle belt or line of any globular or nearly globular body that has some sort of polarity. [See **equal**]
■ **equatorial** /ek-wə-tö'ri-əl or ēk-/ *adj* of, relating to, of the nature of, or in the neighbourhood of an equator. ◆ *n* an equatorial telescope. **equato'rially** *adv* so as to have motion or direction parallel to the equator.
❏ **equatorial telescope** *n* a telescope mounted on an axis, capable of moving parallel to the equator and so following a star in any part of its diurnal course.

equerry /ek'wə-ri or ik-wer'i/ *n* an official who is the personal attendant of a member of the royal family; royal stables (*obs*); an officer responsible for the royal stables (*archaic*). [Fr *écurie*, from LL *scūria* a stable]

equestrian /i-kwes'tri-ən/ *adj* of or relating to horsemanship; on horseback; relating to the **eq'uitès**, a class of people in ancient Rome, *orig* cavalry soldiers, but later having a political and administrative function. ◆ *n* a horse-rider; a performer on horseback. [L *equester*, *equestris*, from *eques* a horseman, from *equus* a horse]
■ **eques'trianism** *n* horsemanship. **equestrienne'** *n* (*pseudo-Fr*) a female horse-rider.

equi- /ē-kwi- or ek-wi-/ *pfx* denoting equal. [L *aequus* equal]

■ **equian'gular** *adj* having equal angles (**equiangular spiral** a curve whose radius vector makes a constant angle with the tangent or *logarithmic spiral*). **equiangular'ity** *n*. **equibal'ance** *n* and *vt* equipoise. **equidiff'erent** *adj* having equal differences. **equidis'tance** *n*. **equidis'tant** *adj* equally distant. **equidis'tantly** *adv*. **equifi'nal** *adj* having the same result. **equifinal'ity** *n*. **equifi'nally** *adv*. **equilat'eral** *adj* (L *latus*, -*eris* side) having all sides equal. **equimul'tiple** *n* a number multiplied by the same number as another. **equipo'tent** *adj* of equal power. **equipoten'tial** *adj* of equal power, capability, potential or potentiality. ◆ *n* (*phys*) an equipotential line or surface. **equiprobabil'ity** *n*. **equiprob'able** *adj* equal in degree of probability. **e'quivalve** *adj* having valves of similar size and form.

Equidae /ek'wi-dē/ *n pl* a family of hoofed mammals consisting of the genus *Equus* (horse, ass and zebra) and various fossil forms. [L *equus* horse]
■ **e'quid** *n* a member of the family Equidae.

equidifferent...to...**equilateral** see under **equi-**.

equilibrium /ēk-, ek-wi-lib'ri-əm/ *n* balance; the state of even balance; a calm and composed state of mind; a state in which opposing forces or tendencies neutralize each other. [L *aequilībrium*, from *aequus* equal, and *lībra* balance]
■ **equilibrate** /ēk-wi-lib'rāt, -lib'rāt or -kwil'/ *vt* and *vi* to balance; to counterpoise. **equilibrā'tion** *n*. **equil'ibrator** (or /-lib'/) *n* a balancing or stability device, *esp* an aeroplane fin. **equilib'rial** *adj*. **equil'ibrist** (or /-lib'-, -līb'/) *n* someone who does balancing tricks. **equilib'rity** *n*.

equimultiple see under **equi-**.

equine /e' or ē'kwīn/ *adj* relating to or of the nature of a horse or horses (also **equinal** /e- or ē-kwīn'əl/). ◆ *n* a horse or other member of the horse family. [L *equīnus*, from *equus* a horse]
■ **equinia** /i- or ē-kwin'i-ə/ *n* glanders. **equin'ity** *n* equine nature.
❏ **equine infectious anaemia** *n* another name for **swamp fever** (see under **swamp**).

equinox /ek' or ēk'wi-noks/ *n* either of the two annual occasions when the sun crosses the equator, making the night equal in length to the day, about 21 March and 23 September; an equinoctial point. [L *aequus* equal, and *nox*, *noctis* night]
■ **equinoc'tial** *adj* relating to the equinoxes, the time of the equinoxes, or to the regions about the equator. ◆ *n* an equinoctial gale; the celestial equator or **equinoctial line**. **equinoc'tially** *adv* in the direction of the equinox.
❏ **equinoctial gales** *n pl* high gales popularly supposed to prevail about the times of the equinoxes (the belief is unsupported by scientific observation). **equinoctial point** *n* either of the two points in the heavens where the equinoctial line cuts the ecliptic. **equinoctial year** see under **year**.

equip /i-kwip'/ *vt* (**equipp'ing**; **equipped'**) to fit out; to supply with everything needed. [Fr *équiper*, prob from ON *skipa* to set in order, and *skip* a ship; partly influenced by confusion with L *equus* horse]
■ **equipage** /ek'wi-pāj/ *n* something with which one is equipped (*archaic*); the apparatus required for any operation, eg making tea (*archaic*); a carriage and attendants; retinue. ◆ *vt* (*obs*) to equip. **equip'ment** *n* the act of equipping; the state of being equipped; things used in equipping or furnishing; outfit; a set of tools, machines, clothes, etc necessary for a particular purpose. **equipp'er** *n*.

equiparate /i-kwip'ə-rāt/ (*obs*) *vt* to regard or treat as equal or the same; to put on an equal footing. ◆ *adj* equal or the same. [L *aequiparāre*]
■ **equiparā'tion** *n*.

équipe /ā-kēp'/ (*Fr*) *n* (in motor-racing and other sports) a team.

equipoise /ek'wi-poiz/ *n* a state of balance; a counterpoise. ◆ *vt* to balance; to counterpoise. [L *aequus* equal, and **poise¹**]

equipollent /ēk- or ek-wi-pol'ənt/ *adj* having equal power or force; equivalent. ◆ *n* an equivalent. [L *aequus* equal, and *pollēns*, *pollentis*, prp of *pollēre* to be strong, able]
■ **equipoll'ence** or **equipoll'ency** *n*.

equiponderate /ēk- or ek-wi-pon'də-rāt/ *vi* to be equal in weight; to balance. ◆ *adj* /-ət/ equal in weight. [L *aequus* equal, and *pondus*, *ponderis* weight]
■ **equipon'derance** *n*. **equipon'derant** *adj*.

equipotent...to...**equiprobable** see under **equi-**.

equisetum /ek-wi-sē'təm/ *n* a plant of the *Equisetum* genus, the only surviving genus of the family **Equisetā'ceae**, constituting the **Equisetī'nae** or **Equisetā'les**, a class of pteridophytes, stiff herbaceous plants with almost leafless articulated and whorled stems and branches (also **horsetail**, **scouring-rush** or **Dutch rush**). [L *equus* a horse, and *sēta* a bristle]
■ **equisetā'ceous** *adj*. **equiset'ic** *adj*. **equisēt'iform** *adj*.

equitation /ek-wi-tā'shən/ *n* the art of riding on horseback. [L *equitāre* to ride, from *equus* a horse]

■ **eq'uitant** adj riding; straddling or overlapping; of leaves, folded lengthwise over succeeding leaves (bot).

equity /ek'wi-ti/ n right as founded on the laws of nature; moral justice, of which laws are the imperfect expression; the spirit of justice which enables us to interpret laws rightly; a system of law which along with the common law is the main historical source of English law, a body of legal principles designed to ensure natural justice or 'fair play' (no longer administered by separate courts); fairness; an equitable right; the value of property in excess of any charges upon it; the part of a company's financing that comes from its shareholders, equivalent to the value of the company's assets less its liabilities; (in pl) ordinary shares; (with cap) the trade union for the British acting profession. [OFr equité, from L aequitās, -ātis, from aequus equal]

■ **equitabil'ity** n. **eq'uitable** adj possessing or showing or in accordance with equity; held or exercised in equity; relating to a concept or rule of law which has its origin in the law of equity; fair or just. **eq'uitableness** n. **eq'uitably** adv.

❑ **equity finance** n capital subscribed by ordinary shareholders. **equity release** n the borrowing of money against the value of a property, which is sold on the death of the borrower to recoup the debt.

equivalent /i-kwiv'ə-lənt/ adj equal in value, power, meaning, etc; interchangeable; of similar valency (chem). ◆ n an equivalent thing or amount, etc; an equivalent weight (chem). [Fr, from L aequus equal, and valēns, valentis prp of valēre to be worth]

■ **equiv'alence** or **equiv'alency** n. **equiv'alently** adv.

❑ **equivalent weight** n (chem) that weight which displaces or combines with or otherwise represents a standard unit, atomic weight, or atomic weight divided by valence.

equivalve see under **equi-**.

equivocal /i-kwiv'ə-kl/ adj capable of meaning two or more things; of doubtful meaning; capable of a double explanation; suspicious; questionable. [L aequus equal, and vōx, vōcis the voice or a word]

■ **equivocal'ity** n. **equiv'ocally** adv. **equiv'ocalness** n. **equiv'ocāte** vi to use equivocal or doubtful words in order to mislead or to avoid answering a question. **equivocā'tion** n the use of equivocal or doubtful words; an instance of this; a fallacy caused by ambiguity (logic). **equiv'ocātor** n. **equiv'ocatory** adj containing or characterized by equivocation. **equivoke** or **equivoque** /ek'wi-vōk/ n an equivocal expression; equivocation; a quibble; a pun.

ER abbrev : Edwardus Rex (New L), King Edward; Elizabeth Regina (New L), Queen Elizabeth (**EIIR** Queen Elizabeth II); emergency room (N Am).

Er (chem) symbol : erbium.

er /ûr/ interj expressing hesitation.

-er¹ /-ər/ sfx marks the agent (person or thing); designates people according to occupation (eg writer), or place of origin or abode (eg Londoner). [OE -ere ; some similar-looking words, eg grocer and officer, are from Fr -ier (L -arius)]

-er² /-ər/ sfx marks the comparative degree of some adjectives (longer) and some adverbs (faster). [OE -ra (adj), and -or (adv)]

ERA abbrev : earned run average (baseball); Equal Rights Amendment.

era /ē'rə/ n a series of years reckoned from a particular point, or that point itself; an important date; an age; a main division of geological time. [LL aera a number, orig counters or pieces of copper used in counting, pl of aes copper]

■ **ē'rathem** n (geol) the stratigraphical unit of rock strata corresponding to a geological era.

eradiate /i- or ē-rā'di-āt/ vt and vi to shoot out like a ray of light. [L ē- from, and radius a ray]

■ **eradiā'tion** n.

eradicate /i-rad'i-kāt/ vt to destroy or get rid of; to root out; to pull up by the roots. [L ērādīcāre, -ātum to root out, from ē from, and rādix, -īcis a root]

■ **erad'icable** adj. **erad'icant** n something that eradicates. **erad'icāted** adj completely eliminated; rooted up; (of a tree, or part of a tree) torn up by the roots (heraldry). **eradicā'tion** n the act of eradicating; the state of being eradicated. **erad'icātive** adj serving to eradicate or drive thoroughly away. **erad'icātor** n.

erase /i-rāz'/ vt to rub or scrape out; to efface; to destroy; to destroy a recording on audio or video tape; to replace the data of a storage area with characters representing zero (comput). [L ērādere, from ē from, and rādere, rāsum to scrape]

■ **erā'sable** adj. **erased'** adj rubbed out; effaced; torn off, so as to leave jagged edges (heraldry). **erā'ser** n someone who or something which erases, eg ink-eraser. **erā'sion** /-zhən/, **erase'ment** or **era'sure** /-zhər/ n the act of erasing; a rubbing out; scraping away; the place where something written has been rubbed out.

❑ **erasable programmable read only memory** n (comput) a chip containing a program which it will hold until it is erased by exposure to ultraviolet light and which can then be reprogrammed (abbrev

EPROM). **erasable read only memory** n (comput) a chip similar to the above, but which cannot be reprogrammed (abbrev **EROM**).

Erasmus /i-raz'məs/ abbrev : European Community Action Scheme for the Mobility of University Students.

Erastian /e-ras'ti-ən/ or -tyən/ n a follower of Thomas Erastus (1524–83), a Swiss physician, who denied the church the right to inflict excommunication and disciplinary penalties; a person who would subordinate the church jurisdiction to the state (a position not held by Erastus at all). ◆ adj relating to the Erastians or their doctrines.

■ **Eras'tianism** n control of the church by the state.

erathem see under **era**.

Erato /er'ə-tō/ (Gr myth) n the Muse of lyric love poetry. [Gr Eratō]

erbium /ûr'bi-əm/ n a rare metallic element (symbol **Er**; atomic no 68) found in gadolinite at Ytterby, near Stockholm.

■ **er'bia** n erbium oxide.

ERDF abbrev : European Regional Development Fund.

Erdgeist /ārt'gīst/ (Ger) n earth-spirit.

ere¹ /ār/ (usu literary) adv, prep and conj before. [OE ær ; cf Du eer]

❑ **ere long** or **erelong'** adv before long; soon. **ere now** or **erenow'** adv before this time. **erewhile'** adv (archaic) formerly; before.

ere² same as **ear³**.

e-reader /ē'rēd-ər/ n a portable device on which electronic versions of books can be stored and read.

Erebus /er'i-bəs/ (myth) n the dark and gloomy cavern between earth and Hades; the lower world or hell. [L, from Gr Erebos]

erect /i-rekt'/ adj upright; directed upward; right end up, not inverted; not decumbent (bot); of the penis, clitoris or nipples, enlarged and rigid. ◆ vt to set upright; to set erect; to set at right angles; to raise; to build; to exalt; to establish. [L ērigere, ērēctum to set upright, from ē from, and regere to direct]

■ **erect'able** adj. **erect'ed** adj. **erect'er** or **erect'or** n someone who or something which erects or raises; a muscle which assists in erecting a part or an organ; an attachment to a compound microscope for making the image erect instead of inverted. **erect'ile** /-īl/ adj that may be erected; capable of becoming erect. **erectility** /e- or ē-rek-til'i-ti/ n. **erec'tion** n the act of erecting; the state of being erected; exaltation; anything erected; a building of any kind; an enlarging and hardening of the penis usu in response to sexual stimulation; an erect penis. **erect'ive** adj tending to erect. **erect'ly** adv. **erect'ness** n.

eremacausis /er-i-mə-kö'sis/ (chem) n very slow oxidation. [Gr ērema quietly or slowly, and kausis burning, from kaiein to burn]

eremic /e-rē'mik/ adj of or belonging to deserts. [Gr erēmikos, from erēmiā desert or solitude]

eremite /er'i-mīt/ n a recluse who lives alone, esp from religious motives; a hermit. [LL erēmīta, from Gr erēmītēs, from erēmos desert]

■ **eremi'tal** adj. **eremitic** /-mit'ik/ or **eremit'ical** adj. **er'emītism** n.

e re nata /ē rē nä'tə or ā rā nä'ta/ (LL; law) according to the exigencies of the case.

erepsin /e-rep'sin/ n an enzyme of the small intestine, acting upon casein, gelatine, etc. [L ēripere, ēreptum, from ē from, and rapere to snatch]

erethism /er'e-thi-zm/ n excitement or stimulation of an organ; abnormal irritability. [Gr erethismos]

■ **erethis'mic** adj. **erethis'tic** adj. **erethit'ic** adj.

Erewhon /er'e-(h)won/ n the imaginary country of Samuel Butler's satirical Utopian romances Erewhon (1872) and Erewhon Revisited (1901). [Formed from nowhere spelt backwards]

■ **Erewhō'nian** n and adj.

erf /ûrf/ (S Afr) n (pl **er'ven**) a garden plot or small piece of ground. [Du; cf OE erfe inheritance]

erg¹ /ûrg/ n the CGS unit of work, equal to 10^{-7} joules. [Gr ergon work]

■ **er'gogram** n a record by ergograph. **er'gograph** n an instrument for measuring and recording muscular work. **ergomā'nia** n abnormal desire to work, addiction to work. **ergomā'niac** n. **ergom'eter** n an instrument for measuring work done, a dynamometer. **ergonom'ic** adj. **ergonom'ically** adv. **ergonom'ics** n sing (Gr nomos, from nemein to manage) the scientific study of man in relation to his physical working environment; the adaptation of machines and general conditions to fit the individual so that he or she may work at maximum efficiency. **ergon'omist** n. **ergopho'bia** n abnormal dislike of work.

❑ **erg'-nine**, **erg'-ten'**, etc n an erg multiplied by ten to the power of nine, ten, etc.

erg² /ûrg/ n (pl **ar'eg** or **ergs**) a Saharan area of shifting sand dunes. [Fr, from Ar 'irj]

ergates /ûr'gə-tēz/ or **ergate** /ûr'gāt/ n a worker ant, an undeveloped female. [Gr ergatēs workman, from ergon work]

■ **ergatan'dromorph** *n* (Gr *andromorphos* of male form) an ant combining characteristics of males and workers. **ergataner** /*ûr-gə-tā'nər* or *-tä'nər*/ *n* (Gr *anēr* man) a worker-like wingless male ant. **er'gative** *adj* (*grammar*) of a grammatical case which, in certain languages, eg Inuktitut and Basque, indicates the subject of a transitive verb (also **ergative case**). ◆ *n* an ergative word. **ergativ'ity** *n*. **ergatoc'racy** *n* (Gr *kratos* power) rule by the workers. **ergatogyne** /*-jī'nē*/ *n* (Gr *gynē* woman) a worker-like wingless female ant. **er'gatoid** *adj* worker-like, wingless but sexually perfect. **er'gatomorph** *n* an ergatoid ant. **ergatomorph'ic** *adj*.

ergo /*ûr'gō*/ (*logic*) *adv* therefore (used to introduce the conclusion of a syllogism). [L *ergō* therefore]
■ **er'gotize** or **-ise** *vi* to wrangle (see also **ergot**).

ergocalciferol /*ûr-gō-kal-sif'ə-rol*/ same as **calciferol**.

ergodic /*ər-god'ik*/ (*maths*) *adj* of or relating to the probability that in a system any state will occur again. [Gr *ergon* work, and *hodos* way]
■ **ergodic'ity** /*-dis'*/ *n*.

ergogram, etc see under **erg**[1].

ergon /*ûr'gon*/ or **er'gon** (*Gr*) *n* work or business.

ergonomic, etc see under **erg**[1].

ergosterol see under **ergot**.

ergot /*ûr'got*/ *n* a disease of grasses (*esp* rye) and sedges due to *Claviceps purpurea*; a seed so diseased; the fungus that produces this disease, now an important source of alkaloid drugs; the horny protuberance on a horse's fetlocks. [Fr]
■ **ergos'terol** *n* an unsaturated sterol obtained from ergot. **ergotamine** /*ûr-got'ə-mēn*/ *n* an alkaloid derived from ergot, used to treat migraine. **er'gotism** *n* poisoning caused by eating bread made of rye diseased with ergot. **er'gotize** or **-ise** *vt* to affect with ergot or with ergotism (see also **ergo**).

erhu /*ûr'hoo*/ *n* a Chinese two-stringed musical instrument, played with a bow. [Chin *èr* two, and *hú* bowed instrument]

ERI *abbrev*: *Edwardus Rex Imperator* (*New L*), Edward, King (and) Emperor.

eric /*er'ik*/ *n* the blood-fine paid by a murderer to his victim's family in old Irish law (also **er'iach** or **er'ick**). [Ir *eiric*]

erica /*er'i-kə*/ *n* a plant of the heath genus *Erica*. [L, from Gr *ereikē* heath]
■ **ericaceous** /*er-i-kā'shəs*/ *adj* belonging to plants of the family **Erica'ceae**; heathlike. **er'icoid** *adj* with heatherlike leaves.

erigeron /*e-rij'ə-ron*/ *n* a plant of the flea-bane genus *Erigeron* of composite plants. [Gr *ērigeron* groundsel, from *ēri* early, and *gerōn* old]

erinaceous /*er-i-nā'shəs*/ *adj* of, relating to, or resembling a hedgehog. [L *erinaceus* hedgehog]

eringo same as **eryngo**.

erinite /*er'i-nīt*/ *n* a basic arsenate of copper found in Cornwall and Ireland. [*Erin* Ireland]

Erinys /*e-rin'is*/ *n* (pl **Erinyes** /*e-rin'i-ēz*/) a Fury. [Gr *Erīnys*, pl *Erīnyes*]

erio- /*er-i-ō*- or *-o-*/ *combining form* denoting wool or fibre. [Gr *erion* wool]
■ **Eriocaulon** /*-ō-kö'lon*/ *n* (Gr *kaulos* stalk) the pipewort genus, giving name to the **Eriocaul(on)ā'ceae**, a family of monocotyledons, related to the Bromelias. **Eriöden'dron** *n* (Gr *dendron* tree) the silk-cotton genus of trees (family Bombacaceae). **eriometer** /*-om'ət-ər*/ *n* (Gr *metron* measure) an optical instrument for measuring small diameters, eg of fibres. **er'ionite** *n* a mineral which occurs in white wool-like crystals. **eriophorum** /*-of'ər-əm*/ *n* (Gr *phoros* carrying) a plant of the cotton-grass or cotton-sedge genus *Eriophorum*. **eriophorous** /*-of'ər-əs*/ *adj* very cottony.

eristic /*e-ris'tik*/ *adj* of or relating to controversy or argument (also **eristical** /*-is'ti-kl*/). ◆ *n* a person given to controversy or debate. [Gr *eristikos*, from *eris* strife]
■ **eris'tically** *adv*.

Eritrean /*er-i-trā'ən*/ *adj* of or relating to the country of *Eritrea* in NE Africa, or its inhabitants. ◆ *n* a native or citizen of Eritrea.

erk /*ûrk*/ (*RAF sl*) *n* an aircraftman. [From *airk*, for aircraftman]

Erlenmeyer flask /*ûr'lən-mī-ə fläsk*/ *n* a conical flask for use in a laboratory. [Emil *Erlenmeyer* (1825–1909), German chemist]

erl-king /*ûrl'king*/ *n* for German *Erlkönig*, a mistranslation (alder-king) of the Danish *ellerkonge* (from *elverkonge* king of the elves).

ERM *abbrev*: Exchange Rate Mechanism.

erm /*ûrm*/ *interj* expressing hesitation or doubt. [Imit]

ermelin /*ûr'mə-lin*/ (*archaic*) *n* ermine.

ermine /*ûr'min*/ *n* the stoat; a white fur, the stoat's winter coat in northern lands, used with the black tail-tip (or an imitation) attached for the ceremonial robes of royalty, the nobility, judges and magistrates; a moth of the genus *Spilosoma*, with dark spots on its light-coloured wings (also called **ermine moth**). [OFr *ermine* (Fr *hermine*), perh from L (*mūs*) *Armēnius*, literally, (mouse) of Armenia, whence it was brought to Rome; but according to some from OHGer *harmin* (Ger *Hermelin*) ermine-fur]
■ **er'mined** *adj* trimmed or decorated with ermine.

ern an old spelling (*Milton*) of **earn**.

erne[1] /*ûrn*/ *n* an eagle, *esp* the sea-eagle. [OE *earn*; cf ON *örn*, Du *arend*]

erne[2] /*ûrn*/ (*Spenser*) same as **yearn**[1].

Ernie /*ûr'ni*/ *n* the computer which picks random numbers to be used as winning numbers on premium bonds. [Abbrev of *e*lectronic *r*andom *n*umber *i*ndicator *e*quipment]

erode /*i-* or *e-rōd'*/ *vt* to eat away or wear away; to form or shape by wearing away. ◆ *vi* to become eaten or worn away. [L *ē* from, and *rōdere*, *rōsum* to gnaw]
■ **erö'ded** or **erose** /*-rōs'*/ *adj* irregularly notched as if bitten. **erö'dent** *adj* and *n* caustic. **erod'ible** *adj* able to be eroded.

erodium /*e-rō'di-əm*/ *n* a plant of the stork's-bill genus *Erodium* of the family Geraniaceae. [Gr *erōdios* a heron]

erogenic /*e-rō-jen'ik*/ or **erogenous** /*e-roj'ə-nəs*/ *adj* producing erotic desire or gratification. [**Eros**]
❑ **erogenous zone** *n* one of a number of areas of the body that are sensitive to sexual stimulation.

EROM /*ē'rom*/ (*comput*) *abbrev*: erasable read only memory (see under **erase**).

Eros /*ē'ros* or *er'os*/ *n* the Greek love-god, identified by the Romans with Cupid; an asteroid discovered in 1898, notable for its near approach to the earth. [Gr *Erōs*, *-ōtos*, the Greek love-god]

erose same as **eroded** (see under **erode**).

erosion /*i-* or *e-rō'zhən*/ (*geol*) *n* eating away or wearing down; the denuding action of weathering, water, ice, wind, etc. [Ety as for **erode**]
■ **ero'sional** *adj*. **erosive** /*-rō'ziv*/ *adj*.

erostrate /*ē-ros'trāt*/ (*bot*) *adj* beakless. [L *ē* from, and *rōstrum* a beak]

erotema /*er-ō-tē'mə*/, **eroteme** /*er'ō-tēm*/ or **erotesis** /*er-ō-tē'sis*/ *n* a rhetorical question. [Gr *erōtēma*, *erōtēsis*, from *erōtaein* to question]
■ **erotetic** /*-tet'ik*/ *adj* interrogatory.

erotic /*e-rot'ik*/ *adj* (also (*rare*) **erot'ical**) relating to or arousing sexual desire; amatory; amorous. ◆ *n* a person who is particularly susceptible to sexual arousal; an amatory poem or composition. [**Eros**]
■ **erot'ica** *n pl* erotic literature or art. **erot'ically** *adv*. **erot'icism** /*-sizm*/ *n* amorous temperament or habit; erotism. **erot'icist** *n*. **eroticīzā'tion** or **-s-** *n*. **erot'icize** or **-ise** *vt* to make erotic; to arouse sexually. **er'otism** *n* sexual desire; the manifestations of sex in its widest application. **erotogenic** /*er-ət-ō-jen'ik*/ or **erotogenous** /*-oj'*/ *adj* producing erotic desire or gratification. **erotol'ogy** *n* the study of sexual behaviour and erotic material. **erōtomā'nia** *n* an obsessive condition in which someone believes that another person is in love with them (also **De Clerambault('s) syndrome**); unhealthily strong sexual passion. **erōtomā'niac** *n*. **erōtophō'bia** *n* fear of or aversion to any form of sexual involvement.

err /*ûr*/ *vi* (**erring** /*ûr'ing*, *er'ing*/; **erred** /*ûrd*/) to make a mistake; to miss the mark; to be inaccurate; to sin; to wander (*archaic*); to wander from the right way (*archaic*); to go astray (*archaic*). [L *errāre* to stray; cognate with Ger *irren* and *irre* astray]
■ **err'able** /*er'*/ *adj* (*obs*) capable of erring. **err'ancy** /*er'*/ *n* a tendency to err. **err'ing** *adj* wandering (*archaic*); straying from the truth or right conduct. ◆ *n* wandering (*archaic*); straying (*archaic*); making mistakes. **err'ingly** *adv*. **erroneous** /*i-rō'ni-əs*/ *adj* erring; full of errors; wrong; mistaken; wandering or straying (*archaic*). **errō'neously** *adv*. **errō'neousness** *n*. **error** /*er'ər*/ *n* a blunder or mistake; wrongdoing; the state of being mistaken; the difference between a quantity obtained by observation and the true value; a fault or mistake causing the failure of a computer program or system to produce expected results; mistaken opinion; deviation from the right way (*archaic*); a wandering, a winding course (*archaic*). **err'orist** *n* (*archaic*). **err'orless** *adj*.
❑ **error message** *n* (*comput*) a message displayed on a computer screen to alert the user to an error, rarely suggesting a remedy.

errand /*er'ənd*/ *n* a commission to say or do something usually involving a short journey; a verbal message (*archaic*); a mission (*archaic*); (in *pl*) shopping (*dialect*). [OE *ǣrende* a message (*archaic*); ON *eyrindi*; prob connected with Gothic *āirus*, ON *ārr* a messenger]
❑ **errand boy** or **errand girl** *n*.
■ **a fool's errand** or **a sleeveless errand** a futile journey. **make an errand** to invent a reason for going. **once'-errand**, **yince'-errand** or **ance'-errand** (*Scot*) for the express purpose and nothing else. **run errands** to be sent to convey messages or perform small pieces of business.

errant /er'ənt/ adj wandering in search of adventure; roving; quixotic; thorough (obs; cf **arrant**); erring. ◆ n a knight errant. [ME errant, from OFr prp of errer to travel, from LL iterāre, confused with prp of errer to err, from L errāre]
■ **err'antly** adv. **err'antry** n an errant or wandering state; a rambling about like a knight errant.

erratic /e-rat'ik/ adj irregular; capricious or unpredictable in behaviour; wandering; having no certain course; not stationary. ◆ n a wanderer; an erratic block or boulder. [L errāticus, from errāre to stray]
■ **errat'ical** adj (archaic). **errat'ically** adv. **errat'icism** n. **erratum** /e-rä'tum/ n (pl **errata** /e-rä'tə/) an error in writing or printing, esp one noted in a list in a book.
❑ **erratic block** or **boulder** n a mass of rock transported by ice and deposited at a distance.

errhine /er'īn/ adj and n (something) causing sneezing or running of mucus from the nose. [Gr errīnon, from en in, and rhīs, rhīnos the nose]

erroneous, error, etc see under **err**.

ers /ûrs/ n the bitter vetch. [Fr, from L ervum]

ersatz /er'zats, ûr' or er-zats'/ n a substitute; a supplementary reserve from which waste can be made good (milit). ◆ adj substitute; fake. [Ger]

Erse /ers or ûrs/ n formerly, and still occasionally, the name given by Lowland Scots to the language of the people of the West Highlands, as being of Irish origin; sometimes used for Irish Gaelic, as opposed to Scottish Gaelic. [Variant of **Irish**]

erst /ûrst/ adv at first; formerly. [OE ǣrest, superl of ǣr; see **ere**[1]]
❑ **erst'while** or **erstwhile'** adv formerly. ◆ adj former.

erubescent /er-ŭ-bes'ənt/ adj growing red; blushing. [L ērubēscere to grow red; see **rubescent** and **ruby**]
■ **erubesc'ence** or **erubesc'ency** n. **erubesc'īte** n the mineral bornite.

Eruca /i-roo'kə/ n a genus of herbs of the family Cruciferae. [L ērūca rocket (see **rocket**[2]); see also **eruciform**]
❑ **erucic acid** /i-roo'sik/ n a crystalline fatty acid found in rapeseed, wallflower seed and mustard seed, used in some edible oils.

eruciform /e-roo'si-förm/ adj like a caterpillar. [L ērūca caterpillar, and förma form]

eruct /i-rukt'/ or **eructate** /i-ruk'-tāt/ vt to belch out (eg wind from the stomach; also vi; also fig); (of a volcano) to emit (fumes and ash or lava). [L ēructāre, -ātum, from ē from, and ructāre to belch forth]
■ **eructa'tion** /ē-/ n.

erudite /er'ŭ-dīt or -ū-/ adj learned. ◆ n a learned person. [L ērudītus, from ērudīre, ērudītum to free from ignorance, from ē from, and rudis ignorant]
■ **er'uditely** adv. **erudi'tion** n the state of being learned; knowledge gained by study; learning, esp in literature.

erumpent /i-rum'pənt/ (bot) adj esp of fungal hyphae, breaking out from under a substrate. [Ety as for **erupt**]

erupt /i-rupt'/ vi to break out or through, eg of a volcano, a tooth from the gum or a rash on the skin; to break out suddenly and violently. ◆ vt to cause (rocks, etc) to burst out. [L ērumpere, ēruptum, from ē from, and rumpere to break]
■ **erup'tion** n a breaking or bursting out; something which bursts out; a breaking out of spots on the skin; the action of a volcano. **erup'tional** adj. **erupt'ive** adj breaking out; attended by or producing eruption; produced by eruption. **erupt'iveness** or **eruptiv'ity** n.

eruv /ār'oov or er-/ (Judaism) n an area within which certain activities normally forbidden in public on the Sabbath are permitted. [Hebrew]

ERV abbrev : endogenous retroviruses, RNA viruses that have become integrated into the genome of the host.

ervalenta see **revalenta**.

erven see **erf**.

ERW abbrev : enhanced radiation weapon.

eryngo /e-ring'gō/ n (pl **eryn'gos** or **eryn'goes**) the sea-holly, a superficially thistle-like umbellifer; its candied root formerly prepared as a sweetmeat. [Gr ēryngos]
■ **eryn'gium** /-jī-əm/ n a bristly plant of the genus Eryngium (family Umbelliferae).

Erysimum /e-ris'i-məm/ n the treacle-mustard genus of Cruciferae. [Latinized from Gr erysimon hedge-mustard]

erysipelas /e-ri-sip'i-ləs/ n an inflammatory disease, generally in the face, marked by a bright redness of the skin (popularly called **St Anthony's fire**). [Gr; prob from root of erythros red, and pella skin]
■ **erysipelatous** /-el'ə-təs/ adj. **erysip'eloid** n infective dermatitis of the hands.

erythema /e-ri-thē'mə/ n redness of the skin. [Gr erythēma, from erythainein to redden, from erythros red]
■ **erythemal** /er-ith'/ adj. **erythemat'ic** adj. **erythem'atous** adj.

erythro- or **erythr-** /e-ri-thr(ō)-/ combining form denoting red. [Gr erythros red]
■ **erythrī'na** n a plant of the kaffirboom genus Erythrina, tropical and subtropical trees with brilliant red flowers. **eryth'rism** n red colouring, esp exceptional or abnormal. **eryth'rīte** n a reddish hydrous arsenate of cobalt. **erythrit'ic** adj. **eryth'ritol** n a compound extracted from certain algae and lichens and used medicinally to dilate blood vessels. **eryth'roblast** /-bläst/ n (Gr blastos a sprout) a cell in bone marrow that develops into an erythrocyte. **erythroblast'ic** adj. **erythroblastō'sis** n the abnormal presence of erythroblasts in the blood. **eryth'rocyte** n (Gr kytos case) a red blood corpuscle. **erythrocytic** /-sit'ik/ adj. **erythroleukae'mia** n a malignant disorder of the blood characterized by an abnormal presence of erythroblasts and myeloblasts in the blood. **erythromycin** /-mī'sin/ n (Gr mykēs fungus) a broad-spectrum antibiotic of the macrolide group. **erythrō'nium** n a plant of the genus Erythronium, the dogtooth violet. **erythropē'nia** n diminution below normal of the number of red cells in the blood. **erythrophō'bia** n a fear of blushing; a neurotic tendency to blush; an aversion to red. **erythropoiesis** /-poi-ēs'is/ n (Gr poiēsis making) the formation of red blood cells. **erythropoiēt'ic** adj. **erythropoi'etin** n a hormone which increases the rate of formation of red blood cells; a drug with the same effect.

Erziehungsroman /er-tsē'ŭng(g)s-rō-män/ (Ger) same as **Bildungsroman**.

ES abbrev : El Salvador (IVR).

Es (chem) symbol : einsteinium.

es /es/ n the nineteenth letter of the modern English alphabet (S or s); anything of that shape (also **ess**).

ESA abbrev : Employment and Support Allowance; Environmentally Sensitive Area; European Space Agency.

ESB abbrev : electrical stimulation of the brain.

ESC abbrev : Economic and Social Committee.

Esc abbrev : escudo.

ESCA abbrev : electron spectroscopy for chemical analysis.

escabeche /es-kə-bech'e/ n a spicy, orig Spanish, cold marinade of olive oil, vinegar and herbs, used to season and preserve cooked meat and fish; a dish made with this. [Sp, from Ar sakbā]

escadrille /es-kə-dril'/ n a French squadron of aircraft; a flotilla. [Fr, flotilla]

escalade /es-kə-lād'/ n the scaling of the walls of a fortress by means of ladders (also **escalā'dō** (pl **escalā'does**)). ◆ vt to scale; to mount and enter by means of ladders. [Fr, from Sp escalada, from escala a ladder, from L scāla]

escalate /es'kə-lāt/ vi to increase rapidly in scale or intensity; orig to ascend or descend on an escalator. ◆ vt to cause to increase rapidly. [escalate is a back-formation from escalator, orig a trademark, prob from **escalade** and elevator]
■ **escalā'tion** n. **es'calātor** n a moving staircase; short form of **escalator clause** below. **es'calātory** adj.
❑ **escalator clause** or **escalation clause** n a clause in an agreement allowing for adjustment up or down according to change in circumstances, as in cost of material in a work contract or in cost of living in a wage agreement.

escalier /es-ka-lyā'/ (Fr) n a staircase.
❑ **escalier dérobé** /dā-ro-bā/ n a private staircase.

escallonia /es-ka-lō'ni-ə/ n a shrub of the Central and S American genus Escallonia. [Discovered by Escallon, an 18c Spanish traveller]

escallop /is-kal'əp/ n a variant of **scallop**.
■ **escall'oped** adj (heraldry) covered with scallop-shells.

escalop a variant of **scallop** except in heraldry.

escalope /es'ka-lop/ n a boneless slice of meat, cut thin and often beaten out still thinner. [Fr]

escamotage /es-ka-mo-täzh'/ (Fr) n juggling.

ESCAP same as **UNESCAP**.

escape /is-kāp'/ vt to free oneself from; to pass out of danger from; to evade or elude. ◆ vi to come off or come through in safety; to emerge into or gain freedom; to flee; to slip out; to issue; to leak. ◆ n the act of escaping; a means of escaping; the avoidance of danger or harm; flight; flight from reality; an outlet; an escape valve; a leakage; an accidental or inadvertent emission; an outburst; a person or thing that has escaped; a garden plant maintaining itself wild; the escape key on a computer keyboard (abbrev **esc**); a sally; a prank (obs); a venial offence (obs); a transgression (obs). ◆ adj of literature, providing escape from reality. [OFr escaper (Fr échapper), from LL ex cappā (literally) out of one's cape or cloak]

escap'able *adj.* **escapade** /es'kə-pād/ or /-pād'/ *n* an exciting, *esp* mischievous, adventure; an escape (*archaic*). **escapado** /-ä'dō/ *n* (*pl* **escapā'does**) an escaped villain; an escapade (Sp *escapada*). **escapee'** *n* a person who has escaped, *esp* from prison. **escape'less** *adj.* **escape'ment** *n* part of a clock or watch connecting the wheelwork with the pendulum or balance, and allowing a tooth to escape at each vibration; the clearance in a piano between the string and the hammer after it has struck the string, while the key is held down; an escape (*archaic*). **escāp'er** *n.* **escāp'ism** *n* escape from (*esp* unpleasant) reality. **escāp'ist** *n* someone who seeks escape, *esp* from reality (also *adj*). **escapol'ogist** *n.* **escapol'ogy** *n* the study or use of methods of escape from any sort of constraint or confinement; (*loosely*) escapism.
□ **escape character** *n* (*comput*) a control character that often terminates an action, etc; (in *pl*) a special sequence of control characters used to control a printer. **escape clause** *n* a clause in a contract, etc that releases one from that contract under certain circumstances. **escape hatch** *n* an emergency means of escape from a ship, submarine, etc. **escape key** *n* a function key on some computer keyboards, used to cancel commands, to leave a program, etc. **escape mechanism** *n* (*psychol*) a mental process by which a person avoids something unpleasant. **escape road** *n* a short track leading off a road on a steep hill, sharp bend, etc, for vehicles going out of control. **escape sequence** *n* (*comput*) a sequence of characters, *usu* beginning with an escape character, that gives or initiates a command. **escape valve** *n* a valve to let steam, etc escape when wanted. **escape velocity** *n* (*phys*) the minimum velocity needed to escape from the gravitation field of a body. **escape wheel** *n* the wheel that the pallets act upon in a clock.

escargot /es-kar-gō'/ (*Fr*) *n* an edible snail.

escarmouche /e-skär'mūsh/ (*obs*) *n* a skirmish. [Fr]

escarole /es'ka-rōl/ or /-rōl/ *n* a broad-leaved, non-curly endive. [Fr]

escarp /is-kärp'/ *vt* to make into a scarp or sudden slope. ◆ *n* a scarp or steep slope; the side of the ditch beside the rampart (*fortif*). [Fr *escarper* to cut steeply, from the root of **scarp**[1]]
■ **escarp'ment** *n* the precipitous side of a hill or rock; escarp.

ESCB *abbrev*: European System of Central Banks.

eschalot see **shallot**.

eschar /es'kär/ (*pathol*) *n* a slough or portion of dead or disorganized tissue, *esp* an artificial slough produced by caustics. [L, from Gr *eschara* a hearth, or the mark of a burn]
■ **escharot'ic** *adj* tending to form an eschar; caustic. ◆ *n* a caustic substance.

eschatology /es-kə-tol'ə-ji/ (*theol*) *n* the doctrine of the last or final matters, such as death, judgement and the state after death. [Gr *eschatos* last, and *logos* a discourse]
■ **eschatolog'ic** or **eschatolog'ical** *adj.* **eschatol'ogist** *n.*

escheat /is-chēt'/ *n* property that falls to the feudal lord or to the state for lack of an heir or by forfeiture; the reversion of property in this way; plunder or gain (*obs*; *Spenser* **excheat'**). ◆ *vt* to confiscate. ◆ *vi* to fall to the lord of the manor or the state. [OFr *eschete*, from *escheoir* (Fr *échoir*), from L *ex* from, and *cadere* to fall]
■ **escheat'able** *adj.* **escheat'age** *n.* **escheat'ment** *n.* **escheat'or** *n* (*hist*) an official who watched over escheats.

Escherichia /esh-ə-rik'i-ə/ *n* a genus of rod-shaped, Gram-negative bacteria of the family Enterobacteriaceae. [T *Escherich* (died 1911), German physician]
□ **Escherichia coli** *n* the type species of this genus, occurring naturally in the intestines of vertebrates and sometimes pathogenic (*abbrev* **E. coli**).

eschew /is-choo'/ *vt* to shun; to flee from (*obs*); to abstain from. [OFr *eschever*; cognate with Ger *scheuen* to shun]
■ **eschew'al** *n.* **eschew'er** *n.*

eschscholtzia or **eschscholzia** /e-sholt'si-ə/ *n* a plant of the genus *Eschscholzia* of the family Papaveraceae, including the Californian poppy, a showy garden annual. [JF von *Eschscholtz*, a member of the expedition that discovered the poppy in 1821]

Esc key /esk kē/ (*comput*) short for **escape key**.

escolar /es-kō-lär'/ *n* an Atlantic and southern fish of spectacled appearance. [Sp, scholar]

escopette /es-kō-pet'/ (*US*) *n* a carbine. [Sp *escopeta*]

escort /es'kört/ *n* anyone or anything accompanying another or others for protection, guidance, courtesy, etc; an armed guard; a police officer accompanying a person under arrest, in order to prevent escape; a man who accompanies a woman on an evening out; a person, usually of the opposite sex, hired to accompany someone to entertainments, etc; a member of an aircraft, etc crew whose duty is to look after children travelling alone; attendance. ◆ *adj* of or relating to an escort. ◆ *vt* /es-kört'/ to accompany or attend as escort.

[Fr *escorte*, from Ital *scorta*, from *scorgere* to guide, from L *ex* out, and *corrigere* to set right]
■ **escort'age** *n* (*US*).
□ **escort agency** *n* one which provides people to act as hired escorts. **escort carrier** *n* a small aircraft-carrier used for escorting naval convoys or in support of military landings.

escot /e-skot'/ (*Shakesp*) *vt* to pay for or maintain. [OFr *escoter*, *escot* a tax; of Gmc origin; cf **scot** and **shot**[1]]

escribano /ä-skrē-bä'nō/ (*Sp*) *n* (*pl* **escriba'nos**) a notary.

escribe /ē-skrīb'/ (*geom*) *vt* to draw (a circle) so as to touch one side of a triangle externally, the others (produced) internally. [L *ē* out, and *scrībere* write]

escritoire /es-krē-twär'/ *n* a writing desk. [Fr *escritoire*, from LL *scrīptōrium*, from L *scrībere, scrīptum* to write]
■ **escritō'rial** (or /-ör'/) *adj.*

escroc /es-krō'/ (*Fr*) *n* a swindler.

escroll or **escrol** /es-krōl'/ *n* an escrow; a scroll (*heraldry*). [Anglo-Fr *escroele, escroe*; see **scroll**]

escrow /es-krō'/ *n* a deed in the hands of a third party, to take effect when a condition is fulfilled (*law*); an encryption system for which a third party has the key (*comput*). ◆ *vt* to put into such a system (*comput*); to place in escrow (*law*). [See **escroll** and **scrow**]

escuage /es'kū-ij/ *n* scutage. [Anglo-Fr; see **scutage**]

escudo /es-koo'dō/ *n* (*pl* **escu'dos**) a former unit of currency in Portugal, replaced by the euro; a coin representing this; the standard monetary unit of Cape Verde (100 centavos); a coin or currency unit of various values formerly used in other countries. [Port and Sp, shield]

Esculapian see **Aesculapian**.

esculent /es'kū-lənt/ *adj* eatable; fit to be used for human food. ◆ *n* something that is eatable. [L *esculentus* eatable, from *esca* food, from *edere* to eat]

escutcheon /es-kuch'ən/ *n* a shield on which a coat of arms is represented; a family shield; the part of a vessel's stern bearing her name; a shield-shaped object or ornament, etc as a shield over a keyhole. [OFr *escuchon*, from L *scūtum* a shield]
■ **escutch'eoned** *adj* having an escutcheon.
□ **escutcheon of pretence** *n* (*heraldry*) an escutcheon placed with the arms of an heiress in the centre of her husband's coat.
■ **a blot on the escutcheon** a stain on one's good name.

ESCWA *abbrev*: Economic and Social Commission for Western Asia.

Esd. (*Bible*) *abbrev*: (the Apocryphal Books of) Esdras.

Esda /ez'də/ *abbrev*: electrostatic document analysis (or apparatus), a forensic test (or the equipment for this) used to reveal impressions on paper or evidence of amendments to documents.

ESE *abbrev*: east-south-east.

-ese /-ēz/ *sfx* denoting country or region of origin, as in *Japanese, Maltese*; the literary style, jargon, etc of a specified group, as in *journalese, officialese*.

esemplastic /es-əm-plas'tik/ *adj* unifying. [Gr *es* into, *hen* (neuter) one, and *plastikos* moulding]
■ **esemplas'tically** *adv.* **esemplasy** /es-em'plə-si/ *n* the unifying power of imagination.

eserine /es'ə-rēn/ *n* another name for **physostigmine**. [Fr *ésérine*, from Efik *esere* Calabar-bean, and **-ine**[1]]

ESF *abbrev*: European Social Fund.

esile /ā'sil/ (*obs*) same as **eisel**.

esker or **eskar** /es'kər/ (*geol*) *n* a ridge of gravel and sand laid down by a subglacial stream or one which issues from a retreating glacier, a kame. [Ir *eiscir* a ridge]

Eskimo /es'ki-mō/ *n* (*pl* **Es'kimos** or **Es'kimo**) one of a people inhabiting arctic America with its islands, Greenland, and the nearest Asiatic coast (now usually referred to as *Inuit* or *Yupik*); Inuktitut, their language. ◆ *adj* of or relating to the Eskimos or their language. [Poss from a Native American word meaning eaters of raw flesh]
□ **Eskimo dog** *n* one of a breed of powerful dogs with a double coat of hair, widely distributed in the Arctic regions and used for pulling sledges (also called **malamute**). **Eskimo roll** *n* (*canoeing*) a complete roll through 360°, enabling recovery after capsizing.

Esky® /es'ki/ (*Aust*) *n* a portable insulated container for keeping drinks, etc cool. [Prob from **Eskimo**]

ESL *abbrev*: English as a second language.

esloin or **esloyne** /es-loin'/ (*obs*) same as **eloin**.

ESN *abbrev*: educationally subnormal, formerly used to describe people with special educational needs; electronic serial number, a unique, unchangeable number embedded in a mobile phone to identify it.

esne /ez'ni/ (*hist*) *n* a domestic slave in Anglo-Saxon times. [OE]

esnecy /es'nə-si/ (obs) n the eldest daughter's right of first choice in dividing an inheritance. [OFr ainsneece (Fr aînesse)]

ESOL abbrev : English for speakers of other languages.

ESOP abbrev : employee share ownership plan.

esophagus a chiefly N American spelling of **oesophagus**.

esoteric /es-ō-ter'ik/ adj inner; secret; mysterious; taught to a select few, opp to exoteric (philos). [Gr esōterikos, from esōterō, compar of esō, eisō within]
■ **esoter'ica** n pl esoteric objects, etc. **esoter'ically** adv. **esoter'icism** /-i-sizm/ or **esoterism** /es-ot'ər-izm/ n the holding of esoteric opinions. **esoter'icist** n. **es'otery** n (rare) secret doctrine.
❏ **esoteric Buddhism** n theosophy.

ESP abbrev : electro-selective pattern (photog); electrostatic precipitator; English for special (or specific) purposes; extrasensory perception.

esp. or **espec.** abbrev : especially.

espada /e-spä'dha/ (Sp) n a sword; a swordfish; a matador.

espadrille /e-spə-dril'/ n a rope-soled shoe. [Fr, from Provençal espardillo, from espart esparto]

espagnole /e-span-yol'/ or **espagnole sauce** /sös/ n a brown sauce flavoured with tomatoes and sherry (also (Fr) **sauce espagnole** /sōs es-pan-yol/). [Fr, Spanish (sauce)]

espagnolette /e-span-yō-let'/ n the fastening of a French window. [Fr, dimin of espagnol Spanish]

espalier /e-spal'yər/ n a latticework of wood to train trees across; a fruit tree trained on stakes; a row of trees trained in this way (obs). ◆ vt to train as an espalier. [Fr, from Ital spalliera a support for the shoulders, from spalla a shoulder, from L spatula broad blade; cf **epaule**]

esparto /e-spär'tō/ n (pl **espar'tos**) a strong grass (Stipa tenacissima and others) grown in Spain, N Africa, etc, and used for making paper, baskets, cordage, etc (also called **esparto grass**). [Sp, from L spartum, from Gr sparton a kind of rope]

espec. see **esp.**

especial /i-spesh'l/ adj special; particular; principal; distinguished. [OFr, from L speciālis, from speciēs species]
■ **espec'ially** adv.
■ **in especial** (archaic) in particular.

esperance /es'pə-rəns/ (Shakesp) n hope. [Fr espérance, from L spērāre to hope]

Esperanto /e-spə-ran'tō/ n an international language devised by Dr LL Zamenhof in 1887 (also adj). [Inventor's pseudonym, (literally) the hoping one]
■ **Esperan'tist** n a speaker of Esperanto.

espial see under **espy**.

espiègle /e-spē-eg'l/ adj roguish or playful; arch. [Fr, from Ger Eulenspiegel; see **owl**]
■ **espièg'lerie** n roguishness; playfulness.

espionage /es'pi-ə-näzh, -näj or -nij/ n spying; use of spies. [Fr espionner, from espion spy]

esplanade /es-plə-nād', -näd', also es'/ n a level space for walking or driving in, esp by the sea; orig a level space between a citadel and the first houses of the town. [Fr, from Sp esplanada, from L explānāre, from ex out, and plānus flat]

espouse /i-spowz'/ vt to give or take in marriage or betrothal; to take upon oneself or embrace (eg a cause). [OFr espouser (Fr épouser), from L spōnsāre to betroth, from spondēre, spōnsum to vow]
■ **espous'al** n the act of espousing or betrothing; the taking upon oneself of eg a cause; (in pl) a contract or mutual promise of marriage; a wedding; a formal betrothal. **espous'er** n.

espressivo /es-pre-sē'vō/ (music) adj and adv in an expressive way. [Ital]

espresso /e-spres'ō/ n (pl **espress'os**) coffee made by forcing hot water under pressure through ground coffee beans; the machine for making this. [Ital, pressed]

ESPRIT abbrev : European Strategic Programme of Research in Information Technology, a European Union initiative to develop fifth-generation computer techniques.

esprit /e-sprē'/ (Fr) n wit or liveliness.
❏ **esprit de corps** /es-prē də kor/ n (Fr corps body) regard for the honour of the body to which one belongs; loyalty of a member to the whole. **esprit de l'escalier** /də-les-kal-yā/ (or sometimes incorrectly **d'escalier**) n (Fr escalier staircase) thinking of an apt or witty retort after the opportunity of making it is past; the retort itself. **esprit fort** /for/ n (Fr fort strong) a freethinker.

esprit follet /e-sprē fo-le/ (Fr) n mischievous goblin.

espumoso /e-spoo-mō'sō/ (Sp) n (pl **espumo'sos**) a sparkling wine.

espy /e-spī'/ (archaic or literary) vt (**espy'ing; espied'**) to watch; to see at a distance; to catch sight of; to observe; to discover unexpectedly. [OFr espier; see **spy**]
■ **espi'al** n the act of espying; observation.

Esq., esq. or **Esqr.** abbrev : esquire.

-esque /-esk/ sfx forming adjectives from nouns, esp proper names, and denoting in the style or manner of or similar to, eg Kiplingesque, statuesque.

Esquimau /es'ki-mō/ n (pl **Esquimaux** /es'ki-mōz/) a French spelling of Eskimo.

esquire /es-kwīr'/, sometimes es'/ n a general title of respect in addressing letters (abbrev **Esq., esq.** or **Esqr.**); orig a squire or shield-bearer; an attendant on a knight (archaic); a landed proprietor; a title of dignity next below a knight; a gentleman acting as escort. [OFr esquier (Fr écuyer), from L scūtārius, from scūtum a shield]
■ **esquir'ess** n (hist; rare) a female esquire.

esquisse /es-kēs'/ (Fr) n a sketch or outline.

ESR abbrev : electrical skin resistance, a measurable skin characteristic which indicates levels of anxiety, relaxation, etc; electron spin resonance (phys); erythrocyte sedimentation rate (med).

ESRC abbrev : Economic and Social Research Council.

ESRO /ez'rō/ abbrev : European Space Research Organization, which became part of ESA in 1975.

ESS abbrev : evolutionarily stable strategy.

ess /es/ see **es**.
■ **collar of esses** a chain of links (also written SS) in the form of the letter S, worn by various dignitaries.

-ess /-es/ sfx denoting the female of a specified species, occupation, etc, eg lioness, princess, poetess. [OFr -esse, from LL -issa, from Gr -issa]

essay /es'ā/ n a written composition less elaborate than a dissertation or treatise; an attempt; a tentative effort; a first draft (archaic); a trial (archaic); an experiment (archaic). ◆ vt /es-ā'/ (**essay'ing; essayed'**) to try; to attempt; to make experiment of (archaic). [OFr essai, from L exagium weighing, from exagere to try or examine]
■ **essay'er** n. **essayette'** n a little essay. **ess'ayish** adj. **ess'ayist** n a writer of essays; a person who essays (archaic). **essayis'tic** adj.

esse /es'i/ (philos) n actual existence; essence. [L esse to be]
■ **in esse** in existence, opp to in posse.

essence /es'əns/ n the inner distinctive nature of anything; the qualities which make any object what it is; a being; an alcoholic solution of a volatile or essential oil; a perfume of such composition; a concentrated extract containing the active constituents of a drug, plant, etc; (also **Essen'cia**) a particularly fine variety of Tokay wine. [Fr, from L essentia, from essēns, essentis assumed prp of esse to be]
■ **essential** /is- or es-en'shl/ adj indispensable or important in the highest degree; relating to, constituting or containing the essence; necessary to the existence of a thing; highly rectified; pure; (of eg a disease) having no known cause. ◆ n something necessary; a leading principle. **essen'tialism** n an educational theory that concentrates on teaching basic skills; a philosophical doctrine that distinguishes between the essence of material objects and their existence or appearance. **essen'tialist** n. **essentiality** /is-en-shi-al'i-ti/ n the quality of being essential; an essential quality or element. **essen'tially** adv. **essen'tialness** n.
❏ **essential minerals** n pl those whose presence is considered necessary to entitle a rock to the name it bears, opp to accessory minerals. **essential oils** n pl oils which give plants their fragrance, used in cosmetics, toiletries, etc and in aromatherapy (also called **ethereal oils** or **volatile oils**). **essential organs** n pl (bot) stamens and carpels.
■ **in essence** basically, fundamentally. **of the essence** of the utmost importance.

Essene /e-sēn' or es'ēn/ n one of a small religious fraternity among the ancient Jews leading retired ascetic lives and holding property in common. [Gr essēnos; origin doubtful]
■ **Ess'enism** n.

essential, etc see under **essence**.

Essex /es'iks/ adj belonging to the English county of Essex.
❏ **Essex Girl** n (inf) an archetypal SE English working-class female with lowbrow tastes and supposedly limited intelligence. **Essex Man** n (inf) an archetypal SE English working-class male without cultural interests or good taste but with a large disposable income which he spends freely, mainly on consumer goods and entertainment.

essive /es'iv/ (grammar) adj denoting a state of being. ◆ n the essive case. [Finn essivi, from L esse to be]

essoin or **essoyne** /e-soin'/ n an excuse for not appearing in court (law); an excuse (Spenser). ◆ vt to offer an essoin for. [OFr essoine (Fr exoine), from es, from L ex out of, and soin care]
■ **essoin'er** n.

essonite /es'ə-nīt/ or **hessonite** /hes'ə-nīt/ n cinnamon stone (qv). [Gr *hēssōn* inferior (ie in hardness, to hyacinth which it resembles)]

EST abbrev : Eastern Standard Time; electric shock treatment; Estonia (IVR).

Est. abbrev : Estate (in addresses, etc); estuary.

est /est/ n a philosophical and psychological programme designed to raise awareness and develop human potential, originated in California by Werner Erhard (born 1935) and used by some business organizations. [*E*rhard *S*eminars *T*raining]

est. abbrev : established; estimated.

-est /-əst/ sfx marks the superlative degree of adjectives (eg *longest*) and some adverbs (eg *fastest*). [OE *-est* or *-ost*]

establish /i- or e-stab'lish/ vt to settle or fix; to set up; to place in fixed position, possession, or power; to make good; to cause to be accepted; to confirm (*archaic*); to prove; to ordain; to found; to set up in business; to institute by law as the recognized state church, and to recognize officially. [OFr *establir*, prp *establissant*, from L *stabilīre*, from *stabilis* firm, from *stāre* to stand]
■ **estab'lished** adj fixed; ratified; instituted by law and backed by the state. **estab'lisher** n. **estab'lishment** n the act of establishing; a fixed state; something which is established; a permanent civil or military force; permanent staff; a person's residence, household and style of living; a business; a settlement; the church established by law; (with *the* and *cap*; often *derog*) the class in a community or in a field of activity who hold power, *usu* because they are linked socially, and who are *usu* considered to have conservative opinions and conventional values. ◆ adj relating to an establishment or the Establishment. **establishmentār'ian** adj maintaining the principle of church establishment; favouring or upholding the Establishment. ◆ n a person of establishmentarian principles. **establishmentar'ianism** n.

estacade /es-tə-kād'/ n a series of stakes in a morass, river, etc as a defensive measure. [Fr, from Sp *estacada*]

estafette /es-tə-fet'/ n a military courier or express. [Fr, from Ital *staffetta*, from *staffa* stirrup; cf OHGer *stapho* a step]

estaminet /e-stam'ē-nā/ n a small bar or café. [Fr]

estancia /e-stän'sya/ n a Spanish-American cattle-estate. [Sp, station, from L *stāre* to stand]
■ **estanciero** /-syä'rō/ n (pl **estancie'ros**) a farmer on such an estate.

estate /i- or e-stāt'/ n property, *esp* landed property of some size; a piece of land built over either privately or by a local authority, with houses (**housing estate**) or factories (**trading** or **industrial estate**); *orig* state (*archaic*); rank; worldly condition; total possessions; a piece of land given over to the cultivation of a particular crop; an order or class of people in the body politic; a chair or canopy of state, or a dais (*obs*); an estate car (see below). ◆ vt to give an estate to (*archaic*); to bestow upon (*archaic*). [OFr *estat* (Fr *état*), from L *status* a state]
❑ **estate agency** n. **estate agent** n someone who values, buys and sells, and leases and manages property for clients; the manager of landed property. **estate'-bottled** adj of wine, bottled on the estate where it has been made. **estate car** n a car designed to carry passengers and goods, *usu* with a large area behind the seats for luggage, etc, and a rear door. **estate duty** n death duty. **estates'man** n (*N Eng*) a small landholder.
■ **man's estate** the state of manhood. **personal estate** see **person**. **real estate** see **real**[1]. **the estates of the realm** the three divisions of the body politic, Lords Spiritual, Lords Temporal and Commons; often misused for the legislature, ie king, lords and commons; the ancient parliament of Scotland consisted of the king and the **three estates**, ie (1) archbishops, bishops, abbots and mitred priors, (2) the barons and the commissioners of shires and stewartries, (3) the commissioners from the royal burghs; in France, the nobles, clergy and **third estate** (*tiers état*) remained separate down to 1780. **the fourth estate** (*inf*) the press.

ESTEC abbrev : European Space Research and Technology Centre.

esteem /i- or e-stēm'/ vt to set a high estimate or value on; to regard with respect or friendship; to consider or think. ◆ n high estimation or value; favourable regard; estimation of worth. [Fr *estimer*, from L *aestimāre*]
■ **esteemed'** adj respected; in commercial correspondence, a colourless complimentary word.

ester /es'tər/ n a compound formed by the condensation of an alcohol and an acid, with elimination of water. [Named by Leopold Gmelin (1788–1853), prob from Ger *Essig* vinegar, and *Ä*th*er* ether]
■ **es'terase** n any of a number of enzymes that catalyse the hydrolysis of an ester. **esterificā'tion** /-ter-/ n. **ester'ify** (or /es'/) vt.

Esth, Esthonian see **Estonian**.

Esth. (*Bible*) abbrev : (the Book of) Esther.

esthesia, **esthesiogen**, etc US spellings of **aesthesia**, **aesthesiogen**, etc.

esthete, **esthetic**, etc US spellings of **aesthete**, **aesthetic**, etc.

estimate /es'ti-māt/ vt to judge the worth of; to ascertain how much is present of; to calculate roughly. ◆ n /-mət/ a valuing in the mind; judgement or opinion of the worth or size of anything; a rough calculation; a preliminary statement of the probable cost of a proposed undertaking; reputation (*Shakesp*); estimation. [Ety as for **esteem**]
■ **es'timable** adj that can be estimated or valued; worthy of esteem; deserving our good opinion. **es'timably** adv. **estimā'tion** n an act of estimating; a reckoning of value; esteem or honour; importance (*archaic*); conjecture; judgement, opinion. **es'timātive** adj. **es'timātor** n.
■ **hold in estimation** to esteem highly. **the estimates** accounts laid before parliament, etc, showing the probable expenditure for the year.

estipulate see **exstipulate**.

estival, etc US spelling of **aestival**, etc.

estoc /e-stok'/ n a short sword. [Fr]

estoile /es-twäl'/ (*heraldry*) n a star with wavy points. [OFr *estoile* (Fr *étoile*) a star]

Estonian or **Esthonian** /es-t(h)ō'ni-ən/ adj of or belonging to *Estonia*, a Baltic republic, until 1918 a province of Russia, incorporated in 1940 as a republic of the USSR and declaring itself fully independent in 1991. ◆ n a native or citizen thereof; its language.
■ **Esth** n an Estonian of the original Finnish stock.

estop /e-stop'/ vt (**estopp'ing**; **estopped'**) to stop or bar (*archaic*); to hinder or preclude (*law*). [OFr *estoper*, from *estoupe*, from L *stuppa* flax; see **stop** and **stuff**]
■ **estopp'age** n (*law*) the state of being estopped. **estopp'el** n (*law*) a judicial bar to alleging or proving that a fact is otherwise than it appears to be.

estover /e-stō'vər/ (*law*) n a right to necessaries allowed by law, such as wood to a tenant for necessary repairs, etc. [OFr *estover* to be necessary, necessaries]
■ **common of estovers** the right of taking necessary wood from another's estate for household use and the making of implements of industry.

estrade /e-sträd'/ n a low platform. [Fr, from Sp *estrado*]

estramazone same as **stramazon**.

estrange /i-strānj'/ vt to cut off or remove; to alienate, *esp* from friendship; to divert from its original use or possessor. [OFr *estranger* (Fr *étranger*), from L *extrāneāre*, from *extrāneus*; see **strange**]
■ **estranged'** adj alienated; disaffected. **estrang'edness** n. **estrange'ment** n. **estrang'er** n.

estrapade /es-tra-pād'/ n a horse's attempt to throw its rider. [Fr]

estray /e-strā'/ n a beast found within a manor or lordship, wandering from its owner. ◆ vi to stray. [See **stray**]

estreat /e-strēt'/ (*law*) n a true extract, copy or note of some original writing or record, *esp* of fines and amercements to be levied by bailiffs or other officers. ◆ vt to extract from the records of a court (eg a forfeited recognizance); to levy or exact. [OFr *estraite*, from L *extrahere*, from *ex* from, and *trahere* to draw; see **extract**]
■ **estreat'ment** n.

estrepe /es'trēp/ (*law*) vt (of a tenant) to lay waste to lands, eg by cutting down trees, etc. [MFr *estreper*, from L *exstirpāre* to root out]
■ **estrepe'ment** n.

estrich /es'trich/ or **estridge** /es'trij/ (*obs*) n the ostrich.

Estrildidae /e-stril'di-dē/ n pl a family of oscinine birds, the weaver finches. [From *astrilda*, the name of a particular species in Linnaeus's classification]
■ **estril'did** adj and n.

estro /es'trō/ (*Ital*) n enthusiasm or height of poetic inspiration.

estrogen, **estrus**, etc N American spellings of **oestrogen**, **oestrus**, etc.

estuary /es'tū-ə-ri/ n the wide lower tidal part of a river. [L *aestuārium*, from *aestus* burning, boiling, commotion or tide]
■ **estūarial** /-ā'ri-əl/ adj. **estūā'rian** adj. **es'tūarine** /-ə-rīn/ adj.
❑ **Estuary English** n a form of English influenced by Cockney, spoken in the Thames Estuary and surrounding areas.

Estyn /es'tin/ n a body regulating education in Wales. [Welsh, to reach out, lengthen]

ESU abbrev : English-Speaking Union; (also without *caps*) electrostatic unit.

esurient /es-ū'ri-ənt/ adj hungry; rapacious. [L *ēsuriēns*, *-entis*, prp of *ēsurīre* to be hungry, from the desiderative of *edere* to eat]
■ **esū'rience** or **esū'riency** n greedy hunger; needy rapacity. **esū'riently** adv.

■ words derived from main entry word; ❑ compound words; ■ idioms and phrasal verbs

ET *abbrev*: Eastern Time; Egypt (IVR); embryo transfer; ephemeris time; extraterrestrial.

Et (*chem*) *symbol*: ethyl.

ETA *abbrev*: estimated time of arrival; /et'ə/ *Euskadi ta Askatasuna* (*Basque*), Basque Homeland and Freedom, a militant Basque separatist organization.

eta¹ /ē'tə or ā'tə/ *n* the seventh letter of the Greek alphabet, long *e* (H or η); as a numeral η' = 8, ‚η = 8000. [Gr *ēta*]
■ **etacism** /ā'tə-sizm/ *n* the pronunciation of eta as close *e* (in this dictionary represented in the respelling as /ā/), *opp* to *itacism*.

eta² /ä'tə/ (also with *cap*) *n esp* formerly, a member of the lowest Japanese class, which did work considered menial or degrading. [Jap]

etaerio /et-ē'ri-ō/ (*bot*) *n* (pl **etae'rios**) an aggregated fruit, a group of achenes or drupels. [Fr *étairion*, from Gr *hetaireiā* association]

étage /ā-täzh'/ (*Fr*) *n* a floor or storey.

étagère /ā-ta-zher'/ (*Fr*) *n* a display stand with shelves for small objects or ornaments, etc.

e-tailer /ē'tā-lər/ *n* an entrepreneur who sells goods through the Internet. [e- as abbreviation of electronic, and **retailer**]
■ **e'-tailing** *n*.

et al *abbrev*: *et alibi* (L), and elsewhere; *et alii, aliae* or *alia* (L), and other (people or things).

étalage /ā-ta-läzh'/ (*Fr*) *n* a display, *esp* of goods in a shop window.

etalon /ā'tə-lon/ (*phys*) *n* an interferometer used to measure wavelengths, consisting of an air film enclosed between half-silvered plane-parallel glass or quartz plates. [Fr, from MFr *estalon* standard of weights and measures, from OFr *estal* place]

etanercept /i-tan'ər-sept/ *n* a cytokine inhibitor, used in the treatment of rheumatoid arthritis.

étape /ā-tap'/ (*Fr*) *n* a storehouse; a halting-place; a day's march; rations; forage.

état /ā-ta'/ (*Fr*) *n* state or rank.
■ **étatisme** /ā-ta-tēzm'/ *n* extreme state control over the individual citizen. **étatiste** /-tēst/ *adj* and *n*.
□ **état-major** /ma-zhor/ *n* the staff of an army, regiment, etc.

États-Généraux /ā-ta zhā-nā-rō'/ (*Fr*) *n pl* the States-General.

ETB *abbrev*: Engineering and Technology Board; English Tourist Board (now known as **ETC**).

ETC *abbrev*: English Tourism Council.

etc *abbrev*: et cetera or et ceteri.

et cetera /et set'ə-rə/ or **etcetera** and the rest, and so on (*abbrev* **etc** or **&c**). *n* something in addition, which can easily be understood from the context. [L *et* and, and *cetera*, neuter pl, the rest of the things]
■ **etcet'eras** *n pl* additional people or things.

et ceteri /et set'ə-rē/ and the other people, and the rest (*abbrev* **etc** or **&c**). [L *et* and, and *ceteri*, masc pl, the rest of the people]

etch /ech/ *vt* and *vi* to design on metal, glass, etc by eating out the lines with an acid; to eat away or corrode; to cut or carve. ◆ *vt* (*usu* in *passive*) to make a deep or irremovable impression. ◆ *n* the act or process of etching. [Ger *ätzen* to corrode by acid; from same root as Ger *essen*; see **eat**]
■ **etch'ant** *n* an acid or corrosive used in etching. **etch'er** *n* a person who etches. **etch'ing** *n* the act or art of etching or engraving; the impression from an etched plate.
□ **etching ground** *n* the coating of wax or varnish on a plate prepared for etching. **etching needle** *n* a fine-pointed steel instrument used in etching.

ETD *abbrev*: estimated time of departure.

eten or **ettin** /et'ən/ (*archaic*) *n* a giant. [OE *eten, eoten*; ON *jötunn*]

etepimeletic /et-ep-i-me-let'ik/ (*animal behaviour*) *adj* of a type of social behaviour shown by young animals to elicit epimeletic behaviour. [See **epimeletic**]

eternal /i- or ē-tûr'nl/ *adj* (also (*archaic*) **eterne'**) without beginning or end of existence; everlasting; ceaseless; unchangeable; unchanging; seemingly endless, occurring again and again (*inf*). [Fr *éternel*, from L *aeternus*, from *aevum* an age]
■ **eter'nalist** *n* someone who thinks that matter has existed eternally. **eternal'ity** or **eter'nalness** *n*. **eternaliza'tion** or **-s-, eterniza'tion** or **-s-** *n*. **eter'nalize** or **-ise, eter'nize** or **-ise** (or /ē' tər-nīz/) *vt* to make eternal; to immortalize with fame. **eter'nally** *adv*. **eter'nity** *n* eternal duration; the state of being eternal; the state or time after death; an extremely long time (*inf*).
□ **eternal triangle** *n* a sexual relationship, full of tension and conflict, involving three people, *usu* a married couple and a third party. **eternity ring** *n* a ring set all round with stones, symbolizing continuity and everlasting love.

■ **The Eternal** God. **the Eternal City** Rome. **the eternal feminine** the spiritualizing and purifying influence of women in social and literary matters. **the eternities** the eternal reality or truth.

etesian /e-tē'zh(y)ən or -zyən/ *adj* periodical; blowing at stated seasons, such as certain winds, *esp* the NW winds of summer in the Aegean. [L *etēsius*, from Gr *etēsios* annual, from *etos* a year]

ETF *abbrev*: European Training Foundation; exchange-traded fund (*finance*).

ETH *abbrev*: Ethiopia (IVR).

eth or **edh** /edh/ *n* a letter (or ð), a barred D, used in Old English without distinction from thorn for voiced or voiceless *th*, in Icelandic and by phoneticians used for the voiced *th*, thorn standing for the voiceless *th*.

ethal /ē'thal/ same as **cetyl alcohol** (see under **cetyl**).

ethambutol /e-tham'bū-tol/ *n* a drug used in the treatment of tuberculosis. [*ethylene, amine* and *but*anol]

ethane /ē'thān or eth'ān/ *n* a colourless, odourless hydrocarbon gas (H₃CCH₃) of the alkane series. [**ether**]
■ **eth'anal** /-al/ *n* acetaldehyde. **eth'anediol** /-dī-ol/ *n* ethylene glycol. **eth'anol** *n* ethyl alcohol. **ethanol'amines** *n pl* derivatives of ethanol used in detergents and cosmetics.
□ **ethanoic acid** /eth-ə-nō'ik/ *n* acetic acid.

ethe see **eath**.

ethene see under **ethyl**.

Etheostoma /e-thi-os'to-mə/ *n* a genus of small American freshwater fishes related to perch. [Gr *ētheein* to sift, and *stoma* mouth]
■ **etheos'tomine** *adj*.

ether /ē'thər/ *n* the clear, upper air; a medium, not matter, assumed in the 19c to fill all space and transmit electromagnetic waves (in these senses also **aether**); (*specif* **ethyl ether** or **diethyl ether**) a colourless, transparent, volatile liquid (C₂H₅OC₂H₅) of great mobility and high refractive power, used as a solvent, an anaesthetic, and in the preparation of explosives; extended to the class of compounds in which two alkyl or other groups are united with an oxygen atom. [L *aethēr*, from Gr *aithēr* the heavens, from *aithein* to light up]
■ **ethe'real** or **ethe'rial** *adj* consisting of ether; heavenly; airy; spirit-like. **ethereal'ity** *n*. **etherealizā'tion** or **-s-** *n*. **ethe'realize** or **-ise** *vt* to convert into ether, or the fluid ether; to render spirit-like. **ethe'really** *adv*. **ethe'reous** (*Milton*), **etheric** /ē-ther'ik/ or **ether'ical** *adj* ethereal. **etherifica'tion** /-ther-/ *n*. **ether'ify** *vt* to convert into ether. **ethe'rion** *n* a very light gas once supposed to exist in air. **e'therism** *n* the condition induced by using ether; addiction to the taking of ether. **e'therist** *n* someone who takes or who administers ether. **etheriza'tion** or **-s-** *n*. **e'therize** or **-ise** *vt* to convert into ether; to stupefy with ether. **etheromā'nia** *n* addiction to the taking of ether. **etheromā'niac** *n*.
□ **ethereal oils** *n pl* essential oils. **Eth'ernet** *n* (*comput*) a system for networking computers.

ethercap see **ettercap**.

ethic /eth'ik/ (now *rare*) *adj* ethical. ◆ *n* (more commonly **eth'ics** *sing*) the science of morals, that branch of philosophy which is concerned with human character and conduct; a system of morals or rules of behaviour; a treatise on morals. [Gr *ēthikos*, from *ēthos* custom or character]
■ **eth'ical** *adj* relating to morals, the science of ethics or professional standards of conduct; relating to, or in accord with, approved moral behaviour; (of advertising) decent, honest and informative, not misleading, dishonest or unscrupulous; denoting a proprietary pharmaceutical not advertised to the general public and only available to the general public on doctor's prescription (also *n*); (of investment, funds, etc) not involving the abuse of natural resources or the exploitation of people or animals. **ethical'ity** or **eth'icalness** *n*. **eth'ically** *adv*. **eth'icism** *n* the tendency to moralize or ethicize; great interest in ethics or passion for ethical ideals. **eth'icist** *n* an expert on or student in ethics; a person who detaches ethics from religion. **eth'icize** or **-ise** /-sīz/ *vt* to make ethical; to treat as ethical. **ethico-** *combining form* denoting something ethical or of ethics.
□ **ethical dative** or **ethic dative** *n* (*esp* in Greek and Latin) a dative implying an indirect interest in the matter, used to give a livelier tone to the sentence. **ethical genitive** *n* a genitive implying interest (eg *talking as usual about his jazz*).
■ **situation ethics** ethics based on the proposition that no conduct is good or bad in itself and that one must determine what is right or wrong in each situation as it arises.

Ethiopian, also (*archaic*) **Aethiopian** /ē-thi-ō'pi-ən/ *adj* of or belonging to *Ethiopia* or its people or their languages; of or belonging to the countries south of Egypt (*archaic*); (of people) black. ◆ *n* a native of Ethiopia; an Ethiopian language; a black person (*archaic*). [Gr *Aithiops*, from *aithein* to burn, and *ops*, *ōps* face]

■ **Ē'thiop** /-op/ n (archaic). **Ēthiop'ic** adj belonging to Ethiopia, to the Ethiopian church, or to a group of Semitic languages including Ge'ez, Amharic and Tigre. ◆n the Ge'ez language. **ē'thiops** n in old chemistry, a name given to various dull, dingy or black compounds.
▫ **Ethiopian pepper** n see **Negro pepper** under **pepper**. **Ethiopian region** n a biological region consisting of Africa and Arabia south of the Tropic of Cancer.

ethmoid /eth'moid/ adj like a sieve. ◆n the ethmoid bone. [Gr ēthmos a sieve, and eidos form]
■ **ethmoid'al** adj.
▫ **ethmoid bone** n one of the bones forming the front part of the braincase.

ethnic /eth'nik/ adj (also **eth'nical**) concerning nations or races; relating to gentiles or heathens; relating to the customs, dress, food, etc of a particular racial group or cult; belonging or relating to a particular racial group; foreign; exotic; between or involving different racial groups. ◆n (esp US) a member of a racial or cultural minority group; a gentile or heathen (obs). [Gr ethnos a nation]
■ **eth'narch** /-närk/ n (Gr archos leader) a ruler or governor of a people. **eth'narchy** n. **eth'nically** adv. **eth'nicism** /-sizm/ n (obs) heathenism; gentile religion. **ethni'city** /-si-ti/ n the state of belonging to a particular racial or cultural group. **ethnobotan'ic** or **ethnobotan'ical** adj. **ethnobotan'ically** adv. **ethnobot'anist** n. **ethnobot'any** n (the study of) traditional plant-lore, plant classification, plant use, etc. **ethnocen'tric** adj. **ethnocen'trically** adv. **ethnocentri'city** /-si-ti/ or **ethnocen'trism** n belief in the superiority of one's own cultural group or society and corresponding dislike or misunderstanding of other such groups. **eth'nocide** /-sīd/ n (L caedere to kill) the extermination of a racial or cultural group. **ethnog'rapher** n. **ethnograph'ic** or **ethnograph'ical** adj relating to ethnography; of objects useful in the study of ethnography. **ethnograph'ica** n pl (a collection of) ethnographic objects; (loosely) exotica. **ethnograph'ically** adv. **ethnog'raphy** n the scientific description of the races of the earth. **eth'nolinguist** n. **ethnolinguist'ic** adj. **ethnolinguist'ics** n sing the study of the relationship between language and cultural behaviour. **ethnolog'ic** or **ethnolog'ical** adj. **ethnolog'ically** adv. **ethnol'ogist** n. **ethnol'ogy** n cultural anthropology; the science concerned with the varieties of the human race (obs). **ethnomethodolog'ical** adj. **ethnomethodol'ogist** n. **ethnomethodol'ogy** n the study of communication in the language of everyday conversation. **ethnomusicolog'ic** or **ethnomusicolog'ical** adj. **ethnomusicol'ogist** n a person who makes a study of music and/or musical instruments in relation to the cultures in which they are found. **ethnomusicol'ogy** n. **ethnosci'ence** n ethnography.
▫ **ethnic cleansing** n the removal from an area by the militarily superior ethnic group, either by extermination or forced migration, of members of the other ethnic groups, esp and orig in the former Yugoslavia. **ethnic minority** n a section of a society whose members belong to a different racial group than the majority of the population.

et hoc genus omne /et hok jē'nəs om'nē or gen'ŭs om'ne/ (L) and all that sort of thing (also **et id genus omne**).

ethos /ē'thos/ n the distinctive habitual character and disposition of an individual, group, race, etc; moral significance. [Gr ēthos custom or character]
■ **etholog'ic** or **etholog'ical** adj. **etholog'ically** adv. **ethol'ogist** n. **ethol'ogy** n the science of character; bionomics (see under **bio-**); the scientific study of the function and evolution of animal behaviour patterns.

ethoxyethane /eth-ok-si-ē'thān/ n diethyl ether (see under **ether**).

ethyl /ē'thīl or eth'il/ n the base (C₂H₅) of common alcohol, ether, etc; (**Ethyl**®) an antiknock compound containing lead tetraethyl Pb(C₂H₅)₄ (US); petrol using this compound (US). [ether and Gr hylē matter]
■ **eth'ylamine** /-ə-mīn/ n a substance (NH₂C₂H₅) resembling ammonia, with one atom of hydrogen replaced by ethyl. **eth'ylate** vt to introduce an ethyl group into (a molecule). **eth'ylene** (also **eth'ene**) n an oil-forming gas, hydrogen combined with carbon (C₂H₄).
▫ **ethyl acetate** n an ester used in perfumes and as a solvent. **ethyl alcohol** n ordinary alcohol. **ethylene glycol** n a thick liquid alcohol used as an antifreeze. **ethyl ether** see **ether**.

ethyne /eth'īn or ē'thīn/ n acetylene.

ETI abbrev : Education and Training Inspectorate (a regulatory body of Northern Ireland).

e-ticket /ē'ti-kit/ n a paperless travel authorization issued online (in full **electronic ticket**); a computerized system issuing e-tickets.
■ **e-tick'eting** n.

etiolate /ē'ti-o-lāt/ vt to cause to grow pale with small yellow leaves due to lack of light, to blanch (bot); to make pale. ◆vi to become pale. [Fr étioler to become pale, to grow into stubble, from éteule stubble, from L stipula a stalk, straw]
■ **e'tiolated** adj. **etiola'tion** n. **e'tiolin** n a yellow pigment found in etiolated plants.

etiology an alternative (esp US) spelling of **aetiology**.

etiquette /et'i-ket or -ket'/ n forms of civilized manners or decorum; ceremony; the conventional laws of courtesy observed between members of the same profession, sport, etc. [Fr étiquette ; see **ticket**]

etna /et'nə/ n a vessel for heating liquids in a saucer of burning alcohol. [After Mount Etna, volcano in Sicily]
■ **Etnē'an** or **Aetnē'an** adj of, relating to, resembling or characteristic of Mount Etna.

étoile /ā-twal'/ (Fr) n a star; a star-shaped object.

Eton /ē'tən/ n a town in S England with an old-established public school; (in pl) an Eton suit.
■ **Etonian** /ē-tōn'i-ən/ n a person educated at Eton College (also adj).
▫ **Eton collar** n a boy's broad starched turned-down collar; a similar-shaped collar on a woman's jumper, etc. **Eton crop** n a short sleek women's hairstyle. **Eton jacket** n a boy's black dress coat, without tails. **Eton mess** n a dessert of crushed meringue, strawberries and cream. **Eton suit** n an Eton jacket with matching waistcoat and trousers.

étourdi, fem **étourdie** /ā-toor-dē'/ (Fr) adj thoughtless, foolish or frivolous.
■ **étourderie** /ā-toor-drē/ n heedlessness or stupid blundering.

étranger /ā-trä-zhā'/, fem **étrangère** /-zher'/ (Fr) adj foreign. ◆n a foreigner.

étrenne /ā-tren'/ (Fr) n (usu in pl) a New Year's gift.

étrier /ā-trē-yā'/ n a small rope ladder of 1–4 rungs used as a climbing aid by mountaineers. [Fr, stirrup]

Etruria /i-troo'ri-ə/ n an ancient state in Italy north of the Tiber; part of Hanley, Stoke-on-Trent in England where Josiah Wedgwood made the china known as Etruria ware. [L Etrūria]
■ **Etru'rian** n and adj Etruscan. **Etruscan** /i-trus'kən/ adj relating to Etruria, or to the language, culture, etc of the Etruscans. ◆n a person inhabiting or from Etruria; the non-Indo-European language of the Etruscans. **Etruscol'ogist** n. **Etruscol'ogy** n.

ETS abbrev : Educational and Training Services, a branch of the Adjutant Generals Corps of the British Army.

et seq. or **et sq.** abbrev : et sequens (L), and what follows (pl **et seqq.** or **et sqq.**).

et sic de ceteris /et sik dē set'ə-ris or et sēk dā kā'te-rēs/ (LL) and so about the rest.

et sic de similibus /et sik dē si-mil'i-bəs or et sēk dā si-mil'i-bŭs/ (L) and so of the like.

et sq. see **et seq.**

ETSU abbrev : Energy Technology Support Unit, an organization which evaluates research on renewable energy (now known as Future Energy Solutions).

-ette /-et/ sfx forming nouns denoting: (1) female, as usherette ; (2) small, as kitchenette ; (3) esp in tradenames, imitation or substitute, as Leatherette.

ettercap /et'ər-kap/ or **ethercap** /edh'ər-kap/ n Scots forms of **attercop**.

ettin see **eten**.

ettle /et'l/ (Scot) vt to purpose or intend; to aim; to aspire. ◆n purpose or intent. [ON ætla to think]

ETUC abbrev : European Trade Union Confederation.

étude /ā-tüd'/ (music) n a composition intended either to train or to test the player's technical skill. [Fr, study]

étui or **etwee** /ā-twē' or et-wē'/ n a small case for holding sewing articles. [Fr étui a case or sheath]

ety abbrev : etymology.

etym. or **etymol.** abbrev : etymological.

etymon /et'i-mon/ n (pl **et'yma** or **et'ymons**) the true origin of a word; an original root; the genuine or literal sense of a word (rare). [Neuter of Gr etymos true]
■ **etym'ic** adj. **etymolog'ical** adj. **etymolog'ically** adv. **etymolog'icon** or **etymolog'icum** n an etymological dictionary. **etymol'ogist** n. **etymol'ogize** or **-ise** vi to inquire into or discuss etymology. ◆vt to trace or suggest an etymology for. **etymol'ogy** n the science or investigation of the derivation and original signification of words; an etymon.

■ words derived from main entry word; ▫ compound words; ■ idioms and phrasal verbs

etypic /ē-tip'ik/ or **etypical** /-əl/ adj not conformable to type. [L ē from, and Gr typos type]

EU abbrev : European Union; Evangelical Union.

Eu (chem) symbol : europium.

Eubacteriales /ū-bak-tē-ri-ā'lēz/ n pl an order of Schizomycetes, nonfilamentous, unbranched bacteria. [Gr eu well, and **bacteria**]
■ **eubactē'rial** adj. **eubactē'rium** n (pl **eubactē'ria**) a member of the Eubacteriales; any typical bacterium.

eucaine or **eucain** /ū-kā'in, -kā'īn or -kān'/ (med) n a safer substitute for cocaine as a local anaesthetic. [Gr eu well, and **cocaine**]

eucalyptus /ū-kə-lip'tas/ n (pl **eucalyp'tuses** or **eucalyp'tī**) a tree or shrub of the large characteristically Australian genus Eucalyptus of the myrtle family, forest trees, some gigantic, and mallee scrub, with leathery often glaucous leaves turned edgewise to the sun, many yielding timber, and some giving oils and gum; the timber of the eucalyptus; eucalyptus oil. [Latinized from Gr eu well, and kalyptos covered]
■ **eu'calypt** n a eucalyptus. **eucalyp'tol** or **eucalyp'tole** n cineol, a constituent of the various oils obtained from eucalyptus leaves.

eucaryon, eucaryot, eucaryote, eucaryotic same as **eukaryon**, etc.

eucharis /ū'kə-ris/ or **ū-kar'is**/ n a plant of the Eucharis genus of S American bulbous plants with fragrant white flowers. [Gr, charming, from eu well, and charis grace]

Eucharist /ū'kə-rist/ (Christianity) n the sacrament of the Lord's Supper; the elements of the sacrament, bread and wine. [Gr eucharistiā thanksgiving, from eu well, and charizesthai to show favour, from charis grace or thanks]
■ **Eucharist'ic** or **Eucharist'ical** adj.

euchlorine /ū-klö'rēn/ n a highly explosive green-coloured gas, a mixture of chlorine with chlorine peroxide. [Gr eu well, and chlōros green]
■ **euchlo'ric** adj.

euchologion /ū-ko-lö'ji-on/ n a formulary of prayers, primarily that of the Greek Church (also **euchology** /-kol'ə-ji/). [Gr euchologion, from euchē a prayer, and logos, from legein to speak]

euchre /ū'kər/ n a N American card game for two, three, or four players, with the 32, 28 or 24 highest cards of the pack. If a player fails to make three tricks they are euchred and their opponent scores against them; an instance of euchring or being euchred. ◆ vt to score over, as above; to outwit. [Ety unknown]
■ **eu'chred** adj (Aust and NZ sl; usu with out) exhausted, at the end of one's tether.

euchromatin /ū-krö'mə-tin/ (biol) n chromatin, lightly stained during interphase, which contains most of the active and transcribable DNA, opp to heterochromatin. [Gr eu well, and **chromatin**]
■ **euchromat'ic** adj.

euclase /ū'klās/ (mineralogy) n a hydrated beryllium aluminium silicate occurring in pale-green transparent crystals. [Fr, from Gr eu well, and klasis breaking]

Euclidean /ū-klid'i-ən or ū-kli-dē'ən/ adj relating to Euclid, a geometrician of Alexandria c.300BC, or to space according to his theories and assumptions.
❑ **Euclidean geometry** n a geometry based on the theories and assumptions of Euclid.

eucrite /ū'krīt/ (mineralogy) n a gabbroitic rock composed of lime-feldspar, pyroxenes and olivine. [Gr eu well, and kritos distinguished]
■ **eucritic** /-krit'ik/ adj.

eucryphia /ū-krif'i-ə/ n a shrub or small tree of the genus Eucryphia, with dark green leaves and white flowers. [Gr eu well, and kryphios hidden, from kryptein to hide]

eucyclic /ū-sī'klik/ (bot) adj having the same number of floral leaves in each whorl. [Gr eu well, and kyklos wheel]

eudaemonism or **eudemonism** /ū-dē'mə-ni-zm/ n a system of ethics that makes happiness the test of rectitude (whether egoistic as Hobbes's or altruistic as Mill's). [Gr eudaimoniā happiness, from eu well, and daimōn a spirit]
■ **eudaemon'ic** adj conducive to happiness. **eudaemon'ics** n sing. **eudae'monist** n. **eudaemonist'ic** adj. **eudae'mony** or **eudaemō'nia** n happiness or wellbeing; in Aristotelian philosophy, a full, active life governed by reason.

eudialyte /ū-dī'ə-līt/ (mineralogy) n a silicate of zirconium, sodium, calcium and iron, occurring in Greenland, easily dissolved by acids. [Gr eu well, and dialyein to dissolve]

eudiometer /ū-di-om'i-tər/ n an apparatus for gas analysis, a graduated tube holding the gas over mercury, usu with wires for sparking. [Gr eudios clear or fine (as weather), and metron measure]
■ **eudiomet'ric** or **eudiomet'rical** adj. **eudiom'etry** n.

euge /ū'jē/ interj well!, well done! [Gr euge]

eugenia /ū-jē'ni-ə/ n any plant of the clove genus Eugenia of the family Myrtaceae. [Named after Prince Eugene of Savoy (1663–1736)]
■ **eugenol** /ū'jin-ol/ n the chief constituent of oil of cloves ($C_{10}H_{12}O_2$; also **eugenic** /-jen'ik/ **acid**).

eugenic[1] /ū-jen'ik/ adj relating to genetic improvement of a race (esp human) by judicious mating and helping the better stock to prevail. [Gr eugenēs of good stock]
■ **eugen'ically** adv. **eugen'ics** n sing the science of genetic improvement of esp the human race. **eu'genism** /-jin-/ n. **eu'genist**, **eugen'ecist** or **eugen'icist** n.

eugenic[2] see eugenol under eugenia.

eugh, eughen and **ewghen** obsolete spellings (Spenser and Shakesp) of **yew** and **yewen**.

euglena /ū-glē'nə/ n an aquatic unicellular organism of the genus Euglena, with a single flagellum and reddish eye-spots. [Gr eu well, and glēnē eyeball]
■ **eugle'noid** n and adj.

Eugubine /ū'gū-bin or -bīn/ adj relating to the ancient town of Eugubium or Iguvium (now Gubbio) or to its famous seven tablets of bronze, the chief monument of the ancient Umbrian language.

euharmonic /ū-här-mon'ik/ (music) adj resulting in perfect harmony. [Gr eu well, and harmoniā harmony]

Euhemerism /ū-hē'mə-ri-zm/ n the theory which explains mythology as growing out of real history, its deities as merely larger-than-life people. [From Euhēmerus, Gr Euēmeros, a 4c BC Sicilian philosopher]
■ **euhē'merist** n and adj. **euhemeris'tic** adj. **euhemeris'tically** adv. **euhē'merize** or **-ise** vt and vi.

euk /ūk/ see yuke.

eukaryon, also **eucaryon** /ū-kar'i-ən/ (biol) n the highly organized cell nucleus, surrounded by a membrane, characteristic of higher organisms (cf **prokaryon**). [Gr eu well, and karyon kernel]
■ **eukar'yote** /-ōt/ or **eukar'yot** /-ət/ n an organism whose cells have such nuclei (also adj). **eukaryot'ic** adj.

eulachon /ū'lə-kən/ n the N Pacific candlefish, so oily that it is dried for use as a candle (also **eulachan, oolakan, oulakan, oulachon, ulicon, ulichon** and **ulikon**). [Chinook Jargon ulâkân]

eulogium /ū-lō'ji-əm/ or **eulogy** /ū'lə-ji/ n (pl **eulō'gia, eulō'giums** or **eu'logies**) praise; a speech or writing in praise; a funeral oration. [LL eulogium, from Gr eulogion (classical eulogiā), from eu well, and logos a speaking]
■ **eu'logist** n a person who extols another, esp a dead friend, etc. **eulogist'ic** or **eulogist'ical** adj full of praise. **eulogist'ically** adv. **eu'logize** or **-ise** vt to extol.

eumelanin /ū-mel'ə-nin/ n any melanin pigment of darker type. [eu-good or most typical, from Gr eu well]

Eumenides /ū-men'i-dēz/ (Gr myth) n pl a euphemistic name for the Erinyes or Furies (see under **fury**). [Gr, literally, the gracious ones, from eu well, and menos disposition]

eumerism /ū'mə-ri-zm/ (biol) n aggregation of similar parts. [Gr eu well, and meros part]

Eumycetes /ū-mī-sē'tēz/ (bot) n pl the higher fungi, Ascomycetes and Basidiomycetes. [Gr eu well, and **mycetes**]

eunuch /ū'nək/ n a castrated man, esp one in charge of a harem, or a high-voiced singer; an ineffectual person, lacking in some way in force or power (fig). [Gr eunouchos, from eunē bed, and echein to have (charge of)]
■ **eu'nuchism** n the condition of being a eunuch. **eun'uchize** or **-ise** vt (lit and fig). **eu'nuchoid** n and adj. **eu'nuchoidism** n a condition in which there is some deficiency of sexual development and in which certain female sex characteristics, eg high voice, are often present.

euoi see evoe.

euonymus /ū-on'i-məs/ n a plant of the spindle-tree and burning bush genus Euonymus (family Celastraceae). [Gr euōnymos spindle-tree]
■ **euon'ymin** n an extract of bark of burning bush.

euouae see evovae.

eupad /ū'pad/ n an antiseptic powder containing hypochlorous acid. [Edinburgh University Pathology Department, where it originated]

eupatrid /ū-pat'rid/ n a member of the aristocracy in ancient Greek states. [Gr eupatridēs, from eu well, and patēr father]

eupepsy /ū-pep'si/ or **eupepsia** /-pep'si-ə/ n good digestion, opp to dyspepsia. [Gr eupepsiā digestibility, from eu well, and pepsis digestion, from peptein to digest]
■ **eupep'tic** adj relating to or having good digestion; cheerful (fig). **eupepticity** /-tis'i-ti/ n.

Euphausia /ū-fö'zi-ə/ n a genus of shrimplike malacostracan crustaceans of the family **Euphausiidae** /-i'i-dē/, order **Euphausiacea** /-ā'si-ə/, common in plankton. [Gr *eu* well, *phainein* to show, and *ousiā* substance]
■ **euphausia'cean** n. **euphaus'iid** or **euphaus'id** adj and n (a creature) belonging to the Euphausiidae or to the Euphausiacea.

euphemism /ū'fi-mi-zm or -fə-/ n a figure of rhetoric by which an unpleasant or offensive thing is described or referred to by a milder term; such a term. [Gr *euphēmismos*, from *euphēmizein* to speak words of good omen, from *eu* well, and *phanai* to speak]
■ **euphemist'ic** adj. **euphemist'ically** adv. **eu'phemize** or **-ise** vt to express by a euphemism. ♦ vi to use euphemistic terms.

euphenics /ū-fen'iks/ n sing the science concerned with the physical improvement of human beings by modifying their development after birth (cf **eugenics**). [By analogy, from **eugenics** and **phenotype** (Gr *eu* well, and *phainein* to show)]

euphobia /ū-fō'bi-ə/ n a fear of good news. [Gr *eu* well, and *phobos* fear]

euphony /ū'fə-ni/ or (obs) **euphonia** /-fō'ni-ə/ n an agreeable sound; a pleasing, easy pronunciation, often created by modification of the original sounds. [Gr *euphōniā*, from *eu* well, and *phōnē* sound]
■ **eu'phon** n a form of glass harmonica invented by Ernst Chladni in 1790. **euphonic** /-fon'ik/, **euphon'ical** or **euphō'nious** adj agreeable in sound. **euphō'niously** adv. **eu'phonism** n the use or custom of using euphonious words or phrases. **euphō'nium** n a member of the saxhorn family, often played in brass bands; the euphon. **eu'phonize** or **-ise** vt to make euphonious.

euphorbia /ū-för'bi-ə/ n a plant of the spurge genus *Euphorbia*, giving name to the **Euphorbiā'ceae**, an isolated family of archichlamydeous dicotyledons. [*Euphorbos*, Greek physician to Juba, 1CBC king of Mauretania]
■ **euphorbiā'ceous** adj. **euphor'bium** n a gum resin obtained from some spurges.

euphoria /ū-fō'ri-ə or -fö'/ or (rare) **euphory** /ū'fə-ri/ n an exaggerated feeling of wellbeing, esp irrational or groundless. [Gr *euphoriā*]
■ **euphor'iant** adj inducing euphoria. ♦ n a drug which does this. **euphoric** /-for'ik/ adj. **euphor'ically** adv.

euphrasy /ū'frə-si or -zi/ or **euphrasia** /ū-frā'zi-ə/ (bot) n eyebright (genus *Euphrasia*) once used to treat disorders of the eyes. [Gr *euphrasiā* delight, from *euphrainein* to cheer, from *eu* well, and *phrēn* the mind]

euphroe /ū'frō/ (naut) n the wooden block through which the lines used to support an awning are passed (also **ū'phroe**). [Du *juffrouw*, from *jong* young, and *vrouw* woman]

Euphrosyne /ū-froz'i-nē or -fros'/ (Gr myth) n one of the three Charites or Graces. [Gr *Euphrosynē*, from *euphrōn* cheerful]

Euphuism /ū'fū-izm/ n the affected and bombastic literary style brought into vogue by John Lyly's romance *Euphues* (1579–80); (without cap) a high-flown expression in this style. [Gr *euphyēs* graceful or goodly]
■ **eu'phuist** n. **euphuist'ic** adj. **euphuist'ically** adv. **eu'phuize** or **-ise** vi.

euploid /ū'ploid/ (biol) n a cell or individual with a complete set of chromosomes. [Gr *eu* well, and **-ploid**]
■ **eu'ploidy** n.

Eur. abbrev : euro; Europe; European.

Eur- see Euro-.

Euraquilo /ū-rak'wi-lō/ n see **Euroclydon**.

Eurasian, Euratom see under **Euro-**.

eureka, rarely **heureka** /(h)ū-rē'kə/ interj announcing a discovery. ♦ n a brilliant discovery; (**eureka**; elec eng) an alloy of nickel and copper, having a high resistivity and almost negligible temperature coefficient, used in resistance wire (also **constantan**). [Gr *heurēka* I have found, perfect tense of *heuriskein* to find, the cry of Archimedes when he thought of a method of detecting the adulteration of the gold in Hiero's crown]

eurhythmy or **eurythmy** /ū-rith'mi or -ridh'/ n rhythmical movement or order; harmony of proportion; (usu with cap) an artistic, therapeutic and educational system based on rhythmic body movement correlated to poetry, music, etc, created by Rudolf Steiner (1861–1925). [Gr *eurythmiā*, from *eu* well, and *rhythmos* rhythm]
■ **eurhyth'mic** or **eurhyth'mical** adj. **eurhyth'mics** n sing the art or system of rhythmic movement expounded by E Jaques-Dalcroze (1865–1950). **eurhyth'mist** n.

euripus /ū-rī'pəs/ n an arm of the sea with strong currents, specif that between Euboea and Boeotia in classical Greece; a ditch round the arena in a Roman amphitheatre. [L, from Gr *euripos*]

euro¹ /ū'rō/ n (pl **eu'ro** or **eu'ros**) the official standard monetary unit of many states in the European Union (100 cent). [Short for *Europe* or *European*]
❑ **euro area** n (the area comprising) the countries that are members of the European Economic and Monetary Union and use the euro as their currency (also (inf) **Eu'roland** or **Eu'rozone**).

euro² /ū'rō/ (Aust) n (pl **eu'ros**) a wallaroo, any of several types of large kangaroo. [From an Aboriginal language]

Euro- /ū-rō-/ or **Eur-** /ūr-/ combining form of or relating to Europe, Europeans or the European Union.
■ **Euraf'rican** adj relating to Europe and Africa, or Europe and N Africa, jointly; of a race common to Europe and N Africa, the Mediterranean race; of mixed European and African parentage or descent. ♦ n a person of Eurafrican race in either sense. **Eurā'sian** adj of mixed European and Asian parentage or descent; of, or relating to, Europe and Asia (**Eurasia**) considered as one continent. ♦ n a person of mixed European and Asian parentage. **Eurat'om** /ū-rat'əm/ n the European Atomic Energy Community (set up in 1958), an association for joint peaceful development of nuclear energy. **Eu'ro-Amer'ican** n an American of European descent (also adj). **Eu'robabble** n (inf) pretentious or meaningless jargon talked about the European Union or by its officials. **Eu'robond** n a borrowing in Eurocurrency by a company from subscribers, which may or may not be sellable and for which the rate and life may be either fixed or variable; a security on which the named currency is not the currency of the country in which it has been issued. **Eurocent'ric** adj of history, culture, etc, concentrating on Europe, sometimes to the exclusion of other influences. **Eurocentri'city** or **Eurocent'rism** n. **Eu'rocheque** n a special type of cheque drawn on the user's own bank which may be cashed in banks and used for making purchases in any of a number of European and non-European countries. **Eurocomm'unism** n the theory of communism professed by Communist parties in W Europe, more pragmatic than that of the (former) Soviet Union and asserting independence from it. **Eurocomm'unist** n. **Eu'rocorps** n a multinational army corps composed of troops from member states of the European Union. **Eurocracy** /ū-rok'rə-si/ n. **Eu'rocrat** n an official concerned with the administration of any organization within the European Union, a European bureaucrat. **Eurocrat'ic** adj. **Eu'rocurrency** n a currency traded on the foreign currency markets of the European Union. **Eu'ro-dollars** n pl US dollars deposited in European banks to facilitate financing of trade between the USA and Europe. **Euroland** n see **euro area** under **euro¹**. **Eu'romarket** or **Eu'romart** n the European Common Market; the European money market; one of the W European stock exchanges. **Eu'ro-MP** n a member of the European Parliament, an MEP. **Eu'ronet** n an information network linking various European databanks. **Eu'ro-Parliament** n the European Parliament. **Eu'ropassport** n a standard form of passport issued to all eligible citizens of the European Union. **Eu'rophile** n (Gr *philos* friend) a lover of Europe, esp a supporter of the European Union (also adj). **Eu'rophobe** n (Gr *phobos* fear) someone who dislikes Europe, or is opposed to the European Union (also adj). **Eu'rophobia** n. **Eu'ropol** n an organization aiming to improve co-operation between the police forces of member states of the European Union, eg in combating terrorism and drug trafficking. **eu'ropop** n a form of simple yet infuriatingly catchy pop music, performed by European artists. **Euroscep'tic** n a person, esp a politician, who is sceptical about the desirability of devolving powers from national governments to the European Union (also adj). **Euroscep'ticism** n. **Eu'roseat** n a constituency in the European Parliament. **Eu'rospeak** n (facetious) the jargon used by European Union officialdom. **Eu'rostat** n the Statistical Office of the European Union. **Eu'rosterling** n sterling as part of Eurocurrency. **eu'roterminal** n the end station of a railway line, coach-route, etc that operates a direct service from the UK into Europe. **Eu'rotunnel** n the Channel tunnel. **Eu'rovision** n the European television network. **Eurozone** n see **euro area** under **euro¹**.

Euroclydon /ū-rok'li-don/ n the tempestuous wind by which St Paul's ship was wrecked (Bible, Acts 27.14). [Gr *Euroklydōn*, as if from *Euros* east wind, and *klydōn* a wave; supposed to be a wrong reading for *Eurakylōn*, L *Euraquilō*, from *Eurus* (Gr *Euros*) and *Aquilō* north wind]

Eurocommunism...to...**Europassport** see under **Euro-**.

European /ū-rō-pē'ən/ adj belonging or relating to Europe; belonging or relating to the European Union; showing or favouring a spirit of co-operation between the countries of Europe, esp those of the EU. ♦ n an inhabitant or native of Europe; a member of the pale-skinned race of man characteristic of Europe; a Europeanist. [Gr *Eurōpē*]
■ **Europē'anism** n. **Europē'anist** n a person who favours the European Union and seeks to uphold or develop it. **Europeaniza'tion** or **-s-** n. **Europē'anize** or **-ise** vt to assimilate or convert to European character or ways; to integrate into the European Union.
❑ **European Commission** n an executive body composed of members of the European Union countries, which is responsible for

the formulation of community policy and which initiates and drafts most community legislation. **European Community** *n* an economic and political free-trade association of European states, formed in 1967 by the amalgamation of the EEC, ECSC and Euratom, and extended in 1993 to become the European Union (*abbrev* **EC**; see also **European Union** below). **European Court of Auditors** *n* an institution of the European Union, responsible for management of its finances. **European Court of Justice** *n* the court of the European Union whose jurisdiction covers the hearing of disputes on issues of European Union law. **European Currency Unit** see **ECU** (*n*). **European Economic and Social Committee** *n* a consultative committee of the European Union, consisting of representatives from various economic and social groups. **European Economic Community** *n* the common market formed in 1957 under the Treaty of Rome by France, West Germany, Italy, Belgium, the Netherlands and Luxembourg, which become an institute of the European Community in 1967 (*abbrev* **EEC**; see also **European Union** below). **European Free Trade Association** *n* a free trade area created in 1960, now comprising Iceland, Liechtenstein, Norway and Switzerland (*abbrev* **EFTA**). **European Monetary Fund** *n* the managing body of the former European Monetary System (*abbrev* **EMF**). **European Monetary System** *n* a former system linking the values of EU countries' currencies in order to limit fluctuations and support weaker currencies (*abbrev* **EMS**). **European Monetary Union** *n* the adoption of a single currency by all the member states of the European Union. **European Ombudsman** *n* a body of the European Union responsible for investigating complaints from citizens against any European Union institution or body. **European Parliament** *n* the legislative assembly of the European Union. **European plan** *n* (*US*) in hotels, the system of charging for lodgings and service without including meals (cf **American plan**). **European Space Agency** *n* a European organization promoting international co-operation in space research and technology (*abbrev* **ESA**). **European Union** *n* an economic and political free-trade association of European states formed in 1993 from the European Community (*abbrev* **EU**).

Europhile, Europhobe see under **Euro-**.

europium /ū-rō'pi-əm/ *n* a rare-earth metallic element (symbol **Eu**; atomic no 63) discovered spectroscopically by Demarçay in 1896. [*Europe*]

Europocentric /ū-rō-pō-sen'trik/ *adj* same as **Eurocentric** (see under **Euro-**).

Europol...to...**Eurovision** see under **Euro-**.

Eurus /ū'rəs/ (*Gr myth*) *n* the south-east or, less exactly, east wind. [L, from Gr *Euros*]

euryhaline /ū-ri-hā'līn/ *adj* (of marine animals) tolerating a wide variation in salinity. [Gr *eurys* wide, and *hals* salt]

Eurypharynx /ū-ri-far'ingks/ *n* the pelican-fish genus. [Gr *eurys* wide, and *pharynx* pharynx]

Eurypterus /ū-rip'tə-rəs/ *n* a genus of **Eurypterida**. [Gr *eurys* wide, and *pteron* wing]
■ **euryp'terid** *n* any member of the Eurypterida. **Eurypterida** /-ter'i-də/ *n pl* a Palaeozoic fossil order of Arachnida, scorpion-like aquatic animals, sometimes over six feet long, with the last (sixth) pair of appendages expanded. **euryp'teroid** *adj* like or of the Eurypterida. ◆ *n* a eurypterid.

eurytherm /ū'ri-thûrm/ (*biol*) *n* an organism which tolerates a wide variation in temperature. [Gr *eurys* wide, and *therme* heat]
■ **eurytherm'al, eurytherm'ic** or **eurytherm'ous** *adj*.

eurythmy, etc an alternative, *esp* American, spelling of **eurhythmy**.

eurytopic /ū-ri-top'ik/ *adj* able to survive in a wide range of environmental conditions. [Gr *eurys* wide, and *topos* place]

Eusebian /ū-sē'bi-ən/ *adj* relating to *Eusebius* of Caesarea, father of ecclesiastical history (died 340), or to the Arian *Eusebius* of Nicomedia (died 342).

Euskarian /ū-skā'ri-ən/ *adj* Basque. [Basque *Euskara* the Basque language]

eusocial /ū-sō'shl/ *adj* denoting a type of behaviour, eg of ants, in which labour is divided, with different social groups performing different tasks. [Gr *eu* well, and **social**]
■ **eusocial'ity** *n*.

eusol /ū'sol/ *n* an antiseptic solution obtained by treating eupad with water. [*E*dinburgh *U*niversity *sol*ution of *l*ime]

eusporangiate /ū-spo-ran'ji-āt/ (*bot*) *adj* of a group of ferns, having each sporangium derived from a group of cells, *opp* to *leptosporangiate*. [Gr *eu* well, and **sporangium**]

Eustachian /ū-stā'shən or ū-stā'ki-ən/ *adj* relating to the Italian physician Bartolommeo *Eustachio* (died 1574).

▫ **Eustachian tube** *n* the tube leading from the middle ear to the pharynx. **Eustachian valve** *n* the rudimentary valve at the entrance of the inferior vena cava in the heart.

eustasy or **eustacy** /ū'stə-si/ *n* changes in world shoreline level, probably caused by rise or fall of the sea-level and not by subsidence or elevation of the land. [Gr *eu* well, and *stasis* standing or *statikos* causing to stand]
■ **eustat'ic** *adj*. **eustat'ically** *adv*.

eustyle /ū'stīl/ *adj* with columns spaced at about two diameters and a quarter. ◆ *n* a colonnade or building so proportioned. [Gr *eustŷlos* well intercolumniated, from *eu* well, and *stŷlos* column]

eutaxy /ū'tak-si/ *n* good order. [Gr *eu* well, and *taxis* arrangement]
■ **eutax'ite** *n* a volcanic rock with banded structure. **eutaxit'ic** *adj* having such a structure.

eutectic, eutectoid see under **eutexia**.

Euterpe /ū-tûr'pē/ (*Gr myth*) *n* the Muse of music and lyric poetry; a genus of palms. [Gr *Euterpē*, from *eu* well, and *terpein* to delight]
■ **Euter'pean** *adj* relating to Euterpe or to music.

eutexia /ū-tek'si-ə/ (*phys*) *n* the property of being easily melted. [Gr *eutēktos* easily melted, from *eu* well, and *tēkein* to melt]
■ **eutec'tic** *n* a mixture in such proportions that the melting point (or freezing point) is as low as possible, the constituents melting (or freezing) simultaneously; the eutectic point. ◆ *adj* of maximum ease of fusibility; relating to a eutectic. **eutec'toid** *n* an alloy similar to a eutectic but involving formation of two or three constituents from another solid (not melted) constituent (also *adj*). ▫ **eutectic point** *n* the temperature at which a eutectic melts or freezes.

euthanasia /ū-thə-nā'z(h)i-ə, -zhə/ or (*rare*) **euthanasy** /-than'ə-si/ *n* the act or practice of putting painlessly to death, *esp* in cases of incurable suffering; an easy mode of death (*archaic*). [Gr *euthanasiā*, from *eu* well, and *thanatos* death]
■ **euthanā'siast** *n* a supporter of or believer in euthanasia. **eu'thanize** or **-ise** *vt* to perform euthanasia on (also **eu'thanase**).

euthenics /ū-then'iks/ *n sing* the science concerned with the improvement of living conditions. [Gr *euthēneein* to flourish]
■ **euthen'ist** *n*.

Eutheria /ū-thē'ri-ə/ *n pl* the placental mammals. [Gr *eu* well, and *thēr* a beast]
■ **euthē'rian** *n* and *adj*.

Euthyneura /ū-thi-nū'rə/ *n pl* a subclass of gastropods in which the visceral nerve-loop is not twisted. [Gr *euthys* straight, and *neuron* nerve]

eutrophy /ū'trə-fi/ *n* healthy nutrition; the state (of a body of water) of being eutrophic. [Gr *eutrophiā*]
■ **eutrophic** /ū-trof'ik/ *adj* relating to healthy nutrition; (of a body of water) over-rich in nutrients either naturally or as a result of artificial pollutants, and hence having an over-abundant growth of water plants and depleted oxygen levels, leading to the death of aquatic animals. **eutroph'icate** *vt* and *vi*. **eutrophica'tion** *n* the process of becoming or making (a body of water) eutrophic.

eutropy /ū'trə-pi/ *n* regular variation of the crystalline form of a series of compounds with the atomic number of the element. [Gr *eu* well, and *tropos* a turn]
■ **eutropic** /-trop'ik/ *adj* according to eutropy; turning sun-wise (*bot*). **eu'tropous** *adj*.

Eutychian /ū-tik'i-ən/ *adj* of or relating to the doctrine of *Eutyches*, a 5c archimandrite of Constantinople, who held that Christ's human nature was merged in the divine. ◆ *n* a follower of Eutyches.

EUW *abbrev*: European Union of Women.

euxenite /ūk'sə-nīt/ *n* a mineral, niobate and titanate of yttrium, erbium, cerium and uranium. [Gr *euxenos* hospitable, as containing many rare elements]

EV (*Bible*) *abbrev*: English version.

eV *abbrev*: electronvolt.

EVA (*astronautics*) *abbrev*: extravehicular activity.

evacuate /i- or ē-vak'ū-āt/ *vt* to throw out the contents of; to discharge, empty or void; to withdraw; to move or remove eg from a place of danger; to clear out troops, inhabitants, etc from; to create a vacuum in (*phys*); to nullify (*law*). ◆ *vi* to move away (from a place of danger, *usu* temporarily); to void excrement, empty the bowels. [L *ē* from, and *vacuāre*, *-ātum* to empty, from *vacuus* empty]
■ **evac'uant** *adj* and *n* (a) purgative or laxative. **evacua'tion** *n* an act of evacuating; withdrawal or removal; the material discharged, excreted, etc. **evac'uative** *adj* and *n* evacuant. **evac'uator** *n*. **evacuee'** *n* a person moved or removed in an evacuation.

evade /i- or ē-vād'/ *vt* to escape or avoid by cunning; to shirk; to avoid answering; to baffle or elude (*fig*). ◆ *vi* (*rare*) to escape or slip away. [L *ēvādere*, from *ē* from, and *vādere* to go]
■ **evā'dable** *adj*. **evād'er** *n*.

evagation /ē- or e-va-gā'shən/ n wandering; a digression. [L ēvagārī, from ē from, and vagārī to wander]

evaginate /i- or ē-vaj'i-nāt/ vt to turn outside in (med); to evert; to remove from a sheath. ◆ adj without a sheath. [L ēvāgināre, -ātum to unsheathe, from ē from, and vāgīna a sheath]
■ **evagina'tion** n.

evaluate /i- or ē-val'ū-āt/ vt to determine or estimate the value of. [Fr évaluer]
■ **evalua'tion** n. **eval'uative** adj tending or serving to evaluate, or functioning as an evaluation. **eval'uator** n.

Evan. or **evan.** abbrev : evangelical.

evanescent /ev-ən-es'ənt/ adj fleeting or passing; vanishing. [L ēvānēscēns, -entis, from ē from, and vānēscere to vanish, from vānus empty]
■ **evanesce'** vi to fade away or vanish. **evanesc'ence** n. **evanesc'ently** adv.

Evang. or **evang.** abbrev : evangelical.

evangel /i-van'jəl/ n the Christian gospel; orig good news (poetic); a doctrine set up as a saving principle, esp in morals or politics; an evangelist (N Am). [L evangelicus, from Gr euangelikos, from eu well, and angellein to bring news]
■ **evangeliar** /ev-ən-jel'/, **evangeliā'rion**, **evangeliā'rium** or **evangel'iary** n a book of passages from the Gospels to be used at mass or in other services. **evangelical** /ev- or ēv-an-jel'ik-əl/ or (archaic) **evangel'ic** adj of or relating to the Christian Gospel; relating to the four Gospels; according to the doctrine of the Gospel; maintaining or promoting the teaching of the Gospel; Protestant; of the school of religious belief that insists especially on the total depravity of unregenerate human nature, the justification of the sinner by faith alone, the free offer of the Gospel to all, and the plenary inspiration and exclusive authority of the Bible; believing in and inspired by the necessity of carrying the Christian faith to those not already within the community of the Christian church; active and ardent in one's advocacy of some principle or cause. **evangel'ical** n a person inspired by evangelical beliefs of any kind; a person who belongs to the evangelical school of religious belief. **evangel'icalism** n. **evangel'ically** adv. **evangel'icalness** n. **evangel'icism** /-sizm/ n evangelical principles. **evan'gelism** n evangelizing; evangelicalism. **evan'gelist** n a person who evangelizes, religiously or otherwise; (with cap) an author of a Gospel, esp Matthew, Mark, Luke or John; an assistant of the apostles; a person who is authorized to preach but who is without responsibility for a fixed area; an itinerant preacher; an active and keen advocate of some principle or cause. **evangelis'tary**, also **evangelistā'rion** n a book of the Gospels or of passages from them to be read at divine service; a table of such passages. **evangelis'tic** adj tending or intended to evangelize, religiously or otherwise. **evangelizā'tion** or **-s-** /i-van-jəl-/ n the act of proclaiming the Gospel; Christianization; the attempt to persuade others of the rightness of some principle or cause. **evan'gelize** or **-ise** vt to make acquainted with the Gospel; to convert to Christianity. ◆ vi to preach the Gospel from place to place; to try to persuade others to support some principle or cause. **evan'gelizer** or **-s-** n. **evan'gely** n (obs) the Gospel.
□ **Evangelical Union** see **Morisonian**.

evanish /i-van'ish/ (chiefly poetic) vi to vanish; to die away. [OFr evanir, evaniss-, from L ex from, and vānus empty; cf evanesce]
■ **evan'ishment** n. **evanition** /ev-ə-nish'ən/ n.

evaporate /i-vap'ə-rāt/ vi to change into vapour; to pass into an invisible state; to depart, vanish or disappear (fig). ◆ vt to convert into vapour; to dry by evaporation; to draw moisture off (a metal) in vapour form. [L ē from, and vapōrāre, -ātum, from vapor vapour]
■ **evaporabil'ity** n. **evap'orable** adj able to be evaporated or converted into vapour. **evaporā'tion** n the act of evaporating or drawing off moisture in the form of steam or gas; the process by which a substance changes into vapour. **evap'orative** adj. **evap'orator** n. **evaporim'eter** or **evaporom'eter** n an instrument for measuring the rate of evaporation. **evap'orite** n a sedimentary rock formed by the evaporation of salt water. **evap'orograph** n a device giving direct or photographic images of objects in darkness by focusing infrared radiations from them onto an oil-film, which evaporates in proportion to the amount of radiation and leaves an image.
□ **evaporated milk** n milk thickened by evaporation of some of its water content, unsweetened.

evapotranspiration /i-vap-ō-tran-spə-rā'shən/ n the return of water into the atmosphere as vapour, by evaporation (from soil, water bodies, etc) and emissions or transpiration (from plants); the total amount converted by this process. [**evaporate** and **transpiration**]

evasion /i-vā'zhən/ n the act of evading or eluding; an attempt to escape the point of an argument or accusation; an excuse. [L ēvādere, ēvāsum; see **evade**]

■ **evasible** /i-vā'zi-bl/ adj capable of being evaded. **evā'sive** /-siv/ adj evading or attempting to evade; elusive; devious, not straightforward; shuffling (archaic). **evā'sively** adv. **evā'siveness** n.
■ **take evasive action** to move or act in such a way as to avoid an object or consequence.

eve see under **even**².

evection /i- or ē-vek'shən/ (astron) n a lunar inequality, the combined effect of the irregularity of the point of the moon's orbit at which it is nearest to Earth and the alternate increase and decrease of the eccentricity of the moon's orbit. [L ēvectiō, -ōnis, from ē from, and vehere, vectum to carry]

evejar see under **even**².

even¹ /ē'vn/ adj flat; level; smooth; calm or unexcited; uniform; in a straight line or plane; straightforward (Shakesp); balanced equally; equal; fair or just; exact; (of people) not owing each other anything; divisible by two without a remainder; denoted by such a number. ◆ vt to make even or smooth; to put on an equal basis; to compare; to make (scores, etc) equal; to act up to (Shakesp). ◆ vi (often with up) to become even. ◆ adv (also archaic **e'en**) exactly (inf); nearly; indeed, in fact; so much as; still, yet, emphasizing a comparative, as in even better; used when speaking or writing of something extreme or completely unexpected, as in even an idiot would know. [OE efen; Du even, Ger eben]
■ **ev'ener** n. **ev'enly** adv. **ev'enness** n. **ev'ens** n pl even money. ◆ adj and adv quits.
□ **even chance** n an equal probability (of success or failure, etc). **ev'en-Chris'tian** n (obs) a fellow Christian. **even date** n the same date. **ev'en-down** adj (dialect or archaic) straight-down (of rain); downright or honest. ◆ adv thoroughly. **ev'en-ev'en** adj denoting nuclei in which there are an even number of protons and also of neutrons. **even-hand'ed** adj impartial; just or fair. **even-hand'edly** adv. **even-hand'edness** n. **even-mind'ed** adj having an even or calm mind; equable. **even money** n in betting odds, considered extremely likely to win or happen, and paying out only the equal of the stake. **ev'en-odd'** adj denoting nuclei in which there are an even number of protons and an odd number of neutrons. **ev'en-stev'ens** or **ev'en-stev'en** adj and adv (inf) (of two sides or parties) having no debts or credits on either side; (of two sides in a game, contest, etc) having equal scores. **even-tem'pered** adj of placid temperament, calm.
■ **be even with** to be revenged on (also **get even with**); to be quits with. **even as** at that or this very moment when. **even now** a very little while ago (archaic); after all that has happened. **even on** (Scot) without intermission. **even out** to become even or equal. **even so** nevertheless. **even up on** to requite or come square with. **on an even keel** see under **keel**¹.

even² /ē'vn/ or **e'en** /ēn/ (obs, poetic or dialect) n evening; eve. [OE ǣfen, ǣfnung]
■ **eve** /ēv/ n evening (poetic); the night or the whole day before a festival or notable event; the time just preceding an event. **evening** /ēv'ning/ n the close of the day; the decline or end (of something, eg life); an evening party, gathering or entertainment; an evening newspaper. **eve'nings** adv (esp N Am) in the evening (on a number of occasions).
□ **eve'jar** n (dialect) the nightjar. **ev'enfall** n early evening, twilight. **evening class** n a class held in the evenings, usu for people who work during the day. **evening dress** n the (men's or women's) dress conventionally appropriate to formal social functions in the evening. **evening primrose** n a N American plant (genus Oenothera) with pale yellow flowers that open in the evening. **evening primrose oil** n an essential oil obtained from the seeds of this plant. **evening star** n a planet, usu Venus or Mercury, seen in the western sky and setting soon after the sun. **ev'eningwear** n clothing intended for wearing during the evening, esp on formal occasions. **ev'ensong** n evening prayers, the Anglican form of service appointed to be said or sung at evening; the time appropriate for these prayers. **ev'entide** n (poetic) evening or the time of evening. **eventide home** n a residential home for old people.

événement /ā-ven-mã'/ (Fr) n an event or happening; specif a political strike or demonstration.

event /i-vent'/ n anything which happens; result; any incident or occurrence, esp a memorable one; contingency or possibility of occurrence; an item in a programme (of sports, etc); a type of horse-riding competition, often held over three days (**three-day event**), consisting of three sections, ie dressage, cross-country riding and showjumping; fortune or fate (obs); an organized activity at a particular venue, eg for sales promotion, fund-raising, etc. ◆ vi to ride in a horse-riding event. [L ēventus, from ēvenīre to come out or happen, from ē from, and venīre to come]
■ **event'er** n a horse trained to take part in events; the rider of such a horse, eg **three-day eventer**. **event'ful** adj full of events; memorable, momentous. **event'fully** adv. **event'fulness** n. **event'ing** n taking

part in riding events; the sport of horse-riding in three-day events. **event'less** adj. **event'lessness** n. **event'ual** adj happening as a consequence; final, after a time. **eventual'ity** n an occurrence or happening; a contingency; the faculty of observing the order or chronology of events (phrenology). **event'ūalize** or **-ise** vi to happen; to come into being. **event'ūally** adv finally; at length, after some time. **event'ūate** vi to turn out. **eventūā'tion** n.

◻ **event horizon** n (astron) the boundary of a black hole, from inside which no normal energy can escape.

■ **at all events** or **in any event** no matter what happens, anyway. **in the event** as things turn or turned out; if it should turn out (that). **in the event of** in the case of (a specified thing happening).

eventration /ē-ven-trā'shən/ n the act of opening the belly; the protrusion of an organ from the abdomen. [Fr éventration, from L ē from, and venter belly]

■ **even'trate** vt.

ever /ev'ər/ adv always; eternally; at all times; continually; at any time; on record, in history or in the world (eg the biggest ever); in any degree; at all or possibly; very or extremely (sl, orig N Am; used as part of an interjection or statement, eg was I ever hungry). ◆ sfx giving complete generality to relative adverbs and pronouns, eg whatever, etc. [OE ǣfre]

◻ **ev'ergreen** adj in leaf throughout the year; always fresh and green; unfading; never failing, retaining one's (or its) vigour, freshness, popularity, interest, etc for ever. ◆ n a tree or shrub that is green throughout the year; a person, piece of music, etc which retains freshness, popularity, etc through the years. **evergreen oak** n same as **holm-oak** (see under **holm²**). **everlast'ing** adj endless; perpetual; unceasing; eternal; wearisomely long (inf). ◆ n (with the) eternity; (with cap and the) God; a flower (of Helichrysum, Antennaria or other genus) that may be kept for years without much change of appearance; a very durable type or cloth. **everlast'ingly** adv. **everlast'ingness** n. **ev'er-living** adj (Shakesp) immortal; deathless. **evermore'** (or /ev'/) adv for all time to come (also **for evermore**); ever; unceasingly.

■ **ever and anon** (archaic and poetic) from time to time. **ever so** to a very great extent; to any extent (archaic). **ever such a** (inf) a very. **for ever** for all eternity, always; for a long time (inf).

Everest /ev'ə-rəst/ n the name of the highest mountain in the world, in the Himalayas; anything extremely difficult to accomplish or conquer, the height of ambition. [Sir George Everest (1790–1866), British Surveyor-General of India]

◻ **Everest pack** n a light aluminium frame, carried on the back, with camping equipment strapped to it.

everglade /ev'ər-glād/ n a large shallow lake or marsh; (with cap; chiefly in pl) such a marsh in southern Florida, enclosing thousands of islets covered with dense thickets. [Perh **ever** and **glade**]

evert /ē- or i-vûrt'/ vt to turn inside out; to turn outwards. [L ēvertere, from ē from, and vertere, versum to turn]

■ **ever'sible** adj. **ever'sion** n. **evert'or** n a muscle that turns a limb, etc outwards.

every /ev'ri/ adj each of a number or collection, all taken separately; the best possible (eg every chance of winning). [OE ǣfre ever, and ǣlc each]

◻ **ev'erybody** or **ev'eryone** pronoun every person. **ev'eryday** adj of or happening every day, daily; common or usual; (esp of clothes) relating to or appropriate for weekdays, not Sunday. **ev'erydayness** n. **Ev'eryman** n (also without cap) the hero of an old morality play, representing mankind; everybody or anybody. **ev'eryplace** adv (US) everywhere. **ev'erything** pronoun all things taken singly; all; the most important thing (eg money isn't everything). **ev'eryway** adv in every way or respect. **ev'erywhen**, **ev'erywhence** or **ev'erywhither** adv (all rare). **ev'erywhere** adv in or to every place.

■ **every bit** or **whit** the whole, all of it; quite or entirely. **every here and there** all over, in various places. **every last** (emphatically) every. **every man Jack** or **every mother's son** everyone without exception. **every now and then** or **every now and again** at intervals, periodically. **every other** every second or alternate. **every so often** at intervals or periodically. **every which way** (US) in every direction or by every method; in disorder. **have everything** (inf) to be well-endowed with possessions, attractiveness, etc.

evet /ev'it/ n same as **eft¹**.

Eve teasing /ēv tē'zing/ (Ind) n sexual harassment of women. [Eve, the first woman, according to the Book of Genesis]

evgs abbrev : evenings.

evhoe see **evoe**.

evict /i- or ē-vikt'/ vt to expel (usu from a dwelling); to dispossess by law. [L ēvictus, pap of ēvincere to overcome]

■ **evic'tee** n a person who is evicted. **evic'tion** n the act of evicting from house or lands; the dispossession of one person by another having a better title to property or land. **evic'tor** n.

◻ **eviction order** n a court order by which a person may be evicted.

evident /ev'i-dənt/ adj that can be seen; clear to the mind; obvious. ◆ n that which serves as evidence. [L ēvidēns, -entis, from ē from, and vidēre to see]

■ **ev'idence** n that which makes anything evident; means of proving an unknown or disputed fact; support (eg for a belief); indication; information in a law case; testimony; a witness or witnesses collectively. ◆ vt to make evident, apparent or visible; to attest or prove; to indicate. **evidential** /-den'shəl/ or **eviden'tiary** adj providing evidence; tending to prove. **evidential'ity** n. **eviden'tially** adv. **ev'idently** adv visibly (Bible); obviously; manifestly; apparently.

■ **in evidence** received by the court as competent testimony; plainly visible, conspicuous or present (adopted from the Fr en évidence). **turn Queen's** or **King's evidence** or (US) **turn State's evidence** to give evidence for the prosecution against an accomplice in a crime.

evil /ē'v(i)l/ adj wicked or bad; mischievous; very disagreeable or angry; harmful; very unpleasant (inf); unfortunate (rare or archaic). ◆ adv (usu in compounds) in an evil manner; badly or terribly. ◆ n something which produces unhappiness or misfortune; harm; wickedness or depravity; sin; illness, disease or curse (eg king's evil). [OE yfel; Du euvel; Ger übel; cf **ill**]

■ **evilly** /ē'vil-li/ adv in an evil manner; badly or terribly. **e'vilness** n the state of being evil; wickedness.

◻ **e'vil-doer** n a person who does evil. **e'vil-doing** n. **evil eye** n a supposed power to cause harm by a look; a look or glance, superstitiously thought to cause harm. **e'vil-eyed** adj. **evil-fā'voured** adj having a repulsive appearance; ugly. **evil-fā'vouredness** n (Bible) ugliness; deformity. **evil-mind'ed** adj inclined to evil; malicious; wicked. **evil-mind'edly** adv. **evil-mind'edness** n. **evil-speak'ing** n the speaking of evil; slander. **evil-starred'** adj (Tennyson) born under the influence of an unpropitious star, unfortunate. **evil-tem'pered** adj bad-tempered, unpleasant or spiteful. **e'vil-worker** n someone who does evil.

■ **speak evil of** to slander. **the Evil One** the Devil.

evince /i-vins'/ vt to prove beyond doubt; to show clearly; to make evident; to give indication of; to overcome or overpower (archaic). [L ēvincere to vanquish, from ē- (intens), and vincere to overcome]

■ **evince'ment** n. **evinc'ible** adj. **evinc'ibly** adv. **evinc'ive** adj tending to evince, prove or demonstrate.

evirate /ē'vi- or ev'i-rāt/ vt to castrate; to make weak or unmanly. [L ēvirāre, from ē from, and vir a man]

eviscerate /ē- or i-vis'ə-rāt/ vt to tear out the viscera or bowels of; to gut (lit and fig). [L ē from, and viscera the bowels]

■ **eviscerā'tion** n. **evisc'erator** n.

evitable /ev'i-tə-bl/ adj avoidable. [L ēvitāre, -ātum, from ē from, and vītāre to shun]

■ **evitā'tion** n the act of shunning or avoiding. **evite** /i-vīt'/ (archaic) and **ev'itate** (Shakesp) vt to avoid.

eviternal /ē-vi-tûr'nl/ adj eternal. [L aeviternus; see **eternal**]

■ **eviter'nally** adv. **eviter'nity** n.

evocation, etc see under **evoke**.

evo-devo /ē'vō-dē'vō/ (inf) n the study of the role of developmental processes in evolution. [Short for evolutionary-developmental biology]

evoke /i-vōk'/ vt to call out; to draw out or bring forth; to call up or awaken (esp memories) in the mind. [L ēvocāre, from ē from, and vocāre to call]

■ **evocable** /i-vok'ə-bl/ adj. **evocate** /ev'ō-kāt/ vt to evoke; to call up from the dead. **evocā'tion** n. **evocative** /i-vok'ə-tiv/ or **evoc'atory** adj. **evoc'atively** adv. **evoc'ativeness** n. **evocator** /e'vō-kā-tər/ n. **evok'er** n.

évolué /ā-vo-lü-ā'/ n a member of a primitive group of people who has been educated to the standards of a more advanced civilization (also adj). [Fr, developed]

evolution /ē- or e-və-loo'shən/ n the cumulative change in the genetic composition of a population of an organism over succeeding generations, resulting in a species totally different from remote ancestors; the act of unrolling or unfolding (archaic); the giving off (of heat, etc); gradual working out or development; a series of things following in sequence; the calculation of roots (maths); (usu in pl) orderly movements eg of a body of troops, flock of birds, etc. [L ēvolūtiō, -ōnis, from ēvolvere; see **evolve**]

■ **ev'olute** n (maths) an original curve from which another curve (the involute) is described by the end of a thread gradually unwound from the former. ◆ adj rolled back. ◆ vt and vi to develop by evolution. **evolu'tional** adj. **evolu'tionally** adv. **evolu'tionarily** adv. **evolu'tionary** adj of or relating to evolution. **evolu'tionism** n the doctrine of evolution. **evolu'tionist** n a person who believes in evolution as a principle in science; a person skilled in evolutions or military movements. ◆*adj* of or relating to evolutionists. **evolutionis'tic** *adj*. **ev'olutive** *adj*.

❏ **evolutionarily stable strategy** *n* (*biol*) a strategy that, if most members of a population adopt it, would give a reproductive fitness higher than any mutant strategy (*abbrev* **ESS**).

evolve /i- or ē-volv'/ *vt* to unroll; to disclose; to develop; to give off (heat, etc); to unravel. ◆*vi* to change gradually, *esp* according to the theory of evolution; to become apparent gradually; to result (with *into*). [L ēvolvere, from ē- from, and volvere, volūtum to roll]

■ **evolv'able** *adj* that can be drawn out. **evolve'ment** *n*. **evolv'ent** *adj* evolving. **evol'ver** *n*.

evovae /i-vō'vē/ or **euouae** /ū-oo'ē/ (*music*) *n* names for a Gregorian cadence, obtained from 'seculorum (formerly written SECVLORVM) Amen' in the doxology 'Gloria Patri'.

EVR *abbrev* : electronic video recording and reproduction.

evulgate /ē- or e-vul'gāt/ *vt* to divulge; to publish. [L ēvulgāre, -ātum, from ē out, and vulgus the people]

evulse /i- or ē-vuls'/ *vt* to pluck out. [L ēvellere, ēvulsum, from ē from, and vellere, vulsum to pluck]

■ **evul'sion** *n*.

evzone /ev'zōn/ *n* a soldier in an élite Greek infantry regiment. [Mod Gr euzōnos, from Gr, girt for action, from eu well, and zōnē girdle]

e-waste /ē'wāst/ *n* discarded electrical equipment (in full **electronic waste**).

ewe /ū/ *n* a female sheep. [OE ēowu; cf L ovis, Gr oïs, Sans avi a sheep]

❏ **ewe'-cheese** *n* cheese made from the milk of ewes. **ewe'-lamb** *n* a female lamb; a poor man's only possession, one's dearest possession (in reference to Bible, 2 Samuel 12). **ewe'-milk** *n*. **ewe'-neck** *n* of horses, a thin concave neck. **ewe'-necked** *adj*.

ewer /ū'ər/ *n* a large water jug with a wide spout. [Through Fr from L aquārium (neuter of aquārius of water), from aqua water]

ewest /ū'ist/ (*Scot*) *adj* or *adv* near. [Appar from OE on nēaweste in the neighbourhood, wrongly divided as on ewest]

ewftes /ūfts/ (*Spenser*) *n pl* efts. [See **eft¹**]

ewghen an old spelling of **yewen** (see **yew**).

ewhow /ā'(h)wow'/ (*Scot*) *interj* expressing regret.

Ewigkeit /ā'vihh-kīt/ (*Ger*) *n* eternity.

ewk see **yuke**.

EWS *abbrev* : English, Welsh and Scottish Railway.

ewt see **newt**.

Ex. (*Bible*) *abbrev* : (the Book of) Exodus.

ex¹ /eks/ *n* the twenty-fourth letter of the modern English alphabet (X or x).

ex² /eks/ *prep* direct from (as ex works or ex warehouse ; *commerce*); without (as ex dividend, without the next dividend); used when stating the former name of a ship. [L, out of or from]

ex. /eks/ *abbrev* : examination or examined; example; except, excepted or exception; exchange; excursion or excursus; executed; executive; export; express; extra.

ex- /eks-/ *pfx* former (as ex-emperor); formerly employed, etc by; outside (as ex-directory).

■ **ex** *n* (*pl* **ex's** or **ex'es**) (*inf*) someone who is no longer what he or she was, *esp* a person's former husband or wife.

exa- /ek-sə- or ek-sa-/ *combining form* denoting 10^{18}.

ex abundantia /eks a-bən-dan'shi-ə or a-bŭn-dan'ti-ä/ (L) out of abundance.

■ **ex abundanti cautela** /-dan'tī kö-tē'lə or -dan'tē kow-tā'lä/ from excessive caution.

ex accidenti /eks ak-si-den'tī or a-ki-den'tē/ (LL) accidentally (as opposed to essentially).

exacerbate /ik-sas' or ig-zas'ər-bāt/ *vt* to make (eg an awkward situation or a disease) worse, more violent or more severe; to embitter; to provoke. [L exacerbāre, -ātum, from ex and acerbāre, from acerbus bitter]

■ **exacerbā'tion** or (*archaic*) **exacerbesc'ence** *n* increase of irritation or violence, *esp* the increase of a fever or disease; embitterment.

exact /ig-zakt'/ *vt* to force out; to compel payment of; to demand and obtain; to extort; to require as indispensable or prerequisite. ◆*vi* to practise extortion. ◆*adj* precise; rigorous; accurate; absolutely correct; finished; consummate; strict in correctness of detail. [L exigere, exāctum to demand or to weigh strictly, from ex from, and agere to drive]

■ **exact'able** *adj*. **exact'ing** *adj* compelling full payment; unreasonable in making demands; demanding much, challenging or difficult. **exact'ingly** *adv*. **exact'ingness** *n*. **exac'tion** *n* the act of

exacting or demanding strictly; an oppressive demand; something which is exacted, as (excessive) work or tribute. **exact'itude** *n* exactness; correctness. **exact'ly** *adv*. **exact'ment** *n*. **exact'ness** *n* the quality of being exact or precise; accuracy. **exact'or** or **exact'er** *n* (also *fem* **exact'ress**) a person who exacts; an extortionist; someone who claims rights, often too strictly.

❏ **exact sciences** *n pl* the mathematical sciences, whose results are precisely measurable.

■ **not exactly** not altogether; not at all (*inf* or *ironic*).

ex aequo /eks ē'kwō or ī'/ (LL) equally or equitably.

exaggerate /ig-zaj'ə-rāt/ *vt* to magnify unduly; to overstate; to represent too strongly; to intensify. ◆*vi* to speak hyperbolically, to overstate the case. [L exaggerāre, -ātum, from ex-, and aggerāre to heap up, from agger a heap]

■ **exagg'erated** *adj*. **exagg'eratedly** *adv*. **exaggerā'tion** *n* extravagant overstatement; a statement displaying this. **exagg'erative** or **exagg'eratory** *adj* containing exaggeration or tending to exaggerate. **exagg'erātor** *n*.

exalbuminous /eks-al-bū'mi-nəs/ (*bot*) *adj* without albumen.

exalt /ig-zölt'/ *vt* to place in a high position (of respect, etc); to elate or fill with the joy of success; to extol or praise; to refine or subtilize (*old chem*). [L exaltāre, from ex-, and altus high]

■ **exalta'tion** /egz-öl-/ *n* elevation in rank or dignity; high estate; elation or rejoicing; a planet's position of greatest influence (*astrol*); a collective noun for larks, a flight. **exalt'ed** *adj* elevated or high; lofty; dignified; exaggerated; extremely happy. **exalt'edly** *adv*. **exalt'edness** *n*.

exam /ig-zam'/ *n* short form of **examination**.

examine /ig-zam'in/ *vt* to test; to inquire into; to question; to look closely at or into; to inspect. [Fr examiner, from L exāmināre, from exāmen the tongue of a balance]

■ **exā'men** *n* examination, *esp* of one's conscience, as a Roman Catholic religious exercise. **examinabil'ity** *n*. **exam'inable** *adj*. **exam'inant** *n* an examiner; someone who is being examined. **exam'inate** *n* someone who is examined. **examinā'tion** *n* careful search or inquiry; close inspection; trial; a test of capacity and knowledge (*inf* short form **exam'**); formal interrogation in court of a witness or accused person (*law*). **examina'tional** *adj*. **examinee'** *n* a person under examination. **exam'iner** or **exam'inātor** *n* a person who examines. **exam'inership** *n*. **exam'ining** *adj*.

❏ **examinā'tion-in-chief** *n* (*law*) questioning of one's own witness (cf **cross-examination**). **exam'ine-in-chief** *vt*.

■ **need one's head examined** (*sl*) to be crazy, stupid, etc.

example /ig-zäm'pl/ *n* a specimen or sample; an illustration; a copy of a book; a person or thing to be imitated or not to be imitated; a pattern; a warning; an instance. ◆*vt* (*rare*) to exemplify; to instance. [OFr, from L exemplum, from eximere to take out, from ex out of, and emere, emptum to take]

■ **exam'plar** *n* (*archaic*) an exemplar.

■ **for example** for instance; as an illustration. **make an example of** to punish severely as a warning to others.

exanimate /eg- or ig-zan'i-māt/ *adj* lifeless; spiritless; depressed. [L exanimātus from ex, and anima breath]

■ **exanimā'tion** *n*.

ex animo /eks an'i-mō/ (L) from the mind or earnestly.

ex ante /eks an'ti/ based on prediction and extrapolation. [L, from before]

exanthem /ek-san'thəm/ or **exanthema** /ek-san-thē'mə/ (*med*) *n* (*pl* **exan'thems** or **exanthe'mata**) a skin eruption, *esp* accompanied by fever; a disease characterized by these symptoms. [Gr exanthēma, -atos, from ex- out, and antheein to blossom]

■ **exanthemat'ic** or **exanthē'matous** *adj*.

exarate /ek'sə-rāt/ *adj* containing grooves or furrows; used of pupae in which the wings and legs are free. [L exarātus, from exarāre to plough up or to trace letters on a tablet]

■ **exarā'tion** *n* (*rare*) the act of writing; composition.

exarch¹ /eks'ärk/ *n* a Byzantine provincial governor, *esp* of Italy (*hist*); a metropolitan bishop (*Orthodox church*); a bishop ranking between a patriarch and a metropolitan bishop (*Orthodox church*); the head of the Bulgarian church; a bishop's representative; an ecclesiastical inspector; a legate. [Gr exarchos leader]

■ **exarch'al** *adj*. **exarch'ate** (or /eks'/) or **ex'archy** *n* the office, jurisdiction or province of an exarch. **exarch'ist** (or /eks'/) *n* a supporter of the Bulgarian exarch.

exarch² /eks'ärk/ (*bot*) *adj* having the protoxylem on the outer edge. [Gr ex- out, and archē beginning, origin]

exasperate /ig-zä'spə-rāt/ *vt* to make very angry; to irritate to a high degree; to infuriate; to make more grievous or more painful; to make rough or harsh (*obs*). ◆*adj* irritated; rough with hard points (*bot*). [L ex- (intens), and asperāre to make rough, from asper rough]

■ **exas'peratedly** adv. **exas'perating** adj. **exas'peratingly** adv. **exasperā'tion** n. **exas'perative** adj. **exas'perator** n.

ex auctoritate mihi commissa /eks ök-to-ri-tä'tē mī'hī kə-mis'ə or owk-tō-ri-tä'te mǐ'hi ko-mǐ'sa/ (L) by the authority entrusted to me.

Exc. abbrev : Excellency.

exc. abbrev : excellent; except; exception; excursion.

Excalibur /eks-kal'i-bər/ n the name of King Arthur's sword. [OFr Escalibor, for Caliburn; cf Caladbolg, a famous sword in Irish legend]

excambion /eks-kam'bi-on/ (Scots law) n exchange of lands (also **excam'bium**). [LL excambiāre; cf cambist, **cambium**, **exchange**] ■ **ex̌camb'** vt to exchange.

excarnate /eks-kär'nāt/ vt to remove the flesh from. [LL excarnāre, -ātum, from L ex from, and carō, carnis flesh] ■ **excarna'tion** n.

ex cathedra /eks kə-thē'drə or eks kath'ə-dra/ (LL) from the chair of office, esp the Pope's throne in the Consistory or a professor's chair; hence authoritatively or judicially. adj (with hyphen) spoken with or as if with authority; implying authoritativeness; (of papal decree) to be obeyed completely, esp by Roman Catholics.

excaudate /eks-kö'dāt/ (zool) adj having no tail. [L ex- without, and cauda tail]

excavate /eks'kə-vāt/ vt to dig out; to lay open by digging; to hollow or scoop out. [L excavāre, from ex- out, and cavus hollow] ■ **excavā'tion** n the act of excavating; a hollow or cavity made by excavating; an archaeological site, a dig. **ex'cavātor** n a person who excavates; a machine used for excavating.

exceed /ik-sēd'/ vt to go beyond the limit or measure of; to surpass or excel. ◆ vi to be outstanding; to go beyond a given or proper limit (archaic); to be intemperate (archaic). [L ex- beyond, and cēdere, cēssum to go] ■ **exceed'ance** n. **exceed'ing** adj surpassing; excessive; very great; projecting beyond a neighbouring member (bot). ◆ adv (Bible) exceedingly. **exceed'ingly** adv extremely; very much; greatly.

excel /ik- or ek-sel'/ vt (**excell'ing**; **excelled'**) to be superior to or better than; to surpass; to exceed (Milton). ◆ vi to have good qualities in large measure; to perform exceptional actions; to be superior or better; to be exceptionally good at (with in or at). [L excellere, from ex- out or up, and celsus high] ■ **excellence** /eks'ə-ləns/ or **exc'ellency** n the state or quality of being extremely good; great merit; any excellent quality; worth; greatness. **Exc'ellency** n a title of honour given to persons high in rank or office. **exc'ellent** adj extremely good; surpassing others in some good quality; of great virtue, worth, etc. **exc'ellently** adv. **excel'sior** interj (L compar adj, taller, loftier) higher still (after Longfellow). ◆ n (sometimes with cap; orig US) a trade name for wood shavings for packing. ■ **excel oneself** (often ironic) to do better than usual or previously.

excellence /ek-se-lãs'/ (Fr) n excellence. ■ **par excellence** as an example of excellence; superior to all others of the same sort.

excentric same as **eccentric** in mechanical senses.

except /ik-sept'/ vt to take out or leave out; to exclude. ◆ vi to object (usu with to or against). ◆ prep leaving out; not including; but. ◆ conj (archaic) unless. [L excipere, exceptum, from ex from, and capere to take] ■ **except'ant** adj and n. **except'ing** prep with the exception of, except. **excep'tion** n the act of excepting; something which is excepted; exclusion; objection; offence. **excep'tionable** adj objectionable. **excep'tionably** adv. **excep'tional** adj unusual (esp in a good sense). ◆ n (finance) an entry in a profit and loss account to which the company wishes to draw attention as being unusual. **excep'tionalism** n. **exceptional'ity** n. **excep'tionally** adv. **excep'tious** adj (archaic) disposed to take exception. **excep'tive** adj including, making or being an exception. **except'less** adj (Shakesp) making no exception, usual. **excep'tor** n. ■ **except for** apart from; not including or counting. **take exception to** object (to). **the exception proves the rule** the existence of an exception to a supposed rule proves the general truth of the rule (often used in argument when no such conclusion is justified); a distorted translation of a part of a legal Latin phrase meaning 'the making of an exception proves that the rule holds in cases not excepted'.

exceptis excipiendis /ik-sep'tis ik-sip-i-en'dis or eks-kep'tēs eks-ki-pi-en'dēs/ (LL) excepting what is to be excepted; with proper exceptions.

excerpt /ek'sûrpt or ek-sûrpt'/ n a passage selected from a book, opera, etc, an extract. ◆ vt /ek-sûrpt'/ to select extracts from; to extract. [L excerptum, pap of excerpere, from ex from, and carpere to pick] ■ **excerpt'ible** adj. **excerpt'ing** n. **excerp'tion** n. **excerp'tor** n.

excerpta /ik-sûrp'tə or eks-kerp'ta/ (L) n pl (sing **excerp'tum** /-təm or -tŭm/) extracts, selections.

excess /ik-ses' or ek'ses/ n a going beyond what is usual or proper; intemperance; something which exceeds; the degree or amount by which one thing exceeds another; usury (Shakesp); (usu in pl) an outrageous or offensive act. ◆ adj more than usual, proper, allowed, etc; additional. [L excēssus, from excēdere, excēssum to go beyond] ■ **excess'ive** adj beyond what is usual or right; immoderate; extreme. ◆ adv excessively. **excess'ively** adv. **excess'iveness** n. ❑ **excess capacity** n the operating situation of a firm or industry when output is below the level at which all its productive resources are fully employed. **excess demand** n a situation in which the quantity of a product or service which buyers wish to buy at the prevailing price exceeds that which sellers are prepared or able to sell. **excess fare** n payment for distance travelled beyond, or in a higher class than, that allowed by the ticket. **excess luggage** or **baggage** n luggage above the weight allowed free. **excess postage** n payment due from the addressee when insufficient stamps have been put on a letter or packet. **excess profits tax** n a tax on profits in excess of those for a specified base period or over a rate adopted as a reasonable return on capital. **excess supply** n the operating situation of a firm or industry in which the quantity of a product or service which sellers wish to sell at the prevailing price exceeds the quantity which buyers wish to buy. ■ **carry to excess** to do (something) too much. **in excess of** more than. **to excess** immoderately.

exch. abbrev : exchange; exchequer.

exchange /iks-chānj'/ vt to give or give up in return for something else; to receive in return for something else (obs); to give and take mutually; to barter; to change (obs). ◆ vi to transfer in mutual ownership, position, etc. ◆ n the giving and taking of one thing for another; barter; the thing exchanged; a conversation or argument, esp a brief one; a process by which accounts between distant parties are settled by bills instead of money; money-changing business, trade; exchanging currency of one country for that of another (also **foreign exchange**); the difference between the value of money in different places; a stock exchange, etc; the building or other place where merchants, etc meet for business; a central office where telephone lines are connected; a bar-room (old US sl); in chess, the taking by both players of an opposing piece in consecutive moves; see **Employment Service** under **employ**. [OFr eschangier (Fr échanger), from LL excambiāre, from L ex from, and LL cambiāre to barter] ■ **exchangeabil'ity** n. **exchange'able** adj that may be exchanged. **exchange'ably** adv. **exchan'ger** n a person who exchanges money, goods, etc, esp professionally; a moneychanger or banker (Bible). ❑ **exchangeable disk drive** n (comput) a disk drive that can be removed for storage or use on the same or a compatible machine. **exchange control** n the official control of the level of a country's foreign exchange transactions so as to conserve its holding of foreign currency and to protect the stability of the national currency. **exchange rate** (or **rate of exchange**) n the ratio at which one currency can be exchanged for another. **Exchange Rate Mechanism** n a former arrangement to regulate exchange rate fluctuations between participating currencies in the EMS by fixing their rates, and limiting fluctuation, against the ECU (abbrev **ERM**). **exchange student** or **teacher** n a student or teacher spending some time at a school, college or university in a foreign country while one from that country attends his or her school, etc, or a school, etc in his or her country. **exchange'-traded fund** n (finance) a type of investment fund that is administered so as to achieve the same return as a particular stock-market index (abbrev **ETF**). ■ **exchange words** or **blows** to quarrel verbally or physically. **force the exchange** in chess, to play so as to force one's opponent to take one piece for another. **in exchange for** in return for. **win** (or **lose**) **the exchange** in chess, to gain (or lose) a rook in exchange for a bishop or knight.

excheat /eks-chēt'/ (Spenser) n same as **escheat**.

exchequer /iks- or eks-chek'ər/ n (also with cap) a department of state having charge of revenue, so named from the chequered cloth which orig covered the table on which the accounts were reckoned; the Court of Exchequer (see below); a national treasury; one's funds, finances or purse (joc). ◆ vt (rare) to proceed against in the Court of Exchequer. [See **chequer**, **check** and **chess**[1]] ❑ **exchequer bill** n a bill issued by the Exchequer, as security for money advanced to the government. ■ **Chancellor of the Exchequer** see under **chancellor**. **Court of Exchequer** in England orig a revenue court developed out of the judicial branch of the Exchequer, which acquired a general common-law jurisdiction by a legal fiction, became a division of the High Court of Justice in 1875, and is now merged in the Queen's (or King's) Bench Division; in Scotland a revenue court abolished in 1886, when its jurisdiction transferred to the Court of Session.

excide /ek-sīd'/ (*archaic*) *vt* to cut off. [L *excīdere*, from ex from, and *caedere* to cut]

excimer /ek'sī-mər/ (*phys*) *n* an excited dimer in which one of the two bound atoms is in a higher energy state. [Blend of **excited** and **dimer**]

excipient /ek-sip'i-ənt/ *n* a substance mixed with a medicine to give it consistency, or used as a means of its administration. [L *excipiēns*, *-entis*, prp of *excipere* to take out or receive, from ex from, and *capere* to take]

excise[1] /ek'sīz or -sīz'/ *n* a tax on certain home commodities, and on licences for certain trades (also **excise tax** or **excise duty**); the department in the civil service concerned with this tax. ◆ *vt* to subject to excise duty. [MDu *excijs*, from OFr *acceis* tax, from LL *accensāre* to tax, from *ad* to, and *cēnsus* a tax]
■ **excīs'able** *adj* liable to excise duty.
□ **excise law** *n* (*US*) a liquor law or licensing law. **ex'ciseman** (or /-sīz'/) *n* an officer charged with collecting excise duty.

excise[2] /ek-sīz'/ *vt* to cut off or out. [L *excīdere* to cut out, from ex from, and *caedere* to cut]
■ **excision** /ek-sizh'ən/ *n* a cutting out or off of any kind; a complete removal, purging.
□ **excision repair** *n* an enzymatic DNA repair process in which a mismatching DNA sequence is removed, the gap being filled by synthesis of a new sequence complementary to the remaining strand.

excite /ik-sīt'/ *vt* to cause to become active; to stir up (people, feelings of any kind, etc); to rouse, *esp* sexually; to energize; to produce electric or magnetic activity in (*phys*); to sensitize; to stir emotionally; to raise (a nucleus, atom, molecule, etc) to an excited state. [Fr *exciter*, from L *excitāre*, *-ātum*, from *exciēre*, from *ex-* out, and *ciēre* to set in motion]
■ **excitabil'ity** *n*. **excit'able** *adj* capable of being excited; responsive to stimulus (*phys*); easily excited. **excit'ableness** *n*. **excit'ably** *adv*. **excitancy** /ek'si-tən-si/ *n* the power to excite. **excitant** /ek'si- or ek-sī'/ *n* something which excites or rouses the vital activity of the body; a stimulant (*med*); the electrolyte in an electric cell. ◆ *adj* exciting; stimulating. **excita'tion** /ek-si- or sī-/ *n* the act of exciting; a means of or reason for excitement; a state of excitement. **excit'ative** or **excit'atory** *adj* tending to excite. **excit'ed** *adj* agitated; roused emotionally or sexually; in a state of great activity; having energy higher than that of the ground, or normal, state (*phys*). **excit'edly** *adv*. **excit'edness** *n*. **excite'ment** *n* the state of being excited; agitation; something which excites emotionally. **excit'er** *n* someone who or something which excites; an auxiliary machine supplying current for another machine; a sparking apparatus for producing electric waves. **excit'ing** *adj* tending to excite; stirring or thrilling. **excit'ingly** *adv*. **excit'ingness** *n*. **excit'on** (or /ek'si-ton/) *n* (*phys*) a bound hole-electron pair in a semiconductor. **excī'tor** *n* an exciter; a nerve bringing impulses to the brain, stimulating a part of the body.

excl. *abbrev* : exclamation; excluding; exclusive.

exclaim /iks-klām'/ *vt* and *vi* to cry out (in shock, surprise, indignation or other strong emotion); to utter or speak boldly or sharply. ◆ *n* (*rare*) an exclamation or outcry. [Fr *exclamer*, from L *exclāmāre*, *-ātum*, from *ex-* out, and *clāmāre* to shout]
■ **exclamation** /eks-klə-mā'shən/ *n* a sharp cry or other utterance; outcry; an uttered expression of surprise, etc; the mark expressing this (!) (also **exclamation mark** or (*US*) **point**); an interjection. **exclama'tional** *adj*. **exclamative** /eks-klam'ə-tiv/ or **exclam'atory** *adj* containing or expressing exclamation.

exclaustration /eks-klö-strā'shən/ *n* the return of a monk or nun to the outside world on release from his or her vows. [L ex out, and *claustrum* an enclosed place]

exclave /eks'klāv/ *n* a part of a country, province, etc, disjoined from the main part, being enclosed in foreign territory. [See **enclave**]

exclosure /eks-klō'zhər/ *n* an area shut off from intrusion, *opp* to enclosure. [L *ex-* from, and **close**[1]]

exclude /iks- or eks-klood'/ *vt* to shut out; to push out, eject; to prevent from entering; to omit; to prevent from taking part; to except or leave out; to exempt (from a law, regulation, etc); to preclude or make impossible; to hatch. [L *exclūdere*, *-clūsum*, from *ex-* out, and *claudere* to shut]
■ **exclud'able** or **exclud'ible** *adj*. **exclud'ed** *adj* (*bot*) exserted. **excludee'** *n* someone who is excluded. **exclud'er** *n*. **exclud'ing** *prep* not counting; without including. **exclu'sion** /-zhən/ *n* a shutting or putting out; ejection; exception; prevention from inclusion or entry. **exclu'sionary** *adj*. **exclu'sionism** *n*. **exclu'sionist** *n* someone who excludes, or wishes to exclude, another from a privilege (also *adj*). **exclu'sive** /-siv/ *adj* able or tending to exclude; (mutually) incompatible; preventing from participation; of the nature of monopoly; socially inaccessible or aloof; sole or only; not to be had elsewhere or from another source; select, fashionable, few; without taking into account (*esp* with *of*); not included. ◆ *n* an exclusive product; a news story published by one newspaper, TV channel, etc

only; one of a number who exclude others from their society. **exclu'sively** *adv*. **exclu'siveness** or **exclusiv'ity** *n*. **exclu'sivism** *n* the practice of being exclusive. **exclu'sivist** *n* and *adj*. **exclu'sory** *adj* acting or tending to exclude.
□ **excluded employee** *n* one who is not qualified to make a claim under certain employment legislation, eg one who has reached retirement age. **exclusion clause** *n* a contractual term or other notice which attempts to exclude a person from liability which would otherwise arise, eg certain risks being excluded from an insurance policy. **exclusion order** *n* an order prohibiting the presence in, or entry to, Britain of any person known to be concerned in acts of terrorism. **exclusion principle** or **Pauli** /pow'li/ **exclusion principle** *n* (*phys*) a fundamental law of quantum mechanics that no two particles of a group called fermions can exist in identical quantum states ie have the same set of quantum numbers (this constraint explains the electronic structure of atoms and also the general nature of the periodic table). **exclusion zone** *n* a zone into which entry is forbidden, *esp* by ships or aircraft belonging to particular nations. **Exclusive Brethren** see **Close Brethren** under **close**[1]. **exclusive dealing** *n* the act of abstaining deliberately from any business or other transactions with people of opposite political or other convictions to one's own; boycotting (*euphem*). **exclusive reckoning** *n* the usual modern method of counting, in which either the first or the last term is counted, but not both (cf **inclusive reckoning**). **exclusive zone** or **exclusive economic zone** *n* territorial waters within a certain limit in which foreign exploitation is totally banned.
■ **law** (or **principle**) **of excluded middle** (*logic*) the principle that everything is either true or false. **to the exclusion of** so as to exclude.

excogitate /eks-koj'i-tāt/ *vt* to discover by thinking; to think out earnestly or laboriously. [L *excōgitāre*, *-ātum*, from *ex-* out, and *cōgitāre* to think]
■ **excog'itator** *n*. **excogita'tion** *n* laborious thinking; invention by thinking out; contrivance. **excog'itative** *adj*.

excommunicate /eks-kə-mū'ni-kāt/ *vt* to forbid or expel from the communion of (any branch of) the church; to deprive of church privileges. ◆ *adj* (or /-kit/) excommunicated. ◆ *n* (or /-kit/) a person who has been excommunicated. [From LL *excommūnicāre*, from L ex out, and *commūnis* common]
■ **excommun'icable** *adj*. **excommun'icant** *n* an excommunicated person. **excommunica'tion** or (*Milton*) **excommun'ion** *n* the act of expelling from the communion of (a branch of) the church. **excommun'icator** *n*. **excommun'icatory** or **excommun'icative** *adj* of or relating to excommunication.

ex concessis /eks kən-ses'is or kon-kā'sēs/, also **ex concesso** /kən-ses'ō or kon-kā'sō/ (*LL*) from what has been conceded.

ex consequenti /eks kon-si-kwen'tī or -se-kwen'tē/ (*LL*) by way of consequence.

ex converso same as **e converso**.

excoriate /eks-kō'ri-āt or -kō'ri-/ *vt* to strip the skin from; to criticize severely. [L *excoriāre*, *-ātum*, from ex from, and *corium* the skin]
■ **excoria'tion** *n* the act of excoriating; the state of being excoriated.

excorticate /eks-kör'ti-kāt/ *vt* to strip the bark off. [L ex from, and *cortex*, *-icis* bark]
■ **excortica'tion** *n*.

excrement[1] /eks'krə-mənt or -kri-/ *n* waste matter discharged from the digestive system, faeces; dregs. [L *excrēmentum*, from *excernere*, from *ex-* out, and *cernere* to sift]
■ **excremental** /-ment'l/, **excrementitial** /-men-tish'l/ or **excrementi'tious** *adj* relating to or containing excrement.

excrement[2] /eks'kri-mənt/ (*Shakesp*) *n* a growth of facial hair. [L *excrēmentum*, from *ex-* out, and *crēscere* to grow]
■ **excremental** /-ment'l/ *adj*.

excrementa /eks-kri-men'tə or -kre-men'ta/ (*L*) *n pl* (sing **excrementum** /-təm or -tŭm/) waste matter or rubbish.

excrescence /iks-kres'əns/ *n* an outgrowth or projection, *esp* abnormal, grotesque or offensive; a wart or tumour; a superfluous or unattractive part; outbreak. [L *excrēscere*, from *ex-* out, and *crēscere* to grow]
■ **excresc'ency** *n* the state of being excrescent; an excrescence. **excresc'ent** *adj* growing out; superfluous; (of a sound or letter) added to a word for euphony, etc without etymological justification. **excrescential** /eks-kri-sen'shl/ *adj*.

excrete /eks-krēt'/ *vt* to discharge, *esp* from the bowels, bladder, sweat glands, etc; to eject in a similar or analogous manner. [L ex from, and *cernere*, *crētum* to separate]
■ **excrē'ta** *n pl* waste products discharged from the body. **excrē'tal** *adj*. **excrē'ter** *n*. **excrē'tion** *n* the excreting of waste matter from an organism; that which is excreted. **excrē'tive** *adj* able to excrete; concerned with excretion. **excrē'tory** (or /eks'kri-tər-i/) *adj* having the quality or power of excreting. ◆ *n* a duct that helps to receive and excrete matter.

excruciate /iks- or eks-kroo'shi-āt/ vt to torture; to rack; to inflict severe pain; to irritate greatly. [L excruciāre to torture, from ex- out, and cruciāre, -ātum to crucify, from crux, crucis a cross]
■ **excru'ciating** adj extremely painful; racking; torturing; agonizing; intensely irritating (fig). **excru'ciatingly** adv. **excrucia'tion** n torture; irritation or annoyance.

excubant /eks'kū-bənt/ adj on guard. [L excubāns, -antis, prp of excubāre to sleep out or lie on guard, from ex out, and cubāre to lie]

excudit /eks-kū'dit or -koo'/ (L) (he or she) struck, hammered, forged or printed (this).

exculpate /eks'kul-pāt, also -kul'/ vt to clear from the charge of a fault or crime; to absolve; to vindicate. [L ex from, and culpa a fault]
■ **excul'pable** adj. **exculpa'tion** n. **excul'patory** adj freeing from the charge of fault or crime.

ex curia /eks kū'ri-ə or koo'ri-ä/ (L) out of court.

excurrent /eks-kur'ənt/ adj flowing outwards (zool); carrying an outgoing current; having the main stem reaching to the top (bot); having the midrib reaching beyond the lamina (bot). [L ex from, and currēns, -entis, prp of currere to run]

excursion /iks-kûr'shən or iks-kûr'zhən/ n a pleasure trip; a group of people on a pleasure outing; a going out or forth; a deviation from the normal course; a wandering from the main subject; rapid increase of reactor power above set operation level (nuclear eng); a digression; an escapade; a raid; a sally. ♦ vi to make or go on an excursion. [L ex-out, and currere, cursum to run]
■ **excurse'** vi (archaic) to digress. **excur'sionist** n someone who goes on a pleasure trip. **excur'sionize** or **-ise** vi (rare) to go on an excursion. **excur'sive** adj rambling; deviating from the main point or topic. **excur'sively** adv. **excur'siveness** n. **excur'sus** n (pl **excur'suses**) a dissertation or discussion on some particular matter appended to the main body of a book or chapter.
❑ **excursion fare** n a special cheap fare allowed on certain journeys by public transport. **excursion ticket** n. **excursion train** n a special train, usu with reduced fares, for people making an excursion esp for pleasure.

excuse /iks- or eks-kūz'/ vt to free from blame or guilt; to exonerate; to overlook or forgive; to pardon or condone (in small matters); to free (from an obligation); to release or dispense with temporarily; to allow to go out of one's presence; to seek to explain or justify (a person or their actions); to make an apology or ask pardon for. ♦ vi (archaic) to make excuses. ♦ n /iks-kūs'/ a plea offered in extenuation or explanation, in order to avoid punishment; pardon or forgiveness; indulgence. [L excūsāre, from ex from, and causa a cause or accusation]
■ **excūsable** /iks-kūz'ə-bl/ adj. **excūs'ableness** n. **excūs'ably** adv. **excūs'al** n. **excūs'atory** adj making or containing excuses; apologetic. **excus'er** n. **excusive** /eks-kūs'iv/ adj.
❑ **excuse-me** or **excuse-me dance** n a dance during which one may change partners.
■ **be excused** to leave a room, etc; to go to the lavatory to relieve oneself (euphem). **excuse for** /iks-kūs'/ a very poor example of. **excuse me** an expression used as an apology for any slight or apparent impropriety, esp as a request to pass, leave, interrupt or catch someone's attention or for contradicting a statement that has been made, or (US) when correcting oneself. **excuse oneself** to ask permission and then leave; to explain and seek pardon (for a misdeed). **make one's excuses** to apologize for leaving or for not attending.

ex debito justitiae /eks deb'i-tō jə-stish'i-ē or dā'bi-tō ū-sti'ti-ī/ (LL) from what is due to justice.

ex delicto /eks di-lik'tō or dā-lik'tō/ (LL) owing to a crime.

ex-directory /eks-dī-rek'tə-ri or -di-/ adj (of a telephone number) not listed in a directory; (of a person) having such a number. [**ex²** and **directory** (see **direct**)]

ex div /eks div/ (also with hyphen) short form of **ex dividend**, denoting a purchase of stocks and shares in which the seller and not the purchaser is entitled to the next payment of interest or dividends. [L extra dividendum without dividend]

ex dono /eks dō'nō/ (L) by gift, as a present from.

exeat /ek'si-at/ n formal leave of absence, esp for a student to be out of college for more than one night; permission granted by a bishop to a priest to move on to another diocese. [L, let him or her go out, 3rd pers sing pr subjunctive of exīre]

exec /eg-zek'/ (inf) n an executive or executive officer. [Short form of **executive**]

exec. /eg-zek'/ abbrev : executive; executor.

execrate /ek'si-krāt/ vt to curse; to utter evil against; to denounce; to detest. [L exsecrārī, -ātus to curse, from ex from, and sacer sacred]
■ **ex'ecrable** adj deserving execration; detestable; accursed; very bad or of low quality. **ex'ecrableness** n. **ex'ecrably** adv. **execrā'tion**

n the act of execrating; a curse pronounced; something which is execrated. **ex'ecrative** adj of or belonging to execration. **ex'ecratively** adv. **ex'ecratory** adj.

execute /ek'si-kūt/ vt to perform; to produce; to give effect to; to carry into effect; to make valid by signing (law); to put to use or bring into action; to put to death by law; to carry out the instructions in (a compiled version of a program), to run (a program) (comput). [L exsequī, exsecūtus, from ex out, and sequī to follow]
■ **execūtable** /eks'i-kūt-ə-bl/ or ek-sek'ūt-ə-bl/ adj that can be executed; that can be run by a computer. ♦ n (comput) an executable file or program. **execūtancy** /eg-zek'/ n technique in music. **execūtant** /eg-zek'/ n someone who executes or performs; a technically accomplished performer of music. ♦ adj performing. **execūter** /eks'/ n. **execū'tion** n the act of, or skill in, executing or performing; accomplishment; completion; the infliction of capital punishment; the carrying into effect of the sentence of a court of law; the warrant for doing so. **execū'tioner** n a person who executes, esp one who carries out a sentence of death. **executive** /eg-zek'ū-tiv/ adj concerned with performance, administration or management; qualifying for or relating to the execution of the law; administrative; for the use of business executives; hence (loosely) expensive or sophisticated; active; designed or fitted to execute or perform. ♦ n the power or authority in government that carries the laws into effect; the persons who administer the government or an organization; a person in an executive position in government or business; (also **chief executive**) the head of an executive, eg a president, governor, mayor, etc (US). **exec'ūtively** adv. **execūtor** /eg-zek'/ n a person who executes or performs; a person appointed by a testator to see a will carried into effect (law). **execūtō'rial** adj. **exec'ūtorship** n. **exec'ūtory** adj executing official duties; designed to be carried into effect. **exec'ūtrix** n (pl **exec'ūtrixes** or **execūtrī'cēs**) a female executor (also **exec'utress**). **exec'ūtry** n executorship; moveable or heritable estate and effects (Scots law).
❑ **execution error** n (comput) a programming error which comes to light when the program is run (also called **run-time error**). **Executive Council** n a ministerial council headed by the Governor(-General) (Aust and NZ); (without caps) a council with executive power. **executive officer** n an officer with executive power; (in certain countries, eg US) a naval officer responsible for the general administration of a ship. **executive program** n (comput) a program which controls the use of a computer and the running of compiled programs. **executive session** n (US) a meeting of the Senate for executive business, usu held in private; any meeting in private. **executive toy** n a mechanism or gadget with little practical use, intended primarily as a diversion for business executives.

exedra, also **exhedra** /ek'si-drə/ n (pl **exedrae** or **exhedrae**) a portico, hall or vestibule; a room with seats; a columned recess in classical Greek and Roman architecture, containing a continuous semicircular bench, used for holding discussions in; any outdoor bench in a recess; an apse, recess or niche. [L, from Gr exedrā, from ex- out, and hedrā seat]

exeem or **exeme** /ek-sēm'/ (obs Scot) vt to release or exempt. [L eximere, from ex from, and emere to take]

exegesis /ek-si-jē'sis/ n a critical interpretation of a text, esp Biblical. [Gr exēgēsis, from exēgeesthai to explain, from ex- out, and hēgeesthai to guide]
■ **ex'egēte** or **exegēt'ist** n a person who interprets or expounds. **exegetic** /-jet'ik/ or **exeget'ical** adj relating to exegesis; explanatory. **exeget'ically** adv. **exeget'ics** n sing the science of exegesis.

exeme see **exeem**.

exempla see **exemplum**.

exemplar /eg-zem'plər or -plär/ n a person or thing to be imitated; the ideal model; a type; an example; a copy of a book or other text. [L exemplar, from exemplum example]
■ **exem'plarily** adv. **exem'plariness** n. **exemplarity** /-plar'/ n exemplariness; exemplary conduct. **exem'plary** adj worthy of imitation or notice; serving as a model, a specimen, an illustration or a warning.
❑ **exemplary damages** n pl (law) damages in excess of the value needed to compensate the plaintiff, awarded as a punishment to the offender (also called **punitive damages**).

exemple /eg-zä'pl'/ (Fr) n an example or a model.
■ **par exemple** for example.

exemplify /ig-zem'pli-fī/ vt (**exem'plifying**; **exem'plified**) to be a typical example of; to illustrate by example; to make an attested copy of; to prove by an attested copy. [L exemplum example, and facere to make]
■ **exem'plifiable** adj. **exemplificā'tion** n the act of exemplifying; something which exemplifies; an attested copy or transcript. **exemp'lificative** adj. **exemp'lifier** n.

exempli gratia /ig-zem'plī grä'shi-ə or ek-sem'plē grä'ti-ä/ (L) by way of example, for instance (*abbrev* **eg**).

exemplum /ig-zem'pləm/ *n* (*pl* **exem'pla** /-plə/) an example; a short story or anecdote illustrating a moral. [L, example]

exempt /ig-zempt' or -zemt'/ *vt* to free, or grant immunity (from); to set apart (*Milton*). ◆ *adj* taken out; (often with *from*) not liable (for) or subject (to); of goods and services, carrying no value-added tax, but on which tax charged by suppliers, etc cannot be reclaimed. ◆ *n* an exempt person or organization; an officer who commanded in absence of his superiors, exempted on this account from ordinary duties (*hist*). [Fr, from L *eximere*, *exemptum*, from *ex* from, and *emere* to buy]
■ **exemp'tion** *n* the act of exempting; the state of being exempt; freedom from any service, duty, burden, etc; immunity.
❑ **exemption clause** *n* a contractual term or notice which attempts to exclude or restrict a person's liability. **exempt rating** *n* a rating by which a business is exempted from charging or reclaiming VAT on the goods it supplies, the goods concerned being themselves exempted from VAT (see also **zero-rating** under **zero**). **exempt supplies** *n pl* goods or services supplied by a business on which VAT is not allowed to be charged.

exenterate /ek-sen'tə-rāt/ (*obs*) *vt* to disembowel. ◆ *adj* /-it/ disembowelled. [L *exenterāre*, from Gr *exenterizein*, from *ex* from, and *enteron* intestine]
■ **exenterā'tion** *n*.

exequatur /ek-si-kwä'tər/ *n* an official recognition of a consul or commercial agent given by the government of the country in which he or she is to be based. [L *exequātur* let him execute, from the opening word]

exequy /ek'si-kwi/ *n* (*usu* in *pl* **exequies** /-kwiz/) a funeral procession; funeral rites. [L *exequiae*, from *ex* from, and *sequī* to follow]
■ **exequial** /eks-ē'kwi-əl/ *adj*.

exercise /ek'sər-sīz/ *n* exertion of the body for health or amusement or the acquisition of a skill; a similar exertion of the mind; a task designed or prescribed for these purposes; a putting in practice; a written school task; a study in music; a set of problems, passages for translation, etc in a text-book; an academic disputation; accomplishment (*Shakesp*); (in *pl*) military drill or manoeuvres; a ceremony or formal proceeding (*N Am*); an act of worship or devotion; a discourse, *esp* the discussion of a passage of Scripture, giving the coherence of text and context, etc (the *addition* giving the doctrinal propositions, etc); a meeting of a presbytery for this purpose; hence, formerly, the presbytery itself. ◆ *vt* to put in practice; to use; to train by use; to improve by practice; to give exercise to; to trouble, concern or occupy the thoughts of; to wield. ◆ *vi* to take exercise; to drill. [OFr *exercice*, from L *exercitium*, from L *exercēre*, *-citum*, from *ex-* and *arcēre* to shut up or restrain]
■ **ex'ercisable** *adj*. **ex'erciser** *n* someone or something which exercises; a device, *usu* with elasticated cords, to help in exercising the muscles.
❑ **exercise bicycle** or **bike** *n* a machine like a bicycle without wheels, used for indoor exercise. **exercise book** *n* a book for writing school exercises in; a book containing exercises to practise. **exercise price** *n* (*stock exchange*) same as **striking price** (see under **strike**).
■ **the object of the exercise** the purpose of a particular operation or activity.

exercitation /eg-zûr-si-tā'shən/ *n* putting into practice; employment; exercise; a discourse. [L *exercitātiō*, *-ōnis*, from *exercēre* to exercise]

exergaming /eks'ər-gā-ming/ *n* the playing of video games that involve physical exercise. [**exercise** and **game**[1]]

exergonic /ek-sûr-gon'ik/ *adj* of a biochemical reaction, accompanied by the release of energy and therefore capable of proceeding spontaneously. [Ety as for **exergue**]

exergue /ek' or ek-sûrg'/ *n* a part on the reverse of a coin, below the main design, often filled up by the date, etc. [Fr, from Gr *ex* out of, and *ergon* work]
■ **exer'gual** *adj*.

exergy /ek'sər-ji/ (*phys*) *n* a measure of the maximum amount of work that can theoretically be obtained from a system. [Ety as for **exergue**]

exert /ig-zûrt'/ *vt* to cause (oneself) to make a strenuous (*esp* physical) effort; to bring into active operation; to put forth (*obs*); to do or perform (*obs*). [L *exserere*, *exsertum*, from *ex* from, and *serere* to put together]
■ **exer'tion** *n* a bringing into active operation; striving; strenuous activity. **exert'ive** *adj* having the power or tendency to exert; using exertion.

exes /ek'səz/ (*inf*) *n pl* expenses; see also **ex** under **ex-**.

exeunt /ek'si-unt or -ŭnt/ (*stage direction*) (they) go out or leave the stage. [L; see **exit**]
■ **exeunt omnes** /om'nēz or -nās/ all go out.

exfiltrate /eks'fil-trāt or -fil'/ *vt* to remove (troops, agents, etc) from a hostile area by secret means. [Modelled on **infiltrate**; from L *ex* out of]
■ **exfiltrā'tion** *n*.

exfoliate /eks-fō'li-āt/ *vt* to cause (skin, bark, rocks, etc) to be shed or come apart in flakes or layers; to remove in flakes, etc; to scrub (part of the body) with a gritty substance to remove dead skin. ◆ *vi* to come off in flakes; to separate into layers. [L *exfoliāre*, *-ātum* to strip of leaves, from *ex* from, and *folium* a leaf]
■ **exfō'liant** *n* a cosmetic preparation for removing dead layers of skin. **exfoliā'tion** *n*. **exfō'liative** *adj*. **exfō'liātor** *n* an exfoliating agent.
❑ **exfoliative cytology** *n* (*biol*) the study of cells shed from a tissue for diagnostic purposes.

ex gratia /eks grā'shi-ə or grä'ti-ä/ (L) as an act of grace; given or made as a favour, not out of obligation, and with no acceptance of liability, as *ex gratia payment* (*abbrev* **ex gr.**).

exhale[1] /eks-hāl' or eg-zāl'/ *vt* to breathe forth; to emit or send out (a vapour, smell, etc); to cause or allow to evaporate; to emit through a membrane (*pathol*). ◆ *vi* to breathe out; to rise or come off as a vapour, smell or emanation; to evaporate; to ooze out. [L *exhālāre*, from *ex* from, and *hālāre*, *-ātum* to breathe]
■ **exhāl'able** *adj*. **exhāl'ant** *adj* exhaling; emitting vapour or liquid. ◆ *n* an organ or vessel that emits vapour or liquid. **exhalation** /eks- or egz-ə-lā'shən/ *n* the act or process of exhaling; evaporation; anything exhaled, vapour, effluvium or emanation; a mist; a meteoric phenomenon, a meteor (*archaic*).

exhale[2] /eks-hāl'/ (*Shakesp*) *vt* to hale or draw out. [**ex-** and **hale**[2]]

exhaust /ig-zöst'/ *vt* to draw off; to draw out the whole of; to use the whole strength of; to use up; to empty; to wear or tire out; to treat or develop completely (an idea, theme, etc). ◆ *vi* of exhaust gases in an engine, to be emitted. ◆ *n* an outward current, or means of producing it; the exit of gases or fluids as waste products from the cylinder of an engine, a turbine, etc; the period of discharge of the gases or fluids; the gases or fluids so escaping (**exhaust gas** or **exhaust steam**); the part or parts of an engine, etc through which the waste gases escape. [L *exhaurīre*, *exhaustum*, from *ex* from, and *haurīre* to draw]
■ **exhaust'ed** *adj* drawn out; emptied; consumed; tired out. **exhaust'edly** *adv*. **exhaust'er** *n* someone or something that exhausts. **exhaustibil'ity** *n*. **exhaust'ible** *adj* that can be exhausted. **exhaust'ing** *adj*. **exhaust'ingly** *adv*. **exhaustion** /-öst'yən/ *n* the act of exhausting or consuming; the state of being exhausted; extreme fatigue. **exhaust'ive** *adj* tending to exhaust; investigating all parts or possibilities; thorough. **exhaust'ively** *adv*. **exhaust'iveness** *n*. **exhaust'less** *adj* that cannot be exhausted.
❑ **exhaust pipe** or **exhaust valve** *n* the pipe or valve through which exhaust gases pass out.

exhedra see **exedra**.

exheredate /eks-her'i-dāt/ (*rare*) *vt* to disinherit. [L *exhērēdāre*, from *ex* out, and *hērēs*, *-ēdis* heir]
■ **exheredā'tion** *n*.

exhibit /ig-zib'it/ *vt* to hold forth or display; to present formally or publicly; to show or manifest (a quality, etc); to administer as a remedy (*med*; *archaic*). ◆ *n* a document or object produced in court to be used as evidence (*law*); something exhibited; an article at an exhibition. [L *exhibēre*, *-itum*, from *ex-* out, and *habēre*, *-itum* to have]
■ **exhib'iter** *n*. **exhibition** /eks-i-bish'ən/ *n* presentation to view; display; showing off; a public show, *esp* of works of art, manufactured goods, etc; that which is exhibited; a public performance at the end of a school year; a grant or gift; an allowance towards support, *esp* to students at a university; the administration of a remedy (*archaic*). **exhibi'tioner** *n* a student who has been awarded an exhibition at a university. **exhibi'tionism** *n* extravagant behaviour aimed at drawing attention to oneself; perversion involving public exposure of one's sexual organs (*psychiatry*). **exhibi'tionist** *n*. **exhibitionist'ic** *adj*. **exhibitionist'ically** *adv*. **exhib'itive** /igz-/ *adj* serving for exhibition; representative. **exhib'itively** *adv*. **exhibitor** /igz-ib'i-tər/ *n*. **exhib'itory** *adj* exhibiting.
■ **make an exhibition of oneself** to behave foolishly, making oneself ridiculous.

exhilarate /ig-zil'ə-rāt/ *vt* to make very happy or cheerful; to raise the spirits of; to refresh the body and mind of; to enliven; to cheer. [L *exhilarāre*, *-ātum*, from *ex-* (intens), and *hīlaris* cheerful]
■ **exhil'arant** *adj* exhilarating; arousing joy, mirth or pleasure. ◆ *n* an exhilarating medicine. **exhil'arāting** *adj* cheering; gladdening. **exhil'arātingly** *adv*. **exhilarā'tion** *n* the state of being exhilarated; joyousness. **exhil'arātive** or **exhil'aratory** *adj*. **exhil'arātor** *n*.

exhort /ig-zört'/ *vt* to urge strongly and earnestly; to counsel. [L *exhortārī*, *-ātus*, from *ex-* (intens), and *hortārī* to urge]
■ **exhortā'tion** /eks- or egz-/ *n* the act of exhorting; language, speech or writing intended to exhort; counsel; a religious discourse.

exhort'ative or **exhort'atory** /igz-/ adj tending to exhort or advise. **exhort'er** n someone who exhorts; in some churches, a layman appointed to give religious exhortation.

exhume /eks-hūm' or ig-zūm'/, also **exhumate** /eks'hū-māt/ vt to take out of the ground or place of burial; to disinter; to bring back into use; to bring to light; to bring up or mention again. [L ex out of, and humus the ground]
■ **exhumā'tion** /eks-/ n. **exhum'er** n.

ex hypothesi /eks hī-poth'ə-sī/ (LL) from the hypothesis.

exies /ek'sāz/ (Scot) n pl a fit, eg of hysterics or ague. [access]

exigent /ek'si-jənt/ adj pressing; urgent; exacting; demanding immediate attention or action. ◆ n extremity (obs); the last strait, the end of all (Shakesp); a needed amount (Browning). [L exigēns, -entis, from prp of exigere, from ex-, and agere to drive]
■ **exigeant** /egz-ē-zhā/ or (fem) **exigeante** /-zhãt/ adj (Fr) exacting. **ex'igence** or **ex'igency** (or /-ij'/) n pressing necessity; emergency; distress. **ex'igently** adv.

exigible /ek'si-ji-bl/ adj liable to be exacted. [See ety for **exact**]

exiguous /eg-zig'-, ek-sig'ū-əs/ adj scanty; slender. [L exiguus, from exigere to weigh strictly; see **exact**]
■ **exigū'ity** /eks-/ n. **exig'uously** adv. **exig'ūousness** n.

exile /ek'sīl or eg'zīl/ n enforced or regretted absence from one's country or home; banishment; (with cap) the captivity of the Jews in Babylon (in these senses formerly /egz-īl'/); someone who is in exile; a banished person. ◆ vt (formerly /egz-īl'/) to expel from one's country, to banish. [OFr exil, from L exsilium banishment, from ex out of, and root of salīre to leap; affected by L exsul an exile]
■ **ex'ilement** n (rare) banishment. **exilic** /egz-il'ik or eks-/ or **exil'ian** adj relating to exile, esp that of the Jews in Babylon.

exility /eg-zil' or ek-sil'i-ti/ (obs) n slenderness or smallness; refinement. [L exīlitās, -ātis, from exīlis slender]

eximious /eg-zim'i-əs/ (archaic) adj excellent or distinguished. [L eximius, from eximere, from ex from, and emere to take]
■ **exim'iously** adv.

ex improviso /eks im-prə-vī'zō or im-prō-vē'sō, also -wē'/ (L) unexpectedly.

exine /ek'sin or -sīn/ see **extine**. [L ex out of]

ex int. (banking) abbrev : ex interest, without interest. [L ex without]

exist /ig- or eg-zist'/ vi to have actual being; to live; to occur; to continue to live, esp in unfavourable circumstances. [L existere, exsistere to stand forth, from ex- out, and sistere to stand]
■ **exist'ence** n the state of existing or being; livelihood; life; anything and everything that exists; being. **exist'ent** adj having being; existing. **existential** /eks-is-ten'shəl/ adj of or relating to (esp human) existence; of or relating to existentialism. **existen'tialism** n a term covering a number of related philosophical doctrines denying objective universal values and holding that people, as moral free agents, must create values for themselves through actions and must accept the ultimate responsibility for those actions in the seemingly meaningless universe. **existen'tialist** n and adj. **existen'tially** adv.
❑ **existential quantifier** n (logic) a formal expression indicating that a statement is true for at least one member of the universe of discourse.

Exit /ek'sit or eg'zit/ n a British organization encouraging voluntary euthanasia, and campaigning for its legalization.

exit /ek'sit or eg'zit/ n the departure of an actor from the stage; any departure; a passage out; a way of departure; death (literary); a place on a motorway where vehicles can leave by a slip road; the last instruction of a subroutine (comput). ◆ vi to make an exit; to leave or depart; to die (literary); to lose the lead deliberately (cards). ◆ vt to make an exit from; to leave or go out of. [Partly from the L stage direction exit (he or she) goes out (in pl exeunt (they) go out), from exīre to go out, from ex- out, and īre, itum to go; partly from L exitus a way out]
■ **ex'itance** n (phys) the amount per unit area of light or other radiation emitted from a surface.
❑ **exit charge** n (stock exchange) a charge made when selling investments, etc. **exit poll** n a poll of a sample of voters, taken as they leave the polling-station, used to give an early indication of voting trends in a particular election. **exit strategy** n a planned method of withdrawal from a situation. **exit value** n (account) the price at which an asset or liability could be sold. **exit wound** n a wound occurring where a bullet, etc leaves the body.

ex libris /eks lī'bris or lī'/ (L) from the books of (used eg on bookplates) (abbrev **ex lib**). n (with hyphen) a name-label pasted into the front of a book, a bookplate.
■ **ex-li'brism** n. **ex-li'brist** n a collector or student of bookplates.

ex mero motu /eks mē'rō mō'tū or mer'ō mō'too/ (L) from his or her own impulse; of his, her or its own accord.

ex natura rei /eks na-tū'rə rē'ī or na-too'ra re'ē/ (LL) from the nature of the case.

ex natura rerum /eks na-tū'rə rē'rəm or rā'rŭm/ (LL) from the nature of things.

ex nihilo /eks nī'hi-lō or nī'/ (L) out of nothing, eg in creation ex nihilo.

exo- /ek-sō- or ek-so-/ combining form (often interchanging with **ecto-**) outside, opp to endo- and ento-. [Gr exō outside]
■ **exobiolog'ical** adj. **exobiol'ogist** n. **exobiol'ogy** n the study of (possible) extraterrestrial life. **ex'ocarp** n (Gr karpos fruit; bot) the outer layer of the part of a fruit which contains the seeds; the epicarp. **ex'ocrine** adj (Gr krīnein to separate; physiol) of glands, secreting through a duct. ◆ n an exocrine gland. **exocytō'sis** n (biol) the discharge of the contents of internal vesicles from a cell. **exocytō'tic** adj. **ex'oderm** n exodermis; ectoderm. **exoderm'al** adj. **exoder'mis** n (Gr dermis skin) the outer cortex layer of a root. **exoen'zyme** n an enzyme that functions outside the cell producing it, an ectoenzyme. **exoergic** /-ûr'jik/ adj (Gr ergon work; nuclear eng) of a process in which energy is released. **exogam'ic** or **exog'amous** adj. **exog'amy** n (Gr gamos marriage) the practice of marrying only outside of one's own group; the union of gametes not closely related (biol). **ex'ogen** n (obs) a dicotyledon, so called because its stem thickens by layers growing on the outside of the wood. **exogenet'ic** adj (med) not genetic, not caused by genetic factors. **exog'enous** adj growing by successive additions to the outside; developing externally; having an external origin. **exog'enously** adv. **exonu'clease** n an enzyme which continuously cleaves nucleotides from one end of a nucleotide chain. **ex'onym** n (Gr onoma a name) a name for a town, country, etc in a foreign language. **exoph'agous** adj. **exoph'agy** n (Gr phagein to eat) the custom among cannibals of eating only the flesh of persons not of their own kin. **ex'oplanet** n a planet that orbits a star other than the sun. **ex'oplasm** n ectoplasm. **exop'odite** or **ex'opod** n (Gr pous, podos foot) the outer branch of a crustacean limb. **exopod'itic** adj. **exoskel'etal** adj. **exoskel'eton** n a hard supporting or protective structure secreted externally by the ectoderm. **ex'osphere** n (Gr sphaira sphere) the outermost layer of the earth's atmosphere, beyond around 500km from the surface of the earth. **exospher'ic** or **exospher'ical** adj. **exospor'al** adj. **ex'ospore** n (Gr sporos a seed) the outer layer of a spore wall; a spore formed by the extrusion of material from the parent cell. **exospor'ous** adj. **exother'mal** or **exother'mic** adj (Gr thermē heat; chem) involving the release of heat, esp during a reaction. **exother'mally** or **exother'mically** adv. **exothermi'city** n. **exotox'ic** adj. **exotox'in** n (biol) a toxin produced by a micro-organism and secreted into the surrounding medium.

Exocet® /ek'sə-set/ n a subsonic tactical missile, launched from a ship, plane or submarine and travelling at low altitude. [Fr, from New L Exocoetus volitans the flying fish]

Exod. (Bible) abbrev : (the Book of) Exodus.

exode /ek'sōd/ n the concluding part of a Greek drama; a farce or afterpiece. [Gr exodion]

exodus /ek'sə-dəs/ n a going out, esp (usu with cap) that of the Israelites from Egypt; (with cap) the second book of the Old Testament. [L, from Gr exodos, from ex- out, and hodos a way]
■ **exodic** /-od'/ adj. **ex'odist** n a person who goes out; an emigrant.

ex officio /eks o-fis'i-ō or -fish', -fik'/ (L) by virtue of office or position (abbrev **ex off.**).

Exon. abbrev : Exonia (L), Exeter; Exoniensis (L), of Exeter.

exon[1] /ek'son/ (biol) n a segment of DNA that encodes part of a protein (cf **intron**). [L ex out of, and Gr neuter sfx -on]
■ **exon'ic** adj.

exon[2] /ek'son/ n one of the four commanding officers of the Yeomen of the Guard. [Appar intended to express the pronunciation of Fr exempt (see **exempt**)]

exonerate /ig-zon'ə-rāt/ vt to free from the burden of blame or obligation; to acquit. [L exonerāre, -ātum, from ex from, and onus, oneris burden]
■ **exonerā'tion** n the act of exonerating. **exon'erative** adj freeing from a burden or obligation. **exon'erator** n.

exophthalmia /ek-sof-thal'mi-ə/, also **exophthalmos** or **exophthalmus** /ek-sof-thal'mas/ (pathol) n a protrusion of the eyeballs. [Gr ex out, and ophthalmos eye]
■ **exophthal'mic** adj.
❑ **exophthalmic goitre** n a form of hyperthyroidism marked by exophthalmia and swelling of the thyroid gland.

exor abbrev : executor.

exorable /ek'sə-rə-bl or eg'zə-/ adj capable of being moved by entreaty. [L exōrāre, from ex- thoroughly, and ōrāre to entreat]
■ **exorabil'ity** n. **exorā'tion** n (obs) entreaty.

exorbitant /ig-zör'bi-tənt/ adj going beyond the usual limits; (esp of prices) excessive. [L exorbitāns, -antis, prp of exorbitāre, from ex out of, and orbita a track, from orbis a circle]

exor'bitance or **exor'bitancy** *n* great excess. **exor'bitantly** *adv*. **exor'bitate** *vi* (*obs*) to stray.

exorcize or **-ise** /*ek'sör-sīz*/ *vt* to call forth or drive away (a spirit); to deliver from the influence of an evil spirit; to command by some holy name. [LL from Gr *exorkizein*, from *ex-* out, and *horkos* an oath]
■ **ex'orcism** /*-sizm*/ *n* the act of exorcizing or expelling evil spirits by certain ceremonies; a formula for exorcizing. **ex'orcist** *n* a person who exorcizes or pretends to expel evil spirits by command (also **ex'orcīzer** or **-s-**); the third of the minor orders (*RC*).

exordium /*eg-zör'di-əm*/ *n* (pl **exor'diums** or **exor'dia**) an introductory part, *esp* of a discourse or composition. [L, from *exordīrī*, from *ex* out of, and *ordīrī* to begin]
■ **exor'dial** *adj* relating to the exordium; introductory.

exosmosis /*ek-sos-mō'sis* or *ek-soz-*/ *n* osmosis outwards, ie away from the solution (also **ex'osmose** /*-mōs*/). [Gr *ex-* out, and **osmosis**]
■ **exosmotic** /*-mot'ik*/ *adj*.

exostosis /*ek-so-stō'sis*/ (*anat*) *n* (pl **exostō'ses** /*-sēz*/) abnormal enlargement of a bone. [Gr *exostōsis*, from *ex-* out, and *osteon* a bone]

exoteric /*ek-sō-ter'ik* or *eg-zō-*/ *adj* external (*obs*); intelligible to the uninitiated; popular or commonplace, *opp* to *esoteric*. [Gr *exōterikos*, from *exōterō* compar of *exō* outside]
■ **exoter'ical** *adj*. **exoter'ically** *adv*. **exoter'icism** /*-sizm*/ *n*.

exotic /*ig-zot'ik*/ *adj* introduced from a foreign country; alien (also *fig*); foreign-looking; outlandish or unusual; romantically strange, rich and showy, or glamorous; relating to striptease or belly-dancing; applied to various high-energy fuels used eg to propel rockets. ◆ *n* anything of foreign origin; something not native to a country, such as a plant, a word or a custom; an exotic dancer. [Gr *exōtikos*, from *exō* outside]
■ **exot'ica** *n pl* exotic objects; theatrical or musical items with an unusual theme or with a foreign flavour. **exot'ically** *adv*. **exot'icism** /*-sizm*/ *n*. **exot'icness** *n*.
❑ **exotic dancer** *n* a striptease artist or belly dancer.

exp. *abbrev* : experiment or experimental; expired; expiry; exponential; export; exporter; express.

expand /*ik-spand'*/ *vt* to spread out; to lay open; to enlarge in bulk or surface area; to develop or bring out in fuller detail; to express at length, as in terms of a series or without contractions. ◆ *vi* to become opened; to increase in volume; to enlarge; to spread; to become communicative (*fig*); to speak or write more fully (on). [L *expandere*, from *ex-* out, and *pandere*, *pānsum* to spread]
■ **expandabil'ity** *n*. **expand'able** *adj*. **expand'ed** *adj* spread out or enlarged; (of plastic) combined with or forming a gas during manufacture to produce a lightweight insulating or packaging material (as in *expanded polystyrene*). **expand'er** or **expand'or** *n* an electronic device which increases the range of amplitude variations in a transmission system; a device used for exercising and developing muscles. **expanse** /*-pans'*/ *n* a wide extent; a stretch; the amount of spread or stretch; the firmament. **expansibil'ity** *n*. **expans'ible** *adj* capable of being expanded. **expans'ibly** *adv*. **expans'ile** /*-īl*/ *adj* capable of expansion. **expan'sion** *n* the act of expanding; the state of being expanded; enlargement; something which is expanded; amount of expanding; territorial extension; immensity; extension. **expan'sional** *adj*. **expan'sionary** *adj* tending to expand. **expan'sionism** *n* the principle or practice of expanding the territory or the economy of a country. **expan'sionist** *n* someone who favours territorial or currency expansion (also *adj*). **expansionist'ic** *adj*. **expans'ive** *adj* widely extended; diffusive; causing expansion; worked by expansion; effusive; talkative or communicative; marked by excessive feeling of wellbeing and delusions of self-importance (*psychiatry*). **expans'ively** *adv*. **expans'iveness** *n*. **expansiv'ity** /*eks-*/ *n*.
❑ **expanded metal** *n* steel, etc stretched to form a mesh, used for reinforcing concrete, etc. **expanding metal** *n* a metal or alloy that expands in the final stage of cooling from liquid. **expanding universe** (**theory**) *n* (*astron*) the theory that the whole universe is constantly expanding and the galaxies moving away from each other. **expansion board** or **card** *n* (*comput*) a printed circuit board which can be inserted into an **expansion slot**, a connector on a computer motherboard which allows extra facilities to be added temporarily or permanently. **expansion bolt** *n* a bolt that expands within a hole, crack, etc, thus providing a firm support, eg in mountaineering. **expansion joint** *n* (*engineering*) a gap left at a joint between eg lengths of rail or sections of concrete, to allow for heat expansion.

ex parte /*eks pär'te* or *pär'te*/ (*law*) *adj* on one side only, or in the interests of one party only; partial; prejudiced. [L *ex* from, and *parte*, ablative of *pars, partis* party or side]

expat /*eks'pat*/ (*inf*) *n* and *adj* short for **expatriate**.

expatiate /*eks-pā'shi-āt*/ *vi* to enlarge in discourse, argument or writing; to walk about (*archaic*); to wander at large (*usu fig*). [L *exspatiārī, -ātus*, from *ex* out of, and *spatiārī* to roam, from *spatium* space]
■ **expatia'tion** *n*. **expā'tiative** or **expā'tiatory** *adj* expansive. **expā'tiātor** *n*.

expatriate /*eks-pat'ri-āt* or *-pā'tri*/ *vt* to send out of one's country; to banish or exile (oneself or another); to deprive of citizenship. ◆ *vi* to settle abroad. ◆ *n* and *adj* /*-tri-ət*/ (a person) living in exile, voluntary or compulsory; (a person) living abroad permanently, for financial or other reasons; (a person) working abroad for a period. [LL *expatriāre, -ātum*, from *ex* out of, and *patria* fatherland]
■ **expatriā'tion** *n* the act of expatriating; exile, voluntary or compulsory.

expect /*ik-spekt'*/ *vt* to think of as likely to come or happen, or as due; to suppose; to await (*obs*). ◆ *vi* (*obs*) to wait. ◆ *n* (*Shakesp*) expectation. [L *expectāre, -ātum*, from *ex* out, and *spectāre* to look, frequentative of *specere* to see]
■ **expect'able** *adj*. **expect'ably** *adv*. **expect'ance** or **expect'ancy** *n* the act or state of expecting; something which is expected; hope. **expect'ant** *adj* looking or waiting for something; in expectation; not yet but expecting to be; pregnant. ◆ *n* a person who expects; a person who is looking for or waiting to receive some title or position. **expect'antly** *adv*. **expecta'tion** /*eks-*/ *n* the act or state of expecting; the prospect of future good; that which is or may fairly be expected; that which should happen, according to general norms of custom or behaviour; the degree of probability; the value of something expected; (in *pl*) prospect of fortune or profit by a will. **expect'ative** *adj* giving rise to expectation; reversionary. ◆ *n* an expectancy; an anticipatory grant of a benefice not yet vacant. **expect'ed** *adj*. **expect'edly** *adv*. **expect'er** *n*. **expect'ing** *n* and *adj*. **expect'ingly** *adv* in a state of expectation.
❑ **Expectation Week** *n* (*Christianity, esp C of E*) the period between Ascension Day and Whit Sunday, commemorating the Apostles' expectation of the Holy Spirit.
■ **be expecting** (*inf*) to be pregnant. **life expectancy** or **expectation of life** the average length of time that one may expect to live.

expectorate /*ek-spek'tə-rāt*/ *vt* to expel from the chest, air-passages or lungs by coughing, etc; to spit out. ◆ *vi* to discharge or eject phlegm from the throat; to spit. [L *expectorāre, -ātum*, from *ex* from, and *pectus, pectoris* breast]
■ **expec'torant** *adj* tending to promote expectoration. ◆ *n* a medicine that promotes expectoration. **expectorā'tion** *n* the act of expectorating; something which is expectorated; spittle or phlegm. **expec'torātive** *adj* having the quality of promoting expectoration. **expec'torātor** *n*.

expedient /*iks-* or *ek-spē'di-ənt*/ *adj* suitable or appropriate; profitable or convenient rather than fair or just; advisable; expeditious (*Shakesp*). ◆ *n* a means suitable to an end; something which serves to promote; contrivance or shift. [L *expediēns, -entis*, prp of *expedīre* (see **expedite**)]
■ **expe'dience** *n* haste or despatch (*Shakesp*); enterprise (*Shakesp*); expediency. **expe'diency** *n* appropriateness; desirableness; conduciveness to the need of the moment; something which is opportune; self-interest. **expēdien'tial** /*-en'shl*/ *adj*. **expedien'tially** *adv*. **expē'diently** *adv*.

expeditate /*eks-ped'i-tāt*/ *vt* to deprive of three claws or of the ball of the foot. [LL *expeditāre, -ātum*, from *ex* from, and *pēs, pedis* foot]
■ **expeditā'tion** *n*.

expedite /*eks'pi-dīt*/ *vt* to free from impediments; to hasten; to send forth; to despatch with speed and efficiency. ◆ *adj* (*obs*) free from impediment; unencumbered; quick; prompt. [L *expedīre, -ītum*, from *ex* from, and *pēs, pedis* a foot]
■ **ex'peditely** *adv*. **ex'pediter** or **ex'peditor** *n*. **expedition** /*-di'shən*/ *n* an organized journey to attain some object, such as hunting, warfare, exploration, etc; the party undertaking such a journey; speed; promptness. **expedi'tionary** *adj* belonging to an expedition; of the nature of an expedition. **expedi'tious** *adj* characterized by speed or rapidity; prompt. **expedi'tiously** *adv*. **expedi'tiousness** *n*. **exped'itive** *adj*.

expel /*ik-spel'*/ *vt* (**expell'ing**; **expelled'**) to drive out; to eject; to discharge in disgrace (from school, etc); to banish; to keep off (*Shakesp*). [L *expellere, expulsum*, from *ex* from, and *pellere* to drive]
■ **expell'able** *adj*. **expell'ant** or **expell'ent** *adj* and *n*. **expellee'** *n* a person who is expelled. **expell'er** *n*.

expend /*ik-spend'*/ *vt* to lay out (money); to employ or consume in any way; to spend. [L *expendere*, from *ex-* out, and *pendere, pēnsum* to weigh]
■ **expendabil'ity** *n*. **expend'able** *adj* that may be expended, *esp* that may be sacrificed to achieve some end (also *n*). **expend'ably** *adv*.

expend'er *n.* **expend'iture** *n* the act of expending; something which is expended; the process of using up; money spent. **expense** /-*pens*'/ *n* expenditure; outlay; cost; a payment, debt or amount of an asset used up in the course of business activity during a particular accounting period; (in *pl*) money from one's own pocket spent in the performance of one's job, etc; such money reimbursed by one's company, etc or an allowance made to cover the amount usually spent; (in *pl*) costs in a lawsuit (*Scots law*). ◆ *vt* to treat as an expense for tax purposes; to charge an item as a cost in a profit and loss account (*bookkeeping*). **expens'ive** *adj* causing or requiring much expense; costly; lavish. **expens'ively** *adv.* **expens'iveness** *n.*
❑ **expendable launch vehicle** *n* (*space flight*) a launch system that is made up of expendable stages and has no recoverable parts (*abbrev* **ELV**). **expense** (or **expenses**) **account** *n* an arrangement by which expenses incurred during the performance of an employee's duties are reimbursed by the employer; a statement of such incurred expenses.
▪ **at the expense of** to the cost or detriment of (often **at someone's expense**); with the loss or sacrifice of. **be at the expense of** to pay the cost of.

experience /*ik-spē'ri-əns*/ *n* practical acquaintance with any matter gained by trial; long and varied observation, personal or general; wisdom derived from the changes and trials of life; the passing through any event or course of events by which one is affected; such an event; anything received by the mind, such as sensation, perception or knowledge; test, trial or experiment (*obs*). ◆ *vt* to have practical acquaintance with; to prove or know by use; to have experience of; to feel, suffer or undergo. [Fr *expérience* and L *experientia*, from *experīrī*, from *ex-* (intens), and old verb *perīrī* to try]
▪ **expē'rienceable** *adj.* **expē'rienced** *adj* taught by experience; having much experience; practised and knowledgeable in sexual matters (*facetious*); skilful; wise. **expē'rienceless** *adj* having little or no experience. **expē'riencer** *n.* **expērien'tial** /-*en'shl*/ *adj* relating to or derived from experience. **expērien'tialism** *n* the philosophical doctrine that all knowledge comes from experience. **expērien'tialist** *n.* **expērien'tially** *adv.*
❑ **experience meeting** *n* a meeting for the relating of religious experiences.

experiment /*ik-sper'i-mənt*/ *n* something done to test a theory or to discover something unknown; a trial; experience (*obs*). ◆ *vi* (also /-*ment*'/) to carry out an experiment or trial; to search by trial. ◆ *vt* (*obs*) to make trial of. [L *experīmentum*, from *experīrī* to try thoroughly; see **experience**]
▪ **experiment'al** *adj* relating to experiment; based on or proceeding by experiment; trying out new styles or techniques; tentative; experienced, having experience (*obs*). **experiment'alism** *n* use of or reliance on experiment. **experiment'alist** *n.* **experiment'alize** or **-ise** *vi.* **experiment'ally** *adv.* **experimentā'tion** *n.* **experiment'ative** *adj.* **exper'imented** *adj* (*obs*) experienced; practised. **exper'imenter** (or /-*ment*'/) or **exper'imentist** *n* a person who carries out experiments.
❑ **experimental psychology** *n* the branch of psychology which deals with the scientific study of the basic mechanisms of the mind, eg memory and perception, and of the responses of individuals to stimuli in controlled situations.

experimentum crucis /*ik-sper-i-men'təm kroo'sis* or *ek-spe-ri-men'toom krük'is*/ (*L*) *n* a crucial test.

expert /*eks'pûrt*/ *n* someone who is skilled in any art or science; a specialist; a scientific or professional witness. ◆ *adj* taught by practice; having a thorough knowledge; having a facility of performance (with *at* or *in*); skilful or adroit (with *at* or *in*). ◆ *vt* (*Spenser*) to experience. [Fr, from L *expertus* skilled, from *experīrī* to try thoroughly; see **experience**]
▪ **expertise** /-*ēz'*/ *n* expert knowledge; expertness; expert appraisal or valuation. **ex'pertize** or **-ise** /-*īz*/ *vi* and *vt* to give an expert opinion (on). **ex'pertly** *adv.* **ex'pertness** *n.*
❑ **expert system** *n* (*comput*) a program which enables a specific field of human knowledge to be stored in the form of facts and rules and uses artificial intelligence techniques to make decisions or solve problems.

expiate /*eks'pi-āt*/ *vt* to make complete atonement for. ◆ *adj* (*Shakesp*) expired or at an end. [L *expiāre*, -*ātum*, from *ex-* (intens), and *piāre* to appease or atone for]
▪ **ex'piable** *adj* capable of being expiated, atoned for or done away with. **expiā'tion** *n* the act of expiating; the means by which atonement is made; atonement. **ex'piator** *n.* **ex'piatory** /-*ə*- or -*ā-tər-i*/ *adj.*

expire /*iks-* or *ek-spīr'*/ *vt* to breathe out; to emit; to bring to an end (*Spenser*). ◆ *vi* to breathe out; to die; to come to an end; to lapse; to become invalid by lapse of time; to fulfil a term (*Spenser*). [Fr *expirer*, from L *ex* from, and *spīrāre*, -*ātum* to breathe]
▪ **expī'rable** *adj* that may expire or come to an end. **expī'rant** *n* someone expiring. **expirā'tion** /*eks-pi-* or -*pī-*/ *n* the act of breathing

out; death (*obs*); end; something which is expired. **expī'ratory** *adj* relating to expiration or the emission of the breath. **expīred'** *adj* dead; extinct; lapsed; obsolete. **expī'ring** *adj* dying; relating to or uttered at the time of dying. **expī'ry** *n* the end or termination, *esp* by lapse of time; expiration.

expiscate /*ek-spis'kāt*/ (*Scot*) *vt* to find out by skilful means or by strict examination. [L *expiscārī*, *expiscātus*, from *ex* from, and *piscārī* to fish, from *piscis* a fish]
▪ **expiscā'tion** *n.* **expis'catory** *adj.*

explain /*ik-splān'*/ *vt* to make plain or intelligible; to unfold and illustrate the meaning of; to expound; to account for. ◆ *vi* to give an explanation. [L *explānāre*, from *ex-* out, and *plānāre* to level, from *plānus* flat or plain]
▪ **explain'able** *adj.* **explain'er** *n.* **explanā'tion** /*eks-plə-nā'shən*/ *n* the act of explaining or clearing from obscurity; that which explains or clears up; the meaning or sense given to anything; a mutual clearing up of matters, reconciliation. **explan'atorily** /*iks-plan'ə-tər-i-li*/ *adv.* **explan'atory** or **explan'ative** *adj* serving to explain or clear up; containing explanations.
▪ **explain away** to modify the force of by explanation, generally in a bad sense.

explantation /*eks-plän-tā'shən*/ *n* the growing in an artificial medium of a part or organ removed from a living individual. [L *explantāre*, from *ex-* out, and *plantāre* to plant]
▪ **explant'** *n* and *vt.*

expletive /*ek-*, *ik-splē'tiv* or *eks'pli-tiv*/ *adj* filling out; added merely to fill up (a line of verse). ◆ *n* a swear-word of any kind; a meaningless oath; a word or anything present merely to fill a gap; a word inserted to fill up a sentence or line of verse; a meaningless word serving a grammatical purpose only. [L *explētivus*, from *ex* out, and *plēre* to fill]
▪ **explē'tory** (also /*eks'pli-*/) *adj* serving to fill up; expletive; supplementary.

explicate /*eks'pli-kāt*/ *vt* to unfold or develop (a theory, etc); to lay open or explain the meaning of. [L *explicāre*, *explicātum* or *explicitum*, from *ex* out, and *plicāre* to fold]
▪ **explic'able** (or /*eks'*/) *adj* capable of being explicated or explained. **explicā'tion** *n* the act of explicating or explaining; explanation. **explic'ative** or **explic'atory** (or /*eks'*/) *adj* serving to explicate or explain. **ex'plicātor** *n.*

explication de texte /*ek-splē-ka-syɔ̃' də tekst'*/ *n* a method of literary criticism based on a detailed analysis of the text of the work. [Fr, (literally) explication of (the) text]

explicit¹ /*ik-splis'it*/ *adj* not merely implied but distinctly stated; plain in language; outspoken; clear; unreserved. [See ety for **explicate**]
▪ **explic'itly** *adv.* **explic'itness** *n.*

explicit² /*eks'pli-sit*/ (*obs*) *n* a conclusion. [From the medieval custom of writing *explicit* at the end of a book or section: orig appar for L *explicitum est* it is completed, later taken to be 3rd pers sing pr indic, and supplied with a plural *expliciunt* ; see **explicate**]

explode /*ik-splōd'*/ *vt* to cause to blow up; to bring into disrepute and reject; to cry down or boo off (eg an actor) (*archaic*). ◆ *vi* to burst with violence and *usu* a loud noise; to burst out or break forth suddenly; of population, to increase suddenly and rapidly. [L *explōdere*, *explōsum*, from *ex* from, and *plaudere* to clap the hands]
▪ **explō'ded** *adj* blown up; (of a theory, etc) rejected because proved false; (of a drawing or diagram of a machine, building, organism, etc) showing the internal structure and separate parts and their relationship. **explō'der** *n.* **explō'sible** *adj* liable to explode. **explō'sion** /-*zhən*/ *n* the act of exploding; a sudden violent burst with a loud noise; an outburst; breaking out of feelings, etc; a great and rapid increase or expansion, as in *population explosion*; release of breath after stoppage in articulating a stop consonant in certain positions. **explō'sive** /-*siv* or -*ziv*/ *adj* causing or liable to cause an explosion; worked, set in place, etc by an explosion; bursting out with violence and noise; likely to result in violence or an outburst of feeling. ◆ *n* something that will explode, *esp* a substance *specif* created to do so; a stop consonant pronounced with explosion (*phonetics*). **explō'sively** *adv.* **explō'siveness** *n.*
❑ **exploding star** *n* a star that flares up, such as a nova or supernova. **explosion shot** *n* a golf stroke to send a ball in a high trajectory out of a bunker by striking the sand behind the ball with a strong swing of the club. **explosion welding** *n* the welding of metals with very different melting points by means of pressure produced by an explosion. **explosive bolt** *n* a bolt that can be blown out of position because it contains a small explosive charge. **explosive rivet** *n* a rivet fixed in inaccessible places by detonation of a small charge in its end.

exploit /*eks'ploit*/ *n* a deed or achievement, *esp* a heroic one; a feat. ◆ *vt* /*iks-ploit'*/ to work or make available; to turn or adapt to use; to benefit from or at the expense of. [OFr *exploit*, from L *explicitum* unfolded; see **explicate**]

■ **exploit'able** *adj*. **exploit'age** *n*. **exploita'tion** /eks-/ *n* the use of industrial processes to acquire natural resources, such as the working of mines, etc; the setting-up and getting into production of an oilfield, mine, etc; the act of using for selfish purposes. **exploit'ative** or **exploit'ive** *adj*. **exploit'er** *n*.

❑ **exploitable girth** *n* the minimum girth at breast height at or above which trees are considered suitable for felling or for other specified purpose.

explore /ik-splör'/ *vt* and *vi* to search or travel through for the purpose of discovery; to examine thoroughly. [Fr, from L *explōrāre*, *-ātum* to search out]

■ **explora'tion** /eks-/ *n* the act of searching or searching for (something) thoroughly; travel for the sake of discovery; examination of a region's geology, etc in a search for mineral resources. **explora'tional** *adj*. **explora'tionist** *n* a scientist engaged in mineral exploration. **explor'ative** or **explor'atory** /-or'/ *adj* serving to explore or investigate; searching out. **explor'er** *n* a person who explores, *esp* a member of a geological, etc exploration; (with *cap*) any of the first series of US satellites. **explor'ing** *adj*.

explosion see under **explode**.

expo /eks'pō/ *n* (*pl* **ex'pos**) an exhibition or public showing. [*exposition*]

exponent /ek-spō'nant/ *n* an interpreter of an art by performance; an example, illustration or type (of); an expounder (of); a symbol showing what power a quantity is raised to, an index (*maths*). ◆ *adj* setting forth; expounding. [L *expōnēns*, *-entis* setting forth, from *ex-* out, and *pōnere* to place]

■ **exponential** /eks-pō-nen'shl/ *adj* relating to or involving exponents; (loosely) of a rate of increase, increasingly steep. ◆ *n* an exponential function. **exponen'tially** *adv*.

❑ **exponential curve** *n* a curve expressed by an exponential equation. **exponential equation** *n* one in which the variable occurs in the exponent of one or more terms. **exponential function** *n* a quantity with a variable exponent, *esp* e^x, where *e* is the base of natural logarithms. **exponential growth** *n* a stage of growth occurring in populations of unicellular micro-organisms when the logarithm of the cell number increases linearly with time. **exponential series** *n* a series in which exponential quantities are developed. **exponential theorem** *n* a theorem that gives a value of any number in terms of its natural logarithm, and from which can at once be derived a series determining the logarithm.

exponible /ek-spō'ni-bl/ *adj* able to be, or requiring to be, explained. [L *expōnere* (see **exponent**)]

export /ek-spört'/ *vt* to carry or send out of a country (eg goods in commerce); to save (a file) in a format that can be used in other programs (*comput*). ◆ *n* /eks'pört/ the act of exporting; something which is exported; a commodity which is or may be sent from one country to another as a business transaction; a type of strong brown beer. [L *exportāre*, *-ātum*, from *ex-* out of, and *portāre* to carry]

■ **exportabil'ity** *n*. **export'able** *adj*. **exporta'tion** *n*. **export'er** *n*.

❑ **Export Credit Guarantee Department** *n* a government department which insures UK exporters against losses arising from exporting goods (*abbrev* **ECGD**). **export multiplier** *n* (*commerce*) the ongoing or multiplying effect on a country's national income of a rise or fall in its exports. **export reject** *n* a manufactured article that is flawed in some way and so not passed for export, often sold at a reduced price on the home market.

■ **invisible exports** such items in a national trade balance as money spent by tourists from abroad, etc (as opposed to **visible exports**, goods sold abroad by traders).

expose /ik-spōz'/ *vt* to lay out to view; to deprive of cover, protection or shelter; to make bare; to abandon (a child or animal); to submit (to an influence, such as light or weather); to put up (for sale); to explain (*archaic*); to disclose; to show up. ◆ *n* (*US*) an exposé. [Fr *exposer*, from L *ex-* out, and *pausāre* to rest, confused with *expōnere* to expose; see **exponent** and **exposition**, and *cf* **pose**¹, **compose**, **repose**, etc]

■ **expōs'able** *adj*. **expōs'al** *n* exposure; exposition. **exposé** /eks-pō'zā/ *n* an article or programme exposing crime, scandal, etc to public notice; a formal statement or exposition; an exposing; a shameful showing up. **exposed'** *adj* unprotected; shelterless. **expōs'edness** *n* the state of being exposed. **expōs'er** *n*. **exposure** /-pō'zhər or -zhyər/ *n* the act of laying open or bare; subjection to an influence; the harmful effects on the body of extreme cold; the act of allowing access of light, or a section of film, etc which has been exposed to light (*photog*); the combination of duration of such access (shutter speed) with lens aperture chosen for the taking of a photograph; the act of showing up an evil; a state of being laid bare; openness to danger; in finance, a vulnerable, overextended

commitment or position; a shelterless state; position with regard to the sun, influence of climate, etc; appearance in public, *esp* on television; the total number of potential viewers, listeners, readers, etc of a particular advertising medium.

❑ **exposure meter** *n* (*photog*) an instrument, now often incorporated in the camera, for measuring the light falling on or reflected from a subject.

■ **expose oneself** to expose one's sexual organs in public.

exposition /eks-pō-zish'ən or -pə-/ *n* the act of exposing; a setting out to public view; the abandonment of a child; a public exhibition; (also **expo**) a large international public exhibition or display, *esp* of industrial products (*commerce*); the act of expounding; explanation; commentary; an expository discourse; the enunciation of themes in a composition; that part of a sonata, fugue, etc in which themes are presented (*music*). [L *expositiō*, *-ōnis*, and *expositor*, *-ōris*, from *expōnere*, *expositum* to expose or set forth; see **expound**]

■ **exposit'ional** *adj*. **expositive** /-poz'/ *adj* serving to expose or explain; explanatory; exegetical. **expos'itively** *adv*. **expos'itor** *n* (also *fem* **expos'itress**) someone who or something which expounds; an interpreter. **expos'itory** *adj* serving to explain; explanatory. **exposture** /-pos'chər/ *n* (*Shakesp*) exposure.

ex post facto /eks pōst fak'tō/ retrospective; retrospectively. [L, literally from what is done or enacted after]

expostulate /iks-pos'tū-lāt/ *vi* to remonstrate; to discuss or reason (with); to discuss (*Shakesp*); to claim (*Milton*). [L *expostulāre*, *-ātum*, from *ex-* (intens), and *postulāre* to demand]

■ **expostulā'tion** *n*. **expost'ūlative** (or /-ə-tiv/) or **expost'ūlatory** (or /-ə-tər-i/) *adj* containing expostulation. **expost'ūlator** *n*.

exposture see under **exposition**.

exposure see under **expose**.

expound /ik-spownd'/ *vt* to expose or lay open the meaning of; to explain; to interpret; to explain in a certain way. ◆ *vi* to speak, talk informatively or pass comment (on), often at length. [OFr *espondre*, from L *expōnere*, from *ex-* out, and *pōnere* to place]

■ **expound'er** *n*.

express /ik-spres'/ *vt* to put into words; to symbolize; to state explicitly; to press or force out; to emit; to represent or make known by a likeness, words, signs, symbols, etc; to reveal; to designate; to dispatch rapidly. ◆ *adj* clearly brought out; exactly representing; directly stated; explicit; clear; intended or sent for a particular purpose; expeditious, *esp* of or sent by special messenger service, etc. ◆ *adv* with haste; specially; by express train or messenger; by express. ◆ *n* a regular and quick conveyance; a system for the speedy transmission of messages or goods; an express train; an express messenger; a messenger or vehicle sent on a special errand; a special message; an express rifle. [L *exprimere*, *expressum*, from *ex* from, and *premere*, *pressum* to press; partly through Fr *exprès*, etc]

■ **express'age** *n* the system of carrying by express; the charge for doing so. **express'er** *n*. **express'ible** *adj*. **expression** /-presh'ən/ *n* the act, mode or power of representing or giving utterance; representation or revelation by language, art, the features, etc; the manner in which anything is expressed; a word or phrase; a symbol; intonation; due indication of feeling in performance of music, etc; the act of forcing out by pressure; the production of protein by a gene (*biol*). **express'ional** *adj* of or relating to expression. **express'ionism** *n* (often with *cap*) in literature and painting, a revolt against impressionism, turning away from the representation of external reality to the expression of the artist's emotions and reactions to experience. **express'ionist** *n* and *adj* (often with *cap*). **expressionis'tic** *adj*. **expressionis'tically** *adv*. **express'ionless** *adj*. **express'ionlessly** *adv*. **express'ionlessness** *n*. **express'ive** *adj* serving to express or indicate; full of expression; vividly representing (with *of*); emphatic; significant. **express'ively** *adv*. **express'iveness** *n*. **expressiv'ity** *n* the quality of being able to express; the amount of protein produced by a gene (*biol*). **express'ly** *adv* explicitly; for the express purpose; definitely. **express'ness** *n*. **expressure** /eks-presh'ər/ *n* pressing out; expression (*Shakesp*); representation (*Shakesp*).

❑ **express agency** or **company** *n* one that undertakes speedy transmission of goods. **express delivery** *n* immediate delivery by special messenger; delivery by express agency. **express fee** *n* a fee for express delivery. **expression mark** *n* a direction written on a piece of music (*usu* in Italian). **expression stop** *n* a stop in a harmonium by which the performer can regulate the air to produce expression. **expression vector** *n* in genetic manipulation, a vector that is specially constructed so that a large amount of the protein product, coded by an inserted sequence, can be made. **express letter**, **packet**, **parcel**, etc *n* one sent by special messenger. **express'man** *n* (*esp old US*) someone working in express delivery. **express messenger** *n* a special messenger delivering goods faster than the standard service. **express rifle** *n* a rifle for big game at short range, with a heavy charge of powder and a light bullet. **express term** n (law) an oral or written undertaking in a contract which has been expressly agreed by the parties. **express train** n a train which travels at high speed and with few stops. **express'way** n (N Am) a motorway.

■ **express oneself** to give expression to one's thoughts, ideas and opinions.

expressis verbis /ek-spres' is vûr' bis or ek-spres'ēs ver' bĕs or wer' / (L) in express terms.

expresso /ek-spres'ō/ n and adj same as **espresso**.

exprobrate /eks'prō-brāt/ (archaic) vt to reproach with; to upbraid. [L exprobrāre, -ātum, from pfx ex- (indicating source), and probrum disgrace]

■ **exprobrā'tion** n. **exprō'brative** adj. **exprō'bratory** adj.

ex professo /eks prə-fes'ō or pro-/ (L) avowedly.

expromission /ek-spro-mish'ən/ (law) n the intervention of a new debtor, substituted for the former one, who is consequently discharged by the creditor. [L exprōmittere, -missum to promise to pay, from ex- (intens), and prōmittere to promise]

■ **expromissor** /-mis'ər/ n.

expropriate /iks- or eks-prō'pri-āt/ vt to dispossess (of property), esp for use by the state. [L expropriāre, -ātum, from ex from, and proprium property]

■ **exprō'priable** adj. **expropriā'tion** n. **exprō'priator** n.

ex propriis /eks prō'pri-is, prō'prē-ēs or pro'/ (L) from one's own resources.

ex proprio motu /eks prō'pri-ō mō'tū or pro'pri-ō mō'too/ (LL) of his or her own accord.

expugn /ik-spūn'/ vt to take by storm; to storm; to overcome. [L expugnāre]

■ **expugnable** /-pug' or -pū'nə-bl/ adj capable of being taken or vanquished. **expugnā'tion** /-pug-/ n.

expulse /ik-spuls'/ (obs) vt to expel forcibly or eject. [L expulsāre, frequentative of expellere (see **expel**)]

■ **expul'sion** n the act of expelling or state of being expelled; banishment. **expul'sive** adj able or serving to expel.

expunge /ik-spunj'/ or (archaic) **expunct** /-pungkt'/ vt to wipe out; to efface; to mark for deletion. [L expungere, -punctum to mark for deletion by a row of dots, from ex- out, and pungere to prick]

■ **expunc'tion** /-pungk'shən/ n. **expunge'ment** n. **expun'ger** n.

expurgate /eks'pûr-gāt, also -pûr'/ vt to purge out or make pure; to revise (a book, etc) by removing anything supposed to be offensive, harmful or erroneous. [L expurgāre, -ātum, from ex- out, and purgāre to purge]

■ **expurgā'tion** n the act of expurgating or purifying; the removal of anything hurtful or evil; bowdlerizing; exculpation. **expurgator** /eks'pûr-gā-tər or eks-pûr'gə-tər/ n someone who expurgates or purifies. **expurgato'rial** /-gə-tö'ri-əl/ or **expur'gatory** adj relating to expurgation; tending to expurgate or purify. **expurge** /-pûrj'/ vt to purify or expurgate.

exquisite /eks-kwiz'it, also eks'/ adj of the most delicate and intricate workmanship; of the highest excellence; attracting the highest admiration; of delicate perception or close discrimination; not easily satisfied; fastidious; intense or extreme, as of pain or pleasure; delicious; far-fetched (Shakesp); abstruse (obs). ◆ n a person who is obsessively or fashionably exact or fastidious in dress; a dandy. [L exquīsītus, from ex out, and quaerere to seek]

■ **exquis'itely** adv. **exquis'iteness** n.

ex quocunque capite /eks kwō-kun'kwi kap'i-tē or kwō-koon'kwe kap'i-te/ (L) from whatever source.

exr abbrev : executor.

ex re nata (L) same as **e re nata**.

exrx abbrev : executrix.

exsanguinous /iks-sang'gwi-nəs/ or **exsanguine** /-gwin/ adj (also **exsang'uined** and **exsanguin'eous**) without blood; anaemic. [L ex- without, and sanguis, -inis blood]

■ **exsang'uinate** vt (med) to drain of blood. **exsanguinā'tion** n. **exsanguin'ity** n.

exscind /ik-sind'/ vt to cut off. [L ex from, and scindere to cut]

exsect /ik-sekt'/ vt to cut out. [L ex from, and secāre, sectum to cut]

■ **exsec'tion** n.

exsert /ik-sûrt'/ vt to protrude. [L exserere, -sertum; see **exert**]

■ **exsert'ed** adj projecting. **exser'tile** /-tīl or (US) -til/ adj. **exser'tion** n.

ex-service /eks-sûr'vis/ adj having formerly served in one of the armed services.

❑ **ex-ser'viceman** or **ex-ser'vicewoman** n.

exsiccate /ek'si-kāt/ vt to dry up. [L exsiccāre, from ex- out, and siccus dry]

■ **exsicc'ant** adj. **exsiccā'tion** n. **exsicc'ative** (or /ek'si-kāt-/) adj. **ex'siccātor** n a drying agent or apparatus.

ex silentio /eks si-len'sh(y)ō or si-len'ti-ō/ (L) based on a lack of contrary evidence.

exstipulate /ik-stip'ū-lāt/ (bot) adj without stipules (also **estip'ulate**).

exsuccous /ik-suk'əs/ adj sapless. [L exsuccus, from ex- out, and succus juice]

ext. abbrev : extension; exterior; external or externally; extinct; extra; extract.

ex tacito /eks tas'i-tō or tak'i-tō/ (L) silently.

extant /iks-tant' or eks'tənt/ adj standing out, or above the rest (archaic); still standing or existing; surviving. [L extāns, -antis, from ex- out, and stāre to stand]

extasy and **extatic** obsolete forms of **ecstasy** and **ecstatic**.

extempore /iks-tem'pə-ri/ adv on the spur of the moment; without preparation; suddenly. ◆ adj composed and delivered or performed impromptu; without the help of written notes; rising at the moment; sudden. ◆ n (obs) an impromptu speech, etc. [L ex out of, and tempore, ablative of tempus time]

■ **extem'poral** adj. **extemporaneity** /-ə-nē'i-ti/ n. **extemporā'neous** adj impromptu; temporary or improvised; (of drugs) prepared in a pharmacy for immediate use. **extemporā'neously** adv. **extemporā'neousness** n. **extem'porarily** adv. **extem'porariness** n. **extem'porary** adj done on the spur of the moment; hastily prepared; speaking extempore; done without preparation; offhand. **extemporizā'tion** or **-s-** n. **extem'porize** or **-ise** vt or vi to speak, or compose and play, extempore or without previous preparation; to make (a speech) without notes; to improvise (a solution, etc).

extend /iks-tend'/ vt to stretch out; to prolong in any direction; to enlarge; to expand; to widen; to unfold; to straighten out; to hold out; to offer or accord; to exert to the full; to seize (law; hist); to value or assess. ◆ vi to stretch or reach; to be continued in space or time. [L extendere, extentum or extēnsum, from ex- out, and tendere to stretch]

■ **extendabil'ity** n. **extend'able** adj. **extend'ant** adj (heraldry) displayed. **extend'ed** adj occupying space; having extension; stretched out; extensive. **extend'edly** adv. **extend'er** n someone or something that extends; a university extension lecture; a substance added to paint to give body, or to food to give extra bulk. **extendibil'ity** n. **extend'ible** adj. **extense** /-tens'/ adj (obs) extensive. **extensibil'ity** n. **extens'ible** or **extensile** /eks-ten'sīl or -sil/ adj that may be extended. **extensificā'tion** n an agricultural policy within the European Union by which land is farmed less intensively and savings made in expenditure on feed, fertilizers and pesticides to balance lower production. **extension** /iks- or eks-ten'shən/ n an act of extending; the condition of being extended; an added piece; a wing or annex of a house; the property of occupying space; the extent of the application of a term or the number of objects included under it, opp to intension (logic); a word or words added to subject, predicate or object (grammar); an extension lead; an additional telephone using the same line as the main one. **exten'sional** adj. **exten'sionalism** or **extensional'ity** n. **exten'sionally** adv. **exten'sionist** n an advocate of extension; a university extension lecturer or student. **extens'ity** n massiveness or spatial quality in sensation from which perception of extension is derived. **extens'ive** adj large; widespread; comprehensive; /eks-/ relating to extension; seeking or deriving a comparatively small crop cheaply from a wide area, opp to intensive (agric). **extens'ively** adv. **extens'iveness** n. **extensivizā'tion** or **-s-** n the extensive method of agriculture (see also **extensification** above). **extensom'eter** or **extensim'eter** /eks-/ n an instrument for measuring small changes in length, etc in metal to which tension has been applied. **exten'sor** n a muscle that extends or straightens any part of the body. **extent'** n the space or degree to which a thing is extended; bulk; compass; scope; degree or amount (as in to some extent); a stretch or extended space; a valuation of property; (before 1947) a writ directing the sheriff to seize the property of a debtor, for the recovery of debts of record due to the Crown (law); seizure (Shakesp); attack (Shakesp); an act of extending (justice, courtesy, etc) (Shakesp). ◆ adj stretched out.

❑ **extended credit** n a form of purchase where the goods become the property of the buyer immediately, as opposed to hire purchase where ownership is not transferred until the last payment is made. **extended family** n a social unit comprising not only a couple and their children but other relatives, eg aunts, uncles and grandparents. **extended memory** n (comput) in MS-DOS, extra memory beyond the first megabyte, accessible through a memory manager. **exten'ded-play** adj (of a gramophone record) giving longer reproduction because of a closer groove and the use of a larger part of its surface area. **extensible markup language** n (comput) text formatting instructions designed to aid data searching and the formatting of results (*abbrev* **XML**). **extension lead** *n* a length of electrical cable with a plug at one end and a socket at the other, which can be used to connect an appliance when the electrical supply is some distance away. **extension tube** *n* a tube fitted between the body of a camera and its lens to allow closer focus.

■ **university extension** the enlargement of the aim of a university, in providing extramural instruction for those unable to become regular students.

extenuate /iks-ten'ū-āt/ *vt* to lessen; to weaken the force of; to palliate; to underrate; to make thin. [L *extenuāre, -ātum*, from *ex-* (intens), and *tenuis* thin]

■ **exten'ūāting** *n* and *adj* palliating. **exten'ūātingly** *adv*. **extenūā'tion** the act of representing anything as less wrong or criminal than it seems; palliation; mitigation. **exten'ūātive** or **exten'ūatory** *adj* tending to extenuate; palliative. **exten'ūātor** *n*.

exterior /eks-tē'ri-ər/ *adj* outer; outward or external; on or from the outside; foreign, involving or dealing with foreign nations. ◆ *n* the outside or outer surface; outward form or presentation; appearance; an outdoor scene in a cinema film, television drama, etc; an outer part (*esp* in *pl*). [L *exterior*, compar of *exter, exterus* outward, from *ex* from]

■ **extēriority** /-or'i-ti/ *n*. **exteriorizā'tion** or **-s-** *n*. **extēr'iorize** or **-ise** *vt* to externalise; to bring an internal part temporarily outside the body (*surg*). **extē'riorly** *adv* outwardly.

□ **exterior angle** *n* (*maths*) the angle between any extended side and the adjacent side of a polygon.

exterminate /iks-tûr'mi-nāt/ *vt* to destroy utterly; to put an end to; to root out; to drive out (*obs*). [L *extermināre, -ātum* to drive beyond the boundary, from *ex* out of, and *terminus* boundary]

■ **exter'minable** *adj* that can be exterminated; illimitable (*Shelley*). **extermina'tion** *n* complete destruction or eradication. **exter'minātive** or **exter'minatory** *adj* serving or tending to exterminate. **exter'minātor** *n*. **exter'mine** *vt* (*Shakesp*) to exterminate.

external /eks-tûr'nəl/ *adj* exterior; lying outside; outward; belonging to the world of outward things; that may be seen; not innate or intrinsic; accidental; foreign or involving foreign nations. ◆ *n* exterior; an external examination or examiner; (in *pl*) the outward parts; (in *pl*) outward or non-essential forms and ceremonies; (in *pl*) outward circumstances or appearances. [L *externus* outward, from *exter* outside]

■ **extern'** or **externe'** *adj* (*obs*) external or outward. ◆ *n* a non-resident, such as a day-scholar, an out-patient, or a non-resident physician or surgeon. **exter'nalism** *n* undue regard to mere externals or non-essential outward forms, *esp* of religion; the doctrine that holds that the content of thoughts depends on relationships with objects external to the mind (*philos*). **exter'nalist** *n* and *adj*. **externality** /-nal'i-ti/ *n* external character; superficiality; undue regard to externals. **externalizā'tion** or **-s-** *n*. **exter'nalize** or **-ise** *vt* to give form or apparent reality to; to give external expression to; to assign (one's feelings) to things outside oneself (*psychol*); to ascribe to causes outside oneself; to regard as consisting of externals only. **exter'nally** *adv*. **externat** /eks-ter-nä/ *n* (*Fr*) a day school.

□ **external-combustion engine** *n* one in which the fuel is burned outside the working cylinder. **external examination** *n* an examination set and marked by an authority outside one's school or university. **external examiner** *n* an examiner from another institution who has had no part in teaching the examinees. **external store** or **storage** *n* (*comput*) any portable storage medium, eg magnetic disks. **external student** *n* one examined (for an **external degree**) by a university in which he or she has not studied.

exteroceptor /eks'tə-rō-sep-tər/ (*zool*) *n* a sensory organ, eg the eye, which receives impressions from outside the body. [L *exterus* exterior, and *receptor*]

■ **exterocep'tion** *n*. **exterocep'tive** *adj*. **exteroceptiv'ity** *n*.

exterritorial, etc /eks-ter-i-tö'ri-əl/ same as **extraterritorial**, etc under **extra-**.

extinct /iks-tingkt'/ *adj* put out; extinguished, quenched or squashed; no longer existing; (of a volcano) no longer erupting; obsolete; dead. [L *ex(s)tinctum* (see **extinguish**)]

■ **extinct'ed** *adj* (*Shakesp*) extinguished. **extinc'tion** *n* the state of being extinct; extinguishing, quenching or wiping out; destruction; suppression; the cutting off of polarized light at certain angles when a section of a doubly refracting mineral is rotated between crossed nicols; the absorbing by the earth's atmosphere of a planet's or star's light (*astron*); the inhibition of a conditioned reflex (*psychol*). **extinct'ive** *adj* tending to extinguish. **extinct'ure** *n* (*Shakesp*) extinction.

extine /eks'tin, -tēn* or *-tīn/ (*bot*) *n* the outer membrane of a pollen grain or spore (also **ex'ine**). [From the root of L *exter, extimus* outer or outermost]

extinguish /iks-ting'gwish/ *vt* to quench or put out; to make extinct; to put an end to; to destroy or annihilate; to obscure by superior splendour; to pay off (a debt) (*law*). ◆ *vi* to die out. [L *ex(s)tinguere, ex(s)tinctum*, from *ex-* out, and *stinguere* to quench]

■ **exting'uishable** *adj*. **exting'uishant** *n* a substance used to extinguish fires. **exting'uisher** *n* someone or something that extinguishes; a small hollow conical instrument for putting out a candle, etc; a device for putting out fire; a conical structure resembling a candle extinguisher. **exting'uishment** *n* the act of extinguishing; putting an end to a right by consolidation or union (*law; hist*).

extirpate /eks'tər-pāt/ *vt* to root out; to destroy totally; to remove surgically; to exterminate (*Spenser, Shakesp* **extirp** /eks-tûrp'/). [L *exstirpāre, -ātum*, from *ex-* out, and *stirps* a stock or root]

■ **extirpable** /eks-tûrp'ə-bl/ *adj*. **extirpā'tion** *n* extermination; total destruction. **ex'tirpative** *adj*. **ex'tirpātor** *n* someone who extirpates; an implement for weeding. **extirpatory** /eks-tûrp'ə-tər-i/ *adj*.

extol /iks-tōl'* or *-tol'/ *vt* (**extoll'ing; extolled'** (*Spenser* **extold'**)) to lift up (*Spenser*); to praise highly. [L *extollere*, from *ex-* up, and *tollere* to lift or raise]

■ **extoll'er** *n*. **extol'ment** *n* the act of extolling; the state of being extolled.

extort /iks-tört'/ *vt* to wring out; to gain or draw out (money, a promise, etc) by compulsion or violence. ◆ *adj* extorted; wrongfully obtained. [L *extorquēre, extortum*, from *ex-* out, and *torquēre* to twist]

■ **extors'ive** *adj* serving or tending to extort. **extors'ively** *adv*. **extort'er** *n*. **extortion** /-tör'shən/ *n* illegal securing of money by compulsion or violence; something which is extorted. **extor'tionary** *adj* relating to or implying extortion. **extor'tionate** *adj* (of a price) extremely high; (of a person) using extortion; oppressive; exacting, demanding too much. **extor'tionately** *adv*. **extor'tionist** or **extor'tioner** *n* someone who practises extortion. **extort'ive** *adj*.

extra¹ /eks'trə/ *adj* beyond or more than the usual or the necessary; extraordinary; additional. ◆ *adv* unusually or exceptionally. ◆ *n* what is extra or additional, such as an item above and beyond the ordinary school curriculum, something over and above the usual course or charge in a bill, etc; a special edition of a newspaper containing later news; a run scored at cricket from a bye, leg-bye, wide or no-ball (not hit); a person temporarily engaged for a minor part in a film, etc, eg to be one of a crowd. [Prob contracted from **extraordinary**]

□ **extra-condensed'** *adj* (*printing*) extremely narrow in proportion to the height. **extra cover** *n* in cricket, a fielding position on the offside between cover point and mid-off, or a player in this position. **extra jam** or **marmalade** *n* under EU regulations, jam or marmalade containing a considerably higher percentage (by weight) of fruit than that in ordinary jam or marmalade. **extra-spec'ial** *adj* very special. ◆ *n* a special late edition of an evening newspaper called for by some news of great importance. **extra time** *n* additional time allowed at the end of a match because of time lost through injury, etc, or to achieve a decisive result when the score is level. **extra virgin** or **extra-virgin** *adj* (of olive oil) of the best quality, extracted by pressing, not by chemical processes.

extra² /eks'trə* or *eks'trä/ (*L*) *prep* outside.

■ **extra modum** /mō'dəm* or *mo'dūm/ beyond measure, extravagant. **extra muros** /mū'rōs* or *moo'rōs/ beyond the walls.

extra- /ek-strə-/ *pfx* outside. [L *extrā* outside]

■ **extra-ax'illary** *adj* (*bot*) not in the axil of a leaf. **extracanon'ical** *adj* not part of the canon of the Bible. **extracell'ular** *adj* (*biol*) outside the cell walls. **extracell'ularly** *adv*. **extracorpor'eal** *adj* outside the body. **extra-curric'ular** *adj* of a subject or activity, outside and additional to the regular academic course; additional to ordinary responsibilities or routine, etc. **extra-curric'ularly** *adv*. **extradō'tal** *adj* not forming part of the dowry. **extradū'ral** *adj* and *n* same as **epidural**. **extraflo'ral** *adj* not in a flower; situated outside a flower. **extraforā'neous** *adj* outdoor. **extragalac'tic** *adj* (*astron*) outside our galaxy. **extra-ill'ustrate** (or /-lus'-/) *vt* to illustrate from other printed books, to grangerize. **extra-illustrā'tion** *n*. **extrajudi'cial** *adj* not made in court, beyond the usual course of legal proceeding. **extrajudi'cially** *adv*. **extralim'ital**, also **extralim'itary** *adj* (*zool*) not found within a given faunal area; lying outside a prescribed area. **extramar'ital** *adj* (of sexual relations, etc) outside marriage. **extramar'itally** *adv*. **extramet'rical** *adj* (*prosody*) in excess of the prescribed number of syllables in the line. **extramun'dane** *adj* beyond the material world. **extramū'ral** *adj* beyond the walls; connected with a university but not under its direct control. **extramū'rally** *adv*. **ex'tranet** *n* (*comput*) an area of an organization's intranet site that may be accessed by certain privileged users outside the organization. **extranū'clear** *adj* (*biol*) outside the nucleus (of a cell or an atom). **extra-parō'chial** *adj* beyond the limits of a parish. **extra-phys'ical** *adj* not subject to physical laws. **extra-profess'ional** *adj* not belonging to a particular profession;

outside the usual limits of professional duty or practice. **extra-provin'cial** adj outside the limits of a particular province. **extra-reg'ular** adj unlimited by rules. **extrasen'sory** adj outside the ordinary senses, as in **extrasensory perception** the ability to perceive without the normal senses (cf **sixth sense**). **extra-sō'lar** adj beyond the solar system. **extraterres'trial** adj outside, or from outside, the earth (also n). **extraterrito'rial** adj outside a territory or territorial jurisdiction (also **exterritor'ial**). **extraterritorial'ity** n the privilege of being outside the jurisdiction of the country one is in (also **exterritorial'ity**). **extratrop'ical** adj outside the tropics. **extra-ū'terine** adj outside the uterus. **extravas'cular** adj (biol) outside the vascular system or a blood vessel. **extravehic'ular** adj situated, used or happening outside a spacecraft.

extract /iks- or eks-trakt'/ vt to draw out by force or otherwise; to choose or select; to find out; to derive (pleasure, etc); to extort; to obtain an officially certified copy of (Scots law); to copy passages from; to publish passages from; to obtain by chemical or physical means from containing or combined matter; to exhaust or treat by extraction; to find (the root of a quantity) by a mathematical process. ◆ adj (obs except Scots law) extracted; derived. ◆ n /eks'trakt/ anything drawn from a substance by heat, distillation, solvents, etc as an essence; a passage taken from a book or writing; an officially certified copy of a court order, decree or deed (Scots law); wool obtained from rags from which cotton has been chemically removed. [L extrahere, extractum, from ex from, and trahere to draw]
■ **extractabil'ity** n. **extract'able** or **extract'ible** adj. **extract'ant** n (chem) a solvent used for extraction. **extrac'tion** n the act of extracting; derivation from a stock or family; birth; lineage; something which is extracted. **extract'ive** adj tending or serving to extract; of the nature of an extract. ◆ n an extract. **extract'or** n someone or something that extracts; (also **extractor fan**) an electric fan which extracts air, gas, etc from a room or building.
□ **extractive industries** n pl those such as mining, forestry, agriculture, etc which draw out natural resources and process them into marketable form for the manufacturing sector of industry. **extractive matter** n the soluble portions of any drug.

extradition /ek-strə-dish'ən/ n a delivering up of an accused person by one government to another. [L ex from, and trāditiō, -ōnis, from trādere, trāditum to deliver up]
■ **extraditable** /-dīt'ə-bl/ adj. **ex'tradite** vt to hand over for trial or punishment to a foreign government.

extrados /ek-strā'dos/ (archit) n the convex surface of an arch; the external curve of the keystone of an arch. [Fr, from L extrā outside, and Fr dos back]

extrait /eks-tre'/ (Fr) n extract.

extraneous /eks-trā'nyəs/ adj external; foreign; not belonging to or dependent on; not essential; irrelevant. [L extrāneus external, extrā outside]
■ **extraneity** /-trə-nē'i-ti/ or **extrān'eousness** n. **extrān'eously** adv.

extraordinaire /ek-strör-di-nār'/ adj outstanding in a particular skill or area (used postpositively, as in self-promoter extraordinaire). [Fr]

extraordinary /eks-trör'di-nə-ri or -din-ri, also eks-trə-ör' or iks-trör'/ adj not usual or regular; remarkable or wonderful; special or additional (eg physician extraordinary in a royal household, and extraordinary professor in a German university, both being subordinate to the ordinary official); for a particular purpose (eg extraordinary general meeting). [L extraordinārius, from extrā outside, and ordō, -inis order]
■ **extraord'inaries** n pl things that exceed the usual order, kind or method. **extraord'inarily** adv. **extraord'inariness** n.
□ **extraordinary ray** n in double refraction, the ray that does not obey the ordinary law of refraction. **extraordinary rendition** n (US; euphem) the covert transporting of individuals, esp terrorist suspects, to undisclosed destinations for the purpose of interrogation.

extrapolate /iks-trap'ō-lāt or -ə-lāt, also eks'/ vt or vi to estimate from observed tendencies the value of (any variable) outside the limits between which values are known; to infer or conjecture from what is known; to forecast (future trends) on the basis of past facts and events; to project into a new area of experience or activity. [L extrā and **interpolate**]
■ **extrapolā'tion** n. **extrap'olātive** or **extrap'olatory** adj. **extrap'olātor** n.

extrapose /ek-strə-pōz'/ (grammar) vt to move an item normally positioned within a phrase or sentence to the end, to focus attention on it. [L extrā outside]
■ **extraposition** /-zish'ən/ n.

extraught /iks-tröt'/ (Shakesp) pap of **extract**.

extravagant /ik-strav'ə-gənt/ adj spending a lot of money; wasteful; excessive; unrestrained; irregular; wandering beyond bounds (archaic). [L extrā beyond, and vagāns, -antis prp of vagārī to wander]
■ **extrav'agance** n excess; lavish expenditure; digression (Milton). **extrav'agancy** n extravagance; vagrancy (Shakesp). **extrav'agantly** adv. **extrav'agate** vi (archaic) to wander; to exceed proper bounds. **extravagā'tion** n.

extravaganza /ik-strav-ə-gan'zə/ n an extravagant or eccentric musical, dramatic or literary production; extravagant conduct or speech. [Ital (e)stravaganza]

extravasate /iks-trav'ə-sāt/ vt to let or force (blood or other fluid) out of the proper vessels; to pour out (lava). ◆ adj extravasated. [L extrā out of, and vās a vessel]
■ **extravasā'tion** n the act of extravasating; the escape of any of the fluids of the living body from their proper vessels.

extravert, **extraversion** and **extraversive** same as **extrovert**, etc.

extreat /eks-trēt'/ (Spenser) n extraction. [estreat]

extreme /iks-trēm' or (archaic) eks'/ adj (superl (rare) **extrēm'est**; compar (rare) **extrēm'er**) outermost; most remote; last; highest in degree; greatest; most violent; (of opinions, etc) not moderate, going to great lengths; stringent. ◆ n the utmost point or verge; end; the utmost or the highest limit or degree; the subject or predicate in a proposition (logic); (in pl) great necessity (obs) [OFr extreme, from L extrēmus, superl of exter, exterus on the outside]
■ **extrēme'ly** adv. **extrēme'ness** n. **extrē'mism** n. **extrē'mist** n someone ready to go to extremes; a holder of extreme opinions; an advocate of extreme action. ◆ adj of or characteristic of extremists. **extremity** /-trem'i-ti/ n the utmost limit; the highest degree; greatest necessity or distress; extreme condition; an end; a hand or foot. **extrēm'ophile** n a micro-organism that is capable of living in hostile conditions or an extreme environment.
□ **extreme fighting** see **ultimate fighting** under **ultimate**. **extremely high frequency** see under **frequent**. **extreme programming** n (also with caps; comput) a method of software development involving the close collaboration of two or more programmers on small components of code whose design may be subject to sudden changes (abbrev **XP**). **extreme sport** n an unconventional sport that exposes the participants to personal danger. **extreme unction** see under **unction**.
■ **go to extremes** to go too far; to use extreme measures. **in the extreme** to the highest degree; extremely. **the last extremity** the utmost misfortune; death.

extricate /eks'tri-kāt/ vt to free from entanglements or perplexities; to disentangle; to set free. [L extricāre, -ātum, from ex from, and trīcae hindrances]
■ **ex'tricable** adj. **extricā'tion** n disentanglement; the act of setting free.

extrinsic /iks-trin'sik/ adj external; not contained in or belonging to a body; foreign; not essential; (of a muscle) running from the trunk to a limb or girdle, opp to intrinsic. [Fr extrinsèque, from L extrīnsecus, from exter outside, sfx -in and secus beside]
■ **extrin'sical** adj. **extrinsical'ity** n. **extrin'sically** adv.

extrorse /iks-trörs'/ or **extrorsal** /iks-trör'səl/ adj turned outward; (of an anther) opening towards the outside of the flower. [Fr, from L extrorsus, from extrā outside, and versus turned]

extrovert /eks'trə- or -trō-vûrt/ vt to turn outward or outside in; to make manifest. ◆ n (psychol) a person interested mainly in the world external to himself or herself, opp to introvert; hence (loosely) a sociable, outgoing, lively person. ◆ adj of or characteristic of an extrovert. [L extrā outside, and vertere to turn; spelling influenced by analogy with **introvert**]
■ **extrover'sion** n. **extrover'sive** adj. **ex'troverted** adj.

extrude /iks-trood'/ vt to force or urge out; to expel; to protrude; to make rods, tubes, etc by extrusion. ◆ vi to protrude. [L extrūdere, extrūsum, from ex- out, and trūdere to thrust]
■ **extrud'able** adj. **extrud'er** n. **extru'sible** adj. **extrusile** /-troo'sīl/ adj. **extrusion** /-troo'zhən/ n the act of extruding, thrusting or throwing out; expulsion; a rock formed by the cooling of magma or lava; the operation of producing rods, tubes, etc of metal or plastic by forcing suitable material through a die by means of a ram. **extrusive** /-troo'siv/ adj (of a rock) formed from molten rock material such as magma or lava. **extru'sory** /-sər-i/ adj.

exuberant /eg- or ig-zū'bə-rənt, also -zoo'/ adj luxuriant; overflowing; abounding; in high spirits; lavish. [L exūberāns, -antis, prp of exūberāre, from ex- (intens), and ūber rich]
■ **exu'berance** or **exu'berancy** n the quality of being exuberant; luxuriance or an overflowing quantity; redundancy; outburst. **exu'berantly** adv. **exu'berate** vi (rare) to be exuberant; to grow profusely.

exude /ig-zūd' or ik-sūd'/ vt to discharge by sweating; to discharge through pores or incisions; to exhibit or show (a feeling, etc). ◆ vi to flow out of a body through the pores; to ooze out. [L *exūdāre*, from *ex* from, and *sūdāre* to sweat]

■ **exudate** /*eks'*/ *n* exuded matter. **exudā'tion** /*eks-*/ *n* the act of exuding or discharging through pores; that which is exuded. **exūd'ative** *adj*.

exul /*ek'sul*/ (*Spenser*) *n* an exile. [L *ex(s)ul*]

exulcerate /*ig-zul'sə-rāt*/ *vt* to exasperate or afflict as if with an ulcer. [L *exulcerāre*, *-ātum*, from *ex-* (intens), and *ulcerāre* to ulcerate]

■ **exulcerā'tion** *n* ulceration; exasperation.

exult /*ig-zult'*/ *vi* to be intensely joyful; to triumph over. [L *ex(s)ultāre*, *-ātum*, from *ex(s)ilīre*, from *ex* out, and *salīre* to leap]

■ **exult'ance** or **exult'ancy** *n* exultation; triumph. **exult'ant** *adj* exulting; triumphant. **exult'antly** *adv*. **exultā'tion** /*egz-*/ *n* triumphant delight; joyousness, *esp* spiritual. **exult'ingly** *adv*.

exurb /*ek'sûrb*/ (*orig US*) *n* a residential area, *esp* a prosperous one, outside the suburbs of a town. [L *ex-* outside, and su*burb*]

■ **exur'ban** *adj*. **exur'banite** *n* and *adj*. **exur'bia** *n* exurbs collectively.

ex utraque parte /*eks ū-trā'kwi pär'tē* or *ŭ-trä'kwe pär'te*/ (*L*) on either side.

exuviae /*ig-zū'* or *ik-sū'vi-ē*/ *n pl* cast-off skins, shells or other coverings of animals; fossil remains of animals (*geol*). [L, from *exuere* to draw off]

■ **exū'vial** *adj*. **exū'viate** *vi* to shed or cast off (a skin). **exuviā'tion** *n* the act of exuviating.

ex voto /*eks vō'tō* or *wō'*/ (*L*) according to one's prayer, by reason of a vow; votive. *n* a votive offering.

EXW *abbrev* : ex works.

eyalet /*ā-yä'let*/ *n* a province in the former Ottoman empire, a vilayet. [Turk, from Ar *iyālah*]

eyas /*ī'as*/ *n* an unfledged hawk. ◆ *adj* (*Spenser*) unfledged. [an *eyas* for a *nyas*, from Fr *niais*, from L *nīdus* nest]

❏ **ey'as-musket** *n* an unfledged male hawk; a child (*Shakesp*).

eye[1] /*ī*/ *n* (pl **eyes**; *archaic* **eyne** /*īn*/; *Scot* **een** /*ēn*/) the organ of sight or vision; the power of seeing; sight; a tinge or suffusion (*Shakesp*); regard; attention; aim; keenness of perception; anything resembling an eye; a central spot; the hole of a needle; the aperture for inserting the bias in a bowl; a round aperture; a mine entrance; a spring of water; a wire loop or ring for a hook; a round hole or window; the seed-bud of a potato; a spot on an egg; a spectacle lens; the central calm area of a cyclone; a private eye (*inf*); (in *pl*) the foremost part of a ship's bows, the hawse-holes. ◆ *vt* (**eye'ing** or **ey'ing**; **eyed** /*īd*/) to look on; to observe narrowly. ◆ *vi* (*Shakesp*) to appear. [OE *ēage*; cf Gothic *augo*, Ger *Auge*, Du *oog*, ON *auga*]

■ **eyed** *adj* having eyes; spotted as if with eyes. **eye'ful** *n* as much as the eye can take in; something worth looking at, eg a fascinating sight or an attractive person (*inf*). ◆ *adj* (*dialect*) sightly; careful, having an eye to. **eye'less** *adj* without eyes or sight; deprived of eyes; blind. **eye'let** *n* see separate entry.

❏ **eye'ball** *n* the ball or globe of the eye. ◆ *vt* (*inf*) to face someone eyeball to eyeball, to confront; to examine closely; to glance over (a page, etc). ◆ *adj* (of a measurement) by eye only, not exact. **eye bank** *n* an organization that procures and distributes eye tissue for transplantation. **eye'bath** *n* a small cup that can be filled with a cleansing or medicinal solution, etc and held over the eye to bathe it. **eye'-beam** *n* a glance of the eye. **eye'-black** *n* mascara. **eye'bolt** *n* a bolt with an eye instead of the normal head, used for lifting on heavy machines, fastening, etc. **eye'bright** *n* a small plant of the genus *Euphrasia* (family Scrophulariaceae) formerly used as a remedy for eye diseases. **eye'brow** *n* the hairy arch above the eye. ◆ *vt* to provide with artificial eyebrows. **eye'browless** *adj* without eyebrows. **eye'brow-raising** *adj* surprising. **eye candy** *n* something or someone that is visually attractive (*inf*); a feature that is visually pleasing but has no information content (*comput*). **eye'-catcher** *n* a part of a building designed specially to catch a person's eye (*archit*); a striking person, *esp* an attractive woman. **eye'-catching** *adj* striking. **eye'-catchingly** *adv*. **eye contact** *n* a direct look between two people. **eye'-cup** *n* (*esp N Am*) an eyebath; an eyepiece. **eye'-drop** *n* a tear (*Shakesp*); (in *pl* without *hyphen*) a medicine for the eyes administered in the form of drops. **eye'-flap** *n* a blinker on a horse's bridle. **eye'-glance** *n* a quick look. **eye'glass** *n* a glass to assist the sight, *esp* a monocle; (in *pl*) spectacles (*usu N Am*); an eyepiece; the lêns of the eye (*Shakesp*). **eye'hole** *n* an eyelet; an eye socket; a peephole. **eye'hook** *n* a hook on a ring at the end of a rope or chain. **eye'lash** *n* the row, or one, of the hairs that edge the eyelid. **eye-leg'ible** *adj* (of headings, etc on microfilm or microprint) able to be read by the naked eye. **eye level** *n* the same height above ground as the average person's eyes (also (with *hyphen*) *adj*). **eye'lid** *n* the lid or cover of the eye; the portion of movable skin by means of which the eye is opened or closed. **eye'liner** *n* a kind of cosmetic used for drawing a line along the edge

of the eyelid in order to emphasize the eye. **eye lotion** *n*. **eye muscle** *n* a muscle controlling the eye or a part of it; a long muscle running down the back beside the spine. **eye'-opener** *n* something that opens the eyes literally or figuratively, *esp* a startling enlightenment; a drink, *esp* in the morning (*inf*). **eye'-opening** *adj*. **eye'patch** *n* a patch worn to protect an injured eye. **eye'piece** *n* the lens or combination of lenses at the eye end of an optical instrument. **eye'-pit** *n* the socket of the eye. **eye'-popping** *adj* (*inf*) startling, sensational or breathtaking. **eye'-rhyme** *n* similarity of words in spelling but not in pronunciation. **eye'-salve** *n* salve or ointment for the eyes. **eye'-servant** *n* someone who does his or her duty only when under the eye of his or her master. **eye'-service** *n* service so performed; formal worship. **eye'shade** *n* a piece of stiff, *usu* tinted, transparent material, worn like the peak of a cap to protect the eyes from the sun or other bright light. **eye'shadow** *n* a coloured cosmetic for the eyelids. **eye'shot** *n* the reach or range of sight of the eye; a glance. **eye'sight** *n* power of seeing; view; observation. **eye socket** *n* either of the two recesses in the skull in which the eyeballs are situated, the orbit. **eye'sore** *n* anything that is offensive to look at. **eye splice** *n* a kind of eye or loop formed by splicing the end of a rope into itself. **eye'-spot** *n* a spot like an eye; any of several diseases of plants causing eye-shaped spots to appear on the leaves and stem; a rudimentary organ of vision. **eye'-spotted** *adj* (*Spenser*) marked with spots like eyes. **eye'stalk** *n* a stalk on the dorsal surface of the head of many Crustacea, bearing an eye. **eye'strain** *n* tiredness or irritation of the eyes. **eye'-string** *n* the muscle that raises the eyelid. **eye tooth** *n* a canine tooth, *esp* in the upper jaw, below the eye. **eye'wash** *n* a lotion for the eye; nonsense (*inf*); deception (*inf*). **eye'-water** *n* water flowing from the eye; a lotion for the eyes. **eye'wear** *n* a collective term for spectacles, sunglasses, goggles, etc. **eye'-wink** *n* (*Shakesp*) a rapid lowering and raising of the eyelid; a glance; the time of a wink. **eye'witness** *n* someone who sees a thing happening or being done.

■ **all my eye** (*sl*) nonsense. **be all eyes** to give complete attention. **be a sheet in the wind's eye** to be intoxicated. **clap, lay** or **set eyes on** (*inf*) to see. **cry one's eyes out** see under **cry**. **electric eye** see **electric**. **eyeball to eyeball** (of a discussion, confrontation, diplomacy, etc) at close quarters, dealing with matters very frankly and firmly (also **eye to eye**). **eye for an eye** retaliation, *lex talionis* (Bible, Exodus 21.24); justice enacted in the same way or to the same degree as the crime. **eye of day** the sun. **eyes down** an interjection used at the start of a bingo game, or of any non-physical contest. **eye up** (*inf*) to consider the (*esp* sexual) attractiveness of. **get** or **keep one's eye in** to become or remain proficient. **give an eye to** to attend to. **give a person the eye** (*inf*) to look at someone in a sexually inviting way. **glad eye, green-eyed** see **glad**[1] and **green**[1]. **have an eye to** to contemplate; to have regard to; to incline towards. **have one's eye on** to keep in mind; to consider acquisitively. **hit one in the eye** to be obvious. **in eye** in sight. **in one's mind's eye** in one's imagination. **in the eyes of** in the estimation or opinion of. **in the wind's eye** against the wind. **keep one's** (or **an**) **eye on** to observe closely; to watch. **keep one's eye** or **eyes skinned** or **peeled** (**for**) to be keenly watchful (for). **make a person open his** or **her eyes** to cause him or her astonishment. **make eyes at** to look at in an amorous way, to ogle. **mind your eye** (*sl*) take care. **my eye** an interjection expressing disagreement. **naked eye** see under **naked**. **one in the eye** a rebuff. **open a person's eyes** to make someone see; to show someone something of which he or she is ignorant. **pick the eyes out of** (*Aust inf*) to choose and take the best parts of. **pipe one's eye** or **put a finger in the eye** to weep. **private eye** see under **private**. **put a person's eye out** to blind someone; to supplant someone in favour. **raise an eyebrow** to be mildly surprised, shocked or doubtful. **see eye to eye** to think alike (from Bible, Isaiah 52.8, *orig* meaning see with one's own eyes). **see with half an eye** to see without difficulty. **shut one's eyes to** to ignore. **throw** or **make sheep's eyes at** to ogle. **turn a blind eye to** to pretend not to see. **under the eye of** under the observation of. **up to the eyes, eyeballs** or **eyebrows** deeply involved (in); extremely busy. **with** or **having an eye to** considering.

eye[2] /*ī*/ (*obs*) *n* a brood, *esp* of pheasants. [an *eye* for a *nye*, from OFr *ni*, from L *nīdus* nest]

eyelet /*ī'lit*/ *n* a small eye or hole to receive a lace or cord, as in garments, sails, etc; the metal, etc ring reinforcing such a hole; a small hole bound with stitching, used as a form of decoration in embroidery; a small hole for seeing through (also **eye'let-hole**); a little eye. ◆ *vt* to make eyelets in. [OFr *oillet*, from L *oculus*, influenced by **eye**[1]]

■ **eyeleteer'** *n* an instrument for making eyelet-holes.

eyeliad, eyliad see **œillade**.

Eyeti, Eyetie or **Eytie** /*ī'tī*/ (*offensive sl*) *n* an Italian.

eyne /*īn*/ (*archaic*) *n pl* eyes. [OE *ēagan*]

eyot /*āt*/ see **ait**[1].

eyra /ī'rə/ *n* a S American wildcat. [Guaraní]

eyre /ār/ (*hist*) *n* a journey or circuit; a court of itinerant justices in the late 12c and 13c. [OFr *eire* journey, from L *iter* a way, a journey, from *īre*, *itum* to go]

eyrie or **eyry** (also **aerie**, **aery** or **ayrie**) /ā'ri, ē'ri or ī'ri/ *n* the nest of a bird of prey, *esp* an eagle; a house or stronghold perched on some high or steep place; any high or inaccessible place; the brood in the nest, or a stock of children (*Shakesp*). [OFr *aire* ; origin unknown]

eyrir /ā'rēr/ *n* (pl **aurar** /ö'rär/) an Icelandic monetary unit, $\frac{1}{100}$ of a krona. [ON, related to L *aureus* golden]

Ez. (*Bible*) *abbrev* : (the Book of) Ezra.

Ezek. (*Bible*) *abbrev* : (the Book of) Ezekiel.

e-zine /ē'zēn/ *n* a journal available only in electronic form on a computer network. [Short for *electronic magazine*]

EZT *abbrev* : Enterprise Zone Trust, a high-risk tax avoidance scheme with potentially high rewards.

Ff

a b c d e f g h i j k l m n o p q r s t u v w x y z

Futura Designed by Paul Renner in 1927. Germany.

F or **f** /ef/ n the sixth letter in the modern English alphabet as in the Roman (ff in medieval script was used instead of a capital F), derived from the Greek *digamma* (C, Ϝ), its sound a voiceless labiodental fricative formed by bringing the lower lip into contact with the upper teeth; the fourth note of the diatonic scale of C major (*music*); the key or scale having that note for its tonic (*music*); in hexadecimal notation, 15 (decimal) or 1111 (binary); anything shaped like the letter F.
□ **F clef** n (*music*) the bass clef. **f'-hole** n either of a pair of holes in the belly of a violin, etc, shaped like an italic f. **F'-layer** n the highest layer of the ionosphere, in which radio signals are transmitted. **f'-number** n (*photog*) the ratio of the focal length to the true diameter of a lens. **f'-stop** n (*photog*) a setting on a camera to show the f-number currently in use.
■ **the three F's** (*hist*) free sale, fixity of tenure, fair rent (objectives of Irish land reformers in the late 19c).

F *abbrev*: Fahrenheit; faraday; Fellow (of a society, etc); fighter plane (as in *F*-15, *F*-16, *F*-111, etc) (*US*); fine (on lead pencils); franc or francs; France (IVR).
□ **f-bomb** (*US sl*) an instance of using the word 'fuck'.
■ **the F-word** (*euphem*) fuck.

F *symbol*: (as a medieval Roman numeral) 40; farad (SI unit); filial generation, thus **F₁** first or **F₂** second filial generation (*genetics*); fluorine (*chem*).

F *symbol*: force.

F̄ *symbol*: (medieval Roman numeral) 40000.

f or **f.** *abbrev*: farthing; fathom or fathoms; female; feminine; femto-; folio; following; foot; forte (*music*); furlong(s).

f *symbol*: frequency.

FA *abbrev*: Faculty of Actuaries; Football Association; fuck all (*sl*). See also **Fanny Adams**.
□ **FA Cup** n an annual football competition organized in England and Wales by the Football Association; the trophy awarded to the winners.

Fa. *abbrev*: Florida (US state).

fa /fä/ (*music*) n the fourth note of the scale in sol-fa notation (also anglicized in spelling as **fah**). [See **Aretinian**]

fa' /fö/ Scots for **fall**.

FAA *abbrev*: Federal Aviation Administration (in the USA); Fleet Air Arm.

fa'ard or **faurd** /färd, förd/ Scots for **favoured**.

fab /fab/ (*sl*) adj excellent, marvellous. [Contraction of **fabulous**]
■ **fabb'y** adj.

fabaceous /fə-bā'shəs/ adj bean-like. [L faba a bean]

Fabergé /fa-ber-zhā or fab-ər-jā'/ n delicate gold and enamel ware made in Russia in the 19c and early 20c. [Peter Carl *Fabergé* (1846–1920)]

Fabian /fā'bi-ən/ adj delaying, avoiding battle, cautious, practising the policy of delay; favouring the gradual introduction and spread of Socialism. ◆ n a member or supporter of the *Fabian Society* founded (1884) for this purpose. [From the Roman hero Quintus *Fabius* Maximus (died 203BC), whose delaying tactics wore out the strength of the Carthaginian general Hannibal]
■ **Fā'bianism** n. **Fā'bianist** n.

fable /fā'bl/ n a narrative in which things irrational and sometimes inanimate are, for the purpose of moral instruction, made to act and speak with human interests and passions; any tale in literary form, not necessarily probable in its incidents, intended to instruct or amuse; the plot or series of events in an epic or dramatic poem (*archaic*); a fiction or myth; a ridiculous story, an old wives' tale; a falsehood; subject of common talk. ◆ vi to tell fictitious tales; to tell lies (*obs*). ◆ vt to feign; to invent; to relate as if true. [Fr *fable*, from L *fārī* to speak]

■ **fā'bled** adj mythical; well-known, celebrated; feigned. **fā'bler** n. **fā'bling** n and adj. **fabular** /fab'ū-lər/ adj. **fab'ulist** n a person who invents fables; a liar. **fab'ulize** or **-ise** vi to write fables or to speak in fables.

fabliau /fab'li-ō/ n (pl **fabliaux** /fab'li-ōz/) a metrical tale similar to those, *usu* coarsely humorous in quality, produced in France in the 12c and 13c. [Fr, from dimin of *fable*]

Fablon® /fab'lon/ n a flexible plastic material with an adhesive backing, used to cover shelves, table tops, etc.

fabric /fab'rik/ n manufactured cloth; any system of connected parts; framework (also *fig*); a building; buildings, stonework, etc; texture; anything created as the result of skill and hard work; the act of constructing. ◆ vt (*Milton*) to construct. [L *fābrica* fabric, from *fāber* a worker in hard materials; partly through Fr *fabrique*]
■ **fab'ricant** n (*archaic*) a manufacturer. **fab'ricate** vt to create with skill and hard work; to manufacture; to produce; to devise falsely. **fabrica'tion** n construction; manufacture; that which is fabricated or invented; a story; a falsehood. **fab'ricative** adj. **fab'ricātor** n.
□ **fabric conditioner** or **softener** n a liquid added to laundry while it is washed, to soften and scent it.

fabular, etc see under **fable**.

fabulous /fab'ū-ləs/ adj immense, amazing; excellent (*inf*); feigned or false; spoken or written about in fable; celebrated in story. [L *fābula*, from *fārī* to speak; see also **fable**]
■ **fabulos'ity** n legendary nature. **fab'ulously** adv. **fab'ulousness** n.

faburden /fab'ər-dən/ (*obs music*) n harmony in thirds and sixths; an early kind of counterpoint; an undersong; a refrain; (in 4-part harmonization) a descant sung to a hymn that has the tune in the tenor. [Fr *faux-bourdon*, from *faux* false, and *bourdon* bourdon]

façade or **facade** /fa- or fə-säd'/ n the exterior front or face of a building; the appearance presented to the world, *esp* if showy and with little behind it (*fig*). [Fr, from *face*, after Ital *facciata* the front of a building, from *faccia* the face]

face /fās/ n the front part of the head, including forehead, eyes, nose, mouth, cheeks, and chin; the outside form or appearance; the front or surface of anything; a flat surface of a solid geometrical figure, crystal, etc; the striking surface of a golf club, etc; the edge of a cutting tool, etc; the front or upper surface, or that usually on view; the exposed surface in a cliff, mine or quarry; a principal cleavage-plane (*geol*); the dial of a watch, etc; the printed surface of a playing card; a style of letter or type (*printing*); special appearance or facial expression; aspect, look, configuration; command of facial expression and bearing; boldness, effrontery; a grimace; presence; anger or favour (*Bible*); (also **baby face**) a wrestler with a crowd-pleasing persona, opp to **heel**. ◆ vt to meet in the face or in front; to stand opposite to or looking towards; to be confronted with; to confront; to stand up to; to brave; to resist; to put an additional face or surface on; to cover in front; to trim. ◆ vi (often with *on*, *to* or *towards*) to direct or turn the face; to take or have a direction; to show a face, *esp* bold or false (*obs*). [Fr *face*, from L *faciēs* form or face; perh from *facere* to make]
■ **faced** adj having a face; having the outer surface dressed; with the front covered with another material. **face'less** adj having no face; (of a person or people concerned in some action) with identity unknown or concealed; robot-like, *esp* of bureaucratic officials who allow no degree of personality to intrude on their decision-making processes. **fac'er** n a tool for smoothing or facing a surface; a severe blow on the face (*sl*); an affront (*inf*); anything that staggers one, a sudden problem or difficulty (*inf*); a person who faces something; a person who puts on a false show (*obs*); a boldfaced person (*obs*). **facial** /fā'shl/ adj of or relating to the face; for the face. ◆ n (*inf*) a beauty treatment to the face. **fa'cialist** n a beautician who specializes in performing facial treatments. **fa'cially** adv. **fac'ing** n a covering in front for decoration or protection; (in *pl*) the collar, lapels and cuffs of a garment, *esp* in a contrasting colour.

■ words derived from main entry word; □ compound words; ■ idioms and phrasal verbs

◻ **face'-ache** n neuralgia in the nerves of the face; an ugly or disagreeable person (sl; usu used as a mild or facetious insult). **Face'book**® n a popular social networking website. **face card** n a playing-card bearing a face (king, queen or jack). **face'-centred** adj (of a crystal structure) with an atom in the centre of the face of each unit cell as well as at each vertex. **face'cloth** or **face flannel** n a cloth used in washing the face; (**facecloth**) a cloth laid over the face of a corpse or living person. **face cream** n a cosmetic cream for the face. **face'-fung'us** n (inf) a moustache or beard. **face'-guard** or **face mask** n a kind of mask to guard or protect the face. **face'-hard'en** vt to harden on the surface, to case-harden (lit and fig). **face'lift** n a surgical operation to smooth and firm the tissues of the face; a renovating process, esp one applied to the outside of a building. **face'man** or **face'worker** n a miner who works at the coalface, as opposed to elsewhere in or at the mine. **face mask** n a face-guard; a face pack. **face'-off** n (in ice-hockey, etc) the dropping of the puck between two players to start the game; a confrontation (fig); see also **face off** below. **face pack** n a creamy cosmetic mixture put onto the face to cleanse and tone the complexion, and removed when dry. **face paint** n paint used to decorate the face. **face painting** n. **face'plate** n a disc on which a piece of wood, etc can be fixed for turning on a lathe; a protective plate in front of a piece of machinery; a flat transparent panel on the front of a protective helmet; the screen or front of a cathode-ray tube. **face powder** n a cosmetic powder for the face. **face'-saver** n a course of action that saves one's face (see below). **face'-saving** n and adj saving one's face (see below). **Face'Time**® n an application enabling video calls to be made over a wireless network. ◆ vt (usu without caps) to communicate with (a person) using this application. **face time** n (orig N Am) time spent dealing with another person face to face; time spent appearing on television. **face value** n the value as stated on the face of a coin, share certificate, etc; the apparent value of anything, which may not be the same as its real value. **facial angle** n (in skull measurement) the angle formed by lines drawn from the middle of the forehead to the upper jaw above the incisor teeth and from the opening of the ear to the opening of the nose. **facial mapping** n a forensic technique for reconstructing the original face beneath a disguise.

■ **face down** to shame or intimidate with stern looks; to confront and make concede. **face off** to start a game (of ice-hockey, etc) by a face-off; to confront each other; to adopt a mutually confrontational attitude. **face out** to carry off by confident appearance; to face down. **face the music** (inf) to accept unpleasant consequences at their worst; to brave a trying situation, hostile reception, etc. **face to face** opposite; in actual presence, in person; in confrontation (**face'-to-face'** adj). **face up to** to face or stand up to; to recognize (a fact or facts) and prepare to endure or act bravely. **fly in the face of** to oppose or defy. **get in** (or **out of**) **someone's face** (inf) to begin (or stop) harassing or obstructing someone. **have two faces** to be two-faced (see under **two**). **in the face of** in defiance of, despite. **in-your-face** or **in-yer-face** (sl) aggressive; direct and provocative. **look (someone) in the face** to look at (someone) without shame or embarrassment. **lose face** to lose prestige. **loss of face** humiliation, loss of dignity. **make** or **pull faces at** to distort one's face into exaggerated expressions in order to amuse, annoy, etc. **off one's face** (sl) drunk or high on drugs; crazy. **on the face of it** on its own showing; as is palpably plain; at first glance. **pull a long face** to look dismal. **put a good** or **brave face on** (**it**) to adopt a good-natured or stoical attitude in a troublesome situation. **put one's face on** (inf) to apply cosmetics to the face. **right face!**, **left face!** or **right about face!** words of command, on which soldiers turn to the side specified. **run one's face** (obs sl) to obtain things on credit by sheer impudence. **save one's face** to avoid humiliation or appearance of climbing down. **set one's face against** to oppose strenuously. **show one's face** to appear. **to one's face** in one's presence, openly.

facet /fas'it or fas'et/ n a small surface, eg of a crystal or gem; an aspect or view; a small flat area on eg a bone (anat); an ommatidium (zool). ◆ vt to cut a facet on, or cover with facets. [Fr facette, dimin of face face]

■ **fac'eted** adj having or formed into facets.

facetious /fə-sē'shəs/, also (archaic) **facete** /-sēt'/ adj humorous in a flippant or inappropriate way, often mildly cutting or deprecating; given to joking, waggish; relating to facetiae. [L facētia, from facētus merry or witty]

■ **face'tiae** /-shi-ē/ n pl witty or humorous sayings or writings; a bookseller's term for improper books, of all degrees of indecency. **face'tiously** adv. **face'tiousness** n.

facia /fash'i-ə, fas'i-ə/ same as **fascia**.

-facient /-fā-shənt/ combining form denoting: producing; causing; making. [L faciēns, -entis, prp of facere to make]

facies /fā'shi-ēz/ n (pl **fā'cies**) general aspect, esp of plant, animal or geological species or formations; facial appearance or expression, esp when characteristic of a disease or condition. [L faciēs face]

facile /fas'īl, -il/ adj easy to accomplish; easy; working with ease; fluent (usu disparagingly); easily said, etc, but unthinkingly stupid; easily persuaded; yielding; having a minor mental incapacity, such that one may easily be persuaded to actions prejudicial to oneself (Scots law); affable (obs). [Fr, from L facilis easy, from facere to do]

■ **fac'ilely** adv. **fac'ileness** n. **facilitate** /fə-sil'/ vt to make easy or easier. **facilitā'tion** n. **facil'itātive** adj. **facil'itātor** n. **facil'ity** n ease in performance or action; fluency; easiness to be persuaded; pliancy; affability (obs); a condition of being facile (Scots law); (esp in pl **facil'ities**) means or opportunities that render anything readily possible; anything specially arranged or constructed to provide a service, recreation, etc; an agreed amount of money made available for borrowing (econ); (in pl) a lavatory (inf).

facile princeps /fas'i-lē prin'seps or fak'i-le prin'keps/ (L) obviously pre-eminent.

facilitate, facility, etc see under **facile**.

façon de parler /fa-sɔ̃ də par-lā'/ (Fr) way of speaking, a mere form of words.

façonné /fa-so-nā', fas-ə-nā' or fas'/ n fabric with a self-coloured pattern of small figures woven into it; the pattern on such a fabric. ◆ adj having such a pattern. [Fr, pap of façonner to work or fashion]

facsimile /fak-sim'i-li/ n (pl **facsim'iles**) an exact copy, eg of handwriting, a coin, a document, etc; accurate reproduction; facsimile telegraph; (also **facsimile transmission**) fax, a system for transmitting exact copies of documents. ◆ adj exactly corresponding. ◆ vt (**facsim'ileing; facsim'iled**) to make a facsimile of, to reproduce. [L fac, imperative of facere to make, and simile neuter of similis like]

■ **facsim'ilist** n. ◻ **facsimile edition** n an edition of a book, etc that is an exact reproduction of an earlier edition. **facsimile telegraph** n the transmission of a still picture over a telegraph circuit and its reproduction.

FACT /fakt/ abbrev: Federation Against Copyright Theft.

fact /fakt/ n anything that happens; a truth; truth; reality, or a real state of things, as distinguished from a mere statement or belief; a piece of information; a deed, act, or anything done (archaic); an assertion of the truth; a crime committed (obs except in **after** and **before the fact**). [L factum, neuter pap of facere to do]

■ **facticity** /-is'i-ti/ n the quality of being a fact, factualness. **fact'ūal** adj relating to facts; actual. **factūal'ity** n. **fact'ūalness** n. **fact'um** n (law) a thing done, a deed. ◻ **fact'-finding** adj appointed to ascertain, or directed towards ascertaining, all the facts of a situation. **fact'-finder** n. **fact sheet** n a paper setting out briefly information relevant to a particular subject. ■ **as a matter of fact** in reality. **facts of life** the details of reproduction, esp human reproduction; the realities of a situation. **in fact** or **in point of fact** indeed. **the fact of the matter** the plain truth about the subject in question.

factice /fak'tis/ n (formerly also **fact'is**) a rubber-like material made from vegetable oils, used as a rubber substitute. [L factīcius, factitīvus, from facere to make]

facticity see under **fact**.

faction[1] /fak'shən/ n a small group of people formed of dissenting members of a larger group, esp in politics, usu used in a negative sense; any rebellious group; dissension. [L factiō, -ōnis, from facere to do]

■ **fac'tional** adj. **fac'tionalism** n. **fac'tionalist** n. **fac'tionalize** or **-ise** vt and vi. **fac'tionary** n a member of a faction. **fac'tionist** n. **fac'tious** adj turbulent; given to faction; proceeding from party spirit; seditious. **fac'tiously** adv. **fac'tiousness** n.

faction[2] /fak'shən/ n a play, programme, piece of writing, etc that is a mixture of fact and fiction; this type of writing, etc. [**fact** and -ion from **fiction**]

factious, etc see under **faction**[1].

factis see **factice**.

factitious /fak-tish'əs/ adj artificial; contrived; made; produced by artificial conditions. [L factīcius, factitīvus, from facere to make]

■ **facti'tiously** adv. **facti'tiousness** n. **fac'titive** adj causative; (of a verb) which can take both a direct object and a complement. **fac'tive** adj (linguistics) making.

factoid /fak'toid/ n an unprovable statement which has achieved unquestioning acceptance by frequent repetition; an individual item of information, often trivial. [**fact** and **-oid**]

factor /fak'tər/ n a doer or transactor of business for another person; a person or organization that buys and sells goods for others, on commission; an agent managing heritable estates for another person (Scot); one of two or more quantities which, when multiplied together, result in the given quantity, eg 6 and 4 are factors of 24 (maths); an element in the composition of anything, or in bringing about a certain result; a fact, etc which has to be taken into account or which affects the course of events; (in heredity) a gene; a blood product given eg to haemophiliacs to aid coagulation. ◆ *vi* to work, act, etc as a factor. ◆ *vt* to factorize; to manage for another person (*Scot*). [L *facere* to do]

■ **factorabil'ity** *n*. **fac'torable** *adj*. **fac'torage** *n* the fees or commission of a factor. **factō'rial** *adj* of or relating to a factor. ◆ *n* the product of all whole numbers from a given number down to one. **fac'toring** *n* the work of a factor; the business of buying up trade debts, or lending money on the security of these. **factorizā'tion** or **-s-** *n*. **fac'torize** or **-ise** *vt* to resolve into factors; to warn not to pay or give up goods (*US*); to attach (the effects of a debtor in the hands of another person, eg of the heir). **fac'torship** *n*.

◻ **factor analysis** *n* in statistics, the use of mathematical techniques to evaluate the variables in a sample. **factor 8** or **factor VIII** *n* one of the proteins which form the clotting agent in blood, absent in haemophiliacs. **factor of production** *n* (*econ*) one of the elements which may contribute to the production of goods, thought of generally as land, capital and labour (and also sometimes the entrepreneur).

■ **factor in** (or **out**) to include (or exclude) as a relevant or influential consideration. **judicial factor** a person appointed by the Court to manage the estate of a person under some incapacity. **safety factor** see under **safe**.

factory /fak'tə-ri/ *n* a place or building where goods are manufactured; a trading settlement in another country (*hist*). [LL *factorium*, ult from L *facere* to do, make]

◻ **Factory Acts** *n pl* laws dealing with working conditions, safety, etc in places of work, enforced by the **factory inspectorate**. **factory farm** *n* one carrying out **factory farming**, farming by methods of feeding and housing animals in which everything is subordinated to achieving maximum production, rapid growth, and qualities in demand on the market. **factory floor** same as **shop floor** (see under **shop**). **factory-gate price** or **charge** *n* the price of goods calculated by the seller exclusive of freight charges to the buyer. **factory ship** *n* a whaling-ship on which whales are processed; a ship which freezes or otherwise processes the catch of a fishing fleet. **factory shop** *n* a shop attached to a factory, *esp* for selling surplus or damaged stock.

factotum /fak-tō'təm/ *n* (pl **facto'tums**) a person employed to do all kinds of work for another. [LL, from L *fac* imperative of *facere* to do, and *tōtum* all]

factual, factuality, factualness and **factum** see under **fact**.

facture /fak'chər/ *n* the act or process of making (*rare*); the result of making, workmanship. [L *factūra*, from *facere* to make]

facula /fak'ū-lə/ *n* (pl **fac'ulae** /-lē/) a spot brighter than the rest of the surface, *esp* as seen on the sun. [L *facula* dimin of *fax* torch]

■ **fac'ular** *adj*.

faculty /fak'əl-ti/ *n* facility or power to act; any particular ability or aptitude; an original power of the mind; any physical or mental capability or function; personal quality or endowment; right, authority or privilege to act; licence or authorization; a department of learning at a university, or the professors and lecturers constituting it; the staff of a school, college or university (*N Am*); the members of a profession; executive ability. [Fr *faculté*, from L *facultās, -ātis*, from *facilis* easy]

■ **fac'ultative** *adj* optional; incidental; of or relating to a faculty; conferring privilege, permission or authority; (eg of anaerobes) able but not obliged to function in the way specified (*zool*). **fac'ultatively** *adv*.

◻ **facultative parasite** *n* (*biol*) a parasite able to live on dead or decaying organic matter as well as on its living host (cf **obligate parasite** under **oblige**).

■ **Court of Faculties** a court established by Henry VIII, whereby authority is given to the Archbishop of Canterbury to grant dispensations and faculties. **Faculty of Advocates** the Scottish college of advocates.

facundity /fə-kun'di-ti/ *n* eloquence. [L *fācunditās, -ātis*]

fad /fad/ *n* a hobby or interest intensely pursued at first, but soon passed over for another; an overriding personal preference or taste, *esp* trifling. [Ety unknown]

■ **fadd'iness** *n*. **fadd'ish** *adj*. **fadd'ishness** or **fadd'ism** *n*. **fadd'ist** *n* a person who is a slave to some fad. **fadd'y** *adj*.

fadaise see under **fade²**.

faddle /fad'l/ (*dialect*) *vi* to trifle. ◆ *n* nonsense, trifling, *usu* in **fiddle-faddle**.

fade¹ /fād/ *vi* to lose strength, freshness, loudness, brightness or colour gradually; to grow pale, dull or faint; to die away; to disappear. ◆ *vt* to cause to fade; to cause to change gradually in distinctness (as in *fade out*, *fade in*); to hit (the ball) intentionally in such a way that it moves from left to right in the air (if right-handed) or from right to left (if left-handed) (*golf*). ◆ *n* a fading; spin imparted on the ball to make it move from left to right in the air for a right-handed player or from right to left for a left-handed player (*golf*); a golf shot that imparts this movement.

◆ *adj* (*archaic*) faded, weak. [OFr *fader*, from *fade*, perh from L *vapidum* dull, insipid]

■ **fā'dable** *adj*. **fā'dedly** *adv*. **fā'dedness** *n*. **fāde'less** *adj* unfading; not liable to fade. **fāde'lessly** *adv*. **fā'der** *n* a sliding control as used eg on audio and lighting equipment to set levels of sound and light. **fād'ing** *n* and *adj*. **fā'dy** *adj* wearing away.

◻ **fade'-away** *n* a gradual disappearance.

■ **fade down** (of sound or light) to fade out (**fade'-down** *n*). **fade in** in films, radio, television, etc, to introduce (sound or a picture) gradually, bringing it up to full volume or clarity (**fade'-in** *n*). **fade out** in films, radio, television, etc, to cause (sound or a picture) to disappear gradually (**fade'-out** *n*). **fade up** (of sound or light) to fade in (**fade'-up** *n*).

fade² /fad/ (*Fr*) *adj* insipid, colourless.

■ **fadaise** /fa-dez'/ *n* a silly saying; twaddle. **fadeur** /fa-dœr'/ *n* dullness.

fadge /faj/ (*archaic*) *vi* to agree, hit it off; to succeed, turn out. [Ety doubtful; not connected with OE *fēgan* to join]

fading /fā'ding/ *n* an old dance, probably Irish; the burden or refrain of a song (*Shakesp*). [Origin unknown]

fado /fä'dŭ/ *n* (pl **fad'os**) a type of melancholy Portuguese folk song or dance. [Port, fate, from L *fātum*]

fae /fā, fi/ (*Scot*) *prep* from.

faeces or (*N Am*) **feces** /fē'sēz/ *n pl* excrement; sediment after infusion or distillation; dregs. [L, pl of *faex, faecis* dregs or grounds]

■ **faecal** or (*US*) **fecal** /fē'kl/ *adj*.

faerie or **faery** /fā'(ə-)ri/ (*archaic*) *n* the world of fairies, fairyland; a fairy. ◆ *adj* of or relating to fairies or fairyland. [A variant of **fairy**]

Faeroese or **Faroese** /fā-rō'ēz/ *adj* relating to the Faeroes or Faroes, a group of islands in the N Atlantic belonging to Denmark. ◆ *n* the language of the Faeroes; a native or inhabitant of the Faeroes (pl **Faeroese** or **Faroese**).

faex populi /fēks pop'ū-lī or fīks pop'ŭ-lē/ (*L*) *n* dregs of the people, the mob.

faff /faf/ (*inf*) *vi* (*usu* with *about* or *around*) to dither, fumble or fuss ineffectually. ◆ *n* a fumbling; a troublesome fuss. [Origin obscure]

fag¹ /fag/ *n* a schoolboy forced to do menial work for another, *usu* older, boy; a tiresome piece of work; drudgery; *orig* an inferior cigarette (for *fag end*), hence any cigarette (*inf*). ◆ *vi* (**fagg'ing** *fagged*) to become weary or tired out (*inf*); to work hard; to be a fag for someone. ◆ *vt* to weary; to use as a fag. [Ety doubtful; perh a corruption of **flag²**]

■ **fagg'ery** *n* drudgery; fagging. **fagg'ing** *n* and *adj*.

◻ **fag end** *n* the stump of a cigarette or cigar (*inf*); the end of a web of cloth that hangs loose; the untwisted end of a rope; the end, remaining or worthless part of a thing.

■ **fagged out** (*inf*) very tired, exhausted.

fag² /fag/ (*sl, orig US, offensive*) *n* a male homosexual. [Short form of **faggot**]

■ **fagg'y** *adj*.

◻ **fag hag** *n* a heterosexual woman who enjoys the company of homosexual men.

faggot or **fagot** /fag'ət/ *n* a roll or ball of minced meat, *esp* pig's liver, mixed with bread and savoury herbs for cooking as food; a bundle of sticks for fuel, etc; a stick; anything like a faggot; a bundle of pieces of iron or steel cut off into suitable lengths for welding; a soldier numbered on the muster roll, but not really existing (*hist*); a voter who has obtained his or her vote expressly for party purposes, on a spurious or sham qualification (*hist*); an old woman (*derog*); a male homosexual (also **fag**; *sl, orig US, offensive*). ◆ *adj* (*hist*) got up for a purpose, as in **faggot vote**. ◆ *vt* to tie together. ◆ *vi* to practise faggoting. [Fr *fagot* a bundle of sticks]

■ **fagg'oting** or **fag'oting** *n* a kind of embroidery in which some of the cross-threads are drawn together in the middle. **fagg'oty** *adj*.

■ **burn one's faggot** to recant a heresy.

Fagin /fā'gin/ *n* a person who trains young thieves, receives stolen goods, etc. [After the character in Charles Dickens' novel *Oliver Twist*]

fagotto /fə-got'ō/ *n* (pl **fagott'i** /-ē/) a bassoon; a soft reed organ stop. [Ital]

■ **fagott'ist** *n* a person who plays the bassoon.

Fagus /fā'gəs/ *n* the beech genus of trees, giving name to the family **Fagā'ceae**. [L *fāgus* beech; cf Gr *phēgos* oak, and OE *bōc* beech]

■ **fagā'ceous** *adj*.

fah see **fa**.

fahlband /fäl'bänt/ *n* in crystalline rocks, a pale band rich in metals. [Ger *fahl* dun-coloured, *Band* band]

■ **fahl'erz** /-erts/ *n* (Ger *Erz* ore) tetrahedrite; also tennantite. **fahl'ore** /-ōr or -ör/ *n* tetrahedrite or tennantite.

Fahrenheit /fa' or fä'rən-hīt/ adj (of a thermometer or thermometer scale) having the freezing point of water marked at 32, and the boiling point at 212 degrees (to convert °F into °C, subtract 32 and take $\frac{5}{9}$ of the remainder). [Named from the inventor, Gabriel D *Fahrenheit* (1686–1736), German physicist]

faible /feb'l/ n a foible; the part of a foil blade between the middle and the point, the weak part. [Fr, weak]

faience or **faïence** /fä-yäs'/ n glazed coloured earthenware. [Fr; prob from *Faenza* in Italy]

faik /fāk/ (*Scot*) vi and vt to abate; to excuse.

faikes see **fakes**.

fail[1] /fāl/ (*Scot*) n a turf, sod. [Perh Gaelic *fàl* a sod]
□ **fail'-dyke** n a turf wall.

fail[2] /fāl/ vi to fall short or be lacking (with *in*); to fall away, to dwindle; to decay; to die; to prove deficient under trial, examination, pressure, etc; not to achieve; to be disappointed or baffled; to become insolvent or bankrupt. ◆ vt not to be sufficient for; to leave undone, omit; to disappoint or desert; to deceive (*Spenser*); to declare unsuccessful or lacking in knowledge after examination. ◆ n a failure, *esp* in an examination. [OFr *faillir*, from L *fallere* to deceive; cf Du *feilen*, Ger *fehlen* and ON *feila*]
■ **failed** adj that has failed; decayed, worn-out; bankrupt. **fail'ing** n a fault, weakness; a foible; failure. ◆ adj that fails. ◆ prep in default of, in the absence of. **fail'ure** n a falling short or cessation; lack of success; omission; decay; bankruptcy; an unsuccessful person.
□ **fail'over** n (*comput*) a procedure by which a system automatically transfers control to a backup system on detection of a failure. **fail'-safe** adj (of a mechanism) incorporated in a system to ensure that there will be no accident if the system does not operate properly; (of a system) designed to revert to a safe condition in the event of failure; certain not to fail.
■ **fail of** to fall short of accomplishing (a purpose). **fail safe** to revert to a safe condition in the event of failure. **without fail** for certain.

faille /fāl, fīl or fä'y'/ n a soft, closely-woven silk or rayon fabric with transverse ribs. [Fr]

failure see under **fail**[2].

fain[1] /fān/ (*archaic* and *poetic*) adj glad or joyful; eager (with *to*); content for lack of anything better; compelled; wont (*Spenser*). ◆ vt (*Spenser*) to delight in; to desire. ◆ adv gladly. [OE *fægen* joyful; cf ON *feginn* glad]
■ **fain'ly** adv gladly. **fain'ness** n eagerness.

fain[2] or **faine** /fān/ (*Spenser*) vt same as **feign**.

fainéant /fen'ā-ä/ adj and n do-nothing, applied *esp* to the later Merovingian kings of France, mere puppets, whose mayors of the palace governed the country. [Fr, as if from *faire* to do, and *néant* nothing; really, from OFr *faignant* prp of *faindre* to skulk]
■ **fai'néance** /-äs/, **fai'neancy** /-ən-si/ or **fainéantise** /-tēz'/ n.

fains /fānz/ (*school sl*) interj a plea for exemption or a truce (also **fain'ites** and **fains I**). [Form of **fen**[2]]

faint /fānt/ adj dim; lacking distinctness; not bright or having any force; lacking in strength (*archaic*); weak in spirit (*archaic*); lacking courage (*archaic*); done in a feeble way; inclined to lose consciousness momentarily; sickly-smelling, oppressive (*archaic*). ◆ vi to lose consciousness momentarily, to swoon; to become feeble or weak (*archaic*); to lose strength, colour, etc (*archaic*); to fade or decay (*archaic*); to vanish (*archaic*); to lose courage or spirit (*archaic*). ◆ vt (*rare*) to render faint. ◆ n a swoon. [OFr *feint* feigned, from L *fingere* to feign]
■ **faint'ed** adj (*Milton*) exhausted. **faint'ing** n and adj. **faint'ish** adj slightly faint. **faint'ishness** n. **faint'ly** adv. **faint'ness** n lack of strength; feebleness of colour, light, etc; dejection. **faints** n pl impure spirit produced at the beginning and end of distillation (also **feints**). **faint'y** adj faintish.
□ **faint'-heart** n and adj. **faint-heart'ed** adj spiritless, lacking courage; timorous. **faint-heart'edly** adv. **faint-heart'edness** n.
■ **not have the faintest** (**idea** or **notion**) (*inf*) not to have the least idea.

fair[1] /fār/ adj bright; clear; clean; free from blemish; pure; pleasing to the eye; beautiful; of a light hue; free from rain, fine, dry; unobstructed; open; smoothly curving; prosperous; impartial; just; equitable; good, pleasing; plausible; civil; specious; reasonable; likely; favourable; pretty good; passable; out-and-out, veritable (*dialect*); a general expression of commendation or courtesy (as in *fair sir*; *archaic*). ◆ n that which is fair; a woman (*archaic*); beauty (*Shakesp*). ◆ vt to make fair. ◆ vi to clear up, as the weather from rain. ◆ adv in a fair manner (in all senses); full, square, directly (eg *hit fair in the centre*); quite (*dialect*). [OE *fæger*]
■ **fair'ing** n adjustment or testing of curves in ship-building; streamlined external fittings on an aeroplane, car, motorcycle, etc, to reduce drag. See also **fair**[2]. **fair'ish** adj somewhat fair; pretty well;

pretty drunk (*dialect*). **fair'ly** adv tolerably; fully, quite; justly; reasonably; plainly; absolutely (*inf*); beautifully (*archaic*); neatly (*archaic*); gently (*obs*). **fair'ness** n.
□ **fair'-and-square'** adj honest (also adv). **fair'-bod'ing** adj (*Shakesp*) auspicious. **fair catch** n (*American football*) an unopposed catch by a member of the team receiving a punt or kick-off. **fair comment** n honest expression of one's views in criticism, not motivated by malice, and therefore not punishable as libel or slander. **fair copy** n a clean copy after correction, *esp* of a legal document. **fair-deal'ing** n. **fair'-faced** adj with a light complexion; beautiful; specious (*archaic*). **fair field** n just conditions. **Fair Funding** n a system of funding for schools in which a Local Education Authority calculates and allocates money to individual schools, who each manage their own budget. **fair game** n a legitimate object for attack or ridicule. **fair'-haired** or **fair'-headed** adj having light-coloured hair. **Fair Isle** n a type of design used in knitwear, named from a Shetland island. **Fair'-Isle** adj. **fair'-lead** or **fair-leader** n a ring, hole or set of holes, etc, or more elaborate device, for guiding a rope, etc so as to reduce friction. **fair'-minded** adj judging fairly. **fair play** n honest dealing; justice. **fair'-seeming** adj appearing fair. **fair-spok'en** adj bland or civil in language and address. **fair trade** n a system of trade involving the payment of fair prices for goods produced in developing countries; smuggling (*old*; *euphem*); a mild form of the protective system, in which the basis of economic policy is supposed to be reciprocity or free trade only with such nations as grant similar privileges. **fair'-trade** adj and adv. **fair'way** n the smooth turf between tee and green, distinguished from the uncut rough and from hazards (*golf*); the navigable channel or usual course of vessels in a river, etc. **fair'-weath'er** adj suitable only for, or found only in, fair weather or (*esp* of friends or supporters) favourable circumstances.
■ **bid fair** see under **bid**[1]. **fair befall** or **fall** (*archaic*) good luck to. **fair dinkum** see under **dinkum**. **fair do's** /dooz/ (*pl* of **do**; *inf*) an expression appealing for, or agreeing to, fair play, strict honesty, etc. **fair enough** expressing acceptance, though not necessarily full agreement. **fair play to him**, **her**, etc credit should be given to him, her, etc. **fair's fair** an expression appealing for, or agreeing to, just treatment. **in a fair way to** see under **way**[1]. **in all fairness** being scrupulously fair. **keep fair with** to keep on amicable terms with. **no fair** (*US inf*) an expression declaring that something is not allowed or is not fair. **speak fair** see under **speak**. **stand fair with** to be in the good graces of. **the fair** or **the fairer sex** (often *patronizing*) the female sex.

fair[2] /fār/ n a large market held periodically for one kind of merchandise, or for the general sales and purchases of a district, with or without amusements; often reduced to a collection of shows, swing-boats, etc; a charity bazaar; a trade show. [OFr *feire*, from L *fēria* holiday]
■ **fair'ing** n a present given at or from a fair; any complimentary gift. See also **fair**[1].
□ **fair'-day** n. **fair'ground** n.
■ **a day after the fair** or **behind the fair** too late. **get one's fairing** (*Scot*) to get one's deserts.

fairnitickle, **fairniticle**, **fairnytickle** or **fairnyticle** see **ferntickle** under **fern**.

fairy /fā'ri/ n a creature of folklore, an imaginary being, generally of diminutive and graceful human form, capable of kindly or unkindly acts towards human beings; fairyland (see also **faerie**); an enchantress; a creature of overpowering charm; a male homosexual (*derog*). ◆ adj like a fairy, fanciful, whimsical, delicate. [OFr *faerie* enchantment, from *fae* (Mod Fr *fée*); see **faerie** and **fay**[1]]
■ **fair'ily** adv. **fair'ydom** n. **fair'yhood** n. **fair'yism** n. **fair'ylike** adj and adv like fairies or like something in fairyland; very delicate and charming.
□ **fair'y-beads** n pl joints of the stems of fossil sea lilies, or crinoids. **fairy-butt'er** n a name applied in N England to certain gelatinous fungi. **fairy cake** n a small sponge cake, *usu* iced or decorated. **fai'ry-cycle** n a small child's bicycle. **fairy godmother** n a benefactress (or, loosely, a benefactor), *esp* an unexpected one. **fair'yland** n the country of the fairies; an enchanting place. **fairy light** n (*usu in pl*) a small light used as decoration, *esp* on Christmas trees. **fair'y-money** or **fairy gold** n money reputedly given by fairies, which changes into withered leaves, slate, stones, etc; money that comes unsought, hence, illusory riches. **fairy moss** n a small floating fern, *Azolla caroliniana*. **fairy penguin** n the smallest of the penguins, *Eudyptula minor* (also called **korora** or **little** (**blue**) **penguin**). **fairy ring** n a ring of darker-coloured grass due to outward spread of a fungus (as the fairy-ring mushroom or champignon, *Marasmius oreades*), attributed to the dancing of fairies. **fairy shrimp** n a small crustacean (genus *Branchinecta*) that lives in fresh or brackish water. **fair'y-stone** n a fossil sea-urchin; a concretion. **fairy story** or **fairy tale** n a story about fairies or other supernatural beings; a folk tale; a romantic tale; an incredible tale; a lie (*euphem*); a marvel. **fairy tale** see **fairy story** above. **fair'ytale** adj beautiful, fortunate, etc, as in a fairy tale. **fairy**

wren *n* a small Australian songbird (genus *Malurus*), the male of which displays colourful plumage.
 ■ **away with the fairies** (*inf*) in a state of abstraction; given to daydreaming.

fait accompli */fe-ta-kɔ̄-plē'/* (*Fr*) *n* an accomplished fact, a thing already done or done in advance, eg of obtaining permission.

faites vos jeux */fet vō zhø'/* (*Fr*) place your stakes (eg in roulette).

faith */fāth/* *n* trust or confidence; belief in the statement of another person; belief in the truth of revealed religion; confidence and trust in God; the living reception of religious belief; that which is believed; any system of religious belief, *esp* the religion one considers true; fidelity to promises; honesty; word or honour pledged; faithfulness.
 ◆ *interj* (*archaic*) by my faith; indeed. ◆ *vt* */fādh/* (*Shakesp*) to believe. [ME *feith* or *feyth*, from OFr *feid*, from L *fidēs*, from *fīdere* to trust] ■ **faith'ful** *adj* full of faith, believing; firm in adherence to promises, duty, friendship, love, etc; loyal; constant; corresponding to truth; worthy of belief; true; exact. **faith'fully** *adv* with confidence; with fidelity; with sincerity; with scrupulous exactitude; solemnly (*inf*); a word customarily used in concluding a letter. **faith'fulness** *n*. **faith'less** *adj* without faith or belief; not believing, *esp* in God or Christianity; not adhering to promises, duty, etc; inconstant, fickle; adulterous; untrustworthy; deceptive. **faith'lessly** *adv*. **faith'lessness** *n*. **faith'worthiness** *n* trustworthiness. **faith'worthy** *adj* worthy of faith or belief.
 ❑ **faith healer** *n*. **faith healing** or **faith cure** *n* a system of belief, based on James 5.15 in the Bible, that sickness may be cured without medical advice or appliances, if the prayer of Christians is accompanied in the sufferer by true faith; cure by suggestion. **faith school** *n* a school that instructs its pupils in a particular religion as part of its curriculum.
 ■ **bad faith** treachery; insincerity or disingenuousness; the breaking of a promise. **Father of the faithful** (in Christianity and Judaism) Abraham; (in Islam) the caliph. **in good faith** with honesty and sincerity; acting honestly. **keep faith** to act honestly, according to one's promise (with). **the Faithful** believers, *esp* Muslims; (without *cap*) adherents, supporters, etc (*inf*).

faitor */fā'tər/* (*obs*) *n* an impostor (often **fai'tour**). [OFr *faitor*, from L *factor, -ōris* a doer]

faix */fāks/* (*dialect*) *interj* faith. [Prob short for *faykins*; see **fay**[2]]

fajitas */fa-hē'təz/* *n pl* a Mexican dish of strips of spiced chicken, beef, etc, served hot, wrapped in flour tortillas. [Mex Sp *fajo* a bundle]

fake[1] */fāk/* *vt* to doctor, cook, pretend or counterfeit; to rob or attack; to filch. ◆ *n* (also **fake'ment**) a swindle, dodge or sham; a person or thing that is not genuine. ◆ *adj* false or counterfeit. [Prob the earlier *feak* or *feague*, Ger *fegen* to furbish up] ■ **fak'er** *n*. **fak'ery** *n*.

fake[2] */fāk/* *vt* to fold, coil. ◆ *n* a coil of rope, etc. [ME *faken*; cf Scot *faik* fold]

fakes or **faikes** */fāks/* *n pl* thin-bedded shaly or micaceous sandstone or sandy shale.

fakie */fā'kē/* *n* (in skateboarding and snowboarding) the movement or act of riding backwards (also *adv*). [Origin unknown]

fakir */fä-kēr'* or *fā'kər/* *n* a religious (*esp* Muslim) mendicant, ascetic or wonder-worker in India, etc. [Ar *faqīr* a poor man] ■ **fakir'ism** (or */fā'/*) *n*.

fa-la */fä-lä'/* *n* an old kind of madrigal. ■ **fa la** (**la**, etc) syllables used as a refrain.

falafel or **felafel** */fə-lä'fəl/* *n* a deep-fried ball of ground dried chickpeas or broad beans, with onions and spices. [Ar *falāfil*]

falaj */fal'aj/* *n* (pl **aflaj'**) a water channel, *specif* one forming part of the ancient irrigation system of Oman. [Ar, stream]

Falange */fä-läng'hhä* (*Sp*), also *fə-lanj'* or *fä'/* *n* the Spanish fascist movement, established in 1933, and the only legal political party under Franco. [Sp, from Gr *phalanx* phalanx] ■ **Falangism** */fə-lan'jizm/* *n* (also without *cap*). **Falan'gist** *n* (also without *cap*).

Falasha */fə-la'shə/* *n* one of a community of black Ethiopian Jews. [Amharic, immigrant]

falbala */fal'bə-lə/* *n* a trimming or flounce. [Ety doubtful; cf **furbelow**]

falcade */fal-kād'* or *fal-käd'/* *n* the motion of a horse when it throws itself on its haunches in a very quick leap or curvet. [Fr, from L *falcāta* (fem) bent]

falcate */fal'kāt/* or **falcated** */fal-kā'tid/* *adj* bent like a sickle. [L *falx, falcis* a sickle] ■ **falcā'tion** *n*. **falciform** */fal'si-förm/* *adj* sickle-shaped. **fal'cūla** *n* a falcate claw. **fal'cūlate** *adj*.

falces see **falx**.

falchion */föl'shən* or *-chən/* *n* a short, broad sword, bent rather like a sickle. [OFr *fauchon*, through LL from L *falx* a sickle]

falciform see under **falcate**.

falciparum */fal-sip'ə-rəm/* *n* (also **falciparum malaria**) a severe form of malaria, caused by the parasite *Plasmodium falciparum*. [L *falx, falcis* a sickle, and *parere* to bear]

falcon */föl'kən, fol'kən, fö'kən* or (*esp US*) *fal'kən/* *n* any of the long-winged birds of prey of the genus *Falco* or related genera; a bird of prey of a kind trained to hunt small game; by falconers confined to the female (*esp* peregrine) falcon (cf **tercel**); a kind of cannon. [OFr *faucon*, from LL *falcō, -ōnis*] ■ **fal'coner** *n* a person who hunts with, or who breeds and trains, falcons or hawks. **fal'conet** *n* a small field gun in use until the 16c. **fal'conine** *adj*. **fal'conry** *n* the art or practice of training, or hunting with, falcons.
 ❑ **fal'con-eyed** *adj* keen-eyed. **falcon-gen'til** or **falcon-gen'tle** *n* the female of the peregrine falcon.

falcula, etc see under **falcate**.

faldage */föl'dij* or *fal'dij/* (*hist*) *n* the right of the lord of a manor of folding his tenant's sheep in his own fields for the sake of the manure; a fee paid by the tenant in lieu of this. [Law L *faldāgium*, from OE *fald* fold]

falderal */fal'də-ral'/*, **folderol** */fol'də-rol'/* or **fal de rol** */fal də rol/* *n* a meaningless refrain in songs; any kind of flimsy trifle.
 ■ **falderal it** to sing meaningless sounds.

faldetta */fäl-det'ə/* *n* a Maltese woman's combined hood and cape. [Ital]

faldstool */föld'stool/* *n* a folding or camp stool; a coronation stool; a bishop's armless seat; a small desk in churches in England, at which the litany is sung or said. [LL *faldistolium* or *faldistorium*, from OHGer *faldstuol*, from *faldan* (Ger *falten*) to fold, and *stuol* (Ger *Stuhl*) stool] ■ **fald'istory** *n* (*obs*) a bishop's seat within the chancel.

Falernian */fa-lûr'ni-ən/* *adj* relating to or associated with a district (*Falernus ager*) in Campania (area around Naples), once famous for its wine.

fall[1] */föl/* *vi* (**fall'ing**; **fell**; **fallen** */fö'lən/*) to descend, *esp* freely and involuntarily by force of gravity; to drop; to drop prostrate; to throw oneself down; to collapse; to become lower literally or figuratively (in position, degree, intensity, value, pitch, etc); to die away; to subside; to abate; to ebb; to decline; to sink; (of the face) to relax into an expression of disappointment or dismay; to flow downwards; to slope or incline down; to hang, dangle or trail down; to be cast or shed; to drop dead or as if dead, *esp* in a fight; to die in battle; to be overthrown; to come to ruin; to lose power, station, virtue or repute; to be degraded; to be taken or captured; to become a victim; to yield to temptation; to pass into any state or action, to become, to begin to be (as in *fall asleep, fall in love, fall a-weeping*); to become pregnant (*dialect*); to rush; to become involved; to take oneself (to); to come to be; to come about; to come by chance or as if by chance; to come in due course; to happen or occur; to chance or light (on); to issue or come forth; to appertain (to); to be apportioned or assigned (to); to come as one's share, lot, duty, etc; to take up a set position; to be found at a specific place; to be disposed; to impinge; to lapse; to terminate; to revert. ◆ *vt* to cause to fall (*archaic* or *US*); to let fall (*archaic*); to get (as what happens to one) (*obs*; *Burns*). ◆ *n* the act, manner, occasion or time of falling or of felling; descent by gravity, a dropping down; that which falls; as much as comes down at one time; onset; overthrow; descent from a better to a worse position; slope or declivity; descent of water; a cascade; length of drop or amount of descent; decrease in value; a sinking of the voice; a cadence; the time when the leaves fall, autumn (chiefly *N Am*); a bout of wrestling; the passing of a city or stronghold to the enemy; a lapse into sin, *esp* that of Adam and Eve, 'the Fall (of Man)'; a falling band, a hanging fringe, flap or ornament; a lot, chance or fortune (*archaic*); a lowering or hoisting rope. [OE *fallan* (WSax *feallan*); Ger *fallen*; prob connected with L *fallere* to deceive] ■ **fall'en** *adj* having fallen; killed, *esp* in battle; overthrown; seduced; in a degraded state, ruined. ◆ *n pl* (*esp literary*; *usu* with *the*) those killed in battle. **fall'er** *n*. **fall'ing** *n*.
 ❑ **fall'-back** *adj* used as a retreat, or second alternative (also *n*). **fallen angel** *n* any of the angels cast out of heaven for rebellion against God. **fallen star** *n* a gelatinous mass of cyanobacteria (*Nostoc*, etc) once popularly thought to be of meteoric origin. **fall'fish** *n* a N American freshwater fish (*Semotilus corporalis*) of the carp family. **fall-in** see **fall in** below. **falling band** *n* a 17c man's collar of fine material turned down on the shoulders. **falling-off'** *n* a decline. **falling-out'** *n* a quarrel. **falling sickness** *n* (*archaic*) epilepsy. **falling star** *n* a meteor. **falling stone** *n* a portion of an exploded meteor. **fall line** *n* the edge of a plateau; (in skiing) the natural line of descent on a slope. **fall'-off** *n* a decrease. **fall'out** *n* a deposit of radioactive dust from a nuclear explosion or plant; the aftermath of any explosive occurrence or situation (*fig*); a by-product or side benefit (*inf*); see also **fall out** below. **fall'-trap** *n* a trap that operates by causing the victim to fall.

■ **fall about** to laugh hysterically, to collapse (with laughter). **fall across** (*archaic*) to meet by chance. **fall among** to find oneself in the midst of. **fall apart** to disintegrate; to fail; to collapse or go to pieces. **fall away** to slope down; to decline gradually; to dwindle or waste away; to lose enthusiasm and so leave (a club, etc); to languish; to grow lean; to revolt or abandon one's beliefs, principles, etc. **fall back** to retreat, give way. **fall back, fall edge** (*obs*) no matter what may happen. **fall back (up)on** to have recourse to as an expedient or resource in reserve. **fall behind** to lag; to be outstripped; to get in arrears. **fall between two stools** to be neither one thing nor the other; to succeed in neither of two alternatives. **fall down on** to fail in. **fall flat** to fail completely, have no effect. **fall flat on one's face** to come to grief or fail dismally. **fall for** (*inf*) to develop a liking or love for (*usu* a person); to be taken in by (a trick, etc). **fall foul of** see under **foul**. **fall in** to (cause to) take places in ranks (*milit*; **fall'-in'** *n*); to become hollowed; to revert; to cave in or collapse. **fall in with** to concur or agree with; to comply with; to meet by chance; to begin to associate with. **fall off** to become detached and drop; to deteriorate; to die away, to perish; to revolt or abandon one's beliefs, principles, etc; to draw back. **fall on** to begin eagerly; to make an attack; to meet (*archaic*). **fall on one's feet** to achieve a successful outcome to a difficult situation; to have unexpected good fortune. **fall out** to quarrel; to happen (that); to turn out; to (cause to) break ranks (*milit*; **fall'-out'** *n*). **fall over** to tumble or trip up (on); to go over to the enemy (*Shakesp*); to go to sleep (*Scot*). **fall over backwards** see under **back**[1]. **fall over oneself** (*inf*) to take a lot of trouble, to be in great haste or eagerness (to do something). **fall short** to turn out to be short or insufficient; to become used up; to fail to attain or reach what is aimed at (with *of*). **fall through** to fail or come to nothing. **fall to** to begin hastily and eagerly; to apply oneself to; to begin to eat. **fall upon** to attack; to rush against; to devolve upon or be the duty of; to chance or come upon. **try a fall** to take a bout at wrestling.

fall² /föl/ *n* a trap. [OE *fealle*, from *feallan* to fall]
❑ **fall guy** *n* (*sl; esp N Am*) a dupe or easy victim; a scapegoat.

fall³ /föl/ *n* the cry given when a whale is sighted or harpooned; the chase of a whale. [Perh from the NE Scottish pronunciation of **whale**]
■ **loose fall** the losing of a whale.

fallacy /fal'ə-si/ *n* an apparently genuine but really illogical argument; deceptive appearance; deception or deceitfulness (*obs*); a wrong but prevalent notion. [L *fallācia*, from *fallāx* deceptive, from *fallere* to deceive]
■ **fallacious** /fə-lā'shəs/ *adj* of the nature of (a) fallacy; deceptive; misleading; not well-founded; causing disappointment. **fallā'ciously** *adv*. **fallā'ciousness** *n*.

fallal /fa-lal'/ *n* a streamer of ribbon; any trifling ornament. ◆ *adj* (*obs*) foppish, trifling.
■ **fallal'ery** *n*. **fallal'ish** *adj*. **fallal'ishly** *adv*.

fallible /fal'i-bl/ *adj* capable of making mistakes, liable to error. [LL *fallibilis*, from *fallere* to deceive]
■ **fall'ibilism** *n* (*philos*) the doctrine that knowledge gained empirically can never be certain. **fall'ibilist** *n* and *adj*. **fallibil'ity** *n* capacity or tendency to make mistakes. **fall'ibly** *adv*.

Fallopian /fə-lō'pi-ən/ *adj* relating to the Italian anatomist Gabriele *Fallopio* (1523–62).
❑ **Fallopian tubes** *n pl* two tubes or ducts through which the ova pass from the ovary to the uterus, perhaps discovered by him.

fallow¹ /fal'ō/ *adj* left unploughed or unsown for a time. ◆ *n* land that is left unploughed or unsown after having been ploughed. ◆ *vt* to plough without seeding. [OE *fealgian* to fallow; *fealh* fallow land]
■ **fall'owness** *n*.
❑ **fall'ow-chat** or **fall'ow-finch** *n* the wheatear.
■ **green fallow** land re-fertilized between crops by sowing a green crop, eg comfrey.

fallow² /fal'ō/ *adj* brownish yellow. [OE *falu* (*fealu*); cf Ger *fahl*, and ON *fölr*]
❑ **fallow deer** *n* a yellowish-brownish deer smaller than the red deer, with broad flat antlers.

false /föls/ *adj* wrong; erroneous; deceptive or deceiving; untruthful; unfaithful (*old*); untrue; not genuine or real, counterfeit; improperly so called; (of teeth, etc) artificial, as opposed to natural; out of tune. ◆ *adv* incorrectly; untruly; dishonestly; faithlessly. ◆ *n* (*obs*) falsehood; untruth. ◆ *vt* (*obs*) to deceive, be false to; to feign; to falsify. [OFr *fals* (Mod *faux*), from L *falsus*, pap of *fallere* to deceive]
■ **false'hood** *n* the state or quality of being false; lack of truth; deceitfulness (*obs*); false appearance (*obs*); an untrue statement; the act of lying; a lie. **false'ly** *adv*. **false'ness** *n*. **fals'er** *n* a falsifier, counterfeiter (*obs*); a deceiver, a liar (*Spenser*). **fal'sies** *n* (*inf*) pads of rubber or other material inserted into a brassière to enlarge or improve the shape of the breasts. **fals'ish** *adj* somewhat false. **fals'ism** *n* a self-evident falsity. **fals'ity** *n* the quality of being false; a false assertion.

❑ **false acacia** *n* one of the shrubs and trees of the N American genus *Robinia*, to which the locust tree also belongs. **false alarm** *n* a warning of danger which turns out to have been unnecessary. **false-bedd'ed** *adj*. **false bedding** *n* (*geol*) irregular lamination running obliquely to the general stratification, due to deposition in banks by varying currents. **false bottom** *n* (eg in a suitcase) a partition cutting off and hiding a space between it and the true bottom. **false card** *n* a card played to deceive. **false-card'** *vi*. **false conception** *n* a uterine growth consisting of non-fetal material. **false dawn** *n* a deceptive appearance simulating dawn (also *fig*). **false face** *n* a mask. **false'-faced** *adj* (*Shakesp*) hypocritical. **false friend** *n* a term in a foreign language that does not mean what it appears to, eg in Italian, *pretendere* does not mean 'to pretend'. **false fruit** *n* a pseudocarp. **false gallop** *n* (*archaic*) a canter. **false'-heart'ed** *adj* treacherous or deceitful. **false hem** *n* a strip of fabric added to the bottom of a garment, etc in order to deepen the hem. **false imprisonment** *n* illegal detention by force or influence. **false leg** *n* the abdominal leg of an insect larva, a proleg. **false memory syndrome** *n* a condition of erroneous memory sometimes attributed to adults who recall childhood experiences, *esp* of sexual abuse, under hypnosis or other medical inducement (*abbrev* **FMS**). **false move** *n* an ill-judged or careless act. **false pregnancy** *n* a psychological disorder in which many of the symptoms of pregnancy are simulated, pseudocyesis (see under **pseud-**). **false pretences** *n pl* deception. **false quantity** *n* pronunciation or use of a long vowel as short or short as long. **false relation** *n* (*music*) occurrence in different parts together or in succession of a tone and a chromatic derivative. **false rib** *n* one that does not reach the breastbone. **false shame** *n* shame felt for something which is not shameful. **false start** *n* a start to a race that is declared invalid, *esp* because a competitor has started before the official signal (*sport*); an unsuccessful attempt to begin an activity. **false step** *n* a stumble; a false move. **false teeth** *n* artificial teeth, dentures. **false topaz** *n* citrine (qv under **citron**). **false vampire** *n* any of various bats wrongly supposed to be blood-suckers. **false'work** *n* a temporary framework used to support a building, etc during construction.
■ **play someone false** to act falsely or treacherously towards a person. **put in a false position** to bring anyone into a position in which he or she will be misunderstood.

falsetto /föl-set'ō/ *n* (*pl* **falsett'os**) (*usu* in a man) a forced (*esp* singing) voice of a range or register above its natural one; a person who uses such a voice; false or strained sentiment. ◆ *adj* and *adv* in falsetto. [Ital *falsetto*, dimin of *falso* false]

falsi crimen /fal-sī krī'mən or fal'sē krē'men/ (*LL*) *n* the crime of falsification, *esp* forgery.

falsify /föl'si-fī/ *vt* (**fals'ifying**; **fals'ified**) to forge or counterfeit; to tamper with; to misrepresent; to prove or declare to be false; to be false to (*obs*); to feign (*obs*). ◆ *vi* (*obs*) to lie. [Fr *falsifier*, from LL *falsificāre*, from L *falsus* false, and *facere* to make]
■ **falsifiabil'ity** *n*. **fals'ifiable** *adj*. **falsificā'tion** *n*. **fals'ifier** *n*.

falsish, falsism and **falsity** see under **false**.

Falstaffian /föl-stäf'i-ən or -staf'/ *adj* like or relating to Shakespeare's *Falstaff*, ie corpulent, jovial, dissolute and irrepressibly impudent.

faltboat /fölt'böt, also folt'/ or **foldboat** /föld'böt/ *n* a small collapsible boat of rubberized sailcloth. [Ger *Faltboot* folding boat]

falter /föl'tər/ *vi* to stumble; to go unsteadily; to hesitate in speech as if taken aback; to flinch; to waver; to flag; to fail. ◆ *vt* to utter falteringly. ◆ *n* unsteadiness. [Prob a frequentative of ME *falden* to fold; connection with *fault* (in which the *l* is late) is not possible]
■ **fal'tering** *n* and *adj*. **fal'teringly** *adv*.

falun gong /fä'lən gong/, also **falun dafa** /dä'fə/ *n* a form of qigong in which, as well as physical and spiritual health, morality of character is promoted; (with *caps*) the movement practising this. [Chin *fǎlún* wheel of dharma, *gōng* exercise, *dàfǎ* great law]

falx /falks/ (*med*) *n* (*pl* **falces** /fal'sēz/) a sickle-shaped or projecting part, as of the dura mater, the outside membrane of the brain and spinal column. [L, a sickle]

fam. *abbrev* : familiar; family.

fame /fām/ *n* renown or celebrity, chiefly in a good sense; public report or rumour (*archaic*). ◆ *vt* (*rare*) to report; to make famous. [Fr, from L *fāma* report, rumour or fame, from *fārī* to speak; cf Gr *phēmē*, from *phanai* to say]
■ **famed** *adj* renowned. **fame'less** *adj* lacking renown.
❑ **fama clamosa** /fam'ə kla-mō'za/ *n* (*Scot*) any notorious rumour ascribing immoral conduct to a minister or office-bearer in a church.
■ **house of ill fame** (*euphem*) a brothel.

familial see under **family**.

familiar /fə-mil'yər or -mil'i-ər/ *adj* well-acquainted or intimate; in the manner of a close friend; intimate to an unwelcome degree, impertinently informal or friendly; free from constraint; unceremonious; having a thorough knowledge; well-known or understood; private or domestic; common or everyday. ◆ *n* a person with whom one is well or long acquainted; a spirit or demon supposed to come to a person, *esp* a witch, etc, at his or her call; a member of a pope's or bishop's household; the officer of the Inquisition who arrested those who were suspected. [OFr *familier*, from L *familiāris*, from *familia* a family]

■ **familiarity** /-*i*-*ar'i*-*ti*/ *n* intimate acquaintanceship; any unusual or unwarrantable freedom in act or speech toward another person, an act of licence (*usu* in *pl*); freedom from constraint. **famil'iarize** or **-ise** *vt* to make thoroughly acquainted with; to make easy by practice or study. **famil'iarly** *adv*.

famille jaune /*fa*-*mē zhōn*/ *n* Chinese porcelain in which the background of the design is yellow, compared with **famille noire** /*nwär*/, in which the background is black, and **famille rose** /*rōz*/ and **famille verte** /*vert*/, which have designs in which respectively pink and green is prominent. [Fr, yellow family]

family /*fam'i-li*/ *n* the household, or all those who live in one house (eg parents, children and servants); parents and their children; the children alone; the descendants of one common ancestor; race; honourable or noble descent; a group of people related to one another, or otherwise connected; a group of animals, plants, languages, etc, often including more than one genus; a collection of curves in the equations of which different values are given to the parameter or parameters (*maths*). ◆ *adj* of or concerning the family; belonging to or specially for a family; suitable for the whole family, or for children as well as parents; large enough for a whole family's needs, family-size. [L *familia*, from *famulus* a servant]

■ **famil'ial** /*fəm-*/ *adj* characteristic of a family. **famil'iar** *adj* see separate entry. **familism** /*fam'*-/ *n* the tendency of a family to cohere as a group; (with *cap*) the principles of the Familists. **Fam'ilist** *n* a member of the 16c mystical sect known as the Family of Love, which based religion upon love independently of faith. **familis'tic** *adj*.
❑ **family allowance** *n* an allowance formerly paid by the state for the support of children, now replaced by child benefit. **family baker, butcher,** etc *n* a small retailer who supplies individual families, not merely institutions. **family Bible** *n* a large Bible for family worship, with a page for recording family events. **family circle** *n* the members of the family taken collectively; one of the galleries in a theatre. **family coach** *n* formerly, a large carriage able to carry a whole family; a parlour game. **family credit** *n* a former payment by the state to a family whose income from employment was below a certain level, replaced in 1999 by a system of income tax credits. **family doctor** *n* a general practitioner. **family fruit tree** or **family tree** *n* a fruit tree bearing different varieties of the same fruit grafted onto it. **family grouping** same as **vertical grouping** (see under **vertical**). **family income supplement** *n* a payment by the state to a family whose income from employment is below a certain level. **family jewels** *n pl* (*usu joc*) everything of value in a household; testicles (*sl*). **family man** *n* a man with a wife and children; a domesticated man; a man dedicated to, and who enjoys sharing activities with, his wife and children. **family name** *n* surname. **family planning** *n* regulating the number and spacing of children, eg by using contraceptives. **family-size** or **family-sized** (of goods) larger than standard. **family tree** *n* a diagram showing the branching of a family.
■ **in a family way** in a familiar or informal manner. **in the family way** (*euphem*) pregnant. **official family** (*US*) the cabinet.

famine /*fam'in*/ *n* extreme general scarcity of food; scarcity of anything; extreme hunger, starvation. [Fr, from L *famēs* hunger]

famish /*fam'ish*/ *vt* to starve. ◆ *vi* (*archaic*) to die of or suffer extreme hunger or thirst. [Obs *fame* to starve, from L *famēs* hunger]
■ **fam'ishment** *n* starvation.
■ **be famished** or **famishing** to feel very hungry.

famous /*fā'məs*/ *adj* renowned; noted; well-known; excellent (*inf*). ◆ *vt* (*archaic*) to make famous. [OFr, from L *fāmōsus*, from *fāma* fame]
■ **fā'mously** *adv*. **fā'mousness** *n*.

famulus /*fam'ū-ləs*/ *n* (*pl* **fam'uli** /-*lī*/) a private secretary or factotum; an attendant, *esp* on a magician or scholar. [L, a servant]

fan[1] /*fan*/ *n* a broad, flat instrument, *esp* used by women to cool themselves, typically in or spreading into the shape of a sector of a circle; a rotating ventilating or blowing apparatus; any fan-shaped structure, eg a deposit of alluvium; anything spreading in a fan shape, eg a bird's wing or tail; a propeller screw or propeller blade; a small sail to keep a windmill to the wind; a whale's tail-fluke; a basket formerly used for winnowing corn by throwing it in the wind; any instrument for winnowing. ◆ *vt* (**fann'ing; fanned**) to move by a fan or the like; to direct a current of air upon; to cool or to kindle with, or as if with, a fan; to fire (a non-automatic gun) by pulling back and releasing the hammer with the other hand; to winnow. ◆ *vi* to move like a fan; to flutter. [OE *fann*, from L *vannus* a basket for winnowing; cf Fr *van*]

■ **fann'er** *n* a fanning apparatus for winnowing, ventilation, etc. **fann'ings** *n pl* the material strained from tea. **fan'wise** *adv* in the manner of a fan.
❑ **fan belt** *n* (in motor vehicles) a continuous belt that drives the alternator and the cooling fan for the radiator. **fan dance** *n* a solo dance in the nude (or nearly so) in which the performer attempts concealment (or nearly so) by tantalizing manipulation of a fan or fans or a bunch of ostrich, etc feathers. **fan'fold** *adj* (of paper) in a continuous strip, scored or perforated so as to fall flat in sections, used for computer print-out. **fan heater** *n* an electric heater containing a fan that drives out heated air. **fan'-jet** *n* (an aeroplane with) an engine in which air is taken in through a fan and some of it, bypassing compressors, combustion chamber and turbines, is added to the exhaust to increase thrust. **fan'light** *n* a window over a door or another window, *orig* resembling an open fan in shape; a skylight. **fan oven** *n* an oven containing a fan that circulates the heated air, making heating uniform and shortening cooking time. **fan palm** *n* any palm with palmate or hand-shaped leaves, *esp* palmetto. **fan'-shaped** *adj* forming a sector of a circle. **fan'tail** *n* a tail shaped like a fan; a variety of domestic pigeon with tail feathers spread out like a fan; a member of various other classes of fantailed birds such as the Australian genus of flycatchers *Rhipidura*; an artificially bred goldfish with double anal and caudal fins; a feature having parts radiating from a centre (*archit*). ◆ *adj* (also **fan'tailed**) having a fan-shaped tail; having parts radiating from a centre (*archit*). **fan tracery** or **fan vaulting** *n* (*archit*) tracery rising from a capital or a corbel, and diverging like the folds of a fan over the surface of a vault. **fan wheel** *n* a wheel with fans on its rim for producing a current of air.
■ **fan out** to fan or spread like a fan from a centre.

fan[2] /*fan*/ *n* a devotee or enthusiastic follower of some sport or hobby or public figure. [From **fanatic**]
■ **fan'dom** *n*. **fan'zine** /-*zēn*/ *n* a magazine by and for amateur enthusiasts, *esp* of science fiction, pop music, or football.
❑ **fan base** *n* the fans of a team, person or thing, considered as a demographic group. **fan'boy** *n* (*inf*) an obsessively enthusiastic fan of an element of popular culture, *esp* comic books or films. **fan club** *n* a group united by devotion to a celebrity. **fan fiction** *n* a style of fiction in which authors take the characters and setting of a favourite book, TV programme, etc and invent new plots and situations for them (short form **fan'fic**). **fan mail** *n* letters from devotees to a celebrity. **fan'site** *n* a website devoted to fans of a particular celebrity, TV programme, etc.

Fanagalo /*fan'ə-gə-lō*/ *n* a South African pidgin language, a mixture of Zulu, Afrikaans and English. [Zulu *fana ka lo* like this, a typical phrase used in southern African mines]

fanal /*fā'nəl*/ (*archaic*) *n* a lighthouse or beacon. [Fr, from Gr *phanos* a lantern, and *phainein* to show]

Fanariot see **Phanariot**.

fanatic /*fə-nat'ik*/ (by some /*fan'ə-tik*/) *n* a person frantically or excessively enthusiastic, *orig* in religion. ◆ *adj* fanatical. [L *fānāticus* belonging to a temple inspired by a god, from *fānum* a temple]
■ **fanat'ical** *adj* extravagantly or unreasonably zealous, *orig* in religious matters; excessively enthusiastic; extravagant (*Shakesp*). **fanat'ically** *adv*. **fanat'icism** /-*i-sizm*/ *n* wild and excessive religious or other enthusiasm. **fanat'icize** or **-ise** /-*i-sīz*/ *vt* to make fanatical. ◆ *vi* to act like a fanatic.

Fanconi's anaemia /*fan-kō'nēz a-nē'mi-ə*/ *n* an inherited form of anaemia which leads to aplastic anaemia and may increase susceptibility to cancer (also called **Fanconi anaemia**). [Guido *Fanconi* (1892–1979), Swiss paediatrician]

fan-cricket same as **fen-cricket** (see under **fen**[1]).

fancy /*fan'si*/ *n* that faculty of the mind by which it recalls, represents, or conjures up past images or impressions, ie imagination, *esp* of a lower, passive, or more trivial kind; an image or representation thus formed in the mind; an unreasonable, lightly-formed or capricious opinion; a whim; a fantasia (*music*); capricious inclination or liking; taste; an individual fancy cake (*Scot*); love (*Shakesp*). ◆ *adj* elaborate; superior; expensive; pleasing to, guided by, or originating in fancy or caprice; fantastic; capriciously departing from the ordinary, the simple, or the plain; ornate; (of flowers) particoloured; (of gems, *esp* diamonds) of a colour other than the normal one. ◆ *vt* (**fan'cying; fan'cied**) to picture in the mind; to imagine; to be inclined to believe; to have a liking for or be sexually attracted to; to consider likely to win; to be pleased with; to breed or cultivate (eg pigeons), with a view to development of conventionally accepted points. ◆ *interj* (also **fancy that**) an exclamation of surprise. [Contracted from **fantasy**]
■ **fan'ciable** *adj* (*inf*) (of a person) sexually attractive. **fan'cied** *adj* formed or conceived by whim, etc; imagined; favoured, *esp* in betting. **fan'cier** *n* a person who fancies; a person who has a liking for anything and is supposed to be a judge of it; a breeder of distinctive varieties. **fan'ciful** *adj* guided or created by fancy; imaginative; whimsical; wild; unreal. **fan'cifully** *adv*. **fan'cifulness** *n*. **fan'ciless** *adj* completely lacking in imagination, etc. **fan'cifully** *adv*. **fan'cily** *adv*.

□ **fancy bread** *n* bread other than plain bread. **fancy cake** *n* a cake decorated with icing, filled with cream, etc. **Fancy Dan** *n* (*inf*) a stylish rather than effective performer. **fancy dress** *n* a costume chosen for fun, *esp* for a party, and *usu* representing a famous type or character; dress arranged according to the wearer's fancy, to represent some character. **fancy dress ball** or **fancy ball** *n* a ball at which fancy dress is worn. **fancy fair** *n* a special sale of fancy articles for some charitable purpose. **fancy-free** *adj* carefree; free of responsibilities; not currently in love. **fancy goods** *n pl* fabrics of variegated rather than simple pattern, applied generally to ornaments and other articles of show. **fancy man** *n* a woman's lover (*derog inf*); a pimp. **fancy monger** *n* (*Shakesp*) a person who makes love, *esp* the love affairs of others, his or her business. **fan'cy-sick** *adj* (*Shakesp*) love-sick. **fancy stitch** *n* a more intricate and decorative stitch than plain stitch. **fancy woman** *n* (*derog inf*) a mistress; a prostitute. **fan'cywork** *n* ornamental needlework.
■ **fancy oneself** (*inf*) to think too highly of oneself. **the fancy** (*old*) sporting characters generally, *esp* boxers; boxing; enthusiasts for a particular sport or pastime. **take a fancy to** to become fond of. **tickle** or **take someone's fancy** to attract someone mildly in some way.

fand¹ */fand/* (*Scot*) *pat* of **find**.

fand² */fand/* or **fond** */fond/* (*obs*) *vi* (*pat* and *pap* **fand'ed, fond'ed** or (*Spenser*) **fond**) to try or attempt; to proceed. [OE *fandian*]

fandangle */fan-dang'gl/* *n* elaborate ornament; nonsense. [Perh from **fandango**]

fandango */fan-dang'gō/* *n* (*pl* **fandang'os** or **fandang'oes**) an old Spanish dance for two, or its music in 3–4 time, with castanets; a gathering for dancing, a ball (*US dialect*). [Sp]

fane¹ */fān/* (*obs*) *n* a flag; a weathercock. [OE *fana* flag; cf Ger *Fahne*; cf **vane** and L *pannus* a cloth]

fane² */fān/* *n* a temple. [L *fānum*]

fanfare */fan'fār/* *n* a flourish of trumpets or bugles; a display of enthusiasm; an elaborate style of bookbinding. ◆ *vt* to herald or acclaim with a fanfare. [Fr, perh from the sound]
■ **fanfarade** */fan-fə-rād'/* *n* a fanfare. **fan'faron** *n* a person who uses bravado; a blusterer or braggart. **fanfarò'na** *n* (*Sp fanfarrona* trumpery; *Walter Scott*) a gold chain. **fanfaronade'** *n* vain boasting; bluster; ostentation. ◆ *vi* to bluster.

fang */fang/* *n* the tooth of a wolf, dog, etc; the venom-tooth of a snake; the embedded part of a tooth, etc; a claw or talon (*obs*); a point (of a tool); a prong; a grip or catch (*Shakesp*); grip or power of suction in a pump (*Scot*). ◆ *vt* (*obs; Shakesp* **phang**) to seize upon or catch; to prime a pump. [OE *fang*, from the same root as *fōn* to seize]
■ **fanged** *adj* having fangs or anything resembling them. **fang'less** *adj*.

fangle */fang'gl/* *n* (*Milton* and *Bunyan*) fancy. ◆ *vt* (*Milton*) to fabricate or decorate in a fancy way. [Mistaken back-formation from **newfangle** or **newfangled**]
■ **fang'led** *adj* (*Shakesp*) foppish.

fango */fang'gō/* *n* (*pl* **fang'os**) a clay or mud from thermal springs in Italy, *esp* at Battaglio, used in the treatment of gout, rheumatism, etc. [Ital, mud, from Gmc]

fanion */fan'yən/* *n* a small flag, *esp* one used in surveying. [OFr *fanion* or *fanon*, from LL *fanō*, *-ōnis* banner, napkin, from OHGer *fano*; cf **fane¹** and **vane**]
■ **fan'on** *n* a cloth for handling holy vessels or offertory bread; a narrow strip of material worn on the left arm by a priest, a maniple (see also **fannel**); a short cape worn by the Pope when celebrating High Mass.

fank¹ */fangk/* (*Scot*) *n* a coil; a noose; a tangle. [Connected with **fang**]

fank² */fangk/* (*Scot*) *n* an enclosure for sheep. [Gaelic *fang*]

fankle */fang'kl/* (*Scot*) *vt* to entangle. ◆ *n* a tangle, muddle. [Connected with **fang**]
■ **fank'led** *adj*.

fannel or **fannell** */fan'əl/* *n* a narrow strip of material worn on the left arm by a priest, a maniple (see also **fanion**). [LL *fanonellus* and *fanula*, dimins of *fanō*; see **fanion**]

fanny */fan'i/* (*sl*) *n* the female genitals (*vulgar*); the buttocks (chiefly *US*). [Origin uncertain]
□ **fanny pack** *n* (chiefly *US*) a bumbag.
■ **fanny about** or **around** to fool about; to waste time.

Fanny Adams */fan'i ad'əmz/* (*sl*) *n* tinned mutton. [The name of a girl murdered and cut up in 1867]
■ **sweet Fanny Adams** or **sweet FA** (*sl*) nothing at all.

fanon see under **fanion**.

fantabulous */fan-tab'ū-ləs/* (*inf*) *adj* superb; wonderful; marvellous. [Blend of **fantastic** and **fabulous**]

fantad see **fantod**.

fan-tan */fan'tan/* *n* a Chinese gambling game where players try to guess the number of objects remaining after some have been removed from the total. [Chin *fǎn tān*]

fantasia */fan-tā'zi-ə, -tä', -zhə* or *-tə-zē'ə/* *n* a musical or other composition not governed by the ordinary rules of form; a piece of music based on a selection of well-known melodies. [Ital, from Gr *phantasiā*; see **fantasy**]

fantasy or **phantasy** */fan'tə-si* or *-zi/* *n* fancy; imagination; mental image; love (*obs*); caprice; fantasia; a story, film, etc not based on realistic characters or setting; this genre; preoccupation with thoughts about unobtainable desires; a mixture of hallucinogenic drugs, *esp* Ecstasy and LSD. ◆ *vt* (**fan'tasying; fan'tasied**) (*archaic*) to fancy or conceive mentally. [OFr *fantasie*, through L from Gr *phantasiā*, from *phantazein* to make visible; cf **fancy** and **fantasia**]
■ **fan'tasied** *adj* filled with fancies. **fan'tasist** *n* a person who creates or indulges in fantasies. **fan'tasize** or **-ise** *vt* and *vi* to indulge in gratifying fantasies; to have whimsical notions. **fan'tasm** *n* same as **phantasm. fantasque** */-task'/* *adj* (*obs*) fantastic. ◆ *n* (*obs*) fantasy. **fan'tast** *n* (*obs*) a person who is prone to fantastic ideas. **fantas'tic** *n* (*obs*) a person who is fantastical; a dandy or fop. **fantas'tical** *adj* fanciful; not real; capricious; whimsical; wild; foppish (*obs*); (**fantastic**) incredible; (**fantastic**) excellent (*inf*). **fantastical'ity** or **fantas'ticalness** *n*. **fantas'tically** *adv*. **fantas'ticate** *vt* and *vi* to fantasize over something; to give fantastic or whimsical treatment to. **fantastica'tion** *n*. **fantas'ticism** */-sizm/* *n*. **fantas'tico** *n* (*pl* **fantas'ticoes**) (*Shakesp; Ital*) a dandy. **fan'tastry** *n*.
□ **fantasy football, cricket**, etc *n* a game or competition in which participants select an imaginary team composed of real-life players from different clubs, and score points according to the actual performance of those players for their respective clubs.

fanteeg see under **fantod**.

Fanti or **Fantee** */fan'tē/* *n* a Ghanaian people; their language.
■ **go Fanti** (*Kipling* and *GK Chesterton*) to adopt the ways of the natives.

fantigue see under **fantod**.

fantoccini */fan-to-chē'nē/* *n pl* marionettes; a marionette show. [Ital, pl of *fantoccino*, dimin of *fantoccio* a puppet, from *fante* a boy, from L *īnfāns*, *-antis*]

fantod */fan'tod/* or **fantad** */-tăd/* (*sl*) *n* a fidgety, fussy person, *esp* a ship's officer; (*usu* in *pl*) fidgets; anxiety.
■ **fantigue** or **fanteeg** */fan-tēg'/* *n* anxiety or agitation.

fantom same as **phantom**.

fantoosh */fan-toosh'/* (*Scot*) *adj* fashionable; pretentious or showy. [Poss connected with Eng dialect *fanty-sheeny* fussy or showy, from Ital *fantoccino* marionette]

fanzine see under **fan²**.

FAO *abbrev* : Food and Agriculture Organization of the United Nations.

fao *abbrev* : for the attention of.

fap */fap/* (*Shakesp*) *adj* fuddled or drunk.

FAQ *abbrev* : Frequently Asked Questions, a list of such questions and their answers, found eg on the Internet.

faq *abbrev* : fair average quality; free alongside quay.

faquir */fā-kēr'/* *n* same as **fakir**.

far */fär/* *adj* (**fur'ther** or **far'ther; fur'thest** or **far'thest**) remote, distant; more distant of two (in *Shakesp* as *compar*); (of an animal) off, right-hand (ie the side furthest from a person leading it); advanced (*obs*). ◆ *adv* to, at, or over a great distance or advanced stage; remotely; in a great degree; very much; long (*obs*). ◆ *vt* (*dialect*) to remove to a distance. —See also **farther**. [OE *feor*; Du *ver*; ON *fiarre* or *feorr*]
■ **far'most** *adv* most distant or remote. **far'ness** *n* the state of being far; remoteness or distance.
□ **far'away** *adj* distant; abstracted or absent-minded. ◆ *n* (*rare*) the distance. **faraway'ness** *n*. **far cry** *n* a long distance. **Far East** *n* China, Korea, Japan, etc; often also the countries from Myanmar (Burma) to Indonesia and the Philippines and, as used by some, the countries of the Indian subcontinent. **far'-fetched'** (*obs* **far'fet**) *adj* fetched or brought from a remote place (*archaic*); forced or unnatural; improbable, unlikely, unconvincing. **far'-flung** *adj* placed or situated far and wide; extensive. **far'-forth** *adv* (*Spenser*) far. **Far North** *n* the Arctic regions. **far'-off** *adj* and *adv* in the distance. **far'-out** *adj* wonderful or amazing (rather *old*); weird; avant-garde; (of jazz or its addicts) more up to date than 'cool'; intellectual; satisfying. **far-reach'ing** *adj* having wide validity, scope, or influence. **far-see'ing** *adj* able to foresee future events. **far-sight'ed** *adj* seeing far; having or exhibiting foresight or shrewdness of judgement; having defective eyesight for near objects. **far-sight'edness** *n*. **far'-sought** *adj* sought at a distance. **Far South** *n* the Antarctic regions. **far'-spent** *adj* far advanced. **Far West** *n* (*esp* formerly) the Great Plains, Rocky

Mountains and Pacific side of N America; (now *usu*) the area between the Rockies and the Pacific.
■ **as far as** to the extent that; up to (a particular place). **by far** in a very great degree. **far and away** by a great deal. **far and near** or **far and wide** everywhere, all about. **far be it** God forbid. **far between** at wide intervals; rare. **far from it** on the contrary. **far gone** well-advanced in time, progress, decline, etc. **go too far** to go beyond reasonable limits, *esp* of tact or behaviour. **I'll see you far** (or **farther**) **first** I will not do it by any means. **in so far as** to the extent that.

farad /*far'əd* or *far'ad*/ *n* a derived SI unit, the unit of electrical capacitance (symbol **F**), defined as that which, when charged by a potential difference of one volt, carries a charge of one coulomb. [Michael *Faraday* (1791–1867), English chemist and physicist]
■ **far'aday** *n* a unit used in electrolysis, equal to 96 500 coulombs. **faradic** /*-ad'ik*/ or **faradaic** /*far-ə-dā'ik*/ *adj* relating to Faraday, *esp* in connection with induced currents. **far'adism** *n* treatment by induced currents. **faradizā'tion** or **-s-** *n*. **far'adize** or **-ise** *vt* (*med*) to stimulate by induced currents.

farand, **farrand** /*far'ənd*, *fär'*/ or **farrant** /*-ənt*/ (*Scot*) *adj* having a certain appearance or manner, *esp* in such compound forms as *auld-farand* old-fashioned, quaint, precocious, sagacious; *fair-farand* goodly, specious. [ME *farand* comely. Origin obscure; prob prp of **fare**]

farandine or **farrandine** /*far'ən-dēn*/ or **ferrandine** /*fer'*/ (*obs*) *n* a cloth or a dress of silk with wool or hair. [Fr *ferrandine*]

farandole /*far-ən-dōl'*/ *n* a Provençal dance in which dancers form a long string; music for it, in 6–8 time. [Provençal *farandoula*]

farborough /*fär'bə-rə*/ or **tharborough** /*thär'*/ *n* Goodman Dull's pronunciation of **thirdborough** in Shakespeare's *Love's Labours Lost* I.1.182.

FARC /*färk*/ *abbrev* : *Fuerzas Armadas Revolucionarias de Colombia* (*Sp*), Revolutionary Armed Forces of Colombia.

farce /*färs*/ *n* comedy of extravagant humour, buffoonery, and improbability; a ridiculous or meaningless display; a hollow formality; stuffing or forcemeat (*cookery*). ◆ *vt* to cram; to stuff, fill with stuffing; to swell out (*Shakesp*). [Fr *farce* stuffing, from L *farcīre* to stuff; the connecting links of meaning seem to be interpolation, theatrical gag, buffoonery; cf **farse**]
■ **farceur** /*fär-sœr'*/ or (*fem*) **farceuse** /*-sœz'*/ *n* (*Fr*) a joker or buffoon; a person who writes or acts in farces. **farci** /*fär-sē'*/ *adj* (*Fr*; *cookery*) stuffed. **far'cical** *adj*. **farcical'ity** *n* farcical quality. **far'cically** *adv*. **far'cify** *vt* to turn into a farce. **farc'ing** *n* (*cookery*) stuffing.

farcy /*fär'si*/ *n* chronic glanders, a disease *esp* of horses (also (*obs*) **far'cin**). [Fr *farcin*, from LL *farcīminum*]
■ **far'cied** *adj*.
❑ **far'cy-bud** *n* a swollen lymphatic gland, as occurs in farcy.

fard /*färd*/ *n* white paint for the face. ◆ *vt* to paint with fard; to gloss over; to trick out. [Fr, of Gmc origin]

fardage /*fär'dij*/ (*naut*; *obs*) *n* wood placed in the bottom of a ship's hold to keep cargo out of the bilge-water, dunnage. [Fr]

fardel¹ /*fär'dl*/ (*obs*) *n* a fourth part. [OE *fēortha dæl*, fourth deal]

fardel² /*fär'dl*/ (*archaic*) *n* a pack; anything cumbersome or irksome; the third stomach of a ruminant, the manyplies or omasum. [OFr *fardel* (Fr *fardeau*), dimin of *farde* a burden, poss from Ar *fardah* a package]
❑ **far'del-bag** *n* the omasum. **far'del-bound** *adj* (*esp* of cattle and sheep), constipated by the retention of food in the omasum.

farden or **farding** /*fär'dən*/ (*obs* or *dialect*) same as **farthing**.

fare /*fär*/ *vi* to get on or succeed; to happen well or badly to; to be in any particular state, to be, to go on; to be fed; to travel (*archaic*). ◆ *n* (*orig* Spenser) a course or passage; the price of passage; a passenger (or passengers); food or provisions for the table. [OE *faran*; Ger *fahren*]
■ **far'er** *n*.
❑ **fare stage** *n* one of a series of divisions of a bus route for which there is a fixed scale of fares; a bus stop that marks such a division. **farewell'** *interj* may you fare well, a parting wish for safety or success; goodbye. ◆ *n* good wishes at parting; the act of departure. ◆ *adj* /*fär'wel*/ parting; said when bidding farewell; final.

farfalle /*fär-fal'ē* or *-i*/ *n pl* pasta in the shape of bow ties or butterflies. [Ital, pl of *farfalla* butterfly]

farfet see **far-fetched** under **far**.

farina /*fə-rī'nə* or *fə-rē'nə*/ *n* ground corn; meal; starch; pollen; a mealy powder. [L *farīna*, from *fār* corn]
■ **farinaceous** /*far-i-nā'shəs*/ *adj* mealy; consisting of cereals. **far'inose** /*-i-nōs*/ *adj* yielding farina.

Faringee see **Feringhi**.

farl or **farle** /*färl*/ (*Scot*) *n* the quarter of a round cake of flour or oatmeal; a cake. [fardel¹]

farm /*färm*/ *n* a tract of land (*orig* one leased or rented) used for cultivation and pasturage, along with a house and other necessary buildings; a farmhouse; a farmstead; a piece of land or water used for breeding animals (eg *mink farm* or *oyster farm*); a place for treatment and disposal (eg *sewage farm*); a place where people are handed over to to be taken care of (eg *baby farm*); a fixed payment (*obs*); a lease (*Spenser*); a fixed payment by way of taxes, etc (*hist*); the letting out of the right to collect rents, taxes, etc in exchange for a fixed sum (*hist*). ◆ *adj* of, belonging to, appropriate to, a farm. ◆ *vt* to cultivate; to rear (animals) for sale; to use as a farm; to arrange for maintenance of at fixed price; to grant or receive the rents, taxes, etc from for a fixed sum; to rent to or from another person. ◆ *vi* to practise the business of a farmer. [LL *firma* a fixed payment, from L *firmus* firm]
■ **farm'able** *adj*. **farmed** *adj* (of animals, esp fish) reared on a farm rather than wild. **farm'er** *n* a person who farms land; the tenant of a farm; a person who receives taxes, etc in return for fixed payment. **far'meress** *n* (*rare*) a female farmer. **farm'ery** *n* the buildings of a farm. **farm'ing** *n* the business of cultivating land.
❑ **farmer general** *n* a member of a group who, in pre-Revolutionary France, had bought the right to receive certain taxes. **Farmer Giles** *n pl* (*Brit* and *Aust* rhyming *sl*) piles, haemorrhoids. **farmer's lung** *n* a lung disease caused by the spores of the fungus actinomycetes which develop in hay baled while it is still damp. **farmers' market** *n* a market where food producers sell their products directly to local consumers. **farm'-gate** price *n* the average price received for a food product by its producer. **farm hand** or **farm labourer** *n* a person who works on a farm for wages. **farm'house** *n* the farmer's house attached to a farm. **farmhouse loaf** *n* an oval or rectangular loaf of white bread with a rounded top. **farm'-in** *adj* (*econ*) acquired by farming into (qv below) a company. **farm'land** *n* land used for farming. **farm'-offices** *n pl* outbuildings on a farm. **farm'-place**, **farm'stead**, **farm steading** or (*Scot*) **farm'-toun** /*-tūn*/ *n* a farmhouse with buildings belonging to it. **farm team** *n* a sports club run with the aim of developing players for a bigger club. **farm'yard** *n* a yard or enclosure surrounded by farm buildings.
■ **buy the farm** (*US sl*) to die. **farm into** to take shares in a company or concern (*usu* of a company obtaining an interest in another). **farm out** to board out for fixed payment; to give (eg work for which one is responsible) to others to carry out or take care of.

farmost see under **far**.

farnesol /*fär'ni-sol*/ *n* an alcohol, $C_{15}H_{25}OH$, found in various essential oils and used in perfumes. [From *Acacia farnesiana*, after Odoardo *Farnese*, 16c Italian cardinal]

faro /*fā'rō*/ *n* a game of chance played by betting on the order of appearance of certain cards. [Perh from *Pharaoh*; reason unknown]

farouche /*fə-roosh'* or *fa-*/ *adj* shy or ill at ease; sullen and unsociable; socially inexperienced and lacking polish. [Fr, wild, shy, savage]

farrago /*fä-rä'gō* or *fə-rā'gō*/ *n* (pl **farragos** or **farrag'oes**) a disordered mixture; a confused mass of objects or people (*obs*). [L *farrāgō*, *-inis* mixed fodder, from *fār* grain]
■ **farraginous** /*fə-raj'in-əs* or *-rāj'*/ *adj* miscellaneous, jumbled.

farrand or **farrant** see **farand**.

farrandine see **farandine**.

farren /*far'ən*/ (*dialect*) *n* a division of land; a right of common (qv under **right¹**). [Origin uncertain]

farrier /*far'i-ər*/ *n* a person who shoes horses; a person who cures horses' diseases (*old*); a person in charge of cavalry horses (*old*). [OFr *ferrier*, from L *ferrum* iron]
■ **farr'iery** *n* the farrier's art; veterinary surgery.

farrow¹ /*far'ō*/ *n* a litter of pigs. ◆ *vi* or *vt* to give birth to (pigs). [OE *fearh*, a pig; Ger (dimin) *Ferkel*; L *porcus*]

farrow² /*far'ō*/ *adj* (of a cow) not pregnant for the time being. [Ety doubtful; cf Flem *verwekoe*, *varwekoe* with *farrow cow*]

farruca /*fa-roo'ka*/ (*Sp*) *n* a Spanish gypsy dance with abrupt variations of tempo and mood.

farse /*färs*/ *n* an explanation of the Latin epistle in the vernacular. ◆ *vt* to extend by interpolation. [**farce**]

Farsi /*fär'sē*/ *n* Modern Persian, an Indo-European language and the official spoken language of Iran. [*Fars* ('Persia'), province of SW Iran]

fart /*färt*/ (*vulgar sl*) *vi* to break wind from the anus. ◆ *n* an act of breaking wind; a worthless person. [OE (assumed) *feortan*; cf Gr *perdesthai*]
■ **fart about** or **around** to fool about; to waste time.

farthel /*fär'dhəl*/ (*Scot*) *n* same as **farl**.

farther /*fär'dhər*/, **farthermore**, **farthermost** and **farthest** same as **further¹**, etc, and sometimes preferred where the notion of distance is more prominent. [A variant (ME *ferther*) of **further¹** that came to be thought a compar of **far**]

farthing /fär'dhing/ n one-fourth of a pre-1971 penny; anything very small; a fourth part (obs); the Gr assarion (L as) and also kodrantēs (L quadrāns), one fourth of an as (Bible). [OE fēorthing a fourth part, from fēortha fourth, and sfx -ing]
■ **far'thingless** adj.
◻ **far'thingland** n a varying area of land. **far'thingsworth** n as much as a farthing will buy.

farthingale /fär'dhing-gāl/ n a kind of crinoline of whalebone for extending a woman's dress outward from the waist. [OFr verdugale, from Sp verdugado hooped, from verdugo rod]

fartlek /färt'lek/ n alternate fast and slow running in one session, done as training work for marathons and other long-distance races. [Swed fart speed, and lek play]

FAS abbrev : Fellow of the Antiquarian Society; Fellow of the Society of Arts; fetal alcohol syndrome; (also **fas**) free alongside ship.

fasces /fas'ēz/ n pl the bundle of rods, with or without an axe, borne before an ancient Roman magistrate. [L fascēs, pl of fascis bundle]

Fasching /fash'ing/ (Ger) n (Shrovetide) carnival.

fascia /fā'shə or fā'shi-ə/ n a board over a shopfront, commonly bearing the name of the shop; (also **fasc'ia-board**) the instrument-board of a motor car; a protective cover over the front of an electronic device, esp a mobile phone; a band or fillet (obs); a broad flat band, as in an architrave, or over a shopfront (archit); any bandlike structure; /fash'i-ə/ connective tissue ensheathing a muscle (zool). [L fascia band, bandage]
■ **fasc'ial** adj. **fasc'iate** or **fasc'iated** adj. **fasciā'tion** n (bot) union of a number of parts side by side in a flat plate. **fasciitis** /fash-i-ī'tis/ n inflammation of the fascia, specif **necrotizing fasciitis**, a bacterial infection that causes rapid decay of the fascia and soft tissue, and **plantar fasciitis**, inflammation of a band of tissue (the plantar fascia) that supports the arch of the foot, causing pain in the heel. **fasciola** /fə-sī'ō-lə/ or **fasciole** /fas'i-ōl/ n a band of colour. **fascioliasis** /fas-i-ō-lī'ə-sis/ n an intestinal infection caused by a liver fluke (Fasciola hepatica).

fascicle /fas'i-kl/, also **fascicule** /-kūl/ or **fasciculus** /-ik'ū-ləs/ n (pl **fasc'icles**, **fasc'icules** or **fascic'ūlī**) a bundle or bunch, esp a bunched tuft of branches, roots, fibres, etc; a part of a book issued in parts. [L fasciculus, dimin of fascis bundle]
■ **fasc'icled**, **fascic'ūlar**, **fascic'ūlate** or **fascic'ūlated** adj. **fascicūla'tion** n.

fascinate /fas'i-nāt/ vt to interest exceedingly, intrigue; to control by the eye like a snake; to hold spellbound; to charm; to captivate; to bewitch, enchant or cast the evil eye upon (obs). [L fascināre, -ātum ; perh related to Gr baskainein to bewitch]
■ **fasc'inating** adj charming, delightful; intriguing, deeply interesting; compelling, irresistible. **fascinā'tion** n the act of fascinating; power to harm, control, allure, or render helpless by looks or spells; the state of being fascinated. **fasc'inātor** n a person who fascinates; a woman's light, soft, head-covering (rare); a woman's ornamental headpiece, typically decorated with feathers, beading, etc.

fascine /fa-sēn'/ n a brushwood bundle, used to fill ditches, protect a shore, etc from attack. [Fr, from L fascīna, from fascis a bundle]

fascio /fä'shō/ n (pl **fasci** /fä'shē/) an organized political group or club. [Ital fascio bundle or group, with a hint of **fasces**]

fasciola and **fascioliasis** see under **fascia**.

Fascism /fash'i-zm/ (Ital **Fascismo** /fä-shēz'mō/) n the authoritarian form of government in Italy from 1922 to 1943, characterized by extreme nationalism, militarism, anti-communism and restrictions on individual freedom; (also without cap) the methods, doctrines, etc of fascists or the Fascists; (usu without cap) rigid and intolerant enforcement of any doctrine. [Ety as for **fascio**]
■ **Fasc'ist** (Ital **Fascista** /fä-shēs'tə/) n (pl **Fasc'ists** (Ital **Fascis'ti** /-tē/)) a member of the ruling party in Italy from 1922 to 1943, or a similar party elsewhere; (also without cap) an exponent or supporter of Fascism or (loosely) anyone with extreme right-wing, nationalistic, etc views or methods. ◆ adj (also without cap) of or relating to Fascists or Fascism. **fascis'tic** adj.

fash /fash/ (Scot) vt to trouble or bother. ◆ vi to be vexed; to take trouble or pains; to annoy. ◆ n pains or trouble; annoyance. [OFr fascher (Fr fâcher), from L fastidium disgust]
■ **fash'ery** n. **fashious** /fash'əs/ adj troublesome or vexatious. **fash'iousness** n.
■ **never fash your thumb** take no trouble in the matter.

fashion /fash'n/ n the make or cut of a thing; form or pattern; vogue or trend; the prevailing mode or shape of dress or that imposed or favoured by those whose lead is accepted; a prevailing custom; manner; sort, type or kind; awareness of, and attention to, the latest trends in dress, behaviour, activities, enthusiasms, etc; high society; appearance. ◆ vt to make; to mould according to a pattern; to suit or adapt. ◆ combining form in the manner of, as in parrot-fashion. [OFr fachon, from L factiō, -ōnis, from facere to make]
■ **fashionabil'ity** n. **fash'ionable** adj according to prevailing fashion; prevailing or in use at any period; observant of the fashion in dress or living; moving in high society; used or frequented by people of fashion. ◆ n a fashionable person. **fash'ionableness** n. **fash'ionably** adv. **fash'ioner** n. **fash'ionist** or **fashionista** /-ēs'ta/ n a follower or setter of fashion.
◻ **fash'ion-forward** adj creating or embracing early the newest fashion trends. **fashion house** n an establishment in which fashionable clothes are designed, made and sold. **fashion jewellery** n costume jewellery. **fash'ionmongering** or **fash'ionmonging** adj (Shakesp) behaving like a fop. **fashion plate** n a picture showing the latest style of (esp formal) dress; a well-groomed, fashionably dressed person. **fashion victim** n (inf) someone who slavishly follows the latest fashions.
■ **after** or **in a fashion** in a way; to a certain extent. **do something**, etc **as though it were going out of fashion** (inf) to do something with extra vigour or enthusiasm, fast and furiously, as though for the last time. **in fashion** currently favoured; fashionable. **in the fashion** in accordance with the prevailing style of dress, etc. **out of fashion** old-fashioned; unfashionable.

fashions /fash'ənz/ (Shakesp) n pl for **farcy**, **farcin**.

fashious, etc see under **fash**.

FAST /fäst/ abbrev : Federation Against Software Theft.

fast[1] /fäst/ adj quick; rapid; (of a clock) showing a time in advance of the correct time; promoting rapid play; for quick-moving traffic, as in fast lane ; (of film) requiring only brief exposure; seeking excitement; rash; dissolute; sexually promiscuous. ◆ adv swiftly; in rapid succession; in advance of the correct time; extravagantly or dissipatedly. [A special use of **fast**[2] derived from Scand sense of urgent]
■ **fast'ish** adj somewhat fast. **fast'ness** n.
◻ **fast'back** n a car whose roof slopes smoothly down towards the rear, giving a streamlined effect; a particular breed of pig which yields lean meat. **fast'ball** n (baseball) a delivery thrown at maximum speed. **fast bowler** n. **fast bowling** n (cricket) bowling in which the ball is delivered fast, pace bowling. **fast-breeder reactor** n a nuclear reactor using fast neutrons which produces at least as much fissionable material as it uses. **Fast'ext** n a facility on some television sets for scrolling through teletext pages faster than normal. **fast food** or **foods** n kinds of food, eg hamburgers, chips, etc, which can be prepared and served quickly. **fast forward** n the facility provided by a cassette recorder, DVD player, etc for moving quickly through recorded material without playing it. **fast-for'ward** vt to advance (a tape, DVD, etc) quickly by this means. ◆ vi (inf) to pass or move on without delay. **fast lane** n a lane on a motorway or dual carriageway that is used to overtake slower vehicles. **fast neutron** n a neutron of very high energy, usu over 10000 electronvolts. **fast reactor** n a nuclear reactor using fast neutrons, and little or no moderator. **fast stream** n (in eg the civil service) a category of personnel who have been selected for rapid promotion to senior posts. **fast'-talk** vt to persuade with rapid, plausible talk. **fast'-talking** adj. **fast track** n (inf) the routine for accelerating the progress of a proposal, etc through its formalities; the quick but competitive route to advancement. **fast'-track** vt to process or promote speedily. ◆ adj relating to or being on a fast track. **fast'-track'er** n. **fast worker** n a person who gains his or her ends quickly and easily, esp by unscrupulous means.
■ **a fast buck** (inf) money quickly and easily obtained. **fast and furious** (or **furiously**) rapidly and vigorously. (**life**) **in the fast lane** (a way of life) full of pressure, excitement and glamour. **pull a fast one** or **put a fast one over** (inf) to gain an advantage by trickery.

fast[2] /fäst/ adj firm; fixed; steadfast; fortified; (of sleep) sound; (of colours) not liable to fade or run. ◆ combining form (esp archaic) denoting firmly fixed, as in lockfast, colourfast. ◆ adv firmly, unflinchingly; soundly or sound (asleep); close or near (archaic or literary). [OE fæst ; Ger fest]
■ **fast'ly** adv (Shakesp) firmly. **fast'ness** n fixedness; a stronghold, fortress, castle.
◻ **fast'-and-loose'** n a cheating game practised at fairs, the dupe being invited to put a stick in the loop of a coiled belt so that it cannot be pulled away (also called **prick-the-garter**). **fast'-hand'ed** adj tight-fisted, mean.
■ **fast by** close to, close by. **hard and fast** (of a rule, etc) unalterable, inflexible, strict. **play fast and loose** (from the cheating game) to be unreliable or shifty; to behave without sense of moral obligation; to trifle (with with).

fast[3] /fäst/ vi to abstain from food completely or restrict one's diet, eg as a religious duty; to go hungry. ◆ vt to deprive of food. ◆ n abstinence from food; special abstinence ordered by the church; the day or time of fasting. [OE fæstan to fast; Ger fasten]
■ **Fast'ens** n (OE fæstenes genitive of fæsten a fast) Shrove Tuesday (also called **Fastens-eve** (Scot **Fasten-e'en** or **Fastern's-e'en**) or

Fastens Tuesday). **fast'er** *n* a person who fasts. **fast'ing** *n* religious abstinence from food.

❑ **fast'-day** *n* a day of religious fasting; a day for humiliation and prayer, *esp* before communion.

fast[4] */fāst/ (Spenser)* a spelling of **faced**.

fasten */fä'sn/ vt* to make fast or firm; to fix securely; to attach. ◆ *vi* to be capable of being fastened; to become fastened; to remain stationary. [**fast**[2]]

■ **fastener** */fäs'nər/ n* a clip, catch, or other means of fastening. **fas'tening** */fäs'ning/ n* a device which fastens.

■ **fasten on** to direct (one's eyes) on; to seize on, eg a fact; to fix the blame, responsibility for, on (a person) (*inf*).

fasti */fas'tī* or *fä'stē/ n pl* same as **dies fasti** (see under **dies**[1]); an enumeration of the days of the year, a calendar; annals. [L]

fastidious */fa-stid'i-əs/ adj* easily repelled or disgusted; meticulous or over-meticulous; difficult to please; exacting in taste, highly discriminating; (of bacteria) having complex requirements for growth. [L *fastīdiōsus*, from *fastīdium* loathing]

■ **fastid'iously** *adv*. **fastid'iousness** *n*.

fastigiate */fa-stij'i-āt/ adj* (of a roof) pointed, sloping to a point or edge; with branches more or less erect and parallel (*bot*); conical. [L *fastīgium* a gable end or roof]

■ **fastig'iated** *adj*. **fastig'ium** *n* the apex of a building; a gable end; a pediment.

FAT (*comput*) *abbrev*: file allocation table, part of a disk giving information about the location of its files.

fat[1] */fat/ adj* (**fatt'er**; **fatt'est**) plump, fleshy; well filled out; thick, full-bodied (as of printing types); corpulent; obese; having much, or of the nature of, adipose tissue or the substance it contains; oily; fruitful or profitable; (of a theatrical role) yielding rich opportunities for displaying one's talent; rich in some important constituent; gross; fulsome. ◆ *n* a substance found in adipose tissue; solid animal or vegetable oil; any member of a group of naturally occurring substances consisting of the glycerides of higher fatty acids, eg palmitic acid, stearic acid, oleic acid (*chem*); the richest part of anything; a piece of work offering more than usual profit for effort; a role or passage that enables an actor or musician to show his or her talent; inclination to corpulence; a fat animal; money (*sl*). ◆ *adv* (in golf) striking the ground before the ball. ◆ *vt* (**fatt'ing**; **fatt'ed**) to make fat. ◆ *vi* to grow fat. [OE *fætt* fatted]

■ **fat'ling** *n* a young animal fattened for slaughter. ◆ *adj* small and fat. **fat'ly** *adv* grossly; lumberingly. **fat'ness** *n* quality or state of being fat; fullness of flesh; richness; fertility; that which makes something fertile. **fatt'ed** *adj* see **kill the fatted calf** below. **fatt'en** *vt* to make fat or fleshy; to enrich; to make fertile. ◆ *vi* to grow fat. **fatt'ener** *n*. **fatt'ening** *n* (also *adj*). **fatt'iness** *n*. **fatt'ish** *adj* somewhat fat. **fatt'ism** *n* discrimination against fat people. **fatt'ist** *n* and *adj*. **fatt'y** *adj* containing fat; having (some of) the qualities of fat. ◆ *n* (*derog*) a fat person.

❑ **fat'back** *n* (*US*) fatty meat from the upper part of a side of pork, *usu* dried and cured with salt. **fat body** *n* an area of fatty tissue in the body of an animal, *esp* an insect, in which energy is stored. **fat'brained** *adj* (*Shakesp*) stupid. **fat camp** *n* (*US*) a residential slimming camp for overweight children. **fat cat** *n* (*orig US sl*) a wealthy, prosperous person, *esp* one who is thought to have gained excessive rewards. **fat'-cat** *adj*. **fat city** *n* (also with *caps*; *US sl*) easy circumstances, prosperous conditions. **fat'-face** or **fat-faced'** *adj* having a fat or broad face. **fat-fing'er** *adj* (*inf*) denoting a computer error caused by the clumsiness of the person inputting the data. **fat'-free** *adj* (of food) containing virtually no fat. **fat'head** *n* (*inf*) a stupid, dim-witted person. **fat-head'ed** *adj*. **fat hen** *n* any one of various thick-leaved plants, *esp* of the goosefoot family. **fat'-lute** *n* a mixture of pipe-clay and linseed oil, for filling joints in wood, *esp* in shipbuilding. **fat mouse** *n* any of several kinds of mouse of the genus *Steatomys*, found in dry regions of Africa, that store fat and are eaten as a delicacy. **fat stock** or **fat'stock** *n* livestock fattened for market. **fat suit** *n* a padded costume worn by an actor to make him or her seem fatter than they really are. **fat'-tailed** *adj* having much fat in the tail, as do certain Asiatic and African sheep. **fatty acids** *n pl* acids which with glycerine form fats, some of which (**essential fatty acids**) cannot be synthesized by the body and must be supplied in the diet. **fatty degeneration** *n* morbid deposition of fat. **fatty heart**, etc *n* fatty degeneration of the heart, etc. **fatty oils** same as **fixed oils** (see under **fix**). **fat'-witted** *adj* dull-witted, stupid.

■ (a) **fat chance** (*sl*) little or no opportunity or prospect. **a fat lot** (*sl*) not much. **kill the fatted calf** see under **calf**[1]. **live off the fat of the land** to live in luxury. **the fat is in the fire** a critical act has precipitated the trouble.

fat[2] */fat/ n* a vessel for holding liquids; a vat; a dry measure of nine bushels. [See **vat**]

Fatah */fat'ə/ n* a Palestinian political organization, now part of the PLO, seeking the liberation of Palestine by use of arms. [Ar, shortening of the movement's name]

fatal */fā'tl/ adj* causing death; mortal; bringing ruin; calamitous; decisive, critical, fateful; destined, unavoidable; belonging to or appointed by fate; announcing fate. [L *fātālis*, from *fātum*; see **fate**]

■ **fat'alism** *n* the doctrine that all events are subject to fate, and happen by unavoidable necessity; acceptance of this doctrine; lack of effort in the face of threatened difficulty or disaster. **fat'alist** *n* a person who believes in fatalism. **fatalist'ic** *adj*. **fatality** */fə-tal'i-ti/ n* a fatal occurrence; a person who has been killed, *esp* in an accident, etc; the state of being fatal or unavoidable; the decree of fate; fixed tendency to disaster or death; mortality. **fat'ally** *adv*.

■ **the fatal sisters** see under **fate**.

fata Morgana */fä'tə mör-gä'nə/* (also with *cap*) *n* a striking kind of mirage seen most often in the Strait of Messina. [Supposed to be caused by the fairy (Ital *fata*) *Morgana* of Arthurian legend]

fate */fāt/ n* inevitable destiny or necessity; appointed lot; destined term of life; ill-fortune; doom; final issue; (in *pl*; with *cap*; *Gr myth*) the three goddesses of fate, Clotho, Lachesis, and Atropos, who determine the birth, life, and death of men and women, **the fatal sisters**. [L *fātum* a prediction, from *fātus* spoken, from *fārī* to speak]

■ **fat'ed** *adj* doomed; destined; invested with the power of destiny (*Shakesp*); enchanted (*Dryden*). **fate'ful** *adj* critical, decisive, having significant consequence; bringing calamity or death; prophetic, portentous; controlled by, or revealing the power of fate. **fate'fully** *adv*. **fate'fulness** *n*.

■ **a fate worse than death** *orig* an ordeal more horrible or degrading than simple death, *esp* rape; (now chiefly *facetious*) any terrible ordeal.

father */fä'dhər/ n* a male parent; a protector who shows the love, concern, etc of a male parent; an ancestor or forefather; a contriver or originator; a title of respect applied to a venerable man, to confessors, monks, priests, etc; a member of certain fraternities; (*usu* in *pl*) a member of a ruling body, such as *conscript fathers*, *city fathers*; the oldest member, or member of longest standing, of a profession or body; any of a group of ecclesiastical writers of the early centuries, *usu* ending with Ambrose, Jerome, and Augustine; (with *cap*) the first person of the Christian Trinity. ◆ *vt* to be the father of, procreate or beget; to adopt; to invent, originate; to acknowledge that one is the father or author of; to ascribe to someone as his offspring or production. [OE *fæder*; Ger *Vater*, L *pater*, Gr *patēr*]

■ **fa'therhood** *n* the state or fact of being a father; fatherly authority (*archaic*). **fa'therless** *adj* having no living father; without a known author. **fa'therlessness** *n*. **fath'erlike** *adj*. **fa'therliness** *n*. **fa'therly** *adj* like a father; paternal. **fa'thership** *n*.

❑ **Father Christmas** same as **Santa Claus**. **father figure** *n* a senior person of experience and authority looked on as a trusted leader or protector. **fa'ther-in-law** *n* (*pl* **fa'thers-in-law**) the father of one's husband or wife; a stepfather (*archaic*). **fa'therland** *n* native land, *esp* Germany (*Vaterland*); the country of one's ancestors. **fa'ther-lash'er** *n* a name applied to two bullhead fish found round the British coasts. **Father's Day** *n* a day on which fathers are honoured, as, in the UK and the USA, the third Sunday in June.

■ **be gathered to one's fathers** (*Bible*) to die and be buried. **Holy Father** the Pope. **like father, like son** said when remarking inherited tendencies. **the father and mother of** see under **mother**[1].

fathom */fadh'əm/ n* (*pl* **fath'om** or **fath'oms**) *orig* the reach of the outstretched arms; now a unit of measurement for the depth of water, equal to 6 feet or 1.8 metres; penetration of mind; a timber measure equal to 216 cubic feet. ◆ *vt* to discover the depth of; to comprehend or get to the bottom of; to measure or encompass with outstretched arms (*archaic*). [OE *fæthm*; Du *vadem*, Ger *Faden*]

■ **fath'omable** *adj*. **fath'omless** *adj* unfathomable.

❑ **fathom'eter** *n* a sonic depth measurer. **fathom line** *n* a sailor's line and lead for taking soundings.

fatidical */fā-* or *fə-tid'i-kl/* (*rare*) *adj* having the power to foretell future events; prophetical. [L *fātidicus*, from *fātum* fate, and *dīcere* to tell]

■ **fatid'ically** *adv*.

fatigue */fə-tēg'/ n* weariness from physical or mental work; toil; lessened power of response to stimulus, resulting from activity (*physiol*); failure under repeated stress, as in metal; fatigue duty (sometimes allotted as a punishment; *milit*); (in *pl*) military overalls. ◆ *vt* (**fatigu'ing**; **fatigued'**) to reduce to weariness; to exhaust the strength or power of recovery of. [Fr *fatigue*, from L *fatīgāre* to weary]

■ **fatigable** or **fatiguable** */fat'ig-ə-bl/ adj* capable of being fatigued; easily fatigued. **fat'igableness** or **fat'iguableness** *n*. **fatigate** */fat'i-gāt/ adj* (*Shakesp*) fatigued. ◆ *vt* (*obs*) to fatigue. **fatigu'ingly** *adv*.

❑ **fatigue dress** *n* soldiers' working dress. **fatigue duty** *n* the nonmilitary part of a soldier's work, such as kitchen duty. **fatigue party** *n* a group of soldiers on fatigue duty.

■ words derived from main entry word; ❑ compound words; ■ idioms and phrasal verbs

Fatimid /fat'i-mid/ n a descendant of Mohammed's daughter *Fatima* and his cousin Ali, *esp* one of a dynasty ruling parts of N Africa from 909 to 1171 (also *adj*).

fatiscent /fa- or fə-tis'ənt/ (*geol*) *adj* gaping with cracks. [L *fatiscēns*, *-entis* prp of *fatīscere* to gape]
■ **fatis'cence** n.

fatsia /fat'si-ə/ n an evergreen spreading shrub of the ivy family, with leathery leaves and clusters of white flowers in the form of umbels. [Perh Jap *yatsude*, the name of this plant]

fatso /fat'sō/ (*derog sl*) n (pl **fat'sos** or **fat'soes**) a fat person. [**fat**[1]]

fatten, **fatter**, **fatty**, etc see **fat**[1].

fattrels /fat'rəlz or fät'/ (*Scot*) n pl ends of ribbon. [OFr *fatraille* trumpery]

fatuous /fat'ū-əs/ *adj* foolish, inane, asinine, *esp* in a cheerfully complacent way. [L *fatuus*]
■ **fatū'itous** *adj*. **fatū'ity** or **fat'ūousness** n complacent stupidity.
❑ **fatuous fire** n ignis fatuus, will-o'-the-wisp.

fatwa or **fatwah** /fat'wə/ n a formal legal opinion or decision issued by a Muslim judicial authority; (non-Muslim) a proclamation of an extreme measure, such as a sentence of death (*fig*). ◆ *vt* (pat and pap **fat'wa'd**) (in a non-Muslim context) to put under threat of terrible revenge. [Ar]

faubourg /fō-boor'/ (*Fr*) n a suburb just beyond the walls or a district recently included within a city.

fauces /fö'sēz/ n pl the upper part of the throat, from the root of the tongue to the pharynx; the throat of a flower. [L *faucēs*]
■ **fau'cal** /-kl/ *adj* of or produced in the fauces, as are certain Semitic guttural sounds. **faucial** /fö'shl/ *adj* of the fauces.

faucet /fö'sit/ n a pipe inserted in a barrel to draw off liquid; a tap (*US*). [Fr *fausset*]

fauchion and **fauchon** /fö'shən or -chən/ n obsolete forms of **falchion**.

faucial see under **fauces**.

faugh /fö/ *interj* expressing disgust.

faulchion and **faulchin** obsolete forms of **falchion**.

fault /fölt, formerly föt/ n a failing or weakness of character; an error; a blemish or flaw; imperfection; a misdeed or slight offence; a dislocation of strata or veins where a fracture has occurred in the earth's crust (*geol*); a defect in an electronic circuit; a stroke in which the player fails to serve the ball properly or into the proper place (*tennis*); a penalty point for failing to hit the correct ball or other error (*snooker* or *billiards*); a penalty point for refusing or failing to clear a fence (*showjumping*); culpability for something which has gone wrong. ◆ *vi* to be faulty; to develop or show a fault (*geol*); to commit a fault; to fall short (*obs*). ◆ *vt* to censure, find fault with; to find a flaw or flaws in; to cause a fault in (*geol*). [OFr *faute*, *falte*, from L *fallere* to deceive]
■ **fault'ful** *adj* (*Shakesp*) full of faults or crimes. **fault'ily** *adv*. **fault'iness** n. **fault'less** *adj* without fault or defect. **fault'lessly** *adv*. **fault'lessness** n. **fault'y** *adj* imperfect, defective; guilty of a fault; culpable.
❑ **fault'-finder** n. **fault'-finding** n criticism, captiousness; the detection and investigation of faults and malfunctions in electronic equipment (**find'-fault** see under **find**). **fault'line** n a fault (*geol*); a surface along which faults have occurred, or are likely to occur (*geol*); an issue or arrangement which is likely to cause disagreements or differences within a group or organization. **fault plane** n (*geol*) a *usu* uncurved surface of rock strata where a fault has occurred. **fault tolerance** n (*comput*) the ability of a system to execute specific tasks correctly regardless of failures and errors.
▣ **at fault** to blame, culpable; guilty; (of dogs) unable to find the scent; at a loss. **find fault** to carp, be critical; (with *with*) to censure for some mistake or defect. **in fault** (*archaic*) to blame. **to a fault** excessively.

faun /fön/ (*Roman myth*) n the protector of shepherds, a rural deity similar to a satyr, having a man's body, with a goat's horns, ears, tail and hind legs. [L *Faunus*, a deity of woods and pastures]

fauna /fö'nə/ n (pl **faun'as** or **faun'ae** /-ē/) the assemblage of all forms of animal life of a region or period, *esp* as distinct from plant life (*flora*); a list or account of this. [L *Fauna* and *Faunus* tutelary deities of shepherds, from *favēre*, *fautum* to favour]
■ **faun'al** *adj*. **faun'ist** n a person who studies faunas. **faunist'ic** *adj*.

faurd see **fa'ard**.

Faustian /fow'sti-ən/ (also without *cap*) *adj* in the manner of *Faust* who, in German legend, made a bargain with the Devil to gain limitless knowledge in exchange for his soul.

faute de mieux /fōt də myø'/ (*Fr*) for want of anything better.

fauteuil /fō-tœ'y', also fō'til/ n an armchair, *esp* a president's chair; the seat of one of the forty members of the French Academy; a theatre stall. [Fr]

fautor /fö'tər/ n a favourer; a patron; an abettor. [L *fautor*, from *favēre* to favour]

Fauve /fōv/ or **Fauvist** /fō'vist/ n a member of a group of expressionist painters at the beginning of the 20c, including Matisse, who viewed a painting as essentially a two-dimensional decoration in colour, not necessarily imitative of nature. [Fr *fauve* wild beast]
■ **Fauv'ism** n this style of painting.

fauvette /fō-vet'/ n a warbler (the bird). [Fr]

faux /fō/ (*Fr*) *adj* false.
❑ **faux ami** /fōz a-mē/ n literally, a false friend (qv). **faux-naïf** /fō-na-ēf'/ n and *adj* (a person) seeming or pretending to be simple and unsophisticated. **faux pas** /fō pä/ n literally, a false step, hence a mistake or blunder, *esp* an offence against accepted standards of politeness, decorum, etc.

fauxbourdon /fō'bər-don or fō-boor-dõ'/ same as **faburden**.

fava bean /fä'və bēn/ (*N Am*) n a broad bean. [Ital *fava*, from L *faba* a bean]

fave /fāv/ n and *adj* (*youth sl*) favourite.

favel or **favell** /fä'vəl/ (*obs*) *adj* light-brown; chestnut. ◆ n (with *cap*) a name for a chestnut horse, *esp* used proverbially to mean craftiness or cunning, from the deceitful but much-courted horse *Fauvel* in the 14c French poem *Roman de Fauvel*; hence **curry favell** (see **curry**[2]).

favela /fä-vā'lə/ n (*esp* in Brazil) a shanty town. [Port]

faveolate /fə-vē'ō-lāt/ *adj* honeycombed. [L *favus* honeycomb]

favicon /fäv'ī'kon/ n a custom-designed image which is displayed on a website, *esp* next to the address, to help create a memorable identity. [**favourites** and **icon**]

favism /fä'vi-zm or fä'vi-zm/ n an acute type of anaemia in which haemolysis is precipitated by contact with broad beans (by ingestion or pollen-inhalation), the original lesion being an enzyme deficiency in the red blood cells. [L *fava* broad bean, and **-ism**]

Favonian /fə-vō'ni-ən/ *adj* relating to the west wind, favourable. [L *Favōnius* the west wind]

favour or (*esp US*) **favor** /fā'vər/ n approval; esteem; goodwill; a kind deed; an act of grace or clemency; indulgence; partiality; advantage; (*usu* in *pl*) sexual intimacy regarded as a pleasure granted by one person to another, *esp* by a woman to a man (*literary* or *facetious*); a knot of ribbons worn, eg at an election, to show one's allegiance; a thing given or worn as a token of favour or love; appearance, face (*archaic*); a letter or written communication (*commercial jargon*); an attraction or grace (*Shakesp*); an object of favour (*Milton*). ◆ *vt* to regard with goodwill; to be on the side of; to show partiality to; to treat indulgently; to give support to; to afford advantage to; to resemble (*inf*); to treat with care or gentleness, *usu* an injured limb, etc; to choose to wear, etc. [OFr, from L *favor*, from *favēre* to favour or befriend]
■ **fā'vourable** or (*esp US*) **fā'vorable** *adj* friendly; propitious; conducive (with *to*); advantageous; satisfactory, promising; (of a wind) following. **fā'vourableness** or (*esp US*) **fā'vorableness** n. **fā'vourably** or (*esp US*) **fā'vorably** *adv*. **fā'voured** or (*esp US*) **fā'vored** *adj* enjoying favour or preference; (of an area, etc) well-liked, convenient; wearing favours; having a certain appearance, featured, as in *ill-favoured*, *well-favoured*. **fā'vouredness** or (*esp US*) **fā'voredness** n. **fā'vourer** or (*esp US*) **fā'vorer** n. **fā'vourite** or (*esp US*) **fā'vorite** /-it/ n a person or thing regarded with special preference; a person unduly loved and indulged, *esp* by a king; a person, horse, etc expected to win; a website that has been bookmarked (qv) on one's computer; a kind of curl of the hair, affected by ladies of the 18c. ◆ *adj* esteemed, preferred, best loved. **fā'vouritism** or (*esp US*) **fā'voritism** n inclination to partiality; preference shown to favourites; the state of being a favourite. **fā'vourless** or (*esp US*) **fā'vorless** *adj* without favour; not favouring (*Spenser*).
❑ **favoured supplier** n a business which has satisfied certain conditions, such as quality and special terms, and is deemed acceptable to a purchaser such as a government department.
▣ **curry favour** see **curry**[2] and **favel**. **favours to come** favours still expected. **in favour** approved of. **in favour of** for; on the side of; for the advantage or benefit of. **out of favour** not approved of.

favrile /fəv-rēl' or fav'rəl/ n a type of iridescent glassware developed in America at the turn of the 20c by LC Tiffany. [Orig trademark, from obs *fabrile*, relating to a craftsman]

favus /fä'vəs/ n a fungal skin disease, chiefly of the scalp, giving a honeycombed appearance. [L *favus* a honeycomb]
■ **favose** /fə-vōs'/ or /fä'vōs/ *adj* honeycombed. **fā'vous** *adj* like a honeycomb; relating to favus.

faw /fö/ n a gypsy. [From the surname *Faa*]

fawn[1] /fön/ n a young deer, *esp* a fallow deer; its colour, light greyish or yellowish brown. ◆ *adj* of this colour. ◆ *vt* and *vi* (of a deer) to give birth to young. [OFr *faon*, through LL from L *fētus* offspring]

fawn[2] /fön/ *vi* to try to please, or flatter, in a servile way (with *on* or *upon*); (of an animal, *esp* a dog) to lick, rub against, jump on, etc, in a show of affection. ◆ *n* (*rare*) a servile action or gesture; cringing flattery. [A variant of **fain**[1], from OE *fægen* glad]
■ **fawn'er** n a person who flatters to gain favour. **fawn'ing** n and *adj*. **fawn'ingly** *adv*. **fawn'ingness** n.

fax /faks/ n a shortening of **facsimile** as in **fax machine**, a machine that scans a document, etc electronically and transfers the information by a telephone or radio link to a receiving machine which reproduces the document; the system for such transfer; a fax machine; a copy produced in this way. ◆ *vt* to send a message or document using a fax machine (also *vi*); to communicate with by fax machine.

fay[1] /fā/ (*poetic*) n a fairy. [OFr *fae*, from LL *fāta*; see **fate**]

fay[2] /fā/ (*Shakesp*) n faith. [OFr *fei*]

fay[3] see **fey**[1].

fay[4] /fā/ (*obs* or *dialect*) *vt* and *vi* to fit or unite closely. [OE *fēgan*; Ger *fügen*]
□ **fay'ing-face** n a prepared surface of contact.

fay[5] or **fey** /fā/ (*dialect*) *vt* to clean out, eg a ditch. [ON *fægja* to cleanse]

fayalite /fā'ə-līt/ or /fā-yä'līt/ n iron-olivine, a silicate of iron found in slag and occurring naturally. [*Fayal* in the Azores, where it was found, prob in ballast]

fayence same as **faience**.

fayne /fān/ (*Spenser*) *vt* see **feign**.

fayre an archaic or archaizing spelling of **fair**[2].

faze /fāz/ *vt* (also **feese**, **feeze**, **phase**, **pheese**, **pheeze** or **phese**) to worry, perturb, unsettle; to drive or drive off (*obs*); to settle the business of (*Shakesp*); to beat (*obs*). ◆ *n* a rush (*dialect*); a rub (*obs*); perturbation, disquiet. [OE *fēsian* to drive away]
■ **fazed**, etc *adj* unsettled, mystified, thrown off balance.

fazenda /fə-zen'də/ n (*esp* in Brazil) a large estate, plantation or cattle ranch. [Port; see **hacienda**]
■ **fazendeiro** /fa-zen-dā'rō/ n (*pl* **fazendei'ros**) a person who owns or runs such a property.

FBA *abbrev* Fellow of the British Academy.

FBI (*US*) *abbrev* : Federal Bureau of Investigation.

FBR *abbrev* : fast-breeder reactor.

FBU *abbrev* : Fire Brigades Union.

FC *abbrev* : football club; Forestry Commission; Free Church.

FCA *abbrev* : Fellow of the Institute of Chartered Accountants in England and Wales, or in Ireland.

FCCA *abbrev* : Fellow of the Association of Chartered Certified Accountants.

FCIB *abbrev* : Fellow of the Chartered Institute of Bankers.

FCII *abbrev* : Fellow of the Chartered Insurance Institute.

FCIS *abbrev* : Fellow of the Institute of Chartered Secretaries and Administrators (formerly known as the Chartered Institute of Secretaries).

FCLIP *abbrev* : Fellow of the Chartered Institute of Library and Information Professionals.

FCMA *abbrev* : Fellow of the Chartered Institute of Management Accountants (formerly known as the Institute of Cost and Management Accountants).

FCMI *abbrev* : Fellow of the Chartered Management Institute.

FCO *abbrev* : Foreign and Commonwealth Office.

fcp or **fcap** *abbrev* : foolscap.

FD *abbrev* : *Fidei Defensor* (L), Defender of the Faith, used *esp* as a title of British monarchs.

FDA *abbrev* : Food and Drug Administration (in the USA); First Division Association, a trade union for senior civil servants.

FE *abbrev* : further education.

Fe (*chem*) *symbol* : iron. [L *ferrum*]

feague /fēg/ (*obs*) *vt* to whip; to perplex. [Cf Du *vegen*, Ger *fegen*]

feal[1] /fēl/ (*obs*) *adj* loyal, faithful. [OFr *feal*, from L *fidēlis*]

feal[2] /fēl/ (*dialect*) *vt* to conceal. [ON *fela*]

feal[3] /fēl/ same as **fail**[1].

fealty /fē'əl-ti/ or /fēl'ti/ n the vassal's obligation of fidelity to his feudal lord (*hist*); loyalty. [OFr *fealte*, from L *fidēlitās*, *-tātis*, from *fidēlis* faithful, from *fīdere* to trust]

fear /fēr/ n a painful emotion excited by danger; apprehension of danger or pain; alarm; solicitude, anxiety; that which causes alarm; risk or possibility; reverence or awe (*relig*); piety towards God (*old relig*). ◆ *vt* to regard with fear, be afraid of; to expect with alarm; to be regretfully inclined to think; to revere (*relig*); to be in fear about (*obs*); to stand in awe of (*relig*); to venerate (*relig*); to terrify (*obs*); to make afraid (*obs*). ◆ *vi* to be afraid; to suspect some danger to (with *for*); (*esp* in *neg*) to be in doubt. [OE *fær*, fear and *færan* to terrify]
■ **feared** /fērd/ *adj* (*archaic* and *Scot*) afraid (also (*Scot*) **feart** /fērt/). **fear'ful** *adj* timorous; producing intense fear; terrible; very great, very bad (*inf*). **fear'fully** *adv*. **fear'fulness** n. **fear'less** *adj* without fear; daring; brave. **fear'lessly** *adv*. **fear'lessness** n. **fear'some** *adj* causing fear, frightful. **fear'somely** *adv*.
□ **fear'nought** n dreadnought cloth, a thick cloth for overcoats, etc.
■ **for fear** in case, lest. **for fear of** in order to avoid. **no fear** (*interj*; *inf*) definitely not. **put the fear of God into** to terrify. **without fear or favour** impartially.

feare see **fere**[1].

feasible /fē'zi-bl/ *adj* practicable, possible; probable, likely (*inf*). [Fr *faisable* that can be done, from *faire*, *faisant*, from L *facere* to do]
■ **feas'ibleness** or **feasibil'ity** n. **feas'ibly** *adv*.
□ **feasibility study** n an investigation to determine whether a particular project, system, etc is desirable, practicable, etc.

feast /fēst/ n a rich and abundant meal; a regularly occurring religious celebration commemorating a person or event, honouring a deity, etc; a pleasurable abundance; (something that supplies) rich gratification of the senses (eg a *feast for the eyes*) or stimulation for the mind. ◆ *vi* to hold a feast; to eat abundantly and well (with *on*); to receive intense delight. ◆ *vt* to provide a feast for; to delight, gratify (one's senses; with *on*). [OFr *feste* (Fr *fête*), from L *fēstum* a holiday, *fēstus* solemn, festal]
■ **feast'er** n. **feast'ful** *adj* (*archaic*) festive, luxurious. **feast'ing** n.
□ **feast'-day** n a day on which a religious festival occurs. **feast'-rite** n a rite or custom observed at religious feasts. **feast'-won** *adj* (*Shakesp*) won or bribed by feasting.
■ **Feast of Dedication** another name for **Hanukkah**. **Feast of Fools** and **Feast of Asses** medieval festivals held between Christmas and Epiphany, in which a mock bishop was enthroned in church, a burlesque mass was said, and an ass driven round in triumph. **Feast of Lots** the Jewish festival of Purim. **Feast of Tabernacles** same as **Sukkoth**. **Feast of Weeks** same as **Shabuoth**. **movable feast** a religious festival of variable date, such as Easter; anything whose date, form, etc is not fixed by custom.

feat /fēt/ n a deed manifesting extraordinary strength, skill or courage, an exploit, achievement; an act or deed (*obs*); art, skill (*Spenser*). ◆ *vt* (*Shakesp*) *perh* to fashion, to make feat or neat. ◆ *adj* (*Shakesp*) neat, deft. [Fr *fait*, from L *factum*, from *facere* to do; cf **fact**]
■ **feat'ly** *adv* (*Shakesp*) neatly; dexterously.

feateous and **feateously** see **featous**.

feather /fedh'ər/ n one of the light growths that form the soft covering of a bird; anything resembling this, eg an ornament; a set of these, or synthetic substitutes, on the end of an arrow, to aid flight; plumage; condition; birds collectively; anything light or trifling; a projecting longitudinal rib or strip; feather-edge; a wedge; a formation of hair, eg on the legs of certain breeds of dog or horse; the act of moving an oar edgewise through the air, to lessen resistance; a foamy wave or wave crest, *esp* that caused by a submarine's periscope. ◆ *vt* to provide, cover or adorn with a feather or feathers; to turn (an oar) parallel to the water, to lessen air-resistance, or to make (a propeller-blade, etc) rotate in such a way as to lessen resistance; to shape (hair) by trimming and thinning; to touch lightly. ◆ *vi* to take on the appearance of a feather; to quiver the tail. [OE *fether*; Ger *Feder*; L *penna*, Gr *pteron*]
■ **feath'ered** *adj* covered or fitted with feathers, or anything featherlike; like the flight of a feathered animal, swift. **feath'eriness** n. **feath'ering** n plumage; the addition of a feather or feathers; a featherlike appearance; an arrangement of small arcs separated by cusps, within an arch (*archit*). **feath'erlike** *adj*. **feath'ery** *adj* relating to, resembling, or covered with feathers or an appearance of feathers.
□ **feather bed** n a mattress filled with feathers or down. **feath'erbed** *vt* to pamper; to protect (an industry, workers, etc) by such practices as overmanning in order to save jobs; to provide with financial inducements (*inf*). **featherbed'ding** n. **feath'er-boarding** same as **weatherboarding** (see under **weather**). **feather-bonn'et** n a Highland soldier's feather-covered headdress. **feath'er-brain** n (also **feath'er-head** or **feath'er-pate** (*archaic*)) a frivolous, silly person. **feath'er-brained** (also **feath'er-headed**) *adj*. **feather cut** n a style of haircut in which the hair is left thin and fine in texture. **feather duster** n a light brush of feathers, used for dusting. **feath'er-edge** n an edge of a board or plank thinner than the other edge. **feath'er-grass** n a perennial grass (genus *Stipa*) with a feathery beard. **feather palm** n any palm with feather-shaped leaves. **feather star** see **crinoid**. **feather stitch** n one of a series of stitches making a zigzag line. **feath'erweight** n the lightest weight that may be carried by a

racehorse; a weight category, applied *esp* in boxing; a sportsperson of the specified weight for the category (eg in professional boxing above bantamweight, **junior featherweight** or **super bantamweight** (maximum 55kg/122lb), **featherweight** (maximum 57kg/126lb), and **super featherweight** or **junior lightweight** (maximum 59kg/130lb)); anyone of little consequence.

■ **a feather in one's cap** an achievement of which one can be proud. **birds of a feather** people of similar character. **feathered friend** (*humorous*) a bird. **feather one's nest** to accumulate wealth for oneself while working for others in a position of trust. **in full** or **high feather** greatly elated or in high spirits. **make the feathers fly** to create a turmoil or uproar. **ruffle someone's feathers** to upset or offend someone. **show the white feather** to show signs of cowardice, a white feather in a gamecock's tail being considered as a sign of degeneracy. **tar and feather** see under **tar**[1]. **you could have knocked me down with a feather** I was astounded.

featous /fē′təs/, **feateous** /-ti-əs/ or **featuous** /-tū-əs/ (*archaic*) *adj* shapely; well-made; handsome; dexterous; neat. [OFr *fetis*, from L *factīcius*, from *facere* to make; cf **factitious**]
■ **feat′eously** *adv* (*Spenser*) dexterously, neatly.

feature /fē′chər/ *n* form, outward appearance; shape of the face; any part of the face, such as the eyes, mouth, etc; an element or prominent trait of anything; a characteristic; (in *pl*) the face; a non-news article in a newspaper; a feature film; anything offered as a special attraction or distinctive characteristic; a phantom (*archaic*); beauty (*obs*). ◆ *adj* being a prominent or distinctive aspect of anything. ◆ *vt* to have as a feature; to make a feature of; to present prominently; to have features resembling (*inf*). ◆ *vi* to play an important part or role (with *in*), be a feature (of). [OFr *faiture*, from L *factura*, from *facere* to make]
■ **-featured** *combining form* having features of a specified type, as in *sharp-featured*. **feat′ureless** *adj* completely lacking in distinct features. **feat′urely** *adj* (*archaic*) handsome. **featurette′** *n* a brief feature, *esp* a short documentary film dealing with an aspect of the making of a feature film and included on a DVD of the feature film. ❑ **feature film** *n* a long film forming the main part of a cinema programme. **feat′ure-length** *adj* (of films) of similar length to a feature film. **feature phone** *n* a mobile phone with features such as Internet access but without the more advanced features of a smartphone. **feature programme** *n* a radio or TV programme that reconstructs dramatically the life of a prominent person, or an important event, or gives a dramatic picture of a profession or activity.

Feb. *abbrev* : February.

feblesse see under **feeble**.

febrifuge /feb′rə-fūj/ (*med*) *n* a medicine, etc that reduces fever. [Med L *febrifugia* feverfew]
■ **febrifugal** /fib-rif′ū-gəl or feb-rə-fū′gəl/ *adj*.

febrile /fē′brī, feb′rīl or -ril/ *adj* relating to fever; feverish. [Med L *febrīlis*, from *febris* fever]
■ **febricity** /fi-bris′i-ti/ *n* feverishness. **febricula** /fi-brik′ū-lə/ or **febricule** /feb′/ *n* a slight short fever. **febrifacient** /fē-bri-fā′shənt/ *adj* (L *faciēns*, -*entis* making) producing fever. **febrif′ic** /fi-/ *adj* febrifacient; feverish. **febril′ity** *n*.

Febronianism /fe-brō′ni-ə-ni-zm/ *n* a system of doctrine antagonistic to the claims of the Pope and asserting the independence of national churches, propounded in 1763 by Johann Nikolaus von Hontheim under the pseudonym Justinus *Febronius*.

February /feb′rū-ə-ri or ′roo-/ *n* the second month of the year. [L *Februārius* (*mēnsis*) the month of expiation, and *februa* the feast of expiation]

fec. *abbrev* : fecit.

feces and **fecal** see **faeces**.

fecht /fehht/ and **fechter** /-ər/ Scots forms of **fight** and **fighter**.

fecial see **fetial**.

fecit /fē′sit or fā′kit/ (L) (he or she) made or did (this).

feck[1] /fek/ *n* (*Scot*) meaning, tenor (*obs*); substance (*obs*); efficacy; quantity, number; the bulk. [Aphetic for **effect**]
■ **feck′less** *adj* feeble, ineffectual; helpless; futile. **feck′lessly** *adv*. **feck′lessness** *n*. **feck′ly** *adv* (*archaic*) mostly; nearly.

feck[2] /fek/ *interj* an Irish euphemism for **fuck**.

fecula /fek′ū-lə/ *n* starch obtained as a sediment; sediment, dregs. [L *faecula* dimin of *faex* dregs]
■ **fec′ulence** or **fec′ulency** *n*. **fec′ulent** *adj* containing or consisting of faeces or sediment; foul; turbid.

fecund /fēk′und or fek′und, also -ūnd or -ənd/ *adj* fruitful; fertile; prolific. [L *fēcundus* fruitful]
■ **fec′undāte** *vt* to make fruitful or fertile; to make pregnant, to fertilize or impregnate. **fecundā′tion** *n*. **fecundity** /fi-kund′i-ti/ *n* fruitfulness, (loosely) fertility; productiveness; the number of young produced by a species or individual (cf **fertility**; *ecology*).

Fed[1] /fed/ (*US sl*) *n* a Federal (agent), ie an agent of the Federal Bureau of Investigation (also without *cap*). [Contraction of **federal**]

Fed[2] *abbrev* : Federal Reserve Board (in the USA); Federal Reserve System (of the USA).

fed /fed/ *pat* and *pap* of **feed**[1].

fedarie, foedarie /fē′də-ri/, **federarie** or **federary** /fed′ə-rə-ri/ *n* Shakespearean words for a confederate accomplice. [L *foedus*, -*eris* treaty; moulded on **feudary**]

fedayee /fə-dä′yē/ *n* (pl **feda′yeen**) an Arab commando or guerrilla, *esp* one involved in the conflict against Israel. [Ar *fidā′i*]

fedelini /fed-ə-lē′nē/ *n* pasta made in long thin cordlike strings. [Ital]

federal /fed′ə-rəl/ *adj* relating to or consisting of a treaty or covenant; confederated, founded upon mutual agreement; (of a union or government) in which several states, while independent in home affairs, combine for national or general purposes, as in the United States (in the American Civil War, *Federal* was the name applied to the states of the North which defended the Union against the *Confederate* separatists of the South); of or relating to the national or central government in such a union, as opposed to any regional or state government. ◆ *n* a supporter of federation; a Unionist soldier in the American Civil War. [L *foedus*, *foederis* a treaty, related to *fīdere* to trust]
■ **fed′eracy** *n*. **fed′eralism** *n* the principles or cause maintained by federalists. **fed′eralist** *n* a supporter of a federal constitution or union. **federalizā′tion** or **-s-** *n*. **fed′eralize** or **-ise** *vt*. **fed′erary** *n* (*Shakesp*) see **fedarie**.
❑ **federal** (or **covenant**) **theology** *n* that first worked out by Cocceius (1603–69), based on the idea of two covenants between God and man, of Works and of Grace (see also **covenant**). **Federal Bureau of Investigation** *n* (in the USA) a bureau or subdivision of the Department of Justice that investigates crimes, such as smuggling and espionage, that are the concern of the federal government. **Federal Reserve Board** *n* (in the USA) the board of governors in charge of the **Federal Reserve System**, which, comprising twelve **Federal Reserve Banks**, controls banking activities and supply of money and credit.

federarie and **federary** see **fedarie**.

federate /fed′ə-rāt/ *vt* and *vi* to join together in a league or federation. ◆ *adj* united in a league; confederated. [L *foederāre*, from *foedus*, *foederis* a treaty]
■ **federā′tion** *n* the act of uniting in a league; a federal union. **fed′erative** *adj* united in a league.
❑ **federated search** *n* (*comput*) a simultaneous search of multiple online databases.

Fed-Ex /fed′eks/ (*US*) *vt* to send (a package) by courier. [After *Federal Express*, US postal delivery service]

fedora /fi-dö′rə/ *n* a brimmed felt hat dented lengthways. [Said to be from Victorien Sardou's play, *Fédora* (1882)]

fee /fē/ *n* the price paid for services, such as to a lawyer or physician; recompense, wages; the sum exacted for any special privilege; a charge payable on entering, joining or taking part; a grant of land for feudal service (*hist*); feudal tenure; service (*obs*); fee simple; inheritance (*obs*); possession (*obs*); ownership (*obs*); cattle, livestock (*obs*); property (*obs*); money (*obs*). ◆ *vt* (**fee′ing**; *feed* or *fee′d*) to pay a fee to; to hire (*Scot*). [Partly OE *feoh* cattle or property; Ger *Vieh*, ON *fé*; related to L *pecus* cattle, and *pecūnia* money; partly Anglo-Fr *fee*, prob ult Gmc and of the same origin]
❑ **fee′-farm** *n* (*Shakesp*) tenure by fee simple at a fixed rent without services. **fee′-grief** *n* (*Shakesp*) a private grief. **fee′ing-market** *n* (*Scot*) a fair or market at which farm-servants are hired for the year or half-year following. **fee simple** *n* unconditional inheritance. **fee tail** *n* an entailed estate, which may descend only to a certain class of heirs.
■ **base fee** qualified fee, a freehold estate of inheritance to which a qualification is annexed. **conditional fee** a fee granted on condition, or limited to particular heirs; the estate of a mortgagee of land, possession of which is conditional on payment. **great fee** the land-holding of a tenant of the Crown.

fée /fā/ (Fr) *n* a fairy.
■ **féerie** /fā-rē/ *n* fairyland; an extravaganza (*theatre*).

feeble /fē′bl/ *adj* very weak, frail; (of a joke, excuse, etc) tame, lame, unconvincing or thin; vacillating, lacking resolve; faint. ◆ *vt* (*Spenser*) to make feeble. [OFr *foible*, for *floible*, from L *flēbilis* lamentable, from *flēre* to weep]
■ **fe′blesse** *n* (*Spenser*). **fee′bleness** *n*. **fee′blish** *adj*. **fee′bly** *adv*.
❑ **feeble-mind′ed** *adj* mentally impaired to the extent of being unable to manage one's affairs with ordinary prudence; lacking resolve; indecisive. **feeble-mind′edly** *adv*. **feeble-mind′edness** *n*.

feed[1] /fēd/ *vt* (**feed′ing**; *fed*) to give, supply, or administer food to; to give as food (with *to*); to nourish; to fatten with nourishing food (with *up*); to provide with necessary material; to foster; to give as food or as material to be used progressively; to furnish (an actor) with cues or opportunities of achieving an effect; in various sports, to pass the ball to. ◆ *vi* to take food; to nourish oneself by eating (with *on* or *off*); to derive strength or sustenance from (with *on* or *off*). ◆ *n* an amount or allowance of food given eg to babies or to cattle; food for livestock feeding; pasture; a plentiful meal (*inf*); material supplied progressively for any operation; the means, channel, motion or rate of such supply; a means of transmitting data over the Internet to several users simultaneously (*comput*); rate of progress of a tool; an actor who feeds another, a stooge. [OE *fēdan* to feed]

■ **feed'able** *adj*. **feed'er** *n* a person who consumes food (*esp* in a specified way, eg a *big feeder*) or provides or administers it to another; an actor who feeds another; something which supplies (water, electricity, ore, paper, etc); any channel of supply to a main system; a transport route linking outlying areas to the trunk line; a tributary; an overhead or underground cable, of large current-carrying capacity, used to transmit electric power between generating stations, substations and feeding points; a container for food for small animals, birds, etc; a feeding bottle; a bib; a primary school from which a secondary school receives regular intakes of pupils; a person who fattens cattle; a shepherd (*obs*); a dependant; a servant (*archaic*). ◆ *adj* secondary, subsidiary, tributary. **feed'ing** *n* the act of eating or supplying with food; that which is eaten; pasture; the placing of the sheets of paper in position for a printing or ruling machine. ❑ **feed'back** *n* return of part of the output of a system to the input as a means towards improved quality or self-correction of error (*negative feedback*) or, when in phase with the input signal, resulting in oscillation and instability (*positive feedback*); used also in speaking of biological, etc self-adjusting systems; response or reaction providing useful information or guidelines for further action or development; (in a public address system, etc) the unintentional returning of some of the sound output back to the microphone, producing a whistle or howl. **feed'-head** *n* a cistern that supplies water to a boiler. **feed'-heater** *n* an apparatus for heating water for a boiler. **feeding bottle** *n* a bottle for supplying liquid food to an infant. **feeding frenzy** *n* a competitive and violent attack on the same prey by a number of predators; a period of violently excited competitive activity (*inf*). **feeding point** *n* (*elec*) the junction point between a feeder and distribution system. **feed'-in tariff** *n* (in Britain) a payment made to an individual household for generating renewable energy. **feed'-line** *n* a line fed to an actor; a cue. **feed'lot** *n* a unit in which cattle are kept indoors and made to put on weight rapidly by means of processed and blended feed supplied to them automatically. **feed'-pipe** *n* a pipe for supplying liquid, such as water to a boiler or cistern. **feed'-pump** *n* a force pump for supplying a boiler with water. **feed'stock** *n* raw material used in an industrial process. **feed'stuff** *n* any type of food for animals, *esp* cattle, pigs, sheep, etc. **feed'through** *n* an electrical conductor connecting two sides of a circuit board, etc; the onward passage of one thing through another. **feed'-water** *n* water supplied to a boiler, etc. ■ **fed to the (back) teeth** (*inf*) fed up. **fed up** (*inf*) jaded; disgruntled; bored; (with *with*) tired of, annoyed by; sated (*obs*). **feed one's face** (*sl*) to eat heartily. **off one's feed** without appetite, disinclined to eat.

feed² /fēd/ *pat* and *pap* of **fee**.

fee-faw-fum /fē'fö'fum'/ or **fee-fi-fo-fum** /fē'fī'fō'fum'/ *interj* expressive of bloodthirstiness, in fairy tales, etc. ◆ *n* words, etc intended to terrify. [From the nursery tale *Jack the Giantkiller*]

feel /fēl/ *vt* (**feel'ing**; **felt**) to perceive by the touch; to investigate by touching or handling; to find (one's way) by groping; to be conscious of; to be keenly sensible of; to have an inward persuasion of, to believe, consider or think; to seem to oneself to be; to caress the genitals of (with *up*; *vulgar sl*). ◆ *vi* to be aware that one is (well, ill, happy, etc); to explore or investigate with one's hand (with *in*, etc); to impart a particular impression when touched, as in *to feel smooth*, *sharp*, etc; to be emotionally affected; to have sympathy or compassion (with *for*). ◆ *n* the sensation of touch; an instinct, touch, knack; an act of feeling something; an impression imparted by something being felt; a general impression or atmosphere associated with something. [OE *fēlan* to feel; Ger *fühlen* ; prob akin to L *palpāri* to stroke]

■ **feel'er** *n* a person, etc that feels; a remark cautiously dropped, or any indirect stratagem, to sound out the opinions of others; a tentacle; a jointed organ in the head of insects, etc capable of a delicate sense, an antenna. **feel'ing** *n* the sense of touch; perception of objects by touch; consciousness of pleasure or pain; an impression received physically or mentally; tenderness; (an) emotion, sensibility, susceptibility, sentimentality; an opinion, sentiment; an instinctive grasp or appreciation (with *for*); mutual or interactive emotion, such as *bad feeling* (resentment or animosity), *good feeling* (friendliness), *ill-feeling*, *fellow feeling*; (in *pl*) the affections or passions; (in *pl*) one's sensibilities, or amour-propre, as in *hurt someone's feelings*. ◆ *adj* expressive of great sensibility or tenderness; easily or strongly affected by emotion; sympathetic; compassionate; pitying; deeply felt. **feel'ingless** *adj*. **feel'ingly** *adv*.

❑ **feel'-bad** or **feel'bad** *adj* (*inf*) causing a feeling of personal unease. **feel-bad factor** *n* the antidote to the feel-good factor (qv below). **feeler gauge** *n* (*engineering*) a thin strip of metal of known thickness, used to measure or set the distance between surfaces or parts. **feel'-good** or **feel'good** *adj* (*inf*) causing or relating to a feeling of personal wellbeing, optimism or (smug) self-satisfaction. **feel-good factor** *n* a sense of optimism sometimes detected by researchers into voting, buying, etc intentions.

■ **bad feeling** resentment or animosity; ill-feeling. **feel after** (*Bible*) to search for. **feelings (are) running high** (there is) a general feeling of anger, emotion, etc. **feel like** to want, have a desire for. **feel oneself** to feel as well as normal. **feel one's feet** or **way** to accustom oneself to a new situation, job, etc. **feel up to** (with *neg*) to feel fit enough to. **get the feel of** to become familiar with or used to. **good feeling** friendly feeling; amicable relations. **no hard feelings** no offence taken.

feer¹ see **fere¹**.

feer² /fēr/ (*Scot*) *vi* to draw the first furrow in ploughing, to mark out the rigs. [Perh OE *fȳrian* to make a furrow, from *furh* furrow]
■ **feer'in** or **feer'ing** *n* a first guiding furrow.

féerie see under **fée**.

feese see **faze**.

feet /fēt/ plural of **foot**.
■ **feet'less** *adj* footless.
■ See also phrases under **foot**.

feeze see **faze**.

fegary /fi-gā'ri/ *n* a variant of **vagary**.

fegs /fegz/ (*dialect*) *interj* in faith, truly. [See **fay²**, **faith** and **faix**]

Fehling's solution /fā'lingz sə-loo'shən or -lū'shən/ (*chem*) *n* a solution of copper sulphate, potassium sodium tartrate and sodium hydroxide used to detect the presence of aldehydes, *esp* sugars. [Hermann von *Fehling* (1812–85), German chemist]

Fehm or **Fehmgericht** same as **Vehm** or **Vehmgericht**.

FEI *abbrev* : *Fédération Équestre Internationale* (*Fr*), International Equestrian Federation.

feign (*Spenser* **fain**, **faine** or **fayne**) /fān/ *vt* to make a show or pretence of, to counterfeit, simulate; to dissemble (*Spenser*); to fashion, shape (*obs*); to invent; to imagine falsely (*obs*); to assume fictitiously; to imagine (*archaic*). [Fr *feindre*, prp *feignant* to feign, from L *fingere*, *fictum* to form]
■ **feigned** *adj* pretended; simulated; imagined (*archaic*); fictitious. **feign'edly** *adv*. **feign'edness** *n*. **feign'ing** *n*.

feijoa /fā-jō'ə or fī-/ *n* any of various evergreen shrubs or trees of the genus *Feijoa* ; the aromatic quince-like fruit they bear. [J da Silva *Feijo*, 19c Brazilian naturalist]

feijoada /fā-zhoo-ad'ə or -zhwad'ə/ *n* a Portuguese dish of beans, meat and vegetables served with rice. [Port, from *feijão*, from L *phaseolus* bean]

feint¹ /fānt/ *n* a mock assault; a deceptive movement in fencing, boxing, etc; a false show; a pretence. ◆ *vi* to make a feint. [Fr *feinte*, from *feindre* to feign]

feint² /fānt/ *adj* a printers' or stationers' word meaning having the faint horizontal rules sometimes printed on stationery. [Altered from **faint**]
■ **feints** *n pl* see **faints** under **faint**.

feis /fesh/ *n* (pl **feiseanna** /fesh'ə-nə/) an ancient Irish assembly for the proclamation of laws and the holding of artistic, intellectual and sports competitions; an Irish festival on the ancient model, including sports events, folk music and dancing. [Ir, festival or assembly]

feisty /fīs'ti/ (*inf*, *orig US*) *adj* excitable, irritable, touchy; spirited. [From old US dialect *fist* a small aggressive dog, from ME *fisten* to break wind]
■ **feist'ily** *adv*. **feist'iness** *n*.

felafel see **falafel**.

felch /felch/ (*sl*) *vi* and *vt* to lick or suck ejaculated semen from the anus of a sexual partner. [Perh imit]

Feldenkrais method /fel'dən-kris meth'əd/ *n* a system of exercises designed to improve posture and efficiency of movement, with both physical and emotional benefits. [M *Feldenkrais* (1904–84), Russian nuclear physicist]

feldgrau /felt'grow/ *n* and *adj* field-grey, the colour of German military uniforms from around 1910–45. [Ger *Feld* field, and *grau* grey]

feldsher /feld'shər or fel'shər/ *n* (in Russia and parts of E Europe) a partly trained person who practises medicine; a person who assists a doctor, *esp* on the battlefield. [Russ *fel'dsher*, from Ger *Feldscher* army surgeon]

feldspar /feld'spär or fel'spär/ or **felspar** /fel'spär/ *n* (also (*obs*) **feld'spath**) any member of the most important group of rock-forming minerals, anhydrous silicates of aluminium along with potassium (such as *orthoclase*, *microcline*), sodium, calcium, or both (the *plagioclases*), or sodium and barium (*hyalophane*). [Swed *feldtspat* a name given in 1740 by D Tilas, from Swed *feldt* or *fält* field, and *spat* spar, apparently because of the abundance of feldspar in tilled fields of SW Finland; confused with Ger *Fels* rock]

■ **feldspathic** or **felspathic** /-*spath*'*ik*/ *adj*. **feld**'**spathoid** or **fel**'**spathoid** *n* any mineral of a group chemically related to feldspar, including nepheline, leucite, sodalite, etc.

Félibre /*fā-lē*'*br*'/ *n* a member of the **Félibrige** /-*brēzh*'/, a Provençal literary brotherhood, founded in 1854 by Joseph Roumanille (1818–91) and six others. [Provençal, perh doctors of the law]

felicia /*fə-lish*'*i-ə*/ *n* any member of a S African genus of herbs and subshrubs of the daisy family, with blue or lilac flowers. [L *fēlix*, -*icis* happy]

feliciter /*fi-lis*'*i-tər* or *fā-lē*'*ki-ter*/ (L) *adv* happily; successfully.

felicity /*fi-lis*'*i-ti*/ *n* happiness; delight; a blessing; a happy event; elegance or aptness of wording or expression. [OFr *felicité*, from L *fēlīcitās*, -*ātis*, from *fēlix*, -*icis* happy]

■ **felicif**'**ic** *adj* producing happiness. **felic**'**itate** *vt* to express joy or pleasure to; to congratulate. **felicita**'**tion** *n* the act of congratulating; (in *pl*) congratulations. **felic**'**itous** *adj* happy; prosperous; delightful; well-chosen, appropriate. **felic**'**itously** *adv*. **felic**'**itousness** *n*.

felid /*fē*'*lid*/ *n* a member of the Felidae, the cat family. [New L *fēlidae*, from L *fēlēs* a cat]

feline /*fē*'*līn*/ *adj* relating to cats or the cat family; like a cat. ◆ *n* any animal of the cat family. [L *fēlīneus*, from *fēlēs* a cat]

■ **felinity** /*fi-lin*'*i-ti*/ *n*. **Fē**'**lis** *n* the cat genus, typical of the family **Fē**'**lidae** and subfamily **Fēlī**'**nae**.

fell[1] /*fel*/ *vt* to cause to fall; to knock down; to bring to the ground; to cut down; to prostrate (eg by illness; *dialect*); to turn under and stitch down the edges of (a seam; *needlework*). ◆ *n* a quantity felled at a time; a number of lambs born at one time; a felled seam. [OE *fǣlla*(*n*), *fella*(*n*) (WSax *fiellan*), causative of *fallan* (*feallan*) to fall]

■ **fell**'**able** *adj*. **fell**'**er** *n*.

fell[2] /*fel*/ *n* a hill; an upland tract of wasteland, pasture or moorland. [ON *fjall*; Dan *fjeld*]

❑ **fell**'**-runner** *n*. **fell**'**-running** *n* the sport of running over fells. **fell**'**-walker** *n*. **fell**'**-walking** *n* the pastime of walking over fells.

fell[3] /*fel*/ *adj* cruel; dire; ruthless; fierce; deadly; keen; doughty; pungent (*Scot*); great, mighty (*Scot*). ◆ *adv* in a fell manner; very (*Scot*); very much (*Scot*). [OFr *fel* cruel, from LL *fellō*, -*ōnis*; see **felon**[1]]

■ **fell**'**ness** *n*. **felly** /*fel*'*li*/ *adv*.

❑ **fell-lurk**'**ing** *adj* (*Shakesp*) lurking with treacherous purpose.

■ **at** (or **in**) **one fell swoop** see under **swoop**.

fell[4] /*fel*/ *n* a skin; a membrane; a covering of rough hair. [OE *fell*; cf Ger *Fell*, L *pellis*, Gr *pella*]

❑ **fell**'**monger** *n* a person who prepares skins for the tanner.

fell[5] /*fel*/ *pat* of **fall**.

fell[6] /*fel*/ (*Spenser*) *n* gall or bitterness. [L *fel*]

fella or **fellah** see **fellow**.

fellah /*fel*'*ə*/ *n* (*pl* **fell**'**ahs**, **fellaheen** or **fellahin** /-*hēn*'/) a peasant, *esp* in Egypt. [Ar *fellāh* tiller]

fellatio /*fe-lā*'*shi-ō*/ *n* (*pl* **fellā**'**tios**) oral stimulation of the penis (also **fellā**'**tion**). [L, from *fellātus*, pap of *fellāre* to suck]

■ **fellate**' *vt* (back-formation) to perform fellatio on.

feller see **fell**[1] and **fellow**.

felloe /*fel*'*ō*/ or **felly** /*fel*'*i*/ *n* a curved piece in the circumference of a wheel; the circular rim of a wheel. [OE *felg*; Ger *Felge*]

fellow /*fel*'*ō*/ *n* (also (*inf*) **fell**'**a**, **fell**'**ah** or **fell**'**er**) a man or boy, sometimes used dismissively; a boyfriend (*inf*); an associate or companion; someone with something in common with one, one's peer or equal in a specified way; one of a pair, a mate; a counterpart; a senior member of a college; a member of the governing body of a university; a postgraduate student receiving a stipend for a stated period of research; (often with *cap*) a member of an academic, scientific or professional society; a worthless or contemptible person. ◆ *adj* denoting one's peer or equal in a specified way. [ME *felawe*, from ON *fēlagi*, a partner in goods, from *fē* (OE *feoh*; Ger *Vieh*) cattle or property, and root *lag*- a laying together, a law. Cf **fee**, **law**, **lay**]

■ **fell**'**owly** *adj* (*Shakesp*) companionable. **fell**'**owship** *n* the state of being a fellow or partner; friendship; communion; an association; an endowment in a college for the support of graduate fellows; the position and income of a university fellow; the reckoning of proportional division of profit and loss among partners.

❑ **fellow citizen** *n* a person belonging to the same city as oneself or another. **fellow-comm**'**oner** *n* at Cambridge and elsewhere, one of a privileged class of undergraduates, dining at the fellows' table. **fellow**

countryman *n* a person from the same country as oneself or another. **fellow creature** *n* a creature like oneself or another. **fellow feeling** *n* a feeling of common interest; sympathy. **fellow heir** *n* a joint heir. **fellow man** *n* a human being like oneself or another. **fellow member** *n* a member of the same organization, etc. **fellow servant** *n* a servant who has the same master or mistress as oneself or another. **fellow townsman** *n* a dweller in the same town. **fellow traveller** *n* a person who travels in the same railway carriage, bus, etc, or along the same route as oneself or another; a person who, though not a party member, holds the same political (*esp* communist) views, a sympathizer (*transl* of *Russ* word).

■ **good fellowship** companionableness. **the right hand of fellowship** the right hand given in welcome, *esp* by one minister or elder to another at an ordination in some churches.

felly[1] see **felloe**.

felly[2] see under **fell**[3].

felo de se /*fē*'*lō dē sē* or *fe*'*lō də sē*/ (*law*) a suicide. [L, literally, felon of himself]

felon[1] /*fel*'*ən*/ *n* a person guilty of a felony; a wicked person (*obs*). ◆ *adj* (*archaic*) wicked or cruel; fell; fierce; mighty. [OFr, from LL *fellō*, -*ōnis* a traitor]

■ **felonious** /*fi-lō*'*ni-əs*/ *adj* relating to a felony; wicked (*archaic*); depraved (*archaic*). **felō**'**niously** *adv*. **felō**'**niousness** *n*. **fel**'**onous** *adj* (*Spenser*) cruel, ruthless, fell. **fel**'**onry** *n* a body of felons. **fel**'**ony** *n* *orig* a crime punished by total forfeiture of lands, etc; a grave crime, formerly classed legally as one more serious than a misdemeanour (still classed as such in the USA because of the harsher punishments imposed).

felon[2] /*fel*'*ən*/ (*archaic*) *n* an inflamed sore. [Perh **felon**[1]]

felsite /*fel*'*sīt*/ *n* a fine-grained mixture of quartz and orthoclase; a devitrified acid igneous rock, characterized by felsitic structure. [**feldspar**]

■ **felsitic** /-*sit*'*ik*/ *adj* consisting of a fine patchy mosaic of quartz and feldspar (also **fel**'**sic**).

felspar see **feldspar**.

felstone /*fel*'*stōn*/ *n* (*old*) felsite. [Ger *Felsstein*, partly anglicized]

felt[1] /*felt*/ *n* a soft fabric formed without weaving, filaments pressed together using the natural tendency of the fibres of wool and certain kinds of hair to interlace and cling together; any material made in a similar way, eg the bituminous matting used to line roofs. ◆ *vt* to make into felt; to cover with felt. ◆ *vi* to become felted or matted. [OE *felt*; cf Du *vilt*, Ger *Filz*]

■ **felt**'**er** *vt* to mat together like felt. **felt**'**ing** *n* the art or process of making felt or of matting fibres together; the felt itself. **felt**'**y** *adj*.

❑ **felt-tip pen**, **felt-tipped pen**, **felt tip** or **felt pen** *n* a pen with a nib of felt or similar fibrous substance.

felt[2] /*felt*/ *pat* and *pap* of **feel**.

felucca /*fe-luk*'*ə*/ *n* a small merchant vessel used on the Nile and in the Mediterranean, with two masts, triangular (lateen) sails, and often a rudder at each end. [Ital *feluca*; cf Ar *falūkah*]

felwort /*fel*'*wûrt*/ *n* a gentian. [OE *feldwyrt*, from *feld* field, and *wyrt* wort]

fem[1] see **femme**.

fem[2] or **fem.** *abbrev*: feminine.

FEMA *abbrev*: Federal Emergency Management Agency (in the USA).

female /*fē*'*māl*/ *n* a woman or girl (sometimes *derog*); any animal or plant of the same sex as a woman. ◆ *adj* (also (*Milton*) **fe**'**mal**) of the sex that produces young or eggs, or (structures containing) spores or seeds; for, belonging to, characteristic of, or fancifully attributed to that sex; womanish (*Shakesp*); of the sex characterized by relatively large gametes (*biol*); (of parts of a mechanism) hollow and adapted to receive a counterpart (*machinery*). [Fr *femelle*, from L *fēmella* a girl, dimin of *fēmina* woman; the second syllable influenced by association with **male**[1]]

■ **fē**'**maleness** *n*. **femality** /*fē-mal*'*i-ti*/ *n*.

❑ **female circumcision** *n* surgical removal of part or all of the clitoris, clitoridectomy. **female condom** *n* a contraceptive consisting of a thin polyurethane pouch that fits inside the vagina. **female genital mutilation** *n* (*disapproving*) procedures involving cutting carried out on the female genitals for cultural or religious reasons. **female thread** *n* a cylindrical hole with a thread cut on the inner surface.

feme /*fem* or *fēm*/ (*law*) *n* a woman. [OFr *feme*]

❑ **feme covert** /*kuv*'*ərt*/ *n* a married woman. **feme sole** *n* a spinster, widow, or married woman legally in the position of an unmarried woman.

femerall /*fem*'*ə-rəl*/ *n* an outlet for smoke in a roof. [OFr *fumeraille*, from L *fūmus* smoke]

femetary see **fumitory**.

femicide /fem'i-sīd/ n the killing of a woman or women. [L *fēmina* woman, and *caedere* to kill]
■ **femici'dal** adj.

feminal /fem'i-nəl/ adj (of a man) thinking and acting in a way traditionally thought of as characteristic of women. [L *fēmina* woman]
■ **feminality** /-al'i-ti/ n.

feminine /fem'i-nin/ adj female; characteristic of, peculiar or appropriate to, women or the female sex; womanish; of that gender to which words denoting females, and in some languages various associated classes of words, belong (*grammar*). ◆ n the female sex or nature; a word of feminine gender. [L *fēminīna*, dimin of *fēmina* woman]
■ **fem'ininely** adv. **fem'ininism** n an idiom or expression supposedly characteristic of women; an addiction to feminine ways. **feminin'ity** n the quality of being feminine (also **femine'ity**, **feminil'ity**, **fem'inineness**, or **femin'ity**).
□ **feminine caesura** n one which does not immediately follow the rhythmical or metrical stress. **feminine ending** n (*prosody*) in French verse, the ending of a line in a mute *e* (the French feminine suffix); the ending of a verse or musical phrase on an unstressed syllable or note. **feminine rhyme** n a two-syllable rhyme, the second syllable being unstressed.

feminism /fem'i-ni-zm/ n advocacy of women's rights, or of the movement for the advancement and emancipation of women. [L *fēmina* woman]
■ **fem'inist** n an advocate or favourer of feminism; a person who studies women. ◆ adj of or relating to feminists or feminism. **feminist'ic** adj.

feminize or **-ise** /fem'i-nīz/ vt and vi to make or become feminine; to (cause a male animal to) develop female characteristics. [L *fēmina* woman]
■ **feminizā'tion** or **-s-** n.

femiter /fem'i-tər/ see **fumitory**.

femme /fam/ (Fr) n a woman, wife; an ostentatiously effeminate person (*inf*); (also **fem**) the more feminine partner in a homosexual relationship (*inf*). See also **feme**.
□ **femme de chambre** /də shã'br'/ n a lady's-maid; a chambermaid. **femme du monde** /dü mõd/ n a woman of the world; a society woman. **femme fatale** /fa-tal'/ n an irresistibly attractive woman who brings difficulties or disaster on men; a siren. **femme incomprise** /ē-kõ-prēz'/ n a woman who is misunderstood or unappreciated. **femme savante** /sa-vãt'/ n a learned woman, a bluestocking.

femto- /fem-tō-/ combining form denoting 10^{-15}. [Dan and Norw *femten* fifteen, from ON *fimmtān*]

femur /fē'mər/ n (pl **fē'murs** or **femora** /fem'ər-ə/) the thigh bone; the third segment of an insect's leg. [L *femur, -oris* thigh]
■ **femoral** /fem'/ adj belonging to the thigh.
□ **femoral artery** n the main artery of the thigh.

fen¹ /fen/ n low marshy land often, or partially, covered with water; a morass or bog. [OE *fenn*; ON *fen*]
■ **fenn'ish** or **fenn'y** adj.
□ **fen'-berry** n the cranberry. **fen'-crick'et** n the mole cricket (see under **mole¹**). **fen'-fire** n the will-o'-the-wisp. **fen'land** n. **fen'man** n a person who lives in fen country. **fen'-sucked** adj (*Shakesp*) drawn out of bogs.

fen² /fen/ (*obs*) vt used only as a prohibitory exclamation in boys' games, to bar an action, right or privilege. [Cf **fend¹**; or perhaps from **feign**]

fen³ /fen/ n a Chinese monetary unit, $\frac{1}{100}$ of a yuan; a coin of this value. [Chin *fēn*]

fence /fens/ n a barrier, *esp* of wood or wood and wire, for enclosing, bounding or protecting land; a barrier of varying design for a horse to jump (*showjumping* and *steeplechasing*); a guard on a machine; a guide on a cutting tool; the art of fencing; defence (*archaic*); a receiver of stolen goods (*criminal sl*); a place where stolen goods are received (*criminal sl*). ◆ vt to enclose with a fence; to fortify; to shield; to keep off; to receive or dispose of (stolen goods) (*criminal sl*). ◆ vi to build fences; to guard; to practise or take part in fencing; to be a receiver or purchaser of stolen goods (*criminal sl*); to answer or dispute evasively; to leap fences. [Aphetic from **defence**]
■ **fenced** adj enclosed with a fence. **fence'less** adj without a fence or enclosure, open. **fenc'er** n a person who takes part in the sport of fencing; a person who makes or repairs fences; a horse trained to jump fences in steeplechasing. **fenc'ible** adj capable of being fenced or defended. ◆ n (*hist*) a militiaman or volunteer soldier enlisted in a crisis, *esp* to fight in a local or regional conflict. **fenc'ing** adj defending or guarding. ◆ n the act of erecting a fence; material for fences; fences collectively; the act of answering or disputing evasively; the leaping of fences; receiving stolen goods (*criminal sl*); the act, art or sport of attack and defence with a foil, sword or similar weapon.
□ **fence'-lizard** n a small American spiny lizard (genus *Sceloporus*) which often suns itself on fences, paths or rocks. **fence'-mending** see

mend one's fences below. **fence month** n close season. **fencing master** or (*fem*) **mistress** n a man or woman who teaches the sport of fencing.
■ **fence the tables** in early, now limited, Scottish usage, to debar the unworthy from taking communion. **mend one's fences** to improve or restore one's relations, reputation or popularity, *esp* in politics (**fence'-mending** n and adj). **sit on the fence** to avoid committing oneself; to remain neutral. **sunk fence** a ditch or watercourse.

fend¹ /fend/ vt to ward (off); to shut out; to defend (*archaic*). ◆ vi to offer resistance; to provide (for). ◆ n (*Scot*) self-support, the effort one makes for oneself. [Aphetic for **defend**]
■ **fend'y** adj (*Scot*) resourceful; thrifty.

fend² /fend/ (*Milton*) same as **fiend**.

fender /fen'dər/ n a guard in front of a hearth to confine the ashes; a protection for a ship's side against piers, etc, consisting of a bundle of rope, etc; a mudguard (*US*); a wing of a car (*N Am*); any structure serving as a guard against contact or impact. [**fend¹**]
□ **fender bender** n (*US inf*) a collision between motor vehicles in which little damage is caused. **fend'er-stool** n a long stool placed beside a fireside fender.

fenestella /fen-i-stel'ə/ n a small window or window-like opening; in a church, a niche containing the piscina, the drain into which the washing water from the sacred vessels was poured; (with *cap*; *biol*) a Palaeozoic genus of lace-like Polyzoa. [L, dimin of *fenestra* a window]

fenestra /fi-nes'trə/ n a window or other wall opening; a perforation; an aperture in a bone or cartilage; a translucent spot, eg that on a moth's wing (*zool*). [L]
■ **fenes'tral** n a window with some other translucent material instead of glass. ◆ adj of or like a window; perforated; with translucent spots. **fenestrate** /fen'is-trit, fi-nes'trit or -trāt/ or **fen'estrated** adj having windows or the appearance of windows (*archit*); pierced; perforated; having translucent spots. **fenestrā'tion** n the arrangement of windows in a building (*archit*); the fact of being fenestrate; perforation; the operation of making an artificial fenestra when the fenestra ovalis has been clogged by growth of bone (*surg*).
□ **fenestra ovalis** or **rotunda** n (*biol*) the oval or round windows, two membrane-covered openings between the middle and the internal ear.

fenfluramine /fen-floo'rə-mēn/ n a drug formerly used to treat obesity (also **fenfluramine hydrochloride**).

feng shui /fung shwē/ n in Chinese philosophy, a discipline that takes into account the influences of energies in the natural environment on a building, placing of furniture, an important event, etc, in order to ensure the optimum happiness and prosperity for the inhabitants, participants, etc. [Chin *fēng* wind, and *shuǐ* water]

feni or **fenny** /fen'i/ n an alcoholic spirit produced in Goa from coconuts or cashew nuts. [Konkani *feni*]

Fenian /fē'nyən/ n a member of an association of Irish people founded in New York in 1857 for the overthrow of the British government in Ireland; a (*esp* Irish) Catholic (*offensive*). ◆ adj belonging to the legendary *fiann*, or to the modern Fenians; Catholic (*offensive*). [Old Ir *Féne*, one of the names of the ancient population of Ireland, confused in modern times with *fiann*, the militia of Finn and other ancient Irish kings]
■ **Fe'nianism** n.

fenitar /fen'i-tər/ see **fumitory**.

fenks /fengks/ or **finks** /fingks/ n the refuse of whale-blubber after its oil has been extracted. [Origin unknown]

fennec /fen'ək/ n a little African fox with large ears. [Ar *fenek*]

fennel /fen'əl/ n a yellow-flowered umbelliferous plant of the genus *Foeniculum*, related to dill, but distinguished by the cylindrical, strongly-ribbed fruit, the seeds and leaves being used for seasoning. [OE *finul*, from L *fēniculum*, *fēnuc(u)lum* fennel, from *fēnum* hay]
□ **fenn'el-flower** n a ranunculaceous plant of the genus *Nigella*.
■ **dwarf**, **Florence**, **French** or **sweet fennel** see **finocchio**. **giant fennel** an umbelliferous plant, *Ferula communis*.

fennish and **fenny¹** see under **fen¹**.

fenny² see **feni**.

fent /fent/ n a slit or crack; a remnant or odd, short or damaged piece of cloth (*N Eng*). [OFr *fente*, from L *findere* to cleave or split]
□ **fent'-merchant** n.

fentanyl /fen'tə-nil/ n a powerful narcotic analgesic.

fenugreek /fen'ū-grēk/ n a plant (*Trigonella foenum-graecum*), related to melilot, the aromatic seeds of which are used as a food flavouring. [L *fēnum graecum* Greek hay]

feod, feodal and **feodary** same as **feud²**, **feudal** and **feudary**.

feoff /fēf or fef/ n a fief. ◆ vt to grant possession of a fief or property in land. [OFr *feoffer* or *fiefer*, from OFr *fief*. See **fee**]

■ **feoffee** /n/ the person invested with the fief. **feoff'er** or **feoff'or** /n/ the person who grants a fief. **feoff'ment** /n/ the gift of a fief.

feracious /fi-rā'shəs/ (*rare*) *adj* fruitful. [L *ferāx*, *-ācis*, from *ferre* to bear]

■ **feracity** /fi-ras'i-ti/ /n/.

ferae naturae /fē'rē nə-tū'rē or fe'rī na-too'rī/ (*law*) (of animals) wild, undomesticated. [L, literally, of wild nature]

feral¹ /fer'əl or fē'rəl/ *adj* wild; untamed; uncultivated (*bot*); run wild; animal (*derog*). [L *fera* a wild beast]

■ **fer'alized** or **-s-** *adj* run wild following domestication. **ferine** /-rīn or -rin/ *adj* relating to or like a wild beast; wild; animal (*derog*). **ferity** /fer'i-ti/ /n/ (*rare*) wildness; uncultivated state; savagery.

feral² /fē'rəl/ (*archaic*) *adj* deadly; funereal. [L *fērālis*]

fer-de-lance /fer'də-läs/ /n/ the lance-headed or yellow viper of tropical America. [Fr, lance-head (literally, iron)]

fere¹, **feare**, **feer**, **fiere** or **pheere** /fēr/ (*archaic*) /n/ a companion; a mate; a spouse; an equal. [OE *gefēra* companion, and *gefēre* company]

■ **in fere** together, in company (also **yfere**).

fere² /fēr/ (*Scot*) *adj* able, sound. [OE *fēre*]

feretory /fer'i-tər-i/ /n/ a shrine for relics, carried in processions; a chapel where shrines are kept. [L *feretrum*, from Gr *pheretron* bier or litter, from *pherein* to bear]

ferial /fē'ri-əl/ *adj* relating to holidays; belonging to any day of the week which is neither a fast nor a festival (*RC*). [L *fēria* a holiday]

ferine and **ferity** see under **feral¹**.

Feringhi or **Feringhee** /fe-ring'gē/ /n/ an Indian name for a European (also **Farin'gee**). [Frank]

ferly /fûr'li/ (*Scot*) *adj* fearful; sudden; peculiar. ◆ /n/ /fâr'li/ a wonder. ◆ *vi* to wonder. [OE *fǣrlic* sudden; cf Ger *gefährlich* dangerous]

ferm /fûrm/ /n/ a farm; lodging (*Spenser*). [Variant of **farm**]

fermata /fûr-mä'tə/ (*music*) /n/ (pl **ferma'tas** or **fermate** /-tē/) a pause. [Ital]

Fermat's principle of least time (*phys*) see **principle of least time** under **principle**.

ferment /fûr'mənt/ /n/ a substance that produces fermentation; internal motion amongst the parts of a fluid; agitation; tumult. ◆ *vt* /-ment'/ to produce fermentation in; to work up or excite. ◆ *vi* to rise and swell by the action of fermentation; (of wine) to undergo alcoholic fermentation; to be in excited action; (of emotions, etc) to agitate in the mind. [Fr, from L *fermentum*, for *fervimentum*, from *fervēre* to boil]

■ **fermentabil'ity** /n/. **ferment'able** *adj* capable of fermentation. **fermentā'tion** /n/ a slow decomposition process of organic substances induced by micro-organisms, or by complex nitrogenous organic substances (*enzymes*) of vegetable or animal origin, *usu* accompanied by evolution of heat and gas, eg alcoholic fermentation of sugar and starch, and lactic fermentation; the act or process of fermenting; restless action of the mind or feelings. **ferment'ative** *adj* causing or consisting of fermentation. **ferment'ativeness** /n/. **ferment'ed** *adj*. **ferment'er** or **ferment'or** /n/ an apparatus in which fermentation is promoted; a substance that causes fermentation. **fermentesc'ible** *adj* capable of being fermented. **fermentitious** /-ish'əs/ *adj*. **ferment'ive** *adj*.

fermi /fûr'mi/ (*phys*) /n/ a unit equal to 10^{-5} angstrom or 10^{-15} metres (also **fem'tometre**). [Enrico *Fermi* (1901–54), Italian physicist]

■ **fer'mion** /n/ one of a group of subatomic particles, such as protons, electrons and neutrons, having half-integral spin and obeying the exclusion principle. **fer'mium** /n/ an artificially produced radioactive transuranic metallic element (symbol **Fm**; atomic no 100).

fern /fûrn/ /n/ one of a class of vascular flowerless plants which reproduce by means of spores, many species of which have featherlike leaves. [OE *fearn*; Ger *Farn*]

■ **fern'ery** /n/ a place for rearing ferns. **fern'ing** /n/ (*med*) (of cervical mucus, etc) a tendency to develop a feathery or fern-like appearance. **fern'y** *adj*.
□ **fernally** /-al'/ /n/ any vascular flowerless plant that is not a true a fern, eg equisetum. **fern'bird** /n/ a small brown-and-white New Zealand bird, *Bowdleria punctata*, related to the warblers, which is found in swamps and marshy scrub and which has somewhat fern-like tail feathers. **fern land** /n/ (in New Zealand) land covered or formerly covered by bracken. **fern'-owl** /n/ the nightjar; the short-eared owl. **fern'-seed** /n/ the spores of ferns, once believed to confer invisibility. **fern'shaw** /n/ a thicket of ferns. **fern'tickled** or **fern'ticled** *adj*.

ferocious /fə-rō'shəs/ *adj* savage, fierce; cruel. [L *ferōx*, *ferōcis* wild, from *ferus* wild]

■ **ferō'ciously** *adv*. **ferō'ciousness** or **ferocity** /-ros'i-ti/ /n/ savage cruelty of temperament; untamed fierceness.

-ferous /-fə-rəs/ or **-iferous** /-i-fə-rəs/ *combining form* bearing, producing or containing, eg *coniferous*, *ferriferous*.

ferrandine see **farandine**.

ferrate /fer'āt/ /n/ a salt of ferric acid. [L *ferrum* iron]
■ **ferr'eous** *adj* relating to, containing, or like iron.

ferrel see **ferrule**.

ferret¹ /fer'it/ /n/ a half-tamed albino variety of the polecat, employed in unearthing rabbits; a diligent searcher or investigator. ◆ *vt* (**ferr'eting**; **ferr'eted**) to drive out of a hiding-place; to search out persistently and indefatigably; to hunt with a ferret. ◆ *vi* to search, rummage; to hunt with a ferret. [OFr *furet* a ferret, dimin, from LL *fūrō*, *-ōnis* robber, from L *fūr* a thief]

■ **ferr'eter** /n/ a person who ferrets. **ferr'ety** *adj* like a ferret in appearance.
□ **ferr'et-badg'er** /n/ a small tree-climbing badger (genus *Melogale*) of SE Asia.

ferret² /fer'it/ /n/ narrow silk or cotton ribbon (also *adj*). [Ital *fioretto*, dimin, from L *flōs*, *flōris* flower]

ferri- /fer-i-/ *combining form* signifying the presence of iron, *usu* in its trivalent form.

■ **ferricy'anide** /n/ a salt of hydroferricyanic acid. **ferricyan'ogen** /n/ the trivalent radical, $Fe(CN)_6$, of the ferricyanides. **ferrimagnet'ic** *adj*. **ferrimag'netism** /n/ iron magnetism in which the magnetic moments of neighbouring ions are non-parallel.

ferriage see under **ferry**.

ferric /fer'ik/ *adj* of iron; containing iron in its trivalent form (**ferric acid** a hypothetical acid H_2FeO_4) (*chem*). [L *ferrum* iron]

■ **ferrif'erous** *adj* bearing or yielding iron.
□ **ferric oxide** /n/ a red crystalline oxide of iron used as a coating on magnetic tape and as a metal polish (also called **jeweller's rouge**).

Ferris wheel /fer'is wēl or hwēl/ (*orig US*) /n/ a fairground attraction, a large upright wheel having seats suspended on the circumference which remain horizontal while the wheel rotates. [GWG *Ferris* (1859–96), American engineer]

ferrite /fer'īt/ /n/ a form of pure iron; any of a number of magnetic materials (generally oxides of iron with other metals, eg barium or manganese) which have high electrical resistivity. [L *ferrum* iron]

■ **ferrit'ic** *adj* consisting mainly of ferrite. **ferr'itin** /n/ a protein in which iron is stored in the liver and spleen.

ferro- /fer-ō-/ *combining form* signifying the presence of iron, *usu* in its divalent form; relating to iron. [L *ferrum* iron]

■ **ferro-all'oy** /n/ an alloy of iron and some other metal. **ferr'ocene** /n/ an orange crystalline compound, $(C_6H_5)_2Fe$, used as a fuel and additive. **ferro-chro'mium** (or **ferro-chrome'**), **ferro-mang'anese**, **ferro-molyb'denum** and **ferro-nick'el** /n/ an alloy of iron with much chromium, manganese, etc. **ferrocon'crete** /n/ reinforced concrete. **ferrocy'anide** /n/ a salt of hydroferrocyanic acid. **ferrocyan'ogen** /n/ the quadrivalent radical, $Fe(CN)_6$, of the ferrocyanides. **ferroelec'tric** *adj* exhibiting electric polarization. ◆ /n/ a ferroelectric substance. **ferroelectric'ity** /n/. **ferrog'raphy** /n/ the technique of studying wear in machinery by measuring magnetically the ferrous content of lubricants, the results being shown by **ferr'ograms**. **ferromagnēs'ian** *adj* containing iron and magnesium. **ferromagnet'ic** *adj* strongly magnetic; formerly, paramagnetic. **ferromag'netism** /n/ the typical form of iron magnetism, with high permeability and hysteresis. **ferr'oprint** /n/ a photograph made by means of iron salts. **ferropruss'iate** /n/ ferrocyanide. **ferrosoferr'ic** *adj* combining ferrous and ferric. **ferr'otype** /n/ an old form of photograph taken using a film on an iron plate.

ferronière or **ferronnière** /fer-on-yer'/ /n/ a jewel held on the forehead by a chain, as in Leonardo da Vinci's 'La Belle Ferronnière'. [Fr *ferronnière*, fem of *ferronnier* ironmonger]

ferrous /fer'əs/ *adj* containing iron; containing iron in its divalent form. [L *ferrum* iron]
□ **ferrous sulphate** /n/ a salt of iron, *usu* used in tanning, etc.

ferruginous /fe-roo'ji-nəs or fə-roo'ji-nəs/ *adj* (also **ferrugin'eous** /fer-/) of the colour of iron-rust; impregnated with iron. [L *ferrūgō*, *-inis* iron-rust, from *ferrum* iron]

■ **ferru'go** /-gō/ /n/ rust disease of plants.
□ **ferruginous duck** /n/ a Eurasian diving duck, the male of which has reddish-brown plumage.

ferrule /fer'ool, -əl/ /n/ (also **ferr'el** or (*Scot*) **virl**) a metal band, ring or cap on the tip of a stick, etc for reinforcing it; a threaded cylindrical fitting for joining two pipes or rods. [OFr *virole*, from L *viriola* a bracelet]

ferry /fer'i/ *vt* (**ferr'ying**; **ferr'ied**) to carry or convey (*esp* over water in a boat or ship, or sometimes an aircraft); to deliver (an aircraft coming from a factory) under its own power. ◆ *vi* to cross by ferry. ◆ /n/ a boat for the conveyance of passengers and *usu* vehicles across a stretch of water (also **ferr'y-boat**); the service thus provided; a place or route of carriage over water; the right of conveying passengers. [OE *ferian* to convey, *faran* to go; Ger *Fähre* a ferry, from *fahren* to go, to carry]

■ **ferr'iage** *n* transport by ferry; the fare paid for it.

❑ **ferr'y-boat** see **ferry** (*n*) above. **ferr'y-house** *n* a ferryman's house; a place of shelter or refreshment at a ferry. **ferr'yman** *n*.

fertile /fûr'tīl or (*US*) -təl/ *adj* able to bear or produce young, fruit, etc abundantly; giving such ability; rich in resources; inventive; capable of breeding, hatching, or germinating; able to become fissile or fissionable (*phys*). [Fr, from L *fertilis*, from *ferre* to bear]

■ **fer'tilely** *adv*. **fertility** /-til'i-ti/ *n* fruitfulness, richness, abundance; the state of being fertile; the ability to produce young; the number or percentage of eggs produced by a species or individual that develop into living young (cf **fecundity**; *ecology*). **fertilization** or **-s-** /-ti-lī-zā'shən/ *n* the act or process of fertilizing. **fer'tilize** or **-ise** *vt* to make fertile or fruitful; to enrich; to impregnate; to pollinate; (of a male gamete, *esp* a sperm cell) to fuse with a female gamete (*esp* an egg cell) to form a zygote. **fer'tilizer** or **-s-** *n* a person or thing that fertilizes. ❑ **Fertile Crescent** *n* a crescent-shaped region stretching from Armenia to Arabia, formerly fertile but now mainly desert, considered to be the cradle of civilization. **fertile material** *n* an isotope (eg uranium-238) that can be readily transformed by the capture of a neutron into fissionable material (plutonium-239). **fertility cult** *n* a religious cult involving ceremonies intended to ensure fruitful harvests. **fertility drug** *n* a drug given to apparently infertile women to induce ovulation.

ferule /fer'ool/ *n* a cane or rod used for punishment. [L *ferula* a giant fennel, from *ferīre* to strike]

■ **fer'ula** *n* a ferule; a staff of command; (with *cap*) the giant fennel genus. **ferulā'ceous** *adj* like a cane, reed or *Ferula*.

fervent /fûr'vənt/ *adj* passionate, ardent; zealous; hot (*archaic*); warm in feeling, friendly or affectionate (*archaic*). [L *fervēre* to boil, *fervēscere*, *fervidus* fiery, glowing, *fervor* violent heat]

■ **fer'vency** *n* heat; eagerness; emotional warmth. **fer'vently** *adv*. **fervescent** /-ves'ənt/ *adj* growing hot. **fer'vid** *adj* very hot; having burning desire or emotion; glowing; zealous. **fervid'ity** *n*. **fer'vidly** *adv*. **fer'vidness** *n*. **Fervidor'** *n* the eleventh month of the French Revolutionary calendar, Thermidor. **fer'vorous** *adj*. **fer'vour** or (*US*) **fer'vor** *n* heat; vehemence, ardour; zeal.

Fescennine /fes'ə-nīn or -nin/ *adj* scurrilous. [The Etruscan town of *Fescennium*]

❑ **Fescennine verses** *n pl* rude extempore verses, generally in Saturnian measure, in which the parties bantered and ridiculed one another.

fescue /fes'kū/ *n* any one of the grasses, closely related to the brome-grasses, of the genus *Festuca*, which includes many pasture and fodder grasses; a pointer used in teaching. [OFr *festu*, from L *festūca* a straw]

fess /fes/ (*US inf*) *vi* (*usu* with *up*) to confess to a crime. [Short form of **confess**]

fesse or **fess** /fes/ (*heraldry*) *n* one of the simple heraldic forms, a horizontal band over the middle of an escutcheon, *usu* one-third of the whole. [Fr *fasce*, from L *fascia* a band]

■ **fesse'-wise** or **fess'-wise** *adv*.

❑ **fesse'-point** *n* the centre of an escutcheon.

fest /fest/ *n* (*usu* in combination) a party or gathering, or (in writing) a collection, *esp* for a particular activity, as in *songfest*; a concentrated period of indulgence in a particular activity, as in *sleaze-fest*. [Ger *Fest* festival]

festa /fes'ta/ (*Ital*) *n* a holiday, festival or saint's day.

festal /fes'tl/ *adj* relating to a feast or holiday; joyous; festive. ◆ *n* a festivity. [See **feast**]

■ **fes'tally** *adv*. **festil'ogy** or **festol'ogy** *n* a treatise on ecclesiastical festivals.

fester /fes'tər/ *vi* to rot or putrefy; to suppurate; to rankle; to worsen and intensify; to be idle (*inf*). ◆ *vt* to cause to fester or rankle. ◆ *n* a sore discharging pus. [OFr *festre*, from L *fistula* an ulcer]

festilogy see under **festal**.

festina lente /fe-stē'na len'ti/ (*L*) make haste slowly.

festinate /fes'ti-nāt/ *vt* (*esp med*) to accelerate. ◆ *adj* (*Shakesp*) hurried, hasty. [L *festīnāre*, *-ātum* to hurry]

■ **fes'tinately** *adv* (*Shakesp*). **festinā'tion** *n* quickening, *esp* of physical movements.

festival /fes'ti-vəl/ *n* a joyful or honorific celebration; a religious feast; a season or series of performances of music, plays, etc. ◆ *adj* of, relating to or characteristic of a festival. [Med L *festivālis* relating to a feast, from *festīvus* festive]

■ **Festival of Dedication** and **Festival of Lights** same as **Hanukkah**.

festive /fes'tiv/ *adj* relating to a feast or holiday; celebratory, joyful. [L *festīvus*, from *festus*]

■ **fes'tively** *adv*. **fes'tiveness** *n*. **festiv'ity** *n* conviviality; joyfulness; gaiety; (in *pl*) joyful celebrations. **fes'tivous** (or /-tī'/) *adj* (*archaic*) festive.

festology see under **festal**.

festoon /fe-stoon'/ *n* a garland suspended between two points; an ornament like a garland (*archit*). ◆ *vt* to adorn, hang or connect with festoons. ◆ *vi* to hang in festoons. [Fr *feston*, appar connected with L *festum* a festival]

■ **festoon'ery** *n* festoons collectively.

❑ **festoon blind** *n* a window blind ruched to fall in festoon-like folds.

festschrift /fest'shrift/ *n* a celebratory publication, commonly a collection of writings presented by their authors and published in honour of some person. [Ger, festival writing]

FET *abbrev* : field-effect transistor.

fet /fet/ *vt* obsolete form of **fetch**[1].

feta /fet'ə/ *n* a crumbly white low-fat cheese originating in Greece and the Middle East, traditionally made from goat's or ewe's milk but now sometimes with cow's milk (also **fett'a**). [Mod Gr *pheta* a slice (ie of cheese), from Ital *fetta*]

fetal see under **fetus**.

fetch[1] /fech/ *vt* to bring; to go and get; to be sold for (a certain price); to cause to come; to call forth; to draw (eg blood, breath); to achieve control over, to take; to derive; to reach or attain; to utter (a sigh or groan); to administer (a blow, etc, *usu* with *indirect object*). ◆ *vi* to make one's way; to arrive; to be effective. ◆ *n* an act of bringing; the distance travelled by a wind or wave without obstruction; a stratagem (*archaic*). [OE *feccan*, appar an altered form of *fetian* to fetch; cf Ger *fassen* to seize]

■ **fetch'er** *n*. **fetch'ing** *adj* fascinating, charming; attractive.

■ **fetch a compass** or **circuit** to go round in a wide curve. **fetch and carry** to perform humble services for another person. **fetch a pump** to pour water in so as to make it draw. **fetch off** to bring out of danger or difficulty; to make away with (*Shakesp*); to fleece (*Shakesp*). **fetch out** to draw forth or develop. **fetch up** to recover; to come to a stop (*inf*); to bring up, rear (eg children) (*US*); to vomit (*inf*).

fetch[2] /fech/ (*archaic*) *n* the apparition, double or ghost of a living person. [Ety unknown]

❑ **fetch'-candle** *n* a nocturnal light, supposed to portend a death.

fête or **fete** /fet or fāt/ *n* an outdoor function with entertainments, stalls, refreshments, etc, often in aid of a charity; a festival; a holiday; the festival of the saint whose name one bears. ◆ *vt* to entertain at a feast; to honour with festivities. [Fr]

❑ **fête champêtre** /shā-pe'tr'/ *n* a rural festival or garden party; an early 18c genre of French painting, typically showing courtly figures in a rural setting (also called **fête galante** /ga-lāt'/), associated mainly with Jean Antoine Watteau (1684–1721). **Fête-Dieu** /dyø/ *n* the festival in honour of the Eucharist, Corpus Christi.

fetial /fē'shəl/ *adj* (also **fē'cial**) relating to the ancient Roman *fētiālēs*, a priestly college of heralds; heraldic, ambassadorial.

fetich, fetiche, etc see **fetish**.

feticide see under **fetus**.

fetid or **foetid** /fet'id or fē'tid/ *adj* stinking; having a strong offensive smell. [L *fētidus*, *fētor*, from *fētēre* to stink]

■ **fē'tidness, foe'tidness, fē'tor** or **foe'tor** *n*.

fetish, fetich or **fetiche** /fet'ish or fē'tish/ *n* an object believed to procure for its owner the services of a spirit lodged within it; an inanimate object to which a pathological sexual attachment is formed; such an attachment; a procedure or ritual followed obsessively; a person who is the object of an obsessive fixation; a fixation; something regarded with irrational reverence. [Fr *fétiche*, from Port *feitiço* magic; a name given by the Portuguese to the gods of W Africa, from Port *feitiço* artificial, from L *factīcius*, from *facere* to make]

■ **fet'ishism** or **fet'ichism** *n* the worship of a fetish; a belief in charms; pathological attachment of sexual interest to an inanimate object. **fet'ishist** or **fet'ichist** *n*. **fetishist'ic** or **fetichis'tic** *adj*. **fet'ishize** or **-ise** or **fet'ichize** or **-ise** *vt* to make a fetish of (a person).

fetlock /fet'lok/ *n* a tuft of hair that grows above a horse's hoof; the part where this hair grows. [History obscure; long considered to be a compound of **foot** and **lock**[2] (of hair); cf Ger *Fissloch*]

■ **fet'locked** *adj* having a fetlock; tied by the fetlock.

fetoscopy see under **fetus**.

fett /fet/ *vt* obsolete form of **fetch**[1].

fetta see **feta**.

fetter /fet'ər/ *n* (*usu* in *pl*) a chain or shackle for the feet; (*usu* in *pl*) anything that restrains. ◆ *vt* to put fetters on; to restrain. [OE *feter*; connected with *fōt* foot]

■ **fett'erless** *adj*.

❑ **fett'erlock** *n* (*heraldry*) a shackle for a horse, as a design on a shield.

■ words derived from main entry word; ❑ compound words; ■ idioms and phrasal verbs

fettle /fet'l/ n condition, trim or form, esp in in fine fettle; a lining of loose sand or ore for a furnace. ◆ vt to make ready, set in order or arrange; to tidy up (dialect); to knock or rub excess material off the edges of (a casting or piece of pottery); to line (a furnace) with loose sand or ore. ◆ vi to potter fussily about. [Prob OE fetel a belt]
■ **fett'ler** n a person who fettles, esp (Aust) a maintenance worker on the railway. **fett'ling** n.

fettuccine, **fettucine** or **fettucini** /fet-oo-chē'nā or -nē/ n pasta made in long ribbons. [Ital]

fetus or (not in scientific use) **foetus** /fē'təs/ n the young animal in the egg or in the womb, after its parts are distinctly formed. [L fētus offspring]
■ **fē'tal** or **foe'tal** adj. **fetici'dal** or **foetici'dal** adj. **fē'ticide** or **foe'ticide** n destruction of a fetus. **fetos'copy** or **foetos'copy** n a procedure for viewing the fetus directly, within the uterus, or for taking a sample of fetal blood from the placenta, by inserting a hollow needle through the abdomen into the uterus, for ascertaining any disorder.
❑ **fetal** or **foetal alcohol syndrome** n the congenital defects characteristic of babies born to mothers whose intake of alcohol is excessive, including short stature, mental retardation, and pixie-like features.

fetwa /fet'wä/ n a variant spelling of **fatwa**.

feu /fū/ (Scot) n a tenure where the vassal, in place of military services, makes a return in grain or in money; a right (abolished in 2004) to the use of land, houses, etc in perpetuity, for a stipulated annual payment (**feu-dū'ty**); a piece of land held in feu. ◆ vt to grant land to a person who undertakes to pay the feu-duty. [OFr feu; see **fee**]
■ **feu'ar** n a person who holds real estate in return for payment of feu-duty. **feud'al** adj relating to a feu.

feud[1] /fūd/ n a war waged by private individuals, families or clans against one another on their own account; a bloody strife; a persistent state of private enmity. ◆ vi to take part in or carry on a feud. [OFr faide, feide, from LL faida, from OHGer fēhida; vowel change unexplained; see **foe**]
■ **feud'ing** n and adj.
■ **right of feud** (law) the right to protect oneself and one's family, and to deal out punishment to those who do one wrong.

feud[2] or **feod** /fūd/ n (hist) a fief or land held on condition of service. [LL feudum; see **fee**]
■ **feud'al** or **feod'al** adj relating to feuds or fiefs; relating to or typical of feudalism. **feud'alism** n the feudal system, a system of social organization prevalent in W Europe in the Middle Ages, in which powerful land-owning lords granted degrees of privilege and protection to lesser subjects holding a range of positions within a rigid social hierarchy; a class-conscious social or political system resembling the medieval feudal system. **feud'alist** n. **feudalis'tic** adj. **feudal'ity** n the state of being feudal; the feudal system. **feudalīzā'tion** or **-s-** n. **feud'alize** or **-ise** vt. **feud'ally** adv. **feud'ary**, **feod'ary** or **feud'atory** adj holding lands or power by a feudal tenure (also n). **feud'ist** n a writer on feuds; a person versed in the laws of feudal tenure.
■ **the feudal system** feudalism.

feudal see under **feu** and **feud**[2].

feu d'artifice /fə dar-tē-fēs'/ (Fr) n (pl **feux d'artifice**) a firework.

feu de joie /fə də zhwä'/ (Fr) n (pl **feux de joie**) a bonfire; (in English, not in French) a firing of guns as a symbol of joy.

feuilleté /fœy-tā'/ (Fr) n puff pastry.

feuilleton /fœy-tɔ̃'/ n in French and other newspapers, a part ruled off the bottom of a page for a serial story, critical article, etc; a contribution of this kind. [Fr, dimin of feuillet a leaf, from L folium]
■ **feu'illetonism** /-tən-izm/ n. **feu'illetonist** n.

feutre same as **fewter**.

fever /fē'vər/ n an abnormally high body temperature, associated with a raised pulse rate and hot, dry skin; any of many, usu infectious, diseases in which this is a marked symptom, such as scarlet fever or yellow fever; an extreme state of excitement or nervousness; a painful degree of anxiety. ◆ vt to put into a fever. ◆ vi (obs) to become fevered. [OE fēfor, from L febris]
■ **fē'vered** adj affected with fever; excited. **fē'verish** adj slightly fevered; indicating fever; restlessly excited; morbidly eager, frenzied. **fē'verishly** adv. **fē'verishness** n. **fē'verous** adj (archaic) feverish; marked by sudden changes; apt to cause fever.
❑ **fē'ver-heat** n the heat of fever; an excessive degree of excitement. **fever pitch** n a state of great excitement or agitation. **fever therapy** n cure by inducement of fever. **fever tree** n a southern African tree of the genus Acacia, usu found in swampy, mosquito-infested places, and hence regarded (esp formerly) as an indicator of malarious spots to be avoided and by some even thought to be itself a cause of malaria; any of various species of trees, such as the Australian

Eucalyptus globulus or the American Pinckneya pubens, which yield substances useful in the treatment of fevers.

feverfew /fē'vər-fū/ n a perennial plant of the daisy family, closely related to camomile, once believed efficacious in reducing fever, now in alleviating headaches. [OE fēferfūge, Med L febrifugia, this plant, from febris fever, and fugare to put to flight]

few /fū/ adj small in number; not many, hardly any. ◆ n and pronoun few people; a small number. [OE fēa, pl fēawe; cf L paucus small]
■ **few'ness** n smallness of number; few words, brevity (Shakesp).
■ **a few** a small number (of), used as a noun, or virtually a compound adjective; also facetiously as an adv, a little. **a good few** or **quite a few** (inf) a considerable number. **every few hours** or **days**, etc at intervals of a few hours, days, etc. **few and far between** very rare. **have had a few** (facetious) to have consumed a large number of alcoholic drinks, to be drunk. **in few** (formal) in a few words, briefly. **no fewer than** as many as (a stated number). **not a few** a good number (of). **some few** an inconsiderable number. **the few** the minority.

fewmet same as **fumet**[1].

fewter or **feutre** /fū'tər/ n (obs) a spear-rest. ◆ vt (Spenser) to set in a rest. [OFr feutre felt or a felt-lined socket]

fewtrils /fū'trilz/ (dialect) n pl little things, trifles. [**fattrels**]

fey[1], **fay** or **fie** /fā/ adj doomed, fated soon to die, under the shadow of a sudden or violent death, imagined to be marked by extravagantly high spirits (chiefly Scot); foreseeing the future, esp calamity (chiefly Scot); eccentric, slightly mad; whimsical; supernatural; fairy-like; elfin. [ME fay or fey, from OE fǣge doomed; cf Du veeg about to die]

fey[2] see **fay**[5].

Feynman diagram /fīn'mən dī'ə-gram/ (phys) n a diagram in which interactions between subatomic particles are represented. [Richard Feynman (1918–88), US physicist]

fez /fez/ n (pl **fezz'es** or **fez'es**) a red brimless truncated conical cap of wool or felt, with a black tassel, worn in Egypt, formerly in Turkey (also called the **tarboosh**). [From Fez in Morocco]
■ **fezzed** /fezd/ adj.

FF abbrev: form feed (comput); French franc or francs.

ff or **ff.** abbrev: fecerunt (L), (they) did it or made it; folios (printing); following pages, lines, etc; fortissimo (music).

fff (music) abbrev: fortississimo.

FGCM abbrev: Field General Court Martial.

FGM abbrev: female genital mutilation.

FHSA abbrev: Family Health Services Authority.

FHSS abbrev: frequency-hopping spread spectrum, a technique for reducing interference in radio broadcasting.

FIA abbrev: Fédération Internationale de l'Automobile (Fr), International Automobile Federation.

fiacre /fē-ak'r'/ (hist) n a hackney coach; a cab. [Fr, from the Hôtel de St Fiacre in Paris, where first used]

fiancé, fem **fiancée** /fē-ã'sā/ n the person one is engaged to be married to, one's betrothed. [Fr]
■ **fiançailles** /fē-ã-sī'y'/ n pl (Fr) betrothal.

fianchetto /fyäng-ket'to/ n (pl **fianchet'ti** /-tē/) in chess, the moving of a bishop onto the square vacated by the adjacent knight's pawn (also vt). [Ital, dimin of fianco flank]

Fianna Fáil /fē'a-nä foil/ n (literally, soldiers of destiny) a political party in the Republic of Ireland.

fiar /fē'ər/ (Scots law) n the owner of the fee simple of a property (in contrast to a life-renter of the property). [**fee**]

fiars /fē'ərz/ (Scot) n pl the prices of grain legally struck or fixed for the year at the Fiars Court, so as to regulate the payment of stipend, rent and prices not expressly agreed upon (usu **fiars prices**). [OFr feor or fuer fixed price or standard, from L forum market]

fiasco /fē-as'kō/ n (pl **fias'cos** or **fias'coes**) a complete failure of any kind; a failure in a musical performance; a flask or bottle. [Ital fiasco bottle, perh from L vasculum a little vessel, from vas a vessel]

fiat /fī'at, or (L) fē'ät/ n a formal or solemn command; a short order or warrant of a judge for making out or allowing processes, letters patent, etc (Spenser flaunt). ◆ vt to sanction. [L fiat (or fiant), let it (or them) be done, 3rd pers sing (pl) present subjunctive of fierī, serving as passive of facere to do]
❑ **fiat money** or **currency** n (esp US) money (paper or coin) made legal tender and assigned a value by government decree, with a commodity value lower than its face value, not convertible into other specie of equivalent value, and generally with a lower purchasing power than nominally equivalent specie.

fib[1] /fib/ n a not very serious lie. ◆ vi (**fibb'ing**; **fibbed**) to tell a fib or lie; to speak falsely. [Perh **fable**]

■ **fibb'er** *n* a person who fibs. **fibb'ery** *n* (*rare*) the habit of fibbing. **fib'ster** *n* a fibber.

fib² /fib/ (*literary*) *vt* (**fibb'ing**; **fibbed**) to punch; to pummel. [Ety unknown]

fiber see **fibre**.

Fibonacci numbers, **sequence** or **series** /fē-bō-nä'chē num'bərz, sē'kwəns or sē'rēz/ *n* a series of numbers in which each term is the sum of the preceding two terms. [Leonardo (*Fibonacci*) of Pisa (c.1170–c.1230)]

fibre or (*US*) **fiber** /fī'bər/ *n* a filament or thread-like cell of animal, vegetable or mineral origin, natural or synthetic; a structure or material composed of such filaments; texture; strength of character; stamina; dietary fibre, roughage. [Fr, from L *fibra* thread or fibre]

■ **fī'brate** *n* (*med*) any of a group of chemical compounds that reduce levels of fats in the body. **fī'bred** or (*US*) **fī'bered** *adj* having fibre. **fī'breless** or (*US*) **fīb'erless** *adj* without fibre, strength or nerve. **fī'briform** *adj* fibre-like. **fī'brin** *n* an insoluble protein precipitated as a network of fibres when blood coagulates. **fibrin'ogen** /-jən/ *n* a protein that forms fibrin. **fī'brinoid** *adj* of or like fibrin. ♦ *n* a natural material that resembles fibrin. **fibrinol'ysin** *n* an enzyme in the blood which causes the breakdown of fibrin in blood clots; a drug having the same effect. **fibrinol'ysis** *n* the enzymatic breakdown of fibrin. **fī'brinous** *adj* of or like fibrin. **fī'brō** *n* (*pl* **fī'bros**) (*Aust*) a building-board of a compressed asbestos and cement mixture (also **Fī'brocement**®); a house constructed of such material. ♦ *adj* (also **Fī'brocement**®) of or relating to fibro or fibros. **fī'broblast** *n* a cell in connective tissue from which fibrous tissue is formed. **fibroblast'ic** *adj*. **fibrocar'tilage** *n* cartilage with embedded fibres. **Fibrocement**® *n* see **fibro** above. **fibrocyst'ic** *adj* of or relating to growth of fibrous tissue with cystic spaces. **fī'brocyte** *n* a normally inactive fibroblast which proliferates following tissue damage. **fī'broid** *adj* of a fibrous nature. ♦ *n* a fibrous benign tumour. **fibroin** /fī'brō-in/ *n* the chief chemical constituent of silk. **fī'broline** /-lēn/ *n* a yarn of flax, hemp and jute waste, used with linen or cotton for the backs of carpets, etc. **fī'brolite** *n* a fibrous variety of the mineral sillimanite. **fibrō'ma** *n* (*pl* **fibrō'mata** or **fibrō'mas**) a benign tumour composed of fibrous tissue. **fibromyal'gia** *n* (*med*) a debilitating condition which causes severe and persistent muscular pain. **fibronec'tin** *n* a protein found in blood, important in cell growth. **fibrose** /fī-brōs'/ *vi* to form fibrous tissue. ♦ *adj* /fī'brōs/ fibrous. **fibrō'sis** *n* a morbid growth of fibrous tissue. **fibrosī'tis** *n* inflammation (*esp* rheumatic) of fibrous tissue. **fibrot'ic** *adj* relating to fibrosis. **fī'brous** *adj* composed of or like fibres. **fibrovas'cular** *adj* composed of fibres and conducting elements.

❑ **fī'breboard** or (*US*) **fī'berboard** *n* a material made from compressed wood fibres. **fī'brefill** *n* synthetic material used for stuffing or insulation in furnishings and garments. **fī'breglass** or (*US*) **fī'berglass** *n* a synthetic fibre made of extremely fine filaments of molten glass, used in textile manufacture, in heat and sound insulation, and in reinforced plastics; plastic reinforced with glass fibres. **fibre optics** *n sing* a technique using **fibre-optic** (or **-optics**) **bundles** or **cables**, bundles of extremely thin flexible glass fibres suitably coated, used in optical instruments to transmit maximum light by total internal reflection, and giving images of maximum clarity, and designed, because of their flexibility, for seeing into otherwise inaccessible places; a technique using fibre-optic cables to transmit multiple simultaneous data messages over long distances. **fi'bre-optic** *adj*. **fibre-optic transceiver** *n* an electronic device which converts electrical data signals into light signals suitable for transmission down a fibre-optic cable and vice versa. **fī'brescope** or (*US*) **fī'berscope** *n* a medical instrument using fibre-optic bundles that allows examination of internal structures, eg the alimentary canal.

■ **to the very fibre of one's being** deeply or fundamentally.

fibril /fī'bril/ *n* a small fibre; a root hair; a minute threadlike structure such as the longitudinal contractile elements of a muscle-fibre. [New L *fibrilla* a little fibre]

■ **fibrill'a** /fī- or fī-/ *n* (*pl* **fibrill'ae** /-ē/) a fibril filament. **fi'brillar**, **fi'brillary** or **fi'brillate** or **fi'brillated** *adj* relating to, of the nature of, or having fibrils or a fibrous structure. **fi'brillate** *vi* and *vt* to (make) undergo fibrillation. **fibrilla'tion** *n* the production or formation of fibrils or fibres; a mass of fibrils; a twitching of muscle fibres; unco-ordinated contraction of muscle-fibres in the heart (*med*). **fi'brillin** *n* a protein found in connective tissue. **fi'brillose** *adj* having, or covered with, small fibres or the appearance of small fibres. **fi'brillous** *adj* relating to or having small fibres.

fibrin, **fibro**, etc see under **fibre**.

fibster see under **fib¹**.

fibula /fib'ū-lə/ *n* a brooch in the shape of a safety pin; the outer and thinner of the two bones from the knee to the ankle in the human skeleton, or a corresponding bone in other animals. [L *fibula* brooch]

■ **fib'ular** *adj*.

-fic /-fik/ *combining form* denoting causing, making or producing, as in *horrific*. [L *-ficus*, from *facere* to make]

fiche /fēsh/ *n* a card or strip of film containing miniaturized data; a shortened form of **microfiche**. [Fr, a slip of paper, etc]

fichu /fish'oo or fē'shü/ *n* a three-cornered cape worn over the shoulders in the 18c and 19c, the ends crossed on the chest; a triangular piece of muslin, etc for the neck. [Fr]

fickle /fik'l/ *adj* inconstant in affections, loyalties or intentions; changeable. ♦ *vt* (*Scot*) to perplex or puzzle. [OE *ficol*; *gefic* fraud]

■ **fick'leness** *n*.

fico /fē'kō/ (*Shakesp*) *n* (*pl* **fic'os**) a fig, as a measure of how little one cares, a whit; a sign of contempt made by placing the thumb between the next two fingers. [Ital, fig]

fictile /fik'tīl, -til/ *adj* used or made by a potter; capable of being moulded, *esp* in clay; relating to pottery. [L *fictilis*, from *fingere* to form or fashion]

fiction /fik'shən/ *n* an invented or false story; a falsehood; romance; the novel or story-telling as a branch of literature; a supposition, for the sake of argument, that a possibility, however unlikely, is a fact (*law*). [Fr, from L *fictiō*, *-ōnis*, from *fictus*, pap of *fingere* to form or fashion]

■ **fic'tional** *adj*. **fictional'ity** *n*. **fic'tionalize** or **-ise** *vt* to give a fictional character to (a narrative dealing with real facts). **fic'tionalized** or **-s-** *adj*. **fic'tionist** *n* (*rare*) a writer of fiction. **fic'tive** *adj* fictitious or imaginary.

fictitious /fik-tish'əs/ *adj* of the nature of fiction; imaginary; not real or authentic; invented. [L *ficticius* counterfeit or feigned]

■ **ficti'tiously** *adv*.

fictor /fik'tər/ *n* (*obs*) a person who makes images from clay, etc. [L *fictor*; see **fiction**]

ficus /fī'kəs or fē'kəs/ *n* any plant of the genus *Ficus*, which includes the fig tree and others. [L]

FID *abbrev* : foreign income dividend.

fid /fid/ *n* a conical pin of hard wood, used by sailors to open the strands of rope in splicing; a square bar, with a shoulder, used to support the weight of the topmast or top-gallant mast. [Origin unknown]

Fid Def *abbrev* : *Fidei Defensor* (*L*), Defender of the Faith, used *esp* on pre-decimal British coins.

fiddious /fid'i-əs/ (*Shakesp*, *Coriolanus* II.1) *vt appar*, to treat as leniently as Coriolanus treated *Aufidius*.

fiddle /fid'l/ *n* a violin, *esp* when used to play folk music; extended (*inf*) to any violin; extended to similar instruments such as *bass fiddle* ; a violin player; a raised rim round a table to keep dishes from sliding off it (*naut*); a swindle, *esp* petty (*inf*); a manually delicate or tricky operation. ♦ *vt* and *vi* to play on a fiddle. ♦ *vt* to swindle; to falsify (records, accounts, etc). ♦ *vi* to trifle or idle (with *about* or *around*); to handle things aimlessly (with *with*). [OE *fithele* ; Ger *Fiedel*; see **viol**]

■ **fidd'ler** *n* a violinist (*inf*); a trifler; a swindler; (also **fiddler crab**) a small crab of the genus *Uca* or *Gelasimus*, from the movements of its enlarged claw. **fidd'ling** *adj* trifling; fiddly. **fidd'ly** *adj* time-consuming; difficult to handle or do because requiring delicate movements of the fingers.

❑ **fidd'le-back** *n* the fiddle-shaped front of a chasuble; a chair with a fiddle-shaped back. **fidd'leback** *n* a wavy grain found in some woods commonly used for the manufacture of violins, and also in woods used for other purposes (also *adj*). **fiddle block** *n* (*naut*) a block having two sheaves of different diameters one above the other. **fidd'le-bow** *n* a bow strung with horsehair, with which the strings of the fiddle are played. **fidd'le-de-dee** *interj* (*archaic*) nonsense. **fidd'le-faddle** *vi* to trifle or idle. ♦ *n* trifling talk or behaviour. ♦ *adj* fussy, trifling. ♦ *interj* nonsense. **fidd'le-faddler** *n*. **fidd'le-faddling** *adj*. **fidd'lehead** *n* an ornament at a ship's bow, over the prow or cutwater, consisting of a scroll turning aft or inward; the edible coiled frond of certain ferns (*N Am*). **fiddle pattern** *n* a design of cutlery involving a violin-shaped handle. **fidd'le-pattern** *adj*. **fiddler's green** *n* the sailors' heaven, full of wine, women and song. **fiddler's money** *n* (*archaic*) small coins, such as sixpences. **fidd'lestick** *n* a violin bow (*inf*); a mere nothing, a trifle (*derisive*). **fidd'lesticks** or **fidd'lestick** *interj* nonsense. **fidd'le-string** *n* a string for a fiddle. **fidd'lewood** *n* (the valuable hard wood of) a tropical American tree (genus *Citharexylum*; family Verbenaceae).

■ **a face like a fiddle** a long or dismal face. **as fit as a fiddle** (*inf*) in the best of condition. **fiddle while Rome burns** to occupy oneself with trifles during a crisis. **on the fiddle** involved in swindling. **play first** or **second fiddle** to act as a first violin or a second violin player in an orchestra; to take a leading, or (*esp* unwillingly) a subordinate, part in anything. **Scotch fiddle** (*archaic sl*) scabies (from the motion of the fingers against the palm).

fiddley /fid'li/ (*naut*) *n* an iron framework round a hatchway opening. [Origin obscure]

FIDE *abbrev*: *Fédération Internationale des Échecs* (*Fr*), the World Chess Federation.

fideism /fē'dā-izm/ *n* the doctrine that knowledge depends on faith rather than reason. [L *fīdere* to trust]
■ **fi'deist** *n*. **fideist'ic** *adj*.

fidelity /fi-del'i-ti/ *n* faithfulness; sexual faithfulness to a husband, wife or partner; honesty; firm adherence; accuracy in reproduction. [L *fidēlitās, -ātis*, from *fidēlis* faithful, from *fīdere* to trust]
□ **fidelity insurance** *n* insurance covering an employer for the negligence of an employee.

fides /fī'dēz or fi'dāz/ (*L*) *n* faith, fidelity.
□ **fides implicita** /im-plis'i-tə or im-plik'i-ta/ *n* implicit unquestioning faith. **fides Punica** /pū'ni-kə or poo'ni-ka/ *n* Punic faith, treachery.
■ **fide et amore** /fī'dē et a-mö'rē or fī'dā et a-mö're/ by faith and love. **fide et fiducia** /fi-dū'shi-ə or fi-doo'ki-ä/ by faith and confidence. **fide et fortitudine** /for-ti-tū'di-nē or for-ti-too'di-ne/ by faith and fortitude. **fidei defensor** /fī'dē-ī di-fen'sör or fi-dā'ē dā-fen'sör/ defender of the faith (qv under **defence**; see also **Fid Def**). **fide non armis** /non är'mis or ar'mēs/ by faith, not arms. **fides et justitia** /jus-tish'i-ə or ūs-tī'ti-a/ fidelity and justice.

fidget /fij'it/ *vi* (**fidg'eting; fidg'eted**) to move about restlessly; to touch and handle things aimlessly (with *with*). ♦ *vt* to cause to feel restless and uneasy. ♦ *n* a person who fidgets; restlessness; (in *pl*) general nervous restlessness, an inability to keep still. [Perh related to **fike**]
■ **fidge** *vi* (*dialect*) to move about restlessly; to be eager. **fidg'etiness** *n*. **fidg'ety** *adj* restless; uneasy.

Fido /fī'dō/ *n* a method of dispersing airfield fog by burning petrol, used *esp* in World War II. [*F*og *I*nvestigation and *D*ispersal *O*peration]

fi donc! /fē dõ'/ (*Fr*) for shame!

fiducial /fi-dū'shyəl or -shəl/ *adj* (of a point or line) serving as a basis of reckoning (*phys* and *surveying*); showing confidence or reliance; of the nature of trust. [L *fīdūcia* confidence, from *fīdere* to trust]
■ **fidū'cially** *adv*. **fidū'ciary** *adj* of the nature of a trust; depending upon public confidence; held in trust. ♦ *n* a person who holds anything in trust; a person who depends for salvation on faith alone, without adherence to the moral law, an antinomian (*obs theol*).
□ **fiduciary issue** *n* (*finance*) the part of an issue of banknotes that is not backed by gold.

fidus Achates see under **Achates**.

fidus et audax /fī'dəs et ö'daks or fīd'ŭs et ow'däks/ (*L*) faithful and bold.

fie¹ /fī/ (*old* or *facetious*) *interj* denoting disapprobation or disgust, real or feigned. [Cf Fr *fi*; L *fī*; ON *fý* or *fei*; Ger *pfui*]
■ **fie upon** an expression of disapprobation of the thing or person named.

fie² see **fey¹**.

fief /fēf/ *n* (*hist*) land held in return for feudal service or on condition of military service; an individual's own area of operation or control. [Fr, from LL *feudum*; see **fee** and **feoff**]
■ **fief'dom** *n* a piece of land held as a fief (*hist*); any area of influence autocratically controlled by an individual or organization.

field /fēld/ *n* country or open country in general; a piece of ground enclosed for cultivation or pasture; the range of any series of actions or energies; speciality; an area of knowledge, interest, etc; a region of space in which forces are at work (*phys*); the locality of a battle; the battle itself; an area of ground reserved and marked out for playing games, etc; a place removed from the classroom, office, etc where practical experience is gained; a wide expanse; the area visible to an observer at one time (eg in a microscope); one of the two interlaced sets of scanning lines making up the picture (*TV*); one scanning of a field from top to bottom and back (*TV*); an area of land in which a mineral, etc is mined; the surface of a shield (*heraldry*); the background of a coin, flag, etc; those taking part in a hunt; the entries collectively against which a contestant has to compete; all parties collectively, the entire set of competitors, runners, etc (as in *to bet on the field* in a horse race); disposition of fielders (*cricket* or *baseball*); a system or collection of elements upon which binary operations of addition, subtraction, multiplication and division can be performed except that division by 0 is excluded (*maths*); a unit of information (eg a name) constituting part of a database record (*comput*); an area in a database, program or screen display in which information may be entered (*comput*). ♦ *vt* to catch (the ball) or stop and return it to the principal playing area (*cricket* or *baseball*); to handle skilfully (*esp* questions); to put into the field for play, military action or (*fig*) other form of contest. ♦ *vi* (*cricket* or *baseball*) to stand in position for catching or stopping the ball. [OE *feld*; cf Du *veld* the open country, Ger *Feld*]

■ **field'ed** *adj* (*Shakesp*) encamped. **field'er** *n* a person who fields. **field'ing** *n* playing in the field at cricket as distinguished from batting. **field'ward** or **field'wards** *adv* towards the fields.

□ **field allowance** *n* (*milit*) a small extra payment to officers on active service. **field ambulance** *n* a medical unit on the field of battle. **field artillery** *n* mobile ordnance for active operations in the field. **field battery** *n* a battery of field artillery. **field bed** *n* a camp or trestle bed; a bed for use in the open air. **field book** *n* the notebook used by a surveyor in the field. **field'boots** *n pl* knee-length boots. **field botany, field geology**, etc *n* botany, geology, etc pursued in the open air. **field capacity** *n* (*geol*) the water-retaining capacity of soil. **field club** *n* a club of field naturalists. **field colours** *n pl* small flags used for marking the position for companies and regiments in the field; hence, any regimental headquarters' flags. **field cornet** *n* the magistrate of a township (*S Afr hist*); a rank equivalent to lieutenant, *assistant field cornet* equal to second lieutenant (*S Afr milit*). **field'craft** *n* the knowledge and skill needed to live in the wild. **field day** *n* a day when troops are taken out for instruction in field exercises; a day spent on outdoor activities; any period of great activity, success or enjoyment. **field'-dew** *n* (*Shakesp*) dew of the fields. **fielded panel** *n* a panel, sometimes subdivided into smaller panels, raised above or recessed into surrounding woodwork. **field-effect transistor** *n* one in which current is controlled by a variable electric field. **field emission** *n* (*electronics*) emission from a metallic surface as a result of an intense electric field at the surface. **field-emission microscope** *n* a microscope in which the positions of the atoms in a surface are shown by the electric field emitted when the surface is made positive in a high-voltage discharge tube containing argon at very low pressure. **field event** *n* an athletic event other than a race. **field'fare** *n* (*ety doubtful*) a species of thrush, having a grey head, a reddish-yellow throat and breast spotted with black. **field glass** or **glasses** *n* a binocular telescope for use in the field or open air. **field goal** *n* in basketball, a score made from normal play, rather than from a free throw; in American football, a score worth three points, made by kicking the ball through the goalposts, *usu* on the fourth down. **field gray** or **grey** *n* a grey (*Feldgrau*) adopted for uniforms in the German Army in World War I; a German soldier dressed thus. **field guide** *n* an illustrated book used to identify birds, animals, plants, etc in the field. **field gun** *n* a light cannon mounted on a carriage. **field hand** *n* an outdoor farm labourer. **field hockey** *n* (*N Am*) hockey played on grass, as opposed to ice hockey. **field hospital** *n* a temporary hospital near the scene of battle. **field ice** *n* ice formed in the polar seas in large surfaces, as distinguished from icebergs. **field-ion microscope** *n* a modification, with greater resolving power, of the field-emission microscope, in which ions of a gas (*usu* helium) which is adsorbing on the metal point are repelled and produce the image on the screen; used in conjunction with an instrument such as a mass spectrometer to identify the atoms, it is known as an **atom-probe-field-ion microscope**. **field kitchen** *n* portable cooking equipment for troops, or the place where it is set up. **field lark** *n* an American bird (genus *Sturnella*) of the Icteridae (see under **icterus**), not a lark. **field mark** *n* a visible characteristic useful in distinguishing birds, animals, etc in the wild. **field marshal** *n* an army officer of highest rank. **field meeting** *n* a secret religious meeting, a conventicle. **field'mouse** or **field'vole** *n* a name for various species of mouse and vole that live in the fields. **field mushroom** see **mushroom**. **field naturalist** *n* a person who studies natural history out of doors. **field night** *n* a night marked by some important gathering, discussion, etc. **field notes** *n pl* data noted in the field, to be worked up later. **field officer** *n* a military officer above the rank of captain, and below that of general. **field of honour** *n* the site of a duel or battle. **field of view** or **vision** *n* what is visible to one at any given moment. **field'piece** *n* a cannon or piece of artillery used in the field of battle. **field preacher** *n* an open-air preacher. **field preaching** *n*. **field'-sequential** *adj* (*TV*) relating to the association of individual primary colours with successive fields. **fields'man** *n* (*cricket*) a fielder. **field sports** *n pl* sports of the field, such as hunting, racing, etc. **field'stone** *n* (chiefly *US*) stone used for building, taken from a nearby field. **field strength** *n* the intensity of an electric or magnetic field. **field test** *n* (also **field trial**) a test in practice, as distinct from one under laboratory conditions. **field'-test** *vt*. **field train** *n* a department of the Royal Artillery responsible for the safety and supply of ammunition during war. **field trial** see **field test** above. **field trip** *n* an expedition (*esp* by students) to observe and study something at its location. **field'vole** see **fieldmouse** above. **field'work** *n* farm work in fields; work (scientific surveying, etc) in the field, as opposed to in a laboratory, office, etc; (often in *pl*) a temporary fortification erected by troops in the field, either for protection or to cover an attack on a stronghold. **field'worker** *n* a practical research worker.

■ **hold the field** to remain supreme. **keep the field** to keep the campaign going; to maintain one's ground. **lead the field** to be foremost. **play the field** see under **play**. **take the field** to assemble on a playing field; to begin warlike operations.

fiend /fēnd/ n a devil; a person driven by the most intense wickedness or hate; an addict; a devotee. [OE *fēond* enemy, orig prp of *fēon* to hate; Ger *Feind*, Du *vijand*]
■ **fiend'ish** adj like a fiend; devilishly cruel; extremely difficult or unpleasant. **fiend'ishly** adv. **fiend'ishness** n. **fiend'like** adj like a fiend; fiendish.

fient /fēnt or fint/ (Scot) n a fiend or devil; often used, like *devil* in English, as an emphatic negative (eg *fient ane*, devil a one, not one). [Ety as for **fiend**]

fierce /fērs/ adj savage; ferocious; (of competition or opposition) strong or intense; violent; severe. [OFr *fers* (Fr *fier*), from L *ferus* wild, savage]
■ **fierce'ly** adv. **fierce'ness** n.

fiere see **fere**[1].

fieri facias /fī'ə-rī fā'shi-as or fē'e-rē fak'i-äs/ (law) the name of a writ commanding a sheriff to distrain the defendant's goods. [LL, literally, cause to be done]

fiery /fīr'i/ adj like or consisting of fire; ardent; impetuous; irritable; (of food) hot-tasting; (of ground in games) dry, hard, fast. [**fire**]
■ **fier'ily** adv. **fier'iness** n.
□ **fiery cross** n a charred cross dipped in blood, formerly carried round in the Scottish Highlands as a call to arms; a burning cross, symbol of the Ku Klux Klan. **fiery mine** n (*mining*) a mine in which there is a possibility of explosion from gas or coal dust.

fiesta /fē-es'tə/ n a saint's day; a holiday; a carnival or festivity. [Sp]

FIFA /fē'fə/ abbrev : *Fédération Internationale de Football Association* (*Fr*), International Football Federation.

fife /fīf/ n a smaller variety of the flute. ◆ vi to play on the fife. [Ger *Pfeife* pipe, or Fr *fifre* fifer, both from L *pīpāre* to cheep]
■ **fif'er** n a fife-player.
□ **fife'-ma'jor** n (*obs*) the chief fifer in a regiment. **fife rail** n (*naut*) the rail round the mainmast, where a fifer sat while the anchor was being heaved.

Fifish /fī'fish/ adj cranky or eccentric (supposed qualities of **Fif'ers**, inhabitants of *Fife*, Scotland).

FIFO /fī'fō/ abbrev : first in, first out (eg of redundancies or computer inputs and outputs).

fifteen /fif'tēn or fif-tēn'/ n and adj five and ten. ◆ n a set, group or team of fifteen (such as, formerly, the Court of Session); (**15**) a certificate designating a film passed as suitable only for people of fifteen years and over. [OE *fiftēne* ; see **five** and **ten**]
■ **fifteen'er** n (*rare*) a verse of fifteen syllables. **fifteenth'** (or /fif'/) adj last of fifteen; next after the fourteenth; equal to one of fifteen equal parts. ◆ n a fifteenth part; a person or thing in fifteenth position; a double octave (*music*); an organ stop sounding two octaves above the basic pitch. **fifteenth'ly** adv.
■ **the Fifteen** the Jacobite rebellion of 1715.

fifth /fifth/ adj last of five; next after the fourth; equal to one of five equal parts. ◆ n one of five equal parts; a person or thing in fifth position; an interval of four (conventionally called five) diatonic degrees (*music*); a tone at that interval from another; a combination of two tones separated by that interval; (with *cap*) the Fifth Amendment (*US*). [OE *fīfta*, assimilated to other ordinals in *-th*]
■ **fifth'ly** adv in the fifth place.
□ **Fifth Amendment** n an amendment to the US constitution which allows a person on trial not to testify against himself or herself and forbids a second trial if a person has been acquitted in a first. **fifth column** n people within a country, etc who sympathize, and will act, with its enemies (expression used by a Spanish insurgent general when four columns were advancing upon Madrid). **fifth columnist** /kol'əm-ist/ n. **fifth generation** n (*comput*) the type of computer which incorporates aspects of artificial intelligence. **fifth'-generātion** adj. **Fifth'-monarchism** n. **Fifth'-monarchist** n. **Fifth-monarchy men** n pl (*hist*) an extreme sect at the time of the Puritan revolution, who looked for a new reign of Christ on earth in succession to Daniel's four great monarchies of Antichrist. **fifth wheel** n the spare wheel of a four-wheeled vehicle; a coupling on an articulated vehicle that allows the towing of a trailer; a superfluous or useless person or thing (*inf*).
■ **plead** or **take the Fifth** (*US inf*) to refuse to testify, in accordance with the Fifth Amendment.

fifty /fif'ti/ n and adj five times ten. [OE *fīftig*, from *fīf* five and *-tig*, the sfx *-ty*]
■ **fif'ties** n pl the numbers fifty to fifty-nine; the years so numbered (of a life or century); a range of temperatures from fifty to just less than sixty degrees. **fif'tieth** adj last of fifty; next after the forty-ninth; equal to one of fifty equal parts. ◆ n a fiftieth part; a person or thing in fiftieth position. **fif'tyish** adj apparently about fifty years old.
□ **fif'ty-fif'ty** n, adj and adv half-and-half; fifty per cent of each of two things; share and share alike; equals either way.

FIG abbrev : *Fédération Internationale de Gymnastique* (*Fr*), International Gymnastics Federation.

fig[1] /fig/ n any of a genus (*Ficus*) of tropical and subtropical trees and shrubs of the mulberry family which produce a soft pear-shaped false fruit packed with seeds; the false fruit itself, often eaten dried; a thing of little or no consequence, a negligible amount, a jot; piles (*obs*). ◆ vt (**figg'ing; figged**) (*Shakesp*) to subject to an insulting gesture made by putting the thumb between the next two fingers. [Fr *figue*, from L *fīcus* a fig or fig tree]
□ **fig'-bird** n any Australian oriole (genus *Sphecotheres*) feeding on figs, etc. **fig leaf** n the leaf of the fig tree; a representation of such a leaf for veiling the genitals of a statue or picture; any scanty clothing (from the Bible, Genesis 3.7); any prudish evasion; a substitute or makeshift; something intended to conceal the reality of actions or motives, *esp* political or international. **fig'-pecker** n the beccafico, a garden warbler. **fig tree** n any tree which produces figs. **fig wasp** n any wasp of the family Agaontidae that lays eggs in wild fig flowers. **fig'wort** n (*bot*) any species of *Scrophularia* ; pilewort.
■ **not give** or **care a fig** (*inf*) to be completely unconcerned.

fig[2] /fig/ (*inf*) n figure; dress; form. ◆ vt (**figg'ing; figged**) to dress or get up (with *out*); (of a horse) to display in an artificially lively condition (with *out* or *up*). [Perh **figure**]
■ **figg'ery** n dressy ornament.
■ **in full fig** in full dress or array.

fig. abbrev : figurative; figuratively; figure.

fight /fīt/ vi (**fight'ing; fought** /föt/) to strive or struggle; to contend in war or in single combat; to quarrel. ◆ vt to engage in conflict with; to contend against; to maintain or contend for, or oppose, by combat, legal action, etc; to conduct (a battle, war, campaign, etc); to achieve by struggle; to cause to contend or enter into conflict. ◆ n a struggle; a combat; a strong disagreement; a battle or engagement; fighting spirit; inclination to fight; a screen to cover the men in a naval fight (*Shakesp*). [OE *fehtan* (WSax *feohtan*); Ger *fechten*]
■ **fight'able** adj able to be fought. **fight'er** n a person, etc who fights; a boxer; a relatively small military aircraft equipped to attack targets which are either in the air or on the ground; a person who does not give in easily. **fight'ing** adj engaged in, eager for, or fit for war or strife. ◆ n the act of fighting or contending.
□ **fighting chance** n a chance of success given supreme effort. **fighting cock** n a gamecock; a pugnacious person. **fighting fish** n a small freshwater fish of Thailand (*Betta pugnax*), kept for its extraordinary readiness for fighting, bets being laid on the outcome. **fighting fund** n a fund of money intended to be used for a specific campaign. **fighting talk** or **words** n pl (*inf*) spirited words issuing a challenge or provoking a fight.
■ **fight back** to retaliate; to counter-attack (**fight'back** n). **fighting drunk** drunk and very aggressive. **fighting fit** in good physical condition. **fight it out** to struggle on until the end. **fight off** to resist or repel. **fight shy of** to avoid owing to mistrust. **fight to the finish**, **to the ropes** or **to the last ditch** to fight until completely exhausted. **live like fighting cocks** to habitually get the best available food and drink.

figment /fig'mənt/ n a fabrication or invention. [L *figmentum*, from *fingere* to form]

figo /fē'gō/ (*Shakesp*) n (pl **fig'os**) a sign of contempt, a fico. [OSp]

figuline /fig'ū-līn or -lin/ (*rare*) adj of earthenware; fictile. ◆ n an earthenware vessel. [L *figulīnus*, from *figulus* potter]

figure /fig'ər, also (*N Am* and *dialect*) -yər or (*old*) fig'ūr/ n the form of anything in outline; appearance; a shape; a geometrical form; a diagram; a horoscope (*Shakesp*); a design; an illustration; bodily shape; a human form or representation of it; a personality, personage or character; an impressive, noticeable, important, ludicrous or grotesque person; a written character denoting a number; amount; value or price; a deviation from the ordinary mode of expression (*rhetoric*); the form of a syllogism with respect to the position of the middle term (*logic*); a group of notes felt as a unit (*music*); a series of steps or movements in a dance or in skating; an emblem. ◆ vt to make an image of; to represent; to mark with figures or designs; to imagine; to reckon, work out (often with *out*); to come to understand (often with *out*); to note by figures. ◆ vi to make figures; to appear as a figure, make an appearance or show; to follow as a logical consequence, be expected (*inf*); to form or shape (*obs*); to symbolize (*archaic*); to foreshow (*obs*). [Fr, from L *figūra*, from *fingere* to form]
■ **figurabil'ity** n the quality of being figurable. **fig'urable** adj. **fig'ūral** adj represented by a figure or figures. **figurant** /fig'ū-rənt/ or **figurante** /fēg-oo-rän'tā/ n (*Ital*) a ballet-dancer, one of those who form a background for the solo dancers. **fig'ūrate** adj of a certain definite form; florid (*music*). **figūrā'tion** n the act of giving figure or form; representation by or in figures or shapes, *esp* significant, typical or emblematic figures; a figure of this kind; ornamentation with a design; consistent use of a particular melodic or harmonic series of notes (*music*); florid treatment (*music*). **fig'ūrative** adj representing by, containing or filled with figures of speech (*rhetoric*); metaphorical;

representing a figure; emblematic or symbolic; of a style of painting, sculpture, etc characterized by the realistic depiction of people, objects, etc (as opposed to abstract art). **fig'uratively** *adv.* **fig'urativeness** *n.* **fig'ured** /-*ərd*/ *adj* having a figure; marked or adorned with figures; delineated in a figure; in the form of figures. **fig'urine** /-*ēn* or *-ēn'* / *n* a small carved or moulded figure. **fig'urist** *n* a person who uses, or interprets, by figures.

□ **figurate numbers** *n pl* a series of numbers such that if each be subtracted from the next, and the series so formed be treated in the same way, by a continuation of the process equal differences will ultimately be obtained. **fig'ure-caster** *n* an astrologer (*obs*); a person who prepares casts of figures. **fig'ure-casting** (*obs*); the art of preparing casts of animal or other forms. **fig'ure-dance** *n* a dance consisting of elaborate formalized movements. **figured bass** *n* a bass with numerals added to indicate chords. **fig'urehead** *n* the figure or bust under the bowsprit of a ship; a merely nominal head, eg of an organization or a government. ◆ *adj* nominal, but lacking real power. **fig'ure-hugging** *adj* denoting a tight piece of clothing which emphasizes the contours of the body. **figure of eight** *n* see under **eight**. **figure of fun** *n* a person who is an object of ridicule. **figure of merit** *n* (*elec eng*) a general parameter which describes the quality of performance of eg an instrument or a circuit. **figure of speech** *n* any of various devices (such as simile or metaphor) for using words in such a way as to make a striking effect. **figure skater** *n*. **figure skating** *n* skating in prescribed patterns on ice. **fig'ure-weaving** *n* the weaving of figured fancy fabrics. **fig'urework** *n* counting or calculation using numbers.

■ **cut a figure** to make a bold impression through one's appearance. **figure on** to count upon or expect; to plan (*US*). **go figure** (*US inf*) to make an effort to understand something puzzling.

Fijian /*fi-jē'ən* or *fē-*/ *adj* of or relating to the republic of *Fiji* in the S Pacific, or its inhabitants. ◆ *n* a native or citizen of Fiji.

fike /*fīk*/ (*Scot*) *vi* to fidget restlessly. ◆ *n* restlessness; any annoying requirement or detail in work; a pernickety exacting person. [Prob ON *fīkja*]

■ **fīk'ery** *n* fuss. **fīk'ish** or **fīk'y** *adj*.

fil see **fill²**.

filabeg see **filibeg**.

filaceous /*fi-lā'shəs*/ *adj* composed of threads. [L *fīlum* a thread]

filacer /*fil'ə-sər*/ *n* formerly, an officer who filed writs (also **fil'azer**). [OFr *filacier*, from *filace* a file for papers, from apparently L *fīlum* a thread]

filaggrin /*fil'ə-grin*/ *n* a protein that helps the skin function as a protective barrier against foreign organisms. [*fila*ment-*aggr*egating pro*tein*]

filagree see **filigree**.

filament /*fil'ə-mənt*/ *n* a slender or threadlike object; a fibre; the stalk of a stamen (*bot*); a chain of cells; a thread of high resistance in an incandescent lamp or thermionic valve (*elec*). [L *fīlum* a thread]

■ **filamentary** /-*ment'ə-ri*/ *adj* like a filament. **filament'ous** *adj* threadlike; of some bacteria, viruses, etc, having long strands of similar cells (*biol*).

filander /*fi-land'ər*/ *n* a threadlike intestinal worm in hawks; (in *pl*) the disease it causes. [OFr *filandre*, from L *fīlum* thread]

filar /*fī'lər*/ (*optics*) *adj* having threads or wires. [L *fīlum* a thread]

Filaria /*fi-lā'ri-ə*/ *n* a genus of nematode worms of the family Filarioidea, introduced into the blood by mosquitoes; (without *cap* (*pl* **filariae** /*fi-lā'ri-ē*/)) any worm of the genus. [L *fīlum* thread]

■ **fila'rial** *adj*. **filariasis** /-*lə-rī'ə-sis*/ *n* a disease caused by the presence of filariae in the blood, inflammation of the lymphatic vessels.

filasse /*fi-las'*/ *n* vegetable fibre prepared for manufacture. [Fr, from L *fīlum* thread]

filature /*fil'ə-chər*/ *n* the putting of silk onto reels, or the place where it is done. [Fr, from L *fīlum* a thread]

■ **fil'atory** *n* a machine for forming or spinning threads.

filazer same as **filacer**.

filbert /*fil'bərt*/ *n* (the nut of) the cultivated hazel (also (*obs*) **fil'berd**). [Prob from St *Philibert*, whose day (22 August) fell in the nutting season (OSax)]

filch /*filch*/ *vt* to steal; to pilfer. [Ety unknown]

■ **filch'er** *n* a thief. **filch'ing** *n* and *adj*. **filch'ingly** *adv* (*rare*).

file¹ /*fīl*/ *n* any contrivance for keeping papers in order, *orig* a line or wire on which papers were strung; a collection of papers arranged for reference; a collection of data in any form, *esp* on computer; a roll or list (*Shakesp*); a line of soldiers, chessboard squares, etc ranged one behind another; a small body of soldiers; a thread (*obs*). ◆ *vt* to put upon a file; to arrange in an orderly way; to put on record; to bring

before a court; to deposit or lodge (a complaint, etc). ◆ *vi* to march in file. [L *fīlum* a thread]

■ **fil'ed** *adj*. **fil'er** *n* a person or thing that files; a filing clerk (*inf*). □ **file allocation table** *n* (*comput*) a list which maps a file to blocks of data storage on a disk. **file copy** *n* a copy filed for reference; an editor's copy of a book in which errors, possible changes, etc are noted. **file extension** *n* (*comput*) a series of characters that follows the dot in a filename and identifies the file type. **file'-leader** *n* the person at the head of a file. **file'name** *n* (*comput*) a name used to refer to a given collection of data. **file server** *n* (*comput*) a computer in a network that stores files and makes them available to users in a network. **file sharing** *n* (*comput*) the activity of making files freely available for other users on a computer network while also downloading files made available by others. **filing cabinet** *n* a cabinet for storing files.

■ **file off** to wheel off at right angles to the original or previous direction. **file with** (*archaic*) to rank with or be equal to. **on file** on record, catalogued. **single file** or **Indian file** one behind another.

file² /*fīl*/ *n* an instrument with sharp-edged furrows for smoothing or rasping metals, etc; a small metal or emery paper instrument for shaping or smoothing finger- or toenails, a nail file; a shrewd or cunning person (*obs*); a pickpocket (*obs*). ◆ *vt* to cut or smooth with, or as if with, a file; to polish or improve, *esp* of a literary style. [OE *fȳl* (WSax *fēol*); Ger *Feile*; Du *vijl*]

■ **filed** *adj* polished or smooth. **fil'er** *n* a person or thing that files. **fil'ing** *n* (*usu* in *pl*) a particle rubbed off with a file. □ **file'-cutter** *n* a maker of metal files. **file'fish** *n* a fish of the *Balistes* or a related genus, with skin granulated like a file.

file³ /*fīl*/ (*Shakesp* or *Scot*) *vt* to defile or pollute. [OE *gefylan*; cf **foul**]

filemot /*fil'i-mot*/, also **philamot** or (*Addison*) **philomot** /-*ə-*/ *adj* of a dead-leaf colour, dull brown. ◆ *n* the colour itself. [Fr *feuillemorte* dead leaf]

filet /*fē-le'*/ (*Fr*) *n* undercut of beef, tenderloin; a boned whole, or thick boneless slice of, fish; a kind of lace consisting of embroidery on a square-mesh net.

filet mignon /*fē-le mē-nyõ'*/ (*Fr*) *n* a small boneless cut of beef from the underside of a sirloin.

filfot see **fylfot**.

filial /*fil'i-əl*/ *adj* relating or appropriate to a son or daughter; in the relation of a child. [Fr, from LL *fīliālis*, from L *fīlius* a son]

■ **fil'ially** *adv*.

filiate and **filiation** same as **affiliate** and **affiliation**.

filibeg, **filabeg** or **fillibeg** /*fil'i-beg*/ *n* the kilt (also **philabeg**, **phillabeg**, **philibeg** or **phillibeg**). [Gaelic *feileadhbeag*, from *feileadh* pleat or fold, and *beag* little]

filibuster /*fil'i-bus-tər*/ *n* a pirate or buccaneer (*hist*); a military adventurer or revolutionary; a person who obstructs legislation by making lengthy speeches, introducing motions, etc; obstruction by such means in a legislative body. ◆ *vi* to act as a filibuster. [Sp *filibustero*, through Fr *flibustier* or *fribustier*, from Du *vrijbuiter* (cf Eng **freebooter** (see under **free**), Ger *Freibeuter*), from *vrij* free, and *buit* booty]

■ **filibus'terer** *n*. **filibus'tering** *n*. **filibus'terism** *n*. **filibus'terous** *adj*.

Filices /*fil'i-sēz*/ (*bot*) *n pl* the ferns, *esp* the true (homosporous leptosporangiate) ferns. [L *filix*, *-icis* fern]

■ **Filicales** /-*kā'lēz*/ or **Filicineae** /-*sin'i-ē*/ *n pl* the ferns, leptosporangiate and eusporangiate, with or without water ferns. **filicin'ean** *adj*.

filicide /*fil'i-sīd*/ *n* the murder of one's own child; a person who murders his or her child. [L *fīlius*, *fīlia* son or daughter, and *caedere* to kill]

filiform /*fil'i-förm*/ *adj* threadlike. [L *fīlum* a thread]

filigree /*fil'i-grē*/, also **filagree** /-*ə-*/ *n* (earlier forms **fil'igrain** and **fil'igrane**) a kind of ornamental metallic lacework of gold and silver, twisted into convoluted forms, joined and partly consolidated by soldering; a delicate structure resembling this. [Fr *filigrane*, from Ital *filigrana*, from L *fīlum* thread, and *grānum* a grain]

■ **fil'igreed** *adj* ornamented with filigree.

filing see under **file²**.

filiopietistic /*fi-li-ō-pī-ə-tis'tik*/ *adj* marked by an excess of filial piety, or excessive veneration of one's ancestors. [See **filial** and **piety**]

filioque /*fil-i-ō'kwi*/ *n* the clause inserted into the Nicene Creed at Toledo in 589, which asserts that the Holy Ghost proceeds from the Son as well as from the Father, a doctrine not accepted by the Eastern Church. [L, and from the son]

filipendulous see under **filiform**.

Filipino /*fil-i-pē'nō*/ or (*fem*) **Filipina** /-*pē'nə*/ *n* (*pl* **Filipi'nos** or **Filipi'nas**) a native of the *Philippines* (also *adj*; see also **Philippine**). [Sp]

filius /fil'i-əs or fē'li-ŭs/ (L) n son; (following a name) junior.
□ **filius nullius** /nul'i-əs or noo'li-ŭs/ n (law) a son of nobody, a bastard. **filius populi** /po'pū-lī or po'pū-lē/ n a son of the people. **filius terrae** /te'rē or te'rī/ n son of the soil, a person of low birth.

fill[1] /fil/ vt to make full; to put into until all the space is occupied; to supply abundantly; to satisfy; to glut; to perform the duties of; to take up (a vacant post); to increase the bulk of (soap, cotton fabrics, etc) by mixing in a lower-grade substance; to put amalgam, gold, etc into (a cavity in a tooth); to fulfil or carry out (esp US); to make up (a prescription). ◆ vi to become full; to become satiated. ◆ n as much as fills or satisfies; a full supply; the fullest extent; a single charge of anything; anything used to fill. [OE fyllan, from full full]
■ **fill'er** n a person or thing that fills, eg any of various paste-like substances used to fill cracks in wood, plaster, etc; a vessel from which liquid is poured into a bottle; any item used to fill a gap in eg a page of newsprint or a broadcasting schedule; a word or sound which fills a pause in an utterance without adding to the meaning, such as like in her father is, like, really old; a substance added to various materials to impart desired qualities. **fill'ing** n anything used to fill up, stop a hole, to complete, etc, such as amalgam, etc in a tooth, or the woof in weaving; (in pl) the quantity of new whisky spirit that a blender puts into store for maturation in eg a year, or the output of a distillery supplied for such purposes. ◆ adj substantial, satisfying.
□ **filler cap** n a device for closing the filling pipe of a petrol tank in a motor vehicle. **filler metal** n (engineering) the metal required to be added at the weld in welding processes. **filler rod** n (engineering) same as **welding rod** (see under **weld**[1]). **fill'-in** n something used to fill in (time or space); a substitute; fill-in flash. **fill-in flash** n usu weak flash lighting used to compensate for strong back-lighting or heavy shadow in outdoor photography. **filling station** n a roadside installation where petrol and oil are sold to motorists. **fill light** n a supplementary light source in photography, used to soften or eliminate shadows. **fill-up** see **fill up** below.
■ **fill in** to occupy (time); to add what is necessary to complete (eg a form); to act as a temporary substitute (for; inf); to supply someone with information. **fill one's boots** see under **boot. fill out** to make or become more substantial, larger or fuller; to complete (a form), etc. **fill someone in** (inf) to give someone detailed information about a situation; to thrash or beat up someone (sl); to murder someone (sl). **fill the bill** to be adequate. **fill up** to fill, or be filled, by addition of more; to have one's eyes fill with tears (inf); to fill in (n **fill'-up**). **fill up with** to stuff with (lit and fig). **have one's fill of** to have enough of, esp something unpleasant or tiresome.

fill[2] or **fil** /fil/ (Shakesp) n a thill or shaft of a vehicle. [See **thill**[1]]
□ **fill'-horse, phil'horse** or **pil'horse** n (Shakesp) a thill-horse, the horse nearest the carriage in a team.

fille /fē'y'/ (Fr) n a girl; a daughter.
□ **fille de chambre** /də shā-br'/ n a chambermaid. **fille de joie** /zhwä/ n (euphem) a prostitute. **fille d'honneur** /do-nær'/ n a maid of honour.

filler[1] /fil'ər/ n (pl **fill'er**) a monetary unit in Hungary, $\frac{1}{100}$ of a forint. [Hung fillér]

filler[2] see under **fill**[1].

fillet /fil'ət/ n meat or fish boned and rolled; a piece of meat without bone, esp the fleshy part of the thigh or the undercut of the sirloin; a boned whole, or thick boneless slice of, fish; a narrow piece of wood, metal, etc; a band for the hair; a small space or band used along with mouldings (archit); a line impressed into a book cover as decoration; the tool used for this. ◆ vt (**fill'eting; fill'eted**) to bone; to make into fillets; to bind or adorn with a fillet. [Fr filet, dimin of fil, from L filum a thread]
□ **fillet weld** n a weld at the junction of two parts at right angles to each other, a fillet of welding material being laid down in the angle created by the intersection of the surfaces of the parts.

fillibeg see **filibeg**.

fillip /fil'ip/ n a stimulus, esp of encouragement, a boost; a jerk of the finger from the thumb. ◆ vt (**fill'iping; fill'iped**) to incite or stimulate; to strike with the fingernail released from the ball of the thumb with a sudden jerk, to flick. [A form of **flip**]

fillipeen US form of **philopena**.

fillister /fil'i-stər/ (woodwork) n a kind of rabbeting plane. [Origin unknown]

filly /fil'i/ n a young mare; a lively girl or young woman (old inf). [Dimin of **foal**; prob from ON]

film /film/ n a coating of a sensitive substance for taking a photograph; a sheet or strip of Celluloid or a similar plastic prepared with such a coating for use in still or cinema photography; a motion picture, a series of images photographed (and usu sounds recorded) on such a strip which, when projected in succession and at speed, or broadcast, onto a screen, tell a story, present a subject, etc; (often in pl) this technique of storytelling, etc as an art form, a medium of communication, or an industry, the cinema; a thin skin or membrane;

a thin layer or coating; a pellicle or scum on liquids; a gauze of very slender threads; a mistiness; a thin sheet of usu plastic-based material used for wrapping. ◆ vt to photograph or record on film; to make a motion picture of; to adapt and enact for the cinema; to cover with a film. ◆ vi to make a motion picture; to become covered with a film. [OE filmen membrane, connected with fell skin]
■ **film'able** adj suitable for making a film of. **film'dom** or **film'land** n the cinema industry. **film'ic** adj relating to the cinema, film or cinematography. **filmi'ness** n. **film'ish** adj having a flavour of the cinema. **filmog'raphy** n a list of the films of a particular actor or director. **film'y** adj composed of or like a film; covered with a film; gauzy or semi-transparent; clouded.
□ **film badge** n a badge containing sensitive film worn by those risking exposure to radioactivity to detect and usu indicate the amount of exposure. **film colour** n a vague textureless area of colour, such as the sky or that seen with closed eyes, as opposed to colour seen on the surface of an object. **film fan** n a devotee of the cinema. **film'goer** n. **film'-maker** n a producer or director of cinema films. **film'-making** n. **film noir** /nwär/ n a style of cinema film, popular in American cinema in the 1940s and 50s, in which the darker side of human nature is presented, in a bleak, often starkly urban setting. **film set** n the scenery, furniture, etc arranged for the scene of a cinema film. **film'set** vt (printing) to set by a process of filmsetting. **film'setting** n typesetting by exposing type onto film which is then transferred to printing plates. **film star** n a famous cinema performer. **film'strip** n a film consisting of a series of stills to be shown separately and consecutively. **filmy ferns** n pl a family of ferns with very thin leaves, the Hymenophyllaceae.
■ **sheet film** film in the same sizes as photographic plates and superseding plates, used in printing and in large-format cameras.

FILO /fī'lō/ abbrev : first in, last out.

filo /fē'lō/ n a type of (orig Greek) pastry made in thin sheets (also **phy'llo**). [Gr phyllon a leaf]

filo- /fīl-ō-/ (biol) combining form denoting thread, hair. [L filum a thread]
■ **fil'oplume** n a slender hairlike feather. **filopo'dium** n (pl **filopo'dia**) (Gr pous, podos foot) a long filamentous spike containing actin filaments, found at the surface of some cells. **fil'ovirus** n any of a group of filamentous viruses causing high fever and severe haemorrhaging, as in Ebola disease and Marburg disease.

Filofax® /fī'lə-faks/ n a small, loose-leaf personal filing system containing a diary and a selection of information, eg addresses, maps, indexes, to assist the user to organize his or her time, business, etc.

filose /fī'lōs/ adj threadlike; having a threadlike end. [L filum a thread]

filoselle /fil-ō-sel'/ n coarse floss silk. [Ital filosello, from LL folexellus cocoon; infl by Ital filo thread]

fils[1] /fēs/ (Fr) n son; (following a name) junior.

fils[2] /fils/ n (pl **fils**) a monetary unit in several Middle-Eastern countries, with varying value. [From Ar fals, a small copper coin]

filter /fil'tər/ n an apparatus for purifying a fluid of solid matter by pouring it through porous material; a device for wholly or partly eliminating undesirable frequencies from light, radio or electric currents; a filter tip (qv below); a program, or part of one, that alters data systematically (comput); (at a road junction) an auxiliary traffic light in the form of a green arrow which allows one lane of traffic to move while the main stream is held up. ◆ vt to pass through a filter; to separate by a filter (esp with out). ◆ vi to pass through a filter; to percolate; to pass gradually and dispersedly through obstacles; to join gradually a stream of traffic; (of a lane of traffic) to move in the direction specified by the filter; to become known gradually (fig). [OFr filtre, from LL filtrum felt]
■ **filterabil'ity** or **filtrabil'ity** n. **fil'terable** or **fil'trable** adj able to pass through a filter (see **filter-passer** below); capable of being filtered. **fil'trate** vt and vi to filter or percolate. ◆ n a filtered liquid. **filtra'tion** n (an) act or process of filtering.
□ **filter bed** n a bed of sand, gravel, clinker, etc used for filtering water or sewage. **filter cake** n a mass of material trapped by a filter. **filter coffee** n coffee made by allowing water to pass through a filter paper containing ground coffee. **fil'ter-feeder** n an aquatic animal that filters its food from the water. **fil'ter-feeding** n. **filter paper** n porous paper for use in filtering. **fil'ter-passer** or **filterable virus** n terms used formerly for a virus in the sense of submicroscopic disease agent. **filter tip** n a cigarette with a filter at the mouth end, to reduce the smoker's ingestion of impurities. **fil'ter-tipped'** adj.

filth /filth/ n repellent dirtiness, or any foul matter; anything that defiles, physically or morally; obscenity; (with the) the police (derog sl). [OE fylth, from fūl foul]
■ **filth'ily** adv. **filth'iness** n. **filth'y** adj foul; unclean; impure; obscene; extremely unpleasant.
■ **filthy lucre** (humorous) money; sordid gain. **filthy rich** (disgustingly) wealthy.

filtre (*Fr*) see **café filtre** under **café**.

fimble /fim'bl/ *n* the male plant of hemp, weaker and shorter in fibre than **carl-hemp** (see under **carl**). [Du *femel* female]

fimbria /fim'bri-ə/ *n* (*anat*) a fringing filament. [L *fimbriae* fibres or fringe]
■ **fim'briate** *adj* fringed (*anat*); having a narrow border (*heraldry*). ◆ *vt* (*anat*) to fringe; to hem. **fim'brial** *adj*. **fim'briated** *adj*. **fimbria'tion** *n*.

fimicolous /fī-mik'ə-ləs/ (*bot*) *adj* growing on dung. [L *fimus* dung, and *colere* to inhabit]

FIN *abbrev*: Finland (IVR).

fin[1] /fin/ *n* an organ by which an aquatic animal steers, balances or swims; a swimmer's flipper; a fixed vertical surface on the tail of an aeroplane; a portion of a mechanism like a fish's fin in shape or purpose; a thin projecting edge or plate; a hand or arm (*sl*). ◆ *vt* (**finn'ing**; **finned**) to provide with fins; to remove the fins from. ◆ *vi* to swim using flippers. [OE *finn*; L *pinna* a feather or a fin]
■ **fin'less** *adj*. **finned** *adj* having fins. **finn'er** *n* a finback. **finn'y** *adj* finned.
□ **fin'back** or **fin whale** *n* a rorqual. **fin'fish** *n* a true fish, bearing fins and breathing through gills, as opposed to other aquatic animals such as shellfish. **fin'foot** *n* a grebe-like water bird. **fin'-foot'ed** *adj* webfooted; having fringed toes. **fin keel** *n* a fin-shaped keel. **fin'-ray** *n* a horny rod supporting a fin. **fin'-toed** *adj* having lobate or fringed toes.

fin[2] /fin/ (*US sl*) *n* a five-dollar bill. [Yiddish *finf* five]

FINA /fē'nə/ *abbrev*: *Fédération Internationale de Natation* (*Fr*), International Swimming Association (formerly known as *Fédération Internationale de Natation Amateur*).

finable see under **fine**[2].

finagle /fi-nā'gəl/ (*inf*) *vt* and *vi* to obtain by guile or swindling, to wangle; to cheat (a person; *usu* with *out of*). ◆ *n* an instance of finagling. [Eng dialect *fainaigue* cheat or shirk]
■ **fina'gler** *n*.

final /fī'nl/ *adj* last; decisive or conclusive; relating to or constituting an end or motive; (of a judgement) ready for execution. ◆ *n* the last of a series (eg of letters in a word, games in a contest, examinations in a curriculum, etc); in the old church modes, the keynote or tonic, the lowest note in the authentic modes, a fourth above it in the plagal; (in *pl*) final examinations; (in *pl*) the deciding rounds of a sports competition; (in *pl*) final approach (*inf*; *aeronautics*). [Fr, from L *fīnālis*, from *fīnis* an end]
■ **fi'nalism** *n* (*philos*) teleology, interpretation in terms of purpose; belief that an end has been reached. **fi'nalist** *n* a person who reaches the final stage in a competition; a student taking his or her final examinations; a teleologist (*philos*); a person who believes that finality has been reached (*philos*). **finality** /-al'i-ti/ *n* the state of being final; completeness or conclusiveness; a final or conclusive act; the principle of final cause (*philos*); that which is final. **fi'nalize** or **-ise** *vt* to complete a commercial agreement, transaction, etc; to decide on the definitive version of; to put the finishing touches to; to put an end to completely. **fi'nally** *adv*.
□ **final approach** *n* (*aeronautics*) the part of the landing procedure from when the aircraft turns into line with the runway until the flare-out is started (*inf* **fi'nals**). **final cause** *n* (*philos*) the end or objective for which a thing is done, *esp* the design of the universe. **final demand** or **final notice** *n* a last bill rendered before legal action is taken to recover a debt.
■ **the final solution** (*hist*) the English version of the name (Ger *Endlösung*) for the German Nazi policy and process, from 1941, of exterminating European Jews.

finale /fi-nä'lā or -li/ *n* the end or climax; the last movement in a musical composition; the concluding part of any performance, eg the last song in a stage musical, *usu* impressively energetic or lavish. [Ital *finale* final, from L *fīnālis*]

finance /fī'nans, or fi-, fī'-, fə-nans'/ *n* money affairs or revenue, *esp* of a ruler or state; money, *esp* public money; the art of managing or administering public money; a loan to pay for something; (in *pl*) money resources. ◆ *vt* to manage financially; to provide or support with money. ◆ *vi* to engage in money business. [Fr, from OFr *finer* to settle, from L *fīnis* an end]
■ **finan'cial** /-shəl/ *adj* relating to finance; (*Aust* and *NZ sl*) having money, solvent. **finan'cialist** *n* a financier. **finan'cially** *adv*. **finan'cier** /-si-ər or (*US*) fin-an-sēr'/ *n* a person engaged in large financial transactions; a person who administers the public revenue. ◆ *vi* and *vt* /-sēr'/ to finance; to swindle.
□ **finance company** or **house** *n* a company specializing in lending money against collateral, *esp* to finance hire-purchase agreements. **financial year** *n* any annual period for which accounts are made up; the annual period ending 5 April, functioning as the income-tax year, over which the Government's financial policies and estimates are made; the annual period ending, for many public bodies, on 31 March.

finasteride /fi-nas'tə-rīd/ *n* a drug, an enzyme inhibitor, used to treat enlarged prostates and male baldness.

finback see under **fin**[1].

finch /finch, -sh/ *n* a name applied to many passerine or perching birds, *esp* to those of the genus *Fringilla* or family Fringillidae, including the bullfinch, chaffinch, goldfinch, etc. [OE *finc*; Ger *Fink*]
■ **finched** *adj* finch-backed.
□ **finch'-backed** *adj* striped or spotted on the back.

find /fīnd/ *vt* (**find'ing**; **found**) to come upon or meet with; to discover or arrive at; to come to perceive; to experience; to regain (a former position, state, etc); to determine after judicial inquiry; to supply or succeed in getting; to manage to reach, hit, land on, etc. ◆ *vi* to come upon game. ◆ *n* an act of finding; something found, *esp* something of value or interest. [OE *findan*; Ger *finden*]
■ **find'able** *adj*. **find'er** *n* a person who finds; a small telescope attached to a larger one, or a lens attached to a camera, to facilitate the directing of it at the object viewed. **find'ing** *n* the act of any person who finds; that which is found; a judicial verdict; (*usu* in *pl*) a conclusion of research or investigation; (in *pl*) the tools which some workmen have to supply themselves, *esp* (of shoemakers) everything except leather (*esp US*); (in *pl*) accessories such as buttons and zips (*US*).
□ **find'-fault** *n* (*Shakesp*) a person who finds fault with another.
■ **finders keepers** (*inf*) those who find something are entitled to keep it. **find one's account in** to find satisfactory profit or advantage in. **find oneself** to feel, as regards health, happiness, etc (*formal*); to come to terms with oneself; to discover one's true personality, vocation or interests. **find one's feet** to become able to stand or able to cope readily with new conditions. **find out** to discover or detect. **find someone in** (*obs*) to supply someone with.

fin de siècle /fɛ̃ d' sye'kl'/ (*Fr*) *n* the end of a century or of an era. ◆ *adj* characteristic of the ideas, etc of the end of a century, *esp* the decadent elegance of the late 19c.

findon haddock and **findram** see **finnan**.

fine[1] /fīn/ *adj* excellent (often *ironic*); beautiful or handsome; not coarse or heavy; consisting of small particles; subtle; slender; sharp; keen; exquisite; nice; delicate; sensitive; over-refined; over-elaborate (*obs*); pretentious (*obs*); showy; splendid; striking or remarkable; egregious, distinguished (*archaic*); pure; refined; containing so many parts of pure metal out of twenty-four (as 22 carats, or ounces, fine, 22/24 gold or silver), or out of a thousand. ◆ *vt* to make fine; to refine; to purify; to change by imperceptible degrees (*esp* with *away* or *down*). ◆ *adj* and *adv* at a more acute angle with the line of flight of the ball (eg *fine leg*); (of a snooker, etc stroke) making very slight contact. ◆ *adv* well or well enough (*inf*); narrowly; with little to spare; into fine pieces. [Fr *fin*, prob a back-formation from L *fīnītus* finished, pap of *fīnīre* to finish, from *fīnis* an end]
■ **fine'ish** (also **fin'ish**) *adj* somewhat fine. **fine'ly** *adv*. **fine'ness** *n* state, fact or degree of being fine; state of subdivision; (of gold or silver) number of parts in a thousand. **fin'er** *n* a refiner. **fin'ery** *n* splendour; showy adornments; a place where anything is fined or refined; a furnace for making iron malleable. **fines** *n pl* material (ore, coal, etc) in a fine state of division, separated out by screening. **fin'ing** *n* the process of refining or purifying; (often in *pl*) a clarifying agent (*winemaking*).
□ **fine art** or **arts** see under **art**[1]. **fine chemicals** *n pl* chemicals produced in small quantities *usu* of high purity, *opp* to *heavy chemicals*. **fine'-draw** *vt* to draw or sew up so finely that no seam can be seen; to draw out finely or too finely. **fine'-drawn** *adj*. **fine gentleman** or **lady** *n* an idle person, *usu* ostentatiously fashionable, sometimes refined. **fine leg** *n* (*cricket*) a fielder, or a fielding position, on the legside boundary at a more acute angle to the batsman than long leg. **fine metal** *n* comparatively pure cuprous sulphide obtained from coarse metal. **fine print** same as **small print** (see under **small**). **fine'-spoken** *adj* using fine phrases. **fine'spun** *adj* finely spun out; over-subtle. **fine-tooth** (or **fine-toothed**) **comb** or **fine comb** *n* a comb with slender teeth set close together. **fine-tune'** *vt* to make delicate adjustments to. **fine-tun'ing** *n*. **fine writing** *n* literary matter or style which is pretentiously ornate. **fīn'ing-pot** *n* a vessel used in refining.
■ **cut it fine** to do something with little time or space to spare. **go over** or **through with a fine-tooth** (or **fine-toothed**) **comb** to investigate very thoroughly.

fine[2] /fīn/ *n* a monetary penalty; an end or conclusion (*obs* except in the phrase *in fine*); a final settlement; (before 1833) a fictitious suit as a means of conveying property or barring an entail (*law*); a composition or percentage accepted by a bankrupt's creditors, given by money payment; a fee paid on some particular occasion. ◆ *vt* to impose a fine on; to punish by fine; to bring to an end (*Shakesp*); to pledge or pawn (*Shakesp*). [L *fīnis* an end]

■ **fin'able** or **fine'able** *adj* liable to a fine. **fine'less** *adj* (*Shakesp*) endless.

■ **foot of fine** see under **foot**.

fine³ /fēn/ *n* ordinary French brandy. [Fr]
❑ **fine Champagne** /shã-pa'ny'/ *n* brandy distilled from wine made from grapes grown in the Charente area of France.

fineer¹ /fi-nēr'/, an old form of **veneer** (*n* and *vt*).

fineer² /fi-nēr'/ (*obs*) *vi* to get goods on credit by fraud or deception. [Prob Du; cf **finance**]

Fine Gael /fē'nə gāl/ *n* (literally, Family of Gaels) a moderate political party in the Republic of Ireland.

fines herbes /fēn-zerb'/ (*Fr*; *cookery*) *n pl* a mixture of herbs used as a garnish or, chopped, as a seasoning.

finesse /fi-nes'/ *n* subtlety of invention or design; sophisticated accomplishment; skill or expertise; tact; an attempt by a player holding a higher card to take the trick with a lower card, risking loss (*bridge*). ◆ *vt* and *vi* to play a finesse. ◆ *vi* to use subtle intention of design. ◆ *vt* to manage or administer with finesse, to manipulate subtly to a desired conclusion. [Fr]
■ **finess'er** *n*. **finess'ing** *n*.

fingan /fin-gän'/ *n* a small coffee cup without a handle, used in the Middle East with an ornamental holder called a zarf (also **finjan** /-jän'/). [Egyp *fingān*, Ar *finjān*]

finger /fing'gər/ *n* one of the five terminal parts of the hand, or *usu* of the four other than the thumb; anything shaped like this; the part of a glove that covers such a part; the breadth of a person's finger, *esp* as a rough measure of alcoholic spirit poured into a glass; touch; agency (*esp* of God); share or interest; (in *pl*) grip or control. ◆ *vt* to handle or perform with the fingers; to pilfer; to toy or meddle with; to make or indicate choice of fingers in performing (*music*); to indicate or identify a guilty person (*sl*); to locate another computer user by means of a special program (*inf*). ◆ *vi* to use or move the fingers. [OE *finger*]
■ **fing'ered** *adj* having fingers, or anything like fingers, or indication of fingering. **fing'ering** *n* act or manner of touching with the fingers; the choice of fingers in playing a musical instrument; the written or printed indication of this. **fing'erless** *adj* having no, or only rudimentary or short, fingers. **fing'erling** *n* a very diminutive being or thing (*archaic*); a fish no bigger than a finger, *esp* a salmon parr or young trout less than a year old.
❑ **fing'er-alphabet** *n* an alphabet for the deaf or hard of hearing. **fing'er-and-toe'** *n* a disease of turnips in which the taproot branches; another turnip disease, anbury. **fing'erboard** *n* the part of a violin, etc against which the strings are stopped by the fingers. **fing'erbowl** or **fing'erglass** *n* a bowl for water to clean the fingers at table. **fing'er-breadth** or **fing'ers-breadth** *n* the breadth of a finger, a digit, as a unit of measurement (1.4cm or ¾ of an inch). **finger buffet** *n* a buffet consisting of **finger foods**, food (such as sandwiches) which may be eaten with the fingers as opposed to a knife and fork. **fing'er-dry** *vt* to style (one's) hair by running the fingers through it while it is drying. **fing'er-end** or **fing'er's-end** *n*. **fing'er-grass** *n* a grass of the genus *Digitaria*, with finger-like spikes. **fing'erguard** *n* the crosspiece of a sword-handle. **fing'erhold** *n* a grasp by the fingers; something by which the fingers can hold on (also *fig*). **fing'erhole** *n* a hole in a wind instrument closed by the finger to modify the pitch. **fing'erlickin'** *adv* or *adj* (*sl*) (of food eaten with the fingers) extremely (good). **fing'ermark** *n* a mark, *esp* a dirty one, made by a finger. **fing'ernail** *n*. **fing'er-paint** *n* a somewhat thick gelatinous paint used *esp* by children and applied with the hands and fingers rather than with a brush (also *vt*). **fing'er-painting** *n*. **fing'erpick** *n* a small plectrum attached to the fingertip. ◆ *vt* and *vi* to play using fingerpicks. **fing'erplate** *n* a decorative plate, *usu* of metal, to protect a door from dirty fingers. **fing'er-pointer** *n* an accuser. **fing'er-pointing** *n*. **fing'erpost** *n* a post with a finger pointing the way to a destination. **fing'erprint** *n* an impression of the ridges of the fingertip, unique to each human being and used as a means of identification, *esp* of criminals; an accurate and unique identification feature or profile produced by chemical analysis, genetic analysis, etc (*fig*); the basic features (*fig*). ◆ *vt* to take the fingerprints of (also *fig*). **fing'erprinting** *n* (also *fig*). **finger roll** *n* a small thin bread roll. **fing'erstall** *n* a covering for protecting a finger. **fing'ertip** *n* the tip of one's finger. ◆ *adj* using the fingertips, hence delicate. **finger wave** *n* a wave in hair made using the fingers.
■ **a finger in the pie** a share in the doing of anything (often said of annoying meddling). **be all fingers and thumbs**, **have one's fingers all thumbs**, etc see under **thumb**. **burn one's fingers** or **get one's fingers burnt** see under **burn**¹. **cross one's fingers** see under **cross**. **get** or **pull the** (or **one's**) **finger out** (*inf*) to start working hard or doing one's job properly or efficiently. **give someone** (or **get**) **the finger** (chiefly *N Am sl*) to make, or be the target of, an obscene gesture of contempt made by extending the middle finger vertically. **have a finger in every pie** to have an involvement in many different affairs. **have at one's finger-ends**, **finger's-ends** or **fingertips** to be

master of (a subject). **keep one's fingers crossed** see under **cross**. **lay** or **put a finger on** to touch. **not lift a finger** to take no action. **point the finger at** to call attention to in accusation. **put** or **lay one's finger on** to indicate, comprehend and express, or recall, precisely. **put the finger on** (*inf*) to identify as a guilty person. **snap one's fingers** to make a short loud clicking sound with the middle finger and thumb, *usu* to attract attention or show defiance, contempt, etc. **to one's fingertips** completely; in all respects. **twist**, **wind** or **wrap someone round one's little finger** to control someone completely, or influence someone to a great extent.

fingering¹ see under **finger**.

fingering² /fing'gə-ring/ *n* a woollen yarn of two or more strands, used in hand-knitting, *orig* and *esp* for stockings. [Perh Fr *fin grain* fine grain]

fini /fē-nē'/ (*Fr*) *adj* finished or completed; ruined or broken.

finial /fin'i-əl/ *n* a decoration on the top of a gable, spire, etc, often in the form of a spike or a bunch of leaves. [L *fīnis* end]

finical /fin'i-kl/ *adj* affectedly or excessively precise in unimportant matters; foppish. [Prob connected with **fine**¹]
■ **finicality** /-kal'i-ti/ *n* the state of being finical; something finical. **fin'ically** *adv*. **fin'icalness** or **fin'icking** *n* fussiness and fastidiousness. **finick'ety**, **fin'icking**, **fin'icky** or **fin'ikin** *adj* particular about unimportant matters; (**finicky**) (of a job) intricate, tricky, fiddly, requiring attention to small details, delicate manipulations, etc.

fining see under **fine**¹.

finis /fin'is or fī'nis/ (*L*) *n* (pl **fi'nēs**) the end; the conclusion.

finish /fin'ish/ *vt* to end; to complete the making of; to use the last of; to perfect; to give the last touches to; to give a particular treatment to the surface of; to complete the education of, *esp* for life in polite society; to complete the course of (a race); to put an end to or destroy. ◆ *vi* to come to an end; to complete the course of a race. ◆ *n* something which finishes or completes; the end of a race, hunt, etc; the last touch, elaboration or polish; the last coat of plaster, paint, etc; surface texture; the flavour that lingers after wine has been swallowed or spat out; (applied to cattle and sheep) the amount of flesh and fat on an animal. [Fr *finir*, *finissant*, from L *fīnīre* to end]
■ **fin'ished** *adj* brought to an end or to completion; having no further prospect of success; complete; consummate; perfect. **fin'isher** *n* a person who finishes; a person who completes or perfects, *esp* in crafts; a finishing or knockout blow. **fin'ishing** *n* and *adj*.
❑ **finishing post** *n* the post marking the end of a race (*esp* for horses). **finishing school** *n* an expensive establishment where some girls complete their education, with emphasis on social refinements, etc rather than academic achievement. **finishing touch** or **stroke** *n* (often in *pl*) the last minor improvement needed to achieve perfection.
■ **finish off** to complete, put the finishing touches to; to eat or drink the last of; to complete the defeat or destruction of; to administer a final killing blow to; to end. **finish up** to finish; to end up, be or become in the end. **finish with** to end relations or dealings with; to come to the end of one's need or use for.

finite /fī'nīt/ *adj* having an end or limit; subject to limitations or conditions, *opp* to **infinite**. [L *fīnītus*, pap of *fīnīre* to limit]
■ **fī'nitely** *adv*. **fī'niteness** or **finitude** /fin'i-tūd or fīn'/ *n*.
❑ **finite verb** *n* a verb limited by person, number, tense or mood, as opposed to an infinitive, gerund or participle.

finjan see **fingan**.

fink /fingk/ (*sl*) *n* a strikebreaker; an informer; loosely, an unpleasant person. ◆ *vi* (often with *on*) to inform on. [Origin uncertain]

finks same as **fenks**.

finlit /fin'lit/ *n* financial literacy.

Finn /fin/ *n* a member of a people living in Finland and adjacent regions; more generally, a member of the group of peoples speaking Finnic languages. [OE *finnas* Finns]
■ **Fin'lander** *n* a native or citizen of Finland. **Finlandizā'tion** or **-s-** *n* a policy towards a superior power of accommodation rather than confrontation, as in the relations between Finland and the former Soviet Union. **Finn'ic** *adj* of or relating to one of the two branches of the Finno-Ugrian family of languages, which includes Finnish, Estonian and Lapp, or to the peoples who speak these languages. **Finn'ish** *adj* pertaining to the Finns, or to Finland, or its language. ◆ *n* the Finno-Ugrian language of Finland.
❑ **Finno-Ugrian** /fin'ō-ū'gri-ən or -oo'gri-ən/ or **Finno-Ugric** /-grik/ *adj* belonging to the NW group of Ural-Altaic languages and peoples, including Finnish, Estonian, Lapp, Cheremiss, Mordvin, Zyrian, Votyak, etc (also **U'gro-Finn'ic**).

Finn. *abbrev* : Finnish.

finnac or **finnack** see **finnock**.

finnan /fin'ən/ or (obs) **findram** /fin'rəm/ n a kind of smoked haddock, prob named from Findon, Kincardineshire, not from the Findhorn river (also **finnan** or **findon haddock** or **haddie**).

finnesko /fin'e-skō/, **finnsko** or **finsko** /fin'skō/ n (pl **finn'eskō**, etc) a reindeer-skin boot with the hair on. [Norw finnsko, from Finn Lapp, and sko shoe]

finnock, **finnack** or **finnac** /fin'ək/ n a young sea trout. [Gaelic fionnag, from fionn white]

fino /fē'nō/ n (pl **fi'nos**) a dry sherry. [Sp, fine or excellent]

finocchio, **finnochio** or **finochio** /fi-nok'i-ō/ n a dwarf variety of fennel, Foeniculum (vulgare) dulce, the leaf stalks of which are used in stews, salads, etc (also called **dwarf**, **Florence**, **French** or **sweet fennel**). [Ital, fennel]

finsko see finnesko.

fiord see fjord.

fiorin /fī'ə-rin/ n a variety of creeping bent grass (Agrostis stolonifera). [Ir fíorthán]

fioritura /fyor-i-too'rə/ (music) n (pl **fioriture** /-rā/) a florid embellishment. [Ital, flowering, from L flōs, flōris]

fippence /fip'əns/ (inf) n a shortened form of **fivepence** (see under five).

fipple /fip'l/ n the underlip (dialect); (in wind instruments) the plug in the mouthpiece, often together with the sharp edge against which it directs the wind. [Cf ON flipi a horse's lip]
□ **fipple flute** n a flute with a fipple, a recorder or flageolet.

fiqh /fēk/ (Islam) n (the study of) religious law. [Ar]

fir /fûr/ n the name of several conifers, esp of the genera Abies and Picea, resinous trees valuable for their timber. [OE fyrh; cf Ger Föhre]
■ **firr'y** adj having many firs; of fir.
□ **fir cone** n. **fir tree** n. **fir'wood** n.

fire /fīr/ n a substance formerly reckoned to be one of the four principal elements out of which all living things were made; the heat and light of burning; a mass of burning matter, such as fuel in a grate; flame or incandescence; a conflagration; the discharging of a firearm; fuel; a heating apparatus; heat or light from sources other than burning; lightning (poetic); volcanic or subterranean heat; great heat; the heat of fever or inflammation; glowing appearance; a sparkle of light; discharge of firearms (also fig); enthusiasm; ardour; passion; spirited vigour or animation; refraction of light in a gemstone. ◆ vt to ignite; to cause to explode; to expose to heat; to bake (pottery); to cauterize (farriery); to fuel; to affect as if by fire; to discharge (a firearm); to send or direct (eg questions) forcefully or rapidly, as if from a firearm; to launch (a missile); to drive out; to dismiss (from employment, etc); to inflame; to animate; to rouse to passion of any kind. ◆ vi to catch fire; to shoot with firearms; to become inflamed; to break out in anger; to make a fast, direct shot aimed merely at displacing an opponent's bowls (bowls); (of a car, engine, etc) to start. [OE fŷr; Ger Feuer; Gr pŷr]
■ **fired** adj affected, or having the appearance of having been affected, with fire; baked (pottery); ignited; kindled; discharged. **fire'less** adj. **fir'er** n a person who fires, in any sense. **fir'ing** n ignition; discharge of guns, etc; simultaneous ringing of a peal of bells; fuelling; firewood; fuel; cautery; injury by overheating; subjection to heat.
□ **fire alarm** n an apparatus for giving warning of fire; a warning of fire. **fire ant** n a tropical American ant that inflicts a painful sting. **fire'arm** n à weapon discharged by explosion (usu in pl). **fire'-arrow** n a dart or arrow with an ignitable head. **fire'back** n a red-backed Sumatran pheasant; the back wall of a fireplace; an ornamental plate of iron placed there. **fire'ball** n a burning meteor, a bolide; ball lightning; an incendiary or illuminating projectile; a flaming ball of burning gases; the luminous sphere of hot gases at the centre of a nuclear explosion; a lively energetic person (inf). **fire'-balloon** n a balloon carrying fire and raised by the heating and rarefaction of air; a balloon discharging fireworks in the air. **fire'-bar** n a bar of a fire-grate; a heating element in an electric radiator. **fire'-basket** n a portable fire-grate, a brazier. **fire'-bird** n the Baltimore oriole, or other bird of orange and red plumage. **fire blanket** n a blanket of non-flammable material for extinguishing small fires. **fire'-blast** n a blight of hops, due to a mite, giving a scorched appearance. **fire'-blight** n a bacterial disease of fruit trees, giving a scorched appearance. **fire'bomb** n an incendiary bomb. ◆ vt to attack with incendiary bombs. **fire'bombing** n. **fire'-bote** n (hist) a tenant's right to cut wood for fuel. **fire'box** n a chamber for the fire in a steam engine, etc. **fire'brand** n a burning piece of wood; an energetic person; a person who stirs up trouble. **fire'brat** n a small insect found in bakehouses and other warm places. **fire'break** n a strip of land kept clear to stop the spread of a fire (also fig). **fire'brick** n a brick resistant to fire, used for furnace linings, grates, etc. **fire brigade** n a body of firefighters. **fire bucket** n a bucket containing sand or water for putting out fires. **fire'bug** n (inf) an arsonist. **fire clay** n a clay poor in lime and iron, suitable for making fire-resistant pottery and firebricks. **fire control** n a system of controlling artillery fire, esp the whole gunfire of a ship from one centre. **fire'cracker** n a device for making a noise, a cylinder of paper or cardboard containing an explosive and a fuse. **fire'crest** or **fire-crested wren** n a bird closely related to the goldcrest. **fire'damp** n a combustible gas given off by coal, etc, chiefly methane. **fire department** n (N Am) same as **fire brigade** above. **fire'dog** n an andiron. **fire door** n a fire-resistant door to prevent the spread of fire within a building; an emergency exit. **fire'drake** n a fire-breathing dragon (literary and German myth); a luminous phenomenon (archaic); a kind of firework, a rocket. **fire drill** n a primitive instrument for making fire by twirling a stick; a practice in putting out or escaping from a fire. **fire'-eater** n a juggler who seems to eat fire; a person who looks for quarrels. **fire'-edge** n (dialect) a cutting edge hardened by fire; crispness in a newly baked cake; first eagerness. **fire engine** n a vehicle which carries firefighters and equipment to put out fires. **fire escape** n a fixed or movable way of escape from a burning building. **fire extinguisher** n a portable device for spraying water, chemicals, foam, etc onto a fire to put it out. **fire'-eyed** adj (Shakesp) having fiery eyes. **fire'fight** n an intense exchange of gunfire. **fire'fighter** n a person whose job is the putting out of fires and the rescuing of people and animals in danger. **fire'fighting** n the job of a firefighter; dealing with events as they arise, without long-term planning (fig). **fire'-flag** or **fire'-flaught** n (literary) a flash of fire, lightning, etc. **fire'float** n a boat or raft used in harbours for extinguishing fires. **fire'fly** n any of various nocturnal insects which emit phosphorescent light. **fire'-grate** n a grating to hold a fire. **fire'guard** n a protective wire frame or railing in front of a fireplace. **fire'-hook** n a hook formerly used to tear down burning buildings. **fire hose** n a hose for extinguishing fires. **fire'house** n (obs) a house with a fireplace, a dwelling-house; a fire station (US). **fire insurance** n insurance against loss by fire. **fire irons** n pl fireside implements, ie poker, tongs, shovel, not necessarily of iron. **fire'light** n the light of a (usu domestic) fire. **fire'lighter** n a piece of readily flammable material or other means of lighting a fire. **fire'lock** n a gun discharged by a lock with flint and steel. **fire'man** n a male firefighter; a stoker; a train driver's assistant (stoker on a steam railway engine); a person who looks after safety conditions in a mine; a person who explodes charges; a reporter sent out (esp abroad) to cover a specific event. **fireman's lift** n a method of carrying someone by putting him or her face down over one's shoulder, esp used by firefighters in rescuing unconscious or injured people. **fire'mark** n a metal plate formerly placed by insurance companies to mark an insured building. **fire'-marshal** (US) or **fire'-master** n the head of a fire brigade. **fire'-new** adj fresh from the fire; brand-new. **fire'-office** n a fire insurance office. **fire opal** n a flame-coloured variety of opal. **fire'pan** n a metal vessel for holding fire. **fire'place** n the place for a domestic fire, the chimney-opening and surrounding area. **fire'-plough** (US **fire-plow**) n (archaeol) a stick rubbed in a wooden groove to make fire. **fire'plug** n a hydrant for use against fires. **fire'-policy** n a written document of insurance against fire. **fire'pot** n (hist) an earthen pot full of combustible material, used as a missile. **fire'power** n the amount of ammunition that can be fired with effect in a given time (milit); the total offensive power or materials of a fighting force or any one of its machines or units (milit); the total weight of influence, argument, etc of an individual, organization, etc (fig). **fire practice** same as **fire drill** above. **fire'proof** adj rendered completely immune to the effects of fire; incombustible. ◆ vt to make fireproof. **fire'proofing** n. **fire'-raiser** n an arsonist. **fire'-raising** n arson. **fire'-resistant** or **fire'-resisting** adj immune to the effects of fire up to a required degree. **fire'-risk** n something which is likely to cause a fire, or to be consumed if there is one. **fire'-robed** adj (Shakesp) apparently clothed in fire. **fire sale** n a sale of goods damaged by fire; any quick sale of goods at cheap bargain prices (US; usu fig). **fire'screen** n a screen for intercepting the heat of a fire or masking an unlit fire. **fire'ship** n (hist) a ship carrying combustible materials sent among the enemy's ships. **fire'-shovel** n. **fire'side** n the side of the fireplace; the hearth; home. ◆ adj domestic; familiar. **fire sign** n any of the three signs of the zodiac (Aries, Leo and Sagittarius) believed to have an affinity with fire. **fire station** n a place where fire engines, firefighters, etc are kept in readiness to attend fires. **fire'-step** or **fir'ing-step** n (hist) a ledge on which soldiers stand to fire over a parapet, a banquette. **fire'-stick** n a primitive implement for making fire by friction. **fire'stone** n a rock, esp sandstone, that can withstand great heat. **fire'-storm** n a huge blaze (esp a result of heavy bombing) which fans its own flames by creating its own draught (also fig). **fire'thorn** n (bot) pyracantha. **fire trail** n (Aust and N Am) a road through forest or bush that allows firefighters to reach fires in remote parts. **fire'trap** n a building, etc inadequately provided with fire exits and fire escapes. **fire truck** n (US) a fire engine. **fire'-tube** n a tube through which fire passes, eg in a steam railway engine. **fire'-walk** or **fire'-walking** n the (religious) ceremony of walking barefoot over hot stones, ashes, etc. **fire'-walker** n. **fire'wall** n a fireproof wall in a building intended to prevent a fire from spreading; software that protects a network against unauthorized users (comput; also fig). ◆ vt

to install or create a firewall around. **fire'-warden** *n* (*N Am*) an official responsible for the prevention and extinction of fires. **fire'-watcher** *n* a person who watches out for fires resulting from bombing or in eg forested areas. **fire'-watching** *n*. **fire'water** *n* (*humorous*) strong alcoholic spirits. **fire'weed** *n* the rosebay willowherb, which springs up after forest, etc fires. **Fire'wire**® *n* a serial bus technology used for high-speed data transfer between computers. **fire'woman** *n* a female firefighter. **fire'wood** *n* wood for fuel. **fire'work** *n* a combustible or explosive mixture used in warfare, or a projectile carrying it (*obs*); a device containing combustible chemicals, for producing coloured sparks, flares, etc, often with loud noises; (now only in *pl*) a display of these; (in *pl*) an impressive technical display in music, talk, etc; (in *pl*) a display of temper. **fire'worm** *n* a glow-worm; a firefly. **fire'-worship** *n* worship of fire; loosely, homage to fire (as among Parsees) as a symbol of deity but not itself a god. **fire'-worshipper** *n*. **firing line** *n* an area, or the troops, within range of the enemy for practical purposes; a position of exposure to fierce criticism, etc, *esp* in the phrase *in the firing line*. **firing order** *n* (*motoring*) the sequence in which the cylinders of a multi-cylinder combustion engine fire. **firing party** *n* a detachment detailed to fire over a grave or shoot a condemned prisoner. **firing pin** *n* a pin that strikes the detonator and explodes the cartridge in a rifle. **firing point** *n* the temperature at which a flammable oil catches fire spontaneously. **firing squad** *n* a firing party, a detachment detailed to shoot a condemned prisoner. ■ **between two fires** under attack from two sides. **breathe fire** (*inf*) to speak or behave in an angry or intimidating manner. **catch** or **take fire** to become ignited; to become aroused about something. **fire and brimstone** hell, formerly an exclamation of wrath or extreme irritation; a preacher's evocation of eternal damnation (**fire'-and-brim'stone** *adj*). **fire and sword** military devastation. **fire away** (*usu imperative*; *inf*) to go ahead; to begin. **fire in one's belly** ardour or passion in speaking, etc; drive or ambition. **fire off** to discharge; to ask or utter in rapid succession. **fire out** (*Shakesp*) to expel. **fire up** to start a fire; to fly into a passion; to excite or enthuse. **go on fire** (*Scot* or *Irish*) to catch fire. **go through fire and water** see under **go¹**. **hang fire** see under **hang**. **on fire** in a state of fiery combustion; in a lively or excited state (*inf*). **open fire** see under **open**. **play with fire** to expose oneself to unnecessary risk; to treat lightly a situation which could prove dangerous. **St Anthony's fire** see under **Anthony**. **St Elmo's fire** see under **saint**. **set on fire** or **set fire to** to ignite. **under fire** exposed to the enemy's fire; exposed to criticism.

firk /fûrk/ (*obs*) *vt* to drive; to rouse; to whip or beat (*Shakesp*). [OE *fercian* to conduct]

firkin /fûr'kin/ *n* a measure equal to one-quarter of a barrel (*brewing*); 9 gallons (*brewing*); 56lb of butter. [With dimin sfx *-kin*, from ODu *vierde* fourth]

firlot /fûr'lǝt/ *n* an old Scottish dry measure, one-quarter of a boll. [Earlier *ferthelot*; cf ON *fiôrthe hlotr* fourth lot]

firm¹ /fûrm/ *adj* fixed; compact; strong; not easily moved or disturbed; unshaken; resolute; decided; (of prices, commodities, markets, etc) steady or stable (*commerce*). ◆ *adv* in a firm manner. ◆ *vt* to make firm. ◆ *vi* to become firm; to become stable or rise slightly (*commerce*). [OFr *ferme*, from L *firmus*]
■ **firm'less** *adj* (*obs*) wavering. **firm'ly** *adv*. **firm'ness** *n*.
❏ **firm'ware** *n* (*comput sl*) software or similar instructions forming a more or less permanent and unerasable part of a computer's memory.
■ **firm down** to make (ground, etc) firm or firmer. **firm up** (of prices, etc) to firm (*commerce*); to make (a promise, etc) firm or firmer.

firm² /fûrm/ *n* a business house or partnership, a company. [Ital *firma*, from L *firmus*; see **farm**]

firmament /fûr'mǝ-mǝnt/ *n* the solid sphere in which the stars were formerly thought to be fixed; the sky. [L *firmāmentum*, from *firmus* firm]
■ **firmamental** /-ment'l/ *adj*.

firman /fûr'man, fer-män'/ *n* a decree or judicial decision. [Pers *fermān*]

firmer /fûr'mǝr/ or **firmer chisel** /chiz'l/ *n* a carpenter's or woodworker's woodcutting chisel. [Fr *fermoir*, an alteration of *formoir*, from *former* to form]

firn /firn or fûrn/ *n* snow on high glaciers while still granular. [Ger *firn* of last year; cf obs Eng *fern* former]

firring same as **furring** (see under **fur¹**).

first /fûrst/ *adj* foremost; in front of or before all others; most eminent; chief; referring to the speaker or writer (*grammar*). ◆ *n* a person or thing that is first or of the first class; a place in the first class; an academic degree of the first class; first gear; the first time that something has happened or been done (*inf*). ◆ *adv* before anything or anyone else; for the first time. [OE *fyrst*, superl; cf *fore* before]
■ **first'ling** *n* (*rare*) the first produce or offspring, *esp* of animals. **first'ly** *adv* in the first place.

❏ **first aid** *n* immediate treatment of a wounded or sick person before full medical attention. **first-aid'er** *n*. **first-attack'** same as **first-strike** below. **first'-begotten** *adj* born first; eldest. **first'-born** *adj* born first. ◆ *n* the first in order of birth; the eldest child. **first'-class'** *adj* of the first class, rank or quality. ◆ *adv* by first-class mail, transport, etc. **first-class mail** or **post** *n* mail sent at a dearer rate to obtain quicker delivery. **first'-day** *n* (*obs*) Sunday. **first-day cover** *n* an envelope with stamps postmarked on their first day of issue. **first degree burn**, **first degree murder** see under **degree**. **first finger** *n* the finger next to the thumb. **first fix** *n* (*building*) the part of joinery, plumbing or electrical work that must be done as soon as the framework of a building is complete (cf **second fix**). **first floor** see under **floor**. **first'-foot'** *n* (*Scot*) the first person to enter a house after the beginning of the new year. ◆ *vt* to visit as first-foot. ◆ *vi* to go around making visits as first-foot. **first'-foot'er** *n*. **first'-foot'ing** *n*. **first'-fruit'** or **first-fruits'** *n* the fruits first gathered in a season; first products or effects of anything; payment in the form of first crops of a season, or annates, to a superior. **first gear** see under **gear**. **first generation** *adj* (*comput*) of the early type of calculating and computing machine, using thermionic valves. **first'-hand** *adj* obtained directly, or in order to obtain (information, etc) directly, without an intermediary. **first-hand'** *adv*. **first lady** *n* the wife of the chief executive of a city, state or country, *esp* of the president of the USA, or any woman chosen by him to carry out official duties as hostess, etc (*US*; often with *caps*); a prominent or leading woman in any field, profession, etc. **first lieutenant** *n* (in the Royal Navy) the executive officer, not necessarily a lieutenant, of a ship or naval establishment; (in the US Army, Air Force and Marine Corps) an officer next below a captain. **first light** *n* the time when daylight first appears in the morning. **First Minister** *n* the title given to the leader of the devolved administrations in Scotland, Northern Ireland and Wales. **first name** *n* a person's Christian name, or the name that comes first in a full name. **first night** *n* the first public performance of a theatrical production. **first-night'er** *n* a person who habitually goes to the theatre on first nights. **first offender** *n* a person convicted for the first time. **first'-past'-the-post'** *adj* denoting or relating to a system of voting in which each voter casts only one non-transferable vote, the candidate receiving the most votes being declared the winner. **first person** *n* (*grammar*) the writer or speaker. **first'-person** *adj*. **first post** *n* (*milit*) the first of two bugle calls denoting the time for retiring for the night (cf **last post** under **last¹**). **first'-rate** *adj* of highest rank or excellence; pre-eminent in quality, size or estimation. ◆ *n* a warship so rated. **first-rate'** *adv* excellently. **first refusal** *n* the chance to buy (*esp* property) before it is offered to others. **first school** *n* a school for children aged five to eight, nine or ten. **first strike** *n* a pre-emptive attack on an enemy, intended to destroy their nuclear weapons before they can be brought into use. **first'-strike** *adj*. **first'-time** *adj* immediate; carrying out an action, eg the purchase of a house, for the first time. **first water** *n* the first or highest quality, or purest lustre, of diamonds and pearls (also *fig*). **First World** *n* the richest and most technologically developed countries of the world. **first year allowance** *n* an amount of capital expenditure which can be set against tax in the accounts relating to the actual year of spending.
■ **at first** at the beginning, in the early stages, etc. **first cab off the rank** (*inf*) the first choice, the first to do something. **first in, first out** (*comput*) denoting a list for which insertions are made at one end and deletions at the other. **first thing** before doing anything else. **not know the first thing about** to know nothing about.

firth¹ /fûrth/ *n* an arm of the sea, *esp* a river mouth (also **frith** /frith/). [ON *fiörthr*; Norw *fjord*]

firth² see **frith³**.

FIS *abbrev*: Family Income Supplement; *Fédération Internationale de Ski* (*Fr*), International Ski Federation.

FISA /fē'sǝ/ *abbrev*: *Fédération Internationale des Sociétés d'Aviron* (*Fr*), International Rowing Federation; Finance Industry Standards Association.

fisc or **fisk** /fisk/ (*obs*) *n* the state treasury; the public revenue; one's purse. [Ety as for **fiscal**]

fiscal /fis'kǝl/ *adj* relating to the public treasury or revenue. ◆ *n* a treasurer (*obs*); a public prosecutor, chief law officer of the crown under the Holy Roman Empire (*hist*); (in Scotland) an officer who prosecutes in criminal cases in local and inferior courts (in full, **procurator fiscal**). [L *fiscus* a basket or purse]
■ **fis'cally** *adv*.
❏ **fiscal cliff** *n* (*inf*) an economic crisis brought about by a sudden increase in taxation combined with cuts in public spending. **fiscal drag** *n* the means by which the inland revenue automatically benefits from any increase in earned income without any actual increase in taxation rates. **fiscal year** *n* (*esp US*) a financial year.
■ **the fiscal question** (*econ*) the question of whether to encourage free trade or protection.

fisgig see **fizgig**.

fish[1] /fish/ n (pl **fish** or **fish'es**) a member of a large group of cold-blooded vertebrates that live in water and breathe through gills; loosely, any exclusively aquatic animal; the flesh of fish as food; a person, as in a *queer fish*; (in pl with *cap* and *the*) Pisces; a fish-dive. ◆ vi to catch or try to catch or obtain fish, or anything that may be likened to a fish (such as seals, sponges, coral, compliments, information or husbands; often with *for*); to search, rummage; to serve the purpose of fishing. ◆ vt to catch and bring out of water; to bring up or out from a deep or hidden place, obscurity, etc; to elicit (with *out*); to practise the fisherman's craft in; to ransack; to hoist the flukes of (*naut*). [OE *fisc*; Ger *Fisch*; ON *fiskr*; L *piscis*; Gaelic *iasg*]

■ **fish'able** adj. **fish'er** n a fisherman (now *rare*); an inappropriate name for the pekan or woodshock, a type of marten. **fish'ery** n the business of catching fish; a place for catching fish; a place where fish are reared for sale; a right of fishing. **fish'ful** adj (*obs*) containing many fish. **fish'ify** vt (*Shakesp*) to turn into fish, or make fish-like. **fish'iness** n. **fish'ing** adj used in fishing. ◆ n the art or practice of catching fish; a fishing ground or stretch of water where one fishes. **fish'y** adj consisting of fish; like a fish; containing many fish; dubious, as of a story; equivocal, unsafe.

❑ **fish'ball** see **fish cake** below. **fish'-bell'ied** adj swelled out downwards like the belly of a fish. **fish'-bone** n. **fish'burger** n a flat cake, similar to a hamburger, made of minced fish. **fish cake** or **fish'ball** n a ball or cake of chopped fish and mashed potatoes, fried. **fish'-carv'er** or **fish'-trowel** n a large flat implement for carving fish at table. **fish'-creel** n an angler's basket; a fishwife's basket. **fish'-day** n a day on which fish is eaten rather than meat. **fish'-dive** n (*sl*) a ballerina's leap into a partner's outstretched arms. **fish eagle** n any of various fish-eating eagles, *esp* the African fish eagle (*Haliaeetus vocifer*) of central and southern Africa. **fish eaters** n pl (*rare*) a knife and fork for eating fish with. **fish'erman** n a person who fishes for sport or as a business. **fisherman's luck** n getting wet and catching no fish. **fisherman's ring** n a signet ring, with the device of St Peter fishing, used in signing papal briefs. **fish'erwoman** n. **fish'eye** n (*sl*) an unfriendly, suspicious stare. **fisheye lens** n (*photog*) an ultra-wide-angle lens covering up to 180°. **fish'-fag** n (*archaic*) a woman who sells fish. **fish farm** n. **fish farmer** n. **fish farming** n rearing fish in ponds or tanks, for sale. **fish finger** n a fairly small oblong cake of fish coated in batter or breadcrumbs. **fish'-garth** n an enclosure on a river for the preserving or taking of fish (also **fish'-weir**). **fish'-glue** n isinglass, or any other glue made from the skins, air-bladders, etc of fish. **fish'-god** n a deity wholly or partly like a fish in form, like the Philistine Dagon. **fish'-guano** n fish-manure. **fish'-guts** n pl. **fish'-gutter** n. **fish'-gutting** n. **fish'-hatchery** n a place for the artificial rearing of fish. **fish'-hawk** n an osprey. **fish'-hook** n a barbed hook for catching fish. **fish'ing-frog** n the devilfish. **fishing ground** n an area of water, *esp* of the sea, where fish are caught. **fish'ing-line** n (a) fine strong *usu* nylon filament used (eg with a rod, hooks, etc) to catch fish. **fish'ing-rod** n a long slender rod to which a line is fastened for angling. **fish'ing-tack'le** n tackle, such as nets, lines, etc, used in fishing. **fish kettle** n a long oval dish for boiling or poaching fish. **fish knife** n a knife with a broad, blunt-edged, *usu* decorated blade for eating fish with; a broad-bladed knife for cutting and serving fish with. **fish'-ladd'er** or (*N Am*) **fish'way** n an arrangement of steps and shelters enabling fish to pass around artificial river barriers such as dams, weirs, etc. **fish louse** n a copepod or other crustacean which is a parasite on fishes. **fish'-manure** n fish used as a fertilizer. **fish'meal** n dried fish, ground to meal; a meal of fish (*Shakesp*); an abstemious, sparing diet. **fish'monger** n a dealer in fish. **fish'-net** adj woven as a fine net. **fish'-oil** n oil obtained from fish and other marine animals. **fish'-packing** n. **fish pond** n a pond in which fish are kept (formerly also **fish'-stew**). **fish'-salesman** n a person who receives consignments of fish for sale by auction to retail dealers. **fish'-scrap** n fish or fishskins from which oil or glue has been extracted. **fish'skin** n the skin of a fish; (also **fishskin disease**) ichthyosis. **fish slice** n a flat implement for carving fish at table; a broad, flat implement for turning fish, etc in the frying-pan. **fish'-spear** n a spear or dart for catching fish. **fish'-stew** n (*obs*) a fish pond. **fish stick** n (*N Am*) a fish finger. **fish'-strainer** n a metal colander for taking fish from a boiler. **fish'tail** adj shaped like the tail of a fish. ◆ vi to swing the tail of an aircraft from side to side to reduce speed while gliding downwards; (of the back of a vehicle) to swing or skid from side to side. **fish-torpē'do** n a self-propelling torpedo. **fish'way** n (*N Am*) a fish-ladder. **fish'-weir** n a fish-garth. **fish'wife** or **fish'-woman** n a woman who carries fish about for sale; a coarse, loud-mouthed woman.

■ **a fish out of water** a person in an unaccustomed, unsuitable situation which makes him or her ill at ease. **big fish** (*sl*) an important or leading person. **drink like a fish** to drink (*usu* alcohol) to excess. **fish in troubled waters** to take advantage of disturbed times to further one's own interests. **have other fish to fry** to have something else to do or attend to. **make fish of one and flesh** (or **fowl**) **of another** to make offensive distinctions. **neither fish nor flesh** (**nor good red herring**) or **neither fish, flesh, nor fowl** neither one thing nor another.

odd fish or **queer fish** a person of odd habits, or of a nature with which one is not in sympathy. **pretty kettle of fish** see under **kettle**[1].

fish[2] /fish/ n a piece of wood placed alongside another to strengthen it (*naut*); a counter in various games. ◆ vt to strengthen with a fish or fishplate. [Prob Fr *fiche* peg or mark]

❑ **fish'-joint** n a place where things are joined by fishplates. **fish'plate** n an iron plate used in pairs to join railway rails.

fishgig see **fizgig**.

fisk[1] /fisk/ (*obs*) vi to frisk; to gad about. [Prob a frequentative of OE *fȳsan* to hurry, or of *fȳsian* to feeze]

fisk[2] see **fisc**.

fisnomie /fiz'no-mi/ (*Shakesp*) n physiognomy.

fissicostate /fi-si-kos'tāt/ adj having divided ribs. [L *fissus*, from *findere* to cleave, and *costa* rib]

fissile /fis'īl or -il/ adj readily split; capable of nuclear fission. [**fissure**]
■ **fissility** /-il'-/ n ability to be split.

fissilingual /fi-si-ling'gwəl/ adj with cloven tongue. [L *fissus*, from *findere* to cleave, and *lingua* tongue]

fission /fish'ən/ n a cleaving; reproduction by dividing; the splitting of the nucleus of an atom into two roughly equal parts accompanied by enormous release of energy. ◆ vi to undergo nuclear fission. [**fissure**]
■ **fiss'ionable** adj capable of nuclear fission. **fiss'ive** adj.
❑ **fission bomb** n a bomb deriving its energy from nuclear fission. **fission fungus** n a bacterium. **fission reactor** n a reactor in which nuclear fission takes place. **fission spectrum** n the wide range of elements and isotopes formed in fission. **fission-track dating** n gauging the date of a mineral by counting tracks made in it by uranium fission products.

fissiparous /fi-sip'ə-ras/ adj reproducing by fission. [L *fissus*, from *findere* to cleave, and *parere* to bring forth]
■ **fissip'arism, fissipar'ity** or **fissip'arousness** n. **fissip'arously** adv.

fissiped /fi-si-ped'/ or **fissipede** /-pēd'/ adj with digits separate. ◆ n an animal with digits separate. [L *fissus*, from *findere* to cleave, and *pēs, pedis* foot]

fissirostral /fi-si-ros'trəl/ adj with deep-cleft or gaping beak. [L *fissus*, from *findere* to cleave, and *rōstrum* beak]

fissle /fis'l/ (*Scot*) vi to rustle. [Imit]

fissure /fish'ər/ n an act of cleaving; a narrow opening, a chasm, cleft or groove; a sulcus, *esp* one of the furrows on the surface of the brain, such as the longitudinal fissure separating the hemispheres; a small abnormal crack in the mucous membrane. ◆ vt to crack, cleave or divide. [L *findere, fissum* to cleave]
■ **fiss'ured** adj cleft or divided.

fist /fist/ n the closed or clenched hand; handwriting (*inf*); an index (*printing*). ◆ vt to strike or grip with the fist. ◆ vi and vt (*vulgar sl*) to stimulate the vagina or anus (of) by inserting the whole hand. [OE *fȳst*; Ger *Faust*]
■ **fist'ful** n a handful. **fistiana** /-ä'nə, -ā'nə/ n pl (*facetious*) anecdotes about boxing and boxers. **fist'ic** or **fist'ical** adj (*facetious*) pugilistic. **fist'y** adj.
❑ **fist bump** n a form of greeting in which two people briefly touch clenched fists. **fist'fight** n a fight in which only the bare fists are used. **fist'icuff** n a blow with the fist; (in pl; often *facetious*) boxing; (in pl; often *facetious*) a fight with fists. **fist'-law** n the law of brute force. **fist'mele** /-mēl/ n (**meal**[1] in sense of *measure*; *hist*) the breadth of a fist with the thumb extended, *esp* as used as the measure of the correct distance between the string and the handle of a braced bow.
■ **make a good, a reasonable, not a bad, etc fist of** to do (something) fairly well, not badly, etc.

fistula /fis'tū-la/ n (pl **fist'ulae** /-lē/ or **fist'ulas**) a narrow passage or duct; an artificially made opening (*med*); a long narrow pipe-like ulcer (*pathol*); a tube through which the wine of the Eucharist was once sucked from the chalice (*Christianity*; also **calamus**). [L *fistula* pipe]
■ **fist'ular, fist'ulose** or **fist'ulous** adj.

fit[1] /fit/ adj (**fitt'er, fitt'est**) suitable; in suitable condition; meeting required standards; of suitable ability; convenient; befitting, appropriate; well trained and ready; in good condition; in good health; having a high level, or the required level, of stamina, suppleness or other athletic strength; highly attractive, sexually desirable (*inf*). ◆ n success in fitting; adjustment and correspondence in shape and size; a thing (*esp* a garment) that fits. ◆ vt (**fitt'ing; fitt'ed** or (*N Am*) **fit**) to make suitable or able; to alter or make so as to be in adjustment; to adjust; to piece together; to be suitable or becoming for; to be of such size and shape as to adjust closely to; to be in agreement or correspondence with; to furnish or supply; to install; to drive by fits (*Shakesp*). ◆ vi to be suitable or becoming; to go into place with accurate adjustment to space; to be of such size and shape as to be able to do so. [Origin obscure]

■ **fit′ly** *adv* (**fit′lier; fit′liest**) suitably; well. **fit′ment** *n* an article of furniture or equipment; a fitting; a due (*Shakesp*); something fitted to an end (*Shakesp*). **fit′ness** *n* the state of being suitable or (*esp* referring to health) fit; the average contribution of one allele or genotype to the next generation, compared with that of other alleles or genotypes (*biol*; cf **Darwinian fitness** and **inclusive fitness** below). **fitt′ed** *adj* (of a cover, clothing, etc) made, cut, sewn, etc to fit exactly; (of a carpet) covering the whole of the floor; (of a cupboard, etc) constructed to fit a particular space and attached to, or built into, the wall of a room; (of a room) fully furnished with (matching) fitted cupboards, etc. **fitt′er** *n* a person or thing that fits or makes fit; a person who fits on clothes; a person who assembles or repairs the parts of a machine, etc. **fitt′ing** *adj* fit; appropriate. ◆ *n* anything used in fitting up, *esp* (in *pl*) equipment accessories; a fixture; a device used for supporting or containing a lamp, together with its holder and its shade or reflector (*elec eng*); the work of a fitter; the act or time of trying on an article of clothing so that it can be adjusted to fit the wearer. **fitt′ingly** *adv*. **fitt′ingness** *n*.

❑ **fitness walker** *n* someone who walks for exercise as well as (or instead of) pleasure. **fit′-out** *n* (*obs*) outfit. **fitt′ing-out** *n* a supply of things fit and necessary. **fitting-out basin** or **dock** *n* a dock where a ship is completed after launching. **fitt′ing-room** *n* a room in a clothes shop where customers may try on clothes before deciding whether or not to buy them. **fitt′ing-shop** *n* a shop in which pieces of machinery are fitted together. **fit′-up** *n* temporary, improvised stage and properties (*theatre*); a frame-up or false criminal charge, *esp* by the police (*sl*).

■ **Darwinian fitness** (*biol*) the number of offspring of an individual that live to reproduce in the next generation. **fit for purpose** in suitable condition to carry out its proper function. **fit in** to find enough room or time for (someone or something); to be, or cause to be, in harmony (with). **fit on** to try on; to try a garment on (a person). **fit out** to provide or equip. **fit the bill** to be adequate. **fit up** to provide with fittings; to frame (*sl*). **inclusive fitness** (*biol*) Darwinian fitness, with the addition of those genes that the individual shares with its relatives and that are passed on by them.

fit² /fit/ *n* an attack of illness, *esp* epilepsy; a convulsion or paroxysm; a temporary attack or outburst of anything, eg laughter; a sudden effort or motion; a mood or passing humour; the approach of death (*Spenser*); a painful experience (*Spenser*); a crisis (*obs*). ◆ *vi* to suffer an epileptic fit. ◆ *vt* (*Shakesp*) to wrench or cause to start with a sudden movement. [OE *fitt* a struggle]

■ **fit′ful** *adj* marked by sudden impulses; unpredictably intermittent; spasmodic. **fit′fully** *adv*. **fit′fulness** *n*.

■ **fit of the face** (*obs*) a grimace. **fits and starts** spasmodic and irregular bursts of activity. **have** or **throw a fit** to suffer a fit; to become very angry (*inf*). **in fits** laughing uncontrollably.

fit³, also **fitt, fitte** or **fytte** /fit/ (*archaic*) *n* a song; a division of a poem, a canto; a strain of music. [OE *fitt* a song]

FITA /ˈfēˈtə/ *abbrev*: *Fédération Internationale de Tir à l'Arc* (*Fr*), International Archery Federation.

fitch¹ /fich/ *n* a polecat; polecat fur; a paintbrush of polecat hair; a small hog's-hair brush. [MDu *visse* and OFr *fissle, fissau*, from the root of Du *visse* nasty]

■ **fitch′et** or **fitchew** /fich′ōō/ *n* the polecat or its fur.

fitch² /fich/ *n* vetch; in the Bible (Isaiah 28.25), black cumin (*Nigella sativa*); in the Bible (Ezekiel 4.9), a species of wheat, spelt. [**vetch**]

fitché or **fitchée** /fich′ā/ (*heraldry*) *adj* cut to a point (also **fitch′y**). [Fr *fiché*, pap of *ficher* to fix]

fitt and **fitte** see **fit³**.

fitz- /fits-/ *pfx* son of; used in England, *esp* of the illegitimate sons of kings and princes, as in *Fitzclarence*, etc. [Anglo-Fr *fiz* (Fr *fils*), from L *fīlius*]

FIV *abbrev*: feline immunodeficiency virus.

five /fīv/ *n* the cardinal number next above four; a symbol representing that number (5, v, etc); a set of five things or people; a score of five points, strokes, tricks, etc; an article of a size denoted by 5; a playing card with five pips; the fifth hour after midnight or midday; the age of five years. ◆ *adj* of the number five; five years old. [OE *fīf*; Ger *fünf*; Gothic *fimf*; Welsh *pump*; L *quinque*; Gr *pente, pempe*; Sans *pañca*]

■ **five′fold** *adj* and *adv* in five divisions; five times as much; folded in five thicknesses. **fiv′er** *n* (*inf*) a five-pound note; a five-dollar bill (*N Am*). ❑ **five′-a-day** *n* (the consumption of) the five items of fruit or vegetables considered necessary to a healthy daily diet. **five′-and-dime′** *n* (*US*) a shop selling cheap goods (*orig* costing five or ten cents). **Five Articles** or **Five Points** *n pl* statements of the distinctive doctrines of the Arminians and Calvinists respectively, the former promulgated in 1610, the latter sustained by the Synod of Dort in

1619 (see **Calvinism**). **five′-a-side′** *n* a form of association football with five players on each side, instead of eleven (also *adj*). **five′-bar** *adj* (of a gate) having five bars. **five-day week** *n* a week, five days of which are working days. **five-eighth′** *n* (*rugby, esp Aust* and *NZ*) a stand-off (**second five-eighth** an inside centre, a player positioned on the outside of the five-eighth). **five′finger** or **five′fingers** *n* a name for various plants (cinquefoil, oxlip, etc) that have leaves with five lobes or flowers with five petals; a starfish. **five′-finger** *adj* (of eg a piano exercise) for five fingers. **five Ks** see under **K**. **Five Nations** *n pl* (*hist*) a confederacy of northern Iroquoian peoples, comprising the Cayuga, Mohawk, Oneida, Onondaga and Seneca nations. **five-o'clock shadow** *n* (*inf*) the new growth of hair that becomes noticeable on a man's shaven face in the late afternoon. **five′-parted** *adj* in five parts; divided into five nearly to the base (*bot*). **five′pence** *n* the value of five pennies. **five′penny** *adj*. **five′pins** *n sing* a game with five 'pins', resembling ninepins and tenpins (**five′pin** *adj* as in *fivepin bowling alley*). **fives′-and-threes′** *n* a variety of the game of dominoes. **five′-square** *adj* (*Bible*) regularly pentagonal. **five′-stones** *n sing* the game of dibs or jacks played with five stones.

■ **bunch of fives** (*sl*) the fist. **give someone five** (*sl*) to shake hands, or slap hands above one's head (**high five**) with someone in congratulation or greeting.

fives¹ /fīvz/ (*Shakesp*) *n* same as **vives**.

fives² /fīvz/ *n pl* a ball game similar to squash played with the (gloved) hand (or a bat) in a walled court. [Origin obscure]

■ **Rugby fives** see under **rugby**.

fix /fiks/ *vt* to make firm or fast; to establish; to drive in; to settle; to make or keep permanent, solid, rigid, steady or motionless; to fasten or attach; to put to rights or mend; to arrange or attend to (a matter, sometimes by means of trickery); to prepare; to castrate or spay; to prevent from causing further trouble (*inf*); to get even with (*inf*); to chastise (*inf*). ◆ *vi* to settle or remain permanently; to become firm, stable or permanent. ◆ *n* a difficulty (*inf*); a dilemma (*inf*); the position of an aircraft, a ship, etc as calculated from instrument readings; the establishment of a position by any means; a shot of heroin or other drug (*sl*); a dose or experience of anything seen as or felt to be addictive (*inf*); something fraudulently or covertly arranged (*inf*); a solution, *esp* when expedient or temporary, as in *quick fix* (*inf*). [L *fīgere, fīxus* to fix, prob through LL *fīxāre*]

■ **fix′able** *adj* capable of being fixed. **fix′ate** *vt* to fix or make stable; to direct (the eyes) on an object; to arrest the emotional development of (*psychol*); to preoccupy. ◆ *vi* to become preoccupied. **fixā′ted** *adj*. **fixā′tion** *n* the act of fixing or state of being fixed; steadiness, firmness; a state in which a body does not evaporate; conversion of atmospheric nitrogen into a combined form; emotional arrest of personality; instinctive forces maintaining their earlier channels of gratification; loosely, an abnormal attachment or an obsession; the process whereby biological specimens are chemically preserved for examination. **fix′ative** *n* (*esp photog*) a fixing agent. **fix′ature** *n* a gummy preparation for fixing the hair. **fixed** *adj* settled; not apt to evaporate; steadily directed; fast, lasting, permanent; not varying or subject to alteration; (with *for*) disposed (in terms of); used substantively for fixed stars (*Milton*). **fix′edly** *adv*. **fix′edness** *n*. **fix′er** *n* a fixing agent (*photog*); a person who makes (often illegal) arrangements. **fix′ing** *n* the act or process of making fixed; arrangement; the process of removing unreduced silver halides after development of an emulsion (*image technol*); (in *pl*) adjuncts or trimmings; (in *pl*) equipment. **fix′ity** *n* fixedness. **fix′ive** *adj*. **fix′ture** *n* fixing; a movable thing that has become fastened to land or to a house; a fixed article of furniture; a thing or person permanently established in a place; a fixed or appointed time or event, such as a horse-race. **fix′ure** *n* (*Shakesp*) stability, position or firmness.

❑ **fixed air** *n* the name given by Dr Joseph Black in 1756 to what in 1784 was named by Lavoisier carbonic acid. **fixed assets** *n pl* (*commerce*) long-lived assets such as plant and buildings, brands, processes, patents and financial investments. **fixed capital** see under **capital¹**. **fixed charges** *n pl* overheads such as interest payments, allowance for depreciation, and fixed costs, which do not vary with the volume of business done. **fixed costs** *n pl* overheads such as rent and rates which do not vary with the volume of business done. **fixed idea** *n* a monomania. **fixed income** *n* one which does not increase or decrease, such as income from a fixed-interest investment. **fixed-in′terest** *adj* having an invariable rate of interest. **fixed odds** *n pl* a betting method whereby a stated amount per unit stake is offered for a certain result or combination of results. **fixed oils** *n pl* those which, on the application of heat, do not volatilize without decomposition. **fixed-pen′alty** *adj* of or relating to an offence, such as illegal parking, the penalty for which is invariable and obligatory, eg a fine which may be imposed and paid without the offender appearing in court. **fixed′-price** *adj* (of a menu, contract, etc) having a price that cannot be varied. **fixed′-rate** same as **fixed-interest** above. **fixed satellite** *n* a geostationary satellite. **fixed stars** *n pl* stars which appear always to occupy the same position in the heavens, as opposed to planets.

───
■ words derived from main entry word; ❑ compound words; ■ idioms and phrasal verbs

fixed-wheel bicycle *n* a bicycle in which the pedals are so connected to the back wheel that freewheeling is impossible, and on which only the front wheel has a conventional brake. **fixed-wing aircraft** *n* an aircraft in which the wings are attached to the fuselage, as opposed to eg a helicopter with rotating 'wings' or propellers. **fix'er-upper** *n* (*chiefly US inf*) a house or flat purchased cheaply with the intention of renovating it.

■ **fix on** to single out or decide upon. **fix up** to arrange or make arrangements for; to settle; to put to rights or attend to; to provide (with).

fizgig or **fisgig** /*fiz'gig*/ (*archaic*) *n* a giddy or flirtatious girl; a firework of damp powder; a gimcrack, whimsy or trifle; a harpoon (also **fish'gig**); (**fiz'gig**, also **fizz'gig**) a police informer (*obs Aust sl*). [**gig**[1]]

fizz or **fiz** /*fiz*/ *vi* (**fizz'ing**; **fizzed**) to make a hissing or sputtering sound; to produce bubbles; (also **be fizzing**) to be very angry (*inf*). ◆ *n* a sputtering sound; bubbly quality; a frothy drink, *esp* champagne (*inf*); vivacity. [Formed from the sound]

■ **fizz'er** *n* something which fizzes; anything excellent (*inf*); a disappointment, fiasco (*Aust inf*); a very fast ball in cricket. **fizz'iness** *n*. **fizz'ing** *n* and *adj*. **fizz'le** *vi* to hiss or sputter; to go out with a sputtering sound (often with *out*); to come to nothing, be a fiasco or fail (often with *out*). ◆ *n* an abortive effort. **fizz'y** *adj*.

fizzen and **fizzenless** see **foison**.

FJI *abbrev*: Fellow of the Institute of Journalists; Fiji (IVR).

fjord or **fiord** /*fē'örd* or *fi-örd'*, also *fyörd*/ *n* a long narrow rock-bound inlet. [Norw *fjord*]

FL *abbrev*: Florida (US state); Liechtenstein (ie *Fürstentum Liechtenstein*; IVR).

Fl (*chem*) *symbol*: flerovium.

fl. *abbrev*: floor; florin; *floruit* (*L*), flourished; fluid.

FLA *abbrev*: Fellow of the Library Association (now replaced by **FCLIP**); Finance and Leasing Association.

Fla. *abbrev*: Florida (US state).

flabbergast /*flab'ər-gäst*/ (*inf*) *vt* to stun or confound. [Prob connected with **flabby** and **gast** to astonish]

flabby /*flab'i*/ *adj* soft or yielding, eg of muscles; (of people) having flabby muscles or flesh; overweight; hanging loose; inefficient; feeble. [**flap**]

■ **flab** *n* (*inf*) excess body fat. **flabb'ily** *adv*. **flabb'iness** *n*.

flabellum /*flə-bel'əm*/ *n* (pl **flabell'a**) a fan, traditionally used to drive away flies from the chalice during the celebration of the Eucharist (*RC church*); a fan-like structure (*biol*). [L, a fan]

■ **flabell'ate** *adj* (*biol*) fan-shaped. **flabellation** /*flab-ə-lā'shən*/ *n* the action of fanning. **flabell'iform** *adj*.

flaccid /*flas'id* or *flak'sid*/ *adj* limp; flabby; lax; easily yielding to pressure; soft and weak. [L *flaccidus*, from *flaccus* flabby]

■ **flac'cidly** *adv*. **flac'cidness** or **flaccid'ity** *n*.

flack /*flak*/ (*N Am sl*) *n* a person who handles publicity and public relations; a press agent. ◆ *vt* and *vi* to act as a flack. [Origin uncertain; poss from **flak**]

flacker /*flak'ər*/ (*dialect*) *vi* to flap or flutter. [Cf OE *flacor* fluttering]

flacket /*flak'it*/ (*dialect*) *n* a flask or bottle. [OFr *flasquet*]

flacon /*fla-kõ'*/ *n* a scent bottle, etc. [Fr]

flaff /*flaf*/ (*Scot*) *vi* to flap; to pant. ◆ *n* a flutter of the wings; a puff. [Imit]

■ **flaff'er** *vi* to flutter.

flag[1] /*flag*/ *n* a piece *usu* of bunting or other cloth with a design, used as an emblem for military or naval purposes, signalling, decoration, display, propaganda, etc; a conspicuous sign to mark a position, eg a golf-hole, or to convey information, such as that a taxi is available for hire; a marker; a flagship (*hist*); a bushy tail. ◆ *vi* (**flagg'ing**; **flagged**) to indicate or inform by flag-signals. ◆ *vt* to decorate with flags; to inform by flag-signals; to mark (eg a passage or item in a book) for attention, by means of a bookmark, pen or pencil mark, etc; to draw attention to; to indicate or code (material on computer tape, etc) so that particular items or classes of data may be found or extracted. [Origin unknown; cf Dan *flag*; Du *vlag*, Ger *Flagge*]

■ **flagg'y** *adj* like a banner; spreading, flabby.

□ **flag'-captain** *n* the captain of a flagship. **flag day** *n* a day on which collectors solicit contributions to a charity in exchange for small flags or stickers as badges to secure immunity for the rest of the day; (with *caps*) 14 June, anniversary of the adoption of the Stars and Stripes (*US*). **flag'-lieutenant** *n* an officer in a flagship, corresponding to an aide-de-camp in the army. **flag'man** *n* a person who signals with a flag. **flag of convenience** *n* a foreign flag under which a shipping company registers its tonnage to avoid taxation or other burdens at home. **flag of distress** *n* a flag displayed by a vessel as a signal of distress, *usu* upside down or at half-mast. **flag'-officer** *n* a naval officer privileged to carry a flag denoting his rank of admiral, vice-admiral, rear-admiral or commodore. **flag of truce** *n* a white flag

displayed during a battle when some peaceful communication is desired. **flag'pole**, **flag'staff** or **flag'stick** *n* a pole, etc for displaying a flag. **flag rank** *n* the rank of a flag-officer. **flag'ship** *n* the ship carrying an admiral and flying his flag; anything of great importance or pre-eminence (*fig*; also *adj*). **flag'-wagging** *n* signalling by flag; aggressive patriotism or imperialism (also **flag'-waving**). **flag'-waver** *n*. **flag'-waving** *adj* serving merely to show (superficial) support for or allegiance to eg a nation or a political party.

■ **black**, **red**, **white** and **yellow flag** see under **black**, **red**[1], **white** and **yellow** respectively. **dip the flag** to lower the flag and then hoist it as a token of respect. **flag down** to signal (eg a taxi) to stop. **flag up** to draw attention to. **show**, **carry** or **fly the flag** or **keep the flag flying** to (continue to) show support for or allegiance to one's own country, organization, etc; to put in an appearance or otherwise ensure that one, or the nation, firm, etc one represents, is not overlooked. **strike** or **lower the flag** to pull down the flag as a token of relinquishment of command, or in respect, submission, or surrender.

flag[2] /*flag*/ *vi* (**flagg'ing**; **flagged**) to droop; to flap feebly; to grow languid or spiritless. [Perh OFr *flac*, from L *flaccus*; prob influenced by imit forms, such as **flap**]

■ **flagg'iness** *n*. **flagg'y** *adj* limp or drooping; flabby.

flag[3] /*flag*/ *n* a stone that separates in slabs; a flat paving-stone (also **flag'stone**). ◆ *vt* (**flagg'ing**; **flagged**) to pave with flagstones. [ON *flaga* a slab]

■ **flagg'ing** *n* flagstones; a pavement constructed from them. **flagg'y** *adj*.

flag[4] /*flag*/ *n* an iris; reed-grass (*Bible*). [Ety obscure; cf Du *flag*]

■ **flagg'iness** *n*. **flagg'y** *adj* having many flags.

□ **flag'-basket** *n* a reed basket for tools. **flag iris** *n*. **flag'-worm** *n* a worm or grub bred among flags or reeds.

flagellum /*flə-jel'əm*/ *n* (pl **flagell'a**) a whip or scourge; a long runner (*bot*); a long hair-like extension from the cell surface whose movement is used for locomotion (*biol*). [L *flagellum*, dimin of *flagrum* a whip]

■ **flag'ellant** *adj* scourging. ◆ *n* a person who whips, *esp* himself or herself in religious discipline or sexual gratification. **flag'ellantism** *n*. **Flagellata** /*flaj-ə-lā'tə*/ *n pl* unicellular organisms with flagella. **flag'ellate** *vt* to whip. ◆ *n* any member of the Flagellata. ◆ *adj* having a flagellum or flagella; whiplike. **flag'ellated** *adj*. **flagellā'tion** *n*. **flag'ellator** *n*. **flag'ellatory** *adj*. **flagellif'erous** *adj*. **flagell'iform** *adj*. **flagellōmā'nia** *n* excessive enthusiasm for beating and flogging. **flagellōmā'niac** *n* and *adj*.

flageolet[1] /*flaj-ō-let'*/ *n* a small pale green bean which is a type of kidney bean. [Corruption of Fr *fageolet*; L *faseolus*]

flageolet[2] /*flaj-ō-let'* or *flaj'*/ *n* a small high-pitched flute with two thumb holes. [Fr, dimin of OFr *flageol*, *flajol* a pipe; not L *flauta* flute]

flagitate /*flaj'i-tāt*/ *vt* to entreat or importune. [L *flagitāre*, *-ātum*]

■ **flagitā'tion** *n*.

flagitious /*flə-jish'əs*/ *adj* grossly wicked; guilty of heinous crimes. [L *flāgitiōsus*, from *flāgitium* a disgraceful act, from *flagrāre* to burn]

■ **flagi'tiously** *adv*. **flagi'tiousness** *n*.

flagon /*flag'ən*/ *n* a large lidded jug for wine; a large bottle in which alcohol, *esp* wine or cider, is sold, *specif* one containing two pints or 1.13 litres. [Fr *flacon*, from *flascon*, from LL *flascō*, *-ōnis*; see **flask**]

flagrant /*flā'grənt*/ *adj* notorious; outrageous or conspicuous; burning or raging (*archaic*). [L *flagrāns*, *-antis*, prp of *flagrāre* to burn]

■ **flā'grance** or **flā'grancy** *n*. **flā'grantly** *adv*.

flagrante bello /*flə-gran'tē bel'ō* or *fla-gran'te*/ (*L*) while war is raging.

flagrante delicto /*flə-gran'tē di-lik'tō* or *fla-gran'te dā-lik'tō*/ (*L*) in the very act (literally, while the crime is blazing); in the act of (illicit) sexual intercourse (*inf*).

flagship see under **flag**[1].

flail /*flāl*/ *n* an implement for threshing corn, consisting of a wooden bar (the *swingle*) hinged or tied to a handle; a medieval weapon with a spiked iron swingle. ◆ *vt* to strike with, or as if with, a flail. ◆ *vi* to move like a flail (often with *about*). [OE *fligel*, influenced by OFr *flaiel*, prob from L *flagellum* a scourge]

flair /*flār*/ *n* intuitive discernment; a faculty for nosing out; popularly and loosely, a natural aptitude; stylishness. [Fr, sense of smell, from *flairer* to smell, from LL *flagrāre*, from L *fragrāre* to emit a smell]

flak /*flak*/ *n* anti-aircraft fire (*milit sl*); adverse criticism (*inf*); heated disagreement or dissension. [Initials of Ger *Flieger-* (or *Flug-*) *abwehrkanone* anti-aircraft cannon]

□ **flak jacket** *n* a heavy protective jacket reinforced with metal.

flake[1] /*flāk*/ *n* a small flat scale or layer; a very small loose mass, eg of snow; a spark or detached flame; a flash (*Spenser*); an eccentric, a crazy person (*N Am inf*); cocaine (*sl*). ◆ *vt* to form into flakes; to sprinkle with, or as if with, flakes. ◆ *vi* to come off in flakes. [Perh connected with ON *flōke* flock of wool; OHGer *floccho*]

■ **flak'iness** n. **flak'y** adj formed of, or tending to form, flakes; (of pastry) formed of thin, crumbly layers; stupid, inept, incompetent (inf); crazy, eccentric (US inf). ◆ n (sl) an angry outburst, a fit of temper. ◻ **flake'-white** n the purest white lead for painting, made in the form of scales or plates.
■ **flake out** to collapse from weariness or illness.

flake² /flāk/ n a movable hurdle for fencing; a stage hung over a ship's side for caulking, etc (naut); a frame or rack for storing or drying food. [Cf ON flake; Du vlaak]

flake³ same as **fake²**.

flam¹ /flam/ n a whim (archaic); an idle fancy (archaic); a falsehood; a trick. ◆ vt (**flamm'ing**; **flammed**) to deceive; to get, manage, etc by deception. [Perh **flimflam** or **flamfew**]

flam² see **flawn**.

flam³ /flam/ n a drumbeat in which both sticks strike almost simultaneously. [Prob imit]

flambé /fläm'bā or flä-bā/ adj in cookery, prepared or served with a dressing of flaming liquor, usu brandy (also **flambéed** /fläm'bād/); (of a Chinese ceramic glaze) dense and iridescent with streaky colour effect (usu red and blue) produced by irregular application or uneven firing; decorated with such a glaze. [Fr, pap of flamber to flame or singe]

flambeau /flam'bō/ n (pl **flam'beaux** or **flam'beaus** /-bōz/) a flaming torch; a large candlestick. [Fr, from OFr flambe, from L flamma]

flamboyant /flam-boi'ənt/ adj gorgeously coloured or decorated; (of a person, style, action, etc) ostentatious, colourful or extravagant; late French Gothic (15c–16c) with flame-like tracery (archit); wavy in form. ◆ n (also **flamboy'ante**) a tropical tree of the Caesalpinia family (Poinciana regia) with flame-coloured flowers. [Fr, prp of flamboyer to blaze]
■ **flamboy'ance** or **flamboy'ancy** n. **flamboy'antly** adv.
◻ **flamboy'ant-tree** or **flamboy'ante-tree** n.

flame /flām/ n the visible flickering luminous streams produced by a gaseous matter undergoing combustion; the gleam or blaze of a fire; rage; ardour of temper; vigour of thought; warmth of affection; love or its object, esp in the phrase an old flame; an insulting, rude, or controversial email message (comput). ◆ vi to burn as flame; to break out in passion. ◆ vt to set aflame. ◆ vi and vt (comput) to send a flame (to). [OFr flambe, from L flamma]
■ **flamed** adj (Spenser) inflamed. **flame'less** adj. **flame'let** n a small flame. **flame'out** n the extinction of the flame in a jet engine, causing it to lose power (see **flame out** below). **flam'er** n. **flam'ing** adj blazing; brilliantly red; gaudy; violent; furious; often used intensively or to express irritation, etc (inf). **flam'ingly** adv. **flammabil'ity** n. **flamm'able** adj capable of being set on fire. **flammif'erous** adj producing flame. **flam'y** adj relating to, or like, flame.
◻ **flame'-coloured** adj of the colour of flame, bright reddish-yellow. **flame-grill'** n. **flame-grilled'** adj cooked on a grill over a direct flame, esp produced by solid fuel rather than gas. **flame gun** n a type of flame-thrower used to destroy weeds. **flame'-leaf** n (bot) a Poinciana tree. **flame of the forest** n any of various tropical trees with bright red flowers. **flame'proof** adj treated so as to be non-flammable; (of dishes, pots, etc) able to be used when cooking with direct heat. ◆ vt to make flameproof. **flame'-retardant** adj burning very slowly, if at all. **flame'-thrower** n a weapon of war that releases a powerful jet of burning liquid. **flame'-tree** n a thick-stemmed Australian tree, Brachychiton acerifolium, with glossy leaves and scarlet bell-shaped flowers; applied to various other trees, specif the flamboyant-tree (see under **flamboyant**), the yellow-flowered Acacia farnesiana of SW USA, the scarlet-flowered Butea frondosa of India and Myanmar, and the Nuytsia floribunda of W Australia, which has orange flowers. **flame war** n (comput) an acrimonious exchange of email messages.
■ **fan the flames** to intensify a strong emotion, worsen an already tense situation. **flame out** of a jet engine, to lose power when the flame dies out; to fail dramatically (inf, esp N Am).

flamen /flā'mən/ n (in ancient Rome) a priest serving one particular god. [L flāmen, -inis]
■ **flamin'ical** adj.

flamenco /flä-meng'kō/ n (pl **flamen'cos**) a type of emotionally intense gypsy song, or the dance performed to it, orig from the S Spanish region of Andalusia. [Sp, Flem, gypsy]

flamfew /flam'fū/ (obs) n a fantastic trifle or gewgaw. [Fr fanfelue]

Flamingant /flä-mē-gä'/ n a person who favours the Flemish language or Flemish nationalism. [Fr]

flamingo /flə-ming'gō/ n (pl **flaming'os** or **flaming'oes**) a large tropical or subtropical wading bird of a pink or bright-red colour, with long legs and neck and a downward-curving bill. [Sp flamengo (now flamenco)]

flamm see **flawn**.

flammability and **flammable** see under **flame**.

Flammenwerfer /fläm'ən-ver-fər/ (Ger) n a flame-thrower.

flammiferous see under **flame**.

flammule /flam'ūl/ n a little flame, such as in a picture of a Japanese god. [L flammula, dimin of flamma flame]
■ **flamm'ūlāted** adj ruddy. **flammūla'tion** n flame-like marking.

flan /flan/ n a flat open tart filled with a sweet or savoury mixture; the blank metal disc on which a design is stamped to produce a coin. [**flawn**]

flanch¹ /flanch, flänch, flansh or flänsh/ n a flange; a design formed on each side of a shield by the segment of a circle (heraldry). [Prob related to **flank**]
■ **flanched** adj having a pair of flanches.

flanch² /flanch, flänch, flansh or flänsh/ or **flaunch** /flönch or flönsh/ vi to widen, esp outwards or upwards, to flare (often with out). ◆ vt to cause to slope in towards the top (often with up). [Ety obscure]
■ **flanch'ing** or **flaunch'ing** n the action or state of the verb; (**flaunching**) a sloping piece of cement, eg round the base of a chimney pot.

flanconade /flang-kə-nād'/ (fencing) n a thrust in the flank or side. [Fr, from flanc the side]

flâneur /flä-nær'/ n a person who saunters about, a stroller. [Fr flâner to lounge]
■ **flânerie** /flän-rē/ n idling.

flange /flanj/ n a projecting or raised edge or flank, such as of a wheel or rail, used to give strength or to make a connection or attachment secure. ◆ vi to widen out. ◆ vt to put a flange on. [Perh connected with **flank**]
■ **flanged** adj.

flank /flangk/ n the side of an animal from the ribs to the thigh; a cut of beef from this part of the animal; loosely, the corresponding part of the human body; the side or wing of anything, esp of an army or fleet; a body of soldiers on the right or left extremity. ◆ vt to be on, pass round, attack, threaten or protect the flank of. [Fr flanc]
■ **flank'er** n one of a detachment of soldiers responsible for guarding the flank; a fortification that commands the flank of an attacking force; (also **flank forward** or **wing forward**) either one of the two outside men of the back row of the scrum (rugby). ◆ vt (obs) to defend by flankers; to attack sideways.
■ **do**, **pull** or **work a flanker** (sl, orig milit) to trick, deceive, cheat, etc someone.

flannel /flan'əl/ n a light woollen textile used for clothing; a piece of this or other cloth used for washing or rubbing, now esp a piece of towelling for washing the face, a facecloth; flattery, soft soap, words intended to hide one's ignorance, true opinions, etc (inf); (in pl) trousers, esp of flannel or a similar cloth. ◆ vt to wrap in flannel; to rub with a flannel; to flatter, to soft-soap, to utter flannel to (inf; also vi). [Poss OFr flaine blanket, or Welsh gwlanen, from gwlan wool]
■ **flannelette'** n a cotton imitation of flannel, widely used to make bed linen, nightwear, etc. **flann'elled** adj. **flann'elly** adj. **flann'en** n (obs or dialect) flannel.
◻ **flann'elboard** or **flann'elgraph** n a display board covered with flannel or felt, on which letters, pictures, etc backed with material will stick when pressed against it. **flann'el-flower** n an Australian perennial plant with daisy-like flowers.

flap /flap/ n the movement of a broad object hanging loose, or the action or sound of it striking a surface; anything broad and flexible hanging loose, such as material covering an opening; skin or flesh detached from the underlying part for covering and growing over the end of an amputated limb; a fluster, a panic (inf); any surface attached to the wing of an aircraft which can be adjusted in flight to alter the lift as a whole; an 'r' sound produced by a single light tap of the tongue against the alveolar ridge or uvula (phonetics). ◆ vt (**flapp'ing**; **flapped**) to beat or move with a flap; to fluster. ◆ vi to move, as of wings; to hang like a flap; to get into a panic or fluster (inf). [Prob imit]
■ **flapp'able** adj (inf) not unflappable, easily perturbed, agitated, irritated, flustered, etc. **flapp'er** n a person or thing that flaps; a flipper (biol); a young wild duck or partridge; a girl nearing womanhood (obs sl); in the 1920s, a flighty young woman, esp one ostentatiously unconventional in dress or behaviour (sl). **flapp'erhood** n. **flapp'erish** adj. **flapp'ing** adj moving with or like a flap; (of or relating to races, animals, etc) not subject to Jockey Club or National Hunt Committee regulations (horse-racing) or not registered under the National Greyhound Racing Club (greyhound racing). ◆ n the action of the verb; racing at flapping meetings (horse-racing or greyhound racing). **flapp'y** adj (inf) in a state of nervousness or panic; in a fluster.
◻ **flap'-dragon** n a game in which small edible items such as raisins are snatched from burning brandy, and swallowed. **flap'-eared** adj (Shakesp). **flap'jack** n a kind of broad, flat pancake (Shakesp and US); a biscuit or cake made with rolled oats and syrup; a flat face powder compact; an apple-puff (dialect). **flap'-mouthed** adj. **flap'track** or **flapping track** n a racetrack for flapping.

flare /flār/ vi to spread; to widen out like a bell; to burn with a glaring, unsteady light; to glitter or flash; to blaze up, literally or in anger (with *up*). ◆ vt to display glaringly; to dispose of (superfluous gas or oil) by burning (with *off*; *chem eng*). ◆ n a widening out, as in the bell of a horn, a bowl, or a skirt; an unsteady glare; an unshaded flame; a sudden blaze; a torch; a signalling light; (the flame or light produced by) a device composed of combustible material, activated to give warning, illumination, etc or to signal for help, eg at sea; a device for the safe disposal of superfluous gas, oil, etc by burning in the open (*chem eng*); a solar flare (qv under **solar¹**); undesirable extra light in a photographic image caused by reflection within the camera. [Poss connected with Norw *flara* to blaze]
■ **flares** n pl trousers that widen (greatly) below the knee, *orig* popular in the late 1960s and early 1970s. **flār'ing** adj. **flā'ringly** adv. **flā'ry** adj.
❑ **flare'-out** n (*aeronautics*) the controlled approach path of aircraft immediately prior to landing. **flare path** n a path lit up to enable an aircraft to land or take off when natural visibility is insufficient. **flare stack** n (*chem eng*) a tall chimney with an automatic igniter at the top, for the safe disposal of superfluous gas, etc by burning. **flare star** n a star, *usu* a red dwarf, which has a periodical sudden and unpredictable increase in brightness. **flare'-up** n a sudden bursting into flame; a sudden outbreak of violence, anger, etc.

flaser /flä'zər/ (*geol*) n irregular streaky lenticular structure developed in metamorphic rocks. [Ger, streak]

flash¹ /flash/ n a momentary gleam of light; a sudden, short-lived flare or flame; (the momentary illumination from) a flashbulb or flashgun (*photog*); a sudden burst, eg of merriment; a moment or instant; a fleeting glimpse or exposure; a sudden rush of water; a board for directing or modifying a stream of water; a bright garter or ribbon worn on the hose with knickerbockers or kilt, a small portion showing below the part folded over; a distinctive mark on a uniform; a sticker or overprinted label on a piece of merchandise advertising a reduction in price, etc; a brief news announcement; in a film, a scene inserted by way of explanation or comment, *esp* a scene of the past, a flashback; vulgar ostentation (*inf*); a thin surplus piece of metal at the sides of a forging or casting, or a similar extrusion in other materials; excess material forced out of a mould; (**Flash®**) a computer program for viewing animated images on the Internet. ◆ adj sudden, quick; showy; vulgar; of, like, or relating to criminals (*sl*); fashionable (*archaic*). ◆ vi to burst out, as a sudden light (*lit* and *fig*); to emit flashes of light; to sparkle brilliantly; to blaze out; to break out into intellectual brilliance; to burst out into violence; to move like a flash; to expose oneself indecently in public (*sl*). ◆ vt to cause to flash; to expand (eg blown glass) into a disc; to send by some startling or sudden means; to show briefly; to display ostentatiously (often with *about* or *around*). [Prob imit; cf Swed dialect *flasa* to blaze]
■ **flash'er** n a person or thing that flashes; a device for turning off and on lights eg in advertising, warning, etc signs; the signs themselves; (on a vehicle) a direction-indicator; a person in the habit of indecently exposing himself or herself in public (*sl*). **flash'ily** adv. **flash'iness** n. **flash'ing** n the act of blazing; a sudden burst, eg of water; (a method of producing) irregular colouring of bricks (by periodically stopping air supply in burning them, or other means); a thin metal strip put over a junction between roof tiles, slates, etc to make it watertight; the practice of indecently exposing oneself in public (*sl*). ◆ adj emitting flashes; sparkling. **flash'y** adj dazzling for a moment; showy but empty; vapid (*Milton*); gaudy; tawdry.
❑ **flash'back** n (in a film, novel, etc) a scene of the past, inserted as comment or explanation; an echo of the past; a recurrence of the effect of a hallucinogenic drug, *esp* LSD. ◆ vi to experience a flashback. **flash blindness** n blindness caused by the flash of the explosion of a powerful bomb, etc. **flash'board** n one of a set of boards set up at the sides of a water channel to deepen it. **flash'bulb** n an oxygen-filled electric bulb in which aluminium or other foil or filament may be fired to provide a brilliant flash, *esp* for illuminating a photographic subject. **flash burn** n one sustained as the result of exposure to a flash of intense heat, eg from a nuclear explosion. **flash card** n a card on which a picture or word is printed or written, to be shown briefly to a child as an aid to learning; one of a set of large brightly-coloured cards each held up by an individual eg in a sports stadium and together forming a picture or message. **flash chip** see **flash memory** below. **flash'cube** n (*photog*) a plastic cube containing four flashbulbs, rotated as the film is wound on. **flash drive** n (*comput*) a portable storage device that can be connected to a computer through a serial port. **flash fiction** n fiction in the form of very short stories. **flash fire** n a sudden extensive (increase in) fire caused eg by flash-over. **flash flood** n a sudden, severe, brief flood caused by a heavy rainstorm. **flash flooding** n. **flash forward** n (in a film, novel, etc) a scene of the future, inserted as comment or explanation; a vision of the future. **flash'-forward** vi to shift one's train of thought to a later time. **flash'-freeze** vt to freeze very quickly. **flash'-frozen** adj. **flash'gun** n a device holding and firing a flashbulb.

flash Harry n (*inf*) an ostentatiously flashy or showy person. **flash'-house** n (*obs*) a brothel. **flash'light** n a light that flashes periodically; light produced by flashbulbs, used to take photographs; an electric torch (*esp N Am*). **flash memory** or **flash chip** n a form of non-volatile computer memory which can be erased and rewritten electrically. **flash mob** n a group of people who arrange to assemble briefly in a public place to perform some activity, often of a humorous or surreal nature. **flash'-over** n an electric discharge over the surface of an insulator (*elec eng*); instant combustion of material that has reached a high temperature (in a burning building, etc) as soon as oxygen reaches it. **flash paper** n a form of nitrocellulose popular in magic tricks and theatrical effects for its properties of burning very quickly and brightly and leaving no ash. **flash photolysis** n the brief exposure of a gas to intense light in order to study the photochemical reactions of its constituents. **flash'point** n the temperature at which a liquid gives off enough flammable vapour to ignite when a light is applied to it; a point in the development of a tense situation when violent action takes place; a place in the world where an outbreak of hostilities may occur at any time as a result of tension. **flash ROM** n (*comput*) ROM that can be updated. **flash tube** n a gas-filled tube that produces a brilliant flash when current is passed through it, used for photographic illumination.
■ **flash in the pan** see under **pan¹**.

flash² /flash/ (*obs* or *dialect*) n a pool, pond or marshy place. [Onomatopoeic; perh infl by Fr *flache* a hollow or pool]

flask /fläsk/ n a narrow-necked container for liquids; a bottle; a *usu* flat pocket-bottle; a vacuum flask (qv); a moulding box of wood, cast iron or pressed steel for holding the mould in which a casting is made; a lead case for storing or transporting radioactive sources (also **cask** or **coffin**); a container for the transport of irradiated nuclear fuel (also **cask** or **coffin**); a horn or metal vessel for carrying powder. [OE *flasce*; Ger *Flasche*; prob from LL *flascō*, from L *vasculum* a flask]
■ **flask'et** n (*hist*) a dish in which food is served; a basket (*Spenser*).

flat /flat/ adj (**flatt'er**; **flatt'est**) smooth; level; lacking points of prominence or interest; shallow; spread out; monotonous; uniform; fixed, unvarying; exact; vapid, no longer brisk or sparkling; defeated; failing in effect; dejected; downright, out-and-out, sheer; (of drink) having lost all effervescence; (of feet) having little or no arch; (of shoes) not having a raised heel; low relative to the semitone above (*music*); below the right pitch (*music*); having flats in the key-signature (*music*); voiced (*phonetics*); (of a battery) dead, unable to generate; (of paint) matt, not glossy. ◆ n a level part; a plain; (often in pl) an area of land covered by shallow water; something broad; a storey or floor of a house, *esp* one, or part of one, used as a separate residence; the floor of a particular compartment (*naut*); a flat piece of scenery slid or lowered onto the stage (*theatre*); an insipid passage (*music*); a simpleton or dupe (*inf*); a character (w) that lowers a note a semitone (*music*); a note so lowered (*music*); a punctured tyre (*inf*); (in pl) flat shoes (*inf*). ◆ adv in or to a flat position; evenly; too low in pitch; without qualification; exactly (used in giving time taken for eg a race). ◆ vi (**flatt'ing**; **flatt'ed**) (*Aust* and *NZ*) to live in a flat (together). [ON *flatr* flat]
■ **flat'let** n a small flat of two or three rooms. **flat'ling**, **flat'lings** or **flat'long** adv (*Spenser* or *Shakesp*) with the flat side; flat side on; not edgewise; prostrate. **flat'ly** adv. **flat'ness** n. **flatt'ed** adj made flat (*obs*); divided into flats. **flatt'en** vt to knock flat; to knock to the ground (*inf*); to knock out (*inf*); to amaze (*inf*). ◆ vi to become flat; (with *out*) to return to a horizontal position. **flatt'ing** n painting leaving a non-glossy finish. **flatt'ish** adj somewhat flat. **flatt'y** n (*inf*) a flat object, *esp* a light flat shoe. **flat'ways** or **flat'wise** adj or adv with or on the flat side.
❑ **flat'back** n a pottery figure with a flat back, designed to stand on a mantelpiece, etc and so be viewed only from the front. **flat'bed**, **flatbed lorry** or (*esp N Am*) **flatbed truck** n a lorry with a flat sideless platform for its body. **flatbed scanner** n (*comput*) an apparatus which has a flat sheet of glass onto which documents are placed for scanning by a light beam. **flat'boat** n a large flat-bottomed boat for transporting goods on a river, canal, etc. **flat'bread** n bread in flat *usu* unleavened loaves. **flat cap** n a low-crowned hat worn by London citizens in the 16c and 17c; hence, a London citizen or apprentice; a cloth cap, an unstiffened cap of wool or other soft cloth, with a peak, widely regarded as a symbol of the working-class man. **flat'car** n (*N Am*) a railway freight wagon without roof or sides. **flat-chest'ed** adj having small breasts. **flat-earth'er** n a person who maintains that the earth is flat. **flat file** n (*comput*) a file without hypertext links. **flat'fish** n a marine fish that habitually lies on one side, and has an unsymmetrical flat body, eg flounder, turbot, etc. **flat'-foot** n a condition in which the arch of the instep is flattened; a policeman (*derog sl*). **flat'-footed** adj having flat feet; resolute (*US*); ponderous (*inf*); unimaginative (*inf*); uninspired (*inf*); unprepared (*N Am*). **flat-foot'edness** n. **flat'head** adj having an artificially flattened head; (with *cap*) of or designating a Native American people of Montana (once mistakenly believed to practise flattening children's skulls, as did the neighbouring Chinook;

also *n*). ◆ *n* (*US sl*) a person of low intelligence; any of various species of edible flat-skulled fish of the Pacific and Indian Oceans. **flat'iron** *n* an old-fashioned iron for pressing clothes, heated on a stove, etc. **flat'land** *n* a plain. **flat'line** *vi* to generate a non-oscillating reading on a heart monitor and hence be dead; (eg of shares) to remain at a constant value. **flat'liner** *n*. **flat'mate** *n* a person with whom one shares a flat. **flat'pack** *n* an item of furniture or equipment sold in a flat pack for the purchaser to assemble. **flat-panel** see **flat-screen** below. **flat race** *n* a race over open or clear ground, without jumps. **flat racing** *n*. **flat rate** *n* a fixed uniform rate (eg of charge or payment). **flat'-screen** or **flat'-panel** *adj* denoting a television system or computer screen using a flat-faced cathode ray tube to produce a sharper and better defined picture. **flat'share** *n* the practice of sharing a flat by two or more tenants. **flat spin** *n* rotation in a horizontal plane about a vertical axis; confused excitement (*inf*). **flat tyre** *n* a punctured tyre. **flat'ware** *n* domestic cutlery (*N Am*); plates and saucers. **flat white** *n* a white coffee made by adding steamed milk to a shot of espresso. **flat'worm** *n* a tapeworm or other member of the Platyhelminthes. **flat'-wo'ven** *adj* (of a rug or carpet) woven with no pile. ■ **flat broke** (*inf*) having no money whatsoever. **flat out** at full speed; using every effort. **flatten out** to bring (an aeroplane) into a horizontal position. **that's flat** I tell you plainly. **the flat** flat racing.

flatter /flat'ər/ *vt* to treat with insincere praise and servile attentions, *esp* in order to gain some advantage; to please with false hopes or undue praise; to overpraise; to represent over-favourably; to coax; to gratify. [Connected with OFr *flater* (Fr *flatter*); Gmc; cf ON *flathra*] ■ **flatt'erer** *n*. **flatt'ering** *adj*. **flatt'eringly** *adv*. **flatt'erous** *adj* (*archaic*) flattering. **flatt'erously** *adv* (*archaic*). **flatt'ery** *n* exaggerated or insincere praise.

flatus /flā'təs/ *n* (pl **fla'tuses**) a puff of wind or blast; a breath; gas generated in the stomach or intestines. [L *flātus*, *-ūs* a blowing, from *flāre* to blow] ■ **flatulence** /flat'ū-ləns/ or **flat'ulency** *n* distension of the stomach or bowels by gases formed during digestion; windiness; emptiness of utterance; pretentiousness. **flat'ulent** *adj*. **flat'ulently** *adv*. **flat'ūous** *adj*.

flaught[1] /flöt or (*Scot*) flöhht/ *n* a flight or a flapping. [Related to **flight**] ■ **flaugh'ter** *vi* to flutter or flicker.

flaught[2] /flöt or (*Scot*) flöhht/ *n* a flake (of snow); a skin or hide; a tuft (of hair, wool, etc); a gust; a flash (of lightning); a spark; a turf. ◆ *vt* to strip or skin; to card (wool). [Cf **flake**[1], **flaw**[2], **flay**[1]] ■ **flaugh'ter** *vi* to cut turfs, etc. ◆ *n* a paring of turf; a spade (**flaugh'ter-spade**) for cutting turfs.

flaunch a variant of **flanch**[2].

flaune see **flawn**.

flaunt /flönt/ *vt* to display ostentatiously; to show off. ◆ *vi* to wave in the wind; to move or wave ostentatiously; to have a gaudy or saucy appearance. ◆ *n* (*Shakesp*) anything displayed for show. [Prob Scand] ■ **flaunt'er** *n*. **flaunt'ing** or **flaunt'y** *adj*. **flaunt'ingly** *adv*.

flautist /flö'tist/ or (*esp US*) **flutist** /floo'tist/ *n* a flute player. [Ital *flautista*]

flava /flā'və/ (*sl*) *n* a special style, flavour or feeling. [Altered spelling of **flavour**]

flavescent /flə- or flā-ves'ənt/ *adj* yellowish or turning yellow. [L *flāvēscēns*, *-entis*, prp of *flāvēscere* to become yellow, from *flāvus* yellow]

Flavian /flā'vi-ən/ *adj* of or relating to *Flavius* Vespasian and his sons Titus and Domitian, known collectively as the Flavian emperors of Rome (69–96AD).

flavin /flā'vin/ or **flavine** /flā'vēn/ *n* a yellow dye made from the bark of quercitron, a N American oak; any of various antiseptic substances, of which acriflavine is one. [L *flāvus* yellow] ■ **flavone** /flā'vōn/ *n* a crystalline compound occurring in certain plants, eg primroses; any of a class of yellow pigments derived from this. **flā'vonoid** *n* a secondary metabolite of plants, occurring as pigments, insecticides, etc. **flavopro'tein** *n* a protein which serves as an electron carrier in the electron transfer chain.

flavivirus /flā-vi-vī'rəs/ *n* a virus of the Flaviridae family, which includes the virus responsible for yellow fever. [L *flavus* yellow, and **virus**]

flavour or (*US*) **flavor** /flā'vər/ *n* that quality in food and drink perceived by the mouth, the joint response of the senses of taste and smell; the pleasantness or degree of this quality; a smack or relish; characteristic quality or atmosphere (*fig*); (in particle physics) any of the five, or probably six, types of quark. ◆ *vt* to impart flavour to. [OFr *flaur*; prob influenced by **savour**] ■ **flā'vorous** *adj*. **flā'vourful** or (*US*) **flā'vorful** *adj*. **flā'vouring** or (*US*) **flā'voring** *n* any substance used to give a flavour to food.

flā'vourless or (*US*) **flā'vorless** *adj*. **flā'voursome** or (*US*) **flā'vorsome** *adj*.

□ **flavour** or (*US*) **flavor enhancer** *n* a chemical substance added to food to intensify its flavour, eg monosodium glutamate. ■ **flavour** or (*US*) **flavor of the week**, **month**, etc the favourite person or thing at a given time.

flaw[1] /flö/ *n* a break or crack; a defect; a flake, fragment or splinter (*Shakesp*). ◆ *vt* to crack or break; to make defective. [ON *flaga* a slab] ■ **flawed** *adj*. **flaw'less** *adj*. **flaw'y** *adj*.

flaw[2] /flö/ *n* a gust of wind; a sudden rush; an outburst of passion; uproar. [Cf Du *vlaag*, Swed *flaga*]

flawn or **flaune** /flön/, **flam** or **flamm** /flam/ (*archaic*) *n* a custard; a pancake. [OFr *flaon*, from LL *flado*, *-ōnis*, from OHGer *flado*]

flax /flaks/ *n* the fibres of the plant *Linum*, which are woven to make linen cloth; the plant itself. [OE *flæx* (WSax *fleax*); Ger *Flachs*] ■ **flax'en** *adj* made of or resembling flax; (*esp* of hair) light yellow. **flax'y** *adj* like flax; of a light colour. □ **flax'-bush** or **flax-lil'y** *n* a New Zealand plant (genus *Phormium*) of the lily family, yielding a valuable fibre, **New Zealand flax**. **flax'-comb** *n* a toothed instrument or hackle for cleaning the fibres of flax. **flax'-dresser** *n* a person who prepares flax for the spinner by the successive processes of rippling, retting, grassing, breaking, and scutching. **flax'-mill** *n* a mill for making flax into linen. **flax'seed** *n* linseed. **flax'-wench** *n* (*hist*) a woman or girl who spins flax. ■ **purging flax** a small wild species of flax (*Linum catharticum*).

flay[1] /flā/ *vt* (**flay'ing**; **flayed**) to strip off the skin from; to flog; to subject to savage criticism. [OE *flēan*; ON *flā* to skin] ■ **flay'er** *n*. □ **flay'-flint** *n* (*archaic*) a skinflint.

flay[2] see **fley**.

flea /flē/ *n* any wingless, very agile, parasitic, bloodsucking insect of the order Siphonaptera. [OE *flēah*; cf Ger *Floh*, Du *vloo*] ■ **flea'some** *adj*. □ **flea'-bag** *n* (*sl*) a sleeping bag; a distasteful place, *esp* used of lodgings; a scruffy, apparently flea-bitten, old woman or animal (*inf*). **flea'-bane** *n* a name for various composite plants (*Erigeron*, *Pulicaria*, etc) whose strong smell is said to drive away fleas. **flea'-beetle** *n* a jumping beetle that infests various vegetables, eg turnips and cabbages. **flea'-bite** *n* the bite of a flea; a small mark caused by the bite; a trifle, an only slight inconvenience (*fig*). **flea'-bitten** *adj* bitten by fleas; shabby, badly looked after; mean (*fig*); having small reddish spots on a lighter background, *esp* of horses. **flea circus** *n* a show of performing fleas. **flea collar** *n* a specially impregnated collar worn by domestic animals to deter or kill fleas. **flea market** *n* (*inf*) a shop, collection of stalls, etc selling second-hand goods, *orig esp* clothes. **flea'pit** *n* (*inf*) a shabby public building, *esp* a cinema, supposedly infested with vermin. **flea'wort** *n* any of several European and Eurasian plants, some of which were formerly used to drive away fleas. ■ **a flea in one's ear** a stinging rebuff or rejoinder.

fleadh /flä/ *n* a festival of Irish traditional music, dancing, etc. [Ir]

fleam /flēm/ *n* an instrument for bleeding diseased cattle. [OFr *flieme* (Fr *flamme*), from Gr *phlebotomon* a lancet, from *phleps*, *phlebos* a vein, and *tomē* a cut]

flèche /flesh/ *n* a spire; a slender spire rising from the intersection of the nave and transepts in some large churches (*archit*); a parapet with two faces forming a salient angle at the foot of a glacis or slope (*fortif*); a point on a backgammon board. [Fr, arrow]

fléchette or **flechette** /flā-shet'/ *n* a steel dart dropped or thrown from an aeroplane, *esp* in World War I; a dart fired from a gun. [Fr, dart, dimin of *flèche* arrow]

fleck /flek/ *n* a spot or speckle; a little bit of a thing. ◆ *vt* (also **fleck'er**) to spot, streak or speckle. [ON *flekkr* a spot; Ger *Fleck*, Du *vlek*] ■ **flecked** *adj* spotted or dappled. **fleck'less** *adj* without a spot or spots.

flection a less common spelling of **flexion**.

fled /fled/ pat and pap of **flee**[1].

fledge /flej/ *vt* to provide with feathers or wings; to bring up (a young bird) until it is ready to fly. ◆ *vi* to acquire feathers for flying. ◆ *adj* (*Milton*) fledged. [ME *fligge*, *flegge*, from an assumed OE (Kentish) *flecge*; cf OE *unflycge* unfledged; see **fly**] ■ **fledged** *adj*. **fledg'ling** or **fledge'ling** *n* a bird just fledged; a very immature or inexperienced person; a recently formed organization, etc (also *fig*). ◆ *adj* young or inexperienced; new, recently formed. **fledg'y** *adj* (*Keats*) feathery.

flee[1] /flē/ *vi* (**flee'ing**; **fled**) to run away, eg from danger; to disappear. ◆ *vt* to keep at a distance from; to run away from or leave hurriedly. [OE *flēon*; Ger *fliehen*; not related to *fly*, but influenced by it, the *f* representing an earlier *th*] ■ **flē'er** *n*.

flee[2] /flē/ n and vi Scots form of **fly**.

fleece /flēs/ n a sheep's coat of wool; the wool shorn from a sheep at one time; anything like a fleece in appearance or texture; a garment of fluffy acrylic thermal fabric worn like a jacket or pullover. ◆ vt to shear; to plunder; to charge (a person) exorbitantly (inf); to cover with or as if with wool. [OE *flēos*; Du *vlies*, Ger *Fliess*, now *Vlies*]
■ **fleeced** adj having a fleece. **fleece'less** adj. **fleec'er** n (inf) a person who strips, plunders or charges exorbitantly. **fleec'y** adj woolly; like a fleece in appearance or texture.
❑ **fleece'-wool** n the wool cut from a sheep at any of its clippings subsequent to its first, or yearling, clipping.

fleech /flēch/ (Scot) vt and vi to flatter, coax or beg. [Origin obscure]
■ **fleech'ing** or **fleech'ment** n.

fleer[1] /flēr/ (literary) vi to make wry faces in contempt; to jeer. ◆ vt to mock. ◆ n mockery; a gibe. [Cf Norw *flira*, Swed *flissa* to titter]
■ **fleer'er** n. **fleer'ing** n and adj. **fleer'ingly** adv.

fleer[2] see under **flee**[1].

fleet[1] /flēt/ n a number of ships, aircraft, motor cars, etc owned by the same company or otherwise associated; a navy; a division of a navy under an admiral. [OE *flēot* a ship, from *flēotan* to float; connected with Du *vloot* and Ger *Flotte*]
❑ **Fleet Air Arm** n the airborne forces of the Royal Navy.

fleet[2] /flēt/ adj swift (literary); nimble (literary); transient (obs). [Prob ON *fliótr* swift; but ult cognate with **fleet**[3]]
■ **fleet'ly** adv. **fleet'ness** n.
❑ **fleet'-foot** adj (Shakesp) nimble or swift of foot. **fleet'footed** adj.

fleet[3] /flēt/ vi to flit or pass swiftly (literary); to float (obs); to flow (Spenser). ◆ vt (Shakesp) to cause to pass quickly. ◆ adj (dialect) shallow. [OE *flēotan* to float]
■ **fleet'ing** adj passing quickly; transient; temporary. **fleet'ingly** adv.

fleet[4] /flēt/ n (dialect) a shallow creek, bay, brook or drain, as in *Northfleet*, *Fleet-ditch*, etc. [OE *flēot* an inlet]
❑ **Fleet Prison** or **the Fleet** n (hist) a London jail near the Fleet river, in use until 1842, notorious as a place of confinement for debtors, and in which clandestine marriages were solemnized until 1754 by **Fleet parsons**, broken-down clergymen imprisoned for debt. **Fleet Street** n journalism or its ways and traditions, from the street in London in which many newspaper offices were formerly situated.

fleg /fleg/ (Scot) n a fright. ◆ vt to frighten. [OE *flecgan* to put to flight]

flehmen /flā'mən/ or **flehmen reaction** /rē-ak'shən/ (animal behaviour) n a response to a stimulus in some mammals, esp felines, taking the form of a grimace in which air is sucked in, allowing trace quantities of chemicals, esp pheromones, to be detected by an accessory olfactory organ in the roof of the mouth. [Coined by Karl-Max Schneider (1887–1955), German zoologist]

fleme /flēm/ (Scot) vt (pap and pat **flēm'it**) to put to flight. [OE *flieman*]

Flemish /flem'ish/ adj of or belonging to the Flemings, or to Flanders. ◆ n the Flemings as a people; one of the two languages of Belgium, virtually identical with Dutch. ◆ vt (without cap; naut) to flemish down. [Du *Vlaamsch*]
■ **Flem'ing** n a native of Flanders; a Flemish-speaking Belgian.
❑ **Flemish bond** n a bricklayer's bond of alternate headers and stretchers in every course (cf **English bond**). **Flemish coil** n (naut) a flat coil of rope with the end in the centre. **Flemish school** n a school of painting formed by the brothers Van Eyck, reaching its height in Rubens, Van Dyck and Teniers. **Flemish stitch** n a stitch used in making certain kinds of point-lace.
▨ **flemish down** (naut) to stow (a rope) in a Flemish coil.

flench /flench/, **flense** /flens/ or **flinch** /flinch/ vt to cut up the blubber of (eg a whale); to flay. [Dan *flense*]

flerovium /fli-rō'vi-əm/ n an artificially produced radioactive transuranic element (symbol Fl; atomic no 114). [Named after the *Flerov* Laboratory in Russia, where it was discovered]

flesh /flesh/ n muscular tissue; all the living substance of the body of similar composition to muscle; the soft substance that covers the bones of animals; the bodies of animals and (sometimes) birds, but not fish, used as food; the body, not the soul; animals, or animal nature; human bodily nature; humankind; kindred; one's own family; bodily appetites; excess weight; the soft substance of fruit or vegetables, esp the part fit to be eaten. ◆ vt to reward with flesh; to train to have an appetite for flesh (esp dogs for hunting); to inure or harden (eg to warfare or killing); to use on flesh (eg a sword); to use for the first time; to gratify with fleshly indulgence; to put flesh upon or fatten; to scrape flesh from. [OE *flǣsc*; cognate forms in all Gmc languages; Ger *Fleisch*, etc]
■ **fleshed** /flesht/ adj having flesh; fat. **flesh'er** n an instrument for scraping hides; a butcher (esp Scot). **flesh'hood** n (Elizabeth Barrett Browning) the state of being in the flesh. **flesh'iness** n. **flesh'ings** n pl actors' flesh-coloured tights. **flesh'less** adj without flesh; lean. **flesh'liness** n. **flesh'ling** n a sensualist. **flesh'ly** adj corporeal; carnal;

not spiritual. ◆ adv carnally. **flesh'ment** n (Shakesp) the act of fleshing or initiating; excitement arising from success. **flesh'y** adj of or relating to flesh; fat; pulpy; plump.
❑ **flesh'-broth** n broth made by boiling meat. **flesh'-brush** n a brush used for rubbing the skin to stimulate circulation. **flesh'-colour** n the normal colour of the skin of a member of a white-skinned race. **flesh'-coloured** adj. **flesh'-eater** n. **flesh'-fly** n a fly (esp *Sarcophaga*) whose larvae feed on damaged flesh. **flesh'-hook** n a hook for lifting meat from a pot. **flesh'-market** n a market where meat is sold. **flesh'-meat** n flesh of animals used for food. **flesh'monger** n a person who deals in flesh; a whoremonger (Shakesp); a procurer, pimp or slave-dealer. **flesh pot** n high living (usu in pl); a place where entertainment of a sexual nature is on offer, eg a striptease club; a city known to provide an abundance of this kind of entertainment; a pot or vessel in which meat is cooked (hist); abundance of flesh (obs). **flesh'-pottery** n (literary) sumptuous living. **flesh'-pressing** see press flesh under **press**[1]. **flesh'-tint** n a tint or colour that represents the normal colour of the skin of a member of a white-skinned race. **flesh'worm** n (archaic) a worm or maggot that feeds on flesh. **flesh wound** n a wound not reaching beyond the flesh.
■ **an arm of flesh** (Bible) human strength or help. **flesh and blood** bodily or human nature. **flesh out** to give substance to or elaborate on (an idea, etc). **in flesh** in good condition; fat. **in the flesh** in bodily life, alive; incarnate; in person, actually present. **make someone's flesh creep** to arouse a feeling of horror in someone. **one flesh** (relig) united in marriage. **one's own flesh and blood** one's own relations. **pound of flesh** see under **pound**[1]. **press flesh** see under **press**[1]. **proud-flesh** see under **proud**.

fletch /flech/ vt to feather (an arrow). [Fr *flèche* an arrow, OFr *flecher* a fletcher]
■ **fletch'er** n a person who makes arrows. **fletch'ing** n the feathers of an arrow.

fletton /flet'ən/ n a type of brick made near *Fletton* in Cambridgeshire, of a mottled yellow and pink colour, with sharp arrises or edges.

fleur /flær/ (Fr) n a flower.
■ **fleuret** /floor'ət/ n an ornament like a small flower (also **fleurette** /flæ-ret'/); /-et'/ a fencing foil. **fleuron** /flæ-rɔ̃'/ n a flower-like ornament, in architecture, printing, etc. **fleury** /floo'ri/ adj (heraldry) having fleurs-de-lis (also **flo'ry** /flö'ri/).
■ **fleur de coin** /kwē/ mint condition of a coin.

fleur-de-lis or **fleur-de-lys** /flær-də-lē'/ or -lēs'/ n (pl **fleurs-de-lis** or **fleurs-de-lys** /flær-/) the iris; an ornament and heraldic design of disputed origin (an iris, three lilies, etc), borne by the kings of France. —Also **flower delice**, **flower-delice**, **flower-de-luce**, **flower deluce** or **flower-deluce**. [Fr; *lis* being OFr *liz*, from L *lilium* lily]

flew[1] /floo/ pat of **fly**; informally used for **fled** (pat).

flew[2] /floo/ n the pendulous upper lip of a bloodhound or similar dog (usu in pl). [Ety unknown]
■ **flewed** adj (Shakesp).

flew[3] see **flue**[3].

flex /fleks/ vt and vi to bend; to contract (a muscle). ◆ n a bending; a flexible cord or line, esp of insulated electrical cable. [L *flectere*, *flexum* to bend]
■ **flexibil'ity** n. **flex'ible** adj easily bent; pliant; adaptable; docile. **flex'ibleness** n (rare). **flex'ibly** adv. **flex'ile** /-īl/ or (esp N Am) -əl/ adj flexible. **flexion** /flek'shən/ n a bend; a fold; the action of a flexor muscle; inflexion (grammar). **flexograph'ic** adj. **flexog'raphy** n (Gr *graphein* to write) (printed matter, esp on plastic, produced by) a method of rotary printing using flexible rubber plates and spirit-based inks. **flex'or** n a muscle that bends a joint, opp to extensor. **flex'ūose** or **flex'ūous** adj full of windings and turnings; undulating. **flexural** /flek'shər-əl/ adj. **flex'ure** n a bend or turning; the curving of a line or surface (maths); the bending of loaded beams; obsequious bowing (Shakesp).
❑ **flex'-fuel** n a fuel consisting of a mixture of petrol and ethanol. ◆ adj denoting an engine or vehicle that can run on such fuel or on either of two different kinds of fuel. **flexible disk** n (comput) a floppy disk. **flexible drive** n a means of conveying rotational motion along a flexible cable, or the cable itself.
■ **flex one's muscles** to cause the muscles of one's arms, shoulders, etc to contract, in order to display them, test them as a preliminary to a trial of strength, etc (often fig).

flexi- /flek-si-/ combining form flexible. [Contraction of **flexible**]
■ **flex'i-cover** n (a book with) a flexible, plasticized cover offering greater durability than paper covers (also adj). **flex'ihours** n pl hours of working under flexitime. **flex'itime** or **Flex'time**® n a system of flexible working hours in which an agreed total of hours may be worked at times to suit the worker, often with the proviso that on each day certain hours (**core times**) are included.

flexitarian /flek-si-tā'ri-ən/ (inf) n a person who follows a mainly vegetarian diet but occasionally eats meat. [*flexi*ble *vegetarian*]

fley or **flay** /flā/ vt (Scot) to cause to flee; to frighten. ◆ vi to be frightened. [ME flayen, from OE flēgan (as in compound āflēgan, āflīegan to put to flight); cf ON fleyja, Gothic flaugjan]

flibbertigibbet /flib'ər-ti-jib'it/ n a flighty, gossipy or mischievous person; an imp. [Poss imit of meaningless chatter]

flic /flēk/ (Fr; sl) n a policeman.

flichter /flihh'tər/ (Scot) n a flutter. ◆ vt and vi to flutter or quiver.

flick[1] /flik/ vt to move or touch lightly and quickly; to strike lightly, eg with a lash or a fingernail. ◆ n a stroke of this kind. [Echoic]
□ **flick'-knife** n a knife the blade of which springs out when a button in the handle is pressed.
■ **flick through** to turn the pages of (a book, etc) idly, or in order to get a rough impression of it.

flick[2] /flik/ (inf) n a cinema film; (in pl) the cinema. [**flicker**[1]]

flicker[1] /flik'ər/ vi to flutter and move the wings like a bird; to burn unsteadily, as of a flame; to appear and quickly disappear. ◆ n an act of flickering, a flickering movement or light. [OE flicorian; imit]
■ **flick'ering** adj. **flick'eringly** adv.
□ **flicker noise** see **shot noise** under **shot**[1]. **flick'ertail** n (N Am) a ground squirrel.

flicker[2] /flik'ər/ n an American woodpecker. [Echoic]

flier and **flies** see **fly**.

flight[1] /flīt/ n a passing through the air; a soaring; distance flown; (of a ball in sports) pace or trajectory; a wandering or digression, eg of imagination or fancy; a series (of steps); a flock of birds flying together; a group of birds born in the same season; a volley; a long-distance arrow (Shakesp); a device attached to the blunt end of an arrow or dart, made of plastic or feathers, to stabilize its trajectory; the power of flying; the art or the act of flying with wings or in an aeroplane or other machine; a unit of the air force equivalent to a platoon in the army; a regular air journey, numbered and at a fixed time; an aircraft making such a journey; a journey of a spacecraft; a line of hurdles across a race track. ◆ vt to cause (birds) to fly up; to shoot (wildfowl) in flight; to put a feather or feathers in (an arrow); to send (a ball) into the air in an arcing trajectory (sport). ◆ vi (of birds) to rise or migrate in a flock. [OE flyht, from flēogan to fly]
■ **flight'ed** adj (Milton) flying. **flight'ily** adv. **flight'iness** n. **flight'less** adj unable to fly. **flight'y** adj swift (Shakesp); fanciful; changeable; giddy-minded, irresponsible; flirtatious.
□ **flight attendant** n a member of the cabin crew on an aeroplane, a steward or stewardess. **flight bag** n a bag suitable for stowing in an aircraft locker during a flight. **flight crew** n the members of an aircraft crew whose responsibility is operation and navigation. **flight data recorder** see **flight recorder** below. **flight deck** n the deck of an aircraft-carrier where the planes take off or land; the compartment for the crew in an aircraft. **flight engineer** n a member of an aircraft crew whose responsibility is looking after the engines and other systems. **flight envelope** n the range of limits, eg in speed, to which an aircraft is theoretically subject. **flight'-feather** n a quill of a bird's wing. **flight lieutenant** n a Royal Air Force officer of rank corresponding to naval lieutenant or army captain. **flight line** n an area of an airfield where aircraft are parked and serviced; line of flight. **flight path** or **flight'path** n the course (to be) taken by an aircraft, spacecraft, etc. **flight plan** n a statement of the proposed schedule of an aircraft flight. **flight recorder** n a device which records on tape or other electronic medium information about the functioning of an aircraft and its systems, used in determining the cause of an air crash (also **flight data recorder** or **crash recorder**). **flight test** n a trial flight of an aircraft. **flight'-test** vt.
■ **flight of fancy** an instance of rather free speculation or indulgence in imagination. **in the first** or **top flight** in the highest class.

flight[2] /flīt/ n an act of fleeing. [Assumed OE flyht; cf flēon to flee]
■ **put to flight** to make flee. **take (to) flight** to flee; to disappear quickly (fig).

flimflam /flim'flam/ n a trick or deception; idle, meaningless talk; nonsense. [Cf **flam**[1]]

flimsy /flim'zi/ adj thin; lightweight; without solidity, strength or reason; weak. ◆ n transfer paper or tracing-paper; a banknote (sl); reporters' copy written on thin paper; a (carbon) copy on thin paper. [First in 18c; prob suggested by **film**]
■ **flim'sily** adv. **flim'siness** n.

flinch[1] /flinch or flinsh/ vi to shrink back, out of pain, fear, etc; to fail (in a duty, etc; often with from). [Prob connected with ME fleechen, OFr flechir, L flectere to bend]
■ **flinch'er** n. **flinch'ing** n and adj. **flinch'ingly** adv.

flinch[2] same as **flench**.

flinder /flin'dər/ (rare) n (usu in pl) a splinter or small fragment. [Norw flindra a splinter]

flindersia /flin-dûr'si-ə/ n any plant of the Australian genus Flindersia, valuable trees of the family Rutaceae. [From the English explorer Matthew Flinders (1774–1814)]
□ **Flinders bar** n a bar of soft iron kept near a compass to counter possible deviation caused by local magnetic fields. **Flinders grass** n a native pasture grass of Australia.

fling /fling/ vt (**fling'ing**; **flung**) to throw, cast or toss; to send forth; to dart, to send suddenly; to cause to fall; to throw out (inf). ◆ vi to throw the body about; to kick or throw (out); to dash or rush, throw oneself impetuously; to throw missiles. ◆ n a cast or throw; a try; a passing attack; a gibe or taunt; a brief period of complete freedom, full enjoyment of pleasure; a brief sexual relationship (inf); a lively Scottish country dance. [Cf ON flengja; Swed flänga]
■ **fling'er** n.
■ **fling mud at** see under **mud**. **fling out** to break out in impetuous plain speaking. **fling to the winds** see under **wind**[1]. **full fling** at the utmost speed, recklessly.

flint /flint/ n a hard mineral, a variety of quartz, which sparks easily when struck with steel; a concretion of silica; a piece of flint, esp one from which sparks are struck, or one manufactured into an implement before (or after) the use of metals; a small piece of an iron alloy, used to produce a spark in cigarette lighters; anything proverbially hard; a tailor or other worker demanding full union rates of pay, opp to **dung** (obs sl). ◆ adj made of flint; hard. [OE flint; Dan flint; Gr plinthos a brick]
■ **flint'ify** vt to turn to flint. **flint'ily** adv. **flint'iness** n. **flint'y** adj consisting of, containing a lot of, or like flint; hard; cruel; obdurate.
□ **flint corn** n a variety of maize with particularly hard grains. **flint glass** n a very fine and pure lead glass, orig made of calcined flints. **flint'-heart** or **flint-heart'ed** adj (Shakesp) having a hard heart. **flint'-knapper** n a person who flakes or chips flints. **flint'-knapping** n. **flint'lock** n a gunlock or gun with a flint from which a spark is struck to ignite the powder.

flip /flip/ vt and vi (**flipp'ing**; **flipped**) to flick with the fingernail suddenly released from the ball of the thumb; to spin in the air; to turn (over); to flap; (of a member of parliament) to switch from one property to another its official designation as a second home required for the fulfilment of parliamentary duties, esp to claim upkeep allowances for which it is eligible or to avoid capital gains tax. ◆ vi (sl; often with out) to become very excited or enthusiastic; to go mad. ◆ n a flick; a hot drink of beer and spirits sweetened, or any similar concoction; a somersault; a trip in an aeroplane, a pleasure-flight (inf). ◆ adj flippant; pert, over-smart. [Cf **fillip** and **flap**]
■ **flipp'er** n an animal's limb adapted for swimming; a hand (inf); a rubber foot-covering imitating an animal's flipper, worn by swimmers, divers, etc. **flipp'ing** n the verbal noun of flip. ◆ adj and adv used as an intensifier (euphem inf).
□ **flip chart** n a large blank pad, bound at the top, on which information can be displayed in sequence during a presentation, etc. **flip'-dog** n an iron for heating flip (the drink). **flip'-flop'** adv with repeated flapping (also **flip'-flap'**). ◆ n (orig, and still US and comput) a bistable pair of valves, transistors or circuit elements, the two stable states being switched by pulses; in Britain, a similar circuit with one stable state temporarily achieved by pulse; a type of flimsy sandal, esp one held on the foot by a thong between the toes; a fruit-seller's dance (hist); a form of somersault; a reversal of policy (US); a firework; the sound of regular footfalls; a flighty woman; a revolving apparatus for public amusement. ◆ vi to move with a flapping sound; to reverse a policy (US). ◆ vt (US) to transpose. **flipp'erty-flopp'erty** adj (rare) loose or dangling. **flip phone** n a mobile phone with a hinged cover that protects it when it is not in use. **flip'side** n the reverse of something; a less familiar aspect of anything; orig the side of a record carrying the song, etc of lesser importance, the reverse of the side on whose merits the record was expected to sell. **flip'-top** adj having a hinged lid which can be flipped up. ◆ n a flip-top device or container.
■ **flip one's lid** (inf) to go mad. **flip out** (inf) to lose control, to become violently angry.

flippant /flip'ənt/ adj pert and frivolous in speech; showing disrespectful levity; nimble (obs); playful (obs). [Cf **flip** and ON fleipa to prattle]
■ **flipp'ancy** or **flipp'antness** n pert fluency of speech; impertinence; levity. **flipp'antly** adv.

flirt /flûrt/ vi to play at courtship, to indulge in light-hearted amorous or sexual banter (with); to trifle, toy or dally (with); to move briskly about. ◆ vt to jerk; to cause to move about quickly; to flick or rap. ◆ n a pert, giddy girl; a person who behaves flirtatiously. [Origin obscure; perh connected with Fr fleureter to talk sweet nothings]
■ **flirta'tion** n the act of flirting; a light-hearted and short-lived amorous attachment. **flirta'tious** adj (inf) given to flirting; representing a light-hearted sexual invitation. **flirta'tiously** adv. **flirt'ing** n. **flirt'ingly** adv. **flirt'ish** adj (obs) indicative of a flirt. **flirt'y** adj flirting, flirtatious.
□ **flirt'-gill** /-jil/ n (Shakesp) a pert or wanton woman.

■ **flirt with** to treat (death, danger, etc) lightly, by indulging in dare-devil behaviour, etc; to entertain thoughts of adopting (an idea, etc) or joining (a movement, etc).

flisk /flisk/ (*Scot*) *vi* to skip or caper about; to be restive. ◆ *n* a whim. [Onomatopoeic]
■ **flisk'y** *adj*.

flit¹ /flit/ *vi* (**flitt'ing**; **flitt'ed** or (*Spenser*) **flitt**) to move about lightly; to fly silently or quickly; to be unsteady or easily moved; to move house (*inf, esp Scot*); to do this stealthily in order to avoid creditors, etc. ◆ *vt* to remove or transfer. [ON *flytja*; Swed *flytta*]
■ **flitt'ing** *n*.

flit² or **flitt** /flit/ (*obs*) *adj* fleet; fleeting; light. [**fleet²**]

flitch /flich/ *n* a side of pork salted and cured; a piece of timber cut from a tree trunk. [OE *flicce*; ON *flikki*]

flite same as **flyte**.

flitt see **flit¹,².**

flitter¹ /flit'ər/ *vi* to flutter. [**flit¹**]
❑ **flitt'er-mouse** *n* (*archaic*) a bat.

flitter² /flit'ər/ *n* (*usu* in *pl*, sometimes collectively in *sing*) a fragment, tatter or strip. [Connected with **flitter¹**]

flittern /flit'ərn/ (*dialect*) *n* an oak sapling.

flivver /fliv'ər/ (*old sl*) *n* a failure; a small cheap motor car or aeroplane; a small destroyer. [Origin uncertain]

flix¹ /fliks/ *n* fur or beaver-down. [Origin uncertain]

flix² /fliks/ an old form of **flux**.
❑ **flix'-weed** *n* a species of hedge-mustard, possibly so called from its use in treating the bloody flux or dysentery.

float /flōt/ *vi* to be supported on or suspended in a fluid; to be buoyed up; to move lightly, supported by a fluid; to seem to move in such a way; to be free from the usual attachment; to drift about aimlessly; (of an employee) to move between different tasks according to short-term requirements; to flow (*Milton*); to be flooded (*Spenser* and *Pope*); (in weaving) to pass threads without interweaving with them; to use a float; (of a currency) to be free to fluctuate in value in international exchange (*econ*). ◆ *vt* to cause to float; to cover with liquid (*obs*); to convey on floats; to levitate; to separate by flotation; to smooth; to pare off (eg turf); to launch (eg a scheme); to circulate (eg a rumour); to offer (stocks, etc) for sale to raise capital; to launch (a company) by drawing up various documents and raising cash by selling shares; to negotiate (a loan); to put forward for consideration. ◆ *n* a contrivance for floating or for keeping something afloat, eg a raft, the cork or quill of a fishing-line, the ball of a ballcock, etc; a blade in a paddle wheel or water wheel; a floating indicator attached to a fishing-line, that moves when a fish takes the bait; a tool for smoothing; a plasterer's trowel; a low cart for carrying cattle, milk, etc or decorated as an exhibit in a street parade, etc; a footlight or the footlights collectively; money in hand for a purpose such as to give change to customers, to provide for expenses, etc; state of floating (*Keats*, etc); a wave (*lit* and *fig*; *obs*); a soft fizzy drink with ice-cream floating on the top. [OE *flotian* to float; ON *flota*]
■ **float'able** *adj*. **float'age** or **flō'tage** *n* buoyancy; anything which floats; flotsam; the part of a ship above the waterline. **float'ant** *n* an agent that causes something to float. **floatā'tion** *n* same as **flotation** (see under **flote**). **floatel** *n* see **flotel**. **float'er** *n* a person or thing that floats; a vagrant, or a person who drifts from job to job or allegiance to allegiance; a person who performs different tasks as required (*esp N Am*); a blunder (*sl*); a floating policy (*US*); a meat pie floating in pea soup (*Aust*); a dark speck that appears to float before one's eyes, caused by dead cells and fragments of cells in the lens and vitreous humour. **float'ing** *adj* that floats, in any sense; not fixed; fluctuating; circulating; not clearly committed to one side or the other (*politics*). ◆ *n* the action of the verb; the spreading of plaster on the surface of walls; flotation therapy (see under **flote**). **float'ingly** *adv*. **float'y** *adj* (of a garment or fabric) light and delicate.
❑ **float'-board** *n* a board of an undershot water wheel or a paddle wheel. **float chamber** *n* a chamber in a carburettor in which a float controls the level of fuel. **float glass** *n* glass hardened while floating on the surface of molten tin. **float grass** or **floating grass** *n* floating meadow-grass (*Glyceria fluitans*). **floating battery** *n* a vessel or hulk which is heavily armed, used in the defence of harbours or in attacks on marine fortresses. **floating bridge** *n* a bridge supported on pontoons. **floating capital** *n* (*econ*) goods, money, etc; capital not permanently invested. **floating charge** *n* (*law* and *econ*) a fluctuating borrowing facility secured on the total assets of a company. **floating crane** *n* a large crane carried on a pontoon, used in docks. **floating currency** *n* (*econ*) a national (unit of) currency whose value is allowed to fluctuate freely in the international trading market. **floating debt** *n* (*econ*) (an) unfunded debt or short-term government loan. **floating dock** *n* a floating structure that can be sunk by admitting water to its air chambers, and raised again carrying a vessel to be

repaired. **floating island** *n* a floating mass of driftwood, or of vegetation buoyed up from the bottom by marsh gas, or anything similar; a dessert consisting of meringues floating in custard. **floating kidney** *n* an abnormally mobile kidney. **floating light** *n* a lightship. **floating-point notation** *n* (*comput*) the expressing of numbers as a fractional value (the mantissa) followed by an integer exponent of the base, eg 70.34791×10^3. **floating-point number** *n* (*comput*) a number so expressed. **floating-point operation** *n* (*comput*) the addition, subtraction, multiplication or division of two floating-point numbers. **floating policy** *n* an insurance policy covering movable property irrespective of its location. **floating rib** see under **rib¹**. **floating vote** *n* the votes of electors who are not permanently attached to any one political party. **floating voter** *n*. **float plane** *n* a seaplane. **float'-stone** *n* a porous spongelike variety of silica, so light as to float for a while on water; a bricklayer's smoothing tool. **float tank** see **flotation therapy** under **flote**.

floccus /flok'əs/ *n* (*pl* **flocci** /flok'sī/) a tuft of woolly hair; a tuft, *esp* at the end of a tail; the covering of unfledged birds. [L *floccus* a lock or trifle; dimin *flocculus*]
■ **floc** *n* a woolly mass of particles. **floccillā'tion** /flok-si-/ *n* (*med*) fitful plucking at the bedclothes by a delirious patient. **flocc'ose** (or /-ōs'/) *adj* woolly. **flocc'ular** *adj*. **flocc'ulate** *adj*. ◆ *vt* and *vi* to collect or mass together in tufts, flakes or cloudy masses. **floccūlā'tion** *n*. **flocc'ule** *n* a flocculus. **flocc'ūlence** *n* flocculated condition. **flocc'ūlent** *adj* woolly; flaky; flocculated. **flocc'ūlus** *n* (*pl* **flocculi** /flok'ū-lī/) a small flock, tuft or flake; a small outgrowth of the cerebellum (*med*); a light or dark patch on the sun's surface, *usu* near sunspots, caused by calcium or hydrogen vapour.

flock¹ /flok/ *n* a company of animals, eg sheep, birds, etc; a company generally; a church congregation, considered as the charge of a minister. ◆ *vi* to gather or go in flocks or in crowds. [OE *flocc* a flock or company; ON *flokkr*]
❑ **flock'-master** *n* an owner or overseer of a flock; a sheep-farmer.

flock² /flok/ *n* a lock of wool; a tuft; cloth refuse, waste wool (also in *pl*); a woolly-looking precipitate (also in *pl*); fine particles of wool or other fibre applied to cloth to give a raised velvety surface or pattern. [OFr *floc*, from L *floccus* a lock of wool]
❑ **flock'-bed** *n* a bed stuffed with wool. **flock'-paper** or **flock wallpaper** *n* a wallpaper dusted over with flock.

floe /flō/ *n* a field of floating ice. [Prob Norw *flo* layer, from ON *flō*]

flog /flog/ *vt* (**flogg'ing**; **flogged**) to beat or strike; to lash; to chastise with blows; to sell (*inf*). ◆ *vi* and *vt* to move or progress toilingly. [17c cant; prob an abbrev of **flagellate**]
■ **flogg'er** *n*. **flogg'ing** *n*.
■ **flog a dead horse** (*inf*) to waste time and energy on a lost or impossible cause. **flog to death** (*inf*) to persist in talking about or advertising something until doing so has no further effect.

flokati /flə-kä'tē/ *n* a hand-woven Greek rug with a very thick shaggy wool pile. [Gr *phlokatē* a peasant's blanket]

flong /flong/ (*printing*) *n* papier-mâché for making moulds in stereotyping. [Fr *flan*]

flood /flud/ *n* a great flow of water; an inundation; a deluge; a condition of abnormally great flow in a river; a river or other water (*poetic*); the rise of the tide; any great inflow or outflow, eg of light, tears or visitors; a floodlight (*inf*). ◆ *vt* to submerge (land) in water; to overflow; to inundate; to supply in excessive quantity; to supply (an engine) with too much petrol, thus preventing it from starting. ◆ *vi* (of land) to be submerged in water; to overflow; to flow (in) in great amounts; (of a woman) to bleed profusely, as after childbirth or in exceptionally heavy menstruation. [OE *flōd*; Du *vloed*, Ger *Flut*; cf **flow²**]
■ **flood'ed** *adj*. **flood'ing** *n* a flood or the process of producing a flood; a haemorrhage in the uterus.
❑ **flood'gate** *n* a gate for allowing or stopping the flow of water, a sluice or lock gate. **flood lamp** *n* a floodlight. **flood'light** *n* lighting of a large area or surface by illumination from lamps situated at some distance (also **floodlighting**); one of the lamps providing such lighting. ◆ *vt* (*pat* and *pap* **flood'lit** or **flood'lighted**) to illuminate (an area) with floodlights. **floodlight projector** *n* housing and support for a floodlight lamp with a reflector for directing the light into a suitable beam. **flood'mark** *n* the mark or line to which the tide or a flood has risen. **flood plain** *n* an extensive level area beside a river, formed of deposits of sediment brought downstream and spread by the river in flood. **flood'tide** *n* the rising tide. **flood'wall** *n* a wall built as protection against floods. **flood'water** *n*. **flood'way** *n* an artificial passage for floodwater.
■ **flooded out** forced to leave a building because of a flood. **the Flood** the deluge, described in the Old Testament (Genesis 6–8), that covered the whole Earth, and from which Noah and his family and livestock escaped in the ark. **open the floodgates** to remove all restrictions or controls.

floor /flōr, flör/ n the lower supporting surface of a room, etc; a platform; all the rooms in a building on the same level; a bottom surface; that on which anything rests or any operation is performed; a levelled area; the ground (inf); the part of a legislative assembly where members sit and make speeches; the (part of a hall, etc accommodating) members of the public at a meeting, etc; the right to speak at a meeting, esp in the phrases *have* and *be given the floor* ; the part of a stock, etc exchange on which dealers operate; a lower limit of prices, etc; a quantity of grain spread out to germinate. ◆ vt to furnish with a floor; to throw or place on, or knock to, the floor; to defeat or stump (inf). [OE flōr ; Du vloer a flat surface, Ger Flur flat land; Welsh llawr]

■ **floored** adj. **floor'er** n (inf) a knock-down blow; a decisive retort, etc; an examination question one cannot answer. **floor'ing** n material for floors; a platform.

❑ **floor'board** n one of the narrow boards making up a floor. **floor'cloth** n a covering for floors, esp of linoleum or the like; a cloth for washing floors. **floor'head** n the upper end of a ship's floor timber. **flooring saw** n a saw curved towards the toe with extra teeth on the back above the toe, used for cutting along the cracks between floorboards, etc. **floor lamp** n (US) a standard lamp. **floor leader** n (US) the leader of a party in a legislative body. **floor limit** n an amount above which a credit card sale must be authorized by the card company, varying from one shop, etc to another. **floor manager** n a stage manager of a television programme; a supervisor in a department store. **floor pan** n the underside of a car, on which the body shell, doors, etc are built up. **floor plan** n a diagram showing the layout of rooms, etc on one storey of a building. **floor price** n a fixed lowest limit to the possible price of something. **floor show** n a performance on the floor of a ballroom, nightclub, etc, not on a platform. **floor timber** n a timber placed immediately across a ship's keel, on which her bottom is framed. **floor'walker** n (N Am) a supervisor in a large store, who attends to customers' complaints, etc.

■ **cross the floor** (of a member of parliament, etc) to change one's allegiance from one party to another. **first floor** the floor in a house above the ground floor, the second storey; the ground floor (N Am) (**first'-floor** adj). **hold the floor** to dominate a meeting by speaking at great length; to speak too much, boringly. **take the floor** to rise to address a meeting; to take part in a dance; to begin a performance. **wipe the floor with** to defeat ignominiously.

floordrobe /flōrd'rōb/ (sl) n a pile of discarded clothes on the floor of a room. [floor and wardrobe]

floozie, floosie or **floozy**, also **floosy** /floo'zi/ (sl) n a young woman of doubtful sexual morals; a prostitute. [Origin uncertain]

flop¹ /flop/ n a limp, heavy, flapping movement, fall or sound; a collapse; a fiasco or failure (inf); a place to sleep (N Am sl); a short pitch shot with a very high trajectory (golf); a set of three community cards, dealt face up at the same time (poker). ◆ adv with a flop. ◆ vt and vi (**flopp'ing; flopped**) to move with a flop; to drop heavily; to change over in nature or politics (US). ◆ vi to collapse; to fail dismally (inf); to go to bed or sleep (inf). [A form of **flap**]

■ **flopp'ily** adv. **flopp'iness** n. **flopp'y** adj limp; flexible. ◆ n (comput) a floppy disk.

❑ **flop'house** n (orig US) a cheap hotel; a dosshouse. **floppy disk** or **disc** n (comput) a storage device in the form of a thin, flexible disc, encased in a stiff plastic cover.

flop² /flop/ (comput) n a floating-point operation (see under **float**).

floptical /flop'ti-kəl/ (comput) adj denoting a type of read-write head using a laser device. [**floppy** (computing sense) and **optical**]

Flor. abbrev : Florida (US state).

flor /flōr/ n a yeasty growth which is allowed to form on the surface of sherry wines after fermentation and which gives them a nutty taste. [Sp, flower or mould, from L flōs, flōris a flower]

flor. abbrev : florin; floruit (L), flourished.

flora /flō'rə or flö'-/ n (pl **flo'ras** or **flo'rae**) the assemblage of all forms of vegetable life of a region or age, esp as distinct from animal life (fauna); a list or descriptive enumeration of these. [L Flōra, goddess of flowers; flōs, flōris a flower]

■ **flo'ral** adj relating to the goddess Flora, to floras, or to flowers. **flo'rally** adv. **Floréal** /flō-rā-äl/ n (Fr) the 8th month of the French revolutionary calendar, the month of flowers, about 20 April–20 May. **florescence** /flor-es'əns/ n a bursting into flower; a time of flowering (bot). **floresc'ent** adj bursting into flower. **floret** /flor'it/ n a small flower; one of the single flowers in the head of a composite flower; one of the branches in the head of a cauliflower or broccoli. **flo'riated** or **flo'reated** adj (archit) decorated with a floral ornament. **floribunda** /flor-, flōr- or flör-i-bun'də/ n a plant, esp a rose, whose flowers grow in clusters. **floricul'tural** /flor- or flör-/ adj. **flor'iculture** n the growing of flowers or plants. **floricul'turist** n. **florif'erous** adj bearing or producing flowers. **flo'riform** adj flower-shaped. **flor'igen** /-i-jən/ n

(Gr gennaein to produce) a postulated flower-forming hormone. **florilegium** /-lē'ji-əm/ n (pl **florilē'gia**) (L legere to gather) an anthology or collection of choice extracts. **flor'ist** n a seller, or grower, of flowers; /flō' or flō'rist/ a person who studies flowers or floras. **florist'ic** adj. **florist'ically** adv. **florist'ics** n sing the study of floras. **flor'istry** n the art of cultivating, arranging or selling flowers. **flo'ry** adj having fleur-de-lys (heraldry); showy or conceited (Walter Scott).

❑ **floral dance** n the annual dance at Helston in S England (properly called **furry** or **furry dance**). **floral diagram** n a figure showing the arrangement of the parts of a flower in ground plan.

floreat /flō'rē-at or flö'rā-at/ (L) may (he, she or it) flourish.

Florentine /flor'ən-tīn/ adj of or relating to Florence in Tuscany; (sometimes without cap) (cookery) containing spinach. ◆ n a native or inhabitant of Florence; (without cap) a durable silk textile fabric (also **flor'ence**); a pie with no crust beneath the meat; (also without cap) a biscuit covered on one side with fruit and nuts on a chocolate base. [L Flōrentīnus, from Flōrentia]

❑ **Florence fennel** see under **finocchio**. **Florence flask** n a long-necked round flask. **Florentine iris** see **orris¹**.

florescent, floret, floribunda, etc see under **flora**.

florid /flor'id/ adj bright in colour; flushed with red; (of a complexion) ruddy, often unhealthily so; characterized by flowery rhetoric, melodic figures, or other ornamentation; over-adorned; richly ornamental; flowery; having many flowers (obs). [L flōridus flowery, from flōs, flōris a flower]

■ **florid'ity** n. **flor'idly** adv. **flor'idness** n.

Florideae /flo-rid'i-ē/ (bot) n pl a large subclass of the Rhodophyceae or red seaweeds. [L flōridus florid]

■ **florid'ean** n and adj. **florid'eous** adj.

florin /flor'in/ n orig a Florentine gold coin with a lily stamped on one side, first struck in the 13c; a former British silver or cupronickel coin worth one-tenth of a pound, first minted in 1849 (a **double florin** was coined in 1887); in the Netherlands and Suriname, the guilder. [Fr, from Ital fiorino, from fiore a lily, from L flōs, flōris]

florist, etc see under **flora**.

floruit /flō'rū-it, flō'rū-, flor'ū- or -ū-/ n a period during which a person flourished, was most active, produced most works, etc. ◆ vi he or she flourished (at a certain date). [L, 3rd pers sing perf indicative of flōrēre to flourish]

flory see under **flora** and **fleur**.

floscule /flos'kūl/ n a floret (see under **flora**). [L flōsculus, dimin of flōs a flower]

■ **flos'cular** or **flos'culous** adj.

floss /flos/ n the rough outside of the silkworm's cocoon, and other waste from silk manufacture; fine silk in spun strands not twisted together, used in embroidery and (**dental floss**) tooth-cleaning; any loose downy or silky plant substance; fluff (also **flosh**). ◆ vi and vt to use dental floss (on). [Prob OFr flosche down, or from some Gmc word cognate with **fleece**; cf ON flos nap]

■ **floss'ing** n. **floss'y** adj made of, like, or relating to floss; showy or overdressed (inf).

❑ **floss silk** or **flox silk** n.

flota /flō'tə/ n a commercial fleet; formerly, the fleet which annually conveyed the produce of America to Spain. [Sp]

flote /flōt/ n (obs) a wave. [See **float**]

■ **flo'tage** n see **floatage** under **float**. **flo'tant** adj (heraldry) floating in air or in water. **flota'tion** n the act of floating; the science of floating bodies; the act of starting a business, esp a limited liability company, by drawing up various documents and raising capital by selling shares; (also **froth flotation**) a method of separating ore from the rock in which it is embedded by forming a froth, the ore particles clinging to the bubbles.

❑ **flotation therapy** n (med) an alternative therapy for stress in which the patient floats for about an hour in a sealed salt-water-filled capsule (a **flotation tank** or **float tank**), sometimes with music piped in.

■ **plane** or **line of flotation** the plane or line in which the horizontal surface of a fluid cuts a body floating in it.

flotel or **floatel** /flō-tel'/ n a platform or boat containing the sleeping accommodation and eating, leisure, etc facilities for workers on oil rigs. [**float** and **hotel**]

flotilla /flo-til'ə/ n a fleet (of small ships). [Sp, dimin of flota a fleet]

flotsam /flot'səm/ n goods lost by shipwreck and found floating on the sea (see also **jetsam**). [Anglo-Fr floteson (Fr flottaison), from OFr floter to float]

■ **flotsam and jetsam** unclaimed odds and ends.

flounce¹ /flowns/ vi to move abruptly, impatiently or disgustedly. ◆ n an impatient or disgusted fling, flop or movement. ◆ adv with a flounce. [Prob cognate with Norw *flunsa* to hurry, and Swed dialect *flunsa* to plunge]

flounce[2] /flowns/ *n* a hanging strip gathered and sewn to the skirt of a dress by its upper edge. ◆ *vt* to provide with flounces. [See **flounce**[1]] ■ **floun'cing** *n* material for flounces. **floun'cy** *adj* decorated with flounces.

flounder[1] /flown'dər/ *vi* to struggle with violent and awkward movements; to stumble helplessly in thinking or speaking. ◆ *n* an act of floundering. [Prob an onomatopoeic blending of the sound and sense of earlier words like **founder** and **blunder**]

flounder[2] /flown'dər/ *n* a name given to a number of species of flatfish of the family Pleuronectidae, in Europe *Platichthys flesus*, in the USA certain species of *Pseudopleuronectes*, *Limanda*, etc. [Anglo-Fr *floundre*, OFr *flondre*, most prob of Scand origin; cf ON *flythra*; Swed *flundra*]

flour /flowr/ *n* the finely ground meal of wheat, or of any other grain; the fine soft powder of any substance. ◆ *vt* to reduce into or sprinkle with flour. ◆ *vi* (of mercury) to break up into fine globules in the amalgamation process. [Same word as **flower**] ■ **flour'y** *adj* covered with flour; like flour. ❏ **flour bolt** *n* a machine for separating flour from bran. **flour mill** *n* a mill for making flour. **flour moth** *n* a moth whose larvae feed on flour and grain.

flourish /flur'ish/ *vi* to grow luxuriantly; to thrive; to be in full vigour; to be prosperous; to use copious and flowery language; to move in fantastic patterns; to display ostentatiously; to play or sing ostentatious passages, or ostentatiously (*music*); to play a fanfare; to make ornamental strokes with the pen; to show off; to bloom (*obs* and *Scot*). ◆ *vt* to adorn with fantastic patterns or ornaments; to make attractive (*Shakesp*); to brandish in show, triumph or exuberance of spirits. ◆ *n* showy splendour; a figure made by a bold stroke of the pen; the waving of a weapon or other object; a flowery passage of words; a showy, fantastic or highly ornamental passage of music; a mass of blossom on a fruit tree (*dialect*); decoration (*obs*). [OFr *florir*, *floriss-*, from L *flōs*, *flōris* flower] ■ **flour'ished** *adj* decorated with flourishes. **flour'isher** *n*. **flour'ishing** *adj* thriving; prosperous; making a flourish. **flour'ishingly** *adv*. **flour'ishy** *adj* full of flourishes. ❏ **flourishing thread** *n* thread used in ornamental needlework. **flourish of trumpets** *n* a fanfare heralding an important person or people; any ostentatious introduction.

flouse /flows/ (*dialect*) *vt* and *vi* to splash (also **floush** /flowsh/). [Cf **flush**[1]]

flout /flowt/ *vt* to jeer at, to mock; to treat with contempt; to reject or defy (orders, etc). ◆ *vi* to jeer (with *at*). ◆ *n* a jeer; a contemptuous act or speech. [Prob a specialized use of *floute*, ME form of **flute**, to play on the flute; cf Du *fluiten*] ■ **flout'ingly** *adv*. ❏ **flout'ingstock** *n* (*Shakesp*) a person or thing that is flouted.

flow[1] /flō/ *vi* (pat and pap **flowed**; *pap* (*Shakesp* and *Milton*) **flown** /flōn/) (of water, etc) to run; to move or change form like a fluid; (of the tide) to rise or come in; to move in a stream; to glide smoothly; to abound or run over; to run in smooth lines; to issue or proceed smoothly and effortlessly; to stream or hang, loose and waving; to melt (*obs*). ◆ *vt* to cover with water. ◆ *n* a stream or current; movement of, or like that of, a fluid; anything which flows or has flowed; mode of flowing; the setting in of the tide; copious fluency; menstruation (*old*). [OE *flōwan*] ■ **flow'age** *n* (an) act of flowing; the state of being flooded. **flow'ing** *adj* moving, as a fluid; fluent; smooth and continuous; falling or hanging in folds or waves. **flow'ingly** *adv*. **flow'ingness** *n*. ❏ **flow chart**, **diagram** or **sheet** *n* a chart pictorially representing the nature and sequence of operations to be carried out, eg in a computer program or an industrial process. **flow cytometry** *n* (*biol*) a technique for sorting single cells or chromosomes which are stained and then directed in drops past a beam of light which sorts the drops into the appropriate vessel. **flow'meter** *n* a device for measuring, or giving an output signal proportional to, the rate of flow of a fluid in a pipe. **flow'-on** *n* (*Aust*) the process by which a wage or salary increase awarded to one group of workers results in a similar increase for other workers; such an increase. **flow-sorted chromosomes** *n pl* those sorted on the basis of size by flow cytometry. **flow'stone** *n* a mineral precipitation from flowing water, *usu* of calcium carbonate. ■ **go with the flow** (*inf*) to be content to react to events and trends.

flow[2] /flōw, flow/ (*Scot*) *n* a morass; a flat, moist tract of land; a quicksand; a moorland pool; a sea basin or sound. [Cf Icel *flói* a marshy moor; Norw dialect *floe* pool in a swamp; ON *flóa* to flood]

flower /flow'ər or flowr/ *n* the reproductive organs of a seed plant; the blossom of a plant, or the state of being in blossom; any plant that produces blossoms, *esp* one grown for its blossom; the prime of life; the best of anything; the person or thing most distinguished; the

embodiment of perfection; a figure of speech; ornament of style; a term of endearment; (in *pl*) menstrual discharge (*obs*); (in *pl*) a sublimate (eg *flowers of sulphur*; *chem*); (often in *pl*) a fungal growth. ◆ *vi* to blossom; to flourish; to reach a peak. ◆ *vt* to adorn with flowers or a floral design. [OFr *flour* (Fr *fleur*), from L *flōs*, *flōris* a flower] ■ **flower'age** *n* (*rare*) flowers collectively; the flowering state of a plant. **flower'ed** *adj* decorated with flower designs; decorated with fleurs-de-lis (*heraldry*). **flower'er** *n* a plant that flowers; an embroiderer of floral designs. **flower'et** *n* a little flower; a floret (see under **flora**). **flower'iness** *n*. **flower'ing** *n* and *adj*. **flower'less** *adj*. **flower'y** *adj* full of or adorned with flowers; highly embellished or florid. ❏ **flower'-bed** *n* a garden bed for flowers. **flower'-bell** *n* a blossom shaped like a bell. **flower'-bud** *n* a bud with the unopened flower. **flower child** *n* one of the Flower People. **flower'-clock** *n* a collection of flowers so arranged that the time of day is indicated by their times of opening and closing. **flower-de-leuce**, **flower-deluce**, **flower deluce** /-di-loos'/, **flower-delice**, **flower delice** /-di-lēs', -lis' or -del'is/ *n* old names for the iris, or for the fleur-de-lis. **flower essence** *n* one of a number of essences extracted from flower petals, used therapeutically in situations of mental or physical disharmony. **flower'-garden** *n*. **flower girl** *n* a girl or woman who sells flowers in the street; a young girl carrying flowers in a bride's retinue at a wedding. **flower'-head** *n* a close inflorescence in which all the florets grow together at the tip of the stem, rather than on separated stalks. **flowering rush** *n* a monocotyledonous plant (genus *Butomus*), with large linear three-edged leaves and an umbel of rose-coloured flowers. **flower of Jove** *n* a campion with heads of purple or scarlet flowers, and leaves with silky-white hairs. **flower'pecker** *n* any of various small birds found from India to Australia which feed on nectar and berries. **Flower People** *n* (also without *caps*) colourfully dressed adherents of a movement (**Flower Power**; also without *caps*) arising in the mid-1960s which rejected materialism and advocated peace and universal love. **flower'pot** *n* a pot in which a plant is grown. **flower'-service** *n* a church service where offerings of flowers are made. **flower show** *n* an exhibition of flowers. **flower'-stalk** *n* the stem that supports the flower. **flowery-kir'tled** *adj* (*Milton*) with a flowery petticoat. ■ **the flowery land** (*archaic*) China.

flown /flōn/ *pap* of **fly**; old *pap* of **flow**[1]. ❏ **flown cover** *n* (*philately*) an envelope which has been carried by air over at least part of its delivery route.

flox silk same as **floss silk** (see under **floss**).

fl. oz. *abbrev*: fluid ounce or ounces.

flu or (*rare*) **flue** /floo/ *n* a shortened form of **influenza**. ■ **flu'ey** *adj* (*inf*).

fluate /floo'āt/ (*obs*) *n* a fluoride.

flub /flub/ (*N Am inf*) *vt* (**flubb'ing**; **flubbed**) (often with *up*) to botch, make a mess of (also *vi*). ◆ *n* a gaffe; a mistake; a person given to making mistakes. [Ety unknown]

fluctuate /fluk'tū-āt/ *vi* to vary this way and that; to go up and down or to and fro; to move like a wave. ◆ *vt* to throw into fluctuation. [L *fluctuāre*, *-ātum*, from *fluctus* a wave, from *fluere* to flow] ■ **fluc'tuant** *adj*. **fluc'tuating** *adj*. **fluctuā'tion** *n* rise and fall; motion to and fro; wavelike motion; alternate variation, vacillation.

flue[1] /floo/ *n* a pipe for conveying hot air, smoke, flame, etc; a small chimney; a flue pipe (*music*); the opening by which the air escapes from the foot of a flue pipe. [Origin uncertain] ❏ **flue'-cure** *vt* to cure (tobacco) by heat introduced through flues. **flue'-cured** *adj*. **flue pipe** *n* a pipe, *esp* in an organ, in which the sound is produced by air passing across an edge. **flue stop** *n* a stop controlling the flue pipes in an organ. **flue'work** *n* (in an organ) the flue pipes collectively.

flue[2] /floo/ *n* light fluff, such as collects in unswept places; soft down or fur. [Origin doubtful] ■ **flu'ey** *adj*.

flue[3] or **flew** /floo/ (*dialect*) *adj* shallow or flat; flared; splayed. [Origin uncertain]

flue[4] same as **flu**.

fluellin /floo-el'in/ *n* a name given to various speedwells (*esp Veronica serpyllifolia* and *Veronica officinalis*) and toadflaxes (*esp Linaria elatine* and *Linaria spuria*). [Welsh *llysiau Llewelyn* Llewelyn's herbs]

fluent /floo'ənt/ *adj* able to speak and write a particular language competently and with ease (*usu* with *in*); spoken or written competently and with facility; voluble; marked by copiousness; (of a movement) smooth, easy or graceful. ◆ *n* (*maths*) the variable quantity in fluxions. [L *fluēns*, *fluentis*, prp of *fluere* to flow] ■ **flu'ence** (*Milton*), **flu'ency** or **flu'entness** *n*. **flu'ently** *adv*.

fluey see under **flu** and **flue**[2].

fluff /fluf/ *n* a soft down from cotton, etc; anything downy; a fault in performing (a play, piece of music, etc) (*inf*); a misplayed stroke at golf, etc (*inf*). ◆ *vt* to make fluffy (often with *up*). ◆ *vt* and *vi* (*inf*) to make a mistake, in sport, musical or dramatic performance, etc. [Perh connected with **flue²**]

■ **fluff'iness** *n*.

❑ **fluff'y** *adj* soft and downy; (of food) soft and light; lacking intelligence or depth (*inf*).

■ **a bit of fluff** (*sl*, often *offensive*) a sexually attractive woman.

flügel or **flugel** */flü'gəl* or *floo'gl/ n* a grand piano. [Ger, wing]

❑ **flü'gelhorn** or **flu'gelhorn** *n* a brass instrument, similar to the keybugle and saxhorn. **flü'gelhornist** or **flu'gelhornist** *n*. **flugelman** */floo'gl-man/ n* same as **fugleman**.

fluid */floo'id/ n* a substance whose particles can move about with freedom; a liquid or gas. ◆ *adj* that flows; unsolidified; of, using or relating to fluids; likely or tending to change; easily changed; (of a movement) smooth and graceful. [L *fluidus* fluid, from *fluere* to flow]

■ **flu'idal** *adj*. **fluid'ic** *adj*. **fluid'ics** *n sing* the science and technology of using a flow of liquid or gas for certain operations in place of a flow of electrons. **fluid'ify** *vt*. **fluid'ity** or **flu'idness** *n*. **fluidizā'tion** or **-s-** *n*. **flu'idize** or **-ise** *vt* to make fluid; to cause (fine particles) to move as a fluid, eg by suspending them in a current of air or gas; to fill with a specified fluid.

❑ **fluid drive** *n* a system of transmitting power smoothly, through the medium of the change in momentum of a fluid, *usu* oil. **fluidized bed** *n* (*chem eng*) a bed of solids which has been fluidized by an upward flow of liquid or gas. **fluid mechanics** *n sing* the mechanics of liquids and gases. **fluid ounce** see under **ounce¹**.

fluke¹ */flook/ n* an accidental success. ◆ *vt* to make, score, etc by a fluke. [Origin unknown]

■ **fluk'ey** or **fluk'y** *adj*. **fluk'ily** *adv*. **fluk'iness** *n*.

fluke² */flook/ n* a flounder (*N Am* or *dialect*); a trematode, parasitic worm, *esp* that which causes liver rot in sheep, so called because of its resemblance to a miniature flounder (also **fluke'-worm**); a variety of kidney potato. [OE *flōc* a plaice; cf ON *flōke*]

fluke³ */flook/ n* the barb of an anchor; a barb; a lobe of a whale's tail. [Prob a transferred use of **fluke²**]

■ **fluk'y** *adj*.

flume */floom/ n* a chute with flowing water down which people slide to a swimming pool; an artificial channel for water, for use in industry or as an amusement on which rides, *usu* in special boats, can be taken; a ravine with a stream flowing through it. [OFr *flum*, from L *flūmen* a river, from *fluere* to flow]

■ **be** or **go up the flume** (*rare*) to come to grief, to be done for.

flummery */flum'ə-ri/ n* a pudding made from the husks of oats, the Scots sowens; blancmange; anything insipid; empty compliment, humbug or pretentiousness. [Welsh *llymru*, from *llymrig* harsh, raw, from *llym* sharp or severe]

flummox */flum'əks/ (inf*) *vt* to perplex or puzzle. [Ety unknown]

flump */flump/ (inf*) *vt* to throw down heavily. ◆ *vi* to move or fall with a flop or thud. ◆ *n* the dull sound so produced. [Imit]

flung */flung/ pat* and *pap* of **fling**.

flunk */flungk/ (sl, esp N Am* and *NZ*) *vi* to fail in an examination; to be dismissed from college, etc for such a failure (with *out*). ◆ *vt* to fail (an examination or course). ◆ *n* a failure. [Perh combined **flinch¹** and **funk²**]

flunkey or **flunky** */flung'ki/ n* a uniformed servant or footman; any servant; a servile person. [Perh originally *flanker* a person who runs alongside]

■ **flun'keydom** *n*. **flun'keyish** *adj*. **flun'keyism** *n*.

Fluon® */floo'on/ n* a proprietary name for **polytetrafluoroethylene** (see under **poly-**).

fluor */floo'ər* or *-ör/ n* fluorite. [L *fluor* flow, from its use as a flux]

■ **fluoresce** */-ar-es'/ vi* to demonstrate fluorescence. **fluorescein** */-es'ē-in/ n* a fluorescent dyestuff, $C_{20}H_{12}O_5$. **fluoresc'ence** *n* the property of some substances (eg fluor) of emitting, when exposed to radiation, rays of greater wavelength than those received; the radiation thus emitted. **fluoresc'ent** *adj*. **fluoric** */-or'ik/ adj*. **flu'oridate**, **flu'oridize** or **-ise** *vt* to add a fluoride to (a water or milk supply). **fluoridā'tion** *n*. **flu'oride** *n* a compound of fluorine with another element or radical; loosely, sodium fluoride or sodium monofluorophosphate as the active ingredient in toothpaste. **flu'orinate** *vt* to introduce fluorine into a chemical compound. **fluorinā'tion** *n*. **flu'orine** */-ēn/ n* a pale greenish-yellow gaseous element (symbol **F**; atomic no 9). **fluorite** */floo'ər-īt/ n* a mineral, calcium fluoride, commonly purple, also green, colourless, etc, crystallizing in cubes and octahedra, found abundantly in Derbyshire. Its coloured varieties may fluoresce strongly in ultraviolet light.

❑ **fluorescence microscopy** *n* (*biol*) light microscopy in which the specimen is irradiated at wavelengths which will excite the natural or artificially introduced fluorochromes. **fluorescent lighting** *n* brighter lighting obtained for the same consumption of electricity, by using

fluorescent material to convert ultraviolet radiation into visible light. **fluorescent screen** *n* a screen coated on one side with a fluorescent material that can display X-ray images. **fluorescent tube** *n* the tube of a fluorescent electric light. **fluorimeter** see **fluorometer** below. **flu'orocarbon** *n* (*chem*) an alkane in which hydrogen atoms are replaced by fluorine atoms, any of a series of compounds of fluorine and carbon (corresponding to the hydrocarbons) highly resistant to heat and chemical action. **flu'orochrome** *n* (*chem*) a molecule or chemical group which fluoresces on irradiation. **fluorog'raphy** *n* photography using fluorescence, *esp* in medical analysis. **fluorom'eter** or **fluorim'eter** *n* an instrument for measuring intensity of fluorescence. **fluoromet'ric** or **fluorimet'ric** *adj*. **flu'oroscope** *n* an instrument for X-ray examination by means of a fluorescent screen. **fluoroscop'ic** *adj*. **fluoros'copy** *n*. **fluorō'sis** *n* chronic poisoning by fluorine. **flu'orotype** *n* (*obs*) photography by means of fluorides. **fluorouracil** */-ō-ūr'ə-sil/ n* an antimetabolite used in the treatment of cancer. **flu'orspar** *n* fluorite.

Fluothane® */floo'ō-thān/ n* a proprietary name for **halothane**.

fluoxetine */floo-ok'sə-tēn/ n* an antidepressant drug that increases the levels of serotonin in the central nervous system.

flurry */flur'i/ n* a sudden blast or gust; agitation; a sudden commotion; bustle; the death-agony of the whale; a fluttering collection or mass of things, eg snowflakes. ◆ *vt* (**flurr'ying**; **flurr'ied**) to agitate or confuse. ◆ *vi* to fall or move in flurries. [Prob onomatopoeic, suggested by **flaw²**, **hurry**, etc]

■ **flurr** */flûr/ (rare*) *vt* to scatter. ◆ *vi* to fly up.

flush¹ */flush/ n* a sudden flow; a flow of blood to the skin, causing redness; a suffusion of colour, *esp* red; the device on a lavatory which is operated to release a flow of water to clean the pan; a sudden growth; a renewal of growth; a rush of feeling; a puddle (*obs*); a watery place near a spring, etc (*obs*); bloom, freshness or vigour; abundance. ◆ *vi* to glow; to become red in the face; to flow swiftly, suddenly or copiously. ◆ *vt* to cleanse by a copious flow of water (as in a lavatory); to clear by a blast of air; to cause to glow; to elate or excite the spirits of. ◆ *adj* overflowing; abounding; well supplied, *esp* with money (*inf*); in full bloom (*Shakesp*); flushed. [Prob **flush⁴** influenced by **flash¹** and **blush**]

■ **flushed** *adj* suffused with ruddy colour; excited. **flush'er** *n* a person who flushes sewers. **flush'ing** *n*. **flush'ness** *n*. **flush'y** *adj* reddish.

❑ **flush'-box** *n* a tank for flushing a lavatory, a cistern.

■ **in the** (or **one's**) **first flush** young or youthful. **in the first flush of** in the early stages of (*esp* youth), when one is at a peak of vigour, enthusiasm, etc.

flush² */flush/ vt* to make even; to fill up to the level of a surface (often with *up*). ◆ *adj* having the surface in the same plane as the adjacent surface (with *with*); (of a deck) having the same level throughout the ship's length; (of type) having an even margin. ◆ *adv* so as to be even or level. [Prob related to **flush¹**]

■ **flush'ness** *n*.

flush³ */flush/ (cards*) *n* a hand in which all the cards or a specified number are of the same suit. ◆ *adj* consisting of cards all of the same suit. [Prob Fr *flux*, from L *fluxus* flow; influenced by **flush¹**]

■ **busted flush** a potential flush that is never completed; something that has to be abandoned as a failure (*fig*). **straight flush** a sequence of five cards of the same suit (**royal flush**, if headed by the ace).

flush⁴ */flush/ vi* to start like an alarmed bird. ◆ *vt* to rouse and cause (*esp* birds) to move off; to force out of concealment (with *out*). ◆ *n* the act of starting (*esp* birds); a bird or a flock of birds so started (*Spenser*). [Prob onomatopoeic; suggested by **fly**, **flutter** and **rush¹**]

fluster */flus'tər/ n* hurrying; flurry; heat (*obs*); confused agitation. ◆ *vt* to confuse; to make hot and flurried; to fuddle with drink. ◆ *vi* to bustle; to be agitated or fuddled. [ON *flaustr* hurry]

■ **flus'terment** *n*. **flus'tery** *adj* confused. **flus'trate** *vt* (*obs*) to fluster. **flustrā'tion** *n* (*obs*).

Flustra */flus'trə/ n* one of the commonest genera of Polyzoa, a division of aquatic animals. [Ety unknown]

flute */floot/ n* a woodwind instrument, *esp* either of two types consisting of a wooden or metal tube with holes stopped by the fingertips or by keys, one type blown from the end through a fipple, the other (also called **transverse flute**) held horizontally and played by directing the breath across a mouth-hole; (in organ-building) a stop with stopped wooden pipes, having a flute-like tone; a longitudinal groove, such as on a pillar (*archit*); a tall, narrow wineglass; a shuttle in tapestry-weaving, etc. ◆ *vi* to play the flute; to make fluty sounds. ◆ *vt* to play or sing in soft flute-like tones; to form flutes or grooves in (*archit*). [OFr *fleûte*; ety dubious]

■ **flut'ed** *adj* ornamented with flutes, channels or grooves. **flut'er** *n*. **flutina** */-tē'/ n* a kind of accordion. **flut'ing** *n* flute-playing or similar sounds; longitudinal grooving. **flut'ist** *n* same as **flautist**. **flut'y** *adj* like a flute in tone.

■ words derived from main entry word; ❑ compound words; ■ idioms and phrasal verbs

❏ **flûte-à-bec** /flüt-ä-bek'/ n (Fr) a fipple flute, a recorder or flageolet. **flute bird** n an Australian bird of the family Artamidae, a type of piping crow (qv). **flute'mouth** n a fish (genus Fistularia) similar to the sticklebacks.

flutter /flut'ər/ vi to move about nervously, aimlessly or bustlingly; (of a bird) to flap wings; (of a flag, etc) to flap in the air; to fall slowly and unsteadily; to vibrate or, eg of a pulse, to beat irregularly; to be agitated or uncertain; to be frivolous (obs); to toss a coin (archaic). ◆ vt to throw into disorder; to move in quick motions. ◆ n quick, irregular motion; agitation; confusion; a bet or wager (inf); a small speculation (inf); a technique used in playing a wind instrument, rapid movement of the tongue as for a rolled 'r' (also **flutt'er-tonguing**); (in sound reproduction) undesirable variation in pitch or loudness; abnormal oscillation of a part of an aircraft. [OE flotorian to float about, from the root of flēotan to float]

■ **flutt'ery** adj.

fluvial /floo'vi-əl/ adj of, belonging to, found or occurring in rivers. [L fluviālis, from fluvius a river, and fluere to flow]

■ **flu'vialist** n a person stressing the role of rivers in the explanation of phenomena. **fluviat'ic** or **flu'viatile** /-tīl or -til/ adj belonging to or formed by rivers.

❏ **fluvioglā'cial** adj relating to glacial rivers.

flux /fluks/ n (an) act of flowing; a flow of matter; a state of flow or continuous change; a discharge generally from a mucous membrane (med); matter discharged; excrement (euphem); an easily fused substance, esp one added to another to make it more easily soldered; the rate of flow of mass, volume or energy (phys). ◆ vt to melt; to apply flux to when soldering. ◆ vi to flow; to fuse. [OFr, from L fluxus, from fluere to flow]

■ **fluxion** /fluk'shən/ n a flowing or discharge; excessive flow of blood or fluid to any organ (med); a difference or variation; the rate of change of a continuously varying quantity (maths); (in pl) the name given by Newton to that branch of mathematics which with a different notation (developed by Leibniz) is known as differential and integral calculus. **flux'ional** or **flux'ionary** adj (archaic) variable; inconstant. **flux'ionist** n a person skilled in fluxions. **flux'ive** adj (Shakesp) flowing with tears.

❏ **flux density** n (phys) the number of photons (or particles) passing through a unit area normal to a beam, or the energy of the radiation passing through this area.

■ **in a state of flux** in an unsettled, undetermined state.

fly /flī/ vi (prp **fly'ing**; pat **flew** /floo/; pap **flown** /flōn/; 3rd sing present indicative **flies**) to move through the air, esp on wings or in aircraft; to operate an aircraft; to move swiftly; to hurry; to pass quickly; to flee; to burst quickly or suddenly; to flutter. ◆ vt to avoid or flee from; to cause (eg a kite, aircraft, etc) to fly; to conduct or transport by air; to cross or pass by flying. ◆ n (pl **flies**) any insect of the order Diptera; often so widely used, esp in composition (eg butterfly, dragonfly, mayfly) as to be virtually equivalent to insect; a fish-hook dressed so as to imitate a fly; collectively, an insect pest; butterfly stroke (swimming); a familiar spirit (archaic); an attendant parasite (obs); a flight; a flap, esp a tent-door; a flap of material covering eg a trouser opening; a trouser fastener, eg a zip; the free end of a flag, or anything similar; a fast stagecoach (hist); a light vehicle on hire, at first drawn by a man, later by a horse (hist); a flywheel; (in pl) the large space above the proscenium in a theatre, from which the scenes, etc are controlled. ◆ adj (sl) knowing; surreptitious or sly; stylish, fashionable (N Am). [OE flēogan to fly, pat flēah; flēoge fly or insect; Ger fliegen, Fliege]

■ **flier** or **flyer** /flī'ər/ n a person who flies or flees; an aircraft pilot; an object, eg a train, moving at top speed; an ambitious person, esp one for whom fast promotion in the workplace is assured (also **high-fli'er** or **high-fly'er**); a usu risky financial speculation (sl); a part of a machine which moves rapidly; a mishit ball that travels further than intended (golf); a rectangular step in stairs; a flying leap (see below); a flying start (inf); a (usu single-sheet) promotional leaflet used (esp as an insert to other printed material) for advertising purposes. **fly'able** adj (of weather) in which it is safe to fly; (of an aircraft) able, or fit, to be flown. **fly'ing** n the action of the verb fly. ◆ adj that flies or can fly; moving or passing very rapidly; organized for speedy action or transfer to any location as the need arises; (of a visit) very brief.

❏ **fly agaric** n a poisonous type of toadstool, Amanita muscaria, used in the production of flypaper and having hallucinogenic properties. **fly ash** n fine particles of ash released into the air during eg the burning of fossil fuels in power stations, also used in brickmaking and as a partial substitute for cement in concrete. **fly'away** adj streaming; flighty; (of hair) too fine to hold a style for long. **fly'back** n the return of the scanning beam in a cathode-ray tube to the point where scanning starts. **fly'bait** n anything that attracts flies; a corpse (sl). **fly ball** n (baseball) a ball hit high into the air. **fly'bane** n poison for flies; a name for various plants used for this. **fly'belt** n a belt of country infested by tsetse fly. **fly'-bitten** adj marked by, or as if by, the bites of flies. **fly'blow** n the egg of a fly, esp when found in meat. **fly'blown**

adj tainted with flies' eggs or maggots (also fig). **fly'boat** n a long, narrow, swift boat used on canals. **fly'book** n a case like a book for holding fishing-flies. **fly'bridge** see flying bridge below. **fly'-by** n a flight, at low altitude or close range, past a place, or a body in space, for observation. **fly'-by-night** n a person who gads about at night; an absconding debtor; an irresponsible person. ◆ adj irresponsible, esp in business matters; unreliable; transitory. **fly-by-wire'** adj (of the control systems of an aircraft) controlled by computer and operated electronically, not mechanically. **fly'catcher** n a name for various birds that catch flies on the wing. **fly cemetery** n (humorous) a cake, biscuit or pastry containing currants. **fly'-dressing** n fly-tying. **fly'-drive** n a package holiday in which the rental of a car, etc is included and the vehicle collected at the destination (also adj). **fly'-dumping** n fly-tipping. **fly'-fish** vi to fish using artificial flies as lure. **fly'-fisher** n. **fly'-fishing** n. **fly'-flap** n a fly swat (see below). **fly'-flapper** n. **fly front** n a concealed fastening on a jacket, shirt, etc. **fly-front'ed** adj. **fly'-hack** n fly-kick. **fly half** n (rugby) a stand-off half. **flying bedstead** n a testing framework resembling a bedstead in shape, that can be raised vertically from the ground by a jet engine. **fly'ing-boat** n a seaplane with a boat's body. **flying bomb** n a bomb in the form of an unpiloted jet-propelled aeroplane. **flying bridge** n a ferry-boat moving under the combined forces of a river or stream and the resistance of a long cable; a pontoon bridge; (also **flybridge**) the highest bridge of a ship. **flying buttress** n (archit) an arch-shaped prop. **flying camp** or **flying column** n a body of troops for rapid deployment from one place to another. **flying colours** n pl unfurled flags; triumphant success. **Flying Corps** n the precursor (1912–18) of the Royal Air Force. **flying doctor** n a doctor, esp orig in the remote parts of Australia, who can be called by radio, etc and who flies to visit patients. **flying dragon** n a flying lizard (see below). **Flying Dutchman** n a black ghostly Dutch ship, or its captain, condemned to sweep the seas around the Cape of Good Hope for ever. **flying fish** n a fish that can leap out of the water and glide in the air for a short time on its long pectoral fins, as if flying. **flying fox** n a large fruit-eating bat. **flying frog** n an Asian frog with large webs between its toes that enable it to glide between trees. **flying jib** n in a ship with more than one jib, the one set furthest forward. **flying leap** n a leap made from a running start. **flying lemur** n an animal (not in fact a lemur) of the genus Cynocephalus of the islands of SE Asia, whose fore and hind limbs are connected by a fold of skin, included in the Insectivora or made a separate order, Dermoptera. **flying lizard** n a dragon or Komodo lizard. **flying machine** n a power-driven aircraft. **flying officer** n an officer in the Royal Air Force of rank equivalent to sublieutenant in the Navy and lieutenant in the Army (formerly called **observer**). **flying party** n a small body of soldiers, equipped for rapid movements, used to harass an enemy. **flying phalanger** n a general name for animals similar to the phalangers with a parachute of skin between fore and hind legs. **flying picket** n one of a mobile group of pickets available for reinforcing the body of local pickets during a strike. **flying saucer** n any of several disc-like flying objects reported to have been seen by various people and alleged to be craft from outer space. **flying shore** n a horizontal baulk or shore. **flying shot** n a shot at something in motion. **flying snake** n a SE Asian snake with a semicircular membrane supported by movable ribs on either side of the body that enables it to glide between trees. **flying squad** n a body of police, etc with special training, available for duty where the need arises, or one organized for fast action or movement. **flying squid** n a squid with broad lateral fins by which it can spring high out of the water. **flying squirrel** n a name for several kinds of squirrels with a parachute of skin between the fore and hind legs; also applied to the flying phalanger. **flying start** n (in a race) a start given with the competitors already in motion; an initial advantage; a promising start. **flying suit** n a pilot's one-piece suit; a similar fashion garment, worn esp by women. **flying wing** n an arrowhead-shaped aircraft designed to minimize drag at very high speeds. **fly'-kick** n a kick made while running. **fly'leaf** n a blank leaf at the beginning or end of a book. **fly line** n a line for angling with an artificial fly. **fly'maker** n a person who ties artificial flies for angling. **fly'man** n a person who works the ropes in theatre flies; a person who drives a fly (hist). **fly orchis** n an orchid (Ophrys muscifera or O. insectifera) with a fly-like flower. **fly'over** n a road or railway line carried over the top of another one at an intersection; a processional flight of aircraft, a flypast (US). **fly'paper** n a sticky or poisonous paper for attracting and killing flies. **fly'past** n a ceremonial flight analogous to a march past; a fly-by in space. **fly'pitch** n (inf) a market stall for which the operator has no licence. **fly'pitcher** n. **fly'poster** n a person who carries out flyposting; an illegal poster. **fly'posting** n the practice of sticking political, advertising, etc bills illegally, on walls, etc. **fly powder** n a powder used for killing flies. **fly rail** n a leg that turns out to support the leaf of a table. **fly rod** n a light flexible rod used in fly-fishing, usu in three pieces: butt, second-joint and tip. **fly'sheet** n a piece of canvas that can be fitted to the roof of a tent to give additional protection from rain; a handbill. **fly slip** n (cricket) a fielder some distance behind the batsman on the offside. **fly'-slow** adj (Shakesp; doubtful reading and sense) slow-flying. **fly'-speck** *n* a small spot of flies' excrement. **fly'spray** *n* (an aerosol containing) an insecticide. **fly swat** or **swatter** *n* a device with which to hit or drive away flies. **fly'-tipping** *n* unauthorized disposal of waste materials. **fly'-tower** *n* a central tower in a modern theatre from which the flies can be hung over the stage. **fly'trap** *n* a trap to catch flies; a plant that traps flies, *esp* the American dogbane and Venus flytrap. **fly'-tying** *n* making artificial flies for angling. **fly'-under** *n* a road or railway line carried under another one at an intersection. **fly'way** *n* a migration route used by birds. **fly'weight** *n* a weight category, applied *esp* in boxing; a sportsperson of the specified weight for the category (eg in professional boxing the lowest weight (**mini flyweight, minimum weight** or **straw'weight** (under 48kg/105lb), **light flyweight** or **junior flyweight** (maximum 49kg/108lb), **flyweight** (maximum 51kg/112lb), and **super flyweight** or **junior bantamweight** (maximum 52kg/115lb)). **fly'wheel** *n* a large wheel with a heavy rim, applied to machinery to equalize the effect of the driving effort. **fly whisk** see under **whisk**[1]. ■ **a fly in the ointment** some slight flaw which corrupts a thing of value (from the Bible, Ecclesiastes 10.1); a minor disadvantage in otherwise favourable circumstances. **a fly on the wall** the invisible observer that one would like to be on certain occasions (**fly'-on-the-wall** *adj*). **fly a kite** see **kite-flying** under **kite**[1]. **fly at** or **upon** to attack suddenly. **fly high** to aim high or be ambitious. **fly in the face of** to insult (*obs*); to oppose or defy; to be at variance with. **fly off the handle** (*inf*) to lose one's temper. **fly open** to open suddenly or violently. **fly out** to break out in a rage. **let fly** to attack (also *fig*); to throw or send off. **like flies** (dying, etc) in vast numbers, with as little resistance as insects. **make the feathers fly** see under **feather**. **no flies on** no lack of alertness or astuteness in. **not harm** or **hurt a fly** not to do anyone the least injury. **on the fly** as one goes along, improvised.

Flymo® /flī'mō/ *n* a proprietary name for a type of lawnmower which hovers on a cushion of air.

flype /flīp/ *vt* to strip back; to turn partly outside in. [Prob Scand; cf Dan *flip* a flap]

Flysch or **flysch** /flish/ *n* a great Alpine mass of Cretaceous and Lower Tertiary sandstone with shales. [Swiss Ger]

flyte or **flite** /flīt/ (*Scot*) *vi* to quarrel; to brawl. ◆ *vt* to scold; to rail at. [OE *flītan* to strive; Ger *befleissen*] ■ **flyte** or **flyt'ing** *n* an open debate; a contest in the exchange of (poetic) abuse (*hist*).

FM *abbrev* : Field Marshal; First Minister; frequency modulation.

Fm (*chem*) *symbol* : fermium.

fm *abbrev* : fathom; femtometre.

FMA *abbrev* : Fund Managers Association (now replaced by **IMA**).

FMCGs *abbrev* : fast-moving consumer goods.

FMD *abbrev* : foot-and-mouth disease.

FMS *abbrev* : flexible manufacturing system.

FMV *abbrev* : full motion video.

FO *abbrev* : Faroe Islands (ie *Føroyar* ; IVR); Field Officer; Flying Officer; Foreign Office; Full Organ.

fo. or **fol.** *abbrev* : folio.

foal /fōl/ *n* the young of any animal of the horse family. ◆ *vi* and *vt* to give birth to (a foal). [OE *fola* ; Ger *Fohlen*, Gr *pōlos* ; L *pullus*] ❑ **foal'foot** *n* (*bot*) coltsfoot. ■ **in foal** or **with foal** (of a mare) pregnant.

foam /fōm/ *n* bubbles on the surface of liquid; a suspension of gas in a liquid; frothy saliva or perspiration; any of many light, cellular materials, rigid or flexible, produced by aerating a liquid, then solidifying it; the sea (*poetic*). ◆ *vi* to gather, produce or be full of foam; to be furious (*inf*). ◆ *vt* to pour out in foam; to fill or cover with foam. [OE *fām* ; Ger *Feim*, prob related to L *spūma*] ■ **foam'ily** *adv*. **foam'iness** *n*. **foam'ing** *n* and *adj*. **foam'ingly** *adv*. **foam'less** *adj*. **foam'y** *adj*. ❑ **foam glass** *n* a very lightweight material made by firing crushed glass with carbon, used as a heat insulator, a construction material, and a filling in lifebelts, etc. **foam** or **foamed plastics** *n pl* cellular plastics, soft and flexible like sponges, or rigid, with excellent heat-insulation properties. **foam rubber** *n* rubber in cellular form, used chiefly in upholstery. ■ **foam at the mouth** to produce frothy saliva; to be extremely angry (*inf*).

fob[1] /fob/ *n* (*archaic*) a trick. ◆ *vt* (*archaic* except with *off*) to cheat; to give as genuine; to put off; to foist or palm. [Cf Ger *foppen* to jeer]

fob[2] /fob/ *n* a small watch pocket in a waistcoat or the waistband of trousers; a chain attaching a watch to a waistcoat, etc; a decoration hanging from such a chain; a small electronic tab used to gain access through a controlled-entry door; a decorative tab on a key ring. [Perh connected with LGer *fobke* little pocket, HGer dialect *fuppe* pocket] ❑ **fob'-watch** *n*. ◆ *vt* (*obs*) to pocket.

fob *abbrev* : free on board.

FOC *abbrev* : father of the chapel (in a trade union).

foc *abbrev* : free of charge.

focaccia /fə-kach'ə/ *n* a flat loaf of Italian bread made with olive oil and topped with salt, herbs etc. [Ital]

focal, foci and **focimeter** see **focus**.

fo'c'sle /fōk'sl/, contracted form of **forecastle**.

focus /fō'kəs/ *n* (pl **foci** /fō'sī/ or **fo'cuses**) a fixed point such that the distances of a point on a conic section from it and from the directrix have a constant ratio (*geom*); a point in which rays converge after reflection or refraction, or from which (**virtual focus**) they seem to diverge (*optics*); any central point; the point or region of greatest activity or interest; the point of origin (eg of an earthquake); the position, or condition, of sharp definition of an image. ◆ *vt* and *vi* (**fo'cusing** or **fo'cussing**; **fo'cused** or **fo'cussed**) to bring or adjust to a focus; to adjust so as to get a sharp image of; to concentrate. [L *focus* a hearth] ■ **fo'cal** *adj* of, belonging or relating to a focus. **focaliza'tion** or **-s-** *n*. **fo'calize** or **-ise** *vt* (*technical*) to focus. **fo'cally** *adv*. **focimeter** /fō-sim'i-tər/ *n* an instrument for measuring the focal length of a lens. **fo'cusing** *n* a psychotherapeutic technique involving self-awareness. ❑ **focal distance** *n* focal length. **focal infection** *n* a localized bacterial infection, eg of a gland, etc. **focal length** *n* the distance between the centre of a lens and its focus. **focal plane** *n* the plane, at right angles to the principal axis of a lens, in which the image is formed. **focal-plane shutter** *n* a camera shutter in the form of a blind with a slot, which is pulled rapidly across, and as close as is practicable to, the film or plate, speed being varied by adjusting the width of the slot. **focal point** *n* focus (*optics*); a centre of attraction for some event or activity. **focus fund** *n* an investment fund containing shares in a relatively small number of companies. **focus group** *n* a small number of people assembled to discuss a topic, new product, etc so that researchers may benefit from their opinions. **focusing cloth** *n* a cloth thrown over a photographic camera and the operator's head and shoulders to exclude extraneous light when focusing. ■ **conjugate foci** (*optics*) two points such that each is the focus for rays proceeding from the other. **in focus** placed or adjusted so as to secure distinct vision, or a sharp, definite image. **principal focus** (*optics*) the focus for rays parallel to the axis.

fodder /fod'ər/ *n* food supplied to cattle; food (*sl*); people seen, callously, as a plentiful and expendable commodity (as in *cannon fodder*); any constant resource (*inf*). ◆ *vt* to supply with fodder. [OE *fōdor*, Ger *Futter* ; cf **food**[1] and **feed**[1]] ■ **fodd'erer** *n*. **fodd'ering** *n*.

FOE or **FoE** *abbrev* : Friends of the Earth.

foe /fō/ (*literary* or *archaic*) *n* (pl **foes**; (*Spenser*) **fone** or **foen** /fōn/) an enemy. [ME *foo*, from OE *fāh, fā* (adj) and *gefā* (noun)] ❑ **foe'man** *n* (pl **foe'men**) an enemy in war.

foedarie see **fedarie**.

foederatus /fed-ə-rā'təs or foi-de-rä'tŭs/ (*L*) *n* (pl **foederati** /-rä'tī or -rä'tē/) a (conquered) ally of Rome; an auxiliary soldier fighting for the Romans.

foehn see **föhn**.

foetid and **foetor** see **fetid**.

foetus see **fetus**.

fog[1] /fog/ *n* (a) thick cloudlike mist near the ground; cloudy obscurity; confusion or bewilderment; blurring on a negative, print or transparency (*photog*). ◆ *vt* (**fogg'ing**; **fogged**) to shroud in fog; to obscure; to confuse; to produce fog on (*photog*). ◆ *vi* to become coated, clouded, blurred or confused (*esp* with *up* or *over*); to be affected by fog (*photog*). [Origin obscure; perh connected with **fog**[2]; perh with Dan *fog*, as in *snee-fog* thick falling snow] ■ **fogged** /fogd/ *adj* clouded, obscured; bewildered. **fogg'er** or **fog'man** *n* a person who sets railway fog signals. **fogg'ily** *adv*. **fogg'iness** *n*. **fogg'y** *adj* misty; damp; fogged; clouded in mind; stupid. **fog'less** *adj* without fog, clear. ❑ **fog bank** *n* a dense mass of fog like a bank of land. **fog'-bell** *n* a bell rung by waves or wind to warn sailors in fog. **fog'bound** *adj* impeded or brought to a standstill by fog. **fog'-bow** *n* a whitish arch like a rainbow, seen in fogs. **fog'-dog** *n* a whitish spot seen near the horizon in fog. **fog'horn** *n* a horn used as a warning signal by or to ships in foggy weather; a siren; a big bellowing voice (*inf*). **fog index** *n* a formula for calculating the readability of a text, used *esp* for children's books. **fog lamp** or **fog light** *n* a lamp, *esp* on a vehicle, used to improve visibility in fog. **fog signal** *n* a detonating cap or other audible warning used in fog. **fog'-smoke** *n* fog. ■ **not have the foggiest** (*inf*) not to have the least idea.

fog[2] /fog/ or **foggage** /fog'ij/ *n* grass that grows after the hay is cut; moss (*Scot*). ◆ *vi* to become covered with fog. [Origin unknown; Welsh *ffwg* dry grass, is borrowed from English] ■ **fogg'y** *adj*.

■ words derived from main entry word; ❑ compound words; ■ idioms and phrasal verbs

fogash /fog'osh/ n the pike-perch. [Hung *fogas*]

fogey see **fogy**.

foggage see **fog²**.

fogou /fō'goo or foo'goo/ (*archaeol*) n a man-made underground passage or chamber, found in Cornwall. [From a Cornish word]

fogy or **fogey** /fō'gi/ (*derog*) n (pl **fo'gies** or **fo'geys**) an old person, *esp* one with old-fashioned views (also **old fogy** or **old fogey**). [Prob from **foggy** moss-grown]
■ **fo'gram** (*archaic*) adj antiquated. ◆n a fogy. **fō'gramite** or **fogram'ity** n. **fō'gydom** or **fo'geydom** n. **fō'gyish** or **fo'geyish** adj. **fō'gyism** or **fo'geyism** n.
■ **young fogy** or **young fogey** (*derog*) a young person who adopts old-fashioned opinions, appearance, etc.

foh /fō/ (*archaic*) interj expressing disgust or contempt (also **pho** or **phoh**).

föhn or **foehn** /fœn/ n a hot dry wind blowing down a mountain valley, *esp* in the Alps. [Ger, from Romansch *favugn*, from L *Favōnius* the west wind]

foible /foi'bl/ n a weakness; a penchant; a failing; a faible (*fencing*). [OFr *foible* weak; cf **faible** and **feeble**]

foid /foid/ n an internationally agreed term for **feldspathoid** (see under **feldspar**). [feldspath*oid*]

foie gras /fwä grä'/ (Fr) n fattened liver of duck or goose, eaten whole or made into **pâté de foie gras** (or **foies gras**).

foil¹ /foil/ vt to defeat; to baffle; to frustrate; to beat down or trample with the feet (*obs*); to destroy a trail by crossing (*hunting*). ◆n a check, repulse or frustration (*obs*); an incomplete fall in wrestling; a blunt fencing sword with a button on the point. [OFr *fuler* to stamp or crush, from L *fullō* a fuller of cloth]
■ **put on the foil** to overcome or bring to nothing.

foil² /foil/ n a leaf or thin plate of metal, eg tinfoil; a mercury coating on a mirror; metal-coated paper; a thin leaf of metal put under a precious stone to show it to advantage; anything that serves to set off something else; a small arc in tracery; an aerofoil or hydrofoil. [OFr *foil* (Fr *feuille*), from L *folium* a leaf]
■ **foiled** adj. **foil'ing** n.
□ **foil'borne** adj (of a craft) lifted up from, or travelling along, the water on hydrofoils.

foin /foin/ (*archaic*) vi to thrust with a sword or spear. ◆n a thrust with a sword or spear. [OFr *foine*, from L *fuscina* a trident]
■ **foin'ingly** adv.

foison /foi'zn/ n plenty (*archaic*); plentiful yield (*archaic*); strength, vitality or essential virtue (also **fushion**, **fusion** /füzh'ən, fizh'ən/ or **fizz'en**; *Scot*). [OFr, from L *fūsiō, -ōnis*, from *fundere, fūsum* to pour forth]
■ **foi'sonless** adj (also **fush'ionless**, **fu'sionless** or **fizz'enless**) weak or feeble (*Scot*).

foist /foist/ vt to pass off (*on* or *upon* the person affected); to insert wrongfully (*in* or *into* the thing affected); to bring in by stealth. [Prob Du dialect *vuisten* to take in hand; *vuist* fist]
■ **foist'er** n.

fol. abbrev : folio; followed; following.

folacin /fō'lə-sin/ n folic acid.

folate see under **folic acid**.

fold¹ /fōld/ n a doubling of anything upon itself; a crease; the concave side of anything folded; a part laid over on another. ◆vt to lay in folds or double over; to enclose in a fold or folds or wrap up; to embrace. ◆vi to become folded; to be capable of being folded; to yield (*obs*); (of a business, etc) to collapse or cease functioning (also with *up*; *inf*). [OE *faldan* (WSax *fealdan*) to fold; Ger *falten*]
■ **fold'able** adj. **fold'er** n a person or thing that folds; a flat knifelike instrument used in folding paper; a folding case for loose papers; a folded circular; another name for a directory (*comput*). **fold'ing** adj that folds or that can be folded. ◆n a fold or pleat; the bending of strata, *usu* as the result of compression (*geol*).
□ **fold'away** adj that can be folded and put away. **foldboat** see **faltboat**. **folded mountains** n pl (*geol*) mountains produced by folding processes. **folding door** n a door consisting of two parts hung on opposite jambs. **fold'ing-machine** n a mechanism that automatically folds printed sheets. **folding money** n (*inf*) paper money. **fold'out** adj and n (a large page, eg containing a diagram) folded to fit into a book, and to be unfolded for reading (also **gate'fold**).
■ **fold in** (*cookery*) to mix in carefully and gradually, without stirring.

fold² /fōld/ n an enclosure for protecting domestic animals, *esp* sheep; a flock of sheep; a church or its congregation (*fig*); the Christian Church (*fig*). ◆vt to confine in a fold. [OE *falod, fald* a fold or stall]
■ **fold'ing** n.

-fold /-fōld/ sfx (with numbers) times, as in *tenfold*. [Ety as for **fold¹**]

folderol see **falderal**.

foley /fō'li/ n the technique of adding sound effects to a cinema film after it has been shot. [Jack *Foley* (1891–1967), US inventor of the process]
□ **foley artist** n a person whose job is to add effects in this way.

foliage /fō'li-ij/ n leaves collectively; a mass of leaves; plant forms in art. [L *folium* a leaf; cf **blade**; Gr *phyllon*]
■ **fōliā'ceous** /-ā'shəs/ adj leaflike; like a foliage leaf; leaf-bearing; laminated. **fō'liaged** adj having foliage; worked like foliage. **fō'liar** adj relating to leaves; resembling leaves. **fō'liate** adj leaflike; having leaves. ◆vt orig to beat into a leaf; to cover with leaf metal; to number the leaves (not pages) of. ◆vi to split into laminae (*med*); (of a plant) to grow leaves. **fō'liated** adj beaten into a thin leaf; decorated with leaf ornaments or foils; consisting of layers or laminae. **fōliā'tion** n the production of leaves, *esp* in plants; the act of beating a metal into a thin plate, or of spreading foil over a piece of glass to form a mirror; the numbering of leaves (not pages) in a book (see **folio**); the alternation of more or less parallel layers or folia of different mineralogical nature, of which the crystalline schists are composed (*geol*); decoration with cusps, lobes or foliated tracery (*archit*). **fō'liature** n foliation. **fō'liolate** or **fō'liolose** adj (*bot*) composed of or relating to leaflets. **fō'liole** n a leaflet of a compound leaf (*bot*); a small leaflike structure. **fō'liose** adj leafy; leaflike. **fō'lium** n (pl **fō'lia**) a leaf; a lamina or lamella (*med*).
□ **foliage leaf** n an ordinary leaf, not a petal, bract, etc. **foliage plant** n one grown for the beauty of its foliage. **foliar feed** n a plant food applied in solution to the leaves.

folic acid /fō'lik or fol'ik as'id/ n an acid in the vitamin B complex (tetrahydrofolate), found in leaves, liver, etc, or a similar acid, deficiency of which causes fetal abnormalities and some of the symptoms of pernicious anaemia (see also **pterin**). [L *folium* a leaf (because occurring in green leaves)]
■ **fo'late** adj of or relating to folic acid. ◆n (a salt of) folic acid.

folie /fo-lē'/ (Fr) n madness, insanity; folly.
□ **folie à deux** /a dø/ n a form of mental illness in which two people, generally close to one another, share the same delusion. **folie de doute** /də doot/ n mental illness characterized by inability to make decisions, however trifling. **folie de grandeur** /grã-dœr'/ n delusions of grandeur.

folio /fō'li-ō/ n (pl **fō'lios**) a leaf (two back-to-back pages) of a book; a leaf of paper in a manuscript, numbered on the front only and blank on the verso; a sheet of paper folded once; a large-format book of such sheets; the size of such a book; one of several sizes of paper adapted for folding once into well-proportioned leaves; a body of written work submitted as part of an examination; a page in an account book, or two opposite pages numbered as one (*bookkeeping*); a certain number of words taken as a basis for computing the length of a document (*law*); a page number in a book (*printing*); a wrapper for loose papers. ◆adj consisting of paper folded only once; of the size of a folio. ◆vt (**fō'lioing**; **fō'lioed**) to number the leaves or pages of; to mark off the end of every folio of, in law copying. [L *in foliō* on leaf (so-and-so), used in references; L *folium* a leaf or a sheet of paper]
■ **in folio** in sheets folded once; in the form of a folio.

foliolate...to...**folium** see under **foliage**.

folk /fōk/ n people, collectively or distributively; a nation or people; the people or commons (*archaic*); those of one's own family, relations (*inf*); now generally used as a pl (either **folk** or **folks**) to mean people in general; folk music. ◆adj as practised, etc by ordinary people, and handed down by tradition (found also in *folk art*, *folk-craft*, *folk medicine*, etc). [OE *folc*; ON *folk*; Ger *Volk*]
■ **folk'ie** n (*inf*) a lover of folk music; a folk musician. **folk'siness** n. **folk'sy** adj (chiefly *US*) everyday; friendly; sociable; of ordinary people; (artificially) traditional in style.
□ **folk dance** n a dance handed down by tradition of the people. **folk etymology** n popular unscientific attempts at etymology. **folk'-free** adj (*archaic*) having the rights of a freeman. **folk hero** n a hero in the eyes of the ordinary people, or in the traditions of a people. **folk'land** n (OE *folcland*) in Anglo-Saxon times, probably land held by folk-right, as opposed to *bócland* (bookland). **folk'lore** n the ancient observances and customs, the notions, beliefs, traditions, superstitions and prejudices of the common people; the study of these observances, etc, the science of the survival of archaic belief and custom in modern ages (a name suggested by WJ Thoms in 1846). **folk'lóric** adj. **folk'lórist** n a person who studies folklore. **folk-mem'ory** n a memory of an event that survives in a community through many generations; the power of remembering as attributed to a community. **folk'moot** n an assembly of the people among the Anglo-Saxons. **folk music** n the music (*esp* song) handed down in the popular tradition of the people, or contemporary music of a similar style. **folk'-right** n the common law or right of the people. **folk rock** n a form of popular music which adapts folk melodies to the rhythm of rock music. **folk'-singer** n. **folk song** n any song or ballad (frequently anonymous) originating among

the people and traditionally handed down by them; a modern song composed and performed in the same idiom (*esp* by a singer-songwriter). **folk'-speech** *n* the dialect of the common people of a country, in which ancient idioms are embedded. **folk story** or **folk tale** *n* a popular story handed down by oral tradition from a more or less remote antiquity. **folk tune** *n* a tune handed down among the people. **folk'way** *n* (*usu* in *pl*) a traditional way of thinking, feeling or acting, followed unreflectingly by a social group. **folk'-weave** *n* a loosely woven fabric.

Folketing /fŏl'kə-ting/ *n* the lower house of the Danish parliament or Rigsdag. [Dan, from *folk* the people, and ON *thing* assembly]

folksonomy /fŏk-son'ə-mi/ *n* any data-classification system that employs terms formed naturally by the users of the data rather than terms decided by an official body. [**folk** and **taxonomy**]

follicle /fol'i-kl/ *n* a fruit formed from a single carpel containing several seeds, splitting along the ventral suture only (*bot*); a Graafian follicle (*zool*); any small sac-like structure, eg the pit surrounding a hair-root (*anat*). [L *folliculus*, dimin of *follis* a windbag]
■ **follic'ulated**, **follic'ular**, **follic'ulose** or **follic'ulous** *adj*.
□ **follicle-stimulating hormone** *n* a hormone secreted in the pituitary gland, which stimulates growth of the Graafian follicles of the ovary, and sperm production (*abbrev* **FSH**).

follow /fol'ō/ *vt* to go after or behind; to keep along the line of; to come after or succeed; to pursue; to attend; to support (eg a team or sportsperson); to believe in (eg a religious leader or teaching); to imitate; to obey (eg orders); to adopt (eg an opinion); to keep the eye or mind fixed on; to grasp or understand the whole course or sequence of; to result from, as an effect from a cause; (on Twitter) to regularly read and respond to posts made by a particular individual; to strive to obtain (*Bible*). ◆ *vi* to come after; to result; to be the logical conclusion. ◆ *n* a stroke that causes the ball to follow the one it has struck (commonly **follow-through'**; *billiards* and *snooker*); a second helping. [OE *folgian, fylgan*; Ger *folgen*]
■ **foll'ower** *n* a person who comes after; a person who copies; a disciple, supporter or devotee; a retainer or attendant; (on Twitter) a person who regularly reads and responds to posts made by a particular individual; a servant-girl's sweetheart (*old*); a part of a machine driven by another part. **foll'owing** *n* a body of supporters. ◆ *adj* coming next after; to be next mentioned; (of a wind) blowing in the same direction as a boat, aircraft, etc is travelling. ◆ *prep* after.
□ **foll'ow-board** *n* (in moulding) the board on which a pattern is laid. **follow-my-lead'er** *n* a game in which all other players have to mimic whatever the leader does. **follow-on'** *n* an act of following on; a second innings following immediately after the first (*cricket*). **follow-through'** *n* an act of following through.
■ **follow home** to follow to the point aimed at, to the heart of the matter. **follow on** to continue endeavours (*Bible*); to start a second innings immediately after the first, as the result of scoring a total that is lower than that of the opposing team by more than a predetermined amount (*cricket*); to follow immediately (*inf*); to start where another (person, etc) left off (*inf*). **follow out** to carry out (eg instructions); to follow to the end or conclusion. **follow suit** to play a card of the same suit as the one which was led (*cards*); to do what another person has done. **follow through** to complete the swing of a stroke after hitting the ball (*sport*); to carry any course of action to its conclusion. **follow up** to pursue an advantage closely; to pursue a question that has been started (**foll'ow-up** *n* and *adj*).

folly /fol'i/ *n* silliness or weakness of mind; a foolish thing; sin (*obs*); a monument of folly, such as a great useless structure, or one left unfinished, because it was begun without establishing the cost; a building constructed merely for ornamental purposes, such as a mock ruin. ◆ *vi* (**foll'ying; foll'ied**) (*archaic*) to act with folly. [OFr *folie*, from *fol* foolish]

Fomalhaut /fŏ'məl-howt, -hŏt, -ə-lŏt/ *n* a first-magnitude star in the constellation of the Southern Fish. [Ar *fam-al-hūt* the whale's mouth]

foment /fō-ment'/ *vt* to foster (*usu* evil); to apply a warm lotion to; to treat or relieve by applying heat or moisture (*obs*). [L *fōmentum* for *fovimentum*, from *fovēre* to warm]
■ **fomentā'tion** *n* instigation; the application of a warm lotion or a warm, moist preparation such as a poultice, to reduce inflammation and pain (extended sometimes to a dry or cold application); the lotion, etc so applied. **fomen'ter** *n*.

fomes /fō'mēz/ (*med*) *n* (*pl* **fomites** /fō'mi-tēz/) a substance capable of carrying infection. [L *fōmes, -tis* touchwood]

fon /fon/ (*obs*) *n* a fool. ◆ *vi* to be foolish or play the fool. ◆ *vt* (**fonn'ing; fonned**) to fool (someone); to toy with. [**fond**[1]]
■ **fon'ly** *adv* foolishly.

fonctionnaire /fŏ-ksyo-ner'/ (*Fr*) *n* an official; a civil servant.

fond[1] /fond/ *adj* prizing highly (with *of*); very affectionate; kindly disposed; weakly indulgent; foolish, *esp* foolishly tender and loving (*archaic*); credulous or foolishly hopeful (*archaic*). ◆ *vi* (*obs*) to dote. [Pap of *fon*, from ME *fonnen* to act foolishly, and *fon* a fool]
■ **fond'ly** *adv*. **fond'ness** *n*.
□ **fond hope** *n* a desire that is held dear but unlikely to be realised.

fond[2] /fond/ (*Spenser*) *pat* of **fand**[2] and *pat* and *pap* of **find**.

fond[3] /fɔ̃/ (*Fr*) *n* basis, foundation or background.

fonda /fon'dä/ (*Sp*) *n* a tavern.

fondant /fon'dənt/ *n* a soft sweet made with flavoured sugar and water, that melts in the mouth. [Fr, from *fondre* to melt, from L *fundere*]

fondle /fon'dl/ *vt* to handle with fondness; to caress. [Ety as for **fond**[1]]
■ **fond'ler** *n*. **fond'ling** *n* a pet (*obs*); a fool (*obs*); the action of the verb.

fonds /fɔ̃/ (*Fr*) *n* landed property; capital; money; fund (*lit* and *fig*).

fondue /fon'doo or fɔ̃-dü'/ *n* a sauce made by heating a mixture of cheese and wine, etc, eaten by dipping pieces of bread, etc in the mixture (also **Swiss fondue**); a dish consisting of small cubes of meat cooked at the table on forks in hot oil and served with piquant sauces (also **fondue bourguignonne** /boor-gē-nyon'/); a soufflé with bread or biscuit crumbs. [Fr, from fem pap of *fondre* to melt]

fone see **foe**.

fons et origo /fons et o-rī'gō, -rē'/ (*L*) the source and origin.

font[1] /font/ *n* a vessel for baptismal water (*relig*); a fount, origin or fountain (*poetic*). [OE *font*, from L *fōns, fontis* a fountain]
■ **font'al** *adj* relating to a font or origin. **font'let** *n* a little font.
□ **font name** *n* (*relig*) baptismal name. **font'-stone** *n* (*relig*) a baptismal font made of stone.

font[2] /font/ see **fount**[1].

fontanelle or **fontanel** /fon-tə-nel'/ *n* a membrane-covered gap between the immature parietal bones in the skull of a fetus or infant; an opening for discharge (*med*). [Fr dimin, from L *fōns, fontis* a fountain]

fontange /fɔ̃-täzh'/ (*hist*) *n* a tall headdress worn in the 17th and 18th centuries. [Fr, from *Fontanges* the territorial title of one of Louis XIV's mistresses]

Fontarabian /fon-tə-rā'bi-ən/ *adj* of or relating to *Fontarabia* or Fuenterrabia at the west end of the Pyrenees (confused by Milton with Roncesvalles).

fonticulus /fon-tik'ū-ləs/ *n* (*pl* **fontic'ulī**) the depression just over the top of the breastbone. [L *fonticulus*, dimin of *fōns* fountain]

Fontina /fon-tē'nə/ *n* a mild Italian cheese made from cow's milk. [Ital]

fontinalis /fon-ti-nā'lis/ *n* a moss of the *Fontinalis* genus of aquatic mosses allied to *Hypnum*. [L *fontinālis* of a spring, from *fōns*]

food[1] /food/ *n* a substance, or substances, that a living thing feeds on; a substance which, when digested, nourishes the body; anything that nourishes or promotes growth or activity; substances produced by plants from raw materials taken in (*bot*). [OE *fōda*; Gothic *fōdeins*, Swed *föda*]
■ **food'ful** *adj* (*rare*) able to supply food abundantly. **food'ie** or **food'y** *n* (*inf*) a person who is greatly (even excessively) interested in the preparation and consumption of good food. **food'ism** *n* great interest in or concern over food. **food'less** *adj* without food.
□ **food bank** *n* a place where a charitable organization dispenses free food to the needy. **food canal** *n* the alimentary canal. **food'-card** *n* a card entitling its holder to obtain his or her quota of rationed foodstuffs. **food chain** *n* a series of organisms connected by the fact that each forms food for the organism above it in the series. **food'-controller** *n* an official who controls the storing, sale and distribution of food in time of emergency. **food conversion ratio** *n* the ratio of the weight of foodstuffs which a cow, pig, chicken, etc consumes, to its own bodyweight. **food court** *n* an area, as in a shopping mall or an airport, containing a variety of (fast-)food booths and a section of communal seating and tables for the customers. **food'-fish** *n* an edible fish. **food hall** *n* an extensive area in a department store where a wide variety of food is sold. **food miles** *n pl* the distance travelled from the place where food is produced to the place where it is eaten, considered in terms of the environmental damage that transporting it entails. **food poisoning** *n* a gastrointestinal disorder caused by the ingestion of foods naturally toxic to the system or of foods made toxic by contamination with bacteria or chemicals. **food processor** *n* an electrical appliance for cutting, blending, mincing, etc food, *esp* in the home. **food'stuff** *n* a substance used as food. **food values** *n pl* the relative nourishing power of foods. **food web** *n* (*ecology*) an interconnected pattern of food chains.

food[2] /food/ *n* (*Spenser*) same as **feud**[1].

fool[1] /fool/ *n* a person lacking in wisdom, judgement or sense; a weak-minded person (*obs*); a jester (*hist*); a dupe or victim; a vague term of endearment (*obs*); a person with a weakness (with *for*). ◆ *vt* to deceive; to cause to appear foolish; to obtain by fooling. ◆ *vi* to play the fool; to trifle. ♦ *adj* (*Scot* and *US*) foolish. [OFr *fol* (Fr *fou*), from L *follis* a windbag]

■ **fool'ery** *n* an act of folly; habitual folly; fooling. **fool'ing** *n* playing the fool; acting the jester (*hist*); a characteristic streak of jesting (*hist*); trifling. **fool'ish** *adj* lacking intellect; lacking discretion; unwise, ill considered; ridiculous, idiotic, silly; marked by folly; paltry (*archaic*). **fool'ishly** *adv*. **fool'ishness** *n*.
◻ **fool'begged** *adj* (*Shakesp*) perh foolish enough to be begged for a fool (qv under **beg**[1]); in allusion to the custom of seeking the administration of a lunatic's estate for one's own advantage). **fool'-born** *adj* (*Shakesp*) born of a fool or of folly. **fool'-happy** *adj* happy or lucky without contrivance or judgement. **foolhard'iness** *n* (*Spenser*) **foolhardize** or **-ise** /-īz/ or **-härd'/** *n*. **fool'hardy** *adj* foolishly bold; rash or incautious. **fool'ish-witt'y** *adj* (*Shakesp*) wise in folly and foolish in wisdom. **fool'proof** *adj* infallible; guaranteed not to cause damage or injury if misused. **fool's cap** *n* a jester's headdress, *usu* having a coxcomb hood with bells. **fool's errand** *n* a silly or fruitless enterprise; a search for what cannot be found. **fool's gold** *n* iron pyrites. **fool's mate** *n* in chess, the simplest of the checkmates (in two moves by each player). **fool's paradise** *n* a state of happiness based on fictitious hopes or expectations. **fool's parsley** *n* a poisonous umbelliferous plant (*Aethusa cynapium*) that a great enough fool might take for parsley.

■ **All Fools' Day** see under **all**. **fool about** or **around** to waste time; to mess about; to trifle with someone's affections, or to be unfaithful to them with a reckless attitude; to have sex, or indulge in sexual frolicking. **fool away** to squander to no purpose or profit. **fool with** to meddle with officiously, irresponsibly or thoughtlessly. **make a fool of** to cause (someone) to look ridiculous or stupid; to humiliate or dupe; to disappoint. **nobody's fool** a sensible, shrewd person. **play** or **act the fool** to behave like a fool; to be reckless or foolish; to be exuberantly comical or high-spirited.

fool[2] /*fool*/ *n* a purée of fruit scalded or stewed, mixed with cream or custard and sugar (eg *gooseberry fool*). [Prob a use of **fool**[1] suggested by *trifle*]

foolscap /*fool'skap*/ *n* a (now little-used) size of long folio writing or printing paper, generally $13\frac{1}{2}$ by 17 inches (or by $8\frac{1}{2}$ as a single sheet), *orig* bearing the watermark of a *fool's cap* and bells.

foosball also **fusball, fussball** /*foos'böl*/ *n* table football. [Ger *Fussball* football]

foot /*fut*/ *n* (pl **feet**; also, as a measure, **foot**; in some compounds and in sense of dregs, or footlights, **foots**) the part of its body on which a human or animal stands or walks; the part on which anything stands; the base; the lower or less dignified end; a measure equal to 12 inches (0.3048m), *orig* the length of a man's foot; the corresponding square or cubic unit (square foot = 144 square inches/0.0929 square metres; cubic foot = 1728 cubic inches/0.0086 cubic metres); foot soldiers; a division of a line of poetry; a manner of walking; a part of a sewing machine that holds the fabric in place under the needle; a muscular development of the ventral surface in molluscs; the absorbent and attaching organ of a young sporophyte (*bot*). ♦ *vt* and *vi* (**foot'ing; foot'ed**) (*esp* with *it*) to dance (*obs*); to walk; to sum up. ♦ *vt* to kick; to pay (the bill) (*inf*); to add a foot to; to grasp with the foot. [OE *fōt*, pl *fēt*; Ger *Fuss*, L *pēs, pedis*, Gr *pous, podos*, Sans *pad*]

■ **foot'age** *n* measurement or payment by the foot; the length of organ pipe giving the lowest note; an amount (ie length) of cinema or TV film. **foot'ed** *adj* provided with a foot or feet; having gained a football (*Shakesp*). ♦ *combining form* having a specified number of feet; having a specified manner of walking. **foot'edness** *n* the tendency to use one foot rather than the other. **-footedness** *combining form*. **foot'er** *n* a line of type or any information (eg a page number) printed at the foot of a page (*printing; comput*); football (*inf*). ♦ *combining form* something of a specified length in feet, *usu* a boat (eg *he sails a twenty-four-footer*). **foot'ie** or **foot'y** *n* football (*inf*); footsie (see **play footsie** below). **foot'ing** *n* a place for the foot to rest on, *esp* a secure and stable one; standing; terms; a place of installation; a fee charged on the installation of a person to a new position (*archaic*); a foundation or basis; the lower part of a column or wall, immediately above the foundation; position or rank; a track or surface; a tread; a dance; plain cotton lace. **foot'less** *adj* having no feet; very drunk (*inf*).
◻ **foot-and-mouth disease** *n* a contagious disease of cloven-footed animals, characterized by vesicular eruption, *esp* in the mouth and in the clefts of the feet. **foot'ball** *n* a large ball for kicking about in sport; a game played with this ball, *esp* soccer (see **association football** under **associate**); a bargaining-point, point of controversy, etc that is tossed around (*esp* a *political football; fig*). **foot'ballene** *n* (*chem*) buckminsterfullerene. **foot'baller** or (*rare*) **foot'ballist** *n* a football player. **foot'balling** *adj* of or relating to football. **foot'bar** *n* the bar, controlled by the pilot's feet, for operating the rudder in aircraft. **foot'bath** *n* an act of bathing the feet; a bowl, etc for this purpose. **foot'board** *n* a support for the feet in a carriage or elsewhere; the footplate of a locomotive engine; an upright board at the foot of a bed. **foot'boy** *n* a young boy attendant in livery. **foot'brake** *n* a brake

operated by the foot. **foot'breadth** *n* the breadth of a foot. **foot'bridge** *n* a bridge for pedestrians. **foot'-candle** *n* a former unit of incident light, equivalent to one lumen per sq foot (= 10.764 lux). **foot'cloth** *n* a packhorse cloth reaching to the feet of the horse. **foot'-dragging** see **drag one's feet** under **drag**. **foot'fall** *n* the sound of a footstep; the number of customers who enter a shop or shopping centre (*commerce*). **foot fault** *n* (*tennis*) a fault made by stepping over the baseline when serving. **foot'fault** *vt* and *vi*. **foot'gear** see **footwear** below. **foot'guards** *n pl* (*milit*) guards that serve on foot. **foot'hill** *n* a minor elevation below a higher mountain or range (*usu* in *pl*). **foot'hold** *n* a place to fix the foot in, eg when climbing; a grip; a firm starting position. **foot-in-the-mouth'** *adj* of or relating to a verbal faux pas. **foot'-jaw** (*zool*) a maxilliped. **foot-lam'bert** *n* a former unit of emitted or reflected light, equivalent to one lumen per sq foot (= 10.764 lux). **foot-land'-raker** *n* (*Shakesp*) a footpad. **foot'-licker** *n* a fawning, slavish flatterer. **foot'light** *n* one of a row of lights along the front of a theatre stage; (in *pl*) the theatre as a profession. **foot'loose** *adj* free or unhampered by (eg family) ties; (of an industry) not dependent on factors of production found only in a certain location. **foot'man** *n* (*pl* **foot'men**) a person who goes on foot; a servant or attendant in livery; a foot soldier; a servant running before a coach or rider; a low stand for fireside utensils. **foot'mark** see **footprint** below. **foot'muff** *n* a muff for keeping the feet warm. **foot'note** *n* a note of reference or comment at the foot of a page; something relatively unimportant. **foot'pace** *n* (*obs*) a walking pace; a dais. **foot'pad** *n* (*archaic*) a highwayman on foot. **foot'page** *n* a boy attendant. **foot passenger** *n* one who travels on foot. **foot'path** *n* a way for walkers only; a side pavement. **foot'-patrol** *n* a patrol on foot. **foot'plate** *n* a platform for **foot'platemen** or **foot'platewomen** (*sing* **foot'plateman** or **foot'platewoman**), train driver and assistant (on a steam locomotive, the stoker). **foot'post** *n* a post or other messenger that travels on foot. **foot'-pound** or **foot-pound force** *n* the energy needed to raise a mass of one pound through the height of one foot in normal gravity. **foot-pound-sec'ond** *adj* applied to a system of scientific measurement with the foot, pound and second as units of length, mass and time. **foot'print** *n* the mark left on the ground or floor by a person's or animal's foot (also **foot'mark**); the area over which any object is effective (*fig*); extent of influence (*fig*). **foot'pump** *n* a pump held or operated by the foot. **foot'-race** *n* a race on foot. **foot'-racing** *n*. **foot'rest** *n* a support for the foot. **foot'-rope** *n* a rope stretching along under a ship's yard for the crew to stand on when furling the sails; the rope to which the lower edge of a sail is attached. **foot rot** *n* ulceration of the coronary band, or any other infection of the feet in sheep or cattle. **foot'rule** *n* a rule or measure a foot in length or measured off in feet. **foot'slog** *vi* to march or tramp. **foot'slogger** *n*. **foot'slogging** *n*. **foot soldier** *n* a soldier serving on foot. **foot'sore** *adj* having sore or tender feet, *usu* from much walking. **foot'stalk** *n* (*bot*) the stalk or petiole of a leaf. **foot'-stall** *n* a side-saddle stirrup. **foot'step** *n* a tread; a footfall; a footprint; a raised step for ascending or descending; (in *pl; fig*) a path or example. **foot'stool** *n* a stool for placing one's feet on when sitting. **foot'stooled** *adj*. **foot'-tapping** *adj* (of music) that makes one tap, or want to tap, one's feet in time with it. **foot'-ton** or **foot-ton force** *n* a unit of work or energy equal to the work done in raising one ton one foot against normal gravity, 2240 foot-pounds. **foot'wall** *n* the layer of rock immediately underlying a vein of ore, mineral deposit or fault. **foot'-warmer** *n* a device for keeping the feet warm. **foot'way** *n* a path for people on foot; a mineshaft with ladders. **foot'wear** or **foot'gear** *n* a collective term for boots, shoes, socks, etc. **foot'well** *n* either of the hollows for the feet in front of the seats of a vehicle. **foot'work** *n* the use or management of the feet, as in sport; skilful manoeuvring (*fig*). **foot'worn** *adj* footsore; showing signs of much wear by feet.
■ **a foot in the door** a first step towards a *usu* difficult desired end. **at the feet of** in submission, homage, supplication or devotion to or under the spell of. **catch on the wrong foot** to catch (someone) unprepared. **cover the feet** (*Bible*) to defecate. **drag one's feet** see under **drag**. **foot of fine** (*law; hist*) the bottom part (preserved in the records) of a tripartite indenture in case of a fine of land. **foot the bill** (*inf*) to pay a bill in full. **get off on the wrong foot** to make a bad beginning. **have one foot in the grave** (*inf*) to be not far from death. **have one's feet on the ground** to act habitually with practical good sense. **have the ball at one's feet** to have nothing to do except seize one's opportunity. **my foot!** (*inf*) an interjection expressing disbelief, *usu* contemptuous. **on foot** walking or running; in progress. **on the back foot** (*inf*) in a defensive position; at a disadvantage. **play footsie (with)** (*inf*) to rub one's foot or leg against (another person's), *usu* with amorous intentions; to make furtively flirtatious advances towards (*fig*); to collaborate secretly (*fig*). **put a** (or **one's**) **foot wrong** (*usu* in *neg*) to make a mistake or blunder. **put one's best foot forward** to make one's best effort. **put one's feet up** (*inf*) to take a rest. **put one's foot down** (*inf*) to take a firm decision, *usu* against something. **put one's foot in it** (*inf*) to spoil anything by some tactless blunder or remark. **set foot in** to enter. **set on foot** (*archaic*) to originate, start. **shoot oneself in the foot** see under **shoot**[1].

footer[1] see under **foot**.

footer[2] see **fouter**.

footle /fōo'tl/ vi to trifle, waste time or potter (with *about* or *around*). ◆ n (*rare*) silly nonsense. [Origin obscure]
■ **foot'ling** n and adj.

footra see **fouter**.

footsal see **futsal**.

Footsie /fŭt'si/ see **FTSE**.

footsie see **play footsie** under **foot**.

footy[1] /fŭt'i/ (*dialect*) adj mean. [Origin obscure]

footy[2] see **footie** under **foot**.

foo yung or **foo yong** see **fu yung**.

foozle /fōo'zl/ (*inf*) n a tedious person; a bungled stroke at golf, etc. ◆ vi to fool away one's time. ◆ vi and vt to bungle. [Cf Ger dialect *fuseln* to work badly or potter]
■ **fooz'ler** n. **fooz'ling** n and adj.

fop /fop/ n an affected dandy. [Cf Ger *foppen* to hoax]
■ **fop'ling** n a vain affected person. **fopp'ery** n vanity in dress or manners; affectation; folly. **fopp'ish** adj vain and showy in dress; affectedly refined in manners. **fopp'ishly** adv. **fopp'ishness** n.

for /för or fər/ prep in the place of; in favour of; wanting or wishing to have; on account of; in the direction of; having as goal or intention, in quest of; with respect to; in respect of; by reason of; appropriate or adapted to, or in reference to; beneficial to; notwithstanding, in spite of; in recompense of; during; in the character of; to the extent of. ◆ conj because. [OE *for*]
■ **as for** as far as concerns. **be for it** or **be in for it** (*inf*) to have something unpleasant about to happen, *esp* a scolding. **for all** (**that**) notwithstanding. **for that** (*obs*) because. **for to** (*archaic* or *dialect*) in order to; to. **for why** (*obs* or *dialect*) why; because. **there is nothing for it but** (**to**) there is no other possible course of action but (to). **what is he for a man?** (*obs*) what kind of man is he?

for abbrev : free on rail.

for- /för- or fər-/ pfx (1) in words derived from Old English, used to form verbs with the senses: (a) away or off; (b) against; (c) thoroughly or utterly (intensive); (d) exhaustion; (e) destruction. (2) used in words derived from Old English to form adjectives with superlative force. (3) a contraction of *fore-*. (4) in words derived from L *foris* outside, *forās* forth or out. No longer a living prefix.

fora see **forum**.

forage /for'ij/ n fodder, or food for horses and cattle; provisions; the act of foraging. ◆ vi to go about and forcibly carry off food for horses and cattle; to rummage about (for what one wants); to search for edible plants growing wild. ◆ vt to plunder. [Fr *fourrage*, OFr *feurre* fodder, of Gmc origin; cf **fodder**]
■ **for'ager** n.
❑ **forage cap** n the undress cap worn by infantry soldiers.

foramen /fō-rā'mən or fö-/ (*zool* or *anat*) n (pl **foramina** /-ram'i-nə/) a small opening. [L *forāmen*, from *forāre* to pierce]
■ **foram'inal** adj. **foram'inated** or **foram'inous** adj pierced with small holes; porous. **foraminifer** /for-ə-min'i-fər/ n any member of the **Foraminif'era** /-am-* or -ām-/ an order of rhizopod protozoa with a shell *usu* perforated by pores. **foraminif'eral** or **foraminif'erous** adj.
❑ **forāmen magnum** n the great hole in the occipital bone through which the spinal cord joins the medulla oblongata.

forane /fo-rān'/ adj a form of **foreign**, outlying or rural, as in *vicar-forane* (qv).

forasmuch /för- or fər-əz-much'/ (*archaic* or *formal*) conj because or since (with *as*).

foray /for'ā/ n a raid; a venture or attempt; a journey. ◆ vt and vi to raid; to forage. [Ety obscure, but ult identical with **forage**]
■ **for'ayer** n.

forb /förb/ (*bot*) n any herb which is not, or does not resemble, a grass. [Gr *phorbē* food]

forbad and **forbade** see **forbid**.

forbear[1] /för- or fər-bār'/ vi (pat **forbore**'; pap **forborne**') to keep oneself in check; to abstain or refrain. ◆ vt to abstain or refrain from; to avoid voluntarily; to spare or withhold; to give up (*obs*). [OE *forberan*, pat *forbær*, pap *forboren*; see **for-** (1a), and **bear**[1]]
■ **forbear'ance** n the exercising of patience or restraint; command of temper; clemency. **forbear'ant** (*obs*) or **forbear'ing** adj long-suffering; patient. **forbear'ingly** adv.

forbear[2] /för'bār/ same as **forebear** (see under **fore-**).

forbid /fər- or för-bid'/ vt (pat **forbade** /-bad'/ or sometimes -bād'/ or **forbad**'; pap **forbidd'en**) to prohibit; to command not to; to deny access. [OE *forbēodan*, pat *forbēad*, pap *forboden*; see **for-** (1a) and **bid**[1,2]; cf Ger *verbieten*]

■ **forbidd'al** or **forbidd'ance** n (*obs*) prohibition; command or edict against a thing. **forbidd'en** adj prohibited; unlawful; not permitted, *esp* in certain scientific rules; (of a combination of symbols) not in an operating code, ie revealing a fault (*comput*). **forbidd'enly** adv (*Shakesp*) in a forbidden or unlawful manner. **forbidd'er** n. **forbidd'ing** n the action of the verb *forbid*. ◆ adj uninviting; sinister; unprepossessing; threatening or formidable in appearance. **forbidd'ingly** adv. **forbidd'ingness** n. **forbode** /för-bōd'/ n (*archaic*) prohibition.
❑ **forbidden degrees** see under **degree**. **forbidden fruit** n the fruit forbidden to Adam in the Bible (Genesis 2.17); anything tempting and prohibited; (also **Adam's apple**) a name fancifully given to the fruit of various species of *Citrus*, *esp* to one having tooth-marks on its rind.
■ **over God's forbode** (*archaic*) God forbid.

forbore and **forborne** see **forbear**[1].

forby, **forbye** or (*Spenser*) **foreby** /fər-bī'/ adv and prep near (*obs*); past (*obs*); by (*obs*); besides (*Scot*). [**for**, adv, and **by**]

forçat /för-sä'/ (Fr) n a convict condemned to hard labour.

force[1] /förs or förs/ n strength, power or energy; efficacy; validity; influence; vehemence; violence; coercion; a group of people assembled for collective action (eg *police force*); (in pl; sometimes with *cap*) a navy, army or air force; an armament; any cause which changes the direction or speed of the motion of a portion of matter (*phys*). ◆ vt to draw or push by strength; to thrust; to compel; to constrain; to overcome the resistance of by force; to achieve or bring about by force; to break or break open by force; to ravish; to take by violence; to cause to grow or ripen rapidly (*hortic*); to strain or work up to a high pitch; to induce or cause (someone) to play in a particular way (*cards*); to cause the playing of (*cards*); to strengthen (*Shakesp*); to attribute importance to (*obs*). ◆ vi to strive (*obs*); to make way by force; to care (*obs*). [Fr, from LL *fortia*, from L *fortis* strong]
■ **forced** adj accomplished by great effort, eg a *forced march*; strained, excessive or unnatural; artificially produced. **forc'edly** adv. **forc'edness** n the state of being forced; constraint; unnatural or undue distortion. **force'ful** adj full of force or strength; energetic; driven or acting with power. **force'fully** adv. **force'fulness** n. **force'less** adj weak. **forc'er** n a person or thing that forces, *esp* the piston of a force pump. **forc'ible** adj having force; done by force. **forc'ibleness** or **forcibil'ity** n. **forc'ibly** adv.
❑ **force de frappe** /fors də frap/ n (Fr) a strike force, *esp* a nuclear one. **forced labour** n compulsory hard labour, as a punishment for a crime. **forced landing** n (*aeronautics*) a landing at a place where no landing was originally planned, necessary because of some mishap or emergency. **force'-feed** vt (pap and pat **force'-fed**) to feed (a person or animal) forcibly, *usu* by the mouth; to impose (an opinion or belief) on (a person) (*fig*). **force'-feeding** n. **force field** n that part of any space where a measurable force can exert an effect (*phys*); an imaginary invisible protective barrier of energy. **force'-land** vi to make a forced landing. **force majeure** /fors mä-zhør'/ n (Fr) superior power; an uncontrollable course of events, excusing one from fulfilling a contract (*law*). **force pump** or **forc'ing-pump** n a pump that delivers liquid under pressure greater than its suction pressure; a pump for cleaning out pipes by blowing air through. **forcible detainer** or **entry** n taking property into custody or forcing an entry into it by violence or intimidation. **forcible feeble** n (*Shakesp*) a weak man with a pretence of valour. **forc'ing-house** n a hothouse for forcing plants, or a place for hastening the growth of animals. **forc'ing-pit** n a frame sunk in the ground over a hotbed for forcing plants.
■ **force and fear** (*Scot*) that amount of constraint or compulsion that is enough to annul an obligation entered into under its influence. **force the pace** to bring and keep the speed up to a high pitch by competition. **in force** operative or legally binding; in great numbers.

force[2] /förs or förs/ or **foss** /fos/ n a waterfall. [ON *fors*]

force[3] /förs or förs/ (*cookery*) vt to stuff (eg fowl). [For **farce**]
❑ **force'meat** n meat chopped fine and highly seasoned, used as a stuffing or alone.

forceps /för'seps/ n (pl **for'ceps** (also **for'cepses** or **for'cipēs** /-si-pēz/)) a pincer-like instrument with two blades, for holding, lifting or removing (eg in surgery). [L, from *formus* hot, and *capere* to hold]
■ **for'cipāte** or **for'cipated** adj formed and opening like a forceps. **forcipā'tion** n torture by pinching with forceps.

forcible, etc see under **force**[1].

ford /förd or förd/ n a place where water may be crossed by wading. ◆ vt to wade across. [OE *ford-faran* to go; cf Ger *furt-fahren*, Gr *poros*, L *portus*, and **fare**, **ferry** and **far**]
■ **ford'able** adj.

fordo /för- or fər-dōo'/ (*archaic*) vt (**fordo'ing**; **fordid**'; **fordone** /-dun'/) to destroy; to ruin; to overcome; to exhaust. [OE *fordōn*; Ger *vertun* to consume]
■ **fordone**' adj exhausted.
❑ **from fordonne** n (*Spenser*) from being fordone.

fore /fōr/ or /för/ *adj* in front; former or previous (*obs*). ◆ *adv* at or towards the front; previously. ◆ *n* the front; the foremast. ◆ *interj* (*golf*) a warning cry to anybody in the way of the ball. [OE *fore*, radically the same as **for**, prep]

■ **foremost** /fōr'mōst* or för'/ *adj* (double *superl*, from OE *forma* first, *superl* of *fore*, and *superl* suffix -*st*) first in place; most advanced; first in rank and dignity.

❑ **fore'-and-aft'** *adj* and *adv* lengthwise (*orig* of a ship); without square sails. **fore-and-aft'er** *n* a schooner, etc with a fore-and-aft rig; a hat peaked at the front and the back. **fore-and-aft sail** *n* any sail not set on yards and lying fore-and-aft when untrimmed. **fore'bitt** *n* one of the bitts, posts for fastening cables, at the foremast. **fore'bitter** *n* a ballad sung at the forebitts.

■ **at the fore** displayed on the foremast (of a flag). **to the fore** at hand; in being or alive (*Scot*); loosely, prominent, towards the front.

fore- /för-, för-/ *pfx* before or beforehand; in front. [OE *fore* ; Ger *vor*]
■ **fore-admon'ish** *vt* to admonish beforehand. **fore-advise'** *vt* to advise beforehand. **fore'arm** *n* the part of the arm between the elbow and the wrist. **forearm'** *vt* to arm or prepare beforehand. **forebear** or **forbear** /för'bār or för'/ *n* (*orig Scot*) an ancestor (from **be** and -**er**[1]). **forebode'** *vt* to predict or foretell; to have a premonition of (*esp* of evil). **forebode'ment** *n* a feeling of coming evil. **forebod'er** *n*. **forebod'ing** *n* a perception beforehand; apprehension of coming evil. **forebod'ingly** *adv*. **fore'-body** *n* (*naut*) the part in front of the mainmast. **fore'-brace** *n* a rope attached to the fore yardarm, for changing the position of the foresail. **fore'brain** *n* the front part of the brain, the prosencephalon. **foreby** *prep* (*Spenser*) same as **forby**. **fore'cabin** *n* a cabin in a ship's forepart. **fore'caddy** *n* (*golf*) a caddy posted up ahead so as to see where the balls go. **fore'car** *n* a small car carrying a passenger in front of a motorcycle. **fore'carriage** *n* the front part of a carriage, with an arrangement for independent movement of the fore-wheels. **fore'cast** *vt* (*pat* and *pap* **fore'cast** (sometimes **fore'casted**)) to assess or calculate beforehand; to foresee; to predict. ◆ *vi* to devise beforehand. ◆ *n* a previous calculation; foresight; a prediction; a weather forecast (see under **weather**). **fore'caster** *n*. **forecastle** or **fo'c's'le** /fōk'sl* or sometimes *för'käs-l* or *för'/ *n* a short raised deck at the fore-end of a ship; the forepart of a ship under the maindeck, the quarters of the crew. **fore'check** *n* (in ice hockey) a check made to an opponent in his or her own defensive area. **forechos'en** *adj* chosen beforehand. **fore-ci'ted** *adj* quoted before or above. **fore'cloth** *n* a cloth that hangs over the front of an altar, an antependium. **fore'course** *n* a foresail. **fore'court** *n* a court in front of a building; an outer court; the front area of a garage or filling station, where the petrol pumps are situated; the part of a tennis court between the net and the service line. **foredate'** *vt* to mark (eg a cheque) with a date earlier than the true date. **fore'-day** *n* (*Scot*) forenoon. **fore'deck** *n* the forepart of a deck or ship. **foredoom'** *vt* to doom beforehand. **fore'-edge** *n* the outer edge of a book, furthest from the spine, placed outward in a medieval library. **fore'-end** *n* the early or fore part of anything. **fore'father** *n* an ancestor. **forefeel'** *vt* to feel beforehand. **forefeel'ingly** *adv*. **forefelt'** *adj*. **fore'finger** *n* the finger next to the thumb. **fore'foot** *n* (*pl* **fore'feet**) either of the front feet of a quadruped (*zool*); the foremost end of the keel, where the stem is found (*naut*). **fore'front** *n* the front or foremost part. **fore'gleam** *n* (*literary*) a glimpse into the future. **forego'** *vt* and *vi* (*prp* **forego'ing** (or /för'* or *för'/); *pat* (*rare*; formerly also *pap*) **forewent'**; *pap* **foregone** (or /för'* or *för'/)) to go before or precede (see also **forgo**). **forego'er** *n* or *för'/*. **forego'ing** *n*. **fore'gone** *adj* (**foregone conclusion** a conclusion come to before examination of the evidence; an obvious or inevitable conclusion or result). **foregone'ness** *n*. **fore'ground** *n* the part of a picture or field of view nearest the observer's eye (cf **background**) (also *fig*). ◆ *vt* (*orig US; fig*) to spotlight or emphasize. **fore'gut** *n* the front section of the digestive tract of an embryo or of an invertebrate animal, from which the forepart of the alimentary canal develops. **fore'-hammer** *n* a sledgehammer. **fore'hand** *n* the upper hand, advantage or preference; the part of a horse that is in front of its rider; the front position or its occupant (*tennis*); the part of the court to the right of a right-handed player or to the left of a left-handed player (*tennis*); a stroke played forehand (*tennis*). ◆ *adj* done beforehand; anticipating or of anticipation (*Shakesp*); with the palm in front, *opp* to backhand (*sport*); (of an arrow) for shooting point-blank (*Shakesp*). ◆ *adv* with the hand in the forehand position. **fore'handed** *adj* done beforehand, as payment for goods before delivery, or for services before rendered; seasonable; planning ahead, with thought or provision for the future (*US*); well-off (*US*); forehand (*US; tennis*); (of a horse, etc) shapely in the foreparts. **forehead** /for'id, -ed, för'hed or för'hed/ *n* the front of the head above the eyes, the brow; confidence or audacity (*obs*). **fore'hock** *n* a cut of bacon or pork from the foreleg. **fore'-horse** *n* the foremost horse of a team. **forejudge'** *vt* to judge before hearing the facts and proof (see also **forjudge**). **forejudg'ement** or **forejudg'ment** *n*. **fore'king** *n* (*Tennyson*) a preceding king. **foreknow'** /för- or *för-/ *vt* to know beforehand; to foresee. **foreknow'able** *adj*. **foreknow'ing** *adj*. **foreknow'ingly** *adv*.

foreknowledge /-*nol'ij*/ *n*. **foreknown'** *adj*. **fore'land** *n* a point of land running forward into the sea, a headland; a front region. **forelay'** *vt* to devise or plan beforehand; to wait for in ambush; to hinder; *pat* of **forelie**. **fore'leg** *n* a front leg. **forelend'** or **forlend'** *vt* (*pat and pap* (*Spenser*) **forelent'** or **forlent'**) (*archaic*) to grant or resign beforehand. **forelie'** *vt* (*pat* **forelay'**) (*Spenser*) to lie in front of. **forelift'** *vt* (*Spenser*) to raise in front. **fore'limb** *n*. **fore'lock** *n* the lock of hair on the forehead (**pull, touch** or **tug the forelock** to raise one's hand to the forehead in sign of respect, subservience, etc; **take time by the forelock** (*literary*) to seize an opportunity quickly); a cotter-pin. **fore'man** *n* (*pl* **fore'men**) the first or chief man, one appointed to supervise, or act as spokesman for, others; an overseer. **fore'mast** *n* the mast that is forward, or nearest to the bow of a ship. **fore'mastman** *n* any sailor below the rank of petty officer. **foremean'** *vt* (*archaic*) to intend beforehand. **fore'men'tioned** *adj* mentioned before in writing or speech. **fore'mother** *n* a female ancestor. **fore'name** *n* the first or Christian name. **fore'named** *adj* mentioned before. **fore'night** *n* (*Scot*) the early part of the night before bedtime, the evening. **forenoon** /för'-noon', för-, för'noon or *för'/ *n* (chiefly *Scot* and *Irish*) the morning; the part of the day before midday, as opposed to early morning. ◆ *adj* /för'* or *för'/ relating to this time. **fore'-notice** *n* notice of anything in advance of the time. **foreordain'** *vt* to arrange or determine beforehand; to predestine. **foreordina'tion** *n*. **fore'part** *n* the front; the early part. **fore'past** *adj* (*obs*) bygone. **fore'paw** *n* a front paw. **fore'payment** *n* payment beforehand. **fore'peak** *n* the narrow part of a ship's hold, close to the bow. **fore'person** *n* a chief person; a supervisor; a spokesperson; an overseer. **foreplan'** *vt* to plan beforehand. **fore'play** *n* sexual stimulation before intercourse. **forepoint'** *vt* to foreshadow. **fore'quarter** *n* the front portion of a side of meat, *incl* the leg; (in *pl*; of an animal, *esp* a horse) the forelegs and shoulders, and the body areas adjoining them. **fore-quo'ted** *adj* quoted or cited before. **foreran'** *vt pat* of **forerun**. **fore'-rank** *n* the front rank. **forereach'** *vi* (*naut*) to glide ahead, *esp* when going in stays (with *on*). ◆ *vt* to sail beyond. **foreread'** *vt* (*pat* **foreread** /-*red'*/) to foretell. **fore'reading** *n*. **fore-reci'ted** *adj* (*Shakesp*) recited or named before. **forerun'** *vt* to run or come before; to precede. **fore'runner** *n* a person or thing coming before another, a precursor; a forewarning or omen; *orig* a runner or messenger sent before. **fore'said** *adj* already mentioned (see also **foresay** below). **foresail** /för'sl*, *för'* or -*sāl*/ *n* the chief and lowest square sail on the foremast; a triangular sail on the forestay. **foresay'** *vt* to predict or foretell; to ordain (*Shakesp*); see also **forsay**. **foresee'** *vt* and *vi* (*pat* **foresaw'**; *pap* **foreseen'**) to see or know beforehand. **foreseeabil'ity** *n*. **foresee'able** *adj*. **foresee'ing** *adj*. **foresee'ingly** *adv*. **foreshad'ow** *vt* to give, or have, some indication of in advance; to shadow or typify beforehand. **foreshad'owing** *n*. **fore'sheet** *n* a rope attached to a corner of a foresail; (in *pl*) the part of a boat nearest the bow. **foreshew** *vt* see **foreshow** below. **fore'ship** *n* the forepart of a ship. **fore'shock** *n* an earth tremor preceding an earthquake. **fore'shore** *n* the space between high and low water marks. **foreshort'en** *vt* to draw or cause to appear as if shortened, by perspective; to make shorter. **foreshort'ening** *n*. **foreshow** or **foreshew** /för-shō'* or *för-/ *vt* (*pat* **foreshowed** or **foreshewed'** /-*shōd'*/; *pap* **foreshown** or **foreshewn** /-*shōn'*/), also (*Spenser*) **foreshewed'**) (*archaic*) to show or represent beforehand; to predict. **fore'side** *n* the front side; outward appearance (*Spenser*). **fore'sight** *n* the act or power of foreseeing; wise forethought or prudence; the sight on the muzzle of a gun; a forward reading on a graduated levelling staff (*surveying*). **fore'sighted** *adj*. **fore'sightful** *adj*. **fore'sightless** *adj*. **foresig'nify** *vt* (*archaic*) to give a sign of beforehand; to foreshow; to typify. **fore'skin** *n* the retractable skin that covers the glans penis, the prepuce. **fore'skirt** *n* (*Shakesp*) the loose front part of a coat. **forespeak'** *vt* to predict; to engage beforehand (*Scot*); see also **forspeak**. **forespend'** *vt* (*pat* **forespent'**) to spend beforehand (see also **forspend**). **fore-spurr'er** *n* (*Shakesp*) a person who rides in advance. **fore'stair** *n* (*Scot*) an outside stair at the front of a house. **forestall** /för-stöl'* or *för-/ *vt* (OE *foresteall* ambush, literally, a place taken beforehand, from *steall* a stand or station) *orig* to buy up before reaching the market, so as to sell again at higher prices; to anticipate; to hinder by anticipating; to bar. **forestall'er** *n*. **forestall'ing** or **forestal'ment** *n*. **fore'stay** *n* a rope reaching from the foremast-head to the bowsprit-end to support the mast. **fore'taste** *n* a taste before buying, etc; a brief encounter with or exposure to something to be experienced, presented, etc in full at a later time; anticipation. **foretaste'** *vt* to taste before possession; to anticipate; to taste before another. **foreteach'** *vt* (*pap and pat* **foretaught'**) (*archaic*) to teach beforehand. **foretell'** *vt* (*pap and pat* **foretold'**) to tell before; to prophesy. ◆ *vi* to utter prophecy. **foretell'er** *n*. **forethink'** *vt* (*pap and pat* **forethought'**) to anticipate in the mind; to have foreknowledge of. **forethink'er** *n*. **fore'thought** *n* thought or care for the future; anticipation; thinking beforehand. **forethought'ful** *adj*. **fore'time** *n* past time. **fore'token** *n* a token or sign beforehand. **foreto'ken** *vt* to signify beforehand. **foreto'kening** *n* and *adj*. **fore'tooth** *n* (*pl* **fore'teeth**) a tooth in the forepart of the mouth. **fore'top** *n* the platform at the head of the foremast (*naut*); the forepart of the crown of the head (*obs*); a lock of hair (*usu* upright) over the forehead; an appendage to a shoe (*obs*). **foretop'mast** *n* the mast erected at the head of the foremast, at the top of which is the **fore'top-gallant-mast**. **forevouched'** *adj* (*Shakesp*) affirmed or told before. **fore'ward** *n* (*archaic*) an advance guard; the front (*Shakesp*). **forewarn'** *vt* to warn beforehand; to give previous notice; see also **forwarn**. **forewarn'ing** *n*. **foreweigh'** *vt* (*archaic*) to estimate beforehand. **forewent'** *pat* (*Spenser* also *pap*) of **forego** above (see also **forgo**). **fore'-wheel** *n* either of the pair of front wheels of a wheeled vehicle. **fore'wind** *n* a favourable wind. **fore'wing** *n* either of an insect's front pair of wings. **fore'woman** *n* (*pl* **fore'women**) a woman overseer, a headwoman or a spokeswoman for a group (eg for a jury). **fore'word** *n* a preface. **fore'yard** *n* the lowest yard on a foremast.

foreanent see **fornent**.

forearm...to...**forebear** see under **fore-**.

forebitt, etc see under **fore**.

forebode...to...**fore-cited** see under **fore-**.

foreclose /fōr-klōz', för-/ *vt* to bar the right of redeeming (a mortgage, etc); to close beforehand; to preclude; to prevent; to stop. [OFr *forclos*, pap of *forclore* to exclude, from L *forīs* outside, and *claudere, clausum* to shut]
■ **foreclos'able** *adj*. **foreclosure** /-klō'zhər/ *n* the process by which a mortgagor, failing to repay the money lent on the security of a property, is compelled to forfeit his or her right to redeem it (*law*); any act or instance of foreclosing.

forecloth...to...**forecourt** see under **fore-**.

foredamned /fōr-dam'ned/ (*obs*) *adj* utterly damned (or *poss* damned beforehand). [**for-** (1c), (or possibly **fore-**)]

foredate...to...**forefront** see under **fore-**.

foregather see **forgather**.

foregleam and **forego**[1], etc see under **fore-**.

forego[2] see **forgo**.

foreground...to...**forehead** see under **fore-**.

forehent see **forhent**.

forehock and **fore-horse** see under **fore-**.

foreign /for'in/ *adj* belonging to another country; from abroad; relating to, characteristic of or situated in another country; alien; extraneous; not belonging; unconnected; not appropriate. [OFr *forain*, from LL *forāneus*, from L *forās* out of doors]
■ **for'eigner** *n* a person belonging to, or from, another country; a stranger or outsider; a job done privately by an employee without the employer's knowledge (*inf*). **for'eignism** *n* a mannerism, turn of phrase, etc, typical of a foreigner. **for'eignness** *n* the quality of being foreign; lack of relation to something; remoteness.
❑ **foreign aid** *n* financial or other aid given by richer to poorer countries. **foreign bill** or **draft** *n* a bill or draft payable in a different country, state, etc from that in which it was drawn. **foreign-built'** *adj* built in a foreign country. **foreign correspondent** *n* a newspaper correspondent working in a foreign country in order to report its news, etc. **foreign exchange** *n* (the exchange, conversion, etc of) foreign currencies. **foreign legion** *n* an army unit consisting of foreigners; (with *caps*) a French army unit, consisting of soldiers of all nationalities, serving outside France. **Foreign Office** *n* the British government department dealing with foreign affairs (now officially **Foreign and Commonwealth Office**).

forejudge[1] see under **fore-**.

forejudge[2] see **forjudge**.

foreknow, etc see under **fore-**.

forel /for'əl/ (*archaic*) *n* a kind of parchment for covering books. [OFr *forrel*, dimin of *forre, fuerre* sheath]

foreland...to...**forementioned** see under **fore-**.

foremost see under **fore**.

foremother...to...**fore-notice** see under **fore-**.

forensic /fə-ren'sik/ *adj* of or relating to sciences or scientists connected with legal investigations; belonging to courts of law, *orig* held by the Romans in the forum; used in law pleading; appropriate or adapted to argument. [L *forēnsis*, from *forum* market-place or forum]
■ **forensical'ity** *n*. **foren'sically** *adv*. **foren'sics** *n sing* the art or study of public debate; a forensic medicine or science department (*inf*).
❑ **forensic medicine** *n* medical science or techniques used to provide information in a lawcourt. **forensic science** *n* certain branches of science, *esp* biology and medicine, that are used to provide information in a lawcourt.

forensis strepitus /fo-ren'sis strep'i-təs or -tŭs/ (*L*) the clamour of the forum.

foreordain...to...**foresay**[1] see under **fore-**.

foresay[2] see **forsay**.

foreshadow...to...**foreskirt** see under **fore-**.

foreslack see **forslack**.

foreslow see **forslow**.

forespeak[1] see under **fore-**.

forespeak[2] see **forspeak**.

forespend[1] see under **fore-**.

forespend[2] see **forspend**.

fore-spurrer see under **fore-**.

FOREST /for'ist/ *abbrev*: Freedom Organization for the Right to Enjoy Smoking Tobacco.

forest /for'ist/ *n* a large uncultivated tract of land covered with trees and undergrowth; woody ground and rough pasture; a royal preserve for hunting, governed by a special code called the **forest law** (*hist*); any area resembling a forest because thickly covered with tall, upright objects. ◆ *adj* of, relating to, or consisting of (a) forest; sylvan; rustic. ◆ *vt* to cover with trees; to cover thickly with tall, upright objects. [OFr *forest* (Fr *forêt*), from LL *forestis* (*silva*) the outside wood, as opposed to the *parcus* (park) or walled-in wood, from L *forīs* out of doors]
■ **for'estage** *n* an ancient duty paid by foresters to the king; the rights of foresters. **for'estal** or **foresteal** /fər-est'i-əl/ *adj*. **foresta'tion** *n* tree-planting on a large scale, afforestation. **for'ested** *adj*. **for'ester** *n* a person who has charge of a forest; a person who has care of growing trees; (with *cap*) a member of the Ancient Order of Foresters or a similar friendly society; an inhabitant of a forest (*obs*); a *usu* green diurnal woodland moth of the Zygaenidae; a large kangaroo (*Aust*). **for'estine** *adj*. **for'estry** *n* the science and art of planting, tending and managing forests; forest country; an expanse of trees.
❑ **for'est-born** *adj* (*Shakesp*) born in a forest. **for'est-bred** *adj*. **for'est-fly** *n* a two-winged insect (*Hippobosca equina*) that annoys horses. **Forest Marble** *n* (*geol*) a Middle Jurassic fissile limestone of which typical beds are found in Wychwood Forest, Oxfordshire. **for'est-oak** *n* a species of *Casuarina*, a mainly Australian tree. **for'est-tree** *n* a large tree, *esp* a timber tree, that grows in forests.

forestair see under **fore-**.

forestal see under **forest**.

forestall, etc see under **fore-**.

forestation see under **forest**.

forestay see under **fore-**.

forester...to...**forestry** see under **forest**.

foretaste...to...**foretopmast** see under **fore-**.

forever /fə-rev'ər/ *adv* for ever, for all time to come; eternally; everlastingly; continually. ◆ *n* an endless or indefinite length of time, or one that seems so.
■ **forev'ermore'** *adv* for ever hereafter.

forevouched...to...**foreward** see under **fore-**.

forewarn[1] see under **fore-**.

forewarn[2] see **forwarn**.

foreweigh...to...**foreyard** see under **fore-**.

forex /for'eks/ *abbrev*: foreign exchange.

forfair /fər-fār'/ *vi* (*obs*) to perish or decay. [OE *forfaran*]
■ **forfairn'** *adj* (*Scot*) worn-out; exhausted.

forfaiting /för'fā-ting/ *n* a method of export finance whereby debts on exported goods are bought and then sold on to banks, etc. [Fr *forfait* forfeit or contract]
■ **for'faiter** *n* a person who, or company which, buys and sells such debts.

forfeit /för'fit/ *n* something to which a right is lost; a penalty for a crime, or breach of some condition; a fine; (*esp* in *pl*) a game in which a player surrenders some item (a **forfeit**) which can be redeemed only by performing a task, or fulfilling a challenge, set by the others; a penalty incurred in such a game. ◆ *adj* forfeited. ◆ *vt* to lose the right to (something) by some fault or crime; to confiscate (*archaic*); to penalize by forfeiting; loosely, to give up voluntarily. —Also (*obs*) **forfault** by association with **fault**. [OFr *forfait*, from LL *forisfactum*, from L *forīs* outside, and *facere* to make]
■ **for'feitable** *adj*. **for'feiter** *n* (*Shakesp*) a person who incurs punishment by forfeiting his or her bond. **for'feiture** *n* act of forfeiting; the state of being forfeited; the thing forfeited. —Also (*obs*) **forfaultable**, etc.

forfend /fər-fend'/ (*archaic*) *vt* to ward off or avert. [**for-** (1a) and **fend**[1]]

forfex /för'feks/ *n* a pair of scissors or pincers; the pincers of an earwig, etc (*zool*). [L *forfex, -icis* shears or pincers]
■ **for'ficate** *adj* (*ornithol*) deeply forked, *esp* of certain birds' tails. **Forfic'ula** *n* the common genus of earwigs. **forfic'ulate** *adj* like scissors.

forfoughten /fər-fö'tən/ (*Scot* **forfoughen** /fər-fohh'ən/, **forfeuchen** /-fŭhh'/) (*dialect*) *adj* exhausted. [**for-** (1c)]

forgat see **forget**.

forgather or **foregather** /för- or fər-gadh'ər/ vi to assemble; to meet; to fraternize (with *with*). [**for-** (1c)]

forgave see **forgive**.

forge[1] /förj or förj/ n the workshop of a person who works in iron, etc; a furnace, *esp* one in which iron is heated; a smithy; a place where anything is shaped or made. ◆ vt to form by heating and hammering, by heating and pressure, or by pressure alone (in the last case, often **cold forge**); to form or fashion (an object or, *fig*, a link or connection); to fabricate; to counterfeit for purposes of fraud; to form by great pressure, electricity or explosion. ◆ vi to commit forgery. [OFr *forge*, from L *fabrica*, from *faber* a workman]
■ **forge'able** *adj*. **forg'er** n a person who forges, *esp* illegally. **forg'ery** n fraudulently making or altering anything, *esp* anything printed; anything which is forged or counterfeited; deceit (*obs*). **forg'etive** *adj* (*Shakesp*) creative. **forg'ing** n a piece of metal shaped by hammering; the act of a criminal forger.
❑ **forge'man** n a worker in an iron workshop, etc.

forge[2] /förj or förj/ vi to move steadily on (*usu* with *ahead*). [Origin obscure]

forge[3] /förj or förj/ vi (of a horse) to click the hind shoe against the fore. [Origin obscure]

forget /fər-get'/ vt (forgett'ing; pat forgot' (*archaic* forgat'); pap forgott'en (also, now *rare*, *dialect* or *US*, but otherwise *archaic*, forgot')) to lose or drop from the memory; to fail to remember or think of; to leave behind accidentally; to neglect; to dismiss from the mind. ◆ vi to fail to remember. [OE *forgetan* (*forgietan*), from pfx *for-* away, and *getan* (*gietan*) to get]
■ **forget'ful** *adj* apt to forget; inattentive. **forget'fully** *adv*. **forget'fulness** n. **forgett'able** *adj*. **forgett'er** n. **forgett'ing** n and *adj*. **forgett'ingly** *adv*. **forgott'en** *adj*. **forgott'enness** n.
❑ **forget'-me-not** n a plant with clusters of small blue flowers (genus *Myosotis*), regarded as an emblem of loving remembrance.
■ **forget it** (*inf*; *esp* in *imperative*) used to state that there is no need to offer apologies, thanks, etc, or to say or do anything further about a particular matter; used to deny a request, or dismiss a suggestion, out of hand. **forget oneself** to lose one's self-control or dignity, to descend to words and deeds unworthy of oneself.

forgive /fər-giv'/ vt (pat forgave'; pap forgiv'en) to pardon; to overlook; to pardon a debt or offence (*Shakesp*); to give up (*Spenser*). ◆ vi to show mercy or compassion, or give a pardon. [OE *forgiefan*, from pfx *for-* away, and *giefan* to give; cf Ger *vergeben*]
■ **forgiv'able** *adj* capable of being forgiven. **forgive'ness** n pardon; remission; a readiness to forgive. **forgiv'er** n. **forgiv'ing** *adj* ready to pardon; merciful; compassionate.

forgo or **forego** /för-, för- or fər-gō'/ vt (forgo'ing or forego'ing; forgone' or foregone'; forwent' or forewent') to give up or relinquish; to do without; to refrain from using or benefiting from; to forfeit (*archaic*); to leave (*obs*). ◆ vi to go or pass away. —See also **forego** under **fore-**. [OE *forgān* to pass by or abstain from, from pfx *for-* away, and *gān* to go]

forgot and **forgotten** see **forget**.

forhaile /för-hāl'/ (*Spenser*) vt to distract. [**for-** (1a)]

forhent or **forehent** /för-hent'/ vt (pap (*Spenser*) forhent') to overtake; to seize. [**for-** (1c)]

forhow /för-how'/ vt to despise (*obs*); (also **forhoo** /fər-hoo'/ or **forhooie** /fər-hoo'ē/) to desert or abandon (*Scot*). [OE *forhogian*, from pfx *for-* away, and *hogian* to care]

forinsec /fə-rin'sek or -'sik/ *adj* (of feudal service) due to the lord's superior. [L *forīnsecus* from without, from *forīs* out of doors, and *secus* following]
■ **forin'secal** *adj* (*obs*) foreign; alien; extrinsic.

forint /for'int/ n the standard monetary unit of Hungary (100 fillér). [Hung, from Ital *fiorino* florin]

forisfamiliate /fō- or fo-ris-fə-mil'i-āt/ (*law*) vt to emancipate from paternal authority; (of a father) to put (a son) in possession of land which is accepted as the whole portion of the father's property. ◆ vi (of a son) to renounce one's title to a further share. [LL *forīsfamiliāre*, *-ātum*, from L *forīs* out of doors, and *familia* a family]
■ **forisfamilia'tion** n.

forjeskit /fər-jes'kit/ or **forjaskit** /-jas'-/ (*Scot*) *adj* tired out. [**for-** (1c); cf **disjaskit**]

forjudge or **forejudge** /för-juj' or för-/ (*law*) vt to deprive of a right, object, etc by a judgement. [OFr *forjugier*, from *fors*, from L *forīs* out, and *jugier* (Fr *juger*) to judge]

fork /förk/ n any pronged instrument (such as an eating implement or garden tool) for spiking and lifting, etc; anything that divides into prongs or branches; a branch or prong; the space or angle between branches, *esp* on a tree or between the legs; a confluent, tributary or branch of a river; one of the branches into which a road divides; a dividing into two branches, a bifurcation; a place of bifurcation; a barbed arrowhead; the part of a bicycle to which a wheel is attached; the appearance of a flash of lightning; the bottom of a sump in a mine; in chess, a simultaneous attack on two pieces by one piece. ◆ vi to branch; to follow a branch road. ◆ vt to form as a fork; to move or lift with a fork; to stab or dig with a fork; in chess, to attack (two pieces) simultaneously; to pump dry. [OE *forca*, from L *furca*]
■ **forked** *adj* shaped like a fork; insincere or deceitful (as in *forked tongue*). **fork'edly** *adv*. **fork'edness** n. **fork'er** n. **fork'ful** n (pl **fork'fuls**) as much as a fork will hold. **fork'iness** n. **fork'y** *adj*.
❑ **fork'-chuck** n a forked lathe-centre in wood-turning. **forked lightning** n lightning in the form of zigzag flashes. **fork'head** n an arrowhead (*Spenser*); the forked end of a rod, holding a connecting pin. **fork'it-tail** or **fork'y-tail** n (*dialect*) an earwig. **fork-lift truck** n (short form **fork'-lift**) a power-driven truck with an arrangement of steel prongs which can lift, raise up high and carry heavy packages and stack them where required (often used with a pallet). **fork lunch** or **fork luncheon**, **fork supper**, etc n a buffet-type meal suitable for eating with a fork only. **fork'tail** n a name for various fish and birds with forked tails, eg the kite. **fork'-tailed** *adj*.
■ **fork out**, **over** or **up** (*sl*) to hand or pay over, *esp* unwillingly.

forlana /för-lä'nə/ or **furlana** /foor-/ n a Venetian dance in 6–8 time. [Ital *Furlana* Friulian]

forlend see **forelend** under **fore-**.

forlorn /fər-lörn'/ *adj* quite lost; forsaken; neglected; wretched. ◆ n (*Shakesp*) a forsaken person; a forlorn hope. [OE *forloren*, pap of *forlēosan* to lose, from pfx *for-* away, and *lēosan* to lose; Ger *verloren*, pap of *verlieren* to lose]
■ **forlorn'ly** *adv*. **forlorn'ness** n.

forlorn hope /fər-lörn' hōp/ n orig, a body of soldiers selected for some service of especial danger; a desperate enterprise of last resort; a vain or faint hope (from association with hope, in the sense of expectation). [Du *verloren hoop* lost troop]

form[1] /förm/ n shape; a mould; something that holds or shapes, eg a piece of formwork (see below); a species or kind; a pattern or type; a way of being; a manner of arrangement; order; regularity; system, eg of government; beauty (*obs*); style and arrangement; structural unity in music, literature, painting, etc; a prescribed set of words or course of action; ceremony; behaviour; condition of fitness or efficiency; a schedule to be filled in with details; a specimen document for imitation; the inherent nature of an object (*philos*); that in which the essence of a thing consists (*philos*); a complete set of crystal faces similar with respect to the symmetry of the crystal (*crystallog*); forme (*printing*); a long seat or bench; a school class; the bed of a hare, shaped by the animal's body; a criminal record (*sl*); the condition of fitness of eg a horse or athlete; a record of past performance of an athlete, horse, etc; (with *the*) the correct procedure (*inf*); (with *the*) the situation or position (*inf*). ◆ vt to give form or shape to; to bring into being; to make; to contrive; to conceive in the mind; to go to make up; to constitute; to establish. ◆ vi to assume a form. [L *fōrma* shape]
■ **form'able** *adj*. **form'ative** *adj* giving form, determining, moulding; capable of development; growing; serving to form words by derivation or inflection, not radical (*grammar*). ◆ n (*grammar*) a derivative (*old*); a formative element; any grammatical element from which words and sentences are constructed. **formed** *adj*. **form'er** n someone or something that forms, shapes or moulds; a tool for giving a coil or winding the correct shape (*elec eng*). **form'ing** n. **form'less** *adj*. **form'lessly** *adv*. **form'lessness** n.
❑ **formative assessment** n (*educ*) the use of continuous assessment to provide feedback on a pupil's progress and development. **form class** n (*linguistics*) a class of forms (words and phrases) that will fit into the same position in a construction. **form critic** n. **form criticism** n biblical criticism that classifies parts of scripture according to literary form and relates literary forms to historical background. **form feed** n (*comput*) a control character used to eject paper from a printer or to move the paper to the next page. **form genus** n a group of species with similar morphological characters, but which are not certainly known to be related in descent. **form horse** n the favourite, the expected winner (*horse-racing*; also *fig*). **form letter** n a letter with a fixed form and contents, used *esp* when writing to a number of people about the same or essentially similar matters. **form teacher** or **tutor** n (*esp* in a secondary school) the teacher who is responsible for the administration, welfare, etc of a particular form or class. **form'work** n shuttering to contain concrete.
■ **good** or **bad form** good or recognized, or bad or unaccepted, social usage.

form[2] see **forme**.

-form /-förm/ or **-iform** /-i-förm/ *combining form* (used to mean) having a specified form or number of forms. [L *fōrma* form]

formal /för'məl/ *adj* according to form or established style; relating to form; ceremonious, punctilious or methodical; of, or suitable for, an

fāte; fär; mē; fûr; mīne; mōte; för; mūte; pŭt; dhen (then); el'ə-mənt (element) • For other sounds see detailed chart of pronunciation important or serious occasion; having the outward form only; sane (*Shakesp*); having the power of making a thing what it is; essential; (of a logical system) using precisely defined conventions to enable deductions to be made. ◆ *n* a social event, *esp* for students, at which formal dress is worn (*inf*); a garment suitable for an important occasion, *esp* a woman's evening dress (*US*). [**form**¹]

■ **form'alism** *n* excessive observance of form or conventional usage, *esp* in religion; stiffness of manner; concentration on form or technique at the expense of social or moral content (*art*). **form'alist** *n* a person having exaggerated regard to rules or established usages; a person who practises formalism (*art*). ◆ *adj* of or relating to formalists or formalism. **formalist'ic** *adj*. **formal'ity** *n* the precise observance of forms or ceremonies; a matter of form; a ceremonious observance; stiffness or conventionality; mere convention at the expense of substance. **formalīzā'tion** or **-s-** *n*. **form'alize** or **-ise** *vt* to make formal; to make official or valid; to make precise or give a clear statement of. ◆ *vi* to be formal. **form'ally** *adv*.
❑ **formal verdict** *n* (*law*) one in which the jury follows the judge's directions; in a fatal accident inquiry, a finding that involves no apportioning of blame (*Scot*).

formaldehyde /fȯr-mal'di-hīd/ *n* a formic aldehyde, formalin.

formalin /fȯr'mə-lin/ or **formol** /fȯr'mol/ *n* a formic aldehyde used as an antiseptic, germicide or preservative. [**formic**]

formaliter /fȯr-mal'i-tər or -ter/ (*LL*) *adv* formally or in respect of the formal element.

formant /fȯr'mənt/ *n* a component of a speech sound determining its particular quality (*acoustics*); anything that determines, limits or defines. [Ger *Formant*, from L *formāns, -antis*, prp of *formāre* to form]

format /fȯr'mat or (*rare*) fȯr'mä/ *n* (of books, etc) the size, form or shape in which they are issued; the style, arrangement and contents of eg a radio or television programme; (the description of) the way data is, or is to be, arranged in a file, on a card, disk, tape, etc (*comput*). ◆ *vt* (**form'atting**; **form'atted**) to arrange (a book, etc) into a specific format; to arrange (data) for use on a disk, tape, etc (*comput*); to prepare (a disk, etc) for use by dividing it into sectors (*comput*). [Fr]
■ **form'atter** *n* (*comput*) a program for formatting a disk, tape, etc.

formate¹ /fȯr-māt'/ *vi* (of aircraft) to join, or fly, in formation; to form (*obs*); to state precisely or formulate (*obs*). [**form**¹]

formate² see under **formic**.

formation /fȯr-mā'shən/ *n* a making or producing; something formed or made, a structure; an arrangement (of eg troops, aircraft or players); a group of strata used as a basis for rock mapping (*geol*); a plant community (*bot*). [L *formātiō* a forming]
■ **formā'tional** *adj*.
❑ **formation dancing** *n* ballroom dancing in which a number of couples perform the same sequence of movements.

forme /fȯrm/ (*printing*) *n* metal type and blocks from which an impression is to be made, assembled and secured in a chase or frame ready for printing (also **form**). [**form**¹]

former /fȯr'mər/ *adj* (*compar* of **fore**) before in time; past; first mentioned (of two); beforehand or first (of two) (*Shakesp*). [Formed late on analogy of ME *formest* foremost, by adding compar sfx *-er* to base of OE *forma* first, itself superl]
■ **form'erly** *adv* in former times; before this time.

formic /fȯr'mik/ *adj* relating to ants; containing or derived from formic acid. [L *formīca* an ant]
■ **for'mate** *n* a salt of formic acid (also **for'miate**). **for'micant** *adj* crawling like an ant; (of a pulse) very small and unequal. **formicā'rium** or **for'micary** *n* (*pl* **formicā'ria** or **for'micaries**) an ant-hill, ants' nest, or colony. **for'micate** *adj* resembling an ant. **formicā'tion** *n* a sensation like that of ants creeping on the skin.
❑ **formic acid** *n* a fatty acid, HCOOH, found in ants and nettles (also **methanoic acid**).

Formica® /fȯr-mī'kə/ *n* a brand of plastic laminates used to provide hard, heat-resistant, easily-cleaned surfaces.

formidable /fȯr'mid-ə-bl or -mid'/ *adj* causing fear; inspiring awe; redoubtable; dauntingly difficult. [Fr, from L *formīdābilis*, from *formīdō* fear]
■ **formidabil'ity** or **for'midableness** *n*. **for'midably** *adv*.

formol see **formalin**.

formula /fȯr'mū-lə/ *n* (*pl* **formulae** /fȯrm'ū-lē/ or **form'ūlas**) a prescribed form, *esp* a fixed phrase or set of phrases traditionally used on a ceremonial, etc occasion; a formal statement of doctrines; a recipe; a milk substitute (prepared from dried ingredients) for bottle-feeding babies; a statement of joint aims or principles worked out for practical purposes by diplomats of divergent interests; a solution or answer worked out by different sides in a dispute, etc; a technical specification governing *orig* cars entered for certain motor-racing events, now also applied to other racing vehicles or craft; a general expression for solving problems (*maths*); a set of symbols expressing

the composition of a substance (*chem*); a list of ingredients of a patent medicine. [L *fōrmula*, dimin of *fōrma*]
■ **form'ūlable** *adj*. **formulaic** /-lā'ik/ *adj*. **form'ūlar** or **formūlaris'tic** *adj*. **formūlarīzā'tion** or **-s-** or **formūlā'tion** *n*. **form'ūlarize** or **-ise** *vt*. **form'ūlary** *n* a formula; a book of formulae or precedents. ◆ *adj* prescribed; ritual. **form'ūlate** or **form'ūlize** or **-ise** *vt* to reduce to or express in a formula; to state or express in a clear or definite form. **form'ūlātor** *n*. **form'ūlism** *n* excessive use of, or dependence on, formulae. **form'ūlist** *n*.

formyl /fȯr'mīl/ (*chem*) *adj* denoting the chemical group HCO, derived from formic acid. [**formic** and **-yl**]

fornent /fər-nent'/ (*Scot*) *adv* and prep (also **foreanent'** or **fornenst'**) right opposite to (in location). [**fore** and **anent**]

fornicate¹ /fȯr'ni-kāt/ *vi* to commit fornication. [L *fornicārī, -ātus*, from *fornix* a vault or brothel]
■ **fornicā'tion** *n* voluntary sexual intercourse between unmarried people, sometimes extended to cases where only one of the pair concerned is unmarried (*law*); adultery (*Bible*); idolatry (*fig*). **for'nicātor** *n*. **for'nicātress** *n*.

fornicate² /fȯr'ni-kāt/ *adj* arched (*archit*); arching over (*bot*). [L *fornicātus*, from *fornix* a vault or arch]
■ **fornicā'tion** *n*.

fornix /fȯr'niks/ *n* (*pl* **for'nices** /-ni-sēz/) something resembling an arch (*archit*); an arched formation of the brain (*med*). [L]
■ **for'nical** *adj*.

forpine /fȯr-pīn'/ *vi* (*Spenser*) to waste away. [**for-** (1c)]

forpit or **forpet** /fȯr'pət/ (*Scot*) *n* a fourth part (now of a peck measure). [*fourth part*]

forrad /for'əd/ or (*dialect*) **forrit** /for'ət or fȯ'rit/ (*Scot*) *adv* (*compar* **forr'ader**) forms of **forward**.

forray /fo-rā'/ *n* and *vt* (*Spenser*) foray.

forren /for'in/ (*Milton*) *adj* foreign.

forsake /fər-sāk' or fȯr-/ *vt* (**forsāk'ing**; **forsook'**; **forsāk'en**) to desert; to abandon. [OE *forsacan*, from *for-* away, and *sacan* to strive]
■ **forsāk'en** *adj*. **forsāk'enly** *adv*. **forsāk'enness** *n*. **forsāk'er** *n*. **forsāk'ing** *n* abandonment.

forsay or **foresay** /fȯr-sā'/ *vt* to forbid (*obs*); to renounce (*Spenser*); to banish (*Spenser*). [OE *forsecgan*, from *for-* against, and *secgan* to say]

forset-seller see **fosset-seller**.

forslack or **foreslack** /fȯr-slak'/ *vi* (*obs*) to be or become slack or neglectful. ◆ *vt* (*Spenser*) to harm by slackness. [**for-** (1c)]

forslow, forsloe or **foreslow** /fȯr-slō'/ *vt* (*Spenser*) to delay. ◆ *vi* (*Shakesp*) to delay. [OE *forslāwian*, from *for*, intensive, and *slāwian* to be slow]

forsooth /fər-sooth' or fȯr-/ *adv* in truth; certainly (now only *ironic*). [*for sooth*]

forspeak or **forespeak** /fər-spēk' or fȯr-/ *vt* to forbid (*obs*); to speak against (*Shakesp*); to bewitch (*Scot*). [**for-** (1b)]

forspend or **forespend** /fər-spend'/ (*archaic*) *vt* (*pap* and *pat* **forspent'**) to wear out physically; to exhaust (resources). [**for-** (1c)]

forsterite /fȯr'stə-rīt/ *n* a variety of olivine. [JR *Forster* (1729–98), German naturalist]

forswatt /fȯr-swot'/ (*Spenser*) *adj* covered with sweat. [**for-** (1c) and *swat*, old pap of **sweat**]

forswear /fər-swār' or fȯr-/ *vt* (*pat* **forswore'**; *pap* **forsworn'**) to deny or renounce upon oath. ◆ *vi* to swear falsely. [**for-** (1b)]
■ **forsworn'** *adj* perjured, having forsworn oneself. **forsworn'ness** *n*.
■ **forswear oneself** to swear falsely.

forswink /fər-swingk' or fȯr-/ (*obs*) *vt* to exhaust by labour. [**for-** (1b) and OE *swincan* to labour]
■ **forswunk'** or (*Spenser*) **forswonck'** *adj* overworked.

forsythia /fȯr-sī'thi-ə or -si'/ *n* any shrub of the genus *Forsythia*, a popular garden plant producing clusters of yellow jasmine-like flowers in the spring. [William *Forsyth* (1737–1804), Scottish botanist]

fort /fȯrt or fȯrt/ *n* a small fortress; an outlying trading-station (*N Am hist*). ◆ *vt* to fortify. [Fr, from L *fortis* strong]
■ **hold the fort** to take temporary charge.

fortalice /fȯr'tə-lis/ (*hist*) *n* a fortress; a small outwork of a fortification. [LL *fortalitia*, from L *fortis*]

forte¹ /fȯrt', now usu for the first meaning fȯr'ti or 'tā/ *n* the thing in which one excels; the upper half of a sword or foil blade, the strong part. [Fr *fort* strong]

forte² /fȯr'ti or 'tā/ (*music*) *adj* and *adv* loud, loudly. ◆ *n* a loud passage. [Ital]
■ **fortissimo** /-tēs'si-mō or -tis'i-/ *adj* and *adv* very loud. ◆ *n* (*pl* **fortis'simos**) a very loud passage. **fortissis'simo** *adj* and *adv* as loud as possible.

■ words derived from main entry word; ❑ compound words; ■ idioms and phrasal verbs

❑ **fortepi'anist** n a player of the fortepiano. **fortepia'no** adj and adv loud with immediate relapse into softness. ◆ n the 18c name for an early type of piano; a fortepiano note.

forth /fōrth or fŏrth/ adv (archaic) forward; onward; out; into the open; in continuation; abroad. ◆ prep (Shakesp) out of or forth from. [OE forth, from fore before; Du voort, Ger fort]

■ **forthcome'** vi (obs) to come forth. **forthcom'ing** adj about to appear or happen; available on request; (of a person) friendly, communicative; just coming forth (archaic); approaching (archaic); at hand, ready to be produced (archaic). **forth'going** n (obs) a going forth. **forth'-putting** n the action of putting forth (obs); undue forwardness (US; archaic). ◆ adj (US) forward. **forth'right** (or /-rīt'/) adv (obs) straightforward; at once. ◆ n (Shakesp) a straight path. ◆ adj straightforward; downright. **forth'rightly** adv. **forth'rightness** n. **forthwith** /-with', -widh' or fŏrth'/ adv immediately.

■ **and so forth** and so on, et cetera.

forthink /fər-thingk'/ vt (Spenser) to be sorry for or regret; to rethink. ◆ vi (dialect) to change one's mind. [From OE forthencan, from OE for- and thencan to think or thyncan to seem]

forthy /fŏr-dhī'/ (Spenser) adv therefore; for that. [OE forthȳ, from for and thȳ, instrumental case of thæt that]

forties and **fortieth** see under **forty**.

fortify /fŏr'ti-fī/ vt (for'tifying; for'tified) to strengthen with forts, etc against attack; to invigorate; to confirm; to strengthen (esp certain wines) by adding alcohol; to enrich (a food) by adding eg vitamins. ◆ vi to put up fortifications. [Fr fortifier, from LL fortificāre, from fortis strong, and facere to make]

■ **for'tifiable** adj. **fortificā'tion** n the art of strengthening a military position by means of defensive works; (often in pl) the work so constructed; something which fortifies. **for'tifier** n.

fortilage /fŏr'ti-lāj or fŏr'-/ (Spenser) n a variant of **fortalice**.

fortis /fŏr'tis/ (phonetics) adj (of a consonant) articulated with relatively great muscular effort and pressure of breath, opp to lenis. ◆ n (pl **fortēs**) such a consonant. [L, strong]

fortissimo, fortississimo see **forte²**.

fortiter et recte /fŏr'ti-tər et rek'tē or for'ti-ter et rek'te/ (L) bravely and uprightly.

fortitude /fŏr'ti-tūd/ n courage in endurance; strength (obs). [L fortitūdō, -inis, from fortis strong]

■ **fortitū'dinous** adj.

fortlet /fŏrt'lət or fŏrt'/ n a little fort.

fortnight /fŏrt'nīt/ n two weeks or fourteen days. [OE fēowertȳne niht fourteen nights]

■ **fort'nightly** adj and adv once a fortnight. ◆ n a magazine, etc appearing fortnightly.

Fortran /fŏr'tran/ n a problem-orientated computer language widely used in scientific work. [Formula translation]

fortress /fŏr'tras or fŏr'-/ n a fortified place; a defence. ◆ vt (Shakesp) to guard. [OFr forteresse, another form of fortelesce (see fortalice)]

fortuitous /fŏr-tū'i-təs or (US) -too'-/ adj happening by chance; fortunate. [L fortuītus]

■ **fortu'itism** n belief in evolution by chance variation. **fortu'itist** n. **fortu'itously** adv. **fortu'itousness** or **fortu'ity** n.

fortune /fŏr'chən/ n whatever comes by lot or chance; luck; the arbitrary ordering of events; the lot that falls to one in life; a prediction of one's future; success; a great accumulation of wealth; a large amount of money (inf); an heiress (obs). ◆ vi (obs) to befall. ◆ vt (obs) to determine the fortune of. [Fr, from L fortūna]

■ **for'tunate** adj happening by good fortune; lucky; auspicious; felicitous. **for'tunately** adv in a fortunate way; by good luck; I'm glad to say or happy to report. **for'tunateness** n. **for'tuned** adj (archaic) supplied by fortune. **for'tuneless** adj without a fortune; luckless. **for'tunize** vt (Spenser) to make fortunate or happy.

❑ **fortune book** n a book for use in fortune-telling. **fortune cookie** n a piece of dough wrapped and cooked around a piece of paper which has a (supposed) horoscope or a maxim on it, served esp in Chinese homes and restaurants. **for'tune-hunter** n (derog) a person who hunts for a wealthy marriage. **for'tune-tell** vi (back-formation). **for'tune-teller** n a person who professes to foretell one's fortune. **for'tune-telling** n.

■ **a small fortune** (inf) quite a large amount of money.

forty /fŏr'ti/ n and adj four times ten. ◆ n (with cap and the) the French Academy. [OE fēowertig, from fēower four, and -tig ten (as sfx)]

■ **for'ties** n pl the numbers forty to forty-nine; the years so numbered (of a life or century); a range of temperature from forty to just less than fifty degrees; (with cap and the) the sea area lying between NE Scotland and SW Norway, with a minimum depth of 40 fathoms. **for'tieth** adj the last of forty; next after the thirty-ninth; equal to one of

forty equal parts. ◆ n one of forty equal parts; a person or thing in fortieth position. **for'tyish** adj apparently about forty years old.

❑ **for'ty-five'** n a gramophone record played at a speed of 45 revolutions per minute; (with cap and the) the Jacobite rebellion of 1745. **for'ty-nin'er** n a prospector in the 1849 gold rush in California. **forty-ninth parallel** n the parallel of latitude 49°N, along which lies part of the border between the USA and Canada. **forty winks** n pl (inf) a short nap, esp after dinner.

■ **roaring forties** the tract of stormy west winds south of 40°S latitude (occasionally also in the Atlantic north of 40°N).

forum /fō'rəm or fö'/ n (pl **fo'rums** or **fo'ra**) orig a marketplace, esp that in Rome where public business was transacted and justice dispensed; the courts of law as opposed to Parliament (rare); a meeting to discuss topics of public concern; a publication, regular meeting, etc serving as a medium for debate; a location on the World Wide Web where people may exchange views and information, usu about a specific subject. [L forum, related to forās out of doors]

forwander /fər-won'dər/ vi to wander until wearied (archaic); to stray far (Spenser). [**for-** (1d)]

■ **forwan'dered** adj (archaic) strayed.

forward /fŏr'wərd/ adj near or at the front; in advance; well advanced; ready; too ready; lacking due modesty or respect, presumptuous; officious; earnest (archaic); early ripe. ◆ vt to help on; to send on. ◆ adv (also **for'wards**) towards what is in front; onward; progressively; /fŏr'əd/ towards or in the front part of a ship. ◆ n a player positioned in front of the other members of the team (sport); a forward contract (inf). [OE foreward (WSax foreweard), from fore, and -ward (-weard) signifying direction; the s of forwards is a genitive ending (cf Ger vorwärts)]

■ **for'warder** n a person or company engaged in forwarding. **for'warding** n the act or business of despatching merchandise, etc. **for'wardly** adv. **for'wardness** n.

❑ **forward contract** n an agreement to buy or sell a fixed amount of a currency or a commodity at a fixed price at a specified future date. **forward delivery** n delivery of goods at a future date. **for'ward-looking** adj having regard to the future; progressive. **forward market** n a market in which commodities, etc are contracted to be bought and sold at a future date at an agreed price (**forward price**). **forward pass** n (rugby) an illegal pass in which the ball is thrown forward towards the opponents' goal-line. **forward pricing** n trading of unit trusts on the price to be set at the next valuation (cf **historic pricing**).

forwarn or **forewarn** /fər- or fŏr-wörn'/ vt to forbid. [**for-** (1b), against, and **warn¹**]

forwaste /fŏr-wāst'/ (Spenser) vt to waste utterly. [**for-** (1c)]

forweary /fər or fŏr-wē'ri/ (Spenser) vt to weary out. [**for-** (1c)]

forwent /fər- or fŏr-went'/ see **forgo**.

forwhy /fŏr-(h)wī'/ (archaic) conj because. ◆ adv why. [**for** and **why**]

forworn /fər-wörn' or -wörn'/ (Spenser) adj much worn. [**for-** (1c)]

forzando and **forzato** same as **sforzando**.

Fosbury flop /foz'bə-ri flop/ n a method of high-jumping in which the athlete goes over the bar horizontally on his or her back. [R Fosbury (born 1947), US athlete]

foss¹ or **fosse** /fos/ n a ditch, moat, trench or canal. [Fr fosse, from L fossa, from fodere, fossum to dig]

■ **fossed** adj. **fossette'** n (anat) a small hollow.

❑ **Foss Way** or **Fosse Way** n the Roman road that runs between Exeter and Lincoln; (without cap) any of the British Roman roads having a fosse on either side.

foss² see **force²**.

fossa¹ /fos'ə/ (anat) n (pl **foss'ae** /-ē/) a pit or depression. [L, a ditch]

■ **foss'ula** n (pl **foss'ulae** /-ē/) a small depression or groove. **foss'ulate** adj.

fossa² /fos'ə/ or **foussa** /foos'ə/ n a Madagascan animal (Cryptoprocta ferox) more or less similar to the civets; (**Fossa**) a genus of Madagascan civets. [Malagasy]

fosse see **foss¹**.

fosset-seller /fos'it-sel'ər/ (Shakesp) n apparently, a person who sells faucets (another reading is **for'set-seller**). [fosset and forset, obs forms of **faucet**]

fossette see under **foss¹**.

fossick /fos'ik/ (Aust) vi to search for gold, on the surface or in abandoned workings; to rummage. ◆ vt to dig out. [Perh connected with Eng dialect fossick a troublesome person]

■ **foss'icker** n. **foss'icking** n.

fossil /fos'l or -il/ n a relic or trace of a former living thing preserved in rock (geol); a rock or mineral substance dug from the earth (obs); an antiquated, out-of-date, or unchanging person or thing (fig; derog). ◆ adj dug out of the earth; in the condition of a fossil; antiquated. [Fr fossile, from L fossilis, from fodere to dig]

---

fāte; fär; mē; fûr; mīne; mōte; fŏr; mūte; pŭt; dhen (then); el'ə-mənt (element) • For other sounds see detailed chart of pronunciation

■ **fossilif'erous** adj bearing or containing fossils. **fossiliza'tion** or **-s-** n. **foss'ilize** or **-ise** vt to convert into a fossil (also fig). ◆ vi to become a fossil; to look for fossils (inf).
❑ **foss'il-fired** adj (of a power station, etc) burning fossil fuel. **fossil fuel** n coal, oil, etc produced in the earth by a process of fossilization. **fossil water** n water which has been trapped in an underground reservoir since a previous geological age.

fossor /fos'ǝr/ n (archaic) a grave-digger. [L fossor, from fodere to dig]
■ **fossorial** /-ō'ri-ǝl or -ō'/ adj (zool) adapted for digging.

fossula and **fossulate** see under **fossa**[1].

foster[1] /fos'tǝr/ vt to bring up or nurse (esp a child not one's own); to put (a child) into the care of someone not its parent; to treat (eg the elderly) in a similar fashion; to encourage; to promote; to cherish. ◆ vi to care for a child or elderly person in a foster-home. ◆ adj of or concerned with fostering. [OE fōstrian to nourish, from fōster food]
■ **fos'terage** n the act or custom of fostering or nursing; the condition or relation of foster-child; the care of a foster-child; the act of encouraging or cultivating. **fos'terer** n. **fos'tering** n. **fos'terling** n (archaic) a foster-child. **fos'tress** n (archaic) a female fosterer.
❑ **fos'ter-brother** n a male child nursed or brought up with a child or children of different parents. **fos'ter-child** n a child nursed or brought up by someone who is not its parent. **fos'ter-daughter** n. **fos'ter-father** n a man who brings up a child in place of its father. **fos'ter-home** n. **fos'ter-mother** n a woman who brings up a child in place of its mother; an apparatus for rearing chickens. **fos'ter-nurse** n. **fos'ter-parent** n. **fos'ter-sister** n. **fos'ter-son** n.

foster[2] /fos'tǝr/ (Spenser) n a forester.

fother[1] /fodh'ǝr/ vt to cover (a sail, etc) with yarn and oakum, as stopping for a leak. [Perh Du voederen (modern voeren), or LGer fodern to line]

fother[2] /fodh'ǝr/ n a load or quantity (dialect); a cartload (dialect); a definite weight, specif of lead, 19½ hundredweight (obs). [OE fōther; Ger Fuder]

fother[3] /fodh'ǝr/ n a dialect variant of **fodder**.

fothergilla /fo-dhǝr-gil'ǝ/ n any plant of the Fothergilla genus of N American deciduous shrubs of the witch-hazel family (Hamamelidaceae), also called **witch-alder**. [Dr John Fothergill, 18c British physician and botanist]

fou[1] /foo/ (Scot) adj full; drunk.

fou[2] /foo/ (obs Scot) n a bushel. [Perh **full**]

fouat or **fouet** /foo'ǝt/ (Scot) n the house leek.

Foucault current /fŭk'ō kur'ǝnt/ same as **eddy current** (see under **eddy**).

Foucault's pendulum /fŭk'ōz pen'dū-lǝm/ (astron) n an instrument, consisting of a heavy metal ball suspended by a very long fine wire, devised by JBL Foucault in 1851 to demonstrate the rotation of the Earth.

foud /fowd/ n a bailiff or magistrate in Orkney and Shetland. [ON fógeti; Ger Vogt; from L vocātus, from vocāre to call]
■ **foud'rie** n his or her jurisdiction.

foudroyant /foo-droi'ǝnt or -drwä'yä/ adj thundering (archaic); dazzling (archaic); sudden and overwhelming (pathol). [Fr, prp of foudroyer, from foudre lightning]

fouet see **fouat**.

fouetté /fwet'ā/ n a ballet-step in which the foot makes a whiplike movement. [Fr]

fougade /foo-gäd'/ or **fougasse** /foo-gäs'/ (milit) n a piece of improvised artillery, a small pit charged with powder or shells and loaded with stones. [Fr]

fougasse /foo-gas'/ n a flat loaf of French bread made with olive oil, sometimes topped with salt, anchovies, etc. [Fr]

fought /föt/ pat and pap of **fight**.

foughten /fö'tn/ old pap of **fight**.

foughty /fow'ti or foo'ti/ (dialect) adj musty; mouldy; tainted. [OE fūht moist]

foul /fowl/ adj filthy; dirty; disfigured; untidy; loathsome; obscene; impure; shameful; gross; in bad condition; stormy; unpleasant; unfavourable; unfair; of little worth; choked up; entangled (naut); full of errors (printing); ugly (Shakesp); bad (inf). ◆ vt to make foul; (of an animal) to defecate on or in (a footpath or other public place); in games or contests, to tackle in a way that constitutes a breach of the rules; to collide with or come into accidental contact with; to obstruct. ◆ vi to collide. ◆ n the act of fouling; any breach of the rules in games or contests. ◆ adv in a foul manner; unfairly. [OE fūl; Ger faul, Gothic fūls]
■ **foul'ly** adv. **foul'ness** n.
❑ **foul'-brood** n a bacterial disease of bee larvae. **foul'-fish** n fish during the spawning season. **foul'mart** see **foumart**. **foul'-mouthed** or **foul'-spok'en** adj addicted to the use of foul or profane language.

foul'-mouth'edness n. **foul play** n unfair action in any game or contest; dishonest dealing generally; violence or murder. **foul'-up** see **foul up** below.
■ **cry foul** to assert that a rule has been broken, and claim the penalty. **fall foul of** to come into accidental contact with; to clash with; to assail. **foul befall** or **foul fall** (obs) bad luck to. **foul up** to make dirty; to (cause to) be or become blocked or entangled; to spoil (inf); to cause to fail or break down (inf); to bungle or make a mistake in (inf; **foul'-up** n). **make foul water** (naut) to come into such shallow water that the keel throws up mud.

foulard /foo-lärd' or -lär'/ n a soft untwilled silk fabric; a silk handkerchief or scarf. [Fr]

foulder /fowl'dǝr/ (Spenser) vi to thunder. [OFr fouldre, from L fulgur lightning]

foulé /foo-lā'/ (Fr) n fulled cloth, esp a light woollen smooth-surfaced dress material.

foumart /foo'märt or -mǝrt/ n a polecat (also **foul'mart**). [ME fulmard, from OE fūl foul, and mearth a marten]

found[1] /fownd/ vt to lay the bottom or foundation of; to establish on a basis; to originate; to endow; to merit (obs). ◆ vi to rely (with on). [Fr fonder, from L fundāre, -ātum to found, from fundus the bottom]
■ **founda'tion** n the act of founding; (often in pl) the base of a building; the groundwork or basis of anything; a permanent fund for a benevolent purpose or for some special objective; an institution; a cosmetic preparation used as a base for facial make-up; a priming substance applied to a canvas or board as a base for oil-painting. **founda'tional** adj. **founda'tioner** n a person supported from the funds or foundation of an institution. **found'er** n (also fem **found'ress**) a person who founds, establishes or originates; an endower.
❑ **foundation course** n an introductory course of study. **foundation degree** n a skills-based vocational higher education qualification. **foundation garment** n a woman's undergarment for supporting or controlling the figure. **foundation hospital** n a hospital managed by a foundation trust (qv below). **founda'tion-muslin**, **founda'tion-net** n gummed fabrics used for stiffening dresses, etc. **foundation school** n a state school whose governors are responsible for the property, for the appointing of staff and for managing the admissions. **founda'tion-stone** n one of the stones forming the foundation of a building, esp a stone laid with public ceremony. **founda'tion-stop** n any organ stop whose sounds are those belonging to the keys, or differing by whole octaves only; a fundamental flue stop denoting principal and flute ranks. **foundation subject** n any of the subjects which form the National Curriculum in England and Wales. **foundation trust** n an organization within the National Health Service that has more autonomy than other hospital trusts. **founder member** n one of those members of a society who were instrumental in its foundation. **founders' shares** n pl same as **deferred shares** (see under **defer**[1]). **founding father** n a person who forms or establishes an institution, organization, etc.

found[2] /fownd/ vt to make (esp metals) by melting and allowing to harden in a mould; to cast. [Fr fondre, from L fundere, fūsum to pour]
■ **found'er** n. **found'ing** n. **found'ry** n the art of founding or casting; a place where founding is carried on; articles produced by founding.

found[3] /fownd/ pat and pap of **find**.
■ **found'ling** n a little child found deserted.
❑ **found money** n financial gain obtained for nothing. **found object** n a natural or man-made object displayed as a work of art, either exactly as found or touched up ('composed').
■ **all found** see under **all**.

founder /fown'dǝr/ vi (of a building) to subside; to collapse in ruins (also fig); to go to the bottom (of the sea); (of a ship) to fill with water and sink; (of a horse) to stumble or go lame; to stick in mud. ◆ vt to cause to founder. ◆ n a collapse; inflammation of a horse's hoof, laminitis. [OFr fondrer to fall in, from fond, from L fundus bottom]
■ **found'erous** adj causing to founder.

foundling see under **found**[3].

foundry see under **found**[2].

fount[1] /font or fownt/ (printing) n a complete assortment of types of one sort, with all that is necessary for printing in that kind of letter (also **font**). [Fr fonte, from fondre, from L fundere to cast]

fount[2] /fownt/ n a spring of water (poetic); a source. [L fōns, fontis]
■ **fount'ful** adj (poetic) full of springs.

fountain /fown'tin/ n a spring of water, a jet; a structure for supplying drinking water or other liquid; an ornamental structure with jets, spouts and basins of water; a reservoir from which oil, ink, etc flows, as in a lamp or pen; the source of anything. ◆ vi to spring up or gush, eg from a fountain. [Fr fontaine, from LL fontāna, from L fōns, fontis a spring]
■ **fount'ainless** adj.

❏ **fount'ainhead** n the head or source; the beginning. **fountain pen** n a pen with a reservoir or cartridge for supplying ink to the nib.

four /fōr or för/ n the cardinal number next above three; a symbol representing that number (4, iv, etc); a set of four things or people (syllables, leaves, rowers, etc); a four-oar boat; a score of four points, strokes, tricks, etc; an article of a size denoted by 4; a playing card with four pips; a four-cylinder engine or car; (in pl) a snack taken at four o'clock (also **fours'es**; dialect); the fourth hour after midnight or midday; the age of four years. ◆ adj of the number four; four years old. [OE fēower; Ger vier]

■ **four'fold** adj and adv in four divisions; folded in four thicknesses; four times as much. **four'foldness** n. **four'some** n a group of four; an activity involving four people; a golf match played between two pairs of players, in which each pair plays only one ball, players taking alternate strokes.

❏ **four'-ale** n ale sold at fourpence a quart (obs); cheap ale. **four'ball** n (golf) a match played between two pairs of players, in which only the lower score of each pair for each hole is counted. **four'-by-four'** or **4 x 4** n a vehicle with four-wheel drive. **four'-by-two'** n the piece of cloth in a rifle pull-through; an army biscuit; a piece of wood, etc four (inches, etc) by two (inches, etc). **four-col'our** adj (photog or printing) involving or using four colours (magenta, cyan, yellow and black) as primary. **four-dimen'sional** adj having four dimensions, esp length, breadth and depth with the addition of time. **four'-eyes** n sing the fish Anableps (also **four-eyed fish**); a person wearing spectacles (derog sl). **four'-figure** adj running into four figures; expressed to four decimal places. **four'-flush** n four cards of the same suit in a five-card poker hand. ◆ vi to bluff with a four-flush; to bluff generally. ◆ adj bluffing; not genuine. **four-flush'er** n. **four'-foot** adj measuring four feet (**four-foot way** in British and some other railways, the space of 4 feet 8½ inches (1.435m) between rails); having the pitch of an open organ pipe four feet long, or having that pitch for its lowest note. **four'-footed** adj having four feet. **four-function calculator** n an electronic calculator which can add, subtract, multiply and divide. **four'-handed** adj having four hands; played by four players (cards). **four'-horse** adj drawn by four horses. **four-hours** /fowr'oorz/ n (Scot) a refreshment taken about four o'clock. **four'-inched** adj (Shakesp) four inches wide. **four'-in-hand** n a coach drawn by four horses, two by two, driven by one person; the team drawing it; a necktie tied with a flat slip-knot, with dangling ends. **four-leaf clover** n a clover leaf with four leaflets rather than three, supposedly bringing good luck. **four'-leaved**, **four'-leafed** or **four'-legged** adj. **four'-legged** (also /-leg'id/) adj. **four-letter word** n any of a number of vulgar short words, esp of four letters, referring to sex or excrement. **four'-oar** n a boat rowed with four oars. **four'-o'clock** n a brightly-coloured flowering plant (Mirabilis jalapa), also known as the **marvel of Peru**; a similar red-flowered plant (Mirabilis laevis) found in California; the friarbird, an Australian honeyeater. **four'-pack** n (inf) four cans of drink packaged together and sold as a single item. **four'-part** or **four-part'ed** adj in four parts; divided into four nearly to the base. **four'pence** n the value of four pennies. **four'penny** n an old silver coin worth fourpence. ◆ adj sold or offered for fourpence. **fourpenny one** n (old sl) a blow or punch. **four-post'er** n a large bed with four curtain posts. **four-pound'er** n a gun that fires a four-pound shot; a four-pound object, eg a loaf. **four'score** adj (archaic) eighty. **four'scorth** adj (obs) eightieth. **four'-seater** n a vehicle with seats for four. **four'-square'** adj (also adv) square; presenting a firm bold front; frank, honest and forthright. **four-stroke cycle** n (in an internal-combustion engine) a recurring series of four strokes of the piston, comprising an out-stroke drawing the mixed gases into the cylinder, an in-stroke compressing them, an out-stroke impelled by their explosion and working the engine, and an in-stroke driving out the burnt gas. **four'-wheel** adj acting on or by means of four wheels. **four-wheel drive** n a system in which the driving power of a vehicle is transmitted to all four wheels (abbrev **4WD**). **four'-wheel-drive'** adj. **four'-wheeled** adj. **four'-wheel'er** n a horse-drawn cab or other vehicle with four wheels.

■ **on all fours** on four feet, or hands and feet, or hands and knees; analogous or strictly comparable (with with; law). **the Four Freedoms** the four essential human freedoms as proclaimed by US President Franklin D Roosevelt in 1941, ie freedom of speech, freedom of worship, freedom from want and freedom from fear. **the four hundred** (US) the exclusive social set. **the four seas** see under **sea**.

fourchette /foor-shet'/ n anything forked; a forked piece between glove fingers, uniting the front and back parts; a combination of the card next above and that next below the one just played; the furcula or wishbone of a bird; an animal's web foot; part of the external female genitals, a membrane at the posterior junction of the labia minora. [Fr, dimin of fourche, from L furca fork]

Fourcroya /foor-kroi'ə/ same as **Furcraea**.

fourgon /foor-gɔ̃/ n a baggage-wagon. [Fr]

Fourier analysis /foo'ri-ā ə-nal'i-sis/ n the determination of the harmonic components (the terms of which form the **Fourier series**

that represents the waveform) of a complex waveform. [JBJ Fourier (1768–1830), French mathematician]

Fourierism /foo'ri-ə-ri-zm/ n the socialistic system of FM Charles Fourier (1772–1837), in which society is re-organized into small co-operative communities, or phalanges, allowing free development to human talent and emotions.

■ **Fou'rierist** n and adj. **Fourieris'tic** adj.

Fourier principle /foo'ri-ā prin'si-pl/ n the principle showing that all repeating waveforms can be resolved into sine wave components consisting of a fundamental frequency and a series of harmonics at multiples of this frequency. [Ety as for **Fourier analysis**]

fou rire /foo rēr'/ (Fr) n wild laughter, helpless giggling.

fourniture see **furniture**.

fourteen /fōr-, för-tēn' or för' or för'tēn/ n and adj four and ten. [OE fēowertēne (-tīene); see **four** and **ten**]

■ **fourteen'er** n a verse line of fourteen syllables. **four'teenth** (or /-tēnth'/) adj last of fourteen; next after the thirteenth; equal to one of fourteen equal parts. ◆ n a fourteenth part; a person or thing in fourteenth position. **fourteenth'ly** adv.

fourth /fōrth or förth/ adj last of four; next after the third; equal to one of four equal parts. ◆ n one of four equal parts, a quarter; a person or thing in fourth position; an interval of three (conventionally called four) diatonic degrees (music); a tone at that interval from another (music); a combination of two tones separated by that interval (music). [OE fēowertha, fēortha]

■ **fourth'ly** adv.

❏ **fourth dimension** n that of time, as opposed to the three spatial dimensions; anything which is beyond ordinary experience. **fourth-dimen'sional** adj. **fourth estate** n a group of people other than the lords, commons and clergy, who influence a country's politics; the press. **fourth official** n (football) an official who has responsibility for off-the-field activities such as substitutions, indicating additional time to be played, etc. **Fourth of July** n the anniversary of the adoption of the Declaration of Independence, a public holiday in the USA. **fourth'-rate** adj of the fourth order; inferior. **fourth wall** n an idea of the naturalistic theatre, that the open front of the stage-set represents as solid a wall as the other three sides. **Fourth World** n the poorest and least developed of the poor countries of the world; the poorest people in the developed countries.

foussa see **fossa²**.

fousty /foo'sti/ (Scot) adj mouldy or damp; having a musty smell; fusty.

fouter, footer or **foutre** /foo'tər/, also (Shakesp) **footra** or **foutra** /-tra/ n a fig (as a type of worthlessness); a worthless despicable fellow (Scot). ◆ vi (Scot) to mess around aimlessly. [OE foutre, from L futuere to copulate with]

fouth or **fowth** /fūth/ (Scot) n abundance. [**full** and sfx -th]

fovea /fō'vi-ə/ (anat) n (pl fō'veae /-vi-ē/) a depression or pit. [L fovea]

■ **fō'veal** adj of or like a fovea; of the fovea centralis. **fō'veate** adj pitted. **fovē'ola**, also **fō'veole** n a small depression.

❏ **fovea centralis** /sen-trā'lis or -rā'/ n a fovea in the centre of the back of the retina, the place where vision is sharpest.

fowl /fowl/ n (pl fowls or fowl) a bird; a bird of the poultry kind, a cock or hen; its flesh as food. ◆ vi to kill or try to kill wildfowl. [OE fugol; Ger Vogel]

■ **fowl'er** n a person who fowls. **fowl'ing** n.

❏ **fowl'ing-net** n a net for catching birds. **fowl'ing-piece** n a light gun for small shot, used in fowling. **fowl'-pest** n an acute contagious virus disease of birds (also **fowl'-plague**); another similar disease, Newcastle disease.

fowth see **fouth**.

fox /foks/ n a wild animal related to the dog, having upright ears, a pointed snout, red or grey fur, and a long bushy tail; its fur; extended to other animals, eg black-fox (pekan) and flying fox; anyone notorious for cunning (inf); an attractive young person, esp a woman (N Am inf); a kind of sword (obs). ◆ vt (inf) to baffle, deceive or cheat. ◆ vi (inf) to act cunningly; to cheat. ◆ vi and vt (of paper) to discolour, showing brownish marks. [OE fox; Ger Fuchs]

■ **foxed** adj (of books) discoloured; drunk (archaic); baffled (inf). **fox'ie** n (Aust and NZ inf) a fox terrier. **fox'iness** n craftiness; decay; a harsh, sour taste; discoloration as in books. **fox'ing** n the act of a person who foxes; discoloration (as of paper). **fox'ship** n (Shakesp) the character of a fox, craftiness. **fox'y** adj of foxes; fox-like; cunning (inf); reddish brown; sexually attractive (N Am inf).

❏ **fox'-bat** n a flying fox, a fruit bat. **fox'berry** n the bearberry, a type of heather (bot); the cowberry or red whortleberry. **fox'-brush** n the tail of a fox. **fox'-earth** n a fox's burrow. **fox'-evil** n (archaic) alopecia, baldness. **fox'fire** n a phosphorescence produced by certain fungi on rotting wood. **fox'glove** n a tall plant (genus Digitalis) with spikes of drooping (typically purple) bell-shaped flowers and leaves from which the drug digitalis was produced. **fox'-grape** n an American grape (*Vitis labrusca*; also *V. rotundifolia*). **fox'hole** n a fox's earth; a small entrenchment (*milit*). **fox'hound** n a hound used for chasing foxes. **fox hunt** n. **fox'hunter** n. **fox'hunting** n. **fox'-mark** n a brownish mark on paper that has foxed. **fox'shark** n a large long-tailed shark, the thresher. **fox'-tail** n a fox's brush; a genus (*Alopecurus*) of grasses, with a head like a fox's tail. **fox terrier** n a terrier of a breed *orig* trained to unearth foxes. **fox'-trap** n. **fox'trot** n a ballroom dance to syncopated music; a tune to which this is danced; (**fox'-trot**) a horse's pace with short steps, as in changing from trotting to walking; see also separate entry **Foxtrot**. ◆ vi (**fox'trotting**; **fox'trotted**) to dance the foxtrot.

■ **fox and geese** a game, played with pieces on a board, in which the object is for certain pieces called the geese to surround or corner a piece called the fox, or to prevent it from passing.

Foxtrot or **foxtrot** /fok'strot/ n (in international radio communication) a code word for the letter *f*.

foy[1] /foi/ (*Spenser*) n allegiance. [Fr *foi* faith]

foy[2] /foi/ (*dialect*) n a parting entertainment or gift. [Du *fooi*]

foyer /foi'ā, foi'ər or (Fr) fwä-yā/ n in theatres, a public room, an anteroom; the entrance hallway of a hotel, etc; a residential centre for disadvantaged young people, where they receive support and are encouraged to find employment and develop an independent lifestyle. [Fr, from L *focus* hearth]

foyle and **foyne** Spenserian spellings of **foil**[1,2] and **foin**.

fozy /fō'zi/ (*Scot*) adj spongy; lacking in freshness; fat; slow-witted. [Cf Du *voos* spongy]

■ **fōz'iness** n softness; lack of spirit.

FP abbrev: fireplug; former pupil; Free Presbyterian.

fp abbrev: fortepiano (*music*); freezing point.

FPA or **fpa** abbrev: Family Planning Association.

FPC abbrev: Financial Planning Certificate, a basic qualification for financial advisers.

FPD abbrev: *Freie Partei Deutschlands*, the German Free Democratic Party.

fps abbrev: feet per second; (also **FPS**) foot-pound-second; frames per second.

Fr or **Fr.** abbrev: Father (*relig*); franc or francs; France; French; Friar; Friday.

Fr (*chem*) symbol: francium.

fr abbrev: fragment; franc; frequently.

fra /frä/ (*Ital*) n brother or friar.

frabjous /frab'jəs/ adj perh joyous; surpassing. [Invented by Lewis Carroll]

■ **frab'jously** adv.

fracas /frak'ä or frä-kä'/ n (pl **fracas** /-käz/) uproar; a noisy quarrel. [Fr, from Ital *fracasso*, from *fracassare* to make an uproar]

frack[1] /frak or fräk/ (*Scot*) adj prompt; eager; lusty. [OE *fræc, frec*]

frack[2] see under **fracking**.

fracking /frak'ing/ (*mining*) n the process of forcing liquid containing sand or other material into the strata round a well bottom to split them and prevent them closing; the process of forcing liquid into shale at high pressure in order to release gas. [Shortened from *hydraulic fracturing*]

■ **frack** vi and vt (back-formation) to engage in fracking. **frack'er** n.

fract /frakt/ vt to break; to violate (*Shakesp*). [L *frangere, frāctum* to break (partly through Fr)]

■ **fract'ed** adj broken; violated; having a part displaced, as if broken (*heraldry*).

fractal /frak'təl/ n an apparently irregular or chaotic geometric entity generated by repeating, according to a mathematical formula, ever-diminishing subdivisions of a basic geometric shape, much used in computer graphics. ◆ adj of, relating to or produced by such a generative process. [Fr, from L *frāctus*, pap of *frangere* to break]

■ **fractal'ity** n.

fraction /frak'shən/ n a fragment or small piece; any part of a unit (*maths*; see **decimal** and **vulgar**, **proper** and **improper**); a breach of friendly relations (*Shakesp*); a portion separated by fractionation, eg a mixture of hydrocarbons with similar boiling points obtained by fractional distillation in a refinery; the breaking of the bread in the Eucharist (*Christianity*); a group of Communists acting as a unit within a larger non-Communist body; a faction or schismatic group within the Communist party. [Ety as for **fract**]

■ **frac'tional** adj belonging to a fraction or fractions; of the nature of a fraction; tiny, insignificant. **frac'tionalism** n the state of consisting of discrete units; the action of forming a fraction within the Communist party. **frac'tionalist** n a breaker-up of political unity. **fractionalīzā'tion** or **-s-** n. **frac'tionalize** or **-ise** vt to break up into parts. **frac'tionally** adv. **frac'tionary** adj fractional; fragmentary. **frac'tionate** vt to break up into smaller units; to separate the components of by distillation or otherwise. **fractionā'tion** n. **frac'tionātor** n a plant for carrying out fractional distillation. **fractionīzā'tion** or **-s-** n. **frac'tionize** or **-ise** vt to break up into fractions. **frac'tionlet** n a small fraction.

❑ **fractional distillation** n a distillation process for the separation of the various constituents of liquid mixtures by means of their different boiling points.

fractious /frak'shəs/ adj ready to quarrel; cross. [L *frangere* to break]

■ **frac'tiously** adv. **frac'tiousness** n.

fractography /frak-tog'rə-fi/ n the microscopic study of fractures in metal surfaces. [Ety as for **fract**, and **-graphy**]

fracture /frak'chər/ n (a) breaking; the breach or part broken; the surface of breaking, other than cleavage; the breaking of a bone. ◆ vt and vi to break through; to crack. [Ety as for **fract**]

❑ **Colles' fracture** see separate entry. **comminuted fracture** a fracture in which the bone is splintered. **compound fracture** the breaking of a bone, communicating with a coexisting skin wound. **greenstick fracture** a fracture where the bone is partly broken, partly bent, occurring *esp* in limbs of children. **impacted fracture** a fracture in which the ends of bone are driven into each other. **simple fracture** a fracture of a bone without a wound in the skin.

frae see **fro**.

fraenum same as **frenum**.

frag /frag/ (*N Am milit slang*) vt (**fragg'ing**; **fragged** /fragd/) to kill with a fragmentation grenade (*esp* as in the Vietnam War). [**fragment**]

Fragaria /frə-gā'ri-ə/ n the strawberry genus. [L *frāgum* the strawberry]

fragile /fraj'īl (US) -əl/ adj easily broken; frail; delicate. [Fr, from L *fragilis*, from *frangere, frāctum* to break]

■ **fra'gilely** adv. **fragility** /frə-jil'/ or **fra'gileness** n the state of being fragile.

❑ **fragile X syndrome** n a genetic condition in which an abnormally easily damaged X-chromosome leads to mental impairment.

fragment /frag'mənt/ n a piece broken off; a usu small piece of something broken or smashed; an unfinished portion (eg of a writing). ◆ vt and vi /frag-ment'/ to break into fragments. ◆ vi /frag-ment'/ (*comput*) of a file, to split into separate sections on a hard disk. [L *fragmentum*, from *frangere, frāctum* to break]

■ **fragmental** /-ment'/ (also /frag'mən-təl/) adj composed of fragments of older rocks; in fragments. **frag'mentarily** adv. **frag'mentariness** n. **frag'mentary** or **fragment'ed** adj consisting of fragments; broken; in fragments; existing or operating in separate parts, not forming a harmonious unity. **fragmentā'tion** n division into fragments; cell division without mitosis (*biol*).

❑ **fragmentation bomb** or **grenade** n one which shatters into small destructive fragments on explosion.

fragor /frā'gör/ (*obs*) n a crash. [L]

fragrant /frā'grənt/ adj sweet-scented. [L *frāgrāns, -antis*, prp of *frāgrāre* to smell]

■ **fra'grance** n pleasantness of smell; a perfume or cologne; sweet or pleasant influence (*fig*). ◆ vt to perfume or give a fragrance to. **fra'grancy** n. **fra'grantly** adv. **fra'grantness** n.

fraîcheur /fre-shœr'/ (*Fr*) n freshness or coolness.

frail[1] /frāl/ adj very easily shattered; feeble and infirm (*esp Scot*); decrepit; morally weak; unchaste (*euphem*); tender (*Spenser*). ◆ n (*old sl*) a woman. [OFr *fraile*, from L *fragilis* fragile]

■ **frail'ish** adj somewhat frail. **frail'ly** adv. **frail'ness** or **frail'ty** (*Spenser* **fra'iltee**) n weakness; infirmity; a flaw, shortcoming.

frail[2] /frāl/ n a rush (*bot*); a basket made of rushes. [OFr *frayel*]

fraim see **fremd**.

fraise[1] /frāz/ n a horizontal or nearly horizontal palisade (*fortif*); a tool for enlarging a drillhole; a 16c ruff. ◆ vt to fence with a fraise. [Fr]

fraise[2] /frāz/ (*dialect*) n commotion.

fraise[3] /frāz/ see **froise**.

Fraktur /fräk-toor'/ n a German black-letter typeface. [Ger, from L *frāctūra* breaking]

framboesia, also (*N Am*) **frambesia** /fram-bē'zi-ə/ n a tropical skin disease, yaws. [Fr *framboise* raspberry]

frame /frām/ vt to form; to shape; to put together; to plan, adjust or adapt; to contrive, devise or concoct; to bring about; to articulate; to direct (one's steps); to set about; to enclose in a frame or border; to make (someone) the victim of a frame-up (*inf*). ◆ vi (*rare*) to make one's way; to resort; to pretend (*dialect*); to make a move; to give promise of progress or success; to contrive (*Bible*). ◆ n the body; a putting together of parts; a structure; a case made to enclose, border or support anything; the skeleton of anything; the rigid part of a bicycle; a structure on which embroidery is worked; a stocking-making machine; a loom (*obs*); a structure on which bees build a honeycomb;

a structure for the cultivation or sheltering of plants; state (of mind) or mood; act of devising (*Shakesp*); the individual unit picture in cinema film or in a (still or movie) photographic film, cartoon strip, etc; formerly, the British term for field (*TV*); the total TV picture; a triangular support in which the balls are grouped for the break (*snooker*, etc); the balls so grouped (*snooker*, etc); in the jargon of certain games, a definite part of a game, a game, or a definite number of games. [OE *framian* to be helpful, related to *fram* forward]
■ **framed** *adj*. **fram'er** *n* a person who forms or constructs; a person who makes frames for pictures, etc; a person who devises; a person who formulates (eg law). **fram'ing** *n* the act of constructing; a frame or setting.
❑ **frame'-breaker** *n* (*hist*) a person who broke stocking-frames on their introduction in protest against the unemployment they caused. **frame'-house** *n* a house consisting of a skeleton of timber, with boards or shingles laid on. **frame'-maker** *n* a maker of picture frames. **frame'-saw** *n* a thin saw stretched in a frame. **frame'-up** *n* (*inf*) a trumped-up affair, *esp* a false criminal charge against an innocent person; a staged or preconcerted event. **frame'work** *n* the work that forms the frame; the skeleton or outline of anything.
■ **frame of reference** a set of axes with reference to which the position of a point, etc is described; any set of limits or standards as a context within which to place a specific action, event, behaviour type, etc.

frampold /*fram'pōld* or *-pold*/ (*obs*) *adj* (also (*Walter Scott*) **fram'pal**) peevish or intractable; fiery. [Ety obscure]
■ **fram'pler** *n* (*Walter Scott*) a brawler.

franc /*frangk*/ *n* a former unit of currency in France, Belgium and Luxembourg, replaced by the euro; the standard monetary unit of several countries, including Switzerland, Liechtenstein and some former French and Belgian dependencies. [OFr *franc*, from the inscription *Francorum rex* ('King of the French') on the first coins]

franchise[1] /*fran'chīz* or *-shīz*/ *n* liberty; a privilege or exemption by prescription or grant; the right to vote, *esp* for a representative in a national government; voting qualification; a commercial concession by which a retailer is granted by a company the generally exclusive right of retailing its goods or providing its services in a specified area, with use of the company's expertise, marketing, trademark, etc; a similar concession granted by a public authority to a broadcasting company; a percentage below which the underwriter incurs no responsibility (*insurance*); a professional sports team (*N Am*). ◆ *vt* (*obs*) to grant a franchise to. [OFr, from *franc* free]
■ **franchisee'** *n* a person to whom a franchise is granted. **fran'chisement** /*-chiz-* or *-shiz-*/ *n* (*obs*) liberation. **fran'chiser** or **fran'chisor** *n* a voter; a firm, etc which grants a commercial concession.
❑ **franchise player** *n* an American football player paid at a premium rate and not eligible to be signed by other teams.

franchise[2] /*frä-shēz'*/ (*Fr*) *n* candour or frankness.

Franciscan /*fran-sis'kən*/ *adj* belonging to the order of mendicant friars in the Roman Catholic Church, founded by St *Francis* of Assisi (1182–1226). ◆ *n* a friar of this order. [L *Franciscus* Francis]

francium /*fran'si-əm*/ *n* an unstable radioactive metallic element (symbol **Fr**; atomic no 87) present in uranium ore. [Named after *France*, the country of its discoverer, Marguerite Catherine Perey (1909–75)]

franco /*fräng'kō*/ (*Ital*) *adj* and *adv* post-free; franked.

Franco- /*frangk-ō-*/ *combining form* French, *esp* jointly French and something else, as in eg *Franco-German*.
■ **Francoma'nia** *n* (also without *cap*) a mania for French ways. **Franc'ophil** or **Franc'ophile** *n* (also without *cap*) a person who is friendly to, or has a fondness for, France or what is French. **Franc'ophobe** *n* (also without *cap*) a person who dislikes or fears France or what is French. **Francophō'bia** *n* (also without *cap*). **Franc'ophone** *adj* (also without *cap*) French-speaking (used eg of Africans for whom French is a second mother-tongue, or of French-speaking Canadians).

francolin /*frang'kō-lin*/ *n* a bird of the *Francolinus* genus of partridges. [Fr]

franc-tireur /*frä tē-rœr'*/ (*Fr*) *n* a sniper; a guerrilla.

frangible /*fran'ji-bl*/ (*formal*) *adj* easily broken. [L *frangere* to break; see **fract**]
■ **frangibil'ity** *n*.

frangipane /*fran'ji-pān*/ *n* a cream made with crushed almonds, used in various pastries, desserts, sweets, etc; frangipani (the perfume). [frangipani]

frangipani /*fran-ji-pä'nē*/ *n* the red jasmine or other species of *Plumeria*, tropical American shrubs of the dogbane genus with scented flowers; a perfume made from or imitating red jasmine; frangipane. [From the Marquis *Frangipani*, 16c inventor of the perfume]

Franglais /*frä-gle'*/ (*usu humorous*; also without *cap*) *n* French with many English words and forms; a jocular cross between English and French. [Fr *Français* and *Anglais*]

franion /*fran'yən*/ *n* a boon companion (*obs*); a loose woman (*Spenser*). [Ety dubious]

Frank /*frangk*/ *n* a German from a confederation in Franconia of which a branch conquered Gaul in the 5c, and founded France; (in the East) a Western European. [See **frank**[1]]
■ **Frank'ish** *adj*.

frank[1] /*frangk*/ *adj* free or open; liberal (*obs*); open or candid in expression; unrestrained (*obs*); unmistakable or true (*med*; as in frank pus or asthma). ◆ *vt* to sign or mark so as to ensure free carriage, eg at a post office; to send thus signed or marked; to mark by means of a **frank'ing-machine** to show that postage has been paid. ◆ *n* the signature of a person who had the right to frank a letter; the mark left by a franking-machine; a franked envelope. [OFr *franc*, from LL *francus*; OHGer *Franko* Frank, hence a free man]
■ **frank'ly** *adv* to be frank; in a frank manner. **frank'ness** *n*.
❑ **frank'-fee** *n* (*feudal law*) tenure in fee simple. **frank'-pledge** *n* (*feudal law*) a mutual suretyship by which the members of a tithing were made responsible for one another. **frank'-tenement** *n* (*feudal law*) freehold.

frank[2] /*frangk*/ (*Shakesp*) *n* a pigsty. ◆ *vt* to shut up in a sty; to cram or fatten. [OFr *franc*]

frankalmoign /*frang'kal-moin*/ (*Eng law*) *n* a form of land tenure in which no obligations were enforced except religious ones, eg praying. [OFr *franc* free, and *almoigne* alms]

Frankenia /*frang-kē'ni-ə*/ *n* the sea-heath genus, constituting a family **Frankeniā'ceae**, related to the tamarisk family. [Named after John *Frankenius* (1590–1661), Swedish physician and botanist]

Frankenstein /*frang'kən-stīn*/ *n* the hero of Mary Shelley's novel of that name, who by his skill creates an animate being like a man, only to his own torment; hence, by confusion, any creation that brings disaster to its maker, *esp* a monstrous-looking humanoid creature.
❑ **Frankenstein food** *n* (*inf*; also **Frank'enfood**) a foodstuff made or derived from genetically modified plants or animals.

frankfurter /*frangk'fûr-tər* or *-fûr-tər*/ *n* a small smoked sausage. [Short for Ger *Frankfurter Wurst* Frankfurt sausage]

frankincense /*frang'kin-sens*/ *n* olibanum, a sweet-smelling resin from Arabia, used as incense; spruce resin. [OFr *franc encens* pure incense]
■ **herb frankincense** laserwort, one of a genus of perennial herbs.

franklin /*frang'klin*/ (*hist*) *n* an English freeholder, free from feudal servitude to a subject-superior. [LL *francus*; see **frank**[1]]

franklinite /*frang'kli-nīt*/ *n* a zinc-manganese mineral, mined at *Franklin Forge*, New Jersey, USA.

frantic /*fran'tik*/ *adj* mad or furious; wild, *esp* with anxiety; marked by hurried activity or frenzy. [OFr *frenetique*, from L *phrenēticus*, from Gr *phrenētikos* mad, from *phrēn* the mind; see **frenetic** and **frenzy**]
■ **fran'tically** or (*Shakesp*) **fran'ticly** *adv*. **fran'ticness** *n* the state of being frantic.
❑ **fran'tic-mad** *adj* (*obs*) raving mad.

franzy /*fran'zi*/ (*dialect*) *adj* cross; peevish. [Variant of **frenzy**]

frap /*frap*/ *vt* (**frapp'ing**; **frapped**) to strike (now *dialect*); to secure by many turns of a lashing (*naut*). [Fr *frapper* to strike]

frape /*frāp*/ (*sl*) *vt* to alter the personal details on a social media account without the owner's knowledge. [Facebook *rape*]

frappant /*fra-pä'*/ (*Fr*) *adj* striking; affecting.

frappé /*frap'ā*/ *adj* (also *fem* **frapp'ée**) (of coffee or other drinks) iced; artificially cooled. ◆ *n* an iced drink. [Fr, pap of *frapper* to strike]

Frappuccino® /*fra-pu-chē'nō*/ *n* a blend of coffee, milk, crushed ice and flavourings. [**frappé** and **cappuccino**]

frascati /*fra-skä'ti*/ (also with *cap*) *n* a white wine from the region of *Frascati* in N Italy.

frass /*fras*/ *n* excrement or other refuse of wood-boring larvae. [Ger, from *fressen* to eat; cf **fret**[1]]

frat /*frat*/ *abbrev*: fraternize; fraternity.

fratch /*frach*/ (*dialect*) *n* a quarrel or brawl. [Perh imit]
■ **fratch'ety** or **fratch'y** *adj*. **fratch'ing** *adj*.

frate /*frä'tā*/ (*Ital*) *n* (pl **fra'ti** /*-tē*/) a friar, a mendicant Franciscan.

frater[1] /*frä'tər*/ (*hist*) *n* (also **fra'ter-house** or **frä'try**) a refectory; sometimes applied in error to a monastic common room or to a chapterhouse (by confusion with **frater**[2]). [OFr *fraitur* for *refreitor*, from LL *refectōrium*]

frater[2] /*frä'tər*/ *n* a friar; a comrade. [L, a brother]
■ **fratry** /*frät'ri*/ or **frät'ery** *n* a fraternity; a convent of friars (see also **frater**[1]).

Fratercula /*fra-tûr'kū-lə*/ *n* the puffin genus. [Ety as for **fraternize**]

fraternal /frə-tûr'nl/ adj belonging to a brother or brethren; brotherly; (of twins) dizygotic, not identical. [Ety as for **fraternize**]
■ **frater'nally** adv.

fraternity /frə-tûr'ni-ti/ n the state of being brothers; a brotherhood; a society formed on a principle of brotherhood; an all-male N American college association; any set of people with something in common. [Ety as for **fraternize**]
□ **fraternity house** or (inf) **frat house** n (US) a college fraternity lodging-house.

fraternize or **-ise** /frat'ər-nīz/ vi to associate as brothers; to seek brotherly fellowship; to come into friendly association (with). [L frāter a brother; cf **brother**, Gr phrātēr a clansman, Sans bhrātr]
■ **fraternīzā'tion** or **-s-** n associating as brothers. **frat'ernizer** or **-s-** n.

fratricide /frat'ri-sīd or frāt'/ n a person who kills his or her brother; the murder of a brother. [Fr, from L frāter, frātris, and caedere to kill]
■ **fratricī'dal** adj.

frau or **Frau** /frow/ n (pl **Frau'en** /frow'=n) a (usu married) woman (often derog); a wife; (used of or to a German or German-speaking woman) Mrs or Ms. [Ger]
■ **fräulein** or **Fräulein** /froi'līn/ n (old) an unmarried woman; often used as a professional title, such as of a German governess; (used of or to a German or German-speaking woman) Miss.

fraud /fröd/ n deceit; impersonation with intent to deceive; criminal deception done with the intention of gaining an advantage; a snare (Milton); a deceptive trick; a cheat or swindler (inf); a fraudulent item. [OFr fraude, from L fraus fraud]
■ **fraud'ful** adj (rare) deceptive. **fraud'fully** adv (rare). **frauds'man** n a person involved in criminal fraud. **fraud'ster** n a swindler. **fraud'ūlence** or **fraud'ūlency** n. **fraud'ūlent** adj using fraud. **fraud'ūlently** adv.
□ **fraudulent bankruptcy** n bankruptcy in which the insolvent is implicated in the misappropriation of the funds owing to his or her creditors.

Frauendienst /frow'ən-dēnst/ (Ger) n courtly love.

fraught /fröt/ adj having or causing (esp something bad or undesirable, eg danger; with with); feeling or making anxious or distressed; tension-filled; filled (with); freighted or laden (obs). ◆ n (obs) a load or cargo; the freight of a ship. ◆ vt (obs) to load. ◆ vi (Shakesp) to form the freight of a vessel. [Prob ODu vracht; cf **freight**]
■ **fraught'age** or **fraut'age** n (Shakesp) loading or cargo.

fräulein see under **frau**.

Fraunhofer's lines /frown'hō-fərz līnz/ see under **line**¹.

fraus pia /frös pī'ə or frows pē'a/ (L) a pious fraud.

Fraxinus /frak'si-nəs/ n the ash genus of trees. [L]
■ **fraxinell'a** n an aromatic plant, dittany (from its ash-like leaves).

fray¹ /frā/ vt to wear off by rubbing; to unravel the end or edge of; to cause a strain on (eg nerves, temper, etc). ◆ vi to become frayed; (of deer, etc) to rub off the velvet from the new antlers. [Fr frayer, from L fricāre to rub]
■ **fray'ing** n the action of the verb; frayed-off material.
■ **fray at the edges** to wear, (fig) become problematic or unmanageable, or (of someone's patience or temper) begin to run out.

fray² /frā/ n an affray; a brawl; a scene of lively action. ◆ vt to frighten. [Aphetic from **affray**]

frazil /fraz'il or frā'zil/ (N Am) n ground-ice; ice in small spikes and plates in rapid streams. [Can Fr frasil; prob Fr fraisil cinders]

frazzle /fraz'l/ vt to fray or wear out. ◆ n the state of being worn-out; a shred. [Origin unknown]
■ **burnt, etc to a frazzle** completely burnt, etc.

FRC abbrev: Financial Reporting Council.

FRCA abbrev: Fellow of the Royal College of Anaesthetists.

FRCP abbrev: Fellow of the Royal College of Physicians (**-Edin**, of Edinburgh; **-Lond**, of London; **-Irel**, of Ireland).

FRCPS Glasg abbrev: Fellow of the Royal College of Physicians and Surgeons of Glasgow.

FRCS abbrev: Fellow of the Royal College of Surgeons (**-Ed**, of Edinburgh; **-Eng**, of England; **-Irel**, of Ireland).

freak¹ /frēk/ n a caprice (obs); an abnormal production of nature, a monstrosity; an eccentric (inf); a weirdly unconventional person (inf); a person who is wildly enthusiastic about something (as in film freak, football freak or Jesus freak; inf); a person who is devoted or addicted to a particular drug (as in acid freak; inf). ◆ adj capricious (obs); wildly unusual. ◆ vi (inf) to freak out. [A late word; cf OE frīcian to dance]
■ **freak'iness** or **freak'ishness** n. **freak'ing** adj and adv used as an intensifier (euphem inf, esp N Am). **freak'ish**, **freak'ful** or **freak'y** adj apt to change the mind suddenly; very unusual, odd. **freak'ishly** adv.
□ **freak'-out** n (sl) a (drug-induced) hallucinatory or (loosely) wildly exciting or unconventional experience or occurrence.

■ **freak out** (inf) to have or cause to have such an experience, etc; to have a strong fit of anger, anxiety, etc.

freak² /frēk/ vt to spot or streak (Milton); to variegate (Milton). ◆ n (obs) a streak of colour. [Perh the same as **freak**¹]

freckle /frek'l/ vt to spot; to colour with spots. ◆ n a small brownish spot on the skin esp of fair-haired people; any small spot. [ON freknur (pl), Dan fregne]
■ **freck'ling** n a little spot. **freck'ly** or **freck'led** adj covered in freckles.

fredaine /frə-den'/ (Fr) n an escapade or prank.

free /frē/ adj (freer /frē'ər/; freest /frē'ist/) not bound; at liberty; not under arbitrary government; not strict, or bound by rules; not literal; unimpeded; unconstrained; readily cut, separated or wrought; ready, esp in the phrase free to confess; guiltless; frank; lavish; uncombined; (of a morpheme) able to stand alone as a word, opp to bound (linguistics); unattached; exempt (with from); not suffering from or encumbered with (with of or from); having a franchise (with of); without, or not necessitating, payment; bold; indecent. ◆ adv freely; without payment; without obstruction. ◆ vt (**free'ing**; **freed**) to give liberty to; to deliver from whatever confines (something); (often with up) to release someone from a commitment in order for them to take on another; to rid (with from or of). ◆ combining form free from, as in trouble-free. [OE frēo; Ger frei; ON frī]
■ **free'bie** n (orig US; sl; also **free'bee**) something supplied free of charge (also adj). **free'dom** n liberty; frankness; outspokenness; unhampered boldness; separation; privileges connected with a city (often granted as a merely symbolic honour); improper familiarity; licence. **free'ly** adv. **free'ness** n. **freer** /frē'ər/ n a liberator.
□ **free agency** n the state or power of acting freely, or without necessity or constraint upon the will. **free agent** n. **free-and-eas'y** n an informal public-house club (see also **free and easy** below). **free'-arm** adj with the arm unsupported. **free association** n a technique in psychoanalysis based either on the first association called forth by each of a series of words or on a train of thought suggested by a single word. **free atom** n an unattached atom assumed to exist briefly during certain chemical reactions. **free'base** n (sl) cocaine refined for smoking by being heated with ether, often also inhaled during the process. ◆ vt to refine (cocaine) in this way. ◆ vi to smoke freebase. **free'-bench** n (hist) a widow's right to an endowment out of her husband's lands. **free'board** n the distance between waterline and the deck or the upper edge of the side of a vessel (naut); a strip of land outside a fence, or a right to this. **free'booter** n a person who roves about freely in search of booty (Du vrijbuiter). **free'bootery** n. **free'booting** adj and n. **free'booty** n. **free'born** adj born free. **Free Church** n that branch of the Presbyterians in Scotland which left the Established Church in the Disruption of 1843; the small minority of that group who refused to combine with the United Presbyterians in the **United Free Church** (see **United Presbyterian Church** under **Presbyterian**); in England, a Nonconformist church generally. **free'-city** n a city constituting a state in itself. **free climbing** n rock climbing using ropes but no spikes, ladders or other fixed aids. **free collective bargaining** n collective bargaining (see under **collect**) without government-imposed or other restrictions. **free companion** n (hist) a member of a **free company**, a medieval band of mercenaries ready for any service. **free'-cost** n freedom from charges. **free'-diver** n a skin-diver. **free'-diving** n skin diving. **freed'man** or (fem) **freed'woman** n (pl **freed'men** or **freed'women**) (hist) a man or woman who has been a slave and has been freed. **freedom fighter** n a person who fights in an armed movement for the liberation of a nation, etc from a government considered unjust, tyrannical, etc. **free drop** n a ruling allowing one to lift a golf ball from its resting place and drop it elsewhere without penalty. **free energy** n (chem) the capacity of a system to perform work. **free enterprise** n the conduct of business without interference from the state. **free fall** n the motion of an unpropelled body in a gravitational field, eg that of a spacecraft in orbit; the part of a parachute jump before the parachute opens; any fast, uncontrolled descent (fig). **free'-fall** adj of or relating to free fall or to a parachute jump which is partly a free fall. ◆ vi to fall with one's parachute kept closed. **free-fall'ing** n. **free fight** n a confused, haphazard or indiscriminate fight. **free'-fisher** n a person who has a right to take fish in certain waters. **free flight** n the flight of a rocket, etc when its motor is no longer producing thrust. **free-float'ing** adj not attached; uncommitted; (of anxiety) not attributable to a specific cause (psychiatry). **Free'fone**® n a British Telecom service allowing callers eg to a business or organization to make their calls free of charge, the charges being paid by the business or organization concerned (also, loosely, **free'phone**). **free'-food'er** n an opponent of taxes on food. **free'-footed** adj (Shakesp) not restrained in movement. **free'-for-all** n a contest open to anybody (also adj); a public brawl. **free'-form** adj flowing freely; unstructured. **free gift** n something given free with a product as an incentive to buy. **free'hand** adj executed by the unguided hand. **free hand** n complete freedom of action. **free'-hand'ed** adj open-handed; liberal. **free'-hand'edness** n. **free'-**

heart'ed adj open-hearted; liberal. **free'-heart'edness** n. **free'hold** n (law) a property held by fee simple, fee tail, or for life; the holding of property in any of these ways. ◆ adj being or relating to a freehold. **free'holder** n a person who possesses a freehold. **free house** n a public house that is not tied to a particular supplier. **free kick** n (football) a kick for which no defender may approach within ten yards of the ball, awarded eg after the opposing side has committed a foul. **free labour** n voluntary, not slave, labour; (the labour of) workers who do not belong to a trade union. **free'lance** n anyone who works for himself or herself, employed or paid by others only for particular, usu short-term, assignments (also **free'lancer**); an unattached politician, etc; orig one of the mercenary knights and men-at-arms who after the Crusades wandered about Europe (hist). ◆ adj being or relating to a freelance. ◆ vi to work as a freelance. ◆ adv in the role of a freelance. **free list** n the list of people admitted without payment to a theatre, etc, or of those to whom a book, etc is sent. **free-liv'er** n a person who freely indulges his or her appetite for eating and drinking; a glutton. **free-liv'ing** adj (biol) not parasitic or symbiotic. **free'load** vi (esp US; inf) to eat at someone else's expense; to sponge; to gain from others' efforts. ◆ n a free meal. **free'loader** n. **free'loading** n and adj. **free love** n (the claim to) freedom in sexual relations, unshackled by marriage. **free-lov'er** n a person who advocates, or is thought to advocate, free love, eg (with cap) a Perfectionist (see under **perfect**). **free lunch** n (inf) something given with apparently no strings attached, but usu received with suspicion. **free'man** or (fem) **free'woman** n (pl **free'men** or **free'women**) a person who is free or enjoys liberty; a person who holds a particular franchise or privilege. **free market** n a capitalist economic system where prices are allowed to fluctuate solely according to supply and demand. **free'-market** adj. **free-marketeer'** n. **free'mason** n in the Middle Ages, a stonemason of a superior grade; (often with cap) a member of a secret male fraternity, united in lodges for social enjoyment and mutual assistance. **freemason'ic** adj. **freemā'sonry** n (also with cap) the institutions, practices, etc of freemasons; instinctive understanding and sympathy. **free-mind'ed** adj with a mind free or unperplexed; without a load of care. **free pardon** n an unconditional pardon to someone convicted of a crime. **freephone** see **Freefone**® above. **free port** n a port open on equal terms to all traders; a free-trade zone adjacent to a port or airport, allowing duty-free import and re-export of goods. **Free'post**® n a Royal Mail service which allows inquirers or potential customers to write to a business or organization free of charge, the postage costs being paid by the business or organization concerned. **free radical** n a group of atoms containing at least one unpaired electron existing briefly during certain chemical reactions. **free'-range** adj (of poultry) allowed some freedom to move about, not kept in a barn or battery; (of eggs) laid by free-range hens. **free'-reed** adj (music) having a reed that does not touch the side of the aperture. **free'ride** or **freeride skiing** n an extreme form of skiing in which participants attempt difficult jumps and turns. **free ride** n (inf) the ability to benefit from a situation, etc without having to bear any of its costs and responsibilities. **free-rid'er** n (inf) a person who enjoys benefits obtained for workers by a trade union without being a member of that trade union; anyone who benefits from an economic situation without paying for the privilege. **free running** n an extreme sport in which participants run through an urban area using techniques from gymnastics, martial arts and climbing to negotiate obstacles. **free school** n a school where no tuition fees are exacted; (in England) a school that is funded by the government but run independently of the local authority. **free'-select** vi (Aust) to take up crown land under a scheme making land available for small farms. **free'-selection** (or -/lek'shən/) n the process of doing so; the land so taken. **free'-selector** (or /-lek'tər/) n. **free'sheet** n a newspaper distributed free. **free'-shot** n (Ger Freischütz) a legendary hunter and marksman who gets a number of bullets (Freikugeln) from the Devil, six of which always hit the mark, while the seventh remains at the Devil's disposal. **free skating** n competitive figure skating in which the skater selects movements from an officially approved list of jumps, spins, etc. **free'-soil** adj in favour of free territory and opposed to slavery. **free-soil'er** n. **free'-space** adj (of a radio, etc) able to operate only where there is **free space**, ie where the radio waves are not affected by surrounding objects such as buildings, hills, etc. **free speech** n the right to express one's opinions freely in public. **free spirit** n a person of an independent and individualistic turn of mind. **free-spōk'en** adj accustomed to speaking without reserve. **free-spōk'enness** n. **free'-standing** adj not supported by or attached to anything else. **Free States** n pl in America, before the Civil War of 1861–65, those of the United States in which slavery did not exist, opp to Slave States. **free'stone** n any easily wrought building stone without a tendency to split into layers; a freestone fruit. ◆ adj (of a type of peach, etc) having a stone from which the pulp easily separates, opp to clingstone. **free'style** adj (of a (eg swimming or skiing) race or competition) in which a competitor is free to choose which style or method to use or which movements to perform; (of wrestling) all-in; (of a competitor) taking part in freestyle competitions, etc; (of music, acting, etc)

improvised. ◆ n freestyle competitions; (in swimming now usu) the front crawl (see under **front**). ◆ vi to perform freestyle rap. **free'styler** n a competitor in freestyle competitions; a performer of freestyle rap. **free'-swimming** adj swimming about, not attached. **free'thinker** n a person who rejects authority in religion; a rationalist. **free'thinking** n and adj. **free'-thought** n. **free throw** n (basketball) a throw at a basket without interference, as a penalty against the opposing side for an infringement. **free-to-air'** or **free-to-view'** adj denoting a television channel for which no extra subscription is required, opp to pay television. **free'-tongued** adj free-spoken. **free trade** n free or unrestricted trade; free interchange of commodities without protective duties. **free-trad'er** n a person who practises or advocates this; a smuggler (obs); a smuggling vessel (obs). **free verse** n verse that has no regularity of metre, rhyme, length of lines, etc; rhythmic prose arranged as irregular verses. **free'-verser** n a writer of free verse, a verslibrist. **Freeview**® n a digital terrestrial television service supplied free of charge. **free vote** n a vote left to individual choice, free from party discipline. **free'ware** n (comput sl) a program that can be copied without charge but not sold. **free'way** n a toll-free road for high-speed traffic (US); a motorway (S Afr). **free'wheel** n the mechanism of a bicycle by which the rear-wheel may be temporarily disconnected and set free from the driving-gear. **freewheel'** vi to cycle with the rear wheel so disconnected; (of a motor vehicle or its driver) to coast; to move, act or live without restraint or concern (fig). **freewheel'ing** n and adj. **free will** n freedom of the will from restraint; freedom of choice; the power of self-determination. **free'-will** adj spontaneous; voluntary. **freewoman** see **freeman** above. **Free World** n the collective name used of themselves by non-communist countries esp during the Soviet era to differentiate themselves from communist states.

■ **feel free** (inf) to regard oneself as permitted. **for free** (inf) given without desire for payment or other return. **free alongside ship** delivered to the quayside free of charge, but exclusive of the cost of loading onto the ship (abbrev **fas**). **free and easy** unconstrained; cheerfully tolerant. **free on board** delivered on a vessel or other conveyance at no charge at all (abbrev **fob**). **free on rail** delivered to a railway station and loaded onto a train free of charge (abbrev **for**). **it's a free country** (inf) there is no objection to or law against the carrying-out of whatever action has been proposed. **make free with** to be familiar with or take liberties with; to help oneself liberally to. **make so free as to** to venture to.

freebie, **Freefone**®, etc see under **free**.

freecycle /frē-sī'kl/ vi and vt to recycle an unwanted product by giving it free to someone who can use it. [free and recycle]

freegan /frē'gən/ n a person who expresses opposition to materialism and consumerism by retrieving and using discarded food, clothes, etc. [From **free**, modelled on **vegan**]

freemartin /frē'mär-tin/ n the female of a pair of twin calves which has internal male organs and external and rudimentary internal female organs; a similar animal of another species. [Ety unknown; perh connected with Ir mart a heifer]

freesia /frē'zi-ə or frē'zhə/ n a plant of the S African genus Freesia of scented plants of the iris family. [FHT Freese or HT Frees, German physicians, or, according to some, EM Fries, Swedish botanist]

freet and **freety** see **freit**.

freeze /frēz/ vi (freez'ing; frōze or (Milton) freez'd; frōz'en or (obs or dialect) frōze, frōre or frōrn) to become ice; to become solid owing to fall of temperature; to be at a temperature at which water would freeze; to be very cold; to become motionless, stiff, attached or stopped by, or as if by, cold. ◆ vt to cause to freeze; to fix; to stabilize; to prevent the use of or dealings in; to stop at or not develop beyond a particular state or stage; to put a temporary stop to; to stop (a moving film) at a particular frame; to preserve (esp food) by freezing and storing below freezing point; to anaesthetize (a part of the body). ◆ n a frost; a period of very cold weather; a stoppage; a period of strict control of wages, prices, etc. [OE frēosan, pap froren; Du vreizen, Ger frieren]

■ **freez'able** adj. **freez'er** n a freezing apparatus; anything that freezes; a compartment in a refrigerator for freezing fresh foods; an apparatus or room for storing food, etc below freezing point, a deep-freeze. **freez'ing** n the action of the verb. ◆ adj very cold. □ **freeze'-dry** vt. **freeze-dry'ing** n rapid freezing and evaporation to dryness in a vacuum for preservation or storage of a substance. **freeze'-frame** n a frame of a cinema film repeated, or a frame of a DVD or video film held, to give a still picture; the facility to do this on a DVD player or video recorder. ◆ vi to pause a film to give a still picture. **freeze'-out** see **freeze out** below. **freeze'-up** n (N Am) the period when ice forms on lakes, etc, at onset of winter. **freez'ing-down** n lowering of the body temperature. **freezing mixture** n a mixture, eg of pounded ice and salt, cold enough to freeze a liquid by the rapid absorption of heat. **freezing point** n the temperature at

which a liquid solidifies, that of water being 32° Fahrenheit, 0° Celsius (centigrade).
■ **freeze down** to lower the body temperature in preparation for heart and other operations. **freeze out** (*inf*) to oblige to leave; to exclude (**freeze'-out** *n*).

freight /frāt/ *n* the lading or cargo, *esp* of a ship; the transport of goods by a vehicle; goods transported; the charge for transporting goods. ◆ *vt* to transport by vehicle; to load (*esp* a ship); to hire or let out. ◆ *adj* (*obs*) freighted; fraught. [Prob ODu *vrecht*, a form of *vracht*]
■ **freight'age** *n* money paid for freight; freighted goods. **freight'er** *n* a person who freights a vessel; a cargo-carrying boat, etc; a transporting agent (*US*).
❑ **freight'-car** *n* (*US*) a luggage van; a goods van or wagon. **Freight'liner**® *n* a train having specially designed containers and rolling stock and used for rapid transport of goods. **freight shed** *n* a goods shed or warehouse. **freight ton** see under **ton**[1]. **freight'-train** *n* a goods train.

freit or **freet** /frēt/ (*Scot*) *n* an omen. [ON *frětt* news]
■ **freit'y** or **freet'y** *adj* superstitious.

fremd /fremd or frāmd/, **fremit** /frem'it or frā'mit/ or **fraim** /frām/ (*Scot*) *adj* foreign; strange; not related or similar; estranged, cold or unfriendly. ◆ *n* (also (*Spenser*) **frenne** /fren/) a stranger; people to whom one is not related, strangers. [OE *fremde*; cf Ger *fremd*]

fremescent /frə-mes'ənt/ (*rare*) *adj* growling or muttering. [L *fremere* to growl]
■ **fremesc'ence** *n*.

fremit see **fremd**.

fremitus /frem'i-təs/ (*pathol*) *n* a palpable vibration, eg of the walls of the chest. [L, a murmur]

frena see **frenum**.

French /french or -sh/ *adj* belonging to *France* or its people; originating in France (sometimes without *cap*). ◆ *n* the people of France; the language of France, also an official language in Belgium, Switzerland, Canada and other countries; French vermouth; oral sex, fellatio (*vulgar sl*). [OE *Frencisc*, from L *Francus*, from OHGer *Franko*]
■ **Frenchifica'tion** *n*. **French'ify** *vt* to make French or Frenchlike; to infect with the manner of the French. **French'iness** *n* (*inf*) an exaggerated French manner. **French'ness** *n* the quality of being French. **French'y** (*inf*) *adj* with an exaggerated French manner. ◆ *n* a contemptuous name for a French person.
❑ **French bean** *n* the common kidney or haricot bean (*Phaseolus vulgaris*) eaten, pods and all, as a table vegetable. **French berry** *n* the berry of a species of buckthorn, used as a yellow dye. **French bread** *n* crusty bread baked in a long narrow shape with tapered ends. **French-Cana'dian** *adj* of or from the French-speaking part of Canada. ◆ *n* a French-Canadian person; the French language of Canada. **French chalk** *n* soapstone, *esp* as used to mark out patterns in dressmaking. **French cricket** *n* a game (*esp* of children) in which players throw a ball at a batsman from the place where it is fielded, the batsman being out if the ball strikes his or her leg below the knee. **French cuff** *n* a cuff of double thickness, *usu* fastened by a cuff link, formed by folding back the band at the end of a shirtsleeve, etc. **French curve** *n* a thin plate, *usu* of plastic, with the outlines of various curves on it, used for drawing curves. **French door** *n* (*N Am*) a French window (qv below). **French dressing** *n* a salad dressing consisting of oil and vinegar or lemon juice, and *usu* seasoning. **French fry** or **French fried potato** *n* (*pl* **French fries** or **French fried potatoes**) a potato chip, *esp* thin and long. **French heel** *n* a way of turning the heel in knitting; a high curved heel for women's shoes. **French horn** *n* the orchestral brass horn. **French kiss** *n* a kiss in which the tongue is inserted into one's partner's mouth. **French kissing** *n*. **French knickers** *n pl* a type of wide-legged knickers. **French leave** see **take French leave** below. **French letter** *n* (*sl*) a condom. **French loaf** *n* a loaf of French bread. **French'man** or (*fem*) **French'woman** *n* a native of France. **French pitch** *n* (*music*) a standard pitch established by the French government in 1859, and later widely adopted, being 435 cycles per second at 15°C for A (see **international (concert) pitch** under **international**). **French pleat** see **French roll** below. **French plum** *n* a prune or dried plum. **French polish** *n* a varnish for furniture, consisting chiefly of shellac dissolved in spirit. **French-pol'ish** *vt* to treat with French polish. **French-pol'isher** *n*. **French-pol'ishing** *n*. **French pox** *n* (*obs*) syphilis. **French roll** or **pleat** *n* a hairstyle in which the hair is formed into a vertical roll at the back of the head. **French roof** *n* a modified mansard roof, really N American. **French sash** *n* a French window (see below). **French seam** *n* a seam stitched on the right side then on the wrong side to enclose raw edges. **French stick** *n* a very narrow French loaf. **French toast** *n* bread dipped in egg (and milk) and fried. **French vermouth** *n* a dry vermouth. **French White** see **China White** under **white**. **French window** *n* a window of floor-to-ceiling height, acting as a door. **Frenchwoman** see **Frenchman** above.

■ **Free French** (from 1942 **Fighting French**) continuers under General de Gaulle of resistance to Germany in World War II after the French capitulation of 1940. **pardon** or **excuse my French** (*inf*) pardon my bad language. **take French leave** to depart without notice or permission; to disappear suspiciously.

frenemy /fren'i-mi/ (*sl*) *n* a friend who is also a rival; an enemy who masquerades as a friend. [friend and **enemy**]

frenetic /fri-net'ik, formerly fren'/ *adj* (also (*rare*) **phrenetic**) delirious; frantic; frenzied; mad; distracted. ◆ *n* (*archaic*) a madman. [OFr *frénétique*, from L *phrenēticus*, from late Gr *phrenētikos*, from Gr *phrenītis* delirium, from *phrēn* heart or mind; see **phrenesiac**]
■ **frenet'ical** or **phrenet'ical** *adj*. **frenet'ically** or **phrenet'ically** *adv*.

frenne /fren/ (*Spenser*) see **fremd**.

frenum or **fraenum** /frē'nəm/ *n* (*pl* **fre'na** or **frae'na**) a ligament restraining the motion of a part of the body. [L *frēnum* a bridle]
■ **fren'ulum** *n* (*pl* **fren'ula**) a small stiff hair on the hind wing of some insects, serving to bond hind and front wings during flight.

frenzy /fren'zi/ *n* a state of violent excitement, agitation, hurry, etc; a paroxysm of madness. ◆ *vt* to drive to frenzy. [OFr *frenesie*, from L and late Gr *phrenēsis*, from Gr *phrenītis*; see **frenetic**]
■ **fren'zical** or **fren'zied** *adj*. **fren'ziedly** *adv*.

Freon® /frē'on/ *n* any of the family of chemicals containing fluorine, used as refrigerants, etc.
❑ **Freon-12'** *n* dichlorodifluoromethane (CCl_2F_2), formerly widely used in household refrigerators.

frequent /frē'kwənt/ *adj* coming or occurring often; crowded (*obs*); addicted (*Shakesp*). ◆ *vt* /fri-kwent'/ to visit (a place) often; to associate with; to resort to (*obs*); to crowd (*obs*). [L *frequēns*, *frequentis*; connected with *farcīre* to stuff]
■ **frē'quence** *n* a crowd or assembly (*Milton*); frequency. **frē'quency** *n* commonness of recurrence; the number of vibrations, cycles or other recurrences in unit time (in ascending order, high, very high, ultra-high, extremely high, super-high frequency); a broadcasting wavelength; resort (*obs*). **frēquenta'tion** *n* the act of visiting often. **frequentative** /fri-kwent'ə-tiv/ (*grammar*) *adj* denoting the frequent repetition of an action. ◆ *n* a verb or affix expressing this repetition. **frequent'er** *n*. **frē'quently** *adv*. **frē'quentness** *n*.
❑ **frequency distribution** *n* a set of statistical data showing numerical values for the frequencies of different scores or results. **frequency modulation** *n* modulation in radio transmission by varying the frequency of the carrier wave, giving greater fidelity than amplitude modulation and (almost) freedom from atmospherics (*abbrev* **FM**).
■ **high frequency** a radio frequency of between 3 and 30 megahertz. **low frequency** a radio frequency of between 30 and 300 kilohertz. **medium frequency** a radio frequency of between 300 kilohertz and 3 megahertz. **superhigh frequency** a radio frequency of between 3000 and 30000 megahertz.

frère /frer/ (*Fr*) *n* a brother.

frescade /fre-skād'/ *n* a cool walk. [Fr, from Ital *frescata*]

fresco /fres'kō/ *n* (*pl* **fres'coes** or **fres'cos**) a mode of painting on walls covered with damp freshly-laid plaster (*true fresco*), or partly-dried plaster (*dry fresco* or *fresco secco*); a picture painted in this way. ◆ *vt* to paint in fresco. [Ital *fresco* fresh]
■ **fres'coed** /-kōd/ *adj*. **frescoer** /fres'kō-ər/ *n*. **fres'coing** *n*. **fres'coist** *n*.

fresh /fresh/ *adj* in a state of activity and health; in new condition; not stale, faded or soiled; new or recently added; raw or inexperienced; in youthful bloom; cool and invigorating; brisk; amorously over-free or cheeky (*inf*); without salt; not preserved by pickling, drying, salting, etc; not frosty, thawing (*Scot*); cheeky or pert (*inf*). ◆ *adv* freshly; afresh; newly. ◆ *n* time of freshness; a small stream of fresh water (*Shakesp*); a thaw or open weather (*Scot*). ◆ *vt* (*obs*) to freshen. [OE *fersc*; cf Ger *frisch*]
■ **fresh'en** *vt* to make fresh; to take the saltness from; to refill (a glass or drink) (*US*). ◆ *vi* to grow fresh or (of wind) stronger. ◆ *vt and vi* to make (oneself) fresh by washing, etc (often with *up*). **fresh'ener** *n*. **fresh'er** *n* a university or college student in his or her first year, a freshman. **fresh'erdom** *n*. **fresh'et** *n* a stream of fresh water; a flood. **fresh'ish** *adj*. **fresh'ly** *adv* with freshness; newly; anew. **fresh'ness** *n*.
❑ **fresh'-blown** *adj* newly blossomed, as a flower. **fresh breeze** *n* (*meteorol*) a wind of force 5 on the Beaufort scale, reaching speeds of 19 to 24mph. **fresh'man** *n* a newcomer; a fresher. **fresh'manship** *n*. **fresh'-new** *adj* (*Shakesp*) quite new. **fresh'-run** *adj* (of eg a salmon) newly come up from the sea. **fresh'water** *adj* of or relating to, or living in, fresh water, not salt water; accustomed to sailing only on fresh water. **freshwater college** *n* (*US*) a provincial college.

fresnel /frā'nəl/ *n* a unit of optical frequency, equal to 10^{12}Hz (= 1 terahertz). [AJ *Fresnel* (1788–1827), French physicist]
❑ **Fresnel ellipsoid** *n* a method, used in crystal optics, of representing the doubly refracting properties of a crystal. **Fresnel lens** *n* (*image technol*) a lens having a surface of stepped concentric circles, thinner

and flatter than a conventional lens of equivalent focal length. **Fresnel zones** *n pl* (*phys*) zones into which a wavefront is divided according to the phase of the radiation reaching any point from it.

fret[1] /*fret*/ *vi* (**frett'ing; frett'ed**) to vex oneself; to worry; to chafe; to wear away; (of a liquid) to work or ferment (*dialect*). ◆ *vt* to wear away by rubbing; to rub or chafe; to eat into; to corrode; to ripple or disturb; to vex or irritate. ◆ *n* agitation of the surface of a liquid; irritation; worry; a worn or eroded spot; sea fret. [OE *fretan* to gnaw, from pfx *for-* intens, and *etan* to eat; Ger *fressen*]
■ **fret'ful** *adj* peevish. **fret'fully** *adv*. **fret'fulness** *n*. **frett'ing** *adj* vexing. ◆ *n* peevishness.

fret[2] /*fret*/ *n* any of the wooden or metal ridges on the neck of a guitar or other instrument which divide the fingerboard into spaces producing different notes. ◆ *vt* (**frett'ing; frett'ed**) to provide with frets. [Prob same as **fret**[3]]
■ **fret'less** *adj*.
□ **fret'board** *n* a fretted fingerboard on a guitar or other instrument.

fret[3] /*fret*/ *vt* (**frett'ing; frett'ed**) to ornament with interlaced work; to variegate. ◆ *n* ornamental network; a type of decoration originating in ancient Greece, for a cornice, border, etc, consisting of lines meeting *usu* at right angles, the pattern being repeated to form a continuous band (also called **grecque key** or **grecque meander**); bendlets, dexter and sinister, interlaced with a mascle (*heraldry*). [OFr *freter* to adorn with interlaced work and *frete* trelliswork; prob influenced by or confused with OE *frætwa* ornament]
■ **frett'ed** or **frett'y** *adj* ornamented with frets.
□ **fret'saw** *n* a saw with a narrow blade and fine teeth, used for fretwork, scrollwork, etc. **fret'work** *n* ornamental work consisting of a combination of frets; perforated woodwork.

Freudian /*froi'di-ən*/ *adj* relating to Sigmund Freud (1856–1939), his theory of the libido, or his method of psychoanalysis. ◆ *n* a follower of Freud.
□ **Freudian slip** *n* an error or unintentional action, *esp* a slip of the tongue, supposed to reveal an unexpressed or unconscious thought.

FRG *abbrev* : Federal Republic of Germany, the former West Germany.

Fri. *abbrev* : Friday.

friable /*frī'ə-bl*/ *adj* apt to crumble; easily reduced to powder. [Fr, from L *friābilis*, from *friāre, friātum* to crumble]
■ **frī'ableness** or **frīabil'ity** *n*.

friand /*frē-ã'*/ or (*fem*) **friande** /*frē-ãd'*/ (*Fr*) *adj* dainty or delicate. ◆ *n* an epicure.

friar /*frī'ər*/ *n* a member of one of the active religious orders of men in the Roman Catholic Church, ie the Franciscans (**Friars Minor** or **Grey Friars**), Dominicans (**Friars Preachers** or **Black Friars**), Carmelites (**White Friars**), Augustinians (**Austin Friars**), and others; a pale patch on a printed page. [OFr *frere*, from L *frāter* a brother]
■ **fri'arly** *adj* like a friar. **fri'ary** *n* a convent of friars.
□ **fri'arbird** *n* an Australian honeyeater with featherless head. **friar's balsam** *n* a tincture of benzoin, storax, tolu and aloes used as an inhalant. **friar's cap** *n* (*bot*) a type of aconite, wolf's-bane. **friar's cowl** *n* (*bot*) wake-robin. **friar's lantern** *n* the will-o'-the-wisp.

fribble /*frib'l*/ (*obs*) *vi* to trifle. ◆ *n* a trifler. [Onomatopoeic; prob influenced by **frivol**]
■ **fribb'ler** *n*. **fribb'ling** or **fribb'lish** *adj* trifling.

fricadel see **frikkadel**.

fricandeau /*frik-ən-dō'* or *frik'*/ *n* (*pl* **fricandeaux** /-*dōz*/) a thick slice of veal, etc, larded. [Fr]

fricassee /*frik-ə-sē'*/ *n* a dish of fowl, rabbit, etc cut into pieces and served in sauce. ◆ *vt* (**fricassee'ing; fricasseed'**) to prepare as a fricassee. [Fr *fricassée*, fem pap of *fricasser* to cook chopped food in its own juice]

fricative /*frik'ə-tiv*/ *adj* produced by friction; relating to, or being, a fricative. ◆ *n* (*phonetics*) a consonant produced by the breath being forced through a narrow opening. [L *fricāre, frictum* to rub]

fricht see **fright**.

FRICS *abbrev* : Fellow of the Royal Institution of Chartered Surveyors.

friction /*frik'shən*/ *n* rubbing; a resisting force met by one body moving against the surface of another; disagreement or jarring. [L *fricāre, frictum* to rub]
■ **fric'tional** *adj*. **fric'tionless** *adj*.
□ **friction tape** *n* (*N Am*) insulating tape (*usu* the cloth variety). **friction welding** *n* welding in which the necessary heat is produced by means of friction, eg by rotating one part and forcing the parts together.

Friday /*frī'dā* or *-di*/ *n* the sixth day of the week. [OE *Frīgedæg* the day of Frīg, the goddess of married love, corresponding to L *diēs Veneris* the day of Venus]
■ **Fri'days** *adv* on Fridays.

■ **Black Friday** Good Friday, from the black vestments of the clergy and altar in the Western Church; any Friday marked by a great calamity. **Good Friday** the Friday before Easter, kept in commemoration of Christ's Crucifixion. **Holy Friday** one of the three fast-days in each church quarter (also **Golden Friday**), sometimes used for Good Friday itself. **Man Friday, Girl Friday**, and **Person Friday** see under **man**[1], **girl** and **person**.

fridge[1] /*frij*/ (*inf*) *n* short form of **refrigerator**.
□ **fridge-freez'er** *n* a refrigerator and a freezer constructed as a single unit.

fridge[2] /*frij*/ (*Sterne*) *vt* to rub or fray. [Prob imit]

fried see **fry**[1].

Friedreich's ataxia /*frē'drīhhs a-tak'si-ə*/ *n* an inherited degenerative disease affecting the nervous system, causing muscle weakness, speech disorders, etc. [Nikolaus *Friedreich* (1825–82), German physician who described it]

friend /*frend*/ *n* a person loving or attached to another; a person with whom one is connected on a social networking site; a close or intimate acquaintance; a favourer, well-wisher or supporter; a member of a society so named; a relative (*Scot*); a lover (*obs* or *euphem*). ◆ *vt* to add someone to one's list of friends on a social networking website; to befriend (*archaic*). [OE *frēond* (orig a prp; cf *frēon* to love); Ger *Freund*]
■ **friend'ed** *adj* (*archaic*) supplied with friends. **friend'ing** *n* (*Shakesp*) friendliness. **friend'less** *adj* without friends; destitute. **friend'lessness** *n*. **friend'lily** *adv*. **friend'liness** *n*. **friend'ly** *adj* like a friend; having the disposition of a friend; favourable; amicable; (of a sports match, etc) played for amusement or practice rather than in a competition; relating to the Society of Friends or Quakers; able to handle small variations in the input format and/or enabling the easy correction of input errors (*comput*). ◆ *n* (*pl* **friend'lies**) a sports match played for amusement or practice. ◆ *combining form* easy and convenient for, compatible with, helpful to or in sympathy with. **friend'ship** *n* attachment from mutual esteem; friendly assistance.
□ **friendly fire** *n* (*milit*) accidental firing upon one's allies rather than one's enemies. **friendly lead** *n* (*archaic*) an entertainment for the benefit of a person in need. **friendly numbers** *n pl* (*maths*) pairs of numbers each of which is the sum of the factors of the other, including unity (also called **amicable numbers**; cf **perfect number**). **friendly society** *n* a benefit society, an association for relief in sickness, old age or widowhood, by provident insurance. **Friends of the Earth** *n pl* an organization of conservationists and environmentalists. **friend zone** *n* (*inf*) a state of friendship that acts as a barrier to a romantic or sexual relationship.
■ **be friends with** to be on good terms with or well-disposed towards. **friends with benefits** (*sl*) two friends who have a casual sexual relationship. **have a friend at court** to have a friend in a position where his or her influence is likely to prove useful. (**Religious**) **Society of Friends** the proper designation of a sect of Christians better known as Quakers.

frier[1] and **fries** see **fry**[1].

frier[2] /*frī'ər*/ (*Milton*) *n* a friar.

Friesian see under **Frisian**.

frieze[1] /*frēz*/ *n* the part of the entablature between the architrave and cornice, often ornamented with figures (*classical archit*); a decorated band along the wall of a room (*archit*). ◆ *vt* to put a frieze on. [OFr *frise*; Ital *fregio*; perh L *Phrygium* (*opus*) Phrygian (work)]

frieze[2] /*frēz*/ *n* a rough, heavy woollen cloth. [Fr *frise*]
■ **friezed** *adj* having a nap.

frig[1] /*frig*/ (*vulgar sl*) *vi* and *vt* (**frigg'ing; frigged**) to masturbate; loosely, to have sexual intercourse with; (often with *about*) to potter about. ◆ *n* masturbation. [Late ME *friggen*, from L *fricāre* to rub]
■ **frigg'ing** *n* masturbation; pottering about. ◆ *adj* and *adv* as an intensive, to a great extent or very; often used as a colourless descriptive.
■ **frig off** (*usu* in *imperative*) to go away.

frig[2] /*frij*/ (*inf*) *n* short for **refrigerator**.

frigate /*frig'it*/ (*navy*) *n* formerly, a vessel in the class next to ships of the line; now denoting an escort vessel. [OFr *fregate*, from Ital *fregata*; ety dubious]
■ **frigatoon'** *n* a small Venetian vessel with a square stern and two masts.
□ **frigate bird** *n* a large tropical seabird (genus *Fregata*) with very long wings and a forked tail.

frigger /*frig'ər*/ *n* a glass ornament. [Origin unknown]

fright /*frīt*/ *n* sudden fear; terror; a figure of grotesque or ridiculous appearance (*inf*). ◆ *vt* (now *rare*, except as Scot **fricht** /*frihht*/) to frighten. [OE *fyrhto*; cf Ger *Furcht* fear]
■ **fright'en** *vt* (*pap* **fright'ened** or (*dialect*) **frit**) to make afraid; to alarm; to drive by fear. **fright'ened** *adj*. **fright'eners** *n pl* (*sl*; also in

sing) something intended to frighten, *esp* for criminal purposes. **fright'ening** *adj.* **fright'eningly** *adv.* **fright'ful** *adj* terrible; horrible; unpleasant (*inf*); great or huge (*inf*). **fright'fully** *adv* dreadfully; very (*inf*). **fright'fulness** *n* the quality of being frightful; terrorism. **fright'some** *adj* frightful; feeling fright. **frit** *adj* (*dialect*) frightened. ◻ **fright wig** *n* a wig with hair that stands up or sticks out dramatically. ■ **put the frighteners on someone** (*sl*) to frighten someone into (not) doing something, *esp* for criminal purposes. **take fright** to become afraid.

frigid /frij'id/ *adj* frozen or stiffened with cold; cold; chillingly stiff; without spirit or feeling; unanimated; leaving the imagination untouched; (*usu* of a woman) sexually unresponsive. [L *frigidus*, from *frigere* to be cold, from *frigus* cold] ■ **frigid'ity** *n* coldness; coldness of affection; lack of animation; sexual unresponsiveness. **frig'idly** *adv.* **frig'idness** *n*. ◻ **frigid zones** *n pl* the parts of the earth's surface within the polar circles.

frigidarium /frij-i-dār'i-əm or frig-i-där'i-ŭm/ *n* the cooling room of a Roman public baths, often with a swimming-bath. [L]

frigorific /frig-ə-rif'ik/ *adj* causing cold; freezing. [L *frigus, -oris* cold, and *facere* to make] ■ **frigorif'ico** *n* (*pl* **frigorif'icos**) (*Sp*) a slaughtering and meat-freezing establishment.

frigot /frig'ət/ (*Spenser*) *n* same as **frigate**.

frijol or **frijole** /frē'hhōl or frē-hhōl'/ *n* (*pl* **frijoles** /-les/) (in Mexican cookery) the kidney bean, or any species of *Phaseolus*. [Sp *fríjol, frijol* or *fréjol*]

frikkadel or **fricadel** /frik'ə-del/ (*S Afr*) *n* a fried ball of minced meat. [Afrik, from Fr; cf **fricandeau**]

frill /fril/ *n* a ruffle; a ruffled or crimped edging; superfluous ornament (*fig*); (in *pl*) affected airs and graces. ◆ *vt* to provide with a frill. ◆ *vi* (*archaic*) to ruffle, as a hawk ruffles its feathers, when shivering. [Origin unknown] ■ **frill'ies** *n pl* (*inf*) light and pretty underwear for women. **frill'ing** *n.* **frill'y** *adj.* ◻ **frilled lizard** *n* a large Australian lizard (genus *Chlamydosaurus*) with an erectile frill around its neck. ■ **no frills** or **without frills** (in a manner, form, etc which is) straightforward, clear, without posturing, with no superfluous additions, etc.

Frimaire /frē-mär'/ *n* the third month of the French revolutionary calendar, about 21 November–20 December, the frosty month. [Fr *frimas* hoarfrost]

fringe /frinj/ *n* a border of loose threads; hair falling over the brow; a border; anything bordering on or additional to an activity. ◆ *vt* to adorn with a fringe; to border. ◆ *adj* bordering, or just outside, the recognized or orthodox form, group, etc as in *fringe medicine, fringe theatre*; unofficial or not part of the main event, as in *fringe meeting*; less important or popular, as in *fringe sports*. [OFr *frenge*, from L *fimbriae* threads, related to *fibra* a fibre] ■ **fringed** *adj.* **fringe'less** *adj.* **fring'y** *adj* decorated with fringes. ◻ **fringe benefit** *n* something in addition to wages or salary that forms part of the regular remuneration from one's employment. **fringe'-dweller** *n* (*Aust*) a person, *esp* an Aborigine, who lives, *usu* in poverty and squalor, on the edge of a town or community. **fringe effect** *n* (*image technol*) see **border effect** under **border**. **fringe medicine** *n* unorthodox and not generally accepted medical techniques. **fringe tree** *n* a large American shrub (*Chionanthus virginica*) of the family Oleaceae, whose very numerous snow-white flowers have long narrow corolla-segments. ■ **lunatic fringe** any (*usu* small) group of fanatics or extremists within a political party, pressure group, etc.

fringillaceous /frin-ji-lā'shəs/ *adj* relating to the finches or Fringill'idae. [L *fringilla* a finch] ■ **fringill'id, fringill'iform** or **fringill'ine** *adj.*

fripon /frē-põ'/ (*Fr*) *n* a knave or scamp. ■ **friponnerie** /frē-pon-ə-rē'/ *n* knavery.

frippery /frip'ə-ri/ *n* tawdry finery; foppish triviality; useless trifles; cast-off clothes (*obs*); an old-clothes shop, or the old-clothes trade (*obs*). ◆ *adj* (*obs*) useless; trifling. [OFr *freperie*, from *frepe* a rag] ■ **fripp'er** or **fripp'erer** *n* (*archaic*) an old-clothes dealer.

fris /frish/ or **friska** /frish'kö/ *n* the quick dance movement of a Hungarian csárdás. [Hung]

Frisbee® /friz'bi/ *n* a plastic saucer-shaped disc which can be made to skim through the air, used in various catching-games, etc.

frisée /frē-zā'/ (*Fr*) *n* a variety of curly endive.

frisette /frē-zet'/ (*Fr*) *n* a fringe of curls on the forehead. ■ **friseur** /frē-zær/ *n* a hairdresser. **frisure** /frē-zür/ *n* a mode of curling.

Frisian /friz'i-ən or frē'zhən/ *n* a native of the Dutch province of Friesland; the Low German language of Friesland. ◆ *adj* of or from Friesland, its people, or their language. ■ **Friesian** /frēz'/ *adj* Frisian, *esp* of a heavy breed of dairy cattle. ◆ *n* a Frisian; a Friesian bull or cow. **Fries'ic** or **Fries'ish** *adj.*

frisk /frisk/ *vi* to gambol; to leap playfully. ◆ *vt* to search (a person or his or her pockets) (*sl*); to search for radioactive radiation by contamination meter. ◆ *n* a frolicsome movement; a search of a person or his or her pockets (*sl*). [OFr *frisque*] ■ **frisk'er** *n.* **frisk'ful** *adj* brisk or lively. **frisk'ily** *adv.* **frisk'iness** *n.* **frisk'ing** *n* and *adj.* **frisk'ingly** *adv.* **frisk'y** *adj* lively; jumping with gaiety; frolicsome.

friska see **fris**.

frisket /fris'kit/ (*printing*) *n* the light frame between the tympan and the forme, to hold in place the sheet to be printed. [Fr *frisquette*]

frisson /frē-sõ'/ *n* a shiver; a shudder; a thrill. [Fr]

frist /frist/ (*obs*) *n* delay or respite. ◆ *vt* to postpone; to grant time, eg for payment. [OE *first* time or respite]

frisure see under **frisette**.

frit¹ /frit/ *n* the mixed materials for making glass, pottery glazes, etc. ◆ *vt* (**fritt'ing; fritt'ed**) to fuse partially. [Fr *fritte*, from Ital *fritta*, from L *frigere, frictum* to roast] ◻ **frit porcelain** *n* an artificial soft-paste English porcelain (from its vitreous nature).

frit² /frit/ *n* a small fly destructive to wheat and other cereal crops (also **frit'fly**). [Ety unknown]

frit³ see under **fright**.

frith¹ see **firth**¹.

frith² /frith/ (*obs* or *hist*) *n* peace; sanctuary. [OE *frith* peace; Ger *Friede*] ◻ **frith'borh** /-borhh/ *n* a surety for keeping the peace, frank-pledge. **frith'gild** *n* a union of neighbours pledged to one another for the preservation of peace. **frith'soken** *n* (OE *frithsōcn*) sanctuary or asylum. **frith'stool** *n* (OE *frithstōl*) a chair of sanctuary, placed near the altar in a church, as at eg Hexham and Beverley.

frith³ /frith/ or **firth** /fûrth/ *n* wooded country; brushwood; underwood. [OE (*ge*)*fyrhthe*]

fritillary /frit'i-lə-ri or fri-til'ə-ri/ *n* a member of the genus (*Fritillaria*) of the lily family, the best-known species having chequered purple flowers; a name for several butterflies of similar pattern. [L *fritillus* a dice-box]

frittata /fri-tä'tə/ *n* (in Italian cookery) a thick omelette containing chopped vegetables or meat. [Ital]

fritter¹ /frit'ər/ *n* a piece of fruit, etc fried in batter. [OFr *friture*, from L *frigere, frictum* to fry]

fritter² /frit'ər/ *vt* to squander piecemeal (often with *away*); to break into fragments (*obs*). ◆ *n* (*obs*) a fragment. [Perh OFr *freture*, from L *fractura*, from *frangere, fractum* to break] ■ **fritt'erer** *n* a person who wastes time.

fritto misto /frē'tō mē'stō/ (*Ital*) *n* a mixed dish of fried food.

friture /frē-tür'/ (*Fr*) *n* a dish of fried food; a fritter.

fritz /frits/ (*US inf*) *n* (with *the*) a state of disrepair, *esp* in the phrase **on the fritz** out of order. [Origin unknown]

frivolous /friv'ə-ləs/ *adj* trifling; lacking (due) seriousness, silly. [L *frīvolus*] ■ **friv'ol** *vt* and *vi* (back-formation; *rare*) to trifle. **frivolity** /-ol'/ *n* a trifling habit or nature; levity. **friv'olously** *adv.* **friv'olousness** *n.*

frize obsolete form of **freeze** or **frieze**¹·².

frizz or **friz** /friz/ *vt* to curl tightly. ◆ *n* a curl; frizzed hair. [OFr *friser* to curl; perh connected with **frieze**²] ■ **frizzed** *adj* having the hair crisped into frizzes. **frizz'y** *adj.*

frizzante /frē-dzan'tā/ (*Ital*) *adj* (of wine) sparkling.

frizzle¹ /friz'l/ *vt* and *vi* to fry; to scorch. [Perh onomatopoeic adaptation of **fry**¹, from sputtering noise]

frizzle² /friz'l/ *vt* to form in small short curls. ◆ *vi* to go into curls. ◆ *n* a curl; frizzled hair. [Related to **frizz** and **frieze**²] ■ **frizz'ly** *adj.*

fro /frō/ *prep* (*obs* except in Scots form **frae** /frā/) from. ◆ *adv* away, only used in **to and fro** (see under **to**). [ON *frā*]

'fro /frō/n an informal shortening of **Afro** (the hairstyle).

frock /frok/ *n* a woman's or child's dress; a monk's wide-sleeved garment; a frock-coat; a smock-frock; an undress regimental coat; a sailor's jersey (*archaic*); a wearer of a frock (*obs*). ◆ *vt* (*rare*) to provide with a frock; to invest with priestly office. [OFr *froc* a monk's frock, from LL *frocus*, from L *floccus* a flock of wool; or from LL *hrocus*, from OHGer *hroch* (Ger *Rock*) a coat]

■ **frocked** *adj* clothed in a frock. **frock'ing** *n* cloth suitable for frocks, coarse cotton twill. **frock'less** *adj*.
❑ **frock'-coat** *n* a double-breasted full-skirted coat for men, now worn only for very formal occasions.

froe /frō/ *n* a cutting tool with a blade at right angles to the handle, used *esp* for splitting wood. [**froward**]

Froebelian /frœ-bē'li-ən/ *adj* relating to Friedrich *Froebel*, German educationist (1782–1852) or to his system (the **Froebel system**) of kindergarten schools.
■ **Froe'belism** *n*.

frog[1] /frog/ *n* a tailless webfooted amphibian, *esp* one of the genus *Rana*, more agile than a toad; a swelling (in the throat); (with *cap*) a contemptuous name for a French person; (on a railway) a structure in the rails allowing passage across or to another track; a depression made in the face(s) of a brick; the block by which the hair is attached to the heel of a violin, etc bow. [OE *frogga*; also *frox*; cognate with ON *froskr*; Ger *Frosch*]
■ **frogg'ery** *n* frogs collectively; a place where frogs abound or are kept. **frogg'y** *adj* frog-like; having or abounding in frogs. ◆ *n* (with *cap*) a contemptuous name for a French person. **frog'let** or **frog'ling** *n* a little frog.
❑ **frog'bit** *n* a small aquatic plant (*Hydrocharis morsus-ranae*), related to the water soldier, but with floating leaves. **frog'-eater** *n* a person who eats frogs; a contemptuous name for a French person. **frog'fish** *n* a name for various fishes, *esp* the angler-fish. **frog'-hopper** *n* any insect of the Cercopidae or Aphrophoridae, whose larvae live surrounded by froth (cuckoo-spit) on plants. **frog'man** *n* an underwater swimmer fitted with a rubber suit, flippers and breathing apparatus. **frog'march** *vt* (sometimes **frog's'-march**) *orig* to carry an unco-operative or drunken prisoner, etc face downwards between four people, each holding a limb; now *usu* to seize from behind and force forwards while holding firmly by the arms or clothing; (sometimes) to propel backwards between two people, each holding an arm. ◆ *n* the act or process of frogmarching. **frog'mouth** *n* any Australian and S Asian bird of the family Podargidae, related to the goatsuckers. **frog's'-mouth** *n* antirrhinum or snapdragon. **frog'spawn** *n* a mass of frogs' eggs encased in a protective nutrient jelly. **frog'-spit** *n* cuckoo-spit. **frog test** *n* (*med*) a formerly used pregnancy test in which the woman's urine is injected into the dorsal lymph sac of the platanna frog, deemed to be positive if frog spermatozoa are present in the frog's urine within three hours.
■ **a frog in the** (or **one's**) **throat** hoarseness.

frog[2] /frog/ *n* an ornamental fastening or tasselled or braided button; an attachment to a belt for carrying a weapon. [Perh Port *froco*, from L *floccus* a flock or lock]
■ **frogged** *adj* having ornamental stripes or workings of braid or lace, mostly on the breast of a coat. **frogg'ing** *n*.

frog[3] /frog/ *n* a V-shaped band of horn on the underside of a horse's hoof. [Perh same as **frog**[1]. Gr *batrachos* means frog in both senses; also influenced by Ital *forchetta* dimin of fork]

froideur /frwu-dûr'/ *n* coolness in personal relationships. [Fr]

froise /froiz/ or **fraise** /frāz/ *n* a thick pancake, often with slices of bacon. [Origin unknown]

frolic /frol'ik/ *n* gaiety; a prank; a gambol; a merrymaking. ◆ *adj* (*archaic*) merry; pranky. ◆ *vi* (**frol'icking**; **frol'icked**) to play wild pranks or light-hearted tricks; to gambol. [Du *vrolijk* merry; cf Ger *fröhlich* joyful or merry]
■ **frol'icsome** *adj* merry; sportive. **frol'icsomely** *adv*. **frol'icsomeness** *n*.

from /from *or* frəm/ *prep* out of; away, to or at a greater distance relatively to; springing out of; beginning at; apart relatively to; by reason of. [OE *fram*, *from*; related to Gothic *fram* and ON *frā*]

fromage frais /from'äzh frā *or* frō'mäzh fre/ *n* a light creamy cheese with a consistency similar to thick yoghurt, sold in tubs. [Fr, literally, fresh cheese]

fromenty see **frumenty**.

frond /frond/ *n* a leaf, *esp* of a palm or fern; a leaflike thallus or plant body, or a leaflike organ of obscure morphological nature. [L *frōns*, *frondis* a leaf]
■ **frond'age** *n* fronds collectively. **frond'ed** *adj* having fronds. **frond'ent** *adj* leafy. **frondesc'ence** *n* the development of leaves. **frondesc'ent** *adj* leaflike; leafy; springing into leaf. **frondif'erous** *adj* bearing or producing fronds. **frond'ose** *adj* leaflike; leafy.

Fronde /frōnd *or* frɔd/ *n* a rebellious movement established in opposition to Mazarin and the court in France during Louis XIV's minority. [Fr, sling, from L *funda* sling]
■ **frondeur** /frön-dûr' *or* frɔ̃-dær'/ *n* a member of the Fronde; an irreconcilable or a dissident.

front /frunt/ *n* the forehead (*poetic*); the face or appearance; the forepart of anything; the side open to view; the face of a building, *esp* the principal face; the part facing the sea or other water; a seaside promenade; the foremost line (of soldiers or battle); the scene of hostilities; the direction in which troops are facing when lined up (*milit*); a combined face presented against opponents; a group of people, organizations or parties having the same or broadly similar (*esp* political or revolutionary) outlook and aims, who act together against opponents, as in *popular front* (see under **popular**); a set of false curls for the forehead (*obs*); the breast of a man's shirt, a dickey; the middle part of the tongue; the auditorium of a theatre; the bounding surface between two masses of air of different density and temperature (*meteorol*); the apparent or nominal leader behind whom the really powerful person works anonymously (also **front man**); (something acting as) a cover or disguise for secret or disreputable activities; boldness; impudence. ◆ *adj* of, relating to, or in, the front; articulated with the front of the tongue (*phonetics*). ◆ *vt* to stand in front of or opposite; to face towards; to meet or oppose face to face; to add a front to; to serve as a front to; to change into or towards a front sound (*phonetics*); to act as the front man of; to act as the compère or frontman of; to stand, perform, etc in front of or at the front of, as eg the singer with a band. ◆ *vi* to be foremost (*Shakesp*); to face; to act as a front for someone else or as a cover for something secret or illicit. [L *frōns*, *frontis* the forehead]
■ **front'age** *n* the front part of a building; extent of front; ground in front. **front'ager** *n* (*law*) a person who owns or occupies property along a road, river or shore. **front'al** /frunt'l/ (also */front'l/*) *adj* of or belonging to the front, or the forehead; relating to a front (*meteorol*). ◆ *n* the façade of a building; something worn on the forehead or face; a pediment over a door or window (*obs*); a hanging of silk, satin, etc embroidered for an altar, now *usu* covering only the top, the *superfrontal*, formerly covering the whole of the front, corresponding to the *antependium*. **front'ed** *adj* formed with a front; changed into or towards a front sound (*phonetics*). **front'less** *adj* lacking a front; devoid of shame or modesty (*archaic*). **front'lessly** *adv*. **front'let** *n* a band or phylactery worn on the forehead. **frontogen'esis** *n* (Gr *genesis* generation; *meteorol*) the formation or intensification of a front. **frontol'ysis** /-is-is/ *n* (Gr *lysis* dissolution; *meteorol*) the weakening or disappearance of a front. **front'ward** or **front'wards** *adv* towards the front. **front'ways** or **front'wise** *adv* with face or front forward.
❑ **front'-bench** *adj* sitting on a **front bench** in parliament, as a minister, or an opposition member of similar standing. **front-bench'er** *n*. **front crawl** *n* (*swimming*) the crawl stroke performed face down. **front door** *n*. **front'-end'** *n* the aspects involved in the running of an operation, eg a website, that involve interaction with the public. **front-end computer** or **processor** *n* a subsidiary computer which receives and processes data before passing it to a more powerful computer for further processing. **front-end load** *n* an initial charge made to a person taking on a long-term savings or investment plan. **front-end loaded** or **front'-loaded** *adj*. **front-end loading** or **front'-loading** *n* the taking of a large part of the total costs and commission of an investment or insurance policy out of the early payments or profits made; any similar weighting of borrowing, deduction, etc towards the early stages of a financial transaction or accounting period. **front-end system** *n* that part of a computerized printing system which receives the matter to be printed and provides the input to the typesetter. **front line** *n* the battle positions closest to the enemy; the most active, exposed or dangerous position or role in any activity or situation, *esp* a conflict (*fig*). **front'-line** *adj* of or relating to the front line; of or relating to a state bordering on another state in which there is an armed conflict, and often involved in that conflict. **front-loaded** see **front-end loaded** above. **front'-loader** *n* a washing machine which is loaded through a door at the front. **front'-loading** *adj* (see also **front-end loading** above). **front'man** *n* the person who appears on television as presenter of a programme, *esp* a documentary programme; the leader of a rock band, *usu* the lead singer; a forward (*football*). **front man** see *n* above. **front office** *n* (*N Am*) the part of an organization where the senior administrative staff work; the senior administrative staff of an organization. **front'-of-house** *adj*. **front of (the) house** *n* (in a theatre) the collective activities such as box office and programme selling carried on in direct contact with the public. **front'-page** *adj* suitable for the front page of a newspaper; important. ◆ *vt* to print a (story) on the front page of a newspaper. **front'-rank** *adj* of foremost importance. **front'-ranker** *n*. **front row** *n* (*rugby*) the players in the front row of the scrum (also **front-row forwards**). **front'-runner** or **front'runner** *n* (in a race) a person who runs best while leading the field or one who sets the pace for the rest of the runners; a person or thing that is most popular, most likely to succeed, etc, *esp* in some kind of competition. **front'-running** *n* a form of insider dealing on the Stock Exchange in which traders make deals for themselves before placing customer orders that are large enough to affect prices. **front'-wheel drive** *n* a system in which the driving power is transmitted to the front wheels of a vehicle as opposed to the rear wheels.

■ **come to the front** to become noticeable; to attain an important position. **front up** (*inf*) to make an appearance. **in front** or **in front of** before.

frontier /frunt' or fron'tēr, -tyər or -tēr'/ n the border of a country; the border of settled country, *esp* in the USA, the advancing limit of the West pioneered in the 19c; an outwork (*fortif*; *Shakesp*); (in *pl*) the extreme limit (of knowledge and attainment) in a particular discipline or line of inquiry. ◆ *adj* belonging to a frontier; bordering. ◆ *vt* (*Spenser*) to border. [OFr *frontier*, from L *frōns*, *frontis*] ❏ **front'iersman** or **front'ierswoman** (or /-tērz'/) n a dweller on a frontier.

frontispiece /frun'tis-pēs or fron'/ n an illustration at the front of a book facing the title page; the principal face of a building (*archit*); a decorated pediment over a door, gate, etc (*archit*). ◆ *vt* to put as a frontispiece; to provide with one. [Fr *frontispice*, from LL *frontispicium*, from *frōns*, *frontis* forehead, and *specere*, *spicere* to see; not connected with **piece**]

fronton[1] /frun'tən/ (*archit*) n a pediment (also **frontoon** /-toon'/). [Fr, from Ital *frontone*]

fronton[2] /fron'tən or fron-ton'/ n the wall against which the game of pelota is played. [Sp *frontón*, from L *frōns*, *frontis* forehead]

frore /frōr or frör/ (*obs*, *dialect* or *poetic*), also (*obs* or *dialect*) **froren** /frōr'ən/, **frorne** or **frorn** /frörn/ adj frozen or frosty. [OE *froren*, pap of *frēosan* to freeze]
■ **frō'ry** adj (*Spenser*) frozen.

frost /frost/ n a state of freezing; temperature at or below the freezing point of water; frozen dew, or *hoarfrost*; a disappointment or failure (*sl*); coldness of manner or relations (*fig*). ◆ *vt* to affect with frost; to cover with hoarfrost; to make like hoarfrost; to sharpen (the points of a horse's shoe) so that it does not slip on ice; to bleach individual strands of (a person's hair) to create a mottled effect; to top or coat (a cake) with icing (*esp US*). ◆ *vi* to assume a frostlike appearance. [OE *frost*, *forst*, from *frēosan*; cf Ger *Frost*]
■ **frost'ed** adj covered by frost; having a frostlike appearance (eg a cake or Christmas card by sprinkling, or glass by roughening); damaged by frost; (of a cake) topped or coated with icing (*esp US*). **frost'ily** adv. **frost'iness** n. **frost'ing** n a coating of hoarfrost; material or treatment to give the appearance of hoarfrost; icing (*esp US*). **frost'less** adj free from frost. **frost'like** adj. **frost'y** adj producing, characterized by, or covered with, frost; chill (*lit* and *fig*); frostlike. ❏ **frost'bite** n inflammation, sometimes leading to gangrene, in a part of the body, caused by exposure to cold. ◆ *vt* to affect with frost. **frost'bitten** adj bitten or affected by frost (*lit* and *fig*); suffering from frostbite. **frost'bound** adj bound or confined by frost. **frost line** n the underground limit to the penetration of frost into the earth. **frost'-nail** n a projecting nail in a horseshoe serving to prevent slipping on ice (also **ice'-calk**). ◆ *vt* to provide with frost-nails. **frost'-smoke** n a vapour frozen in the atmosphere, and having a smoke-like appearance. **frost'work** n tracery made by frost, eg on windows; work resembling frost tracery, etc.

froth /froth/ n foam; chatter (*fig*); something frivolous or trivial. ◆ *vt* to cause froth on. ◆ *vi* to make froth. [ON *frotha*; Dan *fraade*]
■ **froth'ery** n mere froth. **froth'ily** adv. **froth'iness** n. **froth'less** adj. **froth'y** adj full of or like froth or foam; empty; insubstantial. ❏ **froth'-blower** n (*sl*) a beer-drinker. **froth flotation** see **flotation** under **flote**. **froth'-fly** or **froth'-hopper** n a frog-hopper (qv under **frog**[1]). **froth-fo'my** adj (*Spenser*) foaming.

frottage /fro-täzh'/ n rubbing; the use of rubbing or rubbings to obtain texture effects in a work of art; a work of art made by this means; a type of sexual activity in which sexual pleasure, and often orgasm, is obtained by rubbing against someone or something. [Fr]
■ **frotteur** /fro-tœr'/ n a person who practises sexual frottage.

frou-frou /froo'froo/ n the rustling of silk; elaborate trimmings, eg frills; fussy decoration. [Fr]

froughy same as **frowy**.

frounce[1] /frowns/ (*obs*) vt to plait; to curl; to wrinkle up. ◆ *vi* to wrinkle; to frown. ◆ *n* a wrinkle, plait or curl; affected ornament. [OFr *froncier*; see **flounce**[2]]

frounce[2] /frowns/ (*obs*) n a disease of the mouth in hawks. [Origin unknown]

frow /frow/ (*archaic*) n a Dutchwoman. [Du *vrouw*]

froward /frō'ərd/ (*archaic*) adj turned away; self-willed; perverse; unreasonable, *opp* to **toward**. ◆ *adv* (*Spenser*) in an adverse direction. ◆ *prep* (also **fro'wards**) in a direction away from. [**fro** and sfx *-ward*]
■ **fro'wardly** adv. **fro'wardness** n.

frown /frown/ vi to wrinkle the brow, eg in anger; to look angry, gloomy or threatening; to show disapproval. ◆ *vt* to express, send or force by a frown. ◆ *n* a wrinkling or contraction of the brow in displeasure, etc; a stern look. [From OFr *froignier* (Fr *refrogner*) to knit the brow; origin unknown]

■ **frown'ing** adj gloomy; disapproving; threatening. **frown'ingly** adv.
■ **frown on** or **upon** to disapprove of.

frowst /frowst/ vi (*obs*) to luxuriate in hot stuffiness and stupefaction. ◆ *n* hot stuffy fustiness; a spell of frowsting (*obs*). [Origin unknown]
■ **frowst'er** n. **frowst'iness** n. **frowst'y** adj fusty; close-smelling; foul-smelling.

frowy or **froughy** (*Spenser* **frowie**) /frō'i or frow'i/ adj musty or rancid (*Spenser*); (of timber) soft and brittle (*dialect*). [Prob OE *thrōh* rancidity]

frowzy or **frowsy** /frow'zi/ (*dialect*) adj fusty; stuffy or offensive; unkempt. [Origin unknown]
■ **frow'ziness** or **frow'siness** n.

froze /frōz/ pat of **freeze**.

frozen /frō'zn/ adj pap of **freeze**; preserved by keeping at a low temperature; very cold; stiff and unfriendly; (of assets, bank accounts, etc) prevented from being accessed by the owner or account holder. ❏ **frozen shoulder** n (*med*) a shoulder joint which has become stiff owing to enforced immobilization, or to injury to the joint or its surrounding tissue.

FRPharmS *abbrev*: Fellow of the Royal Pharmaceutical Society of Great Britain.

FRPS *abbrev*: Fellow of the Royal Photographic Society.

FRS *abbrev*: Fellow of the Royal Society; Financial Reporting Standard.

FRSA *abbrev*: Fellow of the Royal Society of Arts (officially the Royal Society for encouragement of Arts, Manufactures and Commerce).

FRSE *abbrev*: Fellow of the Royal Society of Edinburgh.

fructans /fruk'tənz/ n a polymer of fructose, found in grasses and some vegetables. [L *frūctus* fruit]

fructed /fruk'tid/ adj (*heraldry*) bearing fruit. [L *frūctus* fruit]
■ **fructif'erous** adj bearing fruit. **fructifica'tion** n fruit-production; a fruiting body (*bot*). **fruc'tify** vt to make fruitful; to fertilize. ◆ *vi* to bear fruit. **fruc'tive** adj productive or fruitful. **fructiv'orous** adj (L *vorāre* to devour) fruit-eating. **fruc'tuary** n a person enjoying the fruits of anything. **fruc'tuate** vi to come to fruit; to fructify. **fructuā'tion** n coming to fruit or bearing of fruit. **fruc'tuous** adj fruitful.

Fructidor /frük-tē-dör'/ n the twelfth month in the French revolutionary calendar, the month of fruit, about 18 August–16 September. [Fr, from L *frūctus* fruit, and Gr *dōron* a gift]

fructose /fruk'tōs or frŭk'/ n a water-soluble simple sugar found in honey and fruit. [L *frūctus* fruit]

frugal /froo'gl/ adj economical in the use of anything; sparing; meagre; thrifty. [L *frūgālis*, from *frūx*, *frūgis* fruit]
■ **fru'galist** n a person who is frugal. **frugality** /-gal'/ n economy; thrift. **fru'gally** adv.

frugi- /froo-ji-/ *combining form* denoting fruit. [L *frūx*, *frūgis* fruit]
■ **frugif'erous** adj (L *ferre* to bear) fruit-bearing. **frug'ivore** n (L *vorāre* to eat) an animal that feeds on fruits or seeds. **frugiv'orous** adj.

fruit (*obs* **fruict**) /froot/ n the produce of the earth, which supplies the needs of humans and animals; an edible part of a plant, generally sweet, acid and juicy, *esp* a part that contains the seed, but sometimes extended to include other parts (eg the flower-stalk in a strawberry), and popularly distinguished from the vegetable, its savoury, firm-fleshed counterpart; a fructification, *esp* the structure that develops from the ovary and its contents after fertilization, sometimes including also structures formed from other parts of the flower or axis (*bot*); the offspring of animals (*archaic*); (often in *pl*) product, effect or advantage; a male homosexual (*derog sl*, *esp US*). ◆ *vi* to produce fruit. [OFr *fruit*, *fruict*, from L *frūctus*, from *fruī*, *frūctus* to enjoy]
■ **fruit'age** n (*archaic*) fruit collectively; fruits. **fruita'rian** n a person who lives on fruit (also *adj*). **fruit'ed** adj containing fruit; having produced fruit. **fruit'er** n a fruiterer (now *dialect*); a tree, etc as a producer of fruit, as in *good fruiter*; a fruit-grower. **fruit'erer** n a person who deals in fruit. **fruit'eress** n (*rare*) a female fruiterer. **fruit'ery** n a place for storing fruit; fruitage. **fruit'ful** adj productive. **fruit'fully** adv. **fruit'fulness** n. **fruit'iness** n. **fruit'ing** n the process of bearing, or coming into, fruit. **fruit'less** adj barren, sterile; without profit; useless; in vain. **fruit'lessly** adv. **fruit'lessness** n. **fruit'let** n a small fruit; one of the small fruit-like parts that forms an aggregate or multiple fruit. **fruit'y** adj like, or tasting like, fruit; rich; (of a voice) mellow or resonant; salacious, saucy or smutty (*inf*); crazy (*US inf*); homosexual (*inf*, *esp US*). ❏ **fruit bat** n any bat of the suborder Megacheiroptera, large fruit-eating bats of the Old World. **fruit body** see **fruiting body** below. **fruit'-bud** n a bud that produces fruit. **fruit cage** n an enclosure with mesh sides and a roof to protect growing fruit and vegetables from birds, etc. **fruit'cake** n a cake containing dried fruit; a slightly mad person (*inf*). **fruit cocktail** n a fruit salad, *esp* one of small, *usu* diced, pieces of fruit. **fruit fly** n a fly of the genus *Drosophila* that feeds on decaying fruit. **fruiting body** n (*bot*) a seed or spore-bearing structure,

eg the large spore-bearing structures of many fungi (also **fruit body**). **fruit'-knife** *n* a small knife with a blade of silver, etc for cutting fruit. **fruit machine** *n* a coin-operated gaming machine found in amusement arcades, pubs, etc in which chance must match with any of a variety of stated winning combinations the pictures, traditionally of different fruits, on a set of revolving wheels. **fruit salad** *n* a mixture of pieces of fruit, fresh or preserved. **fruit sugar** *n* fructose. **fruit tree** *n* a tree yielding edible fruit. **fruit'wood** *n* the wood of a fruit tree (also *adj*).
■ **bear fruit** (*fig*) to have eventual success. **bush fruits** small fruits growing on woody bushes. **first-fruits** see under **first** and see **annates. in fruit** bearing fruit. **old fruit** see under **old. small** or **soft fruit** or **fruits** strawberries, blackcurrants, etc.

fruition /froo-ish'ən/ *n* enjoyment; maturation, fulfilment or completion; use or possession, *esp* accompanied with pleasure; bearing fruit, fruiting. [OFr *fruition*, from L *fruī* to enjoy]
■ **fru'itive** *adj*.

frumentation /froo-mən-tā'shən/ *n* a gift of grain bestowed on starving or rebellious people in ancient Rome. [L *frūmentātiō*, *-ōnis*, from *frūmentārī* to provide with corn, from *frūmentum* corn]
■ **frumentā'ceous** *adj* made of or resembling wheat or other grain. **frumentā'rious** *adj* relating to corn.

frumenty /froo'mən-ti/ *n* hulled wheat boiled in milk, sometimes flavoured with spices, eggs, rum, etc (also **frō'menty, fur'menty, fur'mety** or **fur'mity** /fûr'/). [OFr *frumentee*, from *frument*, from L *frūmentum*]

frump /frump/ *n* a dowdy woman; a jeer or snub (*obs*). ◆ *vt* (*obs*) to snub.
■ **frump'ish** or **frump'y** *adj* ill-dressed or dowdy.

frumple /frum'pl/ (*dialect*) *vt* to wrinkle.

frusemide /froo'sə-mīd/ *n* another name for **furosemide**.

frush[1] /frush/ *vt* (*Shakesp*) to break or bruise. ◆ *adj* (*Scot*) brittle; crumbly. ◆ *n* (*Scot*) a crash; splinters. [OFr *froissier* to bruise, from L *frustum* fragment]

frush[2] /frush/ (*dialect*) *n* the frog of a horse's foot; a disease in that part of a horse's foot (cf **thrush**[2]). [Origin uncertain; cf OE *forsc* frog (animal); see **frog**[3]]

frust /frust/ *n* (*Sterne*) a fragment. [L *frustum* a bit]
■ **frust'ule** *n* (*bot*) the siliceous two-valved shell of a diatom alga, with its contents. **frust'um** *n* (*pl* **frust'ums** or **frust'a**) (*geom*) a slice of a solid body; the part of a cone or pyramid between the base and a parallel plane, or between two planes.

frustrate /fru-strāt' or frus'trāt/ *vt* to make useless or of no effect; to bring to nothing; to balk; to thwart. ◆ *adj* /frus'/ (*archaic*) useless or ineffectual; balked. [L *frustrārī*]
■ **frustra'ted** *adj* thwarted; having a sense of discouragement and dissatisfaction; sexually unfulfilled. **frustra'ting** *adj*. **frustra'tingly** *adv*. **frustrā'tion** *n*.
❑ **frustrated export** *n* an article *orig* intended for export which for some reason has to be offered for sale on the home market.

frutex /froo'teks/ (*bot*) *n* (*pl* **fru'tices** /-ti-sēz/) a shrub. [L *frutex*, *-icis* a shrub]
■ **fru'ticose** *adj* shrubby.

frutify /froo'ti-fī/ (*Shakesp, Merchant of Venice*) *vt* Launcelot Gobbo's blunder for **notify** or **specify**.

fry[1] /frī/ *vt* (**fry'ing; fried**) to cook in oil or fat, *esp* in a pan; to burn or scorch (often *fig*); to execute by electrocution (*US sl*); to torture with heat (*sl*). ◆ *vi* to undergo frying; to be executed by electrocution (*US sl*); to foam (*Spenser*). ◆ *n* a dish of anything fried, *esp* the offal of a pig, lamb, etc; (in *pl*) fried potato chips. [Fr *frire*, from L *frīgere*; cf Gr *phrȳgein*]
■ **fri'er** or **fry'er** *n* a person who fries (*esp* fish); a pan or container for frying; a fish or chicken suitable for frying. **fry'ing** *n* and *adj*.
❑ **fried'cake** *n* (*US*) a cake fried in deep fat; a doughnut. **fry'ing-pan** *n* a broad, shallow pan for frying food in. **fry'-up** *n* (*inf*) mixed fried foods, or the frying of these.
■ **fry in one's fat** to suffer the consequences of one's behaviour. **out of the frying-pan into the fire** out of one difficult situation into a worse.

fry[2] /frī/ *n* young, collectively; a swarm of young, *esp* of fishes just spawned; young salmon in their second year; a number of small things. [ON *friō* seed; Dan and Swed *fro*]
■ **small fry** small things collectively, people or things of little importance; children.

FSA *abbrev*: Fellow of the Society of Antiquaries; Financial Services Authority; Food Standards Agency.

FSAScot *abbrev*: Fellow of the Society of Antiquaries of Scotland.

FSAVC *abbrev*: free-standing additional voluntary contribution, an extra pension contribution that is made independently of any AVC organized by an employer.

FSB *abbrev*: *Federalnaya Sluzhba Bezopasnosti* (*Russ*), the Russian Federal Security Service; Federation of Small Businesses.

FSC *abbrev*: Friendly Societies Commission (now replaced by **FSA**).

FSH *abbrev*: follicle-stimulating hormone; (of a car; often without *caps*) full service history.

FSS *abbrev*: Forensic Science Service.

FST *abbrev*: flat-screen television.

FT *abbrev*: Financial Times (newspaper).

Ft *abbrev*: Fort.

ft *abbrev*: feet; foot.

FTA *abbrev*: Free Trade Agreement; Freight Transport Association.

fth or **fthm** *abbrev*: fathom.

FT Index *abbrev*: Financial Times (Industrial Ordinary Share) Index.

FTP (*comput*) *abbrev*: File Transfer Protocol, a program primarily used for the transfer of files across a network.

FTSE, FT-SE 100 or **FT-SE** *abbrev*: Financial Times Stock Exchange 100-Share Index, which records the share prices of the top 100 UK public companies (often (*inf*) **Foot'sie**).

fub /fub/ *vt* (**fubb'ing; fubbed**) (*archaic*) to put off; to fob. [See **fob**[1]]
■ **fubb'ery** *n* (*obs*) a deception.
■ **fub off** (*Shakesp*) to put off or evade by a trick or a lie.

fubar /foo'bär/ (*sl*) *adj* in a state characterized by extreme disorder, confusion or ineptitude. [Orig US military slang, from fouled (or fucked) up beyond all repair (or recognition)]

fubby /fub'i/ or **fubsy** /fub'zi/ (*dialect*) *adj* chubby; squat. [Ety dubious]

fuchsia /fū'shə/ *n* any plant of a S American genus (*Fuchsia*) of the family Onagraceae, with long pendulous flowers typically red or purple; a reddish-purple colour. ◆ *adj* of a reddish-purple colour. [Named after Leonard *Fuchs* (1501–66), German botanist]
■ **fuchsine** /fooks'ēn/ or **fuchsin** /fooks'in/ *n* the dyestuff magenta, a green solid, purplish-red in solution (from its colour, similar to that of the flower).

fuchsite /fook'sīt/ *n* a brilliant green chromium mica. [JN von *Fuchs* (1774–1856), German mineralogist]

fuci see **fucus**.

fuck /fuk/ (*offensive sl*) *vi* to have sexual intercourse; (with *about* or *around*) to play around or act foolishly; (with *off*) to go away (also *interj*); (with *with*) to trifle, meddle or act disrespectfully. ◆ *vt* to have sexual intercourse with; (with *about* or *around*) to deal inconsiderately with; (with *up*) to botch, ruin, damage or break (**fuck'-up** *n*). ◆ *n* an act of sexual intercourse; a person considered as a (good, poor, etc) partner in sexual intercourse; something of very little value; used in various phrases expressing displeasure, emphasis, etc, as in *what the fuck?, not give a fuck*; a term of abuse, a fucker. ◆ *interj* an expression of displeasure, etc (often with an object, as in *fuck him!*). [Ety doubtful; perh Ger *ficken* to strike or copulate with]
■ **fucked** *adj* exhausted; broken; spoiled; useless; in trouble; defeated. **fuck'er** *n* a person who fucks; a term of abuse; a person. **fuck'ing** *n* sexual intercourse. ◆ *adj* expressing scorn or disapprobation; often used as an intensifier or meaningless qualification. ◆ *adv* very or to a great extent.
❑ **fuck buddy** *n* (*inf*; *orig US*) a person one meets regularly for no other reason than sexual intercourse. **fuckhead** see **fuckwit** below. **fuck'-me** *adj* sexually alluring, or perceived as such, as in *fuck-me boots*. **fuck'-off** *adj* great; impressive; often used as an intensifier. **fuck'wit** or **fuck'head** *n* a contemptibly stupid person.
■ **sweet fuck all** or **fuck all** nothing at all.

fucus /fū'kəs/ *n* (*pl* **fu'ci** /-sī/ or **fū'cuses**) paint for the face, cosmetics (*obs*); any brown alga of the *Fucus* or bladderwrack genus of seaweeds, the type genus of the family Fucaceae. [L *fūcus* the red dye orchil or rouge; Gr *phȳkos*]
■ **fū'coid** *adj* like, relating to or containing bladderwrack, or seaweed, or seaweed-like markings. ◆ *n* a marking like a fossil seaweed; a seaweed of the genus *Fucus*. **fūcoid'al** *adj*. **fū'cused** *adj* painted.
❑ **fucoxanthin** /fū-kō-zan'thin/ *n* a brown carotenoid pigment found in certain algae.

fud /fud/ (*Scot*) *n* a rabbit's or hare's tail; the buttocks.

fuddle /fud'l/ *vt* (**fudd'ling; fudd'led**) to stupefy, eg with drink; to confuse. ◆ *vi* to drink to excess or habitually. ◆ *n* confusion; intoxication; a drinking bout; intoxicating drink (*obs*). [Origin obscure]
■ **fudd'ler** *n* a drunkard. **fudd'ling** *n* and *adj* tippling.
❑ **fudd'le-cap** *n* (*obs*) a hard drinker.

fuddy-duddy /fud'i-dud-i/ (*inf*) *n* an old fogy or stick-in-the-mud; a fault-finder. ◆ *adj* old-fogyish; old-fashioned; stuffy; prim; censorious. [Origin unknown]

fudge[1] /fuj/ *n* a soft sweet made from butter, cream and sugar, often flavoured with vanilla, rum, etc; a thick chocolate sauce used as a topping for ice cream or as a cake filling (*N Am*); stuff, nonsense, humbug (*archaic*). ◆ *interj* (*archaic*) bosh. [Origin obscure]

fudge² /*fuj*/ *vi* to cheat; to fail; to dodge; to fadge (*archaic*). ◆ *vt* to patch up; to fake; to distort; to dodge; to obscure or cover up. ◆ *n* an inserted patch in a newspaper, or space reserved for it; the act of fudging; distortion; evasion. [Variant of **fadge**]

Fuehrer same as **Führer**.

fuel /*fū'əl*/ *n* material for burning as a source of heat or power; something that maintains or intensifies emotion, etc (*fig*); food, as maintaining bodily processes; fissile material for a nuclear reactor. ◆ *vt* (**fū'elling**; **fū'elled**) to provide with fuel; to incite, encourage or stimulate (*esp* anger, hate, violence, etc). ◆ *vi* to take or get fuel. [OFr *fowaille*, from LL *focāle*, from L *focus* a fireplace]
■ **fū'eller** *n*.
◻ **fuel assembly** *n* a group of nuclear fuel elements forming a single unit for purposes of charging or discharging a reactor. **fuel cell** *n* a cell generating electricity for an external circuit as part of a chemical reaction between an electrolyte and a combustible gas or vapour supplied from outside the cell (the reaction taking place at more or less ordinary temperatures). **fuel'-injected** *adj* having **fuel injection**, a system of operating an internal-combustion engine in which vaporized liquid fuel is introduced under pressure directly into the combustion chamber, so dispensing with a carburettor. **fuelling machine** see **charge(-discharge) machine** under **charge**. **fuel oil** *n* heavy oil distillates used as fuel. **fuel reprocessing** the processing of nuclear fuel after use to remove fission products, etc and to recover fissile and fertile materials for further use (also **reprocessing**). **fuel rod** *n* a unit of nuclear fuel in rod form for use in a reactor.
■ **add fuel to the fire** or **fires** to make an angry person angrier, a heated discussion more heated, etc.

fuero /*fwā'rō*/ *n* (*pl* **fue'ros**) a code or body of law or privileges, *esp* in the Basque provinces, a constitution. [Sp, from L *forum*]

fuff /*fuf*/ (*Scot*) *n* a puff; the spitting of a cat; a burst of anger. ◆ *vt* and *vi* to puff; to spit like a cat. [Imit]
■ **fuff'y** *adj* light and soft.

fug /*fug*/ (*inf*) *n* a very hot, close, often smoky state of atmosphere; a person who fugs; dusty fluff. ◆ *vi* (**fugg'ing**; **fugged**) to sit or revel in a fug. ◆ *vt* to cause a fug in. [Origin unknown]
■ **fugg'iness** *n*. **fugg'y** *adj*.

fugacious /*fū-gā'shəs*/ *adj* inclined to run away or flee (*literary*); fleeting (*literary*); (of petals, etc) readily shed. [L *fugāx*, -*ācis*, from *fugere* to flee]
■ **fugā'ciousness** or **fugacity** /-*gas'*-/ *n*.

fugal, **fugato** and **fughetta** see under **fugue**.

-fuge /-*fūj*/ *combining form* denoting: (1) dispelling, expelling; (2) disliking, hating. [L *fugāre* to put to flight, and *fugere* to flee]

fugitive /*fū'ji-tiv*/ *adj* inclined to run away, fleeing; fleeting; occasional, written for some passing occasion. ◆ *n* a person who flees or has fled; a person difficult to catch; an exile. [L *fugitīvus*, from *fugere* to flee]
■ **fū'gie** *n* (*Scot*) a cock that will not fight; a runaway. **fūgita'tion** *n* (*Scots law*; *obs*) absconding from justice; sentence of outlawry. **fū'gitively** *adv*. **fū'gitiveness** *n*.
◻ **fū'gie-warr'ant** *n* (*Scot*) a warrant to apprehend a debtor supposed to be about to abscond, *prob* from the phrase *in meditatione fugae*.

fugleman /*fū'gl-mən*/ *n* a soldier who stands before a company at drill as an example; a ringleader or mouthpiece of others. [Ger *Flügelmann* the leader of a file, from *Flügel* a wing, and *Mann* man]
■ **fū'gle** *vi* (*Carlyle*) to act like a fugleman.

fugly /*fug'li*/ (*offensive sl*) *adj* extremely ugly. [Contraction of the phrase *fuck ugly*]

fugu /*foo'goo*/ *n* a variety of globe fish eaten in Japanese cuisine after poisonous parts have been removed. [Jap]

fugue /*fūg*/ *n* a form of composition in which the subject is given out by one part and immediately taken up by a second (in *answer*), during which the first part supplies an accompaniment or counter-subject, and so on (*music*); a form of amnesia which is a flight from reality (*psychiatry*). [Fr, from Ital *fuga*, from L *fuga* flight]
■ **fū'gal** *adj*. **fū'gally** *adv*. **fugato** /*fū-gä'tō* or (*Ital*) *foo-gä'tō*/ *adj* and *adv* (*pl* **fuga'tos**) in the manner of a fugue without being strictly a fugue (also *n*). **fughetta** /*fū-get'ə* or (*Ital*) *foo-get'ta*/ *n* a short fugue. **fuguist** /*fūg'ist*/ *n* a person who writes or plays fugues.

Führer /*fū'rər* or (*Ger*) *fü'rər*/ *n* the title taken by Hitler as dictator of Nazi Germany. [Ger, leader or guide]

Fujian flu /*foo-jen'* *floo*/*n* a virulent strain of influenza. [*Fujian* province in China]

Fujita scale /*foo-jē'tə skāl*/ *n* a scale for the force of tornados, from F0 for the weakest to F5 for the strongest. [T T *Fujita* (1920–98) Japanese-born US meteorologist]

fulcrum /*ful'krəm* or *fūl'*-/ *n* (*pl* **ful'crums** or **ful'cra**) the prop or fixed point on which a lever moves or pivots (*mech*); a support; a means to an end (*fig*). [L *fulcrum* a prop, from *fulcīre* to prop]
■ **ful'crate** *adj* supported with fulcrums.

fulfil or (*US*) **fulfill** /*fŭl-fil'*/ *vt* (**fulfill'ing**; **fulfilled'**) to complete; to accomplish; to carry into effect; to bring to consummation; to develop and realize the potential of; to fill full (*archaic*). [OE *fullfylla*, from *full* full, and *fyllan* to fill]
■ **fulfill'er** *n*. **fulfill'ing** or **fulfil'ment** *n* full performance; completion; accomplishment.

fulgent /*ful'jənt*/ (*literary*) *adj* shining; bright. [L *fulgēns*, -*entis*, prp of *fulgēre* to shine, *fulgidus* shining, *fulgor* brightness]
■ **ful'gency** *n*. **ful'gently** *adv*. **ful'gid** *adj* flashing. **ful'gor** or **ful'gour** /-*gör* or -*gər*/ *n* splendour. **ful'gorous** *adj* flashing.

fulgurate /*ful'gū-rāt*/ *vi* (*literary*) to flash like lightning. [L *fulgur* lightning]
■ **ful'gural** *adj* relating to lightning. **ful'gurant** *adj* flashing like lightning. **fulgūra'tion** *n* flashing; (in assaying) the sudden and final brightening of the fused globule; the destruction of tissue, *esp* tumours, by electric sparks (*med*). **ful'gūrite** *n* a tube of vitrified sand formed by lightning. **ful'gūrous** *adj* resembling lightning.

fulham /*fūl'əm*/ (*gambling*) *n* a die loaded at the corner to ensure that certain numbers are thrown (also **full'am** or **full'an**). [Prob the place name *Fulham* in London]

fuliginous /*fū-lij'i-nəs*/ (*literary*) *adj* sooty; dusky. [L *fūlīgō*, -*inis* soot]
■ **fūliginos'ity** *n*. **fūlig'inously** *adv*.

full¹ /*fŭl*/ *adj* (**full'er**; **full'est**) holding all that can be contained; having no empty space; replete; abundantly supplied or furnished; abounding; copious; filling; containing the whole matter; complete; perfect; maximum; strong; clear; intense; swelled or rounded; protuberant; having an excess of material; at the height of development or end of course; (with *of*) unable to think or talk of anything but; drunk (*inf*). ◆ *n* the completest extent, eg of the moon; the highest degree; the whole; the time of full moon. ◆ *vt* to make with gathers or puckers. ◆ *vi* to become full. ◆ *adv* quite; thoroughly or truly; directly. [OE *full*; Gothic *fulls*, ON *fullr*, Ger *voll*]
■ **full'ish** *adj* inclined to fullness. **full'ness** or **ful'ness** *n* the state of being full; the moment of fulfilment; plenty or wealth (*Shakesp*). **full'y** *adv* completely; entirely; quite.
◻ **full'-a'corned** *adj* (*Shakesp*) full-fed with acorns. **full'-aged** *adj* having reached majority. **full back** *n* in various sports, a player positioned towards the back of the field, *usu* with a defensive role; see also **back¹**. **full beam** *n* the strongest, undipped, setting of a vehicle's headlights. **full blast** *n* full operation. **full'-blast'** *adv* with maximum energy and fluency. **full'-blood** *n* an individual of unmixed descent. **full'-blood'ed** *adj* having a full supply of blood; vigorous, using maximum force or energy; thoroughbred or of unmixed descent; related through both parents. **full'-blown** *adj* fully expanded, as a flower; beyond the first freshness of youth; fully qualified, developed or admitted; puffed out to fullness. **full board** *n* (in hotels, etc) the providing of bed and all meals. **full'-bod'ied** *adj* with much body, flavour or substance. **full'-bore** *adj* (of a firearm) of larger calibre than small-bore. **full'-bottom** *n* a full-bottomed wig. **full'-bott'omed** *adj* having a full or large bottom, eg of a wig. **full'-bound** *adj* (*bookbinding*) with the boards covered as well as the back. **full brother** or **sister** *n* a son or daughter of the same parents as another. **full'-charged** *adj* fully loaded (*lit* and *fig*). **full'-cir'cle** *adv* round in a complete revolution; so as to return to an original position, state, etc. **full'-cock'** *n* the position of a gun cock drawn fully back, or of a tap fully open. ◆ *adv* in that position. **full'-cocked'** *adj*. **full-court press** *n* the aggressive tactic of confronting opponents in all areas of the court rather than only in one's own defensive area (*basketball*); maximum effort (*US inf*). **full cousin** *n* the son or daughter of an uncle or aunt, a first cousin. **full'-cream'** *adj* (of milk) not skimmed; made with unskimmed milk. **full'-dress** *adj* in or requiring the dress (**full dress**) worn on occasions of state or ceremony. **full-dress debate** *n* a set debate of some importance in which the leaders take part. **full'-eyed** *adj* with large prominent eyes. **full'-face** or **full'-faced** *adj* facing straight towards the viewer; having a full or broad face; (of type) boldfaced. **full-fashioned** see **fully-fashioned** below. **full'-fed** *adj* fed to plumpness or satiety. **full-fledged** see **fully-fledged** below. **full'-fraught** *adj* (*Shakesp*) fully charged, equipped or endowed, all-round. **full'-front'al** *adj* of the front view of a completely naked man or woman (also **full'-front**); with no detail left unrevealed (*fig*); unrestrained (*fig*). ◆ *n* such a view or picture. **full'-grown** *adj* grown to full size. **full hand** see **full house** below. **full'-hand'ed** *adj* bearing something valuable, eg a gift. **full'-heart'ed** *adj* full of heart or courage; fraught with emotion. **full'-hot** *adj* (*Shakesp*) heated to the utmost. **full house** *n* a performance at which every seat is taken (*theatre*); (also **full hand**) three cards of a kind and a pair (*poker*); (in bingo) all the numbers needed to win; a complete set (of anything). **full'-length'** *adj* extending the whole length. ◆ *n* a portrait showing

the whole length of a person. ◆ *adv* stretched to the full extent. **full'-manned** *adj* (*Shakesp*) having a full crew. **full marks** *n pl* the maximum marks possible in an examination (also used as an expression of approval). **full moon** *n* the moon with its whole disc illuminated, when opposite the sun; the time when the moon is full. **full motion video** (also **full-motion video**) *n* a system that provides moving video images and sound on a computer, used in computer games, video playback, etc. **full'-mouthed** *adj* (*archaic*) having a full set of teeth; having food in plenty; loud; sonorous. **full nelson** *n* a type of wrestling hold, a nelson. **full'-on** *adj* (*inf*) out-and-out; explicit, blatant, aggressive. **full'-orbed** *adj* (*archaic*) having the orb or disc fully illuminated, as the full moon; round. **full organ** *n* the organ, or great organ, with all or most of the stops in use. **full'-out** *adj* at full power; total. **full'-page** *adj* occupying a whole page. **full'-pelt'**, **full'-speed'**, **full'-split'** or **full-tilt'** *adv* with highest speed and impetus. **full pitch** or **full toss** *n* (*cricket*) a ball which does not or would not bounce before passing or hitting the batsman's wicket. **full point** same as **full stop** below. **full'-rigged'** *adj* having three or more masts square-rigged. **full'-sailed** *adj* having all sails set; having sails filled with wind; advancing with speed and momentum. **full'-scale** *adj* of the same size as the original; involving full power or maximum effort. **full score** *n* a complete musical score with a staff or line for every part. **full service history** *n* the complete details of repairs and servicing done to a vehicle from new (*abbrev* **FSH** or **fsh**). **full sister** see **full brother** above. **full-speed, full-split** see **full-pelt** above. **full stop** *n* a point marking the end of a sentence; an end or halt. **full'-summed** *adj* (*archaic*) complete in all its parts. **full'-throat'ed** or **full'-voiced** *adj* singing, etc with the whole power of the voice. **full-tilt** see **full-pelt** above. **full time** *n* the end of a football, rugby, etc match. **full'-time** *adj* occupied during or extending over the whole working day, week, etc. **full'-tim'er** *n*. **full toss** see **full pitch** above. **full-voiced** see **full-throated** above. **full'-winged** *adj* (*Shakesp*) having wide, strong wings. **fully'-fashioned** or **full'-fashioned** *adj* (of garments, *esp* stockings) shaped to fit the body closely. **fully'-fledged** or **full'-fledged** *adj* completely fledged; having attained full rank or membership. ■ **at the full** at the height, eg of one's good fortune, etc. **full and by** (*naut*) close-hauled to the wind. **full-line forcing** the supplying of a particular product by a company to a customer only on condition that the customer takes the whole range of the company's product. **full of oneself** having a high or exaggerated opinion of one's own importance, etc (also **full of one's own importance**), too much the subject of one's own conversation. **full of years** (*archaic*) old or aged; at a good old age. **full sail** see under **sail¹**. **full steam ahead** see under **steam**. **full up** full to the limit; sated or wearied (*inf*). **in full** without reduction or omission. **in full cry** (*esp* of hounds) in hot pursuit. **in full rig** (*naut*) with maximum number of masts and sails. **in full swing** at the height of activity. **in the fullness of time** at the due or destined time. **the full monty** /*mon'ti*/ (*inf*) everything that there is or that one needs. **to the full** in full measure or completely.

full² /*fʊl*/ *vt* to scour and beat, as a means of finishing or cleansing woollens; to scour and thicken in a mill. [OFr *fuler* (see **foil¹**) and OE *fullere* fuller, both from L *fullō* a cloth-fuller]
■ **full'age** *n* the charge for fulling cloth. **full'er** *n* a person who fulls cloth.
❏ **fuller's earth** *n* an earthy hydrous aluminium silicate, used to absorb grease and as a filter; (with *caps*) a division of the English Jurassic (*geol*). **full'er's-herb** *n* a tall herb, soapwort. **full'ing-mill** *n* a mill in which woollen cloth is fulled.

fullam and **fullan** see **fulham**.

fuller¹ see under **full²**.

fuller² /*fʊl'ər*/ *n* a blacksmith's tool used in shaping iron. [Origin uncertain]

fullerene /*fʊl'ə-rēn*/ (*chem*) *n* a ball-shaped molecule consisting of carbon atoms. [**buckminsterfullerene**]

fulmar /*fʊl'mär* or *-mər*/ *n* a gull-like bird of the petrel family. [Perh ON *fúll* foul, and *mār* gull]

fulminate /*fʊl'mi-nāt*/ *vi* to thunder or make a loud noise (*literary*); to detonate; to issue decrees with violence or threats; to inveigh; to flash (*literary*). ◆ *vt* to cause to explode; to utter or publish (eg a denunciation); to denounce. ◆ *n* (*chem*) a salt of fulminic acid (often dangerously detonating). [L *fulmināre*, *-ātum*, from *fulmen*, *-inis* lightning, from *fulgēre* to shine]
■ **ful'minant** *adj* fulminating; developing suddenly or rapidly (*pathol*). ◆ *n* a thunderbolt; an explosive. **ful'mināting** *adj* detonating. **fulmina'tion** *n* an act of thundering, denouncing or detonating; a denunciation. **ful'minatory** *adj*. **fulmine** /*fʊl'min*/ *vt* and *vi* (*Spenser* and *Milton*) to fulminate. **fulmin'eous** or **ful'minous** *adj* relating to thunder and lightning.
❏ **fulminating gold** *n* a green powder made from auric (gold) oxide and ammonium hydroxide. **fulminating mercury** *n* fulminate containing bivalent mercury. **fulminating silver** *n* a black solid made from silver oxide and ammonium hydroxide. **fulmin'ic acid** *n* an acid isomeric with cyanic acid.

fulness see under **full¹**.

fulsome /*fʊl'səm*/ *adj* sickeningly obsequious; nauseatingly affectionate, admiring or praiseful; loosely, copious or lavish; excessive; (eg of a voice or a woman's figure) well-developed, well-rounded. [**full¹** and affix *-some*]
■ **ful'somely** *adv*. **ful'someness** *n*.

fulvous /*fʊl'vəs*/ *adj* dull yellow; tawny. [L *fulvus* tawny]
■ **ful'vid** *adj*.

fum see **fung**.

fumado /*fū-mä'dō*/ *n* (*pl* **fumā'does** or **fuma'dos**) a smoked fish, *esp* a pilchard. [Sp, smoked, from L *fūmāre* to smoke]

Fumaria /*fū-mā'ri-ə*/ *n* the fumitory genus, giving name to the **Fumariā'ceae**, a family related to the poppies. [L *fūmus*; see **fumitory**]
❏ **fumaric acid** /*fū-mar'ik*/ *n* an acid isomeric with maleic acid, found in *Fumaria* and other plants.

fumarole /*fū'mə-rōl*/ *n* a hole emitting gases in a volcano or volcanic region (also **fum'erole**). [Fr *fumerolle* or Ital *fumaruola*, from L *fūmus* smoke]
■ **fumarol'ic** *adj*.

fumatorium and **fumatory** see under **fume**.

fumble /*fum'bl*/ *vi* to grope about awkwardly; to make bungling or unsuccessful attempts; to drop or mishandle the ball, eg in American football; to mumble (*obs*). ◆ *vt* to handle, manage or effect awkwardly or bunglingly; to drop or mishandle (the ball), eg in American football; to huddle (*archaic*); to mumble (*obs*). ◆ *n* an act of fumbling; a dropped or fumbled ball, eg in American football. [Cf Du *fommelen* to fumble; Dan *famle*; ON *fálma* to grope about]
■ **fum'bler** *n*. **fum'blingly** *adv*.

fume /*fūm*/ *n* smoke or vapour, often odorous (often in *pl*); any volatile matter; rage or fretful excitement; a passionate person (*archaic*); anything unsubstantial, a pointless conceit. ◆ *vi* to smoke; to give off vapour; to come off in fumes; to be in a rage. ◆ *vt* to treat with fumes; to give off; to offer incense to. [L *fūmus* smoke]
■ **fūm'age** *n* hearth-tax. **fumato'rium** or **fūm'atory** *n* (*pl* **fumato'riums** or **fumato'ria** or **fūm'atories**) a place for smoking or fumigation. **fūmos'ity** *n* (*archaic*) a fuming condition; an exhalation; breath stinking of food or drink. **fūm'ous** or **fūm'y** *adj*.
❏ **fume chamber** or **fume cupboard** or **fume hood** *n* a ventilated case or enclosure for laboratory operations that give off fumes. **fumed oak** *n* oak darkened by ammonia fumes. **fuming sulphuric acid** see **oleum** under **oleate**.

fumet¹ or **fewmet** /*fū'mit*/ (*archaic, usu* in *pl*) *n* the dung of deer, hares, etc. [Appar Anglo-Fr, from L *fimāre* to defecate]

fumet² or **fumette** /*fū-met'*/ *n* the scent of game when it is high; a strongly-flavoured stock, *esp* obtained from cooking game or fish. [Fr *fumet*]

fumetto /*foo-met'tō*/ (*Ital*) *n* (*pl* **fumetti** /*-tē*/) a cartoon or comic strip; a balloon in a cartoon.

fumigate /*fū'mi-gāt*/ *vt* to expose to fumes, *esp* for purposes of disinfecting, or destroying pests; to perfume (*archaic*). [L *fūmigāre*, *-ātum*]
■ **fūm'igant** *n* a source of fumes, *esp* a substance used for fumigation. **fūmigā'tion** *n*. **fūm'igator** *n* a fumigating apparatus. **fūm'igatory** *adj*.

fumitory /*fū'mi-tə-ri*/ *n* any plant of the genus *Fumaria*, *esp* one formerly used to treat scurvy (also **fen'itar**, **fem'etary** or (*Shakesp*) **fem'iter**). [OFr *fume-terre*, literally, earth-smoke, from L *fūmus* smoke, and *terra* earth; so called because its rapid growth was thought to resemble the dispersal of smoke]

fun /*fun*/ *n* pleasure, enjoyment, merriment; frivolity or sport; a source of merriment or amusement; a hoax or trick (*obs*). ◆ *vt* (**funn'ing**; **funned**) (*obs*) to trick. ◆ *vi* to play. ◆ *adj* providing amusement; enjoyable or full of fun. [Prob a form of obs *fon* to befool]
❏ **fun'board** *n* in windsurfing, a special board that affords greater speed. **fun'fair** *n* a fair with sideshows, rides and other amusements. **fun fur** *n* an artificial or inexpensive (sometimes dyed) fur, *esp* for casual wear. **fun park** *n* an outdoor place of entertainment with various amusements. **fun run** *n* a long-distance race, not *usu* covering the full distance of a marathon, undertaken for amusement, or for charitable fund-raising, rather than serious athletic competition. **fun runner** *n*.
■ **all the fun of the fair** all the amusements of the occasion. **be great fun** to be very amusing. **fun and games** amusement; excitement; trouble (*facetious*). **in fun** as a joke, not seriously. **like fun** (*inf*) rapidly or frenziedly; not at all. **make fun of** or **poke fun at** to ridicule.

funambulist /*fū-nam'bū-list*/ *n* a rope-walker or rope dancer. [L *fūnambulus* a rope-walker, from *fūnis* rope, and *ambulāre* to walk]

■ **fūnam'būlate** *vi.* **fūnambūlā'tion** *n.* **fūnam'būlātor** *n.* **fūnam'būlatory** *adj.*

funckia /fung'ki-ə/ *n* any plant of an E Asiatic genus allied to the day lilies formerly called *Funckia*, now *Hosta* (see **hosta**). [From the German botanist, HC *Funck* (1771–1839)]

function /fungk'shən *or* fung'shən/ *n* an activity appropriate to any person or thing; duty peculiar to any office or job; faculty or the exercise of faculty; the peculiar office of anything; a profession (*obs*); a solemn service; a ceremony; a social gathering; a set of logical operations which can be called from another program or system and which returns a value to the caller (*comput*); a variable so connected with another that for any value of the one there is a corresponding value for the other (*maths*); a correspondence between two sets of variables such that each member of one set can be related to one particular member of the other set (*maths* or *logic*); an event, etc dependent on some other factor or factors; the technical term for the vital activity of an organ, tissue, or cell (*physiol*); the part played by a linguistic form in a construction, or by a form or form class in constructions in general (*linguistics*); the doing of a thing (*obs*); performance (*obs*); activity (*obs*). ◆ *vi* to perform a function; to act; to operate, *esp* to expected standards; to work. [OFr, from L *functiō*, *-ōnis*, from *fungī*, *functus* to perform]

■ **func'tional** *adj* relating to or performed by functions (*maths*); (of disease) characterized by impairment of function, not of organs; designed with special regard to purpose and practical use, often to the detriment of decorative qualities; serving a function. **func'tionalism** *n* the theory or practice of adapting method, form, materials, etc primarily with regard to the purpose in hand; the theory or practice of assessing social institutions, customs, etc in terms of the part they play in maintaining the social system. **func'tionalist** *n.* **functional'ity** *n* the capacity to be functional or practical; purpose; a specific application of a computer program. **func'tionally** *adv.* **func'tionary** *n* a person who discharges any duty; a person who holds an office. **func'tionate** *vi* (*obs*) to perform a function. **func'tionless** *adj* having no function. ◻ **functional food** *n* food with additives providing extra nutritional value. **functional group** *n* (*chem*) the group of atoms in a compound that determines its chemical behaviour. **function key** *n* (*comput*) one of a series of keys that will perform a particular function in a program. **function word** *n* (*linguistics*) a word, such as an article or auxiliary, which has little or no meaning apart from the grammatical concept it expresses.

functor /fungk'tər/ *n* a function, an operator (*maths*); a function word (qv). [From **function**; modelled on **factor**, etc]

functus officio /fungk'təs o-fish'i-ō, fŭngk'tŭs o-fik'i-ō/ (*L*) *adj* having fulfilled an office, or out of office; no longer having official power to act; (of a power) that can no longer be exercised.

fund /fund/ *n* a sum of money on which some enterprise is founded or financially supported; a supply or source (of money); a store laid up; a supply; (in *pl*) permanent government debts paying interest; (in *pl*) money available to an organization for a project, etc, or (*inf; usu facetious*) available to an individual. ◆ *vt* to convert into a long-term debt at a fixed rate of interest; to place in a fund; to provide (an organization, project, etc) with money. [L *fundus* the bottom]

■ **fund'able** *adj* capable of being converted into a fund or into bonds; capable of being funded. **fund'ed** *adj* invested in public funds; existing in the form of bonds. **fund'er** *n* a person who provides money for a project, etc; a financial backer. **fund'ing** *n* the action of providing money for a project, etc; financial backing or funds. **fund'less** *adj* completely lacking supplies or money. ◻ **fund'holder** *n* a person who has money in public funds; a general practitioner or medical practice that is assigned a budget. **fund'holding** *adj.* **fund of funds** *n* (*finance*) an investment fund whose assets consist of holdings in several other investment funds. **fund'raise** *vi* to act as a fundraiser. **fund'-raiser** *n* a person who raises funds; an event staged to raise funds. **fund'-raising** *n* the raising of money for an organization, project, etc (also *adj*). ■ **in funds** having plenty of money.

fundamental /fun-də-men'tl/ *adj* basic; serving as foundation; essential; primary; important. ◆ *n* anything which serves as a basis; an essential; the root of a chord or of a system of harmonics (*music*). [L *fundāmentum* foundation, from *fundāre* to found]

■ **fund'ament** /-mənt/ *n* (*facetious*) the buttocks or anus. **fundamen'talism** *n* belief in the literal truth of the Bible, against evolution, etc; adherence to strictly orthodox religions or (*fig*) other, eg political, doctrines. **fundamen'talist** *n* a person who professes such a belief or (*fig*) other, eg political, beliefs considered fundamental (also *adj*). **fundamental'ity** *n.* **fundamen'tally** *adv.* ◻ **fundamental particle** same as **elementary particle** (see under **element**). **fundamental unit** *n* any of a number of arbitrarily defined units in a system of measurement, such as metre, second or candela, from which the other quantities in the system are derived.

fundamentum relationis /fun-də-men'təm ri-lā-shi-ō'nis *or* fŭn-dä-men'tŭm re-lä-ti-ō'nis/ (*LL*) the basis of relation, the principle or nature of the connection.

fundi /fŭn'dē/ (*S Afr*) *n* an expert. [Bantu *umfundisi* a teacher]

fundie *or* **fundy** /fun'dē/ (*inf*) *n* a fundamentalist, *esp* in religion or politics; a member of the radical wing of the German Green Party (cf **realo**). [Short form]

fundus /fun'dəs/ *n* (*pl* **fun'di** /-ī/) the bottom of anything; the upper end of the uterus in pregnant women (*med*); the rounded bottom of a hollow organ (*anat*). [L]

funebral and **funebrial** see under **funeral**.

funèbre /fü-ne'br'/ (*Fr*) *adj* mournful.

funeral /fü'nə-rəl/ *n* disposal of the dead, with related ceremonies or observances; the appropriate ceremony; a procession to the place of burial or cremation, etc; death (*Spenser* and *Shakesp*); tomb (*Spenser*). ◆ *adj* relating to the disposal of the dead or to funerals. [LL *fūnerālis* and L *fūnerārius*, *fūnebris*, *fūnereus*, from L *fūnus*, *fūneris* a funeral procession]

■ **fūne'bral** *or* **fūne'brial** *adj* funereal. **fū'nerary** *adj* relating to or suiting a funeral. **fūne'real** *adj* relating to a funeral; dismal; mournful. **fūne'really** *adv.* ◻ **funeral director** *n* an undertaker. **funeral home** *n* (*US*) an undertaker's place of business with facilities for funerals. **funeral parlour** *n* a room that can be hired for funeral ceremonies; a funeral home. ■ **it's your, my,** etc **funeral** (*inf*) it's your, my, etc affair or look-out.

funest /fü-nest'/ (*obs*) *adj* deadly; lamentable. [Fr, from L *fūnestus* destructive]

fung /fung/ *or* **fum** /fum/ *n* a legendary Chinese bird, sometimes called the phoenix. [Chin *fung*, *fêng*, *fĕng*]

fungible /fun'ji-bl/ *adj* interchangeable; exchangeable for something similar. ◆ *n* something that is interchangeable, or exchangeable for something similar; (in *pl*) movable effects which are consumed by use, and which are estimated by weight, number and measure (*law*); (in *pl*) oil products which are interchangeable and can therefore be mixed during transport (*mining*). [LL *fungibilis*, from L *fungī* to perform; see **function**]

■ **fungibil'ity** *n.*

fungo /fung'gō/ *n* (*pl* **fung'oes**) (in baseball) a ball struck high into the air for fielders to practise catching; (also **fungo bat**) a special lightweight bat used for this. [Origin uncertain]

fungus /fung'gəs/ *n* (*pl* **fungi** /fun'jī, -ji, -gī/ *or* **fung'uses**) a plant of one of the lowest groups, thallophytes lacking chlorophyll and reproducing by spores, including mushrooms, toadstools, mould, yeasts, etc; a soft, morbid growth (*pathol*). [L *fungus* a mushroom; cf Gr *sphongos*, *spongos* a sponge]

■ **fung'al** *adj* relating to, caused by, or resembling fungus. **fungicīd'al** *adj* fungi-destroying; relating to a fungicide. **fungicide** /fun'ji-sīd/ *n* a substance which kills fungi. **fungiform** /fun'ji-förm/ *adj* mushroom-shaped. **fungistatic** /fun-ji-stat'ik/ *adj* inhibiting the growth of fungi. **fungistat'ically** *adv.* **fung'oid** /-goid/ *or* **fungoid'al** *adj* fungus-like; of the nature of a fungus. **fungos'ity** *n* the quality of being fungous. **fung'ous** *adj* of or like fungus; soft; spongy; growing suddenly; ephemeral (*obs*). ◻ **fung'us-gall** *n* a malformation in a plant caused by a fungal attack.

funicle /fü'ni-kl/ *n* a small cord or ligature (*esp anat*); a fibre; the stalk by which the ovule (and seed) is attached to the placenta in angiosperms (*bot*). [L *fūniculus*, dimin of *fūnis* a rope]

■ **funic'ular** *adj* relating to a funicle; relating to a string or cable. **fūnic'ulate** *adj.* **fūnic'ulus** *n* the umbilical cord; a funicle. ◻ **funicular railway** *n* a railway on which the carriages are pulled along a cable.

funk¹ /fungk/ *n* a strong unpleasant smell, *esp* of smoke (*obs* or *US dialect*); pop or jazz music with a strong rhythm and a soulful quality (*inf*). ◆ *vt* to stifle with smoke. ◆ *vi* to smoke and/or cause a strong unpleasant smell. [Ety dubious]

■ **funk'y** *adj* with a strong, musty, or bad smell (*US dialect*); (of jazz, pop music, etc) unsophisticated, earthy and soulful, like early blues music in style, emotion, etc (*inf*); in the latest fashion, trendy (*inf*); kinky (*inf*); odd or quaint (*inf*).

funk² /fungk/ (*inf*) *n* a state of fear; panic; shrinking or shirking from loss of courage; a person who funks. ◆ *vi* to flinch; to draw back or hold back in fear. ◆ *vt* to balk at or shirk from fear. [Poss Flem *fonck*]

■ **funk'iness** *n.* **funk'y** *adj.* ◻ **funk'hole** *n* (*sl, orig milit*) a place of refuge, a dugout; a place to which one can retreat for shelter, etc (*fig*); a job that enables one to avoid military service. ■ **blue funk** see under **blue¹**.

funk³ /fungk/ *n* decayed wood used for tinder, touchwood; a spark. [Cf Du *vonk*]

funky see under **funk**[1] and **funk**[2].

funnel[1] /fun'l/ n a utensil, usu a cone ending in a tube, for pouring fluids into narrow-necked bottles or other containers; a passage for the escape of smoke, etc, esp on a ship. ◆ vt (**funn'elling** or (N Am) **funn'eling**; **funn'elled** or (N Am) **funn'eled**) to pour, pass, transfer, etc through, or as if through, a funnel. [Prob through Fr or Port from L infundibulum, from fundere to pour]
■ **funn'elled** or (N Am) **funn'eled** adj having a funnel; funnel-shaped.
□ **funnel cloud** n a funnel-shaped cloud found in a tornado or waterspout. **funn'el-net** n a net shaped like a funnel. **funn'el-web** or **funnel-web spider** n a venomous spider (genus Atrax) of E Australia which constructs a tube-shaped or funnel-shaped lair.

funnel[2] /fun'l/ (dialect) n the offspring of a stallion and a she-ass. [Origin unknown]

funny[1] /fun'i/ adj full of fun; droll; amusing, mirth-provoking; queer or odd. ◆ n a joke (inf); (in pl) comic strips, or the comic section of a newspaper (esp N Am). [**fun**]
■ **funn'ily** adv. **funn'iness** n.
□ **funny bone** n (inf) the bone at the elbow with the comparatively unprotected ulnar nerve which, when struck, shoots a tingling sensation down the forearm to the fingers (a pun on its medical name humerus). **funny business** n (inf) tricks or deception; amusing behaviour, joke-telling, etc. **funny farm** n (old inf) a hospital or asylum for the mentally ill. **funny man** n (inf) a comedian. **funny money** n (inf) any currency or unit of account considered in some way less real or solid than 'ordinary' money, or a sum of money similarly regarded as in some way unreal. **funny paper** n (US) the comic section of a newspaper, the funnies. **funny stuff** n funny business.
■ **funny ha-ha** (inf) funny meaning 'amusing', as opposed to **funny peculiar** meaning 'queer or odd'.

funny[2] /fun'i/ n a light racing-boat, with a pair of sculls. [Perh from **funny**[1]]

funster /fun'stər/ (inf) n a person who causes merriment; a joker or prankster. [**fun**]

Funtumia /fun-tū'mi-ə/ n an African genus of tree related to dogbane, yielding a type of rubber. [From a Ghanaian name]

fur[1] /fûr/ n the thick, soft, fine hair of certain animals; the skin with this hair attached; a garment of fur; furred animals, opp to feather; a patched or tufted tincture (heraldry); a coating on the tongue; a crust formed by hard water in boilers, etc; a strengthening piece nailed to a rafter (archit). ◆ vt (**furr'ing**; **furred**) to clothe, cover, coat, trim or line with fur; to coat. ◆ vi to become coated. [OFr forrer (Fr fourrer) to line or encase, from forre, fuerre a sheath]
■ **furred** adj. **furr'ier** n a dealer or worker in furs. **furr'iery** n furs in general; trade in furs. **furr'iness** n. **furr'ing** n fur trimmings; a coating on the tongue; (also **firr'ing**) strips of wood fastened to joists, etc; a lining to a wall to carry laths, provide an air-space, etc. **furr'y** adj consisting of, like, covered with or dressed in fur.
□ **fur fabric** n a fabric with a fur-like pile. **fur seal** n a sea bear, an eared seal with dense fur under its long hairs.

fur[2] or **furr** /fûr/ (Scot) n a form of **furrow**.

fur. abbrev: furlong.

furacious /fū-rā'shəs/ (obs) adj thievish. [L fūrāx, -ācis, from fūr thief]
■ **fūrā'ciousness** or **fūracity** /-ras'i-ti/ n.

fural see **furfural** under **furfur**.

furan /fū'ran or fū-ran'/, also **furane** /-rān/ n a colourless liquid heterocyclic compound, C_4H_4O, obtained from wood tar or synthesized, and used in tanning and nylon production (also **fur'furan** /-fū- or -fə-/); any of a group of heterocyclic compounds derived from furan. [L furfur bran]

furbelow /fûr'bi-lō/ (archaic) n a plaited border or flounce; a superfluous ornament. ◆ vt to decorate with a furbelow. [Fr, Ital, and Sp falbala; of unknown origin]

furbish /fûr'bish/ vt to purify or polish; to rub up until bright; to renovate. [OFr fourbir, fourbiss-, from OHGer furban to purify]
■ **fur'bisher** n.

furcate /fûr'kāt/ vi to fork. ◆ adj (also **furcated** /-kā-tid/) forked. [L furca fork]
■ **fur'cal** adj. **furcā'tion** n. **furciferous** /-sif'-/ adj bearing a forked appendage; rascally (facetious; in allusion to the furca or yoke of criminals). **fur'cūla** n the joined clavicles of a bird, the wishbone. **fur'cūlar** adj furcate; shaped like a fork.

Furcraea /fûr-krē'ə/ or **Fourcroya** /foor-kroi'ə/ n a tropical American genus of plants related to Agave, yielding Mauritius hemp. [AF de Fourcroy (1755–1800), French chemist]

furder /fûr'dər/ an obsolete form (Milton) of **further**[1].

fureur /fū-rœr'/ (Fr) n extravagant admiration.

furfur /fûr'fûr/ or -fər/ (Browning, **furfair**) n dandruff or scurf. [L furfur bran]
■ **furfuraceous** /fûr-fū-rā'shəs/ adj branny; scaly; scurfy. **furfural** /fûr'fū-ral/ or -fə-ral/ or in full **furfural'dehyde** n a liquid (C_4H_3OCHO) obtained by heating bran with dilute sulphuric acid (also called **fūr'al, fur'fūrol, furfurole, fūr'ol** or **furole**). **furfurous** /fûr'fū-rəs/ or -fə-rəs/ adj furfuraceous.

furfuran see **furan**.

furibund /fū'ri-bund/ (obs) adj raging. [L furibundus, from furia rage]

furioso /foo-ri-ō'sō, fū-/ n (pl **furiō'sōs**) a furious or mad person. ◆ adj and adv (music) with fury. [Ital; cf **furious**]

furious see under **fury**.

furl /fûrl/ vt and vi to roll up. [Perh **fardel**[2]]

furlana /foor-lä'nə/ same as **forlana**.

furlong /fûr'long/ n a measure of distance, 40 poles, one-eighth of a mile, now little used except in horse-racing. [OE furlang, from furh furrow, and lang long]

furlough /fûr'lō/ n leave of absence, esp from military duty. ◆ vt to grant furlough to. [Du verlof; cf Ger Verlaub]

furmenty, furmety and **furmity** see **frumenty**.

furnace /fûr'nis/ n an enclosed structure in which great heat is produced for any of a number of industrial processes; a time or place of great heat, affliction or torment (fig). ◆ vt to exhale like a furnace; to subject to the heat of a furnace. [OFr fornais, from L fornāx, -ācis, from fornus an oven]

furniment /fûr'ni-mənt/ (Spenser) n furnishing.

furnish /fûr'nish/ vt to equip (a house, etc) with furniture, carpets, curtains, etc; to fit up or supply completely, or with what is necessary; to supply or provide; to equip. ◆ n paper pulp, with any added ingredients, before it goes into the paper-making process. [OFr furnir, furniss-; of Gmc origin; cf OHGer frummen to further]
■ **fur'nished** adj equipped; stocked with furniture. **fur'nisher** n. **fur'nishings** n pl fittings of any kind, esp articles of furniture, etc within a house; any incidental part (Shakesp). **fur'nishment** n.

furniture /fûr'ni-chər/ n movables, either for use or ornament, with which a house is equipped; equipment (Shakesp); the trappings of a horse; decorations (Shakesp); the necessary equipment in some arts or trades; accessories; metal fittings for doors and windows; the piece of wood or metal put round pages of type to make margins and fasten the type in the chase (printing); (also **four'niture**) a type of organ stop. [Fr fourniture]
□ **furniture beetle** n a beetle of the Anobium genus whose larvae bore into dead wood. **furniture van** n a long, high-sided van for transporting furniture, etc, eg when moving house.

furol and **furole** see **furfural** under **furfur**.

furor /fū'rör/ n fury; excitement or enthusiasm. [L]
□ **furor loquendi** /fū'rör lok-wen'dī or fū'ror lok-wen'dē/ n a passion for speaking; the urge to speak. **furor poeticus** /pō-et'ik-əs or po-āt-ik-ūs/ n poetic frenzy; a passion for writing poetry. **furor scribendi** /skri-ben'dī or skrē-ben'dē/ n a passion for writing; the urge to write.

furore /fū-rör', -rör' or fū-rö'rē/ or (N Am) **furor** /fū'rör/ n a craze; wild enthusiasm; wild excitement; public indignation. [Ital]

furosemide /fū-rö'sə-mīd/ n a synthetic diuretic drug used esp in treating oedema. [Altered from **furan**, sem- (of unknown origin), and -**ide**]

furphy /fûr'fi/ (Aust) n a water cart; a rumour or false report. [John Furphy, an Australian manufacturer of water carts (at which gossip would be exchanged)]

furr see **fur**[2].

furrier and **furring** see under **fur**[1].

furrow /fur'ō/ n the trench made by a plough; a groove; a wrinkle. ◆ vt to form furrows in; to groove; to wrinkle. [OE furh; cf Ger Furche, L porca ridge]
■ **furr'owy** adj.
□ **furr'ow-weed** n (Shakesp) a weed common on ploughed land.

furry[1] see under **fur**[1].

furry[2] /fur'i/ n an annual festival and dance (also **furry dance**) held at Helston in Cornwall, S England, on 8 May. See also **floral dance** under **flora**. [Perhaps connected with L feria festival]

furth /fûrth/ (Scot) adv forth; outside. [Variant of **forth**]
□ **furthcom'ing** n (Scots law) an action brought by an arrester against the arrestee and the common debtor after an arrestment in order that the arrested money or property be delivered to the arrester.
■ **furth of** outside; beyond the bounds of.

further[1] /fûr'dhər/ adv at or to a greater distance or degree; in addition. ◆ adj more distant; additional, more or other. [OE furthor (adv), furthra (adj), from fore or forth with compar sfx -ther]

■ **fur'thermore** *adv* in addition to what has been said, moreover or besides. **fur'thermost** *adj* most remote. **fur'thest** *adv* at or to the greatest distance. ♦ *adj* most distant.
◻ **further education** *n* post-school education that is below degree-level (cf **higher education** under **high¹**). **further outlook** *n* (*meteorol*) a general forecast given for a longer or more distant period than that covered by a more detailed forecast.
■ **further to** following on from. **see someone further** to see someone hanged, or similar.

further² /fûr'dhər/ *vt* to promote or help forward. [OE *fyrthran*]
■ **fur'therance** *n* a helping forward. **fur'therer** *n* a promoter or advancer. **fur'thersome** *adj* (*obs*) helpful; advantageous; rash.

furtive /fûr'tiv/ *adj* stealthy; secret. [L *fūrtīvus*, from *fūr* a thief]
■ **fur'tively** *adv*. **fur'tiveness** *n*.

furuncle /fū'rung-kl/ (*pathol*) *n* a boil. [L *fūrunculus*, literally, a little thief]
■ **fūrun'cūlar** or **fūrun'cūlous** *adj*. **fūrunculō'sis** *n* the condition of having many boils; a highly infectious disease of salmon and related fish.

fury /fū'ri/ *n* rage; violent passion; madness; (with *cap*) in mythology, any one of the three goddesses of vengeance, the Erinyes, or *euphem* Eumenides, namely Tisiphone, Alecto and Megaera (in *Milton* a Fate); hence, a passionate, violent woman. [Fr *furie*, from L *furia*, from *furere* to be angry]
■ **fūrios'ity** *n* madness. **furious** /fū'ri-əs/ *adj* full of fury or extremely angry; violent or raging; frenzied. **fū'riously** *adv*. **fū'riousness** *n*.
■ **fast and furious** see under **fast¹**. **like fury** (*inf*) furiously.

furze /fûrz/ *n* gorse. [OE *fyrs*]
■ **furz'y** *adj* overgrown with furze.

fusain /fū-zān'/ *n* an important constituent of coal, resembling charcoal and consisting of plant remains from which the volatiles have been eliminated (also /fū'zān/); artists' fine charcoal; a drawing done with this. [Fr, the spindle tree, or charcoal made from it]

fusarium /fū-zā'ri-əm/ *n* (*pl* **fūsār'ia**) any fungus of the large genus *Fusarium*, *esp* any of several species that cause serious disease in plants. [Mod L, from L *fūsus* spindle]

fusarole or **fusarol** /fū'sə-rōl or -zə-/ (*archit*) *n* an astragal moulding, a semicircular moulding round a column, etc. [Fr *fusarolle*, from Ital *fusaruolo* spindle whorl, from L *fūsus* spindle]

fuscous /fus'kəs/ *adj* (also (*Lamb*) **fusc**) brown; dingy. [L *fuscus*]

fuse¹ /fūz/ *vt* to melt; to liquefy by heat; to join by, or as if by, melting together; to cause to fail by the melting of a fuse (*elec*). ♦ *vi* to be melted; to be reduced to a liquid; to melt together; to blend or unite; (of an electric appliance) to fail by the melting of a fuse. ♦ *n* a piece of fusible metal, with its mounting, inserted as a safeguard against overloading in an electric circuit. [L *fundere, fūsum* to melt]
■ **fūsibil'ity** *n* the degree of ease with which a substance can be fused. **fūs'ible** *adj* able to be fused or easily fused. **fūsile** /fū'zīl, -sīl or -zil/ or (*Milton*) **fū'sil** /fū'zil/ *adj* cast; fusible; molten.
◻ **fuse box** *n* a box containing the switches and fuses for an electrical system. **fuse wire** *n* thin metal wire used in electrical fuses. **fusible metal** *n* any of numerous alloys containing bismuth, lead and tin (sometimes with mercury or cadmium) with low melting points, *esp* in the range 60° to 180°C. **fusing point** *n* melting point.
■ **blow a fuse** to cause or suffer the melting of an electrical fuse through overloading; to lose one's temper (*inf*).

fuse² or (*esp US*) **fuze** /fūz/ *n* a train of combustible material in a waterproof covering, used with a detonator to initiate an explosion; any device used to explode a mine, bomb, etc under specified circumstances or at a specified time. [Ital *fuso*, from L *fūsus* a spindle]
■ **a short fuse** a quick temper.

fusee¹ or **fuzee** /fū-zē'/ *n* the spindle in a watch or clock on which the chain is wound; a match with a long, oval head, for outdoor use; a fuse for firing explosives. [OFr *fusée* a spindleful, from L *fūsus* a spindle]

fusee² same as **fusil²**.

fuselage /fū'zə-läzh' or fū'zi-lij/ *n* the body of an aeroplane. [Fr *fuseler* to shape like a spindle, from L *fūsus* a spindle]

fusel-oil /fū'zl-oil/ *n* a nauseous mixture of alcohols in spirits distilled from potatoes, grain, etc. [Ger *Fusel* bad spirits]

fushion and **fushionless** see **foison**.

fusidic acid /fū-sid'ik as'id/ *n* an antibiotic steroid, $C_{31}H_{48}O_6$. [From the fungus *Fusidium coccineum*, from which it was first isolated]

fusiform /fū'zi-förm/ (*bot* and *zool*) *adj* spindle-shaped. [L *fūsus* a spindle, and *fōrma* shape]

fusil¹ /fū'zil/ (*heraldry*) *n* an elongated rhomboidal figure. [OFr *fusel*, from L *fūsus* a spindle]

fusil² /fū'zil/ *n* (*hist*) a flintlock musket (also **fusee**). [OFr *fuisil* a flint-musket, same as Ital *focile*, from LL *focile* steel (to strike fire with), dimin of L *focus* a fireplace]
■ **fusilier'** or **fusileer'** *n* formerly a soldier armed with a fusil, now simply a historical title borne by a few regiments; a member of such a regiment. **fusillade** /-ād'/ *n* a simultaneous or continuous discharge of firearms; anything assaulting one in a similar way, a barrage (*lit* and *fig*). ♦ *vt* to assault by fusillade. **fusillā'tion** *n* (*obs*) death by shooting.

fusil³ and **fusile** see under **fuse¹**.

fusilli /fū-zil'i/ *n pl* pasta in the form of short, thick spirals. [Ital]

fusion¹ /fū'zhən/ *n* fusing; melting; the state of fluidity from heat; a close union of things, as if melted together; coalition (*US*); nuclear fusion (see under **nucleus**). [Ety as for **fuse¹**]
■ **fū'sionism** *n* a policy that favours union or coalition. **fū'sionist** *n*.
◻ **fusion bomb** *n* one deriving its energy from the fusion of atomic nuclei, eg the hydrogen bomb. **fusion cones** same as **Seger cones**. **fusion cooking** *n* cooking that mixes ingredients and styles from different cuisines. **fusion energy** *n* energy released by the process of nuclear fusion. **fusion music** *n* music in which two or more different styles are combined. **fusion reactor** *n* a nuclear reactor operating by nuclear fusion. **fusion welding** *n* a process in which the weld is carried out solely by the melting of the metals to be joined, without any mechanical pressure.

fusion² and **fusionless** see **foison**.

fuss /fus/ *n* a bustle; flurry; (a) commotion, *esp* over trifling matters; petty ostentatious activity or attentions. ♦ *vi* to be in a fuss or agitate about trifling matters. ♦ *vt* to agitate or flurry. [Origin obscure]
■ **fuss'er** *n*. **fuss'ily** *adv*. **fuss'iness** *n*. **fuss'y** *adj* given to making a fuss; finicky; requiring careful attention; over-elaborate.
◻ **fuss'pot** or (*US*) **fuss'budget** *n* (*inf*) a person who fusses.
■ **make a fuss** to complain. **make a fuss of** to give much (genuinely or apparently) affectionate or amicable attention to. **not fussed** or **not fussy** (*inf*) without a strong preference; unconcerned.

fuss-ball see under **fuzz**.

fust /fust/ *n* a mouldy or musty smell; the shaft of a column. ♦ *vi* to mould; to smell mouldy; (of wine, etc) to taste of the cask. [OFr *fust* (Fr *fût*) cask, from L *fūstis* a cudgel]
■ **fustilā'rian, fustilir'ian** or **fustillir'ian** *n* (*Shakesp*) a term of abuse. **fust'ilugs** *n* (*obs*) a gross overgrown person, *esp* a woman.

fustanella /fus-tə-nel'ə/ *n* a white kilt sometimes worn by Greek and Albanian men. [Mod Gr *phoustanella*, dimin of *phoustani*, Albanian *fustan*, from Ital *fustagno* fustian]

fustet /fus'tət/ *n* the Venetian sumach tree or shrub (*Rhus cotinus*) or its wood, source of the dye called *young fustic*. [Fr, from Provençal *fustet*, from Ar *fustuq*; see **fustic**]

fustian /fus'chən/ *n* a kind of coarse, twilled cotton fabric including the varieties moleskin, velveteen, corduroy, etc; a pompous and unnatural style of writing or speaking; bombast; an alcoholic drink made of white wine with egg yolks, lemon, spices, etc. ♦ *adj* made of fustian; bombastic. [OFr *fustaigne* (Fr *futaine*), from Ital *fustagno*, from LL *fustāneum*, prob from *El-Fustāt* (Old Cairo) where it may have been made]
■ **fust'ianist** *n* a person who writes bombast. **fust'ianize** *vi* (*Oliver Wendell Holmes*) to write bombastically.

fustic /fus'tik/, also **fustoc** /-tok/ *n* formerly, fustet (now called **young fustic**); now, the wood of a tropical American tree (*Chlorophora tinctoria*), yielding a yellow dye (also **old fustic**); this yellow dye (*obs*). [Fr *fustoc*, from Sp *fustoc*, from Ar *fustuq*, from Gr *pistakē* pistachio]

fustigate /fus'ti-gāt/ (*obs*) *vt* to cudgel. [L *fūstīgāre, -ātum*, from *fūstis* a stick]
■ **fustigā'tion** *n*.

fustilugs see under **fust**.

fustily, fustiness see under **fusty**.

fustoc see **fustic**.

fusty /fus'ti/ *adj* stale; musty; stuffy; old-fashioned; lacking freshness; (of wine) smelling of the cask. [From **fust**]
■ **fust'ily** *adv*. **fust'iness** *n*.

Fusus /fū'səs/ *n* a genus of gastropods related to whelks, the spindle shells. [L *fūsus* a spindle]

fut. *abbrev*: future.

futchel /fuch'əl/ *n* a piece of timber lengthwise in a carriage, supporting the splinter bar and the pole. [Origin obscure]

futhork or **futhorc** /foo'thörk/ or **futhark** /-thärk/ *n* the Runic alphabet. [From the first six letters, *f, u, Þ* (th), *o* or *a, r, k*]

futile /fū'tīl (*US*) -təl/ *adj* ineffectual; pointless; trifling; tattling (*obs*). [L *fūtilis* leaky or futile, from *fundere* to pour]

■ **fu'tilely** *adv.* **futilitā'rian** *n* a person who devotes himself or herself to profitless pursuits; a person who believes everything to be futile. **futil'ity** /-til'it-i/ *n* uselessness.

futon /foo'ton/ *n* a type of sofa bed of Japanese design, a simple low frame with a mattress laid loosely on top; more properly, the mattress alone. [Jap]

futsal or **footsal** /fūt'söl/ *n* a form of association football played indoors with five players on each side on a pitch without side walls. [Blend of Sp *futbol* football and *sala* indoor]

futtock /fut'ək/ (naut) *n* one of the curved timbers of a wooden ship, a rib. [Perh for *foot-hook*]

□ **futt'ock-plate** *n* an iron plate with deadeyes, for the topmast or topgallant rigging. **futt'ock-shrouds** *n pl* short pieces of rope or chain securing the futtock-plates to a band round a lower mast.

future /fū'chər/ *adj* about to be; that is to come; expressive of time to come (*grammar*). ◆ *n* time to come; life, fate or condition in time to come; prospects or likelihood of future success; the future tense (*grammar*); (in *pl*) commodities or securities traded at an agreed price, to be delivered and paid for at a specified future date. [Fr *futur*, from L *futūrus*, used as future participle of *esse* to be]

■ **fut'ureless** *adj* without prospects. **fut'urism** *n* (*art*) a movement claiming to anticipate or point the way for the future, *esp* a 20c revolt against tradition. **fut'urist** *n* a person whose chief interests are in what is to come; a believer in futurism. **futurist'ic** *adj* of or relating to futurism; so modern (in design, concept, etc) as to appear to belong to some future time. **futurit'ion** *n* future existence; accomplishment; futurity. **futurity** /fū-tū'ri-ti/ *n* time to come; an event, or state of being, yet to come. **futurolog'ical** *adj.* **futurol'ogist** *n.* **futurol'ogy** *n* the science and study of sociological and technological developments, values and trends, with a view to planning for the future.

□ **future perfect** *adj* (*grammar*) expressive of action viewed as past in reference to an assumed future time, in English formed using *will have* or *shall have*. ◆ *n* the future perfect tense; a verb in that tense. **fu'tureproof** *adj* able to withstand and cope with future developments and technological advances. **future shock** *n* a state of stress created by rapid change. **future studies** *n sing* futurology.

futz /futs/ (chiefly *US inf*) *vi* (often with *around* or *about*) to behave fussily or indecisively. [Yiddish]

fu yung /foo yŭng/ *n* a Chinese dish or sauce based on eggs with bean sprouts, onion, meat, etc (also **foo yung** or **foo yong** /yong/). [Chin *fú yóng* hibiscus]

fuze see **fuse²**.

fuzee see **fusee¹**.

fuzz /fuz/ *n* light fine particles or fibres, eg of dust; fluff; blur; police (*sl*). ◆ *vi* to disintegrate in fuzz. ◆ *vt* to make fuzzy. [Origin doubtful]

■ **fuzz'ily** *adv.* **fuzz'iness** *n.* **fuzz'y** *adj* covered with fuzz; fluffy; with many small tight curls; blurred.

□ **fuzz'-ball** or **fuss'-ball** *n* a puff-ball fungus. **fuzz'box** *n* an electronic device used to distort the sound of eg an electric guitar. **fuzz'y-haired'** *adj.* **fuzzy logic** *n* a form of logic used in computers in which truth values carry probabilities so that the rules of inference are approximate. **fuzz'y-wuzz'y** *n* (*offensive*) a Sudanese soldier (*old inf*, *esp milit*); a dark-skinned native of any of various countries, *esp* if fuzzy-haired (*sl*).

fuzzle /fuz'l/ (*dialect*) *vt* to fuddle.

fwd *abbrev* : forward; four-wheel drive; front-wheel drive.

FX *abbrev* : (sound or special) effects.

fy /fī/ *interj* same as **fie¹**.

fya *abbrev* : first-year allowance.

fyi or **FYI** *abbrev* : for your information.

fyke¹ same as **fike**.

fyke² /fīk/ (*US*) *n* a bag-net for keeping fish in. [Du *fuik*]

fyle a Spenserian form of **file¹,²**.

fylfot or **filfot** /fil'fot/ *n* a swastika, *esp* one turned counter-clockwise. [Prob from misunderstanding of a manuscript, *fylfot* = fill-foot, really meaning a device for filling the foot of a painted window]

fynbos /fän'bös/ (*Afrik*) *n* (an area of) low shrubs. [Afrik, from Dutch *fijn* fine or delicate, and *bosch* bush]

fyrd /fûrd/ or /fĕrd/ *n* any of the local militia of Anglo-Saxon times, in which service was compulsory for many. [OE *fyrd* army]

fytte see **fit³**.

fz (*music*) *abbrev* : (s)forzando.

Gg

abcdefghijklmnopqrstuvwxyz

Garamond Designed by Claude Garamond in 1532. France.

G or **g** /jē/ *n* the seventh letter in the modern English alphabet as in the Roman; *orig* a form of C, inserted in the place of the disused Z, its ordinary sound (as in Latin) a voiced velar stop, but in some words in English the same as J; the fifth note of the diatonic scale of C major (*music*); the key or scale having that note for its tonic (*music*); anything shaped like the letter G.
□ **G clef** *n* (*music*) the treble clef. **G'-string** *n* the lowest string on the violin, tuned to the note of G, or a string tuned to G on another instrument (*music*); a string worn round the waist supporting a strip worn between the legs; the strip itself or any similar covering for the genitals.

G or **G.** *abbrev* : Gabon (IVR); Gauss; German (as in **G-agents** below); giga-; good; gourde; Government (as in **G-man** below); grand (1000 dollars); Group of (as in **G5**, etc below).
□ **G'-agents** *n pl* highly effective poisonous gases developed by the Nazis for possible military use. **G5**, **G7**, **G8**, **G10**, **G20**, etc *n* Group of Five, Seven, Eight, Ten, Twenty, etc (qv under **group**). **G'-man** *n* (*US*) an agent of the Federal Bureau of Investigation. **G'-spot** *n* (short for **Gräfenberg spot**, after Ernst Gräfenberg, German-born gynaecologist, 1881–1957) an exceptionally sensitive and erogenous area of the front wall of the vagina; any area of great sensitivity.

G *symbol* : (as a medieval Roman numeral) 400; (also *G*) the constant of gravitation, the factor linking force with mass and distance; (also *G*) conductance (*phys*); general intelligence.

Ḡ *symbol* : (medieval Roman numeral) 400000.

g or **g.** *abbrev* : gallon(s); good; gram(s) or gramme(s).

g *symbol* : acceleration due to gravity.
□ **g'-suit** *n* a close-fitting suit with cells that inflate to prevent flow of blood away from the head, worn by airmen as a defence against blackout due to high acceleration and resultant great increase in weight.

GA *abbrev* : General Assembly; general average; Georgia (US state; also **Ga.**).

Ga (*chem*) *symbol* : gallium.

GAAP (*finance*) *abbrev* : generally accepted accounting principles.

gab¹ /gab/ (*inf*) *vi* (**gabb'ing**; **gabbed**) to chatter or prate. ◆ *n* idle or fluent talk; the mouth. [Origin doubtful; poss variant of **gob¹**]
■ **gabb'er** *n* a chatterer. **gabb'y** *adj* garrulous.
□ **gab'fest** *n* (*sl*; chiefly *US*) a gathering characterized by much talk or gossip; a prolonged conversation, discussion, etc.
■ **the gift of the gab** a talent (or propensity) for talking.

gab² /gab/ (*obs*) *n* mockery; a jest; a vaunt or boast. ◆ *vi* to brag. [OFr *gabber* to mock]

gab³ /gab/ *n* a Scots form of **gob¹**.

GABA *abbrev* : gamma-aminobutyric acid, a neurotransmitter that occurs naturally in the brain.

gabardine see **gaberdine**.

gabba /gab'ə/ *n* a style of electronic dance music with a very fast heavy rhythm. [Poss imit]

gabbart /gab'ərt/ (*esp Scot*) *n* a barge (also **gabb'ard**). [Fr *gabare*, from Provençal and Ital *gabarra*]

gabble /gab'l/ *vi* to talk inarticulately; to chatter; to cackle like geese. ◆ *n* a noise as of unintelligible chatter. [Perh frequentative of **gab¹**, perh MDu *gabbelen*; imit]
■ **gabb'ler** *n*. **gabb'ling** or **gabb'lement** *n*.

gabbro /gab'rō/ *n* (*pl* **gabb'ros**) a coarsely crystalline igneous rock composed of labradorite or similar plagioclase and pyroxene, often with olivine and magnetite. [Ital]
■ **gabbro'ic** or **gabbroitic** /-it'ik/ *adj*. **gabb'roid** *adj* resembling gabbro.

gabelle /ga-bel'/ *n* a tax, *esp* formerly in France, on salt. [Fr *gabelle*, from LL *gabella*, *gablum*; of Gmc origin]
■ **gabell'er** *n* a collector of gabelle.

gaberdine or **gabardine** /gab-ər-dēn'/ or /gab'ər-dēn/ *n* a closely woven twill fabric, *esp* of cotton and wool; a coat of this material; *orig* a loose cloak, worn *esp* by Jews (*hist*). [OFr *gauvardine* a loose garment; perh MHGer *wallevart* pilgrimage, whence also Sp *gabardina*, etc]

gaberlunzie /gab-ər-lün'i or -yi, and later -lun'zi/ (*Scot*) *n* a beggar's pouch; a strolling beggar, *orig* a bluegown (qv under **blue¹**).

gabfest see under **gab¹**.

gabion /gā'bi-ən/ *n* a wickerwork or wire basket of earth or stones used for embankment work, etc in fortification and engineering; a small curiosity (*Walter Scott*). [Fr, from Ital *gabbione* a large cage, from *gabbia*, from L *cavea* a cage]
■ **gā'bionade** *n* a fortification made from gabions. **gā'bionage** *n* gabions collectively. **gā'bioned** *adj* furnished with gabions.

gable /gā'bl/ (*archit*) *n* (also *Scot*) **gā'vel**) the triangular part of an exterior wall of a building between the top of the side-walls and the slopes on the roof; a gable-shaped structure over a window or door. [The northern form *gavel* is prob ON *gafl*; Swed *gafvel*, Dan *gavl*; the southern form *gable* is prob through OFr *gable*, from ON *gafl*]
■ **gā'bled** *adj*. **gā'blet** *n* (*dimin*) a small gable over a niche, buttress, tabernacle, etc.
□ **gable end** *n* the end wall of a building on the side where there is a gable. **gable window** *n* a window in a gable end; a window with its upper part shaped like a gable.

gabnash /gab'nash/ (*Scot*) *n* prattle; chatter; a cheeky chatterbox. [Cf **nashgab**]

Gabonese /gab-ə-nēz'/ *adj* of or relating to the republic of *Gabon* in W Africa, or its inhabitants. ◆ *n* (*pl* **Gabonese'**) a native or citizen of Gabon.

gaboon /gə-boon'/ *n* a W African hardwood of the genus *Aucoumea*. [*Gaboon*, former name of Gabon]
□ **gaboon viper** *n* an extremely venomous African snake (*Bitis gabonica*).

gaby /gā'bi/ (*dialect*) *n* a simpleton. [Origin unknown]

gad¹ /gad/ *n* a miner's wedge or chisel; a metal spike or pointed bar (*obs*); a spear (also **gade** or **gaid** /gād/; *obs*); an engraver's stylus (*Shakesp*); a rod or stick (*obs*); a goad (*dialect*); a bar across a Scottish condemned cell, to which the shackles were fastened (*hist*). [ON *gaddr* a spike; confused with OE *gād*; see **goad**]
■ **gad'ling** *n* (*obs*) one of the spikes on the knuckles of a gauntlet.
■ **upon the gad** (*Shakesp*) on the spur of the moment.

gad² /gad/ *interj* (also with *cap*) a euphemistic form of **God**.
□ **gadzooks'** *interj* (*archaic*) an obsolete mild oath (*appar* for *God's hooks*; see **gadso**).

gad³ /gad/ *vi* (**gadd'ing**; **gadd'ed**) to wander about, often restlessly, idly or in pursuit of pleasure (often with *about*); to straggle; to rush here and there in a wayward uncontrolled manner (*obs*). ◆ *n* wandering, gadding about. [Back-formation from OE *gædeling* companion, later vagabond]
■ **gadd'er** *n*.
□ **gad'about** *n* a person who wanders restlessly from place to place, or who goes about idly looking for amusement, etc.

Gadarene /gad'ə-rēn/ *adj* indicative of mass panic and headlong flight towards disaster. [From the swine of *Gadara*, Bible, Matthew 8.28]

gade see **gad¹** and **Gadus**.

gadfly /gad'flī/ *n* a bloodsucking fly (genus *Tabanus*) that attacks cattle; sometimes applied to a botfly; a mischievous gadabout; someone who provokes and irritates, *esp* deliberately. [**gad¹** or OE *gād* (see **goad**) and **fly**]

gadge /gaj/ (*Browning*) *n* an instrument of torture.

gadget /gaj'it/ *n* any small ingenious device; a what-d'you-call-it; a widget whose use is restricted to certain websites (*comput*). [Origin obscure]

■ words derived from main entry word; □ compound words; ■ idioms and phrasal verbs

■ **gadgeteer**¹ *n* someone who delights in gadgets. **gad'getry** *n* gadgets; the making of gadgets. **gad'gety** *adj*.

gadgie, **gadje** /gaj'i/, **gaudgie** or **gauje** /gö'ji/ (*dialect*; *usu derog*) *n* a person. [Orig variants of **gorgio**]

Gadhel /gad'əl/ *n* a Gael, a Celt of the branch to which the Irish, the Scottish Highlanders, and the Manx belong (see also **Gael** and **Goidel**). [Ir *Gaedheal* (pl *Gaedhil*)]
■ **Gadhelic** /-el'ik, -ēl'ik or gad'/ *adj* relating to the Gaels (the Celts of Ireland, the Highlands of Scotland, and the Isle of Man) or their languages. ◆*n* the Q-Celtic languages of this group; the Celtic language group to which Irish, Scottish Gaelic and Manx belong.

gadi /gä'dē or gud'ē/ *n* an Indian throne. [Marathi *gādī*, Bengali *gadī*]

Gadidae see **Gadus**.

gadje see **gadgie**.

gadling¹ /gad'ling/ (*obs*) *n* a vagabond. [OE *gædeling*, orig companion]

gadling² see under **gad**¹.

gado-gado /gä'dō-gä'dō/ *n* a SE Asian dish of mixed vegetables, hard-boiled egg and peanut sauce. [Malay, mixed up, disorderly]

gadoid see under **Gadus**.

gadolinite /gad'ə-lin-īt/ *n* a silicate of yttrium, beryllium and iron. [J *Gadolin* (1760–1852), Finnish chemist]
■ **gadolin'ium** *n* a rare-earth element (symbol **Gd**; atomic no 64).

gadroon or **godroon** /gə-droon'/ *n* an embossed, bead- or cable-like decoration used as an edging on silverware, etc. [Fr *godron*]
■ **gadrooned**¹ or **godrooned**¹ *adj*. **gadroon'ing** or **godroon'ing** *n*.

gadsman /gadz'mən/ (*obs Scot*) *n* a person who drives horses at the plough. [**gad**¹, or OE *gād* (see **goad**), and **man**]

gadso /gad'sō/ (*archaic*) *interj* expressing surprise. [Ital *cazzo* the penis, assimilated to **gad**²]

Gadus /gā'dəs/ *n* the cod genus, typical of the family **Gadidae** /gad'i-dē/. [Latinized from Gr *gados* the hake or similar fish]
■ **gade** or **gad'oid** *n* a fish of the genus *Gadus*, to which the cod and hake belong. **gad'oid** *adj* belonging to, or resembling, this genus.

gadwall /gad'wöl/ *n* a northern freshwater duck. [Origin unknown]

gadzooks see under **gad**².

gae¹ /gā/ a Scots form of **go**¹.

gae² see **gie**¹.

Gaea /gī'ə or jē'ə/, **Gaia** /gī'ə or gä'ə/ or **Ge** /gä or jē/ *n* in Greek mythology, the goddess or personification of Earth, mother of Uranus and (by him) of Oceanus, Cronus and the Titans; (*usu* **Gaia**) Earth apprehended as a living entity within the solar system. [Gr]
❏ **Gaea** or **Gaia hypothesis** *n* the hypothesis stating that natural life systems find their own balances.

Gaekwar, **Gaikwar** or **Guicowar** /gī'kwär/ *n* the title given to the ruler of the former Indian state of Baroda. [Marathi *gāekwār* cowherd]

Gael /gāl/ *n* a Celt of the Scottish Highlands, Ireland or the Isle of Man, *esp* one who speaks Gaelic (see also **Goidel**). [Scottish Gaelic *Gaidheal*]
■ **Gael'dom** *n*. **Gaelic** /gāl'ik or gal'ik/ *adj* relating to the Gaels or their languages; relating to sports, such as shinty and hurling, played especially in, or originating in, Ireland and the Scottish Highlands. ◆*n* any of the Celtic languages of Ireland, the Scottish Highlands and the Isle of Man, *esp* (*usu* /gal'ik/) that of the Scottish Highlands. **gael'icism** /-sizm/ *n*. **gael'icize** or **-ise** /-sīz/ *vt*.
❏ **Gaelic coffee** same as **Irish coffee** (see under **Irish**). **Gaelic football** *n* a form of football, played mainly in Ireland, between teams of fifteen players, using a round ball which may be kicked, bounced or punched, but not thrown or run with.

Gael. *abbrev*: Gaelic.

Gaeltacht /gāl'tähht/ *n* the Irish-speaking districts of Ireland. [Ir *gaedhealtacht*]

gaff¹ /gaf/ *n* a hook used *esp* for landing large fish; the spar to which the head of a fore-and-aft sail is fastened (*naut*). ◆*vt* to hook or bind by means of a gaff. [Fr *gaffe*]
❏ **gaff'-rigged** *adj* (of a vessel) having a gaff. **gaff sail** *n* a sail attached to the gaff. **gaff'-topsail** *n* a small sail, the head of which is extended on a small gaff which hoists on the top mast, and the foot on the lower gaff.

gaff² /gaf/ (*sl*) *n* humbug, nonsense. [Prob connected with **gab**² or **gaffe**; cf OE *gegaf-spræc* scurrility]
■ **blow the gaff** to disclose a secret, blab.

gaff³ /gaf/ (*sl*) *n* a low-grade or cheap theatre; a fair; a house or other building, *orig* as the site of a burglary; one's private accommodation, apartment, flat, room, etc. [Origin obscure]

gaff⁴ see **gaffe**.

gaff⁵ /gaf/ (*sl*) *vi* to gamble. [Origin obscure]
■ **gaff'er** *n*. **gaff'ing** *n*.

gaffe or (*rare*) **gaff** /gaf/ *n* a blunder. [Fr *gaffe*]

gaffer¹ /gaf'ər/ *n orig* a word of respect applied to an old man, now *archaic*, *dialect* or *derog* in this sense (*fem* **gammer**); the foreman of a squad of workmen; loosely applied to any manager; (*orig US*) the senior electrician responsible for the lighting in a television or film studio; a master glass-blower. [**grandfather** or **godfather**]
❏ **gaffer tape** *n* a type of strong adhesive tape.

gaffer², **gaffing** see under **gaff**⁵.

gag¹ /gag/ *vt* (**gagg'ing**; **gagged**) to stop up the mouth of forcibly; to silence; to prevent free expression by (the press, etc); to choke up. ◆*vi* to choke; to retch. ◆*n* something put into the mouth or over it to enforce silence (also *fig*), or to distend jaws during an operation; the closure applied in a debate; a nauseous mouthful, boiled fat beef (*Lamb*). [Prob imitative of sound made in choking]
■ **gagg'er** *n* a person who gags.
❏ **gag'-bit** *n* a powerful bit used in breaking horses. **gagging order** *n* a court order forbidding the public discussion or reporting in the media of a current case. **gag'-rein** *n* a rein arranged so as to make the bit more powerful.
■ **gagging for** (*inf*) eagerly desirous of.

gag² /gag/ (*inf*) *n* a joke; a hoax; an actor's (*esp* comic) interpolation or improvisation of his or her part. ◆*vi* (**gagg'ing**; **gagged**) to introduce a gag; to joke, make gags. ◆*vt* to introduce a gag into. [Poss **gag**¹]
■ **gag'ster** *n* (*inf*) a person who tells jokes, a comedian.
❏ **gag'man** *n* a person who writes gags; a comedian.

gag³ /gag/ (*sl*) *vt* to deceive. ◆*vi* to practise deception or fraud. ◆*n* a made-up story, lie. [Poss **gag**¹]

gaga /gä'gä/ (*sl*) *adj* fatuous; in senile dotage; (with *about* or *over*) wildly enthusiastic. [Fr]

gagaku /gä-gä'koo or gä'gä-/ *n* a type of Japanese classical music played mainly on ceremonial occasions at the Japanese court. [Jap, from *ga* graceful, noble, and *gaku* music]

gage¹ /gāj/ *n* a pledge (*archaic*); something thrown down as a challenge, *esp* a glove (*hist*). ◆*vt* to bind by pledge or security (*obs*); to offer as a guarantee (*obs*); to stake, wager (*obs* or *archaic*). [OFr *guage*; Gmc; see **wage**, **wed**]

gage² see **gauge**.

gage³ /gāj/ *n* same as **greengage**.

gage⁴ /gāj/ (*drug sl*) *n* marijuana (also **gauge**).

G-agents see under **G** (*abbrev*).

gaggle /gag'l/ *n* a flock of geese on water or land, in contrast to a *skein* in the air; a group or knot, *usu* of garrulous or animated people. ◆*vi* to cackle. [Prob imit]
■ **gagg'ling** *n* cackling. ◆*adj* garrulous.

gag-tooth /gag'tooth/ *n* a projecting tooth.
■ **gag'-toothed** *adj*.

gahnite /gä'nīt/ *n* (*mineralogy*) a zinc spinel. [JG *Gahn* (1745–1818), Swedish chemist]

Gaia see **Gaea**.

gaid see **gad**¹.

Gaidhealtachd /gä'yal-tähht/ *n* the Gaelic-speaking districts of Scotland. [Gaelic]

gaiety see under **gay**.

gaijin /gī'jēn or -jin/ (*Jap*) *n* (pl **gai'jin**) a foreigner.

Gaikwar see **Gaekwar**.

gai lan /gī län/ *n* a type of cabbage similar to broccoli (also called **Chinese broccoli**, **Chinese kale**). [Chin (Cantonese)]

gaillard or **gaillarde** /gal'yərd/ obsolete spellings of **galliard**.

gaillardia /gā-lär'di-ə/ *n* a N American plant of the genus *Gaillardia*. [*Gaillard* de Marentonneau, 18c French botanist]

gaily see under **gay**.

gain¹ /gān/ *vt* to obtain to one's advantage; to earn; to win; to be successful in; to increase (eg speed, weight, height, momentum); to attract to one's own group or side; to reach. ◆*vi* to profit; to become or appear better, progress; (of a clock, etc) to go fast by so much in a given time. ◆*n* that which is gained; profit; an instance of gaining, a win; the ratio of actual power delivered to that which would be delivered if an amplifier were not used (*telecom*); the ratio of output and input voltages (*telecom*); (also **gain control**) a volume control in an amplifier or receiving set, *usu* a potentiometer (*telecom*). [OFr *gain*, *gaain*, *gaigner*, *gaaignier*, from Gmc, as in OHGer *weidenen* to graze, to seek forage, and *weida* pasture]
■ **gain'able** *adj*. **gain'er** *n*. **gain'ful** *adj* lucrative; profitable; engaged in for pay, paid. **gain'fully** *adv*. **gain'fulness** *n*. **gain'ings** *n pl*. **gain'less** *adj*. **gain'lessness** *n*.

❏ **gain'-sharing** *n* a scheme which rewards employees for improved company performance. **gain'-up** *n* a switch on a camcorder or video camera used in poor light to increase the exposure. ■ **gain ground** to grow in influence, become more widely accepted. **gain on** or **upon** to get closer to, catch up on; to overtake by degrees; to increase one's advantage against. **gain time** to get extra time by delaying.

gain² /gān/ (*dialect*) *adj* near, straight; convenient. [ON *gegn*]

gaingiving /gān'gi-ving/ (*Shakesp*) *n* misgiving.

gainly /gān'li/ (*dialect*) *adj* shapely; comely; graceful. [**gain²**]

gainsay /gān'sā or gān-sā'/ *vt* (*prp* **gain'saying** (or /-sā'/); *pat* and *pap* **gainsaid** /gān' or gān-sād', -sed'/; *3rd pers sing pres indicative* **gainsays** /-sāz/) to contradict; to deny; to dispute. ◆ *n* denial. [OE *gegn* against, and **say¹**] ■ **gainsay'er** *n* (*Bible*) an opposer. **gainsay'ing** *n*.

gainst or **'gainst** /genst/ a poetic abbreviation of **against**.

gainstrive /gān-strīv'/ (*obs*) *vt* to strive against. ◆ *vi* to resist.

gair /gār/ (*Scot*) *n* a gore (of cloth or land). [See **gore²**]

gairfowl same as **garefowl**.

gait¹ /gāt/ *n* a way of walking; the pattern of leg movements used by a horse in trotting, cantering, galloping, etc. ◆ *vt* to teach (a horse) its gaits. [**gate²**] ■ **-gaited** *combining form* having a particular gait, eg *slow-gaited*.

gait² /gāt/ (*dialect*) *n* a sheaf of corn set on end.

gait³ or **gaitt** (*Walter Scott*) spellings of **get** (a child) and **gyte²**.

gaita /gī'tə/ *n* a Spanish bagpipe. [Sp and Port]

gaiter /gā'tər/ *n* a covering for the (lower leg and) ankle, fitting over the upper of the shoe. [Fr *guêtre*] ■ **gait'ered** *adj*.

gaitt see **gait³**.

gajo see **gorgio**.

gak /gak/ (*sl*) *n* cocaine. [Perh from earlier *gack*, a disgusting substance; cf **guck**]

Gal. (*Bible*) *abbrev* : (the Letter to the) Galatians.

gal¹ /gal/ dialect for **girl**. ❏ **gal pal** *n* a female friend.

gal² /gal/ (*phys*; also with *cap*) *n* a unit of acceleration, one centimetre per second per second. [*Gal*ileo; see **Galilean¹**]

gal. *abbrev* : gallon(s).

gala /gä'lə or gā'lə/ *n* a festivity; a sporting occasion, with competitions, etc. ◆ *adj* of the nature of, or suitable for, a great occasion or festivity. [Fr *gala* show, from Ital *gala* finery] ❏ **ga'la-dress** *n* festive costume for a gala day.

galabiah, galabiyah see **gallabea(h)**.

galactic¹ /gə-lak'tik/ *adj* (*med*) relating to or obtained from milk. [Gr *gala, galaktos* milk] ■ **galac'tagogue** /-tə-gog/ *n* (Gr *agōgos* bringing) a medicine that promotes secretion of milk. **galactom'eter** *n* (Gr *metron* measure) an instrument for calculating the specific gravity of milk. **galactoph'orous** *adj* (Gr *phoros* bringing; *zool*) milk-carrying. **galactopoiet'ic** *adj* (Gr *poiētikos* productive) milk-producing. **galactorrhoea** /-rē'ə/ *n* (Gr *rhoiā* a flow; *med*) a too abundant flow of milk. **galactosaemia** /-sēm'i-ə/ *n* (*med*) the presence of galactose in the blood. **galac'tose** *n* a sugar ($C_6H_{12}O_6$) obtained by hydrolysis from lactose.

galactic² see under **galaxy**.

galactico /gə-lak'ti-kō/ (*inf*) *n* (*pl* **galac'ticos**) an internationally famous footballer. [Sp, galactic]

galage /gə-lāj'/ an obsolete form of **galosh** (*n*).

galago /gä-lä'gō/ *n* (*pl* **gala'gos**) a large-eared, long-tailed nocturnal African loris of the genus *Galago*, a bushbaby. [Perh Wolof *golokh* monkey]

galah /gə-lä'/ *n* an Australian cockatoo with a grey back and pink underparts; a fool (*Aust sl*). [From an Aboriginal language]

Galahad /gal'ə-had/ *n* a person notable for nobility and integrity of character. [From Sir *Galahad* in Arthurian legend, the noblest knight of the Round Table]

Galam butter /gä-läm' but'ər/ *n* shea butter. [*Galam*, a district in Senegal]

galanga, galangal see **galingale**.

galant /gə-länt'/ *adj* of a musical style, current in the 18c, characterized by lightness, elegance and technical accomplishment. [Fr]

galantamine /ga-lan'tə-mēn/ *n* a tertiary amine compound, *orig* derived from flowers, *esp* daffodils and snowdrops, used as a drug in treating dementia. [*Galanthus*, snowdrop genus, and **amine**]

galantine /gal'ən-tēn or -tin/ *n* a dish of poultry, veal, etc served cold in jelly. [Fr; see **gelatine**]

galanty show /gə-lan'ti shō/ *n* a performance of shadow puppets. [Prob Ital *galanti*, pl of *galante*; see **gallant**]

galapago /gə-lap'ə-gō/ *n* (*pl* **galap'agos**) a tortoise. [Sp]

galatea /gal-ə-tē'ə/ *n* a cotton fabric *usu* with coloured stripe. [After HMS *Galatea*, 19c ship]

galaxy /gal'ək-si/ *n* (with *cap* and *the*) the disc-shaped system, composed of spiralling arms of stars, that contains our solar system near its edge; any similar system; a splendid assemblage. [Through Fr and L, from Gr *galaxias* the Milky Way (*orig* also the meaning of **galaxy**), from *gala, -aktos* milk] ■ **galac'tic** *adj* relating to a galaxy or galaxies. ❏ **galactic halo** *n* (*astron*) an aggregation of stars, globular clusters, dust and gas surrounding a galaxy. **galactic plane** *n* the plane that passes through the centre of the bulging disc formed by the spiral arms of the Galaxy.

galbanum /gal'bə-nəm/ *n* an aromatic gum-resin obtained from several umbelliferous Asian plants. [L, from Gr *chalbanē*, prob from an Asian language]

galdragon /gal'drə-gən/ (*Walter Scott*) *n* an obsolete Shetland word for a sorceress or witch. [ON *galdra-kona*, from *galdr* crowing, incantation, witchcraft, and *kuna* woman]

gale¹ /gāl/ *n* a wind of force 8 on the Beaufort scale, reaching speeds of 39 to 46mph (*meteorol*); a gentle wind (*old poetic*); a wafted smell (*old poetic*); an outburst (*fig*). [Origin obscure]

gale² /gāl/ *n* (*usu* **sweet'-gale**) bog myrtle. [Prob OE *gagel*; cf Ger *Gagel*]

gale³ /gāl/ *n* a periodic payment of rent; a mining licence; the piece of land for which the licence is granted. [Perh **gavel²**]

galea /gal'i-ə or gā'li-ə/ (*biol*) *n* a helmet-shaped structure. [L *galea* a helmet] ■ **gal'eate** or **gal'eated** *adj*.

galena /gə-lē'nə/ *n* lead sulphide, the commonest ore of lead, occurring as grey cubic crystals (also **galē'nite**). [L *galēna* lead ore] ■ **galē'noid** *adj*.

galengale see **galingale**.

Galenic /gə-len'ik/ *adj* relating to *Galen*, the 2c Greek physician, or to his methods and theories. ■ **Galen'ical** *adj* Galenic. ◆ *n* a remedy such as Galen prescribed, a vegetable simple. **Galenism** /gā'lən-izm/ *n*. **Gā'lenist** *n*.

galenite, galenoid see **galena**.

Galeopithecus /gā-li-ō-pi-thē'kəs or -pith'/ *n* the flying lemur (qv). [Gr *galeē* weasel, marten, and *pithēkos* ape] ■ **galeopithe'cine** /-sīn/ or **galeopithē'coid** *adj*.

galère /ga-ler'/ *n* a group of (*esp* undesirable) people; an unpleasant situation. [Fr, literally, galley]

galette /gə-let'/ *n* a round, flat, sweet or savoury cake; a savoury buckwheat crêpe. [Fr]

Galia melon /gä'li-ə mel'ən/ *n* a small melon with sweet, juicy flesh. [Origin uncertain]

Galician /gə-lith'i-ən, -lis' or -lish'/ *adj* of or relating to the former kingdom, now an autonomous region, of *Galicia* in NW Spain; (not /-lith'/) of or relating to *Galicia*, a region in E central Europe, now partly in Poland, partly in Ukraine. ◆ *n* a native or citizen of Galicia; the dialect language of Galicia in NW Spain, closely related to Portuguese.

Galilean¹ /gal-i-lē'ən/ *adj* of or relating to *Galilee* (L *Galilaea*, Gr *Galilaiā*), one of the Roman divisions of Palestine. ◆ *n* a native of Galilee; a Christian (*archaic*).

Galilean² /gal-i-lē'ən/ *adj* relating to or associated with *Galileo*, the great Italian mathematician (1564–1642).

galilee /gal'i-lē/ (*archit*) *n* a porch or chapel at the west end of some churches, in which penitents were placed, and where ecclesiastics met women who had business with them. [Perh suggested in Bible by Mark 16.7, or Matthew 4.15] ❏ **galilee porch** *n* a galilee in direct communication with the exterior.

galingale /gal'ing-gāl/ *n* (also **galangal** /gal'ən-gal/, **gal'engale** or **galang'a**) the aromatic rootstock of certain East Indian plants of the ginger family (genera *Alpinia* and *Kaempferia*), used like ginger; the rootstock of a sedge (*Cyperus longus*), of ancient medicinal repute; also the whole plant. [OFr *galingal*, from Ar *khalanjān*, from Chin *gāoliàngjiāng*, from *Gāoliàng*, a district near Canton, and *jiāng* ginger]

galiongee /gal-yən-jē'/ n a Turkish sailor. [Turk qālyūnjī, derivative of qālyūn, from Ital galeone galleon]

galiot see **galliot**.

galipot /gal'i-pot/ n the turpentine that exudes from the cluster pine. [Fr]

gall[1] /göl/ n bile, the greenish-yellow fluid secreted from the liver (old); bitterness; ill-will; assurance, presumption, impudence. [OE galla, gealla gall; cf Ger Galle, Gr cholē, L fel]
■ **gall'-less** adj without gall; mild; free from rancour.
▫ **gall bladder** n a muscular sac close to or at the edge of the liver in vertebrates, which stores and concentrates bile, and releases it into the intestine. **gall duct** n a tube for conveying bile or gall. **gall'sickness** or **gall'-sickness** n (Du galziekte ; S Afr) a tick-borne disease affecting the livers of cattle, sheep and goats. **gall'stone** n a concretion in the gall bladder or biliary ducts.

gall[2] /göl/ n an abnormal growth on a plant caused by a parasite such as an insect or fungus, or by bacteria. [Fr galle, from L galla oak-apple]
■ **gallate** /gal'āt/ n a salt of gallic acid.
▫ **gallfly** /göl'/ or **gall wasp** n an insect of the hymenopterous family Cynipidae that causes galls by depositing its eggs in plants. **gall midge** n a Cecidomyia or similar gall-making midge. **gall'nut** n a nut-like gall produced on an oak by a gall wasp, used esp formerly for making ink. **gall wasp** see **gallfly** above.

gall[3] /göl/ n a painful swelling, esp in a horse; a sore due to chafing; a state or cause of irritation; a chafed place; a bare place (archaic); a flaw (archaic; Scot); a geological fault or dyke (mining). ◆ vt to hurt by rubbing; to irritate. ◆ vi to become chafed; to scoff (Shakesp). [OE galla, gealla a sore place]
■ **gall'ing** adj irritating. **gall'ingly** adv.

gall. abbrev : gallon(s).

gallabea(h), gallabia(h), gallabieh, gallabiya(h), gallabiyeh, also **galabea(h), galabia(h)**, etc /ga-lä'bi-ya or -bē'a/ n a loose-fitting cloak worn esp by Arabs; a djellaba. [See **djellaba**]

gallant /gal'ənt/ adj brave; noble; gay, splendid, magnificent (rare); attentive (esp formally or obsequiously) to ladies; amorous (sometimes /gə-lant'/ in the last two senses). ◆ n a dashing, debonair young man; a person of fashion (archaic); a lover (also /gə-lant'/ in this sense). [Fr galant, from OFr gale a merrymaking; prob Gmc; cf **gala**]
■ **gall'antly** adv. **gall'antness** n. **gall'antry** n bravery; intrepidity; attention or devotion to ladies; a chivalrous attention or remark; amorous intrigue; gallants collectively (Shakesp).
■ **the honourable and gallant member** a mode of referring in parliament to a member who is an officer in the fighting services.

galleass /gal'i-as/ (hist) n a vessel built like a galley, but larger and heavier (also **gall'iass**). [OFr galeace, from Ital galeazza, augmentative from galea galley]

galleon /gal'i-ən/ n a large vessel with a high stem and stern, mostly used formerly by Spaniards for carrying treasure. [Sp galeón; cf **galley**]

galleria /gal-ə-rē'ə/ n a shopping arcade. [Ital, arcade]

gallery /gal'ə-ri/ n a covered walk; a long balcony; a long passage; a long, narrow room; an upper floor of seats, esp in a theatre, usu the highest; the occupants of the gallery; a body of spectators; a room or building for the exhibition of works of art; a photographer's studio; in a television studio, a soundproof room overlooking the action, for the director or lighting engineer; an underground passage, drift or level. ◆ vt to tunnel. [OFr galerie (Ital galleria)]
■ **gall'eried** adj furnished with, or made in the form of, a gallery or arcade. **gall'eryite** n a person who frequents the gallery in the theatre.
■ **play to the gallery** to play for the applause of, or seek popularity with, the least cultured and least sophisticated section of one's audience.

gallet /gal'ət/ (building, etc) n a small pebble or stone chip. ◆ vt (**gall'eting**; **gall'eted**) to fill in mortar joints with gallets. [Fr galet a pebble, from OFr gal]

galley /gal'i/ n a long, low-built ship with one deck, propelled by oars and sails; a Greek or Roman warship; a large open rowing boat; the cooking area on board a ship, boat or aircraft; a flat oblong tray for type that has been set up (printing); a galley proof (printing). [OFr galie, galee, from LL galea]
▫ **gall'ey-foist** n (obs) a state barge. **galley kitchen** n a kitchen longer than it is wide, with cupboards and appliances on both sides. **galley proof** n the first proof taken after text has been typeset (traditionally from type on a galley) and before it is made up into pages, a slip-proof; in photocomposition, an early proof before make-up. **galley slave** n a person condemned to work as a slave at the oar of a galley (hist; also fig); a drudge. **gall'ey-worm** n a myriapod.

galley-west /gal-i-west'/ (US sl) adv into confusion or unconsciousness. [Eng dialect collywest, perh from the Northamptonshire village of Collyweston]

galliambic /gal-i-am'bik/ adj in or of a metre (⌣⌣-⌣-⌣--/⌣⌣--⌣⌣) said to have been used by the Phrygian priests of Cybele, best known from the Attis of Catullus. [Gr galliambikos, from Gallos a priest of Cybele, and iambos an iamb]
■ **galliam'bics** n pl galliambic verses.

Galliano® /gal-yä'nō/ n an Italian liqueur flavoured with anise. [Giuseppe Galliano, 19c Italian soldier]

galliard /gal'yərd/ adj (archaic) brisk, lively. ◆ n a spirited dance for two, in triple time, common in the 16c and 17c; a lively, fashionable person (archaic). [OFr gaillard]
■ **gall'iardise** /-ēz or -īz/ n (archaic) gaiety; a merry trick.

galliass see **galleass**.

galli-bagger, -beggar, etc see under **gally**.

Gallic /gal'ik/ adj relating to France or the French; relating to Gaul or the ancient Gauls. [L Gallus a Gaul; Gallicus Gaulish]
■ **Gall'ican** adj of or relating to Gallicanism; esp relating to the Roman Catholic Church in France, regarded as national and more or less independent. ◆ n a person holding Gallican doctrines. **Gall'icanism** n the spirit of nationalism within the French Church, as opposed to **Ultramontanism** the absolute subjection of everything to the personal authority of the Pope. **Gallice** /gal'i-sē, gal'i-kā/ adv (L) in French. **Gall'icism** n (also without cap) an expression or idiom peculiar to French occurring as a use in another language. **Gall'icize** or **-ise** vt and vi (also without cap) to assimilate or conform to French habits, etc.

gallic /gal'ik/ adj of, from, relating to, occurring in, etc plant galls. [Fr gallique, from galle **gall**[2]]
▫ **gallic acid** n a crystalline substance present in gallnuts, tea, and various plants, and obtained by hydrolysis from tannin.

galligaskins /gal-i-gas'kinz/ n pl wide hose or breeches worn in the 16c and 17c; leggings. [OFr garguesque, from Ital grechesco Greekish, from L graecus Greek]

gallimaufry /gal-i-mö'fri/ n any inconsistent or absurd medley; a miscellaneous gathering. [Fr galimafrée a ragout, hash]

gallinaceous /gal-in-ā'shəs/ adj of or relating to the order of birds that includes grouse, pheasants and the domestic fowl. [L gallīna a hen, from gallus a cock]

gallinazo /gal-i-nä'zō/ n (pl **gallina'zos**) a turkey buzzard or other vulture. [Sp, from gallina, from L gallīna hen]

galling see under **gall**[3].

gallinule /gal'i-nūl/ n a waterhen, moorhen. [L gallīnula a chicken, from gallīna a hen]

Gallio /gal'i-ō/ n (pl **Gall'ios**) a person who keeps himself or herself free from trouble and responsibility. [From Gallio, Bible, Acts 18.12–17]

galliot or **galiot** /gal'i-ət/ n a small galley; an old Dutch cargo boat. [Fr galiote, from LL galea galley]

gallipot /gal'i-pot/ n a small glazed pot, esp for medicine. [Prob a **pot** brought in a **galley**]

gallise, gallisize see **gallize**.

gallium /gal'i-əm/ n a metallic element (symbol **Ga**; atomic no 31), as gallium arsenide an important semiconductor. [L gallus a cock, from the discoverer's name, Lecoq de Boisbaudran, or Gallia Gaul, France, his country]

gallivant /gal'-i-vant or gal-i-vant'/ vi to spend time frivolously, esp in flirting; to gad about. [Perh **gallant**]

gallivat /gal'i-vat/ n a large two-masted Malay boat. [Port galeota; see **galliot**]

galliwasp /gal'i-wosp/ n a West Indian lizard. [Origin unknown]

gallize or **-ise** /gal'īz/ vt (in wine-making) to bring to standard proportions by adding water and sugar to inferior must (also **gall'isize** or **-ise**). [Ger gallisieren, from the name of the inventor, Ludwig Gall (1791–1863)]

gallnut see under **gall**[2].

Gallo- /gal-ō-/ combining form signifying France or Gaul, as in Gallo-Roman. [**Gallic**]
■ **Galloma'nia** n enthusiasm for things French, Francomania. **Gall'ophil** or **Gall'ophile** n a person who has a fondness for what is French, a Francophile. **Gall'ophobe** n a person who dislikes or fears what is French, a Francophobe. **Gallophō'bia** n.

galloglass or **gallowglass** /gal'ō-glas/ n a soldier or armed retainer of a chief in ancient Ireland and other Celtic countries. [Ir gallóglach, from gall foreign, and óglach soldier]

gallon /gal'ən/ n a unit of capacity, in Britain equal to 4.546 litres (277.4 cubic inches), also called **imperial gallon**, in the USA equal to 3.785 litres (231 cubic inches). [ONFr galun, galon (OFr jalon)]
■ **gall'onage** n an amount in gallons; the rate of use in gallons.

galloon¹ /gə-*loon*'/ n a kind of lace; a narrow tapelike trimming or binding material, sometimes made with gold or silver thread. [Fr *galon, galonner*; prob cognate with **gallant**]
■ **gallooned**' adj adorned with galloon.

galloon² /gə-*loon*'/ (obs) n a variant of **galleon**.

gallop /*gal*'əp/ vi to go at a gallop; to ride a galloping animal; to move very fast. ◆ vt to cause to gallop. ◆ n the fastest pace of a horse, etc, at each stride of which all four feet are off the ground; a ride at a gallop; a fast pace (fig); a track for galloping or exercising horses. [OFr *galoper, galop*; prob Gmc; cf **wallop**]
■ **gall'oper** n someone who, or that which, gallops; an aide-de-camp (old milit); (esp in pl) a fairground merry-go-round with wooden horses that rise and fall in imitation of galloping. **gall'oping** adj proceeding at a gallop; advancing rapidly, as in *galloping consumption* (fig).
❑ **galloping inflation** n hyperinflation.
▪ **Canterbury gallop** a moderate gallop of a horse (see **canter**).

gallopade /gal-ə-*pād*'/ n a quick kind of dance; the music appropriate to it; a sideways gallop. ◆ vi to move briskly; to perform a gallopade. [Fr]

Gallophil, Gallophile, Gallophobe, etc see under **Gallo-**.

Gallovidian /gal-ō-*vid*'i-ən/ adj belonging to Galloway in Scotland. ◆ n a native of Galloway. [*Gallovidia*, Latinized from Welsh *Gallwyddel*]

gallow /*gal*'ō/ (Shakesp) vt to frighten. [OE *āgælwan* to frighten, to astonish]

Galloway /*gal*'ō-wā/ n a small strong horse, 13–15 hands high; a pit pony (NE Eng); a breed of large black hornless cattle, orig from *Galloway* in Scotland.

Gallowegian see **Galwegian**.

gallowglass see **galloglass**.

gallows /*gal*'ōz or (old) *gal*'əs/ n sing (pl **gall'owses**) a wooden frame for hanging criminals; a person who deserves the gallows (Shakesp and literary); the look of someone destined to hang (Shakesp and literary); any contrivance with posts and a crossbeam for suspending things (obs); a rest for the tympan of a hand printing press (obs); the main frame of a beam-engine; (also **gallows frame**) a headframe; one of a pair of trouser braces (dialect). —The plural form **gal'owses** is used by Shakespeare in the first sense above; various Scottish and dialect spellings of the plural are found, eg **gall'uses** for trouser braces. ◆ adj (often **gall'us**) deserving the gallows; villainous (Scot and dialect); mischievous, wild, unmanageable (Scot and dialect); impudent, saucy, tiresome (Scot and dialect); plucky, daring (Scot and dialect); perky, spirited, sprightly (Scot and dialect); in some dialects, a mere intensive. ◆ adv (often **gall'us**) (dialect) damnably, confoundedly. [Orig pl, from ME *galwes*, from OE *galga*; Ger *Galgen*]
■ **gall'owsness** or usu **gall'usness** n (dialect) recklessness, perversity.
❑ **gall'ows-bird** n a person who deserves hanging or has been hanged. **gall'ows-foot** n the space at the foot of the gallows. **gall'ows-free** adj free from the danger of hanging. **gallows humour** n grim, sardonic humour. **gall'ows-lee** n the place of hanging. **gall'ows-maker** n. **gall'ows-ripe**' adj ready for the gallows. **gallows'-tree** n a gallows.
■ **cheat the gallows** to deserve but escape hanging.

gallstone see under **gall**¹.

gallumph see **galumph**.

Gallup poll /*gal*'əp *pōl*/ n a method of gauging public opinion by questioning suitably distributed sample individuals, devised by George Horace *Gallup* (1901–84).

gallus /*gal*'əs/ an old, Scottish or dialect spelling of **gallows**.

gally /*gal*'i/ (dialect or whaling) vi to scare, daze. [**gallow**]
❑ **gall'y-bagger, -beggar** or **-crow** n (dialect; also **galli-**) a scarecrow.

galoche see **galosh**.

galoot /gə-*loot*'/ (sl, orig and esp US) n a clumsy or inept fellow; an inexperienced soldier or marine. [Orig nautical slang]

galop /*gal*'əp or gə-*lop*'/ n a lively dance or dance tune in double time; a lively sideways slipping step used in dancing. ◆ vi to dance a galop; to perform a lively sideways slipping step. [Fr; cf **gallop**]

galopin /*gal*'ə-pin/ (obs) n an errand boy (Walter Scott); a kitchen boy. [Fr]

galore /gə-*lōr*' or -*lör*'/ adv in abundance. [Ir *go* (an adverbializing particle) and *leór* sufficient]

galosh, golosh or **galoche** /gə-*losh*'/ n a piece running round a shoe or boot above the sole; an overshoe; a rustic shoe, sandal or clog (obs). ◆ vt to provide (a shoe, etc) with a galosh. [Fr *galoche*, from prob LL *gallicula* small Gaulish shoe]

galowses same as **gallowses** (see **gallows**).

galravage, galravitch see **gilravage**.

galtonia /göl-*tō*'ni-ə or *gal*-/ n any bulbous plant of genus *Galtonia*, native to southern Africa, esp *G. candicans*, the Cape hyacinth. [Named after Sir Francis *Galton* (1822–1911), British scientist]

galumph or **gallumph** /gə-*lumf*'/ vi to stride along exultantly; to bound about in a noisy, ungainly way. [A coinage of Lewis Carroll]
■ **galum'pher** n.

galut or **galuth** /gä-*loot*' or gö'ləs/ n (often with cap) a forced exile of Jews, esp (diaspora) from Palestine. [Heb *gālūth* exile]

galvanism /*gal*'və-ni-zm/ n the production of an electric current by chemical means, as in a battery; medical treatment by electric currents; current electricity (obs). [Luigi *Galvani* (1737–98), Italian discoverer of galvanism]
■ **galvanic** /-*van*'/ adj relating to the production of an electric current by chemical means, esp the action of an acid on a metal; (of a response, behaviour, etc) sudden, startling or convulsive, as though produced by an electric shock; of, producing or produced by galvanism (obs). **galvan'ically** adv. **gal'vanist** n. **galvanizā'tion** or **-s-** n. **gal'vanize** or **-ise** vt to subject to the action of an electric current; to stimulate to spasmodic action by, or as if by, an electric shock; to confer a false vitality upon; to coat with metal by an electric current; to coat with zinc without using a current. **gal'vanizer** or **-s-** n. **galvanom'eter** n an instrument for measuring electric currents. **galvanomet'ric** adj. **galvanom'etry** n. **galvanoplas'tic** adj (obs). **galvanoplas'ty** n (obs) electrodeposition. **galvan'oscope** n an instrument for detecting electric currents.
❑ **galvanic battery** or **cell** n (obs) an electric battery or cell. **galvanic belt** n (obs) a belt supposed to benefit the wearer by producing an electric current. **galvanic skin response** n a change in the electrical conductivity of the skin, recorded by a polygraph, due to any of various emotional stimuli. **galvanized iron** n iron coated with zinc to deter rust.

Galwegian /gal-*wē*'ji-ən/ adj belonging to Galloway in Scotland (also **Gallowē'gian**), or of Galway in Ireland. ◆ n a native of either place. [On the analogy of *Norwegian*]

gam¹ /gam/ n a collective noun for whales, a school; a social visit (esp between whalers) at sea (old US). ◆ vi to associate in a gam. ◆ vt (old US; specif of whalers) to call on, exchange courtesies with. [Ety dubious]

gam² /gam/ (Scot) n a tooth or tusk; the mouth.

gam³ /gam/ (sl) n a human leg, esp female. [Perh Fr dialect *gambe* leg]

gam⁴ /gam/ (vulgar sl) n and vi (to practise) oral sex. [Fr *gamahuche* or *gamaruche*, term popularized through the Services]

-gam- /-*gam*-/ or **gamo-** /*gam*-ō- or *gam*-o-/ combining form signifying: marriage; union; reproduction or fertilization. [Gr *gamos* marriage]
■ **gamogen'esis** n sexual reproduction. **gamopet'alous** adj with petals united. **gamophyll'ous** adj with perianth leaves united. **gamosep'alous** adj with sepals united. **gamotrop'ic** adj. **gamot'ropism** n the tendency of gametes to attract each other. **-gamous** adj combining form denoting: having a stated number of spouses, as in *bigamous*; relating to a stated means of fertilization or reproduction, as in *allogamous*. **-gamy** n combining form denoting: marriage, or supposed marriage, to a stated number of spouses; a stated means of fertilization or reproduction.

gama grass /*gä*'mə gräs/ n a tall N American forage grass (*Tripsacum dactyloides*). [Perh Sp *grama*]

gamash /gə-*mash*'/ (archaic and dialect) n a kind of legging (also **gramash**' or (Walter Scott) **gramoche** /-*osh*'/). [Fr (now dialect) *gamache*, Provençal *garamacha*, appar from *Ghadamis*, in Libya, famous for leather]

gamay /ga-*mā*'/ , also /*gam*'ā/ n a variety of red grape used in making dry red wine, esp of the Beaujolais district; a wine made from this grape. [*Gamay* village in the Beaune district, Côte d'Or, France]

gamb /gamb/ (heraldry) n a beast's whole foreleg. [LL *gamba* a leg]

gamba /*gam*'bə/ (music) n short for **viola da gamba**; an organ stop of stringlike quality. [From *viola da gamba* a cello-like instrument]
■ **gam'bist** n a gamba-player.

gambado¹ /gam-*bā*'dō/ n (pl **gambā'does** or **gambā'dos**) a leather covering or boot attached to a saddle. [Ital *gamba* leg]

gambado² /gam-*bā*'dō/ n (pl **gambā'does** or **gambā'dos**) a bound or spring of a horse (dressage); a fantastic movement, a caper. ◆ vi to frolic, caper. [Sp *gambada*; cf **gambol**]

gambeson /*gam*'bi-sən/ (hist) n an ancient leather or quilted cloth coat worn under the habergeon. [OFr, from OHGer *wamba* belly]

gambet /*gam*'bit/ or **gambetta** /gam-*bet*'ə/ (rare) n the redshank. [Ital *gambetta* ruff; *gambetta fosca* spotted redshank]

Gambian /*gam*'bi-ən/ adj of or relating to The *Gambia* in W Africa, or its inhabitants. ◆ n a native or citizen of The Gambia.

gambier or **gambir** /gam'bēr/ n an astringent substance prepared from the leaves of *Uncaria gambir*, a rubiaceous climbing shrub of the East Indies, used in tanning and dyeing. [Malay]

gambist see under **gamba**.

gambit /gam'bit/ n in chess, the (offer of a) sacrifice of a piece for the sake of an advantage in timing or position in the opening stages of a game (**gam'bit-pawn** or **-piece** one so offered); an initial move in any strategy or battle of wits, *esp* one with an element of trickery. ◆ *vt* in chess, to sacrifice or offer for sacrifice in a gambit. [Sp *gambito*, from Ital *gambetto* a tripping up, from *gamba* leg]

gamble /gam'bl/ *vi* to play for money, *esp* for high stakes; to take a chance (with *on*); to engage in wild financial speculations; to take great risks for the sake of possible advantage. ◆ *vt* to squander or lose by staking. ◆ *n* a transaction depending on chance. [Frequentative of **game**[1]]

■ **gam'bler** *n* a person who gambles, *esp* professionally. **gam'bling** *n*. ◻ **gambling house** or (now *rare*) **hell** a building where organized gambling takes place.

gambo /gam'bō/ (*Welsh* and *dialect*) *n* (pl **gam'boes**) a simple farm cart or hay-wagon.

gamboge /gam-bōj', -bōzh'* or *-boozh'* / *n* a yellow gum resin, obtained from any number of Asian trees, chiefly *Garcinia morella*, used as a pigment and in medicine. [From *Cambodia*, from where it was brought about 1600]

■ **gambogian** /-bōj'/ or *-booj'* / or **gambogic** /-bōj'* / *adj*.

gambol /gam'bl/ *vi* (**gam'bolling**; **gam'bolled**) to leap; to skip playfully. ◆ *n* a playful skipping movement; a frolic. [Formerly *gambold*, from OFr *gambade*, from Ital *gambata* a kick, from LL *gamba* leg]

gambrel /gam'brl/ *n* the hock of a horse; a crooked stick used by butchers for hanging carcases on; a gambrel roof. [OFr *gamberel*; cf Fr *gambier* a hooked stick]

◻ **gambrel roof** *n* in the UK, a hipped roof in which the upper parts of the hipped ends take the form of a small vertical gable end; in the USA, a roof with the lower part at a steeper pitch than the upper (called a *mansard-roof* in the UK).

gambroon /gam-broon'/ *n* a twilled cloth of worsted and cotton, or linen. [Prob *Gambrun* (now Bandar Abbas) in Iran]

gambusia /gam-bū'zē-ə/ *n* a fish of the genus *Gambusia*, members of which give birth to live young and feed on mosquito larvae. [New L, from Am Sp *gambusino*]

game[1] /gām/ *n* a sport of any kind; (in *pl*) (an event consisting of competitions in) athletic sports; a contest for recreation; a competitive amusement played according to a system of rules; the state of a game; manner of playing a game; form in playing; the requisite number of points to be gained to win a game; a bout or contest in a series; a spell or set period of playing a game; a bit of fun, a jest; any object of pursuit; a scheme or method of seeking an end, or the policy that would be most likely to attain it; business, activity, operation; fighting spirit (*archaic*); gallantry (*Shakesp*); (*usu* with *the*) prostitution (*sl*); (with *the*) thieving (*sl*); the spoil of the chase; wild animals hunted for sport; the flesh of such animals; a flock of swans (formerly of other animals) kept for pleasure. ◆ *adj* of or belonging to animals hunted as game; having the spirit of a fighting cock (*inf*); plucky, courageous (*inf*); having the necessary spirit and willingness for some act (*inf*). ◆ *vi* to gamble; to play a computer game. [OE *gamen* play; ON *gaman*, Dan *gammen*]

■ **game'ly** *adv*. **game'ness** *n*. **gam'er** *n* a person who plays games; a dedicated player of computer games; an enthusiastic and persistent competitor (*US*). **game'some** *adj* playful. **game'someness** *n*. **game'ster** *n* a gambler; a lewd person (*Shakesp*); a spirited, playful person (*obs*). **game'sy** *adj* keen on sports. **gā'miness**, **gā'myness** or **gā'meyness** *n* the condition or quality of being gamy. **gam'ing** *n*. **gā'my** or **gā'mey** *adj* having the flavour of game, *esp* after being kept for a long time; savouring of scandal, sensational; spirited, plucky, lively (*inf*).

◻ **game bag** *n* a bag for holding a hunter's game. **game ball** see **game point** below. **game bird** *n* a bird hunted for sport. **Game Boy**® *n* a hand-held battery-operated device for playing computer games. **game call** *n* (*bridge*) a bid (and contract) which, if successful, will win a game. **game-changer** *n*. **game-changing** *adj* bringing about a significant new development. **game'-chicken** or **game'cock** *n* a cock of a breed trained to fight, a fighting cock. **game chips** *n pl* thinly cut (*usu* disc-shaped) potato chips served with game. **game'-dealer** *n*. **game face** *n* (*inf*) a serious, businesslike expression, *esp* in the phrase *have one's game face on*. **game fish** *n* any freshwater fish of the salmon family except the grayling (cf **coarse fish**). **game fishing**. **game'keeper** *n* a person who looks after game on an estate, etc (also *fig*). **game laws** *n pl* laws relating to the protection of game. **game licence** *n* a licence to kill, or to sell, game. **game plan** *n* the strategy or tactics used by a football team, etc; any carefully devised strategy. **game'play** *n* (in computer games) the techniques or manner of playing a particular game, as opposed to its graphics, sound effects, etc. **game point** or **game ball** *n* the stage at which the next point wins the game. **game preserve** *n* a tract of land stocked with game preserved for sport or with protected wild animals. **game preserver** *n* a person who preserves game on his or her land. **game show** *n* a television show with contestants competing for prizes. **games'manship** *n* (*facetious*; title of humorous book by Stephen Potter, 1947) the art of winning games or, generally, of scoring points by talk or conduct aimed at putting one's opponent off. **game tenant** *n* a person who rents the right to shoot or fish over a particular area. **game** (or **games**) **theory** *n* (*maths*) the theory concerned with analysing the choices and strategies available in a game or eg business conflict in order to choose the optimum course of action (used eg in training and selection procedures). **game warden** *n* a person who looks after game, *esp* in a game preserve. **gaming contract** *n* a wager upon any game (eg a horse race or football match). **gaming house** *n* a gambling house. **gam'ing-table** *n* a table used for gambling.

■ **ahead of the game** in a more advanced or advantageous position than expected. **big game** the larger animals hunted. **die game** to keep up courage to the last. **give the game away** to disclose a secret; to give up, abandon (a game or contest) (*Aust*). **have a game with** or **make game of** to make sport of, to ridicule. **off one's game** playing badly. **on one's game** playing well. **on the game** (*inf*) working as a prostitute. **play a waiting game** see under **wait**[1]. **play games with** to amuse oneself by causing inconvenience to (someone). **play the game** to act in a fair, honourable, straightforward manner. **red game** grouse. **round game** a game, eg at cards, in which the number of players is not fixed. **the game is not worth the candle** see under **candle**. **the game is up** the scheme has failed, all is revealed.

game[2] /gām/ *adj* lame. [Origin obscure]

gamelan /gam'ə-lan/ *n* an instrument resembling a xylophone; an orchestra of SE Asia consisting of percussion (chiefly), wind instruments and stringed instruments. [Javanese]

gamete /gam'ēt or gə-mēt'/ *n* a sexual reproductive cell; an egg cell or sperm cell. [Gr *gametēs* husband, *gametē* wife, from *gameein* to marry]

■ **gamet'al** (or *-ēt'* /) or **gametic** /-et'* or *-ēt'* / *adj*. **gametangium** /gam-it-an'ji-əm/ *n* (pl **gametan'gia**) a cell or organ in which gametes are formed. **game'tocyte** *n* (Gr *kytos* vessel) a cell that divides to produce gametes. **gametogen'esis** *n* the formation of gametes. **game'tophyte** (or /gam'* /) *n* (Gr *phyton* plant) in alternation of generations, a plant of the sexual generation, producing gametes.

◻ **gamete intra-Fallopian transfer** *n* an infertility treatment involving direct transfer of eggs and sperm into the woman's Fallopian tubes, where conception may occur (*abbrev* **GIFT**).

Gamgee tissue® /gam'jē tish'oo, -ū or tis'ū/ *n* (sometimes without *cap*) a type of wound-dressing consisting of cotton wool between two layers of gauze. [JS *Gamgee* (1828–86), English surgeon who invented it]

gamic /gam'ik/ *adj* sexual; sexually produced. [Gr *gamikos*, from *gamos* marriage]

gamin /gam'in or ga-mē/ *n* a street urchin, a precocious and mischievous imp of the pavement. ◆ *adj* boyish or impish. [Fr]

■ **gamine** /-mēn'/ *n* a girl of a pert, boyish, impish appearance and disposition. **gaminerie** /gam'in-ri or gam-ēn-(ə-)rē/ *n*. **gaminesque'** *adj* like or resembling a gamin or gamine.

gamma /gam'ə/ *n* the third letter of the Greek alphabet (Γ, γ = G, g); as a numeral γ' = 3, ͵γ = 3000; in classification, the third or one of the third grade, (one of) the grade below beta; the third element in a series. [Gr]

◻ **gamma camera** *n* a device which detects gamma radiation and which is used to produce images of parts of the body into which radioactive material has been introduced. **gamma globulin** *n* any of a group of globulins occurring in blood plasma which contain antibodies that protect against various diseases. **gamma radiation** or **rays** *n* a penetrating radiation given off by radium and other radioactive substances. **gamma securities** or **stocks** *n pl* (*stock exchange*) stocks which are relatively inactive, as of small companies rarely traded.

gammadion /ga-mā'di-on/, also **gammation** /-mā'ti-on/ *n* (pl **gammā'dia** or **gammā'tia**) a figure composed of Greek capital gammas, *esp* a swastika. [Late Gr, little gamma]

gamme /gam/ (*obs*) *n* a musical scale; range, spectrum, gamut. [Fr, from Gr *gamma*; cf **gamut**]

gammer /gam'ər/ (*archaic* or *dialect*; *derog*) *n* an old woman (*masc* **gaffer**). [**grandmother** or **godmother**]

gammerstang /gam'ər-stang/ (*dialect*) *n* a tall, awkward person, *esp* a woman; a wanton girl. [Perh **gammer** and **stang**[1]]

Gammexane® /ga-mek'sān/ *n* a powerful insecticide. [γ-hexachlorocyclohexane]

gammock /gam'ək/ (*dialect*) *n* a frolic, fun. ◆ *vi* to frolic, lark.

gammon[1] /gam'ən/ *n* the cured meat from the hindquarters and leg of a pig; the back part of a side of bacon. [ONFr *gambon, gambe* leg]

gammon[2] /gam'ən/ *n* backgammon (*archaic*); a double game at backgammon, won by removing all one's men before one's opponent removes any; patter, chatter, *esp* that of a thief's accomplice to divert attention, as in *to give gammon* (*sl*); nonsense, humbug. ◆ *vt* to defeat by a gammon at backgammon; to hoax, impose upon. ◆ *vi* to talk gammon; to feign or cheat (*obs*). [Prob OE *gamen* a game]
- ■ **gamm'oner** *n*. **gamm'oning** *n*.

gammon[3] /gam'ən/ (*naut*) *n* the lashing of the bowsprit. ◆ *vt* to lash (the bowsprit).

gammy /gam'i/ (*inf*) *adj* lame; maimed. [Cf **game**[2]]

gamo-, -gamous see **-gam-**.

gamp /gamp/ (*inf*) *n* a large, untidily rolled-up umbrella; an umbrella. [From Mrs Sarah *Gamp*, in Dickens's *Martin Chuzzlewit*]
- ■ **gamp'ish** *adj* (of an umbrella) bulging.

gamut /gam'ət/ *n* the note G on the first line of the bass stave (*obs music*); Guido of Arezzo's scale of six overlapping hexachords, reaching from that note up to E in the fourth space of the treble (*obs music*); any recognized scale or range of notes; the whole range of a voice or instrument; the full range or compass of anything, eg the emotions. [From *gamma*, the Gr letter G, adopted when it was required to name a note added below the A with which the old scale began, and *ut* the Aretinian (qv) syllable]

gamy see under **game**[1].

-gamy see under **-gam-**.

gan /gan/ *pat* of **gin**[5].

ganache /gə-nash'/ *n* a mixture of chocolate and cream in equal parts, used to make truffles and as a filling in cakes and biscuits. [Fr]

ganch /gänsh/ or **-ch/** or **gaunch** /gönsh/ or **-ch/** *vt* (*obs*) to impale; to lacerate. ◆ *n* impaling apparatus (*hist*); a wound from a boar's tusk (*archaic*). [OFr *gancher*, from Ital *gancio* a hook]

ganciclovir /gan-sī'klə-vēr/ *n* an anti-herpes prodrug, used in the treatment of HIV.

gander /gan'dər/ *n* the male of the goose; a simpleton (*inf*); a look or glance (*sl*); a man living apart from his wife (*old US*). [OE *ganra, gandra*; Du and LGer *gander*]
- ■ **gan'derism** *n* behaviour of or suited to a gander.
- ❑ **gan'der-moon** or **-month** *n* (*old US dialect*) the month of a wife's lying-in, confinement to bed prior to childbirth. **gan'der-mooner** *n* (*old US dialect*) a husband during his gander-moon.
- ■ **take a gander at** (*sl*) to have a quick look at.

Gandhian /gan'di-ən/ *adj* of, relating to or representative of (the policies, etc) of Mohandâs K *Gandhi* (1869–1948), Indian leader.
- ■ **Gandh'i-ism** or **Gandh'ism** *n*. **Gandh'ist** *n* and *adj*.

G and S or **G&S** *abbrev* : Gilbert and Sullivan.

g and t, G and T or **G&T** *abbrev* : gin and tonic.

gane /gān/ a Scots form of **gone**.

Ganesh /gən-āsh'/, **Ganesa** or **Ganesha** /gən-ā'sha/ *n* the elephant-headed Hindu god of wisdom and success.

gang[1] /gang/ *n* a band of delinquents or criminals; a number of people or animals (*esp* elk) associating together; a number of labourers working together; a set of children who habitually play together; a set of tools, etc used together. ◆ *vt* and *vi* to associate in a gang or gangs. ◆ *vt* to adjust in co-ordination; to arrange or connect (electric components) so that they can be operated by a single control; to attack as a gang (*N Am inf*). [OE *gang* (Dan *gang*, Ger *Gang*), from *gangan* to go]
- ■ **ganger** /gang'ər/ *n* the foreman of a gang of labourers. **gang'ing** *n*. **gang'ster** *n* a member of a gang of delinquents or criminals. **gang'sterdom** *n*. **gang'sterism** *n*.
- ❑ **gang'-bang** *n* (*sl*) successive sexual intercourse with one, *usu* unwilling, female by a group of males. ◆ *vt* to subject (a woman) to a gang-bang. **gang-banger** *n* (*US inf*) a member of a street gang (often shortened to **banger**). **gang'buster** *n* (*US*) a special police agent working to combat criminal gangs, typically by means of strong, swift, effective operations (**like gangbusters** (*US inf*) with great speed, impact or effectiveness). **gang'busting** *n*. **gang'land** or **gang'sterland** *n* the domain of gangsters, the world of (*esp* organized) crime. **gang'master** *n* a person who provides and organizes teams of casual labourers, *esp* in the agricultural industry. **gang mill** *n* a sawmill with gang saws. **Gang of Four** *n* a term applied to a group of four of Chairman Mao's leading advisers after their political downfall; (also *without caps*; sometimes *facetious*) any similar group in politics, etc. **gang plug** *n* an electrical adaptor with a row of sockets. **gang'-punch** *vt* (*comput*) to punch (the same information) in a number of cards, or to punch (a number of cards) with the same information. **gang rape** *n* a number of successive rapes

committed by members of a group on one victim on one occasion. **gang'-rape** *vt*. **gang saw** *n* a saw fitted in a frame with others. **gangs'man** *n* the foreman of a gang. **gangsterland** see **gangland** above. **gang switches** *n pl* a number of electrical switches connected so that they can be operated simultaneously.
- ■ **gang up on** to make a concerted attack on. **gang up with** to join in the (dubious) activities of.

gang[2] /gang/ *vi* and *vt* (*prp* **gang'ing** (*rare*); *pat* and *pap* not in use) (*Scot*) to go. ◆ *n* (*Scot*) the range of pasture allowed to cattle. [OE *gangan* to go]
- ■ **gang'er** *n* a walker (*Scot*); a fast horse (*dialect*). **gang'rel** *n* (*Scot*) a vagrant; a child beginning to walk (*rare*).
- ❑ **gang'board** *n* (*naut*) a gangway, plank or platform for walking on. **gang'-bye** *n* (*Scot*) the go-by. **Gang Days** *n pl* (*obs Scot*) Rogation Days. **gang'plank** *n* a wooden board used to form a bridge to give access onto or out of a ship, or onto another ship. **gang'-there-out** *adj* (*archaic Scot*) vagrant. **gang'way** *n* (OE *gangweg*) a gangplank, *usu* with sides for the protection of users, giving access onto or out of a ship; an opening in a ship's side to take a gangway; any passageway on a ship; an aisle between rows of seats, *esp* the cross-passage about halfway down the House of Commons (ministers and ex-ministers with their immediate followers sitting *above the gangway*). ◆ *interj* make way; make room to pass.

gang[3] see **gangue**.

gangling /gang'gling/ *adj* loosely built, lanky (also **gangly** /gang'gli/). [Orig Scot and Eng dialect; OE *gangan* to go]

ganglion /gang'gli-ən/ *n* (*pl* **gang'lia** or **gang'lions**) a tumour in a tendon sheath (*pathol*); a nerve centre, collection of nerve cells (*anat*); a centre of energy or activity (*literary*). [Gr]
- ■ **gang'liar** or **ganglionic** /-on'ik/ *adj* relating to a ganglion. **gang'liate** or **gang'liated** *adj* having a ganglion or ganglia. **gang'liform** *adj*.

gangplank, gangrel see under **gang**[2].

gangrene /gang'grēn/ (*pathol*) *n* necrosis of part of the body, with decay of body tissue, resulting from a failure in the blood supply to the part. ◆ *vt* to mortify; to cause gangrene in. ◆ *vi* to become gangrenous. [Gr *gangraina* gangrene]
- ■ **gangrenous** /gang'grin-əs/ *adj* mortified, affected with gangrene.

gangsta /gang'stə/ *n* a style of rap music with aggressive and often misogynistic lyrics; a singer of this music; a member of a criminal gang (*US sl*). [Altered spelling of **gangster**]

gangster, etc see under **gang**[1].

gangue or **gang** /gang/ *n* rock in which ores are embedded. [Fr, from Ger *Gang* a vein]

gangway see under **gang**[2].

ganister or **gannister** /gan'i-stər/ *n* a hard, close-grained siliceous stone, found in the Lower Coal Measures of N England. [Origin uncertain; poss from quarries at *Gannister*, Cheshire]

ganja /gän'jə/ *n* an intoxicating preparation, the female flowering tops of Indian hemp, ie marijuana. [Hindi *gajā*]

gannet /gan'ət/ *n* a large white seabird of the family Sulidae, with black-tipped wings; a greedy person (*inf*). See also **solan**. [OE *ganot* a sea-fowl; Du *gent*]
- ■ **gann'etry** *n* a breeding-place of gannets.

gannister see **ganister**.

ganoid /gan'oid/ *adj* (of fish scales) having a hard glistening outer layer over bone; (of fishes) belonging to an order **Ganoid'ei** /-i-ī/ in which such scales are a common feature, which includes the sturgeon and many fossil forms. ◆ *n* a ganoid fish. [Gr *ganos* brightness, and *eidos* appearance]
- ■ **ganoin** or **ganoine** /gan'ō-in/ *n* a calcareous substance, forming an enamel-like layer on ganoid scales.

gansey /gan'zi/ *n* a woollen sweater, a jersey. [From the island of *Guernsey*]

gant /gänt/ or **gaunt** /gönt/ (*Scot*) *vi* to yawn. ◆ *n* a yawn. [Prob frequentative of OE *gānian* to yawn]

gantlet (*obs*) same as **gauntlet**[1,2].

gantline /gant'līn/ (*naut*) *n* a rope used in a single-block hoist. [Variation of **girt** or **girth**[1], and **line**[2]]

gantlope /gant'lōp/ see **gauntlet**[2].

gantry /gan'tri/ *n* a stand for barrels (also **gauntry** /gön'tri/ or **gaun'tree**); the shelving, racks, etc in which drinks are displayed in a bar; a platform or bridge for a travelling crane, railway signals, etc; the servicing tower beside a rocket on its launching pad. [Perh OFr *gantier*, from L *cantērius* a trellis, from Gr *kanthēlios* a pack-ass]
- ❑ **gantry crane** *n* a crane in bridge form with vertical supports running on parallel tracks.

Gantt chart /gant chärt/ n a form of bar chart used to show progress in a production system, showing predicted production figures over a fixed period of time, and updated with actual figures for comparison. [Henry L Gantt (1861–1919), US management consultant]

Ganymede /gan'i-mēd/ n a cupbearer or serving boy; a catamite. [From Ganymēdēs, the beautiful youth who succeeded Hebe as cupbearer to Zeus]

GAO (US) abbrev : General Accounting Office.

gaol, etc see **jail**, etc.

GAP abbrev : gross agricultural product.

gap /gap/ n an opening or breach; a cleft; a passage; a notch or pass in a mountain ridge; a gorge (US); a break in continuity; an interval; an unfilled space, a lack; a divergence, disparity; the space between discharge electrodes, over which a spark can jump (also **spark gap**; elec eng); a break in the magnetic circuit of the recording or erasing head of a tape recorder, which allows the signal to interact with the oxide film (electronics). ◆ vt to make a gap in; to notch (rare, dialect). [ON]
■ **gapp'er** n (inf) a person taking a gap year. **gapp'y** adj full of gaps. ❑ **gap analysis** n (marketing) a method of discovering gaps in the market for possible new products, by checking off consumer wants against qualities of products available and noting where these do not coincide. **gap funding** n money provided by the government to private concerns in order to ensure that the development of unused and unattractive sites is profitable. **gap junction** n (biol) a junction which allows direct communication between cells by molecules which can diffuse through pores in the junction. **gap site** n a piece of land in a built-up area lying empty because the building which once stood on it has been demolished. **gap'-toothed** adj with teeth set wide apart. **gap year** n a year spent by a student between school and university doing non-academic activities such as voluntary work abroad.
■ **bridge**, **close**, **fill** or **stop the gap** to supply what is lacking.

gape /gāp/ vi to open the mouth wide; to yawn; to stare with open mouth; to be wide open; to bawl (Shakesp). ◆ n an act of gaping; the extent to which the mouth can be opened; the angle of the mouth; a wide opening, parting, fissure, chasm, or failure to meet; in a fish-hook, the width between the point and the shank; (in pl) a yawning fit; (in pl) a disease of birds of which gaping is a symptom, caused by a threadworm (Syngamus, or **gape'worm**) in the windpipe and bronchial tubes. [ON gapa to open the mouth; Ger gaffen to stare]
■ **gā'per** n a person who gapes; a mollusc (genus Mya) with a shell gaping at each end; a sea-perch (genus Serranus); an easy catch (cricket sl). **gā'ping** n and adj. **gā'pingly** adv.
❑ **gape'seed** n (dialect) an imaginary commodity that the gaping starer is supposed to be seeking or sowing; hence, the act of staring open-mouthed, or the object stared at.

gapó /gä-pō'/ n (pl **gapós'**) an area of riverside forest that is periodically flooded. [Port (i)gapó, from Tupí igapó, ygapó]

GAR (US) abbrev : Grand Army of the Republic, an association of Union veterans of the Civil War.

gar[1] see **garfish**.

gar[2] /gär/ (chiefly Scot) vt (pat and pap **garred** or **gart**) to cause, to compel (also (Spenser) **garre**). [Norse ger(v)a to make; cf **yare**]

garage /gar'äzh, gar'ij or gə-räzh'/ n a building for housing motor vehicles; an establishment where motor vehicles are tended, repaired, bought and sold; an establishment where petrol, etc is sold, a filling station; a type of unsophisticated rock music; a form of house music (qv). ◆ vt to put into or keep in a garage. ◆ adj (of music) of the kind played by a garage band. [Fr, from garer to secure; cf **ware**[3]]
■ **gar'agey** adj in the garage style of music. **gar'aging** n accommodation for cars, etc. **gar'agist** or **gar'agiste** n a garage proprietor or owner; a garage employee.
❑ **garage band** n an unsophisticated rock group. **garage sale** n a sale of various items held on the seller's premises, esp in the garage.

garam masala /gar'əm mə-sä'lə/ n a mixture of spices, incl cumin, cardamom and coriander, used in Indian cookery. [Hindi, hot mixture]

Garamond /gar'ə-mond/ n a form of typeface like that designed by Claude Garamond (died 1561).

Garand rifle /gar'ənd or gə-rand' rī'fl/ n a semi-automatic, gas-operated, clip-fed, .30 calibre, US army rifle (also called **M1**). [JC Garand (1888–1974), its American inventor]

garb[1] /gärb/ n fashion of dress; dress, clothing; semblance, appearance (fig); external appearance (obs). ◆ vt to clothe, array. [Ital garbo grace; of Gmc origin; cf **gear**]

garb[2] or **garbe** /gärb/ (heraldry) n a sheaf of wheat. [OFr garbe; of Gmc origin]

garbage /gär'bij/ n refuse, such as (orig) animal offal; any worthless matter; household food and other refuse; nonsense; extraneous matter or invalid data (comput). [Of doubtful origin]
❑ **garbage can** n (N Am) a bin for food waste, etc, a dustbin. **gar'bageman** n (N Am) a dustman.
■ **garbage in, garbage out** (comput, etc) see **GIGO**.

garbanzo /gär-ban'zō/ n (pl **garban'zos**) a chickpea. [Sp]

garble /gär'bl/ vt to misrepresent or falsify by suppression and selection; to mangle, mutilate, distort, jumble; to select what may serve one's own purpose from, esp in a bad sense (rare); to cleanse, sift (obs). [Ital garbellare, from Ar ghirbāl a sieve, perh from LL crībellum, dimin of crībrum a sieve]
■ **gar'bled** adj. **gar'bler** n. **gar'bling** n.

garbo /gär'bō/ (Aust inf) n (pl **gar'bos**) a dustman, garbage-collector; rubbish. [garbage]

garboard /gär'börd/ (naut) n the first range of planks or plates laid on a ship's bottom next to the keel (also **garboard strake**). [Du gaarboord]

garboil /gär'boil/ (obs) n disorder, uproar. [OFr garbouil, from Ital garbuglio, connected with L bullīre to boil]

garbologist /gär-bol'ə-jist/ (US) n a dustman, garbage-collector (facetious); someone who studies a society's waste materials in order to make deductions about the lifestyles of its people. [garbage]
■ **garbol'ogy** n.

garbure /gär-bür'/ n a substantial type of soup made with vegetables, pulses, ham or other meat, and usu served with bread. [Fr]

garcinia /gär-sin'i-ə/ n a tropical evergreen tree of the Garcinia genus of Guttiferae, yielding gamboge, kokum butter, and mangosteen. [Laurent Garcin (1683–1752), French botanist]

garçon /gär-sɔ̃/ n a boy; a male servant, now usu a waiter in a restaurant (usu used vocatively). [Fr]

garda /gär'də or gör'də/ n (pl **gardai** /gör'dē/) an Irish policeman or guard. [Ir gárda]
❑ **Garda Siochana** /shē'hhə-nə/ n (literally, guard of peace; Ir síochāin peace) the Irish police force.

gardant (heraldry) obsolete spelling of **guardant** (see under **guard**).

garden /gär'dən/ n a piece of ground on which plants, etc are cultivated, adjoining a house; (often in pl) a usu public area laid out with walks, flower-beds, lawns, trees, etc; a similar smaller place where food and drink are served outdoors; a pleasant spot; a fertile region; (in pl; with cap) used in street names. ◆ adj of, used in or grown in a garden or gardens. ◆ vi to cultivate or work in a garden. [OFr gardin (Fr jardin); from Gmc; cf **yard**[2] and **garth**]
■ **gar'dener** n a person who gardens, or is skilled in gardening; a person employed to tend a garden. **gar'dening** n the laying out and cultivation of gardens; the prodding of the wicket by a batsman in order to remedy perceived unevenness (cricket sl).
❑ **garden centre** n an establishment where plants, gardening equipment, etc are sold. **garden city**, **suburb** or **village** n a model town, suburb or village, laid out with broad roads, public parks, trees, and spacious gardens between the houses. **gardener's garters** n variegated garden ribbon-grass. **garden flat** n a flat with access to a garden. **gar'den-glass** n a bell-glass for covering plants. **garden gnome** see **gnome**[1]. **gar'den-house** n a summerhouse (Shakesp and literary); a house in a garden; a house kept for sensual indulgence (obs). **garden leave** or **gardening leave** n (inf) compulsory paid leave to be taken in the time preceding the formal termination date of employment. **Garden of Eden** same as **Eden**. **garden party** n a social gathering held in the garden of a house. **garden patch** n (US) a plot of ground to be used for a garden. **garden path** n. **garden seat** n. **garden stuff** n edible garden produce (archaic). **gar'den-variety** adj (US) ordinary. **garden warbler** n a warbler (Sylvia borin) common to European woodlands.
■ **everything in the garden is lovely** or **rosy** all is, or appears to be, well. **hanging garden** a garden formed in terraces rising one above another. **lead someone up the garden path** to mislead someone, esp to make someone the victim of an elaborate scheme of deception. **market garden**, etc see under **market**. **philosophers of the garden** followers of Epicurus, who taught in a garden.

gardenia /gär-dē'ni-ə/ n (with cap) a genus of the madder family, Old World tropical and subtropical trees and shrubs with fragrant, usu white flowers of a waxy appearance; (a flower from) a member of the genus. [Alex Garden (c.1730–91), American botanist]

garderobe /gär'drōb/ n (hist) a wardrobe or its contents; an armoury; a private room; a privy. [Fr; cf **wardrobe**]

gare /gār/ (Scot) adj greedy, miserly. [ON gerr; cf **yare**]

garefowl /gār'fowl/ n the great auk. [ON geirfugl]

garfish /gär'fish/ n (also called **gar** and **gar'pike**) a pike-like fish (genus Belone) with a long slender beaked head; the bony pike, an

American ganoid river-fish (genus *Lepidosteus* or *Lepisosteus*); any of various similar Australian fish. [OE *gār* spear]

garganey /gär'gə-ni/ *n* a small duck of Europe and Asia, the male having a curved white stripe over the eye. [Ital *garganello*]

Gargantuan /gär-gan'tū-ən *or* 'tshoo-/ *adj* like or worthy of Rabelais's hero *Gargantua*, a giant of vast appetite; (without *cap*) enormous, prodigious.
■ **Gargan'tuism** *n*. **Gargan'tuist** *n*.

gargarism /gär'gə-ri-zm/ (*obs*) *n* a gargle.
■ **gar'garize** *or* **-ise** *vt* and *vi*.

garget /gär'git/ (*obs*) *n* inflammation of the throat or udder in cows, swine, etc (*vet*); (also **garget plant**) pokeweed (*US*). [Appar from *garget* throat, from ME, from MFr *gargate*; ult echoic]
■ **gar'gety** *adj* (*vet*) affected by, or relating to, garget.

gargle /gär'gl/ *vt* and *vi* to swill (a liquid) round the back of one's throat, *usu* for medicinal purposes, avoiding swallowing it by breathing out through it. ◆ *n* a liquid for gargling; an act of gargling. [OFr *gargouiller*, from *gargouille* the throat]

gargoyle /gär'goil/, also **gurgoyle** /gûr'/ *n* a grotesquely carved head or figure, projecting from a roof-gutter and acting as a rainwater spout; any grotesque figure or person (*fig*). [OFr *gargouille*, from LL *gurguliō* throat]
■ **gar'goylism** *n* (*med, old*) a rare condition characterized by physical deformity and severe mental disablement.

garial see **gharial**.

garibaldi /gar-i-böl'di *or* -bol'di, also -bal'di/ *n* a woman's loose blouse, an imitation of the red shirts worn by followers of *Garibaldi*; a biscuit with a layer of currants. [G *Garibaldi* (1807–82), Italian patriot, appar arbitrarily for the biscuit]

garigue see **garrigue**.

garish¹ /gā'rish/ *adj* showy; gaudy; (of colours) glaring. [Formerly also *gaurish, gawrish*, perh from obs *guare* to stare, perh a frequentative of obs *gaw* to stare; cf ON *gā* to heed]
■ **gar'ishly** *adv*. **gar'ishness** *n*.

garish² see **guarish**.

garjan see **gurjun**.

garland /gär'lənd/ *n* a wreath of flowers or leaves; a book of selections in prose or poetry; a crown (*obs*); ornament, glory (*Spenser; Shakesp*); (*usu* in *pl*) a rope (or iron, etc) band used for various purposes, such as for retaining shot in a ship's hold, etc (*naut, also milit*). ◆ *vt* to deck with a garland. [OFr *garlande*]
■ **gar'landage** *n* (*Tennyson*) a decoration of garlands. **gar'landless** *adj*. **gar'landry** *n* (*rare*) garlands collectively.

garlic /gär'lik/ *n* a plant (*Allium sativum*) whose bulb has a pungent taste and very strong smell; extended to others of the same genus, such as **wild garlic** (ramsons). [OE *gārlēac*, from *gār* a spear, and *lēac* a leek]
■ **gar'licky** *adj* like, or redolent of, garlic.
❑ **garlic mustard** *n* a tall cruciferous hedge plant (*Alliaria petiolata*) with a garlicky smell.

garment /gär'mənt/ *n* any article of clothing; a covering. ◆ *vt* to clothe or cover. [OFr *garniment*, from *garnir* to furnish]
■ **gar'mented** *adj*. **gar'mentless** *adj*. **gar'menture** *n* clothing.

garms /gärmz/ (*sl*) *n* clothes. [Short form of *garments*]

Garnacha /gär-nä'chə/ *n* the name used in Spain for **Grenache**.

garner /gär'nər/ (*literary*) *vt* to (gather up and) store. ◆ *vi* (*Tennyson*) to accumulate. ◆ *n* (*old or poetic*) a granary; a store of anything. [OFr *gernier* (Fr *grenier*) (noun), from L *grānārium* (*usu* in *pl*) a granary]

garnet¹ /gär'nit/ *n* a mineral, in some varieties a precious stone, generally red, crystallizing in dodecahedra and icositetrahedra, a silicate of di- and trivalent metals. [OFr *grenat*, from LL *grānātum* pomegranate; or LL *grānum* grain, cochineal, red dye]
■ **garnetif'erous** *adj*.
❑ **gar'net-paper** *n* abrasive paper similar to glasspaper. **gar'net-rock** *n* a rock composed of garnet with hornblende and magnetite.

garnet² /gär'nit/ (*naut*) *n* a hoisting tackle. [Origin obscure]

garnet³ /gär'nit/ *n* a T-shaped hinge (now only as **cross-garnet**). [Poss OFr *carne*, from L *cardō, -inis* hinge]

garni /gär-nē'/ (*Fr; cookery*) *adj* trimmed, garnished.

garnierite /gär'ni-ə-rīt/ *n* a green hydrated nickel, magnesium silicate. [Jules *Garnier* (1839–1904), French geologist who discovered it in New Caledonia]

garnish /gär'nish/ *vt* to adorn, decorate, trim; to furnish, kit out, supply (*obs*); to add herbs, etc to a dish for flavour or decoration; to garnishee (*law*). ◆ *n* a gift of money, *esp* that formerly paid to fellow prisoners on entering prison or sometimes by workmen on starting a new job (*hist*); something placed round a principal dish at table, whether for embellishment or relish; decoration, embellishment. [OFr *garniss-*,

stem of *garnir* to furnish (old form *warnir*), from a Gmc root seen in OE *warnian*, Ger *warnen*; cf **warn¹**]
■ **garnishee'** *n* (*law*) a person warned not to pay money owed to another, because the latter is indebted to the garnisher who gives the warning. ◆ *vt* (*law*) to attach (a debt) in this way; to serve (a debtor) with a garnishee order. **garnishee'ment** *n*. **gar'nisher** *n* a person who garnishes. **gar'nishing** *n*. **gar'nishment** *n* that which garnishes or embellishes; ornament; a garnisheement. **gar'nishry** *n* (*Browning*) adornment. **gar'niture** *n* that which garnishes or embellishes; trimming, decoration (on clothes); apparel; ornamentation, *esp* a set of ornaments, eg vases; a set of armour.
❑ **garnishee order** *n* (*law*) a court order which creates a charge over a debtor's bank account in favour of a creditor who has sued and obtained a court judgement against that debtor.

garotte see **garrotte**.

garpike see **garfish**.

garran see **garron**.

garre see **gar²**.

garret /gar'it/ *n* a room just under the roof of a house, an attic room; a turret or watchtower (*obs*). [OFr *garite* a place of safety, *guarir, warir* to preserve (Fr *guérir*), from the Gmc root seen in **ware¹**]
■ **garr'eted** *adj* provided with garrets; lodged in a garret (*rare, literary*). **garreteer'** *n* (*archaic*) a person who lives in a garret, *esp* a poor author.
❑ **garr'et-master** *n* a cabinetmaker, locksmith, etc working on his own account for the dealers.

garrigue *or* **garigue** /ga-rēg'/ *n* uncultivated open scrubland of the Mediterranean region; the scrub growing on it. [Fr, from Provençal *garriga* stony ground]

garrison /gar'i-sn/ *n* a body of troops stationed in a town, fortress, etc to defend it; a fortified place. ◆ *vt* to furnish (a town, etc) with a garrison; to station (troops) as a garrison; to defend by fortresses manned with troops. [OFr *garison*, from *garir, guerir* to furnish; Gmc; see **garret**]
❑ **garrison town** *n* a town in which a garrison is stationed.

garron *or* **garran** /gar'ən/ *n* a small type of horse, used *esp* in Ireland and Scotland. [Ir *gearran*]

garrot¹ /gar'ət/ *n* a name for various ducks, but *esp* the golden-eye. [Fr]

garrot² /gar'ət/ (*surg*) *n* (also **garr'otte** *or* **gar'otte**) a tourniquet. [Fr; see **garrotte**]

garrotte, garotte *or* (*US*) **garrote** /gä-rot' *or* gə-rot'/ *n* a length of wire or cord used to strangle someone; a Spanish mode of putting criminals to death (*hist*); the apparatus for the purpose, *orig* a string round the throat tightened by twisting a stick, later a brass collar tightened by a screw, whose point enters the spinal marrow. ◆ *vt* (**garrott'ing, garott'ing** *or* **garrot'ing; garrott'ed, garott'ed** *or* **garrot'ed**) to execute by the garrotte; suddenly to render unconscious by semi-strangulation in order to rob. [Sp *garrot(t)e*; cf Fr *garrot* a stick]
■ **garrott'er** *or* **garott'er** *n*. **garrott'ing** *or* **garott'ing** *n*.

garrulous /gar'oo-ləs, also -ə- *or* -ū-/ *adj* talkative; loquacious; wordy, voluble. [L *garrulus*, from *garrīre* to chatter]
■ **garrulity** /-oo'li-ti *or* -ū'/ *n* loquacity. **garr'ulously** *adv*. **garr'ulousness** *n*.

garrya /gar'i-ə/ *n* a N American ornamental catkin-bearing evergreen shrub of the genus *Garrya*. [Named after N *Garry* (1781–1856) of the Hudson's Bay Company]

garryowen /ga-ri-ō'ən/ (*rugby*) *n* a high kick forward together with a rush towards the landing-place of the ball (also (*esp rugby league*) **up-and-un'der**). [Named after the *Garryowen* Rugby Club in Limerick]

gart see **gar²**.

garter /gär'tər/ *n* a band used to support a stocking; a suspender (*N Am*); (with *cap*) (the badge of) the highest order of knighthood in Great Britain. ◆ *vt* to put a garter on; to support, bind, decorate, or surround with a garter. [OFr *gartier* (Fr *jarretière*), from OFr *garet* (Fr *jarret*) ham of the leg, prob Celtic, as Breton *gar* shank of the leg]
❑ **Garter King-of-Arms** *n* the chief herald of the Order of the Garter. **gar'ter-snake** *n* in N America, any snake of the genus *Thamnophis*, non-venomous, longitudinally striped; in S Africa applied to two venomous snakes, with black and red rings (see **Elaps**). **gar'ter-stitch** *n* a plain stitch in knitting; horizontally ribbed knitting made by using plain stitches only.

garth /gärth/ *n* an enclosure or yard (now *dialect*); a garden (now *dialect*); a courtyard within a cloister; (also **fish'-garth**) a weir in a river for catching fish. [ON *garthr* a court; cf **yard²**, **garden**]

■ words derived from main entry word; ❑ compound words; ■ idioms and phrasal verbs

garuda /gar'ə-də or gə-roo'də/ (also with *cap*) *n* a Hindu demigod, part man, part bird. [*Sans*]

garum /gā'rəm/ (*hist*) *n* a thick sauce prepared from pickled fish, very popular amongst the ancient Romans. [L, from Gr *garos, garon*]

garvie /gär'vi/ (*Scot*) *n* a sprat (also **gar'vock**). [Gaelic *garbhag* is perh from Scot]

gas /gas/ *n* (*pl* **gas'es**) a substance in a condition in which it has no definite boundaries or fixed volume, but will fill any space; often restricted to such a substance above its critical temperature (qv); a substance or mixture which is in this state in ordinary terrestrial conditions; coal gas, or other gas for lighting or heating, or one used for attack in warfare; gaslight; laughing gas (see under **laugh**); firedamp; empty, boastful, frothy, garrulous, or pert talk (*inf*); something delightful, impressive, exciting (*inf*); short for gasoline (petrol) (*N Am, Aust* and *NZ*). ◆ *vt* (**gass'ing; gassed**) to supply, attack, light, inflate or treat with gas; to poison or asphyxiate with gas; to deceive, impose on by empty talk (*old US sl*); to impress or thrill (*US sl*). ◆ *vi* to emit gas; to chatter, *esp* vapidly (*inf*). [A word invented by JB van Helmont (1577–1644); suggested by Gr *chaos*]
■ **gasahol** see **gasohol** below. **gasalier', gaselier'** or **gasolier'** *n* a hanging frame with branches for gas jets (formed on false analogy after *chandelier*). **gase'ity** *n* gaseous state, character or condition. **gaseous** /gāz', gäs', gas'* or *gaz'i-əs*, also *gā'shəs* or *gash'əs/ adj* in the form of gas; of, like, or relating to, gas. **gas'eousness** *n*. **gasifica'tion** *n* conversion into gas. **gas'ifier** *n*. **gas'iform** *adj*. **gas'ify** *vt* to convert into gas. **gasogene** see **gazogene**. **gas'ohol** or **gas'ahol** *n* a mixture of 8 or 9 parts petrol and 1 or 2 parts alcohol, used as a fuel. **gas'olene** or **gas'oline** /-ə-lēn/ *n* a low-boiling petroleum distillate; the ordinary word for petrol (*N Am*). **gasolier** see **gasalier** above. **gasom'eter** *n* a storage tank for gas. **gasomet'ric** or **gasomet'rical** *adj* relating to the measurement of gas. **gasom'etry** *n* the measurement of amounts of gas. **gass'er** *n* an oil well that produces natural gas; something exceptional or remarkable, very successful or funny (*US sl*). **gass'iness** *n*. **gass'ing** *n* poisoning by gas; idle or vapid chattering. **gass'y** *adj* full of gas; abounding in or emitting gas; gaseous; verbose; given to vapid or boastful talk (*inf*). ◻ **gas'bag** *n* a talkative person (*inf*); a bag for holding gas, *esp* in a balloon or airship. **gas black** *n* soot produced by burning natural gas. **gas'-bottle** *n* a steel cylinder for holding compressed gas. **gas'-bracket** *n* a gas pipe projecting from the wall of a room for lighting purposes. **gas'-buoy** *n* a floating buoy carrying a supply of gas to light a lamp fixed on it. **gas'-burner** *n* the perforated part of a gas-fitting where the gas issues and is burned. **gas cap** *n* gas found in the highest part of oil-containing rock. **gas-car'bon** *n* a hard dense carbon deposited in coal-gas retorts. **gas centrifuge** *n* a centrifuge for separating gases. **gas chamber** *n* an enclosed place designed for killing by means of gas (also **gas oven**). **gas chromatography** *n* a widely used form of chromatography in which a gas is passed down the column which contains the mixture to be separated and a solvent. **gas'-coal** *n* any coal suitable for making gas; cannel-coal. **gas'-coke** *n* coke made in gas retorts. **gas'-condenser** *n* an apparatus for freeing coal gas from tar. **gas constant** *n* (*phys*) the constant of proportionality in the equation of state for 1 mole of an ideal gas. **gas cooker** *n* a cooking stove using gas as fuel. **gas'-cooled** *adj* cooled by a flow of gas. **gas-discharge tube** *n* any tube in which an electric discharge takes place through a gas. **gas engine** *n* an engine worked by the explosion of gas. **gaseous diffusion** *n* (*nuclear eng*) an isotope separation process based on differences in molecular diffusion. **gaseous diffusion enrichment** *n* (*phys*) the enrichment of uranium isotopes using gaseous uranium hexafluoride passing through a porous barrier. **gas escape** *n* a leakage of gas. **gas'field** *n* a region in which natural gas occurs. **gas'-filled** *adj* filled with gas. **gas fire** *n* a room-heating apparatus in which gas is burned. **gas'-fired** *adj* fuelled, or heated, by gas(es). **gas'-fitter** *n* a person whose job is to fit up the pipes, etc for gas appliances. **gas'-fittings** *n pl* gas pipes, etc for lighting and heating by gas. **gas'-furnace** *n* a furnace of which the fuel is gas. **gas gangrene** *n* gangrene resulting from infection of a wound by certain bacteria which form gases in the flesh. **gas giant** *n* (*astron*) a large planet with a gaseous atmosphere that makes up most of its mass. **gas'-globe** *n* a glass used to enclose and shade a gaslight. **gas gun** *n* a gun in which gas is the fuel or propellant. **gas'-guzzler** *n* (*inf, orig US*) a car that consumes large amounts of petrol. **gas'-guzzling** *adj* (*inf; esp N Am*) consuming large amounts of petrol. **gas heater** *n* any heating apparatus in which gas is used. **gas helmet** *n* a gas mask in the form of a helmet completely covering the head. **gas'holder** *n* a storage tank for storing gas; a gasometer. **gas jar** *n* a tall, narrow, cylindrical glass vessel for collecting and holding a gas in chemical experiments. **gas jet** *n* a jet of gas; a gas-flame; the perforated part of a gas-fitting where the gas issues and is burnt, a burner. **gas lamp** *n* a lamp that burns gas. **gas lift** *n* a method of extracting oil from the bottom of an oil well by injecting compressed liquid gas there. **gas'light** *n* light produced by combustion of gas; a gas jet, burner or lamp. ◆ *adj* of, concerned with, or for use by,

gaslight. **gas'-lime** *n* lime that has been used in purifying gas. **gas'-liquor** *n* a solution of ammonia and ammonium salts derived from gas-making. **gas'lit** *adj* illuminated by gaslight. **gas main** *n* a principal gas pipe from the gasworks. **gas'man** *n* a man employed in gas-making, in repairing or installing gas-fittings, or in the reading of meters. **gas mantle** *n* a gauze covering, chemically prepared, enclosing a gas jet, and becoming incandescent when heated. **gas mask** *n* a respiratory device (covering nose, mouth and eyes) as a protection against poisonous gases. **gas meter** *n* an instrument for measuring gas consumed. **gas'-motor** *n* a gas engine. **gas oil** *n* a petroleum distillate, intermediate between kerosene and lubricating oil, used as (*esp* heating) fuel. **gas oven** *n* the oven of a gas cooker; a gas chamber. **gas-per'meable** *adj* (of hard contact lenses) allowing oxygen to penetrate through to the eye. **gas pipe** *n* a pipe for conveying gas. **gas'-plant** *n* dittany (see **burning bush** under **burn¹**). **gas plasma display** same as **plasma screen** (see under **plasm**). **gas poker** *n* a poker-shaped gas appliance with gas jets, that can be inserted into fuel to kindle a fire. **gas'-retort** *n* a closed heated chamber in which gas is made. **gas ring** *n* a hollow ring with perforations serving as gas jets. **gas shell** *n* an artillery shell that gives off a poisonous gas or vapour on bursting. **gas stove** *n* an apparatus in which coal gas is used for heating or cooking, a gas cooker. **gas tank** *n* a reservoir for coal gas; the petrol tank of a motor vehicle (*N Am, Aust* and *NZ*). **gas tap** *n*. **gas'-tar** *n* coal tar. **gas'-tight** *adj* impervious to gas. **gas trap** *n* a trap in a drain to prevent escape of foul gas. **gas turbine** *n* a machine consisting of a combustion chamber, to which air is supplied by a compressor stage and in which the air is heated at constant pressure, and a turbine driven by the hot expanding gases. **gas'-water** *n* water through which coal gas has been passed in scrubbing; gas- or ammoniacal liquor. **gas well** *n* a boring from which natural gas issues. **gas'works** *n* a factory where gas is made.
■ **gas and gaiters** nonsense. **ideal gas** see under **ideal**. **natural gas** see **natural**. **step on the gas** (ie gasoline) (*inf*) to press the accelerator pedal of a motor car; to speed up, hurry.

gasahol, gasalier see under **gas**.

Gascon /gas'kən/ *n* a native of *Gascony* in France; (without *cap*) a boaster (*literary*). ◆ *adj* of Gascony.
■ **gasconade'** *n* (*literary*) boasting talk. ◆ *vi* (*literary*) to boast extravagantly. **gasconàd'er** *n*. **gas'conism** *n* boastfulness.

gaseity, gaselier, gaseous see under **gas**.

gash¹ /gash/ *vt* to cut deeply into. ◆ *n* a deep, open cut. [Formerly *garse*, from OFr *garser* to scarify, from LL *garsa* scarification, poss from Gr *charassein* to scratch]

gash² /gash/ (*sl*) *adj* spare, extra. ◆ *n* (*orig* and *esp naut*) rubbish, waste.

gash³ /gash/ (*Scot*) *adj* talkative. ◆ *vi* to tattle.

gash⁴ /gash/ (chiefly *Scot*) *adj* ghastly, hideous (also **gash'ful** or **gash'ly**). [Perh **ghastful** or **ghastly** (see under **ghast**)]
■ **gash'liness** *n*. **gash'ly** *adv*.

gasification, gasify, etc see under **gas**.

gasket /gas'kit/ or (*rare*) **gaskin** /-kin/ *n* a canvas band used to bind the sails to the yards when furled (*naut*); a strip of tow, etc for packing a piston, etc; a layer of packing material, *esp* a flat sheet of asbestos compound, sometimes between thin copper sheets, used for making gas-tight joints between engine cylinders and heads, etc. [Cf Fr *garcette*, Ital *gaschetta*; ety dubious]
■ **blow a gasket** (*inf*) to become extremely angry.

gaskins /gas'kinz/ (*obs; literary*) same as **galligaskins**.

gasohol, gasolene, gasolier, gasoline, gasometer, etc see under **gas**.

gasp /gäsp/ *vi* to pant, or breathe with pain or difficulty (often *gasp for breath*); to breathe in sharply, in astonishment, horror, etc; to desire eagerly (with *for*). ◆ *vt* (sometimes with *out*) to breathe, pant; to utter with gasps. ◆ *n* the act of gasping; a sharp, noisy intake of breath (in astonishment, horror, etc). [ON *geispa* to yawn; cf *geip* idle talk]
■ **gasp'er** *n* a person who gasps; a cheap cigarette (*sl*). **gasp'iness** *n*. **gasp'ing** *n* and *adj*. **gasp'ingly** *adv*. **gasp'y** *adj*.
■ **the last gasp** the point of death; the last minute.

gaspereau /gas'pə-rō/ (*Can*) *n* a type of herring, the alewife. [Fr *gasparot* a kind of herring]

gasser see under **gas**.

gast /gäst/ *vt* (*Shakesp*) to make aghast, to frighten or terrify. [OE *gǣstan*; cf **aghast**]
■ **gastfull** *adj* (*Spenser*) same as **ghastful** (see under **ghast**). **gast'ness** or **gast'nesse** *n* (*Shakesp*) dread.

Gastarbeiter /gast'ar-bī-tər/ (*Ger*) *n* a migrant worker, *esp* one who does menial work. [Literally, guest-worker]

gaster /gas'tər/ (zool) n in hymenopterous insects, the abdomen proper, to the rear of the first (often constricted) abdominal segment. [Gr gastēr belly]

gastero- /gas-tər-ō-/ combining form denoting stomach or belly. [Gr combining form of gastēr belly]

■ **Gasteromycetes** /gas-tər-ō-mī-sē'tēz/ n pl (Gr mykētes, pl of mykēs mushroom) an order of fungi that includes puffballs, stinkhorns, etc. **gasteropod,** etc see **gastropod,** etc under **gastro-**.

Gasthaus /gast'hows/ or **Gasthof** /-hōf/ (Ger) n a hotel, guest-house.

gastr- combining form see **gastro-**.

gastraea /ga-strē'ə/ (zool) n a hypothetical ancestor of the Metazoa, like a gastrula, proposed by E Haeckel. [New L, from Gr gastēr belly]

gastraeum /ga-strē'əm/ (zool) n the undersurface of the body, esp in birds. [Gr gastēr belly]

gastralgia, gastrectomy see under **gastro-**.

gastric /gas'trik/ adj belonging to, relating to, or in the region of, the stomach. [Gr gastēr belly]

□ **gastric balloon** n an uninflated balloon placed in the upper part of the stomach which, when inflated, reduces the capacity of the stomach for food. **gastric band** n a restrictive band placed around the upper part of the stomach, reducing the capacity of the stomach for food. **gastric fever** n typhoid. **gastric flu** n a popular term for any of several disorders of the stomach and intestinal tract, with symptoms of nausea, diarrhoea, abdominal cramps and fever. **gastric juice** n a thin clear acid fluid secreted by the stomach to effect digestion. **gastric mill** see **mill**[1].

gastrin /gas'trin/ (biol) n a hormone which stimulates production of gastric juice. [**gastr-** and **-in** (1)]

gastritis /ga-strī'tis/ (med) n inflammation of the lining of the stomach. [Gr gastēr belly, and sfx -itis inflammation]

gastro- or often before a vowel **gastr-** /gas-tr(ō)-/ combining form denoting (of or like) the stomach or belly. [Gr gastēr belly]

■ **gastral'gia** n (Gr algos pain; med) pain in the stomach. **gastrec'tomy** n (Gr ek out, and tomē cutting) surgical removal of the stomach, or part of it. **gastrocnemius** /gas-trok-nē'mi-əs/ n (pl **gastrocne'mii**) (Gr knēmē lower leg) the muscle that bulges the calf of the leg. **gastroenter'ic** adj gastrointestinal. **gastroenterī'tis** n (med) inflammation of the lining of the stomach and intestines. **gastroenterol'ogist** n. **gastroenterol'ogy** n (med) the study of the stomach and intestines. **gastrointest'inal** (or /-īn'l/) adj of, relating to, or consisting of, the stomach and intestines. **gastrol'oger** n. **gastrolog'ical** adj. **gastrol'ogy** n cookery, good eating. **gastromancy** /gas'trō-man-si/ n (Gr manteiā soothsaying) divination by sounds from the belly, ie ventriloquism; divination by large-bellied glasses. **gastronome** /gas'trə-nōm/ or **gastronomer** /-tron'ə-mər/ n (Gr nomos law) a lover and connoisseur of good food and wines, an epicure. **gastronomic** /-nom'ik/ or **gastronom'ical** adj. **gastron'omist** n. **gastron'omy** n the art or science of good eating; (also **gastronom'ics**) the style of cooking typical of a country or region. **gastropare'sis** n a disorder, often associated with diabetes, in which paralysis of the stomach muscles delays the passage of food through the stomach. **gas'tropod** or **gas'teropod** n (Gr pous, podos foot; zool) any of the **Gastrop'oda** or **Gasterop'oda**, a class of asymmetrical molluscs, including the limpets, whelks, snails and slugs, in which the foot is broad and flat, and the shell, if any, in one piece and conical. **gastrop'odous** or **gasterop'odous** adj. **gas'tropub** n a pub that specializes in providing food and wine of a standard more typical of a fine restaurant than a traditional pub. **gas'troscope** n an instrument for inspecting the interior of the stomach. **gas'trosoph** n (Gr sophos wise) a person skilled in matters of eating. **gastros'opher** n. **gastros'ophy** n. **gastros'tomy** n (Gr stoma mouth) the making of an opening to introduce food into the stomach. **gastrot'omy** n (Gr tomē a cut) the operation of cutting open the stomach or abdomen.

gastrula /gas'trŭ-lə/ (zool) n an embryo at the stage in which it forms a two-layered cup by the invagination of its wall. [New L, a little stomach]

■ **gastrula'tion** n formation of a gastrula.

gat[1] /gät/ n in Indian music, the second and usu final section of a raga (also **gath**). [Sans gāth]

gat[2] /gat/ (Bible) pat of **get**.

gat[3] /gat/ (sl, chiefly US) n a gun, revolver. [**gatling gun**]

gat[4] /gat/ n an opening between sandbanks; a strait. [Perh ON]

gate[1] /gāt/ n a passage into a city, enclosure, or any large building; a narrow opening or defile; a frame for closing an entrance; an entrance, passage or channel; an obstacle consisting of two posts, markers, etc between which competitors in a slalom, etc must pass; (at an airport) any of the numbered exits from which to board or leave an aircraft; the people who pay to see a game, hence, the number attending; the total amount of money paid for entrance (also **gate'-money**); a starting gate; an electronic circuit which passes signals when permitted by another independent source of similar signals; an electronic circuit with one or more inputs and one output (comput); the part of a projector, printer or camera which holds the film flat behind the lens; an H-shaped series of slots for controlling the movement of a gear lever in a gearbox. ◆ vt to supply with a gate; to punish (students or schoolchildren) by imposing a curfew or by confinement to school precincts. [OE geat a way; Du gat, ON gat]

■ **gat'ed** adj having a gate or gates (also in combination, as hundred-gated); punished by gating. **gate'less** adj. **gāt'ing** n.

□ **gate control therapy** n a theory of pain control based on the selective stimulation of different nerve fibres. **gate'crash** vi and vt to enter without paying or invitation. **gate'crasher** n. **gated community** n a residential area into which the entry of non-residents is controlled by gates, security systems, etc. **gate fever** n (prison sl) a neurotic or restless condition affecting long-term prisoners near the end of their prison sentence. **gate'-fine** n the fine imposed upon the gated for disobedience. **gate'fold** n an oversize page in a book, etc that has to be folded in on both sides, and opened out like a gate, a foldout. **gate'house** n (archit) a building over or at a gate. **gate'keeper** n a person who watches over a gate and supervises the traffic through it (also **gate'man**); someone or something that acts to prevent undesirable elements from entering a system; any of several large butterflies with brown or orange wings. **gate'-legged** or **gate'leg** adj (of a table) having a hinged and framed leg that can swing out to support a leaf to extend the table. **gate-money** see n above. **gate net** n a net hung across a gateway for catching hares. **gate of horn** see **ivory gate** below. **gate of justice** n a gate, eg of a city, temple, etc, where a sovereign or judge sat to dispense justice. **gate'post** n a post from which a gate is hung, or against which it shuts. **gate'-tower** n a tower beside or over a gate. **gate valve** n (in a pipeline) a valve with a movable barrier or gate for regulating the flow. **gate'-vein** n (obs or fig) the great abdominal vein. **gate'way** n the way through a gate; a structure at a gate; a connection between computer networks, or between a computer network and a telephone line; any entrance or means of entrance (also as adj; often fig).

■ **break gates** (formerly at Oxford and Cambridge Universities) to enter college after the prescribed hour. **ivory gate** and **gate of horn** (or in Spenser **silver**) in Greek legend and poetical imagery, the gates through which false and true dreams respectively come. **stand in the gate** (Bible) to occupy a position of defence.

gate[2] /gāt/ (Scot and N Eng dialect) n a way, path, street (often in street names, such as Cowgate, Kirkgate); a manner of doing. See also **gait**[1]. [ON gata; Dan gade, Ger Gasse]

gate[3] /gāt/ (Spenser) n an obsolete Scot and N Eng form of **goat**.

-gate /-gāt/ sfx attached to the name of a person or place to denote a scandal connected with that person or place. [On the analogy of **Watergate**]

gateau or **gâteau** /gat'ō or gä-tō/ n (pl **gateaus** /gat'ōz/ or **gâteaux** /gat'ōz or gä-tō/) a rich cake, filled with cream, decorated with icing, etc. [Fr]

gath see **gat**[1].

gather /gadh'ər/ vt to collect; to assemble; to amass; to harvest; to pick up; to draw together; to pull someone or something close to oneself; (in sewing) to draw into puckers by passing a thread through and pulling it tight; to arrange (signatures of a book) in sequence for binding; to learn by inference; to have increase in (eg speed). ◆ vi to assemble or muster; to increase; to suppurate; to make way (naut); to arrange signatures of a book in correct sequence for binding. ◆ n a pleat or fold in cloth, made by drawing threads through; (in pl) that part of the dress which is gathered or drawn in. [OE gaderian, gæderian; (tō)gædere together; geador together, and gæd fellowship]

■ **gath'erer** n a person who collects, amasses, assembles or harvests; a worker who collects molten glass on the end of a rod preparatory to blowing. **gath'ering** n the action of someone or something that gathers; a crowd or assembly; a series of gathers in material; a narrowing; a number of leaves of paper folded one within another; the assembling of the sheets of a book; a suppurating swelling, boil or abscess (inf).

□ **gath'ering-coal** or **-peat** n a coal, or peat, put into a fire to keep it alive until morning. **gath'ering-cry** n a summons to assemble for war. **gath'ering-ground** n a catchment area.

■ **gather breath** to recover wind. **gather ground** to gain ground. **gather oneself together** to collect all one's powers, like one about to leap. **gather to a head** to ripen; to come into a state of preparation for action or effect. **gather way** (naut) to begin to make headway by sail or steam so as to answer the helm.

gatling gun /gat'ling gun/ n a machinegun with a cluster of rotating barrels, invented by RJ Gatling about 1861.

gator /gā'tər/ (inf, chiefly US) n short for **alligator**.

GATS /gats/ abbrev : General Agreement on Trade in Services.

Gatso® /gat'sō/ n an automatic photographic device used to identify vehicles exceeding the speed limit. [Maurice *Gatsonides* (1911–98), Dutch racing driver]

GATT /gat/ *abbrev*: General Agreement on Tariffs and Trade, an international treaty to promote trade and economic benefits, and to simplify and standardize international trading procedures (now replaced by **WTO**).

gau /gow/ n a territorial district of ancient Germany; (under the Nazi regime) a German political district. [Ger *Gau* district]

gauche /gōsh/ *adj* clumsy; tactless; awkward. [Fr, left]
■ **gaucherie** /gōsh'ə-rē or -rē'/ n clumsiness; (an instance of) social awkwardness.

Gaucher's disease /gō'shāz di-zēz'/ n a rare hereditary disease characterized by the accumulation of certain fats in the liver and spleen. [P *Gaucher* (1854–1918), French physician]

gaucho /gow'chō/ n (pl **gau'chos**) a cowboy of the pampas, *usu* of mixed Spanish and native descent; (in *pl*) women's knee-length wide trousers. [Sp]
■ **gauches'co** *adj* of a type of Spanish poetry inspired by the life, language and customs of the gauchos.

gaucie, gaucy, gawcy or **gawsy** /gö'si/ (*Scot*) *adj* portly, jolly. [Origin unknown]

gaud /göd/ n a large ornamental bead on a rosary (*obs*); a prank (*obs*); an ornament; a piece of finery; showy ceremony; festivity (*obs*). ◆ *vi* (*obs*) to make merry. ◆ *vt* to adorn with gauds (*obs*); to paint, eg the cheeks (*obs*; *Shakesp*). [In part appar from OFr *gaudir*, from L *gaudēre* to be glad, or *gaudium* joy; in part directly from L]
■ **gaudeā'mus** (in Scotland /gow-di-ä'müs/) n (L, let us be glad, the opening word of a students' song; *obs*) a joyful celebration among students. **gaud'ery** n finery. **gaud'ily** *adv*. **gaud'iness** n. **gaud'y** n an entertainment or feast, *esp* in certain English colleges. ◆ *adj* showy; merry, gay; vulgarly bright.
❑ **gaud'y-day** or **gaud'y-night** n a day or night on which a feast is held.

gaudeamus igitur /gö-di-ä'məs ij'i-tər or gow-de-ä'müs ig'i-tŭr/ (L) let us therefore rejoice.

gaudgie see **gadgie**.

gaudium certaminis /gö'di-əm sùr-tam'i-nis or gow'di-oom ker-tä'mi-nis/ (L) joy of combat.

gaudy see under **gaud**.

gaudy-green /gö'di-grēn/ (*obs*) n and adj yellowish-green. [OFr *gaude* weld, dyer's rocket]

gaufer see **gofer**².

gauffer, gauffering see **goffer**.

gaufre see **gofer**².

gauge, also **gage** /gāj/ n a measuring apparatus; a standard of measure; a means of limitation or adjustment to a standard; a measurement, such as the diameter of a wire, calibre of a tube, or width of a row of slates; the distance between a pair of wheels or rails; a means of estimate; the width of film or magnetic tape; (*usu* **gage**) the relative position of a ship to another vessel and the wind (see **lee**¹, **weather**). ◆ *vt* to measure; to estimate; to adjust to a standard. ◆ *vi* to measure the contents of casks. [OFr *gauge* (Fr *jauge*)]
■ **gauge'able** *adj* capable of being gauged. **gaug'er** n a person who gauges; a person who works in excise. **gaug'ing** n the measuring of casks holding excisable liquors.
❑ **gauge boson** n (*phys*) a type of particle that mediates the interaction between two fundamental particles. **gauge glass** n a tube to show height of water. **gauge theory** n any one of the theories in particle physics that attempts to describe the various types of interaction between fundamental particles. **gaug'ing-rod** n an instrument for measuring the contents of casks.
■ **broad-** or **narrow-gauge** in railway construction, respectively greater or less than **standard gauge**, in Britain 1.435 metres (56½ inches).

gauje see **gadgie**.

Gaul /göl/ n a name given to ancient France; an inhabitant of Gaul. [Fr *Gaule*, from L *Gallia*, *Gallus*; perh connected with OE *wealh* foreign]
■ **Gaul'ish** *adj* of or relating to Gaul or the Gauls. ◆ n the Celtic (Brythonic) language of the Gauls.

gauleiter /gow'lī-tər/ n a chief official of a district under the Nazi regime; an overbearing wielder of petty authority (*inf*, *fig*). [Ger *Gau* district, and *Leiter* leader]

Gaullist /gō'list/ n a follower or supporter of the French soldier and statesman Charles de *Gaulle* (1890–1970). ◆ *adj* of or relating to the Gaullists.
■ **Gaull'ism** n the political principles and policies of Gaullists.

gault /gölt/ n (with *cap*) a series of beds of clay and marl between the Upper and the Lower Greensand (*geol*); brick-earth; a brick of gault clay. [Origin obscure]
■ **gault'er** n a person who digs gault.

gaultheria /göl-thē'ri-ə/ n a plant of the *Gaultheria* genus of evergreen aromatic plants of the family Ericaceae, which includes the American wintergreen and salal. [JF *Gaultier* (1708–56), Canadian botanist]

gaum¹ /göm/ or **gorm** /görm/ (now *dialect*) *vt* to smear; to daub; to clog; to handle clumsily (*obs*). ◆ n a smear; a daub; a shiny lustre as on new varnish; stickiness; a sticky mass. [Ety doubtful, perh variant of **gum**²]
■ **gaum'y** or **gorm'y** *adj* (*rare*) dauby.

gaum² /göm/ or **gorm** /görm/ (*dialect*) n notice, heed, regard, attention; understanding. ◆ *vt* to pay attention to, heed; to understand. [ON *gaumr* heed, attention]
■ **gaum'less** or **gorm'less** *adj* stupid, witless, vacant.

gaun /gön/ a Scots form of **going**².

gaunch see **ganch**.

gaunt¹ /gönt/ *adj* thin; of a pinched appearance; haggard; (of a place) barren and desolate. [ME, poss from Scand; cf Norw dialect *gand* thin stick, lanky person; OFr *gauntet* yellowish, also suggested]
■ **gaunt'ly** *adv*. **gaunt'ness** n.

gaunt² see **gant**.

gauntlet¹ /gönt'lit/ n the iron glove of armour, formerly thrown down in challenge and taken up in acceptance; a heavy glove with a long, wide cuff covering the wrist; the cuff of such a glove, covering the wrist. [Fr *gantelet*, dimin of *gant* glove, of Gmc origin; cf Swed *vante* a mitten, glove, ON *vöttr* a glove, Dan *vante*]
■ **gaunt'leted** *adj* wearing a gauntlet or gauntlets.
❑ **gaunt'let-guard** n a guard of a sword or dagger, protecting the hand very thoroughly.
■ **throw down** and **take up the gauntlet** respectively, to give and to accept a challenge.

gauntlet² /gönt'lit/ or (now *rare*) **gantlope** /gant'lōp/ n the former military (or naval) punishment of having to run through a lane of soldiers (or sailors) who strike one as one passes. [Swed *gatlopp*, from *gata* lane (cf **gate**²), and *lopp* course (cf **leap**); confused with **gauntlet**¹]
■ **run the gauntlet** to undergo the punishment of the gauntlet; to expose oneself to hostile treatment, harsh criticism or public disgrace.

gauntree, gauntry see **gantry**.

gaup, gauper, gaupus see **gawp**.

gaur /gowr/ n a species of large, wild ox inhabiting some mountainous parts of India (also called **Indian bison**). [Hindustani]

gauss /gows/ n (pl **gauss**) the CGS unit of magnetic flux density (formerly used for other magnetic units), equal to 10^{-4} teslas.
■ **Gauss'ian** *adj* (also without *cap*) of or due to Johann Karl Friedrich *Gauss* (1777–1855), German mathematician and physicist.
❑ **Gaussian distribution** n (*stats*) normal distribution (qv under **norm**).

gauze /göz/ n a thin, transparent fabric; an openwork fabric or fine mesh. [Fr *gaze*, dubiously referred to *Gaza* in Palestine]
■ **gauz'iness** n. **gauz'y** *adj*.
❑ **gauze'-tree** n a West Indian tree, the lacebark. **gauze'-winged** *adj* having gauzy wings.

gavage /gä-väzh'/ n feeding by stomach-tube (*med*); force-feeding of poultry. [Fr *gaver*, from *gave* bird's crop]

gave /gāv/ pat of **give**.

gavel¹ /gav'l/ n a mallet; a chairman's, auctioneer's or judge's hammer. [Orig US; origin uncertain]

gavel² /gä'vl/ a dialectal form of **gable**.

gavel³ /gav'l/ (*hist*) n tribute or rent. [OE *gafol* tribute; connected with *giefan* to give]
❑ **gav'elkind** n a tenure long prevailing in Kent by which lands descended from the father to all sons (or, failing sons, to all daughters) in equal portions, and not by primogeniture. **gav'elman** n a tenant holding land in gavelkind.

gavelock /gav'ə-lək/ (*hist* or *dialect*) n a javelin; a crowbar. [OE *gafeluc*]

gavial same as **gharial**.

gavotte /gä-vot'/ n a dance, somewhat like a country dance, *orig* a dance of the *Gavots*, people of the French Upper Alps; the music for such a dance in common time, often occurring in suites.

gawcy see **gaucie**.

gawd /göd/ (*Shakesp*) n same as **gaud**.

gawk /gök/ n a person who is awkward or ungainly, *esp* from tallness, shyness or simplicity; a person who stares and gapes. ◆ *vi* to stare and gape. [Ety obscure: perh altered from (obs) *gaw* to gape, stare; prob not Fr *gauche* left]

■ **gawk'er** *n*. **gawk'ihood** *n*. **gawk'iness** *n*. **gawk'y** *adj* awkward; ungainly. ◆ *n* a tall awkward person; a gawk.

gawp or **gaup** /göp/ (*inf*) *vi* to gape stupidly or rudely. [From obs *galp*; cognate with **yelp**]

■ **gawp'er** or **gaup'er** *n*. **gawp'us** or **gaup'us** *n* (*dialect*) a silly person.

gawsy see **gaucie**.

gay /gā/ *adj* (**gay'er**; **gay'est**) lively; bright, colourful; playful, merry; pleasure-loving, dissipated (as in **gay dog** (a rake) (*archaic*); of loose life, whorish (*obs*); showy; spotted, speckled (*dialect*); in modern use, homosexual (*orig prison sl*); relating to or frequented by homosexuals (as *gay bar*); inferior or unfashionable (*sl*); (*usu* **gey** /gī/) great, considerable (*Scot*); often by hendiadys instead of an adv, as in **gey and easy** easy enough; unduly familiar (*old US*). ◆ *adv* (*Scot*; **gey**) rather, fairly, considerably. ◆ *n* a homosexual; a gallant (*obs*). [OFr *gai*, perh from OHGer *wāhi* pretty]

■ **gai'ety** *n* gayness (but not used in sense of homosexuality). **gai'ly** *adv*. **gay'ness** *n*. **gay'some** *adj* (*rare*) gladsome.

□ **gay'-bashing** *n* (*inf*) violent victimization of homosexuals by heterosexuals. **gay deceiver** *n* (*old*) a libertine; (in *pl*) a foam-padded brassière (*sl*). **gay gene** *n* (*inf*) a gene thought to influence a person's tendency to be homosexual. **Gay Gordons** *n* a traditional Scottish dance that involves a walking movement and a polka alternately. **gay liberation** *n* the freeing of homosexuals from social disadvantages and prejudice. **gay plague** *n* (*old offensive sl*) AIDS. **gay rights** *n pl* the rights of homosexuals to equal treatment with heterosexuals. **gay science** *n* (*hist*) a rendering of *gai saber*, the Provençal name for the art of poetry.

gayal or **gyal** /gā'əl or gä'yäl/ *n* an Indian domesticated ox, related to the gaur, with curved horns. [Hindi]

gaydar /gā'där/ (*inf*) *n* the supposed ability of a person, *esp* a homosexual, to sense whether or not someone else is homosexual. [**gay** and **radar**]

Gay-Lussac's law see **Charles's law** under **law**[1].

gay-you /gī'ū or gä'ū/ *n* a narrow flat-bottomed Vietnamese boat with outrigger and masts. [Viet *ghe hầu*]

gaz. *abbrev*: gazette; gazetteer.

gazal see **ghazal**.

gazania /gə-zā'ni-ə/ *n* any plant of the genus *Gazania* of the southern hemisphere with bright yellow or orange composite flowers. [Theodore of *Gaza* (1398–1478), who translated the botanical works of Theophrastus]

gazar /gə-zär'/ *n* a stiff silk fabric. [Fr, from *gaze* gauze]

gaze /gāz/ *vi* to look fixedly, or long and steadily, *esp* in admiration or abstraction. ◆ *n* a fixed or long steady look; the object gazed at. [Prob cognate with obs *gaw* to stare; cf ON *gā* to heed; Swed dialect *gasa* to stare]

■ **gaze'ful** *adj* (*Spenser*) looking intently. **gaze'ment** *n* (*Spenser*). **gā'zer** *n*. **gā'zy** *adj* (*rare*) affording a wide prospect; given to gazing. □ **gaze'-hound** *n* (*usu hist*) a hound that pursues by sight. **gaz'ing-stock** *n* an object or person exposed to public view, generally unpleasantly.

■ **at gaze** (*obs*) in the attitude of gazing.

gazebo /gə-zē'bō/ *n* (*pl* **gazē'bos** or **gazē'boes**) a summerhouse or other small structure giving a commanding view of the landscape, a belvedere. [Perh connected with **gaze**, as a sham Latin construction (after model of *videbo* I shall see)]

gazelle /gə-zel'/ *n* any of various small, large-eyed antelopes (*specif Gazella dorcas*) of N Africa and SW Asia. [Fr, from Ar *ghazāl* a wild goat]

gazette /gə-zet'/ *n* (with *cap*) an official newspaper containing lists of government appointments, legal notices, despatches, etc; a title used for some newspapers. ◆ *vt* (**gazett'ing**; **gazett'ed**) to publish or mention in a gazette; to announce or confirm (a person's appointment or promotion), *esp* in an official gazette. [Fr, from Ital *gazzetta* a small coin; or from Ital *gazzetta*, dimin of *gazza* magpie]

■ **gazetteer'** /gaz-/ *n* a geographical dictionary, a reference book containing alphabetical entries for places of the world, with maps, etc; *orig* a writer for a gazette, an official journalist. ◆ *vt* to describe in a gazetteer. **gazetteer'ish** *adj*.

□ **gazetted officer** *n* one of a higher grade who is listed in an official gazette.

■ **appear** (or **have one's name**) **in the Gazette** (*obs*) to be mentioned in one of the official newspapers, *esp* of bankrupts.

gazillion /gə-zil'yən/ *n* an indefinite very large number. [Coinage based on **million**]

gazogene /gaz'ə-jēn/ or **gasogene** /gas'ə-/ *n* an apparatus for carbonating water, etc. [Fr *gazogène*, from *gaz* gas, and Gr sfx *-genēs*, from root of *gennaein* to generate]

gazon or **gazoon** /gə-zoon'/ (*obs*) *n* turf used in fortification; used erroneously by James Hogg for a compact body of men. [Fr, turf]

gazoo, gazooka see **kazoo**.

gazpacho /ga-spä'chō or gəz-pä'chō/ *n* (*pl* **gazpach'os**) a spicy Spanish vegetable soup, served cold. [Sp]

gazump /gə-zump'/ (*inf*) *vt* and *vi* (of a seller) to raise the price of property, etc, after accepting an offer from (a buyer), but before the contract has been signed. [Prob Yiddish *gezumph* to swindle; cf thieves' slang *gessump*, *gazumph*, etc to rob by deception]

gazunder[1] /gə-zun'dər/ (*inf*) *vt* and *vi* (of a buyer) to lower the sum offered to (the seller of a property) just before contracts are due to be signed. [**gazump** and **under**]

gazunder[2] /gə-sun'dər/ (*inf*, chiefly *Aust*) *n* a chamberpot; a low ball in cricket. [*goes under*, contracted as in informal speech]

gazy see under **gaze**.

GB *abbrev*: gigabyte (also **Gb**); Great Britain (also IVR).

Gb (*phys*) *abbrev*: gilbert.

GBA *abbrev*: (Great Britain) Alderney, Channel Islands (IVR).

GBE *abbrev*: (Knight or Dame) Grand Cross of the British Empire.

GBG *abbrev*: (Great Britain) Guernsey, Channel Islands (IVR).

GBH or **gbh** *abbrev*: grievous bodily harm.

GBJ *abbrev*: (Great Britain) Jersey, Channel Islands (IVR).

GBL *abbrev*: gamma-butyrolactone, a colourless liquid used as a solvent and sometimes as a recreational drug.

GBM *abbrev*: (Great Britain, Isle of) Man (IVR).

GBZ *abbrev*: (Great Britain) Gibraltar (IVR).

GC *abbrev*: George Cross.

GCA *abbrev*: ground control (or controlled) approach system, or ground control apparatus (*aeronautics*); Guatemala, Central America (IVR).

GCB *abbrev*: (Knight or Dame) Grand Cross of the (Order of the) Bath.

GCE *abbrev*: General Certificate of Education.

GCH *abbrev*: (Knight) Grand Cross of Hanover.

GCHQ *abbrev*: Government Communications Headquarters.

GCM *abbrev*: General Court Martial; (also **gcm**) greatest common measure.

GCMG *abbrev*: (Knight or Dame) Grand Cross of (the Order of) St Michael and St George.

GCP *abbrev*: good clinical practice.

GCSE *abbrev*: General Certificate of Secondary Education.

GCVO *abbrev*: (Knight or Dame) Grand Cross of the (Royal) Victorian Order.

Gd (*chem*) *symbol*: gadolinium.

GDA *abbrev*: guideline daily amount.

g'day /gə-dā'/ (*Aust inf*) *interj* a form of the common greeting *Good day*.

GDC *abbrev*: General Dental Council.

Gde *abbrev*: gourde.

Gdns *abbrev*: Gardens (in street names, etc).

GDP *abbrev*: gross domestic product.

GDR *abbrev*: German Democratic Republic (the former East Germany).

GE *abbrev*: General Electric; Georgia (IVR).

Ge see **Gaea**.

Ge (*chem*) *symbol*: germanium.

geal /jēl/ (*obs* or *dialect*) *vt* and *vi* to congeal. [Fr *geler*]

gealous, gealousy (*Spenser*) same as **jealous, jealousy**.

gean /gēn/ *n* the European wild cherry. [OFr *guigne*]

geanticline /jē-an'ti-klīn/ *n* an anticline on a great scale. [Gr *gē* earth, and **anticline**]

■ **geanticli'nal** *adj*.

gear /gēr/ *n* equipment; accoutrements; tackle; clothes, *esp* (*inf*) young people's fashion clothes; personal belongings (*inf*); illicit drugs (*sl*); armour (*obs*); a harness; an apparatus; a set of tools or a mechanism for some particular purpose; household stuff; stuff, matter (*archaic*); an affair, business, doings (often contemptuous) (*obs*); any moving part or system of parts for transmitting motion, eg levers, gearwheels; connection by means of such parts; the actual gear ratio in use, or the gearwheels involved in transmitting that ratio, in an automobile

gearbox, *first gear* being the lowest; *landing gear*; *working connection*; *working order*; the diameter in inches of a wheel whose circumference equals the distance a bicycle would go for one turn of the pedals. ◆ *vt* to harness; to put (eg machinery) in gear; to connect in gear; to adjust in accordance with the requirements of a particular plan, etc (with *to*). ◆ *vi* to be in gear; to have a (high or low) gearing (*econ*). ◆ *adj* (*old sl*) unusually good, or (later) very up to date. [ME *gere*, prob ON *gervi*; cf OE *gearwe*, OHGer *garawi*; **yare**, **gar**[2]]
■ **geared** *adj*. **gear'ing** *n* harness; working implements; means of transmission of motion, *esp* a series of toothed wheels and pinions; (in a company's capital) the proportion of debt finance to equity finance (*econ*). **gear'less** *adj*.
❑ **gear'box** *n* the box containing the apparatus for changing gear; (in a motor vehicle) the apparatus itself. **gear'-case** *n* a protective case for the gearing of a bicycle, etc. **gear'-change** or **gear'change** *n* a change of gear; the mechanism with which one changes gear. **gear-lever**, **gear'-stick** or (*N Am*) **gear'shift** *n* a device for selecting or engaging and disengaging gears. **gear ratio** *n* the ratio of the driving to the driven members of a gear mechanism. **gear train** *n* two or more gearwheels, transmitting motion from one shaft to another. **gear'wheel** *n* a wheel with teeth or cogs which impart or transmit motion by acting on a similar wheel or a chain.
■ **change gear** to select a higher or lower gear. **gear down** to make the speed of the driven part lower than that of the driving part; to prepare for decreased production, fewer demands, etc. **gear up** to make the speed of the driven part higher than that of the driving part; to prepare for increased production, new demands, etc; to raise the gearing of (a company). **high gear** a gear ratio giving a high number of revolutions of the driven part relative to the driving part (**high'-gear** *adj*); maximum speed and efficiency, peak performance (*fig*). **highly geared** (of a company or its capital) having a high ratio of borrowing in relation to owners' capital, or of debt to equity. **low gear** a gear ratio giving a low number of revolutions of the driven part relative to the driving part (**low'-gear** *adj*). **multiplying gearing** a combination of cogwheels for imparting motion from wheels of larger to wheels of smaller diameter, by which the rate of revolution is increased. **straight gear** the name given to a set of geared wheels when the planes of motion are parallel (cf **bevel gear** under **bevel**). **three-speed gear**, **two-speed gear** and **variable gear** a contrivance for changing gear at will; see also **synchromesh**.

geare /gēr, jēr/ (*Spenser*) same as **gear**, **jeer**.

geason /gē'zn/ (*obs*) *adj* rare; out of the way; wonderful. [OE *gǣne*, *gēsne* wanting, barren]

geat /jēt/ *n* the hole in a mould through which the metal is poured in casting. [**jet**]

gebur /gə-boor' or yə-boor'/ (*hist*) *n* a tenant-farmer. [OE *gebūr*]

GEC *abbrev*: General Electric Company.

geck /gek/ (*Scot and N Eng dialect*) *n* a dupe; an object of scorn; a derisive gesture; scorn. ◆ *vt* to mock. ◆ *vi* to scoff; to toss the head; to show disdain. [Prob LGer *geck*; Du *gek*, Ger *Geck*]

gecko /gek'ō/ *n* (pl **geck'os** or **geck'oes**) any lizard of the genus *Hemidactylus*, mostly thick-bodied, dull-coloured animals with adhesive toes and vertebrae concave at both ends. [Malay *gēkoq*; imit of its cry]

ged /ged/ (*Scot and N Eng dialect*; *zool*) *n* the pike or luce. [ON *gedda*]

geddit /ged'it/ (*sl*) *interj* (do you) get it?, do you see (the joke, point, etc)?; *usu* used in speech, or as though in speech, to reinforce or draw attention to a preceding pun, joke or irony. [*get it?* (informal, *esp* US, pronunciation expressed phonetically)]

gee[1] /jē/ *vi* (**gee'ing**; **geed**) (of horses) to move to the right, to move on, or move faster.
❑ **gee'-gee** *n* (*inf*) a child's word for a horse; (in *pl*) horses in terms of racing and betting.
■ **gee up** to go faster; to encourage, stimulate; an interjection commanding a horse to move on or go faster (also **gee hup**).

gee[2] /jē/ (*inf*) *interj* expressing surprise, sarcasm, enthusiasm, etc; sometimes used only for emphasis. [Perh **Jesus**]
■ **gee whiz** *interj* expressing surprise, admiration, etc.

gee[3] /jē/ *n* the seventh letter of the modern English alphabet (G or g).

gee[4] /gē/ (*Scot and N Eng dialect*) *n* a fit of perversity.

gee[5] /jē/ (*US dialect* or *sl*) *vi* to go, suit, get on well.

gee[6] /jē/ *n* a radio-navigation system in which three ground stations, A (master), B and C (slave), give for AB and AC two sets of intersecting hyperbolas which, charted, give an equipped aircraft its geographical position over a few hundred miles' range from A. [ground electronics engineering]

geebung /jē'bung/ *n* an Australian proteaceous tree (genus *Persoonia*) or its fruit. [From an Aboriginal language]

geechee /gē'chē/ (*US*, chiefly *black*, *sl*) *n* Gullah dialect; a Gullah; a rural Southern black. [Origin uncertain]

geegaw /jē'gö/ same as **gewgaw**.

gee-gee see under **gee**[1].

geek[1] /gēk/ (*N Am sl*) *n* a circus or carnival freak; a strange or eccentric person, a creep or misfit; someone who is obsessively enthusiastic, *esp* about computers. [British dialect *geck* a fool]
■ **geek'y** *adj*.
❑ **geek chic** *n* a casual fashion style considered typical of young technology enthusiasts.

geek[2] /gēk/ (*Aust inf*) *n* a look, *esp* a good long look. [British dialect, a peep or peer]

geep /gēp/ *n* a creature produced by artificially combining DNA from a goat and sheep.

geese plural of **goose**.

gee-string same as **G-string** (see under **G** (*n*)).

Ge'ez /gē-ez', gē'ez or gēz/ or **Giz** /gēz/ *n* the ancient language of Ethiopia, a Semitic tongue closely related to Arabic.

geezer /gē'zər/ (*sl*) *n* a man; an old man; a crafty or unscrupulous person. [**guiser**]

GEF *abbrev*: Global Environment Facility, an international environmental organization.

gefilte fish or **gefüllte fish** /gə-fil'tə fish/ *n* a cooked mixture of fish, eggs, breadcrumbs or matzo meal, and seasoning, served as balls or cakes or stuffed into a fish. [Yiddish, literally, filled fish]

gefuffle /gə-fuf'l/ form of **carfuffle**.

gefüllte fish see **gefilte fish**.

gegenschein /gā'gən-shīn/ (*astron*) *n* a glow of zodiacal light seen opposite the sun. [Ger *gegen* opposite, and *Schein* glow, shine]

Gehenna /gi-hen'ə/ *n* the valley of Hinnom, near Jerusalem, in which the Israelites sacrificed their children to Moloch, and to which, at a later time, the refuse of the city was conveyed to be burned; hence hell (*Bible*); a place of torment. [Heb *Ge-hinnōm* valley of Hinnom]

Geiger counter /gī'gər kown'tər/ or **Geiger-Müller counter** /-mül'ər/ *n* an instrument for detecting and measuring radioactivity by registering electrical output pulses caused by ionization of particles in a gas-filled tube. [Hans *Geiger* (1882–1945) and W *Müller* (1905–79), German physicists]

geisha /gā'shə/ *n* (pl **gei'sha** or **gei'shas**) (also **geisha girl**) a Japanese girl trained to provide entertainment (eg conversation, performance of dances, etc) for men; a Japanese prostitute. [Jap]

Geissler pump /gī'slər pump/ (*chem*) *n* a vacuum pump that operates from the water supply. [Heinrich *Geissler* (1814–79), the inventor]

Geissler tube /gī'slər tūb/ (*chem*) *n* a gas-filled discharge tube with two electrodes and a capillary section for concentrated illumination. [Ety as for **Geissler pump**]

geist /gīst/ *n* spirit, any inspiring or dominating principle. [Ger]

geit same as **get**, a child.

geitonogamy /gī-tən-og'ə-mi/ (*bot*) *n* pollination from another flower on the same plant. [Gr *geiton* neighbour, and *gamos* marriage]
■ **geitonog'amous** *adj*.

gel[1] /jel/ *n* a jelly-like apparently solid colloidal solution; (also **hair gel**) such a substance used to style hair or fix it in place; a transparent substance, or a sheet of this, used in theatre and photographic lighting to produce light of different colours (short for **gelatine**); an inert matrix in which molecules can be separated by electrophoresis. ◆ *vi* (**gell'ing**; **gelled**) to form a gel; to use gel to style hair; (also **jell**) to come together, begin to work, take shape (*inf*). ◆ *vt* to style using gel. [**gelatine**]
■ **gelā'tion** *n* see separate entry.

gel[2] /gel/ *n* a facetious rendering of an upper-class pronunciation of **girl**.

gelada /jel'ə-də or gel', ji-lä'də or gi-/ *n* an Ethiopian baboon, with a long mane. [Poss from Ar *qilādah* collar, mane]

gelati see **gelato**.

gelatine or **gelatin** /jel'ə-tēn or -tin/ *n* a colourless, odourless and tasteless glue, prepared from albuminous matter, eg bones and hides, used for foodstuffs, photographic films, glues, etc. [Fr, from Ital *gelatina*, *gelata* jelly, from L *gelāre* to freeze]
■ **gelatinate** /ji-lat'i-nāt/, **gelat'inize** or **-ise** *vt* to make into gelatine or jelly; to coat with gelatine or jelly. ◆ *vi* to be converted into gelatine or jelly. **gelatinā'tion**, **gelatiniza'tion** or **-s-** *n*. **gelat'inizer** or **-s-** *n*. **gelat'inoid** *n* a substance resembling gelatine (also *adj*). **gelat'inous** *adj* resembling or formed into gelatine or jelly.

■ **blasting gelatine** a violently explosive rubbery substance composed of nitroglycerine and nitrocotton.

gelation /jel-ā'shən/ n a solidification by cooling; the formation of a gel from a sol. [Partly L *gelātiō, -ōnis*, from *gelāre* to freeze; partly **gel**[1]]

gelato /je-lä'tō/ (*esp Aust*) n (pl **gela'ti** /-tē/) a type of whipped ice cream made from cream, milk and/or water and flavoured with fruit or nuts. [Ital]

geld[1] /geld/ vt (pat and pap **geld'ed** or **gelt** (*archaic* or *dialect*)) to emasculate, castrate; to spay; to deprive of anything essential, enfeeble, deprive; to expurgate (*obs*). [ON *gelda*; Dan *gilde*]
■ **geld'er** n. **geld'ing** n the act of castrating; a castrated animal, *esp* a horse.

geld[2] /geld/ (*Eng hist*) n a tax paid by landholders to the crown in late Anglo-Saxon and Norman times. ◆ vt to tax. [OE *geld, gyld* payment; ON *giald* money; cf **yield**]

gelder rose obsolete form of **guelder rose**.

gelid /jel'id/ adj icy cold; chilly, icy. [L *gelidus*, from *gelū* frost]
■ **gel'idly** adv. **gel'idness** or (*obs*) **gelid'ity** n.

gelignite /jel'ig-nīt/ n a powerful explosive used in mining, made from nitroglycerine, cellulose nitrate, potassium nitrate and wood pulp. [**gelatine** and L *ignis* fire]

gelliflowre (*Spenser*) same as **gillyflower**.

gelly[1] /jel'i/ (*inf*) n gelignite (also **jelly**).

gelly[2] /jel'i/ (*obs*) adj jellied.

gelosy (*Spenser*) same as **jealousy** (see under **jealous**).

gelsemium /jel-sē'mi-əm/ n the so-called yellow or Carolina jasmine, an American climbing plant of the Loganiaceae. [Ital *gelsomino* jasmine]
■ **gel'semine** /-səm-ēn/ and **gelseminine** /-sem'/ n two alkaloids yielded by the gelsemium rhizome and rootlets.

gelt[1] /gelt/ (*sl*) n money; profit. [Yiddish, from Ger *Geld*, Du *geld*]

gelt[2] /gelt/ (*archaic* or *dialect*) pat and pap of **geld**[1].

gelt[3] /gelt/ (*Spenser*) n a madman. [Ir *geilt*]

gelt[4] /gelt/ an obsolete non-standard form of **geld**[2]; same as **gilt**[1] (*Spenser*).

gem /jem/ n any precious stone, *esp* when cut (also **gem'stone**); a person or thing regarded as extremely admirable or flawless; an old size of type smaller than diamond (*printing*); a bud (*obs*). ◆ vt (**gemm'ing**; **gemmed**) (*obs*) to bud; to adorn with gems; to bespangle. [OE *gim*; OHGer *gimma*, from L *gemma* a bud; later remodelled on L or reintroduced]
■ **gemm'ate** vt (*obs*) to deck with gems. ◆ vi (*bot*) see under **gemma**. **gemm'eous** /-i-əs/ adj relating to gems; like a gem. **gemm'ery** n (*rare*) gems generally. **gemm'y** adj full of gems; brilliant. **gemolog'ical** or **gemmolog'ical** adj. **gemol'ogist** or **gemmol'ogist** n a person with special knowledge of gems. **gemol'ogy** or **gemmol'ogy** n the science of gems.
❑ **gem'-cutting** n the art of cutting and polishing precious stones. **gem'-engraving** n the art of engraving figures on gems. **gemstone therapy** n the therapeutic use of energies or vibrations emanating from precious or semi-precious stones.

Gemara /gə-mä'rə/ (*Judaism*) n the second part of the Talmud, consisting of a commentary on and complement to the first part, the Mishnah. [Aramaic, completion]

gematria /gə-mä'tri-ə/ n a cabbalistic method of interpreting the Hebrew Scriptures by interchanging words whose letters have the same numerical value when added. [Rabbinical Heb *gēmatriyā*, from Gr *geōmetriā* geometry]

gemcitabine /jem-sī'tə-bēn/ n a synthetic cytotoxic drug used to treat various cancers.

Gemeinschaft /gə-mīn'shäft/ (*Ger*) n a social group held together by ties such as friendship, kinship, etc.

gemel /jem'əl/ n a twin (*obs*); a gimmal (type of ring) (*hist*); a hinge (*obs*); a pair of bars placed close together (*heraldry*). [OFr *gemel* (Fr *jumeau*), from L *gemellus*, dimin of *geminus* twin]
❑ **gem'el-ring** same as **gimmal ring** (see **gimmal**).

gemfish /jem'fish/ n an edible marine fish (*Rexea solandri*) found off the S Australian and New Zealand coasts, formerly known as **kingfish** or **hake**.

geminate /jem'i-nāt/ vt to double; to arrange in pairs. ◆ adj (*bot*) in pairs. [L *gemināre* to double, from *geminus* twin]
■ **gemina'tion** n a doubling. **gem'inous** adj (*bot*) double, in pairs. **gem'iny** n (*Shakesp*) a pair, *esp* of eyes. ◆ interj (perhaps a separate word) expressing surprise, spelt also **gemini** (*obs*), **gemony** (*obs*) and (the sole current form) **jiminy**.

Gemini /jem'i-nī/ n pl the Twins, a constellation containing the two bright stars Castor and Pollux, giving its name to, and formerly

coinciding with, a sign of the zodiac (*astron*); the third sign of the zodiac, between Taurus and Cancer (*astrol*); (used as a *sing* with pl **Gem'inis**) a person born between 21 May and 21 June, under the sign of Gemini (*astrol*). [L, pl of *geminus* twin]
■ **Gemini'an** n and adj (relating to or characteristic of) a person born under the sign of Gemini. **Gem'inid** n a meteor of a swarm whose radiant is in the constellation Gemini.

gemma /jem'ə/ n (pl **gemm'ae** /-ē/) a small multicellular body produced vegetatively, capable of separating and becoming a new individual (*bot*); a bud or protuberance from the body that becomes a new individual (*zool*); a plant bud, *esp* a leaf-bud (*rare*). [L, a bud]
■ **gemmā'ceous** adj bud-like; relating to gemmae. **gemm'ate** adj having or reproducing by buds or gemmae. ◆ vt see under **gem**. ◆ vi to reproduce by gemmae. **gemmā'tion** n budding or gemma-formation. **gemm'ative** adj relating to gemmation. **gemmif'erous** adj bearing gemmae. **gemmip'arous** adj reproducing by gemmae. **gemmūlā'tion** n (*biol*) formation of gemmules. **gemm'ule** n a hypothetical particle thought by Darwin to be produced by each part of the body as a vehicle of heredity; a plumule (*bot*); an internal bud in sponges (*zool*).
❑ **gemm'a-cup** n a liverwort cupule.

gemman /jem'ən/ (*archaic inf*) n (pl **gemmen** /jem'ən/) a corruption of **gentleman**. [**gentleman**]

gemmate, gemmation, etc see under **gem, gemma**.

gemmeous, gemmery see under **gem**.

gemmiferous, gemmiparous see under **gemma**.

gemmologist, etc see under **gem**.

gemmulation, gemmule see under **gemma**.

gemmy[1] see under **gem**.

gemmy[2] see **jemmy**[2].

gemologist, etc see under **gem**.

gemony see under **geminate**.

gemot /gə-mōt'/ or /yə-mōt'/ (*Eng hist*) n a meeting or assembly; *specif* an Anglo-Saxon legislative or judicial assembly. [OE *gemōt*; cf **moot**]

Gems /jemz/ abbrev : Global Environment Monitoring System (set up by the United Nations Environment Programme).

gemsbok /hhemz'bok (*S Afr*), or *gemz'bok*/ n a S African antelope (*Oryx gazella*) about the size of a stag, with long straight horns. [Du, male chamois, from Ger *Gemsbock*]

gemshorn /gemz'hörn/ (*music*) n a chamois horn, as an early wind instrument; an organ stop made with conical metal pipes, having a soft fluty tone. [Ger, chamois horn]

gemütlich /gə-müt'lēhh/ (*Ger*) adj amiable; comfortable; cosy.
■ **Gemüt'lichkeit** /-kīt/ n kindness; comfort; cosiness.

Gen. abbrev : General; (the Book of) Genesis (*Bible*).

gen /jen/ (*sl*) n general information; the low-down or inside information.
■ **gen up** (**genning up**; **genned up**) to learn (with *on*).

gen. abbrev : genitive.

-gen /-jən/ or **-gene** /-jēn/ combining form used to denote: (1) producing or produced, as in *oxygen*, *phosgene* (*chem*); (2) growth, as in *endogen* (*bot*). [Gr *-genēs* born]

gena /jē'nə/ (*anat* and *zool*) n the cheek or side of the head. [L]
■ **gē'nal** adj.

genappe /jə-nap'/ n a smooth worsted yarn used with silk in fringes, braid, etc. [From *Genappe* in Belgium, where it was first made]

gendarme /zhä'därm/ n (pl **gen'darmes**, or occasionally **gens'darmes**) orig a man-at-arms, a horseman in full armour; since the French Revolution, a member of a corps of armed French police; a similar policeman elsewhere; a rock-pillar on a mountain. [Fr *gendarme*, sing from pl *gens d'armes* men-at-arms, from *gens* people, *de* of, and *armes* arms]
■ **gendarm'erie** /-ə-rē/ n an armed police force; a police station or barracks.

gender[1] /jen'dər/ n a distinction of words roughly corresponding to the sex to which they refer (*grammar*); the quality of being male or female, sex; kind, sort (*obs*). [Fr *genre*, from L *genus* kind]
■ **gen'dered** adj gender-specific. **gen'derless** adj not having or indicating gender; not indicating differences in sex, suitable for either sex.
❑ **gender bender** n (*inf*) a person who for deliberate effect, publicity or amusement adopts a sexually ambiguous public image and style (in dress, hairstyle, make-up, etc). **gen'der-bending** n (*inf*) the blurring of the distinctions between the sexes through sexual ambiguity or bisexuality in behaviour or dress. **gender person** n (*esp N Am*) an overtly non-sexist term for a human being of either sex. **gender reassignment** n the process of changing the sex of a person using surgery and hormone treatment. **gender role** n (*behaviourism*) the set of attitudes and behaviour considered appropriate by a given culture

---

for each sex. **gender-specif'ic** *adj* belonging to or limited to either males or females.

gender² /jen'dər/ *vt* to beget (*archaic*); to generate (*obs*). ◆ *vi* (*obs*) to copulate. [Fr *gendrer*, from L *generāre*]

gene /jēn/ (*biol*) *n* the hereditary determinant of a specified difference between individuals, shown by molecular analysis to be a specific sequence or parts of a sequence of DNA. [Ger *Gen*, from Gr *-genēs* born]

■ **gen'ic** *adj* of or relating to a gene.

❏ **gene amplification** *n* (*biol*) the formation of multiple copies of a particular gene or DNA sequence. **gene bank** *n* a collection of genetic material stored as cloned DNA fragments for plant and animal breeding programmes, genetic manipulation, etc. **gene flow** *n* the passing of genes to succeeding generations. **gene frequency** *n* (*biol*) the frequency of a particular allele of a gene in a population. **gene locus** *n* the site on a chromosome occupied by a gene. **gene mapping** see under **map**. **gene pool** *n* the stock of genes found in an interbreeding population. **gene splicing** *n* the artificial introduction of DNA from one organism into the genetic material of another, in order to produce a desired characteristic in the recipient. **gene therapist** *n*. **gene therapy** *n* the treatment or prevention of (*esp* heritable) diseases by genetic engineering.

gêne /zhen/ (*Fr*) *n* embarrassment (also **gene**).

-gene see **-gen**.

genealogy /jē-ni-al'ə-ji or jen'i-/ *n* the history of the descent of families; the pedigree of a particular person or family. [Gr *geneālogiā*, from *geneā* race, and *logos* discourse]

■ **genealogical** /-ə-loj'i-kl/ or **genealog'ic** *adj*. **genealog'ically** *adv*. **geneal'ogist** *n* a person who studies or traces genealogies or descents. **geneal'ogize** or **-ise** *vi* to investigate or discuss genealogy. ❏ **genealogical tree** *n* a table of descent in the form of a tree with branches.

genera plural of **genus**.

generable see under **generate**.

general /jen'ə-rəl/ *adj* relating to a genus or whole class; including various species; not special; not restricted or specialized; relating to the whole or to all or most; universal; nearly universal; common; prevalent; widespread; public; vague; (after an official title, etc) chief, of highest rank, at the head of a department (as in *director-general*, *postmaster-general*); socially accessible and familiar with all (*obs*). ◆ *adv* (*Shakesp*) generally. ◆ *n* the universal as opposed to the particular; an army officer between a field marshal and lieutenant-general in rank; the head of a religious order, such as the Jesuits; the chief commander of an army in service; a person acting as leader, planning tactics or management; the head of the Salvation Army; a general servant (*obs*); the public, the vulgar (*archaic* and *Shakesp*); the total (*obs*); the most part, majority (*obs*). ◆ *vt* (**gen'eralling**; **gen'eralled**) to act as general of. [OFr, from L *generālis*, from *genus*]

■ **gen'eralate** *n* the office of a general; the district or domain under the charge of a general. **generālē** (or /gen-er-ā'le/) *n* (*L*) general principles, *esp* in *pl* **generā'lia**. **generaliss'imo** *n* (*pl* **generaliss'imos**) (*Ital superl*) supreme commander of a great or combined force. **gen'eralist** *n* a person or thing whose knowledge, activity, etc is not restricted to any particular field, *opp* to *specialist*. **general'ity** *n* a statement having general application; the state of being general; broadness or vagueness; the majority; the general public. **gen'eralīzable** or **-s-** *adj*. **generalīzā'tion** or **-s-** *n*. **gen'eralize** or **-ise** *vt* to make general; to include under a general term; to reduce to a general form; to comprehend as a particular case within a wider concept, proposition, definition, etc; to represent or endow with the common characters of a group without the special characters of any one member; to bring to general use or knowledge; to infer inductively. ◆ *vi* to make general statements; to form general concepts; to depict general character; to reason inductively. **gen'erally** *adv* in a general or collective manner or sense; in most cases; on the whole. **gen'eralship** *n* the position of a military commander; the art of manipulating armies; tactical management and leadership.

❏ **general anaesthetic** see under **anaesthesia**. **General Assembly** see under **assemble**. **General Certificate of Education** *n* in secondary education in England and Wales, a certificate obtainable at Ordinary (formerly), Advanced, and Special levels for proficiency in one or more subjects. **General Certificate of Secondary Education** *n* in England and Wales, a certificate based on coursework as well as examinations, designed to suit a wide range of academic ability. **general degree** same as **pass degree** (see under **pass**). **general delivery** *n* (*US*) poste restante. **general election** *n* an election of all the members of a body (eg House of Commons, House of Representatives) at once. **general epistles** see under **catholic**. **general journal** *n* (*bookkeeping*) a book of initial entry for miscellaneous transactions. **general ledger** *n* (*bookkeeping*) a book which contains nominal accounts; the central database of a

bookkeeping system (*US*). **general line** *n* the party line. **general meeting** *n* a meeting of members of an organization whose decisions are legally binding. **general officer** *n* (*milit*) an officer above the rank of colonel. **general paralysis of the insane** *n* general paresis (qv under **paresis**). **general post** *n* formerly, dispatch of mail to all parts, as opposed to local twopenny or penny post; the main daily delivery of letters; a general change of positions, etc (from a parlour game). **general post office** *n* formerly, an office receiving letters for the general post; (now) the head post office of a town or district. **general practice** *n* the work of a **general practitioner**, a doctor who treats patients for most illnesses or complaints, referring other cases to specialists. **general principle** *n* a principle to which there are no exceptions within its range of application. **gen'eral-purpose** *adj* generally useful, not restricted to a particular function. **general reserve** *n* (*account*) profits which have been set aside for retention in the business but not for any specified purpose. **general servant** *n* a servant whose duties embrace domestic work of every kind. **general staff** *n* military officers who advise senior officers on policy, administration, etc. **General Synod** see under **synod**.

▣ **in general** as a generalization; mostly, as a general rule.

generate /jen'ə-rāt/ *vt* to produce; to bring into life or being; to evolve; to originate; to trace out (*geom*). [L *generāre*, *-ātum*, from *genus* a kind]

■ **gen'erable** *adj* that may be generated or produced. **gen'erant** *n* a begetter, producer, parent (*obs*); a line, point or figure that traces out another figure by its motion (*geom*). **gen'erātor** *n* a begetter or producer; an apparatus for producing gases, etc; an apparatus for turning mechanical into electrical energy; a fundamental tone, the first or lowest in a chord or harmonic series (*music*). **generā'trix** *n* (*pl* **generā'trices** /-tri-sēz/) a mother (*obs*); a generant (*geom*). ❏ **generating station** *n* a plant where electricity is generated.

generation /jen-ə-rā'shən/ *n* production or originating; a single stage of natural descent; the people of the same age or period; descendants removed by the same number of steps from a common ancestor; the ordinary time interval between the births of successive generations (*usu* reckoned at 30 or 33 years); any of a number of stages, levels or series, generally in which each stage, etc is seen as a development of or improvement on the preceding one; a term used in describing the development of computers (see **first generation** under **first**, **fifth generation** under **fifth**); any series of files, each one an amended and updated version of the previous one (*comput*); offspring or progeny (*obs*); a race, kind, class, family (*obs*); (in *pl*) genealogy, history (*Bible*). [L *generātiō*, *-ōnis*, from *generāre* (see **generate**)]

■ **genera'tional** *adj*. **genera'tionism** *n* traducianism.

❏ **generation gap** *n* lack of communication and understanding, or the observable differences in attitudes, ideals or outlook, between one generation and the next. **Generation X** *n* the people who became adults in the early 1990s, considered apathetic or sceptical about traditionally held beliefs and values, *esp* relating to work and the family. **Generation X'er** *n* a member of Generation X.

▣ **alternation of generations** see under **alternate**. **spontaneous generation** the origination of living from non-living matter.

generative /jen'ə-rə-tiv/ *adj* having the power of, or concerned with, generating or producing. [**generate**]

❏ **generative grammar** *n* (*linguistics*) a description of a language as a finite set of grammatical rules able to generate an infinite number of grammatical sentences.

▣ **motion generative** (*Shakesp*) a male puppet, or perhaps someone who is a mere puppet so far as engendering is concerned.

generic /jə-ner'ik/ *adj* general, applicable to any member of a group or class; of or belonging to a genus; (of a drug, etc) not patented or sold as a proprietary name; (of the name of a brand) that has come to be used as a general name for that type of product (eg *Biro* for ballpoint pen, *Hoover* for vacuum cleaner); of or belonging to the same family of computers, software, etc. ◆ *n* a generic drug, etc; a product sold without a brand name, in plain packaging, and with no promotion or advertising; a generic brand name. [Fr *générique*, from L *genus* (see **genus**)]

■ **gener'ical** *adj* general, applicable to any of a group or class; of or belonging to a genus. **gener'ically** *adv*. **genericīzā'tion** or **-s-** *n*. **genericize** or **-ise** /jə-ner'i-sīz/ *vt* to use (a proprietary term) as a generic brand name.

❏ **generic name** *n* the name of the genus, placed first in naming the species, thus *Equus caballus* (horse), *Equus asinus* (ass), *Equus zebra*, etc are species of the genus *Equus*, and *Equus* is the generic name, always written with a capital and in italics (*biol*); the name of a generic drug, product, etc.

generous /jen'ə-rəs/ *adj* liberal; bountiful; ample; kind; of a noble nature (*archaic*); courageous (*obs*); (of eg wine) invigorating in its nature; nobly born (*obs*). [L *generōsus* of noble birth, from *genus* birth]

■ **generos'ity** or **gen'erousness** *n* liberality of nature, the quality of being free and unstinting with one's possessions, money, time;

nobleness of nature, magnanimity; a generous act; nobility of birth (*archaic*). **gen'erously** *adv*.

genesis /jen'i-sis/ *n* (pl **gen'esēs**) generation, creation, development or production; (with *cap*) the first book of the Bible, telling of the Creation. ◆ *combining form* denoting creation or development, as in *parthenogenesis, pathogenesis*. [Gr]
■ **Genesiac** /ji-nē'si-ək/, **Genē'siacal** or **Genesitic** /jen-ə-sit'ik/ *adj* relating to Genesis.

genet[1] /jen'it/ or **genette** /ji-net'/ *n* a carnivorous animal (genus *Genetta*) related to the civet; its fur, or an imitation. [Fr *genette*, from Sp *gineta*, from Ar *jarnait*]

genet[2] see **jennet**.

genetic /ji-net'ik/ or **genetical** /-əl/ *adj* causal, relating to origin; of or relating to genes or genetics. ◆ *combining form* productive of, as in *pathogenetic*. [**genesis**]
■ **genet'ically** *adv*. **genet'icist** /-i-sist/ *n* a student of genetics. **genet'ics** *n sing* the branch of biology dealing with heredity and variation; inherited characteristics of an organism; origin; development.
❑ **genetically modified** *adj* altered through genetic engineering (*abbrev* **GM**). **genetically significant dose** *n* (*radiol*) the dose of radiation that, if given to every member of a population prior to conception of children, would produce in the children the same genetic or hereditary harm as the actual doses received by the various individuals. **genetic code** *n* the rules which relate the four bases of DNA (adenine, guanine, cytosine, thymine) or RNA (adenine, guanine, cytosine, uracil) with the 20 amino acids found in proteins. **genetic counselling** *n* advice, based on chromosomal and amniotic fluid investigation, etc, given to prospective parents on possible heritable defects in their children. **genetic drift** *n* a change in the genetic structure of organisms caused by factors other than natural selection. **genetic engineering** *n* another name for genetic manipulation. **genetic fingerprint** *n* the particular DNA configuration exclusive to an individual human or animal or its offspring. **genetic fingerprinting** *n* the identification of genetic fingerprints (eg in forensic science, to identify or eliminate a specific individual). **genetic marker** *n* an identifiable DNA sequence that can be inherited and readily traced. **genetic manipulation** *n* the procedures with which it is possible to combine DNA sequences from widely different organisms in vitro, often with great precision, thus in the long term making possible the control of hereditary defects and, currently, the mass production of useful biological substances (eg insulin and human growth hormone). **genetic parents** *n pl* the 'natural' parents, those whose genes the child carries. **genetic screening** *n* the testing of high-risk sections of the population for signs of hereditary disease. **genetic spiral** *n* (*bot*) a hypothetical line through the centres of successive leaf primordia at the shoot apex.

genetotrophic /jen-ə-tō-trō'fik or -trof'/ *adj* denoting deficiency diseases which have an underlying genetic, and a direct nutritional, cause and which are treatable by dietary means. [*geneto-*, combining form from **genetic**, and **trophic**]

genetrix see **genitor**.

genette see **genet**[1].

geneva /ji-nē'və/ *n* a spirit distilled from grain and flavoured with juniper berries, a gin, made chiefly in the Netherlands (also called **Hollands** or **Hollands gin**; see **gin**[1]). [ODu *genever*, OFr *genevre*, from L *jūniperus* juniper; confused with town of *Geneva*]
■ **genevrette** /jen-əv-ret'/ *n* a wine made from wild fruits flavoured with juniper berries.

Genevan /ji-nē'vən/ *adj* relating to or associated with *Geneva*, in Switzerland. ◆ *n* an inhabitant of Geneva; an adherent of Genevan or Calvinistic theology.
■ **Genē'vanism** *n* (*obs*) Calvinism. **Genevese** /jen'i-vēz/ *adj* and *n*.
❑ **Geneva bands** *n pl* the two strips of white linen hanging down from the neck of some clerical robes. **Geneva Bible** *n* a version of the Bible, long popular, produced by English Protestant exiles in Geneva in 1560. **Geneva Convention** *n* an international agreement of 1864, with subsequent revisions, concerning the status and treatment in wartime of the sick and wounded, prisoners of war, etc. **Geneva cross** *n* a red cross on a white background displayed for protection in war of people serving in hospitals, etc. **Geneva gown** *n* the long dark preaching gown of the early Geneva reformers, and still the common form of pulpit-gown among Presbyterians. **Geneva movement, mechanism**, etc *n* (*engineering*) a mechanism which converts continuous into intermittent motion by means of slots on the driven wheel. **Genevan theology** *n* Calvinism, the theology of Calvin or his followers, so called from Calvin's residence in Geneva and the establishment of his doctrines there.

genevrette see under **geneva**.

genial[1] /jē'ni-əl/ *adj* (of a climate) mild, pleasant, favouring growth; cheering; kindly; sympathetic; healthful; relating to marriage and procreation (*archaic*). [L *geniālis*, from *genius* the tutelary spirit]
■ **gēniality** /-al'i-ti/ or **gē'nialness** *n*. **gē'nialize** or **-ise** *vt* to impart geniality to. **gē'nially** *adv*.

genial[2] /jə-nī'əl/ (*anat*) *adj* of or relating to the chin. [Gr *geneion* chin, from *genys* jaw]

genic see under **gene**.

-genic /-jen-ik or -jēn-ik/ *combining form* signifying: (1) productive of, generating, as in *pathogenic, carcinogenic*; (2) ideal or suitable for, as in *photogenic*; (3) caused by, as in *iatrogenic*. [**-gen** and sfx *-ic*]

geniculate /jə-nik'yū-lāt/ *adj* (also **genic'ulated**) bent like a knee; jointed; knotted. ◆ *vt* to form joints in. [L *geniculātus*, from *geniculum* a little knee, from *genū* the knee]
■ **genic'ulately** *adv*. **genicula'tion** *n*.

genie /jē'ni/ *n* a jinnee (see **jinn**); a magical being who carries out a person's wishes. [Fr *génie*, from L *genius*, adopted because of its similarity to the Ar word]

genii see **genius**.

genipap /jen'i-pap/, also **genip** /-ip/ *n* a large rubiaceous tree of Central and S America (*Genipa americana*); its orange-sized, wine-flavoured fruit. [From Tupí]

genista /jə-nis'tə/ *n* a plant belonging to the *Genista* genus of shrubby, papilionaceous plants, with simple leaves and yellow flowers, eg green-weed and petty whin. [L *genista* broom]

genistein /jen'i-stān or jen'i-stēn/ *n* a plant oestrogen, found in soya, thought to be effective in fighting cancer.

genit. *abbrev*: genitive.

genital /jen'i-təl/ *adj* belonging to biological generation or the act of reproducing; of, relating to, or affecting, the genitals, or genital area; relating to the stage of mature psychosexual development. [L *genitālis*, from *gignere, genitum* to beget]
■ **genital'ic** or **genitā'lial** *adj*. **gen'itals** or **genitā'lia** *n pl* the organs of generation, the (*esp* external) sexual organs.

genitive /jen'i-tiv/ *adj* of or belonging to a case expressing origin, possession, or similar relation (*grammar*); relating to procreation (*obs*). ◆ *n* (*grammar*) the genitive case; a word in the genitive case. [L *genitīvus* (from *gignere, genitum* to beget) for Gr *genikē* (*ptōsis*), properly, generic (case), from *genos* a class]
■ **geniti'val** *adj*. **geniti'vally** or (*rare*) **gen'itively** *adv*.

genito- /jen-i-tō-/ *combining form* denoting genital.
■ **genito-ūr'inary** *adj* relating to genital and urinary organs or functions.

genitor /jen'i-tər/ (now *rare*) *n* a father; (also *fem* **gen'etrix** or **gen'itrix**) a parent; a progenitor. [L]
■ **gen'iture** *n* engendering; birth (*astrol; obs*).

genius /jē'nyəs or jē'ni-əs/ *n* (pl **ge'niuses** or, in sense of spirit, **genii** /jē'ni-ī/) consummate intellectual, creative, or other power, more exalted than talent; a person endowed with this; the special inborn faculty of any individual; a special taste or natural disposition (*obs*); a good or evil spirit, supposed to preside over every person, place and thing, and *esp* to preside over a person's destiny from his or her birth; a person who exerts a power, influence (whether good or bad) over another; prevailing spirit or tendency; type or generic exemplification. [L *genius*, from *gignere, genitum* to beget]

genius loci /jē'ni-əs lō'sī or gen'i-oos lok'ē/ (L) *n* literally, the spirit of the place; a local presiding spirit or deity; the distinctive atmosphere or aura of a place.

genizah /gə-nē'zə/ *n* a room adjoining a synagogue for the safekeeping of old or damaged books, documents or valuables. [Heb]

Genl *abbrev*: General.

genlock /gen'lok/ (*image technol*) *n* a device for synchronizing locally generated signals with those transmitted from a distance. [*generator* and **lock**[1]]

gennaker /jen'ə-kər/ (*naut*) *n* a sail that combines the features of a *genoa* and a *spinnaker*, used for sailing downwind.

gennel see **ginnel**.

gennet see **jennet**.

genoa or **Genoa** /jen'ō-ə or jə-nō'ə/ *n* (*naut*) a large jib which overlaps the mainsail. [*Genoa* in Italy]
❑ **Genoa cake** *n* a rich cake containing fruit, with almonds on the top.

genocide /jen'ə-sīd/ *n* the deliberate extermination of a racial, national, religious or ethnic group; a person who exterminates, or approves extermination of, a race, etc. [Gr *genos* race, and L *caedere* to kill]
■ **genocī'dal** *adj*.

Genoese /jen'ō-ēz or -ēz'/ or **Genovese** /-vēz/ adj relating to Genoa, seaport in NW Italy. ◆ n (pl **Genoese'** or **Genovese'**) an inhabitant, citizen or native of Genoa. [L Genua, Ital Genova Genoa]

genome /jē'nōm/ n (also formerly **genom**) the complete set of chromosomes of an individual; the total number of genes in such a set. [gene and chromosome]
■ **genomic** /-nom'ik/ adj. **genom'ics** n sing the study of genomes. ❑ **genomic library** n a DNA library derived from a whole, single genome.

genophobia /jen-ō-fō'bi-ə/ n pathological fear of sex. [geno- (combining form, from Gr genos begetting, producing) and **phobia**]

genotoxic /jen-ō-tok'sik/ adj harmful to genetic material, esp in causing genetic mutation. [**gene** and **toxic**]

genotype /jen'ə-tīp or jē'nə-tīp/ n the particular alleles at specified loci present in an individual; the genetic constitution; a group of individuals all of whom possess the same genetic constitution. [**gene**, -o- (linking element in compounds) and **type**]
■ **genotypic** /-tip'ik/ adj. **genotyp'ically** adv. **genotypic'ity** n.

genouillère /zhə-noo-yer'/ n the jointed knee-piece in armour. [Fr]

genre /zhon'rə or (Fr) zhä'r'/ n kind; a literary or artistic type or style; a style of painting scenes from familiar or rustic life. ◆ adj relating to or working in a specific genre. [Fr, from L genus]

Genro /gen'rō/ (hist) n pl the Japanese Elder Statesmen, who advised the emperor in the early 20c. [Jap]

gens¹ /jenz or gäns/ n (pl **gen'tēs**) (in ancient Rome) a clan including several families descended from a common ancestor; a tribe or clan, group of families (anthrop). See also **Gentile**. [L gēns, gentis]
❑ **gens togata** /tō-gä'tə/ n the toga-wearing nation, ie the Romans.

gens² /zhã/ (Fr) n pl people.
❑ **gens de bien** /də byē/ n pl honest, respectable people. **gens de condition** /də kõ-dēs-yõ/ n pl people of rank. **gens d'église** /dā-glēz/ n pl churchmen and churchwomen. **gens de guerre** /də ger/ n pl military men. **gens de lettres** /də letr/ n pl men and women of letters. **gens de loi** /də lwa/ n pl lawyers. **gens de peu** /də pø/ n pl people of humble condition. **gens du monde** /dü mõd/ n pl people of fashion.

gensdarmes see gendarme.

gent¹ /jent/ n (pl **gents**) short for **gentleman**; a man who imitates the style and behaviour of a gentleman (old inf).
■ **gents** n a public lavatory for men.

gent² /jent/ (Spenser) adj noble; gentle. [OFr, from L genitus born]

genteel /jen-tēl'/ adj well-bred; graceful in manners or in form; fashionable (archaic); now used mainly with mocking reference to a standard of obsolete snobbery or false refinement. [Fr gentil, from L gentīlis; see **gentle**]
■ **genteel'ish** adj. **genteel'ism** n a word or phrase used in place of an accustomed one, where this is felt to be coarse or vulgar. **genteel'ize** or **-ise** vt to make genteel or falsely refined. **genteel'ly** adv. **genteel'ness** n.

gentes see gens¹.

gentian /jen'shən/ n any plant of the genus Gentiana, herbs, usu blue-flowered, abounding chiefly in alpine regions, typical of the family **Gentianaceae** /-ā'si-ē/; the root and rhizome of the yellow gentian used as a tonic and stomachic. [L gentiāna, according to Pliny from Gentius, king of Illyria, who introduced it in medicine (2c BC)]
■ **gentianā'ceous** adj of, relating to or belonging to the Gentianaceae. **gentianell'a** n a name for several species of gentian, esp Gentiana acaulis, with deep-blue flowers.
❑ **gentian violet** n in the British pharmacopoeia, crystal violet; sometimes, methyl violet; now generally a mixture of crystal violet, methyl violet and methyl rosaniline, used as an antiseptic, esp for burns.

Gentile or **gentile** /jen'tīl/ n anyone who is not a Jew; anyone who is not a member of a specified religious group, esp the Mormons; a heathen or pagan. ◆ adj (without cap) of or belonging to a gens or clan (rare); belonging to the Gentiles; denoting a race or country (grammar). [L gentīlis, from gēns a nation, clan]
■ **gentilic** /-tīl'ik/ adj tribal. **gen'tilish** adj (obs) heathenish. **gen'tilism** /-til- or -tīl-/ n paganism, or the quality of being a Gentile. **gentilitial** /jen-ti-lish'l/, **gentili'tian** or **gentili'tious** adj relating to a gens.

gentilesse /jen-ti-les'/ (obs) n the quality of being gentle, courtesy. [Fr, from gentil (see **genteel**)]

gentilhomme /zhã-tē-yom'/ (Fr) n (pl **gentilshommes**) a nobleman; a gentleman.

gentility /jen-til'i-ti/ n good birth or extraction; good breeding; respectability; courtesy; signs or characteristics of any of these; now used mockingly to refer to artificial politeness; genteel people. [OFr gentilite (Fr gentilité), from L gentīlitās, from gentīlis; see **gentle**]

gentilize or **-ise** /jen'ti-līz/ (archaic) vt to raise to the class of gentleman. [OFr (Fr) gentil; see **gentle**]

gentle /jen'tl/ adj mild and refined in manners; mild in disposition or action; amiable; soothing; moderate; gradual; well-born, from a good family (archaic). ◆ vt to ennoble (obs); to make gentle; to handle gently. ◆ n a well-born person (obs); a trained falcon; hence a peregrine falcon (masc **ter'cel-gen'tle**; fem **fal'con-gen'tle**); a soft maggot used as bait in angling. [OFr (Fr) gentil, from L gentīlis belonging to the same gens or clan, later, well-bred; see **genteel**]
■ **gen'tlehood** n (archaic) position or character attaching to good birth. **gen'tleness** n. **gen'tlenesse** n (obs) same as **gentilesse**. **gent'ly** adv.
❑ **gentle breeze** n (meteorol) a wind of force 3 on the Beaufort scale, reaching speeds of 8 to 12mph. **gen'tlefolk** n pl people of good family. **gentle-heart'ed** adj having a gentle or kind disposition. **gen'tleman** n see separate entry. **gentle reader** n courteous reader, an old-fashioned phrase common in the prefaces of books. **gen'tlewoman** n see separate entry.
■ **the gentle craft** shoemaking (obs); angling.

gentleman /jen'tl-mən/ n (pl **gen'tlemen**) a man of good birth or high social standing; a man of refined manners; a man of good feeling and instincts, courteous and honourable; a well-to-do man of no occupation; a polite term used for man in general; a man who without a title bears a coat of arms (hist); more generally, any man above the rank of yeoman, including members of the nobility (hist); a personal attendant (Shakesp).
■ **gen'tlemanhood** or **gen'tlemanship** n the condition or character of a gentleman. **gen'tlemanlike** adj like or characteristic of a gentleman. **gen'tlemanliness** n. **gen'tlemanly** adj befitting a gentleman; well-bred, refined, generous. **gentlemanship** see gentlemanhood above.
❑ **Gen'tleman-at-arms** n a member of the royal bodyguard, instituted in 1509, and now composed of military officers of service and distinction only. **gen'tleman-cadet'** n a student in a military college. **gen'tleman-comm'oner** n formerly, at Oxford and Cambridge, an undergraduate with special privileges. **gentleman farmer** n a landowner who lives on his estate superintending the cultivation of his own soil; a gentleman who owns a farm and employs a farm manager and other staff to work it on his behalf. **Gentleman of the Chapel Royal** n a lay singer who assists the priests in the choral service of the royal chapel. **gentleman's** (or **-men's**) **agreement** n an agreement resting on honour, not on formal contract; a contract made by word of mouth and without drawing up any legal documents, ie not legally binding but resting on honour alone (business). **gentleman's gentleman** n a valet. **Gentleman's Relish®** n a savoury paste made from anchovies, for spreading on sandwiches, etc. **gentleman usher** n (pl **gentlemen ushers**) a gentleman who serves as an usher at court, or as an attendant on a person of rank. **gentlemen's agreement** see gentleman's agreement above.

gentlewoman /jen'tl-wům-ən/ n (pl **gen'tlewomen**) a personal attendant on a lady of rank (hist); a woman of good breeding and refinement, a lady (archaic).
■ **gen'tlewomanliness** n. **gen'tlewomanly** adj like, or characteristic of, a refined and well-bred woman.

gentoo /jen'too or jen-too'/ n a species of penguin with a white stripe across its head; (with cap) (a speaker of) Telugu (obs); (with cap) a non-Christian from India, a Hindu (hist). ◆ adj (with cap) of or relating to the Gentoos or the Telugu language. [Port gentio a Gentile]

gentry /jen'tri/ n the class of people next below the rank of nobility; nobility, aristocracy; people of a particular, esp an inferior, sort (inf); rank by birth (archaic); the rank of gentleman (archaic); good manners and courtesy (Shakesp). [OFr genterise, gentelise, formed from adj gentil gentle]
■ **gen'trice** /-tris/ n (archaic) good birth; good breeding. **gentrifica'tion** n the movement of middle-class people into a formerly working-class area with the consequent change in the character of the area; the modernizing of old, badly equipped property, usu with a view to increasing its value. **gen'trifier** n. **gen'trify** vt.

genty /jen'ti/ (Scot) adj neat, dainty; graceful.

genu /jen'oo or jen'ū/ (anat) n the knee; a knee-like bend or structure. [L, knee]

genuflect /jen'ū-flekt/ vi to bend the knee in worship or respect. [L genū the knee, and flectere, flexum to bend]
■ **genūflex'ion** or **genūflec'tion** n.

genuine /jen'ū-in/ adj natural; native; not spurious; real; pure; sincere; running consistently up to full ability (horse-racing). [L genuīnus, from gignere to beget]
■ **gen'uinely** adv. **gen'uineness** n.
❑ **genuine material difference** n (law) (in an equal pay claim) a defence brought by an employer to show that on a balance of probabilities the variation in terms and conditions is due to a genuine

material difference other than sex (eg grading scheme, age, experience). **genuine occupational qualification** *n* an attribute of a person of a particular sex or racial origin which makes them more suited to a particular job, allowing an employer to choose them for the job in preference to someone of another sex or race.

genus /*jē'nəs* or *jen'əs*/ *n* (pl **genera** /*jen'ə-rə*/ or **gē'nuses**) a taxonomic group of lower rank than a family, consisting of closely related species, in extreme cases of one species only (*biol*); a class of objects comprehending several subordinate species (*logic*). [L *genus*, *generis* birth; cognate with Gr *genos*]

-geny /*-jə-ni*/ *combining form* signifying production, development, origin. [Gr *-geneia*, from *-genēs* born]

Geo. *abbrev* : George.

geo or **gio** /*gyō*/ (*Orkney* and *Shetland*) *n* (pl **geos** or **gios**) a gully, creek. [ON *gjā*]

geo- /*jē-ō-*/ *combining form* denoting the earth. [Gr *gē* the earth]

geocaching /*jē'ō-kash-ing*/ *n* a leisure pursuit in which an object is hidden at a grid reference for searchers to find using a Global Positioning System. [**geo-** and **cache**]

geocarpy /*jē-ō-kär'pi*/ (*bot*) *n* the production, or ripening, of fruit underground. [Gr *gē* earth, and *karpos* fruit]
■ **geocarp'ic** *adj*.

geocentric /*jē-ō-sen'trik*/ *adj* (also **geocen'trical**) having the earth for centre; as viewed or reckoned from the centre of the earth (*astron*); taking life on earth as the basis for evaluation. [Gr *gē* the earth, and *kentron* point, centre]
■ **geocen'trically** *adv*. **geocen'tricism** /*-sizm*/ *n* the belief that the earth is the centre of the universe.

geochemistry /*jē-ō-kem'i-stri*/ *n* the study of the chemical composition of the earth. [**geo-**]
■ **geochem'ical** *adj*. **geochem'ically** *adv*. **geochem'ist** *n*.

geochronology /*jē-ō-kro-nol'ə-ji*/ *n* the science of measuring geological time. [**geo-**]
■ **geochronolog'ical** *adj*. **geochronol'ogist** *n*.

geocode /*jē'ō-kōd*/ (*comput*) *vt* to assign geographical co-ordinates to (a digital data set). [**geo-**]

geodata /*jē'ō-dā-tə*/ (*comput*) *n pl* information about the geographical location of objects. [**geo-**]

geode /*jē'ōd*/ *n* a rock cavity lined with crystals that have grown inwards, a druse (*geol*); a rock or stone having this (*geol*); a rounded hollow nodule of ironstone (*mining*). [Fr *géode*, from Gr *geōdēs* earthy, from *gē* earth, and *eidos* form]
■ **geod'ic** *adj*.

geodemographics /*jē-ō-dem-ō-graf'iks*/ *n sing* the study of demographic data in terms of geographical area.

geodesy /*jē-od'i-si*/ *n* (also **geodetics** /*jē-ō-det'iks*/) earth measurement on a large scale; surveying with allowance for the earth's curvature. [Gr *geōdaisiā*, from *gē* the earth, and *daisis* division]
■ **geodesic** /*jē-ō-des'ik* or *-dē'sik*/ *adj* relating to or determined by geodesy; constructed from a grid of identical shapes. ◆ *n* a geodesic line (see below). **geodes'ical** *adj* geodesic. **geod'esist** *n* someone skilled in geodesy; a geodesic surveyor. **geodet'ic** or **geodet'ical** *adj* geodesic. **geodet'ically** *adv*.
❑ **geodesic dome** *n* a light strong dome made by combining a grid of triangular or other straight-line elements with a section of a sphere. **geodesic** (or **geodetic**) **line** *n* the shortest line on a surface between two points on it. **geodetic surveying** *n* geodesy, surveying large areas with allowance for the earth's curvature.

Geodimeter® /*jē-ō-dim'i-tər*/ *n* an instrument which measures distances by means of a beam of light, calculating on the basis of the speed of light.

geoduck /*jē'ō-duk*/ *n* a large edible bivalve shellfish (*Panope generosa*) of the coast of NW America. [From Salish]

geodynamics /*jē-ō-dī-nam'iks*/ *n sing* the study of the dynamic processes and forces within the earth. [**geo-**]
■ **geodynam'ic** or **geodynam'ical** *adj*.

geoengineering /*jē-ō-en-jin-ēr'ing*/ *n* the use of technology to counter changes in the global climate. [**geo-**]

geofact /*jē'ō-fakt*/ (*archaeol*) *n* a rock or other object altered (eg chipped) by the action of nature in such a way that it looks like an artefact. [**geo-** and *artefact*]

geog. *abbrev* : geographic, geographical; geography.

geogeny /*jē-oj'ə-ni*/ *n* the science or theory of the formation of the earth's crust. [**geo-** and **-geny**]

geognosy /*jē-og'nə-si*/ *n* knowledge of the general structure, condition and materials of the earth (also (*rare*) **geognosis** /*jē-əg-nō'sis*/). [Fr *géognosie*, from Gr *gē* the earth, and *gnōsis* knowledge]

■ **gē'ognost** *n*. **gēognostic** /*-nos'tik*/ or **gēognost'ical** *adj*. **gēognost'ically** *adv*.

geogony /*jē-og'ə-ni*/ *n* the science or theory of the formation of the earth. [Gr *gē* the earth, and *gonē* generation, production]
■ **geogonic** /*jē-ō-gon'ik*/ *adj*.

geography /*jē-og'rə-fi* or *jog'*/ *n* the science of the surface of the earth and its inhabitants; the features or the arrangement of a place; a book containing a description of the earth. [Gr *geōgraphiā*, from *gē* earth, and *graphein* to write]
■ **geog'rapher** *n*. **geographic** /*jē-ō-graf'ik*/ or **geograph'ical** *adj*. **geograph'ically** *adv*.
❑ **geographical concentration** *n* (*marketing*) the degree to which the market for a particular product or service is limited to one geographical area. **geographical distribution** *n* the branch of science concerned with the range and dispersal of animals and plants around the world. **geographical filing** *n* (eg in a company sales or transport department) a filing classification system where files are kept according to geographical district. **geographical mile** see under **mile**.
■ **physical** and **political geography** see under **physic** and **politic**.

geoid /*jē'oid*/ *n* the shape produced if the earth's mean sea-level surface is assumed to be continued under the land, approximately an oblate spheroid. [Gr *geōdēs*, *geoeidēs* earthlike, from *gē* earth, and *eidos* form]
■ **geoid'al** *adj*.

geol. *abbrev* : geologic, geological; geology.

geolatry /*jē-ol'ə-tri*/ (*rare*) *n* earth-worship. [Gr *gē* earth, and *latreiā* worship]

geolinguistics /*jē-ō-ling-gwis'tiks*/ *n sing* the study of language in relation to geography. [**geo-**]

geolocation /*jē-ō-lō-kā'shən*/ *n* the act of identifying the geographical location of an object. [**geo-**]

geology /*jē-ol'ə-ji*/ *n* the science relating to the history, development and structure of the earth's crust; the geological features of a particular place or another planet. [Fr *géologie*, from Gr *gē* earth, and *logos* a discourse]
■ **geologic** /*-loj'ik*/ or **geolog'ical** *adj*. **geolog'ically** *adv*. **geol'ogist**, also (now *rare*) **geologian** /*jē-ə-lō'ji-ən*/ or **geol'oger** *n*. **geol'ogize** or **-ise** *vi* to work at geology in the field. ◆ *vt* to investigate the geology of.
❑ **geological column** *n* a diagram showing the subdivisions of part or all of geological time or the stratigraphical sequence in a particular area. **geological survey** *n* a survey of the geology of an area, *esp* to locate coal, oil, etc. **geological time** *n* time before written history, divided into epochs in each of which one of the great rock systems was formed.
■ **dynamical** or **dynamic geology** the study of the work of natural agents in shaping the earth's crust (wind, frost, rivers, volcanic action, etc). **structural geology** the study of the arrangement and structure of rock masses.

geomagnetism /*jē-ō-mag'nə-ti-zm*/ *n* the magnetism of the earth, earth's magnetic field; the study of this. [**geo-**]
■ **geomagnet'ic** *adj*. **geomag'netist** *n*.

geomancy /*jē'ō-man-si*/ *n* divination by shapes formed, eg when earth is thrown down onto a surface; divination by shapes formed by linking random dots made on paper. [Gr *gē* earth, and *manteiā* divination]
■ **gē'omancer** *n*. **gē'omant** *n* (*rare*). **geoman'tic** *adj*.

geomatics /*jē-ō-mat'iks*/ *n sing* the mathematical study of geographical data. [**geo-** and *mathematics*]

geomedicine /*jē-ō-med'sin*/ *n* the study of diseases as influenced by geographical environment. [**geo-**]
■ **geomed'ical** *adj*.

geometry /*jē-om'i-tri* or *jom'*/ *n* that part of mathematics which deals with the properties of points, lines, surfaces and solids, either under classical Euclidean assumptions, or (in the case of **elliptic geometry**, **hyperbolic geometry**, etc) involving postulates not all of which are identical with Euclid's; any study of a mathematical system in which figures undergo transformations, concerned with discussion of those properties of the figures which remain constant; a textbook of geometry (*archaic*). [Gr *geōmetriā*, from *gē* earth, and *metron* a measure]
■ **geom'eter** *n* a geometrician; a geometrid caterpillar or moth. **geometric** /*-met'-*/ or **geomet'rical** *adj* relating to or according to geometry; (eg of a pattern, design or composition) consisting of or using simple figures such as geometry deals with. **geomet'rically** *adv*. **geometrician** /*-me-trish'ən*/ *n* a person skilled in geometry. **geom'etrid** *n* any moth of the family or superfamily **Geomet'ridae** whose caterpillars are loopers. **geom'etrist** *n*. **geometriza'tion** or **-s-** *n*. **geom'etrize** or **-ise** *vt* and *vi* to work geometrically; to show in geometric form.

■ words derived from main entry word; ❑ compound words; ■ idioms and phrasal verbs

◻ **geometric(al) progression** *n* a series of quantities each of which has the same ratio to its predecessor. **geometric mean** see under **mean**[3].

geomorphic /jē-ō-mör'fik/ *adj* of or relating to the surface of the earth. [**geo-**]

geomorphogeny /jē-ō-mör-foj'ə-ni/ *n* the scientific study of the origins and development of land forms. [**geo-**]
■ **geomorphogē'nic** *adj.* **geomorphog'enist** *n*.

geomorphology /jē-ō-mör-fol'ə-ji/ *n* the morphology and development of landforms, including those under the sea; the study of this. [**geo-**]
■ **geomorpholog'ic** or **geomorpholog'ical** *adj* of or relating to this subject. **geomorpholog'ically** *adv.* **geomorphol'ogist** *n*.

Geomys /jē'ō-mis/ *n* the typical genus of **Geomyidae** /-mī'i-dē/, the pouched rats, a family of American burrowing rodents with outward-opening cheekpouches. [Gr *gē* earth, and *mȳs* mouse]
■ **geomy'oid** *adj.*

geophagy /jē-of'ə-ji/ (*biol*) *n* earth-eating, the practice of feeding on soil (also **geoph'agism**). [Gr *gē* earth, and *phagein* to eat]
■ **geoph'agist** *n.* **geoph'agous** /-gəs/ *adj.*

geophilous /jē-of'i-ləs/ (*biol*) *adj* living in or on the ground; geocarpic; having a short stem with leaves at ground level. [Gr *gē* earth, and *phileein* to love]
■ **geophil'ic** *adj.*

geophone /jē'ə-fōn/ *n* (*usu* in *pl*) a device for detecting sound waves, shock waves, etc in the ground. [Gr *gē* earth, and *phōnē* voice, sound]

geophysics /gē-ō-fiz'iks/ *n sing* the physics of the earth, the study of the earth's physical properties. [**geo-**]
■ **geophys'ical** *adj.* **geophys'icist** /-i-sist/ *n.*

geophyte /jē'ō-fīt/ (*bot*) *n* a plant that survives the winter by having subterranean buds, eg bulbs, corms or rhizomes. [Gr *gē* earth, and *phyton* plant]
■ **geophytic** /-fit'ik/ *adj.*

geopolitics /jē-ō-pol'i-tiks/ *n sing* a science concerned with problems of states, such as frontiers, as affected by their geographical environment; worldwide politics; the special combination of geographical and political considerations in a particular state; a Nazi doctrine justifying expansion by necessity for Lebensraum, etc. [Ger *Geopolitik*; see **geo-**]
■ **geopolit'ical** *adj.* **geopolit'ically** *adv.* **geopoliti'cian** *n.*

geoponic /jē-ō-pon'ik/ or **geoponical** /-əl/ *adj* agricultural. [Gr *geōponikos*, from *gē* earth, and *ponos* labour]
■ **geopon'ics** *n sing* the science of agriculture.

Geordie /jör'di/ *n* a native of Tyneside; the dialect of Tyneside; a Scotsman (*Aust* and *NZ*); a coalminer; a coal-carrying boat; a guinea, from the figure of St *George*; a safety lamp for miners invented by *George* Stephenson. ◆*adj* relating to Tyneside, its people, dialect, accent or culture. [Dimin of **George**]

George /jörj/ *n* a jewelled figure of St *George* slaying the dragon, worn by Knights of the Garter; a guinea or Geordie (qv) (*obs*); the automatic pilot of an aircraft (*RAF sl*).
◻ **George Cross** *n* an award (instituted during World War II) for outstanding courage or heroism given in cases where a purely military honour is not applicable. **George Medal** *n* an award for gallantry given to civilians and members of the armed forces.
■ **St George's cross** the Greek cross of England, red on a white background.

georgette /jör-jet'/ *n* a thin silk fabric. [From *Georgette* de la Plante, French dressmaker]

Georgian /jör'ji-ən/ or /jör'jən/ *adj* relating to, typical of, or contemporary with the reigns of any of the various *Georges*, kings of Great Britain, *esp* the first four, who ruled from 1714 to 1830; belonging to Georgia (*Gurjestan, Gruzia*) in the Caucasus, its people, language, etc; of or relating to the American State of *Georgia*; relating to or following Henry *George*, Lloyd *George*, or another person of that surname. ◆*n* a person of any of the Georgian periods; a native or citizen of Georgia; the language of Georgia.
◻ **Georgian planet** *n* (*obs*) a name given to Uranus by its discoverer, Sir William Herschel (in honour of George III).

georgic /jör'jik/ *adj* (*obs*) relating to agriculture or rustic affairs. ◆*n* a poem on husbandry or rural affairs, after Virgil's poetic work on that theme, the *Georgics*. [L *geōrgicus*, from Gr *geōrgikos*, from *geōrgiā* agriculture, from *gē* earth, and *ergon* work]

geoscience /jē'ō-sī-əns/ *n* any of the scientific disciplines, such as geology or geomorphology, which deal with the earth, or all of these collectively. [**geo-**]
■ **geoscientif'ic** *adj.*

geosequestration /jē-ō-sek-wes-trā'shən/ (*chiefly Aust*) *n* a technique for reducing levels of atmospheric carbon dioxide by converting it into liquid and pumping it underground (also **geological sequestration**). [**geo-**]

geosphere /jē'ō-sfēr/ *n* the non-living part of the earth, including the *lithosphere, hydrosphere* and *atmosphere*; the solid part of the earth, distinguished from *atmosphere* and *hydrosphere*. [Gr *gē* earth, and *sphaira* sphere]

geostatic /jē-ō-stat'ik/ *adj* (of a construction) capable of sustaining the pressure of earth from all sides. [Gr *gē* the earth, and *statikos* causing to stand]
■ **geostat'ics** *n sing* the statics of rigid bodies.

geostationary /jē-ō-stā'shə-nə-ri/ *adj* (of a satellite, etc) orbiting the earth in time with the earth's own rotation, ie circling it once every 24 hours, so remaining above the same spot on the earth's surface. [**geo-**]

geostrategy /jē-ō-strat'ə-ji/ *n* global strategy, strategy dealing with geopolitical concerns. [**geo-**]
■ **geostratē'gic** or **geostratē'gical** *adj.*

geostrophic /jē-ō-strof'ik/ *adj* of a virtual force used to account for the change in direction of the wind relative to the surface of the earth arising from the earth's rotation; of a wind whose direction and force are partly determined by the earth's rotation. [Gr *gē* earth, and *strophē* a turn]

geosynchronous /jē-ō-sing'krə-nəs/ *adj* (of a satellite, etc) geostationary. [**geo-**]

geosyncline /jē-ō-sin'klīn/ (*geol*) *n* a syncline on a great scale. [**geo-**]
■ **geosyncli'nal** *adj.*

geotag /jē'ō-tag/ (*comput*) *n* a digital code that assigns geographical co-ordinates to an item of data. ◆ *vt* to apply geotags to (data). [**geo-**]

geotaxis /jē-ō-tak'sis/ (*biol*) *n* the response of an organism to the stimulus of gravity. [Gr *gē* earth, and *taxis* arrangement]
■ **geotact'ic** or **geotact'ical** *adj.* **geotact'ically** *adv.*

geotechnics /jē-ō-tek'niks/ *n sing* the application of scientific and engineering principles to the solution of civil-engineering and other problems created by the nature and constitution of the earth's crust. [**geo-**]
■ **geotech'nic** or **geotech'nical** *adj.* **geotechnolog'ical** *adj.* **geotechnol'ogy** *n* the application of science and technology to the extraction and use of the earth's natural resources.

geotectonic /jē-ō-tek-ton'ik/ *adj* relating to the structure of rock masses. [Gr *gē* earth, and *tektōn* a builder]
■ **geotecton'ics** *n sing* structural geology (qv under **geology**).

geothermic /jē-ō-thûr'mik/ or **geothermal** /-thûr'məl/ *adj* relating to or heated by the internal heat of the earth. [Gr *gē* earth, and *thermē* heat]
■ **geothermom'eter** *n* an instrument for measuring subterranean temperatures.
◻ **geothermal energy** *n* energy extracted from the earth's natural heat, ie from hot springs and certain kinds of rock. **geothermal gradient** *n* the rate at which the temperature of the earth's crust increases with depth.

geotropism /jē-ot'rə-pi-zm/ (*bot*) *n* geotaxis, either downwards, towards the centre of the earth (**positive geotropism**) or upwards, away from the centre of the earth (**negative geotropism**). [Gr *gē* earth, and *tropos* a turning]
■ **geotrop'ic** *adj.* **geotrop'ically** *adv.*

Ger. *abbrev*: German; Germany.

ger or **gur** /gûr/ *n* in Mongolia, a light tent of skins. [Mongolian; related to **yurt**]

ger. *abbrev*: gerund; gerundive.

gerah /gē'rä/ (*ancient hist*; *Bible*) *n* the smallest Hebrew weight and coin, $\frac{1}{20}$ of a shekel. [Heb *gērāh*]

geraniol /jə-rā'ni-ol/ or **-räl**/ *n* an alcohol ($C_{10}H_{18}O$) forming a constituent of many of the esters used in perfumery. [Ger; *geranium* and **-ol**[1]]

geranium /ji-rā'nyəm/ *n* a plant of the genus *Geranium* with seed vessels like a crane's bill, typical of the family **Geraniaceae** /-i-ā'si-ē/; (loosely) any cultivated plant of the genus *Pelargonium*. [L, from Gr *geranion*, from *geranos* a crane]

geratology /ger-ə-tol'ə-ji/ *n* same as **gerontology** (see under **gerontic**). [Gr *gēras* old age, and *logos* a discourse]

gerbe /jûrb/ *n* a wheat sheaf (*obs* or *heraldry*); a fountain or firework resembling a wheat sheaf (*obs*). [Fr *gerbe*; cf **garb**[2]]

gerbera /gûr'bə-rə or jûr'-/ *n* a plant belonging to the *Gerbera* genus of composite plants of S Africa, etc. [T *Gerber* (died 1743), German naturalist]

gerbil /jûr'bil/ n a small desert-dwelling rodent capable of causing great damage to crops but often kept as a pet (also **jer'bil** and (esp formerly) **ger'bille**). [Fr gerbille]

gere (Spenser) same as **gear**.

gerent /jē'rənt or jer'/ (rare) n a controller, ruler. [L gerēns, -entis, prp of gerere to manage]

gerenuk /ger'ə-nook/ n a long-legged, long-necked antelope of E Africa (Litocranius walleri). [From the Somali name]

gerfalcon see **gyrfalcon**.

geriatrics /jer-i-at'riks/ n sing medical care of the old. [Gr gēras old age, and iātros physician]
■ **geriat'ric** adj of, for, or relating to old people; (loosely) ancient, worn-out, past it (used eg of objects or machines, etc) (inf; facetious). ◆ n an old person. **geriatrician** /-ə-trish'ən/ or **geriatrist** /-at'rist/ n.

gerle (Spenser) same as **girl**.

germ /jûrm/ n a micro-organism, esp a harmful one; a rudimentary form of a living thing, whether plant or animal; a shoot; that from which anything springs, the origin or beginning; a first principle; that from which a disease springs; a plant ovary (obs). ◆ vi to put forth buds, sprout. [Partly through Fr germe, from L germen, -inis a sprout, bud, germ, from germināre, -ātum to sprout]
■ **germicī'dal** adj. **germ'icide** n a substance which kills germs (also adj). **germ'inable** adj that can be germinated. **germ'inal** adj relating to a germ or rudiment; in germ, or (fig) in the earliest stage of development; seminal (fig). **germ'inant** adj sprouting; budding; capable of developing. **germ'inate** vi (esp of a seed or spore) to begin to grow. ◆ vt to cause to sprout. **germinā'tion** n. **germ'inative** adj.
◻ **germ cell** n a gamete, a sperm or ovum, or a cell from which it springs. **germ layer** n a primary cell-layer in an embryo, ie ectoderm, mesoderm, or endoderm. **germ line** n (biol) the cells whose descendants give rise to the gametes. **germ'-line therapy** n a form of gene therapy that treats the reproductive cells of the body. **germ plasm** n in early theories of inheritance, the name given to the heritable material, which is now known to be the chromosomes. **germ theory** n the theory that all living organisms can be produced only from living organisms, by the growth and development of germ cells; the theory that micro-organisms cause all infectious diseases. **germ warfare** n warfare in which bacteria or viruses are used as weapons.

germain, germaine (Shakesp) see **germen**.

German /jûr'mən/ n a native or citizen of Germany, or one of the same linguistic or ethnological stock (pl **Ger'mans**); the German language, esp High German. ◆ adj of or from Germany, or the Germans; German-speaking. [L Germānus German]
■ **Germanesque'** adj marked by German characteristics. **Germanic** /-man'ik/ adj of Germany; of the linguistic family to which German, English, Norwegian, etc belong, Teutonic. ◆ n an extinct Indo-European language which differentiated into **East Germanic** (Gothic and other extinct languages), **North Germanic** or Scandinavian (Norwegian, Danish, Swedish, Icelandic) and **West Germanic** (English, Frisian, Dutch, Low German, High German). **German'ically** adv. **Ger'manish** adj somewhat German. **Ger'manism** n a German idiom; German ideas and ways. **Ger'manist** n an expert in German philology or other matters relating to Germany. **Germanis'tic** adj relating to the study of German. **Germaniza'tion** or **-s-** n. **Ger'manize** or **-ise** vt to make German. ◆ vi to become German; to adopt German ways. **German'ophil** n a person who admires the Germans and things German, now usu **German'ophile**. **Germanophil'ia** n. **German'ophobe** n a person who fears or hates the Germans and things German.
◻ **German band** n street musicians, orig from Germany. **German flute** n the ordinary modern flute. **German measles** n sing rubella. **German Ocean** n (archaic) the North Sea. **German shepherd** or **German shepherd dog** n the Alsatian dog. **German silver** n an alloy of copper, nickel and zinc, white like silver, and first made in Germany. **German sixth** n (music) a chord with major third, perfect fifth, and augmented sixth.
■ **High German** the literary language throughout Germany, orig the speech of High or S Germany. **Low German** Plattdeutsch, the language or dialects of Low or N Germany; formerly applied to all the W Germanic dialects except High German.

german /jûr'mən/ adj of the first degree, full (see **brother**, **cousin**); closely related (obs); germane, relevant (obs). ◆ n (obs) a full brother or sister; a near relative. [OFr germain, from L germānus having the same parents or kin]

germander /jər-man'dər/ n a labiate herb (genus Teucrium) with aromatic, bitter and stomachic properties. [LL germandra, from Late Gr chamandrya, from Gr chamaidrȳs, from chamai on the ground, and drȳs oak]
◻ **germander speedwell** n a bright-blue-flowered veronica (Veronica chamaedrys).

germane /jer-mān'/ adj closely related (to); relevant, appropriate (to). [Ety as for **german**]
■ **germane'ly** adv. **germane'ness** n.

Germanesque, Germanic, etc see under **German**.

Germanice /jûr-man'i-sē or ger-man'i-ke/ (L) adv in German.

Germanish...to...**Germanistic** see under **German**.

germanium /jər-mā'ni-əm/ n a metalloid element (symbol **Ge**; atomic no 32) much used in diodes, transistors and rectifiers for its properties as a semiconductor. [Discovered and named by a German chemist, CA Winkler (1838–1904)]

Germanize, etc see under **German**.

germen /jer'mən/ or **germin** /jer'min/ (Shakesp **germain** or **germaine** /-mān/) n a rudiment, germ; a shoot (obs); the ovary in a flower (obs). [L germen, -inis; see **germ**]

germicidal, germicide, germinable see under **germ**.

Germinal /zher-mē-nal'/ (hist) n the seventh month of the French revolutionary calendar, about 21 March to 19 April. [See **germ**]

germinal...to...**germinative** see under **germ**.

gerne /gûrn/ (Spenser) vi to grin or gape. [**grin¹**]

Geronimo /jə-ron'i-mō/ (orig and esp US) interj a war cry used by paratroopers on jumping into action; used facetiously as a stirring shout at the moment of attack upon some venture or activity (inf). [Geronimo (1829–1909), Apache chieftain who campaigned against US troops to preserve tribal lands]

gerontic /ge- or je-ron'tik/ adj (biol) relating to the senescent period in the life history of an individual. [Gr gerōn, -ontos old man]
■ **gerontoc'racy** n government by old men or old people. **geron'tocrat** n. **gerontocrat'ic** adj. **gerontolog'ical** adj. **gerontol'ogist** n. **gerontol'ogy** n the scientific study of the processes of growing old. **geron'tophil** or **geron'tophile** /-fil or -fīl/ n a person who experiences **gerontophilia** /-fil'i-ə/, a sexual attraction towards old people. **geron'tophobe** /-fōb/ n a person who experiences **gerontophō'bia**, an irrational fear of old people and old age. **gerontotherapeut'ics** n sing the science of medical treatment of the diseases of old age.

geropiga /jer-ō-pē'gə/ n a port substitute, a mixture consisting chiefly of grape juice and brandy, sometimes illicitly mixed with real port. [Port]

Gerry see **Jerry**.

gerrymander /jer'i-man-dər, also ger'/ vt to rearrange (voting districts) in the interests of a particular party or candidate; to manipulate (facts, arguments, etc) so as to reach undue conclusions. ◆ n an arrangement of the above nature. [Formed from the name of Governor Elbridge Gerry (1744–1814) and salamander, from the likeness to that animal of the gerrymandered map of Massachusetts in 1812]
■ **gerryman'derer** n.

Gerson therapy /gûr'sən ther'ə-pi/ n an extreme diet therapy used primarily for the treatment of chronic illnesses. [Max Gerson (1881–1959), German-born US doctor]

gertcha /gûr'chə/ (sl) interj get away (along, off) with you!, come off it!; clear off!, get out of that (or there)! [Corruption and contraction of spoken phrase]

gerund /jer'ənd/ n a part of a Latin verb with the value of a verbal noun, such as amandum (= loving); in English, a noun with the ending -ing formed from a verb and having some of the qualities of a verb, such as the possibility of governing an object, etc, and often preceded by a possessive (eg My leaving her was unwise). [L gerundium, from gerere to bear]
■ **gerundial** /ji-rund'i-əl/ or **gerundival** /jer-ən-dī'vl/ adj. **gerundive** /ji-rund'iv/ adj relating to a gerund. ◆ n a Latin verbal adjective expressing necessity, such as amandus (= deserving or requiring to be loved).

Gesellschaft /gə-zel'shäft/ (Ger) n an association of people, eg a commercial company, united by individual commitment to a common cause.

gesneria /je-snē'ri-ə/ n a plant of the tropical American genus Gesneria, typical of the **Gesneriä'ceae**, a family closely related to the Scrophulariaceae. [Named after Konrad von Gesner (1516–65), Swiss botanist and scholar]
■ **gesne'riad** n any plant of the family.

gessamine (Milton) same as **jasmine**.

gesse (Spenser) same as **guess¹**.

gesso /jes'ō/ n (pl **gess'oes**) plaster of Paris; a plaster surface prepared as a ground for painting. [Ital, from L gypsum; see **gypsum**]

gest¹ /jest/ (Shakesp) n the time fixed for a stay in a place. [OFr giste a stopping-place]

■ words derived from main entry word; ◻ compound words; ■ idioms and phrasal verbs

gest² or **geste** /jest/ (obs) n an exploit; a tale of adventure, a romance. [OFr geste, from L gesta things done, from gerere, gestum to bear, behave; cf **jest**]

gest³ or **geste** /jest/ n (obs) bearing; a gesture. [Fr geste, from L gestus, from gerere, gestum to bear, behave]
  ■ **gest'ic** adj of or relating to movement or gesture of the body, esp in dance.

Gestalt or **gestalt** /gə-shtält'/ n form, shape, pattern; an organized whole or unit; Gestalt therapy. [Ger]
  ■ **gestalt'ism** n Gestalt psychology. **Gestalt'ist** n.
  ❑ **Gestalt psychology** n the outlook or theory based on the concept that the organized whole is something more than the sum of the parts into which it can be logically analysed. **Gestalt therapy** or **psychotherapy** n a therapy that works towards self-discovery and liberation through a combination of existentialism, realism, self-expression, self-acceptance and regular self-analysis.

gestant see under **gestate**.

Gestapo /gə-stä'pō/ n the secret police in Nazi Germany; (without cap; pl **gesta'pos**) any such secret police organization associated with harsh and unscrupulous methods. ◆ adj of, relating to or characteristic of the Gestapo. [From Ger Geheime Staatspolizei, secret state police]

gestate /je-stāt'/ vt to carry in the womb during the period from conception to birth; to conceive and develop slowly in the mind. ◆ vi to be in the process of gestating. [L gestāre, -ātum to carry, from gerere to bear]
  ■ **ges'tant** adj (rare) laden (also fig). **gestation** /jes-tā'shən/ n the process of gestating (biol and fig); being carried in a vehicle, a boat, etc (archaic). **gestā'tional** or **gest'ative** adj of carriage, esp in the womb. **gestatō'rial** or **ges'tatory** adj (archaic) relating to carrying.
  ❑ **gestatorial chair** n a ceremonial chair on which the Pope is carried in procession.

gesticulate /je-stik'ū-lāt/ vi to make vigorous gestures, esp when speaking. ◆ vt to express by means of gestures. [L gesticulāri, -ātus, from gesticulus, dimin of gestus gesture, from gerere to carry, behave]
  ■ **gesticulā'tion** n. **gestic'ulative** or **gestic'ulatory** adj. **gestic'ulātor** n.

gesture /jes'chər/ n an action, esp of the hands, expressive of sentiment or passion or intended to show inclination or disposition; the use of such movements; an action dictated by courtesy or diplomacy, or by a desire to impress or create an impression, eg of willingness (also adj); a posture, or movement of the body (obs); behaviour (Shakesp). ◆ vi to make a gesture or gestures. ◆ vt to express by gesture(s). [LL gestūra, from L gestus, from L gerere to carry, behave]
  ■ **ges'tural** adj.
  ❑ **gesture politics** n political activity aimed primarily at satisfying public opinion.

Gesundheit /gə-zŭnt'hīt/ (Ger) interj your health (said to someone who has just sneezed).
  ■ **auf Ihre Gesundheit** /owf ē'rə/ (said to a drinking companion) here's to your health.

get /get/ vt (prp **gett'ing**; pat **got**, obs **gat**; pap **got**, archaic, Scot and US **gott'en**) to obtain; to acquire; to procure; to receive; to attain; to come to have; to catch; to answer (a door or telephone) (inf); to grasp or take the meaning of (often in the informal phrase **get it?**, of a joke, irony, etc); to learn; to commit to memory; to hit (inf); to descry, discern, make out; to succeed in making contact with (eg a radio station); to have the better of, gain a decisive advantage over (inf); to baffle (inf); to irritate (inf); to grip emotionally, take, captivate, hit the taste of exactly; to induce; to cause to be, go, or become; to betake, take (oneself); to beget (archaic except when used of animals, esp horses); to attack or injure, esp in revenge (inf); to prepare (a meal) (inf). ◆ vi (with preposition, adverb, infinitive, etc) to arrive, to bring or put oneself (in any place, position or state); (with adjective, etc) to become; to become richer (obs); to clear out (inf; orig US). ◆ n that which is got (obs); a (usu difficult) shot successfully reached and returned (tennis); output (obs); (of animals) offspring; (also **gait**, **gaitt**, **geit** /get/; see also **git**, and **gyte²**) a child, brat (Scot derog); begetting (obs). [ON geta; cognate with OE -gietan (in compounds)]
  ■ **gett'able** adj. **gett'er** n (esp in combination) someone who, or something which, gets, attains, collects; a material used, when evaporated by high-frequency induction currents, for evacuation of gas left in vacuum valves after sealing during manufacture (electronics). ◆ vt to evacuate (a valve) using a getter; to remove (gas) using a getter. ◆ vi to use a getter. **gett'ering** n evacuation using a getter. **gett'ing** n the action of the verb; a gaining, anything gained (archaic); procreation (archaic).
  ❑ **get-at'-able** adj easily accessible. **get'away** n an escape; a start; breaking cover. ◆ adj used in a getaway. **get'-go** n (US) the beginning or start of something. **get'-out** n (inf) a way of escape or avoidance

(also adj); the dismantling, packing up and moving of props, scenery, costumes, etc at the end of a production run (theatre); the total cost of a production for one week (theatre). **get'-rich'-quick'** adj (inf) wanting, or leading to, easy prosperity. **get'-together** n a social gathering; an informal conference. **get'-up** n (style of) equipment, outfit, make-up. **get'-up-and-go'** n (inf) energy.
  ■ **as all get-out** (inf) as can be. **be getting on** to grow older; (of time) to grow late. **get about** or **around** to travel, go visiting; to be mobile and active. **get across** (inf) to communicate successfully. **get ahead** to make progress, advance. **get a life** see under **life**. **get along** to get on (see below). **get around** see **get about** above. **get at** to reach, attain; to poke fun at (sl); to mean (inf); to begin (inf; orig US); to attack verbally (sl); to influence by underhand or unlawful means (inf). **get away** to escape, make a successful departure; (as imperative) go away, be off, get back; an interjection expressing disbelief. **get away with (something)** to pull something off; to carry a thing through successfully or with impunity. **get back at** to have one's revenge on. **get by** to succeed in passing; to elude notice and come off with impunity, manage satisfactorily, be sufficiently good (inf). **get down** to alight; to depress (inf); to disport oneself with abandon (sl); to complete the hole (golf). **get down to** to set to work on, tackle seriously. **get in** (to manage to) enter; to be elected; to gather; to send for; to manage, succeed in doing (as in We got the gardening in before the rain). **get in on** (inf) to join in, become a participant in. **get it on** or **off (with)** (sl) to have sexual intercourse (with); to get high (on a drug). **get it up** (sl) to achieve an erection. **get off** to escape; to go, to set off (on a journey); to fall asleep (inf); to learn, memorize; to gain the affection of, or have a sexual encounter with, someone of the opposite sex (with with; inf). **get off on** (sl) to get excitement from. **get on** to proceed, advance; to prosper; to agree, associate harmoniously; to fare, manage. **get one's own back** (inf) to have one's revenge (on). **get out** to produce; to extricate oneself (with of); to take oneself off. **get over** to surmount; to recover from; to make an impression on an audience. **get round** to circumvent; to persuade, talk over. **get round to** to bring oneself to do (something). **get (something) over with** to accomplish (an unpleasant task, etc) as quickly as possible. **get there** (sl) to achieve one's object, succeed. **get through** to finish; to reach a destination; to receive approval, or to obtain it for (something); to obtain a connection by telephone; to communicate with, reach the comprehension of (with to). **get together** to meet socially or for discussion. **get up** to rise, esp from bed; to ascend; to arrange, dress, prepare (oneself); to learn up for an occasion; to commit to memory. **have got** (inf) to have. **have got to** to be obliged to. **tell someone where to get off** (inf) to deal summarily or dismissively with someone. **you've got me there** (inf) I don't know the answer to your question.

geta /gā'tə/ n (pl **ge'ta** or **ge'tas**) a Japanese wooden sandal with a thong between the big toe and the other toes. [Jap]

geum /jē'əm/ n an avens, a plant of the Geum genus of the family Rosaceae. [L]

GeV (phys) abbrev : giga-electronvolt, a unit of particle energy (in US sometimes **BeV**).

gewgaw /gū'gö/ n a toy; a trifling object, a bauble. ◆ adj showy without value. [Origin unknown]

Gewürztraminer /gə-voortz'trə-mē-nər/ n a variety of white grape grown esp in the Alsace region; a wine, typically medium-dry, aromatic and with a spicy flavour, made from this grape. [Ger, from Gewürz spice, and Traminer a grape variety (after Tramin wine-growing region in S Tyrol)]

gey /gī/ (Scot) see **gay**.
  ■ **geyan** /gī'ən/ adv for **gey and**.

geyser /gā', gē' or gī'zər/ n a spring that periodically spouts hot water and steam into the air; (usu /gē'/) an apparatus that heats domestic water as the tap is turned on. [Geysir a geyser in Iceland, from Icel geysa, ON göysa to gush]
  ■ **gey'serite** n sinter.

gf abbrev : girlfriend.

GH abbrev : Ghana (IVR); growth hormone.

Ghanaian /gä-nā'yən/ adj of or relating to Ghana, a W African republic. ◆ n a native or citizen of Ghana.

gharial, garial /gur'i-əl/ or **gavial** /gā'vi-əl/ n an Asian crocodile (genus Gavialis) with a very long slender muzzle. [Hindi ghariyāl crocodile]

gharri or **gharry** /gar'i/ n (esp in India) a wheeled vehicle, generally for hire. [Hindi gārī a cart]

ghast /gäst/ vt (Shakesp) to cause to be aghast; to frighten. [OE gǣstan; cf **gast**]
  ■ **ghast'ful** or **ghast'full** adj (Spenser) dreary, dismal. **ghast'fully** adv (obs) frightfully. **ghast'liness** n. **ghast'ly** adj deathlike; hideous;

deplorable (*inf*); very ill (*inf*). ◆ *adv* (*archaic*) in a ghastly manner. **ghast'ness** *n* dread.

ghat or **ghaut** /göt/ *n* (in India) a mountain pass; a landing-stair on a riverside; a place of cremation (**burning ghat**). [Hindi *ghāt* descent]

ghazal /gaz'al/ *n* a Persian and Arabic verse form, of not more than eighteen couplets, the first two lines and the even-numbered lines thereafter rhyming together, used *esp* for poems of an amatory or bacchanalian nature (also **gazal**, **ghazel**). [Ar *ghazal*]

ghazi /gä'zē/ *n* a veteran Muslim warrior, slayer of infidels; a high Turkish title. [Ar *ghāzi* fighting]

GHB *abbrev*: gamma hydroxybutyrate, a designer drug with anaesthetic properties (also called (*inf*) **GBH**, **fantasy**).

Gheber or **Ghebre** /gä'bər or gē'bər/ *n* same as **Guebre**.

ghee or **ghi** /gē or ghē/ *n* clarified butter, *esp* made with milk from the Asiatic buffalo. [Hindi *ghī*]

gherao /ge-row'/ *n* (*pl* **gheraos'**) (in India) the surrounding or trapping of a person (eg an employer) in a room, building, etc until he or she meets one's demands (also *vt*). [Hindi, siege, from *gherna* to surround, besiege]

gherkin /gûr'kin/ *n* a small cucumber used for pickling. [From an earlier form of Du *augurk(je)* a gherkin; appar from Slav]

ghesse (*pat* and *pap* **ghest** or **ghessed**; *Spenser*) same as **guess**[1].

ghetto /get'ō/ *n* (*pl* **ghett'oes** or **ghett'os**) a quarter, *esp* poor, inhabited by any racial or other identifiable group; a section marked out as distinct, set apart to contain some group regarded as non-mainstream (*fig*); *orig* the Jews' quarter in an Italian or other city, to which they used to be confined. [Ital *ghetto* foundry, after one which previously occupied the site of the Venetian Jewish ghetto]
▪ **ghett'oize** or **-ise** *vt* to make into a ghetto; to confine to or put into a ghetto.
❑ **ghett'o-blaster** *n* (*inf*) a *usu* fairly large portable hi-fi with built-in speakers. **ghetto fabulous** *adj* relating to a highly flamboyant and ostentatious style of dress adopted by some members of urban American society.

ghi see **ghee**.

Ghibelline or **Ghibeline** /gib'ə-lēn, -līn or -lin/ *n* a member of a medieval Italian party, *orig* supporters of Hohenstaufen emperors against the Guelfs and the Pope. [Ital *Ghibellino*, appar from *Waiblingen* a Hohenstaufen town]

ghilgai see **gilgai**.

ghillie see **gillie**.

ghost /gōst/ *n* a spirit; the soul of a person; a spirit appearing after death; a dead body (*Shakesp*); a person who writes (eg speeches) on behalf of another credited as author; a faint or false appearance; a semblance; a person on the payroll who does no actual work (*business*, etc); a person counted on an attendance register who is not actually present; a duplicated image due to additional reception of a delayed similar signal which has covered a longer path (*TV*). ◆ *vt* to haunt as or like a ghost; to transfer (a prisoner) quickly and secretly overnight. ◆ *vi* to be a ghost (*business*); to fail to declare income from a job; to disappear, vanish like a ghost; to progress by sail despite very little wind (*naut*). ◆ *vi* and *vt* to work, *esp* write, on behalf of another person credited as the creator or author. [OE *gāst*; Ger *Geist*; the *h* from Caxton (Flemish *gheest*)]
▪ **ghost'ing** *n*. **ghost'like** *adj*. **ghost'liness** *n*. **ghost'ly** *adj* relating to apparitions; ghostlike; faint; spiritual (*obs*); religious (*obs*). **ghost'y** *adj*.
❑ **ghost'buster** *n* (*inf*) a person supposed to be able to drive away ghosts; an employee of the Inland Revenue responsible for detecting and pursuing people who have not paid tax on their incomes. **ghost crab** *n* a nocturnal shore-dwelling crab of the genus *Ocypode*. **ghost gum** *n* an Australian tree (*Eucalyptus papuana*) with smooth white bark. **ghost moth** *n* a moth (*Hepialus humuli*), the male of ghostly white appearance, the caterpillar destructive to hop-gardens. **ghost story** *n* a story in which ghosts figure. **ghost town** *n* one which once flourished owing to some natural resource in the vicinity but which is now deserted since the natural resource has been exhausted. **ghost train** *n* a funfair entertainment consisting of a ride in open railcars through a darkened room with special eerie effects. **ghost word** *n* a word that has originated in a copyist's or printer's error. **ghost'-write** *vi* and *vt* to write for another as a ghost. **ghost'-writer** *n*.
▪ **give up the ghost** to die. **Holy Ghost** the Holy Spirit, the third person in the Christian Trinity. **not to have a ghost** (**of a chance**) not to have the least chance of success. **the ghost walks** (*theatre sl*) money is available, the wages can be paid.

ghoul /gool/ *n* in Arab folklore, a demon that preys on the dead; a gruesome fiend; a person of gruesome or revolting habits or tastes. [Ar *ghūl*]
▪ **ghoul'ish** *adj*. **ghoul'ishly** *adv*. **ghoul'ishness** *n*.

GHQ *abbrev*: General Headquarters.

ghrelin /grel'in/ *n* an appetite-stimulating hormone produced in the stomach wall. [growth-*h*ormone-*rel*easing peptide, and **-in**]

ghubar numeral same as **gobar numeral**.

ghyll /gil/ *n* see **gill**[3].

GHz *abbrev*: gigahertz.

GI /jē-ī'/ *n* a soldier in the US Army (also *adj*). [Abbrev of *government* (or *general*) *issue*]

GI *abbrev*: glycaemic index.

gi see **gie**[2].

giambeux (*Spenser*) same as **jambeaux** (see **jambeau** under **jamb**).

giant /jī'ənt/ *n* (also *fem* **gī'antess**) a huge mythical being of more or less human form; a person of abnormally great stature; anything much above the usual size of its kind; someone with much greater powers than the average person. ◆ *adj* gigantic. [OFr *geant* (Fr *géant*), from L *gigās*, from Gr *gigās*, *gigantos*]
▪ **gi'anthood** *n* the quality or character of a giant; the race of giants. **gi'antism** *n* the occurrence of giants; gigantism. **gi'antly** *adj* giant-like. **gi'antry** *n* giants collectively; giant stories or mythology. **gi'antship** *n*.
❑ **giant fibres** *n pl* the enlarged nerve fibres in the ventral nerve cord of many invertebrates which transmit impulses very rapidly and initiate escape behaviour. **gi'ant-killer** *n* someone who defeats a far superior opponent. **gi'ant-killing** *n*. **giant panda** see **panda**. **giant powder** *n* a kind of dynamite. **giant rude** *adj* (*Shakesp*) enormously rude or uncivil. **giant's-kett'le** *n* a large pothole believed to have been formed by subglacial water. **giant slalom** *n* a skiing event similar to a slalom but skied over a longer distance with greater intervals between the gates. **giant star** *n* (*astron*) a star of great brightness and low mean density. **giant** (or **giant's**) **stride** *n* a gymnastic apparatus enabling one to take great strides around a pole.

giaour /jowr/ (*archaic*) *n* an infidel, a term applied by the Turks to non-Muslims. [Through Turk, from Pers *gaur*; see **Guebre**]

Giardia /jē-är'di-ə/ *n* a genus of parasitic protozoa which commonly infect the small intestine of mammals, including humans. [A *Giard* (1846–1908), French biologist]
▪ **giardī'asis** *n* intestinal infestation with protozoa of the *Giardia* genus, a disease, often with diarrhoea, nausea, etc, contracted through drinking contaminated water.

GIB (*finance*) *abbrev*: guaranteed income bond.

Gib /jib/ (*inf*) *n* Gibraltar.

gib[1] /jib or gib/ *n* a wedge-shaped piece of metal holding another in place, etc. ◆ *vt* (**gib'bing**; **gibbed**) to fasten with a gib. [Origin obscure]

gib[2] /gib/ (*obs*) *n* a tomcat, *esp* a castrated one (also (*archaic* and *dialect*) **gib'-cat**); a term of reproach. [From the name *Gilbert*]

gibber[1] /jib'ər/ *vi* to utter senseless or inarticulate sounds. [Imit]

gibber[2] /gib'ər/ (*Aust*) *n* a stone; a boulder. [From an Aboriginal language]

Gibberella /jib-ə-rel'ə/ *n* a genus of fungi found *esp* on grasses, eg wheat scab. [New L, dimin of L *gibbus* hump]
▪ **gibberell'in** *n* any of several plant-growth regulators produced by a fungus of the genus.
❑ **gibberellic** /-el'ik/ **acid** *n* an acid having similar effects.

gibberish /jib'ə-rish or gib'-/ *n* rapid, gabbling talk; meaningless words. ◆ *adj* meaningless, nonsensical. [Imit]

gibbet /jib'it/ *n* a gallows, *esp* one on which criminals were suspended after execution; the projecting beam of a crane. ◆ *vt* to expose on, or as on, a gibbet. [OFr *gibet* a stick; origin unknown]

gibble-gabble /gib'l-gab'l/ *n* senseless chatter. [**gabble**]

gibbon /gib'ən/ *n* a SE Asian anthropoid ape (of several species) with very long arms. [Fr, used by Comte de Buffon, supposedly from an Ind word]

Gibbonian /gi-bō'ni-ən/ *adj* relating to or associated with the English historian Edward *Gibbon* (1737–94).

gibbous /gib'əs/, also **gibbose** /-ōs/ *adj* hump-backed; humped; swollen or pouched; (of the moon or a planet) between half and full, unequally convex on two sides. [L *gibbōsus*, from *gibbus* a hump]
▪ **gibbos'ity** or **gibb'ousness** *n*. **gibb'ously** *adv*.

gibbsite /gib'zīt/ *n* hydroxide of aluminium, Al(OH)$_3$, an important constituent of bauxite. [George *Gibbs* (1776–1833), American mineralogist]

gibe or **jibe** /jīb/ *vi* to scoff; to flout, jeer. ◆ *vt* to scoff at; to taunt. ◆ *n* a flout; a taunt. [Origin obscure]
▪ **gī'ber** or **jī'ber** *n*. **gī'bingly** *adv*.

gibel /gib'əl/ n a common European and N Asian carp, without barbules, similar to a wild form of goldfish (also called **Prussian** or **Crucian carp**). [Ger *gibel, giebel*]

Gibeonite /gib'i-ə-nīt/ (*Bible*) n a slave's slave (from Joshua 9).

giblets /jib'lits/ n pl the internal eatable parts of a fowl, etc; entrails. [OFr *gibelet* a game stew; origin uncertain]
■ **gib'let** adj made of giblets.

Gibraltarian /jib-röl-tā'ri-ən/ n and adj (an inhabitant) of *Gibraltar*, a British colony at the southern tip of Spain.
□ **Gibraltar board**® n (NZ) a type of plasterboard.

gibus /jī'bəs/ n a collapsible top hat. [Fr, from the maker's name]

gid /gid/ n sturdy, a disease of sheep. [**giddy**]

giddap /gi-dap'/ or /gid'ap/, **giddup** /gi-dup'/ or /gid'up/ or **giddy-up** /gid-i-up'/ or /gid'i-/ (*inf*) *interj* used to urge on a horse or other animal; hurry up, get along (often *playful* or *joc*). [From inf pronunciation of **get up**]

giddy /gid'i/ adj not able to stand steadily, dizzy; causing giddiness; whirling; light-headed; flighty. ◆ vi and vt to make or become giddy. [OE *gidig, gydig* insane, possessed by a god]
■ **gidd'ily** adv. **gidd'iness** n.
□ **gidd'y-headed** adj thoughtless, frivolous. **gidd'y-paced** adj (*Shakesp*) moving irregularly.
■ **play the giddy goat** to act the fool.

giddy-up see **giddap**.

Gideon /gid'i-ən/ n a member of an organization of Christian businessmen, founded in the USA in 1899, best known for putting Bibles (**Gideon Bibles**) in hotel rooms, etc. [Named after *Gideon*, the judge of Israel (Bible, Judges 6 ff)]

gidgee or **gidjee** /gij'ē/ (*Aust*) n a small acacia tree, the foliage of which at times emits an unpleasant odour. [From an Aboriginal language]

gie[1] /gē/ v (pat **gied** /gēd/ or **gae** /gā/; pap **gien** /gēn/) a Scots form of **give**[1].

gie[2] or **gi** /gē/ n a judo or karate costume. [Jap *ki* clothing]

gien see **gie**[1].

gier-eagle /jēr ē'gl/ (*Bible*) n a vulture. [Du *gier*]

GIF /gif/ (*comput*) abbrev : graphic interchange format, a standard image file format.

gif /gif/ conj an obsolete form of **if**.

Giffen good /gif'ən gŭd/ (*econ*, etc) n a foodstuff of relatively low quality which forms an important part of the diet of low-income households, demand for which (contrary to the normal rule) increases when its price rises and decreases when it falls. [Scottish economist Sir Robert *Giffen* (1837–1910) noted this effect in regard to potatoes]

giff-gaff /gif'gaf'/ (*Scot*) n give and take. [**give**[1]]

GIFT abbrev : gamete intra-Fallopian transfer, an infertility treatment involving direct transfer of eggs and sperm into the woman's Fallopian tubes, where conception may occur.

gift /gift/ n a thing given; a quality bestowed by nature, a talent; the act of giving; something easily obtained, understood, etc (*sl*); a bribe (*obs*). ◆ vt to endow, *esp* with any power or faculty; to present, give as a gift (*esp Scot*). [See **give**[1]]
■ **gift'ed** adj highly endowed by nature with talents, abilities, etc; (*esp*) of a child, exceptionally clever. **gift'edly** adv. **gift'edness** n.
□ **Gift Aid** n a UK government scheme allowing charities to reclaim the tax paid on donations. **gift'-book** n a book suitable or intended for presentation. **gift horse** n a horse given as a present (see also below). **gift'shop** n a shop selling articles suitable for presents. **gift token** or **voucher** n a printed card that can be used in payment or exchange for buying certain products to the value of the amount shown. **gift'-wrap** vt to wrap (a present) in coloured paper, with ribbons, etc.
■ **in one's gift** within one's power to bestow. **look a gift horse in the mouth** to criticize, delay or niggle over a gift or lucky opportunity (*orig* to look at a gift horse's teeth to tell its age).

gig[1] /gig/ n a light, two-wheeled carriage; a long, light boat; a machine for raising the nap on cloth (in full, **gig mill**); a whipping-top (*obs*); a flighty girl (*obs*); sport, fun (*dialect*). [ME *gigge* a whirling thing (cf **whirligig**); origin obscure]
■ **gigg'it** vt and vi (*old US*) to convey or move rapidly.
□ **gig'-lamps** n pl the lamps fixed on either side of a gig (carriage); spectacles (*old sl*). **gig'man** n a man who drives or keeps a gig; a narrow middle-class philistine (*Carlyle*). **gigman'ity** n.

gig[2] /gig/ (*sl*) n an engagement, *esp* of a band or pop group for one performance only; such a performance. ◆ vi (**gigg'ing**; **gigged**) to play a gig. [Ety unknown]

gig[3] /gig/ (*comput*) n short form of **gigabyte**.

gig[4] /gig/ n a pronged spear for fishing, a fishgig. [**fizgig**]

giga see **gigue**.

giga- /gī'gə-, gig-ə-, jī'gə-* or *jig-ə-/ combining form denoting 10^9, or loosely (*comput*) 2^{30}. [Gr *gigas* giant]
■ **gi'gabit** n (*comput*) a thousand million bits; (loosely) 2^{30} bits. **gi'gabyte** n (*comput*) a thousand million bytes or a thousand megabytes; (loosely) 2^{30} bytes. **giga-elec'tron-volt** n a unit equal to a thousand million electronvolts. **gi'gaflop** n (*comput*) a unit of processing speed equal to 10^9 floating-point operations per second. ◆ adj able to perform at this speed, as in *gigaflop computer*. **gi'gahertz** n. **gi'gawatt** n.

gigantic /jī-gan'tik/ adj (also **gigantē'an**) of, like or characteristic of a giant; huge. [L *gigās, gigantis*, Gr *gigās, -antos* a giant]
■ **gigantesque'** adj befitting or suggestive of a giant. **gigan'tically** adv. **gigan'ticide** n the act of killing a giant. **gigant'ism** n (of a business concern, etc) hugeness; excessive overgrowth, *usu* owing to overactivity of the pituitary gland (*med*); abnormal increase in size, often associated with polyploidy (*bot*). **gigantol'ogy** n giant-lore. **giganto'machy** /-ki/ or **gigantomachia** /-tō-māk'i-ə/ n (Gr *machē* fight) a war of giants, *esp* against the gods.

giggle /gig'l/ vi to laugh with short catches of the breath, or in a silly manner. ◆ n a laugh of this kind; an amusing person or thing, a laugh (*inf*); (in pl) uncontrollable giggling. [Echoic]
■ **gigg'ler** n. **gigg'lesome** or **gigg'ly** adj inclined to giggle. **gigg'ling** n.

GIGO /gig'ō, gī'gō or gē'gō/ (*comput*, etc) abbrev : garbage in, garbage out, ie incorrect input results in incorrect output.

gigolo /jig'-ə-lō/ n (pl **gig'olos**) a professional male dancing partner or escort; a young man living at the expense of an older woman, *esp* one to whom he gives sexual favours in return. [Fr]

gigot /jig'ət/ n a leg of mutton, etc; a leg-of-mutton sleeve. [Fr]

gigue /zhēg/ or (*Ital*) **giga** /jē'ga/ (*music*) n a lively dance form *usu* in 6–8 or 12–8 time, often used to complete 18c dance suites. [Fr; cf **jig**]

gila /hhē'lə/ (in full **gila monster**) n either of the two *Heloderma* species, the only venomous lizards known. [After the *Gila* River in SW USA]

gilbert /gil'bərt/ n the CGS unit of magnetomotive force. [William *Gilbert* (1540–1603), English physician and physicist]

Gilbertian /gil-bûr'ti-ən/ adj whimsically or paradoxically humorous. [Sir WS *Gilbert* (1836–1911), English librettist, playwright, poet, etc]

Gilbertine /gil'bûr-tīn/ or /-tin/ (*hist*) n a member of the order of canons and nuns founded (c.1148) by St *Gilbert* of Sempringham (also adj).

gilcup see **giltcup** under **gilt**[1].

gild[1] /gild/ vt (**gild'ing**; **gild'ed** or **gilt**) to cover or overlay with gold or with any gold-like substance; to gloss over, give a specious appearance to; to adorn with lustre; to smear with blood (*obs*); to flush, redden, suffuse with colour (*obs*); to supply with gold or money (*obs*). [OE *gyldan*, from *gold*; see **gold**[1]]
■ **gild'er** n a person who coats articles with gold. **gild'ing** n the task or trade of a gilder; gold or imitation gold laid on a surface.
□ **Gilded Chamber** n the House of Lords. **gilded spurs** n pl an emblem of knighthood. **gilded youth** n rich young people of fashion.
■ **gild the lily** see under **lily**. **gild the pill** to make a disagreeable thing seem less so.

gild[2] see **guild**.

gilden or **gylden** /gil'dən/ (*obs*) orig adj golden, adopted later (as *Spenser*) as a pap of **gild**[1]. [OE *gylden*]

gilder[1] see **guilder**.

gilder[2] see under **gild**[1].

gilet /zhē-lā/ n a waistcoat; in a woman's dress, a front part shaped like a waistcoat; a quilted sleeveless jacket; in ballet dress, a bodice shaped like a waistcoat. [Fr]

gilgai or **ghilgai** /gil'gī/ (*Aust*) n a saucer-shaped depression forming a natural reservoir. [From an Aboriginal language]

gilgie or **jilgie** /jil'gi/ (*Aust*) n a yabby, a small freshwater crayfish. [From an Aboriginal language]

gill[1] /gil/ n a membranous organ for breathing in water, *usu* in the form of a thin platelike or branched filamentous structure (*zool*); the wattle below the bill of a fowl; one of the radiating plates on the underside of the cap of a mushroom or toadstool; a projecting rib of a heating surface; the flesh round a person's jaw, as in *green* or *white round the gills* (ie sickly-looking). ◆ vt to gut (fish); to catch (fish) by the gills in a net. [Cf Dan *giælle* ; Swed *gäl*]
□ **gill arch** n (in fish) the incomplete jointed skeletal ring supporting a single pair of gill slits. **gill cover** n a fold of skin, *usu* with bony plates, protecting the gills. **gill net** n a type of fishing-net in which fish are caught by their gills. **gill pouch** n one of a pair of outgrowths on the wall of the pharynx, found in cyclostomes and present at the

embryonic stage in all vertebrates, developing, in fish, into openings (**gill slits**) containing the gills.

gill² /jil/ n a small measure, having various values; in recent times $=\frac{1}{4}$ pint. [OFr *gelle*]
 □ **gill'-house** n (*obs*) a bar selling alcoholic drinks.

gill³ or **ghyll** /gil/ n a small ravine, a wooded glen; a brook. [ON *gil*]

gill⁴ /jil/ n a girl (also **jill**; *obs*); a female ferret (also **jill**; *inf* or *dialect*); a policewoman (*sl*); ground ivy (*dialect*); beer with an infusion of ground ivy (also **gill ale**, **gill beer** *obs*). [*Gillian* or *Juliana* (from *Julius*), a woman's name]
 ■ **gill'et** or **jill'et** n (*Scot*) a skittish, flighty, or loose young woman.
 □ **gill'flirt** or **jill'flirt** n (*archaic*) a wanton girl.

gill⁵ /jil/ (*dialect*) n a two- or four-wheeled cart for carrying timber (also **jill**). [Origin uncertain]

gillaroo /gil-ə-roo'/ n an Irish trout with a thickened muscular stomach. [Ir *giolla ruadh* red lad]

Gilles de la Tourette's syndrome /zhēl də la too-ret' sin'drōm/ n same as **Tourette's syndrome**.

gillet see under **gill⁴**.

gillie, ghillie or **gilly** /gil'i/ n a Highland chief's attendant (*hist*); an attendant on or guide of hunting and fishing sportsmen. ◆ vi to act as gillie. [Gaelic *gille* a lad, Ir *giolla*]
 □ **gillie-wet'foot** (*obs*) or **-white'-foot** n (*obs*) a barefoot Highland lad, *esp* a messenger or chief's attendant.

gillion /jil'yən or gil'/ (*old*) n (in Britain) a thousand million, 10⁹, equivalent of a modern billion. [**giga-** and **million**]

gillravage, gillravitch see gilravage.

gilly see gillie.

gillyflower /jil'i-flowr/ (*Shakesp* **gillyvor** /-vər/) n a flower that smells like cloves, *esp* **clove'-gillyflower** and **stock'-gillyflower** (see **clove¹** and **stock¹**). [OFr *girofle*, from Gr *karyophyllon* the clove-tree, from *karyon* a nut, and *phyllon* a leaf]

gilpy or **gilpey** /gil'pi/ (*Scot*) n a boisterous girl or (formerly) boy.

gilravage, gillravage, galravage, or **gilravitch, gillravitch, galravitch** /gəl-rav'ij or -rā'vij/ (*Scot*) n a noisy frolic; riotous merrymaking. ◆ vi to behave riotously.
 ■ **gilrav'ager** n.

gilsonite see **uintaite**.

gilt¹ /gilt/ pat and pap of **gild¹**. adj gilded; gold-coloured. ◆ n gilding; money (*old sl*); a gilt-edged security; glitter, glamour, superficial attractiveness.
 □ **gilt'cup** or **gil'cup** n (*dialect*) a buttercup. **gilt'-edged** adj having the edges gilt; of the highest quality (**gilt-edged securities**, also called **gilts**, those stocks (such as government stocks) regarded as very safe investments, having a comparatively low fixed rate of interest but guaranteed repayment). **gilt'-head** n a name for several fishes, *esp* a sparoid fish with a half-moon-shaped gold spot between the eyes. **gilt'-tail** n a yellow-tipped worm (*Dendrobaena subrubicunda*) found in old dung-hills. **gilt'wood** adj made of wood and covered with gilt.

gilt² /gilt/ (*dialect*) n a young sow (in various conditions locally). [ON *gyltr*; cf OE *gilte*]

gimbal /jim'bl/ n a gimmal (*obs*); (in *pl*) a contrivance with self-aligning bearings for keeping eg hanging objects, nautical instruments, etc horizontal (*sing* in combination, eg *gimbal ring*). [See **gemel**]

gimcrack or **jimcrack** /jim'krak/ n a dodge, trick; a trivial mechanism; a worthless knick-knack; a paltry, poorly made, flimsy article. ◆ adj worthless, shoddy. [ME *gibecrake* poss inlay]
 ■ **gimcrack'ery** n.

gimel /gē'māl/ n the third letter of the Hebrew alphabet. [Heb]

gimlet /gim'lit/ n a small hand tool with a pointed screw-tip for boring holes in wood; a cocktail made of gin or vodka, with lime-juice. ◆ vt to pierce as with a gimlet; to turn like a gimlet. [OFr *guimbelet*, from Gmc; cf **wimble¹**]
 □ **gim'let-eyed** adj having a piercing look or stare.

gimmal /jim'l/ n a ring that can be divided into two (or three) rings (also **gimmal ring**); a joint or part in any mechanism (also *obs* or *dialect* **gimm'er**; *Shakesp* **gimm'or**). [See **gemel**]
 ■ **gimm'alled** (*Shakesp* **jymold**) adj jointed, hinged.

gimme /gim'i/ (*sl*) contracted form of *give me*. n in golf, a short putt that one's opponent is sportingly excused from playing, there being little likelihood of missing it (*inf*); (*usu* in *pl*, as **the gimmes**) avarice (*US sl*).
 □ **gimme cap** or **hat** n (*US sl*) a peaked cap printed with a company logo or a trademark, distributed among the public as advertising.

gimmer¹ /gim'ər/ (*Scot*) n a young ewe; a woman (*derog*). [ON *gymbr*; cf Swed *gimmer*, Dan *gimmer*]

gimmer² see **gimmal**.

gimmick /gim'ik/ n a device (often peculiar to the person adopting it) to catch attention or publicity; a secret device for performing a trick; an ingenious mechanical device. ◆ vt to provide, use or devise a gimmick for or in, to accomplish by means of a gimmick. [Orig US slang; origin unknown]
 ■ **gimm'ickry** n gimmicks in quantity; use of gimmicks. **gimm'icky** adj relating to a gimmick; designed to catch attention or publicity; (loosely) of little worth or importance.

gimmor (*Shakesp*) see **gimmal**.

gimp¹, also **guimp** or **gymp** /gimp/ n a yarn with a hard core; a trimming made of this; a fishing-line bound with wire; a coarse thread in lace-making. ◆ vt to make or furnish with gimp. [Fr *guimpe*, appar from OHGer *wimpal*; cf **wimple**; perh confused with Fr *guipure*; see **guipure**]

gimp² /gimp/ (*sl*, chiefly *US*) n a lame person; a limp; a weak or submissive person; a person who obtains sexual pleasure from being submissive, and by wearing a rubber costume with zips and chains. ◆ vi to limp. [Ety uncertain; Norw dialect *gimpa* to tip over, has been suggested, or perh a corruption of **gammy**]
 ■ **gimp'y** adj.

gimp³ /jimp/ (*rare* or *dialect*) vt to scallop, notch; to corrugate.

gin¹ /jin/ n a spirit distilled from grain or malt and flavoured with juniper berries or other aromatic substances, made chiefly in Britain and the USA; geneva. [Contracted from **geneva**]
 ■ **ginn'y** adj flavoured with, under the influence of, containing or relating to gin.
 □ **gin fizz** n a drink of gin, lemon juice, carbonated water, etc. **gin palace** n (*derog*) a showily pretentious public house. **gin'shop** n (*archaic*) a bar or shop selling mostly gin. **gin sling** n an iced gin and water, sweetened and flavoured, with *usu* lemon or lime.
 ■ **gin and it** gin and *It*alian vermouth.

gin² /jin/ n a scheme, artifice, contrivance (*Spenser*); a snare or trap; a machine, *esp* one for hoisting (*engineering, mining*, etc); a cotton gin; an instrument of torture (*Spenser*). ◆ vt (**ginn'ing**; **ginned**) to trap or snare; to clear of seeds by a cotton gin. [**engine**]
 ■ **ginn'er** n a person who gins cotton. **gin'ery** or **gin'house** n a place where cotton is ginned.
 □ **gin trap** n a powerful spring trap fitted with teeth.

gin³ /jin/ (*Aust*) n an Australian Aboriginal woman. [From an Aboriginal language]

gin⁴ /jin/ or **gin rummy** /rum'i/ n a type of rummy in which a player whose unmatched cards count ten or less may stop the game. [Origin uncertain]

gin⁵ /gin/ (*archaic*) vt and vi (pat **gan**, used poetically in the sense of *did*) to begin. [Aphetic from OE *beginnan* or *onginnan* to begin]

gin⁶ /gin/ (*Scot*) prep by (the time of). [ME *gain*, appar from ON *gegn* against]

gin⁷ /gin/ (*Scot*) conj if. [Perh pap of **give** as a substitute for **gif**; perh from **gin⁶**]

ging /ging/ (*obs*) n a gang or company. See **gang¹**.

gingal, gingall see **jingal**.

gingelly see **gingili**.

ginger /jin'jər/ n the rootstock of *Zingiber officinale*, or another species of the genus (family Zingiberaceae) with a hot taste, used as a condiment, etc, *esp* dried and ground, or preserved eg in syrup as a sweet; ginger beer; a redhead (*inf*); stimulation (*sl*); mettle (*sl*). ◆ adj (*esp* of hair) sandy, reddish. ◆ vt to put ginger into; to make spirited, to enliven (often with *up*). [ME *gingivere*, from OFr *gengibre*, from LL *gingiber*, from L *zingiber*, from Gr *zingiberis*, from Prakrit, from Sans *srnga* horn, and *vera* body; Malayalam *inchiver*]
 ■ **gin'gerous** adj (*Dickens*) sandy, reddish. **gin'gery** adj of or like ginger; sandy in colour; (of remarks) critical, cutting.
 □ **gingerade'** or **ginger ale** n a carbonated soft drink flavoured with ginger. **ginger beer** n a mildly alcoholic sparkling drink made with fermenting ginger; ginger ale. **ginger beer plant** n a symbiotic association of a yeast and a bacterium, by which ginger beer can be prepared, also called **Californian bees**. **ginger cordial** n a cordial made of ginger, lemon peel, raisins, water, and sometimes spirits. **ginger group** n a group within eg a political party seeking to inspire the rest with its own enthusiasm and activity. **ginger nut** n a small thick gingersnap. **ginger pop** n (*inf*) weak ginger beer. **gin'gersnap** n a gingerbread biscuit. **ginger wine** n an alcoholic drink made by fermenting sugar and water, and flavoured with various spices, chiefly ginger.

gingerbread /jin'jər-bred/ n a cake flavoured with treacle and *usu* ginger; (with *cap*) a self-help support group for one-parent families. ◆ adj (of ornamental work) cheap and tawdry, overelaborate. [OFr *gingimbrat*, from LL *gingiber*; see ety for **ginger**; confused with **bread**]
 □ **gingerbread man** n a ginger biscuit shaped like a human form.
 ■ **take the gilt off the gingerbread** to destroy the glamour.

---

gingerly /jin'jər-li/ adv and adj with soft steps; with extreme wariness and delicate gentleness. [Poss OFr gensor, compar of **gent²**]

gingham /ging'əm/ n a kind of cotton cloth, woven from coloured yarns into stripes or checks; an umbrella (obs inf). [Fr guingan, orig from Malay ginggang striped]

gingili, **gingelly** or **jinjili** /jin'ji-li/ n a species of sesame; an oil obtained from its seeds. [Hindi jinjalī, prob from Ar juljulān]

gingival /jin-jī'vl/ adj relating to the gums. [L gingīva gum]
■ **gingivec'tomy** n the cutting back of inflamed or excess gum. **gingivī'tis** n inflammation of the gums.

gingko see **ginkgo**.

gingle an obsolete variant of **jingle**.

ginglymus /jing'gli-məs (or ging')/ n (pl **ging'lymī**) a joint that permits movement in one plane only, a hinge joint. [Latinized from Gr ginglymos]
■ **ging'limoid** adj.

gink /gingk/ (sl) n a person, esp one considered odd. [Origin unknown]

ginkgo /gingk'gō/ or **gingko** /ging'kō/ n (pl **gink'goes** or **ging'koes**) the maidenhair tree, an ornamental Chinese fan-leaved tree, holy in Japan, the only species in the **Ginkgoā'les** of Gymnosperms. [Jap ginkyo, from Chin yín silver, and xìng apricot]

ginn see **jinn**.

ginnel /gin'əl/ (Scot and N Eng dialect) n a narrow alley or path between high walls or buildings (also **genn'el**). [A voiced form of **kennel²**]

ginny see under **gin¹**.

ginormous /jī-nör'məs/ (inf) adj huge, altogether enormous. [gigantic and enormous]

ginseng /jin'seng/ n a plant of the araliaceous genus Panax, cultivated esp in the Far East; its root, believed to have important restorative and curative properties. [Chin rénshēn perh image of man, from the shape of the root]

gio see **geo**.

giocoso /jo-kō'sō/ (music) adj and adv (played) in a lively or humorous manner. [Ital]

Giorgi system /jör'jē sis'tim/ n a system of units proposed in 1904 and later adopted as the **MKSA system** having the metre, kilogram, second and ampere as units of length, mass, time and current respectively. [Giovanni Giorgi (1871–1950), Italian physicist]

gip /jip/ n same as **gyp¹,³**.

gippo or **gyppo** /jip'ō/, also **gippy**, **gyppie** or **gyppy** /jip'i/ (offensive sl) n (pl **gipp'os**, **gypp'os**, **gipp'ies** or **gypp'ies**) an Egyptian, esp a native Egyptian soldier; a gypsy; a cook (milit sl). [Egypt; see also ety for **gypsy**]
❑ **gippy** (or **gyppy**) **tummy** n (inf) diarrhoea, severe upset stomach, thought of as a hazard of holidaying in hot countries.

gippy see **gippo**.

gipsen /jip'sən/ (Spenser) n an obsolete form of **gypsy**.

gipsy see **gypsy**.

giraffe /ji-räf'/ n an African ruminant mammal with a remarkably long neck and forelegs and a brown-patched gingery coat. [Ar zarāfah]
■ **giraff'id**, **giraff'īne** or **giraff'oid** adj.

girandole /jir'ən-dōl/ or **girandola** /-and'ə-lə/ n a branched chandelier or similar structure; a pendant, etc with small jewels attached around it; a rotating firework; a number of linked mines (milit). [Fr, from Ital girandola, from girare, from L gȳrāre to turn round, from gȳrus, from Gr gȳros a circle]

girasol /jir'ə-sol/ or **girasole** /-sōl/ n a fire opal or other stone that seems to send a firelike glow from within in certain lights; the plant heliotrope (obs); the sunflower (obs). [Ital, from girare (see ety for **girandole**) and sole, from L sōl the sun]

gird¹ /gûrd/ vt (pat and pap **gird'ed** and **girt**) to bind round; to secure by a belt or girdle; to encompass; to surround; to clothe, furnish. [OE gyrdan; cf Ger gürten]
■ **gird'er** n a large beam, simple or built up, of wood, iron or steel, to take a lateral stress, eg to support a floor, wall, or the roadway of a bridge; a strip of strengthening tissue (bot). **gird'ing** n that which girds.
❑ **girder bridge** n a bridge whose load is sustained by girders resting on supports.
■ **gird oneself** to tuck up loose garments under the girdle (so as to be better able to run or act quickly); to brace the mind for any trial or effort; see also **loin**.

gird² /gûrd/ (Scot and N Eng dialect) vi to gibe, jeer (with at). ◆ vt (obs) to taunt. ◆ n a blow, stroke (obs); a taunt, dig or gibe (archaic). [Origin obscure; not from OE gyrd, gierd rod]

gird³ /gird/ (Scot) n a hoop (also **girr** /gir/). [A form of **girth¹**]

girdle¹ /gûr'dl/ n a waistbelt; a cord worn around the waist by a monk, etc; anything that encloses like a belt; a woman's lightweight, close-fitting undergarment, a form of corset, reaching from waist to thigh; a bony arch to which a limb is attached (anat); a worm's clitellum; a ring-shaped cut around a tree; the rim of a brilliant-cut gem. ◆ vt to bind or enclose with a girdle, or as if with a girdle; to cut a ring round (a tree, etc); to cut a circular outline around (a gemstone). [OE gyrdel, from gyrdan to gird]
■ **gird'led** adj. **gird'ler** n a person who or thing which girdles; a maker of girdles.
❑ **girdle'stead** n (obs) the waist.

girdle² see **griddle**.

girkin /gûr'kin/ (obs) n same as **gherkin**.

girl /gûrl/ n a female child; a daughter; a young unmarried woman (often offensive); a woman irrespective of age (inf, often offensive); a girlfriend, sweetheart (inf); a maidservant. [ME gerle, girle, gurle boy or girl, perhaps related to LGer gör, göre child]
■ **girl'hood** n the state or time of being a girl. **girl'ie** or **girl'y** adj (of magazines, photographs, etc) showing nude or scantily clad young women; of, relating to or stereotypically characteristic of girls. ◆ n a girl, esp used as a patronizing form of address; a young woman who embodies stereotypical female characteristics. **girl'ish** (also **girl'y**) adj of or like a girl. **girl'ishly** adv. **girl'ishness** n. **girly** see **girlie** and **girlish** above.
❑ **Girl Friday** n a young female general office worker. **girl'friend** n a sweetheart, or a girl who is one's regular companion; a girl's or woman's female friend. **Girl Guide** n formerly, the name for a Guide (see **guide**). **girl power** n (inf) the social and economic importance of young women. **Girl Scout** n a member of an American organization similar to the Guides.
■ **old girl** a female former pupil; an elderly woman (inf); an amicably disrespectful mode of address or reference to a female of any age or species.

girlond obsolete form of **garland**.

girn /gûrn/ (dialect) vi to grin, snarl; to grimace, make a grotesque face; to complain peevishly. ◆ n an act or manner of girning. [**grin¹**]
■ **girn'er** n. **girn'ie** adj ill-tempered, peevish.

girnel /gûr'nl/ (Scot) n a granary (obs); a large chest or vat for storing grain. [Variant of **garner**]

giro /jī'rō/ n (pl **gī'ros**) (also with cap) a banking system, organized by Girobank plc, by which money can be transferred direct from the account of one holder to that of another person (or to those of others); a social security payment by giro cheque (inf). [Ger, transfer, from Gr gyros ring]
❑ **giro cheque**, **order**, etc n one issued through the giro system.

girolle /jē-rōl'/ n another name for the chanterelle mushroom. [Fr]

giron see **gyron**.

Girondist /ji-ron'dist/ (hist) n a member of the moderate republican party during the French Revolution, so called because its earliest leaders were deputies for the Gironde department (also **Giron'din**).
■ **Giron'dism** n.

gironic see **gyron**.

girosol same as **girasol**.

girr see **gird³**.

girt /gûrt/ adj the past participle of **gird¹** in all senses; (of a ship) moored so taut by her cables to two oppositely placed anchors as to be prevented from swinging to the wind or tide. ◆ vt to gird; to girth. ◆ vi to girt.

girth¹ /gûrth/ n the belly-band of a saddle; a circumferential measure of thickness. ◆ vt to put a girth on; to measure the girth of; to encircle (archaic). ◆ vi to measure in girth. —Also (now obs or dialect as n, rare as v) **girt**. [ON gjörth]
❑ **girth'line** or **girt'line** n (naut) a gantline.

girth² see **grith**.

GIS abbrev: Geographical Information System, a computer system used to process geographically referenced information.

gisarme /ji-zärm'/, also **zhi-** or **gi-/** (hist) n a type of long-staffed battle-axe carried by foot soldiers. [OFr guisarme, prob OHGer getan to weed, and īsarn iron]

gism see **jism**.

gismo or **gizmo** /giz'mō/ (inf) n (pl **gis'mos** or **giz'mos**) a gadget, thingumajig. [Origin unknown]
■ **gismol'ogy** or **gizmol'ogy** n gadgetry, technology involving (strange, baffling or daunting) devices generally.

gist /jist/ n the main point or pith of a matter. [OFr gist (Fr gît), from OFr gesir (Fr gésir) to lie, from L jacēre]

git /git/ (sl) n a person (derog); a fool; a bastard. See also under **get** (n). [**get** offspring, brat]

gitano /jē-tä'nō or hhē-/ (Sp) n (pl **gitan'os**) a male gypsy.
■ **gitan'a** n a female gypsy.

gite or **gîte** /zhēt/ n in France, a farmhouse, cottage, etc; simple holiday accommodation in such a farmhouse, etc; a resting place (archaic). [Fr gîte, from OFr giste; see **gest**[1]]

gittern /git'ərn/ n a kind of guitar, a cither. ◆ vi (obs) to play on the gittern. [OFr guiterne, connected with Gr kitharā; see **cithern** under **cithara**, **guitar**, **zither**]

giust /just/ (Spenser, Walter Scott) n and vi same as **joust**.

giusto /joo'stō/ (music) adj suitable; regular; strict. ◆ adv in strict time; at a reasonable speed. [Ital, from L jūstus just]

give[1] /giv/ vt (**giv'ing**; **gāve**; **given** /giv'n/) to bestow; to impart; to yield; to grant; to donate; to permit; to afford, provide; to pay or render (thanks, etc); to pronounce (a judgement or decision); to show (a result); to apply (oneself); to allow or admit. ◆ vi to yield to pressure; to begin to melt or soften; to grow soft; to open, or give an opening or view, to lead (with upon, on or into, a gallicism); to donate. ◆ n yielding; elasticity. [OE gefan (WSax giefan), the back g prob owing to Scand influence; ON gefa, Swed gifva, Dan give, Gothic giban, Ger geben]
■ **giv'en** adj bestowed; specified; addicted, disposed (with to); granted; admitted. ◆ n something that is assumed to be the case. **giv'enness** n. **giv'er** n a person who or thing which gives or bestows. **giv'ing** n the act of bestowing; the thing given. ◆ adj that gives; generous, liberal.
❑ **give'away** n a betrayal, revelation, esp if unintentional; something given free or at a greatly reduced price, esp something offered with a product or service with the aim of increasing sales. **given name** n the name given to the individual, not that of the family, ie the first or Christian name, distinguished from the surname.
■ **give and take** reciprocity in concession; mutually compensatory variations; fair exchange of repartee. **give as good as one gets** to retort in equal measure in words or action. **give away** to give for nothing; to betray; to bestow ceremonially (eg a bride). **give birth to** to bring forth, produce; to originate, begin, generate. **give chase** to pursue. **give ear** (archaic) to listen (to). **give forth** to emit; to publish; to expatiate, talk at length (inf). **give ground** or **place** to give way, yield. **give head** see under **head**. **give in to** (obs **give into**) to yield to. **give it to** (**someone**) (inf) to scold or beat (someone) severely. **give it up for** (inf) to show one's appreciation to (a person) by cheering or applause. **give line, head, rein**, etc to give more liberty or scope (the metaphors from angling and horse-riding). **give me** (inf) I would choose if I had the choice. **give off** to emit (eg a smell). **give oneself away** to betray one's secret unawares. **give or take** allowing for an error of (a certain amount). **give out** to report, announce; to emit; to distribute to individuals; to expire; to relinquish (Shakesp). **give over** to transfer; to desist from, to cease (Scot and N Eng dialect). **give over to** to set (a period of time) aside for a particular purpose. **give place** see **give ground** above. **give rein** see **give line** above. **give the lie to** to accuse openly of falsehood; to prove wrong. **give tongue** see under **tongue**. **give up** to abandon; to surrender; to desist from. **give up the ghost** see under **ghost**. **give way** to fall back, yield, withdraw; to break, snap or collapse under strain; to begin rowing (usu as a command to a crew); to allow traffic in a direction crossing one's path to proceed first. **give way to** to yield to, submit to; to allow to take precedence, give priority to; to succumb to (eg grief). **what gives?** (inf) what's new?; what's happening?

give[2] same as **gyve**.

Giz same as **Geëz**.

gizmo, gizmology see **gismo**.

gizz or **jiz** /jiz/ (Scot) n a wig. [Origin unknown]

gizzard /giz'ərd/ n a muscular stomach, esp the second stomach of a bird. [ME giser, from OFr guiser, supposed to be from L gigeria (pl) cooked entrails of poultry]
■ **stick in someone's gizzard** to be more than someone can accept or tolerate.

gizzen /giz'n/ (Scot) vi to shrink from dryness so as to leak; to wither. ◆ adj leaky; shrivelled. [ON gisna]

gju see **gue**.

Gk abbrev : Greek.

GKS (comput) abbrev : Graphical Kernel System, an international standard for computer graphics programming.

GLA abbrev : gamma linolenic acid; Greater London Authority.

glabella /glə-bel'ə/ (anat) n (pl **glabell'ae** /-bel'ē/) the part of the forehead between the eyebrows and just above their level. [L glaber bald, smooth]
■ **glabell'ar** adj.

glabrous /glā'brəs/ or **glabrate** /glā'brāt or -brət/ (med, zool, bot) adj hairless, smooth. [L glaber]

glacé /glas'ā/ adj frozen, or with ice; iced with sugar; candied; glossy, lustrous, esp of a thin silk material or kid leather. ◆ vt (**glac'éing**; **glac'éed**) to ice with sugar; to candy. [Fr]

glacial /glā'syəl, glā'si-əl or -shəl/ adj icy; frozen; readily or ordinarily solidified (as **glacial acetic acid** practically pure acetic acid; chem); relating to ice or its action; (of progress) ponderously slow, like that of a glacier; (of manner, etc) distant, hostile; extremely cold (inf). ◆ n a glacial period, an ice age. [L glaciālis icy, glaciāre, -ātum to freeze, from glaciēs ice]
■ **glā'cialist** or **glaciol'ogist** n a person who studies the geological action of ice. **glā'cially** adv. **glaciate** /glas' or glāsh'/ vt to polish by ice action; to subject to the action of land ice; to freeze. **glā'ciated** adj. **glaciā'tion** n. **glaciolog'ical** adj. **glaciologist** see **glacialist** above. **glaciol'ogy** n the study of the geological nature, distribution and action of ice.
❑ **glacial deposits** n pl rock material deposited by glaciers or glacier-associated streams and lakes. **Glacial Period** n the Ice Age, or any ice age.

glacier /glas'yər or -i-ər, glā'syər or glā'shər/ n a mass of ice, fed by snow on a mountain, slowly creeping downhill to where it melts or breaks up into icebergs. [Fr, from glace ice, from L glaciēs ice]

glaciology see under **glacial**.

glacis /glās-ē, glas'is or glā'sis/ n (pl **glacis** /glās-ē, glas'iz or glās'iz/ or **glac'ises**) a gentle slope, esp in fortification. [Fr, orig a slippery place, from L glaciēs ice]

glad[1] /glad/ adj pleased, happy; cheerful; giving pleasure; bright (obs). ◆ vt (**gladd'ing**; **gladd'ed**) (archaic) to make glad, gladden. [OE glæd; Ger glatt smooth, ON glathr bright, Dan glad]
■ **gladd'en** vt to make glad; to cheer. **glad'ful** adj (archaic; Spenser). **glad'fulness** n (archaic). **glad'ly** adv. **glad'ness** n. **glad'some** adj (archaic) glad; joyous. **glad'somely** adv (archaic). **glad'someness** n (archaic).
❑ **glad eye** n (sl) an ogle, esp in the phrase to give someone the glad eye. **glad hand** n (US) the hand of welcome or of effusive or excessive greeting. **glad'-hand** vi and vt to extend the glad hand to; to behave in this manner. **glad'-hander** n (US) a person who is excessively friendly to all and sundry (esp of a vote-seeking politician). **glad'-handing** n. **glad rags** n pl (inf) best clothes, dress clothes.
■ **glad of** glad to have; glad because of.

glad[2] /glad/ or **gladdie** /glad'i/ (inf) n short for **gladiolus**.

gladdon /glad'ən/ (dialect) n an iris. [Origin obscure]

glade /glād/ n an open space in a wood. [Ety obscure; poss connected with **glad**[1] bright]
■ **glā'dy** adj having glades.

gladiate /glad'i-ət or -āt, also glād'/ (bot) adj sword-shaped. [New L gladiatus, from L gladius sword]

gladiator /glad'i-ā-tər/ n in ancient Rome, a combatant in fights or displays held for public entertainment; a fierce or contentious fighter or debater (fig). [L, from gladius sword]
■ **gladiator'ial**, (obs) **gladiator'ian** or **glad'iatory** adj. **glad'iātorship** n.

gladiolus /glad-i-ō'ləs, rarely glə-dī'o-ləs/ n (pl **gladiō'lī** or **gladiō'luses**) any plant of a genus (Gladiolus) of the family Iridaceae, with sword-shaped leaves and long spikes of brightly coloured flowers (also **glad'iole**); the middle part of the sternum (anat). [L, dimin of gladius sword]

gladius /glad'i-əs or glā'di-əs/ n a cuttle-bone; a sword (rare). [L, sword]

Gladstonian /glad-stō'ni-ən/ adj relating to or associated with WE Gladstone (1809–98), four times British prime minister. ◆ n a follower of Gladstone.
❑ **Gladstone bag** n a travelling bag or small portmanteau, opening out flat, named in his honour. **Gladstone sherry** n (hist) cheap sherry (referring to reduction in duty, 1860).

glady see under **glade**.

Glagolitic /glag-ō-lit'ik/ adj relating to or written in Glagol, an ancient Slavonic alphabet, apparently derived from the cursive Greek of the 9c; relating to Roman Catholics of the Slavonic rite, who retained the Slavonic alphabet in their service books. [Old Slav glagolu a word]

glaik /glāk/ n (obs Scot; usu in pl) a flash; dazzling; mocking deception; a trick; a puzzle-game. [Origin obscure]
■ **glaik'it** or sometimes **glaik'et** adj (Scot) giddy; foolish; stupid, daft. **glaik'itness** (Scot) levity, giddiness; stupidity, ineptitude.
■ **fling the glaiks in folk's een** (obs Scot) to throw dust in people's eyes, dazzle or deceive.

glair /glār/ n the clear part of an egg used as a varnish or adhesive; any viscous, transparent substance. ◆ vt to varnish with white of egg. [Fr glaire, perh from LL clāra (ōvī) white (of egg), from L clārus clear]

■ **glair'in** *n* organic matter in mineral waters. **glair'y** (*med, pathol,* etc), **glair'eous** or **glär'eous** *adj* (*archaic*) of or like glair; slimy, viscous.

glaive /glāv/ (*obs*) *n* a sword; a spear; a long-shafted weapon like a halberd, its edge on the outer curve; (also **gleave** /glēv/) a pronged fish-spear (*dialect*). [OFr *glaive*]
■ **glaived** *adj*.

glam[1] see under **glamour**.

glam[2] /glam/ (*inf*) *n* a greying, leisured, affluent married person, a class of woopie (qv).

glamour or *US* **glamor** /glam'ər/ *n* allure, magnetism; an excitingly or fascinatingly attractive quality; groomed beauty and studied charm; the supposed influence of a charm on the eyes, making them see things as fairer than they are (*archaic*); enchantment; witchery (*archaic*). ◆ *vt* (*archaic*) to enchant, bewitch, cast a spell over; (with *up*) to glamorize. [**gramary**]
■ **glam** *adj* (*sl*) glamorous; relating to glam rock. ◆ *vt* to glamorize (often with *up*). **glam'my** *adj*. **glamoriza'tion** or **-s-** *n*. **glam'orize** or **-ise** *vt* to make glamorous; to romanticize. **glam'orous** *adj* full of glamour; bewitching, alluring. **glam'orously** *adv*.
❑ **glamour boy** or **girl** *n* (*inf, often derog*) a man or woman considered to be very glamorous. **glam'ourpuss** *n* (*inf*) a glamorous person, *esp* female. **glam rock** *n* a type of rock music popular in Britain in the 1970s, memorable more for the outrageous clothes, hairstyles and make-up of the performers than for the music itself. **glam-rock'** *adj*.

glance[1] /gläns/ *vi* to fly (off) obliquely on striking; to make a passing allusion, *esp* unfavourable (with *at*); to snatch a momentary view (with *at*); to dart a reflected ray, to flash. ◆ *vt* to catch a glimpse of; to cause (eg a ball or other object) to glance; to direct glancingly; to deflect; to glance at (*obs*). ◆ *n* an oblique impact or movement; a sudden shaft of reflected light; a darting of the eye; a momentary look; a deliberate stroke in which the ball is deflected only slightly from its line of flight (*cricket*); a passing allusion, *esp* satirical (*obs*). [ME *glenten*, poss nasalized form of *glace* to glance, from OFr *glacier* to slip, slide]
■ **glanc'ing** *n* and *adj*. **glanc'ingly** *adv*.
■ **at a glance** immediately, at a first look. **glance at** or **over** or **through** to read quickly or cursorily.

glance[2] /gläns/ *n* a black or grey mineral with metallic lustre, *usu* a sulphide, selenide or telluride, eg redruthite or **copp'er-glance**, galena or **lead'-glance**, argentite or **sil'ver-glance**. [Ger *Glanz* glance, lustre]
❑ **glance'-coal** *n* anthracite.

gland[1] /gland/ (*biol*) *n* a secreting structure in plants and animals. [L *glans, glandis* an acorn]
■ **glandif'erous** *adj* bearing acorns or nuts. **glan'diform** *adj* resembling a gland; acorn-shaped. **gland'ūlar** or rarely **gland'ūlous** *adj* containing, consisting of, or relating to glands. **gland'ūlarly** or **gland'ūlously** *adv*. **glan'dūle** *n* a small gland. **glandūlif'erous** *adj* bearing small glands.
❑ **glandular fever** *n* infectious mononucleosis, a disease characterized by slight fever, enlargement of glands, and increase in the white cells of the blood.

gland[2] /gland/ (*engineering*) *n* a device for preventing leakage at a point where a rotating or reciprocating shaft emerges from a vessel containing fluid under pressure; a sleeve or nut used to compress the packing in a stuffing box (qv). [Origin unknown]

glanders /glan'dərz/ *n sing* a malignant, contagious and fatal disease of horses and asses (also communicable to humans), showing itself *esp* on the mucous membrane of the nose, on the lungs, and on the lymphatic system. [OFr *glandre* a gland]
■ **gland'ered** or **gland'erous** *adj* affected with glanders.

glandiferous, glandular, glandule, etc see under **gland**[1].

glans /glanz/ *n* (pl **glan'des** /-dēz/) an acorn or similar fruit; a glandular structure of similar shape (*anat*). [L, acorn]
❑ **glans clitoris** *n* the extremity of the clitoris. **glans penis** *n* the extremity of the penis.

glare /glār/ *n* an oppressive or unrelieved dazzling light (also *fig*); excessive luminance emitted from a VDU screen, or by light reflecting off a terminal (*comput*); overpowering lustre (*archaic*); cheap or showy brilliance; a fierce stare; a glassy or icy surface (*US*). ◆ *adj* (*US*) glassy (of ice). ◆ *vi* to emit a hard, fierce, dazzling light; to be obtrusively noticeable, intense or strong, eg to shine dazzlingly; to stare fiercely. ◆ *vt* to send out or express with a glare. [ME *glāren* to shine; cf **glass**, OE *glær* amber, LGer *glaren* to glow]
■ **glar'ing** *adj* bright and dazzling; flagrant or conspicuous. **glar'ingly** *adv*. **glar'ingness** *n*. **glar'y** *adj* glaring; shining harshly.

glareous /glā'ri-əs/ *adj* growing on gravel (*bot*); gravelly (*obs*). See also **glair**. [L *glārea* gravel]
■ **glā'real** *adj* (*bot*) growing on dry exposed ground.

glasnost /glas' or glaz'nost/ *n* the policy of openness and forthrightness followed by the Soviet government under Mikhail Gorbachev in 1988–91. [Russ, speaking aloud]
■ **glasnos'tian** or **glasnos'tic** *adj* of, relating to, or in the spirit of, glasnost.

glass /gläs/ *n* a hard, amorphous, brittle substance, a bad conductor of electricity, *usu* transparent, made by fusing together one or more of the oxides of silicon, boron or phosphorus with certain basic oxides (eg sodium, magnesium, calcium, potassium), and cooling the product rapidly to prevent crystallization; an article made of or with glass, *esp* a drinking vessel, a mirror, a lens, the cover of a watch face, a weather glass, a telescope, etc; such articles collectively; the quantity of liquid a glass holds; any fused substance like glass, with a vitreous fracture; a rock, or portion of rock, without crystalline structure; (in *pl*) spectacles. ◆ *adj* made of glass. ◆ *vt* to furnish or fit with glass; to reflect in glass; to put in, under, or behind glass (*rare*); to glaze, cover with a glassy surface (*obs*); to polish highly (*rare*); to attack (someone) with a broken glass or bottle (*inf*). [OE *glæs*]
■ **glass'en** *adj* (*archaic*) of or like glass. **glass'ful** *n* (pl **glass'fuls**) as much as a glass will hold. **glass'ify** *vi* to become glass or like glass. ◆ *vt* to cause to become glass or like glass. **glass'ily** *adv*. **glassine** /-ēn'/ *n* a transparent, glazed, greaseproof paper, used for book covers. **glass'iness** *n*. **glass'like** *adj*. **glass'y** *adj* like glass; (of eyes) expressionless.
❑ **glass'-blower** *n*. **glass'-blowing** *n* the process of making glassware by inflating semi-molten glass. **glass case** *n* a display case made at least partly of glass. **glass ceiling** *n* an indistinct yet unmistakable barrier on the career ladder, through which certain categories of employees (*usu* women) find they can see but not progress. **glass chin** or **glass jaw** *n* a chin or jaw exceptionally vulnerable to punches, used chiefly of boxers. **glass'-cloth** *n* a cloth for drying glasses; a material woven from glass threads; a polishing cloth covered with powdered glass. **glass'-coach** *n* (*obs*) a coach (*esp* one for hire) having glazed windows. **glass cockpit** *n* an aircraft cockpit in which an array of glass-screened displays presents computer-generated information. **glass'-crab** *n* the transparent larva of the spiny lobster. **glass'-cutter** *n* a tool for cutting sheets of glass; a person who does cut-glass work. **glass'-cutting** *n* the act or process of cutting, shaping and ornamenting the surface of glass. **glass eye** *n* an artificial eye made of glass; (in *pl*) spectacles (*obs*); a form of blindness in horses. **glass'-faced** *adj* (*Shakesp*) reflecting the sentiments of another, as in a mirror. **glass fibre** *n* glass melted and then drawn out into extremely fine fibres, which are later to be spun, woven, etc (also called **fibreglass**). **glass'-gall** *n* a scum formed on fused glass. **glass'-gazing** *adj* (*Shakesp*) addicted to looking in a mirror. **glass'-grinding** *n* the ornamenting of glass by rubbing with sand, emery, etc. **glass harmonica** *n* the musical glasses (see **harmonica** under **harmony**). **glass'house** *n* a house made of glass or largely of glass, *esp* a greenhouse; military detention barracks (from one with a glass roof at Aldershot; *sl*); a glass factory. **glass jaw** see **glass chin** above. **glass'man** *n* a maker or seller of glass; a beggar hawking glass as a pretext (*hist*). **glass'-painting** *n* the art of producing pictures on glass by means of staining it chemically. **glass'paper** *n* paper coated with finely pounded glass, used like sandpaper. **glass'-rope** *n* a siliceous sponge (genus *Hyalonema*) with a long anchoring tuft. **glass snake** *n* a legless lizard (genus *Ophisaurus*) with a brittle tail. **glass soap** *n* manganese dioxide or other substance used by glass-makers to remove colouring from glass. **glass'ware** *n* articles made of glass. **glass wool** *n* glass spun into woolly fibres. **glass'work** *n* furnishings or articles made of glass; (*usu* in *pl*) a glass factory. **glass'worker** *n*. **glass'wort** *n* a name for plants of the genera *Salicornia* and *Salsola* yielding soda, once used in making glass. **glass'yheaded** *adj* (*Tennyson*) with a shiny bald head.
■ **live in a glass house** to be open to attack or retort. **musical glasses** see **harmonica** under **harmony**. **water** or **soluble glass** sodium or potassium silicate.

Glassite /glä'sīt/ *n* a follower of John Glas (1695–1773), who was deposed in 1728 from the ministry of the Church of Scotland for maintaining that a congregation with its eldership is, in its discipline, subject to no jurisdiction but that of Jesus Christ (also *adj*).

Glaswegian /glaz-, gläz-, glas- or gläs-wēj'(y)ən/ *n* a native or citizen of Glasgow. ◆ *adj* of or relating to Glasgow or Glaswegians. [Modelled on *Norwegian*]

glauberite /glö'bə-rīt/ *n* a greyish-white mineral, sodium calcium sulphate, found chiefly in rock salt. [Johann Rudolf *Glauber* (1604–68), German chemist]
❑ **Glauber** /glow'bər or glö'bər/ (or **Glauber's**) **salt** *n* hydrated sodium sulphate.

glaucescence, glaucescent see under **glaucous**.

glaucoma /glö- or glow-kō'mə/ n an insidious disease of the eye, marked by increased pressure within the eyeball and growing dimness of vision. [Gr *glaukōma* cataract; see **glaucous**]
■ **glaucomatous** /-kōm'ə-təs or -kom'/ adj.

glauconite /glö'kə-nīt/ n a mineral forming in the sea, a hydrated potassium iron and aluminium silicate, which gives a green colour to some of the beds of the Greensand. [Gr *glaukos* bluish-green]
■ **glauconitic** /-nit'ik/ adj. **glauconītīzā'tion** or **-s-** n conversion into glauconite.

glaucous /glö'kəs/ adj sea-green; greyish-blue; covered with a powdery greenish or bluish bloom (bot). [L *glaucus*, from Gr *glaukos* bluish-green or grey (orig gleaming)]
■ **glaucescence** /-ses'əns/ n. **glaucesc'ent** adj (bot) somewhat glaucous.

Glaucus /glö'kəs/ n a genus of translucent blue nudibranch gastropods of warm seas. [Gr *glaukos* bluish-green]

glaum /glöm/ (Scot) vi to clutch or grab (with at).

glaur /glör/ (Scot) n mire. [Origin unknown]
■ **glaur'y** adj.

Glaux /glöks/ n the generic name of sea milkwort or black saltwort, a fleshy seaside plant of the primrose family, with pink sepals and no petals, once used in soda-making. [Gr *glaux* wart cress]

glaze /glāz/ vt to furnish or set with glass; to cover with a thin surface of glass or something glassy; to cover with a layer of thin semitransparent colour; to give a glassy surface to; to apply a thin wash containing eg milk, eggs, or sugar to (eg pastry), to give a shiny appearance. ◆ vi to become glassy (often with over). ◆ n the glassy coating applied to pottery; a thin coat of semitransparent colour; any shining exterior; a thin wash of eggs, milk, sugar, etc for glazing food. [ME *glasen*, from *glas* glass; see **glass**]
■ **glazed** adj. **glā'zen** adj (obs) glassy; glazed. **glā'zer** n a person who glazes pottery, paper, etc. **glā'zier** /-zyər/ n a person who sets glass in window frames, etc. **glā'zing** n the act or art of setting glass; glass windows; the art of covering with a vitreous substance; semitransparent colours put thinly over others to modify the effect (art). **glā'zy** adj.

GLBT abbrev : gay, lesbian, bisexual and transgender.

GLC abbrev : Greater London Council (abolished in 1986).

GLCM abbrev : Graduate of the London College of Music.

Gld abbrev : guilder.

gleam /glēm/ vi to glow or shine, usu not very brightly. ◆ vt to flash. ◆ n a faint or moderate glow; a small stream of light; a beam; brightness; a brief manifestation (eg a gleam of hope) (fig). [OE *glæm* gleam, brightness; see **glimmer**[1]]
■ **gleam'ing** n and adj. **gleam'y** adj casting gleams; in or of gleams.

glean /glēn/ vt to learn by laboriously scraping together pieces of information; to collect (what is thinly scattered, neglected or overlooked); to pick up (facts or information); orig to follow the harvester(s) gathering any residue. ◆ vi to gather the corn left by a reaper or anything that has been left by others; to gather facts bit by bit. ◆ n (obs or dialect) that which is gleaned; the act of gleaning. [OFr *glener* (Fr *glaner*), through LL *glenāre*; origin unknown]
■ **glean'er** n. **glean'ing** n. **glean'ings** n pl things gleaned, esp bits of information from various sources.

gleave see **glaive**.

glebe /glēb/ n the soil (archaic or poetic); a clod (obs); a field (archaic or poetic); (also **glebe land**) the land attached to a parish church. [L *glēba* a clod]
■ **glē'bous** (rare) or **glē'by** adj (archaic) cloddy, turfy.
❑ **glebe'-house** n a manse.

glede /glēd/ or **gled** /gled/ (Bible; now Scot or N Eng) n the common kite. [OE *glida*, from *glīdan* to glide]

gledge /glej/ (Scot) vi to squint; to cast an eye around; to look cunningly. ◆ n a knowing look; a side-glance; a glimpse. [Cf **gley**[1]]

glee[1] /glē/ n joy; mirth and gaiety; impish enjoyment; a form of short part-song, strictly one without an accompaniment, popular from the mid-17c to the 19c (music); appar glitter (proverbially coupled with gold; Spenser). [OE *glēo*, *glīw* mirth; ON *glȳ*]
■ **glee'ful** or (archaic) **glee'some** adj merry. **glee'fully** adv. **glee'fulness** n.
❑ **glee club** n (chiefly N Am) a club or choir for singing glees, part-songs, etc. **glee'maiden** n (obs) a female minstrel. **glee'man** n (obs) a minstrel.

glee[2] see **gley**[1].

gleed[1] /glēd/ (archaic or dialect) n a hot coal or burning ember. [OE *glēd*; cf Du *gloed*, Ger *Glut*, Swed *glöd*]

gleed[2] see under **gley**[1].

gleek[1] /glēk/ (obs) n a jest or gibe, a trick. ◆ vi to gibe (with at); to jest. ◆ vt to play a trick upon. [Cf **glaik**]

gleek[2] /glēk/ n an old card game for three players, each having twelve cards, and eight being left for the stock. [OFr *glic*, *ghelicque*, poss from MDu *ghelic* alike]

gleet /glēt/ (med and pathol) n a viscous, transparent discharge from a mucous surface. ◆ vt to discharge gleet. [OFr *glette*, *glecte* a flux]
■ **gleet'y** adj.

gleg /gleg/ (Scot and N Eng) adj clever; apt; alert; keen, sharp. [ON *gleggr* clever; cf OE *glēaw* wise, Ger *glau* clear]

glei see **gley**[2].

Gleichschaltung /glīhh'shäl-tŭng/ (Ger) n elimination of all opposition, enforcement of strict conformity, in politics, culture, etc. [Literally, co-ordination, from *gleich* like, and *schalten* to govern]

glen /glen/ n a narrow valley with a stream, often with trees; a depression, usu of some extent, between hills. [Gaelic *gleann*; cf Welsh *glyn*]

glendoveer /glen-dō-vēr'/ (Southey) n a heavenly spirit. [Fr *grandouver*]

glengarry /glen-gar'i/ (Scot) n a Highlander's cap of thick-milled woollen cloth, generally rising to a point in front, with ribbons hanging down behind. [*Glengarry* in the Highlands, Scotland]

glenoid /glē'noid/ adj socket-shaped; slightly cupped. ◆ n a cup-shaped cavity. [Gr *glēnoeidēs*, from *glēnē* a socket]
■ **gle'noidal** adj.

glent /glent/ vt, vi, and n an earlier form of **glint**.

gley[1] /glī, glē/ or **glee** /glē/ (Scot) vi to squint. [Origin obscure; cf **gledge**]
■ **gleyed** or **gleed** adj squint-eyed.

gley[2] or **glei** /glā/ n a bluish-grey sticky clay found under some types of very damp soil. [Russ *gley* clay]

glia /glī'ə or glē'ə/ n (anat) neuroglia. [Gr *glia* glue]
■ **gli'adin** or **gli'adine** n prolamine, a protein in gluten. **gli'al** adj. **gliō'ma** n (pl **gliō'mata** or **gliō'mas**) (med) a tumour of the neuroglia in the brain and spinal cord. **gliomatō'sis** n (med) diffuse overgrowth of neuroglia in the brain or spinal cord. **gliō'matous** adj. **gliō'sis** n (med) excessive growth of fibrous tissue in the neuroglia.

glib[1] /glib/ adj easy; facile; fluent and plausible; smooth, slippery (archaic or dialect). ◆ adv (archaic) glibly. ◆ vt (archaic) to make glib. [Cf Du *glibberig* slippery]
■ **glibb'ery** adj (obs) slippery. **glib'ly** adv. **glib'ness** n.

glib[2] /glib/ (hist) n a bush of matted hair hanging over the brow and eyes, a style formerly common in Ireland. [Ir]

glib[3] /glib/ (Shakesp) vt to castrate. [Cf **lib**[2]]

glidder /glid'ər/ (dialect) adj slippery (also **glid** (Scot; obs) or **glidd'ery**). [OE *glidder*]

glide /glīd/ vi to slide smoothly and easily; to flow gently; to pass smoothly or stealthily; to travel through the air without expending power; to travel by glider. ◆ n an act of gliding; a transitional sound produced in passing from one speech sound to another (phonetics); a portamento (music); a glance stroke (cricket); a smooth and sliding dance step; an inclined plane or slide; a stretch of shallow gliding water. [OE *glīdan* to slip; Ger *gleiten*]
■ **glīd'er** n someone who, or that which, glides; an aircraft like an aeroplane without an engine (a **powered glider** has a small engine); a hydroplane; a flying phalanger. **glīd'ing** n the action of the verb in any sense; the sport of flying in a glider. **glīd'ingly** adv.
❑ **glide slope** or **path** n the slope along which aircraft are assumed to come in for landing, marked out eg by a radio beam. **gliding plane** n (crystallog) in minerals, a plane of molecular weakness along which movement can take place without actual fracture.

gliff /glif/ or (obs) **glift** /glift/ (Scot) n a fright, scare; a glimpse or other transient experience; a moment. [Ety dubious]
■ **gliff'ing** n a moment.

glike /glīk/ (Shakesp) n same as **gleek**[1].

glim /glim/ n a glimpse (Scot); a scrap (Scot); a light or lantern (sl); an eye (sl). [Cf **gleam**, **glimmer**[1] and Ger *Glimm* a spark]

glimmer[1] /glim'ər/ vi to burn or shine faintly or intermittently. ◆ n a faint light; feeble rays of light; an inkling, faint sign, hint. [ME *glemern*, frequentative from root of **gleam**]
■ **glimm'ering** n a glimmer; an inkling. **glimm'eringly** adv. **glimm'ery** adj.

glimmer[2] /glim'ər/ n mica. [Ger]

glimpse /glimps/ n a momentary view; a passing appearance; a short gleam (archaic). ◆ vi (archaic) to glimmer; to appear intermittently. ◆ vt to get a glimpse of. [ME *glymsen* to glimpse]

---

glint /glint/ vi to flash with a glittering light. ◆ vt to reflect. ◆ n a gleam; a momentary flash. [Earlier glent ; prob Scand]

glioblastoma /glī-ō-bla-stō'mə/ (pathol) n a very malignant tumour of the central nervous system. [**glia** and **blastoma**]

glioma, etc see under **glia**.

Glires /glī'rēz/ n pl a division of mammals including the typical rodents (eg the genus **Glis**, Old World dormice), etc. [L glis, glīris dormouse]

glisk /glisk/ (Scot) n a glimpse. [Perh from the same root as OE glisian to shine]

glissade /gli-säd' or -sād'/ vi to slide or glide down. ◆ n the act of sliding down a slope in a standing or squatting position, often with the aid of an ice axe (mountaineering); a gliding movement in ballet. [Fr]

glissando /glis-an'dō/ (music) n (pl glissan'dos or glissan'di /-dē/) the effect produced by sliding the finger along keyboard or strings; a similar effect on the trombone, etc. [Ital, formed from Fr glissant sliding]

glisten /glis'n/ vi to gleam or shimmer as a wet or oily surface does. ◆ n gleam. [ME glistnen, from OE glisnian to shine; cf Du glisteren]
■ **glist'ening** adj.

glister /glis'tər/ (archaic) vi to sparkle, glitter. [ME glistren ; cf **glisten** and Du glisteren]
■ **glis'tering** adj. **glis'teringly** adv.

glit /glit/ (obs) n sticky, slimy or greasy material; gleet. [**gleet**]

glitch /glich/ n a sudden, usu brief malfunction in a spacecraft or other equipment, esp a minute change in voltage on an electronic circuit; any minor error or mishap, hiccup or temporary difficulty (inf).

glitter /glit'ər/ vi to sparkle with light; to be splendid, brilliantly ornamented (usu with with); to be showy. ◆ n sparkle; showiness; tiny pieces of sparkly material, used for decoration. [ME gliteren ; cf ON glitra, Ger glitzern]
■ **glitt'erand** adj (Spenser) glittering. **glitt'ering** n and adj. **glitt'eringly** adv. **glitt'ery** adj.
❑ **glittering generality** n (US) a cliché or banality.

glitterati /glit-ə-rä'tē/ (inf) n pl the current fashionable set, ie famous, glamorous, rich and beautiful people.

glitzy /glit'si/ (sl, orig N Am) adj (glitz'ier; glitz'iest) showy, garish or gaudy; glittering. [Perh from Ger glitzern to glitter]
■ **glitz** n (back-formation) showiness, garishness. **glitz'ily** adv. **glitz'iness** n.

gloaming /glō'ming/ (poetic) n twilight, dusk. [Appar from a short-vowelled derivative of OE glōmung, from glōm twilight]

gloat /glōt/ vi to eye with intense, usu malicious, satisfaction (esp with over); generally, to exult (over). ◆ n an act of gloating. [Perh ON glotta to grin]
■ **gloat'er** n. **gloat'ingly** adv.

glob /glob/ (inf) n a roundish drop, dollop, etc of a semi-liquid substance. [Origin uncertain, poss **globe** and **blob**]
■ **globb'y** adj.

globe /glōb/ n a ball, round body, sphere; the earth; a sphere representing the earth (**terrestrial globe**), or one representing the heavens (**celestial globe**); an orb, emblem of sovereignty; a light bulb (esp Aust and NZ); a nearly spherical glass vessel; a group, body (of people) (obs). ◆ vt and vi to form into a globe. [L globus]
■ **glōb'al** adj spherical; worldwide; affecting, or taking into consideration, the whole world or all peoples; (of products or companies) having a name that is recognized throughout the world (marketing); comprehensive; involving a whole file of data (comput). **glō'balism** n the opinion or position that puts worldwide, international concerns above national or local; globalization. **glō'balist** n someone who is sensitive to global issues and seeks to promote this in others. **glōbaliza'tion** or **-s-** n. **glō'balize** or **-ise** vt to make global. **glōb'ally** adv. **glōb'ate** or **glōbat'ed** adj globe-shaped. **glōbed** adj globe-shaped; having a globe. **glōb'y** adj (Milton, etc) round.
❑ **global exchange** or **global search and replace** n (comput) a facility enabling a user to search for and replace every occurrence of a fixed pattern in a file (also called **search and replace**). **Global Positioning System** n in navigation, a system for providing, worldwide, velocity information and an extremely accurate three-dimensional position (abbrev **GPS**). **global search** n (comput) a word-processing feature which finds every occurrence of a pre-determined character, word or phrase in a file. **global search and replace** see **global exchange** above. **global variable** n (comput) a variable which applies for the whole of a program, including any subroutine. **global village** n the world, in reference to its apparent smallness due to improved communications, and the way in which changes in one area are likely to affect the rest of the world. **global warming** n the slow increase in the earth's surface air temperature caused by the greenhouse effect (qv under **green**[1]). **globe artichoke**

see **artichoke**. **globe fish** n any fish of the families Diodontidae and Tetrodontidae, capable of blowing itself up into a globe. **globe'flower** n any ranunculaceous plant of the genus Trollius with a globe of large showy sepals enclosing small inconspicuous petals. **globe thistle** n **Echinops** under **echinus**. **globe'-trot** vi (back-formation). **globe'trotter** n a person who travels around the world, esp as a tourist. **globe'trotting** n.

globesity /glō-bēs'i-ti/ (inf) n obesity viewed as a worldwide problem. [global and obesity]

globigerina /glōb-i-jə-rī'nə/ n (pl globigerinae /-ī'nē/) a minute marine invertebrate of the genus Globigerina, with a calcareous shell of globose chambers in a spiral; a shell of this type. [L globus globe, and gerere to carry]
❑ **globigerina ooze** a deep-sea deposit of globigerina shells.

globin /glō'bin/ (biochem) n a protein constituent of haemoglobin, a histone. [L globus globe, sphere, and **-in** (1)]

globoid /glō'boid/ adj globe-shaped. ◆ n (something having) the shape of a globe. [**globe**; L globus]
■ **globose** /glōb-ōs' or glōb'ōs/ or (rare) **glō'bous** adj globoid. **glōbos'ity** n the quality of being globe-shaped.

globular /glob'yŭ-lər or glob'yə-lər/ adj spherical; made up of globules. [L globulus (see **globule**) and adj sfx -ar]
■ **globular'ity** n. **glob'ūlarly** adv.
❑ **globular cluster** n (astron) a symmetrical cluster into which many thousands of stars are gathered.

globule /glob'ūl/ n a little globe or round particle; a drop; a small pill. [Fr, from L globulus, dimin of globus globe]
■ **glob'ūlet** n a tiny globule. **globulif'erous** adj producing or having globules. **glob'ūlous** adj.

globulin /glob'yŭ-lin, glob'yə-lin or lən/ (biochem) n any one of a class of proteins soluble in dilute salt solutions but not in pure water. [**globule** and **-in** (1)]

globulite /glob'yŭ-līt/ (geol) n a minute spheroidal crystallite occurring esp in glassy rocks. [**globule** and **-ite** (3)]

globy see under **globe**.

Glock® /glok/ n a type of semi-automatic pistol. [G. Glock (born 1929), its designer]

glockenspiel /glok'ən-shpēl/ n an orchestral instrument consisting of a set of bells or metal bars struck by hammers, with or (more usually) without a keyboard. [Ger Glocke bell, and Spiel play]

glode /glōd/ (Spenser) pat of **glide**.

glogg /glog/ n a Swedish hot spiced drink, of wine, a spirit and fruit, often served at Christmas. [Swed glögg]

gloire /glwär/ (Fr) n glory.

glom[1] /glom/ (US sl) vt (glomm'ing; glommed) to snatch; to steal. [Variant of esp Scot dialect glaum to grab, from Gaelic glàm to seize, devour]
■ **glom on to** to appropriate; to catch on to.

glom[2] /glom/ (US sl) vt (glomm'ing; glommed) to look at, to eye. [Origin uncertain]

glomerate /glom'ə-rāt/ (bot and anat) vt to gather into a ball. ◆ adj balled; clustered in heads. [L glomerāre, -ātum, from glomus, glomeris a ball of yarn]
■ **glomerā'tion** n. **glomer'ular** adj of a glomerulus. **glomer'ūlate** adj of a glomerule. **glom'erule** /-ool/ n (bot) a little ball of spores; a cluster of short-stalked flowers. **glomer'ūlus** n (pl glomer'ūlī) (anat) a capillary blood-plexus, as in the vertebrate kidney; a nest-like mass of interlacing nerve fibrils in the olfactory lobe of the brain.

glonoin /glo-nō'in/ (chem) n a name for nitroglycerine, as used in medicine. [glycerine, O (oxygen), N_2O_5 (nitric anhydride), and sfx -in]

gloom /gloom/ n partial darkness; cloudiness; a dark place (poetic); heaviness of mind; hopelessness; sullenness; a scowl, a sullen look (Scot). ◆ vi to be or look sullen or dejected; to be or become cloudy, dark or obscure; to scowl (obs). ◆ vt (archaic) to fill with gloom. [ME gloumbe ; see **glum**]
■ **gloom'ful** adj. **gloom'ily** adv. **gloom'iness** n. **gloom'ing** adj (Spenser) shining obscurely. ◆ n twilight, gloaming (poetic); scowling (obs). **gloom'y** adj dim or obscure; dimly lit; low in spirits; dismal.
❑ **gloom'-monger** n.

gloop /gloop/ (inf) vi (of a thick viscous substance) to bubble or plop slowly and heavily, esp with a soft thick plopping or popping sound; to fall, drip or lie in a thick viscous dribble or drop. ◆ n thick viscous liquid, esp a glob, splodge or slow drip or dribble of such; sentimentality, mush or pulp. [Imit]
■ **gloop'y** adj consisting of, falling, bubbling or dripping in gloops; soppy, gooey, mawkish.

glop /glop/ (*US sl*) *n* a soft, gooey or sloppy semi-liquid substance or mush; unpalatable bland food of this consistency; schmaltz. [Perh a combination of **glue** and **slop**[1]]

gloria[1] /glö'ri-a or glö'ri-ə/ (*L*) *n* glory; any doxology beginning with the word 'Gloria'.
■ **gloria in excelsis** /in ek-, ik-seľ'sis, eks-cheľ'sis or eks-keľ'sēs/ glory (to God) on high. **gloria Patri** /pat'rī, 'ri or pät'rē/ glory (be) to the Father.

gloria[2] /glö' or glö'ri-ə/ *n* an aureole; a halo; a type of very closely woven fabric, *usu* of a mixture of silk or nylon and wool or cotton, often used for umbrellas. [L]

glorify /glö'ri-fī/ *vt* (**glo'rifying**; **glo'rified**) to make glorious; to cast glory upon; to honour; to worship; to exalt to glory or happiness; to ascribe honour to; to ascribe great charm, beauty, etc to, *usu* to a markedly exaggerated extent; to add undeserved prestige to, *esp* under a euphemistic or overblown title. [L *glöria* glory, and *facere* to make]
■ **glorifica'tion** *n* an act of glorifying; a doxology; riotous festivity (*inf*); something that has been or is glorified above its due or customary status (*inf*).

gloriole /glö'ri-ōl/ *n* a halo or glory, aureola. [Fr, from L dimin *glōriola* little glory]

gloriosa /glö-ri-ō'sə/ *n* any plant of the tropical genus *Gloriosa*, leaf-climbers of the lily family, with showy colourful flowers. [New L, from L *gloriosus* full of glory]

glorious, etc see under **glory**.

glory /glö'ri/ *n* renown; exalted or triumphant honour; widespread praise; an object of supreme pride; splendour, beauty; resplendent brightness; summit of attainment, prosperity or gratification; (in religious symbolism) a combination of the nimbus and the aureola, but often erroneously used for the nimbus; a ring or glow of light around the moon, the Brocken spectre, or other similar object or phenomenon; boastful or self-congratulatory spirit (*obs*); the presence of God; the manifestation of God to the blessed in heaven; a representation of the heavens opened; heaven. ◆ *vi* (**glo'rying**; **glo'ried**) to exult proudly (*usu* with *in*); to rejoice; to boast (*obs*). ◆ *vt* (*obs*) to glorify. ◆ *interj* (*old*) expressing surprise. [OFr *glorie* and L *glöria*]
■ **glö'rious** *adj* noble; splendid; conferring renown; wonderful, delightful, intensely enjoyable (*inf*); elated, tipsy (*archaic*; *inf*); boastful (*obs*). **glö'riously** *adv*. **glö'riousness** *n*.
❑ **Glorious Twelfth** see under **twelfth**. **glory box** *n* (*Aust* and *NZ*) a box in which a young woman keeps her trousseau, etc, a bottom drawer. **glory of the snow** *n* the plant chionodoxa. **glö'ry-pea** *n* the papilionaceous genus *Clianthus*, consisting of Sturt's desert pea (in Australia) and the parrot-bill (in New Zealand).
■ **glory be** a devout ascription of glory to God; hence, a shout of exultation; an interjection expressing surprise. **Old Glory** the Stars and Stripes.

glory hole /glö'ri hōl/ *n* a room, cupboard or receptacle for miscellaneous odds and ends (*inf*); a steward's room on a ship; a hiding-place or enclosed space; a glass-maker's supplementary furnace; a hole for viewing the inside of a furnace; an excavation, for example a quarry (*N Am*). [Perh ME *glory* to defile, or **glaury** or **glory** and **hole**[1]]

Glos. /glos/ *abbrev* : Gloucestershire.

gloss[1] /glos/ *n* brightness or lustre, as from a polished surface; external show; superficial appearance. ◆ *vt* to make glossy; to give a superficial lustre to; to render plausible; to attempt to disguise by treating superficially. [Cf ON *glossi* blaze, *glöa* to glow; see **glass**]
■ **gloss'er** *n*. **gloss'ily** *adv*. **gloss'iness** *n*. **gloss'y** *adj* smooth and shining; highly polished; superficially attractive. ◆ *n* (*inf*) a glossy magazine.
❑ **gloss paint** *n* paint containing varnish, giving a hard, shiny finish. **glossy magazine** *n* a magazine of an expensive, luxury type, printed on glossy paper, with many colour photographs and advertisements. **glossy starling** *n* any of various African starlings of the *Lamprotornis* genus of the family Sturnidae, having dark glossy plumage.
■ **gloss over** to explain away, render more acceptable.

gloss[2] /glos/ *n* an explanation given in a margin or between lines, eg of an obscure or unusual word; a deceptive or intentionally misleading explanation; a collection of explanations of words, a glossary. ◆ *vt* to give a gloss on; to explain away. ◆ *vi* to comment or make explanatory remarks. [Gr *glössa*, *glötta* tongue, a word requiring explanation]
■ **glossa'tor** or **gloss'er** *n* a writer of glosses or comments, a commentator.

gloss- /glos-/ or **glosso-** /glos-ō-, glos-ə- or glə-so-/, sometimes **glotto-** /glot-ō-, glot-ə- or glə-to-/ *combining form* denoting: the tongue; a tongue, language; a gloss (see **gloss**[2]). [Gr *glössa* tongue]

■ **glossec'tomy** *n* surgical removal of the tongue. **glossi'tis** *n* inflammation of the tongue. **glossodynia** /-ō-din'i-ə/ *n* (Gr *odynē* pain) pain in the tongue. **glossog'rapher** *n*. **glossograph'ical** *adj*. **glossog'raphy** *n* the writing of glosses or comments. **glossolā'lia** (Gr *laleein* to talk) the 'gift of tongues', the speaking of wholly or partly unintelligible utterances thought to form part of an unknown language or languages and considered by (*esp* Early) Christians to be a manifestation of the Holy Spirit. **glossolā'lic** *adj*. **glossolog'ical** *adj*. **glossol'ogist** *n*. **glossol'ogy** *n* (*obs*) comparative philology (also called **glottol'ogy**); terminology. **glottochronol'ogy** *n* a statistical study of vocabulary to determine the degree of relationship between particular languages and the chronology of their independent development. **glottogon'ic** *adj* relating to the origin of language.

glossa /glos'ə/ (*anat* and *zool*) *n* the tongue; in insects, one of an inner pair of lobes in the labium. [Gr *glössa* tongue]
■ **gloss'al** *adj* of, or relating to, the tongue.

glossary /glos'ə-ri/ *n* a collection or list of explanations of words; a dictionary of terms used in a specialized subject area; frequently used words, phrases or paragraphs which can be stored by a word processor and recalled rapidly and easily; a collection of glosses. ◆ *adj* relating to a glossary; of the nature of a glossary; containing explanation. [L *glösärium* a word requiring explanation, from Gr *glössa* tongue]
■ **glossä'rial** *adj*. **glossä'rially** *adv*. **gloss'arist** *n* a writer of a gloss or of a glossary.

glossator see under **gloss**[2].

glossectomy see under **gloss-**.

glosseme /glos'ēm/ (*linguistics*) *n* a unit or feature of a language that in itself carries significance and cannot be further analysed into meaningful units. [**gloss**[2] and *-eme* (after phon*eme*), rather than Gr *glossēma* a word needing explanation]

Glossic /glos'ik/ *n* a phonetic alphabet devised by AJ Ellis (1814–90). [Gr *glössa* tongue]

glossina /glo-sī'nə/ *n* an insect of the genus *Glossina*, the tsetse fly genus. [New L; named for its long proboscis (see **gloss-**)]

glossitis...to...**glossology** see under **gloss-**.

-glot /-glot/ *combining form* denoting speaking or written in a language or languages, as in *monoglot*, *polyglot*. [Gr *glötta* tongue, language]

glottal see under **glottis**.

glottis /glot'is/ (*anat* and *zool*) *n* (*pl* **glott'ises** or **glott'ides** /-i-dēz/) the opening of the larynx or entrance to the windpipe. [Gr *glöttis*, from *glötta* the tongue]
■ **glott'al** *adj* of the glottis. **glott'ic** *adj* relating to the glottis or to the tongue; linguistic. **glottid'ean** *adj*.
❑ **glottal stop** *n* a consonant sound produced by closing and suddenly opening the glottis, occurring as a phoneme in some languages, eg Arabic, and as a feature of others, and sometimes heard as a substitute for *t* in English.

glottochronology, **glottogonic**, **glottology** see under **gloss-**.

glout /glowt/ (*archaic*) *vi* to be sulky. ◆ *n* a sulky look, the sulks. [Perh a variant of **gloat**]

glove /gluv/ *n* a covering for the hand, with a sheath for each finger; a fingerless covering for the hand worn in sports such as boxing; a protective covering that is shaped to fit over a particular object exactly. ◆ *vt* to cover with, or as if with, a glove. [OE *glöf*, perh connected with **loof**[2]]
■ **gloved** *adj*. **glov'er** *n* a person who makes or sells gloves. **glov'ing** *n* putting on gloves; the practice of making gloves; a glove-maker's craft.
❑ **glove box** *n* a glove compartment; a closed compartment in which radioactive or toxic material may be manipulated by the use of gloves attached to the walls. **glove compartment** *n* a small compartment in the front of a car, *usu* part of the dashboard, in which gloves, etc can be kept. **glove'-fight** *n* (*archaic*) a boxing match in which the hands are gloved. **glove'-money** *n* (*hist*) a gratuity given to servants, officers of a court, etc. **glove puppet** *n* a puppet worn on the hand like a glove and manipulated by the fingers. **glove'-shield** *n* (*hist*) a shield worn by a knight on the left-hand gauntlet to parry blows. **glove'-stretcher** *n* a scissors-shaped instrument for stretching the fingers of gloves.
■ **fit like a glove** to fit exactly. **the gloves are off** (*inf*) now the fight, argument, etc is about to begin in earnest, without qualification or reservation (**gloves'-off** *adj*).

glow /glō/ *vi* to shine with an intense heat; to burn without flame; to emit a steady light; (*esp* of the complexion) to flush or look healthy; to tingle with bodily warmth or with emotion; to be ardent. ◆ *n* a shining with heat; a luminous appearance; a redness or healthy colour of complexion; a feeling of warmth; brightness of colour; warmth of feeling. [OE *glöwan* to glow; Ger *glühen*, ON *glöa* to glow]

glow'ing adj emitting a steady light; extremely complimentary. **glow'ingly** adv.

❑ **glow discharge** n a luminous electrical discharge in gas at low pressure. **glow'lamp** n an incandescent lamp, usually electric. **glow plug** n an electric plug fitted in a diesel engine to make starting easier in cold weather; a similar device that can be switched on to re-ignite the flame in a gas turbine automatically. **glow'stick** n a plastic tube containing chemicals that, when mixed by bending the tube, become temporarily luminescent. **glow'-worm** n a beetle (esp Lampyris noctiluca) whose larvae and wingless females have luminous organs usu near the tip of the abdomen, emitting a greenish glow; any of various luminous insect larvae (N Am).

glower /glow'ər or glowr/ vi to stare frowningly; to scowl. ◆ n a fierce or threatening stare. [Origin obscure]
■ **glow'eringly** adv.

gloxinia /glok-sin'i-ə/ n a plant of the tropical American genus of Gesneriaceae, Gloxinia, with bright bell-shaped flowers; generally applied to related plants of the genus Sinningia. [BP Gloxin (1765–94), German botanist]

gloze /glōz/ (archaic; rare) vi to flatter; to comment. ◆ vt to make glosses on, explain; to excuse by a flawed or insincere explanation; to flatter; to deceive with smooth words. [OFr glose, from L glōssa, from Gr glōssa; see gloss²]
■ **glo'zing** n flattery, deceit.
▨ **gloze over** to explain away falsely or insincerely.

glucagon /gloo'kə-gon/ (biochem) n a polypeptide hormone secreted by the pancreas which accelerates glycogen breakdown in the liver, so increasing blood glucose levels. [Gr glykys sweet]

glucinum /gloo-sī'nəm/, also **glucinium** /gloo-sin'i-əm/ (chem) n former names for beryllium. [Gr glykys sweet, from the taste of its salts]
■ **glucī'na** n beryllia.

glucocorticoid /gloo-kō-kör'ti-koid/ (biochem) n any of a group of steroid hormones which affect glucose metabolism, having an anti-inflammatory effect. [Gr glykys sweet, and **corticoid**]

gluconeogenesis /gloo-kō-nē-ō-jen'ə-sis/ (biochem) n the conversion of non-carbohydrate substances, eg amino acids, into glucose. [Gr glykys sweet, **neo-**, and **genesis**]
■ **gluconeogen'ic** adj.

glucoprotein see **glycoprotein**.

glucose /gloo'kōs/ n any of several forms of naturally occurring sugar, esp dextrose; a yellowish syrup containing glucose, produced by the incomplete hydrolysis of starch, used in confectionery, etc. [Gr glykys sweet]
■ **glucō'samine** n an amino sugar, used as a dietary supplement to alleviate arthritic pain. **glucosic** /-kos'-/ adj. **glu'coside** n any of the vegetable products making up a large group of the glycosides, which, on treatment with acids or alkalis, yield glucose or a similar substance. **glucosid'ic** adj. **glucosū'ria** n sugar in the urine, glycosuria. **glucosū'ric** adj.

glucosinolate /gloo-kō-sin'ō-lāt/ n a natural pesticide found mainly in brassicas such as broccoli and Brussels sprouts.

glue /gloo/ n an impure gelatine produced by boiling animal waste (hooves, hides, bones), used as an adhesive; any of several synthetic substances used as adhesives. ◆ vt (**glu'ing**; **glued**) to join with, or as if with, glue or some other adhesive. [Fr glu, from LL glus, glūtis]
■ **glu'er** n. **glu'ey** adj (**glu'ier**; **glu'iest**) containing glue; sticky; viscous. **glu'eyness** n. **glu'ish** adj (obs) having the nature of glue.
❑ **glue'ball** n a hypothetical subatomic particle consisting exclusively of gluons bound together. **glue ear** n a condition of the ear where middle-ear fluid fails to drain down the Eustachian tube, collecting instead behind the eardrum and causing deafness, infection and discharge. **glue'-pot** n a vessel for melting or holding glue; a sticky place (inf). **glue'-sniffer** n a person who inhales the fumes of certain types of glue to achieve hallucinatory effects, etc. **glue'-sniffing** n the practice (sometimes fatal) of doing this.
▨ **be glued to** (inf) to fix the eyes on (esp a television or computer screen) with intense concentration or interest; to stay very close to. **marine glue** not a glue, but a composition of rubber, shellac and oil, that resists seawater.

glufosinate /gloo-fos'i-nāt/ n a non-selective chemical herbicide that can be used only on crops tolerant to it.

glug /glug/ n a word representing the sound of liquid being poured from a bottle, down one's throat, etc. ◆ vi (**glugg'ing**; **glugged**) (of liquid) to flow making this sound. ◆ vt to drink in large draughts. [Imit]
■ **gluggable** adj (of wine) unexceptional but perfectly suitable for everyday consumption.

glühwein or **Glühwein** /glü'vīn/ n hot, sweetened, spiced red wine, mulled wine as prepared in Germany, Austria, etc. [Ger, from glühen to glow, and Wein wine]

glum /glum/ adj (**glumm'er**; **glumm'est**) sullen; gloomy. [ME glombe, glome to frown]
■ **glum'ly** adv. **glum'ness** n. **glump'ish** adj (archaic or dialect) glum. **glumps** n pl (archaic or dialect) the sulks. **glump'y** adj (archaic or dialect) sulky.

glume /gloom/ (bot) n an outer sterile bract which, alone or with others, encloses the spikelet in grasses and sedges. [L glūma husk, from glūbere to peel]
■ **gluma'ceous** adj like a glume, thin, brownish and papery. **glumell'a** n a palea. **glumif'erous** adj having glumes. **Glumiflō'rae** n pl an order of monocotyledons consisting of grasses and sedges.

glumpish, etc see under **glum**.

gluon /gloo'on/ (phys) n a particle thought of as passing between quarks and so signifying the force that holds them together. [**glue**]

glut /glut/ vt (**glutt'ing**; **glutt'ed**) to gorge; to feed beyond capacity; to saturate; to block or choke up. ◆ n an act or instance of glutting; a surfeit; an oversupply; an excess quantity of a particular item on the market (business). [L gluttīre to swallow]

glutaeus see **gluteus**.

glutamate...to...**glutamine** see under **gluten**.

glutaraldehyde /gloo-tə-ral'di-hīd/ n a toxic oil, soluble in water, used as a disinfectant and a biological tissue fixative. [glutaric acid (an organic acid), and **aldehyde**]

glutathione /gloo-tə-thī'ōn/ n an antioxidant, found in the body's airways and nose, that protects the lungs from the effects of pollutants. [glutamic acid, and **thio-**]

glute /gloot/ n (inf) a gluteus muscle.

gluten /gloo'tən/ n the nitrogenous part of the flour of wheat and other grains, insoluble in water. [L glūten, -inis glue; cf **glue**]
■ **glu'tamate** n a salt of glutamic acid. **glutam'inase** n an enzyme that hydrolyses glutamine. **glu'tamine** /-min or -mīn/ n a neutral amino acid found in proteins. **glu'telin** n any of various simple proteins, found in cereals and soluble only in dilute acids and alkalis. **glu'tenous** adj containing, made from, etc gluten.
❑ **glutam'ic** or **glutamin'ic acid** n an important amino acid, $HOOCCH_2CH_2CH(NH_2)COOH$, a constituent of most proteins.

gluteus or **glutaeus** /gloo'ti-əs or glū-tē'əs/ (anat) n (pl **glu'tēī** or **glutae'ī**) any of three muscles of the buttock and hip, the outermost of which is the **glu'teus max'imus**. [Gr gloutos the rump]
■ **glutē'al** or **glutae'al** adj.

glutinous /gloo'ti-nəs/ adj gluey; sticky. [L glūten, glutinis glue]
■ **glu'tinously** adv. **glu'tinousness** n.

glutton¹ /glut'n/ n a person who eats to excess; someone who is extremely eager (for something, eg hard work). [Fr glouton, from L glūtō, -ōnis, from glūtīre, gluttīre to devour]
■ **glutt'onize** or **-ise** vi to eat to excess. **glutt'onous** or (rare) **glutt'onish** adj given to, or consisting in, gluttony. **glutt'onously** adv. **glutt'ony** n excess in eating.
■ **glutton for punishment** a person who seems excessively eager to seek and perform strenuous or unpleasant work, etc.

glutton² /glut'n/ n a N European carnivore (Gulo gulo) of the Mustelidae, 60–90cm (2–3ft) long, having dark, shaggy fur; a related animal (Gulo luscus) of N America, the wolverine. [Transl of Ger Vielfrass, literally, large feeder, a popular imitation of Norw fjeldfross, literally, mountain cat]

glycaemia or (US) **glycemia** /glī-sē'mi-ə/ n the presence of glucose in the blood. [Gr glykys sweet, and haima blood]
■ **glycae'mic** or (US) **glyce'mic** adj.
❑ **glycaemic index** n a system for categorizing foods according to how quickly their carbohydrates are broken down into blood sugar (abbrev **GI**).

glyceria /glī-sē'ri-ə/ n any plant of the genus Glyceria (family Gramineae) of aquatic and marsh-growing grasses. [New L, from Gr glykeros sweet]

glycerine /glis'ə-rēn/, **glycerin** /-in/ or **glycerol** /-ol/ n a trihydric alcohol, a colourless, viscous, neutral, inodorous fluid, of a sweet taste, soluble in water and alcohol. [Gr glykeros sweet, from glykys]
■ **glycer'ic** adj. **glyc'eride** n an ester of glycerol. **glyc'eryl** n a radical of which glycerine is the hydroxide.
❑ **glyceryl trinitrate** same as **nitroglycerine** (see under **nitro-**).

glycin /glis'in or glī'sin/ or **glycine** /-sēn or -sēn'/ n the simplest amino acid, $CH_2(NH_2)COOH$, present in proteins, a sweetish colourless crystalline solid first prepared from glue. [Gr glykys sweet]

glyco- /glī-kō-/ combining form denoting: sugar; glycogen. [Gr glykys sweet]

glycocoll /glīk'ə-kol or glik'-/ n a former name for glycin. [**glyco-** and Gr kolla glue]

glycogen /glīk'ə-jən or ō-jən/ n animal starch, a starch found in the liver, yielding glucose on hydrolysis. [Gr glykys sweet, and the root of gennaein to produce]
■ **glycogen'esis** n the synthesis of glycogen; the synthesis of sugar from glycogen. **glycogenet'ic** adj. **glycogen'ic** adj of or containing glycogen.

glycol /glī'kol/ n the type of a class of compounds with two hydroxyl groups on adjacent carbon atoms, and so intermediate between alcohol and glycerine. [From glycerine and alcohol]
■ **glycol'ic** or **glycoll'ic** adj.

glycolysis /glī-kol'i-sis/ n the breaking down of glucose into acids, with the release of energy. [glycose and **-lysis**]
■ **glycolyt'ic** adj.

glyconic /glī-kon'ik/ (classical prosody) adj consisting of four feet, one a dactyl, the others trochees. ◆ n a glyconic verse. [Glycon, Greek poet]

glycoprotein /glī-kō-prō'tēn/ or **glucoprotein** /gloo-kō-/ n any of the compounds formed by the conjugation of a protein with a substance containing a carbohydrate group other than a nucleic acid. [**glyco-** and **protein**]

glycose /glī'kōs/ n glucose. [**glyco-**]
■ **gly'coside** n any of a group of compounds derived from monosaccharides, yielding, on hydrolysis, a sugar and usu a non-carbohydrate. **glycosid'ic** adj. **glycosū'ria** n (Gr ouron urine) the presence of sugar in the urine. **glycosū'ric** adj.

glycosyl /glī'kə-sil/ (biochem) n a radical derived from glucose.
■ **glycos'ylate** vt. **glycosylā'tion** n the process that attaches sugar to proteins to make glycoproteins.

glyoxaline see **imidazole**.

glyph /glif/ n an ornamental channel or fluting, usu vertical (archit); a sculptured mark (archit); a small graphic symbol (comput). [Gr glyphē, from glyphein to carve]
■ **glyph'ic** adj carved. **glyph'ograph** n a plate formed by glyphography. **glyphog'rapher** n. **glyphograph'ic** adj. **glyphog'raphy** n a process of taking a raised copy of an engraved plate by electrotype.

glyphosate /glī'fə-sāt/ n a non-selective organophosphate herbicide used to kill weeds in crops. [glycin, and phosphate]

glyptal resins /glip'təl rez'inz/ n pl almost colourless, tacky, adhesive resins made by heating glycerol or another polyhydric alcohol with a polybasic acid, used as bonding materials for mica, and (modified) in the paint and varnish trades.

glyptic /glip'tik/ adj relating to carving, esp gem-carving. [Gr glyptos carved]
■ **glyp'tics** n sing the art of gem-engraving. **glyptograph'ic** adj. **glyptog'raphy** n the art of engraving on precious stones. **glyptothē'ca** n (Gr thēke receptacle) a place for keeping sculpture.

Glyptodon /glip'tō-don/ n an extinct genus of S American mammals of the Edentata, with fluted teeth. [Gr glyptos carved, and odous, odontos tooth]
■ **glyp'todont** n a mammal of this genus.

GM abbrev: (also **G-M**) Geiger-Müller (counter); general manager; General Motors; genetically modified; George Medal; Grand Master; grant-maintained (of schools).

gm abbrev: gram(s) or gramme(s).

G-man see under **G** (abbrev).

GMB abbrev: General and Municipal Boilermakers Union.

GmbH abbrev: Gesellschaft mit beschränkter Haftung (Ger), a limited liability company.

GMC abbrev: General Medical Council.

Gmc abbrev: Germanic.

gmelinite /(g)mel'i-nīt/ (mineralogy) n a sodium aluminium zeolite. [CG Gmelin (1792–1860), German chemist]

GMO abbrev: genetically modified organism.

GMT abbrev: Greenwich Mean Time.

gnamma hole /nam'ə hōl/ (Aust) n a rock hollow in a desert area, perhaps containing water. [From an Aboriginal language]

gnaphalium /na-fā'li-əm/ n any plant of the Gnaphalium genus of composites, to which cudweed belongs. [Latinized from Gr gnaphallion cottonweed]

gnar[1] /när/ vi to snarl or growl (also **gnarr**, **knar**, **gnarl**). [Onomatopoeic; cf OE gnyrran to grind the teeth, creak, Ger knurren, Dan knurre to growl]

gnar[2] see **knar**[1].

gnarl[1] or **knarl** /närl/ n a lump or knot in a tree. [After Shakespeare's gnarled for **knurled**]

■ **gnarled** adj knotty; contorted; rugged, weather-beaten. **gnarl'y** adj (**gnarl'ier**; **gnarl'iest**) gnarled; ill-natured, bad-tempered; difficult, challenging (inf).

gnarl[2], **gnarr** see **gnar**[1].

gnash /nash/ vt and vi to strike (the teeth) together in rage or pain; to bite with a snap or clash of the teeth. ◆ n a snap of the teeth. [ME gnasten; prob from ON, ult onomatopoeic]
■ **gnash'er** n someone who, or that which, gnashes; (usu in pl) a tooth (facetious). **gnash'ing** n. **gnash'ingly** adv.

gnat /nat/ n any small fly of the family Chironomidae, related to the mosquito but not a bloodsucker; a mosquito; extended to other small insects. [OE gnæt]
■ **gnat'ling** n a little gnat; an insignificant person.
□ **gnat'catcher** n any of the insectivorous American songbirds of the genus Polioptila. **gnat's piss** n (vulgar sl) alcoholic drink considered to be unacceptably weak or tasteless. **gnat'wren** n any of the insectivorous S American songbirds of the Microbates or Ramphocaenus genera.

gnathic /nath'ik/ or **gnathal** /nath' or nā'thəl/ (zool and anat) adj of, or relating to, the jaws. [Gr gnathos jaw]
■ **gnath'ite** (or /nā'/) n in arthropods, an appendage used as a jaw. **Gnathobdell'ida** n pl (Gr bdella leech) an order of leeches with (usu) jaws but no proboscis. **-gnathous** adj combining form.

gnathonic /nā-thon'ik/ or **gnathonical** /-əl/ (obs) adj flattering. [From Gnathō, a character in Terence's Eunuchus, from Gr gnathos jaw]
■ **gnathon'ically** adv.

gnaw /nö/ vt and vi (pat gnawed; pap gnawed or gnawn) (with at) to bite with a scraping or nibbling movement; to wear away; to bite in agony or rage; to distress or worry persistently (fig). [OE gnagan; cf **nag**[2]; Du knagen, Mod Icel naga]
■ **gnaw'er** n a person who gnaws; a rodent. **gnaw'ing** adj.

gneiss /nīs/ (geol) n coarse-grained foliated metamorphic rock, usu composed of quartz, feldspar and mica. [Ger Gneis]
■ **gneiss'ic** or **gneissit'ic** adj of the nature of gneiss. **gneiss'oid** adj like gneiss. **gneiss'ose** adj having the structure of gneiss.

Gnetum /nē'təm/ n a tropical genus of trees and shrubs constituting, with Ephedra and Welwitschia, the order **Gnetā'lēs**, gymnosperms differing from conifers in having a perianth, vessels in secondary wood, and no resin canals. [Said to be from gnemon, a name used in the Indonesian island of Ternate]

gnocchi /no'kē or nyōk'kē/ n pl small dumplings made from flour, semolina or potatoes, usu served with a sauce. [Ital]

gnome[1] /nōm/ n a mythical sprite guarding the inner parts of the earth and its treasures; a dwarf or goblin; (also **garden gnome**) a statue of a gnome, esp in a garden as an ornament; an obscure but powerful international financier or banker (facetious). [New L gnomus dwarf, pygmy, coined by Paracelsus, 16c scientist]
■ **gnōm'ish** adj.
■ **the gnomes of Europe**, **Zürich**, etc the powerful international bankers.

gnome[2] /nōm or nō'mē/ n (pl **gnomes** /nōmz or nō'mēz/ or **gnomae** /nō'mē/) a pithy and sententious saying, generally in verse, embodying some moral sentiment or precept. [Gr gnōmē an opinion, maxim]
■ **gnō'mic** adj relating to or characterized by gnomes; (of writers) expressing themselves in gnomes. **gnō'mically** adv. **gnō'mist** n a writer of gnomes.
□ **gnomic aorist** n (grammar) a past tense of the Greek verb, used in proverbs, etc, for what once happened and is generally true.

gnomon /nō'mon/ n the pin of a sundial, whose shadow points to the hour; an upright rod for taking the sun's altitude by its shadow; that which remains of a parallelogram when a similar parallelogram within one of its angles is taken away (geom); a geometrical figure which, added to or subtracted from another, gives a figure similar to the original one; an index or indicator (obs); the nose (obs; joc). [Gr gnōmōn a gnomon, a carpenter's square, from gnōnai (aorist) to know]
■ **gnomonic** or **gnomonical** /-mon'/ adj relating to a gnomon or to the art of gnomonics. **gnomon'ically** adv. **gnomon'ics** n sing (hist) the art of measuring time by the sundial. **gnomonol'ogy** n (rare) a treatise on gnomonics.

gnosis /nō'sis/ n (pl **gnō'sēs**) knowledge, esp spiritual. ◆ combining form /-(g)nō-sis/ denoting knowledge or recognition. [Gr gnōsis knowledge, adj gnōstikos, from gignōskein to know]
■ **gnōseol'ogy** or **gnōsiol'ogy** n the philosophy of knowledge. **gnos'tic** /nos'/ adj having knowledge; knowing, shrewd; (with cap) relating to Gnosticism. ◆ n (with cap) an adherent of Gnosticism. **-gnostic** adj combining form. **gnos'tical** adj having knowledge. **gnos'tically** adv. **-gnostically** adv combining form. **Gnos'ticism** n the eclectic doctrines of the Gnostics, whose philosophy, esp in early Christian times, taught the redemption of the spirit from matter

by spiritual knowledge, and believed creation to be a process of emanation from the original essence or Godhead. **Gnos'ticize** or **-ise** *vi* to profess or believe in Gnosticism.

gnotobiology /nō-tō-bī-ol'ə-ji/ *n* the study of life under germ-free conditions, gnotobiotics. [Gr *gnōtos* known, and **biology**]
■ **gnotobiolog'ical** *adj*. **gnotobio'sis** *n* the condition of being germ-free, or germ-free and then inoculated with known micro-organisms only; the rearing of animals in such a germ-free environment, or in one in which all the living micro-organisms are known. **gnotobiote** /-bī'ōt/ *n* a gnotobiotic animal. **gnotobiot'ic** *adj* in the condition of gnotobiosis. **gnotobiot'ically** *adv*. **gnotobiot'ics** *n sing* the study of gnotobiotic animals.

GNP *abbrev* : gross national product.

GNSS *abbrev* : Global Navigation Satellite System.

gnu /noo, nū or (*humorous*) gnoo/ *n* (pl **gnu** or **gnus**) a large African antelope (genus *Connochaetes*), superficially like a buffalo (also called **wildebeest**). [From Khoikhoi]

GNVQ *abbrev* : General National Vocational Qualification, a two-year vocational course for students aged 16 and over.

go[1] /gō/ *vi* (prp **gō'ing**; pap **gone** /gon/ (see separate entries); pat **went** (supplied from **wend**); *3rd pers sing pres indicative* **goes**) used to express futurity or intent; to pass from one place to another; to be in motion; (of a path, etc) to lead or give access (to); to proceed; to run (in words or notes); (of verse) to flow smoothly; to walk (*obs*); to depart; to work, to be in operation; (of eg a bell or gun) to sound; to make a (specified) noise, as in *go bang*, *go moo*; to take a direction, turn, follow a course; to extend; (with *to*) to attend once or habitually (the cinema, church, etc); (of a rumour, story, etc) to be current; to be valid, hold true; to be reckoned, to be regarded (as); to be known (*by* or *under* a name); to be on the whole or ordinarily; to tend, serve as a means; to be or continue in a particular state (as in *fear*, *in rags*); to elapse; to be sold; to be spent, consumed; to move or act in a way shown or specified; to be assigned or awarded (to); (of colours, etc) to harmonize; to break down, fail; to die; (with *by* or (*up*)*on*) to be directed by, to act according to; (with *on*) to become chargeable to (an account, etc); (with *to*) to subject oneself (to expense, trouble, etc); (of a female) to be (eg a specific number of months) pregnant (*with* child, young, foal, etc); (of a female animal) to copulate (with *to*); to become, or become as if; to be considered generally as a concept; to be compared or ranked with others; to change to a new system, as in *go decimal*, *go metric*; to happen in a particular way; to be accepted as ultimately authoritative; to turn out; to fare; to contribute (to or towards a whole, purpose or result); to be contained; to be able to pass; to be finished or done away with; to give way; to urinate (*inf*); (with an infinitive without *to*) to move off with the intention of doing something, as in *go see* (*N Am*; see also **go and** below). ◆ *vt* to pass through or over; to stake, bet; to call, bid or declare (*cards*); to eat or drink (a specific thing), *usu* in the phrase *I could go a…* (*inf*); to say (used when reporting speech; *dialect*). ◆ *n* (pl **goes**) a going; a success (*inf*); energy, activity (*inf*); a spell, turn, bout (*inf*); a portion supplied at one time (*inf*); an attempt (*inf*); an affair, matter (*inf*; *archaic*); (with *the*) the current fashion (*inf*; *archaic*); a bargain, deal (*inf*; *archaic*); failure to play (*cribbage*); a score for an opponent's failure to play (*cribbage*). ◆ *adj* (*inf*) ready; in perfect condition. ◆ *interj* (called to start a race, etc) begin. [OE *gān* to go; cf Ger *gehen*, Du *gaan*]
■ **gō'er** *n* a lively, energetic person; a sexually promiscuous person, *esp* a woman; used in combination, denoting a person who regularly goes to or attends a particular place, institution, etc, as in *cinema-goer*; something that travels very fast. **gō'ey** *adj* (*inf*) enterprising, go-ahead. **gō'ing** *n* see separate entry.
❑ **go'-ahead** *adj* dashing, energetic; enterprisingly progressive. ◆ *n* permission to proceed. **go'-around** *n* an act or instance of going, taking a route, around something (as in air-traffic control, etc); an evasion, runaround; a round, cycle, sequence (that is repeated). **go'-as-you-please** *adj* not limited by rules; informal. **go'-between** *n* (pl **go'-betweens**) an intermediary. **go'-by** *n* any intentional disregard, as in *give* (*someone*) *the go-by*; (in coursing) the act of passing by or ahead in motion; escape by artifice; evasion. **go'-cart** *n* a wheeled apparatus for teaching children to walk (*archaic*); a form of child's carriage (*archaic*); same as **go-kart** below. **go'-devil** *n* (*oil*) a cylindrical plug with brushes, scrapers and rollers able to move, under the oil pressure, through a pipeline to clean it. **go'-down** *n* a cutting in the bank of a stream allowing animals to get to the water (*US*); see also separate entry **godown**. **go-faster stripes** *n pl* (*inf*; *facetious*) matching horizontal stripes painted along the sides of a car for sporty effect, which unaccountably give (*esp* young male) drivers of cars bearing them a sense of superior power and road skill. **go'-forward** *n* (*inf*) momentum. **go'-getter** *n* (*inf*) a forceful ambitious person, determined to get what he or she wants. **go'-getting** *adj* forcefully ambitious. **go'-kart** *n* a low racing vehicle consisting of a frame with wheels, engine, and steering gear (now often simply **kart**); a child's home-made vehicle for riding on. **go'-off** *n* (*inf*; *old*) start.

go-slow see **go slow** below. **go'-to** *adj* (*inf*) to be resorted to with confidence in an emergency. **go-to-meeting** see under **Sunday**.
■ **all systems go** everything in the spacecraft is operating as it should; everything in readiness. **all the go** (*inf*; *old*) very fashionable. **a pretty go** (*archaic inf*; *ironic*) an awkward turn of events. **as far as it goes** bearing in mind certain limitations. **at one go** in a single attempt or effort, simultaneously. **be going on for** to be approaching (a particular age). **from the word go** from the very beginning. **give it a go** (*inf*) to try, make an attempt at something. **go about** to pass from place to place; to busy oneself with; to seek, endeavour to (with *gerund*); (of a rumour, etc) to circulate; (of a ship) to change course. **go about one's business** to attend to one's own affairs; to be off, to leave or depart. **go abroad** to go to a foreign country or (*old*) out of doors; (of rumour, etc) to circulate. **go against** to turn out unfavourably for; to be repugnant to; to be in conflict with. **go ahead** to proceed at once. **go all out for** to endeavour to achieve with great vigour. **go along with** to agree with, support. **go along with you** (*inf*) none of that!, away with you!, get away! **go and** (*inf*) to be so stupid or unfortunate as to (eg hurt oneself); to go in order to (do something). **go around** (or **round**) **with** to be a regular companion of. **go aside** to err (*archaic*); to withdraw, retire. **go at** to attack vigorously. **go back** to have known someone for a long or specified time. **go back on** to betray, fail to keep (a promise, etc). **go bail** see under **bail**[1]. **go by** to be guided by or act in accordance with. **go down** to sink, decline; to deteriorate; to be swallowed, believed, received or accepted (*esp* with pleasure); (of a computer or other electronic system) to break down; to fail to fulfil one's contract (*bridge*); to leave a university; to happen (*US sl*); to be sent to prison (*sl*); to be defeated in a competition. **go down on** (*vulgar sl*) to perform fellatio or cunnilingus on. **go down the drain**, **the toilet** or **the tubes** (*inf*) to be wasted; to become valueless. **go down with** (*inf*) to contract (an illness). **go Dutch** see under **Dutch**. **go far** to go a long way (*lit* and *fig*); to achieve success. **go for** to assail; to set out to secure; to go to get or fetch; to be attracted by (*inf*); to be true of. **go for broke** see under **broke**. **go for it** (*inf*) to make every effort to succeed in an undertaking. **go for nothing** to have no value. **go great guns** see under **gun**. **go halves** see under **half**. **go hang** (*sl*) to be forgotten, neglected; to be no longer of concern. **go hard** (**with**) see under **hard**[1]. **go in** to enter; (of the sun or moon) to become concealed behind cloud; to begin batting (*cricket*). **go in and out** to come and go freely. **go in for** to make a practice of; to take up as a career or special interest; to take part in (a competition, etc). **go into** to enter; to examine thoroughly, investigate or elaborate on; to adopt as a profession, etc; (of a whole number) to be capable of dividing a number. **go in unto** (*Bible*) to have sexual intercourse with. **go in with** to enter into partnership with; to join, combine with. **go it** to act in a striking or dashing manner (often in *imperative* by way of encouragement). **go it alone** see under **alone**. **go live** /līv/ (*inf*; of a radio station, automation equipment, etc) to go into operation. **go native** to assimilate oneself to an alien culture or to the way of life of a foreign country (*usu* less advanced than one's own). **go off** to leave; to explode; (of an alarm) to sound; to deteriorate; (of food) to become rotten and inedible; to proceed to an expected conclusion; to cease to like or be fond of (a person, etc) (*inf*); to go to sleep; to experience an orgasm (*sl*); to scold, reprimand (with *at*; *Aust sl*); to be raided by the police (*old Aust sl*); to get married (*old Aust sl*); to cease to operate; to die (*Shakesp*). **go off with** to go away with; to remove, take away (*inf*). **go on** to continue, proceed; an exclamation expressing disbelief (*inf*); to behave, conduct oneself (*inf*); to happen, as in *What's going on?*; to talk at length (*inf*); to be capable of being fitted onto; to appear on stage; to fare; to begin to function; to proceed from (as in *nothing to go on*). **go on at** to carp at persistently. **go one better** in some card games, to take a bet and increase the stake (also **go better**). **go one better** (**than**) to outdo, excel; to cap a performance; to achieve something more impressive, effective, etc (than someone or something). **go one's own way**, **go one's way** see under **way**[1]. **go out** to become extinguished; to become unfashionable; to be broadcast; to mingle in society (*old*). **go out with** to have a romantic relationship with. **go over** to examine or check in review; to recall; to revise. **go over to** to transfer allegiance to. **go places** to travel widely; to go far in personal advancement. **go round** to be enough for all. **go slow** (of workers) deliberately to restrict output or effort in order to obtain concessions from employers (**go-slow'** *adj* and *n*). **go slow with** to be sparing with. **go steady** to court romantically, date regularly (with *with*). **go the whole hog** see under **whole**. **go through** to perform to the end, often perfunctorily; to examine in order; to undergo; to be approved; to use up or spend (*inf*). **go through fire and water** to undertake any trouble or risks (from the usage in ancient ordeals). **go through with** to carry out. **go to** (*archaic*) come now (a kind of interjection, like the L *agedum*, the Gr *age nyn*). **go to pieces** see under **piece**. **go to show** (or **prove**) to serve as an illustration for or as evidence of. **go to the country** see under **country**. **go to the wall** see under **wall**. **go under** to become submerged, overwhelmed or ruined, eg (of a business) to fail, fold; to die (*archaic*). **go up** to ascend;

to be erected; to be destroyed by fire or explosion; (of costs, prices, etc) to increase; to enter a university. **go with** to accompany; to agree with, accord with; to court romantically. **go without** to suffer the lack of. **go without saying** to be self-evident (a Gallicism; Fr *cela va sans dire*). **great go** at Cambridge University, a degree examination, contrasted with **little go** (last held in 1961), a preliminary examination; at Oxford University, Greats (*obs*). **have a go** (*inf*) to make an attempt; (of a member of the public) to tackle a criminal. **have a go at** (*inf*) to criticize severely; to attack physically; to tease or pick on. **have something going for one** (*inf*) to enjoy the advantage of something. **I could go** (*inf*) I could do with, I wouldn't mind (a drink, rest, etc). **let go** see under **let¹**. **make a go of** to make a valiant attempt to succeed at something. **no go** not possible; futile; in vain. **no-go area** a part of a city, etc to which normal access is prevented by the erection of barricades, *esp* by local militants, a paramilitary group, etc. **on the go** very active. **to be going on with** (*inf*) for the moment, in the meantime. **to go** (*usu N Am*) (of food or drink from a restaurant or cafe) to be consumed off the premises.

go² /gō/ *n* a game of skill for two players, who take turns to place black or white stones (or counters) on a board, the object being to capture one's opponent's stones and be in control of the larger part of the board. [Jap]

Goa /gō′ə/ *n* a former Portuguese overseas territory on the west coast of India, part of the modern Indian republic since 1961.
■ **Gō′an** *adj* of Goa or its people. ◆ *n* a native of Goa. **Goanese** /gō-ə-nēz′/ *adj* Goan. ◆ *n* (*pl* **Goanese′**) a Goan; (as *pl*) the people of Goa.
❑ **Goa bean** *n* a papilionaceous plant (genus *Psophocarpus*) of tropical Asia and Africa, grown for its beans and root; its bean. **Goa butter** *n* kokum butter. **Goa powder** *n* araroba. **Goa trance** *n* a type of trance music originating in Goa.

goa /gō′ə/ *n* a grey-brown gazelle of Tibet, with backward-curving horns. [Tibetan *dgoba*]

goad /gōd/ *n* a sharp-pointed stick, often tipped with iron, for driving oxen; anything that provokes or incites. ◆ *vt* to drive with a goad; to urge forward; to incite; to provoke (with *into*). [OE *gād*]
■ **goads′man** or (*rare*) **goad′ster** *n* a man who uses a goad.

goaf¹ /gōf/ (*E Anglia dialect*) *n* a rick in a barn. [ON *gólf* floor]

goaf² /gōf/ (*mining*) *n* the space left by the extraction of a coal seam, into which waste is packed. [Origin obscure]

goal (*Milton* **gole**) /gōl/ *n* the end or aim of a person's effort or ambition; a destination; a pair of posts with a crossbar through or over which the ball is driven in some games (eg *football*); a basket used similarly in other sports; the sending of the ball between the goalposts or over the crossbar or into the basket; a score for doing so; (also **goals**) a name given to various outdoor games, eg early versions of hockey and football; a limit, boundary (*obs*); a competition, race (*obs*); the finishing point of a race; the winning post or a similar marker; sometimes used for the starting-post (*obs*); in ancient Rome, a pillar marking the turning point in a chariot race; the target in archery (*obs*). ◆ *vt* (*rugby*) to convert (a try) into a goal. [Origin obscure]
■ **goal′less** *adj* with no goals scored; without goals in life, unambitious.
❑ **goal′ball** *n* a game developed specifically for the blind, played by two teams on a rectangular indoor court using a ball containing bells, the object being to roll the ball past the opposing team into their goal. **goal difference** *n* the difference between the number of goals scored by a football, etc team and the number of those scored against them during a season, used as a factor in deciding league positions. **goal′keeper** *n* a player whose task is to defend the goal (*inf* **goal′ie**). **goal′keeping** *n*. **goal kick** *n* a free kick awarded to a defending player when an opponent has sent the ball over the goal line but not between the posts (*football*); an attempt to kick a goal (*rugby*). **goal′kicker** *n* a player who kicks a goal, or takes a goal kick. **goal′kicking** *n*. **goal line** *n* the boundary marking each end of the field, on which the goals are situated. **goal′mouth** *n* the space between the goalposts and immediately in front of the goal. **goal′post** *n* one of the upright posts forming the goal. **goal′scorer** *n* (*football*) a player who scores goals, *esp* regularly. **goal′-tender** *n* (in some games, *esp* ice-hockey) a goalkeeper. **goal′-tending** *n* the practice of being a goal-tender; in basketball, the illegal touching of the ball on its downward trajectory towards the basket.
■ **change, move** or **shift the goalposts** to alter the rules of a game, conditions of an agreement, etc unfairly after proceedings have begun, or the agreement has been entered into. **own goal** a goal scored against one's own side by a player from one's own team; any self-inflicted disadvantage.

goalie /gō′li/ (*inf*) *n* a goalkeeper.

Goan, Goanese see under **Goa.**

goanna /gō-an′ə/ (*Aust*) *n* any large monitor lizard. [**iguana**]

goary Milton's spelling of **gory.**

goat /gōt/ *n* a horned ruminant animal (genus *Capra*) of Europe, Asia and N Africa, related to the sheep; (with *cap* and *the*) Capricorn; a lecher (*fig*); a foolish person (*inf*); (in *pl*) the wicked (*Bible*). [OE *gāt*; Ger *Geiss*, Du *geit*]
■ **goat′ish** *adj* resembling a goat, *esp* in smell; lustful; foolish. **goat′ishly** *adv*. **goat′ishness** *n*. **goat′ling** *n* a young goat in its second year. **goat′y** *adj*.
❑ **goat′-antelope** *n* a goatlike antelope, or an animal intermediate between goat and antelope, such as the chamois and the goral. **goat′-fig** *n* the wild fig. **goat′fish** *n* (*N Am*) the red mullet. **goat fuck** *n* (*US taboo sl*) a chaotic situation, thoroughly confused muddle. **goat′-god** *n* Pan. **goat′herd** *n* a person who tends goats. **goat′-moth** *n* a large moth whose larvae feed on wood and exude a goatlike smell. **goat′-sallow** or **-willow** *n* the great sallow (*Salix caprea*). **goat's′-beard** *n* a composite plant of the genus *Tragopogon*, John-go-to-bed-at-noon; a herbaceous perennial with ornamental foliage (*Aruncus sylvester*). **goat's′-hair** *n* cirrus clouds. **goat′skin** *n* the skin of the goat; leather, or a wineskin, made from it. **goat's′-rue** *n* a papilionaceous border and fodder plant (*Galega officinalis*). **goat's′-thorn** *n* a shrub of the genus *Astragalus*. **goat′sucker** *n* (chiefly *N Am*) the nightjar, a bird similar to the swift, falsely thought to suck goats' udders for milk. **goat′weed** *n* goutweed. **goat-willow** see **goat-sallow** above.
■ **get someone's goat** (*inf*) to annoy or rile someone. **play** (or **act**) **the (giddy) goat** see under **giddy.**

goatee /gō-tē′/ *n* a small pointed beard on the chin, resembling a goat's beard. [**goat** and -ee, suffix of uncertain meaning]
■ **goateed′** *adj*.

gob¹ /gob/ *n* the mouth (*sl*); spittle (*sl*); a mouthful, lump (*dialect or sl*); a lump or measured portion of molten glass; a space left in a mine by extraction of coal; waste packed into it. ◆ *vi* (**gobb′ing; gobbed**) (*sl*) to spit. [OFr *gobe* mouthful, lump; cf Gaelic *gob* mouth; perh partly from **goaf²**]
■ **gobb′y** *adj* (*sl*) excessively talkative; cheeky.
❑ **gob′shite** *n* (*vulgar sl*) a stupid person. **gob′smacked** *adj* (*sl*) shocked; taken aback; astounded. **gob′stopper** *n* a very large hard round sweet for prolonged sucking.
■ **gobs of** (*N Am inf*) a lot of.

gob² /gob/ (*US sl*) *n* a sailor in the US Navy. [Origin obscure]

gobang /gō-bang′/ *n* a game played on a board of 256 squares, with 50 counters, the object being to get five in a row (also **gomoku** /gomō′koo/). [Jap *goban*]

gobar numeral /gō′bär nū′mə-rəl/ *n* any of a set of numerals forming the stage between ancient Hindu numerals and present-day Arabic numerals. [Ar *ghubār* sanded board]

gobbeline /gob′ə-lēn/ (*Spenser*) *n* same as **goblin.**

gobbet /gob′it/ *n* a lump, *esp* of meat hacked or vomited; an extract from a text, *esp* for translation or comment; a lump to be swallowed; a mouthful (*obs*); a clot (*obs*). [OFr *gobet*, dimin of *gobe*; see **gob¹**]

gobbi see **gobbo.**

gobble /gob′l/ *vt* to swallow in lumps; to swallow hastily (often with *up* or *down*); to snatch, seize eagerly (often with *up*; *inf*); to fellate (*vulgar sl*). ◆ *vi* to eat greedily; (of a turkey) to make a loud gurgling noise in the throat. ◆ *n* an act or instance of gobbling; a rapid straight putt so strongly played that if the ball had not gone into the hole, it would have gone a good way past (*golf*). [OFr *gober* to devour]
■ **gobb′ler** *n* (*N Am*) a turkey cock.

gobbledegook or **gobbledygook** /gob′əl-di-gook/ (*orig US sl*) *n* unintelligible official jargon; rubbish, nonsense. [Imit of pompous utterance]

gobbo /gob′bō/ (*Ital*) *n* (*pl* **gob′bi** /-bē/) a hunchback; a hunchbacked figure.

gobby see under **gob¹**.

Gobelin /gō′bə-lin, gob′(ə)- or go-blī′/ or **Gobelins** /-lin, -linz or -blē/ *n* a rich French pictorial tapestry (also *adj*). [From the *Gobelins*, a famous family of French dyers settled in Paris as early as the 15c]

gobe-mouches /gob-moosh′/ (*Fr*) *n* a flycatcher (bird); an insectivorous plant; a credulous person.

gobi /gō′bi/ (*Ind*) *n* a cabbage or cauliflower. [Hindi and Punjabi]

gobiid, gobioid see under **goby.**

goblet /gob′lit/ *n* a large drinking cup, properly one with a base and a stem and without a handle; a kind of saucepan with a straight handle and (*usu*) bulging sides (*Scot*); the tall bowl forming the top part of a liquidizer. [OFr *gobelet*, dimin of *gobel*, of doubtful origin]
❑ **goblet cell** *n* (*biol*) a goblet- or flask-shaped epithelial gland cell.

goblin /gob′lin/ *n* an unpleasant or mischievous sprite in the form of an old man; a bogy or bogle. [OFr *gobelin*, from LL *gobelīnus*, perh from *cobālus*, from Gr *kobālos* a mischievous spirit]

gobo[1] /gōˈbō/ (chiefly *US*) *n* (pl **gōˈboes** or **gōˈbos**) a device used to protect a camera lens from light; a device for preventing unwanted sound from reaching a microphone. [Origin obscure]

gobo[2] /gōˈbō/ *n* (pl **gōˈbos**) another name (used *esp* in oriental cookery) for burdock. [Jap]

gobony /go-bōˈni/ *adj* same as **compony**.

gobshite, **gobsmacked**, **gobstopper** see under **gob**[1].

goburra /gō-bûrˈə/ *n* same as **kookaburra**.

goby /gōˈbi/ *n* (pl **goˈbies**) any fish of the genus *Gobius* or the family **Gobīˈidae** small fishes with ventral fins forming a sucker. [L *gōbius*, from Gr *kōbios* a fish of the gudgeon kind]
■ **goˈbiid** *adj* of the Gobiidae. ◆ *n* a goby. **gōˈbioid** *adj*.

GOC *abbrev*: General Officer Commanding; General Optical Council.

god /god/ *n* a superhuman being, an object of worship (*fem* **goddˈess**); (with *cap*) the Supreme Being of monotheist religions, the Creator; an idol (*fem* **goddˈess**); an object of excessive devotion (*fem* **goddˈess**); a man of outstandingly fine physique; an extremely influential or greatly admired man (*fem* **goddˈess**); (in *pl*) the (occupants of the) gallery (*theatre*). ◆ *interj* (also **My God!**) an expression of anger, shock, amazement, etc. ◆ *vt* (*pat* **goddˈed**) to deify, treat as a god (*Spenser, Shakesp*, etc); (with *it*) to act as God or a god. [OE *god*; Ger *Gott*, Gothic *guth*, Du *god*; all from a Gmc root *guth-* God, and quite distinct from *good*]
■ **goddˈess-ship** *n* the state or quality of a goddess. **godˈhead** *n* (ME *-hēd, -hēde*, variant of *-hōd*) the state of being a god; divine nature; (with *cap* and *the*) God; a person idolized by the public (*inf*). **godˈhood** *n* (OE *-hād*, ME *-hōd*) the position or state of being divine; a deity (*obs*). **godˈless** *adj* without a god; living without believing in or obeying God; ungodly, immoral. **godˈlessly** *adv*. **godˈlessness** *n*. **godˈlike** *adj* like a god; divine. **godˈlily** *adv* (*archaic*). **godˈliness** *n* the quality of being godly. **godˈling** *n* (*literary*; *Dryden*) a little god. **godˈly** *adj* (**godˈlier**; **godˈliest**) like God in character; pious; according to God's laws. ◆ *adv* (*inf*) in a godly manner. **godˈship** *n* the rank or character of a god; a divinity. **godˈward** *adj* and *adv* towards God. **godˈwards** *adv*.
❑ **God'-almighty** *adj* (*inf*) enormous, excessive, inordinate; god-awful. ◆ *adv* (*inf*) enormously, excessively. **God'-a-mercy** *interj* (*archaic*) thank God; many thanks to. ◆ *n* (*obs*) an expression of thanks. **god-awˈful** *adj* (*inf*) very bad; unpleasant, distasteful. **god'-botherer** *n* (*derog inf*) a clergyman; an excessively pious person. **god'child** *n* a person to whom one is a godparent. **goddˈam**, **goddˈamn** or **god'damned** *adj* (*inf*) damned, accursed, hateful; utter, complete. ◆ *adv* (*inf*) accursedly; utterly. **god'daughter** *n* a female godchild. **god'father** *n* a male godparent; a sponsor (*fig*); the head of a criminal organization, *esp* the Mafia (*inf*); any influential leader or powerful figure (*inf*). **God'-fearing** *adj* being reverent towards God, religious. **god'-forgotten** or **god'-forsaken** *adj* (also with *cap*) remote and desolate; miserable; behind the times. **god game** *n* a computer game in which players create and control the actions of characters in a simulated universe. **God'-gifted** *adj* blessed with a special talent or ability. **God'-given** *adj* given by God; having an undisputed right, as if by divine authority. **god'-king** *n* a king considered to be a god, or thought to possess godlike powers. **god'mother** *n* a female godparent. **god'parent** *n* a person who, at baptism, guarantees a child's religious education or who (loosely) undertakes to bring up the child in the event of the death of its parents. **God particle** *n* an informal name for the **Higgs boson**. **God's acre** *n* a burial ground (imitated from Ger *Gottesacker*). **god'send** *n* a very welcome piece of unexpected good fortune; a person who or thing that provides unexpected but much needed support or help. **God slot** *n* (*inf*) a regular spot during the week's, day's, etc broadcasting reserved for religious programmes. **god'-smith** *n* (*Dryden*) a maker of idols. **god'son** *n* a male godchild. **god'speed** *n* and *interj* (*old*; also with *cap*) a wish for good fortune and a safe journey, expressed at parting. **God squad** *n* (*inf*) any religious group, *esp* an evangelical Christian one, considered excessively zealous in moralizing and attempting to convert others.
■ **for God's sake** an expression of urgent entreaty; an interjection expressing eg annoyance or disgust. **God forbid** may it not happen that. **God knows** God is my (his, etc) witness that; (*flippantly*) it is beyond human understanding; I don't know, I have no idea (*inf*). **God's country** or **God's own country** a particularly well-favoured (*esp* scenically beautiful) region; one's homeland or native region (*esp US*). **God's gift** (*ironic*) someone greatly desired because of being perfect or ideal, as if sent from God. **God's truth** the absolute, solemn truth. **God willing** if circumstances permit. **household gods** among the ancient Romans, the special gods presiding over the family; anything bound up with home interests.

god day /god dā/ (*Spenser*) for **good-day** (see under **good**).

god-den or **godden** /go-denˈ/ a dialect variant of **good-even**.

Gödel's theorem /gŭˈdəlz thēˈə-rəm/ *n* the theorem first demonstrated by the mathematician Kurt *Gödel* in 1931, that in logic and mathematics there must be true statements that cannot be proved or disproved within the system, and also that there can be no proof of the consistency of such a system from within itself.

godet /gōˈdā/ or *-det'/ *n* a triangular piece of cloth inserted in a skirt, etc, eg to make a flare. [Fr]

godetia /gə- or gō-dēˈsh(y)ə/ *n* any plant of the American genus *Godetia*, closely related to the evening primrose. [CH *Godet*, Swiss botanist (1797–1879)]

godown /gō-downˈ/ *n* in Eastern countries, a warehouse, or a storeroom. [Malay *gudang*]

godroon see **gadroon**.

godso (*obs*) *interj* same as **gadso**.

godwit /godˈwit/ *n* a bird (genus *Limosa*) of the plover family, with a long slightly upcurved bill and long slender legs, with a great part of the tibia bare. [Origin obscure]

goe[1] /gō/ (*Spenser*) same as **go**[1], **gone**.

goe[2] /gō/ an earlier variant of **geo** in the sense of gully, creek.

goel /gōˈel or -āl/ (*Jewish hist*) *n* the avenger of blood among the Hebrews, the nearest relative, whose duty it was to hunt down the murderer. [Heb]

goer, **goes** see **go**[1].

goest /gōˈəst/ (*archaic*) 2nd pers sing pres of **go**[1].

goeth /gōˈəth/ (*archaic*) 3rd pers sing pres of **go**[1].

goethite or **göthite** /goeˈtīt/ *n* a mineral, hydrated ferric oxide. [Named in honour of JW von *Goethe* (1749–1832), German poet]

goety /gōˈə-ti/ (*obs*) *n* black magic. [Gr *goēteiā* witchcraft]
■ **goetic** /-et'/ *adj*.

gofer[1] /gofˈər/ (*N Am sl*) *n* a junior employee who is given errands to run by other members of the staff. [Alteration of *go for*]

gofer[2], **gopher**, **gaufer** or **gaufre** /gōˈ or gōˈfər/ (*dialect*) *n* a waffle with a pattern of crossed lines. [Fr *gaufre* honeycomb, waffle]

goff /gof/ an archaic variant of **golf**.

goffer or **gauffer** /gofˈər, gof' or gōfˈər/ *vt* to pleat, crimp, make wavy (paper or material). ◆ *n* an iron used to do this. [Fr *gaufrer*, from *gaufre* a waffle (see **gofer**[2])]
■ **goff'ering** or **gauff'ering** *n* plaits or ruffles, or the process of making them; indented tooling on the edge of a book.

Gog /gog/ (*obs*) *n* used in oaths for **God**.

Gog and Magog /gog' and māˈgog/ *n pl* the nations represented as the forces of Satan at Armageddon (Bible, Revelation 20.8); the last two survivors of a mythical race of giants inhabiting ancient Britain.

goggle /gogˈl/ *vi* to strain or roll the eyes; to stare wide-eyed, in amazement, etc; (of the eyes) to protrude. ◆ *vt* to roll (the eyes). ◆ *adj* (of the eyes) rolling; staring; prominent. ◆ *n* a stare or affected rolling of the eyes; (in *pl*) spectacles with projecting eye tubes; (in *pl*) protective spectacles with side shields, as worn eg by motorcyclists, skiers, underwater divers, welders, etc; (in *pl*) spectacles, *esp* with round lenses (*inf*); (in *pl*) the eyes (*inf*). [Poss related to Ir and Gaelic *gog* to nod]
■ **gogg'led** *adj* wearing goggles. **gogg'ler** *n* a person with goggle eyes (*inf*); an eye (*sl*); an avid television viewer (*inf*). **gogg'ling** *n* and *adj*. **gogg'ly** *adj*.
❑ **gogg'le-box** *n* (*inf*) a television set. **gogg'le-eyed** *adj* having bulging, staring or rolling eyes (also *adv*).

goglet /gogˈlit/ (*Anglo-Ind*) *n* a water cooler. [Port *gorgoleta*]

go-go or **gogo** /gōˈgō/ *adj* active, alert to seize opportunities; full of energy, lively; (of dancing, music, etc) rhythmic, erotic, vigorous; (of clubs, discotheques) featuring go-go dancers and/or music. [à *gogo* infl by Eng **go**]
❑ **go-go dancer** or **girl** *n* a girl, *usu* scantily dressed, employed to dance (*usu* erotically) to music in nightclubs or discotheques.

Goidel /goiˈdəl/ *n* a Gael in the general sense; someone who speaks a Gadhelic language. See also **Gadhel** and **Gael**. [OIr *Góidel*]
■ **Goidelic** /-del'/ *adj* Gadhelic.

going[1] /gōˈing/ *n* the act of moving; a departure; the condition of the ground for eg walking, racing; progress; the situation in general, as in *the going was difficult* (*inf*); course of life (*Bible*); gait (*obs*). ◆ *adj* (for earlier **a-goˈing**) in motion or activity; about, to be had; in existence; current; usual or accepted. [**go**[1]]
❑ **going-away'** dress, outfit, etc *n* that worn by a bride when leaving on the honeymoon. **going concern** *n* a business currently operating (*esp* making a profit) and expected to continue to do so. **going concern concept** *n* (*account*) a concept that allows accounting measurements to be made on the assumption that the business will continue trading in future years. **going forth** *n* (*Bible*) an outlet

or exit. **going-o'ver** n (pl **goings-o'ver**) (inf) a thorough check, examination; a complete treatment; a beating. **going rate** n the current prevailing price that is being charged at the time for a service or product. **goings-on'** n pl behaviour, activities, now esp if open to censure. **goings-out'** n pl (obs) expenditure.

■ **be hard**, **heavy**, **tough**, etc **going** to prove difficult to do, etc.

going² /gō'ing/ adj the present participle of **go¹** in any sense; about or intending (to). ◆ combining form denoting regularly attending, as in the cinema-going public.

■ **going on** (**for**) approaching (an age or time). **going strong** in full activity, flourishing.

goitre or (esp N Am) **goiter** /goi'tər/ (pathol) n abnormal enlargement of the thyroid gland, producing a swelling in front of the throat, sometimes accompanied by exophthalmus. [Fr goître, from L guttur the throat]

■ **goi'tred** adj. **goi'trous** adj.

goji /gō'jē/ n the vitamin-rich berry of a solanaceous Chinese plant (also called **wolfberry**). [Tibetan]

go-kart see under **go¹**.

Golconda /gol-kon'də/ (literary) n a rich source of wealth and, by implication, great success or happiness. [Ruined city near Hyderabad, India, once famous for diamond-cutting]

gold¹ /gōld/ n a heavy yellow element (symbol **Au**; atomic no 79), one of the precious metals, used for coins, etc; articles made of it; money in the form of gold coins; a standard of money value which varies with the price of the metal; the gold standard; riches; anything very precious; the centre of an archery target, coloured gold; a gold medal; yellow, the colour of gold. ◆ adj made of or like gold; golden in colour; (often used to designate a product, service, etc) superior in quality to, improved upon or more sophisticated than the standard version. [OE gold, ON gull, Ger Gold, Gothic gulth]

■ **gold'ish** adj somewhat golden. **gold'less** adj. **gold'y** adj somewhat like gold.

❑ **gold'-beater** n a person whose trade is to beat gold into gold leaf. **gold-beater's skin** n the outer coat of the caecum of an ox, used for separating sheets of gold being beaten into gold leaf. **gold'-beating** n. **gold beetle** n (US) a beetle of the family Chrysomelidae. **gold brick** n a block of gold or (orig US sl) of pretended gold, hence a sham or swindle; a person who shirks duties or responsibilities. **gold-brick'** vt. **gold'-bug** n (US) a gold beetle; someone whose power comes from their wealth, a plutocrat; a person who favours a gold standard; a person who invests in gold bullion. **gold card** n a special-privilege credit card available only to customers in the higher-income bracket. **gold certificate** or **note** n (US) formerly, a US treasury note issued on gold reserves. **gold'-cloth** n cloth of gold (qv). **gold'crest** n a golden-crested bird of the genus Regulus (also **golden-crested wren**). **gold'-digger** n a person who digs for gold; a person who treats an intimate relationship chiefly as a source of material gain. **gold'-digging** n. **gold disc** n a gold replica of a record, presented to the composer, performer, etc to commemorate achieving sales above a certain amount (for a UK album, 100000 copies). **gold dust** n gold in fine particles, as found in some rivers; something very rare and precious, much sought-after (fig; inf); a cultivated evergreen alyssum, Alyssum saxatile, having numerous tiny yellow flowers. **gold-end'-man** n (obs) a dealer in gold-ends' (archaic), broken remnants of gold. **gold-exchange standard** n (obs) a monetary system by which a country not on the gold standard was linked in its exchange rate to another's which was. **gold export point** see **gold point** below. **gold'eye** n a N American freshwater fish (genus Hiodon). **gold-fe'ver** n a mania for seeking gold. **gold'field** n a gold-producing region. **gold'finch** n a European finch (Carduelis carduelis) with black, red, yellow and white plumage, fond of eating thistle seeds; any of several American finches of the genus Spinus, the male being yellow with black wings, tail and crown. **gold'finny** n a kind of small European wrasse. **gold'fish** n a Chinese and Japanese freshwater fish closely related to the carp, golden or (**silverfish**) pale in its domesticated state, brownish when wild. **goldfish bowl** n a spherical glass aquarium for goldfish; a situation entirely lacking in privacy. **gold foil** n gold beaten into thin sheets, but not as thin as gold leaf. **gold'ilocks** n a golden-haired person; a species of buttercup (Ranunculus auricomus); a composite European plant (Aster linosyris) with clustered bright yellow flowers. **gold import point** see **gold point** below. **gold ink** n a writing fluid containing particles of gold or an imitation. **gold lace** n lace made from gold thread. **gold'-laced** adj. **gold leaf** n gold beaten extremely thin, used to decorate books, picture frames, etc. **gold-leaf'** vt. **gold medal** n in athletics competitions, etc, the medal awarded as first prize. **gold mine** n a mine producing gold; a source of great profit. **gold'miner** n. **gold note** see **gold certificate** above. **gold-of-pleas'ure** n a cruciferous plant (Camelina sativa), yellow-flowered, once much cultivated for its oil-rich seeds. **gold paint** n bronze powders mixed with transparent varnish or amyl acetate. **gold plate** n vessels and utensils of gold collectively; metal, esp silver, plated with

gold. **gold-plate'** vt to coat (another metal) with gold. **gold-pla'ted** adj coated with gold; (of investments, etc) secure and sure to be profitable. **gold-pla'ting** n the process of coating with gold; the addition by a lower body of further restrictions to legislation created by a higher authority. **gold point** n (finance; obs) in international transactions, an exchange rate at which it is advisable to export (**gold export point**) or import (**gold import point**) gold bullion rather than settle by bills of exchange. **gold record** n a gold disc (qv above). **gold reserve** n the stock of gold held by a country's central bank, etc to finance any calls that may be made from overseas creditors for the settlement of debt. **gold rush** n a rush of prospectors to a newly discovered goldfield. **gold'sinny** same as **goldfinny** above. **gold'size** n an adhesive, of various kinds, used to attach gold leaf to a surface. **gold'smith** n a worker in gold and silver. **goldsmith beetle** n a beetle with wing-covers of a gold colour. **gold'smithry** or **gold'smithery** n. **gold'spink** n (chiefly Scot, also **gowd'spink**) the goldfinch. **gold standard** n a monetary standard or system according to which the unit of currency has a precise value in gold. **gold'stick** n a colonel of the Life Guards, who carries a gilded wand before the sovereign; the wand or rod so carried. **gold'stone** see **aventurine**. **gold thread** n gold wire used in weaving; silk wound with gilded wire; an evergreen perennial ranunculaceous plant (genus Coptis) with slender yellow roots and white flowers. **gold'-washer** n someone who obtains gold from sand and gravel by washing; a cradle or other implement for washing gold. **gold'-wasp** n any wasp of a family (Chrysididae) with brilliant metallic colouring and telescopic abdomen, whose larvae feed on those of wasps and bees, known also as cuckoo fly, ruby-tail or ruby-wasp. **gold wire** n wire made of or covered with gold. **gold'work** n gold articles collectively.

■ **as good as gold** behaving in an exemplary manner (usu of children). **go gold** (of a record) to sell in quantities sufficient to merit a gold disc. **pot** (or **crock**) **of gold** a distant and usu unattainable reward.

gold² /gōld/, also (Scot) **gool** or **gule** /gool/ or (Spenser) **goold** /goold/ n the marigold (obs); the corn marigold (dialect). [OE golde, appar related to **gold¹**, **gollan** and **gowan**; cf **marigold**]

goidarn /goi'därn/ (US inf) adj and adv a euphemistic alteration of **goddamn** (see under **god**).

Goldbach's conjecture /gōld'bahhs kən-jek'chər/ (maths) n the theory that every even number greater than 2 is the sum of two prime numbers. [C Goldbach (1690–1764), German mathematician]

golden /gōl'dən/ adj of gold; of the colour of gold; bright, shining like gold; most valuable; happy; most favourable; prosperous; of outstanding excellence; denoting a 50th anniversary. ◆ vt (rare) to gild, make golden. ◆ vi (rare) to become golden in colour. [**gold¹** and adj-forming sfx -en like, made of]

■ **gold'enly** adv.

❑ **golden age** n an imaginary past time of innocence and happiness; any time of highest achievement. **gold'enberry** n the Cape gooseberry. **golden bough** n (classical myth) a branch which permitted the bearer of it to visit the underworld. **golden bowler** n (old sl) dismissal from the British Army followed by a job in Whitehall. **golden boy** or **girl** n a young man or woman of outstanding talents, good looks, popularity, etc likely to win renown. **golden bull** n (L bulla aurea) an edict issued by the Emperor Charles IV in 1356, mainly for the purpose of settling the law of imperial elections. **golden calf** see under **calf¹**. **golden chain** n laburnum. **golden-crested** adj (of animals) having a yellow crest or crown. **Golden Delicious** n a sweet eating apple with a yellowish-green skin. **goldendood'le** n a cross between a golden retriever and a poodle. **golden duck** n (cricket sl) an instance of being dismissed by the first ball of one's innings. **golden eagle** n a large eagle found in mountainous regions in northern countries, so called from a slight golden gleam about the head and neck. **gold'en-eye** n a northern sea-duck (genus Bucephala); the lacewing fly. **golden fleece** n (Gr myth) the fleece of the ram Chrysomallus, the recovery of which was the object of the famous expedition of the Argonauts, and which gave its name to a celebrated order of knighthood in Austria and Spain, founded in 1429. **golden girl** see **golden boy** above. **golden goal** n in football, the first goal scored in extra time, which brings immediate victory to the scoring team. **golden goodbye** see **golden handshake** below. **golden goose** n the fabled layer of golden eggs, killed by its over-greedy owner; (also **the goose that lays the golden eggs**) a source of profit (fig). **golden handcuffs** n pl (inf) a substantial personal financial incentive or stake specifically designed by a company to constrain a valued employee into remaining on its staff. **golden handshake** n (inf) a large sum of money, or some equivalent, given to an employee or member who retires or is otherwise forced to leave a firm, etc (also **golden goodbye**). **golden hello** n (inf) a large sum given to a much-wanted new employee on joining a firm. **Golden Horde** n the Kipchaks, a Turkic people, whose empire was founded in central and southern Russia by Batu in the 13c. **golden hour** n (med) the period immediately following a serious injury, when skilled treatment is urgently required. **golden jubilee** *n* a 50th anniversary. **Golden Legend** *n* (L *Legenda Aurea*) a celebrated medieval collection of saints' lives, by Jacobus de Voragine (1230–98). **golden mean** *n* the middle way between extremes; moderation; golden section (qv below). **golden mole** *n* any of several bronze-coloured S African insectivores of the family Chrysochloridae, which look superficially like moles. **golden number** *n* a number marking the position of a year in the Metonic cycle of nineteen years. **golden oldie** *n* (*inf*) a song, recording, motion picture, etc issued some considerable time ago and still popular; a person who remains successful at a relatively advanced age. **golden opportunity** *n* a very favourable one. **golden orfe** *n* an ornamental yellowish-orange freshwater fish, kept in aquariums and ponds. **golden parachute** *n* (*inf*) an unusually lavish cash payment to a senior member of a firm on his or her dismissal following a takeover. **golden pheasant** *n* an *orig* Chinese species of pheasant, the male of which has a golden-yellow crown and lower back and orange-red breast and underparts. **golden plover** *n* a plover with yellow-speckled feathers. **golden rectangle** *n* one in which the ratio of width to length is the same as that of length to the sum of width and length. **golden retriever** *n* a breed of retriever with a thick, wavy, golden-coloured coat. **golden rice** *n* a genetically modified strain of rice, designed to provide increased levels of vitamin A. **gold'enrod** *n* any plant of the composite genus *Solidago*, with rodlike stems and yellow heads crowded along the branches. **golden rose** *n* an ornamental spray of roses made of wrought gold, blessed by the Pope on the fourth Sunday in Lent, sometimes presented to a dignitary or monarch in recognition of a special service. **golden rule** *n* the precept that one should treat others as one would wish to be treated by them; a rule of the first importance, a guiding principle; a rule of statutory interpretation, which allows the court to depart from a strict and literal interpretation of a statute where this would lead to an absurd result (*law*). **golden salmon** *n* the S American dorado. **golden saxifrage** *n* a greenish-yellow plant (genus *Chrysosplenium*) of the saxifrage family. **golden seal** *n* a N American ranunculaceous plant (*Hydrastis canadensis*); its yellow rhizome, used in medicine. **golden section** *n* division of a line so that one segment is to the other as that to the whole. **golden share** *n* a large share in a company, etc held by an institution or (often) a government, which prevents takeover by another company. **Golden State** *n* (*inf*) California. **golden syrup** see under **syrup**. **golden wattle** *n* any of various kinds of yellow-flowered Australian acacia, *esp Acacia pycnantha*. **golden wedding** see under **wed**. **golden years** *n pl* (*inf*) the period of life after one has retired. **golden years** *n pl* a time of great prosperity; the period of one's life after retirement (*euphem*).

gole obsolete (*Milton*, etc) spelling of **goal**.

golem /gōʹlem/ or /-ləm/ *n* in Jewish folklore, a human image brought to life; a robot; a dolt. [Yiddish *goylem*, from Heb *gōlem* a shapeless thing, an embryo]

Golf or **golf** /golf/ *n* (in international radio communication) a code word for the letter g.

golf /golf/ *n* a game played with a club or set of clubs over a prepared stretch of land, the aim being to propel a small ball into a series of holes. ◆ *vi* to play golf. [Origin uncertain; Du *kolf* a club, has been suggested] ■ **golf'er** *n*. **golfiana** /-i-äʹnə/ *n* a collector's or dealer's term for items of golfing interest. **golf'ing** *n*. □ **golf bag** *n* a bag for carrying golf clubs. **golf ball** *n* a small ball used in golf; in certain typewriters, printers, etc a small detachable metal sphere or hemisphere with the type characters moulded onto its surface. **golf cart** *n* a small motorized vehicle in which golfers can drive around a course. **golf club** *n* a club used in golf; a golfing society; its premises with a golf course attached. **golf course** *n* an area of specially prepared, often landscaped, ground on which golf is played. **golf links** *n pl* a golf course, *esp* by the sea, typically open and undulating.

Golgi body /golʹjē bodʹi/ (*biol*) *n* a cytoplasmic organelle consisting of a stack of plate-like cisternae often close to the nucleus, the site of protein glycosylation (also called **Golgi apparatus**). [Camillo *Golgi* (1843–1926), Italian cytologist]

Golgotha /golʹgə-thə/ *n* Calvary; a burial ground; a charnel house; a place littered with bones. [See under **Calvary**]

goliard /gōʹli-ärd/ or /-lyərd/ (*hist*) *n* any of a band of medieval wandering students and scholars noted for their riotous behaviour and *esp* their satirical Latin poems lampooning the Church, most of which were credited to a mythical Bishop *Golias*. [OFr, glutton, from L *gūla* gluttony] ■ **goliardic** /-ärdʹik/ *adj*. **gōʹliardy** or **goliard'ery** *n*. **gōʹlias** *vi* (*Tennyson*) to play Golias, that is, perhaps, to behave riotously, irreverently or irreligiously.

Goliath /gō-līʹəth or gə-/ *n* an unusually large or tall person, a giant; a person or organization of enormous stature or power. [From *Goliath*, the Philistine giant in Bible, 1 Samuel 17] ■ **golī'athize** or **-ise** *vi* to play Goliath, exaggerate extravagantly. □ **goliath beetle** *n* a tropical beetle (genus *Goliathus*) reaching four inches in length. **goliath frog** *n* the largest kind of frog, living in central and W Africa.

gollan or **golland** /golʹən(d)/, also **gowlan** or **gowland** /gowʹlənd/ (*dialect*) *n* a Scot and N Eng name for various yellow flowers (corn marigold, globeflower, marigold, etc). [Perh connected with **gold²**; see **gowan**]

gollar or **goller** /golʹər/ (*Scot*) *n* a loud inarticulate gurgling sound; a thick or guttural bawl. ◆ *vi* to make such a noise. [Imit]

golliwog see **gollywog**.

gollop /golʹəp/ *vt* and *vi* to gulp greedily or hastily. [Perh **gulp**]

golly¹ /golʹi/ *interj* expressing surprise or admiration. [Thought to be orig a modification of **God**]

golly² /golʹi/ *n* a short form of **gollywog**.

gollywog or **golliwog** /golʹi-wog/ *n* a child's soft doll with a black face, bristling hair and bright clothes; a person who has fuzzy or bristling hair (*derog*). [*Golliwogg*, a doll in certain US children's books, the first of which, illustrated by Florence Upton, was published in 1895]

golomynka /go-lo-ming'kə/ *n* a very oily fish found in Lake Baikal, resembling the gobies. [Russ]

golosh see **galosh**.

goloshoes an obsolete spelling of **galoshes** (*pl* of **galosh**).

golp or **golpe** /golp/ (*heraldry*) *n* a purple roundel. [Perh from Sp *golpe* bruise]

GOM *abbrev* : Grand Old Man (*orig* WE Gladstone), used of an elderly and venerated person, *esp* in a particular field of endeavour.

gombeen /gomʹbēn/ (*Irish*) *n* usury. [Ir *gaimbín*] □ **gom'been-man** *n* a grasping usurer; a moneylender.

gombo, **gombro** same as **gumbo**.

gomeril or **gomeral** /gomʹə-rəl/ (*Scot*) *n* a simpleton; a dunderhead. [Origin obscure]

gomoku see **gobang**.

gompa /gomʹpə/ *n* a Buddhist temple or monastery in Tibet. [Tibetan *gömpa* a place of seclusion, a hermitage]

gomphosis /gom-fōʹsis/ (*anat* and *zool*) *n* (*pl* **gompho'ses** /-sēz/) an immovable articulation, as of the teeth in the jaw. [Gr *gomphōsis*, from *gomphos* a bolt]

gomuti /gō-mooʹti/ *n* (also **gomu'to** (*pl* **gomu'tos**)) a palm, *Arenga pinnata* (or *saccharifera*); the black fibre it yields. [Malay *gumuti*]

gon /gon/ (*geom*) *n* a grade. [Gr *gōnia* angle]

-gon /-gon or -gən/ *combining form* used of a figure having a certain number of angles, as in *hexagon*, *polygon*. [Gr *gōnia* angle]

gonad /gōʹnad or gonʹad/ (*biol*) *n* an organ that produces sex cells. [Gr *gonē* generation] ■ **gonadal** /gon-āʹdəl/, **gonadial** /-āʹdi-əl/ or **gonadic** /-adʹ/ *adj*. **gonadotroph'ic** or **gonadotrop'ic** *adj* stimulating the gonads. **gonadotroph'in** or **gonadotrop'in** *n* a substance that does this, used as a drug to promote fertility.

gondola /gonʹdə-lə/ *n* a long, narrow boat used chiefly on the canals of Venice (also (*Spenser*) **gon'delay**); a lighter, large open boat (*US*); a flat railway wagon (*US*); the cabin suspended from an airship or balloon; a cabin resembling this suspended from an earth-supported structure, *esp* on a ski-lift or aerial tramway, etc; a (free-standing) shelved unit for displaying goods in a supermarket, etc. [Venetian dialect; origin obscure] ■ **gondolier** /-lēr/ *n* a man who rows or propels a gondola.

Gondwana /gond-wäʹnə/ (formerly called **Gondwanaland** /gond-wäʹnä-land/) *n* an ancient continent believed to have connected India with S Africa, S America, Antarctica and Australia from Carboniferous to Jurassic times. [*Gondwana* district in India, ie forest of the Gonds]

gone /gon/ *adj* the past participle of **go¹**; in an advanced stage (*esp* in *far gone*); lost, passed beyond help; departed; dead; over the hill, past one's peak; weak, faint, feeling a sinking sensation; pregnant (with specified time, eg *six months gone*); (of the time) past, as in *gone six*; (of an arrow) wide of the mark; enamoured of (with *on*; *sl*); in an exalted, delirious or inspired state (*sl*). ■ **gone'ness** *n* a sinking sensation. **gon'er** *n* (*sl*) a person or animal dead or ruined beyond recovery; a thing beyond hope of recovery. □ **gone goose** or **gosling** *n* (*inf*, *esp US*) a hopeless case. ■ **gone under** ruined beyond recovery.

gonfalon /gonʹfə-lon/ *n* an ensign or standard with streamers, hung from a horizontal bar, used *esp* in certain medieval Italian republics.

[Ital *gonfalone* and OFr *gonfanon*, from OHGer *gundfano*, from *gund* battle, and *fano* (Ger *Fahne*) a flag; cf OE *gūthfana*]

■ **gonfalonier** /-ēr'/ *n* a person who carries a gonfalon; the chief magistrate in some medieval Italian republics. **gon'fanon** *n* (*hist*) a gonfalon; a pennon.

gong /gong/ *n* a metal disc, *usu* rimmed, that sounds when struck or rubbed with a drumstick; an instrument used to sound a call, *esp* to meals; a steel spiral for striking in a clock; a flat bell sounded by a hammer; a medal (*sl*). ◆ *vt* to summon, or call upon to stop, by sounding a gong. [Malay]

■ **gong'ster** *n* a person who gongs.
❑ **gong'-stick** *n*.

Gongorism /gong'go-ri-zm/ *n* a florid, inverted and pedantic style of writing, introduced by the Spanish poet Luis de *Góngora* y Argote (1561–1627), some of whose distinctive features reappeared in Euphuism.

■ **Gong'orist** *n*. **Gongoris'tic** *adj*.

gonia see **gonion**.

goniatite /gō'ni-ə-tīt/ (*palaeontol*) *n* a fossil cephalopod of a group with comparatively simple angular septa. [Gr *gōnia* an angle]

■ **goniatī'toid** *n* and *adj*.

gonidium /go-nid'i-əm/ (*bot*) *n* (pl **gonid'ia**) an algal cell in a lichen. [Gr *gonē* generation, seed]

■ **gonid'ial** or **gonid'ic** *adj*.

gonimoblast /gon'i-mō-bläst/ (*bot*) *n* in the red seaweeds, a spore-bearing filament that springs from the fertilized carpogonium. [Gr *gonimos* productive, and *blastos* a shoot]

goniometer /gōn-i-om'i-tər/ *n* an instrument for measuring angles, *esp* between crystal faces; a direction-finding apparatus, used *esp* to trace radio signals. [Gr *gōnia* an angle, and *metron* measure]

■ **goniometric** /-ə-met'rik/ or **goniomet'rical** *adj*. **goniomet'rically** *adv*. **goniom'etry** *n*.

gonion /gō'ni-on or -ən/ (*anat*) *n* (pl **gō'nia** /-i-ə/) the point of the angle on either side of the lower jaw. [Gr *gōnia* angle]

gonk /gongk/ *n* (**Gonk®**) a cushion-like soft toy, *usu* with arms and legs; a prostitute's client (*derog sl*). [Nonsense word]

gonna /gən'ə/ (*esp* N Am) an informal contraction of **going to**.

gonococcus /gon-ō-kok'əs/ (*med*) *n* (pl **gonococci** /-kok'ī/) the bacterium that causes gonorrhoea. [Gr *gonos* seed, and *kokkos* a berry]

■ **gonococc'al** or **gonococcic** /-kok'ik/ *adj*. **gonococc'oid** *adj*.

gonocyte /gon'ō-sīt/ (*biol*) *n* an oocyte or spermatocyte. [Gr *gonos* seed, and **-cyte**]

gonophore /gon'ə-för/ *n* a prolongation of the axis bearing stamens or carpels (*bot*); a reproductive zooid of a hydrozoan, similar to a medusa but remaining fixed (*zool*). [Gr *gonos* seed, and *phoreein* to bear]

gonorrhoea /gon-ə-rē'ə/ (*med*) *n* a sexually transmitted contagious infection of the mucous membrane of the genital tract (also (*esp* N Am) **gonorrhē'a**). [Gr *gonorroia*, from *gonos* seed, and *rheein* to flow, from a mistaken notion of its nature]

■ **gonorrhoe'al** or **gonorrhoe'ic** (also (*esp* N Am) **gonorrhē'al**, **gonorrhē'ic**) *adj*.

gonys /gon'is/ (*ornithol*) *n* the ridge along and towards the tip of the lower mandible, formed by the junction of its two halves or rami (as in gulls). [New L, prob from Gr *genys* jaw]

gonzo /gon'zō/ (*US sl*) *adj* bizarre, crazy, absurd (*orig* and *esp* used in reference to journalism of a subjective eccentric nature). [Perh from Ital *gonzo* simpleton, or Sp *ganso*, literally, goose]

goo /goo/ (*sl*) *n* any sticky substance; sentimentality. [Origin uncertain]

■ **goo'ey** *adj* (**goo'ier**; **goo'iest**). **goo'iness** *n*.

goober /goo'bər/ *n* (also **goober pea**) a peanut. [African]

good /gud/ *adj* (compar **bett'er**; superl **best**) having suitable or desirable qualities; promoting health, welfare or happiness; virtuous; pious; kind; benevolent; well-behaved; not troublesome; of repute; stout-hearted, able; worthy; commendable; suitable; adequate; thorough; competent; sufficient; valid; sound; serviceable; beneficial; genuine; pleasing; enjoyable; favourable; (of a shot or play in tennis, golf, etc) made accurately; ample, moderately estimated; considerable, as in *a good deal, a good mind*; able to be counted on; financially or commercially safe or advisable; (from a range) of the better or best quality; used in patronizing address or reference, as in *my good man, your good lady* (ie wife). ◆ *n* that which is morally or ethically right; prosperity; welfare; advantage, temporal or spiritual; benefit; use; virtue; possessions (*archaic*); (*usu* in *pl*) moveable property, chattels, merchandise, freight; things bought and sold (eg machinery, clothing, foodstuffs, furniture), excluding currency, livestock, minerals, crops, land, buildings and services (*business*); the subject matter of a contract of sale of goods, which excludes money or

choses in action (qv under **chose²**) (*law*); tangible items produced by firms and in demand by individuals for consumption, or by firms as an input to their production processes (*econ*). ◆ *interj* well; right; so be it. ◆ *adv* (now mainly *US inf*, or *dialect*) well. [OE *gōd*; Du *goed*, Ger *gut*, ON *gōthr*, Gothic *gōths*]

■ **good'iness** *n* weak, priggish or sanctimonious goodness. **good'ish** *adj* pretty good, of fair quality or quantity. **good'liness** *n*. **good'ly** *adj* (**good'lier**; **good'liest**) comely, good-looking (*archaic*); fine; excellent; ample. ◆ *adv* (*Spenser*) graciously; excellently, kindly. **good'lyhead** or **good'lihead** *n* (*Spenser*) goodness. **good'ness** *n* virtue; excellence; benevolence; nourishment in food; substituted for God in certain expressions, such as *for goodness sake*, and as an interjection. **good'-o** or **good'-oh** *interj* expressing pleasure. ◆ *adv* (*Aust*) well; thoroughly. **good'y** *n* (*pl* **good'ies**) (*usu* in *pl*) a delicacy or sweetmeat; (*usu* in *pl*) something pleasant or desirable (*usu facetious*); the hero of a book, film, or any character on the side of justice and fair play, etc (*inf*); a goody-goody; short for **goodwife** (*archaic*). ◆ *interj* expressing (*esp* childish) pleasure. ◆ *adj* goody-goody.

❑ **good afternoon** *n* and *interj* a salutation on meeting or parting in the afternoon. **good breeding** *n* polite manners formed by a good upbringing. **good-broth'er, -fath'er, -moth'er, -sis'ter, -son'** *n* (*Scot*; *archaic* or *dialect*; also **gude-**) a brother-in-law, father-in-law, etc. **goodbye'** *n* or *interj* farewell, a form of address at parting (formed from *God be with you*). **good'-cheap** *adj* (*archaic*) cheap (literally, good-bargain). **good-condi'tioned** *adj* in a good state. **good-dame'** *n* (*obs Scot*; also **gude-dame'** /gūd- or gid-/) a grandmother. **good-day'** *n* or *interj* a traditional salutation at meeting or parting, now rather formal or archaic, but in Australia a common greeting, *usu* shortened to **g'day**. **good-den'** (*obs*; from *good-e'en*), **good-e'en'** (*archaic*), **good-e'ven** (*archaic*) or **good-eve'ning** *n* or *interj* a salutation on meeting or parting in the evening. **good'faced** *adj* (*Shakesp*) having a handsome face. **good faith** see **in good faith** below. **good feeling** *n* friendly feeling; convivial relations. **good'fella** *n* (*N Am inf*) a gangster, *esp* a member of the Mafia. **good'fellow** *n* a jolly or favourite companion; a reveller. **goodfell'owship** *n* merry or pleasant company; conviviality. **good folk** *n pl* good people. **good'-for-nothing** *adj* worthless, useless. ◆ *n* an idle or worthless person. **Good Friday** see under **Friday**. **good grief** *interj* an exclamation of surprise, dismay or exasperation. **good heavens** *interj* an exclamation of surprise. **good humour** *n* cheerful, tolerant mood or disposition. **good-hu'moured** *adj*. **good-hu'mouredly** *adv*. **good-hu'mouredness** *n*. **good-King-Hen'ry** *n* a goosefoot used in cooking and sometimes grown as a pot-herb. **good-lack'** *interj* (*obs*) an expression of surprise or pity (*prob* a variation of *good Lord*, under the influence of **alack**). **good'-liking** see under **like²**. **good-look'er** *n* (*inf*). **good-look'ing** *adj* handsome, attractive. **good looks** *n pl* attractive appearance. **good'man** *n* a yeoman (*obs*); (*usu* with *cap*) formerly prefixed to the name of a man of yeoman's rank (*fem* **good'wife**; *obs*); /gūd-man'/ (*chiefly Scot*; *archaic*; also **gude-**) a householder or husband (*fem* **goodwife'**); the Devil (*euphem*). **goodman's croft** *n* a patch once left untilled in Scotland to avert the malice of the Devil from the crop. **good-morn'ing** or (*archaic*) **good-morr'ow** *n* and *interj* a salutation at meeting or parting early in the day. **good nature** *n* natural goodness and mildness of disposition. **good-na'tured** *adj*. **good-na'turedly** *adv*. **good-na'turedness** *n*. **goodnight'** *n* and *interj* a common salutation on parting at night or well on in the day. **good'-now** *interj* (*obs* or *dialect*) an exclamation of wonder, surprise or entreaty. **good offices** *n pl* mediation; influence, agency. **good oil** *n* (*Aust inf*) credible or reliable information. **good people** or **good folk** *n pl* (*euphem*) the fairies. **good sailor** *n* a person who tends not to suffer from seasickness. **good Samaritan** see **Samaritan**. **goods engine** *n* an engine used for drawing goods trains. **good sense** *n* sound judgement. **goods for own use** *n pl* (*bookkeeping*) stock taken by the owner of a business for his or her own private purposes, the sale price of which is debited to the owner's drawings account and credited to the sales account. **goodsire'**, also **gudesire'** /gūd- or gid-/ or **gutcher** /gut'shər/ *n* (*obs Scot*) a grandfather. **good'-sized** *adj* (fairly) large. **goods on approval** *n pl* (*marketing*) goods delivered and examined for a trial period before a decision to buy them is made. **goods on consignment** *n pl* (*marketing*) goods delivered to an agent by a principal and sold on behalf of the principal. **good-speed'** *n* and *interj* (*archaic*) a contraction of *I wish you good speed* (ie success). **goods received department** *n* (*business*) one that deals with the reception of goods, and is responsible for checking the condition of goods on delivery, etc. **goods received note** *n* (*business*) a document completed by the storekeeper upon receipt of materials or goods from an outside supplier. **goods train** *n* a train of goods wagons. **good-tem'pered** *adj* of a kindly disposition; not easily made angry. **Good Templar** *n* a member of a temperance society, modelled on the Freemasons. **good'time** *adj* pleasure-seeking; (of music) purely for entertainment. **good'-tim'er** *n*. **good turn** *n* something done for someone in a kind and helpful spirit or manner. **good'wife** (or /-wīf'/)

n the *fem* of **goodman**. **goodwill'** *n* benevolence; well-wishing; the established trade, reputation, efficiency, popularity, and valuable personal relationships with customers, of a business or trade, often appearing as one of its (intangible) assets, with a marketable money value; in consolidated accounts, an intangible asset representing the difference between the acquisition price of a subsidiary and the fair value of its assets and liabilities at the time of acquisition (*finance*). **good'will** or (*obs Scot*) **good-will'y** *adj* well-wishing; expressive of goodwill. **good works** *n pl* acts of charity. **goody bag** *n* a bag containing a number of small gifts, given to people attending a party or promotional event. **good'y-good'y** *adj* and *n* (a person) affecting a smug or obsequious show of virtue; (a person who is) insipidly benevolent or pious.

■ **as good as** the same as, no less than; virtually. **be as good as one's word** to fulfil one's promise. **for good** or **for good and all** permanently; irrevocably. **get** (or **have**) **the goods on** (*inf*) to obtain proof of someone's wrongdoing or criminal activity. **good and** (*inf*) very; completely. **good for anything** ready for any kind of work. **good for you** an interjection expressing approval (*Aust inf* **good on you**). **goodness of fit** (*stats*) the extent to which observed data matches the values predicted by a theorem. **goods and chattels** see under **chattel**. **in good faith** honestly and without any intention to deceive (**good-faith'** *adj*). **in someone's good books** in favour with someone. **make good** to fulfil, perform; to compensate; to become successful, *esp* unexpectedly; to do well, redeeming an unpromising false start; to repair; to justify. **no good** useless; futile; worthless. **not, hardly,** etc **good enough** not sufficiently good; mean, unfair, very different from what was expected or promised. **stand good** to be lastingly good; to remain. **the good** virtuous people collectively. **the Good Book** the Bible. **the goods** (*sl*) the real thing; that which is required, promised, etc. **think good** (*obs*) to be disposed, to be willing. **to the good** for the best; on the credit or advantage side. **up to no good** doing something mischievous or wrong.

goodyear /gŭd'yēr/ or **goodyears** (*Shakesp*) *n* the devil, the plague, or the like (a meaningless imprecation). [Of obscure origin, perh orig 'as I hope for a *good year*']

gooey see under **goo**.

goof /goof/ (*sl*) *n* a stupid or awkward person; a blunder. ♦ *vi* to make a blunder; to mess (about or around) (*N Am*); to waste time, behave idly, etc, *esp* when one should be working (*N Am*; with *off*). ♦ *vt* to make a mess of (often with *up*). [Perh Fr *goffe*]
■ **goof'ily** *adv*. **goof'iness** *n*. **goof'y** *adj* foolish or stupid; (of teeth) protruding.
❑ **goof'ball** *n* (*N Am sl*) a barbiturate pill used as an exhilarant; a goofy person.

google /goo'gl/ (*inf*) *vt* to attempt to find out about (someone or something) by entering their name into an Internet search engine. [From *Google*®, a popular search engine]
❑ **Google Doc**® *n* a text document that can be edited by different people on a website.

googly /goo'gli/ (*cricket*) *n* an off break bowled with an apparent leg-break action by a right-arm bowler to a right-handed batsman, or conversely for a left-arm bowler; a deceptive question (*fig*). [Ety dubious]
■ **goog'le** *vi* (of a ball) to spin like a googly.

googol /goo'gol/ *n* 1 followed by a hundred zeros, 10^{100}. [Coined by E Kasner (1878–1955), US mathematician]
■ **goo'golplex** *n* 1 followed by a googol of zeros, 10 to the power of a googol.

gook /gook/ (*offensive sl*) *n* someone of Asiatic race, *esp* a Japanese, Korean or Vietnamese soldier; *esp* formerly in Rhodesia, a guerrilla or terrorist; a tramp or anyone considered offensively dirty or stupid. [Origin uncertain]

gool, goold see **gold**[2].

gooly, gooley or **goolie** /goo'li/ *n* a small stone (*Aust inf*); (in *pl*) the testicles (*vulgar sl*). [Perh Hindi *goli* a bullet, ball]

goombah /goom'bä/ or /gūm'bə/ (*N Am sl*) *n* someone who belongs to a criminal gang, *esp* the Mafia; an associate or close friend. [Prob from Ital *compare* a godfather]

goon /goon/ *n* a hired thug (*US sl*); a stupid person. ['Alice the *Goon*', a character created by American cartoonist EC Segar (1894–1938)]

goonda /goon'də/ *n* (in India and Pakistan) a hired thug, *esp* one in the pay of a political party. [Hindi *goonda* a scoundrel]

gooneybird /goo'nē-bûrd/ *n* an (*esp* black-footed) albatross (also **goon'ey**). [Prob dialect, simpleton, from obs *gony*]

goop[1] /goop/ (*sl*) *n* a fool; a fatuous person; a rude, ill-mannered person (*N Am*). [Cf **goof**]
■ **goop'iness** *n*. **goop'y** *adj*.

goop[2] /goop/ (*US sl*) *n* an unpleasantly sticky or gooey substance. [Connected with **goo, glop**, etc; imit]

■ **goop'iness** *n*. **goop'y** *adj*.
■ **gooped up** clogged or stuck up with goop.

goor an alternative spelling of **gur**.

Goorkha an alternative spelling of **Gurkha**.

gooroo an obsolete spelling of **guru**.

goosander /goo-san'dər/ *n* a large duck of the merganser genus. [Perh *goose*, and ON *önd*, pl *ander* duck]

goose /goos/ *n* (pl **geese** /gēs/ or, of a tailor's goose, **goos'es**) any one of a group of birds of the duck family, intermediate between ducks and swans; a domesticated member of the group, descended mainly from the greylag; the female of such a bird (*masc* **gander**); a tailor's smoothing-iron, from the likeness of the handle to the neck of a goose; a stupid, silly person; a prod in the buttocks (*sl*); a game of chance once common in England, in which the players moved counters on a board, with the right to a double move on reaching a picture of a goose (*obs*). ♦ *vt* (*sl*) to hiss off the stage (*theatre*); to prod (someone) between the buttocks from behind; to grab or poke (a male) in the genitals from behind. [OE *gōs* (pl *gēs*); ON *gās*, Ger *Gans*, L *anser* (for *hanser*), Gr *chēn*]
■ **goos'ery** *n* a place for keeping geese; stupidity. **goos'ey** or **goos'y** *n* a goose; a blockhead. ♦ *adj* like a goose; affected with gooseflesh.
❑ **goose-barnacle** see under **barnacle**[1]. **goose bumps** *n pl* (*inf*) gooseflesh. **goose'-cap** *n* (*obs*) a silly person. **goose'-club** *n* (*old*) an association for saving to buy geese for Christmas, or to raffle for a goose. **goose'-egg** *n* the egg of a goose; a swelling on the head due to an injury (*N Am*); a zero score (*US*). **goose'-fish** *n* (*US*) the angler-fish. **goose'flesh** *n* a knobbly, pimply condition of the skin, like that of a plucked goose or other fowl, due to erection of hairs through cold, horror, etc; the bristling feeling in the skin caused by this condition. **goose'-flower** *n* the pelican-flower, a gigantic species of the genus *Aristolochia*. **goose'foot** *n* (pl **goose'foots**) any plant of the genus *Chenopodium* of the beet family, so named because of the shape of the leaf; also applied to any member of the family Chenopodiaceae. **goose'-girl** *n* a girl who herds geese. **goosegog, goosegob** see under **gooseberry**. **goose'-grass** *n* cleavers, a Eurasian plant (*Galium aparine*) with a bristly stem and fruits that cling to clothes, etc; silverweed. **goose'herd** *n* a person who herds geese. **goose'-neck** *n* a hook, bracket, pipe, etc bent like a goose's neck. **goose'-pimples** *n pl* gooseflesh. **goose'-quill** *n* one of the quills or large wing feathers of a goose, *esp* one used as a pen. **goose'-skin** *n* gooseflesh, horripilation. **goose step** *n* (*milit*) a method of marching (resembling a goose's walk) with knees stiff and soles brought flat on the ground. **goose'-step** *vi* (**goose'-stepping**; **goose'-stepped**). **goose'-wing** *n* (*naut*) one of the clews or lower corners of a ship's mainsail or foresail when the middle part is furled or tied up to the yard. **goose'-winged** *adj* (*naut*) having only one clew set; in fore-and-aft rigged vessels, having the mainsail on one side and the foresail on the other, so as to sail wing-and-wing.
■ **the goose that lays the golden eggs** see **golden goose** under **golden**.

gooseberry /gŭz'bə-ri/ or /gūs'-/ *n* the small oval fruit (*usu* green) of the **goose'berry-bush** (*Ribes grossularia*), a prickly shrub of the family Grossulariaceae; a fermented effervescing drink (in full **goose'berry-wine**) made from gooseberries; an imitation champagne (*joc*); an unwanted third person in the company of a couple or group of couples, *esp* in the phrase *play gooseberry*. [Perh **goose** and **berry**[1]; or *goose* may be from MHGer *krus* (Gr *kraus* crisp, curled); cf OFr *groisele, grosele* gooseberry, Scot *grossart*]
❑ **goose'berry-caterpillar** *n* a creamy looper with orange spots and black dots, feeding on gooseberry leaves, the larva of the **goose'berry-moth** or magpie moth (*Abraxas grossulariata*), a yellow-bodied moth with black-spotted white wings. **gooseberry-fool'** see **fool**[2]. **goose'berry-stone** *n* grossular, a mineral of the garnet group. **goose'gog** or **goose'gob** *n* (*inf* and *dialect*) a gooseberry.
■ **Cape gooseberry** or **gooseberry tomato** see under **cape**[2]. **Chinese gooseberry** a subtropical vine (*Actinidia chinensis*) with brown, hairy, edible fruit, the kiwi fruit. **Coromandel gooseberry** carambola (qv).

GOP (*inf*) *abbrev*: Grand Old Party, the US Republican party.

gopak /gō'pak/ *n* a high-leaping folk dance from the Ukraine, traditionally performed by men. [From Russ]

gopher[1] /gō'fər/ *n* a name applied to various burrowing animals, including the pouched rat, the ground squirrel, the land tortoise of the southern USA, and a burrowing snake (*N Am*); (with *cap*) a browsing facility based on menus (*comput*). ♦ *vi* to burrow; to mine in a small way. [Perh Fr *gaufre* honeycomb]

gopher[2] /gō'fər/ *n* a kind of wood, generally supposed to be cypress (*Bible*); yellow-wood (*Cladrastis lutea*) (*US*). [Heb]

gopher[3] see **gofer**[2].

gopik /gō'pik/ *n* (pl **go'pik** or **go'piks**) a monetary unit of Azerbaijan, $\frac{1}{100}$ of a manat.

gopura /gō'poo-rə/ or **gopuram** /gō'poo-rəm/ n in S India, a pyramidal tower over the gateway of a temple. [Sans *gopura*]

gora /gō'rə/ n (*Ind*) a white male. [Hindi]

goral /gō'rəl/ or /gō'rəl/ n a Himalayan goat-antelope. [Hindi]

goramy see **gourami**.

gorblimey or **gorblimy** /gör-blī'mi/ (*Cockney*) *interj* expressing surprise. ◆ *adj* loud, coarse, vulgar; relating to the common people. ◆ *n* a type of flat army cap. [Altered from *God blind me*]

gorcock /gör'kok/ n the red grouse cock. [Origin obscure]

gorcrow /gör'krō/ (*dialect*) n the carrion crow. [OE *gor* filth, and **crow**]

Gordian /gör'dyən/ or /gör'di-ən/ *adj* relating to or associated with *Gordium* the capital, or *Gordius* the king, of ancient Phrygia, or to the intricate knot he tied which could not be untied; intricate; difficult. ◆ *vt* (*Keats*) to tie up, knot.
   ■ **Gor'dius** n a genus of hairworms.
   ■ **cut the Gordian knot** to overcome a difficulty by violent measures, as Alexander the Great cut the Gordian knot with his sword.

Gordon Bennett /gör'dən ben'it/ *interj* expressing mild surprise, annoyance, etc. [Prob from James *Gordon Bennett* (1841–1918), US journalist]

Gordon setter /gör'dən set'ər/ n an (*orig*) Scottish breed of setter with a black-and-tan coat. [Alexander *Gordon* (1743–1827), Scottish nobleman]

gore[1] /gōr/ or /gör/ n clotted blood; blood; filth (*obs*). [OE *gor* filth, dung; ON *gor* cud, slime]
   ■ **gor'ily** *adv.* **gor'iness** n. **gor'y** *adj* (**gor'ier**; **gor'iest**) involving bloodshed, bloody; like gore; covered with gore; distasteful, as in *the gory details*.
   □ **gore'-blood** n (*Spenser*). **gory dew** n a dark-red slimy film sometimes seen on damp walls, etc, a simple form of vegetable life (*Porphyridium cruentum*).

gore[2] /gōr/ or /gör/ n a triangular piece of land (now *dialect*); a triangular piece let into a garment to widen it; a sector of a curved surface; a sector-like section of a parachute canopy; a skirt (*obs*). ◆ *vt* to shape like or provide with gores; to pierce with anything pointed, such as a spear or horn. [OE *gāra* a pointed triangular piece of land, and *gār* a spear]
   ■ **gored** *adj* made with gores. **gor'ing** n an angular, tapering or obliquely cut piece. ◆ *adj* forming a gore.

Gore-Tex® /gör'teks/ n a water-repellent synthetic fibre which allows air and moisture to permeate out through its pores.

gorge /görj/ n the throat; a deep narrow valley; the entrance to an outwork (*fortif*); a hawk's crop; the stomach, or its contents; a gluttonous feed; a fish-catching device, to be swallowed by the fish. ◆ *vt* to swallow greedily; to glut. ◆ *vi* to feed gluttonously. [OFr]
   ■ **gorged** *adj* having a gorge or throat; glutted; having a crown or coronet around the neck (*heraldry*).
   ■ **heave the gorge** to retch. **one's gorge rises** one is filled with loathing or revulsion (with *at*).

gorgeous /gör'jəs/ *adj* showy; splendid; magnificent; (*loosely*) pleasant, good, beautiful, etc. [OFr *gorgias* gaudy]
   ■ **gor'geously** *adv.* **gor'geousness** n.

gorgerin /gör'jə-rin/ (*archit*) n same as **necking** (see under **neck**). [Fr, from *gorge* throat]

gorget /gör'jit/ n (*hist*) a piece of armour for the throat; a wimple; a neck ornament. [OFr, from *gorge* throat]
   □ **gorget patch** n a patch on the collar of a military uniform.

gorgia /gör'jə/ n an improvised virtuoso passage in 16c and 17c singing. [Obs Ital *gorgia* throat]

gorgio /gör'jō/ or /gör'ji-ō/, also **gajo** /gö'jō/ n (pl **gor'gios** or **ga'jos**) a gypsy word for a non-gypsy. [Romany]

Gorgon /gör'gən/ n one of three female winged monsters (Stheno, Euryale and Medusa), with horrible and petrifying faces and hissing serpents for hair (*Gr myth*); (*usu* without *cap*) anybody, *esp* a woman, who is very ugly or formidable. ◆ *adj* of, relating to or resembling a Gorgon; (without *cap*) very ugly or formidable. [Gr *Gorgō*, pl *-ones*, from *gorgos* grim]
   ■ **gorgoneion** /-ī'on/ n (pl **gorgonei'a**) a mask of a gorgon. **gorgō'nian** *adj.* **gor'gonize** or **-ise** *vt* to turn to stone.

Gorgonia /gör-gō'ni-ə/ n a genus of sea fans or horny corals. [L *gorgonia* coral, from *Gorgō* Gorgon (because of its appearance after petrifying in the air)]
   ■ **gorgo'nian** *adj* of or relating to this genus. ◆ *n* a horny coral.

Gorgonzola /gör-gən-zō'lə/ n a blue-veined cheese made from cow's milk. [From *Gorgonzola*, a small Italian town near Milan]

gori /gō'ri/ n (*Ind*) a white female. [Hindi]

gorilla /go-ril'ə/ n a great African ape, the largest anthropoid; a heavily built thug (*sl*). [Gr *Gorillai* (pl), reported by Hanno the Carthaginian as a tribe of hairy women; supposed to be an Afr word]
   ■ **gorill'ian** or **gorill'ine** *adj.* **gorill'oid** *adj.*

goring see under **gore**[2].

gorm see **gaum**[1,2].

gormand /gör'mənd/ n older form of **gourmand**.
   ■ **gor'mandise** /-dīz/ n gourmandise; gluttony; gormandizing. **gor'mandism** n gluttony. **gor'mandize** or **-ise** *vi* to eat hastily or voraciously. **gor'mandīzer** or **-s-** n. **gor'mandizing** or **-s-** n.

gormless see under **gaum**[2].

gormy see under **gaum**[1].

gorp[1] /görp/ (*N Am*) n a mixture of raisins, nuts, etc providing a high-energy snack for eg hikers. [Origin uncertain]

gorp[2] a variant (*dialect*) spelling of **gawp**.

gorse /görs/ n any prickly papilionaceous shrub of the genus *Ulex*, with yellow flowers (also (*Shakesp*) **gosse**). [OE *gorst*]
   ■ **gors'y** *adj.*

gorsedd /gör'sedh/ n (often with *cap*) a meeting of bards and druids, *esp* such an assembly prior to an eisteddfod. [Welsh, throne]

gorsoon see **gossoon**.

gory see under **gore**[1].

gosh /gosh/ (*inf*) *interj* a mild substitute or euphemism for God.

goshawk /gos'hök/ n a short-winged hawk (*Accipiter gentilis*), once used for hunting wild geese and other fowl and still used in falconry; any of various related hawks. [OE *gōshafoc*, from *gōs* goose, and *hafoc* hawk]

Goshen /gō'shən/ n a happy place of light and plenty. [From the abode of the Israelites during the plague of darkness in Egypt in Bible, Exodus 8.22]

gosht /gosht/ (*Ind* cookery) n meat. [Hindi and Urdu]

goslarite /gos'lə-rīt/ n a rare mineral, hydrated zinc sulphate, found at *Goslar* in the Harz Mountains, central Germany.

gosling /goz'ling/ n a young goose. [OE *gōs* goose, with double dimin *-l-ing*]
   ■ **gos'let** n a pygmy goose (qv).

gospel /gos'pəl/ n the teaching of Christ; a narrative of the life of Christ, *esp* one of those included in the New Testament, Matthew, Mark, Luke and John; the principles laid down in these gospels; the stated portion of these read at a religious service; any strongly advocated principle or system; absolute truth (*inf*); a type of ardently religious music developed from the spirituals of black Americans of the Southern states. ◆ *vt* (*Shakesp*) to instruct in the gospel. [OE *godspel(l)*, a transl of L *evangelium*, from *gōd* good (with shortened vowel being understood as *God* God) and *spel(l)* story]
   ■ **gos'pelize** or **-ise**, also **gos'pellize** or **-ise** *vt* to evangelize (*rare*); to square with the gospel (*obs*). **gos'peller** n a preacher; an evangelist; a Wycliffite, Protestant or Puritan (often in derision; *hist*); a person who reads the gospel in church.
   □ **gospel side** n the north side or gospeller's side of the altar, *opp* to *epistle side*.

Gosplan /gos'plan/ n the former Soviet state economic planning department. [Russ, *Gos*udarstvennaya *Plan*ovaya Comissiya, state planning committee]

gospodar see **hospodar**.

Goss /gos/ (*antiques*) n white china vessels and trinkets bearing the crest of a town, etc, sold as holiday mementos. [WH *Goss* (1833–1906), manufacturer, of Stoke-on-Trent]

goss /gos/ n and vi an informal short form of **gossip**.

gossamer /gos'ə-mər/ n very fine spider-threads that float in the air or form webs on bushes in fine weather; any very thin material. ◆ *adj* light, flimsy. [ME *gossomer*; perh *goose-summer* a St Martin's summer, when geese are in season and gossamer abounds; cf Ger *Sommerfäden* summer-threads, also *Mädchensommer* maiden-summer]
   ■ **goss'amery** *adj* like gossamer; flimsy.

gossan or **gozzan** /gos'ən/ n decomposed rock, largely quartz impregnated with iron compounds, at the outcrop of a vein *esp* of metallic sulphides. [Cornish miner's term; origin unknown]

gosse /gos/ (*Shakesp*) n obsolete spelling of **gorse**.

gossip /gos'ip/ n idle chat; tittle-tattle; scandalous rumours; easy familiar writing; someone who goes about telling and hearing news, or idle, malicious and scandalous tales; a familiar friend (*archaic*; *Spenser* **goss'ib**); a woman friend who comes to attend a birth (*archaic*); a sponsor at baptism (in relation to child, parent, or other sponsor) (*archaic* or *dialect*). ◆ *vi* (pat **goss'iped**) to run about telling idle or malicious tales; to talk a lot, prattle; to chat. ◆ *vt* to tell or spread as gossip; to stand godfather or gossip to (*obs*; *Shakesp* and *Milton*). [OE *godsibb* godfather, one who is *sib* in *God*, ie spiritually related] ■ **goss′iping** *n* and *adj*. **goss′ipry** *n*. **goss′ipy** *adj*. ❏ **gossip column** *n* the newspaper column written by a gossip-writer. **gossip columnist** *n*. **gossip mill** *n* a place or institution where gossip is continually created and circulated. **goss′ip-monger** *n* a person who spreads gossip and rumours. **goss′ip-writer** *n* a journalist who writes articles about the lives and loves of well-known people.

gossoon /*go-soon*′/ or **gorsoon** /*gör*′/ *n* a boy or boy-servant. [Anglo-Irish, from Fr *garçon* boy]

Gossypium /*go-sip′i-əm*/ *n* a tropical genus of the mallow family, yielding cotton. [L *gossypion*] ■ **goss′ypine** *adj* cottony. **goss′ypol** *n* a poisonous substance in cottonseed.

got see **get**.

gotcha /*got′chə*/ (*inf*) *interj* expressing pleasure at having tricked or surprised someone. [Short form of *I've got you*]

Goth /*goth*/ *n* a member of an ancient Germanic people, originally settled on the southern coasts of the Baltic, migrating to Dacia in the 3c, and later founding kingdoms in Italy, S France and Spain; a rude or uncivilized person, a barbarian; a Gothicist (*hist*); (also **goth**) a performer or fan of Gothic music, or the style of music itself. [The native names *Gutans* (sing *Guta*) and *Gutōs* (sing *Guts*), and *Gutthiuda* people of the Goths; Latinized as *Gothī, Gotthī*; Gr *Gothoi, Gotthoi*; OE *Gotan* (sing *Gota*)] ■ **Goth′ic** *adj* of the Goths or their language; barbarous; romantic; denoting the 12c–16c style of architecture in churches, etc, with high-pointed arches, clustered columns, etc (*orig* applied in reproach at the time of the Renaissance); generally, the style, related to this, favoured in all the fine arts during this time; black-letter (*printing*); a square-cut type without serifs (*US*); *orig* applied to 18c tales or novels of mystery with gloomy sinister backgrounds, now denoting psychological horror-tales (also **Goth′ick** or **goth′ic**); lurid, extravagantly macabre, grotesque (*sl*); (of a music and fashion trend originating in the late 1980s) characterized by a blend of punk and heavy metal styles, dark melancholy themes, severe black dress and white make-up. ◆ *n* the language of the Goths, an East Germanic tongue; Gothic architecture or literature; Gothic lettering. **Goth′ically** *adv*. **Goth′icism** /-*sizm*/ *n* a Gothic idiom or style of building; rudeness of manners. **Goth′icist** *n* an adherent or scholar of Gothic style or idiom. **goth′icize** or **-ise** /-*sīz*/ *vt* to make Gothic. **Goth′ick** *n* and *adj* (denoting) a style of architecture (c.1720–1840) in which the Gothic style of the Middle Ages was imitated; (of 18c and modern tales, etc) Gothic. **goth′y** *adj* relating to Gothic music or fashion. ❏ **Gothic revival** *n* the more serious revival of the Gothic style of architecture which followed the Gothick, in Britain and the USA from mid-18c to mid-19c.

Gothamite /*gōt*′ or *got′ə-mīt*/ *n* a simpleton; a wiseacre; /*goth*′ or *gōth*′/ a New Yorker (*US*). [From *Gotham*, a village in Nottinghamshire, with which name are connected many of the simpleton stories of immemorial antiquity] ■ **Goth′amist** *n* (*obs*) /*gōt*′ or *got*′/ a simpleton.

Gothic, Gothicism, Gothick, etc see under **Goth**.

göthite see **goethite**.

gothy see under **Goth**.

gotta /*got′ə*/ (*inf*) a contraction of **got to** and **got a**.

gotten see **get**.

Götterdämmerung /*gœ-tər-dem′ə-rŭng*/ (*Ger myth*) *n* the ultimate defeat of the gods by evil, literally the twilight of the gods.

gouache /*goo-äsh* or *goo′äsh*, or (chiefly N Am) *gwäsh*/ *n* watercolour painting with opaque colours, mixed with water, honey and gum, presenting a matt surface; work painted according to this method; watercolour paint made opaque in such a way. [Fr]

gouch /*gowch*/ (*sl*) *vi* (often with *out*) to enter a state of torpor, *esp* under the influence of a narcotic drug. [Ety unknown]

Gouda /*gow′də*/ *n* a kind of mild cheese *orig* from *Gouda* in the Netherlands.

gouge¹ /*gowj*, also *gooj*/ *n* a chisel with a hollow blade for cutting grooves or holes; an indentation or hole made by gouging. ◆ *vt* to scoop out, as with a gouge; to force out (eg the eye with the thumb); to swindle (*N Am inf*). [OFr, from LL *gubia* a kind of chisel]

gouge² /*gooj*/ (*obs*; *Walter Scott*) *n* a wench. [OFr]

gougère /*goo-jer*′/ *n* a kind of choux pastry, the dough of which has been mixed with grated cheese prior to baking. [Fr]

goujeers /*goo-jērz*′/ *n* an emendation of some Shakespearean editors, supposedly meaning 'venereal disease'. [From spurious Fr *goujère*]

goujons /*goo-zhŏ*′/ *n pl* small strips of fish or meat coated in flour and deep-fried. [Fr]

gouk see **gowk**.

goulash /*goo′lash*/ *n* a stew of beef, vegetables, *esp* onions, and paprika; a re-deal of cards that have been arranged in suits and order of value, so many (as eg five) cards at a time (*bridge*). [Hung *gulyás* (*hús*) herdsman (meat)]

goura /*gö′rə* or *gow′rə*/ *n* (with *cap*) a New Guinea genus of beautifully crested, ground-loving pigeons; a pigeon of the genus. [From a native name]

gourami /*goor-äm′i*/ *n* (also **goram′y, guram′i**) a large freshwater food-fish (*Osphronemus olfax*) of SE Asia; any of a variety of often colourful, smaller fishes, popular as aquarium fishes. [Malay *gurāmī*]

gourd /*goord, görd* or *görd*/ *n* a large hard-rinded fleshy fruit characteristic of the cucumber family; the rind of one used as a bottle, cup, etc; a gourd-bearing plant. [OFr *gourde*, contracted from *cougourde*, from L *cucurbita* a gourd] ❏ **gourd′-worm** *n* a fluke-worm resembling a gourd-seed, *esp* the liver fluke.

gourde /*goord*/ *n* the standard monetary unit of Haiti (100 centimes). [Fr fem of *gourd*, from L *gurdus* dull, stupid]

gourds /*gördz, gördz* or *goordz*/ (*obs*) *n pl* a kind of false dice. [Cf OFr *gourd* swindle]

gourdy /*gör′di*, also *gör′di* or *goor′di*/ *adj* (of a horse) swollen in the legs. [OFr *gourdi* swollen] ■ **gourd′iness** *n*.

gourmand /*goor′mənd* or *-mä*/ *n* a person who eats greedily; a glutton; a lover of good fare. ◆ *adj* voracious; gluttonous. [Fr; cf **gormand**] ■ **gourmandise** /*goor′man-dīz* or *goor-mä-dēz*/ *n* indulgence in good eating; a discerning appreciation of good food and wines; voracious greed (*Spenser*). **gour′mandism** *n*.

gourmet /*goor′mä* or *-me*/ *n* a connoisseur of good food and wines, an epicure. ◆ *adj* of, for or befitting the gourmet or the gourmet's taste. [Fr, a wine merchant's assistant]

goustrous /*gow′strəs*/ (*Scot*) *adj* boisterous, rude.

gousty /*gow′sti*/ (*Scot*) *adj* dreary; desolate; empty.

gout¹ /*gowt*/ *n* a disease in which excess of uric acid in the blood is deposited as urates in the joints, etc, with swelling *esp* of the big toe; a related disease of poultry affecting the viscera; a swelling of the stalk in wheat and other grasses, caused by goutfly larvae; a drop, spot (*archaic*). [OFr *goutte*, from L *gutta* a drop, the disease once supposed to be caused by a defluxion of humours] ■ **gout′iness** *n*. **gout′y** *adj* relating to gout; diseased with or subject to gout. ❏ **gout′fly** *n* a fly (genus *Chlorops*) whose larvae cause gout by boring in wheat, etc. **gout′weed** or **gout′wort** *n* an umbelliferous weed (*Aegopodium podagraria*), long supposed to be good for gout, also called **bish′op(′s)weed** or **goat′weed**.

gout² or properly **goût** /*goo*/ *n* taste; relish. [Fr *goût*, from L *gustus* taste]

goutte /*goot*/ (*Fr*) *n* a drop (of liquid); a droplet shape (*heraldry*). ■ **goutte à goutte** drop by drop.

gouvernante /*goo-ver-nät*′/ (*Fr*) *n* a female ruler (*obs*); a housekeeper (*archaic*); a duenna (*archaic*); a governess (*archaic*).

Gov. *abbrev*: Governor; (also **Govt.**) Government.

gov see **governor** under **govern**.

govern /*guv′ərn*/ *vt* to direct; to control; to rule with authority; to determine; to determine the case of (*grammar*); to require as the case of a noun or pronoun (*grammar*). ◆ *vi* to exercise authority; to administer the laws. [OFr *governer*, from L *gubernāre*, from Gr *kybernaein* to steer] ■ **governabil′ity** *n*. **gov′ernable** *adj*. **gov′ernall** *n* (*Spenser*) government, management. **gov′ernance** *n* government; control; direction; behaviour (*obs*). **gov′ernante** *n* (*obs*) a gouvernante. **gov′erness** *n* a woman entrusted with the care and education of a child or children, *esp* one employed in a private household (**nursery governess** one having charge of young children only, tending as well as teaching them); a female governor (*archaic*; *fig, Milton*). ◆ *vi* to act as governess. ◆ *vt* to be governess to. **gov′ernessy** *adj* like a governess, *esp* prim. **gov′erning** *adj* having control. **government** /*guv′ər(n)-mənt*/ *n* a ruling or managing; control; a system of governing; the body of persons authorized to administer the laws, or to govern a state (often with *cap*, *esp* if applied to that of a specific country); tenure of office of someone who governs; an administrative division (*archaic*); territory (*archaic*); the power of one word in determining the case of another (*grammar*); conduct (*Shakesp*). ◆ *adj* of or pursued by government. **governmental** /-*ment′l*/ *adj* relating to government. **government′ally** *adv*. **gov′ernor** *n* a real or titular ruler, *esp* of a state, province or colony; the head of an institution or a member of its ruling body; the commander of a fortress; (usu /*guv′nər*/) a father, chief or master, applied more generally in kindly, *usu* ironically respectful, address (sometimes shortened to **gov** or **guv** /guv/; sl); a regulator, or device for maintaining uniform velocity with a varying resistance (machinery); a tutor (obs); a pilot (of a vessel) (obs; Bible). **gov'ernorate** n. **gov'ernorship** n.

◻ **governess car** or **cart** n (hist) a light low two-wheeled vehicle with face-to-face seats at the sides. **governing body** n a board in whom is vested the authority to supervise and regulate the affairs of an establishment or of a particular field of activity. **governmental atonement** see under **Grotian**. **government broker** n a stockbroker who buys and sells gilt-edged securities on the Stock Exchange on behalf of the Bank of England. **government expenditure** n that part of public expenditure incurred by central government (as opposed to local government authorities and non-government public offices). **government paper** n savings bonds and other such certificates issued by the government. **government securities** n pl government paper (see above). **government stock** n consols, savings bonds and other gilt-edged securities. **governor-gen'eral** n (pl **governors-gen'eral**) orig the supreme governor of a country, etc, with deputy governors under him; the representative of the British Crown in Commonwealth countries which recognize the monarch as head of state. **governor-gen'eralship** n.

Govt. see **Gov.**

gowan /gow'ən/ (Scot and N Eng dialect) n the wild daisy; the ox-eye daisy (also **horse'-gowan**). [Appar a form of **gollan(d)**]
■ **gow'aned** adj. **gow'any** adj.
■ **luck'engowan** the globeflower.

gowd, **gowdspink** Scots form of **gold¹**, **goldspink**.

gowf /gowf/ (Scot) vt to strike, cuff. ◆ vi to play golf. ◆ n golf. [See **golf**]
■ **gowf'er** n a golfer.
◻ **gowf'-ba'** n a golf-ball.

gowk or **gouk** /gowk/ (Scot and N Eng dialect) n a cuckoo; a fool; an April fool. [ON gaukr; OE gēac]

gowl /gowl/ (Scot and N Eng dialect) vi to cry or howl. [ON gaula]

gowlan(d) see **gollan**.

gown /gown/ n a loose flowing outer garment; a woman's long formal dress; an academic, clerical or official robe; the members of a university as opposed to the townspeople (see under **town**). ◆ vt and vi to dress in a gown. ◆ vt to invest or provide with a gown. [OFr goune, from LL gunna; origin unknown]
■ **gowned** adj.
◻ **gown'boy** n a school foundationer (as of Charterhouse), wearing a gown. **gown'man** or **gowns'man** n someone who wears a gown, eg a cleric or lawyer, or esp a member of an English university; a civilian (as distinct from a soldier) (hist).

gowpen /gow'pən/ (Scot) n the hollow of the two hands held together; a double handful (now usu used in pl). [ON gaupn]
■ **gow'penful** n (pl **gow'penfuls**).

goy /goi/ (sl) n (pl **goy'im** /goi'im/ or **goys**) a Jewish word for a non-Jew, a Gentile. [Heb, (non-Jewish) nation]
■ **goy'ish** or **goyisch** /goi'ish/ adj.

goyle /goil/ (SW Eng dialect) n a ravine. [Cf **gill³**]

gozzan see **gossan**.

GP abbrev : Gallup Poll; General Practitioner; Gloria Patri (L), glory to the Father; graduated pension; Grand Prix.

GPA (US educ) abbrev : grade point average.

GPI abbrev : general paralysis of the insane.

GPL (comput) abbrev : General Public Licence.

GPMU abbrev : Graphical, Paper and Media Union.

GPO abbrev : (until 1969) General Post Office, the UK postal service.

GPRS abbrev : General Packet Radio Service, an advanced packet-switching system.

GPS abbrev : Global Positioning System.

GR abbrev : Georgius Rex (L) (see **GRI**); Greece (IVR).

Gr. abbrev : Greek.

gr. abbrev : grain(s); gram(s) or gramme(s); grey; gross.

Graafian /grä'fi-ən/ adj relating to or associated with the Dutch anatomist Regnier de Graaf (1641–73) who discovered the **Graafian follicles** in which the ova are contained in the ovaries of higher vertebrates.

graal see **grail¹**.

grab¹ /grab/ vt (**grabb'ing**; **grabbed**) to seize or grasp suddenly; to lay hands on; to impress or interest (sl). ◆ vi to clutch (usu with at). ◆ n a sudden grasp or clutch; unscrupulous seizure; a mechanical double scoop hinged like a pair of jaws, used in excavating, etc; anything similar; a simple card game depending upon prompt claiming. [Cf Swed grabba to grasp]

■ **grabb'er** n a person who or thing which grabs; an avaricious person. **grabb'y** adj (N Am inf) greedy, grasping.
◻ **grab'-bag** n a bag or other receptacle for miscellaneous articles; a bag from which gifts are drawn (US; also fig). **grabbing crane** n an excavator consisting of a crane and a large grab, so hinged as to scoop into the earth as it is lifted. **grab handle** n a fixed handle in a passenger vehicle, used for keeping one's balance; a handle fixed to the side of a bathtub, etc to help with getting out.
■ **how does that grab you?** (sl) what's your reaction to that? **up for grabs** (sl) (ready) for the taking, for sale, etc.

grab² /grab/ n an Eastern coasting vessel. [Ar ghurāb]

grabble /grab'l/ vt and vi to grope; to scramble; to struggle with (somebody or something). [Frequentative of **grab¹**]
■ **grabb'ler** n.

graben /grä'bən/ (geol) n a rift valley (qv under **rift¹**). [Ger, ditch]

GRACE /grās/ (telecom) abbrev : group routing and charging equipment (an automatic telephone system by which all calls, trunk as well as local, can be dialled directly by subscribers, and by which all STD calls are charged).

grace /grās/ n easy elegance in form or manner; any unassumingly attractive or pleasing personal quality; favour; kindness, good will; pardon (archaic); the undeserved mercy of God; divine influence; the state of the soul freed from sin and assured of eternal life (theol); a short prayer of thanks before or after a meal; an ornament (eg trill, turn, acciaccatura) consisting of notes additional to the melody or harmony (music); an act or decree of the governing body of an English university; a ceremonious title in addressing a duke or duchess, an archbishop, or formerly a king or queen (usu with cap, as Your Grace, His/Her Grace); a short period of time in hand before a deadline is reached (see **days of grace** below); (in pl) favour, friendship (with good); (with cap in pl) the three sister goddesses in whom beauty was deified (the Greek Charites), Aglaia, Euphrosyne and Thalia (classical myth). ◆ vt to mark with favour; to adorn. [Fr grâce, from L grātia favour, from grātus agreeable]
■ **graced** adj (Shakesp, etc) favoured, endowed with grace or graces, virtuous, chaste. **grace'ful** adj elegant and easy; marked by propriety or fitness, becoming; having or conferring grace, in any sense. **grace'fully** adv. **grace'fulness** n. **grace'less** adj lacking grace or excellence; without mercy or favour (obs); depraved (archaic); indecorous. **grace'lessly** adv. **grace'lessness** n.
◻ **grace-and-fa'vour** adj (of a residence) belonging to the British sovereign and granted rent-free to a person of importance (also with caps). **grace cup** n a cup or health drunk at the end of a feast or meal, after the final grace. **grace note** n (music) a note introduced as an embellishment, not being essential to the harmony or melody.
■ **airs and graces** affectedly elegant and refined manners and behaviour. **days of grace** days allowed for the payment of a note or bill of exchange after it falls due (in England before 1972 legally three days); such an allowable period after which an insurance premium becomes due. **fall from grace** to backslide, to lapse from the state of grace and salvation, or from favour. **saving grace** divine grace so bestowed as to lead to salvation (theol); a compensating virtue or quality (inf). **take heart of grace** (archaic) to pluck up courage (origin of 'of grace' uncertain). **with** (a) **good** (or **bad**) **grace** in amiable (or ungracious) fashion. **year of grace** year of the Christian era, AD.

grâce à Dieu /gräs a dyœ'/ (Fr) thanks to God.

gracile /gras'īl or -il/ adj slender; gracefully slight in form. [L gracilis slender]
■ **gracil'ity** n the quality of being gracefully slender; (of literary style) simplicity.

graciosity see under **gracious**.

gracioso /grä-shi-ō'sō or (Sp) grä-thyō'sō/ n (pl **graciō'sos**) a clown in Spanish comedy; a favourite (obs). [Sp, amusing]

gracious /grā'shəs/ adj full of, or characterized by, grace and kindness; affable; of becoming demeanour; used as an epithet of royal acts or inclination; elegant, tasteful, esp classically so; favourable (archaic); acceptable (obs); proceeding from divine favour (obs). ◆ interj used as a substitute for **God**. [L grātiōsus, from grātia favour]
■ **grā'ciously** adv. **grā'ciousness** or **gracios'ity** n.
◻ **gracious living** n (living in) conditions of ease, plenty, and good taste.
■ **good gracious**, **goodness gracious** (**me**) or **gracious me** exclamations of surprise.

grackle or (rare) **grakle** /grak'l/ n a myna (hill myna) or similar bird; any of various American birds of the family Icteridae, the males of which have iridescent black plumage. [L grāculus jackdaw]

grad /grad/ (inf) n a graduate.

gradate, etc see under **grade**.

■ words derived from main entry word; ◻ compound words; ■ idioms and phrasal verbs

graddan /grad'ən/ (*Scot*) *n* parched grain. ◆ *vt* to parch in the husk. [Gaelic *gradan*]

grade /grād/ *n* a degree or step in quality, rank or dignity; a stage of advancement; a rank; a yearly stage in education (*N Am*); a pupil's mark of proficiency (*orig US*); (in *pl*, with *the*) elementary school, grade school (*N Am*); a position in a scale; a class, or position in a class, according to value, merit, quality; a position in an ablaut series (*philology*); one-hundredth part of a right angle (*maths*); a gradient or slope (chiefly *US*); an inclined or level stretch of road or railway (*US*); a class of animals produced by crossing a breed with one purer; a group of animals of a similar evolutionary stage (*zool*). ◆ *vt* to arrange according to grade; to assign a grade to; to adjust the gradients of; to cross a breed of animal with one purer. ◆ *vi* to change gradually from one grade, level, value, etc to another; (of produce, etc) to take or fall within a (specified) grade (sometimes with *out*). ◆ *adj* of improved stock. [L *gradus* a step, from *gradī* to step]
■ **grādabil'ity** *n*. **grā'dable** *adj* able to be graded; of or relating to a word that can be modified or used in the comparative or superlative (*linguistics*; also *n*). **gradate** /grə-dāt'/ *vt* and *vi* to shade off, change grade, values, etc imperceptibly. ◆ *vt* to arrange according to grades. **gradā'tim** /gra-dā'tim/ *adv* (*L*) step by step. **gradā'tion** *n* a degree or step; a rising step by step; progress from one degree or state to another; a position attained; the state of being arranged in ranks; a gradual shift in grade, etc; a diatonic succession of chords (*music*); a gradual shading off; ablaut (*philology*). **gradā'tional** *adj*. **gradā'tionally** *adv*. **gradā'tioned** *adj* formed by gradations or stages. **gradatory** /grad'ət-ə-ri/ *adj* proceeding step by step; adapted for walking. **grād'er** *n* a person who, or thing which, grades; a machine used to create a flat surface for road-building; (in combination, as eg *sixthgrader*) a school pupil in a specified grade (*N Am*). **grād'ing** *n* a process of assigning grades; the grade assigned.
❑ **grade crossing** *n* (*N Am*) a level crossing. **graded-index fibre** *n* a fibre in an optical-fibre cable, in which the refractive index of the glass decreases gradually or in small steps from the central core to the periphery. **graded post** *n* (in British schools) a post with some special responsibility, and so extra payment. **grade school** *n* (*N Am*) an elementary school corresponding broadly to the British primary school, often with a nursery school element. **grade separation** *n* (*US*) a crossing at which one road, etc, is an underpass or an overpass. **grading system** *n* a system to establish the rate at which an employee will be paid on a company's incremental pay scales (taking eg qualifications, experience and age into account).
■ **at grade** (*US*) on the same level. **make the grade** *orig* to succeed in climbing a steep hill; to overcome obstacles; to succeed; to be up to standard.

gradely /grād'li/, also **graithly** /grāth'-/ (*dialect*) *adj* decent; proper; fit; fine. ◆ *adv* properly; readily (*obs*); very. [See **graith**]

Gradgrind /grad'grīnd/ *n* a person who regulates all human things by rule and compass and the mechanical application of statistics, allowing nothing for sentiment, emotion and individuality. [From Thomas *Gradgrind* in Dickens's *Hard Times*]
■ **Gradgrind'ery** *n*.

gradient /grā'di-ənt/ *n* the degree of slope as compared with the horizontal; the slope of a line or the slope of a tangent to a curve at any point (*maths*); rate of change in any quantity with distance (eg in barometer readings); an incline. ◆ *adj* rising or falling by degrees; walking, taking steps with the feet; sloping uniformly. [L *gradiens, -entis*, prp of *gradī* to step]
■ **grād'ienter** *n* (*US; surveying*) an instrument for determining grades.

gradin /grā'din/ or **gradine** /grə-dēn'/ *n* a rising tier of seats, as in an amphitheatre; a raised step or ledge behind an altar. [Ital *gradino*, dimin of *grado* step]
■ **gradino** /grə-dēn'o/ *n* (*pl* **gradin'i** /-dēn'ē/) (*Ital*) a decoration for an altar gradin.

gradiometer /grā-di-om'ə-tər/ *n* a magnetometer for measuring the gradient of a magnetic field, etc. [*gradient* and **-meter**]

gradual /grad'ū-əl/ *adj* advancing or happening by grades or degrees; (of a slope) gentle, not steep. ◆ *n* (in the Roman Catholic Church) the portion of the mass between the epistle and the gospel, formerly always sung from the steps of the altar; a book containing the sung parts of the mass, also called a **grail**. [Med L *graduālis*, from L *gradus* a step]
■ **grad'ūalism** *n* the principle, policy or phenomenon of proceeding by degrees. **grad'ūalist** *adj* and *n*. **gradualis'tic** *adj*. **gradual'ity** or **grad'ūalness** *n*. **grad'ūally** *adv*.

graduate /grad'ū-āt/ *vt* to divide into regular intervals; to mark by degrees; to proportion; to confer a university, etc degree upon (chiefly *N Am*). ◆ *vi* to pass by grades; to receive a degree from a higher-education institution; to receive a diploma on completing high school (*N Am*). ◆ *n* /grad'ū-ət/ a person who has obtained a degree from a university or college; a person who has completed a course in any educational or training institution (*N Am*). [Med L *graduāri, -ātus* to take a degree, from *gradus* a step]
■ **grad'ūand** *n* a person about to receive a degree from a higher-education institution. **grad'ūated** *adj* (of a thermometer, etc) marked with degrees. **grad'ūateship** *n*. **graduā'tion** *n* division into proportionate or regular sections, for measurement, etc; a mark or all the marks made for this purpose; the gaining or conferring of a degree from a higher-education institution or (*N Am*) high school; the ceremony marking this. **grad'ūator** *n* an instrument for dividing lines at regular intervals; someone who or something which graduates.
❑ **graduated pension scheme** *n* a government pension scheme in addition to the basic old age pension, to which employees make contributions in relation to their earnings, and employers contribute corresponding sums. **graduate school** *n* (*orig* in the USA) a university department for advanced study for graduates.

gradus /grā'dəs/ *n* a dictionary of Greek or Latin with marks showing the quantity of each syllable. [L, from the phrase *Gradus ad Parnassum* a step towards Parnassus (home of the Muses)]

Graeae or **Graiae** /grī'ī/ (*Gr myth*) *n pl* three sea-goddesses, sisters of the Gorgons, having the form of old women who shared between them a single eye and a single tooth. [Gr *graia* old woman]

Graecize or **-ise**, or (*esp N Am*) **Grecize** /grē'sīz/ *vt* to make Greek; to hellenize. ◆ *vi* to become Greek; to conform to Greek ways or idioms; to use the Greek language. [L *Graecus*, from Gr *Graikos*, Greek; *graikizein* to speak Greek]
■ **Grae'cism** or (*esp N Am*) **Gre'cism** *n* a Greek idiom; the Greek spirit; a following of the Greeks. **Graeco-** or (*esp N Am*) **Greco-** /grē-kō- or grek-ō-/ combining form denoting: Greek; Greece.
❑ **Grae'co-Ro'man** or (*esp N Am*) **Gre'co-Ro'man** *adj* of or relating to both Greece and Rome, *esp* the art of Greece under Roman domination; applied to a mode of wrestling imagined to be that of the Greeks and Romans.

Graf /gräf/ (*Ger*) *n* a count, earl.
■ **Gräfin** /grā'fin/ *n* a countess.

graff[1] /gräf/ (*Scot*; now *obs*) *n* a variant of **grave**[1].

graff[2] /gräf/ *n* and *v* an older, now archaic, form of **graft**[1].

graffito /gräf-fē'tō/ *n* a mural scribbling or drawing, as by schoolboys and idlers at Pompeii, Rome, and other ancient cities (*ancient hist*); sgraffito (*art*). [Ital, from Gr *graphein* to write]
■ **graffi'ti** /-tē/ *n pl* or (loosely) *n sing* scribblings or drawings, often humorous, political or indecent, found on public buildings, in lavatories, etc. **graffi'tied** *adj* covered with graffiti. **graffi'tist** *n*.
❑ **graffiti artist** *n*.

graft[1] /gräft/ *n* a small piece of a plant or animal inserted in another individual or another part so as to come into organic union; any transplanted organ or tissue (*med*); the act of inserting a part in this way; the place of junction of stock and scion (*bot*); the double plant composed of stock and scion; a sucker, branch or plant (*obs*). ◆ *vt* to insert a graft in; to insert (an organ, piece of tissue, plant) as a graft; to cuckold (*obs*). ◆ *vi* to insert grafts. [From older *graff*, from OFr *graffe* (Fr *greffe*), from L *graphium*, from Gr *graphion, grapheion* a style, pencil, from *graphein* to write]
■ **graft'er** *n*. **graft'ing** *n* the action of the verb; the correction of a section of a stencil by cutting it to remove the unwanted section and replacing it with a slightly larger piece of new stencil using stencil correcting fluid to glue it to the original; lengthening a timber by jointing another piece onto it.
❑ **graft chimera** *n* (*bot*) a chimera in which the genetically distinct cell types derive from different species. **graft hybrid** *n* a hybrid form produced, as some have believed, by grafting; a patchwork compound of two species propagated from the junction of tissues in a graft, each part retaining the specific character proper to the cells from which it arose. **graft-versus-host disease** *n* a graft-versus-host reaction of transposed or transplanted lymphocytes against antigens belonging to the host, a major complication of bone marrow grafting (*abbrev* **GVHD**). **graft-versus-host reaction** *n* the reaction occurring when lymphocytes in a tissue graft respond to antigens present in the recipient which are not identical with those of the donor, resulting in attack and destruction of the host tissue (*abbrev* **GVH**).

graft[2] /gräft/ *n* a ditch, excavation (*dialect*); a spade's depth; a ditching spade. ◆ *vi* (*dialect*) to dig. [Cf ON *gröftr* digging]
■ **graft'er** *n*.

graft[3] /gräft/ *n* hard work (*inf*); a criminal's special branch of practice (*sl*); illicit profit by corrupt means, *esp* in public life (*sl*); corruption in official life (*sl*). ◆ *vi* to work hard (*inf*); to engage in graft or corrupt practices (*sl*). [Perh **graft**[2] or an extended use of **graft**[1] for something inserted, supplementary]
■ **graft'er** *n*.

Graham /grā'əm/ *n* a Scottish mountain of between 2000 and 2499 feet that has a reascent of 500 feet on all sides. [After Fiona Torbet (née *Graham*), who published a list of these in 1992]

graham flour /grā'əm flowr/ (mainly *US*) *n* a type of wheat flour similar to wholewheat flour, used to make **graham bread** or **crackers**. [S *Graham* (1794–1851), US dietitian]

Graiae see **Graeae**.

grail[1] or (*archaic*) **graal** or **grayle** /grāl/ *n* (often **holy grail** or **Holy Grail**) in medieval legend, the platter (sometimes supposed to be a cup) used by Christ at the Last Supper, in which Joseph of Arimathaea caught his blood at the Cross, said to have been brought by Joseph to Glastonbury, and the object of quests by King Arthur's Knights; a cherished ambition or goal. [OFr *graal* or *grael* a flat dish, from LL *gradālis* a flat dish, ult from Gr *krātēr* a bowl]

grail[2] see **gradual** (*n*).

grail[3] /grāl/ (*poetic*) *n* (also (*Spenser*) **graile** or **grayle**) gravel. [Perh **gravel**; or OFr *graile* (Fr *grêle*) hail, from L *gracilis* slender]

grain[1] /grān/ *n* a single small hard seed; corn, in general; a hard particle; a very small quantity; the smallest British weight (the average weight of a seed of corn) $= \frac{1}{7000}$ of a pound avoirdupois and $\frac{1}{5760}$ of a pound troy; (in *pl*) refuse malt after brewing or distilling; the arrangement, size and direction of the particles, fibres, or plates of stone, wood, etc; texture; a granular surface; the particles in a photographic emulsion which go to compose the photograph; dried bodies of kermes or of cochineal insects, once thought to be seeds (*hist*); the red dye made from these (*hist*); any fast dye (to **dye in grain** is to dye deeply, also to *dye in the wool*; *hist*); dye in general (*obs*); innate quality or character. ◆ *vt* to form into grains, cause to granulate; to paint in imitation of grain; to dye in grain; (in tanning) to take the hair off. [Fr *grain*, collective *graine*, from L *grānum* seed and *grāna* (orig *pl*); similar to **corn**[1]]

■ **grain'age** *n* duties on grain. **grained** *adj* granulated; subjected to graining; having a grain; rough; furrowed. **grain'er** *n* a person who grains; a paintbrush for graining. **grain'ing** *n* (*specif*) painting to imitate the grain of wood; a process in tanning in which the grain of the leather is raised. **grain'y** *adj* having grains or kernels; having large grains, so indistinct (*photog*).

❑ **grain alcohol** *n* alcohol made by the fermentation of grain. **grain amaranth** see **amarant**. **grain leather** *n* leather which has the side with the hair removed (**grain side**) facing outwards. **grains of Paradise** *n pl* the aromatic and pungent seeds of an African plant of the genus *Amomum*.

■ **against the grain** against the fibre of the wood; against the natural temper or inclination. **in grain** in substance, in essence. **take with a grain of salt** see under **salt**[1].

grain[2] /grān/ *n* a branch, prong or fork (*dialect*); (in *pl*, used as *sing*) a kind of pronged harpoon. [ON *grein*]

graine /grān/ *n* silkworm eggs. [Fr]

graining[1] /grā'ning/ *n* (in Lancashire) dace, though once thought a separate species. [Origin unknown]

graining[2], **grainy** etc see under **grain**[1].

graip /grāp/ (*Scot* and *N Eng* dialect) *n* a three- or four-pronged fork used for lifting dung or digging potatoes. [A form of **grope**; cf Swed *grep*, Dan *greb*]

graith /grāth/ (*Scot*) *n* apparatus; equipment. ◆ *vt* (*obs*) to make ready, dress. [ON *greithr* ready; cf OE *geræde* ready]

■ **graith'ly** *adj* and *adv* an older form of **gradely**.

grakle see **grackle**.

Grallae /gral'ē/ or **Grallatores** /-ə-tō'rēz or -tō'/ *n pl* in old classifications, an order of wading birds. [L *grallātor* a stilt-walker, from *grallae* stilts, from *gradī* to step]

■ **grallatō'rial** *adj*.

gralloch /gral'əhh/ *n* a deer's entrails. ◆ *vt* to disembowel (deer). [Gaelic *grealach*]

gram[1] or **gramme** /gram/ *n* a unit of mass in the metric system, formerly that of a cubic centimetre of water at 4°C, now a thousandth part of the International Prototype Kilogram (see **kilogram** under **kilo-**). [Fr *gramme*, from L *gramma*, from Gr *gramma* a letter, a small weight]

❑ **gram-at'om** or **gram-atomic weight**, **gram-mol'ecule** or **gram-molecular weight** *n* the quantity of an element, or a compound, whose mass in grams is equal to its atomic weight and molecular weight respectively (a now discarded concept; see **mole**[4]). **gram-equiv'alent** or **gram-equivalent weight** *n* the quantity of a substance whose mass in grams is equal to its equivalent weight.

gram[2] /gram/ *n* the chickpea; a pulse generally. [Port *grão* (sometimes *gram*), from L *grānum* a grain]

❑ **gram flour** *n* flour made from ground chickpeas.

■ **black gram** see **urd**.

gram[3] /gram/ or **grame** /grām/ (*obs*) *n* anger; grief; trouble. [OE *grama*, anger]

gram[4] /grām/ *n* an Indian village. [Hindi]

-gram /-*gram*/ *combining form* denoting: something written or drawn to form a record; a greetings message delivered by a messenger in a particular costume and in an appropriately absurd, amusing or humorous manner (eg *gorillagram*, *kissogram*, *stripogram*, *Tarzanogram*) to surprise and embarrass the recipient on a special occasion. [Gr *gramma* letter; later use follows 'singing tele*gram*']

grama /grä'mə/ or **grama grass** /gräs/ *n* an American pasture grass (genus *Bouteloua*) with spikelets ranged unilaterally. [Sp, from L *grāmen* grass]

gramary or **gramarye** /gram'ə-ri/ (*archaic*) *n* magic; enchantment. [ME *gramery* skill in grammar, hence magic; see **grammar**, **glamour**]

gramash see **gamash**.

grame see **gram**[3].

gramercy /grə-mûr'si/ (*obs*) *interj* great thanks. ◆ *n* thanks. [OFr *grant merci* great thanks]

gramicidin /gram-i-sī'din/ *n* an antibiotic obtained from certain bacteria, used against Gram-positive bacteria (also **gramicidin D**). [HCJ *Gram* (1853–1938), Danish bacteriologist who devised the method, and L *caedere* to kill]

❑ **Gram-neg'ative** (also **gram-**) *adj* losing a stain of methyl violet and iodine on treatment with alcohol. **Gram-pos'itive** (also **gram-**) *adj* retaining the stain.

Gramineae /grə-, *gra-* or grā-min'i-ē/ *n pl* the grass family. [L *grāmen*, *grāminis* grass]

■ **graminā'ceous** /grā- or gra-/ or **gramin'eous** *adj* of, or relating to, the grass family; grasslike, grassy. **gramin'icide** *n* a herbicide for controlling grasses. **graminiv'orous** /gra-/ *adj* feeding on grass, cereals, etc.

gramma same as **grama**.

grammalogue /gram'ə-log/ *n* a word represented by a single sign, a logogram; a sign for a word in shorthand. [Gr *gramma* a letter, and *logos* a word]

grammar /gram'ər/ *n* (the study of) the morphology and syntax of a particular language, or language in general; (the study of) the whole structure of a language, or of language in general, including phonology and semantics; a description of the grammar of a language; a book containing such a description; a person's internalized knowledge of the structural rules of a language; the production of utterances deemed correct according to actual or imagined rules of syntax and morphology; any elementary work; any system of rules and structure; a grammar school (*inf*). [Gr *gramma*, *-atos* a letter; partly through OFr *gramaire*]

■ **grammā'rian** *n* a person who has made a study of grammar, a teacher of or writer on grammar. **grammat'ical** *adj* belonging to, or according to the rules of, grammar (also formerly **grammat'ic**). **grammatical'ity** *n*. **grammat'ically** *adv*. **grammat'icism** *n* (*rare*) a point of grammar. **grammat'icize** or **-ise** /-sīz/ *vt* to make grammatical. ◆ *vi* to act the grammarian, hold forth on grammatical matters. **gramm'atist** *n* a strict grammarian. **grammatol'ogy** *n* the science or study of systems of writing.

❑ **grammar school** *n* orig a school in which grammar, *esp* Latin grammar, was taught; later, a secondary school in which academic subjects predominate, most of which have now been absorbed into the comprehensive school system; an elementary school (*N Am*). **grammatical meaning** *n* the functional significance of a word, etc within the grammatical framework of a particular sentence, etc.

gramme see **gram**[1].

Grammy /gram'i/ (*US*) *n* (pl **Gramm'ies** or **Gramm'ys**) an award (corresponding to the cinema Oscar) awarded by the National Academy of Recording Arts and Sciences. [From *gramophone*]

Gram-negative see under **gramicidin**.

gramoche /gra-mosh'/ *n* see **gamash**.

gramophone /gram'ə-fōn/ *n* (also (*US*) **Gramophone**®) an instrument (invented by E Berliner in 1887) for reproducing sounds by means of a needle moving along the grooves of a revolving disc, a record player; (loosely) any record player (now *facetiously* or *archaic*). [Improperly formed from Gr *gramma* letter, record, and *phōnē* sound]

■ **gramophonic** /-fon'ik/ *adj* relating to gramophones. **gramophon'ically** *adv*. **gramophonist** /gram-of'ə-nist* or *gram'ə-fōn-ist*/ *n* (*obs*). **gramoph'ony** *n* (*obs*).

Gram-positive see under **gramicidin**.

grampus /gram'pəs/ *n* technically, Risso's dolphin (*Grampus griseus*); a popular name for many whales, *esp* the killer; someone who breathes heavily and loudly, a puffer and blower (*archaic*). [16c *graundepose*, earlier *grapays*, from OFr *graspeis*, from L *crassus* fat, and *piscis* fish, confused with Fr *grand* big]

gran[1] /gran/ (*inf*) *n* short for **granny**.

gran[2] /gran/ (*Ital*) *adj* great.

❑ **gran turismo** /too-rēz'mō/ n a motor car designed for touring in luxury and at high speed (*abbrev* **GT**).

grana see **granum**.

granadilla /gran-ə-dil'ə/ or **grenadilla** /gren'/ n the edible, oblong, fleshy fruit of *Passiflora quadrangularis*, a tropical American passion flower; the edible fruit of various other passion flowers. [Sp]
❑ **granadilla tree** n the cocuswood tree.

granary /gran'ə-ri/ n a storehouse for grain or threshed corn; a rich grain-growing region; (**Granary**®) a make of bread with a nutty flavour, made with malted wheat flour (also *adj*). ◆ *adj* (loosely, of bread) containing whole grains of wheat. [L *grānārium*, from *grānum* seed]

grand[1] /grand/ *adj* exalted; magnificent; dignified; sublime; imposing; would-be-imposing; on a great scale; pre-eminent; supreme; chief; main; in complete form; in full proportions; very good (*inf*). ◆ *n* a grand piano; a thousand dollars or pounds (*sl*). [Fr *grand*, from L *grandis* great]
■ **grand'ly** *adv*. **grand'ness** *n*.
❑ **grand-du'cal** *adj* relating to a grand duke. **grand duchess** *n* the wife or widow of a grand duke; a woman of the same rank as a grand duke in her own right. **grand duke** *n* a title of sovereignty over a **grand duchy**, first created by the Pope in 1569 for the rulers of Florence and Tuscany, later assumed by certain German and Russian imperial princes. **grand juror** *n* a member of a **grand jury**, a special jury in the USA (and until 1933 in Britain) which decides whether there is sufficient evidence to put an accused person on trial. **grand larceny** see **larceny**. **grand march** the processional opening of a ball. **grandmas'ter** *n* *orig* the title given to a chess player winning a major international tournament, now given to a player achieving a high score in three major tournaments; any exceptionally skilled player. **Grand Master** *n* the head of a religious order of knighthood (Hospitallers, Templars, and Teutonic Knights), or of the Freemasons, etc. **Grand Mufti** *n* the head of the Muslim religious community in several Middle-Eastern countries. **Grand National** *n* a steeplechase held annually at Aintree in Liverpool. **grand old man** *n* (*inf*) a person commanding great respect and veneration. **grand opera** see under **opera**[1]. **grand piano** *n* a large harp-shaped piano, with horizontal strings. **grand slam** *n* a contract to win every trick (*bridge*); the winning of all the major championships in a season (*sport*, eg *tennis*, *golf*); a home run hit when there is a runner at each base, scoring four runs (*baseball*). **grand'stand** *n* an elevated structure on a racecourse, etc, with tiered seating, affording a good view for spectators. ◆ *vi* (*inf*) to show off. **grandstand finish** *n* a close and rousing finish to a sporting contest; a supreme effort to win at the close of a sporting contest. **grand style** *n* a style adapted to lofty or sublime subjects. **grand total** *n* the sum of all subordinate sums. **Grand Tour** see under **tour**. **grand touring** same as **gran turismo** (see under **gran**[2]). **Grand Unified Theory** *n* a unified quantum field theory of the electromagnetic, strong and weak interactions of elementary particles (*abbrev* **GUT**).

grand[2] /grã/ (*Fr*) *adj* great.
❑ **grand amateur** /da-ma-tœr/ *n* a collector of beautiful objects on a large scale. **grand atelier** /dat-əl-yā/ *n* a top-ranking fashion house. **grand coup** /koo/ *n* a successful stroke; in bridge or whist, the trumping of a trick that could have been trumped by the winner's partner. **grand cru** /krü/ *n* a wine from a famous vineyard or group of vineyards (also *adj*). **Grand Guignol** see **Guignol**. **grand luxe** /lüks/ *n* great luxury. **grand mal** /mal/ *n* a violently convulsive form of epilepsy (see also **petit mal** under **petit**). **Grand Marnier**® /mär-nyā/ *n* an orange-flavoured liqueur, often with a cognac base. **grand merci** /mer-sē/ *interj* many thanks. **grand monde** /mõd/ *n* high society. **grand prix** /prē/ *n* (*pl* **grands prix**) literally, chief prize; (with *caps*) any of several international motor races; any competition of similar importance in other sports (*orig* Grand Prix de Paris, a famous horse race). **grand seigneur** /sen-yœr/ *n* a dignified aristocratic gentleman or noble (now *usu ironic*).
■ **le Grand Siècle** /syekl'/ the great century, ie the Classical age of French literature during the reign of Louis XIV.

grand- /grand-/ *combining form* signifying (a person) of the second degree of parentage or descent. [**grand**[1]]
■ **gran'dam**, **gran'dame** or **grann'am** *n* (*archaic*) an old dame or woman; a grandmother. **grand'-aunt** *n* a great-aunt. **grand'child** *n* a son's or daughter's child. **grand'dad** or **gran'dad** *n* (*inf*) a grandfather; an old man (**granddad collar** a round collar, not folded over (*orig* intended to take a detachable stud-fastened collar); **granddad shirt** one with a granddad collar). **grand'daddy** or **gran'daddy** *n* (*inf*) a grandfather; a person or thing considered the oldest, biggest, first, etc of its kind. **grand'daughter** *n* a son's or daughter's daughter. **grand'father** *n* a father's or mother's father. ◆ *vt* (*US inf*) to exempt (an activity, person, etc) from a new piece of legislation, restriction or the like (**grandfather clause** (*US inf*) a qualifying clause within a piece of legislation exempting those already

involved in the activity with which the legislation deals; **grandfather** (or **grandfather's**) **clock** an old-fashioned clock (longcase clock) standing on the ground, or a new clock of this style (larger than a **grandmother**('**s**) **clock**). **grand'fatherly** *adj* like a grandfather, kindly. **grand'kid** *n* (*inf*) a grandchild. **grand'ma**, **grand'mama** or **grand'mamma** *n* (*inf*) a grandmother; an old woman. **grand'mother** *n* a father's or mother's mother. **grand'motherly** *adj* like a grandmother; over-anxious, fussy. **grand'-nephew** *n* a great-nephew. **grand'-niece** *n* a great-niece. **grand'pa** or **grand'papa** *n* (*inf*) a grandfather. **grand'parent** *n* a grandfather or grandmother. **grand'sire** *n* a grandfather (*archaic*); any ancestor (*archaic*); a method of ringing changes (*bellringing*). **grand'son** *n* a son's or daughter's son. **grand'-uncle** *n* a great-uncle.

grande /grãd/ (*Fr*) *adj fem* of **grand**[2].
❑ **grande amoureuse** /a-moo-rœz/ *n* a woman greatly involved in love affairs. (**la**) **Grande Armée** /ar-mā/ *n* (*hist*) the great army, ie that led by Napoleon to invade Russia in 1812. **grande cocotte** /ko-kot/ *n* a high-class prostitute, *usu* one kept by a rich lover. **grande dame** /däm/ *n* a great and aristocratic lady, or a socially important and very dignified one; a woman highly revered in her particular profession or field (now, as for *masc* **grand seigneur**, often *ironic*). **grande école** /ā-kol/ *n* a prestigious French higher-education college, to which entry is competitive, specializing *esp* in applied science, engineering and other technical subjects. **grande entrée** /ã-trā/ *n* admission to Court, etc on occasions of state. **grande marque** /märk/ *n* of motor cars, etc, a famous make. **grande passion** /pas-yõ/ *n* a serious love affair or intense attachment. **grande tenue** /tə-nü/ *n* full dress, *esp* military, etc. **grande toilette** /twa-let/ *n* full dress, *esp* women's evening dress. **grande vedette** /və-det/ *n* a leading film or theatre star.

grandee /gran-dē'/ *n* (in Spain and Portugal from the 13c) a noble of the most highly privileged class, the members of the royal family being included; a man of high rank or station. [Sp *grande*]
■ **grandee'ship** *n*.

grandeur /gran'dyər/ *n* vastness; splendour of appearance, magnificence; loftiness of thought or deportment; pretentiousness. [Fr, from *grand* great]
■ **delusions of grandeur** a mistaken belief in one's own importance.

grandiloquent /gran-dil'ə-kwənt/ *adj* speaking, or expressed, bombastically (also (*archaic*) **grandil'oquous**). [L *grandiloquus*, from *grandis* great, and *loquens*, *-entis* speaking]
■ **grandil'oquence** *n*. **grandil'oquently** *adv*.

grandiose /gran'di-ōs or -ōz/ *adj* grand or imposing; bombastic. [Ital *grandioso*, from *grande* great]
■ **gran'diosely** *adv*. **grandios'ity** *n*.

Grandisonian /gran-di-sō'ni-ən/ *adj* beneficent, polite and chivalrous, like Sir Charles *Grandison*, hero of a novel by S Richardson.

granfer /gran'fər/ (*dialect*) *n* contraction of **grandfather** (see under **grand-**).

grange /grānj/ *n* a farmhouse or country house with its stables and other buildings; a granary or barn (*archaic*; *Milton*); a country house (*obs*); a dwelling (*Spenser*); a lodge of the order of Patrons of Husbandry (*US*). [OFr *grange* barn, from LL *grānea*, from L *grānum* grain]
■ **gran'ger** *n* the keeper of a grange; a member of a grange.

Grangerism /grān'jə-ri-zm/ *n* the practice of cutting plates and title-pages out of many books to illustrate one book. [From James *Granger* (1723–76), whose *Biographical History of England* (1769) included blank pages for illustrations]
■ **grangeriza'tion** or **-s-** *n*. **gran'gerize** or **-ise** *vt* to practise Grangerism on.

graniferous /gra-nif'ə-rəs/ (*bot*) *adj* producing grain or a grain-like seed. [L *grānum* grain, and *ferre* to bear]

granita /gra-nē'ta/ *n* a grainy-textured flavoured water ice. [Ital *granito* grainy]

granite /gran'it/ *n* a coarse-grained igneous crystalline rock, composed of quartz, feldspar and mica; hardness, resilience or resolution (of character); a curling-stone. ◆ *adj* of granite; hard like granite; unyielding, resolute. [Ital *granito* granite, literally, grained, from L *grānum* grain]
■ **granit'ic** *adj* relating to, consisting of, or like granite. **granitifica'tion** *n*. **granit'iform** *adj*. **gran'itite** *n* biotite granite. **granitiza'tion** or **-s-** *n*. **gran'itize** or **-ise** *vt*. **gran'itoid** *adj* of the form of or resembling granite. **granodī'orite** *n* a rock resembling diorite but containing quartz. **granolith'ic** *adj* (Gr *lithos* stone) composed of cement and granite chips (also *n*). **gran'ophyre** /-fīr/ *n* (with *-phyre* after *porphyry*) a quartz-porphyry with graphic intergrowth of quartz and orthoclase for groundmass. **granophyric** /-fir'ik or -fīr'ik/ *adj*.
❑ **graniteware** /gran'it-wär/ *n* a kind of speckled pottery resembling granite; a type of enamelled ironware.

granivorous /gra-niv'ə-rəs/ (zool) adj grain-eating; feeding on seeds. [L grānum grain, and vorāre to devour]
■ **gran'ivore** n.

grannam see under **grand-**.

granny or **grannie** /gran'i/ n a grandmother (inf); an old woman (inf); an old-womanish person (inf); a midwife (US dialect); a revolving cap on a chimney pot. ♦ vt (Scot) to defeat totally, whitewash (in a contest). [**grannam** (see under **grand-**)]
❑ **granny bonds** n pl a former name of index-linked National Savings certificates, before 1981 only available to people over 50 years old. **granny dumping** n (inf, esp N Am) the practice of abandoning elderly relatives outside hospitals, etc when caring for them becomes too expensive or difficult. **granny flat, annexe**, etc n a self-contained flat, bungalow, etc built onto, as part of, or close to a house, for a grandmother or other elderly relative. **granny glasses** n pl small, round, gold- or steel-rimmed spectacles. **granny knot** n a knot like a reef knot, but unsymmetrical, apt to slip or jam. **Granny Smith** n a crisp, green, flavoursome, Australasian variety of apple (after Maria Ann Smith of New South Wales, the first cultivator of this variety).

granodiorite see under **granite**.

granola /grə-nō'lə/ (N Am) n a type of crunchy breakfast cereal made with mixed grain, oats, dried fruit, nuts, etc, and honey or brown sugar. [Orig a trademark]

granolithic, granophyre, etc see under **granite**.

grant /gränt/ vt to bestow; to admit as true; to concede. ♦ vi (Shakesp) to consent. ♦ n something bestowed, an allowance; a gift; conveyance of property by deed (Eng law); a granting. [OFr graanter, craanter, creanter to promise, from L crēdere to believe]
■ **grant'able** adj. **grant'ed** adj or conj (often with that) (it is) admitted or accepted. **grantee'** n (law) the person to whom a grant, gift or conveyance is made. **grant'er** or **grant'or** n (law) the person by whom a grant or conveyance is made.
❑ **grant'-aided** adj (of a school, etc) receiving a grant from public funds. **grant'-in-aid'** n an official money grant for a particular purpose, esp from the government to a lesser department, or local authority, for its programme or to ensure high standards. **grant'-maintained** adj (of a school, etc) funded by central and not local government, and self-governing (abbrev **GM**). **grant of arms** n (heraldry) provision of an achievement to a petitioner by a king-of-arms, in exchange for a fee.
■ **take for granted** to presuppose, or assume, esp tacitly or unconsciously; to treat casually, without respect.

Granth /grunt/ or **Granth Sahib** /grunt sä'ib/ n the holy book of the Sikhs (also **Adi'-Granth**). [Hindi granth a book]
■ **Gran'thi** /-ē/ n the guardian of the Granth Sahib and of the gurdwara.

granule /gran'ūl/ n a little grain; a fine particle; (of eg a dehydrated foodstuff) a pellet, crumb-like particle, as opposed to powder. [L grānulum, dimin of grānum grain]
■ **gran'ular** or (archaic) **gran'ulary**, also **gran'ulose** or **gran'ulous** adj consisting of or like grains or granules; containing or marked by the presence of grains or granules. **granular'ity** n granular consistency; fineness of detail. **gran'ularly** adv. **gran'ulate** vt to form or break into grains or small masses; to make rough on the surface. ♦ vi to be formed into grains. ♦ adj granular; having the surface covered with small elevations. **granula'tion** n the act of forming into grains, esp of metals by pouring them through a sieve into water while hot; a granulated texture; (specif) applied decoration made up of grains of metal (esp gold); (in pl) granulation tissue (qv below). **gran'ulative** adj. **gran'ulātor** or **gran'ulāter** n. **granulif'erous** adj. **gran'uliform** adj. **gran'ulite** n (geol) a schistose but sometimes massive aggregate of quartz and feldspar with garnets; a granular-textured metamorphic rock. **granulit'ic** adj of the texture of granulite. **granūlītīzā'tion** or **-s-** n (geol) reduction of the components of a rock to crystalline grains by regional metamorphism. **gran'ūlocyte** /-sīt/ n a blood cell of the leucocyte division. **granūlocytic** /-sit'ik/ adj. **granūlō'ma** n (pl **granūlō'mas** or **granūlō'mata**) (pathol) a localized collection of macrophages or other inflammatory cells, caused by infection or invasion by a foreign body. **granūlō'matous** adj.
❑ **granulated sugar** n white sugar in fairly coarse grains. **granulation tissue** n (med) a new formation of connective tissue which grows in small rounded masses in a wound or on an ulcerated surface, and tends to leave a white scar.

granum /grä'nəm/ (bot) n (pl **gra'na**) a stack of plate-like discs found in the stroma of chloroplasts, containing chlorophyll and the enzymes for the light reactions of photosynthesis. [L, grain]

grape¹ /grāp/ n the small, green- or dark purple-skinned fruit of the grapevine, growing in bunches, used to make wine, dried to make raisins, or eaten raw; a mangy tumour on the legs of horses, or the form of tuberculosis it is indicative of (vet); grapeshot. [OFr grape, grappe a cluster of grapes, from grape a hook; orig Gmc]
■ **grape'less** adj (of wine) without the flavour of the grape. **grā'pery** n a building or place where grapes are grown. **grā'pey** or **grā'py** adj made of or like grapes.
❑ **grape'fruit** n a large, round, yellow-skinned citrus fruit, so called because it grows in large bunches like grapes; the evergreen tree bearing it. **grape hyacinth** n any of several plants of the genus Muscari closely related to the hyacinths, with clusters of small grapelike flowers. **grape ivy** n an evergreen climbing vine (Rhoicissus rhomboidea), popular as a houseplant for its glossy foliage. **grape'louse** n an insect (Viteus vitifolii) which is a serious pest of vines. **grape'seed** n the seed of the vine. **grape'seed-oil** n an oil pressed from grapeseed. **grape'shot** n clustered iron shot that scatters when fired. **grape'stone** n the pip of the grape. **grape sugar** n glucose or dextrose. **grape'tree** n a tropical American tree (Coccoloba uvifera) of the family Polygonaceae, or its edible fruit. **grape'vine** n Vitis vinifera or other species of Vitis ; the bush telegraph, rumour (from its far-stretching branches) (inf).
■ **sea grape** see under **sea**. **sour grapes** saying or pretending that something is not worth having because one cannot have it oneself (from Aesop's fable of the fox and the grapes). **the grape** (usu facetious) wine.

grape² /grāp/ (Scot) vi a dialect variant of **grope**.

graph /gräf/ n a symbolic diagram; a drawing depicting the relationship between two or more variables (sets of numbers or quantities) usu with reference to two axes. ♦ vt to plot on a graph. ♦ combining form denoting a device that writes, records, etc (eg telegraph, seismograph), or the thing written (eg autograph, etc). [Gr graphē writing, from graphein to write]
■ **graphic** /graf'ik/ adj (also **graph'ical**) relating to writing, or to descriptive, delineative, or diagrammatic representation; picturesquely described or describing; vivid. ♦ n a painting, print, illustration or diagram, an example of the graphic arts. **graph'icacy** n accurate understanding of and use of visual information. **graph'ically** or **graph'icly** adv. **graph'icness** n. **graph'ics** n sing graphic means of presenting, or means of reproducing, informational material; designs containing illustrations or drawings; visual data as distinct from text or numbers; the visual arts concerned with representation, illusion, typography, printing, etc on a flat surface, and the methods associated with these techniques; the art or science of mathematical drawing, and of calculating stresses, etc, by geometrical methods. **grapholog'ic** or **grapholog'ical** adj. **graphol'ogist** n a person skilled in, or who practises, graphology. **graphol'ogy** n the art of estimating and analysing character, etc from handwriting; the study of the systems and conventions of writing (linguistics). **graphoman'ia** n an obsession with writing. **graphopho'bia** n a fear of writing.
❑ **graphical user interface** n (comput) the use of mouse-controlled icons and other images on a desktop display (abbrev **GUI**). **graphic artist** n. **graphic arts** n pl painting, drawing, engraving (as opposed to music, sculpture, etc). **graphic design** n the use of the graphic arts in the creation of commercial products. **graphic designer** n. **graphic equalizer** n a device for boosting or cutting frequencies of an audio signal, using faders. **graphic formula** n a chemical formula in which the symbols for single atoms are joined by lines representing valency bonds. **graphic granite** n (geol) a granite with markings like Hebrew characters, owing to intergrowth of quartz and feldspar. **graphic novel** n a novel in comic-book picture form, aimed mainly at adults. **graphics card** n (comput) a printed circuit board that stores visual data and conveys it to the display screen. **graphics character** n (comput) a pictorial character that appears on the screen. **graphics plotter** see **graph plotter** below. **graphics tablet** n (comput) a peripheral input device which digitizes the movements of a pen over the sensitive pad (tablet), so that a traced pattern will appear on the screen. **graph paper** n squared paper suitable for drawing graphs. **graph** (or **graphics**) **plotter** n (comput) a device similar to a printer which provides a hard copy of computer graphics by allowing the computer to control the pen movement.

grapheme /graf'ēm/ (linguistics) n a letter of an alphabet; all the letters or combinations of letters together that may be used to express one phoneme. [Gr graphēma a letter]
■ **graphēm'ic** adj. **graphēm'ically** adv. **graphē'mics** n sing the study of systems of representing speech sounds in writing.

graphene see under **graphite**.

graphic, etc see under **graph**.

Graphis /graf'is/ n a genus of lichens, with fructifications that resemble writing, found on bark. [New L, from L; ult Gr graphein to write]

graphite /graf'īt/ n a soft black or grey mineral composed of carbon, with many commercial and industrial uses, notably as the 'lead' in lead pencils (also called **plumba'go** or **black'lead**). [Ger Graphit, from Gr graphein to write, and **-ite** (3)]
■ **graph'ene** n a film of graphite with a thickness of one atom. **graphit'ic** adj. **graphitizā'tion** or **-s-** n. **graph'itize** or **-ise** vt to

convert wholly or partly into graphite. **graph'itoid** *adj* with the appearance of graphite.

☐ **graphite reactor** *n* (*nuclear eng*) a reactor in which fission is produced principally or substantially by slow neutrons moderated by graphite.

graphium /grafʹi-əm/ *n* a stylus. [L]

graphologist, etc, **graphomania**, **graphophobia** see under **graph**.

-graphy /-grə-fi/ *combining form* denoting either a particular style of writing, drawing, etc (eg *photography, lithography*) or a method of arranging and recording data within a particular discipline (eg *seismography, biography*). [L *-graphia*, from Gr, from *graphein* to write]

graple see **grapple**.

grapnel /grapʹnəl/ *n* a small anchor with several claws or arms; a grappling-iron; a hooking or grasping instrument. [Dimin of OFr *grapin*, from *grape* a hook; of Gmc origin]

GRAPO or **Grapo** /gräʹpō/ *abbrev*: *Grupos de Resistencia Antifascista Primero de Octubre* (*Sp*), First of October Anti-Fascist Resistance Groups, an extreme left-wing terrorist organization.

grappa /grapʹə/ *n* a spirit (*orig* Italian) made from the residue from a winepress. [Ital, grape stalk]

grapple, also (*Spenser*) **graple** /grapʹl/ *n* an instrument for hooking or holding; a grasp, grip, hold or clutch; a state of being held or clutched. ◆ *vt* to seize; to lay fast hold of, grasp or grip. ◆ *vi* to contend in close fight; to wrestle mentally (with). [Cf OFr *grappil*, from *grape* a hook]

■ **grap'lement** *n* (*Spenser*) a close fight. **grapp'ler** *n*.

☐ **grapp'le-plant** *n* a S African herbaceous plant (*Harpagophytum procumbens*) of the family Pedaliaceae, with woody hook-like growths on its fruits. **grapp'ling-iron** or **-hook** *n* an instrument for grappling; a large grapnel for seizing hostile ships in naval engagements (*hist*).

graptolite /grapʹtə-līt/ (*geol*) *n* one of a group of fossil Hydrozoa with one or two rows of hydrothecae on a simple or branched polypary, characteristic Silurian fossils with an appearance almost like writing upon shales. [Gr *graptos* written, from *graphein* to write, and *lithos* stone]

■ **graptolit'ic** *adj*.

GRAS /gras/ (*US*) *abbrev*: generally recognized as safe (used to designate an officially approved food additive).

grasp /gräsp/ *vt* to seize and hold; to take eagerly; to comprehend. ◆ *vi* to endeavour to seize (with *at* or *after*); to seize or accept eagerly (with *at*). ◆ *n* grip; power of seizing; mental power of apprehension. [ME *graspen, graspen*, from the root of *grāpian* to grope]

■ **grasp'able** *adj*. **grasp'er** *n*. **grasp'ing** *adj* seizing; avaricious. **grasp'ingly** *adv*. **grasp'ingness** *n*. **grasp'less** *adj* feeble, relaxed.

■ **grasp the nettle** see under **nettle**[1].

grass[1] /gräs/ *n* any plant of the monocotyledonous family Gramineae, the most important family in the vegetable kingdom to humans, with long, narrow leaves and tubular stems, including wheat and other cereals, reeds (but not sedges), bamboo and sugarcane; common herbage; pasture grasses; an area planted with or growing such grasses, eg a lawn or meadow; pasturage; an informer (*esp* to the police on a fellow criminal) (*sl*); marijuana (*sl*); temporary or casual work in a printing office (*archaic*); the time of new growth of grass, spring and early summer (*archaic* or *dialect*); the surface, ground level, at a mine. ◆ *vt* to cover, sow or turf with grass; to feed with grass; to bring (eg a fish or game bird) on or down to the grass or ground; to inform on (*sl*). ◆ *vi* to inform (on) (*sl*); to do temporary or casual work in a printing office (*archaic*). [OE *gærs, græs*; ON, Du and Gothic *gras*, Ger *Gras*; prob related to **green**[1] and **grow**]

■ **grass'er** *n* an informer (*sl*); an extra or temporary printing worker (*archaic*). **grass'iness** *n*. **grass'ing** *n* bleaching by exposure on grass. **grass'less** *adj*. **grass'-like** *adj*. **grass'y** *adj* covered with or resembling grass, green.

☐ **grass'bird** *n* an Australasian warbler with streaked brown plumage (genus *Megalurus*); also applied to various other birds of the southern hemisphere. **grass box** *n* a receptacle attached to some lawnmowers to catch the grass cuttings. **grass carp** *n* a breed of fish, native to the South China Sea, imported into other areas to control various kinds of weed which it eats in great quantities. **grass characters** see **grass style** below. **grass cloth** *n* a name for various coarse cloths (rarely made of grass), *esp* rami. **grass'cloth plant** *n* the plant (rami). **grass court** *n* a grass-covered tennis court. **grass'-cutter** *n* a mowing machine; (in India) a person who provides fodder for baggage cattle (*perh* really Hindustani *ghāskatā*). **grass'-green** *adj* green with grass; green as grass. **grass'-grown** *adj* grown over with grass. **grass'hook** *n* another name for **sickle**[1]. **grass'hopper** *n* a name for various herbivorous jumping insects of the order Orthoptera, related to locusts and crickets, that chirp by rubbing their wing-covers; a cocktail made with crème de menthe, crème de cacao and cream. **grasshopper mind** *n* a mind which is desultory or unable to concentrate on any one object for long. **grasshopper warbler** *n* a songbird (*Locustella naevia*) whose song resembles a grasshopper's stridulation. **grass'land** *n* permanent pasture. **grass line** *n* a sisal rope, used on boats, that floats on the surface of the water (also **grass rope**). **grass moth** *n* a small light-coloured moth that frequents grass, a veneer-moth. **grass of Parnassus** see under **Parnassus**. **grass'-oil** *n* a name for several volatile oils derived from widely different plants, some of them grasses. **grass'-plot** *n* a plot of grassy ground. **grass'quit** *n* any of various small tropical American songbirds of the finch family. **grass'-rooter** *n*. **grass'-roots** *n pl* (*orig US*) the ordinary people, the rank and file in a country, political party, etc, thought of as voters; the rural areas of a country; the foundation, basis, origin, primary aim or meaning. ◆ *adj* of, belonging to or appealing to the grass-roots. **grass rope** see **grass line** above. **grass sickness** *n* a disease of the bowels affecting horses. **grass snake** *n* the harmless common ringed snake. **grass style** *n* a form of Chinese calligraphy in which the shapes of characters (**grass characters**) are greatly simplified for artistic effect. **grass tree** *n* an Australian plant (genus *Xanthorrhoea*) with shrubby stems, tufts of long wiry foliage at the summit, and a tall flower-stalk, with a dense cylindrical spike of small flowers. **grass widow** *n* a wife temporarily separated from or deserted by her husband. **grass widower** *n*. **grass'wrack** *n* eelgrass.

■ **go** (or **be put out**) **to grass** to be turned out to pasture, *esp* of a horse too old to work; to go into retirement or to live in the country; (of a boxer) to fall violently, be knocked down (*sl*). **grass** (**someone**) **up** (*sl*) to inform on (someone). **hear the grass grow** to have exceptionally acute hearing; to be exceptionally alert. **let the grass grow under one's feet** to loiter or linger, and so lose one's opportunity.

grass[2] /gräs/ (*old sl*) *n* short for **sparrow-grass**, a corruption of **asparagus**.

grassum /graʹsəm/ (*Scots law*) *n* a lump sum paid (in addition to rent or other periodic payment) by a person taking a lease of landed property, called in England 'premium' or 'fine'. [OE *gærsum* treasure, rich gift, etc]

graste /grāst/ (*Spenser*) *pap* of **grace**.

grat see **greet**[2].

grate[1] /grāt/ *vt* to reduce (*esp* food) to small particles or slivers by rubbing against a rough surface; to rub hard, scrape or wear away with anything rough; to grind (the teeth); to emit or utter jarringly. ◆ *vi* to make a harsh sound; to jar or rasp (on or against); to fret or irritate (*usu* with *on* or *upon*). [OFr *grater*, through LL, from OHGer *chrazzōn* (Ger *kratzen*) to scratch, related to Swed *kratta*]

■ **grat'er** *n* an instrument with a rough surface for rubbing (eg cheese) down to small particles. **grāt'ing** *adj* rubbing harshly; harsh; irritating. ◆ *n* a grating sound. **grāt'ingly** *adv*.

grate[2] /grāt/ *n* a framework of bars with spaces between, *esp* one for holding a fire in a fireplace or furnace, or for looking through a door, etc; the fireplace or furnace itself; a cage; a grid. [LL *grāta* a grate, from L *crātis* a hurdle; see **crate**]

■ **grāt'ed** *adj* having a grating. **grāt'ing** *n* the bars of a grate; a perforated cover for a drain, etc; a partition or frame of bars; a surface ruled closely with fine lines which diffract light (*phys*).

grateful /grātʹf(ŏŏ)l/ *adj* thankful; having a due sense of benefits one has received; expressing gratitude; (of a thing) causing pleasure, or acceptable. [OFr *grat*, from L *grātus* pleasing, thankful]

■ **grate'fully** *adv*. **grate'fulness** *n*. **gratifica'tion** /*grat-*/ *n* a pleasing or indulging; that which gratifies; delight, feeling of satisfaction; a recompense, tip or bribe (*archaic*). **grat'ifier** *n*. **grat'ify** *vt* to please; to satisfy; to indulge; to do what is agreeable to. **grat'ifying** *adj*. **grat'ifyingly** *adv*.

graticule /gratʹi-kūl/ (*surveying*) *n* a ruled grating for the identification of points on a map or on the field of a telescope, etc, a reticle. [L *crātīcula*, dimin of *crātis* wickerwork]

■ **graticulā'tion** *n* the division of a design into squares for convenience in making an enlarged or reduced copy.

gratillity /grə-tilʹi-ti/ (*Shakesp*) *n* a small gratuity.

gratin /gratʹē/ (*cookery*) *n* the golden brown crust covering a gratinated food or dish; a dish with such a covering; see **au gratin**. [Fr *gratin* cheese, *gratiner* to cook au gratin]

■ **grat'inate** *vt* to cook with a topping of buttered breadcrumbs and/or cheese browned until crisp, to cook au gratin. **gratiné** or (*fem*) **gratinée** /grat-ē-nā/ *adj* (Fr) cooked or served au gratin.

gratis /grāʹ, gräʹ or grätʹis/ *adv* for nothing; without payment or recompense. ◆ *adj* free; without charge. [L *grātis*, contraction of *grātiīs*, ablative pl of *grātia* favour]

☐ **gratis dictum** /dikʹtəm/ or *-toom/ *n* mere assertion.

gratitude /gratʹi-tūd/ *n* a warm and friendly feeling towards a benefactor; thankfulness. [Fr, from LL *grātitūdō*, from L *grātus* thankful]

grattoir /grat'wär/ (archaeol) n a scraper made of flint. [Fr]

gratuity /grə-tū'i-ti/ n a gift, usu of money, separate from and additional to payment made for a service; a tip or present; a bounty, a payment to a soldier, etc on discharge. [Fr gratuité, from LL grātuitās, -ātis, from L grātus grateful]
■ **gratū'itous** adj without reason, ground or proof; uncalled-for; unnecessary or unjustified; done or given for nothing; voluntary; benefiting one party only (law). **gratū'itously** adv. **gratū'itousness** n.
❑ **gratuitous promise** n (law) a promise (not legally binding) made by one person to another when the latter has not provided any consideration in return (eg a promise of a gift).

gratulate /grat'ū-lāt/ (archaic) vt to congratulate; to welcome; to express joy at. ◆ adj (Shakesp) gratifying.
■ **grat'ulant** adj congratulatory. **gratula'tion** n congratulation. **grat'ulatory** adj congratulatory.

graunch /grönch/ (inf) vi to make a grinding or crunching noise (usu of a mechanism). ◆ vt to grind or crunch (a mechanism). [imit]
■ **graunch'er** n a clumsy, incompetent mechanic; someone who graunches.

graupel /grow'pəl/ n frozen rain or snowflakes. [Ger graupeln to sleet]

gravadlax see **gravlax**.

gravamen /grəv-ā'men, -vä'men or -mən/ n (pl **gravā'mina**) grievance; the substantial or chief ground of complaint or accusation (law); a statement of abuses, grievances, etc in the Church of England sent by the Lower to the Upper House of Convocation. [L gravāmen, from gravis heavy]

grave¹ /grāv/ n a pit dug out, esp one to bury the dead in; any place of burial; the abode of the dead (Bible); death, destruction (fig); a deadly place. ◆ vt (pap **graved** or **grav'en**) to dig (obs); to engrave on a hard substance (archaic); to fix deeply (eg on the mind) (archaic); to bury (obs). ◆ vi (archaic) to engrave. [OE grafan to dig, græf a cave, grave, trench; Du graven, Ger graben]
■ **grave'less** adj (Shakesp). **grāv'er** n an engraving tool, eg a burin; an engraver (archaic). **grāv'ing** n.
❑ **grave'-clothes** n pl the clothes in which the dead are buried. **grave'-digger** n. **grave goods** n pl (archaeol) artefacts (eg pottery, jewellery, weapons) put into a grave along with the corpse. **grave'-maker** n (Shakesp) a grave-digger. **grave'side** n the area around a grave (also adj). **grave'stone** n a stone placed as a memorial at a grave. **grave'-wax** n (obs) adipocere. **grave'yard** n a burial ground. **graveyard shift** n (sl) a work shift starting at midnight or during the night.
■ **dig one's own grave** to do something that brings misfortune on oneself. **turn in one's grave** (of a dead person) to be disturbed from one's rest by an occurrence that would have been particularly distressing to one's living self. **with one foot in the grave** on the brink of death; very ill and/or old.

grave² /grāv/ adj of importance; serious, not gay or showy; sedate; solemn; weighty; calling for anxiety; very dangerous; low in pitch; (also /gräv/) marked with a grave accent. ◆ n (also /gräv/) a grave accent. [Fr, from L gravis]
■ **grave'ly** adv. **grave'ness** n.
❑ **grave accent** /grāv/ n a mark ('), orig indicating a pitch falling somewhat, or failing to rise, now used for various special purposes (as in French).

grave³ /grāv/ vt to clean (by burning, etc) and seal with tar (a wooden ship's bottom). [Perh Fr grave, grève beach]
❑ **graving dock** n a dry dock for the cleaning and repair of ships.

grave⁴ /grä'vā/ (music) adj and adv in a solemn manner. [Ital]

grave⁵ /grāv/ n a count, prefect, a person holding office (now obs except in compounds, such as landgrave, margrave, burgrave). [Du graaf, Ger Graf]

gravel /grav'l/ n a mass of small rounded mixed stones or rock fragments, often with sand; small collections of gravelly matter in the kidneys or bladder (pathol). ◆ vt (**grav'elling**; **grav'elled**) to cover with gravel; to run aground on gravel (obs); to puzzle, perplex; to irritate (inf, esp US). [OFr gravele (Fr gravier); prob Celtic, as in Breton grouan sand, Welsh gro pebbles]
■ **grav'elly** adj of, full of, or like, gravel; (of sound) harsh, rough.
❑ **grav'el-blind** adj (orig Shakesp **high'-grav'el-blind'**) after Shakespeare, punningly, in a state somewhere between sand-blind and stone-blind. **grav'el-pit** n a pit from which gravel is dug. **grav'el-voiced** adj harsh- or rough-voiced. **grav'el-walk** n a footpath covered with gravel.

graven /grāv'n/ adj pap of **grave¹**; engraved (archaic); deeply fixed (eg on the mind or memory).
❑ **graven image** n a sculpted (or engraved) idol; a solemn person (fig).

graveolent /grə-vē'ō-lənt or grav'i-/ (obs except bot) adj rank-smelling, fetid. [L graveolēns, -entis, from gravis heavy, and olēns, prp of olēre to smell]

graver see under **grave¹**.

Graves /gräv/ n a white (or red) table wine from the Graves district in the Gironde department of France; (loosely) any dry or medium-dry white wine.

graves see **greaves**.

Graves' disease /grāvz' di-zēz'/ (med) n exophthalmic goitre, caused by excessive secretion of thyroid hormone. [RJ Graves (1796–1853), Irish physician]

Gravettian /grə-vet'i-ən/ (archaeol) adj relating to the Upper Palaeolithic culture of La Gravette in SW France, characterized by the narrow pointed blades with blunted back edges that were found there. ◆ n the Gravettian period.

gravid /grav'id/ (med and zool) adj pregnant. [L gravidus, from gravis heavy]
■ **gravid'ity** n.

gravimeter /grə-vim'i-tər/ n an instrument for measuring variations in gravity at points on the earth's surface. [L gravis heavy, and Gr metron measure]
■ **gravimetric** /grav-i-met'rik/ or **gravimet'rical** adj relating to measurement by weight. **gravim'etry** n the measurement of the earth's gravitational field at different points on its surface; measurement by weight.
❑ **gravimetric analysis** n the chemical analysis of materials by the separation of the constituents and their estimation by weight.

gravitas /grav'i-tas or -täs/ n seriousness; weight, importance. [L; see ety for **gravity**]

gravitate, etc, **gravitometer**, **graviton** see under **gravity**.

gravity /grav'i-ti/ n weightiness; the force attracting a body towards the centre of the earth or other celestial body, gravitational attraction or acceleration; graveness, solemnity; seriousness, dangerous nature; lowness of pitch. [L gravitās, -ātis, from gravis heavy]
■ **grav'itāte** vi to be acted on by gravity; to tend towards the earth or other body; to be attracted, or move, by force of gravitation; to sink or settle down; to be strongly attracted or move (towards; fig). **gravitā'tion** n the act of gravitating; the force of attraction between masses, this being directly proportional to the product of the masses and inversely to the square of the distances (the Newtonian **constant of gravitation** (symbol **G**) is 6.67×10^{-11} N m² kg⁻²) (phys). **gravitā'tional** adj of, relating to, etc gravity; of the weakest type of interaction between nuclear particles (phys). **gravitā'tionally** adv. **grav'itātive** adj. **gravitom'eter** n an instrument for measuring specific gravities. **grav'iton** n (phys) a hypothetical quantum of gravitational field energy.
❑ **gravitational field** n that region of space in which appreciable gravitational force exists. **gravity cell** n an electric cell having electrolytes of different specific gravities, so that they form separate layers. **grav'ity-fed** adj (of a boiler, plant, system, etc) to which fuel, etc is supplied under the force of gravity alone. **grav'ity-feed** vt and n. **gravity platform** n a drilling platform, used in the oil industry, made from concrete and steel, the weight of which enables it to hold its position on the seabed. **gravity waves** n pl liquid surface waves controlled by gravity and not by surface tension; hypothetical progressive energy-carrying waves whose existence was postulated by Einstein in 1916.
■ **acceleration due to gravity** (symbol **g**) the acceleration of a body falling freely under the action of gravity in a vacuum, on Earth about 9.8m (32.174 ft) per second². **specific gravity** see under **specify**.

gravlax /gräv'laks, grav'laks/, also **gravadlax** /grav'ad-laks/ n a Scandinavian dish of salmon dry-cured with herbs (usu dill), sugar, salt and pepper, sliced on the slant to serve. [Swed gravlax, Norw gravlaks, literally, buried salmon]

gravure /grə-vūr'/ n any process of making an intaglio printing plate, including photogravure; the plate, or an impression from it. [Fr, engraving]

gravy /grā'vi/ n the juices exuded from meat while cooking; a sauce made by thickening and seasoning these juices; a similar sauce made with an artificial substitute; money, profit or pleasure, unexpected or in excess of what one might expect (inf); money or profit obtained by corrupt practices or graft (sl). [Perh gravé a copyist's mistake for OFr grané, from grain a cookery ingredient]
❑ **gravy boat** n a container for gravy. **grav'y-soup** n soup like gravy, made from fresh meat. **gravy train** n (inf) a job or scheme which offers high rewards for little effort.

gray¹ /grā/ n a derived SI unit, the unit of absorbed dose of ionizing radiation (symbol **Gy**), equal to one joule per kilogram. [Louis H Gray (1905–65), British radiobiologist]

■ words derived from main entry word; ❑ compound words; ■ idioms and phrasal verbs

gray² see **grey**.

   ❑ **gray'fly** n (*Milton*) an unidentified insect.

Gray code /grā kōd/ (*comput*) n a type of code for modifying binary numbers (also **reflective binary code**). [Frank *Gray* (1887–1969), American physicist]

grayle see **grail**¹,³.

grayling /grā'ling/ n a silvery-grey fish (genus *Thymallus*) of the salmon family, with a smaller mouth and teeth, and larger scales; a grey satyrid butterfly of the genus *Hipparchia*. [**gray** (see **grey**) and **-ling**¹]

graywacke same as **greywacke**.

graze¹ /grāz/ vt to eat or feed on (growing grass or pasture); to feed or supply with grass. ◆ vi to eat grass; to supply grass; to eat on one's feet and on the move, eg without stopping work, or (straight from the shelves) in a supermarket (*sl*); to browse, skim along or through reading matter, TV or radio programmes, etc (*sl*). [OE *grasian*, from *græs* grass]

   ■ **grāz'er** n an animal that grazes; a person who eats on his or her feet and on the move (*sl*); a person who browses in or skims through (books, TV programmes, etc). **grāz'ier** n a person who pastures cattle and rears them for the market. **grāz'ing** n the action of the verb in any sense; the act of feeding on grass; the feeding or raising of cattle; pasture.

graze² /grāz/ vt to pass lightly along the surface of; to damage or scrape the top surface of (the skin, etc). ◆ n a passing touch or scratch; an area of grazed skin. [Ety doubtful; perh only a special use of **graze**¹; perh from *rase* (Fr *raser*), the g due to the analogy of *grate*]

grazioso /grä-tsē-ō'sō/ (*music*) adj and adv graceful, gracefully. [Ital]

GRCM abbrev : Graduate of the Royal College of Music.

grease /grēs/ n a soft thick animal fat; oily matter of any kind; the condition of fatness; an inflammation in the heels of a horse, marked by swelling, etc (*vet*). ◆ vt (in UK sometimes pronounced /grēz/) to smear with grease; to lubricate; to bribe (*sl*); to facilitate. [OFr *gresse* fatness, *gras* fat, from L *crassus*]

   ■ **grease'less** adj. **greaser** /grēz'ər or grēs'ər/ n a person who greases; a member of a gang of long-haired motorcyclists (*sl*); a ship's engineer (*sl*); a Mexican or a Spanish American or Mediterranean person (*US; offensive sl*); an obsequious person (*Aust and NZ inf*); (of an aircraft) a gentle landing. **greas'ily** adv. **greas'iness** n. **greas'y** adj (in UK sometimes /grēz'i/) of or like grease or oil; smeared with grease; having a slippery coating; fatty; oily; obscene; unctuous or ingratiating. ◆ n (*Aust and NZ inf*) a shearer; a camp-cook in the outback; (in *pl*) fish and chips.

   ❑ **grease'ball** n (*US derog sl*) a person of Latin racial origin, *esp* Mediterranean or Latin American, with dark hair and skin; someone with oily, slicked-back hair; a loose derogatory term, *esp* for someone dirty or unkempt. **grease'band** n (*hortic*) a band of sticky or greasy material put around eg a tree trunk to prevent insects from climbing further up it. **grease cup** n a lubricating device which stores grease and feeds it into a bearing. **grease gun** n a lubricating pump. **grease'-heels** n sing (*vet*) grease (in horses). **grease monkey** n (*sl*) a mechanic. **grease paint** n a tallowy substance used by actors in making up. **grease'proof** adj resistant or impermeable to grease. **grease'wood** n a name for various oily American shrubs of the goosefoot family. **greasy spoon** n (*sl*) a cheap, shabby, often grubby cafe.

   ■ **grease someone's palm** see under **palm**¹. **grease the wheels** (*fig*) to make things go smoothly. **like greased lightning** extremely quickly.

great /grāt/ adj big; large; of a high degree of magnitude of any kind; (of a letter) capital (*archaic*); elevated in power, rank, station, etc; preeminent in genius; highly gifted; much admired and respected; chief; sublime; weighty; outstanding; (with *on*) devoted to or obsessed by a certain thing; much given to, or excelling in the thing in question; favourite; habitual; in high favour or intimacy; in a high degree; on a large scale; excellent (*inf*, often *ironic*); larger in size than others of the same kind, species, etc (*biol*); in combination, indicating one degree more remote in the direct line of descent (as in *great-grandfather*, *great-grandson* and similarly *great-great-grandfather* and so on indefinitely); pregnant, teeming (*archaic*); swelling with emotion (*archaic*). ◆ n someone who has achieved lasting fame; (with *the*) used collectively for those people who have achieved lasting fame; bulk, mass (*obs*); whole (*obs*); wholesale (*obs*). ◆ adv (*inf*) very well. [OE *great*; Du *groot*, Ger *gross*]

   ■ **great'en** vt to make great or greater. ◆ vi (*obs*) to become great. **great'er** adj compar of **great**; (with geographical names) in an extended sense (eg *Greater London*). **great'ly** adv. **great'ness** n. **Greats** n pl the final honours examinations of the School of Literae Humaniores (**Classical Greats**) or of Modern Philosophy (**Modern Greats**) at Oxford University; the course leading to these.

   ❑ **great ape** n any of the larger anthropoid apes, such as the chimpanzee, gibbon, gorilla and orang-utan. **great auk** n a large, flightless auk once common in N Atlantic areas, now extinct.

great'-aunt n a grandparent's sister or a grandparent's brother's wife. **Great Bear** n Ursa Major. **great'-bellied** adj (*archaic; Shakesp*) pregnant. **Great Britain** n England, Scotland and Wales. **great circle** n a circle on the surface of a sphere whose centre is the centre of the sphere. **great'coat** n an overcoat. **Great Dane** n one of a breed of very large smooth- (and short-)haired dogs. **great'-grand'child** n the child of a grandchild. **great'-grand'father** n the father of a grandparent. **great'-grand'mother** n the mother of a grandparent. **great gross** n a unit of quantity equal to 12 gross (1728). **great'-hearted** adj having a great or noble heart; high-spirited; magnanimous. **great-heart'edness** n. **great'-nephew** n the grandson of one's own or one's spouse's brother or sister. **great'-niece** n the granddaughter of one's own or one's spouse's brother or sister. **great primer** see **primer**. **great schism** n (*hist*) the great Eastern schism or the Western schism (see under **schism**). **Great Sea** n (*archaic*) the Mediterranean. **Great Seal** n a seal kept by the Lord Chancellor or Lord Keeper and used on the most important state papers. **great tit** n a kind of tit (see **tit**¹), *Parus major*, with yellow, black and white markings. **great toe** see under **toe**. **great'-uncle** n a grandparent's brother or a grandparent's sister's husband. **Great War** n a term applied *esp* to the war of 1914–18. **Great White Way** n a nickname for Broadway in New York; any brightly lit street with theatres, etc. **great year** n (*astron*) the length of time (about 25 800 years) it takes for the equinoctial points to make a complete revolution.

   ■ **Great Scott!** an exclamation of surprise. **the Great and the Good** (an assembly of) eminent, worthy and respected public figures (often somewhat *ironic* in use). **the greatest** (*inf*) a wonderful, marvellous person or thing; the outstanding performers in their field. **the great unwashed** a contemptuous term for the general populace.

greave¹ /grēv/ n armour for the leg below the knee. [OFr *greve* shin, greave]

greave² /grēv/ (*obs*) n a thicket. [OE *græfa*, *græfe*; cf **grove**]

greave³ same as **grieve**¹,².

greaves /grēvz/ or (*obs*) **graves** /grāvz/ n pl dregs of melted tallow. [LGer *greven*; cf Ger *Griebe* greaves; OE *grēofa* pot]

grebe /grēb/ n a short-winged almost tailless freshwater diving bird (genus *Podiceps*). [Fr *grèbe*]

grebo /grē'bō/ (*derog sl*) n (pl **gre'bos**) a devotee of heavy metal or grunge music, with unkempt hair and clothes. [Perh from *greaser* long-haired motorcyclist, and **bo**³]

grece see under **gree**².

Grecian /grē'sh(y)ən/ adj Greek. ◆ n a Greek; a scholar of Greek language and literature; a hellenizing Jew (*Bible*); a senior boy of Christ's Hospital school; an Irish labourer recently arrived in England (*old sl*). [L *Graecia* Greece, from Gr *Graikos* Greek]

   ❑ **Grecian bend** n a mode of walking with a slight bend forward, at one time affected by a few women in an attempt to imitate the pose of a figure such as the Venus of Milo. **Grecian nose** n a straight nose which forms a continuous line with the forehead.

grecian see under **gree**².

Grecism, Grecize, Greco-Roman see **Graecize**.

grecque /grek/ (*archit*) n a fret pattern. [Fr (fem), Greek]

gree¹ /grē/ n (*Spenser*) goodwill, favour. ◆ vi (*Shakesp*, *archaic* or *Scot*) to agree. [OFr *gre*, from L *grātus* pleasing; the verb may be from OFr *gréer* or aphetic from **agree**]

gree² /grē/ n degree, rank (*obs*); a step (*obs*); superiority (*dialect*); victory (*dialect*); the prize for such (*dialect*). [OFr *gre*, from L *gradus*; see **grade**]

   ■ **grece** /grēs/ n (from the French plural; *obs* or *dialect*) a flight of steps; a step. —Also spelt **grees**, **grese**, **greece**, **greese**, **grice**, **griece**, **gris**, **grise**, **grize**; **grees'ing**, **gress'ing** and even **grē'cian** are obsolete forms. **grieced** adj (*heraldry*) having or placed on steps.

greedy /grē'di/ adj having a voracious appetite; craving or longing eagerly, *esp* too eagerly; eager to increase, or to obtain or keep more than, one's own share; covetous, grasping. [OE *grǣdig*; Du *gretig*]

   ■ **greed** n an eager desire or longing; gluttony; eagerness or longing for more than one's share; covetousness, *esp* excessive. **greed'ily** adv. **greed'iness** n.

   ❑ **greedy guts** n (*inf*) a glutton.

greegree see **grisgris**.

Greek /grēk/ adj of Greece, its people, or its language. ◆ n a native or citizen of Greece, of an ancient Greek state, or of a colony elsewhere of an ancient Greek state; the language of Greece; any language of which one is ignorant, jargon, anything unintelligible (*inf*); a member of the Greek Church; a hellenizing Jew (*Bible*); a cunning rogue (*archaic*); an Irishman (*old sl*). [OE *Grēcas*, *Crēcas* Greeks, or L *Graecus*, from Gr *Graikos* Greek]

   ■ **Greek'dom** n the Greek world; a Greek community. **Greek'ing** or **greek'ing** n (as in desktop publishing, advertising, etc) representation of text and graphics as straight lines, random characters or other graphic convention, to give an overall impression of the page layout. **Greek'ish** *adj*. **Greek'less** *adj* without knowledge of Greek. **Greek'ling** *n* (*archaic*) a contemptible Greek. **Greek'ness** *n*. ❑ **Greek architecture** *n* the style of architecture developed in ancient Greece (Corinthian, Doric, Ionic). **Greek Church** or **Greek Orthodox Church** see **Eastern Church** under **east**. **Greek cross** *n* an upright cross with arms of equal length. **greeked text** *n* (*comput*) a method of displaying very small text in which a simple symbol replaces the actual text in order to reduce the time needed for display while retaining the appearance of the layout. **Greek fire** *n* a substance (of unknown composition) that caught fire when wetted, used in war against enemy ships, long a secret of the Byzantine Greeks. **Greek gift** *n* a treacherous gift (from Virgil's *Aeneid* 2.49). **Greek god** *n* a classic example of male beauty. **Greek key** (**pattern**) *n* a fret pattern. **Greek letter society** (or **Greek-letter**) *n* (in US universities) a social, professional or honorary fraternity or sorority, using a combination of Greek letters as a title, such as Phi Beta Kappa. **Greek love, style** or **way** *n* (*US sl*) anal sex. **Greek nose** *n* a Grecian nose. **Greek salad** *n* a salad with feta, tomatoes, cucumber, onion and olives.

■ **the Greek calends** never (the Greeks having no calends).

green[1] /grēn/ *adj* of the colour usual in leaves, between blue and yellow in the spectrum; growing; vigorous, flourishing; covered with grass, bushes, etc; new; young; unripe; fresh; undried; raw; incompletely prepared; immature; unseasoned; inexperienced; pale, showing signs of nausea; jealous or envious; easily imposed on, gullible; relating to currency values expressing EU farm prices (eg *green pound, green franc, green rate*, etc); concerned with care of the environment or conservation of natural resources, *esp* as a political issue; (of goods, etc) environment-friendly; (of people) environment-conscious. ◆ *n* the colour of green things; a grassy plot, *esp* that common to a village or town, or for bowling, drying of clothes, etc; the prepared ground (**putting green**) round a golf hole; (sometimes with *cap*) a member or supporter of a Green Party, or an environmentalist generally; a green pigment; greenness, a stage of vigorous growth (of plants, as *in the green*); the green colour as a symbol of the Irish republic; (in *pl*) fresh leaves; (in *pl*) green vegetables for food, *esp* of the cabbage kind; (in *pl*) money, *esp* dollar bills (*sl*); (in *pl*) sexual intercourse (*sl*); (in *pl*) low-grade marijuana (*sl*); (in *pl*; with *cap*) a political party at Constantinople, under Justinian, opposed to the Blues. ◆ *vt* and *vi* to make or become green; to introduce trees and parks into urban areas. ◆ *vi* to become environmentally conscious. [OE *grēne*; Ger *grün*, Du *groen* green; ON *grœnn*]

■ **green'er** *n* (*sl*) a newly arrived immigrant. **green'ery** *n* green plants or boughs; fresh, green growth. **green'ie** *n* (*Aust*) an environmentalist (also *adj*); see also **greeny** below. **green'ing** *n* a becoming or making green; a deliberate policy of introducing trees and parks into urban areas; a becoming or making politically green, ecologically and environmentally conscious, or conservationist; a kind of apple green when ripe. **green'ish** *adj*. **green'ishness** *n*. **green'let** *n* any of several greenish songbirds of the American family Vireonidae. **green'ly** *adv* immaturely, unskilfully. **green'ness** *n*. **greenth** *n* (*obs*) greenness, verdure. **green'y** *adj* having a green tinge. ◆ *n* (*sl*) a d1 note (also **green'ie**); (in *pl*) money, cash in notes; a lump of nasal mucus.

❑ **green accounting** *n* an accounting system that accommodates environmental considerations in the calculation of annual profits. **green algae** or **seaweeds** *n pl* the Chlorophyta. **green audit** *n* an assessment of and investigation into a company's green, ie environment-conscious, claims, methods, policies, etc. **green'back** *n* (*inf*) an American banknote (often printed in green on the back); a plant condition in which fruits (eg tomatoes) remain green around the stalk. **green'-bag** *n* a lawyer's bag for documents, etc (formerly of green material); a lawyer (*old sl*). **green ban** *n* (*Aust*) the refusal of trade unions to work on environmentally and socially objectionable projects. **green bean** *n* a French bean, the immature pod of the kidney bean. **green belt** *n* a strip of open land surrounding a town. **Green Beret** *n* (*inf*) a British or American commando. **green'-bone** *n* the garfish; a viviparous blenny. **green'bottle** *n* a metallic-green fly (genus *Lucilia*). **green card** *n* an international motorists' insurance document; an official US work and residence permit (*orig* green) issued to foreign nationals; a card issued by the Manpower Services Commission certifying that the holder is registered disabled under the terms of the Disabled Persons (Employment) Act 1944, and is thus entitled to certain assistance in gaining and carrying out paid work; in hockey, an official warning to a player after a relatively minor offence (signalled by the showing of a green card). **green'cloth** *n* a gaming-table (*inf*); a department of the royal household chiefly concerned with the commissariat (from the green cloth on the table round which its officials sat). **green'-collar** *adj* relating to jobs in the environmental sector. **green corn** same as **sweetcorn** (see under **sweet**). **green crop** *n* a crop of green vegetables, such as grasses, turnips, etc. **Green Cross Code** *n* a code of road-safety rules for children

issued in 1971. **green dragon** *n* a European aroid plant (genus *Dracunculus*); dragonroot (*US*). **green'-drake** *n* a mayfly. **green earth** *n* any green earthy mineral used as a pigment, *usu* a silicate of iron. **green'ery-yall'ery** *adj* (*inf*) in or favouring greens and yellows, hence decadently aesthetic. **green'eye** *n* a small W Atlantic fish with pale green eyes. **green'-eyed** *adj* having green eyes; jealous (**the green-eyed monster** jealousy). **green'field** *adj* applied to a site, separate from existing developments, which is to be developed for the first time. **green'finch** or **green linnet** *n* a finch of a green colour, with some grey. **green-fing'ered** *adj*. **green fingers** (or **thumb**) *n* a knack of making plants grow well. **green flash** or **ray** *n* a flash of green light sometimes seen at the moment of sunrise or sunset. **green'fly** *n* a plant louse or aphid. **green fund** *n* (*finance*) an ethical (qv) fund. **green gland** *n* one of a pair of glands on the head of certain crustaceans. **Green Goddess** *n* a type of fire engine operated by the army in civil emergencies, etc. **green goose** *n* a young goose (*dialect*); a simpleton (*old sl*). **green gown** *n* (*archaic*) a roll on the grass (sometimes but not always understood to imply loss of virginity). **green'grocer** *n* a dealer in fresh vegetables and fruit; a large green cicada (*Aust*). **greengrocer's apostrophe** same as **grocer's apostrophe** (see under **grocer**). **green'grocery** *n* the produce sold by a greengrocer. **green'hand** *n* an inferior sailor. **green'heart** *n* bebeeru (*Nectandra rodiaei*), a S American tree of the family Lauraceae with very hard wood. **green'horn** *n* a raw, inexperienced youth. **green'house** *n* a glasshouse for plants, *esp* one with little or no artificial heating; the cockpit of an aircraft, having transparent sides (*RAF sl*). **greenhouse effect** *n* the warming-up of the earth's surface due to the trapping of solar radiation, which would otherwise be reflected back into space, by carbon dioxide (produced by the burning of fossil fuels, chlorofluorocarbons, natural methane emissions, etc) and other greenhouse gases. **greenhouse gas** *n* a gas (*esp* carbon dioxide, also ozone, methane, nitrous oxide and chlorofluorocarbons) that contributes to the greenhouse effect. **Green** (or **Emerald**) **Isle** *n* Ireland. **green'-keeper** *n* a person who has the care of a golf course or bowling green. **green label, green labelling** same as **eco-label, eco-labelling** (see under **eco-**). **green leek** *n* any of various Australian parrots with green plumage. **green light** *n* a traffic signal indicating that vehicles may advance; permission to go ahead; any signal or indication of consent or encouragement, as in *get the green light* (*inf*). **greenlight'** *vt* to give permission to proceed. **green linnet** see **greenfinch** above. **green'mail** *n* (*US*) a form of business blackmail whereby a company buys a strategically significant block of shares in another company, sufficient to threaten takeover and thus to force the parent company to buy back the shares at a premium. **green'mailer** *n*. **green man** *n* an illuminated green figure at a pedestrian crossing that indicates that it is safe to cross the road; (in British folklore) a figure symbolizing fertility, often depicted with branches and greenery protruding from his mouth. **green manuring** *n* growing one crop (**green manure**) and digging it under to fertilize its successor. **green monkey** *n* a W African long-tailed monkey, *Cercopithecus aethiops* (**green monkey disease** a sometimes fatal filovirus disease with fever and haemorrhaging, *orig* identified among technicians handling green monkeys in Marburg, Germany (also called **Marburg disease**)). **green paper** *n* (often with *caps*) a statement of proposed government policy, intended as a basis for parliamentary discussion. **Green Party** *n* a party principally concerned with the conservation of natural resources and the decentralization of political and economic power. **Green'peace** *n* an environmental pressure group which campaigns *esp* against nuclear power and dumping, and also whaling. **green pepper** see under **pepper**. **green plover** *n* the lapwing. **green pound** *n* the agreed value of the pound used to express EU farm prices in sterling and to measure the level of Britain's contribution under the Common Agricultural Policy. **green ray** see **green flash** above. **green revolution** *n* agricultural advances in developing countries. **green road** or **way** *n* a grassy country track used by walkers. **green'room** *n* in a theatre, a room for actors to relax or entertain guests in, etc backstage, traditionally and typically having the walls coloured green. **green'sand** *n* a sandstone containing much glauconite; (with *cap*) two divisions (Lower and Upper) of the Cretaceous system, separated by the Gault (*geol*). **green screen** *n* (in film, television, etc) a green-coloured background against which material may be shot for superimposition elsewhere. **green'-screen** *adj*. **green seaweeds** see **green algae** above. **green'shank** *n* a large sandpiper with long, somewhat greenish legs. **green shoots** *n pl* signs of regeneration or improvement, as in an economy. **green sickness** *n* chlorosis. **green snake** *n* a harmless colubrine snake common in southern USA. **green'speak** *n* ecological jargon, the terminology of green issues, or that used by green activists and supporters. **greenstick fracture** see under **fracture**. **green stocks** *n pl* (*commerce*) shares of an organization engaged in combating pollution, or professing to avoid it in the manufacture of its products. **green'stone** *n* a vague name for any basic or intermediate igneous rock (*geol*); nephrite. **green'stuff** *n* green vegetables, *esp* of the cabbage kind. **green'sward** *n* (*archaic* or *literary*) land covered with grass. **green tax** *n* a tax imposed with the intention of discouraging activities that may damage the environment. **green tea** *n* tea made from leaves that have been dried without fermentation and retain a light colour. **green turtle** *n* a tropical and subtropical sea turtle (*Chelonia mydas*) with a greenish shell (see **turtle**[1]). **green vitriol** *n* ferrous sulphate. **green'wash** *n* (*facetious*) a specious overlay, or ineffectual display, of concern for the environment (also *vt*). **green way** see **green road** above. **green'weed** *n* a name given to certain half-shrubby species of *Genista*. **green-well'ie** *adj* of, belonging to or relating to the British upper-class country-dwelling set (represented stereotypically as wearing heavy green wellingtons). **green'wood** *n* a leafy wood or forest (also *adj*). **green woodpecker** *n* a Eurasian woodpecker (*Picus viridis*), having green plumage with a red crown.

■ **green about the gills** (*inf*) looking or feeling sick. **something green in one's eye** (*inf*) a sign that one is gullible.

green[2] or (*obs*) **grein** /grēn/ (*Scot*) *vi* to long, yearn. [Cf ON *girna*]

greengage /grēn'gāj/ *n* a green and very sweet variety of plum, or the tree producing it. [Said to be named after Sir W *Gage* of Hengrave Hall, near Bury St Edmunds, before 1725]

Greenland /grēn'lənd/ *adj* of, belonging to, or originating in the island of *Greenland*.
□ **Greenland seal** *n* the harp seal, found in Arctic and N Atlantic waters. **Greenland whale** *n* the Arctic right whale, *Balaena mysticetus* (also called **Greenland right whale**).

greenling /grēn'ling/ *n* an edible spiny-finned fish of the N Pacific (genus *Hexagrammos*). [**green**[1] and **-ling**[1]]

greenockite /grē'nək-īt/ *n* a rare mineral, cadmium sulphide, discovered by Lord *Greenock* (1783–1859).

Greenwich Mean Time /grin'ij (also gren' or -ich) mēn tīm/ *n* mean solar time for the meridian of *Greenwich* (*abbrev* **GMT**; also called **Greenwich Time**).

grees, greese, greesing see under **gree**[2].

greet[1] /grēt/ *vt* (**greet'ing**; **greet'ed**) to acknowledge upon meeting with formal, familiar or customary words, or a customary or friendly gesture; to meet, receive; to become evident to (the eye or ear); to send kind wishes to; to congratulate (*obs*); to offer congratulations on (*Spenser*). ◆ *vi* (*obs*) to meet and salute. [OE *grētan* to greet, to meet; Du *groeten*, Ger *grüssen* to salute]
■ **greet'er** *n* a person who greets, *specif* someone employed to greet visitors eg to a theatre or club. **greet'ing** *n* an expression of acknowledgement, good wishes, kindness or joy; a salutation.
□ **greetings card** *n* a decorated card used to send greetings.

greet[2] /grēt/ (*Scot*; *Spenser* **greete**) *vi* (*pat* **greet'ed** or (*obs Scot*) **grat**; *pap* **greet'ed** or (*obs Scot*) **grutt'en**) to weep. ◆ *n* weeping; a spell of weeping. [OE (Anglian) *grētan*; Gothic *grētan*]
□ **greeting meeting** *n* the last meeting of a town council before an election.

greffier /gref'yā/ (*Channel Islands*, etc) *n* a registrar; a notary. [Fr]

gregale /grā-gä'lā/ *n* a north-east wind in the Mediterranean. [Ital, from L *graecus* Greek]

gregarian, etc see under **gregarious**.

Gregarina /gre-gə-rī'nə/ *n* a genus of Protozoa, typical of the **Gregarinida** group, parasites of insects, molluscs and crustaceans. [New L, after L *gregārius* (see next entry)]
■ **greg'arine** *n* a member of the Gregarinida. ◆ *adj* of or relating to the Gregarinida; of movement, slow and gliding.

gregarious /gri-gā'ri-əs/ *adj* fond of the company of others (*fig*); associating in flocks and herds; growing together but not matted (*bot*). [L *gregārius*, from *grex*, *gregis* a flock]
■ **gregā'rianism** *n* gregariousness. **gregā'riously** *adv*. **gregā'riousness** *n*.

gregatim /gri-gā'tim or gre-gä'tim/ (L) *adv* literally, in flocks.

grège see **greige**.

grego /grā'gō or grē'gō/ *n* (*pl* **gre'gos**) *orig* a hooded jacket or cloak worn in E Mediterranean countries; an overcoat, *esp* a thick hooded seaman's coat. [Port *grego* or other derivative of L *Graecus* Greek]

Gregorian /gri-gō'ri-ən or -gö'/ *adj* belonging to or established by *Gregory*, *esp* Pope Gregory I (6c). ◆ *n* any follower of a person called *Gregory*; a member of an 18c English brotherhood.
□ **Gregorian calendar** *n* the calendar reformed by Pope Gregory XIII in 1582. **Gregorian chant** or **tones** *n* plainsong, introduced by Pope Gregory I. **Gregorian telescope** *n* a reflecting telescope invented by James Gregory (1638–75). **Gregorian wig** *n* a 16c or 17c type of wig attributed to a barber called Gregory. **Gregory's** /greg'ər-iz/ **mixture** or **powder** *n* (also called (*inf*) **Greg'ory**) a laxative powder of rhubarb, magnesia and ginger, formulated by Dr James Gregory (1753–1821).

greige /grāzh/ *adj* (also **grège**) of cloth, undyed; of a greyish-beige colour. [Fr (*soie*) *grège* raw silk]

grein see **green**[2].

greisen /grī'zən/ *n* a rock composed of quartz and mica, often with topaz, formed from granite by fluorine exhalations. [Ger]
■ **greiseniza'tion** or **-s-** *n* the process by which granite is converted to greisen. **greis'enize** or **-ise** *vt*.

greisly (*Spenser* and *Milton*) see **grisly**.

gremial /grē'mi-əl/ *adj* relating to the lap or bosom (*obs*); intimate (*obs*); resident (*hist*); in full membership (*hist*). ◆ *n* a cloth laid on a bishop's knees to keep his vestments clean from oil at ordinations; a full or resident member (*hist*). [L *gremium* the lap]

gremlin /grem'lin/ *n* orig a goblin accused of vexing airmen, causing mischief and mechanical trouble to aircraft; any imaginary mischievous creature. [Origin uncertain; RAF slang, with a poss connection with *Fremlin's* Ale; prob modelled on **goblin**]

gremolata /grem-ə-lä'tə/ (*cookery*) *n* a colourful, flavoursome garnish, as of chopped parsley, lemon or orange peel, garlic, etc. [Ital]

gren /gren/ (*Spenser*) *vi* same as **grin**[1].

Grenache /grə-näsh'/ *n* a type of black grape, *orig* grown in S France and Spain (where it is known as **Garnacha**), used to produce a full-bodied red wine; a wine produced from this grape.

grenade /gri-nād'/ *n* a small bomb thrown by hand or shot from a rifle; a glass projectile containing chemicals for putting out fires, testing drains, dispensing poison gas or tear gas, etc. [Fr, from Sp *granada* pomegranate, from L *grānātus* full of seeds (*grāna*)]
■ **grenadier** /gren-ə-dēr'/ *n* orig a soldier trained in the use of grenades; then, a member of the first company of every battalion of foot soldiers; now used as the title (Grenadier Guards) of part of the Guards Division of infantry; any of various African weaver birds with red and black plumage; a deep-sea fish of the Macrouridae family.

Grenadian /grə-nā'di-ən/ or **Grenadine** /gren'ə-dēn/ *adj* of or relating to the state of *Grenada* in the Caribbean, or its inhabitants. ◆ *n* a native or inhabitant of Grenada.

grenadilla see **granadilla**.

grenadine[1] /gren'ə-dēn/ *n* a pomegranate syrup, or similar, used in certain drinks. [Ety as for **grenade**]

grenadine[2] /gren'ə-dēn/ *n* a thin silk or mixed fabric. [Fr, perh *Granada*]

Grenzgänger /grents'gen-gər/ (Ger) *n* (*pl* **Grenz'gänger**) a person who crosses a national or political border, *esp* (*hist*) from the communist countries to the West.

grese see under **gree**[2].

Gresham's law see under **law**[1].

gressing see under **gree**[2].

gressorial /gre-sö'ri-əl/ (*zool*) *adj* adapted for walking (also **gresso'rious**). [L *gressus*, pap of *gradī* to walk]

greve an obsolete variant of **greave**[1,2].

grew[1] /grōō/ *pat* of **grow**.

grew[2] see under **gruesome**.

grew[3] /grōō/ or **grewhound** /grōō'hownd/ (*Scot* or *N Eng dialect*) *n* a greyhound. [By confusion with obs *Grew* Greek]

grex venalium /greks ve-nā'li-əm or we-nä'li-oom/ (L) *n* the venal crowd or throng. [Literally, the herd of hirelings]

grey or (*esp N Am*) **gray** /grā/ *adj* of a mixture of black and white with little or no hue; dull, dismal; pale; neutral, anonymous; intermediate in character, condition, etc; grey-haired, old, mature; belonging or relating to the elderly. ◆ *n* a grey colour; a grey or greyish animal, *esp* a horse; grey clothing; dull light; grey hair; a middle-aged or old person (*sl*); a dry, colourless, restrained or uninteresting person (*sl*). ◆ *vt* to make grey or dull; to indicate (a menu item) as unavailable (*comput*). ◆ *vi* to become grey or dull. [OE *græg*; cf Ger *grau*]
■ **grey'ing** *adj* becoming grey; becoming older, aging. ◆ *n* the process of becoming grey; (of population) the process or phenomenon of having a growing elderly or retired sector. **grey'ish** *adj* somewhat grey. **grey'ly** *adv*. **grey'ness** *n*.
□ **grey area** *n* an area between two extremes, having (mingled) characteristics of both of them; a situation in which there are no clear-cut distinctions; an area relatively high in unemployment but not classed as a development area (qv). **grey'beard** *n* a person whose beard is grey; an old man; a stoneware jar for liquor, a bellarmine. **grey'-coat** *n* a person who wears a grey coat, *esp* a pupil in certain schools; a Confederate soldier. ◆ *adj* of or relating to a grey-coat. **grey'-coated** *adj*. **grey economy** *n* unofficial or unusual economic activity not reflected in official information and statistics. **grey eminence** see **éminence grise**. **grey'-eyed** *adj*. **grey'-fish** *n* a dogfish (*US*); a young coalfish (*Scot*). **Grey Friar** *n* (also without *caps*) a Franciscan. **grey goose** *n* the greylag goose. **grey-goose quill**,

shaft or **wing** n (archaic) an arrow. **grey-haired'** or **grey-head'ed** adj. **grey'hen** n the female of the **black grouse** (see under **black**). **grey knight** n (stock exchange sl) a third party that makes a counteroffer to buy a company that is subject to an unwanted takeover bid without making its own ultimate intentions clear. **grey'lag** or **greylag goose** n a large greyish European goose (Anser anser) (perhaps from its lateness in migrating). **grey literature** n material published non-commercially, eg government reports. **grey mare** see under **mare¹**. **grey market** n the unofficial and often secret, but not necessarily illegal, selling of goods, etc alongside or in addition to an official or open market; a financial market trading in shares not yet officially listed. **grey matter** n the ashen-grey active part of the brain and spinal cord; intelligence or common sense (inf). **grey'-out** n (aeronautics) a mild or less severe (physical) blackout. **grey owl** n the tawny owl. **grey parrot** n a red-tailed grey African parrot. **grey'scale** n and adj (TV and comput) (of or relating to) a scale consisting of different shades of the colour grey. **grey seal** n a type of seal that populates N Atlantic coastal waters. **grey squirrel** n a N American squirrel naturalized in Britain. **grey'stone** n a grey volcanic rock. **grey water** n waste water from domestic sinks, baths and showers, that can be reused without purification (cf **black water**). **grey-weth'er** n a grey-coloured, rounded block of sandstone or quartzite, a relic of denudation, looking from a distance like a grazing sheep. **grey whale** n a grey baleen whale, Eschrichtius glaucus, with a mottled skin often disfigured by patches of barnacles. **grey wolf** n the N American timber wolf.

■ **the Greys** the Scots Greys (see under **Scots**).

greyhound /grā'hownd/ n a tall, slender breed of dog bred for its great speed and keen sight. [OE grīghund (cf ON greyhundr, or grey)]

greywacke /grā-wak'ə or -wak'i/ (geol) n an indurated sedimentary rock composed of grains (round or angular) and splinters of quartz, feldspar, slate, etc in a hard matrix. [Ger Grauwacke, partly translated, partly adopted]

□ **greywacke-slate'** n a fine-grained fissile greywacke.

grey-wether see under **grey**.

GRI (hist) abbrev: Georgius Rex Imperator (L), George, King and Emperor.

gribble /grib'l/ n a small marine isopod (genus Limnoria) that bores into timber under water. [Perh from grub]

grice¹ /grīs/ (dialect or archaic) n (pl **grices** or **grice**) a little pig (also **gryce**). [ON grīss]

grice² see under **gree²**.

gricer /grī'sər/ n a trainspotter or railway enthusiast. [Origin uncertain]
■ **grī'cing** n.

Grid /grid/ abbrev: the Global Resource Information Database (of the United Nations Environment Programme).

grid /grid/ n a grating; a gridiron; a framework; a network; a network of power transmission lines; a network of lines for finding places on a map, or for some other purpose; a framework above a theatre stage from which scenery and lights may be suspended; a perforated screen or spiral of wire between the filament and the plate of a thermionic valve (electronics). [Back-formation from **gridiron**]
■ **gridd'er** n (US) an American-football player.
□ **grid'lock** n a traffic jam; a situation in which no progress is possible, a standstill. **grid'locked** adj. **grid reference** n a series of numbers and letters used to indicate the location of a place on a map.
■ **off the grid** not using one or more public utilities.

griddle /grid'l/ or (Scot) **girdle** /gûr'dl, gir'dl/ n a flat iron plate placed over heat for making eg drop scones; a flat, heated, metal cooking surface; a wire-bottomed sieve used by a miner (hist). ◆ vt to cook on a griddle; to sieve using a griddle (hist). [Anglo-Fr gridil, from a dimin of L crātis a hurdle]
□ **gridd'le-cake** n a drop scone; a thick pancake (US). **griddle car** n (old) a coach on a train where simple cooked meals can be obtained.

gride or **gryde** /grīd/ (poetic or archaic) vt and vi to pierce; to cut, esp with a grating sound; to graze; to grate. ◆ n a harsh grating sound. [gird² a blow]

gridelin /grid'ə-lin/ n and adj violet-grey. [Fr gris de lin flax grey]

gridiron /grid'ī-ərn/ n a frame of iron bars for broiling over a fire; a frame to support a ship during repairs; a network; an American-football field; the game of American football. ◆ vt to cover with parallel bars or lines. [ME gredire a griddle; from the same source as **griddle** (but the -ire ending became confused with ME ire iron)]

gridlock see under **grid**.

griece, grieced see under **gree²**.

grief /grēf/ n sorrow; distress; great mourning; affliction; a cause of sorrow; trouble, bother (sl); bodily pain (Shakesp). [OFr, from L gravis heavy]
■ **grief'ful** adj full of grief. **grief'less** adj.

□ **grief'-shot** adj (Shakesp) pierced with grief. **grief'-stricken** adj crushed with sorrow.
■ **come to grief** to meet with disaster or mishap; to end in failure.
good grief! an interjection indicating surprise or dismay.

griesie or **griesy** Spenserian forms of **grisy** (see under **gris¹**, **grise¹**).

griesly Spenserian form of **grisly**.

grieve¹ /grēv/ vi to feel grief; to mourn. ◆ vt to cause grief, distress or pain of mind to; to make sorrowful; to vex; to inflict bodily pain on or do bodily harm to (obs); to show grief for, regret bitterly (poetic). [OFr grever, from L gravāre, from gravis heavy]
■ **griev'ance** n a cause or source of grief; a ground of complaint; a formal complaint; a condition felt to be oppressive or wrongful; a burden or hardship; distress (obs); injury (obs); grief (obs). **griev'er** n. **griev'ingly** adv. **griev'ous** adj causing grief or distress; showing grief; extremely serious; burdensome; painful; severe; hurtful (obs). **griev'ously** adv. **griev'ousness** n.
□ **grievous bodily harm** n (law) serious physical injury received by a person attacked by another.

grieve² /grēv/ n a farm overseer (Scot); a governor or sheriff (hist). [Old Northumbrian græfa (WSax gerēfa); cf **reeve¹**]

griff¹ /grif/ (Brit and NZ sl) n (with the) the true facts, accurate information. [Shortened from earlier griffin; origin uncertain]

griff² or **griffe** /grif/ n a claw (rare); (**griffe**) a clawlike architectural ornament; a person of mixed African and European or Native American descent (US dialect); a steep narrow valley (dialect). [Fr griffe]

griffe see **griff²**.

griffin, griffon, gryfon or **gryphon** /grif'in or -ən/ n an imaginary animal with a lion's body and an eagle's beak and wings; a newcomer in India, a novice (Anglo-Ind); a pony never before entered for a race; a grimly or fiercely watchful guardian, esp over a young woman, a duenna (obs); a tip, a signal or warning (sl). [Fr griffon, from L grўphus, from Gr gryps a bird (probably the lammergeier), also a griffin, from grўpos hook-nosed]
■ **griff'inish** adj. **griff'inism** n.
□ **griffon vulture** n a European vulture, Gyps fulvus.

griffon¹ /grif'ən/ n a dog like a coarse-haired terrier. [Prob from **griffin**]
■ **Brussels griffon** a toy dog with a flat face.

griffon² see **griffin**.

grift /grift/ (US sl) vi to swindle (also n). [Perh from **graft²**]
■ **grif'ter** n a con man, swindler.

grig /grig/ n a cricket (dialect); a grasshopper (dialect); a small, lively eel, the sand-eel (dialect); a small, lively person. ◆ vt to tease, irritate. ◆ vi to fish for grigs (eels). [Origin obscure]
■ **merry as a grig** very merry and lively.

grigri see **grisgris**.

grike or **gryke** /grīk/ n a fissure in limestone rock formed or widened by the dissolvent effect of rain (geol); a deep valley, ravine (dialect). [ON kriki a crack]

grill¹ /gril/ vt to cook on a gridiron, under a grill, etc by radiant heat; to brand or mark with a gridiron; to interrogate aggressively; to torment (as though with burning heat); to scallop (oysters, etc). ◆ vi to undergo grilling. ◆ n a grating; a gridiron; a device on a cooker which radiates heat downwards; a grill room; a grilled dish; an act of grilling. [Fr griller, from a gril a gridiron, from a dimin of L crātis a grate]
■ **grillade'** n (obs; cookery) anything grilled. **grill'age** n (building and engineering) a foundation of crossbeams, eg on marshy ground. **grilled** adj cooked under a grill or on a gridiron; embossed with small rectangular indentations as those on certain late-19c postage stamps of the USA and Peru. **grill'er** n. **grill'ing** n.
□ **grill room** n a part of a restaurant where beefsteaks, etc are served grilled to order. **grill'steak** n a large steak-shaped burger of seasoned minced beef, lamb, etc usu stored frozen and grilled without preliminary defrosting.
■ **mixed grill** a dish of several grilled meats usu with mushrooms, tomatoes, etc.

grill² or **grille** /gril/ n a lattice, grating, screen or openwork of metal, generally used to enclose or protect a window, car radiator, shrine, etc, or on a helmet to protect the face; a grating in a convent or jail door, etc; (in real tennis) a square opening in the corner of an end wall of the court. [Fr; see **grill¹**]
□ **grill'work** or **grille'-work** n.

grilse /grils/ n a young salmon on its first return from salt water. [Origin unknown]

grim /grim/ adj (**grimm'er; grimm'est**) forbidding; stern; ghastly, grisly; sullen, dismal; depressing, gloomy; repellent, unappealing; unyielding, harsh; unpleasant; ill (inf); ferocious (obs). [OE grim(m); Ger grimmig, from Grimm fury, Du grimmig, ON grimmr]
■ **grim'ly** adv. **grim'ness** n.
□ **grim'looked** adj (Shakesp) having a grim or dismal aspect.

grimace /grim'əs or gri-mās'/ n a distortion of the face, in fun, disgust, etc; a smirk. ◆ vi to make grimaces. [Fr]
■ **grim'acer** n.

grimalkin /gri-mal'kin or -möl'kin/ n an old (esp female) cat; a cat generally; a bad-tempered or tyrannical old woman (archaic). [**grey** and **malkin**]

grime /grīm/ n ingrained dirt; sooty or coaly dirt; a style of popular music combining elements of dancehall and hip-hop and characterized by the use of electronic sounds and strong basslines. ◆ vt to soil deeply; to cover with grime. [ME, from MDu grīme]
■ **grīm'ily** adv. **grīm'iness** n. **grīm'y** adj.

Grimm's law see under **law**[1].

grimoire /grē-mwär'/ n a magician's book for calling up spirits. [Fr; cf **gramary**]

grin[1] /grin/ vi (**grinn'ing**; **grinned**) to give a broad smile; to set the teeth together and withdraw the lips in pain, derision, etc. ◆ vt to express by grinning; to set (the teeth) in a grin (obs). ◆ n a broad smile. [OE grennian; ON grenja, Ger greinen, Du grijnen to grumble, Scot **girn**; related to **groan**]
■ **grinn'er** n. **grinn'ing** adj and n. **grinn'ingly** adv.
■ **grin and bear it** to endure pain or misfortune stoically.

grin[2] /grin/ (dialect) n a snare or trap (also vt). [OE grīn]

grind[1] /grīnd/ vt (prp **grīnd'ing**; pat **ground** /grownd/ or (obs) **grind'ed**; pap **ground** or (obs) **ground'en**) to reduce to powder or small particles by friction or crushing; to wear down, sharpen, smooth or roughen by friction; to rub together harshly; to force (in, into; lit and fig); (with out) to produce by great effort, or by working a crank; (with down) to oppress or harass; to work by a crank. ◆ vi to be moved or rubbed together; to jar or grate; (with on or away) to continue (to work, etc) relentlessly and doggedly, esp at something tedious; to read or study hard; (with on) to drone or harp on (inf); (of a dancer) to circle the hips erotically (inf). ◆ n the act, sound or jar of grinding; the specific fineness of particles in a ground powder, esp coffee; drudgery, a hard, tedious task; laborious study for an examination, etc; a bore, bother (inf); a student who gives all his or her time to study (US); private tuition (Irish); in dancing, an erotic circling movement of the hips (inf). [OE grindan]
■ **grind'er** n someone who, or that which, grinds; a tooth that grinds food; a coach or crammer of students for examination; a hard-working student or dogged worker. **grind'ery** n a place where knives, etc are ground; shoemakers' materials. **grind'ing** n an act or process of the verb to grind; the act of reducing to powder. ◆ adj for grinding; wearing down; very severe; extortionate; (of sound) harsh; giving a harsh sound. **grind'ingly** adv. **ground'en** adj (archaic) sharpened.
❑ **grind'house** n (US) a genre of film exploiting sex, violence and horror. **grind rail** or **grinding rail** n a long narrow bar, raised above the ground, on which stunts may be performed in skateboarding, etc. **grind'stone** n a circular revolving stone for grinding or sharpening tools. **ground beef** n (N Am) minced beef. **ground glass** n glass fogged by grinding, sandblasting or etching; glass in the form of fine particles, used as an abrasive.
■ **grind the face** (or **faces**) **of** to oppress, esp by taxation. **grind to a halt** to move more and more slowly until finally coming to a standstill (lit and fig). **keep one's** (or **someone's**) **nose to the grindstone** to subject oneself (or someone) to continuous hard work. **take a grinder** (Dickens) to put the left thumb to the nose and to work an imaginary coffee mill round it with the right hand (a gesture of derision).

grind[2] /grind/ (Spenser) pat of **grin**[1].

gringo /gring'gō/ (derog inf) n (pl **grin'gos**) in Spanish-speaking America, someone whose language is not Spanish, esp an English-speaker. [Sp, gibberish, prob from Griego Greek]

griot /grē-ō'/ n in parts of Africa (esp W Africa), a tribal teller of legends and history, a poet, singer and musician; a member of the caste or class of such troubadours, considered of low social status. [Fr, of uncertain origin]

grip[1] /grip/ n a grasp or firm hold, esp with the hand or mind; strength of grasp; the handle or part by which anything is grasped; a method or style of grasping; a particular mode of grasping hands for mutual recognition, a secret handshake; a bag for travel (orig US); a holding or clutching device, eg a clasp for the hair, or a cable-car braking device; power, mastery; a twinge, spasm, pinch of distress; grasp, or power of holding the mind or commanding the emotions; grippe; a stagehand who moves scenery, etc, or a member of a camera crew responsible for manoeuvring the camera (also **grips**); a job or occupation (Aust inf). ◆ vt (**gripp'ing**; **gripped** /gript/) to take or keep a firm hold of; to hold fast the attention or interest of; to command the emotions of. ◆ vi to maintain a firm hold. [OE gripe grasp, gripa handful]
■ **gripp'er** n someone who, or that which, grips; a clutch, claw, or similar device. **gripp'ing** adj holding the attention; exciting.

gripp'ingly adv. **gripp'y** adj inclined to be mean or greedy (Scot); having grip; tenacious.
❑ **grip'sack** n (US) a bag for travel, a grip. **grip'tape** n a rough adhesive tape, used to provide extra grip.
■ **come** or **get to grips** (**with**) to tackle at close quarters, or (fig) seriously and energetically. **the grip** (Scot) the lump (qv under **lump**).

grip[2] /grip/ or (dialect) **gripe** /grīp/ n a small ditch, gutter or trench to carry away surface water, a drain. ◆ vt to trench or ditch. [OE grӯpe ; cf LGer gruppe, grüppe]

gripe[1] /grīp/ vi to keep on complaining (inf); to cause, or to suffer, a painful stomach spasm; to clutch (obs). ◆ vt to cause a painful stomach spasm in; to secure with gripes (naut); to grasp (obs); to seize and hold fast (archaic); to squeeze or pinch; to afflict, oppress. ◆ n a grumble (inf); (esp in pl) severe spasmodic pain in the intestines; a secure hold, grasp; a lashing for a boat on deck; a pain, pang (obs); forcible retention (obs); a usurer (obs sl). [OE grīpan (grāp, gripen); ON grīpa, Ger greifen, Du grijpen]
■ **grīp'er** n. **grīp'ing** adj (of a person) constantly complaining; (of a pain) seizing acutely; avaricious, grasping. **grīp'ingly** adv.
❑ **gripe site** n (inf) a website set up as a forum for people to air their grievances about an organization. **gripe water** or specif **Gripe Water**® n a solution given to infants to relieve colic and minor stomach ailments.

gripe[2] or **grype** /grīp/ (obs) n a griffin; a vulture. [Gr gryps]
❑ **gripe's egg** n a large oval cup.

gripe[3] see **grip**[2].

gripple see **gripple**.

grippe /grēp/ n (an old term for) influenza. [Fr, from gripper to seize]

gripple (Spenser **griple**) /grip'l/ adj gripping, grasping; greedy. ◆ n (obs) a grip, grasp; a hook. [OE gripul, from stem of grīpan (see **gripe**[1])]

Griqua /grē'kwä/ n one of a people of Griqualand, in South Africa; one of a mixed Khoikhoi and European race (Khoikhoi prevailing), living chiefly in Griqualand.

gris[1] /gris/ or **grise** /grīs/ adj (obs) grey. ◆ n (obs) a grey fur. [Fr]
■ **griseous** /griz'- or gris'i-əs/ adj (zool, bot, etc) grey; blue-grey or pearl-grey. **grisy** (Spenser **griesie** or **gryesy**) /all grī'zi/ adj (obs) grey.

gris[2] see under **gree**[2].

grisaille /grē-zāl' or -zä'ē/ n a style of painting on walls or ceilings, in greyish tints in imitation of bas-reliefs; a similar style of painting on pottery, enamel or glass; a work in this style. ◆ adj painted in this style. [Fr, from gris grey]

gris-amber /gris-am'bər/ (obs) n ambergris.
❑ **gris-amb'er-steam'd** adj (Milton) flavoured by steam from melted ambergris.

grise[1] /grīz/ (obs) vt to shudder at; to terrify. ◆ vi to shudder with fear. [From the verb of which OE āgrīsan is a compound; cf **agrise**]
■ **grī'sy** (Spenser **griesy** or **grysie**) adj grim; horrible; grisly.

grise[2] see under **gree**[2].

grise[3] see **gris**[1].

Griselda /gri-zel'də/ n a woman of excessive meekness, from the heroine of an old tale retold by Boccaccio, Petrarch and Chaucer.

grisely see **grisly**.

griseofulvin /griz-i-ō-fŭl'vin/ (med) n an oral antibiotic used as a treatment for fungal infections. [Isolated from the fungus Penicillium griseofulvum dierckx ; L griseus grey, and fulvus reddish-yellow]

griseous see under **gris**[1].

grisette /gri-zet'/ n (esp formerly) a young French female worker; a name given to varieties of eg birds, moths, fungi. [Fr grisette grey dress fabric, the usual garb of such women, from gris grey]

grisgris, **grigri** or **greegree** (also **gris-gris**, etc) /grē'grē/ n (pl **gris'gris**, **gri'gris** or **gree'grees**) an African charm, amulet or spell. [Fr; prob of African origin]

griskin /gris'kin/ (dialect) n lean meat from a loin of pork. [**grice**[1]]

grisled /griz'ld/ same as **grizzled** (see under **grizzle**[2]).

grisly /griz'li/ adj frightful, ghastly (also (rare) adv). —Also **greisly** (Spenser and Milton) and **griesly**, **grisely**, **grysely** or **gryesly** (all Spenser). [OE grislic; cf **grise**[1]]
■ **gris'liness** n.

grison /griz'ən, grīz'ən or -on/ n a grey, carnivorous S American mammal similar to a large weasel (Galictis vittata); a grey carnivorous mammal of a related species (Galictis cuja). [Fr, from gris grey]

grissino /gri-sē'nō/ n (pl **grissi'ni** /-nē/) a long, cylindrical Italian breadstick. [Ital]

grist /grist/ n corn for grinding, or ground; corn for grinding, or ground, at one time; malt for one brewing; supply, portion, quantity (old US);

a measure of the thickness of rope or yarn; profit (*fig*). [OE *grīst*; cf **grind**[1]]

□ **grist'-mill** *n* a mill for grinding grain.

■ **grist to the mill** raw material for feeding a process; anything that can be turned to profit or advantage.

gristle /gris'l/ *n* cartilage, *esp* when present in meat. [OE]

■ **grist'liness** *n*. **grist'ly** *adj*.

grisy see under **gris**[1], **grise**[1].

grit[1] /grit/ *n* small hard particles of sand, stone, etc; gravel (*obs*); a coarse sandstone, often with angular grains (also **grit'stone**); the texture of stone; strength of character, toughness, indomitability; small woody particles in the flesh of a pear. ◆ *vt* and *vi* to grind or clench (one's teeth); to make a grating sound; to spread (eg icy roads, to prevent skidding) with grit. [OE *grēot*; Ger *Griess* gravel]

■ **gritt'er** *n* a person who, or machine or vehicle that, applies grit. **gritt'ily** *adv*. **gritt'iness** *n*. **gritt'y** *adj* having or containing hard particles; of the nature of grit; determined, plucky; uncompromising. □ **grit blasting** *n* a process used in preparation for metal spraying which cleans the surface and gives it the roughness required to retain the sprayed metal particles. **grit'stone** see **grit** (*n*) above.

grit[2] /grit/ *adj* (**gritt'er**; **gritt'est**) a Scottish form of **great**; (of a ewe) in lamb.

grith /grith/ or **girth** /girth/ (*hist*) *n* sanctuary, asylum. [OE *grith*] □ **grith'-stool** *n* a seat in which a fugitive was in sanctuary.

grits /grits/ *n pl* coarsely ground grain, *esp* oats or (*US*) hominy; a boiled dish of this. [OE *grytta*; cf **groats**]

grivet /griv'it/ *n* a NE African guenon monkey (*Cercopithecus aethiops*), a vervet monkey. [Fr; origin unknown]

grize see under **gree**[2].

grizzle[1] /griz'l/ *vi* to grumble; to whimper; to cry fretfully. ◆ *n* a bout of grizzling. [Origin unknown]

■ **grizz'ler** *n*.

grizzle[2] /griz'l/ *n* a grey colour. [ME *grisel*, from Fr *gris* grey]

■ **grizz'led** *adj* (*esp* of hair or a beard) grey, or mixed with grey. **grizz'ly** *adj* of a grey colour. ◆ *n* (*mining*) a set of parallel bars or a grating used for the coarse screening of ores, rocks, etc; the **grizzly bear** (*Ursus horribilis*) of the Rocky Mountains, a fierce brown bear with white-tipped fur.

Gro. *abbrev*: Grove (in street names).

groan /grōn/ *vi* to utter a sustained, deep-toned sound expressive of distress, disapprobation, etc; to complain; to creak loudly; to be weighed down (with *under*, *beneath* or *with*; *esp* of a table *with* food); to be oppressed, suffer (with *under* or *beneath*). ◆ *vt* to utter or express with or by means of a groan. ◆ *n* a deep moan; the sound, or an act, of groaning; a complaint; a grinding rumble. [OE *grānian*]

■ **groan'er** *n*. **groan'ful** (*archaic*; *Spenser* **grone'full**) *adj*. **groan'ing** *n* and *adj*. **groan'ingly** *adv*.

□ **groaning board** *n* (*archaic*) a table weighed down with very generous supplies of food.

groat /grōt/ (formerly *grōt*) *n* an obsolete English silver coin, worth four old pence and after 1662 coined only as Maundy money (the silver fourpenny-piece, coined 1836–56, was not officially called a groat); a very small sum, proverbially. [MDu *groot*, literally, great, ie thick]

■ **groats'worth** *n* (*obs*).

groats /grōts/ *n pl* hulled (and crushed) grain, *esp* oats. [OE *grotan* (pl)]

Grobian /grō'bi-ən/ *n* a boorish rude slovenly person. [Ger *Grobianus*, a character in German satire of the 15c and 16c, from *grob* coarse]

■ **Gro'bianism** *n*.

grocer /grō'sər/ *n* a person who sells food and general household supplies; a grocer's shop. [Earlier *grosser* a wholesale dealer; OFr *grossier*, from LL *grossārius*, from *grossus*; cf **gross**]

■ **grō'cery** *n* the trade, business or premises of a grocer; (*usu* in *pl*) articles sold by grocers; a grocer's shop or food and liquor shop (*US*). **grocete'ria** *n* (*N Am*) a self-service grocery store. □ **grocer's apostrophe** *n* an apostrophe erroneously used to create a plural, as notoriously seen in grocers' handwritten signs.

grockle /grok'l/ (*derog inf*) *n* a tourist or incomer, *esp* in SW England. [Origin unknown]

grody /grō'di/ (*US sl*) *adj* (**grō'dier**; **grō'diest**) sleazy, grotty, inferior, revolting, offensive, disgusting. [Perh a blend of **gross** and **mouldy**]

grog /grog/ *n* formerly, a mixture of spirits and water; any alcoholic drink, *esp* beer (*Aust* and *NZ inf*); bricks or waste from a clayworks broken down and added to clay to be used for brick manufacture (*building*). ◆ *vi* to drink grog; (with *on*) to drink steadily (*Aust inf*). ◆ *vt* to extract the spirit from the wood of empty spirit-casks by soaking with hot water. [From Old *Grog*, the nickname (appar from his *grogram* cloak) of Admiral Vernon, who in 1740 ordered that rum (until 1970 officially issued to sailors) should be mixed with water]

■ **grogg'ery** *n* (*US*; *old*) a disreputable public house. **grogg'ily** *adv*. **grogg'iness** *n* the state of being groggy. **grogg'y** *adj* dazed, unsteady from illness or exhaustion; affected by grog, partially intoxicated (*archaic*); weak and staggering from blows (*boxing*); applied to a horse that bears wholly on its heels in trotting.

□ **grog'-blossom** *n* a redness of the nose due to drinking. **grog'-on** or **grog'-up** *n* (*Aust inf*) a drinking party or drinking session. **grog'-shop** *n* a drinking place of disreputable character (now *rare*); a shop selling alcoholic liquor (*Aust* and *NZ*).

grogram /grog'rəm/ *n* a kind of coarse cloth of silk and mohair. [OFr *gros grain* coarse grain]

groin[1] /groin/ *n* the area between the lower abdomen and the thigh; the genitals, *esp* the testicles (*euphem*); the line of intersection of two vaults, also a rib along the intersection (*archit*). ◆ *vt* to form into groins; to build in groins. [Early forms *grind*, *grine*, perh from OE *grynde* abyss]

■ **groined** *adj*. **groin'ing** *n*.

□ **groin'-centring** *n* the centring of timber during construction.

groin[2] US spelling of **groyne**.

groin[3] /groin/ (*obs*) *vi* to grunt, growl; to grumble. [OFr *grogner*, from L *grunnīre* to grunt]

grok /grok/ or /gräk/ (*sl*) *vt* and *vi* (**grokking**, **groking** or **grocking**; **grokked**, **groked** or **grocked**) to understand fully. [Coined by Robert Heinlein in his novel *Stranger in a Strange Land* (1961) as a Martian word meaning 'to drink']

Grolier /grō'lyā/ *n* a book or a binding from the library of the French bibliophile Jean *Grolier* (1479–1565).

■ **Grolieresque** /grō-lyər-esk'/ *adj* in the style of Grolier's bindings, with geometrical or arabesque figures and leaf-sprays in gold lines.

groma /grō'mə/ *n* a surveying instrument used by the Romans, in which plumb-lines suspended from the arms of a horizontal cruciform frame were used to construct right angles. [L *grōma* a surveyor's pole, measuring rod]

grommet (rarely **gromet**) /grom'it/ or **grummet** /grum'it/ *n* a ring of rope or metal; a rubber or plastic washer to protect or insulate electrical wire passing through a hole; a metal ring lining an eyelet; an eyelet; a hole edged with rope; a washer of hemp and red-lead putty, paint or some other substance; (*usu* **grommet**) a small tube passed through the eardrum to drain the middle ear (*med*); a ring of stiffener inside a (*esp* novice) seaman's or serviceman's cap; (**grommet**) a young or novice surfer or skateboarder (*sl*). [Perh 15c Fr *grom(m)ette* (Fr *gourmette*) curb of a bridle]

□ **grumm'et-hole** *n*.

gromwell /grom'wəl/ *n* any plant of the genus *Lithospermum*, of the borage family, with smooth, stonelike seeds formerly used medicinally; the oyster plant (genus *Mertensia*), also of the borage family. [OFr *gromil*]

grone an obsolete form of **groan**.

groof or (*obs*) **grouf**, **grufe** /groof/ (*Scot*) *n* the front of one's body; one's face. [ON *ā grūfu* face downwards; cf **grovelling**]

groo-groo see **gru-gru**.

groom /groom or grŭm/ *n* a person who looks after horses; a title of several officers in a noble or royal household (eg *groom of the stole*, *grooms-in-waiting*); a bridegroom; a boy or young man, *esp* a servant (*obs*). ◆ *vt* to tend (*esp* a horse); to smarten; of an animal, to clean and maintain (all aspects of its own body surface, or of that of another member of the same species); to prepare for a particular, often political office, stardom, or success in any sphere; to cultivate an apparently harmless friendship, eg on the Internet, with a child whom one intends to subject to sexual abuse (*inf*). [Origin obscure; cf Du *grom* fry, offspring, OFr *gromet* boy (see **gourmet**, **grummet**[2]); encroaching on OE *guma* (as in bride*groom*) a man]

■ **groom'er** *n*.

□ **grooms'man** *n* the attendant on a bridegroom.

groove /groov/ *n* a furrow, or long hollow, *usu* one cut with a tool; the track cut into the surface of a record, along which the needle of the record player moves; a set routine; repeated musical rhythms used in creating dance music; a joyful mood, excellent form (*old sl*); a pleasurable or groovy experience (*sl*). ◆ *vt* to make or cut a groove or furrow in. ◆ *vi* to experience great pleasure (*old sl*); to be groovy (*old sl*); to listen or dance to pop or jazz music (*inf*). [Prob Du *groef*, *groeve* a furrow; cognate with Ger *Grube* a pit, ON *grōf*, Eng **grave**[1]]

■ **grooved** *adj*. **groov'er** *n*. **groov'ily** *adv*. **groov'iness** *n*. **groov'y** *adj* in top form, or in perfect condition, up-to-date in style, or generally, pleasant or delightful (*old sl*); following a set routine (as though set in grooves) (*old inf*); passé, old-fashioned (*sl*).

■ **in the groove** (*old sl*) in excellent form; up-to-date, fashionable.

grope /grōp/ *vi* (often with *for*) to search, feel about, as if blind or in the dark; to search one's mind with uncertainty or difficulty. ◆ *vt* to find (one's way) by feeling; to fondle (someone) for sexual pleasure (*inf*). ◆ *n* (*inf*) an act of sexual fondling. [OE *grāpian*; related to **grab**[1], **gripe**[1]]

■ **grop′er** *n*. **grop′ing** *adj* and *n*. **grop′ingly** *adv*.

groper[1] same as **grouper**[1].

groper[2] see under **grope**.

grosbeak /grōs′bēk/ *n* any of various finches, buntings and weavers with thick, heavy seed-crushing bills, such as the hawfinch, the cardinal, and the rose-breasted grosbeak. [Fr *grosbec*, from *gros* thick, and *bec* beak]

groschen /grō′shən/ *n* a former Austrian and German unit of currency of various values; a small silver coin current in the north of Germany from the 13c to the late 19c, varying in value between $\frac{1}{24}$ and $\frac{1}{36}$ of a thaler. [Ger]

groser /grō′zər/, **grosert** or **grossart** /-zərt/, also **groset** /-zit/ (*Scot*) *n* a gooseberry. [Fr *groseille*]

grosgrain /grō′grān/ *n* a heavy corded silk used *esp* for ribbons and hat bands. [Fr]

gros point /grō point/ *n* a large cross-stitch or tent stitch used in embroidery, covering two vertical and two horizontal threads of the canvas; embroidery composed of this stitch. [Fr]

gross /grōs/ *adj* total, including everything, without deductions; extremely fat, obese; enormous, bulky; stupid, dull, slow; coarse, sensual; obscene; extreme; flagrant, glaring, palpable; crass, boorish; coarse in mind; dense in growth, rank; solid, earthbound, not ethereal; disgusting, repulsive (*inf*); (of pay) before the deduction of income tax, National Insurance, superannuation and other voluntary deductions; (of a horse) naturally large-girthed, as opposed to overweight (*racing*). ◆ *n* (*pl* **gross**) the main bulk; the whole taken together, sum total (revived from *obs*); twelve dozen, 144; the total profit. ◆ *adv* before tax or other contributions have been deducted. ◆ *vt* to make as total income or revenue. [Fr *gros*, from L *grossus* thick]

■ **gross′ly** *adv*. **gross′ness** *n*.

❑ **gross capital employed** *n* (*account*) the capital and other finance used by a business, which is the total value of assets as shown on the balance sheet. **gross circulation** *n* the total sales of a magazine or newspaper before mistakes or the number of unsold copies have been taken into consideration. **gross domestic product** *n* the gross national product less income from foreign investments, the total value of goods and services produced within a country. **gross earnings** *n pl* a person's total income received from all sources. **gross investment** *n* (*econ*) spending on replacement of worn-out and obsolescent buildings, machinery and equipment and on increasing stock of such capital assets. **gross loss** *n* (*bookkeeping*) the loss made when the cost of goods exceeds their sales value. **gross margin** or **profit** *n* (*business*) the difference between the selling price of an article and the cost of the materials and labour needed to produce it. **gross national product** *n* the total value of all goods and services produced in a specified period (*usu* annually) within a country (ie the gross domestic product) plus the income from property held in foreign countries and incomes of domestic residents received from abroad as salaries, dividends or interest, minus similar payments made to residents of other countries. **gross′-out** *n* (*inf*, chiefly *N Am*) something offensive, disgusting, sickening (also *adj*). See also **gross out** below. **gross output** *n* the total selling value of (a firm's) output within a given period, *incl* the value of necessary materials bought to produce that output. **gross profit** see **gross margin** above. **gross profit margin** *n* the gross profit expressed as a percentage of sales. **gross profit mark-up** *n* the gross profit expressed as a percentage of the cost price of goods. **gross redemption yield** *n* the average annual yield on a gilt-edged stock, including dividend payments and any capital gain or loss. **gross weight** *n* (*business*) the combined weight of an article and its packaging.

■ **great gross** a dozen gross (ie 1728). **gross out** (*inf*, chiefly *N Am*) to disgust, shock, offend with indecency or sickening behaviour. **gross up** to convert a net figure into a gross one for the purpose of tax calculation, etc. **in gross** in bulk, wholesale.

grossart see **groser**.

grossièreté /gros-yer-tā′/ (*Fr*) *n* grossness, rudeness, coarseness.

grossular /gros′ū-lər/ or **grossularite** /-īt/ *n* gooseberry-stone, a lime alumina garnet, often green. [Fr *groseille* gooseberry, Latinized as *grossulāria*]

grosz /grosh/, **grōsh** or **grōsh′** *n* (*pl* **gro′szy** or **gro′sze** /-shi/) a Polish monetary unit, $\frac{1}{100}$ of a zloty. [Pol]

grot[1] /grot/ (*inf*) *n* worthless things; rubbish. [Back-formation from **grotty**]

grot[2] /grot/ (*poetic*) *n* a grotto.

grotesque /grō-tesk′/ *adj* extravagantly formed; fantastic; bizarre; ludicrous, absurd. ◆ *n* an extravagant piece of art, featuring animals,

plants, etc, in fantastic or incongruous forms; a bizarre figure or object. [Fr *grotesque*, from Ital *grottesca*, from *grotta* a grotto]

■ **grotesque′ly** *adv*. **grotesque′ness** *n*. **grotesqu′ery** or **grotesqu′erie** *n*.

Grotian /grō′shi-ən/ *adj* of or relating to Hugo *Grotius*, Latin name of Huig de *Groot* (1583–1645), founder of the science of international law.

❑ **Grotian theory** *n* the theory that man is essentially a social being, and that the principles of justice are of perpetual obligation and in harmony with man's nature. **Grotian** or **governmental** (**theory of the**) **Atonement** *n* the theory that Christ paid the penalty of human sin in order that God might for His sake forgive sinners while preserving the law that punishment should follow sin.

grotto /grot′ō/ *n* (*pl* **grott′oes** or **grott′os**) a cave; an imitation cave, *usu* fantastic or fanciful in appearance. [Ital *grotta* (Fr *grotte*), from L *crypta*, from Gr *kryptē* a crypt, vault]

■ **grott′oed** *adj*.
❑ **grott′o-work** *n*.

grotty /grot′i/ (*inf*) *adj* ugly, dirty, in bad condition, or useless; ill. [*grotesque*]

■ **grott′iness** *n*.

grouch /growch/ *vi* to grumble. ◆ *n* a grumbler; a bad-tempered complaint; the cause of such a complaint; a spell of grumbling; sulks. [See **grutch**, **grudge**]

■ **grouch′ily** *adv*. **grouch′iness** *n*. **grouch′y** *adj*.

grouf see **groof**.

grough /gruf/ *n* a deep gully or channel eroded in upland peat moor areas such as the Peak District. [Perh from obs or dialect *groff* rough, coarse; see **gruff**]

ground[1] /grownd/ *n* the solid surface of the earth; a portion of the earth's surface; land; soil; the floor, etc; the solid land underlying an area of water (*naut*); earth (*elec*; *N Am*); position; an area of land or sea associated with some activity (such as *football ground*, *playground*, *battleground*, *fishing ground*); distance covered or to be covered; matters to be dealt with; that on which something is raised (*lit* or *fig*); a foundation; sufficient reason; an advantage; the bottom, *esp* sea-bottom (*obs*); the surface on which a work is represented (*art*); the background in a painting; a first coat of paint or colour; surrounding rock (*mining*); the space behind the popping crease with which the batsman must be in touch by bat or person if he is not to be stumped or run out (*cricket*); short for **ground-bass** below; (in *pl*) an area of land attached to or surrounding a building; (in *pl*) dregs or sediment (eg of coffee); (in *pl*) the basis of justification. ◆ *vt* to fix on a foundation or principle; to put or rest on the ground; to cause to run aground; to instruct in first principles; to cover with a preparatory layer or coating, as a basis for painting, etching, etc; to earth (*elec*; *N Am*); to keep on the ground, prevent from flying (*aeronautics*); to suspend from usual activity (eg as a punishment). ◆ *vi* to come to the ground; to strike the sea-bottom, etc and remain fixed. ◆ *adj* of, relating to, situated or operating on or near the ground; living on or in the ground; low-growing. [OE *grund*; cognate with Ger *Grund*, ON *grunnr*]

■ **ground′age** *n* a charge on a ship in port. **ground′ed** *adj* positioned on the ground; in control of one's emotions, rational; remaining humble and down to earth in spite of having achieved success; (of a child) forbidden to go out to meet friends. **ground′edly** *adv* on good grounds. **ground′er** *n* someone who, or something that, grounds; a ball that keeps low. **ground′ing** *n* a foundation; a sound general knowledge of a subject; the background of embroidery, etc; the act or process of preparing or laying a ground; the act of laying or of running aground; in bioenergetics, the concept of bodily contact, *esp* through the feet, with the earth. **ground′less** *adj* without ground, foundation or reason. **ground′lessly** *adv*. **ground′lessness** *n*. **ground′ling** *n* a fish that keeps near the bottom of the water, *esp* the spinous loach; a low-growing or creeping plant; a person on the ground in contrast to one in an aircraft, etc; formerly, a spectator in the pit of a theatre, and hence a person of the common herd. ◆ *adj* (*Lamb*, etc) base.

❑ **ground′-angling** *n* fishing without a float, with a weight placed a few inches from the hook, bottom-fishing. **ground annual** *n* (*Scots law*) an annual payment forming a burden on land. **ground′-ash** *n* a sapling of ash; a stick made of an ash sapling. **ground′bait** *n* bait dropped to the bottom to attract fish to a general area (also *fig*). **ground′-bass** *n* (*music*) a bass part constantly repeated with varying melody and harmony. **ground′-beetle** *n* any beetle of the Carabidae, a family related to the tiger beetles. **ground′breaking** *n* (*esp US*) the breaking of ground at the beginning of a construction project. ◆ *adj* innovative, breaking new ground. **ground′burst** *n* the explosion of a bomb on the ground (as opposed to in the air). **ground cherry** *n* any of the European dwarf cherries; any of several plants of the genus *Physalis*, also called **husk-tomato**, **Cape gooseberry**, etc; the fruit of these plants. **ground control** *n* the control, by information radioed from a ground installation, of aircraft or spacecraft. **ground controller** *n*. **ground cover** *n* low plants and shrubs growing among the trees in a forest; various low herbaceous plants used to cover an area instead of grass. **ground crew** see **ground staff** below. **ground'-cuckoo** *n* a name for several ground-running birds of the cuckoo family, such as the roadrunner and the coucal. **ground'-dove** or **-pigeon** *n* any of various small American pigeons that spend much of their time on the ground. **ground effect** *n* the extra aerodynamic lift, exploited by hovercraft, etc and affecting aircraft flying near the ground, caused by the cushion of trapped air beneath the vehicle. **ground elder** *n* another name for goutweed. **ground'-feeder** *n* a fish that feeds at the bottom. **ground floor** or **storey** *n* the floor on or near a level with the ground. **ground frost** *n* frost on the surface of the ground; a temperature of 0°C or less registered on a horizontal thermometer in contact with a grass surface. **ground game** *n* hares, rabbits, etc, as distinguished from winged game. **ground'hog** *n* the woodchuck; the aardvark. **Groundhog Day** *n* (in the USA and Canada) 2 February, supposed to mark the end of winter if a groundhog emerging from hibernation on that day does not see its shadow; a day when things seem to happen in exactly the same way as on the previous day (*inf*). **ground'-hold** *n* (*Spenser* and *naut*) ground tackle. **ground'hopper** *n* a small insect of the family Tetrigidae; a football supporter who travels to see games at as many different stadiums as possible (*inf*). **ground ice** *n* the ice formed at the bottom of a body of water. **ground ivy** *n* a British labiate creeping plant (genus *Nepeta*) whose leaves when the edges curl become ivy-like. **ground loop** *n* an abrupt, uncontrolled movement of an aircraft while on the ground. **ground mail** or **grund mail** *n* (*Scot*) payment for right of burial. **groundman** see **groundsman** below. **ground'mass** *n* (*geol*) the fine-grained part of an igneous rock, glassy or minutely crystalline, in which the larger crystals are embedded. **ground moraine** *n* a mass of mud, sand and stones dragged along under a glacier or ice-sheet. **ground'nut** *n* the peanut or monkey nut (genus *Arachis*); the earth-nut. **ground oak** *n* a sapling of oak; various species of *Teucrium*. **ground'-officer** *n* an officer in charge of the grounds of an estate. **ground-pigeon** see **ground-dove** above. **ground pine** *n* a small Eurasian plant (*Ajuga chamaepitys*) with yellow flowers; a N American club moss (*Lycopodium obscurum*). **ground plan** *n* a plan of the horizontal section of the lowest or ground storey of a building; a first plan, general outline. **ground plate** *n* the bottom horizontal timber to which the frame of a building is secured. **ground'plot** *n* the plot of ground on which a building stands; a method of calculating the position of an aircraft by relating the ground speed and time on course to the starting position. **ground-position indicator** *n* an instrument which continuously displays the dead-reckoning position of an aircraft. **ground provisions** *n pl* (*W Indies*) starchy vegetables such as breadfruit and sweet potatoes. **ground'prox** *n* a device, fitted to large passenger aircraft, which warns the pilot when altitude falls below a given level (*ground proximity warning system*). **ground rent** *n* rent paid to a landowner for the right to the use of the ground for a specified term, usually 99 years in England. **ground'-robin** *n* the chewink. **ground rule** *n* a basic rule of procedure; a modifying (sports) rule for a particular place or circumstance. **ground run** *n* the distance that an aircraft travels down the runway before lift-off or after touching down before reaching a stop. **ground'sel**, **ground'sill** or (*obs*) **ground'sell** *n* the lowest timber of a structure, a ground plate, sleeper or soleplate. **ground'sheet** *n* a waterproof sheet spread on the ground in a tent, etc. **groundskeeper** see **groundsman** below. **ground'-sloth** *n* a large extinct ground-dwelling sloth. **grounds'man** or sometimes **ground'man** *n* a person whose job is to take care of a cricket ground or a sportsfield, etc (also (*US*) **grounds'keeper**); an aerodrome mechanic. **ground'speed** *n* (*aeronautics*) the speed of an aircraft relative to the ground. **ground squirrel** *n* the chipmunk or hackee, or any of several burrowing rodents. **ground staff** *n* aircraft mechanics, etc, whose work is on the ground (also **ground crew**); a paid staff of players (*cricket*); people employed to look after a sportsfield. **ground state** *n* the state of a nuclear system, atoms, etc when at their lowest (or normal) energy. **ground storey** see **ground floor** above. **ground stroke** *n* (*tennis*) a return played after the ball has bounced. **ground'swell** *n* a broad, deep undulation of the ocean caused by a distant gale or earthquake; a gathering movement, as of public or political opinion or feeling, which is evident although the cause or leader is not known. **ground tackle** *n* tackle for securing a vessel at anchor. **ground'-to-air** *adj* (of a missile) aimed and fired from the ground at a target in the air. **ground water** *n* water naturally in the subsoil or occupying space in rocks. **ground wave** *n* a radio wave which passes directly between a transmitting antenna and a receiving antenna. **ground'work** *n* that which forms the ground or foundation of anything; the basis; essential preparatory work; the first principle; the ground of painting (*art*). **ground zero** *n* the point on the ground directly under the explosion of a nuclear weapon in the air; a completely new beginning (*fig*).

■ **break ground** to begin working untouched ground; to take the first step in any project. **break new** (or **fresh**) **ground** to be innovative. **cover a lot of ground** to make good progress. **cover the ground** to treat a topic, etc adequately. **cut** or **take the ground from under**

someone or from under someone's feet to anticipate someone's arguments or actions and destroy their force. **down to the ground** see under **down¹**. **fall to the ground** to come to nothing. **forbidden ground** an unmentionable topic. **gain ground** to advance; to become more widely influential; to spread. **give ground** to fall back, retreat (*lit* and *fig*). **go to ground** (of an animal) to enter its burrow, hole, etc; to go into hiding. **hold** or **stand one's ground** to stand firm. **home ground** familiar territory. **into the ground** to the point of exhaustion. **(let in) on the ground floor** (to admit) on the same terms as the original promoters, or at the start (of a business venture, etc). **lose ground** to fall back; to decline in influence, etc. **off the ground** started, under way. **on firm** (or **shaky**) **ground** in a strong (or weak) position. **on one's own** (or **home**) **ground** in circumstances with which one is familiar. **on the ground** in the world of practical reality. **prepare the ground** to ease the way for, facilitate the progress of, something (with *for*). **run to ground** to hunt out, track down. **shift one's ground** to change one's standpoint in a situation or argument.

ground², **grounden** see **grind¹**.

groundsel¹ /*grown(d)'sl*/ *n* a very common yellow-flowered composite weed (*Senecio vulgaris*). [OE *gundeswilge*, appar from *gund* pus, and *swelgan* to swallow, from its use in poultices, infl by *grund* ground]

groundsel², **groundsell**, **groundsill** see under **ground¹**.

group /*groop*/ *n* a number of people or things together; a number of individual things or people related in some definite way differentiating them from others; a clique, school, section of a party; a number of commercial companies combined under single ownership and central control; a division of an air force made up of a number of wings; a division of the US Air Force subordinate to a wing; a US military unit formed of two or more battalions; a scientific classification; a combination of figures forming a harmonious whole (*art*); a system of elements having a binary operation that is associative, an identity element for the operation, and an inverse for every element (*maths*); a vertical column of the periodic table containing elements with similar properties, etc (*chem*); a number of atoms that occur together in several compounds (also **radical**; *chem*); a division in the Scout organization; a pop group. ◆ *vt* to form into a group or groups. ◆ *vi* to form into a group or groups; to fall into harmonious combination; to cluster, mass. [Fr *groupe*, from Ital *groppo* a bunch, knot, from Gmc; cf Ger *Kropf* protuberance]

■ **group'able** *adj*. **group'age** *n* the collection of objects or people into a group or groups. **group'er** *n* (*hist*) a member of the Oxford group. **group'ie** or **group'y** *n* (*sl*) a (*usu* female) fan who follows pop groups, or other celebrities, wherever they appear, often in the hope of having sexual relations with them. **group'ing** *n* (*art*) the act of disposing and arranging figures in a group. **group'ist** *n* an adherent of a group (also *adj*). **group'let** *n* (often *derog*) a small group, a clique or faction. **group'uscule** /*-ɔs-kūl*/ *n* (from Fr; often *derog*) a grouplet. **groupy** see **groupie** above.

❑ **group calling** *n* (with operator-connected extensions) automatic rerouting of incoming telephone calls to other extensions in a predetermined order until the call has been taken. **group'-captain** *n* a Royal Air Force officer of equivalent rank to a colonel or naval captain. **group discussion** *n* a meeting in which a group of people share their opinions on a particular subject (eg as a market research method, etc). **group dynamics** *n sing* (*psychol*) the interaction of human behaviour within a small social group. **group insurance** *n* insurance issued on a number of people under a single policy. **group marriage** *n* a hypothetical primitive relationship by which every man of a group is husband to every woman of a group. **group practice** *n* a medical practice in which several doctors work together as partners. **group selection** *n* a form of natural selection proposed to explain the evolution of behaviour which apparently is to the long-term good of a group or species, rather than to the immediate good of the individual. **group sex** *n* sexual activity in which more than two people take part simultaneously. **group theory** *n* (*maths*) the investigation of the properties of groups. **group therapy** *n* therapy in which a small group of people with the same psychological or physical problems discuss their difficulties under the chairmanship of eg a doctor. **group'think** *n* a philosophy to which all members of an organization are expected to conform, and which stifles individual opinions. **group trading** *n* (*business*) the practice by a number of traders of joining up, eg to improve distribution, cut administration costs, etc. **group'ware** *n* (*comput sl*) software that supports group activity. **group'work** or **group work** *n* work, eg in a school or office, carried out by a number of people acting together.

■ **Group of Five, Seven, Eight, Ten, Twenty**, etc (also **G5, G7, G8, G10, G20** or **G-5, G-7, G-8, G-10, G-20**, etc) various groups of economically powerful countries, all including France, Britain, Germany, United States and Japan, which have met to discuss matters of mutual interest. **pop group** see **pop²**.

grouper[1] /grōō'pər/ (US and Brit) or **groper** /grō'pər/ (Aust) n (pl **group'ers** or **grop'ers**, or (collectively) **group'er** or **grop'er**) any one of many fishes, esp various kinds resembling bass. [Port garoupa]

grouper[2] see under **group**.

grouse[1] /grows/ n (pl **grouse**) a plump reddish game bird (Lagopus lagopus scoticus) with a short curved bill, short legs, and feathered feet, found on Scottish moors and hills and in certain other parts of Britain (also called **red grouse**); extended to other birds of the family Tetraonidae, including the black grouse or blackcock, the willow-grouse and various birds of N America. [Origin uncertain]
□ **grouse'-disease** n a nematode infection of grouse. **grouse moor** n a tract of moorland on which grouse live, breed, and are shot for sport.

grouse[2] /grows/ vi to grumble. ◆ n a grumble. [Cf **grutch**]
■ **grous'er** n.

grouse[3] /grows/ (Aust and NZ inf) adj very good. [Origin unknown]

grout[1] /growt/ n (orig) coarse meal; a thin coarse mortar for filling cracks, etc (also called **cement grout**); a fine plaster for finishing ceilings, filling between tiles, etc; the sediment of liquor; lees. ◆ vt to fill and finish with grout. [OE grūt coarse meal; or perh in part Fr grouter to grout]
■ **grout'er** n. **grout'ing** n filling up or finishing with grout; the material so used. **grout'y** adj (dialect) thick, muddy; sulky (old US).

grout[2] /growt/ vi to root or grub with the snout. [Perh connected with OE grēot grit]

grove /grōv/ n a wood of small size, generally of a pleasant or ornamental character; an avenue of trees; (with cap) used in street names; an erroneous translation of Asherah, the wooden image of the goddess Ashtoreth, also of Hebrew eshel tamarisk, in Genesis 21.33 (Bible); a lodge of a benefit society called Druids. [OE gráf, poss tamarisk]

grovel /grov'l/ vi (**grov'elling** or (US) **grov'eling**; **grov'elled** or (US) **grov'eled**) to humble oneself, behave abjectly, eg in apologizing; to behave obsequiously or sycophantically; to lie face downwards, or crawl, in abject fear, etc. [Back-formation from ME groveling, grofling prone, from ON grúfa and sfx -ling]
■ **grov'eller** or (esp US) **grov'eler** n. **grov'elling** or (esp US) **grov'eling** adj abject, cringing, servile.

grovet /grov'ət/ (wrestling) n a hold in which a wrestler grips the opponent's head between his own chest and forearm, and forces the shoulders to the floor with his other arm.

grow /grō/ vi (pat **grew** /grōō/; pap **grown** /grōn/) to have life; to have a habitat; to become enlarged by a natural process; to advance towards maturity; to increase in size; to tend in a certain direction while growing; to develop; to become greater in any way; to extend; to pass from one state to another; to become; to come by degrees (to love, like, hate, etc). ◆ vt to cause or allow to grow; to produce or to cultivate; (in passive) to cover with growth. [OE grōwan; ON grōa]
■ **grow'able** adj. **grow'er** n. **grow'ing** n the action of the verb; the production of semiconductor crystals by slow crystallization from the molten state. **grown** adj (sometimes in combination) having reached full, or a certain degree of, growth, as in full-grown, half-grown. **growth** n a growing; gradual increase; progress, development; that which has grown; a diseased, abnormal formation; increase in value. ◆ adj characterized by or experiencing growth, esp economic growth. **growth'ist** n a person who is committed to or who is an advocate of growth, esp economic growth (also adj).
□ **grow'-bag** or sometimes **grow'ing-bag** n a large plastic bag containing compost in which seeds can be germinated and plants grown to full size. **growing pains** n pl neuralgic pains sometimes experienced in growing children; initial problems in the establishment and running of an enterprise, etc. **grow'ing-point** n (bot) the meristem at the apex of an axis, where active cell division occurs and differentiation of tissues begins. **grown'-junction** n a semiconductor junction produced by changing the types and amounts of acceptor and donor impurities added during growing. **grown'-up** n and adj (an) adult. **growth area** n (business and marketing) a region with rapidly increasing industrial and commercial activity, usu resulting from incentives offered to employers. **growth factor** n (biol) any substance that influences the growth of an organism or cell. **growth hormone** n a hormone secreted by the anterior lobe of the pituitary gland, that promotes growth in vertebrates; any of several natural or artificial substances that promote growth in plants. **growth industry** n an industry or branch of industry which is developing and expanding (also fig). **growth market** n (marketing) a market in which demand for a product is greatly increasing. **growth'-orientated** adj providing increased capital rather than high income. **growth promoter** n any of various substances which promote growth in plants, such as cytokinin; any of various hormonal substances used to boost the fattening of livestock. **growth ring** n a recognizable increment of wood in a cross-section of a branch or trunk, usu but not necessarily an annual ring. **growth-share matrix** n (marketing) a diagrammatic analysis of a company's portfolio of businesses, arranged according to their rate of market growth and their relative market share. **growth stock** n stock invested for its capital value rather than its yield in dividends. **growth substance** n one of a number of substances (sometimes called **plant hormones**) formed in plants or synthetically, that at low concentrations have specific effects on plant growth or development.
■ **grow into** to grow big enough to fill comfortably. **grow like Topsy** (inf) simply to grow, apparently from nothing (as Topsy in Harriet Beecher Stowe's Uncle Tom's Cabin assumed she did); (loosely) to grow in a random, indiscriminate or unplanned way. **grow on** to gain a greater hold on; to gain in the estimation of, become ever more acceptable to; (of seedlings) to (be stimulated to) develop into mature plants by suitable positioning, treatment, etc. **grow on trees** to be readily available without effort or expense. **grow out of** to issue from, result from; to pass beyond in development; to become too big for. **grow to** to advance to, come to (archaic); (of milk) to stick to the pan and develop a bad taste in heating (so prob Shakesp, Merchant of Venice, II.2; obs). **grow together** to become united by growth. **grow up** to advance in growth, become full-grown, mature or adult; to spring up.

growl /growl/ vi (of a dog) to utter a deep rough murmuring sound in the throat expressive of hostility; (of thunder, etc) to make a sound similar to this; to speak or grumble surlily, snarl. ◆ vt to utter or express by growling. ◆ n a murmuring, snarling sound, as of an angry dog; a surly grumble. [Cf Du grollen to grumble; related to Gr gryllizein to grunt]
■ **growl'er** n someone who or something that growls; a N American river fish, the large-mouthed black bass, so named from the sound it emits; a small iceberg; a four-wheeled horse-drawn cab (old sl); a jug or pitcher used for carrying beer (US inf). **growl'ery** n (archaic) a retreat for times of ill-humour. **growl'ing** n and adj. **growl'ingly** adv. **growl'y** adj.

grown, **growth** see **grow**.

groyne /groin/ n a breakwater, of wood or other material, to check erosion and sand-drifting. [Prob OFr groin snout, from L grunnīre to grunt, but perh the same as **groin**[1]]

GRT or **grt** abbrev: gross registered tonnage, (in shipping) a measurement of cubic capacity.

GRU abbrev: Glavnoye Razvedyvatelnoye Upravleniye (Russ), Chief Intelligence Directorate, the military intelligence organization of the former Soviet Union.

grub /grub/ vi (**grubb'ing**; **grubbed**) to dig, work or search in the dirt (with about or around); to be occupied meanly, toil, slog (with about or around); to eat (sl); (of a horse) to take its feed. ◆ vt to dig or root out of the ground (generally followed by up or out); to dig up the surface of (ground) to clear it for agriculture, etc; to supply with food (sl). ◆ n an insect larva, esp one thick and soft; food (inf); (also **grub'hunter**) a ball that travels along the ground (sport; inf). [ME grobe; origin uncertain]
■ **grubb'er** n someone who, or that which, grubs; an implement for grubbing or stirring the soil; a grub (sport); a grub kick. **grubb'ily** adv. **grubb'iness** n. **grubb'y** adj dirty, soiled, grimy; infested with grubs.
□ **grub kick** n (rugby) a kick which sends the ball low along the ground. **grub screw** n a small headless screw. **grub shop** n (inf) a restaurant. **grub'stake** n (US) an outfit, provisions, etc given to a prospector for a share in finds. ◆ vt to provide with such. **Grub Street** n a former name of Milton Street, Moorfields, London, once inhabited by booksellers' hacks and shabby writers generally; the milieu of hack writers or activity of hack writing. **Grub'street** adj.

grubble /grub'l/ an obsolete variant of **grabble**.

grudge /gruj/ vt to envy (a person something); to give or allow (something to a person) unwillingly; to resent (doing something); to murmur at (obs). ◆ vi (obs) to murmur, show discontent. ◆ n an old cause of quarrel or resentment; a feeling of enmity or envy. [**grutch**]
■ **grudge'ful** adj (rare; Spenser). **grudg'ing** n and adj. **grudg'ingly** adv.
□ **grudge fight** or **match** n a fight or contest arranged to settle a long-standing quarrel.
■ **grudge a thought** (Shakesp) to thank resentfully or grudgingly.

grue see under **gruesome**.

gruel /grōō'əl/ n a thin food made by boiling oatmeal in water; punishment, severe treatment (archaic inf). ◆ vt to subject to any severe or exhausting experience. [OFr gruel (Fr gruau) groats, from LL grūtellum, dimin of grūtum meal, of Gmc origin; cf OE grūt]
■ **gru'elling** or (US) **gruel'ing** n and adj (an experience, ordeal, encounter, defeat, etc that is) punishing, backbreaking, exhausting. **gru'ellingly** adv.

gruesome /grōō'səm/ adj horrible; grisly; macabre. [Cf Du gruwzaam, Ger grausam]

■ **grue** or **grew** *n* (*Scot*) a creeping of the flesh; a shiver; a shudder; a pellicle of ice. ◆ *vi* (*Scot*) to shudder; to feel the flesh creep; (of the flesh) to creep; (of the blood) to curdle. **grue'somely** *adv*. **grue'someness** *n*.

grufe see **groof**.

gruff /*gruf*/ *adj* rough, or abrupt in manner or sound. [Du *grof*; cognate with Swed *grof* and Ger *grob* coarse]
■ **gruff'ish** *adj*. **gruff'ly** *adv*. **gruff'ness** *n*.

grufted /*gruf'tid*/ (*dialect*) *adj* dirty, begrimed. [Dialect *gruft* particles of soil]

gru-gru or **groo-groo** /*groo'groo*/ *n* a name for several tropical American palms related to the coconut palm, yielding oil-nuts; an edible weevil grub (also **gru-gru worm**) found in their pith. [Poss a native name]

grumble /*grum'bl*/ *vi* to murmur with discontent; to express discontent; to mutter, mumble, murmur; to growl, rumble. ◆ *n* the act of grumbling; an instance or spell of grumbling; a cause or occasion for grumbling. [Cf Du *grommelen*, frequentative of *grommen* to mutter; Ger *grummeln*]
■ **grum'bler** *n*. **Grumbletō'nian** *n* (*hist*; *derog*) a member of the country party as opposed to the court party, after 1689. **grum'bling** *n* and *adj*. **grum'blingly** *adv*. **grum'bly** *adj* inclined to grumble.
❑ **grumbling appendix** *n* an intermittent pain in the vermiform appendix, often a precursor of appendicitis.

grume /*groom*/ *n* (*med*) a thick, viscous fluid; a clot. [OFr *grume* a bunch, from L *grūmus* a little heap]
■ **grum'ous** or **grum'ose** *adj* of or like grume; clotted, lumpy; composed of grains (*bot*).

grummet¹ see **grommet**.

grummet² /*grum'it*/ (*hist*) *n* a cabin-boy. [OFr *gromet*; see ety of **gourmet**]

grumose, grumous see under **grume**.

grump /*grump*/ (*inf*) *n* a bad-tempered, surly person; (in *pl*) a fit of bad temper, the sulks. ◆ *vi* to grumble, complain. [Obs *grump* snub, sulkiness]
■ **grum'pily** *adv*. **grum'piness** *n*. **grum'py** *adj* surly. ◆ *n* a bad-tempered person.

grumph /*grumf*/ (*Scot*) *n* a grunt. ◆ *vi* to grunt. [Imit]
■ **grumph'ie** *n* a pig.

grundle /*grun'dl*/ (*US sl*) *n* the perineum. [Origin unknown]

grund mail see **ground mail** under **ground¹**.

Grundyism /*grun'di-i-zm*/ *n* conventional prudery, from the question 'But what will Mrs *Grundy* say?' in Thomas Morton's play, *Speed the Plough* (1798).

grunge /*grunj*/ (*orig US*) *n* dirt, grime, trash; any unpleasant, nasty substance; thrift-shop fashion; its designer equivalent; a style of rock music featuring a discordant guitar sound and lyrics expressing social alienation. [Prob an imit coinage]
■ **grung'y** or **grung'ey** *adj* dirty, messy; unattractive, unappealing; of or relating to grunge fashion or music.

grunion /*grun'yən*/ *n* a small Californian sea-fish which spawns on shore. [Prob Sp *gruñón* grunter]

grunt /*grunt*/ *vi* (of a pig) to make a gruff snorting noise; to produce a short gruff noise in the throat. ◆ *vt* to utter with a grunt. ◆ *n* a sound made by a pig; any similar sound made by a person or animal; power (*inf*); a tropical spiny-finned fish (*Haemulon*, etc) of a family related to the snappers, that grunts when taken from the sea; an infantry soldier (*milit sl*); a labourer, drudge (*US sl*). [OE *grunnettan*, frequentative of *grunian*]
■ **grunt'er** *n* a person who or animal that grunts; a pig; any of several kinds of grunting fish. **grunt'ing** *n* and *adj*. **grunt'ingly** *adv*. **grunt'le** *vi* (*dialect*) to grunt, keep grunting. ◆ *n* (*Scot*) a grunt; a snout.
❑ **grunt work** *n* monotonous and unrewarding work, *esp* of a physical nature.

gruntled /*grun'tǝld*/ (*facetious*) *adj* happy, pleased, in good humour. [Back-formation from **disgruntled**]

gruppetto /*groo-pet'ō*/ (*music*) *n* (pl **gruppett'i** /-*ē*/) a series of short notes. [Ital, a small group]

grutch /*gruch*/ (*Spenser*) *vt* or *vi* to grudge or complain. ◆ *n* a grudge; a complaint. [OFr *groucher*, *grocher*, *gruchier* to grumble]

grutten see **greet²**.

Gruyère /*grü'*, *grwē'yer* or -*yer'*/ *n* a whole-milk cheese, made at *Gruyère* (Switzerland) and elsewhere.

gr. wt. *abbrev*: gross weight.

gryce see **grice¹**.

gryde see **gride**.

gryesly see **grisly**.

gryesy see under **gris¹**.

gryfon see **griffin**.

gryke see **grike**.

grype see **gripe²**.

gryphon see **griffin**.

grypt /*gript*/ (*Spenser*) *prob* for **griped** or **gripped** in the sense of bitten, pierced.

grysbok /*hhräs'bok* (*S Afr*) or *grīs'bok*/ *n* a small S African antelope, ruddy chestnut with white hairs. [Du, greybuck, from *grijs* grey, and *bok* a buck]

grysely see **grisly**.

grysie see under **grise¹**.

GS *abbrev*: General Secretary; General Staff; Grammar School.

gs *abbrev*: gauss; guineas.

GSA (*Brit*) *abbrev*: Girls' Schools Association.

GSM *abbrev*: Global System for Mobile communications (*orig Groupe Spéciale Mobile*), an international standard for mobile telephone services; Guildhall School of Music and Drama.

gsm *abbrev*: gram(me)s per square metre.

GSO *abbrev*: General Staff Officer.

GSOH *abbrev*: good (or great) sense of humour.

G-spot see under **G** (*abbrev*).

GSR *abbrev*: galvanic skin response.

GST *abbrev*: (in Canada, Australia, etc) goods and services tax.

G-string see under **G** (*n*).

g-suit see under **g**.

GT *abbrev*: gran turismo (see **gran²**).
❑ **GTi** *n* gran turismo injection.

Gt or **gt** *abbrev*: Great or great.

gt. (*med*) *abbrev*: gutta, a drop.

GTC *abbrev*: General Teaching Council (**GTCE** for England; **GTC(NI)** for Northern Ireland; **GTCS** for Scotland; **GTCW** for Wales); good till cancelled (on an order for goods, securities, etc); Government Training Centre.

gtd *abbrev*: guaranteed.

G2B *abbrev*: government-to-business.

gu see **gue**.

guacamole /*gwä-kǝ-mō'li* or *gwo-*, *gwa-*/ *n* a dish of mashed avocado with tomatoes, onions and seasoning. [Am Sp, from Nahuatl *ahuacamolli*, from *ahuacatl* avocado, and *molli* sauce]

guacharo /*gwä'chä-rō*/ *n* (pl **gua'charos**) the oilbird, a S American nocturnal fruit-eating bird (genus *Steatornis*) that roosts in caves, similar to the nightjars. [Sp *guacharo*]

guaco /*gwä'kō*/ *n* (pl **gua'cos**) any of several tropical American plants reputedly antidotal against snakebite, *esp* species of *Mikania* (climbing composites), and of *Aristolochia*; the medicinal substance obtained from them. [Am Sp]

guaiacum /*gwī'ǝ-kǝm*/ *n* any of a family of tropical American trees of the genus *Guaiacum*, some yielding lignum vitae; (also **guaiac**) their greenish resin, used in medicine. [Sp *guayaco*, from a Haitian word]

guan /*gwän*/ *n* any of a number of noisy arboreal S American game birds of the curassow family. [Am Sp]

guana /*gwä'nä*/ *n* any large lizard. [For **iguana**]

guanaco /*gwä-nä'kō*/ *n* (pl **guana'co** or **guana'cos**) a wild llama (also **huana'co** /*-wä-*/ (pl **huana'co** or **huana'cos**)). [Quechua *huanaco*]

guanazolo /*gwä-nä-zō'lō*/ *n* a synthetic substance (amino-hydroxy-triazolo-pyrimidine), a guanine analogue used for controlling the growth of tumours.

guango /*gwang'gō*/ *n* (pl **guan'gos**) the rain tree or saman. [Sp, prob from Quechua]

guanine /*gwä'nēn*/ *n* a yellowish-white, amorphous substance, found in guano, liver, pancreas, and other organs of animals, and germ cells of plants, forming a constituent of nucleic acids. [**guano** and **-ine¹**]

guano /*gwä'nō*/ *n* (pl **gua'nos**) the dung of sea-fowl, used as manure; artificially produced fertilizer, *esp* made from fish. [Sp *guano*, *huano*, from Quechua *huanu* dung]
■ **guanif'erous** *adj*.

guar /*gwär*/ *n* a legume grown for forage and for its seeds which yield guar gum; guar gum. [Hindi]
❑ **guar gum** *n* a powder ground from guar seeds, used in the food industry as a thickening agent and stabilizer, as a sizing for paper, etc.

guaraná /*gwä-rä-nä'*/ *n* a Brazilian liana (*Paullinia cupana*, of the family Sapindaceae); a paste made from its seeds which are high in caffeine (**guaraná bread**); a drink or drug made from this, with stimulant and astringent properties, etc. [Tupí]

Guaraní /gwä-rä-nē´/ n a member of a group of tribes of S Brazil and Paraguay (pl **Guaraní**´); their language, closely related to Tupí. ◆ adj of or relating to the Guaraní or their language.

guarani /gwä´rə-ni/ n (pl **gua´ranis**, **gua´rani** or **gua´ranies**) the standard monetary unit of Paraguay (100 céntimos). [Guaraní]

guarantee /gar-ən-tē´/ n a formal promise that something will be done, esp one in writing by the maker of a product to replace or repair it if it proves faulty within a stated period; generally, a promise or assurance; a legally binding agreement to take responsibility for another person's obligation or undertaking; a pledge or surety; someone to whom a guarantee is given, who gives a guarantee, or who acts as guarantor. ◆ vt (**guarantee´ing**; **guaranteed´**) to issue a guarantee in respect of (eg an article or product); to secure (with against or from); to ensure, make certain or definite; to engage or undertake; to undertake as surety for another person. [Anglo-Fr garantie, from garant warrant, and prob Sp garante ; see **warrant¹**]
■ **guar´antor** (or /-tör´/) n a person who makes a guaranty; a person in a guarantee contract who agrees to answer for a debt or default of another. **guar´anty** n a securing, guaranteeing; a written undertaking to be responsible; a person who guarantees; a security. ◆ vt (now rare) to guarantee.
❑ **guarantee company** n a company in which the members undertake to contribute money up to a certain amount if the company is wound up. **guarantee payment** n a payment ordered by statute to be paid to an employee by his or her employer where the employee has been laid off or put on short-time working. **guarantee society** n a fund which undertakes to make good any debts incurred by the people who pay into it.

guard /gärd/ vt to keep watch over; to take care of; to protect from danger or attack; to control passage through (a doorway, etc); in any of several games, to make a move to protect (a piece, etc); to escort (archaic); to protect the edge of, as by an ornamental border; to provide with guards; to trim (lit and fig; Shakesp). ◆ vi to watch; to be wary; to take precautions. ◆ n keeping safe; protection; watch; that which guards from danger; a person or contingent stationed to keep watch, protect, or keep in custody; a person in charge of a railway train or, formerly, a stagecoach; a state of caution; a posture of defence; either of two players positioned away from the basket (basketball); a lineman positioned immediately to the left or right of the center (American football); this position; the position of a batsman's bat relative to the wicket when standing ready to receive a ball (cricket); a part of a sword hilt; a watch chain; a cricketer's or other sportsperson's protective pad or shield; (in a book) a strip for attachment of a plate, map or additional leaf; a trimming, or a stripe (obs); (in pl) household troops (Foot, Horse, and Life Guards). [OFr garder, from OHGer warten ; OE weardian, Mod Eng **ward**]
■ **guard´able** adj. **guard´age** n (Shakesp) wardship. **guard´ant** or **gard´ant** adj (heraldry) having the face turned towards the viewer. ◆ n (Shakesp) protector. **guard´ed** adj wary; cautious; uttered with caution; trimmed, or striped (obs). **guard´edly** adv. **guard´edness** n. **guardee´** n (inf) a guardsman, esp in reference to elegant or dashing appearance. **guard´less** adj without a guard; defenceless.
❑ **guard´-book** n a blank book with guards. **guard cell** n (bot) one of the lips of a stoma, a pair of specialized epidermal cells. **guard dog** n a watchdog. **guard hair** n one of the long coarse hairs which form the outer fur of certain mammals. **guard´house** n a building for the accommodation of a military guard, and where prisoners are confined. **guard of honour** see under **honour**. **guard´rail** n a rail (on a ship, train, etc, or beside a road) acting as a safety barrier; an additional rail fitted to a railway track to improve a train's stability. **guard ring** n a keeper, or finger-ring that serves to keep another from slipping off. **guard´room** n a room having the same function as a guardhouse. **guard´-ship** or **guard´ship** n a ship of war that superintends marine affairs in a harbour and protects it; guardianship (archaic; Swift). **guards´man** or **guards´woman** n a soldier of the Guards, or (US) National Guard. **guard's van** n (on a railway train) the van in which the guard travels.
■ **mount guard** to go on guard. **on** (or **off**) **guard** or **one's guard** on (or not on) the alert for possible danger; wary (or unwary) about what one says or does. **run the guard** to get past a guard or sentinel without detection. **stand guard** to keep watch, act as sentry.

guardian /gär´di-ən/ n a person who guards or takes care of someone or something; a person who has the care of the person, property and rights of another (eg a minor; law); (in England until 1930) a member of a board administering the poor laws. ◆ adj protecting. [Anglo-Fr gardein]
■ **guard´ianship** n.
❑ **guardian angel** n an angel supposed to watch over a particular person; a person specially devoted to the interests of another; (in pl;

with caps) vigilantes patrolling a place (orig the New York subway) to prevent crimes of violence.

guarish or **garish** /gä´rish/ (obs) vt to heal. [OFr guarir (Fr guérir) to heal]

Guatemalan /gwat-ə-mä´lən/ adj of or relating to the Republic of Guatemala in Central America, or its inhabitants. ◆ n a native or citizen of Guatemala.

guava /gwä´və/ n a small tropical American myrtaceous tree of the genus Psidium ; its yellow, pear-shaped fruit, often made into jelly. [Sp guayaba guava fruit; of S American origin]

guayule /gwä-ū´lā/ n a silvery-leaved shrub of the daisy family (Parthenium argentatum), native to Mexico and SW USA; the rubber yielded by it. [Sp; of Nahuatl origin]

gub¹ /gub/ (Scot inf) n the mouth. ◆ vt (**gubb´ing**; **gubbed**) to strike on the mouth; to defeat comprehensively. [Gaelic gob mouth]

gub² /gub/ or **gubbah** /gub´ə/ (Aust inf ; derog) n a white man. [Aboriginal term, meaning 'white demon']

gubbins /gub´inz/ (inf) n sing (pl **gubb´inses**) a trivial object; a device, gadget; a silly person, fool. ◆ n sing or n pl rubbish. [From obs gobbon portion, perh connected with **gobbet**]

gubernaculum /gū-bər-nak´ū-ləm/ n in mammals, the cord supporting the testes in the scrotal sac. [Ety as for **gubernator**]
■ **gubernac´ular** adj.

gubernator /gū´bər-nā-tər/ n (rare) a governor. [L gubernātor a steersman]
■ **guberna´tion** n (rare) control, rule. **gubernatorial** /-nə-tö´ri-əl/ adj (esp US) of, or relating to, a governor.

guck /guk/ n (esp N Am; sl) n slimy, gooey muck; anything unpleasant or unappealing. [Prob goo or gunk and muck]
■ **guck´y** adj slimy, gooey, mucky; slushy, sloppy, sentimental.

guddle /gud´l/ (Scot) vt and vi to fish with the hands by groping under the stones or banks of a stream. ◆ vi to dabble in, play messily with, something liquid. ◆ n a mess, muddle, confusion. [Origin uncertain]

gude or **guid** /gūd or gid/ Scottish forms of **good**.
❑ **gudeman**, **gudesire**, etc see under **good**.

gudgeon¹ /guj´ən/ n an easily caught small carp-like freshwater fish (genus Gobio); a person easily cheated. ◆ adj (archaic) foolish. ◆ vt (archaic) to impose on, cheat. [OFr goujon, from L gōbiō, -ōnis a kind of fish, from Gr kōbios ; see **goby**]

gudgeon² /guj´ən/ n the bearing of a shaft, esp when made of a separate piece; a metallic journal piece let into the end of a wooden shaft; a metal pin into which the pintle of a small craft's rudder fits; a pin. [OFr goujon the pin of a pulley]
❑ **gudgeon pin** n in an internal combustion engine, a pin fastening the piston to the connecting rod.

gue, **gu** or **gju** /goo or gū/ n a kind of viol formerly used in Shetland. [ON gigja]

Guebre or **Gueber** /gä´bər or gē´bər/ n a Zoroastrian in Iran. [Fr guèbre, from Pers gabr ; see **giaour**]

guelder rose /gel´dər rōz/ n a shrub of the genus Viburnum, with large white balls of flowers. [From Geldern in Germany, or from the Dutch province of Gelderland]

Guelf or **Guelph** /gwelf/ (hist) n a member of a papal and popular party in medieval Italy, opposed to the Ghibellines and the emperors. [Guelfo, Italian form of the German family name Welf, said to have been the war cry of Henry the Lion at the battle of Weinsberg (1140) against the Emperor Conrad III]
■ **Guelf´ic** adj relating to the Guelf family or party.

guenon /gen´ən or gə-nɔ̃/ n any species of the genus Cercopithecus, long-tailed African monkeys. [Fr]

guerdon /gûr´dən/ (esp poetic) n a reward or recompense. ◆ vt to reward. [OFr guerdon, gueredon (Ital guiderdone), from LL widerdonum, from OHGer widarlōn (OE witherlēan), from widar against, and lōn reward; or more prob the latter part of the word is from L dōnum a gift]

guereza /ger´ə-zə/ n a large, long-haired, black-and-white African monkey, with a bushy tail; any species of the same genus (Colobus). [Appar of Somali origin]

guéridon /gā-rē-dɔ̃/ or /ger´i-dən/ n a small ornate table or stand. [Fr]

guerilla see **guerrilla**.

guérite /ge-rēt´/ n a turret or sentry box (hist); a type of chair with a back that is elongated and curves over to form a hood. [Fr, from OFr garite ; see **garret**]

guernsey /gûrn´zi/ n (sometimes with cap) a close-fitting knitted woollen jersey, esp worn by sailors; a usu sleeveless football shirt (Aust); (with cap) one of a breed of dairy cattle from Guernsey, in the

Channel Islands; (with *cap*) Channel Island patois derived from Norman-French. ◆ *adj* (sometimes with *cap*) in the style of a guernsey. ❑ **Guernsey lily** *n* a plant of the genus *Nerine*.
■ **get a guernsey** (*Aust*) to be selected for a team; to win approval.

guerre à mort /ger a mör'/ (*Fr*) war to the death.

guerre à outrance /ger a oo-trãs'/ (*Fr*) war to the uttermost, to the bitter end.

guerrilla or **guerilla** /gə-ril'ə/ *n* a member of an irregular force engaging in warfare or in the harassment of an army, etc, *usu* operating in small bands, and often politically motivated. ◆ *adj* of, relating to, or in the manner of guerrillas; (of an action, strategy, etc) aiming to surprise through speed and suddenness. [Sp *guerrilla*, dimin of *guerra* war, from OHGer *werra*; cf **war**[1]; Fr *guerre*]
■ **guerrillero** /-yā'ro/ *n* (*pl* **guerriller'os**) a guerrilla, someone who takes part in guerrilla warfare.

guess[1] /ges/ *vt* to judge on the basis of inadequate knowledge or none at all; to conjecture; to hit on or solve by conjecture; to think, believe, suppose. ◆ *vi* to make a conjecture or conjectures. ◆ *n* a judgement made or opinion formed without sufficient evidence or grounds; a random surmise; a riddle, conundrum (*Scot*). [ME *gessen*; cognate with Du *gissen*; Dan *gisse*, Mod Icel *giska*, *gizka*, for *gitska*, from *geta* to get, think; see **get**, **forget**]
■ **guess'able** *adj*. **guess'er** *n*. **guess'ing** *n* and *adj*. **guess'ingly** *adv*.
❑ **guess'work** *n* the process or result of guessing.
■ **anybody's guess** purely a matter for individual conjecture, impossible for anyone to know. **keep someone guessing** to cause someone to remain in a state of uncertainty.

guess[2] see **othergates**.

guesstimate or **guestimate** /ges'ti-mət/ *n* (*orig facetious*) a *guess*ed *estimate*, or one based on very little knowledge. ◆ *vt* to estimate using a rough guess.

guest /gest/ *n* a visitor received and entertained gratuitously or for payment; a person visiting one's home by invitation, to stay, for a meal, etc; a person paying for accommodation in a hotel, etc; a person honoured with hospitality by a government, organization, etc; an animal inhabiting or breeding in another's nest (*zool*). ◆ *adj* and *n* (an artist, conductor, etc) not a regular member of a company, etc, or not regularly appearing on a programme, but taking part on a special occasion. ◆ *vi* to be a guest artist, etc. ◆ *vt* to have as a guest artist on a show. [OE (Anglian) *gest* (WSax *giest*), perh infl by ON; related to Du *gast* and Ger *Gast*, L *hostis* stranger, enemy]
■ **guest'en** *vi* (*obs*; *Walter Scott*) to stay as a guest. **guest'wise** *adv* (*obs*) in the manner or capacity of a guest.
❑ **guest beer** *n* a beer which is on sale for a limited period in a public house, in addition to its regular beers. **guest'-chamber** (*archaic*; *Bible*) or **guest'-room** *n* a room for the accommodation of a guest. **guest'-house** *n* a small boarding house; a hospice (*archaic*). **guest'-night** *n* a night when non-members of a society are entertained. **guest-room** see **guest-chamber** above. **guest rope** *n* a rope hanging over the side of a vessel to help other vessels drawing alongside, etc. **guest worker** *n* a foreign worker employed temporarily in a country.
■ **be my guest** used to express willingness and approval for a proposed action.

Gueux /gø/ *n pl* the name assumed in 1566 by the confederation of nobles and others to resist the introduction of the Inquisition into the Low Countries by Philip II of Spain. [Fr, beggars]

guff /guf/ *n* nonsense, humbug (*inf*); a smell, stink (*Scot*). [Perh imit; cf Norw *gufs* a puff]
■ **guff'ie** *n* (*Scot*) a pig.

guffaw /gu-fö'/ *vi* to laugh vociferously. ◆ *n* a loud, boisterous laugh. [From the sound]

guga /goo'gə/ (*Scot*) *n* a young gannet, eaten as a delicacy, *esp* in the Hebrides. [Gaelic]

guggle /gug'l/ *vi* to gurgle. ◆ *n* a gurgle. [Cf **gurgle**]

GUI (*comput*) *abbrev*: Graphical User Interface (see under **graph**).

guichet /gē'shā/ *n* a hatch or other small opening in a wall, door, etc; a ticket-office window. [Fr; cf **wicket**]

Guicowar see **Gaekwar**.

guid see **gude**.

guide /gīd/ *vt* to lead, conduct or direct; to regulate, steer, control; to influence. ◆ *vi* to act as a guide. ◆ *n* a person who, or thing which, guides; a person who conducts travellers, tourists, mountaineers, etc; someone who directs another in their course of life; a soldier or other employed to obtain information for an army; (with *cap*) a member of an organization for girls analogous to the Scout Association (also formerly **Girl Guide**); a guidebook; anything serving to direct, show the way, determine direction of motion or course of conduct.

[OFr *guider*; prob from a Gmc root, as in OE *witan* to know, *wīs* wise, Ger *weisen* to show, connected with **wit**[2], **wise**]
■ **guid'able** *adj*. **guid'age** *n* (*obs*) guidance. **guid'ance** *n* direction; leadership. **guide'less** *adj*. **guid'er** *n* a person who guides; a device for guiding; (with *cap*) a captain or lieutenant in the Guides. **guide'ship** *n*. **guid'ing** *n* the action of the verb; (*usu* with *cap*) the activities of a Guide.
❑ **guide'book** *n* a book of information for tourists. **guide card** *n* (in a card index file) a card, *usu* with a protruding tab on its upper edge, used as a divider, eg to indicate the beginning of an alphabetic or numeric division. **guided atmospheric flight** *n* any unpiloted aeronautical flight, as of guided missiles, remotely piloted military aircraft, drones, and radio-controlled model aircraft. **guided missile** *n* a jet- or rocket-propelled projectile carrying a warhead and electronically directed to its target for the whole or part of the way by remote control. **guide dog** *n* a dog trained to lead a blind person. **guide'line** *n* a line drawn, or a rope, etc fixed, to act as a guide; (often *pl*) an indication of the course that should be followed, or of what future policy will be (*fig*). **guide'post** *n* a post to guide the traveller. **guide rail** *n* an additional rail to keep rolling stock on the rails at a bend; a rail designed to guide the movement of any object. **guide rope** *n* a rope for guiding the movement of a thing hoisted, towed or hauled. **guiding light** or **star** *n* a person or thing adopted as a guide or model.

guidon /gī'dən/ *n* a pennant, *usu* with a rounded outer edge, carried by certain cavalry regiments or mounted batteries; the officer who carries it. [Fr, from Ital *guidone*, appar from *guida* guide]

Guignol /gē-nyol'/ *n* the chief puppet in traditional French puppet shows. [Name originated in Lyon in 18c; said to be that of a local 'character']
■ **Grand Guignol** /grã/ a small theatre in Paris that specialized in short plays of horror; horror plays of this type; (without *caps*) something intended to horrify people.

guild or **gild** /gild/ *n* an association for mutual aid; a corporation; a medieval association looking after common (*esp* trading) interests, providing mutual support and protection, and masses for the dead (*hist*); the hall or meeting-place of a guild (*obs*; *Spenser* **gyeld**); a group of plants distinguished by their way of life (eg saprophytes, or parasites; *ecology*). [OE *gield*, infl by ON *gildi*]
■ **guild'ry** *n* (*Scot*) the corporation of a royal burgh; membership of it (*obs*).
❑ **guild'-brother** *n* a fellow member of a guild. **guild'hall** *n* the hall of a guild; a town hall. **guilds'man** *n* a male member of a guild. **Guild Socialism** *n* a form of socialism that would make trade unions or guilds the authority for industrial matters. **guilds'woman** *n* a female member of a guild.

guilder or **gilder** /gil'dər/ *n* a former unit of currency in the Netherlands, replaced by the euro; an old Dutch and German gold coin; the standard monetary unit of Suriname (100 cents); vaguely, a coin (*Shakesp*). [Du *gulden*]

guile or (*Spenser*) **guyle** /gīl/ *n* cunning; deceit; a stratagem or trick (*obs*). ◆ *vt* (*Spenser*) to beguile. [OFr *guile* deceit, perh Gmc; cf **wile**]
■ **guiled** *adj* (*obs*) armed with deceit; treacherous. **guile'ful** *adj* crafty; deceitful. **guile'fully** *adv*. **guile'fulness** *n*. **guile'less** *adj* without deceit; artless. **guile'lessly** *adv*. **guile'lessness** *n*. **guil'er** or **guyl'er** *n* (*Spenser*) a deceiver.

Guillain-Barré syndrome /gē-yē'ba-rā' sin'drōm/ (*med*) *n* acute polyneuritis causing weakness or paralysis of the limbs. [Georges *Guillain* (1876–1961) and Jean *Barré* (1880–1967), French neurologists]

guillemot /gil'i-mot/ *n* a diving bird of the genus *Uria* with a long pointed bill, a member of the auk family. [Fr, dimin of *Guillaume* William, perh suggested by Breton *gwelan* gull]

guilloche /gi-lösh'/ (*art* or *archit*) *n* ornamental borders or mouldings formed of interlacing curved bands enclosing roundels. ◆ *vt* to decorate with intersecting curved lines. [Fr, a guilloching tool; said to be named from one *Guillot*]

guillotine /gil'ə-tēn or -tēn', also gē'yə-/ *n* an instrument for beheading people with a descending heavy angled blade, adopted during the French Revolution; a machine (either manually or electrically operated) with a single heavy blade for cutting or trimming, *esp* a piece of office equipment used for paper or card; a surgical instrument for cutting the tonsils; a specially drastic rule or closure for shortening a parliamentary discussion. ◆ *vt* to behead, crop, or cut short by guillotine. [Joseph Ignace *Guillotin* (1738–1814), French physician, who first proposed its adoption]

guilt[1] /gilt/ *n* the state of having done wrong; sin, sinfulness, or consciousness of it; the painful or uncomfortable emotion or state of mind caused by the awareness or feeling of having done wrong; the state of having broken a law; liability to a penalty (*law*). [Orig a payment or fine for an offence; OE *gylt*]

■ words derived from main entry word; ❑ compound words; ■ idioms and phrasal verbs

■ **guilt'ily** adv. **guilt'iness** n. **guilt'less** adj free from crime; innocent. **guilt'lessly** adv. **guilt'lessness** n. **guilt'y** adj justly chargeable; blameworthy, responsible; wicked, criminal; involving, indicating, burdened with, or relating to guilt. **guilt'y-like** adv (Shakesp) guiltily. ▫ **guilt complex** n a mental preoccupation with one's (real or imagined) guilt. **guilt trip** n (inf) a prolonged feeling of guilt. **guilty party** n a person, organization, etc that is guilty.

■ **guilty of** or (Shakesp) **to** having committed (a criminal or injudicious act); to blame for (a happening; archaic); deserving of (obs; Bible).

guilt² (Spenser) same as **gilt¹**.

guimbard /gim'bärd/ n a Jew's-harp. [Perh from Provençal guimbardo a kind of dance, from guimba to leap, gambol]

guimp see **gimp¹**.

guinea /gin'i/ n an obsolete English gold coin first made of gold brought from Guinea, in Africa; its value (now d1.05), a unit still used by certain professionals in charging fees, and in auctions. ◆ adj priced at a guinea.

■ **Guin'ean** adj of or relating to either of two countries in W Africa (the Republic of Guinea and the Republic of Guinea-Bissau), or to their inhabitants. ◆ n a native or citizen of either of these countries. ▫ **Guinea** (or **guinea**) **corn** n durra (Sorghum vulgare); pearl millet (Pennisetum typhoideum), a cereal. **guinea fowl** n a native African bird (genus Numida) of the pheasant family, ground-dwelling, dark grey with white spots. **Guinea** (or **guinea**) **grass** n a tall African grass of the millet genus (Panicum). **guinea hen** n a guinea fowl, esp a female; a turkey (obs); a courtesan (Shakesp). **guinea pig** n a small S American rodent, the cavy; (also **human guinea pig**) a person used as the subject of an experiment (as the animal commonly is in the laboratory); a do-nothing, token company director, etc (sl). **Guinea** (or **guinea**) **worm** n a very slender threadlike parasitic nematode worm (Dracunculus medinensis), common in tropical Africa.

guipure /gē-pür'/ n a kind of lace having no ground or mesh, the pattern sections being fixed by interlacing threads; a type of gimp. [Fr guipure, from OFr guiper, prob Gmc; cf Gothic weipan to weave]

guiro /gwē'rō/ n (pl **gui'ros**) a notched gourd used as a percussion instrument in Latin America. [Sp, gourd]

guise /gīz/ n a semblance, pretence or mask; external appearance, shape, likeness; dress (archaic); manner, behaviour (obs); custom (obs). ◆ vt (archaic) to dress. ◆ vi to act as a guiser. [OFr guise; cf OHGer wīsa (Ger Weise) a way, guise, OE wīse way, wīs wise]

■ **guis'er** or **guis'ard**, also **quiz'er** n (chiefly Scot) a person in disguise, dressed up in costume; a Christmas (or now usu Hallowe'en and, in Shetland, Up-Helly-Aa) mummer; someone who goes guising. **gui'sing** n esp in Scotland, an activity, developed from the tradition of mumming, whereby children dress up and go from house to house collecting cash in return for some musical performance, etc.

guitar /gi-tär'/ n a fretted musical instrument, usu six-stringed with a waisted body and a flat back. [Fr guitare, from L cithara, from Gr kitharā; see **cithara**]

■ **guitar'ist** n.

▫ **guitar'fish** n a sharklike ray (family Rhinobatidae) with a well-developed tail.

guizer see **guiser** under **guise**.

Gujarati or **Gujerati** /goo-jə-rä'tē/ n an Indic language spoken in the region and state of Gujarat in western India (also **Gujara'thi** or **Gujera'thi**). [Hindi, from Sans Gurjara Gujarat]

gula /gū'lə/ (zool) n the upper part of the throat; the gullet; in some insects, a plate on the underside of the head. [L gula throat]

■ **gū'lar** adj.

gulag /goo'lag/ n formerly, (one of) the system of esp political prisons and forced labour camps in the Soviet Union; any camp for the detention of political prisoners. [Russ acronym of the title of the body administering the system (glavnoe upravlenie ispravitelno-trudovykh lagerei), popularized by Alexander Solzhenitsyn in his novel The Gulag Archipelago]

gulch /gulch/ or **gulsh**/ n (US) a ravine or narrow rocky valley, a gully. ◆ vt (dialect) to swallow greedily. [Origin doubtful]

gulden /gŭl'dən/ n a former Dutch coin, the guilder or florin; a gold or silver coin in Germany in the Middle Ages; the old unit of account in Austria (before 1892). [Ger, literally, golden]

gule (Scot) see **gold²**.

gules /gūlz/ (heraldry) n a red colour, marked in engraved figures by vertical lines. [OFr gueules, perh from L gula the throat]

■ **gū'ly** adj (obs).

gulet /gŭl'it/ n a wooden Turkish sailing boat, traditionally used to carry freight, now used for pleasure trips. [Turk gūlet]

gulf (or obs **gulph**) /gulf/ n a large indentation in the coast; the area of sea or ocean enclosed by it; a deep place; an abyss; a whirlpool (archaic or poetic); anything insatiable, or too large to be bridged (fig);

a wide separation, eg between opponents' viewpoints; (with cap and the) the Arabian or Persian Gulf, or, (loosely) the region of and surrounding this, or the Gulf States; in Oxford and Cambridge examinations, the place of those candidates for honours who are allowed a pass without honours. ◆ vt to engulf. ◆ vi to flow like a gulf. ◆ adj (with cap) of or relating to the Gulf. [OFr golfe, from Late Gr kolphos, from Gr kolpos the bosom]

■ **gulf'y** adj full of gulfs or whirlpools.

▫ **Gulf States** n pl the small Arab states, rich in oil, bordering the Arabian Gulf, ie Bahrain, Kuwait, Qatar and the United Arab Emirates. **Gulf Stream** n the warm ocean current which flows north from the Gulf of Mexico, eventually to merge into the North Atlantic Drift, having a warming influence on NW Europe. **Gulf War syndrome** n a nervous disorder suffered by servicemen who had served in the Gulf War of 1991, thought by some to be associated with their exposure to harmful chemicals. **gulf'weed** n a large olive-brown seaweed (genus Sargassum) that floats unattached in great 'meadows' at the branching of the Gulf Stream and elsewhere in tropical oceans.

gull¹ /gul/ n a common large or medium-sized seabird of the family Laridae, esp of the genus Larus, with grey, white and black plumage. [Prob Welsh gwylan]

■ **gull'ery** n a place where gulls breed.

▫ **gull'-wing** adj (of a car door) opening upwards; (of an aircraft wing) having an upward-sloping short inner section and a long horizontal outer section.

gull² /gul/ (dialect; Shakesp) n an unfledged bird. [Perh ON gulr yellow]

gull³ /gul/ n a dupe or fool; an easily duped person; a hoax (obs). ◆ vt to dupe, deceive, cheat, hoax. [Perh from **gull¹** or **gull²**]

■ **gull'er** n. **gull'ery** n (archaic) deception. **gullibil'ity** n. **gull'ible** adj easily deceived or tricked, credulous (also (archaic) **gull'able**). **gull'ish** adj simple; like a gull.

▫ **gull'-catcher** n (Shakesp) a cheat.

Gullah /gul'ə/ or **gool'ə/ n a member of an African-American people living in islands and coastal districts of SE USA; their language, a creolized English. [Origin uncertain; poss from **Angola**]

gullet /gul'it/ n the passage in the neck by which food is taken into the stomach; the throat; a narrow trench, passage, water channel, or ravine (dialect). [OFr goulet, dimin of goule (Fr gueule), from L gula the throat]

gullible, etc see under **gull³**.

gully¹ or sometimes **gulley** /gul'i/ n (pl **gull'ies** or **gull'eys**) a channel worn by running water, as on a mountainside; a ravine; a ditch; a narrow channel or gutter, eg at the side of a tenpin bowling lane, or as a street drain, etc; a grooved rail, as for a tramway; a fielding position on the offside, between point and slips, or a player in this position (cricket). ◆ vt to wear a gully or channel in. [Prob **gullet**]

■ **gull'ied** adj.

▫ **gull'y-hole** n a passage by which a gutter discharges into a drain. **gull'y-hunter** n a person who picks up things from gutters. **gull'y-raker** n (Aust) a cattle thief.

gully² or **gulley** /gul'i/ n (chiefly Scot) n a big knife.

gulosity /gū-los'i-ti/ (archaic) n gluttony. [L gulōsus gluttonous, from gulō glutton, from gula throat]

gulp /gulp/ vt to swallow quickly, in large amounts, or with effort; to stifle or suppress (with back or down). ◆ vi to make a swallowing movement, eg in surprise, fright, or when drinking or eating hastily. ◆ n a quick or large swallow; a movement as if swallowing; a quantity swallowed at once; capacity for gulping (rare). [Cf Du gulpen gulp]

■ **gulp'er** n a person or thing that gulps; an eel-like fish capable of swallowing large prey.

gulph see **gulf**.

guly see under **gules**.

gum¹ /gum/ n the firm fleshy tissue that surrounds the bases of the teeth; insolence (old sl); nonsense, humbug (old US dialect). ◆ vt to deepen and widen the gaps between the teeth of (a saw) to make it last longer (US); to chew with (toothless) gums; to talk nonsense, to jaw (old US dialect); to dupe, cheat, deceive (US sl). [OE gōma palate; ON gōmr, Ger Gaumen palate]

■ **gumm'ily** adv. **gumm'y** adj toothless.

▫ **gum'boil** n a small abscess on the gum. **gum'shield** n a flexible pad worn by boxers and others to protect the teeth and gums.

gum² /gum/ n a substance that collects in or exudes from certain plants, and hardens on the surface, dissolves or swells in water, but does not dissolve in alcohol or ether; a plant gum or similar substance used as an adhesive, a stiffener, or for other purposes; any gumlike or sticky substance; chewing gum, bubble gum; a gumdrop (qv below); a gum tree; gummosis; a gumboot (US); a beehive, or trough, orig and esp one made from a hollow gum tree (US dialect). ◆ vt (**gumm'ing**; **gummed**) to smear, coat, treat or unite with gum; to spoil, wreck (*esp* with *up*; *sl*, *orig US*). ◆ *vi* to become gummy; to exude gum. [OFr *gomme*, from L *gummi*, from Gr *kommi*; prob from Egyp *kemai*]

■ **gummif′erous** *adj* producing gum. **gumm′iness** *n*. **gumm′ing** *n* the act of fastening with gum; the application of gum in solution to a lithographic stone; gummosis; the process of becoming gummy. **gummos′ity** *n* gumminess. **gumm′ous** or **gumm′y** *adj* consisting of or resembling gum; producing or covered with gum.

❑ **gum ammoniac** *n* ammoniac, a gum resin. **gum arabic** *n* a gum obtained from various acacias, used as an adhesive and in the production of inks and food-thickeners. **gum benjamin** see **benjamin²**. **gum′boot** *n* a rubber boot. **gum′-digger** *n* a person who digs up fossilized kauri gum (*NZ*); a dentist (*old Aust inf*). **gum dragon** or **tragacanth** *n* tragacanth. **gum′drop** *n* a gelatinous type of sweet containing gum arabic. **gum elastic** *n* rubber. **gum juniper** *n* sandarach. **gum′nut** *n* the woody fruit of the eucalyptus. **gum olibanum** same as **olibanum**. **gum resin** *n* a resin mixed with gum. **gum′shoe** *n* (*US*) a rubber overshoe; a shoe with a rubber sole, a sneaker; a detective or policeman (*sl*). ◆ *vi* (*US sl*) to snoop, pry. **gum tree** *n* a tree that exudes gum, or gum resin, kino, etc, *esp* a eucalyptus tree, or an American tree (genus *Nyssa*) of the cornel family.

■ **gum up the works** (*inf*) to make (eg a machine or scheme) unworkable. **up a gum tree** in a difficult situation (from the opossum's preferred place of refuge).

gum³ /*gum*/ *n* material that gathers in the corner of the eye. [Perh OE *gund* matter, pus]

❑ **gum rash** *n* a skin disease, red gum.

gum⁴ /*gum*/ (*dialect*) *n* used in oaths for **God**, as in *by gum!*

gumbo /*gum′bō*/ *n* (pl **gum′bos**) okra or its mucilaginous pods; a soup thickened with okra pods; a dish of okra pods seasoned; a fruit conserve (*US inf*); in central USA, a fine soil which becomes sticky or soapy when wet; (with *cap*) a patois spoken by blacks and Creoles in Louisiana, etc. [Louisiana Fr *gombo*, from Bantu (*ki*)*ngombo*]

gumma /*gum′ə*/ (*pathol*) *n* (pl **gumm′ata**) a syphilitic tumour. [New L, from L *gummi* gum]

■ **gumm′atous** *adj*.

gummiferous, **gumminess**, **gumming** see **gum²**.

gummite /*gum′īt*/ *n* a hydrated oxide of uranium and lead, like gum in appearance. [L *gummi* gum, and **-ite** (3)]

gummosis /*gum-ō′sis*/ (*bot*) *n* the pathological conversion of cell walls into gum; the diseased condition of plants caused by this, with conspicuous secretion of gum. [New L, from L *gummi* gum, and **-osis**]

gummosity, **gummous** see under **gum²**.

gummy see under **gum¹,²**.

gump¹ /*gump*/ (*Scot*) *vt* and *vi* to guddle.

gump² /*gump*/ (*dialect*) *n* a foolish person.

gumphion /*gum′fi-ən*/ (*obs Scot*) *n* a kind of banner formerly carried in funeral processions. [**gonfanon**]

gumple-foisted /*gum′pl-foi-stid*/ (*Walter Scott*) *adj* sulky. [*gumps* sulks (**gump²**); the second element appears in other words as *-faced*, *-feist*, etc]

gumption /*gum(p)′shən*/ *n* sense; shrewdness; courage, enterprise; common sense; the art of preparing painters' colours (*obs*). [Poss connected with ON *gaumr* heed]

■ **gump′tious** *adj*.

gun /*gun*/ *n* a weapon containing a tube from which projectiles are discharged, *usu* by explosion; a cannon, rifle, revolver, etc; a device for spraying, squirting, or otherwise propelling material; a signal by gun; a person who carries a gun, a member of a shooting-party; a professional killer (*US inf*); the throttle of an aircraft (*sl*); the accelerator of a car (*sl*); (*sl*; *usu* in *pl*) a well-developed bicep muscle; an expert or champion, *esp* in shearing (*Aust* and *NZ inf*). ◆ *vt* (**gunn′ing**; **gunned**) to shoot (with *down*); to shoot at; to provide with guns; to open the throttle of, to increase speed (also **give the gun**; *sl*); to rev up (an engine) noisily (*sl*). ◆ *vi* to shoot; to go shooting. ◆ *adj* (*Aust* and *NZ*) expert, pre-eminent. [ME *gonne*, prob from *Gunna* used as a pet name for an engine of war, poss from the woman's name *Gunhild* (ON *gunnr* war, and *hildr* war)]

■ **gun′less** *adj*. **gunn′age** *n* the number of guns carried by a warship. **gunn′er** *n* a person who works a gun; a private in the artillery; a branch officer in charge of naval ordnance (*naut*); an aircraftman who works a gun in a bomber. **gunn′ery** *n* the art of managing guns, or the science of artillery. **gunn′ing** *n*.

❑ **gun barrel** *n* the tube of a gun. **gun′boat** *n* a small vessel of light draught, fitted to carry one or more guns (**gunboat diplomacy** the show or threat of (*orig* naval) force in international negotiation). **gun carriage** *n* a carriage on which a cannon is mounted. **gun′cotton** *n* an explosive prepared by saturating cotton with nitric and sulphuric acids. **gun deck** *n* a deck in old warships carrying guns below the

main deck (earlier below spar deck). **gun dog** *n* a dog trained to work with a shooting-party. **gun′fight** *n* a fight involving two or more people with guns, *esp* formerly in the old American West (also *vi*). **gun′fighter** *n*. **gun′fire** *n* the firing of guns; the bullets fired; the hour at which the morning or evening gun is fired (*milit* and *naut*); an early-morning cup of tea, *esp* one laced with rum (*milit sl*). **gun′flint** *n* a piece of flint fitted to the hammer of a flintlock musket. **gun′house** *n* a protective shelter for a gun, and gunner, on a warship. **gun′layer** *n* a person who sets the sights of a ship's gun. **gun′lock** *n* the mechanism in some guns by which the charge is exploded. **gun′maker** *n*. **gun′man** *n* a man who carries a gun, *esp* an armed criminal. **gun′metal** *n* an alloy of copper and tin or zinc in the proportion of about 9 to 1, once used in making cannon; any of various metals used in imitation of this; any of various colours with a metallic sheen. **gun moll** *n* (*sl*) a woman who associates with criminals; a gangster's moll. **gun′play** *n* the use of guns, *esp* in a fight or display of skill. **gun′point** *n* the muzzle, or directed aim, of a gun (**at gunpoint** see below). **gun′port** *n* a porthole or similar opening for a gun. **gun′powder** *n* an explosive mixture of saltpetre, sulphur and charcoal; a type of green China tea. **gun′room** *n* a room where guns are kept; on board ship, *orig* the gunner's apartment, now a mess-room for junior officers. **gun′runner** *n*. **gun′running** *n* smuggling guns into a country. **gun′ship** *n* an armed ship, helicopter, etc. **gun′shot** *n* a shot fired from a gun; the distance to which shot can be propelled from a gun, the range of a gun. ◆ *adj* caused by the shot of a gun. **gun′-shy** *adj* frightened by guns or by the sound of guns (also *fig*). **gun′sight** *n* a device helping the user of a gun to aim at a target. **gun′slinger** *n* (*inf*) a gunfighter. **gun′smith** *n* a workman who makes or repairs guns or small arms. **gun′stick** *n* a ramrod. **gun′stock** *n* the piece on which the barrel of a gun is fixed. **gun′stone** *n* (*Shakesp*) a stone shot.

■ **as sure as a gun** quite sure, certainly. **at gunpoint** under, or using, the threat of injury or death from a gun. **beat the gun** to jump the gun (see under **jump¹**). **blow great guns** (of wind) to blow tempestuously. **go great guns** (*inf*) to function, be carried out, etc with great success, speed, efficiency, etc. **great gun** a cannon (*obs*); (also **big gun**) a person of great importance (*inf*). **gun for** to seek, try to obtain; to seek to ruin or destroy. **hired gun** (*inf*) a gunman hired to kill for a fee; a mercenary, professional fighter or killer; a person hired to destroy the opposition, or some unwelcome party, on behalf of another. **kiss the gunner's daughter** to be tied to a gun for a flogging. **son of a gun** a soldier's bastard son (*obs*); a rogue, rascal (*sl*); used as an affectionate greeting; an interjection expressing surprise or frustration (*N Am*). **spike someone's guns** see under **spike¹**. **stick** (or **stand**) **to one's guns** to maintain one's position staunchly.

gundy /*gun′di*/ (*Scot*) *n* a toffee made of treacle and spices. [Perh variant of **candy¹**]

gunge /*gunj*/ (*inf*) *n* any dirty, messy or sticky substance. ◆ *vt* to cover or block with gunge (*usu* with *up*). [Perh a combination of **goo** and **sponge**]

■ **gun′gy** *adj*.

gung-ho /*gung-hō′*/ (*sl*; *orig US*) *adj* (excessively or irrationally) enthusiastic, eager or zealous. [Chin *gōng* work and *hé* together]

gunite /*gun′īt*/ *n* a finely graded cement concrete (a mixture of cement and sand) sprayed into position under air pressure by a cement gun. [Orig a trademark]

gunk /*gungk*/ (*inf*) *n* any unpleasant, dirty, sticky material; any semi-solid, *usu* valueless, residue from a chemical process. [Orig the trademark of a grease solvent]

gunnage see under **gun**.

gunnel¹ /*gun′l*/ *n* see **gunwale**.

gunnel² /*gun′l*/ *n* the butterfish (*Pholis gunnellus*), a small eel-like coastal fish of the blenny family. [Origin unknown]

gunnera /*gun′ə-rə*/ *n* a very large-leaved ornamental plant of the *Gunnera* genus. [JE *Gunnerus* (1718–73), Norwegian botanist]

gunnery see under **gun**.

gunny /*gun′i*/ *n* a strong coarse jute fabric; a sack made from this fabric. [Hindi *ganī*, *gonī* sacking, from Sans *gonī* a sack]

gunsel /*gun′səl*/ (*US sl*) *n* a stupid or inexperienced youth; a boy kept for homosexual purposes, a catamite; a gunman. [Yiddish *genzel* gosling, from MHGer *gensel*, dimin of *gans* goose; final sense influenced by **gun**]

gunter /*gun′tər*/ *n* a Gunter's scale; a rig with topmast sliding on rings (from its resemblance to a sliding variety of Gunter's scale) (*naut*). [Edmund *Gunter* (1581–1626), astronomer]

❑ **Gunter's chain** *n* a surveyor's chain of 100 links, 66ft long (10 chains = 1 furlong; 10 sq chains = 1 acre). **Gunter's scale** *n* a scale graduated in several lines for numbers, logarithmic sines, etc, so arranged that trigonometrical problems can be roughly solved by use of a pair of compasses, or in another form by sliding.

gunwale or **gunnel** /gun'l/ n the *wale* or upper edge of a ship's side next to the bulwarks, so called because the upper *guns* were pointed from it.
■ **full** or **packed to the gunwales** (*inf*) absolutely full. **gunwales to** or **under** (*naut*) with gunwales at or below the surface of the water.

gunyah /gun'yə/ (*Aust*) n an Australian Aborigine's hut; a roughly made shelter in the bush. [From an Aboriginal language]

Günz /günts/ n the first (Pliocene) stage of glaciation in the Alps (also *adj*). [From a Bavarian tributary of the Danube]
■ **Günz'ian** *adj*.

gup[1] /gup/ (*obs*) *interj* expressing remonstrance or derision. [Prob **go up**]

guppy /gup'i/ n (pl **gupp'ies**; also called **millions**) a small brightly coloured fish (genus *Lebistes*) that multiplies very rapidly and feeds on mosquito larvae, algae, etc. [RJL *Guppy* (1836–1916), Trinidadian clergyman who first sent a specimen of it to the British Museum]

guqin /goo-chin'/, also **qin** /chin/ n a traditional Chinese musical instrument with seven strings. [Chin *gŭ* ancient, and *qín* stringed instrument]

gur[1] or **goor** /gŭr or goor/ n an unrefined sweet cane sugar. [Hindi, coarse sugar, from Sans *guda*]

gur[2] see **ger**.

gurami see **gourami**.

gurdwara /gŭr' or goor'dwär-ə/ n a Sikh place of worship which includes a place where the scripture is housed. [Punjabi *gurduārā*, from Sans *guru* teacher, and *dvāra* door]

gurge /gûrj/ n (*literary*; *Milton*) a whirlpool. [L *gurges*]
■ **gurgitā'tion** n surging.

gurgle /gûr'gl/ vi to flow in an irregular noisy current; to make a bubbling sound; (of a baby, etc) to make a low gargle-like bubbling sound in the throat; to utter with a gurgle. ◆ n a gurgling sound. [Imit; cf Ital *gorgogliare*]

gurgoyle see **gargoyle**.

gurjun /gûr'jən/ n a S Asian tree (genus *Dipterocarpus*) yielding timber and a balsamic liquid once used to treat leprosy (also **gar'jan**). [Hindi *garjan*]

Gurkha or **Goorkha** /gûr'kə or goor'kə/ n a member of the dominant people of Nepal, claiming Hindu origin, but Mongolized, from whom regiments in the British and Indian armies were formed.
■ **Gurkhali** /gûr-kä'lē or goor-kä'lē/ n the Indo-European language spoken by Gurkhas.

gurl /gûrl/ (*Scot*) n a growl. ◆ vi to growl. [Cf **growl**]
■ **gur'ly** *adj* grim; lowering; rough; surly.

gurlet /gûr'lit/ n a pickaxe with a head pointed at one end, bladed at the other. [Fr]

Gurmukhi /goor'moo-kē/ n the script in which the sacred texts of the Sikhs are written, which is used also for modern secular writing and printing. [Punjabi *Gurmukhī*, literally, from the mouth of the *guru* or teacher]

gurn /gûrn/ (*dialect*) a variant of **girn**.

gurnard /gûr'nərd/ or **gurnet** /-nit/ n a fish (genus *Trigla*, *Eutrigla* or *Aspitrigla*) with a large, bony-plated angular head and three finger-like walking rays in front of the pectoral fin. [OFr *gornard*, related to Fr *grogner* to grunt, from L *grunnīre* to grunt; from the sound they emit when caught]

gurney /gûr'ni/ (*N Am*) n a wheeled stretcher or cart (as used in a hospital, etc). [Origin uncertain; perh from the personal name]

gurrah /gur'ə/ n a coarse Indian muslin. [Hindi *gārhā* thick]

gurry /gur'i/ (*chiefly US*) n whale offal; fish offal. [Origin unknown]

guru or (*obs*) **gooroo** /goo'roo/ n in Hinduism, a spiritual teacher; one of the leaders and teachers of early Sikhism; a revered instructor, mentor or pundit (often *facetious*). [Hindi *gurū*, from Sans *guru* venerable]
■ **gu'rudom**, **gu'ruism** or **gu'ruship** n the state of being a guru.

gush /gush/ vi to flow out with violence or copiously; to be over-effusive, or highly sentimental. ◆ vt to pour forth copiously. ◆ n that which flows out; a sudden, violent issue of a fluid; sentimentality, effusiveness. [ME *gosshe*, *gusche*; the connection, if any, with ON *gusa*, *gjōsa*, and Du *gudsen*, is not clear]
■ **gush'er** n a person who or thing that gushes; an oil well that does not have to be pumped. **gush'ing** *adj*. **gush'ingly** *adv*. **gush'y** *adj* effusively sentimental.

gusla /goo'slə/, **gusle** /-sle/ or **gusli** /-slē/ n a one-stringed Balkan musical instrument; a Russian instrument with several strings. [Bulgarian *gusla*, Serb *gusle*, Russ *gusli*]
■ **guslar'** n a gusla player.

gusset /gus'it/ n an angular piece inserted in a garment to strengthen or enlarge some part of it or give freedom of movement; a strengthening bracket or plate at a joint where two plates meet, or between connecting members of a structure (*civil eng*); the piece of chain mail covering a join in armour, as at the armpit. ◆ vt to make with a gusset; to insert a gusset into. [OFr *gousset*, from *gousse* pod, husk]
■ **guss'eting** n.

gussie /gus'i/ (*old Aust inf*) n an effeminate man. [From dimin of the personal name *Augustus*]

gussy up /gus'i up/ (*sl*) vt to smarten up. [Poss connected with **gussie**]

gust[1] /gust/ n a sudden blast of wind; a burst of smoke, fire, etc; a violent burst of passion, outburst. ◆ vi to blow in gusts. [ON *gustr* blast]
■ **gust'ful** (*rare*) or **gust'y** *adj* blowing in gusts, squally; stormy; fitfully irritable or emotional. **gust'iness** n.
□ **gust'-lock** n a mechanism on an aeroplane which prevents damage to the elevators by gusts of wind when the aeroplane is stationary.

gust[2] /gust/ n the sense of pleasure of tasting (*archaic*); relish (*archaic*); gratification (*archaic*); taste experience (*obs*); flavour (*archaic*). [L *gustus* taste; cf Gr *geuein* to make to taste]
■ **gust'able** *adj* and n (*archaic*). **gustā'tion** n the act of tasting; the sense of taste. **gust'ative** or **gust'atory** *adj* of or relating to the sense of taste. **gust'ful** *adj* (*archaic*) savoury, tasty; enjoyable. **gust'ie** or **gust'y** *adj* (*Scot*) savoury; appetizingly flavoured.

gusto /gus'tō/ n exuberant enjoyment, zest. [Ital, from L *gustus* taste]

gusty see under **gust**[1,2].

GUT (*phys* and *astron*) *abbrev* : Grand Unified Theory.

gut /gut/ n the alimentary canal, *esp* the lower part; the stomach; the belly, paunch (*inf*); (in *pl*) the viscera; sheep's or other intestines or silkworm's glands prepared for use as violin strings, etc; (in *pl*) the inner or essential parts; (in *pl*) stamina, toughness of character, tenacity, staying power, endurance, forcefulness (*inf*); a narrow passage; a strait or channel; a lane. ◆ *adj* (*inf*) (of feelings or reactions) strong, deeply personal, basic or instinctive; (of issues, etc) having immediate impact, arousing strong feelings. ◆ vt (**gutt'ing**; **gutt'ed**) to take out the guts of; to remove the contents of; to reduce to a shell (by burning, dismantling, plundering, etc); to extract what is essential from. [OE *guttas* (pl); cf *geotan* to pour; dialect Eng *gut*, Ger *Gosse* a drain]
■ **gut'ful** or **guts'ful** n (*Aust* and *NZ inf*) one's fill, more than enough. **gut'less** *adj* cowardly, lacking strength of character. **gut'lessly** *adv*. **gut'lessness** n. **guts** vi and vt (**gut'sing**; **gutsed**) to eat greedily. **gutser** see **gutzer** below. **gutsful** see **gutful** above. **guts'ily** *adv* (*Scot* and *inf*). **guts'iness** n (*Scot* and *inf*). **guts'y** *adj* having pluck or nerve (*inf*); lusty, passionate (*inf*); gluttonous (*Scot*). **gutt'ed** *adj* (*inf*) extremely shocked, upset or disappointed. **gutt'le** vt and vi to eat greedily. **gut'zer** or **gut'ser** n (*Aust* and *NZ*) a glutton; a heavy fall (**come a gutser** to take a heavy fall; to fail or crash).
□ **gutbucket** /gut'buk-it/ n a rhythmically simple, raucous, earthy and emotional style of playing jazz; a fat or gluttonous person (*inf*). **gut flora** same as **intestinal flora** under **intestine**. **gut'rot** n (*inf*) rough, cheap alcohol; a stomach upset. **gut'-scraper** n (*facetious*) a fiddler, violinist. **gut'-wrenching** *adj* (*inf*) highly emotional.
■ **bust a gut** (*inf*) to make a great deal of strenuous effort. **guts it out** to endure discomfort with fortitude. **hate someone's guts** (*inf*) to have a violent dislike for someone. **have had a gutful (of)** (*inf*) to be thoroughly fed up (with), have had as much as, or more than, one is prepared to tolerate (of). **have someone's guts (for garters)** (*inf*) to inflict severe punishment or harm on someone (*usu* used as a threat). **work**, **sweat** or **slog one's guts out** (*inf*) to work extremely hard.

gutcher see **goodsire** under **good**.

gutta[1] /gut'ə/ n (pl **gutt'ae** /-ē/) a drop (*med*); a small droplike ornament on the underside of a mutule or a regula of the Doric entablature (*archit*); a small round colour-spot (*zool*). [L, drop]
■ **gutt'ate** *adj* (also **guttā'ted**) containing drops; having droplike markings; spotted. ◆ vi to exude liquid by guttation. **guttā'tion** n the exudation of drops of liquid from an uninjured part of a plant. **Guttif'erae** n pl (*bot*) a family of archichlamydeous dicotyledons with abundant oil glands and passages, and entire exstipulate opposite leaves, including mangosteen, mammee apple, and St John's wort. **guttif'erous** *adj* exuding drops (of sap, gum, etc); belonging to the Guttiferae.
□ **gutta serena** n (*med*) amaurosis.

gutta[2] /gut'ə/ n the coagulated milky latex of sapotaceous and other tropical trees, *esp* gutta-percha; a hydrocarbon (empirically $C_{10}H_{16}$) found in gutta-percha; a solid gutta-percha golf ball, as used in the 19c, also called (*inf*) **gutt'y**. [Malay *getah* gum]
□ **gutta-percha** /-pûr'chə/ n a strong, waterproof substance, like rubber but harder and not extensible, obtained chiefly from the latex of Malaysian trees of the family Sapotaceae (also *adj*).

guttate, guttation, etc see under **gutta**[1].

gutter[1] /gut'ər/ n a channel for conveying away water, *esp* at the roadside or at the eaves of a roof; a furrow, groove; the blank strip separating the two halves of a sheet of stamps (*philately*); a grooved piece, used to separate pages of type in a forme (*printing*); (sometimes in *pl*) the space comprising the fore-edges of pages lying together internally in a forme (*printing*); the blank space (ie the inner margins) between two facing pages in a book, magazine, etc; (with *the*) slum life, social degradation or sordidness; (in *pl*) mud, dirt (*Scot*). ◆ *vt* to cut or form into small hollows. ◆ *vi* (of a candle) to run down in a stream or channel of drops; (of a flame) to be blown downwards, or threaten to go out; to become hollowed; to trickle or stream. [OFr *goutiere*, from *goute*, from L *gutta* a drop]

■ **gutt'ering** n gutters collectively; material for gutters.
❑ **gutt'erblood** n (*Scot*) a low-born person. **gutter board** same as **snow board** (see under **snow**[1]). **gutter broadcasting**, **gutter** (or **gutter press**) **journalism** n sensationalistic reporting in the media. **gutt'er-man** or **-merchant** n a pavement-side seller of cheap worthless objects. **gutter pair** n (*philately*) a pair of stamps separated by the gutter. **gutter press** n that part of the press which specializes in sensationalistic journalism. **gutt'ersnipe** n a street urchin; a neglected child from a slum area.

gutter[2] see under **gut**.

Guttiferae, guttiferous see under **gutta**[1].

guttle see under **gut**.

guttural /gut'ə-rəl/ adj relating to the throat; formed in the throat; throaty in sound. ◆ n a sound pronounced in the throat or (loosely) by the back part of the tongue (*phonetics*); a letter representing such a sound. [L *guttur* the throat]

■ **gutt'uralize** or **-ise** vt to sound gutturally; to make guttural. **gutt'urally** adv.

gutty[1] see **gutta**[2].

gutty[2] /gut'i/ (*US inf*) adj (**gutt'ier**; **gutt'iest**) forceful, powerful; gritty, gutsy, spirited, plucky. [**gut** and **-y**[1]]

gutzer see under **gut**.

guv see **governor** under **govern**.

GUY abbrev : Guyana (IVR).

guy[1] /gī/ n a rope, cord, etc used to steady something, *esp* a tent, or hold it in position. ◆ vt to keep in position by a guy or guys. [OFr *guis*, *guie*; Sp *guia* a guide]
❑ **guy'-rope** n.

guy[2] /gī/ n an effigy of *Guy* Fawkes, dressed up grotesquely on the anniversary of the Gunpowder Plot (5 November); an oddly dressed figure; a fellow (*inf*); a person generally (often used in *pl* when referring to or addressing any group of people; *inf*, *orig US*); a joke, lark (*archaic* or *dialect*); flight, decamping (*archaic* or *dialect*). ◆ vt (*sl*) to turn to ridicule, make fun of. ◆ vi (*archaic* or *dialect*) to decamp.

Guyanese /gī-ə-nēz'/ adj of or relating to the republic of *Guyana* in S America, or its inhabitants. ◆ n (pl **Guyanese'**) a native or citizen of Guyana.

guyle, guyler Spenserian forms of **guile**, **guiler**.

guyot /gē'ō/ n a flat-topped underwater mountain. [AH *Guyot* (1807–84), Swiss-born American geologist]

guyse a Spenserian form of **guise**.

guzzle /guz'l/ vt and vi to swallow (food, or *esp* drink) greedily or immoderately. ◆ n a bout of guzzling. [Perh connected with Fr *gosier* throat]
■ **guzz'ler** n.

GVH abbrev : graft-versus-host (reaction) (see under **graft**[1]).

GVHD abbrev : graft-versus-host disease (see under **graft**[1]).

GVW abbrev : gross vehicle weight.

GW or **Gw** abbrev : gigawatts.

GWR abbrev : formerly, Great Western Railway.

gwyniad or **gwiniad** /gwin'i-ad/ n a whitefish (*Coregonus pennantii*), found *esp* in Bala Lake in Wales. [Welsh *gwyniad*, from *gwyn* white]

Gy symbol : gray (SI unit).

gyal see **gayal**.

gybe or sometimes **jibe** /jīb/ vi (of a sail) to swing over from one side to the other; to alter course in this way. ◆ vt to cause to gybe. ◆ n an act or the action of gybing. [Origin obscure; see **jib**[1]]
❑ **gybe mark** n a marker on a yacht-race course indicating a turning point at which yachts must gybe.

gyeld a Spenserian form of **guild**.

gylden see **gilden**.

gym /jim/ n and adj a familiar shortening of **gymnasium**, **gymnastic** and **gymnastics**.

❑ **gym shoe** n a plimsoll. **gym slip** or **tunic** n a pinafore dress worn (*esp* formerly) by schoolgirls.

gymbal same as **gimbal**.

gymkhana /jim-kä'nə/ n a public meeting in which (*esp* amateur) riders compete against each other in various equestrian sports; formerly, a public place providing athletics facilities, etc (*Anglo-Ind*); a meeting for athletic sports, etc; an autocross event (*US*). [Hindi *gend-khāna* (ball-house), racket-court, remodelled on *gym*nastics]

gymmal same as **gimmal**.

gymnasium /jim-nā'zi-əm/ n (pl **gymnā'siums** or **gymnā'sia**) a place, hall, building or school for gymnastics; *orig*, in ancient Greece, a public place or building where youths exercised, with areas for running and wrestling, baths, and halls for conversation; (*usu* /gim-nä'zi-oom/; pl also **gymnasien** /gim-nä'zi-ən/) a top-grade secondary school in many European countries, *esp* Germany, which prepares pupils for higher education, *esp* in academic rather than vocational subjects. [Latinized from Gr *gymnasion*, from *gymnos* naked]

■ **gymnā'sial** adj. **gymnā'siarch** /-ärk/ n (Gr *archos* chief) the head of a gymnasium. **gymnā'siast** n a pupil in a gymnasium; a gymnast (*archaic*). **gymnā'sic** adj (*rare*). **gym'nast** /-nast/ n a person skilled in gymnastics. **gymnas'tic** n a system of training by exercise (*archaic*); (in *pl* used as *sing*) exercises and activities devised to strengthen the body and improve agility and co-ordination, *incl* exercises using apparatus and floor; (in *pl*) feats or tricks of agility. ◆ adj (also (*archaic*) **gymnas'tical**) relating to athletic exercises or (*specif*) gymnastics; athletic, vigorous. **gymnas'tically** adv.

gymnic /jim'nik/ (*archaic*; Milton) adj gymnastic. [Gr *gymnikos*, from *gymnos* naked]

gymno- or (before a vowel) **gymn-** /gim-n(ō)-, jim-n(ō)- or -no-/ combining form denoting (*esp* in biological terms) naked. [Gr *gymnos* naked]

■ **gymnorhi'nal** adj (Gr *rhīs*, *rhīnos* nose) with unfeathered nostrils. **gym'nosoph** (*rare*) or **gymnos'ophist** n (Gr *sophos* wise) an ancient Hindu philosopher who wore little or no clothing, and lived solitarily in mystical contemplation. **gymnos'ophy** n. **gym'nosperm** n (Gr *sperma* seed) any of the lower or primitive group of seed-plants whose seeds are not enclosed in any ovary. **gymnosper'mous** adj.

gymp same as **gimp**[1,3].

gyn- see **gyno-**.

gynae, also **gynie** or **gyny** /gī'ni/ an informal shortening of **gynaecology** or **gynaecological**.

gynaeceum see **gynoecium**.

gynaeco- or (*US*) **gyneco-** /gīn-, jīn-, gin-, jin-ē-kō- or -i-ko-/ combining form denoting woman, female. [Gr *gynē*, *gynaikos* woman]

■ **gynaeco'cracy** n (Gr *kratos* power) government by women or a woman; a country with such a government. **gynaecocrat'ic** adj. **gyn'aecoid** adj womanlike. **gynaecolog'ical** or **gynaecolog'ic** adj. **gynaecolog'ically** adv. **gynaecol'ogist** n. **gynaecol'ogy** n the science or branch of medicine dealing with women's physiology and diseases. **gyn'aecomast** n a man suffering from gynaecomastia. **gynaecomas'tia** or sometimes **gynaecomas'ty** n the abnormal enlargement of a man's breast.

gynney, gynny Shakespearean spellings of **guinea** (**hen**).

gyno- /gī-nō-, gī-nə-, gī-no-, jī- or ji-/, also **gyn-** /gīn-, jīn- or jin-/ combining form denoting female, woman or (*bot*) the female reproductive organ. [Gr *gynē* woman]

■ **gynandrism** n see **gynandry** below. **gynan'dromorph** n (Gr *morphē* form) an organism that combines male and female physical characteristics. **gynandromor'phic** or **gynandromor'phous** adj. **gynandromor'phism** or **gynandromor'phy** n. **gynand'rous** adj with stamen concrescent with the carpel, as in orchids (*bot*); hermaphroditic. **gynan'dry** or **gynand'rism** n (Gr *anēr*, *andros* man, male). **gyniol'atry** n extreme devotion to or regard for women. **gynoc'racy** n gynaecocracy, female rule. **gynocrat'ic** adj. **gynodioe'cious** adj (*bot*) having hermaphrodite and female flowers on different plants. **gynodioe'cism** n. **gynomonoe'cious** adj (*bot*) having hermaphrodite and female flowers on the same plant. **gynomonoe'cism** n. **gynophō'bia** n the fear or dislike of women. **gynophō'bic** adj and n. **gy'nophore** n (Gr *phoros* carrying; *bot*) an elongation of the receptacle of a flower carrying carpels only. **gynostē'mium** n (Gr *stēma* stamen; *bot*) a united gynoecium and androecium, such as the column of an orchid.

gynoecium, gynaecium or (*US*) **gynecium** /jī- or gī-ni-sē'əm/ n the female organs of a flower (*bot*); (chiefly **gynaeceum**) the women's quarters in an ancient Greek or Roman house. [Gr *gynaikeion* women's apartments]

gynomonoecious...to...**gynostemium** see under **gyno-**.

-gynous see under **-gyny**.

gyny see **gynae**.

-gyny /-ji-ni/ combining form denoting: female, woman, as in misogyny; the female organs (bot). [Gr gynē woman]
■ **-gynous** adj combining form.

gyoza /gyō'zə/ n (in Japanese cookery) a small dumpling containing minced pork and vegetables. [Jap, from Chin jiǎozi]

gyp[1] /jip/ (sl) n pain, torture. [**gee up**]
■ **give someone gyp** to cause someone pain.

gyp[2] /jip/ (sl; orig US) n a swindle; a cheat. ◆ vt (**gypp'ing**; **gypped**) to swindle.

gyp[3] /jip/ n a college servant at Cambridge University. [Perh **gypsy**; or perh obs gippo a short jacket, a varlet, from obs Fr jupeau]

gyppie, **gyppo**, **gyppy** see **gippo**.

gypseous, **gypsiferous** see under **gypsum**.

gypsophila /jip-sof'i-lə/ n any plant of the genus Gypsophila, hardy perennials related to the pinks, but of more chickweed-like appearance, with small white or pink flowers. [Gr gypsos chalk, and phileein to love]

gypsum /jip'səm/ or /gip'səm/ n a soft mineral, hydrated calcium sulphate, source of plaster of Paris and other plasters. [L, from Gr gypsos chalk]
■ **gyp'seous** adj. **gypsif'erous** adj producing or containing gypsum. ◻ **gypsum block** n a building block (usu hollow) made of gypsum plaster. **gypsum plasterboard** (or simply **plasterboard**) n building-board consisting of a core of gypsum or anhydrous gypsum plaster between two sheets of paper.

gypsy or **gipsy** /jip'si/ n (with cap) a Romany, a member of a wandering people of Indian origin, living mainly in Europe and the USA; (loosely) a person who lives, or looks, like a Gypsy; (with cap) the Romany language; a cunning rogue (offensive). ◆ adj (with cap) of, or characteristic of, Gypsies; out-of-door (eg of meals, etc); unconventional; operating independently or illegally (US inf). ◆ vi (now rare) to live like a Gypsy, camp out, or picnic. [**Egyptian**, because once thought to have come from Egypt]
■ **gyp'sydom** or **gyp'syism** n (also with cap).
◻ **gypsy moth** n a kind of tussock moth, having whitish wings with dark line markings. **gyp'sywort** n a labiate plant (Lycopus europaeus) with which Gypsies were reputed to stain their skin.

gyrate, etc see under **gyre**.

gyre /jīr/ n a ring, circle (literary); a circular or spiral turn or movement (literary); a rotating ocean current (geog). ◆ vt and vi (in Lewis Carroll pronounced /gīr/) to spin round, gyrate. [L gīrus, from Gr gȳros a circle, ring]
■ **gyr'al** or **gyr'ant** adj. **gyr'ally** adv. **gyrate'** vi to revolve, spin, whirl. ◆ adj /jīr'āt/ curved round in a coil. **gyra'tion** n a whirling motion; a whirl or twist (also fig); a whorl. **gyra'tional** adj. **gyra'tory** adj revolving; spinning round; (of traffic) revolving in one-way lines, or (of traffic systems) designed or working on this principle. ◆ n a gyratory

traffic system. **gyroid'al** adj spiral; rotatory. **gyr'ose** adj having a folded surface; marked with wavy lines or ridges. **gyr'ous** adj.

gyre-carline /gīr'kär-lin/ (Scot) n a witch. [ON gȳgr a witch, ogress, and **carline**]

gyrfalcon or **gerfalcon** /jûr'fö(l)-kn/ n a large northern and Arctic falcon (also **jer'falcon**). [OFr gerfaucon, from LL gyrofalcō, most prob from OHGer gîr a vulture (Ger Geier); see **falcon**]

gyro[1] /jī'rō/ (inf) n a gyrocompass; a gyroscope.

gyro[2] or **giro** /jē'rō/, also **gyros** or **giros** /jē'rōs/ n a Greek dish of thin slices cut from a block of meat grilled on a spit, often served in pitta. [Gr gȳros turn]

gyro- /jī-rō-/ combining form denoting: spiral, ring, circle; gyrating; gyroscope. [Ety as for **gyre**]
■ **gyr'ocar** n a monorail car balanced by a gyroscope. **gyrocom'pass** n a compass which indicates direction by the freely moving axis of a rapidly spinning wheel, owing to the earth's rotation, the axis assuming and maintaining a north and south direction. **gyr'odyne** n a rotorcraft in which the rotor(s) are power-driven for take-off, climbing, landing, etc, but unpowered for cruising flight. **gyr'olite** n a mineral, a hydrated calcium silicate. **gyromagnet'ic** adj relating to magnetic properties of rotating electric charges (**gyromagnetic compass** a compass used in aircraft in which, in order to eliminate errors caused by changes of course and speed (greater in an aircraft than in a ship), a gyroscope is combined with a magnet system). **gyromag'netism** n. **gyr'omancy** n (Gr manteiā divination) divination by walking in a circle and falling from giddiness. **gyr'oplane** or **gyrocop'ter** n a rotorcraft with unpowered rotor(s) on a vertical axis, eg an autogiro. **gyr'oscope** n an apparatus in which a heavy flywheel or top rotates at high speed, the turning movement resisting changes in the direction of axis, used as a toy, an educational device, a compass, etc. **gyroscop'ic** adj. **gyroscop'ically** adv. **gyroscop'ica'tion** or **-s-** n. **gyrostä'bilizer** or **-s-** n a gyroscopic device for countering the roll of a ship, etc. **gyr'ostat** n a gyroscope, esp one fixed in a rigid case. **gyrostat'ic** adj. **gyrostat'ics** n sing the science of rotating bodies. **gyr'ovague** n (Med L gyrovagus) a wandering monk of the Middle Ages.

gyron or (Fr) **giron** /jī'ron/ (heraldry) n a triangular charge consisting of the lower half of a quarter of an escutcheon which has been divided diagonally from the corner to the fesse-point. [Fr giron, older geron; OHGer gêro; cf **gore**[2]]
■ **gyron'ic** or **giron'ic** adj. **gyronn'y** adj.

gyrose, **gyrous** see under **gyre**.

gyrus /jī'rəs/ (med and zool) n a convoluted ridge between two grooves; a convolution on the surface of the brain. [Ety as for **gyre**]

gyte[1] /gīt/ (Scot) adj crazy, mad.

gyte[2] /gīt/ (Scot) n (also **gait**, **geit**) a child; a brat. [**get** (offspring)]

gyve /jīv/, earlier (archaic) gīv/ vt to fetter. ◆ n a shackle; a fetter. [ME gives, gyves]

Hh

a b c d e f g h i j k l m n o p q r s t u v w x y z

Helvetica Designed by Max Miedinger in 1957. Switzerland.

H or **h** /āch/, sometimes spelt out **aitch** n the eighth letter in the modern English alphabet as in the Roman, representing in Old English a guttural sound, gradually softened down to a spirant, and now often silent; in German notation = B natural (*music*); anything shaped like the letter H.
❑ **H'-beam** n a metal girder H-shaped in section.

H abbrev : hearts (*cards*); height; heroin (*sl*); hospital; Hungary (IVR); hydrant.
❑ **H'-hour** n (H for unnamed *hour*) the time fixed for beginning a military operation.

H symbol : (as a medieval Roman numeral) 200; hard (on lead pencils); henry (SI unit); hydrogen (*chem*); magnetic field strength (*phys*).
❑ **H'-bomb** n a hydrogen bomb.

Ħ symbol : (medieval Roman numeral) 200 000.

h abbrev : hecto-; hot; hour; husband.

h (*phys*) symbol : Planck('s) constant.

Ha (*chem*) symbol : hahnium.

ha or **hah** /hä/ interj denoting various emotions or responses, eg surprise, joy, exultation, dismay, enquiry, scepticism, encouragement, hesitation, and when repeated, laughter. [Spontaneous utterance]

ha abbrev : hectare; hoc anno (L), in this year.

ha'¹ /hä or hə/ a shortened form of **have**.

ha'² /hö/ n Scots form of **hall**.

haaf /häf/ (*Orkney* and *Shetland*) n a deep-sea fishing ground. [ON haf sea]
❑ **haaf'-fishing** n.

haaf-net see **halve-net**.

haanepoot see **hanepoot**.

haar /här/ (*East Coast*) n a raw sea-mist. [ON hārr hoary; MDu hare bitter cold; Fris harig misty; cf **hoar**]

HAART abbrev : highly active antiretroviral therapy, a treatment for HIV/AIDS.

Hab. (*Bible*) abbrev : (the Book of) Habakkuk.

habanera /hä-bä-nä'rə/ n a Cuban dance or dance tune in 2–4 time. [*Habana* or Havana, in Cuba]

habañero or **habanero** /(h)ä-bə-nyä'rö or -nä'/ (*N Am*) n the Scotch bonnet pepper. [Am Sp, from *Habana* Havana]

habdabs /hab'dabz/ (*inf*) n pl a state of extreme nervousness (also **ab'dabs**). [Origin uncertain]
■ **screaming habdabs** (*inf*) a bad case of this involving hysterical crying.

Habdalah /häv-dä'lə/ n a Jewish ceremony or prayer that marks the end of the Sabbath (also **Havda'lah**). [Heb habhdālā separation, division]

habeas corpus /hā'bi-əs kör'pəs/ n a writ to a jailer to produce a prisoner in person, and to state the reasons of detention. [L, literally have the body (*ad subjiciendum* to be brought up before the judge)]

haberdasher /hab'ər-dash-ər/ n a seller of small sewing articles, such as ribbons, tape, etc; a men's outfitter (*N Am*). [OFr hapertas; origin unknown]
■ **hab'erdashery** (or /-dash'/) n a haberdasher's goods, business or shop.

haberdine /hab'ər-dēn, -dīn or -dīn/ n dried salt cod. [Old Du abberdaen, also labberdaen; prob from Le iLabourd, or Lapurdum, Bayonne]

habergeon /hab'ər-jən or (*Milton*) ha-bûr'ji-on/ (*hist*) n a sleeveless coat of mail, *orig* lighter than a hauberk. [OFr haubergeon, dimin of hauberc]

Haber process /hä'bər/ n a process for synthesizing ammonia from nitrogen and hydrogen. [Fritz *Haber* (1868–1934), German chemist who devised it with Carl Bosch]

habile /hab'il/ adj fit, suitable (*obs*); competent (*obs*); dexterous, adroit (*rare*). [ME variant of **able**, later associated more closely with Fr habile, L habilis]

habiliment /hə-bil'i-mənt/ n attire (*esp* in *pl*). [Fr habiller to dress, from L habilis fit, ready, from habēre]
■ **hab'ilable** adj (*Carlyle*) capable of being clothed. **habil'atory** adj of clothes or dressing.

habilitate /hə-bil'i-tāt/ vt to qualify; to equip or finance (eg a mine); to attire. ♦ vi to qualify, *esp* as a German university lecturer (Ger habilitieren). [LL habilitāre to enable, from L habilis able]
■ **habilitā'tion** n. **habil'itātor** n.

habit /hab'it/ n ordinary course of behaviour; tendency to perform certain actions; custom; accustomedness; familiarity; bodily constitution; characteristic mode of development; the geometric form taken by a crystal (*crystallog*); outward appearance; official or customary dress, *esp* the costume of a nun or monk; a garment, *esp* a riding habit; an addiction to a drug, etc; a learned behavioural response to particular circumstances (*psychol*). ♦ vt to dress; to inhabit (*archaic*). [L habitus state, dress, from habitāre to dwell]
■ **hab'itaunce** n (*Spenser*) dwelling-place. **hab'ited** adj clothed. **habit'ūal** adj customary; usual; confirmed by habit. ♦ n someone who has a habit; a habitual drunkard, drug-taker, frequenter, etc. **habit'ūally** adv. **habit'ūalness** n. **habit'ūāte** vt to accustom; to settle (in), or to frequent (*archaic*). **habitūā'tion** n the act of accustoming; the process of becoming accustomed; acquired tolerance for a drug, which thereby loses its effect; development of psychological, without physical, dependence on a drug. **hab'itūde** n constitution; characteristic condition; habit; relation (*obs*); familiar acquaintance (*obs*). **habitū'dinal** adj. **habitué** /hab-it'ū-ā or (Fr) a-bē-tü-ā/ n a habitual frequenter. **hab'itus** n physical type, *esp* as predisposing to disease (*med*); characteristic appearance, manner of growth, etc of a plant or animal.
❑ **hab'it-cloth** n a light broadcloth. **hab'it-forming** adj (of a drug) such as a taker will find it difficult or impossible to give up using. **hab'it-maker** n a maker of riding habits.
■ **be in the habit of** or **make a habit of** to do regularly or usually. **habit and repute** (*Scots law*) public knowledge that affords strong and generally conclusive evidence of fact, *esp* of an informal marriage.

habitable /hab'i-tə-bl/ adj able to be lived in; fit to live in. [L habitāre to dwell]
■ **habitabil'ity** or **hab'itableness** n. **hab'itably** adv. **hab'itant** n an inhabitant; /ab-ē-tä/ (Fr) a native of *esp* Canada or Louisiana of French descent (*pl* in this sense sometimes **habitans**). **habita'tion** n the act of inhabiting; a dwelling or residence; a lodge of a society. **habita'tional** adj.

habitat /hab'i-tat/ n the normal abode or locality of an animal or plant (*biol*); the physical environment of any community; the place where a person or thing can usually be found (*facetious* or *inf*); a capsule on the seabed, in which people can live for a prolonged period and from which they can explore their surroundings, the capsule being at the same pressure as the water around it. [L, (it) dwells]
❑ **habitat module** n living accommodation for the crew on a space mission.

habitation see under **habitable**.

habitual, etc, **habituate**, etc, **habitude**, **habitué**, **habitus** see under **habit**.

hable /hā'bl/ (*Spenser*) adj same as **able**.

haboob /ha-boob'/ n a sandstorm. [Ar habūb]

haček /ha'chek or hä'/ n in Slavonic languages, the diacritic (ˇ) placed over a letter to modify its sound. [Czech]

hachis /hä-shē' or ä-shē'/ n hash. [Fr]

■ words derived from main entry word; ❑ compound words; ■ idioms and phrasal verbs

hachure /hash'ūr/ or /ä-shür'/ n shading, in the form of lines, showing a hill or slope on a map; any such line. ◆ vt to shade with hachures. [Fr]

hacienda /has-i-en'də/ n (in Spain or Spanish America) a landed estate; a ranch or farm; a main dwelling-house on an estate; a country house; a stock-rearing, manufacturing or mining establishment in the country. [Sp, from L *facienda* things to be done]

hack¹ /hak/ vt to cut with rough blows; to chop or mangle; to notch; to roughen with a hammer; to kick; to kick or strike the shins of (in some sports, illicitly); to cope with or bear (*inf*). ◆ vi to slash, chop; to cough; to use a computer with great skill; to gain unauthorized access to other computers (often with *into*). ◆ n an act of hacking; a gash (*archaic*); a notch; a chap in the skin (*archaic*); a kick on the shin (*archaic*); a mattock or pick. [Assumed OE *haccian*, found in combined form *tō-haccian*; cf Du *hakken*, Ger *hacken*]
  ■ **hack'able** adj (of a computer, program, phone etc) vulnerable to hacking. **hack'er** n a person who hacks; a skilled and enthusiastic computer operator, *esp* an amateur or a producer of poor-quality computer code (*inf*); now *usu* an operator who uses his or her skill to break into commercial or government computer or other electronic systems (*inf*). **hack'ery** n (*inf*) computer hacking. **hack'ing** n. ◆ adj short and interrupted, used eg of a broken, troublesome cough.
  □ **hack'-log** n a chopping-block. **hack'saw** n a saw for metals. ◆ vi (pat **hack'sawed**; pap **hack'sawed** or (*usu*) **hack'sawn**) to cut with a hacksaw.
  ■ **hack someone off** (*inf*) to make someone thoroughly fed up, disgusted.

hack² /hak/ n a horse (or formerly, and still in the USA, a vehicle) kept for hire, *esp* one in a sorry condition; an ordinary riding horse; a ride on horseback; any person overworked on hire; a literary or journalistic drudge; anything hackneyed (*obs*). ◆ adj hired; mercenary; mediocre; hackneyed. ◆ vt to make a hack of; to use as a hack; to hackney; to hire out (a horse); to ride (a horse) in the countryside for recreation. ◆ vi to work as a hack; to journey on horseback; to ride on horseback in the countryside for recreation. [**hackney**]
  ■ **hackette'** n (*sl*) a woman journalist. **hack'ing** n.
  □ **hacking jacket** or **coat** n a waisted jacket with slits in the skirt and flapped pockets on a slant. **hack'work** n literary drudgery for publishers; literary work of poor quality produced to order.

hack³ /hak/ n a grating or rack, eg for feeding cattle; a rack on which food is placed for a hawk; a bank for drying bricks. [OE *hæce, hæc* grating, hatch; cf **hatch¹** and **heck²**]

hack⁴ /hak/ (*Shakesp*) vi a word of unknown meaning but possibly meaning to take to the highway (or the street), or to have spurs hacked off.

hackamore /hak'ə-mör/ n a halter used *esp* in breaking in foals, consisting of a single length of rope with a loop to serve instead of a bridle; a bridle without a bit, exerting pressure on the horse's muzzle, not its mouth. [Sp *jáquima*]

hackberry /hak'be-ri/ or /hak'bə-ri/ n the hagberry; an American tree (*Celtis occidentalis*) related to the elm; its wood. [See **hagberry**]

hackbolt /hak'bōlt/ n the greater shearwater (also **hag'bolt**, **hag'den**, **hag'don** or **hag'down** /-dən/). [Origin obscure]

hackbut /hak'bət/ or /-but/ or **hagbut** /hag'bət, but/ (*hist*) n an arquebus. [OFr *haquebute*, from ODu *hakebus*; see **arquebus**]
  ■ **hackbuteer'** n.

hackee /hak'ē/ n the chipmunk. [Imit of its cry]

hacker see under **hack¹**.

hackery¹ see under **hack¹**.

hackery² /hak'ə-ri/ n an Indian ox-drawn cart for transporting goods. [Perh Bengali *hākārī* shouting]

hackette see under **hack²**.

hacking see under **hack¹,²**.

hackle /hak'l/ n a comb for flax or hemp; a cock's neck feather; this worn as a decoration in a cap, etc; (in *pl*) the hair of a dog's neck; (in *pl*) hair, whiskers; an angler's fly made of a cock's hackle, or its frayed-out part. ◆ vt to comb with a hackle. [Cf **hatchel**, **heckle**; Du *hekel*; Ger *Hechel*; perh partly from OE *hacele, hæcele* cloak, vestment]
  ■ **hack'ler** n. **hack'ly** adj rough and broken, as if hacked or chopped; jagged and rough (*mining*).
  ■ **make someone's hackles rise** to make someone angry.

hacklet /hak'lit/ or **haglet** /hag'lit/ n the kittiwake; also perhaps the shearwater. [Origin unknown]

hackmatack /hak'mə-tak/ n an American larch; its wood. [Native American word]

hackney /hak'ni/ n a horse for general use, *esp* for hire; a horse with a high-stepping action, bred to draw light carriages; a vehicle kept for hire; a person hired for drudgery (*obs*). ◆ vt to carry in a hackney

coach; to use to excess; to make commonplace. [OFr *haquenée* an ambling nag; poss from *Hackney* in East London, where horses were pastured]
  ■ **hack'ney** adj let out for hire. **hack'neyed** adj devoted to common use; trite; dulled by excessive use.
  □ **hackney cab**, **carriage** or **coach** n formerly, any horse-drawn vehicle serving as a taxi; (only **hackney carriage**) the official term used to describe a *usu* black London-style taxi. **hackney-coach'man** n. **hack'neyman** n someone who keeps hackney horses.

hacktivism /hak'ti-vi-zm/ n (*inf*) the practice of hacking into and sabotaging a computer system, *esp* a government or military one, in order to make a political protest. [**hack¹** and **activism**]
  ■ **hack'tivist** n.

Hacky Sack® /hak'i sak/ n a game in which players attempt to kick a small bag filled with plastic pellets without letting it touch the ground; the bag used in this.

hac lege /hak lē'jē/ or /häk lā'ge/ (L) with this law, under this condition.

hacqueton same as **acton**.

had¹ /had/ pat and pap of **have**.

had² /häd, höd/ or /hud/ (pap **hadden** /häd'n/ or /hud'n/) a Scots form of **hold¹**.

hadal see under **Hades**.

haddock /had'ək/ n a N Atlantic sea fish (*Melanogrammus aeglefinus*) of the cod family (also (*Scot*) **hadd'ie**). [ME *haddok*; ety unknown]

hade /hād/ (*mining*) n the angle between the plane of a fault, etc, and a vertical plane. ◆ vi to incline from the vertical. [Origin obscure]

Hades /hā'dēz/ n another name for the god Pluto (*Gr myth*); the underworld roamed by the souls of the dead (*Gr myth*); the abode of the dead; hell (*Bible*). [Gr *Aidēs, Haidēs* the god of the underworld; the abode of the dead]
  ■ **hā'dal** adj forming or belonging to the levels of the ocean deeper than 6000 metres. **Hādē'an** adj of or resembling Hades; of or belonging to the period of time between *approx* 4500 and 3800 million years ago (*geol*; also n).

Hadith /had'ith or hä-dēth'/ n the body of traditions about Mohammed, supplementary to the Koran. [Ar *hadīth*]

hadj, **haj** or **hajj** /häj/ n the annual Muslim pilgrimage to Mecca. [Ar *hajj* effort, pilgrimage]
  ■ **hadj'i**, **haj'i** or **hajj'i** /-i/ n someone who has performed a hadj.

Hadley cell /had'li sel/ (*meteorol*) n an atmospheric cell in which low-level air moves from a latitude of around 30١ N or S towards the equator, where it rises before flowing towards the poles and descending at around 30١. [George *Hadley* (1685–1768), English meteorologist]

hadn't /had'ənt/ contracted form of **had not**.

hadrome /had'rōm/ (*bot*) n the conducting elements and associated parenchyma in xylem. [Gr *hadros* thick]

hadron /had'ron/ n one of a class of subatomic particles, including baryons and mesons. [Gr *hadros* heavy, with *-on* as in **proton**, etc]
  ■ **hadron'ic** adj.

hadrosaur /had'rə-sör/ n the name of a group of herbivorous, bird-hipped, Cretaceous dinosaurs of the ornithopod class, having webbed hands and feet, a duckbill-shaped jaw and a bony crest. [Gr *hadros* thick, and *sauros* a lizard]

hadst see **have**.

hae /hā/ vt a form of **have**, *esp* Scots.

haecceity /hek-sē'i-ti or hēk-/ (*philos*) n Duns Scotus's word for that element of existence on which individuality depends, hereness-and-nowness. [Literally thisness, L *haec*]

haem- /hēm- or hem-/, **haemat-** /-ət-/ or **haemo-** /-ō- or -ə-/ (or *US* **hem-**, **hemat-** and **hemo-**) combining form denoting blood. [Gr *haima, -atos* blood]
  ■ **haem** n (also **hem** and **heme**) the pigment combined with the protein (globin) in haemoglobin. **haemagglutinā'tion** n the clumping together of red blood cells. **haemagglut'inin** n a virus, antibody or other agent causing haemagglutination. **haemal** or **hemal** /hē'məl/ adj of the blood or blood vessels; ventral, *opp* to *dorsal* or *neural* (*old*). **haemangioma** or (*esp US*) **hemangioma** /hi-man-ji-ō'mə/ n an angioma containing blood vessels. **Haeman'thus** n (Gr *anthos* flower) the blood-flower, a S African amaryllid. **haematem'esis** n (Gr *emesis* vomiting) vomiting of blood from the stomach. **haemat'ic** adj relating to blood. **hae'matin** n a brownish substance containing ferric iron obtained from oxyhaemoglobin or from dried blood. **haematin'ic** adj having the effect of increasing the haemoglobin or of stimulating production of red blood cells. ◆ n a substance having this effect. **hae'matite** n a valuable iron ore, Fe_2O_3, often blood-red, with red streak. **hae'matoblast** n (Gr *blastos* a germ) a blood platelet. **hae'matocele** n (Gr *kēlē* a tumour) a cavity containing blood.

hae'matocrit n (Gr kritēs judge) a graduated capillary tube in which the blood is centrifuged, to determine the ratio, by volume, of blood cells to plasma; this ratio. **haematogen'esis** n blood formation. **haematogenous** /-oj'in-əs/ adj producing blood; produced by or arising in the blood; spread through the bloodstream. **hae'matoid** adj blood-like. **haematol'ogist** n. **haematol'ogy** n the study of blood, diseases of blood, and blood-forming tissues. **haematol'ysis** n haemolysis (qv below). **haematō'ma** n a swelling composed of blood effused into connective tissue. **haematophagous** /-tof'ə-gəs/ adj (Gr phagein to eat) feeding on blood. **haematopoiesis** /-poi-ē'sis/ n (Gr poieein to make) the formation of blood. **haematopoiet'ic** adj. **haematō'sis** n the formation of blood; conversion of venous into arterial blood. **haematox'ylin** n a dye obtained from logwood. **Haematox'ylon** n (Gr xylon wood) the logwood genus. **haematū'ria** n (Gr ouron urine) the presence of blood in the urine. **haem'ic** adj haematic (qv above). **hae'min** n the chloride of haematin. **haemochromato'sis** n (see ety for **chroma**, and **-osis**) a disease of the liver characterized by an excessive accumulation of iron and the development of fibrous tissue, and accompanied by bronzing of the skin. **haem'ocoel** n (LL coel, Gr koilos hollow) the central body-cavity of many invertebrates, including arthropods and molluscs. **haemoco'nia** n (Gr koniā dust) blood-dust, small colourless granules in the blood. **haemocy'anin** n (Gr kyanos blue) a blue respiratory pigment with functions similar to haemoglobin, in the blood of crustaceans and molluscs. **hae'mocyte** n a blood cell, esp a red one. **haemocytom'eter** n an instrument for measuring the number of cells in a volume of blood. **haemodial'ysis** n dialysis of the blood using a kidney machine. **haemoglō'bin** n (L globus a ball) the red oxygen-carrying pigment in the red blood corpuscles. **haemoglobinop'athy** n any of various blood disorders caused by changes in the molecular structure of haemoglobin. **haemoglobinū'ria** n (Gr ouron urine) the presence of haemoglobin in the urine. **hae'molymph** n (L lympha water) a fluid found in the haemocoel in most invertebrates, with functions similar to blood. **haemol'ysis** n (Gr lysis dissolution) breaking up of red blood corpuscles. **haemolyt'ic** adj relating to haemolysis (**haemolytic disease of the newborn** a disease of the newborn in which maternal antibodies cause haemolysis of the fetal red blood cells, often resulting in stillbirth, anaemia or jaundice). **hae'mony** n (prob Gr haimōnios blood-red) a plant with sovereign properties against magic, etc in Milton's poem Comus. **haemophil'ia** n (Gr phileein to like) a hereditary disease causing excessive bleeding when any blood vessel is even slightly injured. **haemophil'iac** n someone who suffers from haemophilia. **haemophil'ic** adj. **haemopoiē'sis** same as **haematopoiesis** above. **haemop'tysis** n (Gr ptysis a spitting) the spitting or coughing up of blood from the lungs. **haemorrhage** /hem'ər-ij/ n (Gr haimorrhagiā, from rhēgnynai to burst) a discharge of blood from the blood vessels; a steady and persistent draining away (fig). ◆ vi to lose blood from the blood vessels. ◆ vt to suffer a steady and persistent loss of (blood, resources, etc). **haemorrhagic** /-raj'ik/ adj. **haemorrhoid** /hem'ər-oid/ n (Gr haimorrhois, -idos, from rheein to flow; usu in pl) dilatation of a vein around the anus, piles. **haemorrhoid'al** adj. **haemo'stasis** n stoppage of bleeding or the circulation. **hae'mostat** n an instrument for stopping bleeding; a chemical agent that stops bleeding. **haemostat'ic** n and adj (Gr statikos, or hypothetical states causing to stand) styptic.

haeremai /hī'rə-mī/ (NZ) interj welcome. [Maori, come hither]

haet, **ha'it** or **hate** /hāt/ (Scot) n a whit. [From the phrase deil ha' it devil have it]

haff /haf/ n a lagoon separated from the sea by a long sandbar. [Ger Haff bay]

haffet or **haffit** /haf'it or hä'fit/ (Scot) n the side of the head; the temple; locks of hair on the temple. [half-head; cf OE healf-hēafod the sinciput]

hafflin /hä'flin/ (Scot) n same as **halfling** (see under **half**).

hafiz /hä'fiz/ n a Muslim who has committed the whole of the Koran to memory. [Ar, from hafiza to guard]

hafnium /haf'ni-əm/ n a metallic chemical element (symbol **Hf**; atomic no 72). [L Hafnia Copenhagen, where it was discovered in 1922]

haft /häft/ n a handle, esp on an axe or knife; a winged leaf-stalk. ◆ vt to set in a haft; to establish firmly. [OE hæft; Ger Heft]

Haftorah /häf-tō'rə/ n (also **Haphta'rah**, **Haphtō'rah**) a reading from the Prophets following a reading from the Torah in a synagogue service. [Heb]

Hag. (Bible) abbrev : (the Book of) Haggai.

hag¹ /hag/ n an ugly old woman, orig a witch; an eel-like cyclostomous marine vertebrate, related to the lamprey (also **hag'fish**). [Perh OE hægtesse a witch; cf Ger Hexe]
■ **hagg'ed** adj haglike; haggard. **hagg'ish** adj. **hagg'ishly** adv.
❑ **hag'-ridden** adj tormented by nightmares or driven by obsessions, as though possessed by a witch; henpecked, harried by women

(facetious). **hag'-ride** vt. **hag'-seed** n a witch's offspring. **hag'-taper** n mullein. **hag'-weed** n the common broom plant (a broomstick being a witch's supposed mode of transport).

hag² or **hagg** /hag/ (Scot and N Eng dialect) n any broken ground in a moor, moss or bog; a place from which peat has been dug; a pool or hole in a bog; a relatively high and firm place in a bog; the rough overhanging edge of a peat-hole or stream-bank; brushwood to be cut down. [ON högg a gash, ravine, a cutting of trees]

hag³ /hag/ (Scot) vt and vi (**hagg'ing**; **hagged**) to hack, hew. [ON höggva]

Hagberg falling number test /hag'bûrg/ n a test by which the milling quality of wheat can be determined, a low falling number indicating that the enzyme alpha amylase has begun to break down the starch in the grain, making it less suitable for bread making.

hagberry /hag'be-ri or hag'bə-ri/ n the bird-cherry, a small Eurasian tree with white flowers; the American hackberry tree or its cherry-like fruit. [Cf ON heggr bird-cherry]

hagbolt, hagden, hagdon, hagdown see **hackbolt**.

hagbut see **hackbut**.

hagfish see **hag¹**.

hagg see **hag²**.

Haggadah, also **Haggada** /hə-gä'də or ha-gə-dä'/ and **Agadah** /a-, ə- or ä-gä'də/ n the homiletical and illustrative part of the authoritative book of Jewish civil and religious law and tradition, the Talmud, recited at a ceremonial meal, the Seder, on the first two nights of the Passover; the Passover ritual. [Heb]
■ **Hagga'dic, Haggadist'ic** or **Aga'dic** adj. **Hagga'dist** n.

haggard /hag'ərd/ adj lean; hollow-eyed and gaunt, from weariness, hunger, etc; untamed; intractable. ◆ n an untamed hawk, or one caught when adult, esp a female. [OFr hagard]
■ **hagg'ardly** adv. **hagg'ardness** n.

hagged see under **hag¹**.

haggis /hag'is/ n a Scottish dish made of the heart, lungs and liver of a sheep or calf, etc, chopped up with suet, onions and oatmeal, etc, seasoned and boiled in a sheep's stomach-bag or a substitute. [ME hageys, poss from Anglo-Fr hageis, from haguer to cut up]

haggish see under **hag¹**.

haggle /hag'l/ vi to bargain contentiously or wranglingly; to raise trifling objections; to cavil, quibble. ◆ vt to cut unskilfully; to mangle. ◆ n an instance of haggling. [ON heggra to hew]
■ **hagg'ler** n.

hagi- /hag-i-/ (sometimes haj-i-/) and **hagio-** /-ō-, -o- or -ə-/ combining form signifying holy or denoting saint. [Gr hagios holy]
■ **hag'iarchy** n rule or order of saints or holy persons. **hagioc'racy** n government by holy men. **Hagiog'rapha** n pl those books which with the Law and the Prophets make up the Old Testament. **hagiog'rapher** n one of the writers of the Hagiographa; a writer of hagiography. **hagiograph'ic** or **hagiograph'ical** adj. **hagiog'raphist** n. **hagiog'raphy** n a biography of a saint; a biography that over-praises its subject. **hagiol'ater** n a worshipper of saints. **hagiol'atry** n (Gr latreiā worship). **hagiolog'ic** or **hagiolog'ical** adj. **hagiol'ogist** n a writer of or someone versed in saints' legends. **hagiol'ogy** n. **hag'ioscope** n a squint in a church, giving a view of the high altar. **hagioscop'ic** adj.

haglet same as **hacklet**.

hah /hä/ interj same as **ha¹**.

ha-ha¹ /hä'hä'/ interj in representation of a laugh; /hä-hä'/ an expression of triumph, eg on discovering something. ◆ n the sound of laughter. ◆ vi to laugh. [Imit]

ha-ha² /hä'hä/ or **haw-haw** /hö'hö/ n a ditch or vertical drop often containing a fence, eg between a garden and surrounding parkland, forming a barrier without interrupting the view. [Fr haha]

hahnium /hä'ni-əm/ n a former name for **dubnium**; a former name for **hassium**. [Otto Hahn (1879–1968), German physicist]

haick see **haik¹**.

haiduk or **heyduck** /hī'dūk or hā'duk/ n a brigand; a guerrilla warrior; a liveried servant. [Hung hajduk, pl of hajdú]

haik¹, haick, haique or **hyke** /hīk/ n an oblong cloth worn by Arabs on the head and body. [Ar hayk]

haik² see **heck²**.

haikai see under **haiku**.

Haikh /hīhh/ n and adj Armenian. [Armenian]

haiku /hī'koo/ n (pl **hai'ku** or **hai'kus**) a Japanese poem in three lines of 5, 7 and 5 syllables, developed in the 17c, often incorporating a word or phrase that symbolizes one of the seasons; English verse in imitation of this. [From Jap]

■ **haikai** /hīˈkī/ n (short for *haikai no renga* linked comic verse) *orig* a linked series of haiku forming one poem; a haiku. **hokku** /hoˈkoo/ n *orig* the first half-line of a linked series of haiku; a haiku.

hail[1] /hāl/ n frozen rain, or grains of ice falling from the clouds; a shower or bombardment of missiles, abuse, etc. ◆ vi and vt to shower hail; to shower vigorously or abundantly. [OE *hægl* (*hagol*); Ger *Hagel*]
■ **hail'y** adj.
❏ **hail'shot** n small shot that scatters like hail. **hail'stone** n a ball of hail. **hail'storm** n.

hail[2] /hāl/ vt to greet; to address, accost; to call to from a distance; to summon to stop or come; to acclaim or praise (*esp* in *passive*; *usu* with *as*). ◆ interj of greeting or salutation. ◆ n a call from a distance; a greeting; earshot, *esp* in the phrase *within hail*; health (*obs*). ◆ adj (*obs*) sound, hale. [ON *heill* health, (adj) sound; cf **hale**[1] and **heal**[1]]
■ **hail'er** n.
❏ **hail'-fellow(-well-met')** adj readily or excessively friendly and familiar (also n and adv). **hail Mary** n (a recital of) the English version of the ave Maria.
■ **hail from** to belong to, come from (a particular place).

hail[3] /hāl/ (*Scot*) n (in ball games) a goal; a score. ◆ vt to score (a goal); to put into the goal. [Appar from **hail**[2], from the shout with which the player claimed a goal]

hain /hān/ (*Scot*) vt to save, preserve; to spare. [ON *hegna* to enclose, protect; cf Swed *hägna*; Dan *hegne*]
■ **hained** adj. **hain'ing** n an enclosure.

hainch /hānsh or hānch/ Scots form of **haunch**[1].

haique see **haik**[1].

hair /hār/ n a filament growing from the skin of an animal; an outgrowth of the epidermis of a plant; a fibre; a mass or aggregate of hairs, *esp* that covering the human head; anything very small and fine; a hair's-breadth; type or character (*obs*); a locking spring or other safety contrivance in a firearm. ◆ vt to free from hair; to provide hair for. [OE *hēr*, Ger *Haar*, Du and Dan *haar*, etc; vowel perhaps influenced by Fr *haire* a hair shirt]
■ **haired** adj (*usu* as *combining form*) signifying having hair (of a specified type, length, etc). **hair'iness** n. **hair'less** adj having no hair; very angry (*sl*); desperate (*sl*). **hair'lessness** n. **hair'like** adj. **hair'y** adj of or like hair; covered with hair; dangerous, frightening (*inf*).
❏ **hair'-ball** n a concretion of hair in the stomach, eg in cats as a result of swallowing fur, etc during grooming. **hair'band** n a band, *usu* of or incorporating elastic material, worn over the hair to confine it, or for decoration. **hair'bell** same as **harebell** (see under **hare**). **hair'-brained** adj same as **hare-brained** (see under **hare**). **hairbreadth** see **hair's-breadth** below. **hair'brush** n a brush for the hair. **hair'cloth** n coarse cloth made from horsehair, used in upholstery, etc. **hair'cut** n a cutting of the hair or the style in which this is done; a proportion of the value of an asset paid to the broker when the asset is used as collateral in a transaction (*stock exchange sl*). **hair'do** n (*pl* **hair'dos**) (*inf*) a way in which someone's (*usu* a woman's) hair is styled. **hair'dresser** n someone whose occupation is the cutting, colouring, arranging, etc of hair; a barber. **hair'dressing** n a lotion, etc for the hair; the art or occupation of a hairdresser. **hair'dryer** or **hair'drier** n any of various types of hand-held or other apparatus producing a stream of warm air for drying the hair. **hair'-eel** n a hairworm. **hair extension** n a length of human or artificial hair attached to the wearer's own hair to create a longer or fuller style. **hair gel** see **gel**[1]. **hair'-grass** n a genus (*Aira*) of narrow-stemmed coarse grasses (perhaps only a modification of the generic name). **hair grip** or **hair'grip** n a short, narrow band of metal, bent double, worn in the hair, to keep it in place. **hair'line** n a line made of hair; a very fine line in writing, type, etc; a finely striped cloth; the edge of the hair on the forehead. ◆ adj (of eg a crack) very thin; also *fig*. **hair'net** n a net for keeping (*usu* a woman's) hair in place. **hair oil** n a scented oil for dressing the hair. **hair'-pencil** n a fine paint-brush. **hair'piece** n a length of false hair, or a wig covering only part of the head. **hair'pin** n a U-shaped pin for fastening up the hair. ◆ adj narrowly U-shaped, as a sharp bend on a road. **hair'-powder** n powdered starch formerly dusted on the hair or wig. **hair'-raiser** n a tale of terror. **hair'-raising** adj very exciting, terrifying. **hair restorer** n a preparation claimed to make hair grow on bald places. **hair's'-breadth** or **hair'breadth** n the breadth of a hair; a minute distance. ◆ adj (of an escape, etc) extremely narrow. **hair seal** n a sea-lion, or eared seal with coarse hair only. **hair shirt** n a penitent's garment of haircloth; an intimate or secret affliction (*fig*). **hair slide** n a hinged clasp, often decorative, worn in the hair, *esp* by young girls. **hair space** n (*printing*) the thinnest metal space used by compositors, or its equivalent in photocomposition. **hair'-splitter** n a maker of over-fine distinctions. **hair'-splitting** n and adj. **hair'spray** n lacquer sprayed on the hair to hold it in place. **hair'spring** n a slender spring regulating a watch balance. **hair'streak** n any butterfly of several genera with a fine white band under the wing. **hair stroke** n a hairline in penmanship. **hair'style** n a particular way of cutting and arranging the hair.

hair'stylist n. **hair'-tail** n a fish of the family Trichiuridae, with a whiplike tail. **hair trigger** n a trigger, responding to very light pressure, that releases the hair of a gun. **hair'-trigger** adj having a hair trigger; responding to the slightest stimulus. **hair'-waver** n. **hair'-waving** n. **hair'-work** n work done or something made with (*esp* human) hair. **hair'worm** n a worm, like a horsehair, which when young lives in the bodies of insects. **hairy Mary** n (*angling*) a kind of artificial fly.
■ **against the hair** (*archaic*) against the grain; contrary to inclination. **a hair of the dog (that bit him** or **her**, etc) a smaller dose of that which caused the trouble; a morning drink of the alcohol that caused the hangover as a cure for it, taken as a homeopathic dose. **by the short hairs** or (*inf*) **by the short and curlies** in a powerless position, at someone's mercy. **get in someone's hair** (*inf*) to become a source of irritation to someone. **keep one's hair on** (*inf*) to keep calm. **let one's hair down** to forget reserve and speak or behave freely. **lose one's hair** to grow angry. **make someone's hair curl** to shock someone extremely. **make someone's hair stand on end** to frighten or astonish someone greatly. **not turn a hair** (of a horse) to show no sweat; not to be ruffled or disturbed. **put up one's hair** to dress the hair up on the head instead of wearing it hanging, once the mark of passage from girlhood to womanhood. **split hairs** to make superfine distinctions. **tear one's hair (out)** to display frenzied grief or (*inf*) great irritation. **to a hair** or **to the turn of a hair** exactly.

hairst /hārst/ a Scottish form of **harvest**.
❏ **hairst-rig** n a harvest-field or a section of it, formerly cut in competition.

ha'it see **haet**.

haith /hāth/ (*Scot*) interj by my faith. [faith]

Haitian /ha-ēˈshan or hāˈshan/ adj of or relating to the republic of *Haiti* in the West Indies, its people or its language. ◆ n a native or citizen of Haiti; the creolized form of French spoken in Haiti.

haj or **hajj**, **haji** or **hajji** see **hadj**.

haka /häˈkə/ n a Maori ceremonial war dance; a similar dance performed by New Zealanders, eg by rugby players before a match. [Maori]

hakam /häˈkəm/ n a sage; a rabbinical commentator, *esp* one during the first two centuries AD. [Heb *hākhām* wise]

hake[1] /hāk/ n a gadoid fish resembling the cod. [Prob Scand; cf Norw *hake-fisk*, literally, hook-fish]

hake[2] see **heck**[2].

Hakenkreuz /häˈkən-kroits/ n the swastika. [Ger, hook-cross]

hakim[1] /ha-, ha- or hä-kēmˈ/ n a Muslim physician. [Ar *hakīm*]

hakim[2] /häˈkim/ n a judge, governor or official in Pakistan. [Ar *hakim*]

Halachah, **Halakah** or **Halacha** /hə-lä'hhə or -kə/ n the legal element in the Jewish book of civil and religious obedience, the Talmud. [Heb, from *hālak* to walk]
■ **Halach'ic** adj.

halal or **hallal** /hə-läl', häl'al, ha-läl' or hä-läl'/ vt (**halall'ing** or **hallall'ing**; **halalled'** or **hallalled'**) to slaughter according to Muslim law. ◆ n and adj (denoting or relating to) meat from animals that have been so slaughtered, that may lawfully be eaten by Muslims. [Ar *halāl* lawful]

halala /hə-läl'ə/ n (*pl* **halal'a** or **halal'as**) a Saudi Arabian monetary unit, $\frac{1}{100}$ of a riyal. [Ar]

halation /hə-lä'shən/ n blurring in a photograph by reflection and dispersion of light; a bright area around a bright spot on a fluorescent screen. [halo]

halavah see **halva**.

halberd /hal'bərd/ n a long-shafted axe-like weapon with a hook or pick on its reverse side, used in the 15 and 16c, and in the 18c denoting the rank of sergeant (also **hal'bert**). [OFr *halebard*, from MHGer *helmbarde* (Ger *Hellebarde*), from *Halm* stalk, or *Helm* helmet, and OHGer *barta* (Ger *Barte*) axe]
■ **halberdier** /-dēr'/ n a person armed with a halberd.

Halbstarker /halp'shtär-kər/ (*Ger*) n a juvenile delinquent.

halcyon /hal'si-ən/ adj calm; peaceful; happy and carefree. ◆ n the kingfisher, once believed to make a floating nest on the sea, which remained calm during hatching. [L *halcyōn*, from Gr *alkyōn*, fancifully changed to *halkyōn* as if from *hals* sea, and *kyōn* conceiving]
❏ **halcyon days** n pl a time of peace and happiness.

hale[1] /hāl/ adj healthy; robust; sound of body; whole (*Scot*; also n with definite article). [Scot and N Eng, from OE *hāl*; see **whole**; cf **hail**[2], **heal**[1]]
■ **hale'ness** n. **hayle** n (*Spenser*) welfare.
■ **hale and hearty** in good health.

hale[2] /hāl/ vt to drag. [OFr *haler*; Germanic in origin]

haler /hä'lər/ n (pl **ha'ler**, **ha'lers** or **haleru'**) a monetary unit of the Czech Republic and Slovakia, $\frac{1}{100}$ of a koruna (also **heller** /hel'ər/). [See **heller¹**]

half /häf/ n (pl **halves** /hävz/ or (except for the first definition) **halfs**) one of two equal parts; a half-year or term; half-fare, on a bus, train, etc; a halfback; a halved hole or match in golf; half a pint, *usu* of beer (*inf*); a measure of an alcoholic spirit, *esp* whisky (*Scot*). ◆ *adj* having or consisting of one of two equal parts; partial; incomplete, as measures. ◆ *adv* to the extent of one-half; in part; imperfectly. [OE (Anglian) *half* (WSax *healf*) side, half; cf Ger *halb*; Dan *halv*]

■ **half'en** adj (*Spenser*) half. **half'endeale** adv (*Spenser*) half. **half'lin** or **half'ling** n (*Scot*) a half-grown (*esp* male) person; half a silver penny. ◆ *adj* half-grown. **half'lings** or **half'lins** adv (*Scot*) half; partially. ◆ *adj* half-grown.

❑ **half'-adder** n (*comput*) a circuit having two inputs and outputs, which can add two binary digits and give the sum and the carry digit. **half'-and-half'** n a mixture of two things in equal proportions, traditionally beer or stout and ale. ◆ *adj* and *adv* in the proportion of one to one, or approximately; in part one thing, in part another. **half'-ape** n a lemur. **half'-arsed** or (*US*) **half'-assed** adj (*vulgar sl*) stupid, useless. **half'back** n (in football) a midfield player (*old*); (in rugby) either of two players (the **scrum half** and **stand-off half**) acting as a link between the forwards and the three-quarters; (in American football) a running back positioned in front of the full back. **half'-baked'** adj underdone; incomplete; crude; immature; half-witted. **half'-ball** n (*snooker*, etc) a shot in which the cue ball is aimed at the edge of the object ball. **half'-baptize** or **-ise** vt to baptize privately and hastily. **half'beak** n a fish (Hyporhynchus, etc) with a spearlike under-jaw. **half'-binding** n a bookbinding with only backs and corners of leather or a similar material. **half'-blood** n relation between those who have only one parent in common; a half-breed (*offens*). **half'-blooded** adj. **half'-blue** n (at university) a substitute for a full blue, or the colours awarded him or her. **half board** n (in hotels, etc) the providing of bed, breakfast and one main meal per day, demi-pension; a manoeuvre by which a sailing-ship gains distance to windward by luffing up into the wind (*naut*). **half'-boot** n a boot reaching halfway to the knee. **half'-bound** adj bound in half-binding. **half'-bred** adj poorly bred or trained; mongrel, of mixed breed. **half'-breed** n a person or animal of mixed breed (of people, *usu* with one white and one non-white parent; *offensive*). **half'-brother** n a brother with whom one has only one parent in common. **half'-butt** n (*billiards*, etc) a cue longer than the standard snooker cue. **half'-caf** or **half'-caff** n (*inf*) caffeinated and decaffeinated coffee in equal proportions. **half'-cap** n (*Shakesp*) a cap only partly taken off, a slight salute. **half'-caste** n (*offens*) a person whose parents are from different races, *esp* a Eurasian. **half-cen'tury** n a period of 50 years; (*esp* in cricket, snooker, etc) a score of 50. **half'-chance** n a slight opportunity, *esp* to score in football. **half'-checked** adj (*Shakesp*) with reins attached halfway up the side-piece of the bit, giving little leverage. **half'-cheek** n (*Shakesp*) a face in profile. **half'-close** n (*music*) an imperfect cadence. **half-cock'** n the position of the cock of a gun drawn back halfway and retained by the first notch (**at half-cock** only partially prepared); a stroke made by playing neither forward nor back (*cricket*). ◆ *adv* in that position. **half'-cocked'** adj. **half-crown'** n a coin worth **half-a-crown'** or two shillings and sixpence, from 1970 no longer legal tender; a sum of money equivalent to this (also *adj*). **half-cut'** adj (*inf*) drunk. **half-day'** n a holiday of half a working day; a day on which one works in the morning or afternoon only. **half-dead'** adj (*inf*) very weary, exhausted. **half-doll'ar** n an American coin worth 50 cents (also *adj*). **half'-done** adj partly done; partly cooked. **half'-door** n the lower part of a divided door. **half-doz'en** n and adj six. **half-dū'plex** adj (*comput, telegraphy*, etc) allowing communication or transmission in both directions, but not simultaneously. **halfe-hors'y** adj (*Spenser*) (of the Centaurs) partly of the nature of horses. **half-ev'ergreen** adj having foliage that persists during part of winter; tending to be evergreen in mild areas but deciduous where the climate is more rigorous. **half'-face** n profile. **half'-faced** adj (*Shakesp*) showing only part of the face; thin-faced. **half'-frame** adj (of a photograph) taking up half the normal area of a frame. **half'-hardy** adj able to grow in the open air except in winter. **half-heart'ed** adj lacking in zeal. **half-heart'edly** adv. **half-heart'edness** n. **half hitch** n a simple knot tied round an object. **half-hol'iday** n half of a working day for recreation. **half-hose** see **hose**. **half-hour'** n a period of 30 minutes (also *adj*); a point marking such a period on a clock, etc. **half-hour'ly** adj and adv at intervals of 30 minutes. **half-hunter** see **hunter** under **hunt**. **half-inch'** n half of an inch of length. ◆ vt (*rhyming sl*) to pinch, steal. **half-in'teger** n a number formed by the division of an odd integer by two. **half-in'tegral** adj. **half'-kirtle** n a kind of jacket worn by women in the 16 and 17c. **half'-landing** n a small landing at the bend of a staircase. **half'-leather** n a half-binding for a book, with leather on back and corners. **half'-length** n a portrait showing the upper part of the body. ◆ *adj* of half the whole or ordinary length.

half'-life n the period of time in which activity of a radioactive substance falls to half its original value. **half'-light** n dim light; twilight. **half'-loaf** n a loaf of half the standard weight. **half-mar'athon** n a foot-race just over half the length of a marathon (21.243 km, 13 miles 352 yards). **half mast** n the position of a flag partly lowered, in respect for the dead or in signal of distress. **half-mast'** adv and vt. **half measure** n (often in *pl*) any means inadequate for the end proposed. **half-mil'er** n a runner specializing in races of 800 metres or half a mile. **half-moon'** n the moon at the quarters when half the disc is illuminated; anything semicircular. **half-mourn'ing** n mourning attire less than deep or full mourning; the condition of having one black eye (*sl*). **half nelson** see **nelson**. **half'-note** n (*music*; *N Am*) a minim. **half-one'** n (*golf*) a handicap of one stroke every second hole; same as **half past one** below. **half pay** n reduced pay, as for an officer not on active service. **half'-pay** adj on half pay. **halfpenny** /hāp'ni/ n (pl **halfpence** /hā'pəns/, or **halfpennies** /hāp'niz/) a coin worth half a penny, withdrawn from circulation in 1985; its value; anything very small (*Shakesp*). ◆ *adj* valued at a halfpenny. **halfpennyworth** /hāp'ni-wûrth/ n (also **hap'orth** /hāp'ərth/) as much as is sold for a halfpenny or is worth a halfpenny. **half'-pie** adj (Maori *pai* good; *NZ inf*) not very good; badly done. **half'-pike** n a short-shafted pike; a spontoon. **half'-pint** n (*sl*) a very small person. **half'-pipe** n a U-shaped structure made of concrete or hard snow used by skateboarders or snowboarders in performing stunts. **half'-plate** see **plate**. **half'-pound** n half a pound. ◆ *adj* weighing half a pound. **half-pound'er** n a fish or other thing weighing half a pound; a gun that fires a half-pound shot. **half-price'** n a charge reduced to half. ◆ *adj* and *adv* at half the usual price. **half-round'** n a semicircle. ◆ *adj* (*Milton*) semicircular. **half-roy'al** n a kind of millboard. **half-seas-o'ver** adj and adv halfway across the sea; half-drunk (*inf*). **half'-shell** n one shell or valve of a bivalve. **half'-shift** n a position of the hand in violin-playing giving notes a semitone above the open-string position. **half'-sister** n a sister with whom one has only one parent in common. **half-size'** n any size in clothes, etc halfway between two full sizes. **half'-sole** n the part of a shoe-sole from the instep to the toe. **half-sove'reign** n a gold coin worth **half-a-sov'ereign** or ten shillings. **half-starved'** adj very inadequately fed. **half step** n (*music*; *N Am*) a semitone. **half'-sword** n fighting within half a sword's length, close fighting. **half-term'** n (a holiday taken at) the mid point of an academic term. **half'-text** n handwriting half the size of text (also *adj*). **half'-tide** n the stage midway between flood and ebb. ◆ *adj* uncovered at half-tide. **half-tim'bered** adj built of a timber frame, with spaces filled in. **half-time'** n half of full or whole time; the middle of the whole time; a short break halfway through a game (*sport*); (in industry) half the time usually worked. ◆ *adj* /häf'/ at or for half-time. **half-tim'er** n someone who works half the full time. **half'-tint** n intermediate tone, between light and dark. **half-ti'tle** n a short title preceding the title page or before a section of a book; the page on which this appears. **half'-tone** adj representing light and shade photographically by dots of different sizes. ◆ n a half-tone illustration; a semitone (*music*). **half'-track** n a motor vehicle with wheels in front and caterpillar tracks behind (also *adj*). **half'-truth** n a belief containing an element of truth; a statement conveying only part of the truth. **half volley** see **volley**. **halfway'** (sometimes /häf'wā/) adv midway; at half the distance; imperfectly; slightly, barely (*inf*). **half'way** adj equidistant from two points. **halfway house** n *orig* an inn, etc situated midway between two towns or points on a journey, etc; a midway point or state; a centre offering accommodation and rehabilitation to eg released prisoners, people recovering from mental illness, etc. **half-wellington** see **wellington**. **half'wit** n an idiot (*inf*); a would-be wit (*obs*). **halfwitt'ed** adj foolish, stupid (*inf*); mentally defective (*obs*). **half'-year** n half of a year, six months. **half-year'ly** adj occurring or appearing every half-year. ◆ *adv* twice a year. ◆ n a half-yearly publication.

■ **by half** by a long way. **by halves** incompletely; half-heartedly. **cry halves** to claim half. **go halves** to share equally. **half past one, two**, etc, **half after one, two**, etc (*inf*) thirty minutes after one o'clock, two o'clock, etc. **how the other half lives** (*facetious*) other (*esp* richer or poorer) people's way of life. **not half** (*sl*) not moderately; not even half; not at all; very much, exceedingly. **one's other** (or **better**) **half** one's spouse or partner.

halfa /hal'fə/ or **alfa** /al'fə/ n a N African esparto grass. [Ar *halfā*]

halfpace /häf'pās/ n a landing or broad step; a raised part of a floor. [OFr *halt* (Fr *haut*) high, and *pas* step]

halibut /hal'i-bət/ n a large flatfish, more elongated than flounder or turbot (also **hol'ibut**). [Appar *holy butt* as much eaten on holy days; see **holy** and **butt⁵**; cf Du *heilbot*, Ger *Heilbutt*]

halicore /hə-lik'ə-rē or hal-i'kə-rē/ n the dugong. [Gr *hals* sea, and *korē* girl]

halide /hāl' or hal'īd/ n a compound of a halogen with a metal or radical. [Gr *hals* salt]

halidom /hal'i-dəm/ (*archaic*) n holiness; a holy place or thing, *esp* in an oath. [OE *hāligdōm*, from *hālig* holy]

halieutic /hal-i-ū'tik/ adj relating to fishing. [Gr halieutikos, from halieus fisher, from hals sea]
■ **halieu'tics** n sing the art of fishing; a treatise on fishing.

halimot or **halimote** /hal'i-mōt/ n a non-standard form of **hall-moot** (as if a holy or church court).

haliotis /hal-i-ō'tis/ n (pl **haliō'tis**) any gastropod of the family **Halio'tidae**, with a perforated ear-shaped shell lined with mother-of-pearl; (with cap) the genus to which they belong. [Gr hals sea, and ous, ōtos ear]

halite /hal'īt/ n rock salt. [Gr hals salt]

halitus /hal'i-təs/ n a vapour. [L]
■ **halitō'sis** n foul breath. **halitō'tic** adj. **hal'itous** adj vaporous.

hall /höl/ n a large room entered immediately by the front door of a house; a passage or lobby at the entrance of a house; the main room in a great house; a building containing such a room; a manor-house; the main building of a college; in some cases the college itself; an unendowed college; a licensed residence for students; a college dining room; hence, the dinner itself; a place for special professional education, or the conferring of diplomas, licences, etc; the headquarters of a guild, society, etc; a servants' dining room and sitting room (servants' hall); a building or large chamber for meetings, concerts, exhibitions, etc; a clear space (archaic). [OE hall (heall); Du hal, ON höll, etc]
❑ **hall-bed'room** n (US) a bedroom partitioned off at the end of an entrance hall. **hall'-door** n a front door. **hall'mark** n the authorized stamp impressed on gold, silver or platinum articles at Goldsmiths' Hall or some other place of assaying, indicating date, maker, fineness of metal, etc; any mark of authenticity or good quality. ◆ vt to stamp with such a mark. **hall'-moot** n the court of the lord of a manor; the court of a guild. **hall of fame** n a gallery of busts, portraits, etc of celebrated people; the ranks of the great and famous. **hall of residence** n a building providing residential accommodation for students at a university, etc. **hall'stand** n a tall piece of furniture fitted with hooks on which hats, coats and umbrellas can be left. **hall tree** n (N Am) a hallstand. **hall'way** n an entrance hall.
■ **a hall, a hall** (archaic) a cry at a masque for room for the dance, etc. **bachelor's hall** any place in which a man is free from the restraining presence of a wife; the state of having such freedom, often in the phrase to keep bachelor's hall. **Liberty Hall** a place where everyone may do as they please. **the halls** music halls.

hallal see halal.

hallali /hal'ə-lē/ n a bugle-call.

hallaloo /hal-ə-loo'/ (Fielding) n halloo.

hallan /hal'ən/ (Scot) n a partition or screen between the door and fireplace in a cottage. [Perh hall]
❑ **hallan-shāk'er** (or /-shäk'ər/) n a beggar; a vagrant; a shabby, sorry creature.

hälleflinta /hel'ə-flin-tə/ n a very compact rock composed of minute particles of quartz and feldspar. [Swed, hornstone]

hallelujah or **halleluiah** /hal-ə-loo'yə/, also **alleluia** /al-ə-loo'yə/ interj expressing praise to God. ◆ n a shout of hallelujah; a song of praise to God; a musical composition based on the word. [Heb hallelū praise ye, and Jāh Jehovah]

hallian see hallion.

halliard see halyard.

halling /hal'ing or hö'ling/ n a Norwegian country dance in 2–4 time, or its tune. [Perh Hallingdal, NW of Oslo]

hallion, hallian or **hallyon** /hal'yən/ n a lout; a lazy rascal. [Origin unknown]

hallo see hello.

halloo /hə-loo'/ or **halloa** /hə-lō'/ n a cry to urge on a chase or to call attention. ◆ vi to urge on a pack of hounds; to raise an outcry. ◆ vt to encourage with halloos; to hunt with halloos. [Imit]
■ **don't halloo till you're out of the wood** keep quiet until you are sure you are safe.

halloumi /ha-loo'mi/ n a mild cheese made in Cyprus, often eaten fried or grilled. [Mod Gr]

hallow /hal'ō/ vt to make holy; to consecrate (archaic); to reverence. ◆ n (archaic) a saint. [OE hālgian to hallow, hālga a saint, from hālig holy]
■ **hall'owed** adj holy, revered. **Hallowe'en'** n the eve of or the evening before All Saints Day, celebrated by masquerading and the playing of pranks by children. **Hall'owmas** n the feast of All Hallows or All Saints, 1 November.

halloysite /ha-loi'zīt/ n a clayey mineral, a hydrated aluminium silicate. [Omalius d'Halloy (1783–1875), Belgian geologist]

Hallstatt /häl'shtät/ adj relating to a European culture transitional between Bronze Age and Iron Age. [From finds at Hallstatt in upper Austria]

hallucinate /hə-loo'si-nāt or hə-lū'si-nāt/ vt to affect with hallucination. ◆ vi to experience hallucination. [L hallūcinārī (better ālūcinārī), -ātus to wander in the mind]
■ **hallucinā'tion** n a perception without objective reality; (loosely) delusion. **hallu'cinative** or **hallu'cinatory** adj. **hallu'cinogen** /-nə-jən/ n a drug that produces hallucinatory sensations. **hallucinogen'ic** adj causing hallucinations. **hallucino'sis** n a mental disorder characterized by the repeated occurrence of hallucinations.

hallux /hal'əks/ n (pl **halluces** /-ū'sēz/) the innermost digit of the hind limb of a bird, mammal, reptile or amphibian (zool); the human big toe (anat); a bird's hindtoe (zool). [Mistaken form of L (h)allex, -icis]

hallyon see hallion.

halm /häm/ same as haulm.

halma /hal'mə/ n in the Greek pentathlon, a long jump with weights in the hands (hist); a game played on a board of 256 squares, in which the pieces are moved into vacant squares immediately behind an opponent's pieces. [Gr, a jump]

halo /hā'lō/ n (pl **hā'loes** or **hā'los**) a ring of light or colour, esp one round the sun or moon caused by refraction by ice-crystals; (in paintings, etc) such a ring round the head of a holy person; an ideal or sentimental glory or glamour attaching to anything. ◆ vt (pap **hā'loed** or **hā'lo'd**) to surround with a halo (lit and fig). [Gr halōs a threshing floor, disc, halo]
❑ **halo effect** n (psychol) the tendency to judge a person (well or ill) on the basis of one or only a few characteristics.

halobiont see under haloid.

halocarbon /hal'ō-kär-bən/ (chem) n a compound consisting of carbon and one or more halogens.

halogen /hal'ə-jən/ n any of the elements in the seventh group of the periodic table, these being fluorine, chlorine, bromine, iodine and astatine (the first four defined in the 19c as forming salts by direct union with metals; astatine discovered in 1940). [Gr hals salt, and -gen (1)]
■ **halogenate** /-oj'/ vt to combine with a halogen. **halog'enous** adj.

haloid /hal'oid/ n a halide. ◆ adj having the composition of a halide. [Gr hals salt]
■ **halobiont** /hal-ō-bī'ont/ n an organism living or growing in a saline habitat. **halobion'tic** or **halobiotic** /-bī-ot'ik/ adj living in the sea. **hal'ophile** /-fīl/ or /-fīl/ n an organism that thrives in very salty conditions, eg the Dead Sea. ◆ adj tolerant of salt; capable of living in salt water. **haloph'ilous** adj halophile. **haloph'ily** n adaptation to life in the presence of much salt. **hal'ophobe** n (bot) a plant that cannot survive in salty soil. **halophyte** /hal'ō-fīt/ n a plant adapted to life in soil or water containing much salt. **halophytic** /-fīt'ik/ adj.

halon /hā'lon/ n any one of a class of halogenated hydrocarbons, used esp in fire extinguishers, and considered detrimental to the ozone layer. [Gr hals salt]

haloperidol /hal-ō-per'i-dol/ n a synthetic tranquillizing drug used in treating psychiatric illnesses. [halogen, piperidine and -ol¹]

Haloragis /ha-lə-rā'jis/ n an Australasian genus of plants giving its name to the family **Haloragidā'ceae**, a reduced offshoot of the evening primrose family, including mare's-tail and water milfoil (also called sea'-berry). [Gr hals sea, and rhāx, rhāgos a berry]

halothane /hal'ə-thān/ n a general, inhalation anaesthetic known proprietarily as Fluothane.

halse¹ /höls/ or (Scot and N Eng dialect) **hause** or **hawse** /hös/ (obs or dialect) n the neck; the throat; a pass, defile, or connecting ridge. ◆ vt (pat **halsed** or (Spenser) **haulst**) to embrace. [OE hals (heals) neck; Ger Hals]
❑ **hause'-bane** n (Scot) collarbone. **hause'-lock** n (Scot) the wool of a sheep's neck.

halse² /häls or hös/ (obs) vt to salute, greet. [OE halsian]

halser /hö'zər/ n same as hawser.

halt¹ /hölt/ vi to come to a standstill; to make a temporary stop. ◆ vt to cause to stop. ◆ n a standstill; a stopping-place; a railway station not fully equipped. [Ger Halt stoppage]
■ **call a halt** (**to**) to stop, put an end (to).

halt² /hölt/ vi to be lame, to limp (archaic); to walk unsteadily; to vacillate; to proceed lamely or imperfectly, to be at fault (eg in logic, rhythm, etc). ◆ adj (Bible; archaic) lame, crippled, limping. ◆ n a limp (archaic); foot rot (dialect); an impediment in speech (Scot). [OE halt (healt) lame; Dan halt]
■ **halt'ing** n and adj. **halt'ingly** adv.

halter /höl'tər/ n a rope for holding and leading an animal, or for hanging criminals; a woman's backless bodice held in place by straps

round the neck and across the back. ◆ *vt* to put a halter on. [OE *hælftre* ; Ger *Halfter*]
❑ **halter neck** *n* a neckline on a dress, etc in the style of a halter. **halt'er-necked** *adj*.

halteres /hal-tē'rēz/ (*zool*) *n pl* the rudimentary hindwings of flies, used to maintain balance in flight. [Gr *haltēres* dumbbells held by jumpers, from *hallesthai* to jump]

halva, **halvah** or **halavah** /häl'və/ *n* a sweetmeat, *orig* Turkish, containing sesame seeds, honey, nuts and saffron. [Yiddish *halva* ; ult from Ar]

halve /häv/ *vt* to divide in half; to reduce by half; (in golf) to play (a hole or match) in the same number of strokes as one's opponent; (in carpentry) to join by cutting away half the thickness of each. ◆ *vi* to be reduced by half. [**half**]
■ **halv'er** *n* someone who halves; a half-share. **halv'ers** *interj* used in claiming half a find.

halve-net /häv'net/ or **haaf-net** /häf'net/ (*dialect*) *n* a net held or set to catch fish as the tide ebbs, now only used in the Solway Firth. [Older Scot *half* such a net; cf Norw dialect *haav*, Swed *håf*, Dan *hov*, ON *háfr*]

halyard or **halliard** /hal'yərd/ *n* a rope or purchase for hoisting or lowering a sail, yard, or flag. [For *halier*, from **hale²**, by association with **yard¹**]

ham¹ /ham/ *n* the back of the thigh or hock; the thigh of an animal, *esp* of a pig salted and dried; the meat from this part. [OE *hamm* ; cf dialect Ger *hamme*]
■ **hamm'y** *adj*.
❑ **ham-fist'ed** or **ham-hand'ed** *adj* (*inf*) clumsy.

ham² /ham/ (*inf*) *n* an actor who rants and overacts; overacting; a part that lends itself to this; an inexpert boxer; an amateur, *esp* an amateur radio operator. ◆ *adj* given to overacting or ranting; amateur; clumsy, coarse, inexpert. ◆ *vi* and *vt* (**hamm'ing**; **hammed**) to overact. [Prob **hamfatter**]
■ **hamm'ily** *adv*. **hamm'y** *adj*.

hamadryad /ham-ə-drī'ad/ *n* (pl **hamadry'ads** or **hamadry'ades** /-ēz/) a wood nymph who died with the tree in which she dwelt (*classical myth*); the king cobra, a large poisonous snake of SE Asia, *Ophiophagus hannah* (also **hamadry'as**); a large Ethiopian baboon. [Gr *hamadryas*, from *hama* together, and *drȳs* (oak) tree]

hamal see **hammal**.

hamamelis /ham-ə-mē'lis/ *n* a shrub of the American witch-hazel genus, giving name to a family, **Hamamelidā'ceae**, related to the planes; (with *cap*) the genus itself. [Gr *hamamēlis* medlar, from *hama* together with, and *mēlon* an apple]

hamarthritis /ham-är-thrī'tis/ *n* gout in all the joints. [Gr *hama* together, and *arthrītis* gout]

hamartia /ha-mär'tē-ə/ *n* (in a literary work) the flaw or defect in the character of the hero that leads to his downfall (*orig* and *esp* in ancient Greek tragedy, as explained in Aristotle's *Poetics*). [Gr *hamartiā* failure, error of judgement, sin]
■ **hamartiol'ogy** *n* that section of theology that deals with sin.

Hamas /ha-mas' or ham'as/ *n* a Palestinian Islamic fundamentalist organization. [Ar *hamas* enthusiasm, as an acronym of *harakat al-Muqawama al-Islamiyya*, Islamic Resistance Movement]

hamate /hä'mət/ *adj* hooked. ◆ *n* (*anat*) a hooked bone in the wrist. [L *hāmātus*, from *hāmus* hook]

hamble /ham'bl/ *vt* to mutilate, make (a dog) useless for hunting (by cutting the balls of its feet). ◆ *vi* (*dialect*) to limp, to stumble. [OE *hamelian*]

Hamburg or **Hamburgh** /ham'bûrg/ or *-b(ə-)rə/ *n* a black variety of grape (often *black Hamburg*); a small blue-legged domestic fowl. [*Hamburg* in Germany]
❑ **Hamburg steak** same as **hamburger**.

hamburger /ham'bûr-gər/ *n* (a bread roll containing) a flat round cake of finely chopped meat fried or grilled (often shortened to **burger**); finely chopped meat. [Orig *Hamburg steak*]

hame¹ /hām/ *n* one of the two curved bars of a draught horse's collar. [Cf Du *haam*, LGer *ham*]

hame² /hām/ Scots form of **home**.
■ **hame'with** *adv* homewards.

hamesucken /hām'suk-n/ (*Scots law*) *n* the assaulting of a man in his own house. [OE *hāmsōcn*, from *hām* home, and *sōcn* seeking, attack; cf Ger *Heimsuchung* affliction]

Hamiltonian /ham-il-tō'ni-ən/ *adj* relating to or associated with: James *Hamilton* (1769–1829), or his method of teaching languages without grammar; the philosopher Sir William *Hamilton* (1788–1856); Sir William Rowan *Hamilton* (1805–65), Irish mathematician; or any other of the name.

Hamite /ham'īt/ *n* a descendant or supposed descendant of *Ham*, son of Noah; a member of a dark-skinned long-headed race of NE Africa (*Galla*, *Hadendoa*, etc), sometimes understood more widely to cover much of N Africa; a speaker of any language of a N African family distantly related to Semitic (ancient Egyptian, Berber, etc).
■ **Hamitic** /-mit'ik/ *adj*.

hamlet /ham'lit/ *n* a cluster of houses in the country; a small village. [OFr *hamelet*, dimin of *hamel* (Fr *hameau*), from Gmc; cf **home**]

hammal or **hamal** /hu-mäl'/ *n* an Eastern porter. [Ar *hammāl*]

hammam /hu-mäm', hum'um or ham'am/ *n* an Oriental bathing establishment, a Turkish bath (also **humm'aum** or **humm'um**). [Ar *hammām*]

hammer /ham'ər/ *n* a tool for beating metal, breaking rock, driving nails, etc; a striking-piece in the mechanism of a clock, piano, etc; the apparatus that causes explosion of the charge in a firearm; the mallet with which an auctioneer announces that an article is sold; a small bone of the ear, the malleus; a metal ball weighing about 7 kg, attached to a long handle of flexible wire, for throwing in competition (*athletics*); a trouncer. ◆ *vt* to beat, drive, shape, or fashion with or as if with a hammer; to contrive or think out by intellectual labour (with *out*); to arrive at (a conclusion) or settle (differences) after much argument (with *out*); to trounce or criticize severely (*inf*); to teach by frequent and energetic reiteration (with *in* or *into*); to declare a defaulter on the Stock Exchange; to beat down the price of (a stock), to depress (a market). ◆ *vi* to use a hammer; to make a noise as of a hammer; to persevere doggedly (with *away*). [OE *hamor* ; Ger *Hammer*, ON *hamarr*]
■ **hamm'ered** *adj* beaten with a hammer; (of a musical instrument) played with hammers; severely beaten (*inf*); drunk (*sl*). **hamm'erer** *n*. **hamm'ering** *n* and *adj*. **hamm'erless** *adj*.
❑ **hammer beam** *n* a horizontal piece of timber in place of a tie-beam at or near the feet of a pair of rafters. **hamm'er-brace** *n* a curved brace supporting a hammer beam. **hammer drill** *n* a drill in which the drill bit strikes rapid blows while boring. **hamm'erhead** *n* a shark with a hammer-shaped head (also **hamm'er-fish** and **hammer-headed shark**); the umbrette, a crested thick-billed African wading bird (also (*Du*) **hamm'erkop**). **hamm'er-headed** *adj* with a head shaped like a hammer; dull in intellect, stupid. **hamm'erlock** *n* (*wrestling*) a hold in which the opponent's arm is twisted upwards behind his or her back. **hamm'erman** *n* someone who wields a hammer, such as a blacksmith, goldsmith, etc. **hamm'er-pond** *n* an artificial pond at a water mill. **hamm'er-toe** *n* a condition in which a toe is permanently bent upwards at the base and doubled down upon itself.
■ **bring to the hammer** to sell, or cause to sell, by auction. (**come**) **under the hammer** (come up) for sale by auction. **give** (or **take**) **a hammering** (*inf*) to beat (or be beaten) severely, to defeat (or be defeated) comprehensively. **hammer and sickle** the crossed hammer and sickle emblem of the former Soviet Union, or of Communism. **hammer and tongs** with great noise and violence. **hammer home** to impress (a fact) strongly and effectively on someone.

hammercloth /ham'ər-kloth/ *n* a cloth covering a coach box. [Origin unknown]

Hammerklavier /ham-ər-kla-vēr'/ (*Ger*) *n* a pianoforte.

hammerkop see **hammerhead** under **hammer**.

hammock /ham'ək/ *n* a cloth or netting hung by the ends, for use as a bed or couch. [Sp *hamaca*, from Carib]

Hammond organ® /ham'ənd ör'gən/ *n orig* a two-manual organ, with tones electromagnetically generated by means of rotating wheels controlled by the keys; (loosely) any two-manual digital organ. [Invented by L *Hammond* (1895–1973), US mechanical engineer]

hamose /hā-mōs' or hā'mōs/ *adj* hooked (also **hā'mous**). [L *hāmus* hook]
■ **hamular** /ham'ū-lər/ *adj* like a small hook. **ham'ulate** *adj* tipped with a small hook. **ham'ulus** *n* (pl **ham'uli** /-lī/) (*anat* and *zool*) a small hook or hook-like process.

hamper¹ /ham'pər/ *vt* to impede the progress or movement of; to distort; to curtail. ◆ *n* a shackle; that which impedes; essential but somewhat cumbrous equipment on a vessel (*naut*). [First, about 1350, in Scot and N Eng writers; cf ON and Mod Icel *hemja* to restrain, Ger *hemmen*]

hamper² /ham'pər/ *n* a large basket, *usu* with a cover; the basket and its contents, *usu* food; a laundry basket (*N Am*). ◆ *vt* to give a hamper to, to bribe. [*hanaper* (see under **hanap**)]

hampster see **hamster**.

hamshackle /ham'sha-kl/ *vt* to shackle by tying head to foreleg; to fetter, restrain. [**shackle**; otherwise obscure]

hamster or **hampster** /ham'stər/ *n* a small Eurasian rodent (genus *Cricetus*) with cheekpouches reaching almost to the shoulders. [Ger]

■ words derived from main entry word; ❑ compound words; ■ idioms and phrasal verbs

hamstring /ham'string/ n (in humans) one of the five tendons at the back of the knee; (in a horse, etc) the large tendon at the back of the knee or hock of the hindleg. ◆ vt (pat and pap **ham'stringed** or **ham'strung**) to lame by cutting the hamstring; to make powerless. [**ham**[1] and **string**]

hamular, **hamulate**, **hamuli**, **hamulus** see under **hamose**.

hamza or **hamzah** /häm'zä or ham'zə/ n in Arabic, the sign used to represent the glottal stop. [Ar hamzah a compression]

Han /hän/ n and n pl (a member of) the native Chinese people, as opposed to the Mongols, Manchus, etc. [Chin Hàn]

han /han/ an old plural (Spenser) of **have**.

hanap /han'əp/ n an ornate medieval drinking goblet, often having a cover. [OFr hanap drinking cup; cf OHGer knapf ; OE hnæpp a bowl]

■ **han'aper** n a case for a hanap; a receptacle for treasure, paper, etc; a former department of Chancery.

hance /häns or hans/, also **haunch** /hönch or hönsh/ n a curved rise from a lower to a higher part (naut); the arc of smaller radius at the springing of an elliptical or many-centred arch (archit). [OFr hauce, haulce rise; cf **enhance**]

hanch[1] /hänsh or hansh/ (Scot) vi and vt to snap (at) with the jaws. [Obs Fr hancher]

hanch[2] see **haunch**[1].

hand /hand/ n (in humans) the extremity of the arm below the wrist; any corresponding member in the higher vertebrates; the forefoot of a quadruped; the extremity of the hind limb when it is prehensile; a pointer or index; a measure of four inches; a division of a bunch of bananas; side, direction, quarter; a worker, esp in a factory or on a ship; a performer; a dealer, author or producer; instrumentality; influence; share in performance; power or manner of performing; style; skill; handiwork; touch; stroke; control; (often in pl) keeping, custody; possession; assistance; style of handwriting; a signature, esp of a sovereign; pledge; consent to or promise of marriage, or fulfilment of such promise; feel, handle (of a textile); the set of cards held by a player at one deal; the play of a single deal of cards; (loosely) a game of cards; a turn, round or innings in a game; in various games, (possession of) service; a round of applause; (in pl) skill in handling a horse's reins. ◆ vt to lay hands on, set hand to, manipulate, handle (obs); to join hands with (rare); to pass with the hand; to lead, escort or help (eg into a vehicle) with the hands; to transfer or deliver (often with over); to furl or lower (a sail, esp a square sail) (naut). ◆ pfx (in combination) denoting: by hand, or direct bodily operation (hand-held, hand-knitted, handmade, hand-painted, hand-sewn, hand-weeded); for the hands (hand lotion, handtowel); operated by hand (hand-punch); held in the hand (hand-basket). [OE hand; in all Gmc tongues, perh related to Gothic hinthan to seize]

■ **hand'ed** adj having hands; with hands joined (Milton). ◆ combining form denoting: using one hand in preference to the other (as in left-handed); having a hand or hands as stated (as in one-handed or neat-handed). **hand'edness** n the tendency to use one hand rather than the other; inherent asymmetry in particles, etc, eg causing twisting in one direction (phys). ◆ combining form as in left-handedness. **hand'er** n someone who hands; a blow on the hand. ◆ combining form used to signify: a blow, etc with the hand or hands as stated (eg right-hander, back-hander); a play with a specified number of characters (eg two-hander). **hand'ful** n (pl **hand'fuls**) enough to fill the hand; a small number or quantity; someone or something that taxes one's powers. **hand'ily** adv. **hand'iness** n. **hand'less** adj without hands; awkward; incompetent. **hand'y** adj (**hand'ier**; **hand'iest**) dexterous; near to hand; convenient; near; easy to use.

❑ **hand'bag** n a bag for small articles, carried esp by women; a light travelling bag. ◆ vt (inf) to attack, destroy, wreck, undermine (orig used of Margaret Thatcher). **hand'bagging** n. **handbag music** n a form of house music with long piano breaks and vocal solos. **hand'ball** n a game between goals in which the ball is struck with the palm of the hand; a game similar to fives in which a ball is struck with the gloved hand against a wall or walls (usu four); /-böl'/ (in football) the offence of touching or striking the ball with one's hand. **hand'-barrow** n a wheelless barrow, carried by handles; a handcart. **hand'-basket** n. **hand'bell** n a small bell with a handle, rung by hand. **hand'bill** n a light pruning hook; a bill or loose sheet bearing an announcement. **hand'book** n a manual; a guidebook; a bookmaker's book of bets (US). **hand'brake** n a brake applied by a hand-operated lever. **handbrake turn** n a sharp U-turn on the spot in a motor car, achieved by applying the handbrake at speed. **hand'breadth** or **hand's breadth** n the breadth of a hand. **hand'car** n (US) a workman's small, open-sided railway car, motorized or propelled by hand-pumping a lever. **hand'cart** n a light cart drawn by hand. **hand'clap** n a clap of the hands. **hand'clasp** n (US) a handshake.

hand'craft n handicraft. ◆ vt to make skilfully by hand. **hand'crafted** adj. **hand'cuff** n (esp in pl) a shackle locked on the wrist. ◆ vt to put handcuffs on. **hand'fast** n (archaic) a firm grip; custody; a handle (dialect); a contract, esp a betrothal. ◆ adj (archaic) bound; espoused; tight-gripping. ◆ vt (archaic) to betroth; to join by handfasting. **hand'fasting** n (archaic) betrothal; probationary marriage; private marriage. **hand'-feeding** n feeding of animals or machinery by hand. **hand gallop** n an easy gallop, restrained by the bridle-hand. **hand glass** n a glass or glazed frame to protect plants; a mirror or a magnifying glass with a handle. **hand grenade** n a grenade to be thrown by hand. **hand'grip** n a grasp with the hand; something for the hand to grasp; (in pl) close struggle. **hand'gun** n a gun that can be held and fired in one hand. **hand'-held** adj (also without hyphen) held in the hands rather than mounted on some support. **hand'held** n any piece of equipment designed to be carried in the hand, esp a personal digital assistant. **hand'hold** n a hold by the hand; a place or part that can be held by the hand. **hand'-horn** n an early form of musical horn without valves. **hand'icuffs** n pl fisticuffs. **hand'-in** n (badminton, etc) the player who is serving. **hand'job** n (sl) an act of manually stimulating the penis of another person. **hand'knit** n and adj (a garment) knitted by hand. **hand'-knit'** vt. **hand'-knitted** adj. **hand line** n a fishing-line without a rod. ◆ vi to fish with such a line. **hand'list** n a list without detail, for handy reference. **hand'-loom** n a hand-worked weaving loom. **hand lotion** n. **hand'made** adj. **hand'maid** or **hand'maiden** n (archaic) a female servant or attendant; a person or thing that serves a useful ancillary purpose. **hand mating** n (agric) a system in which the stockman supervises the mating of a specific female to a specific male. **hand'-me-down** adj (of garments) formerly ready-made, usually cheap, now usu second-hand, esp formerly belonging to a member of one's own family. ◆ n a cheap ready-made garment; a second-hand garment. **hand'-mill** n a quern; a coffee mill, pepper-mill, etc worked by hand. **hand'-off** n (rugby) an act or manner of pushing off an opponent. **hand of glory** n see separate entry. **hand organ** n a barrel organ. **hand'out** n a portion handed out, esp to the needy; an issue; a prepared statement issued to the press, people attending a lecture, etc; a usu free leaflet containing information, propaganda, etc. **hand'-out** n (badminton, etc) a player whose side is receiving the service; the situation when the first player on the serving side loses his or her service. **hand'over** n a transfer, handing over. **hand'-painted** adj. **hand'-paper** n paper with a hand for watermark. **hand'-pick** vt to pick by hand; to select carefully for a particular purpose. **hand'play** n dealing of blows. **hand'-post** n a fingerpost. **hand'-press** n a printing or other press worked by hand. **hand'print** n the mark left by a person's hand. **hand-prom'ise** n formerly in Ireland, a solemn form of betrothal. **hand puppet** n a glove puppet. **hand'rail** n a rail to hold for safety, support, etc, as on stairs. **hand relief** n (inf) masturbation. **hand-runn'ing** adv (dialect) consecutively. **hand'saw** n a saw worked by hand, specif with a handle at one end; in Shakespeare, perhaps mistakenly written or copied in place of **heronshaw** (see also **know a hawk from a handsaw** under **hawk**[1]). **hand'-screen** n a screen against fire or sun, held in the hand. **hand'-screw** n a clamp; a jack for raising weights. **hand'set** n on a telephone, the part held by the hand, containing the mouthpiece and earpiece; a remote-control device for a television set, DVD player, etc. **hand'-sewing** n. **hand'-sewn** adj. **hands'-free** adj not involving manual operation, eg of a telephone apparatus that incorporates a microphone and speaker so that the user need not hold the handset when making a call. ◆ n an apparatus that can be operated without using the hands. **hand'shake** n a shaking of hands in greeting, etc (also **hand'shaking**); a golden handshake or the like; an exchange of signals (on a separate line) between two or more devices, which synchronizes them in readiness for the transfer of data (comput). **hand'shaking** n (comput) the process of performing a handshake. **hands-off'** adj not touching with the hands; operated by remote control; that cannot be touched; not favouring active involvement. **hands-on'** adj operated by hand; favouring active involvement; involving practical rather than theoretical knowledge, experience, method of working, etc; (of museums, etc) with exhibits that can be handled; (of a therapeutic technique) involving specific positioning of the hands. **hand'spike** n a bar used as a lever. **hand'spring** n a cartwheel or somersault with hands on the ground. **hand'staff** n (pl **hand'staves** or **hand'staffs**) a staff-like handle, eg of a flail; a staff as a weapon; a javelin. **hand'stand** n an act of balancing one's body on the palms of one's hands with one's trunk and legs in the air. **hands'turn** or **hand's turn** n (usu with a negative) a single or least act of work. **hand'towel** n. **hand'-weeded** adj. **hand'work** n work done by hand. **hand'worked** adj made or done by hand. **hand'writing** n writing, script; style of writing; individual style discernible in one's actions. **hand'written** adj written by hand, not typed or printed. **hand'wrought** adj handworked. **hand'yman** n a man employed to carry out, or skilled in doing, odd jobs; a bluejacket.

■ **at any hand** or **in any hand** (Shakesp) at any rate, in any case. **at first hand** directly from the source. **at hand** conveniently near; within easy reach; near in time; at the beginning (*Shakesp*). **at the hand** (or **hands**) **of** by the act of. **bear a hand** to take part, give aid. **bloody** or **red hand** (*heraldry*) the arms of Ulster, a sinister hand erect couped at the wrist gules, borne by baronets in a canton or inescutcheon. **by hand** by use of the hands, or tools worked by the hand, not by machinery or other indirect means; by personal delivery, not by post. **by the strong hand** by force. **change hands** to pass to other ownership or keeping. **come to hand** to arrive; to be received. **come to one's hand** to be found easy; to come to close quarters. **force someone's hand** to compel someone. **for one's own hand** to one's own account. **get one's hand in** to get control of the play so as to turn one's cards to good use; to get into the way or knack. **good hands** a trustworthy source; good keeping; care of those who may be trusted to treat one well. **hand and foot** *orig* with respect to hands and feet; with assiduous attention. **hand and** (or **in**) **glove** on very intimate terms; in close co-operation. **hand down** or **on** to transmit in succession or by tradition. **hand in hand** with hands mutually clasped; with one person holding the hand of another; in close association; conjointly (**hand'-in-hand'** *adj*). **hand it to someone** (*sl*) to admit someone's superiority, *esp* as shown by his or her success in a difficult matter. **hand out** to distribute, pass by hand to individuals (see also **handout** above). **hand over** to transfer; to relinquish possession of. **hand over fist** with steady and rapid gain. **hand over hand** by passing the hands alternately one before or above another, as in climbing a rope or swimming with a certain stroke; progressively; with steady and rapid gain. **hand over head** headlong. **hands down** with utter ease (as in winning a race). **hands off** (as a command) keep off; do not touch or strike. **hands up** (as a command) hold the hands above the head in surrender. **hand to hand** at close quarters (**hand'-to-hand'** *adj*). **hand to mouth** with provision for immediate needs only (**hand'-to-mouth'** *adj*). **handwriting on the wall** see under **write**. **have one's hands full** to be preoccupied, very busy. **hold hands** see under **hold**[1]. **in hand** as present payment; in preparation; under control; of a ball that has to be played from balk (*billiards*). **keep one's hand in** see under **keep**. **lay hands on** to seize; to obtain or find; to subject physically to rough treatment; to bless, or to ordain by touching with the hand(s); to place one's hands on, over or near an ill person in an act of spiritual healing (also **lay on hands**). **laying-on of hands** the touch of a bishop or presbyters in ordination; in spiritual healing, the action of placing hands on, over or near an ill person. **lend a hand** to give assistance. **lift a hand** (*usu* with a negative) to make the least effort (to help, etc). **off one's hands** no longer under one's responsible charge. **old hand** see under **old**. **on all hands** or **on every hand** on all sides; by everybody. **on hand** ready, available; in one's possession. **on one's hands** under one's care or responsibility; remaining as a burden or encumbrance. **on the one hand ... on the other hand...** phrases used to introduce opposing points in an argument, etc. **out of hand** at once, immediately, without premeditation; out of control. **poor hand** an unskilful person or way of handling (*usu* with *at*). **raise one's hand to** (often with a negative) to strike, behave violently towards. **set** or **put one's hand to** to engage in, undertake; to sign. **shake hands with** see under **shake**. **show of hands** a vote by holding up hands. **show one's hand** to expose one's purpose. **sit on one's hands** to take no action. **slow handclap** slow rhythmic clapping showing disapproval. **stand one's hand** (*inf*) to buy a drink for someone else. **take in hand** to undertake; to take charge of in order to educate, discipline, etc. **take off someone's hands** to relieve someone of. **the hand of God** any unforeseen and unavoidable accident, such as lightning or a storm. **throw in the hand** to give up a venture or plan; to concede defeat. **tie someone's hands** to render someone powerless. **to** (**one's**) **hand** in readiness; within easy reach; (of a letter) received. **try one's hand at** to attempt; to test one's prowess at. **under one's hand** with one's proper signature attached. **upper hand** mastery; advantage. **wash one's hands** (**of**) to disclaim responsibility (for) (Bible, Matthew 27.24).

h and c *abbrev* : hot and cold (water laid on).

handicap /han'di-kap/ *vt* (**hand'icapping**; **hand'icapped**) to impose special disadvantages or impediments upon, in order to offset advantages and make a better contest; to place at a disadvantage. ◆ *n* any contest so adjusted, or the condition imposed; the number of strokes by which a golfer's average score exceeds par for the course, this number being subtracted from one's score in strokeplay competitions (*golf*); any physical, mental or social disability; a disadvantage. [Appar *hand i' cap*, from the drawing from a cap in an old lottery game]
■ **hand'icapped** *adj* suffering from some physical or mental disability; disadvantaged in some way. **hand'icapper** *n* an official in some sports who fixes the handicaps of competitors; a punter (*US horse-racing*).

handicraft /han'di-kräft/ *n* a manual craft or art; objects produced by such craft. [OE *handcræft*, from **hand**, and *cræft* craft, assimilated to **handiwork**]

■ **hand'icraftsman** or *fem* **hand'icraftswoman** *n* a man or woman skilled in a manual art.

handiwork or **handywork** /han'di-wûrk/ *n* work done by the hands; performance generally; work of skill or wisdom; creation; doing. [OE *handgewerc*, from *hand* and *gewerc* (*geweorc*) work]

handjar or **hanjar** /han'jär/ *n* a Persian dagger (also **khan'jar**). [Pers and Ar *khanjar*]

handkerchief /hang'kər-chif/ or -chēf/ *n* (pl **hand'kerchiefs** and sometimes **hand'kerchieves**) a cloth or paper for wiping the nose, etc; a neckerchief. —The form **hand'kercher** is now regarded as non-standard. [**hand** and **kerchief**]
■ **throw the handkerchief** to summon to pursuit or call upon to take one's turn, as in children's games and royal harems.

handle /han'dl/ *vt* to hold, move about, feel freely, etc with the hand; to make familiar by frequent touching; to manage (*esp* successfully); to discuss; to deal with, treat; to cope with, take in one's stride (*inf, esp N Am*); to pass through one's hands; to trade or do business in. ◆ *vi* to respond to control (in a specified way). ◆ *n* a part by which a thing is held, opened or picked up; anything affording an advantage or pretext to an opponent; feel, as of a textile; the total takings from betting on a horse race, etc; one's name (*sl*). [OE *handle, handlian* from *hand*]
■ **hand'led** *adj* having a handle. **hand'ler** *n* someone who handles; a boxer's trainer or second; someone who trains, holds, controls, incites, or shows off an animal at a show, fight, etc; someone who trains and uses a dog or other animal that works for the police or an armed service. **hand'ling** *n*.
□ **hand'lebar** *n* the steering-bar of a cycle, or one half of it. **handlebar moustache** *n* a wide, thick moustache with curved ends thought to resemble handlebars.
■ **a handle to one's name** a title. **fly off the handle** see under **fly**. **get a handle on** to understand, grasp.

handsel or **hansel** /han'səl/ *n* an inaugural gift, eg a present on Handsel Monday, a coin put in the pocket of a new coat, or the like; something thought of as an inauguration or beginning, such as the first money taken, earnest-money, a first instalment, the first use of anything; apparently payment or penalty (*Spenser*). ◆ *vt* (**hand'selling** or **han'selling**; **hand'selled** or **han'selled**) to give a handsel to; to inaugurate; to make a beginning on; to cut off, kill (*Chatterton*, from a blundering reading of a dictionary explanation, 'to cut off a first slice'). [OE *handselen* hand-gift, giving; or ON *handsal*]
□ **Handsel Monday** *n* (*Scot*) the first Monday after New Year's Day, when handsels were given.

handsome /han'səm/ *adj* good-looking; well-proportioned; dignified; liberal or noble; generous; ample; suitable, becoming, gracious (*archaic*); convenient, handy (*obs*). [**hand** and **-some**[1]; cf Du *handzaam*]
■ **hand'somely** *adv* generously, amply; graciously (*archaic*); carefully (*naut*). **hand'someness** *n*.

handy see under **hand**.

handy-dandy /han'di-dan'di/ *n* a children's game of guessing which hand a thing is in. ◆ *interj* (*Shakesp*) the formula used in the game. [**hand**]

handywork see **handiwork**.

hanepoot /hä'nə-pōt/ (*S Afr*) *n* a kind of grape (also **haan'epoot** and **hon'eypot**). [Du *haane-poot*, from *haan* cock, and *poot* foot]

hang /hang/ *vt* (pat and pap **hung** /hung/ (in all senses) or **hanged** (by the neck)) to support from above against gravity; to suspend; to decorate (eg a wall) with pictures, tapestry, etc; to fasten, to stick (wallpaper, etc); to exhibit (pictures, etc); to fix, to fit (a door, etc); to put to death by suspending by the neck; to cause to be brought to justice; to prevent (a jury) from coming to a decision; to suspend (meat or game) until mature; (in the *imperative* and *passive*) a euphemism for damn. ◆ *vi* to be suspended, so as to allow free sideways motion; to be put to death by suspending by the neck; to be brought to justice; to weigh down, to oppress (with *on* and *over*); to cling (with *on* or *onto*); to drape (well, badly, etc); to be exhibited; (of a jury) to be undecided; to be in suspense; to hover; to impend; to linger; to hold back; to depend for outcome (on); to have things hanging; to be in a state of paying extremely close attention (with *on*); (of a computer) to stop working at a particular stage, allowing no input or output; (often with *with*) to spend time relaxing or doing something enjoyable, hang out (*N Am inf*). ◆ *n* the action or mode of hanging; principle of connection, plan; knack of using; meaning; a declivity; a slackening of motion; a hanging mass; a euphemism for damn. [OE *hangian*, pat *hangode*, pap *hangod* (intransitive) and *hōn*, pat *heng*, pap *hangen* (transitive), and ON *hanga* and *hengja*; cf Du and Ger *hangen*]
■ **hangabil'ity** *n*. **hang'able** *adj* liable to be hanged; punishable by hanging. **hang'er** *n* someone who hangs; that on which anything is hung; (in placenames) a wood on a hillside (OE *hangra*); a short sword. **hang'ing** *adj* suspending; suspended; drooping; downcast;

deserving or involving death by hanging. ◆ *n* death by the noose; (*esp* in *pl*) that which is hung, eg drapery or decorations. **hung** *adj* (of a vote, election, etc) not decisive, producing no viable majority for any one party; (of a parliament, etc) having no party with a working majority; (of a jury) unable to agree on a verdict; (of a situation) unable to be settled or solved; (of a man) genitally endowed in a specified way, as in *well-hung* (*inf*).
❑ **hang'bird** *n* a Baltimore oriole (from its pensile nest). **hang'dog** *n* a contemptible person. ◆ *adj* with a cowed, dejected or guilty look. **hanger-on'** *n* (*pl* **hangers-on'**) a person who hangs around or sticks to a person or place for personal gain; an importunate acquaintance; a dependant. **hang'fire** *n* delay in explosion. **hang'-glide** *vi*. **hang'-glider** *n* an apparatus for hang-gliding, or the person using it. **hang'-gliding** *n* a sport in which one glides from a cliff-top, etc hanging in a harness from a large kite. **hanging basket** *n* a container in which flowering plants are grown, suspended by chains from a hook on the outer wall of a building. **hanging buttress** *n* a buttress supported by a corbel or the like. **hanging committee** *n* a committee that chooses the works of art to be shown in an exhibition. **hanging drop preparation** *n* a preparation for a microscope in which the specimen, in a drop of medium on the lower surface of the coverslip, is suspended over the depression in a hollow-ground slide. **hanging garden** see under **garden**. **hanging matter** *n* a crime leading to capital punishment; a serious matter (*inf*). **hanging valley** *n* (*geog*) a tributary valley not graded to the main valley, a product of large-scale glaciation. **hang'man** *n* a public executioner; a word-guessing game involving the drawing of a gibbet with victim. ◆ *adj* rascally. **hangnail** *n* see separate entry. **hang'nest** *n* a hangbird. **hang'out** *n* (*inf*) a haunt. **hang'over** *n* a survival (from another time); after-effects, *esp* of drinking alcohol (see also **hung over** below). **hang time** *n* (*inf*) the length of time a person or thing is able to remain in the air after jumping or being projected before returning to the ground. **hang'-up** *n* (*inf*) a problem about which one is obsessed or preoccupied; an inhibition (see also **hung up** below). **hung'-beef** *n* beef cured and dried. **hung jury** *n* a jury that fails to agree.
■ **get the hang of** (*inf*) to grasp the principle or meaning of. **hang about** or **around** to loiter; to associate habitually (*with* someone; *inf*); to stay, remain, persist. **hang a left** or **right** (*inf*) to turn left or right (*esp* when driving). **hang back** to show reluctance; to lag behind. **hang by a thread** to depend upon very precarious conditions, a most slender chance, etc (from the sword of Damocles). **hang, draw and quarter** to hang (a person), cut him or her down while still alive, disembowel and cut him or her into pieces for exposure at different places (earlier, **draw, hang and quarter** to drag on a hurdle or otherwise to the place of execution, then hang and quarter). **hang fire** to be a long time in exploding or discharging; to be slow in taking effect; to hesitate, delay. **hang in** (*sl*) to wait; to persist (also **hang in there**). **hang in the balance** to be in doubt or suspense. **hang loose** (*sl*) to do nothing; to be relaxed. **hang off** to let go; to hold off. **hang on** (*inf*) to wait; to persist. **hang one's head** to look ashamed or sheepish. **hang on someone's lips** or **words** to give close, admiring attention to someone. **hang out** to hang up outside; to display (eg a sign); to put outside on a clothes-line; to lodge or reside (*inf*); to spend time relaxing or doing something enjoyable (*inf*). **hang out for** to insist on. **hang out with** (*inf*) to associate habitually with. **hang over** to project over or lean out from; (of an unresolved problem, decision, etc) to overshadow, threaten. **hang together** to keep united; to be consistent; to connect. **hang tough** (*US*) to stay resolute or determined. **hang up** to suspend; to delay; to replace a telephone receiver and so break off communication. **hang up one's hat** to take up one's abode. **hung over** suffering from a hangover. **hung up** (*inf*) in a state of anxiety, obsessed (with *about* or *on*). **let it all hang out** (*inf*) to be completely uninhibited, relaxed.

hangar /hang'ər or hang'gər, -gär/ *n* a large shed or building for aircraft, carriages, etc. [Fr]

hangi /hang'i/ (*NZ*) *n* a pit in which food is cooked outdoors; food cooked in this way; a social gathering at which food is cooked. [Maori]

hangnail /hang'nāl/ *n* a torn shred of skin beside the fingernail (also **ag'nail**). [OE *angnægl*, corn, from *ange, enge* compressed, painful, and *nægl* nail (for driving in), confused with *hang* and (finger)*nail*]

Hang Seng index /hang seng in'deks/ *n* the indicator of relative prices of stocks and shares on the Hong Kong Stock Exchange.

hanjar see **handjar**.

hank /hangk/ *n* a coil or skein of a specified length, varying with the type of yarn; a loop; a tuft or handful, eg of hair; a ring for attaching a luff to a sail (*naut*); a restraining hold (*dialect*). ◆ *vt* to catch, as on a loop. ◆ *vi* to catch, be entangled. [ON *hanki* a hasp]

hanker /hang'kər/ *vi* to yearn (with *after* or *for*); to linger about (*dialect*). ◆ *n* a yearning. [Perh connected with *hang*; cf Du *hunkeren*]
■ **hank'ering** *n*.

hankie or **hanky** /hang'ki/ (*inf*) *n* diminutive form of **handkerchief**.

hanky-panky /hang'ki-pang'ki/ (*inf*) *n* funny business, underhand trickery, jugglery; goings-on; faintly improper (*esp* sexual) behaviour. [Arbitrary coinage]

Hanoverian /han-ə-vē'ri-ən/ *adj* relating to or associated with *Hanover* (Ger *Hannover*); relating to the dynasty that came from Hanover to the British throne in 1714. ◆ *n* a native of Hanover; a supporter of the house of Hanover, *opp* to *Jacobite*.

Hansa see **Hanseatic league**.

Hansard /han'särd/ *n* the printed reports of debates in parliament, from Luke *Hansard* (1752–1828), whose descendants continued to print them down to 1889.
■ **han'sardize** or **-ise** *vt* to confront (someone) with his or her former recorded opinions.

Hanseatic league /han-si-at'ik lēg/, **Hanse** /hans/ or **Hansa** /han'sə or -zə/ *n* a league of German commercial cities, operating in the 14c and 15c. [OHGer *hansa* a band of men (MHGer *hanse* merchants' guild)]

hansel see **handsel**.

Hansen's disease /han'sənz di-zēz'/ *n* leprosy. [Gerhard *Hansen* (1841–1912), Norwegian physician]

hansom /han'səm/ *n* a light two-wheeled horse-drawn cab with the driver's seat raised behind (also **han'som-cab**). [Joseph A *Hansom* (1803–82), its inventor]

ha'n't /hänt/ an informal contraction of **have not** or **has not**.

hantavirus /han'tə-vī-rəs/ *n* a virulent and often fatal virus with flu-like early symptoms. [After the *Hantaan* River in Korea, where it was first identified]

hantle /han'tl or hän'tl/ (*Scot*) *n* a good many; a good deal. [Poss **hand** and **tale** number]

Hants. /hants/ *abbrev* : Hampshire. [*Hantsharing*, orig name of county]

Hanukkah, **Chanukah** or **Chanukkah** /hä'nə-kə, hä'nŭ-kä or hhä'nŭ-kä/ *n* the Jewish festival of lights commemorating the re-dedication of the temple in 165BC. [Heb, consecration]

hanuman /han-oo-män'/ *n* the entellus monkey, a long-tailed sacred monkey of India. [*Hanumān* Hindu monkey god]

haoma /hō'ma or how'ma/ *n* a drink prepared from the **haoma vine**, used in Zoroastrian ritual; (with *cap*) a deity, personification of haoma. [Avestan; see **soma²**]

hap¹ /hap/ *n* chance; fortune; accident. ◆ *vi* (**happ'ing**; **happed**) to chance, happen. [ON *happ* good luck]
■ **haphaz'ard** *n* and *adj* random; chance. ◆ *adv* at random. **haphaz'ardly** *adv*. **haphaz'ardness** *n*. **hap'less** *adj* unlucky; unhappy. **hap'lessly** *adv*. **hap'lessness** *n*. **hap'ly** *adv* by hap; perhaps; it may be.

hap² /hap/ (*Scot* and *E Anglia*) *vt* (**happ'ing**; **happed**) to cover up; to wrap up. ◆ *n* a wrap. [Origin unknown]

hapax legomenon /hap'aks le-gom'ə-non/ (*Gr*) *n* (literally) said once; a word or phrase that is found once only.

ha'pence /hā'pəns/ short for **halfpence** (see under **half**).

ha'penny /hāp'ni/ short for **halfpenny** (see under **half**).

haphazard, **hapless** see under **hap¹**.

Haphtarah, **Haphtorah** same as **Haftorah**.

haplo- /hap-lō-, hap-lə- or hap-lo-/ *combining form* denoting single. [Gr *haploos* single, simple]
■ **haplodip'loid** *adj* (*biol*) denoting a species in which one sex has haploid cells and the other has diploid cells. **haplodip'loidy** *n*. **haplography** /hap-log'rə-fi/ *n* the inadvertent writing once of what should have been written twice. **hap'loid** *adj* (*biol*) having the reduced number of chromosomes characteristic of the species in question, as in germ cells, *opp* to *diploid*. **haploid'y** *n*. **haplol'ogy** *n* omission in an utterance of a word of a sound resembling a neighbouring sound (as *idolatry* for *idololatry*). **hap'lont** *n* (Gr *on, ontos*, prp of *einai* to be; *biol*) an organism in which only the gametes are haploid, meiosis occurring at their formation and the vegetative cells being diploid, *opp* to *diplont*. **haplon'tic** *adj*. **haploste'monous** *adj* (Gr *stēmōn* thread; *bot*) with one whorl of stamens. **hap'lotype** *n* (*genetics*) a set of linked alleles inherited by an individual from a single parent.

haply see under **hap¹**.

hap'orth /hā'pərth/ short for **halfpennyworth** (see under **half**).

happen /hap'ən/ *vi* to turn out; to come to pass; to take place, occur; to chance. ◆ *adv* (*N Eng*) perhaps. [**hap¹**]
■ **happ'ening** *n* an event, occurrence; a partly improvised performance, often outdoors, *usu* demanding audience participation (*theatre*). ◆ *adj* (*inf*) fashionable, up-to-the-minute. **happ'enstance** *n* chance; a chance circumstance.
■ **happen into**, **on** or **upon** to meet or come across by chance.

---

happy /hap'i/ adj lucky; fortunate; expressing, full of, or characterized by contentment, wellbeing, pleasure, or good; apt; felicitous; carefree; confident; mildly drunk (inf). ◆ combining form denoting: drunk with, irresponsibly delighted by the possession of or use of, as in power-happy, bomb-happy; dazed as result of. ◆ vt (happ'ying; happ'ied) (Shakesp) to make happy. [hap[1]]

■ **happ'ily** adv in a happy manner; in happiness; contentedly; by chance; perhaps; I'm glad to say, luckily. **happ'iness** n.

❑ **happ'y-clapp'y** adj (inf, usu derog) denoting any form of demonstratively enthusiastic Christian worship, esp involving chanting and hand-clapping. **happy dispatch** n a euphemism for hara-kiri. **happy event** n (usu facetious or joc) a euphemism for the birth of a baby. **happy families** n sing a children's card game played with a set of 36 cards, each depicting one of a four-member family, the object being to collect all four cards for as many families as possible. **happ'y-go-luck'y** adj easy-going, carefree; taking things as they come. ◆ adv in any way one pleases. **happy hour** n (in a club, bar, etc) a time, usu in the early evening, when drinks are sold at reduced prices. **happy hunting-ground** n (also in pl) the Paradise of the Native American; any place that one frequents, esp to make acquisitions or to profit in any way. **happy medium** n a prudent or sensible middle course. **happy slapping** n (sl) the practice of physically attacking an unsuspecting victim while an accomplice records the incident on a camera-equipped mobile phone.

■ **happy as Larry** (inf) completely happy.

hapten /hap'tən/ (immunol) n a substance, usu a molecule, that can combine with an antibody but can initiate an immune response only when it is attached to a carrier molecule. [Gr haptein to fasten, grasp]

hapteron /hap'tə-ron/ (biol) n a holdfast or attachment organ of a plant thallus. [Gr haptein to fasten]

■ **haptoglo'bin** n a protein that combines with free haemoglobin in the blood and prevents its filtration through the kidney. **haptotrop'ic** adj (Gr tropos turning) curving in response to touch, as a tendril. **haptot'ropism** n.

haptic /hap'tik/ adj relating to the sense of touch. [Gr haptein to fasten]

■ **hap'tics** n sing the science of studying data obtained by means of touch.

hapu /hä'poo/ (NZ) n a social unit of Maori people, a division of a tribe. [Maori]

haqueton /hak'tən/ same as **acton**.

hara-kiri /hä-rə-ki'rē/ n ceremonial Japanese suicide by ripping open the belly with a sword. [Jap hara belly, and kiri cut]

haram[1] or **haraam** /ha'ram or ha-ram'/ adj forbidden under Islamic religious law. [Ar harām forbidden]

haram[2] see **harem**.

harambee /ha- or hə-ram-bē'/ n and interj a rallying cry used in Kenya, meaning 'let's organize together'. [Swahili]

harangue /hə-rang'/ n a loud, aggressive speech addressed to a crowd; a pompous or wordy address. ◆ vi (haranguing /-rang'ing/; harangued /-rangd'/) to deliver a harangue. ◆ vt to address by a harangue. [OFr arenge, harangue, from OHGer hring (Ger Ring) ring (of listeners)]

■ **harangu'er** n.

harass /har'əs or hə-ras'/ vt to distress, wear out; to beset constantly; to annoy, pester. [OFr harasser; prob from harer to incite a dog]

■ **har'assed** (or /hə-rast'/) adj. **harass'edly** adv. **harass'er** (or /har'/) n. **harass'ing** (or /har'/) n and adj. **harass'ingly** (or /har'/) adv. **harass'ment** (or /har'/) n.

harbinger /här'bin-jər/ n a forerunner, a thing which tells of the onset or coming (of something); a pioneer; a host (obs); someone sent ahead to provide lodging (obs). ◆ vt to precede as harbinger. [ME herbergeour host; see **harbour**]

harbour or N Am **harbor** /här'bər/ n a refuge or shelter; a shelter, natural or artificial, for ships; a haven. ◆ vt to lodge, shelter, entertain, or give asylum to; to have or keep in the mind (feelings, esp unfriendly ones); to put (a ship) into harbour; to trace to its lair. ◆ vi to take shelter. [ME herberwe, from OE hereteorg, from here army, and beorg protection; cf Ger Herberge, ON herbergi]

■ **har'bourage** or (N Am) **har'borage** n a place of shelter; the act of harbouring. **har'bourer** or (N Am) **har'borer** n. **har'bourless** or (N Am) **har'borless** adj.

❑ **harbour-bar'** n a sandbank at a harbour's mouth. **harbour dues** n pl charges for the use of a harbour. **har'bour-light** n a guiding light into a harbour. **harbour master** n a person who has charge of a harbour. **harbour seal** n a small seal, Phoca vitulina, found in Atlantic waters.

■ **harbour of refuge** a harbour constructed to give shelter to ships; protection in distress.

hard[1] /härd/ adj not easily penetrated or broken; unyielding to pressure; firm, solid; difficult to scratch (mining); difficult; strenuous; laborious; vigorous; bodily fit; coarse and scanty; stingy, niggardly; difficult to bear or endure; difficult to please; unfeeling; insensitive; severe; rigorous; stiff; tough; constrained; intractable; obdurate; troublesome; (of coal) anthracitic; (of water) difficult to lather owing to calcium or magnesium salt in solution; harsh; brilliant and glaring; over-sharply defined; live, reverberating; lacking in finer shades; used as a classification of pencil-leads to indicate durability in quality and faintness in use; (of drink) alcoholic or extremely so; (of a drug) habit-forming; (of news) definite, substantiated; (of consonants) representing a guttural, not a sibilant sound; voiceless (obs phonetics); (of radiation) penetrating; (of photographic paper) giving a high degree of image contrast; (of a person) tough; (of a space, hyphen or carriage return in typesetting or word processing) compulsory, not fortuitously required by a particular piece of typesetting, as, for instance, is the hyphen used to break a word at the end of a justified line, opp to soft. ◆ n hardship; hard state; hard ground; a firm beach or foreshore; a layer of gravel or similar material laid down on swampy or wet ground to provide passage on foot; hard labour; an erection of the penis (inf). ◆ adv with urgency, vigour, etc; earnestly, forcibly; uneasily; in excess; severely; to the full extent (as hard aport); with difficulty; harshly; close, near, as in hard by. [OE hard (heard); Du hard, Ger hart, Gothic hardus; allied to Gr kratys strong]

■ **hard'en** vt to make hard, harder or hardy; to make firm; to strengthen; to confirm in wickedness; to make insensitive. ◆ vi to become hard or harder (lit or fig); (of a market or prices) to stop fluctuating, esp to rise. **hard'ened** adj made hard; unfeeling; obdurate. **hard'ener** n. **hard'ening** n the act or fact of making or becoming hard; a substance added to harden anything; sclerosis of the arteries. **hard'ish** adj somewhat hard. **hard'ly** adv with difficulty; scarcely, not quite; severely, harshly. ◆ interj I shouldn't think so, it seems unlikely. **hard'ness** n the quality of being hard; power of, and resistance to, scratching (mining). **hard'ship** n a thing, or conditions, hard to bear; privation; an instance of hard treatment (obs).

❑ **hard-a-lee'** adv close to the lee-side, etc. **hard-and-fast'** adj (of a rule, etc) rigidly laid down and adhered to. **hard-and-fast'ness** n. **hard'back** n a book with rigid covers (also adj). **hard'backed** adj. **hard'bake** n almond toffee. **hard'ball** n no-nonsense, tough tactics used for (esp political) gain. **hard'beam** n the hornbeam. **hard'-billed** adj having a hard bill or beak. **hard'-bitten** adj given to hard biting, tough in fight; ruthless, callous. **hard'board** n compressed board made from wood fibre. **hard-boiled'** adj (of eggs) boiled until solid; (of a person) callous, brazen or cynical (inf); practical. **hard bop** n a type of jazz, developed in the late 1950s, with less complex rhythms than bop. **hard card** n (comput) a hard disk on a card for use with a personal computer. **hard case** n (sl) a person difficult to deal with or reform. **hard cash** n coin; ready money. **hard cheese** n (sl) bad luck (chiefly as interj). **hard coal** n anthracite. **hard copy** n (comput) output printed on paper, legible to the human reader, as distinct from material which is coded or stored on disk. **hard'-copy** adj. **hard core** n a durable, unyielding central part; (usu **hard'-core**) the rubble and other material used in the foundation of roadways; something very resistant to change, as, eg the most loyal or the most diehard members of a group. **hard'-core** adj relating to a hard core; blatant; (of pornography) explicit, very obscene; (of rock music) consisting of short fast songs with minimal melody and aggressive delivery. **hard court** n a tennis court laid with asphalt or concrete, etc, not grass. **hard'cover** same as **hardback** above. **hard'-cured** adj (of fish) thoroughly cured by drying in the sun. **hard currency** n metallic money; a currency with a high, stable or improving exchange rate, not subject to depreciation; a currency backed by bullion. **hard disk** n (comput) a metal disc with a magnetic coating, in a sealed rigid container, having a higher recording density than a floppy disk. **hard'-drawn** adj (of wire, etc) drawn when cold to give the required thickness. **hard drinker** n someone who drinks alcohol persistently and excessively. **hard drive** or **hard disk drive** n (comput) a disk drive that controls the recording and reading of data on a hard disk. **hard'-earned** adj earned through hard work or with difficulty. **hard edge** adj (of a style of abstract painting) using bright areas of colour with sharply defined edges. **hard'face** n a soullessly relentless person. **hard'-faced** adj tough-looking; uncompromising; unsympathetic; unsentimental. **hard facts** n pl undeniable, stubborn facts. **hard-fav'oured** or **hard-feat'ured** adj having hard, coarse, or forbidding features. **hard'-fav'ouredness** n. **hard-feat'uredness** n. **hard feelings** n pl hostility, resentment. **hard'-fern** n the northern fern (Lomaria or Blechnum). **hard-fist'ed** adj having hard or strong fists or hands; close-fisted; niggardly. **hard'-fought** adj determinedly contested. **hard'-got** or **hard'-gotten** adj obtained with difficulty. **hard'-grained** adj having a close firm grain; forbidding. **hard'grass** n cocksfoot or other coarse grass. **hard'hack** n an American spiraea. **hard-hand'ed** adj having hard hands; rough; severe. **hard hat** n a bowler hat; a protective helmet worn by building workers, etc; a worker who typically wears one; an obstinately conservative person. **hard'head** n knapweed; a fish of various kinds (eg gurnard,

menhaden, father-lasher). **hard-head'ed** *adj* shrewd; pitiless. **hard-heart'ed** *adj* unfeeling; cruel. **hard-heart'edly** *adv.* **hard-heart'edness** *n.* **hard-hit'** *adj* seriously hurt, as by a loss of money, the death of a loved one, etc; deeply smitten with love. **hard-hitt'ing** *adj* duly condemnatory; frankly condemnatory, pulling no punches. **hard house** *n* a form of house music (qv) with a particularly strong beat. **hard labour** *n* physical labour as an additional punishment to imprisonment, abolished in 1948. **hard landing** *n* one made by a spacecraft, etc in which the craft is destroyed on impact. **hard launch** *n* (*commerce*) the official introduction of a new product the general public. **hard left** or **hard right** *n* the extremes of political thought, allegiance, etc, favouring the left (socialist) or right (conservative) views. **hard line** *n* a hardline attitude or policy. **hard'line** *adj* (of an attitude or policy) definite and unyielding; having such an attitude or policy. **hardlin'er** *n.* **hard lines** *n pl* a hard lot; bad luck (*usu* as *interj*). **hard luck** *n* hard lines, bad luck. **hard-luck story** *n* a person's (*esp* false or exaggerated) account of his or her own bad luck and suffering, *usu* intended to gain sympathy. **hard man** *n* (*inf*) a criminal specializing in acts of violence; generally, a tough man. **hard'-metal** *n* sintered tungsten carbide, used for the tip of high-speed cutting tools. **hard'mouthed** *adj* (of a horse) with a mouth insensible to the bit; not easily managed. **hard'nosed** *adj* (*inf*) tough, unsentimental. **hard on** or **hard'-on** *n* (*vulgar sl*) an erection of the penis. **hard pad** *n* once considered to be a neurotropic virus disease of dogs, now recognized as a symptom of distemper, causing hardness of the pads of the feet. **hard palate** *n* the bony front part of the palate. **hard'-pan** *n* a hard layer often underlying the superficial soil; the lowest level. **hard'parts** *n pl* the skeletal material in an organism. **hard'-paste** *adj* (of porcelain) made of china clay and altered granite. **hard'-pressed** or **hard'-pushed** *adj* in difficulties; under pressure; closely pursued. **hard radiation** *n* the more penetrating types of X-rays, beta rays and gamma rays. **hard-rid'ing** *adj* strenuously riding. **hard right** see **hard left** above. **hard rock** *n* a style of rock music, *usu* structurally and rhythmically simple and highly amplified. **hard-rock geology** *n* (*inf*) the geology of igneous and metamorphic rocks. **hard roe** see **roe**[1]. **hard rubber** *n* ebonite. **hard'-ruled** *adj* (*Shakesp*) ruled with difficulty. **hard'-run** *adj* greatly pressed. **hard sauce** *n* a sauce made with butter and sugar, and flavoured with rum or other liquor. **hard science** *n* any of the physical or natural sciences. **hard'scrabble** *adj* (chiefly *US*) *esp* of a place, barren and impoverished. **hard-sec'tored** *adj* (*comput*; now *obs*) of a floppy disk, formatted by a set of holes punched near the hub of the disk, each hole marking the start of a sector. **hard sell** *n* an aggressive and insistent method of promoting, advertising or selling. **hard'-set** *adj* beset by difficulty; rigid; obstinate. **hard'shell** *adj* having a hard shell; rigidly orthodox; uncompromising. **hardshell clam** *n* the quahog. **hard shoulder** *n* a surfaced strip forming the outer edge of a motorway, used when stopping in an emergency. **hard-stand'ing** *n* a hard (concrete, etc) surface on which cars, aircraft, etc may be parked. **hard stocks** *n pl* bricks that, though sound, are overburnt and of bad shape or colour. **hard stuff** *n* (*inf*) strong alcohol, spirits; important information. **hard swearing** *n* persistent and reckless swearing (by a witness); (often) perjury. **hard'tack** *n* ship biscuit, a hard biscuit formerly used as food on sailing ships. **hard'tail** *n* (*inf*) a motorcycle or bicycle with no suspension at the rear. **hard time** *n* an unpleasant experience; a difficult task. **hard'top** *n* a rigid roof on a motor car; a motor car with such a roof. **hard-up** *adj* short of money, or of anything else (with *for*). **hard-vis'aged** *adj* of a hard, coarse or forbidding face. **hard'ware** *n* domestic goods (*esp* tools, etc) made of the baser metals, such as iron or copper; mechanical equipment including war equipment; mechanical, electrical or electronic components of a computer (cf **software**). **hard'wareman** *n.* **hard-wear'ing** *adj* lasting well in use, durable. **hard wheat** *n* wheat having a hard kernel with a high gluten content. **hard'wire** *vt* (*comput*) to incorporate (a feature) into a system in such a way that it cannot subsequently be modified. **hard'-wired** *adj* (of a computer function) depending on its circuitry, which cannot therefore be modified by software. **hard'-won** *adj* won with toil and difficulty. **hard'wood** *n* timber of deciduous trees, whose comparatively slow growth produces compact hard wood; such a tree. **hard words** *n pl* words that give difficulty to a half-educated reader; harsh words; angry words. **hardwork'ing** *adj* diligent, industrious.
■ **be hard going** see under **going**[1]. **die hard** see under **die**[1]. **go hard but** be almost certain that. **go hard with** turn out badly for. **hard as nails** very hard; callous; very tough. **hard at it** working hard, very busy. **hard done by** badly treated. **harden off** to accustom (a plant) to outdoor conditions by gradually increasing exposure to the weather. **hard of hearing** somewhat deaf. **hard on the heels of** following immediately after. **hard put to it** in dire straits or difficulty. **hold hard** to stop. **no hard feelings** no offence taken, no animosity (as a result of a defeat, etc). **put the hard word on** (*Aust*) to ask, particularly for a loan or (*esp* sexual) favour. **the hard way** through personal endeavour or salutary experience.

hard[2] /härd/ (*Spenser* and *Scot*) form of **heard** (see under **hear**).

harden[1], etc, **hardish**, **hardly**, **hardness** see under **hard**[1].

harden[2] see under **hards**.

hardoke /här'dok/ (*Shakesp*) *n* a word found in the folio edition of *King Lear*, perhaps meaning burdock (cf **hordock**). [Prob OE *hār* hoary, and **dock**[3]]

hards /härdz/ or **hurds** /hûrdz/ *n pl* coarse or refuse flax or hemp; tarred rags used as torches (*Walter Scott*). [OE *heordan*]
■ **hard'en**, **herd'en** or **hurd'en** *n* a coarse fabric made from hards.

hardship see under **hard**[1].

hardy /här'di/ *adj* daring, brave, resolute; confident; impudent; able to bear cold, exposure, or fatigue. [OFr *hardi*, from OHGer *hartjan* to make hard]
■ **hard'ihead** (*archaic*) or **hard'ihood** *n* boldness; audacity; robustness (*rare*). **hard'ily** *adv.* **hard'iment** *n* (*archaic*) hardihood; an act of hardihood. **hard'iness** *n.*
□ **hardy annual** *n* an annual plant that can survive frosts; a story or topic of conversation that comes up regularly (*facetious*).

Hardy-Weinberg Law /här-di-wīn'bûrg lö/ *n* the law stating that, provided mating is random and there is no selection, migration or mutation, the gene frequencies in a large population remain constant from generation to generation. [GH *Hardy*, English mathematician (1877–1947), and W *Weinberg*, German physician (1862–1937), who independently of one another formulated the law]

hare /hār/ *n* a common very timid and very swift mammal of the order Rodentia or in some classifications the order Lagomorpha (*esp* of the genus *Lepus*), in appearance like, but larger than, a rabbit. ◆ *vi* (*sl*) to run like a hare, hasten (with *along*, etc). [OE *hara*; Du *haas*, Dan *hare*, Ger *Hase*]
■ **har'ish** *adj* somewhat like a hare.
□ **hare and hounds** *n* a paper chase. **hare'bell** or **hair'bell** *n* a slender-stemmed plant with a hanging blue bell-shaped flower, the Scottish bluebell (*Campanula rotundifolia*). **hare'-brained**, sometimes **hair'-brained** *adj* giddy, silly, stupid; heedless; headlong. **hare'-foot** *adj* swift of foot. **hare'-lip** *n* a cleft upper lip like that of a hare. **hare'-lipped** *adj*. **hare's'-ear** *n* an umbelliferous plant (*Bupleurum*, various species) with yellow flowers. **hare's'-foot** or **hare's-foot trefoil** *n* a variety of clover with long soft fluffy heads. **hare's'-tail** *n* a grass with silky flower-heads. **hare-stane** see **hoar-stone** under **hoar**.
■ **first catch your hare** make sure you have a thing first before you think what to do with it (from a direction in Mrs Glasse's cookery-book, where catch was a misprint for *case* meaning to skin). **hold with the hare and run with the hounds** to run with the hare and hunt with the hounds (qv below). **raise** or **start a hare** to introduce an irrelevant topic, line of inquiry, etc. **run with the hare and hunt with the hounds** to play a double game, to be on both sides at once.

hareem see **harem**.

Hare Krishna /hä'rä krish'nə/ *n* the chant used by members of a sect of the Hindu religion called Krishna Consciousness; the sect itself; a member of the sect. [Hindi *hare* O god, and *Krishna* an incarnation of the god Vishnu]

hareld /har'ld/ *n* the long-tailed duck, *Clangula hyemalis*. [Mod Icel *havella*, from *hav* sea]

harem /hä'rəm or hä-rēm'/, also **haram** /-ram'/, **hareem** and **harim** /-rēm'/ *n* women's quarters in a Muslim house; a set of wives and concubines; the equivalent in the society of certain animals; any Muslim sacred place. [Ar *harīm*, *haram*, anything forbidden, from *harama* to forbid]
□ **harem skirt** *n* an early 20c divided skirt in imitation of Turkish trousers.

harewood /hār'wŭd/ *n* stained sycamore wood, used for making furniture. [Ger dialect *Ehre*, from L *acer* maple]

haricot /har'i-kō/ or -kot/ *n* (*usu* **haricot bean**) the kidney bean or French bean (plant or seed); a kind of ragout or stew of mutton and beans or other vegetables. [Fr]

harigalds or **harigals** /har'i-gəlz/ (*Scot*) *n pl* viscera.

Harijan /har'i-jən/ *n* one of the caste of untouchables, the name proposed by Gandhi. [Sans *Hari* a name of Vishnu, and *jana* person]

hari-kari /hä'rē-kä'rē/ an incorrect form of **hara-kiri**.

harim see **harem**.

hariolate /har'i-ō-lāt/ *vi* to divine. [L *hariolārī*, *-ātus*]
■ **hariolā'tion** *n.*

harish see under **hare**.

harissa /hə-ris'ə/ *n* a hot paste made from chillis, spices and olive oil, used in N African cuisine. [Ar]

hark /härk/ *vi* to listen; to listen (to; also with *at*); to go (away, forward, etc); to go in quest, or to follow (with *after*). ◆ *vt* (*archaic*) to listen to. ◆ *n* (*Scot*) a whisper. [See **hearken**]
□ **hark'-back** *n* a going back again (*lit* and *fig*).

■ **hark away**, **back** or **forward** cries to urge hounds and hunters. **hark back** to revert to, or be reminiscent of (an earlier topic, etc).

harken /här'kən/ vi same as **hearken**.

harl¹ /härl/ or **herl** /hûrl/ n a fibre of flax, etc; a barb of a feather, esp one used in making an artificial fly for angling; such a fly. [ME herle, from LGer]

harl² /härl/ (Scot) vt to drag along the ground; to roughcast. ◆ vi to drag oneself; to troll for fish. ◆ n the act of dragging; a small quantity, a scraping of anything; a haul; roughcast.
■ **har'ling** n.

Harleian /här-lē'ən or här'li-ən/ adj relating to Robert Harley, Earl of Oxford (1661–1724), and his son Edward, or the library collected by them.
□ **Harley Street** n in London, a favourite abode of consultant or specialist physicians and surgeons, often used symbolically.

harlequin /här'lə-kwin/ n a pantomime character, in tight spangled costume, with visor and magic wand; a buffoon; a breed of small spotted dogs. ◆ adj brightly-coloured; variegated. ◆ vi to play the harlequin. [Fr harlequin, arlequin (Ital arlecchino), prob the same as OFr Hellequin a devil in medieval legend, perh of Gmc origin]
■ **harlequināde'** n part of a pantomime in which the harlequin plays a chief part; buffoonery.
□ **harlequin duck** n a variegated northern sea duck, Histrionicus histrionicus.

Harley Davidson® /här'li dā'vid-sən/ n a large powerful motorcycle, produced by the Harley-Davidson Motor Company (inf short form **Harley**®). [WS Harley (1880–1943) and A Davidson (1881–1950), who produced the first model in the USA in 1903]

harlot /här'lət/ n a whore (archaic); a prostitute (archaic); a general term of opprobrium applied to a man or woman (obs). ◆ adj lewd (archaic); base (obs). [OFr herlot, arlot base fellow; ety dubious]
■ **har'lotry** n prostitution; unchastity; meretriciousness; a harlot (obs). ◆ adj (obs) base, foul.

harm /härm/ n injury, physical, mental or moral. ◆ vt to injure. [OE herm (hearm); Ger Harm]
■ **harm'ful** adj hurtful. **harm'fully** adv. **harm'fulness** n. **harm'less** adj not harmful or objectionable, innocent; unharmed. **harm'lessly** adv. **harm'lessness** n.
□ **harm'doing** n.
■ **out of harm's way** in a safe place.

harmala /här'mə-lə/ n the so-called African or Syrian rue (Peganum harmala) of the bean caper family (also **har'mel**). [Gr, from Semitic; cf Ar harmil]
■ **har'malin**, **har'maline**, **har'min** or **har'mine** n alkaloids derived from its seeds.

harmattan /här-mat'ən, formerly här'mə-tən/ n a dry, dusty north-east wind from the desert in W Africa. [Fanti harmata]

harmel, **harmin**, **harmine** see **harmala**.

harmony /här'mə-ni/ n a fitting together of parts so as to form a connected whole; agreement in relation; in any art, a normal and satisfying state of completeness and order in the relations of things to each other; a simultaneous and successive combination of aesthetically agreeable sounds (music); the whole chordal structure of a piece, as distinguished from its melody or its rhythm (music); concord, agreement; music in general; a collation of parallel passages to demonstrate agreement, eg of Gospels. [Gr harmoniā, from harmos a joint fitting]
■ **harmonic** /här-mon'ik/ adj in harmony; in aesthetically pleasing proportion; relating to (good) harmony; musical; concordant; in accordance with the physical relations of sounds in harmony or bodies emitting such sounds (maths). ◆ n a component of a sound whose frequency is an integral multiple of the fundamental frequency; an overtone; a flute-like sound produced on a stringed instrument by lightly touching a string at a node; one of the components of what the ear hears as a single sound; (in television broadcasting) a reflected signal received on a different channel from that on which the main signal is received; (see also **harmonics** below). **harmon'ica** n a mouth organ; the musical glasses, an instrument consisting of drinking-glasses (or revolving glass basins in Benjamin Franklin's mechanized version) filled to different levels with water, and touched on the rim with a wet finger to produce sounds of different pitch; an instrument composed of a soundbox and hanging strips of glass or metal, struck by a hammer. **harmon'ical** adj. **harmon'ically** adv. **harmon'ichord** n a keyboard instrument of violin tone, in which the strings are rubbed by rosined wheels. **harmon'icon** n a harmonica; an orchestrion; a pyrophone (as in chemical harmonicon). **harmon'ics** n sing the science or study of musical acoustics. **harmonious** /-mō'ni-əs/ adj in, having or producing harmony; in agreement; aesthetically pleasing to the ear or eye; concordant; congruous. **harmōn'iously** adv. **harmōn'iousness** n. **harmoniphone** or **harmoniphon** /-mon'i-fōn or -fon/ n a keyboard

wind instrument with reeds. **har'monist** n a person skilled in harmony (in theory or composition); a reconciler; a person who seeks to reconcile apparent inconsistencies; (with cap) a member of a Second Adventist celibate sect (also **Har'monite**) founded by George Rapp (died 1847), from its settlement at Harmony, Pennsylvania. **harmonist'ic** adj. **harmōn'ium** n a reed organ, esp one in which the air is forced (not drawn) through the reeds. **harmōn'iumist** n. **harmonization** or **-s-** /här-mən-ī-zā'shən or -i-/ n any action of the verb harmonize; (in the EU) the progressive introduction of norms and standards applicable in all EU countries. **har'monize** or **-ise** vi to be or get in harmony; to sing in harmony; to agree; to be compatible (orally, visually, or fig). ◆ vt to bring into harmony; to reconcile (eg points of view); to provide non-unison parts to (eg a song or tune) (music). **har'monizer** or **-s-** n. **harmonogram** /-mon'/ n a curve drawn by a harmonograph. **harmon'ograph** n an instrument for tracing curves representing vibrations. **harmonom'eter** n an instrument for measuring the harmonic relations of sounds.
□ **harmonic analysis** n (maths) the process of measuring or calculating the relative amplitudes of all the significant harmonic components present in a complex waveform, frequently presented as a Fourier series. **harmonic conjugates** n pl two points dividing a line internally and externally in the same ratio. **harmonic division** n division by such conjugates. **harmonic mean** n the middle term of three in harmonic progression (qv below). **harmonic minor** n a minor scale with minor sixth and major seventh, ascending and descending. **harmonic motion** n (maths) the motion along a diameter of a circle of the foot of a perpendicular from a point moving uniformly round the circumference. **harmonic pencil** n (maths) a pencil of four rays that divides a transversal harmonically. **harmonic progression** n a series of numbers whose reciprocals are in arithmetical progression, such numbers being proportional to the lengths of strings that sound harmonics. **harmonic proportion** n the relation of successive numbers in harmonic progression. **harmonic range** n a set of four points in a straight line such that two of them divide the line between the other two internally and externally in the same ratio. **harmonic receiver** n a receiver for electric waves, in harmony with the impulses producing them. **harmonic series** n harmonic progression (qv above); the combination or series of notes produced when a string or column of air is vibrated. **harmonic triad** n (music) an old name for the common chord. **harmonic wave** n (phys) a wave whose profile is a sine curve.
■ **harmony of the spheres** see under **sphere**. **pre-established harmony** the divinely established relation, according to Leibniz, between body and mind, with the movements of monads and the succession of ideas being in constant agreement like two clocks.

harmost /här'most/ n a Spartan governor of a subject city or province. [Gr harmostēs]
■ **har'mosty** n the office of harmost.

harmotome /här'mə-tōm/ n a zeolite, hydrated silicate of aluminium and barium. [Gr harmos joint, and tomē a cut]

harn /härn/ n a coarse linen fabric. [See **harden** under **hards**]

harness /här'nis/ n tackle; gear; equipment, esp now the reins of a draught animal; armour for man or horse (archaic); an arrangement of straps, etc for attaching a piece of equipment to the body, such as a parachute harness, a child's walking reins, a seat belt, etc; the wiring system of a car, etc when built separately for installing as a unit. ◆ vt to equip with armour; to put (a) harness on; to attach by harness; to control and make use of. [OFr harneis armour]
□ **har'ness-cask** n (naut) a cask for salt meat for daily use. **harnessed antelope** n any antelope of the striped genus Tragelaphus. **har'ness-maker** n. **harness race** n. **harness racing** n trotting or pacing races between specially bred horses harnessed to sulkies (two-wheeled, one-person light carriages). **har'ness-room** n.
■ **in harness** occupied in the routine of one's daily work, not on holiday or retired; working together.

harns /härnz/ (Scot) n pl brains. [OE hærn, prob from ON hjarne; cf Ger Hirn; Gr krānion]
□ **harn'-pan** n the cranium.

haro see **harrow²**.

haroset, **haroseth**, **charoset** or **charoseth** /ha-rō'set, -seth or hha-/ n (in Judaism) a mixture of finely chopped apples, nuts, spices, etc mixed with wine, and eaten with bitter herbs at the Passover meal, and symbolizing the clay from which the Israelites made bricks in Egypt. [Heb, from charsit clay]

harp /härp/ n a musical instrument played by plucking strings stretched from a curved neck to an inclined soundboard; a harmonica, mouth organ (inf); term of abuse for an Irish American Roman Catholic. ◆ vi to play on the harp. ◆ vt to render on or to the harp; to lead, call, or bring by playing the harp; to give voice to (archaic); to guess at (obs). [OE hearpe; Ger Harfe]

■ words derived from main entry word; □ compound words; ■ idioms and phrasal verbs

■ **harp'er** or **harp'ist** n a player on the harp. **harp'ings** n pl (naut) the forepieces of the wales at the bow.
❑ **harp seal** n the Greenland seal, a grey animal with dark bands curved like an old harp. **harp'-shell** n a genus (*Harpa*) of gastropods with ribs suggesting harp-strings.
■ **harp on about** (inf) to dwell tediously or repeatedly on in speech or writing. **harp on one string** to dwell constantly on one topic.

harpoon /här-poon'/ n a barbed dart or spear, esp for killing whales. ♦ vt to strike, catch or kill with a harpoon. [Fr *harpon* a clamp, from L *harpa*, from Gr *harpē* sickle]
■ **harpoon'er** or **harpooneer'** n.
❑ **harpoon'-gun** n.

harpsichord /härp'si-körd/ n a keyboard instrument in which the strings are plucked by quills or leather plectrum-like devices. [OFr *harpechorde*; see **harp** and **chord**]
■ **harp'sichordist** n.

harpy /här'pi/ n a rapacious and filthy monster, part woman, part bird (*myth*); a large S American eagle (also **harpy eagle**); a grasping, greedy woman. [Gr *harpyia*, literally, snatcher, in Homer a personification of the storm-wind, from *harpazein* to seize]

harquebus, harquebuse, harquebuss /här'kwi-bəs/ n same as **arquebus**.

harridan /har'i-dən/ n a sharp-tongued, scolding or bullying old woman. [Prob OFr *haridelle* a lean horse, a jade]

harrier[1] /har'i-ər/ n a medium-sized keen-scented dog for hunting hares; a cross-country runner. [**hare** or **harry**]

harrier[2] see under **harry**.

Harris tweed /har'is twēd/ n a variety of tweed woven on the island of Lewis and Harris in the Hebrides.

Harrovian /ha-rō'vi-ən/ adj relating to the town of *Harrow* in S England, or the famous school there. ♦ n a person educated at Harrow school.

harrow[1] /har'ō/ n a spiked frame or other contrivance for breaking up or levelling soil, covering seeds, etc. ♦ vt to draw a harrow over; to distress or harass. [ME *harwe*]
■ **harr'owing** adj acutely distressing. **harr'owingly** adv.
■ **harrowing** (or **harrying**) **of hell** Christ's delivery of the souls of patriarchs and prophets from hell into heaven.

harrow[2] or **haro** /har'ō or har-ō'/ interj alas (*archaic*); out upon it (*archaic*); (in the Channel Islands) a cry announcing a claim to legal redress. [OFr *haro, harou*; not an appeal to *Rou* or Rollo]

harrumph /hə-rumf'/ vi to make a noise as of clearing the throat, esp self-importantly; to disapprove. [Imit]

harry /har'i/ vt (**harr'ying; harr'ied**) to plunder; to ravage; to destroy; to harass. [OE *hergian*, from *here* army; Ger *Heer*]
■ **harr'ier** n someone who or something that harries; a kind of hawk (genus *Circus*), with long wings and tail, that preys on small animals.
■ **harrying of hell** see **harrow**[1].

harsh /härsh/ adj rough; jarring on the senses or feelings; rigorous, severe. [ME *harsk*, a Scot and N Eng word; cf Swed *härsk* and Dan *harsk* rancid, Ger *harsch* hard]
■ **harsh'en** vt. **harsh'ly** adv. **harsh'ness** n.

harslet see **haslet**.

hart[1] /härt/ n a male deer (esp red deer) esp over five years old, when the crown or surroyal antler begins to appear. [OE *heort*]
❑ **hart of grease** n (*archaic*) a fat hart. **harts'horn** n the antler of the red deer; a solution of ammonia in water, orig a decoction of the shavings of hart's horn (**spirit of hartshorn**). **hart's tongue** n a fern (*Scolopendrium vulgare*) with strap-shaped leaves.

hart[2] (*Spenser*) for **heart**.

hartal /här'tal or hûr'täl/ (*Ind*) n a stoppage of work in protest or boycott. [Hindi *hartāl*]

hartebeest /här'tə-bēst/ or (*Afrik*) **hartbees** /härt'bēs/ n a large S African antelope. [S Afr Du, hart-beast]
■ **bastard hartebeest** the sassaby.

hartely, harten and **hartlesse** Spenserian forms of **heartily, hearten** and **heartless** (see under **heart**).

hartie-hale see under **heart**.

hartshorn see under **hart**[1].

harum-scarum /hā'rəm-skā'rəm/ adj scatty, disorganized; rash, reckless. ♦ n a giddy, rash person. [Prob from obs *hare* to harass, and **scare**]

haruspex /ha-rus'peks/ n (pl **harus'pices** /-pi-sēz/) (in ancient Rome, orig among the Etruscans) a person who foretold events from inspection of the entrails of animals. [L, perhaps from an Etruscan word and L *specere* to view]

■ **harus'pical** or **harus'picate** adj. **harus'picate** vi. **haruspication** /-kā'shən/ or **harus'picy** /-si/ n.

Harvard classification /här'vəd klas-i-fi-kā'shən/ (*astron*) n a method of classifying stars according to their spectra, orig used at *Harvard* University, and now universally.

harvest /här'vist/ n the time of gathering in crops; crops gathered in; fruits; the product or result of any labour or act; autumn·(*obs* and *dialect*). ♦ vt to reap and gather in (crops); to gather or reap (benefits, etc); to remove (a body part) from a donor prior to transplantation. ♦ vi to gather a crop. [OE *hærfest*; Ger *Herbst*, Du *herfst*]
■ **har'vester** n a person who harvests; a reaping machine; any member of the Opiliones, a class of Arachnida with very long legs (also **har'vestman** or **harvest spider**).
❑ **harvest bug, louse, mite** or **tick** n a minute larval form of mites of the Trombiculidae and Tetranychidae, abundant in late summer. **har'vest-feast** n. **harvest festival** n a church service of thanksgiving for the harvest. **har'vest-field** n. **har'vest-fly** n (in the USA) a cicada of various kinds. **har'vest-goose** n a goose eaten at a harvest home feast. **harvest home** n (a celebration of) the bringing home of the harvest. **harvest lady, harvest lord** n the head reapers at the harvest. **har'vestman** n a harvester. **harvest moon** n the full moon nearest the autumnal equinox, rising nearly at the same hour for several days. **harvest mouse** n a very small mouse that nests in the stalks of corn. **harvest queen** n the corn-maiden; the harvest lady. **harvest spider** n a harvester.

Harvey Smith /här'vi smith/ n a V-sign (qv) with palm inwards, signifying derision or contempt (also **Harvey Smith salute, wave**, etc). [From the British showjumper *Harvey Smith*, who made such a gesture during a show (1971)]

Harvey Wallbanger /här'vi wöl'bang-ər/ n a cocktail containing Galliano, vodka and orange juice. [Origin uncertain]

has /haz/ see **have**.
❑ **has'-been** n (pl **has'-beens**) a person or thing no longer as popular, influential, useful, etc as before.

hash[1] /hash/ vt to hack; to mince; to chop small. ♦ n something that is hashed; a mixed dish of meat and vegetables in small pieces; a mixture and preparation of old matter; a mess; a stupid person (*Scot*). [Fr *hacher*, from *hache* hatchet]
■ **hash'y** adj.
❑ **hash browns** or **hash brown potatoes** n pl pre-cooked potatoes, diced or mashed, mixed with chopped onion, seasoned, and fried until brown.
■ **hash out** (inf) to arrive at by debate, thrash out. **make a hash of** (inf) make a mess of. **settle someone's hash** (sl) to silence or subdue someone.

hash[2] /hash/ (sl) n short for **hashish**.

hash[3] /hash/ or **hashmark** /hash'märk/ n the symbol #, used in particular to mean: (1) number, eg apartment number (esp N Am); (2) space, eg in proofreading and marking up copy for printing. [Cf **hatch**[3] and **hachure**]
■ **hash'ing** n (*comput*) the process of converting items of data into numbers (**hash totals**) which are then used as index numbers or storage addresses.
❑ **hash'tag** n a word or name preceded by the hash symbol, used to indicate the subject of message on a social media site.

hashish or **hasheesh** /hash'ish or -ēsh/ n cannabis resin, smoked or swallowed as an intoxicant. [Ar *hashīsh*]

Hasid, also **Hassid, Chasid** or **Chassid** /has'id or hhä'sid/ n (pl **Hasidim**, etc /has'id-im or hhä-sē'dim/) a very pious Jew; a member of any of a number of extremely devout and often mystical Jewish sects existing at various times throughout history. [Heb *hāsid* (someone who is) pious]
■ **Hasid'ic, Hassid'ic, Chasid'ic** or **Chassid'ic** adj. **Has'idism, Hass'idism, Chas'idism** or **Chass'idism** n. **Has'idist** n.

hask /hask/ (*Spenser*) n a fish basket. [Cf **hassock**]

haslet /häz'lit, also häs' or häs'/ or **harslet** /här'slit/ n edible entrails, esp of a pig, shaped into a loaf and cooked. [OFr *hastelet* roast meat, from *haste* spit, from L *hasta* a spear]

hasn't /haz'ənt/ contracted form of **has not**.

hasp /häsp/ n a clasp; a hinged plate with a hole through which a staple fits and is secured by a padlock, eg for fastening a gate; a skein of yarn (*dialect*). ♦ vt to fasten with a hasp. [OE *hæpse*; Ger *Haspe*, Dan *haspe*]

Hassaniya /has-a-nē'ə/ n a dialect of Arabic spoken in Mauritania and Western Sahara (also **Sahrawi**). [Ar *Hassānīya* language of the descendants of Hassan]

hassar /has'ər/ n a S American nest-building land-walking catfish. [Native American origin]

Hassid, Hassidic, etc see **Hasid**.

---

fāte; fär; mē; fûr; mīne; mōte; för; mūte; pût; dhen (then); *el'ə-mənt* (element) ♦ For other sounds see detailed chart of pronunciation

hassium /has'i-əm/ n an artificially produced radioactive transuranic element (symbol **Hs**; atomic no 108), formerly called **unniloctium** and **hahnium**. [L *Hassias* Hesse, Germany, where it was first produced]

hassle /has'l/ (*inf*) *vt* to harass, annoy persistently; to argue with, bother, make trouble with. ◆ *vi* to be involved in a struggle or argument. ◆ *n* bother, fuss; a difficulty, problem; something requiring trouble or effort; a struggle; an argument. [Ety dubious]

hassock /has'ək/ n a tuft or tussock of grass, rushes, etc; a firmly stuffed cushion for kneeling on in church; a footstool (*US*); (in Kent) a soft calcareous sandstone. [OE *hassuc*]
■ **hass'ocky** *adj*.

HAST *abbrev*: Hawaii-Aleutian Standard Time.

hast see **have**.

hasta /ä'stä/ (*Sp*) *prep* and conj until.
■ **hasta la vista** /lä vē'stä/ until we meet again. **hasta luego** /lū-ā'gō/ see you later. **hasta mañana** /män-yän'ä/ see you tomorrow.

hastate /has'tāt/ or **hastated** /has'tā-tid/ adj spear-shaped; with basal lobes turned outwards (*bot*). [L *hastātus*, from *hasta* spear]

haste /hāst/ n urgency calling for speed; hurry; inconsiderate or undue speed. ◆ *vt* and vi (*obs*) to hasten. [OFr *haste* (Fr *hâte*), from Gmc; cf OE *hǽst*, Du *haast*, Ger *Hast*]
■ **hasten** /hās'n/ *vt* to speed up; to hurry on; to drive forward. ◆ *vi* to move with speed; to hurry; to be quick to, make an immediate move to (do something), as in *I hasten to say that....* **hastener** /hās'n-ər/ n. **hastily** /hāst'i-li/ adv. **hast'iness** n hurry; rashness; irritability. **hast'ings** n pl (*dialect*) early fruit or vegetables, *esp* peas. **hast'y** adj speedy; quick; rash; eager; irritable.
□ **hasty pudding** n a simple porridge of flour or oatmeal and water. **hast'y-witted** adj (*obs*) rash.
■ **make haste** to hasten.

hat /hat/ n any covering for the head, *esp* one with a crown and brim; the office of cardinal, from the red hat formerly worn; a salutation by lifting the hat (*Scot* or *obs*). ◆ *vt* (**hatt'ing**; **hatt'ed**) to provide with or cover with a hat; to lift one's hat to (*archaic*). ◆ *vi* (*Aust*) to work alone. [OE *hæt*; Dan *hat*]
■ **hat'ful** n (pl **hatfuls**) as much as will fill a hat. **hat'less** adj. **hat'lessness** n. **hatt'ed** adj provided or covered with a hat. **hatt'er** n a maker or seller of hats; a miner or other who works by himself, one whose 'hat covers his family' (*Aust*). **hatt'ing** n. **hatt'ock** n (*archaic Scot*) a little hat.
□ **hat'band** n a ribbon round a hat. **hat'box** n. **hat'brush** n. **hat'guard** n a string for keeping a hat from being blown away. **hat'peg** n a peg on which to hang a hat. **hat'pin** n a long pin for fastening a hat to the hair. **hat'-plant** n the sola plant, used for making topees. **hat'rack** n a set of hatpegs. **hat'stand** n a piece of furniture with hatpegs. **hat tip** n (*inf*) an acknowledgement of respect. **hat trick** n a conjurer's trick with a hat; (in cricket) the taking of three wickets with consecutive balls (*orig* considered as deserving a new hat); a corresponding feat (such as three goals scored by the same player) in other games; three successes in any activity.
■ **a bad hat** (*inf*) a rascal, an unscrupulous person. **hang up one's hat** see **hang**. **hats off to** (give) all honour to. **horse and hattock** to horse (traditionally a signal of witches or fairies). **mad as a hatter** completely mad (*poss* from the odd behaviour of some hatters due to mental and physical disorders caused by the mercury in the chemicals used in the making of felt hats). **my hat!** an exclamation of surprise or disbelief. **pass** or **send round the hat** to take up a collection, solicit contributions. **take off one's hat to** to acknowledge in admiration (*fig*); to praise. **talk through one's hat** to talk wildly or nonsensically. **throw one's hat into the ring** see under **ring**¹. **under one's hat** in confidence. **wear several hats**, **another hat**, etc to act in several capacities, another capacity, etc.

hatch¹ /hach/ n a half-door; a small gate (*dialect*); the covering of a hatchway; a hatchway. ◆ *vt* to close as with a hatch. [OE *hæcc*, *hæc* grating, half-gate, hatch; cf **hack**³, **heck**²; Du *hek* gate]
□ **hatch'back** n (a car with) a sloping rear door which opens upwards. **hatch beams** n pl timber balks across a hatch on which the hatch covering planks rest. **hatch boat** n a kind of half-decked fishing-boat. **hatch coamings** same as **coamings** (see **coaming**). **hatch'way** n an opening with a hinged or sliding door in a deck, floor, wall or roof.
■ **down the hatch** (*inf*) said when about to drink something, *esp* alcohol, meaning 'your health', 'cheers'. **under hatches** below deck, *esp* in confinement; hidden, out of sight; in servitude or a depressed state; dead.

hatch² /hach/ *vt* to bring out from the egg; to breed; to originate, develop or concoct (eg a plan). ◆ *vi* to bring young from the egg; to come from the egg; to develop into young; to develop. ◆ *n* the act of hatching; brood hatched. [Early ME *hacchen*, from an assumed OE *hæccean*]

■ **hatch'er** n. **hatch'ery** n a place for artificial hatching, *esp* of fish eggs. **hatch'ling** n a bird or reptile newly hatched.
■ **count one's chickens before they are hatched** see under **chick**¹. **hatches, matches and dispatches** (*inf*) newspaper announcements of births, marriages and deaths.

hatch³ /hach/ *vt* to mark with fine (*usu* diagonal) lines, incisions, or inlaid or applied strips. [OFr *hacher* to chop]
■ **hatch'ing** n shading in fine lines.

hatchel /hach'əl/ n and v same as **hackle**.

hatchet /hach'it/ n a small axe for use in one hand. [Fr *hachette*, from *hacher* to chop]
■ **hatch'ety** adj like a hatchet.
□ **hatch'et-faced** adj having a narrow face with a sharp profile like a hatchet. **hatchet job** n (*inf*) the (attempted) destruction of a person's reputation or standing; a severely critical attack; a severe reduction. **hatchet man** n (*inf*) a gunman; a severely critical journalist; a person who does illegal, unpleasant or destructive work for a politician or political party or other boss or company; a person who destroys or attempts to destroy another's reputation or standing.
■ **bury the hatchet** to end a war or dispute (from a custom of Native N Americans).

hatchettite /hach'i-tīt/ n mountain tallow, a natural waxy hydrocarbon. [Charles *Hatchett* (died 1847), English chemist]

hatchment /hach'mənt/ (*heraldry*) n the arms of a deceased person within a black lozenge-shaped frame, formerly placed on the front of his house. [**achievement**]

hate¹ /hāt/ *vt* to dislike intensely. ◆ *n* extreme dislike; hatred; an object of hatred. [OE *hete* hate, *hatian* to hate; Ger *Hasz*]
■ **hat'able** or **hate'able** adj deserving to be hated. **hate'ful** adj provoking hate; odious; detestable; feeling or manifesting hate. **hate'fully** adv. **hate'fulness** n. **hate'less** adj. **hate'lessness** n. **hat'er** n. **hate'rent** n (*Scot*) hatred. **hate'worthy** adj. **hāt'red** n extreme dislike; enmity; malignity.
□ **hate crime** n a crime motivated by hatred of the victim on the grounds of race, religion, sexual orientation, etc. **hate mail** n correspondence containing anything from insults to death threats, etc. **hate'-monger** n someone who stirs up hatred.

hate² same as **haet**.

hath see **have**.

hatha yoga see under **yoga**.

hatred see under **hate**¹.

hatter¹ see under **hat**.

hatter² /hat'ər/ *vt* to trouble, annoy (*archaic*); to batter (*dialect*). [Poss onomatopoeic]

Hatteria /ha-tē'ri-ə/ (*zool*) n the *Sphenodon* genus of reptiles, the tuatara. [Origin unknown]

hatting see under **hat**.

hatti-sherif /hat'i-she-rēf'/ (*hist*) n a decree signed by the Sultan of Turkey. [Pers *khatt-i-sharīf* noble writing, from Ar]

hattock see under **hat**.

hauberk /hö'bərk/ n a long coat of chain mail sometimes ending in short trousers; *orig* armour for the neck. [OFr *hauberc*, from OHGer *halsberg*, from *hals* neck, and *bergan* to protect]

haud /höd/ n and v (pap **hudd'en**) a Scottish form of **hold**¹.

haugh /höhh or hähh, (*esp* in place names) hö or hä/ (*Scot*) n a riverside meadow or flat. [OE *halh* (WSax *healh*) corner]

haughty /höt'i/ adj proud; arrogant; contemptuous; bold (*archaic*); high (*Spenser*). [OFr *halt*, *haut* high, from L *altus* high]
■ **haught, hault** or **haut** /höt/ adj (*Shakesp, Spenser, Milton*) haughty; exalted. **haught'ily** adv. **haught'iness** n.

haul /höl/ *vt* to drag; to pull with violence or effort; to transport by road. ◆ *vi* to tug, to try to draw something; to alter a ship's course; (of a ship) to change direction. ◆ *n* an act of pulling, or of pulling in; the contents of a hauled-in net or nets; a take, gain, loot (from a robbery); a hauled load; distance (to be) covered in hauling or travelling. [A variant of **hale**²]
■ **haul'age** n the act of hauling; the business of transporting goods, *esp* by heavy road transport; charge for hauling. **haul'er** n. **haulier** /höl'yər/ n a man who conveys coal from the workings to the foot of the shaft; a person or firm employed in transporting goods, *esp* by road.
■ **haul over the coals** see under **coal**. **haul round** or **off** to turn a ship's course away from an object. **haul up** to come or bring to rest after hauling; to call to account. **long haul** see under **long**¹.

hauld /höld/ n a Scottish form of **hold**¹, as in the dialect phrase **out of house and hauld** homeless.

haulm or **halm** /höm or häm/ n a strawy stem; a culm; straw, or stems of plants collectively. [OE *halm* (*healm*)]

haulst see **halse**[1].

hault see under **haughty**.

haunch[1] /hönch or hönsh/, also (old) **hanch** /hänsh/ n the expansion of the body at and near the pelvis; the hip and buttock taken together; the leg and loin (of venison, etc); the side or flank of an arch between the crown and the springing (archit); the rear (Shakesp); a jerked underhand throw (dialect). ◆ vt (dialect) to throw with an underhand movement. [OFr hanche, prob of Gmc origin; cf OHGer anchâ leg] ◻ **haunch bone** n the innominate bone.

haunch[2] see **hance**.

haunt /hönt/ vt to frequent, visit frequently; to associate a great deal with; to intrude upon continually; (of a ghost) to inhabit or visit; to cling or keep coming back into the memory of. ◆ vi to be often around, to visit frequently (with about, etc). ◆ n a place frequently visited; resort, habit of frequenting (Shakesp); a ghost (US dialect). [OFr hanter] ■ **haunt'ed** adj frequented or infested, esp by ghosts or apparitions; obsessed; worried. **haunt'er** n. **haunt'ing** n a visitation by a ghost. ◆ adj making a moving and lasting impression; poignant. **haunt'ingly** adv.

haurient or **hauriant** /hö'ri-ənt/ (heraldry) adj rising as if to breathe. [L hauriēns, -entis, prp of haurīre to draw up, drink]

Hausa /how'sə or -zə/ n a people living mainly in N Nigeria; a member of this people; their language, widely used in commerce throughout W Africa.

hause see **halse**[1].

hausfrau /hows'frow/ n a housewife, esp a woman exclusively interested in domestic matters. [Ger]

haustellum /hö-stel'əm/ n (pl **haustell'a**) a sucking proboscis or its sucking end, as in flies. [L haurīre, haustum to draw up, drink] ■ **haus'tellate** adj having a haustellum. **haustō'rium** n (pl **haustō'ria**) the part by which a parasitic plant fixes itself and derives nourishment from its host.

haut[1] see under **haughty**.

haut[2] /ō/ (Fr) adj high. ◻ **haut monde** /mɔ̃d/ n high society. **haut pas** /pä/ n a dais. **haut relief** /rə-lyef/ n high relief. **haut ton** /tɔ̃/ n high fashion. ■ **de haut en bas** /də ō tä bä/ downwards, or from top to bottom (literary); with an air of superiority, contemptuously.

hautboy /hō'boi or ō'boi/ n an archaic name for **oboe**; a large kind of strawberry (also **haut'bois**). [Fr hautbois, from haut high, and bois wood]

haute /ōt/ (Fr) adj feminine form of **haut**[2]. ◻ **haute bourgeoisie** /boor-zhwä-zē/ n the richer, more influential part of the middle class. **haute couture** /koo-tür/ n fashionable, expensive dressmaking and dress designing. **haute cuisine** /kwē-zēn/ n cookery of a very high standard. **haute école** /ā-kol/ n horsemanship of the most difficult kind. **haute époque** /ā-pok/ n (in relation to architecture, furniture, etc) the period during which Louis XIV, XV and XVI reigned in France. **haute politique** /po-lē-tēk/ n the higher reaches of politics. **haute vulgarisation** /vül-gar-ēz-as-yɔ̃/ n popularization of scholarly subjects.

hauteur /ō'tər or ō-tær/ n haughtiness; arrogance. [Fr]

haüyne /hö'in or hä'win/ n a blue mineral, in composition like nosean, with calcium. [René J Haüy (1743–1822), French mineralogist]

Havana /hə-van'ə/ n a fine-quality cigar, made in Havana or Cuba generally.

Havdalah same as **Habdalah**.

have /hav/ vt (prp **hav'ing**; 2nd pers sing (archaic and dialect) **hast**; 3rd pers sing **has** or (archaic) **hath**; pl **have**; pres subjunctive **have**; pat and pap **had**; 2nd pers pat (archaic or dialect) **hadst**; pa subjunctive **had**) to hold; to keep; to possess; to own; to hold in control; to bear; to be in a relation which is analogous to, if not quite the same as, ownership, as in to have a son, to have an assistant, to have no government; to be characterized by; to be given the use or enjoyment of; to experience; to know; to entertain in the mind; to grasp the meaning or point of; to hold as information; to put, assert or express; to suffer, endure, tolerate; to hold or esteem; to cause or allow to (do something; esp N Am); to convey, take, cause to go; to accept, take; to remove (with off or out); to cause to be removed; to get; to obtain; to give birth to; to get the better of, hold at a disadvantage or in one's power in a dilemma; to take in, deceive (usu in passive); to entertain in one's home (with back, in, round, etc; inf); to ask to do a job in one's house, etc (with in, round, etc; inf); to have sexual intercourse with (vulgar sl); as an auxiliary verb, used with the pap in forming the perfect tenses. ◆ n (pl **haves**) a person who has possessions; a trick, swindle (old sl). [OE habban, pat hæfde, pap gehæfd; Ger haben, Dan have]

■ **hav'er** n a person who has or possesses, a holder; the person in whose custody a document is (Scots law). **hav'ing** n act of possessing; possession, estate; (esp in pl /hāv'ingz/) behaviour, good manners (Scot). ◆ adj greedy. ◻ **have-a-go'** adj willing to attempt something, esp to stop a criminal in the act. **have-at'-him** n (Shakesp) a thrust. **have'-not** n (pl **have'-nots**) a person who lacks possessions. **have-on'** n a deception, a hoax; a piece of humbug or chaff.

■ **had as good** (archaic) might as well. **had as lief** (archaic) would as willingly. **had better** or **had best** would do best to. **had like** see under **like**[1]. **had rather** would prefer. **have at** (let me) attack; here goes. **have done** see under **do**[1]. **have had it** (inf) to be ruined; to have missed one's opportunities; to be doomed, beyond hope; to have been killed; (also **have had that**) not to be going to get or do (something). **have it** to prevail; to exceed in any way; to get punishment, unpleasant consequences. **have it away** (sl) to escape; to have sexual intercourse (with). **have it coming (to one)** (inf) to deserve the bad luck, punishment, etc that one is getting or will get. **have it in for (someone)** (inf) to have a grudge against (someone). **have it in one** to have the courage or ability within oneself (to do something). **have it off** or **away (with)** (vulgar sl) to have sexual intercourse (with). **have it out** to discuss a point of contention, etc explicitly and exhaustively. **have on** to wear; to take in, hoax, chaff; to have as an engagement or appointment. **have to** to be obliged to. **have to be** (inf) to surely be. **have to do with** see under **do**[1]. **have up** to call to account (before a court of justice, etc). **have what it takes** to have the necessary qualities or capabilities (to do something). **have with you** (archaic) I am ready to go with you. **I have it** I have found the answer (to a problem, etc). **let (someone) have it** to attack (someone) with words, blows, etc. **not be having any (of that)** to be unwilling to accept, tolerate, etc the thing proposed or mentioned.

havelock /hav'lək/ n a white cover for a military cap, with a flap over the neck. [General Sir Henry Havelock (1795–1857)]

haven /hā'vn/ n an inlet affording shelter to ships; a harbour; any place of retreat, protection, peace or asylum. ◆ vt to shelter. [OE hæfen; Du haven, Ger Hafen] ■ **hā'vened** adj.

haven't /hav'ənt/ contracted form of **have not**.

haveour see **haviour**.

haver[1] /hā'vər/ vi to talk nonsense or foolishly (Scot and N Eng dialect); to waver, to be slow or hesitant in making a decision. ◆ n (usu in pl; Scot and N Eng dialect) foolish talk; nonsense. ■ **hav'erel** n (Scot and N Eng dialect) a foolish person. **haver'ings** n pl (Scot and N Eng dialect) havers.

haver[2] /hav'ər/ n (Scot and N Eng) oats; the wild oat (grass). [ON (pl) hafrar; cf Ger Hafer, Haber oats] ■ **hav'ersack** n a bag worn over one shoulder for carrying provisions, etc (orig horse's oats) on a journey.

haver[3] see under **have**.

Haversian canals /hav-vûr'shən kə-nalz/ (zool) n pl small channels containing blood vessels and pervading compact bone. [C Havers (1650–1702), English physician and anatomist]

haversine /hav'ər-sīn/ (maths) n half the versed sine of an angle.

havildar /hav'il-där/ n an Indian sergeant. [Pers hawāl-dār]

having see under **have**.

haviour or **haveour** /hāv'yər/ n possession (obs); behaviour (Spenser). [Partly OFr aveir possession, partly **behaviour**]

havoc /hav'ək/ n general destruction; devastation; chaos. ◆ vt (**hav'ocking; hav'ocked**) to lay waste. ◆ interj an ancient war cry, a signal for plunder. [Anglo-Fr havok, from OFr havot plunder; prob Gmc] ■ **play havoc with** see under **play**.

haw[1] /hö/ vi to speak with hesitation or drawl, natural or affected; to make indecisive noises, as in hum and haw (qv under **hum**[1]). [Imit] ■ **haw'-haw'** adj affectedly superior in enunciation. ◆ n a hesitation or affectation of superiority in speech; loud vulgar laughter. ◆ vi to guffaw, to laugh boisterously.

haw[2] /hö/ n the fruit of the hawthorn; a hedge (hist); an enclosure (hist); a messuage (hist). [OE haga a yard or enclosure, a haw; Du haag a hedge, Ger Hag a hedge, ON hagi a field] ◻ **haw'buck** n a bumpkin. **haw'finch** n the common grosbeak (Coccothraustes coccothraustes). **haw'thorn** n a small tree of the rose family, widely used for hedges.

haw[3] /hö/ (zool) n the nictitating membrane; a disease of the nictitating membrane. [Origin unknown]

Hawaii-Aleutian Standard Time or **Hawaii Standard Time** /hə-wī'ē(-ə-loo'shən) stan'dərd tīm/ n one of the standard times used in N America, being 10 hours behind Greenwich Mean Time (abbrev **HAST** or **HST**).

Hawaiian /ha-wīˈən/ adj relating to Hawaii, state of the USA, to its citizens, or to its language. ◆ n a citizen or native of Hawaii; the Polynesian language spoken in Hawaii.
◻ **Hawaiian goose** n the nene (qv). **Hawaiian guitar** n a guitar, usu held horizontally, on which the required notes and esp glissandos are produced by sliding a metal bar or similar object along the strings while plucking.

haw-haw see **ha-ha²** and **haw¹**.

hawk¹ /hök/ n a name given to many birds of prey of the family Accipitridae (related to the falcons) which includes the eagles and buzzards, esp to those of the sparrowhawk and goshawk genus (Accipiter); (in the USA) applied also to some falcons; (in pl) all members of the Accipitridae (biol); a hawk moth; a predatory or a keen-sighted person; (in politics, industrial relations, etc) a person who advocates war, aggressiveness or confrontation rather than peace and conciliation, opp to dove. ◆ vt and vi to hunt with trained hawks; to hunt on the wing. [OE hafoc; Du havik, Ger Habicht, ON haukr]
■ **hawk'er** n a person who hunts with a hawk. **hawk'ing** n falconry. ◆ adj practising falconry; hawklike, keen (Shakesp). **hawk'ish** adj. **hawk'ishly** adv. **hawk'ishness** n. **hawk'like** adj.
◻ **hawk'-beaked** or **-billed** adj with a beak, or nose, like a hawk's bill. **hawk'bell** n a small bell attached to a hawk's leg. **hawk'bit** n a plant (genus Leontodon) closely related to the dandelion. **hawk'-eyed** adj sharp-sighted. **hawk moth** n any member of the Sphinx family, heavy moths with hovering flight. **hawk'-nosed** adj having a hooked beak or nose. **hawk owl** n a long-tailed owl resembling a hawk in flight. **hawks'beard** n a plant (genus Crepis) very like hawkweed. **hawks'bill** n a hawk-beaked turtle. **hawk'weed** n (bot) a genus (Hieracium) of yellow-headed ligulate-flowered composites.
■ **know a hawk from a handsaw** (prob for heronshaw) to be able to judge between things pretty well. **watch like a hawk** to keep a close eye on.

hawk² see under **hawker²**.

hawk³ /hök/ vt to force up (phlegm, etc) from the throat. ◆ vi to clear the throat noisily. ◆ n the act of doing so. [Prob imit]

hawk⁴ /hök/ n a plasterer's slab with a handle underneath. [Origin uncertain; a connection with **hawk¹** has been suggested, because of how the slab is held]

hawked /hökt/ or (Scot) **hawkit** /höˈkit/ adj streaked; white-faced. [Origin obscure]
■ **hawk'ey** or **hawk'ie** n a cow with a white-striped face.

hawker¹ see under **hawk¹**.

hawker² /höˈkər/ n a person who goes round houses or streets offering goods for sale, using a beast of burden or vehicle (distinguished from a pedlar, who carries his wares bodily). [Cf LGer and Ger Höker, Du heuker]
■ **hawk** vt to carry around for sale; to cry (one's wares) while doing this.

hawkey see **hockey²**, **hawked**.

Hawk-Eye® /hökˈī/ n a computerized system that uses cameras to track the path of a ball, used to help arbitration of decisions in tennis, cricket, etc. [Named after Paul Hawkins (born 1974), British scientist who invented it; infl by **hawk-eyed** (see under **hawk¹**)]

hawkie see under **hawked**.

hawking, hawkish see under **hawk¹**.

Hawking radiation /höˈking rā-di-āˈshən/ (astron) n a type of radiation predicted to emerge continuously from black holes. [Stephen Hawking (born 1942), British physicist]

hawkit see **hawked**.

hawklike see under **hawk¹**.

hawm /höm/ (dialect) vi to lounge about. [Ety dubious]

hawse¹ /höz/ n part of a vessel's bow in which the hawseholes are cut; the distance from the head of an anchored vessel to the anchor itself. [ON hāls neck]
◻ **hawse'hole** n a hole for a ship's cable. **hawse'pipe** n a tubular casting, fitted to a ship's bows, through which the anchor chain or cable passes.

hawse² see **halse¹**.

hawser /höˈzər/ n a small cable, a large rope used in tying a ship to a quayside, etc; a hawser-laid rope. [OFr haucier, haulser to raise, from LL altiāre, from L altus high]
◻ **haw'ser-laid** adj composed of strands with a left-handed twist twisted together to the right hand.

hawthorn see **haw²**.

Hawthorne effect /höˈthörn i-fektˈ/ n the effect on the behaviour of people being studied of their awareness that this is being done.

[Hawthorne, a plant of the Western Electric Company in Chicago, where first observed]

hay¹ /hā/ n grass, etc, cut down and dried for fodder or destined for that purpose. ◆ vt and vi to make hay. [OE hīeg, hīg, hēg; Ger Heu, Du hooi; ON hey]
■ **hay'ing** n the making or harvesting of hay. **hay'sel** n (OE sæl season) the hay season.
◻ **hay'band** n a rope of twisted hay. **hay'box** n an airtight box of hay used to continue the cooking of dishes already begun. **hay'cock** n a conical pile of hay in the field. **hay fever** n irritation by pollen of the nose, throat, etc, with sneezing and headache (also (rare) **hay asthma**). **hay'field** n a field where hay is made. **hay'fork** n a long-handled fork used in turning and lifting hay. **hay knife** n a broad knife with a handle set crosswise at one end, used for cutting hay from a stack. **hay'loft** n a loft in which hay is kept. **hay'maker** n someone who makes hay; a machine for shaking and breaking hay to dry it; a wild swinging blow (sl); (in pl) a kind of country dance. **hay'making** n. **hay'mow** n a rick of hay; a mass of hay stored in a barn. **hay'rake** n a large rake for collecting hay. **hay'rick** n a haystack. **hay'ride** n a pleasure ride in a hay wagon. **hay'seed** n grass seed dropped from hay; a rustic, traditionally a stupid person (inf). **hay'stack** n a large built-up pile of hay. **hay'wire** n wire for binding hay. ◆ adj and adv (inf) tangled; crazy; all awry.
■ **hit the hay** (sl) to go to bed. **make hay** to toss and turn cut grass; to throw into confusion (with of). **make hay while the sun shines** to seize an opportunity while it lasts.

hay² /hā/ (archaic) n a hedge, fence. [OE hege, from haga a hedge]
◻ **hay'-bote** n hedge-bote. **hay'ward** n a person who had charge of fences and enclosures and prevented cattle from breaking through; a person who herded the common cattle of a town.

hay³ /hā/ (obs) interj used on hitting in fencing. ◆ n (Shakesp) a hit or home-thrust. [Ital hai thou hast (it), from avere, from L habēre to have]

hay⁴ see **hey²**.

Hay diet /hā dīˈət/ n a diet in which carbohydrates and proteins are not eaten at the same time, in order to aid digestion and effect weight loss. [William H Hay (1866–1940), US physician who devised it]

hayle (Spenser) see **hale¹**.

hazan or **hazzan** /hhə- or hə-zänˈ/ n a cantor in a synagogue (also **chazan** /hə-zänˈ/). [Heb]

hazard /hazˈərd/ n anything which might cause an accident, create danger, etc; risk; the thing risked; any obstacle on a golf course, such as a bunker, trees, a road or water; in billiards, the pocketing of the object ball (**winning hazard**), or of the player's own ball after contact (**losing hazard**); the side of the court into which the ball is served (real tennis); each of the winning openings in a real tennis court; an old dice game. ◆ vt to expose to chance; to risk; to venture; to venture to say or utter; to jeopardize. [OFr hasard; prob through Sp from Ar al zār the die; according to William of Tyre from Hasart, a castle in Syria, where the dice game was invented during the Crusades]
■ **haz'ardable** adj. **haz'ardize** n (Spenser) hazard. **haz'ardous** adj dangerous; perilous; uncertain. **haz'ardously** adv. **haz'ardousness** n. **haz'ardry** n (Spenser) playing at games of hazard or chance; rashness.
◻ **hazard pay** n (US) danger money. **hazard (warning) lights** n pl the direction indicator lights on a motor vehicle when set to flash all at once as an indication to other traffic that the vehicle is obstructing the carriageway.

Hazchem /hazˈkem/ abbrev: hazardous chemicals.

haze¹ /hāz/ n vapour, mist or shimmer due to heat, often obscuring vision; mistiness; lack of definition or precision. ◆ vt to make hazy. ◆ vi to form a haze. [Appar not OE hasu, haswe grey]
■ **hā'zily** adv. **hā'ziness** n. **hā'zy** adj thick with haze; ill-defined; not clear; (of the mind) confused.

haze² /hāz/ vt to vex with needless or excessive tasks, rough treatment, practical jokes; to rag; to bully. [OFr haser to annoy]
■ **hā'zer** n. **hā'zing** n.

hazel /hāˈzl/ n a tree (genus Corylus) of the birch family; its wood. ◆ adj made or consisting of hazel; light-brown, like a hazelnut. [OE hæsel; Ger Hasel, ON hasl, L corulus, corylus]
■ **hā'zelly** adj.
◻ **hazel grouse** or **hen** n the ruffed grouse. **hā'zelnut** n the edible nut of the hazel tree.

HAZMAT or **hazmat** /hazˈmat/ abbrev: hazardous materials.

hazzan see **hazan**.

HB abbrev: hard black (on lead pencils).

Hb symbol: haemoglobin.

HBC abbrev: Hudson's Bay Company.

HBM abbrev: Her (or His) Britannic Majesty.

■ words derived from main entry word; ◻ compound words; ■ idioms and phrasal verbs

HBO *abbrev* : Home Box Office; hyperbaric oxygen.

H-bomb see under **H** (*symbol*).

HC *abbrev* : Heralds' College; Holy Communion; House of Commons.

HCF *abbrev* : highest common factor (also **hcf**); Honorary Chaplain to the Forces.

HCFCs *abbrev* : hydrochlorofluorocarbons.

HCG *abbrev* : human chorionic gonadotrophin.

HCM *abbrev* : Her (or His) Catholic Majesty.

hcp *abbrev* : handicap.

HD *abbrev* : heavy-duty; high definition.

HDA *abbrev* : Health Development Agency.

HDD (*comput*) *abbrev* : hard disk drive.

HDL *abbrev* : high-density lipoprotein.

HDMI *abbrev* : high-definition multimedia interface.

hdqrs *abbrev* : headquarters.

HDTV *abbrev* : high-definition television, an advanced TV system in which the image is formed by a much greater number of scanning lines than in standard TV, giving much improved picture quality.

HE *abbrev* : High Explosive; His Eminence; His Excellency.

He (*chem*) *symbol* : helium.

he /hē/, or when unemphatic *hi, ē* or *i*/ *pronoun* (pl **they**) the nominative (also, irregularly, ungrammatically or dialectally, accusative or dative) masculine form of the 3rd person pronoun: the male (or thing spoken of as if male) named before, indicated, or understood. ◆ *n* (pl **hēs**) (*nominative, accusative* and *dative*) a male. ◆ *adj* and *combining form* signifying male, as in *he-goat, he-pigeon.* [OE *hē, he*]
❑ **he'-man** *n* a man of exaggerated or extreme virility, or what some women consider to be virility.

HEA *abbrev* : Health Education Authority (now replaced by **HDA**).

head /hed/ *n* the uppermost part of the human body, or the uppermost or foremost part of an animal's body, in which reside the brain, mouth and principal sense organs; the brain; the understanding; self-possession; a chief or leader; a headteacher, principal; the place of honour or command; the front, upper end or top of anything; a rounded or enlarged end or top; a capitulum; a mass of leaves, flowers, hair, etc; a headdress or dressing for the head (*archaic*); a headache (*inf*); the pegbox and scroll of a violin, etc; the membrane of a drum; the essential part of an apparatus; in a bicycle, the tube in which the front-fork is socketed; an individual animal or person as one of a group; a title, heading; a topic or chief point of a discourse; a source; energy of a fluid owing to height, velocity and pressure; pressure; strength (*archaic*); insurrectionary force (*archaic*); the highest point of anything; culmination; a cape, headland; a froth on liquor (*esp* beer) poured out; a point where pus gathers on the surface of the skin; headway; the length or height of an animal's or person's head; a mine tunnel; (in *pl*) the obverse of a coin; a person who habitually uses drugs (*sl*; often in combination as in *acid-head*); a person who is preoccupied with a particular subject (*sl*; *usu* in combination); (often in *pl*) a ship's toilet (*naut sl*); an electromagnetic device in tape recorders, hard disks, etc for converting electrical signals into a recorded or stored form, or vice versa, or for erasing such material; a round of curling, in which sixteen stones are played. ◆ *adj* of or relating to the head; for the head; chief, principal; at or coming from the front. ◆ *vt* to remove the head or top from; to behead (*obs*); to supply with a head, top or heading; to be the head, or at the head of (also **head up**); to go round the head of; to face; to meet in the face; to cause to face or front; to strike with the head; to be ahead of. ◆ *vi* to form a head; to face, front; to direct one's course, make (for); (of streams, rivers, etc) to rise, originate. [OE *hēafod*; cf Du *hoofd*, Ger *Haupt*]
■ **head'age** *n* a subsidy payable to farmers, based on the number of animals kept. **head'ed** *adj* (*usu* as *combining form*) having a head; **come to a head** (*Shakesp*). **head'er** *n* a person or a machine that removes heads from or supplies heads for casks, etc; a dive head foremost; a brick or stone with the short side showing on the wall surface; the act of heading a ball; a heading for a chapter, article or page (*printing; comput*); a heading at the top of a microfiche, etc, readable with the naked eye; an optional piece of code preceding data, giving details about the data (*comput*); a card attached to the top of a dumpbin giving information such as the name(s) and author(s) of the book(s) displayed; (also **header tank**) a reservoir, etc that maintains an apparatus or system relying on pressure (eg plumbing) or gravity feed. **head'ily** *adv*. **head'iness** *n*. **head'ing** *n* the action of the verb *head* in any sense; a part forming a head; a small passage to be enlarged into a tunnel; words placed at the head of a chapter, paragraph, etc; direction; bearing. **head'less** *adj*. **head'long** *adv* with the head foremost or first; head over heels; without thought, rashly; precipitately, at full speed. ◆ *adj* rash; precipitate, at full speed; precipitous. **head'most** *adj* most advanced or furthest forward.

head'ship *n* the position or office of head or chief. **head'y** *adj* affecting the brain; intoxicating; inflamed; rash; violent; exciting.
❑ **head'ache** *n* a pain in the head; a source of worry (*inf*). **head'achy** *adj*. **head'band** *n* a band (eg of ribbon, or elastic or rigid material) for wearing around the head; a band round the top of trousers, etc; a band of cloth attached to each end of the spine of a book to strengthen it, or for decoration; a thin slip of iron on the tympan of a printing press. **head'bang** *vi* to shake one's head vigorously in time with loud rock music. **head'banger** *n* (*inf*) a person who is crazy, foolish, fanatical, etc; a fan of loud rock music. **head'banging** *n* the act of shaking the head vigorously in time with loud rock music. **head'board** *n* an often ornamental board or panel at the head of a bed. **head'-boom** *n* a jib boom or a flying jib boom. **head'borough** *n* (*hist*) the head of a frank-pledge or tithing; a petty constable. **head boy** *n* the senior boy in a school. **head-bummer** see under **bum³**. **head'-butt** *vt* to strike (a person) violently with the head (also *n*). **head'case** *n* (*inf*) a person who is mad or crazy. **head-centre** see **centre**. **head'chair** *n* a high-backed chair with a headrest. **head'cheese** *n* (*US*) brawn. **head'cloth** *n* a kerchief worn instead of a hat. **head cold** *n* a cold that affects parts of the sufferer's head, such as the eyes or nasal passages. **head count** *n* (*inf*) a count of people, bodies, etc. **head'-crash** *n* (*comput*) the accidental contact of a computer head with the surface of a hard disk, damaging the data stored on it. **head-down display** *n* (*aeronautics*) a display, *usu* visual, mounted inside the cockpit to supplement the head-up display. **head'dress** *n* a (sometimes ceremonial) covering for the head; a mode of dressing the hair (*archaic*). **head'fast** *n* a mooring rope at the bows of a ship. **head'frame** *n* the structure over a mine-shaft supporting the winding machinery. **head'gear** *n* anything worn on the head; apparatus at the head of a mine-shaft. **head girl** *n* the senior girl in a school. **head'-hugger** *n* a woman's close-fitting headgear of kerchief type. **head'hunt** *vi* (*inf*) to (attempt to) deprive a political opponent of power and influence (*US*); (also *vt*) to seek out and recruit (executives, etc) for a business or organization, *esp* to do so professionally as eg a management consultant. **head'hunter** *n*. **head'hunting** *n* the practice of collecting human heads; the practice of trying to undermine one's opponent's power (*US*); the seeking out of senior staff for one's organization. **headlamp** see **headlight** below. **head'land** *n* a point of land running out into the sea; a cape; the border of a field where the plough turns, ploughed separately afterwards. **head'lease** *n* a main or original lease, which can be divided into subleases. **head'light** or **head'lamp** *n* a strong light on the front of a vehicle. **head'line** *n* a line at the top of a page containing title, folio, etc (*printing*); the title of an article, *esp* a main article, in a newspaper, a caption; a news item given very briefly (*radio* and *TV*); (in *pl*) the sails and ropes next to the yards. ◆ *adj* (likely to be) published or broadcast as a headline. ◆ *vt* to give as a headline, mention in a headline; to add a headline to; to publicize. ◆ *vi* to be a headliner. **head'liner** *n* the person whose name is made most prominent in a playbill or programme. **head'lock** *n* a wrestling hold made by putting one's arm round one's opponent's head and tightening the grip by interlocking the fingers of both hands. **head'-lugged** *adj* (*Shakesp*) dragged by the head. **head'man** *n* a chief, a leader (in primitive societies). **head'mark** *n* a peculiar characteristic. **headmas'ter** *n* the principal teacher of a school. **headmas'tership** *n*. **headmis'tress** *n*. **headmis'tress-ship** *n*. **head money** *n* a poll tax; a sum of money paid for each prisoner taken, or each slave delivered; a reward for a proscribed outlaw's head. **head'note** *n* a note placed at the head of a chapter or page, *esp* a condensed statement of points of law involved introductory to the report of a legal decision; a tone produced in the head register (*music*). **head of state** *n* the chief representative of a country, not necessarily the head of government. **head-on** *adj* and *adv* head to head, *esp* (of a collision) with the front of one vehicle, etc hitting the front of another, or (rarely) a stationary object; with head pointing directly forward; directly opposed, confronting each other. **head'phone** *n* (*usu* in *pl*) an audio receiver worn in pairs over the ears, *esp* for listening to a radio, MP3 player, etc. **head'piece** *n* a helmet; a hat; head, skull (*archaic*; *Spenser* **head'peace**); a brain; a man of intelligence; a top part; a decorative engraving at the beginning of a book, chapter, etc (*printing*). **headquar'tered** *adj* having one's headquarters (in a specified place). **headquar'ters** *n pl* and *n sing* the quarters or residence of a commander-in-chief or general; a central or chief office of a company, etc. **head'race** *n* the channel leading to a water wheel or other hydraulically-operated machine. **head'rail** *n* one of the rails at a ship's head. **head'reach** *n* the distance made to windward in tacking. ◆ *vi* to shoot ahead, in tacking. **head register** *n* (*music*) high register; of the voice in which nose and head cavities vibrate sympathetically; (in male voice) falsetto. **head rent** *n* rent payable to the freeholder. **head'rest** *n* a support for the head; (also **head restraint**) a cushioned frame fitted to the top of a seat in a car, etc to prevent the head jerking back in a collision. **head'-rhyme** *n* alliteration. **head'rig** *n* (*Scot*) a headland in a ploughed field. **head'ring** *n* a palm-leaf hair ornament worn by some black S African men as a symbol of manhood.

head'room *n* uninterrupted space below a ceiling, bridge, etc; space overhead, below an obstacle, etc. **head'rope** *n* a rope for tying or leading an animal; part of the bolt rope at the top of a rectangular sail. **head'sail** *n* a sail on a foremast or bowsprit. **head'scarf** *n* (*pl* **head'scarves**) a scarf worn over the head, a headsquare. **head sea** *n* (*naut*) a sea running directly against a ship's course. **head'set** *n* a set of headphones, often with a microphone attached. **head'shake** *n* a significant shake of the head. **head'sheets** *n pl* the forepart of a small vessel or craft. **head'shot** *n* a photograph or television picture of someone's head (and shoulders) only. **head'shrinker** *n* a headhunter who shrinks the heads of his or her victims; a psychiatrist (*inf*). **heads'man** *n* an executioner who cuts off heads. **head'square** *n* a square of fabric worn as a covering for the head. **head'stall** *n* the part of a horse's bridle round the head; a choirstall with its back to the choirscreen (*obs*). **head start** *n* a boost or advantage intended to overcome a disadvantage or give a better chance of success. **head'-station** *n* the dwelling-house, etc, on an Australian sheep or cattle station. **head'stick** *n* (*printing*) formerly a straight piece of furniture placed at the head of a forme, between the chase and the type. **head'stock** *n* (*machinery*) a device for supporting the end or head of a member or part. **head'stone** *n* the principal stone of a building; the main principle; cornerstone; gravestone. **head'-stream** *n* a headwater; a high tributary; the stream forming the highest or remotest source (of a river). **head'strong** *adj* obstinately self-willed. **heads'-up** (*N Am*) *n* a warning that something is going to happen. ◆ *adj* displaying alertness. **head teacher** *n* a headmaster or headmistress. **head'-tire** *n* (*obs*) a headdress. **head-to-head** *adj* directly competing. ◆ *n* a direct meeting or confrontation between two opponents. **head-up display** *n* the presentation of data on the windscreen of an aircraft or car, etc enabling the pilot or driver to see the information without looking down at the instrument panel (*abbrev* **HUD**). **head voice** *n* tones in the head register. **head waiter** *n* the most senior waiter of a restaurant or hotel. **head'wall** *n* (*mountaineering*) a steep rockface at the end of a cirque. **head'water** *n* the highest part of a stream or river before receiving tributaries. **head'way** *n* motion ahead, *esp* of a ship; progress; the time interval or distance between buses, trains, etc travelling on the same route in the same direction. **head'wind** *n* a wind blowing directly against one's course. **head-wo'man** *n* a female leader or chief. **head'word** *n* a word forming a heading eg of an entry in a dictionary or encyclopedia; a word under which other related words are grouped, as in a dictionary. **head'work** *n* mental work. **head'worker** *n*.

■ **above one's head** beyond one's capacity for understanding. **against the head** (of the ball in a rugby scrum, or the scrum itself) won by the team not putting the ball in. **bring** or **come to a head** to (cause to) reach a climax or crisis. **do one's head in** (*inf*) to cause one to become confused, frustrated or angry. **eat one's head off** see under **eat**. **get it into one's head** to conceive the (*esp* wrong or foolish) notion, to believe (with *that*). **get one's head together** (*inf*) to achieve a state of self-possession. **give a horse its head** to let it go as it chooses. **give head** (*vulgar sl*) to perform oral sex (on). **give someone his** or **her head** to increase someone's scope for initiative. **go by the head** (*naut*) to sink head foremost. **go over someone's head** to take a problem, complaint, etc directly to a person more senior than someone. **go to someone's head** to make someone vain or conceited; to make someone confused or dizzy; to make someone drunk. **have a (good**, etc) **head on one's shoulders** to have ability and balance. **have one's head screwed on (the right way)** to be sensible, bright, etc. **head and shoulders** very much, as if taller by a head and shoulders; violently (*archaic*). **head first** or **head foremost** with the head in front. **head off** to get ahead of so as to turn back; to deflect from a path or intention. **head over heels** as in a somersault; completely; completely in love. **heads or tails** an invitation to guess how a coin will fall. **head to head** in direct competition (see also **head-to-head** above). **hit the headlines** to get prominent attention in the press or other media. **hold up one's head** see under **hold¹**. **keep (or lose) one's head** to keep (or lose) one's self-possession, calmness, control. **keep one's head above water** see under **water**. **lay heads together** to confer and co-operate. **off** or **out of one's head** (*inf*) crazy; very drunk or high on drugs. **off the top of one's head** see under **top¹**. **on one's (own) head be it** one must, or will, accept responsibility for any unpleasant or undesirable consequences of one's actions. **out of one's (own) head** spontaneously; of one's own invention; crazy, mad (*inf*); very drunk or high on drugs (*inf*). **over head and ears** deeply submerged or engrossed. **over one's head** beyond one's capacity for understanding; beyond one's control. **put heads together** same as **lay heads together** (see above). **put one's head on the block** (*inf*) to stick one's neck out, run the risk of censure, etc. **show one's head** to allow oneself to be seen. **take it into one's head** to conceive the (*esp* wrong or foolish) notion, believe (with *that*); to conceive the (*esp* misguided) intention of (with *to*). **turn someone's head** see under **turn**.

-head see **head** and **-hood**.

heal¹ /*hēl*/ *vt* to make whole and healthy; to cure; to restore to health or good condition (physical or mental); to remedy, amend. ◆ *vi* to grow sound or healthy again. ◆ *n* (*archaic* and *Scot*) health; soundness; welfare. [OE *hǣlan* (verb), *hǣlu* (noun), from *hāl* whole; cf Ger *heil*, Du *heel*; ON *heill*; **hail²**, **hale¹**, **whole**]

■ **heal'able** *adj*. **heal'er** *n*. **heal'ing** *n* and *adj*. **heal'ingly** *adv*. **heal'some** *adj* (*Scot*) wholesome. ❑ **heal'-all** *n* allheal.

heal² see **hele**.

heald /*hēld*/ same as **heddle**; also an old form of **heel²**.

health /*helth*/ *n* sound physical or mental condition; soundness; condition of wholesomeness; wellbeing; state with respect to soundness; a toast. [OE *hǣlth*, from *hāl* whole]

■ **health'ful** *adj* enjoying, indicating, or conducive to health. **health'fully** *adv*. **health'fulness** *n*. **health'ily** *adv*. **health'iness** *n*. **health'less** *adj*. **health'lessness** *n*. **health'some** *adj* healthy, wholesome. **health'y** *adj* in good health; morally or spiritually wholesome; economically sound; conducive to or indicative of good health; considerable (*inf*). ❑ **health camp** *n* (*NZ*) a camp intended to improve the physical and emotional condition of children who attend it. **health'care** *n* the care of one's own or others' health. **health centre** *n* a centre for clinical and administrative health welfare work. **health club** *n* a place where members are provided with facilities for maintaining fitness, promoting relaxation and improving health, eg a gymnasium, swimming pool, sauna, etc. **health'-conscious** *adj* anxious to maintain (*esp* one's own) good health. **health farm** *n* a place, *usu* in the country, where people go to improve their health by dieting, exercise, etc. **health food** *n* food thought to be particularly good for one's health, *esp* that grown and prepared without artificial fertilizers, chemical additives, etc. **health resort** *n* a place noted for its health-giving conditions, *esp* its salubrious climate. **health salts** *n pl* salts, *esp* magnesium sulphate, taken as a digestive or mild laxative. **health service** *n* a public service providing medical care, *usu* free of charge. **health stamp** *n* (*NZ*) a stamp, part of the cost of which goes to supporting health camps. **health tourism** *n* the practice of travelling to a foreign country in order to receive medical treatment that is superior to or cheaper than that available in one's own country. **health tourist** *n*. **health visitor** *n* a nurse concerned mainly with health education and advice and preventive medicine rather than the treatment of disease, who visits *esp* mothers with young children and the elderly in their own homes.

heame /*hēm*/ (*Spenser*) *adv* form of **home**.

heap /*hēp*/ *n* a mass of things resting one above another; a mound; a company (*Shakesp*); a great number, a great deal (*often in pl*), a collection (*inf*); an old dilapidated motor car; a ruin (*Bible*). ◆ *vt* to throw into a heap; to amass; to load with a heap or heaps; to pile high, or above the rim or brim (*also vi*). [OE *hēap*; cf ON *hōpr*, Ger *Haufe*, Du *hoop*]

■ **heaped** *adj*. **heap'ing** *adj* (*N Am*; of a spoonful, etc) heaped. **heaps** *adv* (*inf*) very much. **heap'y** *adj* full of heaps. ❑ **heap'stead** *n* the buildings and works around a mine-shaft. ■ **knock** or **strike all of a heap** (*inf*) to confound utterly, dumbfound.

hear /*hēr*/ *vt* (pat and pap **heard** /*hûrd*/) to perceive by the ear; to accede to; to listen to; to listen to for the purpose of witnessing ability (or otherwise) to recite lines learned; to try judicially; to be informed; to be a hearer of; to be called (*Milton*, a Latinism). ◆ *vi* to have or exercise the sense of hearing; to listen; to have news (of or from); to be spoken of (*Spenser*, a Graecism). [OE (Anglian) *hēran* (WSax *hīeran*, *hȳran*); Du *hooren*, ON *heyra*, Ger *hören*, Gothic *hausjan*]

■ **heard** /*hûrd*/ *adj*. **hear'er** *n*. **hear'ing** *n* power or act of perceiving sound; an opportunity to be heard; audience; audition; judicial investigation and listening to evidence and arguments, *esp* without a jury; earshot; news; a scolding (*dialect*). ❑ **hearing aid** *n* any device, electrical or other, for enabling a hearing-impaired person to hear better. **hearing dog** *n* a dog trained to alert a deaf person to sounds such as a doorbell or alarm. **hearing-impair'ed** *adj* (now a preferred term for) deaf or hard of hearing. **hear'say** *n* common talk; report; rumour. ◆ *adj* of the nature of or based on report given by others.

■ **hear, hear!** an exclamation of approval from the hearers of a speech. **hear out** to listen to (someone) until he or she has said all he or she wishes to say. **hear tell of** to hear someone speak of. **hear things** see under **thing**. **will** or **would not hear of** will or would not allow or tolerate.

heard¹ see under **hear**.

heard² (*Spenser*) a form of **herd¹,²**.

heare /*hēr*/ and **hearie** (*Spenser*) forms of **hair** and **hairy**.

hearken /*hār'kn*/ (*archaic* or *literary*) *vi* to hear attentively; to listen. ◆ *vt* to listen to, pay attention to, heed (*poetic*); to seek by enquiry (*obs*). [OE *hercnian* (*heorcnian*); cf **hark**, **hear**; Ger *horchen*]
■ **heark'ener** *n*.

hearse or (*Spenser*) **herse** /hûrs/ *n* a vehicle for carrying the dead; *orig* a canopy or frame over a bier, designed to hold candles; a funeral service (*Spenser*); a bier (*obs*). ◆ *vt* to put on or in a hearse. [OFr *herse* (Ital *erpice*), from L *hirpex, -icis* a harrow]

■ **hearse'-like** *adj*. **hears'y** *adj*.
❑ **hearse'-cloth** *n* a pall.

heart /härt/ *n* the organ that circulates the blood through the body; the stomach (*obs*); the innermost part; the core; the chief or vital part; the breast, bosom; the (imagined) place of origin of the affections, understanding, and thought, as opposed to the head, the seat of reason; courage; innermost feelings or convictions; vigour, spirit; cordiality; compassion; a term of endearment or encouragement; a heart-shaped figure or object; a playing card with heart-shaped pips; the centre of cabbage, lettuce, etc; a diseased state of the heart; (in *pl*) a card game in which the object is to avoid taking tricks containing hearts or the queen of spades. ◆ *vt* to fill up a centre space with rubble (*building*); to love (*inf*). ◆ *vi* (of a lettuce) to form a compact head or inner mass. [OE *heorte*; cf Du *hart*, Ger *Herz*; L *cor, cordis*; Gr *kardiā*]

■ **heart'ed** *adj* used in combination to signify having a heart, *esp* of a specified kind (eg *hard-hearted*, etc); seated or fixed in the heart, stored up in the heart. **heart'en** *vt* to encourage, stimulate; to add strength to; to give courage to. ◆ *vi* to take courage. **heart'ening** *adj*. **heart'ikin** *n* (*obs*) a little heart (used euphemistically in an old oath). **heart'ily** *adv* lustily, vigorously; completely (sick, tired, etc). **heart'iness** *n*. **heart'less** *adj* without heart, courage, consideration or feeling; callous. **heart'lessly** *adv*. **heart'lessness** *n*. **heart'let** *n* a little heart, a nucleus. **heart'ling** *n* (*Shakesp*) little heart, used euphemistically in the oath *ods heartlings*, God's heart. **heart'ly** or (*Spenser*) **harte'ly** *adv* heartily. **heart'some** *adj* exhilarating; merry. **heart'y** *adj* full of heart; heartfelt; sincere; cordial; robust; lusty; enthusiastic; unrestrained; in or indicating good spirits, appetite or condition; (of a meal) substantial; sound; in good heart. ◆ *n* a hearty person, *esp* one who goes in for sports, outdoor pursuits, etc, distinguished from an *aesthete*; (in *pl*) an old form of address to fellow sailors.
❑ **hart'ie-hale** *adj* (*Spenser*) good for the heart, healthy. **heart'ache** *n* sorrow; anguish. **heart attack** *n* an occurrence of coronary thrombosis, with the death of part of the heart muscle, or some other sudden malfunction of the heart. **heart'beat** *n* a pulsation of the heart; a throb; an animating force. **heart block** *n* a condition in which the ventricle does not keep time with the atrium. **heart'-blood** or **heart's'-blood** *n* blood of the heart; life, essence. **heart'-bond** *n* (in masonry) a bond in which two headers meet in the middle of a wall and one header overlaps them. **heart'break** *n* a crushing sorrow or grief. ◆ *vt* (*Burns*) to break the heart of. **heart'breaker** *n* a fickle or unfaithful lover; a flirt; a curl, lovelock. **heart'breaking** *adj*. **heart'broken** *adj*. **heart'burn** *n* a burning, acid feeling in the throat or breast, severe indigestion, cardialgia. **heart'burning** *n* discontent; secret grudging. **heart cam** *n* a heart-shaped cam in a stopwatch, etc. **heart cockle** or **heart shell** *n* a mollusc (genus *Isocardia*) or its shell, like a cockle coiled at the bosses. **heart'-dear** *adj* (*Shakesp*) dear to the heart, sincerely beloved. **heart disease** *n* any morbid condition of the heart. **heart'-easing** *adj* bringing peace of mind. **heart failure** *n* stoppage or inadequate functioning of the heart; shock producing faintness. **heart'felt** *adj* felt deeply; sincere. **heart'-free** *adj* having the affections disengaged. **heart'-grief** *n* deep-seated affliction. **heart-heav'iness** *n* depression of spirits. **heart'land** *n* an area of a country that is centrally situated and/or vitally important. **heart-lung machine** *n* a machine used in chest surgery to take over for a time the functions of the heart and lungs. **heart murmur** *n* an abnormal sound from the heart indicating a structural or functional abnormality. **heart of oak** *n* heartwood of the oak tree; a brave, resolute person. **heart of palm** *n* the leaf bud of the cabbage palm eaten as a vegetable. **heartpea** see **heartseed** below. **heart'-quake** *n* trembling, fear. **heart'-rending** *adj* agonizing. **heart'-rot** *n* decay in the hearts of trees, caused by various fungi. **heart's-blood** see **heart-blood** above. **heart'-searching** *n* examination of one's deepest feelings. **heart's'-ease** or **hearts'ease** *n* the pansy. **heart'seed** or **heart'pea** *n* the balloon-vine, from the heart-shaped scar left by the seed. **heart'-service** *n* sincere devotion, *opp* to *eye-service*. **heart'-shaped** *adj* shaped like the conventional representation of the human heart. **heart shell** see **heart cockle** above. **heart'sick** *adj* despondent; greatly depressed. **heart'sickness** *n*. **heart'sink** *n* (*med inf*) a person who causes medical practitioners to become exasperated because he or she makes repeated requests for medical attention, but is not able to be treated effectively (also *adj*). **heart'-sore** *adj* sore at heart; greatly distressed, very sad; caused by soreness of heart (*Shakesp*). ◆ *n* grief; a cause of grief (*Spenser*). **heart'-spoon** *n* (*dialect*) the depression in the breastbone; the breastbone; the pit of the stomach. **heart'-stirring** *adj* rousing; exhilarating. **heart'-strike** *vt* (*pap* **heart'-stricken** or **heart'-struck** (*obs* **-strook**)) (*archaic*) to strike to the heart; to dismay; to drive into the heart. **heart'-string** *n* *orig* a nerve or tendon imagined to brace and sustain the heart; (in *pl*)

affections. **heart'-throb** *n* a sentimental emotion for a person of the opposite sex (*inf*); a person who is the object of great romantic affection from afar (*inf*). **heart'-to-heart'** *adj* candid, intimate and unreserved. ◆ *n* a conversation of this sort. **heart urchin** *n* a sea urchin of the order Spatangoidea, typically heart-shaped. **heart'warming** *adj* emotionally moving; very gratifying, pleasing. **heart'water** *n* a fatal tick-borne viral disease of cattle, sheep and goats, with accumulation of fluid in the pericardium and pleural cavity. **heart'-whole** *adj* sincere at heart; with affections disengaged; undismayed; out-and-out. **heart'wood** *n* the duramen or hard inner wood of a tree.
■ **after one's own heart** exactly to one's own liking. **at heart** in one's real character; substantially. **break one's heart** to die of, or be broken down by, grief or disappointment. **break someone's heart** to cause deep grief to someone; (loosely) to disappoint someone romantically. **by heart** by rote; in the memory. **change of heart** see under **change**. **close to one's heart** being the object of one's warm interest, concern or liking. **cross one's heart** an expression used to emphasize the truth of a statement (often literally, by making the sign of the cross over one's heart). **cry one's heart out** see under **cry**. **dear to one's heart** same as **close to one's heart** (see above). **eat one's heart out** see under **eat**. **find it in one's heart** to be able to bring oneself. **from the bottom of one's heart** most sincerely. **have a heart** (*usu* in *imperative*) to show pity or kindness. **have at heart** to cherish as a matter of deep interest. **have one's heart in it** (often in *neg*) to have enthusiasm for what one is doing. **have one's heart in one's boots** to feel a sinking of the spirit. **have one's heart in one's mouth** to be in trepidation, great fear or anxiety. **have one's heart in the right place** to be basically decent or generous. **have one's heart set on** to desire earnestly. **have the heart** (*usu* in *neg*) to have the courage or resolution (to do something unpleasant). **heart and hand** or **heart and soul** with complete sincerity; with complete devotion to a cause. **heart of hearts** the inmost feelings or convictions; deepest affections. **in a heartbeat** immediately, without hesitation. **in good heart** in sound or fertile condition; in good spirits or courage. **lay** or **take to heart** to store up in the mind for future guidance; to be deeply moved by something. **lose heart** to become discouraged. **lose one's heart to** to fall in love with. **near to one's heart** same as **close to one's heart** (see above). **set one's heart on** or **upon** to come to desire earnestly. **set someone's heart at rest** to render someone easy in mind, to reassure someone. **speak to the heart** (*Bible*) to comfort, encourage. **take heart** to be encouraged. **take heart of grace** see under **grace**. **take to heart** to lay to heart; to come to feel in earnest. **take to one's heart** to form an affection for. **to one's heart's content** as much as one wishes. **wear one's heart on one's sleeve** to show one's deepest feelings openly. **with all one's heart** most willingly or sincerely.

hearth /härth/ *n* the floor of a fireplace or the area of floor surrounding it; the fireside; the house itself; the home circle; the lowest part of a blast-furnace; a brazier, chafing-dish, or firebox. [OE *heorth*; Du *haard*, Ger *Herd*]
❑ **hearth'-brush** *n* a brush for sweeping the hearth. **hearth'-money, -penny** or **-tax** *n* (*hist*) a tax on hearths. **hearth rug** *n* a rug laid over the hearthstone or in front of the hearth or fireplace. **hearth'stone** *n* a stone forming a hearth; a soft stone used for whitening hearths, doorsteps, etc.

heast or **heaste** /hēst/ (*Spenser*) *n* same as **hest**.

heat /hēt/ *n* that which excites the sensation of warmth; the sensation of warmth, *esp* in a high degree; degree of hotness; exposure to intense heat; a high temperature; the hottest time; redness of the skin, *esp* when irritated; vehemence, passion; sexual excitement in animals, or its period, *esp* in the female, corresponding to *rut* in the male; a single eliminating round in a race; a division of a contest from which the winner goes on to a final test; animation; pressure intended to coerce (*inf*); period of intensive search, *esp* by the police for a criminal after a crime has taken place (*inf*); trouble (*orig* with the police; *inf*); the police (*US sl*); a firearm (*US sl*). ◆ *vt* to make hot; to agitate; *perh* to run over, as in a race (*Shakesp*). ◆ *vi* to become hot. [OE *hætu* heat; *hāt* hot; Ger *Hitze*]
■ **heat'ed** *adj* having become or been made hot; angry, agitated or impassioned. **heat'er** *n* someone who or something that heats; an apparatus for heating a room or building; a conductor carrying a current that indirectly heats the cathode in certain types of valve; a gun, pistol (*old esp US sl*). **heat'ing** *n* and *adj*.
❑ **heat apoplexy** *n* sunstroke. **heat barrier** *n* difficulties caused by a thin envelope of hot air which develops round aircraft at high speeds and causes structural and other problems. **heat capacity** same as **thermal capacity** (see under **thermal**). **heat death** *n* the final state of the universe (if it is a closed system) predicted by the Second Law of Thermodynamics, in which heat and energy are uniformly distributed throughout the substance of the universe. **heat engine** *n* an engine that transforms heat into mechanical work. **heat'er-shield** *n* a triangular shield, like the heated plate of an iron. **heat exchanger** *n* a device for transferring heat from one fluid to another without allowing

contact between them. **heat exhaustion** n a condition caused by exposure to intense heat, characterized by dizziness, fatigue and abdominal pain. **heat'proof** adj resistant to or able to withstand heat. **heat pump** n a device (on the refrigerator principle) for drawing heat from water, air, or the earth, and giving it out to warm, eg a room. **heat'-resistant** adj. **heat'-seeking** adj (of a missile) able to detect heat emitted by its target and home in on this. **heat shield** n an object or substance designed to protect against excessive heat, esp that which protects a spacecraft re-entering the earth's atmosphere. **heat sink** n something into which unwanted heat can be directed. **heat'spot** n an area of skin with nerve-ends sensitive to heat; a spot or blotch on the skin caused by heat; a freckle. **heat'stroke** n exhaustion, illness, or prostration due to exposure to heat; sunstroke. **heat treatment** n the therapeutic use of heat in medicine; the use of heat in hardening metals. **heat'wave** n a heated state of atmosphere passing from one locality to another; a hot spell.

■ **heat of formation** (chem) the net quantity of heat evolved or absorbed during the formation of one mole of a substance from its component elements in their standard states. **in heat** or **on heat** (of a female animal) ready to mate. **in the heat of the moment** while subject to passion and without pausing to think. **latent heat** the heat required to change solid to liquid, or liquid to gas, without change of temperature. **mechanical equivalent of heat** the energy required to produce one heat unit. **specific heat** see under **specify**. **take the heat out of** to lessen the vehemence, intensity of emotion, or acrimony of (a situation, etc). **turn on the heat** (inf) to use brutal treatment, mental or physical, esp in order to coerce.

heath /hēth/ n barren open country, esp covered with ericaceous and other low shrubs; any shrub of genus Erica, sometimes extended to Calluna (heather) and others of the family Ericaceae; a butterfly of the Satyridae family. [OE hǣth; Ger Heide, Gothic haithi a waste]

■ **heath'y** adj abounding with heath.

❑ **heath bell** n heather bell; harebell. **heath'bird** or **heath'-fowl** n the black grouse. **heath'cock** n the male black grouse. **heath'-hen** n the grey-hen or female black grouse; an extinct American bird related to the prairie chicken. **heath'-poult** n the black grouse, esp the female or young.

heathen /hē'dhən/ n (pl **hea'then** (collectively) or **hea'thens** (individually)) someone who is not a Christian, Jew or Muslim but who follows another form of religion, esp polytheistic; a pagan; someone who has no religion; someone who is ignorant or unmindful of religion; an uncivilized person (inf). ◆ adj pagan; irreligious; uncivilized (inf). [OE hǣthen; Du heiden]

■ **hea'thendom** or **hea'thenesse** n (archaic) heathenism; the condition of a heathen; those regions of the world where heathenism prevails. **hea'thenish** adj relating to the heathen; rude; uncivilized; cruel. **hea'thenishly** adv. **hea'thenishness** n. **hea'thenism** n any religious system of the heathens; paganism; barbarism. **hea'thenize** or **-ise** vt to make heathen or heathenish. **hea'thenry** n heathenism; heathendom.

heather /hedh'ər/ n ling, a common low-growing evergreen shrub (Calluna vulgaris) of the heath family that grows in carpet-like thickets on exposed ground; sometimes extended to the heaths (genus Erica); an expanse of heather plants. ◆ adj of the purple colour of (red) heather; composed of or from heather. [Older Scot hadder; origin unknown; prob influenced by **heath**]

■ **heath'ery** adj.

❑ **heather ale** n a famous liquor traditionally brewed in Scotland from the bells of heather. **heather bell** n the flower of the cross-leaved heath (Erica tetralix) or of the common heath (Erica cinerea). **heather mixture** n a woollen fabric speckled in colours like heather.

■ **set the heather on fire** to create a disturbance or a sensation. **take to the heather** to become an outlaw.

heather-bleat /hedh'ər-blēt'/ or **heather-bleater** /-blē'tər/ (Scot) n a snipe (also **heather-bluiter**, **heather-blutter** /-blüt' or -blut'/). [OE haefer-blǣte, from hǣfer goat, and blǣtan to bleat, from its cry; influenced by **heather**; cf also Scot bluiter bittern]

Heath-Robinson /hēth-rob'in-sən/ adj used to describe an over-ingenious, ridiculously complicated or elaborate mechanical contrivance. [Heath Robinson (1872–1944), an artist who drew such contraptions]

■ **Heath-Robinsonesque'**, **Heath-Robinsō'nian** or **Heath-Rob'insonish** adj.

heaume /hōm/ (archaic) n a massive helmet. [Fr]

heave /hēv/ vt (pat and pap **heaved**, (naut) **hōve**; pap in sense of swollen **hōv'en**) to lift up, esp with great effort; to throw; to haul; to swell or puff out; to force (a sigh) from the chest; to displace (a vein) (mining). ◆ vi to be raised; to rise like waves; to retch; to strive or strain to lift or move something; to move into a certain position, orig of a ship, now also fig. ◆ n an effort upward; a throw; a swelling; an effort to vomit; a sigh (Shakesp); horizontal displacement (mining); the lifting up of soil and rocks, eg because of the freezing of water below

the surface of the ground; (of spacecraft) movement perpendicular to the direction of travel (cf **surge**[1]); (in pl) broken wind in horses. [OE hebban, pat hōf, pap hafen; Ger heben]

■ **heav'er** n. **heav'ing** n.

❑ **heave'-ho** n (inf) dismissal, rejection (see also below). **heave'-offering** or **heave'-shoulder** n (Bible) an offering, an animal's shoulder, offered in sacrifice with a lifting and lowering of the hands. ■ **give** (or **get**) **the heave** or **the heave-ho** (inf) to dismiss, reject or snub (or be dismissed, rejected or snubbed). **heave ho!** an orig sailors' call to exertion, as in heaving the anchor. **heave in sight** to come into view. **heave the lead** (naut) to take a sounding with a lead, to determine the depth of water. **heave the log** to cast the log into the water in order to ascertain the ship's speed. **heave to** (naut) to come (or bring a vessel) to a standstill.

heaven /hev'n or hevn/ n the vault of sky overhanging the earth (commonly in pl); the upper regions of the air; a very great and indefinite height; any one of the concentric revolving spheres imagined by the old astronomers; (often with cap) the dwelling-place of God or the gods, and the blessed; (often with cap) the Deity as inhabiting heaven; supreme happiness, contentment or pleasure. ◆ interj (in pl) expressing surprise, disbelief, dismay, etc. [OE heofon]

■ **heavenliness** /hev'n-/ n. **heavenly** /hev'n-/ adj of or inhabiting heaven; of or from God or the angels or saints; celestial; pure; supremely blessed; excellent (inf). ◆ adv divinely, exceedingly (archaic); by the influence of heaven (Milton). **heav'enward** adj. **heav'enward** or **heav'enwards** adv.

❑ **heav'en-born** adj descended from heaven. **heav'en-bred** adj (Shakesp) bred or produced in heaven. **heav'en-directed** adj pointing to the sky; divinely guided. **heaven-fallen** /hevn-föln'/ adj (Milton) fallen from heaven. **heaven-gift'ed** adj bestowed by heaven. **heav'en-kissing** adj (Shakesp) as it were, touching the sky. **heavenly bodies** n pl the sun, moon, planets, comets, stars, etc. **heavenly host** n the angels and archangels. **heav'enly-minded** adj with the mind set upon heavenly things; pure. **heavenly-mind'edness** n. **heav'en-sent** adj sent by heaven; very timely.

■ **for heaven's sake** an expression of entreaty; an interjection expressing exasperation or disgust, etc. **good heavens** or **heavens above** expressing surprise, disbelief, dismay, etc. **heaven forbid** or (archaic) **forfend** may it not happen (that). **heaven knows** God knows (qv); it is beyond human knowledge; it is anyone's guess. **heaven of heavens** (Bible) the highest heavens, abode of God. **in** (**the**) **seventh heaven** in a state of the most exalted happiness (from the Cabbalists, who divided the heavens into seven in an ascending scale of happiness up to the abode of God). **move heaven and earth** to do everything possible. **the heavens opened** there was a very heavy shower of rain. **tree of heaven** ailanto.

Heaviside layer see Kennelly-Heaviside layer.

heavy /hev'i/ adj (**heav'ier**; **heav'iest**) weighty; ponderous; laden; abounding; of high specific gravity; not easy to bear; grievous; oppressive; grave; dull, lacking brightness and interest; lacking sprightliness; pedantic; pompous; laborious; sad; in low spirits; drowsy; with great momentum; deep-toned; massive; thick; not easily digested; doughy; impeding the feet in walking; (of the ground) very wet and soft (horse-racing, etc); heavy-armed (milit); (of liquor) strong; dark with clouds; gloomy; relating to grave or serious roles (theatre); (of newspapers) serious, highbrow; tense, emotional, strained (sl); serious, important (sl); (of a market) with falling prices (commerce). ◆ adv heavily. ◆ n the villain on stage or screen; a large, strong man employed for purposes of a violent and often criminal nature or to deter others (sl); (in Scotland) a type of beer similar to, but not as strong as, export; anything particularly large or heavy. [OE hefig, from hebban to heave; OHGer hebîg]

■ **heav'ily** adv. **heav'iness** n.

❑ **heav'ier-than-air'** adj of a greater specific gravity than the air it displaces, esp (of an aircraft) not sustained by a gas-filled bag. **heav'y-armed** adj bearing heavy armour or arms. **heavy breather** n. **heavy breathing** n loud and laboured breathing due to exertion, excitement, etc, or esp sexual arousal, sometimes associated with anonymous obscene telephone calls. **heavy chemicals** n pl those produced on a large scale for use in industry (eg sulphuric acid and sodium carbonate), opp to fine chemicals. **heavy cream** n (N Am) double cream. **heav'y-duty** adj made to withstand very hard wear or use; substantial. **heav'y-hand'ed** adj clumsy, awkward; oppressive. **heav'y-head'ed** adj having a heavy or large head; dull; stupid; drowsy. **heavy-heart'ed** adj weighed down with grief. **heavy horse** n a large draught horse. **heavy hydrogen** n deuterium; also tritium. **heavy industry** see under **industry**. **heavy-lad'en** adj with a heavy burden. **heavy metal** n a metal of high specific gravity, usu above 5; guns or shot of large size; great influence or power; a person to be reckoned with; a particularly loud, simple and repetitive form of hard rock (music). **heavy oil** n a hydrocarbon that is denser than water, esp one derived from coal tar. **heavy particle** n a baryon. **heavy petting** n sexual activity that stops just short of full intercourse. **heavy rock** n *(music)* hard rock. **heavy spar** *n* barytes. **heavy swell** *n* a rough sea. **heavy water** *n* water in which deuterium takes the place of ordinary hydrogen, or a mixture of this and ordinary water. **heav'yweight** *n* a person or thing well above the average weight; someone important or very influential *(inf)*; a competitor in the heaviest class *(sport)*; a weight category, applied *esp* in boxing; a sportsperson of the specified weight for the category (eg in professional boxing above middleweight, **light heavyweight** (maximum 79kg/175lb), **cruis'erweight** (maximum 86kg/190lb), and **heav'yweight** any weight above these). ◆ *adj* of or relating to heavyweights; important or influential *(inf)*. **heavy wet** *n (old sl)* a drink of strong ale, or ale and porter mixed.

■ **be heavily into** *(inf)* to be keen on or an enthusiastic practitioner of. **be heavy going** see under **going**[1]. **heavy marching order** the condition of troops fully equipped for field service. **the heavies** the heavy cavalry *(milit)*; those who play heavy parts *(theatre)*; the more serious, highbrow newspapers and journals, etc *(inf)*; (shares in) the heavy industries.

Heb. or **Hebr.** *abbrev* : Hebrew; (the Letter to the) Hebrews *(Bible)*.

hebdomad */heb'də-mad* or *-mād/ n* a set of seven; a week; in some Gnostic systems, a group of superhuman beings. [Gr *hebdomas, -ados* a set of seven, a week, from *hepta* seven]

■ **hebdomadal** */-dom'ə-dl/ adj* weekly. **hebdom'adally** *adv*. **hebdom'adar** or **hebdom'ader** *n* (in Scottish universities) a senior member appointed weekly for the supervision of student discipline. **hebdom'adary** *adj* weekly. ◆ *n* a member of a chapter or convent taking his or her weekly turn to officiate.

❏ **hebdomadal council** *n* an administrative board of Oxford University, meeting weekly.

Hebe */hē'bē/ n* a daughter of Zeus and Hera, cupbearer of Olympus, a personification of youth *(Gr myth)*; a genus of Australasian and S American shrubby plants with spikes of showy flowers, belonging to the family Scrophulariaceae, in some classifications included in the genus *Veronica*; (without *cap*) a member of the genus. [Gr *hēbē* youth, puberty]

■ **hebephrenia** */hē-bi-frē'ni-ə/ n* (Gr *phrēn* mind) a form of insanity beginning in late childhood, arresting intellectual development, and ending in complete dementia. **hebephrē'niac** or **hebephrenic** */-fren'ik/ adj* and *n*.

heben */heb'n/ n* and *adj* obsolete form of **ebony**.

hebenon */heb'ə-non/* or **hebona** */-nə/ (Shakesp) n* anything (eg a plant or fruit) with a poisonous juice. [Perh *ebony* or *henbane*, or Ger *Eibenbaum* yew tree]

hebephrenia see under **Hebe**.

hebetate */heb'i-tāt/ (literary) vt* to dull or blunt. ◆ *vi* to become dull. ◆ *adj* dull; blunt; soft-pointed. [L *hebetāre, -ātum*, from *hebes, -etis* blunt]

■ **heb'etant** *adj* making dull. **hebetā'tion** *n*. **heb'etude** *n*. **hebetūdinos'ity** *n*. **hebetū'dinous** *adj*.

hebona see **hebenon**.

Hebrew */hē'brōō/ n* a member of an ancient Semitic people; the language of the Hebrews, in which the Old Testament and sacred texts of Judaism are written; unintelligible speech *(inf)*. ◆ *adj* of the Hebrews or their language. [OFr *Ebreu* and L *Hebraeus*, from Gr *Hebraios*, from Aramaic *'ebrai* (Heb *'ibrī*), literally, one from the other side (of the Euphrates)]

■ **Hebraic** */hē-brā'ik/* or **Hebra'ical** *adj* relating to the Hebrews or to their language. **Hebra'ically** *adv* after the manner of the Hebrew language; from right to left. **Hebra'icism** *n*. **Hē'brāism** *n* a Hebrew idiom. **Hē'brāist** *n* a person skilled in Hebrew. **Hebrāist'ic** or **Hebrāist'ical** *adj* of or like Hebrew. **Hebrāist'ically** *adv*. **Hē'brāize** or **-ise** *vt* to make Hebrew. ◆ *vi* to use a Hebrew idiom; to conform or incline to Hebrew ways or ideals. **Hē'brāizer** or **-s-** *n*. **Hē'brewess** *n* *(Bible)* a Jewess. **Hē'brewism** *n*.

❏ **Hebrew year** see under **year**.

Hebridean */heb-ri-dē'ən/* or **Hebridian** */-rid'i-ən/ adj* of the *Hebrides* */heb'ri-dēz/*, islands off the west coast of Scotland. ◆ *n* a native of the Hebrides. [Due to a misprint of L *Hebudēs*, from Gr *Heboudai*]

■ **He'brid** *adj (rare)*.

Hecate */hek'ə-tē/* or *(Shakesp)* **Hecat** */hek'ət/ n* a mysterious goddess, in Hesiod having power over earth, heaven and sea, and afterwards identified with Artemis, Persephone and other goddesses *(Gr myth)*; in Shakespeare, etc, the chief or goddess of witches. [Gr *Hekatē*]

hecatomb */hek'ə-toom, -tōm* or *-tom/ n* a great public sacrifice; any large number of victims. [Gr *hekatombē*, from *hekaton* a hundred, and *bous* an ox]

hech */hehh/ (Scot) interj* an exclamation of surprise, weariness, etc.

hecht */hehht/* Scottish form of the verb **hight**.

heck[1] */hek/ n* and *interj* a euphemism for hell.

heck[2] */hek/*, **haik** or **hake** */hāk/ (dialect) n* the lower part of a door; an inner door; a grating, *esp* in rivers or streams; a rack for animal fodder; a rack or frame for drying cheese, etc; a piece of spinning machinery, for guiding the yarn to the reels. [OE *hec (hæc)* grating, hatch; cf **hack**[3] and **hatch**[1]; Du *hek* gate]

■ **heck and manger** rack and manger.

heckle */hek'l/ vt* to comb out (flax or hemp fibres). ◆ *vt* and *vi (orig Scot)* to interrupt (someone) with embarrassing questions, or shout or jeer abusively or disruptively (at), eg at an election hustings or public lecture. ◆ *n* a hackle. [Cf **hackle** and **hatchel**]

■ **heck'ler** *n*. **heck'ling** *n*.

hecogenin */hek'ō-jen-in, jen'* or *he-koj'ə-nin/ n* a chemical obtained from various plants, eg *Hechtia texensis*, and *esp* from sisal waste, used in the manufacture of cortisone, etc. [*Hechtia texensis*, and suffixes *-gen* and *-in*]

hectare see under **hecto-**.

hectic */hek'tik/ adj* feverish, agitated, rushed *(inf)*; flushed *(Shelley)*; relating to the constitution or habit of body *(old)*; relating to hectic fever *(old)*. ◆ *n* a hectic fever or flush; a consumptive *(archaic)*. [Gr *hektikos* habitual, from *hexis* habit]

■ **hec'tical** *adj*. **hec'tically** *adv*.

❏ **hectic fever** *n (old)* fever occurring in connection with certain wasting diseases of long duration, *esp* tuberculosis, typically producing a flush in the cheeks.

hecto- */hek-tō-* or *hek-tə-/* or **hect-** */hekt-/ combining form* in names of units, denoting a hundred times (10²). [Fr contraction of Gr *hekaton* a hundred]

■ **hectare** */hek'tär* or *-tār/ n* 100 ares or 10 000 sq metres. **hectocot'ylus** *n* (Gr *kotylē* cup, hollow thing) a tentacle used by male octupuses and other cephalopods to transfer sperm to females. **hec'togram** or **-gramme** *n* 100 grams. **hec'tograph** *n* a gelatine pad for printing copies. ◆ *vt* to reproduce in this way. **hectograph'ic** *adj*. **hec'tolitre** *n* 100 litres. **hec'tometre** *n* 100 metres. **hec'tostere** *n* 100 cubic metres or steres.

hector */hek'tər/ vt* to bully; to treat insolently; to annoy. ◆ *vi* to play the bully; to bluster. ◆ *n* a bully, a blusterer. [Gr *Hektōr* the Trojan hero]

■ **hec'torer** *n*. **hec'toring** *n* and *adj*. **hec'torism** *n*. **hec'torly** *adj*. **hec'torship** *n*.

he'd */hēd/* a contraction of **he had** or **he would**.

heddle */hed'l/ (weaving) n* a series of vertical cords or wires, each having in the middle a loop (**hedd'le-eye**) to receive a warp thread, and passing round and between parallel bars. ◆ *vt* to draw through heddle-eyes (also **heald**). [An assumed OE *hefedl*, earlier form of *hefeld*]

heder same as **cheder**.

Hedera */hed'ə-rə/ n* the ivy genus of the Aralia family. [L]

■ **hed'eral** *adj*. **hed'erated** *adj* crowned with a wreath of ivy.

hedge */hej/ n* a close row of bushes or small trees serving as a fence; a barrier, protection *(fig)*; an act of securing, or something that secures, protection against *(esp* financial) loss. ◆ *vt* to enclose with a hedge; to obstruct; to surround; to guard; to protect oneself from loss on, by compensatory transactions, eg bets on the other side. ◆ *vi* to make hedges; to shuffle, be evasive, eg in an argument; to be shifty; to buy or sell something as a financial hedge. ◆ *adj* living in or frequenting hedges; wayside; used by, or only fit for, vagrants; low; debased. [OE *hecg*; Du *hegge*, Ger *Hecke*]

■ **hedg'er** *n* a person who hedges or dresses hedges. **hedg'ing** *n* the work of a hedger; the action of the verb *hedge*. **hedg'y** *adj*.

❏ **hedge'-accen'tor** *n* the hedge sparrow. **hedge'bill** or **hedg'ing-bill** *n* a bill for dressing hedges, a kind of long-handled hatchet. **hedge'-born** *adj* born under a hedge, low-born. **hedge'-bote** *n* a tenant's right to cut wood for repairing hedges or fences. **hedge'-creep'er** *n* a sneaky rogue. **hedge fund** *n* an investment fund based on a complex mathematical model, designed to minimize risk and produce high profits in the long term, but exposing investors to high risk in the short term. **hedge'hog** *n* a small prickly-backed insectivorous animal that lives in hedges and bushes, considered to have a pig-like snout; a prickly fruit, or prickly-fruited plant; someone whose manners keep others at a distance; an offensive person; a small, strongly fortified, defensive position *(milit sl)*. **hedge'-hop** *vi (inf)* to fly low in an aircraft as if hopping over hedges. **hedge'-hyssop** *n* a plant (genus *Gratiola*) of the figwort family. **hedge'-marriage** *n* a clandestine marriage. **hedge'-mustard** *n* a tall stiff cruciferous roadside weed *(Sisymbrium officinale)* with small yellow flowers, or a related species. **hedge'-parsley** *n* a white-flowered umbelliferous roadside weed *(Torilis* or *Caucalis)* with leaves rather like parsley. **hedge'-parson** or **hedge'-priest** *n* a disreputable, vagrant, or illiterate parson or priest. **hedge'pig** *n* a hedgehog. **hedge'row** *n* a line of hedge, often with trees. **hedge'-school** *n* an open-air school, common in Ireland in the 17c and 18c during the ban on Catholic education; a poorly equipped school. **hedge'-schoolmaster** *n*. **hedge sparrow** or formerly also

hedge warbler n the dunnock (*Prunella modularis*), a small bird that frequents hedges, superficially like a sparrow but with a more slender bill. **hedge trimmer** n an electric tool for cutting back hedges, shrubs, etc. **hedge'-writer** n a Grub Street author, a hack.

hedonism /hē'də-ni-zm or hed'/ n (in ethics) the doctrine that pleasure is the highest good; the pursuit of pleasure; a lifestyle devoted to pleasure-seeking. [Gr *hēdonē* pleasure]
▪ **hēdonic** /-don'/ or **hēdonist'ic** adj. **hēdon'ics** n sing that part of ethics or of psychology that deals with pleasure. **hē'donist** n.

-hedron /-hē-drən/ combining form denoting a geometric solid figure or body with a specified number of plane faces, as in *tetrahedron*. [Gr *hedrā* a base]

hedyphane /hed'i-fān/ n a white variety of green lead ore, arsenate, phosphate, and chloride of lead and calcium with barium. [Gr *hēdys* sweet, pleasant, and the root of *phainein* to show]

heebie-jeebies or **heeby-jeebies** /hē'bi-jē'biz/ n pl (with *the* ; sl) a fit of nerves; irritation or depression; the creeps. [A coinage]

heed /hēd/ vt to observe; to look after; to attend to. ◆ vi to mind, care. ◆ n notice; caution; attention. [OE *hēdan* ; Du *hoeden*, Ger *hüten*]
▪ **heed'ful** adj attentive; cautious. **heed'fully** adv. **heed'fulness** n. **heed'iness** n. **heed'less** adj careless; paying no attention. **heed'lessly** adv. **heed'lessness** n. **heed'y** adj (*Spenser*) heedful, careful.

heehaw /hē'hö/ vi (of a donkey, etc) to bray. ◆ n a bray. [Imit]

heel¹ /hēl/ n the hind part of the foot below the ankle; the whole foot (*esp* of animals); the part of a shoe, etc that covers or supports the heel; a spur; the hinder part of anything, such as a violin bow; a heel-like bend, as on a golf club; a knob; the top, bottom or end of a loaf or a cheese; a despicable person, often someone who lets others down (*sl*); a wrestler who cultivates an antagonistic relationship with the audience, *opp* to *face*. ◆ vt to execute or perform with the heel; to strike with the heel; to supply with a heel; to arm with a spur, as a fighting cock; to seize by the heels; to tie by the heels; to follow at the heels of; to supply with a weapon, money, etc. ◆ vi (of a dog) to follow well; to move one's heels to a dance rhythm; to kick the ball backwards out of the scrum with the heel (*rugby*). [OE *hēla* ; Du *hiel*]
▪ **heeled** adj provided with a heel, shod; (as **-heeled**) in combination, signifying (of shoes) having a heel of a specified type (as in *high-heeled*), and used fig in *well-heeled* comfortably off. **heel'er** n someone who heels, in any sense; a person who follows at heel, such as an unscrupulously faithful follower of a party boss; a dog that herds livestock by following and barking at their heels (*Aust*). **heel'ing** n a heel-piece (*Spenser*); the act of making or attaching a heel.
❑ **heel'ball** n a black waxy composition for blacking the edges of heels and soles of shoes and boots, and for taking brass rubbings, etc. **heel'bar** n a shop or counter where shoes, etc are repaired. **heel'-bone** n the calcaneum, the bone that forms the heel of the foot. **heel'-piece** n a piece or cover for the heel. **heel'tap** n a layer of material in a shoe-heel; a small quantity of liquor left in the glass after drinking (*old*).
▪ **Achilles' heel** see under **Achillean**. **at** (or **on** or **upon**) **the heels of** following close behind. **back on one's heels** driven back by an opponent; on the defensive. **bring to heel** to cause or persuade to come to heel. **clap by the heels** same as **lay by the heels** (see below). **come to heel** to come in behind; to obey or follow like a dog; to submit to authority. **cool one's heels** to be kept waiting for some time. **dig in one's heels** to behave stubbornly. **down at heel** having the heels of one's shoes trodden down; slovenly; in poor circumstances. **heel and toe** with strict walking pace, as opposed to running (also vi to use the heel and toe of one foot to operate both the brake and accelerator pedals, eg when driving a racing car). **heel in** to cover the roots of (plants, etc) temporarily with earth to keep them moist (also **hele in**). **heel of Achilles** see under **Achillean**. **heels o'er gowdy** (*Scot*) or **heels over head** (*archaic*) upside down. **kick one's heels** to endure a period of inactivity. **kick up one's heels** to gambol or frisk. **lay by the heels** to fetter; to put in confinement. **out at heel** having one's heels showing through holes in the socks or stockings; shabby. **set by the heels** same as **lay by the heels** (see above). **set (one) back on one's heels** to surprise, astonish one. **show a clean pair of heels** to run off. **take to one's heels** to flee. **tread on someone's heels** to come crowding behind. **trip up someone's heels** to trip up or overthrow someone. **turn on** (or **upon**) **one's heel** to turn sharply round, to turn back or away. **two for his heels** (in cribbage) a score for turning up the jack. **under the heel** crushed, ruled over tyrannically. **walk to heel** (of a dog) to walk obediently at the heels of the person in charge of it, under control.

heel² /hēl/ vi to incline, slope; (of a ship) to lean on one side. ◆ vt to tilt. [Earlier *heeld, hield* ; OE *hieldan* to slope; cf Du *hellen*]

heel³ same as **hele**.

heeze /hēz/ (*Scot*) vt a form of **hoise**. ◆ n a lift; a heave upwards.
▪ **heez'ie** n a lift.

HEFC abbrev : Higher Education Funding Council (**HEFCE** for England; **HEFCW** for Wales).

heft¹ /heft/ n heaving (*obs*); retching (*Shakesp*); weight (*US*); the greater part (*archaic*). ◆ vt to lift; to feel or judge the weight of. [**heave**]
▪ **hef'tily** adv. **hef'tiness** n. **heft'y** adj rather heavy; muscular; sizeable; vigorous; violent; abundant. ◆ adv very.

heft² and **hefte** (*Spenser*) obsolete forms of **heaved** (*pat* and *pap* of **heave**).

heft³ /heft/ (*Scot*) vt to restrain; to retain (milk or urine). [Cf ON *hefta* to bind]

heft⁴ /heft/ n a number of sheets fastened together; an instalment of a serial publication. [Ger]

heft⁵ /heft/ a Scots form of **haft**.

heft⁶ /heft/ vt to accustom sheep to graze in a specific unfenced area. ◆ n an unfenced area of ground for grazing sheep. [Ger *heften* to fasten]

hefty, etc see under **heft¹**.

Hegelian /hā- or he-gāl'i-ən, also -gēl'/ adj relating to or associated with Wilhelm Friedrich Hegel (1770–1831) or his philosophy. ◆ n a follower of Hegel.
▪ **Hegel'ianism** n.

hegemony /hi-gem'ə-ni or -jem', also 'hej-i-mə-ni/ n leadership; preponderant influence, *esp* of one state over others. [Gr *hēgemoniā*, from *hēgemōn* leader, from *hēgeesthai* to lead]
▪ **hegemō'nial**, **hegemon'ic** or **hegemon'ical** adj. **hegem'onism** n. **hegem'onist** n.

hegira, **hejira**, **hejra**, **hijra** or **hijrah** /hej', hij'(i)-rə or hi-ji'rə/ n the exodus of Mohammed from Mecca, 622AD, from which is dated the Muslim era; any exodus. [Ar *hijrah* exodus, from *hajara* to leave]

heh /hā/ n the fifth letter of the Hebrew alphabet. [Heb]

he-he /hē'hē'/ interj representing a high-pitched or gleeful laugh. ◆ n such a laugh. ◆ vi to laugh so. [Imit]

heich-how see under **heigh**.

heid /hēd/ (*Scot*) n a head. [See **head**]

heifer /hef'ər/ n a young cow. [OE *hēahfore, hēahfru, -fre* ; literally prob high-goer, from *faran* to go]

heigh /hā (or hī)/ interj a cry of enquiry, encouragement or exultation. [Imit]
▪ **heigh'-ho** interj an exclamation expressive of weariness. ◆ n (*Scot* also **heich-how** /hēhh'how'/) routine; familiar jog-trot.

height /hīt/ n the condition of being high; degree of highness; distance upwards; angle of elevation; that which is elevated; a hill; a high place; elevation in rank or excellence; the most intense part; utmost degree. [From **highth**, from OE *hīehtho, hēahthu*, from *hēah* high]
▪ **height'en** vt and vi to make or become higher; to make or become brighter or more conspicuous, or (*fig*) stronger or more intense; to elate (*obs*).
❑ **height of land** n a watershed, *esp* if not a range of hills. **height to paper** n (*printing*) the standard height of type, blocks, etc from foot to face (*approx* 0.918in).

heil! /hīl/ (*Ger*) interj hail!

Heimlich manoeuvre or **procedure** /hīm'lihh mə-noo'vər or -nū or prō-sē'dyər/ n an emergency method of dislodging an obstruction from a choking person's windpipe by applying a sharp thrust below the breastbone. [HJ *Heimlich* (born 1920), US physician who devised it]

Heimweh /hīm'vā/ (*Ger*) n homesickness.

heinie /hī'ni/ (*US inf*) n the buttocks. [Altered from **hinder** (see under **hind¹**)]

heinous /hā'nəs or sometimes hē'nəs/ adj outrageously wicked, odious, atrocious. [OFr *haïnos* (Fr *haineux*), from *hair* to hate]
▪ **hei'nously** adv. **hei'nousness** n.

heir /ār/ n (in law) a person who actually succeeds to property, title, etc on the death of its previous holder; (*popularly*) a person entitled to succeed when the present possessor dies; a child, *esp* a first-born son; a successor to a position, eg of leadership; inheritor of qualities, or of social conditions, or the past generally. ◆ vt (*dialect*) to inherit. [OFr *heir*, from L *hērēs* (vulgar accusative *hērem*) an heir]
▪ **heir'dom** n. **heir'ess** n a female heir; a woman who has succeeded or is likely to succeed to a considerable fortune. **heir'less** adj without an heir. **heir'ship** n.
❑ **heir apparent** n an heir whose right to succeed to an estate is conditional only on outliving the present possessor, no matter who may subsequently be born; a person expected to succeed the leader of a party, etc. **heir'-at-law'** an heir by legal right. **heir'-by-cus'tom** a person whose right as heir is determined by customary modes of descent, such as gavelkind, etc. **heir'loom** n any piece of furniture or personal property that descends to the heir-at-law by special custom;

any object that is passed down through a family from generation to generation. **heir'-por'tioner** *n* (*Scots law*) a joint heiress or her representative. **heir presumptive** *n* a person who will be heir if no nearer relative should be born (also *fig*).

■ **fall heir to** to inherit (also *fig*).

Heisenberg('s) uncertainty principle /*hī'zən-bûrg*(*z*) *un-sûr'tən-ti prin'si-pl*/ *n* a more formal name for **uncertainty principle** (see **uncertainty** under **un-**).

heist /*hīst*/ (*sl*) *n* a robbery or theft, *esp* an armed hold-up, or a particularly clever or spectacular theft; a person who robs or steals. ◆ *vt* to steal or rob in a heist. [Variant of **hoist**]

■ **heist'er** *n*.

hei-tiki /*hā-tik'ē*/ *n* a Maori greenstone neck ornament. [Maori *hei* hang and **tiki**]

hejab see **hijab**.

hejira or **hejra** see **hegira**.

HeLa cell /*hē'lə sel*/ *n* a cancerous cell of a strain developed from those taken in 1951 from a patient suffering from cervical carcinoma. [From the name of the patient, reported as *Helen Lane* or *Henrietta Lacks*]

helcoid /*hel'koid*/ *adj* ulcerous. [Gr *helkos* an ulcer]

held *pat* and *pap* of **hold**[1].

Heldentenor /*hel'dən-ten'ər* or *hel'dən-te-nör'*/ *n* (pl **Heldenten'ors** or **Heldentenöre** /*-te-nø'rə*/) (a man with) a powerful tenor voice, particularly suitable for heroic roles in (*esp* Wagnerian) operas. [Ger, hero tenor, from *Held* hero]

hele, **heel** or **heal** /*hēl*/ *vt* (*Spenser*; now *dialect*) to hide, conceal; to cover. [OE *helian* from *hellan* (weak verb) blended with *helan* (strong), both meaning to hide; Ger *hehlen*; L *celāre*; Gr *kalyptein*]

■ **hele in** (*dialect*; *hortic*) to heel in.

helenium /*hə-lē'ni-əm*/ *n* any plant of the genus *Helenium*, commonly with yellow or variegated daisy-like flowers. [L, from Gr *helenion*]

heli- /*hel-i-*/ *combining form* denoting helicopter (as in *helibus*; *helidrome*; *heliman*; *helipilot*, etc). [Gr *helix*, *-ikos* screw]

■ **hel'iborne** *adj*. **hel'icopter** *n* (Gr *pteron* wing) a flying machine sustained by rotating blades revolving on a vertical axis above the machine. ◆ *vt* to take or carry by helicopter. **helicopter view** *n* same as **bird's-eye view** (qv under **bird**). **hel'ideck** *n* a landing deck for helicopters on a ship, drilling platform, etc. **hel'ipad** *n* a landing-place for a helicopter. **hel'iport** *n* the equivalent of an aerodrome for helicopters, *usu* for commercial services. **hel'iscoop** *n* a net let down from a helicopter to rescue people in difficulty. **heli-ski'er** *n*. **heli-ski'ing** *n* the use of helicopters to transport skiers to remote slopes; an extreme sport (qv) in which a skier is dropped by helicopter at the top of a mountain, and skis down to the treeline. **hel'istop** *n* a landing-place for a helicopter.

heliac /*hē'li-ak*/ or **heliacal** /*hi-lī'ə-kəl*/ *adj* solar; coincident with that of the sun, or as nearly as could be observed. [Gr *hēliakos*, from *hēlios* the sun]

■ **heli'acally** *adv*.

□ **heliacal rising** *n* the emergence of a star from the light of the sun. **heliacal setting** *n* its disappearance in it.

Helianthemum /*hē-li-an'thə-məm*/ *n* the rock-rose genus. [Gr *hēlios* sun, and *anthemon* flower]

Helianthus /*hē-li-an'thəs*/ *n* the sunflower genus. [Gr *hēlios* sun, and *anthos* flower]

heliborne see under **heli-**.

helical, etc, **helices** see **helix**.

Helichrysum /*he-li-krī'zəm*/ *n* a genus of composite plants, the flowers of which keep their colour and shape when dried; (without *cap*) a plant of this genus. [Gr *helix* spiral, and *chrysos* gold]

Helicidae, **helicograph**, **helicoid**, etc see under **helix**.

helicon /*hel'i-kon* or *-kən*/ *n* a circular bass tuba. [Poss from Gr *helix* spiral]

heliconia /*hel-i-kō'ni-ə*/ *n* any plant of the tropical American genus *Heliconia*, with large showy flowers. [Named after Mount *Helicon* in Greece (see **Heliconian**)]

Heliconian /*hel-i-kō'ni-ən*/ *adj* relating to *Helicon* (Gr *Helikōn*), a mountain range in Boeotia, favourite seat of the Muses, described as a fountain by some poets.

helicopter see under **heli-**.

helictite /*hel'ik-tīt*/ *n* a twisted, branching stalactite. [Gr *heliktos* twisted, and **stalactite**]

helideck see under **heli-**.

helio- /*hē-li-ō-, hē-li-o-* or *hē-li-ə-*/ *combining form* denoting sun. [Gr *hēlios* the sun]

■ **heliocentric** /*-sen'trik*/ *adj* (Gr *kentron* centre; *astron*) having the sun as centre. **heliocen'trically** *adv*. **he'liochrome** /*-krōm*/ *n* (Gr *chrōma* colour) a photograph in natural colours. **heliochrō'mic** *adj*. **he'liochrōmy** *n*. **he'liograph** *n* (Gr *graphē* a drawing) an apparatus for signalling by flashing the sun's rays; an engraving obtained photographically; an apparatus for photographing the sun; an instrument for measuring intensity of sunlight. ◆ *vt* and *vi* to communicate by heliograph. **heliog'rapher** *n*. **heliograph'ic** or **heliograph'ical** *adj*. **heliograph'ically** *adv*. **heliog'raphy** *n*. **heliogravure** /*-grəv-ūr'* or *-grāv'yər*/ *n* (Fr *héliogravure*) photo-engraving. **heliol'ater** *n* a sun worshipper. **heliol'atrous** *adj*. **heliol'atry** *n* (Gr *latreiā* worship) sun-worship. **heliol'ogy** *n* the science of the sun. **heliom'eter** *n* an instrument for measuring angular distances, such as the sun's diameter. **heliomet'ric** or **heliomet'rical** *adj*. **he'liopause** *n* (Gr *pausis* cessation) the boundary of the heliosphere (qv below). **helioph'ilous** *adj* (Gr *phileein* to love) fond of the sun. **heliopho'bic** *adj* (Gr *phobos* fear) fearing or shunning sunlight. **he'liophyte** *n* (Gr *phyton* a plant) a plant that can live in full exposure to sunlight. **heliosciophyte** /*hē-li-ō-sī'ō-fīt*/ *n* (Gr *skiā* shadow) a plant that can live in shade but does better in the sun. **he'lioscope** /*-skōp*/ *n* (Gr *skopeein* to look at) an apparatus for observing the sun without injury to the eye. **helioscopic** /*-skop'ik*/ *adj*. **heliō'sis** *n* (Gr *hēliōsis*) (over-)exposure to the sun; the spotting of leaves by raindrops, or by greenhouse glass flaws, etc acting as burning-glasses. **he'liosphere** *n* (Gr *sphaira* sphere) the region around the sun (including the earth) that is filled with solar magnetic fields, in which the sun's heat is effective. **heliospher'ic** *adj*. **he'liostat** *n* (Gr *statos* fixed) an instrument on the principle of the coelostat by means of which a beam of sunlight is reflected in an invariable direction, for study of the sun or for signalling. **heliotax'is** *n* (Gr *taxis* arrangement) response of an organism to the stimulus of the sun's rays. **heliother'apy** *n* (Gr *therapeiā* healing) medical treatment by exposure to the sun's rays. **heliotrope** /*hē'li-ō-trōp* or *hel'i-ō-trōp*/ *n* (Gr *hēliotropion*) any plant of the genus *Heliotropium* of the borage family, many species with fragrant flowers, *esp* the *Peruvian heliotrope*, with small fragrant lilac-blue flowers; the colour of its flowers; a kind of perfume imitating that of the flower; a bloodstone (*mining*); a surveyor's heliograph. **heliotropic** /*-trop'ik*/ or **heliotrop'ical** *adj*. **heliotrop'ically** *adv*. **heliot'ropin** *n* piperonal. **heliotropism** /*-ot'rə-pizm*/ or **heliot'ropy** *n* the tendency of stem and leaves to bend towards (*positive heliotropism*), and roots from (*negative heliotropism*), the light. **he'liotype** *n* (Gr *typos* impression) a photograph by heliotypy. **heliotypic** /*-tip'ik*/ *adj*. **he'liotypy** /*-tī-pi*/ *n* a photomechanical process in which the gelatine relief is itself used to print from. **Heliozō'a** *n pl* (Gr *zōion* an animal) sun-animalcules, an order of Protozoa, spherical with radiating processes of living matter. **heliozō'an** *adj* and *n*. **heliozō'ic** *adj*.

heliodor /*hē'li-ə-dōr* or *-dör*/ *n* a variety of clear yellow beryl occurring in SW Africa. [Ger]

heliograph, etc see under **helio-**.

helipad, **heliport**, **heliscoop**, **heli-skiing** see under **heli-**.

helispheric, **helispherical** see under **helix**.

helistop see under **heli-**.

helium /*hē'li-əm*/ *n* a very light inert gaseous element (symbol **He**; atomic no 2) discovered (1868) by Lockyer in the sun's atmosphere, isolated (1895) by Ramsay from cleveite, and found in certain natural gases. [Gr *hēlios* sun]

□ **helium speech** *n* distorted speech such as occurs in a helium atmosphere.

■ **liquid helium** helium in liquid form (below 4.22K), which has remarkable qualities, undergoing a striking change at 2.19K (see **superfluidity** under **superfluid**).

helix /*hē'liks*/ *n* (pl **he'lixes** or **helices** /*hel'i-sēz*/) a screw-shaped coil; a curve on a developable surface (*esp* a right circular cylinder) which becomes a straight line when the surface is unrolled into a plane, distinguished from a spiral, which is a plane curve (*maths*); the rim of the ear (*anat*); a small volute or twist in the capital of a Corinthian column (*archit*); a screw-propeller; (with *cap*) a genus of molluscs including the best-known land snails; one of the genus. [Gr *helix* a spiral, from *helissein* to turn round]

■ **helical** /*hel'ik-əl*/ *adj*. **hel'ically** *adv*. **helicase** /*hē'li-kāz*/ *n* any of a group of enzymes that are able to separate the strands of the double-helix of a DNA molecule. **Helicidae** /*-is'i-dē*/ *n pl* a large family of terrestrial, air-breathing gastropods, including the common snails. **hel'icograph** *n* a drawing instrument for describing spirals on a plane. **hel'icoid** or **hel'icoidal** *adj* like a helix, screw-shaped. **helispher'ic** or **helispher'ical** *adj* loxodromic.

□ **helicobac'ter pylori** /*pī-lö'rī*/ *n* a bacterium that is a cause of inflammation of the stomach lining, often leading to ulcers or cancer. **helicoid cyme** *n* a bostryx.

Hell /*hel*/ *n* the place of the dead in general; the place or state of punishment of the wicked after death; the abode of evil spirits; the powers of Hell; (the following meanings without *cap*) any place of vice or misery; a place of turmoil; (a state of) supreme misery or discomfort; anything causing misery, pain or destruction; ruin, havoc; commotion, uproar; severe censure or chastisement; used in various colloquial phrases expressing displeasure, emphasis, etc (as in *what in hell?, get the hell out of here, I wish to hell he'd go away*); a gambling house; a space under a tailor's board, or other receptacle for waste; the den in certain games. ◆*interj* (*inf*) expressing displeasure or used for mildly shocking effect. ◆*vi* to live or act in a wild or dissolute fashion (usu with *around*). [OE *hel, hell*; ON *hel*, Ger *Hölle*; perh related to *Hel*, Norse goddess of the dead]

■ **hell'er** *n* an obstreperous troublesome person. **hellion** /*hel'yən*/ *n* a troublesome, mischievous child, or other troublesome person (*esp US*; *inf*; possibly related to **hallion**); someone given to diabolical conduct. **hell'ish** *adj* relating to or like hell; very bad, severe, etc; often used to express displeasure (*inf*). **hell'ish** or **hell'ishly** *adv* in the manner of hell; often used intensively (*inf*). **hell'ishness** *n*. **hell'ova** or **hell'uva** *adj* (*inf*) hell of a (see below). ◆*adv* very. **hell'ward** *adj* and *adv* towards hell. **hell'wards** *adv*.

◻ **hell'bender** *n* a large American salamander; a reckless or debauched person. **hell'-bent** *adj* (with *on*) recklessly determined. ◆*adv* with reckless determination. **hell'-black** *adj* (*Shakesp*) black as hell. **hell'-born** *adj* born in hell; of hellish origin. **hell'-box** *n* a receptacle for broken type. **hell'-bred** *adj*. **hell'-broth** *n* (*Shakesp*) a concoction boiled up for malignant purposes. **hell'cat** *n* a malignant hag; a violent-tempered woman. **hell'-fire** or **hell'fire** *n* the fire of hell; punishment in hell. **hell'-gate** *n* the entrance into hell. **hell'-hated** *adj* (*Shakesp*) hated or abhorred as hell. **hell'hole** *n* the pit of hell; an evil, frightening place. **hell'hound** *n* a hound of hell; an agent of hell. **hell'-kite** *n* (*Shakesp*) a kite of infernal breed. **hell'raiser** *n* a person who enjoys boisterous debauchery. **hell'raising** *n* and *adj*. **hell's angel** *n* (often with *cap*) a member of a gang of motorcyclists, *orig* notorious for violent or antisocial behaviour. **hell's bells**, **teeth**, etc *interj* (*inf*) expressions of irritation, surprise, etc.

■ The following phrases are all informal: **all hell breaks** (or **is let**) **loose** there is chaos or uproar. **as hell** absolutely; very. **beat**, **kick**, **knock**, etc (**the**) **hell out of** to beat, etc severely. **come hell or high water** no matter what difficulties may be encountered. **for the hell of it** for fun or adventure. **from hell** considered to be the worst of their kind, as in *neighbours from hell*. **give someone hell** to punish, castigate or rebuke someone severely; to cause someone pain or misery. **hell for leather** at a furious pace. **hell of a** great, terrific, very, as in *at a hell of a speed, a hell of a row*. **hell to pay** serious trouble, unpleasant consequences. **like hell** very much, very hard, very fast, etc; (also **the hell** or **hell**) used to express strong disagreement or refusal (as in *like hell I will!, the hell I will!, will I hell!*). **not have a cat in hell's chance** see under **cat**[1]. **not have a hope in hell** to have no hope at all. **play hell with** see under **play**. **raise hell** see under **raise**[1]. **to hell with** an expression of angry disagreement with or intention to ignore, etc (someone or something). **what the hell** it does not matter; who cares?; used to express surprise.

hell[1] /*hel*/ *vt* obsolete form of **hele**. [See **hele**]

■ **hell'ier** *n* (*dialect*) a slater; a tiler; a thatcher.

hell[2] see **Hell**.

he'll /*hēl*/ contraction for **he will** and **he shall**.

hellacious /*he-lā'shəs*/ (*N Am inf*) *adj* very bad; terrible; enormous; remarkable; excellent (*sl*). [From **Hell** and adj sfx *-acious*]

Helladic /*he-lad'ik*/ *adj* Greek; of the Greek mainland Bronze Age, answering roughly to Minoan. [Gr *Helladikos* Greek, from *Hellas* Greece]

hellbender see under **Hell**.

hellebore /*hel'i-bör*/ *n* any plant of the genus *Helleborus*, of the buttercup family (such as *black hellebore* or Christmas rose, *stinking hellebore, green hellebore*); any plant of the genus *Veratrum* of the lily family (*American, false*, or *white hellebore*, known also as Indian poke or itchweed); the winter aconite (*winter hellebore*); the rhizome and roots of these prepared as a drug. [Gr *helleboros*]

■ **hell'eborine** /*-īn* or *-in*/ *n* an orchid of the genus *Epipactis*.

Hellene /*hel'ēn*/ *n* a Greek. [Gr *Hellēn* a Greek; also the son of Deucalion]

■ **Hellēn'ic** (or /*-en'*/) *adj* Greek. **Hell'enism** *n* a Greek idiom; the Greek spirit; Greek nationality; conformity to Greek ways, *esp* in language. **Hell'enist** *n* someone skilled in the Greek language; a person who adopted Greek ways and language, *esp* a Jew. **Hellenist'ic** or **Hellenist'ical** *adj* relating to the Hellenists; relating to the Greeks, the Greek language and Greek culture, affected by foreign influences after the time of Alexander. **Hellenist'ically** *adv*. **hell'enize** or **-ise** /*-in-īz*/ *vi* (often with *cap*) to conform, or tend to conform, to Greek usage. ◆*vt* to make Greek.

heller[1] /*hel'ər*/ *n* a small coin probably first made at *Hall* in Swabia, formerly used in Austria (worth one hundredth of a crown) and

Germany (worth half a pfennig), and still in use in the Czech Republic (see **haler**).

heller[2] see under **Hell**.

Hellerwork /*hel'ər-wûrk*/ *n* the therapeutic and preventive use of manipulation, exercise and discussion to improve posture, breathing and body movement. [J *Heller* (born 1940), US aerospace engineer]

hellgrammite or **hellgramite** /*hel'grə-mīt*/ *n* a large American neuropterous larva, used as bait by bass-fishers. [Origin unknown]

hellicat /*hel'i-kat*/ (*Scot*) *adj* giddy-headed; flighty. ◆*n* a wicked creature. [Origin obscure]

hellier see under **hell**[1].

hellion, **hellish**, etc, **hell-kite** see under **Hell**.

hello /*hə-* or *he-lō'*/, **hallo** /*hə-* or *ha-lō'*/ or **hullo** /*hə-* or *hu-lō'*/ *interj* used in greeting, answering a telephone, accosting, calling attention; also expressing surprise, discovery, becoming aware, scorn. ◆*n* (pl **hellōs'**, **hallōs'** or **hullōs'**) a call of hello. ◆*vi* to call hello. [Variant of MFr *hola, ho* a cry drawing attention, and *la* there]

hellova, **helluva**, **hellward**, etc see under **Hell**.

helm[1] /*helm*/ *n* steering apparatus; a position of control, *esp* in the phrase *at the helm*. ◆*vt* to direct, steer. [OE *helma*; ON *hjälm* a rudder, Ger *Helm* a handle]

■ **helm'er** *n* (*inf*) the director of a film. **helm'less** *adj*.

◻ **helms'man** *n* a steersman.

helm[2] see **helmet**.

helmet /*hel'mit*/ or (*archaic* or *poetic*) **helm** *n* a covering of armour for the head; any similar protective covering for the head; anything resembling a helmet, such as a cloud on a mountain top, the top of a guinea-fowl's head, the hooded upper lip of certain flowers. [OE *helm*; Ger *Helm*; cf **hele**]

■ **hel'meted** or (*archaic* or *poetic*) **helmed** *adj*.

◻ **hel'met-shell** *n* a gastropod of the genus *Cassis*, having a thick heavy shell with bold ridges.

helminth /*hel'minth*/ *n* a worm. [Gr *helmins, -inthos* a worm]

■ **helminthī'asis** *n* infestation with worms. **helmin'thic** *adj* relating to worms. **helmin'thoid** *adj* worm-shaped. **helmintholog'ic** or **helmintholog'ical** *adj*. **helminthol'ogist** *n*. **helminthol'ogy** *n* the study of worms, *esp* parasitic ones. **helminth'ous** *adj* infested with worms.

Helodea same as **Elodea**.

helot /*hel'ət*/ *n* one of a class of serfs among the ancient Spartans, deliberately humiliated and liable to massacre (*hist*); a serf (*hist*); a plant or animal living symbiotically with another in a subject relationship (*biol*). [Gr *Heilōtēs*, also *Heilōs, -ōtos*]

■ **hel'otage** *n* the state of a helot. **hel'otism** *n*. **hel'otry** *n* the whole body of the helots; any class of slaves.

help /*help*/ *vt* (pat **helped** or (*archaic*) **hōlp**; *pap* **helped** or (*archaic*) **hōlp'en**) to contribute towards the success of, aid or assist; to give means for doing anything; to relieve the wants of; to provide or supply with a portion; to deal out; to remedy; to mitigate; to prevent, to keep from. ◆*vi* to give assistance; to contribute. ◆*n* means or strength given to another for a purpose; assistance; relief; someone who assists; a hired servant, *esp* domestic; an employee. [OE *helpan*, pat *healp* (pl *hulpon*), pap *holpen*; ON *hjälpa*; Ger *helfen*]

■ **help'able** *adj*. **help'er** *n* someone who helps; an assistant; an assistant minister (*archaic*); a biological entity that facilitates the action of another, eg a plasmid that provides a replicative function (*biol*). **help'ful** *adj* giving help; useful. **help'fully** *adv*. **help'fulness** *n*. **help'ing** *adj* giving help or support. ◆*n* a portion served at a meal. **help'less** *adj* without ability to do things for oneself; wanting assistance; destitute (*obs*); giving no help (*Shakesp*); that cannot be helped (*Spenser*). **help'lessly** *adv*. **help'lessness** *n*.

◻ **help'desk** *n* a department of an organization that provides a support service by means of a helpline (qv below). **helper T lymphocyte** or **helper T cell** *n* (*immunol*) a thymus-derived lymphocyte which co-operates with B lymphocytes to enable them to produce an antibody when stimulated by an antigen. **helping hand** *n* assistance; a long-handled device used for reaching and gripping objects that one cannot reach by hand. **help'line** *n* an often free telephone line by means of which people with a particular problem may contact advisers who will help them deal with it. **help'mate** *n* (a modification of **help'meet**, itself formed from the phrase in the Bible (Genesis 2.18), 'an help meet for him') a helper, *specif* a wife.

■ **cannot help** (or **be helped**) cannot avoid (or be avoided). **cannot help oneself** cannot refrain from or resist doing something. **help off with** to aid in taking off, disposing or getting rid of. **help oneself** (**to**) to take for oneself without waiting for offer or authority. **help on with** to help to put on. **help out** to eke out; to supplement; to assist. **more than one can help** (illogically but idiomatically) more than is necessary. **so help me** (**God**) a form of solemn oath; on my word.

■ words derived from main entry word; ◻ compound words; ■ idioms and phrasal verbs

helter-skelter /hel'tər-skel'tər/ adv in a confused hurry; tumultuously. ◆ n a confused medley; disorderly motion; a fairground or playground spiral slide. ◆ adj confused. [Imit]
■ **hel'ter-skel'teriness** n.

helve /helv/ n the handle of an axe or similar tool. ◆ vt to provide with a helve. [OE helfe (hielfe) a handle]
❑ **helve'-hammer** n a tilt hammer.

Helvetic /hel-vet'ik/ or **Helvetian** /hel-vē'shən/ adj Swiss. [L Helvētia Switzerland]
■ **helvé'tium** n a superseded name for astatine.
❑ **Helvetic Confessions** n pl two confessions of faith drawn up by the Swiss theologians in 1536 and 1566.

hem¹ /hem/ n an edge or border; a border doubled down and sewn. ◆ vt (**hemm'ing**; **hemmed**) to form a hem on; to edge. [OE hemm a border]
❑ **hem'line** n the height or level of the hem of a dress, skirt, etc. **hem'stitch** n the ornamental finishing of the inner side of a hem, made by pulling out several threads adjoining it and drawing together in groups the cross-threads by successive stitches. ◆ vt to embroider with such stitches.
■ **hem in** to surround closely.

hem² /hem or hm/ n and interj a sort of half-cough to draw attention. ◆ vi (**hemm'ing**; **hemmed**) to utter this sound. [Sound of clearing the throat]

hem³ /əm or həm/ (obs) pronoun them; to them. [See **'em**]

hem⁴ see **haem** under **haem-**.

hem- see **haem-**.

hemal see **haemal** under **haem-**.

he-man see under **he**.

hemat- see **haem-**.

heme¹ /hēm/ (Spenser) adv same as **home**.

heme² see **haem** under **haem-**.

hemeralopia /hem-ə-rə-lō'pi-ə/ n day-blindness; vision requiring dim light; sometimes misapplied to night-blindness. [Gr hēmerā day, alaos blind, and ōps eye]

Hemerobaptist /hem-ə-rō-bap'tist/ n a member of an ancient Jewish sect that practised daily baptism; a Mandaean. [Gr hēmerā day, and baptistēs a baptizer]

Hemerocallis /hem-ə-rō-kal'is/ n a day lily. [Gr hēmerokalles, from hēmerā day, and kallos beauty]

hemi- /hem-i-/ combining form used to denote half. [Gr hēmi- half]
■ **hemial'gia** n (Gr algos pain) pain confined to one side of the body. **hemianops'ia** n (Gr an-, privative, and opsis sight) blindness in half of the field of vision (also **hemianō'pia**, **hemiō'pia** or **hemiop'sia**). **hemianop'tic** or **hemiop'ic** adj. **hemicellulose** /-sel'ū-lōs/ n a type of polysaccharide, found in plant cell walls, which can be more easily broken down than cellulose. **Hemichordata** /-kör-dā'tə/ or **Hemichorda** /-kör'də/ n pl a group of wormlike marine animals with rudimentary notochord, including Balanoglossus, believed by many to represent the ancestors of the vertebrates. **hemicrania** /-krā'ni-ə/ n (Gr hēmikrāniā, from krānion skull, head) headache confined to one side. **hemicrys'talline** adj (petrology) consisting of crystals in a glassy or partly glassy groundmass. **hem'icycle** n (Gr kyklos wheel) a semicircle; a semicircular structure. **hemicy'clic** adj (bot) having some parts in whorls, some in spirals. **hemidemisem'iquaver** n (music) a note equal in time to half a demisemiquaver. **hemihē'drism** or **hemihē'dry** /-dri/ n (Gr hedrā a seat) a property of crystals of being **hemihē'dral**, or having half the number of symmetrically arranged planes occurring on a holohedron. **hemihē'dron** n. **hemihy'drate** n a hydrate with two parts of the compound for one of water. **hemimetabolous** /-met-ab'əl-əs/ or **hemimetabolic** /-bol'ik/ adj (of insects) developing gradually without a pupal stage. **hemimorph'ic** adj (Gr morphē form) having a polar axis, dissimilar at the two ends. **hemimorph'ism** n. **hemimorph'ite** n the mineral electric calamine, hydrous zinc silicate, which forms crystals whose ends are different in form and pyroelectric property. **hemiō'lia** or **hemiō'la** n (Gr hēmiolios half as much again, from holos whole) (in medieval music) a perfect fifth; also, a triplet. **hemiolic** /-ol'/ adj in or based on the ratio of 3 to 2, as the paeonic foot. **hemionus** /hi-mī'on-əs/ or **hemione** /hem'i-ōn/ n (Gr hēmionos mule, from onos an ass) an Asiatic wild ass, the kiang or the dziggetai. **hemipar'asite** n an organism that is partly parasitic, partly independent; a saprophyte capable of living parasitically. **hemiparasit'ic** adj. **hemiparasit'ically** adv. **hemiplegia** /-plē'ji-ə or -gi-ə/ n (Gr plēgē a blow) paralysis of one side only. **hemiplegic** /-plej'/ or -plēj'/ adj and n. **hem'ipode** n (Gr pous, podos foot) the button quail. **Hemip'tera** n pl (Gr pteron a wing) an order of insects, variously defined, with wings (when present) often half leathery, half membranous, ie the bugs, cicadas, greenfly, cochineal insect, etc. **hemip'teral**, **hemip'teran** or **hemip'terous** adj. **hem'ispace** n the area to one side, either left or right, of the body.

hem'isphere n (Gr hēmisphairion, from sphaira a sphere) a half-sphere divided by a plane through the centre; half of the globe or a map of it (**eastern and western hemispheres** the eastern and western halves of the terrestrial globe, the former traditionally including Europe, Asia and Africa and the latter, the Americas; **northern and southern hemispheres** the northern and southern halves of the terrestrial globe divided by the equator); one of the two divisions of the cerebrum. **hemispher'ic** or **hemispher'ical** adj. **hemisphē'roid** n the half of a spheroid. **hemisphēroi'dal** adj. **hemistich** /hem'i-stik/ n (Gr hēmistichion, from stichos a line) one of the two divisions of a line of verse; half a line, an incomplete or unfinished line; an epodic line or refrain. **hem'istichal** (or /-is'/) adj. **hem'itrope** n (Gr tropos a turn) a form of twin crystal in which one twin is as if rotated through two right angles from the position of the other. **hem'itrope**, **hemitropal** /hem-it'rə-pl/, **hemitropic** /-trop'/ or **hemit'ropous** adj. **hemizy'gous** adj (see **zygote**) having only one representative of a gene or chromosome, as male mammals, which have only one X-chromosome.

hemina /hi-mī'nə/ (obs) n a measure for liquids, about half a pint; a measure for corn, of varying amount. [L, from Gr hēmina, from hēmi- half]

hemlock /hem'lok/ n a poisonous spotted umbelliferous plant (Conium maculatum); the poison obtained from it; extended to other umbelliferous plants, eg water hemlock (genus Cicuta); (also **hemlock spruce**) a N American tree (genus Tsuga) whose branches are thought to resemble hemlock leaves. [OE hymlīce (Kentish hemlīc)]

hemo- see **haem-**.

hemp /hemp/ n a plant (Cannabis sativa), classified by some as belonging to the mulberry family, Moraceae, but by many now placed in a separate family, Cannabinaceae, yielding a coarse fibre, a narcotic drug, and an oil; the fibre itself; the drug; a similar fibre derived from various other plants (eg Manila, sisal, sunn hemp). [OE henep, hænep; cf **cannabis**]
■ **hemp'en** adj made of hemp; relating to the hangman's noose or hanging (archaic). **hemp'y** adj like hemp; roguish; romping. ◆ n (Scot) a rogue; a romp; a tomboy.
❑ **hemp agrimony** n a composite plant (Eupatorium cannabinum) with hemp-like leaves. **hempen caudle** see under **caudle**. **hempen widow** n the widow of a man who has been hanged. **hemp'-nettle** n a coarse bristly labiate weed (genus Galeopsis). **hemp'-palm** n a palmetto (yielding fibre). **hemp'seed** n the oil-yielding seed of hemp, a bird's food; gallows-bird (Shakesp).

hen /hen/ n a female bird; a female domestic fowl; applied (loosely) to any domestic fowl; the female of certain fishes and crustaceans; a woman or girl (facetiously, disrespectfully, or endearingly); a faint-hearted person. ◆ vi (Scot) to lose courage or resolution; to balk. ◆ vt (Scot) to challenge to an act of daring. ◆ adj female; composed of women. [OE henn, fem of hana a cock; Ger Henne (Hahn cock)]
■ **henn'er** n (Scot) a challenge to an act of daring; a somersault or other gymnastic feat. **henn'ery** n a place where fowls are kept. **henn'y** n a hen-like cock. ◆ adj hen-like.
❑ **hen'-and-chick'ens** n a name for various plants, esp a garden daisy with small heads surrounding the main head. **hen'bane** n a poisonous plant (Hyoscyamus niger) of the nightshade family. **hen'bit** n the ivy-leaved speedwell; a species of dead-nettle. **hen'-coop** n a coop for a hen. **hen'-court** n an enclosure for fowls. **hen'-driver** n a hen harrier. **hen'-flesh** n gooseflesh. **hen harrier** n a bird of prey, the common harrier. **hen'-hearted** adj faint-hearted; timid. **hen house** n a house for fowls. **hen night** same as **hen party** below. **hen-pad(d)le** or **hen-paidle** see under **paddle³**. **hen party** or **night** n a party for women only, esp one held for a woman about to be married. **hen'peck** vt (of a wife) to domineer over (her husband). ◆ n a henpecked husband; henpecking. **hen'pecked** adj. **henpeck'ery** n. **hen'-pen** n (Scot) manure from a hen house. **hen roost** n a roosting-place for fowls. **hen run** n an enclosure for fowls. **hen'-toed'** adj with toes turned in. **hen'-wife** n a woman in charge of poultry. **hen'-witted** adj brainless, silly.
■ **hen on a hot girdle** (chiefly Scot) someone who is in a jumpy or nervous state.

hence /hens/ (formal or archaic) adv from this place; from this time onwards; in the future; from this cause or reason; from this origin. ◆ interj away!, begone! [ME hennes, formed with genitive ending from henne, from OE heonan, from the base of **he**; Ger hinnen, hin hence: so L hinc hence, from hic this]
■ **hence'forth** or **hencefor'ward** adv from this time forth or forward.

henchman /hench'mən or hensh'mən/ n (also **hench'person**; fem **hench'woman**) a servant; a page; a right-hand man; an active political partisan, esp from self-interest; a supporter through thick and thin. [OE hengest a horse (Ger Hengst), and man; not connected with **haunch¹**]

hend¹ /hend/ (obs) adj convenient; skilful; gracious; courteous. [Appar OE gehende handy, from hand]

hend² /hend/ (Spenser) vt to seize, to grasp. [OE gehendan or ON henda; cf hand]

hendecagon /hen-dek'ə-gon/ n a plane figure of eleven angles and eleven sides. [Gr hendeka eleven, and gōniā an angle]
■ **hendecagonal** /-ag'ən-l/ adj.

hendecasyllable /hen'dek-ə-sil-ə-bl/ n a metrical line of eleven syllables. [Gr hendeka eleven, and syllabē a syllable]
■ **hendecasyllabic** /-ab'ik/ adj.

hendiadys /hen-dī'ə-dis/ n a rhetorical figure in which a notion, normally expressible by an adjective and a noun, is expressed by two nouns joined by and or another conjunction, as clad in cloth and green for clad in green cloth. [Medieval L, from Gr hen dia dyoin, literally, one by two]

henequen, also **henequin** and **heniquin** /hen'ə-kən/ n a Mexican agave; its leaf-fibre, sisal hemp, used for cordage. [Sp henequén, jeniquén]

henge¹ /henj/ (Spenser) n axis. [hinge]

henge² /henj/ n a circular or oval area enclosed by a bank and internal ditch, often containing burial chambers, or a circular, oval or horseshoe-shaped construction of large upright stones or wooden posts. [Back-formation from Stonehenge, a famous example, in OE Stānhengist hanging stones]

heniquin see **henequen**.

Henle see **loop of Henle** under **loop¹**.

henna /hen'ə/ n a small Oriental shrub (genus Lawsonia) of the loosestrife family, with fragrant white flowers; a red or reddish-orange pigment made from its leaves, used for dyeing the nails and hair and for skin decoration. ◆ vt to dye or stain with henna. [Ar hinnā']
■ **hennaed** /hen'əd/ adj dyed with henna.

henner, etc see under **hen**.

hennin /hen'in/ n a steeple hat with a veil hanging from it, worn by French women in the 15c. [Obs Fr]

henny see under **hen**.

henotheism /hen'ō-thē-i-zm/ n a doctrine, between polytheism and monotheism, involving belief in the existence of more than one god, but with only one supreme or specially venerated as the god of one's household or tribe, etc. [Gr heis, henos one, and theos god]
■ **henothe'ist** n. **henotheist'ic** adj.

henotic /he-not'ik/ adj tending to unify or reconcile. [Gr henōtikos, from heis, henos one]

henpeck, etc see under **hen**.

henry /hen'ri/ n (pl **hen'ries** or **hen'rys**) a derived SI unit, the unit of inductance (symbol **H**), such that an electromotive force of one volt is induced in a circuit by current variation of one ampere per second. [Joseph Henry (1797–1878), American physicist]

hent /hent/ (obs) vt (pap and pat **hent**) to grasp; to take; to snatch away, carry off; to reach. ◆ n a grasp (obs); perhaps a conception, intention, perhaps an opportunity (Shakesp). [OE hentan to seize]

heortology /hē-ör-tol'ə-ji/ n the study of religious feasts. [Gr heortē a feast, and logos discourse]
■ **heortological** /-ə-loj'i-kl/ adj. **heortol'ogist** n.

hep¹ /hep/ (sl) adj (**hepp'er**; **hepp'est**) knowing, informed or well abreast of fashionable knowledge and taste, esp in the field of jazz. [Perh hep left (command in drilling), with ideas of being in step]
❑ **hep'-cat** or **hep'ster** n (sl) a hipster (qv under **hip⁴**).
■ **be** (or **get**) **hep** to to be (or become) informed about.

hep² /hep/ n see under **hip²**.

hepar /hē'pär/ n an old name for liver-coloured compounds of sulphur. [Gr hēpar, hēpatos liver]
■ **heparin** /hep'ə-rin/ n a complex substance formed in tissues of liver, lung, etc that delays clotting of blood, used in medicine and surgery. **hepatec'tomy** n excision of the liver. **hepatic** /hi-pat'ik/ adj relating to or acting on the liver; relating to liverworts; liver-coloured. ◆ n a liverwort; a hepatic medicine. **Hepat'ica** n a genus of plants with three-lobed leaves, once classed as a section of the Anemone genus; the common liverwort Marchantia polymorpha; (in pl) **Hepat'icae** /-sē/ liverworts. **hepat'ical** adj. **hepaticolog'ical** adj. **hepaticol'ogist** n a person who studies liverworts. **hepaticol'ogy** n. **hep'atite** n a variety of barytes with a sulphureous stink. **hepati'tis** n inflammation of the liver usually referring to **viral hepatitis** which can be divided into: (1) **hepatitis A**, which is caused by a virus encountered in contaminated food and drink (also inf **jaundice**); (2) **hepatitis B**, or **serum hepatitis**, which is caused by a virus introduced by contaminated blood products or hypodermic syringes, etc; (3) **hepatitis Non-A, Non-B**, or **Non-A, Non-B hepatitis**, which is

caused by a virus transmitted in contaminated blood products. All these diseases cause fever, jaundice, and general weakness. **hepatization** or **-s-** /-ə-tī-zā'shən/ n a liver-like solidification of tissue as of the lungs in pneumonia. **hep'atize** or **-ise** vt to convert into a substance resembling liver; to impregnate with sulphuretted hydrogen (obs). **hepat'ocyte** n a liver cell. **hepatol'ogist** n a person who specializes in liver diseases. **hepatol'ogy** n. **hepatō'ma** n (pl **hepatō'mas** or **hepatō'mata**) a cancer of the liver. **hepatomeg'aly** n abnormal enlargement of the liver. **hepatos'copy** n divination by inspection of the livers of animals. **hepatotox'ic** (or /-pat'/) adj damaging the liver.

hephthemimer /hef-thi-mim'ər/ (classical prosody) n seven half-feet. [Gr hepta seven, hēmi- half, and meros part]
■ **hephthemim'eral** adj (of a caesura) occurring in the middle of the fourth foot.

Hepplewhite /hep'l-wīt/ adj belonging to a school of graceful furniture design typified by George Hepplewhite (died 1786), who favoured the use of curves, esp in shield-shaped chair-backs.

hepster see under **hep¹**.

hept /hept/ (Spenser) for **heaped**.

hepta- /hep-tə- or hep-ta-/ combining form denoting seven. [Gr hepta seven]
■ **hep'tachlor** /-klör/ n a very toxic pesticide, $C_{10}H_5Cl_7$, which forms the even more toxic **heptachlor epoxide**, $C_{10}H_5Cl_7O$, in the soil and in animal and plant tissue. **hep'tachord** n (Gr chordē string) in Greek music, a diatonic series of seven tones, containing five whole steps and one half step; an instrument with seven strings; an interval of a seventh. **hep'tad** n (Gr heptas, heptados) a group of seven; an atom, radical or element having a combining power of seven (chem). **hep'tagon** n (Gr heptagōnos, from gōniā an angle) a plane figure with seven angles and seven sides. **heptag'onal** adj. **Heptagynia** /-jin'i-ə/ n pl (Gr gynē woman, female) in Linnaean classification, an order of plants (in various classes) having seven styles. **heptag'ynous** adj. **heptahē'dron** n (Gr hedrā a base) a solid bounded by seven plane faces. **Heptam'eron** n (Gr hēmerā a day) a book containing the transactions of seven days, esp the collection of stories told in seven days bearing the name of Queen Margaret of Navarre (1492–1549). **heptam'erous** adj (Gr meros part) having parts in sevens. **heptam'eter** n (Gr metron measure) a verse of seven measures or feet. **Heptan'dria** n pl (Gr anēr, andros a man, male) a Linnaean class of plants having seven stamens. **heptan'drous** adj with seven stamens. **hep'tane** n a hydrocarbon (C_7H_{16}) with many isomers, seventh of the alkane series. **heptapod'ic** adj. **heptap'ody** n (Gr pous, podos foot) a verse of seven feet. **hep'tarch** or **hep'tarchist** n a ruler in a heptarchy. **heptar'chic** adj. **heptarchy** /hep'tär-ki/ n (Gr archē sovereignty) a government by seven persons; a country governed by seven; a misleading term for a once supposed system of seven English kingdoms, these being Wessex, Sussex, Kent, Essex, East Anglia, Mercia, and Northumbria. **heptasyllab'ic** adj seven-syllabled. **Hep'tateuch** /-tūk/ n (Gr teuchos instrument, volume) the first seven books of the Old Testament. **heptateuch'al** adj. **heptath'lete** n a competitor in a heptathlon. **heptath'lon** n (Gr athlon contest) a seven-event contest consisting of 100 metres hurdles, shot put, javelin, high jump, long jump, 200 metres sprint and 800 metres race. **heptaton'ic** adj (Gr tonos tone; music; of a scale) consisting of seven notes.

her¹ /hûr/ pronoun the genitive (or possessive adj), dative and accusative of the pronoun **she**; herself (reflexive; poetic or dialect); she (inf nominative). [OE hire, genitive and dative sing of hēo she]
❑ **her indoors** n (sl) one's wife.

her² /hûr/ (obs; Spenser) pronoun or possessive adj their. [OE hiera, hira, heora, genitive pl of **he**]

her. abbrev: heres (L), heir.

Hera /hē'rə/ (Gr myth) n the wife and sister of Zeus, identified by the Romans with Juno. [Gr]

Heraclean or **Heracleian** /her-ə-klē'ən/ adj relating to or associated with Heracles (Gr Hēraklēs), also known as Hercules.
■ **Her'aclid** n a person claiming such descent. **Heracli'dan** or **Heraclei'dan** adj relating to the Heracleidae or descendants of Heracles, the aristocracy of Sparta.

Heraclitean or **Heracleitean** /her-ə-klī'shē-ən/ adj relating to or associated with Heraclitus, a Greek philosopher of the 5c BC, who held that all things are in a state of flux, continually entering a new state of being.

herald /her'əld/ n (in ancient times) an officer who made public proclamations and arranged ceremonies; (in medieval times) an officer who had charge of all the etiquette of chivalry, keeping a register of the genealogies and armorial bearings of the nobles; an officer whose duty is to read proclamations, blazon the arms of the nobility, etc; a proclaimer; a forerunner; a name given to many newspapers; the red-breasted merganser (usually **her'ald-duck**).

◆ *vt* to be a sign of the approach of; to usher in; to proclaim. [OFr *herault*; of Gmc origin]

■ **heraldic** /*her*- or *hər-al'dik*/ *adj* of or relating to heralds or heraldry. **heral'dically** *adv*. **her'aldry** *n* the art or office of a herald; the science of recording genealogies and blazoning coats of arms. **her'aldship** *n*.

herb /*hûrb*/ or (old-fashioned or *US*) *ûrb*/ *n* a plant with no woody stem above ground, distinguished from a tree or shrub; a plant used in medicine; an aromatic plant used in cookery. [Fr *herbe*, from L *herba*]

■ **herba'ceous** *adj* relating to, composed of, containing, or of the nature of, herbs; like ordinary foliage leaves; *usu* understood to refer to tall herbs that die down in winter and survive in underground parts (*hortic*). **herb'age** *n* herbs collectively; herbaceous vegetation covering the ground; right of pasture. **herb'aged** *adj* covered with grass. **herb'al** *adj* composed of or relating to herbs; relating to the use of plants, eg medicinally. ◆ *n* a book containing descriptions of plants with medicinal properties, *orig* of all plants. **herb'alism** *n* herbal medicine, the use of (extracts of) roots, seeds, etc for medicinal purposes. **herb'alist** *n* a person who studies, collects or sells herbs or plants; a person who practises herbalism; an early botanist. **herb'ar** *n* (*Spenser*) a herb garden, arbour. **herbā'rian** *n* a herbalist. **herbā'rium** *n* (*pl* **herbā'riums** or **herbā'ria**) (a room, building, etc for) a classified collection of preserved plants. **herb'ary** *n* a garden of herbs. **herbed** *adj* flavoured with herbs. **herbicid'al** *adj*. **herb'icide** /-*i-sīd*/ *n* a substance for killing weeds, etc, *esp* a selective weedkiller. **herb'ist** *n* a herbalist. **herbiv'ora** /-*ə-rə*/ *n pl* grass-eating animals, *esp* ungulates. **herb'ivore** /-*vōr*/ *n*. **herbiv'orous** *adj* eating or living on grass or herbage. **herbiv'ory** *n*. **herb'less** *adj*. **herb'let** or **herb'elet** *n* (*Shakesp*) a small herb. **herb'orist** *n* a herbalist. **herborīzā'tion** or **-s-** *n*. **herb'orize** or **-ise** *vi* to botanize. **herb'ose** or **herb'ous** *adj* abounding with herbs. **herb'y** *adj* of or relating to herbs.

❑ **herbal medicine** *n* the therapeutic and restorative use, based on holistic patient assessment, of the healing properties of plants. **herbal tea** see **herb tea** below. **herb'-beer** *n* a substitute for beer made from herbs. **herb bennet** *n* (L *herba benedicta* blessed herb) avens. **herb Christopher** *n* baneberry. **herb garden** *n*. **herb Gerard** *n* ground elder. **herb-(of-)grace'** or **herb-of-repent'ance** *n* the common rue. **herb Paris** *n* a tetramerous plant (*Paris quadrifolia*) of the lily family. **herb Peter** *n* cowslip. **herb Robert** *n* stinking cranesbill (*Geranium robertianum*), a plant with small reddish-purple flowers. **herb tea** or **herbal tea** *n* a drink made by infusing aromatic herbs. **herb-trin'ity** *n* the pansy.

Herbartian /*hər-bärt'i-ən*/ *adj* of Johann Friedrich *Herbart* (1776–1841), German philosopher and paedagogic psychologist.

Herceptin® /*hûr-sep'tin*/ *n* a proprietary name for trastuzumab.

hercogamy or **herkogamy** /*hər-kog'ə-mi*/ (*bot*) *n* the prevention of self-pollination in flowers by the presence of some physical obstacle. [Gr *herkos* fence, and *gamos* marriage]

■ **hercog'amous** *adj*.

Herculean /*hûr-kū-lē'ən* or *-kū'li-ən*/ *adj* relating to or associated with *Hercules* /*hûr'kū-lēz*/ (Gr *Hēraklēs*); (without *cap*) extremely difficult or dangerous, as the twelve labours of Hercules; (without *cap*) of extraordinary strength and size.

❑ **Hercules beetle** *n* a gigantic S American lamellicorn beetle (*Dynastes hercules*), over 6 inches long, with a long horn on the thorax of the male and a smaller one on the head; (loosely) a related species, such as the *Dynastes gideon* of SE Asia. **Hercules' choice** *n* toil and duty chosen in preference to ease and pleasure (from a famous story in Xenophon's *Memorabilia*). **Hercules' club** *n* a stick of great size and weight; a West Indian tree (genus *Xanthoxylum*); a kind of gourd; a species of *Aralia*.

■ **Pillars of Hercules** two rocks flanking the entrance to the Mediterranean at the Strait of Gibraltar.

Hercynian /*hûr-sin'i-ən*/ *adj* of or relating to the forest-covered mountain region between the Rhine and the Carpathians or the mountain chains running NW and SE between Westphalia and Moravia, of Upper Carboniferous to Cretaceous date. [L *Hercynia* (*silva*) the Hercynian (forest)]

■ **her'cynite** *n* black spinel, aluminate of iron.

herd[1] /*hûrd*/ *n* a collective term for a company of animals, *esp* large animals, or of birds that habitually keep together; a group of domestic animals, *esp* cows or pigs, with or without a guardian; a stock of cattle; the people regarded as a mass, as acting from contagious impulse, or merely in contempt; the rabble. ◆ *vi* to associate (as if) in herds; to live like an animal in a herd. ◆ *vt* to put in a herd; to drive together. [OE *heord*; Ger *Herde*; cf **herd**[2]]

■ **herd'er** *n*.

❑ **herd'-book** *n* a pedigree book of cattle or pigs. **herd instinct** *n* the instinct that urges men or animals to act upon contagious impulses or to follow the herd. **herds'man** *n* a keeper of a herd.

herd[2] /*hûrd*/ *n* (*esp* in combination) a keeper of a herd or flock (of a particular animal, as in *goatherd*, *swineherd*, etc). ◆ *vt* to tend; to harbour. ◆ *vi* to act as herd. [OE *hirde*, *hierde*; Ger *Hirte*; cf **herd**[1]]

■ **herd'ess** *n fem* (*rare*).

❑ **herd'boy** *n* a boy who acts as shepherd, cowherd, etc; a cowboy. **herd'-groom** *n* (*archaic*) a herdsman; shepherd boy. **herd'man** *n* (*obs*) a herdsman.

herden /*hûr'dən*/ see under **hards**.

herd grass or **herd's grass** /*hûrd(z) gräs*/ (*US*) *n* timothy; redtop. [From John *Herd*, who observed timothy in New Hampshire, 1700]

herdic /*hûr'dik*/ *n* a low-hung two- or four-wheeled carriage with a back entrance and side seats. [P *Herdic* (1824–88), its inventor]

herdwick /*hûr'dwik*/ *n* a breed of Lake District sheep; a grazing ground (*obs*). [**herd**[2] and **wick**[2]]

here /*hēr*/ *adv* in, at or to this place; in the present life or state; at this point or time. ◆ *interj* calling attention to one's presence, or to what one is going to say. [OE *hēr*, from base of *hē* he; Du and Ger *hier*, Swed *här*]

■ **here'ness** *n* the fact of being here.

❑ **here'about** or **here'abouts** *adv* around or near this place; in this area. **hereaf'ter** *adv* after this, in some future time, life or state. ◆ *n* a future state; the afterlife. **hereat'** *adv* (*archaic*) at or by reason of this. **here'away** *adv* (*inf*) hereabout. **hereby'** *adv* not far off; by this. **herefrom'** *adv* from this; from this place. **herein'** *adv* (*formal*) contained in this letter, document, etc; in this respect. **hereinaf'ter** *adv* (*formal*) afterwards in this (document, etc). **hereinbefore'** *adv* (*formal*) before in this (document, etc). **herein'to** *adv* (*formal*) into this place, thing, matter, etc. **hereof'** *adv* (*formal*) of or concerning this. **hereon'** *adv* (*formal*) on or upon this. **hereto'** *adv* to this (*formal*); until this time (*Shakesp*); for this object. **heretofore'** *adv* (*formal*) before this time; formerly. **hereund'er** *adv* (*formal*) under this; below; following; by the authority of this (document, etc). **here'unto** (also /-*un'*/) *adv* (*formal*) to this point or time. **hereupon'** *adv* on this; immediately after this. **herewith'** *adv* with this; enclosed with this letter, etc.

■ **here and there** in this place, and then in that; in various places; thinly; irregularly. **here goes!** an exclamation indicating that the speaker is about to proceed with some proposed act or narration, etc. **here's to** I drink the health of. **here today, gone tomorrow** a comment on the transient, ephemeral nature of things. **here we are** (*inf*) this is what we are looking for; we have now arrived (at). **here we go again** (*inf*) the same undesirable situation is recurring. **here you are** (*inf*) this is what you want; this is something for you; this way. **neither here nor there** of no special importance; not relevant. **the here and now** the present time.

heredity /*hi-red'i-ti*/ *n* the transmission of recognizable characteristics to descendants; the sum of such characteristics transmitted; heritability. [L *hērēditās*, *-ātis*, from *hērēs*, *-ēdis* an heir]

■ **hereditabil'ity** *n*. **hered'itable** *adj* that may be inherited. **heredit'ament** /*her-id-*/ *n* any property that may pass to an heir. **heredità'rian** (also **heredità'rianist**) *n* an adherent of **heredità'rianism**, the view that heredity is the major factor in determining human and animal behaviour. **hered'itarily** *adv*. **hered'itariness** *n* the quality of being hereditary. **hered'itary** *adj* descending or coming by inheritance; transmitted to offspring; succeeding by inheritance; according to inheritance. **hered'itist** *n* a hereditarian.

Hereford /*her'i-fərd*/ *n* a breed of white-faced red cattle, originating in *Hereford*shire.

herefrom...to...**hereon** see under **here**.

Herero /*hə-rā'rō* or *her'ə-rō*/ *n* (*pl* **Hereros** or **Hereroes**) a Bantu people of Namibia; a member of this people; their language. ◆ *adj* of or relating to the Herero or their language.

heresy /*her'i-si*/ *n* belief contrary to the authorized teaching of the religious community to which one ostensibly belongs; an opinion opposed to the usual or conventional belief; heterodoxy. [OFr *heresie*, from L *haeresis*, from Gr *hairesis* the act of taking, choice, set of principles, school of thought, from *haireein* to take]

■ **heresiarch** /*he-rē'zi-ärk*/ *n* a leader of a heretical movement. **heresiog'rapher** *n* a person who writes about heresies. **heresiog'raphy** *n*. **heresiol'ogist** *n* a student of, or writer on, heresies. **heresiol'ogy** *n*. **heretic** /*her'ə-tik*/ *n* the upholder of a heresy; a person whose views are at variance with those of the majority. **heretical** /*hi-ret'i-kl*/ *adj*. **heret'ically** *adv*. **heret'icate** *vt* to denounce as heretical.

❑ **her'esy-hunt** *n* vexatious pursuit of a supposed heretic. **her'esy-hunter** *n*.

hereto...to...**herewith** see under **here**.

heriot /*her'i-ət*/ (*hist*) *n* a fine due to the lord of a manor on the death of a tenant, *orig* the tenant's best beast or chattel. [OE *heregeatu*, a military preparation, from *here* an army, and *geatwe* equipment]

■ **her'iotable** *adj*.

herisson /her'i-sən/ n a freely revolving beam fitted with spikes, erected for defence (hist); a hedgehog (heraldry). [Fr; see **urchin**]
■ **hérissé** /her'is-ā or ā'rē-sā/ adj (heraldry) bristled.

heritable /her'i-tə-bl/ adj that may be inherited. [OFr (h)eritable, from LL hērēditāre to inherit, from hērēditas; see **heredity**]
■ **heritabil'ity** n. **her'itably** adv. **her'itor** n a person who inherits; (in Scotland) a landholder obliged to contribute to the upkeep of the parish, esp the church. **her'itress** or **her'itrix** (pl **her'itresses**, **her'itrixes** or **heritri'cēs**) n a female heritor.
□ **heritable property** n (Scots law) real property, as opposed to movable property or chattels. **heritable security** n (Scots law) same as English mortgage.

heritage /her'i-tij/ n that which is inherited; inherited lot, condition of one's birth; anything transmitted from ancestors or past ages, esp historical buildings and the natural environment; the children (of God; Bible). [OFr (h)eritage, as **heritable**]
□ **heritage centre** n a museum displaying local artefacts and features of regional history.

herkogamy see **hercogamy**.

herl same as **harl**[1].

herling or **hirling** /hûr'ling/ (dialect) n a young sea trout, a finnock.

herm /hûrm/ or **herma** /hûr'mə/ n (pl **herms** or **hermae** /-ē/) a head or bust (originally of Hermes) on a square base, often double-faced.

hermandad /ûr-män-däd'/ n a confederation of the entire burgher class of Spain for police and judicial purposes, formed in 1282, and formally legalized in 1485. [Sp, brotherhood, from hermano brother, from L germānus]

hermaphrodite /hûr-maf'rə-dīt/ n a human being, animal or plant with the organs of both sexes, whether normally or abnormally; a compound of opposite qualities. ◆ adj uniting the characters of both sexes; combining opposite qualities. [Gr Hermaphrodītos, the son of Hermēs and Aphroditē, who grew together with the nymph Salmacis into one person]
■ **hermaphrodit'ic** or **hermaphrodit'ical** adj. **hermaphrodit'ically** adv. **hermaph'roditism** n the union of the two sexes in one body.
□ **hermaphrodite brig** n a brig square-rigged forward and schooner-rigged aft.

hermeneutic /hûr-mə-nū'tik/ or **hermeneutical** /-nū'tik-l/ adj interpreting; concerned with interpretation, esp of Scripture. [Gr hermēneutikos, from hermēneus an interpreter, from Hermēs]
■ **hermeneu'tically** adv. **hermeneu'tics** n sing the science of interpretation, esp of Scriptural exegesis; the study of human beings in society (philos). **hermeneu'tist** n.

Hermes /hûr'mēz/ n the herald of the Greek gods, patron of herdsmen, arts, eloquence, and thieves (Gr myth); the Egyptian god Thoth, identified with the Greek Hermes; a herm. [Gr Hermēs, identified by the Romans with Mercury]

hermetic /hûr-met'ik/ or **hermetical** /-met'ik-l/ adj perfectly closed, completely sealed; belonging in any way to the beliefs current in the Middle Ages under the name of Hermes, the Thrice Great; belonging to magic or alchemy, magical; obscure, abstruse. [Medieval L hermēticus, from Hermēs Trismegistos Hermes the thrice-greatest, the Greek name for the Egyptian Thoth, god of science, esp alchemy]
■ **hermet'ically** adv. **hermetic'ity** n. **hermet'ics** n sing the philosophy contained in the **hermetic books**, esoteric science; alchemy.
□ **hermetically sealed** adj closed completely; made airtight by melting the glass.

hermit /hûr'mit/ n a solitary religious ascetic; a person who lives a solitary life; a beadsman; a kind of hummingbird; a hermit crab. [ME eremite, through Fr and L from Gr erēmītēs, from erēmos solitary]
■ **her'mitage** n a hermit's cell; a retreat, a secluded abode; a secluded place; /er-mē-täzh/ a wine produced near Valence (Drôme) in France, where there was a supposed hermit's cell. **her'mitess** n a female hermit. **hermit'ical** adj.
□ **hermit crab** n a soft-bodied crustacean that inhabits a mollusc shell. **hermit thrush** n a N American thrush.

hern[1] /hûrn/ same as **heron**.

hern[2] /ûrn/ a dialect form for **hers**. [Appar from **her**, on the analogy of **mine**[1], **thine**]

hernia /hûr'ni-ə/ n a protrusion of an organ through the wall of the cavity containing it, esp of part of the viscera through the abdominal cavity; a rupture. [L]
■ **her'nial** adj. **her'niated** adj. **hernior'rhaphy** n (Gr rhaphē stitching, suture) the surgical repair of a hernia by an operation involving suturing. **herniot'omy** n (Gr tomē a cut) a cutting operation for the repair of a hernia.

hernshaw /hûrn'shö/ n see **heronshaw**.

Hero /hē'rō/ abbrev: Hazards of Electro-Magnetic Radiation to Ordnance, the danger that a missile warhead might explode, due to the accidental triggering of the electrical fuse by some form of electromagnetic discharge.

hero /hē'rō/ n (pl **hē'roes**) a man of distinguished bravery; any illustrious person; a person reverenced and idealized; the principal male figure, or the one whose life is the thread of the story, in a history, work of fiction, play, film, etc; orig a man of superhuman powers, a demigod. [Through OFr and L from Gr hērōs; poss related to L vir, OE wer a man, Sans vīra a hero]
■ **heroic** /hi-rō'ik/ adj befitting a hero; of or relating to heroes; epic; supremely courageous; using extreme or elaborate means to obtain a desired result, such as the preserving of life; on a superhuman scale, larger-than-life. ◆ n a heroic verse; (in pl) extravagant phrases, bombast; (in pl) unduly bold behaviour. **herō'ical** adj. **herō'ically** (or Milton **herō'icly**) adv. **herō'icalness** n. **herō'icness** n. **heroism** /her'ō-izm/ n the qualities of a hero; courage; boldness. **hē'roīze** or **-ise** vt to treat as a hero, make a hero of; to glorify. **hērō'on** n a temple dedicated to a hero; a temple-shaped tomb or monument. **hē'roship** n the state of being a hero.
□ **heroic age** n any semi-mythical period when heroes or demigods were represented as living among men. **heroic couplet** n a pair of rhyming lines of heroic verse. **herō'i-comic** or **herō'i-comical** adj consisting of a mixture of heroic and comic; high burlesque. **heroic poem** n an epic; a compromise between epic and romance which flourished in the 16c and 17c. **heroic remedy** n treatment that may kill or cure. **herō'ic-size** adj (in sculpture) larger than life-size, but less than colossal. **heroic verse** n the form of verse in which the exploits of heroes are celebrated (in classical poetry, the hexameter; in English, the iambic pentameter, esp in couplets; in French, the alexandrine). **he'ro-worship** n the worship of heroes; excessive admiration of the great, or of anyone. ◆ vt to worship a hero or heroes; to admire (someone) excessively.

heroin /her'ō-in/ n a derivative of morphine used in medicine, but highly addictive and commonly abused (also called **diacetylmor'phine**). [Said to be from Gr hērōs a hero, from its exhilarating effect]
□ **heroin chic** n (inf) a trend in the fashion industry in which models are used who portray a pale emaciated appearance thought to resemble that of heroin addicts.

heroine /her'ō-in/ n a woman of heroic character, a female hero; a woman admired and idealized; the central female character in a story, play, film, etc. [Fr héroïne, from Gr hērōīnē, fem of hērōs hero]

heroism, **heroize**, etc see under **hero**.

heron /her'ən/ n a large long-legged, long-necked wading bird, commonly grey or white in colour (Ardea or related genus). [OFr hairon, from OHGer heigir]
■ **her'onry** n a place where herons breed.

heronshaw, **heronsew** or **hernshaw** /her'ən-, hern'- or hûrn'shö or -shoo/ n a young heron; (esp dialect) a heron. [OFr herounçel, confounded with **shaw**[1]]

heroon, **heroship** see under **hero**.

herpes /hûr'pēz/ n a skin disease of various kinds, with spreading clusters of vesicles, or watery blisters, on an inflamed base. [Gr herpēs, from herpein to creep]
■ **herpetic** /-pet'ik/ adj relating to or resembling herpes; creeping.
□ **herpes simplex** n a sexually transmitted disease. **herpes virus** n any of various DNA viruses that cause herpes, shingles, etc. **herpes zoster** n shingles.

Herpestes /hûr-pes'tēz/ n the ichneumon or mongoose genus. [Gr herpēstēs, from herpein to creep]

herpetology /hûr-pi-tol'ə-ji/ n the study of reptiles and amphibians. [Gr herpeton a reptile, from herpein to creep]
■ **her'petofauna** n reptiles and amphibians. **her'petoid** adj reptile-like. **herpetolog'ic** or **herpetolog'ical** adj. **herpetolog'ically** adv. **herpetol'ogist** n.

Herr /her/ n (pl **Herr'en**) lord, master, the German term of address equivalent to sir, or (prefixed) Mr. [Ger]
□ **Herrenvolk** /her'en-fölk/ n (in Nazi politics) the master race.

herring /her'ing/ n a small silvery sea fish (Clupea harengus) of great commercial value, found moving in great shoals in northern waters. [OE hæring, hēring; cf Ger Hering]
■ **herr'inger** /-ing-ər/ n a person or boat employed in herring fishing.
□ **herr'ingbone** adj like the spine of a herring, applied to a kind of masonry in which the stones slope in different directions in alternate rows, to a zigzag stitch crossed at the corners, and to a crossed strutting, etc; (in skiing) of a method of climbing a slope, the skis being placed at an angle and leaving a herringbone-like pattern in the snow. ◆ vt to make in herringbone work; to make or mark with a herringbone pattern. ◆ vt and vi to climb (a slope) on skis by herringbone steps. **herr'ing-buss** n (hist) see under **buss**[2]. **herr'ing-fishery** n. **herring**

■ words derived from main entry word; □ compound words; ■ idioms and phrasal verbs

gull *n* a large white gull with silver-grey black-tipped wings. **herring pond** *n* (*facetious*) the ocean, *esp* the Atlantic.

■ **dead as a herring** quite certainly dead (because a herring out of water soon dies). **neither fish nor flesh nor good red herring** see under **fish**[1]. **packed like herring** (**in a barrel**) very closely packed. **red herring** see under **red**[1].

Herrnhuter /hûrn'hoo-tər/ *n* one of the Moravians or United Brethren, so called from their settlement in 1722 at *Herrnhut* in Saxony.

herry[1] see **hery**.

herry[2] /her'i/ (*Scot*) *vt* to harry. [**harry**]
■ **herr'iment** or **herr'yment** *n* spoliation; plunder.

hers /hûrz/ *pronoun* possessive of **she** (used without a noun).

hersall /hûr'səl/ (*Spenser*) *n* rehearsal.

herse /hûrs/ (*obs*) *n* a harrow; a spiked portcullis; a form of battle array; a hearse in various senses. [**hearse**]
■ **hersed** *adj* arranged in harrow form.

herself /hûr-self'/ *pronoun* an emphatic form for **she** or **her**[1]; the reflexive form of **her**; predicatively (or *n*) a woman in her real character; having command of her faculties; sane; in good form or normal condition; alone, by herself (*Scot*); the mistress of a house, owner of an estate, etc (*Scot*). [See **her** and **self**]

hership /hûr'ship/ (*Scot*) *n* plundering; plunder. [OE *here* army, or *hergan* to harry; cf ON *herskapr* warfare]

herstory /hûr'stə-ri/ *n* history regarded from a feminist point of view. [**her**[1] and **history**]

Herts. /härts/ *abbrev* : Hertfordshire.

hertz /hûrts/ *n* (pl **hertz**) a derived SI unit, the unit of frequency (symbol **Hz**), that of a periodic phenomenon of which the periodic time is one second (sometimes called **cycle per second** in the UK). [Heinrich *Hertz* (1857–94), German physicist]
■ **Hertz'ian** *adj* connected with Heinrich *Hertz* (see above).
❑ **Hertzian waves** *n pl* electromagnetic waves used in communicating information through space.

Hertzsprung-Russell diagram /hûrt'sprüng-rus'l dī'ə-gram/ (*astron*) *n* a graphical representation of the correlation between spectral type and luminosity for a sample of stars. [E *Hertzsprung* (1873–1967), Danish astronomer, and H Norris *Russell* (1877–1957), American astronomer]

hery, herye or **herry** /her'i/ (*Spenser*) *vt* to praise, to regard as holy. [OE *herian* to praise]

hes /hēz/ *n pl* plural of **he**.

he's /hēz/ a contraction of **he is** or **he has**.

Heshvan see **Hesvan**.

hesitate /hez'i-tāt/ *vi* to hold back or delay in making a decision; to be in doubt; to stammer. ◆ *vt* (*rare*) to express or utter with hesitation. [L *haesitāre, -ātum*, frequentative of *haerēre, haesum* to stick]
■ **hes'itance, hes'itancy** or **hesita'tion** *n* wavering; doubt; stammering; delay. **hes'itant** *adj* hesitating. **hes'itantly** *adv*. **hes'itatingly** *adv*. **hes'itative** *adj* showing hesitation. **hes'itator** *n*. **hes'itatory** *adj* hesitating.
❑ **hesitation form** *n* (*linguistics*) a sound used in speech when stammering or pausing, such as *er, eh* or *um*. **hesitation waltz** *n* a kind of waltz into which a pause and gliding step are introduced at intervals.

hesp /hesp/ a Scots form of **hasp**.

Hesper /hes'pər/ or **Hesperus** /-əs/ *n* Venus as the evening star. [Gr *hesperos* evening, western]
■ **Hesperian** /-pē'ri-ən/ *adj* western (*poetic*); Italian (from the Greek point of view); Spanish (from the Roman); of the Hesperides; of the skipper butterflies. ◆ *n* a westerner; a skipper butterfly. **hes'perid** /-pər-id/ *n* one of the Hesperides; a skipper butterfly. **Hesperides** /-per'i-dēz/ *n pl* (*Gr myth*) the sisters who guarded in their delightful gardens in the west the golden apples which Hera, on her marriage with Zeus, had received from Gaea. **hesperid'ium** *n* (*bot*) a fruit of the orange type. **Hesperiidae** /-ī'i-dē/ *n pl* a family of moth-like butterflies, the skippers. **Hes'peris** *n* the dame's-violet genus of Cruciferae, generally fragrant in the evening.

Hessian /hes'i-ən, sometimes hesh'(i-)ən/ *adj* relating to or associated with *Hesse* in Germany; mercenary (from the use of German mercenaries by the British Army in the American War of Independence) (*US*). ◆ *n* a native or citizen of Hesse; (without *cap*) a cloth made of jute; short for **Hessian boot**, a kind of long boot first worn by Hessian troops.
❑ **Hessian fly** *n* a midge whose larvae attack wheat stems in America, once believed to have been introduced in straw for the Hessian troops.

hessonite an amended form of **essonite**.

hest /hest/, also (*Spenser*) **heast** or **heaste** /hēst/ (*archaic*) *n* behest, command; vow. [OE *hæs* a command, from *hātan* to command]

hesternal /he-stûr'nəl/ *adj* of yesterday. [L *hesternus*]

Hesvan /hes'vän/ or **Heshvan** /hesh' or hhes(h)'/ *n* the second month of the Jewish civil year and the eighth month of the Jewish ecclesiastical year (also **Chesh'van** or **Ches'van**). [Heb]

Hesychast /hes'i-kast/ *n* a member of a 14c quietist sect of the Greek Church. [Gr *hēsychastēs*, from *hēsychos* quiet]
■ **Hes'ychasm** *n* their doctrines and practice. **Hesychas'tic** *adj* keeping silence.

het[1] /het/ *adj* a Scots form of **hot**[1]. [OE *hāt*]

het[2] /het/ (*Brit* and *N Am dialect*) *pap* for **heated**.
■ **het up** agitated; angry.

het[3] /het/ (*sl*) *n* and *adj* (a) heterosexual.

hetaera /hi-tē'rə/ or **hetaira** /he-tī'rə/ *n* (pl **hetae'rae, -rē/, hetae'ras, hetai'rai** /-rī/ or **hetai'ras**) in ancient Greece, a woman employed in public or private entertainment, for flute-playing, dancing, etc; a paramour; a prostitute or courtesan, *esp* of a superior class. [Gr *hetairā*, fem of *hetairos* companion; *hetair(e)iā* a club]
■ **hetae'rism** or **hetai'rism** *n* concubinage; the system of society that admitted hetaerae; a supposed primitive communal marriage. **hetaeris'mic** or **hetairis'mic** *adj*. **hetai'ria** *n* (*hist*) a club or society. **hetae'rist** or **hetai'rist** *n*.

hete see **hight**.

heter- /het-ər-/ or **hetero-** /het-ə-rō-, het-ə-rə- or -ro-/ *combining form* signifying other, different; one or other, often *opp* to *homo-* or *auto-*. [Gr *heteros* other, one or other]
■ **heterauxē'sis** *n* (Gr *auxēsis* growth; *bot*) unsymmetrical growth. **heteroblast'ic** *adj* (Gr *blastos* bud, germ) derived from different kinds of cells; showing indirect development. **het'eroblasty** *n* heteroblastic condition. **heterocarp'ous** *adj* (Gr *karpos* fruit) bearing fruit of more than one kind. **Heterocera** /-os'ər-ə/ *n pl* (Gr *keras* horn) a loose term for moths, distinguished from *Rhopalocera* (butterflies). **heterocercal** /-sûr'kl/ *adj* (Gr *kerkos* tail) having the vertebral column passing into the upper lobe of the tail, which is usually larger than the lower, as in sharks. **heterocercal'ity** or **het'erocercy** *n*. **heterochlamydeous** /-klə-mid'i-əs/ *adj* (Gr *chlamys, -ydos* mantle) having calyx and corolla distinctly different. **heterochromat'ic** or **heterochromous** /-krō'məs/ *adj* (Gr *chrōma* colour) having different or varying colours. **heterochromat'in** *n* (*biol*) relatively dense chromatin visible by microscopy in eukaryotic cell nuclei, which generally contains DNA sequences inactive in transcription. **heterochron'ic** *adj*. **heteroch'ronism** *n*. **heterochronist'ic** *adj*. **heteroch'ronous** *adj*. **heterochrony** /-ok'rə-ni/ *n* (Gr *chronos* time; *biol*) divergence from the normal time sequence in development. **het'eroclite** /-klīt/ *adj* (Gr *heteroklitos*, from *klitos* inflected, from *klīnein* to inflect; *grammar*) irregularly inflected; irregular; having forms belonging to different declensions. ◆ *n* a word irregularly inflected; anything irregular. **heteroclit'ic** or **heteroc'litous** *adj*. **heterocont** *n* see **heterokont** below. **heterocyclic** /-sī'klik/ *adj* (Gr *kyklos* a wheel) having a closed chain in which the atoms are not all alike (*chem*); having different numbers of parts in different whorls (*bot*). **heterodactyl** /-dak'til/ *n* (Gr *daktylos* toe) a heterodactylous bird. **heterodac'tylous** *adj* having the first and second toes turned backwards, as in trogons, and not the first and fourth as in parrots. **het'erodont** *adj* (Gr *odous, odontos* a tooth) having different kinds of teeth. **het'erodox** *adj* (Gr *heterodoxos* from *doxa* opinion, from *dokeein* to think) holding an opinion other than or different from the one generally received, *esp* in theology; heretical. **het'erodoxy** *n* heresy. **heterodu'plex** *adj* (**heteroduplex DNA** laboratory made double-stranded DNA in which some of the bases cannot pair). **het'erodyne** /-ō-dīn/ *adj* (Gr *dynamis* strength) in radio communication, applied to a method of imposing on a continuous wave another of slightly different length to produce beats (also *vt*). **heteroecious** /-ē'shəs/ *adj*. **heteroecism** /-ē'sizm/ *n* (Gr *oikos* a house; *biol*) a form of parasitism that requires two (*usu* unrelated) host species to complete the parasite's life cycle. **heterogametic** /-gə-met'ik/ *adj* (**heterogametic sex** the sex that is heterozygous for the sex-determining chromosome, the male in mammals, the female in birds). **heterog'amous** *adj*. **heterog'amy** *n* (Gr *gamos* marriage) alternation of generations (*biol*); reproduction by unlike gametes (*biol*); the presence of different kinds of flower (male, female, hermaphrodite, neuter, in any combination) in the same inflorescence (*bot*); indirect pollination (*bot*). **heterogenē'ity** *n*. **heterogeneous** /-jē'ni-əs/ *adj* (Gr *heterogenēs*, from *genos* a kind) different in kind; composed of parts of different kinds, *opp* to *homogeneous*. **heteroge'neously** *adv*. **heteroge'neousness** *n*. **heterogenesis** /-jen'i-sis/ *n* (Gr *genesis* generation; *biol*) the alternation of generations. **heterogenetic** /-ji-net'ik/ *adj*. **heterogeny** /-oj'ən-i/ *n* a heterogeneous group or assemblage; heterogenesis. **heterogonous** /-og'ə-/ *adj* (Gr *gonos* offspring, begetting) having flowers differing in length of stamens (*bot*); reproducing both sexually

and asexually (*biol*). **heterog'ony** *n*. **het'erograft** *n* a graft of tissue from a member of one species to a member of another species. **het'erokont** or **het'erocont** *n* (Gr *kontos* a punting pole) any member of the **Heterocont'ae** or yellow-green algae (eg the common *Conferva*), a class usually characterized by the pair of unequal cilia on the motile cells. **heterokont'an** *adj*. **heterologous** /-*ol'ə-gəs*/ *adj* not homologous; different; of different origin; abnormal. **heterol'ogy** *n* lack of correspondence between apparently similar structures due to different origin. **heterom'erous** *adj* (Gr *meros* part) having different numbers of parts in different whorls (*bot*); (of lichens) having the algal cells in a layer (*bot*); having unlike segments (*zool*). **heteromor'phic** or **heteromor'phous** *adj* (Gr *morphē* form) deviating in form from a given type; of different forms. **heteromor'phism** or **het'eromorphy** *n*. **heteron'omous** *adj* (Gr *nomos* law) subject to different laws; subject to outside rule or law, *opp* to *autonomous*. **heteron'omy** *n*. **het'eronym** *n* a word of the same spelling as another but of different pronunciation and meaning. **heteroousian** /het-ər-ō-oo'si-ən or -ow'/ or **heterousian** /-oo', -ow' or -ō-oo'/ *adj* (often with *cap*) (Gr *ousiā* being) of unlike essence; believing the Father and Son to be of different substance. ◆ *n* (often with *cap*) a holder of such belief. **heterophyllous** /-fil'əs/ *adj* (Gr *phyllon* a leaf) having different kinds of foliage leaf. **het'erophylly** *n*. **heteroplasia** /-plā'z(h)i-ə or -si-ə/ *n* (Gr *plasis* a forming) development of abnormal tissue or tissue in an abnormal place. **heteroplastic** /-plas'tik/ *adj*. **het'eroplasty** *n* heteroplasia; grafting of tissue from another person. **het'eropod** *n*. **Heterop'oda** *n pl* (Gr *pous, podos* a foot) pelagic gastropods in which the foot has become a swimming organ. **heteropō'lar** *adj* having alternating or opposite polarity. **Heterop'tera** *n pl* (Gr *pteron* a wing) a suborder of insects, the bugs, Hemiptera with fore and hind wings (when present) markedly different. **heterop'teran** *n* and *adj*. **heterop'terous** *adj*. **heteroscian** /het-ər-osh'i-ən/ *n* (Gr *skiā* a shadow) a dweller in a temperate zone, whose noon-shadow is always thrown one way, either north or south. **heterosex'ism** *n* the belief that homosexuality is a perversion, used as grounds for discrimination against homosexuals. **heterosex'ist** *n* someone who discriminates against homosexuals (also *adj*). **heterosex'ual** *adj* having or relating to sexual attraction towards the opposite sex. ◆ *n* a person who is sexually attracted to the opposite sex. **heterosexual'ity** *n*. **heterō'sis** *n* (*biol*) cross-fertilization; the increased size and vigour (relative to its parents) often found in a hybrid. **Heterosō'mata** *n pl* (Gr *sōma* (pl *sōmata*) a body) the flatfishes. **heterosō'matous** *adj*. **heterospecif'ic** *adj* (of blood or serum) belonging to different groups; derived from different species. **heterosporous** /-os'por-əs, or -pōr' or -pör'/ *adj* having different kinds of asexually-produced spores. **heteros'pory** *n*. **heterostroph'ic** *adj* (Gr *strophē* a turning) consisting of unequal strophes; coiled contrary to the usual direction. **heteros'trophy** *n*. **het'erostyled** or **heterosty'lous** *adj* having styles of different length in different flowers. **heterostyl'ism** *n*. **het'erostyly** *n*. **heterotact'ic** *adj*. **heterotax'is** or **het'erotaxy** *n* (Gr *taxis* arrangement) anomalous arrangement of eg parts of the body, etc. **heterothall'ic** *adj* (Gr *thallos* a shoot; *bot*) (of certain fungi) having two physiologically different types of mycelium, called plus and minus, comparable to male and female. **heterothall'ism** or **het'erothally** *n*. **heterother'mal** *adj* (Gr *thermos* heat) of animals, with a body temperature like that of its surroundings. **heterot'ic** *adj* relating to or showing heterosis. **heterotō'pia** *n* displacement of an organ of the body. **heterotop'ic** *adj*. **het'erotroph** *n* a heterotrophic organism. **heterotroph'ic** *adj*. **heterot'rophy** *n* (Gr *trophē* livelihood; *bot*) dependence (immediate or ultimate) upon green plants for carbon (as in most animals, fungi, etc). **heterotyp'ic** *adj* differing from the normal condition; relating to the first (reductional) division in meiosis (*biol*), see also **homotypic** under **homo-**. **heterousian** *adj* see **heteroousian** above. **heterozygos'ity** *n* the mixed ancestry of heterozygotes. **heterozygote** /-zī'gōt/ *n* (Gr *zygōtos* yoked, from *zygon* yoke) a zygote or individual formed from gametes differing with respect to some pair of alternative characters. **heterozy'gous** *adj*.

hetero /het'ə-rō/ (*inf*) *adj* and *n* (pl **het'eros**) (a) heterosexual. [Short form]

hether and **hetherward** (*Spenser*) same as **hither** and **hitherward**.

hetman /het'man/ (*hist*) *n* (pl **het'mans**) a Polish officer; the head or general of the Cossacks. [Pol, from Ger *Hauptmann* captain]
■ **het'manate** *n*. **het'manship** *n*.

heuch or **heugh** /hūhh/ (*Scot*) *n* a crag; a ravine or steep-sided valley; a quarry-face; an excavation, *esp* for coal. [OE *hōh* heel; cf **hoe**[2]]

heuchera /hū'kə-rə or hoi'/ *n* any plant of the N American *Heuchera* genus of the Saxifragaceae family with stems of many small flowers and heart-shaped leaves. [Johann *Heucher* (1677–1747), German botanist]

heulandite /hū'lən-dīt/ *n* a zeolite like stilbite. [H *Heuland* (1777–1856), English mineralogist]

heureka see **eureka**.

heuristic /hū-ris'tik/ *adj* serving or leading to find out; encouraging the desire to find out; (of method, argument, etc) depending on assumptions based on past experience; consisting of guided trial and error. ◆ *n* the art of discovery in logic; the method in education by which the pupil is set to find out things for himself or herself; (in *pl*) principles used in making decisions when all possibilities cannot be fully explored. [Irreg formed from Gr *heuriskein* to find; cf **eureka**]
■ **heuret'ic** *n* (*logic*) heuristic. **heur'ism** *n* the heuristic method or principle in education. **heuris'tically** *adv*.
❑ **heuristic program** *n* (*comput*) one which attempts to improve its own performance as a result of learning from previous actions within the program.

hevea rubber /hē'vē-ə rub'ər/ *n* rubber from the S American tree **hevea** (*Hevea brasiliensis*), used in electrical insulators for its good electrical and mechanical properties.

hew[1] /hū/ *vt* (pat **hewed**; *pap* **hewed** or **hewn**) to cut with blows; to shape, fell or sever with blows of a cutting instrument. ◆ *vi* to deal blows with a cutting instrument. ◆ *n* (*Spenser*) hacking. [OE *hēawan*; Ger *hauen*]
■ **hew'er** *n* a person who hews. **hew'ing** *n* and *adj*. **hewn** *adj*.
■ **hew to** (*N Am*) to conform to.

hew[2] (*Spenser*) see **hue**[1].

hewgh /hū/ (*Shakesp*) *interj* imitating the whistling of an arrow.

hex[1] /heks/ *n* a witch; a wizard; a spell; something that brings bad luck. ◆ *vt* to bring misfortune, etc to by a hex; to bewitch. [Pennsylvania Dutch *hex*, from Ger *Hexe* (*fem*), *Hexer* (*masc*)]
■ **hex'ing** *n*.

hex[2] /heks/ (*inf*) *n* uranium hexafluoride, a compound used in separating uranium isotopes by gaseous diffusion.

hex[3] /heks/ *abbrev* : hexadecimal.

hex- /heks-/ or **hexa-** /heks-ə- or heks-a-/ *combining form* denoting six. [Gr *hex* six; cf L *sex*, and **six**]
■ **hexachlo'rophene** or **hexachlo'rophane** (or /-ör'/) *n* a bactericide, $CH_2(C_6HCl_3OH)_2$ used in antiseptic soaps, deodorants, etc. **hex'achord** /-körd/ *n* a diatonic series of six notes having a semitone between the third and fourth. **hex'act** /-akt/ *adj* (Gr *aktīs, -īnos* ray) six-rayed. ◆ *n* a six-rayed sponge spicule. **hexacti'nal** (or /-ak'ti-nl/) *adj* six-rayed. **hexactinell'id** *n* and *adj*. **Hexactinell'ida** *n pl* a class of sponges whose spicules have three axes and therefore (unless some are suppressed) six rays. **hexad** /heks'ad/ *n* (Gr *hexas, -ados*) a series of six numbers; a set of six things; an atom, element, or radical with a combining power of six units (*chem*). **hexadactyl'ic** or **hexadact'ylous** *adj* (Gr *daktylos* finger, toe) six-fingered; six-toed. **hexadec'imal** *n* and *adj* (of a number system using the base 16 with the ten digits from 0 to 9 and the letters from A to F (also **hexadecimal notation**). **hexad'ic** *adj* relating to a hexad. **hexaëmeron** /heks-ə-ē'mer-on/ *n* (Gr *hēmerā* day) a period of six days, *esp* that of the creation, according to Genesis; a history of the six days of creation. **hex'afoil** *n* a pattern with six leaf-like lobes or sections (also *adj*). **hex'agon** *n* (Gr *hexagōnon*, from *gōniā* an angle) a figure with six sides and six angles. **hexagonal** /-ag'ən-l/ *adj* of the form of a hexagon; of the **hexagonal system**, a crystal system with three axes at 60° to each other and a fourth perpendicular to their plane (*crystallog*) (**hexagonal chess** a kind of chess played on hexagonal boards). **hexag'onally** *adv*. **hex'agram** *n* (Gr *gramma* figure) a figure of six lines, *esp* a stellate hexagon; any of 64 possible combinations of six lines in the I Ching. **Hexagynia** /-jin'i-ə/ *n pl* (Gr *gynē* woman) a Linnaean order of plants (in various classes) having six styles. **hexagyn'ian** or **hexagynous** /-aj'i-nəs/ *adj*. **hexahē'dral** *adj*. **hexahē'dron** *n* (pl **hexahē'drons** or **hexahē'dra**) (Gr *hedrā* a base) a solid with six sides or faces, *esp* a cube. **hexam'erous** *adj* (Gr *meros* part) having six parts, or parts in sixes. **hexam'eter** *n* (Gr *metron* measure) a line of verse of six measures or feet; (in Greek and Latin verse) such a line where the fifth is almost always a dactyl and the sixth a spondee or trochee, the others dactyls or spondees. ◆ *adj* having six metrical feet. **hexamet'ric** or **hexamet'rical** *adj*. **hexam'etrist** *n* a writer of hexameters. **hexam'etrize** or **-ise** *vi* to write hexameters. **Hexan'dria** *n pl* (Gr *anēr, andros* a man, male; *bot*) a Linnaean class of plants having six stamens. **hexan'drian** *adj*. **hexan'drous** *adj* having six stamens. **hexane** /heks'ān/ *n* a hydrocarbon (C_6H_{14}) with five isomers, sixth member of the alkane series. **hex'apla** *n* (Gr *hexaplā*, contracted pl neuter of *hexaploos* sixfold) an edition (*esp* of the Bible) in six versions. **hex'aplar** *adj*. **hexaplār'ian** *adj*. **hexaplar'ic** *adj*. **hex'aploid** *adj* of or having six times the ordinary number of chromosomes. ◆ *n* a hexaploid cell, individual, species, etc. **hex'apod** *n* (Gr *pous, podos* a foot) an animal with six feet; an insect. **Hexap'oda** *n pl* insects. **hexap'odal** *adj*. **hexap'ody** *n* a line or verse of six feet. **hexarch** /heks'ärk/ *adj* (Gr *archē* beginning; *bot*) having six vascular strands. **hexastich** /heks'ə-stik/ *n* (Gr *hexastichos*, adj, from *stichos* a line) a poem or stanza of six lines. **hexastichal** /-as'tik-l/ *adj* having six lines or rows. **hexastyle** /heks'ə-stīl/ *adj* (Gr *hexastȳlos*, from *stȳlos* a pillar) having six columns.

◆ *n* a building or portico having six columns in front. **Hexateuch** /heks'ə-tūk/ *n* (Gr *teuchos* tool, afterwards book) the first six books of the Old Testament. **hexateuch'al** *adj*. **hexavā'lent** *adj* having a valency of six. **hex'ose** *n* a sugar (of various kinds) with six carbon atoms to the molecule. **hexyl** /hek'sil/ *n* a radical derived from hexane. **hexylene** /heks'i-lēn/ or **hex'ene** *n* (Gr *hȳlē* matter) an unsaturated hydrocarbon (C_6H_{12}) of the ethylene series.

hexobarbitone sodium /heks-ō-bär'bi-tōn sō'di-əm/ *n* a derivative of barbituric acid, formerly used intravenously and intramuscularly as a basic anaesthetic.

hey¹ /hā/ *interj* expressing joy, irritation or interrogation; used also in calling attention or in greeting. [Imit]
■ **hey'day** *interj* (*archaic*) expressive of frolic, exultation or wonder. ❑ **hey'-go-mad** *interj* (*dialect*) expressing a high degree of excitement. **hey presto** or (*old*) **hey pass** *interj* and *n* a conjuror's expression, as on successfully accomplishing a trick.
■ **hey for** now for; off we go for. **like hey-go-mad** helter-skelter.

hey² or **hay** /hā/ *n* a winding country dance. ◆ *vi* to dance this dance. [Obs Fr *haye*]
❑ **hey'-** or **hay'-de-guy** /-gī'/, **-guise** or **-guyes** *n* such a dance popular in the 16c and 17c.

heyday /hā'dā/ *n* culmination or climax of vigour, prosperity, gaiety, etc; flush or full bloom; high spirits (*archaic*). [Origin obscure]

heyduck see **haiduk**.

Hezbollah see **Hizbollah**.

HF *abbrev*: high frequency.

Hf (*chem*) *symbol*: hafnium.

hf *abbrev*: half.

HFC *abbrev*: hydrofluorocarbon.

HFEA *abbrev*: Human Fertilization and Embryology Authority.

HG *abbrev*: High German; His or Her Grace.

Hg (*chem*) *symbol*: mercury. [L *hydrargum*]

hg *abbrev*: hectogram(s).

HGH *abbrev*: human growth hormone.

HGV *abbrev*: heavy goods vehicle (now replaced by **LGV** in official use).

HH *abbrev*: His or Her Highness; His Holiness.

HH or **2H** *symbol*: very hard (on lead pencils).

hh *abbrev*: hands.

HI *abbrev*: Hawaii (US state); Hawaiian Islands.

hi /hī/ *interj* calling attention; hey; hello. [Cf **hey¹**]

hiant /hī'ənt/ *adj* gaping. [L *hiāns*, *-antis*, prp of *hiāre* to gape]

hiatus /hī-ā'təs/ *n* (pl **hiā'tuses**) a gap; an opening; a break in continuity, a defect; a concurrence of vowel sounds in two successive syllables (*phonetics*). [L *hiātus*, *-ūs*, from *hiāre*, *hiātum* to gape]
■ **hiā'tal** *adj*.
❑ **hiatus hernia** *n* a hernia in which a part of a viscus protrudes through a natural opening, *esp* part of the stomach through the opening in the diaphragm intended for the oesophagus.

Hib /hib/ *n* a bacterium of the genus *Haemophilus* that can cause meningitis and other serious illnesses in young children. [*Haemophilus influenzae* type *B*]

hibachi /hi-bä'chi/ *n* (pl **hiba'chi** or **hiba'chis**) a portable barbecue for cooking food out of doors. [Jap *hi* fire, and *bachi* bowl]

hibakusha /hi-bä'kū-shə/ *n* (pl **hiba'kusha**) a survivor of the 1945 atomic bombings of Hiroshima and Nagasaki. [Jap]

hibernate /hī'bər-nāt/ *vi* to winter; to pass the winter in a dormant state; to be inactive. [L *hibernāre*, *-ātum*, from *hibernus* wintry, from *hiems* winter]
■ **hi'bernacle** *n* winter quarters; a hibernaculum. **hibernac'ūlum** *n* (pl **hibernac'ūla**) a winter retreat; a bud in Polyzoa that regenerates the colony after winter (*zool*); a winter bud, bulb, etc by which a plant survives the winter (*bot*). **hiber'nal** *adj* belonging to winter; wintry. **hiberna'tion** *n*.
❑ **hibernation anaesthesia** *n* freezing-down.

Hibernian /hī-bûr'ni-ən/ *adj* relating to *Hibernia*, an ancient and poetic name for Ireland; Irish; characteristic of Ireland. ◆ *n* an Irishman. [L *Hibernia* Ireland]
■ **Hiber'nianism** or **Hiber'nicism** /-sizm/ *n* an Irish idiom or peculiarity; a bull in speech. **Hiber'nically** *adv*. **hiber'nicize** or **-ise** /-sīz/ *vt* (often with *cap*) to render Irish. **hiberniza'tion** or **-s-** *n*. **hi'bernize** or **-ise** *vt* to hibernicize.

Hibiscus /hi-bis'kəs/ *n* a genus of malvaceous plants, mostly tropical trees or shrubs with large colourful flowers; (without *cap*) a plant of this genus. [L, from Gr *ibiskos* marsh-mallow]

hic¹ /hik/ *interj* representing a hiccup.

hic² /hik or hēk/ (L) *demonstrative pronoun* this.
■ **hic et ubique** /et ū-bī'kwē or oo-bē'kwe/ here and everywhere. **hic jacet** /jā'set or yä'ket/ here lies (frequently preceding the name of the dead person on older grave monuments). **hic sepultus** /sə-pul'tus or se-pool'tŭs/ or *se-pool'tŭs*/ here buried (frequently preceding the name of the dead person on older grave monuments).

hiccatee or **hicatee** /hik-ə-tē'/ *n* a West Indian freshwater tortoise. [From a native name]

hiccough see **hiccup**.

hiccup or **hiccough** /hik'up/ *n* the involuntary contraction of the diaphragm while the glottis is spasmodically closed; the sound caused by this; (in *pl*, often with *the*) an attack of these spasms at intervals of a few seconds; a temporary (and *usu* minor) difficulty or setback (*fig*). ◆ *vi* (**hicc'uping** or **hicc'oughing**; **hicc'uped** or **hicc'oughed**) to produce a hiccup (*lit* and *fig*); to falter or malfunction (*inf*). ◆ *vt* to say with a hiccup. [Imit; an early form was *hicket*; cf Du *hik*, Dan *hik*, Breton *hik*. The spelling *hiccough* is due to a confusion with *cough*]
■ **hicc'upy** *adj* marked by hiccups.

hick /hik/ (*derog*) *n* a person from the country; any unsophisticated or unintelligent person. ◆ *adj* relating to, or suggestive of, a hick; rural and uncultured. [A familiar form of *Richard*]

hickery-pickery /hik'ə-ri-pik'ə-ri/ see **hiera-picra**.

hickey /hik'i/ (*N Am inf*) *n* a gadget; a doodah; a thingummy; a love bite; an imperfection or error in printed matter. [Origin obscure]

hickory /hik'ə-ri/ *n* a N American genus (*Carya*) of the walnut family, yielding edible nuts and heavy strong tenacious wood; one of these trees; their wood; a walking-stick made from hickory wood. [Earlier *pohickery*; of Algonquian origin]

hickwall /hik'wöl/ (*dialect*) *n* the green woodpecker. [Origin obscure]

hid, **hidden** see **hide¹**.

hidage see under **hide³**.

hidalgo /hi-dal'gō/ *n* (pl **hidal'gos**) a Spanish nobleman of the lowest class; a gentleman. [Sp *hijo de algo* son of something]
■ **hidal'ga** *n* a Spanish noblewoman of the lowest class; a lady. **hidal'goish** *adj*. **hidal'goism** *n*.

hiddenite /hid'ə-nīt/ *n* a green spodumene, discovered by WE *Hidden* (1853–1918).

hidder /hid'ər/ (*Spenser*) *n* a young male sheep (cf **shidder**). [Perh **he** and **deer**]

hide¹ /hīd/ *vt* (pat **hid** /hid/; pap **hidden** /hid'n/ or **hid**) to conceal; to keep in concealment; to keep secret or out of sight. ◆ *vi* to go into, or to stay in, concealment. ◆ *n* a hiding-place; a concealed place from which to observe wild animals, etc. [OE *hȳdan*; cf MLGer *hûden*, and (doubtfully) Gr *keuthein*]
■ **hidd'en** *adj* concealed; kept secret; unknown. **hidd'enly** *adv* in a hidden or secret manner. **hidd'enmost** *adj* most hidden. **hidd'enness** *n*. **hi'der** *n*. **hid'ing** *n* concealment; a place of concealment.
❑ **hidden agenda** *n* concealed or secret intentions behind a person's actions or statements. **hidden economy** see **black economy** under **black**. **hide-and-seek'** or **hide'-and-go-seek'** *n* a game in which one person seeks the others, who have hidden themselves. **hide'away** *n* a place of concealment; a refuge; a fugitive. ◆ *adj* that hides away. **hide'out** *n* a retreat. **hid'ing-place** *n*. **hid'y-hole** or **hid'ey-hole** *n* (*Scot* and *US*) a hiding-place.
■ **hide one's head** (*inf*) to hide or keep out of sight, from shame, etc (*usu fig*).

hide² /hīd/ *n* the skin of an animal, *esp* the larger animals, sometimes used derogatorily or facetiously for human skin. ◆ *vt* (**hīd'ing**; **hīd'ed**) to flog or whip (*inf*); to skin. [OE *hȳd*; Ger *Haut*, L *cutis*]
■ **hīd'ing** *n* (*inf*) a thrashing.
❑ **hide'bound** *adj* stubborn, bigoted, obstinate (*derog*); (of animals) having the hide attached so closely to the back and ribs that it is taut, not easily moved, as a result of incorrect feeding; (in trees) having the bark so close that it impedes the growth.
■ **hide nor** (or **or**) **hair of** the slightest trace of (something or someone). **on a hiding to nothing** (*inf*) in a situation in which one is bound to lose, in spite of all one's efforts. **tan someone's hide** (*inf*) to whip or beat someone.

hide³ /hīd/ *n* (in old English law) a variable unit of area of land, enough for a household. [OE *hīd*, contracted from *hīgid*; cf *hīwan*, *hīgan* household]
■ **hid'age** *n* a tax once assessed on every hide of land.

hide⁴ /hīd/ (*Spenser*) *pat* of **hie¹**.

hi-def /hī'def'/ (*inf*) *adj* (of a television system, camera, etc) providing high-definition images. ◆ *n* same as **HDTV**.

hideous /hid'i-əs/ adj frightful; horrible; ghastly; extremely ugly; huge (obs). [OFr hideus, hisdos, from hide, hisde dread, poss from L hispidus rough, rude]
■ **hideos'ity** or **hid'eousness** n. **hid'eously** adv.

hiding see under hide[1,2].

hidlings, hidlins or **hidling** /hid'lin(g)(z)/ (Scot) adv in secrecy. ◆ adj secret. ◆ n a hiding-place or hiding-places; secrecy. [hid, and adv sfx -ling]

hidrosis /hi-drō'sis/ (med) n sweating, esp in excess. [Gr hidrōs, -ōtos sweat]
■ **hidrotic** /-drot'ik/ n and adj sudorific.

HIE abbrev : Highland and Islands Enterprise.

hie[1] /hī/ (archaic or poetic) vi (**hie'ing** or **hy'ing**; **hied**) to hasten. ◆ vt to urge (on); to pass quickly over (one's way). ◆ n (obs) haste. [OE hīgian]

hie[2] or **high** /hī/ (Scot) n and interj the call to a horse to turn to the left (cf **hup**). ◆ vt and vi to turn to the left (of or to a horse or plough-ox).

hielaman /hē'lə-mən/ n an Australian Aboriginal narrow shield of bark or wood. [Aboriginal word hīlaman]

Hieland /hē'lənd/, also **Hielan'** /-lən/ or **Hielant** /-lənt/ (Scot) adj of or relating to the Scottish Highlands; sometimes used with pejorative meanings, eg foolish, clumsy, etc, esp in neg, as in **no sae Hieland** not altogether absurd, not so bad as might be.

hiems /hī'emz/ (Shakesp) n winter. [L hiems]
■ **hī'emal** adj.

hieracium /hī-ə-rā'shi-əm/ n any plant of the genus Hieracium, the hawkweed genus of Compositae. [Latinized from Gr hierākion hawkweed, from hierāx hawk]

hiera-picra /hī'ə-rə-pik'rə/ n a purgative drug made from aloes and canella bark (also **hick'ery-pick'ery** or **hig'ry-pig'ry**). [Gr hierā (fem), sacred, and pikrā (fem), bitter]

hierarch /hī'ə-rärk/ n a ruler in holy things; a chief priest; a prelate; an archangel (Milton); any senior person in a hierarchy. [Gr hierarchēs, from hieros sacred, and archein to rule]
■ **hī'erarchal, hierarch'ic** or **hierarch'ical** adj. **hierarch'ically** adv. **hī'erarchism** n. **hī'erarchize** or **-ise** vt. **hī'erarchy** n a body or organization classified in successively subordinate grades; (loosely) in an organization so classified, the group of people who control that organization; classification in graded subdivisions; graded government amongst priests or other religious ministers; the collective body of angels, grouped in three divisions and nine orders of different power and glory: (1) seraphim, cherubim, thrones; (2) dominations or dominions, virtues, powers; (3) principalities, archangels, angels; each of the three main classes of angels.

hieratic /hī-ə-rat'ik/ adj priestly; applying to a certain kind of ancient Egyptian writing which consisted of abridged forms of hieroglyphics; also to certain styles in art bound by religious convention. [L hierāticus, from Gr hierātikos, from hieros sacred]
■ **hierat'ica** n the finest papyrus.

hierocracy /hī-ə-rok'rə-si/ n government by priests or other religious ministers. [Gr hieros sacred, and krateein to rule]
■ **hi'erocrat** n. **hierocrat'ic** adj.

hierodule /hī'ə-rō-dūl/ n in ancient Greece and Rome, any of various groups of slaves in the service of a temple, including female prostitutes obliged to give up some or all of their gains. [Gr hieros sacred, and doulos a slave]

hieroglyph /hī'ə-rō-glif/ n a sacred character used in ancient Egyptian picture-writing or in picture-writing in general. ◆ vt to represent by hieroglyphs. [Gr hieroglyphikon, from hieros sacred, and glyphein to carve]
■ **hieroglyph'ic** or **hieroglyph'ical** adj. **hieroglyph'ic** n a hieroglyph; (in pl) hieroglyphic writing; (in pl) writing that is difficult to read. **hieroglyph'ically** adv. **hieroglyphist** /-og'/ n a person skilled in hieroglyphics.

hierogram /hī'ə-rō-gram/ n a sacred or hieroglyphic symbol. [Gr hieros sacred, and gramma a character, from graphein to write]
■ **hierogramm'at** or **hierogramm'ate** n a writer of sacred records. **hierogrammat'ic** or **hierogrammat'ical** adj. **hierogramm'atist** n. **hi'erograph** n a sacred symbol. **hierog'rapher** n a sacred scribe. **hierograph'ic** or **hierograph'ical** adj relating to sacred writing. **hierog'raphy** n a description of sacred things.

hierolatry /hī-ə-rol'ə-tri/ n the worship of saints or sacred things. [Gr hieros sacred, and latreiā worship]

hierology /hī-ə-rol'ə-ji/ n the science of sacred matters, esp ancient writing and Egyptian inscriptions. [Gr hieros sacred, and logos discourse]
■ **hierologic** /-ə-loj'ik/ or **hierolog'ical** /-kəl/ adj. **hierol'ogist** n.

hieromancy /hī-ə-rō-man'si/ n divination by observing the objects offered in sacrifice. [Gr hieros sacred, and manteiā divination]

Hieronymic /hī-ə-rō-nim'ik/ adj relating to or associated with St Jerome (also **Hieronym'ian**). [L Hierōnymus, Gr Hierōnymos Jerome]
■ **Hieron'ymite** n a member of any of a number of hermit orders established in the 13c and 14c.

hierophant /hī'ə-rō-fant/ n a person who shows or reveals sacred things; a priest; an expounder. [Gr hierophantēs, from hieros sacred, and phainein to show]
■ **hierophant'ic** adj.

hieroscopy /hī-ə-ros'kə-pi/ n hieromancy. [Gr hieros sacred, and skopeein to look at]

Hierosolymitan /hī-ə-rō-sol'i-mī-tən/ adj of or relating to Jerusalem. [L and Gr Hierosolyma Jerusalem]

hierurgy /hī'ə-rûr-ji/ n a sacred performance. [Gr hierourgiā, from hieros sacred, and ergon work]
■ **hierur'gical** adj.

hi-fi or (rare) **Hi-Fi** /hī'fī/ n high-fidelity sound reproduction; equipment for this, comprising a tape deck, amplifier, CD player, etc; the use of such equipment, esp as a hobby. ◆ adj having or relating to high-fidelity sound reproduction, or the equipment used for this.

higgle /hig'l/, also **higgle-haggle** /hig'l-hag'l/ vi to make difficulties in bargaining; to chaffer. [Prob a form of **haggle**]
■ **higg'ler** n a person who higgles; in Jamaica, a market trader dealing in hand crafted wares. **higg'ling** n and adj.

higgledy-piggledy /hig'l-di-pig'l-di/ (inf) adv and adj haphazard; in confusion. [Origin obscure]

Higgs boson /higz bō'zon/ or **particle** /pär'ti-kl/ (phys) n a massive meson with zero spin, predicted by the electroweak theory and discovered in 2012. [Peter Higgs (born 1929), British physicist]

high[1] /hī/ adj elevated; lofty; tall; far up from a base, such as the ground, sea level, low tide, the mouth of a river, the zero of a scale, etc; advanced in a scale, esp the scale of nature; reaching far up; expressible by a large number; of a height specified or to be specified; of advanced degree of intensity; advanced, full (in time, eg high season or high summer); (of a period) at its peak of development, as in High Renaissance ; of grave importance; advanced; exalted, as in high drama ; excellent; eminent; dignified; chief (as in high priestess); noble; haughty; arrogant; extreme in opinion; powerful; angry; loud; violent; tempestuous; acute in pitch; luxurious (as in the high life); elated; drunk; over-excited, nervy; under the influence of a drug; standing out; difficult, abstruse; (of a price) dear; for heavy stakes; remote in time; (of meat, etc) slightly tainted or decomposed, or, in the case of game, ready to cook; pronounced with some part of the tongue well raised in the mouth (phonetics); (of latitude) far from the equator; (of an angle) approaching a right angle; (of facial colouring) florid. ◆ adv at or to an elevated degree; in or into a raised position; aloft; shrilly; arrogantly; eminently; powerfully; extremely; luxuriously; dear; for heavy stakes. ◆ n that which is high; an elevated region; the highest card; a high level; the maximum, highest level; an anticyclone; (inf) a euphoric or exhilarated frame of mind, esp under the influence of a drug; something that promotes such a frame of mind; a high school. [OE hēah ; Gothic hauhs, ON hār, Ger hoch]
■ **high'er** adj compar of **high**. ◆ n (with cap; also **Higher grade**) (in Scotland, a pass in) an examination generally taken at the end of the fifth or sixth year of secondary education (also adj). ◆ vt to raise higher; to lift. ◆ vi to ascend. **high'ermost** (rare) or **high'est** adj superl of **high**. **high'ish** adj somewhat high. **high'ly** adv in or to a high degree; in a high position. **high'most** adj. **high'ness** n the state of being high; dignity of rank; (with cap) a title of honour given to princes, princesses, royal dukes, etc. **hight** /hīt/ or **highth** /hīth/ n obsolete forms of **height**.
❑ **high admiral** n a high or chief admiral of a fleet. **high altar** see under **altar**. **high-alumina cement** n a type of quick-hardening cement, made of bauxite and chalk or limestone, found to lose strength through time under certain conditions. **high bailiff** n (obs) an officer who served writs, etc in certain franchises, exempt from the ordinary supervision of the sheriff. **high'ball** n (N Am) whisky (or other alcoholic spirit) and soda with ice in a tall glass. ◆ vi to go at great speed. ◆ vt to drive very fast. **high'-battled** adj (Shakesp; also **hye-battel'd**) appar in command of proud battalions. **high'binder** n (US) a member of a Chinese criminal secret society; a conspirator; a rowdy, ruffian or blackmailer. **high-blest'** adj (Milton) supremely blest or happy. **high'blooded** adj of noble lineage. **high'-blown** adj swelled with wind; inflated, as with pride (orig Shakesp). **high'-born** adj of noble birth. **high'boy** n (N Am) a tallboy. **high'-bred** adj of noble breed, training or family. **high'brow** n and adj (an) intellectual. **high'browism** n. **high camp** see under **camp[2]**. **high'chair** n a baby's or young child's tall chair, usu fitted with a tray, used esp at mealtimes. **High Church** adj of a section within the Church of England that exalts the authority of the episcopate and the priesthood, the saving grace of sacraments, etc; of similar views in other churches. **High-Church'ism** n. **High-Church'man** n. **high'-class** adj superior;

typical of or belonging to an upper social class. **high-col'oured** *adj* having a strong or glaring colour; (of a complexion) ruddy; over-vivid. **high comedy** *n* comedy set in refined sophisticated society, characterized more by witty dialogue, complex plot and good characterization than by comical actions or situations. **high command** *n* the commander-in-chief of the army together with his staff, or the equivalent senior officers of any similar force. **High Commission, High Commissioner** see under **commission**. **high court** *n* a supreme court. **high cross** *n* a town or village cross. **high day** *n* a holiday or festival; /dā/ broad daylight; /hī/ heyday (*non-standard*). ◆ *adj* befitting a festival. **high-definition television** see HDTV. **high-defini'tion** *adj* providing exceptional visual clarity. **high-den'sity** *adj* (*comput*) (of a disk) having very large data-storage capacity. **high'-dried** *adj* brought to an advanced stage of dryness; of fixed and extreme opinions. **High Dutch** see under **Dutch**. **high'-end** *adj* most expensive; typical of or appealing to the wealthy. **high-energy physics** *n sing* (*phys*) same as **particle physics** (see under **particle**). **higher criticism** *n* the inquiry into the composition, date and authenticity of a text, *esp* of the Bible, from historical and literary considerations. **higher education** *n* education at a level beyond that of secondary education, eg at a university or college. **Higher grade** see **higher** above. **higher mathematics** *n sing* mathematics at an advanced level, eg number theory. **high'er-up** *n* (*inf*) a person occupying an upper position. **high explosive** *n* a detonating explosive (eg dynamite, TNT) of great power and exceedingly rapid action. **high'-explo'sive** *adj*. **highfalutin** or **highfaluting** /-loot'/ (*inf*) *adj* affected; pompous. ◆ *n* bombastic discourse. **high fashion** *n* haute couture. **high feather** *n* high spirits; happy state. **high'-fed** *adj* fed highly or luxuriously; pampered. **high'-feeding** *n*. **high fidelity** *n* good reproduction of sound (see also **hi-fi**). **high-fidel'ity** *adj*. **high five** *n* **high-five'-sign** *n* a sign of greeting or celebration, *esp* popular in N America, consisting of the slapping of raised right palms. **high-five'** *vi* and *vt*. **high'-flī'er** or **high'-fly'er** *n* a bird that flies high; someone prone to extravagance of opinion or action; an ambitious person, or one naturally equipped to reach prominence; (with *cap*; *hist*) a High-Churchman, or, in Scotland, an Evangelical. **high'-flown** *adj* extravagant; elevated; turgid. **high'-fly'ing** *adj* extravagant in conduct or opinion; ambitious or prominent. **high frequency** see under **frequent**. **high'-functioning** *adj* used *esp* of a person with autism, able to perform sophisticated tasks. **high gear** see under **gear**. **High German** *n* of upper or southern Germany; the standard form of the German language, as it is written and spoken amongst educated people; that form of Germanic language affected by the second consonant shift, including the literary language of Germany. **high'-grade** *adj* superior; rich in metal. ◆ *vt* to steal rich ore from. **high'-grown** *adj* (*Shakesp*) covered with a high growth. **high hand** *n* arbitrary arrogance. **high'-hand'ed** *adj* overbearing; arbitrary. **high'-hand'edness** *n*. **high'-hat'** *n orig* a wearer of a top hat; a snob or aristocrat (*inf*); a person who puts on airs (*inf*); /hī'hat/ a pair of cymbals on a stand, the upper one operated by a pedal so as to strike the lower one (also **hi'-hat**). ◆ *adj* affectedly superior. ◆ *vi* to put on airs. ◆ *vt* to adopt a superior attitude towards or to ignore socially. **high'-heart'ed** *adj* full of courage. **high'-heeled** *adj* having or wearing high heels. **High Holidays** or **High Holy Days** *n pl* the Jewish festivals of Rosh Hashanah and Yom Kippur. **high hurdles** *n sing* a hurdle race in which the obstacles are 107cm (42in) high. **high'-im'pact** *adj* (of a material such as plastic) strong enough to withstand great impact; denoting exercises, *esp* aerobics, in which both feet leave the ground at the same time. **highjack, highjacker** see under **hijack**. **high jinks** *n pl* boisterous play, jollity; an old Scottish tavern game in which people played various parts under penalty of a forfeit. **high jump** *n* (a field event consisting of) a jump over a high bar; punishment, a severe reproof, *esp* in the phrase *be for the high jump*. **high'-key** *adj* (of paintings and photographs) having pale tones and very little contrast. **high kick** *n* a dancer's kick high in the air, *usu* with a straight leg. **high'-kilt'ed** *adj* having the skirt tucked up high; indecorous. **high'land** *n* a mountainous district; (with *cap*; in *pl*) the north-west of Scotland, bordered geologically by the great fault running from Dumbarton to Stonehaven, or, ethnologically, the considerably narrower area in which Gaelic is, or was until recently, spoken. ◆ *adj* belonging to or characteristic of a highland, *esp* (*usu* with *cap*) the Highlands of Scotland. **Highland cattle** *n pl* a shaggy breed of cattle with very long horns. **Highland dress** or **costume** *n* kilt, plaid and sporran. **high'lander** *n* an inhabitant or native of a mountainous region, *esp* (with *cap* or **High'landman**) of the Highlands of Scotland. **Highland fling** *n* a lively solo dance of the Scottish Highlands. **Highland Games** *n pl* an event consisting of competitions in athletic sports, bagpiping, traditional dancing, etc held in the Scottish Highlands or by Scots in other places. **high'-lev'el** *adj* at a high level, *esp* involving very important people. **high-level language** *n* (*comput*) a computer-programming language that allows a user to employ instructions in a form similar to natural language rather than using machine code. **high-level waste** *n* nuclear waste requiring continuous cooling to remove the heat produced by

radioactive decay. **high life** *n* the life of fashionable society; the people of this society; a blend of traditional W African music and N American jazz, popular in W Africa. **high'light** *n* an outstanding feature; (in *pl*) the most brightly-lit spots; the most memorable moments; (*usu* in *pl*) a portion or patch of the hair that reflects the light or that is artificially made lighter than the rest of the hair. ◆ *vt* (*pap* and *pat* **high'lighted**) to throw into relief by strong light; to draw attention to or point out; to overlay (parts of a text) with a bright colour, for special attention; to add highlights to (a person's hair). **high'lighter** *n* a broad-tipped felt pen for highlighting parts of a text, etc; a cosmetic used to emphasize features on the face. **high living** *n* luxurious living. **high'-lone** *adv* (*Shakesp*) quite alone. **high'-low** *n* (*archaic*; often *pl*) an ankle-high shoe fastened in front. **highly-strung'** *adj* nervously sensitive, excitable. **highly tried** *adj* (*horse-racing*) tested in experienced company. **high'-main'tenance** *adj* requiring a high degree of care to remain in working order; demanding of care and attention (*inf*). **high'man** *n* (*pl* **high'men**) a loaded die. **High Mass** *n* a mass celebrated with music, ceremonies and incense. **high'-mett'led** *adj* high-spirited, fiery. **high'-mind'ed** *adj* having a high, proud or arrogant mind (*rare*); having lofty principles and thoughts. **high'-mind'edness** *n*. **high-muck-a-muck** *n* see separate entry. **high'-necked'** *adj* (of a garment) covering the shoulders and neck. **high noon** *n* exactly noon; the peak (*fig*). **high-occupancy vehicle** *n* a vehicle carrying two or more people, sometimes entitled to preferential toll rates or to use dedicated road lanes. **high'-oc'tane** *adj* (of petrol) of high octane number and so of high efficiency (also *fig*). **high'-pitched'** *adj* acute in sound, tending towards treble; (of a roof) steep; lofty-toned. **high'-place** *n* (*Bible*) an area of high ground on which idolatrous rites were performed by the Jews, hence the idols, etc themselves. **high'-placed** *adj* having a high place; placed high. **high places** *n pl* positions of importance and *usu* influence. **high point** *n* the most memorable, pleasurable, successful, etc moment or occasion; a high spot. **high polymer** *n* a polymer of high molecular weight. **high'-pow'ered** *adj* very powerful; very forceful and efficient. **high'-press'ure** *adj* making or allowing use of steam or other gas at a pressure much above that of the atmosphere; involving intense activity, stressful; forceful, persuasive. **high'-priced'** *adj* costly. **high priest** *n* a chief priest. **high priestess** *n*. **high'-priest'hood** *n*. **high'-priest'ly** *adj*. **high'-prin'cipled** *adj* of high, noble or strict principle. **high profile** *n* a conspicuous position. **high'-pro'file** *adj* prominent, public. **high'-proof** *adj* proved to contain much alcohol; highly rectified. **high'-raised** or **-reared** *adj* raised aloft; elevated. **high'-ranker** *n*. **high'-ranking** *adj* senior; eminent. **high'-reach'ing** *adj* reaching upwards; ambitious. **high relief** *n* bold relief, standing out well from the surface. **high'-resolu'tion** *adj* (of a computer monitor, TV screen, etc) showing an image in great detail by using a large number of dots per unit area. **high'-rise** *adj* (of modern buildings) containing a large number of storeys. ◆ *n* such a building. **high'-risk'** *adj* vulnerable to some sort of danger; potentially dangerous. **high'road** *n* one of the public or chief roads; a road for general traffic. **high'-roll'er** *n* a plunging spendthrift; a person who gambles for high stakes. **high'-roll'ing** *n*. **high school** *n* a secondary school, often one that was formerly a grammar school. **high seas** *n pl* the open ocean. **high season** *n* the peak tourist period. **high'-sea'soned** or **high'ly-sea'soned** *adj* made rich or piquant with spices or other seasoning. **high'-set** *adj* placed or pitched high. **high shoe** *n* (*archaic*) a boot not reaching far above the ankle. **high'-sight'ed** *adj* (*Shakesp*) looking upwards, supercilious. **high sign** *n* (*N Am*) a signal, often surreptitious, of warning or indicating that it is safe to proceed. **high society** *n* fashionable, wealthy society. **high'-souled** *adj* having a high or lofty soul or spirit. **high'-sound'ing** *adj* pompous; imposing. **high spec** *adj* of a high standard of design and workmanship. **high'-speed** *adj* working, or suitable for working, at a great speed. **high-speed steel** *n* an alloy that remains hard when red-hot, suitable for metal-cutting tools. **high'-spir'ited** *adj* having a high spirit or natural fire; bold; daring; cheerful. **high spirits** *n pl* a happy, exhilarated frame of mind. **high spot** see under **spot**. **high'-stepp'er** *n* a horse that lifts its feet high from the ground; a person of imposing bearing or fashionable pretensions. **high'-stepp'ing** *adj*. **high'-stick'ing** *n* the offence in ice hockey of wielding the blade of the hockey stick above the height allowed. **high'-stom'ached** *adj* (*Shakesp*) proud-spirited, lofty, obstinate. **High Street** *n* (sometimes without *caps*) a common name for the main, or former main, shopping street of a town; (with *the*) shops generally, the everyday marketplace. **high'-street** *adj* typical of or readily found in high streets. **high'-strung** *adj* (*esp* N Am) highly-strung. **high table** *n* the dons' table in a college dining-hall. **high'tail** *vi* to hightail it (see below). **high'-tap'er** *n* hag-taper, the great mullein. **high'-tast'ed** *adj* having a strong, piquant taste or relish. **high tea** *n* an early-evening meal comprising a hot dish followed by cakes, etc and tea. **high tech** or **hi tech** *n* a style or design of furnishing, etc imitative of or using industrial equipment. **high'-tech** or **hi'-tec** *adj*. **high technology** *n* advanced, sophisticated technology in specialist fields, eg electronics, involving high investment in research and development.

high'-ten'sion *adj* high-voltage. **high'-test** *adj* (of petrol) boiling at comparatively low temperature and so of high performance. **high tide** *n* high water; a tide higher than usual; a great festival (*rare*). **high time** *n* quite time (that something were done); a time of jollity. **high toby** see under **toby**. **high'-toned** *adj* high in pitch; morally elevated; superior, fashionable. **high'-top** *n* (*Shakesp*) a masthead. **high tops** *n pl* training shoes which extend above the ankles. **high treason** *n* treason against the sovereign or state. **high'-up** *n* someone in high position (also *adj*). **high-vac'uum** *adj* (*electronics*) (of a system) so completely evacuated that the effect of ionization on its subsequent operation may be neglected. **high'-veloc'ity** *adj* (of shells) propelled at high speed with low trajectory. **high'-viced** *adj* (*Shakesp*) enormously wicked. **high'-vol'tage** *adj* of or concerning a high voltage, one great enough to cause injury or damage. **high water** *n* the time at which the tide or other water is highest; the greatest elevation of the tide. **high'-wa'ter mark** *n* the highest line so reached; a tidemark; highest point. **high'way** *n* a public road on which all have right to go; the main or usual way or course; a road, path or navigable river (*law*); see **bus** (*comput*). **Highway Code** *n* (the booklet containing) official rules and guidance on correct procedure for road users. **high'wayman** *n* a robber who attacks people on the public way. **highway patrol** *n* (*N Am*). **high-wing monoplane** *n* an aircraft with the wing mounted on or near the top of the fuselage. **high wire** *n* a tightrope stretched exceptionally high above the ground. **high words** *n pl* angry altercation. **high'wrought** *adj* wrought with exquisite skill; highly finished; elaborate; worked up, agitated. ■ **for the high jump** (*inf*) about to be reprimanded or chastised; about to be hanged. **from on high** from a high place, heaven, or (*facetiously*) a position of authority. **high and dry** up out of the water; stranded, helpless. **high and low** rich and poor; up and down; everywhere. **high and mighty** (*ironic*) exalted; arrogant. **high as a kite** (*inf*) over-excited, drunk, or very much under the influence of drugs. **high life below stairs** servants' imitation of the life of their employers. **high old time** (*inf*) a time of special jollity or enthusiasm. **hightail it** (*inf, esp N Am*) to hurry away. **hit the high spots** to go to excess; to reach a high level. **on high** aloft; in heaven. **on one's high horse** in an attitude of fancied superiority; very much on one's dignity. **on the high ropes** (*inf*) in an elated or highly excited mood. **running high** see under **feel**.

high² see **hie²**.

high-muck-a-muck /*hī-muk-ə-muk'*/ (*N Am inf*) *n* an important, pompous person. [Chinook Jargon *hiu* plenty, and *muckamuck* food]

hight /*hīt*/, also (*Scot*) **hecht** /*hehht*/ and (*obs*) **hete** /*hēt*/ *vt* (pat (*archaic*) **hight**, (*Scot*) **hecht**, (*Spenser*) **hot** or **hote**; pap (*archaic*) **hight**, (*Scot*) **hecht**, (*obs*) **hō'ten**) to promise, assure, vow (*Scot*); to call, name (*archaic*); to command (*obs*); to mention (*Spenser*); to commit (*Spenser*); to direct, determine, intend (*Spenser*). —The Spenserian senses are not found elsewhere. ◆ *vi* (*archaic*, and only in pat; *orig passive*) to be called or named, to have as a name. [OE *hēht* (*hēt*), reduplicated pat of *hātan* (pap *hāten*) substituted for the present and for the last surviving trace of the inflected passive in English, *hātte* is or was called; cf Ger *ich heisse* I am named, from *heissen* to call, be called, command]

highty-tighty /*hī'ti-tī'ti*/ same as **hoity-toity**.

higry-pigry /*hig'ri-pig'ri*/ see **hiera-picra**.

HIH *abbrev*: His or Her Imperial Highness.

hi-hat see **high-hat** under **high¹**.

hijab or **hejab** /*hi-jab'* or *he-jäb'*/ *n* a covering for a Muslim woman's hair and neck, sometimes reaching the ground. [Ar and Pers]

hijack or **highjack** /*hī'jak*/ *vt* and *vi* to stop and rob (a vehicle); to steal in transit; to force a pilot to fly (an aeroplane) to a destination of the hijacker's choice; to force the driver to take (a vehicle or train) to a destination of the hijacker's choice (also *fig*). [Origin obscure] ■ **hi'jacker** or **high'jacker** *n* a highwayman (*hist*); a robber or blackmailer of rum runners and bootleggers; a person who hijacks. **hi'jacking** or **high'jacking** *n*.

hijinks same as **high jinks** (see under **high¹**).

hijra, hijrah same as **hegira**.

hike /*hīk*/ *vi* to tramp; to go walking, *esp* wearing boots and carrying camping equipment, etc in a backpack; to hitch; (of shirts, etc) to move up out of place (with *up*). ◆ *vt* (*usu* with *up*; *inf*) to raise up with a jerk; to increase (eg prices), *esp* sharply and suddenly. ◆ *n* a walking tour, outing or march; an increase (in prices, etc). [Perh **hitch**] ■ **hi'ker** *n*. ■ **take a hike** (*US inf*) to go away (often as *imperative*).

hikikomori /*hi-kē-kō-mō'ri* or *-mö'ri*/ *n* (*pl* **hikikomo'ri**) (in Japan) complete withdrawal from society for a prolonged period; a person, *usu* an adolescent male, who does this. [Jap, pulling away]

hila, hilar see **hilum**.

hilarious /*hi-lā'ri-əs*/ *adj* extravagantly merry; very funny. [L *hilaris*, from Gr *hilaros* cheerful] ■ **hila'riously** *adv*. **hilarity** /*hi-lar'*/ *n* gaiety; pleasurable excitement.

Hilary term /*hil'ə-ri tûrm*/ *n* the Spring term or session of the High Court of Justice in England; also the Spring term at Oxford and Dublin universities. [St *Hilary* of Poitiers (died c.367)]

hilch /*hilsh*/ (*Scot*) *vi* to hobble. ◆ *vt* to lift. ◆ *n* a limp.

hild /*hild*/ (*Shakesp, Spenser*) same as **held**.

Hildebrandism /*hil'də-bran-di-zm*/ *n* the spirit and policy of *Hildebrand* (Pope Gregory VII, 1073–1085), unbending assertion of the power of the Church, etc. ■ **Hildebrand'ic** *adj*.

hilding /*hil'ding*/ (*archaic*) *n* a mean, cowardly person, a dastard; a worthless beast. ◆ *adj* cowardly, spiritless. [Prob connected with **heel²**]

hill /*hil*/ *n* a high mass of land, smaller than a mountain; a mound; an incline on a road. ◆ *vt* to form into a hill; to bank up (sometimes for **hele**). [OE *hyll*; cf L *collis* a hill, *celsus* high] ■ **hilled** *adj* having hills. **hill'iness** *n*. **hill'ock** *n* a small hill. **hill'ocky** *adj*. **hill'y** *adj* full of hills. ❏ **hill'billy** *n* (*N Am*) a rustic of the hill country; any unsophisticated person; country music. ◆ *adj* of or relating to hillbillies. **hill'-digger** *n* a rifler of sepulchral barrows, etc. **hill'folk** or **hill'men** *n pl* people living or hiding among the hills; the Scottish sect of Cameronians; the Covenanters generally. **hill'-fort** *n* a fort on a hill; a prehistoric stronghold on a hill. **hill'-pasture** *n*. **hill'side** *n* the slope of a hill. **hill station** *n* a government station in the hills, *esp* of N India. **hill'top** *n* the summit of a hill. **hill'walker** *n*. **hill'walking** *n*. ■ **hill and dale** (*obs*; of a gramophone record) with vertical groove undulations. **old as the hills** (*inf*) immeasurably old. **over the hill** (*inf*) past one's highest point of efficiency, success, etc; on the downgrade; past the greatest difficulty. **up hill and down dale** vigorously and persistently.

hillo (*archaic*) same as **hello**.

hilt /*hilt*/ *n* the handle, *esp* of a sword or dagger (sometimes in *pl*). ◆ *vt* to provide with a hilt. [OE *hilt*; MDu *hilte*; OHGer *helza*; not connected with **hold**] ■ **(up) to the hilt** completely, thoroughly, to the full.

hilum /*hī'ləm*/ *n* (*pl* **hi'la**) the scar on a seed where it joined its stalk (*bot*); the depression or opening where ducts, vessels, etc enter an organ (*anat*). [L *hīlum* a trifle, 'that which adheres to a bean'] ■ **hi'lar** *adj*. **hi'lus** *n* (*pl* **hi'li**) (*anat*) a hilum.

HIM *abbrev*: (His or) Her Imperial Majesty.

him /*him*/ *pronoun* the dative and accusative (objective) case of **he**; the proper character of a person (as in *that's not like him*). [OE *him*, dative sing of *hē* he, and *hit* it]

Himalaya /*him-ə-lā'ə* or *hi-mä'lyə*/ or **Himalayan** /*-n*/ *adj* relating to the *Himalayas*, a vast mountain range in S Asia.

himation /*hi-mat'i-on*/ *n* the ancient Greek outer garment, a rectangular cloak thrown over the left shoulder, and fastened either over or under the right. [Gr]

himbo /*him'bō*/ (*sl, usu derog* or *joc*) *n* (*pl* **him'bos**) a man who is attractive but dull and unintelligent; a male bimbo. [**him** and **bimbo**]

himself /*him-self'*/ *pronoun* the emphatic form of **he** or **him**; the reflexive form of **him** (*dative* and *accusative*); predicatively (or *n*) a man in his real character; having command of his faculties; sane; in normal condition; in good form; alone, by himself (*Scot*); the head of an institution or body of people (eg a husband; *Scot*). [See **him** and **self**]

Himyarite /*him'yə-rīt*/ *n* a member of an ancient South Arabian people. [*Himyar* a traditional king of Yemen] ■ **Himyaritic** /*-it'ik*/ *n* and *adj*.

hin /*hin*/ *n* a Hebrew liquid measure containing about four or six English quarts. [Heb *hīn*]

Hinayana /*hin-ə-yä'nə*/ *n* Theravada, one of the two main systems of practice and belief into which Buddhism split, the 'Little or Lesser Vehicle' (*orig* so called derogatorily by Mahayana Buddhists), the form of Buddhism found in Sri Lanka and SE Asia, holding more conservatively than Mahayana Buddhism to the original teachings of the Buddha and the practices of the original Buddhist communities. ◆ *adj* relating to or characteristic of this form of Buddhism. [Sans *hīna* little, lesser, and *yāna* vehicle]

hind¹ /*hīnd*/ *adj* placed in the rear; relating to the part behind; backward, *opp* to **fore**. [OE *hinder* backwards; Gothic *hindar*, Ger *hinter* behind; cf OE *hindan* (adv), back; **behind**] ■ **hinder** /*hīn'dər* or (*Scot*) *hin'ər*/ *adj* hind; last (*Scot*; as in *this hinder nicht* last night). **hind'erlings**, **hind'erlins**, or less correctly **hinderlands** or **hinderlans** /*hin'ər-lənz*/ *n pl* (*Scot*) the buttocks.

---

hīnd'ermost or **hīnd'most** adj farthest behind. **hīnd'ward** adj and adv.

❑ **hīnd'brain** n the cerebellum and medulla oblongata. **hind'cast** n a test of the accuracy of a predictive model by checking whether it can predict a known historical outcome from the events known to have preceded it. ◆ vt and vi (pat and pap **hind'cast** (sometimes **hind'casted**)) to test (a predictive model) in this way. **hin'der-end** /hin'ər-en'/ or -end¹/ n (Scot) the latter end; buttocks. **hīnd'foot** n. **hīndfore'most** adv with the back part in the front place. **hīnd'-gut** n the posterior part of the alimentary canal. **hīnd'head** n the back of the head, the occiput. **hīnd'leg** n. **hīndquar'ters** n pl the rear parts of an animal. **hīnd'sight** n the ability or opportunity to understand and explain an event after it has happened; the rear sight on a gun, etc. **hīnd'-wheel** n. **hīnd'wing** n.

hind² /hīnd/ n the female of the red deer. [OE hind; Du hinde, Ger Hinde]

■ **hind'berry** n the raspberry.

hind³ /hīnd/ (now Scot) n a farm-servant, with a cottage on the farm, formerly bound to supply the landowner with a female field-worker (bondager); a rustic. [OE hīna, hīwna, genitive pl of hīwan members of a household]

hindberry see under **hind²**.

hindbrain, hindcast see under **hind¹**.

hinder¹ /hin'dər/ vt to keep back; to stop, or prevent, progress of. ◆ vi to be an obstacle. [OE hindrian; Ger hindern]

■ **hin'derer** n. **hin'deringly** adv. **hin'drance** or **hin'derance** n act of hindering; that which hinders; prevention; an obstacle.

hinder², hinder-end see under **hind¹**.

hinderland /hin'dər-land/ an anglicized form of **hinterland**. [See also under **hind¹**]

hinderlands, hinderlans, hinderlings, hinderlins, hindermost see under **hind¹**.

Hindi /hin'dē/ n a group of Indo-European languages of N India, including Hindustani; a recent literary form of Hindustani, with terms from Sanskrit, one of the official languages of India. ◆ adj relating to Hindi or the Hindi group of languages. [Hindi Hindī, from Hind India]

hindleg…to…hindquarters see under **hind¹**.

hindrance see under **hinder¹**.

hindsight see under **hind¹**.

Hindu or formerly **Hindoo** /hin'doo or hin-doo'/ n a member of any of the races of Hindustan or India (archaic); specif an adherent of Hinduism; a believer in a form of Brahmanism. ◆ adj of or relating to Hindus or Hinduism. [Pers Hindū, from Hind India]

■ **Hin'duism** n the aggregation of religious values and beliefs and social customs dominant in India, including the belief in reincarnation, the worship of several gods and the arrangement of society in a caste system. **Hin'duize** or **-ise** vt and vi.

Hindustani or formerly **Hindoostanee** /hin-doo-stä'nē/ n a form of Hindi containing elements from other languages, used as a lingua franca in much of India and Pakistan (also adj).

hindward…to…hindwing see under **hind¹**.

hing /hing/ n asafoetida. [Hindi hīg, from Sans higu]

hinge /hinj/ n the hook or joint on which a door or lid turns; a joint as of a bivalve shell; the earth's axis (Milton); a small piece of gummed paper used to attach a postage-stamp to the page of an album (also **stamp hinge**); a cardinal point; a principle or fact on which anything depends or turns. ◆ vt (**hinging** /hinj'ing/; **hinged** /hinjd/) to provide with a hinge or hinges; to bend. ◆ vi to hang or turn as on a hinge; to depend (with on). [Related to **hang**]

❑ **hinge'-bound** adj unable to move easily on a hinge. **hinge joint** n (anat) a joint that allows movement in one plane only.

■ **off the hinges** disorganized; out of gear.

Hinglish /hing'glish/ (inf) n a mixture of Hindi and English.

hinky /hing'ki/ (US sl) adj (**hink'ier; hink'iest**) anxious; arousing suspicion. [Scot henk, hink a limp, hesitation]

hinny¹ /hin'i/ n the offspring of a stallion and a female ass or donkey. [L hinnus, from Gr ginnos, later hinnos a mule]

hinny² /hin'i/ n a Scot or N Eng variant of **honey** (the term of endearment).

hinny³ /hin'i/ vi (**hinn'ying; hinn'ied**) to neigh, whinny. [Fr hennir, from L hinnīre]

hint /hint/ n a distant or indirect indication or allusion; slight mention; insinuation; a helpful suggestion or tip; a small amount, suggestion; moment, opportunity (obs). ◆ vt to intimate or indicate indirectly. ◆ vi to give hints. [OE hentan to seize]

■ **hint'ingly** adv.

■ **hint at** to give a hint, suggestion, or indication of.

hinterland /hin'tər-land/ or (Ger) -länt/ n a region lying inland from a port or centre of influence; an area dependent on a centre of influence; an area of which little is known (fig). [Ger]

HIP abbrev: home information pack, a set of documents containing details about a house, which a seller must make available to prospective buyers.

hip¹ /hip/ n the haunch or fleshy part of the thigh; the hip joint; the external angle formed by the sides of a roof when the end slopes backwards instead of terminating in a gable (archit). ◆ vt (**hipp'ing; hipped** or **hipt**) to sprain or hurt the hip of; to throw over the hip; to carry on the hip (US); to construct with a hip (archit). [OE hype; Gothic hups, Ger Hüfte]

■ **hipped** adj having a hip or hips; (of a roof) sloping at the end as well as at the sides. **hipp'en, hipp'in** or **hipp'ing** n (Scot) a baby's nappy (wrapped around the hips). **hipp'y** adj having large hips. **hip'sters** n pl (also N Am **hip'-huggers**) trousers (for men or women) designed to fit on the hips, not the waist.

❑ **hip bath** n a bath to sit in. **hip'-belt** n the 14c sword-belt, passing diagonally from waist to hip. **hip bone** n the innominate bone. **hip flask** n a flask, esp one containing alcoholic spirit, carried in a hip pocket. **hip'-girdle** n the pelvic girdle; a hip-belt. **hip'-gout** n sciatica. **hip-huggers** see **hipsters** above. **hip joint** n the articulation of the head of the thigh bone with the ilium. **hip joint disease** n a disease of the hip joint with inflammation, fungus growth, caries, and dislocation. **hip'-knob** n an ornament placed on the apex of the hip of a roof or of a gable. **hip'-lock** n in wrestling, a form of cross-buttock. **hip pocket** n a trouser pocket behind the hip. **hip replacement** n operative replacement of the hip joint, performed esp in cases of severe osteoarthritis. **hip-roof'** n a hipped roof. **hip'-shot** adj having the hip out of joint.

■ **have** or **catch on the hip** to get an advantage over someone (from wrestling).

hip² /hip/ or **hep** /hep/ n the fruit of the dog rose or other rose. [OE hēope]

hip³ /hip/ interj an exclamation invoking and forming the first part of a united cheer, as in hip-hip-hurray.

hip⁴ /hip/ (inf) adj (**hipp'er; hipp'est**) knowing, informed about, or following the latest trends in music, fashion, political ideas, etc. [A later form of **hep¹**]

■ **hip'ness** n. **hip'pie** or **hipp'y** n one of the **hippies**, successors of the beatniks as rebels against the values of middle-class society, orig in the 1960s stressing the importance of love, organizing to some extent their own communities, and wearing colourful clothes. **hipp'iedom** or **hipp'ydom** n the lifestyle or community of hippies. **hipster** /hip'stər/ n a person who knows and appreciates up-to-date jazz; a member of the beat generation (1950s and early 1960s); (derog) a member of the generation born in the 1980–90s who look down on their native middle-class culture, and self-consciously adopt a bohemian lifestyle and mode of dress.

❑ **hip'-hop** adj and n (relating to or characteristic of) a popular culture movement developed in the USA in the early 1980s and comprising rap music, breakdancing and graffiti (of, relating to or characteristic of) the rap music associated with this movement.

hip⁵ or **hyp** /hip/ n (archaic) hypochondria. ◆ vt (**hipp'ing; hipped**) to render melancholy; to offend. [**hypochondria** (see under **hypo-**)]

■ **hipped** adj melancholy; peevish, offended, annoyed; obsessed. **hipp'ish** adj.

hip bath…to…hip-lock see under **hip¹**.

HIPC abbrev: highly indebted poor countries.

hipness see under **hip⁴**.

hipp- /hip-/ or **hippo-** /hip-o-/ combining form denoting a horse. [Gr hippos a horse]

■ **hipp'ophile** n a lover of horses. **hipp'ophobe** n a hater of horses.

hipparch /hip'ärk/ n in ancient Greece, a cavalry commander. [Gr hipparchos]

Hipparion /hi-pā'ri-on/ n a fossil genus of Equidae. [Gr hipparion, dimin of hippos a horse]

hippeastrum /hip-i-as'trəm/ n any plant of the S American genus Hippeastrum, bulbous, with white or red flowers. [Gr hippeus horseman, and astron star]

hipped see under **hip¹,⁵**.

hippen see under **hip¹**.

hippety-hoppety /hip'ə-ti-hop'ə-ti/ adv hopping and skipping.
■ **hipp'ety-hop'** n and adv.

hippiatric /hip-i-at'rik/ adj relating to the treatment of the diseases of horses. [Gr hippiātrikos, from hippos horse, and iātros a physician]
■ **hippiat'rics** n sing. **hippiatrist** /-ī'ət-rist/ n. **hippiatry** /-ī'ət-ri/ n.

hippic /hip'ik/ adj relating to horses. [Gr hippikos, from hippos horse]

hippie, hippiedom see under **hip⁴**.

hippin see under **hip**[1].

hipping see under **hip**[1].

hippish see under **hip**[5].

hippo /hip'ō/ n (pl **hipp'os**) a shortened form of **hippopotamus**.

hippo- see **hipp-**.

hippocampus /hip-ō-kam'pəs/ n (pl **hippocamp'ī**) a fish-tailed horse-like sea monster (myth); a genus of small fishes (family Syngnathidae) with horse-like head and neck, the seahorse; a raised curved trace on the floor of the lateral ventricle of the brain (anat). [Gr hippokampos, from hippos a horse, and kampos a sea monster]
■ **hippocamp'al** adj (anat).

Hippocastanaceae /hip-ō-kas-tə-nā'si-ē/ n pl the horse chestnut family. [**hippo-**, and Gr kastanon chestnut tree]

hippocentaur /hip-ō-sen'tör/ n same as **centaur**. [Gr hippokentauros, from hippos a horse, and kentauros]

hippocras /hip'ō-kras/ n an old English drink of spiced wine, formerly much used as a cordial. [ME ypocras Hippocrates]

Hippocratic /hip-ō-krat'ik/ adj relating to or associated with the Greek physician Hippocrates (5c BC).
■ **Hippoc'ratism** n. **Hippocratize** or **-ise** /-ok'rə-tīz/ vi to imitate or follow Hippocrates.
□ **Hippocratic face**, **look**, etc n sunken, livid appearance, eg near death, described by Hippocrates. **Hippocratic oath** n an oath taken by a doctor binding him or her to observe the code of medical ethics contained in it (first drawn up, perhaps by Hippocrates, in 4c or 5c BC).

Hippocrene /hip-ō-krē'nē or hip'ō-krēn/ (myth) n a fountain on the northern slopes of Mount Helicon, sacred to the Muses and Apollo, attributed to a kick of Pegasus. [Gr hippokrēnē, from hippos a horse, and krēnē a fountain]

hippodame /hip'ō-dām/ n (Spenser, wrongly) the sea horse. [**hippo-** and Gr damaein to tame]
■ **hippodamist** /hip-od'ə-mist/ n a horse-tamer. **hippod'amous** adj horse-taming.

hippodrome /hip'ə-drōm/ n (in ancient Greece and Rome) a racecourse for horses and chariots; a circus; a variety theatre. [Gr hippodromos, from hippos a horse, and dromos a course]
■ **hippodromic** /-drom'ik/ adj.

hippogriff or **hippogryph** /hip'ō-grif/ n a fabulous medieval animal, a griffin-headed winged horse. [Fr hippogriffe, from Gr hippos a horse, and gryps a griffin]

hippology /hi-pol'ə-ji/ n the study of horses. [**hippo-** and Gr logos discourse]
■ **hippol'ogist** n.

hippomanes /hip-om'ə-nēz/ n an ancient philtre obtained from a mare or foal. [**hippo-** and Gr maniā madness]

hippophagy /hip-of'ə-ji or -gi/ n feeding on horseflesh. [**hippo-** and Gr phagein (aorist) to eat]
■ **hippoph'agist** n an eater of horseflesh. **hippoph'agous** /-gəs/ adj horse-eating.

hippophile, **hippophobe** see under **hipp-**.

hippopotamus /hip-ō-pot'ə-məs/ n (pl **hippopot'amus**, **hippopot'amuses** or **hippopot'ami** /-mī/) a large African artiodactyl ungulate of aquatic habits, with very thick skin, short legs, and a large head and muzzle. [L, from Gr hippopotamos, from hippos a horse, and potamos a river]
■ **hippopotamian** /-tām'/ or **hippopotamic** /-tam'/, also -pot'/ adj like a hippopotamus, clumsy.

hippuric /hip-ū'rik/ adj denoting an acid, first obtained from the urine of horses, occurring in the urine of many animals, particularly in that of herbivores and rarely in that of human beings. [**hipp-** and Gr ouron urine]

Hippuris /hi-pū'ris/ n the mare's-tail genus of Haloragidaceae. [**hipp-** and Gr ourā a tail]
■ **hipp'ūrite** n a Cretaceous fossil lamellibranch (**Hippuri'tes**) with one conical valve and one flat one. **hippurit'ic** adj.

hippus /hip'əs/ (med) n clonic spasm of the iris. [New L, from Gr hippos a horse]

hippy see under **hip**[1,4].

hippydom see under **hip**[4].

hipster, **hipsters** see under **hip**[1,4].

hipt see **hip**[1].

hirable see under **hire**.

hiragana /hēr-ə-gä'nə/ n the more widely used of the two Japanese systems of syllabic writing (the other being **katakana**; both based on Chinese ideograms). [Jap, flat kana]

hircine /hûr'sīn/ adj goat-like; having a strong goatish smell. [L hircus a he-goat]
■ **hircosity** /-kos'i-ti/ n goatishness.
□ **hircocervus** /hûr-kō-sûr'vəs/ n a fabulous creature, half goat, half stag.

hirdy-girdy /hûr'di-gûr'di/ (Scot) adv in confusion or tumult.

hire /hīr/ n wages for service; the price paid for the use of anything; an arrangement by which use or service is granted for payment. ◆ vt to procure the use or service of, at a price; to engage for wages; to grant temporary use of for payment (often with out). [OE hȳr wages, hȳrian to hire]
■ **hir'able** or **hire'able** adj. **hir'age** or **hire'age** n (NZ) the fee for hiring something. **hired** adj. **hire'ling** n (derog) a hired servant; a mercenary; a person activated solely by material considerations. **hir'er** n a person who obtains use or service for payment; (now Scot or obs) a person who lets out something on hire. **hir'ing** n the act or contract by which an article or service is hired; (also **hiring fair**) a fair or market where servants are engaged (archaic).
□ **hire car** n a rented car, usu one rented for a short period. **hire-pur'chase** n a system by which a hired article becomes the hirer's property after a stipulated number of payments (also adj).
■ **on hire** for hiring; for hire.

hi-res /hī'-rez'/ a shortened form of **high-resolution** (see under **high**[1]).

Hiri Motu /hē'ri mō'too/ n a pidgin form of the Motu language, spoken in Papua New Guinea.

hirling see **herling**.

hirple /hûr'pl or hir'pl/ (Scot) vi to walk or run as if lame. ◆ n a limping gait.

hirrient /hir'i-ənt/ adj roughly trilled. ◆ n a trilled sound. [L hirriēns, -entis, prp of hirrīre to snarl]

hirsel /hûr'sl or hir'sl/ (Scot) n a stock of sheep; a multitude; the ground occupied by a hirsel of sheep. ◆ vt to put in different groups. [ON hirzla safekeeping, from hirtha to herd]

hirsle /hûr'sl or hir'sl/ (Scot) vi to slide or wriggle on the buttocks; to shift or fidget in one's seat; to move forward with a rustling sound. [Cf ON hrista to shake]

hirstie /hir'sti or hûr'sti/ (obs Scot) adj dry; barren.

hirsute /hûr'sūt or hər-sūt'/ adj hairy; rough; shaggy; having long, stiffish hairs (bot). [L hirsūtus, from hirsus, hirtus shaggy]
■ **hirsute'ness** n. **hirsut'ism** n excessive hair growth on a woman's face and body.

hirudin /hi-roo'din/ n a substance present in the salivary secretion of the leech which prevents blood clotting. [L hirūdō, -inis a leech]
■ **Hirudinea** /-in'i-ə/ n pl a class of worms, the leeches. **hirudin'ean** n and adj. **hirud'inoid** adj. **hirud'inous** adj.

hirundine /hi-run'dīn or -din/ adj of or relating to the swallow. [L hirundō, -inis a swallow]

his /hiz/ pronoun, genitive of **he**, or (obs) of **it**[1] (or possessive adj). [OE his, genitive of hē, he he, and of hit it]
■ **hisn** or **his'n** pronoun dialectal forms on the analogy of **mine**[1], **thine**.

hish /hish/ a variant form of **hiss**.

Hispanic /hi-span'ik/ adj Spanish; of or relating to a Spanish-speaking country. ◆ n a person of Latin American descent, esp living in the USA. [L Hispānia Spain]
■ **Hispan'ically** adv. **hispan'icism** n a Spanish phrase. **hispan'icize** or **-ise** /-i-sīz/ or **hispan'iolize** or **-ise** vt (often with cap) to render Spanish. **His'panist** n a person skilled in Spanish.
□ **Hispanic American** n a US citizen of Latin American descent.

Hispano- /hi-spa-nō or hi-spä-nō, also hi-spə-nō/ combining form denoting Spanish, as in Hispano-American. [L hispānus]
■ **Hispan'ophile** n and adj (someone who is) friendly to the Spanish or attracted by Spanish culture.

hispid /his'pid/ (bot and zool) adj rough with, or covered with, strong hairs or bristles. [L hīspidus]
■ **hispid'ity** n.

hiss /his/ vi to make a sibilant sound like that represented by the letter s, the sound made by a goose, snake, gas escaping from a narrow hole, a disapproving audience, etc. ◆ vt to condemn by hissing; to utter in an urgent or angry whisper; to drive by hissing. ◆ n a sibilant; a hissing sound. [Imit]
■ **hiss'ing** n and adj. **hiss'ingly** adv.
□ **hiss'y fit** n (inf, orig US) a tantrum; a display of petulance.

hisself /his-self'/ pronoun a dialect form for **himself**.

hist /hist or st/ interj demanding silence and attention; hush; silence. ◆ vt (hist) to urge or summon, as by making the sound. ◆ vi to be silent. [Imit]

hist. abbrev: histology; historian; history.

---

hist- /hist-/, **histio-** /hist-i-ō-/ or **histo-** /hist-ō- or -o-/ *combining form* denoting: animal or plant tissue; sail. [Gr *histos* and *histion* a web]

■ **histaminase** /-am'i-nāz/ *n* an enzyme that breaks down histamine. **hist'amine** /-ə-mēn/ *n* a base (C₅H₉N₃), formed in vivo by the decarboxylation of histidine and released during allergic reactions, large releases of which cause the contraction of nearly all smooth muscle and dilatation of capillaries, with a fall of arterial blood pressure and shock. **histamin'ic** *adj*. **hist'idine** /-i-dēn/ *n* an amino acid, a component of proteins. **histiocyte** /-i-ō-sīt'/ *n* a macrophage. **histiocyt'ic** *adj*. **hist'ioid** or **hist'oid** *adj* like ordinary tissue. **histiol'ogy** *n* same as **histology** below. **histioph'oroid** *adj*. **Histioph'orus** or **Istioph'orus** *n* (Gr *phoros* bearer) a genus of swordfishes with a sail-like dorsal fin. **hist'oblast** *n* a cell or group of cells, forming the precursor of tissue. **histochem'ical** *adj*. **histochem'ist** *n*. **histochem'istry** *n* the chemistry of living tissues. **histocompatibil'ity** *n* (*genetics*) the factor determining the acceptance or rejection of cells. **hist'ogen** *n* (*bot*) a more or less well-defined region within a plant where tissues undergo differentiation. **histogenesis** /-jen'i-sis/ *n* (*biol*) the formation or differentiation of tissues. **histogenetic** /-ji-net'ik/ *adj*. **histogenet'ically** or **histogen'ically** *adv*. **histogen'ic** *adj*. **histogeny** /his-toj'i-ni/ *n* histogenesis. **hist'ogram** *n* a statistical graph in which frequency distribution is shown by means of rectangles. **histolog'ic** or **histolog'ical** *adj*. **histolog'ically** *adv*. **histologist** /-tol'/ *n*. **histol'ogy** *n* the study of the microscopic structure of the tissues and cells of organisms. **histol'ysis** *n* (Gr *lysis* loosing) the breakdown of organic tissues. **histolytic** /-ō-lit'ik/ *adj*. **histolyt'ically** *adv*. **his'tone** *n* any of a group of five simple proteins, strongly basic, present in chromosomes and involved in the packaging of DNA in the eukaryotic nucleus to form chromatin. **histopathol'ogist** *n* a pathologist who studies the effects of disease on tissues of the body. **histopatholog'ical** *adj*. **histopathol'ogy** *n*. **histoplasmō'sis** *n* a disease of animals and humans due to infection by the fungal organism *Histoplasma capsulatum*.

histie same as **hirstie**.

history /his'tə-ri/ *n* an account of an event; a systematic account of the origin and progress of the world, a nation, an institution, a science, etc; the knowledge of past events; the academic discipline of understanding or interpreting past events; a course of events; a life-story; an eventful life, a past of more than common interest; a drama representing historical events. ◆ *vt* (**his'torying**; **his'toried**) (*Shakesp*) to record. [L *historia*, from Gr *historiā*, from *histōr* knowing]

■ **historian** /his-tö'ri-ən/ *n* a writer of history (*usu* in the sense of an expert or an authority on). **histo'riäted** *adj* decorated with elaborate ornamental designs and figures (also **sto'riated**). **historic** /-tor'ik/ *adj* famous or important in history. **histor'ical** *adj* relating to history; containing history; derived from history; associated with history; according to history; authentic. (Formerly *historic* and *historical* were often used interchangeably). **histor'ically** *adv*. **histor'icism** or **hist'orism** *n* a theory that all sociological phenomena are historically determined; a strong or excessive concern with and respect for the institutions of the past. **histor'icist** *n* and *adj*. **historicity** /hist-ər-is'i-ti/ *n* historical truth or actuality. **histor'icize** or **-ise** /-sīz/ *vt* to make or represent as historical. **historiette'** *n* a short history or story. **histor'ify** *vt* to record in history. **historiog'rapher** *n* a writer of history (*esp* an official historian). **historiograph'ic** or **historiograph'ical** *adj*. **historiograph'ically** *adv*. **historiog'raphy** *n* the art or employment of writing history. **historiol'ogy** *n* the knowledge or study of history. **historism** *n* see **historicism** above.

◻ **historical linguistics** *n sing* the study of the history of languages. **historical materialism** *n* the Marxist theory that all historic processes and forms of society are based on economic factors. **historical method** *n* the study of a subject in its historical development. **historical novel** *n* a novel having as its setting a period in history and involving historical characters and events. **historical painting** *n* the painting of historic scenes in which historic figures are introduced. **historical present** *n* the present tense used for the past, to add life and reality to the narrative. **historical school** *n* those scholars, *esp* in the fields of economics, legal philosophy and ethnology, who emphasize historical circumstance and evolutionary development in their researches and conclusions. **historic cost** or **historical cost** *n* (*account*) the actual price paid (cf **current-cost**). **historic pricing** *n* trading of unit trusts on the price set at the latest valuation.

■ **be history** (*inf*) to be finished, gone, dead, etc, as in *he's history*. **go down in history** to be remembered and commented on for many years. **make history** to do that which will mould the future or have to be recognized by future historians; to do something never previously accomplished.

histrionic /his-tri-on'ik/ or **histrionical** /his-tri-on'i-kəl/ *adj* of or relating to the stage or actors; stagy, theatrical; affected; melodramatic; hypocritical. [L *histriōnicus*, from *histriō* an actor]

■ **his'triö** (from L) or **his'trion** (from Fr) *n* (*pl* **his'triös** or **his'trions**) (*archaic*) an actor. **histrion'ically** *adv*. **histrion'icism** or **his'trionism**

n acting; theatricality. **histrion'ics** *n pl* play-acting; stagy action or speech; insincere exhibition of emotion.

hit /hit/ *vt* (**hitt'ing**; **hit**) to strike; to reach with a blow or missile (also *fig*); to come into forceful contact with; to knock (eg oneself, one's head); to inflict (a blow); to drive by a stroke; to move onto (a road), reach (a place); to go to (a place) to enjoy oneself, as in *hit the town* (*inf*); (of news) to be published in (*inf*); to come, by effort or chance, luckily (upon); to suit (with) (*obs*); to imitate exactly; to suit, fit or conform to; to hurt, affect painfully (*fig*); to make a request or demand of (*N Am inf*); to murder (*sl*). ◆ *vi* to strike; to make a movement of striking; to come in contact; to arrive suddenly and destructively; (of an internal combustion engine) to ignite the air and fuel mixture in the cylinders; to inject a dose of a hard drug (*sl*). ◆ *n* an act or occasion of striking; a successful stroke or shot; a lucky chance; a surprising success; an effective remark, eg a sarcasm, witticism; something that pleases the public or an audience; a stroke that allows the batter to reach at least first base safely (*baseball*); at backgammon, a move that throws one of the opponent's men back to the entering point, or a game won after one or two men are removed from the board; a murder by a gang of criminals (*sl*); a dose of a hard drug (*sl*); an instance of a computer file, *esp* a website, being contacted. [OE *hyttan*, appar ON *hitta* to light on, to find; Swed *hitta* to find, Dan *hitte* to hit upon]

■ **hitt'er** *n*.

◻ **hit'-and-miss'** *adj* hitting or missing, according to circumstances; random. **hit'-and-run'** *adj* (eg of an air-raid) lasting only a very short time; (of a driver) causing injury and driving off without reporting the incident; (of an accident) caused by a hit-and-run driver. ◆ *n* such an event or accident. **hit list** *n* (*sl*) a list of people to be killed by gangsters or terrorists; any list of targeted victims. **hit'man** *n* (*inf*) someone employed to kill or attack others (also *fig*). **hit'-or-miss'** *adj* hit-and-miss. **hit parade** *n* a list of currently popular songs (*old*); a list of the most popular things of any kind (*fig*). **hit squad** *n* (*sl*) a group of assassins working together. **hitt'y-miss'y** *adj* random, haphazard.

■ **a hit or a miss** a case in which either success or complete failure is possible. **hard hit** gravely affected by some trouble, or by love. **hit a blot** in backgammon, to capture an exposed man; to find a weak place. **hit at** to aim a blow, sarcasm, gibe, etc at. **hit back** to retaliate. **hit below the belt** see under **belt**. **hit it** to find, often by chance, the right answer. **hit it off** to agree, be compatible and friendly (sometimes with *with*). **hit it up** (*sl*) to inject a drug. **hit off** to imitate or describe aptly (someone or something). **hit on** or **upon** to come upon, discover, devise; to single out; to make sexual advances to, flirt with (*inf*). **hit out** to strike out, *esp* with the fist; to attack strongly (absolute or with *at*). **hit the bottle** (*sl*) to drink excessively. **hit the ceiling** or **roof** to be seized with or express violent anger. **hit the ground running** (*inf*) to react instantly, functioning at full speed and efficiency immediately. **hit the hay** or **sack** (*sl*) to go to bed. **hit the high spots** see under **high¹**. **hit the nail on the head** see under **nail**. **hit the road** (*sl*) to leave, go away. **hit the sack** see **hit the hay** above. **hit wicket** the act, or an instance, of striking the wicket with the bat or part of the body and dislodging the bails, and thus being out (*cricket*). **make** or **score a hit with** to become popular with; to make a good impression on.

hitch /hich/ *vi* to move jerkily; to hobble or limp; to catch on an obstacle; to connect with a moving vehicle so as to be towed (*orig N Am*); to travel by getting lifts, to hitch-hike. ◆ *vt* to jerk; to hook; to catch; to fasten; to tether; to harness to a vehicle; to make fast; to throw into place; to bring in (to verse, a story, etc), *esp* with obvious straining or effort; to obtain (a lift) in a passing vehicle. ◆ *n* a jerk; a limp or hobble; a catch or anything that holds; a stoppage owing to a small or passing difficulty; a type of knot by which one rope is connected with another, or to some object (*naut*); a means of connecting a thing to be dragged; a mode or act of harnessing a horse or horses, a team, or a vehicle with horses (*US*); a lift in a vehicle; a slight fault or displacement in a bed of sedimentary rock (*mining*); a recess cut in rock to support a timber (*mining*); a term of service or imprisonment (*N Am inf*). [Ety obscure]

■ **hitch'er** *n*. **hitch'ily** *adv*. **hitch'y** *adj*.

◻ **hitch'-hike** *vi* to hike with the help of lifts in vehicles (also *n*). **hitch'-hiker** *n*. **hitch'-hiking** *n*. **hitching post** *n* a post, etc to which a horse's reins can be tied. **hitch kick** *n* a technique in long jumping in which the legs are moved as if running while in the air (see also **hitch and kick** below).

■ **clove hitch** a type of knot by which a rope is attached to a pole, spar or rope thicker than itself. **get hitched** (*sl*) to get married. **hitch and kick** a technique in high jumping whereby the athlete springs from, kicks with, and lands on the same foot. **hitch up** to harness a horse to a vehicle; to jerk up; to marry (*sl*). **timber hitch** a knot for tying a rope round a log, etc for hauling.

hi tech see **high tech** under **high¹**.

hithe /hīdh/ *n* a small haven or port, *esp* a landing-place on a river. Now *obs* except in historical use or in place names. [OE *hȳth*]

hither /hidh'ər/ (*literary, formal* or *archaic*) *adv* to this place. ◆ *adj* on this side or in this direction; nearer. ◆ *vi* to come, chiefly in the phrase **hither and thither** to go to and fro. [OE *hider*; Gothic *hidrē*, ON *hethra*]

■ **hith'ermost** *adj* nearest on this side. **hith'erside** *n* the nearer side. **hith'erto** *adv* up to this time; to this point or place (*archaic*). **hith'erward** or **hith'erwards** *adv* towards this place.

■ **hither and thither** to and fro; this way and that.

Hitler /hit'lər/ (*inf*) *n* a person similar in character to Adolf *Hitler* (1889–1945), German Nazi dictator, overbearing or despotic (also (*derog*) **little Hitler**).

■ **Hitlerism** /hit'lər-izm/ *n* the principles, policy, and methods of Adolf Hitler, ie militant anti-Semitic nationalism, subordinating everything to the state. **Hit'lerist** or **Hit'lerite** *n* and *adj*.

Hitopadesa /hē-tō-pä-dā'shə/ *n* a collection of fables and stories in Sanskrit literature, a popular summary of the *Panchatantra*. [Sans *Hitopadeśa*]

Hittite /hit'īt/ *n* one of the Khatti or Heth, an ancient people of Syria and Asia Minor; an extinct language belonging to the Anatolian group of languages and discovered from documents in cuneiform writing. ◆ *adj* of or relating to the Hittites or their language. [Heb *Hitti*; Gr *Chettaios*]

hitty-missy see under **hit**.

HIV *abbrev*: human immunodeficiency virus, identified in two strains, **HIV-1** and **HIV-2**.

❑ **HIV positive** *adj* carrying the virus.

hive /hīv/ *n* a box or basket in which bees live and store up honey; a colony of bees; a scene of great industry; a teeming multitude or breeding-place; a hat of plaited straw shaped like an old beehive (*obs*). ◆ *vt* to collect into a hive; to lay up in store (often with *away* or *up*). ◆ *vi* (of bees) to enter or take possession of a hive; to take shelter together; to reside in a body. [OE *hȳf*]

■ **hive'less** *adj*. **hive'like** *adj*. **hiv'er** *n* someone who hives. **hive'ward** *adj* and *adv*. **hive'wards** *adv*.

❑ **hive bee** *n* the common honey-producing bee, *Apis mellifica*. **hive'-honey** *n*. **hive'-nest** *n* a large nest built and occupied by several pairs of birds in common.

■ **hive off** to withdraw as if in a swarm; to assign (work) to a subsidiary company; to divert (assets or sections of an industrial concern) to other concerns (**hive'-off** *n*).

hives /hīvz/ *n* a popular term for nettle rash and similar diseases or for laryngitis. [Origin unknown]

hiya /hī'yə/ (*sl*) *interj* a greeting developed from *how are you*.

Hizbollah, **Hizbullah** /hiz-bə-lä'/ or **Hezbollah** /hez-/ *n* an organization of militant Shiite Muslims. [Ar, party of God]

Hizen /hē-zen'/ (also without *cap*) *adj* of a type of richly decorated Japanese porcelain (also *n*). [*Hizen*, former province in Kyushu, Japan]

hizz /hiz/ (*Shakesp*) *vi* to hiss. [Echoic]

HK *abbrev*: Hong Kong (not in official use; IVR); House of Keys (the Manx parliament).

HKJ *abbrev*: Hashemite Kingdom of Jordan (IVR).

HL *abbrev*: House of Lords.

hl *abbrev*: hectolitres.

HM *abbrev*: (His or) Her Majesty('s).

hm *abbrev*: hectometre.

h'm or **hmm** *interj* see **hum³**.

HMA (*comput*) *abbrev*: High Memory Area, the first 64 kilobytes of extended memory.

HMAS *abbrev*: (His or) Her Majesty's Australian Ship.

HMC *abbrev*: (His or) Her Majesty's Customs; Headmasters' and Headmistresses' Conference.

HMCS *abbrev*: (His or) Her Majesty's Canadian Ship.

HMG *abbrev*: (His or) Her Majesty's Government.

HMI *abbrev*: (His or) Her Majesty's Inspector or Inspectorate; Horizontal Motion Index (*comput*).

HMIE *abbrev*: Her Majesty's Inspectorate of Education (a Scottish regulatory body).

HMIP *abbrev*: (His or) Her Majesty's Inspectorate of Pollution (now replaced by **EA**).

HMP *abbrev*: (His or) Her Majesty's Prison; *hoc monumentum posuit* (*L*), erected this monument.

HMRC *abbrev*: (His or) Her Majesty's Revenue and Customs.

HMS *abbrev*: (His or) Her Majesty's Service or Ship.

HMSO *abbrev*: (His or) Her Majesty's Stationery Office (now replaced by **OPSI**).

HN *abbrev*: Honduras (IVR).

HNC *abbrev*: Higher National Certificate.

HND *abbrev*: Higher National Diploma.

HO *abbrev*: hostilities only, used to designate service in the Royal Navy during wartime.

Ho (*chem*) *symbol*: holmium.

ho¹, **hoa** or **hoh** /hō/ *interj* a call to excite attention, to announce destination or direction, to express exultation, surprise, or (*esp* if repeated) derision or laughter; hullo; hold; stop. ◆ *n* (pl **hos, hoas** or **hohs**) cessation; moderation. ◆ *vi* (*obs*) to stop. [Cf ON *hō*, Fr *ho*]

ho² /hō/ (*US sl*) *n* (pl **hos** or **hoes**) a prostitute; a disrespectful term for any woman. [African-American form of **whore**]

ho. *abbrev*: house.

hoa see **ho**.

hoactzin see **hoatzin**.

hoagie /hō'gē/ (*N Am*) *n* another name for **submarine sandwich** (see under **submarine**).

hoar /hör/ *adj* white or greyish-white, *esp* with age or frost (*poetic*); mouldy (*obs*). ◆ *n* hoariness; age. ◆ *vi* (*Shakesp*) to become mouldy. ◆ *vt* (*Shakesp*) to make hoary. [OE *hār* hoary, grey; ON *hārr*]

■ **hoar'ily** *adv*. **hoar'iness** *n*. **hoar'y** *adj* white or grey with age; ancient; old and hackneyed; covered with short, dense, whitish hairs (*biol*).

❑ **hoar'frost** *n* rime or white frost, the white particles formed by the freezing of the dew. **hoar'head** *n* a hoary-headed old man. **hoar'-headed** *adj*. **hoar'-stone** (*Scot* **hare'-stane**) *n* an old hoary stone; a standing stone or ancient boundary stone. **hoary marmot** *n* a greyish-brown N American marmot.

hoard¹ /hörd/ *n* a store; a hidden stock; a treasure; a place for hiding anything (*obs*). ◆ *vt* to store, *esp* in excess; to treasure up; to amass and deposit in secret. ◆ *vi* to store up; to collect and form a hoard. [OE *hord*; ON *hodd*, Ger *Hort*]

■ **hoard'er** *n*.

hoard² /hörd/ (*old*) *n* a hoarding. [OFr *hurdis*, from *hurt*, *hourt*, *hourd* a palisade]

hoarding /hör'ding/ *n* a screen of boards, *esp* for enclosing a place where builders are at work, or for display of bills, advertisements, etc. [**hoard²**]

hoarhound see **horehound**.

hoarse /hörs/ *adj* rough and husky; having a rough husky voice, as from a cold; harsh; discordant. [ME *hors*, *hoors*, from OE *hās*, inferred *hārs*]

■ **hoarse'ly** *adv*. **hoars'en** *vt* and *vi*. **hoarse'ness** *n*.

hoast /hōst/ (*dialect*) *n* a cough. ◆ *vi* to cough. [ON *hōste*; cf OE *hwōsta*; Du *hoest*]

hoastman /hōst'mən/ *n* a member of an old merchant guild in Newcastle, with charge of coal-shipping, etc. [OFr *hoste*, from L *hospes* stranger, guest]

hoatzin /hō-at'sin/ or **hoactzin** /-akt'-/ *n* a S American bird (genus *Opisthocomus*), forming an order by itself, with an occipital crest, large crop, peculiar sternum, and, in the tree-climbing and swimming young, clawed wings (also **stink'bird**). [Nahuatl *uatsin*]

hoax /hōks/ *n* a deceptive trick played as a practical joke or maliciously (also *adj*). ◆ *vt* to trick, by a practical joke or fabricated tale, for fun or maliciously. [Appar **hocus** (see under **hocus-pocus**)]

■ **hoax'er** *n*.

hob¹ /hob/ *n* a hub; a surface beside a fireplace, on which anything may be laid to keep hot; any flat framework or surface, eg on top of a gas cooker, on which pots and pans are placed to be heated; a game in which stones are thrown at coins on the end of a short stick; the stick used; a gear-cutting tool. [Cf **hub**]

❑ **hob'nail** *n* a nail with a thick strong head, used in horseshoes, heavy workshoes, etc. ◆ *vt* to furnish with hobnails; to trample upon with hobnailed shoes. **hob'nailed** *adj*.

hob² /hob/ *n* a rustic; a lout; a supernatural creature or fairy, such as Robin Goodfellow (*folklore*); a clownish person; a male ferret; mischief. [Perh from *Robert*] [For *Robert*]

■ **Hobb'inoll** *n* a rustic (from Spenser's *Shepheards Calender*). **hobb'ish** *adj* clownish. **hob'goblin** *n* a mischievous fairy; a frightful apparition. **hobgob'linism** or **hobgob'linry** *n*.

■ **play hob** or **raise hob** to cause confusion.

hob-a-nob and **hob-and-nob** same as **hobnob**.

Hobbesian /hobz'i-ən/ or **Hobbian** /hob'i-ən/ *adj* relating to Thomas Hobbes (1588–1679) or his political philosophy. ◆ *n* a follower of Hobbes.

■ **Hobbes'ianism**, **Hobb'ianism** or **Hobb'ism** *n*. **Hobb'ist** *n* and *adj* (a) Hobbesian.

hobbit /hob'it/ n one of a race of imaginary beings, half human size, hole-dwelling and hairy-footed, invented by JRR Tolkien in his novel *The Hobbit* (1937).
- **hobb'itry** n.

hobble /hob'l/ vi to walk with short unsteady steps; to walk awkwardly; (of action, verse, speech, etc) to move irregularly. ◆ vt to fasten the legs of (a horse) loosely together; to hamper; to perplex. ◆ n an awkward hobbling gait; a difficulty, a scrape (*archaic*); anything used to hamper the feet of an animal, a clog or fetter. [Cf Du *hobbelen*, *hobben* to toss, and **hopple**]
- **hobb'ler** n someone who hobbles; an unlicensed pilot, a casual labourer in docks, etc; a man who tows a canal-boat with a rope. **hobb'ling** n. **hobb'lingly** adv.
- **hobb'le-bush** n the N American wayfaring tree (*Viburnum alnifolium*), a small shrub with white flowers and straggling branches that impede movement among them. **hobble skirt** n a narrow skirt that hampers walking.

hobbledehoy /hob'l-di-hoi'/ n an awkward youth, a stripling, neither man nor boy. [Origin obscure]
- **hobbledehoy'dom**, **hobbledehoy'hood** or **hobbledehoy'ism** n. **hobbledehoy'ish** adj.

hobbler /hob'lər/ (*obs*) n a person required to keep a hobby (horse) for military service; a horseman employed for light work, such as reconnoitring, etc; a horse. [OFr *hobeler*, from *hobin* a small horse]

hobby[1] /hob'i/ n a favourite pursuit followed as an amusement; a small or smallish strong, active horse; a pacing horse; a hobby-horse; an early form of bicycle. [ME *hobyn*, *hoby*, prob *Hob*, a by-form of the name *Rob*, for *Robert*. OFr *hobin*, *hobi* (Fr *aubin*), is from the English]
- **hobb'yism** n. **hobb'yist** n someone who pursues or rides a hobby. **hobb'yless** adj.
- **hobb'y-horse** n a stick or figure of a horse straddled by children; one of the chief parts played in the ancient morris dance; the wooden horse of a merry-go-round; a rocking horse; a dandy-horse; a loose and frivolous person, male or female (*Shakesp*); a hobby; a favourite topic or obsession, *esp* in the phrase *to be on one's hobby-horse*. **hobby-hors'ical** adj whimsically given to a hobby.

hobby[2] /hob'i/ n a small species of falcon. [OFr *hobé*, *hobel*, perh related to MDu *hobbelen*, to roll, turn]

hobday /hob'dā/ vt to cure a breathing impediment (in a horse) by surgical operation. [Sir Frederick *Hobday* (1869–1939), British veterinary surgeon]
- **hob'dayed** adj.

hobgoblin see under **hob**[2].

hobjob /hob'job/ (*dialect*) n an odd job. ◆ vi to do odd jobs.
- **hob'jobber** n. **hob'jobbing** n.

hobnail see under **hob**[1].

hobnob /hob'nob/ adv at random; hit-or-miss; with alternate or mutual drinking of healths. ◆ vi (**hob'nobbing**; **hob'nobbed**) to associate or drink together familiarly; to talk informally (with). ◆ n a sentiment in drinking (*obs*); mutual healthdrinking; a familiar private talk. [Prob *hab nab* have or have not (ne have); cf Shakespeare, *Twelfth Night* III.4, 'Hob, nob, is his word; give 't or take 't']
- **hob'nobby** adj.

hobo /hō'bō/ n (pl **ho'boes** or **ho'bos**) an itinerant workman, *esp* unskilled (*N Am*); a homeless, penniless person; a tramp. ◆ vt to travel as a hobo. [Origin unknown]
- **ho'bodom** or **ho'boism** n.

Hobson-Jobson /hob'sən-job'sən/ n festal excitement, *esp* at the Moharram ceremonies; the modification of names and words introduced from foreign languages, which the popular ear assimilates to already familiar sound, as in the case of the word Hobson-Jobson itself. [Ar *Yā Hasan*, *Yā Hosain* a typical phrase of Anglo-Indian argot at the time adopted as an alternative title for Yule and Burnell's *Glossary of Anglo-Indian Colloquial Words and Phrases* (1886)]

Hobson's choice see under **choice**.

hoc /hok or hōk/ (*L*) adj and pronoun this.
- **hoc anno** /an'ō/ in this year. **hoc genus omne** /jēn'əs or gen'ŭs om'ne/ all that sort. **hoc loco** /lōk' or lok'ō/ in this place. **hoc tempore** /tem'pə-rē or -po-re/ at this time.

hock[1] /hok/ or **hough** /hok or (*Scot*) hohh/ n a joint on the hindleg of a quadruped, between the knee and fetlock, and sometimes on the leg of a domestic fowl, corresponding to the ankle joint in humans; a piece of meat extending from the hock joint upwards; in humans, the back part of the knee joint; the ham. ◆ vt to hamstring. [OE *hōh* the heel]
- **hock'er** n.

hock[2] /hok/ n properly, the wine made at *Hochheim*, on the Main, in Germany; now applied to all white Rhine wines. [Obs *Hockamore*, from Ger *Hochheimer*]

hock[3] /hok/ (*sl*) vt to pawn. ◆ n the state of being in pawn. [Du *hok* prison, hovel]
- **in hock** in debt; in prison; having been pawned, in pawn (*inf*).

hock[4] /hok/ vt to subject to Hock-tide customs. ◆ vi to observe Hock-tide. [Origin unknown]
- **Hock'-day** or **Hock Tuesday** n an old English festival held on the second Tuesday after Easter Sunday, one of the chief customs being the seizing and binding of men by women until they gave money for their liberty. **Hock'-days** n pl Hock Tuesday and the preceding day (**Hock Monday**) on which the men seized the women in the same way. **Hock'-tide** n the two Hock-days.

hockey[1] /hok'i/ n a ball game played by two teams of eleven players, each with a club or stick curved at one end, a development of shinty (also (*old*) **hook'ey**); a hockey stick (*N Am*); ice hockey. [Prob OFr *hoquet* a crook]

hockey[2] /hok'i/ (*dialect*) n harvest home, the harvest supper (also **hawk'ey** or **hork'ey**). [Origin unknown]
- **hock'-cart** n the cart that brings home the last load of the harvest.

hockey[3] see **oche**.

hocus-pocus /hō'kəs-pō'kəs/ n skill in conjuring; deception; mumbo-jumbo; a juggler (*obs*); a juggler's trick or formula. ◆ vi (**hō'cus-pō'cusing** or **hō'cus-pō'cussing**; **hō'cus-pō'cused** or **hō'cus-pō'cussed**) to juggle. ◆ vt to play tricks on. [Conjuror's sham Latin, once conjectured to be a corruption of *hoc est corpus* this is my body, Christ's words used in the communion service at the consecration of the bread]
- **hoc'us** vt (**hō'cusing** or **ho'cussing**; **hō'cused** or **hō'cussed**) to cheat; to stupefy with drink; to drug (drink).

hod[1] /hod/ n a V-shaped stemmed trough for carrying bricks or mortar on the shoulder; a coal scuttle; a pewterer's blowpipe. [Cf dialect *hot*, *hott*, MHGer *hotte*, obs Du *hodde*, Fr *hotte* a basket]
- **hod carrier** or **hod'man** n a man who carries a hod; a bricklayer's or mason's labourer.

hod[2] /hod/ (*Scot*) vi (**hodd'ing**; **hodd'ed**) to bob; to jog.
- **hodd'le** vi (*Scot*) to waddle.

hodden /hod'n/ n coarse, undyed homespun woollen cloth, made from a mixture of black and white wool and so grey in appearance. ◆ adj of or clad in hodden; rustic. [Origin unknown]
- **hodd'en-grey** n hodden; a homely unpretentious person.

hoddy-doddy see under **hodmandod**.

Hodge /hoj/ n a countryman, rustic. [For *Roger*]

hodgepodge see **hotchpotch**.

hodge-pudding /hoj'pŭd-ing/ (*Shakesp*) n a pudding made of a mass of ingredients mixed together.

Hodgkin's disease /hoj'kinz di-zēz'/ n a disease in which the spleen, liver and lymph nodes become enlarged, and progressive anaemia occurs (also **Hodgkin's lymphoma**). [Thomas *Hodgkin* (1798–1866), British physician]

hodiernal /hō-di-ûr'nəl/ (*rare*) adj of or relating to the present day. [L *hodiernus*, from *hodiē* today = *hōc diē* on this day]

hodja see **khoja**.

hodmandod /hod'mən-dod/ n a snail. [Cf **dodman**]
- **hodd'y-dodd'y** n (*obs*) a dumpy person; a duped husband; a simpleton.

hodograph /hod'ə-gräf/ (*maths*) n a curve whose radius vector represents the velocity of a moving point. [Gr *hodos* a way, and *graphein* to write]

hodometer, **hodometry** see **odometer**.

hodoscope /hod'ə-skōp/ (*phys*) n any apparatus for tracing the paths of charged particles. [Gr *hodos* a way, and *skopeein* to see]

hoe[1] /hō/ n a long-handled instrument with a narrow blade used for scraping or digging up weeds and loosening the earth. ◆ vt (**hoe'ing**; **hoed**) to scrape, remove or clean with a hoe; to weed. ◆ vi to use a hoe. [OFr *houe*, from OHGer *houwâ* (Ger *Haue*) a hoe]
- **hō'er** n.
- **hoe'-cake** n (*US*) a thin cake of ground maize (*orig* baked on a hoe-blade). **hoe'down** n (*esp US*) a country dance, *esp* a square dance; hillbilly or other music for it; a party at which such dances are performed.

hoe[2] /hō/ n a promontory or projecting ridge (now only in place names). [OE *hōh* heel; cf **heuch**]

Hof /hōf/ (*Ger*) n yard; manor; court.

hog[1] /hog/ n a general name for swine; a castrated boar; a pig reared for slaughter; a yearling sheep not yet shorn (also **hogg**); the wool from such a sheep; a yearling of other species; a shilling (*old sl*); a low filthy fellow; a greedy person; an inconsiderate boor; a person of coarse manners; a frame or brush that is hauled along a ship's bottom to clean it. ◆ vt and vi (**hogg'ing**; **hogged**) to eat hoggishly; to arch or hump like a hog's back, *esp* of the hull of a ship. ◆ *vt* to take or use selfishly; to cut like a hog's mane; to behave like a hog or a road hog towards. [OE *hogg*]

■ **hogged** /*hogd*/ *adj.* **hogg'erel** *n* a yearling sheep. **hogg'ery** *n* hogs collectively; hoggishness of character; coarseness. **hogg'et** *n* a yearling sheep or colt. **hogg'ish** *adj.* **hogg'ishly** *adv.* **hogg'ishness** *n.* **hog'hood** *n* the nature of a hog.

❑ **hog'back** or **hog's'-back** *n* a hill-ridge, an ancient monument, or other object, shaped like a hog's back, ie curving down towards the ends. **hog badger** *n* an Asian badger with an elongated snout. **hog'-cholera** *n* swine fever. **hog'-deer** *n* a small Indian deer. **hog'fish** *n* a fish of N Atlantic waters, with bristles on its head. **hog'-frame** *n* a frame built to resist vertical flexure. **hog heaven** *n* (*US inf*) a condition of supreme happiness, contentment or pleasure. **hog'-mane** *n* a mane clipped short or naturally short and upright. **hog'-maned** *adj.* **hog'nose** *n* any of various species of short-bodied, harmless American snakes (genus *Heterodon*). **hog'nut** *n* the earth-nut. **hog'-pen** *n* a pigsty. **hog'-plum** *n* a West Indian tree (genus *Spondias*) of the cashew family, the fruit of which is relished by pigs. **hog'-rat** *n* the hutia, a West Indian rodent (genus *Capromys*). **hog'-reeve** or **hog'-constable** *n* an officer whose duty was to round up stray swine. **hog'-ringer** *n* a person who puts rings into the snouts of hogs. **hog'-shouther** /*-shoo'dhər*/ *vt* (*Scot*) to jostle with the shoulder. **hog'-skin** *n* leather made of the skin of pigs, pigskin. **hog's pudding** *n* a hog's entrails stuffed with various ingredients. **hog'tie** *vt* to tie (a person) up so as to prevent any movement of the arms or legs; to thwart, stymie, frustrate, impede. **hog'ward** /*-wörd*/ *n* a swineherd. **hog'wash** *n* the refuse of a kitchen, brewery, etc given to pigs; thin worthless stuff; insincere nonsense. **hog'weed** *n* the cow parsnip; applied also to many other coarse plants.

■ **bring one's hogs to a fine market** to make a complete mess of something. **go the whole hog** see under **whole**. **hog in armour** a boor in fine clothes. **hog it** (*sl*) to eat greedily; to live in a slovenly fashion.

hog² /*hog*/ *n* (in curling) a stone that does not pass the hog-score. ◆ *vt* (**hogg'ing**; **hogged**) to play a hog. [Perh **hog¹**]

❑ **hog'-line** or **hog'-score** *n* a line drawn across the rink short of which no stone counts.

hog³ /*hog*/ (*dialect*) *n* a mound of earth and straw in which potatoes, etc, are stored. ◆ *vt* (**hogg'ing**; **hogged**) to store (potatoes, etc) in such a heap. [Origin obscure]

hogan¹ /*hō'gən*/ *n* a log hut, *usu* covered with earth, built by the Navajo tribe of Native Americans. [Navajo]

hogan² see under **hogen-mogen**.

hogg, hogged see **hog¹**.

hogger /*hog'ər*/ (*Scot*) *n* a footless stocking worn as a gaiter; a short connecting-pipe. [Origin obscure]

hoggerel, hoggery, hogget see under **hog¹**.

hoggin or **hogging** /*hog'in*/ *n* sifted gravel; a mixture containing gravel. [Origin uncertain]

hoggish see under **hog¹**.

hogh a Spenserian spelling of **hoe²**.

Hogmanay /*hog-mə-nā'*/ (*Scot*) *n* the last day of the year, New Year's Eve; something to eat and/or drink or a gift begged or bestowed then. [Prob from North Fr dialect *hoginane*, from 16c *aguillanneuf* (*-l'an neuf*) a gift at the New Year]

hog-mane see under **hog¹**.

hogshead /*hogz'hed*/ *n* a large cask (Shakesp); a measure of capacity = $52\frac{1}{2}$ imperial gallons, or 63 old wine gallons; *of beer* = 54 gallons; *of claret* = 46 gallons; *of tobacco* (*US*) = 750 to 1200lb. [Appar **hog¹**, and **head**; reason unknown]

hogtie, hogward, hogwash, hogweed see under **hog¹**.

hoh /*hō*/ see **ho**.

ho-hum /*hō'hum'*/ (*inf*) *adj* dull, apathetic; boring, routine. ◆ *interj* used to express boredom or resignation.

hoi /*hoi*/ see **hoy²**.

hoick or **hoik** /*hoik*/ *n* a jerk. ◆ *vt* and *vi* to hitch up; (*esp* of aeroplanes) to jerk upwards. [Poss a variant of **hike**]

hoicks /*hoiks*/ *interj* a cry to urge hounds. ◆ *vt* to urge on with cries. ◆ *vi* to shout hoicks; to hark back.

hoiden see **hoyden**.

hoik see **hoick**.

hoi polloi /*hoi pə-loi'*/ (*derog*) *n* the many; the masses; the rabble, the vulgar. [Gr]

hoise /*hoiz*/ (*archaic*) *vt* (pat and pap **hoised** or **hoist**) to hoist. [Perh Old Du *hijssen*, Du *hijschen* to hoist]

hoisin sauce /*hoi'zin* or *hoi'sin sös*, also (chiefly *N Am*) *hoi-sin'*/ *n* a dark sweet sauce made from soy beans and spices and used in Chinese cookery. [Chin]

hoist /*hoist*/ *vt* to lift; to heave upwards; to raise or move with tackle; to steal (*sl*). ◆ *n* act of lifting; the height of a sail; that part of a flag next to the mast; a set of signal flags flying on a single line; tackle for lifting heavy objects. [Pat and pap of **hoise**]

■ **hoist'er** *n* someone who or something that lifts; a shoplifter (*sl*).

❑ **hoist'man** *n* a person who works a hoist. **hoist'way** *n* a hoist shaft.

■ **hoist with one's own petard** caught in one's own trap.

hoisting /*hō'sting*/ (*Walter Scott*) same as **hosting** (see under **host²**).

hoity-toity /*hoi'ti-toi'ti*/ *adj* giddy, noisy; huffy; superciliously haughty. ◆ *interj* an exclamation of surprise or disapprobation. [From *hoit* (*obs*) to romp; origin uncertain]

hojatoleslam or **hojatolislam** /*hoj-ə-tol'ez-läm, -iz-läm*/ *n* an Iranian rank and title lower than ayatollah.

hoke, hokey see under **hokum**.

hokey cokey /*hō'ki kō'ki*/ *n* a Cockney song whose lyrics dictate a pattern of accompanying movements, *usu* performed by several people in a circle; these dance-type movements.

hokey-pokey see **hoky-poky**.

hoki /*hō'ki*/ *n* a food-fish with white flesh found in the waters of the southern hemisphere, eg around the Falkland Islands and around New Zealand (also **whiptail hake**).

hokku see under **haiku**.

hokum /*hō'kəm*/ (*N Am sl*) *n* something done for the sake of applause; claptrap; pretentious or over-sentimental rubbish. [Appar **hocus-pocus** combined with **bunkum**]

■ **hoke** *vt* to overact (a part in a play); to give an impressive facade or appearance to (*usu* with *up*). ◆ *n* hokum. **hokey** /*hōk'i*/ *adj* overdone, contrived; phoney; over-sentimental.

hoky-poky or **hokey-pokey** /*hō'ki-pō'ki*/ *n* hocus-pocus; a kind of ice-cream sold on the streets (*old inf*).

Holarctic /*ho-lärk'tik*/ *adj* of the north temperate and Arctic biological region, including Palaearctic and Nearctic. [Gr *holos* whole, and *arktikos* northern, from *arktos* a bear, the Great Bear constellation]

hold¹ /*hōld*/ *vt* (**hōld'ing**; *pat* **held**; *pap* **held**, and *obs* **hōld'en**) to keep; to have; to grasp; to have in one's possession, keeping or power; to sustain; to defend successfully; to maintain; to assert authoritatively; to think, believe; to occupy; to pass on a title to; to bind; to contain; to have a capacity of; to enclose; to confine; to restrain; to detain; to retain; to reserve; to keep the attention of; to catch; to stop; to continue; to persist in; to celebrate, observe; to conduct; to carry on; to convoke and carry on; to esteem or consider; to aim, direct; to endure; to bet (*archaic*). ◆ *vi* to grasp; to remain fixed; to be true or unfailing; to continue unbroken or unsubdued; to remain valid; to continue, to persist; to adhere; to derive right; when making a telephone call, to wait, without replacing the receiver, eg to be connected to a person one wants to speak to (also **hold the line**). ◆ *n* an act or manner of holding; grip; power of gripping; tenacity; a thing held; a place of confinement; custody; stronghold; (a sign for) a pause (*music*); an order to keep in reserve (a room, etc) or to suspend (operations) (*N Am*); a means of influencing or controlling. [OE *haldan* (WSax *healdan*); OHGer *haltan*, Gothic *haldan*]

■ **hold'er** *n.* **hold'ing** *n* anything held; a farm managed for its owner; hold; influence; intensive embracing and prolonged eye contact as a technique for developing intimacy between parent (*esp* mother) and child, claimed by some to be a cure for autism (*psychiatry*); stacking (of aircraft waiting to land); tenure (*Scots law*); the burden of a song (Shakesp); (in *pl*) property owned (eg land or investments).

❑ **hold'all** *n* an accommodating receptacle for clothes, etc, *esp* a large strong bag. **hold'back** *n* a check; a strap joining the breeching to the shaft of a vehicle; something withheld, *esp* money (see also **hold back** below). **hold 'em** see **Texas hold 'em** under **Texas**. **hold'erbat** *n* (*building*) a metal collar formed from two semicircular parts which can be clamped together round a pipe, with a projecting piece for fixing to a wall. **hold'fast** *n* that which holds fast; a long nail; a catch; a plant's fixing organ other than a root. **holding company** *n* an industrial company that owns and controls part or all of one or more other companies, *usu* without having a direct hand in production. **holding ground** *n* any part of the seabed where an anchor will hold. **holding operation** *n* a course of action designed to preserve the status quo. **holding pattern** *n* a specific course which aircraft are instructed to follow when waiting to land. **hold'out** *n* (*inf*) refusal to agree to something or to take part in an activity; a person who refuses in this way. **hold'over** *n* (*N Am*) someone or something held over; a leftover, relic. **hold'-up** *n* an attack with a view to robbery; a highwayman; an act or state of holding up; a stoppage; (in *pl*) women's stockings worn without a suspender belt, supported by elasticated tops.

■ words derived from main entry word; ❑ compound words; ■ idioms and phrasal verbs

■ **get hold of** to obtain; to get in touch with. **hold a call** or **put a call on hold** to delay completing a direct connection between a caller and the telephone number or person that they are trying to reach, keeping the caller waiting, eg until the line is clear, or the person sought can come to a telephone. **hold against** (*inf*) to remember as a failing or as a misdemeanour on the part of. **hold back** to restrain; to hesitate; to keep in reserve (**hold`back** *n*). **hold by** to believe in; to act in accordance with. **hold down** to restrain; to keep (a job) by carrying out its duties efficiently, *esp* in spite of difficulties. **hold forth** to put forward; to show; to speak in public, to declaim. **hold good** to remain the case. **hold hands** (of two people) to be hand in hand or clasping both of each other's hands; (of several people) each to clasp the hand of the person on either side, thus forming a line, circle, etc. **hold hard!** stop! **hold in** to restrain, check; to restrain oneself. **hold it!** keep the position exactly!; stop! **hold of** (*Prayer Book*) to regard. **hold off** to keep at a distance; to refrain (from). **hold on** to persist in something; to continue; to cling; to keep (with *to*); stop (*imperative*); to wait a bit. **hold one's hands up** to admit one is at fault. **hold one's own** to maintain one's position; (in the course of an illness) not to fail or lose strength. **hold one's peace** or **one's tongue** to keep silence. **hold out** to endure, last; to continue resistance; to offer. **hold out for** to wait determinedly for (something one wants or has asked for). **hold out on** (*inf*) to keep information, money, etc from. **hold over** to postpone; to keep possession of (land or a house beyond the term of agreement). **hold (someone) in hand** to amuse in order to gain some advantage. **hold the line** see **hold** (*vi*) above; to persist or maintain one's position while under pressure. **hold the road** (of a vehicle) to remain stable and under the driver's control, eg in wet weather, at high speeds or on bends. **hold to** or **hold someone to** to keep, or make someone keep (a promise), adhere to (a decision), etc. **hold together** to remain united; to cohere. **hold up** to raise; to keep back; to endure; to bring to, or keep at, a standstill; to stop and rob; to rob by threatening assault. **hold up one's head** to face the world with self-respect. **hold water** see under **water**. **hold with** to take sides with, support; to approve of. **keep hold of** to maintain one's possession of or grip on. **no holds barred** not observing any rules of fair play (**no`-holds-barred`** *adj*). **on hold** postponed; in abeyance; waiting to be connected.

hold² /hōld/ *n* the interior cavity of a ship used for the cargo. [**hole¹**, with excrescent *d*]

hole¹ /hōl/ *n* a hollow place; a cavity; an aperture; a gap; a breach; a pit; a subterfuge; a means of escape; a difficult situation; a scrape; a place of hiding, a mean lodging, a secret room for some disreputable business; an animal's excavation or place of refuge; a miserable or contemptible place; a cylindrical hollow $4\frac{1}{4}$ inches in diameter, into which golf balls are played; the distance, or the part of the game, between tee and hole (*golf*); the score for playing a hole in fewest strokes (*golf*); a vacancy in an energy band, caused by removal of an electron, which moves and is equivalent to a positive charge (*electronics*); (*vulgar sl*) the anus or vagina. ◆ *vt* to form holes in; to put, send or play into a hole. ◆ *vi* to go or play into a hole. [OE *hol* a hole, cavern; Du *hol*, Dan *hul*, Ger *hohl* hollow; connected with Gr *koilos* hollow]

■ **holey** /hōl'i/ *adj* full of holes. **hol'ing** *n* and *adj*.
□ **hole`-and-cor'ner** *adj* secret; underhand; in obscure places. **hole card** *n* (in stud poker) the card dealt face down in the first round. **hole`-in-the-wall`** *adj* (*inf*) small, insignificant, difficult to find. **hol'ing-axe** *n* a narrow axe for cutting holes in posts. **hol'ing-pick** *n* a pick used in undercutting coal.
■ **a hole in one's coat** a stain on a person's reputation. **hole in one** (in golf) a shot from the tee that goes into the hole, and so completes the hole with a single stroke. **hole in the heart** imperfect separation of the left and right sides of the heart. **hole in the wall** (*inf*) a small insignificant place; a cash dispenser. **hole out** (*golf*) to play the ball into the hole. **hole up** (*inf*) to go to earth, hide (also *fig*). **in holes** full of holes. **make a hole in** (eg one's pocket) to use up a large amount of (eg money). **pick holes in** see under **pick¹**. **toad in the hole** meat, *esp* sausages, baked in batter.

hole² an earlier (and etymological) spelling (*Spenser*) of **whole**.
■ **hole`som(e)** *adj* wholesome.

holey see under **hole¹**.

Holi /hō'lē/ *n* a Hindu spring festival characterized by boisterous revelry. [Hindi *holī*, from Sans *holikā*]

holibut see **halibut**.

holiday /hol'i-dā/ *n* orig a religious festival; a day or (*esp* in *pl*) a season of rest and recreation; (often in *pl*) a period of time spent away from home, for recreation; (*US*, usu in *pl*) the holiday season. ◆ *vi* to go away from home for a holiday. ◆ *adj* befitting a holiday; cheerful. [**holy** and **day**]
□ **holiday camp** *n* an area, often at the seaside, with chalets, hotels, entertainments, etc for holidaymakers. **hol'idaymaker** *n* someone on holiday away from home; a tourist. **holiday season** *n* (*US*) the period between Thanksgiving and the New Year, during which both Christmas and Hanukkah are celebrated.

holing, etc see under **hole¹**.

holism /hol'i-zm or hō'li-zm/ *n* the theory that the fundamental principle of the universe is the creation of wholes, ie complete and self-contained systems from the atom and the cell by evolution to the most complex forms of life and mind; the theory that a complex entity, system, etc, is more than merely the sum of its parts. [Gr *holos* whole; coined by JC Smuts (1870–1950), South African general and statesman]
■ **hol'ist** *n*. **holist'ic** *adj*. **holist'ically** *adv*.
□ **holistic medicine** *n* a form of medicine that considers the whole person, physically and psychologically, rather than treating merely the diseased part.

holla /hol'ə or hol'ä/ *interj* (*naut*) ho, there!, attend!, the usual response to *ahoy!*◆ *n* a loud shout. [Fr *hola*; cf **hello**]
■ **holl'a-ho!** or **holl'a-hoa!** *interj*.

holland /hol'ənd/ *n* a coarse linen fabric, unbleached or dyed brown, which is used for covering furniture, etc; *orig* a fine kind of linen first made in *Holland*.
■ **Holl'ander** *n* a native or citizen of *Holland*; a Dutch ship. **Holl'andish** *adj*. **Holl'ands** *n* gin made in Holland.
■ **sauce hollandaise** /sōs ol-ä-dez/ (Fr) or **hollandaise sauce** /hol-ən-dāz'** or *hol'ən-dāz sōs*/ a sauce made with egg yolks, melted butter and lemon juice or vinegar.

holler /hol'ər/ (*N Am* and *dialect*) *n*, *vi* and *vt* same as **hollo**.

Hollerith code /hol'ə-rith kōd/ (*comput*) *n* a code for transforming letters and numerals into a pattern of holes, formerly used in punched cards. [H *Hollerith* (1860–1929), US inventor]

hollidam see under **holy**.

hollo /hol'ō/ *n* and *interj* (pl **holl'oes** or **holl'os**) a shout of encouragement or to call attention; a loud shout. ◆ *vt* and *vi* to shout. [Cf **holla** and **hello**]

holloa /ho-lō'/ same as **hello**.

hollow /hol'ō/ *n* a hole; a cavity; a depression; a valley; a vacuity; an emptiness; a groove; a channel. ◆ *adj* having an empty space within or below, not solid; concave; sunken; unsound, unreal, fleeting, deceptive; insincere; echoing, as if coming from a hollow. ◆ *vt* (often with *out*) to make a hole or cavity in; to make hollow; to excavate. ◆ *adv* completely, as in *beat* (ie defeat) *someone hollow*; clean. [OE *holh* a hollow place, from *hol*; see **hole¹**]
■ **holl'owly** *adv* with a hollow sound; in a hollow or insincere manner. **holl'owness** *n* the state of being hollow; a cavity; insincerity; treachery.
□ **holl'ow-eyed** *adj* having sunken eyes. **holl'ow-ground** *adj* ground so as to have concave surface(s). **hollow-ground slide** *n* a microscope slide having a depression in the centre, used in hanging drop preparations. **holl'ow-heart'ed** *adj* having a hollow heart; faithless; treacherous. **holl'ow-ware** or **holl'oware** *n* hollow articles of iron, china, etc, eg pots and pans.

holly /hol'i/ *n* an evergreen shrub (*Ilex aquifolium*; family Aquifoliaceae) having leathery, shining, spinous leaves and scarlet or yellow berries, much used for Christmas decorations. [OE *holegn*; cf Welsh *celyn*, Ir *cuileann*]
□ **holl'y-fern** *n* a spiny-leaved fern. **holl'y-oak** *n* the holm-oak.

hollyhock /hol'i-hok/ *n* a plant (genus *Althaea*) of the mallow family, with flowers of many colours, brought into Europe from the Holy Land. [ME *holihoc*, from *holi* holy, and OE *hoc* mallow]

Hollywood /hol'i-wŭd/ *adj* of or belonging to *Hollywood*, a suburb of Los Angeles in California and the centre of American cinema; typical of or resembling films made there, brash and romantic, presenting the image of an affluent and often artificial society.
■ **Holl'ywoodize** or **-ise** *vt* to refurbish or trivialize in the Hollywood manner.

holm¹ /hōm/ *n* (in place names) an islet, *esp* in a river; rich flat land beside a river. [OE *holm*; Ger *Holm*, etc]

holm² /hōm/ (*Spenser*) *n* holly; the holm-oak. [ME *holin*; see **holly**]
□ **holm'-oak** *n* the evergreen oak (*Quercus ilex*), not unlike holly.

HOLMES /hōmz/ *n* Home Office Large and Major Enquiry System, a computer database of information. [Acronym]

Holmesian /hōm'zi-ən/ *adj* relating to, or in the manner of, the detective Sherlock *Holmes*, in the stories by A Conan Doyle (1859–1930). ◆ *n* a devotee of Holmes.

holmium /hōl'mi-əm/ *n* a metallic element (symbol **Ho**; atomic no 67). [New L *Holmia* Stockholm]
■ **hol'mia** *n* its oxide. **hol'mic** *adj*.

holo- /hol-ō-, hol-ə- or hə-lo-/ or **hol-** /hol-/ combining form denoting: whole; wholly. [Gr *holos* whole]

■ **holobenth'ic** *adj* (*zool*) passing the whole life cycle in the depths of the sea. **holoblast'ic** *adj* (Gr *blastos* a shoot, bud) (of egg) segmenting completely. **hol'ocrine** *adj* (Gr *krinein* to separate, decide) producing a secretion of disintegrated cells. **holocrys'talline** *adj* wholly crystalline in structure, without glass. **holodisc'us** *n* a genus of deciduous shrubs (family Rosaceae) grown for their summer flowers. **holoen'zyme** *n* an enzyme that has a protein and non-protein component. **holohē'dral** *adj* (Gr *hedrā* base). **holohēd'rism** *n* (*maths*) the property of having the full number of symmetrically arranged planes crystallographically possible. **holohē'dron** *n* a geometrical form possessing this property. **holometabol'ic** *adj.* **holometab'olism** *n* (of an insect) complete metamorphosis. **holometab'olous** *adj.* **holophōt'al** *adj* (Gr *phōs, phōtos* light). **hol'ophote** *n* an apparatus by which all the light from a lighthouse is thrown in the required direction. **hol'ophrase** *n* a single word expressing a sentence or phrase. **holophras'tic** *adj.* **hol'ophȳte** /-*fīt*/ *n*. **holophytic** /-*fit'ik*/ *adj* (Gr *phyton* a plant) obtaining nutriment wholly in the manner of a green plant. **holophytism** /-*fīt'izm*/ *n*. **holoplank'ton** *n* organisms which remain as plankton throughout their life cycle. **holop'tic** *adj* having the eyes meeting in front. **Holostei** /*hol-os'ti-ī*/ *n pl* (Gr *osteon* bone) an order of fishes including *Lepidosteus*. **holosteric** /-*ster'ik*/ *adj* (Gr *stereos* solid) wholly solid; having no liquids (eg an aneroid barometer). **hol'otype** *n* (*zool*) the original type specimen from which the description of a new species is established. **holotypic** /-*tip'ik*/ *adj.* **holozoic** /-*zō'ik*/ *adj* (Gr *zōion* an animal) obtaining nutrition wholly in the manner of an animal, ie from other organisms live or dead.

holocaust /*hol'ə-köst*/ *n* a huge slaughter or destruction of life; the cause of such, eg a major fire; a disaster (*inf*); (with *cap*) the mass murder of Jews by the Nazis during World War II; a sacrifice, in which the whole of the victim was burnt. [Gr *holokauston*, from *kaustos* burnt]

■ **holocaust'al** or **holocaust'ic** *adj.*

❑ **holocaust denial** *n* the act of denying that mass murder of Jews took place during World War II.

Holocene /*hol'ə-sēn*/ (*geol*) *adj* of or belonging to the most recent epoch of the Quaternary period, starting 10 000 years ago and approximating to the period since the last glaciation (also *n*). [**holo-** and Gr *kainos* new]

holocrine, holocrystalline, holodiscus, holoenzyme see under **holo-**.

hologram /*hol'ə-gram*/ *n* a photograph made without use of a lens, by means of interference between two parts of a split laser beam, the result appearing as a meaningless pattern until suitably illuminated, when it shows as a 3-D image (a number of pictures can be stored on the same plate or film). [**holo-** and **-gram**]

■ **hol'ograph** /-*gräf*/ *n* a document wholly written by the person from whom it comes (also *adj*). ◆ *vt* to make a hologram of. **holographic** /-*graf'ik*/ *adj.* **holog'raphy** *n* (the technique or process of) making or using holograms.

holohedron...to...**holosteric** see under **holo-**.

holothurian /*hol-ō-thū'ri-ən*/ *n* any member of the genus **Holothu'ria** or family **Holothuroid'ea**, a class of wormlike unarmoured echinoderms, the sea cucumbers (also *adj*). [Gr *holothourion* a kind of sea animal]

holotype...to...**holozoic** see under **holo-**.

holp /*hōlp*/ and **holpen** /-*ən*/ (*old*) *pat* and *pap* of **help**.

hols /*holz*/ (*inf*) *n pl* holidays.

Holstein /*hōl'stīn*/ (*N Am*) *adj* and *n* same as **Frisian**. [Region of Germany]

holster /*hōl'stər*/ *n* a pistol-case, slung on a saddle or belt; a similar case for a tool, eg a torch or an axe used in mountaineering. ◆ *vt* to put into a holster. [Perh Du *holster* pistol-case; cf OE *heolster* hiding-place]

■ **hol'stered** *adj.*

holt¹ /*hōlt*/ *n* a hold, grasp (*Brit* and *US dialect*); a stronghold (*obs*); a refuge; an otter's den. [**hold¹**]

holt² /*hōlt*/ *n* (in place names) a wood or woody hill; an orchard. [OE *holt* a wood; ON *holt* a copse, Ger *Holz*]

holus-bolus /*hō'ləs-bō'ləs*/ (*archaic*) *adv* all at once; altogether. [Sham L; perh from Eng *whole bolus* or Gr *holos* and *bōlos* lump, bolus]

holy /*hō'li*/ *adj* perfect in a moral sense; pure in heart; religious; associated with God or gods; set apart for a sacred use; regarded with awe (often *ironic*); saintly; sanctimonious, simulating holiness. ◆ *n* a holy object, place or (*obs*) person. [OE *hālig*, literally, whole, from *hāl* sound; connected with **hail²**, **heal¹**, **whole**]

■ **ho'lily** *adv.* **ho'liness** *n* sanctity; (with *cap*) a title of the Pope and of patriarchs in Eastern Churches; (with *cap*) a title of respect applied in non-Christian religions to a person believed to have achieved a high degree of spiritual enlightenment. **holydam, holydame** or **hollidam** *n* (*Shakesp*), used for **halidom**.

❑ **ho'lier-than-thou'** *adj* offensively sanctimonious and patronizing. ◆ *n* such an attitude; someone who has such an attitude. **ho'ly-ale** *n* (conjectured in Shakespeare's *Pericles* I.1.6, for rhyme's sake) a church festival. **Holy Alliance** *n* a league formed after the fall of Napoleon (1815) by the sovereigns of Austria, Russia and Prussia, professedly to regulate all national and international relations in accordance with the principles of Christian charity. **holy city** *n* depending upon religion: Jerusalem; Rome; Mecca; Benares; Allahabad, etc; (in Christianity) heaven. **holy coat** *n* the seamless robe of Jesus, claimed to be kept at Trier, Germany. **ho'ly-cru'el** *adj* (*Shakesp*) cruel through holiness. **holy day** *n* a religious festival (see also **holiday**). **Holy Family** *n* the infant Christ with Joseph, Mary, etc. **Holy Ghost** see **Holy Spirit** below. **holy grail** see under **grail¹**. **holy grass** *n* a sweet-smelling grass sometimes strewn on church floors on festival days. **holy Joe** *n* (*sl*) a parson; a pious person. **Holy Land** *n* Biblical Palestine. **Holy Office** *n* the Inquisition; a former title of the Sacred Congregation for the Doctrine of the Faith, the RC doctrinal court. **holy of holies** *n* the innermost chamber of the Jewish temple in Jerusalem; a very sacred place. **Holy One** *n* God; Christ; the one who is holy, by way of emphasis; a person, eg a monk, living a cloistered life in the service of God. **holy orders** see under **order**. **Holy Roller** *n* (*derog*) a preacher or follower of an extravagantly emotional religious sect. **Holy Roman Empire** *n* the unification of Europe with papal blessing, under a Christian emperor, 800–814AD and 962–1806AD. **ho'ly-rood** (as a place name /*hol'*/) *n* Christ's cross; a cross, *esp* in Roman Catholic churches over the entrance to the chancel (for **Holy-rood Day** see under **rood**). **Holy Saturday** *n* the Saturday before Easter Sunday. **Holy See** *n* the Roman Catholic bishopric of Rome, ie the Pope's see. **Holy Sepulchre** *n* the tomb in which the body of Christ was laid after the crucifixion. **Holy Spirit** or **Holy Ghost** *n* the third person of the Christian trinity. **ho'lystone** *n* a sandstone used by seamen for cleansing the decks, said to be named from cleaning the decks for Sunday, or from kneeling in using it. ◆ *vt* to scrub with a holystone. **holy terror** *n* (*inf*, *esp joc*) a formidable person, or someone given to causing commotion or agitation. **Holy Thursday** *n* Maundy Thursday. **holy war** *n* a war waged for the eradication of heresy or a rival religion; a Crusade. **holy water** *n* water blessed for religious uses. **Holy Week** *n* the week before Easter. **Holy Willie** *n* a religious hypocrite (after Burns's poem). **holy writ** *n* the Scriptures. **Holy Year** *n* in the Roman Catholic Church, a jubilee year.

homage /*hom'ij*/ *n* a vassal's acknowledgement that he is the man of his feudal superior (*hist*); a body of vassals or tenants; anything done or rendered as an acknowledgement of superiority; reverence, *esp* shown by outward action. ◆ *vt* to do or pay homage to. [OFr *homage*, from LL *homināticum*, from L *homō* a man]

■ **hom'ager** *n* a person who does homage.

homaloid /*hom'ə-loid*/ *n* Euclidean space, analogous to a plane. [Gr *homalos* even, and *eidos* form]

■ **homaloid'al** *adj* flat; of the nature of a plane.

hombre /*om'brā*/ (*Sp*) *n* a man.

Homburg /*hom'bûrg*/ *n* a man's hat, of felt, with a narrow brim and crown, and a depression in the top. [First worn at *Homburg*, town in western Germany]

home /*hōm*/ *n* a habitual dwelling-place, or the place felt to be such; the residence of one's family; the scene of domestic life, with its emotional associations; a separate building occupied by a family, a house; one's own country; the mother country; seat; habitat; natural or usual place of anything; the den or base in a game; the goal; the inner table in backgammon; the plate in baseball (also **home plate**); an institution affording refuge, asylum or residence for strangers, the afflicted, poor, etc; a private hospital; a place where cats, dogs, etc are received and boarded; in football pools, a match won by a team playing on their own ground; a home signal. ◆ *adj* relating or belonging to, or being in, one's own dwelling, country, playing-ground, etc; domestic; near the dwelling or headquarters; coming or reaching home; effective, searching; made or done at home, not in a factory, abroad, etc. ◆ *adv* to one's home; at home; to the innermost, most significant or final place or position; effectively. ◆ *vi* to go home; to find the way home; to dwell; to be guided to a target or destination (*usu* with *in*). ◆ *vt* to send home; to provide with a home; to guide to a target or destination (*usu* with *in* on). [OE *hām*; Du *heim*, Ger *Heim*, Gothic *haims*]

■ **home'less** *adj* without a home; of or relating to people who, having no permanent place of residence, live and sleep rough in public places, or in squats or doss-houses. ◆ *n pl* (with *the*) homeless people. **home'lessness** *n*. **home'like** *adj* like a home; familiar; easy; comfortable. **home'lily** /-*li-li*/ *adv*. **home'liness** *n*. **home'ly** *adj* relating to home; comfortable; familiar; plain; unpretentious; (*usu* of people) ugly (*N Am*). **hom'er** *n* a pigeon of a breed that can readily be trained to find its way home from a distance; any person or animal so skilled; a home run (*baseball*); a job done at home or away from the usual work place (*inf*). **home'ward** or **home'wards** *adv*. **home'ward** *adj* in the direction of home. **home'y** *adj* (also **hom'y**) homelike; homely. ◆*n* (also **hom'ie**; *sl*) a homeboy. **hom'ing** *adj* returning home (also *n*); (*esp* of pigeons) trained to return home; guiding home; (of a navigational device on a missile, etc) guiding itself to the target or destination.

❑ **home'-and-home'** or **home'-and-away'** *adj* (of sports events) played alternately on one's own and one's opponents' home grounds. **home banking** or **home and office banking system** *n* a system offered by some banks allowing a person at home, in an office, etc to gain access to information about his or her own account(s), transfer funds, etc, via the Internet or by telephone. **home base** *n* (*baseball*) the home plate (qv below). **home bird** or **home body** *n* a person who likes to stay at home, whose interests are in the home. **home'-born** *adj* originating at home or in the home; native, not foreign. **home'bound** *adj* homeward bound; fixed to the home. **home'boy** *n* (*US sl*) a male acquaintance from one's own neighbourhood or town; a member of a youth gang. **home'-bred** *adj* bred at home; native; domestic; plain; unpolished. **home'-brewed** *adj* brewed at home or for home use (**home'-brew'** *n*); also *fig*. **home'buyer** *n* a person in the process of arranging to buy his or her own home. **home cinema** *n* a set of digital equipment for watching DVDs with high-quality reproduction at home. **home circuit** *n* (*law*) the south-eastern circuit of Assize with boundaries changed at various times. **home'-comer** *n*. **home'coming** *n* arrival at home; return home; an annual event at schools, colleges or universities at which graduates are welcomed (*US*). **homecoming queen** *n* (*US*) a female student elected to preside over a homecoming. **home counties** *n pl* the counties over and into which London has extended, ie Middlesex, Essex, Kent, Surrey (and sometimes also Herts and Sussex). **home'craft** *n* household skills; skills practised at home or concerned with home life. **home'-croft** *n* a cottage with a small piece of land for an industrial worker to grow his or her own food. **home'-crofter** *n*. **home'-crofting** *n*. **home-defence'** *n* defence of a country by a force of its own people within it. **Home Department** *n* the official title, now rarely used, of the Home Office (qv below). **home economics** *n sing* domestic science, household skills and management. **home economist** *n*. **home farm** *n* the farm attached to and near a large house. **home'felt** *adj* felt in one's own breast; inward; private. **home'-fire** *n* the domestic hearth, with its activities and connections. **home fries** *n pl* (*US*) sliced pieces of potato fried in oil or butter. **home'girl** *n* (*US sl*) a female acquaintance from one's own neighbourhood or town; a member of a youth gang. **home'-grown** *adj* produced in one's own country, or garden. **home guard** *n* a member of a volunteer force for the defence of a country; (with *caps*) a force of this kind (first formed in Britain in the war of 1939–45). **home help** *n* a person employed by the local authority to help disabled or elderly people with domestic work. **home'-keeping** *adj* staying at home. **home'land** *n* native land, fatherland; mother country; formerly in South Africa, the formal name for an area reserved for black African peoples (also **Bantustan**). **home'-life** *n* domestic life. **home loan** *n* a mortgage. **home'-made** *adj* made at home; made in one's own country; plain. **home'maker** *n* a housewife or house-husband. **home'making** *n*. **home market** *n* the market for goods in the country that produces them. **home movie** *n* a motion picture made at home, *usu* by an amateur. **home nurse** *n* a district nurse. **Home Office** *n* the government department broadly responsible for the domestic civil affairs of the United Kingdom as a whole. **home'owner** *n* someone who owns his or her own home. **home page** *n* (*comput*) the first or main page of an Internet website. **home plate** *n* (*baseball*) the final point which a batter must reach in order to score a run. **home port** *n* the port at which a boat is registered. **home'-produced'** *adj* produced within the country in question, not imported. **home range** *n* the area within which an animal normally confines its activities. **home report** *n* a statement of the condition of a dwelling-house that is for sale, made available by the seller to prospective buyers. **Home Rule** (also without *caps*) *n* self-government, such as that claimed by Irish, Scottish and Welsh Nationalists, including a separate parliament to manage internal affairs. **home'-rul'er** *n* an advocate of Home Rule. **home run** *n* (*baseball*) a hit that goes far enough to allow the batter to make a complete circuit of all four bases; the score made in this way. **home-school** *vt* (of parents) to teach (their children) at home rather than send them to school. **Home Secretary** *n* the head of the Home Office (qv above). **home shopping** *n* buying products and services by means of telecommunications such as the Internet or cable television. **home'sick** *adj* pining for home. **home'sickness** *n*. **home'-sig'nal** *n* a signal at the beginning of a section of railway line showing whether or not the section is clear. **home'spun** *adj* spun or made at home; not made in foreign countries; plain, unadorned; simple, artless, rustic; inelegant. ◆*n* cloth made at home; an unpolished person (*Shakesp*). **home'stall** *n* (*obs*) a homestead; a farmyard. **home'stead** *n* a dwelling-house with outhouses and enclosures immediately connected with it; a piece of public land allotted under special laws to

a settler (*US* and *Aust*); the house occupied by the owner or manager of a sheep or cattle station (*Aust* and *NZ*). **home'steader** *n*. **home'steading** *n* (*orig US*) a scheme by which people are permitted to buy, or live rent-free in, semi-derelict buildings and improve them with the help of Government grants, etc. **home straight** or **home stretch** *n* the last stretch of a racecourse; the final or winning stage of anything. **home'-thrust** *n* in fencing, a hit that goes home where it is aimed; a pointed remark that goes home. **home time** *n* the end of the formal school day at a day school. **home town** *n* the town where one's home is or was. **home truth** *n* a pointed, *usu* unanswerable, typically wounding, statement made direct to the person concerned. **home unit** *n* (*Aust* and *NZ*) a flat or apartment. **home video** *n* a home movie made with a video camera. **home'ward-bound'** *adj* bound homeward or to one's native land. **home'work** *n* work or preparation to be done at home, *esp* for school; paid work, *esp* piecework, done at home. **home'worker** *n* a person who works from home, *esp* someone who is linked to an office by computer, and under terms and conditions similar to those of conventional office workers. **home'working** *n*. **home zone** *n* a residential street or area where traffic-calming measures, the provision of benches, children's play areas, etc are intended to create a safer social environment and encourage pedestrian use.

■ **at home** in one's own house; ready to receive a visitor; feeling the ease of familiarity with a place or situation (see also under **at¹**). **bring home to** to prove to, in such a way that there is no way of escaping the conclusion; to impress upon. **do one's homework** (*inf*) to prepare oneself, eg for a discussion by acquainting oneself with the relevant facts. **eat someone out of house and home** (*inf*) to live at the expense of another person so as to ruin him or her. **go** or **strike home** (of a remark, etc) to impress itself duly on the mind of the person addressed. **home and dry** having arrived or achieved one's aim, etc; safe, successful, secure. **home from home** a place where one feels comfortable and at ease. **long home** the grave. **make oneself at home** to be as free and unrestrained as in one's own house. **not at home** out of one's house; not receiving visitors. **nothing to write home about** (*inf*) not very exciting or attractive. **pay home** to strike to the quick; to retaliate.

homelyn /*hom'ə-lin* or *hōm'lin*/ *n* the spotted ray. [Origin unknown]

homeo- or **homoeo-** /*hom-i-ō-*, *hom-i-ə-*, *hom-i-o-* or *hō-*/ or **homoio-** /*-moi-*/ *combining form* denoting: like, similar. [Gr *homoios* like, similar]

■ **hom'eobox** or **hom'oeobox** *adj* (of genes) that regulate the development of multicellular animals and plants. **homeomeric** or **homoeomeric** /*-mer'ik*/ *adj* homeomerous. **homeom'erous**, **homoeom'erous** or **homoiom'erous** *adj* (Gr *meros* part) composed of similar parts; (of lichens) having the algal cells distributed throughout the thallus; (in metameric animals) having all the somites alike. **homeom'ery** or **homoeom'ery** *n*. **hom'eomorph** or **hom'oeomorph** *n* (Gr *morphē* form) a thing similar in form to another but essentially different, *esp* a different chemical substance with similar crystalline form. **homeomorph'ic** or **homoeomorph'ic** *adj* of or relating to a homeomorph; of two geometrical figures, such that one can be converted into the other by distortion (*maths*). **homeomorph'ism** or **homoeomorph'ism** *n*. **homeomorph'ous** or **homoeomorph'ous** *adj*. **homeomorph'y** or **homoeomorph'y** *n*. **homeopath** or **homoeopath** /*hom'* or *hōm'i-ə-path*/ or **homeopathist** or **homoeopathist** /*-op'ə-thist*/ *n* (Gr *pathos* feeling) a person who believes in or practises homeopathy. **homeopathic** or **homoeopathic** /*-path'* / *adj*. **homeopath'ically** or **homoeopath'ically** *adv*. **homeopathy** or **homoeopathy** /*-op'ə-thi*/ *n* the system of treating diseases by small quantities of drugs that produce symptoms similar to those of the disease. **homeosis** or **homoeosis** /*hom-i-ō'sis*/ *n* (Gr *homoiōsis* a becoming like; *biol*) assumption of the character of a corresponding member of another whorl or somite. **homeostasis** or **homoeostasis** /*hom-i-os'tə-sis*/ *n* (Gr *stasis* a standing still) the tendency for the internal environment of the body to remain constant in spite of varying external conditions; a tendency towards health or stable physical conditions. **homeostat'ic** or **homoeostat'ic** *adj*. **homeoteleuton** or **homoeoteleuton** /*hom-i-ō-tel-ū'ton*/ *n* (Gr *homoioteleuton*, from *teleutē* ending) the use or occurrence of similar word endings. **homeotherm'al**, **homoeotherm'al**, **homeotherm'ic**, **homoeotherm'ic**, **homeotherm'ous** or **homoeotherm'ous**, also **homoi'other'mal**, etc *adj* homothermal (see under **homo-**). **homeot'ic** or **homoeot'ic** *adj* showing, depending on, or characterized by homeosis; (of a mutant) effecting large-scale changes in development, eg in Drosophila, the substitution of a leg for a wing. **homoiousian** /*hom-oi-oo'si-ən* or *-ow'*/ *adj* (Gr *ousiā* being) of similar (as distinguished from identical) essence; believing God the Father and God the Son to be of similar (not identical) essence. ◆*n* a holder of such belief, a semi-Arian.

homer¹ /*hō'mər*/ *n* a Hebrew measure of capacity, roughly 11 bushels. [Heb *khōmer* heap, from *khāmar* to swell up]

homer[2] see under **home**.

Homeric /hō-mer'ik/ adj relating to or associated with the Greek poet *Homer* (fl c.800BC); attributed to Homer; resembling Homer or his poetry; worthy of Homer; in the heroic or epic manner; relating to Bronze Age Greece. [Gr *homērikos*, from *Homēros* Homer]

■ **Homerid** /hō'mər-id/ n one of the **Homer'idae** /-i-dē/, Chian reciters of the Homeric poems, claiming descent from him.

❏ **Homeric laughter** n loud inextinguishable laughter (Gr *asbestos gelos*, from *Iliad*, 1.599). **Homeric question** the question of whether a single author wrote the *Iliad* and the *Odyssey*, disputed by some authorities.

homey see under **home**.

homicide /hom'i-sīd/ n manslaughter or murder; a person who kills another. [L *homicīdium* manslaughter, and *homicīda* a man-slayer, from *homō* a man, and *caedere* to kill]

■ **homici'dal** adj relating to homicide; murderous; bloody.

homie see under **home**.

homily /hom'i-li/ n a plain explanatory sermon, practical rather than doctrinal; a talk giving advice and encouragement. [Gr *homīlia* an assembly, a lecture or sermon, from *homos* the same, and *īlē* a company]

■ **homilet'ic** or **homilet'ical** adj. **homilet'ically** adv. **homilet'ics** n sing the art of preaching. **hom'ilist** n.

homing see under **home**.

hominid /hom'i-nid/ (zool) n an animal of the family **Homin'idae**, comprising humans and their close, now extinct, bipedal ancestors, but more recently taken to include all the great apes (also adj). [L *homō*, *-inis* man]

■ **hom'inin** n any member of the taxonomic tribe **Homin'inī**, usu taken to comprise humans and their direct ancestors, but sometimes taken also to include chimpanzees.

hominoid /hom'i-noid/ (zool) n a member of the superfamily **Hominoid'ea**, comprising humans and modern apes and their extinct ancestors (also adj). [L *homō*, *-inis* man]

hominy /hom'i-ni/ n maize hulled, or hulled and crushed; a kind of porridge made by boiling this. [Native American origin]

homme /om/ (Fr) n a man.

❏ **homme d'affaires** /da-fer'/ n a business man; an agent, steward. **homme de bien** /də byẽ/ n a man of worth, a good man. **homme de lettres** /də letr'/ n a man of letters. **homme d'épée** /dā-pā/ n a military man. **homme d'esprit** /des-prē/ n a man of wit. **homme d'état** /dā-tä/ n a statesman. **homme du monde** /dü mɔ̃d/ n a man of fashion. **homme moyen sensuel** /mwa-yẽ sä-sü-el/ n the ordinary man; the man in the street. **homme sérieux** /sā-ryø/ n a serious, earnest man.

hommock see **hummock**.

homo- /hom-ō-, hom-ə-, hə-mo- or hō-/ combining form denoting the same. [Gr *homos* same]

■ **homoblast'ic** adj (Gr *blastos* a germ; zool) derived from similar cells; showing direct embryonic development. **hom'oblasty** n. **homocentric** /-sen'trik/ adj (Gr *homokentros*, from *kentron* centre, point) concentric; proceeding from or diverging to the same point; (of rays) either parallel or passing through one focus (phys). **homocercal** /-sûr'kəl/ adj (Gr *kerkos* tail) (of fishes) having the upper and lower lobes of the tail-fin alike. **homochlamydeous** /-klə-mid'i-əs/ adj (Gr *chlamys*, *-ydos* cloak; bot) with calyx and corolla similar. **homochromat'ic** adj monochromatic. **homochromous** /-krō'məs/ adj (Gr *chrōma* colour) alike in colour; of the same colour. **homochromy** /-ok' or -krōm'/ n protective coloration. **homocyclic** /-sīk'lik/ adj (Gr *kyklos* a ring; chem) having a closed chain of similar atoms. **homocysteine** /-sis'tēn, -tin/ n an oxidized form of cysteine that occurs as a by-product of the metabolism of protein, thought to be an indicator of heart disease when present in high levels. **homodont** /hom'ə-dont/ adj (Gr *odous, odontos* tooth) having teeth all alike. **homodyne** /hom'ə-dīn/ adj (Gr *dynamis* power; radio telephony) applied to the reception of waves strengthened by the imposition of a locally generated wave of the same length. **homoerot'icism** or **homoerot'ism** n orientation of the libido towards someone of the same sex. **homoerot'ic** adj. **homogamet'ic** adj. **homogamic** /-gam'ik/ or **homogamous** /hom-og'ə-məs/ adj. **homogamy** /hom-og'ə-mi/ n (Gr *gamos* marriage) breeding of like with like; inbreeding; the condition of having all the flowers of an inflorescence sexually alike (bot); simultaneous ripening of stamens and stigmas (bot). **homogenate** /-oj'ə-nāt/ n a substance produced by homogenizing (see **homogenize** below). **homogeneity** /hom-ō-ji-nē'i-ti/ n the state or fact of being homogeneous. **homogeneous** /hom-ō-jēn'i-əs, also hōm-* or *-jen'/ adj (Gr *homogenēs*, from *genos* kind) of the same kind or nature; having the constituent elements similar throughout; (of the same degree or dimensions in every term (maths); (of radiation) of constant wavelength or constant quantum energy. **homogē'neousness** n. **homogenesis** /-jen'i-sis/ n (Gr *genesis* birth;

biol) a mode of reproduction in which the offspring is like the parent, and passes through the same cycle of existence. **homogenet'ic** or **homogenet'ical** adj homogenous. **homogeniza'tion** or **-s-** n. **homog'enize** or **-ise** (or /hom'o-jən-īz/) vt to make homogeneous; to make (milk) more digestible by breaking up fat globules, etc; to produce (milk) synthetically by mixing its constituents. **homog'enizer** or **-s-** n. **homogenous** /hom-oj'ən-əs/ adj similar owing to common descent. **homog'eny** n similarity owing to common descent or origin. **homograft** /hom'ō-gräft/ n (med) a graft of tissue from one individual to another of the same species (also **allograft**). **homograph** /hom'ə-gräf/ n (Gr *graphein* to write) a word of the same spelling as another, but of different meaning, pronunciation or origin. **homol'ogate** vt (LL *homologāre*, *-ātum*, from Gr *homologeein* to agree, from *logos* speech) to confirm; to approve; to consent to; to ratify. ◆ vi to agree. **homologa'tion** n (Scots law) confirming and ratifying by subsequent act. **homological** /-loj'/ adj. **homolog'ically** adv. **homol'ogize** or **-ise** /-jīz/ vt and vi. **homologoumena** or **homologumena** /hom-ol-o-goo'mi-nə/ n pl (Gr *homologoumena* things granted, neuter pl of prp passive (contracted) of *homologeein*) the books of the New Testament whose authenticity was universally acknowledged in the early Church, opp to *antilegomena*. **homologous** /hom-ol'ə-gəs/ adj agreeing; of the same essential nature, corresponding in relative position, general structure, and descent (med or biol); (of chromosomes) pairing with each other during meiosis, so that one member of each pair is carried by every gamete; (of a series of organic compounds) with each successive member having one more of a chemical group in its molecule than the preceding member. **hom'ologue** or (US) **hom'olog** /-ə-log'/ n anything that is homologous to something else, such as a human arm, a whale's flipper and a bird's wing. **homol'ogy** /-ə-ji/ n (Gr *homologos*) the quality of being homologous; affinity of structure and origin, apart from form or use. **hom'omorph** n (Gr *morphē* form) a thing having the same form as another. **homomorph'ic** or **homomorph'ous** adj alike in form, esp if essentially different otherwise; uniform. **homomorph'ism** n. **homomorphō'sis** n regeneration of a lost part in the original form. **hom'onym** n (Gr *homōnymos*, from *onyma* name) a word having the same sound and perhaps the same spelling as another, but a different meaning and origin, sometimes extended to words having a different sound and the same spelling; a name rejected as already used for another genus or species (biol); a namesake. **homonym'ic** adj relating to homonyms. **homon'ymous** adj having the same name; having different significations and origins but the same sound; ambiguous; equivocal. **homon'ymously** adv. **homon'ymy** n. **homonym'ity** n. **homoousian** or **homousian** /hom-ō-oo'si-ən, ho-moo' or -ow'/ adj (Gr *ousiā* being) of the same essence; believing God the Son to be of the same essence as God the Father. ◆ n a holder of such belief (according to the Nicene Creed). **hom'ophile** n (rare) a homosexual. **hom'ophobe** /-fōb/ n (Gr *phobos* fear) a person with a strong antipathy to homosexuals. **homophō'bia** n. **homophō'bic** adj. **homophone** /hom'ə-fōn/ n (Gr *phōnē* sound) a character representing the same sound as another; a word that is pronounced the same as another but is different in spelling and meaning. **homophonic** /-fon'/ adj sounding alike, in unison; in the monodic style of music, in which one part or voice carries the melody and the others accompany it. **homophonous** /-of'/ adj. **homoph'ony** n. **homophyly** /-of'i-li/ n (Gr *phȳlon* a race; biol) resemblance due to common ancestry. **hom'oplasmy** /-plaz-mi/ or **homop'lasy** n the quality or fact of being homoplastic. **homoplast'ic** adj (Gr *plastikos* plastic, *plasma* a mould; biol) similar in structure and development but not descended from a recent common source. **homopō'lar** adj (chem) having an equal distribution of charge, as in a covalent bond. **homopolar'ity** n. **homopol'ymer** n a DNA or RNA strand whose nucleotides are all of the same kind. **Homoptera** /-op'/ n pl (Gr *pteron* a wing) an order of insects (or suborder of Hemiptera) having wings of a uniform texture, eg cicadas, frog-hoppers, greenfly, scale insects, etc. **homop'terous** adj. **Homorelaps** n see under **Elaps**. **homosex'ual** adj having or relating to sexual attraction to members of one's own sex. ◆ n a person sexually attracted only to others of the same sex. **homosex'ualism** n. **homosex'ualist** n. **homosexual'ity** n. **homosporous** /-os'por-əs*, or *-ō-spō'rəs or -spō'/ adj (Gr *sporos* seed; bot) having spores all of one kind. **homotax'ial** or **homotax'ic** adj. **homotax'is** n (Gr *taxis* arrangement; geol) coincidence in order of organic succession but not necessarily in time; similarity in geological age, while not necessarily strict contemporaneity. **homothall'ic** adj (bot) having only one type of mycelium, opp to *heterothallic*. **homothall'ism** or **hom'othally** n. **homotherm'al**, **homotherm'ic** or **homotherm'ous** adj (Gr *thermē* heat) keeping the same temperature, warm-blooded. **homotonic** /-ton'/ or **homot'onous** adj (Gr *tonos* tone) of the same tenor or tone. **homot'ony** n. **homotypal** /-tīp'l/ or **homotypic** /-tip'ik/ adj conforming to normal type; (homotypic; biol) relating to the second (equational) division in meiosis (cf **heterotypic** under **heter-**). **hom'otype** /-ō-tīp/ n (Gr *typos* type) that which has the same fundamental structure as something else. **homotypy** /hom'ō-tī-pi or *hom-ot'i-pi/ n.* **homousian** *n* see **homoousian** above. **homozygōs'is** *n* the condition of having inherited a given genetic factor from both parents, so producing gametes of only one kind as regards that factor; genetic stability as regards a given factor. **homozy'gote** *n* a zygote that is formed as a result of homozygosis. **homozygot'ic** *adj.* **homozy'gous** *adj.*

homo[1] /hō'mō/ *n* humankind generically; (with *cap*; *zool*) the human genus. [L *homō, -inis* man, human being]
❏ **Homo erectus** *n* (formerly known as *Pithecanthropus erectus*) a name given to a type of erect hominid between *Australopithecus* and *Homo sapiens*, represented by Java man and Peking man. **Homo habilis** *n* a name given to a much earlier hominid, thought also to walk upright. **Homo neanderthalensis** see under **Neanderthal**. **Homo sapiens** *n* the one existing species of humans.

homo[2] /hō'mō/ (*inf*; *usu derog*) *n* (pl **ho'mos**) and *adj* (a) homosexual. [**homo-**]

homunculus /hō- or ho-mung'kyū-ləs/, also **homuncule** /-kūl/ or **homuncle** /-mung'kl/ *n* (pl **homunc'ulī**, **homunc'ules** or **homunc'les**) a tiny man capable of being produced artificially according to Paracelsus, endowed with magical insight and power; a dwarf, manikin; a dwarf of normal proportions (*med*); a minute human form believed by the spermatist school of preformationists to be contained in the spermatozoon. [L *homunculus*, dimin of *homō* a man]
■ **homunc'ūlar** *adj.*

homy see under **home**.

Hon. *abbrev* : honorary; Honourable (see under **honour**).

hon /hun/ (*inf*) *n* short for **honey** as a term of endearment.

honcho /hon'chō/ (*US sl*) *n* (pl **hon'chos**) a boss, a leader, a manager. ◆ *vt* (**hon'choing**; **hon'choed**) to lead or manage. [Jap *han'cho* squad leader]

hond /hond/ *n* an obsolete form of **hand**.

Honduran /hon-dū'rən/ *adj* (also **Hondūr'as**) of or relating to the Republic of *Honduras* in Central America, or its inhabitants. ◆ *n* a native or citizen of Honduras.
❏ **Honduras bark** *n* cascara amarga (qv).

hone[1] /hōn/ *n* a smooth stone used for sharpening instruments. ◆ *vt* to sharpen on or as if on a hone. [OE *hān*; ON *hein*; related to Gr *kōnos* a cone]
■ **ho'ner** *n.*
❏ **hone'-stone** *n* a hone; any hard fine-grained stone suitable for honing, *esp* novaculite.

hone[2] /hōn/ (*dialect*) *vi* to pine, moan, grieve (for or after). [Perh Fr *hogner* to grumble]

honest /on'ist or -əst/ *adj* truthful; full of honour; honourable; just; fair-dealing; upright, upstanding; the opposite of thieving; free from fraud or trickery; candid, frank; ingenuous; unpretentious; seemly; respectable (now *patronizing*); chaste (*archaic*). ◆ *adv* honestly (*inf*). [OFr *honeste*, from L *honestus*, from *honor*]
■ **hon'estly** *adv* in an honest way; in truth. ◆ *interj* expressing annoyance, disbelief, etc. **hon'esty** *n* the state of being honest; integrity; candour, frankness, truthfulness; a cruciferous garden plant (*Lunaria biennis*) with shining silver or satiny white dissepiments; decorum (*obs*); chastity (*Shakesp*).
❏ **honest broker** *n* an impartial mediator in a dispute. **hon'est-to-God'** or **hon'est-to-good'ness** *adj* genuine, out-and-out, complete (also *adv*). **honesty bar** *n* an unattended bar where patrons are expected to leave money to pay for their drinks. **honesty box** *n* a receptacle for money due for goods taken when no attendant is present.
■ **honest Injun** (*inf*) upon my honour. **make an honest woman of** (now *usu facetious*) to marry, where the woman has first been seduced.

honewort /hōn'wərt/ *n* a name given to various umbelliferous plants. [Poss *obs hone* a tumour, and **wort**[1]]

honey /hun'i/ *n* a sweet, thick fluid elaborated by bees from the nectar of flowers; its colour, golden brown; nectar of flowers; anything sweet like honey; a term of endearment; a person or thing that is excellent, pleasant or delightful (*inf*). ◆ *vt* (**hon'eying**; **hon'eyed** /-id/) to sweeten; to make agreeable. ◆ *vi* (*Shakesp*) to talk endearingly. ◆ *adj* (*Shakesp*) sweet. [OE *hunig*; Ger *Honig*; ON *hunang*]
■ **hon'eyed** or **hon'ied** *adj* covered with honey; (often falsely) sweet; seductive; flattering. **hon'eyless** *adj.*
❏ **honey ant** *n* one of several types of ant, *esp* of the genus *Myrmecocystus*, that feed on honey, and store it in the worker-ants, who disgorge it as necessary. **honey badger** *n* the ratel, a badger-like animal from India and Africa. **hon'ey-bag** *n* an enlargement of the alimentary canal of the bee in which it carries its load of honey. **honey bear** *n* the kinkajou, which robs the nests of wild bees; the sloth bear; the Malayan bear. **honey bee** *n* any of the varieties of bee

living in hives and producing honey. **hon'ey-bird** *n* a honey guide; a honey-sucker. **hon'ey-blob** *n* (*dialect*) a sweet yellow gooseberry. **hon'eybun** or **hon'eybunch** *n* terms of endearment. **honey buzzard** *n* a hawk (*Pernis apivorus*) that feeds on the larvae and honey of bees, wasps, etc. **hon'ey-cart**, **hon'ey-waggon** or **-wagon** *n* a truck for offensive refuse. **hon'ey-chile** *n* (*US dialect*) a term of endearment. **hon'eycomb** /-kōm/ *n* a comb or mass of waxy cells formed by bees in which they rear their young and store honey, pollen, etc; anything like a honeycomb; a bewildering maze (of rooms, cavities, etc). ◆ *vt* to make like a honeycomb; to spread into all parts of. **hon'eycombed** /-kōmd/ *adj.* **hon'eycombing** *n* honeycomb stitch. **hon'eycomb-moth** *n* a bee-moth. **honeycomb stitch** *n* an embroidery stitch used to hold the gathers made when smocking. **honey creeper** *n* any of several kinds of small, brightly-coloured S American birds which feed on nectar. **hon'ey-crock** *n* a crock or pot of honey. **hon'eydew** *n* a sugar secretion from aphids or plants; ambrosia; a fine sort of tobacco moistened with molasses. **honeydew melon** *n* a sweet-flavoured melon with smooth green or orange rind. **hon'eyeater** *n* any bird of a large Australian family, the Meliphagidae, which feeds on nectar. **honey fungus** or **mushroom** *n* a kind of honey-coloured edible mushroom (*Armillaria mellea*), a parasite on the roots of trees and shrubs, which it can kill. **honey guide** *n* a species of bird of a mainly African family (Indicatoridae) which guides humans and ratels to honey bees' nests by hopping from tree to tree with a peculiar cry; a marking on a flower said to show the way to the nectaries. **honey locust** *n* an ornamental N American tree (genus *Gleditsia*). **hon'eymoon** (*obs* **hon'eymonth**) *n* the first weeks after marriage, commonly spent on holiday, before settling down to the business of life; such a holiday; a holiday reminiscent of a honeymoon (also **second honeymoon**); a period of (unusual) harmony at the start of a new business relationship, term of office, etc (*fig*). ◆ *vi* to spend one's honeymoon (with *in*). **hon'eymooner** *n.* **hon'ey-mouse** *n* (*obs*) the honey possum. **hon'ey-mouthed** *adj* having a honeyed mouth or speech; soft or smooth in speech. **honey mushroom** see **honey fungus** above. **honey possum** *n* a long-snouted Australian marsupial (genus *Tarsipes*) that feeds on honey and insects (also **honey phalanger**). **hon'eypot** *n* a container for honey; anything that attracts people in great numbers (*fig*); (in *pl*) a children's game; see also **hanepoot** (*S Afr*). **hon'ey-sac** *n* a honey-bag (see above). **hon'ey-seed** or **hon'y-seed** *n* (*Shakesp, 2 Henry IV*) the Hostess's blunder for **homicide**. **hon'ey-stalk** *n* (*Shakesp*) probably the stalk or flower of the clover. **hon'ey-stone** *n* mellite, a very soft yellow mineral found with lignite. **hon'ey-sucker** *n* a honeyeater. **hon'eysuckle** *n* a climbing shrub (genus *Lonicera*) with mainly cream-coloured flowers, so named because honey is readily sucked from the flower (by long-tongued insects only); applied also to clover and many other plants; the rewarewa (*NZ*). **hon'ey-suckle** or **hon'y-suckle** *adj* (*Shakesp, 2 Henry IV*) the Hostess's blunder for **homicidal**. **hon'ey-sweet** *adj* sweet as honey. **hon'ey-tongued** *adj* soft, pleasing, persuasive, or seductive in speech; eloquent. **hon'ey-trap** *n* a scheme used to entrap someone, involving seduction or some other sexual act that could shame the person involved if the subsequent threat of exposure were carried out. **honey-wagon** see **honey-cart** above.
■ **virgin honey** honey that flows of itself from the comb. **wild honey** honey made by wild bees.

honeypot /hun'i-pot/ see under **honey** and **hanepoot**.

hong[1] /hong/ *n* a Chinese warehouse; a foreign mercantile house in China; one of the multinational trading and financial companies based in Hong Kong. [Chin *háng* row, range]

hong[2] /hong/ obsolete form of **hang**, **hung**.

hongi /hong'i/ *n* a traditional Maori greeting involving touching nose to nose. [Maori]

honied see **honeyed** under **honey**.

Honiton /hon'i-tən or (locally) hun'/ *adj* of a kind of pillow lace with sprigs, made at *Honiton*, Devon. ◆ *n* such lace.

honk /hongk/ *n* the cry of the wild goose; the noise of a motor horn. ◆ *vi* to make such a sound; to smell unpleasantly (*sl*); to vomit (*sl*). ◆ *vt* to sound (a horn). [Imit]
■ **honk'er** *n.* **honk'ing** *adj.*

honky or **honkie** /hong'ki/ (*derog sl, orig US*) *n* a white person (also *adj*). [Origin uncertain]

honky-tonk /hong'ki-tongk/ *n* a low drinking haunt (*N Am sl*); cheap entertainment; a style of jangly piano music. ◆ *adj* cheap and unsophisticated; (of piano music) having a jangly sound. [Ety dubious]

honor see **honour**.

honorand /on'ə-rand/ *n* a person receiving an honour, *esp* an honorary degree. [L *honōrandus*, gerundive of *honōrāre* to honour, from *honor, -ōris* honour]

honorarium /on-ə-rā'ri-əm/ *n* (pl **honorā'ria** or **honorā'riums**) a voluntary fee paid, *esp* to a professional person for his or her services.

[L *honōrārius*, *honōrārium* (*dōnum*) honorary (gift), from *honor*, *-ōris* honour]

honorary /on'ə-rə-ri/ *adj* conferring honour; (holding a title or office) without performing services or without reward. ◆ *n* an honorarium. [Ety as for **honorarium**]

honorific /(h)on-ə-rif'ik/ *adj* attributing or giving honour or respect. ◆ *n* an honorific form of title, address or mention. [L *honōrificus*, from *honor*, *-ōris* honour, and *facere* to do, make]
■ **honorif'ical** *adj*. **honorif'ically** *adv*.

honoris causa /(h)on-ō'ris or -ō̆' kow'zä or kö'zə/ or **honoris gratia** /grä'shi-ə or grä't(s)i-ä/ (*LL*) as an honour, as a token of respect.

honour or *US* **honor** /on'ər/ *n* the esteem due or paid to a worthy person, body, etc; respect; high estimation; veneration; that which rightfully attracts esteem; that which confers distinction or does credit; integrity; a fine and scrupulous sense of what is right; chastity; virginity; distinction; exalted rank; any mark of esteem; privilege; a title or decoration; a title of respect in addressing or referring to judges, etc; a prize or distinction; (in *pl*) privileges of rank or birth; an ornament or decoration (*poetic*); (in *pl*) civilities, respects paid; (in *pl*; in universities, etc) a higher grade of distinction for meritorious, advanced or specialized work; the right to play first from the tee (*golf*); any one of four best trumps in whist; (in bridge) an ace, king, queen, jack or ten in trumps, or an ace in a no-trump hand; (in *pl*) a score for holding these; a group of manors held by one lord. ◆ *vt* to hold in high esteem; to respect; to adorn (*obs*); to exalt; to do honour to; to confer honour(s) upon; to grace (eg with one's presence); to accept and pay when due; to fulfil (a promise, agreement, etc). [Anglo-Fr (h)onour, from L *honor*, *-ōris*]
■ **hon'ourable** *adj* worthy of honour; illustrious; governed by principles of honour, good, honest, etc; conferring honour; befitting people of exalted rank; (with *cap*; written **Hon.**) prefixed to the names of various people as a courtesy title. **hon'ourableness** *n* eminence; conformity to the principles of honour; fairness. **hon'ourably** *adv*. **hon'oured** *adj*. **honouree'** *n* a person who is honoured. **hon'ourer** *n*. **hon'ourless** *adj*.
❑ **hon'our-bound'** same as **in honour bound** below. **hon'or-guard** *n* (*US*) a guard of honour. **honour killing** *n* the killing by a member of a family of another family member whose actions are seen as bringing dishonour on the family as a whole. **hon'our-point** *n* (*heraldry*) the point just above the fesse-point. **honours list** *n* a list of people who have received or are to receive a knighthood, order, etc from the monarch for eg service to their community or country. **hon'ours-man** *n* (*old*) one who has taken a university degree with honours. **honours of war** *n pl* the privileges granted to a surrendering force of marching out with their arms, flags, etc. **honour system** *n* a system under which it is assumed that people will be honest, as in an unsupervised shop or examination.
■ **affair of honour** a duel. **birthday honours** honours granted to mark the monarch's birthday. **Companions of Honour** an order instituted in 1917 for those who have rendered conspicuous service of national importance. **Court of Honour** a court regulating affairs of honour. **debt of honour** see under **debt**. **do the honours** (*inf*) to perform a task, *esp* the duties of a host. **guard of honour** a body of soldiers serving as a ceremonial escort. **guest of honour** the most important or distinguished guest (at a party, etc). **honour bright** (*old school sl*) an oath or appeal to honour. **honours easy** see under **ease**. **in honour bound** (or *adj* **hon'our-bound'**) obliged by duty, conscience, etc (to). **in honour of** out of respect for; celebrating. **last honours** funeral rites. **laws of honour** the conventional rules of honourable conduct, *esp* in the conduct of duels. **maid of honour** a lady in the service of a queen or princess; a small almond-flavoured cake, or a kind of cheesecake; a bridesmaid (*N Am*). **matron of honour** a married woman in the service of a queen or princess; a married woman performing the duties of a bridesmaid, *esp* the chief bridesmaid. **military honours** ceremonial tokens of respect paid by troops to royalty, or at the burial of an officer, etc. **person of honour** (*obs*) a titled person. **point of honour** any scruple caused by a sense of duty, honour, self-respect, etc; the obligation to demand and to receive satisfaction for an insult, *esp* by duelling. **upon my honour** an appeal to one's honour in support of a statement. **word of honour** a promise that cannot be broken without disgrace.

hony-seed, **hony-suckle** see **honeysuckle** under **honey**.

hoo /hoo/ (*Shakesp*) *interj* expressing boisterous emotion (also **hoo-oo'**).

hooch[1] or **hootch** /hooch/ *n* whisky or any strong liquor, *esp* if illicitly made or acquired; *orig* a drink made by north-western Native Americans from fermented dough and sugar. [Said to be from *Hoochinoo*, a Native Alaskan people]

hooch[2] /hoohh/ *interj* a Highland dancer's shout.

hood[1] /hŭd/ *n* a flexible covering for the head and back of the neck, *esp* one attached to a coat, jacket or cloak; a covering for a hawk's head; a distinctively coloured ornamental fold of material, derived from a hood, worn on the back over an academic gown; a folding roof for a car, carriage, etc; a chimney-cowl; an overhanging or protective cover; the expansion of a cobra's neck; a hood-moulding; a car bonnet (*N Am*). ◆ *vt* to cover with a hood; to blind. [OE *hōd*; Du *hoed*, Ger *Hut*]
■ **hood'ed** *adj*. **hood'ie** *n* a hoodie crow; (the following meanings *inf*; also **hoody**) a hooded jacket or sweatshirt; a young person, *esp* a member of a gang, who wears such a garment. **hood'less** *adj* having no hood.
❑ **hooded seal** *n* a large seal (*Cystophora cristata*) of the N Atlantic, which has an inflatable sac over the nose region. **hoodie crow** *n* the hooded crow (*Corvus cornix*). **hood'man** *n* (*obs*) the person blindfolded in blindman's buff. **hood'man-blind** *n* (*Shakesp*) blindman's buff. **hood'-mould** or **hood'-moulding** *n* an uppermost projecting moulding over a door, window or arch.

hood[2] /hŭd/ (*sl*) *n* a hoodlum, a violent criminal.

hood[3] or **'hood** /hŭd/ (*US inf*) *n* a shortened form of **neighbourhood**.

hood[4] /hŭd/ (*Spenser*) *n* condition. [OE *hād*]

-hood /-hŭd/ *n sfx* indicating: state or nature, as in *hardihood*, *manhood* (also **-head** /-hed/ as in *Godhead*); a group of people, as in *priesthood*, *sisterhood*. [OE *hād*, Ger *-heit* state]

Hoodia /hŭd'i-ə/ *n* a genus of S African succulents whose leaves contain sap used as an appetite suppressant. [Van *Hood*, 19c English horticulturalist]

hoodlum /hood' or hŭd'ləm/ *n* a rowdy, street bully; a small-time criminal or gangster. [Origin uncertain]

hoodman see under **hood**[1].

hoodoo /hoo'doo/ *n* voodoo; a bringer of bad luck; a jinx; foreboding of bad luck; bad luck; a rock-pinnacle (*geol*). ◆ *vt* (**hoo'dooing**; **hoo'dooed**) to bewitch; to bring bad luck to. [Appar **voodoo**]

hoodwink /hŭd'wingk/ *vt* to deceive, cheat; to blindfold; to cover up, hide (*Shakesp*). [**hood**[1] and **wink**[1]]

hoody see under **hood**[1].

hooey /hoo'i/ (*inf*) *n* nonsense.

hoof /hoof or hŭf/ *n* (*pl* **hooves** or **hoofs**) the horny part of the feet of certain animals, eg horses; a hoofed animal; a foot (*inf*). ◆ *vt* to strike with the hoof, to kick; to expel; (with *it*) to walk (*sl*); (with *it*) to dance (*sl*). [OE *hōf*; Ger *Huf*; ON *hōfr*]
■ **hoofed** *adj*. **hoof'er** *n* (*sl*) a professional dancer. **hoof'less** *adj*.
❑ **hoof'beat** *n* the sound of a hoof striking *esp* a hard road. **hoof'-bound** *adj* having a contraction of the hoof causing lameness. **hoof'-mark** or **hoof'print** *n* the mark of a hoof on the ground, etc. **hoof'rot** *n* foot rot.
■ **on the hoof** (of animals) still alive, *esp* (of cattle) not yet slaughtered; on the move, moving (*inf*).

hoo-ha or **hoo-hah** /hoo'hä'/ (*sl*) *n* a noisy fuss. [Imit]

hook /hŭk/ *n* an object bent so that it can catch or hold something; a sharply bent line; a snare, trap, attraction, etc; an advantageous hold; a curved instrument for cutting grain, branches, etc; a spit of land with a hooked end; a boxer's swinging blow made with the elbow bent; the curve of a ball in flight (*sport*); an inadvertent stroke causing the ball to move in the air from right to left (for a right-handed player) or from left to right (for a left-handed player) (*golf*); an attacking stroke played with a horizontal bat sending the ball from shoulder height or above onto the leg-side behind the wicket (*cricket*); an act of hooking; in pop music, a catchy phrase; a twist or interesting point in a story (*sl*); an excuse or pretext (*sl*). ◆ *vt* to catch, fasten, or hold with or as if with a hook; to form into a hook; to make with a hook; to make (a **hooked rug**) by drawing yarn through a prepared backing with a hooked tool; to ensnare, trap; to attract; to hit (the ball) so that it inadvertently moves in the air from right to left (for a right-handed player), or from left to right (for a left-handed player) (*golf*); to hit (the ball) with a horizontal bat from shoulder height or above onto the leg-side behind the wicket (*cricket*); to punch with a swinging blow, with the elbow bent; to obtain possession of (the ball) in the scrum by using the foot to kick it backwards (*rugby*). ◆ *vi* to bend; to be curved; to pull abruptly; to act as hooker (*rugby*); (of a ball) to move in the air from right to left (for a right-handed player), or from left to right (for a left-handed player) (*golf*). [OE *hōc*; Du *hoek*]
■ **hooked** /hŭkt/ *adj* curved like a hook; physically dependent (on drugs); (with *on* or *by*) addicted (to a drug, activity or indulgence); enthralled. **hook'edness** *n*. **hook'er** *n* someone who hooks; the forward in the front row whose task it is to hook the ball (*rugby*); a prostitute (*inf*). **hook'y** *adj*.
❑ **hook'-climber** *n* a climbing plant that clings to its support by means of hooks. **hook'-nosed** *adj*. **hook'-pin** *n* an iron pin with a hooked head used for pinning the frame of a floor or roof together. **hook shot** *n* (*basketball*) a shot made by a player side-on to the basket by curving up the farther-away arm. **hook'-tip** *n* a moth with forewings

that have hooked ends. **hook'-up** *n* a connection; a temporary linking up of separate broadcasting stations for a special transmission. **hook'worm** *n* a parasitic nematode with hooks in the mouth; the disease it causes, ankylostomiasis or miner's anaemia.

■ **by hook or by crook** by one method or another. **hook and eye** a contrivance for fastening garments by means of a hook that catches in a loop or eye. **hook into** (*inf*) to form a connection or association with. **hook it** (*sl*) to decamp, make off. **hook, line and sinker** complete or completely. **hook up** to fasten or be fastened with a hook or hooks; to connect or be connected electronically; to meet, *esp* by arrangement (*inf*). **off the hook** ready-made; out of difficulty or trouble; (of a telephone handset) not on its rest, so that incoming calls cannot be received. **off the hooks** out of gear; superseded; dead. **on one's own hook** on one's own responsibility, initiative or account. **sling** or **take one's hook** (*sl*) to get out, run away, make off.

hookah or **hooka** /*hŭk'ə*/ *n* the tobacco pipe of Arabs, Turks, etc with which smoke is inhaled through water. [Ar *huqqah* bowl, casket]

hooker¹ /*hŭk'ər*/ *n* a two-masted Dutch or Irish fishing-vessel; a small fishing-smack. [Du *hoeker*]

hooker² see under **hook**.

Hooke's law see under **law¹**.

hookey¹ or **hooky** /*hŭk'i*/ (*US inf*) *n* truant, in the phrase *play hookey*.
■ **blind hookey** a gambling card game. **Hookey Walker** see under **walk¹**.

hookey² see **hockey¹**.

hooky see under **hook, hookey¹**.

hoolachan /*hoo'lə-hhən*/ or **hoolican** /*hoo'li-kən*/ (*Scot*) *n* a Highland reel, *esp* the reel of Tulloch. [Gaelic (*ruidhle*) *Thulachain* the reel of Tulloch, in Strathspey]

hooley /*hoo'li*/ (chiefly *Irish*) *n* a boisterous party, *usu* with singing and dancing. [Origin unknown]

hooligan /*hoo'li-gən*/ *n* a street tough, vandal; a (young) violent, rude person. [Said to be the name of a leader of a gang, poss *Houlihan* or *Hooley's gang*]
■ **hool'iganism** *n*.

hoolock /*hoo'lək*/ *n* a small gibbon of NE India. [Said to be a native name, *hulluk*]

hooly /*hül'i*/ or **hūl'i**/ (*Scot*) *adv* softly, carefully (also *adj*). [Perh ON *hōfliga* fitly, or *hōgliga* gently]
■ **hooly and fairly** fair and soft, gently.

hoon /*hoon*/ (*Aust* and *NZ inf*) *n* a lout, yob; a pimp (*obs*). ◆ *vi* to act loutishly.

hoo-oo see **hoo**.

hoop¹ /*hoop*/ *n* a ring or circular band, *esp* for holding together the staves of casks, etc; any large ring, eg for a child to roll, for leaping through, for holding wide a skirt; a ring; a croquet arch. ◆ *vt* to bind with hoops; to encircle. [OE *hōp*; Du *hoep*]
■ **hoop'er** *n* a person who hoops casks; a cooper.
□ **hoop'-ash** *n* a kind of ash used for making hoops; the nettle-tree (genus *Celtis*). **hooped'-pot** *n* a drinking-pot with hoops to mark the amount each person should drink. **hoop'-la** *interj orig* used at a circus when a performer jumped through a hoop. ◆ *n* a fairground game in which small hoops are thrown over prizes; great activity, excitement or disturbance; pointless activity, nuisance, nonsense (*US sl*). **hoop'-snake** *n* any of several harmless snakes, once erroneously believed to be capable of forming themselves into a hoop and rolling over the ground.
■ **go through the hoop** to suffer an ordeal, undergo punishment. **jump through hoops** to go through complicated procedures in order to please or satisfy.

hoop², **hooper¹** and **hooping-cough** see **whoop**.

hooper² see under **hoop¹**.

hoopoe /*hoo'poo*/ *n* a crested bird with salmon-coloured plumage (*Upupa epops*), an occasional visitor to Britain. [Earlier *hoop*, from OFr *huppe*, partly remodelled on L *upupa*; cf Gr *epops*]

hoor /*hoor*/ *n* a Scots and Irish form of **whore**; a difficult or unpleasant thing or person (*inf*).
■ **cute hoor** (*Irish inf*) an astute, devious person.

hooray¹ or (*old*) **hoorah** same as **hurrah**.
□ **Hooray** (or **Hoorah**) **Henry** *n* (*inf*) a young upper-class man with an affectedly ebullient manner.

hooray² /*hū-rā'*/ or **hooroo** /*-roo'*/ (*Aust*) *interj* goodbye, cheerio.

hoord an obsolete form of **hoard¹**.

hoosegow or **hoosgow** /*hoos'gow*/ (*US sl*) *n* a prison, jail. [Sp *juzgado* tribunal, courtroom, from *juzgar* to judge, from L *jūdicāre*]

hoosh¹ /*hoosh*/ *interj* used in driving away animals. ◆ *vt* to drive or shoo away. [Imit]

hoosh² /*hoosh*/ *n* a thick soup.

Hoosier /*hoo'zhi-ər* or *-zhər*/ (*US*) *n* a native of the state of Indiana.

hoot /*hoot*/ *vi* (of an owl) to give a hollow cry; to make a sound like an owl, *usu* expressing hostility or scorn; to laugh loudly; to sound a motor-horn, siren, or the like (also *vt*). ◆ *vt* to greet or drive with such sounds. ◆ *n* the sound of hooting; the note of an owl, motor-horn, etc; a jot, a care (often in the phrase *not give two hoots*); a hilarious performance, escapade, person, etc (*inf*). ◆ *interj* (*old Scot*; often **hoots**) expressing incredulity, irritation, annoyance, etc (also **hoot'-toot'** or **hoots'-toots'**). [Imit, prob immediately Scand; cf Swed *hut* begone]
■ **hoot'er** *n* someone who hoots; a siren or steam-whistle at a factory, mine, etc; a nose, *esp* a large or ugly one (*sl*); (in *pl*) breasts (*N Am vulgar sl*).

hootch see **hooch¹**.

hootenanny, **hootananny** or **-ie** /*hoo'tə-na-nē*/ or **hootnanny** or **-ie** /*hoot'na-nē*/ *n* thingummy (*US dialect*); a party with folk-singing and sometimes dancing, *esp* an informal concert with folk music (*N Am inf*).

hoove¹ /*hoov*/ *n* a disease of cattle and sheep, marked by distension of the abdomen by gas (also **wind dropsy** or **drum-belly**). [Cf **heave**]
■ **hoov'en** or **hō'ven** *adj*.

hoove² see **hove²**.

Hoover® /*hoo'vər*/ *n* a vacuum cleaner. ◆ *vt* and *vi* (*usu* without *cap*) to clean with (or suck up, etc as if with) a vacuum cleaner; to eat quickly and greedily. [WH *Hoover* (1849–1932), US businessman who bought the patent]

hooves see **hoof**.

hop¹ /*hop*/ *vi* (**hopp'ing**; **hopped**) to leap on one leg; to move in jumps like a bird; to walk lame; to limp; to move smartly (in or out); to fly (in aircraft) (*inf*). ◆ *vt* to cause to hop; to jump or fly over; to jump from; to board when in motion (*US*). ◆ *n* a leap on one leg; a jump; a spring; a dance, dancing party (*inf*); one stage in a journey by aeroplane. [OE *hoppian* to dance; Ger *hopfen*, *hüpfen*]
■ **hopp'er** *n* someone who hops; a hopping or leaping animal, *esp* (*US*) a grasshopper; a jack or sticker of a piano; a shaking or moving receiver, funnel or trough (*orig* a shaking one) in which something is placed to be conveyed or fed, as to a mill; a barge with an opening in its bottom for discharging refuse; a railway wagon with an opening in the bottom for discharging its cargo; a container in which seed corn is carried for sowing; a device in early computers that held and passed on punched cards to a feed mechanism. **-hopping** *combining form* denoting: making quick journeys between, *usu* by air, as in *island-hopping*; (of an aircraft) skimming, as in *hedge-hopping*.
□ **hop-off'** *n* the start of a flight. **hop'-o'-my-thumb** *n* (ie on my thumb) a pygmy. **hop'scotch** *n* a game in which children hop over lines scotched or scored on the ground.
■ **hop it** (*sl*) to take oneself off, go away. **hopping mad** (*inf*) extremely angry. **hop, skip** (or **step**) **and jump** a leap on one leg, a skip, and a jump with both legs as an athletic event, the triple jump. **hop the twig** (*sl*) to escape one's creditors; to die. **on the hop** in a state of restless activity; in the act, unawares, at the very moment.

hop² /*hop*/ *n* a plant (*Humulus lupulus*) of the mulberry family with a long twining stalk; (in *pl*) its bitter catkin-like fruit-clusters used for flavouring beer and in medicine; opium (*old US sl*); any narcotic (*old sl*). ◆ *vt* (**hopp'ing**; **hopped**) to mix or flavour with hops. ◆ *vi* to gather hops. [Du *hop*]
■ **hopped** *adj* impregnated with hops. **hopp'er** *n* (also **hop'-picker**) a person who picks hops; a mechanical contrivance for stripping hops from the bines. **hopp'ing** *n* the act of gathering hops; the time of the hop harvest. **hopp'y** *adj* tasting of hops.
□ **hop'bind** or **hop'bine** *n* the stalk of the hop. **hop'-bitters** *n* a drink like ginger beer, flavoured with hops. **hop'dog** *n* the tussock moth caterpillar; a tool for pulling out hop-poles. **hop'-flea** *n* a small beetle that damages hops. **hop'-fly** *n* a greenfly that damages hops. **hop'-garden** *n* a field of hops. **hop'head** *n* (*derog sl*) a drug addict; a drunkard (*Aust* and *NZ*). **hop'-oast** *n* a kiln for drying hops. **hopped'-up** *adj* (*US sl*) drugged; under an exhilarating drug; excited, agitated; artificially stimulated; made to seem exciting; given added power. **hop'-picker** *n* a hopper. **hop pillow** *n* a pillow stuffed with hops, said to aid sleep. **hop'-pocket** *n* coarse sack for hops; an amount of hops equal to *approx* 75 kilos or 1½cwt. **hop'-pole** *n* a pole supporting a hopbine. **hop'-sack** or **hop'sack** *n* a sack for hops. **hop'sack** or **hop'-sacking** *n* sacking for hops; coarse fabric of hemp and jute, or woollen fabric with a roughened surface. **hop'-tree** *n* an American rutaceous shrub (*Ptelea trifoliata*) with bitter fruit, a substitute for hops. **hop'-tre'foil** *n* a yellow clover. **hop'-vine** *n* hop-plant; its stem. **hop'-yard** *n* a field where hops are grown.
■ **hop up** (*old sl*) to excite, artificially stimulate; to drug.

hope[1] /hōp/ vi to cherish a desire (that something good will happen), with some expectation of success or fulfilment; to have confidence; to be hopeful. ◆ vt to desire, with belief in the possibility of fulfilment; to expect, fear (obs). ◆ n a desire for something good, with a certain expectation of obtaining it; confidence; anticipation; that on which hopes are grounded; an embodiment of hope; the event, object, etc that is hoped for. [OE hopian, from hopa hope; Du hopen, Ger hoffen]

■ **hope'ful** adj full of hope; having qualities that excite hope; promising good or success. ◆ n a promising young person; a (usu young) person of ambition. **hope'fully** adv in a hopeful manner; if all goes well (inf). **hope'fulness** n. **hope'less** adj without hope; giving no reason to expect good or success; incompetent; incurable; unhoped-for (Spenser). **hope'lessly** adv. **hope'lessness** n. **hōp'er** n. **hōp'ingly** adv (archaic).

❑ **hope chest** n (N Am) a place, often a trunk or chest, for things stored by a woman for her marriage, a bottom drawer.

■ **hope against hope** to continue to hope when there is no (longer any) reason for hope. **it is hoped** (inf) if all goes well. **no'-hop'er** (inf) a racehorse that is not good enough to have a chance of winning; any person or thing that has absolutely no chance of success (**no'-hope'** adj). **some hope**, **what a hope** or **not a hope** (ironic) that will never happen.

hope[2] /hōp/ n an enclosure; the upper end of a narrow mountain-valley; (in place names) a combe (usu pronounced /-əp/); an inlet. [OE -hop (in compounds), or ON hōp]

hope[3] see **forlorn hope**.

Hopi /hō'pē/ n (pl **Hō'pi** or **Hō'pis**) a member of a Pueblo people living chiefly in NE Arizona; the Uto-Aztec language of this people. ◆ adj of the Hopi or their language. [Hopi Hópi peaceful ones]

hoplite /hop'līt/ n a heavily-armed Greek foot soldier. [Gr hoplītēs]

hoplology /hop-lol'ə-ji/ n the study of weapons. [Gr hoplon tool, weapon]

■ **hoplol'ogist** n.

hopped, **hopped-up** see under **hop**[2].

hopper, **hopping** see **hop**[1,2].

hopple /hop'l/ vt to restrain by tying the feet together. ◆ n (chiefly in pl) a fetter for horses, etc when left to graze. [Cf obs Flem hoppelen; also **hop**[1] and **hobble**]

hoppus foot or **hoppus cubic foot** /hop'əs (kū'bik) fŏŏt/ n a unit of volume for round timber. [Edward Hoppus, English surveyor who devised it in 1736]

hoppy see under **hop**[2].

hopscotch see under **hop**[1].

hora or **horah** /hō'rə/ n a Romanian or Israeli dance performed in a circle; music for this. [Romanian horă, Heb hōrāh]

horae canonicae /hō' or hō'rē kən-on'i-kē, or hō'rī kan-on'i-kī/ (L) n pl the canonical hours.

horal /hō'rəl/ adj relating to hours; hourly. [L hōra an hour]

■ **ho'rary** adj (archaic) relating to an hour; noting the hours; hourly; continuing for an hour.

Horatian /hor-ā'shən/ adj relating to Horace, the Roman poet (65–8BC), or to his manner or verse.

horde /hörd/ n a migratory or wandering tribe or clan; a multitude. ◆ vi to live together as a horde; to come together to form a horde. [Fr, from Turk ordu camp]

■ **Golden Horde** see under **golden**.

Hordeum /hör'di-əm/ n the barley genus. [L, barley]

■ **hordein** /hör'di-in/ n a protein found in barley grains. **hordeolum** /-dē'/ n a sty on the eyelid.

hordock /hör'dok/ n a variant reading for **hardoke**.

hore (Spenser) same as **hoar**.

horehound or **hoarhound** /hör'hownd/ n a hoary labiate plant (Marrubium vulgare) once popular as a remedy for coughs (also called **white horehound**). [OE hār hoar, and hūne horehound]

■ **black horehound** or **stinking horehound** a darker-coloured related weed (Ballota nigra). **water horehound** gypsywort.

horizon /hə-rī'zən/ n the line at which earth and sky seem to meet (called the **sensible**, **apparent** or **visible horizon**); a plane through the earth's centre parallel to the sensible horizon (called the **rational horizon**), or the great circle in which it meets the heavens (**celestial horizon**; astron); a horizontal reflecting surface, eg of mercury, used as a substitute for the horizon in taking an observation (an **artificial horizon**); a stratigraphical level, characterized generally by some particular fossil or fossils (geol), by a different physical property of the soil (soil science), or by artefacts characteristic of a particular culture or period (archaeol); a level line or surface (anat); (often pl) the limit of one's experience or mental vision. [Fr, from L, from Gr horizōn

(kyklos) bounding (circle); horizōn, -ontos, prp of horizein to bound, from horos a limit]

■ **horizontal** /hor-i-zont'l/ adj relating to the horizon; parallel to the horizon; level; near the horizon; measured in the plane of the horizon; applying equally to all members of a group, aspects of an activity, etc; of relationships between separate groups of equal status or stage of development; denoting a balance sheet in which assets are set out in one column, and equity and liabilities in another, side by side (account). ◆ n a horizontal line, position or object; (also **horizontal scrub**) a large Tasmanian shrub, whose stem and branches ascend and then grow horizontally to form a dense mass of boughs and foliage. **horizontal'ity** n. **horizon'tally** adv.

❑ **horizontal bar** n (gym) a steel bar used for swinging and vaulting exercises.

horkey see **hockey**[2].

Horlicks® /hör'liks/ n a proprietary malt drink. [After the original manufacturers, J and W Horlick]

■ **make a Horlicks of** (sl) to make a complete mess of.

horme /hör'mē/ (psychol) n goal-directed or purposive behaviour. [Gr hormē animal impulse]

❑ **hormic theory** n theory stressing the importance of instinctive impulses and purposive striving.

hormesis /hör-mē'sis/ (med) n a phenomenon whereby substances that are toxic in large doses have a beneficial effect when absorbed in very small doses. [Gr, from hormaein to excite]

■ **hormetic** /-met'ik/ adj.

hormone /hör'mōn/ n an internal secretion that, on reaching some part of a plant or animal body, exercises a specific physiological action; a synthetic compound with the same function. [Gr hormōn, contracted prp of hormaein to stir up]

■ **hormon'al** adj. **hormon'ally** adv. **hormon'ic** (or /-mōn'/) adj.

❑ **hormone replacement therapy** n a treatment for post-menopausal women involving the artificial provision of a hormone that is no longer produced naturally after the menopause, thereby reducing the risk of brittle bones in later life.

horn /hörn/ n a hard outgrowth on the head of an animal, sometimes confined to the hollow structure on an ox, sheep, goat, etc, sometimes extended to a deer's antler, the growth on a giraffe's head, on a rhinoceros's snout, etc; a beetle's antenna; a snail's tentacle; any projection resembling a horn; a cusp; a crescent tip; either of the pair of outgrowths supposed to spring from a cuckold's forehead; the material of which horns are composed, keratin; an object made of or like a horn, eg a drinking vessel; a funnel-shaped mouthpiece; a primitive musical instrument consisting of an animal's horn, blown through to produce sound; any of various brass instruments consisting of a tube tapering to a mouthpiece; an apparatus on motor vehicles for making a noise warning of approach; a Jewish symbol of strength; (cap; with the) Cape Horn, in S America; an erection of the penis (vulgar sl); the telephone (US sl); see also **horn balance** below. ◆ adj made of horn. ◆ vt to furnish with horns, real or cuckold's; to dishorn; to outlaw (obs Scots law); to gore; to butt or push. ◆ vi to play or blow the horn; to butt. [OE horn; Scand horn, Ger Horn, Gaelic and Welsh corn, L cornū, Gr keras]

■ **horned** adj having a horn or horns; curved like a horn. **horn'er** n a person who works or deals in horns; a horn player; a cuckold-maker (obs). **horn'ful** n. **Horn'ie** n (Scot) the Devil, usu represented with horns. **horn'iness** n. **horn'ing** n appearance of the moon when in its crescent form; a mock serenade with tin horns and any discordant instruments, a shivaree (US dialect); putting to the horn (obs Scots law; see below); cuckold-making (obs). **horn'ish** adj like horn; hard. **horn'ist** n a horn player. **horn'less** adj without horns. **horn'let** n a little horn. **horn'y** adj like horn; of horn; hard; callous; sexually aroused or arousing (sl); lecherous, lustful (sl).

❑ **horn balance** n a forward extension of an aircraft control surface to assist its operation. **horn'beak** n (dialect) the garfish. **horn'beam** n a tree (genus Carpinus) resembling a beech, with hard tough wood. **horn'bill** n a bird (of family Bucerotidae) with a horny excrescence on its bill. **horn'book** n (hist) a first book for children, which consisted of a single leaf set in a frame, with a thin plate of semitransparent horn in front to preserve it. **horn'bug** n (US) a stag beetle. **horned cairn** n (archaeol) a long barrow with a pair of curved projecting arms at one end, or at both. **horned horse** n the gnu. **horned owl** or **horn owl** n an owl with hornlike tufts of feathers on its head. **horned poppy** n a poppy (genus Glaucium) with a horned seed vessel. **horned toad** n a spiny American lizard (genus Phrynosoma; also **horned lizard**); a S American toad (Ceratophrys) with a bony shield on the back. **horned viper** n a viper of N African and Near Eastern deserts with a horn-like spine above each eye. **horn'-footed** adj hoofed. **horn gate** n gate of horn (see under **gate**[1]). **horn'geld** n (hist) cornage. **horn'-mad** adj (archaic) mad to the point of goring anybody; enraged like a cuckold. **horn'-madness** n (Browning). **horn'-maker** n (Shakesp) a cuckold-maker. **horn mercury** *n* native mercurous chloride or calomel. **horn'-nut** *n* water chestnut. **horn of plenty** *n* see **cornucopia**; a trumpet-shaped edible fungus, *Craterellus cornucopoides*. **horn-pout, horned-pout** see under **pout²**. **horn'-rimmed** *adj* (*esp* of spectacles) having rims of horn, or material resembling horn. **horn'-rims** *n pl* spectacles with rims of dark horn, or material resembling horn. **horn silver** *n* cerargyrite. **horn spoon** *n* a spoon made of (*usu* a sheep's) horn. **horn'stone** *n* (*mineralogy*) a flinty chalcedony; hornfels. **horn'tail** *n* a hymenopterous insect, often with a stout ovipositor. **horn'work** *n* an outwork having angular points or horns, and composed of two demi-bastions joined by a curtain (*fortif*); work in horn; cuckoldry (*obs*). **horn'worm** *n* a hawk moth caterpillar. **horn'wort** *n* a rootless water plant (genus *Ceratophyllum*) with much-divided submerged leaves that turn translucent and horny. **horn'wrack** *n* the sea mat. **horn'y-hand'ed** *adj* with hands hardened by toil. **horn'yhead** *n* an American cyprinoid fish with hornlike processes on its head.

■ **horn in** (*sl*) to interpose, butt in (on). **horns of a dilemma** see under **dilemma. horns of the altar** the projections at the four corners of the Hebrew altar. **letters of horning** (*Scots law*; *obs*) letters running in the sovereign's name, and passing the signet, instructing messengers-at-arms to charge the debtor to pay, on his failure a caption or warrant for his apprehension being granted. **make a spoon or spoil a horn** to attempt something at the risk of failure. **pull** or **draw in one's horns** to moderate one's ardour or pretensions; to curtail or restrict one's activities, spending, etc. **put to the horn** (*obs Scots law*) to outlaw by three blasts of the horn at the Cross of Edinburgh.

hornblende /hörn'blend/ *n* a rock-forming mineral, one of the amphiboles, essentially silicate of calcium, magnesium and iron, generally green to black, with a cleavage angle of about 561. [Ger; cf **horn** and **blende**]
■ **hornblend'ic** *adj*.

horned, horner see under **horn**.

hornet /hör'nit/ *n* a large kind of wasp. [OE *hyrnet*, appar from *horn* horn]
■ **stir up a hornet's** (or **hornets'**) **nest** to do something that causes a violent reaction.

hornfels /hörn'fels/ (*mineralogy*) *n* a compact type of rock composed of lime silicates. [Ger, from *Horn* horn, and *Fels* rock]

hornful, horngeld, Hornie, horniness, horning, hornish, hornist see under **horn**.

hornito /hör-nē'tō/ *n* (*pl* **horni'tos**) a low oven-shaped fumarole. [Sp, dimin of *horno*, from L *furnus* an oven]

hornless, hornlet see under **horn**.

hornpipe /hörn'pīp/ *n* an old Welsh musical instrument like a clarinet, probably sometimes having a horn mouthpiece or bell; a lively English dance, usually by one person, traditionally popular amongst sailors; a tune for the dance. [**horn** and **pipe¹**]

hornstone see under **horn**.

hornswoggle /hörn'swo-gl/ (*inf*; *orig* and *esp US*) *vt* to trick, deceive; to cheat. [Ety unknown]

horntail...to...**hornwrack, horny** see under **horn**.

horography /hor-og'rə-fi/ *n* the art of constructing sundials, clocks, etc. [Gr *hōrā* an hour, and *graphein* to describe]
■ **horog'rapher** *n*.

horologe /hor'ə-loj/ *n* any instrument for telling the time. [L *hōrologium*, from Gr *hōrologion*, from *hōrā* an hour, and *legein* to tell]
■ **horologer** /-ol'ə-jər/ or **horol'ogist** *n* a maker of clocks, etc. **horolog'ic** or **horolog'ical** *adj*. **horolog'ium** *n* a horologe (*obs*); (with *cap*) a southern constellation (*astron*). **horol'ogy** *n* the science of the measurement of time; the art of clock-making; the office-book of the Greek Church for the canonical hours (also **horologium**).

horometry /hor-om'i-tri/ *n* time measurement. [Gr *hōrā* an hour, and *metron* a measure]
■ **horometrical** /-met'/ *adj*.

horoscope /hor'ə-skōp/ *n* a map of the heavens at the hour or on the day of a person's birth, by which an astrologer predicts the events of a person's life; such a prediction; a representation of the heavens for this purpose; any similar prediction about the future. [Gr *hōroskopos*, from *hōrā* an hour, and *skopeein* to observe]
■ **horoscopic** /-skop'ik/ *adj*. **horoscopist** /-os'kə-pist/ *n* an astrologer. **horos'copy** *n* the art of predicting the events of a person's life from his or her horoscope; the aspect of the stars at the time of birth.

horrendous /ho-ren'dəs/ (*inf*) *adj* dreadful; frightful; horrible. [L *horrendus*, gerundive of *horrēre* to bristle]
■ **horren'dously** *adv*. **horren'dousness** *n*.

horrent /hor'ənt/ *adj* (*literary*) bristling. [L *horrēns, -entis*, prp of *horrēre* to bristle]

horrible /hor'i-bl/ *adj* producing horror; dreadful; detestable, foul (*inf*). [L *horribilis*, from *horrēre* to shudder]
■ **horr'ibleness** *n*. **horr'ibly** *adv*.

horrid /hor'id/ *adj* nasty, repellent, detestable (*inf*); shaggy, bristling, rough (*archaic* or *poetic*); horrible (*archaic*). [L *horridus*, from *horrēre* to bristle]
■ **horr'idly** *adv*. **horr'idness** *n*.

horrify /hor'i-fī/ *vt* (**horr'ifying; horr'ified**) to produce a reaction of horror in (a person). [L *horrificus*, from root of *horrēre* to shudder, with *facere* to make]
■ **horrif'ic** *adj* producing horror; frightful, awful. **horrif'ically** *adv*. **horrificā'tion** *n*. **horr'ifyingly** *adv*.

horripilation /hor-i-pi-lā'shən/ *n* a contraction of the cutaneous muscles causing erection of the hairs and gooseflesh. [L *horripilātiō, -ōnis*, from root of *horrēre* to bristle, and *pilus* a hair]
■ **horrip'ilant** *adj*. **horrip'ilate** *vt* and *vi*.

horror /hor'ər/ *n* intense repugnance or fear; the power of producing such feelings; a source of such feelings; any person or thing that is mildly objectionable, ridiculous, grotesque or distasteful (*inf*); shagginess, raggedness (*obs*); a shuddering (*obs*). [L *horror* a shudder, bristling, etc]
❑ **horror comic, horror film, horror novel**, etc *n* a comic (ie strip cartoon), film, novel, etc having gruesome, violent, horrifying, or bloodcurdling themes. **horror story** *n* a story (often true) of one disaster after another; such a sequence of events, a chapter of accidents. **horr'or-stricken** or **horr'or-struck** *adj*.
■ **the horrors** extreme depression, frightening thoughts; delirium tremens.

hors /or/ (*Fr*) *prep* out of, outside.
■ **hors concours** /k3-koor/ not in competition. **hors de combat** /də k3-ba/ unfit to fight, disabled. **hors de saison** /də se-z3/ out of season. **hors d'œuvre** (*pl* **d'œuvre** or **d'œuvres** /dæ-vr'/) a savoury snack, eg olives, canapés, etc to whet the appetite before a meal. **hors la loi** /la lwa/ in outlawry, outlawed. **hors série** /sā-rē/ excluded from a series, added later. **hors texte** /tekst/ an illustration inset separately into a book.

horse /hörs/ *n* (*pl* **horses**, or sometimes **horse**) a solid-hoofed ungulate (*Equus caballus*) with flowing tail and mane, widely domesticated for riding and as a draught animal; any member of the genus *Equus* (horse, ass, zebra, etc) or the family Equidae; a male adult of the species; cavalry (*collectively*); a wooden frame on which soldiers used to be mounted as a punishment (also **timber-mare**); a gymnastic apparatus for vaulting over, etc; a horselike apparatus or support of various kinds (such as *saw-horse, clothes-horse*); a crib or translation, a pony (*US sl*); a mass of barren country interrupting a lode (*mining*); heroin (*sl*). ◆ *vt* to mount or set on, or as if on, a horse; to provide with a horse; to sit astride; to carry on the back; (of a stallion) to copulate with (a mare); to urge to work tyrannically. ◆ *vi* to get on horseback; to travel on horseback; to charge for work before it is done (with *it*). [OE *hors*; ON *hross*; OHGer *hros* (Ger *Ross*)]
■ **horse'less** *adj* without a horse; mechanically driven, motorized. **hors'ey** or **hors'y** *adj* of or relating to horses; horselike, *esp* in appearance (*derog* of people); devoted to horses, horse-racing or -breeding; (*esp* of a woman) affectedly refined in speech or manner, in a way stereotypically associated with the upper classes, traditionally fond of equestrian pursuits. **hors'iness** *n*. **hors'ing** *n* (*archaic*) birching of a person mounted on another's back.
❑ **horse'-and-bugg'y** *adj* (*N Am*) hopelessly out of date. **horse artillery** *n* field artillery with comparatively light guns and the gunners mounted. **horse'back** *n* the back of a horse. **horse bean** *n* a variety of broad bean; applied also to other beans. **horse block** *n* a mounting block. **horse boat** *n* a boat for carrying horses, or towed by a horse. **horse bot** *n* a botfly. **horse box** *n* a road trailer or railway car designed to carry horses; a stall or compartment on a ship; a high-sided church pew (*facetious*). **horse'-boy** *n* a stable boy. **horse brass** *n* a *usu* brass ornament of a kind hung on the harness of a horse. **horse'-bread** *n* a coarse bread for feeding horses. **horse'-breaker** or **horse-tamer** *n* a person who breaks or tames horses, or teaches them to pull or carry; a courtesan who appears on horseback (*obs*). **horse'car** *n* (*US*) a streetcar drawn by horses. **horse chestnut** *n* a smooth, brown, bitter seed or nut, perhaps so called from its coarseness, contrasted with the edible chestnut; the tree that produces it (*Aesculus hippocastanum*). **horse'-cloth** *n* a cloth for covering a horse. **horse'-collar** *n* a stuffed collar for a draught horse, carrying the hames. **horse'-coper** or (*Scot*) **horse'-couper** /-kow- or -koo-/ or **horse'-dealer** *n* a person who deals in horses. **horse'-courser** *n* (*obs*) a jobbing dealer in horses. **horse'-dealing** *n* horse-trading. **horse'-doctor** *n* a veterinary surgeon. **horse'-drench** *n* a dose of medicine for a horse. **horse'-faced** *adj* having a long horselike face. **horse fair**

n a fair or market for sale of horses. **horse'feathers** *n pl* and *interj* (*US*) nonsense. **horse'flesh** *n* the flesh of a horse, *esp* when eaten as meat, or traded on the hoof; horses collectively. ◆ *adj* of a reddish-bronze colour. **horseflesh ore** *n* bornite or erubescite (from its colour). **horse'fly** *n* the forest-fly or other large fly that stings or bites horses. **horse'-foot** *n* coltsfoot (*obs*); a kingcrab. **horse-god'mother** *n* (*dialect*) a fat clumsy woman. **horse'-gowan** *n* (*Scot*) the ox-eye daisy. **horse guards** *n pl* cavalry soldiers employed as guards; (with *cap*) the cavalry brigade of the British household troops, *esp* the *Royal Horse Guards*, or *Blues*, a regiment raised in 1661; (with *cap*) their headquarters in Whitehall, London, once the seat of the departments of the army commander-in-chief; the military authorities. **horse'hair** *n* a hair from a horse's mane or tail; a mass of such hairs; a fabric woven from horsehair. ◆ *adj* made of or stuffed with horsehair. **horsehair worm** same as **hairworm** (see under **hair**). **horse'hide** *n*. **horse hoe** *n* a hoe drawn by horses. **horse'-knacker** *n* someone who buys and slaughters worn-out horses. **horse latitudes** *n pl* two zones of the Atlantic Ocean (about 30 1N and 30 1S, *esp* the former) noted for long calm periods. **horse'laugh** *n* a harsh, boisterous laugh. **horse'leech** *n* a horse-doctor (*obs*); a large species of leech, supposed to fasten on horses; a bloodsucker (Bible, Proverbs 30.15). **horseless carriage** *n* (*archaic*) a motor car. **horse'-litter** *n* a litter or bed borne between two horses; bedding for horses. **horse mackerel** *n* the scad or any related fish; the tunny; applied to various other fishes. **horse'man** *n* a rider; a person skilled in managing a horse; a mounted soldier; a person who has charge of horses; a kind of carrier pigeon; a kind of land crab. **horse'manship** *n* the art of riding and of training and managing horses. **horseman's word** *n* (*Scot hist*) a ploughman's secret word to control horses; a magic word used against one's enemy, imparted by the Devil in exchange for service in hell. **horse marine** *n* a person quite out of his element; a member of an imaginary corps. **horse'meat** *n* food for horses; horseflesh used as food. **horse mill** *n* a mill turned by horses. **horse'-milliner** *n* (*archaic*) someone who provides the trappings for horses. **horse'mint** *n* any wild mint; the American *Monarda punctata*, or any of several other species of *Monarda*; (**sweet horsemint**) the common dittany. **horse mushroom** *n* a large coarse mushroom. **horse mussel** *n* a mollusc (genus *Modiolus*) similar to the common mussel but much bigger. **horse nail** *n* a nail for fastening a horseshoe to the hoof. **horse opera** *n* (*facetious*) a Wild West film. **horse pistol** *n* a large pistol formerly carried in a holster by horsemen. **horse'play** *n* rough, boisterous play. **horse'pond** *n* a pond for watering horses at. **horse'power** *n* the power a horse can exert, or its conventional equivalent (taken as 745.7 watts, or **metric horsepower** taken as 735.5 watts). **horse race** *n* a race by horses. **horse'-racing** *n* the practice of racing or running horses in matches. **horse'radish** *n* a plant related to scurvy-grass with a pungent root, used in the preparation of a sharp-tasting condiment; the condiment itself (also **horseradish sauce**). **horseradish tree** *n* a tree (*Moringa pterygosperma*) cultivated in tropical countries for its edible capsules and its seeds, ben-nuts, which yield oil of ben (the roots tasting like horseradish); an Australian tree (*Codonocarpus cotinifolius*) with leaves of horseradish flavour. **horse rake** *n* a rake pulled by horses. **horse'-rider** *n*. **horse'-riding** *n*. **horse sense** *n* (*inf*) plain common sense. **horse'shoe** *n* a metal plate for horses' feet, consisting of a curved piece of iron nailed to the underside of the hoof; anything of similar shape; a representation of it, *esp* as a symbol of good luck. ◆ *adj* shaped like a horseshoe. **horseshoe bat** *n* a bat with a horseshoe-shaped appendage on the nose. **horseshoe crab** *n* a large marine arachnid (genus *Limulus*) with a convex horseshoe-shaped armoured body. **horse'shoeing** *n*. **horse'shoer** /*-shoo'ər*/ *n* a person who makes or fits horseshoes. **horse'-sickness** or **African horse-sickness** *n* a serious disease of horses, due to a virus. **horse's neck** *n* a cocktail consisting of brandy, ginger ale and a twist of lemon peel. **horse soldier** *n* a cavalry soldier. **horse'tail** *n* a horse's tail; a Turkish standard, marking rank by number; any plant of the genus *Equisetum* (scouring-rush) with hollow rushlike stems, constituting with related fossils a class of fern-allies, Equisetinae. **horse'-thief** *n*. **horse'-trading** *n* hard bargaining. **horse'-trainer** *n* a person who trains horses for racing, etc. **horse'way** *n* a road along which a horse may pass. **horse'whip** *n* a whip for driving horses. ◆ *vt* to thrash with a horsewhip; to lash. **horse'-woman** *n* a woman who rides on horseback, or who rides well. **horse-wrangler** see under **wrangle**.

■ **dark horse** see under **dark**. **flog a dead horse** to try to work up excitement about a subject in which others have lost interest. **from the horse's mouth** see **straight from the horse's mouth** below. **gift horse** see under **gift**. **high horse** see **on one's high horse** under **high¹**. **hold your horses** not so fast; wait a moment. **horse and hattock** see under **hat**. **horse around** (*inf*) to fool about, play boisterously. **horse of a different colour** another thing altogether. **horses for courses** phrase expressing the view that each racehorse will do best on a certain course which peculiarly suits it (also *fig* of people). **metric horsepower** see **horsepower** above. **put the cart before the horse** see under **cart**. **straight from the horse's mouth** from a very trustworthy source (of information). **take horse** to mount

on horseback. **white horse** see under **white**. **willing horse** a willing, obliging worker.

horson (*Shakesp*) same as **whoreson** (see under **whore**).

horst /*hörst*/ (*geol*) *n* a block of the earth's crust that has remained in position while the ground around it has either subsided or been folded into mountains by pressure against its solid sides. [Ger]

horsy see under **horse**.

hortative /*hör'tə-tiv*/, also **hortatory** /*hör'tə-tə-ri*/ *adj* inciting; encouraging; giving advice. [L *hortārī*, *-ātus* to incite]
■ **hortā'tion** *n*. **hort'atively** or **hort'atorily** *adv*.

horticulture /*hör'ti-kul-chər*/ *n* the art of gardening. [L *hortus* a garden, and *cultūra*, from *colere* to cultivate]
■ **horticul'tural** *adj*. **horticul'turalist** or **horticul'turist** *n* an expert in the art of cultivating gardens.

hortus siccus /*hör'təs sik'əs* or *hor'tŭs sik'ŭs*/ (*L*) *n* a collection of dried plants; a herbarium.

Horus /*hō'rəs* or *hö'rəs*/ *n* the Egyptian sun-god, son of Isis and Osiris, *usu* depicted with a falcon's head. [Egyp *hur* hawk]

Hos. (*Bible*) *abbrev*: (the Book of) Hosea.

hosanna /*hō-zan'ə*/ *n* an exclamation of praise to God. [Gr *hōsanna*, from Heb *hōshī'āh nnā*, *hōshīā'* save, and *nā* I pray]

hose /*hōz*/ *n* (*pl* **hos'es**) a flexible pipe for conveying water, etc; a socket for a shaft; (*pl* **hose** or (*archaic*) **hos'en**) an old-fashioned covering for the legs or feet; stockings; socks (also **half-hose**); close-fitting breeches or drawers (*obs*). ◆ *vt* to direct a hose at; to wash (*down*) with water from a hose; to provide with hose (*archaic*). [OE *hosa*, *pl hosan*, Du *hoos*, Ger *Hose*]
■ **hosed** *adj*. **hosier** /*hōzh'(y)ər* or *hōz'yər*/ *n* a dealer in or a maker of hosiery. **hō'siery** *n* hose collectively; knitted goods, *esp* underwear. ❑ **hose'man** *n* a fireman who directs the stream of water. **hose'-net** *n* (*Scot*) a stocking-shaped net. **hose'pipe** *n*. **hose reel** *n* a large revolving drum for carrying hoses.

hosel /*hō'zl*/ *n* the socket for the shaft in the head of a golf club. [Dimin of **hose**]

hospice /*hos'pis*/ *n* a home for the care of the terminally ill; a house of lodging for travellers, *esp* one kept by monks (*hist*); a hostel (*obs*); a home of refuge (*obs*). [Fr, from L *hospitium*, from *hospes*, *-itis* a stranger, guest]

hospitable /*hos'pi-tə-bl* or *ho-spit'ə-bl*/ *adj* kind to strangers; welcoming and generous towards guests. [LL *hospitāgium*, from L *hospes*, *-itis* stranger, guest]
■ **hos'pitableness** (or /*-pit'-*/) *n*. **hos'pitably** (or /*-pit'-*/) *adv*. **hospitage** /*hos'pit-ij*/ *n* (*Spenser*) behaviour expected of a guest.

hospital /*hos'pi-tl*/ *n* an institution for the treatment of the sick or injured; a building for any of these purposes; formerly a charitable institution for the old or destitute, or for taking in (and educating) the needy young; a hostel for travellers (*obs*). [OFr *hospital*, from LL *hospitāle*, from *hospes*, *-itis* a guest]
■ **hos'pitale** /*-āl*/ *n* (*Spenser*) lodging. **hospitalizā'tion** or **-s-** *n*. **hos'pitalize** or **-ise** *vt* to send to hospital; to injure so badly that hospital treatment is needed. **hos'pitaller** or (*US*) **hos'pitaler** *n* a member of a charitable brotherhood for the care of the sick in hospitals; one of the Knights of St John (otherwise called Knights of Rhodes, and afterwards Knights of Malta), an order that built a hospital for pilgrims at Jerusalem.
❑ **hospital corner** *n* a neat triangular fold used in tucking bedclothes under the mattress on either side of a bed, as in hospitals. **hospital pass** *n* (*sport sl*) a pass to a teammate who is about to be tackled and may thereby receive an injury. **hospital ship** *n* a ship fitted out exclusively for the treatment and transport of the sick and wounded, *esp* in time of war. **hospital trust** *n* a self-governing trust set up with national funding to run a hospital or group of hospitals within the National Health Service.

hospitality /*hos-pi-tal'i-ti*/ *n* (friendly welcome and) entertainment of guests (also *fig*); a room or suite where guests, delegates, etc are welcomed and entertained, *usu* being offered free drinks (also **hospitality suite**). [Ety as for **hospital**]

hospitium /*ho-spish'i-əm*/ *n* (*pl* **hospi'tia**) a lodging place. [L; cf **hospice**]

hospodar /*hos'po-där*/ (*hist*) *n* a prince or governor, *esp* of Moldavia or Wallachia (also **gos'podar**). [Romanian *hospodár*, of Slav origin]

hoss /*hos*/ (*esp US inf* and *dialect*) *n* a horse.

host¹ /*hōst*/ *n* a person who entertains a stranger or guest at his or her house without (or with) reward; an innkeeper or publican; a person who introduces performers or participants, who chairs discussions, etc on a programme or show; a place acting as the venue for (an event), *usu* implying some involvement in the organization of the event and the welcoming of the participants; an organism on which another lives as a parasite (also *fig*); a person or animal that has received transplanted tissue or a transplanted organ; a host computer (see below). ◆ *vt* to receive and entertain guests at (an event); to act as or be the chairperson, compère, etc of (a show, programme, event, etc). ◆ *vi* (*Spenser, Shakesp*) to lodge, to be a guest. [OFr *hoste*, from L *hospes, hospitis*]

■ **hōst'ess** *n* a female host; a paid female partner at a dance hall, nightclub, etc; a prostitute (*euphem*). ◆ *vt* and *vi* to act as a hostess (to). **hōst'ess-ship** *n* the character or office of a hostess. **hōst'lesse** *adj* (*Spenser*) inhospitable. **hōst'ry** *n* (*Spenser*) lodging.

❑ **host computer** *n* a computer attached to and in control of a multi-terminal computer system, or one attached to a multi-computer network and able eg to provide access to a number of databases. **hostess trolley** *n* a trolley with electronically heated compartments for keeping food warm while it is brought to the table.

■ **air hostess** see under **air**. **lie at host** (*Shakesp*) to be lodged. **reckon** or **count without one's host** to count up one's bill without reference to the landlord; to fail to take account of some important possibility, such as the action of another.

host² /hōst/ *n* an army (*archaic*); a great multitude. [OFr *host*, from L *hostis* an enemy]

■ **hōst'ing** *n* a battle (*Milton*); a muster, a military expedition (*Spenser*).

■ **a host in himself** a man of great strength, skill or resources within himself. **Lord of hosts** a favourite Hebrew term for Jehovah, considered as head of the hosts of angels, the hosts of stars, etc.

host³ /hōst/ *n* a sacrificial victim (*obs*); (often with *cap*) in the Roman Catholic Church, the consecrated wafer of the Eucharist. [L *hostia* a victim]

hosta /hos'tə/ *n* any plant of the *Hosta* genus of decorative perennial herbaceous plants (family Liliaceae) from Asia with ribbed basal leaves and blue, white and lilac flowers. [NT *Host* (1761–1834), Austrian botanist]

hostage /hos'tij/ *n* a person kept prisoner by an enemy as security. [OFr *hostage* (Fr *ôtage*), from L *obses, obsidis* a hostage]

■ **hostages to fortune** the people or things one values most (from Bacon's essay *Of Marriage and Single Life*); hence, things of which the loss would be particularly painful; (in *sing*) a remark that might expose one to attack in the future.

hostel /hos'təl/ *n* an inn; in some universities, an extra-collegiate hall for students; a residence for students or for some class or society of people, *esp* one run charitably or not for profit; a youth hostel. [OFr *hostel, hostellerie*, from L *hospitāle*; cf **hospital**]

■ **hos'teler** or **hos'teller** *n* hospitaller (*archaic*); the keeper of a hostel; a person who lives in or uses a hostel, *esp* a youth hostel. **hos'telling** *n* holidaying in youth hostels. **hos'telry** *n* (now *esp joc*) an inn.

hostess see under **host¹**.

hostile /hos'tīl/ or (*US*) -təl/ *adj* relating to an enemy; showing enmity or unfriendliness, or angry opposition; resistant (*esp* to new ideas, changes, etc); (of a place or conditions) inhospitable, harsh; engaged in hostilities; relating to hostilities. ◆ *n* a hostile person, an enemy. [L *hostilis* from *hostis*]

■ **hos'tilely** *adv*. **hostilities** /-til'/ *n pl* (acts of) warfare. **hostil'ity** *n* enmity, unfriendliness.

❑ **hostile bid** *n* (*commerce*) a bid not welcomed by the company whose shares are to be bought. **hostile witness** *n* (*law*) a witness who gives evidence against the party he or she was called by.

hostler /hos'lər/ or (*obs*) *os'ler*/ *n* an ostler (now *US*); a maintenance worker who services railway wagons, locomotives, etc (*US*).

hostlesse, hostry see under **host¹**.

hot¹ /hot/ *adj* (**hott'er; hott'est**) having a high temperature; very warm; fiery; pungent; powerful; giving a feeling suggestive of heat; animated; ardent; vehement; violent; passionate; sexually excited (*sl*); lustful; sexually attractive (*sl*); dangerously charged with electricity; dangerous; near the object sought (eg in the game of hide-and-seek); (of news) fresh, exciting; (of jazz, etc) intensely played with complex rhythms and exciting improvisations; skilful (*inf*); currently fashionable, sought-after, most wanted (*inf*); recently stolen or obtained dishonestly (*inf*); highly radioactive (*inf*). ◆ *adv* hotly. ◆ *vt* (**hott'ing; hott'ed**) (*inf*) to heat. [OE *hāt*; Ger *heiss*, Swed *het*]

■ **hot'ly** *adv*. **hot'ness** *n*. **hott'er** *n* (*inf*) a (*usu* young) car thief who attempts displays of dangerous stunts in powerful cars. **hott'ie** or **hott'y** *n* a hot-water bottle (*inf*); a sexually attractive person (*N Am sl*). **hott'ing** *n* (*inf*) attempting high-speed stunts in stolen powerful cars, often as a display. **hott'ish** *adj*.

❑ **hot air** *n* empty talk. **hot'-air** *adj* making use of heated air; boastful, empty. **hot-air balloon** *n* one containing air that is heated by a flame to maintain or increase altitude. **hot'-and-hot'** *adj* cooked and served up at once in hot dishes (also *n*). **hot'bed** *n* a glass-covered bed heated by a layer of fermenting manure for bringing forward plants rapidly; a place, or conditions, favourable to rapid growth or development, *usu* of a bad kind (*fig*). **hot blast** *n* a blast of heated air.

hot'-blood'ed *adj* having hot blood; homothermous; passionate; ardent; high-spirited; irritable. **hot'-brain** *n* (*archaic*) a hothead. **hot'-brained** *adj* (*archaic*). **hot button** *n* (*orig US; politics*) an emotive topic, a sensitive issue. **hot'-butt'on** *adj*. **hot-cock'les** *n* an old game in which a person with eyes covered guesses who strikes him or her. **hot coppers** see under **copper¹**. **hot cross bun** *n* a bun bearing a cross, customarily eaten on Good Friday. **hot date** *n* a social engagement with a person to whom one is sexually attracted. **hot-desk'ing** *n* the practice of allocating a desk only to a worker who needs it at the time rather than to each worker as a matter of course. **hot dog** *n* a hot sausage in a long soft roll. **hot'-dog** *n* (*inf; esp N Am*) a person who performs clever manoeuvres, such as spins and turns, while surfing, skate-boarding, etc. ◆ *vi* (*inf; esp N Am*) to perform such clever manoeuvres; to show off. **hot'-dogger** *n*. **hot'-dogging** *n*. **hot favourite** *n* (in sports, races, etc) the one (considered) most likely to win (also *fig*). **hot flue** *n* (*obs*) a drying-room. **hot flush** (also (*US*) **hot flash**) *n* a sudden sensation of heat experienced by a menopausal woman. **hot'foot** *adv* in haste (**hotfoot it** (*inf*) to rush). **hot gospeller** *n* a loud, forceful proclaimer of a vigorously interactive kind of religious faith; a fanatical propagandist. **hot gospelling** *n*. **hot hatch** *n* (*inf*) a more powerful version (often designated **GT**, etc) of a standard hatchback car. **hot'-hatch** *adj*. **hot'head** *n* an impetuous headstrong person; one who is easily angered. **hot'headed** *adj*. **hot'house** *n* a greenhouse kept hot for the rearing of tropical or tender plants; any heated chamber or drying-room, *esp* that where pottery is placed before going into the kiln; a hot-bathing establishment (*obs*); a brothel (*Shakesp*); any establishment promoting the development of skills, etc (*fig*). ◆ *adj* (of a plant) suitable for rearing only in a greenhouse; (too) delicate, unable to exist in tough, or even normal, conditions (*fig*). ◆ *vt* to educate intensively, *esp* to a precocious level. **hot'housing** *n*. **hot key** *n* (*comput*) a key or combination of keys that activates a program, etc. **hot line** or **hot'line** *n* a special telephone and teleprinter link, *orig* one between the Kremlin and Washington, DC; any line of speedy communication ready for an emergency. **hot'-liv'ered** *adj* (*Milton*) hot-tempered. **hot melt, hot-melt glue** or **hot-melt adhesive** *n* an adhesive that is applied hot and which sets as it cools. **hot metal** *n* (*printing*) machines or methods using type made from molten metal. **hot'-met'al** *adj*. **hot money** *n* funds transferred suddenly from one country to another because conditions make transfer financially advantageous. **hot'-mouthed** *adj* (*obs*) (of a horse) restive, as when the bit hurts. **hot pants** *n pl* women's very brief shorts; sexual desire (for) (*sl*). **hot'plate** *n* the flat top surface of a stove for cooking; a similar plate, independently heated, for keeping things hot. **hot'pot** *n* a dish of chopped mutton, beef, etc seasoned and stewed together with sliced potatoes. **hot potato** see under **potato**. **hot press** *n* a device consisting of hot plates between which paper, cloth, etc are pressed to produce a glossy surface; an airing cupboard (*Irish*). **hot'-press** *vt*. **hot property** *n* (*inf*) a person regarded as a great asset or success. **hot rod** *n* a motor car converted for speed by stripping off non-essentials and heightening in power. **hot-rod'der** *n* the owner of a hot rod; a reckless youth. **hot seat** *n* the electric chair (*US sl*); any uncomfortable or tricky situation (*fig*); a position of responsibility. **hot shoe** *n* a socket on a camera for attaching flash or other apparatus (also **accessory shoe**). **hot'-short** *adj* brittle when heated. **hot'shot** *n* (*esp US*) a person who is (*esp* showily) successful, skilful, etc (also *adj*). **hot-spir'ited** *adj* having a fiery spirit. **hot'spot** *n* an area of (too) high temperature in an engine, etc; a region of the earth where there is evidence of isolated volcanic activity due to hot material rising through the earth's mantle; a popular nightclub (*inf*); an area of potential trouble, *esp* political or military; a place of very high radioactivity; an area of a web page that activates a hyperlink when clicked on with a mouse (*comput*); an area where a portable computer equipped for wireless Internet connection can gain access to a local area network. **hot spring** *n* a spring of water that has been heated underground, occurring *esp* in volcanic regions. **Hot'spur** *n* a violent, rash man, *orig* applied to Henry Percy (1364–1403). **hot stuff** *n* (*inf*) any person, thing, or performance that is outstandingly remarkable, excellent, vigorous or attractive. **hotted-up** see **hot up** below. **hot-tem'pered** *adj* having a quick temper. **hot ticket** *n* (*inf*) a highly popular person or thing. **hot'-trod** *n* (*Scot*) the chase in hot pursuit (see below) in old Border forays. **hot tub** *n* a large bath, *esp* outdoors, kept filled with hot water. **hot wall** *n* a wall enclosing passages for hot air, affording warmth to fruit trees. **hot war** *n* real war, not cold war. **hot water** *n* (*inf*) a state of trouble. **hot-water bottle** *n* a (now *usu* rubber) container for hot water, used to warm a bed, or sometimes parts of the body. **hot well** *n* a spring of hot water; in a condensing engine, a reservoir for the warm water drawn off from the condenser. **hot-wire** *vt* to start the engine of (a vehicle), *usu* illegally, without a key by manipulating the wiring. **hot'-working** *n* (*engineering*) the process of shaping metals by rolling, extrusion, forging, etc at elevated temperatures. **hot yoga** same as **Bikram yoga**.

■ **go** or **sell like hot cakes** to disappear or be sold promptly. **have the hots for** (*vulgar sl*) to be sexually attracted to, desire sexually. **hot and bothered** anxious and confused; agitated. **hot on** (*inf*) very fond of, interested in; good at, well-informed about. **hot on the heels of** (*inf*) following or pursuing closely. **hot to trot** (*inf*) eager to begin. **hot under the collar** (*inf*) indignant; embarrassed. **hot up** (*inf*) to increase in excitement, energy, performance, etc (**hotted-up**' *adj*). **in hot pursuit** pursuing at full speed. **make it hot for** (*inf*) to make it unpleasant or impossible for.

hot² /*hot*/ or **hote** /*hōt*/ (*Spenser*) *vt* named; was called. [Pat active and passive of **hight**]

hotch /*hoch*/ (*Scot*) *vt* and *vi* to hitch, jog; to fidget with eagerness. [Cf Du *hotsen*, Fr *hocher*]
■ **hotch with** to swarm, seethe with.

hotchpotch /*hoch'poch*/, **hotchpot** /*hoch'pot*/ or **hodgepodge** /*hoj'poj*/ *n* a confused mass of ingredients shaken or mixed together in the same pot; a kind of mutton-broth with vegetables of many kinds; a jumble; (**hotchpot**) a commixture of property in order to secure an equable division amongst children. [Fr *hochepot*, from *hocher* to shake, and *pot* a pot; cf Du *hutspot*]

hote see **hight**.

Hotel or **hotel** /*hō-tel'*/ *n* (in international radio communication) a code word for the letter *h*.

hotel /*hō-tel'* or (*old*) *ō-tel'*/ *n* a commercial building with rooms for the accommodation of the paying public; an inn; a public house (*Aust*); in France, also a public office, a private townhouse, a palace. [Fr *hôtel*, from L *hospitālia* guest-chambers, from *hospes*]
■ **hotelier** /*hō-tel' yэr*/ (Fr **hôtelier** /*ōt- э-lyā*/) *n* a person who owns or runs a hotel.
❑ **hôtel de ville** (Fr /*ō-tel dэ vēl*/) *n* a town hall. **hôtel-Dieu** (Fr /*ō-tel-dyø*/) *n* a hospital. **hotel'-keeper** *n*. **hotell'ing** or (*US*) **hotel'ing** *n* (in an office where hot-desking is practised) the advance booking of a desk by an employee.

hoten see **hight**.

hotly see under **hot¹**.

HOTOL /*hō'tol*/ (*aeronautics*) *abbrev* : *h*orizontal *t*ake-*o*ff and *l*anding. [Cf **VTOL**]

Hotspur, **hotted** see **hot¹**.

Hottentot /*hot'n-tot*/ *n* an old name (now considered offensive) for the **Khoikhoi**; the Khoikhoi language; a barbarian; a member of any dark-skinned people (*old derog*); (without *cap*) a small fish (*Pachymetopon blochii*). ◆ *adj* (*old*) of or relating to the Khoikhoi or their language; dark-skinned (*derog*). [Du imit; the language was unintelligible to them and sounded staccato]
❑ **Hottentot fig** *n* a S African plant (*Carpobratus edulis*) with daisy-like flowers; its edible fruit. **Hottentot** (or **Hottentot's**) **god** *n* praying mantis. **Hottentot's bread** *n* elephant's-foot.

hotter¹ /*hot'эr*/ (*Scot*) *vi* to vibrate; to tremble; to clatter; to totter; to jolt; to swarm. ◆ *n* vibration; commotion; swarming. [Cf Flem *hotteren*]

hotter², **hottest** see **hot¹**.

hottie, **hotting**, **hottish** see under **hot¹**.

houdah see **howdah**.

houdan /*hoo'dэn*/ *n* a black-and-white five-toed domestic fowl of a breed *orig* from *Houdan* near Paris.

Houdini act /*hoo-dē'ni akt*/ *n* a remarkable feat of escape. [Harry *Houdini* (1874–1926), US escapologist]

houf, **houff** see **howf**.

hough /*hok*/ or (*Scot*) *hohh*/ see **hock¹**.

hommos, **houmous**, **houmus** see **hummus**.

hound¹ /*hownd*/ *n* a dog (*inf*); a dog of a kind used in hunting; a pursuer in a paper chase; a contemptible scoundrel; a hunter, tracker or assiduous seeker of anything; an addict or devotee (often as *combining form*). ◆ *vt* to set on in chase; to drive by harassing; to harass. [OE *hund*; Gr *kyōn*, *kynos*, L *canis*, Sans *sva*]
❑ **hound'fish** *n* a dogfish. **hounds'-berry** *n* dogwood. **hounds'-foot** *n* (Ger *Hundsfott*, -*futt* dog's vulva; *obs*) a scoundrel. ◆ *adj* (*Walter Scott*) scoundrelly. **hound's'-tongue** *n* a plant (genus *Cynoglossum*) of the borage family (from its leaf). **hound's'-tooth** *n* a textile pattern of broken checks (also *adj*). **hound'-trailing** *n* speed competition between hounds trained to follow an aniseed trail.
■ **Gabriel** (or **Gabriel's**) **hounds** (*inf*) the yelping noise made by flights of wild geese, ascribed to damned souls whipped on by the angel Gabriel. **master of hounds** the person responsible for looking after a pack of hunting hounds, associated hunting equipment, etc. **ride to hounds** to hunt foxes (on horseback).

hound² /*hownd*/ *n* one of a pair of bars supporting and strengthening the chassis of a horse-drawn vehicle; either of a pair of supports for the topmast (*naut*). [ME *hune*, *hownde* related to ON *hunn* knob, cube]

hour /*owr*/ *n* 60 minutes, or the 24th part of the day; the time as indicated by a clock, etc; an hour's journey, or (*old*) three miles; a

time or occasion; an angular unit (151) of right ascension; (in *pl*) the goddesses of the seasons and the hours (*myth*); (in *pl*) set times of prayer, the *canonical hours*, the offices or services prescribed for these, or a book containing them, often illustrated (also **book of hours**); (in *pl*) the prescribed times for doing business. [OFr *hore* (Fr *heure*), from L *hora*, from Gr *hōrā*]
■ **hour'ly** *adj* happening or done every hour; frequent. ◆ *adv* every hour; frequently; by the hour.
❑ **hour'-angle** *n* (*astron*) the angle (*usu* measured as time) between the declination circle of a body observed and the observer's meridian. **hour'-circle** *n* (*astron*) a great circle passing through the celestial poles; the equivalent of a meridian; the circle of an equatorial which shows the right ascension. **hour'glass** *n* an instrument for measuring the hours by the running of sand through a narrow neck. ◆ *adj* having the form of an hourglass; constricted; slim-waisted. **hour hand** *n* the hand that shows the hour on a clock, etc. **hour'long**' *adj* and *adv* lasting an hour. **hour'plate** *n* a timepiece dial.
■ **after hours** after the normal hours of business. **at all hours** at irregular hours, *esp* late hours. **at the eleventh hour** at the last moment (Bible, Matthew 20.6,9). **in a good** (or **evil**) **hour** under a fortunate (or an unfortunate) impulse (from the old belief in astrological influences). **keep good hours** to go to bed and to rise early; to lead a quiet and regular life. **on the hour** at exactly one, two, etc o'clock.

houri /*hoo'ri* or *how'ri*/ *n* a nymph of the Muslim paradise; a voluptuously alluring woman. [Pers *hūrī*, from Ar *hūriya* a black-eyed girl]

house /*hows*/ *n* (*pl* **houses** /*howz'iz*/) a building for living in; a building in general; a dwelling-place; an inn; a public house; a household; a family in line of descent; kindred; a trading establishment; one of the twelve divisions of the heavens in astrology; a legislative or deliberative body or its meeting-place; a convent; a school boarding house; the pupils belonging to it (*collectively*); a section of a school; an audience, auditorium or performance; the workhouse (*old inf*); the circle around the tee within which stones must lie to count (*curling*); (**the House**) at Oxford, Christ Church (*Aedes Christi*), in London, the Stock Exchange or the Houses of Parliament; bingo, *esp* when played for money (*esp army sl*); (*usu* with *cap*) house music (qv below). ◆ *adj* domestic; of a restaurant, hotel, etc or its management, as in *house rules*; (of wine) unnamed and cheaper than those listed on a menu, etc by name or region. ◆ *vt* /*howz*/ to protect by covering; to shelter; to store; to provide houses for. ◆ *vi* to take shelter; to reside. ◆ *interj* /*hows*/ an exclamation made by the first player to finish a game of bingo. [OE *hūs*; Gothic *hūs*, Ger *Haus*]
■ **house'ful** *n* (*pl* **house'fuls**). **house'less** *adj* without a house or home; having no shelter. **hous'ey** *adj* typical of house music (qv below). **housing** /*how'zing*/ *n* houses, accommodation or shelter, or the provision of any of these (also *adj*); a cavity into which a timber fits; anything designed to cover, protect or contain machinery, etc; a housing joint (see below).
❑ **house agent** *n* a person who arranges the buying, selling and letting of houses. **house arrest** *n* confinement, under guard, to one's house, or to a hospital, etc instead of imprisonment. **house'boat** *n* a barge with a deck-cabin that may serve as a dwelling-place. **house'-bote** *n* (*law*) a tenant's right to wood to repair his or her house. **house'bound** *adj* confined to one's house, eg because of illness, responsibilities towards young children, etc. **house'boy** *n* a male domestic servant, *esp* in Africa or India. **house'breaker** *n* a person who breaks into and enters a house for the purpose of stealing; someone whose work is demolishing old houses. **house'breaking** *n*. **house'-broken** *adj* house-trained. **house call** *n* a visit made by a professional person, *esp* a doctor, to a client or patient at home. **house'-carl** *n* (*hist*) a member of a king's or noble's bodyguard. **house church** or **house group** *n* a group of Christians meeting, *usu* in a house, for worship, prayer, Bible study, etc, *usu* in addition to Sunday church worship. **house'coat** *n* a woman's *usu* long coatlike dressing-gown, worn at home. **house'craft** *n* skill in domestic activities. **house'-dog** *n* a dog kept in a house; a watchdog. **house'-dúty** or **house'-tax** *n* a tax laid on inhabited houses. **house'-factor** *n* (*Scot*) a house agent. **house'-father** *n* the male head of a household or community; a man in charge of children in an institution. **house flag** *n* the distinguishing flag of a shipowner or shipping company. **house'fly** *n* the common fly. **house group** see **house church** above. **house guest** *n* a guest in a private house. **house'hold** *n* those who are held together in the same house, and compose a family; a single person living alone or a group of people living together (*econ*). ◆ *adj* relating to the house and family; well-known to the general public, as in *household name*, *household word*. **Household Cavalry** *n* the two cavalry regiments, the Life Guards and the Royal Horse Guards, responsible for guarding the British sovereign. **house'holder** *n* the holder or tenant of a house. **household gods** see under **god**, **lar**, **penates**. **household suffrage** or **franchise** *n* the right of

---

householders to vote for members of parliament. **household troops** *n pl* Guards regiments whose particular duty is to attend the sovereign and defend the metropolis. **household word** *n* a familiar saying or name. **house'-hunt** *vi* to look for a house to live in. **house'-hunter** *n*. **house'-hunting** *n*. **house'-husband** *n* a married man or live-in male partner who looks after the house and family and does not have a paid job. **house'keeper** *n* a person employed to run a household; a person who has the chief care of a house; someone who stays much at home (*archaic*); a dispenser of hospitality (*obs*); a watchdog (*obs*). **house'keeping** *n* the keeping or management of a house or of domestic affairs; the money used for this; hospitality (*obs*); operations carried out on or within a computer program to ensure the efficient functioning of the program. ◆ *adj* domestic. **house leek** *n* a plant (*Sempervivum tectorum*) of the stonecrop family with succulent leaves, often growing on roofs. **house lights** *n pl* (*theatre*) the lights illuminating the auditorium. **house'-line** *n* (*naut*) a small line of three strands, for seizings, etc. **house longhorn beetle** see **longhorn** under **long¹**. **house'maid** *n* a maid employed to keep a house clean, etc. **housemaid's knee** *n* an inflammation of the sac between the kneecap and the skin, to which those whose work involves frequent kneeling are especially liable. **house'man** *n* a house officer (qv below). **house martin** *n* a kind of black-and-white swallow (*Delichon urbica*) with a slightly forked tail, often building its nest on a house wall. **house'master** or **house'mistress** *n* (in schools) the male or female head of a (boarding-)house, *esp* in connection with a public school. **house'-mate** *n* one person sharing a house with another. **house'-mother** *n* the mother of a family, the female head of a family; a woman in charge of children in an institution. **house mouse** *n* a brownish-grey mouse (*Mus musculus*) that is a pest in human houses. **house music** *n* (also with *cap*) a type of electronically produced dance music with a strong 4–4 beat, often incorporating edited fragments of other recordings. **house of call** *n* a house where the journeymen of a particular trade call when out of work; a house that one often visits. **house of cards** *n* a situation, etc that is as unstable as a pile of playing cards. **House of Commons** see under **common**. **house of correction** *n* a jail. **house officer** *n* a recent graduate in medicine holding a junior resident post in a hospital. **house of God**, **house of prayer** or **worship** *n* a place of worship. **house of ill fame** or **house of ill repute** *n* a brothel. **House of Keys** see under **Keys**. **House of Lords** see under **lord**. **House of Peers** see under **peer¹**. **House of Representatives** see under **represent**. **house'parent** *n* a man or woman in charge of children in an institution. **house party** *n* a company of guests spending some days in a private house, *esp* one in the country. **house plant** *n* a plant that can be grown indoors as decoration. **house'-proud** *adj* taking a pride (often an excessive and fussy pride) in the condition of one's house. **house'room** *n* room or place in a house (also *fig*). **house'-sit** *vi*. **house'-sitting** *n* looking after a house by living in it while the owner is away, on holiday, etc. **house sparrow** see under **sparrow**. **house'-steward** *n* a steward who manages the household affairs of a great family. **house style** *n* the particular forms of type, layout, presentation, etc preferred by a publisher or other business. **house surgeon** *n* a resident surgeon in a hospital (also **house physician**). **house-tax** see **house-duty** above. **house'-to-house'** *adj* performed or conducted by calling at house after house. **house'top** *n* the top or roof of a house. **house'-train** *vt*. **house'-trained** *adj* (of animals) taught to urinate and defecate outdoors, or in a place provided for the purpose; (of human beings) clean and well-mannered (*facetious*). **house'-warming** *n* a party given after moving into a new house. **housewife** /hows'wīf, formerly huz'if/ *n* the mistress and manager of a house; a married woman who looks after the house and family and does not have a paid job; /huz'if/ a pocket sewing-outfit. **house'wifely** *adj*. **housewifery** /hows'wif-ri, -wīf-ri or huz'if-ri/ *n*. **house'wifeship** or (*Scot*) **house'wifeskep** *n*. **house'work** *n* domestic work. **house'y-house'y** *n* a game in which numbers are drawn at random and marked off on players' boards until one is clear (now *usu* called **bingo**). **housing association** *n* a non-profit-making organization that owns, maintains and lets houses at reasonable rents. **housing estate** *n* a planned residential area, *esp* one built by a local authority. **housing joint** *n* a joint where the end of one board fits into a groove cut across another board. **housing scheme** *n* a plan for the designing, building and provision of houses, *esp* by a local authority; sometimes applied to an area coming under such a plan.

■ **bring the house down** to evoke very loud applause in a place of entertainment. **full house** see under **full¹**. **House or Council of States** the upper house of the Indian parliament. **House of the People** the lower house of the Indian parliament. **Inner House** the higher branch of the Court of Session, its jurisdiction chiefly appellate (**Outer House** the lower branch of the Court of Session). **keep a good house** to keep up a plentifully supplied table. **keep house** to maintain or manage an establishment. **keep open house** to give entertainment to all comers. **keep the house** to remain indoors; to take charge of the house or be on watch for the time being; to be confined to the house. **like a house on fire** (or **afire**) with astonishing rapidity; very well or successfully.

on the house (of drinks) at the publican's expense; free, with no charge. **put** or **set one's house in order** to settle one's affairs. **set up house** to start a domestic life of one's own. **the Household** the royal domestic establishment.

housel /how'zəl/ *n* the Eucharist; the act of taking or administering it. ◆ *vt* (pap **hous'elled**) to administer the Eucharist to. [OE *hūsel* sacrifice]

■ **hous'elling** *n*. **hous'ling** *adj* (*Spenser*) sacramental.

housing¹ see under **house**.

housing² /how'zing/ *n* an ornamental covering for a horse; a saddle-cloth; (in *pl*) the trappings of a horse. [OFr *houce* a mantle, of Gmc origin]

hout, **hout-tout**, **houts-touts** same as **hoot**, etc.

houting /how'ting/ *n* a European food-fish with white flesh. [Du, MDu *houtic*]

Houyhnhnm /hwin'əm or win'əm/ *n* one of the noble and rational race of horses in Swift's *Gulliver's Travels*. [Imit; cf **whinny**]

HOV *abbrev*: high-occupancy vehicle.

Hova /huv'ə or hō'və/ *n* (pl **Hov'a** or **Hov'as**) a member of the dominant race in Madagascar, *esp* of the middle class.

hove¹ /hōv or hoov or (*Scot*) hüv/ *vt* to swell. ◆ *vi* to swell; to rise (*Spenser*). [Perh a form of **heave**]

hove² or **hoove** /hoov/ (*Spenser*) *vi* to hover; to loiter, linger. [Origin unknown]

hove³ *pat* and *pap* of **heave**.

hovel /hov'əl or huv'əl/ *n* a small or wretched dwelling; a shed; a framework for a corn-stack (*dialect*). ◆ *vt* (**hov'elling** or US **hov'eling**; **hov'elled** or US **hov'eled**) to put in a hovel; to shelter; to build like a hovel or shed, as a chimney with a side opening. [Origin doubtful]

❑ **hov'el-post** *n* a post for supporting a corn-stack.

hoveller /hov'ə-lər, hov'lər, huv'ə-lər or huv'lər/ *n* a boatman acting as an uncertificated pilot or doing any kind of occasional work on the coast; a small coasting vessel. [Ety dubious]

hoven¹ /hō'vən/ see under **hoove¹**.

hoven² see **heave**.

hover /hov'ər or huv'ər/ *vi* to remain aloft flapping the wings; to remain suspended; to remain undecided (with *between*); to linger, *esp* nervously or solicitously; to move about nearby; to hold the pointer over a particular area on a screen (*comput*). ◆ *vt* to brood over. ◆ *n* an act or state of hovering; a helicopter (*US*); an apparatus for keeping chicks warm. ◆ *combining form* denoting vehicles or stationary objects that move or rest on a cushion of air, eg *hover-car, hover-mower*. [Perh from **hove²**]

■ **hov'eringly** *adv*.

❑ **hov'er-bed** *n* a bed that supports a patient on a cushion of warm air. **hover box** *n* (*comput*) a box containing supplementary information which appears onscreen when the pointer is held over a particular area on a web page, etc. **hov'ercraft** *n* a craft able to move at a short distance above the surface of sea or land supported by a down-driven blast of air. **hov'erfly** *n* a syrphid or other wasp-like fly that hovers and darts. **hov'erport** *n* a port for hovercraft. **hov'ertrain** *n* a train that moves supported by a cushion of air, like a hovercraft.

how¹ /how/ *adv* and *conj* in what manner; to what extent; by what means; in what condition; for what reason; to what extent, in what degree; that. ◆ *n* manner, method. [OE *hū*, prob an adverbial form from *hwā* who]

❑ **how'-to** *adj* (of books, etc) showing how to do things (also *n*).

■ **and how!** (*orig N Am inf*) yes, certainly; very much indeed; I should think so indeed. **how about...?** what do you think of...?; would you like (something)?; are you interested in (doing something)? **how are you?** a conventional greeting to an acquaintance; sometimes specifically referring to his or her state of health. **how come?** (*inf*) how does that come about? **how-do-you-do** see under **do¹**; see also **howdy**. **how now?** what is this?; why is this so? **how so?** (*archaic*) how can this be so?, why? **how's that** /how-zat'/ (*cricket*; sometimes written **howzat'**) the appeal of the fielding side to the umpire to give the batsman out. **how's your father** (*facetious*) amorous frolicking; sexual intercourse; nonsense, foolish activity. **the how and the why** the manner and the cause.

how² or **howe** /how/ (*Scot*) *n* a hollow. [**hole¹**]

how³ or **howe** /how/ (*dialect*) *n* a low hill; a tumulus or barrow. [ON *haugr*; cf OE *hēah* high]

how⁴ /how/ *interj* a greeting thought to have been used by Native N Americans. [From Siouan word, related to Dakota *háo*]

howbeit /how-bē'it/, also (*Spenser*) **howbe** /how-bē'/ (*archaic* or *formal*) *conj* be it how it may; notwithstanding; yet; however. [**how¹**, **be** and **it¹**]

howdah or **houdah** /how'də/ n a pavilion or seat fixed on an elephant's back. [Ar haudaj]

howdie or **howdy** /how'di/ (Scot) n a midwife. [Poss OE hold gracious]

howdy /how'di/ interj (chiefly N Am) an informal form of the common greeting, How do you do?
  □ **how'-d'ye-do'** or **how'dy-do'** n a troublesome state of affairs.

howe see **how**^{2,3}.

however /how-ev'ər/ or (poetic) **howe'er** /how-ār'/ adv in whatever degree or manner. ◆ conj nevertheless; at all events. [how¹ and ever]

howf, howff, houf or **houff** /howf/ (Scot) n a place in which one is often to be found, a haunt, often a public house. ◆ vi to go often to a place. [Poss OE hof a house]

howitzer /how'it-sər/ n a short, squat gun, used for shelling at a steep angle, esp in siege and trench warfare. [Ger Haubitze, from Czech houfnice a sling]

howk /howk/ (Scot) vt and vi to dig. [Earlier holk; cf LGer holken]

howker /how'kər/ n same as **hooker¹**.

howl /howl/ vi to yell or cry, like a wolf or dog; to utter a long, loud, whining sound; to wail; to roar; to laugh (inf); to cry (inf). ◆ vt to utter through a shriek or wail. ◆ n a loud, prolonged cry of distress; a mournful cry; a loud peal of laughter; a loud sound like a yell, made by the wind, a radio, etc; the loud high noise produced in a loudspeaker by feedback. [OFr huller, from L ululāre to shriek or howl, from ulula an owl; cf Ger heulen, Eng **owl**]
  ■ **howl'er** n someone who howls; a S American monkey, with prodigious power of voice; a glaring and amusing blunder (inf). **howl'ing** adj filled with howlings, as of the wind, or of wild beasts; tremendous (inf). ◆ n a howl.
  ■ **howl down** to drown out (a speaker) with angry cries.

Howleglass see under **owl**.

howlet /how'lit/ n an owlet; (also (Scot) /hool'it/) an owl. [**owlet**]

howre an obsolete form of **hour**.

howso /how'sō/ (obs) adv howsoever.

howsoever /how-sō-ev'ər/ adv in what way soever; although; however. [how¹, so¹ and ever; and ME sum as]

how-to see under **how¹**.

howtowdie /how-tow'di/ (Scot) n a dish of boiled chicken. [OFr hetoudeau, estaudeau a young chicken prepared for eating]

howzat see **how's that** under **how¹**.

hox /hoks/ (Shakesp) vt to hock or hamstring. [OE hōhsinu hock-sinew]

hoy¹ /hoi/ n a large one-decked boat, commonly rigged as a sloop. [MDu hoei; Du heu, Flem hui]

hoy², also **hoi** /hoi/ interj used to attract attention ◆ vt to incite, drive on.

hoya /hoi'ə/ n a plant of the Australasian Hoya genus of plants of the Asclepiadaceae, including the wax plant. [Thomas Hoy (died 1821), English gardener]

hoyden or (old) **hoiden** /hoi'dən/ n a tomboy, a romp (formerly also masc). [Perh Du heiden a heathen, a gypsy, from heide heath]
  ■ **hoy'denhood** n. **hoy'denish** adj. **hoy'denism** n.

HP abbrev : half pay; high pressure; High Priest; hire purchase; Houses of Parliament.

hp abbrev : horsepower.

HPC abbrev : Health Professions Council.

HPV abbrev : human papilloma virus.

HQ or **hq** abbrev : headquarters.

HR abbrev : Croatia (ie Hrvatska; IVR); Home Rule; House of Representatives (US); human resources.

hr abbrev : hour.

HRE abbrev : Holy Roman Emperor or Empire.

HRH abbrev : His or Her Royal Highness.

HRT abbrev : hormone replacement therapy.

hryvna /hriv'nə/, also **hryvnya** or **hryvnia** /-nyə/ n the standard monetary unit of Ukraine (100 kopiyok).

HS abbrev : High School; Home Secretary.

Hs (chem) symbol : hassium.

hs abbrev : hoc sensu (L), in this sense.

HSE abbrev : Health and Safety Executive.

Hse abbrev : House (in addresses or place names).

HSH abbrev : His or Her Serene Highness.

HSM abbrev : His or Her Serene Majesty.

HST abbrev : Hawaii Standard Time; high-speed train; Hubble Space Telescope.

HT abbrev : high tension.

ht abbrev : height.

HTLV abbrev : human T-cell lymphotrophic virus.

HTML (comput) abbrev : hypertext mark-up language, the language used to create World Wide Web documents.

HTTP (comput) abbrev : hypertext transfer protocol, the standard by which hypertext documents are transferred over the Internet and the first part of an Internet address.

HTTPS abbrev : hypertext transfer protocol secure, used in addresses of Internet sites that are protected by encryption.

huanaco same as **guanaco**.

huaquero /wä-kā'rō/ n a person who steals antiquities and relics from tombs in Latin America. [Am Sp, from Quechua huaca holy place]

huarache /wə-rä'chi/ n a Mexican sandal with uppers of leather thongs. [Mexican Sp]

hub /hub/ n the centre of a wheel, the nave; a mark at which quoits, etc are thrown; an important centre or focus of activity, as applied (archaic and facetious) to Boston, USA, esp in the phrases hub of the universe or hub of the solar system; the focal point (of a discussion, problem, etc); a unit that connects network components together (comput). [Prob a form of **hob¹**; origin unknown]
  □ **hub'-brake** n a brake acting on the hub of a wheel. **hub'-cap** n a metal covering over the hub of a wheel.

hubba hubba /hub'ə hub'ə/ (N Am inf) interj expressing approval, enthusiasm, pleasure, etc.

hubble-bubble /hub'l-bub'l/ n a bubbling sound; tattle; confusion; a crude kind of hookah. [Reduplication from **bubble**]

Hubble constant /hub'l kon'stənt/ or **Hubble's constant** /hub'lz/ (astron) n the constant factor in **Hubble's law** that the velocity of a galaxy is proportional to its distance from us, giving the rate of increase of velocity with distance in the expanding universe. [EP Hubble (1889–1953), US astronomer]

hubbub /hub'ub/, also **hubbuboo** /hub'u-boo/ or (Shakesp) **whoobub** /hoo'bub/ n a confused sound of many voices; riot; uproar. [Appar of Irish origin]

hubby /hub'i/ (inf) n husband. [Dimin of **husband**]

hubris /hū'bris/ or **hybris** /hī'bris/ n insolence; over-confidence; arrogance, such as invites disaster or ruin (ancient drama); overweening. [Gr hybris]
  ■ **hubris'tic** adj. **hubris'tically** adv.

huck see **huckle**.

huckaback /huk'ə-bak/ n a coarse linen or cotton fabric with a raised surface, used for towels, etc. [Origin unknown]

huckle /huk'l/, also **huck** /huk/ n the haunch; the hip. ◆ vt (Scot inf) to force roughly. [Poss connected with **hook**]
  □ **huck'le-backed** adj having a rounded back; humpbacked. **huck'le-shoul'dered** adj round-shouldered. **huckle'-bone** n the hip bone; the astragalus, the talus or ankle-bone of a quadruped.

huckleberry /huk'l-bə-ri/ or -be-ri/ n a N American shrub (genus Gaylussacia) related to the whortleberry; its fruit; extended to species of whortleberry. [Appar for hurtleberry whortleberry]
  ■ **huck'leberrying** n.

huckster /huk'stər/ n a retailer of small wares, a hawker or pedlar; an aggressive seller; a mercenary person. ◆ vi to hawk or peddle (also vt); to haggle meanly or sell aggressively. [Origin obscure]
  ■ **huck'sterage** n. **huck'steress** or **huck'stress** n. **huck'stery** n.

HUD abbrev : head-up display.

hudden see **haud**.

huddle /hud'l/ n a confused mass; a jumble; confusion; perfunctory haste; a gathering together of the team behind their line of scrimmage so as to receive instructions, signals, etc before the next play (American football); a secret conference (inf); a period of deep consideration of a problem. ◆ vt to jumble; to hustle, bundle, to drive, draw, throw or crowd together in disorder; to put hastily; to perform perfunctorily and hastily; to hustle out of sight, hush up (obs). ◆ vi to crowd in confusion; to crowd closely together, eg because of cold (sometimes with up); to form or gather into a huddle (American football). [Poss connected with **hide¹**]
  ■ **hudd'led** adj jumbled; crowded closely together; in a heap; crouching.

huddup /hud-up'/ (US) interj get up (to a horse).

Hudibrastic /hū-di-bras'tik/ adj similar in style to Hudibras, a metrical burlesque on the Puritans by Samuel Butler (1612–80); mock-heroic.
  ■ **Hudibras'tics** n pl verses of the form used in Hudibras, a burlesque cacophonous octosyllabic couplet with extravagant rhymes.

hue¹ or (Spenser) **hew** /hū/ n appearance; (brilliance of) colour; tint; dye. [OE hīow, hēow (WSax hīw, hīew); Swed hy complexion]

■ **hued** *adj* having a hue, often in combination, as in *dark-hued*. **hue'less** *adj*.

hue² /hū/ *n* a shouting, clamour. [Imit; perh Fr *huer*]
■ **hu'er** *n* a pilchard fishermen's lookout man.
■ **hue and cry** an outcry calling upon all to pursue someone who is to be made prisoner (*hist*); a proclamation or publication to the same effect (*hist*); the pursuit itself; a loud clamour about something.

huff /huf/ *n* a fit of anger, sulks or offended dignity, *esp* in the phrase *in a huff* (*inf*); in draughts, an act of huffing; a puff of wind (*obs*); bluster (*obs*); a blusterer, bully (*obs*). ◆ *vt* to hector; to give offence; to remove from the board for failing to make a possible capture (*draughts*); to puff up (*obs*). ◆ *vi* to blow, puff, swell (*obs*); to take offence; to bluster. [Imit]
■ **huff'ish** or **huff'y** *adj* given to huff; touchy; ready to take offence. **huff'ishly** or **huff'ily** *adv*. **huff'ishness** or **huff'iness** *n*. **huff'kin** *n* (*dialect*) a type of muffin or bun.
❑ **huff'-cap** *adj* (*obs*) (of liquor) heady; blustering.
■ **huffing and puffing** loud talk, noisy objections.

hug /hug/ *vt* (**hugg'ing**; **hugged**) to clasp close with the arms; to embrace; to cherish; to keep close to or skirt. ◆ *n* a close embrace; a particular grip in wrestling. [Ety obscure]
■ **hugg'able** *adj*.
❑ **hug'-me-tight** *n* a close-fitting knitted garment.
■ **hug oneself** to congratulate oneself.

huge /hūj/ *adj* vast; enormous. [OFr *ahuge*]
■ **huge'ly** *adv* very; vastly. **huge'ness** *n*. **huge'ous** *adj* (*archaic*) huge. **huge'ously** *adv* (*archaic*). **huge'ousness** *n* (*archaic*). **hu'gy** *adj* (*archaic*).

hugger-mugger /hug'ər-mug'ər/ *n* secrecy; confusion. ◆ *adj* secret; disorderly. ◆ *adv* in secrecy or disorder. [Origin obscure]

HUGO /hū'gō/ *abbrev* : Human Genome Organization.

Huguenot /hū'gə-not or -nō/ (*hist*) *n* a French Protestant (also *adj*). [Fr, from earlier *eiguenot*, from Ger *Eidgenoss* confederate, assimilated to the name *Hugues* Hugh]

huh /hu/ *interj* expressing disgust, disbelief, enquiry, etc. [Imit]

hui /hoo'i/ (NZ) *n* (pl **hu'i** or **hu'is**) a Maori gathering; any social gathering (*inf*). [Maori]

huia /hoo'yə or hoo'i-ə/ *n* a New Zealand bird (*Heteralocha acutirostris*) related to the crows and starlings, now probably extinct. [Maori; imit]

huissier /wē-syā'/ (Fr) *n* a doorkeeper, usher; a bailiff.

huitain /wē-tān'/ *n* a group of eight lines of verse. [Fr, from *huit* eight]

hula-hula /hoo'lə-hoo'lə/ *n* a Hawaiian dance (also **hu'la**). [Hawaiian]
❑ **hula hoop** *n* a light hoop used in the game of keeping the hoop in motion around the waist by a swinging movement of the hips. **hula skirt** *n* a grass skirt as worn by hula dancers.

hule same as **ule**.

hulk /hulk/ *n* an unwieldy ship; a dismantled ship; a big ungainly or awkward person (*derog inf*); anything unwieldy; often by confusion, a hull; (in *pl* with *the*) old ships formerly used as prisons. [OE *hulc*, cf Gr *holkas* a towed ship, from *helkein* to draw]
■ **hulk'ing** or **hulk'y** *adj* big and clumsy.

hull¹ /hul/ *n* the frame or body of a ship; part of a flying-boat in contact with the water; the heavily-armoured body of a tank, missile, rocket, etc. ◆ *vt* to pierce the hull of. ◆ *vi* (Shakesp) to float or drift, as a mere hull, to float about. ◆ *adj* (of a ship, etc) floating and moving on the hull, as opposed to being raised on hydrofoils, etc. [Perh same word as **hull²**, modified in meaning by confusion with Du *hol* a ship's hold, or with **hulk**]
❑ **hull'-down** *adv* and *adj* so far away that the hull is below the horizon.

hull² /hul/ *n* a husk or outer covering. ◆ *vt* to separate from the hull; to husk. [OE *hulu* a husk, as of corn, from *helan* to cover; Ger *Hülle* a covering, from *hehlen* to cover]
■ **hull'y** *adj* having husks or pods.

hullabaloo /hul-ə-bə-loo'/ *n* an uproar. [Perh *halloo* or possibly rhyming on Scot *baloo* lullaby]

hullo /hu-lō'/ *v*, *n* and *interj* same as **hello**.

Hulsean /hul'si-ən/ *adj* relating to or associated with John *Hulse* (1708–90), founder of a series of divinity lectures at Cambridge.

hum¹ /hum/ *vi* (**humm'ing**; **hummed**) to make a sound like bees or that represented by *m*; to sing with closed lips without words or articulation; to pause in speaking and utter an inarticulate sound; to stammer through embarrassment; to be audibly astir; to have a strong unpleasant smell (*sl*); to be busily active. ◆ *vt* to render by humming; to applaud (*obs*). ◆ *n* the noise of bees; a murmurous sound; an inarticulate murmur; the sound of humming; a strong unpleasant smell (*sl*). [Imit; cf Ger *hummen, humsen*]

■ **humm'able** *adj*. **humm'er** *n* a person or thing that hums, such as a bee, a hummingbird, or a top; a person who makes things hum (see below). **humm'ing** *n* and *adj*.
❑ **humming ale** *n* ale that froths up well, or that makes the head hum. **humm'ingbird** *n* any member of the tropical family Trochilidae, very small birds of brilliant plumage and rapid flight (from the humming sound of the wings). **humm'ing-top** *n* a top that produces a humming sound as it spins.
■ **hum and haw** or **hum and ha** to make inarticulate sounds when at a loss; to shilly-shally. **make things hum** to set things going briskly.

hum² /hum/ *vt* (**humm'ing**; **hummed**) to impose on; to hoax. ◆ *n* an imposition; a hoax. [Contraction of **humbug**]

hum³ /hum/ *interj* expressing doubt or reluctance to agree (also **h'm**, **hmm**).

huma /hoo'mə/ *n* a fabulous restless bird. [Pers *humā* phoenix]

human /hū'mən/ *adj* belonging to, relating to, or of the nature of, people or humankind; having the qualities of a person or the limitations of people; humane; not invidiously superior; genial, kind. ◆ *n* a human being. [Fr *humain*, from L *hūmānus*, from *homō* a human being]
■ **humane** /hū-mān'/ *adj* having the feelings proper to human beings; kind; tender; merciful; humanizing, as *humane letters*, classical, elegant, polite. **humane'ly** *adv*. **humane'ness** *n*. **hū'manism** *n* literary culture; classical studies; any system that puts human interests and the human mind paramount, rejecting the supernatural, belief in a god, etc; pragmatism (*philos*); a critical application of the logical method of pragmatism to all the sciences. **hū'manist** *n* a person who studies polite literature; at the Renaissance, a person who studies Greek and Roman literature; a person who studies human nature; advocate of any system of humanism; a pragmatist. ◆ *adj* of or relating to humanism or humanists. **hūmanist'ic** *adj* of or relating to humanism; emphasizing observation of one's own feelings and reactions to others as a basis for a greater understanding of the self (*psychol* and *psychiatry*). **humanīzā'tion** or **-s-** *n*. **humanize** or **-ise** /hū'mən-īz/ *vt* to render human or humane; to soften; to impart human qualities to, to make like that which is human or of humankind. ◆ *vi* to become humane or civilized. **hū'mankind** *n* the human species. **hū'manlike** *adj*. **hū'manly** *adv* in a human manner; by human agency; having regard to human limitations; humanely. **hū'manness** *n*. **hū'manoid** *adj* and *n* (of) any of the earlier creatures from which modern humans are directly descended and to which they are immediately related, more closely than to *anthropoid* creatures; (of) any creature with the appearance or characteristics of a human being.
❑ **human being** *n* any member of the human race; a person. **human bowling** *n* a game like bowling, in which people get inside large balls and are rolled towards a set of pins. **human capital** *n* the knowledge and skill of employees regarded as a business asset. **human chain** *n* a number of people passing something from one to another in a line. **human chorionic gonadotrophin** see **chorionic gonadotrophin** under **chorion**. **human engineering** *n* the development of human labour as a resource, *esp* in relation to machines and technology. **humane killer** *n* a device for killing animals painlessly. **humane society** *n* a society promoting humane behaviour, *usu* to animals. **human immunodeficiency virus** *n* a virus that breaks down the human body's natural immune system, often causing AIDS (*abbrev* **HIV**). **human interest** *n* (in newspaper articles, broadcasts, etc) reference to people's lives and emotions. **human nature** *n* the nature of humankind; the qualities of character common to all humans that differentiate them from other species; irrational or less than saintly behaviour (often *facetious*). **human resources** *n pl* people collectively regarded in terms of their skills and knowledge; the workforce of an organization. **human rights** *n pl* the right each human being has to personal freedom, justice, etc. **human shield** *n* a person or people (civilian, POW, etc) deliberately deployed in strategic sites (during hostilities) to deter enemy attack upon them; this use of people, as a tactic in war.

humanity /hū-man'i-ti/ *n* the nature peculiar to a human being; humanness; humaneness; the kind feelings of human beings; humankind collectively; (in some Scottish universities) Latin language and literature; (in *pl*) non-scientific subjects of study, such as literature and history, so called from their humanizing effects. [Fr *humanité*, from L *hūmānitās*, from *hūmānus*, from *homō* a man]
■ **humanitarian** /hū-man'i-tā'ri-ən/ *n* someone who denies Christ's divinity, and holds him to be a mere man; a philanthropist. ◆ *adj* of, belonging to, or worthy of humanity or human beings, *esp* benevolent. **humanitā'rianism** *n*.

humble¹ /hum'bl/ (old-fashioned *um'bl*) *adj* low; lowly; modest; unpretentious; having a low opinion of oneself or of one's claims; abased. ◆ *vt* to bring down to the ground; to lower; to abase; to mortify; to degrade. [Fr, from L *humilis* low, from *humus* the ground]
■ **hum'bleness** *n*. **hum'blesse** *n* (Spenser). **hum'bling** *adj* and *n*. **hum'blingly** *adv*. **hum'bly** *adv*.

❑ **hum'blebrag** n (inf) an apparently self-effacing statement that contains a boastful allusion to one's wealth or lifestyle. **hum'ble-mouthed** adj humble in speech.
■ **your humble servant** an old formula used in subscribing a letter.

humble² /hum'bl/ same as **hummel**.

humble-bee /hum'bl-bē/ n the bumblebee (genus Bombus). [Perh from humble, frequentative of **hum¹**; cf Ger Hummel]

humbles /hum'blz/ n pl same as **umbles**.
❑ **humble pie** n a pie made from the umbles of a deer.
■ **eat humble pie** (punningly) to humble or abase oneself, to eat one's words, etc.

humbucker /hum'bu-kər/ n an electric guitar pick-up with two coils, designed to prevent unwanted noise. [**hum¹** and **buck¹** (in sense of 'oppose')]

humbug /hum'bug/ n hollowness, pretence, fraud, deception; an imposter; a lump of toffee; a peppermint drop, or the like. ◆ vt (**hum'bugging**; **hum'bugged**) to deceive; to hoax; to cajole. ◆ vi to potter about. [Appears about 1750; origin unknown]
■ **humbugg'able** adj. **hum'bugger** n. **hum'buggery** n.

humbuzz /hum'buz/ (dialect) n a cockchafer; a bull-roarer. [**hum¹** and **buzz¹**]

humdinger /hum-ding'ər/ (sl) n an exceptionally excellent person or thing; a smooth-running engine; a swift vehicle or aircraft. [Prob **hum¹** and **ding²**]

humdrum /hum'drum/ adj dull; droning; monotonous; commonplace. ◆ n a stupid fellow; monotony; tedious talk. [**hum¹** and perh **drum¹**]

humdudgeon /hum-duj'ən/ n an unnecessary outcry (Scot); low spirits (dialect). [**hum¹** and **dudgeon¹**]

Humean or **Humian** /hū'mi-ən/ adj relating to or associated with David Hume (1711–76) or his philosophy. ◆ n a follower of Hume.
■ **Hūm'ism** n. **Hūm'ist** n.

humect /hū-mekt'/ vt and vi to make or become moist (also **humect'ate**). [L (h)ūmectāre, from ūmēre to be moist]
■ **humect'ant** adj and n. **humectā'tion** n. **humect'ive** adj and n.

humefy see **humify²**.

humerus /hū'mə-rəs/ n (pl hū'merī) the bone of the upper arm. [L (h)umerus shoulder]
■ **hū'meral** adj belonging to the shoulder or the humerus. ◆ n (also **humeral veil**) an oblong vestment worn on the shoulders.

humf see **humph²**.

humhum /hum'hum/ n a kind of plain, coarse cotton cloth used in the East Indies.

Humian see **Humean**.

humic see under **humus¹**.

humid /hū'mid/ adj moist; damp; rather wet. [L (h)ūmidus, from (h)ūmēre to be moist]
■ **humidifica'tion** n. **humid'ifier** n a device for increasing or maintaining humidity. **humid'ify** vt to make humid. **humid'istat** n a device for controlling humidity. **humid'ity** n moisture, esp in the air; a moderate degree of wetness. **hu'midly** adv. **hu'midness** n. **hum'idor** n a box or a chamber, etc for keeping anything moist, such as cigars; a contrivance for keeping the air moist.

humify¹ /hū'mi-fī/ vt and vi to make or turn into humus. [**humus¹**]
■ **humifica'tion** n.

humify² /hū'mi-fī/ vt to moisten (also (obs) **hu'mefy**). [L (h)ūmificāre]
■ **humifica'tion** n.

humiliate /hū-mil'i-āt/ vt to humble; to mortify, injure the self-respect or pride of. [L humiliāre, -ātum]
■ **humil'iant** adj humiliating. **humil'iating** adj. **humilia'tion** n. **humil'iative** adj. **humil'iātor** n. **humil'iatory** /-ə-tər-i/ adj.

humility /hū-mil'i-ti/ n the state or quality of being humble; lowliness of mind; modesty. [OFr humilite, from L humilitās, from humilis low]

HUMINT /hū'mint/ abbrev: Human Intelligence, that branch of military intelligence concerned with obtaining information about individuals (cf **COMINT**, **ELINT**).

Humism, Humist see under **Humean**.

humite /hū'mit/ (mineralogy) n an orthorhombic magnesium orthosilicate also containing magnesium hydroxide, found in impure marbles. [Sir Abraham Hume, 19c mineral collector]

humlie see under **hummel**.

hummable see under **hum¹**.

hummaum see **hammam**.

hummel /hum'l/ or **humble** /hum'bl or hum'l/ (Scot) adj hornless; awnless. ◆ n a hornless stag. ◆ vt (**humm'elling** or **hum'bling**;

humm'elled or **hum'bled**) to make hummel. [Cf LGer hummel, hommel]
■ **hum'lie** n (Scot) a polled or hornless cow, ox, etc. **humm'eller** n (dialect) a machine for removing barley awns.
❑ **hummel bonnet** (or usu **hummle bonnet**) n a type of Scottish cap worn by Highland regiments before the introduction (1851) of the glengarry.

Hummer /hum'ər/ (inf) n a Humvee®.

hummer, humming, hummingbird see under **hum¹**.

hummock /hum'ək/ or (archaic) **hommock** /hom'ək/ n a hillock; a pile or ridge of ice. [Origin unknown: at first nautical]
■ **humm'ocked** adj. **humm'ocky** adj.

hummum same as **hammam**.

hummus /hum'əs or hŭm'əs/ n a Middle-Eastern hors d'œuvre of puréed chickpeas with garlic and lemon and sometimes tahini (also **houmm'os, houm'ous** or **houm'us**). [Turk]

humogen /hū'mō-jən/ n a fertilizer composed of peat treated with a culture of nitrogen-fixing bacteria. [L humus soil, and Gr gennaein to produce]

humongous or **humungous** /hū' or ū'mung-gəs/ (inf, orig N Am) adj huge, enormous; exceptionally bad. [Origin uncertain]

humour or US **humor** /hū'mər or ū'mər/ n a mental quality that apprehends and delights in the ludicrous and mirthful; that which causes mirth and amusement; the quality of being funny; playful fancy; temperament or disposition of mind; state of mind (as in good humour, ill humour); disposition; caprice; in Corporal Nym's vocabulary in Merry Wives of Windsor and Henry V (also as adj and vt, and **hū'moured** adj) a word of any meaning, down to no meaning at all (Shakesp); moisture (archaic); a fluid (med); a fluid of the animal body, esp formerly any one of the four that in old physiology were held to determine temperament. ◆ vt to go along with the humour of; to gratify by compliance. [OFr humor (Fr humeur), from L (h)ūmor, from (h)ūmēre to be moist]
■ **hū'moral** adj relating to or proceeding from a body fluid. **hū'moralism** n the state of being humoral; the old doctrine that diseases have their seat in the humours. **hū'moralist** n someone who favoured the doctrine of humoralism. **hū'morally** adv. **hūmoresk'** or **hūmoresque'** n a humorous piece of music; a musical caprice. **hū'morist** n someone possessed of a sense of humour; a writer of comic stories; a person whose conduct and conversation are regulated by humour or caprice (archaic); a person who studies or portrays the humours of people. **hūmoris'tic** adj humorous. **hū'morous** adj full of humour; exciting laughter; governed by humour (archaic); capricious (archaic); irregular (archaic). **hū'morously** adv. **hū'morousness** n. **hū'mourless** or (US) **hu'morless** adj. **hū'moursome** adj capricious, petulant. **hū'moursomeness** n.
❑ **humoral immunity** n an acquired immunity in which antibodies circulating in body fluids play the major part.
■ **comedy of humours** the comedy of Ben Jonson and his school in which the characters, instead of being conceived as rounded individuals, are little more than personifications of single qualities. **out of humour** displeased, in a bad mood.

humous see under **humus¹**.

hump /hump/ n a rounded projection in the back due to spinal deformity; a fatty protuberance on the back of a camel, etc; a protuberance; a rounded mass, eg of earth; a long walk with one's possessions in a bundle on one's back (obs Aust); despondency or annoyance, esp in the phrase have (or give someone) the hump (inf); the sulks (inf). ◆ vt to bend in a hump; to hunch; to exert oneself (inf); to hurry (sl); to vex or annoy (sl); to shoulder, to carry on the back (orig Aust); to carry, to heave (heavy loads) (inf); to have sexual intercourse with (someone) (vulgar sl). ◆ vi to put forth effort; to have sexual intercourse (vulgar sl). [Origin obscure]
■ **humped** adj having a hump. **hum'per** n (inf) someone who carries heavy loads, eg a porter in a market. **hump'y** adj full of humps or protuberances; having a hump or humps; sulky, irritable (inf).
❑ **hump'back** n a back with a hump or hunch; a person with a humpback; a Pacific species of salmon; a whale with a humplike dorsal fin. **hump'-back** or **hump'-backed** adj having a humpback. **humpback bridge** n a bridge with a sharp rise in the middle.
■ **hump the bluey** (Aust) to travel on foot, carrying a bundle of possessions. **over the hump** (inf) past the crisis or difficulty.

humpen or **Humpen** /hŭm'pən/ n a type of usu cylindrical enamelled or painted glass drinking vessel made in Germany from the 17c. [Ger]

humper see under **hump**.

humph¹ /humf, hmh, huh or hmf/ interj expressive of reserved doubt or dissatisfaction.

humph² or **humf** /humf/ (Scot) n a hump. ◆ vt to carry (something cumbersome, heavy or awkward). [**hump**]

Humphrey see **dine with Duke Humphrey** under **dine**.

humpty /*hump'ti* or *hum'ti*/ *n* a low padded seat, a pouffe. [*humpty* hunchbacked; perh connected with **Humpty-Dumpty**]

Humpty-Dumpty /*hump'ti-dump'ti* or *hum'ti-dum'ti*/ *n* a short, squat, egg-like character of nursery folklore; (without *caps*) a short stout person; a gypsy drink, ale boiled with brandy. ◆ *adj* short and broad.

humpy[1] /*hum'pi*/ (*Aust*) *n* an Aboriginal hut. [Aboriginal word *oompi*]

humpy[2] see under **hump**.

humstrum /*hum'strum*/ (now *dialect*) *n* a hurdy-gurdy or other musical instrument. [**hum**[1] and **strum**, with imit effect]

humungous see **humongous**.

humus[1] /*hū'məs*/ *n* decomposed organic matter in the soil. [L *humus*; cf Gr *chamai* on the ground]
■ **hū'mic** or **hū'mous** *adj*. **hum'usy** *adj* having much humus.

humus[2] same as **hummus**.

Humvee® /*hum'vē*/ (*US*) *n* a military vehicle similar to but larger than a Jeep (also *inf* **Humm'er**). [From *HMMWV*, abbrev of its full name, *High-Mobility Multipurpose Wheeled Vehicle*]

Hun /*hun*/ *n* a member of a powerful savage nomad race of Asia who moved westwards, and under Attila (433–453) overran Europe; in USA formerly a Hungarian (*derog*); a barbarian; a German (*orig* World War I *sl*, now *derog sl*). [OE (pl) *Hūne, Hūnas*; L *Hunni*; Gr *Ounnoi, Chounnoi*]
■ **Hunn'ic** or **Hunn'ish** *adj*.

hunch /*hunch* or *hunsh*/ *n* a hump; a lump; a premonition; a hint; an intuitive feeling. ◆ *vt* to hump, bend. ◆ *vi* (often with *up*) to sit with the body bent forward or curled up. [Origin obscure]
□ **hunch'back** *n* a person whose spine is convexly curved to an abnormal degree. **hunch'backed** *adj*.
■ **play one's hunch** to act on one's hunch (as a gambler might).

hundred /*hun'drəd*/ *n* (pl **hundreds** or, when preceded by a numeral, **hundred**) ten times ten; a hundred pounds, dollars, etc; (in *pl*) an unspecified large number; a division of a county in England *orig* supposed to contain a hundred families (chiefly *hist*). ◆ *adj* being a hundred in number; hundredth (*obs* or *dialect*); also used indefinitely, very many (*inf*). [OE *hundred*, from old form *hund* a hundred, with sfx *-red* a reckoning]
■ **hun'dreder** or **hun'dredor** *n* (*hist*) the bailiff or an inhabitant of a hundred. **hun'dredfold** *adj, adv* and *n* folded a hundred times; in a hundred divisions; a hundred times as much. **hun'dredth** *adj* last of a hundred; next after the ninety-ninth; equal to one of a hundred equal parts. ◆ *n* one of a hundred equal parts; a person or thing in hundredth position.
□ **hun'dred-per-cent'** *adj* out-and-out; thorough-going (**not a hundred per cent** not in perfect health). **hun'dred-percent'er** *n* (*US*) an uncompromising patriot. **hun'dreds-and-thou'sands** *n pl* little sweets used as decoration. **hun'dredweight** *n* $\frac{1}{20}$ of a ton, or 112lb avoirdupois (50.80kg; also called **long hundredweight**); *orig* and still in US, 100lb (45.3kg; also called **short hundredweight**); 50kg (also called **metric hundredweight**; *abbrev* **cwt**).
■ **Chiltern Hundreds** a district of Buckinghamshire, whose stewardship is a nominal office under the Crown, the temporary acceptance of which by a member of parliament enables him or her to vacate his or her seat. **great** or **long hundred** usually 120; sometimes some other number greater than ten tens (eg of herrings, 132 or 126). **Hundred Years' War** the struggle between England and France, from 1337 down to 1453. **not a hundred miles from** (*inf*) at, very near. **Old Hundred** see under **old**. **one, two**, etc **hundred hours** one, two, etc o'clock (from the method of writing hours and minutes 1.00, 2.00, etc). **the Hundred Days** the time between Napoleon's return from Elba and his final downfall after Waterloo (the reign lasted exactly 95 days, March 20-June 22, 1815).

Hung. *abbrev*: Hungarian; Hungary.

hung *pat* and *pap* of **hang**.

Hungarian /*hung-gā'ri-ən*/ *adj* relating to *Hungary* in central Europe or its inhabitants. ◆ *n* a person of Hungarian birth, descent or citizenship; the Magyar or Hungarian language. [Cf **Ugrian**]
□ **Hungary** /*hung'gə-ri*/ **water** *n* oil of rosemary distilled with alcohol (said to have been used by a queen of Hungary).

hunger /*hung'gər*/ *n* craving for food; need or lack of food; strong desire for anything. ◆ *vi* to crave food; to long (*for*). [OE *hungor* (noun), *hyngran* (verb); cf Ger *Hunger*, Du *honger*, etc]
■ **hung'erful** *adj* hungry. **hung'erly** *adj* (*Shakesp*) hungry. ◆ *adv* (*Shakesp*) hungrily. **hung'rily** *adv*. **hung'ry** *adj* having an eager desire for food (or anything else); greedy, desirous, longing (with *for*); stingy, mean (*Aust*); lean; poor; used in combination to signify eager for, in need of (as in *land-hungry*).
□ **hung'er-bitten** *adj* bitten, pained or weakened by hunger. **hunger march** *n* a procession of unemployed or others in need, as a demonstration. **hung'er-marcher** *n*. **hunger strike** *n* prolonged

refusal of all food by a prisoner, etc as a form of protest, or a means to ensure release. **hung'er-strike** *vi*. **hung'er-striker** *n*.
■ **go hungry** to remain without food.

hung over, **hung up**, etc see under **hang**.

hunk[1] /*hungk*/ *n* a lump; a strong or sexually attractive man (*inf*). [Same as **hunch**]
■ **hunk'y** *adj* (*inf*; of a man) strong or sexually attractive.

hunk[2] /*hungk*/ *n* (*US*) goal or base in boys' games. ◆ *adj* safe, secure. [Du *honk*]
■ **hunk'y** (*US*) or **hunk'y-do'ry** (*orig US*) *adj* (*inf*) in a good position or condition; excellent; all right.

hunker[1] /*hung'kər*/ (*US*) *n orig* a member of the conservative section of the New York Democratic party (1845–8); a conservative person. [Origin obscure]

hunker[2] /*hung'kər*/ *vi* to squat (often with *down*). [Origin obscure; perh connected with ON *hūka* to squat]
■ **hunk'ers** *n pl* (*inf*) the hams or haunches.

hunks /*hungks*/ *n sing* a miserly curmudgeon. [Ety dubious]

hunky[1] /*hung'ki*/ (*N Am*) *n* a derogatory name for a person of E European descent, *esp* an unskilled workman. [For **Hungarian**]

hunky[2] see under **hunk**[1,2].

hunky-dory see under **hunk**[2].

Hunnic, Hunnish see under **Hun**.

hunt /*hunt*/ *vt* to chase or go in quest of for prey or sport; to seek or pursue game over (land, etc); to ransack; to use in the hunt; to search for; to pursue; to hound or drive; to drive away, dismiss (chiefly *Aust*). ◆ *vi* to go out in pursuit of game; to search; to oscillate or vary in speed (*mech*); (of a bell) to move its order of ringing through a set of changes (**hunt up** to be rung progressively earlier; **hunt down** to be rung progressively later). ◆ *n* a chase of wild animals; a search; a pack of hunting hounds; an association of huntsmen; the district hunted by a pack; game killed in a hunt (*Shakesp*); a huntsman (*obs*). [OE *huntian*; prob connected with *hentan* to seize]
■ **hunt'ed** *adj* fearful; harassed. **hunt'er** *n* a person or animal that hunts (*fem* **hunt'ress**); a horse used in hunting, *esp* foxhunting; a watch whose face is protected with a metal case (a **half-hunt'er** if that case has a small circle of glass let in). **hunt'ing** *n* the pursuit of wild game, the chase; the moving of the order of ringing a bell through a set of changes (also *adj*).
□ **hunt'away** *n* (*NZ*) a dog trained to drive sheep from behind. **hunt ball** *n* a ball given by the members of a hunt. **hunt'-counter** *n* (*Shakesp*) perhaps one who hunts counter (qv below). **hunt'er-gath'erer** *n* (*anthrop*) a member of a society that lives by hunting and gathering fruit, etc, as opposed eg to cultivating crops. **hunt'er-kill'er** *n* a surface craft or submarine designed to hunt down and destroy enemy vessels. **hunter's moon** *n* a full moon following the harvest-moon. **hunt'ing-box, -lodge** or **-seat** *n* temporary accommodation for hunters. **hunt'ing-cap** *n* a form of cap often worn in the hunting-field. **hunt'ing-cat** *n* a cheetah. **hunt'ing-cog** *n* an extra cog in one of two geared wheels, by means of which the order of contact of cogs is changed at every revolution. **hunt'ing-crop** or **-whip** *n* a short whip with a crooked handle and a loop of leather at the end, used in the hunting-field. **hunt'ing-field** *n* the scene or sphere of hunting, *esp* foxhunting; the assemblage of huntsmen. **hunt'ing-ground** *n* a place or region for hunting (**happy hunting-ground** see under **happy**). **hunt'ing-horn** *n* a horn used in hunting, a bugle. **hunt'ing-knife** or **-sword** *n* a knife or short sword used to dispatch the game when caught, or to skin and cut it up. **hunt'ing-leopard** *n* a cheetah. **hunt'ing-mass** *n* (*obs*) a hasty and abridged mass said for impatient hunters. **hunt'ing-song** *n*. **hunting spider** *n* a wolf spider. **hunt'ing-tide** *n* the season of hunting. **hunting-whip** see **hunting-crop** above. **hunt saboteur** *n* a person opposed to all blood sports, *esp* foxhunting, who, *usu* as part of an organized group, takes action to thwart the activities of hunters. **hunts'man** *n* a person who hunts; a person who manages the hounds during the chase. **hunts'manship** *n* the qualifications of a huntsman. **huntsman spider** *n* (*Aust*) any spider of the many varieties belonging to the Heteropodidae (or Sparassidae) family, *esp* those of the genus *Isopoda*, typically large and flat-bodied, inhabiting tree bark. **hunt's'-up** *n* (*Shakesp*) a tune or song intended to arouse huntsmen in the morning; hence, anything calculated to arouse. **hunt'-the-gowk** *n* (*Scot*) the making of an April fool; (also **hunt'iegowk**) a fool's errand, a deception or a hoax, appropriate to the First of April. ◆ *vt* to make an April fool of. **hunt'-the-slipp'er** *n* a game in which a person in the middle of a ring of people tries to catch a shoe passed round surreptitiously by the others.
■ **good hunting!** (*inf*) good luck! **hunt after** or **for** to search for. **hunt counter** to follow the scent backwards. **hunt down** to pursue to extremities; to persecute out of existence; see also **hunt** (*vi*) above. **hunt out** or **up** to seek out. **hunt the letter** to affect alliteration. **hunt up** see **hunt** (*vi*) above.

Hunterian /hun-tē'ri-ən/ adj relating to or associated with the surgeon John *Hunter* (1728–93), to his anatomical collection, nucleus of the Hunterian Museum in London, or to the annual Hunterian Oration at the Royal College of Surgeons; of or relating to his elder brother, William *Hunter* (1718–83), anatomist and obstetrician, or his museum in Glasgow.

huntiegowk see **hunt-the-gowk** under **hunt**.

hunting see under **hunt**.

Huntingdonian /hun-ting-dō'ni-ən/ n and adj (a member) of the Countess of Huntingdon's Connection, a denomination of Calvinistic Methodists founded by George Whitefield (1714–70) with Selina, Countess of *Huntingdon* (1707–91).

huntingtin /hun'ting-tin/ n a protein produced by the gene that causes Huntington's disease. [*Huntingt*on's and **-in** (1)]

Huntington's disease /hun'ting-tənz di-zēz'/ or **Huntington's chorea** /ko-rē'ə/ n an inherited and fatal disease, marked by progressive mental deterioration. [Dr G *Huntington* (1851–1916), US neurologist who described it]

huntress, **huntsman**, **huntsmanship** see under **hunt**.

Huon pine /hū'on or hū'ən pīn/ n a Tasmanian conifer (*Dacrydium*, or *Lagerostrobus*, *franklinii*), found first on the *Huon* river.

hup /hup/ vi to shout 'hup'; (of a horse) to go on, to go faster; to turn to the right. ◆ vt to turn (a horse) to the right. ◆ n a cry of 'hup'. ◆ interj (to a horse) to go faster or to turn to the right. ■ **neither hup nor wind** (*Scot*) to do neither one thing nor another, be unmanageable.

hupaithric /hū-pā'thrik/ adj hypaethral.

huppah see **chuppah**.

hurcheon /hûr'chən/ a Scots form of **urchin**.

hurden see under **hards**.

hurdies /hûr'diz/ (*Scot*) n pl the buttocks; the thighs. [Origin unknown]

hurdle /hûr'dl/ n a frame of twigs or sticks interlaced; a movable frame of timber or iron for gates, etc (*agric*); (in certain races) a portable barrier over which runners jump; a rude sledge on which criminals were drawn to the gallows (*hist*); an obstacle to be surmounted, difficulty to be overcome; (in pl) a hurdle-race. ◆ vt to enclose with hurdles; to jump over (a hurdle, an obstacle, etc). ◆ vi to jump as over a hurdle; to run a hurdle-race. [OE *hyrdel*; Ger *Hürde*] ■ **hurd'ler** n a maker of hurdles; an athlete who takes part in hurdles events. **hurd'ling** n. ❑ **hur'dle-race** n a race in which hurdles have to be cleared. **hur'dle-racer** n. **hur'dle-racing** n. **hurdle rate** n (*finance*) the minimum rate at which annual assets must grow before the achievement of specified results.

hurds see **hards**.

hurdy-gurdy /hûr'di-gûr'di/ n a stringed musical instrument, whose strings are sounded by the turning of a wheel; a barrel organ (*inf*). [Imit]

hurl /hûrl/ vt to fling with violence; to wheel (*Scot*); to convey in a wheeled vehicle (*Scot*). ◆ vi to dash; to travel in a wheeled vehicle (*Scot*); to play hurley; to vomit (*sl*). ◆ n act of hurling; a trip or journey in a wheeled vehicle (*Scot*). [Cf LGer *hurreln* to hurl, precipitate; influenced by **hurtle** and **whirl**] ■ **hurl'er** n. **hurl'ey** or **hurl'ing** n a game similar to hockey, of Irish origin, played by teams of 15, with broad-bladed sticks (**hurl'eys**) and a hide-covered cork ball. **hurl'y** n (*Scot*) a large two-wheeled barrow. ❑ **hurl'barrow** n (*Scot*) a wheelbarrow. **hurl'bat** see **whirlbat** under **whirl**. **hurl'ey-house** n (*Scot*) a house in a state of disrepair. **hurl'y-hacket** n (*Scot*) a carriage, gig; an improvised sledge; sledging.

hurly¹ /hûr'li/ n commotion; tumult. [Perh from **hurl**] ❑ **hurly-burly** /hûr'li-bûr'li/ n tumult; confusion. ◆ adj confused or tumultuous (also adv).

hurly² see under **hurl**.

Huronian /hū-rō'ni-ən/ (*geol*) n and adj upper Precambrian of Canada, well exemplified north of Lake *Huron*.

hurrah, **hurra** /hŭ-rä' or hu-rä'/ or now usually **hurray** or **hooray** /hŭ-rä'/ interj an exclamation of approbation or joy (also n and vi). [Cf Norw, Swed, Dan *hurra*, Ger *hurrah*, Du *hoera*]

hurricane /hur'i-kin or -kān/ n a West Indian cyclonic storm of great violence; a wind of force 12 to 17 on the Beaufort scale, reaching speeds of 73mph or more (*meteorol*); anything tempestuous, a tumult, commotion; a social party, a rout (*obs*); (with cap) a type of fighting aeroplane used in World War II. [Sp *huracán*, from Carib] ■ **hurricà'no** n (pl **hurricà'noes**) (*obs*) a hurricane; a waterspout (*Shakesp*). ❑ **hurricane deck** n a light partial deck over the saloon of some ships. **hurricane lamp** n an oil lamp encased so as to defy strong wind; a protected electric lamp.

hurry /hur'i/ vt (**hurr'ying**; **hurr'ied**) to urge forward; to hasten. ◆ vi to move or act with haste, *esp* perturbed or impatient haste. ◆ n a driving forward; haste; flurried or undue haste; commotion; a rush; need for haste; a tremolo passage for strings, or a drum roll, in connection with an exciting situation (*music*). [Prob imit; cf Old Swed *hurra* to whirl round] ■ **hurr'ied** adj. **hurr'iedly** adv. **hurr'iedness** n. **hurr'ying** n and adj. **hurr'yingly** adv. ❑ **hurr'y-scurr'y** or **-skurr'y** n confusion and bustle. ◆ adv confusedly. ■ **hurry up** to make haste; to hasten. **in a hurry** in haste, speedily; soon; easily; willingly.

hurst /hûrst/ n a wood, a grove; a sand bank. [OE *hyrst*]

hurt /hûrt/ vt (pap and pat **hurt**) to cause pain to; to damage; to injure; to wound (a person's feelings, etc). ◆ vi to give pain; to be the seat or source of pain; to be injured (*inf*, *esp* N Am). ◆ n a wound; injury. ◆ adj injured; pained in body or mind. [OFr *hurter* (Fr *heurter*) to knock, to run against] ■ **hurt'er** n that which hurts; a beam, block, etc to protect a wall from wheels; the shoulder of an axle against which the hub strikes. **hurt'ful** adj causing hurt or loss; harmful, *esp* emotionally. **hurt'fully** adv. **hurt'fulness** n. **hurt'less** adj without hurt or injury, harmless. **hurt'lessly** adv. **hurt'lessness** n.

hurtle /hûr'tl/ vi to move rapidly with a clattering sound; to rattle; to clash (*archaic*). ◆ vt to dash; to hurl; to brandish (*Spenser*). [Frequentative of **hurt** in its original sense]

hurtleberry /hûr'tl-ber-i/ n same as **whortleberry**.

husband /huz'bənd/ n a man to whom someone is married; a husbandman (*obs*); a manager; a thrifty manager. ◆ vt to manage with economy; to conserve; to supply with a husband (*archaic*); to become, be or act as a husband to (*archaic*); to cultivate (*archaic*). [OE *hūsbonda*, ON *hūsbōndi*, from *hūs* a house, and *būandi* inhabiting, prp of ON *būa* to dwell; cf **boor**, **bower**¹ and Ger *bauen* to till] ■ **hus'bandage** n allowance or commission of a ship's husband. **hus'bandless** adj. **hus'bandlike** adj. **hus'bandly** adj frugal, thrifty; relating to or befitting a husband. **hus'bandry** n the business of a farmer; tillage; economical management; thrift. ❑ **hus'bandland** n (*hist*) a manorial tenant's holding; two oxgangs. **hus'bandman** n a working farmer; a man who labours in tillage. ■ **ship's husband** an owner's agent who manages the affairs of a ship in port.

hush /hush/ interj silence; be still. ◆ n a silence, *esp* after noise; a rush of water or its sound (*dialect*); the washing away of surface soil to lay bare bedrock (*mineralogy*). ◆ adj silent (*archaic*); quiet (*archaic*); for the purpose of concealing information (eg *hush money*) (*inf*). ◆ vi to become silent or quiet. ◆ vt to make quiet; to calm; to procure silence or secrecy about (sometimes with *up*); to pour in a stream (*dialect*); to wash away or to pour in order to expose bedrock (*mining*). [Imit; cf **hist** and **whist¹**] ■ **hush'aby** /-ə-bī/ n (*archaic*) a lullaby used to soothe babies to sleep (also vt and interj). **hushed** adj silent, still. **hush'-hush** or **hush'y** adj (*inf*) secret. ❑ **hush'-boat** n (*obs*) a ship travelling in secret. **hush kit** n (*inf*) a device fitted to the jet engine of an aeroplane to reduce noise. **hush money** n (*inf*) money paid to ensure that someone with secret knowledge will not disclose it. **hush puppy** n (*US*; *usu* in pl) a ball or balls of maize dough, deep-fried (from its occasional use as dog food). ■ **hush up** to stifle, suppress; to be silent.

husher /hush'ər/ another spelling of **usher**.

Hush Puppies® /hush pup'iz/ n pl a make of light soft (*esp* suede) shoes.

husk /husk/ n the dry, thin covering of certain fruits and seeds; a case, shell or covering, *esp* one that is worthless or coarse; (in pl) refuse, waste; huskiness; bronchitis in cattle caused by parasitic nematodes; a supporting frame. ◆ vt to remove the husk or outer integument from. [Perh connected with **house**] ■ **husked** adj covered with a husk; stripped of husks. **husk'er** n someone who husks maize, *esp* at a husking-bee; apparatus (such as a glove) for the same purpose. **husk'ily** adv. **husk'iness** n. **husk'ing** n the stripping of husks; a festive gathering to assist in husking maize (also **husk'ing-bee**). **husk'y** adj full of husks; of the nature of husks; like a husk; dry; sturdy like a corn husk; (of a voice) dry and almost whispering, as if there were husks in the throat; (of words) spoken in a husky voice. ◆ n (N Am) a big strong man.

husky¹ see under **husk**.

husky² /hus'ki/ n a sledge-dog of the Arctic; an Inuit; the Inuit language. [Appar from **Eskimo**]

huso /hū'sō/ n (pl **hu'sos**) the great sturgeon. [OHGer *hûso*]

huss /hus/ n any of various kinds of dogfish, when used as food. [ME *husk*, *huske*]

hussar /hū-zär' or hə-/ n a soldier of a light cavalry regiment; *orig* a soldier of the national cavalry of Hungary in the 15c. [Hung *huszar*, through Old Serb, from Ital *corsaro* a freebooter]

hussif /hus'if/ dialect form of **housewife**, in the sense of pocket sewing-kit.

Hussite /hus'īt or hūs'īt/ n a follower of the Bohemian reformer John Hus, martyred in 1415.
■ **Huss'itism** n.

hussy /hus'i or huz'i/ n an impudent girl; a promiscuous or worthless girl or woman; a housewife (*obs*); a hussif (*obs*). [**housewife**]

hustings /hus'tingz/ n *sing* electioneering; the booths where the votes were formerly taken at an election of an MP, or the platform from which the candidates gave their addresses; *orig* the principal court of the city of London. [OE *hūsting* a council (used in speaking of the Danes), from ON *hūsthing*, from *hūs* a house, and *thing* an assembly]

hustle /hus'l/ vt to shake or push together; to crowd with violence; to jostle; to thrust hastily; to hasten roughly; to exert pressure on; to sell (*esp* aggressively); to obtain (money) illicitly (*sl*). ◆ vi to act strenuously or aggressively; to earn money illicitly (eg as a prostitute; *sl*). ◆ n frenzied activity; a swindle, fraud (*sl*); a type of lively disco dance with a variety of steps. [Du *hutselen* to shake to and fro; cf **hotchpotch**]
■ **hus'tler** n a lively or energetic person; a swindler (*sl*); a prostitute (*sl*). **hus'tling** n.

huswife /hus'if/ obsolete form of **housewife**.

hut /hut/ n a small, mean or crudely built house; a small temporary dwelling or similar structure. ◆ vt (**hutt'ing**; **hutt'ed**) to quarter (troops) in or furnish with a hut or huts. ◆ vi to dwell in a hut or huts. [Fr *hutte*, from OHGer *hutta* (Ger *Hütte*); cf **hide**[1]]
■ **hut'ment** n an encampment of huts (*milit*); lodging in huts. **hutt'ing** n material for making huts.
❑ **hut'-cir'cle** n (*archaeol*) the remains of a prehistoric circular hut, a pit lined with stones, etc.

hutch /huch/ n a box, a chest; a coop or cage for small animals, *esp* for rabbits; a small, cramped house (*inf*); a baker's kneading-trough; a trough used with some ore-dressing machines; a low wagon in which coal is drawn up out of the pit. ◆ vt (*Milton*) to hoard up. [Fr *huche* a chest, from LL *hūtica* a box; prob Gmc]

Hutchinsonian /huch-in-sōn'i-ən/ n a follower of John Hutchinson (1674–1737), who held that the Hebrew Scriptures contain typically the elements of all rational philosophy, natural history and true religion.

hutia /hoo-tē'ə/ n the hog-rat. [Sp *hutia*, from Taino]

Huttonian /hu-tō'ni-ən/ adj relating to the teaching of James *Hutton* (1726–97), *esp* expounding the importance of geological agencies still at work, and the igneous origin of granite and basalt. ◆ n a follower of Hutton.

Hutu /hoo'too/ n a member of a Bantu-speaking people in Rwanda and Burundi. [Bantu]

hutzpah see **chutzpah**.

huzoor /hu-zoor'/ n an Indian potentate, or (loosely) any person of rank or importance. [Ar *hudūr* the presence]

huzza /hu-zä' or hu-zä'/ interj and n hurrah; a shout of joy or approbation. ◆ vt (**huzza'ing**; **huzzaed** or **huzza'd** /-zäd'/) to attend with shouts of joy. ◆ vi to utter shouts of joy or acclamation. [Perh Ger *hussa*; cf **hurrah**]

huzzy /huz'i/ dialect variant of **hussy**.

HV or **hv** *abbrev*: high voltage.

HWM *abbrev*: high water mark.

hwyl /hū'il/ n divine inspiration in oratory; emotional fervour. [Welsh]

hyacine /hī'ə-sīn/ (*Spenser*) n hyacinth (the stone).

hyacinth /hī'ə-sinth/ n a flower (a bluebell or blue larkspur) that sprang from the blood of Hyacinthus, a youth accidentally killed by Apollo (Gr *myth*); a bulbous genus (*Hyacinthus*) of the lily family, cultivated; extended to others of the family, such as **wild hyacinth** (the English bluebell), **grape hyacinth** (genus *Muscari*), and **Cape hyacinth** a species of *Galtonia* (*G. candicans*) with white flowers; a blue gemstone of the ancients (*perh* aquamarine); a red, brown or yellow zircon-jacinth; cinnamon stone; a purple colour, of various hues. [Gr *hyakinthos* a species of *Scilla*, blue larkspur, or a blue stone; cf **jacinth**]
■ **hyacin'thine** adj consisting of or resembling hyacinth; very beautiful, like Hyacinthus; of a colour variously understood as golden, purple-black, or a blue or purple of some kind.

Hyades /hī'ə-dēz/ or **Hyads** /hī'adz/ n pl a cluster of five stars in the constellation of the Bull, supposed by the ancients to bring rain when they rose with the sun. [Gr *Hyades*, *Hyades*, explained by the ancients as from *hyein* to rain; more prob little pigs, from *hys* a pig]

hyaena see **hyena**.

hyaline /hī'ə-lin or -līn/ adj glassy; of or like glass; clear; transparent; free from granules (*biol*). ◆ n (*Milton*) a glassy transparent surface. [Gr *hyalos* glass]
■ **hy'alin** n a translucent substance formed by degeneration of certain tissues. **hyaliniza'tion** or **-s-** n. **hy'alinize** or **-ise** vt, vi (*med*) (of tissue) to change to a firm, glassy consistency. **hy'alite** n transparent colourless opal. **hy'aloid** adj (*anat*) hyaline, transparent. **hyalom'elane** or **hyalom'elan** /-ān or -an/ n (Gr *melās*, *-anos* black) tachylite. **hyalonē'ma** n (Gr *nēma* thread) the glass-rope sponge. **hy'alophane** n (root of Gr *phainesthai* to seem) a feldspar containing barium. **hy'aloplasm** n the clear fluid part of protoplasm.
❑ **hyaline cartilage** n a translucent bluish-white cartilage, eg covering bones at points of articulation. **hyaline degeneration** n hyalinization. **hyaline membrane disease** n a condition of newborn babies in which the lungs are unable to expand properly and hyaline material forms in them. **hyaloid membrane** n the transparent membrane that encloses the vitreous humour of the eye. **hyaluron'ic acid** n (Gr *ouron* urine) a natural polysaccharide that occurs in body tissues and synovial fluid and often binds with proteins.

Hyblaean /hī-blē'ən/ adj relating to ancient *Hybla* in Sicily, noted for its honey.

hybrid /hī'brid/ n an organism that is the offspring of a union between different races, species, genera or varieties; a mongrel; a word formed of elements from different languages; anything produced by combining elements from different sources. ◆ adj (also **hyb'ridous**) produced from different species, etc; mongrel; (of a circuit) consisting of transistors and valves; (of an integrated circuit) having integrated circuit(s) and other components attached to a ceramic base. [L *hibrida* offspring of a tame sow and wild boar; with associations of Gr *hybris* insolence, overweening]
■ **hy'bridism** or **hybrid'ity** n the state of being hybrid. **hybridiz'able** or **-s-** adj. **hybridiza'tion** or **-s-** n a technique for determining the similarity of two DNA or RNA strands from different sources by annealing them to form hybrid molecules, whose stability is a measure of their relatedness. **hy'bridize** or **-ise** vt to cause to interbreed. ◆ vi to interbreed. **hybridiz'er** or **-s-** n. **hybridō'ma** n a hybrid cell produced from a cancer cell and an antibody-producing cell.
❑ **hybrid bill** n (*politics*) a parliamentary public bill that affects certain private interests. **hybrid computer** n one that combines features of digital and analogue computers. **hybrid vehicle** n a vehicle able to be powered by more than one type of energy, *esp* one that can run using internal combustion and electricity. **hybrid vigour** n heterosis.

hybris see **hubris**.

hydathode /hī'dəth-ōd/ (*bot*) n an epidermal water-excreting organ. [Gr *hydōr*, *hydatos* water, and *hodos* way]

hydatid /hī'də-tid/ n a water cyst or vesicle in an animal body, *esp* one containing a tapeworm larva; the larva itself; hydatid disease. ◆ adj containing or resembling a hydatid. [Gr *hydatis*, *-idos* a watery vesicle, from *hydōr*, *hydatos* water]
■ **hydatid'iform** adj resembling a hydatid.
❑ **hydatid disease** n an infection, *esp* of the liver, caused by tapeworm larvae, giving rise to expanding cysts. **hydatidiform mole** n (*med*) an affection of the vascular tufts of the fetal part of the placenta whereby they become greatly enlarged.

hydatoid /hī'də-toid/ adj watery. [Gr *hydōr*, *-atos* water, and *eidos* form]

Hydnocarpus /hid-nō-kär'pəs/ n a genus of trees related to the chaulmoogra, yielding an oil containing chaulmoogric acid. [Gr *hydnon* truffle, and *karpos* fruit]

hydr- see **hydro-**[1].

Hydra /hī'drə/ n a water monster with many heads, which when cut off were succeeded by others (*myth*); a large southern constellation; (without *cap*) any manifold evil; (without *cap*) a freshwater hydrozoon of the genus *Hydra*, remarkable for power of multiplication on being cut or divided. [Gr *hydrā*, from *hydōr* water, related to Sans *udra* an otter]

hydraemia, **hydragogue**, **hydrangea**, etc see under **hydro-**[1].

hydrargyrism /hī-drär'ji-ri-zm/ n mercurial poisoning. [Gr *hydrargyros* mercury, from *argyros* silver; *hydrargyrum* is modern L on analogy of *argentum*, etc, L *hydrargyrus*]
■ **hydrar'gyral** adj. **hydrar'gyrum** n mercury.

hydrate, **hydration** see under **hydro-**[1].

hydraulic /hī-drö'lik or -drol'ik/ adj relating to hydraulics; conveying water; worked by water or other liquid in pipes; setting in water. ◆ vt (**hydraul'icking**; **hydraul'icked**) (*mining*) to excavate and wash out by powerful jets of water. [Gr *hydōr* water, and *aulos* a pipe]
■ **hydraul'ically** adv. **hydraul'ics** n *sing* the science of hydrodynamics in general, or its practical application to water pipes, etc.

❏ **hydraulic belt** *n* an endless belt of absorbent material for raising water. **hydraulic brake** *n* a brake in which the force is transmitted by means of a compressed fluid. **hydraulic cement** *n* a cement that will harden under water. **hydraulic jack** *n* a lifting apparatus in which oil, etc, is pumped against a piston. **hydraulic mining** *n* hydraulicking. **hydraulic press** *n* a press operated by forcing water into a cylinder in which a ram or plunger works. **hydraulic ram** *n* a device whereby the pressure head produced when a moving column of water is brought to rest is caused to deliver some of the water under pressure. **hydraulic seeding** *n* sowing seed by spraying it, mixed with nutrients, etc, on the ground. **hydraulic suspension** *n* a system of car suspension using hydraulic units.

hydrazine /hī′drə-zēn/ *n* a fuming corrosive liquid, $H_2N.NH_2$, a powerful reducing agent, used as a rocket fuel; any of a class of organic bases derived from it. [From **hydr-** and **azo-**]

■ **hy′drazides** *n pl* a class of chemical compounds derived from hydrazine.

❏ **hydrazoic** /-zō′ik/ **acid** *n* HN_3, a colourless, foul-smelling liquid that combines with lead and other heavy metals to produce explosive salts (azides).

hydria /hī′dri-ə or hid′ri-ə/ *n* a large ancient Greek water-vase. [Gr *hydriā*]

hydro /hī′drō/ *n* (pl **hy′dros**) short form of **hydroelectricity** or **hydropathic** (see under **hydro-**[1]).

hydro-[1], also **hydr-** /hī-dr(ō)-, hī-dr(ə)- or hī-dr(o)-/ *combining form* denoting of, like or by means of water. [Gr *hydōr* water]

■ **hydraemia** or (*esp N Am*) **hydremia** /hī-drē′mi-ə/ *n* (Gr *haima* blood) wateriness of the blood. **hydragogue** /hī′drə-gog, -gōg/ *adj* (Gr *agōgos* bringing; *med*) removing water or serum. ◆ *n* a drug with that effect. **hydrangea** /hī-drān′jə or hī-drān′jyə/ *n* (Gr *angeion* vessel) a plant of the *Hydrangea* genus of shrubby plants of the family **Hydrangeā′ceae**, with large globular clusters of showy flowers, natives of China and Japan. **hydrant** /hī′drənt/ *n* a connection for attaching a hose to a water main or a fireplug. **hydranth** /hī′dranth/ *n* (Gr *anthos* flower) a nutritive polyp in a hydroid colony. **hydrarthrō′sis** *n* (*med*) swelling of a joint caused by the accumulation in it of watery fluid. **hy′drate** *n* a chemical combination of a substance and water which can be expelled without affecting the composition of the substance; an old word for a **hydroxide** (see under **hydro-**[2]). ◆ *vt* to combine with water; to cause to absorb water (**hydrated electron** a very reactive free electron released in aqueous solutions by the action of ionizing radiations; **hydrated ion** an ion surrounded by molecules of water which it holds in a degree of orientation). **hydrā′tion** *n*. **hydrē′mia** *n* mainly N American form of **hydraemia**. **hy′dric** *adj* relating to an abundance of moisture; see also under **hydrogen**. **hy′drically** *adv*. **hydride** *n* see under **hydrogen**. **hydro-ae′roplane** (*N Am* **hydro-air′plane**) *n* a seaplane. **hydrobiolog′ical** *adj*. **hydrobiol′ogist** *n*. **hydrobiol′ogy** *n* the biology of aquatic animals and plants. **hy′drocele** /-sēl/ *n* (Gr *kēlē* a swelling; *med*) a swelling containing serous fluid, *esp* in the scrotum. **hydrocell′ūlose** *n* a gelatinous material obtained by hydration of cellulose, used in paper-making, etc. **hydrocephal′ic** or **hydroceph′alous** *adj*. **hydrocephalus** /-sef′ə-ləs or -kef′/ *n* (Gr *kephalē* head) an accumulation of serous fluid within the cranial cavity, either in the subdural space or the ventricles; water in the head; dropsy of the brain. **Hydrocharis** /hī-drok′ə-ris/ *n* (Gr *charis*, *-itos* grace) the frogbit genus, giving name to the **Hydrocharitā′ceae**, a family of water plants related to the pondweeds. **hy′drochore** /-kōr/ *n* (Gr *chōreein* to make room, spread about) a plant disseminated by water. **hydrochoric** /-kor′ik/ *adj*. **hydrocoll′oid** *n* a substance that forms a gel when mixed with water. **Hydrocoralli′nae** *n pl* an order of Hydrozoa, massive reef-builders, the millepores, etc. **hydrocor′alline** *n* and *adj*. **hydrodynamic** /-dīn-am′ik/ or **hydrodynam′ical** *adj* (Gr *dynamis* power). **hydrodynam′icist** *n*. **hydrodynam′ics** *n sing* the science of the motions and equilibrium of a material system partly or wholly fluid (called **hydrostatics** when the system is in equilibrium, **hydrokinetics** when it is not). **hydroelast′ic** *adj* (**hydroelastic suspension** a system of car suspension in which a fluid provides interconnection between the front and rear suspension units). **hydroelec′tric** *adj*. **hydroelectric′ity** *n* electricity produced by means of water, *esp* by water power. **hydroextract′or** *n* a drying machine that works centrifugally. **hy′drofoil** *n* a device on a boat for raising it from the water as its speed increases; a boat fitted with this device; a corresponding device on a seaplane to aid its take-off (also **hy′drovane**); a seaplane with hydrofoils. **hy′drogel** *n* a gel formed with water. **hydrogeol′ogist** *n*. **hydrogeol′ogy** *n* the branch of geology dealing with ground water. **hy′drograph** *n* a graph showing seasonal variations in level, force, etc of a body of water. **hydrog′rapher** *n* (Gr *graphein* to write). **hydrographic** /-graf′ik/ or **hydrograph′ical** *adj*. **hydrograph′ically** *adv*. **hydrog′raphy** *n* the investigation of seas and other bodies of water, including charting, sounding, study of tides, currents, etc. **hy′droid** *adj* like a Hydra; polypoid. ◆ *n* a hydrozoan; a hydrozoan in its asexual generation.

hydrokinet′ic *adj* relating to hydrokinetics; relating to the motion of fluids; relating to fluids in motion; operated or operating by the movement of fluids. **hydrokinet′ics** *n sing* see **hydrodynamics** above. **hy′drolase** *n* an enzyme that catalyses hydrolysis. **hydrolog′ic** or **hydrolog′ical** *adj*. **hydrolog′ically** *adv*. **hydrol′ogist** *n*. **hydrol′ogy** *n* the study of water resources in land areas of the world; the study of underground water resources (*US*). **hydrol′ysate** /-i-sāt/ *n* a substance produced by hydrolysis. **hydrolyse** or (*N Am*) **-yze** /hī′drō-līz/ *vt* to subject to hydrolysis (also *vi*). **hydrolysis** /hī-drol′i-sis/ *n* (Gr *lysis* loosing) chemical decomposition or ionic dissociation caused by water. **hy′drolyte** /-līt/ *n* a body subjected to hydrolysis. **hydrolytic** /-lit′ik/ *adj*. **hydromagnet′ic** *adj*. **hydromagnet′ics** *n sing* magnetohydrodynamics. **hy′dromancy** /-*n* (Gr *manteiā* divination) divination by water. **hydromā′nia** *n* a craving for water. **hydromant′ic** *adj*. **hydromechan′ics** *n sing* hydrodynamics. **hydromedū′sa** *n* a hydrozoan in its sexual generation. **Hydromedū′sae** *n pl* the class Hydrozoa. **hydromedū′san** or **hydromedū′soid** *adj* (also *n*). **hy′dromel** (Gr *hydromeli*, from *meli* honey) a beverage made of honey and water; mead. **hydromet′allurgy** (or /-met-al′ər-ji/) *n* the extraction of metal from ore by treatment with water or other fluids. **hydromē′teor** *n* (Gr *meteōron* a meteor) any weather phenomenon depending on the moisture content of the atmosphere. **hydrometeorol′ogy** *n*. **hydrom′eter** *n* (Gr *metron* a measure) an instrument for measuring specific gravity. **hydrometric** /-met′/ or **hydromet′rical** *adj*. **hydrom′etry** *n* the science of the measurement and analysis of water, including the methods, techniques and instrumentation used in hydrology. **Hydromys** /hī′drō-mis/ *n* (Gr *mȳs* mouse) an Australasian genus of aquatic rodents. **hy′dronaut** *n* a person trained to work in an underwater vessel, eg a submarine. **hydronephrō′sis** *n* distension of the kidney with urine held up as a result of obstruction in the urinary tract. **hydronephro′tic** *adj*. **hydropathic** /hī-drō-path′ik or hī-drə-/ *adj* of, for, relating to or practising hydropathy. ◆ *n* (in full **hydropathic establishment**; *inf* **hy′dro** (pl **hy′dros**)) a hotel (with special baths, etc, and often situated near a spa) where guests can have hydropathic treatment. **hydropath′ical** *adj*. **hydropath′ically** *adv*. **hydrop′athist** *n* a person who practises hydropathy. **hydrop′athy** *n* (Gr *pathos* suffering) the treatment of disease by water, externally and internally. **hydrophane** /hī′drō-fān/ *n* (Gr *phanos* bright) a translucent opal transparent in water. **hydrophanous** /-drof′ən-əs/ *adj* transparent on immersion. **Hydrophidae** /hī-drof′i-dē/ *n pl* (Gr *ophis* snake) a family of venomous sea snakes. **hydrophil′ic** *adj* (*chem*) attracting water. **hydroph′ilite** *n* native calcium chloride (a very hygroscopic mineral). **hydroph′ilous** *adj* water-loving; pollinated by agency of water (*bot*). **hydroph′ily** *n* (Gr *phileein* to love) water-pollination. **hydrophō′bia** *n* (Gr *phobos* fear) horror of water; inability to swallow water owing to a contraction in the throat, a symptom of rabies; rabies itself. **hydrophō′bic** (or /-fob′/) *adj* relating to hydrophobia; repelling water (*chem*). **hydrophobic′ity** *n*. **hydrophobous** /-drof′ə-bəs/ *adj* (*obs*). **hy′drophone** /-fōn/ *n* (Gr *phōnē* voice) an apparatus for listening to sounds conveyed by water. **hy′drophyte** /-fīt/ *n* (Gr *phyton* plant) a plant growing in water or in very moist conditions. **hydrophytic** /-fīt′ik/ *adj*. **hydrophyton** /hī-drof′i-ton/ *n* the coenosarc of a hydroid colony. **hydroph′ytous** *adj*. **hydrop′ic** *adj* (*non-standard* **hydrop′tic**; see **hydropsy** below) dropsical; thirsty; charged or swollen with water. **hy′droplane** *n* a light, flat-bottomed motorboat which, at high speed, skims along the surface of the water; a hydro-aeroplane or seaplane (*non-standard*). ◆ *vi* (of a boat) to skim like a hydroplane; (of a vehicle) to skid on a wet road. **hydropneumat′ic** *adj* utilizing water and air acting together. **hydropol′yp** *n* a hydrozoan polyp. **hydropon′ic** *adj*. **hydropon′ically** *adv*. **hydroponics** /hī-drō-pon′iks/ *n sing* (Gr *ponos* toil) the art or practice of growing plants in (sand or gravel containing) a chemical solution without soil. **hy′dropower** *n* hydroelectric power. **hy′dropsy** *n* (Gr *hydrōps* dropsy; *archaic*) dropsy. **Hydropterid′eae** /-i-ē/ *n pl* (Gr *pteris*, *-idos* male-fern) the water ferns or heterosporous ferns. **hydroptic** *adj* see **hydropic** above. **hy′dropult** *n* (modelled on **catapult**) a hand force pump. **hydroquinone** /-kwin-ōn′, or *kwin′* or *-kwīn′*/ *n* quinol. **hy′droscope** *n* (Gr *skopeein* to view) a kind of water clock, a graduated tube, from which the water escaped (*hist*); an instrument for viewing under water. **hy′droski** /-skē/ *n* a kind of hydrofoil used on seaplanes as a source of hydrodynamic lift, and on aeroplanes to make them amphibious. **hydrosō′ma** or **hy′drosome** /-sōm/ *n* (pl **hydrosō′mata** or **hy′drosomes**) (Gr *sōma* body) a hydroid colony. **hydrosō′mal** or **hydrosō′matous** *adj*. **hy′drospace** or **hydrosphere** /hī′drō-sfēr/ *n* (Gr *sphaira* sphere) the water on the surface of the earth, the seas and oceans. **hy′drostat** *n* (Gr *-statēs* causing to stand) a contrivance for indicating the presence of water. **hydrostat′ic** or **hydrostat′ical** *adj* (**hydrostatic balance** a balance for weighing bodies in water to determine their specific gravity; **hydrostatic drive** or **transmission** (in a vehicle) a drive consisting of a system transmitting power through oil, under pressure; **hydrostatic extrusion** (*metallurgy*) a form of extrusion in which the metal to be shaped is preshaped to fit a die forming the lower end of a high-pressure container that is filled with a pressure-transmitting liquid, the pressure being built up in the liquid by a plunger until the metal is forced through the die; **hydrostatic paradox** the principle that any quantity of fluid, however small, may balance any weight, however great; **hydrostatic press** a hydraulic press). **hydrostat'ics** *n sing* see **hydrodynamics** above. **hydrostat'ically** *adv.* **hydrotac'tic** *adj.* **hydrotax'is** *n* (Gr *taxis* arrangement) response of an organism to the stimulus of water. **hydrothē'ca** *n* (Gr *thēkē* case) the horny cup of a hydranth. **hydrotherapeu'tic** *adj.* **hydrotherapeu'tics** or **hydrother'apy** *n* treatment of disease by the external use of water, eg treatment of disability by developing movement in water. **hydrother'mal** *adj* relating to or produced by the action of heated or superheated water, *esp* in dissolving, transporting and redepositing mineral matter. **hydrothorax** /-thö'/ *n* (Gr *thōrax* chest) oedema in the chest. **hydrotrop'ic** *adj.* **hydrot'ropism** *n* (Gr *tropos* a turn) the turning of a plant root towards (*positive*) or away from (*negative*) moisture. **hydrous** /-hī'dras/ *adj* (*chem* and *mineralogy*) containing water. **hydrovane** *n* see **hydrofoil** above. **hydrozincite** /-zingk'īt/ *n* basic zinc carbonate. **Hydrozō'a** *n pl* (Gr *zōion* an animal) a class of Coelenterata, chiefly marine organisms such as the zoophytes, millepores, etc, in which alternation of generations typically occurs, the hydroid phase colonial giving rise to the medusoid phase by budding; sometimes extended to include the true jellyfishes; (without *cap*) hydrozoans. **hydrozō'an** *n* and *adj.* **hydrozō'on** *n* (*pl* **hydrozō'a**) a coelenterate of the Hydrozoa.

hydro-², also **hydr-** /hī-dr(ō)-, hī-dr(a)- or hī-dr(o)-/ *combining form* denoting: a chemical compound containing hydrogen; a chemical process using hydrogen. [Contraction of **hydrogen**]
■ **hydriodic** /hī-dri-od'ik/ *adj* of an acid composed of hydrogen and iodine, hydrogen iodide. **hydrobrō'mic** *adj* applied to an acid composed of hydrogen and bromine, hydrogen bromide. **hydrocar'bon** *n* a compound of hydrogen and carbon with nothing else, occurring notably in oil, natural gas and coal. **hydrochloric** /-klor'ik or -klör'/ *adj* applied to an acid composed of hydrogen and chlorine, hydrogen chloride, still sometimes called *muriatic acid*. **hydrochlor'ide** *n* a compound of hydrochloric acid with an organic base. **hydrochlorofluorocar'bon** *n* a chlorofluorocarbon that contains hydrogen and is therefore more easily broken down. **hydrocor'tisone** *n* one of the corticosteroids, 17-hydroxy-corticosterone, a synthesized form of which is used to treat rheumatoid arthritis, etc. **hy'drocracking** *n* cracking of petroleum, etc in the presence of hydrogen. **hydrocyanic** /-sī-an'ik/ *adj* denoting an acid (*prussic acid*) composed of hydrogen and cyanogen. **hydroferricyanic** /-fer-i-sī-an'ik/ and **hydroferrōcyan'ic** *adj* applied to two acids composed of hydrogen, iron and cyanogen, hydroferricyanic acid, $H_3Fe(CN)_6$, having an atom of hydrogen less than hydroferrocyanic, $H_4Fe(CN)_6$. **hydrofluor'ic** *adj* applied to an acid composed of fluorine and hydrogen, hydrogen fluoride. **hydrofluorocar'bon** *n* an alkane in which some of the hydrogen atoms are substituted by fluorine atoms (cf **fluorocarbon**; *abbrev* HFC). **hydrogasificā'tion** *n* production of methane from coal by treatment with hydrogen at high temperature and pressure. **hydrosul'phide** *n* a compound formed by action of hydrogen sulphide on a hydroxide. **hydrosul'phite** *n* a hyposulphite (*esp* sodium hyposulphite). **hydrosulphū'ric** *adj* formed by a combination of hydrogen and sulphur. **hydrox'ide** *n* a chemical compound that contains one or more hydroxyl groups. **hydrox'y** *adj* (of a compound) containing one or more hydroxyl groups (often as *combining form*). **hydroxyap'atite** *n* a mineral that is a major constituent of bone and tooth enamel. **hydrox'yl** *n* (Gr *hýlē* matter) a compound radical consisting of one atom of oxygen and one of hydrogen; sometimes loosely applied to hydrogen peroxide. **hydroxyl'amine** *n* a basic substance composed of a hydroxyl group and an amino group (NH_2OH). **hydrox'ylate** *vt* to introduce hydroxyl into. **hydroxyurē'a** *n* a compound derived from urea used as an antimetabolite in treating cancer.

hydrogen /hī'dra-jan/ *n* a gaseous element (symbol **H**; atomic no 1) which in combination with oxygen produces water, is the lightest of all known substances, and very inflammable, and (in water or heavy water) is of great importance in the moderation (slowing down) of neutrons. [Coined by English chemist Henry Cavendish (1731–1810) from Gr *hydōr* water, and *gennaein* to produce]
■ **hy'dric** *adj* of or containing hydrogen. **hy'dride** *n* a compound of hydrogen with an element or radical. **hy'drogenase** *n* an enzyme that catalyses reduction by hydrogen. **hydrogenate** /hī'drō-jan-āt or hī-droj'an-āt/ *vt* to (cause to) combine with hydrogen, as in the hardening of oils by converting an olein into a stearin by addition of hydrogen in the presence of a catalyst such as nickel or palladium. **hydrog'enated** *adj.* **hydrogenā'tion** *n.* **hydrog'enize** or **-ise** *vt* to hydrogenate. **hydrog'enous** *adj.*
❑ **hydrogen bomb** or **H'-bomb** *n* a bomb in which an enormous release of energy is achieved by converting hydrogen nuclei into helium nuclei in a fusion, not fission, process started by great heat (the

first H-bomb was exploded by the USA in November 1952). **hydrogen bond** *n* a strong inter- or intra-molecular force, important in water molecule self-association and in polypeptide chain arrangement in proteins, resulting from the interaction of a hydrogen atom bonded to an electronegative atom with a lone pair of electrons on another electronegative atom and similarly in the bonding of the base pairs in the two strands of DNA. **hydrogen cyanide** *n* a toxic gas, HCN, which when dissolved in water forms hydrocyanic acid. **hydrogen ion** *n* an atom of hydrogen carrying a positive charge, a proton, *esp* an ion formed in a solution of acid in water. **hydrogen peroxide** see under **peroxide**. **hydrogen sulphide** *n* a compound of hydrogen and sulphur, H_2S. **hydronium ion** *n* a hydrated hydrogen ion, such as H_3O^+.
■ **heavy hydrogen** see under **heavy**. **hydrogenation of coal** conversion of coal to liquid fuels by hydrogenation.

hydyne /hī'dīn/ *n* an American rocket-launching fuel.

hye an obsolete form of **hie¹** and **high**.

hyena or **hyaena** /hī-ē'na/, also (*Shakesp*) **hyen** /hī'en/ *n* a carrion-feeding carnivore (genus *Hyaena*, part of the family **Hyaenidae**) with a long thick neck, coarse mane and sloping body. [L *hyaena*, from Gr *hyaina*, from *hŷs* a pig]
❑ **hyena dog** *n* an African wild dog (*Lycaon pictus*), with blotched markings like that of a hyena.
■ **spotted hyena** an animal (genus *Crocuta*) resembling a hyena, that produces a sound like a hysterical laugh.

hyetal /hī'i-tl/ *adj* rainy; relating to rain or rainfall. [Gr *hyetos* rain]
■ **hy'etograph** *n* a rain chart; a self-registering rain gauge. **hyetograph'ic** or **hyetograph'ical** *adj.* **hyetograph'ically** *adv.* **hyetog'raphy** *n.* **hyetol'ogy** *n* a branch of meteorology dealing with rainfall. **hyetom'eter** *n* a rain gauge. **hyetomet'rograph** *n* a self-registering rain gauge, hyetograph.

Hygeian /hī-jē'an/ *adj* relating to Hygieia or to health and its preservation. [Gr *Hygieia*, later *Hygeia* goddess of health, daughter of Asklēpios (Aesculapius)]

hygiene /hī'jēn/ *n* the science or art of preserving health, *esp* through cleanliness; sanitary principles and practices. [Fr *hygiène*, from Gr *hygieinē* (*technē*) hygienic (art), from *hygieia* health, *hygiēs* healthy]
■ **hygienic** /hī-jēn'ik/ *adj.* **hygien'ically** *adv.* **hygien'ics** *n sing* principles of hygiene. **hygien'ist** /hī'jēn-ist/ *n* a person skilled in hygiene; a dental hygienist.

hygristor /hī-gris'tar/ *n* an electronic component whose resistance varies with humidity. [**hygro-** and res*istor*]

hygro- /hī-grō-, hī-gra- or hī-gro-/ *combining form* signifying wet, moist. [Gr *hygros* wet]
■ **hygrochas'tic** *adj.* **hygrochasy** /hī-grok'a-si/ *n* (Gr *chasis* a gape) dehiscence on moistening. **hy'grodeik** /-dīk/ *n* (Gr *deiknynai* to show) a psychrometer with an index and scale. **hy'grograph** *n* an instrument, a development of a hygroscope, for recording the humidity of the air. **hygrograph'ic** or **hygrograph'ical** *adj.* **hygrol'ogy** *n* the study of the humidity of the air or other gases. **hygrom'eter** *n* an instrument for measuring the humidity of the air or of other gases. **hygrometric** /-met'rik/ or **hygromet'rical** *adj* of or belonging to hygrometry; hygroscopic. **hygrom'etry** *n* measurement of the humidity of the air or of other gases. **hy'grophil** or **hygrophilous** /-grof'/ *adj* (Gr *phileein* to love) moisture-loving; living where there is much moisture. **hy'grophobe** *adj* (Gr *phobeein* to fear) growing best where moisture is scanty. **hy'grophyte** /-fīt/ *n* (Gr *phyton* plant) a plant adapted to plentiful water supply. **hygrophytic** /-fīt'ik/ *adj.* **hy'groscope** *n* an instrument that shows, without measuring, changes in the humidity of the air. **hygroscopic** /-skop'ik/ or **hygroscop'ical** *adj* relating to the hygroscope; readily absorbing moisture from the air; (of eg some movements of plants) indicating or caused by absorption or loss of moisture (**hygroscopic salt** a salt, *esp* calcium chloride, that absorbs moisture from other substances). **hygroscopicity** /-skop-is'i-ti/ *n.* **hy'grostat** *n* an apparatus that produces constant humidity.

hying /hī'ing/ *prp* of **hie¹'²**.

hyke /hīk/ *n* see **haik¹**.

Hyksos /hik'sos or -sös/ *n* a foreign line of kings (the 15th and 16th dynasties, called the shepherd kings) who ruled Egypt c.1674–c.1550BC. [Gr *Hyksōs*, from Egyp *Hiku-khasut* princes of the desert, appar misunderstood as shepherd princes]

hyla /hī'la/ *n* a common tree frog of the Hylidae. [**hyle**]

hylding (*Spenser*) same as **hilding**.

hyle /hī'lē/ *n* wood, matter. [Gr *hýlē* wood, matter]
■ **hy'lic** *adj* material; corporeal. **hy'licism** or **hy'lism** *n* materialism. **hy'licist** or **hy'list** (also wrongly **hy'loist**) *n.* **hy'lobate** *n* a gibbon (genus **Hylob'atēs**; from the root of Gr *bainein* to go). **hylogen'esis** *n* the origin of matter. **hylomor'phic** *adj.* **hylomor'phism** *n* (*philos*) the

doctrine that matter is the first cause of the universe. **hylop'athism** *n* (Gr *pathos* feeling) the doctrine that matter is sentient. **hylop'athist** *n*. **hyloph'agous** *adj* (Gr *phagein* to eat) wood-eating. **hy'lophyte** *n* (Gr *phyton* plant) a woodland plant. **hy'lotheism** *n* (Gr *theos* god) the doctrine that there is no God but matter and the universe. **hy'lotheist** *n*. **hylot'omous** *adj* (Gr *tomē* a cut) woodcutting. **hylozo'ical** or **hylozoist'ic** *adj*. **hylozō'ism** *n* (Gr *zōē* life) the doctrine that all matter is endowed with life. **hylozō'ist** *n*.

Hymen /hī'men/ or -mən/ *n* the god of marriage (*myth*); marriage (*archaic*). [Gr wedding-cry, perh also a god]
■ **hymenē'al** or **hymenē'an** *adj* (also **hymenae'al** or **hymenae'an**). **hymenē'al** *n* wedding hymn; (in *pl*) nuptials (*archaic*).

hymen /hī'mən/ *n* a membrane; a thin membrane partially closing the vagina of a virgin. [Gr *hymēn* membrane]
■ **hy'menal** *adj* relating to the hymen. **hymē'nial** *adj* relating to the hymenium. **hymē'nium** *n* (*pl* **hymē'nia**) the spore-bearing surface in fungi. **Hymenomycetes** /hī-mən-ō-mī-sē'tēz/ *n pl* an order of fungi with exposed hymenium from an early stage eg toadstools, etc. **Hymenophyllā'ceae** or the filmy ferns. **hymenophyllā'ceous** *adj*. **hy'menoplasty** *n* plastic surgery to reconstruct a ruptured hymen. **Hymenop'tera** *n pl* an order of insects with four transparent wings eg ants, bees, wasps, etc. **hymenop'teran** *n* and *adj*. **hymenop'terous** *adj*.

hymn /him/ *n* a song of praise, *esp* to God, but also to a nation, etc. ◆ *vt* (**hymning** /him'ing/ or him'ning/; **hymned** /himd/ or him'nid/) to celebrate in song; to worship by hymns. ◆ *vi* to sing in adoration. [Gr *hymnos*]
■ **hym'nal** or **hym'nary** *n* a hymn-book (also *adj*). **hym'nic** *adj*. **hym'nist** or **hym'nodist** *n* a person who composes hymns. **hym'nody** *n* hymns collectively; hymn-singing; hymnology. **hymnog'rapher** *n*. **hymnog'raphy** *n* the art of writing hymns; the study of hymns. **hymnol'ogist** *n*. **hymnol'ogy** *n* the study or composition of hymns.
❑ **hymn'-book** *n* a book of hymns.

hynde a Spenserian spelling of **hind²**.

hyoid /hī'oid/ *adj* having the form of the Greek letter upsilon (υ), applied to a bone at the base of the tongue. [Gr *hȳoeidēs*, from *hȳ* the letter upsilon, and *eidos* form]

hyoplastron /hī-ō-plas'tron/ *n* (*pl* **hyoplas'tra**) in a turtle's plastron, a plate between the hypoplastron and the entoplastron. [Gr *hȳ* the letter upsilon]
■ **hyoplas'tral** *adj*.

Hyoscyamus /hī-ō-sī'ə-məs/ *n* the henbane genus. [Gr *hyoskyamos*]
■ **hy'oscine** /-sēn/ or -sən/ (also called **scopolamine**; used as a truth drug, for travel sickness, etc) and **hyoscy'amine** *n* two poisonous alkaloids similar to atropine, obtained from henbane.

hyp see **hip⁵**.

hyp. *abbrev* : hypotenuse; hypothesis; hypothetical.

hypabyssal /hip-ə-bis'l/ (*petrology*) *adj* moderately deep-seated, not quite abyssal, intermediate between plutonic and eruptive. [Gr *hypo* beneath]

hypaesthesia or (*US*) **hypesthesia** /hip-es-thē'zi-ə or hip-ēs- or hīp-/ *n* a diminished susceptibility to physical stimuli. [Gr *hypo* under, and **aesthesia**]
■ **hypaesthēs'ic** or **hypesthēs'ic** *adj*.

hypaethral /hi-pē'thrəl or (*esp N Am*) hī-/ *adj* roofless, open to the sky. [Gr *hypo* beneath, and *aithēr* upper air, sky]
■ **hypae'thron** *n* an open court.

hypalgesia /hīp-al-jē'si-ə, -zi-ə or hīp'/ *n* diminished susceptibility to pain (also **hypal'gia**). [Gr *hypo* under, and *algēsis, algos* pain]
■ **hypalgē'sic** *adj*.

hypallage /hi-pal'ə-je or hī-/ (*rhetoric*) *n* a figure of speech in which the relations of words are mutually interchanged, as in *pouring wind and gusting rain*. [Gr *hypo* under, and *allassein* to exchange]
■ **hypallact'ic** *adj*.

hypanthium /hi- or hī-pan'thi-əm/ *n* the flat or concave receptacle of a perigynous flower. [Gr *hypo* under, and *anthos* flower]

hypate /hip'ə-tē/ (*Gr music*) *n* the lowest string of the lyre, or its tone. [Gr *hypatē* highest (fem), prob as having the longest string]

hype¹ /hīp/ (*inf*) *n* intensive or artificially induced excitement about or enthusiasm for something or someone; a sales gimmick, etc; a publicity stunt; the person or thing promoted by such a stunt; a deception. ◆ *vt* (often with *up*) to promote or to advertise extravagantly. [Origin uncertain]
■ **hyp'er** *n* someone who or something that hypes.
❑ **hyped-up'** *adj* excessively promoted; artificial, fake.

hype² /hīp/ (*sl*) *n* a hypodermic needle; a drug addict; something that stimulates artificially, *esp* a drug. ◆ *vi* (*esp* with *up*) to inject oneself

with a drug. ◆ *vt* (often with *up*) to stimulate artificially. [Short form of **hypodermic**]
■ **hyp'er** *adj* over-excited; over-stimulated.
■ **hyped up** artificially stimulated; highly excited.

hyper- /hī-pər- or hī-pûr-/ *combining form* signifying: over; excessive; more than normal. [Gr *hyper* over]
■ **hyperaccūm'ūlator** *n* a plant that absorbs large amounts of heavy metals from the soil. **hyperacid'ity** *n* excessive acidity, *esp* in the stomach. **hyperact'ive** *adj* (*med*) abnormally or pathologically active. **hyperactiv'ity** *n*. **hyperacusis** /-ə-kū'sis/ *n* (Gr *akousis* hearing) abnormally increased power of hearing. **hyperacute'** *adj*. **hyperacute'ness** *n*. **hyperadrē'nalism** *n* excessive activity of the adrenal gland. **hyperaemia** or (*N Am*) **hyperemia** /-ē'mi-ə/ *n* (Gr *haima* blood) congestion or excess of blood in any part. **hyperae'mic** or (*N Am*) **hypere'mic** *adj*. **hyperaesthesia** /-ēs-thē'zi-ə/ or (*N Am*) **hyperesthesia** /-is-thē'/ *n* (Gr *aisthēsis* perception) excessive sensitivity to stimuli; an abnormal extension of the bodily senses assumed to explain telepathy and clairvoyance; exaggerated aestheticism. **hyperaesthē'sic, hyperaesthetic** or (*N Am*) **hyperesthetic** /-thet'ik/ *adj* overaesthetic; abnormally or morbidly sensitive. **hyperalgē'sia** /-si-ə or -zi-ə/ *n* (Gr *algēsis* pain) heightened sensitivity to pain. **hyperalgē'sic** *adj*. **hyperbar'ic** *adj* having specific gravity greater than that of cerebrospinal fluid (*spinal anaesthesia*); relating to conditions of high atmospheric pressure with a greater concentration of oxygen than normal, as in a **hyperbaric chamber** a chamber containing oxygen at high pressure. **hyperbat'ic** *adj*. **hyperbat'ically** *adv*. **hyper'baton** *n* (Gr, from the root of *bainein* to go; *rhetoric*) a figure of speech in which the customary order of words is reversed. **hyper'bola** *n* (*pl* usually **hyper'bolas**) (Gr *hyperbolē* overshooting, from *ballein* to throw; *geom*) one of the conic sections, the intersection of a plane with a cone when the plane cuts both branches of the cone. **hyperbole** /hī-pûr'bə-lē/ *n* a rhetorical figure which produces a vivid impression by extravagant and obvious exaggeration. **hyperbol'ic** or **hyperbol'ical** *adj* of a hyperbola or hyperbole (**hyperbolic functions** (*maths*) a set of six functions (sinh, cosh, tanh, etc) analogous to the trigonometrical functions; **hyperbolic geometry** that involving the axiom that through any point in a given plane there can be drawn more than one line that does not intersect a given line; **hyperbolic logarithms** natural logarithms; **hyperbolic paraboloid** a saddle-shaped surface represented by the equation $x^2/a - y^2/b = z$; **hyperbolic spiral** a spiral of polar equation $p\theta = k^2$). **hyperbol'ically** *adv*. **hyper'bolism** *n*. **hyper'bolize** or **-ise** *vt* to represent hyperbolically. ◆ *vi* to speak hyperbolically or with exaggeration. **hyper'boloid** *n* a solid figure in which some of the plane sections are hyperbolas. **hyperborean** /-bö'/ *adj* (Gr *Hyperboreoi* a people supposed to live in sunshine beyond the north wind, from *Boreas* the north wind) belonging to the extreme north. ◆ *n* an inhabitant of the extreme north. **hypercalcae'mia** or **hypercalce'mia** *n* an abnormally high concentration of calcium in the blood. **hypercatalect'ic** *adj* (*prosody*) having an additional syllable or half-foot after the last complete dipody. **hypercatalex'is** *n*. **hy'percharge** *n* the strangeness of a particle plus its baryon number. ◆ *vt* /-chärj'/ to charge excessively; to overload. **hypercholesterolae'mia** *n* a condition characterized by an abnormally high level of blood cholesterol. **hy'percolour** *n* a dye that causes a fabric to change colour with a change of temperature. **hypercon'scious** *adj* more than normally aware (of). **hypercorrect'** *adj* over-correct; very critical; due to or showing hypercorrection. **hypercorrec'tion** *n* a correction made in the mistaken belief that nonstandard linguistic usage is being thus avoided, eg the erroneous use of *I* in the place of *me* in phrases such as *between you and I*. **hypercorrect'ness** *n*. **hypercrit'ic** *n* someone who is over-critical; a carper. **hypercrit'ic** or **hypercrit'ical** *adj* over-critical, *esp* of very small faults. **hypercrit'ically** *adv*. **hypercrit'icism** *n*. **hypercrit'icize** or **-ise** /-sīz/ *vt*. **hy'percube** *n* (*maths*) a theoretical solid in four or more dimensions, all sides being equal and all angles right angles. **hyperdac'tyl** *adj* (Gr *daktylos* finger, toe). **hyperdac'tyly** *n* possession of more than five fingers or toes. **hyperdorian** /-dö'/ *adj* (Gr *hyperdōrios*; *music*) above the Dorian mode; applied in ancient Greek music to a mode having as its lower tetrachord the upper tetrachord of the Dorian (as: *b c d e ; e f g a ; b*). **hy'perdrive** *n* (in science fiction) an engine or power source that enables matter to be transported through hyperspace. **hyperdulia** /-doo-li'ə/ *n* see under **dulia**. **hyperem'esis** *n* (Gr *emesis* vomiting) excessive vomiting. **hyperemet'ic** *adj*. **hyperemia, hyperesthesia** *n* see **hyperaemia, hyperaesthesia** above. **hypereutec'tic** *adj* (of a compound) containing more of the minor component than an eutectic compound. **hyperextend'** *vt* to extend (a limb) beyond its normal range, causing injury. **hyperexten'sion** *n*. **hyperfine'** *adj* (**hyperfine structure** (*phys*) the splitting of spectrum lines into two or more very closely spaced components). **hyperfocal distance** /-fō'kəl/ *n* (*photog*) the distance in front of a lens focused at infinity beyond which all objects are acceptably in focus. **hyper'gamous** *adj* relating to hypergamy.

hypergamy /hī-pûr'gə-mi/ n (Gr gamos marriage) a custom that allows a man but forbids a woman to marry a person of lower social standing; now sometimes more generally marriage of one person with another of higher social rank. **hyperglycaemia** or (US) **hyperglycemia** /-glī-sē'mi-ə/ n an abnormally high concentration of sugar in the blood. **hypergolic** /-gol'ik/ adj (of two or more liquids) spontaneously explosive on mixing. **hyperhidrō'sis**, **hyperhydrō'sis** or **hyperidrō'sis** n excessive sweating. **hyperinflā'tion** n (econ) rapid inflation uncontrollable by normal means. **hyperinō'sis** n (Gr īs, īnos strength, fibre) excess of fibrin in the blood. **hyperinot'ic** adj. **hyperkalae'mia** n an abnormally high concentration of potassium in the blood. **hyperkeratō'sis** n the abnormal thickening of the outer layer of the skin. **hyperkinē'sia** or **hyperkinē'sis** n abnormal movement in muscle; hyperactivity. **hyperkinetic** /-net'ik/ adj. **hyperlink'** n a form of cross-reference in computer-readable text which allows instant access to related material. ◆ vt to link in this way. **hyperlipae'mia** or (US) **hyperlipe'mia** n an abnormally high level of fat in the blood (also **hyperlipidae'mia** or (US) **hyperlipidē'mia**). **hyperlydian** /-lid'i-ən/ adj (Gr hyperlydios) above the Lydian mode; applied in ancient Greek music to a mode having as its lower tetrachord the upper tetrachord of the Lydian (as: g a b c; c d e f; g). **hyperman'ia** n (psychiatry) an extreme form of mania. **hyperman'ic** adj. **hy'permarket** or **hy'permart** n a very large self-service store with a wide range of goods. **hypermē'dia** n (comput) a system linking information stored as text, graphics, audio and video. **hypermet'rical** adj (prosody) beyond or exceeding the ordinary metre of a line; having or being an additional syllable. **hypermetrō'pia** n (Gr metron measure, and ōps eye) long-sightedness (also **hyperō'pia**). **hypermetrop'ic** adj. **hypermnē'sia** n abnormal power of memory. **hypernatraemia** /-nə-trē'mi-ə/ n (natrium (see **natron**) and Gr haima blood) an abnormally high concentration of sodium chloride (salt) in the blood, esp in infants. **hypernō'va** n (pl **hypernō'vae** /-vē/ or **hypernō'vas**) (astron) a star that collapses to form a black hole, emitting very large quantities of light and gamma radiation. **hy'pernym** n (Gr onyma name) a superordinate word representing a class or family of which several other words can be members, as flower is a hypernym of rose and daisy. **hyper'nymy** n. **hy'peron** n any baryon that is not a neutron. **hyperopia** n see **hypermetropia** above. **hyperpar'asite** n a parasite living on another parasite. **hyperparathy'roidism** n an abnormally high level of parathyroid hormone in the blood. **hyperphagia** /-fā'ji-ə/ n bulimia. **hyperphrygian** /-frij'i-ən or -frij'ən/ adj (Gr hyperphrygios) above the Phrygian; applied to a mode of ancient Greek music having as its lower tetrachord the upper tetrachord of the Phrygian (as: a b c d; d e f g; a). **hyperphys'ical** adj beyond physical laws; supernatural. **hyperplasia** /-plā'zi-ə or -zhə/ n (Gr plasis a forming; pathol) overgrowth of a part due to excessive multiplication of its cells. **hyperplastic** /-plas'/ adj. **hyperpyretic** /-pir-et'ik/ adj (Gr pyretikos feverish). **hyperpyrex'ia** n abnormally high body temperature. **hypersarcō'ma** or **hypersarcō'sis** n (Gr hypersarkōma, hypersarkōsis, from sarx flesh; pathol) proud or fungous flesh. **hypersens'itive** adj excessively sensitive. **hypersens'itiveness** n. **hypersensitiv'ity** n. **hypersensitizā'tion** or **-s-** n. **hypersens'itize** or **-ise** vt to increase the sensitivity of. **hypersen'sual** adj beyond the scope of the senses. **hypersom'nia** n (L somnus sleep) a pathological tendency to sleep excessively. **hyperson'ic** adj (L sonus sound) (of speeds) greater than Mach 5; (of aircraft) able to fly at such speeds; (of sound waves) having a frequency greater than 1000 million Hz. **hyperson'ics** n pl. **hy'perspace** n space having more than three dimensions (maths); (in science fiction) a theoretical fourth dimension. **hypersthene** /hī'pər-sthēn/ n (Gr sthenos strength, because harder than hornblende) rock-forming orthorhombic pyroxene, anhydrous silicate of magnesium and iron, generally dark green, brown, or raven-black with a metallic lustre. **hypersthē'nia** n (pathol) a morbid condition marked by excessive excitement of all the vital phenomena. **hypersthenic** /-sthen'ik/ adj of hypersthene or of hypersthenia. **hypersthē'nite** n a rock consisting almost entirely of hypersthene; an aggregate of labradorite and hypersthene (obs). **hy'perstress** n excessive stress. **hyperten'sion** n blood pressure higher than normal; a state of great emotional tension. **hyperten'sive** adj suffering from hypertension. ◆ n a victim of hypertension. **hy'pertext** n (comput) a system that contains key words that act as links to other text, etc (also adj). **hypertherm'al** adj. **hypertherm'ia** n (dangerous) overheating of the body. **hyperthy'roid** adj. **hyperthyroidism** /-thī'roid-izm/ n overproduction of thyroid hormone by the thyroid gland, and the resulting condition. **hypertō'nia** n a hypertonic condition. **hyperton'ic** adj (of muscles) having excessive tone; tensed to an abnormally high degree; (of a solution) having a higher osmotic pressure than a specified solution. **hypertroph'ic**, **hypertroph'ical**, **hyper'trophied** or **hyper'trophous** adj (Gr trophē nourishment). **hyper'trophy** n overnourishment (of an organ, etc) causing abnormal enlargement. **hyperveloc'ity** n very great speed, as of nuclear particles. **hyperven'tilate** vi. **hyperventilā'tion** n abnormally

increased speed and depth of breathing. **hy'pervisor** n a device that enables two operating systems to run concurrently on a computer. **hypervitaminō'sis** n the condition resulting from too much of any vitamin (esp vitamin D).

Hypericum /hī-per'i-kəm/ n the St John's wort genus of plants, shrubs with yellow five-petalled flowers, giving name to the family **Hypericā'ceae**. [Gr hyperikon or hypereikos, from hypo under, and ereikē heath]
■ **hyper'icin** /-sin/ n a compound with antidepressant properties, found in St John's wort.

Hyperion /hī-pē'ri-on/ (Gr myth) n a Titan, son of Uranus and Ge, and father of Helios, Selene and Eos; Helios himself, the incarnation of light and beauty; a satellite of Saturn. [Gr Hyperiōn]

hypesthesia see **hypaesthesia**.

hypha /hī'fə/ (bot) n (pl **hy'phae** /-fē/) a thread of fungus mycelium. [Gr hyphē web]
■ **hy'phal** adj.

hyphen /hī'fən/ n a short stroke (-) joining two syllables or words. ◆ vt to hyphenate. [Gr hyphen, from hypo under, and hen one]
■ **hy'phenate** vt to join or separate by a hyphen. ◆ adj hyphened; hyphenated. ◆ n a hyphenated American. **hy'phenated** adj hyphened; of mixed nationality, expressed by a hyphened word, such as Irish-American (US); of divided or alien national sympathies. **hyphena'tion** n. **hy'phened** adj containing a hyphen. **hyphenic** /-fen'ik/ adj. **hy'phenism** n state of being a hyphenate. **hyphenizā'tion** or **-s-** n hyphenation. **hy'phenize** or **-ise** vt.

hypinosis /hip-i-nō'sis/ n a deficiency of fibrin in the blood, opp to hyperinosis. [Gr hypo under, and īs, īnos fibre]

hypnagogic see under **hypno-**.

hypno- or **hypn-** /hip-n(ō)-, hip-n(ə)- or hip-n(o)-/ combining form denoting: sleep; hypnosis. [Gr hypnos sleep]
■ **hypnagogic** /-goj'ik or -gog'ik/ adj (Gr agōgos bringing) sleep-bringing; ushering in sleep; relating to a state of drowsiness preceding sleep (**hypnagogic** (or **hypnogogic**) **image** hallucination experienced when falling asleep or fatigued). **hyp'nic** adj relating to or inducing sleep. ◆ n a soporific. **hypno-anaesthē'sia** n hypnotic sleep. **hypno-anal'ysis** n analysis of a patient's psychological troubles by obtaining information from him or her while in a state of hypnosis. **hypnogen'esis** or **hypnogeny** /-noj'i-ni/ n production of the hypnotic state. **hypnogenet'ic**, **hypnog'enous** or **hypnogen'ic** adj inducing the hypnotic state, or sleep. **hyp'noid** or **hyp'noidal** adj like sleep; like hypnosis; esp of a state between hypnosis and waking. **hyp'noidize** or **-ise** vt to put in the hypnoidal state. **hypnol'ogy** n the scientific study of sleep. **hyp'none** n an aromatic ketone used in medicine as a hypnotic. **hypnopae'dia** n learning or conditioning, by repetition of recorded sound during sleep (or semiwakefulness). **hypnopomp'ic** adj (Gr pompē a sending) dispelling sleep; relating to a state between sleep and wakefulness. **hypnō'sis** n a sleeplike state in which the mind responds to external suggestion and can recover forgotten memories. **hypnotee'** n a person who has been hypnotized. **hypnother'apist** n. **hypnother'apy** n the use of hypnosis to treat physical and psychological disorders. **hypnot'ic** adj of or relating to hypnosis; soporific (**hypnotic suggestion** suggestion (qv) made to a person under hypnosis). ◆ n a soporific; a person subject to hypnotism or in a state of hypnosis. **hypnot'ically** adv. **hyp'notism** n the science of hypnosis; the art or practice of inducing hypnosis; hypnosis. **hyp'notist** n a person skilled in hypnotism. **hypnotist'ic** adj. **hypnotizabil'ity** or **-s-** n. **hypnotiz'able** or **-s-** adj. **hypnotizā'tion** or **-s-** n. **hyp'notize** or **-ise** vt to put in a state of hypnosis; to fascinate, dazzle, overpower the mind of. **hyp'notizer** or **-s-** n. **hyp'notoid** adj like hypnosis.

Hypnos /hip'nos/ (Gr myth) n the god of sleep.

hypnum /hip'nəm/ n any moss of the large Hypnum genus (often divided), with capsules on special lateral branches. [Latinized from Gr hypnon a kind of lichen]

hypo /hī'pō/ (inf) n (pl **hy'pos**) short for **hyposulphite**, in the sense of sodium thiosulphate, used as a fixing agent (photog); short for **hypodermic syringe** or **injection** (see also **hype²**); short for (an attack of) **hypoglycaemia** (see under **hypo-**). ◆ adj short for **hypodermic**; short for **hypoglycaemic**.

hypo- /hī-pō-, hī-pə- or hī-po- or occasionally hip-ō- or hi-po-/ combining form signifying: under; defective; inadequate. [Gr hypo under]
■ **hypoaeolian** /hī-pō-ē-ō'li-ən/ adj below the Aeolian mode; applied in old church music to a plagal mode extending from e to e, with a for its final. **hypoallergen'ic** adj specially formulated in order to minimize the risk of allergy. **hypoblast** n (Gr blastos bud; zool) the inner germ-layer of a gastrula. **hypoblast'ic** adj. **hypobole** /hip-ob'ə-lē/ n (Gr hypobolē throwing under, suggestion, from ballein to throw; rhetoric) anticipation of objections. **hypocalcaemia** or (US) **hypocalcemia** /hī-pō-kal-sē'mi-ə/ n abnormal reduction of the

calcium content of the blood. **hypocaust** /-köst/ n (Gr hypokauston, from hypo under, and kaiein to burn) a space under a floor for heating by hot air or furnace gases, esp in ancient Roman villas. **hy'pocentre** n the point on the centre of the earth directly below the centre of explosion of a nuclear bomb. **hypochlorite** /-klö'rīt/ n a salt of **hypochlo'rous acid**, an acid (HClO) with less oxygen than chlorous acid. **hypochondria** /-kon'dri-ə/ n orig the plural of **hypochondrium** below; morbid anxiety about health; imaginary illness; a nervous malady, often arising from indigestion, and tormenting the patient with imaginary fears (once supposed to have its seat in the abdomen) (obs). **hypochon'driac** adj relating to or affected with hypochondria; melancholy. ◆ n a sufferer from hypochondria. **hypochondri'acal** adj. **hypochondri'asis**, **hypochondri'acism** or **hypochon'driasm** n hypochondria. **hypochon'driast** n someone suffering from hypochondria. **hypochon'drium** n (Gr hypochondrion, from chondros cartilage; anat) the region of the abdomen on either side, under the costal cartilages and short ribs. **hypocist** /hī'pō-sist/ n (Gr hypokistis, from kistos cistus) an inspissated juice from the fruit of Cytinus hypocistis (Rafflesiaceae), a plant parasitic on cistus roots. **hypocorism** /hī-pok'ə-rizm/ or **hypocorisma** /-iz'mə/ n (Gr hypokorisma, from hypokorizesthai to use child-talk, from koros boy, korē girl) a pet-name; a diminutive or abbreviated name. **hypocorist'ic** or **hypocorist'ical** adj. **hypocorist'ically** adv. **hypocotyl** /-kot'il/ n that part of the axis of a plant which is between the cotyledons and the primary root. **hypocotylē'donary** adj. **hypocretin** /hī-pō-krē'tin/ same as **orexin** (see under **orexis**). **hypocrisy** /hi-pok'ri-si/ n (Gr hypokrisia acting, playing a part) a feigning to be better than one is, or to be what one is not; concealment of true character or belief (not necessarily conscious); an instance or act of hypocrisy. **hypocrite** /hip'ə-krit/ n (Gr hypokritēs actor) a person who practises hypocrisy. **hypocrit'ical** (also **hypocrit'ic**) adj practising hypocrisy; of the nature of hypocrisy. **hypocrit'ically** adv. **hypocycloid** /-sī'kloid/ n a curve generated by a point on the circumference of a circle which rolls on the inside of another circle. **hypocycloid'al** adj. **hypoderm** /-dûrm/, **hypoder'ma** or **hypoder'mis** n (Gr derma skin; bot and anat) the tissue next under the epidermis. **hypoderm'al** adj. **hypoderm'ic** adj relating to the hypodermis; under the epidermis; under the skin, subcutaneous, esp of a method of injecting a drug in solution under the skin by means of a fine hollow needle to which a small syringe is attached. ◆ n a hypodermic injection; a drug so injected; (also **hypodermic syringe**) a syringe for the purpose. **hypoder'mically** adv. **hypodorian** /-dö'ri-ən/ adj (Gr hypodōrios) below the Dorian; applied in ancient Greek music to a mode whose upper tetrachord is the lower tetrachord of the Dorian (as: a; b c d e; e f g a), and in old church music to a plagal mode extending from a to a, with d as its final. **hypoeutec'tic** adj (of a compound) containing less of the minor component than a eutectic compound. **hypogastric** /-gas'trik/ adj (Gr gastēr belly) belonging to the lower median part of the abdomen. **hypogas'trium** n the hypogastric region. **hypogeal** or **hypogaeal** /-jē'əl/, **hypoge'an** or **hypogae'an** /-jē'ən/, **hypoge'ous** or **hypogae'ous** /-je'əs/ adj (Gr hypogeios, -gaios, from gē or gaia the ground; bot) underground; germinating with cotyledons underground. **hypogene** /-jēn/ adj (Gr gennaein to engender; geol) of or relating to rocks formed, or agencies at work, under the earth's surface; plutonic, opp to epigene. **hypogeum** or **hypogaeum** /-jē'əm/ n (pl **hypoge'a** or **hypogae'a**) an underground chamber; a subterranean tomb. **hypoglossal** /-glos'əl/ adj (Gr glōssa the tongue) under the tongue. ◆ n (also **hypoglossal nerve**) the twelfth cranial nerve of vertebrates, running to the muscles of the tongue. **hypoglycaemia** or **hypoglycemia** /hī-pō-gli-sē'mi-ə/ n (med) abnormal reduction of the sugar content of the blood. **hypoglycae'mic** or **hypoglyce'mic** adj. **hypog'nathism** n. **hypognathous** /hīp- or hip-og'nə-thəs/ adj having the lower jaw or mandible protruding. **hypogynous** /hī-poj'i-nəs/ adj (Gr gynē a woman, female; bot) growing from beneath the ovary; having the other floral parts below the ovary. **hypog'yny** n. **hy'poid** adj of a type of bevel gear in which the axes of the driving and driven shafts are at right angles but not in the same plane. **hypohidrō'sis** or **hypohydrō'sis** n abnormal lack of sweating. **hypokalae'mia** n an abnormally low concentration of potassium in the blood. **hypolim'nion** n (Gr limnion, dimin of limnē lake) a lower and colder layer of water in a lake. **hypolydian** /hī-pō-lid'i-ən/ adj below the Lydian mode; applied in ancient Greek music to a mode having as its upper tetrachord the lower tetrachord of the Lydian (as: f; g a b c; c d e f) and in old church music to a plagal mode extending from c to c with f as its final. **hypomagnesaemia** /hī-pō-mag-nə-zē'mi-ə/ n a condition, esp in cattle, characterized by an abnormally low level of magnesium in the blood. **hypomania** /-mā'ni-ə/ n (med) a milder form of mania, a condition marked by overexcitability. **hypomā'nic** (or /-man'ik/) adj. **hypomenorrhea** or **hypomenorrhoea** /-men-ə-rē'ə/ n (med) the condition in which the interval between two menstrual periods is increased to between 35 and 42 days. **hypomixolydian** /hī-pō-mik-sō-lid'i-ən/ adj applied in old church music to a mode extending from d to d with g as its final. **hyponasty**

/-nas-ti/ n (Gr nastos pressed close; bot) increased growth on the lower side causing an upward bend, opp to epinasty. **hyponatrae'mia** n an abnormally low concentration of sodium in the blood. **hyponī'trite** n a salt or ester of **hyponī'trous acid**, a crystalline acid, $H_2N_2O_2$, an oxidizing or reducing agent. **hy'ponym** n (Gr onyma a name) one of a group of terms whose meanings are included in the meaning of a more general term, eg spaniel and puppy in the meaning of dog. **hypon'ymy** n. **hypophosphite** /-fos'fīt/ n a salt of **hypophosphorous acid**, an acid (H_3PO_2) with less oxygen than phosphorous acid. **hypophrygian** /-frij'i-ən/ adj below the Phrygian mode; applied in ancient Greek music to a mode having as its upper tetrachord the lower tetrachord of the Phrygian (as: g; a b c d; d e f g), and in old church music to a plagal mode extending from b to b, with e for its final. **hypophyseal** or **hypophysial** /-fiz'i-əl/ adj. **hypophysec'tomy** n surgical removal of the pituitary gland. **hypophysis** /hī-pof'i-sis/ n (pl **hypoph'ysēs**) (Gr hypophysis an attachment underneath, from phyein to grow) a down-growth (zool); the pituitary gland; an inflated part of the pedicel under the capsule, in mosses (bot); (in flowering plants) a cell between the suspensor and the embryo proper. **hypopitū'itarism** n underproduction of growth hormones by the pituitary gland. **hypoplasia** /-plā'zi-ə or -zhə/ n (Gr plasis a forming; pathol) underdevelopment or immaturity of an organ. **hypoplastic** /-plas'/ adj. **hypoplastron** /-plas'tron/ n (zool) the plate behind the hyoplastron in a turtle's plastron. **hypospadias** /-spā'di-əs/ n (Gr spaein to tear) a congenital deficiency on the floor of the male urethra, causing it to have its opening on the underside of the penis. **hypostasis** /hip- or hīp-os'tə-sis/ n (pl **hypos'tasēs**) (Gr hypostasis, from stasis setting) orig basis, foundation; substance, essence (philos); the essence or real personal subsistence or substance of each of the three divisions of the Trinity; Christ as the union of human and divine qualities (theol); sediment, deposit; passive hyperaemia in a dependent part owing to sluggishness of circulation (med). **hypostasize** or **-ise** vt same as **hypostatize** below. **hypostatic** /-stat'ik/ or **hypostat'ical** adj. **hypostat'ically** adv. **hypos'tatize** or **-ise** vt to treat as hypostasis; to personify. **hyp'ostress** n insufficient stress. **hypostrophe** /hip- or hīp-os'trə-fi/ n (Gr hypostrophē turning back) relapse (med); reversion after a parenthesis (rhetoric). **hypostyle** /hip' or hīp'ō-stīl/ adj (Gr stylos a pillar; archit) having the roof supported by pillars. ◆ n a building with such a roof. **hyposul'phate** n a dithionate. **hyposul'phite** n a salt of **hyposulphurous acid** ($H_2S_2O_4$; also, in older usage $H_2S_2O_3$). **hyposulphūr'ic** adj dithionic. **hypotac'tic** adj. **hypotaxis** /-tak'sis/ n (Gr taxis arrangement; grammar) dependent construction; subordination of one clause to another (cf **parataxis**). **hypoten'sion** n low blood pressure. **hypoten'sive** adj characterized by low blood pressure; reducing blood pressure. ◆ n a person with low blood pressure. **hypotenuse** /hīp-, hip-ot'ən-ūs or -ūz/ or **hypothenuse** /-oth'/ n (Fr hypoténuse, from L hypoténūsa, from Gr hypoteinousa fem participle, subtending or stretching under, from teinein to stretch) the side of a right-angled triangle opposite to the right angle. **hypothalam'ic** adj. **hypothalamus** /-thal'ə-məs/ n (LL; med) the part of the brain that makes up the floor and part of the lateral walls of the third ventricle. **hypothec** /hip- or hīp-oth'ik/ n (Gr hypothēkē a pledge) in Scots law, a lien or security over goods in respect of a debt due by the owner of the goods (**the hale** (or **whole**) **hypothec** (Scot) the whole affair, collection, concern; everything). **hypoth'ecary** adj relating to hypothecation or mortgage. **hypoth'ecate** vt to place or assign as security under an arrangement; to mortgage; to hypothesize (N Am). **hypothecā'tion** n. **hypoth'ecātor** n. **hypotherm'al** adj. **hypothermia** /-thûr'mi-ə/ n (Gr thermē heat) subnormal body temperature, caused by exposure to cold or induced for purposes of heart and other surgery (see **freeze down** under **freeze**). **hypothesis** /hī-poth'i-sis/ n (pl **hypoth'esēs**) (Gr hypothesis, from thesis placing) a supposition; a proposition assumed for the sake of argument; a theory to be proved or disproved by reference to facts; a provisional explanation of anything. **hypoth'esize**, **-ise**, **hypoth'etize** or **-ise** vt and vi. **hypothet'ic** or **hypothet'ical** adj. **hypothet'ically** adv. **hypothy'roid** adj relating to or affected by hypothyroidism. **hypothy'roidism** n insufficient activity of the thyroid gland; a condition resulting from this, cretinism, etc. **hypotòn'ia** n a hypnotic condition. **hypoton'ic** adj (of muscles) lacking normal tone; (of a solution) having lower osmotic pressure than a specified solution. **hypotrochoid** /-trō'koid/ n (Gr trochos wheel, and eidos form) the curve traced by a point on the radius, or radius produced, of a circle rolling within another circle. **hypotyposis** /-tīp-ō'sis/ n (rhetoric) vivid description of a scene. **hypoventilā'tion** n abnormally decreased speed and depth of breathing. **hypovolae'mia** or (US) **hypovolē'mia** n (**volume**, and Gr haima blood; med) abnormal reduction of the volume of blood or blood plasma. **hypovolae'mic** or (US) **hypovolē'mic** adj. **hypoxaemia** or (N Am) **hypoxemia** /-ē'mi-ə/ n deficiency of oxygenation of the blood. **hypoxaem'ic** or **hypoxem'ic** adj. **hypox'ia** n deficiency of oxygen reaching the body tissues. **hypox'ic** adj.

hypso- /hip-sō-, hip-sə- or hip-so-/ combining form signifying height. [Gr hypsos height]
■ **hypsography** /-sog'rə-fi/ n (Gr graphein to write) the branch of geography dealing with the measurement and mapping of heights above sea level; a map showing topographic relief; a method of making such a map. **hypsom'eter** n an instrument for doing this by taking the boiling point of water. **hypsomet'ric** adj. **hypsometry** /hip-som'ə-tri/ n (Gr metron a measure) the art of measuring the heights of places on the earth's surface. **hyp'sophobe** n a person suffering from **hypsophobia** /hip-sō-fō'bi-ə/ (Gr phobos fear) fear of (falling from) high places. **hypsophyll** /hip'sō-fil/ n (Gr phyllon leaf; bot) a bract. **hypsophyll'ary** adj.

hypural /hī-pū'rəl/ adj situated beneath the tail. [Gr hypo under, and ourā tail]

hyrax /hī'raks/ n (pl **hy'raxes** or **hy'races** /-sēz/) a mammal of the genus Procavia or Dendrohyrax, superficially like marmots but more closely related to the ungulates, living among rocks in Africa and Syria, ie the daman, the dassie or rock rabbit, the cony of the Bible, constituting the order **Hyracoid'ea**. [Gr, shrew]
■ **hy'racoid** adj.

hyson /hī'son/ n a very fine sort of green tea. [From Chin xī chūn flourishing spring]
□ **hy'son-skin** n the refuse of hyson tea removed by winnowing.

hyssop /his'əp/ n an aromatic labiate (Hyssopus officinalis) used in perfumery and folk-medicine; an unknown wall plant used as a ceremonial sprinkler (Bible); a holy-water sprinkler. [L hyssōpus, -um, from Gr hyssōpos, -on; cf Heb 'ēzōb]

hyster- /his-tər-/ or **hystero-** /his-tə-rō-, his-tə-rə- or his-tə-ro-/ combining form denoting the womb. [Gr hysterā the womb]
■ **hysterec'tomize** or **-ise** vt. **hysterec'tomy** n (Gr ektomē a cutting out) surgical removal of the uterus. **hysteri'tis** n inflammation of the uterus. **hysterot'omy** n (Gr tomē a cut) surgical incision of the uterus.

hysteranthous /his-tər-an'thəs/ adj having the leaves appearing after the flowers. [Gr hysteros later, and anthos flower]

hysteresis /his-tə-rē'sis/ n the retardation or lagging of an effect behind the cause of the effect; the influence of earlier treatment of a body on its subsequent reaction. [Gr hysterēsis a deficiency, coming late, from hysteros later]
■ **hysterēs'ial** adj. **hysteret'ic** adj.
□ **high-hysteresis rubber** n rubber with less than normal bounce.

hysteria /hi-stē'ri-ə/ n a psychoneurosis in which repressed complexes become split off or dissociated from the personality, forming independent units, partially or completely unrecognized by consciousness, giving rise to hypnoidal states (eg amnesia, somnambulisms), and manifested by various physical symptoms (such as tics, paralysis, blindness, deafness, etc), general features being an extreme degree of emotional instability and an intense craving for affection; (loosely) an outbreak of wild emotionalism. [Gr hysterā the womb, with which hysteria was formerly thought to be connected]
■ **hysteric** /his-ter'ik/ or **hyster'ical** adj relating to, of the nature of, or affected with, hysterics or hysteria; like hysterics; fitfully and violently emotional; (**hyster'ical**) extremely funny (inf). ♦ n (**hyster'ic**) a hysterical person. **hyster'ically** adv. **hyster'icky** adj (inf). **hyster'ics** n pl hysteric fits; (popularly) fits of uncontrollable laughter or crying, or of both alternately. **hysterogen'ic** adj inducing hysteria. **hysterogeny** /-oj'ə-ni/ n. **hys'teroid** or **hys'teroidal** adj like hysteria. **hysteromān'ia** n hysterical mania, often marked by erotic delusions and an excessive desire to attract attention.
□ **hysterical pregnancy** n pseudocyesis. **hysteroid dysphoria** n pathological depression typical of women.

hysteron proteron /his'tə-ron prot'ə-ron/ n a figure of speech in which what would ordinarily follow comes first; an inversion. [Gr, literally, latter former]

hythe same as **hithe**.

Hz symbol : hertz (SI unit).

I i

a b c d e f g h i j k l m n o p q r s t u v w x y z

Isbell Designed by Richard Isbell and Jerry Campbell in 1981. USA.

I[1] or **i** /ī/ *n* the ninth letter in the modern English alphabet as in the Roman, with various sounds, as in d*i*p, m*i*nd, b*i*rd, mach*i*ne; anything shaped like the letter I.
☐ **I'-beam** *n* a metal girder I-shaped in section; an I-shaped cursor on a computer screen.

I[2] /ī/ *pronoun* the nominative singular of the first personal pronoun; the word used in mentioning oneself. ◆ *n* the object of self-consciousness, the ego. [ME *ich*, from OE *ic*; Ger *ich*, ON e*k*, L *ego*, Gr *egō*]
☐ **I'-and-I** *pronoun* a form used *esp* by Rastafarians for **we** or **us**.

I[3] /ī/ *adv* same as **aye**[1].

I or **I.** *abbrev* : independence; independent; institute; international; island or isle; Italy (IVR).
☐ **I'-way** *n* (*inf*) the information superhighway.

I *symbol* : (as a Roman numeral) 1; iodine (*chem*).

I (*phys*) *symbol* : electric current.

i (*maths*) *symbol* : the imaginary square root of − 1.

i' /i/ *prep* a form of **in**.

IA *abbrev* : Institute of Actuaries; International Ångström; Iowa (US state; also **Ia.**).

-ia /-ē-ə/ or **-ya** /-yə/ *sfx* used in naming: (1) a pathological condition; (2) a genus of plants or animals; (3) (as L or Gr neuter *pl*) a taxonomic division; (4) (as *pl*) things relating to (something specified).

IAA *abbrev* : indoleacetic acid.

IAAF *abbrev* : International Association of Athletics Federations.

IAEA *abbrev* : International Atomic Energy Agency.

Iai-do /ē-ī'dō/ *n* Japanese swordsmanship as a martial art. [From Jap]

IAL (*comput*) *abbrev* : International Algebraic Language, an early version of **Algol**[2].

iambus /ī-am'bəs/ *n* (*pl* **iam'buses** or **iam'bī**) (*prosody*) a foot of two syllables, a short followed by a long, or an unstressed by a stressed (also **i'amb**). [L *iambus*, from Gr *iambos*, from *iaptein* to assail, this metre being first used by satirists]
■ **iam'bic** *adj* consisting of iambuses; of the nature of an iambus; using iambic verse. ◆ *n* an iambus; (in *pl*) iambic verse. **iam'bically** *adv*. **iam'bist** or **iambog'rapher** *n*.
☐ **iambic pentameter** *n* a verse form comprising lines each of five feet, each foot containing two syllables, used in blank or heroic verse in English.

-ian or **-ean** /-i-ən/, also **-an** /-ən/ *adj sfx* indicating relationship or similarity, as in *utilitarian*, *Shakespearean*. ◆ *n sfx* denoting a person who is interested or skilled in a specified thing, as in *mathematician*. [L adjectival ending *-iānus*]

-iana see **-ana**.

ianthine /ī-an'thin or -thīn/ *adj* violet-coloured. [Gr *ianthinos*, from *ion* violet, and *anthos* flower]

IAP (*comput*) *abbrev* : Internet access provider.

IAS or **i.a.s.** *abbrev* : immediate access store (*comput*); Immigration Advisory Service; indicated air speed (*aeronautics*); instrument approach system.

-iasis /-ī-ə-sis/ (*med*) *sfx* denoting a diseased condition, as in *pityriasis*, *psoriasis*. [Gr suffix meaning state or condition]

Iastic /ī-as'tik/ (*music*) *adj* Ionian. [Gr *Iastikos* Ionian]
☐ **Iastic mode** *n* the Ionian, hypophrygian or hyperdorian mode of ancient Greek music.

IATA *abbrev* : International Air Transport Association.

-iatric /-i-at-rik/ *adj combining form* relating to care or treatment within a particular specialty, as in *paediatric*, *psychiatric*. [Gr *iātros* physician]
■ **-iatrics** *n sing combining form*. **-iatry** *n combining form*.

iatrochemistry /ī-at-rō-kem'i-stri/ *n* an application of chemistry to medical theory introduced by Franciscus Sylvius (1614–72) of Leyden. [Gr *iātros* physician, and **chemistry**]
■ **iatrochem'ical** *adj*. **iatrochem'ist** *n*.

iatrogenic /ī-at-rō-jen'ik/ *adj* (of a disease or symptoms) induced unintentionally in a patient by the treatment or comments of a physician. [Gr *iātros* a physician, and *-genēs* born]
■ **iatrogenic'ity** *n*. **iatro'geny** *n*.

IB *abbrev* : International Baccalaureate.

ib. or **ibid.** *abbrev* : *ibidem* (L), in the same place.

ibadah /ib'ä-dä/ (Islam) *n* (*pl* **ib'adat** /-dät/) service, worship. [Ar]

Iberian /ī-bē'ri-ən/ *adj* of Spain and Portugal; formerly, of Iberia (now Georgia) in the Caucasus; of the ancient inhabitants of either of these, or their later representatives; of a Mediterranean people of Neolithic culture in Britain, etc. ◆ *n* a member of any of these peoples. [L *Ibēria*, from Gr *Ibēriā*]

iberis /ī-bē'ris/ *n* any plant of the *Iberis* genus of Cruciferae, including the candytuft (*I. sempervirens*). [Gr *ibēris* pepperwort]

ibex /ī'beks/ *n* (*pl* **i'bex**, **i'bexes** or **ibices** /ī'bi-sēz/) any of various wild mountain goats of Europe, N Africa and Asia, with large, ridged, backward-curving horns. [L *ibex, -icis*]

IBF *abbrev* : International Boxing Federation.

Ibibio /i-bib'i-ō/ *adj* and *n* (*pl* **Ibib'io** or **Ibib'ios**) same as **Efik**.

ibidem /i-bī'dəm, ib'i-dəm or i-bē'dem/ (L) *adv* (used in referring to a book, chapter, passage, etc already cited) in the same place (*abbrev* **ib.** or **ibid.**).

ibis /ī'bis/ *n* (*pl* **ibis** or **ibises**) a wading bird of the family Plataleidae, typically having long, thin down-curved bills, long broad wings and short tails, and including the sacred ibis (*Threskiornis aethiopicus*) worshipped by the ancient Egyptians. See also **wood ibis** under **wood**[1]. [L and Gr *ībis*, prob Egyp]

-ible /-ə-bl/ *adj sfx* having similar uses to those of **-able**, *esp* the passive 'capable of being', as in *audible*, *permissible*, *visible*. [L *-ibilis*, from *-bilis* as used with a 2nd-, 3rd- or 4th-conjugation verb]
■ **-ibility** *n sfx*. **-ibly** *adv sfx*.

Iblis see **Eblis**.

IBO *abbrev* : International Boxing Organization.

Ibo see **Igbo**.

ibogaine /i-bō'gə-ēn/ *n* a psychoactive alkaloid derived from an African plant (*Tabernanthe iboga*), used as an experimental treatment for drug and alcohol addiction.

IBRD *abbrev* : International Bank for Reconstruction and Development, ie the World Bank (qv).

IBS (*med*) *abbrev* : irritable bowel syndrome.

Ibsenism /ib'sə-ni-zm/ *n* the dramatic qualities and type of social criticism characteristic of the plays of the Norwegian dramatist, Henrik Ibsen (1828–1906).
■ **Ibsen'ian** *adj* of or in the style of Ibsen. **Ib'senite** *n* a champion or follower of Ibsen.

ibuprofen /ī-bū-prō'fən/ *n* an anti-inflammatory non-steroidal drug used in various over-the-counter painkillers and in the treatment of arthritis and rheumatic pain. [From its full name, *iso*butyl*phen*yl propionic acid]

IC *abbrev* : integrated circuit (*electronics*); internal-combustion.

i/c *abbrev* : in charge; in command.

-ic /-ik/ *adj sfx* denoting: belonging or relating to, as in *academic*, *systematic*; formed with an element in its higher valency, as in *sulphuric* (*chem*). [L *-icus*, from Gr *-ikos*]
■ **-ically** *adv sfx*.

ICA *abbrev* : Institute of Chartered Accountants (**ICAEW** of England and Wales; **ICAI** of Ireland); Institute of Contemporary Arts; Invalid Care Allowance (now replaced by Carer's Allowance).

■ words derived from main entry word; ☐ compound words; ■ idioms and phrasal verbs

-ical /-i-kl/ adj sfx a variant of **-ic**, although not always giving an identical meaning (cf **economic** and **economical**). [L -icalis]

ICANN abbrev: Internet Corporation for Assigned Names and Numbers.

ICAO abbrev: International Civil Aviation Organization.

Icarian /ī-kā'ri-an or i-/ adj of or like Icarus, who, according to Greek mythology, flew from Crete on wings made by Daedalus partly of wax, which melted as he passed too near the sun, plunging him into the sea; see also **daedal**.

ICBM abbrev: intercontinental ballistic missile.

ICC abbrev: International Chamber of Commerce; International Cricket Council; International Criminal Court.

ICD abbrev: interactive compact disc (comput); International Classification of Diseases.

ICE abbrev: in case of emergency; Institution of Civil Engineers; internal combustion engine; intrusion countermeasure electronics (software designed to prevent unauthorized access to computer data).

ice /īs/ n frozen water; any substance resembling this, esp any liquid or gaseous substance reduced to a solid state by freezing; a portion of ice-cream or water ice; reserve, formality; coldness of manner; diamond(s) or other precious stone(s) (sl); an illicit drug, a highly synthesized form of methamphetamine (drug sl). ◆ adj of ice. ◆ vt (**ic'ing**; **iced**) to cool with ice; to cover with icing; to kill (US criminal sl). ◆ vi to freeze; to become covered with ice (with up, over, etc). [OE īs; ON īss; Ger Eis, Dan is]

■ **iced** /īst/ adj covered with or cooled with ice; coated or topped with icing. **i'cer** n a person who makes or applies icing. **ic'ily** adv. **ic'iness** n. **ic'ing** n (a coating of) concreted sugar; the formation of ice, eg on roads, aircraft, ships, etc. **ic'y** adj composed of, covered with, or like ice; frosty; cold; chilling; (of manner) without warmth, distant, hostile. ◆ adv in an icy manner.

❑ **ice'-action** n the action of glaciers and land ice on the earth's surface. **ice age** n (geol) any time when a great part of the earth's surface has been covered with ice, esp (often with caps) that in the Pleistocene epoch. **ice anchor** n an anchor with a single arm for mooring to an ice floe, etc. **ice apron** n a structure on the upstream side of a bridge pier to break or ward off floating ice. **ice axe** n an axe used by mountain-climbers to cut footholds in ice or compacted snow. **ice bag** n a waterproof bag filled with or for carrying ice. **ice'ball** n a game, similar to basketball, played by two teams of players on ice. **ice beer** n beer brewed using a process that freezes the beer and then removes some of the alcoholic content. **ice'berg** n (from Scand or Du) a huge mass of ice, floating in the sea, which has broken away from a glacier, ice barrier, etc; a cold and unemotional person (esp US inf); a type of crisp lettuce with tightly-packed light-green leaves (also **iceberg lettuce**). **ice'blink** n a glare in the sky caused by light reflected from distant masses of ice. **ice block** n (Aust and NZ) an ice lolly. **ice'-blue** n and adj (a) very pale blue. **ice'boat** n a boat for forcing a way through ice, an icebreaker; a craft mounted on runners for moving over ice (also **ice yacht**). **ice'bound** adj (of a ship, etc) covered, surrounded or immobilized by ice. **ice'box** n the freezing compartment of a refrigerator; a refrigerator (old US); an insulated box packed with ice, used for storing and carrying cold food and drink. **ice'breaker** n a ship for breaking channels through ice; anything for breaking ice; something or someone that breaks down reserve between a group or gathering of people. **ice'breaking** adj. **ice bucket** n an insulated container for holding ice cubes to be used in drinks; a receptacle partially filled with ice, used for cooling bottles of wine. **ice'-calk** same as **frost-nail** (see under **frost**). **ice'cap** n a permanent covering of ice over the polar regions of a planet, a mountain-top, etc. **ice'-cold** adj cold as, or like, ice. **ice colours** n pl (chem) dyestuffs produced on cotton fibre by a solution of diazo-salt cooled with ice interacting with a second component. **ice contact slope** n (geol) the steep slope of material deposited at the ice front of a glacier and in contact with it. **ice craft** n skill in travelling over or through ice. **ice cream** n a sweet frozen food containing cream, or one of various substitutes, and flavouring (**ice'-cream soda** carbonated water with ice cream added). **ice cube** n a small cube of ice used for cooling drinks, etc. **ice dance** or **dancing** n a form of ice-skating based on the movements of ballroom dancing. **ice dancer** n. **ice diving** n scuba diving below the surface of frozen water. **iced tea** or **ice tea** n chilled sweetened tea flavoured eg with lemon. **iced water** n drinking water chilled with ice. **ice fall** n a fall of ice; a steep broken place in a glacier. **ice fern** n a fern-like encrustation on a window in frost. **ice'field** n a large flat area of land covered with ice or an area of sea covered with floating ice. **ice fish** n the capelin; any percoid Antarctic fish of the family Channichthyidae. **ice floe** n a large sheet of ice floating in the sea. **ice'-foot** n a belt of ice forming round the coast in Arctic regions (also **ice'-belt** or **ice'-ledge**). **ice'-free** adj without ice. **ice front** n the front face of a glacier. **ice hill** n a slope of ice for tobogganing. **ice hilling** n. **ice hockey** n a game played by two teams on an ice rink, in which players equipped

with skates and long sticks try to drive a flat puck into their opponent's goal. **ice house** n (esp formerly) a building for storing ice in. **ice lolly** n a lollipop consisting of water ice on a stick. **ice machine** n a machine for making ice in large quantities. **ice man** n (esp US) a man who sells or delivers ice; a jewel thief (sl); a professional killer, a hitman (criminal sl). **ice'pack** n drifting ice packed together, pack ice; an ice-filled bag for applying to a part of the body to reduce swelling (med); a gel-filled pack that remains frozen for long periods, for use in a cool box, etc. **ice pan** n a slab of floating ice. **ice pick** n a tool with a pointed end used for splitting ice. **ice plant** n a flowering plant (Mesembrianthemum or Dorotheanthus) whose succulent leaves are covered with fine hairs which give them a glistening, sugary appearance. **ice point** n the temperature (0°Celsius or 32°Fahrenheit) at which ice is at equilibrium with water in liquid form at a pressure of one atmosphere. **ice rink** n a skating rink of ice. **ice run** n a tobogganing slide. **ice sheet** n a thick sheet of ice covering a large area of land, esp an entire region, as in ice ages. **ice shelf** n a floating sheet of ice permanently attached to a land mass and projecting into the sea. **ice show** n an entertainment or exhibition provided by skaters on ice. **ice skate** n a skate for moving on ice (see **skate**[1]). **ice'-skate** vi. **ice'-skater** n. **ice'-skating** n. **ice spar** n a clear glassy orthoclase. **ice'stone** n cryolite under **cryo-**. **ice storm** n a storm of freezing rain. **ice tea** see iced tea above. **ice track** n a frozen track used in speedskating. **ice water** n water formed from melted ice. **ice worm** n a species of oligochaete found on glaciers in Alaska, etc. **ice yacht** see iceboat above. **icing sugar** n sugar in the form of a very fine powder, for icing cakes, etc. **ic'y-pearled** adj (Milton) studded with pearls or spangles of ice.

■ **break the ice** to break through the barrier of reserve or inhibition on first meeting; to move to restore friendly relations after a period of hostility. **cut no ice** to count for nothing; to have no effect. **dry ice** solid carbon dioxide, which changes directly into vapour at −78.5°Celsius, and is chiefly used for refrigeration, but is also exploited in the theatre, the dense, swirling, floor-level white cloud it produces on evaporation creating a spectacular stage-effect. **ice out** (fig) to exclude (someone) from one's company by ignoring him or her. **icing on the cake** anything that is a desirable addition to something already satisfactory. **on ice** (fig) kept, or waiting in readiness; postponed; in prison, esp in solitary confinement (US prison sl). **put on ice** to put into abeyance, to suspend. (**skate**) **on thin ice** (to be) in a delicate, difficult or potentially embarrassing situation. **tip of the iceberg** the top of an iceberg, visible above the water, most of it being invisible below the surface; hence, the small obvious part of a much larger problem, etc (fig).

Iceland /īs'lənd/ adj of, belonging to, or originating in, the island of Iceland.

■ **Ice'lander** (or /īs-land'ər/) n a native or citizen of Iceland. **Icelandic** /īs-land'ik/ adj of or relating to Iceland or its inhabitants. ◆ n the modern language of the Icelanders; Old Norse.

❑ **Ice'land-dog'** n a shaggy white dog with sharply pointed ears originally from Iceland. **Iceland falcon** n a white gerfalcon of Iceland. **Iceland moss** n a lichen (Cetraria islandica) of northern regions, used as a medicine and for food. **Iceland poppy** n a dwarf poppy (Papaver nudicaule) with grey-green pinnate leaves and flowers varying from white to orange-scarlet. **Iceland spar** n a transparent calcite with strong double refraction.

Iceni /ī-sē'nī/ n pl an ancient British tribe that, led by Queen Boudicca, rebelled against the Romans in 61AD.

ICFTU abbrev: International Confederation of Free Trade Unions.

ich[1] /ich/ (Shakesp) vt same as **eche**.

ich[2] see **ch**.

ichabod /ik'ə-bod/ interj the glory is departed. [From Heb; see Bible, 1 Samuel 4.21]

ich dien /ihh dēn/ (Ger) I serve (the motto of the Prince of Wales).

IChemE abbrev: Institution of Chemical Engineers.

I Ching /ī or ē ching/ n an ancient Chinese system of divination, consisting of a set of symbols, 8 trigrams and 64 hexagrams, and the text, the I Ching, used to interpret them. [Chin yìjīng book of changes]

ichneumon /ik-nū'mən/ n any animal of the mongoose genus (Herpestes) of the civet family, esp the Egyptian species that destroys crocodiles' eggs; (in full **ichneumon fly**) any insect of the order Hymenoptera whose larvae are parasitic in or on other insects and their larvae. [Gr ichneumōn, literally, tracker, ichneuein to hunt after, from ichnos a track]

ichnite /ik'nīt/ or **ichnolite** /ik'nə-līt/ n a fossilized footprint. [Gr ichnos a track, footprint]

■ **ichnol'ogy** n the science of fossilized footprints.

ichnography /ik-nog'rə-fi/ n a ground plan; the art of drawing ground plans. [Gr ichnos a track, footprint, and graphein to write]

■ **ichnograph'ic** or **ichnograph'ical** adj. **ichnograph'ically** adv.

ichor /ī'kör/ n the ethereal juice in the veins of the gods (*myth*); colourless matter oozing from an ulcer or wound (*med*). [Gr *īchōr*]
■ **i'chorous** adj.

ichthyic /ik'thi-ik/ or **ichthic** /ik'thik/ adj of, resembling or relating to fish. [Gr *ichthȳs* fish]

ichthyo- /ik-thi-ō-/ or **ichthy-** /ik-thi-/ *combining form* signifying fish. [Gr *ichthȳs* fish]
■ **ichthyocoll'a** n (Gr *kolla* glue) fish-glue; isinglass. **ichthyodor'ūlite** or **ichthyodor'ylite** /-i-līt/ n (Gr *dory* a spear, and *lithos* a stone) a fossilized fish spine. **ichthyol'atrous** adj. **ichthyol'atry** n (Gr *latreiā* worship) the worship of fish. **ich'thyolite** n (Gr *lithos* a stone) a general term for any fossil fish. **ichthyolitic** /-lit'ik/ adj. **ichthyolog'ical** adj. **ichthyol'ogist** n. **ichthyol'ogy** n the study of fishes, their natural history, distribution, etc. **ichthyophagist** /-of'ə-jist/ n a fish-eater. **ichthyoph'agous** /-ə-gəs/ adj (Gr *phagein* to eat) feeding on fish. **ichthyoph'agy** n. **ichthyop'sid** or **ichthyop'sidan** n (Gr *opsis* appearance). **Ichthyop'sida** n pl a group of vertebrates in Huxley's classification comprising amphibians, fishes and fish-like vertebrates. **Ichthyopterygia** /-op-tər-ij'i-ə/ n pl (Gr *pterygion* a fin, dimin of *pteryx* wing) the Ichthyosauria. **ichthyor'nis** n (Gr *ornis* a bird) an extinct Cretaceous sea bird of the genus *Ichthyornis* with reptilian teeth set in sockets. **ichthyosaur** /ik'thi-ō-sör/ or **ichthyosau'rus** n (Gr *sauros* lizard) any Mesozoic extinct marine reptile of the order **Ichthyosau'ria**, with a fish-shaped body and elongated snout similar to dolphins. **ichthyosaur'ian** adj. **ichthyō'sis** n a rare inherited condition in which the skin becomes thickened, scaly and rough, due to an abnormality in the production of keratin (also called **fish skin disease**). **ichthyot'ic** adj.

ichthyoid /ik'thi-oid/ adj (also **ich'thyoidal**) fish-like. ♦n a fish-like vertebrate. [Gr *ichthȳs* fish]

ichthys /ik'this/ n a fish symbolizing Christ or an emblem or motto (ΙΧΘΥΣ), believed to have mystical qualities, being the first letters of the Greek words *Jesous Christos, Theou Uious, Soter* (Jesus Christ, Son of God, Saviour). [Gr *ichthȳs* fish]

ICI abbrev: Imperial Chemical Industries.

icicle /īs'i-kl/ n a hanging, tapering piece of ice formed by the freezing of dropping water. [OE *īsesgicel*, from *īses*, genitive of *īs* ice, and *gicel* icicle]

icing see under **ice**.

-icism see **-ism**.

icker /ik'ər/ (*Scot*) n an ear of corn. [OE (Northumbrian) *eher*, *æhher* (WSax *ēar*)]

icky /ik'i/ (*inf*) adj (**ick'ier**; **ick'iest**) sickly-sweet, cloying; repulsive, distasteful, unpleasant (also **icky poo**). [Perh from **sickly**]

icon or **ikon** /ī'kon/ n in the Eastern Churches, a figure representing Christ, the Virgin Mary or a saint, in painting, mosaic, or low relief sculpture; a symbol, image, picture or representation; anybody or anything venerated or uncritically admired; a picture or symbol in a graphic display, representing a particular facility or operation available to the user, *usu* activated by means of a mouse (*comput*). [L *īcōn*, from Gr *eikōn* an image]
■ **icon'ic** adj. **icon'ically** adv. **icon'ify** vt and vi to reduce (a window) on a computer screen to an icon. **i'conize** or **-ise** vt to venerate or admire uncritically. **icon'oclasm** n (Gr *klaein* to break) the act of destroying images that are the object of veneration; opposition to image-worship. **icon'oclast** n a destroyer of images; a person opposed to image-worship, *esp* those in the Eastern Church, from the 8c; a person who attacks traditional or established beliefs, principles, ideas, institutions, etc. **iconoclast'ic** adj. **iconoclast'ically** adv. **iconog'rapher** n. **iconograph'ic** or **iconograph'ical** adj. **iconog'raphy** n (Gr *graphiā* a writing) the study of the subjects depicted in paintings, etc; pictorial representation of subjects; the symbols used in paintings, etc and their conventional significance; a description, catalogue or collective representation of portraits. **iconol'ater** n an image-worshipper. **iconol'atry** n (Gr *latreiā* worship) image-worship. **iconolog'ical** adj. **iconol'ogist** n. **iconol'ogy** n the study of icons; icons collectively; the study of artistic symbolism. **iconomachist** /-om'ə-kist/ n a person who contends against the use of icons in worship. **iconom'achy** n (Gr *machē* fight) opposition to image-worship. **iconomat'ic** adj using pictures of objects to represent not the things themselves but the sounds of their names, as in a transitional stage of writing between pictorial representation and a phonetic system. **iconomat'icism** /-i-sizm/ n. **iconom'eter** n an instrument for inferring distance from size or size from distance of an object, by measuring its image; a direct photographic viewfinder. **iconom'etry** n. **iconoph'ilism** n a taste for pictures, etc. **iconoph'ilist** n a connoisseur of pictures, etc. **iconom'oscope** n an early form of electron camera. **iconos'tasis** or **icon'ostas** n (pl **iconos'tases** /-ēz/) (Gr *eikonostasis*, from *stasis* placing) in Eastern churches, a screen separating the sanctuary from the nave, on which the icons are placed.

□ **iconic memory** n the persistence of a sense impression after the disappearance of the stimulus.

icosahedron /ī-kos-ə-hē'drən/ (*geom*) n (pl **icosahē'drons** or **icosahē'dra**) a solid with twenty plane faces. [Gr *eikosi* twenty, and *hedrā* a seat]
■ **icosahē'dral** adj. **icositetrahē'dron** n (pl **icositetrahē'drons** or **icositetrahē'dra**) (Gr *tetra* four) a solid figure with twenty-four plane faces.

Icosandria /ī-kō-san'dri-ə/ (*bot*) n pl a Linnaean class of plants with twenty or more free stamens. [Gr *eikosi* twenty, and *anēr, andros* a man (male)]
■ **icosan'drian** adj. **icosan'drous** adj.

ICR (*comput*) abbrev: intelligent character recognition.

ICRF abbrev: Imperial Cancer Research Fund (now known as Cancer Research UK).

-ics /-iks/ n sfx denoting: (1) the study, practice, art or knowledge of a particular subject or type of activity, as in *aeronautics, paediatrics, gymnastics, politics*; (2) the procedures, functions or phenomena involved in, or relating to, a specific activity, as in *mechanics, acoustics, graphics*; (3) the actions, behaviour, etc characteristic of a particular state or condition, as in *hysterics, histrionics*. [Gr *-ika*, neuter pl adj ending]

ICSA abbrev: Institute of Chartered Secretaries and Administrators.

ICSH abbrev: interstitial-cell-stimulating hormone.

ICSI abbrev: intracytoplasmic sperm injection, a method of in vitro fertilization.

ICSID abbrev: International Centre for Settlement of Investment Disputes.

ICSTIS /ik'stis/ abbrev: Independent Committee for the Supervision of Standards for Telephone Information Services.

ICSU abbrev: International Council for Science (formerly known as the International Council of Scientific Unions).

ICT abbrev: information and communication technology.

icterus /ik'tə-rəs/ n jaundice. [Gr *ikteros* jaundice, also a yellowish bird (according to Pliny the golden oriole) the sight of which supposedly cured jaundice]
■ **icteric** /-ter'ik/ or **icter'ical** adj relating to or suffering from jaundice. ♦n a medicine for jaundice. **ic'terid** adj and n (of or resembling) a member of a family of American orioles (**Icter'idae**), mostly yellow and black passerine birds, including the Baltimore oriole, bobolinks, cowbirds and grackles. **ic'terine** /-tər-īn/ or /-in/ adj of or resembling the family **Icter'idae**; yellowish or marked with yellow. **icteritious** /ik-tər-ish'əs/ adj jaundiced; yellow.

ictus /ik'təs/ n (pl **ic'tuses** or L **ic'tūs** /-toos/) rhythmical or metrical stress in contradistinction to the usual stress of a word in prose, etc (*prosody*); a stroke or sudden attack, *esp* an epileptic fit (*med*). [L, a blow]
■ **ic'tal** or **ic'tic** adj.

ICU (*med*) abbrev: intensive care unit.

ID abbrev: Idaho (US state); identification; identity; infectious diseases (*med*); inner diameter (also **i.d.**); intelligence (or information) department; intradermal (also **i.d.**) (*med*).
□ **ID card** n a card which identifies a person, often including a photograph, details of age, membership, etc.

I'd /īd/, contracted from *I would*, or *I had*; also used for *I should*.

id[1] /id/ or **ide** /īd/ n a fish (*Leuciscus idus*), closely related to the chub, inhabiting fresh water in N Europe. [Swed *id*]

id[2] /id/ n in psychoanalytic theory, one of the three parts of the personality, being the unconscious mass of primitive energies from which come instincts for the gratification of basic desires for food, sex, etc, and for the avoidance of pain, modified by the ego and the superego. [L *id* it]

id[3] /id/ (*biol*) n in Weissman's theory, an element in the chromosome carrying all the hereditary characters. [Gr *idios* own, private; appar. suggested by **idioplasm**]
■ **idant** /ī'dənt/ n an aggregation of ids; a chromosome.

id. abbrev: idem.

-id[1] /-id/ adj sfx as in *fluid, stupid, solid, tepid, turgid, gelid*, etc. [L *-idus*]

-id[2] /-id/ sfx used in the names of a particular zoological or racial group, or dynastic line, as in *arachnid, hominid, Fatimid*. [Gr *-idēs* son of]

-id[3] /-id/ n sfx used in names of bodies, formations, particles, etc, as *hydatid, energid*; used in the names of meteors coming from a particular constellation, as in *Perseid, Orionid*. [Gr *-is, -idos* daughter of]

-id[4] see **-ide**.

IDA abbrev: International Development Association.

Ida. *abbrev*: Idaho (US state).

-idae /-i-dē/ *n sfx* used in names of zoological families, as in *Boridae*, *Canidae*. [L, from Gr *-idai*, pl of *-idēs*]

Idaean /ī-dē'an/ *adj* of Mount Ida in Crete, or that near Troy. [Gr *Idaios*]
□ **Idaean vine** *n* the cowberry.

Id al-Adha same as **Eid al-Adha**.

Id al-Fitr same as **Eid al-Fitr**.

Idalian /ī-dā'li-ən/ *adj* relating to *Idalium* in Cyprus, or to Aphrodite, to whom it was sacred.

idant see under **id³**.

IDB (*esp S Afr*) *abbrev*: illicit diamond buying.

IDD (*telecom*) *abbrev*: International Direct Dialling.

IDE (*comput*) *abbrev*: Integrated Drive Electronics, a control system that allows communication between a computer and a device (eg a hard disk); Integrated Development Environment, a software user interface.

ide see **id¹**.

-ide /-īd/ or **-id** /-id/ *n sfx* indicating: (1) a chemical compound composed of two chemical elements, as in *potassium iodide*; (2) a chemical compound derived from another or belonging to a class of compounds, as in *hydroperoxide*, *amide*. [From Ger *-id* (Fr *-ide*), from its first use in *oxide*]

idea /ī-dē'ə/ *n* an image of an external object formed by the mind; a notion, thought, impression, conception, any product of intellectual action, of memory and imagination; a plan; an aim, purpose; in Plato, an archetype of the manifold varieties of existence in the universe, belonging to the supersensible world, in Kant, one of the three products of the reason (the Soul, the Universe, and God) transcending the conceptions of the understanding, and in Hegel, the ideal realized, the absolute truth of which everything that exists is the expression (*philos*). [L, from Gr *ideā*; cf *idein* (aorist) to see]
■ **ide'aed** or **ide'a'd** *adj* provided with an idea or ideas. **ide'aless** *adj* devoid of ideas. **ide'ate** *vt* to form or have an idea of; to imagine; to preconceive. ◆ *vi* to form ideas. ◆ *adj* produced by an idea. ◆ *n* the correlative or object of an idea. **idea'tion** *n* the power of the mind for forming ideas or images; the exercise of such power. **ideā'tional** or **ide'ative** *adj*. **idea'tionally** *adv*.
■ **get** or **have ideas** (*inf*) to become or be overambitious; to have undesirable ideas. **have no idea** to be unaware of what is happening; to be ignorant or naive. **not my idea of** (*inf*) the opposite of my (or the accepted and familiar) conception of. **put ideas into someone's head** to fill someone with unsuitable or over-exalted aspirations. **that's an idea** that plan, suggestion, etc is worth considering. **that's the idea** you have understood the point. **the very idea** the mere thought; (as an ejaculation) that's absurd, outrageous. **what an idea!** that's preposterous. **what's the big idea?** (*sl, usu ironic*) what's the intention, purpose?

ideal /ī-dēl' or ī-dē'əl/ *adj* conceptual; existing in imagination only; highest and best conceivable; perfect, as opposed to the real or the imperfect; theoretical, conforming absolutely to theory. ◆ *n* the highest conception of anything, or its embodiment; a standard of perfection; that which exists in the imagination only; a subring of a ring, any member of which when multiplied by any member of the ring, whether in the subring or not, results in a member of the subring (*maths*). [LL *idealis*, from Gr *ideā*, from *idein* to see]
■ **ide'alism** *n* a tendency towards the highest conceivable perfection, love for or the search after the best and highest; the habit or practice of idealizing; impracticality; the doctrine that in external perceptions the objects immediately known are ideas, that all reality is in its nature psychical. **ide'alist** *n* a person who strives after the ideal; an impractical person; a person who holds the doctrine of idealism. **idealist'ic** *adj* relating to idealists or to idealism. **idealist'ically** *adv*. **ide'ality** /-al'i-ti/ *n* an ideal state; ability and disposition to form ideals of beauty and perfection. **ideāliza'tion** or **-s-** *n*. **ide'alize** or **-ise** *vt* to regard or represent as ideal. ◆ *vi* to form ideals; to think or work idealistically. **id'ealizer** or **-s-** *n*. **ide'alless** *adj* having no ideals. **ide'ally** *adv* in an ideal manner; in ideal circumstances; mentally. **ide'alogue** *n* a misspelling of **ideologue**.
□ **ideal crystal** *n* (*crystallog*) a crystal in which there are no imperfections or alien atoms. **ideal gas** *n* (*chem*) a hypothetical gas which obeys physical laws under all conditions (also **perfect gas**). **ideal point** *n* (*maths*) a hypothetical point where two parallel lines join at infinity. **ideal transducer** *n* (*elec eng*) a transducer which converts without loss of the power supplied to it.

idée /ē-dā'/ (*Fr*) *n* an idea.
□ **idée fixe** /fēks/ *n* a fixed idea, an obsession or monomania. **idée reçue** /rə-sü/ *n* an accepted idea; conventional outlook.

idem /ī'dem or id'em/ (*L*) *pronoun* the same (*abbrev* **id**).

■ **idem quod** the same as (*abbrev* **iq**). **idem sonans** /sō'nanz or so'näns/ sounding the same (used of a word in a legal document which, though misspelt, can be accepted as that for which it clearly stands).

idempotent /ī'dəm-pō-tənt or i-dem'pə-tənt/ (*maths*) *adj* and *n* (of) a quantity which does not change value when multiplied by itself (cf **nilpotent**). [L *idem* the same, and **potent¹**]
■ **ī'dempotency** (or /i-dem'/) *n*.

ident /ī'dent/ *n* a short film or sound sequence used in broadcasting to identify the channel or station. [Shortened from **identification**]

identic /ī-den'tik/ (*diplomacy*) *adj* identical, as in **identic note** or **identic action** an identical note sent by, or identical action taken by, two or more governments in dealing with another, or others. [Med L *identicus*, from L *idem* the same]

identical /ī-den'ti-kl/ *adj* the very same; not different; exactly alike; expressing or resulting in identity (*logic* or *maths*). [Med L *identicus*, from L *idem* the same]
■ **iden'tically** *adv*. **iden'ticalness** *n*.
□ **identical twins** *n pl* twins who are the same sex and look very alike, having developed from one zygote.

identify /ī-den'ti-fī/ *vt* (**iden'tifying**; **iden'tified**) to ascertain or establish the identity of; to assign (a plant, animal, etc) to a species; to associate closely (eg one concept with another, a person with a group, movement, etc); to regard (oneself) as in sympathy (with a group, movement, etc); to see clearly, pinpoint (a problem, etc). ◆ *vi* to be emotionally in sympathy (with eg a character in a book, play, etc). [LL *identificāre*, from *idem* the same, and *facere* to make]
■ **iden'tifīable** *adj*. **identifī'ably** *adv*. **identificā'tion** *n* the act of identifying, eg in establishing a person's name and individuality; the state of being identified; something which proves one's identity; a process by which a person adopts the behaviour, ideas, etc of someone else, particularly someone whom he or she admires (*psychol*). **iden'tifīer** *n* someone or something that identifies; a name or label used to identify a program or file (*comput*).
□ **identification card**, **disc**, etc *n* a card, disc, etc carried on one's person, with one's name, etc on it. **identification parade** *n* a group of people assembled by the police, from among whom a witness tries to identify a suspect (also **identity parade**).

identikit /ī-den'ti-kit/ (*orig (US)* **Identi-Kit**) *n* a device for building up a composite portrait from a large number of different features shown on transparent slips, by means of which a witness is assisted in producing a likeness of someone sought by the police. ◆ *adj* composed from identikit; formulaic and uninteresting (*inf*). [*identity* and **kit¹**]

identity /ī-den'ti-ti/ *n* the state of being the same; sameness; individuality; personality; who or what a person or thing is; (also **old identity**) a long-standing and well-known inhabitant of a place (*Aust* and *NZ inf*); an equation true for all values of the symbols involved (*maths*). ◆ *adj* relating to or involving identity or proof of identity. [LL *identitās*, -*ātis*, from L *idem* the same]
□ **identity bracelet** *n* a bracelet consisting of a flat metal bar, on which the owner's name may be engraved, joined to a chain. **identity card**, **disc**, etc *n* a card, disc, etc bearing the owner's or wearer's name, etc, used to establish his or her identity. **identity crisis** *n* psychological confusion caused by inability to reconcile differing elements in one's personality. **identity element** *n* (*maths*) an element (*e*) in a system of elements such that $e*x = x*e = x$ for every value of *x*, where * denotes a binary operation (in the ordinary number system, $e = 0$ for addition, and 1 for multiplication). **identity parade** *n* see **identification parade** under **identify**. **identity theft** *n* the practice of using another person's name or other personal information to carry out fraudulent monetary transactions.
■ **law** or **principle of identity** (*logic*) a law stating that A is A, that a thing is the same as itself.

ideo- /id- or īd-i-ō-/ *combining form* signifying the mind or mental activity, idea. [Fr *idéo-*, from Gr *ideā*]

ideogram /id'i-ō-gram or īd'/ or **ideograph** /-gräf/ *n* a character or symbol in writing that stands not for a word or sound but for a concept, idea or the thing itself; any sign or symbol used to represent a word. [Gr *ideā* idea, and *gramma* a drawing, or *graphein* to write]
■ **ideographic** /-graf'ik/ or **ideograph'ical** *adj*. **ideograph'ically** *adv*. **ideography** /-og'rə-fi/ *n*.

ideology /īd- or id-i-ol'ə-ji/ *n* the science of ideas, metaphysics; abstract speculation; visionary speculation; a body of ideas, *usu* political and/or economic, forming the basis of a national or sectarian policy; way of thinking. [Gr *ideā* idea, and *logos* discourse]
■ **ideolog'ic** /-loj'/ or **ideolog'ical** *adj* of or relating to an ideology; arising from or concerned with rival ideologies. **ideolog'ically** *adv*. **ideol'ogist** *n* a person occupied with ideas or an idea; a theorist or visionary; a supporter of a particular ideology. **id'eologue** *n* (*usu derog*) a doctrinaire adherent of an ideology.

ideomotor /id-i-ō-mō'tər/ adj describing or relating to a muscular action that is evoked by an idea. [**ideo-** and **motor**]

ideophone /id'i-ō-fōn/ n a word or phrase that is spoken but not written, usu one that is only fully comprehensible in the context in which it is spoken. [Gr ideā idea, and phōnē sound]

ideopraxist /id- or īd-i-ō-prak'sist/ n someone who is impelled to carry out an idea. [Gr ideā idea, and prāxis doing]

Ides /īdz/ (also without cap) n pl in ancient Rome, the 15th day of March, May, July, October, and the 13th of the other months. [Fr ides, from L īdūs (pl)]

id est /id est/ (L) that is, that is to say (abbrev **ie** or **i.e.**).

IDF abbrev : Israel Defence Forces.

idio- /id-i-ō-/ combining form signifying peculiarity to the individual, separateness, isolation. [Gr idios own, private]

idioblast /id' or ī'di-ə-blāst/ n a plant cell that differs from neighbouring cells in the same tissue. [Gr idios own, private, and blastos sprout]
■ **idioblast'ic** adj.

idiocy see under **idiot**.

idioglossia /id-i-ō-glos'i-ə/ n a condition in which pronunciation is so bad as to be quite unintelligible; a private language developed between two or more children, esp twins, etc. [Gr idios own, private, and glōssa tongue]

idiogram see **karyogram** under **kary-**.

idiograph /id'i-ō-gräf/ n a private mark; a trademark. [Gr idios own, private, and graphein to write]
■ **idiographic** /-graf'ik/ adj relating to an individual or to anything unique.

idiolect /id'i-ō-lekt/ n an individual's own distinctive form of speech. [Gr idios own, and **dialect**]
■ **idiolec'tal** or **idiolec'tic** adj.

idiom /id'i-əm/ n a mode of expression peculiar to a language; a distinctive expression whose meaning is not determinable from the meanings of the individual words; a form or variety of language; a dialect; a characteristic mode of artistic expression of a person, school, etc. [Gr idiōma, from idios own]
■ **idiomat'ic** or **idiomat'ical** adj. **idiomat'ically** adv. **idioticon** /-ot'i-kon/ n a vocabulary of a particular dialect or district.
□ **Idiom Neutral** n an international language that is a simplified version of Volapük.

idiomorphic /id-i-ō-mör'fik/ adj (of minerals) having the faces belonging to its crystalline form, as a mineral that has had free room to crystallize out. [Gr idios own, and morphē form]

idiopathic /id-i-ō-path'ik/ adj (of a state or experience) peculiar to the individual; (of a disease, etc) arising spontaneously from some unknown cause, primary. [Gr idios own, and pathos suffering]
■ **idiopath'ically** adv. **idiop'athy** n.

idiophone /id'i-ō-fōn/ (music) n a percussion instrument made entirely of a naturally resonant material. [Gr idios own, and phōnē voice]

idioplasm /id'i-ō-plazm/ n that part of the protoplasm that was once thought to determine hereditary character. [Gr idios own, private, and plasma mould]

idiorrhythmic or **idiorhythmic** /id-i-ō-ridh'mik or -rith'/ adj self-regulating; allowing each member to regulate his or her own life. [Gr idios own, and rhythmos order]

idiosyncrasy /id-i-ō-sing'krə-si/ n peculiarity of temperament or mental constitution; any characteristic of a person; hypersensitivity exhibited by an individual to a particular food, drug, etc (med). [Gr idios own, and synkrāsis a mixing together, from syn together, and krāsis a mixing]
■ **idiosyncratic** /-krat'ik/ or **idiosyncrat'ical** adj. **idiosyncrat'ically** adv.

idiot /id'i-ət or id'yət/ n a foolish or unwise person; a person having the lowest level of intellectual ability, ie having an intelligence quotient of less than 20 (now obs). ◆ adj afflicted with idiocy; idiotic. [Fr, from L idiōta, from Gr idiōtēs a private person, ordinary person, one who holds no public office or has no professional knowledge, from idios own, private]
■ **id'iocy** /-ə-si/ or (rare) **id'iotcy** n the state of being an idiot; imbecility; folly. **idiotic** /-ot'ik/ or **idiot'ical** adj relating to or like an idiot; foolish. **idiot'ically** adv. **id'iotish** adj idiotic. **id'iotism** n the state of being an idiot (archaic); an idiom (obs).
□ **idiot board** n a mechanical device used to prompt a speaker or performer on television, an autocue. **idiot box** n (sl) a television set. **idiot card** n a large card with words, etc, for the same purpose as an idiot board. **idiot light** n (N Am inf) a light that comes on, eg on the dashboard of a car, when a fault is detected. **id'iot-proof** adj (of a tool, device, machine, method of working, etc) so simple that even an idiot cannot make a mistake. **idiot tape** n (comput) a continuous

unjustified tape for controlling a typesetting or filmsetting machine, which contains only paragraph break signals and needs processing to suit a particular page size.

idiothermous /id-i-ō-thûr'məs/ adj warm-blooded, ie having a body temperature of one's own, independent of surroundings. [Gr idios own, and thermē heat]

idioticon see under **idiom**.

idiot savant /ē-dyō sa-vā or id'i-ət sav'ənt/ n a mentally subnormal individual who demonstrates remarkable talent in some restricted area such as memorizing or rapid calculation. [Fr, literally, knowing idiot]

idle /ī'dl/ adj unemployed; disliking work, lazy; not occupied; not in use or operation; useless; unimportant; unedifying; vain; baseless, without foundation; trifling. ◆ vt to pass or spend in idleness; to make (an engine, etc) idle. ◆ vi to be idle or unoccupied; (of machinery) to run without doing work; (of an engine) to run slowly when disengaged from the transmission. [OE īdel; Du ijdel, Ger eitel]
■ **i'dlehood** n (archaic). **i'dleness** n. **i'dler** n a person who wastes time or is reluctant to work; an idle pulley or idle wheel. **id'lesse** n (poetic) idleness. **i'dly** adv.
□ **i'dle-head'ed** adj foolish. **idle money** n (econ) that part of the total money supply that is neither being used to finance current transactions nor being lent out on the money market. **idle pulley** n a pulley which rotates freely and guides, or controls the tension of, a belt (also **i'dler**). **idle time** n a period or periods when a machine, eg a computer, is able to function properly but is not being used for productive work. **idle wheel** n a wheel placed between two others for transferring the motion from one to the other without changing the direction (also **i'dler**). **idle worms** n pl (inf) worms once jocularly supposed to be bred in the fingers of lazy maidens.

IDN abbrev : in Dei nomine (L), in the name of God.

Ido /ē'dō/ n an auxiliary international language developed (since 1907) from Esperanto. [Ido, offspring, from Gr -idos daughter of]
■ **Id'ist** or **I'doist** n.

idocrase /īd', id'ō-krās or -krāz/ n another name for the mineral vesuvianite. [Gr eidos form, and krāsis mixture]

idol /ī'dl/ n an image of a god; an object of worship; an object of love, admiration or honour in an extreme degree; an idolum; a fantasy, a phantom (archaic); an impostor, a sham (obs); an image or semblance (obs); a figure or effigy (obs); a false notion or other erroneous way of looking at things to which the mind is prone as classified by Bacon in Novum Organum (also **Idō'lon** or **Idō'lum**; pl **Idō'la**). [L īdōlum, from Gr eidōlon, from eidos form, from idein (aorist) to see]
■ **i'dolism** n the worship of idols; great reverence or admiration; a fallacy (Milton). **i'dolist** n. **idolizā'tion** or **-s-** n. **i'dolize** or **-ise** vt to worship as an idol; to admire or revere greatly. ◆ vi to worship idols. **i'dolizer** or **-s-** n. **idoloclast** /-dol'/ n a destroyer of idols.

idolater or **idolator** /ī-dol'ə-tər/ n (also fem **idol'atress**) a worshipper of idols; a besotted admirer. [Fr idolâtre, from Gr eidōlolatrēs, from eidōlon idol, and latreuein to worship]
■ **idol'atrize** or **-ise** vt and vi to worship as an idol; to adore. **idol'atrous** adj. **idol'atrously** adv. **idol'atry** n the worship of an image held to be the abode of a superhuman personality; excessive adoration of or devotion to someone or something.
■ **(on) this side of idolatry** stopping short of excessive adulation.

idolize, idoloclast see under **idol**.

idolum /ī-dō'ləm/ or **idolon** /ī-dō'lon/ n (pl **idō'la**) a mental image; a fallacy (logic). [L, from Gr eidolon phantom]

idoxuridine /ī-dok-sū'ri-dēn/ n a drug containing iodine used to treat some skin infections.

IDP (comput) abbrev : integrated data processing.

idyll or sometimes US **idyl** /id'il, īd'il or -əl/ n a short pictorial poem, chiefly on pastoral subjects; a story, episode, or scene of happy innocence or rustic simplicity; a work of art of this character in any medium. [L īdyllium, from Gr eidyllion, dimin of eidos image]
■ **idyll'ic** or (rare) **idyll'ian** adj. **idyll'ically** adv. **id'yllist** n.

IE abbrev : Indo-European.

ie or **i.e.** abbrev : id est (L), that is, that is to say.

-ie /-ē or -i/ (esp Aust) sfx variant of, and forming nouns in the same way as, **-y³**, as in nightie, hippie, movie, barbie, tinnie.

IEC abbrev : International Electrotechnical Commission.

IED abbrev : improvised explosive device.

IEE abbrev : Institution of Electrical Engineers.

IEGMP abbrev : Independent Expert Group on Mobile Phones.

-ier /-ēr or -i-ər/ sfx forming nouns denoting an occupation or interest in a specified area, as in bombardier, chocolatier.

IF abbrev : intermediate frequency (also **i.f.**).

if /if/ conj on condition that; provided that; supposing that; whether; though; whenever; in surprise or irritation, as in if it isn't John!, if that

isn't the doorbell again!◆ n a condition; a supposition; an uncertainty. [OE *gif*; cf Du *of*, ON *ef*]
- **iff'iness** *n*. **iff'y** *adj* (**iff'ier**; **iff'iest**) (*inf*) dubious, uncertain, risky. ■ **as if** as it would be if; even supposing that, although, accepting that; an interjection expressing incredulity. **if only** see under **only**. **if only to** if for no other reason than to. **ifs and ans** things that might have happened, but which did not. **ifs and buts** objections. **if you like** if you want, if you approve; to use another expression, to put it a different way.

IFA *abbrev* : Independent Financial Adviser.

IFAD or **Ifad** *abbrev* : International Fund for Agricultural Development.

IFC *abbrev* : International Finance Corporation.

-iferous see **-ferous**.

iff /*if*/ (*logic*) *conj* used to express *if and only if*.

iffy see under **if**.

-iform see **-form**.

IFP *abbrev* : Inkatha Freedom Party (in South Africa).

IFPI *abbrev* : International Federation of the Phonographic Industry.

IFR (*aeronautics*) *abbrev* : instrument flying regulations (or rules).

IFS *abbrev* : Institute for Fiscal Studies; Irish Free State (*hist*).

ifs *abbrev* : Institute of Financial Services.

iftar /*if'tər*/ (*Islam*) *n* the meal, taken after sunset, that breaks the daily fast during Ramadan. [Ar]

IG *abbrev* : Indo-Germanic.

igad /*i-gad'*/ same as **egad**.

igapó same as **gapó**.

igarapé /*ē-gä-rä-pā'*/ *n* a canoe waterway in Brazil. [Tupí]

Igbo /*ē'bō*/ *n* (also **Ibo** /*ē'bō*/) a people of E Nigeria; a member of this people (*pl* **Ig'bo** or **Ig'bos**); their language, widely used in S Nigeria. ◆ *adj* of or relating to the Igbo or their language.

IGC *abbrev* : intergovernmental conference (*esp* in the European Union).

IGCSE *abbrev* : International General Certificate of Secondary Education.

igloo /*ig'lōō*/ *n orig* a dome-shaped Inuit house made of blocks of hard snow; now *usu* a dwelling made of other materials; a dome-shaped place of storage or container for goods; a hollow in the snow made by a seal over its breathing hole in the ice. [Inuit *igdlu*, *iglu* house]

ign. *abbrev* : *ignotus* (*L*), unknown.

ignaro /*ig-nä'rō*/ or /*ē-nyä'rō*/ *n* (*pl* **igna'roes** or **igna'ros**) (*archaic*) an ignorant person. [Prob from Spenser's character (*Faerie Queene* I.8) whose only answer is 'He could not tell', from Ital *ignaro*, from L *ignārus* ignorant]

Ignatian /*ig-nā'shən*/ *adj* relating to or associated with St *Ignatius*, first-century bishop of Antioch (applied to the Epistles attributed to him), or Saint *Ignatius* Loyola, the Spanish founder of the Society of Jesus. ◆ *n* a Jesuit.
- ■ **St Ignatius's bean** see under **saint**.

igneous /*ig'ni-əs*/ *adj* of or like fire; formed by solidification of the earth's internal molten magma (*geol*). [L *igneus* fiery, from *ignis* fire]

ignescent /*ig-nes'ənt*/ *adj* emitting sparks when struck. ◆ *n* an ignescent substance. [L *ignēscēns, -entis*, prp of *ignēscere* to catch fire]

ignimbrite /*ig'nim-brīt*/ *n* a hard rock formed by fusion of the volcanic fragments and dust of a nuée ardente. [L *ignis* fire, from *imber, imbris* a shower of rain, and **-ite** (3)]

ignipotent /*ig-nip'ə-tənt*/ (*poetic*) *adj* presiding over fire. [L *ignipotens* powerful in fire, from *ignis* fire, and *potens* powerful]

ignis fatuus /*ig'nis fat'ū-əs* or *fat'ŭ-ŭs*/ *n* (*pl* **ignes fatui** /*ig'nēz fat'ū-ī* or *ig'nās fat'ŭ-ē*/) will-o'-the-wisp, the light produced by combustion of marsh-gas, which may lead a traveller into danger; any delusive ideal or hope that may lead one astray. [L *ignis* fire, and *fatuus* foolish]

ignite /*ig-nīt'*/ *vt* to set on fire; to heat to the point at which combustion occurs. ◆ *vi* to catch fire. [L *ignīre, ignītum* to set on fire, to make red-hot, from *ignis* fire]
- ■ **ignītabil'ity** or **ignītibil'ity** *n*. **ignīt'able** or **ignīt'ible** *adj*. **ignīt'er** *n* someone who or something that ignites, eg an apparatus for firing an explosive or explosive mixture. **ignition** /*-nish'ən*/ *n* an act of igniting; a means of igniting; the state of being ignited; the firing system of an internal-combustion engine. **ig'nitron** (or /*ig-nī'tron*/) *n* a device for conducting current in which an electrode dips into a pool of mercury and draws up an arc to start ionization.
- ❑ **ignition key** *n* in a motor vehicle, the key which is turned to operate the ignition system. **ignition temperature** *n* the temperature at which a substance will ignite in air.

ignoble /*ig-nō'bl*/ *adj* mean or worthless; unworthy; base; dishonourable; of low birth. [Fr, from L *ignōbilis*, from *in-* not, and (g)*nōbilis* noble]
- ■ **ignōbil'ity** or **ignō'bleness** *n*. **ignō'bly** *adv*.

ignominy /*ig'nə-min-i* or *-nō-*/, also (*Shakesp*) **ignomy** /*-nə-mi*/ *n* loss of good name; public disgrace; humiliation; dishonour, infamy. [L *ignōminia*, from *in-* not, and (g)*nōmen, -inis* name]
- ■ **ignomin'ious** *adj* disgraceful; humiliating. **ignomin'iously** *adv*. **ignomin'iousness** *n*.

ignoramus /*ig-no-rā'məs* or *-nə-*/ *n* (*pl* **ignorā'muses**) an ignorant person. [L *ignōrāmus* we are ignorant, in legal use, we ignore, take no notice, 1st pers pl pres indicative of *ignōrāre*]

ignorant /*ig'nə-rənt*/ *adj* lacking knowledge, ill-educated; uninformed; having no understanding or awareness (with *of*); showing or arising from lack of knowledge; discourteous, rude, ill-bred; keeping back knowledge (*Shakesp*); unknown (*obs*). ◆ *n* (*rare*) an ignorant person. [Fr, from L *ignōrāns, -antis*, prp of *ignōrāre*; see **ignore**]
- ■ **ig'norance** *n* lack of knowledge, awareness, education or enlightenment; the state of being ignorant. **ig'norantly** *adv*.

Ignorantine /*ig-nō-ran'tīn, -nō-* or *-tin*/ (*RC*) *n* a member of a religious congregation of men devoted to the instruction of the poor (inaccurately applied to *Brethren of the Christian Schools*).

ignoratio elenchi /*ig-nə-rā'shō il-eng'kī* or *ig-nō-rä'ti-ō e-leng'kē*/ (*logic*) *n* the fallacy of appearing to refute a proposition by proving a proposition that is irrelevant to the point at issue. [L, literally ignorance of proof, from Gr *elenchou agnoia*]

ignore /*ig-nōr'* or *-nör'*/ *vt* to disregard; to refuse to take notice of; to pay no heed or attention to; to waive or set aside. [L *ignōrāre* not to know, from *in-* not, and the root of (g)*nōscere*, to know]
- ■ **ignor'able** *adj*. **ignorā'tion** *n*. **ignor'er** *n*.

ignotum per ignotius /*ig-nō'təm pûr ig-nō'shyəs, -shəs* or *ig-nō'tŭm per ig-nō'ti-ŭs*/ (*L*) the unknown by means of the even less known, ie an explanation that is more complex and obscure than the thing to be explained.

iguana /*i-gwä'nə*/ *n* (*pl* **igua'nas** or **igua'na**) a large thick-tongued grey-green arboreal lizard of tropical America, having a row of spines along its back; loosely extended to others of the same family **Igua'nidae** (also **igua'nid**); in South Africa, a monitor lizard of the genus *Varanus*. [Sp, from Arawak *iwana*]

iguanodon /*i-gwä'nə-don*/ *n* a large, bipedal, bird-hipped herbivorous dinosaur of the Jurassic and Cretaceous periods, with teeth like those of the iguana. [**iguana**, and Gr *odous, odontos* tooth]

Iguvine /*ig'ū-vīn*/ *adj* Eugubine.

IHC or **IHS** *abbrev* : *Iesous* (*Gr*), Jesus, using Greek capital iota, capital eta, and capital sigma (written as C or S), the first two and last letters of the name (used as a Christian symbol).

ihram /*ē-räm'* or *ēhh'räm'*/ *n* the seamless white cotton garment worn by Muslim pilgrims to Mecca; the holy state it betokens or bestows. [Ar *ihrām*]

IHT *abbrev* : Inheritance Tax.

IIP *abbrev* : Office of International Information Programs (in the USA).

IIS *abbrev* : Institute of Information Scientists (now replaced by **CILIP**).

ijtihad /*ij-tə-häd'*/ *n* the use of reasoning in Islamic law. [Ar, exerting oneself]

ikat /*ik'at*/ *n* a technique of tie-dyeing yarn prior to weaving, resulting in a fabric with a geometric pattern of colours; this fabric. [Malay-Indonesian *mengikat* to tie]

IKBS (*comput*) *abbrev* : intelligent knowledge-based system.

ikebana /*ē'ke-bä'nə*/ *n* the Japanese art of flower arranging. [Jap, living flowers, arranged flowers]

ikon same as **icon**.

IL *abbrev* : Illinois (US state); Israel (IVR).

il- /*il-*/ *pfx* same as **in-**, the form used with words beginning with *l*, as in *illegible*.

ilang-ilang same as **ylang-ylang**.

ileac or **ileal** see under **ileum** and **ileus**.

ileo- /*il-*/ or /*īl-i-ō-*/ or **ile-** /*il-i-* or *īl-i-*/ combining form denoting the ileum.

ileum /*il'* or *īl'i-əm*/ *n* (*pl* **il'ea**) the lowest part of the small intestine, between the jejunum and the ileocaecal valve. [LL *īleum*, L *īlia* (pl) the groin, flank, intestines]
- ■ **il'eac** or **il'eal** *adj*. **ileitis** /*il-* or *īl-i-ī'tis*/ *n* inflammation of the ileum. **ileos'tomy** *n* a surgical operation in which the ileum is brought through an artificial opening in the abdominal wall through which the contents of the intestine may be discharged.

ileus /*il'* or *īl'i-əs*/ *n* (*pl* **il'euses**) obstruction of the intestine with severe pain, vomiting, etc. [L *īleos*, from Gr *īleos* or *eileos* colic]
- ■ **il'eac** or **il'eal** *adj*.

ilex /ī'leks/ *n* (*pl* **i'lexes** or **ilices** /ī'li-sēz/) the holm-oak (*Quercus ilex*); a shrub or tree of the genus *Ilex*, to which the holly belongs. [L *īlex* holm-oak]

ilia see **ilium**.

Iliac and **iliac** see under **Ilium** and **ilium**.

iliacus /i-lī'ə-kəs/ (*anat*) *n* a triangular muscle in the groin which, acting with the psoas muscle, flexes the thigh. [New L, from L *īlia* (pl); see **ileum**]

Iliad /il'i-ad or -əd/ *n* a Greek epic ascribed to Homer, on the siege of Troy; a long story or series of woes. [Gr *Ilias, -ados*, from *Ilios* or *Ilion* Ilium, Troy]

ilices see **ilex**.

ilio- /il-i-ō-/ or **ili-** /il-i-/ *combining form* denoting the ilium.

Ilium /il'i-əm or īl'/ *n* Troy. [L *Īlium*, from Gr *Ilion* Troy]
■ **Il'iac** or **Il'ian** *adj*.

ilium /īl' or il'i-əm/ *n* (*pl* **il'ia**) a wide bone that is fused with the ischium and pubis to form the hip (or innominate) bone; the haunch bone. [L *īlium* (in classical L only in pl *īlia*); see **ileum**]
■ **il'iac** *adj*.

ilk[1] /ilk/ *n* type, kind. ◆ *adj* (*Scot*) same. [OE *ilca* same]
■ **of that ilk** of that same, ie of the estate of the same name as the family (*Scot*); of that class, type or kind (*non-standard*).

ilk[2] /ilk/ (*Scot*) *adj* each, *usu* combined with the article as **ilk'a** /-ə or -ä/. [OE *ǣlc* each, and *ān* one]
■ **ilk'aday** *n, adj* and *adv* every day, every day but Sunday.

Ill. *abbrev* : Illinois (US state).

I'll /īl/ a contraction of **I will** or **I shall**.

ill /il/ *adj* (*compar* **worse**; *superl* **worst**) ailing, sick; evil, bad, wicked; producing evil; hurtful, harmful; unfortunate; unfavourable; difficult; reprehensible; incorrect, incompetent; (of temper, etc) peevish; grieved, distressed (*Scot*); severe (*Scot*). ◆ *adv* (*compar* **worse**; *superl* **worst**) badly; not well; not rightly; wrongly; unfavourably; amiss; with hardship; with difficulty. ◆ *n* evil; wickedness; misfortune; harm; ailment. [ON *illr* ; not connected with OE *yfel*, evil, but formerly confused with it, so that *ill* is often (esp in Scot) to be read where *evil* is written]
■ **ill'ness** *n* sickness; disease. **illth** *n* (*Ruskin*, etc) the contrary of wealth or wellbeing. **illy** /il'i/ *adv* (*rare*) ill.
□ **ill-advised'** *adj* imprudent; ill-judged. **ill-advis'edly** *adv*. **ill-affect'ed** *adj* not well-disposed. **ill-assort'ed** *adj* incompatible; not matching. **ill-behaved'** *adj* behaving badly, ill-mannered. **ill'-being** *n* the state of being poor or in bad health. **ill-beseem'ing** *adj* (*Shakesp*) unbecoming. **ill blood** or **ill feeling** *n* resentment, enmity. **ill-bod'ing** *adj* (*literary*) inauspicious. **ill-bred'** *adj* badly brought up or badly educated; uncivil. **ill breeding** *n*. **ill-condit'ioned** *adj* in bad condition; churlish (*archaic*). **ill-consid'ered** *adj* badly thought out; misconceived. **ill-deed'ly** *adj* (*Scot*; *archaic*) mischievous. **ill-defined'** *adj* having no clear outline; vague, imprecise, hazy. **ill-disposed'** *adj* unfriendly; unsympathetic. **ill-equipped'** *adj* insufficiently provided with tools, etc. **ill'-faced** (*Spenser* **ill-faste**) *adj* (*poetic*) ugly-faced. **ill fame** *n* disrepute. **ill-fa'ted** *adj* unlucky. **ill-fa'voured** (*Scot* **ill-faurd**) *adj* unattractive, ugly. **ill-fā'vouredly** *adv*. **ill-fā'vouredness** *n*. **ill feeling** *n* resentment, animosity, bad feeling. **ill fortune** *n* bad luck. **ill-found'ed** *adj* without foundation, baseless. **ill'-gotten** or (*archaic*) **ill'-got** *adj* procured by dishonest or unworthy means. **ill-haired'** *adj* (*Scot*) cross-grained. **ill-head'ed** (*Spenser* **ill-hedd'ed**) *adj* (*archaic*) not clear in the head. **ill health** *n* poor health. **ill-hu'mour** *n*. **ill-hu'moured** *adj* bad-tempered. **ill-hu'mouredly** *adv*. **ill-informed'** *adj* ignorant. **ill-judged'** *adj* foolish, unwise, ill-timed. **ill-look'ing** *adj* having an evil look; ugly. **ill luck** *n* bad luck. **ill-manned'** *adj* (*archaic*) provided with too few men. **ill-mann'ered** *adj* rude, discourteous; coarse, uncouth. **ill-matched'** *adj* not suited to one another; not matching well. **ill nature** *n*. **ill-na'tured** *adj* bad-tempered; spiteful, malevolent, mean. **ill-na'turedly** *adv*. **ill-na'turedness** *n*. **ill-off'** *adj* (*rare*) in bad circumstances, badly off. **ill-o'mened** *adj* unfortunate, unlucky; inauspicious, doomed. **ill-spent'** *adj* misspent, wasted, squandered. **ill-starred'** *adj* born under the influence of an unlucky star; unlucky, ill-fated. **ill success** *n* lack of success, failure. **ill temper** *n*. **ill-tem'pered** *adj* bad-tempered; morose; badly tempered, ill-mixed, distempered (*Shakesp*). **ill-tem'peredly** *adv*. **ill-timed'** *adj* said or done at an unsuitable time; inappropriate, ill-judged. **ill-treat'** *vt* to treat badly or cruelly; to abuse. **ill-treat'ment** *n*. **ill turn** *n* an act of unkindness or enmity. **ill-u'sage** or **ill-use'** *n*. **ill-use'** *vt* to ill-treat. **ill-used'** *adj* badly treated. **ill-versed'** *adj* having scanty knowledge or skill (with *in*). **ill-will'** *n* unkind feeling; enmity, hostility. **ill'-wisher** *n* a person who wishes harm to another. **ill-wrest'ing** *adj* (*Shakesp*) misinterpreting to disadvantage.

■ **go ill with** to result in danger or misfortune to. **ill at ease** uneasy; embarrassed. **ill become** to do someone no credit. **take it ill** to be offended. **with an ill grace** ungraciously.

illapse /i-laps'/ *n* a sliding in. ◆ *vi* to glide in. [L *illābī, illāpsus*, from *il-* (*in-*) in, and *lābī* to slip, to slide]

illaqueate /i-lak'wi-āt/ *vt* to ensnare. [L *illaqueāre, -ātum*, from *il-* (*in-*) into, and *laqueus* a noose]
■ **illaq'ueable** *adj*. **illaqueā'tion** *n*.

illation /i-lā'shən/ *n* the act of inferring from premises; inference; conclusion. [L *illātiō, -ōnis*, from *illātus*, used as pap of *inferre* to infer, from *il-* (*in-*) in, and *lātus* carried]
■ **illative** /il'ə-tiv or il-ā'tiv/ *adj* relating to, of the nature of, expressing, or introducing an inference; denoting a case in some Finno-Ugric languages expressing direction into or towards (*grammar*). ◆ *n* the illative case; a word in this case. **ill'atively** (or /-ā'/) *adv*.

illaudable /il-ö'də-bl/ *adj* not praiseworthy. [**il-** (**in-** (2))]
■ **illau'dably** *adv*.

illawarra /il-ə-wor'ə/ *n* a breed of shorthorn dairy cattle. [*Illawarra*, coastal district of E Australia]

Illecebrum /i-les'i-brəm/ *n* a genus of plants of one species found in Devon and Cornwall, for which the name **Illecebrā'ceae** is used for its family in some classification systems, whilst in others it is regarded as belonging to the Paronychiaceae, the Corregiolaceae or the Caryophyllaceae families. [Said to be from L *illecebra* allurement, 'as enticing the simpler into bogs and marshes']

illegal /il-ē'gl/ *adj* prohibited by law, unlawful. ◆ *n* a person who has entered a country illegally. [**il-** (**in-** (2))]
■ **illēgality** /-gal'i-ti/ *n* the quality or condition of being illegal. **illē'galize** or **-ise** *vt*. **illē'gally** *adv*.

illegible /il-ej'i-bl/ *adj* impossible or very difficult to read. [**il-** (**in-** (2))]
■ **illegibil'ity** or **illeg'ibleness** *n*. **illeg'ibly** *adv*.

illegitimate /il-i-jit'i-mit/ *adj* born of parents not married to each other at the time; (of a birth) happening outside marriage; unlawful, improper; not properly inferred or reasoned (*logic*); not recognized by authority or good usage. ◆ *n* a person born outside marriage. ◆ *vt* /-māt/ to pronounce or render illegitimate. [**il-** (**in-** (2))]
■ **illegit'imacy** /-mə-si/ or **illegit'imateness** *n*. **illegit'imately** *adv*. **illegitimā'tion** *n*.
□ **illegitimate pollination** *n* in dimorphic flowers, pollination of long style from short stamen, or short from long. **illegitimate recombination** *n* recombination, facilitated by the casual presence of duplicate sequences, between species whose DNA shows little or no homology.

illiad a Shakespearean form of **œillade**.

illiberal /il-ib'ə-rəl/ *adj* narrow-minded, intolerant or prejudiced; niggardly, ungenerous; narrow in opinion or culture, unenlightened. [**il-** (**in-** (2))]
■ **illiberality** /-al'i-ti/ *n*. **illib'eralize** or **-ise** *vt*. **illib'erally** *adv*.

illicit /il-is'it/ *adj* not allowable; unlawful; unlicensed. [L *illicitus*, from *il-* (*in-*) not, and *licitus*, pap of *licēre* to be allowed]
■ **illic'itly** *adv*. **illic'itness** *n*.
■ **illicit process of the major** or **minor** (*logic*) the fallacy of distributing the major or minor term in the conclusion when it is not distributed in the premise.

illimitable /il-im'i-tə-bl/ *adj* not able to be limited, infinite. [**il-** (**in-** (2))]
■ **illimitabil'ity** or **illim'itableness** *n*. **illim'itably** *adv*. **illimitā'tion** *n*. **illim'ited** *adj*.

illinium /i-lin'i-əm/ (*chem*) *n* former name for **promethium** (see under **Promethean**). [*Illinois* University, where its discovery was claimed]

illipe /il'i-pi/ or **illupi** /i-lŭ'pi/ *n* the mahwa tree (family Sapotaceae), producing **illipe nuts** and **illipe oil**. [Tamil *illuppai*]

illiquation /il-i-kwā'shən/ *n* the melting of one thing into another. [**il-** (**in-** (1))]

illiquid /il-ik'wid/ *adj* (of assets, etc) not readily converted into cash; deficient in liquid assets. [**il-** (**in-** (2))]
■ **illiquid'ity** *n*.

illision /i-lizh'ən/ *n* the act of striking against something. [L *illīsiō, -ōnis*, from *illīdere*, from *in* into, and *laedere* to strike]

illite /il'īt/ (*mineralogy*) *n* a white or pale clay mineral found in shales and sediments, having a similar structure to the micas. [US state of *Ill*inois, and **-ite** (3)]

illiterate /il-it'ə-rit/ *adj* unable to read and write; ignorant, uneducated; displaying ignorance of, or contravening the accepted standards of, writing and speech; ignorant in a particular field or subject, as in *mathematically illiterate*. ◆ *n* an illiterate person. [**il-** (**in-** (2))]
■ **illit'eracy** /-ə-si/ or **illit'erateness** *n*. **illit'erately** *adv*.

■ words derived from main entry word; □ compound words; ■ idioms and phrasal verbs

illocution /il-ə-kū'shən/ (*philos*) *n* an act which is performed by a speaker actually speaking the words, as an order or a promise (cf **perlocution**). [**il- (in-** (1))]
■ **illocu'tionary** *adj*.

illogical /il-oj'i-kəl/ *adj* contrary to the rules of logic; regardless or incapable of logic; senseless, unreasonable, crazy. [**il- (in-** (2))]
■ **illog'ic** *n*. **illogicality** /-kal'i-ti/ or **illog'icalness** *n*. **illog'ically** *adv*.

illude /il-ood' or -ūd'/ *vt* to trick. [L *illūdere*, from *in* on, and *lūdere*, *lūsum* to play]

illume /il-ūm' or -oom'/ *vt* a shortened poetic form of **illumine**.

illuminance /il-ū'mi-nəns or -oo'-/ (*phys*) *n* the luminous flux incident on a given surface per unit area, expressed in lux (also **illumina'tion**).

illuminate /il-ū'mi-nāt or -oo'-/ *vt* to light up; to make bright, fill with light; to enlighten, clarify; to illustrate, elucidate; to adorn with coloured lettering or illustrations. ◆ *adj* /-āt or -ət/ enlightened; claiming special enlightenment; made bright or clear with light. ◆ *n* a person who claims to have special enlightenment. [L *illūmināre*, *-ātum*, from *lumen* light]
■ **illu'minant** *adj* enlightening; giving off light. ◆ *n* a means of lighting. **illu'minating** *adj*. **illu'minatingly** *adv*. **illumina'tion** *n* the act or state of illuminating or being illuminated; an act of lighting up; a source of light; the strength or intensity of light; intellectual or spiritual enlightenment; clarification, elucidation; (in *pl*) a decorative display of lights; the adorning of books with coloured lettering or illustrations; such lettering or illustrations; illuminance (*phys*). **illu'minative** /-ə-tiv or -ā-tiv/ *adj*. **illu'minātor** *n* a decorator of manuscripts, etc; a person who provides clarification or enlightenment.

Illuminati /il-loo-mi-nä'tē/ *n pl* the enlightened, a name given to various religious sects, and *esp* to a society of German Free-thinkers at the end of the 18c; (without *cap*) people who claim to have special enlightenment, *esp* in philosophical or religious matters. [L, pl of *illuminato*, *-us*]
■ **illu'minism** *n* the doctrines or principles of the Illuminati; belief in or claim to an inward spiritual light. **illu'minist** *n*.

illumine /il-ū'min or -oo'-/ *vt* a literary form of **illuminate**. [L *illūmināre*, from *in* in, upon, and *lūmināre* to cast light]
■ **illu'minable** *adj*. **illu'miner** *n*.

illuminism, illuminist see under **Illuminati**.

illupi see **illipe**.

illusion /il-oo'zhən or -ū'-/ *n* deceptive appearance; an apparition; a false conception or notion; delusion; a false perception due to misinterpretation of stimuli from an object (*psychol*; cf **hallucination**); a very fine transparent gauze or tulle used for veils, dresses, trimmings, etc; a mocking (*obs*). [L *illūsio*, *-ōnis*, from *illūdere* to mock, make sport of]
■ **illu'sionary** or **illu'sional** *adj*. **illu'sionism** *n* the doctrine that the external world is illusory (*philos*); the production of illusion, *esp* the use of artistic techniques, such as perspective, etc, to produce an illusion of reality. **illu'sionist** *n* a believer in or practitioner of illusionism; a person who produces illusions, a conjurer, prestidigitator. **illusionis'tic** *adj*. **illu'sive** /-siv/ or **illu'sory** /-sər-i/ *adj* misleading by false appearances; false, deceptive, unreal. **illu'sively** or **illu'sorily** *adv*. **illu'siveness** or **illu'soriness** *n*.

illustrate /il'ə-strāt/ *vt* to elucidate and amplify by pictures, examples, etc; to provide or create pictures for (a book, etc); to demonstrate, show clearly; to make bright, adorn (*obs*); to enlighten (*archaic*); to show in a favourable light (*obs*); to give distinction or honour to (*obs*). ◆ *vi* to provide an example, etc. ◆ *adj* /-lus'/ (*archaic*) illustrious; renowned. [L *illūstrāre* to light up, prob from *lūx* light]
■ **ill'ustrated** (or /-us'/) *adj* having pictorial illustrations. ◆ *n* an illustrated periodical. **illustrā'tion** *n* the act of illustrating or process of being illustrated; something that serves to illustrate; exemplification; an example; a picture or diagram elucidating or accompanying text. **illustrā'tional, illustrative** /il'əs-trā-tiv, -trə- or il-us'trə-tiv/ or **illus'tratory** *adj* serving to clarify, explain or adorn. **ill'ustratively** (or /il-us'/) *adv*. **ill'ustrātor** *n*.

illustrious[1] /il-us'tri-əs/ *adj* distinguished, renowned; noble, glorious; luminous (*obs*). [L *illūstris* lustrous, or renowned; see also **illustrate**]
■ **illus'triously** *adv*. **illus'triousness** *n*.

illustrious[2] /il-us'tri-əs/ (*Shakesp*) *adj* dull (*perh* for *illustrous*, not lustrous).

illustrissimo /ēl-loo-strē'sē-mō/ (*Ital*) *adj* most illustrious.

illuvium /i-loo'vi-əm/ *n* material, including mineral salts, fine clay and silt particles, dissolved or suspended in water and transported from one layer of soil to a lower layer where they are deposited. [New L, from **il-** (*in-*) in, into, and *-luvium* (see **alluvium**), from L *luēre* to wash]
■ **illu'vial** *adj*. **illuviā'tion** *n* the process of deposition of illuvium.

Illyrian /i-lir'i-ən/ *adj* of or relating to *Illyria*, an ancient region to the east of the Adriatic Sea, its inhabitants, or their (*prob* Indo-European) language. ◆ *n* a native or citizen of Illyria; their language.

illywhacker /il'i-hwak-ər or il'i-wak-ər/ (*Aust sl*) *n* a con man, a trickster. [Origin unknown]

ilmenite /il'mə-nīt/ *n* a black mineral $FeTiO_3$, composed of iron, titanium and oxygen. [From the *Ilmen* Mountains in the Urals]

ILO *abbrev*: International Labour Organization, a United Nations body.

il penseroso /ēl pen-se-rō'zō/ *n* the pensive (or melancholy) man. [Ital *pensieroso*]

ILS *abbrev*: instrument landing system.

IM *abbrev*: nt messaging; Institute of Management (now known as **CMI**); intramuscular(ly) (also **i.m.**).

I'm /īm/ a contraction of **I am**.

im- /im-/ *pfx* same as **in-**, but the form used with words beginning with *b*, *m* or *p*, as in *imbalance*, *immodest*, *implant*.

IMA *abbrev*: Investment Management Association.

image /im'ij/ *n* a likeness or representation of a person or thing; a statue, an idol; a person or thing that closely resembles another; a representation in the mind, an idea; a mental picture or representation resulting from thought or memory rather than sensory perception (*psychol*); (a person who is) the epitome or personification of a quality; the figure of any object formed by rays of light reflected or refracted (*real* if the rays converge upon it, *virtual* if they appear to diverge from it) (*optics*); an analogous figure formed by other rays (*optics*); the element of a set that is associated with an element in a different set when one set is a function or transformation of the other (*maths*); a figure of speech, *esp* a metaphor or simile (*rhetoric*); the character or attributes of a person, institution, business, etc as regarded by the general public; a favourable self-representation created by a public figure, corporation, etc; an exact copy of an area of store held either in another storage device or in another area of the same device (*comput*). ◆ *vt* to form an image of; to form a likeness of in the mind; to mirror; to imagine; to portray; to typify; to produce a pictorial representation of (a part of the body) for diagnostic medical purposes. [OFr, from L *imāgō* image; cf *imitārī* to imitate]
■ **im'ageable** *adj*. **im'ageless** *adj*. **im'ager** *n* a device that records images. **imagery** /im'ij-ri or -ə-ri/ *n* the products of the imagination; mental pictures; figures of speech; images in general or collectively. **im'aging** *n* image formation. **im'agism** *n* (sometimes with *cap*) an early 20c school of poetry aiming at concentration, clear and simple language, and freedom of form and subject. **im'agist** *n* and *adj*. **imagist'ic** *adj*.
❑ **image breaker** *n* an iconoclast. **image converter** *n* an instrument that converts infrared or other invisible images into visible images. **image enhancement** *n* a method of enhancing the definition of an image using a computer program to convert shades of grey into either black or white. **image intensifier** *n* an electronic device for increasing the brightness of an optical image, such as the fluoroscopic image in X-ray examinations. **im'age-maker** *n* a person whose job is to enhance the public image of another person, *esp* a politician. **image orthicon** *n* a television camera tube that converts the images it receives into electronic impulses which are transmitted as television signals. **image printer** *n* a printer in which all the parts of a page, text and graphics, are processed before being sent to the optical and mechanical components of the printer. **image processing** *n* (*comput*) techniques for filtering, storing and retrieving graphics images. **image processor** *n*. **im'age-worship** *n*.

imaginal see under **imago**.

imagine /im-aj'in/ *vt* to form a mental image of; to conceive; to think; to believe falsely, fancy; to conjecture, suppose; to contrive or devise. ◆ *vi* to form mental images; to exercise imagination. [OFr *imaginer*, from L *imāginārī*, from *imāgō* an image]
■ **imag'inable** *adj*. **imag'inableness** *n*. **imag'inably** *adv*. **imag'inal** *adj* of or relating to an image. **imag'inarily** *adv*. **imag'inariness** *n*. **imag'inary** *adj* existing only in the imagination; not real, illusory; of or containing an imaginary number (*maths*); non-existent. **imagina'tion** *n* the act of imagining; the faculty of forming mental images; the creative power of the mind; resourcefulness, contrivance. **imag'inative** /-ə-tiv or -ā-tiv/ *adj* full of or endowed with imagination; done or created with, or showing, imagination. **imag'inatively** *adv*. **imag'inativeness** *n*. **imagineer'** *n* someone who designs and creates a new and imaginative product or piece of technology (*orig* a person doing such work at a Disney theme park). ◆ *vt* to design and create something new and imaginative. **imag'iner** *n*. **imag'ining** *n* (in *pl*) things imagined. **imag'inist** *n* (*Austen*) a person with an active imagination and a tendency to speculate or wonder.
❑ **imaginary numbers** or **quantities** *n pl* non-existent quantities involving the square roots of negative quantities.

imagism, **imagist** see under **image**.

imago /i-mā'gō/ or -mä'/ n (pl **imagines** /i-mā'jin-ēz, -mä'gin- or -mä'/, **ima'gos** or **ima'goes**) the last or perfect stage of an insect's development; an image or optical counterpart of a thing; an elaborated representation of an important or influential person (esp a parent) in an individual's life, persisting in the unconscious (psychol). [L imāgō, -inis image]
■ **imaginal** /i-maj'/ adj.

imam /i-mäm'/ or **imaum** /i-möm'/ n the officer who leads the devotions in a mosque; (with cap) a title for various Muslim potentates, founders and leaders. [Ar imām chief]
■ **imam'ate** n the (period of) office of an imam; the territory under the jurisdiction of an imam.

IMAP /ī'map/ abbrev : Internet Message Access Protocol.

IMarEST abbrev : Institute of Marine Engineering, Science and Technology (formerly known as **IMarE**, Institute of Marine Engineers).

imaret /i-mä'ret or im'ə-ret/ n (in Turkey) an inn or hospice for travellers. [Turk, from Ar 'imārah building]

Imari /ē-mä'ri/ (also without cap) adj and n (of) a type of Japanese porcelain, richly decorated in red, green and blue. [Imari, seaport in Japan from where such porcelain was exported]

imaum see **imam**.

IMAX® /ī'maks/ n a system of widescreen cinema presentation using 70 mm film projected on a large screen that fills the audience's field of vision. [From image and maximum]

imbalance /im-bal'əns/ n a lack of balance between corresponding things; lack of equilibrium. [**im-** (**in-** (2))]

imbar, etc see **embar**, etc.

imbark /im-bärk'/ (poetic) vt to enclose in bark. [**im-** (**in-** (1))]

imbase same as **embase**.

imbecile /im'bə- or im'bi-sēl, -sil, -sīl/ n a person of very low intelligence (from birth or an early age) whose mental ability is of a greater degree than idiocy, but who is incapable of managing adequately his or her own affairs (now obs); (loosely) a foolish, unwise or stupid person. ◆ adj extremely feeble-minded; foolish, fatuous. [Fr imbécille (now imbécile), from L imbēcillus weak, feeble]
■ **imbecilic** /im-bi-sil'ik/ adj. **imbecil'ity** n.

imbed same as **embed**.

imbibe /im-bīb'/ vt to drink; to absorb, drink in; to receive into the mind, assimilate. ◆ vi (often facetious) to drink alcohol. [L imbibere, from in in, into, and bibere to drink]
■ **imbīb'er** n. **imbibition** /im-bib-ish'ən/ n the absorption or adsorption of a liquid by a solid or gel (chem); the uptake of water by germinating seeds (bot); the transfer of dye to an absorbing layer, eg gelatine, to produce a dye image (image technol). **imbibit'ional** adj.

imborder see **emborder**.

imbosk and **imboss** see **emboss**².

imbrast (Spenser) same as **embraced** (see **embrace**¹).

imbrex /im'breks/ n (pl **im'brices** /-bri-sēz/) in Roman buildings, one of a series of usu curved tiles fixed over the joins of flat tiles. [L]

imbricate /im'bri-kāt/ vt to lay one overlapping another, as tiles on a roof. ◆ vi to be so placed. ◆ adj /-kət or -kāt/ (of fish scales, leaves, layers of tissue, teeth, etc) overlapping like roof tiles. [L imbricāre, -ātum to cover with overlapping tiles, from imbrex a pantile]
■ **im'bricately** adv. **imbrica'tion** n.

imbroccata /im-bro-kä'tə/ (fencing) n a thrust. [Ital]

imbroglio, also **embroglio** /im-brō'lyō/ n (pl **imbro'glios** or **embro'glios**) a confused mass or heap; an intricate or perplexing situation, a tangle; an embroilment; an ordered confusion (music). [Ital, confusion, from imbrogliare to confuse, embroil]

imbrue or **embrue** (Spenser **embrewe**) /im-broo'/ (literary) vt to wet or moisten; to soak; to drench; to stain or dye. [OFr embreuver, from bevre (Fr boire), from L bibere to drink]
■ **imbrue'ment** or **embrue'ment** n.

imbrute or **embrute** /im-broot'/ (archaic) vt or vi to degrade, or sink, to the state of a brute. [**im-** (**in-** (1))]

imbue /im-bū'/ vt to fill, permeate, inspire (eg the mind) (with with); to moisten; to tinge deeply. [OFr imbuer, from L imbuere, from in, and root of bibere to drink]

imburse /im-bûrs'/ (rare) vt to put in a purse or in one's purse; to pay, refund. [**im-** (**in-** (1)), and L bursa a purse]

IMechE abbrev : Institution of Mechanical Engineers.

IMEI abbrev : International Mobile Equipment Identity, an identification number for a mobile phone.

IMF abbrev : International Monetary Fund.

IMHO or **imho** abbrev : in my humble opinion.

imidazole /i-mid'ə-zōl/ (chem) n any of a group of heterocyclic compounds produced by substitution in a five-membered ring containing two nitrogen atoms on either side of a carbon atom (also called **glyoxaline**). [**imide** and **azole**]

imide /im'īd/ (chem) n any of a class of organic compounds formed from ammonia or a primary amine by replacing two hydrogen atoms by a metal or acid radical. [Alteration of **amide**]
■ **imid'ic** adj.

IMinE abbrev : Institution of Mining Engineers.

imine /im'īn or i-mīn'/ n a highly reactive nitrogen-containing organic substance having a carbon-to-nitrogen double bond. [Alteration of **amine**]

imipramine /i-mip'rə-mēn/ n an antidepressant drug. [From dimethylpropylamine]

imit. abbrev : imitation; imitative.

imitate /im'i-tāt/ vt to strive to be like or produce something like; to copy or take as a model; to mimic. [L imitārī, -ātus]
■ **imitability** /-ə-bil'i-ti/ or **im'itableness** n. **im'itable** adj. **im'itancy** n (Carlyle) the tendency to imitate. **im'itant** n (rare) an imitation. **imitā'tion** n the act of imitating; that which is produced as a copy, or counterfeit; a performance in mimicry; the repeating of the same passage, or the following of a passage with a similar one in one or more of the other parts (music). ◆ adj sham, counterfeit; produced as a substitute, by a cheaper method in cheaper materials, etc. **im'itātive** adj inclined to imitate; formed after a model; mimicking; (of words) onomatopoeic. **im'itātively** adv. **im'itātiveness** n. **im'itātor** n.

immaculate /im-ak'ū-lit/ adj clean, spotless; perfectly groomed; flawless; unstained; pure. [L immaculātus, from in- not, and maculāre to spot]
■ **immac'ulacy** n. **immac'ulately** adv. **immac'ulateness** n.
❑ **Immaculate Conception** n the Roman Catholic dogma that the Virgin Mary was conceived without original sin, first proclaimed as an article of faith in 1854 (not the same as the Virgin Birth).

immanacle /im-an'ə-kl or im-man'/ (Milton) vt to put in manacles, to restrain or confine. [**im-** (**in-** (1))]

immanation /im-ə-nā'shən/ n a flowing in. [L in in, and mānāre, -ātum to flow]

immane /im-ān'/ (archaic) adj huge; cruel, savage. [L immānis huge, savage]
■ **immane'ly** adv. **immanity** /im-an'i-ti/ n monstrous cruelty.

immanent /im'ə-nənt/ adj dwelling within; pervading; inherent. [L in in, and manēre to remain]
■ **imm'anence** or **imm'anency** n the pervasion of the universe by the intelligent and creative principle, a fundamental conception of pantheism. **immanental** /-ent'l/ adj. **imm'anentism** n belief in an immanent God. **imm'anentist** n.

immanity see under **immane**.

immantle /im-(m)an'tl/ vt to envelop in a mantle. [**im-** (**in-** (1))]

Immanuel see **Emmanuel**.

immarcescible /im-är-ses'i-bl/ adj unfading; imperishable. [L in- not, and marcēscere to languish]

immarginate /im-är'ji-nāt/ (bot) adj without a distinct margin. [**im-** (**in-** (2))]

immask /im-mäsk'/ (Shakesp) vt to mask or disguise. [**im-** (**in-** (1))]

immaterial /im-ə-tē'ri-əl/ adj not consisting of matter; incorporeal; unimportant, irrelevant. [**im-** (**in-** (2))]
■ **immatē'rialism** n (philos) the doctrine that there is no material substance, that material things do not exist outside the mind. **immatē'rialist** n. **immateriality** /-al'/ n the quality of being immaterial or of not consisting of matter. **immatē'rialize** or **-ise** vt to separate from matter, to make immaterial. **immatē'rially** adv.

immature /im-ə-tyŭr' or -choor'/ adj not fully grown; not yet ripe; not fully developed (mentally, physically, etc); (of behaviour, attitudes, etc) childish. [**im-** (**in-** (2))]
■ **immature'ly** adv. **immature'ness** or **immatur'ity** n.

immeasurable /im-ezh'ə-rə-bl/ adj too great to be measured. [**im-** (**in-** (2))]
■ **immeas'urableness** n. **immeas'urably** adv. **immeas'ured** adj (Spenser) immeasurable.

immediate /im-ē'di-it, -dyət, -dyit or -jət/ adj done or happening without delay; direct, with nothing intervening; next, nearest or closest; involving, or resulting from, nothing other than direct knowledge or intuitive understanding (philos). [**im-** (**in-** (2))]
■ **immē'diacy** n the state of being immediate; directness or freshness of appeal; an immediate problem, requirement, etc. **immē'diately** adv without delay; directly, with nothing intervening. ◆ conj as soon as. **immē'diateness** n. **immē'diatism** n the policy of action at once, esp (US hist) in abolition of slavery.

❑ **immediate access store** *n* (*comput*) the main memory of a computer, which holds programs and data during execution (*abbrev* **IAS**). **immediate constituent** *n* any meaningful constituent forming part of a linguistic construction which may be used to analyse structure, eg in a sentence the subject and predicate are immediate constituents.

immedicable /im-med'i-kə-bl or im-ed'/ (*formal*) *adj* incurable. [**im-** (**in-** (2))]

Immelmann turn /im'əl-mən tûrn/ (*aeronautics*) *n* a manoeuvre involving a half loop and a half roll, carried out to achieve greater height and reverse the direction of flight. [Max *Immelmann* (1890–1916), German aviator]

immemorial /im-i-mō'ri-əl or -mö'/ *adj* ancient beyond the reach of memory. [**im-** (**in-** (2))]
■ **immemō'rially** *adv*.

immense /i-mens'/ *adj* vast in extent or degree; very large, enormous; fine, very good (*sl*). [Fr, from L *immēnsus*, from *in-* not, and *mēnsus*, pap of *metīrī* to measure]
■ **immense'ly** *adv*. **immense'ness** or **immens'ity** *n* a measureless expanse; vastness.

immensurable /im-men'shūr-ə-bl, im-en', -syūr- or -syər-/ *adj* too great to be measured, immeasurable. [**im-** (**in-** (2))]
■ **immensurabil'ity** *n*.

immerge /im-mûrj' or im-ûrj'/ (*rare*) *vt* and *vi* to dip or plunge into liquid, to immerse. [**im-** (**in-** (1))]

immeritous /im-mer'it-əs/ (*archaic*) *adj* undeserving. [L *immeritus*, from *in-* not, and *meritus* deserving]

immerse /im-ûrs'/ *vt* to dip or plunge under the surface of a liquid; to baptize by immersion; to engage or involve deeply, to engross. [See **immerge**]
■ **immersed'** *adj* embedded in another part (*bot* or *zool*); growing entirely submerged in water (*bot*). **immer'sible** *adj*. **immer'sion** *n* the act of immersing; the process or state of being immersed; deep absorption or involvement; baptism by immersing all or part of a person's body in water; the disappearance of a celestial body, eg in eclipse or occultation (*astron*); a method of teaching a foreign language by giving the learner intensive practice in a situation in which all communication is in the language concerned; an immersion heater (*inf*). **immer'sionism** *n*. **immer'sionist** *n* a person who favours or practises baptism by immersion. **immer'sive** *adj*.
❑ **immersion foot** *n* another name for **trench foot** (see under **trench**). **immersion heater** *n* an electrical apparatus directly immersed in the liquid, used for heating water. **immersion lens** *n* a microscope object-glass that works with a drop of oil or water between it and the cover glass.

immesh see **enmesh**.

immethodical /i-mi-thod'ik-əl/ *adj* without method or order, disorganized; irregular. [**im-** (**in-** (2))]
■ **immethod'ically** *adv*.

immew see **emmew**.

immigrate /im'i-grāt/ *vi* to migrate into a country with the intention of settling in it. [L *immigrāre*, from *in* into, and *migrāre*, *-ātum* to remove]
■ **imm'igrant** *n* a person who immigrates; an animal or plant living or growing in an area to which it has migrated. **immigrā'tion** *n* the act or process of immigrating; the immigration checkpoint at an airport, port, etc (*inf*).

imminent /im'i-nənt/ *adj* impending, approaching, forthcoming; looming, threatening; jutting, overhanging (*obs*). [L *imminēns*, *-entis*, from *in* upon, and *minēre* to project, jut]
■ **imm'inence** or **imminency**; impending evil (*Shakesp*). **imm'inency** *n* the state or fact of being imminent. **imm'inently** *adv*.

immingle /im-ming'gl or im-ing'/ (*rare*) *vt* and *vi* to mingle together, to mix. [**im-** (**in-** (1))]

imminute /im'i-nūt/ (*archaic*) *adj* lessened. [L *imminutus*, pap of *imminuere*, from *in-* (intensive), and *minuere* to lessen]
■ **imminū'tion** *n* lessening.

immiscible /im-mis'i-bl or im-is'/ *adj* not capable of being mixed, eg as oil and water. [**im-** (**in-** (2))]
■ **immiscibil'ity** *n*. **immisc'ibly** *adv*.

immiseration /im-iz-ə-rā'shən/ *n* progressive impoverishment or degradation (also **immiserīzā'tion** or **-s-**). [**im-** (**in-**(1)), and *misery*]
■ **immis'erize** or **-ise** *vt*.

immit /im-mit' or im-it'/ (now *obs*) *vt* (**immitt'ing**; **immitt'ed**) to insert, infuse; to introduce; to inject. [L *immittere*, from *in* into, and *mittere*, *missum* to send]
■ **immission** /-ish'ən/ *n*.

immitigable /im-it'i-gə-bl/ *adj* incapable of being mitigated. [**im-** (**in-** (2))]
■ **immitigabil'ity** *n*. **immit'igably** *adv*.

immix /im-miks' or im-iks'/ (*archaic*) *vt* to mix in (with *with*); to commingle. [**im-** (**in-** (1))]
■ **immix'ture** *n*.

immobile /im-ō'bīl, -bēl or (*US*) -bil/ *adj* immovable; not readily moved; unable to move; motionless; stationary. [**im-** (**in-** (2))]
■ **immob'ilism** *n* a political policy characterized by extreme lack of action. **immobil'ity** *n*. **immobilīzā'tion** or **-s-** *n*. **immob'ilize** or **-ise** *vt* to render immobile; to put or keep out of action or circulation. **immob'ilizer** or **-s-** *n* anything that renders something immobile, *esp* a device that prevents a motor vehicle from being started without the proper key.

immoderate /im-od'ə-rit/ *adj* excessive; extravagant; unrestrained. [**im-** (**in-** (2))]
■ **immod'erately** *adv*. **immoderā'tion**, **immod'erateness** or **immod'eracy** *n*.

immodest /im-od'ist/ *adj* shamelessly indecent, improper; too self-assertive, boastful. [**im-** (**in-** (2))]
■ **immod'estly** *adv*. **immod'esty** *n*.

immolate /im'ō-lāt or im'ə-lāt/ *vt* to offer or kill as a sacrifice; to give up or sacrifice (something highly valued) in exchange for, or for the sake of, something else. [L *immolāre*, *-ātum* to sprinkle meal (on a victim), hence, to sacrifice, from *in* upon, and *mola* meal]
■ **immolā'tion** *n*. **imm'olātor** *n*.

immoment /im-mō'mənt/ (*Shakesp*) *adj* of no value, trifling. [**im-** (**in-** (2))]
■ **immome'ntous** *adj*.

immoral /im-or'əl/ *adj* inconsistent with accepted moral principles or standards, wrong; evil, unscrupulous; sexually improper; promiscuous, licentious, dissolute. [**im-** (**in-** (2))]
■ **immor'alism** *n* the denial or rejection of morality. **immor'alist** *n* a person who practises or advocates immorality. **immorality** /im-or- or im-ər-al'i-ti/ *n* the quality or state of being immoral, *esp* promiscuity or licentiousness; an immoral act or practice. **immor'ally** *adv*.

immortal /im-ör'tl/ *adj* exempt from death; living in perpetuity without fading or decaying; imperishable; never to be forgotten, famous or remembered throughout time. ◆ *n* a being who will never cease to exist; a person whose greatness will never fade, or whose genius will be revered for all time; (in *pl*; often with *cap*) a god, *esp* of the ancient Greeks and Romans; (in *pl*; *usu* with *cap*) the forty members of the French Academy. [**im-** (**in-** (2))]
■ **immortality** /im-ör- or im-ər-tal'i-ti/ *n*. **immortalīzā'tion** or **-s-** *n*. **immor'talize** or **-ise** *vt* to make immortal; to give everlasting fame to. **immor'tally** *adv*.
■ **the Immortal Memory** a toast in memory of the Scottish poet, Robert Burns, *usu* on the anniversary of his birth, 25 January.

immortelle /im-ör-tel'/ *n* an everlasting flower; a china replica of flowers, as a graveyard monument. [Fr (*fleur*) *immortelle* immortal (flower)]

immotile /im-ō'tīl, im-mō' or (*US*) -til/ *adj* (of living organisms) not motile. [**im-** (**in-** (2))]
■ **immotil'ity** *n*.

immovable /im-oo'və-bl/ *adj* impossible to move; steadfast; unyielding; impassive; motionless; unalterable; (commonly **immove'able**) not liable to be removed (*law*); real, not personal (*law*). ◆ *n* (*law*; *usu* in *pl* **immove'ables**) immoveable property. [**im-** (**in-** (2))]
■ **immov'ableness** or **immovabil'ity** *n*. **immov'ably** *adv*.

immune /im-ūn'/ *adj* exempt (with *from*); free from obligation (with *from*); not liable to danger, protected (with *to*); protected against a disease or infection because of the presence of specific antibodies which act against the antigens concerned; unaffected, not susceptible (with *to*). ◆ *n* someone who, or something that, is immune. [L *immūnis*, from *in-* not, and *mūnis* serving]
■ **immunifa'cient** *adj* producing immunity. **immun'ity** *n* the condition of being immune. **immunīzā'tion** or **-s-** *n*. **imm'unize** or **-ise** *vt* to render immune, *esp* to make immune from a disease by injecting or exposing to disease-germs or their poisons (either active or rendered harmless). **imm'unizer** or **-s-** *n*. **immunolog'ic** or **immunolog'ical** *adj*. **immunolog'ically** *adv*. **immunol'ogist** *n*. **immunol'ogy** *n* the scientific study of immunity and the defence mechanisms of the body.
❑ **immune body** *n* an antibody. **immune response** *n* the production of antibodies in the body as a defensive response to the presence of antigens, foreign tissue, etc. **immune system** *n* the process within an organism whereby antigenic or foreign matter is distinguished and neutralized through antibody or cytotoxic action. **immunological memory** *n* the ability of the immune system to mount a larger and more rapid response to an antigen that has already been encountered, mediated by long-lived cells stimulated on first exposure to the antigen. **immunological tolerance** *n* the failure of the body to recognize antigens with consequent absence of antibody production.

immuno- /i-mū-no- or im-/ *combining form* denoting immune, immunity. [**immune**]

■ **immunoass'ay** (or /-ə-sā'/) *n* any of the various methods used to determine levels of antibody and antigen in a tissue. **immunoblot'** *n* a technique used to transfer the pattern of proteins separated by electrophoresis to a medium in which they can be further analysed by immunological procedures (also called **western blotting**). **immunochem'ical** *adj*. **immunochem'ically** *adv*. **immunochem'istry** *n* the chemistry of antibodies, antibody reactions, etc. **immunocom'petence** *n* the capacity of the immune system to distinguish and neutralize antigenic or foreign matter. **immunocom'petent** *adj*. **immunocom'promised** *adj* (*med*) having an impaired immune system. **immunocytochem'ical** *adj*. **immunocytochem'ically** *adv*. **immunocytochem'istry** *n* the study of the chemical aspects of cellular immunity. **immunodefi'ciency** *n* deficiency in immune response due to depletion or inactivity of lymphoid cells. **immunodiagnos'tics** *n sing* diagnostics relating to immunology. **immunoelectrophorē'sis** *n* identification of antigens in serum by electrophoresis. **immunoelectrophoret'ically** *adv*. **immunofluoresc'ence** *n* a technique used to detect antibodies or antigens in which the antibodies or antigens are marked with a fluorescent dye. **immū'nogen** *n* same as **antigen**. **immunogenet'ics** *n sing* the study of inherited characteristics of immunity. **immunogen'ic** *adj* capable of producing an immune response. **immunogenic'ity** *n*. **immunoglō'bulin** *n* one of a group of highly variable antibody proteins in humans. **immunopatholog'ical** *adj*. **immunopatholog'ically** *adv*. **immunopathol'ogy** *n* the study of immune factors associated with disease. **immunophorē'sis** *n* a technique for identifying an (unknown) antigen or testing for a specific antibody in serum, which makes use of the precipitin reaction of known antibodies. **immunosuppress'** *vt* and *vi*. **immunosuppress'ant** *n* a drug which inhibits the body's immune response, used to ensure that transplanted organs are not rejected, and in the treatment of various auto-immune diseases. **immunosuppress'ion** *n*. **immunosuppress'ive** *adj* and *n*. **immunother'apy** *n* the treatment or prevention of disease, *esp* cancer, by the use of agents which stimulate the patient's own natural immunity. **immunotox'ic** *adj*. **immunotox'in** *n* a toxin with immunosuppressive effects. **immunotransfū'sion** *n* the transfusion of blood or plasma containing in high concentration the appropriate antibodies for the infection from which the patient is suffering.

immure /im-ūr'/ *vt* to enclose as if within walls, to wall in; to shut up; to imprison; to confine. ◆ *n* (*obs; Shakesp* **emure'**) an enclosing wall. [L *in* in, and *mūrus* a wall]
■ **immure'ment** *n*.

immutable /im-ū'tə-bl/ *adj* unchangeable; changeless. [**im- (in-** (2))]
■ **immūtabil'ity** or **immūt'ableness** *n*. **immūt'ably** *adv*.

IMO *abbrev*: in my opinion (also **imo**); International Maritime Organization; International Miners' Organization.

iMode® /ī'mōd/ *n* a technology enabling the Internet to be accessed from cellular phones.

Imp. *abbrev*: *Imperator* (L), Emperor; *Imperatrix* (L), Empress; Imperial.

imp /imp/ *n* a mischievous child; a little devil or wicked spirit; a shoot, scion, graft (*obs*); a scion of a family (*obs*). ◆ *vt* to graft, engraft (*obs*); to engraft (a hawk or falcon's wing or tail) with new feathers in order to repair broken feathers or improve flight (*falconry*). [OE *impa*, from LL *impotus* a graft, from Gr *emphytos* engrafted]
■ **imp'ish** *adj* like or characteristic of an imp, teasingly mischievous. **imp'ishly** *adv*. **imp'ishness** *n*.

impacable /im'pa-kə-bl/ (*rare*) *adj* not to be quieted or appeased, implacable. [L *in-* not, and *pācāre* to quiet]

impact /im-pakt'/ *n* the blow of a body in motion impinging on another body; the impulse resulting from collision; the impulse resulting from a new idea or theory; strong effect, influence, eg (*marketing*) the effect of an advertisement, promotion, etc on a potential customer. ◆ *vt* to drive (an object) with force into something else; to drive or press (two objects) together with force; to have an impact or effect on. ◆ *vi* to come into contact forcefully. [L *impactus*, pap of *impingere*; see **impinge**]
■ **impact'ful** *adj* creating an impact; effective or impressive. **impac'tion** *n* the act of pressing together, or of fixing a substance tightly in a body cavity; the condition so produced. **impact'ite** *n* a glassy type of rock formed as a result of the impact (and heat) of a meteorite on the earth's surface. **impact'ive** *adj*. **impact'or** *n* a spacecraft designed to collide into the surface of a celestial body. ❑ **impact adhesive** *n* a glue that forms a bond when two surfaces, each coated with the adhesive, are brought together. **impacted faeces** *n pl* faeces that are so hard or dry that they cannot be evacuated through the anus. **impacted fracture** see under **fracture**. **impacted tooth** *n* a tooth, *esp* a wisdom tooth, wedged between the jawbone and another tooth and thus unable to erupt through the gum. **impact parameter** *n* (*nuclear phys*) the distance at which two

particles which collide would have passed if no interaction had occurred between them. **impact printer** *n* any device in which printed characters are formed on the paper by means of a hammer striking the ribbon, eg dot matrix printers, line printers.

impaint /im-pānt'/ (*Shakesp*) *vt* to paint or depict. [**im- (in-** (1))]

impair¹ /im-pār'/ *vt* to diminish in quantity, value, or strength; to injure, damage or spoil; to weaken. ◆ *vi* (*obs; Spenser* **empaire'**, **empare'** or **empayre'**) to become worse; to decay. [OFr *empeirer* (Fr *empirer*), from L *im-* (intensive), and *pējōrāre* to make worse, from *pējor* worse]
■ **impaired'** *adj* damaged, weakened; (of a driver or driving) under the influence of drugs or alcohol (*Can*). **impair'er** *n*. **impair'ing** *n*. **impair'ment** *n*.

impair² /im-pār'/ (*Shakesp*) *adj* perhaps unsuitable, unfit, inferior. [Fr, from L *impār*, from *in-* not, and *par* equal]

impala /im-pä'lə/ *n* (*pl* **impa'la** or **impa'las**) an African antelope (*Aepyceros melampus*), with horns curved in the shape of a lyre and capable of prodigious leaps. [Zulu *i-mpāla*]

impale or **empale** /im-pāl'/ *vt* to pierce with something pointed, eg a sharp stake; to fix on a sharp stake thrust through the body; to transfix; to juxtapose (two coats of arms) on a single vertically divided shield (*heraldry*); to shut or fence in, to surround with pales (*archaic*). [Fr *empaler*, from L *in* in, and *pālus* a stake]
■ **impale'ment** or **empale'ment** *n* the act or punishment of impaling; the marshalling side by side of two escutcheons combined in one (*heraldry*); an enclosed space (*archaic*). **impal'er** or **empal'er** *n*.

impalpable /im-pal'pə-bl/ *adj* not perceivable or detectable by touch; not capable of being comprehended or grasped; extremely fine-grained. [**im- (in-** (2))]
■ **impalpabil'ity** *n*. **impal'pably** *adv*.

impaludism /im-pal'ū-di-zm/ *n* a disease carried by insects, affecting inhabitants of marshy areas. [L *in* in, and *palus*, *palūdis* a marsh]

impanation /im-pə-nā'shən or -pā-/ *n* a local union of the body of Christ with the consecrated bread in the Eucharist; later specially used of Luther's consubstantiation. [From LL *impānāre*, *-ātum*, from *in* in, and *pānis* bread]
■ **impanate** /im-pān'āt or im'pən-āt/ *adj* embodied in bread.

impanel and **impannel** see **empanel**.

impar- /im-par-/ or **impari-** /im-par-i-/ *combining form* signifying unequal. [L *impār*, from *in-* not, and *pār* equal]
■ **imparidigitate** /-dij'i-tāt/ *adj* (*zool*) having an odd number of fingers or toes on each limb. **imparipinn'ate** *adj* (*bot*) (of pinnate leaves) with a terminal unpaired leaflet. **imparisyllab'ic** *adj* (of a noun or verb) having differing numbers of syllables in different inflected forms. **imparity** /im-par'i-ti/ *n* inequality, disparity.

imparadise, also **emparadise** /im-par'ə-dīs/ (chiefly *literary*) *vt* to transport to a state of blissful happiness, as if in paradise; to enrapture; to make a paradise of (a place). [**im- (in-** (1))]

impark /im-pärk'/ (*archaic*) *vt* to enclose in, or as, a park. [**im- (in-** (1))]
■ **imparkā'tion** *n*.

imparl or **emparl** /im-pärl'/ (*obs except law*) *vi* to hold a consultation; to parley. ◆ *vt* to talk over. [Obs Fr *emparler*, from *em-* (L *in-*), and *parler* to talk]
■ **imparl'ance** (*Spenser* **emparl'aunce**) *n* parleying, conference; delay in pleading, ostensibly for amicable adjustment.

impart or (*Spenser*) **empart** /im-pärt'/ *vt* to give (something abstract); to communicate, make known, relate. [OFr *empartir*, from L *impartīre*, from *in* on, and *pars*, *partis* a part]
■ **impart'able** *adj*. **impartā'tion** *n*. **impart'er** *n*. **impart'ment** *n*.

impartial /im-pär'shl/ *adj* not favouring one more than another, unbiased; fair, just; partial (*Shakesp; non-standard*). [**im- (in-** (2))]
■ **impartiality** /-shi-al'i-ti/ or **impar'tialness** *n*. **impar'tially** *adv*.

impartible /im-pär'ti-bl/ (now chiefly *law*) *adj* not partible; incapable of, or not subject to, partition; indivisible. [**im- (in-** (2))]
■ **impartibil'ity** *n*. **impart'ibly** *adv*.

impassable /im-pä'sə-bl/ *adj* not capable of being passed, traversed or travelled through. [**im- (in-** (2))]
■ **impassabil'ity** or **impass'ableness** *n*. **impass'ably** *adv*.

impasse /am-pas' or ĕ-pas/ *n* a situation from which further progress is impossible; a deadlock, stalemate. [Fr, from *in* in, and *passer* to pass]

impassible /im-pas'i-bl/ (*rare*) *adj* incapable of suffering or experiencing pain, unfeeling; incapable of emotion, impassive. [Church L *impassibilis*, from *in-* not, and *patī*, *passus* to suffer]
■ **impassibil'ity** or **impass'ibleness** *n*. **impass'ibly** *adv*.

impassion /im-pash'ən/ *vt* to arouse the passions of; to make passionate. [Ital *impassionare*, from L *in* in, and *passiō*, *-ōnis* passion]
■ **impass'ionate** (*Spenser* **empass'ionate**) *adj* impassioned; dispassionate (*rare*). **impass'ioned** (*Spenser* **empass'ioned**) *adj* moved by or filled with passion; fiery; ardent. **impass'ionedly** *adv*. **impass'ionedness** *n*.

impassive /im-pas'iv/ adj not showing feeling or emotion; imperturbable; not capable of feeling or emotion; having no sensation. [im- (in- (2))]
■ **impass'ively** adv. **impass'iveness** or **impassiv'ity** n.

impaste /im-pāst'/ vt to lay paint or colours thickly on. [LL impastāre, from in into, and pasta paste]
■ **impastation** /im-pas-tā'shən/ n. **impāst'ed** adj. **impasto** /im-päs'tō/ n (pl **impast'os**) in painting, paint or pigment applied thickly, esp when used to achieve surface texture; the technique of laying paint on thickly in this way. **impast'oed** or **impast'o'd** adj.

impatiens /im-pā'shi-enz/ n (pl **impā'tiens**) any of various plants of the genus Impatiens, including busy lizzie, touch-me-not and balsam. [L, impatient, because the ripe seed capsules burst at a touch]

impatient /im-pā'shənt/ adj not able to endure or to wait; fretful; restless; intolerant (of). [L impatiēns, -entis impatient, from in- not, and patiēns patient]
■ **impā'tience** n. **impā'tiently** adv.

impave /im-pāv'/ (Wordsworth) vt to depict or set in pavement, as mosaic. [im- (in- (1))]

impawn /im-pön'/ (archaic) vt to put in pawn; to pledge; to risk. [im- (in- (1))]

impeach or (Spenser) **empeach** /im-pēch'/ vt to disparage; to find fault with; to call in question or cast doubt on; to arraign (esp when a lower legislative house charges a high officer with grave offences before the upper house as judges); to turn king's evidence against (law); to bring an accusation against; to charge (a public official) with an offence committed in office (esp N Am); to hinder, impede, prevent (obs); to impair (obs). ◆n hindrance, prevention (obs); damage, impairment, detriment (obs); calling in question (Shakesp). [OFr empech(i)er to hinder (Fr empêcher), from L impedicāre to fetter]
■ **impeach'able** adj. **impeach'er** n. **impeach'ment** n.

impearl /im-pûrl'/ (poetic) vt to decorate with, or as if with, pearls; to make pearl-like. [im- (in- (1))]

impeccable /im-pek'ə-bl/ adj faultless; without flaw or error; incapable of sin. [im- (in- (2))]
■ **impeccabil'ity** n. **impecc'ably** adv. **impecc'ancy** n. **impecc'ant** adj free from sin.

impecunious /im-pi-kū'ni-əs or -nyəs/ adj without money, penniless; short of money. [im- (in- (2))]
■ **impecunios'ity** or **impecun'iousness** n. **impecun'iously** adv.

impede /im-pēd'/ vt to hinder or obstruct. [L impedīre, from in in, and pēs, pedis a foot]
■ **impe'dance** n hindrance; the measurement, in ohms, of opposition to an alternating current (elec); a similar measurement of resistance to vibrations of alternating effects as in sound (acoustic impedance) or as caused by applied forces (mechanical impedance). **impediment** /-ped'/ n an obstacle; a defect preventing fluent speech. **impediment'a** n pl (L impedīmenta) military baggage; baggage or luggage generally; encumbrances. **impedimen'tal** or **imped'itive** adj hindering. **impē'ding** adj. **impē'dingly** adv.

impel /im-pel'/ vt (**impell'ing**; **impelled'**) to urge forward; to excite to action; to instigate. [L impellere, impulsum, from in on, and pellere to drive]
■ **impell'ent** adj impelling or driving on. ◆n an impelling agent or power. **impell'er** n someone who, or something that, impels; a rotor for transmitting motion in a compressor, centrifugal pump, etc.

impend /im-pend'/ vi to be about to happen; to threaten, loom; to overhang (obs). [L impendēre, from in on, and pendēre to hang]
■ **impend'ence** or **impend'ency** n (obs). **impend'ing** or (now rare) **impend'ent** adj.

impenetrable /im-pen'i-trə-bl/ adj incapable of being penetrated; impervious; inscrutable; occupying space exclusively (phys). [im- (in- (2))]
■ **impenetrabil'ity** n. **impen'etrably** adv.

impenetrate /im-pen'i-trāt/ vt to permeate; to penetrate thoroughly. [im- (in- (1))]
■ **impenetrā'tion** n.

impenitent /im-pen'i-tənt/ adj not repenting. ◆n someone who does not repent; a hardened sinner. [im- (in- (2))]
■ **impen'itence** n. **impen'itency** n. **impen'itently** adv.

impennate /im-pen'ət/ adj (of birds) featherless, wingless (applied to birds with small wings adapted for swimming, such as penguins). [im- (in- (2))]

imper. abbrev : imperative.

imperative /im-per'ə-tiv/ adj expressive of command, advice or request (grammar); urgently necessary; calling out for action; obligatory; authoritative; peremptory. ◆n that which is imperative; the imperative mood (grammar); a verb in the imperative mood. [L imperātīvus, from imperāre to command, from in in, and parāre to prepare]
■ **imperatī'val** adj (grammar). **imper'atively** adv. **imper'ativeness** n.
❑ **imperative mood** n the form of a verb expressing command, advice or request.
■ **categorical imperative** see under **category**.

imperator /im-pə-rä'tər or im-pe-rä'tor/ n a commander; a ruler; an emperor. [L imperātor a general, later an emperor, from imperāre to command]
■ **imperatorial** /im-per-ə-tö'ri-əl or -tö'/ adj.

imperceable see **impierceable**.

imperceptible /im-pər-sep'ti-bl/ adj not discernible by the senses; very small, slight or gradual. [im- (in- (2))]
■ **imperceptibil'ity** n. **impercep'tibleness** n. **impercep'tibly** adv. **impercep'tive** or **impercip'ient** adj not perceiving; having no power to perceive. **impercep'tively** or **impercip'iently** adv. **impercep'tiveness** or **impercip'ience** n failure to perceive.

imperf. abbrev : imperfect.

imperfect /im-pûr'fikt/ adj incomplete, deficient; defective, faulty; falling short of perfection; lacking any normal part, or the full normal number of parts; lacking some necessary sanction, formality, etc and therefore incapable of being legally enforced (law); expressing continued or habitual action in past time (grammar); of or relating to the intervals of the third and sixth (music); (in mensural notation) a note value containing two of the next lower note values (music). ◆n the imperfect tense; a verb in the imperfect tense. [im- (in- (2))]
■ **imperfectibil'ity** n. **imperfect'ible** adj. **imperfection** /-fek'shən/ n the state of being imperfect; a defect. **imperfec'tive** adj (grammar) denoting the aspect of the verb which indicates that the action described is in progress. ◆n the imperfective aspect, or a verb in this aspect. **imperfec'tively** adv (grammar). **imper'fectly** adv. **imper'fectness** n.
❑ **imperfect cadence** n (music) a cadence which is not resolved to the tonic key, esp one passing from tonic to dominant chord. **imperfect competition** n (econ) the market condition that exists between the extremes of perfect competition and absolute monopoly. **imperfect flower** n a flower in which stamens or carpels are lacking or non-functional. **imperfect fungus** n a fungus of the order Fungi Imperfecti of which no sexual stage is known.

imperforate /im-pûr'fə-rət/ or **imperforated** /-rā-tid/ adj not pierced through or perforated; having no opening; lacking an opening, esp as a result of abnormal development, as in imperforate anus (med); without perforations as a means of separation, as a sheet of postage stamps. [im- (in- (2))]
■ **imper'forable** adj. **imperforā'tion** n.

imperial /im-pē'ri-əl/ adj relating to, or of the nature of, an empire or emperor; sovereign; supreme; commanding, imperious, august; (of products, etc) of superior quality or size. ◆n an emperor or empress or a member of an imperial family; a supporter of an emperor; a small beard or tuft of hair under the lower lip as popularized by Napoleon III; a domed roof shaped to a point at the top (archit); the top of a coach or carriage, or a trunk designed to be carried there; a size of paper, in Britain 22 × 30in (56 × 76cm), in USA 23 × 33in (58 × 84cm); a size of slates, 33 × 24in (838 × 610mm); a stag with fourteen points on its antlers; an obsolete Russian gold coin. [L imperium sovereignty]
■ **impē'rialism** n the power or authority of an emperor; the policy, practice or advocacy of extension of a nation's power or influence over other territories; the spirit or character of an empire. **impē'rialist** n a soldier or partisan of an emperor; a believer in, or advocate of, imperialism (also adj). **impērialist'ic** adj. **impērialist'ically** adv. **impēriality** /-al'i-ti/ n imperial power, right or privilege. **impē'rialize** or **-ise** vt to make imperial. **impē'rially** adv. **impē'rious** adj assuming command; haughty; tyrannical; overbearing, domineering, dictatorial; imperial (obs). **impē'riously** adv. **impē'riousness** n.
❑ **imperial city** n Rome. **Imperial Conference** n a former periodical conference (orig Colonial Conference) of the prime ministers and other representatives of the United Kingdom and the self-governing Dominions. **imperial measure** or **weight** n non-metric standard of measure or weight (**imperial gallon**, **yard** and **pound**) as fixed by parliament for the United Kingdom (final act 1963). **imperial octavo** n a book size, in Britain $7\frac{1}{2}$ × 11in, in USA $8\frac{1}{4}$ × $11\frac{1}{2}$in. **Imperial Parliament** n the parliament of the United Kingdom. **imperial preference** n (hist) the favouring of trade within the British Empire by discriminating tariffs.

imperil /im-per'il/ (formal) vt (**imper'illing**; **imper'illed**) to endanger. [im- (in- (1))]
■ **imper'ilment** n.

imperious, etc see under **imperial**.

imperishable /im-per'i-shə-bl/ adj not perishable, not subject to decay or deterioration, indestructible; everlasting, enduring. [**im-** (**in-** (2))]
■ **imperishabil'ity** n. **imper'ishableness** n. **imper'ishably** adv.

imperium /im-pēr'i-əm or -per'/ n (pl **imper'ia**) absolute sovereignty, the power to command; the area, or extent, of absolute sovereignty. [L imperium]
■ **imperium in imperio** /in im-pēr'i-ō or -per'/ absolute authority within the sphere of higher authority.

impermanence /im-pûr'mə-nəns/ n lack of permanence, transitoriness. [**im-** (**in-** (2))]
■ **imper'manency** n. **imper'manent** adj. **imper'manently** adv.

impermeable /im-pûr'mi-ə-bl/ adj (of a substance, membrane, etc) not permitting passage, esp of fluids or gases; impervious. [**im-** (**in-** (2))]
■ **impermeabil'ity** n. **imper'meableness** n. **imper'meably** adv.

impermissible /im-pər-mis'i-bl/ adj not permissible; not allowed. [**im-** (**in-** (2))]
■ **impermissibil'ity** n. **impermiss'ibly** adv.

impers. abbrev : impersonal.

imperseverant /im-pər-sev'ə-rənt/ adj lacking the power to perceive; lacking perseverance. [**im-** (**in-** (2)), and **perceive** or **persevere**]

impersistent /im-pər-sis'tənt/ adj not persistent; not enduring. [**im-** (**in-** (2))]

impersonal /im-pûr'sə-nəl/ adj having no personality, or personal touches; (of a verb) used only in the third person singular (in English usu with it as subject; grammar); (of a pronoun) not referring to a particular person (grammar); without reference to any particular person; objective, uncoloured by personal feeling, cold. [**im-** (**in-** (2))]
■ **impersonality** /-al'i-ti/ n. **impersonaliza'tion** or **-s-** n. **imper'sonalize** or **-ise** vt. **imper'sonally** adv.

impersonate /im-pûr'sə-nāt/ vt to assume the character of (another person); to pretend to be (another person); to personify (archaic); to embody, incarnate (obs). [L in in, and persōna person; see **personate**]
■ **impersona'tion** n. **imper'sonator** n.

impertinent /im-pûr'ti-nənt/ adj saucy, impudent; intrusive, presumptuous; not pertinent (archaic or law). [**im-** (**in-** (2))]
■ **imper'tinence** or **imper'tinency** n that which is impertinent; impudence, disrespectful behaviour; intrusion, presumptuousness; matter introduced into an affidavit, etc not pertinent to the matter (law). **imper'tinently** adv.

imperturbable /im-pər-tûr'bə-bl/ adj that cannot be disturbed or agitated; serene, unruffled. [L imperturbābilis, from in- not, and perturbāre to disturb; see **perturb**]
■ **imperturbabil'ity** n. **impertur'bably** adv. **imperturbā'tion** n.

impervious /im-pûr'vi-əs/ or **imperviable** /-pûr'vi-ə-bl/ adj not able to be penetrated; not easily influenced by ideas, arguments, etc, or moved or upset (with to). [**im-** (**in-** (2))]
■ **imperviabil'ity** n. **imper'viableness** n. **imper'viously** adv. **imper'viousness** n.

impeticos /im-pet'i-kos/ (Shakesp) vt a word coined by the fool in Twelfth Night II.3, perhaps meaning **impocket**, or perhaps to bestow on (the wearer of) a petticoat.

impetigo /im-pi-tī'gō/ n (pl **impetigines** /-tij'i-nēz/ or **impetī'gos**) a contagious bacterial skin infection characterized by clusters of small pustules which join to form crusty yellow sores. [L impetigō, from impetere to rush upon, attack]
■ **impetiginous** /-tij'/ adj.

impetrate /im'pi-trāt/ vt to obtain by entreaty or request, esp by prayer. [L impetrāre, -ātum, from in on, and patrāre to bring about]
■ **impetrā'tion** n. **im'petrātive** or **im'petrātory** adj.

impetuous /im-pet'ū-əs/ adj tending to act in a rash or impulsive manner or without due consideration; (of an action) rash, impulsive; rushing on with great force or violence (poetic). [L impetus (pl impetūs), from in into, on, and petere to seek]
■ **impetuosity** /-os'i-ti/ n. **impet'uously** adv. **impet'uousness** n.

impetus /im'pi-təs/ n (pl **im'petuses**) momentum; impulse; incentive. [Ety as for **impetuous**]

imp. gal. or **imp. gall.** abbrev : imperial gallon(s).

impi /im'pi/ (S Afr) n (pl **im'pis** or **im'pies**) a group of armed southern African native warriors. [From Zulu]

impictured /im-pik'chərd/ (Spenser) adj painted. [**im-** (**in-** (1))]

impierceable /im-pēr'sə-bl/ (obs; Spenser **imperceable** /im'pər-sə-bl/) adj not pierceable. [**im-** (**in-** (2))]

impiety /im-pī'ə-ti/ n lack of piety or veneration; any impious act. [L impietās, -ātis, from in- not; cf **piety**]

impignorate /im-pig'nə-rāt/ (formal and Scot) vt to pledge, pawn or mortgage (also adj). [L in in, into, and pignus, -oris, -eris pledge]
■ **impignorā'tion** n.

impinge /im-pinj'/ vi (prp **imping'ing**) (with on, upon or against) to encroach, infringe; to strike, collide with; to make an impression on (the mind, senses, etc). ◆ vt to strike, drive or fix upon or against something else. [L impingere, from in against, and pangere to fix, drive in]
■ **impinge'ment** n. **imping'ent** adj. **imping'er** n.

impious /im'pi-əs or im-pī'əs/ adj irreverent, lacking respect; lacking veneration, as for gods, etc. [L impius, from im- (in-) not, and pius; cf **pious**]
■ **im'piously** adv. **im'piousness** n.

impish see under **imp**.

implacable /im-plak'ə-bl or -plāk'/ adj incapable of being placated or appeased; inexorable. [**im-** (**in-** (2))]
■ **implacabil'ity** or **implac'ableness** n. **implac'ably** adv.

implacental /im-plə-sen'tl/ adj aplacental, having no placenta. [**im-** (**in-** (2))]

implant /im-plänt'/ vt to engraft; to plant firmly, to embed; to fix in; to insert; to instil or inculcate; to plant (ground, etc with). ◆ n /im'/ anything implanted or inserted which has a specialized function; something implanted in body tissue, such as a graft, a pellet containing a hormone, an artificial pacemaker, etc. [**im-** (**in-** (1))]
■ **implant'able** adj. **implantā'tion** n the act or process of implanting; the attachment of an embryo to the lining of the uterus (also **nidation**).

implate /im-plāt'/ vt to put a plate or covering on; to sheathe. [**im-** (**in-** (1))]

implausible /im-plö'zi-bl/ adj not plausible. [**im-** (**in-** (2))]
■ **implausibil'ity** or **implaus'ibleness** n. **implaus'ibly** adv.

impleach or **empleach** /im-plēch'/ (poetic) vt to intertwine. [**im-** (**in-** (1))]

implead /im-plēd'/ (law, now rare) vt to take legal action against, to sue. [**im-** (**in-** (1))]
■ **implead'er** n.

impledge /im-plej'/ vt to pledge. [**im-** (**in-** (1))]

implement /im'pli-mənt/ n a piece of equipment, a requisite (archaic); something that serves to achieve a purpose; a tool or instrument of labour; the fulfilment of an obligation (Scots law). ◆ vt (often /-ment'/) to give effect to, to carry out; to fulfil, complete or perform. [LL implēmentum, from L in in, and plēre to fill]
■ **implemen'tal** adj instrumental; effective. **implementā'tion** n performance, fulfilment; the various steps involved in producing a functioning data-processing or control system from a design (comput). **im'plementer** n.

implete /im-plēt'/ (archaic) vt to fill. ◆ adj filled up, replete. [L implēre, -ētum, from in in, and plēre to fill]
■ **impletion** /-plē'shən/ n filling; fullness; fulfilment.

implex /im'pleks/ adj not simple; involved, complicated. ◆ n (zool) in arthropods, an inturning of the integument where muscles are attached. [L implexus, from in into, and plectere to twine]
■ **implexion** /im-plek'shən/ n. **implex'ūous** adj.

implicate /im'pli-kāt/ vt to involve; to entangle; to imply; to show to be, or to have been, a participator; to entwine together; to enfold. ◆ n a thing implied. ◆ adj /-kit/ intertwined. [L implicāre, -ātum, also -itum, from in in, and plicāre, -ātum or -itum to fold]
■ **implicā'tion** n the act of implicating or implying; that which is implied; the relation between two propositions in a sentence or statement such that the sentence or statement is only true when both propositions are true, or, if the first proposition is true the second proposition must be true (logic). **implicā'tional** adj. **im'plicative** (or /im-plik'ə-tiv/) adj tending to implicate. **im'plicatively** adv. **implic'ature** n the act of implying a meaning other than the literal meaning of a statement, as in he's a well-behaved student to convey that his academic work is poor; a meaning so conveyed. **implicit** /im-plis'it/ adj not explicit; implied but not expressly stated; absolute, relying entirely, unquestioning; present without being visible or realized (with in); entangled, intertwined (obs). **implic'itly** adv. **implic'itness** n.

implied, etc see **imply**.

implode /im-plōd'/ vt and vi to (cause to) collapse inwards suddenly and violently; to pronounce or sound by implosion (phonetics). [L in in, and plōdere (plaudere) to clap]
■ **implōd'ent** n an implosive sound. **implosion** /-plō'zhən/ n a collapsing inwards; in the formation of voiceless stops, compression of enclosed air by simultaneous stoppage of the mouth parts and the glottis (phonetics); inrush of air in a suction stop (phonetics); (in behaviour therapy) a method of treating phobias in which the patient is exposed intensively to the object of fear (also called **flooding**;

psychol). **implosive** /-*plōs'iv* or *-plōz'*/ *adj* of or relating to implosion.
◆ *n* (*phonetics*) an implosive consonant; a suction stop or (sometimes) a click.

implore /*im-plōr'* or *-plör'*/ *vt* and *vi* to ask or beg earnestly; to entreat. [L *implōrāre* to invoke with tears, from *in* in, and *plōrāre* to weep]
■ **implorā'tion** *n*. **implor'ator** *n* (*Shakesp*). **imploratory** /-*plor'ə-tə-ri*/ *adj*. **implōr'er** *n*. **implōr'ing** *adj*. **implōr'ingly** *adv*.

implosion, implosive see under **implode**.

implunge /*im-plunj'*/ *vt* to plunge, submerge (also (*Spenser*) **emplonge'**). [**im-** (**in-** (1))]

impluvium /*im-ploo'vi-əm*/ *n* (*pl* **implu'via**) in ancient Roman houses, the square basin in the atrium that received the rainwater from the open space in the roof. [L *impluvium*, from *in* in, into, and *pluere* to rain]

imply /*im-plī'*/ *vt* (**imply'ing**; **implied'**) to express indirectly; to insinuate, to hint; to signify, to mean; to include in reality; to enfold (*obs*). [OFr *emplier*, from L *implicāre* to involve]
■ **implī'edly** *adv*.

impocket /*im-pok'it*/ (*archaic*) *vt* to put in one's pocket. [**im-** (**in-** (1))]

impolder or **empolder** /*im-pōl'dər*/ *vt* to make a polder of. [Du *impolderen*; see **polder**]

impolite /*im-pə-līt'*/ *adj* having rough manners; bad-mannered, rude. [**im-** (**in-** (2))]
■ **impolite'ly** *adv*. **impolite'ness** *n*.

impolitic /*im-pol'i-tik*/, also (*obs*) **impolitical** /-*it'i-kl*/ *adj* not politic; inexpedient. [**im-** (**in-** (2))]
■ **impol'icy** *n* an act or nce of being impolitic. **impolit'ically** *adv* (*rare*). **impol'iticly** *adv*. **impol'iticness** *n*.

imponderable /*im-pon'də-rə-bl*/ *adj* not able to be weighed or evaluated (also *n*). [**im-** (**in-** (2))]
■ **imponderabil'ity** or **impon'derableness** *n*. **impon'derables** or (*L*) **imponderabil'ia** *n pl orig* supposed fluids with no detectable weight, such as heat, light, electricity, magnetism; factors in a situation whose influence cannot be gauged or evaluated. **impon'derably** *adv*. **impon'derous** *adj* weightless; very light.

impone /*im-pōn'*/ *vt* and *vi* to impose. ◆ *vt* to stake as a wager (*Shakesp*; *perh* an error for **impawn**). [L *impōnere*, from *in* on, and *pōnere* to place]
■ **impōn'ent** *adj* that which imposes, or is competent to impose, an obligation. ◆ *n* a person who imposes an obligation, duty, etc.

import /*im-pōrt'* or *-pört'*/ *vt* to bring in from an outside source; to bring in from abroad; to convey, as a word; to signify; to portend; to load (a file, *esp* one of a different format) for processing in an application (*comput*); to be of consequence to (*archaic*); to behove (*archaic*). ◆ *n* /*im'*/, formerly /-*pōrt'* or *-pört'*/ something that is brought from abroad; importing; meaning; importance; tendency. [L *importāre, -ātum*, from *in* in, and *portāre* to carry]
■ **import'able** *adj*. **import'ance** *n* (also (*obs*) **import'ancy**) the fact of being important; extent of value or significance; weight, consequence; appearance of dignity; import, significance (*archaic*); importunity (*obs*). **import'ant** *adj* of great import or consequence; momentous; significant; pompous. **import'antly** *adv*. **importā'tion** *n* the act of importing; a commodity or service imported. **import'er** *n*.
❑ **import duty** *n* a tax levied on goods which enter one country from another. **import licence** *n* an official licence which permits the trader, etc to import certain goods which are otherwise restricted from entry into a country.
■ **invisible imports** services bought from foreign countries, such as money spent by tourists abroad, etc (cf **invisible exports** under **export**). **visible imports** goods and raw materials bought from foreign countries.

importable /*im-pōr'tə-bl*, *Spenser im'*/ (*obs*) *adj* unbearable; irresistible. [L *importābilis*, from *im-* (**in-**) not, and *portāre* to bear]

importune /*im-pör-tūn'* or *-pör'*/ *vt* to press or urge with repeated requests; to harass with troublesome insistence; to solicit for immoral purposes, make improper advances to; to annoy (*obs*); to import, signify (*Spenser*; *non-standard*). ◆ *vi* to press, urge or solicit importunately. ◆ *adj* importunate; inopportune, untimely (*obs*); burdensome (*obs*); urgent, resistless (*obs*). [L *importūnus* inconvenient, from *im-* (**in-**) not, and *portus* a harbour; cf **opportune**]
■ **impor'tunacy** (or (*Shakesp*) /-*tūn'*/) or **import'unateness** *n*. **impor'tunate** /-*it* or *-āt*/ *adj* troublesomely persistent or demanding; pressing, insistent, annoying; inopportune (*obs*); burdensome (*obs*). **impor'tunately** *adv*. **importune'ly** (or /-*pör'*/) *adv*. **importun'er** *n*. **importun'ing** *n*. **importun'ity** *n*.

impose /*im-pōz'*/ *vt* to place upon something; to lay on; to lay (the hands) on the head of a candidate for ordination or in certain sacraments; to enjoin; to set as a burden or task; to set up in, or by, authority; to pass off unfairly or deceptively; to arrange or place in a chase, as pages of type (*printing*). ◆ *vi* (with *on* or *upon*) to mislead,

deceive; to burden by taking undue advantage of one's good nature; to act with constraining effect. ◆ *n* (*Shakesp*) command, charge. [Fr *imposer*; see **compose**]
■ **impos'able** *adj*. **impos'er** *n*. **impos'ing** *adj* commanding, impressive; adapted to impress forcibly; specious, deceptive (now *rare*). **impos'ingly** *adv*. **impos'ingness** *n*.
❑ **imposing stone** or **table** *n* (*printing*) a heavy table upon which metal type is imposed.

imposex /*im'pō-seks*/ *n* the superimposition of male sexual characteristics onto female gastropods, caused by pollutants such as tributyltin (qv). [**impose** and **sex**]

imposition /*im-pə-zish'ən*/ *n* an act or nce of imposing or laying on; the act of laying on hands in ordination and certain sacraments; something imposed, a burden; a punishment task; the assembling of pages and locking them into a chase (*printing*). [L *impositiō, -ōnis*, from *in* on, and *pōnere, positum* to place]

impossible /*im-pos'i-bl*/ *adj* that cannot be; that cannot be done or dealt with; that cannot be true; out of the question; hopelessly unsuitable or difficult to deal with (*inf*); beyond doing anything with. ◆ *n* a person or thing that is impossible. [**im-** (**in-** (2))]
■ **imposs'ibilism** *n* belief in or advocacy of an impracticable policy. **imposs'ibilist** *n*. **impossibil'ity** *n*. **imposs'ibly** *adv*.

impost[1] /*im'pōst*/ *n* a tax, *esp* on imports; the weight carried by a horse in a handicap race (*inf*). [OFr *impost* (Fr *impôt*), from L *impōnere, impositum* to lay on]

impost[2] /*im'pōst*/ (*archit*) *n* the upper part of a pillar in vaults and arches, on which the weight of the building is laid; a horizontal block resting on uprights. [Fr *imposte*, from Ital *imposta*, from L *impōnere, impositum*]

imposter see **impostor**.

imposthume see **impostume**.

impostor or **imposter** /*im-pos'tər*/ *n* someone who assumes a false character or impersonates another in order to deceive. [LL, from L *impōnere, impositum* to impose]
■ **impos'ture** /-*chər*/ *n* an imposition, fraud.

impostume or **imposthume** /*im-pos'tūm*/ (*archaic*) *n* an abscess. [OFr *empostume* from *aposteme*, from Gr *apostēma* abscess, from *apo* from, and the root of *histanai* to set; the form due to confusion with *posthumous*, which itself is due to confusion]
■ **impos'tumate** or **impos'thumate** *vt* and *vi* to affect with or form into an impostume. **impostumā'tion** or **imposthumā'tion** *n*. **impos'tumed** or **impos'thumed** *adj*.

imposture see under **impostor**.

impot /*im'pot*/ (*school sl*) *n* an imposition.

impotent /*im'pə-tənt*/ *adj* powerless; helpless; incapable of having sexual intercourse, owing to inability to achieve or maintain an erection; unable to control (with *of*; *obs*); without self-control, unrestrained (*poetic*; *obs*). [**im-** (**in-** (2))]
■ **im'potence** or **im'potency** *n*. **im'potently** *adv*.

impound /*im-pownd'*/ *vt* to confine, as within a pound; to restrain within limits; to take legal possession of; to hold up in a reservoir. [**im-** (**in-** (1)) and **pound**[2]]
■ **impound'able** *adj*. **impound'age** *n*. **impound'er** *n*. **impound'ment** *n*.

impoverish /*im-pov'ə-rish*/ *vt* to make poor (*lit* or *fig*). [From OFr *empovrir, -iss-*, from L *in* in, and *pauper* poor]
■ **impov'erishment** *n*.

impracticable /*im-prak'ti-kə-bl*/ *adj* not able to be done or put into practice; not able to be used; unmanageable (*archaic*). [**im-** (**in-** (2))]
■ **impracticabil'ity** *n*. **imprac'ticableness** *n*. **imprac'ticably** *adv*.

impractical /*im-prak'ti-kl*/ *adj* not practical. [**im-** (**in-** (2))]
■ **impracticality** /-*kal'*/ *n*. **imprac'tically** *adv*. **imprac'ticalness** *n*.

imprecate /*im'pri-kāt*/ *vt* to call down by prayer (*esp* something evil); to invoke evil upon, to put a curse on. ◆ *vi* to curse or blaspheme. [L *imprecāri*, from *in* upon, and *precāri, -ātus* to pray]
■ **imprecā'tion** *n* the act of imprecating; a curse. **im'precatory** /-*kə-tə-ri, -kā-* or *kā'*/ *adj*.

imprecise /*im-pri-sīs'*/ *adj* not precise; inexact. [**im-** (**in-** (2))]
■ **imprecise'ly** *adv*. **imprecise'ness** *n*. **imprecis'ion** *n*.

impregn /*im-prēn'*/ (*poetic*; *archaic*) *vt* to impregnate. [Ety as for **impregnate**]
■ **impregnant** /*im-preg'nənt*/ *adj* impregnating (*archaic*); impregnated (*obs*).

impregnable /*im-preg'nə-bl*/ *adj* that cannot be captured, broken into or taken by force; which cannot be overcome, unassailable. [Fr *imprenable*, from L *in-* not, and *prendere, prehendere* to take]
■ **impregnabil'ity** *n*. **impreg'nably** *adv*.

impregnate /im'preg-nāt/ or -preg'/ vt to make pregnant; to make fertile; to fill, saturate or imbue (with the particles or qualities of another substance); to saturate (also *fig*). [LL *impraegnāre, -ātum*, from *in* in, and *praegnāns* pregnant]
■ **impregnā'tion** n.

impresa /im-prā'zə/ or **imprese** /im'prēz/ or (*Milton*) im-prēz'/ (*obs*) n an emblematic device, often with a motto; a motto. [Ital *impresa*]

impresario /im-pre-sä'ri-ō or -zä'/ n (pl **impresa'rios** or **impresa'ri** /-rē/) the manager of an opera company, etc; a producer or organizer of entertainments; a showman. [Ital, from *impresa* undertaking, enterprise]

imprescriptible /im-pri-skrip'ti-bl/ (*law*) adj not liable to be lost by prescription or lapse of time; inalienable. [**im-** (**in-** (2))]
■ **imprescriptibil'ity** n.

imprese see **impresa**.

impress¹ /im-pres'/ vt to press; to apply with pressure, *esp* so as to leave a mark; to mark by pressure; to produce by pressure; to stamp or print; to fix deeply in the mind; to affect the mind; to produce a profound effect upon, or upon the mind of; to apply (a voltage) to (*electronics*). ◆ vi to be impressive, make a good impression. ◆ n /im'/ the act or process of impressing; that which is made by pressure; stamp; distinctive mark. [L *imprimere, -pressum*, from *in premere*; see **press¹**]
■ **impressibil'ity** n. **impress'ible** adj susceptible, easily impressed. **impression** /im-presh'ən/ n the act or result of impressing; pressure; a difference produced in a thing by action upon it; a single printing of a book, or a reprint from the same plates or type setting; the effect of anything on the mind; a profound effect on the emotions; a vague uncertain memory or inclination to believe; belief, generally ill-founded; (the mould formed by) the pressing of an elastic substance, eg wax or silicone, on the teeth and/or gums, which is then used in the making of dentures, etc (*dentistry*); an impersonation. **impressionabil'ity** n. **impress'ionable** adj able to receive an impression; very susceptible to impressions. **impress'ional** adj. **impress'ionism** n (often with *cap*) a 19c movement in painting, originating in France, aiming at the realistic representation of the play of light in nature, purporting to render faithfully what the artist actually saw, dispensing with the academic rules of composition and colouring; any similar tendency in other arts. **impress'ionist** n (often with *cap*) an exponent of impressionism (also *adj*); an entertainer who impersonates people. **impressionis'tic** adj. **impressionist'ically** adv. **impressive** /-pres'/ adj exerting or tending to exert pressure; likely to impress others; solemn. **impress'ively** adv. **impress'iveness** n. **impressure** /im-presh'ər/ n (*archaic*) impression.
■ **be under the impression** to think or believe without certainty.

impress² /im-pres'/ vt to force into service, *esp* government service; to pressgang. ◆ n /im'/ or (*Shakesp*) /im-pres'/ the act of impressing or seizing for service, *esp* government service (also **impress'ment**). [**im-** (**in-** (1)), and cf **press²**]

impress³ or **impresse** /im'pres/ (*obs*) n an impresa.

impress⁴ obsolete variant of **imprest**.

imprest /im'prest/ n a loan or advance of money, *esp* from government funds for some public purpose; formerly, an advance of wages to soldiers and sailors. [**im-** (**in-** (1)) and **prest²**]
□ **imprest system** n (*commerce*) a method of maintaining a cash fund, eg petty cash, in which a fixed amount or float is regularly topped up from central funds, reimbursing the fund for incidental expenses.

imprimatur /im-pri-mā'tər/ n a licence or permission to print a book, etc. [L *imprimātur*, let it be printed, subjunctive passive of *imprimere*, from *in* on, and *premere* to press]

imprimis /im-prī'mis/ adv in the first place. [L *imprīmis*, from *in prīmīs* (ablative pl), *in* in, and *prīmus* first]

imprint /im-print'/ vt to print; to stamp; to impress; to fix in the mind; to cause (a young animal) to undergo imprinting (*usu* with *on*). ◆ n /im'print/ that which is imprinted; any characteristic mark, stamp, etc; the name of the publisher, time and place of publication of a book, etc, printed *usu* on the back of the title page or at the end of the book; the printer's name on the back of the title page or at the end of the book. [**im-** (**in-** (1))]
■ **imprint'ing** n a learning process in young animals in which their social preferences become restricted to their own species, or a substitute for this.

imprison /im-priz'n/ vt to put in prison; to shut up; to confine or restrain. [**im-** (**in-** (1))]
■ **impris'onable** adj liable to be, or capable of being, imprisoned; (of an offence) likely to lead to imprisonment. **impris'onment** n.

improbable /im-prob'ə-bl/ adj unlikely. [**im-** (**in-** (2))]
■ **improbabil'ity** n. **improb'ably** adv.

improbation /im-prō-bā'shən/ (*Scots law*; *obs*) n an action for the purpose of declaring some instrument false or forged. [**im-** (**in-** (2))]

improbity /im-prōb'i-ti or -prob'/ n lack of probity; dishonesty or unscrupulousness. [**im-** (**in-** (2))]

impromptu /im-promp'tū/ adj improvised, spontaneous, unrehearsed; makeshift. ◆ adv without preparation; on the spur of the moment. ◆ n an extempore witticism or speech; an improvised composition; a musical composition with the character of an extemporization. [L *impromptū* for *in promptū* (ablative), *in* in, and *promptus* readiness]

improper /im-prop'ər/ adj not strictly belonging; not properly so called; not suitable; unfit; unbecoming; unseemly; indecent. [L *im-* (*in-*) not, and *proprius* own]
■ **improp'erly** adv. **imprōprī'ety** n.
□ **improper fraction** n a fraction in which the numerator has a greater value or degree than the denominator.

impropriate /im-prō'pri-āt/ vt to appropriate to private use; to place (ecclesiastical property) into the hands of a layman. ◆ adj /-ət/ transferred into the hands of a layman. [LL *impropriātus*, from L *in* in, and *proprius* one's own]
■ **imprōpriā'tion** n. **imprō'priātor** n a layman who is in possession of a benefice or its revenues.

impropriety see under **improper**.

improv /im'prov/ (*inf*) n improvisation. [Abbrev]

improve /im-proov'/ vt to make better; to make more valuable (*esp* by cultivating or building); to make good use of (*archaic*); to make use of (land, etc), to occupy (*US; archaic*); to increase (*obs*). ◆ vi to become better; to make progress; to make improvements; to grow in price or value; to follow up with something better (with *on* or *upon*); to increase (*obs*). [Anglo-Fr *emprower*, from OFr *en prou, preu* into profit]
■ **improvabil'ity** or **improv'ableness** n. **improv'able** adj. **improv'ably** adv. **improve'ment** n the act of improving; a change for the better; a thing changed, or introduced in changing, for the better; a better thing substituted for, or following, one not so good (often with *on*). **improv'er** n someone or something that improves; an apprentice in the last year of his apprenticeship. **improv'ing** adj tending to cause improvement; instructive; edifying; uplifting. **improv'ingly** adv.
■ **improve the occasion** to seize an opportunity for edification or other purpose; to draw a moral from what has happened. **on the improve** (*Aust*) improving.

improvident /im-prov'i-dənt/ adj not provident or prudent; lacking foresight; thoughtless. [**im-** (**in-** (2))]
■ **improv'idence** n. **improv'idently** adv.

improvise /im-prō-vīz', -prə- or im'/, also (*obs*) **improvisate** /im-prov'i-zāt/ vt to compose and recite, or perform, without preparation; to bring about suddenly; to make or contrive without preparation or in emergency. ◆ vi to perform extempore; to do anything without proper materials or preparation. [Fr *improviser*, from L *in-* not, and *prōvīsus* foreseen; see **provide**]
■ **improvīsā'tion** (or /-prov'iz-/) n the act of improvising; something (eg a performance) which is improvised. **improvīsā'tional** adj. **improvisator** /im-prov'iz-ā-tər or im'prov-īz-/ (*Ital* **improvvisatore** /im-prov-vē-sä-tō'rä/) n someone, *esp* a performer, who improvises. **improvisatō'rial** /-iz-ə-/ adj. **improvisatory** /-iz' or -īz'/ adj. **improv'isātrix** (*Ital* **improvvisatrice** /-trē'chä/) n (*archaic*) a female improvisator. **improvīs'er** n.

imprudent /im-proo'dənt/ adj lacking foresight or discretion; incautious; inconsiderate. [**im-** (**in-** (2))]
■ **impru'dence** n. **impru'dently** adv.

impsonite /imp'sə-nīt/ (*mineralogy*) n an organic compound of the asphaltite group. [*Impson* valley, Oklahoma, where it is chiefly found, and **-ite** (3)]

impudent /im'pū-dənt/ adj shamelessly bold; impertinent; disrespectful; insolent; immodest (*obs*). [L *im-* (*in-*) not, and *pudēns, -entis*, prp of *pudēre* to be ashamed; and *pudīcus* modest]
■ **im'pudence** n. **im'pudently** adv. **impudicity** /-dis'i-ti/ n (*rare*) immodesty.

impugn /im-pūn'/ vt to oppose; to attack by words or arguments; to call in question, criticize. [L *impugnāre*, from *in* against, and *pugnāre* to fight]
■ **impugnable** /-pūn'/ adj. **impugnā'tion** n. **impugn'er** n. **impugn'ment** n.

impuissant /im-pū'is-ənt, -pū-is', -pwis' or -pwēs'/ (*archaic*) adj powerless, feeble, impotent. [**im-** (**in-** (2))]
■ **impuiss'ance** (or /-pū'/) n.

impulse /im'puls/ n the act of impelling; the effect of an impelling force; force suddenly and momentarily communicated; a beat; a single blow, thrust or wave; a disturbance travelling along a nerve (**nerve impulse**) or a muscle; an obsolete term for **pulse¹**

■ words derived from main entry word; □ compound words; ■ idioms and phrasal verbs

(*electronics*); an outside influence on the mind; a sudden inclination, whim or desire. ◆ *vt* to give an impulse to. [L *impulsus* pressure, from *impellere* ; see **impel**]

■ **impul'sion** /-*shən*/ *n* a driving or impelling force; the act of impelling or state of being impelled. **impuls'ive** *adj* having the power of impelling; acting or actuated by impulse; not continuous; tending or likely to act on impulse. **impuls'ively** *adv.* **impuls-iveness** or **impulsiv-ity** *n.*

❑ **impulse buy** *n.* **impulse buyer** *n.* **impulse buying** *n* the buying of goods on a whim rather than because of previous intent.

impundulu /*im-pŭn'dū-lŭ*/ (*S Afr*) *n* a mythical bird with magical powers, often identified with the secretary bird. [Bantu *mpundulu*]

impunity /*im-pū'ni-ti*/ *n* freedom or safety from punishment or recrimination. [L *impūnitās, -ātis*, from *in-* not, and *poena* punishment]

impure /*im-pūr'*/ *adj* mixed with something else; containing some unclean or extraneous substance; tainted, adulterated; unchaste, lewd; unclean ritually or ceremonially. [**im-** (**in-** (2))]

■ **impure'ly** *adv.* **impure'ness** *n.* **impur'ity** *n* an impure or unclean thing or constituent; the quality or state of being impure.

❑ **impurity level** *n* (*electronics*) an abnormal energy level arising from slight impurities, resulting in conduction in semiconductors.

impurple /*im-pûr'pl*/ same as **empurple**.

impute /*im-pūt'*/ *vt* to ascribe (*usu* something evil, dishonest, etc); to charge; to attribute (grief, righteousness, etc) vicariously to (*theol*); to reckon or take into account. [Fr *imputer*, from L *imputāre, -ātum*, from *in* in, and *putāre* to reckon]

■ **imputabil'ity** *n.* **imput'able** *adj* capable of being imputed or charged; open to accusation; ascribable, attributable. **imput'ableness** *n.* **imput'ably** *adv.* **imputā'tion** *n* the act of imputing or charging; censure; reproach; the reckoning as belonging. **imput'ative** *adj* imputed. **imput'atively** *adv.* **imput'er** *n.*

❑ **imputation system** *n* a method of taxation whereby some or all of the corporation tax on a company is offset by the income tax paid by shareholders on dividends.

IMRO *abbrev* : Investment Management Regulatory Organization (now replaced by **FSA**).

imshi or **imshy** /*im'shi*/ (*old milit sl*) *interj* go away. [Ar]

IN *abbrev* : Indiana (US state).

In (*chem*) *symbol* : indium.

in¹ /*in*/ *prep* expressing the relation of a thing to that which surrounds, encloses, includes or conditions it, with respect to place, time or circumstances, or to that which is assumed, held, maintained, or the relation of a right or possession to the person who holds or enjoys it; at; among; into; within; during; consisting of; by way of; because of; by or through; by the medium or method of; among the characteristics or possibilities of; wearing; belonging to; concerned or involved with; being a member of; with (*obs*). ◆ *adv* within; not out; at home or at one's place of business; on the spot; in or into a position within or inward; in or into a centre or central point; in or into office, parliament, etc; in favour; in a position of assured success; in intimacy, on good terms (with); in or into fashion; in the market; in season; into concealment; being in the middle of an innings (*cricket*); as an addition or inclusion; alight; in pocket. ◆ *n* a member of the party in office; a reflex angle; a turning in of anything upon itself. ◆ *adj* inward; proceeding inwards; that is fashionable, much in use (as in *in-word, in-thing*); within a small group. ◆ *vt* to take in; to enclose; to gather in harvest. ◆ *n combining form* indicating a (public) gathering of a group of people in one room, building, etc, *orig* as a form of protest (as in *sit-in, work-in*), now for any joint purpose (as in *love-in, teach-in*). [OE *in* ; Du, Ger *in*, ON *ā* ; Welsh *yn*, L *in*, Gr *en*; OE also had *innan* within; cf OHGer *inanna*, Swed *innan*]

❑ **in'-and-in'** *adj* and *adv* (of breeding) carried out repeatedly within a closely related group of individuals of the same species to ensure continuity of certain characteristics, etc; with constant and close interaction. **in'-box** *n* (*comput*) a file for storing incoming electronic mail. **in'-built** *adj* built in, integral. **in'-car** *adj* existing, situated or operating within a car, as in *in-car entertainment*. **in-com'pany** *adj* happening or existing within a company. **in'-depth** *adj* (of a survey, research, etc) detailed or penetrating; thorough, comprehensive, not superficial. **in'-fighting** *n* fighting or bitter rivalry, between individuals or within a group, that is kept secret from, or is not apparent to, outsiders; see also separate entry **infighting**. **in'-flight** *adj* provided during an aeroplane flight. **Ingathering, Feast of** see **Feast of Tabernacles** under **tabernacle**. **in'group** *n* a social group of people having the same interests and attitudes. **in'-house'** *adj* and *adv* within a particular company, establishment, etc. **in'-joke** *n* a joke to be fully appreciated only by members of a particular limited group. **in-line'** *adj* denoting a linked series of operations or processes; arranged in a line; (of a computer program) being an integral part. **in'-line skate** *n* a type of roller skate with wheels set in a line (also *vi*). **in'-line skating**

n. **in'-off'** *n* (*snooker*, etc) a stroke in which the cue ball falls into a pocket after striking another ball. **in'-patient** *n* a patient living and being treated in a hospital (cf **out-patient**). **in'-service** *adj* carried out while continuing with one's ordinary employment, eg *in-service training*. **in'shore** *adj* close to the shore; moving towards the shore. **in'-source** *vt* to obtain (goods or parts) from, or contract work with, a supplier within the same organization. **in'-sourcing** *n.* **in'-store** *adj* provided within a shop. **in'-tray** *n* a shallow container for incoming letters, etc still to be dealt with.

■ **be in it** to participate (*Aust inf*); to be involved (*esp* in dishonest or illegal activities). **in as far as, in so far as** or **insofar as** to the extent that. **in as much as** or **inasmuch as** considering that. **in for** doomed to receive (*esp* unpleasant consequences); involved to the extent of; entered for; (see also **go in for** under **go¹**). **in for it** in for trouble; committed to a certain course. **in it** enjoying success; in the running. **in itself** intrinsically, apart from relations. **in on** (*inf*) participating in; privy to. **ins and outs** (or **outs and ins**) turnings this way and that; nooks and corners; the complete details of any matter; those who repeatedly enter and leave. **in that** for the reason that. **in with** friendly with, associating much with; enjoying the favour of. **nothing in it** no truth, no importance, no difficulty in the matter; no important difference, no significant gap, six of one and half a dozen of the other. **on the in** (*sl*) on the inside, ie in prison.

in² /*in*/ (*obs*) *n* see **inn**.

in. *abbrev* : inch(es).

in- /*in-*/ *pfx* (1) in words derived from Latin and Old English, used to form verbs with the sense in, into; sometimes used to form other parts of speech with this sense; sometimes used as an intensive or almost meaningless prefix; (2) in words derived from Latin, used to form negatives. See also **il-, im-** and **ir-**.

-in /-*in*/ (*chem*, etc) *n sfx usu* indicating: (1) a neutral substance such as a protein, fat or glycoside, eg *albumin, stearin, insulin* ; (2) certain enzymes, eg *pepsin* ; (3) an antibiotic or other pharmaceutical drug, eg *penicillin, aspirin*. [Variant of **-ine¹**]

inability /*in-ə-bil' i-ti*/ *n* lack of sufficient power or means; incapacity. [**in-** (2)]

in absentia /*in ab-sen'shyə* or *ab-sen'ti-ä*/ (*L*) in (his, her, their, etc) absence.

inabstinence /*in-ab'sti-nəns*/ *n* lack of abstinence. [**in-** (2)]

in abstracto /*in ab-strak'tō*/ (*L*) in the abstract.

inaccessible /*in-ak-ses'i-bl* or *-ak-*/ *adj* not able to be reached, obtained or approached. [**in-** (2)]

■ **inaccessibil'ity** or **inaccess'ibleness** *n.* **inaccess'ibly** *adv.*

inaccurate /*in-ak'ū-rit*/ *adj* not accurate; incorrect; erroneous. [**in-** (2)]

■ **inacc'uracy** /-*ə-si*/ *n* the state or condition of being inaccurate; an error or mistake. **inacc'urately** *adv.* **inacc'urateness** *n.*

inactive /*in-ak'tiv*/ *adj* not active; (of personnel or equipment) not in active service (*milit*); not functioning; dormant; inert; having no power to move; sluggish; idle; lazy; having no effect; having no reactivity (*chem*); optically neutral in polarized light. [**in-** (2)]

■ **inac'tion** *n.* **inact'ivate** *vt* to render inactive. **inactiva'tion** *n.* **inact'ively** *adv.* **inactiv'ity** *n* inaction; inertness; idleness.

inadaptable /*in-ə-dap'tə-bl*/ *adj* that cannot be adapted. [**in-** (2)]

■ **inadaptā'tion** /-*ad-*/ *n.* **inadap'tive** *adj.*

inadequate /*in-ad'i-kwət*/ *adj* insufficient; short of what is required; incompetent. ◆ *n* an incompetent person. [**in-** (2)]

■ **inad'equacy** /-*kwə-si*/ or **inad'equateness** *n* insufficiency. **inad'equately** *adv.*

inadmissible /*in-əd-mis'i-bl*/ *adj* not allowable. [**in-** (2)]

■ **inadmissibil'ity** *n.* **inadmiss'ibly** *adv.*

inadvertent /*in-əd-vûr'tənt*/ *adj* unintentional; inattentive. [**in-** (2)]

■ **inadvert'ence** or **inadvert'ency** *n* negligence; oversight. **inadvert'ently** *adv.*

inadvisable /*in-ad-vī'zə-bl*/ *adj* not advisable, unwise; another form of **unadvisable** which is still the form preferred by some. [**in-** (2)]

■ **inadvisabil'ity** or **inadvis'ableness** *n.*

inaidable /*in-ā'də-bl*/ (*Shakesp*) *adj* that cannot be aided. [**in-** (2)]

inalienable /*in-ā'lyə-nə-bl* or *-li-ə-nə-bl*/ *adj* not capable of being transferred or removed. [**in-** (2)]

■ **inalienabil'ity** *n.* **inal'ienably** *adv.*

inalterable /*in-öl'tə-rə-bl*/ *adj* not alterable. [**in-** (2)]

■ **inalterabil'ity** *n.* **inal'terableness** *n.* **inal'terably** *adv.*

inamorata /*in-am-o-rä'tə*/ and **inamorato** /-*tō*/ *n* (*pl* **inamora'tas** and **inamora'tos**) respectively, a woman and man in love or beloved. [Ital *innamorata, -to*, from LL *inamorāre* to cause to love, from L *in* in, and *amor* love]

inane /*in-ān'*/ *adj* empty, void; vacuous; senseless; characterless. [L *inānis*]

■ **inane'ly** *adv.* **inane'ness** *n.* **inanition** /*in-ə-nish'ən*/ *n* exhaustion due to lack of nutrients in the blood, resulting from starvation or intestinal disease. **inanity** /*in-an'i-ti*/ *n* senselessness; mental vacuity; emptiness; an insipid frivolous utterance.

inanga /*ē'nan-gə* or *ē'näng-ä*/ *n* a small silvery Australasian fish (*Galaxias maculatus*) whose young are caught as whitebait. [Maori]

inanimate /*in-an'i-mət*/ *adj* without animation; without life; dead; spiritless; dull. [in- (2)]
■ **inan'imately** *adv.* **inan'imateness** *n.* **inanimā'tion** *n.*

inappeasable /*in-ə-pē'zə-bl*/ *adj* that cannot be appeased. [in- (2)]

inappellable /*in-ə-pel'ə-bl*/ *adj* incapable of being appealed against or challenged. [in- (2); see **appeal**]

inappetent /*in-ap'i-tənt*/ *adj* lacking desire or appetite. [in- (2)]
■ **inapp'etence** or **inapp'etency** *n.*

inapplicable /*in-ap'li-kə-bl* or *in-ə-plik'ə-*/ *adj* not applicable. [in- (2)]
■ **inapplicabil'ity** or **inapplic'ableness** *n.* **inapplic'ably** *adv.*

inapposite /*in-ap'ə-zit*/ *adj* not apposite, suitable or pertinent. [in- (2)]
■ **inapp'ositely** *adv.* **inapp'ositeness** *n.*

inappreciable /*in-ə-prē'shə-bl* or *-shyə-bl*/ *adj* too small or slight to be noticed or to be important; negligible; priceless (*obs*). [in- (2)]
■ **inapprē'ciably** *adv.* **inappreciation** /*-shi-ā'shən*/ *n.* **inapprē'ciative** /*-shi-ə-tiv* or *-shi-ā-tiv*/ *adj* not valuing justly or at all. **inapprē'ciatively** *adv.* **inapprē'ciativeness** *n.*

inapprehensible /*in-ap-ri-hen'si-bl*/ *adj* not apprehensible; that cannot be grasped by the intellect or senses. [in- (2)]
■ **inapprehen'sion** *n.* **inapprehen'sive** *adj* not apprehensive; untroubled; without apprehension. **inapprehen'siveness** *n.*

inapproachable /*in-ə-prō'chə-bl*/ *adj* unapproachable; inaccessible. [in- (2)]
■ **inapproachabil'ity** *n.* **inapproach'ably** *adv.*

inappropriate /*in-ə-prō'pri-it*/ *adj* not appropriate, not suitable. [in- (2)]
■ **inappro'priately** *adv.* **inappro'priateness** *n.*

inapt /*in-apt'*/ *adj* not apt; unfit or unqualified. [in- (2)]
■ **inapt'itude** or **inapt'ness** *n* unfitness, awkwardness. **inapt'ly** *adv.*

inarable /*in-ar'ə-bl*/ *adj* not arable. [in- (2)]

inarch /*in-ärch'*/ (*rare*) *vt* to graft (a plant) by uniting without separating from the original stem (also **enarch'**). [in- (1)]

inarm /*in-ärm'*/ *vt* to embrace. [in- (1)]

inarticulate /*in-är-tik'ū-lit*/ *adj* not uttered with the distinct sounds of spoken language; indistinctly uttered or uttering; incapable of clear and fluent expression; *orig* not jointed or hinged. [in- (2)]
■ **inartic'ulacy** *n.* **inartic'ulately** *adv.* **inartic'ulateness** or **inarticulā'tion** *n* indistinctness of sounds in speaking.

in articulo mortis /*in ärt-ik'ū-lō mör'tis* or *ärt-ik'ū-lö/* (*L*) at the point (or moment) of death.

inartificial /*in-är-ti-fish'əl*/ *adj* not artificial; simple. [in- (2)]
■ **inartific'ially** *adv.*

inartistic /*in-är-tis'tik*/ *adj* not artistic; not appreciative of art. [in- (2)]
■ **inartis'tically** *adv.*

inasmuch /*in-az-much'* or *-əz-*/ see under **in**[1].

inattentive /*in-ə-ten'tiv*/ *adj* careless; not paying attention; neglectful. [in- (2)]
■ **inatten'tion** *n.* **inatten'tively** *adv.* **inatten'tiveness** *n.*

inaudible /*in-ö'di-bl*/ *adj* not loud enough to be heard. [in- (2)]
■ **inaudibil'ity** *n.* **inaud'ibleness** *n.* **inaud'ibly** *adv.*

inaugurate /*in-ö'gū-rāt*/ *vt* to induct formally into an office; to cause to begin; to make a public exhibition of for the first time. [L *inaugurāre, -ātum* to inaugurate with taking of the auspices; see **augur**]
■ **inau'gural** *adj* relating to, or done at, an inauguration. ♦*n* an inaugural address. **inaugurā'tion** *n.* **inau'gurātor** *n.* **inau'guratory** /*-ə-tər-i*/ *adj.*

inaurate /*in-ö'rāt*/ (*rare*) *adj* gilded; having a golden lustre. [L *inaurāre, -ātum* to gild, from *in* in, on, and *aurum* gold]

inauspicious /*in-ö-spish'əs*/ *adj* not auspicious; ill-omened; unlucky. [in- (2)]
■ **inauspic'iously** *adv.* **inauspic'iousness** *n.*

inauthentic /*in-ö-then'tik*/ *adj* not authentic; not genuine; untrue. [in- (2)]
■ **inauthen'tically** *adv.* **inauthenticity** /*-tis'i-ti*/ *n.*

in banco /*in bang'kō*/ (*LL*; *law*) in full court.
■ **in banco regis** /*rē'jis* or *rä'gis*/ in the King's Bench.

inbd *abbrev* : inboard.

inbeing /*in'bē-ing*/ *n* inherent existence; inherence; inner nature. [in- (1)]

inbent /*in'bent*/ *adj* bent inwards. [in- (1)]

in-between /*in-bi-twēn'*/ *adj* intervening; intermediate. ♦*n* an interval; an intermediary; any thing or person that is intermediate.

in bianco /*in byang'kō* or *bē-äng'kō*/ (*Ital*) in blank, in white.

inboard /*in'börd* or *-börd*/ *adv* and *adj* within the hull or interior of a ship; between the wing tip and fuselage (of an aircraft). [in- (1)]

in-bond /*in'bond*/ *adj* (of goods, raw materials, etc) not subject to import/export duties, held in bond. [in- (1)]
❑ **in-bond shop** *n* (*W Indies*) a duty-free shop.

inborn /*in'börn*/ *adj* born in or with one; innate; implanted by nature. [in- (1)]

inbound /*in'bownd*/ *adj* coming in. [in- (1)]

inbreak /*in'brāk*/ (*rare*) *n* a violent rush in; irruption. [in- (1)]

inbreathe /*in-brēdh'* or *in'brēdh*/ *vt* to breathe in, inhale; to imbue. [in- (1)]

inbreed /*in'brēd* or *in-brēd'*/ *vt* to breed or generate within. ♦ *vt* and *vi* to breed from closely related parents. [in- (1)]
■ **in'bred** *adj* innate; bred from closely related parents. **in'breeding** *n.*
❑ **inbred line** *n* (*biol*) a strain that has been inbred over many generations, its members being genetically identical or nearly so.

inbring /*in-bring'*/ (*obs*) *vt* to bring in; to bring into court. [in- (1)]
■ **in'bringing** *n.* **inbrought'** *adj.*

inburning /*in-bûr'ning*/ (*Spenser*) *adj* burning within. [in- (1)]

inburst /*in'bûrst*/ (*rare*) *n* an irruption. [in- (1)]

inby or **inbye** /*in-bī'*/ (*Scot*) *adv* toward the interior; near; near the house. ♦*adj* situated near the house. [in- (1)]

inc. *abbrev* : including; inclusive; incorporated.

Inca /*ing'kə*/ *n* a member of a S American people of Peru before the Spanish conquest in the 16c, who had a complex civilization and empire; the language of the Incas; a member of the Incan royal family; a king or emperor of the Incas. ♦ *adj* of or relating to the Incas or their language. [Sp, from Quechua *inka* ruler, king]
■ **In'can** *adj.*

incage see **encage**.

incalculable /*in-kal'kū-lə-bl*/ *adj* not calculable or able to be reckoned; too great to calculate; unpredictable. [in- (2)]
■ **incalculabil'ity** *n.* **incal'culableness** *n.* **incal'culably** *adv.*

incalescent /*in-ka-les'ənt* or *-kə-*/ (*chem*) *adj* growing warm. [L *incalēscēns, -entis,* prp of *incalēscere,* from *in* in, and *calēscere,* inceptive of *calere* to be warm]
■ **incalesc'ence** *n.*

in-calf /*in-käf'*/ *adj* pregnant (with calf). [in[1] and calf[1]]

in camera see under **camera**.

incandesce /*in-kan-des'*/ *vt* and *vi* to make or become luminous by heat. [L *in* in, and *candēscere,* from *candēre* to glow]
■ **incandesc'ence** *n* a white heat. **incandesc'ent** *adj* white-hot. **incandesc'ently** *adv.*
❑ **incandescent lamp** *n* one whose light is produced by heating something to white heat, such as a filament resisting an electric current or a mantle heated by a flame.

incantation /*in-kan-tā'shən*/ *n* a formula of words said or sung for purposes of enchantment, a magic spell; recitation of magic spells. [L *incantāre* to sing a magical formula over]
■ **incantā'tional** *adj.* **in'cantātor** *n.* **incan'tatory** /*-tə-tə-ri*/ *adj.*

incapable /*in-kā'pə-bl*/ *adj* not capable; unable (with *of*); incompetent; helplessly drunk; disqualified; unable to receive or keep (with *of*; *obs*). ♦ *n* an incompetent person; a person who is helplessly drunk. [in- (2)]
■ **incapabil'ity** *n.* **incā'pably** *adv.*

incapacious /*in-kə-pā'shəs*/ *adj* not large, narrow; of small capacity. [L *incapāx, -ācis*]
■ **incapā'ciousness** *n.* **incapacitant** /*-pas'-*/ *n.* **incapac'itate** *vt* to disable; to make unfit (for); to disqualify legally. **incapacitā'tion** *n* (a) disqualifying. **incapac'ity** *n* lack of capacity; inability; disability; legal disqualification.
❑ **Incapacity Benefit** *n* an allowance paid to someone who is incapable of working because of sickness or disability.

Incaparina /*in-kap-ə-rē'nə*/ *n* a high-protein dietary supplement developed by the *I*nstitute of *N*utrition of *C*entral *A*merica and *P*anama. [*I.N.C.A.P* and *-arina,* from Sp *fariña* powdered manioc, from L *farina* flour]

in capite /*in kap'i-tē* or *kap'i-te*/ (*LL*) in chief; holding directly from the Crown (*feudal law*).

incapsulate /*in-kap'sū-lāt*/ *vt* to enclose as in a capsule; to enclose (a modifying element) between other elements of a word. [in- (1)]

incarcerate /*in-kär'sə-rāt*/ *vt* to imprison; to confine. [L *in* in, and *carcer* a prison]

■ words derived from main entry word; ❑ compound words; ■ idioms and phrasal verbs

■ **incarcera'tion** *n* imprisonment; obstinate constriction or strangulation (*surg*). **incar'cerātor** *n*.

incardinate /*in-kär'di-nāt*/ *vt* to attach or transfer (a priest, etc) to the jurisdiction of a (new) bishop. ◆ *adj* Sir Andrew Aguecheek's blunder for *incarnate* (Shakesp, *Twelfth Night* V.1). [LL *incardināre* to ordain as chief priest]
■ **incardinā'tion** *n* the official acceptance of a priest or member of the clergy into a new diocese.

incarnadine /*in-kär'nə-dīn* or *-din*/ *vt* to dye red. ◆ *adj* carnation-coloured; flesh-colour; blood-red. [Fr *incarnadin*, from Ital *incarnadino* carnation, flesh-colour]

incarnate /*in-kär'nāt* or *in'*/ *vt* to embody in flesh, give human form to; to personify (*fig*). ◆ *vi* to form flesh, heal. ◆ *adj* /*-kär'nit* or *-nat*/ invested with flesh; personified. [LL *incarnāre, -ātum*, from L *in* in, and *carō, carnis* flesh]
■ **incarnā'tion** *n* the act of embodying in flesh, *esp* of Christ (often with *cap*); an incarnate form; manifestation, visible embodiment; the process of healing, or forming new flesh (*surg*).

incarvillea /*in-kär-vil'i-ə*/ *n* any plant of the genus *Incarvillea*, of the family Bignoniaceae typically having trumpet-shaped flowers borne in clusters on erect stems. [Pierre d'*Incarville* (1706–57), French missionary to China]

incase and **incasement** see **encase**.

incatenation /*in-kat-i-nā'shən*/ *n* harnessing; chaining together; linking. [L *in* in, and *catēna* chain]

incautious /*in-kö'shəs*/ *adj* not cautious or careful. [**in-** (2)]
■ **incau'tion** *n*. **incau'tiously** *adv*. **incau'tiousness** *n*.

incave same as **encave**.

incavo /*in-kä'vō*/ *n* (*pl* **inca'vi** /*-vē*/) the incised part in an intaglio. [Ital, from L *in* in, and *cavus* hollow]

incede /*in-sēd'*/ (*rare*) *vi* to advance majestically. [L *incēdere*; see Virgil, *Aeneid* I.46]
■ **incēd'ingly** *adv*.

incendiary /*in-sen'di-ə-ri*/ *n* a person who maliciously sets fire to property; a person who inflames passions or stirs up trouble; an incendiary bomb. ◆ *adj* relating to incendiarism; adapted or used for setting buildings, etc on fire; tending to stir up trouble. [L *incendiārius*, from *incendium*, from *incendere* to set on fire]
■ **incen'diarism** *n* the malicious burning of property.
❑ **incendiary bomb** *n* a bomb containing a highly inflammable substance and designed to burst into flames on striking its objective.

incendivity /*in-sen-div'i-ti*/ *n* the power of causing ignition. [L *incendere* to set on fire]

incense[1] /*in'sens*/ *n* material burned or volatilized to give fragrant fumes, *esp* in religious rites, *usu* a mixture of resins and gums, etc (eg olibanum, benzoin, styrax, cascarilla bark); the fumes so obtained; any pleasant smell; homage, adulation (*fig*). ◆ *vt* to perfume or fumigate with incense; to offer incense to. [OFr *encens*, from L *incēnsum*, from *incendere* to set on fire]
■ **incensā'tion** *n*. **in'censer** or **in'censor** (or /*-sens'*/) *n* a burner or offerer of incense; a flatterer. **in'censory** (or /*-sens'*/) *n* a censer or thurible.
❑ **in'cense-boat** *n* a boat-shaped vessel for feeding a censer with incense. **in'cense-breathing** *adj* (*Gray*) exhaling fragrance. **in'cense-burner** *n* a stationary vessel for burning incense.

incense[2] /*in-sens'*/ *vt* to inflame with anger, to enrage; to incite, urge; to kindle (*obs*). [OFr *incenser*, from L *incendere, incēnsum* to kindle]
■ **incense'ment** *n*. **incen'sor** *n* (*obs*) an instigator or inciter.

incentive /*in-sen'tiv*/ *adj* inciting, encouraging; igniting (*Milton*). ◆ *n* that which incites to action, a stimulus. [L *incentīvus* striking up a tune, from *incinere*, from *in* in, and *canere* to sing]
■ **incentivizā'tion** or **-s-** *n*. **incent'ivize** or **-ise** *vi* to have or be given an incentive, *esp* to work more efficiently, productively, etc.

incentre /*in'sen-tər*/ *n* the centre of an inscribed circle or sphere. [**in-** (1)]

incept /*in-sept'*/ *vt* to take into the body, ingest; to begin (*obs*). ◆ *vi* formerly, to complete the taking of a master's or doctor's degree at a university. [L *incipere, inceptum* to begin, from *in* in, on, and *capere* to take]
■ **incep'tion** *n* beginning. **incep'tive** *adj* beginning or marking the beginning; inchoative (*grammar*). ◆ *n* (*grammar*) an inchoative verb. **incep'tor** *n*.

incertain /*in-sûr'tən*/ (*obs*) *adj* uncertain. [**in-** (2)]
■ **incer'tainty** (*obs*) or **incer'titude** *n* (*archaic*).

incessant /*in-ses'ənt*/ *adj* uninterrupted; continual. [L *incessāns, -antis*, from *in-* not, and *cessāre* to cease]
■ **incess'ancy** *n*. **incess'antly** *adv* unceasingly; immediately (*obs*). **incess'antness** *n*.

incest /*in'sest*/ *n* sexual intercourse between people who are so closely related that marriage is prohibited. [L *incestum*, from *in-* not, and *castus* chaste]
■ **incest'ūous** *adj* relating to, or characterized by, incest; turned inward on itself, or of, or within, a small closely-knit group (*fig*). **incest'uously** *adv*. **incest'uousness** *n*.
❑ **incest taboo** *n* (*behaviourism*) a strong negative social sanction that forbids sexual relations between members of the same immediate family.

inch[1] /*inch* or *insh*/ *n* the twelfth part of a foot, equal to 2.54cm; the amount of eg rainfall that will cover a surface to the depth of one inch (now measured in millimetres); the amount of atmospheric pressure needed to balance the weight of a column of mercury one inch high (now measured in millibars); proverbially, a small distance or degree; (in *pl*) stature. ◆ *vt* and *vi* to move by slow degrees. [OE *ynce* an inch, from L *uncia* a twelfth part; cf **ounce**[1]]
■ **inched** *adj* marked with inches.
❑ **inch'-tape** *n* a measuring tape divided into inches. **inch'-worm** *n* a looper caterpillar.
■ **at an inch** (*Shakesp*) ready at hand. **by inches** or **inch by inch** by small degrees. **every inch** entirely, thoroughly. **inch out** to defeat by a small amount; to measure or dispense in tiny amounts. **within an inch of** very close to. **within an inch of someone's life** to the point where there is danger of death.

inch[2] /*insh*/ (*Scot* and *Irish*) *n* an island; a low-lying meadow beside a river. [Gaelic *innis* island]

incharitable /*in-char'i-tə-bl*/ (*old*) *adj* lacking charity. [**in-** (2)]

inchase /*in-chās'*/ same as **enchase**.

inchmeal /*inch'mēl* or *insh'mēl*/ *adv* inch by inch; little by little. [**inch**[1] and ME *-mele*, from OE *maelum* measure or quantity taken at one time]

inchoate /*in-kō'āt* or *in'kō-āt*/ *adj* only begun; unfinished, rudimentary; not established. ◆ *vt* /*in'*/ to begin. [L *inchoāre* (for *incohāre*), *-ātum* to begin]
■ **inchoately** /*-kō'* or *in'*/ *adv*. **incho'ateness** *n*. **inchoā'tion** *n* beginning; rudimentary state. **inchoative** /*in-kō'ə-tiv* or *in-kō-ā'tiv*/ *adj* incipient; denoting the beginning of an action, inceptive (*grammar*). ◆ *n* (*grammar*) an inchoative verb.

incident /*in'si-dənt*/ *adj* falling (on something); liable to occur; naturally belonging (to); consequent. ◆ *n* that which happens; an event; a subordinate action; an episode; that which naturally belongs to or is consequent on something else; a minor event showing hostility and threatening more serious trouble; a brief violent action, eg a bomb explosion. [L *incidēns, -entis*, from *in* on, and *cadere* to fall]
■ **in'cidence** *n* the frequency or range of occurrence; the fact or manner of falling; the falling of a ray on a surface; the falling of a point on a line, or a line on a plane (*geom*). **incidental** /*-dent'l*/ *adj* incident; striking or impinging; liable to occur; naturally attached; accompanying; concomitant; occasional, casual. ◆ *n* anything that occurs incidentally. **incident'ally** *adv* in an incidental way; (loosely) by the way, parenthetically, as a digression. **incident'alness** *n*.
❑ **incidental music** *n* music accompanying the action of a play, film, television programme, etc. **incident centre**, **office** or **room** *n* a temporary establishment set up near the scene of a crime, disaster or unrest, etc by the police or army in order to collect information and monitor the situation.
■ **angle of incidence** (*phys*) the angle between an incident ray and the normal to the surface it falls on.

incinerate /*in-sin'ə-rāt*/ *vt* to reduce to ashes. [L *incinerāre, -ātum*, from *in*, in, and *cinis, cineris* ashes]
■ **incinerā'tion** *n*. **incin'erātor** *n* a furnace for burning anything to ashes.

incipient /*in-sip'i-ənt*/ *adj* beginning, coming into existence; nascent. [L *incipiēns, -entis*, prp of *incipere* to begin]
■ **incip'ience** *n*. **incip'iency** *n*. **incip'iently** *adv*.

incipit /*in-sip'it* or *in-kip'it*/ (*L*) (here) begins (commonly used as an introduction in medieval manuscripts).

incise /*in-sīz'*/ *vt* to cut into; to cut or gash; to engrave. [Fr *inciser*, from L *incidere, incīsum*, from *in* into, and *caedere* to cut]
■ **incised'** *adj* cut; engraved; cut to about the middle (*bot*). **incis'iform** *adj* (*zool*) shaped like an incisor tooth. **incision** /*in-sizh'ən*/ *n* the act of cutting in, *esp* (*surg*) into the soft tissues of the body; a cut; a gash; a notch; trenchancy. **incisive** /*-sīs'*/ *adj* having the quality of cutting in; trenchant; acute; sarcastic. **inci'sively** *adv*. **inci'siveness** *n*. **incisor** /*-sīz'ər*/ *n* a tooth at the front of the mouth, a cutting tooth. **incisorial** /*-sis-ō'ri-əl, -sīs-* or *-ö'*/ or **incisory** /*-sīs'* or *-sīz'ər-i*/ *adj*. **incisure** /*-sizh'ər*/ *n* (*surg*) a cut, incision.

incite /*in-sīt'*/ *vt* to move or provoke to action; to instigate. [Fr, from L *incitāre*, from *in* in, and *citāre* to rouse, from *ciēre* to put in motion]
■ **incitant** /*in'sit-ənt* or *in-sīt'ənt*/ *n* that which incites; a stimulant. **incitā'tion** /*-sit-* or *-sīt-*/ *n* the act of inciting or rousing; an incentive.

incitative /-sīt'ə-tiv/ adj and n. **incite'ment** n. **incit'er** n. **incit'ingly** adv.

incivil /in-siv'il/ adj an old form of **uncivil**. [**in-** (2)]
■ **incivil'ity** n lack of civility or courtesy; impoliteness; (often in pl) an act of discourtesy.

incivism /in'si-vi-zm/ n neglect of duty as a citizen, conduct unbecoming a good citizen. [Fr incivisme]

incl. abbrev : including; inclusive.

inclasp /in-kläsp'/ same as **enclasp**.

incle see **inkle**[1].

inclement /in-klem'ənt/ adj severe; stormy; harsh. [**in-** (2)]
■ **inclem'ency** n. **inclem'ently** adv.

incline /in-klīn'/ vi to lean forward or downward; to bow or bend; to deviate or slant; to slope; to tend; to be disposed; to have some slight desire. ◆ vt to cause to bend downwards; to turn; to cause to deviate; to slope; to tilt; to direct; to dispose. ◆ n /in'klīn or in-klīn'/ a slope; a sloping tunnel or shaft (mining). [L inclīnāre to bend towards, from in into, and clīnāre to lean]
■ **inclīn'able** adj. **inclīn'ableness** n. **inclination** /-klin-ā'shən/ n the act of inclining; a bend or bow; a slope or tilt; a deviation; an angle with the horizon or with any plane or line; tendency; disposition, esp favourable; natural aptness; preference; affection. **inclinā'tional** adj. **inclīnato'rium** n the dipping-needle. **inclīn'atory** adj. **inclīned'** adj bent; sloping; oblique; having a tendency; disposed. **inclīn'er** n. **inclīn'ing** n inclination; party, following (Shakesp). **inclinom'eter** /-klin-/ n an instrument for measuring slopes or the inclination of the axis of an aeroplane.
□ **inclined plane** n one of the mechanical powers, a slope or plane up which one can raise a weight one could not lift.

inclip /in-klip'/ (archaic) vt to embrace, enfold. [**in-** (1)]

inclose and **inclosure** see **enclose**.

include /in-klood'/ vt to comprise as a part, contain; to classify, or reckon as part; to take in; to enclose; to conclude (Shakesp). [L inclūdere, inclūsum, from in in, and claudere to shut]
■ **includ'able** or **includ'ible** adj. **includ'ed** adj comprised; enclosed; not protruding (bot). **includ'ing** prep (or prp merging into prep) with the inclusion of. **inclusion** /-kloo'zhən/ n the act of including; that which is included; a foreign body (gas, liquid, glass or mineral) enclosed in a mineral groundmass; a particle, etc distinct from the substance surrounding it (biol). **inclusive** /-kloo'siv/ adj comprehensive; including everything; including the stated limits or extremes (with of); included; enclosing. **inclu'sively** adv. **inclu'siveness** or **inclusiv'ity** n.
□ **inclusion bodies** n pl (pathol) particles found in the nucleus and cytoplasm of cells infected with a virus. **inclusive fitness** see under **fit**[1]. **inclusive language** n language that attempts to avoid excluding anyone, esp on the basis of gender. **inclusive reckoning** n a system of counting in which both the first and the last terms are included (ie Monday–Wednesday is 3 days). **inclusive transcription** n any phonetic transcription allowing more than one pronunciation of the transcribed words.
■ **include in** or **out** (inf) to include or exclude.

incoagulable /in-kō-ag'ū-lə-bl/ adj incapable of coagulation. [**in-** (2)]

incoercible /in-kō-ûr'si-bl/ adj that cannot be coerced; that cannot be liquefied by pressure. [**in-** (2)]

incog. abbrev : incognito.

incogitable /in-koj'i-tə-bl/ adj unthinkable. [L in- not, and cōgitāre to think]
■ **incogitabil'ity** n. **incog'itancy** n. **incog'itant** adj unthinking; thoughtless. **incog'itātive** adj.

incognisable, **incognisance**, **incognisant** see **incognizable**.

incognito /in-kog'ni-tō or in-kog-nē'tō/ adj unknown, unidentified; disguised; under an assumed name or title. ◆ adv under an assumed name; with concealment of identity. ◆ n (pl **incognitos**) a person concealing his or her identity; an assumed identity. [Ital, from L incognitus, from in- not, and cognitus known, from cognōscere to recognize, come to know]

incognizable or **incognisable** /in-kog'ni-zə-bl/ adj that cannot be known or distinguished. [See **cognition** and **recognize**]
■ **incog'nizance** or **-s-** n failure to recognize. **incog'nizant** or **-s-** adj unaware (with of).

incoherent /in-kō-hē'rənt/ adj not coherent; loose; rambling. [**in-** (2)]
■ **incohēr'ence** or **incohēr'ency** n. **incohēr'ently** adv.

incombustible /in-kəm-bus'ti-bl/ adj incapable of combustion; incapable of being burnt. [**in-** (2)]
■ **incombustibil'ity** or **incombust'ibleness** n. **incombust'ibly** adv.

income /in(g)'kum or kəm/ n profit, or interest from anything; revenue; that which comes in, inflow; arrival, entrance (archaic); a disease, tumour, etc without known cause (Scot and N Eng dialect). [**in-** (1)]

incomer /in'kum-ər/ n a person who comes in, esp one who comes to live in a place, not having been born there. **in'coming** adj coming in; accruing; ensuing, next to follow. ◆ n the act of coming in; revenue.
□ **income bond** n a type of savings bond paying monthly or annual interest (without deducting tax at source). **income group** n a group within a population having incomes within a certain range, eg middle income group. **incomes policy** n a government policy of curbing inflation by controlling wages. **income support** n in Britain, a social security payment made to people on low incomes. **income tax** n a tax directly levied on income or on income over a certain amount. **income unit** n a type of unit trust in which a regular dividend is paid to the holder instead of accumulating in the capital fund.
■ **negative income tax** a type of Government subsidy in which low-paid workers are paid an additional sum instead of having tax deducted from their wages.

in commendam see **commendam** under **commend**.

incommensurable /in-kə-men'shə-rə-bl or -shū-/ adj having no common measure; not reaching the same standard; disproportionate. ◆ n (maths) a quantity that has no common factor with another, esp with rational numbers. [**in-** (2)]
■ **incommensurabil'ity** or **incommen'surableness** n inability to be measured. **incommen'surably** adv.

incommensurate /in-kə-men'shə-rət/ adj disproportionate (with to or with); inadequate; incommensurable. [**in-** (2)]
■ **incommen'surately** adv. **incommen'surateness** n.

incommiscible /in-kə-mis'i-bl/ adj that cannot be mixed together. [L in- not, and commiscēre to mix]

incommode /in-kə-cōd'/ vt to cause trouble or inconvenience to. [Fr incommoder, from L incommodāre, from in- not, and commodus commodious]
■ **incommō'dious** adj inconvenient; (of eg a house) cramped, poky; troublesome (obs); unsuitable (with to or for ; obs). **incommō'diously** adv. **incommō'diousness** n. **incommodity** /-od'/ n inconvenience; anything that causes inconvenience.

incommunicable /in-kə-mūn'i-kə-bl/ adj that cannot be communicated or passed on to others. [**in-** (2)]
■ **incommunicabil'ity** or **incommun'icableness** n. **incommun'icably** adv. **incommun'icative** adj uncommunicative. **incommun'icatively** adv. **incommun'icativeness** n.

incommunicado, also **incomunicado** /in-kə-mūn-i-kä'dō/ adj and adv without means of communication; in solitary confinement. [Sp incomunicado]

incommutable /in-kə-mū'tə-bl/ adj that cannot be commuted or exchanged. [**in-** (2)]
■ **incommutabil'ity** or **incommut'ableness** n. **incommut'ably** adv.

incomparable /in-kom'pə-rə-bl/ adj not admitting comparison; matchless. [**in-** (2)]
■ **incomparabil'ity** or **incom'parableness** n. **incom'parably** adv. **incompared** /in-kom-pā'red/ adj (Spenser) peerless.

incompatible /in-kəm-pat'i-bl/ adj not consistent; contradictory; incapable of existing together in harmony, or at all; incapable of combination, co-operation, or functioning together; mutually intolerant or exclusive; irreconcilable. ◆ n a thing incompatible with another; (in pl) things which cannot coexist. [**in-** (2)]
■ **incompatibil'ity** n the state of being incompatible; an incompatible feature, element, etc; a difference, usu physiological, which prevents completion of fertilization (bot); a difference in physiological properties between a host and parasite which limits the development of the latter (bot); the mismatch which leads to a graft or a blood transfusion being rejected. **incompat'ibleness** n. **incompat'ibly** adv.

incompetent /in-kom'pi-tənt/ adj unable to function; without the proper legal qualifications; lacking ability or skill for one's work. ◆ n an incompetent person. [**in-** (2)]
■ **incom'petence** n the state or condition of being incompetent; (in the veins, heart, etc) a condition in which the proper function of the valves is impaired, allowing blood to leak backwards (med). **incom'petency** n. **incom'petently** adv.

incomplete /in-kəm-plēt'/ adj imperfect; unfinished; lacking calyx, corolla, or both (bot); (in American football) denoting a pass that is not caught by a receiver. [**in-** (2)]
■ **incomplete'ly** adv. **incomplete'ness** n. **incomplē'tion** n.
□ **incomplete reaction** n (chem) a process in which a reversible reaction is allowed to reach equilibrium and from which a mixture of reactants and reaction products is obtained.

incompliance /in-kəm-plī'əns/ n refusal to comply; an unaccommodating disposition; inflexibility. [**in-** (2)]
■ **incomplī'ant** adj.

incomposed /in-kəm-pōzd'/ (poetic; obs) adj discomposed. [**in-** (2)]

incomposite /in-kom'pə-zit/ adj simple; ill-constructed. [**in-** (2)] □ **incomposite numbers** n pl prime numbers.

incomprehensible /in-kom-pri-hen'si-bl/ adj not capable of being understood; not to be contained within limits, limitless (archaic and theol). [**in-** (2)]
■ **incomprehensibil'ity** or **incomprehens'ibleness** n inability to be comprehended. **incomprehens'ibly** adv. **incomprehen'sion** n. **incomprehens'ive** adj. **incomprehens'iveness** n.

incompressible /in-kəm-pres'i-bl/ adj incapable of being compressed into smaller bulk. [**in-** (2)]
■ **incompressibil'ity** or **incompress'ibleness** n.

incomputable /in-kəm-pū'tə-bl/ or /in-kom'/ adj that cannot be computed or reckoned. [**in-** (2)]

incomunicado see **incommunicado**.

inconceivable /in-kən-sē'və-bl/ adj that cannot be conceived by the mind; incomprehensible; involving a contradiction in terms; physically impossible; taxing belief or imagination (inf). ♦ n (rare) an inconceivable thing. [**in-** (2)]
■ **inconceivabil'ity** or **inconceiv'ableness** n. **inconceiv'ably** adv.

inconcinnity /in-kən-sin'i-ti/ n lack of congruousness or proportion. [**in-** (2)]
■ **inconcinn'ous** adj.

inconclusive /in-kən-kloo'siv/ adj not settling a point in debate; indeterminate, indecisive. [**in-** (2)]
■ **inconclusion** /-kloo'zhən/ n lack of a definite conclusion. **inconclus'ively** adv. **inconclus'iveness** n.

incondensable /in-kən-den'sə-bl/ adj incapable of being condensed. [**in-** (2)]

incondite /in-kon'dit/ or /-dīt/ adj not well put together, poorly constructed, irregular, unfinished. [L inconditus, from in- not, and condere, conditum to build]

incongruous /in-kong'grü-əs/ or **incongruent** /-grü-ənt/ adj inconsistent; out of keeping; unsuitable. [**in-** (2)]
■ **incongruity** /-kong-** or /-kən-groo'/ n the fact of being incongruous; an incongruous thing. **incong'ruously** or **incong'ruently** adv. **incong'ruousness** or **incong'ruence** n.

inconie see **incony**.

inconnu /ē-ko-nü'/ (Fr) n an unknown person (also fem **inconnue**); a large food-fish (Stenodus leucichthys) of NW Canada.

inconscient /in-kon'shyənt/ or /-shənt/ adj unconscious; abstracted; not controlled by, or arising from, consciousness. [**in-** (2)]
■ **incon'sciently** adv. **incon'scious** adj unconscious.

inconscionable /in-kon'shə-nə-bl/ adj unconscionable. [**in-** (2)]

inconsecutive /in-kən-sek'ū-tiv/ adj not succeeding or proceeding in regular order; not consecutive. [**in-** (2)]
■ **inconsec'utively** adv. **inconsec'utiveness** n.

inconsequent /in-kon'si-kwənt/ adj not following from the premises (logic); illogical; irrelevant; disconnected; unrelated; unimportant. [**in-** (2)]
■ **incon'sequence** n. **inconsequential** /-kwen'shl/ adj not following from the premises (logic); of no consequence or value. **inconsequential'ity** n. **inconsequen'tially** adv. **inconsequen'tialness** n. **incon'sequently** adv.

inconsiderable /in-kən-sid'ə-rə-bl/ adj not worthy of notice; unimportant; of no great size. [**in-** (2)]
■ **inconsid'erableness** n. **inconsid'erably** adv.

inconsiderate /in-kən-sid'e-rit/ adj without care or regard for others; thoughtless; rash, imprudent. [**in-** (2)]
■ **inconsid'erately** adv. **inconsid'erateness** or **inconsiderā'tion** n.

inconsistent /in-kən-sis'tənt/ adj not consistent; not suitable or agreeing; intrinsically incompatible; self-contradictory; changeable, fickle. [**in-** (2)]
■ **inconsist'ence** or **inconsist'ency** n. **inconsist'ently** adv.

inconsolable /in-kən-sō'lə-bl/ adj not able to be comforted. [**in-** (2)]
■ **inconsol'ability** or **inconsol'ableness** n. **inconsol'ably** adv.

inconsonant /in-kon'sə-nənt/ adj not agreeing or in harmony with. [**in-** (2)]
■ **incon'sonance** n. **incon'sonantly** adv.

inconspicuous /in-kən-spik'ū-əs/ adj not conspicuous. [**in-** (2)]
■ **inconspic'uously** adv. **inconspic'uousness** n.

inconstant /in-kon'stənt/ adj subject to change, variable; fickle. [**in-** (2)]
■ **incon'stancy** n. **incon'stantly** adv.

inconstruable /in-kən-stroo'ə-bl/ adj which cannot be construed; impossible to interpret or understand. [**in-** (2)]

inconsumable /in-kən-sū'mə-bl/ adj that cannot be consumed or wasted. [**in-** (2)]
■ **inconsum'ably** adv.

incontestable /in-kən-tes'tə-bl/ adj too clear to be called in question; undeniable. [**in-** (2)]
■ **incontestabil'ity** n. **incontest'ably** adv.

incontiguous /in-kən-tig'ū-əs/ adj not adjoining or touching. [**in-** (2)]
■ **incontig'uously** adv. **incontig'uousness** n.

incontinent[1] /in-kon'ti-nənt/ adj unable to control urination or defecation; lacking self-restraint, esp in sexual matters; lacking control over (with of). [L incontinēns, -entis, from in- not, and continēns; see **continent**]
■ **incon'tinence** or **incon'tinency** n. **incon'tinently** adv.

incontinent[2] /in-kon'ti-nənt/ (archaic) adv straight away, immediately (also **incon'tinently**). [Fr, from LL in continenti (tempore) in unbroken (time)]

incontrollable /in-kən-trō'lə-bl/ adj uncontrollable. [**in-** (2)]
■ **incontroll'ably** adv.

incontrovertible /in-kon-trə-vûr'ti-bl/ adj incontestable; indisputable. [**in-** (2)]
■ **incontrovertibil'ity** n. **incontrovert'ibly** adv.

in contumaciam /in kon-tū-mash'i-əm, in kon-tū-mä'ki-am/ (L) as an act of contumacy.

inconvenient /in-kən-vē'nyənt/ adj not convenient, unsuitable; inopportune; causing trouble, difficulty or uneasiness; incommodious. [**in-** (2)]
■ **inconvēn'ience** vt to trouble or incommode. ♦ n the state of being inconvenient; something causing difficulty or giving trouble. **inconvēn'iently** adv.

inconversable /in-kən-vûr'sə-bl/ adj indisposed to conversation, unsocial. [**in-** (2)]

inconversant /in-kon'vər-sənt/ or (rare) /-kən-vûr'/ adj not versed (with with or in). [**in-** (2)]

inconvertible /in-kən-vûr'ti-bl/ adj that cannot be changed or exchanged. [**in-** (2)]
■ **inconvertibil'ity** n. **inconvert'ibly** adv.

inconvincible /in-kən-vin'si-bl/ adj not capable of being convinced. [**in-** (2)]

incony or **inconie** /in-kun'i/ (Shakesp) adj fine, delicate, pretty. [Origin unknown]

inco-ordinate /in-kō-ör'di-nit/ or /-örd'nit/ adj not co-ordinate (also **incoord'inate**). [**in-** (2)]
■ **inco-ordination** /-i-nā'shən/ n lack or failure of co-ordination, eg the inability to combine the muscular movements necessary to perform an action (also **incoordinā'tion**).

incoronate /in-kor'ə-nāt/ or /-nit/ or **incoronated** /-nā-tid/ (formal) adj crowned. [**in-** (1)]
■ **incoronā'tion** n.

incorporal or **incorporall** /in-kör'pə-rəl/ (archaic) adj incorporeal. [L incorporālis bodiless, from in- not, and corporālis, from corpus, -oris body]

incorporate[1] /in-kör'pə-rāt/ vt to form into a body; to combine into one mass; to merge; to absorb; to form into a corporation; to admit to a corporation. ♦ vi to unite into one mass; to form a corporation. ♦ adj /-ət/ incorporated. [L incorporāre, -ātum, from in in, into, and corpus, -oris body]
■ **incor'porated** adj united in one body; constituted as an incorporation. **incor'porāting** adj (linguistics) combining the parts of a sentence in one word, polysynthetic. **incorporā'tion** n the act of incorporating; the state of being incorporated; the formation of a legal or political body; an association; an incorporated society. **incor'porative** /-ə-tiv/ or /-ā-tiv/ adj. **incor'porātor** n a person who incorporates; a member, or original member, of an incorporated company (US); a member of a university admitted to membership of another.

incorporate[2] /in-kör'pə-rit/ or /-rāt/ adj without a body; incorporeal. [L incorporātus, from in- not, and corporātus, from corpus, -oris body]

incorporeal /in-kör-pö'ri-əl/ adj having no material form or body; spiritual or metaphysical; intangible; of, relating to, or constituting a legal right which attaches to something without a physical existence (eg copyright, patents, easement). [L incorporeus, from in- not, and corpus, -oris body]
■ **incorporeal'ity** or **incorpore'ity** n. **incorpo'really** adv.

incorpse /in-körps'/ (archaic) vt to incorporate. [**in-** (1)]

incorrect /in-kə-rekt'/ adj containing faults; not accurate; not correct in manner or character, improper; not regulated or corrected (obs). [**in-** (2)]
■ **incorrect'ly** adv. **incorrect'ness** n.

incorrigible /in-kor'i-ji-bl/ adj beyond correction or reform (also n). [**in-** (2)]
■ **incorrigibil'ity** or **incorr'igibleness** n. **incorr'igibly** adv.

incorrosible /in-kə-rō'si-bl/ or **incorrodible** /in-kə-rō'di-bl/ adj incapable of being corroded; not readily corroded. [**in-** (2)]

incorrupt /in-kə-rupt'/ adj free from corruption; pure; not decayed; not depraved or defiled; free from error; not able to be influenced by bribes. [**in-** (2)]
■ **incorruptibil'ity** or **incorrupt'ibleness** n. **incorrupt'ible** adj incapable of corruption; not capable of decay; that cannot be bribed; honest; just. **incorrupt'ibly** adv. **incorrup'tion** or **incorrupt'ness** n. **incorrupt'ive** adj. **incorrupt'ly** adv.

incrassate /in-kras'āt/ vt and vi (obs) to thicken. ◆ adj incrassated. [LL incrassāre, -ātum, from L in in, and crassus thick]
■ **incrass'ated** adj (esp biol) thickened or swollen. **incrassā'tion** n. **incrass'ative** /-ə-tiv/ adj.

increase /in-krēs'/ vi to grow in size or number; to become richer or more powerful (archaic); to have a syllable more in the genitive than in the nominative (L grammar). ◆ vt to make greater in size or number; to make richer or more powerful (archaic). ◆ n /in'/ growth; increment; addition to the original stock; profit; produce; progeny (archaic). [ME encressen, from Anglo-Fr encresser, from L incrēscere, from in, crēscere to grow]
■ **increas'able** adj. **increase'ful** adj (Shakesp) fruitful, productive. **increas'er** n. **increas'ing** n and adj. **increas'ingly** adv.
■ **on the increase** becoming greater.

increate /in-krē-āt'/ (archaic) adj uncreated, never having been created. [**in-** (2)]

incredible /in-kred'i-bl/ adj unbelievable; difficult to believe in; very great; unusually good, amazing (inf). [**in-** (2)]
■ **incredibil'ity** or **incred'ibleness** n. **incred'ibly** adv.

incredulous /in-kred'ū-ləs/ adj unwilling to believe, sceptical; unbelieving; expressing disbelief; unbelievable (obs). [**in-** (2)]
■ **incredū'lity** /-krid-/ or **incred'ulousness** n. **incred'ulously** adv.

incremate /in'kri-māt/ (obs) vt to burn; to cremate. [**in-** (1)]
■ **incremā'tion** n.

increment /ing'/ or /in'kri-mənt/ n increase; the amount of increase, eg in wages and salaries; an amount or thing added; the finite increase of a variable quantity (maths); an adding of particulars towards a climax (rhetoric); a syllable in excess of the number of the nominative singular or the second person singular present indicative (grammar). ◆ vt (in computer programming) to add 1 to the value in a storage location (cf **decrement**). [L incrēmentum, from incrēscere to increase]
■ **incremental** /-ment'l/ adj and n. **increment'ally** adv.
□ **incremental backup** n (comput) a copy containing files altered since the last backup. **incremental plotter** n (comput) a device which plots graphs from data specifying increments to its current position, rather than from data specifying co-ordinates (cf **digital plotter**).
■ **unearned increment** any exceptional increase in the value of land, houses, etc not due to the owner's labour or outlay.

increscent /in-kres'ənt/ (esp heraldry) adj (of the moon) waxing. [**in-** (1)]

incretion /in-krē'shən/ (physiol) n secretion directly into the bloodstream, eg of a hormone from an endocrine gland. [**in-** (1) and **secretion**]

incriminate /in-krim'i-nāt/ vt to charge with a crime or fault; to implicate, involve in a charge. [**in-** (1)]
■ **incrim'inating** or **incrim'inatory** adj. **incriminā'tion** n.

incross /in'kros/ n a plant or animal produced by crossing two inbred individuals of different lineage but of the same breed (also vt). [**in-** (1)]
■ **incross'bred** n a plant or animal produced by crossing two inbred individuals of different breeds. **incross'breed** vt.

incrust and **incrustation** see encrust.

incubate /in'/ or /ing'kū-bāt/ vi to brood eggs; to hatch; to undergo incubation; to brood, foment (fig). ◆ vt to hatch; to foster the development of (as bacteria, etc); to brood or ponder over (fig). [L incubāre, -ātum (or usu -itum), from in on, and cubāre to lie, recline]
■ **incubā'tion** n the act of sitting on eggs to hatch them; hatching (natural or artificial); fostering (as of bacteria, etc); brooding or fomenting (fig); (also **incubation** or **latent period**) the period between infection with disease and the appearance of symptoms (med). **in'cubātive** or **in'cubātory** adj. **in'cubātor** n an apparatus for hatching eggs by artificial heat, for rearing prematurely born babies, or for developing bacteria; a brooding hen; an organization that offers office facilities, advice, and often capital to newly formed businesses. **in'cubous** adj (bot) (of a liverwort) having the upper leaf-margin overlapping the leaf above.

incubus /in'/ or /ing'kū-bəs/ n (pl **in'cubuses** or **in'cubi** /-bī/) a devil supposed to assume a male body and have sexual intercourse with women in their sleep (cf **succubus**); a nightmare; any oppressive person, thing or influence. [L incubus nightmare, from in on, and cubāre to lie]

incudes see incus.

in cuerpo see en cuerpo.

inculcate /in'kul-kāt or -kul'/ vt to instil by frequent admonitions or repetitions. [L inculcāre, -ātum, from in into, and calcāre to tread, from calx heel]
■ **inculcā'tion** n. **inculc'ative** /-ə-tiv/ adj. **in'culcātor** n. **inculc'atory** adj.

inculpable /in-kul'pə-bl/ adj free from guilt; blameless. [L inculpābilis, from in- not, and culpābilis; see **culpable**]
■ **incul'pably** adv.

inculpate /in'kul-pāt or -kul'/ vt to blame; to incriminate; to charge. [LL inculpāre, -ātum, from in in, and culpa a fault]
■ **inculpā'tion** n. **incul'patory** /-pə-tə-ri/ adj.

incult /in-kult'/ (rare) adj uncultivated; coarse, uncultured. [**in-** (2)]

incumbent /in-kum'bənt/ adj imposed on, or laid on or upon, someone as a duty; obligatory; lying, resting or weighing on something; overlying (geol); leaning over (archaic); overhanging (archaic); lying along a surface, as a moth's wings at rest; (of a radicle) lying along the back of one cotyledon (bot). ◆ n a person who holds an ecclesiastical benefice, or any office. [L incumbēns, -entis, prp of incumbere to lie upon]
■ **incum'bency** n the state or fact of being incumbent or an incumbent; a duty or obligation; the holding of an office; an ecclesiastical benefice. **incum'bently** adv.

incumber see encumber.

incunabula /in-kū-nab'ū-lə/, also **incunables** /-kū'nə-blz/ n pl (sing **incūnab'ūlum** or **incūn'able**) early printed books, esp those printed before the year 1501; the cradle, birthplace, origin of a thing. [L incūnābula swaddling-clothes, infancy, earliest stage, from in in, and cūnābula, dimin of cūnae a cradle]
■ **incūn'able** adj. **incūnab'ūlar** adj. **incūnab'ūlist** n a student or collector of incunabula.

incur /in-kûr'/ vt (**incurr'ing**; **incurred'**) to become liable to; to bring upon oneself; to suffer. [L incurrere, incursum, from in into, and currere to run]
■ **incurr'able** adj. **incurr'ence** n.

incurable /in-kū'rə-bl/ adj unable to be cured or remedied. ◆ n someone beyond cure or who does not respond to treatment. [**in-** (2)]
■ **incurabil'ity** or **incur'ableness** n. **incur'ably** adv.

incurious /in-kū'ri-əs/ adj not curious or inquisitive; inattentive; uninterested; indifferent; not fastidious, uncritical (obs); not exquisite (obs); uninteresting (archaic). [**in-** (2)]
■ **incurios'ity** n. **incū'riously** adv. **incū'riousness** n.

incurrent /in-kur'ənt/ adj running or flowing in or inward; carrying an inflowing current. [L in into, and currēns, -entis, prp of currere to run]

incursion /in-kûr'shən/ n a hostile inroad; the action of leaking or running in; a sudden attack, invasion; an intrusion. [L incursiō, -ōnis, from incurrere to run into]
■ **incur'sive** adj making inroads; aggressive; invading; intruding.

incurve /in-kûrv'/ vt and vi to curve; to curve inward. ◆ n /in'/ a curve inwards. ◆ adj curved inward. [L incurvāre to bend in, and incurvus bent]
■ **incur'vate** (or /in'/) vt and vi to bend, esp inwards. ◆ adj curved, esp inward (also **incur'vāted**). **incurvā'tion** n bending; bowing, kneeling, etc; an inward bend or growth. **incur'vature** n a curve or curvature, esp inward. **incurved'** (or /in'/) adj curved; curved inward. **incur'vity** n.

incus /ing'kəs/ n (pl **incudes** /ing-kū'dēz or ing'/) one of the small bones in the middle ear articulated with the malleus and the stapes, so called because it is considered to resemble an anvil in shape. ◆ adj anvil-shaped. [L incūs, incūdis an anvil; see **incuse**]

incuse /in-kūz'/ vt to impress (eg a coin) with a design, or a design on a coin, etc, by stamping. ◆ adj hammered. ◆ n an impression, a stamp. [L incūsus, pap of incūdere, from in on, and cūdere to strike, to work on the anvil]

incut /in'kut/ adj set in by, or as if by, cutting; inserted in spaces left in the text (printing). [**in**[1] and **cut**]

IND abbrev : in nomine Dei (L), in the name of God; India (IVR).

Ind /ind or īnd/ (poetic) n India.

Ind. abbrev : Independent; India; Indian; Indiana (US state).

indaba /in-dä'bə/ n an important tribal conference; an international Scout conference; a problem, a matter of concern (S Afr inf). [Zulu]

indagate /in'də-gāt/ (archaic) vt to search out. [L indāgāre, -ātum to trace]
■ **indagā'tion** n. **in'dagātive** adj. **in'dagātor** n. **in'dagātory** adj.

indamine /in'də-mēn/ *n* any organic base whose salts are unstable blue or green dyes. [From **indigo** and **amine**]

indapamide /in-dap'ə-mīd/ *n* a synthetic thiazide drug used in the treatment of high blood pressure and oedema. [From **indole** and **amide**]

indart see **endart**.

indebted /in-det'id/ *adj* owing money; owing gratitude to another for something received, obligated. [**in-** (1)]
■ **indebt'edness** *n*.

indecent /in-dē'sənt/ *adj* offensive to common modesty; unbecoming; gross, obscene. [**in-** (2)]
■ **inde'cency** *n* the quality of being indecent; anything violating modesty or seemliness. **indē'cently** *adv*.
□ **indecent assault** *n* a sexual assault not involving rape. **indecent exposure** *n* the offence of indecently exposing part of one's body (*esp* the genitals) in public.

indeciduous /in-di-sid'ū-əs/ *adj* not deciduous. [**in-** (2)]
■ **indecid'uate** *adj* not deciduate.

indecipherable /in-di-sī'fə-rə-bl/ *adj* incapable of being deciphered; illegible. [**in-** (2)]
■ **indecipherabil'ity** or **indecī'pherableness** *n*. **indecī'pherably** *adv*.

indecision /in-di-sizh'ən/ *n* lack of decision or resolution; hesitation; wavering. [**in-** (2)]
■ **indecisive** /-sī'siv/ *adj* inconclusive; undecided; vacillating; hesitant. **indecī'sively** *adv*. **indecī'siveness** *n*.

indeclinable /in-di-klī'nə-bl/ (*grammar*) *adj* not varied by inflection. [**in-** (2)]
■ **indeclin'ably** *adv*.

indecomposable /in-dē-kəm-pō'zə-bl/ *adj* that cannot be decomposed. [**in-** (2)]

indecorous /in-dek'ə-rəs, sometimes -di-kō' or -kö'/ *adj* unseemly; violating good manners. [L *indecōrus*]
■ **indec'orously** *adv*. **indec'orousness** or **indecō'rum** *n* improper or impolite behaviour; a breach of decorum.

indeed /in-dēd'/ *adv* (emphasizing an affirmation, marking a qualifying word or clause, a concession or admission, or, as an interjection expressing surprise, interrogation, disbelief or mere acknowledgement) in fact, in truth, in reality. [**in**[1] and **deed**[1]]

indef. *abbrev* : indefinite.

indefatigable /in-di-fat'i-gə-bl/ *adj* untiring; unflagging; unremitting in effort. [Fr (obs), from L *indēfatīgābilis*, from *in-* not, *dē* from, and *fatīgāre* to tire]
■ **indefatigabil'ity** or **indefat'igableness** *n*. **indefat'igably** *adv*.

indefeasible /in-di-fē'zi-bl/ *adj* not to be annulled, forfeited or made void. [**in-** (2)]
■ **indefeasibil'ity** *n*. **indefeas'ibly** *adv*.

indefectible /in-di-fek'ti-bl/ *adj* incapable of defect, flawless; unfailing. [**in-** (2)]

indefensible /in-di-fen'si-bl/ *adj* untenable, that cannot be defended (*lit* or *fig*); that cannot be excused or justified. [**in-** (2)]
■ **indefensibil'ity** or **indefens'ibleness** *n*. **indefens'ibly** *adv*.

indefinable /in-di-fī'nə-bl/ *adj* that cannot be defined; hard to identify or describe. [**in-** (2)]
■ **indefin'ableness** *n*. **indefin'ably** *adv*.

indefinite /in-def'i-nit/ *adj* without clearly marked outlines or limits; not clearly distinguished in character; not precise, unclear; undetermined; (of a determiner or pronoun) not referring to a particular person or thing (*grammar*; see also **article**); not distinguishing between complete and incomplete active, as the Greek aorist (*grammar*); not fixed in number (*bot*); not terminating in a flower (*bot*); racemose or centripetal (*bot*). [**in-** (2)]
■ **indef'initely** *adv*. **indef'initeness** *n*.

indehiscent /in-di-his'ənt/ (*bot*) *adj* not dehiscent; (of fruits) not opening when mature. [**in-** (2)]
■ **indehisc'ence** *n*.

indelible /in-del'i-bl/ *adj* unable to be erased or blotted out; (of ink, etc) making an indelible mark. [L *indēlēbilis*, from *in-* not, and *dēlēre* to destroy]
■ **indelibil'ity** or **indel'ibleness** *n*. **indel'ibly** *adv*.

indelicate /in-del'i-kit/ *adj* immodest or verging on the immodest; tactless; in poor taste; coarse. [**in-** (2)]
■ **indel'icacy** *n*. **indel'icately** *adv*.

in deliciis /in də-lis'i-ēs, dā-lik'i-ēs/ (L) as favourites.

indemnify /in-dem'ni-fī/ *vt* (**indem'nifying**; **indem'nified**) to secure (with *against*); to compensate; to free, exempt (with *from*). [L *indemnis* unhurt (from *in-* not, and *damnum* loss), and *facere* to make]

■ **indemnification** /-fi-kā'shən/ *n* the act of indemnifying; the state of being indemnified; the amount paid as compensation. **indem'nifier** *n*.

indemnity /in-dem'ni-ti/ *n* security from damage or loss; compensation for loss or injury; legal exemption from incurred liabilities or penalties. [Fr *indemnité*, from L *indemnis* unharmed, from *damnum* loss]
■ **Act of Indemnity** an act or decree for the protection of public officers from any technical or legal penalties or liabilities they may have been compelled to incur.

indemonstrable /in-dem'ən-strə-bl/ or *in-di-mon'/ adj* that cannot be demonstrated or proved. [**in-** (2)]
■ **indemonstrabil'ity** *n*. **indemon'strably** *adv*.

indene /in'dēn/ *n* a double-ring liquid hydrocarbon (C_9H_8) obtained from coal tar and used in making resins. [**indigo**]

indent /in-dent'/ *vt* to begin farther in from the margin than the rest of a paragraph; to cut into zigzags; to divide along a zigzag line; to notch; to indenture, apprentice; to draw up (as a deed, contract, etc) in exact duplicate; to impress; to make a dent or dint in. ◆ *vt* and *vi* to make out a written order with counterfoil or duplicate; to order (*esp* from abroad); to requisition; (of a coastline, etc) to penetrate, form recesses. ◆ *vi* to move in a zigzag course (*archaic*); to bargain (*obs*); to make a compact (*obs*). ◆ *n* /in'dent, also in-dent'/ a cut or notch; a recess like a notch; the amount of space left at the beginning of a line, indentation; an indenture; an order for goods (*esp* from abroad); an (*orig* Indian) official requisition for goods; a dent or dint. [Two different words fused together: (1), from LL *indentāre*, from L *in* in, and *dēns, dentis* a tooth; (2), from Eng **in** and **dint**, **dent**[2]]
■ **indentā'tion** *n* a hollow or depression; the act or process of indenting or notching; a space left at the beginning of a line; the act or process of creating or leaving such a space; a notch; a recess. **indent'ed** *adj* having indentations; serrated; zigzag. **indent'er** or **indent'or** *n*. **inden'tion** *n* indentation; a blank space left at the beginning of a line.

indenture /in-den'chər/ *n* the act of indenting, indentation; a deed under seal, with mutual covenants, where the edge is indented to enable authenticity to be confirmed (*law*); a written agreement between two or more parties, *esp* (in *pl*) between an apprentice and an employer; a contract. ◆ *vt* to bind by indentures; to indent. [Anglo-Fr *endenture*, from LL *indentāre* ; see **indent**]
■ **inden'tureship** *n*.

independent /in-di-pen'dənt/ *adj* not dependent or relying on others (with *of*); not subordinate or subject to control by others; completely self-governing, autonomous; (of a business, etc) not affiliated or merged with a larger organization; capable of thinking or acting for oneself; too self-respecting to accept help; not subject to bias; having or affording a comfortable livelihood without necessity of working or help from others; (of a quantity or function) not depending on another for its value (*maths*); (with *cap*) belonging to the Independents. ◆ *n* (with *cap*) a person who in ecclesiastical affairs holds that every congregation should be independent of every other and subject to no superior authority, a Congregationalist; a person not committed to any group or (*esp* political) party. [**in-** (2)]
■ **independ'ence** *n* the state of being independent; a competency (*law*). **independ'ency** *n* the state of being independent, independence; a sovereign state; an independent income; (with *cap*) Congregationalism. **independ'ently** *adv*.
□ **Independence Day** *n* a day when a country becomes self-governing or the anniversary of this event (often celebrated with an annual national holiday). **independent clause** see under **clause**. **independent financial adviser** *n* a professional adviser on life insurance, pensions and investment who is not employed by an institution selling such services (*abbrev* **IFA**). **independent particle model** *n* (*phys*) a model of a nucleus in which each nucleon is assumed to act separately in a common field to which they all contribute. **independent school** *n* a public school, a school not part of the state education system. **independent suspension** *n* (*motoring*) a suspension system in which the wheels are mounted independently on the chassis, so as to be capable of independent movement. **independent variable** *n* a variable in a statement that determines the value of another variable or variables (*maths*); a variable manipulated in an experiment to observe its effect on another variable (*stats*).
■ **Declaration of Independence** the document proclaiming with reasons the secession of the thirteen colonies of America from the United Kingdom, reported to the Continental Congress on 4 July 1776, the anniversary of this being observed in the USA as a national holiday.

in deposito /in də-poz'i-tō or dā-pos'ē-tō/ (LL) on deposit, as a pledge.

indescribable /in-di-skrī'bə-bl/ *adj* that cannot be described; that is too bad, severe or extreme to be satisfactorily described. ◆ *n* (*old sl*; in *pl*) trousers. [**in-** (2)]
■ **indescribabil'ity** or **indescrib'ableness** *n*. **indescrib'ably** *adv*.

indesignate /in-dez'ig-nāt or -nət/ (logic) adj without any indication of quantification. [**in-** (2)]

indestructible /in-di-struk'ti-bl/ adj that cannot be destroyed. [**in-** (2)] ■ **indestructibil'ity** or **indestruc'tibleness** n. **indestruc'tibly** adv.

indetectable /in-di-tek'tə-bl/ adj which cannot be detected (also **indetect'ible**). [**in-** (2)]

indeterminable /in-di-tûr'mi-nə-bl/ adj incapable of being ascertained or fixed; (of an argument, etc) that cannot be settled. [**in-** (2)] ■ **indeter'minableness** n. **indeter'minably** adv. **indeter'minacy** n. **indeter'minate** adj not determinate or fixed; uncertain; having no defined or fixed value; (of growth of a plant) continuing indefinitely (bot). **indeter'minately** adv. **indeter'minateness** or **indetermina'tion** n lack of determination; absence of fixed direction. **indeter'mined** adj not determined; unsettled. **indeter'minism** n (philos) the theory that denies determinism. **indeter'minist** n. **indeterminist'ic** adj.
□ **indeterminacy principle** n another name for **uncertainty principle** (see **uncertainty** under **un-**). **indeterminate vowel** n (phonetics) a schwa.

indew (obs) same as **endue**.

index /in'deks/ n (pl of a book usu **in'dexes**; other senses **indices** /in'di-sēz/) the forefinger (also **in'dex-finger**), or the corresponding digit in animals; a pointer or hand on a dial or scale, etc; a moving arm, as on a surveying instrument; the gnomon of a sundial; the finger of a fingerpost; a figure of a pointing hand, used to draw attention (printing); the nose (old sl); anything giving an indication; a table of contents or other preliminary matter in a book (obs); hence a preface, prologue, introduction (Shakesp; fig); an alphabetical register of subjects dealt with in the text of a book, etc, usu located at the end, with page or folio references; a similar list of other things; a list of prohibited books; a direct, or indication of the first notes of the next page or line (music; obs); a symbol denoting a power (maths); a number, commonly a ratio, expressing some relation (as refractive index, the ratio of sines of angles of incidence and refraction or cranial index, the breadth of a skull as a percentage of its length); a numerical scale showing the relative changes in the cost of living, wages, etc, with reference to some predetermined base level; the reciprocal of intercept with parameter as unit (crystallog). ◆ vt to provide with or place in an index; to link to an index, index-link. [L index, indicis, from indicāre to show]
■ **index'al** adj. **indexa'tion** or **in'dexing** n a system by which wages, rates of interest, etc are directly linked (**index-linked'**) to changes in the cost of living index. **in'dexer** n. **index'ical** adj. **in'dexless** adj.
□ **index auctorum** n (L) index of authors. **index case** n (med) the first identified case of a disease. **Index Expurgatorius** n (L; RC) formerly, a list of books from which certain passages must be expurged before the books may be read by Roman Catholics. **index fossil** n a fossil species that characterizes a particular geological horizon. **index fund** n an investment fund that imitates the composition of a particular stock market index. **index learning** n superficial knowledge gleaned from book indexes. **Index Librorum Prohibitorum** n (L; RC) (until 1966) a list of books prohibited to Roman Catholic readers. **index-link'** vt. **index-link'ing** n indexation. **index locorum** n (L) an index of places. **index mineral** n (geol) a mineral whose appearance marks a particular grade of metamorphism in progressive regional metamorphism. **index number** n a figure showing periodic movement up or down of a variable compared with another figure (usu 100) taken as a standard. **index rerum** n (L) an index of matters or subjects; a reference notebook. **in'dex-tracking** adj (of a fund) aiming to follow a stock exchange index. **index verborum** n (L) an index of words.

indexterity /in-dek-ster'i-ti/ n lack of dexterity. [**in-** (2)]

India or **india** /in'di-ə/ n (in international radio communication) a code word for the letter i.

Indian /in'di-ən/ adj of or belonging to India (with various boundaries) or its native population, or to the Indies (East or West), or to the indigenous peoples of America, or to the Indians of South Africa. ◆ n a member of one of the races of India; formerly a European long resident in India; a member of any of the indigenous peoples of America; in South Africa, a person belonging to the Asian racial group; any of the Native American Languages (old); a person who carries out orders, a worker, etc, as opposed to a leader or organizer, as in chiefs and Indians; an Indian restaurant or meal (inf). [L India, from Indus (Gr Indos), the Indus (Pers Hind, Sans sindhu a river)]
■ **In'dianist** n a person who has a scholarly knowledge of Indian languages, history, etc. **Indianiza'tion** or **-s-** n. **In'dianize** or **-ise** vt to make Indian; to assimilate to what is Indian; to cause to be done, controlled, etc by Indians. ◆ vi to become Indian or like an Indian.
□ **In'diaman** n (pl **In'diamen**) a large ship employed in trade with India. **Indian agent** n in USA and Canada, an official who represents the government in the administration of native Indian affairs, esp on reservations. **Indian berry** n the fruit of Anamirta cocculus (see

cocculus indicus under **coccus**). **Indian bison** n a gaur. **Indian bread** n maize bread; a Virginian fungus said to have been eaten by the Native Americans. **Indian buffalo** n an Asiatic buffalo (see **buffalo**). **Indian club** n a bottle-shaped block of wood, swung in various motions by the arms to develop the muscles. **Indian corn** n maize, so called because brought from the West Indies. **Indian cress** n a garden plant (Tropaeolum majus, popularly nasturtium) from Peru, with orange flowers. **Indian fig** n the banyan-tree; the prickly pear. **Indian file** see under **file**[1]. **Indian fire** n a firework used as a signal light, consisting of sulphur, realgar, and nitre. **Indian gift** n (N Am inf) a gift that is given and then taken back, or for which a return gift is expected. **Indian giver** n. **Indian giving** n giving with the expectation of reciprocation. **Indian head massage** n a system of head massage that follows the principles of ayurveda, intended to reduce stress and improve the condition of the hair. **Indian hemp** n Cannabis sativa (Cannabis indica is a variety), source of the drug variously known as hashish, marijuana, etc; a perennial American plant (Apocynum cannabinum) formerly used to make rope. **indian ink** or (N Am) **india ink** see under **ink**. **Indian liquorice** n the jequirity or crab's-eye plant (Abrus precatorius) whose root is used as a substitute for liquorice. **Indian mallow** n a tall N American weed (Abutilon theophrasti) with small yellow flowers. **Indian meal** n ground maize. **Indian medicine** see **ayurveda**. **Indian millet** n durra. **Indian pink** n any of several American flowering plants, esp Spigelia marilandica. **Indian pipe** n a woodland plant (Monotropa uniflora) of N America, with a solitary drooping flower, not unlike a tobacco pipe. **Indian poke** n an American plant, white hellebore. **Indian red** n red ochre, or native ferric oxide, formerly imported from the East as a red pigment, also made artificially. **Indian rice** see **zizania**. **Indian rope-trick** n the supposed Indian trick of climbing an unsupported rope. **Indian runner** n a breed of domestic duck. **Indian shot** n a cosmopolitan tropical plant of the genus Canna, much cultivated for its flowers. **Indian sign** n a magic spell bringing bad luck. **Indian summer** n (orig in America) a period of warm, dry, calm weather in late autumn; a time of particular happiness, success, etc towards the end of a life, era, etc (fig). **Indian tobacco** n an American flowering plant (Lobelia inflata) with inflated seed pods. **Indian turnip** n an American araceous plant with a starchy tuber. **Indian wrestling** n a trial of strength in which contestants lie on their backs side by side, head to toe, with one leg and arm interlocking, the object being to force the opponent's leg down; a trial of strength with contestants standing face to face with one arm interlocking and outsides of corresponding feet braced against each other, the object being to unbalance the opponent; arm wrestling. **Indian paper** n a thin soft absorbent paper, of Chinese or Japanese origin, used in taking the finest proofs (**India proofs**) from engraved plates; a thin tough opaque paper used for printing Bibles. **india-rubb'er** or **India rubber** n an elastic gummy substance, the inspissated juice of various tropical plants; a piece of this material, esp one used for rubbing out pencil marks. **India rubber tree** n a rubber plant. **India shawl** n a Kashmir shawl.
■ **East India Company** a great chartered company formed for trading with India and the East Indies, the English Company, incorporated in 1600 and (having lost its power by 1858) dissolved in 1874. **East Indian** an inhabitant or native of the East Indies, usu applied to a Eurasian. **East Indies** the Indian subcontinent, SE Asia, and the Malay archipelago (hist); Sumatra, Borneo, Java and the other islands of Indonesia, by some, but not generally, taken to include the Philippines and New Guinea. **Red Indian** (now considered offensive) a member of the indigenous peoples of (esp North) America, a Native American. **West Indian** a native or an inhabitant of the West Indies. **West Indies** an archipelago stretching from Florida to Venezuela.

Indic /in'dik/ adj originating or existing in India; of the Indian branch of Indo-European languages. ◆ n the languages that form this branch.

indic. abbrev : indicative.

indican /in'di-kən/ n a glucoside, $C_{14}H_{17}NO_6$, that occurs in the indigo plant and is a source of the dye indigo; a compound, $C_8H_7NO_4S$, excreted in the urine of mammals as a detoxification product of indoxyl. [L indicum indigo, and **-an**]

indicate /in'di-kāt/ vt to point out; to show; to give some notion of; to be a mark or token of; to give ground for inferring; to point to as suitable treatment (med), also (usu in passive) as a desirable course of action in any sphere. ◆ vi to use an indicator when driving. [L indicāre, -ātum, from in in, and dicāre to proclaim]
■ **in'dicant** adj indicating. ◆ n something which indicates. **indica'tion** n the act of indicating; a mark; a token; a reading on a gauge, dial, etc; suggestion of treatment; a sign; a symptom. **indicative** /in-dik'ə-tiv/ adj pointing out; giving intimation; applied to the mood of the verb that expresses fact (grammar). ◆ n the indicative mood; a verb in the indicative mood. **indic'atively** adv. **in'dicātor** n someone who or which indicates; something that provides an indication; a pointer; a device in a motor vehicle that activates a flashing light to show that the driver intends to move in a certain direction; a diagram showing names and directions of visible objects, as on a mountain top; a

---

■ words derived from main entry word; □ compound words; ■ idioms and phrasal verbs

substance showing chemical condition by change of colour; a measuring contrivance with a pointer or the like; any device for exhibiting condition for the time being; (with *cap*) a genus of birds, the honey guides. **in'dicatory** (or /-*dik'*/) *adj*.

❑ **indicated horsepower** *n* (of a reciprocating engine) the horsepower developed by the pressure-volume changes of the working agent within the cylinder, exceeding the useful or brake horsepower at the crankshaft by the power lost in friction and pumping. **indicator diagram** *n* a graphical representation of the pressure and volume changes undergone by a fluid in performing a work-cycle in the cylinder of an engine on compression, the area representing, to scale, the work done during the cycle. **indicator species** *n* (*biol*) a species whose presence or absence indicates particular conditions in a habitat.

indices see **index**.

indicia /in-dish'i-ə or in-dik'i-a/ *n pl* (*sing* **indicium**) indicating marks or signs, symptoms. [L *indicium* sign, notice]
■ **indic'ial** *adj*.

indicolite /in-dik'ə-līt/ or **indigolite** /-*dig'*/ (*mineralogy*) *n* a pale blue or bluish-black variety of tourmaline. [**indigo** and **-ite** (3)]

indict /in-dīt'/ *vt* to charge with a crime formally or in writing. [With Latinized spelling (but not pronunciation) from Anglo-Fr *enditer*, from L *in* in, and *dictāre* to declare, frequentative of *dicere* to say]
■ **indict'able** *adj*. **indictee'** *n* a person who is indicted. **indict'er** *n*. **indict'ment** *n* a formal accusation; the written accusation against someone who is to be tried by jury; the form under which one is put to trial at the instance of the Lord Advocate (*Scots law*).
❑ **indictable offence** *n* an offence that must be tried before a jury in the Crown Court.
■ **find an indictment** (of a grand jury in the USA) to be satisfied that there is a *prima facie* case, and endorse the bill *a true bill*.

indiction /in-dik'shən/ *n* a proclamation; a decree of the emperor, fixing land tax valuation (*Roman hist*); the tax itself (*Roman hist*); a recurring period of fifteen years, instituted by Constantine the Great for fiscal purposes, and adopted by the popes as part of their chronological system; a year bearing a number showing its place in a fifteen years' cycle, reckoning from 24 September (or other day), 312AD (*Roman hist*). [L *indictiō, -ōnis*, from *indīcere* to appoint]

indie /in'di/ (*inf*) *n* an independent record company, *esp* one that produces music outside the mainstream of popular music; an independent film or television production company; a type of music produced predominantly by indie labels. ♦ *adj* (of music, films, etc) made by an independent company, and often catering to non-mainstream tastes. [**independent**]

indifferent /in-dif'(ə-)rənt/ *adj* without importance; uninteresting; mediocre; not very good, inferior; in poor health (*dialect*); apathetic; neutral; unconcerned. ♦ *n* (now *rare*) a person who is indifferent, apathetic or neutral; that which is indifferent. [**in-** (2)]
■ **indiff'erence** or **indiff'erency** *n*. **indiff'erentism** *n* indifference; the doctrine that religious differences are of no importance (*theol*); the doctrine of absolute identity, ie that to be in thought and to exist are one and the same thing (*philos*). **indiff'erentist** *n*. **indiff'erently** *adv* in an indifferent manner; tolerably; passably; without distinction, impartially.

indigenous /in-dij'i-nəs/ *adj* native born; originating or produced naturally in a country, not imported, *opp* to *exotic*. [L *indigena* a native, from *indu-* in, and *gen-*, root of *gignere* to produce]
■ **in'digene** /-jēn/ *n* and *adj* (a) native, aboriginal. **indigenizā'tion** or **-s-** *n*. **indi'genize** or **-ise** *vt* to adapt or subject to native culture or influence; to increase the proportion of indigenous people in administration, employment, etc. **indig'enously** *adv*. **indig'enousness** *n*.

indigent /in'di-jənt/ *adj* impoverished; in need, *esp* of means of subsistence. ♦ *n* a person so poor as to lack means of subsistence. [Fr, from L *indigēns, -entis*, prp of *indigēre*, from *indu-* in, and *egēre* to need]
■ **in'digence** or **in'digency** *n*. **in'digently** *adv*.

indigest /in-di-jest'/ *adj* not digested; shapeless. ♦ *n* a crude mass; a disordered state of affairs. [L *indigestus* unarranged, from *in-* not, and *dīgerere* to arrange, digest]
■ **indigest'ed** *adj* not digested; unarranged; not methodized. **indigestibil'ity** *n*. **indigest'ible** *adj* not digestible; not easily digested (*lit* and *fig*). **indigest'ibly** *adv*. **indigestion** /in-di-jes'chən/ *n* difficulty in digesting, or inability to digest, food; pain, flatulence, etc caused by this. **indigest'ive** *adj* dyspeptic.

indign /in-dīn'/ (*archaic* or *poetic*) *adj* unworthy; disgraceful, unseemly. [L *in-* not, and *dīgnus* worthy]

indignant /in-dig'nənt/ *adj* feeling or showing justifiable anger (often mixed with scorn) at perceived unjust treatment. [L *indīgnus* unworthy, from *in-* not, and *dīgnus* worthy]

■ **indig'nance** *n* (*archaic*) indignation; contemptuous impatience. **indig'nantly** *adv*. **indignā'tion** *n* righteous anger at injustice, etc; feeling caused by an unjustified slight, etc to oneself; a thing, eg a weapon, indicating anger (*Shakesp*). **indig'nify** *vt* to treat insultingly (*archaic*); to disgrace (with inadequate praise) (*obs*). **indig'nity** *n* disgrace; dishonour; unmerited contemptuous treatment; incivility with contempt or insult; indignation (*archaic*); unworthiness (*obs*).

indigo /in'di-gō/ *n* (*pl* **in'digos** or **in'digoes**) a violet-blue dye obtained from the leaves of the indigo plant, from woad, or produced synthetically; the colour of this dye; indigotin; the indigo plant, any of various species of *Indigofera*, a tropical genus of Papilionaceae. ♦ *adj* deep blue. [Sp *índico, índigo*, from L *indicum*, from Gr *Indikon* Indian (neuter adj)]
■ **in'digoid** *adj* of, relating to or resembling indigo or its colour. ♦ *n* any of various synthetic dyes related in chemical structure to indigo. **in'digotin** (or /in-dig'/) or **indigo blue** *n* the blue colouring matter of indigo obtained from indican by hydrolysis. **indirubin** /in-di-roo'bin/ or **indigo red** *n* an isomer of indigotin, obtained from natural indigo.
❑ **indigo bird**, **bunting** or **finch** *n* an American finch (*Passerina cyanea*) of which the male is blue. **indigo carmine** *n* a blue dye administered by injection to test kidney function. **indigo snake** *n* a large non-venomous snake of N America (*Drymarchon corais*) with smooth blue-back skin.

indigolite see **indicolite**.

indigotin see under **indigo**.

indinavir /in-din'ə-vīr/ *n* a protease inhibitor used as a drug in the treatment of HIV.

indirect /in-di-rekt'/ or -*dī*-/ *adj* not direct or straight; not lineal or in direct succession; not related in the natural way, oblique; not straightforward or honest. [**in-** (2)]
■ **indirec'tion** *n* (*Shakesp*) indirect course or means, dishonest practice. **indirect'ly** *adv*. **indirect'ness** *n*.
❑ **indirect address** *n* (*comput*) an instruction which specifies a location which contains the required address. **indirect evidence** or **testimony** *n* circumstantial or inferential evidence. **indirect immunofluorescence** *n* a technique for detecting the presence of an antigen in which a specific antibody is bound to the antigen and then a second antibody, which is labelled with a fluorochrome and is specific to the first antibody, is used to detect the antigen using a fluorescence microscope. **indirect lighting** *n* a system of lighting in which the light emitted from the fittings is reflected upwards or diffused. **indirect object** *n* (*grammar*) a noun, pronoun or noun phrase affected by the action of the verb but not itself directly acted upon, as *the man* in *Give the man your seat*. **indirect question** *n* (*grammar*) a question in indirect speech, as in *She asked whether he was leaving*. **indirect speech** *n* a person's words reported with adjustment of the necessary person and time, as in *He said he was leaving*. **indirect tax** *n* one collected not directly from the taxpayer but through an intermediate agent, as eg a customs duty or sales tax. **indirect taxation** *n*.

indirubin see under **indigo**.

indiscernible /in-di-sûr'ni-bl or -zûr'/ *adj* not discernible. [**in-** (2)]
■ **indiscern'ibleness** or **indiscernibil'ity** *n*. **indiscern'ibly** *adv*.

indiscerptible /in-di-sûrp'ti-bl/ *adj* not able to be separated or disunited; not discerptible. [**in-** (2)]
■ **indiscerptibil'ity** *n*.

indiscipline /in-dis'i-plin/ *n* lack of discipline. [**in-** (2)]
■ **indisc'iplinable** *adj*. **indisc'iplined** *adj*.

indiscoverable /in-dis-kuv'ə-rə-bl/ *adj* not discoverable. [**in-** (2)]

indiscreet /in-dis-krēt'/ *adj* not discreet; imprudent; injudicious. [**in-** (2)]
■ **indiscreet'ly** *adv*. **indiscreet'ness** *n*. **indiscretion** /-kresh'ən/ *n* lack of discretion; rashness; an indiscreet act, or one apparently so; (*esp* formerly) an imprudent or immoral act.

indiscrete /in-dis-krēt' or -dis'/ *adj* not separated or distinguishable in parts; homogeneous. [**in-** (2)]
■ **indiscrete'ly** *adv*. **indiscrete'ness** *n*.

indiscriminate /in-dis-krim'i-nit/ *adj* lacking discrimination; choosing or chosen at random; promiscuous. [**in-** (2)]
■ **indiscrim'inately** *adv*. **indiscrim'inateness** *n*. **indiscrim'ināting** *adj* undiscriminating. **indiscriminā'tion** *n*. **indiscrim'inative** /-ə-tiv/ *adj* not discriminative.

indispensable /in-dis-pen'sə-bl/ *adj* that cannot be dispensed with; absolutely necessary; (of a law, etc) that cannot be set aside. [**in-** (2)]
■ **indispensabil'ity** or **indispens'ableness** *n*. **indispens'ably** *adv*.

indispose /in-dis-pōz'/ *vt* to render indisposed, averse, unwilling or unfit. [**in-** (2)]
■ **indisposed'** *adj* averse, unwilling; unwell, sick. **indispos'edness** *n*. **indisposition** /-pə-zish'ən/ *n* the state of being indisposed; disinclination; the state of being unwell or unfit.

---

indisputable /in-dis-pū'tə-bl, also -dis'/ adj beyond doubt or question. [**in-** (2)]
■ **indisputabil'ity** or **indisput'ableness** n. **indisput'ably** adv.

indissociable /in-dis-ō'shyə-bl or -shə-bl/ adj incapable of being separated. [**in-** (2)]

indissoluble /in-dis-ol'ū-bl or -dis'əl-/ adj that cannot be broken or dissolved; inseparable; binding permanently. [**in-** (2)]
■ **indissol'ubleness** or **indissolubility** /-ol-ū-bil'/ n. **indissol'ubly** adv.

indissolvable /in-di-zol'və-bl/ (archaic) adj that cannot be dissolved. [**in-** (2)]

indissuadable /in-dis-wā'də-bl/ adj not able to be dissuaded. [**in-** (2)]
■ **indissuad'ably** adv.

indistinct /in-dis-tingkt'/ adj not distinct; not plainly marked; confused; not clear to the mind or senses; dim. [**in-** (2)]
■ **indistinc'tion** n (rare) confusion; absence of distinction, sameness. **indistinct'ive** adj not constituting a distinction; not discriminating. **indistinct'ively** adv indiscriminately. **indistinct'iveness** n. **indistinct'ly** adv. **indistinct'ness** n.

indistinguishable /in-dis-ting'gwi-shə-bl/ adj that cannot be told apart, identical; indiscernible. [**in-** (2)]
■ **indistinguishabil'ity** or **indistin'guishableness** n. **indistin'guishably** adv.

indistributable /in-dis-trib'ū-tə-bl/ adj not distributable. [**in-** (2)]

indite /in-dīt'/ (archaic) vt to compose or write; to dictate. [OFr enditer ; see **indict**]
■ **indite'ment** n. **indit'er** n.

indium /in'di-əm/ n a soft malleable silver-white metallic element (symbol **In**; atomic no 49). [From two indigo-coloured lines in the spectrum]

indiv. abbrev : individual.

indivertible /in-di-vûr'ti-bl/ adj not capable of being turned aside. [**in-** (2)]

individable /in-di-vī'də-bl/ (archaic) adj indivisible. [**in-** (2)]

individual /in-di-vid'ū-əl/ adj not divisible without loss of identity; subsisting as one; relating to one only or to each one separately of a group or kind; single, separate; distinctive; inseparable (obs). ◆ n a single person, animal, plant or thing considered as a separate member of its species or as having an independent existence; a person (inf). [L indīviduus, from in- not, and dīviduus divisible, from dīvidere to divide]
■ **individ'ualism** n individual character; independent action as opposed to co-operation; that theory which opposes interference of the state in the affairs of individuals, opp to socialism or collectivism; the theory that looks to the rights of individuals, not to the advantage of an abstraction such as the state; the doctrine that individual things alone are real; the doctrine that nothing exists but the individual self. **individ'ualist** n a person who thinks and acts with independence; someone who advocates individualism. ◆ adj of or relating to individualists or individualism. **individualist'ic** adj. **individualist'ically** adv. **individuality** /-al'i-ti/ n separate and distinct existence; oneness; distinctive character. **individualizā'tion** or **-s-** n. **individ'ualize** or **-ise** vt to stamp with individual character; to particularize. **individ'ually** adv. **individ'uate** vt to individualize; to give individuality to. ◆ adj undivided; inseparable; individuated. **individuā'tion** n the act or process of individuating or individualizing; individual existence; essence; continued identity; the sum of the processes of individual life; synthesis into a single organic whole. **individ'uum** n an indivisible entity; an individual person or thing; a member of a species.

indivisible /in-di-viz'i-bl/ adj not divisible, incapable of being divided; (of a number) incapable of being divided without leaving a remainder (maths). ◆ n (maths) an indefinitely small quantity. [**in-** (2)]
■ **indivisibil'ity** or **indivis'ibleness** n. **indivis'ibly** adv.

Indo- /in-dō-/ combining form denoting Indian.

Indo-Aryan /in-dō-ā'ri-ən/ adj Indic (also n).

Indo-Chinese /in-dō-chī-nēz'/ adj of or relating to Indo-China, the south-eastern peninsula of Asia.

Indocid® /in'do-sid/ n a proprietary name for **indomethacin**.

indocile /in-dō'sīl or in-dos'il/ adj (also **indō'cible**) not docile; not willing to be instructed or disciplined. [**in-** (2)]
■ **indocil'ity** n.

indoctrinate /in-dok'tri-nāt/ vt to instruct in any doctrine; to imbue with any opinion. [**in-** (1)]
■ **indoctrinā'tion** n. **indoc'trinātor** n.

Indo-European /in-dō-ū-rō-pē'ən or in'/ (philology) adj of the family of languages, also called **In'do-German'ic** and sometimes Aryan, whose great branches are Aryan proper or Indian, Iranian, Armenian,

Greek or Hellenic, Italic, Celtic, Tocharian, Balto-Slavic, Albanian, Germanic, and probably Anatolian. ◆ n the hypothetical parent-language of this family (also called **Proto-Indo-European**).

Indo-Germanic /in-dō-jûr-man'ik/ (philology) adj Indo-European (also n).

Indo-Iranian /in'dō-i-rān'i-ən, -ī- or -rän'/ adj and n (of) the Indic and Iranian languages, constituting a subfamily of Indo-European.

indole or **indol** /in'dōl/ (chem) n a crystalline chemical compound (C_8H_7N), forming the basis of the indigo molecule and found in some plants, coal tar, and present in urine and faeces of mammals (being a product of decomposition of the amino acid tryptophan). [**indigo** and L oleum oil]
□ **indoleacetic acid** n a naturally-occurring plant growth hormone ($C_8H_6NCH_2CO_2H$), the commonest growth hormone of the auxin type. **indolebutyric acid** n a synthetic plant growth regulator ($C_8H_6N(CH_2)_3COOH$), with auxin-like action, used in rooting compounds.

indolent /in'də-lənt/ adj disliking activity; lazy; causing little or no pain (med); (of an ulcer, etc) slow to heal (med). [L in- not, and dolēns, -entis, prp of dolēre to suffer pain]
■ **in'dolence** or **in'dolency** n. **in'dolently** adv.

Indology /in-dol'ə-ji/ n the study of Indian history, literature, philosophy, etc.
■ **Indol'ogist** n.

indometacin /in-dō-met'ə-sin/ or **indomethacin** /-meth'/ n a non-steroidal, anti-inflammatory, antipyretic and analgesic drug, used in the treatment of arthritic conditions. [indole, methyl, acetic (acid) and **-in** (3)]

in Domino /in dom'i-nō/ (LL) in the Lord.

indomitable /in-dom'i-tə-bl/ adj not to be overcome, unconquerable. [**in-** (2)]
■ **indomitabil'ity** or **indom'itableness** n. **indom'itably** adv.

Indonesian /in-dō-nē'zi-ən, in-də- or -zhən/ adj of the East Indian or Malay Archipelago, specif of the Republic of Indonesia, covering much of this territory; of a short, mesocephalic, black-haired, light-brown race distinguishable in the population of the East Indian Islands; of a branch of the Austronesian family of languages chiefly found in the Malay Archipelago and Islands (Malay, etc). ◆ n an Indonesian national, a member of the race or a speaker of one of the languages; the official language of the Republic of Indonesia, a form of Malay also known as **Bahasa Indonesia**. [Gr Indos Indian, and nēsos island]

indoor /in'dör or in-dör'/ adj practised, used, or being within a building; (of a game or sport) adapted for playing indoors. [**in-** (1)]
■ **indoors'** adv inside a building.
□ **indoor relief** n (hist) support given to paupers in the workhouse or poorhouse, opp to outdoor relief.

Indo-Pacific /in-dō-pə-sif'ik/ adj of the group of approx 700 languages spoken in New Guinea, nearby islands, and Tasmania. ◆ n the languages forming this group.

indorse see **endorse**[1].

indoxyl /in-dok'sil/ (chem) n a crystalline chemical compound (C_8H_7NO), derived from indole, occurring in plants and the urine of mammals and as an intermediate stage in the manufacture of indigo dye.

Indra /in'drə/ n the Hindu god of the firmament and of rain. [Sans]

indraught or **indraft** /in'dräft/ n a drawing in; an inward flow of current or air. [**in**[1] and **draught**]

indrawn /in'drön or in-drön'/ adj drawn in (lit and fig). [**in**[1] and **drawn**]

indrench /in-drench' or -drensh'/ (obs) vt to submerge in water. [**in-** (1)]

indricothere /in-drik'ə-thēr/ or **indricotherium** /-thē'ri-əm/ n another name for **paraceratherium**.

indris /in'dris/ or **indri** /in'dri/ n (pl **in'dris**) a short-tailed lemur (Indri indri) found in the forests of eastern and central Madagascar. [Fr, from Malagasy indry! look! (mistakenly thought to be the animal's name)]

indubious /in-dū'bi-əs/ (archaic) adj not dubious; certain. [**in-** (2)]

indubitable /in-dū'bi-tə-bl/ adj that cannot be doubted; certain. [**in-** (2)]
■ **indūbitabil'ity** or **indū'bitableness** n. **indū'bitably** adv without doubt, certainly.

induce /in-dūs'/ vt to draw on; to prevail on, make, cause, encourage (to do something); to bring into being; to initiate or speed up (labour of childbirth) artificially, as by administering drugs (also vi) (med); to cause, as an electric state, by mere proximity (phys); to infer inductively (logic); to bring in (obs). ◆ vi to reason or draw inferences inductively. —see also **induct** and **induction** below. [L indūcere, inductum, from in into, and dūcere to lead]
■ **induce'ment** n the act of inducing or that which induces; a means of persuasion; incentive, motive; a statement of facts introducing other important facts (law). **induc'er** n someone who, or that which,

induces; an agent which increases the transcription of specific genes (*biol*). **indu'cible** *adj*.

□ **induced abortion** see **abortion** under **abort**. **induced current** *n* (*elec*) a current set in action by the influence of the surrounding magnetic field, or by the variation of an adjacent current. **induced radioactivity** *n* radioactivity induced in non-radioactive elements by neutrons in a nuclear reactor, or protons or deuterons in a cyclotron or linear accelerator. **inducible enzyme** *n* (*bot*) an enzyme produced only in response to an inducing agent, often its substrate.

induciae /*in-dū'si-ē*/ (*Scots law*) *n sing* the time limit within which (after a citation) the defendant must appear in court or reply. [L *indūciae, -tiae* truce, delay]

induct /*in-dukt'*/ *vt* to introduce; to put in possession, as of a benefice, to install; to enlist into military service, to conscript (*N Am*); to induce (*phys*). [See ety for **induce**]

■ **induct'ance** *n* the property of inducing an electromotive force by variation of current in a circuit; a device having inductance. **inductee'** *n* (*N Am*) a person enlisted into military service, a conscript. **induc'tion** *n* a bringing or drawing in; installation in office, benefice, etc; the initiation of labour or abortion artificially, as by administering drugs (*med*); a prelude; an introductory section or scene; the act of inducing (*archaic*); magnetizing by proximity without contact; the production by one body of an opposite electric state in another by proximity; production of an electric current by magnetic changes in the neighbourhood; reasoning from particular cases to general conclusions (*logic*). **induc'tional** *adj*. **induct'ive** *adj*. **induct'ively** *adv*. **induct'iveness** *n*. **inductiv'ity** *n*. **induct'or** *n*.

□ **induction coil** *n* an electrical device consisting of two coils of wire, in which every variation of the current in one induces a current in the other. **induction course** *n* a short course for new employees to familiarize them with the workings of the company, their role, etc. **induction hardening** *n* a process for hardening metal surfaces by induction heating followed by rapid cooling. **induction heating** *n* the heating of a conductive material by means of an induced current passing through it. **induction lighting** *n* a form of lighting that uses long-life, energy-saving, phosphorus-coated **induction lamps** containing not filaments but a magnetic coil and mercury gas. **induction loop system** *n* a method of sound distribution in which signals fed into a wire loop are received via headphones or hearing aids by those inside the area enclosed by the loop. **induction motor** *n* an electric motor in which currents in the primary winding set up an electromagnetic flux which induces currents in the secondary winding, interaction of these currents with the flux producing rotation. **induction port** or **valve** *n* a port or valve by which steam, or an explosive mixture, is admitted to the cylinder of an engine.

■ **induction by simple enumeration** logical induction by enumeration of all the cases singly.

inductile /*in-duk'tīl* or *-til*/ *adj* not ductile. [**in-** (2)]
■ **inductility** /*-til'i-ti*/ *n*.

indue see **endue**.

indulge /*in-dulj'*/ *vt* to yield to the wishes of; to favour or gratify; to treat with favour or undue favour; not to restrain; to grant an indulgence to or on; to grant some measure of religious liberty to (*hist*). ◆ *vi* to gratify one's appetites freely, or permit oneself any action or expression (with *in*); to partake, *esp* of alcohol (*inf*). [L *indulgēre* to be kind to, indulge, from *in* in, and prob *dulcis* sweet]

■ **indulg'ence**, also **indulg'ency** *n* gratification; excessive gratification; favourable or unduly favourable treatment; a pleasure indulged; a grant of religious liberty; forbearance of present payment; (in the Roman Catholic Church) a remission, to a repentant sinner, of the temporal punishment which remains due after the sin and its eternal punishment have been remitted (*plenary* indulgences, which remit all, *partial*, which remit a portion of the temporal punishment due, *temporal*, those granted only for a time, *perpetual* or *indefinite*, those which last until revoked, *personal*, those granted to a particular person or confraternity, *local*, those gained only in a particular place); exemption of an individual from an ecclesiastical law. **indulg'ent** *adj* ready to gratify the wishes of others; compliant; not severe. **indulg'ently** *adv*. **indulg'er** *n*.

■ **Declaration of Indulgence** a name given to proclamations of Charles II and *esp* James II declaring laws restraining religious liberty suspended by the king's will.

induline or **indulin** /*in'dū-lin, -lēn* or *-līn*/ *n* any one of a class of coal tar dyestuffs, giving blues, etc. [**indigo**]

indult /*in-dult'*/ *n* a licence granted by the Pope, authorizing something to be done which the common law of the church does not sanction. [Ety as for **indulge**]

indumentum /*in-dū-men'təm*/ (*biol*) *n* (*pl* **indumen'ta** or **indumen'tums**) a total covering of hair, feathers, etc; the underside of rhododendron leaves. [L *indūmentum* garment, from *induere* to put on]

induna /*in-doo'nə*/ (*S Afr*) *n* a tribal councillor or leader, *esp* of an impi; a black African foreman or overseer. [Zulu *nduna* person of rank]

induplicate /*in-dū'pli-kit*/ or **induplicated** /*-kā-tid*/ (*bot*) *adj* folded inwards. [**in-** (1)]
■ **induplica'tion** *n*.

indurate /*in'dū-rāt*/ *vt* to make hard; to make hardy; to make callous, unfeeling or obdurate. ◆ *vi* to harden; to become hardy. ◆ *adj* indurated. [L *indūrāre, -ātum*, from *in* in, and *dūrāre* to harden]
■ **in'durated** *adj*. **indura'tion** *n*. **in'durative** *adj*.

indusium /*in-dū'zi-əm*/ (*biol*) *n* (*pl* **indu'sia**) a protective membrane or scale, eg that covering a fern sorus; an insect larva case. [L *indūsium* an undergarment, tunic, from *induere* to put on]
■ **indu'sial** *adj* containing fossil insect indusia. **indu'siate** *adj* having indusia.

industry /*in'də-stri*/ *n* the quality of being diligent; assiduity; steady application; habitual diligence; any branch of manufacture and trade, *heavy* industry relating to such basic industries as coalmining, steel-making, shipbuilding, etc, involving heavy equipment, *light* industry to smaller factory-processed goods, eg knitwear, glass, electronics components, etc; all branches of manufacture and trade collectively. [L *industria*, perhaps from the old word *indu* in, within, and *struere* to build up]

■ **industrial** /*-dus'-*/ *adj* relating to, characteristic of or used in industry; (of a region or city) having highly developed industry. ◆ *n* an industrial worker (*rare*); (in *pl*) stocks and shares in industrial concerns. **indus'trialism** *n* devotion to labour or industrial pursuits; that system or condition of society in which industrial labour is the chief and most characteristic feature. **indus'trialist** *n* a person who owns, or holds a powerful position in, an industrial concern or concerns. ◆ *adj* of or characterized by industry. **industrializā'tion** or **-s-** *n*. **indus'trialize** or **-ise** *vt* and *vi* to make or become industrially developed. ◆ *vt* to give a character of industrialism to. **indus'trially** *adv*. **indus'trious** *adj* diligent or active in one's work or in a particular pursuit; skilful (*obs*). **indus'triously** *adv*. **indus'triousness** *n*.

□ **industrial action** *n* any action, such as a strike or go-slow, taken by workers as a means of forcing employers to meet demands, as a protest, etc. **industrial archaeology** *n* the study of industrial machines and buildings of the past. **industrial council** see **Whitley Council**. **industrial democracy** *n* a form of management in which workers' representatives are appointed to the board of a company, or actively participate in the management in some other capacity. **industrial design** *n* the art or process of incorporating aesthetic qualities into manufactured goods. **industrial designer** *n*. **industrial diamond** *n* small diamonds, not of gemstone quality and often synthesized from carbon, used to cut rock in borehole drilling and in abrasive grinding. **industrial disease** *n* a disease or condition caused by one's occupation, eg pneumoconiosis. **industrial engineer** *n*. **industrial engineering** *n* the application of scientific principles to the various factors affecting an industrial or manufacturing process in order to develop the most efficient method of production. **industrial espionage** *n* the practice of obtaining or attempting to obtain trade secrets or other confidential information by underhand or dishonest means. **industrial estate** *n* a planned industrial area, with factories organized to provide varied employment. **industrial melanism** *n* melanism (eg in moths) developed as a response to blackening of trees, etc by industrial pollution. **industrial park** (*N Am*) an industrial estate. **industrial relations** *n pl* relations between management and workers or labour in general. **industrial revolution** *n* the economic and social changes arising out of the change from industries carried on in the home with simple machines to industries in factories with power-driven machinery, *esp* such changes (from about 1760) in Britain, the first country to be industrialized. **industrial school** *n* (*hist*) a school in which pupils were trained for work in industry; a school where neglected or delinquent children were taught technical and vocational subjects. **indus'trial-strength** *adj* suitable for use in industry; extremely strong. **industrial tribunal** *n* a tribunal set up to hear complaints and make judgements in disputes between employers and employees on matters such as industrial relations and alleged unfair dismissal.

■ **Industrial Injuries Disablement Benefit** in Britain, a weekly payment for injury sustained while at work (also **injury benefit**).

induviae /*in-dū'vi-ē*/ (*bot*) *n pl* withered leaves persistent on the stems of some plants. [L *induviae* clothes]
■ **indū'vial** *adj*. **indū'viate** *adj*.

indwell /*in-dwel'*/ (*literary*) *vi* and *vt* (**indwell'ing**; **indwelt'**) to dwell or remain in. [**in-** (1)]
■ **in'dweller** *n* an inhabitant. **in'dwelling** *adj* dwelling within, remaining permanently in the mind or soul. ◆ *n* residence within, or in the heart or soul.

Indy /in'di/ n a form of motor racing in which cars complete many laps of a high-speed oval circuit; a motor race of this kind. [*Indianapolis* in the USA, where the annual Indianapolis 500 race takes place]
❑ **Indy car** n a high-speed supercharged racing car.

-ine¹ /-īn or -in/ (*chem*) n sfx indicating: (1) a basic organic compound containing nitrogen, such as an amino acid or alkaloid; (2) a halogen, such as *chlorine* and *fluorine*; (3) a mixture of compounds, such as *benzine*; (4) a feminine form, such as *heroine*. [L fem adjectival ending -*īna*]

-ine² /-īn/ adj sfx meaning: (1) belonging to, characteristic of, as in *elephantine*; (2) like, similar to, or being, as in *adamantine, crystalline*. [L adjectival ending -*īnus*]

inearth /in-ûrth'/ (*archaic*) vt to inter. [**in-** (1)]

inebriate /in-ē'bri-āt/ vt to make drunk, to intoxicate; to exhilarate greatly. ◆ adj /-it or -ət/ drunk; intoxicated. ◆ n a drunk person; a drunkard. [L *inēbriāre, -ātum*, from *in* (intens), and *ēbriāre* to make drunk, from *ēbrius* drunk]
■ **inē'briant** adj intoxicating (also n). **inēbria'tion** or **inebriety** /in-ē-brī'i-ti or in-ē'/ n drunkenness; intoxication. **inē'brious** adj drunk; causing intoxication (*obs*).

inedible /in-ed'i-bl/ adj not good to eat; not suitable for eating (eg because poisonous or indigestible). [**in-** (2)]
■ **inedibil'ity** n.

inedited /in-ed'i-tid/ adj not edited; unpublished. [**in-** (2)]

ineducable /in-ed'ū-kə-bl/ adj incapable of being educated or of learning. [**in-** (2)]
■ **ineducabil'ity** n.

ineffable /in-ef'ə-bl/ adj not able to be described, inexpressible; not to be uttered. [L *ineffābilis*, from *in-* not, and *effābilis* expressible]
■ **ineffabil'ity** or **ineff'ableness** n. **ineff'ably** adv.

ineffaceable /in-i-fā'sə-bl/ adj that cannot be rubbed out, indelible. [**in-** (2)]
■ **ineffaceabil'ity** n. **inefface'ably** adv.

ineffective /in-i-fek'tiv/ adj not effective; not capable of performing competently, useless. [**in-** (2)]
■ **ineffec'tively** adv. **ineffec'tiveness** n. **ineffec'tual** adj not producing, or not capable of producing, the proper effect; futile; ineffective, weak. **ineffectual'ity** or **ineffec'tualness** n. **ineffect'ually** adv.

inefficacious /in-ef-i-kā'shəs/ adj not having the power to produce an effect, or the desired effect. [**in-** (2)]
■ **ineffica'ciously** adv. **inefficacy** /-ef'i-kə-si/ n lack of efficacy.

inefficiency /in-i-fish'ən-si/ n lack of the power or skill to do or produce something in the best, most economical, etc way. [**in-** (2)]
■ **ineffic'ient** adj not efficient. **ineffic'iently** adv.

inegalitarian /in-i-gal-i-tā'ri-ən/ adj not egalitarian. [**in-** (2)]

inelaborate /in-i-lab'ə-rit or -rāt/ adj not elaborate; simple, *esp* in workmanship. [**in-** (2)]
■ **inelab'orately** adv.

inelastic /in-i-las'tik/ adj not elastic; incompressible; unyielding. [**in-** (2)]
■ **inelasticity** /in-el-əs-tis'i-ti/ n.
❑ **inelastic collision** or **scattering** see under **collide**.

inelegance /in-el'i-gəns/ n lack of grace or refinement (also **inel'egancy**). [**in-** (2)]
■ **inel'egant** adj. **inel'egantly** adv.

ineligible /in-el'i-ji-bl/ adj not qualified for election; not suitable to be available for choice or to be chosen; unsuitable. ◆ n an ineligible person. [**in-** (2)]
■ **ineligibil'ity** n. **inel'igibly** adv.

ineloquent /in-el'ə-kwənt/ adj not eloquent. [**in-** (2)]
■ **inel'oquence** n. **inel'oquently** adv.

ineluctable /in-i-luk'tə-bl/ adj not able to be escaped from or avoided. [L *inēluctābilis*, from *in-* not, *ē* from, and *luctārī* to struggle]
■ **ineluctabil'ity** n. **ineluct'ably** adv.

ineludible /in-i-loo'di-bl/ (*rare*) adj inescapable.
■ **ineludibil'ity** n. **inelud'ibly** adv.

inept /in-ept'/ adj awkward, clumsy; foolish, silly; unsuitable; irrelevant and futile; void (*law*). [L *ineptus*, from *in-* not, and *aptus* apt]
■ **inept'itude** n or **inept'ness** n. **inept'ly** adv.

inequable /in-ek'wə-bl or -ēk'/ (*rare*) adj not equable; uneven, not uniform. [**in-** (2)]

inequality /in-ē-kwol'i-ti or in-i-/ n lack of equality; disparity; difference; inadequacy; incompetence; unevenness; dissimilarity; an uneven place; a statement that two quantities or expressions are not equal (*maths*); a departure from uniformity in orbital motion (*astron*). [**in-** (2)]

inequation /in-ə-kwā'shən or -zhən/ n a mathematical sentence which expresses an inequality. [**in-** (2)]

inequipotent /in-ek-wi-pō'tənt/ (*zool*) adj having different potentialities for development and differentiation. [**in-** (2)]

inequitable /in-ek'wi-tə-bl/ adj unfair, unjust. [**in-** (2)]
■ **ineq'uitableness** n. **ineq'uitably** adv. **ineq'uity** n lack of equity or fairness; an unjust action.

ineradicable /in-i-rad'i-kə-bl/ adj not able to be got rid of, removed completely, or rooted out. [**in-** (2)]
■ **inerad'icableness** n. **inerad'icably** adv.

inerasable /in-i-rā'zə-bl/ adj impossible to erase (also **ineras'ible**). [**in-** (2)]
■ **ineras'ably** or **ineras'ibly** adv.

inerm /in-ûrm/ (*bot*) adj unarmed; without thorns. [L *inermis*, from *in-* not, and *arma* (pl) arms]
■ **ine'rmous** adj.

inerrable /in-er'ə-bl or -ûr'/ adj incapable of erring, infallible. [**in-** (2)]
■ **inerrabil'ity** or **inerr'ableness** n. **inerr'ably** adv. **inerr'ancy** n the quality of being inerrant. **inerr'ant** adj unerring; (of a star) fixed (*astron*).

inert /in-ûrt'/ adj without inherent power of moving, or of active resistance to motion; passive; chemically inactive; not readily changed by chemical means; sluggish; disinclined to move or act. [L *iners, inertis* unskilled, idle, from *in-* not, and *ars, artis* art]
■ **inertia** /in-ûr'shi-ə, -shyə or -shə/ n inertness; the inherent property of matter by which it continues, unless constrained, in its state of rest or uniform motion in a straight line. **iner'tial** adj of or relating to inertia. **inert'ly** adv. **inert'ness** n.
❑ **inert gas** n any of a group of elements whose outer electron orbits are complete, rendering them inert to all the usual chemical reactions. **inertial confinement** n in fusion studies, short-term containment of plasma arising from inertial resistance to outward forces, achieved mainly by using a powerful laser. **inertial control guidance** or **navigation** n an automatic gyroscopic guidance system for aircraft, missiles, etc using data computed from acceleration and the physical properties of the earth, but dispensing with the magnetic compass and independent of ground-based radio aids. **inertia-reel seat belt** n a type of self-retracting seat belt in which the wearer is constrained only when violent deceleration of the vehicle causes the belt to lock. **inertia selling** n sending unrequested goods to householders and attempting to charge for them if they are not returned.

inerudite /in-er'ū-dīt or ŭ-/ adj not erudite; unlearned. [**in-** (2)]

inescapable /in-i-skā'pə-bl/ adj unescapable; inevitable. [**in-** (2)]
■ **inescā'pably** adv.

inesculent /in-es'kū-lənt/ (*archaic*) adj inedible. [**in-** (2)]

inescutcheon /in-i-skuch'ən/ (*heraldry*) n a small shield borne as a charge on a larger escutcheon. [**in¹** and **escutcheon**]

in esse see under **esse**.

inessential /in-i-sen'shl/ adj not essential; not necessary; immaterial. ◆ n an inessential thing. [**in-** (2)]

inessive /in-es'iv/ (*grammar*) adj (in Finnish and related languages) denoting a case in nouns indicating 'place in which'. ◆ n the inessive case. [L *inesse* to be in, on, or at]

inestimable /in-es'ti-mə-bl/ adj not able to be estimated or valued; priceless. [**in-** (2)]
■ **inestimabil'ity** or **ines'timableness** n. **ines'timably** adv.

inevitable /in-ev'i-tə-bl/ adj not able to be evaded or avoided; certain to happen; exactly right, giving the feeling that the thing could not have been other than it is. ◆ n (*esp* with *the*) something inevitable. [L *inēvītābilis*, from *in-* not, *ē* from, and *vītāre* to avoid]
■ **inevitabil'ity** n. **inev'itableness** n. **inev'itably** adv.

inexact /in-ig-zakt'/ adj not precisely correct or true; lax. [**in-** (2)]
■ **inexact'itude** n lack of exactitude, or an example of this. **inexact'ly** adv. **inexact'ness** n.

in excelsis /in ek-sel'sis, ik-, eks-, iks-chel'sis, -kel'sis or -sēs/ (*LL*) on the heights; on high; in the highest degree.

inexcitable /in-ik-sī'tə-bl/ adj not excitable; from which one cannot be roused (*obs*). [**in-** (2)]

inexcusable /in-ik-skū'zə-bl/ adj which cannot be excused; not justifiable; unpardonable. [**in-** (2)]
■ **inexcusabil'ity** n. **inexcus'ableness** n. **inexcus'ably** adv.

inexecrable /in-ek'si-krə-bl/ (*Shakesp*) adj perhaps a misprint for *inexorable*, though interpreted by some as an intensive form of *execrable*.

inexecutable /in-ig-zek'ū-tə-bl, in-ek-sek', -ik- or in-ek-si-kū'tə-bl/ adj incapable of being executed or carried out. [**in-** (2)]
■ **inexecū'tion** n the fact or state of not being executed.

inexhaustible /in-ig-zö'stə-bl/ adj not able to be exhausted or spent; unfailing, tireless; endless. [**in-** (2)]
■ **inexhaust'ed** adj (archaic) unexhausted, not used up or spent. **inexhaustibil'ity** n. **inexhaust'ibly** adv. **inexhaust'ive** adj unfailing (archaic); not exhaustive.

inexistence[1] /in-ig-zis'təns/ (now rare) n non-existence. [**in-** (2)]
■ **inexist'ent** adj.

inexistence[2] /in-ig-zis'təns/ (archaic) n inherence. [**in-** (1)]
■ **inexist'ent** or **inexist'ant** adj indwelling; inherent.

inexorable /in-ek'sə-rə-bl/ adj not to be moved by entreaty or persuasion; unrelenting; unyielding. [LL inexorābilis, from in- not, and exōrāre, from ex out of, and ōrāre to entreat]
■ **inexorabil'ity** or **inex'orableness** n. **inex'orably** adv.

inexpansible /in-ik-span'si-bl/ adj incapable of being expanded. [**in-** (2)]

inexpectant /in-ik-spek'tənt/ adj not expecting; without expectation. [**in-** (2)]
■ **inexpec'tancy** n. **inexpecta'tion** n.

inexpedient /in-ik-spē'di-ənt/ adj contrary to expediency; not in accordance with good policy, impolitic. [**in-** (2)]
■ **inexpe'dience** or **inexpe'diency** n. **inexpe'diently** adv.

inexpensive /in-ik-spen'siv/ adj not costing much; cheap in price. [**in-** (2)]
■ **inexpens'ively** adv. **inexpens'iveness** n.

inexperience /in-ik-spē'ri-əns/ n lack of experience. [**in-** (2)]
■ **inexpe'rienced** adj not having experience; unskilled or unpractised.

inexpert /in-ek'spûrt or in-ik-spûrt'/ adj not expert; unskilled. [**in-** (2)]
■ **inex'pertly** adv. **inex'pertness** n.

inexpiable /in-ek'spi-ə-bl/ adj that cannot be expiated or atoned for; that cannot be appeased. [**in-** (2)]
■ **inex'piableness** n. **inex'piably** adv.

inexplainable /in-ek-splā'nə-bl/ (rare) adj inexplicable.

inexplicable /in-ek'spli-kə-bl or -ik-splik'/ adj incapable of being explained or accounted for; that cannot be disentangled, inextricable (obs). [**in-** (2)]
■ **inexplicabil'ity** or **inexplic'ableness** n. **inexplic'ably** adv.

inexplicit /in-ik-splis'it/ adj not explicit; not clear. [**in-** (2)]
■ **inexplic'itly** adv. **inexplic'itness** n.

inexpressible /in-ik-spres'i-bl/ adj that cannot be expressed; unutterable; indescribable. [**in-** (2)]
■ **inexpress'ibles** n pl (facetious; archaic) trousers. **inexpress'ibly** adv. **inexpress'ive** adj inexpressible (archaic); unexpressive. **inexpress'ively** adv. **inexpress'iveness** n.

inexpugnable /in-ik-spug'nə-bl/ adj not able to be attacked or captured; unassailable, impregnable. [**in-** (2)]
■ **inexpugnabil'ity** or **inexpugn'ableness** n. **inexpug'nably** adv.

inexpungible /in-ik-spun'ji-bl/ adj incapable of being wiped out or effaced. [**in-** (2)]

inextended /in-ik-sten'did/ adj not extended; without extension. [**in-** (2)]
■ **inextensibil'ity** n. **inexten'sible** adj that cannot be extended or stretched. **inexten'sion** n.

in extenso /in ik-sten'sō or ek-sten'/ (LL) at full length.

inextinguishable /in-ik-sting'gwi-shə-bl/ adj that cannot be extinguished, quenched, or destroyed. [**in-** (2)]
■ **inextin'guishableness** n. **inextin'guishably** adv.

inextirpable /in-ik-stûr'pə-bl/ adj not able to be destroyed, exterminated or rooted out. [**in-** (2)]

in extremis /in ik-strē'mis or ek-strā'mēs/ (LL) in the last extremity; at the point of death; at the last gasp; in desperate circumstances.

inextricable /in-ek'stri-kə-bl or -ik-strik'/ adj not able to be escaped from; from which one cannot extricate oneself; not able to be extricated or disentangled; intricately involved, confused. [L inextrīcābilis]
■ **inextricabil'ity** n. **inex'tricably** adv.

INF abbrev : intermediate-range nuclear forces.

inf. abbrev : infantry; inferior; infinitive; informal; information; infra (L), below.

in facie curiae /in fā'shē-ē kū'ri-ē, fā'shē or fak'i-ā/ (LL) in the presence of, or before, the court.

infall /in'föl/ n an inroad; a falling in; a confluence, inlet or junction. [**in**[1] and **fall**[1]]

infallible /in-fal'i-bl/ adj incapable of error; incapable of making a mistake; incapable of failure, or not liable to fail; inevitable. [**in-** (2)]
■ **infall'ibilism** n (RC) the doctrine of the Pope's infallibility. **infall'ibilist** n. **infallibil'ity** n. **infall'ibly** adv.

■ **the doctrine of infallibility** (RC) (defined in 1870) the doctrine that the Pope, when speaking ex cathedra, is kept from error in all that regards faith and morals.

infame /in-fām'/ (archaic) vt to defame. [Ety as for **infamous**]
■ **infamize** or **-ise** /in'fə-mīz/ vt to defame, to brand with infamy (also **infam'onize** or **-ise**).

infamous /in'fə-məs, formerly in-fā'məs/ adj having a very bad reputation; publicly declared guilty; notoriously vile; disgraceful. [L īnfāmāre, from in- not, and fāma fame]
■ **in'famously** adv. **in'famy** n ill repute; public disgrace; an infamous act or happening; extreme vileness.

infancy see under **infant**.

infangthief /in'fang-thēf/ (OE law) n the right of arresting and fining a thief within the boundary of one's own jurisdiction. [OE infangenethēof, from in in, the root of fōn to seize, and thēof thief]

infant /in'fənt/ n a baby; a person under the age of legal maturity (Eng law); a young schoolchild; an infante or infanta; an aristocratic youth (obs). ◆ adj of or belonging to infants; of or in infancy; at an early stage of development. [L īnfāns, infantis, from in- not, and fāns, prp of fārī to speak; cf Gr phanai]
■ **in'fancy** n the state or time of being an infant; childhood; the beginning or an early stage of anything; speechlessness, silence (Milton). **in'fanthood** n. **infantile** /in'fən-tīl or (US) -til, also -fant'/ adj relating to infancy or to an infant; having characteristics of infancy; no better than that of an infant, childish; undeveloped. **infant'ilism** n the persistence of infantile characteristics; a childish utterance or characteristic. **infantility** /-til'/ n. **infant'ilize** vt to treat like a child; to make suitable for children. **infantilīzā'tion** or **-s-** n. **in'fantine** /-īn/ adj infantile.
❑ **infantile paralysis** n poliomyelitis. **infant mortality** (**rate**) n (the rate of) deaths in the first year of life. **infant school** n a school for children up to about the age of seven.

infante /in-fan'tā/ (hist) n a prince of the royal family of Spain or Portugal, esp a son of the king other than the heir apparent. [Sp and Port; from the root of **infant**]
■ **infan'ta** n a princess of Spain or Portugal; the wife of an infante.

infanteer see under **infantry**.

infanticide /in-fan'ti-sīd/ n the killing of newborn children, practised in some societies; the killing of a child, esp by its mother, within twelve months of its birth; loosely, the murder of an infant; someone, esp a mother, who kills an infant. [L īnfanticīdium child-killing, īnfanticīda child-killer, from īnfāns an infant, and caedere to kill]
■ **infanticī'dal** (or /-fant'/) adj.

infantile...to...**infantine** see under **infant**.

infantry /in'fən-tri/ n foot soldiers; a part of an army composed of such soldiers; infants or children collectively (archaic). ◆ adj of or relating to infantry. [Fr infanterie, from Ital infanteria, from infante youth, servant, foot soldier, from L īnfāns, -antis, a youth]
■ **infanteer'** n (Can) an infantryman. **in'fantryman** n (pl **in'fantrymen**) a soldier of the infantry.

infarct /in-färkt'/ n a portion of tissue that is dying because blood supply to it has been cut off. [Med L īnfarctus, from in in, and far(c)tus, from farcīre to cram, stuff]
■ **infarc'tion** n.

infare /in'fār/ n entrance (obs); the act of going in (obs); a house-warming after a wedding (Scot and US). [OE innfær; cf **in**[1] and **fare**]

infatuate /in-fat'ū-āt/ vt to inspire with foolish or unreasoning passion; to cause to behave foolishly or unreasonably; to deprive of judgement. ◆ adj (archaic) infatuated. ◆ n a person who is infatuated. [L īnfatuāre, -ātum, from in in, and fatuus foolish]
■ **infat'uated** adj filled with foolish or unreasoning passion; besotted; deprived of judgement. **infatuā'tion** n.

infauna /in-fö'nə/ n the class of animals that inhabit ocean and river beds. [**in-** (1) and **fauna**]
■ **infau'nal** adj.

infaust /in-föst'/ (rare) adj unlucky; ill-omened. [L īnfaustus, from in- not, and faustus propitious]

infeasible /in-fē'zi-bl/ adj not feasible. [**in-** (2)]
■ **infeasibil'ity** or **infeas'ibleness** n.

infect /in-fekt'/ vt to taint, esp with disease; to introduce pathogenic microorganisms into; to corrupt; to spread to; to affect successively; to inflict with a virus (comput). ◆ adj (obs) tainted. [L inficere, īnfectum, from in into, and facere to make]
■ **infec'tion** /-shən/ n the act or process of infecting; that which infects or taints; an infectious disease. **infec'tious** /-shəs/ or **infec'tive** /-tiv/ adj (of a disease) able to be transmitted by infection; caused by infection; corrupting; apt or likely to spread to others. **infec'tiously**

adv. **infec'tiousness** *n.* **infect'ively** *adv.* **infect'iveness** or **infectiv'ity** *n.* **infect'or** *n.*
❑ **infectious mononucleosis** *n* glandular fever.

infecundity /*in-fi-kun'di-ti*/ *n* lack of fecundity or fertility; unfruitfulness. [**in-** (2)]
■ **infecund** /*-fek'* or *-fēk'*/ *adj.*

infeft /*in-feft'*/ (*old Scots law*) *vt* (*pap* **infeft'** or (*rare*) **infeft'ed**) to invest with heritable property. [**enfeoff**]
■ **infeft'ment** *n* the symbolical giving possession of land in completion of the title.

infelicitous /*in-fi-lis'i-təs*/ *adj* not felicitous or happy; inappropriate, inapt. [**in-** (2)]
■ **infelic'itously** *adv.* **infelic'ity** *n* something that is inappropriate or inapt; misfortune, or an instance of this.

infelt /*in'felt*/ *adj* inwardly felt, heartfelt. [**in-** (1)]

infer /*in-fûr'*/ *vt* (**inferr'ing**; **inferred'**) to bring on (*Spenser* and *Shakesp*); to render (*Milton*); to derive from what has gone before; to arrive at as a logical conclusion, to deduce; to conclude; (*usu* of a thing or statement) to entail or involve as a consequence, to imply (often condemned as a misuse, but generally accepted for over four centuries). [L *ĭnferre*, from *in* into, and *ferre* to bring]
■ **in'ferable** (also /*-fûr'*/), **inferr'able** or **inferr'ible** *adj* that may be inferred or deduced. **in'ference** *n* that which is inferred or deduced; the act of drawing a conclusion from statements of fact; consequence; conclusion. **inferential** /*-en'shl*/ *adj* relating to inference; deducible or deduced by inference. **inferen'tially** *adv.*

infere /*in-fēr'*/ (*obs*) *adv* for **in fere**, together. [See **fere**[1]]

inferiae /*in-fē'ri-ē* or *ēn-fe'ri-ī*/ (L) *n pl* offerings to the spirits of the dead.

inferior /*in-fē'ri-ər*/ *adj* lower in any respect; subordinate; poor or poorer in quality; set slightly below the line (*printing*); (of an ovary) having the other parts above it (*bot*); (of the other parts) below the ovary (*bot*); (of a planet) revolving within the earth's orbit (*astron*). ◆ *n* a person who is lower in rank or station; an inferior character (*printing*). [L *ĭnferior*, compar of *ĭnferus* low]
■ **inferiority** /*-or'*/ *n.* **infe'riorly** *adv* in an inferior manner.
❑ **inferior conjunction** *n* (*astron*) a conjunction when a celestial body, such as a planet, passes between the sun and the earth. **inferiority complex** *n* a complex involving a suppressed sense of personal inferiority (*psychol*); popularly, a feeling of inferiority.

infernal /*in-fûr'nəl*/ *adj* belonging to the regions below the earth, the underworld; resembling or suitable to hell; outrageous, very unpleasant (*inf*); extremely annoying (*inf*). [L *ĭnfernus*, from *ĭnferus*]
■ **infernality** /*-nal'*/ *n.* **infer'nally** *adv.* **infer'no** *n* (*pl* **infer'nos**) (also with *cap*) hell (*Ital*); a place or situation of horror and confusion, *esp* a conflagration.
❑ **infernal machine** *n* a contrivance made to resemble some ordinary harmless object, but charged with a dangerous explosive.

infertile /*in-fûr'tīl* or (*US*) *-til*/ *adj* not fertile; not capable of producing offspring, sterile; not productive; barren. [**in-** (2)]
■ **infertility** /*-til'*/ *n.*

infest /*in-fest'*/ *vt* to swarm over, cover or fill, in a troublesome, unpleasant or harmful way; to invade and live on or in as a parasite; to disturb or harass. ◆ *adj* (*obs*) hostile; troublesome. [L *ĭnfestāre*, from *ĭnfestus* hostile]
■ **infesta'tion** *n* attack, or the condition of being attacked, *esp* by parasites; molestation (*obs*).

infeudation /*in-fū-dā'shən*/ *n* the putting of an estate in fee, enfeoffment; a deed of enfeoffment; the granting of tithes to laymen. [**in-** (1) and **feud**[2]]

infibulate /*in-fib'ū-lāt*/ *vt* to fasten with a clasp. [**in-** (1) and L *fibula* a clasp]
■ **infibula'tion** *n* the act of confining or fastening, *specif* the fastening or partial closing-up of the prepuce or the labia majora by a clasp, stitches or the like to prevent sexual intercourse.

infidel /*in'fi-del* or *-dl*/ *n* someone who rejects a religion, *esp* Christianity or Islam; loosely, someone who disbelieves in a particular theory, etc. ◆ *adj* unbelieving; sceptical; disbelieving a religion. [OFr *infidèle*, from L *ĭnfidēlis*, from *in-* not, and *fĭdēlis* faithful, from *fĭdēs* faith]
■ **infidel'ity** *n* lack of faith or belief; disbelief in religion; unfaithfulness, *esp* in marriage; an instance of this; treachery.

infield /*in'fēld*/ *n* the space enclosed within the baselines (*baseball*); the part of the field near the wicket (*cricket*); the players stationed in the infield; formerly, land near a farmhouse, kept constantly manured and under tillage (also *adj*). [**in**[1] and **field**]
■ **in'fielder** *n* a player on the infield.

in fieri /*in fī'ə-rī*/ (L; *law*) in course of completion; pending.

infighting /*in'fī-ting*/ *n* boxing at close quarters when blows from the shoulder cannot be given (see also under **in**[1]). [**in**[1] and **fighting**]

infilling /*in'fi-ling*/ *n* filling up or in; something used to fill up or in; material used to fill up or level (*building*); infill housing. [**in**[1] and **fill**[1]]
■ **in'fill** *vt* to fill in. ◆ *n* material for infilling; infill housing (qv below).
❑ **infill housing** or **development** *n* new houses, buildings, etc built in the gaps between existing ones.

infiltrate /*in'fil-trāt* or *-fĭl'*/ *vt* to cause to filter; to cause to filter into; to permeate. ◆ *vi* to permeate gradually; to sift or filter in. ◆ *vt* and *vi* (of troops, agents, etc) to enter (a hostile area) secretly and for subversive purposes. ◆ *n* any substance permeating a solid. [**in-** (1)]
■ **infiltrā'tion** *n* the process of infiltrating; gradual permeation or interpenetration; gradual accession or introduction of a new element, as of population or troops; a deposit or substance infiltrated. **in'filtrative** *adj.* **in'filtrator** *n* someone who becomes accepted as a member of a group towards which he or she has hostile or subversive intentions.

infima species /*in'fi-ma spē'shēz* or *ēn'fi-ma spek'i-ās*/ (LL) *n* (*pl* **infimae** /*-ē*/ **species**) the lowest species included in a genus or class.

infimum /*in-fī'məm*/ (*maths*) *n* the greatest lower bound (cf **supremum**; *abbrev* inf). [L, neuter of *infimus*, superl of *inferus* lower]

infin. *abbrev*: infinitive.

infinite /*in'fi-nit*, in church singing also *in'fi-nīt*/ *adj* without end or limit; greater than any quantity that can be assigned (*maths*); extending to infinity; vast; in vast numbers; inexhaustible; infinitated (*logic*); (of part of a verb) not limited by person or number. ◆ *n* something that has no determinate bounds, and for which there is no possible bound or limit; the Absolute, the Infinite Being or God. [**in-** (2)]
■ **infin'itant** *adj* (*logic*) denoting merely negative attribution. **infin'itary** *adj* relating to infinity. **infin'itate** *vt* to make infinite; to turn into a negative term (*logic*). **in'finitely** *adv.* **in'finiteness** *n.* **infinitesimal** /*-es'*/ *adj* infinitely small; (loosely) extremely small; (of a variable) having values that are close to zero (*maths*). ◆ *n* an infinitely small quantity; an infinitesimal variable (*maths*). **infinites'imally** *adv.* **infin'itude** *n* infinity. **infin'ity** *n* the state or quality of having no limits or bounds; an infinite quantity or distance; vastness, immensity; a countless or indefinite number; the reciprocal of zero (*maths*).
❑ **infinite canon** *n* (*music*) a canon that can be repeated indefinitely. **infinite loop** *n* (*comput*) a logical loop in a program from which there is no exit other than by terminating the run. **infinite set** *n* (*maths*) a set that can be put into a one-one correspondence with part of itself. **infinitesimal calculus** *n* differential and integral calculus. **infinity pool** *n* a swimming pool constructed so that the water appears to extend as far as the horizon.

infinitive /*in-fin'i-tiv*/ (*grammar*) *adj* expressing, or in the mood that expresses, the verbal idea without reference to person, number or time, as *stop* in *Make him stop*, or, in English, the *to* + *verb* form generally. ◆ *n* the infinitive mood; a verb in the infinitive mood. [L *infīnītīvus*, from *in-* not, and *fīnīre* to limit]
■ **infiniti'val** *adj.* **infiniti'vally** *adv.* **infin'itively** *adv.*
❑ **infinitive marker** *n* a word that is used with a verb in the infinitive, such as *to* in *to sing*.

infinity see under **infinite**.

infirm /*in-fûrm'*/ *adj* sickly; weak; frail; unstable. [L *ĭnfirmus*, from *in-* not, and *firmus* strong]
■ **infirm'ity** *n.* **infirm'ly** *adv.* **infirm'ness** *n.*

infirmarian /*in-fər-mā'ri-ən*/ (*hist*) *n* an officer in a medieval monastery who was in charge of the infirmary (also **infirm'arer**). [See **infirmary**]

infirmary /*in-fûr'mə-ri*/ *n* a hospital or place for the treatment of the sick. [Med L *infirmaria*; see **infirm**]

infix or (*archaic*) **enfix** /*in-fiks'*/ *vt* to fix in; to drive or fasten in; to set in by piercing; to insert an affix within (a root) (*philology*). ◆ *n* /*in'fiks*/ (*philology*) an element or affix inserted within a root or word, as *m* in the Gr *lambanō*, from the root *lab*. [L *ĭnfīxus*, from *in* in, and *fīgere*, *fīxum* to fix]
❑ **infix notation** *n* a form of algebraic notation in which the operators are placed between the operands, as in *A* + *B* (cf **postfix notation** under **post-**).

infl. *abbrev*: influenced.

in flagrante (delicto) /*in flə-gran'ti (di-lik'tō)* or *flä-gran'te (dä-lik'tō)*/ same as **flagrante delicto**.

inflame /*in-flām'*/ *vt* to cause to burn; to make hot; to make red; to cause inflammation in; to arouse strong emotions in; to anger; to exacerbate. ◆ *vi* to burst into flames; to become hot, painful, red, excited or angry; to suffer inflammation. [OFr *enflammer*, from L *ĭnflammāre*; see ety for **inflammable**]
■ **inflam'able** *adj* (*obs*) inflammable. **inflamed'** *adj.* **inflam'er** *n.*

inflammable /in-flam'ə-bl/ adj capable of being set on fire (see **flammable** under **flame**); easily excited or angered. ◆ n an inflammable substance. [L *īnflammāre*, from *in* into, and *flamma* a flame]

■ **inflammabil'ity** n. **inflamm'ableness** n. **inflamm'ably** adv. **inflammation** /-flə-mā'shən/ n the state of being in flames or inflamed; heat of a part of the body, with pain, redness, and swelling; arousal of the passions. **inflamm'atory** adj tending to inflame; inflaming; tending to stir up strong emotion, *esp* anger or hostility.

inflate /in-flāt'/ vt to cause to swell up with air or gas; to puff up; to expand unduly; to increase excessively; to elate. ◆ vi to become full of air or gas; to distend. [L *īnflāre, -ātum*, from *in* into, and *flāre* to blow] ■ **inflat'able** n and adj (any object) that can be inflated. **inflat'ed** adj swollen or blown out; turgid; pompous; hollow, filled with air (*bot*); (of prices) artificially increased. **inflat'edly** adv. **inflat'ingly** adv. **inflation** /in-flā'shən/ n the act of inflating; the condition of being inflated; undue increase in quantity of money in proportion to buying power, as on an excessive issue of fiduciary money; a progressive increase in the general level of prices; turgidity of style; afflatus; inspiration (*rare*). **infla'tionary** adj. **infla'tionism** n the policy of inflating currency. **infla'tionist** n and adj. **inflat'ive** adj causing inflation; tending to inflate. **inflat'or** or **inflat'er** n someone who, or something that, inflates; a cycle pump. **inflat'us** n (L) inspiration.
❑ **inflationary universe** n (*astron*) a model of the very early universe (10^{-44} seconds after the Big Bang) in which the universe expands momentarily much faster than the speed of light. **infla'tion-proof** adj (of investments, etc) protected, *esp* by indexation, against inflation. **infla'tion-proofing** n.

inflect /in-flekt'/ vt to bend in; to turn from a direct line or course; to modulate (eg the voice); to vary the endings of (a word) (*grammar*). [L *īnflectere*, from *in* in, and *flectere, flexum* to bend, *flexiō, -ōnis* a bend]
■ **inflec'tion** or **inflex'ion** n a bending or deviation; modulation of the voice; variation in word-ending to express the relations of case, number, gender, person, tense, etc (*grammar*); a suffix added to a word when inflecting (*grammar*). **inflec'tional** or **inflex'ional** adj. **inflec'tionally** or **inflex'ionally** adv. **inflec'tionless** or **inflex'ionless** adj. **inflect'ive** adj subject to inflection. **inflexed'** adj (*esp biol*) bent inward; bent; turned. **inflexure** /in-flek'shər/ n an inward bend or fold.

inflexible /in-flek'si-bl/ adj not flexible; incapable of being bent; unyielding; rigid; obstinate; unbending. [**in-** (2)]
■ **inflexibil'ity** or **inflex'ibleness** n. **inflex'ibly** adv.

inflexion and **inflexional** see under **inflect**.

inflict /in-flikt'/ vt to lay on (a blow, etc); to impose (eg punishment or pain; *usu* with *on* or *upon*); to afflict (*Shakesp*). [L *īnflīgere, īnflīctum*, from *in* against, and *flīgere* to strike]
■ **inflict'able** adj. **inflic'ter** or **inflic'tor** n. **inflic'tion** n the act of inflicting or imposing; something inflicted. **inflict'ive** adj.

infliximab /in-flik'si-mab/ n a therapeutic antibody used to treat Crohn's disease and some types of arthritis. [*inflammation*, *xi* (denoting a chimaeric antibody), and *monoclonal antibody*]

inflorescence /in-flo-res'əns or -flə-/ (*bot*) n a specialized branching stem or axis of a plant bearing a flower or flowers; the arrangement of flowers on an axis, a flower cluster; the process of producing flowers, blossoming. [L *īnflōrēscere* to begin to blossom]

inflow /in'flō/ n the act of flowing in, influx; the rate of flowing in; something that flows in. [**in-** (1)]
■ **in'flowing** n and adj.

influence /in'flū-əns/ n the power of producing an effect, *esp* unobtrusively; the effect of power exerted; something having such power; someone exercising such power; domination, often hidden or inexplicable; exertions of friends who have useful connections and are able to secure advantages for one; the occult power or virtue supposed to flow from stars and planets, thought to affect a person's personality, actions, future, etc (*astrol*); a spiritual influx; inflow (*obs*). ◆ vt to have or exert influence upon; to affect. [OFr, from LL *influentia*, from L *in* into, and *fluere* to flow]
■ **in'fluenceable** adj. **in'fluencer** n. **in'fluent** adj flowing in; exerting influence. ◆ n a tributary stream; an organism that has a major or modifying effect on an ecological community. **influential** /-en'shl/ adj of the nature of influence; having a great deal of influence; effectively active (in bringing something about). **influen'tially** adv.
■ **under the influence** (*inf*) suffering from the effects of (too much) alcohol, drunk.

influenza /in-flū-en'zə/ n a highly contagious viral infection characterized by headache, fever, muscular aches and pains and inflammation of the respiratory passages; any of several diseases of *esp* domestic animals which attack the respiratory system.

[Ital, *influence, influenza* (as a supposed astral visitation), from LL *īnfluentia*; see **influence**]
■ **influen'zal** adj.

influx /in'fluks/ n a flowing in, *esp* of a large number of people or things; accession; that which flows in, eg a river or stream. [L *īnfluxus*, from *īnfluere*]
■ **influxion** /in-fluk'shon/ n.
❑ **influx control** n formerly in South Africa, a government control which prevented black Africans entering urban areas without permits (cf **pass laws**).

info /in'fō/ n an informal short form of **information**.
❑ **in'fobahn** n the information (super)highway; the Internet. **infograph'ic** n an illustration or diagram that conveys information. **infoma'nia** n enthusiasm for or obsession with gathering (*esp* electronic) information. **infomer'cial** n a short film which is in fact an advertising medium. **infopreneur'ial** adj of or relating to the industry concerned with the development, manufacture and sale of *esp* computerized or electronic equipment for the distribution of information. **in'fosphere** n the business of collecting (*esp* electronic) information. **infotain'ment** n the presentation of serious subjects or current affairs as entertainment. **in'fotech** n an informal short form of **information technology**.

in-foal /in-fōl'/ adj pregnant (with foal). [**in**[1] and **foal**]

infobahn see under **info**.

infobahn, infographic see under **info**.

infold[1] see **enfold**.

infold[2] /in'fold/ n a fold inwards. [**in-** (1)]
■ **in'folding** n.

infomania...to...**infopreneurial** see under **info**.

inforce same as **enforce**.

inform[1] /in-förm'/ vt to pass on knowledge to; to tell; to animate or inspire; to give a quality to; to direct or educate (*obs*); to give form to (*obs*). ◆ vi to give information, make an accusation (with *against* or *on*); to take shape or form (*obs*). [OFr *enformer*, from L *īnfōrmāre*, from *in* into, and *fōrmāre* to form, *fōrma* form]
■ **inform'ant** n someone who informs or communicates information. **informati'cian** n someone engaged in informatics. **informa'tics** n *sing* information science; information technology. **information** /in-fər-mā'shən/ n the act of informing; intelligence given; knowledge; an accusation made before a magistrate or court; data (*comput*); directory enquiries (*N Am*). **informat'ional** adj. **inform'ative** adj having the power to form; instructive. **inform'atively** adv. **inform'ativeness** n. **inform'atory** adj instructive; giving information. **informed'** adj knowing, intelligent, educated. **inform'er** n a person who gives information; a person who informs against another; an animator or inspirer (*literary*).
❑ **information highway** see **information superhighway** below. **information retrieval** n the storage, classification, and subsequent tracing of (*esp* computerized) information. **information science** n (the study of) the processing and communication of data, *esp* by means of computerized systems. **information scientist** n. **information superhighway** or **highway** n a collective name for digital electronic telecommunication systems, including computer networks (*esp* the Internet), cable and satellite television, and telephone links. **information technology** n the (*esp* computerized or electronic) technology related to the gathering, recording and communicating of information (*abbrev* IT). **information theory** n mathematical analysis of the efficiency with which communication channels are employed.

inform[2] /in-förm'/ (*archaic*) adj formless, unformed; misshapen, deformed. [Ety as **informal**]

informal /in-för'məl/ adj not of a formal or conventional nature; characterized by lack of ceremony or formality; relaxed, friendly, unceremonious; (*esp* of clothes) appropriate to everyday or casual use; (of speech or writing) having vocabulary, idiom, etc characteristic of conversational speech; (of a vote) invalid (*Aust* and *NZ*). [L *in-* not, and *fōrma* form; *infōrmis* formless, misshapen]
■ **informal'ity** n. **inform'ally** adv.

in forma pauperis /in för'mə pö'pə-ris or för'mä pow'pe-ris/ (L) as a pauper; as a poor person, not liable to costs (*law*).

informidable /in-för'mi-də-bl/ (*rare*) adj not formidable. [**in-** (2)]

in foro conscientiae /in fö'rō kon-shi-en'shi-ē or kōn-ski-en-ti-ī/ (L) in the court of conscience; judged by one's own conscience.

infortune /in-för'tūn/ n misfortune (*rare*); a malevolent influence or planetary aspect (*astrol*). [**in-** (2)]

infosphere, infotainment, infotech see under **info**.

infra /in'frə or ēn'frä/ (L) adv below; lower down on the page, or further on in the book.

infra dignitatem /dig-ni-tā'təm/ or /-tä'tem/ beneath one's dignity; unbecoming (*inf* short form **infra dig**).

infracostal /in-frə-kos'tl/ (*anat*) *adj* beneath the ribs. [L *īnfrā* below, and *costa* a rib]

infraction /in-frak'shən/ *n* violation, *esp* of law; a breach. [L *īnfringere*, *īnfrāctum*, from *in* in, and *frangere*, *frāctum* to break]
▪ **infract'** *vt* to infringe. **infract'ed** *adj* broken; interrupted; bent in. **infrac'tor** *n*.

infra dig see **infra dignitatem** under **infra**.

infragrant /in-frā'grənt/ *adj* not fragrant, malodorous. [**in-** (2)]

infrahuman /in-frə-hū'mən/ *adj* lower than human (also *n*). [L *īnfrā* below]

Infralapsarian /in-frə-lap-sā'ri-ən/ *n* a believer in Infralapsarianism (also *adj*). [L *īnfrā* below, after, and *lāpsus* a fall]
▪ **Infralapsār'ianism** *n* the common Augustinian and Calvinist doctrine, that God for his own glory determined to create the world, to permit the fall of man, to elect some to salvation and leave the rest to punishment, distinct both from *Supralapsarianism* and *Sublapsarianism*; also sometimes used as equivalent to Sublapsarianism.

inframaxillary /in-frə-mak'si-lə-ri/ *adj* situated under the jaw; belonging to the lower jaw. [L *īnfrā* below, and *maxilla* jaw]

infrangible /in-fran'ji-bl/ *adj* not able to be broken; not to be violated. [L *in-* not, and *frangere* to break]
▪ **infrangibil'ity** or **infran'gibleness** *n*. **infran'gibly** *adv*.

infraorbital /in-frə-ör'bi-tl/ *adj* situated below the orbit of the eye. [L *īnfrā* below]

infraposed /in'frə-pōzd/ *adj* placed below something else (cf **superposed**).
▪ **infraposi'tion** *n*.

infrared /in'frə-red'/ *n* infrared radiation; the infrared region of the spectrum. ◆ *adj* between the red end of the visible spectrum and microwaves; using infrared radiation; sensitive to this radiation. [L *īnfrā* below]
❑ **infrared astronomy** *n* the study of radiation from celestial bodies, such as nascent stars, in the infrared wavelength range. **infrared photography** *n* photography using film specially sensitized to infrared radiation, with applications in conditions without visible light, camouflage and forgery detection, and aerial surveys. **infrared radiation** *n* electromagnetic radiation between the visible and microwave regions of the spectrum, ie with wavelengths from 0.75 to 1000 micrometres.

infrasonic /in-frə-son'ik/ (*acoustics*) *adj* (of frequencies) below the usual audible limit; of, using or produced by infrasonic vibrations or pressure waves. [L *īnfrā* below]
▪ **in'frasound** *n*.

infraspecific /in-frə-spə-sif'ik/ (*biol*) *adj* included within or affecting a species.

infrastructure /in'frə-struk-chər/ *n* inner structure, structure of component parts; a system of communications and services as backing for military, commercial, etc operations. [L *īnfrā* below]
▪ **infrastruc'tural** *adj*.

infrequent /in-frē'kwənt/ *adj* seldom occurring; rare; uncommon. [**in-** (2)]
▪ **infre'quency** or **infre'quence** *n*. **infre'quently** *adv*.

infringe /in-frinj'/ *vt* to violate, *esp* a law; to neglect to obey. ◆ *vi* to encroach or trespass (with *on* or *upon*). [L *īnfringere*, from *in* in, and *frangere* to break]
▪ **infringe'ment** *n*. **infring'er** *n*.

infructuous /in-fruk'tū-əs/ *adj* not fruitful (*lit* and *fig*). [L *īnfrūctuōsus*, from *in-* not, and *frūctuōsus* fruitful]
▪ **infruc'tuously** *adv*.

infula /in'fū-lə/ *n* (*pl* **in'fulae** /-ē/) a white-and-red band of woollen cloth, worn on the forehead by the ancient Romans in religious rites; one of the lappets in a bishop's mitre. [L *īnfula*]

infundibulum /in-fun-dib'ū-ləm/ *n* (*pl* **infundib'ula**) a funnel or funnel-shaped part, *esp* the funnel-shaped stalk that connects the pituitary gland to the brain. [L, a funnel, from *in* in, and *fundere* to pour]
▪ **infundibular** /in-fun-dib'ū-lər/ *adj* (also **infundib'ulate**) funnel-shaped; having an infundibulum. **infundib'uliform** *adj*.

infuriate /in-fū'ri-āt/ *vt* to enrage, anger; to madden. ◆ *adj* /-it or -āt/ enraged, furiously angry; mad. [L *in* in, and *furiāre, -ātum* to madden, from *furere* to rave]
▪ **infur'iating** *adj*. **infur'iatingly** *adv*. **infuria'tion** *n*.

infuscate /in-fus'kāt/ or /-kit/ *adj* clouded or tinged with brown. [L *in* in, and *fuscus* brown]

infuse /in-fūz'/ *vt* to pour in; to instil; to soak in liquid without boiling; to imbue; to shed or pour (*obs*). ◆ *vi* to undergo infusion. ◆ *n* (*Spenser*) infusion. [L *īnfundere*, *īnfūsum*, from *in* into, and *fundere*, *fūsum* to pour]
▪ **infus'er** *n* a device for making an infusion, *esp* of tea. **infus'ible** *adj*. **infusion** /in-fū'zhən/ *n* pouring in; something poured in or introduced; the pouring of water over any substance in order to extract its active qualities; a solution in water of an organic, *esp* a vegetable, substance; the liquid so obtained; inspiration; instilling. **infusive** /-fū'siv/ *adj* having the power of infusion, or of being infused.

infusible /in-fū'zi-bl/ *adj* that cannot be fused; having a high melting point. [**in-** (2)]
▪ **infusibil'ity** *n*.

infusoria /in-fū-zō'ri-ə, -zō', -sō'ri-ə or -sō'/ (*obs*) *n pl orig* minute organisms found in stagnant infusions of animal or vegetable material; (with *cap*) the Ciliophora, a former class of Protozoa with cilia throughout life (Ciliata) or in early life (Suctoria). [Neuter pl of New L *īnfūsorius*; see **infuse**]
▪ **infūsō'rial** or **infū'sory** *adj* composed of or containing infusoria. **infūsō'rian** *n* and *adj*.
❑ **infusorial earth** *n* diatomite.

ing /ing/ (*dialect, esp N Eng*; often in *pl*) *n* a meadow, *esp* one beside a river. [ON *eng* meadow]

-ing¹ /-ing/ *sfx* forming: (1) the present participle of verbs, as in *jumping, waiting, talking*; (2) adjectives from participles, as in *a crying baby, a moving vehicle*; (3) adjectives not derived from verbs, as in *sodding, swashbuckling*. [ME *-ing, inde*, from OE *-ende*]

-ing² /-ing/ *sfx* forming: (1) nouns, signifying something consisting of, made from, or used in making, as in *wiring, matting, scaffolding*; (2) *sing* and *pl* nouns from verbs, signifying a result of an action or process, as in *etching(s), drawing(s)*; (3) nouns, signifying an activity or area of activity as a whole, as in *skiing, banking, mining, engineering*.

-ing³ /-ing/ *sfx* forming nouns, denoting a person or thing of a specified quality or kind, as in *sweeting* (see also **-ling¹**). [ME, from OE, related to OHGer *-ing* belonging to]

ingan /ing'ən/ *n* a Scots and dialect form of **onion**.

ingate¹ /in'gāt/ *n* an inlet for molten metal in founding. [**in¹** and **gate¹**]

ingate² /in'gāt/ (now *Scot* and *N Eng* dialect) *n* a way in, (an) entrance. [**in¹** and **gate²**]

ingather /in-gadh'ər/ *vt* to gather in; to harvest. [**in-** (1)]
▪ **ingathering** /in'gadh-ər-ing/ *n* collection; securing of the fruits of the earth; harvest.
▪ **Feast of Ingathering** see **Feast of Tabernacles** under **tabernacle**.

ingeminate /in-jem'i-nāt/ (*formal*) *vt* to reiterate; to redouble. [L *ingemināre, -ātum*, from *in* in, and *geminus* twin]
▪ **ingeminā'tion** *n*.

ingener /in'jə-nər/ (*Shakesp*) *n* same as **engineer** (see under **engine**).

ingenerate¹ /in-jen'ə-rāt/ *vt* to generate or produce within. ◆ *adj* /-it/ inborn; innate. [**in-** (1)]

ingenerate² /in-jen'ə-rit or -rāt/ *adj* not generated, self-existent. [**in-** (2)]

ingenious /in-jē'nyəs or -ni-əs/ *adj* skilful in invention or contriving; skilfully contrived; of good natural abilities, *esp* having or displaying great intelligence (*obs*). [L *ingenium* mother-wit]
▪ **ingē'niously** *adv*. **ingē'niousness** *n* great inventiveness and imagination; skill in combining ideas; cleverly contrived or unconventional design. **ingē'nium** *n* (*obs*) mentality; talent or genius.

ingénue /ɛ̃-zhä-nü'/ (*Fr*) *n* an artless, naïve or inexperienced young woman, *esp* an actress portraying such a type.
▪ **ingénu'** *n* an inexperienced young man.

ingenuity /in-ji-nū'i-ti/ *n orig* ingenuousness; now (by confusion with **ingenious**) ingeniousness. [L *ingenuitās, -ātis*; see ety for **ingenuous**]

ingenuous /in-jen'ū-əs/ *adj* candid, frank; honourable; free from deception, artless; freeborn (*obs*). [L *ingenuus* freeborn, ingenuous]
▪ **ingenu'ity** *n* (see previous entry). **ingen'uously** *adv*. **ingen'uousness** *n*.

ingest /in-jest'/ *vt* to take (eg food) into the body. [L *ingerere, ingestum* to carry in, from *in* in, and *gerere* to carry]
▪ **ingest'a** *n pl* nourishment taken into the body through the alimentary canal via the mouth. **ingest'ible** *adj*. **ingestion** /in-jes'chən/ *n*. **ingest'ive** *adj*.

ingine /in-jīn'/ (*obs*) *n* ability; genius. [L *ingenium*]

ingle¹ /ing'gl/ or (*Scot* and *dialect*) /ing'l/ *n* a fire in a room; a fireplace. [Poss Gaelic *aingeal*; or L *igniculus*, dimin of *ignis* fire]
❑ **ing'le-cheek** *n* the jamb of a fireplace. **ing'lenook** or (*Scot*) **ing'leneuk** *n* an alcove by a large open fire, a chimney-corner. **ing'le-side** *n* a fireside.

---

ingle² /ing'gl/ (*obs*) *n* a catamite; a friend (*Walter Scott*; *non-standard*). [Origin obscure]

inglobe /in-glōb'/ (*Milton*) *vt* to englobe, form into a sphere. [**in-** (1)]

inglorious /in-glō'ri-əs or -glö'/ *adj* shameful, disgraceful; not glorious; unhonoured. [**in-** (2)]
  ■ **inglo'riously** *adv*. **inglo'riousness** *n*.

ingluvies /in-gloo'vi-ēz/ *n* the crop or craw of birds. [L *ingluviēs*]
  ■ **inglu'vial** *adj*.

ingo /in'gō/ (*Scot*) *n* (*pl* **in'goes**) an entrance; a reveal, the inner sides of a recess or opening, eg a doorway; entry into or taking on of a new tenancy. [**in¹** and **go¹**]

ingoing /in'gō-ing/ *n* a going in; an entrance; a reveal (*Scot*). ◆ *adj* going in; entering as an occupant; thorough, penetrating. [**in¹** and **go¹**]

ingot /ing'gət or -got/ *n* a mass of unwrought metal, *esp* gold or silver, cast in a mould. [Perh OE *in* in, and the root *got*, as in *goten*, pap of *gēotan* to pour; Ger *giessen*, Gothic *giutan*]

ingraft see **engraft**.

ingrain /in-grān'/ *vt* (also **engrain'**) to dye in a fast or lasting colour; to fix a dye firmly in; to instil (a habit or attitude) deeply in. ◆ *adj* (or /in'grān/) ingrained. [Orig to dye in grain, ie with grain, the dye]
  ■ **ingrained'** or **engrained'** (or /in'/) *adj* dyed in grain; deeply coloured or permeated; deep-rooted and established, eg *ingrained laziness*; thorough-going (*fig*). **ingrain'er** or **engrain'er** *n*.

ingram or **ingrum** /ing'rəm/ (*obs*) *adj* ignorant. [**ignorant**]

ingrate /in-grāt' or in'grāt/ (*archaic*) *adj* ungrateful; unpleasing (*obs*). ◆ *n* an ungrateful person. [L *ingrātus*, from *in-* not, and *grātus* pleasing, grateful]
  ■ **ingrate'ful** *adj*. **ingrate'ly** *adv*.

ingratiate /in-grā'shi-āt/ *vt* to commend (*usu* oneself) persuasively to someone's favour (followed by *with*). [L *in* into, and *grātia* favour]
  ■ **ingra'tiating** *adj*. **ingra'tiatingly** *adv*. **ingratia'tion** *n*.

ingratitude /in-grat'i-tūd/ *n* lack of gratitude or thankfulness. [LL *ingrātitūdō*, from L *ingrātus* unthankful]

ingravescent /in-grə-ves'ənt or ing-grə-/ *adj* (of a disease or medical condition) becoming more severe. [L *ingravescere* to become heavier, from L *gravis* heavy]
  ■ **ingravesc'ence** *n*.

ingredient /in-grē'di-ənt/ *n* something that is put into a mixture or compound; a component. [L *ingrediēns*, *-entis*, prp of *ingredī*, from *in* into, and *gradī* to walk]

in gremio /in grēm' or grem'i-ō/ (LL) in the bosom.
  ■ **in gremio legis** /lē'jis/ in the bosom of the law; under the protection of the law.

ingress /in'gres/ *n* (an) entrance; power, right or means of entrance. [L *ingressus*, from *ingredī*; see ety for **ingredient**]
  ■ **ingression** /in-gresh'ən/ *n*. **ingress'ive** *adj* of or relating to ingress; (of speech sounds) pronounced with inhalation rather than exhalation of breath (*phonetics*). ◆ *n* an ingressive speech sound.

ingroove see **engroove**.

ingross /in-grōs'/ (*archaic*) *vt* same as **engross**.

ingroup see under **in¹**.

ingrowing /in'grō-ing/ *adj* growing inwards; growing into the flesh; growing in or into. [**in-** (1)]
  ■ **in'grown** *adj*. **in'growth** *n* growth within or inwards; a structure formed in this way.

ingrum see **ingram**.

inguinal /ing'gwi-nəl/ *adj* in, of or relating to the groin. [L *inguinālis*, from *inguen*, *inguinis* the groin]

ingulf and **ingulph** see **engulf**.

ingurgitate /in-gûr'ji-tāt/ *vt* to swallow up (food) greedily. [L *ingurgitāre*, *-ātum*, from *in* into, and *gurges*, *-itis* a whirlpool]
  ■ **ingurgita'tion** *n*.

inhabit /in-hab'it/ *vt* to dwell in; to occupy. ◆ *vi* (*archaic*) to dwell. [L *inhabitāre*, from *in* in, and *habitāre* to dwell]
  ■ **inhabitabil'ity** *n*. **inhab'itable** *adj* capable of being inhabited; fit to live in; see also separate entry. **inhab'itance** or **inhab'itancy** *n* the act or a period of inhabiting; abode or residence. **inhab'itant** *n* a person who or an animal which inhabits a particular place; a resident. ◆ *adj* resident. **inhabita'tion** *n* the act or a period of inhabiting; dwelling-place; population (*archaic*); *perh* the inhabited world (*Milton*). **inhab'iter** *n* an inhabitant (*rare*); a colonist, settler (*obs*). **inhab'itiveness** *n* (*phrenology*) love of locality and home. **inhab'itor** *n* (*Bible*) an inhabitant. **inhab'itress** *n* (*archaic*) a female inhabitant.

inhabitable /in-hab'i-tə-bl/ (*obs*) *adj* not habitable, uninhabitable (see also under **inhabit**). [L *inhabitābilis*, from *in-* not, and *habitābilis*]

inhale /in-hāl'/ *vt* and *vi* to breathe in; to draw in. [L *in* upon, and *hālāre* to breathe (L *inhālāre* means to breathe upon)]
  ■ **inhā'lant** *adj* inhaling; drawing in. ◆ *n* a medicinal preparation to be inhaled; an inhaling organ, structure or apparatus. **inhalation** /in-hə-lā'shən/ *n* the act of drawing into the lungs; something to be inhaled. **inhalator** /in'hə-lā-tər or -lā'/ *n* an apparatus for enabling one to inhale a gas, vapour, etc. **inhalatorium** /in-hāl-ə-tō'ri-əm or -tör'/ *n* an institution or department for administering inhalations. **inhā'ler** *n* a person who inhales; a smoker who fully inhales tobacco smoke; a device for administering a medicinal preparation by inhalation, eg to relieve asthma, etc; a respirator or gas mask.

inharmonious /in-här-mō'ni-əs/ *adj* discordant, unmusical; disagreeing; marked by disagreement and discord. [**in-** (2)]
  ■ **inharmonic** /in-här-mon'ik/ or **inharmon'ical** *adj* lacking harmony; inharmonious. **inharmonic'ity** /-nis'-/ *n* the quality or phenomenon of being inharmonious. **inharmō'niously** *adv*. **inharmō'niousness** *n*. **inharmony** /in-här'mən-i/ *n*.

inhaul /in'höl/ or **inhauler** /-ər/ (*naut*) *n* a rope or line for hauling in something, eg a sail. [**in¹** and **haul**]

inhaust /in-höst'/ (*archaic*) *vt* to drink in. [L *in* in, and *haurīre*, *haustum* to draw]

inhearse or **inherce** /in-hûrs'/ (*Shakesp*) *vt* (also **enhearse'**) to enclose as in a hearse; to bury. [**in-** (1)]

inhere /in-hēr'/ *vi* (with *in*) to stick, remain firm in something; to be inherent. [L *inhaerēre*, *inhaesum*, from *in* in, and *haerēre* to stick]
  ■ **inhēr'ence** or **inhēr'ency** *n* a sticking fast; existence in something else; a fixed state of being in another body or substance; the relation between a quality or attribute and its subject (*philos*). **inhēr'ent** *adj* existing in and inseparable from something else; innate; natural; sticking fast (*archaic*). **inhēr'ently** *adv*.
  ❑ **inherent floatability** *n* (*mining*) the natural tendency of some mineral species to repel water and to become part of the float, as opposed to the froth, in the froth flotation process.

inherit /in-her'it/ *vt* to get possession of as heir; to possess by transmission from past generations; to have at secondhand from anyone (*inf*); to have by genetic transmission from ancestors; to make heir (*Shakesp*); to be the heir of, succeed as heir (*archaic*). ◆ *vi* to succeed. [OFr *enhériter* to put in possession as heir, from LL *inhērēditāre* to inherit, from L *in* in, and *hērēs*, *hērēdis* an heir]
  ■ **inheritabil'ity** *n*. **inher'itable** *adj* same as **heritable**. **inher'itance** *n* that which is or may be inherited; the right to inherit; the act of inheriting; hereditary descent. **inher'itor** *n* (also *fem* **inher'itress** or **inher'itrix**) someone who inherits or may inherit; an heir.
  ❑ **inherited error** *n* (*comput*) an error occurring in one stage of a calculation which is then carried over as an initial condition to a subsequent stage. **inheritance tax** *n* a tax (replacing **death duty** (see under **death**)) levied on inheritors according to their relationship to the testator (with exemption for spouses in the UK) when the estate exceeds a specified allowance.

inhesion /in-hē'zhən/ same as **inherence** (see under **inhere**).

inhibit /in-hib'it/ *vt* to hold in or back; to keep back; to restrain or check; to restrict or prevent. [L *inhibēre*, *-hibitum*, from *in* in, and *habēre* to have]
  ■ **inhib'ited** *adj* tense and reticent because of mental restraint. **inhib'itedly** *adv*. **inhibi'tion** *n* the act of inhibiting or restraining; the state of being inhibited; something that restricts, prevents or debars; a writ from a higher court to an inferior judge to stop, suspend or postpone proceedings (*obs*); a restraining action of the unconscious will; the blocking of a mental or psychophysical process by another set up at the same time by the same stimulus; stoppage or retardation of a physical process by some nervous influence. **inhib'itive** *adj*. **inhib'itor** *n* something which inhibits (also **inhib'iter**); a substance that interferes with a chemical or biological process. **inhib'itory** *adj* prohibitory.

inholder /in-hōl'dər/ (*obs*) *n* an inhabitant (*Spenser*); a container. [**in-** (1)]

inhomogeneous /in-hom-ō-jē'ni-əs/ *adj* not homogeneous. [**in-** (2)]
  ■ **inhomogeneity** /-jən-ē'i-ti/ *n*.

inhoop /in-hoop'/ (*Shakesp*) *vt* to confine, as in a hoop or enclosure. [**in-** (1)]

inhospitable /in-hos'pit-ə-bl or -pit'/ *adj* not kind or welcoming to strangers; (of a place) barren, not offering shelter, food, etc. [**in-** (2)]
  ■ **inhos'pitableness** or **inhospital'ity** *n*. **inhosp'itably** *adv*.

in-house see under **in¹**.

inhuman /in-hū'mən/ *adj* not human; brutal; cruel; without human feeling. [**in-** (2)]
  ■ **inhumanity** /in-hū-man'i-ti/ *n* the state of being inhuman or inhumane; an inhuman or inhumane act; brutality; cruelty. **inhū'manly** *adv*.

inhumane /in-hū-mān'/ adj lacking humane feelings, cruel. [**in-** (2)]
■ **inhumane'ly** adv.

inhume /in-hūm'/ vt to bury in the earth, to inter (also **inhumate** /in' or -hūm'/). [L inhumāre, from in in, and humus the ground]
■ **inhuma'tion** n the act or process of depositing in the ground; (a) burial. **inhum'er** n.

inia see **inion**.

inimical /in-im'i-kl/ adj unfriendly; hostile; unfavourable; opposed. [L inimīcālis, from inimīcus enemy, from in- not, and amīcus friend]
■ **inim'ically** adv. **inim'icalness** or **inimical'ity** n. **inimicitious** /-sish'əs/ adj (Sterne) unfriendly.

inimitable /in-im'i-tə-bl/ adj that cannot be imitated; exceptionally good or remarkable. [**in-** (2)]
■ **inimitabil'ity** or **inim'itableness** n. **inim'itably** adv.

inion /in'i-ən/ (anat) n (pl **in'ia**) the external occipital protuberance. [Gr īnion the occiput]

iniquity /in-ik'wi-ti/ n lack of fairness and justice; gross injustice; wickedness, sin; a crime; (with cap) one of the names of the Vice, the established buffoon of traditional medieval morality plays (hist). [Fr iniquité, from L inīquitās, -ātis, from inīquus unequal, from in- not, and aequus equal]
■ **iniq'uitous** adj unjust; scandalously unreasonable; wicked, sinful. **iniq'uitously** adv. **iniq'uitousness** n.

inisle same as **enisle**.

initial /i-nish'l/ adj beginning; of, at, or serving as the beginning; original. ◆ n the letter beginning a word, esp a name. ◆ vt (**init'ialling** or N Am **init'ialing**; **init'ialled** or N Am **init'ialed**) to put the initials of one's name to, esp when acknowledging or agreeing to something. [L initiālis, from initium a beginning, from inīre, initum, from in into, and īre, itum to go]
■ **init'ialism** n an abbreviation in which each letter is pronounced separately; an acronym (N Am). **initializa'tion** or **-s-** n. **init'ialize** or **-ise** vt to assign initial values to variables, eg in a computer program; to return a device (eg a computer or a printer) to its initial state. **init'ially** adv.
❑ **initial cell** n (bot) a cell that remains meristematic and gives rise to many daughter cells from which permanent tissues are formed. **initial public offering** n a sale of new shares in a company on a stock exchange (abbrev **IPO**). **Initial Teaching Alphabet** n a 44-character alphabet in which each character corresponds to a single sound or phoneme of English, sometimes used in the teaching of reading.

initiate /i-nish'i-āt/ vt to begin, start; to introduce (to) (eg knowledge); to admit, esp with rites, (eg to a secret society, a mystery). ◆ vi to perform the first act or rite. ◆ n /-it/ someone who is initiated. ◆ adj initiated; belonging to someone newly initiated. [L initiāre to originate or initiate, from initium a beginning; see ety for **initial**]
■ **initia'tion** n. **init'iative** /-i-ə-tiv/ adj serving to initiate; introductory. ◆ n the lead, first step, often considered as determining the conditions for oneself or others; the right or power of beginning; energy and resourcefulness enabling one to act without prompting from others; the right to originate legislation, or a constitutional method of doing so. **init'iator** n someone who or something that initiates; a substance that starts a chain reaction (chem); an explosive used in a detonator. **init'iatory** /-i-ə-tə-ri/ adj tending or serving to initiate; introductory. ◆ n an introductory rite.
❑ **initiation rite** n a rite of passage. **initiator codon** n (biochem) the first codon of the coding region in messenger RNA and the point at which translation usu starts.
■ **on one's initiative** using one's own resources and without prompting from others.

inject /in-jekt'/ vt to force in; to inspire or instil; to fill or introduce into by injection. ◆ vi to inject a narcotic drug into one's body. [L injicere, injectum, from in into, and jacere to throw]
■ **injec'table** adj able to be injected (also n). **injec'tion** /-shən/ n the act of injecting, introducing or forcing in, esp a liquid; something injected, esp a liquid injected into the body with a syringe or similar instrument; a magma injected into a rock (geol); the spraying of fuel into the cylinder of a compression-ignition engine by an injection pump (motoring); the putting of a man-made craft or satellite into orbit (also **insertion**); an amount of money added to an economy in order to stimulate production, expansion, etc; a mapping function in which each element in a set corresponds to only one element in another set (maths). **injec'tive** adj (maths) of or relating to injection. **injec'tor** n a person who injects; something used for injecting, esp an apparatus for forcing water into a boiler.
❑ **injec'tion-moulded** adj. **injection moulding** n the moulding of thermoplastics by squirting the material from a heated cylinder into a water-chilled mould. **injection string** n (mining) a pipe run in addition to the production string in the borehole to allow the passage of additives or of drilling mud to stop the well (also called **kill string**).

injera /in-jer'ə/ n a type of Ethiopian bread made from soured tef flour. [Ahmaric]

injoint /in-joint'/ (Shakesp) vi to join. [**in-** (1)]

injudicious /in-jū-dish'əs/ adj not judicious; ill-judged, imprudent. [**in-** (2)]
■ **injudic'ial** adj not according to legal forms. **injudic'ially** adv. **injudic'iously** adv. **injudic'iousness** n.

Injun /in'jən/ (inf) n a Native American (also adj). [Colloquial pronunciation of **Indian**]
■ **honest Injun** see under **honest**.

injunction /in-jungk'shən/ n the act of enjoining or commanding; an order, command; a precept; an exhortation; an inhibitory writ by which a superior court stops or prevents some inequitable or illegal act being carried out, called in Scotland an interdict; conjunction (Milton). [LL injunctiō, -ōnis, from in in, and jungere, junctum to join]
■ **injunct'** vt to prohibit, restrain by means of an injunction. **injunc'tive** adj. **injunc'tively** adv.

injure /in'jər/ vt to harm; to damage; to wrong; to hurt. [L injūria injury, from in- not, and jūs, jūris law]
■ **in'jurer** n. **injurious** /in-joo'ri-əs/ adj tending to injure; wrongful; hurtful; damaging to reputation. **inju'riously** adv. **inju'riousness** n. **injury** /in'jər-i/ n that which injures; physical damage, a wound; hurt; wrong; impairment; annoyance; insult, offence (obs).
❑ **injury benefit** see **Industrial Injuries Disablement Benefit** under **industry**. **injury time** n (in ball games) extra time allowed for play to compensate for time lost as a result of injury stoppages during the game.

injustice /in-jus'tis/ n the violation or withholding of another's rights or dues; the fact or an act of being unjust; wrong; iniquity. [**in-** (2)]

ink /ingk/ n a black or coloured liquid used in writing, printing, etc; a dark liquid ejected by cuttlefishes, etc. ◆ vt to mark, daub, cover, blacken or colour with ink. [OFr enque (Fr encre), from LL encaustum the purple-red ink used by the later Roman emperors, from Gr enkauston, from enkaiein to burn in; see **encaustic**]
■ **ink'er** n someone who inks; a pad or roller for inking type, etc. **ink'iness** n. **ink'y** adj (**ink'ier**; **ink'iest**) consisting of or resembling ink; very black; blackened with ink; drunk (esp Aust sl; also **inked**).
❑ **ink'-bag** or **ink'-sac** n a sac in some cuttlefishes, containing a black viscid fluid. **ink'berry** n (the fruit of) any of various N American shrubs, esp Ilex glabra of the holly family and Phytolacca americana, pokeweed. **ink'-blot** n (psychol) a standardized blot of ink used in the Rorschach test to identify personality traits and disorders. **ink-blot test** same as **Rorschach test**. **ink'-bottle** n a bottle for holding ink. **ink'-cap** n any mushroom of the genus Coprinus, such as C. comatus, the shaggy ink-cap. **ink'-eraser** n an eraser of india-rubber treated with fine sand, used for rubbing out ink marks. **ink'-feed** n the passage by which ink is fed to the nib of a fountain pen. **ink'-fish** n a cuttlefish or squid. **ink'holder** n a container for ink; the reservoir of a fountain pen. **ink'horn** n formerly an ink-holder, made of horn; a portable case for ink, etc. ◆ adj pedantic, bookish, obscure. **ink'horn-mate** n (Shakesp; derog) a bookish person, a scribbler. **ink'ing-roll'er** n a roller covered with a substance for inking printing type. **ink'ing-ta'ble** n a table or flat surface used for supplying the inking-roller with ink during the process of printing. **ink-jet printer** n a printer which produces characters on paper by squirting a fine jet of ink that is vibrated, electrically charged and deflected by electrostatic fields. **ink'pad** n a pad of inked cloth used in rubber-stamping, fingerprinting, etc. **ink pencil** n a copying pencil, a pencil made from a substance whose marks when moistened look like ink and can be copied by a printing press. **ink plant** n a European shrub (Coriaria myrtifolia) or a related species native to New Zealand (C. thymifolia). **ink'pot** n an ink-bottle, or pot for dipping a pen in. **ink'-slinger** or US **ink'-jerker** n (derog sl) a professional author or journalist; a scribbler; a controversialist. **ink'spot** n a small ink stain. **ink'-stained** adj. **ink'stand** n a stand or tray for ink bottles and (usu) pens. **ink'stone** n a kind of stone containing sulphate of iron, used in making ink. **ink'well** n a container for ink fitted into, or standing on, a desk, etc.
■ **China ink**, **Chinese ink** or **Indian ink**, (US) **India ink** (sometimes without caps) a mixture of lamp black and size or glue, usu kept in solid form and rubbed down in water for use; a liquid suspension of the solid ink. **ink in** to fill in (eg a pencil drawing) in ink; to apply ink to (a printing roller). **invisible** or **sympathetic ink** a kind of ink that remains invisible on the paper until it is heated. **marking-ink** see under **mark¹**. **printing ink** see under **print**. **sling ink** (derog sl) to write; to earn one's living by writing; to engage in controversy.

Inkatha /in-kä'tə/ n a South African Zulu cultural and political movement, orig a paramilitary organization, seeking liberation from white minority rule. [Zulu, a plaited grass coil used for carrying loads on the head]

inkhosi see **inkosi**.

inkle[1] /ing'kl/ (obs) n a kind of broad linen tape (also **inc'le**). [Poss Du enkel single]

inkle[2] see under **inkling**.

inkling /ing'kling/ n a slight hint; an intimation; a faint notion or suspicion. [ME inclen to hint at; origin unknown]
- **ink'le** vi to have or give a hint of.

in-kneed /in'nēd'/ adj bent inward at the knees; knock-kneed. [**in-** (1)]

inkosi /ing-kō'si/ n (pl **inko'sis** or **amakosi** /am-ə-kō'si/) a traditional leader of a Zulu clan (also **inkho'si**). [Zulu]

INLA abbrev : Irish National Liberation Army.

inlace same as **enlace**.

inlaid see under **inlay**.

inland /in'land or in'lənd/ n the interior part of a country; the populated part of a country, or part near the capital (archaic). ◆ adj of the interior of a country, remote from the sea; operating or produced within a country; confined to a country; sophisticated, refined (Shakesp). ◆ adv (also /in-land'/) landward; away from the sea; in an inland place. [OE inland a domain, from in and land]
- **in'lander** n a person who lives inland.
◻ **inland bill** n a bill of exchange that is (designated as being) payable in the same country, state, etc as it is drawn (cf **foreign bill**). **inland navigation** n the passage of boats or vessels on rivers, lakes, or canals within a country. **inland revenue** n internal revenue, derived from direct taxes such as income tax and stamp duty; (with caps) the government department responsible for collecting such taxes.

in-law /in'lö/ (inf) n (pl **in'-laws**) a relative by marriage, eg mother-in-law, brother-in-law.

inlay /in'lā' or in-lā'/ vt (**inlaying**; **inlaid**) to insert, embed; to insert a page of text, an illustration, etc into a space cut in a larger page; to ornament by laying in or inserting pieces of metal, ivory, etc; to insert a substance or piece of tissue) to replace or correct a defect in tissue (med); to mix images electronically, using masks (TV). ◆ n /in'lā/ inlaying; inlaid work; material inlaid; a shaped filling for a tooth cavity (dentistry). [**in-** (1)]
- **inlaid**' (or /in'lād or in-lād'/) adj inserted by inlaying; decorated with inlay; consisting of inlay; having a pattern set into the surface. **inlayer** /in'lā-ər or in-lā'ər/ n. **in'laying** n.

inlet /in'let or -lət/ n a small bay or opening in a coastline; a piece let in or inserted; an entrance; a passage by which anything is let in; a place of entry. [**in**[1] and **let**[1]]

inlier /in'lī-ər/ (geol) n an outcrop of older rock surrounded by younger. [**in**[1] and **lie**[2]]

in limine /in lim'i-nē or lē'mi-ne/ (L) on the threshold.

in loc. abbrev : in loco (L), in its place.

in loc. cit. abbrev : in loco citato (L), in the place cited.

inlock /in-lok'/ vt same as **enlock**.

in loco parentis /in lō'kō (or lok'ō) pə- or pä-ren'tis/ (L) in the place of a parent.

inly /in'li/ (poetic) adv inwardly; in the heart; thoroughly, entirely. [**in**[1]]

inlying /in'lī-ing/ adj situated inside or near a centre. [**in**[1] and **lying**]

in malam partem /in mä'ləm pär'təm or mal'am pär'tem/ (L) in an unfavourable manner.

inmarriage /in'ma-rij/ n endogamy (qv under **endo-**). [**in-** (1)]

INMARSAT or **Inmarsat** abbrev : International Maritime Satellite.

inmate /in'māt/ n a person who lodges in the same house with others (obs); a person confined in an institution, esp a prison. ◆ adj (obs) dwelling in the same place. [**in**[1] or **inn** and **mate**[1]]

in medias res /in mē'di-əs rēz or mä'di- or med'i-äs räs/ (L) into the midst of things.

in memoriam /in me-mö'ri-am, mō'/ (L) in memory of. [L, into memory]

inmesh same as **enmesh**.

inmost see **innermost** under **inner**.

inn /in/ n a small hotel open to the public for food, drink and accommodation; a hotel; loosely, a public house; (also (Spenser) **in**; often in pl) a dwelling-place, abode (obs). ◆ vt and vi (archaic) to lodge, put up. [OE inn an inn, house, from in, inn within (adv), from the prep in in]
◻ **inn'keeper** n a person in charge of an inn. **inn sign** n a painted or otherwise decorated panel outside an inn, illustrating its name. **inn'yard** n the courtyard round which an old-fashioned inn was built.
▪ **Inns of Court** the buildings of four voluntary societies that have the exclusive right of calling to the English bar (Inner Temple, Middle Temple, Lincoln's Inn and Gray's Inn); hence, the societies themselves; the **Inns of Chancery** were the buildings of minor societies, residences of junior students of law.

innards /in'ərdz/ (inf) n pl entrails; internal parts of a mechanism; interior. [**inwards**]

innate /in'āt or i-nāt'/ adj inborn; instinctive; inherent; (of an anther) attached by the base to the tip of the filament (bot). [L innātus, from in-in, and nāscī, nātus to be born]
- **inn'ately** (or /-nāt'/) adv. **inn'ateness** (or /-nāt'/) n. **innā'tive** adj (archaic) native.

innavigable /in-nav'i-gə-bl/ adj unnavigable. [**in-** (2)]
- **innav'igably** adv.

inner /in'ər/ adj (compar of **in**) farther in; interior. ◆ n (archery) (a hit on) that part of a target next to the bull's-eye. [OE in, compar innera, superl innemest]
- **inn'erly** adv. **inn'ermost** or **in'most** adj (superl of **in**) farthest in; most remote from the outside. **inn'erness** n.
◻ **inner bar** n (law) Queen's or King's counsel as a whole. **inner child** n the supposed part of the psyche in which adults retain a conception of themselves as a child (psychol); an adult's ability to react and experience things as a child would (fig). **inner city** n the central part of a city, esp with regard to its special social problems, eg poor housing, poverty. **inn'er-city** adj. **inner dead centre** n the piston position, when the crank pin is nearest to the centre, at the beginning of the outstroke of a reciprocating engine or pump (also **top dead centre**). **inner-direc'ted** adj (psychol) guided by one's own principles, values, etc rather than by external influences. **inner-direc'tion** n. **inner ear** n (anat) the internal structure of the ear, encased in bone and filled with fluid, consisting of the cochlea, the semicircular canals and the vestibule. **inner light** n (often with caps) a divine presence in the soul believed, esp by Quakers, to guide one and unite one with Christ. **inner man** or **inner woman** n the soul; the mind; the stomach or appetite (facetious). **inner part** or **voice** n (music) a voice part intermediate between the highest and the lowest. **inner planet** n any of the planets in the solar system whose orbits lie within the asteroid belt. **inner space** n the undersea region regarded as an environment; the unconscious human mind. **inner tube** n the rubber tube inside a tyre, which is inflatable. **inn'erwear** n underwear. **inner woman** see **inner man** above.

innervate /in'ər-vāt or in-ûr'vāt/ vt to supply (an area or organ of the body) with nerves or nervous stimulus (also **innerve**'). [**in-** (1)]
- **innervā'tion** n.

inning /in'ing/ n ingathering, esp of crops; a turn at batting for both teams in baseball, etc; (in pl) lands recovered from the sea. [**in**[1] or **inn**]
- **inn'ings** n sing a team's or individual batsman's turn at batting in cricket, etc; hence, the time during which a person or a party is in possession of anything, a spell or turn.
▪ **a good innings** (inf) a long life.

innit /in'it/ interj an informal contraction of **isn't it**, used as a tag question or as mere oral punctuation. [Phonetic respelling of colloquial pronunciation]

innocent /in'ə-sənt/ adj not hurtful; inoffensive; pure; harmless; guileless; simple-minded; ignorant of evil; imbecile (dialect); not legally guilty; not responsible or to blame; devoid (with of); not malignant or cancerous, benign (med). ◆ n someone having no fault; someone having no knowledge of evil; a child; a foolish, simple-minded person; an idiot. [OFr, from L innocēns, -entis, from in- not, and nocēre to hurt]
- **inn'ocence** n harmlessness; blamelessness; guilelessness; simplicity; freedom from legal guilt. **inn'ocency** n (archaic) the quality of being innocent. **inn'ocently** adv.
◻ **Innocents' Day** see **Childermas**.

innocuous /in-ok'ū-əs/ adj harmless. [L innocuus, from in- not, and nocuus hurtful, from nocēre to hurt]
- **innocū'ity** or **innoc'uousness** n. **innoc'uously** adv.

innominate /i-nom'i-nāt or -nit/ adj having no name. [L in- not, and nōmināre, -ātum to name]
- **innom'inable** adj unnamable. ◆ n (in pl; obs facetious) trousers.
◻ **innominate artery** n the first large artery rising from the arch of the aorta, dividing at the lower neck to form the right common carotid and right subclavian arteries (also called **brachiocephalic artery**). **innominate bone** n the hip bone, formed by fusion in the adult of the ilium, ischium, and pubis. **innominate vein** n one of two large veins on either side of the lower part of the neck formed by the union of the external jugular and sub-clavian veins (also called **brachiocephalic vein**).

innovate /in'ō-vāt or in'ə-vāt/ vt to introduce as something new; to renew, alter (rare). ◆ vi to introduce novelties; to make changes. [L innovāre, -ātum, from in in, and novus new]
- **innovā'tion** n the act of innovating; a thing introduced as a novelty; revolution (Shakesp); substitution of one obligation for another (Scots law); a season's new growth (bot). **innovā'tional** adj. **innovā'tionist** n. **inn'ovative** adj. **inn'ovātor** n. **inn'ovatory** adj.

innoxious /in-ok'shəs/ adj not noxious. [in- (2)]
■ innox'iously adv. innox'iousness n.

innuendo /in-ū-en'dō/ n (pl innuen'dos or innuen'does) insinuation; an indirect reference or intimation; a part of a pleading in cases of libel and slander, pointing out what and who was meant (law). ◆ vt to insinuate by innuendo; to interpret as innuendo. ◆ vi to make insinuations. [L innuendō by nodding at (ie indicating, to wit, from its use in old legal documents to introduce a parenthetic indication), ablative gerund of innuere to nod to, indicate, from in to, and nuere to nod]

Innuit see **Inuit**.

innumerable /i-nū'mər-ə-bl or in-nū'/ adj too many to be numbered; countless. [in- (2)]
■ innūmerabil'ity n. innū'merableness n. innū'merably adv. innū'merous adj (archaic) without number; innumerable.

innumerate /i-nū'mər-ət or in-nū'/ adj having little or no knowledge or understanding of mathematics, esp calculating or arithmetic (also n). [Coined in 1959 by British journalist Sir Geoffrey Crowther (on analogy of illiterate), from L numerus number]
■ innum'eracy n.

innutrition /in-nū-trish'ən or i-nū-/ n lack of nutrition; the failure to give proper nourishment. [in- (2)]
■ innū'trient adj not nutrient. innūtritious /-trish'əs/ adj not nutritious.

ino- /ī-nō-/ combining form denoting fibrous tissue or muscle, as in inotropic. [Gr is, inos muscle, fibre]

inobedient /in-ō-bē'dyənt/ adj disobedient. [in- (2)]
■ inobe'dience n. inobe'diently adv.

inobservant /in-əb-zûr'vənt/ adj unobservant; heedless. [in- (2)]
■ inobser'vable adj incapable of being observed. inobser'vance n lack of observance. inobservā'tion /-ob-/ n.

inobtrusive /in-əb-troo'siv/ adj unobtrusive. [in- (2)]
■ inobtru'sively adv. inobtru'siveness n.

inoccupation /in-ok-ū-pā'shən/ n lack of occupation. [in- (2)]

inoculate /in-ok'ū-lāt/ vt to introduce (eg bacteria, a virus) into an organism; to give a mild form of a disease to in this way, esp for the purpose of safeguarding against subsequent infection; to insert as a bud or graft; to graft; to imbue. ◆ vi to practise inoculation. [L inoculāre, -ātum, from in into, and oculus an eye, a bud]
■ inoculabil'ity n. inoc'ulable adj. inoculā'tion n the act or practice of inoculating; the communication of disease by the introduction of a germ or virus, esp that of a mild form of the disease to produce immunity; the analogous introduction of anything, eg nitrogen-fixing bacteria into soil or seed, or a crystal into a supersaturated solution to start crystallization; the insertion of the buds of one plant into another. inoc'ulative /-ə-tiv or -ā-tiv/ adj. inoc'ulātor n. inoc'ulatory adj. inoc'ulum n (pl inoc'ula) any material used for inoculating.

inodorous /in-ō'də-rəs/ adj having no smell. [in- (2)]
■ ino'dorously adv. ino'dorousness n.

inoffensive /in-ə-fen'siv/ adj giving no offence; harmless. [in- (2)]
■ inoffen'sively adv. inoffen'siveness n.

inofficious /in-ə-fish'əs/ adj disobliging (obs); regardless of duty (law); inoperative. [in- (2)]
■ inoffi'ciously adv. inoffi'ciousness n.

inoperable /in-op'ə-rə-bl/ adj that cannot be operated on successfully, or without undue risk (med); not workable. [in- (2)]
■ inoperabil'ity or inop'erableness n. inop'erably adv. inop'erative adj not in action; producing no effect. inop'erativeness n.

inoperculate /in-o-pûr'kū-lāt/ (esp zool) adj without an operculum or lid. [in- (2)]

inopinate /in-op'i-nāt/ (obs) adj not thought of; unexpected. [L inopīnatus]

inopportune /in-op'ər-tūn or -tūn'/ adj badly timed; inconvenient. [in- (2)]
■ inopp'ortunely (or /-tūn'/) adv. inopp'ortuneness (or /-tūn'/) or inopportun'ity n.

inorb /in-örb'/ (poetic) vt to set in an orb; to encircle. [in- (1)]

inordinate /in-ör'di-nit or -örd'nit/ adj excessive; unrestrained; immoderate. [L inordinātus, from in- not, and ordināre, -ātum to arrange, regulate]
■ inor'dinacy or inor'dinateness n. inor'dinately adv. inordinā'tion n deviation from rule; irregularity.

inorganic /in-ör-gan'ik/ adj not organic, not of animal or vegetable origin; of or relating to compounds which do not contain carbon (chem); not belonging to an organism; of accidental origin; not developed naturally. [in- (2)]
■ inorgan'ically adv. inorganizā'tion or -s- n lack of organization. inor'ganized or -s- adj unorganized.

□ **inorganic chemistry** n the chemistry of all substances except carbon compounds, generally admitting a few of these also (such as oxides of carbon and carbonates).

inornate /in-ör-nāt' or -ör'nit/ adj not ornate; simple. [in- (2)]

inosculate /in-os'kū-lāt/ (physiol) vt and vi to join together by interconnecting ducts or openings, so as to allow a flow from one into the other, as a connection between blood vessels; to anastomose. [L in in, and osculārī, -ātus to kiss]
■ inosculā'tion n.

inositol /in-os'i-tol/ n a lipid that is essential for the formation of cell membranes. [Gr īs, īnos a sinew, muscle, and -ite and -ol²]

inotropic /in-ə-trop'ik or īn-/ (med) adj affecting or controlling muscular contraction, esp in the heart. [Gr īs, īnos tendon, and tropos a turn]

in pace /in pā'sē, pä'chä or pä-ke/ (L) in peace.

in partibus infidelium /in pär'ti-bəs in-fi-dē'li-əm or pär'ti-bŭs ēn-fi-dā'li-ŭm/ (L) in the lands of the unbelievers, a phrase applied to titular bishops in countries where no Catholic hierarchy had been set up, or to those bearing the title of an extinct see.

in-patient see under **in¹**.

inpayment /in'pā-mənt/ n the payment of money into a bank account; the amount paid in. [in¹ and payment]

in pectore /in pek'to-rē or pek'to-re/ (L) in secret; undisclosed; in reserve; in petto.

in personam /in pər-sō'nam or per-/ (L; law) against a specific person, used of a proceeding, enforceable rights, etc (see also in rem).

in petto /ēn or in pet'tō/ (Ital) within the breast; in one's own mind but not yet divulged; in secret; in reserve.

inphase /in-fāz'/ adj in the same phase. [in¹ and phase¹]

in pleno /in plē'nō or plä'nō/ (L) in full.

in posse /in pos'i/ (L) potentially; in possibility (see also in esse under esse).

inpouring /in'pö-ring, -pö' or -pō-/ n a pouring in; addition. [in¹ and pouring]

in principio /in prin-sip'i-ō or -kip'/ (L) in the beginning.

in propria persona /in prō-pri-ə pûr-sō'nə or pro'pri-ä per-sō'nä/ (LL) in person; personally.

in puris naturalibus /in pū'ris na-tū-rā'li-bəs or poo'rēs/ (LL) stark naked.

input /in'pŭt/ n amount, material or energy, that is put in; power, or energy, or coded information, stored or for storage; information available in a computer for dealing with a problem; the process of feeding in data; the place where or device by which a signal is applied (electronics); contribution (Scot). ◆ adj relating to computer input. ◆ vt (inputt'ing; input') to feed (data, etc) into eg a computer. [in¹ and put¹]
■ inputt'er n.
□ **input area** or **block** n (comput) an area of memory reserved for data input from a backing store or peripheral. **input device** n (comput) a piece of equipment used to transfer data into memory, eg a keyboard, light pen, etc. **in'put/out'put** adj relating to the passage of data into or out of a computer. **input-output analysis** n (econ) a method of studying an economy as a whole by analysing the relationship between the input and output of each industry. **input program** or **routine** n (comput) part of a program that controls transfer of data to an input area.

inqilab /in'ki-läb/ n (in India, Pakistan, etc) revolution. [Urdu]

inquere /in-kwēr'/ (Spenser) vi and vt to inquire. [inquire]

in querpo see **en cuerpo**.

inquest /in'kwest, formerly in-kwest'/ n a judicial inquiry before a jury into any matter, esp any case of violent or sudden death; the body of people appointed to hold such an inquiry; an inquiry or investigation. [OFr enqueste, from LL inquesta, from L inquīsīta (rēs), from inquīrere to inquire]

inquietude /in-kwī'i-tūd/ n uneasiness; disturbance. [in- (2)]
■ inquī'et adj (archaic) unquiet, disturbed. ◆ vt (rare) to disturb. inquī'etly adv.

inquiline /in'kwi-līn/ adj living in the home of or in close association with another. ◆ n an animal living in this way. [L inquilīnus tenant, lodger, from incola inhabitant, from in in, and colere to inhabit]
■ inquil'ic adj and n. in'quilinism or inquilin'ity n. inquilī'nous adj.

inquinate /in'kwi-nāt/ vt to defile or corrupt. [L inquināre, -ātum to defile]
■ inquinā'tion n.

inquire or **enquire** /in-kwīr'/ vi to ask a question; to make an investigation (often with into). ◆ vt to ask; to seek (obs); to make an examination regarding (*obs*); to call (*archaic*). ◆ *n* (*archaic*) inquiry. [OFr *enquerre* (Fr *enquérir*), from L *inquīrere*, from *in* in, and *quaerere*, *quaesītum* to seek]

■ **inquirā'tion** (*Dickens*) or **enquirā'tion** *n* (*dialect*) inquiry. **inquir'er** or **enquir'er** *n*. **inquir'ing** *adj* tending to inquire; eager to acquire information; (of eg a look) expressing inquiry. **inquir'ingly** *adv*. **inquir'y** or **enquir'y** (or *esp US* /*ing'kwi-ri*/) *n* the act of inquiring; a search for knowledge; (an) investigation; a question.

■ **inquire after** to ask about the health, etc of. **writ of inquiry** a writ appointing an inquest.

inquirendo /*in-kwī-ren'dō*/ (*law*) *n* (*pl* **inquiren'dos**) authority to inquire into something, eg for the benefit of the Crown. [L, by inquiring]

inquisition /*in-kwi-zish'ən*/ *n* a searching examination; an investigation; a judicial inquiry; (with *cap* and *the*) a Roman Catholic tribunal established from 1232 to 1820 to preserve the supremacy of Catholicism in Europe by suppressing heresy, notably in Spain (the **Spanish Inquisition**) where the torture and execution of disbelievers was not uncommon. [L *inquīsītiō*, *-ōnis*; see ety for **inquire**]

■ **inquisit'ional** *adj* searching, often unduly vexatiously, in inquiring; relating to inquisition or the Inquisition. **inquisitive** /*-kwiz'i-tiv*/ *adj* eager to know; apt to ask questions, *esp* about other people's affairs; curious. **inquis'itively** *adv*. **inquis'itiveness** *n*. **inquis'itor** *n* someone who inquires, *esp* with undue pertinacity or searchingness; an official inquirer; a member of the Inquisition tribunal. **inquisitō'rial** (or /*-tör'*/) *adj* relating to an inquisitor or inquisition; unduly pertinacious in interrogation; used of criminal proceedings in which the prosecutor is also judge, or in which the trial is held in secret (*law*). **inquisito'rially** *adv*. **inquisito'rialness** *n*. **inquis'itress** *n* (*archaic*) a female inquisitor. **inquisitū'rient** *adj* (*Milton*) eager to act as inquisitor.

■ **Grand Inquisitor** the head of a court of Inquisition.

inquorate /*in-kwö'rət*/ *adj* not making up a quorum. [**in-** (2) and **quorum**]

in re /*in rē* or *rā*/ (*L*) in the matter (of); concerning.

in rem /*in rem*/ (*L*; *law*) against a thing or property, used of a proceeding, an enforceable right, etc against all persons or against property, such as the arrest of a ship in the enforcement of a maritime lien (see also **in personam**).

in rerum natura /*in rē'rəm nə-tū'rə* or *rā'rŭm na-too'rä*/ (*L*) in the nature of things.

INRI *abbrev*: *Jesus Nazarenus Rex Judaeorum* (*L*), Jesus of Nazareth, King of the Jews.

in rixa /*in rik'sə*/ (*L*; *law*) in a quarrel; (said) in the heat of the moment, used as a defence in cases of defamation.

inro /*in'rō*/ *n* (*pl* **in'rō**) a small Japanese container for pills and medicines, once part of traditional Japanese dress. [Jap, seal-box]

inroad /*in'rōd*/ *n* an incursion into an enemy's country; a raid; encroachment. [**in**[1] and **road** in sense of riding; cf **raid**[1]]

■ **make inroads into** to make progress with; to use up large quantities of.

inrush /*in'rush*/ *n* an inward rush. [**in**[1] and **rush**[1]]

■ **in'rushing** *n* and *adj*.

INS *abbrev*: Immigration and Naturalization Service (*US*); inertial navigation system; International News Service.

ins. *abbrev*: inches (also in); insurance.

in saecula saeculorum /*in sāk'yŭ-lə sāk-yŭ-lör'əm*, or *sek(')-*, *-lör'*, also *sī'kŭ-lä sā'kŭ-lö'rŭm*/ (*L*) for ever and ever.

insalivate /*in-sal'i-vāt*/ *vt* to mix with saliva. [**in-** (1)]

■ **insalivā'tion** *n*.

insalubrious /*in-sə-loo'bri-əs* or *-lū'*/ *adj* not salubrious; unhealthy. [**in-** (2)]

■ **insalu'briously** *adv*. **insalu'brity** *n*.

insalutary /*in-sal'ū-tə-ri*/ *adj* unwholesome. [**in-** (2)]

insane /*in-sān'*/ *adj* not sane or of sound mind; crazy; mad; utterly unwise; senseless; causing insanity. [L *īnsānus*]

■ **insane'ly** *adv*. **insane'ness** *n* insanity; madness. **insan'ie** *n* (*Shakesp* an emendation of the reading *infamie*) insanity. **insanity** /*in-san'i-ti*/ *n* lack of sanity; a degree of mental illness causing one to act against the social or legal demands of society or in which one is held to be not responsible for one's actions under law; madness; extreme stupidity.

❑ **insane root** *n* (*Shakesp*) *prob* a root mentioned by Plutarch, *Life of Antony*, *perh* hemlock, henbane or belladonna.

insanitary /*in-san'i-tə-ri*/ *adj* not sanitary; dirty and unhealthy. [**in-** (2)]

■ **insan'itariness** *n*. **insanitā'tion** *n*.

insatiable /*in-sā'shə-bl* or *-shi-ə-bl*/ *adj* not capable of being satiated or satisfied. [**in-** (2)]

■ **insātiabil'ity** or **insa'tiableness** *n*. **insā'tiably** *adv*. **insā'tiate** *adj* not sated; insatiable. **insā'tiately** *adv*. **insā'tiateness** *n*. **insatiety** /*in-sə-tī'i-ti*/ *n* the state of not being, or of being incapable of being, sated.

inscape /*in'skāp*/ *n* (in poetry, literature, etc) the essential inner nature or distinctive form of a person, object, etc (see also **instress**). [Coined by English poet Gerard Manley Hopkins (1844–89), from **in**[1] and **-scape**]

inscient[1] /*in'shənt* or *-shi-ənt*/ (*archaic*) *adj* having little or no knowledge, ignorant. [L *īnsciēns*, *-entis*, from *in-* not, and *scīre* to know]

■ **in'science** *n*.

inscient[2] /*in'shənt* or *-shi-ənt*/ (*archaic*) *adj* having insight or inward knowledge. [L *in* in, and *sciēns*, *-entis*, prp of *scīre* to know]

insconce (*Shakesp*) same as **ensconce**.

inscribe /*in-skrīb'*/ *vt* to engrave or mark in some other way; to engrave or mark on; to enter in a book or roll; to dedicate; to describe within another figure so as either to touch all sides or faces of the bounding figure or to have all angular points on it (*geom*); to rewrite (data on a document) in a form which may be read by a character recognition device (*comput*). [L *īnscrībere*, *īnscrīptum*, from *in* upon, and *scrībere* to write]

■ **inscrīb'able** *adj*. **inscrīb'er** *n*. **inscription** /*in-skrip'shən*/ *n* the act of inscribing; that which is inscribed; a dedication; a record inscribed on stone, metal, clay, etc. **inscrip'tional** or **inscrip'tive** *adj*. **inscrip'tively** *adv*.

inscroll /*in-skrōl'*/ (*Shakesp*) *vt* to write on a scroll.

inscrutable /*in-skroo'tə-bl*/ *adj* that cannot be scrutinized or searched into and understood; mysterious, enigmatic, inexplicable. [L *īnscrūtābilis*, from *in-* not, and *scrūtārī* to search into]

■ **inscrutabil'ity** or **inscrut'ableness** *n*. **inscrut'ably** *adv*.

insculp /*in-skulp'*/ *vt* to engrave, to cut or carve upon something (*Shakesp*); to carve; to form by carving (*archaic*). [L *īnsculpere*, from *in* in, and *sculpere* to carve]

■ **insculpt'** *adj* engraved (*Shakesp*); having depressions in the surface (*bot*). **insculp'ture** *n* anything engraved (*Shakesp*); an inscription (*archaic*). ◆ *vt* (*archaic*) to carve on something.

in se /*in sā*/ (*L*) in itself.

inseam[1] /*in'sēm*/ *n* an inner seam in a shoe or garment.

inseam[2] same as **enseam**[3].

insect /*in'sekt*/ *n* a word loosely used for a small invertebrate creature, *esp* one with a body divided into sections; a member of the Insecta (*zool*); a small, wretched, insignificant person (*fig*). ◆ *adj* of insects; like an insect; small, insignificant. [L *īnsectum*, pap of *īnsecāre*, from *in* into, and *secāre* to cut]

■ **Insec'ta** *n pl* a subphylum of arthropods having a distinct head, thorax and abdomen, with three pairs of legs attached to the thorax, usually winged in adult life, breathing air by means of tracheae, and commonly having a metamorphosis in the life history. **insectār'ium** or **in'sectary** *n* (*pl* **insectār'iums** or **in'sectaries**) a vivarium for insects. **insecticī'dal** *adj*. **insec'ticide** /*-i-sīd*/ *n* a substance that kills insects. **insec'tiform** *adj*. **insec'tifuge** *n* a substance that drives away insects. **insec'tile** or **insec'tan** *adj*. **Insectiv'ora** *n pl* an order of mammals, mostly terrestrial, insect-eating, nocturnal in habit, and small in size, including shrews, moles, hedgehogs, etc. **insect'ivore** *n* a member of the Insectivora; any animal or plant deriving nourishment from insects. **insectiv'orous** *adj* feeding on insects; of or relating to the Insectivora. **insectol'ogist** *n*. **insectol'ogy** *n* the study of insects.

❑ **insect net** *n* a light hand-held net for catching insects. **insect powder** *n* powder for stupefying and killing insects; an insecticide or insectifuge. **insect repellent** *n* a substance which keeps off (*esp* biting) insects.

insection /*in-sek'shən*/ *n* an incision; a notch; division into segments. [L *insecāre*]

insecure /*in-si-kūr'*/ *adj* apprehensive of danger or loss; anxious because not well-adjusted to life; lacking in confidence; exposed to danger or loss; unsafe; uncertain; not fixed or firm. [**in-** (2)]

■ **insecure'ly** *adv*. **insecur'ity** *n*.

inseem (*Shakesp*) same as **enseam**[2].

inselberg /*in'zəl-bûrg* or *in'səl-berg*/ (*geol*) *n* (*pl* **in'selberge** /*-gə*/) a steep-sided round-topped mount, *usu* of granite or gneiss, rising above the general level of plain eroded bedrock, often found in the semi-arid regions of tropical countries. [Ger, island mountain]

inseminate /*in-sem'i-nāt*/ *vt* to impregnate (a female) *esp* artificially; to sow; to implant; to introduce (ideas, philosophies, attitudes, etc) into people's minds. [L *īnsēmināre*, from *in* in, and *sēmen*, *-inis* seed]

■ **inseminā'tion** *n*. **insem'inator** *n*.

insensate /*in-sen'sāt* or *-sit*/ *adj* without sensation, inanimate; having little or no sensibility or moral feeling; having little or no good sense.

[L *īnsēnsātus*, from *in-* not, and *sēnsātus* intelligent, from *sēnsus* feeling]
■ **insen'sately** *adv*. **insen'sateness** *n*.

insensible /in-sen'si-bl/ *adj* not having feeling; not capable of emotion; callous; dull; unconscious; not capable of being sensed. [**in-** (2)]
■ **insensibil'ity** or **insen'sibleness** *n*. **insen'sibly** *adv*.

insensitive /in-sen'si-tiv/ *adj* not sensitive; unfeeling, inconsiderate, crass. [**in-** (2)]
■ **insen'sitively** *adv*. **insen'sitiveness** or **insensitiv'ity** *n*.

insensuous /in-sen'sū-əs/ or *-shū-əs/ adj* not sensuous. [**in-** (2)]

insentient /in-sen'shənt/ or *-shi-ənt/ adj* not having perception; incapable of sensation. [**in-** (2)]
■ **insen'tience** or **insen'tiency** *n*.

inseparable /in-sep'ə-rə-bl/ *adj* incapable of being separated; (of eg friends or siblings) unwilling to be separated; (of a prefix) not existing as a separate word (*grammar*). ◆ *n* (*usu* used in *pl*) an inseparable companion. [**in-** (2)]
■ **insep'arableness** or **inseparabil'ity** *n*. **insep'arably** *adv*. **insep'arate** *adj* (*archaic*) not separate or separable.

insert /in-sûrt'/ *vt* to put in; to introduce (into). ◆ *n* /in'/ something inserted; a loose sheet placed within the folds of a newspaper or periodical, as a supplement or containing advertising material; insert mode. [L *īnserere, īnsertum*, from *in* in, and *serere* to join]
■ **insert'able** *adj*. **insert'ed** *adj* (*bot*) attached to or growing out of another member. **insert'er** *n*. **insertion** /in-sûr'shən/ *n* the act of inserting; something inserted; the mode or condition of being inserted; the part of a muscle by which it is attached to the part to be moved, eg the point or place of attachment to a bone (*anat*); a piece of embroidery, lace, etc inserted in a dress, etc; the putting of a man-made craft or satellite into orbit (also **injection**). **inser'tional** *adj*.
❏ **insert key** *n* (*comput*) a key that switches between insert and overwrite modes. **insert mode** *n* a word processing facility whereby typed characters are added without replacing existing characters.

in-service see under **in¹**.

insessorial /in-se-sö'ri-əl/ *adj* (of eg birds' claws) adapted for perching; (of a bird) having claws of this type. [L *īnsessor*, pl *-ōrēs*, besieger (of the roads), highwayman, adopted with the meaning percher, from *īnsidēre*, from *in* on, and *sedēre* to sit]

INSET *abbrev*: in-service education and training (for schoolteachers).

inset /in'set/ *n* something set in, an insertion or insert, *esp* a loose sheet inserted between the pages of a magazine, book, etc; a small map or figure inserted in a spare corner of another; a piece let in to a garment, etc; the setting in of a current. ◆ *vt* /-set'/ (*prp* **insett'ing**; *pap* and *pat* **inset'**) to set in, to infix or implant. [**in** and **set**]
■ **insett'er** *n*.

inseverable /in-sev'ə-rə-bl/ *adj* that cannot be severed or separated. [**in-** (2)]

inshallah /in-shä'lä/ *interj* (among Muslims) if Allah wills, equivalent to 'God willing'. [Ar *in shā'llāh*]

insheathe see **ensheath**.

inshell /in-shel'/ (*Shakesp*) *vt* to draw in or withdraw, as into a shell. [**in-** (1)]

inshelter /in-shel'tər/ *vt* to place in shelter. [**in-** (1)]

inship /in-ship'/ (*Shakesp*) *vt* to ship, to embark. [**in-** (1)]

inshore /in'shōr' or *-shōr'/ adv* and *adj* near or towards the shore from the water. ◆ *adj* /in'shōr or *-shōr/* situated, carried on, or operating on the water close to the shore, as fishing grounds, fishing, or fishermen.

inshrine /in-shrīn'/ same as **enshrine**.

inside /in'sīd' or *in'sīd/ n* the side, space or part within; the side of a road or pavement nearest to buildings, etc; (often in *pl*) the entrails; inner nature; that which is not visible at first sight; (in *pl*) the inner quires of a ream of paper; the inside track; a position affording exclusive information or advantage (*inf*). ◆ *adj* being within; interior; indoor; working indoors; from within; from a secret or confidential source; (of a criminal activity) carried out by, or with the help of, someone trusted and/or employed by the victim (*inf*); of a position nearer or near the centre of the field (*rugby*, etc). ◆ *adv* in, to or near the interior; indoors; on the inner side; in or into prison (*inf*). ◆ *prep* within; into; on the inner side of; in a position nearer the centre of the field than (*rugby*, etc). [**in¹** and **side¹**]
■ **insi'der** *n* a person who is inside; someone within a certain organization, etc, *esp* one with access to exclusive information about it; someone possessing some particular advantage.
❏ **in'side-car** *n* an Irish horse-drawn buggy in which the passengers face one another. **inside edge** see under **edge**. **inside left** or **inside right** *n* in some games, a forward between the centre and outside. **insider dealing** or **trading** *n* the criminal offence of using information not publicly available to deal on the Stock Exchange. **inside track** *n*

the inner side of a race-track, being the most advantageous position (also *fig*).
■ **inside of** (*esp US*) in less than, within. **inside out** with the inner side turned outwards. **know** (**something**) **inside out** (*inf*) to know (something) thoroughly.

insidious /in-sid'i-əs/ *adj* developing or advancing gradually and imperceptibly; deceptively attractive; cunning and treacherous. [L *īnsidiōsus*, from *īnsidiae* an ambush, from *īnsidēre*, from *in* in, and *sedēre* to sit]
■ **insid'iously** *adv*. **insid'iousness** *n*.

insight¹ /in'sīt/ *n* the power of discerning and understanding things; imaginative penetration; practical knowledge; enlightenment; a view into anything; awareness, often of one's own mental condition (*psychol*); the apprehension of the principle of a task, puzzle, etc (*psychol*). [**in¹** and **sight¹**]
■ **insight'ful** *adj*.
❏ **insight learning** *n* direct learning without the process of trial and error.

insight² /in'sīt/ or *in'sihht/* (*Scot*) *n* household goods, furniture (also *adj*). [Origin unknown]

insignia /in-sig'ni-ə/ *n pl* (in US treated as *sing*) signs or badges of office, honour, membership, occupation, etc; marks by which anything is known. [L, neuter pl of *īnsignis*, from *in* in, and *signum* a mark]
■ **insigne** /in-sig'ni/ *n* (*rare*) a sign or badge.

insignificant /in-sig-nif'i-kənt/ *adj* having no meaning; having no effect; unimportant; small in size, amount, etc; petty. [**in-** (2)]
■ **insignif'icance** or **insignif'icancy** *n*. **insignif'icantly** *adv*. **insignif'icative** *adj* not significative or expressing by external signs.

insincere /in-sin-sēr'/ *adj* not sincere, hypocritical. [**in-** (2)]
■ **insincere'ly** *adv*. **insincerity** /-ser'i-ti/ *n*.

insinew /in-sin'ū/ *vi* (*Shakesp*) to be joined as with sinews. [**in-** (1)]

insinuate /in-sin'ū-āt/ *vt* to hint or indirectly suggest (*usu* something unpleasant); to introduce or insert gently or artfully (with *into*); (with *into*) to work (*esp* oneself) into (someone's favour). [L *īnsinuāre, -ātum*, from *in* in, and *sinus* a curve]
■ **insin'uating** *adj*. **insin'uatingly** *adv*. **insinuā'tion** *n*. **insin'uative** *adj* insinuating; using insinuation. **insin'uator** *n*. **insin'uatory** /-ə-tər-i/ *adj*.

insipid /in-sip'id/ *adj* without a satisfying or definite flavour, tasteless; lacking spirit or interest; dull. [LL *īnsipidus*, from L *in-* not, and *sapidus* well-tasted, from *sapere* to taste]
■ **insip'idly** *adv*. **insip'idness** or **insipid'ity** *n*.

insipience /in-sip'i-əns/ (*archaic*) *n* lack of wisdom. [L *īnsipientia*, from *in-* not, and *sapiēns* wise]
■ **insip'ient** *adj*. **insip'iently** *adv*.

insist /in-sist'/ *vi* (often with *on*) to maintain very firmly; to persist in demanding; to take no refusal. ◆ *vt* to maintain persistently. [L *īnsistere*, from *in* upon, and *sistere* to stand]
■ **insist'ence** or **insist'ency** *n*. **insist'ent** *adj* urgent; compelling attention; insisting; (of a bird's hind-toe) touching the ground with the tip only. **insist'ently** *adv*.

in situ /in sī'tū or sit'oo/ (L) in the original, intended or designated position; in position; (of a cancer) not having undergone metastasis to invade surrounding tissue (*med*).
❏ **in-situ hybridization** *n* (*biol*) a technique, using a radioactive nucleic acid probe and autoradiography, for locating the position of a specific DNA sequence on a chromosome.

Ins key /ins kē/ (*comput*) short for **insert key**.

insnare same as **ensnare**.

insobriety /in-sō-brī'ə-ti/ *n* lack of sobriety, drunkenness. [**in-** (2)]

insociable /in-sō'shə-bl/ *adj* unsociable; incompatible (*obs*). [**in-** (2)]
■ **insociabil'ity** *n*.

insofar see **in as far as** under **in¹**.

insolate /in'sō-lāt or in-sō'lāt/ *vt* to expose to the sun's rays; to treat by exposure to the sun's rays. [L *īnsōlāre, -ātum*, from *in* in, and *sōl* the sun]
■ **insolā'tion** *n* exposure to the sun's rays; solar radiation falling upon a given surface.

insole /in'sōl/ *n* the inner sole of a boot or shoe; a sole of some material placed inside a shoe for warmth, dryness or comfort. [**in¹** and **sole¹**]

insolent /in'sə-lənt/ *adj* disrespectful and rude; impudent. [L *īnsolēns, -entis*, from *in-* not, and *solēns*, prp of *solēre* to be accustomed]
■ **in'solence** *n*. **in'solently** *adv*.

insolidity /in-so-lid'i-ti/ *n* lack of solidity. [**in-** (2)]

insoluble /in-sol'ū-bl/ *adj* not capable of being dissolved; not capable of being solved or explained. [**in-** (2)]

■ words derived from main entry word; ❏ compound words; ■ idioms and phrasal verbs

■ **insolubil'ity** or **insol'ubleness** n. **insol'ubilize** or **-ise** vt to make insoluble. **insol'ubly** adv.

insolvable /in-sol'və-bl/ adj not solvable. [**in-** (2)]
■ **insolvabil'ity** n. **insol'vably** adv.

insolvent /in-sol'vənt/ adj not able to pay one's debts; bankrupt; concerning insolvent people. ◆ n a person unable to pay his or her debts. [**in-** (2)]
■ **insolv'ency** n bankruptcy.

insomnia /in-som'ni-ə/ n sleeplessness; prolonged inability to sleep. [L *īnsomnis* sleepless]
■ **insom'niac** n a person who suffers from insomnia. ◆ adj suffering from, causing, or caused by, insomnia. **insom'nious** adj. **insom'nolence** n.

insomuch /in-sō-much'/ adv to such a degree (with as or that); inasmuch (with as); so.

insooth /in-sooth'/ (archaic) adv in sooth, indeed. [**in** and **sooth**]

insouciant /in-soo'si-ənt/ or /ɛ̃-soo-sē-ā̃/ adj indifferent, unconcerned, nonchalant; heedless; apathetic. [Fr, from *in-* not, and *souciant*, prp of *soucier*, from L *sollicitāre* to disturb]
■ **insouciance** /in-soo'si-əns/ or /ɛ̃-soo-sē-ās/ n. **insouciantly** /in-soo'si-ənt-li or ɛ̃-soo-sē-āt'li/ adv.

insoul see **ensoul**.

inspan /in-span'/ or /in'span/ (esp S Afr) vt (**inspann'ing**; **inspanned'**) to yoke to a vehicle; to bring or force into service. ◆ vi to prepare to depart. [Du *inspannen* to yoke, from *in* in, and *spannen* to tie]

inspect /in-spekt'/ vt to look into; to examine; to look at closely, officially or ceremonially. ◆ n /in'/ (obs) inspection. [L *īnspectāre*, frequentative of *īnspicere*, *īnspectum*, from *in* into, and *specere* to look]
■ **inspect'ingly** adv. **inspec'tion** n the act of inspecting or looking into; careful or official examination. **inspec'tional** adj. **inspec'tive** adj. **inspec'tor** n a person who inspects; an examining officer; a police officer ranking below a superintendent; an officer in any of several charities or humane societies. **inspec'torate** n a district for which an inspector is responsible; the office of inspector; a body of inspectors. **inspectō'rial** adj. **inspec'torship** n the office of inspector. □ **inspector general** n the head of an inspectorate; a military officer who conducts investigations.

insphere and **insphear'd** see **ensphere**.

inspire /in-spīr'/ vt to infuse into (the mind), esp with an encouraging or exalting influence; (of divine influence, etc) to instruct or guide; to instruct or affect with a particular emotion; to bring about, cause to occur; to animate; orig to breathe in or blow in (air, etc); to draw or inhale into the lungs. ◆ vi to draw in the breath. [L *īnspīrāre*, from *in* in, into, and *spīrāre* to breathe]
■ **inspīr'able** adj able to be inhaled. **inspirā'tion** /in-spər-, -spīr- or -spīr-/ n the act of inspiring; instruction, dictation, or stimulation by a divinity, a genius, an idea or a passion; an inspired condition; an object or person that inspires; an inspired thought or idea; breathing in; a breath. **inspirā'tional** adj. **inspirā'tionally** adv. **inspirā'tionism** n. **inspirā'tionist** n a person who maintains that the writers of the Scriptures were directly and divinely inspired. **inspirative** /in-spīr'ə-tiv or in'spīr-ā-tiv/ adj tending to inspire. **inspirator** /in'spīr-ā-tər/ n an inspirer; an apparatus for injecting or drawing in vapour, liquid, etc. **inspiratory** /in-spīr'ə-tər-i, in-spīr' or in'spir-/ adj belonging to or aiding inspiration or inhalation. **inspīred'** adj actuated or directed by divine influence; influenced by elevated feeling; prompted by superior, but not openly declared, knowledge or authority; actually authoritative; (of a guess, etc) unexpectedly accurate. **inspīr'er** n. **inspīr'ing** adj. **inspīr'ingly** adv.

inspirit /in-spir'it/ vt to infuse spirit into, encourage. [**in-** (1)]
■ **inspir'iting** adj. **inspir'itingly** adv.

inspissate /in-spis'āt/ vt to thicken, condense. ◆ adj thickened or hardened by absorption or evaporation. [L *in* in, and *spissāre*, from *spissus* thick]
■ **inspiss'ated** adj. **inspissā'tion** n. **in'spissātor** n.

Inst. abbrev : Institute; Institution.

inst. abbrev : instant, ie the present month (used in formal correspondence).

insta- /in-stə-/ (inf) combining form instant or instantly, as in *instacheck*. [Contracted form]
■ **In'stagram**® n an Internet application for sharing photographs and videos.

instability /in-stə-bil'i-ti/ n lack of stability, physical or mental. [**in-** (2)]
■ **insta'ble** adj unstable.

install (also **instal**) /in-stöl'/ vt (**install'ing**; **installed'**) to set up and put in use; to place in an office or order; to place in a certain position; to invest with any charge or office with the customary ceremonies; to load (software) onto a computer. ◆ n the process of loading software

onto a computer in an orderly fashion. [LL *īnstallāre*, from *in* in, and *stallum* a stall, from OHGer *stal* (Ger *Stall*, Eng **stall**[1])]
■ **install'ant** n someone who installs another in an office, etc. **installā'tion** n the act of installing; the act of fitting something in position for use; apparatus placed in position for use; the complete apparatus for electric lighting, or the like; a large-scale work in an art gallery, often involving video or mixed media; a military base, etc. **install'er** n. **install'ment** n instalment (US); a knight's stall (Shakesp); installation (archaic).

instalment or US **installment** /in-stöl'mənt/ n one of a series of partial payments; a portion (eg of a serial story) supplied or completed at one time; the act of installing. [Anglo-Fr *estaler* to fix, set; prob influenced by **install**]
□ **instalment** or **installment plan** n (N Am) hire purchase.

instance /in'stəns/ n an example; an occurrence; an occasion; solicitation, urging; process, suit (law); the description of the parties to the case in the heading of a court writ (Scots law); the quality of being urgent (archaic); motive, cause (archaic); evidence, proof (Shakesp). ◆ vt to mention as an example. [L *īnstāns*, *īnstantis*, prp of *īnstāre* to be near, press upon, urge, from *in* upon, and *stāre* to stand]
■ **in'stancy** n insistency; urgency; imminence. **in'stant** adj immediate; instantaneous; without delay; present, current; of the current month (used in formal correspondence); (esp of food or drink) pre-prepared so that little has to be done to it before use; urgent (archaic). ◆ n the present moment of time; a very brief period of time, a moment; a particular moment or point of time; the present month (used in formal correspondence); an instant drink (inf). **instantaneity** /in-stant-ə-nē'i-ti/ n. **instantaneous** /in-stənt-ā'ni-əs/ adj done in an instant; momentary; occurring or acting at once or very quickly; for the instant; at a particular instant. **instantān'eously** adv. **instantān'eousness** n. **instan'ter** adv (law) without delay. **instantial** /in-stan'shl/ adj (rare). **instan'tiate** vt to be or provide an example of. **instantiā'tion** n. **in'stantly** adv at once; at this very time (Shakesp); importunately, zealously (Bible). **in'stants** n pl scratchcards (affording instant awareness of success if any) forming part of the National Lottery system.
□ **instant messaging** n a process for exchanging electronic messages on the Internet using a computer or mobile phone (abbrev **IM**). **instant photography** n a system which rapidly produces, sometimes by processing within an **instant camera**, a positive picture from the original exposed material. **instant replay** n action replay.
■ **at the instance of** at the urging or request of. **court of first instance** a lower court in which a legal case is first heard, whose decision may be appealable to a higher court. **for instance** as an example. **in the first instance** firstly, originally. **on the instant** immediately. **this instant** immediately.

instar[1] /in'stär/ n the form of an insect between moult and moult. [L *īnstar* image]

instar omnium /in' or ēn'stär om'ni-əm or -ŭm/ (L) worth all of them, as Cicero described Plato in relation to all other men.

instate /in-stāt'/ vt to put in possession; to install. [**in-** (1) and **state**]
■ **instate'ment** n.

in statu pupillari /in stā'tū pū-pi-lä'rī or stat'oo poo-pi-lä'rē/ (LL) in a state of wardship; as a pupil.

in statu quo /in stā'tū or stat'oo kwō/ (L) in the same state as formerly; in the same state as at present, unchanged.

instauration /in-stö-rā'shən/ (rare) n restoration; renewal. [L *īnstaurātiō*, *-ōnis*]
■ **in'staurātor** n.

instead /in-sted'/ adv in the stead, place or room (of); as an alternative or substitute. [**in**[1] and **stead**]

instep /in'step/ n the prominent arched part of the human foot, between the ankle and the toes; the corresponding part of a shoe, stocking, etc; (in horses) the hindleg from the ham to the pastern joint. [Origin obscure]

instigate /in'sti-gāt/ vt to urge on, incite; to initiate, bring about. [L *īnstīgāre*, *-ātum*]
■ **in'stigatingly** adv. **instigā'tion** n the act of inciting, esp to do wrong or cause trouble. **in'stigative** adj. **in'stigātor** n an inciter, generally in a bad sense.

instil or **instill** /in-stil'/ vt (**instill'ing**; **instilled'**) to infuse slowly into the mind; to drop in. [L *īnstillāre*, from *in* in, and *stillāre* to drop]
■ **instillā'tion** or **instil'ment** n the act of infusing slowly into the mind; the act of instilling or pouring in by drops; the application of medication drop by drop; that which is instilled or infused; a medication applied drop by drop.

instinct /in'stingkt, formerly in-stingkt'/ n impulse; an involuntary prompting to action; intuition; the natural impulse by which animals are guided apparently independently of reason or experience; a complex co-ordination of reflex actions by which an organism successfully adapts to its environment without foresight or experience. ◆ *adj* /*in-stingkt'*/ instigated or incited; moved; animated; charged; imbued. [L *īnstinctus*, from *īnstinguere* instigate]

■ **instinct'ive** *adj* prompted by instinct; involuntary; acting according to or determined by natural impulse. **instinc'tively** *adv*. **instinctiv'ity** *n* (*rare*). **instinc'tual** *adj* concerning instincts. **instinc'tually** *adv*.

institorial /*in-sti-tō'ri-əl* or *-tō'ri-*/ (*law*) *adj* relating to an agent or factor. [L *īnstitōrius*, from *īnstitor* an agent, broker]

institute /*in'sti-tūt*/ *vt* to set up, establish; to originate, inaugurate; to order (*obs*); to educate (*obs*). ◆ *n* anything instituted or formally established; an institution; a literary and philosophical society or organization for education, research, etc; the building in which such an organization is housed; a foundation for further education, *esp* in technical subjects; established law; precept or principle; a brief course of instruction, *esp* for teachers (*US*); the person first nominated as heir (distinguished from the *substitutes* who follow) (*Scots law*); (in *pl*) a book of precepts, principles or rules; the act of instituting (*obs*). [L *īnstituere, -ūtum*, from *in* in, and *statuere* to cause to stand, from *stāre* to stand]

■ **institution** /*-tū'shən*/ *n* the act of instituting or establishing; that which is instituted or established; foundation; established order; enactment; a society or organization established for some object, *esp* cultural, charitable or beneficent, or the building housing it; a custom or usage, *esp* one familiar or characteristic; the act by which a bishop commits a cure of souls to a priest; appointment of an heir; a system of principles or rules (*obs*); that which institutes or instructs (*obs*). **institū'tional** *adj* concerning an institution, institutions or institutes; being, or of the nature of, an institution; depending on or originating in institution; associated with, or typical of, institutions, routine, uninspiring. **institū'tionalism** *n* the system or characteristics of institutions or institution life; belief in the merits of institutions and institution life. **institū'tionalist** *n* a writer on institutes; a person who sets a high value on institutionalism. **institutionaliz'ation** or **-s-** *n*. **institū'tionalize** or **-ise** *vt* to make an institution of; to confine to an institution; (*usu* in *passive*) as a result of such confinement, to cause to become apathetic and dependent. **institū'tionally** *adv*. **institū'tionary** *adj* institutional; educational (*obs*). **in'stitūtist** *n* a writer of institutes or elementary rules. **in'stitūtive** *adj* able or tending to establish; depending on an institution. **institū'tively** *adv*. **in'stitūtor** or **in'stitūter** *n* a person who institutes; an instructor (*obs*). ❑ **institutional church** *n* one that is active through social organizations.

instreaming /*in'strē-ming*/ *n* an influx (also *adj*). [**in**[1] and **streaming**]

instress /*in'stres*/ *n* the force or energy which sustains an inscape, the sensation of inscape (also *vt*). [Coined by Gerard Manley Hopkins, from **in**[1] and **stress**]

instruct /*in-strukt'*/ *vt* to inform; to teach; to direct; (of a judge) to give (a jury) guidance concerning the legal issues of a case; to give (a lawyer) the facts concerning a case; to engage (a lawyer) to act in a case; to order or command; to prepare (*obs*). ◆ *adj* (*Milton*; *obs*) instructed, taught. [L *īnstruere, īnstructum*, from *in* in, and *struere* to pile up]

■ **instruct'ible** *adj*. **instruc'tion** *n* (the art of) instructing or teaching; information; direction; command; an element in a computer program or language that activates a particular operation; (in *pl*) special directions for performing a specific task. **instruc'tional** *adj* relating to instruction; educational. **instruc'tive** *adj* providing instruction; conveying knowledge; denoting, as in Finnish, 'by means of' (*grammar*). **instruc'tively** *adv*. **instruc'tiveness** *n*. **instruc'tor** *n* (also *fem* **instruc'tress**) a teacher; a college or university lecturer, below assistant professor in rank (*N Am*). **instruc'torship** *n*.

instrument /*in'strə-mənt*/ *n* a tool or utensil; a contrivance for producing musical sounds; a document constituting or containing a contract; a formal record; a person or thing used as a means or agency; a term generally employed to denote an indicating device but also other pieces of small electrical apparatus. ◆ *vt* /*-ment'*/ to score (a piece of music) for instruments; to equip with indicating, measuring or control, etc apparatus. ◆ *adj* for instruments; by means of instruments (as in *instrument flight*). [L *īnstrūmentum*, from *īnstruere* to instruct; see **instruct**]

■ **instrumental** /*-ment'l*/ *adj* acting as an instrument or means; serving to promote an object; helpful; of, for, belonging to, or produced by, musical instruments; relating to or done with an instrument; denoting a type of learning process in which a particular response is always associated with a reinforcement, the response then intensifying (*psychol*); serving to indicate the instrument or means (*grammar*). ◆ *n* the instrumental case or a word in this case (*grammar*); a piece of music for instruments only, ie without a vocal part. **instrument'alism** *n* (*philos*) a form of pragmatism associated with John Dewey. **instrument'alist** *n* a person who plays a musical instrument; a person skilled in the making of instruments; a person who believes in or advocates instrumentalism. **instrumentality** /*-ment-al'i-ti*/ *n* agency.

instrument'ally *adv*. **instrumentā'tion** *n* the use or provision of instruments; the arrangement of a composition for performance by different instruments, orchestration (*music*). **instrumen'ted** *adj* equipped with electronic, etc instruments.

❑ **instrument flying** *n* navigation of aircraft in poor visibility by means of instruments only. **instrument landing** *n* landing of aircraft in poor visibility by means of instruments and ground radio devices only. **instrument panel** or **board** *n* a panel, eg in a car, on which instruments, dials, etc are mounted.

insubjection /*in-səb-jek'shən*/ *n* lack of subjection. [**in-** (2)]

insubordinate /*in-səb-ör'di-nit* or *-örd'nit*/ *adj* refusing to submit to authority; disobedient, rebellious. [**in-** (2)]

■ **insubord'inately** *adv*. **insubordinā'tion** *n*.

insubstantial /*in-səb-stan'shəl*/ *adj* not substantial; tenuous, flimsy; not real. [**in-** (2)]

■ **insubstantiality** /*-shi-al'i-ti*/ *n*. **insubstan'tially** *adv*.

insucken /*in'suk-n*/ (*Scots law*; *hist*) *adj* relating to a sucken. [**in**[1] and **sucken**]

insufferable /*in-suf'ə-rə-bl*/ *adj* not able to be endured; detestable. [**in-** (2)]

■ **insuff'erableness** *n*. **insuff'erably** *adv*.

insufficient /*in-sə-fish'ənt*/ *adj* not sufficient; inadequate; lacking (*obs*). [**in-** (2)]

■ **insuffic'iency** *n* the state of being insufficient (also *rare* **insuffic'ience**); the inability of an organ or part to function normally (*med*). **insuffic'iently** *adv*.

insufflate /*in'suf-lāt* (or *-suf'*)/ *vt* to blow in; to breathe on. [L *īnsufflāre*, from *in* in, on, and *sufflāre* to blow]

■ **insufflā'tion** *n* the act of breathing on anything, *esp* in baptism or exorcism; the act of blowing air, power, etc into a cavity or on a surface; the act of blowing gas or a medication in powder form into a body cavity. **in'sufflātor** *n* an instrument or device for insufflation.

insula /*in'sū-lə*/ (L *ēn'sū-la*)/ *n* (*pl* **in'sulae** /*-lē*/) a block of buildings (*ancient Rome*); an apartment house (*ancient Rome*); a small lobe of the cerebrum hidden in the fissure of Sylvius (also called **Reil's island**; *anat*). [L, an island]

insular /*in'sū-lər*/ *adj* belonging to an island; surrounded by water; standing or situated alone; remaining, *esp* seeking to remain, isolated, detached or aloof; hence, narrow, prejudiced. [LL *insulāris*, from L *insula* an island]

■ **in'sūlarism** *n*. **insūlarity** /*-lar'i-ti*/ *n* the state of being insular. **in'sūlarly** *adv*.

insulate /*in'sū-lāt*/ *vt* to cut off from connection or communication; to prevent the passing of heat, sound, electricity, etc from (a body, area, etc) to another; to place in a detached situation. [L *insulātus* made into an island, from *insula* island]

■ **insūlā'tion** *n* material which insulates or is a non-conductor of electricity; the process of insulating. **in'sūlātor** *n* someone who, or that which, insulates; a non-conductor of electricity; a device for insulating a conductor; a stand for a piano leg.

❑ **insulating board** *n* (*building*) fibreboard of low density to reduce heat loss and give a degree of soundproofing. **insulating tape** *n* (also (*N Am*) **friction tape**) a *usu* adhesive tape made from, or impregnated with, water-resistant insulating material, used for covering joins in electrical wires, etc.

insulin /*in'sū-lin*/ *n* a protein hormone produced in the islets of Langerhans in the pancreas, important in the regulation of glucose in the blood, and used in the treatment of diabetes mellitus. [New L *insula* islet, and **-in**]

■ **in'sulinase** *n* an enzyme, present in the tissues of the liver and kidneys, which breaks down insulin in the body.

❑ **insulin shock** or **reaction** *n* a state of collapse produced by an overdose of insulin.

insulse /*in-suls'*/ (*rare*) *adj* lacking wit; dull, stupid; tasteless, insipid. [L *insulsus*, from *in-* not, and *salere* to salt]

■ **insul'sity** *n* stupidity.

insult /*in-sult'*/ *vt* to treat with indignity or contempt; to affront; to triumph insolently or exultantly over; to attack physically, assault (*obs*). ◆ *vi* (*obs*) to make an attack; to behave with boastful insolence. ◆ *n* /*in'*/ an offensive remark or action; abuse; an affront; injury, damage (*med*, *esp US*). [L *insultāre*, from *insilīre* to spring at, from *in* upon, and *salīre* to leap]

■ **insult'able** *adj*. **insult'ant** *adj* (*rare*) insulting. **insult'er** *n*. **insult'ing** *adj*. **insult'ingly** *adv*. **insult'ment** *n* (*Shakesp*) insult.

■ **add insult to injury** to treat an affronted person with further indignity; to make matters worse.

insuperable /*in-sū'pə-rə-bl* or *-soo'*/ *adj* not capable of being overcome or surmounted. [L *insuperābilis*, from *in-* not, and *superāre* to pass over, from *super* above]

■ **insuperabil'ity** or **insu'perableness** *n*. **insu'perably** *adv*.

---

insupportable /in-sə-pōr'tə-bl or -pör'| adj unbearable, intolerable, insufferable; not sustainable or defensible; irresistible (Spenser). [**in-** (2)]
- **insupport'ableness** n. **insupport'ably** adv.

insuppressible /in-sə-pres'i-bl/ adj not capable of being suppressed or concealed. [**in-** (2)]
- **insuppress'ibly** adv.

insure /in-shoor'/ vt to make an arrangement for the payment of a sum of money in the event of loss or injury to; to guarantee; to make sure or secure. ◆ vi to effect or undertake insurance. [OFr enseurer, from en, and seur sure; see **ensure** and **sure**[1]]
- **insurabil'ity** n. **insur'able** adj capable of being insured. **insur'ance** n the act, practice or business of insuring; a contract of insurance, a policy; protection offered by such a contract; the premium paid for insuring; the sum to be received; means of avoiding risk, loss, damage, etc. **insur'ancer** n (obs). **insur'ant** n someone who obtains or holds an insurance policy. **insured'** n (usu with the) an insured person or organization. ◆ adj covered by insurance. **insur'er** n either party to a contract of insurance (now, strictly the insurance company).

insurgent /in-sûr'jənt/ adj rising in revolt; rising; rushing in. ◆ n a person who rises in opposition to established authority; a rebel. [L īnsurgēns, -entis, from in upon, and surgere to rise]
- **insur'gence** or **insur'gency** n a rising up or against; rebellion; insurrection.

insurmountable /in-sər-mown'tə-bl/ adj not surmountable; not capable of being overcome. [**in-** (2)]
- **insurmountabil'ity** or **insurmount'ableness** n. **insurmount'ably** adv.

insurrection /in-sə-rek'shən/ n a rising or revolt. [L īnsurrēctiō, -ōnis, from īnsurgere ; see **insurgent**]
- **insurrec'tional** or **insurrec'tionary** adj. **insurrec'tionary** or **insurrec'tionist** n. **insurrec'tionism** n.

insusceptible /in-sə-sep'ti-bl/ adj not susceptible (also **insuscep'tive**). [**in-** (2)]
- **insusceptibil'ity** n. **insuscep'tibly** or **insuscep'tively** adv.

inswathe same as **enswathe**.

inswing /in'swing/ n an inward swing or swerve. [**in**[1] and **swing**]
- **inswinger** /in'swing-ər/ n a ball bowled so as to swerve to leg (cricket); a ball kicked so as to swing in towards the goal or the centre of the pitch (football).

Int. abbrev : International.

int. abbrev : interest; interior; internal; international.

intact /in-takt'/ adj untouched; unimpaired; whole; undiminished. [L intactus, from in- not, and tangere, tactum to touch]
- **intact'ness** n.

intaglio /in-tä'lyō/ n (pl **intagl'ios**) a figure cut into any substance; a stone or gem in which the design is hollowed out, opp to cameo; the production of such figures, stones or gems; a countersunk die; a method of printing in which the image area is sunk into the surface of the plate, opp to relief. ◆ vt to form or represent by an intaglio. —See also **cavo-rilievo**. [Ital, from in into, and tagliare to cut, from L tālea a cutting, layer]
- **intagl'iated** adj incised, engraved.

intake /in'tāk/ n amount, quantity, etc taken in; an act of taking in; an airway in a mine; a place where water, gas, etc is taken in; a narrowing in a pipe; decrease by knitting two stitches together; the place where contraction occurs; the setting back of a wall-face; a body of people taken into an organization, eg new recruits, or new pupils at a school; the point at which the fuel mixture enters the cylinder of an internal-combustion engine; a cheat or cheater (dialect). [**in**[1] and **take**]

Intal® /in'tal/ n a drug (sodium cromoglycate), usu administered by inhaler and used to control certain types of asthma and allergic bronchitis.

intangible /in-tan'ji-bl/ adj not tangible or perceptible to touch; insubstantial; (of eg a business asset) having value but no solid physical existence; eluding the grasp of the mind. ◆ n something intangible, eg a supplementary asset such as goodwill. [**intact**]
- **intangibil'ity** or **intan'gibleness** n. **intan'gibly** adv.

intarsia /in-tär'si-ə/ n (also **tar'sia**) a form of decorative wood inlay work, developed in Italy during the 15c; coloured geometrical patterning in knitting, reminiscent of this. ◆ adj decorated in this style. [Ital intarsio]

integer /in'ti-jər/ n any positive whole number, any negative whole number, or zero (maths); a whole. [L, from in- not, and root of tangere to touch]

Integra® /in-teg'rə/ n an artificial skin, consisting of silicon on collagen sponge, laid on injured tissue to encourage cell growth.

integral /in'tə-grəl, also in-teg'rəl/ adj entire or whole; intrinsic, belonging as a part to the whole; unimpaired, intact; not fractional; not involving fractions; relating to integrals. ◆ n a whole; the whole as made up of its parts; the value of the function of a variable whose differential coefficient is known (maths). [LL integralis; see ety for **integer**]
- **integral'ity** n. **in'tegrally** adv.
- ❑ **integral calculus** see under **calculus**. **integral function** n (maths) a function which does not include the operation of division in any of its parts.

integrand /in'ti-grand/ (maths) n a function to be integrated. [L integrandus gerundive of integrare]

integrant /in'ti-grənt/ adj making part of a whole; necessary to form an integer or an entire thing. ◆ n an integrant thing or component. [Fr intégrant]

integrate /in'ti-grāt/ vt to make up as a whole; to make entire; to combine, amalgamate; to incorporate (one person or thing) into another; to desegregate; to find the integral of (maths); to find the total value of. ◆ vi to become integral; to perform integration. ◆ adj made up of parts; complete; whole. [L integrāre to make whole]
- **integrabil'ity** n. **in'tegrable** adj capable of being integrated. **integrā'tion** n the act or process of integrating (maths); unification into a whole, eg of diverse elements (such as racial variety) in a community; the state of being integrated; the formation of a unified personality (psychol). **integrā'tionist** n someone who favours racial and/or cultural integration (also adj). **in'tegrative** adj integrating, tending to integrate. **in'tegrator** n a person who integrates; an instrument for finding the results of integrations (maths).
- ❑ **integrated circuit** n a circuit consisting of an assembly of electronic elements in a single structure which cannot be subdivided without destroying its intended function. **integrated services digital network** see **ISDN**.
- ❑ **monolithic integrated circuit** an integrated circuit formed in or on a single crystal of semiconductor, usu silicon.

integrin /in-teg'rin/ (biol) n any of a superfamily of cell surface proteins that bind to components of the extracellular matrix, facilitating cell adhesion and signalling. [**integer** and **-in** (1)]

integrity /in-teg'ri-ti/ n uprightness; honesty; purity; entireness, wholeness; the unimpaired state of anything. [**integer**]

integument /in-teg'ū-mənt/ n an external covering; either of the two protective outer coats that surrounds an ovule (bot); a covering layer of tissue, such as the skin, exoskeleton, etc (zool). [L integumentum, from in upon, and tegere to cover]
- **integumental** /-men'tl/ or **integument'ary** adj.

intel /in'tel/ (milit sl) n information about an enemy's plans and movements. [Short form of intelligence]

intellect /int'i-lekt/ n the mind, in reference to its rational powers; the thinking principle; someone with a highly-developed intellect. [L intellēctus, -ūs, from intelligere, intellēctum to understand, from inter between, and legere to choose]
- **in'tellected** adj (Cowper) endowed with intellect. **intellec'tion** n the act of understanding; apprehension or perception (philos). **intellec'tive** adj able to understand; produced or perceived by the understanding. **intellectual** /-lek'tū-əl/ adj of or relating to the intellect; perceived or performed by the intellect; having the power of understanding; endowed with a superior intellect; appealing to, or (thought to be) intended for, intellectuals; intelligible only to a person with a superior intellect. ◆ n a person of superior intellect or enlightenment (often used to suggest doubt as to common sense or practical skills); a person who uses his or her intellect to earn a living, esp a writer, philosopher, etc; a member of the intelligentsia; (in pl) intellectual matters (archaic); (in pl) mental powers (archaic); intellect (obs). **intellect'ualism** n the doctrine that derives all knowledge from pure reason; the culture (esp exclusive or unbalanced) of the intellect. **intellect'ualist** n. **intellectuality** /-al'i-ti/ n intellectual power. **intellect'ualize** or **-ise** vi to reason intellectually. ◆ vt to endow with intellect; to give an intellectual character to. **intellect'ually** adv.
- ❑ **intellectual property** n (law) property such as copyright, trademarks and patents, having no tangible form but representing the product of creative work or invention.

intelligent /in-tel'i-jənt/ adj endowed with the faculty of reason; having or showing highly developed mental faculties; alert, bright, quick of mind; well-informed; capable of performing some of the functions of a computer (technol); knowing, aware (with of; archaic); communicative (Shakesp). [L intelligēns, -entis, prp of intelligere ; see ety for **intellect**]
- **intell'igence** n intellectual skill or knowledge; mental brightness; information communicated; news; intelligence department; an intelligent person or being. **intell'igencer** n (archaic) a spy; a source of information or news, an informant; a newspaper (usu as a title).

intelligential /-jen'shl/ adj concerning the intelligence. **intell'igently** adv.

❏ **intelligence department** or **service** n a department of state or armed service for securing and interpreting information, *esp* about an enemy. **intelligence quotient** n the ratio, commonly expressed as a percentage, of a person's mental age to his or her chronological age (*abbrev* **IQ**). **intelligence test** n a test by questions and tasks to determine a person's mental capacity, or the age at which his or her capacity would be normal. **intelligent design** n the creation of the universe by a rational agent, rather than by random processes. **intelligent terminal** n (*comput*) a terminal incorporating a microprocessor, capable of performing simple tasks independently of the larger computer to which it is connected.

intelligentsia or (formerly) **intelligentzia** /in-tel-i-jent'si-ə or (formerly) -gent'/ n the intellectual or cultured classes, *orig* in Russia, the intellectual élite. [Russ, from L *intelligentia* intelligence]

intelligible /in-tel'i-jə-bl/ adj capable of being understood, comprehensible; easy to understand, clear; capable of being apprehended by the understanding only, not by senses (*philos*). [L *intelligibilis*]
■ **intelligibil'ity** or **intell'igibleness** n. **intell'igibly** adv.

Intelpost /in'tel-pōst/ n an international communications system using electronic fax and telex systems to send text and graphics. [*inter*national *electronic post*]

Intelsat /in'tel-sat/ n a worldwide satellite service dealing with communications such as television exchange, business messages, etc. [*Inter*national *Tele*communications *Sat*ellite Consortium]

intemerate /in-tem'ə-rit/ (now *rare*) adj pure; undefiled; inviolate. [L *intemerātus*, from *in-* not, and pap of *temerāre* to violate]
■ **intem'erately** adv.

intemperance /in-tem'pə-rəns/ n lack of due restraint; excess of any kind; habitual overindulgence in alcohol. [L *intemperans* intemperate]
■ **intem'perant** n a person who is intemperate. **intem'perate** adj indulging to excess in any desire or passion; given to an immoderate use of alcohol; exceeding the usual degree; immoderate. **intem'perately** adv. **intem'perateness** n.

intempestive /in-tem-pes'tiv/ (*literary*) adj unseasonable; untimely; inopportune. [L *intempestīvus*, from *in-* not, and *tempestās* season, from *tempus* time]
■ **intempest'ively** adv. **intempestiv'ity** n.

intenable /in-ten'ə-bl/ (*obs*) adj untenable. [**in-** (2)]

intend /in-tend'/ vt to have as a purpose, plan; to mean or express; to design or destine; to direct or turn (the attention, etc) (*archaic*); to stretch out, extend (*obs*); to expand (*obs*); to strain (*obs*); to intensify (*obs*). ◆ vi to set out for or proceed towards a particular destination (with *for*; *obs*); to be present, attend (*obs*); to listen (with *to*; *obs*). [OFr *entendre*, from L *intendere*, *intentum* and *intensum*, from *in* towards, and *tendere* to stretch]
■ **intend'ed** adj planned. ◆ n (*inf*) a fiancé or fiancée. **intend'edly** adv with intention or design. **intend'ment** n the true meaning or intention of something, *esp* a law.

intendant /in-ten'dənt/ n an administrative official (eg a provincial or colonial governor) of France, Portugal and Spain (*hist*); an official who superintends some public business in certain countries; a superintendent, director or manager. [Fr, from L *intendens, -dentis*, prp of *intendere*; see ety for **intend**]
■ **intend'ancy** n the office, term of office, or sphere of an intendant; a body of intendants; management, superintendence (also **intend'ance**).

intender see **entender**.

intenerate /in-ten'ə-rāt/ (*rare*) vt to make tender; to soften. [L *in* in, to, and *tener* tender]
■ **intenerā'tion** n.

intenible /in-ten'i-bl/ adj incapable of holding or retaining. [L *in-* not, and *tenēre* to hold]

intensative see **intensive**.

intense /in-tens'/ adj strained; concentrated, dense; extreme in degree; (of person, manner, etc) earnestly or deeply emotional, or affecting to have deep feeling; (of a photographic negative) opaque. [OFr *intensive*, from L *intensus*]
■ **intens'ate** vt (*rare*) to intensify. **intense'ly** adv. **intense'ness** or **inten'sity** n. **intensifica'tion** n the act of intensifying. **intens'ifier** n an utterance that lends force and emphasis (*grammar*); a person or thing that intensifies; an image intensifier. **intens'ify** vt to make more intense. ◆ vi to become intense.

intension /in-ten'shən/ n straining; intentness; intensity; intensification; the sum of the qualities by which a general name is determined (*logic*). [Ety as for **intend**]
■ **inten'sional** adj. **inten'sionally** adv.

intensitive see **intensive**.

intensive /in-ten'siv/ adj concentrated, intense; strained; unremitting; relating to intensity or to intension; using large amounts of capital or labour to increase production; intensifying; intensified; (also (*rare*) **inten'sative** or **inten'sitive**) giving force or emphasis (*grammar*). ◆ n an intensifier. ◆ *combining form* signifying having, using or requiring a great deal of something, as in *labour-intensive*, *capital-intensive*. [**intend**]
■ **inten'sively** adv. **inten'siveness** n.
❏ **intensifying screen** n (*radiol*) a layer or screen of fluorescent material placed adjacent to a photographic film, so that registration by incident X-rays is augmented by local fluorescence; a thin layer of lead which performs a similar function for high-energy X-rays or gamma-rays. **intensive care** n specialized, closely-monitored health care for the critically ill in a specially designed hospital unit (**intensive care unit**). **intensive culture** or **intensive farming** n obtaining the maximum yield from the soil of a limited area.

intent /in-tent'/ adj fixed with close attention; diligently applied; concentrating on a particular aim or purpose (*usu* with *on* or *upon*). ◆ n the thing aimed at or intended; purpose, intention, design; meaning or connotation; intentness (*obs*). [Ety as for **intend**]
■ **inten'tive** adj (*archaic*) attentive. **intent'ly** adv earnestly; diligently. **intent'ness** n.
■ **to all intents (and purposes)** in every important aspect; virtually. **with intent** (*law*) deliberately, with the intention of doing the harm, etc that is or was done.

intention /in-ten'shən/ n design; purpose, aim; application of thought to an object; a concept; (in *pl*) purpose with respect to marriage (*inf*); a plan of treatment (*med*); a process of healing (see also below); application or direction of the mind (*obs*). [**intend**]
■ **inten'tional** adj with intention; intended; designed; directed towards, or relating to the mind's capacity to direct itself towards, objects and states of affairs (*philos*). **intentional'ity** n. **inten'tionally** adv with intention; on purpose. **inten'tioned** adj having a certain intention.
❏ **intention tremor** n a tremor that occurs when an individual with a chronic disease affecting the central nervous system (eg multiple sclerosis) tries to touch an object.
■ **first intention healing** healing by which the edges of a wound are brought together directly and granulation occurs. **second intention healing** healing in which the edges of a wound are separated and the gap is filled first by granulation tissue and then covered by epithelial tissue from the wound edges. **third intention healing** healing in which ulceration occurs and scar tissue is formed at the wound site. **well-** (or **ill-**)**intentioned** having good (or evil) intentions; meaning well (or meaning harm).

inter /in-tûr'/ vt (**interr'ing**; **interred'**) to bury. [Fr *enterrer*, from LL *interrāre*, from L *in* into, and *terra* the earth]
■ **inter'ment** n burial.

inter- /in-tər-* or *in-tûr-/ pfx denoting: between, among, in the midst of; mutual, reciprocal; together. [L *inter*]

interact[1] /in-tər-akt'/ vi to act on one another. [**inter-**]
■ **interac'tant** n a substance, etc which interacts. **interaction** /-ak'shən/ n mutual action. **interac'tional** adj. **interac'tionism** n (*philos*) the theory that mind and body act on each other (as distinct from psychophysical parallelism and epiphenomenalism). **interac'tionist** n. **interac'tive** adj allowing or capable of mutual action; allowing two-way communication between a computer and its user or another computer or device. **interac'tively** adv. **interactiv'ity** n. **interac'tome** n the complete set of interactions between the molecules in a cell.
❏ **interactive compact disc** n a CDI. **interactive television** n a television system in which the viewer can choose, from a range of options, what is shown on the screen, eg camera angle, action replay, etc.

interact[2] /in'tər-akt/ n an interlude; an entr'acte; the interval between acts. [**inter-**]

inter alia /in'tər or -ter ā'li-ə or al'i-a/ (L) among other things.
■ **inter alios** /ā'li-ōs or a'li-ōs/ among other people.

interallied /in-tər-al'īd or -ə-līd/ adj between or among allies. [**inter-**]

interambulacrum /in-tər-am-bū-lā'krəm/ n (*pl* **interambulā'cra**) (in sea urchins) a radial band between two ambulacra. [**inter-**]
■ **interambulā'cral** adj.

interatomic /in-tər-ə-tom'ik/ adj existing, happening, etc between atoms. [**inter-**]

interbank /in'tər-bangk/ adj between or among banks. [**inter-**]

interbedded /in-tər-bed'id/ (*geol*) adj interstratified. [**inter-**]
■ **interbedd'ing** n.

interbrain /in'tər-brān/ n the diencephalon.

■ words derived from main entry word; ❏ compound words; ■ idioms and phrasal verbs

interbreed /in-tər-brēd'/ vt and vi (pat and pap **interbred'**) to breed together, esp of different races. [**inter-**]
■ **interbreed'ing** n.

intercalate /in-tûr'kə-lāt/ vt to insert between others (eg a day in a calendar); to interpolate. [L intercalāre, -ātum, from inter between, and calāre to proclaim; see **calends**]
■ **inter'calar** /-lər/ (obs) or **inter'calary** adj inserted between others. **inter'calated** adj. **intercalā'tion** n. **inter'calative** /-lā-tiv or -lə-tiv/ adj.

intercede /in-tər-sēd'/ vi to act as peacemaker between two parties, mediate; to plead (for). [L intercēdere, -cēssum, from inter between, and cēdere to go]
■ **intercēd'ent** adj. **intercēd'er** n.

intercellular /in-tər-sel'ū-lər/ (biol) adj placed, situated or occurring between cells. [**inter-**]

intercensal /in-tər-sen'səl/ adj between censuses. [Irregularly formed from L inter and **census**]

intercept /in-tər-sept'/ vt to stop and seize on the way from one place to another; to cut off; to stop, alter, or interrupt the progress of; to take or comprehend between (maths). ◆ n /in'/ that part of a line that is intercepted (maths); the act of intercepting. [L intercipere, -ceptum, from inter between, and capere to seize]
■ **intercep'ter** or **intercep'tor** n a person or thing which intercepts; a light, swift aeroplane for pursuit. **intercep'tion** n. **intercep'tive** adj.

intercession /in-tər-sesh'ən/ n the act of interceding or pleading on behalf of another; an intercessional prayer (Christianity). [**intercede**]
■ **intercess'ional** adj. **intercessor** /-ses'ər/ n a person who intercedes; a bishop who acts during a vacancy in a see. **intercessōrial** /-ōr'/ or -ör'/ or **intercess'ory** adj interceding.
□ **intercession of saints** n prayer offered on behalf of Christians on earth by saints.

interchain /in-tər-chān'/ vt to chain together. [**inter-**]

interchange /in-tər-chānj'/ vt to give and take mutually; to exchange. ◆ vi to succeed alternately. ◆ n /in'/ mutual exchange; alternate succession; a road junction or series of junctions designed to prevent streams of traffic crossing one another. [**inter-**]
■ **interchange'able** adj capable of being interchanged; following each other in alternate succession (obs). **interchange'ableness** or **interchangeabil'ity** n. **interchange'ably** adv. **interchange'ment** n (Shakesp) exchange, mutual transfer. **interchang'er** n.
□ **interchange fee** n one charged by the issuer of a debit or credit card for processing a transaction made with it.

interchapter /in'tər-chap-tər/ n an intercalary chapter in a book, not numbered in the general sequence. [**inter-**]

intercipient /in-tər-sip'i-ənt/ (obs) adj intercepting. ◆ n the person or thing that intercepts. [L intercipiēns, -entis, prp of intercipere ; see **intercept**]

intercity /in-tər-sit'i/ adj between cities. ◆ n (**Intercity®**) a fast train running between cities. [**inter-**]

interclude /in-tər-klood'/ vt to block; to enclose; to cut off. [L interclūdere, from inter between, and claudere to shut]
■ **interclusion** /-kloo'zhən/ n.

intercollegiate /in-tər-kə-lē'ji-āt or -ət/ adj between colleges. [**inter-**]

intercolline /in-tər-kol'īn/ adj lying between hills. [**inter-**]

intercolonial /in-tər-kə-lō'ni-əl/ adj between colonies. [**inter-**]
■ **intercolo'nially** adv.

intercolumniation /in-tər-kə-lum-ni-ā'shən/ (archit) n the spacing of, or distance between, columns, measured in terms of the lower diameter. [**inter-**]
■ **intercolum'nar** adj placed between columns.

intercom /in'tər-kom/ n a telephone system within a building, aeroplane, tank, etc. [Internal communication]

intercommune /in-tər-kə-mūn'/ vi to commune mutually or together; to hold discussions, have dealings. [**inter-**]
■ **intercomm'unal** adj existing between communities. **intercommun'ion** or **intercommunica'tion** n mutual communion or relation, esp between churches; the permitting of members of one denomination to receive Holy Communion in the churches of another denomination. **intercommun'ity** n the state of being or having in common.
■ **letters of intercommuning** an ancient writ issued by the Scottish Privy Council warning people not to harbour or have any dealings with those named, on pain of being held accessory.

intercommunicate /in-tər-kə-mū'ni-kāt/ vt and vi to communicate mutually or together; to have free passage from one to another. [**inter-**]
■ **intercommun'icable** adj. **intercommunica'tion** n.

interconnect /in-tər-kə-nekt'/ vt to connect (things) with each other. ◆ vi to be mutually connected. [**inter-**]
■ **interconnec'tedness**, **interconnec'tion** or **interconnex'ion** n. **interconnectiv'ity** n the ability of different parts of a system to operate together. **interconnec'tor** n a device or feeder by which electricity generated in an area or country may be exported to another area or country.

intercontinental /in-tər-kon-ti-nen'təl/ adj between or connecting different continents. [**inter-**]
□ **intercontinental ballistic missile** n a ballistic missile capable of carrying a nuclear bomb over 5500 km (abbrev **ICBM**).

interconversion /in-tər-kən-vûr'shən/ n the conversion of two things or more into one another, mutual conversion. [**inter-**]
■ **interconvert'** vt (back-formation) to convert (two or more things) into one another. **interconvert'ible** adj mutually convertible; interchangeable; exactly equivalent.

intercooler /in'tər-koo-lər/ n a heat exchanger in a turbocharger, used eg in supercharged internal-combustion engines. [**inter-** and **cool**]
■ **intercool'ed** adj.

intercostal /in-tər-kos'təl/ adj between the ribs or the leaf-veins. [L inter between, and costa a rib]
■ **intercos'tally** adv.

intercourse /in'tər-kōrs or -körs/ n connection or dealings between people; communication; commerce; communion; coition, sexual intercourse. [OFr entrecours, from L intercursus a running between, from inter between, and currere, cursum to run]

intercrop /in-tər-krop'/ vt and vi (**intercropp'ing**; **intercropped'**) to grow or cultivate in alternate rows. ◆ n /in'/ a crop grown in the rows between another crop. [**inter-**]

intercross /in-tər-kros'/ vt and vi to cross and recross; to cross mutually; to place or lie crosswise; to crossbreed. ◆ n /in'/ a crossing of breeds; an intercrossed animal. [**inter-**]

intercrural /in-tər-kroo'rəl/ adj situated or relating to (the area) between the crura or legs. [**inter-**]

intercurrent /in-tər-kur'ənt/ adj running between, intervening; going on at the same time; supervening. [L inter between, and currere to run]
■ **intercurr'ence** n.

intercut /in-tər-kut'/ (film) vt to alternate (contrasting shots) within a sequence by cutting. [**inter-**]

interdash /in-tər-dash'/ vt to intersperse with dashes. [**inter-**]

interdeal /in'tər-dēl/ (archaic) n (also (Spenser) **enterdeale**) mutual dealings; negotiations. ◆ vi to have mutual dealings. [**inter-**]
■ **interdeal'er** n.

interdenominational /in-tər-di-nom-i-nā'shə-nl or -nāsh'nl/ adj common to, or with the participation of, various religious denominations; independent of denomination. [**inter-**]
■ **interdenomina'tionally** adv.

interdental /in-tər-den'tl/ adj between the teeth; relating to the surfaces of the teeth where they adjoin (dentistry); pronounced with the tip of the tongue between upper and lower teeth (phonetics). [**inter-**]
■ **interdent'ally** adv.

interdepartmental /in-tər-dē-pärt-men'tl/ adj existing or occurring between departments. [**inter-**]
■ **interdepartment'ally** adv.

interdepend /in-tər-di-pend'/ vi to depend on one another. [**inter-**]
■ **interdepend'ence** or **interdepend'ency** n. **interdepend'ent** adj. **interdepend'ently** adv.

interdict /in-tər-dikt'/ vt to prohibit; to forbid; to forbid (someone) to take communion (RC); to destroy (lines of communication, supply, etc) by firepower (milit). ◆ n /in'/ prohibition; a prohibitory decree; a prohibition of the Pope restraining the clergy from performing divine service. [L interdīcere, -dictum, from inter between, and dīcere to say]
■ **interdic'tion** /-shən/ n. **interdic'tive** or **interdic'tory** adj containing interdiction; prohibitory. **interdic'tor** n.

interdigital /in-tər-dij'i-tl/ adj between digits. [**inter-**]
■ **interdig'itate** vt and vi to interlock by finger-like processes, or in the manner of the fingers of clasped hands; to interstratify or be interstratified. **interdigitā'tion** n.

interdisciplinary /in-tər-di-si-plin'ə-ri/ adj involving two or more fields of study. [**inter-**]
■ **interdisciplinar'ity** n.

interess or **interesse** /in'tər-es or -es'/ (obs) n interest. ◆ vt (pap (Shakesp) **interest'**) to interest. [Anglo-Fr interesse, from LL interesse compensation, interest, from L interesse (infinitive) to concern]

interest /int'ə-rest, int'rəst or -rist/ n advantage, benefit; premium paid for the borrowing of money; any increase; concern, importance;

personal influence; a right to some advantage; claim to participate or be concerned in some way; stake, share; partisanship or side; the body of people whose advantage is bound up in anything; regard to (*esp* personal) advantage; a state of engaged attention and curiosity; disposition towards such a state; the power of arousing it; a subject or activity to which one willingly devotes time and attention, a hobby. ◆ *vt* to concern deeply; to cause to have an interest; to engage the attention of; to awaken concern in; to excite the curiosity of. [From *interess*, influenced by OFr *interest*, L *interest*, it concerns, 3rd person singular present indicative of *interesse*, from *inter* between, among, and *esse* to be]

■ **in'terested** *adj* having an interest or concern; affected or biased by personal considerations, self-interest, etc. **in'terestedly** *adv*. **in'terestedness** *n*. **in'teresting** (*old* /-*est'*/) *adj* engaging or apt to engage the attention or regard; exciting emotion or passion. **in'terestingly** *adv*. **in'terestingness** *n*.
❑ **interest-free'** *adj* and *adv* with no interest charged on money borrowed. **interest group** *n* a number of people grouped together to further or protect a common interest. **interest rate** *n* a charge made on borrowed money, *usu* expressed as a percentage to be repaid annually.
■ **compound interest** see under **compound¹**. **in an interesting condition**, **state** or **situation** old-fashioned euphemisms for pregnant. **in the interest(s) of** with a view to furthering or to helping. **make interest for** (*obs*) to secure favour for. **simple interest** see under **simple**.

interface /in'tər-fās/ *n* a surface forming a common boundary; a meeting-point or area of contact between objects, systems, subjects, etc; the connection or junction between two systems or two parts of the same system (*comput*); the physical connection between computer and user; the surface of separation between phases (*chem*). ◆ *vt* to connect by means of an interface. ◆ *vi* (*esp comput*) to interact or operate compatibly (with). [**inter-**]
■ **interfacial** /-fā'shl/ *adj* between plane faces; of an interface.

interfacing /in'tər-fā-sing/ *n* firm material sewn between layers of fabric to shape and stiffen a garment. [**inter-**]

interfaith /in'tər-fāth/ *adj* occurring, carried out or organized between (members, representatives, etc of) different religious faiths. [**inter-**]

interfascicular /in-tər-fə-sik'ū-lər/ *adj* between vascular bundles. [**inter-**]

interfemoral /in-tər-fem'ə-rəl/ *adj* situated between the thighs, connecting the hind limbs. [**inter-**]

interfenestration /in-tər-fen-i-strā'shən/ *n* spacing of windows. [L *inter* between, and *fenestra* a window]

interfere /in-tər-fēr'/ *vi* to intervene; to come in the way, obstruct; to interpose; to meddle; (of a horse) to strike a foot against the opposite leg in walking; (of waves, rays of light, etc) to act reciprocally. [OFr *entreferir*, from L *inter* between, and *ferīre* to strike]
■ **interfer'ence** *n* the act of interfering; the effect of combining similar rays of light, etc (*phys*); the distortion of a wireless or television signal by others or by natural disturbances. **interferential** /-fər-en'shl/ *adj*. **interfer'er** *n*. **interfēr'ing** *adj*. **interfēr'ingly** *adv*. **interfēr'ogram** *n* (*phys*) a photographic or diagrammatic record of interference. **interfērom'eter** *n* an instrument which, by observing interference fringes, makes precision measurements of wavelengths, wave speeds, angles, distances, etc; a radio telescope (**radio interferometer**) using two or more antennas spaced at known intervals and linked to a common receiver, one of its applications being the precise determination of the position of sources of radio waves in space. **interfēromet'ric** *adj*. **interfēromet'rically** *adv*. **interfērom'etry** *n*. **interfēr'on** *n* any of several proteins produced by cells infected with a virus and having the ability to inhibit viral growth.
❑ **interference figure** *n* a figure observed when a crystal section is viewed between crossed nicols. **interference fit** *n* (*engineering*) a fit between two parts which requires force on assembly to expand the outer or contract the inner. **interference fringes** *n pl* alternate light and dark bands seen when similar beams of light interfere. **interference microscopy** *n* a method of microscopy in which the phase changes caused by differences in the optical path within the specimen can be measured or made visible.
■ **interfere with** to meddle in; to get in the way of, hinder; to assault sexually. **run interference** (chiefly *N Am*) in team sports, to hinder opposing players while a teammate is in possession of the ball or puck; to assist someone by obstructing his or her opponents.

interfertile /in-tər-fûr'tīl/ or (*US*) -*təl*/ *adj* capable of interbreeding. [**inter-**]

interfile /in-tər-fīl'/ *vt* to place among other items in a file; to combine in one file. [**inter-**]

interflow /in'tər-flō/ *n* intermingling. ◆ *vi* to flow into one another or between. [**inter-**]

interfluent /in-tûr'flū-ənt/ *adj* flowing between or together (also **inter'fluous**). [L *interfluēns*, -*entis*, fr9om *inter* between, and *fluere* to flow]
■ **inter'fluence** *n*.

interfluve /in'tər-floov/ *n* an area of land dividing two river valleys. [L *inter* between, and *fluvius* river]
■ **interflu'vial** *adj*.

interfold /in-tər-fōld'/ *vt* to fold one into the other. [**inter-**]

interfoliate /in-tər-fō'li-āt/ *vt* to interleave. [L *inter* between, and *folium* a leaf]

interfretted /in-tər-fret'id/ (*heraldry*) *adj* interlaced. [**inter-**]

interfrontal /in-tər-frun'tl/ or -*fron'tl*/ *adj* between the frontal bones. [**inter-**]

interfuse /in-tər-fūz'/ *vt* to cause to mix or fuse. ◆ *vi* to mix or fuse, mingle. [**inter-**]
■ **interfusion** /-fū'zhən/ *n*.

intergalactic /in-tər-ga-lak'tik/ *adj* between, or among, galaxies. [**inter-**]
■ **intergalac'tically** *adv*.

intergenerational /in-tər-jen-ə-rā'shun-əl/ *adj* between different generations. [**inter-**]

interglacial /in-tər-glā'si-əl/ or -*glā'shəl*/ (*geol*) *adj* occurring between two periods of glacial action. ◆ *n* a retreat of ice between glaciations. [**inter-**]

Interglossa /in-tər-glos'ə/ *n* an international language based on well-known Greek and Latin roots, devised by Lancelot Hogben (1943). [L *inter* between, and Gr *glōssa* tongue]

intergrade /in-tər-grād'/ *vi* to merge in or shade off into something else through a series of intermediate forms. ◆ *n* /in'/ an intermediate grade. [**inter-**]
■ **intergradation** /-grə-dā'shən/ *n*.

intergrow /in-tər-grō'/ *vt* to grow into or among each other. [**inter-**]
■ **intergrown'** *adj*. **in'tergrowth** *n*.

interim /in'tər-im/ *n* the time between or intervening; the meantime; (with *cap*) in the history of the Reformation, the name given to certain edicts of the German emperor for the regulation of religious and ecclesiastical matters, until they could be decided by a general council, such as the Augsburg Interim (1548). ◆ *adj* temporary, provisional. ◆ *adv* (*rare*) meanwhile. [L]
❑ **interim accounts** *n pl* a set of financial statements for part of a financial year, *usu* six months. **interim dividend** *n* (*finance*) a dividend, not voted on by shareholders, distributed part of the way through a company's financial year.

interior /in-tē'ri-ər/ *adj* inner; remote from the frontier or coast; inland; domestic rather than foreign; situated within or further in (sometimes with *to*); devoted to mental or spiritual life. ◆ *n* the inside of anything; the inland part of a country; a picture of a scene within a house; the home affairs of a country; inner nature or character. [L, compar of assumed *interus* inward]
■ **interiority** /-or'i-ti/ *n*. **inter'iorly** *adv*.
❑ **interior angle** *n* the angle between two adjacent sides of a polygon. **interior decoration** or **design** *n* the construction and furnishing of the interior of a building. **interior decorator** or **designer** *n* a person or company that specializes in the design and furnishing of interiors. **interior grate** *n* an open grate with built-in boiler. **interior monologue** *n* a literary representation of a person's inner thoughts and feelings before they take coherent grammatical form. **inter'ior-sprung** *adj* (of a mattress, etc) containing springs.

interj. *abbrev* : interjection.

interjacent /in-tər-jā'sənt/ *adj* lying between; intervening. [L *interjacēns*, -*entis*, prp of *interjacēre*, from *inter* between, and *jacēre* to lie]
■ **interjā'cency** *n*.

interjaculate /in-tər-jak'ū-lāt/ *vt* to ejaculate in interruption. [L *inter* between, and *jaculārī* to throw]
■ **interjac'ulatory** /-ū-lə-tə-ri/ *adj*.

interject /in-tər-jekt'/ *vt* to exclaim in interruption or parenthesis; to insert; to interpose; to throw between. ◆ *vi* to throw oneself between. [L *inter(j)icere*, *interjectum*, from *inter* between, and *jacere* to throw]
■ **interjec'tion** /-shən/ *n* an act of interjecting; a syntactically independent word or phrase of an exclamatory nature, *usu* expressing strong or sudden emotion (*grammar*). **interjec'tional**, **interjec'tionary** or **interjec'tural** *adj*. **interjec'tionally** *adv*. **interjec'tor** *n*. **interjec'tory** *adj*.

interjoin /in-tər-join'/ (*Shakesp*) *vt* to join together. [**inter-**]

interkinesis /in-tər-kī-nē'sis/ or -*ki*-/ (*biol*) *n* the resting stage between two divisions of mitosis (see also **interphase**). [L *inter* between, and Gr *kinēsis* movement]

■ words derived from main entry word; ❑ compound words; ■ idioms and phrasal verbs

interknit /in-tər-nit'/ vt to knit into each other. [**inter-**]

interlace /in-tər-lās'/ vt to lace, weave or entangle together. ◆ vi to intermix. [**inter-**]
■ **interlace'ment** n.
❑ **interlaced scanning** n in television, the alternate scanning of an image in two sets of alternate lines.

interlaminate /in-tər-lam'i-nāt/ vt to insert between layers; to arrange or apply in alternate layers. [**inter-**]
■ **interlam'inar** adj. **interlaminā'tion** n.

interlanguage /in'tər-lang-gwij/ (linguistics) n a form of a language produced by a person who is not a native speaker of the language at any stage in the process of learning it. [**inter-**]

interlard /in-tər-lärd'/ vt to mix in, as fat with lean; to intersperse (one's speech or writing) with unusual words. [**inter-**]

interlay /in-tər-lā'/ vt to lay between; to interpose. ◆ n /in'/ (printing) layers of tissue, etc placed between a printing plate and its base to achieve the correct type height or printing pressure. [**inter-**]

interleave /in-tər-lēv'/ vt to put a leaf or page between; to insert blank leaves or pages in; to intersperse with alternately. [**inter-**]
■ **in'terleaf** n (pl **in'terleaves**) a leaf or page so inserted.

interleukin /in-tər-lū'kin/ n any of a group of proteins that control the production of blood cells and play an important part in the combating of infection. [**inter-**, leucocyte, and **-in**]
❑ **interleukin 2** n an interleukin that stimulates production of T-lymphocytes, used as an experimental treatment for cancer (abbrev **IL-2**).

interline[1] /in-tər-līn'/ vt to write in alternate lines; to insert between lines; to write between the lines of. [**inter-**]
■ **interlinear** /-lin'i-ər/ adj written between lines. **interlineation** /-lin-i-ā'shən/ or **interlin'ing** n.

interline[2] /in-tər-līn'/ vt to supply (a part of a garment, eg the collar) with an additional lining to reinforce or stiffen it.
■ **interlin'ing** n.

interline[3] /in-tər-līn'/ vi to join an airline route at a point other than its starting-point; to change from one plane (and airline route) during the course of a journey. ◆ adj /in'/ involving or relating to more than one transport (eg air) line or route. [**inter-**]

interlinear and **interlineation** see under **interline**[1].

Interlingua /in-tər-ling'gwə/ n an international language based on the living Latin roots in European languages; (without cap) any artificially devised international language. [L inter between, and lingua tongue]
■ **interlin'gual** adj. **interlin'gually** adv.

interlink /in-tər-lingk'/ vt and vi to link together. [**inter-**]

interlobular /in-tər-lob'ū-lər/ adj between lobes. [**inter-**]

interlocation /in-tər-lō-kā'shən/ n a placing between. [**inter-**]

interlock /in-tər-lok'/ vt to lock or clasp together; to connect so as to work together. ◆ vi to be locked together. ◆ n /in'/ an interlocked condition; any synchronizing mechanism; fabric knitted with closely locking stitches. [**inter-**]
■ **in'terlocker** n. **interlock'ing** adj.

interlocution /in-tər-lo-kū'shən/ n dialogue, conversation; an intermediate decree before a final decision. [L interlocūtiō, -ōnis, from inter between, and loquī, locūtus to speak]
■ **interlocutor** /-lok'ū-tər/ n a person who speaks in dialogue; a judge's decree (Scots law). **interloc'utory** adj. **interloc'utress**, **interloc'utrice** or **interloc'utrix** n a female interlocutor.

interloper /in'tər-lō-pər/ n an intruder; a person who meddles in another's affairs, esp for profit. [Prob L inter between, and **lope**[1]]
■ **interlope'** (or /in'/) vi and vt to intrude into any matter in which one has no fair concern.

interlude /in'tər-lood or -lūd/ n an interval between acts of a play, etc; a short dramatic or comic piece, formerly often performed during this interval; a short piece of music played between the parts of a drama, opera, hymn, etc; an interval, any period of time or any happening different in character from what comes before or after. ◆ vt and vi to interrupt, as an interlude. [L inter between, and lūdus play]
■ **interlu'dial** adj.

interlunar /in-tər-loo'nər or -lū'/ adj belonging to the moon's monthly time of invisibility (also **interlu'nary**). [L inter between, and lūna the moon]
■ **interlunā'tion** /-loo-/ n the dark time between old moon and new.

intermarry /in-tər-mar'i/ vi to marry within one's own family or group; (of groups, races, etc) to mingle by marriage; (of a couple) to marry (law); to marry (with with; law). [**inter-**]
■ **intermarr'iage** n.

intermaxilla /in-tər-mak-sil'ə/ n the premaxilla. [L inter between, and maxilla a jawbone]

■ **intermax'illary** (or /-il'/) adj of the intermaxilla; between the maxillaries. ◆ n the intermaxilla.

intermeddle /in-tər-med'l/ vi to meddle; to interfere improperly. [**inter-**]
■ **intermedd'ler** n.

intermediate /in-tər-mē'dyit or -di-it/ adj placed, occurring or classified between others, or between extremes, limits or stages; (of igneous rocks) between acid and basic in composition; intervening. ◆ n that which is intermediate; any compound manufactured from a primary that serves as a starting material for the synthesis of some other product (chem); a racing-car tyre with tread between that on a slick and a wet tyre; (with cap) in Scotland, (a pass in) an examination more advanced than Standard Grade but less so than Higher. ◆ vi /-di-āt/ to mediate; to act as an agent or go-between. [**inter-**]
■ **intermē'diacy** /-ə-si/ or **intermē'diateness** n the state of being intermediate. **intermē'dial** adj (rare) intermediate; intermediary. **intermē'diary** adj acting as an intermediate; intermediate. ◆ n an intermediate agent. **intermē'diately** adv. **intermēdiā'tion** n the act of intermediating. **intermē'diator** n. **intermē'diatory** /-ə-tə-ri/ adj. **intermē'dium** n (pl **intermē'dia**) an intervening agent or instrument; a small bone in the wrist and ankle.
❑ **intermediate frequency** n (electronics) the output carrier frequency of a frequency changer in a superheterodyne receiver, adjusted to coincide with the frequency band of the intermediate amplifier. **intermediate host** n (zool) an animal that acts as a secondary host to a parasite but in which it does not become sexually mature. **intermediate level waste** n nuclear waste which does not require continuous cooling, as high-level waste does, but does require shielding during storage and transport, unlike low-level waste. **intermediate school** n (NZ) a school for children aged between eleven and thirteen. **intermediate technology** n technology which combines simple, basic materials with modern sophisticated tools and methods. **intermediate vector boson** n (phys) any of three elementary particles (W^+, W^- and Z^0) that carry weak interactions between particles.

interment see under **inter**.

intermetallic /in-tər-mə-tal'ik/ adj (of an alloy or compound) formed from two or more metallic elements. [**inter-**]

intermezzo /in-tər-met'sō, sometimes -med'zō/ n (pl **intermez'zi** /-sē/ or **intermezz'os**) a short dramatic or musical entertainment as entr'acte; a short intermediate movement separating sections of a symphonic work (music). [Ital, from L intermedius]

intermigration /in-tər-mī-grā'shən/ n reciprocal migration. [**inter-**]

interminable /in-tûr'mi-nə-bl/ adj without termination or limit; boundless; endless; tediously long. [**in-** (2)]
■ **inter'minableness** n. **inter'minably** adv.
❑ **interminate decimal** n a decimal fraction that runs to an infinity of places.

intermingle /in-tər-ming'gl/ vt and vi to mingle or mix together. [**inter-**]

in terminis /in tûr'mi-nis/ (L) definitely; in express terms.

intermit /in-tər-mit'/ vt and vi (**intermitt'ing**; **intermitt'ed**) to stop for a time. ◆ vt (obs) to interpose. [L intermittere, -missum, from inter between, and mittere to cause to go]
■ **intermission** /-mish'ən/ n an act of intermitting; an interval; music played during the interval at a theatre, etc; pause; a respite; perh a temporary occupation or recreation (Shakesp). **intermissive** /-mis'iv/ adj coming and going; intermittent. **intermitt'ence** or **intermitt'ency** n. **intermitt'ent** adj intermitting or ceasing at intervals. **intermitt'ently** adv.

intermix /in-tər-miks'/ vt and vi to mix together. [L intermiscēre, -mixtum, from inter among, and miscēre to mix]
■ **intermix'ture** n a mass formed by mixture; something added and intermixed.

intermodal /in-tər-mō'dəl/ adj (of a vehicle, container, system, etc) employing, suitable for, or able to adapt to or be conveyed by, two or more modes of transport. [**inter-**]

intermodulation /in-tər-mod-ū-lā'shən/ (electronics) n unwanted mutual interference between electronic signals, affecting the amplitude of each. [**inter-**]

intermolecular /in-tər-mo-lek'ū-lər/ adj between molecules. [**inter-**]

intermontane /in-tər-mon'tān/ (geol) adj (of a basin) lying between mountain ranges, often associated with a graben. [**inter-**]

intermundane /in-tər-mun'dān/ adj between worlds. [**inter-**]

intermure /in-tər-mūr'/ (obs) vt to wall in. [L inter within, and mūrus a wall]

intern /in'tûrn/ n an inmate, eg of a boarding school; a resident assistant surgeon or physician in a hospital, hence also a trainee gaining practical experience in any profession (also **in'terne**; N Am).

◆ *vi* to serve as an intern. ◆ *vt* /*in-tûrn'*/ to confine to a prescribed area, or imprison (eg an enemy ship or alien, a suspected terrorist), as a precautionary measure. [Fr *interne*, from L *internus* inward]

■ **internee'** *n* a person interned. **intern'ment** *n* confinement of this kind. **in'ternship** *n* (*N Am*) the position or period of being an intern.

internal /*in-tûr'nəl*/ *adj* in the interior; domestic as opposed to foreign; intrinsic; relating to the inner nature or feelings; inner; taking place within, or involving those inside, an organization or institution. ◆ *n* (in *pl*) inner parts. [L *internus*, from *inter* within]

■ **internality** /*-nal'i-ti*/ *n*. **internaliză'tion** or **-s-** *n*. **inter'nalize** or**-ise** *vt* to assimilate (an idea, etc) into one's personality; to withdraw (an emotion, etc) into oneself (rather than express it). **inter'nalized** or **-s-** *adj*. **inter'nally** *adv*.

❏ **internal-combustion engine** *n* an engine in which the fuel is burned within the working cylinder. **internal energy** *n* (*phys*) the kinetic energy of a thermodynamic system due to the energy of its constituent molecules, and the potential energies due to their molecular interactions. **internal evidence** *n* evidence afforded by the thing itself. **internal market** *n* (*business*) a system where semi-autonomous units within an entity behave as though they were competing in a market place within the entity; the single market of the European Union. **internal rhyme** *n* a rhyme occurring within a line of verse. **internal student** *n* one who has studied at the university that examines him or her.

international /*in-tər-nash'ə-nl*/ *adj* between nations or their representatives; transcending national limits; extending to several nations; relating to the relations between nations. ◆ *n* (with *cap*) an international socialist organization, the **First International** formed in London in 1864 with the aim of economic emancipation for the working classes of the world, the **Second International** formed in Paris in 1889 as a successor to it, the **Third International** founded by the Bolsheviks in 1919 to encourage World revolution, the **Fourth International** formed in 1938 as a rival to the Third, by that time dominated by Stalin; a game or contest between players chosen to represent different nations; a player who takes (or has taken) part in an international match. [**inter-**]

■ **Internationale** /*ē̆-ter-na-syŏ-näl'*/ *n* the international communist song, first sung in France in 1871; the Second International. **interna'tionalism** *n*. **interna'tionalist** *n* someone who favours the common interests, or action, of all nations; someone who favours the principles of the International; a player who represents his or her country in international contests; a specialist in international law. **internationalis'tic** *adj*. **international'ity** *n*. **internationaliză'tion** or **-s-** *n*. **interna'tionalize** or **-ise** *vt* to make international; to put under international control. **interna'tionally** *adv*.

❏ **International Atomic Energy Agency** *n* an organization for promoting the peaceful uses of atomic power (*abbrev* **IAEA**). **International Atomic Time** *n* an international standard of time synchronized by atomic clocks (*abbrev* **TAI**). **International Baccalaureate** *n* (a school-leaving examination giving) an international qualification for higher education. **International Bible Students' Association** see **Russellite**. **International Brigade** *n* any of several groups of volunteers raised internationally that fought on the Republican side in the Spanish Civil War. **International Classification of Diseases** *n* a list of all known diseases published by the World Health Organization (*abbrev* **ICD**). **International Confederation of Free Trade Unions** *n* an organization for promoting free trade unionism worldwide, formed in 1949 (*abbrev* **ICFTU**). **International Court of Justice** *n* the World Court. **International Date Line** *n* the line east and west of which the date differs, being the 180th meridian with deviations. **International Development Association** *n* an organization founded in 1960 to lend money at low interest rates to developing countries (*abbrev* **IDA**). **International Finance Corporation** *n* an affiliate of the World Bank that promotes the growth of the private sector in developing countries through loans, etc, founded in 1974 (*abbrev* **IFC**). **International Labour Organization** *n* an agency of the UN, originally founded in 1919 for research and recommendations in labour practices (*abbrev* **ILO**). **international law** *n* the law regulating the relations of states (**public international law**) or that determining which nation's law shall in any case govern the relations of private persons (**private international law**). **international master** *n* (also with *caps*) (a person holding) the second highest international chess title. **international match point** *n* a scoring unit in tournament contract bridge, often shortened to **imp** or **i.m.p. international modern** or **style** *n* a 20c architectural style characterized by the use of modern building materials and techniques, simple geometric shapes and lack of ornament. **International Monetary Fund** *n* an organization, established in 1945 to promote international trade through increased stabilization of currencies, which maintains a pool of money on which member countries can draw (*abbrev* **IMF**). **International Phonetic Alphabet** *n* the alphabet of the International Phonetic Association, a series of symbols representing human speech sounds

(*abbrev* **IPA**). **international** (**concert**) **pitch** *n* since 1939, 440 cycles per second at 20°C for A in the treble clef. **International Space Station** *n* the space station (formerly called 'Freedom') developed by NASA, ESA, Japan and Canada. **international standard atmosphere** *n* a standardized atmosphere adopted internationally for comparing aircraft performance. **international system of units** see **SI**. **International Telecommunication Union** *n* a UN agency promoting international telecommunications collaboration in order to improve worldwide service (*abbrev* **ITU**). **international units** *n pl* internationally recognized units in terms of which pure, or impure, vitamin material can be assayed.

interne see **intern**.

internecine /*in-tər-nē'sīn*/, also **internecive** /*-siv*/ *adj* deadly; murderous; (loosely) mutually destructive; involving conflict within a group. [L *internecīnus*, *-īvus*, from *internecāre*, from *inter* between (used intensively), and *necāre* to kill]

internee see under **intern**.

Internet or **internet** /*in'tər-net*/ *n* an international computer network of digital information linked by telecommunication systems and using a common address procedure (also called **the Net**). [**inter-** and *net*work]

❏ **Internet café** *n* a café or other place where the public can buy access to the Internet (see also **cybercafé**). **Internet of things** *n* a computer network that records physical objects and can be used to monitor the relationships between them. **Internet protocol** *n* (*comput*) a set of rules for transferring packets of data across a network of computers.

interneural /*in-tər-nū'rəl*/ (*anat*) *adj* situated between the neural spines or spinous processes of successive vertebrae. [**inter-**]

interneuron /*in-tər-nū'ron*/ *n* a neuron that connects afferent and efferent neurons in a reflex arc (also **interneu'rone** /*-ōn*/). [**inter-**]

internist /*in-tûr'nist* or *in'tûr-nist*/ *n* a specialist in internal diseases; a physician rather than a surgeon. [*intern*al and **-ist**]

internment see under **intern**.

internode /*in'tər-nōd*/ *n* the space between two nodes, eg in a plant stem or nerve fibre. [L *internōdium*, from *inter* between, and *nōdus* a knot]

■ **internō'dal** or (*obs*) **internō'dial** *adj*.

inter nos /*in'tər* or *-ter nōs*/ (L) between ourselves.

internuncio /*in-tər-nun'shi-ō*/ *n* (*pl* **internun'cios**) a messenger between two parties; the Pope's representative at minor courts. [Ital *internunzio*, Sp *internuncio*, L *internuntius*, from *inter* between, and *nuntius* a messenger]

■ **internun'cial** *adj* relating to an internuncio; interconnecting, as the neurone linking the afferent and efferent neurones of the central nervous system.

interoceanic /*in-tər-ō-shi-an'ik*/ *adj* between oceans. [**inter-**]

interoceptor /*in-tər-ō-sep'tər*/ (*physiol*) *n* a sensory receptor that responds to changes within the body, such as the acidity of the blood. [*interior* and *receptor*]

■ **interocep'tive** *adj*.

interocular /*in-tər-ok'ū-lər*/ *adj* between the eyes. [**inter-**]

interoperable /*in-tər-op'ə-rə-bl*/ (*comput*) *adj* (of hardware or software systems) able to exchange and use information from different computer systems. [**inter-**]

■ **interoperabil'ity** *n*.

interorbital /*in-tər-ör'bi-təl*/ *adj* between orbits. [**inter-**]

interosculation /*in-tər-os-kū-lā'shən*/ *n* interconnection by, or as if by, osculation; possession of characters common to different groups; dovetailing into one another. [**inter-**]

■ **interos'culant** *adj*. **interos'culate** *vt*.

interosseous /*in-tər-os'i-əs*/ *adj* situated between bones (also **inteross'eal**). [**inter-**]

interpage /*in-tər-pāj'*/ *vt* to print on intermediate pages; to insert (intervening pages). [**inter-**]

interparietal /*in-tər-pə-rī'ə-təl*/ *adj* situated between the right and left parietal bones of the skull. [**inter-**]

inter partes /*in'tər* or *-ter pär'tēz* or *pär'tās*/ (L; *law*) between parties.

interpellation /*in-tər-pe-lā'shən*/ *n* a question raised during the course of a debate, *esp* in parliament; interruption (*obs*); intercession (*obs*); a summons (*obs*). [Fr, from L *interpellāre*, *-ātum* to disturb by speaking, from *inter* between, and *pellere* to drive]

■ **interpell'ant** *adj* causing an interpellation. ◆ *n* a person who interpellates. **inter'pellate** (or /*-pel'*/) *vt* to question by interpellation. **inter'pellātor** *n*.

interpenetrate /*in-tər-pen'i-trāt*/ *vt* to penetrate thoroughly; to pervade. ◆ *vt* and *vi* to penetrate each other. [**inter-**]

■ **interpen'etrable** *adj*. **interpen'etrant** *adj*. **interpenetrā'tion** *n*. **interpen'etrātive** *adj*.

interpersonal /*in-tər-pûr'sə-nəl*/ *adj* between persons. [**inter-**]
■ **interper'sonally** *adv*.

interpetiolar /*in-tər-pet'i-ō-lər*/ (*bot*) *adj* between petioles. [**inter-**]

interphase /*in'tər-fāz*/ *n* an interface (*chem*); the period of the cell cycle between one mitosis and the next (also **interkinesis**; *biol*). [**inter-**]

interphone /*in'tər-fōn*/ *n* an intercom. [Gr *phōnē* voice]

interpilaster /*in-tər-pi-las'tər*/ (*archit*) *n* a space between two pilasters. [**inter-**]

interplanetary /*in-tər-plan'i-tə-ri*/ *adj* between planets. [**inter-**]
❑ **interplanetary matter** *n* matter other than planets and their satellites, eg dust particles and gas.

interplant /*in-tər-plänt'*/ *vt* to plant among another crop; to plant (land) with a combination of crops. [**inter-**]

interplay /*in'tər-plā*/ *n* mutual action; interchange of action and reaction. [**inter-**]

interplead /*in-tər-plēd'*/ (*law*) *vi* to discuss adverse claims to property by bill of interpleader. [**inter-**]
■ **interplead'er** *n* a person who interpleads; a form of process in the English courts, by a bill in equity, intended to protect a defendant who claims no interest in the subject matter of a suit, but has reason to know that the plaintiff's title is disputed by some other claimant.

interpleural /*in-tər-ploo'rəl*/ *adj* situated between the right and left pleural cavities. [**inter-**]

inter pocula /*in'tər* or -*ter pok'ū-lə* or *pō'kŭ-la*/ (*L*) literally, over one's cups, hence, in the course of drinking, over drinks.

Interpol /*in'tər-pol*/, the *International Criminal Police* Commission, directed to international co-operation in the suppression of crime.

interpolable see under **interpolate**.

interpolar /*in-tər-pō'lər*/ *adj* between or connecting the poles. [**inter-**]

interpolate /*in-tûr'pō-lāt* or -*pə-lāt*/ *vt* to insert a word or passage in a book or manuscript, *esp* in order to mislead; to tamper with or to corrupt by spurious insertions; to insert, interpose, interject; to fill in as an intermediate term of a series (*maths*). [L *interpolāre*, -*ātum*, from *inter* between, and *polīre* to polish]
■ **inter'polable** *adj*. **interpolā'tion** *n*. **inter'polātive** *adj*. **inter'polātor** or **inter'polater** *n* someone who or something that interpolates; an apparatus for regenerating and retransmitting signals (*telecom*).

interpone /*in-tər-pōn'*/ (*Scots law*) *vt* to interpose. [L *interpōnere*]

interpose /*in-tər-pōz'*/ *vt* to place between; to thrust in; to offer (eg aid or services); to put in by way of interruption. ◆ *vi* to come between; to mediate; to interfere. [Fr *interposer*, from L *inter* between, and Fr *poser* to place; see **pose**[1]]
■ **interpos'al** *n*. **interpos'er** *n*. **interposition** /*in-tər-poz-ish'ən*/ *n* the act of interposing; intervention; mediation; the right of a state to oppose the federal government for encroachment on the prerogatives of the state (*US*); anything interposed.

interpret /*in-tûr'prit*/ *vt* to explain the meaning of, to elucidate, unfold, show the significance of; to translate into intelligible or familiar terms. ◆ *vi* to practise interpretation. [L *interpretārī*, -*ātus*, from *interpres*, -*etis*]
■ **interpretabil'ity** *n*. **inter'pretable** *adj* capable of being explained. **inter'pretate** *vt* and *vi* (*archaic*). **interpretā'tion** *n* the act of interpreting; the sense given by an interpreter; the representation of a dramatic part, performance of a piece of music, etc, according to one's conception of it. **interpretā'tional** *adj*. **inter'pretative** /-*āt-iv* or -*ət-iv*/ or **inter'pretive** *adj* inferred by or containing interpretation. **inter'pretatively** or **inter'pretively** *adv*. **inter'preter** *n* a person who translates orally for the benefit of two or more parties speaking different languages; an expounder; an obsolete machine that prints out information held on a punched card (*comput*); a program which translates and executes a source program one statement at a time (*comput*; cf **compiler**); a translator of written texts (*obs*). **inter'pretership** *n*. **inter'pretress** or (*obs*) **inter'pretess** *n* a female interpreter.
❑ **interpretive centre** *n* a place where visitors to a site of historical or natural interest may find explanatory material about it.

interprovincial /*in-tər-prə-vin'shl*/ *adj* between provinces. [**inter-**]

interproximal /*in-tər-prok'si-məl*/ (*dentistry*) *adj* relating to the surfaces of teeth where they adjoin. [**inter-**]

interpunction /*in-tər-pungk'shən*/ *n* the insertion of punctuation marks in writing (also **interpunctuā'tion**). [**inter-**]
■ **interpunc'tūate** *vt*.

interquartile /*in-tər-kwör'tīl*/ (*stats*) *adj* of or relating to the difference between quartile values in a frequency distribution. [**inter-**]

interracial /*in-tər-rā'shəl* or -*shi-əl*/ *adj* between races. [**inter-**]
■ **interrā'cially** *adv*.

interradial /*in-tər-rā'di-əl*/ *adj* between radii or rays; of or relating to an interradius. [**inter-**]
■ **interrā'dially** *adv*. **interrā'dius** *n* an interradial part; a radius midway between primary radii or perradii.

interrail /*in'tər-rāl*/ *vi* to travel by train through European countries using an **interrail pass**, which allows unlimited travel for a specified time.
■ **in'terrailer** *n*.

interramal /*in-tər-rā'məl*/ *adj* situated between the rami or branches, *esp* of the lower jaw. [L *inter* between, and *rāmus* a branch]
■ **interramificā'tion** /-*ram-*/ *n* interweaving of branches.

interregal /*in-tər-rē'gəl*/ *adj* between kings. [**inter-**]

interregnum /*in-tər-reg'nəm*/ *n* (*pl* **interreg'na** or **interreg'nums**) the time between two reigns; the time between the cessation of one and the establishment of another government; any breach of continuity in order, etc. [L *inter* between, and *regnum* rule]

interrelation /*in-tər-ri-lā'shən*/ *n* reciprocal relation. [**inter-**]
■ **interrela'te** *vt* and *vi*. **interrela'ted** *adj*. **interrelā'tionship** *n*.

interrex /*in'tər-reks*/ *n* (*pl* **interreges** /-*rē'jēz*/) someone who rules during an interregnum; a regent. [L *inter* between, and *rēx* a king]

interrog. *abbrev* : interrogate; interrogation; interrogative; interrogatively.

interrogate /*in-ter'ə-gāt*/ *vt* to question; to examine by asking questions; to transmit a request to a device or program (*comput*); (of a radar set, etc) to send out signals to (a radio-beacon) in order to ascertain position. ◆ *vi* to ask questions. [L *interrogāre*, -*ātum*, from *inter* between, and *rogāre* to ask]
■ **interr'ogable** *adj*. **interr'ogant** *n* a questioner. **interrogatee'** *n* someone who is interrogated. **interrogā'tion** *n* the act of interrogating; a question put; the mark (?) placed after a question (also **interrogation mark** or **point**). **interrogā'tional** *adj*. **interrogative** /*in-tər-og'ə-tiv*/ *adj* denoting a question; expressed as a question. ◆ *n* a word used in asking a question. **interrog'atively** *adv*. **interr'ogator** *n*. **interrog'atory** *n* a question or inquiry. ◆ *adj* expressing a question.

in terrorem /*in te-rō'rem* or -*rō'*/ (*L*) as a warning.

interrupt /*in-tər-upt'*/ *vt* to break in between; to stop or hinder by breaking in upon; to break continuity in. ◆ *vi* to make an interruption. ◆ *adj* interrupted (*obs*); gaping apart (*Milton*). ◆ *n* (*comput*) a signal that causes a break in the current routine, control passing to another routine in such a way that the original one may later be resumed. [L *interrumpere*, -*ruptum*, from *inter* between, and *rumpere* to break]
■ **interrupt'ed** *adj* broken in continuity; irregular in spacing or size of parts (*biol*). **interrupt'edly** *adv* with interruptions; irregularly. **interrup'ter** or **interrup'tor** *n* a person who interrupts; an apparatus for interrupting, eg for breaking an electric circuit. **interrup'tible** *adj*. **interrup'tion** *n* the act of interrupting; hindrance; temporary cessation. **interrup'tive** *adj* tending to interrupt. **interrup'tively** *adv*.
❑ **interrupted cadence** *n* (*music*) a cadence in which some other chord (often the submediant) replaces the expected tonic.

interscapular /*in-tər-skap'ū-lər*/ (*anat*) *adj* between the shoulder blades. [**inter-**]

interscholastic /*in-tər-skə-las'tik*/ *adj* between schools; representative of several schools. [**inter-**]

inter-science /*in-tər-sī'əns*/ *adj* belonging to the examination between matriculation and BSc of London University. [**inter-**]

interscribe /*in-tər-skrīb'*/ (*obs*) *vt* to write between. [L *interscrībere*, from *inter* between, and *scrībere* to write]

inter se /*in'tər* or -*ter sē* or *sā*/ (*L*) between or among themselves.

intersect /*in-tər-sekt'*/ *vt* to cut across; to cut or cross mutually; to divide into parts. ◆ *vi* to cross each other. ◆ *n* /*in'*/ a point of intersection. [L *inter* between, and *secāre*, *sectum* to cut]
■ **intersec'tion** *n* intersecting; the point or line on which lines or surfaces cut each other (*geom*); the set of elements which two or more sets have in common (*maths*); a crossroads. **intersec'tional** *adj*.

interseptal /*in-tər-sep'tl*/ *adj* between septa. [**inter-**]

intersert /*in-tər-sûrt'*/ *vt* (*obs*) to insert between other things, interpolate. [L *interserere*, -*sertum* to interpose, from *inter* between, and *serere* to plant]
■ **intersert'al** *adj* (*petrology*) having interstitial crystalline or glassy matter between feldspar laths.

interservice /*in-tər-sûr'vis*/ *adj* between the armed forces. [**inter-**]

intersex /*in'tər-seks*/ (*biol*) *n* an individual developing anatomical characteristics of both sexes; the condition of being intersexual. [**inter-**]
■ **intersex'ūal** *adj* between the sexes; intermediate between the sexes; relating to an intersex. **intersexūal'ity** *n*.

intersidereal /*in-tər-sī-dē'ri-əl*/ (*rare*) *adj* interstellar. [**inter-**]

interspace /in'tər-spās/ n an interval. ◆ vt /-spās'/ to put intervals between. [**inter-**]
■ **interspatial** /-spā'shl/ adj. **interspa'tially** adv.

interspecific /in-tər-spi-sif'ik/ adj between species. [**inter-**]

intersperse /in-tər-spûrs'/ vt to scatter or set here and there; to diversify. [L interspergere, -spersum, from inter among, and spargere to scatter]
■ **interspers'al** n (rare). **interspersion** /-spûr'shən/ n.

interspinal /in-tər-spī'nəl/ adj between the vertebrae (also **interspī'nous**). [**inter-**]

interstadial /in-tər-stā'di-əl/ (geol) n a retreat of ice during a glacial period, less extensive than an interglacial. ◆ adj of or relating to an interstadial.

interstate /in'tər-stāt or -stāt'/ adj relating to relations, esp political and commercial, between states; between or involving two or more states. ◆ adv (Aust) into or to another state. ◆ n (US) /in'/ an interstate highway. [**inter-**]

interstellar /in-tər-stel'ər/, also **interstellary** /-ə-ri/ adj beyond the solar system or among the stars; in the intervals between the stars. [L inter between, and stella a star]

interstice /in-tûr'stis/ n a small space between things closely set, or between the parts which compose a body; the time interval required by canon law before receiving higher orders (RC); a space between atoms in a lattice where other atoms can be located. [L interstitium, from inter between, and sistere, statum to stand, set]
■ **interstitial** /-stish'l/ adj occurring in an interstice or interstices; containing interstitial atoms or ions (chem); relating to the surfaces of teeth where they adjoin (dentistry); an extra atom in a crystal lattice, causing a defect. **interstit'ially** adv.
❑ **interstitial cells** n pl (anat) the cells between the seminiferous tubules of the testis, that secrete androgens.

interstratification /in-tər-strat-i-fi-kā'shən/ n the state of lying between, or alternating with, other strata. [**inter-**]
■ **interstrat'ified** adj. **interstrat'ify** vt and vi.

intersubjective /in-tər-sub-jek'tiv or -səb-/ adj between subjects; between points of view. [**inter-**]
■ **intersubjec'tively** adv. **intersubjectiv'ity** n.

interswitchboard line /in-tər-swich'bōrd or -bôrd līn/ (telecom) n same as **tie line** (see under **tie¹**).

intertangle /in-tər-tang'gl/ vt and vi to tangle together. [**inter-**]
■ **intertang'lement** n.

intertarsal /in-tər-tär'sl/ (anat) adj between tarsal bones. [**inter-**]

intertentacular /in-tər-ten-tak'ū-lər/ adj between tentacles. [**inter-**]

interterritorial /in-tər-ter-i-tō'ri-əl or -tö'/ adj between territories. [**inter-**]

intertext /in'tər-tekst/ n in literary theory, a text evaluated in terms of its explicit relation (eg by allusion) to other texts. [**inter-**]
■ **intertext'ual** adj. **intertextual'ity** n. **intertext'ualize** or **-ise** vi and vt.

intertexture /in-tər-teks'chər/ n interwoven state. [**inter-**]

intertidal /in-tər-tī'dl/ adj between low-water and high-water mark. [**inter-**]

intertie /in'tər-tī/ n (in roofing, etc) a short timber binding together upright posts. [**inter-**]

intertissued /in-tər-tish'ūd/ adj interwoven (also (Shakesp) **entertiss'ued**). [**inter-**]

intertitle /in'tər-tī-tl/ n (usu in pl) text appearing between scenes or episodes in a film or television programme. [**inter-**]

intertraffic /in-tər-traf'ik/ (obs) n traffic between two or more people or places. [**inter-**]

intertribal /in-tər-trī'bl/ adj between tribes; involving more than one tribe. [**inter-**]

intertrigo /in-tər-trī'gō/ n (pl **intertri'gos**) an inflammation of the skin from chafing or rubbing. [L intertrīgō, from inter between, and terere, trītum to rub]

intertropical /in-tər-trop'i-kl/ adj between the tropics. [**inter-**]
❑ **intertropical convergence zone** n an area of converging trade winds near the equator.

intertwine /in-tər-twīn'/ vt and vi to twine or twist together. ◆ n /in'/ an instance of intertwining. [**inter-**]
■ **intertwine'ment** n. **intertwīn'ing** n and adj. **intertwīn'ingly** adv.

intertwist /in-tər-twist'/ vt to twist together. [**inter-**]
■ **intertwist'ingly** adv.

interunion /in-tər-ū'nyən/ n a blending together. [**inter-**]

interurban /in-tər-ûr'bən/ adj between cities. [L inter between, and urbs, urbis a city]

interval /in'tər-vəl/ n time or space between; a break between acts of a play, parts of a sports match, etc; difference of pitch between any two musical tones (music); a set of real numbers or points between two given numbers or points (maths). [L intervallum, from inter between, and vallum a rampart]
■ **intervallic** /-val'ik/ adj. **intervalom'eter** n (photog) a device for operating the shutter at set intervals.
❑ **interval training** n alternate fast and slow running at measured intervals in one session, done as training work for marathons and other long-distance races.
■ **at intervals** periodically; with prescribed spaces between.

intervale /in'tər-vāl/ (US) n a low level tract of land along a river. [**inter-**]

intervallum /in-tər-val'əm/ adj (of fortifications, etc) between the ramparts. ◆ n (obs) an interval. [Ety as for **interval**]

intervein /in-tər-vān'/ vt to intersect, as with veins. [**inter-**]

intervene /in-tər-vēn'/ vi to come or be between; to occur between points of time; to interrupt; to step in so as to affect the outcome of a situation; to interpose in an action to which one was not at first a party (law). ◆ vt (obs) to separate. [L inter between, and venīre to come]
■ **interven'er** n a person who intervenes (also (law) **interven'or**). **intervenient** /-vē'ni-ənt/ adj (archaic) being or passing between, intervening. **interven'ing** adj coming in between. **intervention** /-ven'shən/ n intervening; interference; mediation; interposition; a system of removing surplus produce from the market and storing it until prices rise. **interven'tional** adj. **interven'tionism** n. **interven'tionist** n someone who advocates interference, esp by a government in economic matters, or in the affairs of a foreign government (also adj). **interven'tor** n a mediator in ecclesiastical controversies.
❑ **intervening sequence** n (biol) an intron. **intervention price** n the market price at which intervention occurs. **intervention stock** n the total stock of surplus produce removed from the market by intervention.

intervertebral /in-tər-vûr'ti-brəl/ adj between vertebrae. [**inter-**]
❑ **intervertebral disc** n a disc of cartilage separating individual vertebrae.

interview /in'tər-vū/ n a formal meeting; a meeting between an employer, board of directors, etc and a candidate to ascertain by questioning and discussion the latter's suitability for a post, etc; a meeting between a journalist, or radio or TV broadcaster, and a notable person to discuss the latter's views, etc for publication or broadcasting; an article or programme based on such a meeting; a mutual view or sight (obs). ◆ vt and vi to conduct an interview (with). [OFr entrevue, from entre between, and voir to see]
■ **interviewee'** n a person who is interviewed. **in'terviewer** n a person who interviews.

intervital /in-tər-vī'tal/ adj between lives, between death and resurrection. [L inter between, and vīta life]

inter vivos /in'tər or -ter vī'vōs or wē'wōs/ (L; law) from one living person to another, among the living.

intervocalic /in-tər-vō-kal'ik/ adj between vowels. [**inter-**]
■ **intervocal'ically** adv.

intervolve /in-tər-volv'/ vt and vi to entwine or roll up one with or within another. [L inter within, and volvere to roll]

interwar /in-tər-wör'/ adj between wars. [**inter-**]

interweave /in-tər-wēv'/ vt and vi to weave together; to intermingle. [**inter-**]

Interweb /in'tər-web/ n (facetious) Internet.

interwind /in-tər-wīnd'/ vt and vi (pat and pap **interwound** /-wownd'/) to wind together or around and among one another. [**inter-**]

interwork /in-tər-wûrk'/ vt and vi to work together; to work into another or one another. [**inter-**]
■ **interwrought** /-röt'/ adj.

interwreathe /in-tər-rēdh'/ vt to wreathe together or into one another. [**inter-**]

interzone /in-tər-zōn'/ or **interzonal** /-zō'nəl/ adj between zones (eg of occupied country). [**inter-**]
■ **in'terzone** n.

intestate /in-tes'tāt or -tit/ adj dying without having made a valid will; (of property) not disposed of by will. ◆ n a person who dies without making a valid will. [L intestātus, from in- not, and testārī, -ātus to make a will]
■ **intes'tacy** /-tə-si/ n the state of someone dying without having made a valid will.

intestine /in-tes'tin/ n (commonly in pl) a part of the digestive system extending from the stomach to the anus, divided into the **small intestine** (comprising duodenum, jejunum and ileum) and the **large intestine** (comprising caecum, colon and rectum). [L intestīnus, from intus within]

■ **intes'tinal** (also /-tīn'/) *adj* relating to the intestines.
❑ **intestinal flora** *n* bacteria normally present in the intestine.

inthral, inthrall see **enthral**.

inti /in'ti/ *n* a former unit of currency in Peru. [Quechua]

intifada /in-ti-fä'də/ *n* the uprising in 1987 and continued resistance by Palestinians to Israeli occupation of the Gaza Strip and West Bank of the Jordan. [Ar, shaking off]

intil /in-til'/ (*Scot*) *prep* into, in, or unto. [**in** and **till**[1]]

intima /in'ti-mə/ (*anat*) *n* (*pl* **in'timae** /-mē/) the innermost coat or membrane of an organ or part, *esp* a blood or lymphatic vessel. [L, short for *tunica intima* innermost coat]
■ **in'timal** *adj*.

intimate /in'ti-mit or -māt/ *adj* innermost; internal; close; deep-seated; private; personal; closely acquainted; familiar; in a sexual relationship; engaging in sex; encouraging informality and closer personal relations through smallness, exclusiveness. ◆ *n* a close friend. ◆ *vt* /-māt/ to hint; to announce. [L *intimāre, -ātum*, from *intimus* innermost, from *intus* within]
■ **in'timacy** /-mə-si/ *n* the state of being intimate; close familiarity; an intimate remark; sexual intercourse. **in'timately** *adv*. **intimā'tion** *n* an indication; a hint; an announcement. **intim'ity** *n* (*archaic*) intimacy.

intime /ɛ̃-tēm'/ *adj* intimate; small and cosy. [Fr]

intimidate /in-tim'i-dāt/ *vt* to strike fear into; to influence by threats or violence. [L *in* into, and *timidus* fearful]
■ **intim'idating** *adj*. **intimidā'tion** *n* the act of intimidating; the use of violence or threats to influence the conduct or compel the consent of another; the state of being intimidated. **intim'idator** *n*. **intim'idatory** *adj*.

intimism /in'ti-mi-zm/ *n* a genre of French impressionist painting of the early 20c, based on subject matter from everyday life. [Fr *intime* ; see ety for **intimate**]
■ **in'timist** (Fr *intimiste* /ɛ̃-tē-mēst/) *n* and *adj*.

intinction /in-tingk'shən/ (*Christianity*) *n* a mode of administering communion by dipping the bread into the wine. [LL *intinctiō, -ōnis*, from L *intingere, intinctum* to dip in]

intine /in'tin, -tēn or -tīn/ (*bot*) *n* the inner membrane of a pollen grain or spore. [L *intus* within]

intire /in-tīr'/ an obsolete form of **entire**.

intitule /in-tit'ūl/ *vt* same as **entitle**, now used only to mean give a title to (a Parliamentary Act, etc). [OFr *intituler*, from L *titulus* title]

into /in'tŭ/ *prep* to a position within; to a state of; used to indicate the dividend in dividing (*maths*); in contact or collision with; interested in or enthusiastic about (*inf*); to part of (*maths*). ◆ *adj* (*maths*) describing a mapping of one set to a second set, involving only some of the elements of the latter. [**in** and **to**]
■ **multiply into** (*rare*) to multiply (one quantity) by (another quantity) to find the product.

intoed or **in-toed** /in'tōd/ *adj* having the toes more or less turned inwards. [**in-** (1)]

intolerable /in-tol'ə-rə-bl/ *adj* too bad, severe, etc to be tolerated; insufferable. [**in-** (2)]
■ **intolerabil'ity** or **intol'erableness** *n*. **intol'erably** *adv*. **intol'erance** *n* the state of being intolerant; inability to tolerate, *esp* a drug. **intol'erant** *adj* not able or willing to endure; not accepting opinions different from one's own; persecuting; easily irritated or angered by the faults of others. ◆ *n* someone opposed to toleration. **intol'erantly** *adv*. **intolera'tion** *n*.

intomb /in-toom'/ obsolete form of **entomb**.

intonaco /in-tō'nə-kō/ (*Ital*) *n* in fresco painting, the finishing coat of lime plaster on which the paint is applied.

intonate[1] /in'tō-nāt or -tə-/ *vt* and *vi* to intone. [LL *intonāre, -ātum*, from L *in* in, and *tonus* tone]
■ **intonā'tion** *n* modulation or rise and fall in pitch of the voice; the opening phrase of any plainsong melody, sung *usu* either by the officiating priest alone, or by one or more selected choristers; pitching of musical notes; intoning. **intonā'tional** *adj*. **in'tonātor** *n* a monochord. **intone** /in-tōn'/ *vt* and *vi* to chant, read or utter in musical tones, singsong, or monotone; to begin by singing the opening phrase; to utter with a particular intonation. **intōn'er** *n*. **intōn'ing** *n* and *adj*. **intōn'ingly** *adv*.

intonate[2] /in'tō-nāt/ (*obs*) *vt* and *vi* to thunder. [L *intonāre, -ātum* to thunder; cf **intonate**[1]]

intorsion or **intortion** /in-tör'shən/ *n* a twist; a twine. [Fr *intorsion*, L *intortiō, -ōnis*, from *in* in, and *torquēre, tortum* to twist]
■ **intort'ed** *adj* twisted inwards; involved.

in totidem verbis /in tō'ti-dem ver'bēs or wer'bēs/ (*L*) in so many words.

in toto /in tō'tō/ (*L*) entirely.

intown /in'toon/ (*Scot*) *adj* infield, near the farmhouse. [**in** and **town**]
❑ **intown multure** *n* (*hist*) payment to the miller by those who are compelled to have their grain ground at the mill.

intoxicate /in-tok'si-kāt/ *vt* to make drunk; to excite to enthusiasm or madness; to elate excessively; to poison (*obs*). [LL *intoxicāre, -ātum*, from *in* in, and *toxicum*, from Gr *toxikon* arrow-poison, from *toxon* a bow]
■ **intox'icant** *adj* intoxicating. ◆ *n* an intoxicating agent. **intox'icating** *adj*. **intox'icatingly** *adv*. **intoxicā'tion** *n* poisoning (*med*); the state of being drunk; high excitement or elation.

Intoximeter® /in-tok'si-mē-tər/ (also without *cap*) *n* a device for measuring the amount of alcohol in the blood of a person who breathes into it, and showing this measurement on a printout.

intra /in'trə or in'trä/ (*L*) within.
■ **intra muros** /mū'rōs or moo'rōs/ within the walls. **intra vires** /vī'rēz, wē' or vē'rās/ within the legal power of. **intra vitam** /vē'tam, vī'tam or wē'täm/ during life.

intra- /in-trä- or -trə-/ *pfx* signifying within. [L *intrā* within]
■ **intra-abdom'inal** *adj* situated within the cavity of the abdomen. **intra-arté'rial** *adj* within an artery. **intra-artic'ular** *adj* in or within a joint. **intracap'sular** *adj* lying within a capsule. **intracar'diac** *adj* within the heart. **intracav'itary** *adj* (*radiol*) applied within or through body cavities, as radium applied in the uterus, or irradiation through natural or artificial body cavities. **intracell'ular** *adj* inside a cell or cells. **intracrā'nial** *adj* within the skull. **intraderm'al** *adj* within, or introduced into the skin. **intrafallō'pian** *adj* within, or introduced into, (either of) the Fallopian tubes. **intramed'ullary** *adj* within the bone marrow. **intramercū'rial** *adj* within Mercury's orbit. **intramolec'ūlar** *adj* within the limits of the molecule; formed by a reaction between different parts of a molecule. **intramun'dane** *adj* within the world. **intramū'ral** *adj* within walls; taking place within, or between groups within, a single (*esp* educational) establishment or institution; within the scope of normal studies. **intramū'rally** *adv*. **intramus'cular** *adj* within a muscle. **intramus'cularly** *adv*. **intranat'ional** *adj* within a nation. **in'tranet** *n* (*comput*) a website that can only be accessed by clients of its host computer, eg within a company. **intraoc'ular** *adj* within the eye. **intraparī'etal** *adj* within walls, private; situated in the parietal lobe of the brain. **intrapet'iolar** *adj* between petiole and stem. **intrasex'ual** *adj* within or between members of the same sex. **intraspecif'ic** *adj* between members of a species. **intraterritō'rial** *adj* within a territory. **intrathē'cal** *adj* within, or introduced into, the sheath of the spinal cord or brain. **intrathē'cally** *adv*. **intravas'cular** *adj* within the blood vessels. **intravē'nous** *adj* within, or introduced into, a vein or veins. **intravē'nously** *adv*. **intrazō'nal** *adj* (of a soil) having a well-developed profile within it.

intractable /in-trak'tə-bl/ *adj* unmanageable; obstinate. [**in-** (2)]
■ **intractabil'ity** or **intract'ableness** *n*. **intract'ably** *adv*.

intrada /in-trä'də/ (*music*) *n* an introductory piece, prelude. [Ital]

intradermal see under **intra-**.

intrados /in-trä'dos/ (*archit*) *n* (*pl* **intra'dos** or **intra'doses**) the soffit or undersurface of an arch or vault. [Fr, from L *intrā* within, and *dorsum* the back]

intrafallopian...to...**intranet** see under **intra-**.

intrans. *abbrev* : intransitive.

in trans. *abbrev* : *in transitu* (*L*), in transit.

intransigent, also (*rare*) **intransigeant** /in-tran'si-jənt, -trän' or -zi-/ *adj* refusing to come to any understanding, irreconcilable; obstinate. ◆ *n* an intransigent person. [Fr *intransigeant*, from Sp *intransigente*, from L *in-* not, and *transigēns, -entis* prp of *transigere* to transact; see **transact**]
■ **intran'sigence** or **intran'sigency** *n*. **intran'sigentism** *n*. **intran'sigentist** *n*. **intran'sigently** *adv*. —Also (now *rare*) **intransigeance, intransigeancy**, etc.

intransitive /in-tran'si-tiv, -trän' or -zi-/ *adj* representing action confined to the subject of the verb, ie having no object (*grammar*); not passing over or indicating passing over. ◆ *n* an intransitive verb. [**in-** (2)]
■ **intran'sitively** *adv*. **intransitiv'ity** *n*.

in transitu /in tran' or trän'si-too/ (*L*) in passage, in transit, on the way.

intransmissible /in-trans-mis'i-bl, -tranz- or -tränz-/ *adj* that cannot be transmitted. [**in-** (2)]

intransmutable /in-trans-mū'tə-bl, -tranz- or -tränz-/ *adj* that cannot be changed into another substance. [**in-** (2)]
■ **intransmutabil'ity** *n*.

intrant /in'trənt/ adj entering; penetrating. ◆ n a person who enters, esp on membership, office or possession. [L intrāns, -antis, from intrāre to enter]

intraocular...to...**intrapetiolar** see under **intra-**.

intrapreneur /in-trə-prə-nœr'/ n a person who initiates commercial ventures within a large organization. [**intra-** and entre*preneur*]
■ **intrapreneur'ial** adj.

intrasexual...to...**intrathecal** see under **intra-**.

intrauterine /in-trə-ū'tə-rīn/ adj within the uterus. [**intra-**]
❑ **intrauterine contraceptive device** see **IUCD**.

intravasation /in-tra-və-zā'shən/ n the entrance of extraneous matter into blood or lymph vessels. [L intrā within, and vās a vessel]

intravascular and **intravenous** see under **intra-**.

intra vires and **intra vitam** see under **intra**.

intrazonal see under **intra-**.

intreat /in-trēt'/ archaic form of **entreat**, etc.

intrench and **intrenchment** see **entrench**.

intrenchant /in-tren'shənt or -tren'chənt/ (Shakesp) adj not able to be cut or wounded, indivisible. [**in-** (2)]

intrepid /in-trep'id/ adj without trepidation or fear; undaunted; brave. [L intrepidus, from in- not, and trepidus alarmed]
■ **intrepid'ity** n firm, unshaken courage; daring. **intrep'idly** adv.

intricate /in'tri-kit or -kāt (also -trik'it)/ adj involved; entangled; complex. [L intrīcātus, from in- in, and trīcāre to make difficulties, from trīcae hindrances]
■ **in'tricacy** /-kə-si (also -trik')/ or **in'tricateness** n. **in'tricately** adv.

intrigue /in'trēg/ n indirect or underhand scheming or plotting; a private scheme; the plot of a play or romance; a secret illicit love affair; beguilement. ◆ vi /-treg'/ to engage in intrigue. ◆ vt to puzzle, to fascinate. [Fr; see **intricate**]
■ **intrigant** or **intriguant** /in'tri-gant or ē-trē-gã/ n (archaic) a person who intrigues (also adj). **in'trigante** or **in'triguante** n a female intrigant (also adj). **intrigu'er** n. **intrigu'ing** adj. **intrigu'ingly** adv.

intrince /in-trins'/ (Shakesp) adj intricate. [See **intrinsicate**]

intrinsic /in-trin'sik/ or **intrinsical** /-əl/ adj inward; genuine; inherent; essential, belonging to the point at issue; (of muscles) entirely contained within the limb and girdle. [Fr intrinsèque, from L intrīnsecus, from intrā within, sfx -in, and secus following]
■ **intrinsicality** /-əl'i-ti/ n (rare). **intrin'sically** adv. **intrin'sicalness** n (rare).
❑ **intrinsic factor** n a protein secreted in the stomach, essential in the absorption of vitamin B$_{12}$.

intrinsicate /in-trin'si-kāt/ (Shakesp) adj intricate. [Apparently Ital intrinsecato familiar, confused with **intricate**]

intro /in'trō/ (inf) n (pl **in'tros**) contraction of **introduction**, used esp of the opening passage of a jazz or popular music piece.

intro- /in'trō- or in-tro-/ pfx within, into. [L intrō]

introd. abbrev : introduction.

introduce /in-trə-dūs'/ vt to bring in, establish; to conduct into a place; to put in, add, insert or inject; formally to make known or acquainted; to give (a person) his or her first experience of, to acquaint with (with to); to preface; to present to an audience (eg a radio broadcast, a theatre entertainment). [L intrōdūcere, -ductum, from intrō inward, and dūcere to lead]
■ **introduc'er** n. **introduc'ible** adj. **introduction** /-duk'shən/ n (an) act of introducing; formal presentation; preliminary matter serving to introduce the text of a book; a preliminary passage or section leading up to a movement (music); a text serving to acquaint the reader with the fundamental principles of a subject or course of study; something introduced. **introductive** /-duk'tiv/ adj promoting introduction. **introduc'torily** adv. **introduc'tory** adj serving to introduce; preliminary; prefatory.

introgression /in-trə-gresh'ən/ n the introduction of the genes of one species into another species. [L intrō inwards, and pap of gradī to step]

introit /in-trō'it, in' or -troit/ n the anthem sung at the beginning of Mass, immediately after the Confiteor, and when the priest has ascended to the altar (RC); in other churches, an introductory hymn, psalm or anthem. [L introitus, from introīre, from intrō inwards, and īre, itum to go]
■ **intrō'itus** n an entrance to a cavity or hollow organ, eg the vagina (anat); an introit.

introjection /in-trō-jek'shən/ n the endowment of inanimate objects with the attributes of living creatures; the taking into the self of persons or things from the outer world so as to experience a oneness with them and to feel personally touched by their fate; the process of believing one possesses the qualities of another person (psychol). [L intrō within, and jacere to throw]
■ **introject'** vt and vi.

introld see **entrold**.

intromit /in-trō-mit' or -trə-/ vt (**intromitt'ing**; **intromitt'ed**) to introduce; to admit; to permit to enter; to insert. ◆ vi to deal with the effects of another (esp Scots law); to have dealings (Scots). [L intrō inward, and mittere, missum to send]
■ **intromission** /-mish'ən/ n introduction; insertion; in Scots law, the assumption of authority to deal with another's property (**legal intromission**, where the party is expressly or impliedly authorized to interfere, **vicious intromission**, where an heir or next of kin, without any authority, interferes with a deceased person's estate); the proceeds of such interference. **intromiss'ive** adj relating to intromission; intromitting. **intromitt'ent** adj intromitting; adapted for insertion, esp (zool) in copulation. **intromitt'er** n.

intron /in'tron/ (biol) n any of the sequences of a eukaryotic gene that do not carry coded information for the peptide sequence of proteins (also known as **intervening sequence**; cf exon[1]). [Perh intervening sequence and -on as in **codon** and **exon**[1]]

introrse /in-trörs'/ adj turned or facing inward; (of an anther) opening towards the centre of the flower. [L introrsus toward the middle, inward, from intrō inward, and versus, from vertere to turn]
■ **introrse'ly** adv.

introspection /in-trō-spek'shən or -trə/ n the observation and analysis of the processes of one's own mind; a viewing of the inside or interior. [L intrō within, and specere to look at]
■ **introspect'** vi to practise introspection. **introspec'tionist** n. **introspec'tive** adj. **introspec'tively** adv. **introspec'tiveness** n.

introsusception /in-trō-sə-sep'shən/ n intussusception. [L intrō inwards]

introvert /in-trō-vûrt' or -trə-/ vt to turn inwards; to turn in upon itself; to turn inside out; to withdraw part within the rest of. ◆ n /in'/ anything introverted; a person interested mainly in his or her own inner states and processes rather than the outside world, opp to extrovert or extravert (psychol); loosely, a shy or reflective person. ◆ adj /in'/ introverted. [L intrō inwards, and vertere, versum to turn]
■ **introvers'ible** adj. **introver'sion** /-shən/ n. **introver'sive** or **introver'tive** adj. **in'troverted** adj.

intrude /in-trood'/ vi to thrust oneself in; to enter uninvited or unwelcome. ◆ vt to force in. [L in in, and trūdere, trūsum to thrust]
■ **intrud'er** n a person or thing that intrudes; a person who enters premises secretly or by force, with criminal intentions; a military aircraft that raids enemy territory alone. **intrusion** /-troo'zhən/ n (an) act of intruding; encroachment; an injection of rock in a molten state among and through existing rocks; a mass so injected. **intru'sionist** n a person who intrudes, esp of those who, before the Scottish Disruption of 1843, refused a parish the right of objecting to the settlement of an obnoxious minister by a patron. **intru'sive** /-siv/ adj tending or apt to intrude; intruded; inserted without etymological justification; entering without welcome or right; (of a rock) which has been forced while molten into cracks and fissures in other rocks. ◆ n an intrusive rock. **intru'sively** adv. **intru'siveness** n.

intrust a variant of **entrust**.

intubate /in'tū-bāt/ vt to insert a tube in; to treat, diagnose or aid by insertion of a tube into, eg the larynx (med). [L in in, and tubus a tube]
■ **intubā'tion** n the act or process of inserting a tube.

intuition /in-tū-ish'ən/ n the power of the mind by which it immediately perceives the truth of things without reasoning or analysis; a truth so perceived, immediate, instinctive knowledge or belief. [L in into or upon, and tuērī, tuitus to look]
■ **intuit** /in-tū'it/ vt and vi to know intuitively. **intu'itable** adj. **intu'ited** adj. **intuitional** /-ish'ən-əl/ adj. **intuit'ionalism** or **intuit'ionism** n the doctrine that the perception of truth is by intuition; a philosophical system which stresses intuition and mysticism as opposed to the idea of a logical universe. **intuit'ionalist** or **intuit'ionist** n and adj. **intu'itive** adj perceived or perceiving by intuition; received or known by simple inspection and direct apprehension. **intu'itively** adv. **intu'itiveness** n. **intu'itivism** n.

intumesce /in-tū-mes'/ vi to swell up. [L in in, and tumēscere to swell]
■ **intumesc'ence** n a swelling or increase in volume, eg of an organ in the body. **intumesc'ent** adj.
❑ **intumescent paint** n fire-retardant paint that on exposure to heat swells to form an insulating barrier that protects the underlying surface.

interbidate /in-tûr'bi-dāt/ vt to render turbid. [L in in, and turbidāre, -ātum to trouble]

intuse /in'tūs/ (Spenser) n a bruise. [L in in, and tundere, tūsum to thump]

intussusception /in-tə-sə-sep'shən/ n the passing or telescoping of part of a tube (esp the bowel) within the adjacent part (med); growth by intercalation of particles. [L intus within, and susceptiō, -ōnis, from suscipere to take up]
■ **intussuscept'** vt. **intussuscept'ed** adj. **intussuscep'tive** adj.

intwine and **intwist** same as **entwine** and **entwist**.

Inuit or **Innuit** /in'ū-it or in'ū-it/ n an indigenous people of Greenland, the arctic and subarctic regions of Canada, and N Alaska; a member of this people; their language. ◆ adj of or relating to the Inuit. [Inuit, people, pl of *inuk* a person]

Inuktitut /in-nŭk'ti-tŭt/ n the Inuit language. [**Inuit**]

inula /in'ū-la/ n a plant of the genus *Inula* of the Compositae, including the elecampane *I. helenium*. [L *inula*, prob from Gr *helenion* elecampane]
■ **in'ulase** /-lās/ n an enzyme that forms fructose from inulin. **in'ulin** n a carbohydrate present in the roots of certain plants.

inumbrate /in-um'brāt/ vt to cast a shadow upon; to shade. [L *inumbrāre, -ātum*, from *in* on, and *umbrāre* to shade, from *umbra* a shadow]

inunction /in-ungk'shən/ n anointing; smearing or rubbing with an ointment or liniment; the ointment used for this. [L *inunctiō, -ōnis*, from *inunguere* to anoint, from *in* in, on, and *ung(u)ere* to smear]

inundate /in'un-dāt, formerly in-un'dāt/ vt (of water) to flow upon or over in waves; to flood; to overwhelm, swamp (*fig*); to fill with an overflowing abundance. [L *inundāre, -ātum*, from *in* in, and *undāre* to rise in waves, from *unda* a wave]
■ **inun'dant** adj overflowing. **inundā'tion** n.

inurbane /in-ûr-bān'/ adj not urbane. [**in-** (2)]
■ **inurbane'ly** adv. **inurbanity** /-ban'i-ti/ n.

inure[1] or **enure** /in-ūr'/ vt to accustom; to habituate; to harden; to use or practise (*obs*); to put into operation (*Spenser* and *Milton* **enure** *obs*); to commit (*obs*). ◆ vi (*law*) to come into operation or effect; to serve to one's use or benefit. [**in-** (1) and **ure[1]**]
■ **inured'ness** or **enured'ness** n. **inure'ment** or **enure'ment** n the act of inuring; the state of being inured; habituation.

inure[2] /in-ūr'/ (*obs*) vt to burn in. [L *inūrere*, from *in* in, and *urere* to burn]

inurn /in-ûrn'/ vt to place in an urn; to entomb. [**in-** (1)]

inusitate /in-ū'zi-tāt/ (*obs*) adj unaccustomed. [L *inūsitātus*, from *in-* not, and *ūsitātus* familiar]
■ **inusitation** /-ā'shən/ n disuse.

inust /in-ust'/ (*obs*) adj burned in. [L *inūrere, inūstum*; see **inure[2]**]
■ **inustion** /in-us'chən/ n burning in; cauterization.

in usum Delphini /in ū'zəm del-fī'nī or oo'sŭm del-fē'nē/ (*L*) literally, for the use of the Dauphin; toned down to suit the young, expurgated.

in utero /in ū'tə-rō or ŭ'te-rō/ (*L*) in the womb.

inutility /in-ū-til'i-ti/ n lack of utility; uselessness; unprofitableness; something useless. [**in-** (2)]
■ **inu'tile** adj.

in utroque iure /in oo'trō-kwā yoo'rā/ (*L*) under both laws (civil and canon).

in utrumque paratus /in ū-trŭm'kwi pə-rā'təs or ŭ-trŭm'kwe pa-rā'tŭs/ (*L*) prepared for either event.

inutterable /in-ut'ə-rə-bl/ adj unutterable. [**in-** (2)]

inv. abbrev : *invenit* (*L*), designed it; invented; invoice.

in vacuo /in vak'ū-ō, vak'ŭ-ō or wak'/ (*L*) in a vacuum; unrelated to a context, without specific application.

invade /in-vād'/ vt to enter by military force; to attack; to encroach upon; to violate; to overrun; to enter; to penetrate; to rush into. [L *invādĕre*, from *in* in, and *vādĕre* to go]
■ **invad'er** n.

in vadio /in vä'di-ō/ (*LL*) in pledge.

invaginate /in-vaj'i-nāt/ vt to ensheath; to dent inwards, push or withdraw within, introvert. ◆ vi to be introverted; to form a hollow cavity by infolding. [**in-** (1) and L *vāgīna* a sheath]
■ **invaginā'tion** n.

invalid /in-val'id/ adj without validity, efficacy, weight or cogency; having no effect; void; null; /in'və-lid or -lēd/ disabled through injury or chronic sickness; suitable for invalids. ◆ n /-id, -ēd or -ēd'/ a feeble, sickly or disabled person; a person disabled during, and no longer fit for, active service, *esp* a soldier or sailor. ◆ vt /-id, -ēd or -ēd'/ to disable or affect with disease; to enrol or discharge as an invalid. ◆ vi (*archaic*) to become an invalid; to be discharged as an invalid. [**in-** (2)]
■ **invalidate** /-val'/ vt to render invalid or ineffective. **invalidā'tion** n. **invalidhood** /in'və-lid-hŭd, -lēd- or -lēd'/ n. **in'validing** n the sending or return home, or to a more healthy climate, of those rendered incapable of active duty by wounds, sickness, etc. **in'validism** /-id-, -ēd- or -ēd'/ n the state of being an invalid; lack of validity. **inval'idly** adv. **inval'idness** n lack of cogency or force.

invaluable /in-val'ū(-ə-)bl/ adj that cannot have a value set upon it; priceless. [**in-** (2)]
■ **inval'uableness** n. **inval'uably** adv.

Invar® /in'vär or in-vär'/ n an alloy of iron and nickel that expands only slightly when heated, used in the making of scientific instruments. [From **invariable**]

invariable /in-vā'ri-ə-bl/ adj not variable; without alteration or change; unalterable; constantly in the same state. [**in-** (2)]
■ **invāriabil'ity** or **invā'riableness** n. **invā'riably** adv. **invar'iance** n invariableness; the theory of the constancy of physical laws. **invā'riant** n and adj (something) that does not change; (an expression or quantity that is) unaltered by a particular procedure (*maths*).

invasion /in-vā'zhən/ n the act of invading; an attack; incursion; an attack on the rights of another; encroachment; penetration; a violation. [Ety as for **invade**]
■ **invasive** /-vā'ziv/ adj invading; aggressive; encroaching; infringing another's rights; entering; penetrating.

inveagle same as **inveigle**.

invecked /in-vekt'/ adj invected.

invected /in-vek'tid/ (*heraldry*) adj having or consisting of a borderline of small convex curves (cf **engrail**). [L *invehere, invectum* to enter]

invective /in-vek'tiv/ n a severe or reproachful accusation or denunciation; an attack with words; abusive language; sarcasm or satire. ◆ adj sarcastic; abusive; satirical. [L *invectīvus* attacking, from *invehi* to assail; see **inveigh**]

inveigh /in-vā'/ vi to make an attack in speech or writing; to rail; to revile. [L *invehi* to assail, launch oneself at]

inveigle /in-vē'gl or in-vā'gl/ vt (older forms **invea'gle** and **envei'gle**) to entice; to persuade by cajolery; to wheedle. [Prob altered from Anglo-Fr *enveogler* (Fr *aveugler*) to blind, from L *ab* from, and *oculus* the eye]
■ **invei'glement** n. **invei'gler** n.

invendible /in-ven'di-bl/ adj unsaleable. [**in-** (2)]
■ **invendibil'ity** n.

invenit /in-vē'nit, in-wā'nit or -vā'/ (*L*) he or she devised or designed (this).

invent /in-vent'/ vt to devise or contrive; to design for the first time; originate; to form or compose by imagination; to fabricate (something false); to find (*obs*). [L *invenīre, inventum*, from *in* upon, and *venīre* to come]
■ **inven'tible** or **inven'table** adj. **inven'tion** n that which is invented; a contrivance; a deceit; the faculty or power of inventing; ability displayed by any invention or effort of the imagination; a short piece working out a single idea (*music*). **inven'tive** adj able to invent, devise or contrive; showing imaginative skill. **inven'tively** adv. **inven'tiveness** n. **inven'tor** n. **inven'tress** n.
❑ **Invention of the Cross** n a festival observed on 3 May in commemoration of the alleged discovery of the true cross at Jerusalem in 326AD by Helena, mother of Constantine the Great.

inventory /in'vən-t(ə)-ri or (chiefly *US*) in'vən-tō-ri/ n a list or schedule of articles, eg furniture in a rented house, items of property comprised in an estate; a catalogue; stock, equipment; stock of a commodity (*US*); stocktaking (*US*); the total quantity of material in a nuclear reactor. ◆ vt to make an inventory of; to amount to. ◆ vi to sum up. [LL *inventōrium* for L *inventārium* a list of things found, from *invenīre* to find]
■ **inventō'rial** adj. **inventō'rially** adv.

in ventre /in ven'trā/ (*L; law*) in the womb.

inveracity /in-və-ras'i-ti/ n lack of veracity; an untruth. [**in-** (2)]

Inverness /in-vər-nes' or in'vər-nes/ adj of or named after the town of *Inverness*, eg of a cloak or overcoat with a cape or tippet (also *n*).

inverse /in'vûrs or in-vûrs'/ adj inverted; upside down; in the reverse or contrary order; opposite; opposite in effect, as subtraction to addition, etc (*maths*); related by inversion. ◆ n an inverted state; the result of inversion; a direct opposite; a proposition formed by immediate inference from another, its subject being the negative of the original subject (*logic*); a point so related to another point that the rectangle contained by their distances from a fixed point collinear with them is constant, or related in some analogous manner (*geom*). [L *inversus*, pap of *invertere, inversum*, from *in* in, and *vertere* to turn]
■ **in'versely** (or /-vûrs'/) adv. **inver'sion** /-shən/ n the act of inverting; the state of being inverted; a change or reversal of order or position; that which results from inverting; a mutation of chromosomes in which certain genes are in reverse order; an inversion layer. **inver'sive** adj.
❑ **inverse proportion** n (*maths*) a process by which one quantity decreases while another increases, their product remaining constant. **inverse ratio** n the ratio of reciprocals. **inverse square law** n (*phys*) a law in which the force, magnitude, etc of a phenomenon is inversely proportional to the square of the distance from the source. **inversion layer** n a layer of air in the atmosphere in which temperature increases with height; such a layer of warm air that lies

over a layer of cooler air and prevents it from rising, so trapping pollutants.

invert /in-vûrt'/ vt to turn in or round; to turn upside down; to reverse; to change the customary order or position of; to form the inverse of; to change or reverse the relative positions of notes in a chord, interval or phrase (*music*); to modify by reversing the direction of motion; to break up (cane sugar) into dextrose and laevulose, thereby (the laevulose prevailing) reversing the direction of rotation of polarized light (*chem*). ◆ n /in'/ an inverted arch; invert sugar; a homosexual or transsexual (*psychol*). [L *invertere, inversum*, from *in* in, and *vertere* to turn]

■ **in'vertase** (or /-vûr'/) n an enzyme that inverts cane sugar. **inver'ted** *adj* turned inwards; upside down; reversed; pronounced with tip of tongue turned up and back (as *r* in SW England). **inver'tedly** *adv*. **inver'ter** or **inver'tor** n. **invertibil'ity** n. **inver'tible** *adj*. **inver'tin** n invertase.

❏ **inverted arch** n an arch with its curve turned downwards. **inverted commas** see under **comma**. **inverted mordent** see **mordent**. **inverted pleat** n a box-pleat with the folded edges on the right side of the fabric. **inverted snob** n a person who prefers (the attitudes and conventions of) the lower classes to (those of) the upper classes. **inverted snobbery** n. **invert sugar** n the mixture obtained by hydrolysis of cane sugar.

invertebrate /in-vûr'ti-brit or -brāt/ *adj* without a vertebral column or backbone; weak, irresolute, spineless; characterless; formless. ◆ n a member of the Invertebrata; an indecisive person. [**in-** (2)]

■ **Invertebra'ta** n pl a collective name for all animals other than vertebrates.

invest /in-vest'/ vt to clothe with insignia of office; to place in office or authority (with *with* or *in*); to give rights, privileges or duties to; to lay out for profit, as by buying property, shares, etc; to put on (*archaic*); to adorn, clothe, cover (*archaic*); to surround, besiege (*milit*). ◆ vi (*inf*) to make a purchase (with *in*). [L *investīre, -ītum*, from *in* on, and *vestīre* to clothe]

■ **inves'table** or **inves'tible** *adj*. **inves'titive** *adj*. **inves'titure** n investing; the ceremony of investing; in feudal and ecclesiastical history, the act of giving corporal possession of a manor, office, or benefice, accompanied by a certain ceremonial, such as the delivery of a branch, a banner, etc, to signify the authority which it is supposed to convey. **invest'ment** n the act of investing; investiture; any placing of money to secure income or profit; that in which money is invested; a blockade (*milit*); (in pl) clothes (*archaic*). **inves'tor** n a person who invests, *esp* money.

❏ **investment bank** n a bank that arranges loans for corporations, handles mergers, manages pension funds, etc. **investment bond** n a single-premium life assurance policy in which a fixed sum is invested in a unit trust. **investment club** n a group of people who regularly pool savings to invest in the stock market. **investment trust** see under **trust**.

investigate /in-ves'ti-gāt/ vt to search or inquire into with care and accuracy. ◆ vi to make a search, examination or inquiry. [L *investīgāre, -ātum*, from *in* in, and *vestīgāre* to track]

■ **inves'tigable** *adj* able to be investigated. **investiga'tion** n the act of examining; a search, examination or inquiry; research. **investiga'tional** *adj*. **invest'igative** or **invest'igatory** *adj*. **invest'igator** n.

❏ **investigative journalism** n journalism involving the investigation and exposure of corruption, crime, inefficiency, etc.

inveterate /in-vet'ə-rit/ *adj* firmly established by usage or custom; deep-rooted, confirmed in any habit; stubborn; rootedly hostile. [L *inveterātus* stored up, long continued, from *in* in, and *vetus, veteris* old]

■ **invet'eracy** or **invet'erateness** n. **invet'erately** *adv*.

invexed /in-vekst'/ (*heraldry*) *adj* arched; concave. [L *in* in, and the root of *vehere* to carry]

inviable /in-vī'ə-bl/ *adj* not viable; unable to survive. [**in-** (2)]

■ **inviabil'ity** n.

invidious /in-vid'i-əs/ *adj* likely to incur or provoke ill-will or resentment; likely to excite envy, enviable; offensively discriminating. [L *invidiōsus*, from *invidia* envy]

■ **invid'iously** *adv*. **invid'iousness** n.

invigilate /in-vij'i-lāt/ vt and vi to supervise, *esp* at examinations. [L *in* on, and *vigilāre, -ātum* to watch]

■ **invigila'tion** n. **invig'ilator** n.

invigorate /in-vig'ə-rāt/ vt to give vigour to; to strengthen; to animate or enliven. [**in-** (1)]

■ **invig'orant** n an invigorating agent. **invig'orating** *adj*. **invig'oratingly** *adv*. **invigora'tion** n. **invig'orator** n.

invincible /in-vin'si-bl/ *adj* that cannot be defeated or overcome; insuperable. [**in-** (2)]

■ **invincibil'ity** or **invin'cibleness** n. **invin'cibly** *adv*.

in vino veritas /in vī'nō ver'i-tas, wē'nō wā'ri-täs or vē'nō vä'ri-täs/ (L) literally, in wine is truth, hence, truth is told under the influence of alcohol.

inviolable /in-vī'ə-lə-bl/ *adj* that must not be dishonoured; that cannot be injured. [**in-** (2)]

■ **inviolabil'ity** or **invī'olableness** n the quality of being inviolable. **invī'olably** *adv*. **invī'olate** /-lit or -lāt/ or **inviolated** /-lāt-id/ *adj* not violated; not dishonoured; uninjured. **invī'olately** *adv*. **invī'olateness** or **invī'olacy** n.

invious /in'vi-əs/ (*rare*) *adj* impassable; trackless. [L *invius*, from *in-* not, and *via* a way]

invis'd /in'vīzd/ *adj* a word used in Shakespeare's *Lover's Complaint*, perhaps meaning unseen or inscrutable. [L *invīsus* unseen]

invisible /in-viz'i-bl/ *adj* incapable of being seen; unseen; relating to services rather than goods (*econ*); not shown in regular statements, as *invisible assets* (see also under **export** and **import**; *finance*). ◆ n an invisible export, etc; (in pl) invisible imports and exports collectively. [**in-** (2)]

■ **invisibil'ity** or **invis'ibleness** n. **invis'ibly** *adv*.

❏ **invisible earnings** n pl profits from invisibles, *esp* invisible exports. **invisible ink** see under **ink**.

invite /in-vīt'/ vt to ask hospitably or politely to come; to express affable willingness to receive or to have done; to request formally or publicly; to encourage or tend to bring on; to offer inducement; to attract. ◆ n /in'/ (*inf*) an invitation. [L *invītāre, -ātum*]

■ **invitation** /in-vi-tā'shən/ n the act of inviting; a request or solicitation; the written or verbal form with which a person is invited; an enticement; the brief exhortation introducing the confession in the Anglican communion office. **invitatory** /in-vīt'ə-tə-ri/ *adj* using or containing invitation. ◆ n a form of invitation to worship, *esp* the antiphon to the Venite or Psalm 95. **invitee'** (or /-vīt'/) n (*rare*) someone who is invited, a guest. **invite'ment** n (*Lamb*) allurement, temptation. **invīt'er** n. **invīt'ing** *adj* alluring; attractive. ◆ n (*archaic*) invitation. **invīt'ingly** *adv*. **invīt'ingness** n attractiveness.

in vitro /in vī'trō, wit'rō or vit'/ (L) in glass; in the test tube, *opp* to *in vivo* (*med*).

❏ **in vitro fertilization** n fertilization of an ovum by mixing with sperm in a culture medium, after which the fertilized egg is implanted in the uterus to continue normal development (*abbrev* **IVF**). **in vitro transcription** n the use of a laboratory medium without the presence of intact cells to obtain specific messenger RNA production from a DNA sequence (also called **cell-free transcription**). **in vitro translation** n the use of pure messenger RNA, ribosomes and other cell extracts to obtain a specific protein product without the presence of intact cells (also called **cell-free translation**).

in vivo /in vī'vō, wē'wō or vē'vō/ (L) in the living organism.

invocation /in-vō-kā'shən/ n the act or the form of invoking or addressing in prayer or supplication; a form of address under which a divinity, etc is invoked; any formal invoking of the blessing or help of a god, a saint, etc; an opening prayer in a public religious service or in the Litany (*relig*); a call for inspiration from a Muse or other deity eg at the beginning of a poem; an incantation or calling up of a spirit; a call or summons, *esp* for evidence from another case (*law*). [L *invocātio*, from *invocāre* to invoke]

■ **invocatory** /in-vok'ə-tə-ri/ *adj* making an invocation.

invoice /in'vois/ n a letter of advice of the despatch of goods, with particulars of their quantity and the amount due for payment. ◆ vt to list (goods) on an invoice; to send an invoice to (a customer). [Prob pl of Fr *envoi*]

invoke /in-vōk'/ vt to call upon earnestly or solemnly; to implore to give assistance; to address in prayer; to conjure up; to resort to. [Fr *invoquer*, from L *invocāre, -ātum*, from *in* on, and *vocāre* to call]

■ **invok'er** n.

involucre /in'və-loo-kər or -lū-/ n an envelope (*anat*); a ring or crowd of bracts around a capitulum, umbel, etc (*bot*). [L *involūcrum*, from *involvere* to involve]

■ **involucel** /in-vol'ū-sel/ n the group of bracts below a partial umbel. **involūcell'ate** *adj* having an involucel. **involu'cral** *adj* of the nature of, or relating to, an involucre. **involu'crate** *adj* having an involucre. **involū'crum** n an involucre; a growth of new bone enclosing a mass of infected or dead bone in osteomyelitis (*med*).

involuntary /in-vol'ən-tər-i or (chiefly *US*) -ter-i/ *adj* not voluntary; not having the power of will or choice; not under control of the will; not done voluntarily. [**in-** (2)]

■ **invol'untarily** *adv*. **invol'untariness** n.

❏ **involuntary muscle** n a muscle that is not controlled consciously, such as the heart.

involute /in'vl-loot or -lūt/ *adj* involved; rolled inward at the margins (*bot*); turned inward; closely rolled; (of gear teeth) having the profile of an involute curve. ◆ n that which is involved or rolled inward; a curve traced by the end of a string unwinding itself from another curve (the *evolute*). ◆ *vt* and *vi* /in-və-loot'/ or -*lūt*'/ to make or become involute. [Ety as for **involve**]

■ **in'voluted** *adj*.

involution /in-və-lū'shən/ or -*loo*'/ *n* the action of involving; the state of being involved or entangled; complicated grammatical construction; raising to a power (*maths*); the condition satisfied by a system of pairs of points in a straight line such that the rectangle contained by their distances from a fixed point in that line (the *centre of involution*) is constant (*geom*); degeneration; return to normal size, as the uterus after birth (*zool*); atrophy of an organ, eg in old age. [Ety as for **involve**]

■ **involu'tional** *adj*.

□ **involutional psychosis** or **melancholia** *n* a psychosis occurring in middle life, with feelings of anxiety, futility, guilt, and, in some cases, with delusions of persecution.

involve /in-volv'/ *vt* to entangle; to complicate; to implicate; to comprehend; to entail or imply, bring as a consequence; to be bound up with; to concern; to raise to a power (*maths*); to make (oneself) emotionally concerned (in or with); to engage the emotional interest of; to engage in a romantic or sexual relationship (with). [L *involvere*, from *in* in, and *volvere*, *volūtum* to roll]

■ **involved'** *adj* implicated; complicated. **involve'ment** *n*.

invulnerable /in-vul'nə-rə-bl/ *adj* that cannot be wounded or damaged; not vulnerable. [**in-** (2)]

■ **invulnerabil'ity** or **invul'nerableness** *n*. **invul'nerably** *adv*.

invultuation /in-vul-tū-ā'shən/ *n* the making or using of an image of a person for the purposes of witchcraft. [LL *invultuātiō*, -*ōnis*, from L *in* in, and *vultus* the face]

inwall see **enwall**.

inward /in'wərd/ *adj* placed, moving, or being within; internal; seated in the mind or soul, not perceptible to the senses; uttered as if within, or with closed mouth; confidential (*archaic*); secret, private (*archaic*). ◆ *n* inside (*Shakesp*); interior (*obs*); an intimate friend (*Shakesp*); (in *pl*; often /in'ərdz/) entrails (also **inn'ards**). ◆ *adv* toward the interior; into the mind or thoughts. [OE *inneweard* (adv)]

■ **in'wardly** *adv* within; in the heart; privately; toward the centre. **in'wardness** *n* internal state; inner meaning or significance; intimacy, familiarity (*Shakesp*). **in'wards** *adv* same as **inward**.

□ **inward investment** *n* investment in production, manufacturing, distribution, etc in an area or country by business organizations based elsewhere, *esp* in foreign countries.

inweave /in-wēv'/ *vt* (*pat* **inwove'**; *pap* **inwo'ven** (*Milton*, etc **inwove'**)) to weave in; to complicate. [**in-** (1)]

inwick /in'wik/ (*curling*) *n* a stroke in which the stone glances off the edge of another stone, and then slides close to the tee. ◆ *vi* to make an inwick. [**in**[1] and **wick**[4]]

inwind see **enwind**.

inwit /in'wit/ (*obs* or *literary archaism*) *n* inward knowledge; conscience. [**in**[1] and **wit**[2]]

inwith /in'with or in-widh'/ (*Scot*) *prep* and *adv* within. [**in**[1] and **with**[2]]

inwork /in-wûrk'/ *vt* and *vi* to work in. [**in-** (1)]

■ **in'working** *n* energy exerted inwardly. **in'wrought** *adj* (as pap /in-röt'/) wrought in or among other things; adorned with figures.

inworn /in'wōrn, in-wōrn' or -wörn/ *adj* worn or worked in, inwrought. [**in-** (1)]

inwove, etc see **inweave**.

inwrap same as **enwrap**.

inwreathe same as **enwreathe**.

inwrought see under **inwork**.

inyala /in-yä'lə/ or **nyala** /n-yä'lə/ *n* a S African antelope. [Bantu]

I/O (*electronics*) *abbrev* : input/output.

io /ī'ō/ *interj* of invocation, or expressing joy or triumph or grief. ◆ *n* (*pl* **ī'os**) a cry of 'io'. [Gr *iō*]

IOC *abbrev* : International Olympic Committee.

iodine /ī'ə-dēn or ī'ō-dēn, also -*dīn* or -*din*/ *n* a halogen element (symbol **I**; atomic no 53) giving a violet-coloured vapour. [Gr *ioeidēs* violet-coloured, from *ion* a violet, and *eidos* form]

■ **i'odate** *n* a salt of iodic acid. **iodic** /ī-od'ik/ *adj* relating to or caused by iodine; applied to an acid (HIO₃) and its anhydride (I₂O₅). **i'odide** *n* a salt of hydriodic acid. **i'odism** *n* iodine poisoning. **i'odize** or **-ise** *vt* to treat with iodine. **iodoform** /ī-od' or -ōd'ə-förm/ *n* a lemon-yellow crystalline compound of iodine (CHI₃) with a saffron-like odour, used as an antiseptic. **iodomet'ric** *adj* (*chem*) measured by iodine. **iodom'etry** *n* a method of determining the quantity of iodine in a substance. **iod'ophile** /-fīl or -fīl/ *adj* staining intensely with iodine. **i'odous** *adj* of, containing, or resembling iodine. **iod'ūret** *n* (*obs*) an iodide.

□ **iodine-131** *n* a short-lived radioactive isotope of iodine present in fallout, widely used in medicine.

iodyrite /ī-od'i-rīt/ *n* a mineral, silver iodide. [**iodine** and **argyrite**]

IoJ *abbrev* : Institute of Journalists (now known as **CIoJ**).

iolite /ī'ō-līt/ *n* cordierite or dichroite, a strongly dichroic transparent gem, a silicate of aluminium, magnesium and iron, violet-blue, grey or yellow according to direction of view by transmitted light. [Gr *ion* violet, and *lithos* stone]

IOLT *abbrev* : Institute of Logistics and Transport.

IOM *abbrev* : Isle of Man.

Io moth /ī'ō moth/ *n* a large N American moth (*Automeris io*) whose larvae give a painful sting. [After *Io* in Gr myth, who was tormented by an insect]

ion /ī'ən or ī'on/ *n* an electrically-charged particle formed by loss or gain of electrons by an atom, effecting by its migration the transport of electricity. [Gr *ion*, neuter prp of *ienai* to go]

■ **ionic** /ī-on'ik/ *adj*. **ī'onīzable** or **-s-** *adj*. **ionīzā'tion** or **-s-** *n*. **ionize** or **-ise** /ī'ən-īz/ *vt* to produce ions in; to turn into ions. **ī'onizer** or **-s-** *n* an electrical apparatus that contributes to clearing the air by restoring to it the negative charges destroyed by pollution, air-conditioning, etc. **ion'omer** *n* the product of ionic bonding action between long-chain molecules, characterized by toughness and a high degree of transparency. **ion'opause** *n* the region of the earth's atmosphere at the outer limit of the ionosphere. **ionophore** /ī'ə-nə-för/ *n* a chemical compound able to combine with an ion and enable it to pass through a cell membrane, etc. **ionophorē'sis** *n* electrophoresis, *esp* of small ions. **ion'osphere** *n* the region of the upper atmosphere that includes the highly ionized Appleton and Kennelly-Heaviside layers. **ionospher'ic** *adj*. **ionotrop'ic** *adj* (*biochem*) denoting a neurotransmitter receptor which affects cell activity by regulating the cell's ion channels (cf **metabotropic** under **metabolism**). **iontophorē'sis** *n* the migration of charged particles, eg of a drug, into body tissue through electric currents; electrophoresis. **iontophoret'ic** *adj*.

□ **ion channel** *n* (*biochem*) a pore in a cell membrane that allows movement of ions into and out of the cell. **ion engine** *n* a space engine in which the thrust is produced by a stream of ionized particles. **i'on-exchange** *n* transfer of ions from a solution to a solid or another liquid, used in water-softening and many industrial processes. **ionic bond** *n* a bond within a chemical compound achieved by transfer of electrons, the resulting ions being held together by electrostatic attraction. **ion implantation** *n* the introduction of ions into a crystalline material by subjecting the material to bombardment with a stream of ions, an important element in the production of integrated circuits. **ion implanter** *n*. **ionization chamber** *n* an instrument used to detect and measure ionizing radiation, consisting of an enclosure containing electrodes between which ionized gas is formed. **ionization potential** *n* the energy, in electronvolts, required to detach an electron from an atom, molecule or radical. **ionizing radiation** *n* any electromagnetic or particulate radiation which can cause ionization.

Ionian /ī-ō'ni-ən/ *adj* Ionic; of or relating to an area off the west coast of Greece, as in *Ionian Islands*, *Ionian Sea*. ◆ *n* an Ionic Greek. [Gr *Iōnios*]

Ionic /ī-on'ik/ *adj* relating to the Ionians, one of the main divisions of the ancient Greeks, to their dialect, or to Ionia, the coastal district of Asia Minor settled by them; relating to an order of Greek architecture characterized by the volute of its capital; relating to a metrical foot of two long and two short syllables (*Ionic a majore*) or two short and two long (*Ionic a minore*) or to verse characterized by the use of that foot; relating to a mode of ancient Greek music (the same as the Iastic, Hypophrygian, or Hyperlydian), or to an old ecclesiastical mode extending from C to C with C for its final. ◆ *n* the Ionic dialect; an Ionic foot or verse; an Ionic philosopher. [Gr *Iōnikos*, *Iōnios*]

■ **Ionicize** or **-ise** /ī-on'i-sīz/ or **Ionize** or **-ise** /ī'ən-īz/ *vt* and *vi* to make or become Ionian; to use the Ionic dialect. **I'onism** *n*. **I'onist** *n*. □ **Ionic dialect** *n* the most important of the three main branches (Ionic, Doric and Aeolic) of the ancient Greek language, the language of Homer and Herodotus, of which Attic is a development. **Ionic school** *n* the representative philosophers of the Ionian Greeks, such as Thales, Anaximander, Heraclitus, Anaxagoras, who debated the nature of the primordial constitutive principle of the cosmic universe.

ionium /ī-ō'ni-əm/ *n* a radioactive isotope of thorium. [**ion**]

ionize...to...**ionomer** see under **ion**.

ionone /ī'ə-nōn/ *n* either of, or a mixture of, two isomeric ketones extracted from certain plants, with an intense odour of violets, used in making perfumes. [Gr *ion* a violet]

ionopause...to...**iontophoretic** see under **ion**.

iopanoic acid /ī-ō-pə-nō'ik as'id/ *n* a compound containing iodine, opaque to X-rays and used in X-ray examination of the gall bladder.

iota /ī-ō'tə/ n the Greek letter I, ι, corresponding to I; as a numeral ι' = 10, ,ι = 10 000; a jot, a very small amount. [Gr *iōta* the smallest letter in the alphabet; Heb *yōd*]
■ **iō'tacism** n /-sizm/ the tendency of vowels and diphthongs to be pronounced /i/.

IOU /ī-ō-ū'/ n a signed slip of paper or other document acknowledging a debt (*esp* of money) to a specified person, stating the date and nature of the debt. [Pronunciation of *I owe you*]

IOW *abbrev* : Isle of Wight.

IP (*comput*) *abbrev* : Internet Protocol.

IPA *abbrev* : India Pale Ale; Institute of Practitioners in Advertising; International Phonetic Alphabet; International Phonetic Association; International Publishers' Association.

iPad® /ī'pad/ n a brand of small personal computer.

IPC *abbrev* : International Publishing Corporation.

IPCC *abbrev* : Intergovernmental Panel on Climate Change.

IPD *abbrev* : Institute of Personnel and Development (now **CIPD**).

ipecacuanha /ip-i-kak-ū-an'ə/ n (sometimes shortened to **ipecac'**) the dried root of various S American plants, used as a purgative, emetic and expectorant; a plant from which this is obtained, chiefly *Cephaelis* or *Uragoga* (family Rubiaceae). [Port, from Tupí]

iPhone® /ī'fōn/ n a brand of smartphone.

IPL *abbrev* : Indian Premier League.

i-Player® /ī'plā-ər/ n a service of the British Broadcasting Corporation that allows programmes to be watched via the Internet.

IPMS *abbrev* : Institution of Professionals, Managers and Specialists (now known as Prospect).

IPO (*stock exchange*) *abbrev* : Initial Public Offering.

iPod® /ī'pod/ n a brand of digital audio player.

ipomoea /ip-ō-mē'ə/ n a plant of the jalap and morning glory genus (*Ipomoea*) of the Convolvulus family. [Gr *īps*, *īpos* a worm, and *homoios* like]

IPPF *abbrev* : International Planned Parenthood Federation.

ippon /ip'on/ (*judo* and *karate*) n a winning score, worth ten points, awarded for a perfectly executed move. [Jap, one point]

ipratropium /ip-rə-trō'pi-əm/ n a bronchodilator drug used in the treatment of certain types of asthma and bronchitis.

iprindole /i-prin'dōl/ n a drug formerly used to treat depression.

ipse dixit /ip'sē dik'sit or ip'se dēk'sit/ (*L*) he himself said it; a dogmatic pronouncement; dictum.

ipsilateral or **ipselateral** /ip-si-lat'ə-rəl/ adj belonging to or affecting the same side of the body (cf **contralateral**). [Irregularly formed from L *ipse* and **lateral**]

ipsissima verba /ip-sis'ə-mə vûr'bə or ip-sis'i-ma ver' or wer'ba/ (*L*) the very words.

ipso facto /ip'sō fak'tō/ (*L*) by that very fact; thereby.

IQ *abbrev* : intelligence quotient.

iq *abbrev* : *idem quod* (*L*), the same as.

IR *abbrev* : Inland Revenue; Iran (IVR).

Ir (*chem*) *symbol* : iridium.

Ir. *abbrev* : Ireland; Irish.

ir *abbrev* : infrared.

ir- /ir-/ *pfx* same as **in-**, the form used with words beginning with *r*, as in *irradiate*.

IRA *abbrev* : Irish Republican Army.

irade /i-rä'de/ (*hist*) n a written decree of the Sultan of Turkey. [Turk, from Ar *irādah* will]

iraimbilanja /i-räm-bi-lan'jə/ n (pl **iraimbilan'ja**) a monetary unit of Madagascar, $\frac{1}{5}$ of an ariary. [Malagasy, literally, one iron weight]

Iranian /i-, ī-rän'i-ən or -rän'/ n a native or inhabitant of *Iran*; the modern Persian language; the branch of Indo-European which includes Persian. ◆ adj of or relating to Iran, its people or language; of or relating to the branch of Indo-European which includes Persian. [Pers *Irān* Persia]

Iraqi /i-rä'kē/ n a native of *Iraq*; the form of Arabic spoken in Iraq. ◆ adj relating to the country of Iraq, its inhabitants or language. [Ar '*Irāqī*]

irascible /i-ras'i-bl or ī-/ adj quick-tempered; irritable. [Fr, from L *īrāscibilis*, from *īrāscī* to be angry, from *īra* anger]
■ **irascibil'ity** n. **irasc'ibly** adv.

irate /ī-rāt'/ adj enraged, angry. [**ire**]
■ **irate'ly** adv. **irate'ness** n.

IRB *abbrev* : International Rugby Board.

IRBM *abbrev* : intermediate range ballistic missile.

IRC (*comput*) *abbrev* : Internet Relay Chat.

ire /īr/ n anger; rage; keen resentment. [L *īra* anger]
■ **ire'ful** adj full of ire or wrath; resentful. **ire'fully** adv. **ire'fulness** n. **ire'less** adj.

irenic /ī-rēn'ik or -ren'/ or **irenical** /-əl/ adj tending to create peace; pacific. [Gr *eirēnē* peace]
■ **iren'ically** adv. **iren'icism** n. **iren'icon** n same as **eirenicon**. **iren'ics** n sing irenical theology, promoting peace between Christian churches, *opp* to *polemics*. **irenology** /ī-rən-ol'ə-ji/ n the study of peace.

irid /ī'rid/ n the iris of the eye; any plant of the iris family. [Ety as for **iris**]
■ **Iridā'ceae** /i-rid-ā'si-ē, ī-/ n pl the iris family, distinguished from lilies by their inferior ovary and single whorl of stamens (also **Irid'eae**). **iridaceous** /i-rid-ā'shəs or ī-/ or **irid'eal** adj belonging to the Iridaceae. **i'ridal**, **irid'ial** or **irid'ian** adj relating to the iris of the eye.

irid- /i-rid- or ī-rid-/ or **irido-** /-dō- or -do-/ *combining form* denoting the iris (of the eye). [Ety as for **iris**]
■ **iridec'tomy** n surgical removal of part of the iris. **iridodiagnos'tics** n sing diagnosis by examination of the iris. **iridol'ogist** n. **iridol'ogy** n study of the visible parts of the eye, *esp* the iris, by which physical and emotional disorders and tendencies may be revealed. **iridot'omy** n surgical incision into the iris of the eye.

iridescence /ir-i-des'əns/ n play of rainbow colours, caused by interference, as on bubbles, mother-of-pearl, some feathers. [Ety as for **iris**]
■ **iridesc'ent** adj coloured like the rainbow; glittering with changing colours. **iridesc'ently** adv.

iridic /ī-rid'ik or i-/ adj containing or consisting of iridium; of or relating to the iris of the eye. [Ety as for **iris**]

iridium /ī-rid'i-əm or i-/ n a very heavy steel-grey metallic element (symbol **Ir**; atomic no 77) with very high melting-point. [Ety as for **iris**]

iridize or **-ise** /īr' or ī'i-dīz/ vt to make iridescent; to tip with iridium. [Ety as for **iris**]
■ **iridization** or **-s-** /ī-rid-īz-ā'shən, ir-id- or -iz-/ n iridescence.

iridosmine /ir-i-doz'min, īr- or -dos'/ or **iridosmium** /ir-i-doz'mi-əm, īr- or -dos/ n a native alloy of iridium and osmium used for pen-points, also called **osmiridium**.

iridovirus /i-rid'ō-vī-rəs/ n a member of the *Iridovirus* genus of viruses which mainly attack aquatic creatures, causing infected larvae to appear iridescent. [*iridescent virus*]

irinotecan /ī-rī-nō-tē'kan/ n a synthetic drug used to treat colon cancer.

iris /ī'ris/ n (pl **irides** /ī'rid-ēz or i'/ or **i'rises**) the contractile curtain perforated by the pupil, and forming the coloured part of the eye; a plant of the genus *Iris* with tuberous roots, long tapering leaves and large showy flowers; an iris diaphragm; an appearance resembling the rainbow. [Gr *Īris*, *-idos* the rainbow goddess]
■ **i'risate** vt to make iridescent. **irisation** /ī-ri-sā'shən/ n. **irised** /ī'rist/ adj showing colours like the rainbow.
❑ **iris diaphragm** n an adjustable stop for a lens, giving a continuously variable hole. **iris recognition** or **iris scanning** n a security system which uses a digital camera to detect the unique marks on a person's iris and map these to information on a database in order to confirm the person's identity.

iriscope /ī'ri-skōp/ n an instrument for exhibiting the prismatic colours. [Gr *īris* rainbow, and *skopeein* to see]

Irish /ī'rish/ adj relating to, produced in, derived from, or characteristic of, *Ireland*; self-contradictory, ludicrously inconsistent (as Irish thought and speech is traditionally supposed to be; *offensive*). ◆ n the Celtic language of Ireland; an Irish commodity, *esp* whiskey; (as pl) the natives or people of Ireland; fiery temper, passion, as in *get one's Irish up* (*derog*).
■ **I'risher** n (now chiefly *US*; often slightly contemptuous) an Irishman. **I'rishism** n an Irish phrase, idiom or characteristic, *esp* an apparently nonsensical one (also (*non-standard*) **I'ricism**). **I'rishman** or **I'rishwoman** n a native of Ireland. **I'rishness** n the qualities or characteristics of Ireland or the Irish. **I'rishry** n the people of Ireland collectively.
❑ **Irish bridge** n a ford or water splash treated so as to be permanent. **Irish car** n a lightweight horse-drawn buggy. **Irish coffee** n a beverage made of sweetened coffee and Irish whiskey and topped with cream. **Irish elk** see under **elk**. **Irish Guards** n pl a regiment formed in 1900 to represent Ireland in the Foot Guards. **Irish moss** n carrageen. **Irish Republican Army** n a militant organization seeking to bring about union between the Republic of Ireland and Northern Ireland, and independence from Britain. **Irish setter** n a breed of setter developed in Ireland, having a long brownish-red coat. **Irish stew** n stewed mutton, onions and potatoes. **Irish terrier** n a breed of dog with rough, wiry, reddish-brown coat. **Irish wolfhound** n a large breed of dog, typically having a shaggy grey coat.

iritis /ī-rī'tis/ n inflammation of the iris of the eye.
■ **irit'ic** adj having iritis; affecting the iris.

■ words derived from main entry word; ❑ compound words; ■ idioms and phrasal verbs

irk /ûrk/ vt (now usu used impersonally) to weary; to disgust; to distress; to annoy, gall. [ME *irken*]

■ **irk'some** adj tedious; burdensome. **irk'somely** adv. **irk'someness** n.

IRL abbrev : Ireland (IVR).

IRO abbrev : Inland Revenue Office; International Refugee Organization.

iroko /i-rō'kō/ n (pl **irō'kos**) either of the two timber trees of the genus *Chlorophora* of central and W Africa; the hard wood of these trees, often used as a substitute for teak. [Yoruba]

iron /ī'ərn/ n a metallic element (symbol **Fe**; atomic no 26), the most widely used of all the metals; a weapon, instrument or utensil made of iron; an appliance for smoothing cloth; a pistol or revolver (sl); a golf club with a metal head; strength; a medicinal preparation of iron; (in pl) fetters, chains; a theatre safety curtain (archaic; orig short for **iron curtain** below); a stirrup; (usu in pl) supports for weak or malformed legs. ◆ adj formed of iron; resembling iron; harsh, grating; stern; not to be broken; robust; insensitive; inflexible. ◆ vt to smooth with an iron; to arm with iron; to hit (a golf ball) with an iron; to fetter; to smooth, clear up (with *out* ; fig). [OE *īren* (*īsern, īsen*) Ger *Eisen*]

■ **i'roner** n a person who irons; an iron for pressing clothes. **i'roning** n the act or process of smoothing with hot irons; clothes, etc that are to be, or have been, ironed. **i'ronlike** adj. **i'rony** adj made, consisting of, rich in iron; like iron; hard.

❑ **Iron Age** n (archaeol) the stage of culture of a people using iron as the material for their tools and weapons. **i'ronbark** n any of several eucalyptus trees with rough bark and yielding durable timber. **i'ron-bound** adj bound with iron; unyielding; rugged, as a coast. **i'ron-cased** adj. **i'ron-clad** adj clad in iron; covered or protected with iron. ◆ n a ship covered with iron plates. **i'ron-clay** n clay-ironstone. **Iron Cross** n a Prussian war medal instituted in 1813, revived in 1870 and 1914 and reinstated by Hitler as a German war medal in 1939. **Iron Crown** n the crown of Lombardy, so named from a thin band of iron said to be made from one of the nails of the Cross. **iron curtain** n the safety curtain in a theatre, orig made of iron (archaic); an impenetrable barrier to observation or communication, esp (with caps) between the former Soviet bloc and the West. **iron-fis'ted** adj exercising strict, despotic control. **i'ron-founder** n a person who founds or makes castings in iron. **i'ron-foundry** n. **i'ron-glance** n specular iron. **iron-gray'** or **-grey'** adj of a grey colour like that of iron freshly cut or broken. ◆ n this colour. **iron hand** n strict, despotic control (the iron hand is sometimes hidden in the *velvet glove*, qv). **iron-hand'ed** adj. **iron-heart'ed** adj having a heart as hard as iron; unfeeling. **iron horse** n a worn-out circumlocution for a railway engine. **i'roning-board** n a smooth board covered with cloth, usu on a stand, on which clothes, etc are ironed. **iron-liq'uor** n iron acetate, a dyers' mordant. **iron lung** n an apparatus consisting of a chamber that encloses a patient's chest, the air pressure within the chamber being varied rhythmically so that air is forced into and out of the lungs, a respirator. **iron maiden** n an old instrument of torture, consisting of a box lined with iron spikes in which a prisoner was fastened. **iron man** n a man of extraordinary strength (esp Aust); (the winner of) a test of endurance at a surf carnival, comprising swimming, surfing and running events (Aust); a pound note (orig Aust inf) or a dollar (US inf). **I'ronman**® n a long-distance triathlon race consisting of a 2.4-mile swim, a 112-mile bicycle ride and a 26.2-mile run. **i'ronmaster** n a proprietor of an ironworks. **i'ron-mine** n. **i'ron-miner** n. **i'ron-mining** n. **i'ronmonger** n a dealer in ironmongery or, loosely, in household goods and equipment generally. **i'ronmongery** n articles made of iron; domestic hardware. **iron mould** (earlier **i'ron-mole**, Scot **i'ron-mail**) n (OE *mal* mole, spot) a spot left on wet cloth after touching iron. **i'ron-on** adj designed to be attached by pressing with a hot iron. **iron ore** n. **iron oxide** n ferric oxide. **iron-pan'** n a hard layer in sand or gravel, due to percolation of water precipitating iron salts. **iron pyrites** n pl common pyrites, sulphide of iron. **iron ration** n a ration of concentrated food, esp for an extreme emergency. **i'ron-red** n a pigment derived from ferric oxide, used as a colorant in ceramics. **i'ron-sand** n sand containing particles of iron ore; steel filings used in fireworks. **i'ron-sick** adj (naut) having the iron bolts and spikes much corroded. **I'ronside** or **I'ronsides** n a nickname for a man of iron resolution (eg Oliver Cromwell); a Puritan cavalryman; a Puritan; (in pl) a name given to Cromwell's cavalry. **iron-sid'ed** adj having a side of, or as hard as, iron; rough; hardy. **i'ronsmith** n a worker in iron, blacksmith. **i'ronstone** n any iron-ore, esp carbonate; hard white earthenware. **i'ronware** n wares or goods of iron. **iron-willed'** adj firmly determined. **iron-witt'ed** adj (Shakesp) unfeeling, insensible. **i'ronwood** n timber of great hardness, and any of various trees producing it. **iron-word'ed** adj (Tennyson) expressed in strong terms. **i'ronwork** n the parts of a building, etc, made of iron; anything of iron, esp artistic work; (often in pl) an establishment where iron is smelted or made into heavy goods.

■ **pump iron** see under **pump¹**. **rule with a rod of iron** to rule with stern severity. **strike while the iron is hot** to seize one's opportunity while the circumstances are favourable. **too many irons in the fire** too many responsibilities, undertakings, etc to cope with at once.

irony¹ /ī'rə-ni/ n orig the Socratic method of discussion by professing ignorance; conveyance of meaning (generally satirical) by words whose literal meaning is the opposite, esp words of praise used as a criticism or condemnation; a situation or utterance (eg in a tragedy) that has a significance unperceived at the time, or by the persons involved (cf **dramatic irony** under **drama**); a condition in which one seems to be mocked by fate or the facts. [L *īrōnīa*, from Gr *eirōneiā* dissimulation, from *eirōn* a dissembler]

■ **ironic** /ī-ron'ik/ or **iron'ical** adj. **iron'ically** adv. **i'ronist** n. **i'ronize** or **-ise** vt and vi.

irony² see under **iron**.

Iroquoian /ir-ə-kwoi'ən/ adj of or belonging to the *Iroquois*, a group of orig five, later six, Native American peoples, now mainly in NE USA and E Canada, who constitute the Iroquois Confederacy (cf **Five Nations** under **five** and **Six Nations** under **six**); of a group of Native American languages including those spoken by the Iroquois, and also Cherokee. ◆ n the Iroquoian group of languages.

IRQ abbrev : Iraq (IVR).

irradiate /ir-ā'di-āt/ vt to shed light or other rays upon or into; to treat by exposure to rays; to expose (perishable food) to electromagnetic radiation to kill bacteria and slow down decomposition; to light up; to brighten; to radiate. ◆ vi to radiate; to shine. ◆ adj adorned with rays of light or with lustre. [**ir-** (**in-** (1))]

■ **irra'diance** or **irra'diancy** n. **irra'diant** adj. **irradiā'tion** n the act of irradiating; exposure to rays; the therapeutic application of electromagnetic radiation; that which is irradiated; brightness; apparent enlargement of a bright object by spreading of the excitation of the retina, or in a photograph by reflections within the emulsion; spread of a nervous impulse beyond the usual area affected; intellectual light. **irra'diative** adj.

irradicate /ir-ad'i-kāt/ vt to fix firmly. [**ir-** (**in-** (1))]

irrational /ir-ash'ə-nəl/ adj not rational; not commensurable with natural numbers; long treated as short, or having such a syllable (indicated W; prosody). ◆ n an irrational syllable or number. [**ir-** (**in-** (2))]

■ **irra'tionalism** n an irrational system; irrationality. **irra'tionalist** n and adj. **irrationalist'ic** adj. **irrational'ity** n. **irra'tionalize** or **-ise** vt to make irrational. **irra'tionally** adv.

❑ **irrational number** n a real number that cannot be expressed as a fraction whose denominator and numerator are both integers.

irrealizable or **irrealisable** /ir-ē-ə-lī'zə-bl/ adj not realizable. [**ir-** (**in-** (2))]

■ **irreality** /-al'i-ti/ n unreality.

irrebuttable /ir-i-but'ə-bl/ adj which cannot be rebutted. [**ir-** (**in-** (2))]

irreceptive /ir-i-sep'tiv/ adj not receptive. [**ir-** (**in-** (2))]

irreciprocal /ir-i-sip'rə-kəl/ adj not reciprocal. [**ir-** (**in-** (2))]

■ **irreciprocity** /ir-es-i-pros'i-ti/ n.

irreclaimable /ir-i-klā'mə-bl/ adj that cannot be claimed back, brought into cultivation, or reformed; incorrigible. [**ir-** (**in-** (2))]

■ **irreclaimabil'ity** or **irreclaim'ableness** n. **irreclaim'ably** adv.

irrecognizable or **irrecognisable** /ir-ek-əg-nī'zə-bl or ir-ek'-/ adj unrecognizable. [**ir-** (**in-** (2))]

■ **irrecognition** /-nish'ən/ n lack of recognition.

irreconcilable /ir-ek-ən-sī'lə-bl or ir-ek'-/ adj incapable of being brought back to a state of friendship or agreement; inconsistent. ◆ n an irreconcilable opponent; an intransigent; any of two or more opinions, desires, etc that cannot be reconciled. [**ir-** (**in-** (2))]

■ **irreconcīlabil'ity** or **irreconcī'lableness** n. **irreconcil'ably** adv. **irrec'onciled** adj not reconciled, esp (Shakesp) with God; not brought into harmony. **irreconcile'ment** n.

irrecoverable /ir-i-kuv'ə-rə-bl/ adj irretrievable; not reclaimable; beyond recovery. [**ir-** (**in-** (2))]

■ **irrecov'erableness** n. **irrecov'erably** adv.

irrecusable /ir-i-kū'zə-bl/ adj that cannot be rejected. [Fr, from LL *irrecūsābilis*]

■ **irrecūs'ably** adv.

irredeemable /ir-i-dē'mə-bl/ adj not redeemable; not subject to be paid at the nominal value. [**ir-** (**in-** (2))]

■ **irredeemabil'ity** or **irredeem'ableness** n. **irredeem'ables** n pl undated government or debenture stock. **irredeem'ably** adv.

Irredentist /ir-i-den'tist/ n a member of an Italian party formed in 1878, its aims to gain or regain for Italy various regions claimed on language and other grounds; (without cap) a person who advocates the redeeming of territory from another state. ◆ adj of or relating to the Irredentists; (without cap) advocating the redeeming of territory from another state. [Ital (*Italia*) *irredenta*

unredeemed (Italy), from L *in-* not, and *redemptus* pap of *redimere* to redeem]
■ **Irredent'ism** *n* the programme of the Irredentist party; (without *cap*) the doctrine of 'redeeming' territory from another state, *esp* where there is some historical claim to the territory or when an ethnic group seeks to rejoin the major part of the ethnic group in another state.

irreducible /*ir-i-dū'si-bl*/ *adj* that cannot be reduced or brought from one degree, form, or state to another; not to be lessened; not to be overcome; unable to be replaced in a normal position by manipulation, as a hernia, etc. [**ir-** (**in-** (2))]
■ **irreducibil'ity, irreduc'ibleness** or **irreductibility** /-*duk-ti-bil'i-ti*/ *n*. **irreduc'ibly** *adv*. **irreduction** /-*duk'shən*/ *n*.

irreflective /*ir-i-flek'tiv*/ *adj* not reflective. [**ir-** (**in-** (2))]
■ **irreflec'tion** or **irreflex'ion** *n*.

irreflexive /*ir-i-flek'siv*/ (*logic*) *adj* denoting a relation that never holds between each member of a domain and itself. [**ir-** (**in-** (2))]

irreformable /*ir-i-för'mə-bl*/ *adj* not reformable; not subject to revision or improvement. [**ir-** (**in-** (2))]
■ **irreform'ably** *adv*.

irrefragable /*ir-ef'rə-gə-bl*/ *adj* incapable of being refuted; unanswerable. [L *irrefrāgābilis*, from *in-* not, *re-* backwards, and *frangere* to break]
■ **irrefragabil'ity** or **irref'ragableness** *n*. **irref'ragably** *adv*.
■ **the Irrefragable Doctor** Alexander of Hales (died 1245) who prepared a system of instruction for the schools of Christendom.

irrefrangible /*ir-i-fran'ji-bl*/ *adj* incapable of refraction. [**ir-** (**in-** (2))]
■ **irrefrangibil'ity** or **irrefran'gibleness** *n*. **irrefran'gibly** *adv*.

irrefutable /*ir-ef'ū-tə-bl*, also *-ū'*/ *adj* that cannot be refuted. [**ir-** (**in-** (2))]
■ **irrefutabil'ity** or **irref'utableness** (or /-*ūt'*/) *n*. **irref'utably** (also /-*ūt'*/) *adv*.

irreg. *abbrev* : irregular; irregularly.

irregular /*ir-eg'ū-lər*/ *adj* not regular; not conforming to rule or to the ordinary rules; disorderly; uneven; unsymmetrical; variable; (of troops) not trained under the authority of a government; (of a marriage) not celebrated by a minister after proclamation of banns or of intention to marry. ◆ *n* an irregular soldier. [**ir-** (**in-** (2))]
■ **irregularity** /-*lar'i-ti*/ *n* a rough place or bump on an even surface; an instance of action, behaviour, etc not conforming to rules or regulations. **irreg'ularly** *adv*.

irrelative /*ir-el'ə-tiv*/ *adj* not relative; irrelevant. [**ir-** (**in-** (2))]
■ **irrelated** /*ir-i-lā'tid*/ *adj*. **irrelā'tion** or **irrel'ativeness** *n*. **irrel'atively** *adv*.

irrelevant /*ir-el'ə-vənt*/ *adj* not relevant. [**ir-** (**in-** (2))]
■ **irrel'evance** or **irrel'evancy** *n*. **irrel'evantly** *adv*.

irreligious /*ir-i-lij'əs*/ *adj* having no religion; regardless of religion; opposed to religion; false in religion (*Shakesp*); ungodly. [**ir-** (**in-** (2))]
■ **irrelig'ion** *n* lack of religion; hostility to or disregard of religion. **irrelig'ionist** *n*. **irrelig'iously** *adv*. **irrelig'iousness** *n*.

irremeable /*ir-em'i-ə-bl* or -*ēm'*/ *adj* which cannot be returned. [L *irremeābilis*, from *in-* not, *re-* back, and *meāre* to go, come]
■ **irrem'eably** *adv*.

irremediable /*ir-i-mē'di-ə-bl*/ *adj* beyond remedy or redress. [**ir-** (**in-** (2))]
■ **irremē'diableness** *n*. **irremē'diably** *adv*.

irremissible /*ir-i-mis'i-bl*/ *adj* not to be remitted or forgiven. [**ir-** (**in-** (2))]
■ **irremissibil'ity** or **irremiss'ibleness** *n*. **irremiss'ibly** *adv*. **irremission** /-*mish'ən*/ *n*. **irremiss'ive** *adj* unremitting.

irremovable /*ir-i-moo'və-bl*/ *adj* not removable; not liable to be displaced. [**ir-** (**in-** (2))]
■ **irremovabil'ity** or **irremov'ableness** *n*. **irremov'ably** *adv*.

irrenowned /*ir-i-now'nid*/ (*Spenser*) *adj* inglorious. [**ir-** (**in-** (2))]

irrepairable /*ir-i-pā'rə-bl*/ (*archaic*) *adj* beyond repair, irreparable. [**ir-** (**in-** (2))]

irreparable /*ir-ep'ə-rə-bl*/ *adj* that cannot be made good or rectified; beyond repair. [**ir-** (**in-** (2))]
■ **irreparabil'ity** or **irrep'arableness** *n*. **irrep'arably** *adv*.

irrepealable /*ir-i-pē'lə-bl*/ *adj* that cannot be repealed or annulled. [**ir-** (**in-** (2))]
■ **irrepealabil'ity** or **irrepeal'ableness** *n*. **irrepeal'ably** *adv*.

irreplaceable /*ir-i-plā'sə-bl*/ *adj* whose loss cannot be made good; without possible substitute. [**ir-** (**in-** (2))]
■ **irreplace'ably** *adv*.

irrepleviable /*ir-i-plev'i-ə-bl*/ or **irreplevisable** /*ir-i-plev'i-sə-bl*/ (*law*) *adj* unable to be replevied. [**ir-** (**in-** (2))]

irreprehensible /*ir-ep-ri-hens'i-bl*/ *adj* beyond blame. [**ir-** (**in-** (2))]
■ **irreprehens'ibleness** *n*. **irreprehens'ibly** *adv*.

irrepressible /*ir-i-pres'i-bl*/ *adj* not able or willing to be restrained, subdued or (loosely) kept out of the limelight. [**ir-** (**in-** (2))]
■ **irrepressibil'ity** or **irrepress'ibleness** *n*. **irrepress'ibly** *adv*.

irreproachable /*ir-i-prō'chə-bl*/ *adj* free from blame; faultless. [**ir-** (**in-** (2))]
■ **irreproachabil'ity** or **irreproach'ableness** *n*. **irreproach'ably** *adv*.

irreproducible /*ir-ē-prō-dū'si-bl*/ *adj* that cannot be reproduced. [**ir-** (**in-** (2))]

irreprovable /*ir-i-proo'və-bl*/ *adj* blameless. [**ir-** (**in-** (2))]
■ **irreprov'ableness** *n*. **irreprov'ably** *adv*.

irresistance /*ir-i-zis'təns*/ *n* lack of resistance; passive submission. [**ir-** (**in-** (2))]
■ **irresistibil'ity** or **irresist'ibleness** *n*. **irresist'ible** *adj* not capable of being successfully opposed; resistless; overpowering; overmastering; fascinating, enticing. **irresist'ibly** *adv*.

irresoluble /*ir-ez'ə-lū-bl* or -*lū'-bl*/ *adj* that cannot be resolved into parts; that cannot be solved; that cannot be got rid of (*archaic*). [**ir-** (**in-** (2))]
■ **irresolubil'ity** *n*. **irres'olubly** *adv*.

irresolute /*ir-ez'ə-lūt* or -*loot*/ *adj* not firm in purpose. [**ir-** (**in-** (2))]
■ **irres'olutely** *adv*. **irres'oluteness** or **irresolution** /-*ū'shən* or -*oo'shən*/ *n* lack of resolution.

irresolvable /*ir-i-zol'və-bl*/ *adj* that cannot be resolved. [**ir-** (**in-** (2))]
■ **irresolvabil'ity** or **irresolv'ableness** *n*. **irresol'vably** *adv*.

irrespective /*ir-i-spek'tiv*/ *adj* (with *of*) not having regard (also *adv*). [**ir-** (**in-** (2))]
■ **irrespec'tively** *adv*.

irrespirable /*ir-es'pi-rə-bl* or -*i-spī'*/ *adj* unfit for respiration. [**ir-** (**in-** (2))]

irresponsible /*ir-i-spon'si-bl*/ *adj* not responsible; without sense of responsibility; feeling no burden of responsibility, light-hearted, carefree; reprehensibly careless; done without feelings of responsibility. [**ir-** (**in-** (2))]
■ **irresponsibil'ity** or **irrespon'sibleness** *n*. **irrespons'ibly** *adv*. **irrespons'ive** *adj* not responding; not readily responding. **irrespons'ively** *adv*. **irrespons'iveness** *n*.

irrestrainable /*ir-i-strā'nə-bl*/ *adj* not restrainable. [**ir-** (**in-** (2))]

irresuscitable /*ir-i-sus'i-tə-bl*/ *adj* incapable of being resuscitated or revived. [**ir-** (**in-** (2))]
■ **irresusc'itably** *adv*.

irretention /*ir-i-ten'shən*/ *n* absence of retention or power to retain. [**ir-** (**in-** (2))]
■ **irreten'tive** *adj*. **irreten'tiveness** *n*.

irretrievable /*ir-i-trē'və-bl*/ *adj* not able to be recovered; irreparable. [**ir-** (**in-** (2))]
■ **irretrievabil'ity** or **irretriev'ableness** *n*. **irretriev'ably** *adv*.

irreverent /*ir-ev'ə-rənt*/ *adj* not reverent; proceeding from irreverence. [**ir-** (**in-** (2))]
■ **irrev'erence** *n* lack of reverence or veneration, *esp* for God. **irreverential** /-*en'shəl*/ *adj*. **irrev'erently** *adv*.

irreversible /*ir-i-vûr'si-bl*/ *adj* not reversible; that cannot proceed in the opposite direction or in both directions; incapable of changing back; not alike both ways; that cannot be recalled or annulled; (involving damage which is) permanent (*med*). [**ir-** (**in-** (2))]
■ **irreversibil'ity** or **irrevers'ibleness** *n*. **irrevers'ibly** *adv*.

irrevocable /*ir-ev'ə-kə-bl*/ *adj* that cannot be recalled or revoked. [**ir-** (**in-** (2))]
■ **irrevocabil'ity** or **irrev'ocableness** *n*. **irrev'ocably** *adv*.

irrigate /*ir'i-gāt*/ *vt* to wet or moisten; to water by means of canals or watercourses; to cause a stream of liquid to flow upon. ◆ *vi* (*sl*) to drink. [L *irrigāre*, -*ātum* to water, and *irriguus* watering, watered, from *in* upon, and *rigāre* to wet]
■ **irr'igable** *adj*. **irrigā'tion** *n* the act or process of irrigating; the washing out of a wound, the eye, or a hollow organ with a flow of water or solution, as in *colonic irrigation* (*med*). **irrigā'tional** *adj*. **irr'igative** *adj*. **irr'igātor** *n* someone who, or something that, irrigates; an appliance for washing a wound, etc. **irrig'ūous** *adj* watered; wet; irrigating.

irritate¹ /*ir'i-tāt*/ *vt* to make angry or fretful; to excite a painful, uncomfortable, or unhealthy condition (eg heat and redness) in; to excite or stimulate; to rouse; to provoke. [L *irritāre*, -*ātum* to annoy, vex]

■ **irritabil'ity** *n* the quality of being easily irritated; the peculiar susceptibility to outside stimuli possessed by living matter. **irr'itable** *adj* that may be irritated; easily annoyed; susceptible to excitement or irritation. **irr'itableness** *n*. **irr'itably** *adv*. **irr'itancy** *n*. **irr'itant** *adj* irritating. ◆ *n* that which causes irritation. **irr'itatedly** *adv*. **irr'itating** *adj*. **irr'itatingly** *adv*. **irritā'tion** *n* the act of irritating or exciting; anger, annoyance; that which irritates; stimulation; the term applied to any discomfort in the organs or tissues not amounting to inflammation but often leading to it (*med*). **irr'itative** *adj* tending to irritate or excite; accompanied with or caused by irritation. **ir'ritātor** *n*.
❏ **irritable bowel syndrome** *n* a condition in which abdominal pain, constipation or diarrhoea occurs, often recurring over a period of years, without there being any significant deterioration in health or underlying disease.

irritate² /ir'i-tāt/ (*Scots law*) *vt* to make void. [L *irritāre*, from *in*- not, and *ratus* valid]
■ **irr'itancy** *n*. **irr'itant** *adj* rendering void.

irrupt /ir-upt'/ *vi* to break in; to carry out a sudden invasion or incursion. [L *irrumpere, irruptum*, from *in* in, and *rumpere* to break]
■ **irruption** /ir-up'shən/ *n* a breaking or bursting in; a sudden invasion or incursion. **irrup'tive** *adj* rushing suddenly in. **irrup'tively** *adv*.

IRS (*US*) *abbrev* : Internal Revenue Service.

irukandji /ir-ə-kan'jē/ *n* an Australasian jellyfish (*Carukia barnesi*) with an extremely poisonous sting. [After the *Irukandji* people of N Queensland]

Irvingite /ûr'ving-īt/ *n* a popular name for a member of the Catholic Apostolic Church (also *adj*). [Edward *Irving* (1792–1834)]
■ **Ir'vingism** *n* the doctrine and practice of the Irvingites.

IS *abbrev* : Iceland (IVR); income support; independent suspension (*mech*); information science (or systems); internal security.

Is. *abbrev* : (the Book of) Isaiah (*Bible*); Island(s) or Isle(s).

is /iz/ used as *3rd pers sing pres* indicative of **be**. [OE *is*; Ger *ist*, L *est*, Gr *esti*, Sans *asti*]

is- see **iso-**.

ISA *abbrev* : Individual Savings Account (*finance*); Industry Standard Architecture, a bus system used in early computers.

Isa. (*Bible*) *abbrev* : (the Book of) Isaiah.

isabel /iz'ə-bel/ *n* and *adj* dingy yellowish grey or drab (also **isabell'a** or **isabell'ine** /-in* or *-īn*/). [Origin unknown: too early in use to be from *Isabella*, daughter of Philip II, who did not change her linen for three years until Ostend was taken; an etymological connection with Isabella of Castile, to whom a similar legend is ascribed, is chronologically possible but by no means certain]

isagogic /ī-sə-goj'ik* or *-gog'ik/ *adj* introductory. [Gr *eisagōgē* an introduction, from *eis* into, and *agein* to lead]
■ **isagoge** /ī'sə-gō-ji* or *-gō'/ *n* an academic introduction to a subject. **isagog'ics** *n sing* that part of theological study introductory to exegesis.

isallobar /ī-sal'* or *ī-zal'ə-bär/ (*meteorol*) *n* the contour line on a weather chart, connecting those places experiencing equal changes in atmospheric pressure over a specified period. [Gr *isos* equal, *allos* other, different, and *baros* weight]

isapostolic /īs-ap-ə-stol'ik/ *adj* equal to the apostles, as bishops of apostolic creation, the first preachers of Christ in a country, etc. [Gr *isos* equal, and *apostolikos* apostolic]

Isatis /ī'sə-tis/ *n* the woad genus of Cruciferae. [Gr *isatis* woad]
■ **ī'satin** or **ī'satine** *n* a substance ($C_8H_5O_2N$) obtained by oxidizing indigo.

ISBA *abbrev* : Incorporated Society of British Advertisers.

ISBN *abbrev* : International Standard Book Number, a number allotted to a book showing area, publisher and individual title.

ISC *abbrev* : Independent Schools Council (**ISCIS** Independent Schools Council Information Service).

ischaemia or **ischemia** /i-skē'mi-ə/ *n* inadequate flow of blood to a part of the body. [Gr *ischein* to restrain, and *haima* blood]
■ **ischaem'ic** or **ischem'ic** *adj*.

ischium /is'ki-əm/ *n* (*pl* **is'chia**) a posterior bone of the pelvic girdle. [Latinized from Gr *ischion* the hip joint]
■ **ischiad'ic, is'chial** or **ischiat'ic** *adj*.

ischuria /i-skū'ri-ə/ *n* a suppression or retention of urine. [Gr *ischein* to hold, and *ouron* urine]
■ **ischuretic** /is-kū-ret'ik/ *adj* and *n*.

ISD *abbrev* : international subscriber dialling.

ISDN *abbrev* : integrated services digital network, an advanced telecommunications network.

-ise see **-ize**.

isenergic /īs-e-nûr'jik/ (*phys*) *adj* denoting equal energy. [Gr *isos* equal, and *energeia* energy]

Isengrim /iz'ən-grim/ or **Isegrim** /ī'zə-grim/ *n* the wolf in the animal fable of *Reynard the Fox*.

isentropic /ī-sen-trop'ik/ (*phys*) *adj* of equal entropy. [Gr *isos* equal, and *entropē* a turning about, from *en* in, and *trepein* to turn]

ish /ish/ (*Scots law*) *n* issue, liberty of going out; expiry. [OFr *issir* to go out, from L *exīre*, from *ex* out of, and *īre* to go]

-ish /-ish/ *sfx* forming adjectives signifying: somewhat, as in *brownish, oldish*; like or similar to (sometimes implying deprecation), as in *outlandish, childish*; roughly, approximately, as in *sixish*; having as a nationality, as in *Scottish*. [OE *-isc*]

Ishmael /ish-mā'əl/ *n* someone like Ishmael (Bible, Genesis 16.15), at war with society.
■ **Ish'maelīte** *n* a descendant of Ishmael; a Bedouin; an Ishmael. **Ishmaelīt'ish** *adj*.

Ishtar see **Astarte**.

Isiac, Isiacal see under **Isis**.

Isidorian /is-* or *iz-i-dō'* (or *-dō'*) *-ri-ən/ *adj* of or relating to St *Isidore* of Seville (c.560–636), or the collection of canons and decretals adopted by him; but *esp* applying to the forged *Pseudo-Isidorian* or *False Decretals*, published (c.845) by *Isidore* Mercator, and ascribed to St Isidore.

isinglass /ī'zing-gläs/ *n* a material, mainly gelatine, obtained from sturgeons' air-bladders and other sources; thin transparent sheets of mica. [Appar from obs Du *huizenblas*, from *huizen* a kind of sturgeon, and *blas* a bladder; Ger *Hausenblase*; cf **huso**]

ISIS or **Isis** *abbrev* : Independent Schools Information Service (now known as **ISCIS** (see **ISC**)).

Isis /ī'sis/ *n* an Egyptian goddess, wife and sister of Osiris. [Gr *īsis*]
■ **Ī'siac, Īsī'acal** *adj*.

Isl. *abbrev* : Island.

Islam /iz'läm, is'läm* or *-läm'/ *n* a monotheistic religion based on the teachings of the prophet Mohammed (also **Is'lamism**); the followers of this religion considered as a group. [Ar *islām* surrender (to God)]
■ **Islamic** /-lam'ik/ *adj*. **Islam'icist** *n* a person who studies Islam, Islamic law, Islamic culture, etc (also *adj*). **Islamicizā'tion** or **-s-** *n*. **Islam'icize** or **-ise** *vt* to Islamize. **Is'lamist** *n* an Islamicist; a person engaged in a political movement seeking to establish a traditional Islamic society (also *adj*). **Is'lamite** *n*. **Islamitic** /-lə-mit'ik/ *adj*. **Islamīzā'tion** or **-s-** *n*. **Is'lamize** or **-ise** *vt* and *vi* to convert to or (cause to) conform to Islam. **Islam'ophobe** *n* (Gr *phobos* fear) a person who fears or hates Islam and its followers (also *adj*). **Islamophō'bia** *n*. **Islamophō'bic** *adj* and *n*.

island /ī'lənd/ *n* a mass of land (not a continent) surrounded with water; anything isolated, detached, or surrounded by something of a different nature; a small raised traffic-free area in a street, *esp* for pedestrians; tissue or cells detached and differing from their surroundings. ◆ *adj* of an island; forming an island. ◆ *vt* to cause to appear like an island; to isolate; to dot as with islands. [ME *iland*, from OE *īegland, īgland, ēgland*, from *īeg, īg, ēg* island (from a root which appears in Angles-ea, Aldern-ey, etc, OE *ēa*, L *aqua* water) and *land*; the *s* is due to confusion with *isle*]
■ **islander** /ī'lənd-ər/ *n* an inhabitant of an island.
❏ **island-hopping** see under **hop¹**. **islands of Langerhans** same as **islets of Langerhans** (see under **isle**). **Islands of the Blest** or **Blessed** *n pl* (Gr *myth*) the abode of the blessed dead, situated somewhere in the far west. **island universe** *n* a spiral nebula regarded as forming a separate stellar system.
■ **Reil's island** see **insula**.

isle /īl/ *n* an island. ◆ *vt* to make an isle of; to set in an isle. ◆ *vi* to dwell in an isle. [ME *ile, yle*, from OFr *isle* (Fr *île*), from L *īnsula*]
■ **isles'man** or **isle'man** *n* an islander, *esp* an inhabitant of the Hebrides. **islet** /ī'lit/ *n* a little isle; any small group of cells differing in nature and structure from surrounding cells.
❏ **Isle of Wight disease** *n* a disease of bees caused by a mite in the spiracles, that appeared in the Isle of Wight in 1906, and spread to other regions. **islets of Langerhans** /läng'ər-häns/ *n pl* groups of epithelial cells in the pancreas that secrete the hormones insulin and glucagon, discovered by Paul *Langerhans*, German pathologist (1847–88).

ISM (*US*) *abbrev* : Institute for Supply Management.

ism /iz'm/ *n* any distinctive doctrine, theory or practice. [From sfx *-ism*]
■ **ismat'ic** or **ismat'ical** *adj* addicted to isms or faddish theories. **ismat'icalness** *n*.

-ism /-i-zm/, **-asm** /-a-zm/ or **-icism** /-i-si-zm/ *sfx* forming abstract nouns signifying condition, system, as *egoism, deism, Calvinism, laconism, pleonasm, Anglicism, witticism*. [L *-ismus, -asmus*, from Gr *-ismos, -asmos*]

Ismaili /is-mä-ē'lē or is-mā'i-li/ n one of a sect of Shiite Muslims that recognizes Ismail, son of the sixth imam, as the true seventh imam (also adj).
■ **Ismailian** /is-mā-il'i-ən/ n and adj. **Is'mailism** n. **Ismailit'ic** adj.

isn't /iz'ənt/ contraction of **is not**.

ISO abbrev: Imperial Service Order; International Organization for Standardization (often used to denote the speed of photographic film).

iso /ī'sō/ (film and TV) n short for **isolated replay**, a facility whereby a section of film can be isolated and the action replayed.

iso- /ī-sō-, -so-/, also **is-** /īs-/ combining form signifying equal; denoting an isomeric substance, as in **iso-oc'tane** one of the isomers of normal octane. [Gr isos equal]

isoagglutination /ī-sō-ə-gloo-ti-nā'shən/ n the agglutination of red blood corpuscles within the same blood group. [**iso-**]
■ **isoagglu'tinin** n an antibody that causes the agglutination of red blood corpuscles in animals of the same species from which it was derived.

isoaminile /ī-sō-am'i-nīl/ n a drug formerly used as an antitussive.

isoantibody /ī-sō-an'ti-bod-i/ n an antibody that occurs naturally against foreign tissue from an individual of the same species. [**iso-**]

isoantigen /ī-sō-an'ti-jən/ n an antigen that stimulates antibody production in different members of the same species. [**iso-**]

isobar /ī'sō-bär/ n a curve running through places of equal pressure; esp one connecting places, or their representations on a map, of equal barometric pressure (meteorol); same as **isobare** (chem). [**iso-** and Gr baros weight]
■ **isobaric** /-bar'ik/ adj. **isobaromet'ric** adj.

isobare /ī'sō-bār/ or **isobar** /ī'sō-bär/ n either of two atoms of different chemical elements but of identical atomic mass (eg an isotope of titanium and an isotope of chromium both of atomic mass 50). [Ety as for **isobar**]

isobase /ī'sō-bās/ (geol) n a contour line of equal upheaval of the land. [**iso-** and Gr basis step]

isobath /ī'sō-bäth/ n a contour line connecting points of equal underwater depth. [**iso-** and Gr bathos depth]
■ **isobath'ic** adj.

isobilateral /ī-sō-bī-lat'ə-rəl/ adj bilaterally symmetrical with upper and undersurfaces alike; symmetrical about two planes (bot). [**iso-**]

isobront /ī'sō-bront/ n a contour line marking simultaneous development of a thunderstorm. [**iso-** and Gr brontē thunder]

isobutylene /ī-sō-bū'tə-lēn/ n an isomer of butylene used in the manufacture of synthetic rubber. [**iso-** and **butylene**]

isochasm /ī'sō-kazm/ n a contour line of equal frequency of auroral displays. [**iso-** and Gr chasma a gap, expanse]
■ **isochasm'ic** adj.

isocheim or **isochime** /ī'sō-kīm/ n a contour line of mean winter temperature. [**iso-** and Gr cheima winter weather, cheimainein to be stormy]
■ **isocheim'al**, **isocheim'enal** or **isochī'mal** adj and n. **isocheim'ic** adj.

isochor or **isochore** /ī'sō-kōr or -kör/ n a curve representing variation of some quantity under conditions of constant volume. [**iso-** and Gr chōrā space]
■ **isochoric** /-kor'ik/ adj.

isochromatic /ī-sō-krō-mat'ik/ adj having the same colour (optics); orthochromatic (photog). [**iso-** and Gr chrōma, -atos colour]

isochronal /ī-sok'rə-nəl/ or **isochronous** /-nəs/ adj of equal time; performed in equal times; performed at the same time; in regular periodicity. [**iso-** and Gr chronos time]
■ **isoch'ronally** or **isoch'ronously** adv. **i'sochrone** n a line on a chart or map joining points associated with a constant time difference, eg in reception of radio signals. **isoch'ronism** n. **isoch'ronize** or **-ise** vt.

isoclinal /ī-sō-klī'nəl/ adj (of stratified rock) folded with nearly the same dip in each limb (geol); in terrestrial magnetism, having the same magnetic dip. ◆n a contour line of magnetic dip. [**iso-** and Gr klīnein to bend]
■ **ī'socline** n an area of rock strata with isoclinal folds; an isoclinal. **isoclinic** /-klin'ik/ adj and n isoclinal.

isocracy /ī-sok'rə-si/ n (a system of government in which all people have) equal political power. [**iso-** and Gr krateein to rule]
■ **isocrat'ic** adj.

isocryme /ī'sō-krīm/ n a contour line of equal temperature during the coldest time. [**iso-** and Gr krȳmos cold]
■ **isocrȳm'al** adj and n.

isocyanide /ī-sō-sī'ən-īd/ n a salt or ester of **isocyanic acid**, a hypothetical acid only known in its compounds. [**iso-**]

isocyclic /ī'sō-sī-klik/ adj (chem) having a closed chain of similar atoms, homocyclic. [**iso-**]

Isodia /ī-sō'di-ə/ n pl the feast of the presentation of the Virgin in the temple at the age of three. [Gr, neuter pl of adj eisodios, from eisodos entrance]

isodiametric /ī-sō-dī-ə-met'rik/ or **isodiametrical** /-əl/ adj of equal diameters; about as broad as long. [**iso-**]

isodiaphere /ī-sō-dī'ə-fēr/ n one of two or more nuclides with the same difference between the totals of neutrons and protons. [**iso-** and Gr diapherein to differ, carry across]

isodicon /ī-sod'i-kon/ (Gr church) n a troparion or short anthem sung while the Gospel is being carried through the church. [Dimin of Gr eisodos entrance]

isodimorphism /ī-sō-dī-mör'fi-zm/ (crystallog) n isomorphism between each of the two forms of a dimorphous substance and the corresponding forms of another dimorphous substance. [**iso-**]
■ **isodimorph'ic** adj. **isodimorph'ous** adj.

isodomon /ī-sod'o-mon/ n (pl **isod'oma**) masonry of uniform blocks in courses of equal height, the vertical joints placed over the middle of the blocks below (also (Latinized) **isod'omum**). [Gr, neuter of isodomos equal-coursed, from isos equal, and domos a course, from demein to build]
■ **isod'omous** adj.

isodont /ī'sō-dont/ or **isodontal** /-əl/ (zool) adj having all the teeth similar in size and form. ◆n an isodontal animal. [Gr isos equal, and odous, odontos tooth]

isodynamic /ī-sō-dī-nam'ik or -dī-/ adj of equal strength, esp of magnetic intensity. ◆n an isodynamic line on the earth or a map, a contour line of magnetic intensity. [**iso-** and Gr dynamis strength]

isoelectric /ī-sō-i-lek'trik/ adj having the same potential. [**iso-**]
□ **isoelectric point** n the pH-value at which the ionization of an ampholyte is at a minimum.

isoelectronic /ī-sō-el-ik-tron'ik/ adj having an equal number of electrons, or similar electron patterns. [**iso-**]

isoenzyme /ī-sō-en'zīm/ n one of several variants of the same enzyme occurring within a single species. [**iso-**]

isoetes /ī-sō'ə-tēz/ n (pl **iso'etes**) a plant of the quillwort genus (Isoetes) constituting a family (**Isoetā'ceae**) of pteridophytes, with short stem, a bunch of quill-shaped leaves in which the sporangia are sunk, and branching roots. [Gr isoetes house leek (an evergreen), from isos equal, and etos a year]

isoflavone /ī-sō-flā'vōn/ n a plant oestrogen, found esp in soy beans, having possible nutritional benefits. [**iso-**]

isogamy /ī-sog'ə-mi/ (biol) n the conjugation of two gametes of similar size and form. [**iso-** and Gr gamos marriage]
■ **isogamete** /ī-sō-gam'ēt or ēt'/ n. **isogamet'ic**, **isogam'ic** or **isog'amous** adj.

isogeny /ī-soj'ə-ni/ n likeness of origin. [**iso-** and Gr genos kind]
■ **isogenetic** /ī-sō-ji-net'ik/, **isogenic** /-jen'ik/ or **isog'enous** adj.

isogeotherm /ī-sō-jē'ō-thûrm/ n a subterranean contour of equal temperature. [**iso-** and Gr gē the earth, and thermē heat, from thermos hot]
■ **isogeotherm'al** or **isogeotherm'ic** adj of equal subterranean temperature. ◆n an isogeotherm.

isogloss /ī'sō-glos/ n a line on a map separating one region from another region which differs from it in a particular feature of dialect. [**iso-** and Gr glōssa tongue]
■ **isogloss'al**, **isoglott'al** or **isoglott'ic** adj.

isogonic /ī-sō-gon'ik/ or **isogonal** /ī-sog'ə-nəl/ adj of equal angles, esp of magnetic declination. ◆n an isogonic line or contour line of magnetic declination. [**iso-** and Gr gōniā an angle]
■ **i'sogon** n an equiangular polygon.

isogram /ī'sō-gram/ n a line drawn on a map or diagram showing all points which have an equal numerical value with respect to a given climatic or other variable (see also **isopleth**). [**iso-** and Gr gramma a letter]

isohel /ī'sō-hel/ n a contour line of equal amounts of sunshine. [**iso-** and Gr hēlios sun]

isohyet /ī-sō-hī'ət/ n a contour line of equal rainfall. [**iso-** and Gr hȳetos rain, from hȳein to rain]
■ **isohy'etal** adj of equal rainfall. ◆n an isohyet.

isoimmunization or **-s-** /ī-sō-im-ū-nī-zā'shən/ n the development of antibodies within an individual against antigens from another individual of the same species. [**iso-**]

isokinetic /ī-sō-ki-net'ik/ adj (of the withdrawal of a fluid sample) accomplished without disturbance to the speed and direction of flow. [**iso-** and Gr kīneein to move]

■ words derived from main entry word; □ compound words; ■ idioms and phrasal verbs

Isokontae /ī-sō-kon'tē/ *n pl* the green algae, whose zoospores *usu* have equal cilia. [**iso-** and Gr *kontos* a (punting) pole]
- i'**sokont** *n*. **isokont'an** *adj* and *n*.

isolate /ī'sō-lāt/ *vt* to place in a detached situation, like an island; to detach; to insulate; to separate (*esp* those with an infectious disease) (*med*); to seclude; to segregate; to obtain in a pure, uncombined state; to establish a pure culture of (a microorganism). ◆ *n* /-lit or lāt/ something isolated, *esp* for individual study or experiment. ◆ *adj* isolated. [Ital *isolare*, from *isola*, from L *īnsula* an island]
- **isolabil'ity** *n*. **i'solable** *adj*. **i'solāted** *adj* standing apart; separate; solitary. **isolā'tion** *n*. **isolā'tionism** *n* the policy of avoiding political entanglements with other countries. **isolā'tionist** *n* and *adj*. **i'solātive** *adj* tending towards isolation; occurring without influence from outside. **i'solātor** *n* someone who or something that isolates; a transparent plastic enclosure in which a patient is kept free of contamination by infective agents (*med*).
- ❑ **isolated replay** see **iso**. **isolating languages** *n pl* those in which each word is a bare root, not inflected or compounded.

isolecithal /ī-sō-les'i-thəl/ *adj* (of the ova of mammals and some other vertebrates) having the yolk distributed evenly through the protoplasm. [**iso-** and Gr *lekithos* egg yolk]

isoleucine /ī-sō-lū'sīn/ *n* an essential amino acid. [**iso-**]

isoline /ī'sō-līn/ same as **isopleth**.

isologue /ī'sō-log/ *n* an organic compound with similar molecular structure to another, but containing different atoms of the same valency. [**iso-** and Gr *logos* ratio]
- **isol'ogous** *adj*.

isomagnetic /ī-sō-mag-net'ik/ *adj* having equal magnetic induction or force. ◆ *n* (also **isomagnetic line**) an imaginary line joining places at which the force of the earth's magnetic field is constant. [**iso-**]

isomer /ī'sō-mər/ (*chem*) *n* a substance, radical, or ion isomeric with another; an atomic nucleus having the same atomic number and mass as another or others but a different energy state. [**iso-** and Gr *meros* part]
- **i'somēre** *n* (*zool*) an organ or segment corresponding to or homologous with another. **isomeric** /-mer'ik/ *adj* (*chem*) identical in percentage composition and molecular weight but different in constitution or structure; (of nuclei) differing only in energy state and half-life. **isom'erism** *n* the property of being isomeric; the existence of isomers. **isomerīzā'tion** or **-s-** *n*. **isomerize** or **-ise** /ī-som'ər-īz/ *vt* and *vi* to change into an isomer. **isom'erous** *adj* (*bot*) having the same number of parts (*esp* in floral whorls).

isomerase /ī-som'ə-rāz or -rās/ *n* an enzyme which speeds up the conversion of one isomeric compound to another isomeric form.

isometric /ī-sō-met'rik/ *adj* (also **isomet'rical**) having equality of measure; relating to isometrics; having the plane of projection equally inclined to three perpendicular axes; (of muscular contraction) not shortening the muscle fibres and not moving a joint; of the cubic system, or referable to three equal axes at right angles to one another (*crystallog*). ◆ *n* (also **isometric line**) a line on a graph showing variations of pressure and temperature at a constant volume. [**iso-** and Gr *metron* measure]
- **isomet'rically** *adv*. **isomet'rics** *n sing* a system of strengthening the muscles and tuning up the body by opposing one muscle to another or to a resistant object. **isom'etry** *n* equality of measure.

isomorph /ī'sō-mörf/ *n* that which shows isomorphism. [**iso-** and Gr *morphē* form]
- **isomorph'ic** *adj* showing isomorphism. **isomorph'ism** *n* similarity in shape or structure in unrelated forms (*biol*); close similarity in crystalline form combined with similar chemical constitution (*crystallog*); a one-to-one correspondence between the elements of two or more sets and between the sums or products of the elements of one set and those of the equivalent elements of the other set or sets (*maths*). **isomorph'ous** *adj*.
- ❑ **isomorphous mixture** *n* a mixed crystal or solid solution in which isomorphous substances are crystallized together by vicarious substitution.

isoniazid /ī-sō-nī'ə-zid/ or **isoniazide** /-zīd/ *n* an anti-tuberculosis drug, used in combination with other such drugs. [*isoni*cotinic acid hydra*zide*]

isonomy /ī-son'ə-mi/ *n* equal law, rights or privileges. [Gr *isonomiā*, from *isos* equal, and *nomos* law]
- **isonom'ic** or **ison'omous** *adj*.

isopach /ī'sō-pak/ or **isopachyte** /-īt/ (*geol*) *n* a contour line connecting points beneath which a stratum has the same thickness. [**iso-** and Gr *pachys* thick]

isoperimeter /ī-sō-pə-rim'i-tər/ *n* a figure with perimeter equal to another. [**iso-** and Gr *perimetron* circumference]
- **isoperimetrical** /ī-sō-per-i-met'ri-kəl/ *adj*. **isoperim'etry** *n*.

isopleth /ī'sō-pleth/ *n* an isogram, *esp* one on a graph showing variations of a climatic element as a function of two variables; cf **nomogram**. [**iso-** and Gr *plēthos* great number]

isopod /ī'sō-pod/ *n* a member of the Isopoda. [**iso-** and Gr *pous, podos* a foot]
- **Isopoda** /ī-sop'ə-də/ *n pl* an order of Crustacea including woodlice, fish lice, etc with no carapace, a depressed body, sessile eyes, seven pairs of nearly equal thoracic legs, and *usu* lamellar uropods. **isop'odan** or **isop'odous** *adj*.

isopolity /ī-sō-pol'i-ti/ *n* reciprocity of rights of citizenship in different communities. [**iso-** and Gr *polīteiā* citizenship]

isoprenaline /ī-sō-pren'ə-lēn/ *n* a drug used to stimulate the heart and to dilate the air-passages in asthma and bronchial conditions.

isoprene /ī'sō-prēn/ (*chem*) *n* a hydrocarbon of the terpene group, which may be polymerized into synthetic rubber. [**iso-**, *propyl* and sfx *-ene*]

isopropyl /ī-sō-prop'il/ *n* the radical $(CH_3)_2CH$, derived from propane. [**iso-** and **propane**]

Isoptera /ī-sop'tə-rə/ *n pl* an order of insects, the termites, having the two pairs of wings (when present) closely alike. [**iso-** and Gr *pteron* a wing]
- **isop'teran** *n* and *adj*. **isop'terous** *adj*.

isopycnic /ī-sō-pik'nik/ *n* a contour line of equal atmospheric density. [**iso-** and Gr *pyknos* thick]

isorhythmic /ī-sō-ridh'mik or -rith'mik/ *adj* (in ancient prosody) equal in the number of time-units for thesis and arsis, as dactyl, spondee, anapaest; (in medieval motets) having a strict scheme of repeated rhythm independent of melodic repetition. [**iso-** and Gr *rhythmos* rhythm]

isosceles /ī-sos'i-lēz/ (*geom*) *adj* (of a triangle) having two equal sides. [Gr *isoskelēs*, from *isos* equal, and *skelos* a leg]

isoseismal /ī-sō-sīz'məl/ *n* a curve or line connecting points at which an earthquake shock is felt with equal intensity. ◆ *adj* of equal seismic intensity (also **isoseis'mic**). [**iso-** and Gr *seismos* a shaking]

isosmotic /ī-soz-mot'ik/ *adj* having the same osmotic pressure. [**iso-**]

isospin /ī'sō-spin/ *n* (in particle physics) a quantum number applied to members of closely related groups of particles to express and explain the theory that such particles (eg protons and neutrons) are in fact states of the same particle differing with regard to electric charge (also **isotopic spin**). [*isotopic spin*]

isosporous /ī-sos'pə-rəs, ī-sō-spō'rəs or -spö'/ (*bot*) *adj* having spores of one kind only, *opp* to *heterosporous*. [**iso-** and Gr *sporos* seed]
- **isos'pory** *n*.

isostasy /ī-sos'tə-si/ (*geol*) *n* a condition of equilibrium held to exist in the earth's crust, equal masses of matter underlying equal areas, whether of sea or land down to an assumed level of compensation. [Gr *isos* equal, and *stasis* setting, weighing, *statikos* relating to weighing]
- **isostatic** /ī-sō-stat'ik/ *adj* in hydrostatic equilibrium from equality of pressure; in a state of isostasy; relating to isostasy. **isostat'ically** *adv*.

isostemonous /ī-sō-stē'mə-nəs/ (*bot*) *adj* having as many stamens as petals. [**iso-** and Gr *stēmōn* a thread]

isosteric /ī-sō-ster'ik/ *adj* (of two different molecules) having the same number of atoms, and the same number and arrangement of valency electrons. [**iso-**]

isosthenuria /ī-sōs-the-nū'ri-ə/ *n* inability to produce urine in different concentrations. [**iso-** and Gr *sthenos* strength, and *ouron* urine]

isotactic /ī-sō-tak'tik/ *adj* of or concerning a polymer with its attached groups of atoms in a regular order on one side of the central chain. [**iso-**]

isothere /ī'sō-thēr/ *n* a contour line of equal mean summer temperature. [**iso-** and Gr *theros* summer, from *therein* to make warm]
- **isotheral** /ī-soth'ər-əl or ī-sō-thēr'əl/ *adj* of equal mean summer temperature. ◆ *n* an isothere.

isotherm /ī'sō-thûrm/ *n* a contour line of equal temperature. [**iso-** and Gr *thermē* heat, from *thermos* hot]
- **isotherm'al** *adj* at constant temperature; relating to isotherms. ◆ *n* an isothermal line, isotherm. **isotherm'ally** *adv*.

isothiocyanate /ī-sō-thī-ō-sī'ə-nāt/ *n* any of a group of sulphur-containing compounds, some of which are produced by cabbages, cress and other cruciferous vegetables and act as herbicides or fungicides. [**iso-**]

isotone /ī'sō-tōn/ *n* one of a number of nuclides having the same number of neutrons in the nucleus with differing numbers of protons. [**iso-** and prob Gr *tonos* tension]

isotonic /ī-sō-ton'ik/ *adj* having the same tone, tension or osmotic pressure; (of muscular contraction) shortening the muscle fibres and moving a joint; (of an energy drink) containing salts and minerals of the same concentration as in the body. [**iso-** and Gr *tonos* tension, tone]

■ **isotonic'ity** *n*.

isotope /ī'sō-tōp/ *n* one of a set of chemically identical species of atom which have the same atomic number but different mass numbers (a natural element is made up of isotopes, always present in the same proportions). [**iso-** and Gr *topos* place (ie in the periodic table)]

■ **isotopic** /-top'ik/ *adj*. **isotop'ically** *adv*. **isotopy** /ī-sot'ə-pi/ *n* the fact or condition of being isotopic.

❑ **isotope separation** *n* the process of altering the relative abundance of isotopes in a mixture. **isotopic number** *n* the excess number of neutrons over protons in a nuclide. **isotopic spin** same as **isospin**.

■ **stable isotope** a non-radioactive isotope found in nature.

isotretinoin /ī-sō-trə-tin'ō-in/ *n* a drug derived from Vitamin A, used in the treatment of severe acne.

isotron /ī'sō-tron/ *n* a device for separating isotopes by accelerating ions by means of an electric field, the velocities attained being in inverse proportion to the masses. [**isotope** and **-tron**]

isotropic /ī-sō-trop'ik/, also **isotropous** /ī-sot'rə-pəs/ *adj* having the same properties irrespective of direction; without predetermined axes (*biol*). [**iso-** and Gr *tropos* turn, direction]

■ **isot'ropism** or **isot'ropy** *n*.

isotype /ī'sō-tīp/ *n* a presentation of statistical information by a row of diagrammatic pictures each representing a particular number of instances. [**iso-** and Gr *typos* form]

isoxsuprine /ī-sok'sə-prēn/ *n* a drug which dilates blood vessels, used, *esp* formerly, to inhibit contractions in premature labour and in the treatment of arteriosclerosis.

isozyme /ī'sō-zīm/ *n* another word for **isoenzyme**.

ISP (*comput*) *abbrev*: Internet Service Provider, a company or organization that provides access to the Internet.

ispaghula /is-pə-goo'lə/ *n* another name for **psyllium**; the dried seeds of this plant, used as a laxative. [Hindi]

I-spy /ī'spī'/ *n* a wordgame, in which one guesses objects in view, whose names begin with a certain letter of the alphabet; a children's game of hide-and-seek, so called from the cry when someone is spied. [**I** and **spy**]

Israeli /iz-rā'lē/ *n* a citizen of the modern state of *Israel*. ◆ *adj* of or relating to Israel or its inhabitants. [See **Israelite**]

Israelite /iz'ri-əl-īt or -rəl-/ *n* a descendant of Jacob (*Bible*); a Jew (*Bible*); one of the elect (*fig*); a member of a Christian sect that observes the Jewish law. [Gr *Israēlitēs*, from *Israēl*, Heb *Yisrāēl* a name given to Jacob, perhaps meaning 'contender with God', from *sara* to fight, and *El* God]

■ **Israelīt'ic** or **Israelīt'ish** *adj*.

ISS *abbrev*: International Space Station; International Social Service.

issei /ē'sā' or ē-sā'/ *n* a Japanese immigrant in the USA, *orig* one to the USA or Canada after 1907, who did not qualify for citizenship until 1952 (cf **nisei** and **sansei**). [Jap, first generation]

ISSN *abbrev*: International Standard Serial Number.

ISSP *abbrev*: Intensive Supervision and Surveillance Programme (for young offenders).

issue /ish'ū or -oo, also is'ū/ *n* a going or flowing out; an outlet; (an) act of sending out; that which flows or passes out; offspring, children; produce, profits; a fine (*obs*); a putting into circulation, giving out for use, as of banknotes; publication, as of a book; a set of things put forth at one time; a single thing given out or supplied (chiefly *milit*); an act or deed (*Shakesp*); ultimate result, outcome; upshot; lucky or successful outcome (*Shakesp*); critical determination; a point in dispute; a point on which a question depends; a question awaiting decision or ripe for decision; a discharge or flux (*archaic med*); an ulcer produced artificially. ◆ *vi* (in *Spenser usu* **issue**) to go, flow or come out; to proceed, as from a source; to spring; to be produced; to come to a point in fact or law (*law*); to turn out, result, terminate. ◆ *vt* to send out; to put forth; to put into circulation; to publish; to give out for use; to supply (*milit*). [OFr *issue*, from *issir* to go or flow out, from L *exīre*, from *ex* out, and *īre* to go]

■ **iss'uable** *adj*. **iss'uably** *adv*. **iss'uance** *n* the act of giving out, promulgation. **iss'uant** *adj* (*heraldry*) issuing or coming up from another, as a charge or bearing. **iss'ueless** *adj* without issue; childless. **iss'uer** *n*.

❑ **issuing house** *n* a corporate bank that handles share issues on behalf of listed companies.

■ **at issue** in disagreement; in dispute. **feigned issue** (*law*) an issue made up for trial by agreement of the parties or by an order of court, instead of by the ordinary legal procedure. **force the issue** to hasten or compel a final decision on a matter. **general issue** (*law*) a simple denial of the whole charge, as 'Not guilty', instead of a **special issue**, an issue taken by denying a particular part of the allegations. **have**

issues to have unresolved points of conflict or grievance. **immaterial issue** (*law*) an issue which is not decisive of any part of the litigation, as opposed to a **material issue**, one which necessarily involves some part of the rights in controversy. **join** (or **take**) **issue** to take an opposite position, or opposite positions, in dispute; to enter into dispute; to take up a point as basis of dispute. **make an issue of** to exaggerate the seriousness of. **side issue** a subordinate issue arising from the main business.

-ist /-ist/ *sfx* denoting the person who is an advocate or believer in a doctrine or practises an art, as *Calvinist*, *chemist*, *novelist*, *artist*, *royalist*. [L *-ista*, from Gr *-istēs*]

ISTC *abbrev*: formerly, Iron and Steel Trades Confederation.

isthmus /is'məs or isth'məs/ *n* a narrow neck of land connecting two larger portions; a narrow part of a structure connecting two larger parts (*anat*); a constriction. [L, from Gr *isthmos*, from root of *ienai* to go]

■ **isth'mian** *adj* relating to an isthmus, *esp* the Isthmus of Corinth. ❑ **Isthmian Games** *n pl* (*Gr hist*) games held on the Isthmus of Corinth, near the Saronic Gulf shore.

Istiophorus same as **Histiophorus** (see under **hist-**).

istle /ist'li/ or **ixtle** /ikst'li/ *n* a valuable fibre obtained from Agave, Bromelia, and other plants. [Mexican Sp *ixtle*, from Nahuatl *ichtli*]

IT *abbrev*: Information Technology.

It. *abbrev*: Italian; Italian vermouth.

it¹ /it/ *pronoun* (*genitive* **its**; *pl* **they** and **them**) the neuter of **he** or **she** and **him** or **her¹** applied to a thing without life, a lower animal, a young child, rarely (except as an antecedent or in contempt) to a man or woman; used as an impersonal, indefinite, or anticipatory or provisional subject or object, as the object of a transitive verb that is normally an intransitive, or a noun; (in children's games) the player chosen to oppose all others; the *ne plus ultra*, that which answers exactly to what one is looking for (*inf*); an indefinable crowning quality, personal magnetism; sex appeal, sexual intercourse or activity (*inf*). [OE *hit*, neuter (nominative and accusative) of *hē*; Du *het*, Gothic *hita*, this; related to Gothic *ita*, Ger *es*, L *id*, Sans *i*]

❑ **It Girl** *n* (*inf*) a young woman who is, or who makes it her business to be, noted in fashionable circles for her charisma, beauty and wealth.

it² /it/ (*inf*) *n* Italian vermouth.

ITA *abbrev*: initial teaching alphabet (also **i.t.a.**).

ita /ē'tə, it'ə/ *n* the miriti palm. [Arawak *ité*]

itacism /ē'tə-si-zm/ *n* the pronunciation of Greek eta as in Modern Greek, like English long e, *opp* to *etacism*; iotacism in pronunciation of various vowels and diphthongs. [Gr *ēta* eta, η]

itacolumite /it-ə-kol'ū-mīt/ *n* a schistose quartzite containing scales of mica, talc and chlorite, often having a certain flexibility. [*Itacolumi*, Brazilian mountain]

itaconic acid /it-ə-kon'ik or īt-, as'id/ *n* a white crystalline solid obtained by fermentation of sugar with Aspergillus mould, used in plastics manufacture. [Anagram of *aconitic*]

ita est /ē'tə est/ (*L*) it is so.

Ital. *abbrev*: Italian; Italy.

ital. *abbrev*: italic.

Itala see **Italic version** under **Italian**.

Italian /i-tal'yən/ *adj* of or relating to *Italy* or its people or language. ◆ *n* a native or citizen of Italy, or a person of the same race; the language of Italy; an Italian restaurant or meal (*inf*). [L *Italiānus* and Gr *Italikos*, from L *Italia*, Gr *Italiā* Italy]

■ **Ital'ianate** *adj* Italian in style (also *vt*). **Ital'ianism** or **Ital'icism** /-sizm/ *n* an Italian idiom or habit; Italian sympathies. **Ital'ianist** *n* a person who has a scholarly knowledge of Italian; a person of Italian sympathies. **Italianīzā'tion** or **-s-** *n*. **Ital'ianize** or **-ise** *vt* to make Italian; to give an Italian character to. ◆ *vi* to become Italian; to play the Italian; to speak Italian; to use Italian idioms; to adopt Italian ways. **Ital'ic** *adj* relating to Italy, *esp* ancient Italy; of or relating to the Italic branch of languages; (*without cap*) of a sloping type introduced by the Italian printer Aldo Manuzio in 1501, used *esp* for emphasis or other distinctive purpose, indicated in manuscripts by single underlining. ◆ *n* a branch of Indo-European *usu* considered to comprise Oscan, Umbrian, Latin and related languages, but sometimes applied to either the Latin group or the Osco-Umbrian group alone; (*without cap, usu in pl*) an italic letter. **italicīzā'tion** or **-s-** *n*. **ital'icize** or **-ise** *vt* to put in, or mark for, italics. **Ital'iot** or **Ital'iote** *n* a Greek of ancient Italy (also *adj*).

❑ **Italian architecture** *n* the style practised by Italian architects of the 15c–17c, which originated in a revival of the ancient architecture of Rome. **Italianate Englishman** *n* an Englishman of the Renaissance, full of Italian learning and vices, proverbially equivalent to a devil incarnate. **Italian garden** *n* a formal garden with statues. **Italian iron** *n* a smoothing iron for fluting. **Italian sixth** *n* (*music*) a chord of a note with its major third and augmented sixth. **Italian sonnet** same as **Petrarchan sonnet** (see under **sonnet**). **Italian vermouth** *n* a sweet vermouth. **Italian warehouseman** *n* (*hist*) a dealer in such groceries as macaroni, olive oil, dried fruits, etc. **Italic version** or **It'ala** *n* a translation of the Bible into Latin, based on the 'Old Latin' version, and made probably in the time of Augustine.

Italic, italic, etc see under **Italian**.

Italo- /i-tal-ō- or it-ə-lō-/ *combining form* signifying Italy or Italian, as in *Italophile*.

ITAR-Tass or **Itar-Tass** /it-ä-tas'/ *n* the official Russian news agency. [Acronym from Russ *Informatsionnoe telegrafnoe agentstvo Rossii* Information Telegraph Agency of Russia, **TASS**]

ITC *abbrev* : (until 2003) Independent Television Commission (now replaced by **Ofcom**).

itch /ich/ *n* an irritating sensation in the skin; scabies, an eruptive disease in the skin, caused by a parasitic mite; a constant teasing desire. ◆ *vi* to have an unpleasant, irritating sensation in the skin; to have a constant, teasing desire. [OE *giccan* to itch; Scot *youk, yuck,* Ger *jucken* to itch]
■ **itch'iness** *n*. **itch'y** (**itch'ier; itch'iest**) *adj* relating to or affected with an itch or itching.
◻ **itching powder** *n* a powder that causes itching when applied to the skin. **itch'-mite** *n* a mite (*Sarcoptes scabiei*) that burrows in the skin causing severe itching leading to scabies. **itch'weed** *n* Indian poke. **itch'y-palmed** *adj* greedy for money.
■ **have an itching palm** to be greedy for financial gain. **have** (or **get**) **itchy feet** to have strong desire to move, travel, or change one's course.

it'd /it'əd/ a contraction of **it had** or **it would**.

-ite /-īt/ *sfx* used to form: (1) names of people, indicating their origin, place of origin, affiliations, loyalties, etc, eg *Semite, Durhamite, Jacobite, Thatcherite*; (2) names of fossil organisms, eg *ammonite*; (3) names of minerals, eg *calcite*; (4) names of salts of acids with sfx **-ous,** eg *sulphite* salt of sulphurous acid; (5) names of bodily parts, eg *somite.* The nouns may be used also as adjectives. [Gr *-itēs*]

item /ī'təm/ *n* a separate article or particular in an enumeration; a piece of news or other matter in a newspaper, magazine, television programme, etc; two people having a romantic or sexual relationship (*inf*). ◆ *vt* to set down in enumeration; to make a note of. ◆ *adv* (*archaic*) likewise; also. [L *item* likewise]
■ **itemizā'tion** or **-s-** *n*. **i'temize** or **-ise** *vt* to give or list by items. **i'temizer** or **-s-** *n*.

iterate /it'ə-rāt/ *vt* to do again; to say again, repeat. [L *iterāre, -ātum,* from *iterum* again]
■ **it'erance** or **iterā'tion** *n* repetition. **it'erant** or **it'erative** /-ə-tiv or -ā-tiv/ *adj* repeating. **it'erātively** *adv*.

iteroparous /it-ə-rō-par'əs/ (*zool*) *adj* (of an animal) capable of producing offspring several times in the course of a lifetime. [L *iterum* again, and *parēre* to bring forth]
■ **iteropar'ity** *n*.

iterum /it'ə-rəm or -e-rŭm/ (*L*) *adv* again; anew.

ithyphallus /ith-i-fal'əs/ *n* an erect phallus; (with *cap*) the stinkhorn genus of fungi. [Gr *īthyphallos,* from *īthys* straight, and *phallos* a phallus]
■ **ithyphall'ic** *adj* of or with an ithyphallus; relating to the processions in honour of Dionysos in which an ithyphallus was carried, or to the hymns sung or the metres used; shameless.

itinerant /i-tin'ə-rənt, also ī-/ *adj* making journeys from place to place; travelling. ◆ *n* someone who travels from place to place, *esp* a judge, a Methodist preacher, a strolling musician, or a pedlar; a wanderer. [L *iter, itineris* a journey]
■ **itin'eracy** /-ə-si/ or **itin'erancy** *n*. **itin'erantly** *adv*. **itin'erary** *adj* travelling; relating to roads or journeys. ◆ *n* a plan or record of a journey; a road book; a route; an itinerant. **itin'erate** *vi* to travel from place to place, *esp* for the purpose of judging, preaching or lecturing. **itinerā'tion** *n*.

-itis /-ī-tis/ *combining form* denoting: an inflammatory disease, as in *bronchitis*; jocularly extended to conditions considered disease-like, as in *jazzitis.* [Gr *-ītis*]

it'll /it'l/ a contraction of **it will** or **it shall**.

ITN *abbrev* : Independent Television News.

its /its/ *possessive* or *genitive* of **it**[1]. (The old form was *his, its* not being older than the end of the 16c. *Its* does not occur in the English Bible of 1611 (in Leviticus 25.5 the possessive *it* was amended to *its* for the 1660 edition) or in Spenser, rarely in Shakespeare, and is not common until the time of Dryden.)
■ **itself** /it-self'/ *pronoun* the emphatic and reflexive form of **it**.
■ **by itself** alone, apart. **in itself** by its own nature.

it's /its/ a contraction of **it is** or **it has**.

itsy-bitsy /it'si-bit'si/ or **itty-bitty** /it'i-bit'i/ (*inf*) *adj* tiny. [Prob a childish reduplicated form of **little** influenced by **bit**[1]]

ITT *abbrev* : International Telephone and Telegraph Corporation.

ITU *abbrev* : intensive therapy unit (*med*); International Telecommunication Union.

iTunes® /ī'tūnz/ *n* a computer application that allows users to download recorded music from the Internet.

ITV *abbrev* : Independent Television.

-ity /-it-i/ *sfx* forming nouns denoting a state or quality, as in *chastity, creativity.* [L *-itas*]

IU *abbrev* : international unit; intrauterine (also **i.u.**).

IUCD or **IUD** *abbrev* : intrauterine (contraceptive) device, a plastic or metal spiral or T-shaped device inserted in the uterus to prevent conception.

IUCN *abbrev* : International Union for the Conservation of Nature.

-ium /-i-əm/ *sfx* forming nouns denoting: a metallic element, as in *plutonium*; a group forming a positive ion, as in *ammonium*; a biological structure, as in *conidium.* [Latinized form of Gr *-ion*]

IUPAC /ū'pak/ *abbrev* : International Union of Pure and Applied Chemistry.

iure /yoo're/ (*L*) *adv* by right or by law.
■ **iure coronae** /ko-rō'nē or -nī/ by right of the crown. **iure divino** /di-vī'nō or dē-wē'nō/ by divine law. **iure humano** /hū-mä'nō or (h)oo-mä'nō/ by human law. **iure mariti** /ma-rē'tē/ by a husband's right. **iure propinquitatis** /prō-ping-kwi-tä'tis/ by right of relationship. **iure sanguinis** /sang'gwi-nis/ by right of blood.

IV *abbrev* : intravenous; intravenous drip; intravenously.

IVA *abbrev* : individual voluntary agreement, an arrangement to repay a percentage of one's debts over a fixed period of time in order to avoid bankruptcy.

IVD *abbrev* : intra vas device, a contraceptive that blocks the path of sperm along the vas deferens.

I've /īv/ a contraction of **I have**.

-ive /-iv/ *sfx* forming adjectives denoting a quality, inclination, action, etc, as in *abrasive, secretive.* [Fr *-if*]

ivermectin /ī-və-mek'tin/ *n* a drug used in the treatment of onchocerciasis.

IVF *abbrev* : in vitro fertilization.

Ivorian /ī-vō'ri-ən/ *adj* of or relating to the *Ivory Coast* (now officially the Republic of Côte d'Ivoire) in W Africa, or its inhabitants. ◆ *n* a native or citizen of the Ivory Coast.

ivory /ī'və-ri/ *n* dentine, *esp* the hard white substance composing the tusks of the elephant, walrus, hippopotamus and narwhal; (in *pl*) objects of, or resembling, ivory, eg piano-keys, dice, teeth, and formerly billiard balls and dominoes (*sl*); the creamy-white colour of ivory. ◆ *adj* made of, resembling, or of the colour of, ivory. [OFr *ivurie* (Fr *ivoire*), from L *ebur, eboris* ivory; Coptic *ebu* elephant, ivory]
■ **i'voried** *adj* made like ivory; supplied with teeth (*sl*). **i'vorist** *n* a worker in ivory.
◻ **i'vory-black** *n* a black pigment, a powder, *orig* made from burnt ivory, but now from bone. **ivory gate** see under **gate**[1]. **i'vory-nut** *n* the nut of the S American palm *Phytelephas* or other palm, yielding **vegetable ivory** a substance like ivory. **i'vory-palm** *n* a low-growing S American palm yielding the ivory nut. **ivory-por'celain** *n* a fine ware with an ivory-white glaze. **ivory tower** *n* (*fig*) a place of retreat from the world and one's fellows; a lifestyle remote from that of most ordinary people, leading to ignorance of practical concerns, problems, etc. **ivory-tow'ered** *adj*. **i'vory-tree** *n* the palay.
■ **show one's ivories** (*sl*) to show the teeth. **tickle the ivories** (*inf*) to play the piano.

IVR *abbrev* : International Vehicle Registration.

ivresse /ē-vres'/ (*Fr*) *n* drunkenness.

ivy /ī'vi/ *n* an araliaceous evergreen plant (*Hedera helix*) that climbs by roots on trees and walls. [OE *īfig,* OHGer *ebah*]
■ **i'vied** (also **i'vy'd**) *adj* overgrown or covered with ivy.
◻ **i'vy-bush** *n* a bush or branch of ivy, *esp,* formerly, one hung at a tavern-door, the ivy being sacred to Bacchus. **Ivy League** *n* a name given to eight eastern US universities of particular academic and social prestige. **i'vy-leaved** *adj* having five-lobed leaves like ivy (as the *ivy-leaved* toadflax). **i'vy-man'tled** *adj* (*poetic*) ivied. **i'vy-tod'** *n* a bush of ivy.
■ **ground-ivy** and **poison ivy** see under **ground**[1] and **poison** respectively.

IW *abbrev* : Isle of Wight.

IWC *abbrev* : International Whaling Commission.

iwi /ē'wi/ (*NZ*) *n* a tribe. [Maori]

iwis or **ywis** /i-wis'/ (archaic) adv certainly, sometimes erroneously written I wis, as if 'I know'. [ME ywis, iwis, from OE gewis certain; Ger gewiss (adv)]

IWW abbrev : Industrial Workers of the World.

ixia /ik'si-ə/ n any plant of the iridaceous genus Ixia, found in southern Africa. [New L, from Gr ixos mistletoe, bird-lime]

ixodiasis /ik-sō-dī'ə-sis/ n a disease caused by or transmitted by ticks. [New L Ixodes the tick genus, and **-iasis**]

ixtle see istle.

Iynx a spelling of the generic name **Jynx**.

Iyyar /ē'yär/ n the eighth month of the Jewish year (second of the ecclesiastical year). [Heb]

izard /iz'ərd/ n a Pyrenean chamois. [Fr isard]

-ize or **-ise** /-īz/, also **-icize** or **-icise** /-i-sīz/ sfx forming verbs from adjectives (meaning to (cause to) become as specified), eg equalize, or from nouns (meaning to practise, or subject to, the thing specified), eg botanize or satirize. [L -izāre, from Gr -izein; Fr -iser]

izvestiya or **izvestia** /iz-ves'ti-ə/ (Russ) n news; information.

izzard /iz'ərd/ (archaic or dialect) n the letter Z.

izzat /iz'ət/ n public esteem; honour, reputation, prestige. [Urdu, from Ar 'izzah glory]

Jj

a b c d e f g h i j k l m n o p q r s t u v w x y z

Jenson Designed by Robert Slimbach in 1996. USA.

J or **j** /jā/ or (*Scot*) jī/ *n* the tenth letter in the modern English alphabet, developed from I, specialized to denote a consonantal sound (*dzh* in English, *y* in German and other languages, *zh* in French, an open guttural in Spanish), I being retained for the vowel sound (a differentiation not general in English books until about 1630); anything shaped like the letter J.
❑ **J'-curve** *n* (*econ*) a small initial deterioration, decrease, etc followed by a larger sustained improvement, increase, etc, appearing on a graph as a J-shaped curve. **J'-pen** *n* a pen with a short broad nib.

J or **J.** *abbrev* : jack (*cards*); Japan (IVR); Japanese; joint (of marijuana) (*inf*); Journal; Judge (*pl* **JJ**); Justice (*pl* **JJ**).

J *symbol* : joule (the SI unit of work, heat and energy).

j *symbol* : (as a Roman numeral) used in old manuscripts and in medical prescriptions instead of *i* final, eg *vj*, six.

j (*maths*) *symbol* : used equally with *i* for the imaginary square root of − 1.

JA *abbrev* : Jamaica (IVR).

jab /jab/ *vt* and *vi* to poke, stab; to strike with a short straight punch. ◆ *n* a sudden thrust or stab; a short straight punch; an injection (*inf*). [Orig Scot variant of **job²**]

jabber /jab'ər/ *vi* to gabble or talk rapidly. ◆ *vt* to say indistinctly. ◆ *n* rapid indistinct speaking. [Imit]
■ **jabb'erer** *n*. **jabb'ering** *n* and *adj*. **jabb'eringly** *adv*.

jabberwock /jab'ər-wok/ *n* a fabulous monster created by Lewis Carroll in his poem *Jabberwocky*; (also **jabb'erwocky**) nonsense, gibberish.

jabble /jab'l/ (*Scot*) *n* an agitation in liquid; a rippling; a quantity of liquid enough to dash about or splash. ◆ *vt* and *vi* to splash; to ripple; to dash; to jumble (*fig*). [Imit]

jabers /jā'bərz/ *n* in the Irish oath *be jabers* probably for **Jesus**.

jabiru /jab'i-roo or -roo'/ *n* a large S American stork; also applied to certain other kinds of stork, eg the saddlebill. [Tupí *jabirú*]

jaborandi /jab-ə-ran'di or jab-ö-/ *n* a sweat- and saliva-inducing Brazilian drug, obtained from the leaflets of rutaceous shrubs (genus *Pilocarpus*) and other sources; the leaflets or plants themselves. [Tupí]

jabot /zhab'ō/ *n* a frill of lace, etc, worn in front of a woman's dress or on a man's shirt-front, *esp* (now) as part of full Highland dress. [Fr]

jacamar /jak'ə-mär/ *n* any one of a S American family (Galbulidae) of long-billed insect-catching birds with *usu* metallic green or bronze plumage. [Fr, from Tupí *jacamá-ciri*]

jaçana /zhä-sə-nä'/ or **jacana** /jak'ə-nə/ *n* a long-toed swamp bird of the tropics. [Port, from Tupí]

jacaranda /jak-ə-ran'də/ *n* a tropical tree of the family Bignoniaceae, with lilac-coloured flowers, fern-like leaves and hard, heavy, fragrant brown wood; any similar tree or its wood. [Port and Tupí *jacarandá*]

jacchus /jak'əs/ *n* a S American marmoset (genus *Callithrix*). [L *Iacchus*, from Gr *Iakchos* Bacchus]

jacent /jā'sənt/ (*obs*) *adj* lying flat; sluggish. [L *jacēns, -entis*, prp of *jacēre* to lie]

jacinth /jas'inth or jās'/ *n orig* a blue gemstone, *perh* sapphire; a reddish-orange variety of transparent zircon, hyacinth (*mineralogy*); a variety of garnet, topaz, quartz, or other stone (*jewellery*); a reddish-orange colour; a slaty-blue fancy pigeon. [LL *iacinthus*, from L *hyacinthus* hyacinth]

jack¹ /jak/ *n* (with *cap*) a familiar form or diminutive of John; (with *cap*) the common man (*obs*); (with *cap*) a contemptuous term for an ordinary man (*obs*); (*usu* with *cap*) an ill-mannered, vulgar or boorish fellow (*obs*); (sometimes with *cap*) an attendant, servant or labourer; (often with *cap*) a sailor; (with *cap*) used in addressing a man whose name is unknown to the speaker (*US sl*); a detective (*sl*); money (*US sl*); nothing at all (also **jack shit**; *US vulgar sl*); a machine or device

which *orig* took the place of a servant, such as a boot-jack for taking off boots, a device for turning a spit (*smoke-jack, roasting jack*), a device for raising heavy weights; a winch; a socket whose connections operate either to complete or break the circuit only when a jack plug is inserted (*telecom*, etc); a figure that strikes the bell in clocks; the male of some animals; a jackass (also **jack donkey**); a jack rabbit; a jackdaw; a jackfish; any of various tropical and subtropical carangid fishes; (in keyboard instruments) part of the action that moves the hammer or carries the quill or tangent; the key itself (*Shakesp*); a contrivance for guiding threads in a loom; a saw-horse; a jack-crosstree (*naut*); a small flag indicating nationality, flown by a ship, *usu* at the bow or the bowsprit; a leather pitcher or bottle; a playing card bearing the picture of a young man, a knave; (in *pl*) the game of dibs (also **jack'stones**); a piece used in this game (also **jack'stone**); the small white ball aimed at in bowls; (with *cap*) a Jacqueminot rose.
◆ *vt* to raise with, or as if with, a jack (with *up*); to act upon with a jack; to throw up or abandon (*usu* with *in* or, formerly, *up*; *sl*); to increase (eg prices) (with *up*); to connect electronically (with *in* or *into*; *inf*); to contrive, organize, or set in motion (with *up*; *NZ inf*). ◆ *vi* (with *up*) to give up (*old sl*); (with *off*) to masturbate (*sl*); (with *up*) to inject oneself, take a fix (*drug sl*); (with *up*) to refuse, resist (*Aust sl*); (with *around*) to waste time, behave irresponsibly (*inf*). ◆ *adj* (*Aust*) tired, fed up. [Appar Fr *Jacques*, once the most common name in France, hence used as a substitute for *John*, once the most common name in England; really = *James* or *Jacob*, from L *Jacōbus*; but possibly partly from *Jackin, Jankin*, dimin of *John*]
■ **Jack'een** or **jack'een** *n* (*Irish derog sl*) a person from Dublin, *esp* one with a parochial attitude. **Jack'y** or **Jack'y-Jacky** *n* (*Aust offensive sl*) a nickname for an Aborigine.
❑ **Jack-a-dan'dy** *n* a dandy or fop, *esp* if diminutive. **Jack-a-lan'tern** *n* a Jack-o'-lantern. **Jack'-a-Lent** *n* (*Shakesp*) a boy (for **Jack of Lent** a kind of puppet formerly used as an Aunt Sally in Lent). **jack bean** *n* a subtropical American climbing bean (genus *Canavalia*). **jack'-block** *n* a block of pulleys used for raising and lowering topgallant-masts. **jack'boot** *n* a large boot reaching above the knee, to protect the leg, *orig* covered with iron plates and worn by cavalry; military rule, *esp* when brutal (*fig*). ◆ *vi* (with *around*; also *vt* with *it*) to behave in an oppressive or brutally authoritarian way, to domineer, throw one's weight around. **jack'booted** *adj*. **jack'-by-the-hedge** *n* (also with *cap*) garlic mustard. **jack-cross'tree** *n* (*naut*) the crosstree at the head of a topgallant-mast. **jack easy** *adj* indifferent, not caring one way or the other. **jack'fish** *n* a young pike. **Jack'-fool** *n* a fool. **Jack Frost** *n* frost or freezing weather personified. **jack'hammer** *n* a hand-held compressed-air hammer drill for rock-drilling (also *vt*). **jack'-high** *adj* and *adv* (in bowls) as far as the jack. **Jack'-in-office** *n* (also without *cap*) a vexatiously self-important petty official. **Jack'-in-the-box** *n* (also without *cap*) a toy figure that springs up from a box when the lid is released. **Jack'-in-the-green** *n* a May-Day dancer enclosed in a green shrubby framework. **Jack'-in-the-pulpit** *n* a N American plant (*Arisaema triphyllum*) like cuckoo pint; also applied to various other plants, *esp* of the genus *Arisaema*. **Jack Ketch** *n* (*hist*) a public hangman, from one so named under James II. **jack'knife** *n* a large clasp knife; a dive in which the performer doubles up in the air and straightens out again. ◆ *vi* and *vt* to double up as a jackknife does; (of articulated vehicles or parts) through faulty control, to form, or cause to form, an angle of 901 or less. **Jack Mormon** *n* (*US*) a non-Mormon living amicably in a Mormon community; an inactive, lapsed or nominal Mormon. **Jack-of-all'-trades** *n* (also without *cap*) someone who can turn a hand to anything. **Jack-o'-lan'tern** *n* (also without *cap*) a will-o'-the-wisp; a lantern made from a hollowed-out pumpkin, turnip, etc with holes cut to resemble eyes, mouth and nose. **jack pine** *n* any of several N American species of pine. **jack plane** *n* a large strong plane used by carpenters. **jack plug** *n* (*telecom*, etc) a one-pronged plug used to introduce an apparatus quickly into a circuit. **jack'pot** *n* a money pool in card games, competitions, etc that can be won only on certain conditions being fulfilled and accumulates until such time as they are (see also **hit the jackpot** below); a prize-money

---

fāte; fär; mē; fûr; mīne; mōte; för; mūte; pŭt; dhen (then); *el'ə-mənt* (element) • For other sounds see detailed chart of pronunciation

fund; *orig* a poker game, played for the pot or pool (consisting of equal stakes from all the players), which must be opened by a player holding two jacks or better; a mess, an awkward situation (*US sl*). **Jack'-priest** *n* (*derog*) a parson. **Jack'-pudding** *n* (*hist*) a professional buffoon, a jester. **jack rabbit** *n* a long-eared American hare. **jack'-rafter** *n* a rafter shorter than the rest, as in a hip-roof. **Jack Russell** or **Jack Russell terrier** *n* a breed of small terrier, introduced by *John Russell*, 19c parson. **Jack'-sauce** *n* (*Shakesp*) an impudent fellow. **jack screw** *n* same as **screw jack** (see under **screw**). **jack shaft** or **jack'shaft** *n* (*engineering*) an intermediate shaft, eg between a motor and the wheels it drives. **jack shit** (*chiefly US sl*) nothing at all. **Jack'-slave** *n* (*Shakesp*) a low servant, a vulgar fellow. **jack'smith** *n* (*obs*) a maker of roasting jacks. **jack'snipe** *n* any of various small species of snipe. **Jack Sprat** *n* a diminutive fellow. **jack'-staff** *n* the staff on a ship on which the jack (flag) is hoisted. **jack'-stays** *n pl* ropes or strips of wood or iron stretched along the yards of a ship to bind the sails to. **Jack Straw** or **jack'-straw** *n* a straw effigy; a man of straw, a lightweight; a straw or slip used in the game of **Jack Straws** or spillikins. **Jack tar** *n* (also without *cap*) a sailor. **Jack the lad** *n* a flashy, cocksure young man. **jack towel** *n* a continuous towel passing over a roller. **jack'-up** *n* an offshore oil rig or accommodation platform, etc secured by legs that are lowered from the platform to the seabed (also **jack'-up rig**); an act of non-co-operation or resistance (*Aust sl*); a swindle or other dishonest arrangement (*NZ inf*). **Jacky-Jacky** see **Jacky** above.
■ **before you can** or **could say Jack Robinson** very quickly. **cheap-Jack** see under **cheap**. **every man Jack** one and all, everybody. **hit the jackpot** to win a jackpot; to have a big success or stroke of good fortune. **I'm all right, Jack** an expression of selfish or indifferent complacency at the misfortunes or difficulties of others. **steeplejack** see under **steeple**. **Union Jack** (not properly a jack) see under **union**¹. **yellow jack** (*sl*) yellow fever.

jack² /jak/ *n* a medieval protective coat, *esp* of leather. [Fr *jaque*, perh from *Jacques* James]
❑ **jack'man** *n* a soldier wearing a jack; a retainer.

jack³ or **jak** /jak/ *n* a tree of S and SE Asia of the breadfruit genus (*Artocarpus*); its fruit. [Port *jaca*, from Malayalam *chakka*]
❑ **jack'-fruit** *n*. **jack'-tree** *n*.

jackal /jak'l/ or /jak'öl/ *n* a wild, carnivorous, gregarious African or Asian animal closely related to the dog, which feeds on the kill of other animals, though formerly and erroneously supposed to act as a lion's provider or hunting scout; someone who does another's dirty work; someone who wants to share the spoil but not the danger. ◆ *vi* (*pap* **jack'alled**) to play the jackal. [Pers *shaghāl*]

jackanapes /jak'ə-nāps/ *n* a cocky, impudent fellow; a cheeky child; an ape or monkey (*archaic*). [Origin uncertain]

jackaroo or **jackeroo** /jak-ə-roo'/ (*Aust inf*) *n* a newcomer, or other person, gaining experience on a sheep or cattle station (also *fem* **jillaroo'**). ◆ *vi* to be a jackaroo. [From an Aboriginal language]

jackass /jak'as/ *n* a male ass; a blockhead, fool; a laughing jackass (*Aust*). [**jack**¹ and **ass**¹]
■ **laughing jackass** the kookaburra.

jackdaw /jak'dö/ *n* a small species of crow with a greyish neck. [**jack**¹ and **daw**²]

jackeen see under **jack**¹.

jackeroo see **jackaroo**.

jacket /jak'it/ *n* a short coat; an animal's coat; the skin (of potatoes); a loose paper cover (of a book, etc); a paper or cardboard envelope or folder (*US*); the outer casing of a boiler, pipe, etc, eg a steam-jacket or water jacket; the steel lattice structure which supports a steel offshore oil platform; the aluminium or zirconium alloy covering of the fissile elements in a reactor. ◆ *vt* to provide or cover with a jacket; to beat (*old sl*). [OFr *jaquet*, dimin of *jaque*; see ety for **jack**²]
■ **jack'eted** *adj* wearing a jacket.
❑ **jacket potato** *n* a potato cooked in its skin.
■ **dust someone's jacket** (*old sl*) to beat someone.

jacks /jaks/ (*Irish sl*) *n* a toilet. [Cf *jakes*, **John**]

jacksie or **jacksy** /jak'si/ (*sl*) *n* the posterior; the anus. [Perh **jack**¹]

Jacky see under **jack**¹.

Jacob /jā'kəb/ *n* (also **Jacob sheep**) a kind of sheep, piebald in colour, with two or four horns, *orig* imported to Britain from Spain. [From Bible, Genesis 30.40]

Jacobean /jak-ō-bē'ən/ *adj* of or characteristic of the period of James I of England (1603–25). ◆ *n* a person who lived in the reign of James I. [L *Jacōbus* James]
❑ **Jacobean lily** *n* (*Sprekelia formosissima*) a Mexican bulbous plant named after St James.

Jacobethan /jak-ō-bē'thən/ *adj* being or containing a combination of Jacobean and Elizabethan styles.

Jacobian /jə-kō'bi-ən/ (*maths*) *n* the matrix or determinant formed from the first partial derivatives of several functions of several variables (also **Jacobian determinant**). [KGJ *Jacobi* (1804–51), German mathematician]

Jacobin /jak'ō-bin/ *n* a French Dominican monk, their order being originally established at St *Jacques*, Paris; one of a society of revolutionists in France, so called from their meeting in the hall of the Jacobin convent (*hist*); an extremist or radical, *esp* in politics; (also without *cap*) a hooded pigeon; (without *cap*) a hummingbird of Central and S America. ◆ *adj* of or relating to the Jacobins. [Fr, from L *Jacōbus* James]
■ **Jacobin'ic** or **Jacobin'ical** *adj*. **Jacobin'ically** *adv*. **Jac'obinism** *n* the principles of the Jacobin revolutionists. **Jac'obinize** or **-ise** *vt*.

Jacobite /jak'ō-bīt/ *n* an adherent of James II of England (James VII of Scotland), and his descendants; a member of a Syrian monophysitic sect, named after the 6c monk *Jacobus* Baradaeus (*church hist*). ◆ *adj* of or relating to the Jacobites. [L *Jacōbus* James]
■ **Jacobit'ic** or **Jacobit'ical** *adj*. **Jac'obītism** *n*.

Jacob's ladder /jā'kəbz lad'ər/ *n* a ladder of ropes with wooden or metal rungs (*naut*); a wild or garden plant (genus *Polemonium*) with ladder-like leaves; an endless chain of buckets used as an elevator. [From the *ladder* seen by *Jacob* in his dream, Bible, Genesis 28.12]

Jacob's staff /jā'kəbz stäf/ *n* a pilgrim's staff (*obs*); any of several different surveying instruments of different periods; a sword-stick (*obs*). [Prob from the pilgrimage to St James (L *Jacōbus*) of Compostela in N Spain]

jacobus /jə-kō'bəs/ (*hist*) *n* (*pl* **jaco'buses**) a gold coin of James I worth 20 to 25 shillings. [L *Jacōbus* James]

jaconet /jak'ə-net/ *n* a cotton fabric, stronger than muslin, different from the fabric originally so named which was imported from *Jagannāth* (Puri) in India; a thin material with waterproof backing used for medical dressings. [See also **Juggernaut**]

jacquard /jak'ärd/ or /jak-ärd'/ (often with *cap*) *n* an apparatus with perforated cards for controlling the movement of the warp threads in weaving intricate designs; a fabric woven by this method; a Jacquard loom. [Joseph Marie *Jacquard* (1752–1834), the French inventor]
❑ **Jacquard loom** *n* a loom with a jacquard, which produces jacquard.

Jacqueminot /jak'mi-nō/ *n* a deep-red hybrid perpetual rose (also **Jacque** and **Jack**). [Jean-François *Jacqueminot* (1787–1865), French general]

Jacquerie /zhä'krē/ *n* the revolt of the French peasants in 1358; (also without *cap*) any peasant revolt. [From *Jacques* Bonhomme, Goodman Jack, a name applied in derision to the peasants]

jactation /jak-tā'shən/ *n* the act of throwing; jactitation (*pathol*); boasting. [L *jactātiō, -ōnis* tossing, boasting, from *jactāre* to throw]

jactitation /jak-ti-tā'shən/ *n* restless tossing in illness (*pathol*); bodily agitation, twitching, jerking, etc (*pathol*); bandying about of words (*obs*); bragging; public assertion, *esp* if ostentatious and false. [LL *jactitātiō, -ōnis*, from L *jactitāre*, frequentative of *jactāre* to throw]
■ **jactitation of marriage** (*law*) malicious pretence of being married to another person.

jaculation /jak-ū-lā'shən/ *n* the act of throwing or hurling, eg a dart. [L *jaculārī, -ātus* to throw eg a dart, from *jaculum* a dart, from *jacere* to throw]
■ **jac'ulate** *vt* to throw. **jac'ulātor** *n* someone who throws eg a javelin; an archerfish. **jac'ulatory** /-ət-ər-i/ *adj* throwing out suddenly; ejaculatory.

Jacuzzi® /jə-koo'zi/ *n* a type of bath or small pool equipped with a mechanism that agitates the water to massage and invigorate the body; (*usu* without *cap*) a bathe in such a bath or pool. [Candido *Jacuzzi* (1902–86), its Italian inventor]

jade¹ /jād/ *n* a hard ornamental stone of varying shades of green and sometimes almost white, existing in two forms: *nephrite* (silicate of calcium and magnesium) and **jade'ite** (silicate of aluminium and sodium), once believed to cure side pains; the colour of this stone. ◆ *adj* made of jade; of the colour of jade. [Fr, from Sp *ijada* the flank, from L *ilia*]

jade² /jād/ *n* a pitiful, worn-out horse; a worthless nag; a woman, *esp* perverse, ill-natured, or not to be trusted (often *ironic*). ◆ *vt* to exhaust or cause to flag from overwork; to satiate or weary from excess. ◆ *vi* to become weary. [Origin unknown; cf ON *jalda* a mare, Scot *yaud*]
■ **jā'ded** *adj*. **jā'dedly** *adv*. **jā'dedness** *n*. **jā'dery** *n* (*obs*) the tricks of a jade. **jā'dish** *adj* (*obs*).

j'adoube /zha-doob'/ *interj* used by chess players to indicate an intention only to adjust a piece on the board without necessarily moving it to a different square. [Fr, I adjust]

Jaeger® /yā'gər/ n woollen material used in making clothes, *orig* containing no vegetable fibre. [Dr Gustav *Jaeger* (1832–1917), German naturalist who believed that no clothing should contain vegetable fibres]

jaeger see **jäger**.

Jaffa /jaf'ə/ n (also **Jaffa orange**) an orange from *Jaffa* in Israel; (without *cap*) a well-bowled ball that is likely to take a wicket (*cricket sl*).

Jag /jag/ (*inf*) n a Jaguar car. [Short form]

jag[1] /jag/ n a notch, slash or dag in a garment, etc; a ragged protrusion; a cleft or division (*bot*); a prick (*Scot*); an inoculation, injection (chiefly *Scot inf*). ◆ vt (**jagg'ing**; **jagged** /jagd/) to cut unevenly or into notches; to prick or pierce. ◆ vi to move at a sharp angle. [Origin unknown]
■ **jagg'ed** *adj* notched, rough-edged, uneven. **jagg'edly** *adv*. **jagg'edness** n. **jagg'er** n a kitchen utensil with a jagged-edged wheel, used for cutting and decorating the edges of pastry (also **jagg'ing-iron**). **jagg'y** *adj* notched; slashed; prickly (*Scot*).

jag[2] /jag/ n a quantity (*US*); a spree, bout of indulgence; one's fill of liquor or narcotics; a spell, fit; a load, bundle (*dialect*); a saddlebag or other bag (*obs*). ◆ vt (*dialect*) to cart; to transport by packhorse.
■ **jagged** /jagd/ *adj* (*US*) drunk. **jagg'er** n (*dialect*) a carter; a packhorseman; a pedlar.

Jagannath /jug-ə-nät'/ and **Jagannatha** /jug-ə-nä'thə/ n corrected forms of **Juggernaut** (the incarnation of Vishnu).

jäger or **jaeger** /yā'gər/ n a (German) huntsman; a German or Austrian rifleman or sharpshooter; an attendant upon an important or wealthy person, dressed in huntsman's costume; (**jaeger**) a skua that chases and robs other seabirds (*N Am*). [Ger, hunter, from *jagen* to hunt]

jaggery /jag'ə-ri/ n a coarse, dark sugar made from palm-sap. [Hindi *jāgrī*, Sans *śarkarā*; cf **sugar, sacchar-**]

jaghir, jaghire or **jagir** /jä-gēr'/ n (formerly in India) the government revenues of a tract of land assigned with power to administer. [Hindi and Pers *jāgīr*]
■ **jaghir'dar** n the holder of a jaghir.

jaguar /jag'ū-är or -ər, also *jag'wär*/ n a powerful feline beast of prey, related to the leopard, native to S America. [Tupí *jaguára*]

jaguarundi or **jaguarondi** /jä-gwə-run'dē or -ron'dē/ n a S American wildcat. [Tupí, from Guaraní]

Jah /yä or jä/ n Jehovah, the Hebrew God. [Heb *Yah*]
■ **Jah'veh** n same as **Yahweh**. **Jah'vism** n the (system of) religion of Yahweh. **Jah'vist** n.

Jai /jī/ (*Ind*) *interj* victory! [Hindi, long live]

jai alai /hī'(ə-)lī or -lī'/ n a game resembling handball but played with a long curved basket strapped to the wrist, a type of pelota. [Sp, from Basque *jai* festival, and *alai* merry]

jail or **gaol** /jāl/ n a prison. ◆ vt to imprison. [OFr *gaole* (Fr *geôle*), from LL *gabiola* a cage, from L *cavea* a cage, from *cavus* hollow]
■ **jail'er, jail'or** or **gaol'er** (also *fem* **jail'eress**, etc) a person in charge of a jail or of prisoners.
□ **jail'bait** n (*sl*) a sexually attractive person who is below the legal age of consent (also *adj*). **jail'bird** or **gaol'bird** n (*inf*) someone who often is, has been, or should be in jail. **jail'break** or **gaol'break** n an escape from prison. ◆ vt to modify (an electronic device) to allow it to use unauthorized software. **jail delivery** or **gaol delivery** n the clearing of a jail by sending all prisoners to trial; deliverance from jail. **jail'-fever** or **gaol'-fever** n typhus fever, once common in jails. **jail'house** n (*US*) a prison.
■ **break jail** or **gaol** to force one's way out of prison. **Commission of Jail Delivery** one of the commissions formerly issued to judges of assize and judges of the Central Criminal Court in England to try all prisoners.

Jain /jīn or jān/ or **Jaina** /jī'na/ n an adherent of an ascetic Indian religion related to Buddhism (also *adj*). [Hindi *jina* conqueror, title of the Jain teachers]
■ **Jain'ism** n. **Jain'ist** n and *adj*.

jak /jak/ n same as **jack**[3].

jake[1] /jāk/ (chiefly *US inf*) *adj* honest; correct; fine, OK, first-rate (also *Aust*).

jake[2] /jāk/ (*US*) n a country lout; a yokel. [Perh from the name, short form of *Jacob*]

jakes /jāks/ (*Shakesp*) n a privy. [Origin unknown]

JAL *abbrev* : Japan Air Lines.

jalap /jal'ap/ n the purgative root of an Ipomoea or *Exogonium*, first brought from *Jalapa* (or Xalapa) in Mexico.
■ **jalap'ic** *adj*. **jal'apin** n a glucoside resin, one of the active constituents of jalap.

■ **false jalap** marvel of Peru (qv), formerly used as a substitute for jalap.

jalapeño /hä-lə-pā'nyō/ or **jalapeño pepper** /pep'ər/ n an especially hot type of capsicum pepper, used in Mexican cooking. [Mex Sp]

jalebi or **jallebi** /jə-leb'i/ n an Asian snack of deep-fried dough covered in syrup. [Sans *jal vallika* watery crescent]

jalfrezi /jal-frā'zi/ *adj* (in Indian cookery) denoting a hot-flavoured dish of meat or vegetables stir-fried with green chillis and spices. [Hindi]

jalopy or **jaloppy** /jə-lop'i/ (*inf*) n a car, *esp* one that is old or worn-out. [Origin obscure]

jalouse /jə-looz'/ (*Scot*) vt and vi to suspect (also **jealouse**, by conflation with **jealous**).

jalousie /zhal-ū-zē' or zhal'/ n an outside shutter with slats. [Fr, from *jalousie* jealousy]
■ **jal'ousied** *adj*.

Jam. *abbrev* : Jamaica.

jam[1] /jam/ n a conserve of fruit boiled with sugar. ◆ vt to spread with jam; to make into jam. [Perh from **jam**[2]]
■ **jamm'y** *adj* covered or filled with jam; smeared or sticky with jam; like jam; lucky, excellent (*inf*).
□ **jam'pot** n a jar for jam (also **jam'jar**); a high collar, *esp* a clergyman's. **jam sandwich** n (*inf*) formerly in the UK, a police car (from the white-and-red livery).
■ **jam tomorrow** better things promised for the future that always remain in the future. **want jam on it** (*inf*) to expect or want too much.

jam[2] /jam/ vt (**jamm'ing**; **jammed**) to press or squeeze tight; to push forcefully or violently (*on or in*); to crowd full; to block by crowding; to bring to a standstill by crowding or interlocking; to interfere with by emitting signals of similar wavelength (*radio*); to interfere or block (signals generally). ◆ vi to become stuck, wedged, etc; to become unworkable; to press or push (eg into a confined space); to play in a jam session. ◆ n a crush or squeeze; a block or stoppage due to crowding or squeezing together; a jammed mass (eg of logs in a river); a jamming of radio messages; a difficult or embarrassing situation (*inf*). [Poss onomatopoeic; connected with **champ**[1]]
■ **jamm'er** n a person or thing that jams something.
□ **jam-packed'** *adj* completely full, crowded, etc. **jam session** n a gathering of musicians (*orig* an informal one) at which live, *esp* improvised music is played.

jamadar same as **jemadar**.

jamahiriya or **jumhouriya** /ja-mä'hē-rē'ya/ n in Libya, the people's or proletariat's state. [Ar, connected with *jumhūrīya* republic, from *jumhūr* people]

Jamaica /jə-mā'kə/ or **Jamaican** /-kən/ *adj* of the island of Jamaica in the W Indies.
■ **Jamai'can** n a native or inhabitant of Jamaica.
□ **Jamaica bark** n Caribbee bark. **Jamaica cedar** n Bastard Barbados cedar (see **cedar**). **Jamaica ebony** n cocuswood. **Jamaica pepper** n allspice. **Jamaica plum** n hog-plum (qv under **hog**[1]). **Jamaica rum** n a slowly-fermented, full-bodied pungent rum.

jamb /jam/ n the sidepiece or post of a door, fireplace, etc; a greave (in this sense also **jambe** /jam/). [Fr *jambe* leg; cf **gamb**]
■ **jambeau** /jam'bō/ n (pl **jam'beaux** or **jam'beux**; *Spenser* **giambeux**) (*obs*) a greave; legging. **jam'ber** or **jam'bier** n (*obs*) a greave.

jambalaya /jum-bə-lī'ə/ (*US*) n a Creole or Cajun dish made with rice mixed with seafood or chicken, seasonings, etc; a mixture generally. [Provençal *jambalaia*]

jambee /jam-bē'/ n a light cane, fashionable in the 18c. [*Jambi* in Indonesia]

jamber, jambeux, jambier see under **jamb**.

jambiya or **jambiyah** /jam-bē'yä/ n a type of Middle-Eastern curved, double-edged dagger. [Ar]

jambo /jam'bō/ *interj* an E African salutation. [From Swahili]

jambok same as **sjambok**.

jambolan, jambolana see **jambu**.

jambone /jam'bōn/ n a lone hand in euchre, played only by agreement, in which the player lays their cards on the table and must lead one chosen by their opponent, scoring eight points if they take all the tricks. [Origin unknown]

jambool see **jambu**.

jamboree /jam-bə-rē'/ n a large and lively gathering, party or celebration, a spree (*inf*); a large Scout or Guide rally; in euchre, a lone hand of the five highest cards, by agreement scoring 16 points for the holder. [Origin uncertain]

jambu /jum'/ or *jam'boo*/ n a S Asian evergreen tree of the family Myrtaceae (also **jambul, jambool** /jum-bool'/, **jam'bolan** and **jambolana** /-bō-lä'nə/). [Sans *jambu, jambū, jambūla*]

jamdani /jäm'dä-nē/ n a variety of Dhaka muslin woven in a flowery design. [Pers *jāmdānī*]

james /jāmz/ n same as **jemmy**[1].

Jamesian /jāmz'i-ən/ adj relating to William *James* (1842–1910), American psychologist, or Henry *James* (1843–1916), his brother, the novelist.

Jamesonite /jïm'i-sən-īt or jäm'sən-īt/ n a mineral compound of lead, antimony and sulphur. [Robert *Jameson* (1772–1854), Scottish mineralogist]

Jamestown weed see **jimson weed**.

jammies /jam'iz/ (inf) n pl pyjamas.

jammy see under **jam**[1].

jamon serrano /ham'on sə-rä'nō/ n a finely cured uncooked ham produced in Spain. [Sp, mountain ham]

jampan /jam'pan/ n an Indian sedan chair. [Bengali *jhāmpān*]
■ **jampanee**' or **jampani** /-ē'/ n its bearer.

Jan. abbrev : January.

Jandal® /jan'dəl/ (NZ) n a thong, a type of sandal.

jane[1] /jān/ (sl, orig and chiefly US) n a woman. [*Jane*, female personal name]
❑ **Jane Doe** see **John Doe** under **John**.

jane[2] /jān/ n a small silver Genoese coin (Spenser); jean (cloth). [LL *Janua*, L *Genua* Genoa]

Janeite /jān'īt/ n a devotee of *Jane* Austen.

JANET® /jan'it/ n a computer network linking UK universities, research institutions, etc. [Abbrev of *Joint Academic Network*]

jangle /jang'gl/ vt and vi to sound with an unpleasant irritating tone, such as a harsh, dissonant metallic or ringing noise. ◆ vt to upset, irritate. ◆ vi (obs) to wrangle or quarrel. ◆ n dissonant clanging; contention. [OFr *jangler*]
■ **jang'ler** n. **jang'ling** n and adj. **jang'ly** adj.

Janian, **Janiform** see under **Janus**.

janissary see **janizary**.

janitor /jan'i-tər/ n a doorkeeper; an attendant or caretaker (also fem **jan'itrix** or **jan'itress**). [L *jānitor*, from *jānua* a door]
■ **janitorial** /-tö'/ adj. **jan'itorship** n.

janizary /jan'i-zə-ri/ n (also **jan'issary** /-zər-i or -sər-i/ or **jan'izar**) a soldier of the old Turkish footguards (c.1330–1826), formed orig of renegade prisoners and of tributary Christian children; a Turkish soldier acting as an escort for travellers in the East (hist); a follower, supporter. [Fr *Janissaire*, supposed to be from Turk *yeni* new, and *çeri* soldiery]
■ **janizā'rian** adj.
❑ **janizary music** n military music with a great deal of percussion.

Janjaweed or **Janjawid** /jan'jə-wēd/ n pl (usu with the) (members of) any of several tribal militias in Sudan. ◆ adj belonging to the Janjaweed. [Ar *jaan* evil, and *jawad* horse]

janker /jang'kər/ (Scot) n a long pole on wheels for transporting large logs suspended from it. [Origin unknown]

jankers /jang'kərz/ (milit sl) n pl defaulters. ◆ n sing punishment, detention, etc for defaulting. [Origin unknown]

jann /jän/ n pl the least powerful order of jinn; (sing) a jinnee. [Ar *jānn*]

jannock[1] /jan'ək/ (dialect) adj straightforward, on the level. [Origin obscure]

jannock[2] /jan'ək/ (N Eng) n bread made from oatmeal. [Origin obscure]

Jansenism /jan'sən-i-zm/ (Christianity) n a system of evangelical doctrine deduced from Augustine by Cornelius *Jansen* (1585–1638), Roman Catholic Bishop of Ypres, essentially a reaction against the ordinary Catholic dogma of the freedom of the will, maintaining that human nature is corrupt, and that Christ died only for the elect, all others being irretrievably condemned to hell.
■ **Jan'senist** n a believer in Jansenism (also adj).

jansky /jan'ski/ (astron) n (pl **jan'skys**) a unit in radio astronomy measuring the power received at the telescope from a cosmic radio source 10^{-26}Wm^{-2}Hz^{-1} (abbrev **Jy**). [Karl G *Jansky* (1905–50), US radio engineer]

jantee see **jaunty**[1].

janty see **jaunty**[1], **jonty**.

January /jan'ū-ə-ri/ n the first month of the year. [L *Jānuārius* (*mēnsis*) the month dedicated to Janus]

Janus /jā'nəs/ n the ancient Roman two-faced god, guardian of doors, whose temple in Rome was closed in time of peace. [L *Jānus*]
■ **Jān'ian** or **Jān'iform** adj (wrongly **Jān'uform**) Janus-faced.

❑ **Jān'us-faced** adj two-faced, facing in two directions; hypocritical, deceitful.

Jap /jap/ (derog inf) n and adj Japanese.
❑ **Jap'-silk** n a thin kind of silk.

Jap. abbrev : Japanese.

jap see **jaup**.

japan /jə-pan'/ adj of Japan; japanned. ◆ n Japanese ware or work; a glossy black varnish or lacquer; a liquid used for paint-grinding and -drying; japanned work. ◆ vt (**japann'ing**; **japanned**') to varnish with japan, esp in imitation of Japanese work; to make black; to ordain (a clergyman) (old sl).
■ **Japanese** /jap-ə-nēz' or jap'/ adj of Japan, its people, or their language. ◆ n (pl **Japanese** (formerly **Japaneses**)) a native or citizen of Japan; the language of Japan. **Japanēs'ery** n Japanese decoration; a Japanese ornament; Japanese bric-à-brac. **Japanesque** /-esk'/ n a design in Japanese style. ◆ adj (also **Japanēs'y**) savouring of the Japanese. **Jap'anize** or **-ise** vt to make Japanese. **japann'er** n. **Japano-** combining form Japanese (esp in combination with another nationality, eg *Japano-Chinese*). **Jap'anophile** n a lover of Japan or the Japanese (also adj).
❑ **Japan Current** n Kuroshio. **japan'-earth** n terra-japonica, gambier. **Japanese beetle** n a small scarabaeid beetle (*Popillia japonica*) introduced accidentally into the eastern USA and now a major plant pest there. **Japanese cedar** n a very tall Japanese conifer (*Cryptomeria japonica*) often dwarfed by Japanese gardeners. **Japanese garden** n a formal garden with water, bridges, rocks, raked gravel and shrubs but without bright flowers. **Japanese knotweed** n a tall fast-growing strain of knotweed. **Japanese lantern** n a collapsible paper lantern, a Chinese lantern. **Japanese maple** n a decorative foliage tree (*Acer palmatum* or *A. japonicum*). **Japanese medlar** n the loquat. **Japanese paper** n a fine soft paper handmade from paper-mulberry bark. **Japanese vellum** n a heavier weight of Japanese paper. **Japan lacquer** n Japan varnish. **Japan laurel** n a shrub (*Aucuba japonica*) of the dogwood family, with spotted yellow leaves. **japanned leather** n patent leather (see under **patent**). **Japan varnish** n a varnish obtained from a species of sumach (*Rhus vernicifera*), extended to various other similar varnishes. **Japan wax** or **tallow** n a fat obtained from the berries of species of sumach.

jape /jāp/ vi to jest, joke. ◆ vt to mock; to seduce (obs). ◆ n a jest, joke, trick. [OFr *japer* to yelp]
■ **jāp'er** n. **jāp'ery** n. **jāp'ing** n.

Japhetic /jə-fet'ik/ (obs) adj of European race; relating to a number of European and Near-Eastern non-Indo-European languages formerly thought to be related and to belong to some pre-Indo-European grouping. [From supposed descent from *Japheth*]

japonaiserie /zha-pə-nez-ri'/ (Fr) n Japanesery.

Japonic /jə-pon'ik/ adj Japanese. [New L *japonicus*, fem *japonica* Japanese]
■ **japon'ica** n the Japanese quince (*Chaenomeles japonica*), camellia, or any of several other Japanese plants.

jar[1] /jär/ n a wide-mouthed wide vessel; as much as a jar will hold; a Leyden jar (qv); a unit of electrical capacitance (obs); an alcoholic drink, esp a glass of beer (inf). ◆ vt to put in jars. [Fr *jarre* or Sp *jarra*, from Ar *jarrah*]
■ **jar'ful** n (pl **jar'fuls**). **jarred** adj (inf) drunk.

jar[2] /jär/ vi (**jarr'ing**; **jarred**) to make a harsh discordant sound; to vibrate from an impact; to give an unpleasant shock; to grate (on); to be discordant or distasteful; to clash; to quarrel; to be inconsistent; to tick (Shakesp). ◆ vt to cause to vibrate or shake; to cause to vibrate painfully; to grate on; to make dissonant. ◆ n a harsh sudden vibration; a dissonance; a grating sound or feeling; clash of interests or opinions; conflict; a tick of a clock (Shakesp). [Imit]
■ **jarr'ing** n the act of jarring; a severe reproof. ◆ adj harshly discordant; grating. **jarr'ingly** adv.

jar[3] /jär/ n a turn (used only in the phrase **on the jar** ajar). [Earlier *char*, from OE *cerr*; cf **char**[2], **ajar**[1]]

jararaca or **jararaka** /jä-rə-rä'kə/ n a venomous S American snake of the family Crotalidae. [Tupí, from Guaraní]

jardinière /zhär-dē-nyer'/ n a container for the display of flowers, growing or cut; a style of drapery (eg curtains) with raised centre and full-length ends; a mixture of diced or sliced cooked vegetables, usu as a garnish for meat; a lappet forming part of an old headdress. [Fr, gardener (fem)]

jargon[1] /jär'gən/ n the terminology of a profession, art, group, etc; an artificial or barbarous language; a pidgin; unintelligible talk, gibberish; chatter, twittering. ◆ vi to twitter, chatter; to speak jargon. [Fr]
■ **jargoneer**' or **jar'gonist** n a person who uses jargon. **jargonist'ic** adj. **jargonīzā'tion** or **-s-** n. **jar'gonize** or **-ise** vt to express in jargon. ◆ vi to speak jargon.

jargon[2], **jargonelle** see **jargoon**.

---

jargoon /jär-goon'/ or **jargon** /jär'gən/ n a brilliant colourless or pale zircon. [Fr *jargon*; prob connected with **zircon**]
■ **jargonelle'** n an early-ripening pear (*orig* a gritty kind).

jark /järk/ (*old sl*) n a seal on a (*usu* counterfeit) document; a pass, safe-conduct. [Origin unknown]
□ **jark'man** n a swindling beggar, a begging-letter writer.

jarl /yärl/ (*hist*) n a Scandinavian noble or chief. [ON; related to **earl**]

Jarlsberg® /yärlz'bûrg/ n a hard yellow cheese made in *Jarlsberg* in Norway.

jarool see **jarul**.

jarosite /jar'ō-sīt/ n a hydrous sulphate of iron and potassium forming hexagonal crystals. [From Barranco *Jaroso*, an area in S Spain]

jarrah /jar'ə/ n a W Australian timber tree, *Eucalyptus marginata*. [From an Aboriginal language]

jarta or **yarta** /yär'tə/ (*Shetland*) n (also (*Walter Scott*) **yar'to**) used as an endearment, literally, heart (also *adj*). [ON *hjarta* heart]

jarul or **jarool** /jə-rool'/ n the Indian bloodwood (genus *Lagerstroemia*), a lythraceous tree. [Bengali *jarūl*]

jarvey or **jarvie** /jär'vi/ (*obs sl*) n a driver of hackney coaches or jaunting cars. [Earlier *Jarvis*, poss from St *Gervase*, whose emblem is a whip]

Jas. *abbrev*: James; (the Letter of) James (*Bible*).

jasey, **jasy** or **jazy** /jā'zi/ (*old inf*) n a wig, *orig* of worsted. [**jersey**]

Jasher or **Jashar** /jā'shər/ n one of the lost books of the ancient Hebrews, quoted twice in the Bible (Joshua 10.13, and 2 Samuel 1.18), most probably a collection of heroic ballads.

jasmine /jaz'min/, also **jessamine** /jes'ə-min/ n a genus (*Jasminum*) of oleaceous shrubs, many with very fragrant flowers. [Fr *jasmin*, *jasemin*, from Ar *yāsmin*, *yāsamīn*, from Pers *yāsmīn*]
■ **red jasmine** frangipani (*Plumeria rubra*), a tropical American shrub related to periwinkle.

jasmonate /jas'mə-nāt or jaz-/ n any of several organic compounds that occur in plants and are thought to control processes such as growth and fruit ripening and to aid the plant's defences against disease and insect attack. [Derived from *jasmone*, a compound found in the jasmine plant]

jasper /jas'pər/ or (*Spenser*) **jasp** /jasp/ n an opaque quartz containing clay or iron compounds, used in jewellery or ornamentation and red, yellow, brown or green in colour; a fine hard porcelain (also **jas'perware**); a precious stone (*obs*). ◆ *adj* made of jasper. [OFr *jaspe*, *jaspre*, from L *iaspis*, *-idis*; and directly from Gr *iaspis*, *-idos*, of Eastern origin]
■ **jaspe** or **jaspé** /jasp or jas'pā/ *adj* mottled, variegated or veined. ◆ *n* cotton or rayon cloth with a shaded effect used for bedspreads, curtains, etc. **jasp'erize** or **-ise** *vt* to turn into jasper. **jasp'erous** or **jasp'ery** *adj*. **jaspid'ean** or **jaspid'eous** *adj*. **jas'pis** n (now *rare*) jasper.

jass see **jazz**.

jasy see **jasey**.

Jat /jät/ n a member of a people inhabiting NW India and Pakistan. ◆ *adj* of or relating to the Jats. [Hindi *jāt*]

jataka /jä'tə-kə/ n (sometimes with *cap*) a collection of stories recording the past lives and rebirths of Buddha. [Sans *jātaka* rebirth, from *jāta* born]

jato /jā'tō/ (*aeronautics*) n (*pl* **jā'tos**) a jet-assisted *t*ake-*o*ff, using a **jato unit** consisting of one or more rocket motors, *usu* jettisoned after use.

jatropha /jat'rə-fə/ n any plant of the genus *Jatropha*, esp *Jatropha curcas*, whose seeds yield an oil that can be used as a biofuel. [New L, from Gr *iātros* a physician, and *trophē* food]

jaunce or **jaunse** /jöns or jäns/ *vi* (*Shakesp*) to prance. ◆ *vt* to cause (a horse) to prance. ◆ *n* prancing (*Shakesp*); a wearisome journey (*dialect*). [Perh from a doubtful OFr *jancer* to cause to prance]

jaundice /jön'dis (rarely jän'dis)/ n a disease in which there is yellowing of the whites of the eyes, skin, etc, by excess of bile pigment, the patient in rare cases seeing objects as yellow; any of various diseases with some similar features; the state of taking an unfavourable, prejudiced view. ◆ *vt* to affect with jaundice, in any sense. [Fr *jaunisse*, from *jaune* yellow, from L *galbinus* yellowish, from *galbus* yellow]
■ **jaun'diced** *adj* affected with jaundice; feeling or showing prejudice, bitterness, distaste or jealousy.

jaunse see **jaunce**.

jaunt /jönt, also jänt/ *vi* to go from place to place, *esp* for pleasure; to make an excursion. ◆ *n* an excursion; a ramble. [Origin obscure, though early meanings correspond with **jaunce**]
■ **jaunt'ing** *adj* strolling; making an excursion.

□ **jaunting car** n a low-set, two-wheeled, open vehicle, traditionally used in Ireland, with side-seats either back to back or facing each other.

jauntie see **jonty**.

jaunty¹ or **janty** /jön'ti (also jän'ti)/ *adj* gentlemanly (formerly **jantee** or **jauntee**) (*obs*); having or showing a cheerful, self-confident manner; smart; stylish. [Fr *gentil*]
■ **jaunt'ily** *adv*. **jaunt'iness** n.

jaunty² see **jonty**.

jaup /jöp or jäp/ or **jap** /jäp/ (*Scot*) *vt* and *vi* to spatter; to splash. ◆ *n* a splash; a spattering. [Origin unknown]

Java /jä'və/ *adj* of the island of *Java*, in Indonesia. ◆ *n* a rich variety of coffee; extended to coffee in general (*N Am inf*); (**Java**®) an object-oriented programming language, widely used in web-based systems (*comput*).
■ **Ja'van** or **Javanese'** *adj* and *n*.
□ **Java man** n the early man formerly known as Pithecanthropus erectus, later redesignated Homo erectus. **Java plum** n the fruit of the jambu tree. **Java sparrow** n a kind of weaver bird.

JavaScript® /jä'və-skript/ n (*comput*) a scripting language used in web-based systems, *esp* to provide access to objects within other systems.

Javel(le) water /zha- or zhə-vel' wö'tər/, also **eau de** /ō də/ **Javel(le)** n a solution of potassium chloride and hypochlorite used for bleaching, disinfecting, etc. [After *Javel*, former town, now part of the city of Paris]

javel /jav'əl/ (*Spenser*) n a worthless fellow. [Origin unknown]

javelin /jav'(ə)lin/ n a light spear for throwing, either as a weapon or in sport. [Fr *javeline*; prob Celtic]
□ **jav'elin-man** n (*hist*) an armed member of a sheriff's retinue or a judge's escort at assizes; a soldier armed with a javelin.

jaw¹ /jö/ n the part of the body used for biting or chewing; one of the bones of a jaw; the lower part of the face around the mouth and chin; one of a pair of parts for gripping, crushing, cutting, grinding, etc; (in *pl*) a narrow entrance; (in *pl*) a dangerous position, on the point of being devoured (*fig*); talkativeness (*inf*); a long talk or lecture (*inf*). ◆ *vt* (*inf*) to scold, lecture. ◆ *vi* to talk, *esp* at excessive length, chat, lecture. [Perh **chaw¹**, modified by Fr *joue* cheek]
■ **jawed** *adj* having jaws. **jaw'ing** n (*sl*) talk, *esp* if unrestrained, abusive or reproving. **jaw'less** *adj*.
□ **jaw'bone** n the bone of the jaw. ◆ *vt* and *vi* (*US sl*) to engage in jawboning, to lecture or scold. **jaw'boning** n (*US sl*) governmental urging of industry to restrict wage increases, accept restraints, etc. **jaw'-breaker** n a heavy-duty rock-breaking machine with hinged jaws (also **jaw'-crusher**); a word hard to pronounce (also **jaw'-twister**; *inf*). **jaw'-breaking** *adj* and *n*. **jaw'-breakingly** *adv*. **jaw'-dropping** *adj* (*inf*) amazing. **jaw'-droppingly** *adv*. **jaw'fall** n a falling of the jaw (*archaic*); depression of spirits (*rare*). **jaw'-fallen** *adj* (*rare*) depressed in spirits; dejected. **jaw'-foot** n (*zool*) a maxilliped. **jaw lever** n an instrument for opening the mouth of a horse or cow to admit medicine. **Jaws of Life**® n *pl* powerful hydraulic pincers used to free people from wreckage after a motor-vehicle accident. **jaw'-tooth** n a molar.
■ **his**, etc **jaw dropped** his, etc mouth fell open in amazement. **hold one's jaw** (*inf*) to stop talking or scolding.

jaw² /jö/ (*Scot*) n a dash or surge of liquid; a portion of liquid so dashed. ◆ *vt* and *vi* to pour suddenly in a body. [Origin unknown]
□ **jaw'box** n a sink. **jaw'hole** n a cesspool; an entrance to a sewer.

jawan /jə-wän'/ n a male Indian police constable or common soldier. [Urdu *javān* young man, from Pers]

jawari see **jowar**.

jawbation /jö-bā'shən/ n variant of **jobation** (see under **Job**). [Influenced by **jaw¹**]

Jawi /jä'wi/ n the version of Arabic script used to write Malay; Malay written in Arabic script. [Malay]

ja wohl /ya vōl'/ (*Ger*) yes indeed.

jay¹ /jā/ n a bird of the crow family with colourful plumage; a flashy, immoral woman (*archaic sl*); a stupid, awkward or easily duped person (*US sl*). ◆ *adj* (*US sl*) stupid, unsophisticated. [OFr *jay*]
□ **jay'walk** *vi*. **jay'walker** n a careless pedestrian whom motorists are expected to avoid running down. **jay'walking** n.

jay² /jā/ n the tenth letter of the modern English alphabet (J or j).

Jaycee /jā-sē'/ (*N Am*, *Aust* and *NZ*) n (sometimes without *cap*) a member of a Junior Chamber of Commerce, an organization that promotes business skills for young people. [Phonetic representation of the initial letters of Junior Chamber]

jazerant see **jesserant**.

jazy see **jasey**.

---

fāte; fär; mē; fûr; mīne; mōte; för; mūte; pŭt; dhen (then); *el'ə-mənt* (element) • For other sounds see detailed chart of pronunciation

jazz /jaz/, also (*obs*) **jass** /jas/ *n* any of various styles of music with a strong rhythm, syncopation, improvisation, etc, originating in black American folk music; an art form and also various types of popular dance music derived from it; flamboyance or garishness; insincere or lying talk, nonsense (*sl, esp US*); sexual intercourse (*US black sl*). ◆ *adj* of or relating to jazz. ◆ *vt* to impart a jazz character to, to enliven or brighten (*usu* with *up*). ◆ *vi* to play or dance to jazz music. ◆ *vt* and *vi* (*US black sl*) to have sexual intercourse (with). [Origin uncertain]

■ **jazz'er** *n* a jazz musician. **jazz'ily** *adv*. **jazz'iness** *n*. **jazz'y** *adj*. ▫ **jazz age** *n* the decade following World War I, *esp* in America. **jazz-funk'**, **jazz-pop'**, **jazz-rock'** *n* music which is a blend of jazz and funk, pop and rock respectively. **jazz hands** *n* the act of shaking both open hands, palm-outwards, as part of a dance routine. **jazz mag** *n* (*sl*) a pornographic magazine. **jazz'man** *n* a jazz musician. **jazz pants** *n pl* trousers made of an elasticated material, worn for dancing.

■ **and all that jazz** (*inf*) and all that kind of thing, and all that palaver.

JC *abbrev*: Jesus Christ; Julius Caesar.

JCB /jā-sē-bē'/ *n* a type of mobile excavator used in the construction industry. [Abbrev of *JC* Bamford, the manufacturer's name]

JCL (*comput*) *abbrev*: job control language.

J-cloth® /jā'kloth/ *n* a brand of disposable cloth used in domestic cleaning. [Initial letter of manufacturers Johnson and Johnson]

JCR *abbrev*: junior common (or combination) room (see under **junior**).

JCS *abbrev*: Joint Chiefs of Staff.

jealous /jel'əs/ *adj* suspicious of, or upset or angered by, rivalry; envious; solicitous, anxiously heedful; mistrustfully vigilant; unable to tolerate unfaithfulness, or the thought of it; caused by jealousy. [OFr *jalous*, from L *zēlus*, from Gr *zēlos* emulation]

■ **jeal'ously** *adv*. **jeal'ousy**, **jeal'oushood** (*Shakesp*) or **jeal'ousness** *n*.

jealouse /jə-looz'/ (*obs except Scot*) *vt* and *vi* see **jalouse**.

Jeames /jēmz/ *n* a flunkey. [From Thackeray's creation C *Jeames* de la Pluche, whose diaries were serialized in *Punch* from 1842]

jean /jēn/ or (*esp formerly*) /jān/ *n* a twilled-cotton cloth (also in *pl*); (in *pl*) trousers or overalls made *orig* of jean; (in *pl*) casual trousers made *esp* of denim, and also of corduroy or other similar material. [OFr *Janne*, from L *Genua* Genoa]

■ **jeanette** /ja-net'/ *n* a light or coarse jean. ■ **satin jean** a smooth, glossy twilled cotton.

jeat /jet/ (*obs*) same as **jet**[1,2].

jebel or **djebel** /jeb'əl/ *n* in Arab countries, a hill or a mountain. [Ar, mountain]

Jebusite /jeb'ū-zīt/ *n* one of a people inhabiting Jerusalem before the Israelites; 17c nickname for a Roman Catholic.

■ **Jebusitic** /-zit'ik/ *adj*.

Jeddart /jed'art/ or **Jethart** /jedh'ərt/ (*Scot*) *n* Jedburgh, in SE Scotland. [OE *Gedwearde*]

▫ **Jeddart justice** *n* hanging first and trying afterwards. **Jeddart staff** *n* (*hist*) a sort of battle-axe with a long head.

jee[1] same as **gee**[1,3].

jee[2] /jē/ (*Scot*) *vi* to stir; to budge. ◆ *vt* to disturb; to set on one side or ajar. ◆ *n* a displacement to the side; a condition of being ajar.

■ **jee** or **jow one's ginger** to bestir oneself, show perturbation.

jeel /jēl/ (*Scot*) *vi* to congeal; to set. ◆ *n* extreme cold; jelly.

■ **jee'lie** or **jee'ly** *n* jelly; jam. ◆ *vi* to set, to jelly.

▫ **jeely nose** *n* (*inf*) a bleeding nose. **jeely piece** *n* a jam sandwich.

Jeep® /jēp/ *n* a light, strong, four-wheel-drive, military vehicle suitable for rough terrain. [From GP, the maker's codename for it]

jeepers /jē'pərz/ or **jeepers creepers** /krē'pərz/ (*US inf*) *interj* expressing surprise. [Euphemism for **Jesus (Christ)**]

jeepney /jēp'ni/ *n* (in the Philippines) a jitney constructed from a Jeep or similar vehicle. [*Jeep* and jit*ney*]

jeer /jēr/ *vi* (*usu* with *at*) to scoff; to deride; to mock. ◆ *vt* to mock; to treat with derision. ◆ *n* a derisive remark; a sarcastic or satirical jest; mockery (*obs*). [Origin unknown]

■ **jeer'er** *n*. **jeer'ing** *n* and *adj*. **jeer'ingly** *adv*.

Jeez or **Jeeze** /jēz/ (*inf*) *interj* expressing surprise, enthusiasm or emphasis. [Euphemism for **Jesus**]

jeff[1] /jef/ (*obs printing sl*) *vi* to gamble with quadrats thrown like dice.

jeff[2] /jef/ (*orig circus sl*) *n* a rope.

Jeffersonian /jef-ər-sōn'i-ən/ *adj* relating to or associated with Thomas *Jefferson* (1743–1826), US President 1801–09; holding Jeffersonian, ie Democratic, political principles. ◆ *n* a Democrat.

jeggings /jeg'ingz/ *n pl* tight-fitting trousers in a lightweight fabric with the colour and appearance of denim. [*jeans* and *leggings*]

jehad see **jihad**.

Jehovah /ji-hō'və/ *n* Yahweh, the name of the Hebrew God revealed to Moses, a name used also by Christians. [Heb; for *Yehōwāh*, ie *Yahweh* with the vowels of *Adōnāi*]

■ **Jehō'vist** *n* a person who held that the vowel points attached by the Masoretes to the Hebrew word *YHWH* are the proper vowels of the word (*obs*); a writer of passages in the Pentateuch in which the name applied to God is Yahweh, a Yahwist. **Jehovist'ic** *adj*.

▫ **Jehovah's Witnesses** *n pl* a religious organization, based on interpretations of the Bible, whose members believe in the imminent return of Jesus to bring peace to the world.

Jehu /jē'hū/ (*inf*) *n* any fast and furious coachman or driver. [The King of Israel renowned for his furious chariot driving, from Bible, 2 Kings 9.20]

jeistiecor /jē'sti-kör/ (*obs Scot*) *n* a close-fitting garment. [Fr *juste au corps* close-fitting to the body]

jejune /ji-joon'/ *adj* naïve, immature, callow; showing lack of information or experience; spiritless, meagre, arid. [L *jejūnus* hungry]

■ **jeju'nal** *adj* of or relating to the jejunum. **jejune'ly** *adv*. **jejune'ness** or **jeju'nity** *n*. **jeju'num** *n* the part of the small intestine between the duodenum and the ileum.

Jekyll and Hyde /jek'il (*or* jē'kil, also *-k*(ə)l) ən(d) hīd/ *n* a split personality exemplifying both good and evil. [From RL Stevenson, *The Strange Case of Dr Jekyll and Mr Hyde* (1886)]

jelab see **djellaba**.

jell see **gel**[1] and **jelly**[1].

jellaba see **djellaba**.

jelly[1] /jel'i/ *n* anything gelatinous; the juice of fruit boiled with sugar; a conserve of fruit, jam (*US* and formerly *Scot*; see also **jeely** under **jeel**); a clear, gelatinous, fruit-flavoured dessert (also (*N Am*) **jell'o**, *orig* a trademark); a savoury gelatinous food obtained by boiling bones or by setting stock with gelatin; a capsule of the drug Temazepam (*sl*); a jellyfish; a sandal made from brightly coloured or transparent flexible plastic. ◆ *vi* to set as a jelly; to congeal. ◆ *vt* to make into a jelly; to set in a jelly. [Fr *gelée*, from *geler*, from L *gelāre* to freeze; cf **gel**[1]]

■ **jell** *vi* and *vt* to jelly; to take distinct shape (*inf*). **jell'ied** *adj* in a state of jelly; enclosed in jelly; under the influence of Temazepam (*sl*). **jellifica'tion** *n*. **jell'iform** *adj*. **jell'ify** *vt* to make into a jelly. ◆ *vi* to become gelatinous.

▫ **jelly baby** *n* a kind of gelatinous sweet in the shape of a baby. **jelly bag** *n* a bag through which fruit juice is strained for jelly. **jelly bean** *n* a kind of sweet in the shape of a bean with a sugar coating and jelly filling. **jell'yfish** *n* a marine coelenterate with jelly-like body; a person who lacks firmness of purpose (*inf*). **jell'y-pan** *n* (*Scot*) a preserving-pan.

jelly[2] /jel'i/ (*inf*) *n* short form of **gelignite**.

jelutong /jel'ŭ-tong/ *n* pontianac, a substitute for gutta-percha; the Bornean apocynaceous tree (*Dyera costulata*) producing it. [Malay]

jemadar or **jemidar** /jem'ə-där/, also **jamadar** /jum'-/ (*Ind*) *n* a former junior rank in the Indian Army; an officer of police, customs, etc. [Urdu *jama'dār*]

jemima /ji-mī'mə/ (*inf*) *n* an elastic-sided boot. [The female name]

jemmy[1] /jem'i/ *n* a burglar's short crowbar; a baked sheep's head (*sl*); an overcoat (*dialect*). ◆ *vt* (**jemm'ying**; **jemm'ied**) (*usu* with *open*) to force open with a jemmy or similar tool. [A form of the name *James*]

jemmy[2] /jem'i/ (*dialect*) *adj* neat, handy (also **gemm'y**). [Cf **jimp**]

■ **jemm'iness** *n* neatness.

Jena glass /yā'nə gläs/ *n* a special type of glass containing borates and free silica, resistant to chemical attack. [From *Jena* in Germany]

je ne sais quoi /zhə nə se kwa/ a special unknown ingredient or quality. [Fr, I don't know what]

Jenkins /jeng'kinz/ (*old inf*) *n* a society reporter; a toady.

jennet, also **gennet** or **genet** /jen'it/ *n* a small Spanish horse; a jenny donkey. [OFr *genet*, from Sp *jinete* a light horseman, perh of Ar origin]

jenneting /jen'i-ting/ *n* a kind of early apple. [Prob St John's apple, from Fr *Jeannet*, dimin of *Jean* John; not from *June-eating*]

Jenny /jen'i/ *n* generic name for a country lass (*Scot*); a womanish man (*Scot*); (the following meanings *usu* without *cap*) a wren or owl regarded as female; a female ass (also **jenny donkey**); a travelling crane; a spinning jenny; an in-off into a middle pocket from near the cushion (*billiards*). [The female name]

▫ **jenny-long'-legs** (*Scot*) or **jenn'y-spinner** *n* (*dialect*) a cranefly. **jenny-wren'** *n* a wren.

jeofail /jef'āl/ (*obs*) *n* an error in pleadings, or the acknowledgment of a mistake. [Anglo-Fr *jeo fail* I mistake]

jeopardy /jep'ər-di/ n hazard, danger; the danger of conviction and punishment faced by the accused on a criminal charge (US law). ◆ vt (rare; also (old US) **jeop'ard**) to jeopardize. [Fr jeu parti a divided or even game, from LL jocus partītus, from L jocus a game, and partītus divided, from partīrī to divide]
■ **jeop'ardize** or **-ise** vt to put in jeopardy, risk losing or damaging. **jeop'arder** n. **jeop'ardous** adj (obs) dangerous; daring. **jeop'ardously** adv (obs).

jequirity /jə-kwir'i-ti/ n the tropical shrub Indian liquorice, the seeds of which are used ornamentally and medicinally, and its root for a liquorice substitute; (also **jequirity bean**) its seed. [Origin obscure]

Jer. (Bible) abbrev : (the Book of) Jeremiah.

jerbil see **gerbil**.

jerboa /jûr-bō'ə/ n a desert rodent (family Dipodidae) that jumps on long hind legs like a kangaroo. [Ar yarbū‘]

jereed see **jerid**.

jeremiad /jer-i-mī'ad/ n a lamentation; a tale of grief, a doleful story. [From Jeremiah, reputed author of the Book of Lamentations]
■ **Jeremī'ah** n a person who continually prophesies doom.

jerepigo /jer-ə-pē'gō/ (S Afr) n (pl jerepi'gos) a heavy, sweet, usu red, dessert wine. [Port jeropiga a mixture added in the making of port]

jerfalcon same as **gyrfalcon**.

Jericho /jer'i-kō/ (humorous) n a remote out-of-the way place, to which one is consigned. [Supposed to refer to Bible, 2 Samuel 10.4–5]

jerid or **jereed** /je-rēd'/ n a wooden javelin, traditionally used in Turkey and Arab countries; a tournament in which it is used. [Ar jarīd]

jerk[1] /jûrk/ n a short movement begun and ended suddenly; a twitch; an involuntary spasmodic contraction of a muscle; a movement in physical exercises; a stroke (obs); a short burst of birdsong (obs); a useless or stupid person (sl); (in weightlifting) a movement lifting the barbell from shoulder height to a position on outstretched arms above the head; (also **clean and jerk**) a weightlifting competition involving such a lift (cf **clean**). ◆ vt to throw or move with a jerk; to utter abruptly (usu with out); to thrash (obs). ◆ vi to move with a jerk. [Imit, related to **yerk**]
■ **jerk'er** n a person who, or thing that, jerks; a hornyhead (fish) (US). **jerk'ily** adv. **jerk'iness** n. **jerk'y** adj moving or coming by jerks or starts, spasmodic.
□ **jerk'-off** n (US vulgar sl) a worthless, contemptible person. **jerk'water** n (US) a train on a branch line. ◆ adj not on a main line; small, insignificant, hick (inf).
■ **jerk around** (inf) to treat badly or unfairly. **jerk off** (vulgar sl) to masturbate.

jerk[2] /jûrk/ vt to make into charqui. ◆ n charqui (also **jerked'-meat** or **jerk'y**); a blend of spices used in charqui. [**charqui**]

jerk[3], etc see **jerque**, etc.

jerkin /jûr'kin/ n a sleeveless jacket, a short coat or close-fitting waistcoat. [Origin unknown]
■ **jirkinet'** n (Scot) a woman's bodice.

jerkinhead /jûr'kin-hed/ (archit) n the combination of a truncated gable with a hipped roof. [Perh from **jerkin**[1]]

jerky see **jerk**[1,2].

jeroboam /jer-ō-bō'əm/ n a very large drinking bowl, a jorum; a large bottle, esp one holding the equivalent of 4 normal bottles of champagne. [Allusion to Bible, 1 Kings 11.28 and 14.16]

jerque or **jerk** /jûrk/ vt to search (eg a vessel) for concealed or smuggled goods; to examine (eg a ship's papers). [Poss Ital cercare to search]
■ **jerqu'er** or **jerk'er** n. **jerqu'ing** or **jerk'ing** n.

Jerry or **Gerry** /jer'i/ (wartime sl) n a German, esp a German soldier; (collectively) the Germans.
■ **jerrican** or **jerrycan** /jer'i-kan/ n a flat-sided can used for storing and transporting liquids, esp petrol, orig a German one.

jerry[1] /jer'i/ (inf) n a chamberpot. [**jeroboam**]

jerry[2] /jer'i/ (inf) n a jerry-builder. ◆ adj constructed hastily and with bad materials. [Prob the personal name]
□ **jerr'y-builder** n someone who builds flimsy houses cheaply and hastily. **jerr'y-building** n. **jerr'y-built** adj. **jerr'y-come-tum'ble** n (dialect) a tumbler, circus performer. **jerr'y-shop** n a pub.

jerrymander a mistaken form of **gerrymander**.

jersey /jûr'zi/ n the finest part of wool; combed wool; a knitted (usu woollen) garment for the upper body; a fine knitted fabric in cotton, nylon, etc; (with cap) a cow of Jersey breed. ◆ adj made of knitted fabric; (with cap) of or pertaining to the Jersey breed of cows. [The island of Jersey]
■ **Jer'sian** n a hybrid obtained by mating a Jersey bull and a Friesian cow.

Jerusalem /jə-roo'sə-ləm/ n a city in Israel, sacred to Christians, Jews and Muslims.
□ **Jerusalem artichoke** see under **artichoke**. **Jerusalem cherry** n a S American plant (Solanum pseudo-capsicum) with reddish cherry-like berries. **Jerusalem cross** n (heraldry) a cross potent. **Jerusalem letters** n pl (hist) letters or symbols tattooed on someone who has made a pilgrimage to Jerusalem. **Jerusalem oak** n a pungent-smelling Mediterranean plant (Chenopodium botrys), naturalized in N America where it is regarded as a weed. **Jerusalem pony** n a donkey. **Jerusalem sage** n a perennial plant (Phlomis fruticosa) found in S Europe, with dense yellow flowers.

jess /jes/ (falconry) n a short strap round the leg of a hawk. ◆ vt to put a jess on (a hawk). [OFr ges, from L jactus a cast, from jacere to throw]
■ **jessed** adj having jesses on.

jessamine see **jasmine**.

jessamy /jes'ə-mi/ (obs) n jasmine; a dandy. [Altered from **jessamine**]

jessant /jes'ənt/ (heraldry) adj overlying; also appar for **issuant** (see under **issue**). [Appar OFr gesant, prp of gesir, from L jacēre to lie]

Jesse /jes'i/ n a genealogical tree of Christ's descent from Jesse; a large branched church candlestick.
□ **Jesse window** n one showing Christ's genealogy in stained glass or carved on the mullions.

jesserant /jes'ə-rənt/ or **jazerant** /jaz'/ (hist) n splint armour (qv). [OFr jaseran(t), jazeran, from Sp jacerina]

Jessie /jes'i/ (Scot inf; also without cap) n an effeminate or namby-pamby man or boy.

jest /jest/ n something spoken in fun; a joke; fun; a taunt or jeer; something ludicrous, an object of laughter. ◆ vi to make a jest; to joke. ◆ vt to jeer at, ridicule; to utter as a jest. [ME geste a deed, a story, from OFr geste, from L gesta things done, doings, from gerere to do]
■ **jestee'** n (Sterne) the object of a jest. **jest'er** n a person who jests; a buffoon; a court fool; a reciter of romances (archaic). **jest'ful** adj given to jesting. **jest'ing** n and adj. **jest'ingly** adv.
□ **jest'book** n a collection of funny stories. **jest'ing-stock** n (obs) a butt for jests.

Jesuit /jez'ū-it/ n a member of the religious order, the Society of Jesus, founded in 1534 by Ignatius Loyola; someone who delights in oversubtle arguments (derog).
■ **Jesuit'ic** or **Jesuit'ical** adj relating to or like the Jesuits; crafty or equivocating (derog). **Jesuit'ically** adv. **Jes'uitism** or **Jes'uitry** n the principles and practices of, or ascribed to, the Jesuits.
□ **Jesuits' bark** n cinchona (brought to Rome by Jesuit missionaries).

Jesus /jē'zəs/ n the founder of Christianity, acknowledged by Christians as the Son of God and Saviour of mankind (also **Jesus Christ**, **Jesus of Nazareth** and (in hymns, etc, esp in the vocative) **Jesu** /jē'zū/). ◆ interj a loose profanity expressing anger, surprise, etc. [Gr Iēsous (vocative and oblique cases Iēsou), from Heb Yēshūa‘, short form of Yehōshūa‘ Joshua]
■ **Jesus wept!** (inf) an interjection expressing amazement, horror, etc.

jésus /zhā'zü/ n a size of paper in France, approx super-royal.
■ **grand jésus** imperial size.

JET abbrev : Joint European Torus, a large tokamak experiment designed to use deuterium and tritium to produce energy by a fusion process.

jet[1] /jet/ n a rich black variety of lignite, taking a high polish, used for ornaments; jet-black. ◆ adj made of jet; jet-black. [OFr jaiet, from L and Gr gagātēs, from Gagas or Gangai, a town and river in Lycia, where it was obtained]
■ **jett'iness** n. **jett'y** adj of the nature of jet, or black as jet.
□ **jet'-black** adj black as jet (also n).

jet[2] /jet/ n a narrow spouting stream; a spout, nozzle or pipe emitting a stream or spray of fluid; a jet plane; a strutting movement (obs). ◆ vt and vi (jett'ing; jett'ed) to spout. ◆ vi to travel by jet plane; to jut (obs); to encroach (Shakesp); to strut (obs). [OFr jetter, from L jactāre to fling]
□ **jet boat** n (NZ) a power boat propelled by a pressurized jet of water. **jet'-driven** adj driven by the backward emission of a jet of gas, etc. **jet engine** n a gas turbine, esp one fitted to an aircraft, which uses jet propulsion to provide thrust. **jet'foil** n a hydrofoil powered by a jet of water. **jet lag** n exhaustion, discomfort, etc resulting from the body's inability to adjust to the rapid changes of time zone caused by high-speed long-distance air travel. **jet'-lagged** adj. **jet'liner** n an airliner powered by a jet engine. **jet pipe** n the exhaust pipe in a jet engine. **jet plane** n a jet-driven aeroplane. **jet'-propelled** adj. **jet propulsion** n. **jet'-setter** n a member of the jet set (see below). **jet'-setting** adj living in the style of the jet set (also n). **jet ski** n a powered craft comparable to a motorbike adapted to plane across water on a ski-like keel. **jet'-ski** vi to ride a jet ski (as a water sport or recreation). **jet'-skier** n. **jet'stream** or **jet stream** n a narrow band of very high-velocity, westerly winds more than 30000ft (c.10000m) above the earth (meteorol); the exhaust of a jet engine or rocket

motor. **Jet'way**® *n* (*US*) a movable enclosed structure in an airport allowing passengers to transfer between an aircraft and the terminal. ■ **the jet set** a wealthy social set whose members travel frequently and widely for pleasure.

jet d'eau /*zhe dō'*/ (*Fr*) *n* a jet of water, eg in an ornamental fountain.

jeté /*zhǝ-tā'*/ (*ballet*) *n* a leap from one foot to the other in which the free leg *usu* finishes extended forward, backward or sideways. [Fr, thrown]

Jethart see **Jeddart**.

jeton see **jetton**.

jetsam /*jet'sǝm*/ *n* (also (*archaic*) **jet'som** and **jet'son**) goods jettisoned from a ship and washed up on shore; according to some, goods from a wreck that remain under water (cf **flotsam**); jettison (*obs*). [Contraction of **jettison**]
■ **flotsam and jetsam** see under **flotsam**.

jettatura /*jet-ǝ-too'rǝ*/ *n* the supposed power to harm others by a look, the evil eye. [Ital *iettatura*, a Neapolitan word, from L *ējectāre*, from *jactāre*, frequentative of *jacere* to throw]

jettiness see under **jet¹**.

jettison /*jet'i-sǝn*/ *n* the act of throwing goods overboard. ◆ *vt* to throw overboard (goods in time of danger); to abandon, reject. [Anglo-Fr *jetteson*, from L *jactātiō, -ōnis* a casting, from *jactāre*, frequentative of *jacere* to throw]

jetton or **jeton** /*jet'ǝn*/ *n* a piece of stamped metal used as a counter in card-playing or other gambling games; a (*usu* metal) token for operating a machine, *esp* a pay telephone. [Fr *jeton*, from *jeter* to throw, from L *jactāre*, frequentative of *jacere* to throw]

jetty¹ /*jet'i*/ *n* a pier, or similar projecting structure. ◆ *vi* (*pap* and *pat* **jett'ied**) (*archit*) to project, jut out. [OFr *jettee* thrown out; see **jet²**]

jetty² see under **jet¹**.

jeu /*zhǝ*/ (*Fr*) *n* a game.
❑ **jeu de mots** /*dǝ mō'*/ *n* (*pl* **jeux de mots**) a play on words, a pun. **jeu de paume** /*pōm*/ *n* real tennis. **jeu d'esprit** /*des-prē'*/ *n* (*pl* **jeux d'esprit**) a witticism.

jeune /*zhœn*/ (*Fr*) *adj* young.
❑ **jeune amour** /*a-moor'*/ *n* young love. **jeune fille** /*fē-y'*/ *n* a girl. **jeune premier** /*prǝ-myā'*/ or (*fem*) **jeune première** /*prǝ-myer'*/ *n* (*theatre*) a juvenile lead.

jeunesse dorée /*zhœ-nes do-rā'*/ (*Fr*) *n* luxurious, stylish, sophisticated young people, (literally) gilded youth.

Jew /*joo*/ *n* a member of a Semitic people practising a monotheistic religion; an Israelite; a usurer, miser, someone who drives a hard bargain (*offensive*). ◆ *adj* (*derog* or *offensive*) Jewish. ◆ *vt* and *vi* (*old*; *offensive*; also without *cap*) to haggle (with) or get the better of in a bargain. [OFr *Jueu*, from L *Jūdaeus*, from Gr *Ioudaios*, from Heb *Yehūdāh* Judah]
■ **Jew'ess** *n* (*offensive* when used by non-Jews) a Jewish woman. **Jew'ish** *adj* of the Jews or their religion; extortionate, money-grubbing (*offensive*). **Jew'ishly** *adv*. **Jew'ishness** *n*. **Jew'ry** *n* the Jewish world, community or religion; Judaea (*archaic*); a district inhabited by Jews (*hist*). ❑ **Jew'-baiting** *n* the persecuting of Jews. **jew'fish** *n* a name for several very large American and Australian fishes. **Jew's'-ear** *n* an ear-like fungus (genus *Auricularia*) parasitic on elder and other trees. **Jew's eye** *n* something of very high value (*Shakesp* 'worth a Jewe's eye'; from the practice of torturing Jews for money). **Jew's-frank'incense** *n* benzoin. **Jew's** or **Jews'-harp'** or **-trump'** *n* (also without *cap*) a small lyre-shaped instrument played against the teeth by plucking a metal tongue with the finger. **Jews' houses** or **leavings** *n pl* in Cornwall, remains of prehistoric miners' dwellings, mine refuse, and tin furnaces. **Jew's mallow** *n* a yellow-flowered plant, *Kerria japonica* (family Rosaceae); (**Jews' mallow**) jute, *Corchorus olitorius*. **Jew's-myr'tle** *n* butcher's broom. **Jew's'-pitch** *n* asphalt. **Jew's'-stone** *n* a large fossil sea-urchin spine. **Jews' thorn** *n* Christ's thorn.
■ **wandering Jew** see under **wander**.

jewel /*joo'ǝl*/ *n* a precious stone; a personal ornament of precious stones, gold, etc; a hard stone (ruby, etc) used for pivot bearings in a watch; an imitation of a gemstone; an ornamental glass boss; anything or anyone highly valued. ◆ *vt* (**jew'elling**; **jew'elled**) to adorn with jewels; to fit with a jewel. [OFr *jouel* (Fr *joyau*); either a dimin of Fr *joie* joy, from L *gaudium* joy, from *gaudēre* to rejoice, or derived through LL *jocāle*, from L *jocārī* to jest]
■ **jew'eller** *n* someone who deals in, or makes, jewels. **jewellery** /*joo'al-ri*/ or **jew'elry** *n* jewels in general.
❑ **jewel case** or **box** *n* a casket for holding jewels; a (*usu* plastic) storage case for a compact disc. **jew'elfish** *n* an African cichlid (*Hemichromis bimaculatus*) popular in aquariums for its bright colours. **jew'el-house** *n* a room in the Tower of London where the crown jewels are kept. **jeweller's rouge** *n* finely powdered ferric oxide, used for polishing metal. **jew'el-weed** *n* any plant of the genus *Impatiens*.

■ **jewel in the crown** *orig* (in *pl*) any or all of the countries of the British Empire, *esp* (in *sing*) India; the best, most highly prized, most successful, etc of a number or collection.

jezail /*jez'īl* or *-āl'*/ *n* (*hist*) a heavy Afghan musket. [Pers *jazā'il*]

Jezebel /*jez'ǝ-bǝl*/ *n* a wicked scheming woman; (formerly often) a shameless painted woman. [From Ahab's wife, see eg 1 Kings 21 and 2 Kings 9.30]

jhala /*jä'lǝ*/ (*Hindu music*) *n* part of the second movement of a raga. [Sans]

-ji /*-jē*/ (*Ind*) *sfx* used after names or titles as a mark of respect. [Hindi]

jiao /*jow*/ *n* a Chinese monetary unit, 10 fen or $\frac{1}{10}$ of a yuan. [Chin *jiǎo*]

jib¹ /*jib*/ *n* a triangular sail stretched in front of the foremast in a ship; the boom of a crane or derrick; the lower lip, the face (*dialect*); a jibbing horse; an act of jibbing, a standstill. ◆ *vt* (**jibb'ing**; **jibbed**) to cause to gybe. ◆ *vi* (*usu* with *at*) to gybe; (of a horse) to balk or shy; to refuse, show objection, boggle. [Origin obscure; perh several different words; cf **gibbet** and **gybe**; the j sound precludes connection with Dan *gibbe*, Du *gijpen*]
■ **jibb'er** *n* a jibbing horse.
❑ **jib boom** *n* a boom or extension of the bowsprit, on which the jib is spread. **jib crane** *n* a crane with an inclined, pivoted arm fixed to the foot of a rotating vertical post, the upper ends connected by a chain, etc, to allow raising and lowering of the arm. **jib sail** *n*. **jib sheet** *n* a rope for trimming the jib.
■ **the cut of someone's jib** (*inf*) someone's appearance.

jib² /*jib*/ (*Scot*) *vt* to milk (a cow) dry; to strip; to fleece (*obs*).
■ **jibb'ings** *n pl* the last milk drawn from a cow.

jibba or **jibbah** /*jib'ǝ*/ see **jubbah**.

jibber¹ same as **gibber¹**.

jibber² see under **jib¹**.

jibber-jabber /*jib'ǝr-jab'ǝr*/ (*inf*) *n* inconsequential chatter. *vi* to chatter inconsequentially. [**jibber¹** and **jabber**]

jib-door /*jib'dör*/ *n* a disguised door, flush with the wall. [Origin unknown]

jibe¹ see **gybe**.

jibe², **jiber** see **gibe**.

jibe³ /*jīb*/ (chiefly *US*) *vi* to agree, accord (with). [Poss related to **chime¹**]

JIC *abbrev*: Joint Intelligence Committee.

jicama /*hē'kǝ-mǝ*/ *n* the fleshy tuber of a plant of the pea family (*Pachyrhizus erosus*), used in Mexican cookery; the plant producing this. [Mex Sp]

jickajog see **jig-jog**.

jiffy /*jif'i*/ (*inf*) *n* an instant (sometimes shortened to **jiff**). [Origin unknown]
❑ **Jiffy bag**® *n* a stout padded envelope in which to post books, etc.

jig /*jig*/ *n* a lively dance, *usu* in 6–8 time; a dance tune for such a dance; a jerky movement; a lure which moves jerkily when drawn through the water (*angling*); an appliance for guiding or positioning a tool; an appliance of various kinds in mechanical processes, eg a jigger in mining; a mocking ballad (*obs*); a jingle or piece of doggerel (*obs*); a farcical afterpiece or interlude sung and danced to popular tunes (*obs*); a jest, a prank (*obs*). ◆ *vt* and *vi* (**jigg'ing**; **jigged**) to jerk; to perform as a jig. ◆ *vt* to work upon with a jig; to equip with jigs. ◆ *vi* to dance a jig; to jump up and down; to fish with a jig. [Origin obscure; Fr *gigue* is from the English word]
■ **jigamaree'** or **jigg'umbob** *n* (*inf*) a what's-its-name; a gadget. **jigg'er** *n* a person or thing that jigs in any sense; any of various kinds of subsidiary appliance, *esp* with reciprocating motion, such as an oscillation transformer, an apparatus for separating ores by jolting them in sieves in water, a simple potter's wheel or a template or profile used with it, and a type of warehouse crane; a golf club, used *esp* formerly, with narrow lofted iron head; a rest for a billiard cue (*old inf*); a light hoisting tackle (*naut*); a small aft sail on a ketch, etc (*naut*); a boat with such a sail (*naut*); a jigger-mast (*naut*); a sail on a jigger-mast (*naut*); a what's-its-name (*N Am inf*); a small measure for alcoholic drinks. ◆ *vt* to jerk or shake; to form with a jigger; to ruin (sometimes with *up*); to damn, blast (*inf*). ◆ *vi* to tug or move with jerks. **jigg'ered** *adj* (*inf*) exhausted; broken; surprised; bewildered; damned. **jigg'ing** *n*. **jigg'ish** *adj*. **jigg'le** *vt* and *vi* to move with vibratory jerks. ◆ *n* a jiggling movement. **jigg'ly** *adj*.
❑ **jig borer** *n* an adjustable precision machine-tool for drilling holes. **jigg'er-mast** *n* a four-masted ship's aftermost mast; a small mast astern. **jig'saw** *n* a jigsaw puzzle; a narrow reciprocating saw for cutting awkward shapes. ◆ *vt* and *vi* (*pap* and *pat* **jig'sawed**) to cut with a jigsaw. **jigsaw puzzle** *n* a picture mounted on wood or card and cut up into pieces (as by a jigsaw) to be fitted together.
■ **the jig is up** (*inf*) the game is up, the trick is discovered, etc.

jigajig, etc see **jig-jog**.

---

jigamaree see under **jig**.

jigger[1] /jig'ər/ n a variant of **chigoe**.

jigger[2], **jiggered** see under **jig**.

jiggery-pokery /jig'ə-ri-pō'kə-ri/ (inf) n trickery; deception. [Cf joukery-pawkery under **jouk**]

jiggety-jog see **jig-jog**.

jiggle, **jiggumbob** see under **jig**.

jig-jog /jig'jog/ adv with a jolting, jogging motion. ◆ n a jolting motion; a jog. —Also **jick'ajog**, **jig'jig'**, **jig'ajig**, **jig'ajog'**, **jigg'ety-jog**. [**jig** and **jog**]
□ **jig'-a-jig**, **jig'-jig** or **jigg'y-jigg'y** n (sl) sexual intercourse (also vi).
■ **get jiggy with** (sl) (often with it) to start dancing energetically; to become excited about or enthusiastically involved with; to have sex with; to become sexually excited about; (often with it) to be stylish, abreast of the latest fashions.

jigot same as **gigot**.

jihad or **jehad** /jē-had'/ n a holy war (for the Islamic faith); a fervent campaign for a cause. [Ar jihād struggle]
■ **jihad'i**, **jehad'i** or **jihad'ist** adj relating to or involved in a jihad. ◆ n (pl **jihad'is**, **jihad'een**, **jehad'is**, **jehad'een** or **jihad'ists**) a person taking part in a jihad.

jilbab /jil'bab/ n (pl **jil'babs** or **jal'abib** /-ə-bēb/) a long outer garment, worn by women in some Islamic communities. [Ar]

jilgie see **gilgie**.

jill[1], etc see **gill**[4].

jill[2] see **gill**[5].

jillaroo see **jackaroo**.

jillet see under **gill**[4].

jillion /jil'yən/ (N Am) n an indefinite but extremely large number (also adj). [Coinage based on **million**; cf **zillion**]

jilt /jilt/ n a person, orig and esp a woman, who encourages and then rejects a lover. ◆ vt to discard abruptly (a lover one had previously encouraged). [Poss **jillet** (see under **gill**[4])]

jimcrack see **gimcrack**.

Jim Crow /jim krō/ (chiefly US sl) n a derogatory name for any black person; racial discrimination against black people; (without caps) a tool for bending or straightening iron rails or bars; a plane or other tool that works in both directions. [From a black minstrel song with the refrain 'Wheel about and turn about and jump Jim Crow']
■ **Jim Crow'ism** n.
□ **Jim Crow car**, **school**, etc n one for black people only.

jim-dandy /jim'dan'di/ (US inf) n a fine or excellent example. ◆ adj fine, excellent, superb. [Prob Jim and **dandy**[1]]

jiminy /jim'i-ni/ see **geminy** under **geminate**.

jimjam /jim'jam/ (inf) n a knick-knack, a gadget; an oddity, peculiarity; (in pl) delirium tremens (sl); (in pl) a state of nervous excitement; (in pl) a child's word for pyjamas. [Origin unknown]

Jimmy[1] /jim'i/ (sl) n an act of urinating (also **Jimmy Riddle**). [Rhyming slang for piddle]

Jimmy[2] /jim'i/ (Scot inf) n term of address for a male stranger.

jimmy /jim'i/ (chiefly US) n a burglar's jemmy. ◆ vt to force open, esp with a jimmy.

jimmy-o'goblin /jim'i-ō-gob'lin/ (sl) n (also with cap(s)) a pound sterling. [Rhyming slang for sovereign]

Jimmy Riddle see **Jimmy**[1].

Jimmy Woodser /jim'i wŭd'sər/ (Aust and NZ inf) n a solitary drinker; a drink taken on one's own.

jimp /jimp/ (Scot) adj slender; elegant; scant. [Origin unknown]
■ **jimp** or **jimp'ly** adv neatly; hardly; scant. **jimp'ness** n. **jimp'y** adj neat.

jimson weed, **jimpson weed** or (obs) **Jamestown weed** /jim'sən wēd/ (N Am) n the thorn apple (Datura stramonium). [Jamestown, Virginia, where it established itself]

jingal, **gingall** or **gingal** /jin(g)'göl or -göl'/ n a large Chinese or Indian swivel-musket. [Hindi janjāl]

jingbang /jing-bang' or jing'bang/ (sl) n company; collection; lot. [Origin unknown]

jingle /jing'gl/ n a succession of clinking, tinkling sounds; something which makes a tinkling sound, esp a metal disc on a tambourine; a catchy, pleasant-sounding arrangement of words which may have very little meaning; a short, simple verse, usu with music, or sometimes a short catchy tune on its own, used to advertise a product, etc; a covered two-wheeled vehicle (obs). ◆ vt and vi to sound with a jingle. ◆ vi to be full of alliteration; to be catchy. [Imit]
■ **jing'ler** n. **jing'let** n a ball serving as the clapper of a sleigh-bell. **jing'ly** adj.

□ **jing'le-jangle** n a dissonant continued jingling; a jingling ornament. **jingling Johnny** n a Chinese pavilion, or musical percussion instrument with little bells. **jingling match** n (obs) a game in which blindfolded players try to catch a player who is holding or wearing bells.

jingo or **Jingo** /jing'gō/ n (pl **jing'oes**) used in the mild oaths 'By jingo', 'By the living jingo' (Scot 'By jing', 'By jings'); from its occurrence in a music-hall song of 1878 that conveyed a threat against Russia, a chauvinistic, sabre-rattling patriot. [Appears first as a conjurer's summoning call; poss from Basque Jinkoa, Jainko(a) God]
■ **jing'o** or **jing'oish** adj chauvinist, sabre-rattling. **jing'oism** n. **jing'oist** n. **jingois'tic** adj characteristic of jingoism. **jingois'tically** adv.

jingo-ring /jing'gō-ring/ n a children's game in which the players dance round one of their number singing 'Here we go round the jingo-ring'. [Connected with **jink**]

jinjili see **gingili**.

jink /jingk/ (orig Scot) vi to dodge nimbly; to make a sudden evasive turn (aeronautics). ◆ vt to elude; to cheat. ◆ n (esp aeronautics and rugby) a quick, deceptive turn. [Imit of the movement]
■ **high jinks** see under **high**[1].

jinker /jing'kər/ (Aust) n a janker; a sulky or other light horse-drawn passenger vehicle. ◆ vt to transport in a jinker. [janker]

jinn /jin/ n pl (sing **jinnee** or **jinni** /jen'i or jin-ē'/) a class of spirits in Muslim theology and folklore, assuming various shapes, sometimes as enormous monstrous men with supernatural powers (also **djinn** (sing **djinni**) or **ginn** (sing **genie**)). —The jinn are often called **genii** by a confusion and **jinns** sometimes occurs as a plural in non-standard use. [Ar jinn (pl), jinnī (sing)]

jinricksha, **jinrickshaw**, **jinrikisha** see **rickshaw**.

Jin Shin Do® /jin shin dō/ n a form of acupressure using extra meridians, resulting in a deeper level of treatment. [Jap, literally, way of the compassionate spirit]

jinx /jingks/ n a person or thing that brings bad luck; an unlucky influence. ◆ vt to bring bad luck to, or put an unlucky spell on. [Appar from **Jynx**, the bird being used in spells, and the name itself coming to mean 'a spell or charm']
■ **jinxed** adj beset with bad luck.

jipyapa or **jippi-jappa** /hē-pi-hä'pə/ n a palm-like tree (Carludovica palmata) of tropical America, the fibre from whose leaves is used for panama hats, etc. [Name of a town in Ecuador]

jirble /jir' or jûr'bl/ (Scot) vt and vi to pour splashingly or unsteadily. [Imit]

jird /jûrd/ n a gerbil of N Africa and Central Asia (genus Meriones). [Berber (a)gherda]

jirga /jēr'gə/ n in Afghanistan, a council of tribal elders, esp the **Loya Jirga** or Grand Council, a traditional consultative or law-making national assembly. [Pashto]

jirkinet see under **jerkin**.

jism, **gism** /jiz'əm/ or **jissom** /jis'əm/ n energy, force (inf, chiefly US); (also **jizz**) semen (vulgar sl). [Origin unknown]

JIT (business) abbrev : just-in-time (see under **just**[1]).

jitney /jit'ni/ (US inf) n a bus or other, smaller, passenger vehicle, usu with low fares; orig a five-cent piece, a nickel. ◆ adj cheap; paltry. [Perh Fr jeton counter]

jitter /jit'ər/ (orig US) vi to behave in a flustered way. ◆ n small rapid variations in an electrical signal.
■ **jitt'ers** n pl a flustered state (usu with the, esp as in **have the jitters** to be on edge, nervous or flustered). **jitt'eriness** n. **jitt'ery** adj.
□ **jitt'erbug** n (US) a type of two-step to jazz music, the standard movements allowing for energetic improvisation; someone who performs this dance; (in Britain, by misunderstanding or extension) a nervous person, scaremonger or alarmist. ◆ vi to dance the jitterbug, esp wildly.

jiu-jitsu see **ju-jitsu**.

jive /jīv/ n a lively style of jazz music, swing; the style of fast dancing done to this music; jargon, orig of Harlem and of jazz musicians (sl). ◆ vi to play or dance jive; to talk jive (also **jive talk**; sl); to talk nonsense (US inf). ◆ vt (US inf) to taunt. ◆ adj (US inf) insincere; deceitful.
■ **jī'ver** n. **jī'vey** adj.
□ **jive'-ass** n and adj (US inf) term of contempt.

jiz see **gizz**.

jizz[1] /jiz/ n the characteristic features which distinguish a bird, animal or plant from other species which resemble it. [Origin uncertain]

jizz[2] see **jism**.

JJ abbrev : Judges; Justices.

jnana /jə-nä'nə/ (*Hinduism*) *n* spiritual knowledge. [Sans *jñāna*, for *jñā* to know]

Jnr or **jnr** *abbrev* : Junior or junior.

jo or **joe** /jō/ (*Scot*) *n* (*pl* **joes**) a beloved one. [An old form of **joy**]

joanna /jō-an'ə/ (*sl*) *n* a piano. [Rhyming slang]

joannes see **johannes**.

Job /jōb/ *n* a person of great patience. [From *Job* in the *Book of Job* in Bible]
■ **jōbā'tion** (also **jawbā'tion**) *n* a tedious scolding. **jobe** /jōb/ *vt* to reprimand tediously.
□ **Job's comforter** *n* someone who aggravates the distress of the unfortunate person they have come to comfort. **Job's news** *n* bad news. **Job's post** *n* the bearer of bad news. **Job's tears** *n pl* the involucres of an Indian grass (*Coix lachryma*) used as beads; round grains of chrysolite.

job¹ /job/ *n* any individual piece of work; any undertaking or employment done for payment or profit; an occupation or post; someone's proper business or responsibility; a task to be performed by an operating system (*comput*); a state of affairs (*inf*); an item or example of a specified kind (*inf*); a transaction in which private gain is sought under pretence of public service; an end accomplished by intrigue or wirepulling; a criminal enterprise, *esp* theft (*inf*); a surgical procedure to improve or enhance a part of the body (*esp* in compounds, such as *nose job*; *inf*); a hired horse or carriage (*obs*); a job lot. ◆ *adj* employed, hired or used by the job or for jobs; bought or sold lumped together. ◆ *vi* to do casual jobs; to buy and sell, as a broker; to practise jobbery. ◆ *vt* to perform as a job; to put or carry through by jobbery; to deal in, as a broker; to hire or let out (*esp* horses). [Origin unknown]
■ **jobb'er** *n* a person who jobs; a person who buys and sells, as a broker; a stock-jobber; someone who turns official actions to private advantage; a person who employs unfair means to secure some private end; a wholesale merchant, *esp* if selling to retailers (*US*). ◆ *combining form* with *first*, *second*, etc, denoting someone in, or seeking, their first, second, etc job. **jobb'ery** *n* jobbing; the abuse of public office for private gain; unfair means employed to secure some private end. **jobb'ie** *n* (*sl*) a lump of excrement. **jobb'ing** *adj* working by the job. ◆ *n* the doing of jobs; miscellaneous printing-work other than books or newspapers; buying and selling as a broker; stock-jobbing; jobbery. **job'less** *adj* having no job. ◆ *n* (with *the*) jobless people. **job'lessness** *n*.
□ **job centre** or **Jobcentre** *n* (also without *cap*) an office run by the government agency **Jobcentre Plus**, which provides information about available jobs. **job club** or **Job'club** *n* an association directed towards helping the jobless to find employment for themselves through learning and using the required skills, motivation, etc. **job control language** *n* (*comput*) a language for writing instructions to control the performance of jobs by an operating system. **job description** *n* a detailed listing of all the duties, responsibilities, tasks, etc necessary to a specific job. **job evaluation** *n* a method of working out the relative postion and appropriate salary for the different jobs in an organization by allocating points for the various aspects of each job as listed in the job description. **job'-hopping** *n* changing job frequently. **job lot** *n* a collection of odds and ends, *esp* for sale as one lot; any collection of inferior quality. **job'-master** *n* a livery-stable keeper who jobs out horses and carriages. **job of work** *n* a task, bit of work. **job rotation** *n* the practice of moving workers from one activity to another in order to provide them with variety and widen their experience. **job'seeker** *n* (also with *cap*) in Britain since 1996, an unemployed person receiving **Jobseeker's Allowance**, a state benefit for those actively seeking work. **job share**, **job'share** or **job sharing** *n* the practice of dividing one job between two part-time workers. **job'-share** *vi*.
■ **a bad** (or **good**) **job** a piece of work badly (or well) done; an unlucky (or lucky) fact. **do the job** to succeed in doing what is required. **give something up as a bad job** to abandon a task, etc as impossible or not worthwhile. **have a job to** (*inf*) to have difficulty in. **job off** to sell (goods) cheaply to get rid of them. **job out** to divide (work) among contractors, etc. **jobs for the boys** jobs given to or created for friends or supporters. **just the job** (*inf*) exactly what is wanted. **make the best of a bad job** to do one's best in difficult circumstances. **odd jobs** see under **odd¹**. **on the job** at work, in activity, busy (**on'-the-job** *adj* happening while one is at work); engaged in sexual intercourse (*inf*).

job² /job/ *n* a sudden thrust with anything pointed, such as a beak. ◆ *vt* and *vi* (**jobb'ing**; **jobbed**) to prod or peck suddenly. ◆ *vt* (*Aust inf*) to punch. [Appar imit; cf **jab**]

jobation, **jobe** see under **Job**.

jobernowl /job'ər-nōl/ (*old inf*) *n* a stupid person. [Appar Fr *jobard* a noodle, and **nowl**, **noll**]

jobsworth /jobz'wûrth/ (*derog sl*) *n* a minor official who regards the rigid enforcement of petty rules as more important than providing a service to the public. [From 'It's more than my *job's worth* to let you...']

Jock /jok/ *n* a Scottish soldier (*inf*); a Scotsman (*inf*); the jack in cards (*Scot*); a male yokel (*Scot*). [Scot variant of **Jack** (see **jack¹**)]

jock¹ /jok/ *n* a jockstrap; a male athlete or sportsman (*US inf*); a macho young man whose clothes accentuate and display his physique. [**jockstrap**]
■ **jock'ish** *adj*.
□ **jock itch** *n* (*inf*) irritation of the skin around the groin, caused by a fungal infection.

jock² /jok/ (*inf*) *n* a disc jockey. [Abbrev]

jockey /jok'i/ *n* a person who rides (*esp* professionally) in horse-races; a horse-dealer (*obs*); someone who takes undue advantage in business. ◆ *vt* to ride (a horse) in a race; to jostle by riding against; to manoeuvre; to trick by manoeuvring. ◆ *vi* (often with *for*) to seek advantage by manoeuvring. [Dimin of **Jock**, ie a lad, jockeys orig being boys]
■ **jockette'** *n* (*facetious*) a female jockey. **jock'eyism** *n*. **jock'eyship** *n* the art or practice of a jockey.
□ **jockey cap** *n* a reinforced cap with a long peak, as worn by jockeys. **Jockey Club** *n* an association for the promotion and regulation of horse-racing; a perfume composed of rose, orris, cassia, tuberose, bergamot, etc. **jockey strap** see **jockstrap**. **jockey wheel** *n* a guiding wheel, *esp* one which allows a trailer or caravan to be manoeuvred when not being towed.

jocko /jok'ō/ *n* (*pl* **jock'os**) a chimpanzee. [Fr, from a W African word *ncheko*]

Jock Scott /jok skot/ (*angling*) *n* a kind of artificial fly.

jockstrap /jok'strap/ *n* a genital support worn *esp* by men participating in athletics (also **jock** or **jockey strap**). [Dialect *jock* the penis, and **strap**]

jockteleg /jok'tə-leg/ (*Scot*) *n* a large clasp knife. [The suggested *Jacques de Liège*, supposedly a famous cutler, lacks confirmation]

joco /jō-kō'/ (*Scot*) *adj* cheerful; pleased with oneself. [**jocose**]

jocose /jō-kōs'/ *adj* full of jokes; facetious; merry. [L *jocōsus*, from *jocus* a joke]
■ **jocose'ly** *adv*. **jocose'ness** or **jocosity** /-kos'i-ti/ *n* the quality of being jocose. **jocosē'rious** *adj* half in jest, half in earnest.

jocular /jok'ū-lər/ *adj* given to or inclined to joking; of the nature of, or intended as, a joke. [L *joculāris*, from *jocus*]
■ **jocularity** /-lar'i-ti/ *n*. **joc'ularly** *adv*.

joculator /jok'ū-lā-tər/ *n* a professional jester or minstrel. [L, from *joculārī* to jest]

jocund /jōk'und, jok'und or -ənd/ *adj* mirthful; merry; cheerful; pleasant. [OFr, from LL *jocundus* for L *jūcundus* pleasant, modified by association with *jocus*]
■ **jocundity** /-kund'i-ti/ or **joc'undness** *n*. **joc'undly** *adv*.

jodel /yō'dl/ same as **yodel**.

jodhpurs /jod'pûrz/ *n pl* riding-breeches, loose round the hip and tight-fitting from the knee to the ankle (also **jodhpur breeches**). [*Jodhpur* in India]
□ **jodhpur boots** *n pl* ankle-high boots worn with jodhpurs for riding.

Joe /jō/ (*sl*) *n* a man, an ordinary fellow, *esp* (*US*) a soldier.
■ **Joey** /jō'i/ *n* a circus clown, *esp* in the English tradition (*Joseph* Grimaldi); a fourpenny bit (*obs*) (*Joseph* Hume, MP, 1836); (sometimes without *cap*) a threepenny bit.
□ **Joe Baxi** /bak'si/ *n* (*rhyming sl*) a taxi. **Joe Blake** *n* (*Aust rhyming sl*) a snake; (in *pl*) the shakes, delirium tremens (*obs*). **Joe Bloggs** *n* (*N Am* and *Aust*) **Joe Blow** *n* the average man in the street. **Joe Miller** *n* an old or stale jest; a joke-book. **Joe Millerism** *n* the habit of telling old jokes (*Joe Miller* (1684–1738), a comedian after whom a joke-book was named). **Joe Public** or (chiefly *US*) **Joe Sixpack** *n* the average man in the street. **Joe Soap** or merely **Joe** *n* (RAF rhyming slang for *dope*) someone imposed on to perform unpleasant tasks.
■ **not for Joe** see under **Joseph**.

joe see **jo**.

joe-pye weed /jō'pī wēd/ *n* a plant of the genus *Eupatorium*, having clusters of small purple flowers. [Origin unknown]

Joey see under **Joe**.

joey /jō'i/ (*inf*) *n* a young animal, *esp* a kangaroo (*Aust*); an opossum (*NZ*). [From an Aboriginal language]

jog /jog/ *vt* (**jogg'ing**; **jogged**) to shake; to push with the elbow or hand; to stimulate, stir up (eg the memory). ◆ *vi* to move by jogs; to run at a slow, steady pace, as a form of exercise; (with *on* or *along*) to move along or progress slowly, steadily, unremarkably. ◆ *n* a slight shake; a push or nudge; a spell of jogging. [Appar imit; perh related to **shog**]

■ **jogg'er** *n* a person who jogs for exercise; a person who moves slowly and heavily (*Dryden*); a piece of mechanical equipment which shakes sheets of paper into alignment ready for stapling, binding, etc; (in *pl*) jog pants. **jogg'ing** *n* running at a slow, steady pace, *esp* for exercise (also *adj*).
□ **jogger's nipple** *n* (*inf*) painful inflammation of a runner's nipple caused by friction against clothing. **jogging bottoms** *n pl* jog pants. **jog pants** or **jog'pants** *n pl* loose-fitting trousers of jersey fabric, elasticated at the waist and ankles, such as are worn for jogging. **jog'trot** *n* a slow jogging trot; a humdrum routine. ◆ *vi* to move at a jogtrot.

joggle¹ /*jog'l*/ *vt* (**jogg'ling**; **jogg'led**) to jog or shake slightly; to jostle. ◆ *vi* to shake. ◆ *n* the act of joggling; a slight jog. [Appar dimin or frequentative of **jog**]

joggle² /*jog'l*/ *n* a tooth, notch or pin to prevent surfaces in contact with each other from slipping; a joint made for this purpose. ◆ *vt* to join with a joggle. [Perh connected with **jag¹**]

johannes /*jō-(h)an'ēz*/ *n* a gold coin of John V of Portugal (also **joann'es**). [L *Jōhannēs*, from *Jōannēs*, from Gr *Iōannēs*, from Heb *Yōchānān* John]
■ **Johann'ean** or **Johann'ine** *adj* of or relating to John, *esp* the Apostle.

Johannisberg /*jō-han'is-bûrg*/ or **Johannisberger** /*-bûrg-ər*/ *n* a white wine produced at *Johannisberg* ('St John's Mountain'), near Wiesbaden.

John /*jon*/ *n* a male proper name; (without *cap*) a lavatory (*inf, esp US*); a prostitute's client (*inf*). [L *Jōhannēs*; see **johannes**]
■ **Johnian** /*jōn'i-ən*/ *n* a member of St *John's* College, Cambridge. **johnn'ie** or **johnn'y** *n* (*inf*) a condom. **Johnn'y** (or **Johnn'ie**) *n* (*inf*) a simpleton, an empty-headed man-about-town; a fellow or chap generally.
□ **John'-a-dreams** *n* (*Shakesp*) a dreamy fellow. **John a-Nokes** or **John a-Stiles** or **-Styles** *n* (*obs*) a fictitious name for a person in a law-suit, or generally. **John'-apple** *n* a kind of apple, apple-John. **John Barleycorn** *n* malt spirits personified. **John Bircher** *n* (*US*) a member of the extreme right-wing anti-communist **John Birch Society**. **john'boat** *n* (*US*) a light flat-bottomed boat with square ends. **John Bull** *n* a generic name for an Englishman, from Arbuthnot(t)'s *History of John Bull*, 1712. **John Bullism** *n* the typical English character, or any act or word expressive of it. **John Canoe** *n* see separate entry. **John Chinaman** *n* (*derog*) a Chinese man; (*collectively*) the Chinese. **John Citizen** *n* a typical citizen. **John Collins** *n* an alcoholic long drink based on gin. **John Company** *n* (*obs*) the East India Company. **John Doe, Jane Doe** *n* names for unidentified male and female characters, *esp* in US detective stories, films. **John Doe and Richard Roe** *n* imaginary plaintiff and opponent in the old legal action for ejectment, proverbial as a legal fiction. **John Dory** see **dory¹**. **John'-go-to-bed-at-noon** *n* the goat's-beard (because it closes early in the day). **John Hancock** *n* (*US inf*) a signature (from *John Hancock*, signatory of the Declaration of Independence). **John Hop** *n* (*old Aust* and *NZ rhyming sl* for *cop*) a policeman. **John Kanoo** see **John Canoe**. **Johnn'y-cake** *n* (also without *cap*) a flat cake made from maize flour (*US*) or wheat flour (*Aust*). **Johnny-come-late'ly** *n* (also without *cap*) an upstart. **Johnny-head'-in-air** or **John o'dreams** *n* a dreamy, impractical person. **Johnn'y-raw** *n* a beginner; a greenhorn. **Johnny Reb** *n* (*US inf*) a Confederate soldier in the Civil War. **John Thomas** *n* (*sl*) the penis.

John Canoe /*jon kə-noo'*/ (*W Indies*) *n* (also **John Kanoo, joncanoe, junkanoo**, etc) a boisterous rhythmic dance performed *esp* as part of Christmas celebrations; the celebrations themselves; any of, or *esp* the leader of, the dancers; the mask or headdress of such a dancer. [From a W African language]

Johne's disease /*yō'nəz di-zēz'*/ *n* an infectious disease of cattle and sheep caused by a mycobacterium. [HA *Johne* (1839–1910), German veterinary surgeon]

Johnsonian /*jon-sō'ni-ən*/ *adj* of or in the manner of Dr Samuel *Johnson*, the lexicographer (1709–84).
■ **John'sonese** *n* Johnsonian style, idiom, diction, or an imitation of it, ponderous English, full of antitheses, balanced triads, and words of classical origin. **Johnsōniana** /*-ä'nə* or *-ā'nə*/ *n pl* matters or miscellaneous items connected with Johnson. **Johnsō'nianism** or **John'sonism** /*-sən-izm*/ *n*.

joie de vivre /*zhwa də vē'vr'*/ (*Fr*) *n* exuberance, literally joy of living.

join /*join*/ *vt* to connect; to unite; to associate; to add or annex; to become a member of; to come into association with or the company of; to go to and remain with, in, or on; to draw a straight line between (*geom*). ◆ *vi* to be connected; to combine, unite; to run into one; to grow together; to be in, or come into, close contact. ◆ *n* a joining; a

place where things have been joined; a mode of joining. [OFr *joindre*, from L *jungere, junctum* to join]
■ **join'able** *adj*. **joind'er** *n* (*esp law*) joining, uniting. **join'er** *n* a worker in wood, *esp* one who makes smaller structures than a carpenter; someone who joins or unites; someone who joins many societies. **join'ery** *n* the art of the joiner; a joiner's work. **join'ing** *n* the act of joining; a seam; a joint. **joint** *n* a joining; the place where, or mode in which, two or more things join; a place where two things (*esp* bones) meet, allowing a hingelike movement; a node, or place where a stem bears leaves, *esp* if swollen; a segment; a piece of an animal's body as cut up for serving at the table; the flexible hinge of cloth or leather connecting the back of a book with its sides; a crack intersecting a mass of rock (*geol*); the place where adjacent surfaces meet; the condition of adjustment at a joint, as in the phrase *out of joint*; a disreputable bar or other meeting-place (*US sl*); a public meeting-place, a place in general (*inf*); a cigarette containing marijuana (*inf*); see also **the joint** below. ◆ *adj* joined, united or combined; shared among more than one; done or made by more than one; sharing with another or others. ◆ *vt* to unite by joints; to provide with joints or an appearance of joints; to fill the joints of with mortar, etc; to divide into joints. ◆ *vi* to fit closely together. **joint'ed** *adj* having a joint or joints; composed of segments; constricted at intervals. **joint'er** *n* a jointer plane; a bricklayer's tool for putting mortar in joints; a worker employed to make joints. **joint'ing** *n*. **joint'less** *adj*. **joint'ly** *adv* in a joint manner; unitedly or in combination; together. **joint'ness** *n*.
□ **joined'-up** *adj* (of handwriting) having the letters linked in cursive style; (of a person) mature or sophisticated (*inf*); coherent and co-ordinated, as in *joined-up thinking, joined-up government*. **join'-hand** *n* (*obs*) cursive handwriting. **joint account** *n* a bank or building-society account held in the name of two or more people, any of whom can deposit or withdraw money. **Joint Chiefs of Staff** *n pl* (in the USA) the chief military advisory body to the President. **jointed cactus** *n* a plant (*Opuntia pusilla*) of the prickly-pear genus, a serious pest in S Africa. **jointer plane** or **jointing plane** *n* the largest kind of plane used by a joiner. **Joint European Torus** *n* see JET. **joint'-fir** *n* any plant of the family Gnetaceae. **joint heir** *n* a person who inherits jointly with another or others. **joint'ing-rule** *n* a long straight-edged rule used by bricklayers. **joint'-oil** *n* synovia. **joint resolution** *n* (*US*) one passed by both Houses of Congress. **joint'-stock** *n* stock held jointly (**joint'-stock company** one whose capital is split into many units, held by different owners). **joint'-stool** *n* (*Shakesp*) a stool made of parts inserted in each other. **joint tenancy** *n*. **joint tenant** *n* a person who is owner of land or goods along with others. **joint venture** *n* a business activity undertaken by two or more companies acting together, sharing costs, risks and profits. **joint'-worm** or **joint'worm** *n* (*US*) a hymenopterous larva that attacks grain-stalks near the first joint. ■ **join battle** see under **battle¹**. **join in** to (begin to) take part. **join issue** to begin to dispute; to take up the contrary view or side. **joint and several liability** (*law*) the responsibility of any one member of a group for the actions or debts of any or all of the others, and the responsibility of the group as a whole for the actions or debts of any one member. **join up** to enlist, *esp* as part of a general movement; to unite (with *with*). **out of joint** dislocated; disordered, awry. **put someone's nose out of joint** to supplant someone in another's love or confidence; to disconcert, rebuff or offend someone. **second joint** the middle piece of a fly-fishing rod; the thigh of a fowl, as opposed to the **first joint**, the leg or drumstick. **the joint** (*US inf*) prison. **universal joint** a device one part of which is able to move freely in all directions, as in the ball-and-socket joint.

jointure /*join'tyər*/ *n* property settled by a husband on his wife at their marriage for her use after her husband's death. ◆ *vt* to settle a jointure upon, arrange a jointure for. [OE, from OFr, from L *junctūra* a joining]
■ **joint'uress** or **joint'ress** *n* a woman on whom a jointure is settled.

joist /*joist*/ *n* a beam supporting the boards of a floor or the laths of a ceiling. ◆ *vt* to fit with joists. [OFr *giste*, from *gesir*, from L *jacēre* to lie]

jojoba /*hō-hō'bə*/ *n* a desert shrub of the box family, native to Mexico, Arizona and California, whose edible seeds yield a waxy oil chemically similar to spermaceti, used in cosmetic preparations, etc; the oil itself. [Mex Sp]

joke /*jōk*/ *n* an amusing quip or story; a witticism; anything said or done for fun; anything that or anyone who provokes a laugh; an absurdity. ◆ *vi* to jest; to tell jokes; to be humorous; to make fun. ◆ *vt* to poke fun at; to chaff. [L *jocus*]
■ **jok'er** *n* a person who jokes or jests; an additional playing card in the pack, used at euchre, poker, etc; an innocent-looking clause insidiously introduced to cripple the effect of a bill or document (*US*); an unforeseen factor affecting a situation; a person, often one viewed with mild, *usu* amicable, amusement (*inf*). **joke'some, jō'key** or **jō'ky** *adj*. **joke'ster** *n* (*US*) a player of jokes. **jō'kily** *adv*. **jō'kiness** *n*. **jok'ingly** *adv* in a joking manner.
□ **joke'smith** *n* (*archaic*) a maker of jokes.

■ **joking apart** or **aside** if I may be serious, seriously. **no joke** a serious or difficult matter.

jokol /yō'köl/ (*Shetland*; *obs*) *adv* yes, (literally) yes carl (also **yo'kul**). [Shetland Norn *jo* yes, and (inferred) *koll*, from ON *karl* carl]

jol /jöl/ (*S Afr sl*) *n* a party or celebration. ◆ *vi* (**joll'ing**; **jolled**) to have a good time. [Afrik]
■ **joll'er** *n*.

jole see **jowl**[1,2].

jolie laide /zho-lē led'/ (*Fr*) *n* (*pl* **jolies laides**) a woman whose ugliness is part of her charm.

joliotium /jo-lē-ō'shi-əm/ *n* a former name for **dubnium**. [Irène and Frédéric *Joliot*-Curie, 20c French physicists]

joll see **jowl**[1,2].

jolley /jol'i/ (*pottery*) *n* a kind of jigger to which the mould for making plates, etc is fixed.
■ **joll'eyer** or **joll'yer** *n*. **joll'eying** or **joll'ying** *n*.

jolly /jol'i/ *adj* merry; expressing, providing or provoking fun and gaiety; entertaining, festive, jovial; healthy, plump; splendid, very agreeable (*inf*). ◆ *vt* to make fun of; (*esp* with *along*) to put or keep in good humour, amuse; encourage; (with *up*) to make cheerful. ◆ *adv* (*inf*) very. ◆ *n* a royal marine (*sl*); a party or celebration (*inf*); an outing, a trip, *esp* at someone else's expense (*inf*). [OFr *jolif*, *joli*, perh connected with ON *jōl* Yule]
■ **jollifica'tion** *n* an occasion of merrymaking or being jolly; noisy festivity and merriment. **joll'ify** *vt* and *vi*. **joll'ily** *adv*. **joll'iment** *n* (*Spenser*) merriment. **joll'iness**, **joll'ity** or (*Spenser*) **joll'yhead** *n*.
□ **Jolly Roger** *n* a black flag with white skull and crossbones, flown by pirate ships.
■ **get one's jollies** (*inf*) to enjoy oneself, have fun.

jollyboat /jol'i-bōt/ *n* a small boat kept hoisted at the stern of a ship. [Origin obscure]

jolt /jōlt or jolt/ *vi* to jostle or proceed with sudden jerks. ◆ *vt* to jostle or knock against; to shake with a sudden shock. ◆ *n* a sudden jerk; a shock; a surprising or activating shock. [Ety obscure]
■ **jolt'er** *n*. **jolt'ingly** *adv* in a jolting manner. **jolt'y** *adj*.

jolterhead /jōl'tər-hed/ or **jolthead** /jōlt'hed/ (*archaic*) *n* a large clumsy head; a blockhead. [Ety obscure]

jomo see **zhomo** under **zho**.

Jon. (*Bible*) *abbrev* : (the Book of) Jonah.

Jonah /jō'nə/ *n* a bringer of bad luck on a ship or elsewhere. [From the biblical prophet *Jonah*, whose disobedience to God provoked a storm at sea, to put an end to which he was thrown overboard]

Jonathan /jon'ə-thən/ *n* the people of the United States, collectively, or a typical specimen (often *Brother Jonathan*) (*archaic*); an American variety of apple. [The male personal name, orig of the son of Saul, king of Israel]

joncanoe see **John Canoe**.

jongleur /zhŏ-glær'/ *n* a wandering minstrel; a mountebank. [Fr, from OFr *jogleor*, from L *joculātor*; cf **juggler** under **juggle**]

jonquil /jong'kwil, formerly jung-kwil'/ *n* a name given to certain species of narcissus with rush-like leaves. [Fr *jonquille*, from L *juncus* a rush]

Jonsonian /jon-sō'ni-ən/ *adj* of or characteristic of the English dramatist Ben *Jonson* (1572–1637) or his works.

jonty /jon'ti/, **jaunty**, **jauntie** or **janty** /jon'ti or jän'ti/ (*sl*) *n* a naval master-at-arms.

jook, etc see **jouk**.

jor /jör/ (*Hindu music*) *n* the second movement of a raga. [Sans]

joram see **jorum**.

Jordan /jör'dən/ *n* the great river of Palestine; death (as a passage into the Promised Land, from the Bible, Numbers 33.51); (*usu* without *cap*) a chamberpot (*Shakesp* and *dialect*).

jordan almond /jör'dən ä'mənd/ (also with *cap*) *n* a large, high-quality almond, often coloured and used in confectionery. [Late ME *jardyne almaund*, from Fr *jardin* garden]

Jordanian /jör-dä'ni-ən/ *adj* of or relating to the kingdom of *Jordan* in SW Asia, or its people. ◆ *n* a native or citizen of Jordan. [See **Jordan**]

jordeloo /jör-di-loo'/ *same as* **gardyloo**.

jorum or **joram** /jö'rəm/ *n* a large drinking bowl; a large drink. [Poss from *Joram* in Bible, 2 Samuel 8.10]

Joseph /jō'zif/ *n* someone whose chastity is above temptation (from the story of *Joseph* and Potiphar's wife in the Bible, Genesis 39); (without *cap*) a caped overcoat worn by women in the 18c for riding (possibly in allusion to *Joseph's* coat, Genesis 37).
■ **not for Joseph** (or **Joe**) not on any account (*prob* from the refrain of a 19c music-hall song).

josephinite /joz'ə-fēn-īt/ *n* a mineral found only in *Josephine* Creek, in Oregon, USA, and believed to have originated at the outer edge of the earth's core and been carried up nearly 2000 miles to the surface.

Josephson junction /jō'zif-sən jung'shən/ (*electronics*) *n* a junction formed from two superconducting metals separated by a thin insulating layer, allowing the unimpeded passage of a current and generating microwaves when subjected to a certain voltage. [BD *Josephson* (born 1940), English physicist]

Josh. (*Bible*) *abbrev* : (the Book of) Joshua.

josh /josh/ (*sl*) *vt* to ridicule; to tease. ◆ *vi* to banter, joke. ◆ *n* a hoax; a derisive or teasing joke.
■ **josh'er** *n*.

Joshua tree /josh'ū-ə trē/ *n* a small tree-shaped yucca, *Yucca brevifolia*, with sword-shaped leaves, native to deserts of SW USA. [Named after *Joshua* (see Bible, Joshua 8.18)]

joskin /jos'kin/ (*old sl*) *n* a clown, yokel. [Thieves' cant]

joss /jos/ *n* a Chinese idol; luck or fate. [Port *deos* god, from L *deus*]
■ **joss'er** *n* (*sl*) a person; a blunderer, a fool; a clergyman (*obs Aust*).
□ **joss house** *n* a temple. **joss stick** *n* a stick which gives off a perfume when burned, used as incense *esp* in India, China, etc.

joss-block /jos'blok/ (*dialect*) *n* a mounting block.

jostle /jos'l/ or **justle** /jus'l/ *vt* and *vi* to shake or jar by collision; to hustle; to elbow. ◆ *vi* (*obs*) to tilt, joust. ◆ *n* an act of jostling. [Frequentative of **joust**]
■ **jos'tlement** or **jos'tling** *n*.

jot /jot/ *n* an iota, a whit, a tittle. ◆ *vt* (**jott'ing**; **jott'ed**) to set down briefly; to make a memorandum of. [L *iōta* (read as *jōta*), from Gr *iōta* the smallest letter in the alphabet, equivalent to *i*; Heb *yōd*]
■ **jott'er** *n* someone who jots; a book or pad for notes. **jott'ing** *n* a memorandum; a brief note.

jota /hhō'tä/ *n* a Spanish dance in triple time. [Sp]

jotun /yō'tən/ or **jötunn** /yæ'tən/ (*Norse myth*; also with *cap*) *n* a giant. [ON *jötunn*]
□ **Jotunheim** /yō'tən-hīm/ *n* the home of the giants.

joual /zhoo-al'/ or -äl'/ (*Can*) *n* a non-standard, chiefly urban, variety of Canadian French. [Appar from the pronunciation of Fr *cheval* horse in this dialect]

jougs /jūgz or jugz/ (*Scot hist*) *n pl* an instrument of punishment consisting of an iron collar attached to a wall or post and put round an offender's neck. [Prob OFr *joug* a yoke, from L *jugum*]

jouisance or **jouysaunce** /joo'i-səns/ (*Spenser*) *n* joyousness. [Fr *jouissance*, from *jouir* to enjoy, from L *gaudēre* to rejoice]

jouk or **jook** /jook/ (*Scot*) *vi* to duck; to dodge; to bow. ◆ *n* an elusive duck or dodging movement; a bow. [Ety obscure]
■ **jouk'ery**, **jook'ery** or **jouk'ery-pawk'ery** *n* (*Scot*) trickery, roguery.

joule[1] /jool/ *n* the derived SI unit of work, energy and heat (symbol **J**), equal to the work done when a force of one newton moves its point of application one metre in the direction of the force. [JP *Joule* (1818–89), English physicist]

joule[2] see **jowl**[2].

jounce /jowns/ *vt* and *vi* to jolt, bump. [Ety uncertain]

jour /zhoor/ (*Fr*) *n* a day.
□ **jour de fête** /də fet/ *n* a feast-day, *esp* a saint's day.

journal[1] /jûr'nəl/ *n* a daily register or diary; a book containing a record of each day's transactions; a newspaper published daily (or otherwise); a magazine; the transactions of any society. ◆ *adj* (*Shakesp*) diurnal. [Fr, from L *diurnālis*; see **diurnal**]
■ **journalese'** *n* the jargon of bad journalism. **journ'alism** *n* the profession of collecting, writing, editing, publishing, etc news reports and other articles for newspapers, journals, television, radio and related media; the style of writing associated with the reporting of news, current affairs and popular interest subjects via a transitory medium; the material produced in this way. **jour'nalist** *n* a person who writes for or manages a newspaper, magazine, or other news-related medium; a person who keeps a journal (*obs*). **journalist'ic** *adj*. **journalist'ically** *adv*. **journaliza'tion** or **-s-** *n*. **jour'nalize** or **-ise** *vi* to write for or in a journal. ◆ *vt* to enter in a journal. **jour'no** *n* (*pl* **jour'nos**) (*inf*) a journalist.
□ **journal proper** *n* (*bookkeeping*) a book in which entries are made for transactions where no other record is available, transfers between accounts, opening entries when a business starts, and corrections for errors.

journal[2] /jûr'nəl/ (*mech*) *n* that part of a shaft or axle which is in contact with and supported by a bearing. ◆ *vt* to provide with or fix as a journal. [Origin unexplained]
□ **jour'nal-box** *n* a box or bearing for a journal.

journal intime /zhoor-nal ē̃-tēm'/ (*Fr*) *n* a diary.

■ words derived from main entry word; □ compound words; ■ idioms and phrasal verbs

journey /jûr'ni/ n (pl **jour'neys**) an act of travelling from one place to another; a tour or excursion; movement from end to end of a fixed course; a day's work or travel (obs); a campaign (obs); the weight of finished coins delivered at one time to the Master of the Mint (also **jour'ney-weight**); a set of colliery trucks. ◆ vi (**jour'neying**; **jour'neyed** /-nid/) to travel. [Fr journée, from jour a day, from L diurnus]
■ **jour'neyer** n.
❑ **jour'ney-bated** adj (Shakesp) worn out by travel. **jour'neyman** n a hired workman, orig one hired by the day; a worker whose apprenticeship is completed; someone who is competent at his trade; an electrically controlled clock or dial. **jour'ney-work** n work done by a journeyman; necessary, routine work.

joust or **just** /jowst/ (less commonly just or joost)/ n a contest between two lance-bearing knights on horseback at a tournament. ◆ vi to take part in such a tournament, to tilt. [OFr juste, jouste, joste, from L juxtā near to]
■ **joust'er** n.

J'Ouvert /zhoo-ver'/ (W Indies) n (also without caps) the eve of Mardi Gras, the day on which the festivities begin. [Fr jour ouvert, literally, day opened]

jouysaunce see **jouisance**.

Jove /jōv/ n another name for the god Jupiter. [Early L Jovis (in the nominative usu Juppiter, Jupiter father Jove) the god Jove or Jupiter, or the planet Jupiter, an auspicious star]
■ **Jō'vian** adj of the god or planet Jupiter.
■ **by Jove** an exclamation of surprise, admiration, etc.

jovial /jō'vi-əl/ adj joyous; full of jollity and geniality; (with cap) of the god or planet or influenced by Jupiter. [**Jove**]
■ **joviality** /-al'i-ti/ or **jō'vialness** n. **jō'vially** adv.

Jovian see under **Jove**.

jovysaunce a misreading of **jouysaunce** (see **jouisance**).

jow /jow/ (Scot) vt and vi to ring, toll; to rock. ◆ n a stroke of a bell. [**jowl²**]
❑ **jowing-in'** n and adj ringing-in.
■ **jow one's ginger** see under **jee²**.

jowar /jow-är'/, **jowari** or **jawari** /-ē/ n durra. [Hindi jawār, jawārī]

jowl¹ /jowl or jōl/ or (obs) **jole** or **joll** /jōl/ n the jaw; the cheek; a pendulous double chin; (in animals) a dewlap or wattle; a head; the head and shoulders of a salmon, sturgeon or ling. [Prob several different words. The development and relations of ME chaul, OE ceafl jaw, ME chol, OE ceolu, ceolur, etc, and the modern forms with j are difficult to make out. Fr joue cheek, or some other word may have added to the confusion]
■ **jowled** adj. **jowl'er** n a heavy-jawed hound. **jow'ly** adj having noticeable heavy or droopy jaws.

jowl², **joll**, **jole** or **joule** /jōl/ (dialect) vt and vi to bump; to beat; to toll. ◆ n a stroke; a knock. [Ety obscure]

joy /joi/ n intense gladness; rapture, delight; rejoicing; a cause of joy; a beloved person, a dear. ◆ vi (**joy'ing**, **joyed**) (obs) to rejoice; to be glad; to exult. ◆ vt (obs) to give joy to; to enjoy (Milton). [Fr joie (cf Ital gioia), from L gaudium]
■ **joy'ance** n (poetic, orig Spenser) gaiety, festivity. **joy'ful** adj full of joy; feeling, expressing or giving joy. **joy'fully** adv. **joy'fulness** n. **joy'less** adj without joy; not giving joy. **joy'lessly** adv. **joy'lessness** n. **joy'ous** adj joyful. **joy'ously** adv. **joy'ousness** n.
❑ **joy'pad** n a device consisting of a pad with buttons on it, used for controlling the motion of objects in a computer game. **joy'pop** vi (sl) to take addictive drugs from time to time without forming an addiction. **joy'ride** n (inf) a drive taken for pleasure, esp if reckless or surreptitious and in a stolen car. ◆ vi to take a joyride. **joy'rider** n. **joy'riding** n. **joy'stick** n the control-lever of an aeroplane, invalid car, video game, etc; a lever controlling the movement of the cursor on a computer screen (comput). **joy'-wheel** n a huge fairground wheel that carries passengers round its axis.
■ (**get** or **have**) **any joy** (inf) (to achieve) satisfaction or success (in an attempt, etc). **no joy** (inf) no news, reply, information, luck or success.

Joycean /joi'sē-ən/ adj of, or in the manner of, James Joyce (1882–1941), Irish writer. ◆ n a student or imitator of James Joyce.

JP abbrev : Justice of the Peace.

JPEG /jā'peg/ (comput) abbrev : Joint Photographic Experts Group, a standard image file format (also **JPG**).

Jr or **jr** abbrev : Junior or junior.

JSA abbrev : Jobseeker's Allowance.

juba /joo'bə/ n an African-American breakdown or rustic dance, in which the participants clap hands, slap their thighs, and sing verses with juba as a refrain.

jubate /joo'bāt/ (zool, etc) adj maned. [L jubātus, from juba mane]

jubbah /jŭb'ə or jub'ə/ n a long loose outer garment worn by Muslims (also **jibba**, **jibbah** or **djibbah**). [Ar jubbah]

jube¹ /joob/ an informal Australian shortening of **jujube** (the sweet).

jube² /joo'bē/ n a rood loft or screen and gallery. [L, imperative of jubēre to command, the first word of the prayer said on or beside it by the deacon]

jubilant /joo'bi-lənt/ adj rejoicing, feeling or expressing great joy; singing or shouting in joy or triumph. [L jūbilāre to shout for joy. Not connected with jubilee]
■ **ju'bilance** or **ju'bilancy** n exultation. **ju'bilantly** adv. **ju'bilate** vi to exult, rejoice. **jubilā'tion** n rejoicing, a feeling or the expression of joy; joyful or triumphal shouting or singing.

jubilate /joo-bi-lā'tē or yoo-bi-lä'te/ n the third Sunday after Easter, so called because the church service began on that day with Psalm 66 (RC); (usu with cap) Psalm 100, used as a canticle, or a setting of this (C of E, RC). [The opening word of both psalms in L, imperative pl of jūbilāre to shout for joy]

jubilee /joo'bi-lē/ n a time, season or circumstance of great joy and festivity; jubilation; the celebration of a 50th or 25th anniversary, eg of a king's accession; a year (every 25th year, ordinary jubilee) of indulgence for pilgrims and others, an extraordinary jubilee being specially appointed by the Pope (RC); every 50th year, a year of release of slaves, cancelling of debts, and return of property to its former owners (Jewish hist). [Fr jubilé, from L jūbilaeus, from Heb yōbēl a ram's horn which was used to proclaim the jubilee year]
❑ **jubilee clip** n a metal loop with a screw fitting, placed round a tube, hose, etc, and tightened to form a watertight connection.
■ **silver**, **golden** and **diamond jubilee** respectively a 25th, 50th and 60th anniversary.

JUD abbrev : Juris Utriusque Doctor (L), Doctor of both laws (ie Canon and Civil).

Jud. (Bible) abbrev : (the Book of) Judges (also **Judg.**); (the Apocryphal Book of) Judith.

jud /jud/ (mining) n a mass of coal holed or undercut ready for final removal. [Origin unknown]

Judaean or **Judean** /joo-dē'ən/ adj of Judaea or the Jews. ◆ n a native of Judaea; a Jew. [L Judaea]

Judaeo- /joo-dā-ō-/ or N Am **Judeo-** /joo-dē-ō-/ combining form denoting Judaic, as in Judaeo-Spanish. [L Judaea]

Judaic /joo-dā'ik/ adj relating to the Jews or Judaism. [L Jūdaicus, from Jūda Judah, a son of Israel]
■ **Judā'ica** n pl the culture of the Jews, their literature, customs, etc, esp as described in books, articles, etc. **Judā'ical** adj Judaic. **Judā'ically** adv. **Ju'daism** n the doctrines and rites of the Jews; conformity to the Jewish rites; the Jewish way of life. **Ju'daist** n someone who holds the doctrines of Judaism. **Judāist'ic** adj. **Judāist'ically** adv. **Judāizā'tion** or **-s-** n. **Ju'dāize** or **-ise** vi to conform to, adopt or practise Jewish customs or Judaism. ◆ vt to imbue with Jewish principles or beliefs. **Ju'dāizer** or **-s-** n.

Judas /joo'dəs/ n a traitor; (also without cap) a Judas hole; (used attrib) denoting an animal or bird used to lure others (as in Judas goat). [Judas Iscariot]
❑ **Ju'das-coloured** adj (of hair) red (Judas traditionally being red-haired). **Judas hole** or **Judas window** n (also without caps) a spyhole in a door, etc. **Judas kiss** n any act of treachery under the guise of kindness (from the Bible, Matthew 26.48–49). **Judas tree** n a tree (genus Cercis) of the Caesalpinia family, with rose-coloured flowers that appear before the leaves (Judas being traditionally believed to have hanged himself on one); also the elder (for the same reason).

judder /jud'ər/ n a strong vibration in an aircraft or other mechanical apparatus; an intense, jerking motion; in singing, a vibratory effect produced by alternations of greater or less intensity of sound. ◆ vi to shake or vibrate. [Prob jar² and shudder]
■ **judd'ery** adj.

Judenhetze /yoo'dən-het-sə/ (Ger) n Jew-baiting.

Judeo- see **Judaeo-**.

Judezmo /joo-dez'mō/ n a mixture of Spanish and Hebrew, Ladino. [Ladino, Jewish]

Judg. see **Jud.**

judge /juj/ vi to act in the capacity of a judge; to point out or declare what is just or law; to try cases and decide questions of law, guiltiness, etc; to pass sentence; to compare facts to determine the truth; to form or pass an opinion; to distinguish. ◆ vt to hear and determine authoritatively; to sit in judgement on; to pronounce on the guilt or innocence of; to sentence; to decide the merits of; to find fault with, to censure, condemn; to decide; to award; to estimate; to form an opinion on; to conclude; to consider (to be). ◆ n a person who judges; a person appointed to hear and settle causes, and to try accused persons; someone chosen to award prizes, to decide doubtful or disputed points in a competition, etc; an arbitrator; someone who can decide upon the merit of anything; (in Jewish history) a supreme magistrate having civil and military powers; someone capable of discriminating well; (with *cap*; in *pl*) the title of the 7th book of the Old Testament. [Anglo-Fr *juger*, from L *jūdicāre*, from *jūs* law, and *dīcere* to say, to declare]

■ **judge'ment** or **judg'ment** *n* the act of judging; the comparing of ideas to find out the truth; the faculty by which this is done, the reason or discernment; the mental act of establishing a relationship between two terms (*logic*); an opinion formed; an estimate; discrimination, good taste; a legal verdict or sentence; condemnation, doom; a misfortune thought to be sent as a punishment from God. **judgement'al** or **judgment'al** *adj* involving judgement; apt to pass judgement. **judgement'ally** or **judgment'ally** *adv*. **judge'ship** *n* the office or function of a judge.

❑ **judge advocate** *n* the crown-prosecutor at a court martial. **Judge Advocate General** *n* (*pl* **Judge Advocates General** or **Judge Advocate Generals**) the civil adviser to the crown on military law, *esp* courts martial. **judge'-made** *adj* (of law) based on decisions of judges. **judgement call** *n* a decision based on subjective judgement rather than on objective evidence. **judge'ment-day** *n* (also **Judgment Day**) the day of God's final judgement on mankind. **judge'ment-debt** *n* a debt validated by a legal judgement. **judge'ment-hall** *n* a hall where a court of justice meets. **judgement of Solomon** *n* a judgement intended to call the bluff of the false claimant, like that of Solomon in the Bible, 1 Kings 3.16–28. **judge'ment-seat** *n* the seat or bench in a court from which judgement is pronounced. **Judges' Rules** *n pl* formerly, in English law, a system of rules governing the behaviour of the police towards suspects, eg the cautioning of a person about to be charged.

■ **against one's better judgement** contrary to what one believes to be right. **judgement reserved** a decision delayed after the close of a trial (in Scotland, 'avizandum made'). **judgement respited** execution of sentence delayed. **sit in judgement** (**on**) to consider oneself responsible for judging.

Judica /joo'di-kə/ (*Christianity*) *n* Passion Sunday. [From the opening words of the introit, '*Judica* me, Deus' (Psalm 43)]

judicature /joo'di-kə-chər or joo-di'/ *n* the power of dispensing justice by legal trial; jurisdiction; the office of judge; the body of judges; a court or system of courts. [L *jūdicāre*, *-ātum* to judge]

■ **ju'dicable** *adj* that may be judged or tried. **judica'tion** *n* judgement. **ju'dicative** *adj* having power to judge. **ju'dicātor** *n* a person who judges. **ju'dicatory** /-kə-tər-i/ *n* judicature; a court. ◆ *adj* relating to a judge or judgement.

judicial /joo-dish'əl/ *adj* relating to a judge, a court of justice or the administration of justice; established by decision of a court; arising from process of law; having the authority to make judgements; of the nature of judgement; forming or expressing judgement; judgelike, impartial; inclined to pass judgement, critical. [L *jūdiciālis*, from *jūdicium*]

■ **judic'ially** *adv*.

❑ **judicial astrology** *n* (*hist*) the study of the influence of the planets, etc on human affairs. **judicial combat** *n* trial by battle. **Judicial Committee of the Privy Council** *n* the final court of appeal for certain Commonwealth countries, and for UK medical tribunals and ecclesiastical courts. **judicial murder** *n* a death sentence which is deemed unjust although passed in accordance with legal procedure. **judicial precedent** *n* the system whereby a court is bound to declare the law in accordance with previous rulings by equivalent or higher courts. **judicial review** *n* a procedure by which a judicial body or commission reviews a decision made by another body, *esp* the government or a court of law. **judicial separation** *n* the separation of two married people by order of court. **judicial trustee** (or *Scot* **factor**) *n* an administrator appointed by the courts to manage the estate of someone in need of such.

judiciary /joo-dish'ə-ri or -i-ə-ri/ *adj* relating to judgement, judges, or courts of law. ◆ *n* the branch of government concerned with the legal system and the administration of justice; a body of judges; a system of courts. [L *jūdiciārius*]

■ **judic'iarily** *adv*.

judicious /joo-dish'əs/ *adj* according to sound judgement; possessing sound judgement, discreet. [Fr *judicieux*, from L *jūdicium*]

■ **judic'iously** *adv*. **judic'iousness** *n*.

judo /joo'dō/ *n* a sport and physical discipline based on unarmed self-defence techniques, a modern variety of ju-jitsu. [Jap *jiu* gentleness, and *do* way]

■ **judogi** /joo'dō-gi or -dō'gi/ *n* the costume (jacket and trousers) worn by a **ju'doist** or **judoka** /joo'dō-kə or -dō'kə/, a person who practises, or is expert in, judo.

Judy /joo'di/ *n* Punch's wife in the street puppet show 'Punch and Judy'; a frump, an odd-looking woman (*obs*); (often without *cap*) a girl (*Aust* and *Brit sl*). [From the personal name *Judith*]

jug¹ /jug/ *n* a vessel for pouring liquids, *usu* with a spout or lip and a handle; a jugful; a container, *esp* a tankard or glass (of beer, etc); (in *pl*) a woman's breasts (*sl*). ◆ *vt* (*pap* and *pat* **jugged**) to boil or stew in a closed pottery jar, or similar. [Origin unknown]

■ **jug'ful** *n* (*pl* **jug'fuls**) as much as a jug will hold. **jugg'ing** *n*. **jug'let** *n* (*archaeol*) a small juglike vessel.

❑ **jug band** *n* a band using jugs and other utensils as musical instruments. **jug'-ears** *n* (*derog inf*) a name for someone with protruding ears. **jugged hare** *n* hare cut in pieces and stewed with wine and other seasoning.

jug² /jug/ (*sl*) *n* prison. ◆ *vt* to imprison. [Cf **jougs**]

jug³ /jug/ *n* the note or sound of the nightingale (also **jug'-jug**). ◆ *vi* to utter the sound. [Imit]

juga see **jugum**.

jugal /joo'gəl/ *adj* relating to a yoke, *esp* that of marriage; malar. ◆ *n* the malar bone. [L *jugālis*, from *jugum* a yoke]

Jugannath see **Juggernaut**.

jugate /joo'gāt/ *adj* paired (*bot*); having the leaflets in pairs (*bot*); side by side or overlapping, like heads shown on a coin, etc. [L *jugāre*, *-ātum* to join, from *jugum* a yoke]

Jugendstil /yoo'gənd-shtēl/ *n* the German term for art nouveau. [Ger *Jugend* youth (the name of a magazine first appearing in 1896), and *Stil* style]

Juggernaut /jug'ər-nöt/ *n* (without *cap*) a very large lorry; (often without *cap*) any relentless destroying force or object of devotion and sacrifice; (also **Jugannath** /jug'u-nät/) an incarnation of Vishnu, whose idol at Puri is traditionally drawn on a processional chariot, beneath which devotees were once believed to throw and crush themselves. [Sans *Jagannātha* lord of the world]

juggins /jug'inz/ (*sl*) *n* a simpleton. [Origin unknown]

juggle /jug'l/ *vi* to throw and manipulate balls or other objects in the air with dexterity (also *fig*); to conjure, practise sleight-of-hand; to perform as an entertainer (*obs*); to practise trickery or deception; to tamper. ◆ *vt* to keep (several different items, activities, etc) in motion, progress or operation simultaneously, *esp* with dexterity; to manipulate or alter by trickery or cheating. ◆ *n* an act of juggling; a fraudulent trick. [OFr *jogler*, from L *joculārī* to jest, from *jocus* a jest]

■ **jugg'ler** *n*. **jugg'lery** /-lə-ri/ *n* the art or act of a juggler; legerdemain; trickery. **jugg'ling** *n* and *adj*. **jugg'lingly** *adv* in a deceptive manner.

jughead /jug'hed/ (*US sl*) *n* an idiot, fool, stupid person. [**jug¹** and **head**]

Juglans /joo'glanz/ *n* the walnut genus, giving the name to the family **Juglandaceae** /-glan-dā'si-ē/, from *Jovis glāns* Jove's acorn]

■ **juglandaceous** /-dā'shəs/ *adj*.

Jugoslav same as **Yugoslav**.

jugular /jug'ū-lər, also joog'/ *adj* relating to the neck or throat; having or denoting ventral fins situated in front of pectoral fins. ◆ *n* one of the large veins on each side of the neck. [L *jugulum* the collarbone, from *jungere* to join]

■ **jug'ūlate** *vt* to cut the throat of; to check (a disease, etc) by drastic means.

■ **go for the jugular** to attack someone at the place liable to cause greatest harm.

jugum /joo'gəm/ *n* (*pl* **ju'ga**) in certain insects, a process on the back edge of the forewing that unites it to the hindwing in flight; a pair of opposite leaves (*bot*). [L, yoke]

juice /joos/ *n* the liquid in fruit and vegetables; the fluid part of animal bodies; characteristic essence, interesting flavour, tasty nourishment (*fig*); vitality, piquancy; electric current, petrol, or other source of power (*inf*); alcoholic drink (*US sl*). ◆ *vt* to squeeze juice from (a fruit); (with *up*) to enliven (*US*). [Fr *jus*]

■ **juiced** *adj* (*sl*; often with *up*) drunk; excited. **juice'less** *adj*. **juic'er** *n* a juice extractor. **juic'ily** *adv*. **juic'iness** *n*. **juic'y** *adj* full of juice; of popular interest, *esp* of a scandalous or sensational kind; profitable.

❑ **juice extractor** *n* an appliance for extracting the juice from fruit, etc.

■ **step on the juice** (*inf*) to accelerate a motorcar.

ju-jitsu or **jiu-jitsu** /joo-jit'sū/ *n* a system of fighting without weapons, developed by the samurai in Japan; a martial art founded on it. [Jap *jū-jutsu*]

ju-ju or **juju** /joo'joo/ *n* an object of superstitious worship in W Africa; a fetish or charm; the supernatural power or taboo of a ju-ju. [Appar Fr *joujou* a toy]

jujube /joo'joob/ *n* a spiny shrub or small tree (genus *Zizyphus*) of the buckthorn family; its dark-red fruit, which is dried and eaten as a sweet; a chewy, fruit-flavoured lozenge or sweet made with sugar and gum or gelatine (also shortened to **jube** (*Aust*)). [Fr *jujube* or LL *jujuba*, from Gr *zizyphon*]

juke /*jook*/ (*sl*) *vi* to dance. [Gullah *juke* disorderly, from W African *dzug* to lead a careless life]

   juke'box *n* (*orig US*) a slot machine that plays musical recordings; a device that selects computer tapes or optical disks for reading. **jukebox musical** *n* (*inf*) a musical based around well-known pop songs. **juke'-joint** *n* a place for dancing and drinking.

jukskei /*yŭk'skī* or *yæk'skā*/ (*S Afr*) *n* an outdoor game similar to quoits, in which bottle-shaped pegs are thrown at stakes fixed in the ground; one of these pegs. [Afrik *yuk* yoke, and *skei* pin (orig yoke pins were thrown)]

Jul. *abbrev* : July.

julep /*joo'ləp*/ *n* a sweet drink, often medicated; an American drink of spirits, sugar, ice and mint (also **mint julep**). [Fr, from Sp *julepe*, from Ar *julāb*, from Pers *gulāb*, from *gul* rose, and *āb* water]

Julian /*joo'lyən* or *joo'li-ən*/ *adj* relating to or associated with *Julius* Caesar (100–44BC).

   Julian calendar *n* that in which a year was set at 365 days with a leap year every 4 years (from which the Gregorian calendar later evolved), instituted by Julius Caesar in 46BC. **Julian year** see under **year**.

Julia set /*joo'li-ə set*/ *n* any of an infinite number of sets of complex numbers for a given power, producing a convoluted fractal boundary when plotted on a graph. [Gaston *Julia* (1893–1978), French mathematician]

julienne /*joo-li-en'* or *zhü'lyen*/ *n* a clear soup, with shredded vegetables; any foodstuff which has been shredded. ◆ *vt* to shred or cut into thin strips. ◆ *adj* (of vegetables) cut into thin strips. [Fr personal name]

Juliet or **juliet** /*joo'li-et*/ *n* (in international radio communication) a code word for the letter *j*.

juliet cap /*joo'li-et kap*/ *n* a round close-fitting women's skullcap worn *esp* by brides. [Prob *Juliet*, in Shakespeare's *Romeo and Juliet*]

July /*joo-lī'*/ *n* the seventh month of the year. [L *Jūlius*, from Gaius Julius Caesar, who was born in it]

July-flower a mistaken form of **gillyflower**.

jumar /*joo'mär*/ (*mountaineering*) *n* a clip which grips the rope when weight is applied, and runs freely along the rope when the weight is taken off (also **jumar clamp**); a climb using these. ◆ *vi* to climb using jumars. [Swiss name]

jumart /*joo'märt* or *-mart*/ (*obs*) *n* the supposed offspring of a bull and a mare, or stallion and cow. [Fr]

jumbal or **jumble** /*jum'bl*/ *n* a thin, crisp, sweet cake, formerly made in the shape of a ring. [Perh **gimmal** or **gimbal**]

jumbie see **jumby**.

jumble¹ /*jum'bl*/ *vt* to mix confusedly; to confuse mentally; to throw together without order; to shake up, jolt (*obs*). ◆ *vi* (*obs*) to be mixed together confusedly; to flounder about. ◆ *n* a confused mixture; confusion; things offered for sale at a jumble sale; a jolting. [Origin obscure]

   ■ **jum'bler** *n*. **jum'blingly** *adv* in a confused or jumbled manner. **jum'bly** *adj*.

   ❑ **jumble sale** *n* a sale of miscellaneous articles, second-hand or home-made, etc, to raise money for a charity or other body.

jumble² see **jumbal**.

jumbo /*jum'bō*/ *n* (*pl* **jum'bos**) anything very big of its kind; an elephant (after a famous large one so named); a jumbo jet. ◆ *adj* huge; colossal; extra-large. [Prob mumbo-*jumbo*; earlier than Jumbo the elephant]

   ■ **jum'boize** or **-ise** /*-bō-īz*/ *vt* to enlarge (a ship) by adding a prefabricated section, eg amidships.

   ❑ **jumbo jet** *n* a large jet airliner.

jumbuck /*jum'buk*/ (*Aust inf*) *n* a sheep. [Origin unknown]

jumelle /*joo-mel'* or *zhü-mel*/ *n* a paired or twinned article, *esp* opera glasses. [Fr, twin; cf **gemel**, **gimmal**]

jumhouriya see **jamahiriya**.

jump¹ /*jump*/ *vi* to spring or leap; to move suddenly or quickly; to move with a jerk, to start, eg with fright; (of a parachutist) to leap out of a plane; to bounce; to rise suddenly; to change or move abruptly or out of sequence from one thing, state, etc to another; to throb, flicker; to be lively or exciting; to agree, coincide (*with*). ◆ *vt* to cause or help to leap; to leap over, from, or onto; to skip over; to drive through (a red) traffic light) (*inf*); to start (a vehicle) using jump leads; to fall off or out of (rails, a groove, etc); to board (a train, etc) so as to travel without paying (*inf*); (eg of game) to spring or start; to appropriate (a claim), on the grounds that the owner has failed to satisfy conditions or has abandoned it; to seize suddenly, catch unawares, ambush (*inf*); (of a

male) to have sexual intercourse with (*vulgar sl*); to make up hastily (*obs*); to risk (*Shakesp*). ◆ *n* an act of jumping; a bound; an obstacle to be jumped over; a height or distance jumped; a jumping contest; a descent by a parachutist; a sudden rise or movement; a jerk or start; (in *pl*) convulsive movements, chorea, delirium tremens, or the like (*sl*); a bounce; an abrupt change; a jump-cut; changing to a branch program (*comput*); venture, hazard (*Shakesp*). ◆ *adv* (*Shakesp*) exactly. [Prob onomatopoeic]

   ■ **jump'able** *adj*. **jump'er** *n* a person, animal or thing that jumps; a jump shot or a player of such (*basketball*); a heavy drill with a jumping motion, used in quarrying, etc; a short section of overhead transmission line conductor forming an electrical connection between two sections of a line (*elec eng*); a multi-core flexible cable connection between the coaches of a multiple-unit train; one of a group of Welsh Methodists (c.1760) who jumped about in worship. **jump'ily** *adv*. **jump'iness** *n*. **jump'y** *adj* nervy, on edge, liable to jump or start; moving jerkily.

   ❑ **jump ball** *n* (*basketball*) a ball thrown up between opposing players by the referee to restart the game. **jump'-cut** *n* (*film*) an abrupt change from one scene or subject to another, across an interval of time (also *vi*). **jumped'-up** *adj* (*inf*) upstart; cocky, arrogant. **jumper cables** *n pl* (*N Am*) jump leads. **jumping bean** *n* the seed of a Mexican euphorbiaceous plant (*esp* genus *Sebastiania*), containing a moth larva which causes it to move or jump. **jumping deer** *n* the black-tailed American deer. **jumping gene** *n* (*inf*) a transposon. **jumping hare** *n* a S African rodent related to the jerboa. **jumping jack** *n* a jointed toy figure whose limbs can be moved by pulling a string; a firework that jumps along the ground; a jumping exercise in which the legs are spread apart then brought together while the arms are swung above the head and back to the sides. **jumping mouse** *n* a genus (*Zapus*) of jumping rodents. **jumping-off place** *n* the terminus of a route, a destination; a starting-point; a place from which one sets out into the wilds, the unknown, etc; somewhere very remote (*US*). **jumping spider** *n* any member of the spider family Salticidae that leap upon their prey. **jump jet** *n* a fighter plane able to land and take off vertically. **jump'-jockey** *n* (*horse-racing*) a jockey who rides in steeplechases. **jump leads** *n pl* two electrical cables for supplying power to start a car from another battery. **jump'-off** *n* (*US*) the start; starting-place; see **jump off** below. **jump rope** *n* (*N Am*) a skipping rope. **jump seat** *n* a movable seat in a car or aircraft; a carriage with a movable seat (*obs*); a folding seat. **jump shot** *n* (*basketball*) a shot at a basket made when the player is in midair. **jump'-start** *vt* to start (a car) by using jump leads; to bump start (a car). ◆ *n* an act of starting a car in this way. **jump suit** or **jump'suit** *n* a one-piece garment for either sex, combining trousers and jacket or blouse. **jump'-turn** *n* (*skiing*) a turn executed in midair. **jump'-up** *n* (*W Indies*) a social dance.

   ■ **for the high jump** see under **high¹**. **have the jump on** (chiefly *US inf*) to have an advantage over. **jump at** to accept eagerly. **jump down someone's throat** to berate or snap at someone angrily and suddenly. **jump off** (*showjumping*) to compete in another, more difficult round, when two or more competitors have an equal score after the first round (**jump'-off** *n*). **jump on** to jump so as to come down heavily upon; to attack physically; to censure promptly and vigorously; to give sudden attention to. **jump (one's) bail** to abscond, forfeiting one's bail. **jump out** to be visually striking; to grab the attention. **jump ship** (*inf*) (of a sailor) to leave one's ship while still officially employed, in service, etc. **jump the gun** (ie the starting-gun in a race) to get off one's mark too soon, act prematurely, take an unfair advantage. **jump the queue** to get ahead of one's turn (*lit* and *fig*). **jump to conclusions** come to a decision prematurely, based upon insufficient facts or consideration. **jump to it!** hurry! **one jump ahead of** in a position of advantage over.

jump² /*jump*/ (*obs*) *n* a short coat; (in *pl*) a kind of female under-bodice. [Perh from Fr *juppe*, now *jupe* a petticoat]

jumper /*jum'pər*/ *n* a knitted upper garment, *orig* one loose at the waist; *orig* a type of overall, slipped over the head; a pinafore dress (*N Am*). [Prob **jump²**]

Jun. *abbrev* : June; Junior.

jun. *abbrev* : junior.

Juncaceae, juncaceous see **juncus**.

juncate (*Spenser*) a variant of **junket**.

junco /*jung'kō*/ *n* (*pl* **junc'oes** or **junc'os**) the reed-bunting (*obs*); a N American snow-bird. [Sp *junco*, from L *juncus* rush]

junction /*jung'shən* or *jungk'shən*/ *n* a joining, a union or combination; a place or point where eg roads, railway lines or wires meet; the contact area between semiconductor material of different electrical properties (*electronics*). [L *junctiō*, *-ōnis*; see ety of **join**]

   ❑ **junction box** *n* a casing for a junction of electrical wires.

juncture /*jungk'chər*/ *n* a joining, a union; a critical or important point of time; a feature of pronunciation which marks the beginning or ending of an utterance or the transition between elements within it (*linguistics*). [L *junctūra*; see ety of **join**, **jointure**]

juncus /*jung'kəs*/ *n* any plant of the genus *Juncus*, the typical genus of rushes, giving name to the **Junca'ceae**, the rush family. [L *juncus* a rush]
■ **juncā'ceous** *adj*.

June /*joon*/ *n* the sixth month of the year. [L *Jūnius*]
■ **Juneteenth** /-*tēnth*/ *n* 19 June, a US holiday commemorating the abolition of slavery.
❑ **June'berry** *n* the serviceberry. **June bug** *n* a large N American flying beetle of the family Scarabaeidae. **June drop** *n* a falling of immature fruit through a variety of causes, at its height around June.

juneating a non-standard form of **jenneting**.

Jungermanniales /*yŭn-gər-man-i-ā'lēz*/ (*bot*) *n pl* one of the main divisions of the Hepaticae, with thallus or leafy stem, and *usu* a capsule opening by four valves. [Ludwig *Jungermann* (1572–1653), German botanist]

Jungian /*jŭng'i-ən*/ *adj* of or according to the theories of the Swiss psychologist, Carl Gustav *Jung* (1875–1961).

jungle /*jung'gl*/ *n* a dense tropical growth of thickets, brushwood, etc; dense tropical forest; a jumbled assemblage of large objects; a confusing mass eg of regulations; a place or situation where there is ruthless competition, or cruel struggle for survival; (also **jungle music**) a fast rhythmic style of dance music. [Hindi *jangal* waste ground, Sans *jāngala* desert]
■ **jun'gled** *adj*. **jungli** /*jung'gli*/ *adj* (*Ind*) inhabiting a jungle; wild and boorish. ◆ *n* an inhabitant of a jungle; an uneducated peasant. **jung'list** *n* a performer or devotee of jungle music (also *adj*). **jung'ly** *adj*.
❑ **jungle fever** *n* a severe malarial fever. **jun'glefowl** *n* any of several Asiatic fowl of the genus *Gallus*, thought to be the wild ancestor of the domestic fowl. **jun'gle-green** *adj* very dark green. **jungle gym** *n* (*N Am*) a climbing-frame. **jungle juice** *n* (*sl*) alcoholic liquor, *esp* if very strong, of poor quality, or home-made.

junior /*joon'yər*/ *adj* younger; less advanced; of lower standing; (of a product) smaller (and often simpler) than the standard; (of boxing weights) lighter than the standard for that weight. ◆ *n* someone younger, less advanced, or of lower standing; (often with *cap*) the young boy in a family (*US*); a bridge-player on the declarer's right; an American student in his or her third year (of four); a British junior school-pupil. [L *jūnior*, compar of *juvenis* young]
■ **juniority** /-*i-or'i-ti*/ *n*.
❑ **junior bantamweight** see **bantamweight** under **bantam**. **junior college** *n* (*N Am*) a college offering only the first two years of a university education. **junior common room** or (*Cambridge University*) **junior combination room** *n* in some universities, a common room for the use of (*esp* undergraduate) students (cf **senior common room** under **senior**, **middle common room** under **middle**; *abbrev* **JCR**). **junior featherweight** see **featherweight** under **feather**. **junior flyweight** see **flyweight** under **fly**. **junior high school** or **junior high** *n* (*N Am*) a school between elementary and senior high, for 12- to 14-year-olds. **junior lightweight** see **lightweight** under **light**[2]. **junior middleweight** see **middleweight** under **middle**. **junior miss** *n* a (clothing size or range suitable for the) teenage girl or young woman. **junior optime** see **optime**. **junior school** *n* a school for children aged between seven and eleven years. **junior service** *n* the Army. **junior soph** *n* (*hist*) a second-year undergraduate at Cambridge. **junior technician** *n* (*RAF*) a rank senior to aircraftman. **junior welterweight** see **welterweight**.

juniper /*joon'ni-pər*/ *n* an evergreen coniferous shrub (genus *Juniperus*) whose berries are used in making gin; any of various other coniferous trees, or, in the Bible, other shrubs. [L *jūniperus*]

junk[1] /*jungk*/ *n* rubbish generally; nonsense; a narcotic, *esp* heroin (*sl*); the tissue inside the head of the sperm whale from which spermaceti is obtained; an old or useless piece of rope (*archaic*); a chunk; salt meat, *perh* because it becomes as hard as old rope (*obs*; *orig naut*). ◆ *vt* to treat as junk; to discard or abandon as useless (*inf*); to cut into junks. ◆ *adj* worthless; (of a communication) unsolicited and undesired, as in *junk email*. [Origin obscure]
■ **junk'ie** or **junk'y** *n* (*inf*) a narcotics addict (also (*obs US*) **junk'er**); (loosely) someone hooked on something, an addict (*usu* in combination, as in *art junkie*, *coffee junkie*). **junk'iness** *n*. **junk'y** *adj* rubbishy; worthless.
❑ **junk bond** *n* a bond offering a high yield but with high risk. **junk'-bottle** *n* (*US*) a thick strong bottle of green or black glass. **junk'-dealer** or **junk'man** *n* a dealer in junk. **junk food** *n* food of little nutritional value, *usu* easily available and quick to prepare. **junk jewellery** *n* fun jewellery, of little value but often quite showy. **junk mail** *n* unsolicited mail such as advertising circulars, etc. **junk'-ring** *n* a metal ring confining the packing of a piston. **junk shop** *n* a shop where assorted second-hand bric-à-brac is sold. **junk'yard** *n* a yard in which junk is stored or collected for sale.

junk[2] /*jungk*/ *n* an E Asian flat-bottomed sailing vessel, with high forecastle and poop, and large squarish sails internally supported by battens. [Port *junco*, appar from Javanese *djong*]

junkanoo see **John Canoe**.

Junker /*yoong'kər*/ *n* a young German noble or squire; an overbearing, narrow-minded, reactionary aristocrat. [Ger, from *jung* young, and *Herr* lord]
■ **Junk'erdom** *n*. **Junk'erism** *n*.

junker see **junkie** under **junk**[1].

junket /*junk'it*/ *n* curds mixed with cream, sweetened and flavoured; a feast or celebration, a picnic, an outing, a spree, now *esp* one enjoyed by officials using public funds; a cream cheese; any sweetmeat or delicacy (*obs*); a rush-basket (*dialect*). ◆ *vi* (**junk'eting**; **junk'eted**) to feast, banquet, or take part in a convivial entertainment or spree; to go on a junket. ◆ *vt* to feast, regale, entertain. [Anglo-Fr *jonquette* rush-basket, from L *juncus* a rush]
■ **junketeer'** or **junk'eter** *n*. **junk'eting** *n* (often in *pl*) merrymaking or entertainment, picnicking.

junkie, junky see under **junk**[1].

Juno /*joo'nō*/ *n* the wife of Jupiter, identified with the Greek Hera, special protectress of marriage and guardian of women (*Roman myth*); a queenly woman; the fourth largest known asteroid. [L *Jūnō, -ōnis*]
■ **Junoesque** /-*esk'*/ *adj* (of a woman) large, buxom, and (*usu*) beautiful. **Junō'nian** *adj* relating to Juno.

Junr or **junr** *abbrev* : junior.

junta /*jun'tə* or *hŭn'tə*/ *n* a government formed by a *usu* small group of military officers following a coup d'état; a meeting or council; a Spanish grand council of state; (in the following meanings also **junto**, *pl* **jun'tos**) a body of people joined or united for some secret intrigue, a confederacy, a cabal or faction. [Sp, from L *jungere, junctum* to join]

jupati /*joo'pə-tē* or -*tē'*/ *n* a species of *Raphia* palm. [Tupí]

Jupiter /*joo'pi-tər*/ *n* the chief god, the counterpart of the Greek Zeus (also **Jove**; *Roman myth*); the largest and, next to Venus, the brightest of the planets, fifth in outward order from the sun. [L *Jūpiter, Juppiter* Father (*pater*) Jove]
❑ **Jupiter's beard** *n* the house leek; a kidney-vetch; a fungus (*Hydnum barba-jovis*).

jupon /*joo'pən*/ *n* a sleeveless jacket or close-fitting coat, extending down over the hips (*hist*); a petticoat. [Fr]

Jura see **Jurassic**.

jura see **jus**[1].

jural /*joo'rəl*/ *adj* relating to law; relating to rights and obligations. [L *jūs, jūris* law]
■ **ju'rally** *adv*.

jurant /*joo'rənt*/ *adj* taking an oath. ◆ *n* someone who takes an oath. [L *jūrāre, -ātum* to swear]
■ **ju'ratory** *adj* relating to an oath.

Jurassic /*joo-ras'ik*/, also **Jura** /*joo'rə*/ (*geol*) *adj* of or belonging to a period of the Mesozoic era, between 200 and 145 million years ago, well developed in the *Jura* Mountains (also *n*).

jurat[1] /*joo'rat*/ *n* a sworn officer, *esp* (*Fr* and *Channel Islands*) a magistrate. [Fr, from Med L *jūrātus* a sworn man, from L *jūrāre* to swear]

jurat[2] /*joo'rat*/ (*law*) *n* the official memorandum at the end of an affidavit, showing the time when and the person before whom it was sworn. [L *jūrātum* sworn, from *jūrāre* to swear]

juratory see under **jurant**.

jure /*joo'rē* or *yoo're*/ (*L*) *adv* same as **iure**.

juridical /*joo-rid'i-kəl*/ or **juridic** /-*rid'ik*/ *adj* relating to the administration of justice; relating to a judge; used in courts of law. [L *jūridicus*, from *jūs, jūris* law, and *dīcere* to declare]
■ **jurid'ically** *adv*.
❑ **juridical days** *n pl* days on which law courts are in session.

jurisconsult /*joo-ris-kon-sult'*/ *n* someone who is consulted on the law; a lawyer who gives opinions on cases put to him or her; a person knowledgeable in law. [L *jūris consultus*, from *jūs, jūris* law, and *consulere, consultum* to consult]

jurisdiction /*joo-ris-dik'shən*/ *n* the distribution of justice; legal authority; extent of power; the district over which any authority extends. [L *jūrisdictiō, -ōnis*]
■ **jurisdic'tional** or **jurisdic'tive** *adj*.

jurisprudence /*joo-ris-proo'dəns*/ *n* knowledge of law; the science or philosophy of law; a body or branch of law; a legal system. [L *jūrisprūdēntia*, from *jūs, jūris* law, and *prūdēntia* knowledge]

■ words derived from main entry word; ❑ compound words; ■ idioms and phrasal verbs

■ **jurispru'dent** *adj* knowledgeable in jurisprudence. ◆ *n* a person who is knowledgeable in jurisprudence. **jurisprudential** /-den'shl/ *adj*.

■ **medical jurisprudence** forensic medicine (see under **forensic**).

jurist /joo'rist/ *n* a person versed in the science of law, *esp* Roman or civil law; a student or graduate of law; a lawyer (*US*). [Fr *juriste*]

■ **jurist'ic** or **jurist'ical** *adj*. **jurist'ically** *adv*.

juris utriusque doctor /joo'ris ū-tri-us'kwē (or yoo'ris ŭ-tri-ŭs'kwe) dok'tör/ (*L*) doctor both of canon and of civil law.

jury /joo'ri/ *n* a group of people sworn to reach a just verdict on the basis of the evidence before them; a committee of adjudicators or examiners. [Anglo-Fr *juree*, from *jurer*, from L *jūrāre* to swear]

■ **ju'ried** *adj* (of an award) adjudicated by a committee of experts. **ju'ror** *n* a person who serves on a jury (also **ju'ryman** and **ju'rywoman** (*pl* **ju'rymen** and **ju'rywomen**)); someone who takes an oath.

□ **jury box** *n* the place in court in which the jury sits during a trial. **jury duty** *n*. **jury of matrons** *n* (*obs*) a jury of women empanelled to give a decision in a case of alleged pregnancy. **jury-pro'cess** *n* a writ summoning a jury. **jury room** *n* the room in which the jury deliberates and comes to a verdict. **jury service** *n*.

■ **the jury is** (still) **out** (*inf*) a decision has yet to be reached.

jury- /joo-ri-/ (*naut*) *combining form* indicating makeshift. [Perh OFr *ajurie* aid, from L *adjūtāre* to aid]

□ **ju'rymast** *n* a temporary mast raised instead of one lost. **ju'ry-rig** *n* a temporary, makeshift rig. **ju'ry-rigged** *adj* rigged in a temporary way. **ju'ry-rudder** *n* a temporary replacement rudder.

jus[1] /jus or yoos/ (*L*) *n* (*pl* **jura** /joo'rə or yoo'ra/) law; a legal right.

□ **jus canonicum** /kə-non'i-kəm or ka-non'ik-ŭm/ *n* canon law. **jus civile** /si-vī'lē, kē-wē'le or -vē'/ *n* civil law. **jus divinum** /di-vī'nəm, di-wē'nŭm or -vē'/ *n* divine right. **jus gentium** /jen'shi-əm or gen'ti-ŭm/ *n* law of nations. **jus mariti** /ma'ri-tī or -rē'tē/ *n* the right of a husband. **jus naturale** /nat-ū-rā'lē or nat-ŭ-rä'le/ *n* natural law; the fundamental shared human conception of what constitutes justice. **jus primae noctis** /prī'mē or prē'mī nok'tis/ *n* the formerly alleged right of a feudal superior to take the virginity of a vassal's bride. **jus sanguinis** /sang'gwi-nis/ *n* the principle that a person's nationality is that of their natural parents. **jus soli** /sō'lī or sō'lē/ *n* the principle that a person's nationality is that of the country in which they were born.

jus[2] /zhüs or (Fr) zhü/ (*cookery*) *n* juice; gravy. [Fr]

jusqu'au bout /zhü-skō boo'/ (Fr) to the very end.

■ **jusqu'auboutisme** /-tēz-m'/ *n* the practice of carrying on to the bitter end. **jusqu'auboutiste** /-tēst/ (also anglicized as **jusqu'aubou'tist** /-boo'tist/) *n*.

jussive /jus'iv/ (*grammar*) *adj* expressing a command. ◆ *n* a grammatical form or construction expressing a command. [L *jubēre*, *jussum* to command]

just[1] /just/ *adj* fair, impartial; according to justice; due, deserved; righteous (*Bible*); in accordance with facts, valid; well-grounded; accurately true; exact; normal (*obs*); close-fitting (*obs*). ◆ *adv* precisely, exactly; so much and no more; barely; barely a moment ago; at this very moment; only, merely; quite, absolutely, indeed (*inf*). [Fr *juste*, or L *justus*, from *jūs* law]

■ **just'ly** *adv* in a just manner; equitably; accurately; by right. **just'ness** *n* equity; fittingness; exactness.

□ **just-in-time'** *adj* relating to a system of manufacture by which components are delivered when they are needed for assembly, to reduce storage costs (*abbrev* **JIT**). ◆ *n* this system of manufacture. **just intonation** *n* (*music*) observance of the true mathematical theoretical pitch, without compromise or temperament.

■ **just about** nearly; more or less. **just about to** see **about to** under **about**. **just now** precisely at this moment; a little while ago; very soon. **just so** exactly, I agree; in a precise, neat manner.

just[2] /just/ see **joust**.

juste milieu /zhüst mēl-yə'/ (Fr) *n* the just mean, the happy medium.

justice /jus'tis/ *n* the quality of being just; integrity; impartiality; rightness; the awarding of what is due; the administration of law; a judge; a magistrate; a justice of the peace. [Fr, from L *justitia*]

■ **jus'ticer** *n* (*obs*) a maintainer or administrator of justice. **jus'ticeship** *n* the office or dignity of a justice. **justiciable** /jus-tish'i-ə-bl/ *adj* liable to trial. **justiciar** /-tish'i-ər/ *n* (*hist*) a judge or administrator of justice; a supreme judge. **justiciary** /-tish'i-ə-ri/ *n* a justiciar (*hist*); the jurisdiction of a justiciar (*Scot*). ◆ *adj* relating to the administration of justice.

□ **Justice of the Peace** *n* a person commissioned to perform certain minor judicial and other functions within a specified locality, in England and Wales (but not in Scotland) called a magistrate (*abbrev* **JP**). **justices' justice** *n* (*ironic*) the (unsatisfactory) kind of justice to be expected from the unpaid and amateur magistracy of England.

■ **bring to justice** to bring to trial and (*usu*) to punish (someone believed to be guilty). **chief justice** in the Commonwealth, a judge

presiding over a supreme court; in the USA, a judge who is chairman of a group of judges in a court. **do justice to** to give full advantage to; to treat fairly; to appreciate (a meal, etc) fully by eating heartily (*inf*). **do oneself justice** to show one's abilities to best advantage. **European Court of Justice** an EU institution whose function is to ensure that the laws embodied in the EU treaties are observed, and to rule on alleged infringements. **High Court of Justice** a section of the English Supreme Court, comprising Chancery and Queen's (or King's) Bench Divisions. **High Court of Justiciary** the supreme criminal court in Scotland. **Lord Chief Justice** the chief judge of the Queen's (or King's) Bench Division of the High Court of Justice. **Lord Justice-Clerk** the Scottish judge ranking next to the Lord Justice-General, presiding over the Second Division of the Inner House of the Court of Session, vice-president of the High Court of Justiciary. **Lord Justice-General** the highest criminal judge in Scotland, called also the Lord President of the Court of Session.

Justicialism /ju-stish'ə-li-zm/ (also without *cap*) *n* the political ideology of Juan Domingo Perón (1895–1974), President of Argentina, which combined Fascism and Socialism. [Sp *justicialismo*, from *justicia* justice]

justify /jus'ti-fī/ *vt* (**jus'tifying**; **jus'tified**) to prove or show to be just, right or reasonable; to vindicate; to show adequate reason or grounds for (one's action) (*law*); to absolve; to punish, *esp* to hang (*obs*); to adjust by spacing to form an even right margin (*printing*; *comput*). [Fr *justifier* and LL *jūstificāre*, from *justus* just, and *facere* to make]

■ **justifiabil'ity** *n*. **jus'tifiable** (or /-fī'/) *adj* that may be justified or defended. **jus'tifīableness** (or /-fī'/) *n*. **jus'tifiably** (or /-fī'/) *adv*. **justification** /jus-ti-fi-kā'shən/ *n* the act of justifying; something which justifies; vindication; absolution; a plea showing sufficient reason for an action (*law*). **jus'tificātive** or **justificatory** /jus-tif'i-kə-tə-ri, jus'ti-fi-kā-tə-ri or -kā'/ *adj* having power to justify. **jus'tificātor** or **jus'tifīer** *n* a person who defends or vindicates; a person who pardons and absolves from guilt and punishment.

□ **justifiable homicide** *n* the killing of a person in execution of sentence of death, in self-defence, or to prevent an atrocious crime. **justification by faith** *n* the doctrine that mankind is absolved from sin by faith in Christ.

justle see **jostle**.

jut /jut/ *vi* (**jutt'ing**; **jutt'ed**) to project or protrude from the main body, *esp* sharply. ◆ *vt* (*usu* with *out*) to cause to project or protrude. ◆ *n* a projection; a jerking movement (*obs*). [A variant of **jet**[2]]

■ **jutt'ing** *adj*. **jutt'ingly** *adv*.

□ **jut'-window** *n* a bay window.

Jute /joot/ (*hist*) *n* a member of a Germanic people *orig* from Jutland, who with the Angles and Saxons invaded Britain in the 5c. [ME, from LL *Jutae* Jutes]

■ **Ju'tish** *adj*.

jute /joot/ *n* the fibre of *Corchorus capsularis* or *C. olitorius* (family Tiliaceae), plants of Bangladesh, etc, used for making sacks, mats, etc; the plant itself. ◆ *adj* made of jute. [Bengali *jhūṭo*, from Sans *jūṭa* matted hair]

■ **China jute** a species of *Abutilon*; its fibre.

jutty /jut'i/ *n* a projecting part of a wall; a pier, a jetty. ◆ *vt* (*Shakesp*) to project beyond. ◆ *vi* (*archaic*) to jut. [Cf **jetty**[1]]

juv. *abbrev* : juvenile.

juve /joov/ (*theatre*) *n* a juvenile lead (also **juve lead**).

juvenal[1] /joo'və-nəl/ (*Shakesp*) *n* a youth. [L *juvenālis* belonging to youth, from *juvenis* young]

juvenal[2] see **juvenile**.

Juvenalian /joo-vi-nā'li-ən/ *adj* of the Roman satirist Juvenal (1c–2c AD); bitterly sarcastic and denunciatory rather than humorous.

juvenescent /joo-və-nes'ənt/ *adj* becoming youthful. [L *juvenēscere* to grow young]

■ **juvenesc'ence** *n*.

juvenile /joo'və-nīl/ *adj* young; relating or suited to youth or young people; having or retaining characteristics of youth; childish; (of plants and animals) immature; (of a bird) having its first plumage of true feathers but sexually immature; of the plumage of such a bird (also (*N Am*) **ju'venal**); originating beneath the surface of a planet, *esp* Earth, and now appearing at the surface for the first time (*geol*). ◆ *n* a young person, *esp* (*law*) one under the age of eighteen; a young animal or bird; a book written for the young; an actor who plays youthful parts. [L *juvenīlis*, from *juvenis* young]

■ **ju'venilely** *adv*. **ju'venileness** *n*. **juvenilia** /-il'yə/ *n pl* writings or works produced in the childhood or youth of the author, artist, etc. **juvenility** /-il'i-ti/ *n* juvenile character; juveniles as a group; (in *pl*) juvenile behaviour. **ju'venilize** or **-ise** /-il-īz/ *vt* to make young or youthful.

□ **juvenile court** *n* a former name for a **youth court** (see under **youth**). **juvenile delinquency** *n* criminal or antisocial behaviour by a juvenile. **juvenile delinquent** or **juvenile offender** *n* a young lawbreaker, between the ages of 10 and 17. **juvenile hormone** *n* a hormone necessary to an insect in immature stages, which must be absent in order for it to change to the adult form.

juvie /joo'vē/ (*US sl*) *adj* juvenile. ◆ *n* a detention centre for juvenile offenders.

juxtaposition /juk-stə-pə-zish'ən/ *n* a placing or being placed close together. [L *juxtā* near, and **position**, **pose**[1]]

■ **jux'tapose** (or /-pōz'/) *vt* to place side by side. **juxtaposi'tional** *adj.* □ **juxtaposition twins** *n pl* (*mineralogy*) crystals joined together face to face without interpenetration.

Jy *abbrev*: jansky (*astron*); July.

jymold see **gimmalled** under **gimmal**.

Jynx /jingks/ (*obs*) *n* the wryneck genus; (without *cap*) a wryneck. [L *iynx*, from Gr *iynx* or *īynx*]

Kk

a b c d e f g h i j k l m n o p q r s t u v w x y z

Kabel Designed by Rudolf Koch in 1927. Germany.

K or **k** /kā/ *n* the eleventh letter in the modern English alphabet, tenth in the Roman, derived from Greek *kappa* (K, κ), its sound a voiceless velar stop formed by raising the back of the tongue to the soft palate; anything shaped like the letter K.
 ■ **the five Ks** the symbols of a Sikh's spiritual and cultural allegiance to Sikhism (**kaccha, kangha, kara, kesh** and **kirpan**), worn by baptized Sikhs.

K or **K.** *abbrev* : Cambodia (formerly Kampuchea; IVR); kaon (*phys*); kilobyte(s) (*comput*); kilometre(s); kina (Papua New Guinea currency); king (in cards and chess); Kirkpatrick (catalogue of Domenico Scarlatti's works); knight; Köchel (catalogue of Mozart's works); krona (Swedish currency); króna (Icelandic currency); krone (Danish and Norwegian currency); kwacha (Malawian and Zambian currency).

K *symbol* : (as a medieval Roman numeral) 250; a thousand; a unit of 1024 words, bytes or bits (*comput*); *kalium* (L), potassium (*chem*); kelvin (SI unit).

K̄ *symbol* : (medieval Roman numeral) 250 000.

k or **k.** *abbrev* : karat or carat; kilo or kilo-.

k *symbol* : Boltzmann constant (*phys*); velocity constant (*chem*).

ka¹ /kä/ (*ancient Egypt*) *n* the spirit or soul within a person, a god, or a statue of a dead person. [Egypt]

ka² or **kae** /kä/ (*obs*) *vt* to serve (in the phrase **ka me, ka thee** one good turn deserves another). [Origin unknown]

ka³ see **kae¹**.

Kaaba /kä'bə/ *n* the cube-shaped holy building at Mecca into which the Black Stone is built, which Muslims face towards when they pray (also **Caaba**). [Ar *ka'bah*, from *ka'b* cube]

kaama /kä'mə/ *n* the hartebeest. [Of Khoikhoi or Bantu origin]

kabab see **kebab**.

kabaddi /kə- or kə-bä'di/ *n* an *orig* Asian version of tag played barefoot by two teams of seven, in which the players in turn make 'raids' into the opposing team's court, ie, for as long as they can hold their breath while chanting 'kabaddi', they try to touch a member of the opposing team and escape to safety without being captured.

kabaka /kə-bä'kə/ *n* a title of the rulers of the Baganda people of S Uganda. [African name]

kabala see **cabbala**.

kabaya /kə- or kə-bä'yə/ *n* a loose tunic. [Malay, from Pers or Ar]

kabbala, kabbalah see **cabbala**.

kabele see **kebele**.

kabeljou or **kabeljouw** /kä'bl-, kob'l-yow/ or (*S Afr*) kä'bl-yō/ *n* a large S African fish, *Argyrosomus hololepidotus*. [Afrik]

Kabinett /ka-bi-net'/ *n* one of the six higher levels of quality-controlled German wine. [Ger *Kabinettwein*, literally, cabinet wine]

kabob see **kebab**.

kabuki /kä-boo-kē' or -boo'kē/ *n* a popular, traditional, stylized form of Japanese drama, with singing and dancing, in which men play all the roles. [Jap, from *ka* song, *bu* dance, and *ki* skill]

Kabyle /ka- or kə-bīl'/ *n* one of the Berber peoples of N Africa; a member of this people; a dialect of Berber. ◆ *adj* of the Kabyles or their language. [Fr, from Ar *qabā'il*, pl of *qabīlah* a tribe]

kaccha /kuch'ə/ *n* the short trousers traditionally worn by Sikhs. [Punjabi]

kacha or **kachcha** same as **cutcha**.

kachahri or **kacheri** /kuch'ə-ri or ku-cher'i/ *n* an Indian magistrate's office or courthouse (also **cutcherr'y**). [Hindi *kachahrī*]

kachina /kə-chē'nə/ *n* any of the ancestral spirits invoked by the Pueblo peoples of N America at ritual ceremonies; a dancer who impersonates the ancestral spirits at these ceremonies. [Hopi *qachina* supernatural]

 □ **kachina doll** *n* a doll representing a kachina given to children by the dancers at these ceremonies.

kachori /kach'ə-ri/ *n* an Indian snack of pastry with a spicy filling. [Hindi *kacaurī*]

kack, etc see **cack**.

kadai /kə-dī'/ same as **karahi**.

kadaitcha same as **kurdaitcha**.

Kaddish /kad'ish/ (*Judaism*) *n* a liturgical prayer used during the mourning period. [Aramaic *qaddīsh*]
 ■ **say Kaddish** to be a mourner.

kade see **ked**.

kadi /kä' or kā'di/ *n* same as **cadi**.

kae¹ /kā/ (*Scot*) *n* a jackdaw (also **ka**). [Cf MDu *ka*, Dan *kaa*]

kae² see **ka²**.

Kaffir or **Kaffer** /kaf'ər/ (*offensive*) *n* (also (formerly) **Caffre** or **Kafir** /ka' or kä'fər/) a black South African; a name applied to certain indigenous peoples of South Africa including the Xhosa, and to the languages spoken by them (*hist*); (in *pl*) South African mining shares (*stock exchange sl*). ◆ *adj* of the Kaffirs or their languages. [Kafir]
 □ **kaff'irboom** *n* (Du *boom* tree) the coral tree (*Erythrina caffra*). **kaffir bread** *n* the pith of South African cycads (genus *Encephalartos*). **kaffir corn** *n* sorghum.

kaffiyeh /kä-fē'ye/, **keffiyeh** or **kufiyah** /kə-fē'yə/ *n* an Arab headdress of cloth, folded and held by a cord around the head. [Ar *kaffīyah*]

kafila see **cafila**.

Kafir /kä'fər or kaf'ər/ *n* an infidel (*offensive*; also without *cap*); a native of Kafiristan (in Afghanistan; also **Caffre**); a Kaffir. [Ar *kāfir* unbeliever]
 ■ **Kaf'iri** *adj* and *n*.

Kafkaesque /kaf-kə-esk'/ *adj* in the style of, or reminiscent of, the ideas, work, etc of the Czech novelist Franz *Kafka* (1883–1924), *esp* in his vision of man's isolated existence in a dehumanized world.

kaftan same as **caftan**.

kago /kä'gō/ *n* (*pl* **kag'os**) a Japanese basketwork palanquin. [Jap]

kagool, kagoul, kagoule see **cagoul**.

kagu /kä'goo/ *n* a ground-dwelling bird (*Rhynochetos jubatus*) with pale grey plumage and a loose crest, found only in New Caledonia. [Native name]

kahal /kä'hal/ *n* any of the Jewish communities scattered across Europe; the local governing body of any of these communities. [Heb *kāhal* congregation, community]

kahawai /kä'wī or ka'ha-wī/ (*Aust* and *NZ*) *n* a large marine fish (*Arripis trutta*) of the perch family but resembling a salmon. [Maori]

kahikatea /kī-kə-tē'ə/ *n* a tall coniferous tree of New Zealand (*Podocarpus dacrydioides*). [Maori]

Kahlúa® /kə-loo'ə/ *n* a Mexican liqueur made from coffee beans, cocoa beans and vanilla.

kai /kä'ē or kī/ (*NZ*, etc) *n* food; a meal. [Maori; also in other Polynesian languages]
 ■ **kai'kai** *n* food; a feast.

kaiak same as **kayak**.

kaid /kä-ēd' or kād/ *n* a N African chief. [Ar *qā'id*; cf **alcaide**]

kaie /kā/ an obsolete form of **key¹,²**.

kaif see **kef**.

kail¹ /kāl/ *n* a ninepin; (in *pl*) the game of ninepins; (in *pl*) skittles. [Cf Du *kegel*, Ger *Kegel*, Fr *quille*]

kail² see **kale**.

kaim see **kame**.

kaimakam /kī-mə-käm'/ n a governor of a province in modern Turkey; an Ottoman lieutenant-colonel or lieutenant governor. [Turk *kaymakam*, from Ar *qā'imaqām*]

kain see **cain**.

kainga /kä-ing'ə/ (NZ) n a Maori village. [Maori]

kainite /kī'nīt, kā'nīt or kā'i-nīt/ n hydrous magnesium sulphate with potassium chloride, found in salt deposits, used as a fertilizer. [Ger *Kainit*, from Gr *kainos* new, recent]

kainogenesis same as **caenogenesis** (see under **caeno-**).

Kainozoic same as **Cainozoic**.

kaisar-i-Hindi /kī'sär-i-hin'di/ n title from 1876 to 1947 of the British monarch as emperor of India. [Pers *qaysari-Hindi*, from L *Caesar*]

kaiser /kī'zər/, also (obs) **kesar** or **keasar** /kē'zər/ n (also with cap) an emperor, esp a German emperor. [Ger, from L *Caesar*]
■ **kai'serdom** n. **kai'serin** n the wife or widow of a kaiser. **kai'serism** n. **kai'sership** n.
■ **the Kaiser's war** the war of 1914–18 (after Kaiser Wilhelm II).

kaizen /kī'zen/ n the Japanese principle of continuously improving industrial and business working practices. [Jap, improvement]

kajawah /kə-jä'wə or kä'jə-wə/ n a camel saddle or pannier. [Pers]

kaka /kä'kä or -kə/ n a green New Zealand parrot (*Nestor meridionalis*); any of several related parrots, many of which are extinct. [Maori *kaka* parrot]
■ **ka'kapo** n (pl **ka'kapōs**) (Maori po night) the rare New Zealand owl-parrot, nocturnal and flightless.
□ **kaka beak** or **bill** n the New Zealand glory-pea (genus *Clianthus*).

kakemono /kak-i-mō'nō/ n (pl **kakemō'nos**) a Japanese wall-picture or calligraphic inscription on a roller. [Jap *kake* to hang, and *mono* thing]

kaki /kä'kē/ n the Japanese persimmon, or Chinese date plum. [Jap]

kakiemon /kä-ki-ā'mon/ (also with cap) n a Japanese porcelain, first made by Sakaida *Kakiemon* in the 17c, recognizable from its characteristic use of iron-red.

kakodyl same as **cacodyl**.

kakuro /kə-koo'rō/ n (pl **kaku'ros**) a type of puzzle in which numbers must be entered into a grid to give a prescribed sum for each row and column. [Jap *kasan* addition, and *kurosu* (Japanese pronunciation of **cross**)]

kala-azar /kä'lä-ä-zär'/ n an often fatal tropical fever, characterized by acute anaemia, etc, caused by a protozoan parasite and usu transmitted by sandfly bites. [Assamese *kālā* black, and *āzār* disease]

Kalamazoo®️ system /ka-lə-mə-zoo' sis'təm/ n a bookkeeping system which uses simultaneous recording, with different forms placed on top of each other interleaved with carbon sheets.

kalamdan /kal'am-dan/ n a Persian writing case. [Pers *qalamdān*, from *qalam* a pen, and *dān* holding]

kalamkari /kal-am-kä'rē/ n a method of colouring and decorating by several dyeings or printings; a chintz fabric treated in this way. [Pers *qalamkārī* writing, painting, etc, from *qalam* pen]

kalanchoe /kal-ən-kō'ē/ n a succulent plant which bears red, yellow or pink flower clusters on long stems. [Fr, from Mandarin]

Kalashnikov /kə-lash'ni-kof/ (also without cap) n a Russian-made submachine-gun. [MT *Kalashnikov* (1919–2013), its Russian designer]

kale or **kail** /kāl/ n a variety of cabbage with open curled leaves; cabbage generally; broth of which kale is a chief ingredient, hence a meal, dinner (Scot); money (US sl). [Scot and N Eng form of **cole**]
□ **kail'-pot** or (Scot) **-pat** n. **kail'-runt** n a cabbage stem. **kail'yard** or (Scot) **-yaird** n a cabbage-patch, kitchen garden. **Kailyard school** n a late 19c to early 20c group of Scottish writers of sentimental stories (one of whom, Ian Maclaren, used the title *Beside the Bonnie Brier Bush*, 1894, in allusion to the Jacobite song 'There grows a bonnie brier bush in our kailyard').
■ **give someone his kale through the reek** (Scot) to reprimand someone severely.

kaleidophone /kə-lī'də-fōn/ n an instrument for demonstrating sound waves by lines of light on a screen. [Gr *kalos* beautiful, *eidos* form, and *phōnē* voice]

kaleidoscope /kə-lī'də-skōp/ n an optical toy in which one sees an ever-changing variety of beautiful colours and forms; a delightfully diverse and unpredictable sequence of sights, events, etc. [Gr *kalos* beautiful, *eidos* form, and *skopeein* to look]
■ **kaleidoscopic** /-skop'ik/ adj relating to a kaleidoscope; showing constant change. **kaleidoscop'ically** adv.

kalendar same as **calendar**.

kalends same as **calends**.

Kalevala /kä'li- or kä'le-vä-lə/ n the great Finnish epic poem, in eight-syllable lines of trochaic verse (imitated by Longfellow in *Hiawatha*) pieced together from oral tradition by Dr Elias Lönnrot from 1835 to 1849. [Finnish *kaleva* a hero, and *-la* denoting place]

Kali /kä'lē/ n a Hindu goddess, Durga, wife of Siva, as goddess of destruction. [Sans]

kali[1] /kal'i or kā'lī/ n the prickly saltwort or glasswort (*Salsola kali*); its ash (obs); an alkali, esp potash (obs). [Ar *qili*, as in root of **alkali**]
■ **kalinite** /kal'in-īt/ n native potash alum. **kā'lium** n potassium.

kali[2] /kä'lē/ n a carpet with long nap; the large carpet covering the centre of a Persian room. [Pers *kālī*]

kalian /käl-yän'/ n a Persian hookah. [Pers]

kalif see **caliph**.

Kaliyuga /kä-li-yŭg'ə/ (Hindu myth) n the present (fourth) age of the world, of universal degeneracy. [Sans]

Kallima /kal'i-mə/ n an Oriental genus of butterflies, mimicking dead leaves. [Gr *kallimos* beautiful]

kallitype /kal'i-tīp/ n a former photographic process in which ferric salts are reduced to ferrous salts. [Gr *kallos* beauty, and *typos* type]

kalmia /kal'mi-ə/ n any shrub of the N American *Kalmia* genus of evergreen shrubs of the heath family, including the mountain laurel or calico-bush. [Peter *Kalm* (1715–79), pupil of Linnaeus]

Kalmuck, **Calmuck** /kal'muk/ or **Kalmyk** /kal'mik/ n a member of a Mongolian people in China and Russia; their language. ◆ adj of the Kalmucks or their language. [Turki and Russ]

kalong /kä'long/ n a large fruit bat. [Malay *kālong*]

kalooki or **kalookie** /kə-loo'ki/ n a card game similar to rummy, using two packs of cards and two jokers. [Origin unknown]

kalotype same as **calotype**.

kalpa /kal'pə/ (Hinduism) n a day of Brahma, a period of 4320 million years (also **cal'pa**). [Sans, formation]

kalpak /käl'päk or -päk'/ n a triangular Turkish or Tatar felt cap (also **calpac** or **calpack**). [Turk *kālpāk*]

kalpis /kal'pis/ n a water-jar. [Gr]

Kalsomine®️ or **calcimine** /kal'sə-mīn or -min/ n a kind of whitewash or colour wash for walls, etc. ◆ vt to cover with Kalsomine. [From L *calx, calcis* lime]

kaluki /kə-loo'ki/ n a N American version of **kalooki**.

kalumpit /kä-lŭm-pēt'/ n a Philippine tree of the myrobalan genus; its edible fruit. [Tagálog]

kalyptra /ka-lip'trə/ n a veil worn by Greek women. [Gr; see also **calyptra**]

kam or **kamme** /kam/ (Shakesp) adj and adv awry (also **cam**). [Cf Welsh, Gaelic and Ir *cam*]

Kama or **Cama** /kä'mä/ (Hinduism) n the god of love in the Puranas (also **Kamadeva** /-dä-vä/); (without cap) earthly desire. [Sans *Kāma*]

kamacite /kam'ə-sīt/ n a variety of nickeliferous iron, found in meteorites. [Ger *Kamacit* (obs), from Gr *kamax, kamakos* vine-pole, shaft]

kamala /kä'mä-lä/, **kamela** /-mä'lä/ or **kamila** /-mē'lä/ n an orange dyestuff obtained from the fruit-hairs of an East Indian tree of the spurge family (*Mallotus philippinensis*), the tree itself. [Sans *kamala*; Hindi *kamēlā, kamīlā*]

Kamasutra or **Kama Sutra** /kä-mə-soo'trə/ n an ancient Sanskrit text on sexual love. [Sans, from *kama* love, and *sūtra* a string, rule]

kame or **kaim** /kām/ n a comb (Scot); a steep irregular ridge like a cock's comb; an esker, a bank or ridge of gravel, sand, etc, eg as associated with the glacial deposits of Scotland (geol); a fortified site (Walter Scott). [Scot and N Eng form of **comb**[1]]

kamees /ka- or kə-mēs'/ same as **camise**.

kameez /ka- or kə-mēz'/ n (in S Asia) a loose tunic with tight sleeves, worn by women (see also **shalwar-kameez** under **shalwar**). [Urdu *kamis*, from Ar *qamīs* (see **camise**)]

kamela see **kamala**.

kamelaukion /ka-me-lö'ki-ən/ n the tall cylindrical hat worn by Orthodox priests. [Mod Gr]

kamerad /kam-ə-räd'/ interj a German shout of surrender. ◆ vi to surrender. [Ger, comrade, from Fr *camarade*]

kami /kä'mi/ (Jap) n a lord; a divine being or object of worship (Shinto). [Jap, superior, lord, god]

kamichi /kä'mē-shē/ n the horned screamer, a S American bird. [Fr, from Carib]

kamik /kä'mik/ n a knee-length sealskin boot. [Inuit]

kamikaze /kä-mi-kä'zē/ n (a Japanese airman, or plane, making) a suicidal attack. ◆ adj of, or relating to, a kamikaze attack or someone who carries it out; of, or of someone or something engaged upon, an act of certain or deliberate self-destruction in pursuit of a particular cause; reckless, foolhardy (*inf*). [Jap, divine wind]

kamila see **kamala**.

kamis /*ka*- or *kə-mēs'*/ same as **camise**.

kamme see **kam**.

kampong /*kam'pong* or *kam-pong'*/ *n* (in Malaysia) an enclosed space or village. [Malay]

kamseen, kamsin see **khamsin**.

Kan. *abbrev* : Kansas (US state).

kana /*kä'nä*/ *n* Japanese syllabic writing (either **hiragana** or **katakana**), as distinguished from Japanese written in Chinese characters (**kanji**). [Jap]

Kanak /*kə-näk'* or -*nak'*/ *n* a Melanesian; a member of the Melanesian population of New Caledonia seeking its independence from France. [Hawaiian *kanaka* a man]

Kanaka /*kə-nak'ä*, -*näk'* or *kan'ə-kä*/ *n* a Hawaiian; (sometimes without *cap*) a South Sea Islander, *esp* an indentured or forced labourer in Australia (*derog*); the Hawaiian language. [Hawaiian, a man]

kanamycin /*ka-nə-mī'sin*/ *n* an antibiotic obtained from a bacterium (*Streptomyces kanamyceticus*) found in soil, used (*esp* formerly) in the treatment of infections caused by Gram-negative bacteria.

Kanarese or **Canarese** /*kan-ə-rēz'*/ *adj* of *Kanara* in W India. ◆ *n* (*pl* **Kanarese** or **Canarese**) one of the people of Kanara; their Dravidian language, now called **Kannada**, related to Telugu.

kanban /*kan'ban*/ *n* a Japanese industrial system based on the use of cards to regulate the stages of a manufacturing process and control costs. [Jap, literally, sign]

kandy /*kan'di*/ *n* see **candy**[2].

kaneh /*kä'ne*/ *n* a Hebrew measure of 6 cubits in length (also **caneh**). [Heb *qāneh* reed, cane]

kang /*kang*/ *n* a Chinese sleeping-platform that can be warmed by a fire underneath. [Chin *kàng*]

kanga or **khanga** /*kang'gə*/ *n* (in E Africa) a piece of cotton cloth, *usu* brightly decorated, wound around the body as a woman's dress. [Swahili]

kangaroo /*kang-gə-roo'*/ *n* a large Australian herbivorous marsupial (family Macropodidae), with short forelimbs, very long hindlegs and great leaping power; an early type of safety bicycle; (in *pl*; with *cap*) the Australian national Rugby League team; (in *pl*) Australian mining shares (*Brit stock exchange*). ◆ *vi* (*inf*) (of a car) to move forward in jerks, because of the driver's poor clutch control. [From an Aboriginal language]
❑ **kangaroo'-apple** *n* the edible fruit of a species of *Solanum*; the plant that yields it. **kangaroo closure** *n* (in parliament) the method of allowing the chairman to decide which clauses shall be discussed and which passed or leapt over. **kangaroo court** *n* a court operated by a mob, by prisoners in jail, or by any improperly constituted body; a tribunal before which a fair trial is impossible; a comic burlesque court. **kangaroo dog** *n* an Australian breed of dog bred to hunt kangaroos. **kangaroo grass** *n* a valuable fodder grass of the southern hemisphere (*Anthistiria* or *Themeda*). **kangaroo'-hop** *vi* to move forward jerkily. **kangaroo justice** *n* the kind of justice dispensed by a kangaroo court. **kangaroo mouse** *n* a small hopping rodent (genus *Microdipodops*), similar to, but smaller than, the kangaroo rat. **kangaroo paw** *n* (*Aust*) a plant of the genus *Anigozanthus*, the flower of which resembles a paw in shape. **kangaroo rat** *n* a N American rodent (genus *Dipodomys*) related to the jerboa; a rat-kangaroo. **kangaroo'-thorn** *n* a prickly Australian acacia (*Acacia armata*). **kangaroo vine** *n* an evergreen climber (*Cissus antarctica*).

kangha /*kung'hə*/ *n* the comb traditionally worn by Sikhs in their hair. [Punjabi]

kanji /*kan'ji*/ *n* (*pl* **kan'ji** or **kan'jis**) in the Japanese writing system, the set of characters derived from Chinese ideographs; one of these characters. [Jap, from Chin *Hànzì* Chinese character; cf **kana**]

Kannada /*kun'ə-də*/ *n* an important Dravidian language (also *adj*). [Kanarese]

Kans. *abbrev* : Kansas (US state).

kans /*käns*/ *n* an Indian grass related to sugar-cane. [Hindi *kās*]

kant see **cant**[2].

kantar /*kan-tär'*/ *n* a varying unit of weight in Turkey, Egypt, etc, *approx* a hundredweight (also **cantar**). [Ar *qintār*; see **quintal**]

kantele /*kan'tə-lä* or *kan'ti-lē*/ *n* a Finnish zither (also **kan'tela**). [Finn *kantele*]

kanten /*kan'tən*/ *n* agar-agar jelly. [Jap]

kantha /*kän'thə*/ *n* an embroidered cloth quilt. [Bengali]

Kantian /*kant'i-ən*/ *adj* relating to the German philosopher Immanuel *Kant* (1724–1804) or his philosophy.
■ **Kan'tianism** or **Kant'ism** *n* the doctrines or philosophy of Kant. **Kant'ist** *n* a disciple or follower of Kant.

kantikoy, canticoy /*kan'ti-koi*/ or **cantico** /-*kō*/ *n* (*pl* **kan'tikoys, can'ticoys** or **can'ticos**) a Native American religious dance; a dancing-match. ◆ *vi* to dance as an act of worship. [From Algonquian]

KANU /*kä'noo*/ *abbrev* : Kenya African National Union.

Kanuck same as **Canuck**.

kanzu /*kan'zoo*/ *n* a long white garment worn by men in central E Africa. [From Swahili]

kaoliang /*kä-ō-li-ang'*/ *n* sorghum grain of several varieties; an alcoholic drink made from it. [Chin *gāoliǎng* tall grain]

kaolin or **kaoline** /*kä'ō*- or *kä'ə-lin*/ *n* china clay, *esp* that composed of kaolinite. [From the mountain *gāolǐng* (literally, high mountain) in Jiangxi province, China]
■ **kaolin'ic** *adj*. **ka'olinite** *n* a hydrated aluminium silicate occurring in minute monoclinic flakes, a decomposition product of feldspar, etc. **kaolinit'ic** *adj*. **ka'olinize** or **-ise** *vt* and *vi* to turn into kaolin. **kaolinō'sis** *n* a disease caused by inhaling kaolin dust.

kaon /*kä'on*/ (*phys*) *n* one of several types of subatomic particle of smaller mass than a proton (see **meson**). [*K* (pronounced /*kā*/) and mes*on*]

kapellmeister /*kə-pel'mī-stər*/ *n* the director of an orchestra or choir, *esp* formerly in the household of a German prince. [Ger *Kapelle* chapel, orchestra, and *Meister* master]

kaph /*kaf*/ *n* the eleventh letter of the Hebrew alphabet. [Heb]

kapok /*kä'* or *kä'pok*/ *n* very light, waterproof, oily fibre covering the seeds of a species of silk-cotton tree, used for stuffing pillows, life-belts, etc. [Malay *kāpoq*]

Kaposi's sarcoma /*ka-pō'sez* (or *kap'ə-sez*) *sär-kō'mə*/ *n* a form of cancer characterized by multiple malignant tumours, *esp* of the skin of the feet and legs, a common feature of AIDS and first described by Hungarian-born dermatologist Moritz *Kaposi* (1837–1902) (*abbrev* **KS**).

kappa /*kap'ə*/ *n* the tenth (earlier eleventh) letter of the Greek alphabet (Κ, κ); as a numeral κ' = 20, ͵κ = 20 000.

kaput or **kaputt** /*kə-pŭt'*/ (*inf*) *adj* ruined; broken; not working; smashed. [Ger]

kara /*kur'ə*/ *n* the steel bangle, signifying the unity of God, traditionally worn by Sikhs. [Punjabi]

karabiner /*ka-rə-bē'nər*/ (*mountaineering*) *n* a steel link with a spring clip in one side (also **carabin'er**). [Ger]

karahi /*kə-rī'*/ *n* a wok-like copper utensil used in Asian cookery; a dish prepared in this. [Hindi]

karait /*kä-rīt'*/ same as **krait**.

Karaite /*kā'rə-īt*/ *n* a member of a strict sect of Jews adhering to the literal interpretation of Scripture as against oral tradition. [Heb *qārā* to read]
■ **ka'raism** *n*.

karaka /*kə-rak'ə*/ *n* a New Zealand tree with edible orange fruit whose seeds are poisonous until treated. [Maori]

karakul or **caracul** /*kä'rə-kool* or -*kool'*/ *n* (often with *cap*) an Asiatic breed of sheep; a fur prepared from the skin of very young lambs of the Karakul or Bukhara breed; a cloth imitating it. [Russ *Kara Kul*, a lake near Bukhara, Uzbekistan]

karaoke /*kar-i-ō'kē*/ *n* the (*orig* Japanese) practice and entertainment, popular at public venues and parties, of singing pop songs to accompanying backing music provided (from a large pre-recorded selection similar to a jukebox system) by a **karaoke machine**, which also enables the singer, using a microphone, to follow the words on a screen. [Jap, literally, empty orchestra]
❑ **karaoke bar** *n* a bar equipped with a karaoke machine, providing karaoke entertainment.

karat a N American spelling of **carat**.

karate /*ka-rä'ti*/ *n* a traditional Japanese form of unarmed self-defence using blows and kicks, now a popular combative sport. [Jap, literally, empty hand]
■ **kara'teist** *n*. **kara'teka** *n* an expert in karate.
❑ **karate chop** *n* a sharp downward blow with the side of the hand. **kara'te-chop** *vt*.

Karen /*kə-ren'*/ *n* a member of a Thai people of E and S Burma (now Myanmar); their language. ◆ *adj* of the Karens or their language.
■ **Karenn'i** *n* (one of) a group of eastern Karen peoples whose women stretch their necks by wearing brass collars.

Karitane /ka-ri-tä'ni/ (NZ) adj (of a nurse, hospital, etc) trained, administered, etc according to the principles of the Royal New Zealand Society for the Health of Women and Children. [*Karitane*, town in the South Island of New Zealand]

karite /kär'i-ti/ n the shea tree. [Native African name]

kark or **cark** /kärk/ (Aust sl) vi (also with *it*) to break down; to die. [Origin uncertain]

Karling /kär'ling/ n and adj (a) Carolingian. [Ger *Karl* Charles, and patronymic sfx *-ing*]

karma /kär'mə or kur'mə/ (Hinduism and Buddhism) n the moral quality of a person's (or animal's) actions regarded as determining the nature of a future existence or incarnation; the concept of such transcendental retribution; the theory of inevitable consequence generally; fate, destiny. [Sans *karma* act]
■ **kar'mic** adj. **kar'mically** adv.

Karman vortex street /kär'mən vör'teks strēt/ (acoustics) n the regular vortex pattern behind an obstacle in a flow where vortices are generated and travel away from the object. [T von *Karman* (1881–1963), Hungarian-born American engineer]

Karmathian /kär-mä'thi-ən/ n a member of a pantheistic socialistic Muslim sect which arose about the close of the 9c. [*Karmat*, its founder]

karmic see under **karma**.

Karoo or **Karroo** /kä-roo'/ n a high inland pastoral tableland (S Afr; also without *cap*); a series of strata in S Africa of the Permian and Triassic periods (geol). [Believed to be of Khoikhoi origin]

karoshi /ka-rosh'ē/ n (in Japan) sudden death as a result of extreme overwork. [Jap]

kaross /kä-ros'/ n a S African garment of animal skins. [Perh a Khoikhoi modification of Du *kuras* cuirass]

karri /kar'ē/ n a W Australian gum tree (*Eucalyptus diversicolor*); its red timber. [From an Aboriginal language]

Karroo see **Karoo**.

karsey see **kazi**.

karst /kärst/ (geol) n rough limestone country with underground drainage (also adj). [From the *Karst* district, near Trieste]
■ **karst'ic** adj. **karstificā'tion** n the development of karstic features. **karst'ify** vt.

karsy see **kazi**.

kart /kärt/ n a go-kart (qv).
■ **kart'er** n. **kart'ing** n go-kart racing.

Kartell /kär-tel'/ n a German spelling of **cartel**.

kary- /ka-ri-/ or **karyo-** /ka-ri-ō- or ka-ri-o-/ (biol) combining form denoting nucleus. [Gr *karyon* kernel]
■ **karyog'amy** n the fusion of cell nuclei during fertilization. **kar'yogram** n a chromosome diagram or karyotype. **karyokinesis** /-kin-ē'sis/ n (Gr *kinēsis* movement) mitosis. **karyol'ogy** n the study of cell nuclei, and *esp* of chromosomes. **kar'yolymph** n a colourless, watery fluid, occupying most of the space inside the nuclear membrane; nuclear sap. **karyol'ysis** n the dissolution of the nucleus by disintegration of the chromatin; the gradual disappearance of the nucleus in a dead cell; the liquefaction of the nuclear membrane in mitosis. **kar'yon** n the cell nucleus. **kar'yoplasm** n the protoplasm of a cell nucleus. **kar'yosome** n a nucleus; an aggregation of chromatin; a type of nucleolus. **kar'yotin** n chromatin. **kar'yotype** n the appearance, number and arrangement of the chromosomes in the cells of an individual; a diagram or photograph of the chromosomes of a cell or cells. ◆ vt to investigate or determine the karyotype of. **karyotyp'ic** or **karyotyp'ical** adj.

karzy see **kazi**.

kasbah /kaz'bä/ n a castle or fortress in a N African town or the area round it, *esp* in Algiers (also **casbah**). [Ar dialect *kasba*]

kasha /kash'ə/ n a porridge or gruel-like dish made from crushed cereal, *usu* buckwheat. [Russ]

Kashmir /kash-mēr'/ n a region in the north-west of the Indian subcontinent; (without *cap*; *obs*; also /kash'/) same as **cashmere**.
■ **Kashmiri** /kash-mēr'i/ adj belonging to Kashmir. ◆ n a native or inhabitant of Kashmir; the Indic language spoken in this region.
❑ **Kashmir goat** n a Himalayan goat whose fine, soft wool is used to make cashmere.

Kashrut, Kashruth /kash-root'/ or **Kashrus** /kash-roos'/ n (also without *cap*) the Jewish system of dietary laws relating to the fitness and preparation of food; the condition of being suitable for ritual use. [Heb, fitness, from *kāshēr* (see **kosher**)]

kat¹ see **khat¹**.

kat² or **khat** /kät/ n the chief ancient Egyptian unit of weight, $\frac{1}{50}$ lb avoirdupois.

kat symbol : katal (SI unit).

kata /kat'a/ (karate) n a formal sequence of practice exercises and movements. [Jap]

katabasis /kə-tab'ə-sis/ n a going down; a military retreat. [Gr]
■ **katabatic** /-ə-bat'ik/ adj (of a wind) blowing down a slope, because of air density differences resulting from overnight cooling, etc.

katabolism see **catabolism**.

katabothron /kat-ə-both'ron/ or **katavothron** /ka-tav'o-thron/ n an underground water channel. [Mod Gr *katabothron*, from Gr *kata* down, and *bothros* hole]

katadromous same as **catadromous**.

katakana /kat-ə-kä'nə/ n one of the two syllabic writing systems in Japanese, based on cursive Chinese ideograms, and used for loan words from languages other than Chinese. [Jap; cf **kana**]

katal /kat'l/ n a derived SI unit, the unit of catalytic activity (symbol **kat**), equal to one mole per second. [Appar from Gr *katalysis* catalysis]

katana /kə-tä'nə/ (Jap) n a long single-edged samurai sword, slightly curved towards the tip. [Jap]

katathermometer /ka-tə-thər-mom'i-tər/ n an alcohol thermometer for measuring the cooling power of the air. [Gr *kata* down, and **thermometer**]

katavothron see **katabothron**.

kathak /kə-thäk'/ n (also with *cap*) a classical dance of N India in which brief passages of mime alternate with rapid, rhythmic dance. [Sans, a professional storyteller, from *katha* story]

kathakali /kä-tə-kä'li, also -thə-/ n (also with *cap*) a classical dance drama of S India. [Malayalam, drama]

katharevousa /ka-thə-rev'ŭ-sə/ n a formal archaizing written form of Modern Greek, based on Ancient Greek. [Mod Gr *kathareuousa*, fem prp of Ancient Gr *kathareuein* to be pure, from *katharos* pure]

katharometer /ka-thə-rom'i-tər/ n an instrument for analysing the concentration of gases by measuring heat loss. [Gr *katharos* pure, and **-meter**]

katharsis same as **catharsis** (see under **cathartic**).

kathode same as **cathode**.

kati see **catty**.

kation see **cation**.

katipo /kat'i-pō/ n a venomous NZ spider. [Maori]

katorga /kä'tər-gə/ (Russ) n penal servitude, hard labour, *esp* in the labour camps of Joseph Stalin.

katti see **catty**.

katydid /kä'ti-did/ n a N American insect related to the grasshopper. [Imit of its distinctive sound]

katzenjammer /kat'sən-jam-ər or -jam'/ (N Am) n a hangover; a similar state of emotional distress; an uproar, clamour. [Ger, literally, cats' misery]

kaugh see **kiaugh**.

kaumatua /kow-mä'too-ə/ (NZ) n a Maori elder. [Maori]

kauri /kow'ri/ or **kauri-pine** /-pīn/ n a tall coniferous forest-tree of New Zealand (*Agathis australis*), source of **kauri gum**, a resin used in making varnish; the timber of this tree. [Maori]

kava /kä'və/ n an aromatic plant of the pepper family (*Piper methysticum*); a narcotic drink prepared from its root and stem (also **a'va**). [Polynesian]

kaval /kə-val'/ n an end-blown flute with eight fingerholes, common in Balkan folk music. [Bulg, from Turk *kav* hollow]

kavass /kä- or ke-väs' or -vas'/ n an armed servant in Turkey (also **cavass'**). [Ar *qawwās*]

kaw see **caw**.

kawaii /ka-wī'ē/ adj (in Japanese culture) the quality of being cute (also adj). [Jap]

kawakawa /kä'wə-kä-wə/ n a New Zealand shrub (*Macropiper excelsum*) with aromatic leaves. [Maori]

Kawasaki disease /kä-wə- or kow-ə-sä'ki di-zēz'/ n a disease of unknown origin in young children, causing a rash and fever and sometimes damaging the heart. [T *Kawasaki*, 20c Japanese physician]

kay¹ /kā/ n the eleventh letter of the modern English alphabet (K or k).

kay² see **quay**.

kayak /kī'ak/ n an Inuit seal-skin canoe; a canvas, fibreglass, etc canoe built in this style. ◆ vi to travel or race in a kayak. [Inuit]
■ **kay'aker** n. **kay'aking** n.

kayle same as **kail¹**.

■ words derived from main entry word; ❑ compound words; ■ idioms and phrasal verbs

kayo or **KO** /kā-ō'/ (*sl*) *n* (*pl* **kayos'**, **kayoes'** or **KOs**) and *vt* (*pat* and *pap* **kayoed'** or **Ko'd'**) knockout, knock out.
■ **kayo'ing** *n*.

kazachoc /ka-zə-chok'/ *n* a Russian folk dance in which high kicks are performed from a squatting position. [Russ, dimin of *kazak* a Cossack]

Kazak, Kazakh /kə-zäk' or kaz'ak/ or **Kazakhstani** /kaz'ak-stän-i/ *n* a member of a Turko-Tatar people of central Asia; the Turkic dialect spoken by this people; a native or citizen of the Republic of Kazakhstan. ◆ *adj* of or relating to Kazakhstan, the Kazaks or their language. [Russ]

kazatzka /kə-zat'skə/ *n* a Slavic folk dance performed by a man and a woman. [Russ *kazachki* Cossack dances]

kazi, khazi, karzy, karsey or **karsy** /kä'zi/ (*sl*) *n* a lavatory (also **cars'ey**). [Said to be from Ital *casa* house or perh Ar *kursi* chair]

kazoo /kə-zoo'/ *n* a musical instrument consisting of a tube with a strip of catgut, plastic, etc, that makes a buzzing sound when hummed into (also **gazoo'** or **gazoo'ka**). [Prob imit]

KB *abbrev* : kilobyte(s) (also **Kb**); King's Bench.

KBE *abbrev* : Knight Commander of the (Order of the) British Empire.

kbyte (*comput*) *abbrev* : kilobyte.

KC *abbrev* : Kennel Club; King's Counsel.

Kc *abbrev* : Czech koruna (unit of currency).

kc *abbrev* : kilocycle(s).

kcal *abbrev* : kilocalorie(s).

KCB *abbrev* : Knight Commander of the (Order of the) Bath.

KCMG *abbrev* : Knight Commander of (the Order of) St Michael and St George.

KCVO *abbrev* : Knight Commander of the (Royal) Victorian Order.

KD *abbrev* : knocked down (*commerce*); Kuwaiti dinar (unit of currency).

KE *abbrev* : kinetic energy.

kea /kē'ə or kä'ə/ *n* a large New Zealand parrot. [Maori]

keasar see **kaiser**.

keavie see **cavie**.

keb /keb/ (*Scot*) *vi* to give birth to a premature or stillborn lamb. ◆ *n* a ewe giving birth to such a lamb. [Cf Ger *Kibbe, Kippe* ewe]

kebab /ki-bab'/ *n* (also **kabab, kabob** /-bob'/, **kebob** or **cabob**; also used in *pl*) small pieces of meat cooked with vegetables, etc; (in full **shish kebab** /shish/; Turk *sis* skewer) such a dish prepared and served on a skewer; (in full **doner kebab** /don'ər or dō'nər/; Turk *döner* rotating) a dish of thin slices cut from a block of minced and seasoned lamb grilled on a spit, eaten in a split piece of unleavened bread. ◆ *vt* (*lit* and *fig*) to skewer. [Ar *kabab*]

kebbie /keb'i/ (*Scot*) *n* a shepherd's crook; a crook-handled walking-stick.

kebbock or **kebbuck** /keb'ək/ (*Scot*) *n* a cheese. [Origin unknown; Gaelic *cabag* (a cheese), may be derived from this word]

kebele /kə-bā'lā/ *n* a self-governing local district association found in Ethiopia (also **kabe'le** /kä-/). [From Amharic]

keblah see **kiblah**.

kebob see **kebab**.

keck¹ /kek/ *vi* to retch, feel sick; to feel disgust or loathing. ◆ *n* a retching. [Imit]

keck² see **kex**.

keckle¹ /kek'l/ *vt* to protect by binding with rope, etc. [Origin unknown]
■ **keck'ling** *n* rope, etc used to keckle cables or hawsers.

keckle² /kek'l/ (chiefly *Scot*) *vi* a variant of **cackle**.

kecks¹, kecksy see **kex**.

kecks² see **keks**.

ked /ked/ or **kade** /kād/ *n* a wingless fly (*Melophagus ovinus*) that infests sheep. [Origin unknown]

keddah see **kheda**.

kedge¹ /kej/ (*naut*) *n* a small anchor for keeping a ship steady, and for warping (qv) the ship. ◆ *vt* to move by means of a kedge, to warp. ◆ *vi* (of a ship) to move in this way. [Origin doubtful]
■ **kedg'er** *n* a kedge.

kedge² /kej/, also **kedgy** /kej'i/ or **kidge** /kij/ (*dialect*) *adj* brisk, lively; pot-bellied. [Cf **cadgy**]

kedgeree /kej'ə-rē/ *n* an Indian dish of rice, cooked with butter and dal, flavoured with spice, shredded onion, etc; a similar British dish made with rice, cooked fish and hard-boiled eggs. [Hindi *khichrī*]

keech /kēch/ (*Shakesp*) *n* a lump of fat. [Perh connected with **cake**]

keek /kēk/ (*Scot* and *N Eng*) *vi* to peep. ◆ *n* a peep. [ME *kyke*; cf Du *kijken*, Ger *kucken*]
■ **keek'er** *n* someone who peeps or spies; an inspector of coal; an eye; a black eye.
□ **keek'ing-glass** *n* a mirror.

keel¹ /kēl/ *n* the part of a ship extending along the bottom from stem to stern, and supporting the whole frame; a ship (*poetic*); a longitudinal member running along the underside of an airship's hull; any similar structure functioning like a ship's keel (*biol*); any narrow prominent ridge. ◆ *vt* or *vi* to turn keel upwards. [ON *kjölr*]
■ **keel'age** *n* dues for a keel or ship in port. **keeled** *adj* keel-shaped (*bot*); having a ridge on the back. **keel'less** *adj*.
□ **keel'boat** *n* a type of yacht with a heavy external keel providing weight to offset that of the sails; see also **keel²**. **keel'haul** *vt* to punish by hauling under the keel of a ship by ropes from the one side to the other; to rebuke severely. **keel'hauling** *n*.
■ **keel over** (of a ship) to capsize; to stagger or fall over. **on an even keel** balanced, not tilting to one side or the other (often *fig*); (of eg business affairs) running smoothly, settled or well-organized.

keel² /kēl/ *n* a low flat-bottomed boat, a barge (also **keel'boat**). [MDu *kiel* ship, cognate with OE *cēol* ship]
■ **keel'er** or **keel'man** *n* someone who works on a barge.

keel³ /kēl/ (*Shakesp*) *vt* to cool. [OE *cēlan* to chill]

keel⁴ /kēl/ (*Scot*) *n* red ochre, ruddle. ◆ *vt* to mark with ruddle. [Origin obscure; Gaelic *cilic* (ruddle), may be from this word]

keelie /kē'li/ (*Scot*) *n* the kestrel or other hawk; an urban tough, *esp* from Glasgow; a boorish lower-class youth or man. [Of uncertain origin; some connect with **gillie**]

keeling /kē'ling/ (*Scot*) *n* a codfish. [Origin unknown]

keelivine or **keelyvine** /kē'li-vīn/ (*Scot*) *n* a lead pencil. [Perh **keel⁴**, but ety uncertain]

keelson /kel' or kēl'sən/ or **kelson** /kel'sən/ *n* a ship's inner keel, which binds the floor timbers to the outer keel. [LGer *kielswīn* keel swine]

keelyvine see **keelivine**.

keema /kē'mə/ (*Ind cookery*) *n* minced beef. [Hindi]

keen¹ /kēn/ *adj* eager; sharp, having a fine edge; piercing; having an acute or penetrating mind; intense; competitive, low (eg of prices); very good, wonderful (*inf*, *esp N Am*). ◆ *vt* to sharpen. [OE *cēne* bold, fierce, keen; cf Ger *kühn* bold, and ON *kœnn* expert]
■ **keen'ly** *adv*. **keen'ness** *n*.
■ **keen on** (*inf*) devoted to; fond of; very interested in, *esp* romantically or sexually; very desirous of.

keen² /kēn/ *n* a lamentation over the dead. ◆ *vi* to wail over the dead. [Ir *caoine*]
■ **keen'er** *n* a professional mourner. **keen'ing** *n* wailing, lamentation.

keep /kēp/ *vt* (**keep'ing; kept** /kept/) to tend, look after; to have or take care or charge of; to guard; to maintain; to manage, conduct, run; to attend to the making of records in; to retain; to retain as one's own; to have in one's custody; to store customarily in a specified place; to have habitually in stock for sale; to support financially, or otherwise supply with necessaries; to have in one's service; to remain in or on (a place or position); to adhere to; to associate with; to continue to follow or hold to; to continue to make; to maintain a hold on or of; to restrain from leaving, to hold back; to prevent; to reserve or withhold; not to divulge (a secret); to be faithful to (a promise); to preserve or cause to remain in a certain state; to observe, celebrate; to conform to the requirements of, to fulfil. ◆ *vi* to remain; to continue to be or go; to be or remain in a specified condition; to remain fresh or good; to last or endure; to be capable of being reserved; to continue; to lodge or reside (*Cambridge University* and *US*); to refrain; to confine or restrict oneself; to keep wicket. ◆ *n* something kept, one's charge (*Spenser*); something that keeps, contains or protects; food, means of subsistence, board; the innermost and strongest part of a castle, the central tower; a stronghold. [OE *cēpan*]
■ **keep'able** *adj*. **keep'er** *n* someone who or something that keeps, in any sense; an attendant in charge of animals in captivity; a custodian of a museum or gallery; a prison guard; a gamekeeper; the title of certain officials, such as *Lord Keeper (of the Great Seal)*, whose office since 1757 has been merged in that of Lord Chancellor; a wicketkeeper; a goalkeeper; a man who keeps a mistress (*obs*); the socket that receives the bolt of a lock; the armature of a magnet; a guard ring; (*inf*, chiefly *US*) a person or thing worth holding on to. **keep'erless** *adj*. **keep'ership** *n* the office of a keeper. **keep'ing** *n* care, custody, charge; preservation; reservation; retention; observance, compliance; just proportion; harmonious consistency; maintenance of, or as, a mistress; maintenance, support (*Shakesp*).
□ **keep fit** *n* a programme of physical exercises designed to keep the muscles, circulation and respiratory system in good condition. **keep-fit'** *adj*. **keep'ing-room** *n* (*dialect*) a sitting room, parlour. **keep'net** *n*

a cone-shaped net suspended in a river, etc, in which fish caught by anglers can be kept alive. **keep'sake** *n* something given, or kept, as a reminder of the giver, or a certain event, time, etc; an annual gift-book (such as *The Keepsake* itself, 1827–56). ◆ *adj* (also **keep'saky**) vapidly pretty. **keep'y-upp'y** *n* the feat of keeping a football from touching the ground by repeatedly flicking it upwards using the foot, knee or head. **kept man** or (*fem*) **kept woman** *n* a man or woman maintained financially by a romantic or sexual partner.

■ **for keeps** for good; permanently; with serious intent. **how are you keeping?** how are you? **in keeping with** in accord with, suitable to. **keep an act** formerly, to hold an academic debate. **keep at** to persist in (anything); to nag, badger (someone to do something) (*inf*). **keep a term** see under **term**. **keep back** to withhold; to keep down, repress. **keep body and soul together** to stay alive. **keep cave**, **company and counsel** see under **cave**², etc. **keep down** to remain low or out of sight; to restrain, repress; to retain (food) in the stomach, not to vomit; to set in lower-case type, avoiding capitals. **keep from** to abstain from; to remain away from. **keep good hours** see under **hour**. **keep house** see under **house**. **keep in** to prevent from escaping; to confine in school after school hours; to conceal; to restrain. **keep in with** to maintain the confidence or friendship of. **keep off** to hinder or prevent from approaching or making an attack, etc; to stay away or refrain from; (of rain, etc) not to start. **keep on** to continue; to retain, continue to employ. **keep on about** to continue talking about. **keep on at** (*inf*) to nag, badger. **keep one's breath to cool one's porridge** to hold one's peace when further talk is clearly in vain. **keep one's countenance** to avoid showing one's emotions. **keep one's distance** see under **distance**. **keep (oneself) to oneself** to avoid the company of others. **keep one's eye on** see under **eye**¹. **keep one's hand in** to retain one's skill by practice. **keep one's head down** to avoid attracting attention to oneself. **keep one's mind on** to concentrate on. **keep one's powder dry** see under **powder**. **keep out** to remain outside; to exclude. **keep someone going in something** to keep someone supplied with something. **keep tabs on** to keep a check on, to keep account of. **keep the peace** see under **peace**. **keep time** to observe rhythm accurately, or along with others; (of a clock or watch) to go accurately. **keep to** to stick closely to; to confine oneself to. **keep under** to hold down in restraint. **keep up** to retain (one's strength or spirit); to support, prevent from falling; to continue, to prevent from ceasing; to maintain in good condition; to continue to be in touch (with); to keep pace (with); to stop, stay (*obs*). **keep up with the Joneses** to keep on an equal social footing with one's neighbours, eg by having possessions of the same quality in the same quantity. **keep wicket** to act as a wicketkeeper.

keeshond /kās'hond or -hont/ *n* a medium-sized dog of the spitz type. [Du, from *kees* terrier, and *hond* dog]

keeve or **kieve** /kēv/ *n* a large tub. [OE *cȳf* vat]

kef /kāf/, **kaif** /kīf/ or **kif** /kif or kēf/ *n* a state of dreamy repose; a drug such as marijuana, smoked to produce this state. [Ar *kaif* pleasure]

keffel /kef'l/ (*dialect*) *n* a horse, nag. [Welsh *ceffyl*; cf **caple**]

keffiyeh see **kaffiyeh**.

kefir or **kephir** /kef'ər/ *n* an effervescent drink made from fermented cow's milk. [Native name in the Caucasus]

keftedes /kef-tedh'ēz/ *n pl* a Greek dish of meatballs made with onions and herbs. [Mod Gr *kephtedes*, pl of *kephtes* pounded meat]

kefuffle see **carfuffle**.

keg /keg/ *n* a small cask; a metal cask in which beer is kept under gas pressure. [Earlier *cag*, from ON *kaggi*]
■ **kegg'er** *n* (*US inf*) a drinking party at which a keg of beer is consumed.
□ **keg beer** *n* any of various types of beer kept in and served from pressurized kegs.

Kegel exercises /kā'gəl ek'sər-sī-ziz/ or **Kegels** /kā'gəlz/ *n pl* exercises for strengthening the pelvic floor muscles, used as a method of controlling incontinence, eg after childbirth. [Arnold *Kegel*, 20c US gynaecologist]

keight /kīt/ (*Spenser*) *vt* for **caught** (*pat* of **catch**).

keir see **kier**.

keiretsu /kā-ret'soo/ (*commerce*) *n* (*pl* **keiret'su**) (in Japan) a group of industrial companies acting in collaboration. [Jap]

keirin /kā'rin/ *n* an 8-lap track cycling event in which the riders follow a motorcycle pacer for the first 5½ laps, sprinting the remaining 2½ laps after the motorcycle has pulled off the track (also **kei'ren**). [Jap]

keister /kē'stər/ (*US sl*) *n* the buttocks, arse; a safe or strong-box; a case or box. [Prob Ger *Kiste* chest, case]

keitloa /kāt'lō-ə/ *n* a two-horned rhinoceros. [Tswana *kgetlwa*]

keks or **kecks** /keks/ (*inf*) *n pl* trousers. [Orig dialect, also attested as *kicks* (pl of **kick**)]

keksye see **kex**.

kelim see **kilim**.

kell /kel/ (*Scot* and *N Eng*) *n* a woman's headdress or hairnet; a film or membrane; a caul. [**caul**]

kellaut see **killut**.

kelly /kel'i/ *n* (in drilling processes) the top pipe of a rotary string of drill pipes, with which is incorporated a flexibly attached swivel through which mud is pumped to the bottom of the hole. [Origin uncertain]

keloid or **cheloid** /kē'loid/ *n* a hard growth of scar tissue in skin that has been injured. [Gr *chēlē* claw]
■ **keloid'al** or **cheloid'al** *adj*.

kelp /kelp/, also sometimes **kilp** /kilp/ *n* any large brown seaweed, wrack; the calcined ashes of seaweed, a source of soda, iodine, etc. [ME *culp*; origin unknown]
■ **Kel'per** *n* (also without *cap*) an inhabitant of the Falkland Islands. ◆ *adj* of or relating to the Falkland Islands.

kelpie or **kelpy** /kel'pi/ *n* a malignant water sprite haunting fords in the form of a horse (*Scot*; *folklore*); an Australian breed of sheepdog. [Origin uncertain]

kelson see **keelson**.

Kelt, etc see **Celt**.

kelt¹ /kelt/ *n* a salmon, etc that has just spawned. [Origin unknown]

kelt² /kelt/ (*Scot*) *n* coarse cloth *usu* made of black and white wool mixed and not dyed. [Origin obscure]
■ **kelt'er** *n* and *adj*.

kelter¹ see **kilter**.

kelter² see under **kelt**².

keltie or **kelty** /kel'ti/ (*Scot*) *n* a bumper or glass filled to the brim, *esp* one imposed as a penalty on someone who does not drain his glass completely.

Kelvin /kel'vin/ *adj* applied to a thermometer scale with absolute zero for zero and centigrade degrees, in which the triple point of water is exactly 273.16K. [Sir William Thomson, Lord *Kelvin* (1824–1907), physicist]
■ **kel'vin** *n* a base SI unit, the unit of thermodynamic temperature (symbol **K**), defined as $\frac{1}{273.16}$ of the thermodynamic temperature of the triple point of water (formerly called **degree Kelvin**); a kilowatt-hour (*rare*).

kemb /kem/ (*obs* and *dialect*) *vt* to comb. [OE *cemban*]
■ **kempt** /kemt or kempt/ *adj* combed; tidy.

kembo same as **kimbo**.

kemp¹ /kemp/ *n* a coarse, rough strand of wool; (in *pl*) knotty hair that will not felt. [ON *kampr* beard]
■ **kem'py** *adj*.

kemp² /kemp/ (*Scot* and *N Eng*) *n* a champion (*archaic*); a contest in reaping or other work. ◆ *vi* to strive for mastery. [OE *cempa* a warrior; cf **champion**]
■ **kem'per** *n* (also **kem'pery-man**) a champion, a knight errant. **kemp'ing** *n*.

kemple /kem'pl/ (*Scot*) *n* forty bundles of hay or straw. [Origin obscure]

kempt see under **kemb**.

Ken. *abbrev*: Kentucky (US state).

ken¹ /ken/ *vt* (*pat* and *pap* **kenned** or **kent**) to know (chiefly *Scot*); to see and recognize at a distance (*archaic*); to cause to know, direct (*obs*). ◆ *n* range of sight or knowledge. [OE *cennan*, causative of *cunnan*, and ON *kenna*; cf **can**¹, **con**²]
■ **kenn'er** *n*. **kenn'ing** *n* range of vision; a small portion, a little bit (*Scot*); a periphrastic formula in Old Norse or other old Germanic poetry. **ken-no** /ken'ə/ *n* (*Scot*, literally, know not) a cheese prepared in ostensible secrecy for the gossips at a birth. **kent** *adj* known.
■ **beyond one's ken** outside the limits of one's knowledge.

ken² /ken/ (*sl*) *n* a house, *esp* a disreputable one. [Perh Pers *khān* a caravanserai, or **kennel**¹; or connected with preceding word]

kenaf /kə-naf'/ *n* a tropical Asian herbaceous plant, the jute-like fibres of which can be used as a substitute for wood pulp in paper-making. [Pers]

Kendal green /ken'dl grēn/ *n* green cloth for foresters made at *Kendal* in Cumbria.

kendo /ken'dō or -dō'/ *n* the Japanese art of swordsmanship practised with bamboo staves, in 18c-style armour, and observing strict ritual. [Jap *kendō* way of the sword]

kennel¹ /ken'l/ *n* a house for a dog or dogs; a pack of hounds; the hole of a fox, etc; a hovel; (in *pl*) an establishment where dogs are boarded or bred. ◆ *vt* (**kenn'elling**; **kenn'elled**) to put or keep in a kennel. ◆ *vi* to live in a kennel. [From an ONFr form corresponding to Fr *chenil*, from L *canīle*, from *canis* a dog]

❑ **kenn'elmaid** or **kenn'elman** n a female or male attendant who looks after dogs.

kennel² /ken'l/ n a street gutter. [ME *canel*, from ONFr *canel*, from L *canālis*; see **canal**]

kennel-coal same as **cannel**.

Kennelly-Heaviside layer or **region** /ken'ə-li-hev'i-sīd lā'ər or rē'jən/ n a strongly ionized region of the upper atmosphere about 60 miles up, in which wireless waves are deflected (also **Kennelly layer**, **Heaviside layer** and **E'-layer**). [AE *Kennelly* (1861–1939) and O *Heaviside* (1850–1925), who inferred its existence]

kenner see under **ken¹**.

kennet /ken'it/ (*obs*) n a small hunting dog. [ONFr *kennet* (dimin) from L *canis* dog]

Kennick /ken'ik/ n a name given to the jargon used by some travelling people. [Romany]

kenning, **ken-no** see under **ken¹**.

keno /kē'nō/ (*N Am, Aust*) n a gambling game similar to bingo. [Fr *quine* five winning numbers]

kenophobia /ken-ō-fō'bi-ə/ n a morbid fear of empty spaces. [Gr *kenos* empty, and **phobia**]

kenosis /ke-nō'sis/ (*theol*) n Christ's renunciation of divine attributes in order to identify with humanity. [Gr *kenōsis* emptying, from Bible, Philippians 2.7]

■ **kenotic** /-ot'ik/ adj. **kenot'icist** /-i-sist/ n a believer in kenosis.

Kensington /ken'zing-tən/ adj (of people) interested exclusively in an artificial city life and in material values. [Part of a London borough]

kent¹ /kent/ (*Scot*) n a long pole for punting or leaping ditches. ◆ vt and vi to punt or pole. [Cf **quant¹**]

kent² see **ken¹**.

kent-bugle /kent'bū'gl/ n an obsolete keybugle. [Supposed to be named after a Duke of Kent]

kente /ken'ti/ n a silk cloth made in Ghana by sewing together long narrow handwoven strips (also called **kente cloth**). [Origin uncertain]

Kentia /ken'ti-ə/ (also without *cap*) n a name formerly applied to many pinnate varieties of palm, but now only to the Howea feather palm. [W *Kent* (died in 1820s), Dutch botanist]

Kentish /kent'ish/ adj of or relating to the English county of *Kent*. ◆ n the dialect of Kent, Essex, etc.
❑ **Kentish fire** n synchronized volleys of applause (probably from anti-Catholic demonstrations in Kent, 1828–9). **Kentish glory** n a moth (*Endromis versicolora*), the male of which has orange hindwings. **Kent'ish-man** n a native of W Kent (one born east of the Medway being a **Man of Kent**). **Kentish rag** or **Kentish ragstone** n a rough limestone from the Lower Greensand of Kent.

kentledge /kent'lij/ n pig iron in a ship's hold for ballast (also **kint'ledge**). [Origin unknown]

Kenyan /ken'yən or kēn'/ adj of or relating to the E African republic of *Kenya* or its inhabitants. ◆ n a native or inhabitant of Kenya.

Kenyapithecus /kē'nyə-pith'ə-kəs or ken'yə-/ n a lower Pliocene genus of fossil anthropoid ape; an example of this genus, first discovered by LSB Leakey in Kenya in 1961. [*Kenya*, and Gr *pithēkos* ape]

kep /kep/ (*Scot* and *N Eng*) vt (*pap* and *pat* **kepp'it**) to catch (an approaching object or falling liquid). ◆ n a catch; an act or opportunity of catching. [**keep**]

kephalic /ki-fal'ik/ same as **cephalic** (see under **cephal-**).

kephalin see **cephalin** under **cephal-**.

kephir see **kefir**.

kepi /kā'pē/ n a flat-topped French military cap with a straight peak. [Fr *képi*]

Keplerian /kep-lē'ri-ən/ adj relating to or associated with the German astronomer Johann *Kepler* (1571–1630).

keppit see **kep**.

kept *pat* and *pap* of **keep**.

keramic /ki-ram'ik/ a rarer form of **ceramic**.

keratin /ker'ə-tin/ n a nitrogenous compound, the essential ingredient of horny tissue, the substance of horns, nails, etc. [Gr *keras*, *-atos* a horn]
■ **keratinizā'tion** or **-s-** n the formation of keratin; a becoming keratinous. **ker'atinize** or **-ise** vt and vi to make or become keratinous. **kerat'inocyte** (also /-ə-tin'/) n a skin cell which produces keratin. **keratinous** /kə-rat'i-nəs/ adj horn-like; horny. **kerati'tis** n inflammation of the cornea. **keratogenous** /-oj'i-nəs/ adj producing horn or keratin. **ker'atoid** adj resembling horn or keratin. **keratom'eter** n an instrument for measuring the curvature of the cornea. **keratomileusis** /-mī-lū'sis/ n (Gr *mileusis* shaping) the surgical reshaping of the cornea to correct defective vision.

ker'atōplasty n grafting of part of a healthy cornea to replace a piece made opaque by disease, etc. **ker'atose** adj (*esp* of certain sponges) having a horny skeleton. **keratō'sis** n (*pl* **keratoses** /-sēz/) a horny growth on or over the skin, eg a wart; a skin condition producing this. **keratot'omy** n surgery of the cornea.

keratophyre /ker'ə-tō-fīr/ (*petrology*) n a fine-grained soda trachyte. [Gr *keras*, *-atos* horn, and *-phyre* from **porphyry**]

keraunograph /kə-rö'nō-gräf/ n an instrument for recording distant thunderstorms. [Gr *keraunos* a thunderbolt, and *graphein* to write]

kerb or (*esp N Am*) **curb** /kûrb/ n a kerbstone, pavement edge; a kerb market; an edging or margin of various kinds. ◆ adj (of a market, of dealing, etc) unofficial, outside official trading hours. [Fr *courbe*, from L *curvus* bent]
❑ **kerb'-crawler** n someone who drives along slowly with the intention of enticing people into the car, *usu* for sexual purposes. **kerb'-crawling** n. **kerb drill** n the procedure for crossing a road safely, recommended for pedestrians. **kerb'-market** n a market in stocks operating separately from the Stock Exchange, *orig* on the pavement. **kerb'-merchant**, **-trader** or **-vendor** n a person who sells on or beside the pavement. **kerb'side** n (also adj). **kerb'stone** n a stone placed edgeways as an edging to a path or pavement. **kerb'stone-broker** n one outside the Stock Exchange. **kerb weight** n the weight (of a car) without passengers and luggage.

kerchief /kûr'chif/ n a square piece of cloth worn to cover the head, neck, etc; a handkerchief (*old*). ◆ vt to cover with a kerchief. [OFr *cuevrechief* (Fr *couvrechef*), from *covrir* to cover, and *chef* the head]
■ **ker'chiefed** adj.

ker-ching /kər-ching'/ interj an exclamation indicating that money is being made or is to be made. ◆ adj involving the making of money. [Imit of the sound made by a cash register]

kerf /kûrf/ n a cut; a notch; the groove made by a saw; a cut place, the face of a cut; a quantity cut at once, as of wool, etc; a single layer of hay, turf, etc cut. [OE *cyrf* a cut]

kerfuffle see **carfuffle**.

Kerguelen cabbage /kûr'gə-lən kab'ij/ n a wind-pollinated plant (*Pringlea antiscorbutica*) related to the cabbage, growing on Kerguelen and nearby islands in the S Indian Ocean.

kerma /kûr'mə/ (*radiol*) n the initial energy, measured in grays, of all the charged ionizing particles released by an uncharged ionizing particle in a given mass of tissue. [*kinetic energy released in material* (or *matter*)]

kermes /kûr'mēz/ n the female bodies of a coccus insect (*Kermes* (or *Coccus*) *ilicis*), used as a red dyestuff; the oak (**kermes oak**; *Quercus coccifera*) on which they breed; a cherry-red mineral, antimony oxysulphide (also **kermes mineral** or **ker'mesite**). [Pers and Ar *qirmiz*]

kermesse /kûr'mis/ n a cycle race held in an urban area. [Flem *kermesse* kermis]

kermis or **kirmess** /kûr'mis/ n a fair in the Low Countries; in N America, an indoor fair, *usu* for charity. [Du *kermis*, from *kerk* church, and *mis* mass]

kern¹ /kûrn/ (*printing*) n part of a type that projects beyond the body and rests on an adjoining letter. ◆ vt to give (a typeface) a kern; to adjust (*esp* by reduction) the space between characters in (a typeface or piece of writing). [Fr *carne* a projecting angle, from L *cardō*, *-inis*]
■ **kern'ing** n.

kern² or **kerne** /kûrn/ n an Irish or highland foot soldier (*hist*); a troop of such (*hist*); a peasant, a boor (*obs*). [From Ir, from Olr; see **cateran**]
■ **ker'nish** adj.

kern³ see **kirn¹**.

kern⁴ /kûrn/ vi to granulate. [Cf **corn¹**]

kernel /kûr'nl/ n a seed within a hard shell; the edible part of a nut; a gland (*rare*); a nucleus; the important, central part of anything. ◆ vi (*rare*) to form kernels. [OE *cyrnel*, from *corn* grain, and dimin sfx *-el*; Ger *Kern* a grain]
■ **ker'nelly** adj full of, or resembling, kernels.

kernicterus /kûr-nik'tə-rəs/ (*pathol*) n a condition of acute neural dysfunction linked with high levels of bilirubin in the blood. [Ger *Kern* nucleus, and Gr *ikteros* jaundice]

kernish see under **kern²**.

kernite /kûrn'īt/ n hydrated oxide of sodium and boron. [*Kern* County, California, where it was discovered]

kero /ker'ō/ (*Aust* and *NZ inf*) n a short form of **kerosene**.

kerogen /ker'ə-jen/ n the organic matter in oil-shale that yields oil on distillation. [Gr *kēros* wax, and root of *gennaein* to generate]

kerosene, also (*esp* in technical use) **kerosine** /ker'ə-sēn/ n paraffin oil obtained from shale or by distillation of petroleum; paraffin (*N Am*). [Gr *kēros* wax]

Kerr effect /kûr'i-fekt'/ (*phys*) *n* one of two effects relating to the optical properties of matter in electric and magnetic fields, the **electro-optical effect** causing some liquids and gases to become double refracting in certain circumstances, the **magneto-optical effect** producing an elliptic polarization in certain circumstances. [J *Kerr* (1824–1907), Scottish physicist]

Kerria /ker'i-ə/ *n* a plant genus comprising a single species, the deciduous yellow-flowering shrub, Jew's mallow; (without *cap*) a plant of this genus. [William *Kerr*, late 18c-early 19c English gardener]

Kerry blue (**terrier**) /ker'i bloo (ter'i-ər)/ *n* a breed of Irish terrier with a long, silky, bluish coat.

kersantite /kûr'sən-tīt/ *n* a dyke rock of black mica and plagioclase. [From *Kersanton*, in Brittany]

kersey /kûr'zi/ *n* a coarse woollen cloth. [Perh from *Kersey* in Suffolk]

kerseymere /kûr'zi-mēr or -mēr'/ *n* a twilled cloth of very fine wool. [For **cassimere**, **cashmere**]

kerve /kûrv/ (*Spenser*) *vt* a variant of **carve**.

kerygma /kə-rig'mə/ (*theol*) *n* (preaching of) the Christian gospel, *esp* in the way of the early Church. [Gr *kērygma* proclamation, preaching] ■ **kerygmat'ic** *adj*.

kesar see **kaiser**.

kesh /kāsh/ *n* the uncut hair and beard traditionally worn by Sikhs. [Punjabi]

kest /kest/ an obsolete variant of **cast**.

kestrel /kes'trəl/ *n* a small species of falcon. [OFr *cresserelle*]

ket[1] /ket/ (*Scot*) *n* carrion. [ON *kjöt*]

ket[2] /ket/ (*Scot*) *n* matted wool. [Anglo-Fr *cot*]

ket- see **keto-**.

keta /kē'tə/ *n* a Pacific salmon, the dog-salmon. [Russ *keta*]

ketamine /ket'ə-mēn or kēt'/ *n* an anaesthetic and analgesic drug (also called (*drug sl*) **Special K**). [**ket-**]

ketch[1] /kech/ *n* a small two-masted sailing vessel, the foremast being the taller. [Earlier *catch*, perh from the verb **catch**]

ketch[2] /kech/ an obsolete variant of **catch**.

ketchup /kech'əp/ *n* a smooth, thick sauce made from tomatoes, mushrooms, etc (also **catch'up** or **cat'sup**). [Malay *kēchap*, perh from Chin]

keto- /kē-tō-/ or **ket-** /kēt-/ *combining form* denoting a ketone compound or derivative. ■ **ke'tene** *n* a highly reactive colourless toxic gas (CH$_2$CO).

ketone /kē'tōn/ *n* an organic compound consisting of a carbonyl group united to two like or unlike alkyl radicals. [Ger *Keton*, from *Aketon* acetone] ■ **ketonaemia** or (*US*) **ketonemia** /-ē'mi-ə/ *n* (*med*) the presence of ketone bodies in the blood, as in diabetes. **ketonic** /ki-ton'ik/ *adj*. **kētonu'ria** *n* the excretion of urine with an abnormally high number of ketone bodies, *esp* as a symptom of diabetes mellitus. **ke'tose** *n* any of a class of monosaccharide sugars that contain a ketone group. **ketō'sis** *n* the excessive formation in the body of ketone bodies, due to incomplete oxidation of fats, as occurs in eg diabetes. **ketot'ic** *adj*. ❑ **ketone body** *n* any of three compounds that are produced when fatty acids are broken down in the liver.

ketoprofen /kē-tō-prō'fən/ *n* a non-steroidal anti-inflammatory drug.

kettle[1] /ket'l/ *n* a container for boiling water, with a spout, a lid and a handle; a metal container for heating liquids or cooking something in liquid; a kettle hole (*geol*); an enclosed area created by cordons of police officers to control public protesters; a kettledrum (*Shakesp*). [ON *ketill*; OE *cetel*, Ger *Kessel*, Gothic *katils*; all perh from L *catillus*, dimin of *catīnus* a deep cooking vessel] ◆ *vt* to contain (protesters) in an enclosed area. ■ **kett'leful** *n*. **kett'ling** *n*. ❑ **kett'ledrum** *n* (*music*) a percussion instrument, consisting of a hollow metal hemisphere with a parchment head, tuned by screws which adjust the tension. **kett'ledrummer** *n*. **kett'le-holder** *n* a cloth, etc for lifting a hot kettle. **kettle hole** *n* (*geol*) a circular hollow in rock caused by the melting of a trapped block of ice. **kett'lestitch** *n* (*bookbinding*) the stitch that is made at the head and tail of each section of a book to interlock the sections. ■ **a kettle of fish** a situation, set of circumstances, *esp* in the ironic phrase **a pretty kettle of fish** an awkward mess; *orig* a riverside picnic at which newly-caught salmon were cooked on the spot (*obs*).

kettle[2] see **kiddle**.

kettle-pins see **kittle-pins**.

Ketubah /ke-too-vä'/ *n* a formal Jewish marriage contract which couples sign before their wedding. [Heb *kethūbhāh* document]

Keuper /koi'pər/ (*geol*) *n* the uppermost division of the Trias (also *adj*). [Ger miners' term]

keV *abbrev* : kilo-electronvolt(s).

kevel /kev'l/ same as **cavel**.

Kevlar® /kev'lär/ *n* a lightweight synthetic fibre of exceptionally high strength and heat resistance, used in aerospace, firefighting equipment, etc.

kewpie doll /kū'pi dol/ *n* a plump baby doll with a topknot of hair. [**Cupid**]

kex /keks/ *n* (also **kecks**, and (false singulars) **keck**, **kecks'y** or **keks'ye**) a dry, often hollow, herbaceous (*usu* umbelliferous) stalk; any tall umbelliferous plant. [Origin unknown]

key[1] /kē, formerly kā/ *n* an instrument for locking or unlocking, winding up, turning, tuning, tightening or loosening; (in musical instruments) a lever or piston-end pressed to produce the sound; a similar lever for other purposes in machines, as in a typewriter, computer or calculator; a system of tones definitely related to one another in a musical scale; a keynote (*obs*); something that gives command of anything or upon which success turns; a scheme or diagram of explanation or identification; a taxonomic system for distinguishing similar species (*biol*); a set of answers to problems; a crib translation; a field or group of characters in each record used for sorting and retrieving (*comput*); that which leads to the solution of a problem; a leading principle; general tone of voice, emotion, morals, etc; a wedge; a peg inserted into eg a keyway to prevent relative motion; a tapered piece of metal for fixing the boss of a wheel, etc to a shaft; a spanner; the middle stone of an arch; a piece of wood let into another piece crosswise to prevent warping; a lever to close or break an electrical circuit; a dry winged fruit, eg of ash or maple, often hanging with others in bunches; a fret pattern; the preparation of a surface to take plaster, glue, etc. ◆ *vt* to provide with a key; to lock or fasten with a key (*obs*); to mark the position on the layout of (something to be printed), using symbols (*printing*); to keyboard; to stimulate (to a state of nervous tension and excitement), raise (in pitch or standard), or increase (with *up*). ◆ *vt* and *vi* to attune (with *to*); to prepare (a surface) eg for plastering; to give (an advertisement) a feature that will enable replies to it to be identified; to scratch (the paintwork of a car) using a key (*inf*). ◆ *adj* vital, essential, crucial. [OE *cæg*] ■ **keyed** *adj* equipped with a key or keys; set to a particular key (*music*); in a state of tension or readiness. **key'less** *adj* without a key or keys; not requiring a key.

❑ **key'board** *n* the manually operated range of keys or levers in a musical instrument, computer, etc (also *adj*); (often in *pl*) *usu* in pop groups, etc, a musical instrument, *esp* electronic, incorporating a keyboard. ◆ *vi* and *vt* to type text, etc by means of a keyboard, *esp* into a computer. **key'boarder** *n* someone who types text on a keyboard. **key'boardist** *n* a person who plays a keyboard instrument, *esp* an electronic one. **key'bugle** or **keyed bugle** *n* a bugle with keys, having a chromatic scale of two octaves. **key'card** *n* a small *usu* plastic card, either punched, having a magnetically coded strip or incorporating a microchip, that electronically operates a mechanism, eg a lock or a cash dispenser. **key'-cold** *adj* (*Shakesp*) cold as a key, lifeless. **key'-desk** *n* the frame enclosing the keyboards, stops, etc of an organ. **keyed bugle** see **keybugle**. **key'-fruit** *n* a winged fruit of a tree. **key grip** *n* the chief grip in a film crew. **key'hole** *n* the hole in which a key of a lock is inserted; any small hole similar in shape or purpose. **keyhole limpet** *n* a mollusc (genus *Fissurella*) with a perforated conical shell. **keyhole saw** *n* a padsaw (qv under **pad**[1]). **keyhole surgery** *n* surgery using endoscopes, etc, performed through small incisions. **key industry** *n* an industry indispensable to others and essential to national economic welfare and independence. **key light** *n* the main light in a TV or film studio or on a stage. **key'line** *n* (*printing*) an outline drawing showing the shape, size, position, etc of an illustration. **keylogging** see **keystroke logging** below. **key man** *n* an indispensable worker, essential to the continued conduct of a business, etc. **key money** *n* a premium, fine or sum additional to rent, demanded for the grant, renewal or continuance of a tenancy. **key'note** *n* the fundamental note or tonic (*music*); any central principle or controlling thought. ◆ *adj* of fundamental importance; (of a speech, etc) expounding the central principle, or setting the tone for a conference, etc. ◆ *vt* and *vi* to give the keynote; to put forward the central principle in an opening address at a convention. **key'pad** *n* a small device with push-button controls, eg a TV remote control unit or pocket calculator; a small keyboard with push-button controls for a specific purpose, eg a numeric keypad (*comput*). **key'pal** *n* (*inf*) a person who is mainly or only known to one as an email correspondent. **key'-plate** *n* a keyhole escutcheon. **key punch** *n* (*comput*) an obsolete device operated by a keyboard, which transfers data onto punch-cards, etc. **key'punch** *vt*. **key ring** *n* a ring for holding a bunch of keys. **key'-seat** *n* a groove for receiving a key, to prevent one piece of machinery from turning on another. **key signature** *n* (*music*) the indication of key by marking sharps, flats or naturals where the key changes or at the beginning of a line.

key stage n (educ) any of the four age-based levels of the National Curriculum in England and Wales. **key'stone** n the stone at the apex of an arch; the chief element; something on which all else depends. ♦ vt and vi to produce a **keystone effect**, ie the distortion of a television picture in which a rectangular pattern is transformed into a trapezoidal pattern. **key'stroke** n a single operation of a key on a typewriter or other machine using keys. **keystroke logging** or **key'logging** n the act of recording the keystrokes made by a computer user, eg to detect sources of error or for surveillance. **key'stroking** n. **key'way** n a groove cut in a shaft or boss to accommodate a key that interlocks with another component so as to prevent relative motion. **key'word** n a headword; a word serving as a key in an index, etc; a word that encapsulates the passage in which it appears; a group of letters or numbers that is used to identify a database record (comput). **key'word-in-context** adj applied to electronic concordances or indexes that supply the keywords alphabetically in a fixed position in the line, preceded and followed by a fixed amount of context. **key'worker** n a person working in the social services who takes responsibility for individual cases and projects. ■ **have the key of the door** (inf) to have reached the age of 21. **have the key of the street** (inf) to be locked out; to be homeless. **key in** (comput) to enter (data) by operating a keyboard. **out of key** out of tune; out of place, incongruous. **power of the keys** the power to loose and to bind, conferred by Christ on Peter (Bible, Matthew 16.19), and claimed by the popes.

key² an old spelling of **quay**.

key³ or **cay** /kē/ n a low island or reef. [Sp cayo]

Keynesian /kānz'i-ən/ adj relating to John Maynard Keynes (1883–1946) or to his economic teaching, esp his advocacy of a measure of public control, within capitalism, of the unrestricted play of economic forces both national and international. ♦ n someone who supports Keynesian financial policies.
■ **Keynes'ianism** n.

Keys /kēz/ n pl (in full **House of Keys**) the lower house of the Manx Court of Tynwald. [Appar **key¹**, not Manx kiare-as-feed four-and-twenty]

KFAT abbrev : formerly, (National Union of) Knitwear, Footwear and Apparel Trades.

KFOR /kā'för/ abbrev : Kosovo Force, a NATO-led peacekeeping force in Kosovo.

KG abbrev : Knight of the (Order of the) Garter.

kg abbrev : keg(s); kilogram(s), kilogramme(s).

kg symbol : kilogram, kilogramme (SI unit).

KGB abbrev : Komitet Gosudarstvennoi Bezopasnosti (Russ), Committee of State Security, the former Soviet secret police.

kgotla /hhö'tlə or kgot'lə/ n an assembly of tribal elders in Botswana; the place of such assembly. [Bantu]

kgy abbrev : kilogray(s).

khaddar /kud'ər/ or **khadi** /kud'i/ n (in India) hand-spun, hand-woven cloth. [Hindi khādar, khādī]

khaki /kä'ki/ adj dust-coloured, dull brownish or greenish yellow; militaristically imperialist (hist). ♦ adv (hist) with war-spirit. ♦ n a cloth of this colour used for military uniforms, etc. [Urdu and Pers khākī dusty]
□ **khaki election** n an election called immediately after a war, or at a time of patriotic military fervour.

khalat see **killut**.

khalif see **caliph**.

khalifa or **khalifah** /kä-lē'fä/ n a caliph; a Senussi leader; the Mahdi's successor. [Ar khalīfah]
■ **khalifat** /käl'i-fat/ or **khalifate** /-fāt/ n the caliphate.

Khalkha or **Khalka** /kal'kə/ n a dialect of Mongolian. [Native word]

Khalsa /kal'sə/ n the order of baptized Sikhs who wear the five Ks. [Hindi, pure]

khamsin, **kamsin** or **kamseen** /kam'sin or -sēn'/ n a hot south or south-east wind in Egypt, which blows for about fifty days from mid-March. [Ar khamsīn from khamsūn fifty]

khan¹ /kän/ n an Eastern inn, a caravanserai. [Ar khan]

khan² /kän/ n in Central Asia, (a title for) a prince or chief; in ancient Persia, (a title for) a governor. [Turki (and thence Pers) khān lord or prince]
■ **khan'ate** n the rank of a khan; a region governed by a khan. **khan'um** /-ŭm/ n (Middle East) (a title for) a lady of rank; Mrs.

khanga see **kanga**.

khanjar see **handjar**.

khansamah or **khansama** /kän'sä-mä/ n a house-steward or butler in India. [Hindi khānsāmān, from Pers khān lord, and sāmān household stores]

kharif /kə-rēf'/ (Ind, etc) n a crop sown before the monsoon to ripen in autumn. [Hindi kharīf, from Ar, gathered]

khat¹, **kat** or **qat** /kat/ n a shrub of E Africa, Arabia, etc, or specif its leaves, chewed or taken as tea for their stimulant effect. [Ar qat]

khat² see **kat²**.

khaya /kä'yə/ n any tree of the African genus Khaya, related to mahogany. [Wolof khaye]

khazi see **kazi**.

kheda or **keddah** /ked'ə/ n an enclosure for catching wild elephants; the operation of catching wild elephants. [Hindi khēdā]

khedive /ke-dēv'/ n (also with cap) the title (1867–1914) of the viceroy of Egypt. [Fr khédive from Turk khidīv, hudīv, from Pers khidīw prince]
■ **khedi'va** n his wife. **khedi'val** or **khedi'vial** adj. **khedi'vate** or **khedi'viate** n the khedive's office or territory.

khidmutgar /kid'mut-gär/ or **khitmutgar** /kit'/ n a table-servant. [Urdu, from Pers khidmat service, and agent sfx -gār]

khilafat /kil'ä-fat or ki-lä'fat/ n caliphate. ♦ adj of an anti-British agitation among Muslims in India after the Treaty of Sèvres, 1920. [Ar khilāfat; cf **caliph**]

khilat see **killut**.

khilim see **kilim**.

khimar /kē'mär/ n a piece of cloth worn by Muslim women to cover the head or face. [Ar]

khitmutgar see **khidmutgar**.

Khmer /kmûr or kmer/ n a member of a people inhabiting Cambodia; their language, the official language of Cambodia. ♦ adj of the Khmers or their language.
□ **Khmer Rouge** /roozh/ n a Communist guerrilla movement formerly active in Cambodia.

Khoikhoi /koi'koi/ n (formerly called **Hottentot**) a nearly extinct race of nomadic people in southern Africa; a member of this people; their language. ♦ adj of the Khoikhoi people or their language. [Khoikhoi, literally, men of men]

Khoisan /koi'sän/ n a family of languages of southern Africa, including Khoikhoi and San (also adj). [**Khoikhoi** and **San**]

khoja or **khodja** /kō'jə/ or **hodja** /hō'jə/ (Middle East) n a title of respect; a professor or teacher in a Muslim school; a member of a Shiite Muslim sect of converts from Hinduism. [Turk and Pers khōjah, khwājah]

khor /kör or kör/ n a dry watercourse; a ravine. [Ar khurr, khorr]

khotbah, **khotbeh** see **khutbah**.

khoum /koom/ n a monetary unit in Mauritania, $\frac{1}{5}$ of an ouguiya. [Ar kūms one fifth]

khud /kud/ (Ind) n a pit, hollow; a ravine. [Hindi khad]

khurta see **kurta**.

khuskhus same as **cuscus³**.

khutbah /kŭt'bä/ n a Muslim sermon delivered in the mosques on Fridays (also **khot'bah** or **khot'beh**). [Ar]

kHz abbrev : kilohertz.

kiaat /ki-ät'/ n an African tree (Pterocarpus angolensis); its wood, used for making furniture, etc. [Afrik, prob from Malay kaju wood]

kiang or **kyang** /kyang or ki-ang'/ n a Tibetan wild ass. [Tibetan rkyang]

kia-ora /kē'ä-ö'rə/ (NZ) interj good health. [Maori]

kiaugh /kyöhh or kyähh/ or **kaugh** /köhh or kähh/ (Scot) n care, trouble.

kibble¹ /kib'l/ n a bucket used in wells or in mining. [Cf Ger Kübel bucket]
□ **kibb'le-chain** n the chain for drawing up a bucket.

kibble² /kib'l/ vt to grind cereal, etc fairly coarsely. ♦ n (N Am) coarsely ground cereal used for feeding pets. [Origin obscure]

kibbutz /ki-bŭts'/ n (pl **kibbutzim** /ki-bŭts-ēm'/) a Jewish communal agricultural settlement in Israel. [Heb]
■ **kibbutz'nik** n a person who lives and works on a kibbutz.

kibe /kīb/ n a chilblain, esp on the heel. [Prob Welsh cibi]

kibitka /ki-bit'kə/ n a Russian covered wagon or sledge; a Central Asian felt tent. [Russ]

kibitzer /kib'it-sər/ (N Am inf) n an onlooker (at cards, etc) who gives unwanted advice; an interferer. [Yiddish]
■ **kib'itz** vi to give unwanted advice, to meddle, comment out of turn.

kiblah /kib'lä/ n the point toward which Muslims turn in prayer, the direction of Mecca (also **keb'lah**. [Ar *qiblah*]

kibosh or **kybosh** /kī'bosh/ (*inf*) n nonsense, rot. ◆ *vt* to dispose of finally. [Ety obscure]

■ **put the kibosh on** to kibosh.

kick /kik/ *vt* to hit with the foot; to put or drive by blows with the foot; to start or work by a foot on a pedal; to achieve by a kick or kicking; to free oneself from (eg a habit) (*inf*). ◆ *vi* to thrust out the foot with violence; to raise the leg high, eg in dancing; to show opposition or resistance; (of a gun, etc) to recoil or jerk violently; (of a ball, etc) to rear up unexpectedly; to move suddenly as if kicked; to put on an extra spurt of speed (*athletics*); to be exposed to kicking, lie around (often with *about*); to be full of vitality (*usu* in *prp*). ◆ *n* a blow or fling with the foot; the recoil of a gun; an unexpected rearing up of a ball; kicking power; resistance; resilience; an extra spurt of speed (*athletics*); stimulus, pungency (*inf*); a thrill (*inf*); an enthusiastic but short-lived interest; a phase of such interest; the fashion (*archaic sl*); the depression in the bottom of a bottle; dismissal (*esp with the* ; *sl*); sixpence (*obs sl*). [ME *kiken*; origin unknown; Welsh *cicio* (to kick) comes from Eng]

■ **kick'able** *adj*. **kick'er** n someone who or something that kicks, eg a horse; (in some sports) a player whose function is to take (*esp* set-piece) kicks; an outboard motor (*N Am*); an unexpected, *esp* disadvantageous, turn of events (*N Am inf*); an unpaired card that determines which of two near-equivalent hands wins the pot (*poker*). **kick'ing** *adj* (*sl*) extremely lively and enjoyable; excellent. ◆ *n* (*inf*) a violent attack (also *fig*). ❑ **kick'about** n an informal game of association football. **kick'-ass** *adj* (*inf*, *esp N Am*) aggressive or domineering, *esp* in management. **kick'back** n part of a sum received paid to another by confidential agreement for favours past or to come; money paid in return for protection; loose material thrown up from the track by a galloping horse (*horse-racing*); a sudden recoil; a strong reaction. **kick'ball** n a game played by children, similar to baseball but using a much larger ball which is kicked not batted. **kick boxer** n. **kick boxing** n a martial art in which the combatants kick with bare feet and punch with gloved fists. **kick'down** n a method of changing gear in a car with automatic gear transmission, by pressing the accelerator pedal right down. **kick'flip** n in skateboarding and snowboarding, a jump into the air which causes the board to rotate before the jumper lands on it. ◆ *vi* to perform a kickflip. **kicking strap** n a strap behind a draught horse's hindquarters to prevent kicking; a rope used on a yacht to prevent the boom from rising. **kick'-off** n the first kick in a game of football; the start of the game; the start of any activity (*inf*). **kick pleat** n a pleat in a narrow skirt from knee-level to hem, which allows the wearer to walk easily. **kick'sorter** n (*telecom*) a device that selects and counts electrical pulses of specified amplitudes. **kick'stand** n a piece of metal attached to a motorcycle, etc, which is kicked into position to hold the machine upright when parked. **kick'-start** n the starting of an engine by a pedal. ◆ *vt* to start (an engine) thus; to get (something) moving, to give a sudden (advantageous) impulse to (*fig*). **kick turn** n a skiing or skateboarding turn through 180°. **kick'-up** n a disturbance; a dance; a depression in the bottom of a bottle.

■ **for a kick-off** for a start. **for kicks** for thrills. **kick about** or **around** to consider; to discuss; to treat harshly (*inf*); (of a person) to wander around doing nothing in particular; (of an object) to lie about serving no useful purpose. **kick arse** or **ass** see under **arse**. **kick back** (of a machine, *esp* a gun) to react strongly, to recoil; to relax (*N Am inf*); to pay as a kickback (*inf*). **kick in** (*inf*) to contribute, pay one's share; to take effect. **kick in the pants** (*inf*) a sharp telling-off intended to make the recipient put in more effort. **kick in the teeth** (*inf*) a mortifying rebuff. **kick off** to start, *esp* a game of football; to open a discussion (*inf*); to die (*sl*). **kick on** (*inf*) to continue with an activity, *esp* with renewed vigour. **kick oneself** (*inf*) to regret something one has done or has failed to do. **kick one's heels** see under **heel**[1]. **kick out** (*inf*) to eject with force; to dismiss. **kick over the traces** to throw off control. **kick** or **strike the beam** to be of little weight or importance (*fig* from the lighter scale in a balance rising so as to strike against the beam). **kick the bucket** see under **bucket**. **kick up a dust, fuss, row** or **stink** to create a disturbance. **kick up one's heels** see under **heel**[1]. **kick upstairs** (*inf*) to promote (*usu* to a less active or less powerful position).

kickie-wickie /kik'i-wik-i/ (*Shakesp*) n a wife. [Altered by editors to *kicksy-wicksy*; perh connected with **kickshaws**]

kickshaws /kik'shöz/ or **kickshaw** /-shö/ n a trinket, a cheap, worthless article; a delicacy (*archaic*). [Fr *quelque chose* something]

kid[1] /kid/ n a young goat; a young antelope or other related animal; a child or young person (*inf*); leather made of kidskin, or a substitute; a glove, shoe or boot made of kid (*archaic*). ◆ *adj* made of kid leather or imitation kid leather; young or younger, still a child, as in *kid sister* (*inf*). ◆ *vt* and *vi* (**kidd'ing**; **kidd'ed**) (of a goat) to give birth to a kid or kids. [ON *kith*; cf Dan *kid*; Ger *Kitze* a young goat]

■ **kidd'o** n (*pl* **kidd'os**) (*sl*) term of address for a young man or woman. **kidd'y** n (*pl* **kidd'ies**) a child (*inf*); a flashy thief (*criminal sl*). **kiddy'wink, kidd'iewink** or **kiddiewink'ie** n (*facetious*) a child. **kid'let** n (*inf*) a young child. **kid'ling** n a young kid. ❑ **kid'-fox** n (*Shakesp*) a young fox. **kid glove** n a glove made of kid leather. ◆ *adj* as if done by someone wearing kid gloves; overnice, delicate; extremely tactful. **kid'skin** n kid leather, typically soft and smooth. **kids' stuff** n (*inf*) something only suitable for young children, *usu* because very tame or very easy. **kid'vid** n (*inf*) television or video entertainment for children.

■ **handle**, etc **with kid gloves** to treat carefully and gently; to deal with very tactfully.

kid[2] /kid/, also **kiddy** /kid'i/ (*inf*) *vt* and *vi* to hoax; to pretend, *esp* as a joke; to tease, delude, deceive as a joke. ◆ *n* a deception. [Perh connected with **kid**[1] a child]

■ **kidd'er** n. **kidd'ingly** *adv*. **kidol'ogist** /-jist/ n (*inf*). **kidology** /kid-ol'ə-ji/ n (*inf*) the art of kidding, sometimes to gain a psychological advantage. ❑ **kid'stakes** n (*Aust inf*) nonsense, humbug. ■ **kid on** to kid (**kid'-on** n and *adj*).

kid[3] /kid/ n a small tub. [Perh a variant of **kit**[1]]

kid[4] /kid/ n a faggot. [Origin unknown; Welsh *cedys* (faggots) is prob from Eng]

kidder /kid'ər/ or **kiddier** /-i-ər/ n a forestaller; a huckster. [Origin obscure]

Kidderminster /kid'ər-min-stər/ n a two-ply or ingrain carpet formerly made at *Kidderminster* (also *adj*).

kiddle /kid'l/ (*hist*) n a stake-fence set in a stream for catching fish (also **kid'el** or **kett'le**). [OFr *quidel*; cf Breton *kidel*]

kiddush /kid'əsh/ n a Jewish blessing that is uttered over wine and bread on holy days. [Heb *qiddūsh* sanctification]

kiddy, etc see under **kid**[1,2].

kidel see **kiddle**.

kidge see **kedge**[2].

kidgie see **cadgy**.

kidling see under **kid**[1].

kidnap /kid'nap/ *vt* (**kid'napping; kid'napped**) to steal (a human being), often for ransom. ◆ *n* an instance of this. [**kid**[1] a child, and **nap**[4]]

■ **kid'napper** n.

kidney /kid'ni/ n either of two rounded flattened organs, in the posterior abdominal area in man, that filter waste from the blood and secrete it as urine; these organs taken from the bodies of certain animals, used as food; temperament, humour, disposition; sort, kind. [ME *kidenei* (pl *kideneiren*), perh a compound of *ei* (pl *eiren*) egg, confused sometimes with *nere* kidney]

❑ **kidney bean** n the French bean; any kidney-shaped variety of bean, *esp* the red variety of runner bean. **kidney machine** n an apparatus used, in cases where the kidney functions badly, to remove harmful substances from the blood by dialysis. **kidney ore** n haematite in kidney-shaped masses. **kidney-potā'to** n a kidney-shaped variety of potato. **kidney stone** n nephrite; a septarian nodule; a hard deposit formed in the kidney. **kidney vetch** n any plant of the papilionaceous genus *Anthyllis*, including lady's fingers.

kidologist, kidology see under **kid**[2].

kidult /kid'ult/ (*inf*) n an adult who enjoys entertainment intended for children. ◆ *adj* intended for both adults and children. [**kid**[1] and **adult**]

kie-kie /kē'kē/ n a New Zealand climbing plant (*Freycinetia banksii*) of the screw-pine family. [Maori]

kielbasa /kēl-bas'ə/ n a highly seasoned Polish sausage. [Pol]

kier or **keir** /kēr/ n a bleaching vat. [Cf ON *ker* tub]

kierie /kē'rē/ (*S Afr*) n a stick. [Prob Khoikhoi]

kieselguhr /kē'zl-goor/ n diatomite. [Ger, from *Kiesel* flint, and *Guhr* fermentation]

kieserite /kē'zə-rīt/ n a mineral, hydrated magnesium sulphate ($MgSO_4.H_2O$), a source of Epsom salts. [DG *Kieser* (1779–1862), German scientist]

kiev /kē'ef, -ev/ or /kē-ef', -ev'/ n a dish made of thin fillets of meat, *esp* chicken (**chicken kiev**), filled with butter, garlic, etc, coated with breadcrumbs, and fried. [*Kiev*, in Ukraine]

kieve see **keeve**.

kif see **kef**.

kight (*Spenser*) same as **kite**[1].

kike /kīk/ (*offensive sl*; *esp N Am*) n a Jew. ◆ *adj* Jewish. [Possibly from the *-ki* ending of many E European Jewish immigrants' names in the USA at the end of the 19c]

kikoi /kē'koi/ n (in E Africa) a piece of striped cloth wound round the waist. [Swahili]

kikumon /kik'ŭ-mon/ n the chrysanthemum badge of the Japanese imperial family. [Jap *kiku* chrysanthemum, and *mon* badge]

Kikuyu /ki- or kē-koo'ū/ n an agrarian people of Kenya; a member of this people; their language. ◆ adj of the Kikuyu or their language.
□ **kikuyu grass** (or simply **kikuyu**) n an African grass (*Pennisetum clandestinum*) grown also in Australia and S America.

kild /kild/ (*Spenser*) variant of **killed**.

kilderkin /kil'dər-kin/ (*obs*) n a small cask; a liquid measure of 18 gallons. [MDu *kindeken*, *kinneken* (Scot *kinken*), dimin of *kintal*, from LL *quintāle* quintal]

kilerg /kil'ûrg/ n a thousand ergs. [Gr *chīlioi* thousand, and **erg**^{1}]

kiley see **kylie**.

kilim /ki-lēm'/ n a pileless woven rug traditionally made in the Middle East (also **kelim** or **khilim**). [Turk, from Pers *kilīm*]

kill^1 /kil/ vt to put to death, to murder or execute; to deprive of life; to destroy; to nullify or neutralize, to make inactive, to weaken or dilute; to reject, discard, defeat; to overwhelm with amazement, admiration, laughter, etc (*inf*); to injure seriously (*Irish*); to spoil; to muffle or still; to extinguish (a light, etc) (*inf*); to stop the flow of oil in (a well) by pumping in mud or other liquid (*oil*); to cause to stop, to turn off (machinery, etc); to exhaust, to overexert (*inf*); to cause severe pain to (*inf*); to consume completely (*inf*); to mark for cancellation, to cut (*printing*); to cancel or suppress (a story) (*press*); to bring (a loose ball) under control (*football*, etc); to play (a shot) so hard that one's opponent cannot play it back again (*tennis*, etc). ◆ vi to commit murder or manslaughter. ◆ n an act or instance of killing, etc; prey or game killed; an act or instance of destroying an enemy plane, tank, etc; the plane, tank, etc so destroyed; a shot impossible to return (*tennis*, etc). [ME *killen* or *cullen*]
■ **kill'er** n a person, creature, organism, chemical, etc that kills; someone who murders readily or habitually; an instrument for killing; a neutralizing agent; an animal intended for slaughter (*Aust* and *NZ inf*); a gruelling task or activity (*inf*). ◆ adj (*sl*) spectacularly impressive, stupendous. **kill'ing** adj depriving of life; destructive; deadly, irresistible; exhausting; fascinating; irresistibly funny (*inf*). ◆ n the act of causing death, slaughter; a large financial gain, *esp* sudden (*inf*); a severe handling. **kill'ingly** adv.
□ **kill-court'esy** n (*Shakesp*) a discourteous person. **kill'cow** n (*obs*) a bully, a swaggerer. **killer cell** n (*immunol*) a lymphocyte that destroys certain tumour cells without evident antigen specificity. **killer whale** n a ferocious black-and-white toothed marine whale; the grampus. **killing field** n a scene of large-scale killing, *esp* in war. **killing time** n (*Scot hist*) the days of the persecution of the Covenanters in the 17c. **kill'joy** n a spoilsport. ◆ adj austere, disapproving. **kill line** n (*mining*) one of the small-bore pipelines, connected through the blow-out preventer stack, that allow denser mud to be pumped into a borehole which has to be shut down because of the danger of a blow-out. **kill string** see **injection string** under **inject**.
■ **dressed to kill** dressed so as to dazzle, attract and impress others. **in at the kill** (*fig*) present at the culminating moment. **kill by inches** to kill gradually, eg by torture. **kill off** to exterminate; (of an author, etc) to write in the death of (a fictional character). **kill the fatted calf** see under **calf**^{1}. **kill time** to occupy oneself with amusements, etc, in order to pass spare time or to relieve boredom (also **kill'-time** n an occupation of this sort). **kill two birds with one stone** see under **bird**. **kill up** (*Shakesp*) to exterminate. **make a killing** (*inf*) to make a lot of money, a large profit.

kill^2 /kil/ (*US dialect*) n a stream, brook; a river; a channel (used chiefly in place names, *esp* in areas *orig* settled by Dutch). [Du *kil*, from MDu *kille* a channel]
□ **kill'ifish** n any of several small freshwater fish used as bait and to control mosquitoes, a topminnow.

killadar /kil'ə-där/ (*Ind*, etc) n the commandant of a fort or garrison. [Hindi (Pers) *qil'adār*]

killas /kil'əs/ (*geol*) n clay-slate. [Cornish miners' term]

killcrop /kil'krop/ n a greedy, insatiable baby; a changeling. [LGer *kīlkrop*; Ger *Kielkropf*]

killdeer /kil'dēr/ n (pl **kill'deer** or **kill'deers**) the largest N American ring-necked plover (also **kill'dee**). [Imit]

killick /kil'ik/ or **killock** /-ək/ n a small anchor; its fluke or barb; in the Royal Navy, a leading seaman (from his badge, bearing the symbol of an anchor). [Origin obscure]

killifish see under **kill**^{2}.

killikinick see **kinnikinick**.

killogie /ki-lō'gi/ (*Scot*) n the space in front of the fireplace of a kiln. [**kiln** and **logie**]

killut /kil'ut/ n (in India) a robe of honour or other ceremonial present (also **kell'aut**, **khal'at** or **khil'at**). [Hindi and Pers *khil'at*]

Kilmarnock /kil-mär'nək/ n a kind of closely-woven broad cap for men, *orig* made at *Kilmarnock* in Scotland.
□ **Kilmarnock cowl** n a kind of nightcap.

kiln /kiln or (now *dialect*) kil/ n a large oven for drying, baking or calcining corn, hops, bricks, pottery, limestone, etc. ◆ vt to dry, fire, etc in a kiln. [OE *cyln*, *cylen*, from L *culīna* a kitchen]
□ **kiln'-dry** vt (*pap* **kiln'-dried**) to dry in a kiln. **kiln'-hole** n the mouth of a kiln.

Kilner jar® /kil'nər jär/ n a glass jar with an airtight lid, used for preserving fruit and vegetables. [From the original manufacturer's name]

Kilo or **kilo** /kē'lō/ n (in international radio communication) a code word for the letter *k*.

kilo /kē'lō/ n (pl **kil'os**) a short form of **kilogram** or sometimes of another word with the prefix **kilo-**.

kilo- /kil-ə-, kil-ō-, kē-lə-, kē-lō- or ki-lo-/ combining form in names of units, denoting a thousand times (10^3), as in *kilobar*; (loosely) in units of computer storage capacity, denoting 1024 (2^{10}). [Gr *chīlioi* a thousand]
■ **kil'obit** n (*comput*) 1000 bits; (loosely) 1024 bits. **kil'obyte** n (*comput*) 1000 bytes; (loosely) 1024 bytes. **kil'ocalorie** n 1000 calories, a Calorie, used to measure energy content of food (see also **calorie**). **kil'ocycle** or **kilocycle per second** n kilohertz (see below). **kil'ogram** or **kil'ogramme** n a base SI unit, the unit of mass (symbol **kg**), defined as the mass of a platinum-iridium cylinder (the **International Prototype Kilogram**) kept in Paris, equal to 2.205lb (**kil'ogram-calorie** same as **kilocalorie** above). **kil'ogray** n 1000 grays (see **gray**^{1}), used to measure the absorbed dose of radiation, eg in food irradiation. **kil'ohertz** n 1000 cycles of oscillation per second, used to measure frequency of sound and radio waves. **kil'ojoule** n 1000 joules, used to measure energy, work and heat. **kil'olitre** n 1000 litres. **kilomega-** combining form (*obs*) same as **giga-**. **kil'ometre** (also /-om'/) n 1000 metres, 0.6214 or about $\frac{5}{8}$ mile. **kilometric** /-met'/ adj. **kil'opond** n a unit of measurement equal to the gravitational force on a mass of one kilogram (cf **pond**^{2}). **kil'oton** or **kil'otonne** n a measure of explosive force equivalent to that of 1000 tons of TNT. **kil'ovolt** n 1000 volts. **kil'owatt** n 1000 watts, the power used by one bar of the average electric fire (**kilowatt hour** the energy consumed by a load of one kilowatt in one hour of use (3.6 megajoules), the unit by which electricity is charged to the consumer).

kilp /kilp/ see **kelp**.

kilt^1 /kilt/ n a pleated knee-length skirtlike garment, *usu* of tartan, traditionally worn by men as part of Highland dress; any similar garment. ◆ vt to tuck up (skirts); to pleat vertically; to hang, string up (*archaic*). ◆ vi (*archaic*) to move lightly and quickly, to trip. [Scand; cf Dan *kilte* to tuck up; ON *kilting* a skirt]
■ **kilt'ed** adj dressed in a kilt; tucked up; vertically pleated. **kilt'y** or **kilt'ie** n (*inf*) a wearer of a kilt.

kilt^2 /kilt/ (*Spenser* and *Irish*, *esp* hyperbole) pap of **kill**^{1}.

kilter /kil'tər/ (*esp US*) n good condition (also (*dialect*) **kelter** /kel'tər/). [Origin unknown]
■ **out of kilter** or **off kilter** out of order, not functioning properly; out of correct condition or shape.

Kimball tag /kim'bl tag/ n a punched tag detached from retail goods when sold, and used as computer input for information on sales, stock control, etc.

kimberlite /kim'bər-līt/ n a mica-peridotite, an intrusive igneous rock, in which the diamonds at *Kimberley* and elsewhere in S Africa were found.

kimbo /kim'bō/ vt to set akimbo.
■ **kim'boed** adj.

kimchi /kim'chi/ n a very spicy Korean dish made with a variety of raw vegetables, *esp* cabbage, radish, cucumber, garlic, ginger, etc. [Korean]

Kimeridgian or **Kimmeridgian** /kim-ə-rij'i-ən/ (*geol*) adj of the middle division of the Upper Jurassic, named from a clay well developed at *Kimmeridge* in Dorset (also n).

kimmer see **cummer**.

kimono /ki-mō'nō/ n (pl **kimo'nos**) a loose robe with wide sleeves, fastening with a sash, a traditional outer garment in Japan; a dressing-gown of similar form. [Jap]
■ **kimo'noed** adj.
□ **kimono sleeve** n a magyar sleeve.

kin^1 /kin/ n people belonging to the same family; one's relatives; relationship; affinity. ◆ adj related. [OE *cynn*; ON *kyn*, Gothic *kuni* family, race; cognate with L *genus*, Gr *genos*]

---

fāte; fär; mē; fûr; mīne; mōte; för; mūte; pŭt; dhen (then); *el'ə-mənt* (element) ◆ For other sounds see detailed chart of pronunciation

■ **kin'less** *adj* without relatives. **kinsfolk** /*kinz'fōk*/ *n* folk or people kindred or related to one another (also, chiefly *N Am*, **kin'folk** or **kins'folks**). **kin'ship** *n* relationship. **kins'man** or **kins'woman** *n* a person of the same kin or race as another.

■ **next of kin** one's closest relatives, among whom one's personal property is distributed if one dies intestate; the person or persons most closely related to an individual by blood, marriage, or a legal ruling. **of kin** related.

kin² /*kin*/ *n* a Japanese and Chinese weight, the catty. [Jap *kin*, Chin *jīn*]

-kin /-*kin*/ *sfx* denoting a diminutive, eg *lambkin* and *manikin*; also in proper names, eg *Jenkin* (from *John*), *Wilkin* (from *William*). [Prob Du or LGer; cf Ger *-chen*]

kina¹ /*kē'nə*/ *n* the standard monetary unit of Papua New Guinea (100 toea). [Native name]

kina², kinakina see **quina**.

kinaesthesis or (*N Am*) **kinesthesis** /*kīn-ēs-thē'sis*, *kin-* or *-es-*/ *n* sense of the body's movement or of muscular effort (also **kinaesthē'sia** or (*N Am*) **kinesthe'sia** /-*zi-ə* or -*zyə*/). [Gr *kīneein* to move, and *aisthēsis* sensation]

■ **kinaesthetic** or (*N Am*) **kinesthetic** /-*thet'ik*/ *adj* relating to kinaesthesis.

kinase /*kī'nāz* or *kin'āz*/ *n* an enzyme that catalyses the phosphorylation of its substrate by adenosine triphosphate (ATP). [*kinetic* and **-ase**]

kinchin /*kin'chin*/ (*criminal sl*) *n* a child. [Appar Ger *Kindchen* little child]

□ **kin'chin-cove** *n* (*obs*) a boy. **kin'chin-lay** *n* the robbing of children. **kin'chin-mort** *n* (*obs*) a girl.

kincob /*king'kəb*/ *n* a rich silk fabric embroidered with gold or silver thread, made in India. [Urdu and Pers *kimkhāb*]

kind¹ /*kīnd*/ *n* related people, a race; sort or species, a particular variety; an individual belonging to a specific variety; fundamental qualities (of a thing); produce, as distinguished from money; either of the Eucharistic elements; nature, the material universe (*archaic*); innate character (of a person) (*archaic*); sex (*obs*). ◆ *adj* disposed to do good to others; benevolent; helpful; agreeable; having or springing from the feelings natural for those of the same family (*obs*). [OE (*ge*)*cynde*, from *cynn* kin]

■ **kind'a** *adv* (*inf*) short for **kind of**, somewhat, sort of. **kind'less** *adj* (*Shakesp*) unnatural, destitute of kindness. **kind'ly** *adv* in a kind manner; a (rather peremptory) substitute for 'please'. ◆ *adj* see separate entry. **kind'ness** *n* the quality or fact of being kind; a kind act.

□ **kind-heart'ed** *adj*. **kind-heart'edly** *adv*. **kind-heart'edness** *n*. **kind-spok'en** *adj* spoken kindly; given to speaking kindly.

■ **after (its) kind** according to (its) nature. **do one's kind** (*Shakesp*) to act according to one's nature. **in a kind** (*archaic*) in a way, to some extent. **in kind** in goods instead of money; tit for tat. **kind of** (*inf*) of a kind, somewhat, sort of, to some extent, as it were, used adjectivally and adverbially.

kind² /*kīnd*/ (*obs*) *vt* (*pap* (*Spenser*) **kynd'ed**) to beget.

kindergarten /*kin'dər-gär-tn*/ *n* (also in short forms **kin'der** (*Aust*) and **kin'dy** or **kin'die** (*Aust* and *NZ*)) a school or class for pre-primary children, in which object lessons and games figure largely; a class for the new intake of children at an elementary school (*US* and *Aust*). [Ger, from *Kinder* children, and *Garten* garden]

■ **kindergart'ener** *n* (also **kindergärtner** /-*gert'nar*/) a teacher in a kindergarten; a pupil of a kindergarten (*US*).

kinderspiel /*kin'dər-spēl* or *-shpēl*/ *n* a children's cantata or play. [Ger, children's sport, child's play, from *Kinder* children, and *Spiel* game, play]

kindle¹ /*kin'dl*/ *vt* to set fire to; to light; to inflame (eg the passions); to provoke, incite. ◆ *vi* to catch fire; to begin to be excited; to be roused. [Cf ON *kyndill* a torch, from L *candēla* candle]

■ **kin'dler** *n*. **kin'dling** *n* the act of causing to burn; materials for starting a fire, such as twigs, dry wood.

kindle² /*kin'dl*/ (*Shakesp*) *vt* and *vi* to bring forth young. ◆ *n* brood, litter. [ME *kindlen*; cf **kind¹**]

■ **in kindle** with young.

Kindle® /*kin'dl*/ *n* the proprietary name of a type of e-reader.

kindless see under **kind¹**.

kindly /*kīnd'li*/ *adj* inclined to kindness; benign; genial; comfortable; natural (*obs*); native (*obs*); native-born (*archaic*). ◆ *adv* in a kind or kindly manner (see also under **kind¹**). [OE *gecyndelic*; cf **kind¹**]

■ **kind'lily** *adv* (*rare*). **kind'liness** *n*.

□ **kind'ly-nā'tured** *adj*. **kindly tenant** *n* (*Scot hist*) a tenant whose family has held lands in succession, from father to son, for several generations.

■ **take it kindly** to feel it as a kindness. **take kindly to** (often in *neg*) to take a favourable view of, or to adopt (a practice) with enthusiasm.

kindred /*kin'drid*/ (*Spenser* **kinred** /*kin'rid*/) *n* relationship by blood, or (less properly) by marriage; relatives; a group of relatives, family, clan; similarity, affinity. ◆ *adj* related; cognate; congenial. [ME *kinrede*, from OE *cynn* kin, and *sfx -rǣden* expressing mode or state]

■ **kin'dredness** *n*. **kin'dredship** *n*.

kine /*kīn*/ (*Bible*) *n pl* cows. [ME *kyen*, a double plural of OE *cū* a cow, the plural of which is *cȳ*; cf Scot **kye**]

kinema /*kin'ə-mə*/ an old form of **cinema**.

kinematics /*kin-i-mat'iks* or *kīn-*/ *n sing* the science of motion without reference to force. [Gr *kīnēma* motion, from *kīneein* to move]

■ **kinemat'ic** or **kinemat'ical** *adj*. **kinemat'ically** *adv*.

kinematograph see **cinematograph**.

kinescope /*kin'i-skōp*/ (*N Am*) *n* a cathode-ray tube for a television.

kinesi- /*kin-ēs-i-* or *kī-*/ or (before a vowel) **kines-** /*kin-ēs-* or *kī-*/ (*med*) *combining form* denoting movement, motion. [Gr *kīnēsis* movement]

■ **kinesiat'ric** or **kinesipath'ic** *adj*. **kinesiat'rics** *n sing* a method of treating disease by means of exercises or gymnastic movements. **kinesiolog'ical** *adj*. **kinesiol'ogist** *n*. **kinesiol'ogy** *n* the study of human movement and posture, including aspects of anatomy, biomechanics and physiology; any of various therapies that use gentle finger pressure to detect blockages and other physical problems as part of a holistic approach to treating disease. **kines'ipath, kinesip'athist** or **kinesither'apist** *n*. **kinesip'athy** or **kinesither'apy** *n* same as **kinesiatrics**.

kinesis /*ki-nē'sis* or *kī-*/ *n* a movement, change of position, *specif* (*biol*) under stimulus, and with the direction not precisely determined. [Gr *kīnēsis* movement]

■ **kinē'sics** *n sing* (the study of) body movements that convey information in the absence of speech.

kinesthesis, etc N American spelling of **kinaesthesis**, etc.

kinetheodolite /*kin-* or *kīn-i-thi-od'ə-līt*/ *n* an improved form of theodolite used in tracking missiles and artificial satellites.

kinetics /*ki-net'iks* or *kī-*/ *n sing* the science of the action of force in producing or changing motion. [Gr *kīnetikos*, from *kīneein* to move]

■ **kinet'ic** or **kinet'ical** *adj* relating to motion or to kinetics; due to motion. **kinet'ically** *adv*. **kinetochore** /*kin-et'ə-kōr*/ *n* (*biol*) a paired structure within the centromere of a chromosome to which spindle microtubules become attached during meiosis and mitosis. **kinet'ograph** *n* an early form of cinematograph camera. **kinet'oplast** *n* a DNA body located near the base of the flagellum in flagellate protozoa. **kinet'oscope** *n* an early form of cinematograph projector; an instrument for the production of curves by combination of circular movements.

□ **kinetic art** or **sculpture** *n* art or sculpture in which movement (produced by air currents, or electricity, or sound, etc) plays an essential part. **kinetic energy** *n* the energy possessed by a body by virtue of its motion. **kinetic theory** *n* a theory that accounts for the bulk properties of gases in terms of the motion of the molecules of the gas.

kinfolk same as **kinsfolk** (see under **kin¹**).

king /*king*/ *n* a male hereditary chief ruler or titular head of a nation; a male monarch; a queen bee (*obs*); a playing card having the picture of a king; in chess, either of two pieces, the most important pieces on each side, *usu* with a top in the shape of a crown, that can move one square at a time in any direction; in draughts, a piece that has been crowned; a man or other male animal who is pre-eminent among his fellows. Cf **queen**. ◆ *vt* to make king; to provide with a king (*obs*). ◆ *combining form* denoting most important. [OE *cyning*, from *cynn* a tribe, with sfx *-ing*; cf ety of **kin¹**]

■ **king'dom** *n* the state or attributes of a king; a monarchical state; a region that was once a monarchical state; the spiritual sovereignty of God; one of the three major divisions of natural history (animal, vegetable, mineral); any of the higher taxonomic ranks, each composed of a number of plant divisions, or animal phyla; an area in which a specified quality or attribute is paramount. **king'domed** *adj* (*Shakesp*) provided with or constituted like a kingdom. **king'domless** *adj*. **king'hood** *n* kingship; kingliness. **king'less** *adj*. **king'let** *n* either of two species of N American bird of the genus *Regulus*, allied to the goldcrest and firecrest. **king'lihood** *n*. **king'like** *adj*. **king'liness** *n*. **king'ling** *n* a petty king. **king'ly** *adj* belonging or suitable to a king; royal; kinglike. ◆ *adv* in the manner of a king. **Kings** *n* the title of two historical books of the Old Testament. **king'ship** *n* the state, office or dignity of a king.

□ **king'-apple** *n* a large red variety of apple. **king'-archon** *n* the second of the nine archons in Athens, successor to the abolished kings in religious functions. **king'bird** *n* an American flycatcher. **king'bolt** or **king'-rod** *n* a metal rod in a roof connecting the tie-beam and the ridge; a kingpin in a mechanical structure. **King Charles's head** *n* a matter that persists in obtruding itself as did King Charles's head in the thoughts of Mr Dick in Dickens's *David*

■ words derived from main entry word; □ compound words; ■ idioms and phrasal verbs

Copperfield. **King Charles spaniel** see under **spaniel**. **king cobra** *n* a large Asiatic species of cobra. **king crab** *n* any of several large decapods valued as a food (also **stone crab**); same as **horseshoe crab** (see under **horse**). **king'craft** *n* (*obs*) the art of governing. **king'-crow** *n* a kind of drongo. **king'cup** *n* the buttercup; the marsh-marigold. **kingdom come** *n* (*inf*) the state after death; some inconceivably far-off time. **King Edward** *n* a popular English variety of potato. **king'fish** *n* the opah; any of various fish notable for their size or value (*N Am* and *Aust*). **king'fisher** *n* a European fish-eating bird with very brilliant blue-green and chestnut plumage, formerly known as the halcyon; any bird of the same family, most species of which are not fish-eating; a brilliant blue colour (also *adj*). **king'-hit** *n* (*Aust sl*) a knockout blow (also *vt*). **King James Bible** (or **Version**) *n* the Authorized Version. **king'klip** *n* (*S Afr*) any of several marine food-fishes. **King Log** *n* a do-nothing king, as opposed to **King Stork**, one who devours his frog-subjects (from Aesop's fable). **king'maker** *n* a person who has the power to create kings or other high officials. **king mob** *n* the vulgar multitude. **king-of-arms** (sometimes **king-at-arms'**) *n* a principal herald (those of England having the designations Garter, Clarencieux, and Norroy and Ulster (includes N Ireland), of Scotland, Lyon). **king of beasts** *n* the lion. **king of birds** *n* the eagle. **king of kings** *n* a powerful monarch with other monarchs subject to him; (with *caps*) God, Christ. **king of metals** *n* gold. **king of terrors** *n* death. **king of the castle** *n* (*orig* from a children's game) the most important, powerful person in a group. **king of the forest** *n* the oak. **king of the herrings** *n* the shad; the oarfish; applied also to various other fishes, such as the opah, the rabbitfish or chimera. **king pair** *n* (*cricket*) an instance of getting out to one's first ball in both innings of a match. **king penguin** *n* a large penguin, smaller than the emperor. **king'pin** *n* a tall pin, or one prominently placed; a pin on which an axle swivels, like that on a motor vehicle's front wheel; the most important person of a group engaged in an undertaking; the key issue. **king'post** *n* a perpendicular beam in the frame of a roof rising from the tie-beam to the ridge. **king prawn** *n* a large prawn, *esp* of the genus *Penaeus*, found around Australia. **king salmon** *n* the largest Pacific salmon, the quinnat. **King's Bench** see **Queen's Bench** under **queen**. **king's bounty** see under **bounty**. **king's'-chair** or **king's-cush'ion** *n* a seat formed by two people clasping wrists. **King's Counsel** see **Queen's Counsel** under **queen**. **king's English** or **queen's English** *n* correct standard speech. **king's evil** *n* a scrofulous disease formerly supposed to be healed by the touch of the monarch. **King's Guide** see **Queen's Guide** under **queen**. **king's highway** *n* the public thoroughfare. **king's'-hood** *n* the second stomach of a ruminant, sometimes humorously for the human stomach. **king'side** *n* in chess, the side of the board where the king stands at the beginning of play. **king'-size** or **king'-sized** *adj* of large or larger-than-standard size. **king's'-man** *n* a royalist; a custom-house officer. **king snake** *n* any non-venomous N American snake of the genus *Lampropeltis*, which feeds on small animals and other snakes. **king's peace** (or **queen's peace**) *n orig* the peace secured by the sovereign for certain people (eg those employed on the king's or queen's business); the peace of the kingdom generally. **King's Proctor** (or **Queen's Proctor**) *n* a legal officer chiefly concerned with establishing collusion in divorce cases. **King's Regulations** see **Queen's Regulations** under **queen**. **King's Scout** see **Queen's Scout** under **queen**. **king's'-spear** *n* an asphodel. **King's Speech** see **Queen's Speech** under **queen**. **King Stork** see **King Log** above. **king's-yell'ow** *n* orpiment as a pigment. **king-vul'ture** *n* a large brilliantly-coloured tropical American vulture. **king'wood** *n* a beautiful Brazilian wood also called **violet-wood**; the papilionaceous tree yielding it, a species of *Dalbergia*.

■ **king it** to play king, act as superior to, or in authority over, others. **take the king's shilling** see under **shilling**. **three kings of Cologne** the three Wise Men of the East, Caspar, Melchior and Balthazar. **turn King's evidence** see under **evident**.

kingle /king'l/ (*Scot*) *n* very hard rock, *esp* sandstone.

kinin /kī'nin/ (*biol*) *n* a plant hormone that promotes cell division and is used commercially as a preservative for cut flowers (also **cytokinin**); any of a group of polypeptides in the blood, causing dilation of the blood vessels and contraction of smooth muscles. [Gr *kīn(ēsis)* movement]

kink¹ /kingk/ *n* a twisted loop in a string, rope, etc; a mental twist or quirk; a crick; a whim; an imperfection; an unusual sexual preference, or a person who has one (*inf*). ◆ *vi* to form a kink. ◆ *vt* to cause a kink in. [Prob Du]

■ **kink'ily** *adv*. **kink'iness** *n*. **kink'le** *n* a slight kink. **kink'y** *adj* twisted; curly; eccentric (*inf*); crazy (*inf*); out of the ordinary in an attractive (*esp* provocative) way (*inf*); with unusual or perverted sexual tastes (*inf*).

kink² /kingk/ (*Scot* and *N Eng*) *vi* to cough loudly; to gasp for breath. ◆ *n* a convulsive cough or gasp. [Scot and N Eng form of **chink³**] ▫ **kink'-cough** or **kink'-host** *n* whooping cough.

kinkajou /king'kə-joo/ *n* a S American tree-dwelling animal related to the raccoon. [Appar from a Native American word misapplied]

kinkle, kinky see under **kink¹**.

kinnikinick /ki-ni-ki-nik'/ or **killikinick** /ki-li/ *n* a mixture used by Native Americans as a substitute for tobacco; a species of cornel or other plant forming part of the mixture. [From Algonquian, mixture]

kino /kē'nō/ *n* (*pl* **kin'os**) an astringent resinous substance that exudes from various tropical trees. [Appar of W African origin]

kinone see **quinone** under **quinol**.

kinred (*Spenser*) see **kindred**.

kinsfolk, kinship, etc see under **kin¹**.

kintledge see **kentledge**.

kiosk /kē'osk or ki-osk'/ *n orig* an Eastern garden pavilion; a small roofed stall for the sale of papers, sweets, etc, either out-of-doors or inside a public building; a bandstand; a public telephone box. [Turk *kösk, keushk*, from Pers *kūshk*]

kip¹ /kip/ (*sl*) *n* a nap; a bed; a lodging-house; a brothel (*Irish*). ◆ *vi* to go to bed, sleep, nap. [Cf Dan *kippe* a low alehouse] ■ **kip down** to go to bed.

kip² /kip/ *n* the skin of a young animal. [Du, bundle of hides, is suggested] ▫ **kip'skin** *n* leather made from the skin of young cattle, intermediate between calfskin and cowhide.

kip³ /kip/ (*Aust*) *n* a short flat stick used to throw up pennies in the game of two-up. [Origin unknown]

kip⁴ /kip/ *n* the standard monetary unit of Laos (100 at). [Thai]

kip⁵ /kip/ (*mining*) *n* a level or slight incline at the end of an underground passage, on which the tubs of coal stand until hoisted up the shaft.

kip⁶ or **kipp** /kip/ *n* anything beaked (*Scot*); a pointed hill (*Scot*); (in gymnastics) a swinging movement that reverses the relative positions of body and legs. [Cf Ger, orig LGer, *Kippe* point, tip]

kip⁷ /kip/ (*Scot*) *vi* to play truant. [Origin uncertain] ■ **play kip** or **play the kip** to play truant.

kip⁸ /kip/ *n* a unit of weight equal to 1000 pounds. [*ki*lo and *p*ound]

kipe /kīp/ (*dialect*) *n* an osier basket for catching pike. [OE *cȳpe*]

Kipp /kip/ *n* a form of generator for hydrogen sulphide or other gas (also **Kipp's apparatus**). [PJ *Kipp* (19c), Dutch founder of a firm of manufacturers of scientific apparatus]

kipp see **kip⁶**.

kippa /kip'ä/ (*Judaism*) *n* a religious skullcap, the yarmulka. [Heb *kipa*]

kippage /kip'ij/ (*Scot*) *n* a state of displeasure or anger. [Fr *équipage* ; see **equipage** under **equip**]

kipper¹ /kip'ər/ *n* a male salmon during the spawning season after spawning; a salmon or (*esp*) herring split open and cured; a person, *esp* if young or small (*sl*); a British person (*obs Aust sl*). ◆ *vt* to cure or preserve (eg a salmon or herring). [Perh OE *cypera* a spawning salmon; or perh from **kip⁶**, from the beaked lower jaw of the male salmon after spawning]

■ **kipp'erer** *n*. ▫ **kipper tie** *n* (*inf*) a very wide, and often garish, necktie.

kipper² /kip'ər/ (*Aust*) *n* an Aboriginal youth initiated into manhood. [From an Aboriginal language]

kipunji /ki-pun'ji/ *n* a long-tailed Tanzanian monkey with a crest of erect hair. [Local name]

kir /kēr/ *n* a drink made of white wine and blackcurrant syrup or liqueur. [F *Kir* (1876–1968), the Frenchman who is said to have invented it]

kirbeh /kir'be/ *n* a water container made from animal hide. [Ar *qirba*]

Kirbigrip®, **kirby grip** or **kirbigrip** /kûr'bi-grip/ *n* a kind of hair-grip, a U-shaped piece of springy metal with one side ridged to prevent slipping. [From *Kirby*, the name of one of the original manufacturers]

Kirghiz same as **Kyrgyz**.

kirimon /kē'ri-mon/ *n* one of the two imperial crests of Japan, bearing three leaves and three flowers of Paulownia. [Jap]

kirk /kirk or kûrk/ (chiefly *Scot*) *n* church, in any sense; sometimes specially applied to the Church of Scotland. ◆ *vt* to church. [Scot and N Eng form of **church**, from ON *kirkja*; OE *cirice*]

■ **kirk'ing** or **kirk'in'** *n* the first attendance at church of a couple after marriage, of a woman after giving birth, or of a magistrate after election. **kirk'ward** *adj* and *adv*. ▫ **kirk session** *n* the lowest court in the Scottish Presbyterian church, minister or ministers and elders as the governing body of a particular congregation. **kirk'ton** or **kirk town** *n* (*Scot*) the village in which the parish church stands. **kirkyard** or **kirkyaird** /-yärd'/ or **kirk'** / *n* a churchyard.

■ **make a kirk or** (or **and**) **a mill of** to do what one pleases or can with. **the Auld Kirk** see under **auld**.

Kirlian photography /kûr′li-ən fə-tog′rə-fi/ n a process of directly recording on photographic film the electrical discharge emitted by an object placed in contact with the film, claimed by some to prove the existence of auras, and also used as a diagnostic tool in alternative medicine. [S and V *Kirlian*, Soviet electricians who discovered the process in 1939]

Kirman /kûr′mən/ n a type of Persian rug or carpet with naturalistic designs (also *adj*). [*Kerman* in SE Iran, where they are made]

kirmess see **kermis**.

kirn[1] /kirn/ or **kern** /kern or kûrn/ (*Scot*) n the cutting of the last sheaf or handful of the harvest; a harvest home. [Origin unknown]
□ **kirn′-ba′by**, **corn′-ba′by**, **kirn′-doll′ie**, **corn′-doll′ie** or **corn′-maiden** n a dressed-up figure made of the last handful of corn cut; (*esp* **corn-dollie**) any of a number of straw decorations *usu* of traditional design.

kirn[2] /kirn/ n a Scot and N Eng form of **churn**.
□ **kirn′-milk** n buttermilk.

kirpan /kər-pän′/ n a small sword or dagger, worn by Sikh men as a symbol of religious loyalty. [Punjabi]

kirri older form of **kierie**.

kirsch /kērsh/ or **kirschwasser** /kērsh′vä-sər/ n a liqueur made from the wild cherry. [Ger *kirschwasser* cherry water]

kirtan /kēr′tän/ n a type of Indian religious music in antiphonal form. [Sans *kīrtanam* praise]

kirtle /kûr′tl/ (*hist*) n a woman′s gown or outer petticoat; a man′s tunic or coat. [OE *cyrtel*; Dan *kjortel*; ON *kyrtill*; appar from L *curtus* short]
■ **kir′tled** *adj*.

kisan /kē′sän/ (*Ind*) n a peasant. [Hindi *kisān*]

kish /kish/ n solid graphite that has separated from, and floats on the top of, a molten bath of cast iron or pig iron which has a high carbon content. [Origin uncertain; poss Ger *Kies* gravel]

kishke /kish′kə/ n (*Jewish*) beef or chicken intestine stuffed with onion, flour meal and fat; (*esp* in *pl*) the guts. [Yiddish]

Kislev, **Chislev** /kis′lef/ or **Kisleu** /kis′li-oo/ n the third (ecclesiastically ninth) Jewish month, parts of November and December. [Heb]

kismet /kiz′met or kis′/ n fate, destiny. [Turk *qismet*, from Ar *qisma*]

kiss /kis/ vt to caress or greet by touching with the lips; (of an inanimate object) to touch gently. ◆ vi to greet by touching with the lips; (of two people) to press their lips together, *esp* as an expression of affection or sexual love; to touch lightly; (of snooker or billiard balls) to touch gently while moving. ◆ n a caress, greeting, etc by touching with the lips; a light touch, *esp* by a moving snooker ball on another; a melt-in-the-mouth biscuit, etc; a drop of sealing wax. [OE *cyssan* to kiss, from *coss* a kiss; Ger *küssen*, Dan *kys*; related to **choose** and **gust**[2]]
■ **kiss′able** *adj*. **kiss′er** n a person who kisses; the mouth (*sl*). **kiss′ogram** or **kiss′agram** n a service whereby a kiss is delivered to a specific person (eg on their birthday) by a **kissogram girl** (or **man**) *usu* in glamorous or unusual costume.
□ **kiss′-curl** n a flat, circular curl at the side of the forehead. **kissing bug** n any of several N and S American biting insects which attack victims′ lips and cheeks. **kiss′ing-com′fit** n a perfumed comfit for sweetening the breath. **kissing cousin** n a more or less distant relation with whom one is on familiar enough terms to kiss on meeting. **kiss′ing-crust** n that part of the upper crust of a loaf which overhangs and touches another. **kissing disease** n (*inf*) glandular fever. **kissing gate** n a gate set in a V- or U-shaped enclosure. **kiss′ing-strings** n pl cap or bonnet strings tied under the chin. **kiss-in-the-ring**′ n an old game in which one person kisses another after a chase round a ring of players. **kiss′-me** or **kiss′-me-quick** n the wild-pansy or other plant; a short veil; a small bonnet. **kiss of death** n (*inf*) something that causes failure, destruction, etc. **kiss-off** n (*sl*) a sudden, *usu* offensive dismissal. **kiss of life** n in first aid, a mouth-to-mouth method of restoring breathing (cf **Schafer′s method**); a means of restoring vitality or vigour (*fig*). **kiss of peace** n a kiss of greeting between the members of the early, and some branches of the modern, Church.
■ **kiss and make up** (*inf*) to become reconciled (also **kiss′-and-make-up** *adj*). **kiss and tell** (*inf*) to give an exposé of one′s sexual adventures (**kiss′-and-tell** *adj*). **kiss goodbye to** (*inf*) to relinquish all hope of. **kiss hands** to kiss the sovereign′s hands on acceptance of office. **kiss off** (*sl*) to dismiss; to kill; to die. **kiss** (**someone′s**) **arse** or (*N Am*) **ass** (*sl*) to be obsequious or sycophantic (towards someone); (in *imperative*; *offensive*) get lost, go away. **kiss the book** to kiss a Bible or New Testament, in England, after taking a legal oath. **kiss the gunner′s daughter** to get a flogging, tied to the breech of a cannon. **kiss the rod** to submit to punishment.

kissel /kis′l/ n a Russian dessert of thickened fruit purée. [Russ *kisel*]

kist /kist/ (*Scot* and *N Eng*) n a chest; a coffin; a cist (*archaeol*). ◆ vt to coffin. [OE *cist* chest, or ON *kista*]
□ **kist o′ whistles** n an organ.

kistvaen or **cistvaen** /kist′vīn/ (*archaeol*) n a cist. [Welsh *cist* chest, and *maen* stone, with lenition of *m*]

kit[1] /kit/ n an outfit; equipment; material, tools, instructions, assembled, *esp* in a container, for some specific purpose; the container itself; a container for fish, or the quantity held (10 stones or 63.6kg); a set of parts or pieces for assembly by the purchaser; a small wooden tub or pail (*dialect*). ◆ vt (sometimes with *out* or *up*) to provide with kit. [Prob MDu *kitte* a hooped container for beer]
□ **kit′bag** n a strong canvas bag for holding one′s kit or outfit (*milit*); a knapsack; a strong canvas grip. **kit′-boat** n or **-car** n a boat or car put together from standard components by an amateur builder.
■ **get one′s kit off** (*inf*) to remove one′s clothes, *esp* so as to display one′s private parts in public. **the whole kit** the whole set or lot (of things or people).

kit[2] /kit/ n a kitten; the young of various small fur-bearing mammals, eg the polecat, ferret, fox.
□ **kit′-cat** n the game of tip-cat.

kit[3] /kit/ (*hist*) n a small pocket violin. [Origin obscure; cf OE *cytere*, Gr *kithara*]

Kit-Cat /kit′kat/ n the name of a London Whig literary club, which existed from about 1688 or 1703 to about 1720, meeting for some time at the pie-shop of Christopher (*Kit*) *Cat* (or *Catling*); (also without *caps*) a portrait 36 by 28 inches in size, like those of the Kit-Cat Club painted by Kneller to fit their later low-ceilinged clubroom.

kitchen /kich′ən/ n a room or building in which food is cooked; the staff of such a room or building; a tea-urn (*obs Scot*); anything eaten as a relish with other food (*esp Scot*); the percussion section of an orchestra (*inf*). ◆ vt to regale in the cookroom (*Shakesp*); to serve as relish to (*Scot*); to make palatable (*Scot*); to use sparingly, make last (*Scot*). [OE *cycene*, from L *coquīna*, from *coquere* to cook]
■ **kitch′endom** n the domain of the kitchen. **kitch′ener** n a person employed in the kitchen; a cooking stove. **kitchenette**′ n a very small kitchen, or part of a room modified as such.
□ **kitchen cabinet** n an informal, unelected group of advisers to a political office-holder. **kitchen Dutch** or **kitchen Kaffir** n (*obs S Afr*) a mixture of Dutch or Kaffir with English, used in speaking to native servants. **kitch′en-fee** n (*obs*) the fat that falls from meat in roasting, a perquisite of the cook. **kitchen furniture** n the furniture of a kitchen; the percussion instruments of an orchestra. **kitchen garden** n a garden where vegetables are cultivated for the kitchen. **kitchen gardener** n. **kitch′en-knave** n (*obs*) a scullion. **kitch′en-maid** n a maid or servant whose work is in the kitchen. **kitchen midden** n (Dan *kjøkkenmödding*) a domestic rubbish heap found on an archaeological site. **kitchen police** n pl (*US milit sl*) soldiers detailed to help with kitchen duties, *esp* as a punishment. **kitch′en-range** n an old-fashioned kitchen grate with oven, boiler, etc attached, for cooking. **kitchen-sink** *adj* (of plays, etc) dealing with banal or sordid real-life situations. **kitch′en-stuff** n material used in kitchens; kitchen refuse, *esp* fat from pots, etc. **kitchen tea** n (*Aust* and *NZ*) a bride′s shower, the gifts being kitchen utensils, etc. **kitchen unit** n one of a set of fitted kitchen cupboards. **kitc′henware** n pots, pans, bowls, gadgets, utensils, etc such as are used in the kitchen. **kitch′en-wench** n (*Shakesp*) a kitchen-maid.
■ **everything except** (or **but**) **the kitchen sink** every conceivable thing.

kite[1] /kīt/ n a long-tailed bird of prey of the hawk family (Accipitridae); a rapacious person; a light frame covered with paper or cloth for flying in the air; a more complicated structure built of boxes (**box kite**), often for carrying recording instruments or a person in the air; a light additional sail, *usu* set high up; a rumour or suggestion given out to see how the wind blows, test public opinion, etc; an accommodation bill, *esp* a mere paper credit; an aircraft (*RAF sl*). ◆ vt to cause to fly like a kite; to write (a cheque) before one has sufficient money in one′s bank to cover it (*inf*). ◆ vi to fly like a kite; to rise sharply. [OE *cyta*; cf Welsh *cud*, Breton *kidel* a hawk]
■ **kit′ing** n kite-flying.
□ **kite′-balloon** n an observation-balloon designed on the principle of the kite to prevent revolving, etc. **kite′boarder** or **kite′surfer** n. **kite′boarding** or **kite′surfing** n the sport of being propelled over water by a large kite while standing upright on a specially designed surfboard (**kite′board**). **kite′-flyer** n a person who takes part in kite-flying. **kite′-flying** n sending up and controlling a kite; the juggling of cheques between accounts so as to create a sham balance of funds on which to draw; testing public opinion by circulating rumours, etc. **Kite mark**, **Kite′mark** or **kite′-mark** n a kite-shaped mark on goods indicating conformity in quality, size, etc, with the specifications of the British Standards Institution. **kite′-marked** *adj* bearing this mark. **kite′surfing** see **kiteboarding** above.

■ words derived from main entry word; □ compound words; ■ idioms and phrasal verbs

■ **fly a kite** to take part in kite-flying (qv above).

kite² or **kyte** /kīt/ (*Scot* and *N Eng*) *n* a paunch, belly. [Ety uncertain]

kitenge /ki-teng'gē/ *n* (in E Africa) a length of brightly-coloured thick cotton cloth, worn *esp* as a woman's dress. [Swahili]

kith /kith/ *n* knowledge (*obs*); native land (*obs*); one's friends or acquaintances (*obs* except in **kith and kin** friends and relatives). [OE *cȳth*, from *cunnan* to know]

kithara /kith'ə-rə/ same as **cithara**.

kithe see **kythe**.

kitling see under **kitten**.

kitsch /kich/ *n* trash; art, literature, fashion, etc dismissed as being of merely popular taste or appeal, vulgar, sentimental or sometimes pretentious. ◆ *adj* trashy or vulgar. [Ger]
■ **kitsch'ily** *adv*. **kitsch'iness** or **kitsch'ness** *n*. **kitsch'y** *adj*.

kitten /kit'n/ *n* a young cat (*dimin* **kitt'y**); sometimes the young of another animal. ◆ *vt* and *vi* (of a cat) to give birth (to). [ME *kitoun*, from ONFr *caton*, dimin of *cat*, from LL *cattus* cat]
■ **kit'ling** *n* (*Scot*) a kitten. **kitt'enish** or **kitt'eny** *adj* frolicsome; skittish; affectedly playful. **kitt'enishly** *adv*. **kitt'enishness** *n*. **kitt'le** *vt* and *vi* (*Scot*) to kitten; to come or bring into being.
❑ **kitten heel** *n* a low, tapering heel on a woman's shoe; (*usu* in *pl*) a shoe having such a heel. **kitt'en-heeled** *adj*. **kitten moth** *n* any of several smaller moths similar to the puss moth.
■ **have kittens** to be in a state of great excitement, anxiety or anger.

kittiwake /kit'i-wāk/ *n* a gull of the genus *Rissa* with long wings and rudimentary hind-toes. [Imit]

kittle¹ /kit'l/ (*esp Scot*) *adj* difficult to deal with, *esp* because touchy, obstinate or intractable; fickle, capricious. ◆ *vt* to tickle; to offend; to puzzle. [Ety obscure]
■ **kitt'ly** *adj* (*Scot*) ticklish; easily offended, sensitive.
❑ **kittle cattle** *n pl* (*fig*) awkward customers. **kitt'ly-bend'ers** *n* (*US*) running on thin bending ice.

kittle² see under **kitten**.

kittle-pins /kit'l-pinz/ *n pl* skittles (also **kett'le-pins**). [Prob alteration of **kail¹**]

kittly see under **kittle¹**.

kittul see **kitul**.

kitty¹ /kit'i/ *n* a pool or fund of money held in common; the jack (*bowls*); a jail (*archaic*). [Origin uncertain]

kitty² see **kitten**.

kitty-cornered /kit'i-kör-nərd/ (*N Am*) *adj* and *adv* same as **catercornered** (see under **cater²**).

kitul or **kittul** /ki-tool'/ *n* the jaggery palm (*Caryota urens*); its fibre. [Sinhalese *kitūl*]

kiva /kē'və/ *n* a partly or wholly underground chamber used for religious ceremonies by Pueblo peoples. [Hopi]

Kiwanis /ki-wä'nis/ *n* a N American social and charitable organization. [Adapted from Ojibwa *nunc kee-wanis* we make a noise]
■ **Kiwan'ian** *n* and *adj*.

kiwi /kē'wē/ *n* a flightless bird of New Zealand, the apteryx; a New Zealander (*inf, esp sport*); a non-flying member of an airfield staff (*inf*); a kiwi fruit. [Maori, from the bird's cry]
❑ **kiwi fruit** *n* the fruit of a subtropical vine (*Actinidia chinensis*) with edible pale green flesh and a furry greyish-brown skin (also called **Chinese gooseberry**).

kJ *abbrev*: kilojoule(s).

KKK *abbrev*: Ku Klux Klan.

KL *abbrev*: Kuala Lumpur, the capital of Malaysia.

kl *abbrev*: kilolitre(s).

Klan, etc see **Ku Klux Klan**.

klang or sometimes **clang** /klang/ (*music*) *n* a complex tone, composed of fundamental and harmonics; timbre. [Ger]
❑ **klang'farbe** /-fär-bə/ *n* tone-colour; timbre.

klatch or **klatsch** /klach/ (*inf, esp N Am*) *n* a coffee party or similar social function. [Ger *Klatsch* gossip]

klavier /klä-vēr'/ *n* a clavier. [Ger, from Fr *clavier*]

klaxon or **Klaxon** /klak'sən/ *n orig* a mechanical horn with a loud rasping sound, of a kind used on early motor vehicles; any electric horn. ◆ *vi* to sound a klaxon. [Name of the manufacturer]

Klebsiella /kleb'zi-el-ə/ *n* a genus of Gram-negative rodlike bacteria, which cause various diseases in man and animals, including pneumonia. [E *Klebs* (1834–1913), German pathologist]

Klebs-Löffler bacillus /klebz-lûf'lər bə-sil'əs/ *n* a rod-shaped Gram-positive bacterium (*Corynebacterium diphtheriae*) that causes diphtheria in humans and similar diseases in other animals. [E *Klebs*

(see ety for **Klebsiella**) and F *Löffler* (1852–1915), German bacteriologist]

Kleenex® /klē'neks/ *n* a trademark for various absorbent paper products, *esp* a kind of soft tissue used as a handkerchief.

kleftiko /klef'ti-kō/ *n* a Greek dish of slowly cooked lamb. [Mod Gr, from *kleftikos* relating to the klephts]

Kleig light see **Klieg light**.

Klein bottle /klīn bot'l/ (*maths*) *n* a one-sided four-dimensional surface, which in three dimensions can be represented as a surface obtained by pulling the narrow end of a tapering tube through the wall of the tube and then stretching the narrow end and joining it to the larger end. [Felix *Klein* (1849–1925), German mathematician]

klendusic /klen-dū'sik/ *adj* (of plants) able to withstand disease by means of some protective mechanism. [Gr *kleidoein* to lock up, from *kleis* a key, and *endusis* entry]
■ **klendū'sity** *n*.

klepht /kleft/ *n* one of the Greeks who took to the mountains in patriotic resistance to the 15c Turkish conquest of Greece, or one of their descendants, by the 19c merely brigands. [Mod Gr *klephtēs*, from ancient Gr *kleptēs* thief, from *kleptein* to steal]
■ **klepht'ic** *adj*. **klepht'ism** *n*.

kleptocracy /klep-tok'rə-si/ *n* government by thieves, a thieves' regime; a country with such a government; a body or order of thieves. [Gr *kleptēs* thief, and **-cracy**]
■ **klept'ocrat** *n*. **kleptocrat'ic** *adj*.

kleptomania or **cleptomania** /klep-tō-mā'ni-ə/ *n* a mania for stealing; a morbid impulse to hide things away. [Gr *kleptein* to steal, and *maniā* madness]
■ **kleptomā'niac** *n* and *adj*.

Kletterschuhe /klet'ər-shoo-ə/ (also without *cap*) *n pl orig* felt-soled, now also Vibram-soled, lightweight rock-climbing boots. [Ger, from *kletter-* climbing, and *Schuhe* shoes]

klezmer /klez'mər/ *n* (*pl* **klezmorim** /-mö-rim/) traditional E European Yiddish music; a player of this music. [Yiddish, from Heb *keley zemer* musical instruments]

Klieg light or **Kleig light** /klēg līt/ *n* a type of incandescent floodlighting lamp for film studio use, the brilliance of which may cause a strain on the eyes (**klieg eyes**). [From *Kliegl* brothers, the inventors]

Klinefelter's syndrome /klīn'fel-tərz sin'drōm/ *n* impaired gonadal development in a male with one or more extra X-chromosomes, resulting in underdeveloped testes, mixed (male and female) secondary sexual characteristics, sterility, and sometimes mild mental retardation. [HF *Klinefelter* (1912–90), US physician]

klinker or **clinker** /kling'kər/ *n* a very hard paving-brick. [Du]

klinostat /klī'nō-stat/ *n* a revolving stand for experimenting with growing plants. [Gr *klīnein* to incline, and *statos* standing]

klipdas /klip'das/ *n* a S African hyrax (*Hyrax capensis*). [Du, literally, rock-badger]

klipspringer /klip'spring-ər/ *n* a small S African antelope. [Du *klip* rock, and *springer* jumper]

KLM *abbrev*: *Koninklijke Luchtvaart Maatschappij* (*Du*), Royal Dutch Airlines.

Klondike or **Klondyke** /klon'dīk/ (also without *cap*) *n* a very rich source of wealth; a card game, a form of patience. ◆ *vt* and *vi* to export (fresh fish, *esp* herring) direct from Scotland to the Continent; to tranship (fish) at sea. [From the gold-rush to *Klondike* in the Yukon, beginning 1896]
■ **klon'dyker** or **klon'diker** *n* a factory ship.

kloof /kloof/ (*S Afr*) *n* a mountain ravine. [Du, cleft]

klootchman or **kloochman** /klooch'mən/ (*NW US and W Can*) *n* (*pl* **-mans** or **-men**) a native American woman or wife (also **klootch** or **klooch**). [Chinook, from Nootka *lhūtsma*]

kludge /kluj/ (*comput; inf*) *n* a botched or makeshift device or program which is unreliable or inadequate in function. ◆ *vt* to patch up using a kludge.
■ **kludg'y** *adj*.

klutz /kluts/ (*N Am sl*) *n* an idiot; an awkward, stupid person. [Ger *Klotz* idiot]
■ **klutz'iness** *n*. **klutz'y** *adj*.

klystron /klis' or klīs'tron/ *n* any of a number of electron tubes (amplifiers, oscillators, etc) in which the velocity of the electron beam is modulated by an ultra-high-frequency field and subsequently imparts energy to it or other UHF fields. [Gr *klystēr* syringe]

KM *abbrev*: Knight of Malta.

km *abbrev*: kilometre(s).

K-meson /kā-mē'zon/ *n* another name for **kaon**.

km/h *abbrev* : kilometres per hour.

kn. *abbrev* : knot(s) (the nautical, etc measure).

knack /nak/ *n* a special unfailing talent, learned or *esp* intuitive; a thing regularly (and *esp* unwittingly or unconsciously) done, a habit; a clever contrivance (*obs*); a toy, ornament or knick-knack (*obs*). [Prob from (*obs*) *knack* a cracking sound (imit); cf Du *knak* a crack, Ger *knacken* to crack]
■ **knack'iness** *n*. **knack'ish** or **knack'y** *adj* cunning, crafty.

knacker¹ /nak'ər/ *n* someone who buys and slaughters old horses; someone who buys and breaks up old houses, ships, etc; a worn-out horse. ◆ *vt* to wear out, exhaust, break or disable (*inf*); to kill; to castrate. [Origin obscure]
■ **knack'ered** *adj* (*inf*) exhausted, worn-out. **knack'ery** *n* a knacker's yard.
□ **knacker's yard** *n* a place where horses are slaughtered; the scrap-heap (*fig*).

knacker² /nak'ər/ *n* anything that makes a snapping or cracking sound; (in *pl*) castanets or clappers, bones; (in *pl*) testicles (*sl*). [Imit]

knackwurst /nak'woorst, -wûrst or (*Ger*) -voorst/ *n* a kind of highly seasoned sausage (also **knock'wurst**). [Ger *knacken* to crack, and *Wurst* sausage]

knag /nag/ *n* a knot in wood; a peg. [Cf Dan *knag*, Ger *Knagge*]
■ **knagg'iness** *n*. **knagg'y** *adj* knotty; rugged.

knaidel or **kneidel** /knā'dl/ (*Jewish cookery*) *n* (*esp* in *pl* **knaidlach** or **kneidlach** /knā'dlähh/) a kind of dumpling *usu* eaten in clear soup. [From Yiddish]

knap¹ /nap/ (*obs* except *dialect*) *n* a protuberance; a hillock; a hill-crest. [OE *cnæpp*]

knap² /nap/ *vt* (**knapp'ing; knapped**) to snap or break with a snapping noise; to break (eg stones) in pieces with repeated blows; to pronounce with a snapping effect; to rap; to bite off, nibble; to steal. [Du *knappen* to crack or crush]
■ **knapp'er** *n* someone who breaks stones, *esp* flint-flakes for gun-flints. **knapp'le** *vi* to nibble.
□ **knap'-bottle** *n* the bladder campion. **knapp'ing-hammer** *n* (*Scot*) a hammer for breaking stones.

knapsack /nap'sak/ *n* a bag made of strong material, with straps for carrying on the back, eg when hiking; a rucksack. [Du *knappen* to crack, eat]

knapskull, knapscull or **knapscal** /nap'skəl/ (*obs Scot*) *n* a kind of helmet. [Origin unknown]

knapweed /nap'wēd/ *n* a composite plant of the genus *Centaurea*, like a spineless thistle. [Earlier *knopweed*; see **knop**]

knar¹ or **gnar** /när/ *n* a knot on a tree. [Cf LGer *knarre*, Du *knar*; also **knur**]
■ **knarred** or **gnarred** *adj* gnarled, knotty.

knar² /när/ see **gnar¹**.

knarl see **gnarl¹**.

knave /nāv/ *n* orig, as in *Shakesp*, a boy; a serving-boy; a dishonest or deceitful man, a rogue (*old*); a jack (*cards*). [OE *cnafa*, *cnapa* a boy, a youth; Ger *Knabe*, *Knappe*]
■ **knav'ery** *n* dishonesty. **knave'ship** *n* (*Scot*) a certain quantity of grain, the due of the miller's servant. **knav'ish** *adj* fraudulent; dishonest. **knav'ishly** *adv*. **knav'ishness** *n*.
□ **knave'-bairn** *n* (*Scot*) a male child.

knawel /nö'əl/ *n* a cornfield weed (genus *Scleranthus*) of the chickweed family. [Ger *Knauel* or *Knäuel*]

knead /nēd/ *vt* to work and press together into a mass (eg flour into dough); to massage. [OE *cnedan*; cf ON *knotha*, Ger *kneten*]
■ **knead'able** *adj*. **knead'er** *n*.
□ **knead'ing-trough** *n* a trough in which to knead.

knee /nē/ *n* the joint between the thigh and shin bones; in a horse's foreleg, the joint corresponding to the human wrist; in a bird, the joint corresponding to the ankle; the part of a garment covering the knee; a root upgrowth by which swamp-growing trees breathe; a piece of timber or metal shaped like a bent knee; a piece of machinery that operates like a knee; a genuflexion (*Shakesp*). ◆ *vt* to press, strike or nudge with the knee; to provide with a knee; to make (trousers, etc) baggy at the knee; to kneel to (*Shakesp*); to achieve by kneeling, or crawl over on the knees (*Shakesp*). ◆ *vi* (*obs*) to kneel. [OE *cnēow*, *cnēo*; Ger *Knie*, L *genu*, Gr *gony*]
■ **kneed** or **knee'd** *adj* having knees or angular joints; (of trousers) baggy at the knees.
□ **knee'-breeches** *n pl* breeches extending to just below the knee. **knee'-cap** or **knee'cap** *n* the patella, a flat round bone on the front of the knee joint; a cap or strong covering for the knees, used chiefly for horses to save their knees in case of a fall. ◆ *vt* to subject to knee-capping. **knee'-capping** or **knee'capping** *n* a form of torture or (terrorist) punishment in which the victim is shot or otherwise injured

in the knee-cap. **knee'-cords** *n pl* knee-breeches of corduroy. **knee'-crooking** *adj* (*Shakesp*) obsequious, fawning. **knee'-deep** *adj* rising or reaching to someone's knees; sunk to the knees; deeply involved (in). **knee'-deep** *adv*. **knee'-drill** *n* directed devotional exercises. **knee'-high** *adj* rising or reaching to someone's knees (also *adv*). ◆ *n* a sock or stocking that reaches to the knee. **knee'hole** *n* the space beneath a desk or bureau for the knees. **knee'-holly** *n* butcher's broom. **knee'-jerk** *n* a reflex throwing forward of the leg when tapped below the knee-cap. ◆ *adj* (of a reaction) automatic, unthinking, predictable. **knee joint** *n* the joint of the knee; a joint with two pieces at an angle, so as to be very tight when pressed into a straight line. **knee'-length** *adj* reaching to the knee. **knee'-pad** *n* a protective cover for the knee. **knee'-pan** *n* the knee-cap. **knee sock** *n* a sock reaching to just below the knee. **knee'-stop** or **-swell** *n* a lever worked by an organist's knee, for regulating the wind supply of a reed organ, etc. **knees'-up** *n* (*inf*) a riotous dance or party. **knee'-timber** *n* timber bent into a shape suitable for a knee in shipbuilding, etc. **knee'-trembler** *n* (*sl*) an act of sexual intercourse in a standing position; loosely, any sexual adventure. **knee'-tribute** *n* (*Milton*) the homage of kneeling.
■ **bend** or **bow the knee** to kneel or submit. **bring someone to his** or **her knees** to make someone admit defeat. **give** or **offer a knee** (*Thackeray*, etc) to act as second in a fight, it being usual for the principal to rest on the second's knee between the rounds. **knee-high to a grasshopper** (*orig US*) very short, with connotation of extreme youth. **on the knees of the gods** awaiting the decision of fate (after Homer). **sit on someone's knee** to sit on the horizontal surface of a seated person's thighs.

kneel /nēl/ *vi* (*pat* and *pap* **kneeled** or **knelt** /nelt/) to rest or fall on a knee or the knees. [OE *cnēowlian*]
■ **kneel'er** *n* a person who kneels; a flat cushion or bench to rest the knees on while kneeling; a hassock.

kneidel and **kneidlach** see **knaidel**.

Kneipe /knī'pə/ (*Ger*) *n* a tavern, a students' beer house or drinking party.

knell /nel/ *n* the sound of a bell, *esp* at a death or funeral; something that signals the end of anything. ◆ *vi* to toll. ◆ *vt* to summon or proclaim as by a tolling bell. [OE *cnyllan* to beat noisily; Du and Ger *knallen*]

knelt *pat* and *pap* of **kneel**.

Knesset /knes'it/ *n* the one-chamber parliament of Israel. [Heb, assembly]

knevell a variant of **nevel**.

knew /nū/ *pat* of **know**.

knicker see **nicker⁴**.

knickerbocker /nik'ər-bok-ər/ *n* (in *pl*) loose breeches gathered in at the knee; (with *cap*) a descendant of one of the original Dutch settlers of New York; (with *cap*) a New Yorker. [From the wide-breeched Dutchmen in *Knickerbocker*'s (ie Washington Irving's) humorous *History of New York*]
□ **knickerbocker glory** *n* a large and extravagant ice-cream sundae.

knickers /nik'ərz/ *n pl* women's or girls' underpants (*inf*); a woman's undergarment covering (and sometimes gathered in at) the thigh; knickerbockers (*N Am*). ◆ *interj* (*inf*) now *usu* a mild expression of exasperation, etc. [**knickerbocker**]
■ **knick'ered** *adj* clad in knickers. **knick'erless** *adj*. **knicks** *n* (*inf*) knickers.
■ **get one's knickers in a twist** (*inf*) to become harassed, anxious or agitated.

knick-knack, also **nick-nack** /nik'nak/ *n* a small, trifling, ornamental or would-be ornamental article. [A doubling of **knack**]
■ **knick-knack'atory** *n* a collection of knick-knacks. **knick-knack'ery** *n* knick-knacks collectively. **knick-knack'et** *n* a knick-knack. **knick'-knacky** *adj*. —Also **nick-nack'atory**, etc.

knickpoint or **nickpoint** /nik'point/ (*geol*) *n* a discontinuity in a river profile, *esp* when caused by the intersection of a new curve of erosion. [Part-translating Ger *Knickpunkt*, from *knicken* to bend, and *punkt* point]

knife /nīf/ *n* (*pl* **knives** /nīvz/) an instrument with a blade for cutting or spreading. ◆ *vt* to cut; to apply with a knife; to stab; to try to defeat by treachery. ◆ *vi* to cut (with *through*) or penetrate (with *into*) as if with a knife. [ME *knif*, from OE *cnīf*]
■ **knife'less** *adj* without a knife; without use of the knife. **knife'like** *adj*. **knif'er** *n*. **knif'ing** *n* the (criminal) act of stabbing someone with a knife.
□ **knife-and-fork'** *n* (*Dickens*) a trencherman. ◆ *adj* involving, or relating to, the use of a knife and fork. **knife'-board** *n* a board on which knives are cleaned; a bench running along the top of an old type of bus (*inf*). **knife'-box** *n* a box for keeping table cutlery in. **knife'-boy** *n* a boy employed in cleaning knives. **knife'-edge** *n* the cutting edge of a knife; a sharp-edged ridge; a sharp piece of steel

---

serving as the axis of a balance, etc (also *fig*, *esp* as *adj* or in phrase **on a knife-edge** critically poised, in the balance). **knife'-grinder** *n* someone who grinds or sharpens knives. **knife'-man** *n* a man wielding or using a knife. **knife'-money** *n* a knife-shaped bronze currency formerly used in China. **knife pleat** *n* a narrow, flat pleat. **knife'-point** *n* the sharp tip of a knife (**at knife-point** under threat of injury by a knife). **knife'-rest** *n* a support for a carving knife or fork. **knife'-switch** *n* a switch in an electric circuit, in which the moving element consists of a flat blade that engages with fixed contacts.
■ **at it like knives** continuously and eagerly occupied with it. **have one's knife in** to bear a grudge against; to be persistently hostile or vindictive towards. **the knives are out for** people are out to get (someone). **twist the knife (in the wound)** to increase someone's distress or embarrassment, eg by making constant reminders of the circumstances that caused it. **under the knife** undergoing a surgical operation. **war to the knife** unrelenting conflict.

knight /nīt/ *n* a man who has been awarded the rank immediately below baronet, with the title 'Sir'; in the Middle Ages, a man who performed mounted military service for his lord in exchange for land; in feudal times, a gentleman, bred to arms, admitted to a certain honourable military rank; a man devoted to the service of a lady, her champion; a member of the equestrian order in ancient Rome; in chess, any of four pieces, two on each side, *usu* shaped like a horse's head, that can move one square forward, backward, or to either side, and one diagonally; formerly used in jocular titles of various professions, as in **knight of the shears** a tailor, and **knight of the whip** a coachman. ◆ *vt* to make a knight. [OE *cniht* youth, servant, warrior; Ger *Knecht* and Du *knecht* servant]
■ **knight'age** *n* knights collectively. **knight'hood** *n* the rank, title or status of knight; the order or fraternity of knights. **knight'less** *adj* (*Spenser*) unbecoming to a knight. **knight'liness** *n*. **knight'ly** *adj* like a knight; befitting a knight; chivalrous; of a knight or knights. ◆ *adv* in the manner of a knight.
❏ **knight bachelor** *n* (*pl* **knights bachelors** or **knights bachelor**) a knight belonging to no special order of knighthood (the lowest form of knight in rank and earliest in origin). **knight banneret** *n* (*pl* **knights bannerets**) a knight who carried a banner and who was superior in rank to the knight bachelor. **knight errant** *n* (*pl* **knights errant**) a knight who travelled in search of adventures; a man or boy who behaves adventurously or chivalrously. **knight errantry** *n*. **knighthood-err'ant** *n* (*Tennyson*) the body of knights errant. **knight marshal** *n* formerly an officer who had jurisdiction over offences within twelve miles of the monarch's abode. **Knight of St John** or **Knight of Malta** *n* a hospitaller (qv under **hospital**). **knight of the road** *n* (*facetious*) a highwayman (*obs*); a commercial traveller; a lorry driver; a tramp. **knight of the shire** *n* a member of parliament for a county district. **knight service** *n* tenure of land by a knight on condition of military service. **knight's fee** *n* a holding of land for which knight service was required. **Knights of Labor** *n pl* (*US*) a secret 19c organization for workers. **knight's progress** *n* in chess, a series of moves in which a knight may visit every square on the board. **Knights Templar** see **Templar**.

kniphofia /nip-hō'fi-ə or nī-fō'fi-ə/ *n* any plant of the African *Kniphofia* genus of the lily family, otherwise called *Tritoma*, the red-hot poker. [Named after JH *Kniphof* (1704–65), German botanist]

knish /knish/ *n* (in Jewish cookery) dough with a potato, meat, etc filling, baked or fried. [Yiddish, from Russ]

knit /nit/ *vt* (**knitt'ing**; **knitt'ed** or **knit**) to make (a garment, etc) by means of knitting needles or a knitting machine; to form (wool, etc) into network by needles or machinery; to do so in plain stitch (cf **purl¹**); to intertwine; to unite closely, to draw together; to contract (the brows, etc); to form into a knot (*archaic*); to tie together (*archaic*). ◆ *vi* to knit something; (of the brows, forehead, etc) to contract in a frown; to grow together. ◆ *n* a style of knitting (*Shakesp*); a knitted fabric or article. [OE *cnyttan*, from *cnotta* a knot]
■ **knitt'er** *n*. **knitt'ing** *n* knitted work; the act or process of producing knitted work; union, junction. ◆ *adj* of, for, or relating to knitting.
❏ **knitting machine** *n* a machine for knitting. **knitting needle** *n* a long needle or wire, without an eye, used for knitting. **knit'wear** *n* knitted clothing.

knitch /nich/ (*dialect*) *n* a faggot, a bundle of wood, etc tied together. [OE *gecnycc* bond]

knittle /nit'l/ *n* a small line made of two or three yarns twisted with the fingers (*naut*); (in *pl*) the halves of two yarns in a rope, twisted for pointing. [OE *cnyttels* sinew, string]

knive /nīv/ *vt* (*rare*) to knife.

knives plural of **knife**.

knob /nob/ *n* a hard protuberance; a hard swelling; a round ornament, button or handle; a small roundish lump of a substance; the penis (*sl*); a stupid person (*sl*); a small group (of wildfowl). [Cf LGer *knobbe*; **knop**]

■ **knobbed** *adj* containing or set with knobs. **knobb'er** *n* a stag in its second year. **knobb'iness** *n*. **knobb'le** *n* a small knob. **knobb'ly** or **knobb'y** *adj* having, or full of, knobs; knotty.
❏ **knob'head** *n* (*vulgar sl*) an idiot; someone despised. **knob'stick** *n* a stick with a knobbed head; a blackleg or scab (*obs sl*).
■ **with (brass) knobs on** (*inf*) with interest, more so.

knobble see under **knob**, **knubble**.

knobkerrie /nob'ke-ri/ *n* a round-headed stick used as a club and a missile by some S African peoples. [**knob** and **kierie**, on the model of Afrik *knopkierie*]

knock /nok/ *vi* to strike hard or heavily; to drive or be driven against something; to strike *esp* a door for admittance; to rap; to make a noise by, or as if by, striking; (of machinery) to rattle or clank regularly; (of an internal-combustion engine) to make the noise caused by detonation. ◆ *vt* to strike; to drive against; to bring to a specified state or position by striking or pushing; to make by striking; to impress strongly, stun, daze, confound (*sl*); to disparage, criticize in a carping way (*inf*); to approach (a specified age) (*inf*); to have sexual intercourse with (*sl*). ◆ *n* a sudden stroke; a rap; the noise of detonation in an internal-combustion engine; a reversal, shock, setback (*inf*); a criticism (*inf*); an innings, a spell at batting (*cricket*); a clock (*Scot*). [OE *cnocian*; perh imit]
■ **knock'er** *n* someone who knocks; a device suspended on a door for making a knock; a carper or critic (*inf*); (in *pl*) a woman's breasts (*sl*); someone who makes unsolicited door-to-door calls on domestic householders, eg hoping to buy valuables from them, or selling, etc; a goblin thought to inhabit a mine who points out the presence of ore by knocks (*dialect*). **knock'ing** *n* a beating on a door; a rap; a noise as if of something that knocks; knock in an internal-combustion engine; the practice of making unsolicited calls on householders, eg hoping to buy valuables from them.
❏ **knock'about** *n* a boisterous performance with horseplay; a performer of such turns; someone who does odd jobs, *esp* on a station (*Aust*); a small yacht without a bowsprit (*N Am*); a small motor car suitable for doing short journeys. ◆ *adj* boisterous (*orig theatre*); suitable for rough use (*obs*). **knock'-back** *n* a setback; a refusal or rejection (*sl*); a refusal of parole from prison (*sl*). **knock'-down** *n* an act or instance of knocking down; an introduction (*US*, *Aust* and *NZ inf*). ◆ *adj* such as to overthrow, powerful; adapted for being taken to pieces; (of prices) very low. **knocked'-down** *adj* supplied in parts or kit form for assembly by the purchaser. **knock'er-up** *n* a person employed to rouse workers in the morning. **knock-for-knock agreement**, **policy**, etc *n* an arrangement between motor insurance companies by which, after an accident involving two cars, each company settles the damage to the car it insures without considering which driver was to blame. **knocking copy** *n* advertising material that denigrates competing products. **knock'ing-shop** or **knocking shop** *n* (*sl*) a brothel. **knock'-knee** *n* the state of being knock-kneed. **knock-kneed'** *adj* having knees that knock or touch in walking; weak (*fig*). **knock'-on** see **knock on** and **knock-on effect** below. ◆ *adj* (*inf*) causing or caused by a series of consequences. **knock'out** *n* the act of knocking out; a blow that knocks out; a conspiracy among dealers at an auction to keep prices artificially low; any person or thing of outstanding attraction or excellence (*inf*); a knockout competition; see also **technical knockout** under **technical**. ◆ *adj* (of a competition) eliminating losers at each round; stunningly attractive or excellent (*inf*). **knockout auction** *n* an auction at which the majority of bidders are dealers in league to keep prices artificially low. **knockout drops** *n pl* (*inf*) a drug put in a drink to make the drinker unconscious. **knock'-rating** *n* the measurement of freedom from knocking of a fuel in an internal-combustion engine, as compared with a standard fuel. **knock'-up** *n* (in tennis, etc) practice immediately before a match.
■ **knock about** or **around** to mistreat physically; to discuss informally; to saunter, loaf about; to be around in the area; to travel about, roughing it and having varied experiences; to be a casual friend of, associate with (with *with*). **knock back** (*inf*) to drink or eat, *esp* swiftly; to cost; to shock, disconcert; to rebuff, reject, turn down. **knock cold** to knock (someone) out; to shock violently. **knock copy** to disparage a rival's products. **knock down** to fell with a blow; to demolish; to assign (an article) with a tap of the auctioneer's hammer (to); to reduce in price (*inf*); to spend (one's resources) on a drinking binge (*Aust* and *NZ sl*); to misappropriate, filch (*US*) (**knock-down** *adj* see above). **knock into a cocked hat** see under **cock¹**. **knock into the middle of next week** (*inf*) to hit (someone) very hard. **knock off** (*inf*) to stop work; to stop, discontinue; to accomplish hastily; to deduct; to steal, rob (*sl*); to copy illegally, to pirate (*sl*); to kill (*sl*); to have sexual intercourse with (*sl*). **knock on** to grow old (*inf*); to knock (the ball) forward with the hand or arm (an infringement of the rules in rugby; **knock'-on** *n*). **knock-on effect** the effect one action or occurrence has on one or more indirectly related matters or circumstances. **knock one's head against a brick wall** to meet with total resistance or refusal to compromise. **knock on the head** (*inf*) to suppress, put an end to. **knock on wood** see **touch wood** under

touch. **knock out** to dislodge by a blow; to strike unconscious or incapable of recovering in time (*boxing*); to defeat in a knockout competition; to overcome, demolish, destroy, disable; to produce, *esp* quickly or roughly (*inf*); to tire (oneself) out (*sl*); to overwhelm with amazement, admiration, etc (*sl*); to disable (a specific gene) in order to study the effect that it has on an organism (*genetics*). **knock sideways** (*inf*) to put off one's usual course. **knock the bottom out of** (*inf*) to make, or show to be, invalid; to make ineffectual, bring to nothing. **knock the (living) daylights out of** see under **day**. **knock together** (*inf*) to get together or construct hastily. **knock under** (*archaic*) to give in, yield. **knock up** to rouse by knocking; to wear out; to construct or arrange hastily; to achieve (a certain score) (*games, esp cricket*); to practise immediately before a match (*tennis*, etc); to make pregnant (*sl*). **on the knocker** on credit (*sl*); immediately, on the nail (*Aust sl*). **up to the knocker** (*obs sl*) up to the required standard of excellence or fashion.

knockwurst see **knackwurst**.

knoll[1] /nōl/ (*Scot* **knowe** /now/) *n* a round hillock; the top of a hill (*dialect*). [OE *cnol*; Ger *Knollen* a knob, lump]

knoll[2] /nōl/ archaic form of **knell**.

knop /nop/ *n* a loop or tuft in yarn; a bud (*archaic*); a knob (*obs*). [Cf ON *knappr*; Du *knop*, Ger *Knopf*]

knosp /nosp/ *n* the unopened bud of a flower; an architectural ornament resembling this. [Ger *Knospe*]

knot[1] /not/ *n* an interlacement of parts of a cord or cords, rope, ribbon, etc, by twisting the ends around each other, and then pulling tight the loops thus formed; any of various specific methods of forming such an interlacement; a piece of ribbon, lace, etc folded or tied upon itself as an ornament, eg *shoulder-knot*, *breast-knot*, etc; anything like a knot in form; a bond of union; an elaborately designed flower-bed (*hist*); a tangle (in string, hair, etc); a difficulty; the main point or central part of a tangle, intricacy, problem or difficulty; a complex of lines, mountains, etc; the base of a branch buried in a later growth of wood; a cross-section of this joint, visible as a darker roundish mark, in a length of wood; a node or joint in a stem, *esp* of a grass; a hard lump; a concretion; a swelling; a knob; a boss; a bud; a hill (*dialect*); a clump or cluster; a specific quantity of yarn; a division of the knot-marked log-line; a nautical mile per hour, used in navigation and meteorology; loosely, a nautical mile; a tight feeling, eg in the stomach, caused by nervousness. ◆ *vt* (**knott'ing**; **knott'ed**) to tie in a knot; to unite closely; to make knotty; to make by knotting; to remove knots from; to cover knots in (wood before painting). ◆ *vi* to form a knot or knots; to knit knots for a fringe. [OE *cnotta*; Ger *Knoten*, Dan *knude*, L *nōdus*]

■ **knot'less** *adj.* **knott'ed** *adj* full of, or having, knots. **knott'er** *n* a person or contrivance that makes or removes knots. **knott'ily** *adv.* **knott'iness** *n.* **knott'ing** *n* the formation or removal of knots; the covering of knots before painting; the sealer used for this; fancywork done by knitting threads into knots. **knott'y** *adj* containing knots; hard, rugged; difficult; intricate.

❑ **knot garden** *n* a garden with intricate formal designs of shrubs, flower-beds, etc. **knot'grass** *n* a much-jointed species of *Polygonum*, a common weed; applied also to various grasses. **knot'hole** *n* a hole in wood where a knot has fallen out. **knot'weed** *n* any of various plants of the genus *Polygonum*. **knot'work** *n* ornamental work made with knots; carving or decoration in interlaced forms.

■ **at a rate of knots** (*inf*) very fast. **get knotted!** (*inf*) an interjection expressing anger, derision, defiance, etc. **porters' knot** (*obs*) a double shoulder-pad with a loop fitting round the forehead, used to help market porters carry their load. **tie someone (up) in knots** to confuse or bewilder someone completely. **tie the knot** (*inf*) to get married.

knot[2] /not/ *n* a small shore bird (*Calidris canutus*) of the sandpiper family. [Origin unknown: the connection with King Cnut is a fancy of English antiquarian William Camden (1551–1623)]

Knotenschiefer /knō'tən-shē-fər/ *n* spotted slate or spotted schist, slightly altered argillaceous rock spotted with little concretions. [Ger, knot slate or schist]

knout /nowt or noot/ *n* a whip formerly used as an instrument of punishment in Russia; punishment inflicted by the knout. ◆ *vt* to flog. [Fr spelling of Russ *knut*]

know /nō/ *vt* (**know'ing**; **knew** /nū or (*N Am*) noo/; **known** /nōn/) to be informed or assured of; to be acquainted with; to be familiar with from having learned or experienced; to recognize; to take notice of, approve (*Bible*); to have sexual intercourse with (*archaic*). ◆ *vi* to possess knowledge, in general or of the matter in hand. ◆ *n* possession of the relevant facts; knowledge (*Shakesp*). [OE *cnāwan*; ON *knā*, L (*g*)*nōscere*, Gr *gignōskein*]

■ **know'able** *adj* capable of being known, discovered or understood. **know'ableness** *n.* **know'er** *n.* **know'ing** *adj* intelligent; skilful; cunning; signifying secret awareness; deliberate. **know'ingly** *adv* in a knowing manner; consciously; intentionally. **know'ingness** *n* the quality of being knowing or intelligent; shrewdness. **known** *adj* widely recognized; identified by the police. ◆ *n* a known fact; (with *the*) that which is known.

❑ **know'-all** *n* someone who thinks they know everything. **know'-how** or **know'how** *n* the faculty of knowing the right thing to do in any contingency; specialized skill. **know'-nothing** *n* someone who is totally ignorant; a member of the (Native) American Party (1854–6), *orig* secret. ◆ *adj* completely ignorant. **know'-nothingism** *n.*

■ **I don't know** I disagree. **I know** or **I know what** I've got an idea. **in the know** (*inf*) in possession of private information; initiated. **I wouldn't know** I am not in a position to know. **know all the answers** to be completely informed on everything, or to think one is. **know better** to be wiser, better instructed (than to do this or that). **know how many beans make five** to be sensible and aware, to have one's wits about one. **knowing to** (*obs*) aware or informed of. **known as** going by the name of. **know the ropes** to understand the detail or procedure. **know what's o'clock** (*obs*) or **know what's what** to have one's wits about one, be on the ball. **know which side one's bread is buttered on** to be looking after one's own interests. **there is no knowing** one cannot tell. **what do you know?** what is the news?; a greeting or expression of incredulity. **you know** (*inf*) used as a conversation filler, marking a pause, sometimes for emphasis but often almost meaningless. **you never know** (*inf*) perhaps.

knowe see **knoll**[1].

knowledge /nol'ij/ *n* that which is known; information, instruction; enlightenment, learning; practical skill; assured belief; acquaintance; cognizance (*law*); (with *the*) the detailed information on which London taxi-drivers are tested before being licensed; sexual intimacy (*archaic*). ◆ *vt* (*obs*) to acknowledge. [ME *knowleche*, where *-leche* is unexplained; see **know**]

■ **knowledgeabil'ity** or **knowledgabil'ity** *n.* **knowl'edgeable** or **knowl'edgable** *adj* possessing knowledge; intelligent; well-informed. **knowl'edgeably** or **knowl'edgably** *adv.*

❑ **knowledge base** *n* (*comput*) a collection of specialist knowledge formulated for use *esp* in expert systems. **knowl'edge-based** *adj* of software systems that store and effectively utilize large amounts of such specialist knowledge. **knowledge box** *n* (*sl*) the head. **knowledge economy** *n* an economic system that is driven by the rapid and widespread dissemination of information. **knowledge engineering** *n* (*comput*) the application of artificial intelligence techniques in constructing expert systems. **knowledge worker** *n* someone whose job involves the accumulation, analysis or dissemination of information.

■ **to one's** or (**to the best of one's**) **knowledge** so far as one knows.

knub or **nub** /nub/ *n* a knob; a small lump; the waste or refuse of silk-cocoons. [Cf LGer *knubbe*]

■ **knubb'le** or **nubb'le** *n* a small lump. **knubb'ly, nubb'ly, knubb'y** or **nubb'y** *adj.*

knubble, nubble /nub'l/ or **knobble** /nob'l/ *vt* to beat with the fists; to knock. [**knob**]

knuckle /nuk'l/ *n* any of the bones that protrude when a finger joint is bent; a joint of veal or pork from the knee downwards (*cookery*). ◆ *vi* to yield (*usu* with *down* or *under*); (in marbles) to touch the ground with the knuckles (*usu* with *down*); to bend the knee inward (*obs golf*). ◆ *vt* to touch or press with the knuckle or knuckles; to shoot (a marble) from the thumb knuckle. [ME *knokel*, not recorded in OE; cf Du *knokkel* (dimin of *knok*), Ger *Knöchel* ankle-bone, knuckle (dimin of *Knochen* bone)]

■ **knuck'ly** *adj.*

❑ **knuck'leball** *n* (*baseball*) a type of pitch with an unpredictable trajectory, caused by gripping the ball with the fingertips. **knuck'leballer** *n* (*baseball*) a pitcher who throws knuckleballs. **knuck'le-bone** *n* any bone with a rounded end; (in *pl*) the game of dibs. **knuck'le-bow** *n* the curved part of a sword-guard that covers the fingers. **knuck'leduster** *n* a metal covering for the knuckles, worn on the hand as a weapon in fist-fighting. **knuck'le-head** *n* (*inf*) an idiot. **knuck'le-headed** *adj.* **knuckle-head'edness** *n.* **knuckle joint** *n* any of the finger joints; a hinged joint in which two pieces of machinery are joined by a pin through eyes at their ends, one piece being forked and enclosing the other (*mech*). **knuckle sandwich** *n* (*inf*) a blow with the fist.

■ **knuckle down (to)** to set oneself to hard work (on); see also *vi* above. **knuckle under** to yield to authority, pressure, etc. **near the knuckle** on the verge of the indecent. **rap someone's knuckles** to reprimand someone.

knur, knurr, nur or **nurr** /nûr/ *n* a knot on a tree; a hard ball or knot of wood. [ME *knurre*; cf Du *knor*, MHGer *knorre*, Ger *Knorren*]

❑ **knur and spell** *n* a game played with a knur, trap (*spell*), and stick, chiefly in N England.

knurl or **nurl** /nûrl/ *n* a small excrescence or protuberance; a ridge or bead, *esp* in series, eg in the milling of a screw-head; a dwarfish person (*Burns*). ◆ *vt* to make knurls on, to mill. [Prob a dimin of **knur**]

■ **knurled** *adj* (spelt **gnarled** in *Shakesp, Measure for Measure* II.2) covered with knurls. **knurl'ing** *n* mouldings or other woodwork elaborated into a series of knobs. **knurl'y** *adj* gnarled.

knut /knut/ *or* /nut/ (*sl*) see **nut**.

KO *or* **k.o.** *abbrev*: kick-off; knockout; knock out. ◆ *vt* /kā-ō'/ (*inf*) (**KO'ing** *or* **k.o.''ing**; **KO'd** *or* **k.o.'d**') to knock out. ◆ *n* (*pl* **KO's** *or* **k.o.'s**') a knockout.

ko /kō/ (*NZ*) *n* (*pl* **kos**) a Maori digging stick. [Maori]

koa /kō'ə/ *n* a Hawaiian acacia. [Hawaiian]

koala /kō-ä'lə/ *n* an Australian marsupial, like a small bear, also called **koala bear** *or* **native bear**. [Aboriginal word *kūlā*]

koan /kō'än/ *n* (in Zen Buddhism) a nonsensical, logically unanswerable question given to students as a subject for meditation. [Jap, a public proposal or plan]

kob /kob/ *n* any of various species of African water-antelope or waterbuck. [Wolof]

koban /kō'ban/ *or* **kobang** /kō'bang/ *n* an obsolete oblong gold Japanese coin, rounded at the corners. [Jap *ko-ban*]

kobo /kō'bō/ *n* (*pl* **ko'bo**) a Nigerian monetary unit, $\frac{1}{100}$ of a naira. [Local pronunciation of **copper**]

kobold /kō'bold/ (*Ger folklore*) *n* a spirit of the mines; a benevolent creature who may secretly help with domestic work. [Ger]

kochia /kō'ki-ə/ *or* /kok'i-ə/ *n* a plant (*Kochia scoparia*) of the goosefoot family whose foliage turns dark red in late summer (also called **burning bush**, **summer cypress**). [WDJ *Koch* (1771–1849), German botanist]

Koch's postulates /kohhs pos'tū-ləts/ *n pl* criteria formulated by German bacteriologist Robert *Koch* (1843–1910) for establishing that a micro-organism is the cause of a disease.

ko cycle /kō sī'kl/ *n* in traditional Chinese medicine, the cycle that balances and controls the interaction of the five basic elements (see also **sheng cycle, wu cycle**).

Kodak® /kō'dak/ *n* a make of camera. ◆ *vt and vi* (*rare*) to photograph with a Kodak. [The trademark name of the Eastman *Kodak* Company]

Kodiak /kō'di-ak/ *or* **Kodiak bear** /bār/ *n* the largest variety of brown bear (*Ursus arctos*), found in Alaska and the Aleutian Islands. [From *Kodiak* Island, Alaska]

koel /kō'əl/ *n* an Asian and Australasian cuckoo of the genus *Eudynamys*. [Hindi, from Sans *kokila*]

koff /kof/ *n* a small Dutch sailing-vessel. [Du *kof*]

kofta /kof'tə/ (*Ind cookery*) *n* minced and seasoned meat or vegetables, shaped into balls and fried.

koftgar /koft'gär/ (*Ind*) *n* someone who inlays steel with gold. [Urdu from Pers *koftgar*]
■ **koftgari** /koft-gur-ē'/ *or* sometimes **koft'work** *n* such work.

kohanga reo /kə-hung'ə rā'ō/ (*NZ*) *n* (*pl* **kohang'a re'os**) an infant class using Maori as the medium of instruction. [Maori, literally, language nest]

kohen /kō'hen *or* kō'ən/ (*Judaism*) *n* (*pl* **ko'hanim**) a member of the priestly class, descended from Aaron, having certain privileges and obligations in the synagogue. [Heb, literally, priest]

kohl /kōl/ *n* a fine powder of native stibnite (formerly known as antimony), black in colour, used (*orig* in the East) to darken the area around the eyes. [Ar *koh'l*]

kohlrabi /kōl-rä'bi/ *n* a variety of cabbage with a turnip-like edible stem. [Ger, from Ital *cavolo rapa*, from L *caulis* cabbage, and *rapa* turnip]

koi /koi/ *n* (*pl* **koi**) a Japanese carp. [Jap]

Koine /koi'nē/ *n* a Greek dialect developed from Attic, in use in the E Mediterranean in Hellenistic and Byzantine times; (often without *cap*) any dialect that has spread and become the common language of a larger area. [Gr *koinē* (*dialektos*) common (dialect)]

koka /kō'kä/ *n* the lowest score awarded for a throw or hold in judo, worth three points. [Jap]

kokako /kō'kə-kō *or* kō'kə-kō/ *n* (*pl* **ko'kakos**) a large New Zealand bird (*Callaeas cinerea*) with dark plumage and two wattles. [Maori]

kokanee /kō-kan'ē/ *n* a small landlocked species of sockeye salmon. [From Salish]

koker /kō'kər/ (*Guyana*) *n* a sluice-gate. [Du]

kokra /kok'rə/ *n* the wood of an Indian tree (genus *Aporosa*) of the spurge family, used for making flutes, clarinets, etc.

kok-saghyz /kok-sä'gēz/ *n* a species of dandelion (*Taraxacum koksaghyz*) from the Tien Shan, grown in Russia, etc for rubber-making. [Russ]

kokum /kō'kəm/ *n* an Indian tree (*Garcinia indica*). [Marathi *kokamb* mangosteen]
□ **kokum butter** *n* an edible fat obtained from its nuts.

kola see **cola**.

Kolarian /kō-lä'ri-ən/ *n* the Munda group of languages (also *adj*). [*Kolar*, ancient name of India]

kolinsky /ko-lin'ski/ *n* a species of mink (*Mustela sibirica*) found in E Asia, or its fur. [Russ *kolinski* of the Kola Peninsula]

kolkhoz /kol-hhoz'/ *n* (*pl* **kolkhoz'**, **kolkhoz'es** *or* **kolkhoz'y**) a collective or co-operative farm in the former USSR. [Russ abbrev of *kollektivnoe khozyaistvo*]

Kol Nidre /kol nē'drä/ (*Judaism*) *n* the opening prayer said at the service on the eve of Yom Kippur; the service itself; the traditional music for this prayer. [Aramaic *kol nidre* all vows, the opening words of the prayer]

kolo /kō'lō/ *n* (*pl* **kō'los**) a Serbian folk dance or dance tune. [Serbo-Croat, wheel]

komatik /kom'ə-tik/ *n* an Inuit sled with wooden runners. [Inuit]

kombu /kom'boo/ *n* an edible brown seaweed, used *esp* for making stock, a species of *Laminaria*. [Jap]

Kominform, **Komintern** alternative forms of **Cominform**, **Comintern**.

komissar same as **commissar**.

komitaji /kō-mē-tä'jē/ *n orig* a member of the Bulgarian Revolutionary Committee in Macedonia; any Balkan guerrilla. [Turk *qomitaji* committee-man, bandit, from *qomite*, from Fr *comité* committee]

Kommers /ko-mers'/ *n* a traditional gathering of a German student fraternity, with drinking and singing. [Ger, from L *commercium* commerce]
■ **Kommers'buch** /-boohh/ *n* a songbook for such occasions.

Komodo dragon *or* **lizard** /kə-mō'dō drag'ən *or* liz'ərd/ *n* a very large monitor lizard (*Varanus komodoensis*) of some Indonesian islands. [From *Komodo* Island, Indonesia]

komondor /kom'ən-dör/ *n* (sometimes with *cap*) a large powerful sheepdog with a long white coat. [Hung]

Komsomol /kom'sə-mol/ *n* the Communist youth organization in the former Soviet Union. [Russ abbrev of *Kommunisticheskii Soyuz Molodezhi* Communist Union of Youth]

kon (*pat* **kond**; *Spenser*) variant of **con**[3].

konfyt /kon-fīt'/ (*S Afr*) *n* a preserve of fruit, in syrup or candied; jam. [Afrik, from Du *konfijt*]

kongoni /kon-gō'ni/ *n* (*pl* **kongo'ni**) an E African hartebeest (*Alcelaphus buselaphus*). [Swahili]

konimeter /ko-nim'i-tər/ *n* an instrument for measuring dust in air. [Gr *konis* dust, and *metron* measure]
■ **koniol'ogy** *n* the study of dust in the air and its effects. **kon'iscope** *n* an instrument for estimating the dustiness of air.

konk same as **conk**[2,3].

koodoo see **kudu**.

kook[1] /kook/ (*sl*) *n* a person who is mad, foolish, or eccentric and amoral. [Prob from **cuckoo**]
■ **kook'ie** *or* **kook'y** *adj* with the qualities of a kook; (of clothes) smart and eccentric. **kook'ily** *adv*. **kook'iness** *n*.

kook[2] see **cook**[3].

kookaburra /koo'kə-bur-ə/ *n* an Australian kingfisher (*Dacelo novaeguineae*) which has a discordant laughing call, the laughing jackass. [From an Aboriginal language]

kookie, **kooky** see under **kook**[1].

koolah /koo'lə/ *n* an obsolete form of **koala**.

koori /kūr'i/ (*Aust*) *n* an Aborigine; a young Aboriginal woman. [From an Aboriginal language]

kop /kop/ *n* a hill (*S Afr*); (with *cap*) a bank of terracing at a football ground, *orig* that at Liverpool's Anfield ground. [from Afrikaans *kopje* little head; from Du *kop* head]
■ **koppie** *or* **kopje** /kop'i/ *n* (*S Afr*) a low hill.

kopasetic see **copacetic**.

kopeck, **kopek** *or* **copeck** /kō-pek' *or* kō'pek/ *n* a Russian coin, the hundredth part of a rouble, no longer having any significant worth. [Russ *kopeika* small lance]

koph /kof, köf *or* kōf/ *n* the nineteenth letter of the Hebrew alphabet. [Heb *qōph*]

kopiyka /ko-pē'ə-kə/ *n* (*pl* **kopi'yok** *or* **kopi'ykas**) a Ukrainian monetary unit, $\frac{1}{100}$ of a hryvna. [Cf **kopeck**]

kopje see under **kop**.

koppa /kop'ə/ n a Greek letter (ϙ) between pi and rho in the alphabet, corresponding to Q in the Roman alphabet, dropped by most Greek dialects but retained as a numeral: ϙ =90, ͵ϙ =90 000. [Gr; cf Heb *qōph*]

koppie see under **kop**.

kora¹ /kō'rə or kō'rə/ n a W African musical instrument similar to a harp. [Native word]

kora² /kō'rə or kö'rə/ n the water cock (genus *Gallicrex*). [Origin uncertain]

Koran /kō-rän' or kö-, sometimes kō'rən or kö'/ n the Muslim Scriptures in Arabic, believed by the faithful to be the true word of God as spoken by Mohammed (also **Qoran**, **Quran** and **Qur'an**). [Ar *qurān* reading]
■ **Koranic** /-rän'ik/ adj.

kore /kö'rə/ n an archaic Greek statue of a draped maiden. [Gr, maiden; cf **kouros**]

Korean /kə-rē'ən/ adj of or relating to North or South *Korea* in E Asia, their people or language. ◆ n an inhabitant or native of North or South Korea; their language.
▫ **Korean chrysanthemum** n a late-flowering hybrid chrysanthemum.

korero /ko-rer'ō/ (*NZ*) n (pl **kore'ros**) a talk, discussion. [Maori]

korfball /körf'böl or körf'böl/ n a game of Dutch origin resembling basketball played by teams of six men and six women a side. [Du *korfbal*, from *korf* basket, and *bal* ball]

korkir see **corkir**.

korma /kör'mə/ n a mild-flavoured Indian dish consisting of meat or vegetables braised in water, stock, yoghurt or cream.

korora /kō'rō-rə/ n the fairy penguin. [Maori]

Korsakoff's psychosis or **syndrome** /kör'sə-kofs sī-kō'sis or sin'drōm/ (*med*) n an illness in which damage to a small area of the brain results in disorientation and absolute loss of recent memory, often caused by alcoholism. [S *Korsakoff* (1854–1900), Russian physician]

koruna /ko-roo'nə/ n the standard monetary unit of the Czech Republic and Slovakia (100 haleru). [Czech, from L *corona* crown]

kos same as **coss**.

kosher /kō'shər/ adj pure or clean according to Jewish law; (of food) prepared according to Jewish dietary law; legitimate, proper, genuine (*inf*). ◆ n kosher food. ◆ vt to prepare (food) in a kosher manner. [Heb *kāshēr* right]

kosmos same as **cosmos¹**.

Kosovar /kos'əvär/ n a native or citizen of Kosovo, a region of the former Yugoslavia that declared unilateral independence in 2008. ◆ adj of or relating to Kosovo.

koss same as **coss**.

koto /kō'tō/ n (pl **ko'tos**) a Japanese musical instrument consisting of a long box with thirteen silk strings. [Jap]

kotow a less common form of **kowtow**.

kottabos /kot'ə-bos/ same as **cottabus**.

kotwal or **cotwal** /kōt'wäl/ n a chief constable or magistrate of an Indian town. [Hindi *kotwāl*]

koulan see **kulan**.

koulibiaca same as **coulibiac**.

koumiss see **kumiss**.

kouprey /koo'prā/ n the very rare SE Asian wild cow, believed to be closely related to the ancestors of modern domestic cattle. [Native name in Cambodia]

kourbash see **kurbash**.

kouros /koo'ros/ n an archaic Greek statue of a nude youth. [Ionic Greek, boy; cf **kore**]

kouskous see **couscous**.

kow see **cow³**.

kowhai /kō'hī, -hwī or -wī/ n a New Zealand tree or shrub of the genus *Sophora*, with golden flowers. [Maori]

kowtow /kow-tow'/, also **kotow** /kō-tow'/ n the old Chinese ceremony of touching the forehead to the ground as a gesture of deference. ◆ vi to perform that ceremony; to abase oneself before (with *to*); to grovel or fawn. [Chin *kē* knock, and *tóu* head]
■ **kowtow'er** n.

KP abbrev : kitchen police; Knight of (the Order of) St Patrick.

kpg abbrev : kilometres per gallon.

kph abbrev : kilometres per hour.

Kr (*chem*) symbol : krypton.

kr abbrev : krona (Swedish currency); króna (Icelandic currency); krone (Danish and Norwegian currency).

kraal /kräl/ n a S African village of huts surrounded by a fence; a corral. ◆ vt to pen. [Du *kraal*, from Port *curral*, from L *currere* to run]

krab /krab/ (*mountaineering*) n short form of **karabiner**.

kraft /kräft/ n a type of strong brown wrapping paper made from pulp treated with a sulphate solution (also **kraft paper**). [Ger *Kraft* strength]

krait /krīt/ n a deadly S Asian rock snake (*Bungarus caeruleus*). [Hindi *karait*]

kraken /krä'kən/ n a fabled sea-monster. [Norw; the -*n* is the definite article]

krakowiak see **cracovienne** under **Cracovian**.

krameria /krä-mē'ri-ə/ n the shrub rhatany, a S American plant with thick roots from which an astringent is prepared; the astringent itself. [JGH and WH *Kramer*, 18c German botanists]

krang see **kreng**.

krantz, kranz /kränts/ or **krans** /kräns/ (*S Afr*) n a crown of rock on a mountain-top; a precipice. [Du *krans* a wreath]

krater see **crater**.

kraut /krowt/ (often with *cap*; *derog sl*) n a German. [From **sauerkraut**]

krav maga /kräv mä'gə or krav mə-gä'/ n a system of unarmed combat originally developed in Israel. [Heb, contact fighting]

kreasote same as **creosote**.

kreatine same as **creatine**.

Krebs cycle /krebz sī'kl/ n (in the mitochondria of cells) the biochemical pathway whereby, in the presence of oxygen, the pyruvic acid formed by glycolysis is broken down to form carbon dioxide and water, with the release of large amounts of energy in the form of ATP (also called **citric acid cycle**, **tricarboxylic acid cycle**). [H *Krebs* (1900–81), German-born British biochemist]

kreese same as **kris**.

kremlin /krem'lin/ n a citadel, *esp* (with *cap*) that of Moscow; (with *cap*) the Russian government, formerly the central government of the Soviet Union. [Russ *kreml'*]
■ **Kremlinol'ogist** n. **Kremlinol'ogy** n the study of the former Soviet government and its policies.

kreosote same as **creosote**.

kreplach /krep'lähh/ n pl small dough dumplings filled with cheese, meat, etc, *usu* served in soup. [Yiddish]

kreutzer /kroit'sər/ n any of various former copper coins of Austria, S Germany, etc, one hundredth of the florin or gulden. [Ger *Kreuzer*, from *Kreuz* cross, because they were at one time stamped with a cross]

krewe /kroo/ (*US*) n an organization that arranges parades and social gatherings at a Mardi Gras carnival. [Altered spelling of **crew¹**]

k'ri /krē/ n a marginal reading in the Hebrew Bible, intended as a substitute for the k'thibh (qv). [Heb *qerē* read (imperative)]

kriegspiel or **kriegsspiel** /krēg'spēl/ n a war game played on a map to train officers; a form of chess in which the players use separate boards and are allowed only limited communication through an umpire. [Ger *Kriegsspiel*, from *Krieg* war, and *Spiel* game]

Krilium® /kril'i-əm/ n a substance added to soil to improve its structure, consisting of synthetic polymers.

krill /kril/ n pl small shrimplike creatures of the genus *Euphausia* (order Euphausiaceae), eaten by whales, etc. [Norw *kril*]

krimmer or **crimmer** /krim'ər/ n tightly curled grey or black fur from a Crimean type of lamb. [Ger *Krim* Crimea]

kris /krēs/ n (pl **kris'es**) a Malay dagger with a wavy scalloped blade (also **crease**, **creese** or **kreese**). ◆ vt to stab with a kris. [Malay]

Krishna /krish'nə/ n a deity in later Hinduism, a form of Vishnu. [Sans]
■ **Krish'naism** n (also called **Krishna Consciousness**) belief in, or worship of, Krishna.

Kris Kringle or **Kriss Kringle** /kris kring'gl/ (*US*) n a traditional name for Santa Claus. [Ger *Christkindl* the Christ child]

kromesky /krō-mes'ki or krə-, also krō' or kro'/ n a croquette wrapped in bacon or calf's udder, and fried. [Pol *kroméczka* little slice]

krona /kroo'nə/ n (pl **kro'nor**) the standard monetary unit of Sweden (100 öre). [Swed, crown]

króna /krō'nə/ n (pl **krónur**) the standard monetary unit of Iceland (100 aurar). [Icel, crown]

krone /krō'nə/ n the standard unit of currency of Denmark and Norway (100 öre) (pl **kro'ner**); a former silver coin of Austria, equal to 100 heller (pl **kro'nen**); a former gold coin of Germany, equal to 10 marks (pl **kro'nen**). [MLGer *krōne* ; cf **crown**]

Kronos /kron'os or krō'nos/ n a supreme god of the Greeks, son of Ouranos and Gaia, dethroned by his son Zeus.

krónur see **króna**.

kroon /kroon/ n (pl **kroons** or **kroo'ni**) the standard monetary unit of Estonia (100 senti). [Estonian, crown]

Kru or **Kroo** /kroo/ n a member of a W African people of the coast of Liberia, noted as seamen; the language of this people. ♦ adj of the Kru or their language.
□ **Kru'-** or **Kroo'-boy** or **-man** n.

Krugerrand /kroo'gər-rand/ n a South African coin, used only for investment, containing one troy ounce of fine gold and bearing a portrait of SJP Kruger (President of the Transvaal 1883–1900) (also **Kruger Rand**, **rand**, or **krugerrand**). [**rand**[1]]

kruller see **cruller**.

krummholz /krum'holts/ n a wood composed of stunted trees growing just above the timber line on a mountain. [Ger, literally, crooked wood]

krummhorn, **krumhorn** or **crumhorn** /krŭm'hörn/ n an old double-reed wind instrument with a curved end; an organ reed stop. [Ger, curved horn]

krumping /krum'ping/ n an energetic style of hip-hop dancing, incorporating punching and kicking movements. [Origin uncertain; perh related to **crunk**]

krunk see **crunk**.

kryometer, etc same as **cryometer**, etc (see under **cryo-**).

krypsis /krip'sis/ n the 17c doctrine that Christ secretly exercised divine powers. [Gr, concealment]

krypton or **crypton** /krip'ton/ n an inert gaseous element (symbol **Kr**; atomic no 36) present in the air in extremely small quantity, used in fluorescent lights and lasers. [Gr kryptein to hide]
■ **kryp'tonite** n someone or something that renders an apparently invulnerable person or thing vulnerable (after the name of the only substance to which the comic-strip character Superman is vulnerable).

krytron /krī'tron/ (technol) n a sophisticated electronic timing device used for detonating nuclear and other explosive charges, and for varied industrial and scientific purposes.

KS abbrev : Kansas (US state); Kaposi's sarcoma; Kyrgyzstan (IVR).

KSA abbrev : Kingdom of Saudi Arabia (IVR).

ksar /ksär/ (Milton) n a variant of **tsar**.

Kshatriya /kshat'ri-ya/ n a member of the second or military caste among the Brahmanic Hindus. [Sans, from kshatra authority]

KStJ abbrev : Knight of (the Order of) St John.

KT abbrev : Knight of the Thistle; Knight Templar.

Kt abbrev : Knight.

kt abbrev : karat (carat); kiloton(s) or kilotonne(s); knot (naut).

k'thibh /kthēv/ n a traditional but erroneous reading retained in the main text of the Hebrew Scriptures. [Heb kethībh written; cf **k'ri**]

Ku (chem) symbol : kurchatovium.

kuccha same as **kaccha**.

kuchcha same as **cutcha**.

Kuchen /koo'hhən/ (Ger) n a cake or cakes.

Kuchipudi /kŭch-i-poo'di/ n a traditional form of dance drama originating in S India. [Named after the village of Kuchipudi]

kudos /kū'dos/ n credit, fame, renown, prestige. [Gr kȳdos glory]

kudu or **koodoo** /koo'doo/ n an African antelope with long spiral horns. [From Khoikhoi]

kudzu /kŭd'zoo/ n an ornamental papilionaceous plant of China and Japan (Pueraria thunbergiana) with edible root tubers and a stem yielding a fibre. [Jap kuzu]

Kufic or **Cufic** /kū'fik/ adj of Al Kūfa, south of Babylon, esp of the lettering of its coins, inscriptions and manuscripts, mainly early copies of the Koran. ♦ n the script formed by this lettering.

kufiyah see **kaffiyeh**.

kugel /koo'gəl/ n (in Jewish cookery) a baked pudding, either sweet or savoury. [Yiddish]

Kuh-horn /koo'hörn/ (Ger) n an alpenhorn.

Kuiper Belt /kī'pər belt/ (astron) n a large ring of icy bodies orbiting the Sun just beyond Neptune. [G Kuiper (1905–73), Dutch-born US astronomer who predicted its existence]

Ku Klux Klan /koo kluks klan/ or **Ku Klux** or **the Klan** n a secret organization founded in the Southern USA after the Civil War of 1861–5 to oppose Northern influence and prevent blacks from enjoying their rights as freemen, and later revived in an attempt to preserve White Protestant supremacy by violent means. [Gr kyklos a circle, and **clan**]
■ **Ku Klux'er** n.
□ **Ku Klux Klann'er** or **Ku Klux Klan'sman** n a member of this organization (also **Klansman**).

kukri /kŭk'rē/ n a sharp, curved Gurkha knife or short sword. [Hindi kukṛ]

kuku /koo'koo/ n a large fruit-eating pigeon of New Zealand (Hemiphaga novaeseelandiae), the wood pigeon. [Maori]

kula /koo'lə/ n a ceremonial exchange of gifts among inhabitants of some Pacific islands to promote good relationships between islands. [Melanesian]

kulak /koo-lak'/ (Russ) n a rich peasant, in the Communist period regarded as an exploiter of others and a class traitor. [Russ, fist]

kulan or **koulan** /koo'län/ n the onager, or a related wild ass of the Kyrgyz Steppe. [Kyrgyz]

kulfi /kŭl'fi/ n an Indian ice-cream dessert. [Hindi]

Kultur /kool-toor'/ (Ger) n culture, civilization, esp German civilization, sometimes used derogatorily to suggest imperialism, militarism and arrogance.
□ **Kultur'geschichte** /-gə-shehh'tə/ n the history of civilization. **Kultur'kampf** /-kampf/ n the war of culture (used by Virchow in 1873 of the conflict between Bismarck and the Roman Catholic Church). **Kultur'kreis** /-krīs/ n an area regarded as a centre of diffusion of cultural elements.

kumara /koo'mə-rə/ n the sweet potato. [Maori]

kumari /kŭ-mar'i/ (Ind) n Miss (as a title of respect).

kumiss or **koumiss** /koo'mis/ n fermented mares' milk. [Russ kumis, from Tatar kumiz]

kumite /koo'mi-tā/ n freestyle fighting in the martial arts. [Jap, literally, sparring]

kümmel /kŭm'l, kim'l or kŭm'l/ n a liqueur flavoured with cumin and caraway seeds. [Ger, from L cumīnum, from Gr kymīnon cumin]

kumquat or **cumquat** /kum'kwot/ n a very small Chinese variety of orange with a sweet rind; the small evergreen shrub or tree that yields this fruit. [Cantonese, gold orange]

kuna /koo'nə/ n (pl **ku'na**) the standard monetary unit of Croatia (100 lipa). [Serbo-Croat, marten]

kung fu /kung foo/ n a martial art (of both armed and unarmed combat and self-defence) developed in ancient China. [Chin gōng fū combat skill]

kunkur /kung'kûr/ or **kunkar** /kung'kər/ n a concretionary limestone in India; a laterite found in Sri Lanka. [Hindi kaṇkar stone]

Kunstlied /kŭnst'lēt/ (Ger) n an art-song.

kunzite /kun'zīt/ n a lilac-coloured variety of spodumene, used as a gemstone. [GF Kunz (1856–1932), US gemologist]

Kuomintang /kwō'min-tang or gwō'min-däng/ n the Chinese nationalist people's party, formed in 1912. [Chin Guómíndǎng national people's party]

Kuo-yü /kwō' or gwō'yü/ n a form of Mandarin taught all over China. [Literally, national language]

Kupferschiefer /kŭp'fər-shē-fər/ n a shale rich in copper in the Permian of Germany. [Ger, copper shale]

kurbash or **kourbash** /koor'bash/ n a hide whip used in the East. ♦ vt to whip with a kurbash. [Ar qurbāsh]

kurchatovium /kûr-chə-tō'vi-əm/ n a former name for **rutherfordium** (see under **rutherford**). [IV Kurchatov (1903–60), Russian physicist]

Kurd /koord or kûrd/ n one of the Islamic people of Kurdistan, a mountainous region of Turkey, Iran and Iraq.
■ **Kurd'ish** adj and n.

kurdaitcha /kə-dī'chə/ n (in Aboriginal tribes of central Australia) the man charged with avenging the death of a kinsman. [From an Aboriginal language]

kurgan /kŭr-gän'/ n a prehistoric burial mound. [Russ, from Tatar]

Kurhaus /koor'hows/ (Ger) n a building in which a spa is housed. [Literally, cure-house]

kuri /kū'ri/ (NZ) n a mongrel; an extinct native dog. [Maori]

Kuroshio /koo-rō'shi-ō/ n a warm current flowing north along the western edge of the Pacific. [Jap, black stream]

kurrajong or **currajong** /kur'ə-jong/ n a name for various Australian trees with fibrous bark. [From an Aboriginal language]

kurre (Spenser) same as **cur**.

Kursaal /koor'zäl/ (Ger) n the reception-room of a spa. [Literally, cure-room]

kurta or **khurta** /kŭr'tä/ n a loose-fitting collarless shirt or tunic worn in India. [Hindi]

kurtosis /kər-tō'sis/ (*stats*) *n* the relative degree of sharpness of the peak on a frequency-distribution curve. [Gr *kyrtōsis* bulging, swelling, from *kyrtos* curved]

kuru /koo'roo/ *n* a progressive and fatal brain disease, related to Creutzfeldt-Jakob disease, found only in certain parts of Papua New Guinea and now thought to be transmissible by prions. [Native word, meaning 'the trembles']

kurus /kə-roosh'/ *n* (*pl* **kurus'**) a Turkish monetary unit, $\frac{1}{100}$ of a lira. [Turk *kurus*]

kurvey /kûr-vā'/ (*obs S Afr*) *vi* to transport goods by ox-wagon. [Du *karwei* work, from Fr *corvée*; cf **corvée**]
■ **kurvey'or** *n* a carrier.

Kushite, etc same as **Cushite**, etc.

kutch same as **cutch²**.

kutcha same as **cutcha**.

Kuwaiti /koo-wā'ti/ *adj* of or relating to the state of *Kuwait* in the Arabian Gulf, or its inhabitants. ◆ *n* a native or citizen of Kuwait.

kuzu /koo'zoo/ *n* a thickening agent made from the starch of the kudzu plant, acceptable in a macrobiotic diet. [See **kudzu**]

kV *abbrev*: kilovolt(s).

kvass /kväs/ *n* an E European rye beer. [Russ *kvas*]

kvetch /kvech/ *vi* to complain, whine, *esp* incessantly. ◆ *n* a complaint; a grumble. [Yiddish]
■ **kvetch** or **kvetch'er** *n* a complainer, fault-finder.

kW *abbrev*: kilowatt(s).

KWAC /kwak/ *abbrev*: keyword and context.

kwacha /kwach'ə/ *n* the standard monetary unit of Zambia (100 ngwee) and Malawi (100 tambala). [Native name, meaning 'dawn']

Kwakiutl /kwä-kē-oo'tl/ *n* a Native American people of Vancouver Island and the mainland coastal area adjacent to it; a member of this people; their language. ◆ *adj* of the Kwakiutls or their language.

kwanza /kwän'zə/ *n* the standard monetary unit of Angola (100 lwei).

Kwanzaa /kwan'zä/ *n* (in the USA) a non-religious seven-day holiday (from 26 December to 2 January) celebrating African-American life, history and culture. [Swahili, literally, first fruits]

kwashiorkor /kwä-shi-ör'kör or kwosh'/ *n* a widespread nutritional disease of newly weaned children in tropical and subtropical regions due to deficiency of protein. [Ghanaian name; perh derived from a reference to the displacement of a child on weaning and arrival of next child]

kwela /kwā'lə/ *n* Zulu folk music resembling jazz. [Bantu, lift (from leaping upward in dancing to the music)]

kWh *abbrev*: kilowatt-hour(s).

KWIC /kwik/ *abbrev*: keyword in context.

KWOC /kwok/ *abbrev*: keyword out of context.

Kwok's disease same as **Chinese restaurant syndrome** (see under **china¹**).

KWT *abbrev*: Kuwait (IVR).

KY *abbrev*: Kentucky (US state; also **Ky.**).

ky see **kye**.

kyang see **kiang**.

kyanite /kī'ə-nīt/ or **cyanite** /sī'/ *n* a mineral, an aluminium silicate, generally sky-blue. [Gr *kyanos* blue]
■ **kyanit'ic** *adj*.

kyanize or **-ise** /kī'ə-nīz/ *vt* to preserve from dry rot by injecting corrosive sublimate into the pores of (wood). [John H *Kyan* (1774–1830)]

kyat /chat/ *n* the standard monetary unit of Myanmar (100 pyas).

kybosh see **kibosh**.

kydst (*Spenser*) see **kythe**.

kye or **ky** /kī/ (*Scot*) *n pl* cows. [See **kine**]

K-Y® jelly /kā'wī jel'i/ *n* a sterile water-soluble lubricant, used in medical procedures and with condoms.

kyle /kīl/ *n* a narrow strait. [Gaelic *caol*]

kylie or **kiley** /kī'li/ (*Aust*) *n* a boomerang. [From an Aboriginal language]

kylin /kē'lin/ *n* a mythical animal illustrated on Chinese and Japanese pottery. [From Chinese *qí lín*]

kylix /kil'* or *kī'iks/ see **cylix**.

kyllosis /ki-lō'sis/ *n* club foot. [Gr *kyllōsis*]

kyloe /kī'lō/ *n* one of the small, long-haired cattle of the Scottish Highlands and Hebrides. [Origin unknown]

kymograph /kī'mō-gräf/ *n* an instrument which creates a graph showing the fluctuation of a measurement over a period of time. [Gr *kȳma* a wave, and *graphein* to write]
■ **ky'mogram** *n* a graph produced by a kymograph. **kymographic** /-graf'ik/ *adj*. **kymog'raphy** *n*.

kynd or **kynde** /kīnd/ (*Spenser*) *n*, *adj* and *vt* same as **kind¹,²**.

kyne (*Spenser*) same as **kine**.

kyogen /kyō-gen'/ *n* a comic interlude between Noh plays. [Jap, play, drama]

kype /kīp/ *n* a hook on the lower jaw of mature male salmon and trout during the breeding season. [Scot *kip* a hooked thing]

kyphosis /kī-fō'sis/ (*pathol*) *n* a hunchbacked condition. [Gr *kȳphōsis*, from *kȳphos* a hump]
■ **kyphotic** /-fot'ik/ *adj*.

Kyrgyz or **Kirghiz** /kir'giz/ *n* (*pl* **Kyr'gyz** or **Kir'ghiz**) a member of an indigenous people of central Asia, inhabiting Kyrgyzstan and part of Siberia; the Turkic language of this people. ◆ *adj* of the Kyrgyz or their language.

Kyrie eleison /kē'ri- or kir'i-ā e-lā'i-son, e-le-ā'son or el-ā-ē'son/ (in short **Kyrie**) *n* a form of prayer in all the ancient Greek liturgies, retained in the Roman Catholic mass, following immediately after the introit (including both words and music); one of the responses to the commandments in the Anglican ante-communion service. [Gr *Kȳrie*, *eleēson* Lord, have mercy]

kyrielle /kē-ri-el'/ *n* a string of short lines in stanzas all ending with the same word or line. [Fr, litany, rigmarole, from Gr *Kȳrie*, *eleēson*; see preceding entry]

kyte see **kite²**.

kythe or **kithe** /kīdh/ (*Scot*) *vt* (*2nd pers sing* (*Spenser*) **kydst**) to make known. ◆ *vi* to show oneself, to appear. [OE *cȳthan* to make known; see **uncouth**]

kyu /kū/ (*judo*) *n* one of the six novice grades, the least experienced being sixth kyu; a novice in one of these grades. [Jap]

KZ *abbrev*: Kazakhstan (IVR).

■ words derived from main entry word; ❑ compound words; ■ idioms and phrasal verbs

L l

L¹ or **l** /el/ n the twelfth letter in the modern English alphabet, eleventh in the Roman, its sound a lateral liquid formed by letting the breath pass the side or sides of the tongue; anything shaped like the letter L.

L² /el/ (US inf) n an elevated railroad.

L or **L.** abbrev : Lake; lambert; Latin; learner (driver); lecturer; left; Liberal; libra (L), pound sterling (usu written **₤**); licentiate; lira or (pl) lire; litre; Loch; Lough; Luxembourg (IVR).
□ **L'-driver** n a learner driver. **L'-plate** n a sign displayed on a motor vehicle driven by a learner-driver, a red 'L' on a white background.

L symbol : (as a Roman numeral) 50.

L symbol : angular momentum (phys); inductance (elec); luminance (phys); molar latent heat (chem).

L̄ symbol : (Roman numeral) 50000.

L- /el-/ pfx denoting: laevo (or levo-); laevorotatory.
□ **L-dopa** see **dopa**.

l or **l.** abbrev : laevorotatory (chem); latitude; league; left; length; libra (L), pound weight (usu written **lb**); line; lira or (pl) lire; litre.

l (chem) symbol : specific latent heat per gramme.

LA abbrev : Legislative Assembly; Library Association (in the UK now replaced by **CILIP**); Literate in Arts; Los Angeles; Louisiana (US state).

La (chem) symbol : lanthanum.

La. abbrev : Lane (in street names, etc); Louisiana (US state).

la¹ /lä/ (music) n the sixth note of the scale in sol-fa notation (also anglicized in spelling as **lah**). [See **Aretinian**]

la² /lä/ interj lo! see! behold! ah! indeed! [Cf **lo** and **law⁵**]

laager /lä'gər/ (Afrik **laer**, not used in South African English) n in South Africa, a defensive ring of ox-wagons; any extemporized fortification; an encampment; a defensive group of people drawn together by similarity of opinion, etc (fig). ◆ vt and vi to arrange or camp in a laager. [Afrik lager, from Ger Lager a camp; Du leger; cf **lair¹**, **layer** and **leaguer**]

laari see **lari**.

Lab. abbrev : Labour; Labrador.

lab /lab/ n a familiar contraction of **laboratory** and **Labrador** (dog).

labanotation /lä-bə-nō-tā'shən/ n a system of ballet notation (also called **Laban system**). [Rudolf von Laban, who proposed it]

labarum /lab'ə-rəm/ n orig a Roman military standard, the imperial standard after Constantine's conversion, with a monogram of the Greek letters XP (ChR), for Christ; a similar ecclesiastical banner carried in processions; any moral standard or guide. [L, from Late Gr labaron, origin unknown]

labda, labdacism see **lambda**.

labdanum see **ladanum**.

labefactation /lab-i-fak-tā'shən/ or **labefaction** /-fak'shən/ n a weakening decay; overthrow. [L labefactātiō, -ōnis, from labāre to totter, and facere to make]

label /lā'bl/ n a small slip of paper or other material placed on or near anything to denote its nature, contents, composition, ownership, destination, etc; a characterizing or classificatory designation (fig); a manufacturer's or retailer's tradename attached to goods to identify them; a strip of material with this or other information on it; the piece of paper on a record, cassette, compact disc, etc giving the maker's production company's tradename and identifying the recorded material; the tradename itself (inf); a character or set of characters indicating the start of an instruction in a program and used elsewhere in the program to refer to that instruction (comput); an element, often a radioactive atom, that is used for the identification and monitoring of a chemical reaction, the presence of molecules in living organisms, etc; a paper appended to a will, such as a codicil (law); a fillet with pendants (an eldest son's cadency mark; heraldry); a dripstone (archit); an attached band or strip (archaic). ◆ vt (**lā'belling**; **lā'belled**) to fix a label to; to describe by or on a label; to replace an atom in (a molecule or compound) by a radioactive isotope, for the purpose of identification (phys). [OFr label, perh from OHGer lappa (Ger Lappen) flap]
■ **la'beller** n.
□ **labelled atom** n a tagged atom. **la'belmate** n a musician whose recordings are issued by the same record company as another.

labellum /lə-bel'əm/ n (pl **labell'a**) the posterior petal, and often the most conspicuous part, of the flower of an orchid; the lower lip of the corolla forming a landing platform for pollinating insects; a lobe at the end of the proboscis in some insects. [L, dimin of labrum lip]
■ **labell'oid** adj.

labial /lā'bi-əl/ adj of or formed by the lips; sounded by the impact of air on a lip-like projection, such as an organ flue pipe (music). ◆ n a sound formed by the lips. [L labium lip]
■ **lā'bialism**, **labializā'tion** or **-s-** n a tendency to labialize. **lā'bialize** or **-ise** vt to make labial; to pronounce with rounded lips. **lā'bially** adv. **Lābiatae** /-ā'tē/ n pl a family of sympetalous dicotyledons with lipped flowers, four-cornered stems and opposite branches, comprising the dead-nettles, mints, etc. **lā'biate** adj lipped; having a lipped corolla; belonging to the Labiatae. ◆ n any plant of the Labiatae. **lābiodent'al** adj and n (a sound) produced by the lips and teeth together, such as f and v. **lābiove'lar** adj and n (a sound) produced by the lips and soft palate together, such as w. **lā'bium** n (pl **lā'bia**) a lip or lip-like part; in insects, the underlip, formed by the partial fusion of the second maxillae.
□ **labia majora**, **labia minora** n pl the two outer and inner folds of skin respectively surrounding the vaginal orifice in human females.

labile /lā'bīl or (esp in US) lā'bəl/ adj unstable; apt to slip or change. [L lābilis, from lābī to slip]
■ **labil'ity** n.

labiodental and **labiovelar** see under **labial**.

labis /lā'bis/ n the cochlear or Eucharistic spoon. [Gr labis handle, from root of lambanein to take]

labium see under **labial**.

lablab /lab'lab/ n a tropical bean (Dolichos lablab) with edible pods. [Ar lablāb]

labor see **labour**.

laboratory /lə-bor'ə-tə-ri or (esp N Am) lab'ə-rə-tə-ri/ n a place for experimental work or research; orig a chemist's workroom. [L labōrāre, from labor work]

labor improbus /lā'bör im-prō'bəs or la'bor im-pro'bŭs/ (L) n persistent, dogged labour.

laborious, etc see under **labour**.

labour or (esp N Am) **labor** /lā'bər/ n physical or mental toil; work, esp when done for money or other gain; pains; duties; a task requiring hard work; effort made toward the satisfaction of needs; workers collectively; supply or services of workers, esp physical workers; (with cap) the Labour Party or its cause, principles or interest (politics); the pains and physical efforts of childbirth; heavy pitching or rolling of a ship (naut); the outcome of toil (archaic); trouble taken (archaic); exertion of influence (archaic). ◆ adj of labour or (with cap) the Labour Party. ◆ vi to experience labour; to work; to take pains; to be oppressed or burdened; to move slowly and with difficulty; to undergo childbirth; to pitch and roll heavily (naut). ◆ vt to strain, over-elaborate or repeat unnecessarily; to elaborate, work out in detail; to spend labour on (archaic); to cultivate (dialect). [OFr labour, labeur, from L labor]
■ **laborious** /lə-bō' or -bö'ri-əs/ adj involving or devoted to labour; strenuous; arduous. **labo'riously** adv. **labo'riousness** n. **lā'boured** adj showing signs of effort in execution; strained; over-elaborated, repeated unnecessarily; cultivated (dialect); worked (archaic). **lā'bourer** n someone who labours; someone who does heavy physical work requiring little skill or training. **lā'bourism** n. **lā'bourist**

n someone who supports or works for the rights of workers. **La'bourite** *n* a member or supporter of the Labour Party. **la'boursome** *adj* (*Shakesp*) laborious.

◻ **labor union** *n* (*US*) a trade union. **labour camp** *n* a penal institution where the inmates are forced to work; temporary accommodation for workers. **Labour Day** *n* a public holiday held in many countries on 1 May in celebration of labour and workers; in N America (**Labor Day**) a holiday held on the first Monday in September; in Australia (**Labor Day**) a holiday held on different days in different states. **Labour Exchange** *n* a former name for a **job centre** (see under **job**[1]). **labour force** *n* the number of workers employed in an industry, factory, etc; the part of the population which is employed or available for work. **la'bour-intens'ive** *adj* requiring a relatively large number of workers for the capital invested, *opp* to *capital-intensive*. **labour of love** *n* work undertaken for its own sake and without hope of any tangible reward. **Labour Party** *n* in Britain, a political party formed in 1900 by trade unions, etc to represent the working community and its interests; its representatives in parliament; a local organization of the party; a similar party in various countries, *esp* (as **Labor Party**) Australia. **la'bour-sav'ing** *adj* intended to supersede or lessen labour.

■ **hard labour** compulsory work imposed in addition to imprisonment, abolished in the UK in 1948. **labour with** to take pains to convince.

labra see **labrum**.

labradoodle /*lab'rə-doo-dl*/ *n* a cross between a Labrador and a poodle, bred for its gentle character traits. [From *Labrador* and *poodle*]

Labrador /*lab'rə-dör*/ *n* a mainland region of Newfoundland and Quebec; a Labrador dog.
■ **labradoresc'ence** *n* a brilliant play of colours shown by some labradorites. **labradoresc'ent** *adj*. **lab'radorite** (or /-*dör'*/) *n* a plagioclase feldspar with fine colours found on the Labrador coast.
◻ **Labrador dog** or **Labrador retriever** *n* a sporting dog about 56cm in height, either black, yellow (from red to fawn) or chocolate in colour. **Labrador tea** *n* a shrub of the heather family (genus *Ledum*) used in Labrador to prepare a medicinal or herbal tea.

labrum /*lā'brəm*/ *n* (*pl* **lā'bra**) a lip; a lip-like part. [L *labrum* a lip]
■ **la'bral** *adj*. **lā'bret** *n* a lip ornament. **lā'brose** *adj* thick-lipped.

Labrus /*lā'brəs*/ *n* the wrasse genus of fishes, of the family **La'bridae**. [L *lābrus*, *lābros* a kind of fish]
■ **la'brid** or **la'broid** /*la'* or *lā'*/ *adj* and *n*.

labrys /*lab'ris* or *lā'bris*/ *n* the double-headed axe, a religious symbol of ancient Crete, etc. [Gr, from Lydian; perh connected with **labyrinth**]

laburnum /*lə-bûr'nəm*/ *n* a small poisonous papilionaceous tree or shrub, a native of the Alps, bearing slim seed-pods and hanging clusters of yellow flowers. [L]

labyrinth /*lab'(i-)rinth*/ *n* orig a building with intricate passages; an arrangement of tortuous paths or alleys (*usu* between hedges) in which it is difficult to find the way out; a maze; a tangle of intricate ways and connections; a perplexity; the cavities of the internal ear (*anat*); a loudspeaker enclosure whose function is to absorb certain unwanted sound waves. [Gr *labyrinthos*, perh connected with *labrys* the double-axe; see **labrys**]
■ **labyrinth'al**, **labyrinth'ian**, **labyrinth'ic**, **labyrinth'ical** or **labyrinth'ine** /-*īn* or -*in*/ *adj*. **labyrinthī'tis** *n* (*med*) inflammation of the inner ear. **labyrinth'odont** *n* (Gr *odous*, *odontos* tooth) an extinct stegocephalian amphibian of Carboniferous, Permian, and *esp* Triassic times, so called from the mazy pattern of a section of the teeth in some (also *adj*).
◻ **labyrinth fish** *n* a freshwater fish of Asia and Africa with a labyrinthine organ on its head enabling it to breathe through the surface of its body.

LAC *abbrev* : leading aircraft(s)man.

lac[1] same as **lakh**.

lac[2] /*lak*/ *n* a dark-red transparent resin used in making shellac, secreted on the twigs of trees in Asia by certain coccid insects (**lac insects**), from which scarlet colouring matters (**lac'-dye** and **lac'-lake**) are obtained. [Hindi *lākh*, from Sans *lākṣā* 100000, hence the (teeming) lac insect]

laccolith /*lak'ō-lith*/ or **laccolite** /*lak'ō-līt*/ (*geol*) *n* a mass of igneous rock that has risen in a molten condition and bulged up the overlying strata to form a dome. [Gr *lakkos* a reservoir, and *lithos* a stone]
■ **laccolithic** /-*lith'ik*/ or **laccolit'ic** *adj*.

lace /*lās*/ *n* a string or cord for passing through holes, eg to tie up a shoe or garment, etc; a delicate ornamental fabric made by looping, knotting, plaiting or twisting threads into definite patterns. ◆ *vt* to fasten with a lace (often with *up*); to put a lace or laces into; to compress or pinch in by lacing; to trim or decorate with lace; to streak with colour (*fig*); to thrash; to reprimand severely; to intermingle, eg coffee with brandy, etc; to intertwine. ◆ *vi* to have

lacing as the means of fastening; to practise tight-lacing. [OFr *las* a noose, from L *laqueus*]
■ **laced** *adj*. **lacet** /*lās-et'*/ *n* a kind of braidwork. **lac'ily** *adv*. **lac'iness** *n*. **lac'ing** *n* ornamental lacework; a beating (*inf*). **lac'y** or (*rare*) **lac'ey** *adj* of or like lace; decorated with lace.
◻ **lace'bark** *n* a tall West Indian tree of the Daphne family, the inner bark like a coarse lace. **lace'-boot** *n* a boot fastened by a lace. **lace bug** *n* a small insect that has a lacy pattern on its wings. **laced mutton** *n* (*Shakesp*) a prostitute. **lace'-frame** *n* a machine used in lace-making. **lace glass** see **lacy glass** below. **lace'-leaf** see **lattice-leaf** under **lattice**. **lace'-man** *n* a dealer in lace. **lace'-paper** *n* paper stamped or cut like lace. **lace'-pill'ow** *n* a cushion held on the knees by lacemakers, on which the lace is worked. **lace'-up** *n* a boot or shoe tied with a lace. ◆ *adj* fastened with a lace or laces. **lace'wing** *n* the golden-eye, a type of green or brown insect with two pairs of gauzy wings and brilliant golden eyes, which feeds on aphids, etc. **lacing course** *n* an arrangement of bricks built into a structure to strengthen it. **lacy glass** or **lace glass** *n* an early form of pressed glass with a lacy design.
■ **lace into** (*inf*) to reprimand (someone); to consume (something) with great appetite or vigour.

lacerate /*las'ə-rāt*/ *vt* to tear or rip; to rend; to wound; to afflict or distress severely. [L *lacerāre*, -*ātum* to tear, from *lacer* torn]
■ **lac'erable** *adj*. **lac'erant** *adj* harrowing. **lac'erate** or **lac'erated** *adj* rent or torn; with edges cut into irregular segments (*bot*). **lacerā'tion** *n*. **lac'erative** *adj* tearing; having the power to tear.

Lacerta /*la-sûr'tə*/ *n* a genus of lizards, including the common lizard; one of the northern constellations, the Lizard. [L]
■ **lacertian** /-*sûr'shyən*/ *adj* of lizards; lizard-like. **Lacertil'ia** *n pl* the lizard order or suborder of reptiles. **lacertil'ian** *adj*. **lacer'tine** *adj*.

lacet and **lacey** see under **lace**.

laches /*lach'iz*/ (*law*) *n* negligence or undue delay in carrying out a legal duty, *esp* until the entitlement period (for a claim, remedy, etc) has expired. [Anglo-Fr *lachesse*]

Lachesis /*lak'i-sis*/ (*Gr myth*) *n* that one of the three Fates who assigned to each mortal his or her destiny, and who spun the thread of life from the distaff held by Clotho; a genus of snakes including the bushmaster. [Gr]

lachrymal, also **lacrymal**, **lacrimal** /*lak'ri-məl*/ *adj* of or for tears. ◆ *n* a bone near the tear-gland; (in *pl*) lachrymal glands; (in *pl*) weeping fits; a tear bottle. [From *lachryma*, a medieval spelling of L *lacrima* tear; cf Gr *dakry*; Eng **tear**; Gr *dakrȳma* may have influenced the spelling]
■ **lach'rymary** or **lach'rymatory** *adj* lachrymal; causing tears to flow. ◆ *n* a tear-bottle. **lachrymā'tion** *n* the secretion of tears; (the act of) weeping. **lach'rymātor** *n* a substance that causes tears to flow, as teargas; a contrivance for releasing such a substance. **lach'rymose** *adj* tearful, given to weeping; lugubrious, mournful. **lach'rymosely** *adv*. **lachrymos'ity** *n*. —Also **lac'rymary**, **lac'rimary**, etc.
◻ **lachryma Christi** /*lak'ri-mə kris'tē*/ *n* (L, Christ's tear) a sweet but piquant wine from grapes grown on Vesuvius. **lachrymal duct** *n* a duct that conveys tear-water from the inner corner of the eye to the nose. **lachrymal gland** *n* a gland at the outer angle of the eye that secretes tears. **lachrymal urn** or **vase** *n* a tear bottle.

lacinia /*lə-sin'i-ə*/ *n* (*pl* **lacin'iae** /-*ē*/) a long narrow lobe in a leaf, etc (*bot*); the inner lobe of the maxilla (*zool*). [L, a lappet or tag]
■ **lacin'iate** or **lacin'iated** *adj* cut into narrow lobes, slashed. **laciniā'tion** *n*.

lack[1] /*lak*/ *n* want, deficiency; something absent or in short supply. ◆ *vt* to be without; to be short of or deficient in; to need; to miss (*obs*). ◆ *vi* (now *usu* in *prp*) to be wanting or absent; to be deficient; to be in want (*obs*). [Cf MLGer and Du *lak* blemish]
■ **lack'ing** *adj*.
◻ **lack'-all** *n* (*archaic*) someone who is destitute. **lack'-beard** *n*. **lack'-brain** *n* (*Shakesp*) a fool. **lack'land** *n* and *adj*. **lack'-Latin** *n* (*obs*; often **Sir John Lack-Latin**) an ignorant priest. ◆ *adj* uneducated, ignorant. **lack'-linen** *adj* (*Shakesp*) without linen. **lack'-love** *n* someone who is deficient in love (also *adj*). **lack'lustre** or *US* **lack'luster** *adj* dull, without brightness, sheen or vitality (also *n*).

lack[2] /*lak*/ *n* see **good-lack** under **good**.

lackadaisical /*lak-ə-dā'zi-kl*/ *adj* listless; languid and ineffectual; indolent; affectedly pensive; shallowly sentimental. [See **alack-a-day**]
■ **lackadai'sically** *adv*. **lackadai'sicalness** *n*. **lack'adai'sy** or **lack'aday** *interj* (*archaic*).

lacker see **lacquer**.

lackey or (*rare*) **lacquey** /*lak'i*/ *n* (*pl* **lack'eys** or **lacqu'eys**) a footman or valet; a servile follower. ◆ *vt* and *vi* to serve or attend as or like a footman or slavish servant. [OFr *laquay* (Fr *laquais*), from Sp *lacayo* a lackey; perh Ar *luka'* servile]

□ **lackey moth** n a moth (*Malacosoma neustria*) of the egger group with a gaudily striped caterpillar, like a footman in livery.

lacmus /lak'məs/ n an obsolete form of **litmus**.

Laconian /lə-kō'nyən or -ni-ən/ or **Laconic** /lə-kon'ik/ adj of Sparta, the chief city of ancient *Laconia*. [Gr *Lakōnikos*]

■ **lacon'ic** or **lacon'ical** adj expressing or expressed in few words (in reference to the succinct style of Spartan speech); sententiously brief. **lacon'ically** adv. **laconism** /lak'/ or **lacon'icism** n a concise style; a short, pithy phrase.

lacquer or **lacker** /lak'ər/ n a solution of film-forming substances in a volatile solvent, esp a varnish of lac and alcohol; a similar substance sprayed on the hair to hold it in place; the juice of the lacquer tree (**Japan lacquer**) or a similar product; a covering of one of these; an article or ware so coated. ◆ vt to cover with lacquer; to varnish. [Fr *lacre*, from Port *lacre*, *laca*; *lacrymal*, see **lac**²]

■ **lacqu'erer** n. **lacqu'ering** n varnishing with lacquer; a coat of lacquer varnish.

□ **lacquer tree** n a tree of the genus *Rhus*. **lacqu'erware** n pieces of decorative art, esp of Asian origin, often inlaid with ivory, mother-of-pearl, etc, and coated with hard shiny lacquer.

lacquey see **lackey**.

lacrimal, etc variants of **lachrymal**, etc.

lacrimoso /la-kri-mō'sō/ (music) adj and adv plaintive or plaintively. [Ital, from L *lacrimōsus* tearful, from *lacrima* a tear]

lacrosse /lə- or lä-kros'/ n a team sport (orig Native American) in which a long-handled, netted stick (**lacrosse stick** or **crosse**) is used to throw, catch and cradle (qv) the ball and drive it through the opponents' goal. [Can Fr]

■ **min'i-lacrosse** and **pop'-lacrosse** simplified versions of lacrosse.

lacteal /lak'ti-əl/ adj of milk; conveying chyle. ◆ n a lymphatic vessel conveying chyle from the intestines to the thoracic ducts. [L *lac*, *lactis* milk; Gr *gala*, *galaktos* milk]

■ **lactal'bumin** n a protein, present in milk, which contains all of the essential amino acids. **lac'tam** n a four-membered heterocyclic ring which is found in penicillin and cephalosporin antibiotics. **lactā'rian** n a vegetarian whose diet includes milk and other dairy products. ◆ adj of or designating such a person or diet. **lactase** /lak'tās/ n an enzyme that acts on lactose. **lac'tate** n a salt of lactic acid. ◆ vi (also /lak-tāt'/) to secrete milk. **lactā'tion** n secretion or yielding of milk; the period of suckling. **lactā'tional** adj. **lac'teous** adj milky. **lactesc'ence** n. **lactesc'ent** adj turning to milk; producing milky juice. **lac'tic** adj derived from or relating to milk. **lactif'erous** adj conveying or producing milk or milky juice. **lactif'ic** adj producing milk or milky juice. **lactif'luous** adj flowing with milk. **lactoglob'ulin** n a globular protein present in milk. **lac'tone** n a cyclic ester which can be formed by the reaction between the hydroxyl group and the carboxyl group in a hydroxycarboxylic acid molecule. **lac'tose** n milk sugar, $C_{12}H_{22}O_{11}$, a crystalline sugar obtained by evaporating whey. **lactosūr'ia** n (Gr *ouron* urine) the presence of lactose in the urine. □ **lactic acid** n an acid obtained from milk, $CH_3CH(OH)COOH$, used as a preservative (also called **hydroxy-propanō'ic acid**).

lacto- /lak-tō-, -tə- or -to-/ combining form denoting milk. [L *lac*, *lactis* milk]

■ **lactobacill'us** n any bacterium of the genus *Lactobacillus*, which converts certain carbohydrates to lactic acid (see also **acidophilus**). **lactoflā'vin** n (L *flāvus* yellow) an earlier name for **riboflavin** (see under **ribose**). **lactogen'ic** adj inducing lactation. **lactom'eter** n a hydrometer for testing the relative density of milk. **lactoprō'tein** n any protein present in milk. **lac'toscope** n an instrument for measuring the purity or richness of milk. **lactovegetā'rian** n and adj (a) lactarian.

Lactuca /lak-tū'kə/ n the lettuce genus of composite plants, with milky juice. [L *lactūca*, from *lac*, *lactis* milk]

lacuna /lə- or la-kū'nə/ n (pl **lacū'nae** /-nē/) a gap or hiatus; an intercellular space (biol); a cavity; a depression in a pitted surface. [L *lacūna* hollow or gap, and *lacūnar*, *-āris* a fretted ceiling]

■ **lacūn'al** adj lacunary. **lacū'nar** n (pl **lacū'nars** or **lacunaria** /lak-ū-nā'ri-ə/) a sunken panel or coffer in a ceiling or a soffit; a ceiling containing these. ◆ adj of, relating to or having a lacunar. **lacūn'ary** or **lacūn'ate** adj relating to or including lacunae. **lacū'nose** adj having lacunae; pitted.

lacustrine /lə-kus'trīn or -trin/ adj relating to lakes; dwelling in or on lakes; formed in lakes. [L *lacus* a lake]

LACW abbrev : leading aircraft(s)woman.

lacy see under **lace**.

lad¹ /lad/ n a boy; a youth; a male companion, workmate, etc (inf); a stableman or -woman; a dashing, high-spirited or extrovert man (inf); a lover (Scot). [ME *ladde* youth or servant; origin obscure]

■ **ladd'ie** n a little lad; a boy (Scot and N Eng). **ladd'ish** adj (of young men) boisterous or aggressive, esp as members of a social group. **ladd'ishness** n. **ladd'ism** n an attitude displayed by certain young men which celebrates drunkenness, aggressive behaviour, devotion to sport and sexism; a culture of laddishness. **ladette'** n a lively young woman who enjoys social behaviour of a kind associated with young men.

□ **lad mag** n (inf) a magazine aimed at young men interested in drink, sport, adventure, etc, usu illustrated by photographs of semi-nude young women. **lad's love** n (dialect) the aromatic plant southernwood.

lad² obsolete form of **led**.

ladanum /lad'ə-nəm/ n a fragrant resin exuded from Cistus leaves in Mediterranean countries (also **lab'danum**). [L *lādanum*, *lēdanum*, from Gr *lādanon*, *lēdanon*, from *lēdon* the Cistus plant, prob from Pers *lādan*]

ladder /lad'ər/ n a piece of equipment, generally portable, with horizontal rungs between two vertical supports, used for going up and down; anything of similar form or pattern, such as a run in knitwear where the breaking of a thread gives an appearance of rungs; an arrangement which enables fish to pass around dams, weirs, etc (fish-ladder or salmon-ladder); a means of attaining a higher status (fig). ◆ vt to cause a ladder to appear in (tights, etc); to provide with a ladder (rare); to scale with a ladder (rare). ◆ vi of knitwear, fabric, etc, to develop a ladder. [OE *hlæder*; Ger *Leiter*]

■ **ladd'ered** or **ladd'ery** adj.

□ **ladd'er-back** n a chair with a back consisting of several horizontal bars between two long uprights (also adj). **ladder tournament** n a tournament in which players are ranked according to performance and can move upwards by defeating a higher-ranked player.

laddie, **laddish** see under **lad**¹.

lade¹ /lād/ vt (pat **lād'ed**; pap **lād'en** or **lād'ed**) to load; to burden; to put on board; to ladle or scoop (now usu technical); to empty or drain, as with a ladle. ◆ vi to take cargo aboard. [OE *hladan*, pat *hlōd*; pap *hlæden*, *hladen* to load, draw water]

■ **lād'en** adj loaded; burdened. **lād'ing** n the act of loading; that which is loaded; cargo; freight.

lade² or **laid** /lād/ Scots forms of **load**.

lade³ /lād/ (Scot) n a millstream. [Perh OE *lād* way or course; cf **lode** and **lead**¹]

laden see **lade**¹.

ladette see under **lad**¹.

la-di-da or **lah-di-dah** /lä-di-dä'/ (inf) adj affectedly elegant or superior, esp in speech or bearing.

ladies, etc see **lady**.

Ladin /lä-dēn'/, also **Ladino** /-dē'nō/ n a Romance language spoken in the upper Inn valley in central Europe; a general name for the Rhaeto-Romanic languages or dialects. [L *Latīnus* Latin]

■ **Ladinity** /-din'i-ti/ n.

Ladino¹ /lä-dē'nō/ n (pl **Ladin'os**) the old Castilian language; the language, Spanish mixed with Hebrew, spoken by Jews in areas near the E Mediterranean (also **Judezmo**); a Latino (see under **Latin**). [Sp, from L *Latīnus* Latin]

Ladino² see **Ladin**.

ladino /lə-dē'nō/ n (pl **ladi'nos**) a variety of clover grown for forage in N America. [Origin uncertain]

ladle /lā'dl/ n a large, usu deep spoon for lifting liquid; the float-board of a millwheel; a long-handled pan or bucket for holding and conveying molten metal; a church collection-box on a long handle (Scot). ◆ vt to transfer or distribute with a ladle. [OE *hlædel*, from *hladan* to lade]

■ **lad'leful** n (pl **lad'lefuls**) as much as a ladle will hold.

■ **ladle out** (inf) to distribute generously.

ladrone /lə-drōn'/ (archaic) n a robber. [Sp *ladrón*, from L *latrō*, *-ōnis*]

lady /lā'di/ (with cap when used as a prefix) n (pl **ladies** /lā'diz/; old genitive **la'dy**) the mistress of a house; used as the feminine of **lord** and of **gentleman**, and ordinarily as a less formal substitute for **dame**¹; any woman with refined manners and instincts; a consort, a term formerly preferred to wife by some who liked to stand upon their dignity (archaic); a lady-love or object of chivalric devotion; a girlfriend, mistress, etc; a feminine prefix with various formal uses, eg for the wife of a knight, baron or baronet; a woman with a particular job, occupation, etc, as in tea lady, bag lady; a size of slates, approx 40.6×20cm (16×7.9in). [OE *hlæfdige*, appar literally 'the bread-kneader', from *hlāf* loaf, and a lost word from the root of **dough**]

■ **la'dies** n a public lavatory for women. **la'dyfied** or **la'dified** adj inclined to affect over-refined manners. **la'dyfy** or **la'dify** vt to make a lady of; to call My Lady or Your Ladyship. **la'dyhood** n the condition or character of a lady. **la'dyish** *adj* having the airs of a fine lady. **la'dyism** *n* affectation of the airs of a fine lady. **la'dykin** (*archaic*) an endearing diminutive of **lady**. **la'dylike** *adj* like a lady in manners; refined; soft, delicate; genteel. **la'dylikeness** *n*. **la'dyship** *n* the title of a lady.

□ **ladies' companion** *n* a small bag used for a woman's needlework. **ladies' fingers** same as **lady's finger** below. **ladies' gallery** *n* a gallery in the House of Commons, once screened off by a grille. **ladies' man** or **lady's man** *n* a man who enjoys the company of women and being attentive to them; a (would-be) seducer of women. **la'dieswear** *n* clothing for women. **la'dybird** *n* any member of the family Coccinellidae, small round beetles, often brightly spotted, which prey on greenfly, etc (also **la'dybug** (*N Am*), **la'dycow** or **la'dyfly**). **Lady Bountiful** *n* (also without *caps*; often *derog*) a rich and generous woman, often applied to one who is ostentatiously or offensively so (from a character in Farquhar's *The Beaux' Stratagem*). **ladyboy** *n* (*inf*) a young male transvestite or transsexual, *esp* in Thailand. **lady chapel** *n* a chapel dedicated to the Virgin Mary, usually behind the high altar, at the end of the apse. **Lady Day** *n* 25 March, the day of the annunciation of the Virgin. **lady fern** *n* a pretty British fern (*Athyrium filix-foemina*), with long bipinnate fronds (imagined by the old herbalists to be the female of the male fern). **la'dy-help** *n* a woman paid to assist in housework, but treated more or less as one of the family. **lady-in-wait'ing** *n* a female attendant to a lady of royal status. **la'dy-killer** *n* a man who is, or fancies himself, irresistible to women. **la'dy-love** *n* a beloved lady or woman; a sweetheart. **Lady Muck** see under **muck**. **lady of the night** *n* a euphemism for a prostitute. **lady's-cu'shion** *n* the mossy saxifrage. **lady's finger** or **fingers** *n* a name for many plants, *esp* the kidney-vetch; okra; a finger-shaped sponge cake. **la'dy's-maid** *n* a lady's female attendant, responsible for her clothes, etc. **lady's-mant'le** *n* a genus (*Alchemilla*) of plants of the rose family with small, yellowish-green flowers and leaves like folded drapery. **lady's-slipp'er** *n* a genus (*Cypripedium*) of orchids with a large slipper-like lip. **la'dy's-smock** or **la'dy-smock** *n* the cuckoo flower (*Cardamine pratensis*), a cruciferous meadow-plant, with pale lilac-coloured flowers. **lady's-thist'le** *n* the milk thistle. **lady's** (or **ladies'**) **tresses** *n* (*sing* or *pl*) an orchid of the genus *Spiranthes* with small white flowers. **la'dy-trifles** *n pl* (*Shakesp*) trifles befitting a lady.

■ **find the lady** see **three-card trick** under **three**. **her ladyship**, **your ladyship** and **my lady** forms of expression used in speaking of or to a person who has the title of Lady. **our Lady** the Virgin Mary. (**Our**) **Lady's bedstraw** see **bedstraw** under **bed**[1].

Laender see **Land**.

laeotropic /lē-ō-trop'ik/ *adj* turning to the left. [Gr *laios* left, and *tropos* a turn]

laer see **laager**.

laesa majestas /lē'zə mə-jes'tas or lī'sa mä-yes'täs/ (*L*) *n* lese-majesty (*qv*), injured majesty.

laesie (*Spenser*) for **lazy**.

laetare /lē-tā'ri or lī-tä're/ *n* the fourth Sunday in Lent. [*laetāre* (the first word of the introit for that day), imperative singular of L *laetārī* to rejoice, from *laetus* joyful]

laevigate a non-standard spelling of **levigate**[1].

laevo- or **levo-** /lē-vō-/ *combining form* denoting on or to the left. [L *laevus* left]

laevorotatory or **levorotatory** /lē-vō-rō'tə-tə-ri or -rō-tā'/ *adj* counter-clockwise; rotating the plane of polarization of light to the left (*optics*). [L *laevus* left, and *rotāre* to rotate]

■ **laevorota'tion** *n*.

laevulose or **levulose** /lev'ū- or lē'vū-lōs/ *n* fructose, a laevorotatory sugar ($C_6H_{12}O_6$). [L *laevus* left]

Laffer curve /laf'ər kûrv/ (*econ*) *n* a curve joining the points on a graph which shows the relationship between tax revenue received by the state and the percentage tax rate imposed by the state. [Arthur *Laffer* (born 1940), US economist]

lag[1] /lag/ *n* a retardation or falling behind; the amount by which one phenomenon is delayed behind another; delay; someone who, or something which, comes behind; the fag end; (*esp* in *pl*) dregs (*obs*). ◆ *vi* (**lagg'ing**; **lagged**) to fall behind; to move or walk slowly; to loiter; to string (*billiards*). ◆ *adj* hindmost (*obs*); behindhand (*rare*); late (*rare*); tardy (*rare*). [Origin unknown]

■ **lagg'ard** *adj* lagging behind. ◆ *n* (also **lagg'er**) a person who lags behind. **lagg'ardly** *adj* and *adv*. **lagg'ardness** *n*. **lagg'ing** *n* and *adj*. **lagg'ingly** *adv*.

□ **lag'-end** (*Shakesp*) the last or long-delayed end. **lag of the tides** *n* the progressive lengthening of the interval between tides as neap tide is approached, *opp* to *priming*.

lag[2] /lag/ *n* an insulating wooden or other lining; a non-conducting covering for pipes, etc; boarding; a wooden stave or lath; a wooden

lining; a non-conducting covering; a perforated wooden strip used instead of a card in weaving. ◆ *vt* to provide with a lag or lagging. [Prob ON *lögg* barrel-rim; cf Swed *lagg* stave]

■ **lagg'er** *n* a person who insulates pipes, machinery, etc against heat loss. **lagg'ing** *n* a non-conducting covering for pipes, etc to minimize loss of heat; boarding, as across the framework of a centre for an arch, or in a mine to prevent ore falling into a passage.

lag[3] /lag/ (*sl*) *vt* to steal; to carry off; to arrest; to imprison; to transport or send to penal servitude. ◆ *n* a convict; a former convict; a term of imprisonment or transportation. [Origin unknown]

lagan /lag'ən/ or **ligan** /lī'gən/ *n* wreckage or goods at the bottom of the sea; now *esp* such goods attached to a buoy with a view to recovery. [OFr *lagan*, perh Scand from the root of **lay**[1] and **lie**[2]; falsely associated with L *ligāmen* a tying]

lagena /lə-jē'nə/ *n* a narrow-necked bottle used in antiquity; (in some vertebrates) a pocket lined by sensory epithelium, developed from the saccule of the ear. [L *lagēna*, from Gr *lagȳna*]

■ **lagē'niform** *adj* flask-shaped.

lager /lä'gər/ *n* (in full **lager beer**) a light beer traditionally matured for up to six months before use. [Ger *Lagerbier*, from *Lager* a storehouse]

□ **lager lout** *n* (*inf*) a youth noted for his boorish, aggressive and unruly behaviour brought on by an excess of lager, beer, etc. **lager loutery** *n* (*inf*) the phenomenon or behaviour of lager louts.

laggard, etc see under **lag**[1].

laggen or **laggin** /lag'ən or lä'gən/ (*Burns*) *n* the angle between the side and bottom of a wooden dish. [Cf **lag**[2] and **leglin**]

□ **lagg'en-gird** *n* a hoop at the bottom of a wooden vessel.

lagger, lagging see **lag**[1,2].

lagniappe or **lagnappe** /lan'yap/ *n* something given beyond what is strictly required; a gratuity. [Louisiana Fr, from Am Sp (Quechua *yápa* addition)]

lagomorph /lag'ə-mörf/ *n* an animal of the order **Lagomor'pha** of gnawing mammals having two pairs of upper incisors, eg hares and rabbits (also *adj*). [Gr *lagōs* hare, and *morphē* form]

■ **lagomor'phic** or **lagomor'phous** *adj*.

lagoon or (*old*) **lagune** /lə-goon'/ *n* a shallow lake, *esp* one near or communicating with the sea or a river; an area of water separated from the sea by earth or sand banks, coral reefs, etc. [Ital *laguna*, from L *lacūna*]

■ **lagoon'al** *adj*.

Lagos rubber /lä'gos rub'ər/ *n* a high-grade rubber yielded by tropical African trees of the genus *Funtumia*. [*Lagos*, in Nigeria]

Lagrangian points /la-grän'ji-ən points/ (*astron* and *space technol*) *n pl* the five points associated with a binary system (*esp* Earth-Moon) where the combined gravitational forces are zero. [From JL *Lagrange* (1736–1813), French mathematician and astronomer]

lagrimoso /lä-gri-mō'sō/ (*music*) *adj* and *adv* plaintive or plaintively. [Ital from L *lacrimōsus* tearful, from *lacrima* a tear]

Lagting or **Lagthing** /läg'ting/ *n* the upper house of the Norwegian parliament; the parliament of the Faeroe Islands (also **Løg'ting**). [Norw *lag*, Faeroese *løg* law, and *ting* (thing) court, parliament]

lagune see **lagoon**.

lah same as **la**[1].

lahar /lä'här/ *n* a mud-lava or other mud-flow. [Javanese]

lah-di-dah see **la-di-da**.

LAIA *abbrev*: Latin American Integration Association.

laic, laical, laicize and **laicity** see under **lay**[3].

laid[1] /lād/ *pat* and *pap* of **lay**[1]. *adj* put down or prostrate; pressed down; spread or set out; flattened by wind and rain.

□ **laid'-back'** or **laid back** *adj* (*inf*) relaxed; easy-going; unhurried. **laid paper** *n* paper that shows the marks of the close parallel wires on which the pulp was laid, *opp* to *wove* paper. **laid work** *n* in embroidery, the simplest kind of couching.

laid[2] /lād/ Scots form of **load**.

laidly /lād'li/ *adj* Scot and N Eng form of **loathly**.

laigh /lāhh/ *adj* and *adv* a Scots form of **low**[1]; low-lying; sunken. ◆ *n* a tract of low-lying or sunken land.

laik see **lake**[4].

laika /lī'kə/ *n* any of several similar breeds of small reddish-brown working dog, originating in Finland. [Russ, from *layat* to bark]

lain *pap* of **lie**[2].

Laingian /lang'i-ən/ *adj* of or relating to the theories or practices of RD *Laing* (1927–89), British psychiatrist, *esp* his view that mental illness is a response to stress caused by a person's family life or by social pressures. ◆ *n* a supporter of Laing's theories and practices.

■ words derived from main entry word; □ compound words; ■ idioms and phrasal verbs

lair¹ /lār/ n the den or retreat of a wild animal; an enclosure for beasts; the ground for one grave in a graveyard (*Scot*). ◆ vt to put in a lair. ◆ vi to lie in a lair; to go to a lair. [OE *leger* a couch, from *licgan* to lie down; Du *leger*, Ger *Lager*]
■ **lair'age** n a place or accommodation where cattle are housed or laired, *esp* at markets and docks.

lair² /lār/ (*Scot*) vt and vi to mire, cover with mud. ◆ n mire. [ON *leir* mud]
■ **lair'y** adj.

lair³ /lār/ n Scots form of **lore¹**.

lair⁴ /lār/ (*obs Aust sl*) n a flashily dressed man.
■ **lai'rize** or **-ise** vi to act the lair. **lair'y** adj loud; aggressive; insolent; flashily dressed.
■ **laired up** dressed flashily.

laird /lārd/ (*Scot*) n an estate landowner. [Scot and N Eng form of **lord**]
■ **laird'ship** n.

lairy see under **lair²,⁴**.

laisse /les/ n a tirade or string of verses on one rhyme. [Fr]

laissez-aller, also **laisser-aller** /le-sā-al'ā or (Fr) -al-ā' / n lack of constraint; relaxed freedom. [Fr, let go]

laissez-faire /le-sā-fer' / n a general principle of non-interference in the concerns of other people or parties (also **laisser-faire'**). [Fr, let do]
■ **laissez-faire'ism** n.

laissez-passer /le-sā-pä-sā' / n a pass, special passport or similar permit, to allow one to travel in a restricted area, etc. [Fr, let pass]

laitance /lā'təns/ n a milky accumulation of fine particles which forms on the surface of newly laid concrete if the concrete is too wet or is vibrated or tamped too much. [Fr, from *lait* milk]

laith /lāth/ adj a Scots form of **loath**.
■ **laithfu'** /lāth'fə/ adj bashful.

laity see under **lay³**.

lake¹ /lāk/ n a large or considerable body of water enclosed by land; a large quantity, an excess, eg of wine, etc (*econ*). [ME *lac*, either from OE *lacu* stream (see **lake³**), confused in sense with L *lacus* lake, or from *lacus* itself, directly or through Fr *lac*]
■ **Lake'land** n and adj (of or belonging to) the Lake District (qv below); (without *cap*) (of or belonging to) any similar area of countryside. **lake'let** n a little lake. **lāk'er** n a fish found in lakes; a boat for lakes; a person who sails on lakes; a Lake poet; a visitor to the Lake District. **lāk'ish** adj resembling or having the characteristics of the Lake poets (see below). **lāk'y** adj.
❑ **lake'-basin** n a hollow now or once containing a lake; the area drained by a lake. **Lake District** n a picturesque and mountainous region in Cumbria (formerly Cumberland, Westmorland and Lancashire) with many lakes. **lake'-dweller** n. **lake dwelling** n a settlement, *esp* prehistoric, built on piles in a lake. **lake herring** see **cisco**. **lake'-law'yer** n (*US*) the bowfin; the burbot. **Lake poets** n pl Wordsworth, Coleridge and Southey, who lived in the Lake District. **lake'side** n and adj.

lake² /lāk/ n a reddish pigment originally derived from lac; a coloured substance derived by combining a dye with a metallic hydroxide; its colour; carmine. ◆ vt and vi to make or become lake-coloured. [**lac²**]
■ **lak'y** adj.

lake³ /lāk/ (*obs*) n a small stream or water channel. [OE *lacu*]

lake⁴ or **laik** /lāk/ (*N Eng*) vi to sport or play; to take a holiday from work; to be unemployed. [OE *lācan*]
■ **lak'er** or **laik'er** n.

lakh or **lac** /lak/ (*Ind* and *Pak*) n the number 100000, *esp* in referring to rupees; an indefinitely vast number. [Hindi *lākh*, from Sans *lakṣa* 100000]

lakin /lā'kin/ (*Shakesp*) n a short form of **ladykin**, *dimin* of **lady**.

Lakota /lə-kō'tə/ n (a member of) a Native American people comprising the westernmost branch of the Sioux; the Siouan language of this people. ◆ adj of or relating to the Lakota or their language.

laksa /lak'sa/ n a dish of rice noodles served in a rich curry sauce. [Malay]

Lakshmi /laksh'mē/ n in Hindu mythology, Vishnu's consort. [Sans]

la-la /lä'la or lä'lä/ vi to sing an accompaniment using syllables such as la-la. [Poss **la¹**]

la-la land /lä'lä land/ (*inf*) n a state of being divorced from reality, *esp* through intoxication by alcohol or drugs; (with *caps*) a nickname for Los Angeles, *esp* used by non-residents to connote a lifestyle based around the entertainment industry, drug abuse, eccentric beliefs, etc (*US*).

lalang /lä'läng/ n a coarse grass, *Imperata arundinacea*, of the Malay archipelago. [Malay]

lalapalooza see **lollapalooza**.

laldie or **laldy** /lal'di/ (*Scot*) n a beating or thrashing (as punishment); vigorous action of any kind. [Perh connected with OE *læl* a whip, weal, bruise]
■ **get laldie** to receive a thrashing. **give it** or **give someone laldie** to do something or punish someone energetically and enthusiastically.

Lalique glass /la-lēk' gläs/ n ornamental glassware, *esp* with bas-relief decoration of figures, flowers, etc. [Named after René *Lalique* (died 1945), French designer of jewellery and glassware]

lallan /lal'ən or lä'lən/ (*Scot*) adj and n a form of **lawland** or **lowland**.
■ **Lall'ans** n the Broad Scots language or dialect; a form of Scots developed by modern Scottish writers. ◆ adj of or relating to this dialect.

lallapalooza see **lollapalooza**.

lallation /la-lā'shən/ n in speech, the pronouncing of *r* like *l*; *orig* childish speech. [L *lallāre* to sing a lullaby]
■ **lall'ing** n babbling.

l'allegro /lä-lā'grō/ (*Ital*) n the merry or cheerful man.

lallygag /lal'i-gag/ or **lollygag** /lol'i-gag/ (*inf, esp N Am*) vi to idle or loiter; to caress, *esp* publicly. [Ety uncertain]

Lam. (*Bible*) abbrev : (the Book of) Lamentations.

lam¹ /lam/ vt to beat. ◆ vi (with *into*) to attack. [Cf OE *lemian* to subdue or lame, ON *lemja* to beat, literally lame]
■ **lamm'ing** n a thrashing.

lam² /lam/ (*US sl*) n escape or hurried flight, *esp* from the police. ◆ vi (with *it*, or *out*, *into*, etc) to escape or flee. [Origin uncertain, perh from **lam¹**]
■ **on the lam** escaping, running away. **take it on the lam** to make an escape or flee.

lama /lä'mə/ n a Buddhist priest or monk in Tibet. [Tibetan *blama*, the *b* silent]
■ **Lamaism** /lä'mə-izm/ n the religion prevailing in Tibet and Mongolia, being Buddhism influenced by Tantrism, and by Shamanism or spirit-worship. **La'maist** n and adj. **lamaist'ic** adj. **la'masery** (or /lä-mä'sə-ri/) or **lamaserai** /-rī/ n a Tibetan monastery.

lamantin /lä-man'tin/ n the manatee. [Fr]

Lamarckism /lä-märk'ki-zm/ n the theory of the French naturalist JBPA de Monet de *Lamarck* (1744–1829) that species have developed by the efforts of organisms to adapt themselves to new conditions (also **Lamarck'ianism**).
■ **Lamarck'ian** adj and n.

lamasery or **lamaserai** see under **lama**.

Lamaze /lə-mäz' / adj and n (relating to) a method of managing childbirth in which the expectant mother is trained in relieving pain through breathing techniques and gives birth without the use of drugs. [Fernand *Lamaze* (1891–1957), French physician]

lamb /lam/ n the young of a sheep; its flesh eaten as a food; lambskin; someone simple, innocent, sweet or gentle as a lamb (*fig*); a dear (*inf*). ◆ vt and vi to give birth to (a lamb or lambs); to tend at lambing. [OE *lamb*; Ger *Lamm*, Du *lam*]
■ **lamb'er** n someone who tends lambing ewes; a lambing ewe. **lamb'ing** n the time when ewes give birth to lambs; the work involved in delivering and caring for newborn lambs. **lamb'kin**, **lamb'ling** (*rare*), or (*Scot*) **lamb'ie** n a little lamb. **lamb'-like** adj like a lamb; gentle.
❑ **lamb'-ale** n a feast at lamb-shearing. **lamb's ears** or **lamb's tongue** n a labiate plant, *Stachys lanata*, with silver woolly leaves. **lamb's fry** n lamb's offal, *esp* lamb's testicles. **lamb'skin** n the skin of a lamb dressed with the wool on; the skin of a lamb dressed as leather; a woollen cloth resembling this; a cotton cloth with raised surface and deep nap. **lamb's lettuce** n corn-salad. **lamb's quarter** n (*US*) another name for **fat hen** (see under **fat¹**). **lamb's'-tails** n pl hazel catkins. **lamb's tongue** n see **lamb's ears** above. **lamb's'wool** n fine wool, *specif* wool obtained from the first shearing of a (yearling) lamb; an old English beverage composed of ale and the pulp of roasted apples, with sugar and spices.
■ **lamb down** (*Aust inf*) to persuade (someone) to squander all his or her money. **like a lamb to the slaughter** meekly, innocently, without resistance. **the Lamb** or **Lamb of God** applied to Christ, in allusion to the paschal lamb and John 1.29.

lambada /lam-bä'də/ n a rhythmic and energetic dance originating in Latin America and popularized in the late 1980s; the music for this style of dancing. [Port]

lambast /lam-bast'/ or **lambaste** /lam-bāst'/ vt to thrash; to reprimand severely. [Perh **lam¹** and **baste³**]

lambda /lam'də/, also (more correctly) **labda** /lab'də/ n the Greek letter (Λ, λ) corresponding to Roman *l*; as a numeral, λ' = 30, λ = 30000; used as a symbol for wavelength; used as a symbol for the lambda particle (*phys*); the meeting of the sagittal and lambdoid sutures of the skull (*anat*). [Gr *lambda*, properly *labda*, from Heb *lāmedh*]

■ **lamb'dacism** or **lab'dacism** *n* a too frequent use of words containing *l*-sounds; faulty pronunciation of the sound of *l*; a defective pronunciation of *r*, making it like *l*. **lamb'doid** or **lambdoid'al** *adj* shaped like or relating to the Greek capital Λ, applied in anatomy to the suture between the occipital and the two parietal bones of the skull.

□ **lambda particle** *n* a sub-atomic particle, the lightest of the hyperons (*phys*); a bacteriophage, an important vector in genetic manipulation, which can either grow in synchrony with its host (*Escherichia coli*) or exist as a multiplying virulent phage (*biol*).

Lambeg drum /*lam'beg drum*/ (also without *cap*) *n* a large drum used *esp* on ceremonial occasions by Protestant communities in Northern Ireland. [From the village of *Lambeg*, near Belfast]
■ **Lam'begger** *n* someone who plays a Lambeg drum.

lambent /*lam'bənt*/ *adj* moving about as if touching lightly like a flame; gliding or playing over; flickering; softly radiant, glowing; (*esp* of wit) light and brilliant; licking. [L *lambere* to lick]
■ **lam'bency** *n* the quality of being lambent; a flicker. **lam'bently** *adv*. **lam'bitive** *adj* (*obs*) of a medicine, taken by licking. ◆ *n* a medicine so taken.

lambert /*lam'bərt*/ (*phys*) *n* a unit of brightness, one lumen per square centimetre. [JH *Lambert* (1728–77), German scientist]

Lambeth degree /*lam'bəth di-grē'*/ *n* a degree conferred by the Archbishop of Canterbury, whose palace is at *Lambeth*.

Lambeth Walk /*lam'bəth wök*/ *n* a dance popularized in the 1930s, named after the London borough of Lambeth.

Lambic beer /*lam'bik bēr*/ *n* a type of Belgian beer brewed using wild yeast. [*Lambeek* in Belgium, where it was first brewed]

lambing see under **lamb**.

lambitive see under **lambent**.

lambkin, lambling, etc see under **lamb**.

lamboys /*lam'boiz*/ (*ancient hist*) *n pl* kilted flexible steel plates worn skirt-like from the waist. [Perhaps Fr *lambeaux* flaps; or a blunder for *jambeaux*]

lambrequin /*lam'bər-kin* or *-bri-kin*/ *n* a veil over a helmet; a strip of drapery over a window, doorway, from a mantelpiece, etc; a stylized representation of such drapery in a coat of arms (*heraldry*). [Fr]

Lambrusco /*lam-broos'kō*/ *n* a variety of white or red grape frequently used in wine-making in Italy; the light sparkling wine made from this kind of grape.

LAMDA /*lam'də*/ *abbrev* : London Academy of Music and Dramatic Art.

lame¹ /*lām*/ *adj* disabled, *specif* in the use of a leg; hobbling; unsatisfactory; imperfect; weak, implausible; conventional, unfashionable (*US sl*). ◆ *n* (*US sl*) an old-fashioned person. ◆ *vt* to make lame; to cripple; to make imperfect (*fig*). [OE *lama* lame; Du *lam*, Ger *lahm*]
■ **lame'ly** *adv*. **lame'ness** *n*. **lam'ish** *adj* a little lame; hobbling. □ **lame'brain** *n* (*inf*) a stupid person, an idiot. **lame'brained** *adj*. **lame duck** see under **duck¹**.

lame² /*lām*/ *n* a thin plate *esp* of metal, as in armour. [Fr, from L *lāmina* a thin plate]

lamé /*lä'mā*/ *n* and *adj* (of) a fabric in which metallic (*usu* gold or silver) threads are interwoven. [Ety as for **lame²**]

lamed or **lamedh** /*lä'mäd*/ *n* the twelfth letter of the Hebrew alphabet. [Heb]

lamella /*lə-mel'ə*/ *n* (*pl* **lamell'ae** /*-ē*/) a thin plate or layer. [L *lāmella*, dimin of *lāmina*]
■ **lamell'ar** (or /*lam'i-*/) *adj*. **lam'ellate** (or /*-el'*/) or **lam'ellated** *adj*. **lamell'iform** *adj*. **lamell'oid** *adj*. **lamell'ose** *adj*.

lamellibranch /*lə-mel'i-brangk*/ *n* any member of the **Lamellibranchiā'ta**, Pelecypoda, or bivalve molluscs (eg the mussel, oyster or clam) with plate-like (nutritive) gills. [New L, from L *lāmella* a thin plate, and *branchia* a gill]
■ **lamellibranch'iate** *adj*.

lamellicorn /*lə-mel'i-körn*/ *n* a member of the **Lamellicorn'ia**, a group of beetles (eg the cockchafer) with flattened plates on the end of their antennae. [New L, from L *lāmella* a thin plate, and *cornu* a horn]

lamellirostral /*lə-mel-i-ros'trəl*/ or **lamellirostrate** /*lə-mel-i-ros'trāt*/ (*zool*) *adj* having transverse lamellae within the edge of the bill. [New L, from L *lāmella* a thin plate, and *rostrum* beak]

lament /*lə-ment'*/ *vi* to cry out in grief; to wail; to mourn. ◆ *vt* to mourn for; to deplore. ◆ *n* sorrow expressed by crying out; an elegy or dirge; a musical composition of a similar character. [L *lāmentārī*]

■ **lamentable** /*lam'ənt-ə-bl*/ *adj* deserving or expressing sorrow; sad; pitiful; pitifully bad (*inf*); worthless (*inf*). **lam'entably** *adv*. **lamentā'tion** *n* the act of lamenting; the audible expression of grief; wailing. **Lamentā'tions** *n* a book of the Old Testament traditionally attributed to Jeremiah. **lament'ed** *adj*. **lament'ing** *n* and *adj*. **lament'ingly** *adv*.

lameter or **lamiter** /*lä'mi-tər*/ (*Scot*) *n* a cripple. [Obscurely derived from **lame¹**]

lamia /*lā'mi-ə*/ *n* in Greek and Roman mythology, a bloodsucking serpent-witch. [Gr and L *lamia*]

lamiger or **lammiger** /*lam'i-jər*/ (*dialect*) *n* a cripple. [Cf **lameter**]

lamina /*lam'i-nə*/ *n* (*pl* **lam'inae** /*-nē*/) a thin plate or layer; a leaf blade; a thin plate of bone; a thin layer of rock (*geol*); a plate of sensitive tissue within a hoof. [L *lāmina* a thin plate]
■ **lam'inable** *adj* suitable for making into thin plates. **lam'inar, lam'inary** or **lam'inose** *adj* consisting of or like thin plates or layers; of or relating to a fluid, streamlined flow. **Laminā'ria** *n* the tangle genus of brown seaweeds, with large expanded leathery fronds. **laminār'ian** *adj*. **lam'inarize** or **-ise** *vt* to make (a surface, etc) such that a flow over it will be laminar. **lam'inate** or **lam'inated** *adj* in laminae or thin plates; consisting of scales or layers, one over another; made by laminating; covered by a thin layer (eg of protective material). **lam'inate** *vt* to make into a thin plate; to separate into layers; to make by bonding layers together; to cover with a thin layer (eg of protective material). ◆ *vi* to separate into thin layers. ◆ *n* a laminated plastic, or other material similarly made. **laminā'tion** *n* arrangement in thin layers; a thin layer; a thin, transparent protective coating, *usu* of plastic, *esp* one that covers a book jacket, certificate, menu, etc. **lam'inator** *n* someone who manufactures laminates. **laminec'tomy** *n* surgical removal of a lamina. **laminī'tis** *n* (*vet*) inflammation of a horse's lamina.
□ **laminar flow** *n* viscous flow; a fluid flow in which the particles move smoothly without turbulence, *esp*, as in aircraft, such a non-impeding flow over a streamlined surface (*phys*). **laminated glass** *n* safety glass. **laminated plastic** *n* sheets of paper, canvas, linen or silk, impregnated with a resin, dried and bonded together, *usu* by means of heat and pressure.

lamington /*lam'ing-tən*/ (*Aust*) *n* a piece of sponge cake, coated in chocolate and coconut. [From Lord *Lamington*, Governor of Queensland (1895–1901)]

laminitis, laminose see under **lamina**.

lamiter see **lameter**.

Lammas /*lam'əs*/ *n* 1st August, an old feast-day celebrating the first fruits of the harvest; a quarter day in Scotland (now fixed as 28 August); the time of year of Lammas. [OE *hlāf-mæsse*, *hlāmmæsse*, from *hlāf* loaf, and *mæsse* feast]
□ **Lamm'as-tide** *n* the season of Lammas.

lammer /*lä'mər*/ or *lam'ər*/ (*Scot*) *n* amber. [Fr *l'ambre* the amber]

lammergeier or **lammergeyer** /*lam'ər-gī-ər*/ *n* the great bearded vulture of S Europe, etc. [Ger *Lämmergeier*, from *Lämmer* lambs, and *Geier* vulture]

lammiger see **lamiger**.

lamp¹ /*lamp*/ *n* any appliance or device containing a source of artificial light, *usu* an electric light bulb; a container with a wick for burning oil, paraffin, etc to give light; any source of light; an eye (*archaic* and *sl*). ◆ *vi* (*Spenser*) to shine. ◆ *vt* (*archaic*) to illumine; to supply with lamps. [Fr *lampe*, and Gr *lampas, -ados*, from *lampein* to shine]
■ **lamp'ad** *n* (*rare* or *poetic*) a lamp, candlestick or torch. **lamp'adary** *n* in the Greek Church, someone who looks after the lamps and carries a lighted taper before the patriarch; a candelabrum. **lampaded'romy** or **lampadephor'ia** (Gr *lampadēdromiā*, *lampadēphoriā*) an ancient Greek torch-race. **lamp'adist** *n* a runner in a torch-race. **lamp'adomancy** *n* (Gr *manteiā* divination) divination by flame. **lamp'ing** *adj* (*poetic*) shining. ◆ *n* the hunting of rabbits, etc by using bright lights to blind them. **lamp'ion** *n* an oil lamp, often in a decorative coloured-glass pot.
□ **lamp'black** *n* soot obtained from a fuel-burning lamp, or from burning substances rich in carbon (eg mineral oil, turpentine, tar, etc) in a limited supply of air; a pigment made from it and used in chemical and industrial processes, etc. ◆ *vt* to blacken with lampblack. **lampbrush chromosome** *n* a chromosome observed during the early stages of meiosis in many eukaryotes, having a characteristic appearance due to the orderly series of lateral loops of chromatin arranged in pairs on either side of the chromosome axis. **lamp'-burner** *n* the part of a lamp from which the flame rises. **lamp chimney** or **lamp'-glass** *n* a glass funnel placed round the flame of a lamp. **lamp'-fly** *n* (*Browning*) perh a glow-worm, or a firefly. **lamp'holder** *n* a socket for an electric bulb. **lamp'hole** *n* a shaft for lowering a lamp into a sewer. **lamp'-hour** *n* the energy required to maintain a lamp for an hour. **lamp'light** *n* the light shed by a lamp or lamps. **lamp'lighter** *n* formerly, a person employed to light

street-lamps; a spill or other means of lighting a lamp (*US*). **lamp'lit** *adj*. **lamp'post** or **lamp'-standard** *n* the pillar supporting a street-lamp. **lamp'-room** *n* a room in which miners' or other lamps are kept, tended, etc; the room at the top of a lighthouse, housing the lamp itself. **lamp'shade** *n* a decorative or protective cover designed to moderate or direct the light of a lamp or light bulb. **lamp'-shell** *n* a brachiopod, *esp Terebratula* or a similar genus, from its shell shaped like an antique lamp.

■ **smell of the lamp** to show signs of great elaboration or study.

lamp² /*lamp*/ (*Scot*) *vi* to run wild, to scamper; to go jauntily, stride along; to walk with long, heavy steps.

lamp³ /*lamp*/ (*sl*) *vt* to punch or thump. [Cf **lam¹**]

lampas¹ /*lam'pas*/ or **lampers** /*lam'pərz*/ (*vet*) *n* a swelling of the roof of the mouth in horses (also (*Shakesp*) **lam'passe**). [Fr *lampas*]

lampas² /*lam'pas*/ *n* a flowered material of silk and wool used in upholstery. [Fr]

lampern /*lam'pərn*/ *n* the European river lamprey. [OFr *lamprion*]

lampion see under **lamp¹**.

lampoon /*lam-poon'*/ *n* a personal satire. ◆ *vt* to attack or ridicule by personal satire. [OFr *lampon*, perh from a drinking-song with the refrain *lampons* let us drink]

■ **lampoon'er** or **lampoon'ist** *n*. **lampoon'ery** *n*.

lamprey /*lam'pri*/ *n* (*pl* **lam'preys**) a type of primitive fish-like vertebrate (genus *Petromyzon* or *Lampetra*) or cyclostome which fixes itself to the fish it preys on and to stones, etc by its sucking mouth. [OFr *lamproie*, from LL *lamprēda*, *lampetra*, explained as from L *lambere* to lick, and *petra* rock, but found also as *naupreda*, *nauprida*]

lamprophyre /*lam'prō-fīr*/ (*mineralogy*) *n* a compact intrusive rock with phenocrysts of black mica, hornblende, etc, but not of feldspar. [Gr *lampros* bright, and *-phyre* from **porphyry**]

■ **lamprophyric** /*-fir'ik*/ *adj*.

lampuki /*lam'pū-ke*/ *n* an edible Mediterranean fish of the genus *Coryphaena*, the dolphinfish (also **lam'puka**). [Maltese]

LAN /*lan*/ (*comput*) *abbrev* : local area network.

lana /*lā'nə*/ *n* the wood of the genipap tree. [S American word]

lanai /*lə-nī'*/ *n* a living area built onto the side of a house. [Hawaiian]

lanate /*lā'nāt*/ or **lanose** /*lā'nōs* or *-nōz*/ (*biol*) *adj* woolly. [L *lānātus*, from *lāna* wool]

Lancashire /*lang'kə-shər* or *-shēr*/ *n* a crumbly, white cheese made *orig* in the county of *Lancashire*.

Lancasterian /*lang-kə-stē'ri-ən*/ (*educ*) *adj* of or relating to Joseph *Lancaster* (1778–1838), or his method of teaching by means of monitors.

Lancastrian /*lang-kas'tri-ən*/ *adj* of or relating to *Lancaster* or Lancashire, or to the dukes or (*hist*) house of Lancaster. ◆ *n* a native of Lancaster or Lancashire; a supporter of the house of Lancaster (*hist*).

lance¹ /*läns*/ or (*Spenser*) **launce** (also /*löns*/) *n* a cavalry weapon with a long shaft, a spearhead, and a small flag; a similar weapon for other purposes, such as hunting; a surgeon's lancet; a blade in a cutting tool to sever the grain in advance of the main blade (*carpentry*); a lancer. ◆ *vt* to pierce, as with a lance; to open or incise with a lancet in order to allow drainage (*med*); to shoot out or fling (*obs*). ◆ *vi* to rush, dart or fling oneself (*obs*). [Fr, from L *lancea*; Gr *lonchē* a lance; cf **launch¹**]

■ **lance'let** *n* any of the narrow, translucent, backboned marine animals of the genera *Branchiostoma* and *Asymmetron*. **lanc'er** *n* a light cavalry soldier armed with a lance, or a soldier of a regiment formerly so armed. **lanc'ers** *n sing* a set of quadrilles, first popular in England about 1820, or its music. **lanc'iform** *adj* shaped like a lance.

❑ **lance corporal** *n* (formed on **lance prisado**) acting corporal; the military rank between private and corporal, the lowest rank of non-commissioned officer in the British Army (*army sl* **lance'jack**). **lance sergeant** *n* a corporal acting as a sergeant. **lance'wood** *n* any of various West Indian, Australian and New Zealand trees with strong, elastic, durable wood.

lance² see **launce¹**.

lancegay /*läns'gā*/ (*obs*) *n* a kind of spear. [OFr, from *lance* a lance, and *zagaye* a pike (as in **assegai**)]

lance-knight and **lance-knecht** non-standard forms of **landsknecht**.

lanceolate /*län'si-ə-lāt*/ or **lanceolated** /*-lā-tid*/ *adj* (also **lan'ceolar**) shaped like a lance-head; lancet-shaped; tapering toward both ends and two or three times as long as broad (*bot*). [L *lanceolātus*, from *lanceola*, dimin of *lancea* lance]

■ **lan'ceolately** *adv*.

lance prisado /*läns pri-zä'dō*/, **prisade** /*pri-zäd'*/, **pesade** /*pi-zäd'*/ or **speisade** /*spē-zäd'*/ (*obs*) *n* a lance corporal. [Ital *lancea spezzata* broken lance, as if meaning an experienced soldier]

lancet /*län'sit*/ *n* a surgical instrument used for opening veins, abscesses, etc; a lancet window; a lancet arch. ◆ *adj* shaped like a lancet, narrow and pointed. [OFr *lancette*, dimin of **lance¹**; see **lance¹**]

■ **lan'ceted** *adj*.

❑ **lancet arch** *n* a high and narrow pointed arch. **lancet fish** *n* a large, elongated marine fish with long sharp teeth. **lancet window** *n* a tall, narrow, acutely arched window.

lanch see **launch¹**.

lanciform see under **lance¹**.

lancinate /*län'si-nāt*/ *vt* to lacerate; to pierce. [L *lancināre*, *-ātum* to tear]

■ **lan'cinating** *adj* (of pain) shooting or darting. **lancinā'tion** *n* sharp, shooting pain.

Lancs. /*langks*/ *abbrev* : Lancashire.

Land /*länt*/ *n* (*pl* **Länder**, sometimes **Laender** /*len'dər*/) a state or province in Germany and Austria functioning as a unit of local government. [Ger *Land* land]

land¹ /*land*/ *n* the solid portion of the surface of the earth; a country; a district; a nation or people; a constituent part of an empire or federation; ground; a piece of ground owned, real estate; soil; a group of dwellings or tenements under one roof and having a common entry (*Scot*); the high part of the bore of a gun that remains after the gun has been rifled. ◆ *combining form* denoting a domain or district frequented or dominated by, as in *gangland*. ◆ *vt* to set on land or on shore; to set down; to deposit, drop or plant; to cause to arrive; to bring ashore; to capture; to secure; to attach to one's interest; to earth up; (with *up*) to silt or to block with earth. ◆ *vi* to come on land or on shore; to alight; to arrive, find oneself or end up being. ◆ *adj* of or on the land; land-dwelling; terrestrial. [OE *land*; Du *land*, Ger *Land*]

■ **land'ed** *adj* possessing land or estates; consisting in or derived from land or real estate. **land'er** *n* someone who, or something which, lands; a heavy blow (*inf*). **land'ing** *n* disembarkation; a coming to ground; alighting; putting ashore; setting down; a place for getting on shore or onto the ground; the level part of a staircase between flights of steps or at the top. ◆ *adj* relating to the unloading of a vessel's cargo, or to disembarking, or to alighting from the air. **land'less** *adj*. **land'lessness** *n*. **land'ward** *adj* lying towards the land; inland; rural (*Scot*). **land'ward** or **land'wards** *adv* towards the land; in the country (*Scot*).

❑ **land agency** *n*. **land agent** *n* a person employed to let farms, collect rents, etc; an agent or broker for the buying and selling of land. **land'-army** *n* a body of women organized for farm work in wartime. **land bank** *n* a bank which finances real estate transactions using the land as security; a stock of land held by a building company for future development. **land'boarding** *n* the sport of being propelled over land by a large kite while standing on a wheeled board. **land breeze** *n* a breeze setting from the land towards the sea. **land bridge** *n* a connection by land allowing terrestrial plants and animals to pass from one region to another (*geol*); a route by land allowing passage between countries or regions previously unconnected. **land crab** *n* any crab that lives much or mostly on land. **landed interest** *n* the combined interest of the land-owning class in a community. **land'fall** *n* an approach to land after a journey by sea or air; the land so approached. **land'fill** *n* the disposal of refuse by burying it under the soil; refuse disposed of in this way; a place where landfill is practised. **land'filling** *n*. **land'-fish** *n* (*Shakesp*) a fish on land, someone who is more fish than man. **land'-flood** *n* an overflowing of land by water; inundation. **land'force** *n* a military force serving on land. **land'form** *n* a feature of the landscape such as a valley or escarpment. **land girl** *n* a girl who does farm work, *esp* in wartime. **land'-grabber** *n* someone who acquires land by harsh and grasping means; someone who is eager to occupy land from which others have been evicted. **land'-grabbing** *n*. **land grant** *n* a grant of public land (to a college, etc). **land'-haul** *vt* to haul (eg a boat) overland. **land'-herd** *n* a herd of land animals. **land'holder** *n* a tenant or proprietor of land. **land'holding** *adj* and *n*. **land'-hunger** *n* the desire to possess land. **land'ing-beam** *n* a radio beam by which an aircraft is guided in to land. **land'ing-carriage** *n* the wheeled structure on which an aeroplane runs when starting or landing. **landing craft** *n* a small, low, open vessel (or vessels) for landing troops and equipment on beaches. **landing field** *n* a field that allows aircraft to land and take off safely. **landing gear** *n* the wheels, floats, etc of an aircraft used in landing. **land'ing-ground** *n* a piece of ground prepared for landing aircraft as required. **landing net** *n* a kind of scoop net for landing a fish that has been hooked. **land'ing-place** *n* a place for landing. **land'ing-ship** *n* a ship whose forward part can be let down in order to put vehicles ashore. **land'ing-speed** *n* the minimum speed at which an aircraft normally lands. **landing stage** *n* a platform, fixed or floating, for landing passengers or goods. **landing strip** *n* a narrow hard-surfaced runway. **land'-jobber** *n* a speculator in land. **land'-jobbing** *n*. **land'lady** *n* a woman who has tenants or lodgers; the manageress or proprietress of a public house or hotel; a hostess (*obs*). **land law** *n* (*usu in pl*) a law concerning property in land. **Land League** *n* an association founded in Ireland in 1879 to procure reduction of rents and to promote peasant-proprietorship, suppressed in 1881. **land'-line** *n* an overland line of communication or transport. **land'locked** *adj* almost or entirely shut in by land; cut off from the sea. **land'lord** *n* a man who has tenants or lodgers; the manager or proprietor of a public house or hotel. **land'lordism** *n* the authority, policy, behaviour or united action of the landowning class; the system of land-ownership. **land'-lubber** *n* (*naut*; *derog*) a landsman. **land'-lubberly** *adj*. **land'man** *n* a countryman; a landsman. **land'mark** *n* any land-boundary mark; any conspicuous object on land marking a locality or serving as a guide; an event of outstanding significance in history, thought, etc. **land'mass** *n* a large area of land unbroken by seas. **land'-measure** *n* a system of square measure used in measuring land. **land'-measuring** *n* the determination of superficial extent of land. **land'mine** *n* a type of bomb laid on or near the surface of the ground, which explodes when trodden on or driven over; a large bomb dropped by parachute. ◆ *vt* to lay with landmines. **land'mining** *n*. **land office** *n* (*US*) an office dealing with the sale of public land. **land of milk and honey** *n* a land of great fertility promised to the Israelites by God (*Bible*); any region of great fertility, abundance, contentment, etc. **land of Nod** *n* the land to which Cain went after killing Abel (*Bible*); sleep (*inf*). **land'owner** *n* someone who owns land. **land'-ownership** *n*. **land'-owning** *adj*. **land'-pilot** *n* (*Milton*) someone skilled in finding his or her way by land. **land'-pirate** *n* a highway robber; someone who swindles sailors in port; a piratical publisher (*obs*). **land'-plane** *n* an aeroplane that takes off from and alights on land. **land'-poor** *adj* (*US*) poor through owning much unprofitable land. **land'race** *n* a large white Danish breed of pig; any locally-developed breed of farm animal, *esp* pig or sheep. **land'rail** *n* the corncrake. **land'-rat** *n* a rat properly so called, not a water rat; a thief by land, distinguished from a pirate. **land'-reeve** *n* a land-steward's assistant. **land reform** *n* the redistribution of agricultural land to landless people. **Land Registry** *n* in England and Wales, the official body which registers title to land. **land'-roll** *n* a machine for breaking up clods of earth. **Land Rover**® *n* a sturdy motor vehicle used for driving on rough ground. **land'-scrip** *n* (*US*) a negotiable government certificate giving title to the acquisition of public land. **land set-aside** *n* (also **set-aside**) the practice of taking arable land out of production, eg for environmental or national economic reasons. **land'-shark** *n* a land-grabber; someone who robs sailors on shore; a lean breed of pig (*old US*). **land'-ship** *n* a land vehicle having certain properties of a ship, eg a tank. **land'side** *adj* and *n* (of, in or relating to) that part of an airport accessible to the general public, *opp to* airside. **land'skip** an archaic form of **landscape**. **land'slide** *n* a landslip (*orig US*); an overwhelming victory in a political election. **land'slip** *n* a fall of land or rock from a hillside or cliff; a portion of land fallen in this way. **lands'man** *n* a man who lives or works on land; a man with no seafaring experience. **land'-spring** *n* a shallow intermittent spring. **land'-steward** *n* the manager of a landed estate. **land'-survey'ing** *n* measurement and mapping of land. **land'-survey'or** *n*. **land tax** *n* a tax on land. **land'-val'ue** *n* (*usu in pl*) the economic value of land as a basis of taxation. **land'-waiter** *n* a customs officer who is present at the landing of goods from ships. **land'wind** *n* a wind blowing off the land. **land-yacht, land-yachting** see under **yacht**. ■ **land with** to encumber with (a burden, difficult situation, etc). **see how the land lies** to find out in advance how matters stand.

land² /land/ (*obs*) *n* same as **laund**.

land³ /land/ (*US*) *n* and *interj* a euphemism for lord.

landamman or **landammann** /land'a-man (Ger länt'ä-män)/ *n* the chief magistrate in some Swiss cantons. [Ger *Landammann*, from *Land* land, and *Amtmann* bailiff, from *Amt* office, and *Mann* man]

landau /lan'dö/ *n* a horse-drawn carriage with a folding top. [*Landau* in Germany, where the carriage is said to have been first made] ■ **landaulet'** or **landaulette'** *n* a motor car with a folding top, a convertible; a small landau.

landdamne /land-dam'/ (*Shakesp*) *vt* said to mean to abuse with violence (*perh* a misprint for *lamdamn* or *lame-damn*).

landdros /lunt'dros/ or **landdrost** /lunt'drost/ (*S Afr hist*) *n* a district magistrate or sheriff. [Du, from *land* land, and *drost* a bailiff]

lande /läd/ *n* a heathy plain or sandy tract (now forested) along the coast in SW France. [Fr]

landgrave /land'gräv/ (*hist*) *n* a German count with jurisdiction over a territory; later a mere title. [Ger *Landgraf*, from *Land* land, and *Graf* count]

■ **landgrä'viate** or **land'gravate** *n* the territory of a landgrave. **landgravine** /land'grə-vēn/ *n* a female landgrave; the wife or widow of a landgrave.

ländler /lent'lər/ *n* a S German and Austrian dance, or the music for it, similar to a slow waltz. [Ger, from *Landl*, a nickname for Upper Austria]

landloper, land-loper /land'lō-pər/ or **land-louper** /land'low-pər/ (now *dialect, esp Scot*) *n* a vagabond or vagrant. [MDu *landlooper*, from *land* land, and *loopen* to ramble; cf Ger *Landläufer*]

landscape /land'skāp/ *n* the appearance of the area of land which the eye can view at once; the aspect of a country, or a picture or photograph representing it; the production of such pictures or photographs. ◆ *vt* to improve by landscape gardening or interior landscaping (also *fig*). ◆ *vi* to work as a landscape gardener. ◆ *adj* (of a page, illustration, etc) wider than it is deep, *opp to* portrait (*printing*). [Du *landschap*, from *land* and *-schap*, sfx = *-ship*] ▫ **landscape gardener** *n*. **landscape gardening** *n* the art or profession of laying out grounds so as to produce the effect of a picturesque landscape. **land'scape-mar'ble** *n* a limestone with dendritic markings. **land'scape-paint'er** or **land'scapist** *n* a painter of landscapes. **land'scape-paint'ing** *n*. ■ **interior landscaping** the supply and display of plants in order to landscape (*esp* office) interiors.

Landseer /land'sēr/ or **Landseer Newfoundland** /nū'fənd-lənd or nū-fownd'lənd/ *n* a type of black-and-white Newfoundland dog, as painted by Sir Edwin Landseer (1802–73).

landsknecht /länts'knehht/ (*hist*) *n* a mercenary foot soldier of the 16c. [Ger, from *Lands*, genitive of *Land* country, and *Knecht* servant, soldier]

Landsmaal or **Landsmål** /läns'möl/ *n* a literary language based on Norwegian dialects, created by Ivar Aasen (1850), now called Nynorsk, new Norse. [Norw from *land* land, and *maal* speech]

Landsting or **Landsthing** /läns'ting/ *n* the upper house of the Danish Rigsdag or parliament; a Swedish provincial council. [Dan and Swed, from *land* land, and *t(h)ing* parliament]

Landsturm /länt'shtoorm/ *n* conscription in time of national emergency; the force so called up. [Ger, from *Land* land, and *Sturm* alarm]

Landtag /länt'tähh/ *n* the legislative assembly of a German state or land; the Diet of the Holy Roman Empire, or of the German Federation; formerly the provincial assembly of Bohemia or Moravia. [Ger, from *Land* country, and *Tag* diet, day]

Landwehr /länt'vär/ *n* an army reserve. [Ger, from *Land* land, and *Wehr* defence]

lane¹ /lān/ *n* a narrow passage or road; a narrow street; a passage through a crowd or between obstructions; a division of a road for a single stream of traffic; a similar division of waterways or airspace; a division of a running track or swimming pool for one competitor; an individual playing area in a bowling alley; a channel; a sluggish stream (*Scot*); a prescribed course. [OE *lane, lone*] ▫ **lane'way** *n* a lane. ■ **Red Lane** (*inf*) the throat, gullet.

lane² /lān/ *adj* a Scots form of **lone**. ■ **my lane**, **his** or **her lane**, etc alone.

lang /lang/ *adj* a Scots form of **long**. ▫ **lang syne** /sīn/ *adv* long since, long ago. ◆ *n* time long past.

lang. *abbrev*: language.

langaha /läng-gä'hə/ *n* a Madagascan wood snake, with a long flexible snout. [Perh Malagasy]

Langerhans see **islets of Langerhans** under **isle**.

langlauf /läng'lowf/ *n* cross-country skiing. [Ger *lang* long, and *Lauf* race, run or leap]

Langmuir trough /lang'mūr trof/ (*mining*) *n* an apparatus in which a rectangular tank is used to measure surface tension of a liquid. [Irving Langmuir (1881–1957), American chemist]

Langobard /lang'gō-bärd/ see **Lombard**.

langouste /lã-goost'/ *n* the spiny lobster. [Fr] ■ **langoustine** /-ēn'/ *n* the Norway lobster, spiny lobster or rock lobster (*Nephrops*; see **lobster**), larger than a prawn but smaller than a lobster.

langrage, langridge /lang'grij/ or **langrel** /lang'grəl/ (*naval warfare*) *n* shot consisting of a canister containing irregular pieces of iron, formerly used to damage sails and rigging. [Origin unknown]

Langshan /lang'shan/ *n* a small black Chinese hen. [From a place near Shanghai]

langspel /läng'späl/ or **langspiel** /läng'spēl/ *n* an old Shetland cither. [Norw *langspill*, from *lang* long, and *spill* play or instrument]

■ words derived from main entry word; ▫ compound words; ■ idioms and phrasal verbs

language /lang'gwij/ n human speech; a variety of speech or body of words and idioms, *esp* that of a nation; mode of expression; diction; any manner of expressing thought or feeling; an artificial system of signs and symbols, with rules for forming intelligible communications, for use in eg a computer; a national branch of one of the religious and military orders, eg the Hospitallers; bad language, swearing (*inf*). ◆ *vt* (*archaic*) to express in language. [Fr *langage*, from *langue*, from L *lingua* the tongue]
■ **lang'uaged** *adj* skilled, rich in or having language. **lang'uageless** *adj* (*Shakesp*) speechless or silent.
❏ **language laboratory** *n* a room in a school, college, etc in which pupils sit in separate cubicles and are taught a language by means of pre-recorded material.
■ **bad language** swearing. **dead language** a language no longer spoken, *opp* to *living language*. **speak the same language** to have the same tastes, understanding, background or way of thinking; to come within one's range of understanding.

langue /lãg/ n language viewed as a general or abstract system, *opp* to *parole* (*linguistics*); a language (qv) of a religious or military order. [Fr, from L *lingua* tongue]

langued /langd/ (*heraldry*) *adj* having a tongue (of this or that tincture). [Fr *langue*, from L *lingua* tongue]

langue de chat /lãg-də-sha'/ n a very thin finger-shaped biscuit or piece of chocolate. [Fr, cat's tongue]

Langue d'oc /lãg dok'/ n a collective name for the Romance dialects of southern France, the language of the troubadours, as opposed to **Langue d'oïl** /lãg do-ēl' or doil'/ (also **Langue d'oui** /dwē'/) the Romance dialect of northern France, the language of the trouvères, the main element in modern French. The name *Langue d'oc* is often used as synonymous with Provençal, one of its chief branches, and has survived in the province *Languedoc*, also giving its name to a class of wines. [OFr *langue*, from L *lingua* tongue, *de* of, and Provençal *oc* yes, from L *hōc* this; cf OFr *oil*, *oui* yes, from L *hōc illud* this (is) that, yes]
■ **Languedocian** /lang-gə-dō'shi-ən/ *adj*.

languescent see under **languid**.

languet or **languette** /lang'gwet, -get or -get'/ n a tongue-like object or part. [Fr *languette*, dimin of *langue* tongue]

languid /lang'gwid/ *adj* slack; flagging; inert; listless; faint; relaxed; spiritless. [L *languidus*, from *languēre* to be weak]
■ **languescent** /-gwes'ənt/ *adj* (*rare*) growing languid. **lang'uidly** *adv*. **lang'uidness** *n*.

languish /lang'gwish/ *vi* to become or be languid, inert or depressed; to lose strength and animation; to pine; to flag or droop; to look languishingly; to spend time in hardship or discomfort. ◆ *n* (*Shakesp*) languishing; languishment. [Fr *languiss-* (serving as participial stem of *languir*), from L *languēscere*, from *languēre* to be faint]
■ **lang'uished** *adj* (*poetic*) overcome by languor. **lang'uisher** *n*. **lang'uishing** *n*. ◆ *adj* expressive of languor, or merely sentimental emotion; lingering. **lang'uishingly** *adv*. **lang'uishment** *n* the act or state of languishing; tenderness of look.

languor /lang'gər/ n languidness; listlessness; weariness or weakness; dreamy inertia; tender softness; pining; affliction (*obs*); a stuffy suffocating atmosphere. [L *languor*, *-ōris*]
■ **lang'uorous** *adj* full of or expressing languor; languishing. **lang'uorously** *adv*. **lang'uorousness** *n*.

langur /lung-goor'/ n the entellus monkey or another of its genus (*Prebytis*). [Hindi *lāgūr*]

laniard see **lanyard**.

laniary /lā'ni-ə-ri/ *adj* of teeth, claws, etc, designed for tearing. [L *laniārius* of a butcher, from *lanius* a butcher]

laniferous /la-nif'ə-rəs/ or **lanigerous** /la-nij'ə-rəs/ *adj* wool-bearing. [L *lānifer*, *lāniger*, from *lāna* wool, and *ferre*, *gerere* to bear]

La Niña /la nē'nya/ n a meteorological phenomenon in which unusually cold ocean temperatures in the tropical Pacific cause extreme weather conditions. [Sp, little girl, on the model of **El Niño**]

lank /langk/ *adj* long and thin; drooping; flaccid; limp; thin; (of hair) long, straight and lifeless. ◆ *vt* and *vi* (*Shakesp*) to make or become lank. [OE *hlanc*]
■ **lank'ily** *adv*. **lank'iness** *n*. **lank'ly** *adv*. **lank'ness** *n*. **lank'y** *adj* lean, tall and ungainly; long and limp.

lanner /lan'ər/ n a kind of falcon native to regions of Africa, SE Asia and the Mediterranean; the female of this species (*falconry*). [Fr *lanier*, poss from L *laniārius* tearing, or from *lānārius* a weaver (a medieval term of reproach)]
■ **lann'eret** *n* (*falconry*) the male lanner.

lanolin /lan'ō-lin/ or **lanoline** /lan'ə-lin or lan'ə-lēn/ n fat from wool, a mixture of palmitate, oleate and stearate of cholesterol, used as a base for certain ointments. [L *lāna* wool, and *oleum* oil]

lanose see **lanate**.

lansoprazole /lan-sop'rə-zōl/ n a drug used in the treatment of gastric ulcers.

lansquenet /lan'skə-net/ n a landsknecht; a card game. [Fr, from Ger *Landsknecht*]

lant¹ /lant/ n stale urine, used in wool-scouring. [OE and ON *hland*]

lant² /lant/ same as **launce**¹.

lantana /lan-tä'nə or -tä'/ n any plant of the *Lantana* genus, tropical American shrubs of the vervain family with flamboyant spikes of yellow or orange flowers.

lanterloo /lan'tər-loo/ (*obs*) n a card game, ancestral form of loo. [Fr *lanturlu* (a meaningless refrain)]

lantern /lan'tərn/ n a case for holding or carrying a light; a lamp or light contained in such a case; the light-chamber of a lighthouse; a magic lantern; an open structure like a lantern, *esp* one surmounting a building, giving light and air. ◆ *vt* to provide with a lantern. [Fr *lanterne*, from L *lanterna*, from Gr *lamptēr*, from *lampein* to give light]
■ **lant'ernist** *n* a person who works a magic lantern.
❏ **lantern fish** *n* a deep-sea fish that emits light from the sides of its body. **lantern fly** *n* any insect of the homopterous family Fulgoridae, with a lantern-like proboscis, formerly thought to give out light. **lan'tern-jawed** *adj* hollow-faced. **lantern jaws** *n pl* long thin jaws. **lantern of the dead** *n* a lighted tower, once common in French cemeteries. **lantern slide** *n* a transparent slide with a picture to be projected by a magic lantern or slide projector. **lantern wheel** or **lantern pinion** *n* a type of cogwheel consisting of pins fastened at each end to circular plates, somewhat like a lantern in appearance.

lanterne rouge /lan'tûrn roozh/ (*inf*) n the last-placed cyclist in a road race. [Fr, red lamp]

lanthanum /lan'thə-nəm/ n a metallic element (symbol **La**; atomic no 57). [Gr *lanthanein* to escape notice, because it lay hidden in rare minerals until 1839]
■ **lan'thanide** *n* a member of the **lanthanide series**, a group of rare-earth elements from atomic number 57 (lanthanum) or 58 to 71.
❏ **lanthanum glass** *n* optical glass used for high-quality photographic lenses, etc.

lanthorn an obsolete spelling of **lantern**, based on folk etymology, from the old use of horn for lanterns.

lantskip /lant'skip/ (*Milton*) n same as **landscape**.

lanugo /la-nū'gō/ n (*pl* **lanū'gos**) down, fine hair; an embryonic woolly coat of hair. [L *lānūgō*, *-inis* down, from *lāna* wool]
■ **lanū'ginose** /-jin-/ or **lanū'ginous** *adj* downy; covered with fine soft hair.

lanx /langks/ (*ancient hist*) n (*pl* **lances** /lan'sēz/) a platter. [L]

lanyard or **laniard** /lan'yərd/ n a short rope used as a fastening or handle (*naut*); a cord for hanging a knife, whistle, etc around the neck. [Fr *lanière*, origin doubtful; confused with **yard**¹]

lanzknecht a non-standard form of **landsknecht** (as if from Ger *Lanze* lance).

LAO *abbrev*: Laos (IVR).

Lao /low/ or **Laotian** /lä-ō'shən/ *adj* of Laos in SE Asia, or of its people. ◆ *n* a native of Laos; the language of these people.

Laodicean /lā-o-di-sē'ən/ *n* and *adj* (a person who is) lukewarm or half-hearted, *esp* in religion, like the Christians of *Laodicea* (Bible, Revelation 3.14–16) (also without *cap*). [Gr *Lāodikeia* Laodicea]
■ **Laodicē'anism** *n*.

Laotian see **Lao**.

lap¹ /lap/ n the fold of the clothes and body from waist to knees of a person sitting down; part of a garment covering this area, *esp* arranged to hold or catch something; a fold; a single circuit of a racetrack, or round of anything coiled; an overlap; the amount of overlap (in slating, over the next but one); a hollow; a place where one is nurtured or where one can rest secure (*fig*; in phrases); a flap; a lobe (of the ear); a polishing disc, cylinder, etc; the length of material needed to go round a drum, etc; a layer or sheet of (cotton, etc) fibres; in a steam-engine, the distance the valve has to move from mid position to open the steam or exhaust port; in euchre, etc, points carried over to another game. ◆ *vt* to wrap, enfold or surround; to lay overlappingly; to get or be a lap ahead of; to traverse as a lap or in laps; to polish with a lap (*rare*); to unite accurately; to hold in the lap (*rare*). ◆ *vi* to lie with an overlap; to overlap; to extend beyond some limit. [OE *læppa* a loosely hanging part; Ger *Lappen* a rag]

■ **lap'ful** *n*. **lapp'er** *n* someone who wraps or folds; a machine that compacts scutched cotton into a fleece on a roller called a **lap'-roller**. **lapp'ing** *n* and *adj*.

❏ **lap belt** *n* a form of vehicle seat belt that passes across the lap only. **lap'-board** *n* a flat wide board resting on the lap, used by tailors and seamstresses. **lap dance** *n*. **lap dancer** *n* a night-club stripper who dances close to clients and sits briefly on their laps. **lap dancing** *n*. **lap dissolve** *n* (*cinematog*) a technique by which one scene in a film fades out while the next scene fades in, so that the two images momentarily overlap. **lap'dog** *n* a dog small enough to be petted in the lap; a pet dog (also *fig*); a devoted, docile, dependent person (*fig*; *usu derog*). **lap'held** same as **laptop** below. **lap joint** *n* a joint formed by overlapping edges. **lap'-joint'ed** *adj*. **lap of honour** *n* a ceremonial circuit of a field, track or show ring, made by the victor or victors in a contest. **lap'stone** *n* a stone held in the lap to hammer leather on. **lap'streak** or **lap'strake** *n* a clinker-built boat (also *adj*). **lap'top** *n* a portable personal computer, small enough to be carried in a briefcase, etc and used on one's lap (also *adj*). **lap'work** *n* lap-jointed work.

■ **in the lap of luxury** in luxurious conditions. **in the lap of the gods** (of a situation) such that the result cannot be predicted or influenced.

lap² /lap/ *vt* (**lapp'ing**; **lapped**) to scoop up with the tongue (often with *up*); to take in greedily or readily (*usu* with *up*; *fig*); to wash or flow against. ◆ *vi* to drink by licking up; to make a sound or movement as of lapping. ◆ *n* a motion or sound of lapping; something which can be lapped; thin liquid food for animals. [OE *lapian*; LGer *lappen*; L *lambere* to lick; Gr *laptein*]

■ **lapp'ing** *n* and *adj*.

lap³ /läp or lap/ (*Scot*) *pat* of **leap¹**.

lap⁴ /lap/ or **lappie** (formerly **lapje**) /lap'i/ (*S Afr*) *n* a rag or piece of cloth. [Afrik, from Du *lap* rag, patch]

laparoscopy /lap-ə-ros'kə-pi/ *n* surgical examination by means of a **laparoscope** /lap'ər-ə-skōp/, a tube-shaped optical instrument which permits examination of the internal organs from outside, also used in female sterilization procedures. [Gr *lapara* flank, and *skopeein* to see]

■ **laparoscopic** /-skop'ik/ *adj*. **laparoscop'ically** *adv*.

laparotomy /lap-ə-rot'ə-mi/ *n* surgical cutting of the abdominal wall. [Gr *lapara* flank, and *tomē* cutting]

lapel (*obs* **lappel**) /lə- or lə-pel'/ *n* part of a coat, jacket, etc folded back as a continuation of the collar. [Dimin of **lap¹**]

■ **lapelled'** *adj*.

lapis /lap'is/ *n* a stone (the Latin word, used in certain phrases only, eg *lapis philosophicus* the philosophers' stone, and *lapis ollaris* potstone). [L *lapis, -idis* a stone]

■ **lapidār'ian** *adj* relating to stones; inscribed on stones; knowledgeable about stones. **lap'idarist** /-ə-rist/ *n* an expert in gems. **lap'idary** /-ə-ri/ *n* a cutter of stones, *esp* gemstones; a treatise on gems (*obs*); an expert in gems (*obs*). ◆ *adj* relating to stones; (of a bee) dwelling in stone-heaps; inscribed on stone; suitable for an inscription, eg on a monument; written in such a style, ie pithy, polished, impressive. **lap'idate** *vt* (*archaic*) to pelt with stones. **lapidā'tion** *n* (*archaic*) stoning. **lapid'eous** *adj* stony. **lapidesc'ence** *n* (*archaic*). **lapidesc'ent** *adj* (*archaic*) becoming stone; petrifying. **lapidic'olous** *adj* (L *colĕre* to inhabit) living under or among stones. **lapidif'ic** *adj* (*archaic*). **lapidificā'tion** *n* (*archaic*). **lapid'ify** *vt* and *vi* (*archaic*) to turn into stone. **lapilli** /lä-pil'lē/ *n pl* (*pl* of Ital *lapillo*; also of L *lapillus*) small fragments (in size from a pea to a walnut) of lava ejected from a volcano. **lapill'iform** *adj*.

❏ **lapis laz'ūlī** *n* a beautiful stone consisting of calcite and other minerals coloured ultramarine by lazurite, haüyne, and sodalite, commonly spangled with iron pyrites (see **azure**, **lazulite** and **lazurite**). **lapis lazuli blue** *n* a deep blue, sometimes veined with gold, used in decoration and in porcelain. **lapis lazuli ware** *n* a pebble ware veined with gold upon blue.

Lapith /lap'ith/ (*Gr myth*) *n* (*pl* **Lap'ithae** /-ē/ or **Lap'iths**) a member of a people of Thessaly who fought the Centaurs.

lapje see **lap⁴**.

Lapp /lap/ or **Laplander** /lap'lən-dər/ *n* a native or inhabitant of Lapland; a person of the race or people inhabiting Lapland.

■ **Lapp**, **Lap'landish** or **Lapp'ish** *adj*. **Lapp** or **Lapp'ish** *n* the language of the Lapps.

lappel see **lapel**.

lapper see **lopper¹**.

lappet /lap'it/ *n* a little lap or flap. [Dimin of **lap¹**]

■ **lapp'eted** *adj*.

❏ **lapp'et-head** *n* (*obs*) a headdress with lappets. **lappet moth** *n* a moth of the Lasiocampidae whose caterpillar has lappets on its sides.

lappie see **lap⁴**.

lapsang /lap'sang/ or **lapsang souchong** /soo-shong' or -chong'/ *n* (also with *caps*) a variety of souchong tea with a smoky flavour. [Chin]

lapse /laps/ *vi* to slip or glide; to pass by degrees; to fall away by ceasing or relaxing effort or cause; to fall from the faith; to fail in virtue or duty; to pass into disuse; to pass or fail owing to some omission or non-fulfilment; to become void. ◆ *vt* to catch in a lapse (*Shakesp*; *perh* with associations of *lap* or *latch*); to allow to pass, fall away or become void. ◆ *n* a slip; passage (of time); a falling away; a failure (in virtue, attention, memory, etc); a vertical gradient, eg of atmospheric temperature; a gliding (*archaic*). [L *lāpsāre* to slip, *lāpsus* a slip, from *lābi, lāpsus* to slip]

■ **laps'able** *adj* liable to lapse. **lapsed** *adj* having slipped or passed or been let slip; *esp* in the Christian Church, fallen away from the faith.

❏ **lapse rate** *n* (*meteorol*) rate of change in temperature in relation to height in the atmosphere.

lapsus /lap'səs or -sŭs/ (*L*) *n* a slip.

❏ **lapsus calami** /kal'ə-mī or ka'la-mē/ *n* a slip of the pen. **lapsus linguae** /ling'gwē or -gwī/ *n* a slip of the tongue. **lapsus memoriae** /me-mōr'i-ē, mōr' or -ri-ī/ *n* a slip of the memory.

Laputa /lä-pū'tə/ *n* a flying island in Swift's *Gulliver's Travels*, inhabited by people who engage in ridiculous projects.

■ **Lapu'tan** or **Lapu'tian** /-shən/ *n* an inhabitant of Laputa. ◆ *adj* absurd; chimerical.

lapwing /lap'wing/ *n* a bird (*Vanellus vanellus*) of the plover family, with iridescent dark upper plumage and a distinctive flapping motion in flight; any bird of the genus *Vanellus*. [ME *lappewinke*, from OE *læpewince*, *hlæpewince*, *hlēapewince*; modified by folk etymology]

laquearia /la-kwi-ā'ri-ə or la-kwe-ā'ri-ə/ *n pl* a panelled ceiling. [L]

LAR *abbrev* : Libya (ie *Libyan Arab Jamahiriya*; IVR).

lar /lär/ *n* (*pl* **lares** /lā'rēz or lä'räs/) the god of a house (*orig prob* a field god). See also **lares et penates**. [L *lar*]

larboard /lär'bōrd, -börd or lä'bərd/ (*obs naut*) *n* and *adj* port or left. [ME *laddeborde*, influenced by **starboard**; origin unknown]

LARC (*med*) *abbrev* : long-acting reversible contraception.

larceny /lär'sə-ni/ *n* the legal term in England and Ireland for stealing; theft. [OFr *larrecin* (Fr *larcin*), from L *latrōcinium*, from *latrō* a robber]

■ **lar'cener** or **lar'cenist** *n* a thief. **lar'cenous** *adj*. **lar'cenously** *adv*.

■ **grand larceny** in England before 1827, larceny of property of the value of one shilling or more, as opposed to **petty larceny**, larceny of property less in value than one shilling. **simple larceny** larceny uncombined with aggravating circumstances, as opposed to **compound larceny**.

larch /lärch/ *n* any tree of the coniferous genus *Larix*, distinguished from cedar by the deciduous leaves. [Ger *Lärche*, from L *larix, -icis*]

■ **larch'en** *adj* (*rare*).

lard /lärd/ *n* the clarified fat of the pig; a *usu* modified form of this, produced *esp* in a solid, white form for use in cookery. ◆ *vt* to smear or enrich with lard; to stuff with bacon or pork; to fatten; to mix with anything; to stuff or load; to interlard, interpenetrate; to garnish or strew. ◆ *vi* (*Shakesp*) to be intimately mixed. [OFr, from L *lāridum, lārdum*; cf Gr *lārīnos* fat, and *lāros* pleasant to taste]

■ **lardā'ceous** *adj*. **lar'don** or **lardoon'** *n* a strip or cube of bacon used for larding. **lar'dy** *adj* like or containing lard; fat or overweight.

❏ **lard'-arse** or (*US*) **lard'-ass** *n* (*derog sl*) an overweight person. **lard'-arsed** or (*US*) **lard'-assed** *adj* (*derog sl*). **lar'dy-cake** *n esp* in S England, a rich sweet cake made of bread dough, with lard, dried fruit, etc.

lardalite see **laurdalite**.

larder /lär'dər/ *n* a place where food is kept; a stock of provisions. [OFr *lardier* bacon-tub; see **lard**]

■ **lard'erer** *n* a person in charge of a larder.

❏ **larder beetle** *n* a beetle of the family Dermestidae, which feeds on a great variety of materials, such as dried meat and cheese, tobacco and leather. **larder fridge** *n* a type of refrigerator without a freezer compartment.

lardon, **lardoon** and **lardy** see under **lard**.

lare /lār/ *n* a Scot and N Eng form of **lore¹**; also a Spenserian form of **lair¹**.

lares et penates /lā'rēz et pe-nā'tēz or lä'räs et pe-nä'täs/ (*L*) *n pl* household gods; valued personal or household objects.

Largactil® /lär-gak'til/ *n* a tranquillizing drug, chlorpromazine.

large /lärj/ *adj* great in size; extensive; bulky; broad; copious; abundant; generous; magnanimous; loftily affected or pretentious; diffuse (*obs*); (of language) free or licentious (*Shakesp*); (of the wind) having a favouring component (*naut*). ◆ *adv* ostentatiously; prominently or importantly; before the wind (*naut*). ◆ *n* (*music*) an obsolete note, equal to two (or in 'perfect' time three) longs. [Fr, from L *largus* abounding]

■ **large'ly** *adv* in a large manner; in great measure; mainly, especially. **lar'gen** *vi* and *vt* (*poetic*) to enlarge. **large'ness** *n*. **larg'ish** *adj* fairly large, rather big.

❑ **large'-hand'ed** *adj* having large hands; grasping (*Shakesp*); profuse. **large'-heart'ed** *adj* having a large heart; of liberal disposition or comprehensive sympathies; generous. **large'-mind'ed** *adj* magnanimous; characterized by breadth of view. **large'mouth** *n* a N American freshwater black bass, a prized game fish. **large paper edition** *n* a special edition of a book, with wider margins. **large'-scale** *adj* (of maps, models, etc) representing a small area in great detail; (of a business enterprise) extensive in size and scope. **large-scale integration** *n* (*electronics*) production of an integrated circuit with more than 100 gates on an integrated chip.

■ **as large as life** actually, really. **at large** at liberty; at random; in general; in full; representing the whole area, not a division (*US*). **large it** or **have it large** (*inf*) to enjoy oneself unrestrainedly or boisterously. **larger than life** exaggerated (**larg'er-than-life'** *adj*).

largess or **largesse** /lär-jes' or lär'jes/ *n* a bestowal or distribution of gifts; generosity, magnanimous spirit or manner. [Fr *largesse* and L *largītiō, -ōnis*, from *largus*]

■ **largition** /lär-jish'ən/ *n* (*archaic*) giving of largess.

largo /lär'gō/ (*music*) *adj* and *adv* broad and slow. ◆ *n* (*pl* **lar'gos**) a movement to be performed in this manner. [Ital, from L *largus*]

■ **larghet'to** *adj* and *adv* somewhat slow; not as slow as largo. ◆ *n* (*pl* **larghet'tos**) a somewhat slow movement.

lari /lä'ri/ *n* (*pl* **la'ri** or **la'ris**) the standard monetary unit of Georgia (100 tetri); (also **laa'ri**) a monetary unit in the Maldives, $\frac{1}{100}$ of a rufiyaa. [Ult from Pers]

Lariam® /lar'i-əm/ *n* a proprietary name for mefloquine, an antimalarial drug. [Altered from **malaria**]

lariat /lar'i-ət/ *n* a lasso or picketing rope. [Sp *la* the, and *reata* picketing rope]

Laridae and **larine** see **Larus**.

lark[1] /lärk/ *n* a bird of the genus *Alauda*, well-known for flying high as it sings; extended to various similar birds. ◆ *vi* to catch larks. [ME *laverock*, from OE *lǣwerce, lāwerce*; Ger *Lerche*]

❑ **lark'-heeled** *adj* having a long hind-claw. **lark'ing-glass** *n* an instrument with mirrors used by bird-catchers to dazzle larks. **lark's'-heel** *n* the Indian cress; the larkspur.

■ **get up with the lark** to rise very early in the morning.

lark[2] /lärk/ *n* a frolic; a piece of mischief; an activity, *esp* a mischievous one. ◆ *vi* to frolic, play about, have fun (now *usu* with *about*). [Perh from the preceding (cf **skylarking**); some connect it with **lake**[4]]

■ **lark'er** *n*. **lark'iness** *n*. **lark'ish** *adj*. **lark'y** *adj* (*inf*).

larkspur /lärk'spûr/ *n* any plant of the genus *Delphinium*, from the spurred flowers. [**lark**[1] and **spur**]

larmier /lär'mi-ər/ *n* a corona or other course serving as a dripstone (*archit*); a tear pit (*zool*). [Fr, from *larme*, from L *lacrima* a tear]

larn /lärn/ (*dialect* or *facetious*) *vt* and *vi* to learn; to teach. [**learn**]

larnax /lär'naks/ *n* (*pl* **larnakes** /lär'nək-ēz/) a chest, coffin, etc of ancient Greece, *usu* made of terracotta and frequently ornamented. [Gr, perh connected with late Gr *narnax* a chest]

larney /lär'ni/ (*S Afr*) *n* a white person; a rich person. ◆ *adj* (of clothes, etc) smart. [Origin uncertain; perh from Hindi *rānī* queen]

laroid see under **Larus**.

LARP /lärp/ *n* *l*ive *a*ction *r*ole *p*laying, a role-playing game in which participants play the parts of particular characters, often in costume. **LARPer** *n*. **LARPing** *n*.

larrigan /lar'i-gən/ *n* a long boot made of oiled leather, worn by lumbermen, etc. [Origin unknown]

larrikin /lar'i-kin/ (*Aust*) *n* a hooligan; someone who is careless of usual social conventions or behaviour. ◆ *adj* characteristic of a larrikin. [Origin doubtful; a connection with '*larking*' about' has been suggested but remains unsubstantiated; also perh Cornish *larrikin* a rowdy youth]

■ **larr'ikinism** *n*.

larrup /lar'əp/ (*inf*) *vt* to flog or thrash. [Cf Du *larpen* thresh with flails]

larum /lar'əm/ (*archaic*) *n* alarm; a noise giving notice of danger. [**alarm**]

❑ **lar'um-bell** *n*.

Larus /lä' or lā'rəs/ *n* the principal genus of the gull family (**Laridae** /lar'i-dē/). [L, from Gr *laros* a bird, prob a gull]

■ **lar'ine** *adj*. **lar'oid** *adj*.

larva /lär'və/ *n* (*pl* **larvae** /lär'vē* or *-vī*/) an animal in an immature but active state markedly different from the adult, eg a caterpillar; a spectre or ghost (*obs*). [L *lārva, lārua* a spectre, a mask]

■ **lar'val** *adj*. **lar'vate** or **lar'vated** *adj* masked, or covered as if masked. **larvicī'dal** *adj* destroying larvae. **lar'vicide** *n*. **lar'viform** *adj*. **larvip'arous** *adj* giving birth to larvae.

larvikite see **laurvikite**.

larynx /lar'ingks/ *n* (*pl* **larynges** /lar'in-jēz* or *lar-in'jēz*/ or **lar'ynxes**) the upper part of the windpipe. [Gr *larynx, -yngos*]

■ **laryngal** /lar-ing'gl/ or **laryngeal** /lar-in'ji-əl/ *adj*. **laryngectomee** /-jek'-/ *n* a person who has undergone a laryngectomy. **laryngectomy** /-jek'-/ *n* surgical removal of the larynx. **laryngismus** /-jiz'məs/ *n* spasm of the larynx. **laryngitic** /-jit'ik/ *adj*. **laryngitis** /-jī'tis/ *n* inflammation of the larynx. **laryngological** /-ing-gə-loj'-/ *adj*. **laryngol'ogist** *n*. **laryngology** /-gol'ə-ji/ *n* the science of the larynx. **laryngophony** /-gof'-/ *n* the sound of the voice as heard through the stethoscope applied over the larynx. **laryng'oscope** *n* a mirror for examining the larynx and trachea. **laryngoscop'ic** *adj*. **laryngos'copist** *n*. **laryngos'copy** *n*. **laryng'ospasm** *n* spasmodic closure of the larynx. **laryngot'omy** *n* the operation of cutting into the larynx.

lasagne /lə-zän'yə, -sän', la- or lə-/ or **lasagna** (also /-ya/) *n pl* flat sheets of pasta; (*n sing*) a baked dish of this with tomatoes, cheese and *usu* meat. [Ital; sing *lasagna*]

lascar /las'kər, -kär or las-kär'/ *n* an Oriental (*orig* Indian) sailor or camp-follower. [Hindi and Pers *lashkar* army, or *lashkarī* a soldier]

lascivious /lə-siv'i-əs/ *adj* wanton; lustful; inclining or tending to lechery. [LL *lascīviōsus*, from L *lascīvus* playful]

■ **lasciv'iously** *adv*. **lasciv'iousness** *n*.

LASEK /lā'sek/ *abbrev*: laser-assisted epithelial keratomileusis (or keratectomy), a surgical procedure in which tissue on the surface of the cornea is reshaped with a laser.

laser[1] /lā'zər/ *n* a device which amplifies an input of light, producing an extremely narrow and intense monochromatic beam which can be used for a range of tasks, eg printing, optical scanning, surgical operations, etc (also *adj*). [*l*ight *a*mplification by *s*timulated *e*mission of *r*adiation]

■ **lase** *vi* (of a crystal, etc) to be, or become, suitable for use as a laser. **la'sing** *adj* and *n*.

❑ **laser-beam machining** *n* (*engineering*) the use of a focused beam of high-intensity radiation from a laser to vaporize and so machine material. **laser card** *n* a plastic card with digital information stored in the same way as on a laser disc. **laser disc** or **disk** *n* a disc on which digitally-recorded data, audio or video material is registered as a series of pits that are readable by laser beam, a compact disc. **laser disc** (or **disk**) **player** *n*. **laser level** *n* (*surveying*) an instrument for accurate single-handed levelling, using a laser beam narrowly confined in the vertical dimension and continuously rotated round an accurately-vertical axis. **laser pen** *n* a pen that incorporates a laser, allowing it to be used as a pointer. **laser printer** *n* a fast, high-quality printer using a laser beam to form characters on paper.

laser[2] /lā'sər/ *n* the juice of laserwort; the plant silphium (*hist*). [L *lāser* the juice of *lāserpīcium*, the silphium plant]

■ **Laserpicium** or **Laserpitium** /las-ər-pish'i-əm/ *n* a genus of umbelliferous perennial herbs of Europe, Asia and N Africa. **laserwort** /läs'ər-wûrt/ *n* any plant of the genus, *esp* herb frankincense (L *latifolium*); also applied to species of *Ferula* and *Thapsia*.

lash[1] /lash/ *n* loosely, the flexible part of a whip, but properly its terminal piece of whipcord; a scourge; an eyelash; a stroke with a whip or anything pliant; a sweep or flick; a stroke of satire. ◆ *vt* to strike with, or as if with, a lash; to dash against; to drive, urge or work by blows of anything flexible (also *fig*); to whisk or flick with a sweeping movement; to secure with a rope or cord; to bind (rope) to prevent unravelling; to scourge with sarcasm or satire; to lavish or squander (*obs*). ◆ *vi* to dash or rush; to make a rapid sweeping or flicking movement; to use the whip. [Perh several different words, with possible connections with **latch**[1], **lash**[2] and **lace**]

■ **lash'er** *n* a person who lashes or whips; a rope for binding one thing to another. **lash'ing** *n* an act of whipping; a rope for making things secure; the binding preventing the unravelling of a rope; (*esp* in *pl*) an abundance of anything (*inf*).

❑ **lash'-up** *n* (*sl*) an improvisation; a mess, fiasco.

■ **lash out** to kick out, fling out or hit out without restraint; to spend extravagantly.

lash[2] /lash/ (*obs* or *dialect*) *adj* slow or slack; soft; insipid. [ME *lasche* slack, from OFr *lasche* (Fr *lâche* cowardly), from L *laxus* lax]

■ **lash'er** *n* a weir; a waterfall from a weir; a pool below a weir.

lashkar /lash'kär/ *n* a body of armed Indian tribesmen, a force; a camp of Indian soldiers (*obs*). [Hindi, army, camp; cf **lascar**]

LASIK /lā'sik/ *abbrev*: laser-assisted in-situ keratomileusis, a surgical procedure in which a flap is created in the cornea and the underlying tissue is reshaped with a laser.

Lasiocampidae /lă-zi-ō-kam'pi-dē or -si-/ n pl a family of moths including eggers and lackey moths. [Gr lasios woolly, and kampē a caterpillar]

lasket /las'kit/ (naut) n a loop at the foot of a sail, used to fasten an extra sail. [Perh **latchet**]

lasque /läsk/ n a flat thin diamond, common in India. [Perh Pers lashk a bit or piece]

lass /las/ n a girl, young woman; a sweetheart; a maid-servant (Scot). [Origin obscure; the association with **lad**[1] may be accidental]
■ **lassie** /las'i/ n (dimin) a Scots word for a girl. **lass'lorn** adj (Shakesp) forsaken by one's mistress. **lass'ock** n (dimin).

Lassa fever /las'ə fē'vər/ n an infectious tropical virus disease, often fatal, transmitted by rodents. [From Lassa, in Nigeria, where it was first recognized]

lassi /las'i/ or lus'i/ (Ind) n a (sweet or savoury) flavoured cold drink made with yoghurt or buttermilk. [Hindi]

lassitude /las'i-tūd/ n faintness; weakness; weariness; languor. [L lassitūdō, from lassus faint]

lasslorn and **lassock** see under **lass**.

lasso /la-soo' or las'ō/ n (pl lassoes' or lassos' (or /las'/)) a long rope with a running noose for catching wild horses, etc. ◆ vt (lasso'ing (or /las'/); lassoed /las-ood' or las'/) to catch with a lasso. [S American pronunciation of Sp lazo, from L laqueus a noose]
■ **lasso'er** (or /las'/) n.

lassu /losh'ŭ/ n the slow movement of a csárdás. [Hung]

last[1] /läst/ adj latest; coming or remaining after all the others; final; immediately before the present; utmost; ending a series; most unlikely, least to be preferred. ◆ adv after all the others; at or in the end, finally; most recently. [OE latost, superl of læt slow, late]
■ **last'ly** adv finally.
▢ **last'-ditch** adj (of an attempt, etc) made at the last moment or in the last resort. **last'-gasp'** adj made, etc when almost at the point of death, defeat, etc. **last heir** n the person to whom lands escheat when other heirs are lacking. **last hurrah** n a final performance. **last'-minute** adj made, done or given at the latest possible time. **last post** n (milit) the second of two bugle-calls denoting the time for retiring for the night; the farewell bugle-call at military funerals. **last rites** n pl religious rites performed for a person close to death. **last straw** n (ie the straw that breaks the camel's back) that small event or factor which, following a series of others, finally makes the situation intolerable or irreparable. **last word** n the final remark in an argument; the final decision; the most up-to-date of its kind (inf).
■ **at last** in the end. **at long last** after long delay. **breathe one's last** to die. **die in the last ditch** to fight to the bitter end. **first and last** altogether. **last but not least** finally but not less importantly. **last thing** after doing everything else; finally before going to bed at night. **on one's last legs** on the verge of utter failure or exhaustion. **put the last hand to** to finish, put the finishing touch to. **see** (or **hear**) **the last of** to see (or hear) for the last time. **the Last Day** and **the Last Judgment** the Day of Judgment. **the Last Supper** the supper taken by Christ and his disciples on the eve of the crucifixion. **the last trump** the trumpet that will sound at the Last Day (Bible, 1 Corinthians 15.52). **to the last** to the end; until death.

last[2] /läst/ vi to continue, endure; to escape failure; to remain fresh or unimpaired; to hold out; to survive. [OE læstan to follow a track, keep on, suffice, last; see **last**[3]]
■ **last'er** n someone who has staying power; a thing that keeps well. **last'ing** adj enduring; durable. ◆ n endurance. **last'ingly** adv. **last'ingness** n.
■ **last out** to last as long as or longer than; to last to the end or as long as is required.

last[3] /läst/ n a shoemaker's model of the foot on which boots and shoes are made or repaired. ◆ vt to fit with a last. [OE læste last, låst footprint]
■ **last'er** n someone who fits the parts of shoes to lasts; a tool for doing so.

last[4] /läst/ n a load or cargo; a varying weight, generally about 4000lb. [OE hlæst, from hladan to lade; Ger Last, ON hlass]
■ **last'age** n the lading of a ship; room for stowing goods in a ship; a duty formerly paid for the right of carrying goods, etc.

Lat. abbrev : Latin.

lat[1] /lat/ n (anat) short form of latissimus dorsi, a muscle in the lower back.
▢ **lat spread** n a body-building exercise which stretches this muscle.

lat[2] /lat/ n (pl **lats** or **lat'i**) the standard monetary unit of Latvia (100 santims). [Shortened from Latvija]

lat[3] /lat/ (inf) n short form of **latrine**.

lat[4] /lät/ n in India, an isolated pillar. [Hindi lat]

lat. abbrev : lateral; latitude.

Latakia /lat-ä-kē'ə/ n a Syrian tobacco from Latakia.

latch[1] /lach/ n a door catch lifted from the outside by a lever or string; a light door lock, opened from the outside by a key. ◆ vt (obs) to seize, take or receive. ◆ vt and vi to fasten with a latch. [OE læccan to catch]
▢ **latch'key** or **latch'string** n a key or string for opening a latched door. **latchkey child** n a child who regularly returns home to an empty house.
■ **latch on to** (inf) to attach oneself to; to gain comprehension of. **on the latch** not locked, but able to be opened by a latch.

latch[2] /lach/ vt (Shakesp) probably to moisten, but possibly to fasten (see **latch**[1]). ◆ n (Scot; also **letch**) a mire; a boggy water channel. [**leach**[1]]

latchet /lach'it/ (obs) n a loop; a thong or lace. [OFr lachet, a form of lacet, dimin of laz; see **lace**]

late /lāt/ adj (**lāt'er**; **lāt'est**) tardy; behindhand; coming, remaining, flowering, ripening, producing, etc after the due, expected or usual time; long delayed; belonging to or happening in the final part of a time, period or series; deceased; departed; out of office; former; not long past; most recent; slow (dialect). ◆ adv after the due, expected or usual time; towards the end; recently. [OE læt slow; Du laat, ON latr, Ger lass weary; L lassus tired]
■ **lāt'ed** adj (Shakesp) belated. **late'ly** adv recently. **lāt'en** vt and vi to make or grow late. **late'ness** n. **lāt'er** adv at some time after or in the near future. ◆ interj (inf, chiefly US) see you later, goodbye (also **lā'ters**). **lāt'est** n (inf; with the) the latest news, fashion, version, etc. **lāt'ish** adj and adv.
▢ **late blight** see **potato blight** under **potato**. **late'comer** n a person who arrives late. **late onset diabetes** n diabetes occurring in older people, in which the insulin lack is only relative. **late wood** n (bot) the wood formed in the later part of a growth ring, usu having smaller, thicker-walled cells than the early wood.
■ **at the latest** not later than (a stated time). **late in the day** (fig) at an unreasonably late stage of development, etc. **of late** recently.

lateen /lə-tēn'/ adj applied to a triangular sail, common in the Mediterranean, the Lake of Geneva, etc; rigged with such a sail. ◆ n a lateen sail; a boat with a lateen rig. [Fr (voile) latine, from L Latīnus Latin]

La Tène /la ten'/ adj of a division of the Iron Age exemplified at La Tène near Neuchâtel in Switzerland, later than Hallstatt.

latent /lā'tənt/ adj hidden; concealed; not visible or apparent; dormant; undeveloped, but capable of development; in Freudian psychoanalysis, applied to that part of a dream's content that is repressed and transformed into the manifest content. [L latēns, -entis, prp of latēre to lie hidden; Gr lanthanein to be hidden]
■ **lā'tence** or **lā'tency** n. **lā'tently** adv. **latesc'ence** n. **latesc'ent** adj becoming latent.
▢ **latent heat** see under **heat**. **latent image** n (photog) the invisible image produced by the action of light on the sensitive chemicals on a film, etc, which becomes visible after development. **latent period** n the time between stimulus and reaction (psychol); the time between the contracting of a disease and the appearance of symptoms (med).

lateral /lat'(ə-)rəl/ adj on, relating to, belonging to, or in the direction of the side or sides; (of a consonant) produced by air passing over one or both sides of the tongue (phonetics). ◆ n a lateral part, movement, consonant, etc; (in American football) a sideways or backwards pass. [L laterālis, from latus, lateris a side]
■ **laterality** /-ral'i-ti/ n the state of belonging to the side; physical one-sidedness, either right or left. **lateraliza'tion** or **-s-** n the specialized development in one or other hemisphere of the brain of the mechanisms controlling some activity or ability. **lat'erally** adv.
▢ **lateral line** n in fishes, a line along the side of the body, marking the position of a sensory organ. **lateral shift** n (geol) the horizontal displacement of outcrops, as a consequence of faulting. **lateral thinking** n thinking which seeks new ways of looking at a problem and does not merely proceed by logical steps from the starting-point of what is known or believed.

Lateran /lat'ə-rən/ adj relating to the Church of St John Lateran at Rome, the Pope's cathedral church, on the site of the splendid palace or basilica of Plautius Lateranus (executed 66AD). [L Laterānus]
▢ **Lateran Councils** n pl five general councils of the Western Church, held in the Lateran basilica (1123, 1139, 1179, 1215, and 1512–17), regarded by Roman Catholics as ecumenical. **Lateran Treaty** n the treaty that restored the Vatican city as an independent papal state in 1929.

laterigrade /lat'ə-ri-grād/ adj running sideways, like a crab. [L latus, -eris side, and gradus step]

laterite /lat'ə-rīt/ n a clay formed by weathering of rocks in a tropical climate, composed chiefly of iron and aluminium hydroxides. [L *later, lateris* a brick]
■ **lateritic** /lat-ə-rit'ik/ *adj* of laterite; similar to laterite in composition. **lateriza'tion** or **-s-** n conversion into laterite.

lateritious /lat-ə-rish'əs/ *adj* brick-red. [L *laterīcius*, from *later, lateris* a brick]

latewake /lāt'wāk/ n a mistaken form of **lykewake**.

latex /lā'teks/ (*bot*) n (*pl* **lā'texes** or **lā'ticēs**) the milky juice of some plants, eg rubber trees; a synthesized form of such juice, widely used in the manufacture of rubber products. [L *latex, laticis*]
■ **laticifer** /lə-tis'if-ər/ n a plant cell containing latex. **laticiferous** /lat-i-sif'ə-rəs/ *adj* containing or conveying latex.

lath /läth/ n (*pl* **laths** /lädhz/ or /läths/) a thin strip of wood; a substitute for such a strip, used in slating, plastering, etc; anything long and thin. ◆ *vt* to cover with laths. [OE *lætt*]
■ **lathen** /läth'ən/ *adj*. **lath'ing** n the act or process of covering with laths; a covering of laths. **lath'like** *adj*. **lath'y** *adj* like a lath.
❑ **lath'-splitter** n someone who splits wood into laths.
■ **dagger of lath** the Vice's weapon in the old morality plays.

lathe[1] /lādh/ n a machine for turning and shaping articles of wood, metal, etc; the swing-frame of a loom carrying the reed for separating the warp threads and beating up the weft. ◆ *vt* to cut or shape with a lathe. [Origin doubtful]
■ **capstan lathe** and **turret lathe** see under **capstan** and **turret**[1] respectively.

lathe[2] /lādh/ (*hist*) n a former division of Kent. [OE *læth* a district; ON *lāth* landed property]

lathee see **lathi**.

lather /ladh'ər or lä'dhər/ n a foam made with water and soap; froth from sweat; a state of agitation (*inf*). ◆ *vt* to spread over with lather; to thrash (*inf*). ◆ *vi* to form a lather. [OE *lēathor*; ON *lauthr*]
■ **lath'ery** *adj*.

lathi or **lathee** /lä-tē'/ (*Ind*) n a long, heavy stick used as a weapon. [Hindi *lāthī*]

lathyrus /lath'i-rəs/ n any plant of the *Lathyrus* genus of Papilionaceae. [L, from Gr *lathyros* the chickling vetch]
■ **lath'yrism** n a neurological disease producing stiffness and paralysis of the legs in humans and animals, apparently due to eating cultivated vetch made poisonous by a freak mixing with some unknown seed.

latices, laticifer and **laticiferous** see **latex**.

laticlave /lat'i-klāv/ (*hist*) n a broad stripe on a Roman senator's tunic. [L *lātus* broad, and *clāvus* a stripe]

latifundia /la-ti-fun'di-ə/ n *pl* great landed estates (also *sing*). **latifun'dium**, (*Ital*) **latifondi** /lä-tē-fon'dē/). [Pl of L *lātifundium*, from *lātus* wide, and *fundus* an estate]

Latin /lat'in/ *adj* relating to ancient Latium (*esp* Rome) or its inhabitants, or its language, or to those languages that are descended from Latin, or to the peoples speaking them, *esp* (*popularly*) the Spanish, Portuguese and Italians or the inhabitants of Central and S America of Spanish, etc extraction; of or denoting the temperament considered characteristic of the Latin peoples, passionate, excitable, volatile; written or spoken in Latin; Roman Catholic. ◆ *n* an inhabitant of ancient Latium; the language of ancient Latium, and *esp* of Rome; a person belonging to a Latin people; a Roman Catholic. [L *Latīnus* belonging to *Latium*, the district round Rome]
■ **Latian** /lā'shyən or -shən/ *adj* of Latium. **Latina** n see **Latino** below. **Lat'inate** *adj* imitating Latin style; (of vocabulary) borrowed from Latin. **Lat'iner** n (*obs*) someone who knows Latin; an interpreter. **Lat'inism** n a Latin idiom; the use or inclination towards use of Latin idioms, words or ways. **Lat'inist** n a person skilled in Latin. **Lat'inity** n the (easy) use of Latin; the quality of one's Latin. **Latiniza'tion** or **-s-** n. **Lat'inize** or **-ise** *vt* to turn into or make Latin or like Latin. ◆ *vi* to use Latin idioms or derivatives. **Lat'inizer** or **-s-** n. **Latino** /la-tē'nō/ or (*fem*) **Lati'na** n and *adj* (a person) of Latin-American descent, *esp* in N America.
❑ **Latin America** n those parts of America where Spanish, Portuguese and French are the official languages, with the exception of French-speaking Canada. **Latin American** *adj* and n. **Latin Church** n the Roman Catholic Church. **Latin cross** n an upright cross with the lowest limb longest. **Latin Empire** n that portion of the Byzantine Empire seized in 1204 by the Crusaders (French and Venetian), and overthrown by the Greeks in 1261. **Latin Kingdom** n the Christian kingdom of Jerusalem ruled by French or Latin kings, and lasting from 1099 to 1187. **Latin Quarter** n the educational and students' quarter of Paris around the Sorbonne (where Latin was spoken in the Middle Ages; Fr *quartier latin*), famous for its unconventional way of life. **Latin square** n (*stats*) a matrix in which no figure occurs more than once in the same row or column. **Latin Union** n a monetary

union (1865–1926) of France, Belgium, Italy and Switzerland, with Greece from 1868.
■ **classical Latin** the Latin of the writers who flourished from about 75BC to about 200AD. **dog Latin** see under **dog**[1]. **Late Latin** the Latin written by authors between 200AD and c.600. **Low Latin** Medieval, or Late and Medieval, Latin. **Middle** or **Medieval Latin** the Latin of the Middle Ages between 600 and 1500. **New** or **Modern Latin** Latin as written between 1500 and the present time, mostly used as a scientific medium. **Silver Latin** see under **silver**. **thieves' Latin** thieves' cant. **Vulgar Latin** colloquial Latin, *esp* that of the period under the emperors.

Latina and **Latino** see under **Latin**.

latirostral /la-ti-ros'trəl/ (*ornithol*) *adj* broad-billed (also **latiros'trate**). [L *lātus* broad, and *rōstrum* beak]

latiseptate /la-ti-sep'tāt/ (*bot*) *adj* having a broad partition. [L *lātus* broad, and *saeptum* a fence (used in pl)]

latitant /lat'i-tənt/ *adj* lurking; lying in wait; hibernating; dormant. [L *latitāre, -ātum* (3rd pers sing present *latitat*), frequentative of *latēre* to be in hiding]
■ **lat'itancy** n. **lat'itat** n a writ based on the supposition that the person summoned is in hiding. **latitā'tion** n.

latitude /lat'i-tūd/ n angular distance from the equator (*geog*); a place of specified angular distance from the equator (*geog*); (also **celestial latitude**) angular distance from the ecliptic (*astron*); width (chiefly *humorous*); a wide extent; range; scope; allowance; breadth in interpretation; extent of meaning or importance; freedom from restraint; laxity. [L *lātitūdō, -inis*, from *lātus* broad]
■ **latitūd'inal** *adj* relating to latitude; in the direction of latitude. **latitūd'inally** *adv*. **latitūdinā'rian** *adj* broad or liberal, *esp* in religious belief; lax. ◆ *n* a member of a school of liberal and philosophical theologians within the English Church in the later half of the 17c; a person with latitudinarian views, *esp* one free from prejudice in religious or church matters. **latitūdinā'rianism** n. **latitūd'inous** *adj* broad or wide, *esp* in interpretation.

latke /lät'kə/ n a traditional Jewish pancake, *esp* one made with grated potato. [Yiddish, from Russ *latka* a pastry]

la trenise see **trenise**.

latria /lə-trī'ə/ n see under **dulia**. [Gr *latreiā*, from *latreuein* to serve]

latrine /lə-trēn'/ n a lavatory, *esp* in barracks, camps, etc. [L *lātrīna*, from *lavātrīna*, from *lavāre* to wash]

latrocinium /la-trō-sin'i-əm/ or **latrociny** /lat'rō-si-ni/ (*obs*) n highway-robbery; Pope Leo I's name for the 'Robber-Council' at Ephesus in 449AD, which upheld the doctrine of Eutyches. [L *latrōcinium* robbery]

latron /lā'tron/ (*obs*) n a robber. [L *latrō, -ōnis*]

-latry /-lə-tri/ *combining form* denoting worship. [Gk *latreiā*, from *latreuein* to serve]

latte /lä'tā or lat'ā/ n espresso coffee with frothed hot milk. [Ital (*caffè*) *latte* milk coffee]
■ **skinny latte** a drink of latte made with low- or non-fat milk.

latten /lat'ən/ n brass or any similar alloy (*old*); tin-plate; metal in thin plates. [OFr *laton* (Fr *laiton*), prob from Old Provençal, from Ar *lātūn* copper, from Turkic; a Germanic origin for the word has also been postulated, cf **lath**]

latter /lat'ər/ *adj* later; coming or existing after; second-mentioned of two; modern; recent; last (*Shakesp*). [OE *lætra*, compar of *læt* slow, late]
■ **latt'erly** *adv* towards the latter end; of late. **latt'ermost** *adj* (OE *lætemest*) last.
❑ **latt'er-born** *adj* (*Shakesp*) younger. **latt'er-day** *adj* modern; recent. **Latter-day Saint** n a Mormon. **latter end** n the final part; the end of life. **latt'ermath** n (*dialect*) aftermath. **latt'er-mint** n (*Keats*) apparently a late kind of mint. **latt'er-wit** n (*old US*) a witty thought after the occasion has passed.

lattice /lat'is/ n a network of crossed laths or bars, also called **latt'icework**; anything of a similar pattern; a window with small, *esp* diamond-shaped panes set in lead, also called **lattice window**; the geometrically regular, three-dimensional arrangement of fissionable and non-fissionable material in an atomic pile; the regular arrangement of atoms in crystalline material; a system of lines for position-fixing overprinted on a navigational chart; a partially-ordered set in which any two elements have a least upper bound and a greatest lower bound (*maths*); a space lattice (qv). ◆ *vt* to form into open work; to provide with a lattice. [Fr *lattis*, from *latte* a lath]
❑ **latt'ice-bridge** n a bridge of lattice-girders. **lattice energy** n (*chem*) energy required to separate the ions of a crystal from each other to an infinite distance. **latt'ice-gird'er** n a girder composed of upper and lower members joined by a web of crossing diagonal bars. **latt'ice-leaf** n the lace-leaf or ouvirandra (*Aponogeton*

fenestrale), a water plant of Madagascar with leaves like open latticework.

■ **red lattice** (*Shakesp*) the sign of an alehouse.

latticinio /la-ti-chē'ni-ō/, also **latticino** /-nō/ *n* (*pl* **lattici'ni** /-nē/) a type of Venetian glassware containing decorative threads of milk-white glass; a piece of such glassware; the white glass itself. [Ital, from L *lacticinium* food made with milk, from *lac, lactis* milk]

latus rectum /lā'təs rek'təm or lat'ŭs rek'tŭm/ (*geom*) *n* a focal chord parallel to the directrix of a conic. [L, right or perpendicular side]

Latvian /lat'vi-ən/ *adj* of or relating to *Latvia* in NE Europe, Lettish. ◆ *n* a native or citizen of Latvia; the language of Latvia, Lettish. [Lettish *Latvija* Latvia or Lettland]

lauch /löhh/ *n* and *v* (*pat* **leuch** or **leugh** /lūhh/; *pap* **leuch'en** or **leugh'en**) a Scots form of **law**[2] (*Walter Scott*) and of **laugh**.

laud /löd/ *vt* to praise; to celebrate. ◆ *n* praise; (in *pl*) one of the hours of the Divine Office, *orig* held at sunrise, now often grouped with matins to form the morning prayer (*RC*). [L *laudāre*, from *laus, laudis* praise]

■ **laud'able** *adj* praiseworthy. **laud'ableness** or **laudabil'ity** *n*. **laud'ably** *adv*. **laudā'tion** *n* praise; honour paid. **laud'ative** or **laud'atory** *adj* containing praise; expressing praise. ◆ *n* (*obs*) a eulogy. **laud'er** *n*.

laudanum /lö'də-nəm or löd'nəm/ *n* tincture of opium. [Coined by Paracelsus; perh **ladanum**, transferred to a different drug]

lauf /lowf/ *n* a run in a bobsleigh contest. [Ger]

laugh /läf/ *vi* to express, by explosive inarticulate sounds of the voice, amusement, joy, scorn, etc, or a reaction to tickling, etc; to be entertained or amused by (with *at*); to make fun of (with *at*); to express scorn for (with *at*); to have a cheerful appearance (*fig*). ◆ *vt* to have an effect on, affect or force into by laughing; to express by laughter; to laugh at, deride (*Spenser*). ◆ *n* an act or sound of laughing; someone who or something that is good fun (*inf*). [OE (Anglian) *hlæhhan* (WSax *hliehhan*); Ger *lachen*, Gothic *hlahjan*]

■ **laugh'able** *adj* ludicrous. **laugh'ableness** *n*. **laugh'ably** *adv*. **laugh'er** *n* someone who laughs; a breed of pigeon which makes a laughing sound; an easily won game, a walkover (*inf, esp N Am*). **laugh'ful** *adj* mirthful. **laugh'ing** *n* and *adj*. **laugh'ingly** *adv*. **laugh'some** *adj* (*archaic*) inclined to laugh; provoking laughter. **laugh'ter** *n* the act or sound of laughing. **laugh'worthy** *adj* deserving to be laughed at. **laugh'y** *adj* (*rare*) inclined to laugh.

❑ **laugh and lie** (or **lay**) **down** *n* an old card game in which a player lays down his or her cards when a winning hand is achieved. **laughing gas** *n* nitrous oxide, which may excite laughter when breathed. **laughing gear** *n* (*sl, orig Aust*) the mouth. **laughing hyena** *n* the spotted hyena (*Crocuta crocuta*; see under **hyena**). **laughing jackass** *n* the kookaburra. **laughing stock** *n* an object of ridicule. **laugh track** or **laughter track** *n* recorded laughter edited into the soundtrack of a TV comedy programme.

■ **be laughing** (*inf*) to have no (further) problems, worries, etc; to be in a favourable or advantageous position. **don't make me laugh** (*inf*) an expression of scornful disbelief. **have the last laugh** to triumph finally after one or more setbacks or defeats; to have one's actions, etc finally vindicated after being scorned. **have the laugh of** to get the better of. **laugh in someone's face** to scorn or mock a person openly. **laugh off** to treat (injuries, etc) as of no importance. **laugh on the other side of one's face** or (*rare*) **on the wrong side of one's mouth** to be made to feel disappointment or sorrow, *esp* after boasting, etc. **laugh someone out of court** to prevent someone getting a hearing by ridicule. **laugh to scorn** to deride or jeer at. **laugh up one's sleeve** or (*rare*) **in one's sleeve** to laugh inwardly. **no laughing matter** a very serious matter.

launce[1] /löns or läns/ or **lance** /läns/ *n* a sand eel (genus *Ammodytes*), an eel-like fish that buries itself in wet sand at ebb-tide (also **lant**). [Perh connected with **lance**[1]]

launce[2] (*Spenser*) same as **lance**[1].

launce[3] /löns or läns/ (*Spenser*) *n* a balance. [L *lanx, lancis* a plate, a scale of a balance]

launcegaye /löns'gā or läns'gā/ same as **lancegay**.

launch[1] /lönch or lönsh/ (*obs* **lanch** or **länch** or **länsh**/) *vt* to throw or hurl; to dart; to send out; to set going; to initiate; to cause or allow to slide into water or to take off from land; to put (a book or other product) on the market, *esp* with attendant publicity, etc; to throw (oneself) freely, venturesomely, or enthusiastically (into some activity) (with *into*); to pierce (*Spenser*); to lance (*obs*). ◆ *vi* to rush, dart, plunge or fling oneself; to be launched; to take off; to throw oneself freely, or in a spirit of adventure (into some activity) (with *out* or *into*); to begin a *usu* long story, speech, etc (with *into*). ◆ *n* the act or occasion of launching; the introduction of a new product or service onto the market (*commerce*); a lancing (*Spenser*). [OFr *lanchier, lancier* (Fr *lancer*); see **lance**[1]]

■ **launch'er** *n* a device for launching, *esp* for sending off a rocket. ❑ **launch'ing-pad** *n* a platform from which a rocket can be launched; a place, event, etc which gives a good start to a career, etc, or at which a project, campaign, etc is launched. **launch'ing-ways** *n pl* the timbers on which a ship is launched. **launch pad** same as **launching-pad** above. **launch vehicle** see under **vehicle**. **launch window** *n* the period of time during which the launching of a spacecraft must take place if the flight is to be successful.

launch[2] /lönch or lönsh/ *n* a large power-driven boat for pleasure or short runs; the largest boat carried by a man-of-war. [Sp *lancha*, perh from Malay *lanchār* swift]

laund /lönd/ (*Shakesp*) *n* a glade; a grassy place. [OFr *launde, lande*; prob Celtic; see **lawn**[1]]

launder /lön'dər/ *vt* to wash and iron (clothes, etc); to clean or cleanse generally (*fig*); to alter (something suspect or unacceptable) so as to improve it, often illicitly; to handle (the transfer of money, goods, etc or the movement of people) in such a way that the identity or illegality of the source, the illegality of the transfer, or the identity or criminality of the people remains undetected (*inf*). ◆ *vi* to wash and iron clothes, etc; to be able to be laundered. ◆ *n* a washerwoman or washerman (*obs*); a trough for conveying water. [ME *lavander*, from OFr *lavandier*, from L *lavandārius*, from the gerundive of *lavāre* to wash]

■ **laun'derer** *n* a woman who washes and irons clothes. **laun'dress** *n* a woman who washes and irons clothes. **laun'dry** *n* a place where clothes, etc are washed and ironed; clothes, etc for or from the laundry; a collection of articles for washing or that have been washed.

❑ **laundry list** *n* a list of items to be laundered; a list of items or matters to be achieved, produced, dealt with, prevented, etc (*fig*). **laun'dry-maid** *n*. **laun'dryman** or **laun'drywoman** *n* a worker in a laundry; a person who runs a laundry; a person who collects and delivers laundry.

launderette /lön-də-ret'/ or **laundrette** /-dret'/ *n* a shop where customers pay to wash clothes in washing machines. [Orig trademark]

Laundromat® /lön'drō-mat or -drə-/ (*N Am*) *n* a launderette.

laura /lö'rə/ or **lavra** /lä'vrə/ *n* a group of recluses' cells. [Gr *laurā* (modern *labra*, with *b* as *v*) alley, lane, monastery]

lauraceous see under **Laurus**.

Laurasia /lö-rā'sh(y)ə, -zh(y)ə/ *n* the ancient landmass thought to have existed in the northern hemisphere, and which subsequently split up to to form N America, Greenland, Europe and northern Asia. [*Laurentia*, the ancient N American landmass, from the Laurentian strata of the Canadian Shield, and *Eurasia*]

■ **Laurā'sian** *adj*.

laurdalite /lör'də-līt/ or **lardalite** /lär-/ (*mineralogy*) *n* a coarse nepheline syenite. [*Laurdal* or *Lardal* in Norway]

laureate /lö'ri-it/ *adj* crowned with laurel; honoured by a distinction. ◆ *n* a person crowned with laurel; a person honoured by a distinction; a poet laureate. ◆ *vt* /-āt/ to crown with laurel, in token of literary merit; to confer a degree upon. [L *laureātus* laurelled, from *laurus* laurel]

■ **lau'reateship** *n*. **laureā'tion** *n* crowning with laurel; graduation. ■ **Poet Laureate** see under **poet**.

laurel /lor'əl or lö'rəl/ *n* the sweet bay tree (*Laurus nobilis*), used in ancient times for making wreaths of honour; another species of *Laurus* found in Madeira and the Canaries; the cherry laurel; in America, any species of Rhododendron or of Kalmia; extended to various trees and shrubs of similar appearance; a crown of laurel; honours gained (often in *pl*). ◆ *adj* made of laurel. ◆ *vt* (**lau'relling**; **lau'relled**) to crown, adorn or cover with laurel. [Fr *laurier*, from L *laurus*]

❑ **lau'rel-wa'ter** *n* a sedative and narcotic water distilled from cherry-laurel leaves. **lauric acid** /lör'ik/ *n* an acid, $CH_3(CH_2)_{10}COOH$, found in the berries of *Laurus nobilis*, etc (also called **dodecanō'ic acid**). **lauryl alcohol** /lor'il or lör'-/ *n* a liquid made from coconut oil or its fatty acids, used in the manufacture of detergents. **lauryl thiocyanate** *n* a salt of lauryl alcohol used as a disinfectant.

■ **cherry laurel, Japan laurel** and **spurge laurel** see under **cherry**[1], **japan** and **spurge** respectively. **look to one's laurels** to be careful not to lose one's pre-eminent position. **rest on one's laurels** (sometimes as a criticism) to be content with one's past successes and the honour they bring, without attempting any further achievements.

Laurentian /lö-ren'sh(y)ən/ *adj* of or relating to *Lorenzo* or *Laurentius* de' *Medici* (1449–92), or to the library founded by him at Florence; of or relating to, or in the style of, the English writer DH *Lawrence* (1885–1930; also **Lawren'tian**); of or relating to the St *Lawrence* river in SE Canada; applied to a series of Precambrian rocks covering a large area in the region of the Upper Lakes of N America.

lauric acid see under **laurel**.

Laurus /lö'rəs/ n the laurel genus, giving its name to the family **Laurā'ceae**, leathery-leaved archichlamydeous dicotyledons. [L]
■ **laurā'ceous** adj.

laurustine /lö'rə-stīn/ or **laurustinus** /lö-rə-stī'nəs/ n a winter-flowering shrub (*Viburnum tinus*). [L *laurus* laurel, and *tīnus* laurustine]

laurvikite /lör'vi-kīt/ or **larvikite** /lär-/ (mineralogy) n a soda syenite composed mainly of feldspar with schiller structure. [*Laurvik* or *Larvik* in Norway]

lauryl alcohol and **lauryl thiocyanate** see under **laurel**.

laus Deo /lös dē'ō or lows dä'ō/ (L) praise to God.

lauwine /lö'win/ (Byron) n an avalanche. [Ger *La(u)wine*, perh from *lau* tepid]

lav /lav/ or **lavvy** /lav'i/ (inf) n short for **lavatory**.

lava /lä'və/ n (pl **la'vas**) molten material discharged in a stream from a volcano or fissure; such material subsequently solidified. [Ital, poss from L *lavāre* to wash, or from L *lābes* a falling down, from *lābī* to slide, fall]
■ **la'vaform** adj in the form of lava.
▫ **lava lamp** n an electric lamp in which a brightly-coloured viscous substance moves around forming ever-changing shapes.

lavabo /lə-vä'bō/ n (pl **lavä'bos** or **lavä'boes**) in the mass, the ritual act of washing the celebrant's fingers while he says *Lavabo inter innocentes* (RC); a monastic lavatory; a fixed basin or washstand; a lavatory. [L, I shall wash (from Psalm 26.6)]

lavage see under **lave**[1].

lava-lava /lä'və-lä'və/ n a rectangular piece of printed cloth worn by both sexes in Polynesia as a kind of skirt. [Samoan, clothing]

lavallière or **lavaliere** /la-va-lyer' or lav'ə-lēr/ n a loosely-tied bow; a jewelled pendant worn round the neck on a chain. [Duchesse de *la Vallière* (1644–1710)]

lavash /lə-vash'/ n a thin, crispy flatbread of Armenian origin. [Armenian]

lavatera /la-va-tē'rə or lə-vä'tə-rə/ n any plant of the genus *Lavatera* of herbs and shrubs (family Malvaceae) with large pink, white or purple mallow-like flowers. [The brothers *Lavater*, 17c and 18c Swiss physicians and naturalists]

lavatory /lav'ə-t(ə-)ri/ n a bowl, usu with a wooden or plastic seat and flushed by water, used for urination and defecation; a room containing a lavatory and often a washbasin; orig a place, room, fixture or vessel for washing; a laundry (obs); a ritual washing; a lotion (obs). [LL *lavatorium*, from *lavare*, *lavatum* to wash]
■ **lavator'ial** adj of or characteristic of lavatories; of humour, etc, scatological (usu derog).
▫ **lavatory paper** n toilet paper.

lave[1] /lāv/ (archaic) vt and vi to wash; to bathe. [L *lavāre*, *-ātum*; Gr *louein* to wash]
■ **lavage** /lav'ij or läv-äzh'/ n (med) irrigation or washing out. **lavation** /lav-ā'shən/ n washing. **lavement** /läv'/ n a washing; a lavage. **lāv'er** n a large vessel for washing, esp ritual washing; the basin of a fountain (*Spenser*); an ablution (*Milton*).

lave[2] /lāv/ (Scot) n remainder. [OE *lāf*; ON *leif*; see **leave**[2]]

lave[3] /lāv/ (obs) vt to pour out; to bale. [OE *lafian* to pour; fused with L *lavāre* to wash]

laveer /lä-vēr'/ (archaic naut) vi to beat to windward. [Du *laveeren*; cf **luff**]

lavender /lav'ən-dər/ n a labiate plant (*Lavandula vera*) with fragrant pale-lilac flowers, yielding an essential oil; sprigs of it dried and used for perfuming clothes, linen, etc; the colour of its blossoms; lavender water. ◆ adj of the colour of lavender flowers. ◆ vt to sprinkle with lavender. [Anglo-Fr *lavendre* (Fr *lavande*), from LL *lavendula*, earlier *livendula*, perh connected with *līvidus* livid]
▫ **lavender cotton** n a species of Mediterranean shrub, santolina. **lavender marriage** n (inf) a marriage of convenience used to disguise the homosexuality of one or both partners. **lavender water** n a perfume composed of spirits of wine, essential oil of lavender, and ambergris.
■ **lay in lavender** to lay by carefully, with sprigs of lavender; to pawn (inf). **oil of lavender** an aromatic oil distilled from lavender flowers and stems, used for its relaxing properties.

laver[1] /lä'vər/ n edible seaweed of various kinds, esp porphyra (*purple laver*) and ulva (*green laver*). [L *laver* a kind of water plant]
▫ **laver bread** or **laverbread** /lä'vər or lä'vər bred/ n a name for a food popular in Wales, the fronds of porphyra boiled, dipped in oatmeal and fried.

laver[2] see under **lave**[1].

laverock /lav'ə-rək, also (Scot) lä'v(ə-)rək/ an archaic and dialectal form of **lark**[1].

lavish /lav'ish/ adj generous or profuse in giving; prodigal or wasteful; extravagant; unrestrained. ◆ vt to expend or bestow profusely; to waste. ◆ n (obs) profusion; over-abundance; extravagant outpouring. [OFr *lavasse*, *lavache* deluge of rain, from *laver*, from L *lavāre* to wash]
■ **lav'ishly** adv. **lav'ishment** n. **lav'ishness** n.

lavolta /la-vol'tə/ or **lavolt** /la-volt'/ (Shakesp) n an old dance in which there was much turning and high leaping. ◆ vi to dance the lavolta. [Ital *la volta* the turn]

lavra see **laura**.

law[1] /lö/ n a rule of action established by authority; a statute; the rules of a community or state; jurisprudence; established usage; that which is lawful; the whole body of persons connected professionally with the law; litigation; a rule or code in any department of action, such as morality, art, honour, arms (including heraldry), a game, etc; a theoretical principle extracted from practice or observation; a statement or formula expressing the constant order of certain phenomena; the Mosaic code or the books containing it (theol); an allowance of time, a start esp in hunting (sport); indulgence (obs). ◆ vt to take to court, go to law with (obs); to determine (Burns); to expedite (obs). ◆ vi (obs) to go to law. [ME *lawe*, from late OE *lagu*, of ON origin, from the same root as **lie**[2] and **lay**[1]]
■ **law'ful** adj allowed by law; rightful. **law'fully** adv. **law'fulness** n. **law'ing** n going to law (archaic); expedition (obs). **law'less** adj not subject to or controlled by law; unruly. **law'lessly** adv. **law'lessness** n. **law'yer** n someone who practises law, esp a solicitor; a person learned or skilled in law; an interpreter of the Mosaic law (Bible); a brier, bramble, or other tenacious trailing or climbing plant (see also **Penang-lawyer**). **law'yerly** adj.
▫ **law'-abiding** adj obedient to and having respect for the law. **law'-abidingness** n. **law agent** n (Scots law; old) a solicitor. **law'-book** n a book dealing with the law or law cases. **law'breaker** n a person who does not observe or who abuses a law. **law'breaking** n and adj. **law'-burrows** n (Scots law) a writ requiring a person to give security against doing violence to another. **law'-calf** n a book-binding in smooth, pale-brown calfskin. **law centre** n an office, usu in a socially deprived area, where free legal advice and assistance are given (also **neighbourhood law centre**). **Law Commission** n a body of judges, solicitors, barristers and academic lawyers, appointed to report to Parliament on areas of possible law reform. **law'court** n a court of justice. **law'-day** n a day when court proceedings may be held in public, a day of open court. **lawful day** n a day on which particular kinds of business may be legally done, not a Sunday or a public holiday. **law'giver** n a person who enacts or imposes laws. **law'giving** adj. **law Latin** n Latin as used in law and legal documents, being a mixture of Latin with Old French and Latinized English words. **law'-list** n an annual book of information about lawyers, courts, etc. **Law Lord** n a common name for a Lord of Appeal in Ordinary (qv under **lord**) or other peer who holds or has held high judicial office and may also sit to hear appeals to the House of Lords in its judicial capacity; in Scotland, a judge of the Court of Session. **law'maker** n a legislator. **law'man** n a sheriff or policeman (US; now chiefly archaic or facetious). **law'-man** n (hist) a member of a select body with magisterial powers in some of the Danish towns of early England. **law'-mer'chant** n (obs) the customs that have grown up among merchants in reference to mercantile documents and business, commercial law. **law'monger** n a trivially contentious lawyer. **law of averages** n see under **average**. **law'-officer** n a legal official and adviser of the government, esp an Attorney-General, Solicitor-General, or Lord Advocate. **law of nations** n now **international law** (see under **international**), orig applied to those ethical principles regarded as obligatory on all communities. **law of nature** n the invariable order of nature; natural law. **law of octaves** n see under **octave**. **law of supply and demand** n the economic theory that the price of an item at a particular time is determined by conditions of supply and demand. **law of the jungle** n the rules for surviving, succeeding, etc in a competitive or hostile situation by the use of force, etc. **law of the land** n the established law of a country. **law of the Medes and Persians** n see under **Median**. **law reports** n pl written records of previous case law which are used during court proceedings to make reference to established legal principles. **Law Society** n the solicitors' governing body for England and Wales. **laws of motion** n pl see under **motion**. **law'-stā'tioner** n a person who sells parchment, documents and other articles needed by lawyers. **law'suit** n a suit or process in law. **law'-writer** n a writer on law; a copier or engrosser of legal papers. **lawyer's wig** n another name for **shaggy cap** (see under **shag**). **lawyer vine** n a spiny Australian vine of the palm family.
■ **be a law unto oneself** or **itself** to act in a way that does not follow established rules or conventions. **Bode's law** (astron) a rule popularized by Johann *Bode* (1747–1826, German astronomer) but first announced by Johann Titius (1729–96), which states that the distances of the planets from the sun in astronomical units is found by adding 4 to the series 0, 3, 6, 12, 24,... and dividing the number

so obtained by 10. **Boyle's law** (also **Mariotte's law**) the law that, for a gas at a given temperature, pressure varies inversely to volume, announced by Robert *Boyle* in 1662, and confirmed by Mariotte (1620–84, French physicist). **Charles's law** the law that all gases have the same value for the coefficient of expansion at constant pressure, stated by JAC *Charles* (1746–1823, French physicist), also called **Gay-Lussac's law** after JL Gay-Lussac (1778–1850, French chemist and physicist). **Dalton's law** (*chem*) the law that, in a mixture of gases, the pressure exerted by each gas is the same as that which it would exert if it were the only gas present. **go to law with** to resort to litigation against. **Gresham's law** the law, formulated by Sir Thomas *Gresham* (1519–79), that of two forms of currency the inferior or more depreciated tends to drive the other from circulation, owing to the hoarding and exportation of the better form. **Grimm's law** the law formulating certain changes undergone by Indo-European stopped consonants in Germanic, stated by Jacob *Grimm* (1785–1863). **have** or **get the law on** (*inf*) or **have the law of** (*archaic*) to enforce the law against. **Hooke's law** the law formulated by Robert *Hooke* (1635–1703), which states that, for an elastic material within its elastic limit, the extension produced by stretching the material is proportional to the force that is producing the extension. **Kepler's laws** three laws of planetary motion discovered by Johann *Kepler* (1571–1630): (1) the orbits of the planets are ellipses with the sun at one focus; (2) the areas described by their *radii vectores* in equal times are equal; (3) the squares of their periodic times vary as the cubes of their mean distances from the sun. **lay down the law** to speak authoritatively or dictatorially. **Mariotte's law** see **Boyle's law** above. **Moore's law** the law formulated by Gordon *Moore* (born 1929), which states that the number of transistors that it is possible to fit onto a silicon chip doubles *approx* every 18 months. **Murphy's law** (*facetious*) the law which states that if anything can go wrong, it will. **Parkinson's law** see separate entry. **Snell's law** the law of refraction discovered by Willebrord *Snel* or *Snell* (1580–1626, Dutch mathematician), which states that the sine of the angle of incidence divided by the sine of the angle of refraction is a constant, known as the refractive index. **Sod's law** see under **sod²**. **take the law into one's own hands** to obtain justice, or what one considers to be justice, by one's own actions, without recourse to the law, the police, etc. **the law** (*inf*) the police; a policeman. **Verner's law** a law stated by Karl *Verner* in 1875, showing the effect of accent in the shifting of Indo-European stopped consonants and *s* in Germanic, and explaining the most important anomalies in the application of Grimm's law.

law² /lö/ (*obs*) *n* share of expense, score. [ON *lag* market-price]
■ **law'ing** or **law'in** *n* (*Scot*) a bill or reckoning, *esp* in a bar or pub.

law³ /lö/ (*Scot*) *n* a hill, *esp* rounded or conical. [Scot and N Eng form of **low³**, OE *hlāw*]

law⁴ /lö/ (*Scot*) *adj* low. [Scot and N Eng form of **low¹**]
■ **law'land** *n* and *adj* lowland.

law⁵ /lö/ *interj* expressing asseveration (*obs*); expressing surprise (*dialect*). [Partly for **la** or **lo**, partly **lord**]

lawin see **law²**.

lawing see **law¹,²**.

lawk /lök/ or **lawks** /löks/ (*dialect*) *interj* expressing surprise. [**lord** or **lack²**]

lawn¹ /lön/ *n* a smooth space of ground covered with grass, generally beside a house; an open space between woods (*archaic*). [**laund**]
■ **lawned** *adj*. **lawn'y** *adj*.
□ **lawn'mower** *n* a machine for cutting grass on a lawn. **lawn party** *n* (*US*) a garden party. **lawn'-sprink'ler** *n* a machine for watering a lawn by sprinkling. **lawn tennis** *n* the modern form of tennis, as opposed to real tennis.

lawn² /lön/ *n* a sort of fine linen or cambric; extended to some cottons. ◆ *adj* made of lawn. [Prob from *Laon*, near Rheims]
■ **lawn'y** *adj*.
□ **lawn sleeves** *n pl* wide sleeves of lawn worn by Anglican bishops.

lawrencium /lö-ren'si-əm/ *n* an artificially produced radioactive transuranic element (symbol **Lr**; atomic no 103). [Ernest O *Lawrence* (1901–58), American physicist]

Lawrentian see **Laurentian**.

lawyer, etc see under **law¹**.

lax¹ /laks/ *adj* slack; loose; soft or flabby; not strict in discipline or morals; careless or negligent; loose in the bowels. [L *laxus* loose]
■ **lax'ative** *adj* stimulating loosening of the bowels; giving freedom (*archaic*); speaking or expressing itself freely (*obs*). ◆ *n* a purgative or aperient medicine. **lax'ativeness** *n*. **laxā'tor** *n* a muscle that relaxes an organ or part. **lax'ism** *n* the view that in morals an opinion only slightly probable may be safely followed. **lax'ist** *n* a person holding

loose notions of moral laws, or of their application. **lax'ity** or **lax'ness** *n*. **lax'ly** *adv*.

lax² /laks/ *n* a salmon (*usu* one caught in Swedish or Norwegian waters). [Revived use, from OE *leax*; OHGer *lahs*, ON *lax*; cf **lox²**]

lay¹ /lā/ *vt* (**lay'ing**; **laid**) to cause to lie; to place or set down; to beat down; to spread on a surface; to spread or set something on; to cover; to apply; to cause to subside; to exorcize; to deposit; to set on the table; to make (a bet), wager; to put forward; to cause to be; to set; to produce and deposit; to station; to locate; to put in (a particular) position; to waylay; to impose; to attribute or impute; to set material in position for making; to form (a rope, etc) by setting in position and twisting; to design or plan; to layer (*hortic*); to cause (a hedge) to grow more thickly by cutting some of the growth halfway through and pressing it diagonally towards the ground; to have sexual intercourse with (*sl*); to put below the horizon by sailing away; to give birth to a child (*obs*); to beset (*Shakesp*). ◆ *vi* to produce eggs; to wager or bet; to deal blows; to lie (*archaic, naut* and *non-standard*). ◆ *n* a situation, a place for lying; an oyster-bed; a way of lying; a disposition, arrangement or plan; a layer; a mode of twisting; laying activity; an act of sexual intercourse (*sl*); a partner, *usu* female, in sexual intercourse (*sl*); a bet (*Shakesp*); a share of profit, *esp* in whaling; a field or method of operation, *esp* in thieving (*sl*). [OE *lecgan* to lay, causative of *licgan* to lie; cf ON *leggja*, Ger *legen*]
■ **layer** /lā'ər or lār/ *n* a course, bed or stratum; someone who or something which lays, eg a hen, a bricklayer, etc; a distinctively coloured space between contour lines on a map; a shoot bent down to earth in order to take root. ◆ *vt* and *vi* to propagate by layers. ◆ *vt* to put in layers; to cut (hair) in layers. ◆ *vi* to be laid flat, lodge. **lay'ered** *adj* in or with layers. **lay'ering** *n* the first coat of plaster; the act or time of laying eggs; the eggs laid.
□ **lay'about** *n* a lazy, idle person, a loafer. **lay'away** *n* goods on which a deposit has been paid, kept for a customer until payment is completed; this system of purchasing goods. **lay'back** *n* in rock climbing, a method of climbing a sharp-edged crack in a horizontal position (also *vi*). **lay'-by** *n* (*pl* **lay'-bys**) a widened area of a roadway to allow vehicles to draw up out of the stream of traffic; (also **lay'-bye**) a deposit against future purchase (*S Afr*); (also **lay'-bye**) a system of reserving the right to purchase goods by making a deposit (*S Afr*). **lay'-down** *n* in card games, *esp* bridge, a hand which cannot fail to take the number of tricks required to win, and which therefore is sometimes exposed to view without any play taking place; the contract made by the holder of such a hand. **layer cake** *n* a cake built up in layers. **lay'-off** *n* a temporary suspension of work introduced by an employer as an economic measure; the act of laying off or period of time during which someone lays off or is laid off. **lay'out** *n* something which is laid out; a display; an outfit; the disposition, arrangement, plan, *esp* of buildings or ground; the general appearance of a printed page, also called *format*; a set, unit or organization. **lay'over** *n* (chiefly *N Am*) a break in a journey. **lay'shaft** *n* an auxiliary geared shaft in a machine, *esp* the secondary shaft in a car's gearbox. **lay'stall** *n* (*obs*) a place for depositing dung, rubbish, etc. **lay'-up** *n* the time or condition of being laid up; (in basketball) a shot taken from near the basket, *esp* one-handed and bouncing off the backboard; (in golf) a shot deliberately played short of a hazard or green.
■ **lay aboard** to run alongside, *esp* in order to board. **lay about one** to deal blows vigorously or on all sides. **lay a course** (*naut*) to succeed in sailing to the place required without tacking. **lay aside** or **lay away** to discard; to put on one side for future use (see also **layaway** above). **lay at** to try to strike. **lay away** to lay eggs in out-of-the-way places (*Scot*, etc); to purchase goods by layaway (qv above). **lay bare** to show clearly, disclose. **lay before** to submit (eg plans) to. **lay by** to keep for future use; to dismiss; to put off. **lay by the heels** see under **heel¹**. **lay down** to give up; to deposit, as a pledge; to apply (eg embroidery; *archaic*); to formulate; to assert (a law or rule); to store; to plant; to record; to lay on (*printing*). **lay hands on** see under **hand**. **lay heads together** (*archaic*) to confer together. **lay hold of** or **on** to seize. **lay in** to get in a supply of. **lay into** to beat thoroughly. **lay it on** to charge exorbitantly; to do anything, eg to exaggerate or flatter, excessively. **lay off** to mark off; to dismiss temporarily from employment as an economic measure; to cease (*inf*); to doff (*archaic*); to harangue volubly; to hedge (*gambling*); to pass (the ball) to a teammate who is in a better position (*football*). **lay of the land** (chiefly *N Am*) same as **lie of the land** (see under **lie²**). **lay on** to install a supply of; to provide; to deal blows with vigour; to arrange made-up pages in the correct order on the imposing surface (also **lay down**; *printing*). **lay oneself open to** to make oneself vulnerable to, or exposed to (criticism, etc). **lay oneself out to** (*archaic*) to make it one's professed object or practice, take great pains, to. **lay on hands** see under **hand**. **lay on load** (*Spenser*) to belabour. **lay on the table** see under **table**. **lay open** to make bare, to show or expose; to cut open. **lay out** to display; to spend (money); to plan; to arrange according to a plan; to prepare for burial; to knock unconscious; to take measures, seek. **lay**

siege to to besiege; to importune. **lay the table** to put dishes, etc on the table in preparation for a meal. **lay to** to apply with vigour; to bring a ship to rest. **lay to heart** see under **heart**. **lay under** to subject to. **lay up** to store up, preserve; (*usu in passive*) to confine to bed or one's room; to put in dock for cleaning, repairs, etc or because no longer wanted for or fit for service; to play a lay-up shot. **lay upon** to wager upon. **lay wait** to lie in wait, or in ambush. **lay waste** to devastate. **on a lay** on shares instead of wages.

lay² /lā/ pat of **lie²**.

lay³ /lā/ adj of or relating to people who not members of the clergy; non-professional; not trumps (*cards*). ◆ *n* the laity; a layman (*obs*). [OFr *lai*, from L *lāicus*, from Gr *lāikos*, from *lāos* the people]
■ **laic** /lā'ik/ adj lay. ◆ *n* a layman. **lā'ical** adj. **lāic'ity** *n* the state of being lay; the nature of the laity; the influence of the laity. **lāiciza'tion** or **-s-** *n*. **laicize** or **-ise** /lā'i-sīz/ *vt* to make laical; to open to the laity. **lā'ity** *n* the people as distinguished from some particular profession, *usu* the clerical; (*usu* with *cap*) *specif* one of the three divisions within the General Synod of the Church of England, the others being the Bishops and the Clergy.
◻ **lay baptism** *n* baptism administered by a layman. **lay brother** or **lay sister** *n* a person under vows of celibacy and obedience, who serves a religious house, but is exempt from the studies and choir duties of monks or nuns. **lay clerk** *n* a singer in the choir of an Anglican cathedral, etc. **lay communion** *n* the state of being in the communion of the church as a layman. **lay'man** *n* one of the laity; a non-professional person; someone who is not an expert. **lay'person** *n*. **lay reader** *n* (in some branches of the Anglican communion) a man or woman who is not ordained but is licensed by a bishop to undertake a range of ecclesiastical duties. **lay sister** see **lay brother** above. **lay vicar** *n* a layman who is vicar-choral in an Anglican cathedral. **lay'woman** *n*.

lay⁴ /lā/ *n* a short narrative poem; a lyric; a song. [OFr *lai*; origin obscure]

lay⁵ /lā/ (*archaic*) *n* law; religious faith. [OFr *lei* (Fr *loi*), from L *lēx, lēgis* law]

lay⁶ /lā/ *n* a form of **lea¹,²,³**.

lay-day /lā'dā/ *n* one of a number of days allowed for loading and unloading of cargo (*commerce*); a day a vessel is delayed in port (*naut*). [Perh formed from **delay¹** and **day**]
◻ **lay'time** *n* the total time in port allowed to a vessel.

layer see under **lay¹**.

layette /lā-et'/ *n* a baby's complete set of clothing, etc. [Fr]

lay-figure /lā'fi-gər/ *n* (earlier **lay'man**) a jointed model used by painters; a living person or a fictitious character lacking in individuality. [Du *leeman*, from *led* (now *lid*) joint, and *man* man]

laylock /lā'lək/ *n* an obsolete form of **lilac**.

layman see under **lay³** and **lay-figure**.

lazar /laz'ər/ *n* a leper; a person with a pestilential disease such as leprosy. [From *Lazarus*, the beggar with leprosy, in the Bible (Luke 16.20)]
■ **Laz'arist** *n* a member of the Roman Catholic Congregation of the Priests of the Mission, founded by St Vincent de Paul in 1624. **la'zar-like** adj or adv.
◻ **lazar house** *n* a lazaretto.

lazaretto /la-zə-ret'ō/, also **lazaret** /laz'ə-ret/ or **lazarette** /la-zə-ret'/ *n* (*pl* **lazarett'os**, **laz'arets** or **lazarettes'**) a hospital for infectious diseases, *esp* leprosy; a place of quarantine; a place for keeping stores on a ship. [Ital *lazzaretto*]

laze, **lazily**, etc see under **lazy**.

lazo same as **lasso**.

lazuli /laz'ū-lī/ see **lapis lazuli** under **lapis**.

lazulite /laz'ū-līt/ *n* a blue mineral, hydrated phosphate of aluminium, magnesium, and iron. [LL *lazulum*, from Pers *lājward*; cf **azure**, **lapis lazuli** and **lazurite**]

lazurite /laz'ū-rīt/ *n* a blue cubic mineral, sodium aluminium silicate with some sulphur, a constituent of lapis lazuli. [LL *lazur*, from Pers *lājward*; cf **azure**, **lapis lazuli** and **lazulite**]

lazy /lā'zi/ adj reluctant to exert oneself; averse to work; sluggish. [Origin unknown]
■ **laze** *vi* (back-formation) to be idle. ◆ *n* an instance of lazing. **la'zily** adv. **la'ziness** *n*.
◻ **la'zy-bed** *n* a bed for growing potatoes, the seed being laid on the surface and covered with earth dug out of trenches along both sides. **la'zybones** *n* (*inf*) a lazy or idle person. **lazy daisy stitch** *n* an embroidery stitch often used to make flower designs. **lazy eye** *n* an apparently healthy eye having, nevertheless, impaired vision; amblyopia. **lazy jack** *n* a jack constructed of compound levers pivoted together. **lazy painter** *n* (*naut*) see under **painter¹**. **lazy Susan** *n* a revolving tray, often with a number of separate dishes or

sections for foods, intended to be placed on a dining table, etc. **lazy tongs** *n pl* a series of diagonal levers pivoted together at the middle and ends, capable of being extended by a movement of the scissors-like handles so as to pick up objects at a distance. ◆ *adj* (with *hyphen*) constructed on the model of lazy tongs.

lazzarone /läd-zä-rō'nā/ or /la-zə-rō'ni/ *n* (*pl* **lazzaro'ni** /-nē/) a Neapolitan beggar. [Ital]

lazzo /läd'dzō/ (*Ital*) *n* (*pl* **laz'zi** /-ē/) a piece of farce or comic dialogue in the commedia dell'arte.

LB abbrev : Liberia (IVR).

lb abbrev : leg before (wicket) (*cricket*); leg bye (*cricket*); libra (L), pound weight.

LBC abbrev : London Broadcasting Company.

lbf abbrev : pound force.

LBO abbrev : leveraged buyout.

LBS abbrev : London Business School.

lbw (*cricket*) abbrev : leg before wicket.

LC (*US*) abbrev : Library of Congress.

lc abbrev : left centre; letter of credit; *loco citato* (L), in the place cited; lower case (*printing*).

LCC abbrev : formerly, London County Council (later known as **GLC**).

LCD abbrev : liquid crystal display; lowest (or least) common denominator (also without *caps*).

LCDT abbrev : London Contemporary Dance Theatre.

LCh or **LChir** abbrev : *Licentiatus Chirurgiae* (L), Licentiate in Surgery.

LCJ abbrev : Lord Chief Justice.

LCM or **lcm** (*maths*) abbrev : least or lowest common multiple.

LCP abbrev : Licentiate of the College of Preceptors.

L/Cpl abbrev : lance corporal.

LCST abbrev : Licentiate of the College of Speech Therapists.

LD abbrev : Lady Day; lethal dosage; Low Dutch.

Ld abbrev : Lord.

LDC abbrev : less developed country.

Ldg (*navy*) abbrev : Leading.

LDL abbrev : low-density lipoprotein.

L-dopa see **dopa**.

LDP abbrev : Liberal Democratic Party.

Ldp or **Lp** abbrev : Lordship.

LDS abbrev : Latter-Day Saints; *laus Deo semper* (L), praise be to God always; Licentiate in Dental Surgery.

LDV abbrev : Local Defence Volunteers (known as the Home Guard from 1940).

LEA abbrev : local education authority.

lea¹ /lē/ *n* open country, meadow, pasture, or arable (also **lay**, **lee**, **ley** /lā or lē/). [OE *lēah*; dialect Ger *lohe, loh*; perh Flem *-loo* in place names, eg Water*loo*; confused with **lease⁴**]

lea² /lē/, also **lay** /lā/ or **ley** /lē or lā/adj and *n* fallow; (of) arable land under grass or pasture. [OE *lǣge*, found in *lǣghrycg* lea-rig]
◻ **lea'-rig** *n* an unploughed rig or grass field. **ley'-farm'ing** *n* pasturing and cropping in alternating periods.

lea³ /lē/, **lay** or **ley** /lā/ *n* a measure of yarn, 80 yards of worsted, 120 of cotton, 300 of linen. [Perh connected with Fr *lier*, from L *ligāre* to bind]

leach¹ /lēch/ *vt* (also **letch**) to allow (a liquid) to percolate through something; to subject (something) to percolation so as to separate the soluble constituent(s); to drain away by percolation. ◆ *vi* to percolate through or out of; to pass out of by the action of a percolating liquid; to lose soluble elements by the action of a percolating liquid. [OE *leccan* to water, irrigate or moisten]
■ **leach'ate** *n* a liquid that has percolated through or out of some substance; a liquid that has been polluted or made toxic by percolating through rubbish; a solution obtained by leaching. **leach'ing** *n*. **leach'y** adj liable to be leached.
◻ **leach'-trough** or **leach'tub** *n* a trough or tub in which ashes are leached.
■ **bacterial leaching** the use of selected strains of bacteria to accelerate the acid leach of sulphide minerals.

leach² a Spenserian form of **leech¹**.

leachour a Spenserian form of **lecher**.

lead¹ /lēd/ *vt* (*pap* and *pat* **led**) to show the way by going first; to precede; to guide by the hand; to direct; to guide; to conduct; to convey; to cart (*dialect*); to induce; to live; to cause to live or experience; to adduce (*Scots law*); to have a principal or guiding part or place in; to play as the first card of a round (*cards*). ◆ *vi* to be first or among the first; to be guide or chief; to act or play (a card) first; to cart crops to the farmyard (often with *in*); to afford a passage (to), or (*fig*) tend towards; (of a newspaper, etc) to have as its main story, feature, etc (with *with*). ◆ *n* first place; precedence; the amount by which one is ahead; direction; guidance; an indication; a precedent or example; a chief role; the player of a chief role; leadership; initiative; the act or right of playing first, or the play of whoever plays first; the first player of a side (*curling*, etc); a leash; a watercourse leading to a mill; a channel through ice; the course of a running rope from end to end; a main conductor in electrical distribution; the distance between successive contours on the same helix of a screw thread measured parallel to the axis of the screw. ◆ *adj* chief; main; leading. [OE *lǣdan* to lead, *lād* a way; Ger *leiten* to lead]

■ **lead'er** *n* a person who leads or goes first; a chief; in an orchestra, the principal first violin; the head of a party, expedition, etc; the leading editorial article in a newspaper (also **leading article**); the principal upward-growing shoot of a tree; a horse or dog in a front place in a team; a tendon; a short blank strip at the beginning and end of a film or tape; a translucent connection between a fishing-line and bait; a line of dots to guide the eye (*printing*); the principal wheel in any machinery; an alternative name for a conductor (of an orchestra, etc) (*US*). **leaderene'** *n* a female leader, *esp* a domineering one (*orig* applied to Margaret Thatcher when UK Prime Minister). **leaderette'** *n* a brief newspaper leader. **lead'erless** *adj*. **lead'ership** *n* the office of leader or conductor; those acting as leaders of a particular organization or group; ability to lead. **lead'ing** *n* guidance; spiritual guidance; leadership; carting (crops, etc). ◆ *adj* acting as leader; directing or controlling; principal; preceding.

❏ **lead'erboard** *n* a scoreboard that lists the names and scores of the current leaders in a sporting, *esp* golf, competition. **lead'erca'ble** *n* a cable on the sea-bottom by which ships with induction-receiving apparatus can find their way into port. **Leader of the House of Commons** or **Lords** *n* a senior member of the government officially responsible for initiating the business of the House. **lead'-in** *n* the part of the groove on a record before the start of the recording, *opp* to *lead-out* (also **lead-in groove**); the cable connecting the transmitter or receiver to the elevated part of an aerial; the introduction to, or introductory passage of, a commercial, discussion, newspaper article, piece of music, etc (also *adj*). **leading aircraftman** or **aircraftsman, aircraftwoman** or **aircraftswoman** *n* the rank above aircraft(s)man or aircraft(s)woman. **leading case** *n* (*law*) a case serving as a precedent. **leading counsel** *n* counsel who takes precedence over another in conducting a case. **leading dog** *n* (*Aust* and *NZ*) a sheepdog trained to control sheep by running ahead of them. **leading edge** *n* the edge first met; the foremost edge of an aerofoil or propeller blade; the rising amplitude portion of a pulse signal (*telecom*); the forefront, *esp* in scientific or technical development (*fig*). **leading lady** or **leading man** *n* the principal actress or actor in a play. **leading light** *n* a very influential member. **leading note** *n* (*music*) the seventh tone of a major or minor scale, which leads the hearer to expect the tonic to follow. **leading question** *n* a question put in such a way as to suggest the desired answer. **leading reins** or **leading strings** *n pl* (*US*) children's walking reins; vexatious care or custody. **lead'-off** *n* a first move (see also **lead off** below). **lead'-out** *n* the part of the groove on a record after the recording has finished, *opp* to *lead-in* (also **lead-out groove**); a wire by which electric current can enter or leave an electronic instrument. **lead time** *n* (*orig US*) the time between the conception or design of a product, factory, alteration, etc and its production, completion, implementation, etc; the time taken for delivery of goods after an order has been placed. **lead'-up** *n* something that introduces or causes something else; the period immediately prior to something happening.

■ **lead apes in hell** imagined to be the lot of old maids in the afterlife. **lead astray** to draw into a wrong course; to seduce from proper conduct. **lead by the nose** to make (someone) follow submissively. **lead in** (*Scot*) to house the harvest. **lead in prayer** to lead the offering up of prayer in an assembly, uniting the prayers of others. **lead off** to begin or take the start in anything. **lead on** to persuade to go on, to draw on; to persuade to do something foolish; to trick or deceive. **lead out** to conduct to execution or a dance; to bring out by preceding; to begin to play (*cards*). **leads and lags** (*commerce*) in international trade, the early payment of bills, dividends, etc to concerns abroad, and the delayed invoicing of foreign customers and delayed conversion of foreign currencies into sterling (in order to take advantage of expected changes in the rate of exchange), which have an effect on the balance of payments situation; any variations in the times of completion of transactions. **lead someone a dance** see under **dance**. **lead the way** to go first and guide others. **lead up to** to bring about by degrees, to prepare for by steps or stages; to happen immediately before; to play in challenge to, or with a view to weakness in (*cards*).

lead² /led/ *n* a heavy soft bluish-grey metallic element (symbol **Pb**; atomic no 82); a plummet for sounding; a thin plate of lead separating lines of type (also **leading**); a pan or cauldron of lead, or

of a kind once made of lead; a strip of lead, U- or H-shaped in cross-section, used to join pieces of stained glass or the panes of a lattice window, a came; blacklead graphite; the core of coloured material in a coloured pencil; a stick of graphite for a pencil; (in *pl*) sheets of lead for covering roofs, or a flat roof so covered; a lead weight or piece of lead shot used at the end of a fishing-line and in cartridges. ◆ *adj* made of lead. ◆ *vt* to cover, weight or fit with lead; to join together (pieces of stained glass or a lattice window) with leads (often with *up*; also *vi*); to separate the lines of with leads (*printing*). [OE]

■ **lead'ed** *adj* fitted or weighted with or set in lead; separated by leads (*printing*); (of petrol) containing tetraethyl lead. **lead'en** *adj* made of lead; lead-coloured; inert; oppressive; depressing; heavy; dull. ◆ *vt* and *vi* to make or become leaden. **lead'enly** *adv*. **lead'enness** *n*. **lead'ing** *n* leads collectively; (also **lead**) the strip of lead separating lines of type (*printing*); the vertical space caused by such a strip. **lead'less** *adj*. **lead'y** *adj* like lead.

❏ **lead acetate** see **sugar of lead** under **sugar**. **lead'-arm'ing** *n* (*naut*) tallow, etc placed in the hollow of a sounding-lead to ascertain the nature of the bottom of the sea, river, etc. **lead colic** see **lead poisoning** below. **lead'en-stepp'ing** *adj* (*Milton*) moving slowly. **lead'-free** see **unleaded** under **un-**. **lead glance** *n* galena. **lead glass** *n* glass containing lead oxide. **lead'-line** *n* a sounding-line (*naut*); any of the lines on a stained glass cartoon indicating where the leads will lie in the finished work. **lead monoxide** *n* a bright yellow solid compound used in pigments and paints. **lead'-paint** *n* paint with red lead or white lead as its base. **lead pencil** *n* a blacklead pencil for writing or drawing. **lead poisoning** *n* plumbism, poisoning by the absorption of lead into the system, its commonest form being **lead colic**, or painter's colic; death by shooting (*sl*). **leads'man** *n* a seaman who heaves the lead or plummet for sounding. **lead tree** *n* Saturn's tree (qv). **lead'wort** same as **plumbago¹**.

■ **eat lead** (*sl*) to be shot, be killed by shooting. **go down like a lead balloon** (*humorous*) to be conspicuously unsuccessful. **red lead** and **white lead** see under **red¹** and **white** respectively. **swing the lead** (*naut* and *milit sl*) to invent specious excuses to evade duties.

leaf /lēf/ *n* (*pl* **leaves** /lēvz/) one of the lateral organs developed from the stem or axis of a plant below its growing-point, *esp* one of those flat green structures that transpire and assimilate carbon; any similar structure, such as a scale or a petal; the condition of having leaves; leaves collectively; anything beaten thin like a leaf; two pages of a book on opposite sides of the same paper; a broad thin part, structure or extension, hinged, sliding or inserted at will, for folding doors, window-shutters, table tops, drawbridges, etc; the tooth of a pinion; marijuana (*sl*). ◆ *vt* (**leaf'ing**; **leafed**) and *vi* (with *through*) to turn the pages of (a book, etc). ◆ *vi* (also **leave**) to produce leaves. ◆ *adj* in the form of leaves. [OE *lēaf*; Ger *Laub*, Du *loof* a leaf]

■ **leaf'age** *n* foliage. **leafed** /lēft/ *adj* having leaves (also **leaved** /lēvd/). **leaf'ery** *n* leafage. **leaf'iness** *n*. **leaf'less** *adj* having no leaves. **leaf'let** *n* a single sheet of printed political, religious, advertising, etc matter, flat or folded, or several sheets folded together; a little leaf; a division of a compound leaf. ◆ *vt* (**leaf'leting**, or less correctly **leaf'letting**; **leaf'leted** or less correctly **leaf'letted**) to distribute leaflets to. ◆ *vi* to distribute leaflets. **leafleteer'** *n*. **leaf'like** *adj*. **leaf'y** or **leav'y** *adj* covered with or having many leaves; abounding with trees and shrubs; leaflike.

❏ **leaf'-base** *n* the base of a leaf-stalk, where it joins the stem. **leaf beetle** *n* any beetle of the family Chrysomelidae, including the Colorado beetle. **leaf'-bridge** *n* a drawbridge with rising leaves swinging on hinges. **leaf'bud** *n* a bud producing a shoot with foliage leaves only (not flowers). **leaf'-climb'er** *n* a plant that climbs by means of its leaves (petioles or tendrils). **leaf curl** *n* a plant disease of various kinds characterized by curling of the leaves. **leaf'-cushion** *n* a swollen leaf-base; a pulvinus that serves as a hinge for leaf movements; a raised scar marking the position of a leaf. **leaf'-cutter** *n* an insect (ant or bee) that cuts pieces out of leaves. **leaf'-cutt'ing** *n* a leaf used as a cutting for propagation. **leaf'-fall** *n* the shedding of leaves; the time of the shedding of leaves, *usu* autumn; premature fall of leaves. **leaf fat** *n* dense fat that forms around the kidneys of some animals, *esp* pigs. **leaf'-green** *n* chlorophyll. **leaf'-hopper** *n* a name for various hopping orthopterous insects that suck plant juices. **leaf insect** *n* an orthopterous insect of the family Phasmidae with wing-covers like leaves. **leaf'-met'al** *n* metal, *esp* alloys imitating gold and silver, in very thin leaves for decoration. **leaf miner** *n* an insect whose larvae bore into and feed on leaves. **leaf monkey** *n* an Asian monkey of the genus *Presbytis*. **leaf mosaic** *n* a name for various virus diseases of potato, tobacco, etc in which the leaf is mottled; the arrangement of leaves so as to avoid shading one another. **leaf mould** or **soil** *n* earth formed from decayed leaves, used with soil as a compost for plants. **leaf'-nosed** *adj* having a leaflike structure on the nose, as certain bats. **leaf roll** *n* a potato disease. **leaf'-scar** *n* a scar left by the fall of a leaf.

---

leaf'-sheath *n* a leaf-base more or less completely enveloping the stem. **leaf spot** *n* any of several plant diseases characterized by the appearance of dark spots on the leaves. **leaf spring** *n* a spring made up of narrow, curved strips of metal of increasing length. **leaf'-stalk** *n* (*bot*) the petiole of a leaf. **leaf trace** *n* a branch from the vascular system of the stem destined to enter a leaf.
■ **take a leaf out of someone's book** see under **book. turn over a new leaf** to begin a new and better course of conduct.

league[1] /lēg/ *n* a bond or alliance; a union for mutual advantage; an association or confederacy; an association of clubs for games; a class or group. ♦ *vt* and *vi* to join in league. [Fr *ligue*, from LL *liga*, from L *ligāre* to bind]
■ **lea'guer** *n* a member of a league; (with *cap*) a member of the league against the Huguenots in the time of Henry III of France, of the Anti-Corn-Law League, or of the Irish Land League (*hist*).
□ **league match** *n* a match between two clubs in the same league. **League of Nations** *n* an international body, formed under a covenant drawn up in 1919, to secure peace, justice, scrupulous observance of treaties, and international co-operation generally, and superseded in 1945 by the United Nations. **league table** *n* a table in which clubs in a league are placed according to their performances, or (*fig*) any grouping made to reflect relative success, importance, etc.
■ **in league with** having made an alliance with, *usu* for a bad purpose. **in the big league** (*inf*) among the most important, powerful, etc people, organizations, etc. **not in the same league as** not of the same calibre, ability, importance, etc as. **top** or **bottom of the league** (*fig*) the highest or lowest in a particular field of achievement, or in quality.

league[2] /lēg/ *n* a nautical measure, $\frac{1}{20}$th of a degree, 3 international nautical miles, 5.556km (3.456 statute miles); an old measure of length, varying from the Roman league, 2.215km (1.376 modern English miles), to the French, 4.448km (2.764 miles), and the Spanish, 6.781km (4.214 miles), in general, eg in poetry, taken to be about 4.828km (3 miles). [LL *leuga, leuca* Gallic mile of 1500 Roman paces; poss Gaulish]

leaguer[1] /lē'gər/ (*archaic*) *n* a camp, *esp* of a besieging army; siege; (by confusion with **ledger**) an ambassador. ♦ *vt* to beleaguer. [Du *leger* a lair]
□ **lea'guer-la'dy** or **lea'guer-lass'** *n* a female camp-follower.

leaguer[2] /lē'gər/ (*obs*) *n* an old Dutch liquid measure; a large cask. [Du *ligger* a tun]

leaguer[3] see under **league**[1].

leak /lēk/ *n* a crack or hole in a vessel or container through which fluid may pass; passage through such an opening; an act of urination (*sl*); a place, means or instance of unintended or undesirable admission or escape (*lit* and *fig*); the *usu* unauthorized, but sometimes only apparently unauthorized, revealing of secret information; a piece of such information; a loss of electricity from a conductor, etc, *usu* because of faulty insulation; a high resistance, *esp* serving as a discharging path for a condenser (*elec*). ♦ *adj* (*obs*) leaky. ♦ *vi* to have a leak; to pass through a leak; to urinate (*sl*). ♦ *vt* to cause to leak; to let out or in by, or (*fig*) as if by, a leak; to divulge (secret information) without, or apparently without, authorization, or to cause this to be done. [OE *hlec* leaky; or perh reintroduced from Du or LGer *lek* leak; or ON *leka* to leak]
■ **leak'age** *n* a leaking; something which enters, escapes or is revealed by leaking; an allowance for leaking. **leak'er** *n*. **leak'iness** *n*. **leak'y** *adj*.
■ **leak out** (of air) to escape; (of secret information) to be divulged to the public without, or apparently without, authorization. **spring a leak** to become leaky. **take a leak** (*sl*) to urinate.

leal /lēl/ (*archaic* or *poetic*) *adj* true-hearted or faithful. [OFr *leel, leiel*; doublet of **loyal**]
■ **leal'ly** *adv*. **lealty** /lē'əl-ti/ *n*.
■ **Land o' the Leal** the home of the blessed after death, heaven.

leam[1] or **leme** /lēm/ (*archaic*) *n* a gleam of light, a glow. ♦ *vi* to shine. [OE *lēoma*]

leam[2] /lēm/ same as **lyam**.

lean[1] /lēn/ *vi* (*pat* and *pap* **leaned** /lēnd/ or **leant** /lent/) to incline; to be or become inclined to the vertical; to rest sideways against something; to bend over; to swerve; to abut; to have an inclination. ♦ *vt* to cause to lean. ♦ *n* an act or condition of leaning; a slope; a thing to lean on (*archaic*). [OE *hlēonian, hlinian*, and causative *hlænan*; Du *leunen*]
■ **lean'ing** *n* and *adj*.
□ **lean'-to** *n* (*pl* **lean'-tos**) a shed, greenhouse, conservatory, etc propped against another building or wall.
■ **lean on** to rely or depend on; to put pressure on, to use force on (a person) (*inf*). **lean over backwards** see under **back**[1].

lean[2] /lēn/ *adj* thin, without (much) flesh; not fat; without fat; unproductive; unprofitable; taking extra time (*printing*); (of a fuel mixture) containing a high proportion of air; (of ore) low grade, of marginal value (*mining*). ♦ *n* meat without fat. [OE *hlǣne*; LGer *leen*]
■ **lean'ly** *adv*. **lean'ness** *n*. **lean'y** *adj* (*Spenser*) lean.
□ **lean'-burn'** *adj* of, using or relating to a fuel-air mixture in which the fuel component is relatively low, so reducing the amount of fuel used and pollution produced. **lean concrete** *n* a non-load-bearing concrete of low cement content. **lean cuisine** *n* cuisine minceur (qv). **lean'-faced** *adj* having a thin face; slender and narrow, eg letters (*printing*). **lean'-witt'ed** *adj* of little sense.

leap[1] /lēp/ *vi* (**leap'ing**; **leaped** /lēpt/ or **leapt** /lept/) to move with bounds; to spring upward or forward; to jump; to rush violently; to pass abruptly or over a wide interval. ♦ *vt* to bound over; to cause to take a leap; of male animals, to mate with, cover. ♦ *n* an act of leaping; a bound; the space passed or covered by leaping; a place of leaping; an abrupt transition; a wide gap or interval. [OE *hlēapan*; cf *lope*[1], *loup*[1], and Ger *laufen* to run]
■ **leap'er** *n* a steeplechaser; someone who or something that leaps.
□ **leap day** *n* an intercalary day in the calendar (29 February). **leap'frog** *n* a game in which two people, *esp* children, take turns in vaulting each other, the one stooping or crouching to become the other's vaulting-horse; any similar vault or jump (also *fig*); a method of advancing against an enemy force in which one part of an army engages with the enemy whilst the rear part advances (*milit*). ♦ *vt* and *vi* (**leap'frogging**; **leap'frogged**) to jump (over) as in leapfrog (also *fig*); to go in advance of each other alternately (*milit*; also *fig*). **leap'ing-house** *n* (*Shakesp*) a brothel. **leap'ing-time** *n* (*Shakesp*) active youth. **leap second** *n* a second added to or subtracted from one scale of time whenever necessary, to bring that scale into harmony with another scale or with the rotation of the earth. **leap year** *n* a year with an intercalary day (*perh* because any anniversary after that day misses or leaps over a day of the week).
■ **by leaps and bounds** by a large amount or extent; very quickly. **leap in the dark** an act of which the consequences cannot be foreseen.

leap[2] /lēp/ (*dialect*) *n* a basket; a wicker net. [OE *lēap*]

leaprous, leaperous and **leaporous** old spellings of **leprous**.

leapt see **leap**[1].

lear[1], **leare, lere** or **leir** /lēr/ *vt* to teach (*archaic* and *Scot*); to learn (*Spenser*). ♦ *n* something which is learned, a lesson; lore; learning (*Scot*). [OE *lǣran* to teach]

lear[2], **leer** or **lehr** /lēr/ *n* a glass-annealing oven. [Ety uncertain]

learn /lûrn/ *vt* (*pat* and *pap* **learned** /lûrnd/ or **learnt** /lûrnt/) to be informed; to get to know; to gain knowledge, skill or ability in; to teach (now *non-standard*). ♦ *vi* to gain knowledge or skill. [OE *leornian*; Ger *lernen*; cf OE *lǣran* (Ger *lehren*) to teach]
■ **learnabil'ity** *n*. **learn'able** *adj* that can be learned. **learned** /lûrn'id/ *adj* having learning; knowledgeable about literature, etc; skilful. **learn'edly** *adv*. **learn'edness** *n*. **learn'er** *n* someone who learns; someone who is still in the early stages of learning. **learn'ing** *n* the gaining of knowledge; what is learned; knowledge; scholarship; skill in languages or science (*obs*).
□ **learned helplessness** *n* (*psychol*) the eventual passive acceptance of consistent violence, failure, oppression, etc, resulting in the cessation of all voluntary activity. **learning curve** *n* a graph used in education and research to represent progress in learning; the rate at which someone becomes familiar with a subject or activity (*inf*). **learning disability** *n* a condition of significant mental impairment in which the subject has difficulty in learning skills and acquiring information. **learning support** *n* a term applied to the education of pupils with learning difficulties. **learning support assistant** *n* a person who helps a teacher in the classroom, often concentrating on a pupil with learning difficulties.
■ **New Learning** the awakening to classical learning in the 16c, led (in England) by Colet, Erasmus, Warham, More, etc. **specific learning difficulty** any of various identifiable particular learning difficulties, such as dyslexia, dyspraxia etc.

leary same as **leery** (see under **leer**[1]).

lease[1] /lēs/ *n* a contract letting or renting a house, farm, etc for a term; tenure or rights under such a contract; the duration of such tenure; a hold upon, or prospect of continuance of, life, enjoyment, health, etc. ♦ *vt* to grant or take under lease. [Fr *laisser* to leave, from L *laxāre* to loosen, *laxus* loose]
■ **leas'able** *adj*. **leas'er** *n* a lessee.
□ **lease'back** *n* an arrangement whereby the buyer of a property leases it back to the seller (also called **sale and leaseback**). **lease'hold** *n* land or property held by the occupier under a lease; a tenure by lease. ♦ *adj* held by lease. **lease'holder** *n*. **lease'-lend** same as **lend-lease** (see under **lend**).
■ **a new lease of life** renewed strength or liveliness.

lease[2] /lēz/ (*dialect*) *vi* to glean. [OE *lesan* to gather]
■ **leas'ing** *n* gleaning.

lease³ /lēs/ n in weaving, a place or way of separating warp threads at the ends. [Perh connected with **leash**]
□ **lease'-band** or **lease'-rod** n a band or rod above and below which the warp threads are placed.

lease⁴ or **leaze** /lēz/ (dialect) n pasture. [See **leasow**]

leash /lēsh/ n a line for holding and controlling a dog, or a hawk; control by a leash, or (fig) as if by a leash; a set of three of anything, esp of animals. ◆ vt to hold by or as if by a leash; to bind. [OFr lesse (Fr laisse) a thong to hold a dog by, from L laxus loose]
■ **straining at the leash** impatient or eager to begin.

leasing /lē'zing/ (dialect) n falsehood, lies; lying. [OE lēasung, from lēasian to lie, from lēas false, loose; Gothic laus, OHGer los]
□ **leas'ing-mak'er** n a speaker of seditious words. **leas'ing-mak'ing** n.

leasow or **leasowe** /lē'sō or -zō/ (dialect) n pasture. ◆ vt and vi to pasture. [Same word as **lease⁴**, from OE læs a meadow, in oblique cases læswe; cf **mead²** and **meadow**]

least¹ /lēst/ adj (used as superl of **little**) little beyond all others; smallest. ◆ adv in the smallest or lowest degree. ◆ n the smallest amount; the lowest degree. [OE læst (adj and adv); compar læssa (adj), læs (adv); no positive]
■ **least'aways**, **least'ways** (dialect) or **least'wise** adv (rare or US) at least; however (used to tone down a preceding statement).
□ **least energy principle** n (phys) the principle stating that a system is in stable equilibrium only under those conditions for which its potential energy is a minimum. **least time principle** see **principle of least time** under **principle**.
■ **at least** or **at the least** at the lowest estimate; at any rate.

least² /lēst/ (Spenser) conj same as **lest¹**.

leasure (Spenser) an obsolete spelling of **leisure**.

leat or **leet** /lēt/ (dialect) n a trench for bringing water to a millwheel, etc. [OE gelæt]

leather /ledh'ər/ n a tanned, tawed, or otherwise dressed skin; a strap or other piece of leather; the ball in certain games; human skin (sl); (in pl) clothes, esp as worn by motorcyclists, or riding breeches made from leather. ◆ adj made of leather. ◆ vt to apply leather to; to thrash (inf). [OE lether leather; Du leder, Ger Leder]
■ **Leatherette'®** n cloth or paper made to look like leather. **leath'ering** n (inf) a thrashing. **leath'ern** adj of or like leather. **leath'ery** adj resembling leather; tough.
□ **leath'erback** n a large variety of sea-turtle (also called **leathery turtle**). **leath'ercloth** n a fabric coated on one face so as to resemble leather (also called **American cloth**). **leath'er-coat** n (Shakesp) an apple with a rough coat, the golden russet. **leath'ergoods** n pl objects and utensils made from leather. **leath'er-head** n a blockhead; an Australian friarbird with a bare head. **leath'erjacket** n a name applied to various fishes; a grub of the cranefly. **leath'er-knife** n a curved knife for cutting leather. **leath'er-lunged** /-lungd/ adj strong-lunged, able to shout vigorously. **leath'er-mouthed** /-mowdhd/ adj of certain fish, having a mouth like leather, smooth and toothless. **leath'erneck** n a sailor's name for a soldier or marine (from the leather neckband once worn), esp now a US marine. **leath'er-winged** adj (Spenser) having wings like leather. **leath'erwood** n a N American shrub or small tree (Cyrilla racemiflora) with tough leathery bark.
■ **artificial leather** any of certain plastic materials treated so as to simulate leather. **fair leather** leather not artificially coloured. **morocco leather** see **morocco**. **patent leather**, also **japanned** or **lacquered leather** see under **patent**. **Russia leather** see under **Russian**. **split leather** leather split by a machine, for trunk-covers, etc. **white leather** tawed leather, having its natural colour.

leave¹ /lēv/ vt (**leav'ing**; **left**) to abandon or resign; to quit or depart from; to have remaining at death; to bequeath; to refer for decision, action, etc; to allow, or cause, to remain. ◆ vi to depart; to desist; to cease. [OE læfan]
■ **leav'er** n someone who leaves, esp leaves school. **leav'ings** n pl things left; relics; refuse.
□ **leav'ing-shop** n (old sl) an unlicensed pawnshop.
■ **be left with** to have remaining. **leave a little** or **leave much** (or **a lot**) **to be desired** to be slightly or very inadequate or unsatisfactory. **leave alone** to let remain undisturbed. **leave be** to leave undisturbed. **leave behind** to forget to bring, or leave intentionally or accidentally; to go away from (also fig). **leave go** (inf) to let go. **leave it at that** to take no further action, make no further comment, etc. **leave it out!** (inf) stop it! **leave off** to desist, to terminate; to give up using. **leave out** to omit. **leave unsaid** to refrain from saying.

leave² /lēv/ n permission; liberty granted; a formal parting; a farewell; permission to depart or be absent; permitted absence from duty; the time of this; holidays. [OE lēaf permission, cognate with lēof dear; see **lief**]
□ **leave of absence** n permission to be absent, or the (time of) permitted absence. **leave'-taking** n bidding farewell.

■ **French leave** see under **French**. **take leave** to assume permission. **take leave of one's senses** to become irrational. **take (one's) leave (of)** to depart (from), say farewell (to).

leave³ /lēv/ (Spenser) vt to levy, to raise. [Fr lever]

leave⁴, **leaved**, **leaves** and **leavy** see **leaf**.

leaven /lev'n/ n the ferment, eg yeast, that makes dough rise; anything that makes a general change. ◆ vt to raise with leaven; to permeate with an influence. [Fr levain, from L levāmen, from levāre to raise, from levis light]
■ **leav'ening** n. **leav'enous** adj containing leaven.

Leavisite /lē'vi-sīt/ n a follower of the English literary critic and editor FR Leavis (1895–1978). ◆ adj of or relating to Leavis or the Leavisites.

leaze see **lease⁴**.

Lebanese /leb-ə-nēz'/ adj of or relating to (the) Lebanon, a republic on the eastern coast of the Mediterranean, or its people. ◆ n a native or citizen of (the) Lebanon.

lebbek /leb'ek/ n an Old World tropical mimosaceous timber tree (Albizzia lebbek). [Origin unknown]

Lebensraum /lā'bənz-rowm/ (Ger) n space inhabited by living things; room to live (and, if necessary, expand); specif territory claimed as necessary for economic growth (as by the Nazis).

lecanora /le-kə-nō'rə or -nö'/ n any lichen of the genus Lecanora, including the edible manna lichen of the steppes and deserts of Asia and Africa. [Gr lekanē a dish]

leccy /lek'i/ (inf) short form of **electricity**.

Le Chatelier's principle /lə sha-tel'yāz prin'si-pl/ n (chem) a principle stating that if any change of conditions is imposed on a system in equilibrium, the system will alter in such a way as to counteract the imposed change. [HL Le Chatelier (1850–1936), French chemist]

lecher /lech'ər/ n an excessively lewd man. ◆ vi to behave in a lewd way. [OFr lecheor, from lechier to lick; OHGer leccón, Ger lecken, Eng **lick**]
■ **lech** /lech/ n (back-formation from **lecher**; inf) a lecher; lust, a lewd desire. ◆ vi to lust. **lech'erous** adj lustful; provoking lust. **lech'erously** adv. **lech'erousness** n. **lech'ery** n.

Lecher wires /lehh'ər wīrz/ n pl two insulated parallel stretched wires, forming a microwave electromagnetic transmission line. [Ernst Lecher, Austrian physicist (1856–1926)]

lechwe /lēch'wē or lech'wä/ n an African antelope, smaller than the waterbuck to which it is related. [Bantu; cf Sotho letsa antelope]

lecithin /les'i-thin/ n any of a group of complex phospholipids that are an important component of biological membranes, found in the yolk of an egg, in the brain, blood, etc. [Gr lekithos egg yolk]
■ **lec'ithinase** n an enzyme which catalyses the hydrolysis of lecithin.

Leclanché cell /lə-klā'shä sel/ (chem) n a primary cell which has a positive electrode of carbon surrounded by a mixture of manganese dioxide and powdered carbon in a porous pot. [G Leclanché (1839–82), French chemist]

lect. abbrev: lecture; lecturer.

lectern /lek'tərn/ n (also (obs) **lec'turn** or **lett'ern**) a reading-desk (esp one from which the lessons are read in a church). [LL lectrīnum, from lectrum a pulpit, from Gr lektron a couch]

lectin /lek'tin/ n any of a number of naturally occurring substances, usu proteins derived from plants, which act like antibodies but are not formed in response to an antigen. [L lectus, pap of legere to choose, select]

lection /lek'shən/ n a reading; a lesson read in church. [L lectiō, -ōnis, from legere, lectum to read]
■ **lec'tionary** n a book of church lessons for each day.

lectisternium /lek-ti-stûr'ni-əm/ n an ancient Roman religious observance at which images of gods were placed on couches as if at a feast. [L, from lectus a couch, and sternere to spread]

lector /lek'tör or -tər/ n a reader, esp in a college; a lecturer who teaches in his own language in a foreign university; someone who has the duty of reading the Scripture lesson in a church service; an ecclesiastic in one of the minor orders, lowest in the Orthodox, second-lowest (next above doorkeeper) in the Roman Catholic. [L lector, -ōris, from legere, lectum to read]
■ **lec'torate** n. **lec'torship** n. **lec'tress** n a female reader. **lectrice** /-trēs'/ n a woman who teaches as a lector.
■ **lector benevole** /bi-nev'ə-li or be-nev'o-le/ kind reader.

lecture /lek'chər/ n a lesson or period of instruction; a discourse on any subject, esp a professorial or tutorial discourse; a long, formal, stern reproof; reading (archaic); an expository and discursive religious discourse; an endowed lectureship, eg the Bampton, Hulsean, etc. ◆ vt to instruct by lectures; to instruct authoritatively; to reprove or scold lengthily and sternly. ◆ *vi* to give a lecture or lectures. [L *lectūra*, from *legere*, *lectum* to read]

■ **lec'turer** *n* a person who lectures; a college or university instructor of lower rank than a professor; one of a class of preachers in the Church of England, supported by voluntary contributions. **lec'tureship** *n* the post or job of a lecturer; the foundation of a course of lectures.

lecturn see **lectern**.

lecythus /*les'i-thəs*/ *n* the Latinized form of **lekythos**. [See **lekythos**] ■ **lecythidā'ceous** *adj*. **Lec'ythis** *n* the monkey pot genus of **Lecythidā'ceae**, a family of tropical trees, including the Brazil nut, cannonball-tree, and anchovy-pear.

LED *abbrev* : light-emitting diode (see under **light**[1]).

led /*led*/ *pat* and *pap* of **lead**[1]. *adj* under leading or control, *esp* of a farm or place held along with another by a non-resident. □ **led captain** *n* an obsequious attendant, a henchman. **led horse** *n* a spare horse led by a servant; a sumpter horse or pack-horse.

ledden /*led'n*/ (*Spenser*) *n* language, dialect or speech. [OE *lēden*, *lēoden*, language, from *lēode* people, confused with *læden* Latin, from L *Latīnum* Latin]

lederhosen /*lā'dər-hō-zən*/ *n pl* short leather trousers with braces. [Ger, leather trousers]

ledge /*lej*/ *n* a shelf-like projection; a ridge or shelf of rocks; a lode or vein (of ore or rock); an attached strip; a raised edge (*obs*). [ME *legge*, prob from the root of **lay**[1]] ■ **ledged** *adj*. **ledg'y** *adj* having many ledges.

ledger /*lej'ər*/, formerly also **lidger** /*lij'ər*/ *n* a document containing the principal financial records of a company, in which details of all transactions, assets and liabilities are kept, and in which the records in all the other books are entered; a register or account book (*US*); a book that lies permanently in one place (*obs*); a horizontal timber in scaffolding; (also **leg'er**) ledger bait, ledger tackle or ledger line (*angling*); a flat grave-slab; (also **leidger**, **lieger** or **leiger**) a resident, *esp* an ambassador (*obs*). ◆ *adj* resident or stationary. ◆ *vi* to fish with a ledger line. [Appar from OE *licgan* to lie, *lecgan* to lay] □ **ledger** or **leger bait** *n* (*angling*) fishing bait that is anchored to the bottom, the **ledger tackle** being weighted. **ledger** or **leger line** *n* a line fixed in one place (*angling*); a short line added above or below the stave where required (*music*).

ledum /*lē'dəm*/ *n* a plant of the Labrador tea genus (*Ledum*) of ericaceous plants. [Latinized from Gr *lēdon* ladanum]

lee[1] /*lē*/ *n* shelter; the sheltered side; the quarter toward which the wind blows; tranquillity (*obs*). ◆ *adj* sheltered; on or towards the sheltered side, *opp* to *windward* or *weather*. [OE *hlēo(w)*, genitive *hlēowes* shelter; ON *hlé*, LGer *lee* ; see also **lew**[1]] ■ **lee'ward** (also (*naut*) /*lū'ərd* or *loo'ərd*/) *adj* relating to, or in, the direction towards which the wind blows. ◆ *adv* towards the lee. ◆ *n* the lee side or quarter. □ **lee'-board** *n* a board lowered on the lee side of a vessel, to lessen drift to leeward. **lee gage** or **gauge** *n* position to leeward, *opp* to *weather gage*. **lee licht of the mune** *n* (in Scottish ballads) *perh* the pleasant moonlight. **lee shore** *n* a shore on a ship's lee side. **lee side** *n* the sheltered side. **lee tide** *n* a tide moving in the same direction as the wind. **lee wave** *n* (*meteorol*) a stationary wave, sometimes dangerous to aircraft, set up under particular conditions in an airstream to the lee of a hill or mountain range over which air is flowing. **lee'way** *n* leeward drift; room to manoeuvre, latitude. ■ **make up leeway** to make up for lost time, ground, etc.

lee[2] /*lē*/ (*Spenser*) *n* a river. [Poss from the River *Lee*]

lee[3] see **lea**[1], **lees** and **lie**[1].
■ **leear** /*lē'ər*/ *n* Scots form of **liar**.

leech[1] /*lēch*/ *n* a bloodsucking annelid worm, *usu* aquatic; someone who attaches himself or herself to another for personal gain; a physician (*archaic*). ◆ *vt* to apply leeches to (a former medical treatment, drawing blood from a patient); to cling to like a leech; to drain. ◆ *vi* (*usu* with *on*) to cling (to). [OE *læce*, *perh* orig two different words] ■ **leech'craft** *n* (*archaic*) the art of medicine. **leech'dom** *n* (*archaic*) a remedy or prescription.

leech[2] /*lēch*/ *n* the side edge of a sail. [Cf ON *līk* ; Dan *lig* ; Swed *lik* a bolt rope]

leechee see **lychee**.

Lee Enfield /*lē en'fēld*/ *n* a type of rifle used by the British Army in the Boer War and World Wars I and II. [From JP *Lee*, US designer (1831–1904), and *Enfield*, the town where it was manufactured]

leek /*lēk*/ *n* a vegetable (*Allium porrum*) of the onion genus, with broad flat leaves and a slim white bulb which extends into a long stem, taken as the national emblem of Wales. [OE *lēac* leek, plant; cf **charlock**, **garlic** and **hemlock**]

■ **eat the leek** (*Shakesp*) to be compelled to take back one's words or put up with insulting treatment.

lee-lane /*lē'lān'* / (*Scot*) *n* used only in phrases (**by**) **my**, **his**, **her**, etc **lee-lane** quite alone (also **lee'some-lane**). [**lee** of obscure origin; see **lone**]

leep[1] /*lēp*/ *vt* to plaster with cow-dung. [Hindi *līpnā*]

leep[2] /*lēp*/ (*dialect*) *vt* to boil, to scald. [Cf ON and Icel *hleypa* to curdle, from ON *hlaupa* to leap]

leer[1] /*lēr*/ *n* a sly, sidelong or lecherous look; complexion or colour (*Shakesp*). ◆ *vi* to look lecherously; to glance sideways. [OE *hlēor* face, cheek] ■ **leer'ing** *n* and *adj*. **leer'ingly** *adv*. **leer'y** *adj* cunning; wary (with *of* or *about*).

leer[2] see **lear**[2].

Leerie /*lē'ri*/ (*Scot*) *n* a nickname for a lamplighter, in full **Lee'rie-licht'-the-lamp**.

lees /*lēz*/ *n pl* sediment that forms during the fermentation or aging of an alcoholic liquor, eg wine; the worst part or parts. [Fr *lie*, from LL *lia*] ■ **lee** *n sing* (*rare*).

leese /*lēz*/ (*Spenser* and *Shakesp*) *vt* (*pat* **lore** /*lōr* or *lör*/; *pap* **lore** or **lorn** in *Spenser*, in the sense of left) to lose. [OE *lēosan* (in compounds) to lose]

leesome-lane see **lee-lane**.

leet[1] /*lēt*/ or **leetspeak** /*lēt'spēk*/ *n* a form of writing used *esp* by young people on the Internet, characterized by unconventional spelling and grammar and the use of numbers and symbols to replace many letters. [Altered from **élite**]

leet[2] /*lēt*/ (*hist*) *n* a court-leet; its jurisdiction or district; the right to hold it. [Anglo-Fr *lete* or Anglo-L *leta*, poss from OE *læth* lathe (of a county)]

leet[3] /*lēt*/ (*Scot*) *n* a selected list of candidates for a position. [Origin uncertain, *perh* Anglo-Fr *litte* a list, or aphetic form of *élite*] ■ **short leet** a select list for the final choice.

leet[4] see **leat**.

leet[5] see **lite**[2].

leetle /*lē'tl*/ an old-fashioned affectation for **little**.

leeward and **leeway** see under **lee**[1].

leeze see **leeze me** under **lief**.

left[1] /*left*/ *adj* on, for, or belonging to that side or part of the body, etc which in man has normally the weaker and less skilful hand, *opp* to *right* ; on that side from the point of view of a person looking downstream, a soldier looking at the enemy, a president looking at an assembly, an actor looking at the audience; on the west side from the point of view of a person looking north; in politics, relatively liberal, democratic, progressive, innovating; inclined towards socialism or communism. ◆ *n* the left side; the region to the left side; the left hand; a blow with the left hand; a glove, shoe, etc for the left hand or foot, etc; a turning to the left; the more progressive, democratic, socialist, radical or actively innovating party or wing (from its sitting in some legislatures to the president's left); a shot from the left barrel of a gun or a bird killed by this. ◆ *adv* on or towards the left. [ME *lift*, *left*, from OE (Kentish) *left* weak, worthless; cf OE *lyftādl* paralysis] ■ **left'ie** or **left'y** *n* (*inf*) a leftist; a left-handed person. **left'ish** *adj*. **left'ism** *n* the principles of the political left. **left'ist** *adj* and *n*. **left'ward** *adj* and *adv* towards the left; on the left side; more left-wing. ◆ *n* (*rare*) the region on the left side. **left'wardly** or **left'wards** *adv*. □ **Left Bank** *n* the artistic quarter of Paris on the south bank of the Seine. **left'-bank** *adj*. **left'-click** *vi* to press and release the left-hand button on a computer mouse. ◆ *n* an act of doing this. **left'-field** *n* in baseball, the area in the outfield to the left facing from the plate. ◆ *adj* (*inf*, *esp US*) out of the ordinary, bizarre. **left'-foot'ed** *adj* performed with the left foot; having more skill or strength in the left foot. **left'-foot'er** *n* (*sl*) a Roman Catholic. **left'-hand** *adj* on the left side; towards the left; with thread or strands turning to the left; performed with the left hand. **left-hand drive** *n* a driving mechanism on the left side of a vehicle which is intended to be driven on the right-hand side of the road; a vehicle with a driving mechanism of this type. **left'-hand'ed** *adj* having the left hand stronger and readier than the right; for the left hand; counter-clockwise; forming a mirror image of the right-handed form; awkward; unlucky; dubious (as in *a left-handed compliment*); (of a marriage) morganatic. ◆ *adv* in the manner of a left-handed person. **left'-hand'edly** *adv*. **left'-hand'edness** *n*. **left'-hand'er** *n* a blow with the left hand; a left-handed person. **left'-hand'iness** *n* awkwardness. **left'-leaning** *adj* tending to hold left-wing political opinions. **left'-of-centre** *adj* in politics, etc, towards the left, but only moderately so. **left wing** *n* the political left; the wing on the left side of an army, football pitch, etc. **left'-wing** *adj* playing on the left wing; belonging to the more leftwardly inclined section; (having opinions which are) progressive, radical, socialist, etc.

left'-wing'er *n* a person with left-wing views or who supports the left wing of a party, etc; a player on the left wing.

■ **have two left feet** to be clumsy or awkward, *esp* in dancing. **left, right and centre** in, from, etc all directions; everywhere. **over the left (shoulder)** (*obs sl*) contrariwise.

left² /*left*/ *pat* and *pap* of **leave¹**.

□ **left'-off** *adj* laid aside or discarded. **left'over** *adj* remaining over from a previous occasion. ◆*n* a thing left over; a survival; food uneaten at a meal (*usu in pl*). **left-luggage office** *n* a room at an airport or a railway or bus station where, for a small fee, one can safely leave one's luggage for a time.

lefte /*left*/ (*Spenser*) *pat* lifted.

leg /*leg*/ *n* a limb used for walking; the human lower limb, or sometimes the part between knee and ankle; a long, slender support of eg a table; a branch or limb of anything forked or jointed, eg a pair of compasses; a single short trunk, as of a fruit bush not managed as a stool (*qv*), from which branches grow (*hortic*); the part of a garment that covers the leg; a distinct part or stage of a course or journey; in sports, one event or part in a contest consisting of two or more parts or events; the legside of a cricket field; a backward movement of the leg in making a bow (*archaic*); a swindler, *esp* at a race-course (for *blackleg*; *old sl*). ◆ *vt* and *vi* to walk briskly, run or dash away (*vt* with *it*); to propel (a barge) through a canal tunnel by pushing with the feet on the wall or roof. ◆ *adj* on the legside of a cricket field. [ON *leggr* a leg; Dan *læg*, Swed *lägg*]

■ **legged** /*legd* or *leg'id*/ *adj* (*usu as combining form*) having (a certain type, number, etc of) legs. **legg'er** *n* a bargeman who legs; a worker or machine that makes stocking-legs. **legg'iness** *n*. **legg'ing** *n* an outer and extra covering for the leg, eg (in *pl*) thick, footless tights, *usu* of wool or knitted fabric, or fashion varieties made in other, thinner materials; an outer and extra covering for the lower leg. **legg'ism** *n* (*archaic*) the character of a blackleg. **legg'y** *adj* having noticeably long slim legs; (of a plant) having a long stem. **leg'less** *adj* having no legs; very drunk (*inf*). **leg'lessness** *n*. **leg'let** *n* any object worn on the leg for decoration.

□ **leg bail** see **give leg bail** under **bail¹**. **leg before** and **leg before wicket** *n* (*cricket*) a way of being given out when the ball has struck the batsman's legs, or another part of his body, without having made contact with the bat, and would otherwise have hit the wicket (*abbrev* **lbw**). **leg break** *n* (*cricket*) a ball that breaks from the legside towards the offside on pitching. **leg'-bus'iness** *n* (*sl*) ballet-dancing. **leg bye** *n* (*cricket*) a run made after the ball has touched any part of the batsman's person except his hands or bat, credited to the batsman's team but not his individual score. **leg'-cutter** *n* (*cricket*) a fast bowler's delivery that moves from leg to off after pitching. **leg'-guard** *n* a cricketer's pad. **leg'-iron** *n* a fetter for the leg. **leg'-man** or **-woman** *n* a person whose work involves journeys outside the office; an assistant who runs errands or gathers information; a newspaper reporter. **leg-of-mutt'on** *adj* shaped like a leg of mutton, eg a triangular sail; (of a sleeve) tight on the lower arm and full between elbow and shoulder. **leg'-over** *n* (*vulgar sl*) an act of sexual intercourse. **leg'-pull** *n* a good-humoured hoax, bluff or practical joke. **leg'-puller** *n*. **leg'-pulling** *n*. **leg'-rest** *n* a support for the legs. **leg'room** *n* space for one's legs, as in a car. **leg'-show** *n* an entertainment depending mainly on the exhibition of women's legs. **leg'side** *n* that half of a cricket field on the side on which the batsman stands when waiting to receive the ball, separated from the offside by an imaginary line drawn from wicket to wicket. ◆ *adj* on the legside. **leg slip** *n* (*cricket*) a fielder or position slightly behind the batsman on the legside. **leg spin** *n* (*cricket*) spin imparted to a ball to cause a leg break. **leg'-spin** *adj*. **leg spinner** *n* (*cricket*) someone who bowls leg breaks. **leg theory** *n* (*cricket*) the policy of bowling short-pitched leg-side balls persistently at the batsman's body with a large number of leg-side fielders close to the wicket; bodyline. **leg warmers** *n pl* long footless socks. **leg'wear** *n* anything worn on the legs, eg socks, stockings, etc. **leg-woman** see **leg-man** above. **leg'work** *n* (*inf*) work involving much travelling, searching, etc.

■ **change the leg** (of a horse) to change the gait. **feel one's legs** to begin to support oneself on one's legs. **find one's legs** to become familiar or accustomed. **fine**, **long**, **short** and **square leg** (*cricket*) see under **fine**, etc. **get one's leg over** (*vulgar sl*; of a man) to have sex. **give someone a leg up** to give someone a help or hoist in mounting, climbing, etc (also *fig*). **in high leg** (*archaic*) in great excitement. **not have a leg to stand on** to have no case at all. **on one's last legs** see under **last¹**. **on one's legs** standing, *esp* while speaking. **pull someone's leg** to make a playful attempt to hoax or deceive someone. **shake a leg** (*inf*) to hurry up. **show a leg** to make an appearance; to get up. **upon one's legs** in an independent position.

leg. *abbrev* : legal; legate; legato; legislation; legislative; legislature.

legacy /*leg'ə-si*/ *n* that which is left to one by will; a bequest of personal property; something handed on by or left unfinished by a predecessor or previous owner. ◆ *adj* (*comput*) denoting software,

data, etc that is outdated or discontinued. [L *lēgāre*, *-ātum* to leave by will]

■ **leg'atary** *n* a legatee. **legatee'** *n* a person to whom a legacy is left. **legator** /*li-gā' tər*/ *n* a person who leaves a legacy.

□ **legacy duty** *n* a duty levied on legacies, varying according to degree of relationship, abolished in 1950. **leg'acy-hunter** *n* a person who courts those likely to leave legacies.

■ **cumulative legacy** an additional legacy to the same person. **demonstrative legacy** a general legacy with a particular fund named from which it is to be satisfied. **general legacy** a sum of money payable out of the assets generally. **residuary legatee** the person to whom the remainder of the property is left after all claims are discharged. **specific legacy** a legacy of a definite thing, such as jewels, pictures, a sum of stock in the funds, etc. **substitutional legacy** a second legacy to the same person instead of the first.

legal /*lē'gl*/ *adj* relating to, or according to, law; lawful; created by law; according to the Mosaic law or dispensation (*theol*). [L *lēgālis*, from *lēx*, *lēgis* law]

■ **legalese'** *n* complicated legal jargon. **lē'galism** *n* strict adherence to law; the doctrine that salvation depends on strict adherence to the law, as distinguished from the doctrine of salvation by grace (*theol*); the tendency to observe letter or form rather than spirit, or to regard things from the point of view of law. **lē'galist** *n* and *adj* (someone) inclined to legalism; (someone) knowledgeable about the law. **legalis'tic** *adj*. **legalist'ically** *adv*. **lēgality** /*-gal' i-ti*/ *n*. **legalizā'tion** or **-s-** *n* a process whereby something previously unlawful is made lawful. **lē'galize** or **-ise** *vt* to make lawful. **lē'gally** *adv*.

□ **legal aid** *n* financial assistance given to those unable to pay the full costs of legal proceedings. **legal eagle** *n* (*inf*) a bright, discerning lawyer. **legal fiction** *n* a fact or point of law that is probably no longer true but is held to be so as a further point of law depends upon it. **legal high** *n* a substance that is not classed as an illegal drug but is consumed to achieve a similar effect. **legal holiday** *n* (*US*) a day established as a holiday by law. **legal separation** *n* another name for **judicial separation** (see under **judicial**). **legal tender** *n* banknotes or coins which by law must be accepted as payment of a debt, or for a product or service; the currency of exchange, notes and coin, in a particular country. **legal year** see under **year**.

legate /*leg' it*/ *n* an ambassador, *esp* from the Pope; a delegate deputy, *esp orig* a Roman general's lieutenant; the governor of a Papal province (*hist*). [L *lēgātus*, from *lēgāre* to send with a commission]

■ **leg'ateship** *n*. **leg'atine** /*-ə-tīn*/ *adj* of or relating to a legate. **legation** /*li-gā'shən*/ *n* a diplomatic mission, body of delegates, or its official quarters; the office or status of a legate; a Papal province (*hist*).

legatee see under **legacy**.

legato /*le-gä'tō*/ (*music*) *adj* and *adv* (*superl* **legatis'simo**) smooth or smoothly, the notes running into each other without a break. ◆ *n* (*pl* **legat'os**) a legato passage or manner. [Ital, bound, tied, from L *ligāre*, *-ātum* to tie]

legator see under **legacy**.

legend¹ /*lej'ənd*/ *n* a traditional story (*orig* a story of a saint's life); an untrue or unhistorical story; a collection of such stories; a body of tradition; a person having a special place in popular opinion for their striking qualities or deeds, real or fictitious; the body of fact and fiction gathered round such a person; a motto, inscription, or explanatory words (with eg a picture); a book of readings from the Bible and saints' lives (*obs*). ◆ *adj* very famous. [Fr *légende*, from LL *legenda* to be read]

■ **leg'endarily** *adv*. **leg'endary** *n* a book or writer of legends. ◆ *adj* relating to, of the nature of, consisting of, or described in, legend; very famous; romantic; fabulous. **leg'endist** *n* a writer of legends. **leg'endry** *n*.

legend² /*lej'ənd*/ (*Shakesp*) *n* for **legion**.

leger¹ /*lej'ər*/ (*obs sl*) *n* someone who sells short weight in charcoal; someone who swindles by scamping work, using bad materials. [Poss Fr *léger* light]

■ **leg'ering** *n*.

leger² see **ledger**.

legerdemain /*lej-ər-də-mān'*/ *n* dexterous trickery or conjuring, sleight-of-hand; jugglery. ◆ *adj* juggling; tricky. [Literally light of hand, from Fr *léger* light, *de* of, and *main* hand]

legerity /*li-jer'i-ti*/ *n* lightness; nimbleness. [Fr *légèreté*, from *léger* light, from assumed LL *leviārius*, from L *levis* light]

legge /*leg*/ (*Shakesp*) *n* dregs of the people. [**lag¹**]

legger, **leggism**, etc see under **leg**.

leghorn /*leg'hörn* or *li-görn'*/ *n* fine straw plait made in Tuscany; a hat made of this; (with *cap*) /*li-görn'*/ a small breed of domestic fowl. [*Leghorn* (Ital *Legorno*, now *Livorno*, L *Liburnus*) in Italy]

legible /lej'i-bl/ adj clear enough to be deciphered; easy to read; readable (rare). [L legibilis, from legere to read]
■ **leg'ibleness** or **legibil'ity** n. **leg'ibly** adv.

legion /lē'jən/ n in ancient Rome, a body of three to six thousand soldiers; a military force, applied esp to several in French history; a very great number. ◆ adj multitudinous. [L legiō, -ōnis, from legere to levy]
■ **le'gionary** adj of, relating to, or consisting of, a legion or legions; containing a great number. ◆ n a member of a legion. **le'gioned** adj set out in legions. **legionell'a** n (pl **legionell'as** or **legionell'ae** /-ē/) a genus of bacteria that can cause respiratory diseases; a disease caused by such bacteria (also called **legionellō'sis**; see also **legionnaire's disease** below). **lēgionnaire** /-när'/ (Fr légionnaire) n a member of the British, Foreign, etc Legion.
❏ **legionnaire's** or **legionnaires' disease** n a severe, sometimes fatal, pneumonia-like disease caused by the bacterium Legionella pneumophilia (so named after an outbreak of the disease at an American Legion convention in Philadelphia in 1976). **Legion of Honour** n a French order instituted in 1802 by Napoleon I.
■ **American Legion** an association of US war veterans. **British Legion** (in full **Royal British Legion**) an ex-servicemen's and -women's association. **Foreign Legion** a legion composed of foreigners, esp that in the French Army organized in 1831. **their name is Legion** they are too many to number (from Bible, Mark 5.9). **Thundering Legion** in Christian tradition, a body of soldiers under Marcus Aurelius, whose prayers brought down a thunderstorm and destroyed the enemy.

legis. abbrev : legislation; legislative; legislature.

legislate /lej'is-lāt/ vi to make laws; to pass law in the form of an Act of Parliament or by delegated legislation. [L lēx, lēgis law, latum serving as supine to ferre to bear]
■ **legislā'tion** n. **leg'islătive** (or /-lə-tiv/) adj law-making; having the power to make laws; relating to legislation. ◆ n a law-making power; a law-making body. **leg'islatively** adv. **leg'islator** n a lawgiver; a member of a legislative body. **legislatorial** /-lə-tö'ri-əl/ adj of or relating to, or of the nature of, a legislator, legislature or legislation. **leg'islatorship** n. **leg'islatress** n (rare) a female legislator. **leg'islature** n a law-making body.

legist /lē'jist/ n a person knowledgeable about the law. [Fr légiste]

legit /li- or lə-jit'/ (inf) adj short form of **legitimate**.

legitim /lej'i-tim/ (Scots law) n that which children are entitled to out of a deceased father's moveable estate (also called **bairn's-part**). [L lēgitima (pars) lawful (part), from lēx law]

legitimate /li-jit'i-mət or (rare) -māt/ adj lawful; born in wedlock, or having the legal status of those born in wedlock; related, derived, or transmitted by birth in wedlock or subsequently legitimated; as used by believers in the theory of divine right, according to strict rule of heredity and primogeniture; logically inferred; following by natural sequence; genuine; conforming to an accepted standard; of or relating to legitimate drama (theatre). ◆ vt /-māt/ to make lawful; to recognize as a legitimate child. [LL lēgitimāre, -ātum, from L lēgitimus lawful, from lēx law]
■ **legit'imacy** /-mə-si/ n the fact or state of being legitimate. **legit'imately** adv. **legit'imateness** n. **legitimā'tion** n the act of making legitimate, esp of conferring the privileges of legitimate birth. **legit'imism** n. **legit'imist** n a person who believes in the right of royal succession according to the principle of heredity and primogeniture. **legitimizā'tion** or **-s-** n. **legit'imize** or **-ise** vt to legitimate.
❏ **legitimate drama** n drama of typical form, normal comedy and tragedy, distinguished from opera, musicals, variety, etc, as well as cinema and television; drama of lasting relevance and value. **legitimate pollination** n in heterostyled plants, pollination of long styles from long stamens, and short from short.

legless, etc, **leglet** see under **leg**.

leglin, leglan or **leglen** /leg'lən/ (Scot) n a milking-pail. [Cf **laggen**]
■ **cast a leglin girth** to have an illegitimate child.

Lego® /leg'ō/ n a toy consisting of small interlocking plastic pieces, principally bricks for constructing model buildings, etc. ◆ adj (fig) of buildings, simply and cheaply constructed, jerry-built. [Dan leg godt play well, invented by Godfred Kirk Christiansen]
❏ **Leg'oland** n (fig) an area of simply and cheaply constructed buildings, from Legoland a model village in Jutland, made with Lego.

leguan or **leguaan** /leg'ū-ən/ (S Afr) n a large monitor lizard of the genus Varanus. [Du, from Fr l'iguane the iguana]

legume /leg'ūm or li-gūm'/ n any plant of the pea or bean family, including lentils; the seed pod of such a plant, esp when eaten as a vegetable. [L legūmen pulse, prob from legere to gather]
■ **legū'min** n a globulin obtained from peas, beans, lentils, etc. **Legūminō'sae** /-sē/ n pl an order of angiosperms characterized by the legume or seed pod, including Papilionaceae, Mimosaceae, and Caesalpiniaceae. **legū'minous** adj relating to pulse vegetables; of or relating to the Leguminosae; bearing legumes.

lehr see **lear²**.

Lehrjahre /lār'yä-rə/ n (sing or pl; also without cap) an apprenticeship (usu fig). [Ger, from lehren to teach, and Jahre years]

lei¹ /lā'ē/ n a garland or wreath, esp of flowers, shells or feathers. [Hawaiian]

lei² see **leu**.

Leibnitzian or **Leibnizian** /līb-nit'si-ən/ adj relating to the great German philosopher and mathematician Gottfried Wilhelm Leibniz (1646–1716).
■ **Leibnitz'ianism** or **Leibniz'ianism** n the philosophy of Leibniz, the doctrine of primordial monads, pre-established harmony, and fundamental optimism on the principle of sufficient reason.

Leicester /les'tər/ adj of a long-woolled breed of sheep that originated in Leicestershire. ◆ n a sheep of that breed.
❏ **Leicester** (or **Leicestershire**) **plan** n a comprehensive school system, started in Leicestershire in 1957, which avoids the use of very large schools and also makes full use of free modern methods of learning.
■ **Red Leicester** a kind of hard cheese orig made in Leicestershire.

Leics. abbrev : Leicestershire.

leidger and **leiger** see **ledger**.

Leip. abbrev : Leipzig.

leipoa /lī-pō'ə/ n any bird of the genus Leipoa of Australian mound-birds. [Gr leipein to leave, and ōon an egg]

Leipzig option /līp-(t)zig op'shən/ n the strategic possibility of toppling a government, regime, etc by mass demonstrations. [From the use of this method in defeating Communism in East Germany in 1989]

leir see **lear¹**.

leish /lēsh/ (Scot) adj active, supple or athletic. [Origin uncertain]

leishmania /lēsh-mā'ni-ə or -man'i-ə/ n (pl **leishman'ia**, **leishman'iae** /-i-ē/ or **leishman'ias**) any protozoan of the genus Leishmania of Protozoa (family Trypanosomidae), or any protozoan of the Trypanosomidae in a non-flagellated form. [Named after Sir William Leishman (1865–1926), who discovered the cause of kala-azar]
■ **leishmaniasis** /lēsh-mən-ī'ə-sis/ or **leishmaniō'sis** n (pl **leishmanī'ases** or **leishmanī'oses**) any of various diseases, such as kala-azar, due to infection with any protozoan of the genus Leishmania.

leisler /līz'lər/ n a small black bat (Nyctalus leisleri) named after the 19c zoologist TP Leisler (also **Leisler's bat**).

leister /lē'stər/ (Scot) n a salmon-spear. ◆ vt to spear with a leister. [ON ljōstr ; Dan lyster]

leisure /lezh'ər or (US and old) lā'zhər/ n time away from work; freedom from occupation, free time; convenient opportunity. ◆ adj free from necessary business; for casual wear; for or relating to leisure, recreational time or pursuits. ◆ vi (archaic) to have leisure. ◆ vt (archaic) to make leisurely. [OFr leisir, from L licēre to be permitted]
■ **leis'urable** adj leisured; leisurely. **leis'urably** adv. **leis'ured** adj having much leisure. **leis'ureliness** n. **leis'urely** adj and adv not hasty or hastily.
❏ **leisure centre** n a centre providing a variety of recreational facilities. **leisure suit** n a loose-fitting garment comprising matching top and trousers made from a soft fabric. **leis'urewear** n comfortable, casual clothing worn on informal or recreational occasions.
■ **at leisure** free from occupation; without hurrying. **at one's leisure** at one's ease or convenience.

leitmotiv or **leitmotif** /līt'mō-tēf or -tēf'/ n (in opera, etc) a musical theme associated with a person or a thought, recurring when the person appears on the stage or the thought becomes prominent in the action; a recurring theme in literature; any recurring theme. [Ger, from leiten to lead, and Motiv a motif]

lek¹ /lek/ n the standard monetary unit of Albania (100 qintars); a coin or note of this value.

lek² /lek/ n the piece of ground on which the blackcocks and cock capercailzies gather to display; the season during which this displaying takes place. ◆ vi to gather and display at a lek. [Appar from Swed leka to play]
■ **lekk'ing** n.

leke Spenserian form of **leak** (adj).

lekker /lek'ə/ (S Afr inf) adj pleasant; enjoyable. [Afrik, from Du, literally, tasty]

lekythos /lē'ki-thos/ (ancient hist) n a narrow-necked Greek flask. [Gr lēkythos]

LEM or **lem** /lem/ abbrev : Lunar Excursion Module.

leman /lem'ən or lē'mən/ (*archaic*) *n* (*pl* **lem'ans**) a lover; a sweetheart; a paramour; later chiefly applied derogatorily to women. [OE *lēof* lief, and *mann* man]

leme see **leam**[1].

lemel or **limail** /lē'mel/ *n* the dust and filings of metal. [ME *lemaille*, from MFr *lemaille*, from OFr *limer* to file, from L *limāre* to file]

lemma[1] /lem'ə/ *n* (*pl* **lemm'as** or **lemm'ata**) a preliminary proposition (*maths*); a premise taken for granted (*maths*); a theme, argument, heading or headword. [Gr *lēmma, -atos*, from the root of *lambanein* to take]
■ **lemmatizā'tion** or **-s-** *n*. **lemm'atize** or **-ise** *vt* to organize (words in a text) so that inflected and variant forms are grouped under the appropriate lemma.

lemma[2] /lem'ə/ (*bot*) *n* (*pl* **lemm'as** or **lemm'ata**) the lower of the two bracts enclosing a floret of a grass. [Gr *lemma* rind, from *lepein* to peel]

lemming /lem'ing/ *n* a northern rodent (of the genus *Lemmus* and others) closely related to voles; a fool, *esp* a person unthinkingly following others to disaster (from the rodent's reputed habit of rushing en masse into the sea to drown when migrating; *inf*). [Norw *lemming*]

Lemna /lem'nə/ *n* the duckweed genus, giving its name to the family **Lemna'ceae**, free-floating spathifloral monocotyledons. [Gr *lemna* water starwort]

Lemnian /lem'ni-ən/ *adj* relating to *Lemnos* in the Aegean Sea.
□ **Lemnian earth** *n* an earthy clay from Lemnos. **Lemnian ruddle** *n* a red ochre found in Lemnos.

lemniscate /lem-nis'kāt/ (*maths*) *n* the locus of the foot of the perpendicular from the centre of a conic upon the tangent. [L *lēmniscātus* ribboned, from Gr *lēmniskos* a ribbon or bandage]

lemon[1] /lem'ən/ *n* a pale yellow oval citrus fruit with sour-tasting flesh; the tree that bears it; a pale yellow colour; something or someone disappointing, worthless, unattractive or defective (*inf*). ◆ *adj* tasting of or flavoured with lemon; (coloured) pale yellow. ◆ *vt* to flavour with lemon. [Fr *limon* (now the lime); cf Pers *līmūn*; cf **lime**[2]]
■ **lemonade'** *n* a drink (still or carbonated) made with lemon juice or flavoured with lemon. **lem'ony** *adj*.
□ **lemon balm** same as **balm** (*Melissa officinalis*). **lemon cheese** or **lemon curd** *n* a soft cooked paste of lemons, eggs, butter and sugar, used as a spread. **lem'on-coloured** *adj*. **lemon drop** *n* a hard lemon-flavoured sweet. **lem'onfish** *n* (*NZ*) shark meat sold as food. **lemon geranium** *n* a pelargonium (*Pelargonium crispum*) with fragrant leaves. **lemon grass** *n* a fragrant perennial grass (*Cymbopogon* or *Andropogon*) of tropical climates, smelling like lemon and yielding an essential oil. **lemon law** *n* (*US*) a law protecting car-buyers against defects within a certain period after purchase. **lemon peel** *n* the skin of lemons, sometimes candied. **lemon squash** *n* a concentrated lemon drink. **lemon squeezer** *n* a small press for extracting the juice of lemons. **lem'on-weed** *n* sea-mat. **lem'onwood** *n* a small New Zealand tree (*Pittosporum eugenioides*). **lem'on-yell'ow** *n* and *adj*.
■ **hand someone a lemon** (*sl*) to swindle someone. **the answer is a lemon** (*inf*) one is given an unsatisfactory answer or no answer at all.

lemon[2] /lem'ən/ *n* a species of sole differing in its markings from the common sole (also **lemon sole** or **sand sole**); a kind of dab resembling a sole (also called **lemon dab**, **lemon sole**, **smear dab** or **smooth dab**). [Fr *limande*]

lempira /lem-pē'rə/ *n* the standard monetary unit of Honduras (100 centavos). [*Lempira*, a department of Honduras named after a native chief]

lemur /lē'mər/ *n* any member of the **Lemuroidea** /lem-ū-roid'i-ə/ or **Prosimiae**, a group of long-tailed mammals related to the monkeys, forest dwellers, mainly nocturnal, common in Madagascar (*pl* **lē'murs**); an ancient Roman ghost of the dead (*pl* **lemures** /lem'ū-rēz/). [L *lemurēs* ghosts]
■ **Lemuria** /li-mū'ri-ə/ *n* (*pl*) an ancient Roman festival (9, 11 and 13 May) when ghosts were exorcized; (*sing*) a hypothetical vanished continent where the Indian Ocean now lies, posited to explain the distribution of lemurs. **lemurian** /li-mū'ri-ən/, **lemurine** /lem'ū-rīn/ or **lem'ūroid** *n* and *adj*.

lend /lend/ *vt* (**lend'ing**; **lent**) to give the use of for a time; to provide, grant or supply in general; to supply (money) at interest; to let for hire. ◆ *vi* to make a loan. ◆ *n* (*Scot*) a loan (often **len'**). [OE *lǣnan*, from *lǣn, lān* a loan]
■ **lend'able** *adj*. **lend'er** *n*. **lend'ing** *n* the act of giving in loan; something which is lent or supplied (*Shakesp*).
□ **lend'-lease** *n* in World War II, an arrangement authorized by Congress in 1941 by which the US President could supply war materials to other countries whose defence he considered vital to the United States (also *adj*).
■ **lend an ear** (*inf*) to listen. **lend itself to** to be able to be used for. **lend oneself to** to adapt oneself to.

lenes see **lenis**.

leng /leng/ (*obs*) *vi* to lengthen; to tarry; to long (*Spenser*). [OE *lengan*]

lenger /leng'gər/ (*Spenser*) *adj* and *adv* longer. [OE *lengra*, compar of *lang* (adj)]

lengest /leng'gist/ (*obs*) *adj* and *adv* longest. [OE, superl of *lang* (adj) and of *lange* (adv)]

length /leng(k)th/ *n* extent from end to end; the quality of being long; the longest measure of anything; long duration; prolixity; time occupied in uttering a vowel or syllable (*phonetics*); the quantity of a vowel; any definite portion of a known extent; a stretch or extent; distance (chiefly *Scot*); a suitable distance for pitching a cricket ball when bowling; the lengthwise measurement of a horse, boat, etc (*racing*). ◆ *combining form* stretching downwards, or sometimes along, as far as, eg *knee-length, arm's-length*. [OE *lengthu*, from *lang* long]
■ **length'en** *vt* and *vi* to increase in length. **length'ful** *adj* (*obs*). **length'ily** *adv*. **length'iness** *n*. **length'ways** or **length'wise** *adv* and *adj* in the direction of the length. **length'y** *adj* of great or tedious length; rather long.
□ **length'man** or **length'sman** *n* someone responsible for the upkeep of a particular stretch of road or railway.
■ **at length** in full; monotonously and tediously; fully extended; at last. **go the length of** to go as far as (also *fig*). **go to great lengths**, **all lengths**, **any length** or **lengths** to do everything possible (sometimes more than is ethical) to achieve a purpose. **length of days** prolonged life.

lenient /lē'nyənt or -ni-ənt/ *adj* mild; tolerant; merciful; softening (*archaic*); soothing (*archaic*). ◆ *n* (*med*; *archaic*) something which softens; an emollient. [L *lēniēns, -entis*, prp of *lēnīre* to soften, from *lēnis* soft]
■ **lē'nience** or **lē'niency** *n*. **lē'niently** *adv*. **lenify** /len' or lēn'/ *vt* (*archaic*) to mitigate or assuage. **lenitive** /len'/ *adj* soothing; mitigating; laxative. ◆ *n* any palliative; an application for easing pain (*med*); a mild purgative (*archaic*). **lenity** /len'/ *n* mildness; clemency.

Leninism /len'i-ni-zm/ *n* the political, economic and social principles and practices of the Russian revolutionary leader, Vladimir Ilyich Ulyanov *Lenin* (1870–1924), *esp* his theory of government by the proletariat.
■ **Len'inist** or **Len'inite** *n* and *adj*.

lenis /lē'nis or len'is/ (*phonetics*) *adj* (of a consonant) articulated with relatively little muscular effort and pressure of breath, *opp* to *fortis*. ◆ *n* (*pl* **lē'nes** /-ēz/) such a consonant. [L, soft]
■ **lenite** /li-nīt'/ *vi* and *vt* to undergo or cause to undergo lenition. **lenition** /li-nish'ən/ *n* a softening of articulation, common in Celtic languages.

lenitive and **lenity** see under **lenient**.

leno /lē'nō/ *n* (*pl* **lē'nos**) a thin muslin-like fabric. [Perh Fr *linon*]

lenocinium /lē-nō-sin'i-əm/ (*Scots law*) *n* connivance at one's wife's adultery. [L *lēnōcinium* enticement, from *lēnō* a pander]

lens /lenz/ *n* (*pl* **lens'es**) a piece of transparent matter (glass, plastic, etc) with one or both surfaces curved to cause regular convergence or divergence of rays passing through it; the refracting structure (*crystalline lens*) between the crystalline and vitreous humours of the eye; a mechanical equivalent of the human lens on a camera, allowing the subject image to fall on the eye or (on the opening of the shutter) the film plane (see also **fisheye lens** under **fish**[1], **telephoto lens** under **telephoto**, and **wide-angle lens** under **wide**); a contact lens; a device to influence the direction of sound waves (**acoustic lens**); (with *cap*) the lentil genus. ◆ *vt* and *vi* (*inf*) to shoot (a cinema film). [L *lēns, lentis* lentil]
□ **lens hood** *n* a piece fitted around or over a camera lens to shield it from a direct source of light. **lens'man** *n* (*inf*) a cameraman.
■ **electron lens** any arrangement of electrodes designed to influence the direction of cathode rays.

Lent /lent/ *n* in the Christian religion, the time from Ash Wednesday to Easter observed in the Western Churches (a longer period in the Eastern Churches) as a time of fasting in commemoration of Christ's fast in the wilderness (Matthew 4.2); a similar observance in other religions; any period of fasting (*fig*); spring (*obs*). [OE *lencten* the spring; Du *lente*, Ger *Lenz*]
■ **Lent'en** *adj* (also without *cap*) of Lent; meagre; fleshless.
□ **lenten rose** *n* a herbaceous perennial, *Helleborus orientalis*, which flowers from February to April. **lent lily** *n* the daffodil.

lent *pat* and *pap* of **lend**.

lentamente, **lentando** and **lenti** see **lento**.

Lenten and **lenten** see under **Lent**.

Lentibulariaceae /len-tib-ū-lā-ri-ā'si-ē/ *n pl* the bladderwort and butterwort family of tubifloral dicotyledons. [Origin obscure]

lentic /len'tik/ (ecology) adj associated with standing water; inhabiting ponds, swamps, etc. [L lentus slow]

lenticel /len'ti-sel/ (bot) n a breathing pore in bark. [New L lenticella, from L lenticula, dimin of lens, lentis lentil]
■ **lenticell'ate** adj.

lenticle /len'ti-kl/ n (geol) a lenticular mass. [L lens, lentis lentil]
■ **lentic'ular** adj shaped like a lens or lentil seed; of or relating to a lens or lenses; double-convex. ◆ n a three-dimensional picture made up of photographs of a scene which have been taken from several different angles, split into strips, juxtaposed, and laminated with corrugated plastic, the corrugations acting as lenses to create an illusion of depth. **lentic'ularly** adv. **lent'iform** or **lent'oid** adj lenticular.

lentiform see under **lenticle**.

lentigo /len-tī'gō/ n (pl **lentigines** /len-tij'i-nēz/) a freckle or (as sing) freckles. [L lentīgō, -inis a freckle, from lēns a lentil]
■ **lentig'inose** or **lentig'inous** adj (bot) minutely dotted.

lentil /len'til/ n a leguminous annual plant (Lens esculenta, or Ervum lens) common near the Mediterranean; its small, flattish, round seed, orange or brown, used for food. [OFr lentille, from L lēns, lentis the lentil]

lentisk or **lentisc** /len'tisk/ n the mastic tree. [L lentiscus]

lentivirus /len'ti-vī-rəs/ n a slow virus. [New L, from L lentus slow, and **virus**]

lento /len'tō/ (music) adj slow. ◆ adv slowly. ◆ n (pl **len'tos** or **len'ti** /-tē/) a slow passage or movement. [Ital, from L lentus slow]
■ **lentamen'te** /-tā/ adv. **lentan'do** adj and adv slowing. **lentiss'imo** adj and adv very slow or slowly.

lentoid see under **lenticle**.

lentor /len'tör/ (archaic) n sluggishness; viscidity. [L lentus slow]
■ **len'tous** adj.

lenvoy /len-voi'/ same as **envoy²**. [Fr l'envoi the envoy]

Lenz's law /lent'siz lö/ (phys) n the law that an induced electromotive force will tend to cause a current to flow in such a direction as to oppose the cause of the induced electromotive force. [HFE Lenz (1804–65), German physicist]

Leo /lē'ō/ n the Lion, a constellation giving its name to, and formerly coinciding with, a sign of the zodiac (astron); the fifth sign of the zodiac, between Cancer and Virgo (astrol); a person born between 24 July and 23 August, under the sign of Leo (astrol; pl **Le'os**). [L leō, -ōnis lion]
■ **Leō'nian** n and adj (relating to or characteristic of) a person born under the sign of Leo. **Lē'onid** /-ə-nid/ n a meteor of a swarm whose radiant is in the constellation Leo. **Lē'onine** adj relating to any of the popes named Leo; of a kind of Latin verse, generally alternate hexameter and pentameter, rhyming at the middle and end (prob from some unknown poet named Leo, Leoninus, or Leonius); (without cap) lionlike. ◆ n a Leonine verse.

leone /lē-ō'nē/ n the standard monetary unit of Sierra Leone (100 cents).

Leonian...to...**Leonine** see under **Leo**.

leontiasis /lē-on-tī'ə-sis/ n a form of leprosy in which the face takes on a lionlike appearance. [Gr leontīāsis, from leōn, -ontos lion]

leopard /lep'ərd/ or (fem) **leopardess** /lep'ər-des/ n a large spotted animal of the cat family found in Africa and Asia, also called the **panther**; in N America, the jaguar or any similar large cat; a lion passant gardant (heraldry). [OFr, from L leopardus, from Gr leopardos (for leontopardos), from leōn lion, and pardos pard]
❑ **leopard cat** n a spotted wildcat of the Indian subcontinent. **leopard moth** n a white moth (Zeuzera pyrina) with black spots on its wings and body. **leop'ard's-bane** n a composite plant, Doronicum. **leop'ard-wood** n letter-wood.
■ **hunting leopard** the cheetah. **snow leopard** a Central Asian relative of the leopard, with pale fur and dark markings, the ounce. **the leopard cannot change its spots** personality traits cannot be changed.

leotard /lē'ə-tärd/ n a skintight garment worn by dancers, acrobats, etc, sleeveless or long-sleeved, with legs varying from none at all to ankle-length. [Jules Léotard, 19th-century French trapeze artist]

lep /lep/ vi (pat (Spenser) **lepp'ed**) a dialect form of **leap¹**, **leaped** or **leapt**.

leper /lep'ər/ n a person affected with leprosy; a spurned person (fig); an outcast; leprosy (obs). [OFr lepre, from L lepra, from Gr leprā; see ety for **lepra**]

lepid /lep'id/ adj pleasant or jocose. [L lepidus]

lepid- /lep-id-/ or **lepido-** /lep-i-dō- or -do-/ combining form denoting scales. [Gr lepis, -idos a scale]

■ **lepidoden'droid** adj and n. **Lepidoden'dron** n (Gr dendron tree) a genus of fossil trees, mainly Carboniferous, of the **Lepidodendrā'ceae**, related to Lycopodiaceae, the stem covered with ovate leaf-scars arranged spirally. **lepid'olite** n (Gr lithos stone) a lithia mica, usu pink. **lepidomelane'** n (Gr melās, -anos black) a black mica rich in iron, occurring in scales. **Lepidop'tera** n pl (Gr pteron wing) an order of insects, with four wings covered with fine scales, the butterflies and moths. **lepidop'teran** n and adj. **lepidop'terist** n a person who studies butterflies and moths. **lepidopterol'ogy** n. **lepidop'terous** adj. **Lepidosī'ren** n (Gr Seirēn a Siren) an Amazon mudfish. **Lepidos'teus** n (Gr osteon a bone) a genus of fishes with rhomboid scales hard like bone, the bony pike. **Lepidos'trobus** n (Gr strobos twist) the fossil fructification of Lepidodendron. **lep'idote** adj (Gr lepidōtos) scaly; scurfy.

leporine /lep'ə-rīn/ adj of or resembling the hare. [L leporīnus, from lepus, leporis the hare]

lepped see **lep**.

LEPRA /lep'rə/ abbrev : Leprosy Relief Association.

lepra /lep'rə/ n leprosy (med); a scurfy, mealy substance on some plants (bot). [Gr leprā, fem of lepros scaly, from lepos or lepis a scale, lepein to peel]
■ **lep'rose** /-rōs/ adj scaly; scurfy.

leprechaun /lep'rə-kön/ (folklore) n a sprite or creature who helps Irish housewives, mends shoes, grinds meal, etc (old form **lep'rechawn**). [Prob OIr luchorpán, from lu small, and corpan, corp a body]

leprose see under **lepra**.

leproserie or **leprosery** /lep'rə-sə-ri/ n a leper hospital. [Fr léproserie]

leprosy /lep'rə-si/ n a chronic skin disease caused by a bacillus and occurring in two forms, tubercular, beginning with spots and thickenings of the skin, and anaesthetic, attacking the nerves, with loss of sensation in areas of skin; a name formerly widely applied to chronic skin diseases; corruption (fig). [Ety as for **leper**]
■ **leprosā'rium** n a hospital for lepers. **leprosity** /-ros'i-ti/ n scaliness. **lep'rous** adj of or affected with leprosy; scaly; scurfy.

-lepsy /-lep-si/ (med) combining form denoting a seizing or seizure, as in catalepsy. [Gr lēpsis, from lambanein to seize, take]
■ **-leptic** adj combining form.

leptin /lep'tin/ n a protein which regulates how much fat is stored by the body. [Gr leptos slender, and **-in** (1)]

lepton /lep'ton/ n any of a group of subatomic particles with weak interactions, incl electrons, negative muons, tau particles and neutrinos, opp to baryon (pl **lep'tons**); a former unit of currency in modern Greece, $\frac{1}{100}$ of a drachma (pl **lep'ta**); the smallest ancient Greek coin, translated 'mite' in the New Testament (pl **lep'ta**). [Gr leptos, neuter lepton slender]
■ **leptocephal'ic** or **leptoceph'alous** adj (Gr kephalē head) narrow-skulled. **leptoceph'alus** n (pl **leptoceph'ali**) the larva of an eel. **leptocerc'al** (Gr kerkos tail) slender-tailed. **leptodac'tyl** n (Gr daktylos finger, toe) a bird or other animal with long slender toes. **leptodac'tylous** adj slender-toed. **lep'tome** n (bot) phloem or bast. **lepton'ic** adj of or relating to leptons. **leptophyll'ous** adj (bot) with long slender leaves. **lep'torrhine** adj (Gr rhīs, rhīnos nose) narrow-nosed. **lep'tosome** n (Gr sōma body) a person with a slight, slender physical build; an asthenic. **leptosō'mic** or **leptosomatic** /-sə-mat'ik/ adj. **leptospīrō'sis** n (Gr speira a coil) a disease of animals or humans caused by bacteria of the genus **Leptospī'ra**. **leptosporan'giate** adj (bot) having each sporangium derived from a single cell, opp to eusporangiate. **lep'totene** /-tēn/ n (biol) the first stage of meiotic prophase in which long, slender, single-stranded chromosomes appear.
❑ **lepton number** n the number of leptons minus the number of antileptons (antiparticles of leptons) in a system.

lere see **lear¹**.

Lerna /lûr'nə/ or **Lerne** /lûr'nē/ (Gr myth) n a swamp near Argos, supposed to be the home of the Hydra killed by Hercules.
■ **Lernaean** or **Lernean** /lûr-nē'ən/ adj.

lerp /lûrp/ n in Australia, a scalelike, waxy, protective, edible secretion produced on the leaves of certain plants by louse larvae. [From an Aboriginal language]

les see **lez**.

lesbian /lez'bi-ən/ adj (of women) homosexual; (with cap) of the island of Lesbos, or Mytilene, home of the poets Alcaeus and Sappho; amatory or erotic. ◆ n a female homosexual.
■ **les'bianism** n. **les'bic** adj lesbian. **lesbo** /lez'bō/ n (pl **les'bos**) (sl, often offensive) a lesbian.
❑ **Lesbian rule** n (fig) an adaptable standard, from the pliable lead rule orig used by Lesbian masons.

lese-majesty or **leze-majesty** /lēz-maj'i-sti/ (also (Fr) **-majesté** /-ma-zhə-stā'/) n an offence against the sovereign power, treason.

—**lese** or **leze**, treated as if it had verbal force, has also been used to form compounds such as **lese'-human'ity** and **leze'-lib'erty**. [Fr *lèse majesté*, transl of L *laesa mājestās* injured majesty, from *laedere* to hurt]

Lesh states /lesh *stāts*/ *n pl* seven levels of relaxation that may be attained through meditation. [T *Lesh*, 20c US physician]

lesion /lē'zhən/ *n* an abnormal change in the structure of body tissue caused by disease or injury, *esp* an injury or wound (*med*); an injury or hurt. [Fr *lésion*, from L *laesiō*, *-ōnis*, from *laedere*, *laesum* to hurt]

less /les/ *adj* (used as *compar* of **little**) smaller (not now used of material things); in smaller quantity (not number); minor; fewer (*archaic* and *inf*); inferior, lower in estimation; younger; more (*Shakesp*, with an expressed or implied negative). ◆ *adv* not so much; in a lower degree. ◆ *n* a smaller portion or quantity. ◆ *conj* (*Milton*) unless (often written **'less**). ◆ *prep* without; with diminution of, minus. [OE *lǣssa* less, *lǣs* (adv); apparently not connected with **little**]
■ **much less** not to mention. **no less** (*usu ironically*) a phrase used to express admiration. **nothing less than** quite as much as; tantamount to; formerly, anything rather than.

-less /-les or -lis/ *adj sfx* free from or lacking, as in *guiltless* or *godless*. [OE *-lēas*, Ger *-los*, Gothic *-laus*]

lessee /le-sē' or les'ē/ *n* the person or business to which a lease is granted. [**lease**[1]]
■ **lessee'ship** *n*.

lessen /les'n/ *vt* to make less, in any sense; to lower in estimation; to disparage; to belittle. ◆ *vi* to become less, shrink. [**less**]

lesser /les'ər/ *adj* less; smaller; inferior; minor. ◆ *adv* (*Shakesp*) less. [Double compar from **less**]

lesson /les'n/ *n* a spell, instalment, or prescribed portion of instruction; a set exercise; an instructive or warning experience or example; a severe reproof; a portion of Scripture read during a religious service; a piece or performance of music (*obs*). ◆ *vt* (*archaic*) to instruct; to train; to rebuke. [Fr *leçon*, from L *lectiō*, *-ōnis*, from *legere* to read]
■ **less'oning** *n* (*archaic*).

lessor /les'ör/ *n* the person or business which grants a lease. [**lease**[1]]

lest[1] /lest/ *conj* so that not; for fear that. [ME *leste*, from OE *thȳ lǣs the* the less that, from *thȳ* instrumental case; see **the**[2]]

lest[2] /lest/ (*Spenser*) *vi* for **list**[4], to listen.

lesula /lə-soo'lə/ *n* a Congolese monkey of the genus *Cercopithecus*. [Local name]

let[1] /let/ *vt* (*prp* **lett'ing**; *pat* **let** or (*Scot*) **loot** /lüt or lüt/; *pap* **let** or (*Scot*) **loot'en**, **litt'en** or **lutt'en**) to give leave or power to, to allow, permit, suffer (*usu* with infinitive without *to*); to allow to go or come; to grant to a tenant or hirer; in the imperative with accusative and infinitive without *to*, often used virtually as an auxiliary with imperative or optative effect; to leave (*Shakesp*); to omit (*Shakesp*); to allow to escape (*archaic*); to behave so as to give an impression, make it appear (*obs*; also *vi*). ◆ *n* a letting for hire. [OE (Anglian) *lētan* (WSax *lǣtan*) to permit, pat *lēt*; pap *lǣten*; Ger *lassen*]
■ **lett'able** *adj* able to be hired out, suitable for letting. **lett'er** *n* a person who lets, *esp* on hire. **lett'ing** *n*.
❑ **let'-alone** *n* (*Shakesp*) absence of restraint, freedom. ◆ *adj* refraining from interference; leaving things to themselves. **let'-down** *n* an act or occasion of letting down; a disappointment. **let'-off** *n* an act or occasion of letting off; a festivity; an outlet; (in games) a failure to take advantage of an opportunity. **let'-out** *n* a chance to escape or avoid keeping an agreement, contract, etc. **lett'er-gae'** *n* (*Scot*) someone who lets go, a precentor. **letting down** *n* (*aeronautics*) the reduction of altitude from cruising height to that required for the approach to landing. **let'-up** *n* end or ceasing; abatement; respite or relief.
■ **let alone** not to mention, much less; to refrain from interference with; (*imperative*) trust (*archaic*). **let be** (*dialect* **let-a-be**) to leave undisturbed; not to mention, to say nothing of (*Scot*). **let blood** to cause to bleed. **let down** to allow to fall; to lower; to make longer; to allow air to escape from; to leave in the lurch, fail to back up when needed, betray trust, disappoint. **let drive** to aim a blow; to discharge a missile. **let fall** to drop; to mention or hint. **let fly** to fling, discharge, shoot; to deliver a blow (also *fig*). **let go** to cease holding; to finish the employment of; to slacken (*naut*). **let in** to allow to enter; to take in or swindle (*archaic*); (with *for*) to involve in or betray into anything unpleasant or troublesome; to insert; to leak inwards. **let in on** (*inf*) to allow to take part in. **let into** to set into the surface of; to admit to the knowledge of; to throw into one with. **let loose** to set free; to let go of restraint, to indulge in unrestrained talk or conduct. **let off** to allow to go free or without exacting all; to fire off, discharge; to break wind from the anus (*inf*). **let on** (*inf*) to allow to be believed, to pretend; to disclose awareness; to reveal, divulge. **let oneself go** (*inf*) to allow one's appearance, lifestyle, etc to deteriorate; to act without restraint. **let out** to allow to go free, or to become known; to emit; to widen, slacken, enlarge; to put out to hire; to leak outwards; to strike out or

kick out (*archaic*). **let someone know** to inform someone. **let up** (*inf*) to become less; to abate. **let up on** (*inf*) to cease to have to do with; to treat less harshly. **let well alone** to let things remain as they are from fear of making them worse. **to let** available for hire.

let[2] /let/ *vt* (*pat* and *pap* **lett'ed** or **let**) (*archaic*) to hinder; to prevent. ◆ *adj* (*archaic*) obstructed. ◆ *n* obstruction by the net, or other ground for cancelling a service (*tennis*, etc); a service affected in such a way; hindrance, obstruction (*archaic*); delay (*archaic*). [OE *lettan* to hinder, from *lǣt* slow]
■ **lett'er** *n*.

-let /-lit or -lət/ *n sfx* used to form diminutives, as in *bracelet*, *leaflet* and *streamlet*.

letch[1] /lech/ *vt* a variant of **leach**[1]. ◆ *n* (*dialect*) a boggy patch of ground (also **latch**). [See **leach**[1]]

letch[2] same as **lech** (see under **lecher**).
■ **letch'ing** *n*.

lethal /lē'thəl/ *adj* deadly; mortal; vicious; death-dealing. [L *lēt(h)ālis*, from *lēt(h)um* death]
■ **lethal'ity** *n*. **le'thally** *adv*. **le'thee** *n* (*Shakesp*) *appar* lifeblood, or death (*prob* with some reminiscence of **Lethe**). **lethif'erous** *adj* carrying death.

lethargy /leth'ər-ji/ *n* heavy unnatural slumber; torpor. [Gr *lēthārgiā* drowsy forgetfulness, from *lēthē* forgetfulness, and *ārgos* idle]
■ **lethargic** /-är'/ or **lethar'gical** *adj* relating to lethargy; unnaturally sleepy; torpid. **lethar'gically** *adv*. **leth'argied** *adj*. **leth'argize** or **-ise** *vt*.
❑ **lethargy of neutrons** *n* the natural logarithm of the ratio of initial and actual energies of neutrons during the moderation process.

Lethe /lē'thē/ *n* a river of the underworld causing forgetfulness in all who drank of it (*Gr myth*); oblivion. [Gr *lēthē* forgetfulness (*lēthēs hydōr* the water or river of forgetfulness), from *lēthein*, a collateral form of *lanthanein* to be hidden]
■ **lethē'an** *adj*. **leth'ied** *adj* (*Shakesp*).

lethee and **lethiferous** see under **lethal**.

Letraset® /let'rə-set/ *n* a transfer lettering system of alphabets, symbols, etc which can be stripped into position on paper, film, etc.

LETS *abbrev* : Local Exchange Trading System, a system in which skills and resources are bartered using a nominal local currency (often named after a local feature, such as bobbins in Manchester and reekies in Edinburgh).

Lett /let/ *n* a member of a people inhabiting **Lett'land** (now Latvia); a native or citizen of Latvia. [Ger *Lette*, from Lettish *latvis* (now *latvietis*)]
■ **Lett'ic** *adj* of the group (also called **Baltic**) of languages to which Lettish belongs, including Lithuanian and Old Prussian. **Lett'ish** *adj*. ◆ *n* the language of Letts.

letter[1] /let'ər/ *n* a conventional mark primarily used to express a sound of speech; often loosely applied to the sound itself; a written or printed message signed and sent, *usu* by post, to an addressee; literal meaning; printing type; (in *pl*) learning, literary culture; an emblem, *usu* a monogram, awarded to a student for achievement in an extracurricular activity, *esp* in sport (*US*). ◆ *vt* to stamp letters upon; to mark with a letter or letters. ◆ *vi* (*US*) to earn a letter for achievement. [Fr *lettre*, from L *littera*, *lītera*]
■ **lett'ered** *adj* marked with letters; educated; knowledgeable in literature; literary. **lett'erer** *n*. **lett'ering** *n* the act of impressing or marking with letters; the letters impressed or marked; their style or mode of formation. **lett'erless** *adj* without letters; illiterate.
❑ **lett'er-board** *n* a board on which material in type is placed for keeping or convenience in handling. **letter bomb** *n* a device inside an envelope which explodes when the envelope is opened. **lett'erbox** *n* a box or slot for receiving mail; a box for posting mail. ◆ *adj* (*cinematog*) of a film shown on television or video, etc, preserving the original widescreen cinematic format, not cut for a television screen. ◆ *vt* to format (a film) in this way. **lett'erboxed** *adj*. **lett'erboxing** *n*. **lett'er-card** *n* a card folded and gummed like a letter, with a perforated margin for opening. **lett'er-carrier** *n* a postman; mail-carrier. **lett'er-clip** *n* a device for gripping letters or papers to keep them together. **lett'er-founder** *n* someone who casts type. **lett'erhead** *n* a printed heading on notepaper, etc; a piece of notepaper with such a heading (also **lett'er-heading**). **letter of comfort** *n* (*law*) a letter sent by a person in authority to provide assurances about intended actions. **letter of credit** *n* a letter authorizing credit or cash to a certain sum to be given to the bearer. **letter of indication** *n* a banker's letter requesting foreign bankers to accept the bearer's circular notes. **letter-of-marque** see under **marque**[2]. **letter-per'fect** *adj* (of an actor, etc) having the words of the part committed accurately to memory, word-perfect. **lett'erpress** *n* a method of printing in which ink on raised surfaces is pressed onto paper; matter printed in this way; printed text as opposed to illustrations; a copying-press. **letter quality** *n* output from a printer where the printing is acceptable for distribution outside

an organization. **lett'er-quality** *adj.* **lett'erset** *n* a method of printing in which ink is transferred from a letterpress plate to paper by means of a rubber-covered cylinder. **letters of administration** see under **administer**. **letters of credence** or **letters credential** *n pl* a diplomat's formal document accrediting him or her to a foreign government. **letters patent** *n pl* a document conferring a patent or privilege, so called because written on open sheets of parchment. **letters requisitory** or **letters rogatory** *n pl* a legal instrument by which a court of one country asks that of another to take a certain evidence on its behalf. **lett'er-stamp** *n* an instrument for cancelling postage-stamps; a stamp for imprinting dates, etc. **lett'er-weight** *n* a paperweight. **lett'er-wood** *n* leopard-wood, a S American tree of the breadnut genus, with dark-brown mottled heartwood. **lett'er-writer** *n* someone who writes letters, *esp* for payment; a book of forms for imitation in writing letters.
■ **the letter of the law** the literal interpretation of the law. **to the letter** exactly, in every detail.

letter² and **letting** see under **let¹,²**.

lettern /let'ərn/ (*obs*) same as **lectern**.

lettre /le'tr'/ (*Fr*) *n* a letter.
□ **lettre de cachet** /də ka-she'/ *n* a letter under the royal signet; a royal warrant for arrest and imprisonment. **lettre de change** /də shāzh'/ *n* a bill of exchange. **lettre de marque** /də märk'/ *n* a letter of marque or of reprisal.

lettuce /let'is/ *n* a composite plant (*Lactuca sativa*) with milky juice, or one of many varieties, whose leaves are used for salad; extended to other (inedible) plants of the genus. [Appar from some form (perh the *pl*) of Anglo-Fr *letue* (Fr *laitue*), from L *lactūca*, from *lac* milk, from the milky juice of the leaves]
■ **frog's lettuce** a kind of pondweed. **lamb's lettuce** corn-salad.

leu /lā'oo/ *n* (*pl* **lei** /lā/) the standard monetary unit of Romania and Moldova (100 bani) (also (*rare*) **ley** /lā/). [Romanian, lion]

leuc- or **leuk-** /lūk-, look-, lūs- or loos-/, also **leuco-** or **leuko-** /lū-kō-, loo-ko- or -ko-/ *combining form* denoting white. [Gr *leukos* white] The letters **c** and **k** are interchangeable in most of these words. Except in the first case, **-k-** forms have not been given below:
■ **leucaemia** or more commonly **leukaemia**, also (*esp N Am*) **leukemia** and, more strictly formed, **leuchaemia** /loo-kē'mi-ə/ *n* (Gr *haima* blood) a sometimes fatal cancerous disease in which too many leucocytes are accumulated in the body, associated with changes in the lymphatic system and enlargement of the spleen. **leucae'mic** *adj.* **leucae'mogen** *n* a substance that encourages the development of leukaemia. **leucaemogen'esis** *n.* **leucaemogen'ic** *adj.* **leucis'tic** *adj* (*biol*) lacking pigmentation in the skin, but differing from an albino in having blue eyes. **leu'co-base** or **leu'co-compound** *n* a colourless reduction product of a dye that can be converted back to the dye by oxidation. **leu'coblast** *n* an immature cell which will develop into a leucocyte. **leucocrat'ic** *adj* of igneous rocks, light in colour, due to a low content of iron and magnesium. **leu'cocyte** /-kō-sīt/ *n* (Gr *kytos* container, used as if cell) a white corpuscle of the blood or lymph. **leucocythaemia** /-sī-thē'mi-ə/ *n* (Gr *haima* blood) leukaemia. **leucocytic** /-sit'ik/ *adj.* **leucocytol'ysis** *n* (Gr *lysis* dissolution) breaking down of the leucocytes. **leucocytopē'nia** *n* (Gr *penia* poverty) leucocyte deficiency. **leucocytopē'nic** *adj.* **leucocytō'sis** *n* the presence of an excessive number of white corpuscles in the blood. **leucocytot'ic** *adj.* **leucoder'ma** or **leucoder'mia** *n* (Gr *derma* skin) a condition in which white patches, surrounded by a pigmented area, appear in the skin. **leucoder'mal** or **leucoder'mic** *adj.* **leucopē'nia** *n* leucocytopenia. **leucopēn'ic** *adj.* **leucoplakia** /lū- or loo-kō-plā'ki-ə/ *n* (Gr *plax, plakos* a flat surface) the stage of a chronically inflamed area at which the surface becomes hard, white and smooth. **leucoplast** /lū' or loo'kō-pläst/ *n* (Gr *plastos* formed, from *plassein* to form; *bot*) a starch-forming body in protoplasm (also **leucoplas'tid**). **leucopoiesis** /lū- or loo-kō-poi-ē'sis/ *n* (Gr *poieein* to make) the production of white blood cells. **leucorrhoea** /lū- or loo-kō-rē'ə/ *n* (Gr *rhoiā*, from *rheein* to flow) an abnormal mucous or muco-purulent discharge from the vagina, the whites. **leucosin** /lū' or loo'kō-sin/ *n* a cereal albumin; a polysaccharide present in some algae. **leu'cotome** /-kō-tōm/ *n* a needle used in leucotomies. **leucotomy** /lū- or loo-kot'ə-mi/ *n* (Gr *tomē* a cutting) a surgical scission of the white association fibres between the frontal lobes of the brain and the thalamus to relieve cases of severe schizophrenia and manic-depressive psychosis.

leuch and **leuchen** see **lauch**.

leucin /lū' or loo'sin/ or **leucine** /-sēn/ *n* an essential amino acid, a product of protein hydrolysis. [Gr *leukos* white]

Leuciscus /lū- or loo-sis'kəs/ *n* a genus of freshwater cyprinoid fishes, including the roach, dace, chub, minnow, etc. [Gr *leukiskos* white mullet]

leucistic see under **leuc-**.

leucite /lū' or loo'sīt/ *n* a whitish mineral (silicate of aluminium and potassium). [Gr *leukos* white]
■ **leucitic** /-sit'ik/ *adj.* **leucitohē'dron** *n* the cubic icositetrahedron, simulated by typical leucite crystals.

leuco- see **leuc-**.

Leucojum /lū- or loo-kō'jəm/ *n* the snowflake genus of amaryllids. [Gr *leukoïon* snowdrop, etc, from *leukos* white, and *ion* violet]

leucoma /lū- or loo-kō'mə/ *n* (*pathol*) a white opacity of the cornea. [Gr *leukōma*, from *leukos* white]

leugh and **leughen** see **lauch**.

leuk- and **leuko-** see **leuc-**.

Lev. or **Levit.** (*Bible*) *abbrev*: (the Book of) Leviticus.

lev or **lew** /lef/ *n* (*pl* **leva** /lev'ä/) the standard monetary unit of Bulgaria (100 stotinki). [Bulgarian, lion]

Levant /li-vant'/ *n* the eastern Mediterranean and its shores; the East (*obs*); (without *cap*) the levanter wind; (without *cap*) a kind of morocco leather. ◆ *adj* (without *cap*; /lev'ənt/) eastern. [Fr *levant* or Ital *levante* east, literally rising, from L *levāre* to raise]
■ **Levant'er** *n* an inhabitant of the Levant; (without *cap*) a boisterous easterly wind in the Levant. **Levant'ine** (or /lev'ən-tīn/) *adj* of or trading to the Levant. ◆ *n* a native or inhabitant of the Levant; (without *cap*) a closely-woven twilled silk cloth.

levant /li-vant'/ *vi* to decamp. [Sp *levantar* to move, from L *levāre* to raise]
■ **levan'ter** *n* someone who absconds, *esp* with gambling debts unpaid.

levator /le-vā'tər* or -tör/ (*anat*) *n* a muscle that raises, *opp* to *depressor*. [L *levātor* a lifter, from *levāre* to raise]

leve see **lief**.

levee¹ /lev'i, also lev'ā or li-vē'/ (*hist* or *archaic*) *n* a morning (or comparatively early) reception of visitors, *esp* by a person of distinction; getting out of bed (*archaic*). ◆ *vt* to attend the levee of. [Fr *levée, lever*, from L *levāre* to raise]

levee² /lev'i or li-vē'/ (*US*) *n* a natural or artificial riverside embankment, *esp* on the Lower Mississippi; a quay. [Fr *levée* raised; see ety for **levee¹**]

levée en masse /lə-vā ā mas'/ (*Fr*) see **levy in mass** under **levy**.

level /lev'l/ *n* a horizontal position; a condition of horizontality; a horizontal plane or line; a nearly horizontal surface or a region with no considerable inequalities; the horizontal plane, literal or figurative, that anything occupies or reaches up to; height; an instrument for testing horizontality; a horizontal mine-gallery; an ascertainment of relative elevation; a levelling survey; natural or appropriate position or rank; a condition of equality; a ditch or channel for drainage, *esp* in flat country; an area of flat, *usu* low-lying farming land that has been drained for agricultural use; the act of aiming (*Shakesp*); the thing aimed at (*Spenser*). ◆ *adj* horizontal; even, smooth; even with anything else; uniform; well-balanced, sound of judgement; in the same line or plane; filled to a level with the brim; equal in position or dignity. ◆ *adv* in a level manner; point-blank. ◆ *vt* (**lev'elling**; **lev'elled**) to make horizontal; to make flat or smooth; to lay low; to raze; to aim; to make equal; to direct; to survey by taking levels. ◆ *vi* to make things level; to aim; to speak honestly, to be frank (*usu* with *with*; *inf*); to guess, estimate. ◆ *vt* and *vi* to change in spelling or pronunciation, making one word or form the same as another. [OFr *livel, liveau* (Fr *niveau*), from L *lībella* a plummet, dimin of *lībra* a balance]
■ **lev'eller** *n* someone who levels in any sense; someone who would like to remove all social or political inequalities, *esp* (with *cap*) one of an ultra-republican party in the Parliamentary army, crushed by Cromwell in 1649. **lev'elling** *n* the act of making level; a change in spelling or pronunciation making one word or form the same as another. **lev'elly** *adv.* **lev'elness** *n.*
□ **level crossing** *n* a place at which a road crosses a railway at the same level. **lev'el-head'ed** *adj* having sound common sense. **lev'elling-rod** or **lev'elling-staff** *n* a graduated rod used in surveying. **levelling screw** *n* a screw for adjusting part of a machine, etc so that it stands level. **level pegging** *n* the equal state of two rivals, contestants, etc (often in the form **be level pegging with**). ◆ *adj* at the same level, equal (also **lev'el-pegg'ed**). **level playing field** *n* (*fig*) a position of equality, from which rivals may compete without either having an unfair advantage.
■ **do one's level best** (*inf*) to do one's utmost. **find one's level** to settle in one's natural position or rank. **level down** or **up** to lower or raise to the same level or status. **level off** to make flat or even; to reach and maintain equilibrium. **level out** to make or become level. **on the level** fair; honestly speaking.

level-coil /lev'l-koil/ (*archaic*) *n* an old Christmas game in which the players changed seats; a hubbub. [Fr *lever le cul* to lift the buttocks]

lever /lē'vər or in US lev'ər/ n a bar turning on a support or fulcrum for imparting pressure or motion from a source of power to a resistance; anything that can be used to gain an advantage. ◆ vt to move with a lever. [OFr leveor, from lever, from L levāre to raise]
■ **le'verage** n the mechanical power gained by the use of a lever; advantage gained for any purpose, eg (in finance) power gained over a resource greater than that one actually owns. ◆ vi and vt to borrow necessary capital (esp for a management buyout) counting on the profits from the deal to cover interest repayment (finance); to make use of something to achieve a further objective. **le'veraged** adj financed by borrowed capital.
□ **lever arch file** n a file in the form of a large loose-leaf folder or book with arch-shaped metal rods on which the papers are secured. **le'ver-watch** n a watch with a vibrating lever in the escapement mechanism.

lever de rideau /lə-vā də rē-dō'/ (Fr) n a curtain-raiser.

leveret /lev'ə-rit/ n a hare in its first year. [OFr levrette (Fr lièvre), from L lepus, leporis a hare]

leviable see under **levy**.

leviathan /le-vī'ə-thən/ n (also with cap) a biblical sea-monster, described in the Bible (Job 41), apparently a crocodile; a huge sea-monster; anything of huge size, esp a ship or a man; (after Hobbes's book, 1651) the state; Satan (obs). ◆ adj gigantic, formidable. [Heb livyāthān]

levigate¹ /lev'i-gāt/ vt to smooth; to grind to a fine powder, esp with a liquid. ◆ adj smooth. [L lēvigāre, -ātum, from lēvis smooth; Gr leios; related to **level**]
■ **lev'igable** adj. **leviga'tion** n.

levigate² /lev'i-gāt/ (obs) vt to lighten. [L levigāre, -ātum, from levis light]

levin /lev'in/ (archaic) n lightning. [ME leuen(e), prob from ON]

levirate /lē'vi- or lev'i-rāt/ n the (ancient Hebrew and other) custom of compulsory marriage with a childless brother's widow. [L lēvir a brother-in-law]
■ **lev'irate** or **leviratical** /-rat'i-kl/ adj. **levirā'tion** n.

Levi's® /lē'vīz/ n pl heavy, close-fitting denim, etc trousers, reinforced at points of strain with copper rivets. [From the US original manufacturer, Levi Strauss]

Levit. see **Lev.**

levitation /lev-i-tā'shən/ n the act of rising by virtue of lightness; the act of making light; the floating of heavy bodies in the air, according to spiritualists; raising and floating on a cushion of air. [On the model of gravitate, from L levis light]
■ **lev'itate** vt and vi to float or cause to float. **lev'itātor** n.

Levite /lē'vīt/ n a descendant of Levi, the third son of Jacob and Leah (Bible); a subordinate priest of the ancient Jewish Church; (also without cap) a clergyman (sl).
■ **levitic** /li-vit'ik/ or **levit'ical** adj. **levit'ically** adv. **Levit'icus** n the third book of the Old Testament.
□ **Levitical degrees** n pl the degrees of kindred within which marriage was forbidden in Leviticus 18.6–18.

levity /lev'i-ti/ n lightness of temper or conduct; thoughtlessness; a trifling or frivolous tendency; fickleness; vain quality; lightness of weight (archaic). [L levitās, -ātis, from levis light]

levo- see **laevo-**.

levodopa /lē-vō-dō'pə/ n another name for **L-dopa** (see **dopa**).

levonorgestrel /lē-vō-nör-jes'trəl/ n a hormone used in oral contraceptives, esp as an emergency contraceptive taken a few hours after intercourse. [The l(a)evorotatory form of the hormone norgestrel]

levulose see **laevulose**.

levy /lev'i/ vt (lev'ying; lev'ied) to raise or collect (eg an army or tax); to call for; to impose; to begin to wage. ◆ n the act of levying; a contribution called for from members of an association; a tax; the amount collected; troops levied. [Fr levée, from lever, from L levāre to raise]
■ **leviable** /lev'i-ə-bl/ adj able to be levied or assessed.
□ **levy in mass** (Fr **levée en masse**) n a levy of all able-bodied men for military service, conscription.
■ **levy war** to make war.

lew¹ /lū or loo/ adj tepid, lukewarm. [OE hlēow]

lew² see **lev**.

lewd /lood or lūd/ adj obscene; sensual; lustful; unchaste; ignorant (obs); bare (Bible); bad (obs). [OE lǣwede ignorant]
■ **lewd'ly** adv. **lewd'ness** n. **lewds'by** or **lewd'ster** n (archaic) someone addicted to lewdness.

lewis /loo'is/ n a dovetail iron tenon, made in three pieces, for lifting blocks of stone (also **lew'isson**); a freemason's son. [Ety uncertain]

Lewis acid /loo'is as'id/ n a substance that can accept an electron pair from a base (**Lewis base**) to form a covalent bond. [GN Lewis (1875–1946), US physical chemist]

Lewis gun /loo'is gun/ n a light machine-gun designed by the American Samuel McLean, c.1908, and perfected by US Army Colonel Isaac Newton Lewis (1858–1931).

lewisia /loo-is'i-ə/ n a perennial herb with pink or white flowers, of the genus Lewisia. [American explorer Meriwether Lewis (1774–1809)]

Lewisian /loo-iz'i-ən or -is'/ adj of Lewis in the Outer Hebrides; Precambrian (geol).

lewisite¹ /loo'i-sīt/ n a vesicant liquid, an arsine derivative, that causes blistering and other irritation, developed for use in chemical warfare. [Named after WL Lewis (1878–1943), US chemist]

lewisite² /loo'i-sīt/ n a yellow or brown cubic mineral containing titanium and antimony. [Named after WJ Lewis (1847–1926), English mineralogist]

lewisson see **lewis**.

Lewy body /loo'i bod'i/ n an abnormal structure in a nerve cell, found in people with Parkinson's disease and a common type of dementia. [FH Lewy (1885–1950), German neurologist]

lex /leks/ (L) n law.
□ **lex non scripta** /non skrip'tə or nōn skrēp'tä/ n unwritten law, ie the common law. **lex scripta** /skrip'tə or skrēp'tä/ n statute law. **lex talionis** /ta-li-ō'nis or tä-/ n the law of talion, or retaliation.

lex. abbrev: lexicon.

lexeme /lek'sēm/ (linguistics) n a word or other essential unit of vocabulary in its most abstract sense. [lexicon and -eme]

lexicon /lek'si-kən/ n a wordbook or dictionary; a vocabulary of terms used in a particular subject; the vocabulary of a language or person. [Gr lexikon a dictionary, from lexis a word, legein to speak]
■ **lex'ical** adj belonging to a lexicon; relating to the words of a language as distinct from its grammar and constructions. **lex'ically** adv. **lexicographer** /-kog'rə-fər/ n. **lexicographic** /-kə-graf'ik/ or **lexicograph'ical** adj. **lexicograph'ically** adv. **lexicog'raphist** n. **lexicog'raphy** n the writing and compiling of dictionaries. **lexicolog'ical** adj. **lexicolog'ically** adv. **lexicol'ogist** n. **lexicol'ogy** n the study of the history and meaning of words.
□ **lexical analysis** n (comput) a stage during the compilation of a program in which standard components of a statement are replaced by internal codes (tokens) which identify their meaning. **lexical meaning** n the meaning of the base word when not inflected.

lexigram /lek'si-gram/ n a sign which represents a word. [Gr lexis a word, and **-gram**]

lexigraphy /lek-sig'rə-fi/ n a system of writing in which each sign represents a word. [Gr lexis word, and graphein to write]
■ **lexigraphic** /-graf'ik/ or **lexigraph'ical** adj.

lexis /lek'sis/ n the way in which a piece of writing is expressed in words, diction; the total stock of words in a language. [Gr, word]

ley¹ /lā or lē/ see **lea**¹,²,³.
□ **ley'-farming** see under **lea²**.

ley² /lā/ n any of the straight lines between features of the landscape, possibly pathways, or perhaps having scientific or magical significance in prehistoric times (also **ley line**). [Variant of **lea¹**]

ley³ see **leu**.

Leyden jar /lā'dən jär/ n a condenser for electricity, a glass jar coated inside and outside with tinfoil or other conducting material. [Leyden in Holland, where it was invented]

Leyland cypress /lā'land sī'prəs/ or **leylandii** /lā-lan'di-ī/ n a fast-growing conifer (Cupressocyparis leylandii), popular for garden hedges. [CJ Leyland (1849–1926), British horticulturalist]

lez, **lezz** or **les** /lez/ or **lezzy** /lez'i/ (inf; often offensive) n short form of lesbian.

leze-majesty, **leze-liberty**, etc see under **lese-majesty**.

LF abbrev: line feed (comput); low frequency (radio).

LG see **LGer**.

lg. or **lge** abbrev: large.

LGA abbrev: Local Government Association.

LGBT abbrev: lesbian, gay, bisexual and transgender.

LGBTI abbrev: lesbian, gay, bisexual, transgender, and intersex.

LGer or **LG** abbrev: Low German.

lgth abbrev: length.

LGU abbrev: Ladies' Golf Union.

LGV abbrev: large goods vehicle.

LH abbrev: luteinizing hormone.

lh abbrev: left hand.

LHA abbrev: Local Health Authority.

Lhasa Apso /lä′sə ap′sō/ n (pl **Lhasa Apsos**) a Tibetan (breed of) small, long-haired dog. [*Lhasa*, the capital of Tibet]

LHD abbrev : *Litterarum Humaniorum Doctor* (L), Doctor of Humanities, literally Doctor of the Humaner Letters.

lhd abbrev : left-hand drive.

iherzolite /lûr′zə-līt/ (mineralogy) n peridotite, consisting essentially of olivine with monoclinic and orthorhombic pyroxenes. [From Lake *Lherz* in the Pyrenees (Ariége)]

LI abbrev : Light Infantry; Long Island (US).

Li (chem) symbol : lithium.

li /lē/ n a Chinese unit of distance, about one-third of a mile. [Chin *li*]

liable /lī′ə-bl/ adj subject to an obligation, esp legally; exposed to a possibility or risk; responsible (for); tending (usu with to); apt; likely (to); subject (Shakesp); fitting, suitable (Shakesp). [Appar from Fr *lier*, from L *ligāre* to bind]
■ **liabil′ity** n the state of being liable; that for which one is liable, a debt, responsibility, etc; someone or something that is a problem or that causes a problem.
■ **employers′ liability** responsibility of employers to their servants for the negligence of those to whom they have delegated their authority. **limited liability** a principle of modern statute law which limits the responsibilities of shareholders in a partnership, joint-stock company, etc by the extent of their personal interest therein. **public liability** responsibility of a business for injury to members of the public through negligence.

liaison /lē-ā′zn or -zō̃ or lye-zō̃′/ n union, or bond of union; connection; a secret or illicit love affair; effective conjunction with another unit or force (milit); in French, the linking in pronunciation of a final (and otherwise silent) consonant to a vowel beginning the next word; a binding agent or thickener. [Fr, from L *ligātiō, -ōnis*, from *ligāre* to bind]
■ **liaise** /lē-āz′/ vi (back-formation) to form a link (with); to be or get in touch (with).
□ **liaison officer** n an officer forming a link with another unit or force.

liana /lē-ä′nə/ or **liane** /lē-än′/ n any climbing plant, esp a twisted woody kind festooning tropical forests. [Fr *liane*, Latinized or Hispanicized as *liana*, appar from *lier*, from L *ligāre* to bind]
■ **lian′oid** adj.

liang /lyang/ n a Chinese ounce or tael, a unit of weight and formerly of currency. [Chin *liǎng*]

liar see under **lie¹**.

liard /lī′ərd/ adj grey; dapple-grey (Scot **lī′art** or **ly′art**). ◆ n /lyär/ an old French coin of low value. [OFr *liard, liart*]

Lias /lī′əs/ (geol) n and adj Lower Jurassic. [A Somerset quarryman's word, appar from OFr *liois* (Fr *liais*) a kind of limestone]
■ **Liassic** /lī-as′ik/ adj.

liatris /lī-at′ris/ n (pl **liat′ris**) a plant of the genus *Liatris*, including the blazing star. [Origin uncertain]

Lib. /lib/ abbrev : Liberal.

lib¹ /lib/ (inf) n short form of **liberation** (see under **liberate**).

lib² /lib/ (now dialect) vt to geld. [Cf Du *lubben*]

lib. abbrev : *liber* (L), book; librarian; library.

libation /li- or lī-bā′shən/ n the pouring forth of wine or other liquid in honour of a god or goddess, or (facetiously) for some other purpose; the liquid poured; an alcoholic drink (facetious). [L *lībāre, -ātum* to pour, sip, touch; Gr *leibein* to pour]
■ **lī′bant** adj (archaic or poetic) sipping; lightly touching. **lī′bate** vt (rare) to make a libation to. **lī′batory** adj.

libbard /lib′ərd/ (archaic) n same as **leopard**.

libber /lib′ər/ (inf) n short form of **liberationist** (see under **liberate**).

lib. cat. abbrev : library catalogue.

Lib Dem abbrev : Liberal Democrat.

libeccio /li-bet′chō/ or (Milton) **libecchio** /-bek′i-ō/ n (pl **libecc′ios** or **libecch′ios**) the south-west wind. [Ital, from L *Libs*; Gr *Lips, Libos*]

libel /lī′bl/ n any malicious defamatory publication or statement; defamation, either written or made for general reception, eg by radio or television (Eng law); distinguished from **slander** or spoken defamation; in Scots law both are slander; a written accusation; the statement of a plaintiff's grounds of complaint. ◆ vt (**lī′belling** or (US) **lī′beling** (and in all such forms); **lī′belled**) to defame by libel; to satirize unfairly; to proceed against by producing a written complaint (law). [L *libellus*, dimin of *liber* a book]
■ **lī′bellant** n a person who brings a libel. **libellee′** n a person against whom a libel is brought. **lī′beller** n a defamer. **lī′belling** n. **lī′bellous** adj containing a libel; defamatory. **lī′bellously** adv.

liber /lī′bər/ (bot; rare) n phloem or bast. [L *liber* bast, book]

liberal /lib′(ə-)rəl/ adj generous; noble-minded; broad-minded; not bound by authority or traditional orthodoxy; looking to the general or broad sense rather than the literal; candid; free; free from restraint; ample; (with cap) of the Liberal Party (see below); of studies or education, directed towards the cultivation of the mind for its own sake, disinterested, opp to *technical* and *professional*; befitting a freeman or a gentleman (archaic); licentious in speech or action (obs).
◆ n a person who advocates greater freedom in political institutions; (with cap) a member of the Liberal Party (see below); a person whose views are liberal. [L *līberālis* befitting a freeman, from *līber* free]
■ **lib′eralism** n the principles of a liberal in politics or religion. **lib′eralist** n and adj. **liberalist′ic** adj. **liberality** /-al′i-ti/ n the quality of being liberal; generosity; magnanimity, broad-mindedness or nobleness of mind; candour; freedom from prejudice. **liberalīzā′tion** or **-s-** n. **lib′eralize** or **-ise** vt and vi to make or become liberal or enlightened. **lib′erally** adv. **lib′eralness** n.
□ **liberal arts** n pl the studies that make up a liberal education; in the Middle Ages, the *trivium* and *quadrivium*. **liberal democracy** n (politics) a state or system which combines the right to individual freedom with the right to representative government. **Liberal Democrat** n a member of the **Liberal Democrats** (formerly called Social and Liberal Democrats), a UK political party formed in 1988 from the Liberal Party and the Social Democratic Party. **Liberal Party** n in the UK, the political party which emerged, as successors to the Whigs, in the mid 19c, splitting into two factions in 1988, the larger and more influential group forming, together with the SDP, the Liberal Democrats; in Australia and Canada, one of the major political parties; generally, a party advocating democratic reform and individual liberty. **Liberal Unionists** n pl a section of the Liberal Party that opposed Gladstone's Home Rule policy (1886) and joined the Conservatives.

liberate /lib′ə-rāt/ vt to set free; to release from restraint, confinement or slavery; to steal or appropriate (facetious); to give off (chem). [L *līberāre, -ātum*, from *līber* free]
■ **liberā′tion** n setting free, releasing; the first stage in ore treatment, in which comminution is used to detach valuable minerals from gangue (mining); freeing, or seeking to free (a group) from social disadvantages, prejudices, injustice or abuse (inf short form **lib**). **liberā′tionism** n. **liberā′tionist** n a person who supports the cause of social freedom and equality for sections of society believed to be underprivileged or discriminated against (inf short form **libb′er**); a person who is in favour of church disestablishment. ◆ adj of or relating to liberationism or liberationists. **lib′erātor** n. **lib′eratory** /-ə-tə-ri/ adj tending to liberate.
□ **liberated woman** n one who rejects the older ideas of woman as the weaker sex, a woman's place being in the home, etc, and believes in living and working on equal terms with men. **liberation theology** n esp in S America, a development of Christian doctrine that demands a commitment to social revolution wherever injustice and exploitation are thought to exist.

Liberian /lī-bē′ri-ən/ adj of Liberia, a republic in W Africa. ◆ n a native or citizen of Liberia. [L *līber* free; the country was orig a homeland for freed slaves]

libero /lē′bə-rō/ (football) n (pl **li′beros**) a footballer who plays behind the backs, acting as the last line in the defence but able to move freely throughout the field, a sweeper. [Ital, free, free man]

liberty /lib′ər-ti/ n freedom from constraint, captivity, slavery or tyranny; freedom to do as one pleases; the unrestrained enjoyment of natural rights; power of free choice; privilege; permission; free range; leisure; disposal; the bounds within which certain privileges are enjoyed; (often in pl) a limited area outside a prison in which prisoners were allowed to live (archaic); presumptuous, improper or undue freedom of speech or action; speech or action violating ordinary civility. [Fr *liberté*, from L *lībertās, -ātis* liberty; L *libertīnus* a freedman, from *līber* free]
■ **libertā′rian** n a believer in free will; a person who believes in the maximum amount of freedom of thought, behaviour, etc. ◆ adj of or relating to libertarians or libertarianism. **libertā′rianism** n. **liberticī′dal** adj. **liber′ticide** n a destroyer of liberty; destruction of liberty. **lib′ertinage** (also /-ûrt′/) n debauchery. **lib′ertine** /-tēn, -tin or -tīn/ n a person who leads a licentious life, a rake or debauchee; orig a freedman; formerly a person who professed free opinions, esp in religion. ◆ adj unrestrained; licentious; belonging to a freedman. **lib′ertinism** n.
□ **lib′erty-boat** n a boat for liberty-men (see below). **liberty bodice** n an undergarment like a vest formerly often worn by children. **liberty cap** n same as **cap of liberty** (see under **cap¹**); a yellowish-brown conical-capped mushroom producing the drug psilocybin. **Liberty Hall** n (inf; also without caps) a place where one may do as one likes. **liberty horse** n a circus horse that, as one of a group and without a rider, carries out movements on command. **lib′erty-man** n a sailor with permission to go ashore. **liberty of indifference** n freedom of the will. **liberty of the press** n freedom to print and publish without

government permission. **liberty ship** n a prefabricated all-welded cargo-ship mass-produced in the USA during World War II.
■ **at liberty** not restrained or constrained; free; unoccupied; available. **civil liberty** freedom of an individual within the law; individual freedom as guaranteed by a country's laws. **take liberties with** to treat with undue freedom or familiarity, or indecently; to falsify. **take the liberty** to venture or presume.

libido /li-bē'dō or li-bī'dō/ n (pl **libid'os**) vital urge, either in general or as of sexual origin (psychol); sexual impulse. [L libīdō, -inis desire, from libet, lubet it pleases]
■ **libidinal** /-bid'-/ adj relating to the libido. **libid'inally** adv. **libid'inist** n a lewd person. **libidinos'ity** or **libid'inousness** n. **libid'inous** adj lustful, lascivious, lewd. **libid'inously** adv.

libken /lib'ken/ (old sl) n a place of abode, a home. [Old slang lib to sleep, and **ken²**]

Lib-Lab abbrev: Liberal-Labour.

LIBOR or **Libor** /lī'bör/ (finance) abbrev: London Inter-Bank Offer Rate.

Libra /lē'bra/ n the Balance, a constellation giving its name to, and formerly coinciding with, a sign of the zodiac (astron); the seventh sign of the zodiac, between Virgo and Scorpio (astrol); a person born between 24 September and 22 October, under the sign of Libra (astrol). [L]
■ **Li'bran** n and adj (relating to or characteristic of) a person born under the sign of Libra.
■ **first point of Libra** the intersection of celestial equator and ecliptic passed by the sun in autumn in the northern hemisphere, now actually in Virgo.

libra /lī' or lē'bra/ n (in ancient Rome) a pound (still used abbreviated to **lb** for the British pound in weight and to d for a pound in money). [L lībra]

libraire /lē-brer'/ (Fr) n a bookseller.
■ **librairie** /lē-bre-rē'/ n bookselling; a bookshop.

library /lī'b(ra-)ri/ n a building or room where a collection of books is kept; a collection of books; a publisher's series; also a collection of records, CDs, films, etc; a collection of computer programs. [L librārium a bookcase, from liber a book]
■ **librā'rian** n someone who works in or is in charge of a library. **librā'rianship** n.
□ **library edition** n an edition of a book with high-quality binding, etc.
■ **lending library** one from which people may take books away on loan.

librate /lī'brāt/ vi to oscillate; to be poised. ◆ vt (obs) to poise; to balance. [L lībrāre, -ātum, from lībra balance]
■ **librā'tion** n balancing; a state of equipoise; a slight swinging motion. **librā'tional** adj. **lī'bratory** adj.
□ **libration of the moon** n a slight turning of the moon to each side alternately so that more than half of its surface is visible.

libretto /li-bret'ō/ n (pl **librett'i** /-ē/ or **librett'os**) the text or book of words of an opera, oratorio, ballet, etc. [Ital dimin of libro, from L liber a book]
■ **librett'ist** n a writer of libretti.

Librium® /lib'ri-əm/ n a proprietary name for chlordiazepoxide, a tranquillizer.

Libyan /lib'i-ən/ adj of Libya in N Africa. ◆n a native or citizen of Libya. [Gr Libyē Libya]

lice /līs/ n pl see **louse**.

licence or (US) **license** /lī'səns/ n being allowed; leave; grant of permission, eg for manufacturing a patented article, developing an area or natural resource, selling intoxicants, driving a motor vehicle, piloting an aeroplane, using a television set, owning a gun; the document by which authority is conferred; excess or abuse of freedom; licentiousness, libertinage or debauchery; a departure from a rule or standard for artistic or literary effect; tolerated freedom. [Fr licence, from L licentia, from licēre to be allowed]
■ **li'censable** adj. **li'cense** (also **li'cence**) vt to grant licence to; to issue with a licence; to permit to depart, dismiss; to authorize or permit. **li'censed** adj holding a (valid) licence; permitted, tolerated; legally allowed to sell alcohol. **licensee'** n a person to whom a licence is granted, esp to sell alcohol. **li'censer** or (chiefly US) **li'censor** n a person who grants licence or permission; a person authorized to license. **li'censure** n the act of licensing or granting of a licence, esp for professional practice. **licentiate** /lī-sen'shi-āt/ n a holder of an academic diploma of various kinds; in some European universities, a graduate ranking between bachelor and doctor; among Presbyterians, a person authorized by a Presbytery to preach. **licen'tiateship** n. **licentious** /-sen'shəs/ adj indulging in excessive freedom; given to the indulgence of the animal passions; dissolute. **licen'tiously** adv. **licen'tiousness** n.

□ **license block** see under **block**. **licensed victualler** n a person licensed to sell food and esp alcoholic drink, for consumption on the premises, a publican. **license plate** n (N Am) a vehicle number plate.
■ **special licence** licence given by the Archbishop of Canterbury permitting the marriage of two specified people without banns, and at a place and time other than those prescribed by law, loosely used in Scotland in speaking of marriage by consent registered by warrant of the sheriff.

licentia vatum /lī-sen'shyə vä'təm or li-ken'ti-ä wä'tŭm, also vä'/ (L) n poetic licence.

lich¹ /lich/ (Spenser) adj a Southern form of **like¹**.

lich² /lich/ n (obs) a body, living or dead. [ME lich, liche (Southern), like (Northern), from OE līc; Ger Leiche corpse]
□ **lich'gate** or **lych'gate** n a roofed churchyard gate, orig to rest a bier under. **lich'-owl** n a screech owl, once thought to be a death-portent. **lich'wake** see **lykewake**. **lich'way** n a path by which the dead are carried to burial.

lichanos /lik'a-nos/ (Gr music) n the string or the note struck by the forefinger. [Gr lichanos forefinger, lichanos, from leichein to lick]

lichee see **lychee**.

lichen /lī'kən or lich'ən/ n a compound plant consisting of a fungus and an alga living symbiotically, forming crusts and tufts on stones, trees and soil; an eruption on the skin. [L līchēn, from Gr leichēn, -ēnos]
■ **li'chened** adj covered with lichens. **li'chenin** n a starch obtained from Iceland moss. **li'chenism** n the association of fungus and alga as a lichen. **li'chenist** or **lichenol'ogist** n a specialist in **lichenol'ogy**, the study of lichens. **li'chenoid** adj. **li'chenose** or **li'chenous** adj relating to, of the nature of, or covered with, lichens or lichen.

lichgate, etc see under **lich²**.

lichi see **lychee**.

licht /lihht/ the Scots form of **light¹,²,³**.

licit /lis'it/ adj lawful, allowable. [L licitus]
■ **lic'itly** adv.

lick /lik/ vt to pass the tongue over (eg to moisten or taste); to take into the mouth using the tongue; to lap; to put or make by passing the tongue over; to pass over or play upon in the manner of a tongue; to flicker over or around; to smear; to beat (inf). ◆ vi to go at full speed (inf); to smoke crack (drug sl). ◆ n an act of licking; a quantity licked up, or such (a small amount) as might be imagined to be licked up; a slight smearing or wash; a place where animals lick salt; a blow or flick (esp Scot in pl a thrashing); vigorous speed (inf); a wag (Scot); in jazz or rock music, a short instrumental passage or flourish (inf). [OE liccian; Ger lecken, L lingere, Gr leichein]
■ **lick'er** n. **lick'ing** n a thrashing.
□ **lick'er-in'** n a toothed cylinder that takes in material to a carding engine. **lick'penny** n (obs) something which licks up, or is a drain upon, one's money. **lick'spittle** or (rare) **lick'-platter** n a toady. **lick'-trencher** n (archaic) a parasite.
■ **a lick and a promise** a perfunctory wash. **lick into shape** to mould into satisfactory form, from the notion that the she-bear gives form to her shapeless young by licking them. **lick one's lips** to look forward, or (archaic) to recall, with pleasure. **lick one's wounds** to retire from a defeat, failure, etc, esp in order to try to recover one's strength, pride, etc. **lick someone's boots** to toady. **lick the dust** to be killed or finished off (inf); to be abjectly servile.

lickerish or **liquorish** /lik'ə-rish/ (obs) adj dainty; tempting; eager to taste or enjoy; lecherous. [Variant of **lecherous**]
■ **lick'erishly** adv. **lick'erishness** n.

lickety-split /lik'ə-ti-split'/ (US inf) adv immediately; very quickly. [**lick** and **split**]

licorice another spelling (chiefly N Am) for **liquorice**.

lictor /lik'tör or -tər/ (hist) n an officer who attended a Roman magistrate, bearing the fasces. [L]

lid /lid/ n a cover, hinged or separate, for the opening and closing of a receptacle; the movable cover of the eye; a temperature inversion in the atmosphere that prevents the mixing of the air above and below the inversion region (meteorol); an effective restraint (fig); a hat (inf). [OE hlid (Du lid), from hlīdan to cover]
■ **lidd'ed** adj having a lid or lids. **lid'less** adj.
■ **flip one's lid** see under **flip**. **put the lid on it** (inf) to end the matter; to be a culminating injustice, misfortune, etc. **take**, **lift** or **blow the lid off** to uncover, reveal (a scandal, etc).

Lide /līd/ (obs or dialect) n the month of March. [OE hlȳda, connected with hlūd loud]

lidger see **ledger**.

lido /lē'dō/ n (pl **lid'os**) a bathing beach; an open-air swimming-pool. [From the Lido at Venice, from L lītus shore]

lidocaine /lī'də-kān/ n US name for **lignocaine**. [acetanilid and cocaine]

LIE (*insurance*) *abbrev* : loss of independent existence.

lie¹ /lī/ *n* a false statement made with the intention of deceiving; anything misleading or of the nature of imposture; (with *the*) an accusation of lying. ♦ *vi* (**ly'ing**; **lied**) to make a false statement with the intention to deceive; to give a false impression. —Also (*Scot*) **lee** /lē/, often referring to an unintentional false statement. [OE *lyge* (noun), *lēogan* (strong verb); Du *liegen*, Gothic *liugan*, Ger *lügen* to lie]

■ **lī'ar** *n* a person who lies, *esp* habitually. **ly'ing** *adj* addicted to telling lies. ♦ *n* the habit of telling lies. **ly'ingly** *adv*.

□ **lie detector** *n* an instrument claimed to detect lying by recording abnormal involuntary bodily reactions in a person not telling the truth.

■ **give someone the lie** (*archaic*, **in his** or **her throat**) to accuse someone directly of lying. **give the lie to** to accuse of lying; to prove false. **lie in one's throat** or **through one's teeth** (*usu facetious*) to lie shamelessly. **white lie** a minor falsehood, *esp* one uttered for reasons of tact, etc.

lie² /lī/ *vi* (*prp* **ly'ing**; *pat* **lay**; *pap* **lain**, (*Bible*) **lī'en**, (*non-standard*) **laid**, by confusion with **lay**¹) to be in a horizontal or nearly horizontal position; to assume such a position; to lean; to press; to be situated; to have a position or extent; to remain; to be or remain passively; to abide; to be still; to be incumbent; to depend; to consist; to be sustainable (*law*); to be imprisoned (*Shakesp*); to lodge, pass the night (*archaic*). ♦ *n* mode or direction of lying; slope and disposition; relative position; general situation; a spell of lying; an animal's lair or resting place; a position from which a golf ball is to be played; a layer (*archaic* or *dialect*); a railway siding. [OE *licgan*; Ger *liegen*; Gothic *ligan*]

■ **lī'er** *n*.

□ **lie'-abed'** *n* someone who lies late in bed (also *adj*). **lie-down** see **lie down** below. **lie'-in'** *n* a longer than usual stay in bed in the morning. **ly'ing-in'** *n* (*pl* **ly'ings-in'**) confinement during childbirth. **lying-in hospital** or **ward** *n* (*old*) a maternity hospital or ward.

■ **lie along** (*archaic*) to be extended at full length. **lie at someone's door** (of something untoward) to be directly attributable to someone. **lie at someone's heart** (*archaic*) to be an object of interest or affection to someone. **lie back** to lean back on a support; to rest after a period of hard work. **lie by** to be inactive; to keep out of the way; to lie to (*naut*). **lie by the heels** (*archaic*) to be in prison. **lie down** to place oneself in a horizontal position, *esp* in order to sleep or rest (**lie'-down'** *n*). **lie hard** or **heavy on**, **upon** or **to** to oppress, burden. **lie in** to stay in bed later than usual; to be in the state of giving birth to a child (*old*). **lie in one** to be in one's power. **lie in the way** to be ready, at hand; to be an obstacle. **lie in wait** to lie in ambush (often with *for*). **lie low** to keep quiet or hidden; to conceal one's actions or intentions. **lie of the land** (*fig*) the current situation. **lie on** or **upon** to be incumbent on. **lie on one's hands** to remain unwanted, unclaimed or unused. **lie on one's oars** see under **oar**. **lie out of** to remain without the good of, without payment of. **lie over** to be deferred to a future occasion. **lie to** (*naut*) to be or become nearly stationary with head to the wind. **lie under** to be subject to or oppressed by. **lie up** to abstain from work; to take to or remain in bed; (of a ship) to go into or be in dock. **lie with** to rest with as a choice, duty, etc; to have sexual intercourse with (*Bible* or *archaic*); to lodge or sleep with (*archaic*). **take it lying down** (*inf*) to endure without resistance or protest.

Liebfraumilch /lēb'frow-milk or -milhh/ *n* a German white wine made with grapes from the Rhine region. [Ger *Liebfrau* the Virgin Mary (after the convent where it was originally made) and *Milch* milk]

Liebig /lē'big/ *n* a beef extract first prepared by the German chemist J von *Liebig* (1803–73).

□ **Liebig condenser** *n* the ordinary water-cooled glass condenser used in laboratory distillations.

Liechtenstein /lik' or lihh'tən-s(h)tīn/ *adj* of or relating to the Principality of *Liechtenstein* in central Europe, or its inhabitants.

■ **Liech'tensteiner** *n* a native or citizen of Liechtenstein.

lied /lēt/ *n* (*pl* **lieder** /lē'dər/) a German lyric or song, *esp* an art-song. [Ger; cf OE *lēoth* a song]

□ **lied ohne worte** /ō'nə vör'tə/ *n* a song without words.

lief /lēf/, also **lieve** or **leve** /lēv/ (*archaic*) *adj* (**lief'er** or **liev'er** (*Scot* **loor**); **lief'est** or **liev'est**) beloved, dear (also *n*). ♦ *adv* willingly. [OE *lēof*; Ger *lieb*]

■ **had as lief** should like as well to. **had liefer** or **liever** had rather. **leeze me** (for *lief is me* ; *Scot*) an expression of affection (*usu* with *on*).

liege /lēj/ (*hist*) *adj* free except as within the relations of vassal and feudal lord; under a feudal tenure. ♦ *n* a person under a feudal tenure; a vassal; a loyal vassal, a subject; a lord or superior (also in this sense, **liege'-lord**). [OFr *lige*, prob from OHGer *ledic* free, and *līdan* to depart]

■ **liege'dom** *n* allegiance. **liege'less** *adj* not subject to a superior.

□ **liege'man** *n* a vassal; a subject.

lieger see **ledger**.

lien¹ /lē'ən or lēn/ (*law*) *n* a right to retain possession of another's property until the owner pays a debt or fulfils a contract. [Fr, from L *ligāmen* tie or band]

lien² /lī'ən/ (*Bible*) *pap* of **lie**².

lien³ /lī'ən/ (*obs*) *n* the spleen. [L *liēn*]

■ **lī'enal** *adj*.

lientery /lī'ən-tə-ri/ *n* a form of diarrhoea with liquid evacuations of undigested food. [Gr *leios* smooth, and *enteron* an intestine]

■ **lienteric** /-ter'ik/ *adj*.

lier see under **lie**².

lierne /li-ûrn'/ (*archit*) *n* a cross-rib or branch-rib in vaulting. [Fr]

lieu /lū or loo/ *n* place or stead, used chiefly in the phrase *in lieu of*. ♦ *adj* in place of, substitute, as in *lieu day* or *lieu holiday*. [Fr, from L *locus* place]

Lieut. *abbrev* : Lieutenant.

lieutenant /lef-, lif- or ləf-ten'ənt/, also (*esp navy*) /le-, lə- or loo-ten', (*archaic*) loot'nənt, (*US*) loo-/ *n* a person representing, or performing the work of, a superior (formerly also *fig*); an officer holding the place of another in his or her absence; a commissioned officer in the army next below a captain, or in the navy next below a lieutenant-commander and ranking with captain in the army; an officer in the police or fire departments next below a captain (*US*); a person holding a place next in rank to a superior, as in the compounds *lieutenant-colonel*, *lieutenant-commander* and *lieutenant-general*. [Fr; see **lieu** and **tenant**]

■ **lieuten'ancy** or **lieuten'antship**, (*Shakesp*) **lieuten'antry** *n* the post or commission of a lieutenant; lieutenants as a group or class.

□ **lieutenant governor** *n* a State governor's deputy (*US and Aust*); a governor subordinate to a governor-general; a governor in the Isle of Man, Jersey and Guernsey. **lieutenant governorship** *n*.

■ **Lord Lieutenant** (*pl* **Lords Lieutenant**, **Lord Lieutenants** or **Lords Lieutenants**) a permanent representative of the Crown in a county, head of the magistracy and the chief executive authority; the title of the viceroy of Ireland (until 1922).

lieve, etc see **lief**.

life /līf/ *n* (*pl* **lives** /līvz/) the state of being alive; conscious existence; animate or vegetative existence; the sum of the activities of plants and animals; continuation or possession of such a state; continued existence, activity, vitality or validity of anything; the period of usefulness of machinery, etc; vitality; union of soul and body; the period between birth and death; any of a number of opportunities of remaining in a game; career; current state of existence; manner of living; moral conduct; animation; liveliness, vivacity; the appearance of being alive; a living being, *esp* human; living things collectively; social state; social vitality; human affairs; a narrative of a life, a biography; eternal happiness; a source of existence or animation; the living form and expression, living semblance; in wines, sparkle; in cut gems, reflection, sparkle; imprisonment for life (*inf*); a person insured against death. ♦ *interj* used as an oath, abbreviated from *God's life*. ♦ *adj* and combining form for the duration of life; of life. [OE *līf* ; ON *līf*, Swed *lif*, Du *liif* body, life; Ger *Leib* body, *leben* to live, *Leben* life]

■ **life'ful** (*Spenser* **lyfull** or **lifull**) *adj* full of vital energy. **life'less** *adj* dead; unconscious; without vigour or vivacity; of food or drink, insipid; sluggish; not able to support living things. **life'lessly** *adv*. **life'lessness** *n*. **life'like** *adj* of something inanimate, like a living person or the copied original. **life'likeness** *n*. **līf'er** *n* a person sentenced to imprisonment for life; a life sentence. **life'some** *adj* (*archaic*) full of life; lively.

□ **life'-affirming** *adj* reinforcing a belief in the worth of human existence. **life'-and-death'** *adj* critical; determining or affecting whether someone lives or dies. **life annuity** *n* a sum paid to a person yearly during his or her life. **life assurance** or **life insurance** *n* insurance providing a sum of money for a specified beneficiary in the event of the policyholder's death, and sometimes for the policyholder if he or she reaches a specified age. **life'belt** *n* a buoyant circular belt for keeping a person afloat in water; any aid to survival (*fig*). **life'blood** *n* the blood necessary to life; anything which gives essential strength or life; a twitching, eg of the eyelid or lip (*archaic*). **life'boat** *n* a boat for saving people in trouble at sea; a measure taken in an attempt to save a business, financial operation, etc (*fig*; also often as *adj*). **life'boatman** *n*. **life'buoy** *n* a float for supporting a person in the water until he or she can be rescued. **life class** *n* an art class in which the students draw or paint the human body from a live model. **life coach** *n* a person whose job is to advise clients on how to achieve success and happiness. **life cycle** *n* the round of changes in the life and generations of an organism, from zygote to zygote (*biol*); the various stages in the life or development of anything, eg a manufactured product (*fig*). **life'-estate'** *n* an estate held during the life of the possessor. **life expectancy** *n* the length of time which any living organism can reasonably be expected to remain alive.

life'-force' *n* a directing principle supposed to be inherent in living things, turning their activities to nature's own purposes. **life'-giving** *adj* imparting life; invigorating. **life'guard** *n* a person employed to rescue bathers in difficulties; a bodyguard. **Life Guards** *n pl* two troops of cavalry, first so called in 1685, amalgamated in 1922 and forming, with the Royal Horse Guards, the Household Cavalry. **life history** *n* the history of a (person's, plant's, animal's, etc) life; the succession of changes from zygote to maturity and death; the life cycle. **life'hold** *adj* held for life. **life instinct** *n* (in psychoanalysis) the instinct for self-preservation and reproduction. **life insurance** see **life assurance** above. **life'-in'terest** *n* an interest lasting during a life. **life jacket** *n* a buoyant jacket for keeping a person afloat in water, a lifebelt. **life'line** *n* a rope for saving or safeguarding life; a line used by a diver for signalling; a vital means of communication; a line on the palm of the hand, taken as showing how long a person will live (*palmistry*). **life'long** *adj* lasting throughout one's life. **life'-mor'tar** *n* a mortar for throwing a line to a ship in distress. **life peer** *n* a peer whose title is not hereditary. **life peerage** *n*. **life peeress** *n* a woman who receives a peerage which cannot be handed down to heirs. **life'-preserv'er** *n* an apparatus for saving someone from drowning; a club or cosh. **life raft** *n* a raft kept on board a ship for use in an emergency. **life'-ren'dering** *adj* (*Shakesp*) yielding up life. **life'-rent** *n* (*Scots law*) a right to use for life. **life'-renter** *n* a person who enjoys a life-rent (also *fem* **life'-rentrix**). **life'-rock'et** *n* a rocket for carrying a line to a ship in distress. **life'-saver** *n* a person who saves another from death, *esp* from drowning; a lifeguard; someone who or something that comes to one's aid at a critical moment (*inf*). **life'-sav'ing** *adj* designed to save life, *esp* from drowning. ◆ *n* the act or skill of rescuing people who are in danger of drowning. **life school** *n* a school where artists work from living models. **life sciences** *n pl* those sciences (biology, medicine, etc) concerned with living organisms. **life scientist** *n*. **life sentence** *n* a prison sentence to last for the rest of the prisoner's natural life (*usu* now lasting *approx* 13 years). **life'-size** or **life'-sized** *adj* of the size of the object represented. **life'span** *n* the length of time for which a person or animal normally lives, or a machine, etc functions. **life story** *n* a biography or autobiography, *esp* as recounted in the media or book form. **life'style** *n* way of living, ie one's material surroundings, attitudes, behaviour, etc; the characteristic way of life of a group or individual. **life-support machine** or **system** *n* a device or system of devices designed to maintain human life in adverse conditions, eg in space, during serious illness, etc. **life table** *n* a table of statistics of probability of life. **life'-tenant** *n* the holder of a life-estate. **life'time** *n* the time during which one is alive. **life'-wear'y** *adj* (*Shakesp*) weary of life; wretched. **life'-work** *n* the work to which one's life is, has been or is to be devoted.

■ **bring to life** to give life to, make alive; to animate. **come to life** to become alive; to become animated. **for life** for the whole period of one's existence; (as if) to save one's life. **for the life of me**, **him**, **her**, etc (*usu* with *can* and a *neg*) try as I, he, she, etc might; though it were to save my, his, her, etc life. **get a life** (*inf*; *usu* in *imperative*) to start to live life to the full and do interesting things. **high life** fashionable society or its (glamorous) manner of living. **line of life** a crease in the palm in which palmists see a promise of longevity. **not on your life** (*inf*) on no account, absolutely not. **see life** to see how other people live, *esp* the less well-off or respectable. **take someone's life** to kill someone. **the life and soul** the person who is the chief source of fun, etc, *esp* at a party. **the life of Riley** /rī'li/ an easy, carefree (and often irresponsible) life. **to the life** very closely like the original; exactly drawn.

LIFFE *abbrev* : London International Financial Futures and Options Exchange.

LIFO /lī'fō/ *abbrev* : last in, first out (a method of pricing goods, controlling stock, storing data in a computer, or determining the likely order of redundancies).

lift¹ /lift/ *vt* to bring or take (often with *up*) to a higher or (with *down*) lower position; to elevate; to take up; to elate, encourage; to take and carry away; to hold up, support; to arrest (*sl*); to steal (*inf*); to plagiarize; to remove or revoke; in a foundry, to remove a pattern from a mould; to take up for burial (*Scot*); to increase (in value, price, etc) (*esp US*). ◆ *vi* to rise. ◆ *n* an act of lifting; lifting power; vertical distance of lifting; an enclosed platform or cagelike structure moving in a vertical shaft to carry people or goods up and down; the shaft in which it works; the component of the aerodynamic force on an aircraft acting upwards at right angles to the drag; something which is to be raised; something which assists in lifting; one of the layers of material in a shoe heel, *esp* an extra one to increase the wearer's height; a mechanism for raising or lowering a vessel to another level of a canal; a step in advancement, promotion, etc; a boost to one's spirits; a feeling of elation; a (*usu* free) journey in someone else's vehicle. [ON *lypta*, from *lopt* the air]

■ **lift'able** *adj*. **lift'er** *n* someone who, or something which, lifts; a thief (*Shakesp*).

□ **lift'back** *n* a car with a sloping rear door lifting up from the bottom, a hatchback. **lift'-boy**, **lift'-girl** or **lift'-man** *n* a person whose job is to operate a lift in a hotel, store, etc. **lift gate** *n* a device at the rear of a lorry, etc for lifting items of cargo to the required height for loading. **lift'ing-bridge** *n* a bridge whose roadway can be raised bodily. **lift'-off** *n* the take-off of an aircraft or rocket; the moment when this occurs. **lift pump** *n* any pump that is not a force pump.

■ **have one's face lifted** to undergo an operation for smoothing and firming the skin of one's face. **lift a finger** or **hand** (**to**) to make the smallest effort (to help, etc). **lift a** or **one's hand** (**to**) to raise it in hostility (to), to threaten physically. **lift off** of a rocket, etc, to take off, be launched.

lift² /lift/ (*Scot*) *n* the air, heavens or sky. [OE *lyft* ; Ger *Luft*, ON *lopt*, Gothic *luftus* the air]

lifull see under **life**.

lig¹ /lig/ (*sl*) *vi* to lie about, to idle; to be a freeloader, *esp* in the entertainment industry. ◆ *n* a party with free refreshments. [Orig dialect for **lie²**]

■ **ligg'er** *n*. **ligg'ing** *n*.

lig² or **ligge** /lig/ *vi* an obsolete or dialect form of **lie²**.

ligament /lig'ə-mənt/ *n* anything that binds; the bundle of fibrous tissue joining bones or cartilages (*anat*); a bond or tie. [L *ligāre* to bind]

■ **ligamental** /-ment'l/, **ligament'ary** or **ligament'ous** *adj*. **ligand** /lig'ənd or lī'/ *n* an atom, molecule, radical or ion which forms a complex with a central atom. **ligase** /lī'gāz/ *n* an enzyme which seals nicks in one strand of a duplex DNA, often used to seal gaps resulting from the artificial insertion of one DNA sequence into another. **ligate** /lī'gāt/ *vt* to tie up. **liga'tion** *n* the act of binding; the state of being bound; the joining together, often facilitated by sticky ends, of two linear nucleic acid molecules (*biol*). **ligature** /lig'ə-chər/ *n* anything that binds; a bandage; a tie or slur (*music*); a character formed from two or more letters, eg æ, ff (*printing*); a cord for tying the blood vessels, etc (*med*); impotence produced by magic (*archaic*). ◆ *vt* to bind with a ligature.

ligan see **lagan**.

ligand, **ligase**, **ligate**, **ligation**, **ligature**, etc see under **ligament**.

liger /lī'gər/ *n* the offspring of a *lion* and female ti*ger*.

ligge see **lig²**.

ligger¹ /lig'ər/ *n* the horizontal timber of a scaffolding; a lower millstone (cf **runner**); a plank bridge; a coverlet for a bed; a kelt or spent salmon; a night-line with float and bait for pike-fishing. [**lig²**, Scot and N Eng form of **lie²**]

ligger² and **ligging** see under **lig¹**.

light¹ /līt/ *n* the agency by which objects are made visible; electromagnetic radiation capable of producing visual sensation; anything from which it originates, such as the sun or a lamp; a high degree of illumination; day; a gleam or shining from a bright source; a gleam or glow in the eye or on the face; the power of vision (*archaic*); an eye (*archaic*); the brighter part of a picture; a means of igniting or illuminating; a lighthouse; mental or spiritual illumination (*fig*); enlightenment; a hint, clue or help towards understanding; knowledge; open view; aspect; a conspicuous person; an aperture for admitting light; a vertical division of a window; in a crossword, the word (or sometimes an individual letter in the word) on the diagram that is the answer to a clue. ◆ *adj* not dark; bright; whitish; well lit. ◆ *vt* (**light'ing**; **light'ed** or **lit**) to shine light on, provide light in; to set fire to; to follow or precede (someone, or his or her path) with a light. ◆ *vi* (*archaic*) to become light or bright. [ME *liht*, from OE (Anglian) *leht*, *lēht* (WSax *lēoht*); Ger *Licht*]

■ **light'er** *n* a person who sets something alight; a means of igniting, *esp* a small device for lighting cigarettes. **light'ful** *adj* (*archaic*) full of light. **light'ing** *n* illumination; ignition, kindling; arrangement or quality of lights. **light'ish** *adj*. **light'less** *adj*. **light'ness** *n*. **light'some** *adj* (*archaic* and *poetic*) full of light.

□ **light'-ball** *n* (*hist*) a combustible ball used to give light in warfare. **light box** *n* a box-shaped device with an internal lamp to facilitate viewing through paper, negatives, etc placed on its translucent surface; a box that produces simulated daylight, used in light therapy. **light bulb** *n* a glass bulb containing a low-pressure gas and a metal filament which glows when an electric current is passed through it, one of the most common methods of electric lighting. **light bulb moment** *n* (*inf*) a moment of inspiration or sudden understanding. **light'-dues** *n pl* tolls from ships, for maintenance of lighthouses. **light-emitting diode** *n* a semiconducting device that emits light when an electric current passes through it, as used for alphanumeric displays in digital clocks, electronic calculators, etc (*abbrev* **LED**). **light'-fast** *adj* (of colour in fabric, or coloured fabric) not liable to fade from prolonged exposure to light. **light'house** *n* a building with a powerful light to guide or give warning to ships or aircraft. **light'houseman** or **light'housekeeper** *n* the person in charge of a lighthouse. **light'ing-up** *n* and *adj*. **lighting-up time** *n* the time of day from which vehicles must have their lights switched on. **light meter** *n* (*photog*) a meter for measuring the level of light present, an exposure meter. **light'-mill** *n* a radiometer. **light'-or'gan** *n* a keyboard instrument that gives a play of light as an organ gives sound. **light pen** *n* (*comput*) a pen-shaped photoelectric device that can communicate directly with a computer, entering or altering data on a screen; a light-sensitive fibre-optic device shaped like a pen, used for reading barcoded labels. **light pollution** *n* the unpleasant effects of excessive artificial lighting, *esp* in large cities. **light'-proof** *adj* impervious to light, light-tight. **light'ship** *n* a ship serving the purpose of a lighthouse. **light show** *n* a colourful spectacle of moving lights that often accompanies rock and pop bands at live performances, *usu* projected onto a large screen. **light table** *n* (*printing*) (a table incorporating a ground-glass surface, illuminated from below, for use when working on lay-out with translucent materials. **light therapy** *n* the use of artificial light to treat depression, fatigue and disorders such as SAD, thought to be caused by insufficient natural light for the body's needs. **light'-tight** *adj* light-proof. **light time** *n* the time taken by light to travel from a heavenly body to the observer. **light'-tower** *n*. **light trap** *n* any mechanical arrangement which permits movement while excluding light, such as the doors and partitions providing access to a darkroom. **light'-year** *n* the distance light travels in a year (about 6 000 000 000 000 miles). ▪ **according to one's lights** as far as one's knowledge, spiritual illumination, etc enables one to judge. **between the lights** in the twilight. **between two lights** under cover of darkness. **bring to light** to reveal. **come to light** to be revealed. **fixed light** in lighthouses, an unchanging light. **floating light** a light at the masthead of a lightship. **go out like a light** to fall sound asleep soon after going to bed. **hide one's light under a bushel** see under **bushel**[1]. **in a good** (or bad) **light** putting a favourable (or unfavourable) construction on something. **inner light** spiritual illumination, *esp* divinely inspired. **in one's** (or **the**) **light** positioned between the speaker or the stated person and the source of illumination; blocking one's chance of success. **in the light of** considering, taking into account. **leading light** see under **lead**[1]. **light at the end of the tunnel** an indication that success, completion, etc is assured, if still distant. **light of nature** intellectual perception or intuition; man's capacity of discovering truth unaided by revelation (*theol*). **lights out** a bugle or trumpet call for the extinction of lights (*milit*); the time at which lights are turned out for the night, in a boarding school, barracks, etc. **light up** to light one's lamp, pipe, cigarette, etc; to turn on the light; to make or become light, bright, happy, etc. **lit** (**up**) drunk. **northern** and **southern lights** aurora borealis and australis respectively. **see the light** to come into view or being; to realize a fact, mistake, etc; to be religiously converted. **see the light of day** to be born, discovered or produced; to come to public notice. **shed**, **throw** or **cast light on** to clarify, help to explain. **stand in one's own light** to hinder one's own advantage. **strike a light!** (*sl*) an exclamation expressing surprise.

light[2] /līt/ *adj* not heavy; of incorrectly low weight; of work, easily performed; easily digested; containing little fat and/or sugar, and so healthier; containing little alcohol; of bread, well risen; not heavily armed; active; not heavily burdened or equipped; unimportant; not dense, copious or intense; slight; scanty; gentle; delicate; nimble; facile; frivolous; unheeding; cheerful or lively; amusing; unchaste; of soil, loose or sandy; giddy or delirious; idle; worthless; in the state of having given birth to a child (in *compar*; *obs*); falling short in the number of tricks one has contracted to make (*bridge*). ◆ *adv* lightly. ◆ *vt* (*obs*) to make lighter. [OE (Anglian) *līht* (WSax *līoht*, *lēoht*); Ger *leicht*, ON *lēttr*; L *levis*] ▪ **light'en** *vt* to make lighter. ◆ *vi* to become lighter. **light'ener** *n* a cosmetic applied to the skin of the face to mask darker areas. **light'er** *n* a large open boat used in unloading and loading ships. **light'erage** *n* loading, unloading and ferrying by lighters; the payment for such service. **light'ish** *adj*. **light'ly** *adv* in a light manner; slightly; easily, readily, unthinkingly (*Shakesp*); not improbably (*archaic*); promptly. ◆ *vt* (*esp* in Scots form **lichtly** /lihht'li/) to slight or make light of. **light'ness** *n*. **lights** *n pl* the lungs of an animal (as lighter than the adjoining parts). **light'some** *adj* light, cheerful, lively, cheering. **light'somely** *adv*. **light'someness** *n*.
❑ **light air** *n* (*meteorol*) a wind of force 1 on the Beaufort scale, reaching speeds of 1 to 3mph. **light'-armed** *adj* (*milit*) armed in a manner suitable for activity. **light breeze** *n* (*meteorol*) a wind of force 2 on the Beaufort scale, reaching speeds of 4 to 7mph. **light engine** *n* one without coaches or trucks attached. **light'erman** *n* a person employed in lighterage. **light'er-than-air** *adj* of aircraft, kept in the air by gas which is lighter than air. **light'-faced** *adj* (*printing*) of type, having thin lines. **light'-fing'ered** *adj* light or active with one's fingers; inclined to steal. **light flyweight** see flyweight under **fly**. **light'-footed** (*archaic* **light'-foot**) *adj* nimble, active. **light'-hand'ed** *adj* with a light, delicate, or dexterous touch; having little in the hand; empty-handed; insufficiently manned. **light'-head'ed** *adj* giddy in the head; delirious; thoughtless; unsteady, *esp* through slight drunkenness. **light'-head'edly** *adv*. **light'-head'edness** *n*. **light'-heart'ed** *adj*

unburdened or merry of heart; free from anxiety; cheerful; inconsiderate (*archaic*). **light'-heart'edly** *adv*. **light'-head'edly** *adv*. **light'-heart'edness** *n*. **light heavyweight** see **heavyweight** under **heavy**. **light'-heeled** *adj* swift of foot; loose, unchaste (*obs*). **light horse** *n* light-armed cavalry. **light horseman** *n*. **light industry** see under **industry**. **light infantry** *n* light-armed-infantry. **light'-legged** *adj* swift of foot. **light literature**, **music**, etc such as calls for little mental effort. **light middleweight** see **middleweight** under **middle**. **light'-mind'ed** *adj* frivolous or unstable; inconsiderate. **light'-mind'edness** *n*. **light'-o'-love** *n* a fickle or wanton woman; in *Shakesp* the name of an old dance tune. **light railway** *n* a railway of light construction. **light'-spir'ited** *adj* having a cheerful spirit. **light water** *n* normal water (H_2O) as opposed to heavy water (qv). **light-water reactor** *n* a reactor using normal water as moderator and coolant (*abbrev* **LWR**). **light'weight** *n* a weight category, applied *esp* in boxing; a sportsperson of the specified weight for the category (eg in professional boxing above featherweight, **junior lightweight** or **super featherweight** (maximum 59kg/130lb), **light'weight** (maximum 61kg/135lb), and **super lightweight** or **junior welterweight** (maximum 63.5kg/140lb)); a person of little importance, authority, etc; a light article of any kind, eg a motorcycle. ◆ *adj* light in weight; lacking substance, earnestness, solemnity, etc (*fig*). **light'-winged** *adj* having light wings; volatile.
▪ **lighten up** (*inf*) to relax, calm down; to become less serious, angry or otherwise emotional. **make light of** to treat as being of little consequence.

light[3] /līt/ *vi* (**light'ing**; **light'ed** or **lit**) (also (*Prayer Book*) **light'en**) to dismount; to come down eg from a horse or vehicle, or from a fall or flight; to alight; to settle; to rest; to come upon by chance (with *on* or *upon*). [OE *līhtan* to dismount, literally to make light; see **light**[2]] ▪ **light into** (*inf*) to attack, with blows or words. **light out** (*inf*) to decamp.

lighten[1] /līt'(ə)n/ *vt* to make light, lighter or brighter; to illuminate. ◆ *vi* to become light, lighter or brighter; to flash as lightning. [Ety as for **light**[1]]
▪ **light'ening** *n* a making or becoming lighter or brighter.

lighten[2] see under **light**[2,3].

lightning /līt'ning/ *n* a flash of light in the sky, caused by electricity being discharged from thunderclouds; a revival or exhilaration supposed to precede death (*Shakesp*). ◆ *adj* characterized by speed and suddenness. [Ety as for **light**[1]]
❑ **light'ning-arrester** *n* an apparatus for protecting electrical apparatus in thunderstorms. **lightning bug** *n* a firefly. **lightning chess** *n* a fast form of chess in which players must complete their moves within a short time period (also called (*US*) **rapid-tran'sit chess**). **lightning conductor** or **lightning rod** *n* a metallic rod for protecting buildings from lightning. **lightning strike** *n* an industrial or military strike without warning. **light'ning-tube** *n* a fulgurite.

lightsome see under **light**[1,2].

lignage /lī'nij/ (*Spenser*) same as **lineage** (see under **line**[1]).

lign-aloes or **lignaloes** /līn-al'ōz or lig-nal'ōz/ (*Bible*) *n* aloes-wood. [L *lignum* wood, and *aloēs*, genitive of L and Gr *aloē* aloe]

ligne /līn (Fr lē'ny')/ *n* a measure of watch movement (Swiss ligne = 2.256mm). [Fr]

ligneous, **lignite**, etc see under **lignum**[1].

lignocaine /lig'nō-kān/ *n* a local anaesthetic used eg in dentistry and also to regulate an unsteady heartbeat. [L *lignum* wood, and co*caine*]

lignum[1] /lig'nəm/ *n* wood. [L *lignum* wood]
▪ **lig'neous** *adj* woody; wooden. **lignifica'tion** *n*. **lig'niform** *adj* resembling wood. **lig'nify** *vt* and *vi* to turn into wood or make woody. **lig'nin** *n* a complicated mixture of substances deposited in the thickened cell walls of plants, making them rigid. **ligniper'dous** *adj* (L *perdere* to destroy) destructive of wood. **lig'nite** /-nīt/ *n* brown coal, a stage in the conversion of vegetable matter into coal. **lignitic** /-nit'ik/ *adj*. **ligniv'orous** *adj* (L *vorāre* to devour) feeding on wood. **lig'nose** *adj* ligneous. ◆ *n* a constituent of lignin.
❑ **lignocell'ulose** *n* any of several compounds of lignin and cellulose occurring in woody tissue. **lignum vitae** /vī'tē, or lig'nŭm wē'tī or vē'/ *n* (L, wood of life) the wood of a tropical American genus of trees, *Guaiacum*.

lignum[2] /lig'nəm/ (*Aust*) *n* a wiry shrub (*Muehlenbeckia cunninghamii*) or any other shrub of the Polygonum family, forming dense masses in swamps and plains in Australia. [For **polygonum**] ❑ **lig'num-scrub'** *n*. **lig'num-swamp'** *n*.

ligroin /lig'rō-in/ *n* a petroleum fraction boiling between 801 and 1201C. [Origin unknown]

ligule /lig'ūl/ *n* (*bot*) a scale at the top of the leaf-sheath in grasses; a similar scale on a petal; a strap-shaped corolla in composite plants. [L *ligula*, dimin of *lingua* a tongue]

■ **lig'ula** n a tongue-like part or organ; the anterior part of an insect's labium or lower lip. **lig'ular** adj. **lig'ulate** adj (bot) like a strap; having ligules. **Liguliflo'rae** n pl a division of the Compositae having all flowers ligulate. **liguliflo'ral** adj. **lig'uloid** adj.

Liguorian /li-gwŏ'ri-ən or -gwō'/ n and adj (a) Redemptorist. [St Alfonso Liguori (1696–1787), Italian bishop and theologian]

ligure /lig'ūr or -yər/ (Bible) n an unknown precious stone, jacinth or amber according to the Revised Version (the New English Bible says turquoise). [Gr ligyrion]

Li-ion battery see lithium-ion battery under lithia.

like¹ /līk/ adj identical, equal, or nearly equal in any respect; similar, resembling; suiting, befitting; characteristic of; used in requesting a description, as in what is it like?; used in combination to form adjectives from nouns, with the force 'resembling', 'suitable to', 'typical of', eg catlike, lady-like; used in combination to form adjectives and adverbs from adjectives, with the force 'somewhat', 'kind of', eg stupid-like (inf); inclined, likely or probable (dialect). ◆ n one of the same kind; the same thing; an exact resemblance. ◆ adv in the same manner; probably (dialect); as it were (dialect); as if about (dialect); nearly (inf); to some extent (dialect); sometimes used meaninglessly (dialect). ◆ conj (Shakesp; another reading as; now non-standard) as; as if. ◆ prep in the same manner as; to the same extent as; such as. ◆ vt (Shakesp) to compare or liken. ◆ vi (obs) to be or seem likely (to), come near (to). [OE līc, seen in gelīc; ON līkr, Du gelijk, Ger gleich (= geleich)]

■ **like'lihood** n probability; promise of success or of future excellence; similitude (obs); semblance (obs); resemblance (obs). **like'liness** n likelihood; likeness (Spenser). **like'ly** adj like the thing required; promising; probable; credible; similar (Spenser); pleasing (dialect); comely (dialect). ◆ adv (inf) probably. **lik'en** vt to represent as like or similar; to compare. **like'ness** n a resemblance; semblance; guise; a person who or thing which has a resemblance; a portrait. **like'wise** adv in the same or similar manner; moreover; too, also.

□ **like'-mind'ed** adj having similar opinions, values, etc. **like'-mind'edness** n.

■ **as likely as not** probably. **compare like with like** to compare only such things as are genuinely comparable. **feel like** to be disposed or inclined towards; used in requesting a description, as in what does it feel like? **had like** (archaic) was likely, came near to. **look like** to show a probability of; to appear similar to; used in requesting a description, as in what does it look like? **not likely** (inf) absolutely not. **something like** (a) a fine specimen, a model of what the thing should be; around, approximately. **such like** of that kind, similar. **the like** (inf) similar things. **the likes of** people such as.

like² /līk/ vt to be fond of; to be pleased with; to approve; to enjoy; to please (obs). ◆ n a liking, chiefly in the phrase likes and dislikes. [Orig impersonal, from OE līcian to please, to be suitable, from līc like, suitable, likely]

■ **likabil'ity** or **likeabil'ity** n. **lik'able** or **like'able** adj inspiring affection; amiable, pleasant. **lik'ableness** or **like'ableness** n. **lik'ably** or **like'ably** adv. **līk'er** n someone who likes. **līk'ing** n affection, fondness; taste or preference; satisfaction; beloved (Milton); condition, plight (obs). ◆ adj (obs) pleasing; in good condition (also (archaic) **good'-liking** or **well'-liking**).

■ **on liking** (archaic) on approval.

like³ /līk/ (Scot) n a corpse; a lykewake. [Scot and N Eng form of lich²]
□ **likewake**, **likewalk** see lykewake.

-like /-līk/ adj sfx combining with nouns to convey senses such as 'having the qualities of', 'similar to'. [like¹]

likin /lē-kēn'/ n formerly, a Chinese transit duty. [Chin lí jīn]

lilac /lī'lək/ n a European tree (Syringa vulgaris) of the olive family, with light-purple or white flowers, or other species of the genus; a light purple colour (also adj). [Fr (obs; now lilas) and Sp, from Ar līlāk, līlak, from Pers līlak, nīlak bluish]

lilangeni /li-lən-gen'i or lē-läng-gä'ni/ n (pl emalangeni /em-ə-lən-gen'i/) the standard monetary unit of Swaziland (100 cents).

liliaceous, **lilied**, etc see under lily.

lill¹ /lil/ (Spenser) vt to loll (the tongue). [Cf loll]

lill² /lil/ (Scot) n a fingerhole of a wind instrument. [Cf Du lul]

Lillibullero /lil-i-bŭ-le'rō or -lē'rō/ n the famous ballad in mockery of the Irish Catholics, which 'sung James II out of three kingdoms' (also **Lilliburlē'ro**). [From the meaningless refrain]

Lilliputian /li-li-pū'sh(y)ən/ n an inhabitant of **Lill'iput** /-put or -pŭt/, an imaginary diminutive country described by Swift in Gulliver's Travels, inhabited by tiny people; a midget. ◆ adj (also without cap) diminutive.

lilly-pilly /lil'i-pil-i/ n an Australian tree of the myrtle family. [Origin unknown]

LILO /lī'lō/ abbrev : last in, last out (a rough guide to likely order of redundancies).

Lilo® /lī'lō/ n an inflatable mattress, often used in camping, etc.

lilt /lilt/ vi to sing or play, esp merrily, or vaguely and absent-mindedly, giving the swing or cadence rather than the structure of the melody; to hum; to do anything briskly or adroitly, eg to hop about (dialect). ◆ vt to sing or play in such a manner. ◆ n a cheerful song or air; cadence, movement of a tune, etc; a springy quality in gait, etc; a lill, a fingerhole (obs). [ME lulte; origin unknown]

lily /lil'i/ n any plant or flower of the genus **Lil'ium**, typical species of **Lilia'ceae**, a family of monocotyledons differing from rushes chiefly in the large conspicuous flowers; extended to other plants of the same family, of the related family Amaryllidaceae, or unrelated; the fleur-de-lis; a person or thing of great purity or whiteness (fig). ◆ adj white; pale. [OE lilie, from L līlium, from Gr leirion lily]

■ **lilia'ceous** adj. **lil'ied** adj adorned with lilies; resembling lilies.

□ **lil'y-liv'ered** adj white-livered; cowardly. **lily of the Nile** n Richardia or Zantedeschia. **lily of the valley** n Convallaria, with two long oval leaves and spikes of white bell-shaped flowers. **lily pad** n a leaf of a water lily. **lil'y-trotter** n another name for the **jaçana**. **lil'y-white** adj pure white; faultless, without blame.

■ **gild** or **paint the lily** to attempt to beautify that which is already beautiful.

Lima or **lima** /lē'mə/ n (in international radio communication) a code word for the letter l.

lima /lē'mə/ n (in full **Lima bean**) a flattened, whitish, edible bean (Phaseolus lunatus), the seed of a tropical American plant related to the French bean, and of which the butter bean is a well-known variety. [Lima in Peru]
□ **li'ma-wood** n a kind of brazil-wood.

limaces, etc see limax.

limail see lemel.

limation /lī-mā'shən/ n filing. [L līma a file]

limax /lī'maks/ n (pl limaces /lī-mā'sēz/) a slug of the common genus Limax, giving its name to the slug family **Limā'ceae**. [L līmāx a slug]

■ **limacel** /lim-ə-sel'/ n a slug's reduced, usu embedded, shell. **limaceous** /lī-mā'shəs/ adj. **limaciform** /lim-as'/ or lī-mās'/ adj slug-like. **limacine** /lim'ə-sīn, lī'/ or -sin/ adj of, resembling or relating to slugs. **limacol'ogist** n. **limacol'ogy** n the study of slugs. **limaçon** /lim'ə-son/ or (Fr) lē-ma-sɔ̃/ n a curve whose polar equation is $r = acos\theta + b$.

limb¹ /lim/ n orig a member or organ of the body, now only an arm, leg or wing; a prudish euphemism for leg; a projecting part; a main branch of a tree, spur of a mountain, etc; a member of a body of people, as in a limb of the law; an imp or mischievous child, as in a limb of Satan. ◆ vt to dismember (archaic); to supply with limbs (Milton). [OE lim; ON limr, Swed lem]

■ **limbed** adj having limbs, esp used in combination, as in long-limbed. **limb'less** adj. **limb'meal** adv (Shakesp) limb by limb.
□ **limb'-girdle** n a bony arch with which a limb articulates.

■ **out on a limb** in a hazardous position on one's own (fig).

limb² /lim/ n an edge or border, eg of the sun, etc; the edge of a sextant, etc; the free or expanded part of a floral or other leaf (bot). [L limbus a border]

■ **lim'bate** adj bordered. **lim'bous** adj overlapping.

limbeck or **limbec** /lim'bek/ (Spenser and Shakesp) n aphetic for **alembic**.

limber¹ /lim'bər/ adj pliant, flexible, supple. ◆ vt to make limber. [Origin uncertain]

■ **lim'berness** n.
□ **lim'berneck** n botulism in birds.

■ **limber up** to loosen up the muscles in preparation for physical effort of some sort.

limber² /lim'bər/ n a detachable two-wheeled vehicle containing ammunition, preceding the gun carriage and forming with it part of a field gun unit (milit); the shaft of a vehicle (dialect). ◆ vt to attach to the limber. [Poss Fr limonière]

limber³ /lim'bər/ (naut) n (usu in pl) a channel or hole on either side of the inner keel for drainage. [Fr lumière, from L lumināria windows]

limbic /lim'bik/ (anat) adj of or relating to the **limbic system** in the brain, the hypothalamus, etc, concerned with basic emotions. [L limbicus, from limbus border]

Limbo or **limbo** /lim'bō/, also **Limbus** /-bəs/ n (pl **Lim'bos**, **lim'bos** or **Lim'bi** /-bē/) the borderland of Hell, reserved for the unbaptized (**Limbus patrum** for the righteous who died before Christ, **Limbus infantum** for children); any unsatisfactory place of consignment or oblivion; an uncertain or intermediate state; prison. [From the Latin phrase in limbo, in in, and ablative of limbus border]

limbo /lim'bō/ n (pl **lim'bos**) a West Indian dance in which the dancer bends backwards and passes under a bar which is progressively lowered. ♦ vi to dance the limbo. [Perhaps **limber**[1]]

Limburger /lim'bûr-gər/ n a white cheese from *Limburg* in Belgium, of strong taste and smell (also **Limburger cheese**).

limburgite /lim'bər-gīt/ n a volcanic rock composed of olivine and augite, etc, in a fine-grained or glassy groundmass. [*Limburg* in Baden, a typical locality]

limbus /lim'bəs/ (anat) n (pl **lim'bi** /-bī/) the edge of an organ or part. [L, edge]

Limbus patrum and **Limbus infantum** see **Limbo**.

lime[1] /līm/ n bird-lime, a sticky substance for catching birds; any slimy or gluey material (*dialect*); the white caustic earth (calcium oxide, quicklime, or caustic lime) obtained by driving off water and carbon dioxide from calcium carbonate (eg in the form of limestone); calcium hydroxide (slaked lime) obtained by adding water to quicklime; loosely, limestone or calcium carbonate. ♦ adj of lime. ♦ vt to cover with lime; to treat with lime; to manure with lime; to ensnare, trap (also *fig*); to cement (*dialect*). ♦ vi (*Shakesp*) to adulterate wine with lime. [OE *līm*; Ger *Leim* glue, L *līmus* slime]
■ **līm'iness** n. **līm'ing** n in the preparation of leather, etc, the soaking of skins in limewater to remove hair; the application of lime. **līm'y** adj glutinous, sticky (*dialect*); smeared with, containing, like or of the nature of, lime.
□ **lime'-burner** n someone who calcines limestone, etc to form lime. **lime'kiln** n a kiln or furnace in which calcium carbonate is reduced to lime. **lime'light** n the glare of publicity (from a type of lamp formerly used in theatre stage lighting, which used heated lime to provide light; light produced by a blowpipe flame directed against a block of quicklime. ♦ vt (*pat* and *pap* **lime'lit** or **lime'lighted**) (*esp fig*) to illuminate by limelight, to subject to the glare of limelight. **lime'pit** n a lime-filled pit in which hides are steeped to remove hair. **lime'stone** n a sedimentary rock of calcium carbonate, sometimes (*magnesian* limestone) with a high dolomite content. **limestone pavement** n (*geol*) a surface of exposed limestone resembling a pavement. **lime'-scale** n an encrustation left inside a kettle etc by the action of hard water (also **scale**). **lime'-twig** n a twig smeared with bird-lime; a snare. **lime'wash** n a milky mixture of slaked lime and water, used for coating walls, etc. ♦ vt to cover with limewash. **lime'water** n a suspension of calcium hydroxide in water, sometimes used as an antacid.

lime[2] /līm/ n a tropical citrus tree, *Citrus aurantifolia*; its small nearly globular fruit, with acid-tasting flesh; the colour of the fruit, a yellowish green. ♦ adj flavoured with lime; (coloured) yellowish-green. [Fr, from Sp *lima*; cf **lemon**[1]]
■ **limeade** /līm-ād'/ n a non-alcoholic drink made from the juice of limes and water, often carbonated. **lime'y** n (*N Am sl*) a British sailor or ship (from the use of lime juice on British ships to prevent scurvy); any British person. **lim'y** adj tasting of lime.
□ **lime green** n a bright, yellowish shade of green, the colour of limes. **lime'-green** adj. **lime juice** n the acid-tasting juice of the lime.

lime[3] /līm/ n the linden tree (*Tilia europaea*), or any other tree of the genus, with heart-shaped leaves and small yellowish flowers. [**lind**]
□ **lime'-tree** n. **lime'-wood** n.

lime[4] and **lime-hound** see **lyam**.

lime[5] /līm/ (*W Indies sl*) vi to loiter, hang about. [Ety unknown]

limen /lī'men/ (*psychol*) n the threshold of consciousness; the limit below which a stimulus is not perceived. [L *līmen, -inis* threshold]
■ **liminal** /lim'* or *lim'in-əl/ adj. **liminality** /-al'i-ti/ n.

limerick /lim'ə-rik/ n a form of humorous verse in a five-line jingle. [Said to be from a refrain referring to *Limerick* in Ireland]

limes /lī'mēz or lē'mes/ n (pl **limites** /lī'mit-ēz or lē'mi-tās/) a boundary or boundary fortification, *esp* of the Roman Empire. [L *līmes, -itis*]

limey see under **lime**[2].

limicolous /lī-mik'ə-ləs/ adj living in mud. [L *līmus* mud, and *colere* to dwell]
■ **lī'mous** adj (*archaic*) muddy; slimy.

liminal and **liminality** see under **limen**.

limit /lim'it/ n a boundary, *esp* one which may not be passed; a restriction; a predetermined price at which a broker is instructed to buy or sell (*stock exchange*); a value, position or figure that can be approached indefinitely (*maths*); a prescribed time (*Shakesp*); something which is bounded, a region or division; (with *the*) the extreme of what may be endured (*inf*). ♦ vt to confine within bounds; to restrict; to appoint or specify (*Shakesp*). [L *līmes, -itis* boundary]
■ **lim'itable** adj. **limitā'rian** n (*theol*) someone who limits salvation to part of mankind. **lim'itary** /-ə-ri/ adj of a boundary; placed at the boundary; confined within limits; licensed as a limiter (*hist*). **limitā'tion** n a limiting; a lack of physical ability, talent, etc (*law*); a specified period within which an action must be brought, etc (*law*).

lim'itātive adj tending to limit. **lim'ited** adj within limits; narrow; restricted. ♦ n a limited company. **lim'itedly** adv. **lim'itedness** n. **lim'iter** n a person, device or circumstance that limits or confines; a friar who had a licence to beg within certain bounds (*hist*). **lim'iting** n and adj. **lim'itless** adj having no limits; boundless; immense; infinite. **lim'itlessly** adv. **lim'itlessness** n.
□ **limited** (or **lim'ited-liabil'ity**) **company** n one whose owners have liability for its debts, etc only according to their financial stake in it. **limited edition** n an edition, *esp* of a book, of which only a certain number of copies is printed or made. **limited express** n (*N Am*) an express railway train carrying a limited number of passengers. **limited liability** see under **liable**. **limited monarchy** n one in which the monarch shares the supreme power with others, constitutional monarchy. **lim'ited-o'ver** adj of a cricket match, in which the number of overs bowled by each side is restricted. **limited war** n one in which the combatants' aim is not the total destruction of the enemy, *esp* one in which nuclear warfare is deliberately avoided. **limit gauge** n (*engineering*) a gauge used to verify that a part has been made to within specified dimensional limits. **limit point** n (*maths*) a point such that every neighbourhood of it includes at least one point of a given set.
■ **off limits** out of bounds. **statute of limitations** an act specifying the period within which certain action must be taken. **within limits** to a limited extent.

limitrophe /lim'i-trōf/ adj near the frontier; border. [L *līmitrophus*, from *līmes, -itis* border, and Gr *trophos* feeder]

limma /lim'ə/ n a pause of one mora (*prosody*); in Pythagorean music, the difference between two whole tones and a perfect fourth; applied also to other minute intervals. [Gr *leimma* a remnant]

limmer /lim'ər/ (*Scot* and *N Eng dialect*) n a rogue or thief; a hussy, an ill-natured woman. [Origin obscure]

limn /lim/ vt and vi (prp **limning** /lim'ing or lim'ning/) (*archaic*) to draw or paint, *esp* in watercolours; *orig* to illuminate with ornamental letters, etc. [OFr *luminer* or *enluminer*, from L *lūmināre* or *illūmināre* to cast light on]
■ **limner** /lim'nər/ n a painter on paper or parchment; a portrait-painter.

Limnaea /lim-nē'ə/ n a genus of pond-snails. [Gr *limnē* a pool or marsh]
■ **limnae'id** n any member of the family **Limnae'idae**, to which this genus belongs. **limnetic** /-net'ik/ adj living in fresh water. **limnolog'ical** adj. **limnol'ogist** n. **limnol'ogy** n the scientific study (embracing physical, geographical, biological, etc characteristics) of lakes and other freshwater bodies. **limnoph'ilous** adj living in ponds or marshes.

limo /lim'ō/ n (pl **lim'os**) short form of **limousine**.

Limoncello /lē-mon-chel'ō/ n (pl **Limoncell'os**) a sweet Italian liqueur flavoured with lemons. [Ital]

limonene /lim'ə-nēn/ n a liquid terpene ($C_{10}H_{16}$) found in lemon, orange, and other essential oils. [New L *limonum* lemon]

limonite /lī'mə-nīt/ n brown iron ore, hydrated ferric oxide, a deposit in bogs and lakes (*bog iron*) or a decomposition product in rocks. [Gr *leimōn* a meadow]
■ **limonitic** /-it'ik/ adj.

limosis /lī-mō'sis/ n an abnormally ravenous appetite. [Gr *līmos* hunger]

limous see under **limicolous**.

Limousin /lē-moo-zē'/ n a breed of cattle. [*Limousin*, a district in France]

limousine /lim'ə-zēn/ n a large closed motor car (*orig* with the driver's seat outside but covered by the roof) which has a partition separating driver and passengers; any large motor car (sometimes used *ironically*). [Fr, after a type of long cloak once worn in the *Limousin* district (see above)]

limp[1] /limp/ vi to walk unevenly, *esp* when one leg is injured; to drag a leg; (of a damaged ship or aircraft) to proceed with difficulty. ♦ n a limping gait. [There is an OE adj *lemp-healt* halting]
■ **limp'ing** n and adj. **limp'ingly** adv.

limp[2] /limp/ adj lacking stiffness; flaccid; drooping; (of a cloth binding for books) not stiffened by boards. [Origin obscure]
■ **limp'ly** adv. **limp'ness** n.
□ **limp-wrist'ed** adj (*sl*) of a man, effeminate.

limpet /lim'pit/ n a gastropod (genus *Patella*, etc) with a conical shell, that clings to rocks; a person not easily got rid of. [OE *lempedu* lamprey]
□ **limpet mine** n an explosive device designed to cling to a surface, *esp* one attached to a ship's hull by a magnet, etc.

limpid /lim'pid/ adj clear; transparent. [L *limpidus*]
■ **limpid'ity** n. **lim'pidly** adv. **lim'pidness** n.

limpkin /limp'kin/ n an American wading bird, *Aramus guarauna*, like a rail. [From its limping gait]

limulus /lim'yŭ-ləs/ n a crustacean of the king crab genus *Limulus*. [L *līmulus*, dimin of *līmus* looking sideways]

limy[1] see under **lime**[1].

limy[2] see under **lime**[2].

lin[1] /lin/ vi (*Spenser*) to cease, to give over. ◆ vt (*obs*) to cease from. [OE *linnan* to cease]

lin[2] see **linn**.

lin. *abbrev* : lineal; linear.

linac /lin'ak/ n a linear accelerator (qv under **line**[1]).

linage see under **line**[1].

linalool /li-nal'ō-ol or lin'ə-lool/ n a fragrant liquid alcohol, used as an ingredient of perfume, obtained from oil of rosewood and other essential oils. [Mex Sp *linalóe* a tree with aromatic wood, from L *lignum aloes* lignaloes]

linch /linch or linsh/ (*dialect*) n (also **linch'et** or **lynch'et**) a boundary ridge or unploughed strip; a terrace or ledge. [OE *hlinc* ridge; cf **link**[3]]

linchpin /linch' or linsh'pin/ n a pin used to keep a wheel on its axle; a person or thing essential to a plan, organization, etc (*fig*). [OE *lynis* axle, and **pin**]

Lincoln green /ling'kən grēn/ n a bright-green cloth once made in *Lincoln*, England; its colour.

lincomycin /ling-kō-mī'sin/ n an antibiotic used against streptococcal and staphylococcal infections, produced from the bacterium *Streptomyces lincolnensis*. [L *lincol*nensis and *-mycin*]

lincrusta /lin-krus'tə/ n a thick, embossed type of wallpaper. [L *līnum* flax, and *crusta* rind, on the analogy of **linoleum**]

Lincs. /lingks/ *abbrev* : Lincolnshire.

linctus /lingk'təs/ n (pl **linc'tuses**) a syrup-like medicine for coughs and sore throats. [L *linctus, -ūs* a licking]
 ■ **linc'ture** n.

lind /lind/ or **linden** /lin'dən/ same as **lime**[3]. [OE *lind*; cf ON *lind*, Ger *Linde*]

lindane /lin'dān/ same as **Gammexane**®.

lindworm /lind'wûrm/ (*myth*) n a wingless dragon. [Adapted from Swed and Dan *lindorm*]

lindy hop /lin'di hop/ n a type of lively dance to swing music, similar to the jitterbug. ◆ vi to dance the lindy hop. [*Lindy*, nickname of US aviator Charles Lindbergh, in whose honour the dance was named in the 1920s]

line[1] /līn/ n a thread, string, cord or rope, *esp* one for fishing, sounding, hanging clothes, or guidance; something which has length without breadth or thickness (*maths*); a long narrow mark; a streak, stroke, or narrow stripe; draughtsmanship; a row; a row of printed or written characters, ships, soldiers, etc; a verse, such as is *usu* written in one row; a series or succession, eg of descendants; a service of ships, buses, etc or a company running them; a course, route or system; a railway or tramway track or route; a stretch or route of telegraph, telephone, or power wires or cables; a connection by telephone; an order given to an agent for goods; such goods received; trade in, or the stock on hand of, any particular product; a lineament; a rank, column of figures, etc; a short letter or note; a wrinkle, *esp* on the face; a trench or other military position; a limit; method; policy; a rule or canon; (with *the*; often with *cap*) the equator; lineage, ancestry; direction; occupation; course; province or sphere of life, interest, or taste; the regular army; line of battle (see below); the chain of command and delegation in an organization; (in a factory, etc) the part of the workforce directly concerned with making a product; an old measurement, the twelfth part of an inch; relevant information (*inf*); glib talk, not always honest (*sl*); in a TV, the path traversed by the electron beam or scanning spot in moving once from side to side (horizontal scanning) or from top to bottom (vertical scanning) of the picture; a queue (*N Am*); a small amount of a powdered drug (*esp* cocaine) laid out in a narrow channel ready for sniffing (*sl*); (*usu* **the line**) the odds, *esp* on football games, set by bookmakers (*N Am*); (in *pl*) a certificate of marriage or church membership; (in *pl*) the words of an actor's part; (in *pl*) one's lot in life (*rare*); (in *pl*) outlines; (in *pl*) military fieldworks; (in *pl*) rows of huts (*milit*); (in *pl*) a school punishment of writing out a phrase or sentence a wearisome number of times; (in *pl*) fits of bad temper (*Shakesp*). ◆ vt to mark out with lines; to cover with lines; to put in line; to form a line along; to give out (a hymn, etc) for public singing line by line; to delineate or sketch (sometimes verbally); to measure with a line (*archaic*). ◆ vi to take a place in line. [Partly from OE *līne* cord (from or cognate with L *līnum* flax), partly through Fr *ligne*, and partly directly from L *līnea*; cf **line**[2]]
 ■ **linage** or **lineage** /līn'ij/ n the number of lines in a piece of printed matter; measurement or payment by the line, eg in newspapers;

aligning (*archaic*). **lineage** /lin'i-ij/, *obs* forms **linage, lignage** or **lynage** /lin'ij/ n ancestry. **lineal** /lin'i-əl/ adj of or belonging to a line or lines, or to one dimension; composed of lines; in the direction of a line; in, of, or transmitted by, direct line of descent, or legitimate descent. **lineality** /-al'i-ti/ n. **lin'eally** adv. **lineament** /lin'i-ə-mənt/ n a feature; a distinguishing mark in the form of anything, *esp* of the face. **linear** /lin'i-ər/ adj of or belonging to a line; in or of one dimension; consisting of, or having the form of, lines; long and very narrow, with parallel sides; capable of being represented on a graph by a straight line; of a narrative, etc, proceeding in a single sequence, without digression, flashback, etc; of a system in which doubling the cause doubles the effect. **linearity** /lin-i-ar'i-ti/ n. **lineariza'tion** or **-s-** n. **lin'earize** or **-ise** vt to make linear. **lin'early** adv. **lin'eate** or **lin'eated** adj marked with lines. **lineā'tion** n marking with lines; arrangement of or in lines. **lined** /līnd/ adj marked with lines; having a line. **lineolate** /lin'i-ə-lāt/ adj marked with fine lines. **līn'er** n a person who makes, marks, draws, paints, or writes lines; a paintbrush for making lines; a line-fisherman; a line-fishing boat; any large passenger-carrying vessel or aircraft of a particular company; cosmetic material used to outline the eyes or lips. **līn'ing** n alignment; the making of a line; use of a line; marking with lines. **līn'y** or **līn'ey** adj.

❑ **line abreast** or **ahead** n naval formation(s) in which all the vessels are side by side or one behind the other. **linear A** n a script, essentially the same as linear B, used with an earlier undeciphered language of Crete. **linear accelerator** n an apparatus in which electrons are accelerated while travelling down a metal tube or tubes, eg by means of electromagnetic waves. **linear aerospike engine** n a rocket engine with a specially designed nozzle (**aerospike nozzle**) that allows the exhaust gases to expand and so to be used most efficiently. **linear B** n an ancient script (c.1400BC) found in Crete, deciphered as a form of Greek seven centuries earlier than any previously known. **linear equation** n an equation with more than two terms, of which none is raised above the power one. **linear motor** n an electric motor which produces direct thrust in a linear, rather than rotational, direction. **linear perspective** n that part of perspective which regards only the positions, magnitudes and forms of the objects delineated. **linear programming** n programming which enables a computer to give an optimum result when fed with a number of unrelated variables, used in determining the most efficient arrangement of eg an industrial process. **line'backer** n (*American football*) a defensive player whose position is just behind the line of scrimmage. **line block** n a printing block consisting of black and white only, without gradations of tone. **line breeding** n the mating of closely related animals in order to preserve the characteristics of a common ancestor. **line dancing** n dancing in which participants form rows without partners and follow a set pattern of steps to country-and-western music. **line drawing** n a drawing in pen or pencil using lines only, without gradations of tone. **line'-engrav'er** n. **line'-engrav'ing** n the process of engraving in lines, steel or copperplate engraving; an engraving done in this way. **line feed** n (*comput*) a control character used to move to the next line on a printer or screen. **line'-fence'** n (*US*) a farm-boundary fence. **line'-fish** n one caught with a line rather than a net. **line'-fish'er** or **line-fish'erman** n. **line'-fish'ing** n. **line-item veto** n (*US*) the power, *esp* of a US President, to reject an individual provision (**line item**) in a piece of proposed legislation without rejecting the bill as a whole. **line judge** n (*sport*) an official whose job is to watch a line to see on which side of it the ball, etc falls. **line'man** n a person who attends to the lines of a railway, telegraph, telephone, or power wires, etc; a player in the line of scrimmage (*American football*). **line management** n a system of management in which each **line manager** is responsible for exercising authority and responsibility within a formalized hierarchy. **line of battle** n arrangement in line to meet the enemy. **line'-of-batt'le-ship** n a ship fit for the line of battle, a battleship. **line of beauty** n a curve like a drawn-out S, as described by the English painter William Hogarth. **line of country** n one's field of study or interest. **line of credit** n the maximum amount of credit that a customer is permitted. **line of fire** n the range or scope of a weapon, etc. **line of force** n a line drawn in a magnetic or electric field so that its direction at every point gives the direction of magnetic or electric force at that point. **line of sight** n the straight line between the eye and the object on which it is focused, or between two objects along which they are visible from each other (also **line of vision**); the straight line along which the eye looks, in any direction; the straight line between a transmitter and the receiving antenna (*telecom*). **line'-out** n (in Rugby Union) a method of restarting play when the ball has gone into touch, the forwards of each team forming a line facing the touch-line and trying to catch or deflect the ball when it is thrown in. **line printer** n a machine for rapid printing of computer output, a line at a time. **line scanning** n (*image technol*) a method of scanning in which the scanning spot sequentially traverses the image in a series of straight lines. **line'-shooter** n (*sl*) someone who shoots a line (see **shoot**[1]). **linesman** /līnz'/ n a lineman; a soldier in a regiment of the line; in football, an official who marks the spot at which the ball goes into touch, rules when a player is offside, etc (officially **assistant referee**); in tennis, an official whose job is to watch a line to see on which side of it the ball falls, a line judge. **line squall** *n* one of a chain of squalls occurring along a travelling line, with rise and sudden change of wind, rise of pressure and fall of temperature. **line'-storm** *n* (*US*) an equinoctial storm. **line'-up** *n* arrangement in line; putting or coming into line; a queue; an identification parade; the bill of artistes appearing in a show; a list of team members.

■ **above the line** (of advertising) through the media and by poster. **all along the line** at every point (*lit* or *fig*). **below the line** (of advertising) by such means as free gifts, direct mailings to households, etc. **bring into line** to cause to conform. **down the line** of a shot in tennis, football, etc, travelling parallel to and close to the side of the court, pitch, etc; in the future (*inf*). **draw the line** see under **draw**. **end of the line** (*fig*) a point beyond which it is useless or impossible to proceed. **fall into line** to conform. **Fraunhofer('s) lines** dark lines crossing the spectrum, from the Bavarian optician Joseph von *Fraunhofer* (1787–1826). **get a line on** (*inf*) to get information about. **give line** (*angling*) to allow apparent freedom in order to secure at last (also *fig*). **hold the line** see under **hold**[1]. **in line** in a straight line; in agreement or harmony (with *with*); in the running (with *for*); in contention (with *for*); in a line of succession (with *to*); under control. **lay it on the line** (*inf*) to speak out firmly and frankly. **lay** or **put on the line** to risk or stake (a reputation, etc). **line up** to bring into alignment; to form a line; to make a stand (*in support of*, or *against*); to gather together in readiness; to secure or arrange (for a person). **on the line** (*art*) hanging on the level of the eyes. **on** or **along the lines of** in a (specified) manner or direction. **out of line** not aligned; impudent; exhibiting unacceptable behaviour. **read between the lines** to infer what is not explicitly stated. **shoot a line** see under **shoot**[1]. **toe the line** see under **toe**.

line[2] /līn/ *n* flax, its fibre, or its seed (*obs*); combed out or heckled flax; yarn spun from good flax; linen thread or cloth (*obs*). ◆ *vt* to cover on the inside; to fill or stuff; to reinforce or strengthen (*esp* books); to be placed all along the side of; to serve as lining for. [OE *līn* flax, cognate with or derived from L *līnum*; cf ety for **line**[1]]

■ **lined** *adj* having a lining. **lin'er** *n* a person who lines; something which serves as a lining; a sleeve of metal, resistant to wear and corrosion, etc, fitted inside or outside a cylinder, tube, etc (*engineering*); a sleeve for a gramophone record, or an insert inside it, or the paper insert that is part of a CD's packaging. **lin'ing** *n* the action of a person who lines; material applied to a surface, *esp* material on the inner surface of a garment, etc; contents; (in *pl*) underclothing, *esp* drawers (*obs* or *dialect*).

❑ **liner notes** *n pl* information printed on the liner of a record or CD, *usu* including credits, acknowledgements, etc.

■ **line one's pocket** or **pockets** to make a profit, *esp* dishonestly.

line[3] /līn/ *vt* (*esp* of a dog or wolf) to copulate with. [Fr *ligner*]

line[4] /līn/ *n* a form of **lind**.

❑ **line'-grove** *n* (*Shakesp*).

lineage, lineal, linear, etc see under **line**[1].

lined see **line**[1,2].

linen /lin'ən/ *n* cloth made of lint or flax; underclothing, *orig* of linen; articles of linen, or of other materials generally, such as cotton, rayon, etc, eg *table-linen, bed linen, body-linen*. ◆ *adj* of or like linen. [OE *līnen* (adj), from *līn* flax; see **line**[2]]

❑ **lin'en-draper** *n* a dealer in linens. **lin'en-fold** or **lin'en-scroll** *n* a decoration in mouldings like parallel folds of linen. **linen paper** *n* paper made of flax fibres, or with a similar texture.

■ **wash one's dirty linen in public** or (*rare*) **at home** to expose, or (*rare*) keep secret, sordid family affairs.

lineolate see under **line**[1].

liner see under **line**[1,2].

ling[1] /ling/ *n* a fish (genus *Molva*) of the cod family. [Prob connected with **long**[1]]

ling[2] /ling/ *n* heather. [ON *lyng*]

■ **ling'y** *adj*.

ling[3] /ling/ *n* Scots form of **line**[1].

■ **sting and ling** see under **sting**[2].

ling. *abbrev* : linguistics.

-ling[1] /-ling/ *sfx* forming nouns and denoting a diminutive, such as *duckling*; hence expressing affection, as in *darling* (OE *dēorling*); sometimes implying deprecation, as in *underling*.

-ling[2] /-ling/ *adv sfx* conveying the senses of direction, condition, position.

Lingala /lin-gä'lə/ *n* a Bantu language spoken in the Democratic Republic of Congo and the Republic of Congo. [Bantu]

lingam /ling'gam/ *n* the Hindu phallus, a symbol of Siva (also **ling'a**). [Sans]

lingel or **lingle** /ling'gl/ or (chiefly *Scot*) ling'l/ *n* a shoe-maker's waxed thread. [OFr *lignoel*, from a dimin from L *līnea*]

linger /ling'gər/ *vi* to remain for long; to be left or remain behind; to delay, in reluctance to leave; to tarry; to loiter; to be protracted; to remain alive, although gradually dying. ◆ *vt* to prolong or protract (*Shakesp*); to pass in tedium or dawdling. [Frequentative from OE *lengan* to protract, from *lang* long]

■ **ling'erer** *n*. **ling'ering** *n* and *adj*. **ling'eringly** *adv*.

lingerie /lẽ̃'/ or lön'zhə-ri or -rä/ *n* women's underclothing; *orig* linen goods. [Fr, from *linge* linen, from L *līnum* flax thread, linen]

lingle see **lingel**.

lingo /ling'gō/ *n* (*pl* **ling'oes**) a language, *esp* one poorly regarded or not understood; the jargon of a profession or class. [Provençal *lengo, lingo*, or some other form of L *lingua* language]

lingoa geral /ling'gwä zhe-räl'/ *n* a trade jargon used in Brazil based on Tupí-Guaraní. [Port, general language]

lingonberry /ling'ən-be-ri/ *n* the cowberry or red whortleberry, *esp* as used in Scandinavian cookery. [Swed *lingon* cowberry]

lingot /ling'gət/ (*obs*) *n* an ingot. [Fr *lingot*, from Eng **ingot**, with the definite article *l'*]

lingua /ling'gwə/ *n* the tongue (*anat*); a tongue-like structure. [L *lingua* (for *dingua*) the tongue]

■ **ling'ual** *adj* relating to the tongue; pronounced using the tongue (*phonetics*); (of a tooth-surface) facing towards the tongue (*dentistry*); relating to language or speech. **ling'ually** *adv*. **ling'uiform** *adj* tongue-shaped. **ling'uist** *n* someone who has an excellent knowledge of languages; someone who studies linguistics; in W Africa, an intermediary between chief or priest and the people. **ling'uister** *n* (*US*) an interpreter (also **link'ster** or **ling'ster**). **linguist'ic** or **linguist'ical** *adj* relating to languages or knowledge or the study of languages. **linguist'ically** *adv*. **linguist'ian** *n* a person who studies linguistics. **linguist'ics** *n sing* the scientific study of language in its widest sense, in every aspect and in all its varieties. **ling'uistry** *n*. **lingula** /ling'gū-lə/ *n* a little tongue-like part; (with *cap*) a narrow-shelled genus of brachiopods; extended loosely to related genera, such as **Lingulell'a**, the characteristic fossil of the Upper Cambrian *Lingula Flags*. **ling'ular** *adj* relating to a lingula. **ling'ulate** *adj* tongue-shaped.

❑ **lingua franca** /ling'gwə frangk'ə/ *n* (*pl* **lingue franche** /ling'gwä frangk'ā/ or **lingua francas**) (Ital, Frankish language) *orig* a mixed Italian trade jargon used in the Levant; a language chosen as a medium of communication among speakers of different languages; any hybrid language used for the same purpose; the familiar conventions of any style, *esp* in music or the arts, readily recognized and understood by devotees. **linguistic atlas** or **map** *n* an atlas or map that charts the spread and distribution of features of a language or dialect, such as pronunciation or vocabulary. **linguistic philosophy** or **linguistic analysis** *n* a term loosely used to cover methods of analysis of philosophically puzzling concepts by the meticulous assembly and scrutiny of the widely-varying expressions of these concepts in ordinary discourse; later extended to a systematic study of the working of language itself.

linguini /ling-gwē'nē/ or **linguine** /-nā/ *n pl* a kind of pasta made in long thin flat pieces. [Ital, pl of *linguino, linguina*, dimins of *lingua* tongue]

linguist, etc, **lingula**, etc see under **lingua**.

linhay, linney or **linny** /lin'i/ (*dialect*) *n* a shed, open in front. [Origin obscure]

liniment /lin'i-mənt/ *n* a thin ointment; an embrocation for relieving muscular stiffness. [L *linīmentum*, from *linīre, linĕre* to smear]

linin /lī'nin/ *n* a substance which forms the network of a cell nucleus. [L *līnum* thread, net]

lining see under **line**[1,2].

linish /lin'ish/ *vt* to give a smooth or clean surface to (metal, etc) by putting it in contact with a moving belt covered with an abrasive. [**linen** and **finish**]

■ **lin'isher** *n*. **lin'ishing** *n*.

link[1] /lingk/ *n* a ring of a chain, chain mail, etc; anything that connects (also *fig*); a unit in a communications system; the $\frac{1}{100}$th part of the surveyor's chain, 7.92 inches (*approx* 20cm); a segment or unit in a connected series; a winding of a river (*Scot*); a cuff link; a hyperlink (*comput*); a connection (*comput*). ◆ *vt* (often with *up*) to connect or join up. ◆ *vi* to be or become connected (often with *up*); to go arm in arm. [Prob from an ON form cognate with OE *hlencan* (pl) armour; Icel *hlekkr*, Ger *Gelenk* a joint]

■ **link'able** *adj*. **link'age** *n* an act or mode of linking; the fact of being linked; a system of links, a connection; a chemical bond; product of magnetic flux by number of coils (*elec*); a system of lines pivoted together, describing definite curves (*maths*); a tendency of genes, or characters, to be inherited together because the genes are on the same chromosome (*biol*). **link'er** *n* (*comput*) a program enabling two or more different machine-language segments to be treated as a unit. ◻ **linked list** *n* (*comput*) a list in which each item contains both data and a pointer to the next (and sometimes the previous) item. **linked verse** *n* a form of Japanese verse alternating three lines of respectively 3, 7 and 5 syllables with two lines of 7 and 7 syllables, different poets supplying succeeding verses. **link man** *n* a person who provides a connection, eg by passing on information, or by holding together separate items of eg a broadcast programme. **link'-mo'tion** *n* the reversing gear of a steam-engine; a system of pieces moving as a linkage. **link'span** *n* a ramp attached to a pier to assist the loading of vehicles onto ferry-boats. **link'-up** *n* a connection, union. **link'work** *n*. ▪ **missing link** any point or fact needed to complete a series or a chain of thought or argument; an intermediate form in the evolution of man from his ape ancestors.

link² /*lingk*/ (*hist*) *n* a torch of pitch and tow; burnt links used as blacking (*Shakesp*). [Origin doubtful] ◻ **link'boy** or **link'man** *n* an attendant carrying a link to light the way in dark streets.

link³ /*lingk*/ *n* (in *pl*, often treated as *sing*) a stretch of flat or gently undulating ground along a seashore; hence a golf course, *esp* one by the sea; a bank (*obs*). [OE *hlinc* a ridge of land, a bank; cf **linch**]

link⁴ /*lingk*/ (*Scot*) *vi* to move nimbly; to trip along briskly. [Cf Norw *linke* to hobble, limp]

linkster see **linguister** under **lingua**.

Link trainer /*lingk trā'nər*/ *n* a flight-simulator training device for pilots and aircrew; a similar device for training motor vehicle drivers. [From E *Link* (1904–81), US inventor]

Linn. /*lin*/ *abbrev*: Linnaean; Linnaeus.

linn or **lin** /*lin*/ *n* a waterfall; a pool at the foot of a waterfall; a deep ravine. [OE *hlynn*, a torrent, combined with Gaelic *linne*, Ir *linn*, Welsh *llyn* pool]

Linnaean or **Linnean** /*li-nē'ən*/ *adj* relating to *Linnaeus* or *Linné*, the Swedish botanist (1707–78), or to his artificial system of classification.

linnet /*lin'it*/ *n* a common finch, *Carduelis cannabina*, feeding on flaxseed. [OFr *linette*, *linot*, from *lin* flax, from L *līnum*; cf OE *līnece* or *līnete*, and **lintie**] ▪ **green linnet** the greenfinch.

linney and **linny** see **linhay**.

lino and **linocut** see **linoleum**.

linoleic acid /*li-nō-lē'ik as'id*/ *n* a highly unsaturated fatty acid obtained from the glycerides of certain fats and oils, such as linseed oil, and used in paints as a drying agent. ▪ **linoleate** /*lin-ō'li-āt*/ *n* a salt or ester of linoleic acid.

linolenic acid /*li-nō-lē'nik as'id* or *-len'ik*/ *n* an essential fatty acid derived from linolenic acid.

linoleum /*li-nō'li-əm* or *-lyəm*/ or (*inf*) **lino** /*lī'nō*/ *n* stiff, hard-wearing floor-covering made by impregnating a fabric with a mixture of oxidized linseed oil, resins, and fillers (*esp* cork). ◆ *adj* made of linoleum. [L *līnum* flax, and *oleum* oil] ◻ **linocut** /*lī'nō-kut*/ *n* a design cut in relief in linoleum; a print made from such a block. **lī'nocutting** *n*. **lino tile** *n* a floor tile made of linoleum or a similar material.

Linotype® /*lī'nō-tīp* or *-nə-*/ *n* a machine for producing stereotyped lines of printer's type; a slug or line of printing-type cast in one piece by this method.

linsang /*lin'sang*/ *n* a civet-like animal of Borneo and Java; applied also to related animals of the Himalayas, Myanmar (Burma) and W Africa. [Javanese *linsan*]

linseed /*lin'sēd*/ *n* lint or flaxseed (also **lint'seed**). [OE *līn* flax, and *sæd* seed] ◻ **lin'seed-cake** *n* the cake remaining when the oil is pressed out of lint or flaxseed, used as a food for sheep and cattle. **lin'seed-meal** *n* the meal of linseed, used for poultices and as a cattle food. **linseed oil** *n* oil extracted from flaxseed, having many industrial applications.

linsey /*lin'zi*/ *n* cloth made from linen and wool (also *adj*). [Perh **line²** wool, and poss **say³**] ◻ **lin'sey-woolsey** /*-wŭl'zi*/ *n* a thin coarse material of linen and wool mixed, or inferior wool with cotton; gibberish (*Shakesp*). ◆ *adj* made of linen and wool; neither one thing nor another, presenting a confusing mixture.

linstock /*lin'stok*/ (*hist*) *n* a staff to hold a lighted match for firing a cannon (also **lint'stock**). [Du *lontstok*, from *lont* a match (cf **lunt**), and *stok* a stick]

lint /*lint*/ *n* flax (*Scot*); scraped linen, or a cotton substitute, for dressing wounds; cotton fibre (*esp* US); raw cotton; small pieces of thread, fluff, etc that cling to clothes and furniture and accumulate in the filters of washing machines and driers and in navels. [ME *lynt*, *lynet* from L *linteus* of linen, from *līnum* flax]

▪ **lin'ter** *n* (*US*) a machine for stripping off short cotton fibre from the ginned seeds; (in *pl*) the fibre so removed. **lint'y** *adj*. ◻ **lint'seed** *n* (*Scot*) flaxseed for sowing. **lint'white** *adj* flaxen.

lintel /*lin'tl*/ *n* a timber or stone over a doorway or window. [OFr *lintel* (Fr *linteau*), from a dimin of L *līmes*, *-itis* border] ▪ **lint'elled** *adj*.

linter, etc see under **lint**.

lintie /*lin'ti*/ or **lintwhite** /*lint'(h)wīt*/ (now chiefly *Scot*) *n* a linnet. [OE *linetwige*, perh literally 'flax-twitcher']

lintseed see **linseed**.

lintstock see **linstock**.

lintwhite see **lint** and **lintie**.

Linux /*lin'əks*, *lē'nəks* or *lī'nəks*, also *-nuks*, *-nŭks*/ *n* a computer operating system similar to Unix, but designed for use on personal computers. [*Linus* Torvalds (born 1969), Finnish computer programmer, and **Unix**]

lion /*lī'ən*/ *n* a large, fierce, tawny, loud-roaring animal of the cat family, the male having a shaggy mane (*fem* **li'oness**); a person of unusual courage (*fig*); (with *cap* and *the*) Leo; any object of interest, *esp* a famous or conspicuous person much sought after (from the lions once kept in the Tower, one of the sights of London); a Scottish coin of James VI, with a lion on the obverse, worth 74 shillings Scots; (with *cap*) a member of an international organization of professional people's clubs (**the Lions**), with charitable, etc aims. [Anglo-Fr *liun*, from L *leō*, *-ōnis*, from Gr *leōn*, *-ontos*] ▪ **li'oncel**, **li'oncelle** or **li'onel** *n* (*heraldry*) a small lion used as a bearing. **li'onet** *n* a young lion. **li'onism** *n* lionizing; a lion-like appearance occurring in leprosy. **lionizā'tion** or **-s-** *n*. **li'onize** or **-ise** *vt* to treat as a hero or celebrity; to go around the sights of; to show the sights to (*rare*). **li'onizer** or **-s-** *n*. **li'onlike** or **li'only** *adj*. ◻ **li'on-cub** *n* a young lion. **li'onhead** *n* a small long-haired breed of rabbit. **li'on-heart** *n* a person with great courage. **li'on-heart'ed** *adj*. **li'on-hunt'er** *n* a hunter of lions; a person who runs after celebrities. **lion's mouth** *n* (*fig*) a dangerous position. **lion's provider** *n* (*archaic*) the jackal, supposed to attend upon the lion, really his hanger-on. **lion's share** *n* the whole or greater part. **li'on-tā'mer** *n*. ▪ **twist the lion's tail** to harass Great Britain.

lip /*lip*/ *n* either of the muscular flaps in front of the teeth, forming the opening to the mouth; any similar structure, such as either of the two divisions of a liplike flower corolla; the edge or rim of an orifice, cavity, deep geographical depression, vessel, etc; part of such a rim bent outwards like a spout; impudent talk, insolence or cheek (*sl*). ◆ *vt* (**lipp'ing**; **lipped**) to touch with the lips; to kiss; to wash, overflow, or overrun the edge of; to lap or lave; to form a lip on; to edge; to turn or notch the edge of (*Scot*); (of a golfer or golf shot) to get the ball to the very edge of (the hole); to utter with the lips. ◆ *vi* to use the lips in playing a wind instrument; to lap at the brim; to have water lapping over. ◆ *adj* of the lip; formed or sounded by the lips. ◆ *combining form* from the lips only, not sincere. [OE *lippa*; Du *lip*, Ger *Lippe*, L *labium*] ▪ **lip'less** *adj*. **lip'like** *adj*. **lipped** /*lipt*/ *adj* having a lip or lips; labiate. **lipp'y** *adj* having a hanging lip; saucy, cheeky (*sl*). ◆ *n* (*inf*; also **lippie**) lipstick. ◻ **lip brush** *n* a brush for applying colouring to the lips. **lip'-deep** *adj* insincere; immersed to the lips. **lip gloss** *n* a substance applied to the lips to give them a glossy appearance. **lip liner** *n* cosmetic material used to outline the lips. **lip microphone** *n* one constructed in the form of a box shaped to fit the face around the mouth, thus reducing extraneous noises, used eg at sporting events. **lip'-read** *vi*. **lip'-reader** *n*. **lip'-read'ing** *n* gathering what a person says by watching the movement of his or her lips. **lip'-rounding** *n* (*phonetics*) rounding of the lips, as in pronouncing o. **lip'salve** *n* ointment for the lips, *esp* to prevent chapping; blandishment. **lip service** *n* insincere praise or worship; professed, not real, respect or loyalty. **lip'-smacking** *adj* (*inf*) delicious, appetizing. **lip'stick** *n* a short stick of cosmetic colouring for the lips. ◆ *vt* and *vi* to paint with (a) lipstick. **lipstick lesbian** *n* a lesbian with a conventionally feminine appearance; a heterosexual woman who experiments briefly with lesbianism. **lip-sync** or **lip-synch** /*lip'singk*/ *n* the synchronization of lip movements with already recorded sound, *esp* by singers making television appearances; the synchronization of the voice with already filmed lip-movements (in dubbing; also *vt* and *vi*). **lip'-syncer** or **lip'-syncher** *n*. ▪ **bite one's lip** to do this to show annoyance or disappointment; to repress laughter, tears, an angry retort, etc. **hang on someone's lips** to listen eagerly to all that someone has to say. **in Lipsburie pinfold** (*Shakesp*) perh between the teeth. (**keep**) **a stiff upper lip** (to show) resolution, with no yielding to emotion. **lip out** (*golf*) to hit the rim of the hole and not fall in. **make a lip** (*Shakesp*) to pout in sullenness or derision. **smack one's lips** to bring the lips together and part them with a smacking noise, as an indication of relish.

lip- /lip-/ or **lipo-** /li-pō-, li-pə- or li-po-, also lī-/ combining form denoting fat. [Gr lipos fat]

■ **lipaemia** or (N Am) **lipemia** /-ē'mi-ə/ n (Gr haima blood) an excess of fat in the blood. **lip'ase** /-ās or -āz/ n an enzyme that breaks up fats. **lipec'tomy** n (Gr ektomē a cutting out) surgical removal of fatty tissue. **lip'id** n (sometimes **lip'ide** /-īd/) any of a group of chemicals found in bodily tissues, including fats, oils and waxes (esters of fatty acids), derivatives of these such as phospholipids (qv under **phosphorus**), and other substances such as steroids and terpenes. **lip'ochrome** /-krōm/ n (Gr chrōma colour) a pigment of butterfat, etc. **lipogen'esis** n (Gr genesis creation) the formation of fat in the body. **lip'oid** adj fat-like. ◆ n a fat-like substance; a lipid. **lipolysis** /li-pol'i-sis/ n (Gr lysis loosing) the breaking down of fat into fatty acids and glycerol. **lipō'ma** n (pl **lipō'mata**) a fatty tumour. **lipomatō'sis** n the excessive growth of fat. **lipō'matous** adj. **lipophil'ic** adj having an affinity for lipids. **lipoprō'tein** n a water-soluble protein found in the blood, which carries cholesterol. **lip'ōsculpture** n a form of liposuction, often using ultrasound, in which the skin is tightened after the removal of fat. **liposō'mal** adj. **lip'ōsome** n (Gr sōma body) a naturally occurring lipid globule in the cytoplasm of a cell; an artificial droplet of an aqueous substance surrounded by a lipid, used in medicine to carry active drugs to their specific site of action. **lip'ōsuction** n a surgical process for the removal of excess, unwanted fat from the body (inf short form **lī'pō**).

lipa /lē'pə/ n (pl **li'pa** or **li'pas**) a Croatian monetary unit, $\frac{1}{100}$ of a kuna. [Serbo-Croat, literally, lime tree]

liparite /lip'ə-rīt/ (mineralogy) n rhyolite. [From the Lipari Islands, where it occurs]

Lipizzaner /lip-it-sä'nər/ n a breed of horses (usu grey or white in colour) particularly suited and trained for displays of dressage (also **Lippiza'ner**, **Lippizza'ner**, **Lippiza'na**, **-nə/** or **Lippizza'na**). [Lipizza (Lippiza or Lippizza), near Trieste, where the horses were originally bred]

lipo-, etc see **lip-**.

lipogram /lip'ō-gram or lī'pō-/ n a piece of writing, esp in verse, from which all words are omitted which contain a particular letter. [Gr leipein to leave, and gramma a letter, graphein to write]

■ **lipogrammat'ic** adj. **lipogramm'atism** n. **lipogramm'atist** n. **lipog'raphy** n accidental omission of a letter or letters in writing.

lippen /lip'n/ (Scot) vi to trust, rely or depend (with to or on). ◆ vt to expect. [Origin obscure]

■ **lipp'ening** adj (Walter Scott) unguarded.

Lippes loop see **loop**[1].

lippitude /lip'i-tūd/ (archaic) n soreness of the eyes. [L lippitūdō, from lippus bleary-eyed]

lippy[1] or **lippie** /lip'i/ n an old Scottish dry measure, the fourth part of a peck. [Dimin from OE lēap a basket; cf **leap**[2]]

lippy[2] see under **lip**.

liq. abbrev : liquid; liquor.

liquate /lik'wāt/ vt to melt; to subject to liquation. [L liquāre, -ātum to liquefy]

■ **liq'uable** adj. **liquā'tion** n melting; separation of metals with different melting-points.

liquefy /lik'wi-fī/ or -wə-/ vt (**liq'uefying**; **liq'uefied**) to make liquid. ◆ vi to become liquid; to drink (facetious). [L liquefacere, from liquēre to be liquid, and facere to make]

■ **liquefacient** /-fā'shənt/ n and adj. **liquefaction** /-fak'shən/ n. **liquefac'tive** adj. **liq'uefiable** adj. **liq'uefier** n.

❑ **liquefied petroleum gas** n propane or butane under moderate pressure, used in some vehicles in place of petrol or diesel fuel (abbrev **LPG**).

liquesce /li-kwes'/ vi to become liquid; to merge. [L liquēscere, from liquēre to be liquid]

■ **liquesc'ence** n. **liquesc'ency** n. **liquesc'ent** adj.

liqueur /li-kūr' or lē-kœr'/ n a potent alcoholic preparation flavoured or perfumed and sweetened, eg chartreuse, cherry brandy, curaçao, benedictine, kümmel or maraschino; a sweet, usu with a chocolate outer shell and a filling that has the flavour of a particular liqueur. ◆ vt to flavour with a liqueur. ◆ adj (of brandy or whisky) that may be drunk as a liqueur. [Fr, from L liquor; see **liquor**]

❑ **liqueur glass** n a very small drinking-glass.

liquid /lik'wid/ adj flowing; fluid; watery; in a state between solid and gas, in which the molecules move freely about one another but do not fly apart (phys); clear; moist; (of sound, etc) free from harshness; indisputable; unfixed; (of assets) readily converted into cash. ◆ n a fluid substance; a flowing consonant sound, such as l or r (phonetics). [L liquidus liquid, clear, from liquēre to be clear]

■ **liq'uidate** vt to clear up or off (esp a debt); to wind up (a commercial firm, etc), bringing its trading to an end; to turn (assets) into cash; to dispose of; to wipe out, do away with (sl); to kill off (sl).

◆ vi to go into liquidation. **liquidā'tion** n. **liq'uidator** n. **liquid'ity** n the state of being liquid; the condition of having liquid assets; the amount of liquid assets a company has; a measure of the ease with which an asset can be turned into cash. **liq'uidize** or **-ise** vt to make liquid; to purée (food). **liq'uidizer** or **-s-** n a machine which purées foodstuffs. **liq'uidly** adv. **liq'uidness** n.

❑ **liquid assets** n pl (finance) assets which are already, or may be easily converted into, cash, such as shares, bank deposits, etc. **liquid crystal** n a liquid which, like a crystal, has different optical properties depending on its polarity, over a definite range of temperature above its freezing point. **liquid crystal display** n a display, esp in electronic instruments, based on the changes in reflectivity of a liquid crystal cell when an electric field is applied, switching it from an opaque to a transparent state. **liquidity ratio** n (finance) the proportion of a bank's assets that can be converted into cash at short notice. **liquid lunch** n (inf) an instance of drinking alcohol at lunch-time instead of eating food.

■ **go into liquidation** (of a commercial firm, etc) to be wound up, cease trading.

Liquidambar /lik-wid-am'bər/ n a genus of balsamiferous trees of the family Hamamelidaceae, found in N America and Asia. [L liquidus liquid, and LL ambar amber]

liquidus /lik'wi-dəs/ n (also **liquidus curve** or **freezing-point curve**) a curve plotted on a graph showing how temperature affects the composition of a melting or solidifying mixture, above which curve the mixture is entirely liquid. [L, liquid]

liquitab /lik'wi-tab/ n a plastic packet containing a portion of detergent for use in a washing machine or dishwasher. [liquid tablet]

liquor /lik'ər/ n a strong alcoholic drink; anything liquid, esp the product of cooking or a similar operation; a liquid secretion; any prepared solution, esp a strong one (chem). ◆ vt to apply liquor or a solution to; to rub with oil or grease (Shakesp). ◆ vi (sl) to drink (alcohol) (esp with up). [OFr licur, licour (Fr liqueur), from L liquor, -ōris]

■ **liqu'ored** adj (sl) drunk.

❑ **liquor laws** n pl laws controlling the sale of intoxicating drinks.

■ **in liquor** (sl) drunk.

liquorice or **licorice** /lik'(ə-)ris (N Am also -rish)/ n a papilionaceous plant (Glycyrrhiza glabra, or other species) of Europe and Asia; its long sweet root used in medicine; an extract from this root; confectionery made with this extract. [Anglo-Fr lycorys, from LL liquirītia, a corruption of Gr glykyrrhīza, from glykys sweet, and rhīza root]

❑ **liquorice allsorts** n pl an assortment of sweets flavoured with liquorice.

■ **Indian liquorice** see under **Indian**. **wild liquorice** a kind of milk vetch (Astragalus glycyphyllus; also **liquorice-vetch**); restharrow.

liquorish /lik'ə-rish/ adj another spelling of **lickerish**; inclined towards liquor.

■ **liqu'orishness** n.

lira /lē'rə/ n (pl **lire** /lē'rā/ or **lir'as**) a former unit of currency in Italy and Malta, replaced by the euro; the standard monetary unit of Turkey (100 kurus). [Ital, from L lībra a pound]

liriodendron /lī-ri-ō-den'dron/ n a tree of the tulip-tree genus Liriodendron. [Gr leirion a lily, and dendron a tree]

lirk /lirk/ (Scot) n a fold; a wrinkle. ◆ vi to wrinkle. [Origin unknown]

lis /lēs/ (heraldry) n (pl **lis** or **lisses** /lēs'iz/) a fleur-de-lis. [Fr]

Lisbon /liz'bən/ n a light-coloured wine from Estremadura in Portugal, shipped from Lisbon.

lisente /li-sen'tē/ plural of **sente**.

lisk /lisk/ (dialect) n the groin; the flank or loin. [ME leske, prob Old Swed livski the joint of the groin]

lisle /līl/ n a long-stapled, hard-twisted cotton yarn (also adj). [Old spelling of Lille, France, where orig manufactured]

LISP or **Lisp** /lisp/ (comput) n a high-level programming language, designed to create complex chains of operations and data, and used in artificial intelligence research. [list processor]

lisp /lisp/ vi to pronounce certain sounds with the tongue against the upper teeth or gums, as th for s or z; to articulate childishly; to utter imperfectly. ◆ vt to utter with a lisp. ◆ n the act or habit of lisping; a defect of speech causing one to lisp. [OE wlisp (adj) stammering; Du lispen, Ger lispeln]

■ **lisp'er** n. **lisp'ing** adj and n. **lisp'ingly** adv.

lispound or **lispund** /lis'pownd or -pŏnd/ (Orkney and Shetland) n a varying weight, 12 to 34 pounds (approx 5.4 to 15.4kg). [LGer or Du lispund, for livschpund Livonian (Livonia, former Baltic province of Russia) pound]

Lissajous figure /lē'sə-zhoo or -zhoo' fig'ər/ (maths) n a plane curve formed by the combination of two sinusoidal waveforms vibrating in perpendicular directions. [JA Lissajous (1822–80), French physicist]

lissencephalous /lis-en-sef'ə-ləs/ (zool) adj with smooth cerebral hemispheres. [Gr lissos smooth, and enkephalon brain]

lissom or **lissome** /lis'əm/ adj lithe, nimble, flexible. [lithesome]
■ **liss'omly** or **liss'omely** adv. **liss'omness** or **liss'omeness** n.

lissotrichous /li-sot'ri-kəs/ (zool) adj smooth-haired. [Gr lissos smooth, and thrix, trichos hair]

list¹ /list/ n a catalogue, roll, or enumeration (of items). ◆ vt to place in a list or catalogue; to make a list of; to enrol (eg soldiers). ◆ vi to enlist (also **'list**, as if for **enlist**). [OFr liste, of Gmc origin, ult same word as **list²**, from the sense of a strip of paper]
■ **list'able** adj. **list'ing** n a list; a position in a list; a print-out of all the data stored in a file or the commands in a program (comput); an official quotation for stock so that it can be traded on the Stock Exchange; (in pl) a guide to currently-running theatrical or other entertainments.
❏ **List D schools** n pl formerly, the name given in Scotland to community homes for young offenders (before 1969 called **approved schools**). **listed building** n one officially listed as being of special architectural or historic interest, which cannot be demolished or altered without (local) government consent. **listed company** n (commerce) a public company which obtains an official listing from the Stock Exchange. **list price** n the recommended price of an article as shown in a manufacturer's catalogue or advertisement, ie before discounts, etc.
■ **active list** the roll of those liable for active service.

list² /list/ n the selvage on woven textile fabrics; a border; a stripe; a strip, esp one cut from an edge; a ridge or furrow made with a lister (also **lister ridge**; old US); material composed of cut-off selvages; a boundary (obs); a destination (Shakesp); (in pl) the boundary of a jousting-ground or similar area, hence the ground itself, combat. ◆ adj made of strips of woollen selvage. ◆ vt to border; to put a list on; to remove the edge from; to plough with a lister (US). [OE līste; Ger Leiste; affected in some senses by OFr lisse (Fr lice, Ital lizza), from LL liciae barrier]
■ **list'ed** adj enclosed for jousting, etc; fought in lists. **list'er** n (US) a double-mould-board plough.
■ **enter the lists** to come forward for contest or to do battle.

list³ /list/ vt (pat **list'ed** or (archaic) **list**; pap **list'ed**; 3rd pers sing prt **lists**, or (archaic) **list** or **list'eth**) to please (impers; archaic); to have pleasure in (pers; archaic); to desire (archaic); to like or please (archaic); to choose (archaic); to cause to heel or lean over (naut). ◆ vi (naut) to heel over. ◆ n the action or degree of heeling over; joy (obs); desire; inclination; choice. [OE lystan, (impers) to please, from lust pleasure]
■ **list'less** adj uninterested; languid; having no desire or wish (archaic). **list'lessly** adv. **list'lessness** n.

list⁴ /list/ (archaic or poetic) vi to listen. ◆ vt to listen to. [OE hlystan]
■ **list'ful** adj attentive.

list⁵ /list/ n a fillet (archit); a division of parted hair (archaic or poetic). [Ital lista, listello; ult the same as **list¹** and **list²**]
■ **list'el** n (archaic) a small fillet.

listen /lis'n/ vi to attempt to hear something or pay attention (to what is being said or to the person saying it); to follow advice. ◆ n an act or period of listening. [OE hlysnan, recorded in the Northumbrian form lysna]
■ **listenabil'ity** n. **list'enable** adj pleasant to listen to. **listener** /lis'nər/ n a person who listens. **list'enership** n the estimated number of listeners to a radio broadcast.
❏ **list'ener-in** n (pl **list'eners-in**). **list'ening-in** n. **listening post** n orig a post where soldiers are stationed to hear what the enemy is doing; a position advantageous for the gathering of information about the affairs of another country, etc.
■ **listen in** to listen (to a radio broadcast); to overhear intentionally a message intended for another person. **listen up** (inf) to pay attention, listen hard.

lister see under **list²**.

listeria /li-stē'ri-ə/ n a bacterium frequently found in certain foods (esp chicken, soft cheeses, etc), which if not killed in cooking can affect the central nervous system, causing meningitis, encephalitis, miscarriage and even death in the very young and elderly; the disease caused by such bacteria (also called **listeriō'sis**). [Lord Joseph Lister (1827–1912), English surgeon]
■ **Listē'rian** adj relating to Lord Lister or to his pioneering system (**Lis'terism**) of antiseptic treatment of surgical wounds. **Lis'terize** or **-ise** vt to treat by Listerism.

listful see under **list⁴**.

listless see under **list³**.

lit pat and pap of **light¹,³**.

lit. abbrev: literal; literally; /lit/ literary; /lit/ literature.

litany /lit'ə-ni/ n a prayer of supplication, esp in processions; an appointed form of responsive prayer in public worship in which the same thing is repeated several times; a long list or catalogue, evocative or merely boring. [LL litanīa, from Gr litaneiā, from litesthai to pray]
❏ **lit'any-desk** or **-stool** n in the Anglican Church, a movable desk at which a priest kneels, facing the altar, while reciting the litany.
■ **lesser litany** the common formula, 'Kyrie eleison, Christe eleison, Kyrie eleison'.

litas /lē'tas/ n (pl **li'tas** or **li'tai** /-tā/) the standard monetary unit of Lithuania (100 centas). [Lithuanian]

LitB see **LittB**.

litchi see **lychee**.

lit crit /lit krit/ n short for literary criticism.

LitD see **LittD**.

lit de justice /lē də zhü-stēs'/ (Fr) see **bed of justice** under **bed¹**.

lite¹ adj (of food and drink) low in calories, alcoholic content, etc. [Advertising simplification of **light²**]

lite² or **lyte** /līt/ (dialect, also **leet**, otherwise obs) n, adj and adv little. [OE lȳt]

lite³ (Spenser) same as **light³**; also as **light²** in the phrase lungs and lites.

lite pendente /lī'tē pen-den'tē or lē'te pen-den'te/ (L; law) pending the suit.

liter US spelling of **litre**.

literacy see under **literate**.

literae humaniores or **litterae humaniores** /lit'ə-rē hū-mā-ni-ō'rēz or -ō', or lit'e-rī hoo-män-i-ō'rās/ (L) n pl the humanities, Latin and Greek, literally the more humane letters; (as sing) the name of the school and examination at Oxford University.

literal /lit'ə-rəl/ adj relating to or consisting of letters of the alphabet; of the nature of a letter; according to the letter, following word for word; not figurative or metaphorical; inclined to use or understand words in a matter-of-fact sense. ◆ n a wrong letter in printed or typed material; a misprint of a letter in a word (printing). [L litterālis, from littera (lītera) a letter]
■ **lit'eralism** n strict adherence to the literal form; interpretation that is not figurative or metaphorical; exact and unimaginative rendering (art). **lit'eralist** n. **literalist'ic** adj. **literalist'ically** adv. **literality** /-al'i-ti/ n. **lit'eralize** or **-ise** vt. **lit'eralizer** or **-s-** n. **lit'erally** adv using the literal, as opposed to the figurative, meaning of a word or phrase; often inappropriately used for mere emphasis. **lit'eralness** n.

literary /lit'(ə)-rə-ri/ adj relating to, of the nature of, knowledgeable about, or practising, literature or the writing of books; bookish; (of language) formal, such as found in (esp older) literature; relating to letters of the alphabet (obs); epistolary (obs). [L līterārius, from lītera (littera) a letter]
■ **lit'erarily** adv. **lit'erariness** n. **lit'eraryism** n a bookish expression.
❏ **literary agent** n a person who deals with the business affairs of an author. **literary criticism** n (the art of making) qualitative judgements on literary works (short form **lit crit**). **literary executor** n a person appointed to deal with unpublished material after an author's death. **literary source** n (law) in English law, a statute or law report, as the place where the law can be physically located.

literate /lit'ə-rət or -it/ adj able to read and write; learned, scholarly; having a competence in or with (often used as combining form, as in computer-literate). ◆ n a person who is literate; an educated person without a university degree, esp a candidate for priestly orders, or formerly a woman holding a certificate from St Andrews University (**LLA** Lady Literate in Arts). [L lītera, līterātus, līterātim, līterōsus, from lītera (littera) letter]
■ **lit'eracy** n the condition of being literate. **lit'erately** adv. **literati** /-ä'tē/ n pl (sing **litterā'tus** (or /-ä'/) (L) or **literato** /-ä'tō/ (Ital)) men and women of letters, the learned. **literā'tim** (or /-ä'/) adv letter for letter; without the change of a letter. **litera'tion** n the representation of sounds by letters. **lit'erātor** n a dabbler in learning; a person of letters, a literary person. **lit'erose** adj affectedly or spuriously literary. **literos'ity** n.

literature /lit'(ə-)rə-chər/ n the art of composition in prose and verse; the whole body of literary composition universally, or in any language, or on a given subject, etc; literary matter; printed matter; humane learning; literary culture or knowledge. [L līterātūra, from lītera (littera) a letter]
■ **lit'eratured** adj (Shakesp) learned, having literary knowledge.

literose see under **literate**.

lith /lith/ (archaic and Scot) n a joint or segment. [OE lith a member; Ger Glied]

lith- /lith-/ or **litho-** /lith-ō-, -ə- or -o-/ combining form denoting: stone; calculus (med). [Gr lithos stone]

■ **lith'ate** *n* (*obs*) a urate. **lithī'asis** *n* (Gr *lithiāsis*) formation of calculi in the body. **lith'ic** *adj* relating to or obtained from stone or calculi. **lithificā'tion** *n*. **lith'ify** *vt* to transform into stone. **lithist'id** *n* any of the **Lithist'ida**, hard stony sponges. **lith'ite** *n* a calcareous body secreted in an animal cell, *esp* with a sensory function. **lithochromatic** /*-ə-krō-mat'ik* or *-krə-*/ *adj*. **lithochromat'ics** *n sing* the art or process of painting in oil on stone and taking impressions from the result. **lith'ochromy** /*-krō-mi*/ *n* (Gr *chrōma*, *-atos* colour) painting on stone; chromolithography. **lith'oclast** *n* (Gr *klaein* to crush) an instrument for crushing bladder-stones. **lith'ocyst** /*-ō-sist*/ *n* (Gr *kystis* a bladder) a sac containing a lithite. **lithodomous** /*-od'ə-məs*/ *adj* (Gr *lithodomos* a mason, from *domos* a dwelling) living in burrows in rocks. **Lithod'omus** *n* the date-shell genus. **lithogenous** /*-oj'i-nəs*/ *adj* rock-building. **lith'oglyph** /*-ə-glif*/ *n* (Gr *glyphein* to carve) an engraving on stone, *esp* a precious stone. **lith'ograph** /*-gräf*/ *n* (Gr *graphein* to write) a print produced by lithography, from stone (**lithographic stone** or **slate** a fine-grained slaty limestone), or a substitute (such as zinc or aluminium), with greasy ink. ♦ *vt* and *vi* to print in this way. **lithographer** /*-og'rə-fər*/ *n*. **lithographic** /*-ə-graf'ik*/ or **lithograph'ical** *adj*. **lithograph'ically** *adv*. **lithog'raphy** *n* a method of printing from a stone or metal plate that makes use of the immiscibility of oil and water, the image to be printed being receptive to the oil-based ink, and the rest of the plate to moisture, so that when ink comes into contact with the dampened plate, only the image prints. **lith'oid** or **lithoid'al** *adj* like stone. **lith'olapaxy** *n* (Gr *lapaxis* evacuation) the operation of crushing stone in the bladder and working it out. **lithol'atrous** *adj*. **litholatry** /*-ol'ə-tri*/ *n* (Gr *latreiā* worship) stone-worship. **litholog'ic** or **litholog'ical** *adj*. **litholog'ically** *adv*. **lithol'ogist** *n*. **lithol'ogy** *n* the science of rocks as mineral masses; the department of medicine concerned with calculi. **lith'omancy** /*-man-si*/ *n* (Gr *manteiā* divination) divination by stones. **lith'omarge** /*-ō-märj*/ *n* (L *marga* marl) a compact china clay. **lithophagous** /*-of'ə-gəs*/ *adj* (Gr *phagein* to eat) stone-swallowing; rock-boring. **lith'ophane** /*-ō-fān*/ *n* (Gr *phainesthai* to appear) porcelain with pictures showing through transparency. **lithophilous** /*-of'i-ləs*/ *adj* (Gr *philos* friend) growing, living or sheltering among stones. **lithophysa** /*-ō-fī'sə*/ *n* (*pl* **lithophy'sae** /*-sē*/) (Gr *phȳsa* bubble) a bladder-like spherulite (also **lith'ophyse**). **lith'ophyte** /*-fīt*/ *n* (Gr *phyton* plant) a plant that grows on rocks or stones; a stony organism, such as coral. **lithophytic** /*-fit'ik*/ *adj*. **lith'opone** /*-ō-pōn*/ *n* (Gr *ponos* work) a white pigment of barium sulphate and zinc sulphide. **lithoprint** /*lī'thō-*/ *n* a print made by lithography. **lith'osol** *n* soil consisting mainly of recently weathered rock fragments. **lith'osphere** /*-ō-sfēr*/ *n* (Gr *sphaira* sphere; *geol*) the rocky crust of the earth. **lithospheric** /*-sfer'ik*/ *adj*. **lith'otome** /*-ō-tōm*/ *n* (Gr *tomia* the operation of cutting) an instrument for lithotomy. **lithotomic** /*-tom'*/ or **lithotom'ical** *adj*. **lithotomist** /*-ot'əm-ist*/ *n* a surgeon who practises lithotomy. **lithot'omous** *adj* boring in rocks, as some molluscs. **lithot'omy** *n* the surgical operation of removing a stone from a bodily organ, *esp* the bladder. **lithotripter**, **lithotrite**, **lithotrity**, etc *n* see under **lithotripsy**.

litharge /*lith'ärj*/ *n* lead monoxide, such as is obtained in the process of refining silver. [Fr, from Gr *lithargyros*, from *lithos* a stone, and *argyros* silver]

lithate see under **lith-**.

lithe[1] /*līdh*/ *adj* supple or limber. [OE *līthe* soft, mild; Ger *lind* and *gelinde*]

■ **lithe'ly** *adv*. **lithe'ness** *n*. **lithe'some** *adj*. **lithe'someness** *n*.

lithe[2] /*līdh*/ (*obs*) *vi* to listen. [ON *hlȳtha* to listen]

lither /*lidh'ər*/ *adj* bad (*obs*); lazy (*obs*); soft, yielding (*Shakesp*). [OE *lȳthre* bad; influenced by **lithe**[1]]

■ **lith'erly** *adj* mischievous. ♦ *adv* idly.

lithia /*lith'i-ə*/ *n* lithium oxide, a white crystalline substance that absorbs carbon dioxide and water vapour (from its mineral origin, unlike soda and potash); lithium in the form of salts, found in mineral waters. [Gr *lithos* stone]

■ **lith'ic** *adj* relating to or obtained from lithium. **lith'ium** /*-i-əm*/ *n* the lightest metallic element (symbol **Li**; atomic no 3), whose salts, *esp* lithium carbonate, are used to treat manic depression and other psychiatric illnesses.

❑ **lithium drifted silicon detector** *n* a detector for ionizing radiation, used for low-energy X-ray and X-ray spectroscopy. **lith'ium-i'on battery** *n* a type of lightweight battery with a high energy capacity, used in wireless communication devices (also **Li'-i'on battery**).

lithic see under **lith-** and **lithia**.

lithium see under **lithia**.

litho /*lī'thō*/ *n* (*pl* **lī'thos**) short form of **lithograph** or **lithography** (see under **lith-**). ♦ *adj* short form of **lithographic** (see under **lith-**). ♦ *vt* and *vi* (**lī'thoing**; **lī'thoed**) short form of **lithograph** (see under **lith-**).

lithology, **lithophyte**, etc see under **lith-**.

lithospermum /*lith-ō-spûr'məm*/ *n* any plant of the genus *Lithospermum* of the borage family. [Gr *lithospermon* gromwell, from *lithos* stone, and *sperma* seed]

lithospheric, **lithotome**, etc see under **lith-**.

lithotripsy /*lith'ō-trip-si*/ or **lithotrity** /*li-thot'ri-ti*/ *n* the surgical operation of crushing a stone in the bladder, kidney or gall bladder, so that its fragments may be passed naturally from the body. [Gr *lithōn* (genitive pl) *thryptika* breakers of stones; reconstructed as from Gr *tripsis* rubbing or L *trītus* rubbing]

■ **lithotrip'ter** or **lithotrip'tor** *n* a device that crushes stones in the bladder, etc by ultrasound (also **lith'otrite**, **lith'otrītor** or **lithontrip'tor**). **lithotritic** /*-trit'ik*/, **lithotrip'tic**, **lithontrip'tic** or **lithonthryp'tic** *adj*. ♦ *n* a medicine producing a similar result. **lithot'ritist**, **lithotrip'tist** or **lithontrip'tist** *n* a surgeon who performs the operation. **lithot'ritize** or **-ise** *vt*.

Lithuanian /*li-thū-ā'ni-ən* or *-thoo-*/ *adj* relating to the republic of *Lithuania* on the Baltic Sea, or its people or their language. ♦ *n* the Lithuanian language; a native or inhabitant of Lithuania.

lit. hum. *abbrev*: literae (or litterae) humaniores.

litigate /*lit'i-gāt*/ *vt* and *vi* to dispute, *esp* by a lawsuit. [L *lītigāre*, *-ātum*, from *līs*, *lītis* strife, and *agere* to do]

■ **lit'igable** *adj*. **lit'igant** *adj* contending at law; engaged in a lawsuit. ♦ *n* a person engaged in a lawsuit. **litigā'tion** *n*. **lit'igā'tor** *n*. **litigious** /*-ij'əs*/ *adj* relating to litigation; inclined to engage in lawsuits; disputable; open to contention; *perh* depending on results of negotiation (*Shakesp*). **litig'iously** *adv*. **litig'iousness** *n*.

litmus /*lit'məs*/ *n* a substance obtained from certain lichens, turned red by acids, blue by alkalis. [ON *litmosi* herbs used in dyeing, from *litr* colour, and *mosi* moss]

❑ **litmus paper** *n* a test paper dipped in litmus solution. **litmus test** *n* a chemical test for relative acidity or alkalinity; an event seen as an indicator of underlying attitudes, factors, etc (*fig*).

litotes /*lī'tō-* or *lit'ō-tēz*/ (*rhetoric*) *n* meiosis or understatement; *esp* affirmation by negation of the contrary, as in *not a little angry* (= furious). [Gr *lītotēs* simplicity, from *lītos* plain]

litre /*lē'tər*/ *n* the metric unit of capacity, 1 cubic decimetre or 1000 cubic centimetres; until 1964, the volume of a kilogram of water at 41C, under standard atmospheric pressure (1.000028cudm). ♦ *combining form* denoting the capacity of the cylinders of a motor vehicle engine (eg *three-litre*). [Fr, from LL *lītra*, from Gr *lītrā* a pound]

■ **li'treage** *n* volume in litres.

LittB or **LitB** *abbrev*: *Lit(t)erarum baccalaureus* (*L*), Bachelor of Letters or of Literature.

LittD or **LitD** *abbrev*: *Lit(t)erarum doctor* (*L*), Doctor of Letters or of Literature.

litten see **let**[1].

litter /*lit'ər*/ *n* rubbish, *esp* rejected food containers, wrappings, etc carelessly dropped in a public place; any scattered or confused collection of objects, *esp* of little value; a state of confusion and untidiness with things strewn about; a stretcher, or bed supported on poles, for transporting a sick person; a couch carried by men or animals (*hist*); a brood of young born to an animal; an occasion of birth of animals; straw, hay, etc provided as bedding for animals (see also **cat litter** under **cat**[1]); materials for a bed (*archaic*). ♦ *vt* to scatter carelessly about; to make untidy by spreading litter or objects about; (of animals) to give birth to; to supply (animals) with litter. ♦ *vi* to produce a litter or brood; to strew rubbish, etc untidily; to lie untidily about. [OFr *litiere*, from LL *lectāria*, from L *lectus* a bed]

■ **litt'ered** *adj*. **litt'ery** *adj* in a condition of litter; addicted to litter.

❑ **litter basket** or **litter bin** *n* a receptacle for rubbish. **litter lout** or (*N Am*) **litterbug** *n* a person who wilfully drops litter. **litt'ermate** *n* a fellow member of a litter.

litterae humaniores see **literae humaniores**.

littérateur /*lē-tā-rä-tœr'*/ *n* a literary person. [Fr]

little /*lit'l*/ *adj* (*compar* **lesser** or **littler**; *superl* **least** or **littlest**) small in size, extent, quantity or significance; petty; small-minded; young; resembling or reminiscent of something else, but on a small or smaller scale. ♦ *n* (or *adj* with a noun understood) that which is small in quantity or extent; a small quantity; a small thing; not much. ♦ *adv* (*compar* **less**; *superl* **least**) in a small quantity or degree; not much; not at all. [OE *lȳtel*]

■ **litt'leness** *n*. **litt'lie** *n* (*Aust* and *NZ*) a small child. **litt'ling** (*Scot* **litt'lin** or **litt'leane**) *n* (OE *lȳtling*) a child.

❑ **Little Bear** or (*N Am*) **Little Dipper** *n* Ursa Minor. **litt'le-ease** *n* (*hist*) a confined space in which a prisoner can neither sit, stand nor lie; the pillory; the stocks. **little end** *n* in an internal-combustion engine, the smaller end of the connecting rod. **Litt'le-end'ian** *n* one of the Lilliputian party who opposed the *Big-endians*, maintaining that boiled eggs should be cracked at the little end (from Swift's *Gulliver's Travels*). **little finger** *n* the fifth and smallest digit of the hand. **little go**

see **great go** under **go¹**. **little green men** *n pl* a type of men imagined as originating in parts of the universe other than our earth. **little magazine** *n* a small highbrow magazine. **little man** *n* a man of no importance, an underdog. **little Mary** *n* (*JM Barrie*) the stomach. **little office** *n* a short service of psalms, hymns, collects, etc. **little owl** *n* a small owl (*Athene noctua*), native to Europe, Asia and Africa. **little people** *n pl* the fairies, or other race of small supernatural beings; a traditional race of pygmies (*archaic*). **Little Russian** *n* (*archaic*) Ukrainian. **little theatre** *n* a small theatre, *usu* one in which experimental plays, and other plays not likely to be a great commercial success, are produced. **little toe** see under **toe**. **little woman** *n* (*facetious*, mainly *old*) one's wife. **litt'leworth** *adj* (*archaic*) worthless.

■ **in little** on a small scale. **little by little** or (*archaic*) **by little and little** by degrees. **make little of** to treat as of little consequence, to belittle; to comprehend only slightly. **not a little** very. **twist**, **wind** or **wrap someone round one's little finger** see under **finger**.

littoral /*lit'ə-rəl*/ *adj* belonging or relating to the seashore or to the shore of a lake, to lands near the coast, the beach, the space between high and low tidemarks, or water a little below low-water mark; inhabiting the shore or shallow water in a lake or sea. ◆ *n* the shore or coastal strip of land. [L *littorālis* for *lītorālis*, from *lītus*, *lītoris* shore]

liturgy /*lit'ər-ji*/ *n* the form of service or regular ritual of a church, strictly that used in the celebration of the Eucharist; the form of service used in the Eastern Orthodox Church in the celebration of the Eucharist; in ancient Greece, personal service to the state. [Gr *leitourgiā*]

■ **liturgic** /*-ûr'jik*/ or **litur'gical** *adj*. **litur'gically** *adv*. **litur'gics** *n sing* the doctrine or study of liturgies. **liturgiolog'ical** *adj*. **liturgiol'ogist** *n*. **liturgiol'ogy** *n* the study of liturgical forms. **lit'urgist** *n* a leader in public worship; a person who adheres to, or who studies, liturgies.

lituus /*lit'ū-əs*/ *n* an augur's curved staff (*hist*); a J-shaped Roman trumpet (*hist*); a curve of similar form with the polar equation $r^2\,\theta = a$ (*maths*). [L *lituus*]

live¹ /*liv*/ *vi* (**liv'ing**; **lived** /*livd*/) to have, or continue in, life, temporal, spiritual, or figurative, to be alive; to enjoy life; to lead one's life in a certain way, eg *live well*, *loosely*, etc; to be supported, subsist, get a living; to survive, remain alive, escape death; to continue, last, escape destruction or oblivion; to reside or dwell. ◆ *vt* to spend or pass; to act in conformity to; to express (eg a set of principles, a creed, etc) by one's life, make one's life the same thing as. [OE *lifian* (WSax *libban*)]

■ **livabil'ity** or **liveabil'ity** *n*. **liv'able** or **live'able** *adj* worth living, capable of being lived; (*usu* followed by *in*) habitable; (*usu* followed by *with* or *in*) such as one could endure to live with or in, bearable. **liv'er** *n*.

❏ **lived'-in** *adj* (of a room, etc) homely with the signs of habitation; (of a face) marked by life's experiences. **live'-in'** *adj* (of an employee) living at the place of work; (of a sexual partner) sharing the same dwelling.

■ **live a lie** to conduct one's life in such a way as to deny or conceal some essential circumstance or aspect of one's character, *usu* shameful. **live and breathe** to be passionately enthusiastic about. **live and learn** to keep learning new and surprising things. **live and let live** to give and expect toleration or forbearance. **live by** to order one's life according to (a principle, etc). **live down** eventually to rehabilitate oneself in people's eyes after (a failure, mistake, etc). **live for** to attach great importance to; to make (something) the chief concern of one's life; to look forward longingly to. **live in** to reside at one's place of employment. **live it up** to go on a spree; to cram one's life with excitement and pleasure. **live off** to be financially supported by; to feed oneself exclusively on (particular foods). **live on** to live by feeding upon, or with expenditure limited to; to continue or last. **live on air** (*facetious*) to have no apparent means of sustenance. **live out** to live (one's life) entirely in a particular way or place; to survive; to fulfil (eg the destiny reserved for one); (of someone in domestic service) to live away from the workplace (*US*); (of eg a hotel worker, hospital doctor, etc) to live away from one's place of employment; (of a student) to have accommodation outside the college or university campus. **live out of** (*inf*) to depend on the limited range of eg food offered by (tins) or clothes contained in (a suitcase). **live through** to experience at first hand and survive (*esp* an unpleasant event). **live to** to live long enough to, come at last to. **live together** to cohabit. **live under** (*archaic*) to be tenant to. **live up to** to behave in a manner worthy of; to fulfil or satisfy (expectations, a promise, etc). **live well** to live luxuriously. **live with** to cohabit with; to accept and adapt to as an inescapable part of one's life. **the living theatre** the live theatre.

live² /*līv*/ *adj* having life; alive, not dead; (of a volcano) active, not extinct; stirring; in operation or motion; current, applicable, relevant; unquarried or unwrought; charged with energy (eg from electricity, explosives or other chemicals, etc) and still capable of discharge; burning; vivid; of the theatre, etc, concerned with living performance as distinct from filming, broadcasting or televising; (of a broadcast)

made directly from the actual event, not from a recording; (of a musical recording, video, etc) made during a concert performance; (of yoghurt) containing live bacteria; fully operational (*comput*); a fishmonger's word for very fresh. ◆ *adv* at, during, or as a live performance. [**alive**]

■ **-lived** /*-līvd*/ or sometimes *-livd*/ *combining form* denoting having life (eg *long-lived*). **liv'en** *vt* to enliven. ◆ *vi* to become lively. **liv'ener** *n*.

❏ **live axle** *n* driving axle. **live bait** *n* a living animal as bait. **live'bearer** *n* a fish that gives birth to live young. **live'-bearing** *adj*. **live birth** *n* birth in a living condition, *opp* to *stillbirth*. **live'blog** *vi* to blog about an event while it is taking place. ◆ *n* a blog in which an event is described as it is taking place. **live'-born** *adj*. **live'-box** *n* a glass box for examining living objects under the microscope; a box for live fish. **live cartridge** *n* one containing a bullet, as opposed to a blank or a spent cartridge. **live cell therapy** *n* the use of specially prepared animal tissue to stimulate regeneration of diseased or damaged human tissue or cells (also called **cellular therapy**). **live centre** *n* a rotating centre in the tailstock of a lathe, turning with the workpiece. **live circuit** *n* a circuit through which an electric current is flowing. **live'-feath'ers** *n pl* those plucked from the living fowl. **live load** *n* a moving weight or variable force on a structure. **live oak** *n* an American evergreen oak, with durable wood. **live'-rail** *n* one carrying electric current (see also **live wire** below). **live shell** *n* a shell still capable of exploding. **live steam** *n* steam at full pressure, direct from a boiler. **live'stock** *n* domestic animals, *esp* horses, cattle, sheep and pigs; domestic or body vermin (*sl*). **live'stream** *vt* to broadcast (an event) on the Internet as it happens. **live'ware** *n* (*comput sl*) all the people working with a computer system, personnel as distinct from hardware or software. **live weight** *n* weight of living animals. **live'-well** *n* the well in a fishing-boat where fish are kept alive. **live wire** *n* a wire charged with an electric current; a person of intense energy or alertness (*fig*).

livelihead see under **lively**.

livelihood /*līv'li-hŭd*/ *n* (also (*Spenser*) **live'lod** or **live'lood**) means of living; occupation or employment as a means of support. [OE *līflād*, from *līf* life, and *lād* course]

livelong¹ /*liv'long*, also *līv'long*/ (*poetic*) *adj* very long; protracted; enduring; of the day or night, complete, entire, in all its pleasant or tedious length. [**lief** dear, used intensively, and **long¹**]

livelong² /*liv'long*/ *n* the orpine, a plant difficult to kill. [**live¹** and **long¹**]

livelood see **livelihood**.

lively /*līv'li*/ *adj* brisk; active; sprightly; spirited; vivid; lifelike; vital (*obs*); oral (*obs*). ◆ *adv* vivaciously; vigorously. [OE *līflic*, from *līf* life]

■ **live'lihead** *n* (*obs*) liveliness; life; living form; livelihood. **live'lily** *adv*. **live'liness** *n*.

■ **look lively!** make haste, hurry up.

liven see under **live²**.

liver¹ /*liv'ər*/ *n* a large gland that secretes bile, stores and filters blood, converts sugar into glycogen and performs other metabolic functions, formerly regarded as the seat of courage, love, etc; this organ taken from an animal's body, used for food; a disordered state of the liver (*inf*); in old chemistry, a sulphide or other liver-coloured substance (*liver of sulphur*, a mixture obtained by heating potassium carbonate with sulphur). ◆ *adj* liver-colour. [OE *lifer*; Ger *Leber*, ON *lifr*]

■ **-livered** *combining form* eg *white-livered* or *lily-livered* (literally, having a pallid, blood-starved liver), cowardly. **liv'erish** or **liv'ery** *adj* (*old*) suffering from a disordered liver; irritable. **liv'erishly** *adv*. **liv'erishness** *n*.

❏ **liv'er-col'our** *n* and *adj* (of) the colour of liver, dark reddish brown. **liv'er-coloured** *adj*. **liver fluke** *n* a trematode worm that infects the bile-ducts of sheep and other animals. **liv'er-grown** *adj* having a swollen liver. **liver rot** *n* a disease caused by liver flukes. **liver salts** *n pl* mineral salts taken to cure indigestion. **liver sausage** *n* a rich sausage made of liver. **liver spot** *n* a liver-coloured mark on the skin appearing in old age. **liv'erwing** *n* a fowl's right wing, which is cooked with the liver. **liv'erwort** /*-wûrt*/ *n* any plant of the Hepaticae, forming with the mosses the Bryophyta, similar to a moss, growing in damp places and having leaves of a liverlike shape, some kinds having once been used medicinally in diseases of the liver. **liv'erwurst** /*-wûrst*/ *n* liver sausage.

liver² see under **live¹**.

liver³ /*lī'vər*/ *n* a fanciful bird on the arms of the city of Liverpool. [Formed from *Liverpool*]

livermorium /*liv-ər-mö'ri-əm* or *-mō'ri-əm*/ *n* an artificially produced transuranic element (symbol Lv; atomic no 116). [Named after the Lawrence *Livermore* National Laboratory in California]

Liverpudlian /*li-vər-pud'li-ən*/ *adj* belonging to Liverpool. ◆ *n* a native of Liverpool. [*Liverpool*, with *-puddle* facetiously substituted for *-pool*]

■ words derived from main entry word; ❏ compound words; ■ idioms and phrasal verbs

livery¹ /liv'ə-ri/ n the feeding, care, and stabling of a horse at a certain rate; the distinctive dress or badge of a great man's household (*hist*); the distinctive dress or uniform of a person's servants, *esp* menservants, or of a body, eg a trade guild; any characteristic garb; the distinctive decoration used for all its aircraft, etc by an airline, etc; the distinctive style of dress or consistent visual appearance of employees, vehicles, communications, etc of a company; a body of liverymen or of livery-servants; a livery-servant (*archaic*); a delivery or handing over (*obs*); a dispensing or allowance of food or clothes to servants and retainers (*hist*). [Anglo-Fr *liveré*, literally, handed over, from *livrer*, from L *līberāre* to free]
■ **liv'eried** *adj* clothed in livery.
□ **livery company** *n* any of the trade guilds of the City of London which assumed a distinctive dress in the 14c. **livery cupboard** *n* a small cupboard used for the temporary storage of food, etc. **liv'eryman** *n* a man who wears a livery; a freeman of the City of London entitled to wear the livery and enjoy other privileges of his company; a person who keeps or works at a livery stable. **livery pot** *n* a flask in which an allowance of wine was formerly given to a servant. **liv'ery-servant** *n* a servant who wears a livery. **livery stable** *n* a stable where horses are kept at livery and for hire.
■ **at livery** of a horse, kept at the owner's expense at a livery stable. **sue one's livery** (*Shakesp*) to ask for the writ delivering a freehold into the possession of its heir.

livery² see under **liver**¹.

lives /līvz/ plural of **life**.

livid /liv'id/ *adj* black and blue; of a lead colour; discoloured; pale, ashen; extremely angry (*inf*). [L *līvidus*, from *līvēre* to be of a lead colour]
■ **livid'ity**, **liv'idness** or **livor** /lī'vər or -vör/ *n* lividness of colour. **liv'idly** *adv*. **liv'idness** *n*.

living /liv'ing/ *adj* live; alive; having vitality; lively; (of a likeness) strikingly exact; currently in existence, activity or use. ◆ *n* means of subsistence; manner of life; a property; a benefice. [Prp of **live**¹]
□ **living death** *n* a life of unrelieved misery. **living-flame** *adj* of a gas fire, simulating the effect of burning solid fuel. **living fossil** *n* an animal or a plant of a group of which most are extinct. **living memory** *n* the memory of anybody or somebody still alive. **living rock** *n* rock still forming part of the bedrock, not detached. **living room** *n* a sitting room for the general use of a family, etc. **living wage** *n* a wage on which it is possible for a wage-earner and his or her family to live adequately. **living will** *n* a document drawn up to state what kind of medical care the signatory would prefer if unable to express his or her own wishes, as in cases of dementia, coma, etc.
■ **the living** those alive at present.

Livingstone daisy /liv'ing-stən dā'zi/ *n* a S African annual succulent plant (*Dorotheanthus bellidiformis* or *Mesembryanthemum criniflorum*), with daisy-like flowers. [Ety unknown]

livor see under **livid**.

livraison /lē-vre-zõ'/ (*Fr*) *n* a number of a book published in parts.

livre /lē'vr'/ *n* an old French coin, superseded by the franc in 1795; an old French weight about 1lb avoirdupois. [Fr, from L *lībra* a pound]

lixiviation /lik-si-vi-ā'shən/ *n* leaching. [L *lixīvium* lye]
■ **lixiv'ial** or **lixiv'ious** *adj*. **lixiv'iate** *vt*. **lixiv'ium** *n* lye.

lizard /liz'ərd/ *n* any member of the Lacertilia or Sauria, an order of scaly reptiles, *usu* differing from snakes in having four legs, movable eyelids, and non-expansible mouths; (with *cap*) the constellation Lacerta (*astron*). [OFr *lesard* (Fr *lézard*), from L *lacerta*]
□ **liz'ardfish** *n* a small marine fish of the family Synodontidae, with a large mouth and lizard-like head. **liz'ard-hipped** *adj* (of dinosaurs) having a pelvis slightly similar to a lizard's, the pubis extending forwards and downwards from the limb socket, saurischian. **lizard orchid** *n* a rare European orchid (*Himantoglossum hircinum*) bearing a fanciful resemblance to a lizard.

LJ *abbrev* : Lord Justice.

LL *abbrev* : Late Latin; Lord Lieutenant; Low Latin.

ll *abbrev* : lines.

'll /l/ short form of **will** and **shall**.

LLA *abbrev* : Lady Literate in Arts (see under **literate**).

llama /lä'mə/ *n* a S American transport animal of the camel family, a domesticated guanaco; its wool; cloth made of this. [Sp, from Quechua]

llano /lyä'nō or lä'nō/ *n* (*pl* **lla'nos**) one of the vast steppes or plains in the northern part of S America. [Sp, from L *plānus* plain]
■ **llanero** /lyä-nä'rō/ *n* (*pl* **llaner'os**) an inhabitant of the llanos.

LLB *abbrev* : *Legum baccalaureus* (L), Bachelor of Laws.

LLCM *abbrev* : Licentiate of the London College of Music.

LLD *abbrev* : *Legum doctor* (L), Doctor of Laws.

LLM *abbrev* : *Legum magister* (L), Master of Laws.

LLW *abbrev* : low-level waste.

LM *abbrev* : long metre; Lord Mayor; lunar module.

lm *symbol* : lumen (SI unit).

LMA *abbrev* : Liabilities Management Authority.

LME *abbrev* : London Metal Exchange.

LMS *abbrev* : local management of schools, a system in which a school's board of governors is responsible for managing its allocated budget, now replaced by **Fair Funding** (see under **fair**¹); formerly, London, Midland and Scottish Railway.

LMSSA *abbrev* : Licence in Medicine and Surgery of the Society of Apothecaries.

LMVD (*NZ*) *abbrev* : Licensed Motor Vehicle Dealer.

LMX (*insurance*) *abbrev* : London Market Excess of Loss.

ln *abbrev* : (natural) logarithm.

LNE or **LNER** *abbrev* : formerly, London and North-Eastern Railway.

LNG *abbrev* : liquefied natural gas.

lo /lō/ (*archaic*) *interj* look; behold. [OE *lā*]
■ **lo and behold** (often *facetious*) used to signal a startling revelation.

loach /lōch/ *n* a small river-fish of a family (Cobitidae) related to the carp, having a long narrow body and spines round its mouth. [Fr *loche*]

load /lōd/ *n* that which is carried; that which may or can be carried at one time or journey; a burden; a charge; a freight or cargo; a definite quantity, varying according to the goods; weight carried; power output of an engine, etc; work imposed or expected; power carried by an electric circuit; a large quantity borne; a burden sustained with difficulty; that which burdens or grieves; a weight or encumbrance; weight of blows (*Spenser*); abundance (*inf, esp* in *pl*). ◆ *vt* (*pat* **load'ed**; *pap* **load'ed** or (*archaic*) **load'en**) to lade or burden; to charge; to put a load on or in; to put on or in anything as a load; to put film in (a camera); to put ammunition in (a gun); to put on too much; to weigh down; to overburden; to supply, present, or assail overwhelmingly or lavishly; to weight or bias; to give weight or body to, by adding something; to mix (colour) with white (*art*); to lay colour on in masses (*art*); to add charges to (*insurance*); to doctor, drug, adulterate or fortify (wine); to transfer (data or a program) to the main memory (*comput*). ◆ *vi* to put or take on a load; to charge a gun; to become loaded or burdened. ◆ *combining form* denoting the goods or people conveyed in a vehicle (as in *busload, coachload, lorryload*). [OE *lād* course, journey, conveyance; meaning affected by the unrelated **lade**³; cf **lode** and **lead**¹]
■ **load'ed** *adj* carrying a load; containing bullets; containing film; rich, wealthy (*sl*); under the influence of drink or drugs (*sl*); weighted in discussion in a certain direction; (of dice, etc) illicitly weighted so as to produce a desired outcome. **load'en** *vt* (*obs* or *dialect*) to load. **load'er** *n* a person or machine that loads (in various senses); a program for controlling the loading of other programs (*comput*). **load'ing** *n* the act of loading; that with which anything is loaded. **loads** *n pl* (*inf*) a lot, heaps. ◆ *adv* very much, as in *loads nicer*.
□ **load'-bearing** *adj* of a wall, etc, supporting a structure, carrying weight. **loaded question** *n* a question designed to make an unwilling answerer commit himself or herself to some opinion, action or course. **load factor** *n* the ratio of an external load to the weight of an aircraft; the actual payload on an aircraft as a percentage of the maximum permissible payload; the ratio of an average load to peak load over a period (*elec eng*). **loading bay** see under **bay**². **loading coil** *n* a coil inserted in an electric circuit to increase inductance. **loading gauge** *n* a suspended bar that marks how high a railway truck may be loaded; the maximum horizontal and vertical space that rolling stock may safely occupy above the track. **load line** *n* a line on a ship's side to mark the depth to which her cargo may be allowed to sink her. **load'master** *n* a member of an aircrew who is in charge of the cargo. **load shedding** *n* temporarily reducing the amount of electricity sent out by a power station.
■ **a load of** a quantity of (something distasteful or senseless, eg *a load of rubbish, a load of tripe*). **a load off one's mind** relief from anxiety. **get a load of** (*sl*) to listen to, look at, pay attention to. **have a load on** (*N Am*) to be drunk. **load the dice** to make one side heavier than the other so as to influence their fall for purposes of cheating. **load the dice against someone** (*fig*) to deprive someone of a fair chance of success.

loadsa- /lōd-zə-/ (*sl*) *combining form* representing *loads of*, chiefly in (and originating as a back-formation from) **load'samoney**, (a person loaded with) wealth accumulated as a result of the economic boom of the 1980s. [*Loadsamoney*, grotesque character invented by comedian Harry Enfield]

loadstar and **loadstone** same as **lodestar** and **lodestone** (see under **lode**).

loaf[1] /*lōf*/ *n* (*pl* **loaves** /*lōvz*/) a portion of bread baked in one mass, *esp* of standard weight; a moulded portion of food, *esp* bread or meat; a conical mass of sugar; bread (formerly, still *Scot*); any lump (*obs*); a cabbage-head; the head, or brains (for *loaf of bread*; *Cockney rhyming sl*). ◆ *vi* (also **loave** /*lōv*/) to form a head, as in a cabbage. [OE *hlāf* bread]

❑ **loaf'-bread** *n* (*Scot*) ordinary plain bread. **loaf'-cake** *n* (*US*) a plain cake like a loaf in form. **loaf sugar** *n* refined sugar moulded into a large cone.

■ **half loaf** a loaf of half the standard weight. **loaves and fishes** temporal benefits, the main chance (from Bible, John 6.26).

loaf[2] /*lōf*/ *vi* to loiter or stand idly about, pass time idly. [Poss from Ger *Landläufer* tramp, vagabond]

■ **loaf'er** *n* someone who loafs; a casual shoe, *esp* one resembling a moccasin. **loaf'erish** *adj*. **loaf'ing** *n* and *adj*.

Loaghtan /*lohh'tən*/ *n* a breed of four-horned sheep with a soft brown fleece, native to the Isle of Man. [Manx *loaghtyn* brown, poss literally mouse-brown, from *lugh* mouse, and *dhoan* brown]

loam /*lōm*/ *n* a soil consisting of a natural mixture of clay and sand, with animal and vegetable matter; a composition basically of moist clay and sand used in making bricks. ◆ *vt* to cover with loam. [OE *lām*; Ger *Lehm*; cf **lime**[1]]

■ **loam'iness** *n*. **loam'y** *adj*.

loan[1] /*lōn*/ *n* anything lent, *esp* money at interest; the act of lending; the condition of being lent; an arrangement for lending; permission to use; a loan word. ◆ *vt* to lend. [ON *lán*; cf **lend**, OE *lǣnan*; Dan *laan*]

■ **loan'able** *adj*. **loanee'** *n*. **loan'er** *n*.

❑ **loan'back** *n* a facility available from some life-assurance companies whereby a person may borrow from the sum he or she has invested. **loan collection** *n* privately-owned works of art lent by their owner for a public exhibition. **loan'-hold'er** *n* a person who holds security for a loan. **loan'-office** *n* a public office at which loans are negotiated, received, or recorded; a pawnshop. **loan shark** *n* (*inf*) a person who lends money at exorbitant rates of interest, a usurer. **loan sharking** *n*. **loan'-society** *n* a society organized to subscribe money to be lent. **loan translation** *n* a compound, phrase, etc that is a literal translation of a foreign expression, such as English *motorway* from German *Autobahn*, German *Fernsehen* from English *television* (also called a **calque**; see under **calk**[3]). **loan word** *n* a word taken into one's own language from another language, generally with slight adaptation.

■ **on loan** given as a loan.

loan[2] /*lōn*/ or **loaning** /*lō'ning*/ (*Scot*) *n* a lane; an open space for passage left between fields of corn; a place for milking cows. [OE *lone, lane*; see **lane**[1]]

loast /*lōst*/ (*Spenser*) see **lose**[2].

loath or **loth** /*lōth*/ *adj* reluctant, unwilling; hateful, repulsive, ugly (*obs*). [OE *lāth* hateful; cf **loathe**]

■ **nothing loath** not at all unwilling.

loathe /*lōdh*/ *vt* to dislike intensely; to feel disgust at. [OE *lāthian*; cf **loath**]

■ **loathed** *adj*. **loath'edness** *n*. **loath'er** *n*. **loath'ful** *adj* exciting loathing or disgust; (*Spenser* **lothefull** or **lothfull**) loathsome; reluctant. **loath'fulness** *n*. **loath'ing** *n* extreme hate or disgust; abhorrence. ◆ *adj* hating. **loath'ingly** *adv*. **loath'liness** *n*. **loath'ly** *adj* (*archaic*) hideous; loathsome. **loathsome** /*lōth'* or *lōdh'səm*/ *adj* exciting loathing or abhorrence; detestable. **loath'somely** *adv*. **loath'someness** *n*. **loathy** /*lōdh'i*/ *adj* (*archaic*).

loave and **loaves** see **loaf**[1].

lob /*lob*/ *n* (in sport) a ball lifted in a high, slow arc; a lump; a clumsy person; a lout; something thick and heavy; a pollack; a lobworm. ◆ *vt* (**lobb'ing**; **lobbed**) to play as a lob; to send a high ball over (an opponent); to droop (*Shakesp*). [Cf Fris and Du *lob* lump]

❑ **Lob's pound** *n* (*dialect*) prison; difficulty.

lobar, **lobate**, etc see under **lobe**.

lobby /*lob'i*/ *n* a small hall or waiting room; a passage serving as a common entrance to several apartments; the antechamber of a legislative hall; a corridor into which members of parliament pass as they vote (also **division lobby**); a group of people who campaign to persuade legislators to make regulations favouring their particular interests. ◆ *vt* to seek to influence (public officials), *esp* in the lobby. ◆ *vi* to frequent the lobby in order to influence members or to collect political intelligence; to conduct a campaign in order to influence public officials. [LL *lobia*, from MHGer *loube* (Ger *Laube*) a portico arbour, from *Laub* a leaf; cf **lodge**]

■ **lobb'yer** *n*. **lobb'ying** *n*. **lobb'yist** *n*.

❑ **lobby correspondent** *n* a reporter on parliamentary affairs. **lobb'y-member** *n* (*US*) formerly, someone who frequented a lobby in the interest of some cause. **lobby system** *n* the giving of political information to lobby correspondents on condition that the source is not revealed.

lobe /*lōb*/ *n* a broad, *esp* rounded, segmental division, branch, or projection; the soft lower part of the ear; a division of the lungs, brain, etc; a division of a leaf. [Gr *lobos* lobe]

■ **lōb'ar** *adj* relating to or affecting a lobe. **lōb'ate**, **lōbed** or **lōb'ose** *adj* having a lobe or lobes. **lōbā'tion** *n* lobing. **lobec'tomy** *n* (*med*) the surgical excision of a lobe of any organ or gland of the body. **lobe'less** *adj*. **lobe'let** *n* a lobule (see below). **lōb'ing** *n* division into lobes; formation of, possession of, or provision with, lobes. **lobiped** *adj* see **lobe-footed** below. **lobotomizā'tion** or **-s-** *n*. **lobot'omize** or **-ise** *vt* to perform a lobotomy on; to render dull, bland or inoffensive (*fig*). **lobot'omy** *n* surgical incision into a lobe of an organ or gland; (*loosely*) leucotomy. **lob'ūlar**, **lob'ūlate** or **lob'ūlated** *adj*. **lobūlā'tion** *n*. **lob'ūle** or **lob'ūlus** *n* (*pl* **lob'ūles** or **lob'ūli** /*-ī*/) a small lobe or lobe-like structure. **lō'bus** *n* (*pl* **lō'bī**) a lobe.

❑ **lobar pneumonia** *n* inflammation of a whole lobe of the lungs, as distinguished from **lobular pneumonia**, which attacks the lungs in patches. **lōbe'-foot** *n* a phalarope. **lōbe'-foot'ed** or **lō'biped** *adj* having lobate feet, ie with lobes along the sides of the toes, as a coot does.

lobelia /*lō-bē'lyə*/ *n* a plant of the genus *Lobelia* giving its name to a family, **Lobelia'ceae**, differing from Campanulaceae in having two carpels and zygomorphic flowers, twisted upside down, including garden plants with red, white, blue, purple or yellow flowers. [Named after the botanist Matthias de *Lobel* (1538–1616)]

■ **lobeline** /*lō'bə-lēn* or *-lin*/ *n* a poisonous alkaloid obtained from *Lobelia inflata*, used as a respiratory stimulant and to discourage tobacco-smoking.

loblolly /*lob'lo-li*/ *n* a name for various American pines (also **loblolly pine**); thick gruel, hence ship's medicine (*dialect*); a lout (*dialect*); a muddy swamp or mire (*US*). [Perh **lob** and **lolly**]

❑ **loblolly bay** *n* an American tree (*Gordonia lasianthus*) of the tea family, the bark of which is used in tanning. **lob'lolly-boy** *n* (*obs*) a ship-surgeon's attendant. **loblolly tree** *n* a name for several American leathery-leaved trees.

lobo /*lō'bō*/ (*US*) *n* a timber wolf. [Sp, wolf, from L *lupus*]

lobola /*lə-bō'lə*/ or **lobolo** /*-lō*/ *n* (in southern Africa) a payment for a bride, sometimes paid in cattle. [Zulu *ilobolo*]

lobose, **lobotomy**, etc see under **lobe**.

lobscouse /*lob'skows*/ *n* a stew or hash with vegetables or biscuit, a sea dish (also **lob's course**). [Origin obscure; cf **lob** and **loblolly**]

lobster /*lob'stər*/ *n* a large strong-clawed edible crustacean (genus *Homarus*), red when boiled; its flesh as food; any of several crustaceans resembling it, eg the **Norway lobster** (genus *Nephrops*), **spiny** or **rock lobster** (genus *Palinurus*); a British soldier (*obs sl*). [OE *loppestre*, from L *locusta* a lobster; cf **locust**]

❑ **lobster moth** *n* a European moth (*Stauropus fagi*) whose larva resembles a lobster. **lobster pot** *n* a basket for trapping lobsters.

lobular, **lobus**, etc see under **lobe**.

lobworm /*lob'wûrm*/ *n* a lugworm; sometimes an earthworm. [**lob** and **worm**]

local /*lō'kl*/ *adj* relating to position in space; of or belonging to a place; confined to a place or places; concerned with a particular place or area; (of a bus or train) serving the community of a particular area, stopping at every stop. ◆ *n* a person belonging to a particular place, an inhabitant; one's nearest pub; an examination (*US*); a local anaesthetic (qv below); a local bus or train; a trade union branch (*US*); a news item of local interest (*N Am press*); a place. [L *locālis*, from *locus* a place]

■ **lo'calism** *n* the state of being local; affection for a place; provincialism; the policy of allowing decisions to be made at a local level. **lo'calist** *n* someone preoccupied with local concerns (also *adj*). **locality** /*lō-kal'i-ti*/ *n* place; position; district. **lo'calizable** or **-s-** *adj*. **localizā'tion** or **-s-** *n*. **lo'calize** or **-ise** *vt* to assign or limit to a place. **lo'calizer** or **-s-** *n* something that localizes, *esp* a radio transmitter used in effecting a blind landing (also *adj* as in **localizer beam**, etc). **lo'cally** *adv*. **lo'calness** *n*.

❑ **local action** *n* (*law*) a legal action that relates to a specific place and must be brought there. **local anaesthesia** *n* anaesthesia affecting only a restricted area of the body. **local anaesthetic** *n* a solution for injecting into any part of the body to anaesthetize it, or an injection of this. **local area network** *n* (*comput*) a computer network operating over a small area such as an office or group of offices, in which a high rate of data transfer is possible (*abbrev* **LAN**). **local authority** *n* the elected body for local government, eg town council, county council. **local call** *n* a telephone call made to another number on the same exchange or group of exchanges; a call made within a certain radius (less than 56km). **local colour** *n* faithful, characteristic details of particular scenery, manners, etc, giving verisimilitude in works of art and fiction; colour of individual items as apart from the general colour scheme in a picture. **local education authority** *n* the department of a local authority which administers state education (*abbrev* **LEA**). **local**

examinations *n pl* examinations of school pupils held in various local centres by universities. **local government** *n* self-administration (in local affairs) by towns, counties, etc, as opposed to national or central government; a local authority (*US*). **Local Group** *n* (*astron*) the family of galaxies to which our own Galaxy and the Andromeda Galaxy belong. **local loop** *n* in a telecommunications system, a pair of wires connecting the customer's premises with the local exchange that serves it. **local management of schools** *n* a system of school management in which the governors and head teacher of a state school are allocated a budget by a local authority. **local option** *n* the right of a town or district to decide whether liquor licences shall be granted within its bounds, or to decide whether or not to enforce (locally) permissive laws and regulations. **local preacher** *n* a Methodist layperson authorized to preach in his or her district. **local radio** *n* radio (programmes) broadcast from a local station to a relatively small area, often on local themes. **local time** *n* the time of a place as measured by the passage of the sun over the meridian passing through that place. **local variable** *n* (*comput*) a variable with its use restricted to a particular subprogram. **local veto** *n* the power of a district to prohibit the sale of liquors in its own area.

locale /lō-käl'/ *n* the scene of some event, etc. [Fr *local*, with *e* to show stress]

locate /lō-kāt'/ *vt* to place; (often *passive*) to set in a particular position, situate; to designate or find the position of; to find or pinpoint. ◆ *vi* (*orig N Am*) to establish oneself in residence or business in an area. [L *locāre* to place]
■ **locāt'able** or **locāte'able** *adj.* **locā'tion** *n* the act of locating, or process of being located; a farm (*Aust*); in South Africa, under apartheid, any of the townships or other areas in which the black or coloured population were obliged to live; position, site; site for filming outside the studio (*film*); a leasing on rent (*law*); a position in a memory which can hold a unit of information, eg a word (*comput*); such a unit of information (*comput*). **locā'tional** *adj.* **locative** /lok'ə-tiv/ *adj* relating to location; denoting a case representing 'place where' (*grammar*). ◆ *n* the locative case; a word in the locative case. **locā'tor** *n.*
■ **on location** outside the studio (of filming or sound-recording).

locavore /lō'kə-vör/ *n* a person who will eat only food produced locally. [Blend of **local** and **carnivore**]

loc. cit. /lok sit/ *abbrev* : *loco citato* (*L*), in the passage or place just quoted.

locellate /lō-sel'āt/ (*bot*) *adj* divided into small compartments. [L *locellus*, dimin of *locus* a place]

loch /lohh/ (*Scot*) *n* a lake; an arm of the sea (also **sea loch**). [Gaelic *loch*; OE (Northumbrian) *luh*]
■ **loch'an** *n* (*Gaelic*) a little loch.

Lochaber axe /lo-hhä'bər aks/ *n* a Highland variety of halberd. [From the *Lochaber* district in NW Scotland]

lochan see under **loch**.

lochia /lok'i-ə or lō'ki-ə/ (*med*) *n pl* a discharge from the uterus after childbirth. [Gr *lochia* (pl)]
■ **lō'chial** *adj.*

loci /lō'kī or -sē/ plural of **locus**.

lock[1] /lok/ *n* a fastening device, *esp* one in which a bolt is moved by mechanism, with or without a key; an immobilizing device that can be operated on machinery, etc; an enclosure on a canal in which water can be adjusted to allow boats to be raised or lowered; the part of a firearm by which it is discharged; a grapple in wrestling or a disabling hold generally; (also **lock forward**) one of the two players in the second row of the scrum (*rugby*); a state of being jammed or immovable; the state of being firmly interlocked or engaged; (*usu* **air'lock**) a bubble blocking the flow of fluid through a pipe, etc; a number of things mutually engaged; a lockful; a lock-keeper; any narrow, confined place; a lock-hospital; locking up; the full extent of the turning arc of the front wheels of a motor vehicle; a certainty (*N Am inf*). ◆ *vt* to fasten (a door, chest, etc) with a lock; to fasten so as to impede motion; to engage; to jam; to shut up, secure; to close fast; to hold closely, eg in an embrace; to construct locks on (a canal); to take (a boat) through a lock. ◆ *vi* to become fixed, to jam; to unite firmly; to become or have the means of becoming locked. [OE *loc*]
■ **lock'able** *adj.* **lock'age** *n* the locks of a canal; the difference in the levels of locks; materials used for locks; water lost by use of a lock; tolls paid for passing through locks. **lock'fast** *adj* firmly fastened by locks. **lock'ful** *n* enough to fill a lock. **lock'less** *adj.*
□ **lock'away** *n* (*finance*) a long-term security (also *adj*). **lock'-chain** *n* a chain for fastening the wheels of a vehicle by tying the rims to some part which does not rotate. **lock'down** *n* an act of confining prisoners to their cells, *esp* as a means of restoring order; any general cessation of activity, *esp* in response to a crisis. **locked in** *adj* securely fixed, not subject to change (*inf*); concentrating and performing at one's best (*sl*). **locked-in syndrome** *n* (*med*) a neurological condition, resulting from

brainstem damage, in which the subject is conscious and aware but unable to move or communicate, other than sometimes through blinking. **lock gate** *n* a gate for opening or closing a lock in a canal, river, or dock-entrance. **lock'-hos'pital** *n* (*archaic*) a hospital for venereal diseases (from one in Southwark, *orig* a lazar-house, probably since specially isolated). **lock'house** *n* a lock-keeper's house. **lock'-in** *n* (*inf*) a period of drinking in a pub after it has officially closed for the night. **lock'jaw** *n* tetanus; loosely, trismus. **lock'-keeper** *n* the attendant at a lock. **lock'man** *n* a lock-keeper; a hangman (*Scot*; *obs*); an undersheriff, or a coroner's summoner (*Isle of Man*). **lock'nut** or **lock'ing-nut** *n* a nut screwed on top of another one to prevent it loosening; a nut designed to lock itself when screwed tight. **lock'out** *n* the act of locking out, *esp* used of the locking out of employees by the employer during an industrial dispute. **lock'pick** *n* a picklock. **locks'man** *n* a turnkey; a lock-keeper. **lock'smith** *n* a person who makes and mends locks. **lock'step** *n* a method of marching in tight formation, with minimum space between one marcher and the one behind (**in lockstep** operating in close conformity). **lock'stitch** *n* a sewing-machine stitch formed by the locking of two threads together. **lock'-up** *n* a cell for locking up prisoners; a lockable shelter for a motor vehicle; a small shop; a locking up; a long-term investment (*finance*). ◆ *adj* capable of being locked up.
■ **lock away** to hide, *usu* by locking up out of sight. **lock horns** to engage in combat, physical or otherwise. **lock in** to confine by locking doors. **lock on (to)** of a radar beam, to track (an object) automatically. **lock out** to keep out by locking doors; to exclude employees from a factory, etc; to prevent other users from accessing (a file) while one user is reading or updating it (*comput*). **lock, stock and barrel** the whole; altogether, entirely. **lock up** to confine; to lock securely; to lock whatever is to be locked; to make inaccessible or unavailable (*fig*); to invest (capital) so that it cannot be readily realized. **under lock and key** locked up; imprisoned.

lock[2] /lok/ *n* a piece, strand, tuft or ringlet of hair; a wisp of wool or cotton; a small quantity, as of hay; a quantity of meal, the perquisite of a mill-servant (*Scots law*; *obs*); a lovelock (*Shakesp*); (in *pl*) hair; (in *pl*) dreadlocks. [OE *locc*; ON *lokkr*, Ger *Locke* a lock]

Lockean or **Lockian** /lok'i-ən/ *adj* relating to the philosophy of John Locke (1632–1704). ◆ *n* (also **Lock'ist**) a follower of Locke.

locker /lok'ər/ *n* a small cupboard that can be locked; a person or thing that locks. [**lock**[1]]
□ **locker room** *n* a room for changing clothes and storing belongings in lockers.
■ **Davy Jones's locker** see under **Davy Jones**. **shot in the locker** see under **shot**[1].

locket /lok'it/ *n* a small ornamental case containing a miniature portrait, photograph or memento, worn on a chain, etc round the neck. [Fr *loquet* latch]

Lockian and **Lockist** see **Lockean**.

lockram /lok'rəm/ *n* a coarse linen said to have been made at *Locronan* (Ronan's cell) in Brittany.

loco[1] /lō'kō/ *n* (*pl* **lō'cos**) a locomotive.
□ **lō'coman** *n* a railway-engine driver.

loco[2] /lō'kō/ (*US*) *adj* of cattle, suffering from loco disease; mad, crazy (*sl*). ◆ *n* (*pl* **lō'cos** or (*rare*) **lō'coes**) *Astragalus* or any other related leguminous plant (also **lo'coweed** or **lo'coplant**). [Sp *loco* mad]
■ **locoed** /lō'kōd/ *adj* poisoned by loco; mad (*sl*).
□ **loco disease** *n* a disease of farm animals, caused by eating loco, with symptoms of disordered vision and paralysis.

loco citato /lō'kō si-tä'tō or lok'ō ki-tä'tō/ (*L*) in the passage cited (*abbrev* **loc. cit.**).

locofoco /lō-kō-fō'kō/ (*US*) *n* (*pl* **lōcōfō'cos**) a match for striking; (*usu* with *cap*) one of the extreme section of the Democratic party of 1835, known as the Equal Rights Party. [Origin unknown]

locomotive /lō-kə-mō'tiv/ *n* a railway engine; a self-propelled engine running on rails, used for pulling trains, and driven by steam, electricity or diesel power; any machine or engine that converts power into movement. ◆ *adj* moving from place to place; capable of, or assisting in, locomotion. [L *locus* a place, and *movēre*, *mōtum* to move]
■ **locomo'bile** /-bil/ *adj* having the power of changing place; self-propelling. ◆ *n* a locomobile vehicle. **locomobil'ity** *n.* **lo'comote** *vi* (back-formation) to move from place to place. **locomotion** /-mō'shən/ *n* the power of moving from place to place. **locomotiv'ity** *n.* **locomo'tor** *n.* **locomo'tor** or **locomo'tory** *adj* relating to locomotion.
□ **locomotor ataxia** *n* (*pathol*) tabes dorsalis, failure of muscle co-ordination in the late stages of syphilis, caused by degeneration of the nerve fibres.

locorestive /lō-kō-res'tiv/ (*Lamb*) *adj* staying in one place. [Humorously modelled on **locomotive**, from L *restāre* to stay still]

Locrian /lō'kri-ən/ adj of Locris in Greece, or its people, the Locri. ♦ n one of the Locri. [Gr Lokros Locrian]
❑ **Locrian mode** n in ancient Greek music, the same as the Hypodorian.

loculus /lok'ū-ləs/ or **locule** /-ūl/ n (pl **loc'uli** /-lī/ or **loc'ules**) a small compartment or chamber (bot, anat and zool); in ancient catacombs, a small recess for holding an urn. [L loculus, dimin of locus a place]
■ **loc'ulament** n (bot) a loculus. **loc'ular** or **loc'ulate** adj having loculi. **loculicidal** /lok-ū-li-sī'dl/ adj (L caedere to cut) dehiscing along the back of the carpel.

locum /lō'kəm/ n (pl **lō'cums**) short for locum tenens or locum tenency. [L lŏcum, accusative of lŏcus a place]
❑ **locum tenency** n. **locum tenens** /lō'kəm tē'nenz or ten'enz/ n (pl **lō'cum tenen'tes** /-tēz/) a deputy or substitute, esp for a doctor or member of the clergy.

locuplete /lok'ū-plēt/ adj well-supplied. [L locuplēs, -ētis]

locus /lō'kəs or lok'ŭs/ n (pl **loci** /lō'sī or lok'ē/) a place, locality, location; a passage in a book, piece of writing, etc; the line or surface constituted by all positions of a point or line satisfying a given condition (maths); the position of a gene on a chromosome (genetics). [L locus place]
❑ **locus classicus** /klas'i-kəs or -kŭs/ n the classical passage, the stock quotation. **locus paenitentiae** /pē-ni-ten'shi-ē or pī-ni-ten'ti-ī/ n room for penitence; time for repentance. **locus standi** /stan'dī or -dē/ n a place for standing; a right to interfere; a right to appear in court (law).

locust /lō'kəst/ n a name for several kinds of migratory winged insects of the family Acrididiae, related to grasshoppers, highly destructive to vegetation; extended to various similar insects; a devourer or devastator (fig); a locust bean; a locust tree. ♦ vi (rare) to lay waste like locusts. [L locusta lobster, locust; cf **lobster**]
■ **locust'a** n (pl **locust'ae** /-ē/) a grass spikelet; (with cap) a genus of grasshoppers of the family **Locust'idae** (not usu classed as locusts). ❑ **locust bean** n the carob bean. **locust bird** n any of several pratincoles that feed on locusts. **locust tree** n the carob; the false acacia (Robinia pseudo-acacia) or its wood; a large West Indian tree (Hymenaea courbaril) of the Caesalpinia family, with buttress roots, valuable wood, and bark exuding resin. **lo'cust-years** n pl years of poverty and hardship (used by Winston Churchill, after an expression in the Old Testament, Joel 2.25).

locution /lo-kū'shən/ n an act or mode of speaking; an expression, word or phrase. [L loquī, locūtus to speak]
■ **locū'tionary** adj of or relating to an utterance. **loc'utory** n a room for conversation, esp in a monastery.

lod /lod/ n in statistics, the logarithm of the odds relating to an event. [Acronym of logarithm odds]

lode /lōd/ n a vein containing metallic ore; a reach of water; an open ditch. [OE lād a course; cf **load**]
❑ **lodes'man** n (old) a pilot. **lode'star** or **load'star** n the star that guides, the Pole Star, often used figuratively. **lode'stone** or **load'stone** n a form of magnetite which exhibits polarity, behaving, when freely suspended, as a magnet; a magnet (often fig).

loden /lō'dən/ n a thick waterproof woollen cloth with a short pile; (also **loden coat**) a coat made of this cloth. [Ger]

lodge /loj/ n a house in the wilds for sportsmen; a gatekeeper's cottage; a college head's residence; a porter's room; an abode, esp if secluded, humble, small or temporary; the meeting-place of a branch of some societies, eg freemasons; the branch itself; a Native American dwelling, esp a teepee or longhouse (qv); the dwelling-place of a beaver, otter, etc; a retreat; a frequently used element in the name of a house or hotel; an accumulation (obs); a loggia; a box in a theatre. ♦ vt to supply with temporary accommodation; to place; to deposit for safety, etc; to infix; to bring (a charge or accusation) against someone; to make (a complaint or objection) officially; to vest (a power, talent, etc) in someone; to settle, fix firmly; to prompt or force to take shelter; (of wind, etc) to blow (eg crops) flat, to lay flat. ♦ vi to stay temporarily, rent accommodation as a lodger; to pass the night; to take shelter; to come to rest in a fixed position; (of crops, etc) be blown flat. [OFr loge, from OHGer lauba shelter; cf **lobby** and **loggia**]
■ **lodg'er** n a person who lodges; a person who lives in a rented room or rooms. **lodg'ing** n temporary accommodation; (often in pl) a room or rooms rented in another person's house; harbour. **lodg'ment** or **lodge'ment** n the act of lodging, or state of being lodged; the depositing of money in a bank account; an accumulation of something that remains at rest, or a blockage caused by it; the occupation and holding of a position within enemy territory by a besieging party, and the fortifications erected to maintain it (milit); the position so occupied.
❑ **lodge'-gate** n a gate with a lodge. **lodge'-keeper** n. **lodge'pole** n a pole used in the construction of a Native American lodge. **lodgepole pine** n either of two fast-growing N American pines (Pinus contorta).

lodging house n a house where lodgings are let; a house other than a hotel where travellers lodge; a house where vagrants may lodge. **lodging turn** n a turn or shift of railway work that requires sleeping away from home.

lodicule /lod'i-kūl/ (bot) n a small scale in a grass flower (also **lodic'ula** (pl **lodic'ulae** /-ē/)). [L lōdīcula, dimin of lōdīx, -īcis coverlet]

lo'e /loo/ Scots form of **love** (v).

loerie /low'ri/ a variant spelling of **lourie**.

loess or **löss** /læs or lō'is/ n a windblown loamy deposit found in river valleys. [Ger Löss]
■ **loessial** /lō-es'i-əl/ or **loessic** /-es'ik/ adj.

L of C abbrev : line of communication.

lofexidine /lō-fek'si-dēn/ n a drug used to alleviate withdrawal symptoms experienced by users of opiates.

lo-fi /lō'fī/ (inf) adj (of sound reproduction) of low quality; loosely applied to anything inferior or deliberately underemphasized; laid-back. [low¹; modelled on **hi-fi**]

loft /loft/ n a room or space immediately under a roof; a gallery in a hall or church; an upper room; an attic or upper floor, usu unfurnished, for storage, etc, eg in a warehouse (US); a room or shed for pigeons; a stroke that causes a golf ball to rise; the degree of angle at which a clubhead is set (golf); the amount of height that a player gives a ball (golf); a lifting action; upper region, sky or height (Spenser); a floor or ceiling (Spenser); a layer (Milton); a fabric's thickness, esp when indicating its insulating properties. ♦ vt to strike (the ball) so that it rises (golf); to toss; to propel high into the air or into space; to provide with a loft (obs); to put or keep in a loft (obs). [Late OE loft, from ON lopt sky, an upper room; OE lyft, Ger Luft the air]
■ **loft'ed** adj sent high into the air; (of a golf club) designed to send the ball on a high trajectory. **loft'er** n a golf iron for lofting. **loft'ily** adv. **loft'iness** n. **loft'y** adj very high in position, character, sentiment, manner or diction; very tall; stately; haughty; (of wool) bulky, springy, supple and soft.
❑ **lofted house** n (Scot) a house of more than one storey.
■ **cock of the loft** the head or chief of a set.

log¹ /log/ n a fallen tree trunk; a bulky piece of wood, used eg as firewood; a clog or impediment; an inert or insensitive person (fig); an apparatus (orig a block of wood), attached to the end of a line thrown overboard, for ascertaining a ship's speed; a record of a ship's, or other, performance and experiences, a logbook; a record produced by a mainframe computer of all the work done over a certain period of time. ♦ adj consisting of or constructed of logs. ♦ vt (**logg'ing**; **logged**) to cut or haul in the form of logs; to enter in a logbook, or record otherwise; to cover a distance of, according to the log; to record the name and punishment of; to punish or fine. ♦ vi to fell timber. [Origin obscure]
■ **logg'at** n a small log or piece of wood; a stake; (in pl) the old game of throwing loggats at a stake. **logged** /logd/ adj reduced to the inactivity or helplessness of a log; waterlogged (naut); cleared of logs. ♦ combining form denoting saturated, permeated, impregnated, entirely filled, as in waterlogged, smoke-logged. **logg'er** n a lumberman; (also **data logger**) a device which automatically records data. **logg'ing** n.
❑ **log'board** n a hinged board on which particulars for entering into a ship's logbook are temporarily chalked. **log'book** n a book containing an official record of a ship's progress and proceedings on board, or of a journey made by an aircraft or car, or of any progress; a headteacher's record of attendances, school events, etc; a record of work done, studies followed, etc; formerly, the registration documents of a motor vehicle (now called **vehicle registration document**). **log cabin** n a hut built of cut or uncut logs. **log'-canoe** n a boat made by hollowing out the trunk of a tree. **log'-chip** n the quadrant-shaped board attached to a logline. **logg'erhead** n (poss from logger a block of wood for hobbling a horse) a blockhead; a dunce; a round piece of timber in a whaleboat, over which the line is passed (naut); (also **loggerhead turtle**) a large-headed type of sea-turtle (Caretta caretta); (also **loggerhead shrike**) a N American shrike (Lanius ludovicianius); an implement consisting of a large metal ball attached to a shaft, heated for melting tar, etc. **logg'erheaded** adj. **log'-glass** n a 14- or 28-second sandglass, used with the logline to ascertain the speed of a ship. **log'-head** n a blockhead. **log'-house** n a log cabin. **log'-hut** n. **log jam** n jamming that brings floating logs to a standstill; congestion of events, etc, leading to a complete cessation of action (fig); such cessation of action, a deadlock, impasse. **log'juice** n (sl) bad port wine, as if coloured with logwood. **log'line** n (naut) the line fastened to the log, and marked for finding the speed of a vessel. **log'-man** n a man who carries logs (Shakesp); someone who cuts and removes logs. **log'-reel** n a reel on which the logline is wound. **log'roll** vt and vi. **log'roller** n. **log'rolling** n a gathering of people to facilitate the collection of logs after the clearing of a piece of land, or for rolling logs

into a stream; the sport of trying to dislodge another person standing on the same floating log; mutual aid among politicians, etc, *esp* trading in votes to secure the passage of legislation. **log'-saw** *n* a bowsaw, a saw with a narrow blade stretched like a bowstring in a bow-like frame. **log'-slate** *n* a double slate which is used as a logboard. **log'wood** *n* a tropical American tree (*Haematoxylon campechianum*) of the Caesalpinia family, exported in logs; its dark-red heartwood; an extract from it used in dyeing.

■ **at loggerheads** at variance, quarrelling (with *with*). **log in** or **on** (*comput*) to gain access to a mainframe or server system, *usu* by means of a code (**login'** or **log-in'** *n*, **logon'** or **log-on'** *n*). **log out** or **off** (*comput*) to exit from a mainframe or server system (**logout'** or **log-out'** *n*, **logoff'** or **log-off'** *n*). **sleep like a log** to sleep very soundly.

log² /*log*/ *n* short form of **logarithm**.
□ **log'-log** *adj* (of graph paper, graphs, etc) having a logarithmic scale on both the *x*-axis and the *y*-axis (also called **double-log** or **-logarithmic**; cf **semi-log** under **semi-**). **log tables** *n pl* a book of tables setting out logarithmic values.

log³ /*lōg*/ or /*log*/ *n* a Hebrew liquid measure, believed to be very nearly a British pint. [Heb *lōg*]

-log /*-log*/ *combining form* US variant of **-logue**.

logan /*log'ən*/ *n* a rocking stone (also **log'an-stone**, **logg'an-stone** or **logg'ing-stone**). [Dialect word *log* to rock; poss connected with Dan *logre* to wag the tail]

loganberry /*lō'gən-ber-i* or *-bə-ri*/ *n* a supposed hybrid between a raspberry and a Pacific coast blackberry, obtained by Judge JH *Logan* (died 1928).

logania /*lō-gā'ni-ə*/ *n* any plant of the *Logania* genus of Australian plants giving name to the **Loganiā'ceae**, related to the gentians. [Named after James *Logan* (1674–1751), botanist, scholar and statesman]

logaoedic /*log-ə-ē'dik*/ (*classical prosody*) *adj* combining dactyls with trochees. [Gr *logos* prose, and *aoidē* song]

logarithm /*log'ə-ri-dhm* or *-thm*/ *n* (short form **log**) a mathematical operation used *esp* before electronic computing, to simplify multiplication and division. The logarithm of a number N to a given base b is the power to which the b must be raised to produce the N, and is written as log$_b$N. [Gr *logos* ratio, reckoning, and *arithmos* number]
■ **logarith'mic** or **logarith'mical** *adj*. **logarith'mically** *adv*.
□ **logarithmic sine**, **cosine**, etc *n* the logarithm of the sine, cosine, etc. **logarithmic spiral** *n* the path of a point travelling along a radius vector with a velocity increasing as its distance from the pole increases, its polar equation being $r=a^\theta$, or $\theta=k\,log r$.

loge /*lozh* or *lōzh*/ *n* a box in the theatre or opera house. [Fr]

loggan-stone see **logan**.

loggat, **logger**, **loggerhead**, etc see under **log¹**.

loggia /*loj'(y)ə*/ *n* (*pl* **loggie** /*loj'ā*/ or **logg'ias**) a covered open arcade. [Ital; cf **lodge**]

logging-stone see **logan**.

Loghtan or **Loghtyn** alternative spellings of **Loaghtan**.

logia /*log'i-ə*/ *n pl* (*sing* **log'ion**) sayings, *esp* early collections of those attributed to Christ. [Gr]

logic /*loj'ik*/ *n* the science and art of reasoning correctly; the science of the necessary laws of thought; the principles of any branch of knowledge; sound reasoning; individual method of reasoning; convincing and compelling force (eg of facts or events); basis of operation as designed and effected in a computer, comprising **logical elements** which perform specified elementary arithmetical functions. [Gr *logikē* (*technē*) logical (art), from *logos* speech, reason]
■ **log'ical** *adj* of or according to logic; reasoning correctly; following necessarily from facts or events; of, or used in, logic circuits (*comput*). **logical'ity** or **log'icalness** *n*. **log'ically** *adv*. **logician** /*loj-ish'ən*/ *n* a person skilled in logic. **log'icism** /*log'i-sizm*/ *n* Gottlob Frege's theory that underlying mathematics is a purely logical set of axioms, mathematics being thus a part of logic. **log'icist** *n*. **log'icize** or **-ise** /*-sīz*/ *vi* to argue.
□ **logical analysis** *n* (*philos*) analysis, the process of stating clearly what our concepts comprise and imply. **logical atomism** *n* (*philos*) the theory that all propositions can be analysed into simple elements. **logical designer** *n* one engaged in the scientific construction of computers. **logical positivism** (or **empiricism**) see under **positive**. **logic bomb** *n* (*comput*) a set of instructions incorporated in a computer program such that a harmful operation will be performed if certain conditions are fulfilled. **logic circuit** *n* (*comput*) an electronic circuit with *usu* two or more inputs and one output, which performs a logical operation, eg *and*, *not*. **logic diagram** *n* (*comput*) a diagram showing logical elements and interconnections without engineering details.
■ **chop logic** see under **chop²**.

logie /*lō'gi*/ (*Scot*) *n* the space in front of a kiln fire. [Origin unknown; cf **killogie**]

logion see **logia**.

logistic /*lo-jis'tik*/ or **logistical** /*lo-jis'ti-kəl*/ *adj* relating to reasoning, to calculation, or to logistics or logistic; proportional. [Gr *logistikos*, from *logizesthai* to compute; influenced by Fr *loger* to lodge]
■ **logis'tic** *n* the art of calculation; sexagesimal arithmetic. **logis'tically** *adv*. **logistician** /*-tish'ən*/ *n* a person skilled in logistics. **logis'tics** *n sing* or *n pl* the art of movement and supply of troops; the handling of the practical detail of any large-scale enterprise or operation.
□ **logistic equation** *n* (*ecology*) an equation describing the typical increase of a population towards an asymptotic value. **logistics vessel** *n* a ship designed for the transport of troops and vehicles, and for their landing directly onto beaches.

loglog /*log'log*/ *n* the logarithm of a logarithm (also **lō'log**).

LOGO /*lō'gō*/ (*comput*) *n* a simple programming language with list processing features and distinctive graphics.

logo /*lō'gō*/ *n* (*pl* **lo'gos** /*lōg'ōz*/) a small design used as the symbol of an organization, etc. [Short for **logotype**]

logodaedalus /*log-ō-dē'də-ləs*/ *n* someone skilled in the manipulative use of words. [Latinized from Gr *logodaidalos*, from *logos* word, and *Daidalos* Daedalus; see ety for **daedal**]
■ **logodaedal'ic** *adj*. **logodae'daly** *n* verbal legerdemain.

logogram /*log'ō-gram*/ or **logograph** /*-gräf*/ (*shorthand*) *n* a single sign standing for a word, phrase or morpheme; a logogriph. [Gr *logos* word, and *gramma* letter]

logographer /*lo-gog'rə-fər*/ *n* in Greek literature, one of the earliest annalists, *esp* those before Herodotus; a professional speech-writer. [Gr *logos* word, and *graphein* to write]
■ **logographic** /*-graf'ik*/ or **logograph'ical** *adj*. **logograph'ically** *adv*. **logog'raphy** *n* a method of printing with whole words cast in a single type.

logogriph /*log'ō-grif*/ *n* a riddle in which a word is to be found from other words made up of its letters, or from synonyms of these. [Gr *logos* word, and *grīphos* a net, riddle]

logomachy /*lo-gom'ə-ki*/ *n* contention about words or in words. [Gr *logomachiā*, from *logos* word, and *machē* fight]
■ **logom'achist** *n*.

logopedics or **logopaedics** /*lo-gə-pē'diks*/ *n sing* speech therapy. [Gr *logos* word, and *paideiā* education]
■ **logope'dic** or **logopae'dic** *adj*.

logophile /*log'ə-fīl*/ *n* a lover of words. [Gr *logos* word, and **-phile**]

Logos /*log'os*/ *n* in the Stoic philosophy, the active principle living in and determining the world; the Word of God incarnate (*theol*). [Gr *logos* word]

logothete /*log'ō-thēt*/ (*hist*) *n* a chancellor, *esp* in the Byzantine Empire and in Norman Sicily. [Gr *logothetēs* an auditor]

logotype /*log'ō-* or *lō'gō-tīp*/ (*printing*) *n* a piece of type representing a word or several letters cast in one piece; a single piece of type comprising a name and/or address, trademark or design; (*usu* **logo**) an identifying symbol consisting of a simple picture or design and/or letters. [Gr *logos* word, and *typos* an impression]

Løgting see **Lagting**.

-logue or (*US*) **-log** /*-log*/ *combining form* denoting: speech or discourse, as in *monologue*, *dialogue*, *travelogue*; compilation, as in *catalogue*; student or enthusiast, as in *ideologue*.

logy /*lō'gē*/ (chiefly *US*) *adj* dull, lethargic. [Poss Du *log* heavy]

-logy /*-lə-ji*/ *combining form* indicating: science, theory; discourse, treatise. [Gr *logos* word, reason]

loid /*loid*/ (*sl*) *n* short for **Celluloid**®. ◆ *vt* to open (a spring lock) with a strip of Celluloid.

loin /*loin*/ *n* meat from the lower part of an animal's back; (*usu* in *pl*) the waist and lower part of the back or the hips and top of the legs; (in *pl*) the genital area, *esp* (*poetic*) as a source of new life. [OFr *loigne*, from L *lumbus* loin]
□ **loin'cloth** *n* a piece of cloth for wearing round the loins.
■ **gird up one's loins** to prepare for energetic action, as if by tucking up one's clothes.

loipe /*loi'pə*/ *n* (*pl* **loi'pen**) a track used for cross-country skiing. [Dan *løjpe*]

loir /*loi(-ə)r*/ *n* a large European species of dormouse. [Fr, from LL *lis*, *liris*, from L *glīs*, *glīris*]

loiter /*loi'tər*/ *vi* to proceed lingeringly; to dawdle; to linger or lurk. [Du *leuteren* to dawdle; Ger dialect *lottern* to waver]
■ **loi'terer** *n*. **loi'tering** *n* and *adj*. **loi'teringly** *adv*.

loke /lōk/ (*dialect*) *n* a short, narrow lane; a cul-de-sac; a private road; a grass-covered track. [ME, from OE *loca* an enclosed place]

Lok Sabha /lok sä'bə/ *n* the lower house of the Indian parliament. [Hindi *lok* people, and *sabha* assembly]

lokshen /lok'shən/ *n pl* noodles. [Yiddish, pl of *loksh* a noodle, from Russ *loksha*]
  ❏ **lokshen pudding** *n* a traditional Jewish pudding made with noodles, egg, sugar, dried fruit and cinnamon. **lokshen soup** *n* a traditional Jewish noodle soup.

lol /lol/ *abbrev* : laugh(ing) out loud; lots of love.

loligo /lō-lī'gō/ *n* the common squid or any other cephalopod mollusc of the *Loligo* genus or related genera. [L *lōlīgō*, *-inis*]

Lolita /lō- or lə-lē'tə/ *n* a young girl who acts in a sexually provocative manner. [From the eponymous character in a novel by Nabokov (1955)]

lolium /lō'li-əm/ *n* any plant of the *Lolium* genus of grasses, including darnel and rye-grass. [L *lōlium* darnel, 'tares']

loll /lol/ *vi* to lie lazily about, to lounge or sprawl; to dangle, hang (now mainly of the tongue). ◆ *vt* to let hang out. [Perh imitative; cf Du *lollen* to sit over the fire]
  ■ **loll'er** *n*. **loll'ingly** *adv*.

lollapalooza /lol-ə-pə-loo'zə/, **lallapalooza** or **lalapalooza** /lal-ə-pə-loo'zə/ (*US sl*) *n* something excellent or wonderful. [Ety unknown]

Lollard /lol'ərd/ (*hist*) *n* a follower of John Wycliffe, the 14c English religious reformer; an idler. [MDu *lollaerd* mutterer or droner, from *lollen* to mew, bawl, mutter; combined with *loller* (see **loll**)]
  ■ **Loll'ardy, Loll'ardry** or **Loll'ardism** *n*.

lollipop /lol'i-pop/ *n* a large boiled sweet which has been allowed to solidify around a stick; a sweet made with sugar and treacle (*dialect*); an ice lolly; (*usu* in *pl*) a sweet in general (also *fig*); (in *pl*; *old*) popular works of classical music. [Perh Scot and N Eng dialect *lolly* tongue]
  ❏ **lollipop man, woman** or **lady** *n* (*inf*) a crossing-warden carrying a pole with a disc on the end.

lollop /lol'əp/ *vi* (**loll'oping**; **loll'oped**) to bound about in an unco-ordinated, puppy-like manner; to lounge or idle. [Poss from **loll**]

lollo rosso /lol'ō ros'ō/ *n* a curly-leaved variety of lettuce. [Ital, literally, red lettuce]

loll-shraub /lol'shröb'/ or **loll-shrob** /-shrob'/ (*Ind*) *n* red wine, claret. [Hindustani *lāl sharāb*, from Pers *lāl* red, and Ar *sharāb* wine]

lolly /lol'i/ (*inf*) *n* a lollipop; an ice lolly; money.

lollygag see **lallygag**.

Lollywood /lol'i-wŭd/ *n* the Pakistani film industry. [From *Lahore* and *Bollywood*]

lolog same as **loglog**.

lolz /lolz/ same as **lulz**.

loma[1] /lō'mə/ (*zool*) *n* a membranous fringe or flap. [Gr *lōma*, *-atos*]

loma[2] /lō'mə/ (*US*) *n* in south-western states, a hill with a broad, flat top. [Sp, back, ridge]

Lombard /lom'bərd, lum'bərd* or *lom'bärd/ *n* an inhabitant of *Lombardy* in N Italy; the dialect of Lombardy; (also **Langobard** /lang'gō-bärd/ or **Longobard** /long'/) one of the Langobardi, or Longobardi, a Germanic tribe which founded a kingdom in Lombardy (568), overthrown by Charlemagne (774); a banker or moneylender, so called from the number of Lombard bankers in London (*obs*). ◆ *adj* (also **Lombardic** /-bärd'ik/) of or relating to the Lombards or their dialect. [OFr, from L *Langobardus*, *Longobardus*]
  ❏ **Lombard architecture** *n* the Romanesque style of N Italy, superseded by the Gothic in the 13c. **Lombardic script** *n* a medieval Italian style of handwriting. **Lombard Street** *n* the chief centre of the banking interest in London; the British money market and banking scene (*fig*). **Lombardy poplar** *n* a variety of black poplar with erect branches.

lome same as **loam**.

lomentum /lō-men'təm/ (*bot*) *n* (*pl* **loment'a**) a pod that breaks in pieces at constrictions between the seeds (also **lō'ment** /-mənt/). [L *lōmentum* bean meal (used as a cosmetic), from *lavāre*, *lōtum* to wash]
  ■ **lomentā'ceous** *adj*.

lompish (*Spenser*) same as **lumpish** (see under **lump**).

lon. or **long.** *abbrev* : longitude.

Lond. *abbrev* : London.

Londin. *abbrev* : *Londiniensis* (*L*), of London.

Londoner /lun'də-nər/ *n* a native or citizen of *London*.
  ■ **Londonese'**, **Londonian** /-dō'ni-ən/, **Lon'donish** or **Lon'dony** *adj*. **Londonese'** *n* cockney speech. **Lon'donism** *n* a mode of speech, etc peculiar to London. **Lon'donize** or **-ise** *vt* and *vi*.

❏ **London Clay** *n* (*geol*) a Lower Eocene formation in SE England. **London Inter-Bank Offered Rate** *n* the rate of interest at which the major clearing banks lend money amongst themselves (*abbrev* **LIBOR**). **London ivy** *n* smoke. **London Pride** or **pride** *n* a hardy perennial saxifrage (*Saxifraga umbrosa*; also **none-so-pretty** and **St Patrick's cabbage**); formerly applied to other plants.

lone /lōn/ *adj* isolated; solitary; unfrequented, uninhabited; unmarried; or widowed. [**alone**]
  ■ **lone'ness** *n*. **lon'er** *n* a person who prefers to act on his or her own and not to have close friends or confidential relationships. **lone'some** *adj* (*esp N Am*) solitary; feeling lonely. **lone'somely** *adv*. **lone'someness** *n*.
  ❏ **lone hand** *n* (in card games) a hand played independently; a player without a partner. **lone pair** *n* (*chem*) a pair of valency electrons unshared by another atom. **lone wolf** *n* (*fig*) a loner.
  ■ **on** or **by one's lonesome** (*inf*) completely alone.

lonely /lōn'li/ *adj* unaccompanied; isolated; uninhabited; unfrequented; uncomfortably conscious of being alone. [**alone**]
  ■ **lone'liness** *n*.
  ❏ **lonely heart** *n* a *usu* unmarried person without close friends and consequently lonely and unhappy, *esp* one in search of a happy relationship. **lone'ly-heart** *adj*.

long[1] /long/ *adj* (**longer** /long'gər/, *obs* **leng'er**; **longest** /long'gist/, *obs* **leng'est**) not short; of a specified (or to be specified) length; extended in space in the direction of greatest extension; far-extending; extended in time; of extended continuance; taking a considerable time to utter or do; distant in time (*rare*); of distant date; requiring much time in utterance or performance; (of a speech sound) of extended duration (*phonetics*); (of a syllable) loosely, accented; (of a vowel) loosely, in a long syllable; (of a dress, etc) coming down to the ankles, full-length; (of the memory) retentive; (of a word) abstruse or grandiose; numerically extensive; (of eg a suit of cards) of more than average number; exceeding the standard value, as in *long dozen*, *long hundred*; having a large holding in a commodity or security, in expectation of a rise in prices (*finance*); (of a chance) remote; tedious. ◆ *n* a long time; a long syllable (*prosody*); a long signal in Morse code; the long summer university vacation (*inf*); an obsolete note equal to two (in 'perfect' time three) breves (also **longa**; *music*); (in *pl*) long trousers; (in *pl*) long-dated securities. ◆ *adv* (*compar* and *superl* as for *adj*) for, during, or by, a great extent of time; throughout the whole time; far in space (*rare*). ◆ *combining form* to yearn (with *for*). [OE *lang*, *long* (adj), *lange*, *longe* (adv); Ger *lang*, ON *langr*; L *longus*]
  ■ **long'a** *n* (*music*) a long. **long'ing** *n* an eager desire, craving. ◆ *adj* yearning. **long'ingly** *adv*. **longish** /long'ish or -gish/ *adj*. **long'ly** *adv* (*Shakesp*) long. **long'ness** *n* (*rare*). **long'some** *adj* (*archaic* and *dialect*) long and tedious. **long'ways** or (*N Am*) **long'wise** *adv* lengthways.
  ❏ **long'-ago'** *adj* of the far past. ◆ *n* the far past. **long'-and-short work** see **longs and shorts** below. **long arm** *n* far-reaching power. **long'board** *n* a surfboard, skateboard, etc of greater than normal length. **long'boat** *n* the largest and strongest boat of a ship; a longship. **long'bow** *n* a bow drawn by hand as distinct from the crossbow. **long'-breathed** (or /-bretht'/) *adj* able to continue violent exercise of the lungs for a long time. **longcase clock** *n* a grandfather clock. **long'-chain** *adj* (*chem*) having a long chain of atoms in the molecule. **long'cloth** *n* a cotton made in long pieces. **long'-clothes** or (*obs*) **long'-coats** *n pl* long garments for a baby. **long corner** *n* (in hockey) a free stroke taken from the corner of the goal line. **long'-da'ted** *adj* of securities, due for redemption in more than fifteen years. **long-day plant** *n* a plant that will only flower after being exposed to conditions of long days and short nights. **long'-descend'ed** *adj* of ancient lineage. **long'-dist'ance** *adj* going or extending to or over a long distance or time; (of a chance) remote. ◆ *adv* over a long distance. **long division** *n* (*maths*) division in which the working is shown in full. **long dozen** *n* thirteen. **long'-drawn-out'** *adj* prolonged; unduly protracted. **long drink** *n* a large thirst-quenching drink (sometimes alcoholic) in a tall glass. **long'-eared** *adj* with long ears or ear-like feather-tufts. **long face** *n* a dismal expression. **long'-faced** *adj* dismal-looking. **long field** *n* (*cricket*) a fielder or position near the boundary on the bowler's side, long off or long on. **long'-firm** *n* a company of swindlers who obtain goods on pretence of being established in business, and then decamp without payment. **long'-hair** *n* a long-haired animal or person; a highbrow (also *adj*). **long'-haired** *adj* having long hair or fur; unconventional, hippy; highbrow. **long'hand** *n* ordinary writing as distinct from *shorthand*. **long haul** *n* a journey over a great distance; any activity requiring lengthy effort (*fig*). **long'-haul** *adj*. **long'-head** *n* a dolichocephal. **long'-headed** *adj* dolichocephalous; shrewd; sagacious. **long'-head'edness** *n*. **long home** *n* the grave. **long hop** *n* (*cricket*) a short-pitched, high-bouncing, ball that is easy to hit. **long'horn** *n* an animal belonging to a breed of cattle with long horns; a longhorn beetle with long antennae (**house longhorn beetle**, a beetle whose larvae are very

destructive to house timbers); a long-eared owl. **long'house** *n* a long communal house, eg in SE Asia or among certain Native American peoples, *esp* the Iroquois; a large oblong hall or dwelling built by the Vikings (*archaeol*). **long hundred** see under **hundred**. **long iron** *n* (*golf*) an iron club used to play long-range shots. **long johns** *n pl* long underpants. **long jump** *n* an athletic contest in which competitors jump as far as possible along the ground from a running start. **long jumper** *n*. **long jumping** *n*. **long'leaf pine** *n* a N American pine tree (*Pinus palustris*). **long leg** *n* (*cricket*) a fielder, or a fielding position, on the boundary behind the batsman on the legside. **long'-legged** *adj* having long legs. **long'-legs** *n* a cranefly. **long lens** *n* a telephoto lens. **long'-life** *adj* (of foodstuffs) treated so as to prolong freshness. **long'-line** *n* a long fishing-line with many hooks attached. ◆ *adj* (of clothing) long or lengthened in shape, as of a brassière or top extending over the ribcage. **long'-liner** *n* a fishing vessel that uses long-lines. **long'-lining** *n* the practice of fishing with long-lines. **long'list** *n* a preliminary list from which a shortlist is subsequently selected. ◆ *vt* to include in a longlist. **long'-lived** */-livd'* or *-līvd'/ adj* having a long life. **long mark** *n* a macron. **long measure** *n* lineal measure; (also **long metre**) quatrains of eight-syllable lines. **long moss** *n* a tropical American rootless epiphyte (*Tillandsia usneoides*) of the pineapple family, resembling bunches of hair. **long'-nine** *n* (*obs US*) a cheap cigar. **long odds** *n pl* in betting, a remote chance, unfavourable odds in terms of risk, favourable in terms of potential gain. **long off** *n* (*cricket*) a fielder, or a fielding position, on the boundary behind the bowler on the offside. **long-oil** see **oil length** under **oil**. **long on** *n* (*cricket*) a fielder, or a fielding position, on the boundary behind the bowler on the onside. **long paddock** *n* (*Aust*) the grass verge of a road, sometimes used for grazing animals on. **long-persistence screen** *n* a cathode-ray tube coated with long afterglow (up to several seconds) phosphor. **long pig** *n* (*old*) human flesh as food for cannibals. **long'-playing** *adj* of a gramophone record, giving length in reproduction because of the extremely fine groove and slow rotation. **long'prim'er** *n* (*printing*) a size of type (about 10-point) intermediate between small pica and bourgeois. **long'-pur'ples** *n* the early purple orchis; purple loosestrife. **long QT syndrome** *n* (*med*) a hereditary disorder affecting the electrical rhythm of the heart (*abbrev* **LQTS**). **long'-range** *adj* (of weapons) long in range, designed to reach remote targets; (of aircraft, etc) covering long distances without having to refuel; (of a forecast) extending well into the future. **long robe** see under **robe**[1]. **long'-run'ning** *adj* continuing over a long period. **longs and shorts** *n pl* Greek or Latin verses; (also **long-and-short work**) masonry of alternate vertical and horizontal blocks, as in quoins and jambs. **long sheep** *n* a long-woolled sheep. **long'ship** *n* (*hist*) a distinctive type of long vessel built by the Vikings. **long shot** *n* (a bet, entry, venture, etc with) a remote chance of success; a shot taken at a distance from the object filmed. **long'-sight'ed** *adj* able to see far but not close at hand; hypermetropic; presbyopic; having foresight; sagacious. **long'-sight'edly** *adv*. **long'-sight'edness** *n*. **long'-six'es** *n pl* (*archaic*) candles weighing six to a pound. **long'-spun** *adj* long-drawn-out, tedious. **long'spur** *n* any bunting of the genera *Calcarius* and *Rhyncophanes* with a long claw on the hind toe. **long'-stand'ing** *adj* of long existence or continuance. **long'-sta'ple** *adj* having a long fibre. **long'-stay** *adj* of eg patients in a hospital, staying permanently or semi-permanently; (of a car park) allowing patrons to leave their cars for days or weeks rather than hours. **long stop** *n* a fielder, or a fielding position (now largely disused), directly behind the wicket to stop balls missed by the wicketkeeper (*cricket*); a person or thing that acts as a final safeguard or check (*fig*). **long'-stop** *vi* to field as long stop. **long'-suff'ering** *adj* enduring long and patiently. ◆ *n* long endurance or patience. **long'-suff'eringly** *adv*. **long suit** *n* the suit with most cards in a player's hand; a particular talent, good quality, or advantage that one has. **long tail** *n* (*commerce*) the phenomenon by which a large number of less popular products can generate more revenue than a small number of highly successful ones. **long'-tail** *n* an animal, *esp* a dog, with an uncut tail (also *adj*); a greyhound. **long'-term** *adj* extending over a long time; (of a policy) concerned with time ahead as distinct from the immediate present. **long'-time** *adj* enduring for a long time. **long-togs**, **long Tom**, **long ton** see under **tog**[1], **tom**[1] and **ton**[1] respectively. **long'-tongued** *adj* having a long tongue; talkative, babbling. **long'-track** (**skating** or) **speedskating** *n* speedskating in which contestants race around a 400-metre track, *usu* in pairs against the clock. **long vacation** *n* a long holiday during the summer, when schools, etc are closed. **long view** *n* the taking into consideration of events, etc in the distant future. **long'-vis'aged** *adj* long-faced; with a rueful countenance. **long'-waist'ed** *adj* of a garment, having a deep or dropped waist; (of a person) long from the armpits to the hips. **long'wall** *n* a long working face in a coalmine (**longwall system** or **working**) a mining technique whereby a seam is exposed along its length then removed, layer by layer). **long'-wave** *adj* (*radio*) of, or using, wavelengths over 1000 metres. **longwear'ing** *adj* of clothes, that may be worn for a long time without wearing out, hard-wearing. **long whist** see under **whist**[2]. **long'-wind'ed** *adj*

long-breathed; tediously wordy and circumlocutory. **long'-wind'edly** *adv*. **long'-wind'edness** *n*.

■ **a long figure** (*sl*) a high price or rate. **a long purse** abundance of money. **as long as** provided only that. **before long** or (*poetic* or *facetious*) **ere long** soon. **draw the long bow** see under **bow**[2]. **go long** (*finance*) to acquire more holdings in commodities or securities in expectation of a rise in prices. **in the long run** see under **run**. **long on** well supplied with. **long since** a long time ago. **make a long arm** (*inf*) to help oneself freely at table. **make a long nose** to cock a snook or put a thumb to the nose as a vulgar gesture. **no longer** not now as formerly. **not by a long shot** not by any means. **not long for this world** near death. **so long** (*inf*) goodbye (*poss* from Ar *salaam* peace, used as a word of farewell). **so long as** provided only that. **the long and the short** (**of it**) or (*esp Shakesp*) **the short and the long** (**of it**) the sum of the matter in a few words.

long[2] */long/* (*Shakesp* and *dialect*) *adj* and *adv* on account. [**along**[2]]

long[3] */long/* (*archaic*) *vi* to belong, pertain or be fitting. [Not found as a verb in OE; *perh gelang* along, beside (as if to go along with)]

long. see **lon.**

longa */long'gə/ n* see **long**[1].

longaeval and **longaevous** see under **longevity**.

longan */long'gən* or *-gan/ n* a tropical Asian tree (*Nephelium longana*) related to the lychee; its fruit. [Chin *lóngyǎn* dragon's eye]

longanimity */long-gə-nim'i-ti/* (*rare*) *n* forbearance. [L *longanimitās*, *-ātis*, from *longus* long, and *animus* spirit]

■ **longanimous** */-gan'/ adj*.

longe see **lunge**[2].

longeron */lon'jə-*, *lon'zhə-ron* or *lɔ̃-zhə-rɔ̃'/ n* a longitudinal member of an aeroplane. [Fr]

longevity */lon-jev'i-ti/ n* great length of life. [L *longaevitās*, *-ātis*, from *longus* long, and *aevum* age]

■ **longaeval**, **longeval**, **longaevous** or **longevous** */-jēv'/ adj*.

longicaudate */lon-ji-kö'dāt/* (*zool*) *adj* long-tailed. [L *longus* long, and *cauda* tail]

longicorn */lon'ji-körn/ n* a longhorn beetle, any of several beetles of the family Cerambycidae, with very long antennae (the larvae feed on wood). ◆ *adj* denoting, or having, long antennae. [L *longus* long, and *cornū* horn]

longinquity */lon-jing'kwi-ti/ n* remoteness. [L *longinquitās*, *-ātis*, from *longus* long]

longipennate */lon-ji-pen'āt/* (*zool*) *adj* having elongated wings or feathers. [L *longus* long, and *penna* feather, wing]

Long Island iced tea */long ī'lənd īst tē/ n* a cocktail containing gin, rum, tequila and vodka. [Prob after *Long Island* in New York]

longitude */lon'ji-tūd* or *long'gi-/ n* the arc of the equator between the meridian of a place and a standard meridian (*usu* that of Greenwich) expressed in degrees East or West; (also **celestial longitude**) the arc of the ecliptic between a star's circle of latitude and the first point of Aries or vernal equinox (21 March), measured eastwards (*astron*); length. [L *longitūdō*, *-inis* length, from *longus* long]

■ **longitūd'inal** *adj* relating to longitude; lengthways. **longitūd'inally** *adv*.

❑ **longitudinal wave** *n* (*acoustics*) a wave in which the particles are displaced in the direction of advance of the wave.

Longobard see **Lombard**.

longshore */long'shör* or *-shör/ adj* existing or employed along the shore. [**along**[1] and **shore**[1]]

❑ **longshore drift** *n* the movement of material along the seashore by a current flowing parallel to the shoreline. **long'shoreman** *n* a stevedore; a person who makes a living along the shore by fishing, etc.

longueur */lɔ̃-gœr'/* (*Fr*) *n* (often in *pl*) a tedious passage, eg in a book; prolixity, long-windedness; a period or instance of dullness or tedium.

lonicera */lo-nis'ə-rə/ n* the honeysuckle, a shrub of the *Lonicera* genus. [A *Lonicerus* (died 1586), German botanist]

Lonrho */lon'rō/ abbrev : London Rho*desian (industrial conglomerate).

Lonsdale belt */lonz'dāl belt/ n* an award in the form of a belt given for gaining the same boxing title three times in succession. [Lord *Lonsdale* (1857–1944), who first presented them]

loo[1] */loo/* (*inf*) *n* a lavatory. [Ety uncertain; *perh* Fr *lieu*, *l'eau* (see **gardyloo**) or **Waterloo**]

❑ **loo roll** *n* a roll of lavatory paper.

loo[2] */loo/ n* a card game. ◆ *vt* to subject to a forfeit at loo. [See **lanterloo**]

❑ **loo'-table** *n* a form of round table, *orig* one for playing loo.

loo[3] */loo/* Scots form of **love** (*v*).

looby /loo'bi/ *n* a clumsy, clownish person. ◆ *adj* clumsy, stupid. [Cf **lob**]
■ **loob'ily** *adv* (*obs*).

loof[1] /loof/ see **luff**.

loof[2] /loof/ or (*Scot*) *lüf/ n* (*pl* **loofs** or **looves**) the palm of the hand. [ON *lōfi*]
■ **loof'ful** (or (*Scot*) /*lüf'fə*/) *n* an open handful.

loofah /loo'fə/ *n* (also **loofa** or **luffa** /*luf'*/) a tropical plant (genus *Luffa*) of the gourd family; the fibrous network of its fruit, used as a hard, rough sponge. [Ar *lūfah*]

look /lōōk/ *vi* to direct one's eyes and attention; to give attention; to face; to seem or appear; to seem to be; to have an appearance; to take care (*archaic* or *dialect*). ◆ *vt* to make sure; to see to it; to ascertain by a look; to look at; to expect; to seem likely; to render by a look; to express by a look; to refer to, turn (with *up*); to give (a look, as cognate object). ◆ *n* an act of looking; view; air; appearance; (in *pl*) beauty, comeliness (also **good looks**). ◆ *interj* see; behold. [OE *lōcian* to look]
■ **look'er** *n* a person who looks; an observer; a person who has good looks (*inf*). **-looking** *combining form* having a specified appearance or expression, as in *sad-looking*. **look'ism** *n* a term formed on the analogy of *racism* and *sexism*, denoting an attitude of prejudice and discrimination against people who look different, eg because of some physical disability.
❑ **look'alike** *n* a person who closely resembles another in personal appearance, a double. **look and say** *n* (*educ*) a method of teaching reading, whereby the pupil is trained to recognize words at a glance, and say them, rather than articulate the letters of the word one by one. **look'-and-say** *adj*. **look'er-on'** *n* (*pl* **look'ers-on'**) an onlooker; a (mere) spectator. **look'-in** *n* a chance of doing anything effectively or of sharing; a short casual call. **look'ing-for** *n* (*Bible*) expectation. **look'ing-glass** *n* a mirror. ◆ *adj* topsy-turvy (alluding to *Through the Looking-Glass* (1872) by Lewis Carroll). **look'out** *n* a careful watch; a place to observe from; a person given the task of watching or keeping watch; prospect; concern. **look'-round** *n* inspection. **look'-see** *n* (*inf*) a look around. **look'up** *adj* (*comput*) denoting a table giving a set of values for a variable.
■ **be looking at** (*inf*) to be able to expect (a possible price, length of time, etc). **look after** to take care of; to seek; to expect (*Bible*). **look alive** (*inf*) to rouse oneself for action. **look down on** to despise. **look down one's nose at** to regard with contempt. **look for** to search for; to expect. **look forward to** to anticipate with pleasure. **look here!** (*inf*) used to draw attention to something, or as an angry response. **look in** to make a short visit. **look into** to inspect closely; to investigate. **look like** to resemble; to promise or threaten (eg rain); used in requesting a description, as in *what does it look like?* **look on** to regard, view or think; to be a spectator. **look out** to be watchful; to be on one's guard; to look for and select; to show or appear (*Shakesp*). **look over** to examine cursorily; to overlook or pass over. **look sharp** (*inf*) be quick about it. **look small** to appear or feel foolish and ashamed. **look the part** to have, or assume, an appearance in keeping with one's role. **look to** to look at or towards; to watch; to take care of; to depend on (with *for*); to expect (to do). **look to be** (*inf*) to seem to be. **look up** to search for, refer to; to take courage; to improve, take a turn for the better; to seek out and call upon, visit (*inf*). **look up to** to feel respect or veneration for. **look you** (*archaic* and *Welsh*) observe, take notice of this. **not much to look at** (*inf*) plain, unattractive.

loom[1] /loom/ *n* a machine for weaving; the shaft of an oar; an electrical wiring assembly complete with insulating covering; a tool, implement (*obs*); a receptacle (*Scot*). [OE *gelōma* a tool]

loom[2] /loom/ *vi* to appear indistinctly or as in a mirage, *esp* in an exaggerated or magnified form; (of an event) to impend, be imminent; to overhang threateningly (with *over*). ◆ *n* an indistinct or mirage-like appearance. [Origin obscure]
■ **loom large** to take over a major part of someone's thoughts, life, etc.

loom[3] see **loon**[2].

loon[1] /loon/, also (*Shakesp*) **lown** or **lowne** /lown/ *n* a simple-minded or eccentric person (*inf*); a low-born person (*archaic*); a rascal; a harlot; in the north-east of Scotland, a boy (also **loon'ie**); (in *pl*) casual trousers that flare widely from the knees (also **loon'-pants**). [Origin unknown]

loon[2] /loon/ or **loom** /loom/ (*esp N Am*) *n* any of an order of northern diving birds, *esp* a sleek-bodied sharp-beaked bird of the genus *Gavia*. [ON *lōmr*]
■ **loon'ie** *n* a Canadian one-dollar coin stamped with a loon on one of its faces. **loon'ing** *n* the cry of the loon.

loony /loo'ni/ (*sl*) *adj* crazy, insane, lunatic. ◆ *n* a mad person, a lunatic. [Short form of **lunatic**, and **-y**[1]]
■ **loon'iness** *n*.

❑ **loony bin** *n* a lunatic asylum. **loony left** *n* (the members of) the extreme left wing of the (*usu* British) political spectrum, whose policies and beliefs are popularly regarded as lunatic.

loop[1] /loop/ *n* the oval-shaped coil made in a piece of string, chain, etc as it crosses back over itself; any similar doubling in the shape or structure of anything; anything of similar form, eg an element in fingerprints; a branch of anything that returns to the main part; a series of instructions within a computer program which is performed repeatedly until a predetermined condition is met, when the computer will exit from the loop and carry on with the next instruction in the main program (*comput*); a closed-circuit round which a signal can pass (*electronics*); an aerobatic manoeuvre in which an aircraft climbs, from level flight, to describe a circle in the sky; any loop-shaped movement or manoeuvre; an intra-uterine contraceptive device shaped like a loop (also called **Lippes loop**). ◆ *vt* to fasten in or with a loop; to ornament with loops; to make a loop of. ◆ *vi* to travel in loops. [Ety dubious]
■ **looped** *adj*. **loop'er** *n* a caterpillar of the Geometridae, so-called from its mode of walking by forming the body into a loop and planting its hinder legs close behind the six 'true' legs; someone or something that makes loops; someone who loops the loop in an aeroplane. **loop'iness** *n* the state or quality of being loopy. **loop'ing** *n* and *adj*. **loop'y** *adj* having loops; crafty (*Scot*); slightly crazy (*inf*).
❑ **loop diuretic** *n* a drug which inhibits resorption from the loop of Henle. **loop'-line** *n* a branch railway that returns to the main line. **loop of Henle** /hen'li/ *n* a loop formed by a tubule in the kidney, identified by Friedrich *Henle* (1809–85), German anatomist.
■ **in** (or **out of**) **the loop** (*inf*) included (or not included) in a group to whom information is made available. **loop the loop** to move in a complete vertical loop or circle, head downwards at the top of the curve.

loop[2] /loop/ or **loophole** /loop'hōl/ *n* a vertical slit in a wall eg of a castle, for looking through, firing through or receiving light and air; a means of escape; a means of evasion, eg an ambiguity in a contract, etc. [Perh MDu *lûpen* to peer]
■ **looped** *adj* (*Shakesp*) full of small openings. **loop'hole** *vt* to make loopholes in.
❑ **loop'-light** *n* a small narrow window.

loor see **lief**.

loord /loord/ (*Spenser*) *n* a lout. [Fr *lourd* heavy]

loos (*Spenser*) see **los**.

loose /loos/ *adj* slack; free; unbound; not confined; not compact; unattached; untied; not close-fitting; not tight; relaxed; (of the joints) freely mobile; (of the bowels) affected by diarrhoea; (of a cough) producing phlegm easily; inexact; indefinite; vague; not strict; unrestrained; lax; licentious; inattentive; dispersedly or openly disposed; not serried; (of the ball) not in the possession of any player (*football*); denoting all play except for the set scrums and line-outs (*rugby*). ◆ *adv* loosely. ◆ *n* loose play (*rugby*); an act or mode of loosing, *esp* an arrow (*archaic*); the loose state (*archaic*); unrestraint (*archaic*); freedom (*archaic*); abandonment (*archaic*); an outbreak of self-indulgence; a course or rush (*obs*); event, upshot, end, as in *at the very loose* (*Shakesp*). ◆ *vt* to make loose; to set free; to unfasten; to untie; to disconnect; to relax; to slacken; to discharge; to solve (*Spenser*). ◆ *vi* to shoot; to weigh anchor (*archaic*). [ON *lauss*; OE *léas*; see **less**]
■ **loose'ly** *adv*. **loos'en** *vt* to make loose; to relax; to make less dense; to open or relieve (the bowels). ◆ *vi* to become loose; to become less tight. **loos'ener** *n* a laxative. **loose'ness** *n* the state of being loose; diarrhoea.
❑ **loose'-bod'ied** *adj* of clothes, flowing, loose-fitting; loose in behaviour. **loose box** *n* a part of a stable where horses are kept untied. **loose cannon** *n* (*fig*) something or someone dangerously uncontrolled, like a cannon that may discharge unpredictably and cause damage to one's own side. **loose change** *n* coins kept about one's person for small expenditures. **loose cover** *n* a detachable cover, eg for an armchair. **loose'-cut** *n* a disease of cereal crops caused by a parasitic fungus, *Ustilago nuda*, that reduces the grains to powder. **loose end** *n* something that has been left unfinished or that has not been explained or decided. **loose fish** *n* a person of irregular, *esp* lax, habits; a prostitute. **loose forward** *n* in Rugby Union, either of the two wing forwards or the number 8 at the back of the scrum; in Rugby League, the player at the back of the scrum. **loose-head prop** *n* (*rugby*) the prop forward on the left of the front row in the scrum. **loose housing** *n* a means of housing cattle whereby the animals have access to shelter but are free to move about in straw-covered yards. **loose-knit** or **loosely-knit** *adj* (of communities, etc) not bound together by close ties. **loose'-leaf** *adj* of a folder, binder, etc, having a cover designed so as to allow leaves to be inserted or removed. **loose'-limbed** or **loose'-joint'ed** *adj* having supple limbs.
■ **be at a loose end** to have nothing to do. **break loose** to escape from confinement. **give a loose to** to give rein or free vent to. **let**

■ words derived from main entry word; ❑ compound words; ■ idioms and phrasal verbs

loose to set at liberty. **loosen up** to become less shy or taciturn; to exercise gently, eg in preparation for athletic effort. **on the loose** indulging in a bout of unrestraint; freed from confinement. **stay loose** (*inf*) keep cool, keep relaxed.

loosestrife /*loos'strīf*/ *n* a plant (*Lysimachia vulgaris*) of the primrose family, or other member of the *Lysimachia* genus (eg yellow pimpernel, creeping Jenny); a tall waterside plant (*Lythrum salicaria*, purple loosestrife). [Intended as a translation of Gr *lȳsimacheion* common loosestrife (as if from *lyein* to loose, and *machē* strife), which may be from the personal name *Lȳsimachos*]

loot[1] /*loot*/ *n* plunder; stolen goods; money (*inf*). ◆ *vt* and *vi* to plunder. [Hindi *lūt*]
■ **loot'er** *n*. **loot'ing** *n*.

loot[2] /*loot*/ (*inf*) *n* short form of **lieutenant**.

loot[3] and **looten** see **let**[1].

looves see **loof**[2].

looyenwork /*loo'yən-wûrk*/ *n* therapy of the body tissues aimed at releasing muscle fibre adhesions and easing physical and emotional tensions. [Named after Ted *Looyen*, who introduced it in 1985]

lop[1] /*lop*/ *vt* (**lopp'ing**; **lopped**) to cut off the top or ends of, *esp* of a tree; to cut away (eg superfluous parts). ◆ *n* twigs or branches of trees cut off; an act of lopping. [OE *loppian*]
■ **lopp'er** *n*. **lopp'ing** *n* a cutting off; the part or parts cut off.

lop[2] /*lop*/ *vi* to hang down loosely. ◆ *n* lopgrass (see below). [Perh connected with **lob**]
❑ **lop'-eared** *adj* of animals, having drooping ears. **lop'grass** *n* soft brome-grass. **lopsid'ed** *adj* leaning to one side, off balance; heavier or bigger on one side than the other. **lopsid'edly** *adv*. **lopsid'edness** *n*.

lope[1] /*lōp*/ *vi* to run with a long stride; to leap. ◆ *n* a bounding run. [ON *hlaupa*; cf **leap**[1] and **loup**[1]]
■ **lō'ping** *adj*.

lope[2] /*lōp*/ (*Spenser*) pat of **leap**[1].

loper /*lō'pər*/ *n* one of *usu* a pair of sliding or hinged pieces of wood, metal, etc which act as supports for a desk top or the extended flap of a table. [Ety unknown]

lopho- /*lof-ō-* or *lof-ō-*/ *combining form* signifying crested or tufted. [Gr *lophos* a crest]
■ **loph'obranch** /*-brangk*/ *n* (Gr *branchia* gills) any fish of the seahorse and pipefish group, characterized by tufted gills (also *adj*). **lophobranch'iate** *adj*. **loph'odont** /*-dont*/ *adj* (Gr *odous*, *odontos* a tooth) having transversely ridged molar teeth. **lophophorate** /*-fŏr'āt*/ *adj* and *n*. **loph'ophore** *n* (Gr *phoros* bearing) a ring of ciliated tentacles round the mouth of some sedentary marine animals.

lopolith /*lop'ə-lith*/ (*geol*) *n* a saucer-shaped intrusion of igneous rock. [Gr *lopas* dish, and *lithos* stone]

lopper[1] /*lop'ər*/ (*dialect*; *Scot* **lapper** /*lä'pər*/) *vi* to curdle. ◆ *vt* to curdle; to clot. ◆ *n* a clot; slush. [ON *hlöypa* to curdle]
❑ **lapp'er-milk'** or **lapp'ered-milk** *n* (*Scot*).

lopper[2] and **lopping** see **lop**[1].

loq. *abbrev*: *loquitur* (L), see separate entry.

loquacious /*lō-kwā'shəs*/ *adj* talkative. [L *loquāx*, *-ācis*, from *loquī* to speak]
■ **loquā'ciously** *adv*. **loquā'ciousness** or **loquacity** /*-kwas'/* *n*.

loquat /*lō'kwot* or *-kwat*/ *n* a Chinese and Japanese ornamental tree (*Eriobotrya japonica*) of the rose family; its small, yellow edible fruit. [Chin (Cantonese) *luh kwat*]

loquitur /*lok'wi-tər* or *-tŭr*/ (L) speaks (3rd pers present indicative), used with a person's name as stage direction, etc (*abbrev* **loq.**).

lor and **lor'** see **lord**.

loral and **lorate** see under **lore**[2].

loran or **Loran** /*lō'* or *lö'rän*/ *n* a long-range radio-navigation system. [For *long-range navigation*]

lorazepam /*lo-raz'ə-pam*/ *n* a benzodiazepine used as a sleeping drug and in the treatment of anxiety.

lorcha /*lör'chə*/ *n* a light vessel of European build, but rigged like a Chinese junk. [Port]

lord /*lörd*/ (with *cap* when used as a prefix) *n* a master; a feudal superior (also **lord'-supe'rior**; *hist*); a ruler; the proprietor of a manor (*hist*); a titled nobleman, duke (not prefixed), marquess, earl, viscount or (*esp*) baron; a peer; by courtesy, the son of a duke or marquess, or the eldest son of an earl; a bishop, *esp* if a member of the House of Lords; a judge of the Court of Session; used in various official titles, such as Lord Chief Justice; (with *cap*) God; (with *cap*) Christ; an owner (*archaic*); a dominant person; a husband, *esp* in the phrase *lord and master* (*archaic* or *facetious*). ◆ *vt* (with *it*) to act like a lord, tyrannize; to address as lord; to make a lord (*archaic*). ◆ *interj* expressing surprise

(*inf* **lor**, **lor'**, **law** or **lord'y**). [ME *lovered*, *laverd*, from OE *hlāford*, from *hlāf* bread, and *ward* (WSax *weard*) keeper, guardian]
■ **lord'ing** *n* (*archaic*) sir (*usu* in *pl*, gentlemen); a petty lord. **lord'less** *adj*. **lord'like** *adj*. **lord'liness** *n*. **lord'ling** *n* a little lord; a would-be lord (also **lord'kin**). **lord'ly** *adj* like, befitting, or in the manner of a lord; magnificent; lavish; lofty; haughty, proud; tyrannical. ◆ *adv* in a lordly manner. **lordol'atry** *n* (*joc*) worship of nobility. **lord'ship** *n* the state or condition of being a lord; the territory of a lord (*hist*); dominion; authority; used in referring to or addressing a lord (with *his* or *your*), or a woman sheriff or judge (with *her* or *your*).
❑ **Lord Advocate** see under **advocate**. **Lord Chancellor** see under **chancellor**. **Lord Chief Justice** see under **justice**. **Lord High Admiral** see under **admiral**. **Lord Lieutenant** see under **lieutenant**. **Lord Mayor** see under **mayor**. **Lord Muck** see under **muck**. **Lord of Appeal in Ordinary** *n* a judge appointed to the House of Lords to hear appeals to the House in its capacity as court of final appeal. **Lord of Misrule** see under **misrule**. **Lord of Session** *n* a judge of the Court of Session. **Lord Provost** see under **provost**. **lords and ladies** *n* (*bot*) common arum. **Lord's Day** *n* Sunday. **Lords Ordinary** *n pl* the judges forming the Outer House of the Court of Session. **Lord's Prayer** *n* the prayer that Christ taught his disciples (Matthew 6.9–13). **Lords Spiritual** *n pl* the archbishops and bishops (and formerly mitred abbots) in the House of Lords. **Lord's Supper** *n* holy communion. **Lord's table** *n* the communion table. **Lords Temporal** *n pl* the lay peers. **lord-superior** see **lord** (*n*) above.
■ **drunk as a lord** extremely drunk. **House of Lords** the upper house of the British parliament. **live like a lord** to live in luxury. **Lord knows** (**who**, **what**, etc) I don't know, and I doubt if anybody knows. **My Lord** /*mi-lörd'* or *mi-lud'*/ used in addressing a judge or other lord; formerly also used as a prefix.

lordosis /*lör-dō'sis*/ *n* abnormal curvature of the spinal column, the convexity towards the front. [Gr *lordōsis*, from *lordos* bent back]
■ **lordot'ic** *adj* affected with or relating to lordosis.

lore[1] /*lör* or *lör*/ *n* learning, *esp* of a special, traditional, or out-of-the-way miscellaneous kind, as in *folklore*, *plant-lore*; that which is learned; teaching (*archaic*); doctrine (*archaic*). [OE *lār*]
■ **lor'ing** *n* (*Spenser*) teaching.

lore[2] /*lör* or (*zool*) *lör*/ *n* the side of the head between eye and bill of a bird; the corresponding area of a reptile or fish; a thong (*obs*). [L *lōrum* thong]
■ **lor'al** *adj*. **lor'ate** *adj* strap-like.

lore[3] see **leese**.

lorel see **losel**.

Lorelei /*lor'ə-lī*/ *n* in German legend, a siren of the Rhine who lured sailors to their death. [Ger *Lurlei* the name of the rock she was believed to inhabit]

Lorentzian /*lə-rent'si-ən*/ (*phys*) *adj* of or relating to HA *Lorentz* (1853–1928), Dutch physicist, or his theories.
❑ **Lorentz force** /*lö'rents*/ *n* the force experienced by a point charge moving with a certain velocity in a field of magnetic induction and in an electric field. **Lorentz transformations** *n pl* the relations between the co-ordinates of space and time of the same event as measured in two inertial frames of reference moving with a uniform velocity relative to one another, and derived from the postulates of the special theory of relativity.

lorette /*lö-ret'*/ *n* a courtesan. [Fr, from the church of their district in Paris, Notre Dame de *Lorette*]

lorgnette /*lör-nyet'*/ *n* spectacles with a handle; an opera glass. [Fr *lorgner* to look sidelong at, to ogle]
■ **lorgnon** /*lörn'yɔ̃*/ *n* an eyeglass; spectacles.

lorica /*lö-*, *lö-* or *lə-rī'kə*/ *n* (*pl* **lori'cae** /*-sē*/) (also **loric** /*lö'* or *lö'rik*/) a leather corslet (*hist*); the case of a protozoan, rotifer, etc (*zool*). [L *lōrīca* a leather corslet, from *lōrum* a thong]
■ **loricate** /*lor'i-kāt*/ *vt* to coat or armour protectively. ◆ *adj* armoured with plates or scales. **lorica'tion** *n*.

lorikeet /*lor-i-kēt'*/ *n* a small lory. [From **lory**, on the analogy of *parakeet*]

lorimer /*lor'i-mər*/ or **loriner** /*-nər*/ *n* a maker of the metal parts of a horse-harness. [OFr *loremier*, *lorenier*, from L *lōrum* a thong]

loring see under **lore**[1].

loriot /*lö'* or *lö'ri-ət*/ *n* the golden oriole. [Fr *loriot*, from *l'* the, and OFr *oriol*, from L *aureolus*, dimin of *aureus* golden, from *aurum* gold]

loris /*lö'* or *lö'ris*/ *n* a small primate of S Asia belonging to the genus *Loris* (**slender loris**) or *Nycticebus* (**slow loris**). [Fr *loris*; said to be from Du]

lorn /*lörn*/ (*archaic*) *adj* lost; forsaken; left (*Spenser*). [OE *loren*, pap of *lēosan* (found in compounds), to lose; see **leese**]

Lorne sausage /lörn sos'ij/ (*Scot*) *n* sausage meat served in large square pieces (also **square sausage**). [Associated with Tommy *Lorne* (1890–1935), Scottish comedian]

lorrell see **losel**.

lorry /lor'i/ *n* a heavily-built motor vehicle for transporting heavy loads by road; a long (*esp* railway) wagon without sides, or with low sides. [Origin uncertain]
□ **lorr'y-hop** *vi* (or *vt* with *it*) to travel by getting lifts on lorries. **lorr'y-hopping** *n*.

lory /lō'/ or /lō'ri/ *n* any parrot of a family with brushlike tongues, natives of New Guinea, Australia, etc; in South Africa, a turaco. [Malay *lūrī*]

los or **loos** /lōs/ (*obs*) *n* praise, reputation. [OFr, from L *laudēs*, pl of *laus* praise]

lose[1] /looz/ *vt* (**los'ing**; **lost** /lost/) to fail to keep or obtain; to be deprived or bereaved of; to cease to have; to cease to hear, see or understand; to confuse or bewilder; to mislay; to waste (eg time); to miss; to be defeated in; to cause the loss or ruin of; to cause to perish; to bring to ruin; to get away from. ◆ *vi* to fail, to be unsuccessful; to suffer waste or loss; (of a clock or watch) to go slow. [OE *losian* to be a loss; apparently influenced in sense by **leese** and in pronunciation by **loose**]
■ **los'able** *adj*. **los'er** *n* someone who or something that loses; someone who is habitually unsuccessful or generally inept (*derog inf*). **los'ing** *n* and *adj*. **los'ingly** *adv*. **lost** /lost/ *adj* parted with; no longer possessed; missing; not able to be found; thrown away; squandered, wasted; ruined; lacking in morals; damned; confused, unable to find the way (*lit* and *fig*).
□ **losing game** *n* a game that is going against one; a game played with the aim of losing. **lost'-and-found**' *adj* relating to an office, official, etc whose function is to trace or take care of lost property, luggage, etc. **lost cause** *n* a hopeless ideal or endeavour. **lost generation** *n* orig the young men who died in World War I; later, a group of US writers whose work explored the disillusionment felt after World War I; any generation which is perceived to have lost or rejected traditional value systems. **lost soul** *n* a damned soul, an irredeemably evil person. **lost tribes** *n pl* the tribes of Israel that never returned after deportation by Sargon of Assyria in 721BC.
■ **get lost!** (*inf*) go away and stay away!; stop annoying or interfering! **lose face** see under **face**. **lose it** (*inf*) to lose one's temper; to suffer a mental breakdown; to suffer a sudden failing of one's powers. **lose oneself** to lose one's way; to become rapt or bewildered; to become totally engrossed. **lose out** (*inf*) to suffer loss or be at a disadvantage; (also with *on*) to fail to acquire something desired. **lose way** (of a boat) to lose speed. **lost to** insensible to.

lose[2] /lōz/, also **losen** /lō'zən/ (*Spenser*) *vt* (*pap* **loast** or **los'te** /lōst/) to loose.

losel /lō'zl/ or /loo'zl/ or **lorel** /lō'/ or /lō'rəl/ (*Spenser* **lozell** or **lorrell**) *n* a worthless person; a rascal. ◆ *adj* good-for-nothing. [Appar from the *pap losen, loren*, of **leese**]

losh /losh/ (*Scot*) *interj* same as **lord**.

loss /los/ *n* losing; diminution; default (*Shakesp*); bereavement; destruction; defeat; deprivation; detriment; something lost. [OE *los*, influenced by **lost**]
■ **loss'less** *adj* (*electronics* and *telecom*) not dissipating energy, said of a dielectric material or of a transmission line which does not suffer attenuation (cf **lossy** below). **loss'y** *adj* (*electronics* and *telecom*) dissipating energy, said of a dielectric material or of a transmission line with high attenuation (cf **lossless** above).
□ **loss adjuster** *n* an assessor employed by an insurance company, *usu* in fire damage claims. **loss'-leader** *n* something sold at a loss to attract other custom. **loss'maker** *n* an organization, business, etc that makes a continual loss.
■ **at a loss** in, or resulting in, deficit; off the scent; at fault; nonplussed; perplexed.

löss see **loess**.

lost see under **lose**[1].

los'te /lōst/ a Spenserian *pap* of **loose** and **lose**[2].

lot /lot/ *n* an object, such as a slip of wood or a straw, drawn or thrown out from among a number in order to reach a decision by chance; decision by this method; sortilege or divination; a prize won through divination; destiny; that which falls to anyone as his or her fortune; a separate portion; a patch of ground; a set; a set of things offered together for sale; the whole; a great deal, large amount; a plot of ground allotted or assigned to any person or purpose, *esp* for building; the area around a film studio used for outside filming; a turn (*obs*); a tax or due (*hist*; see **scot**); a large quantity or number; a batch of horses grouped for daily exercise (*horse-racing*). ◆ *vt* (**lott'ing**; **lott'ed**) to allot; to separate into lots; to divide (a property) into lots, *esp* for selling purposes; to cast lots for (*obs*). [OE *hlot* lot, from *hlēotan* to cast lots]

■ **lots** *n* a large amount. ◆ *adv* by a great deal, as in *lots better*.
■ **a bad lot** an unscrupulous person with a bad reputation. **across lots** (*US*) by short cuts. **cast** or **throw in one's lot with** to choose to share the fortunes of. **cast** or **draw lots** (of two or more people) to draw from a set of different but unseen or superficially indistinguishable objects as a means of singling out one person. **lots of** (*inf*) many. **lots to blanks** (*Shakesp*) any odds. **the lot** the entire number or amount.

lota or **lotah** /lō'tä/ *n* in India, a small brass or copper pot. [Hindi *lotā*]

lote see **lotus**.

lo-tech see **low technology** under **low**[1].

loth see **loath**.

Lothario /lō-thä'ri-ō or -thä'/ *n* (*pl* **Lothar'ios**) a seducer, a rake. [From *Lothario*, in Nicholas Rowe's play, *The Fair Penitent* (1703)]

lothefull or **lothfull** (*Spenser*) see under **loathe**.

loti /loo'/ or /lō'ti/ *n* (*pl* **malō'ti**) the standard monetary unit of Lesotho (100 lisente). [Bantu, from the *Maloti* Mountains of Lesotho]

lotic /lō'tik/ *adj* associated with, or living in, running water. [L *lavāre*, *lōtum* to wash]

lotion /lō'shən/ *n* a liquid preparation for applying to the skin, medicinally or cosmetically; a washing (*obs*). [L *lōtiō, -ōnis* a washing, from *lavāre, lōtum* to wash]

loto see under **lottery**.

Lotophagi and **lotos** see **lotus**.

lottery /lot'ə-ri/ *n* an arrangement for the distribution of prizes by lot; a game of chance (not involving skill) in which prizes are distributed to purchasers of tickets chosen by lot; a matter of chance; a card game of chance. [Ital *lotteria, lotto*, of Gmc origin; cf **lot**]
■ **lott'o** or (*rare*) **lō'to** *n* (*pl* **lott'os** or **lō'tos**) a game played by covering on a card each number drawn until a line of numbers is completed or all of the numbers are covered (also called **housey-housey**, now *usu* **bingo**).

lotus /lō'təs/ *n* (also **lō'tos** or (*archaic*) **lote** /lōt/) an Egyptian or Indian water lily of various species of *Nymphaea* and *Nelumbium*; a N African tree (possibly the jujube), whose fruit induced in the eater a state of blissful indolence and forgetfulness (*Gr myth*); an architectural ornament like a water lily; (with *cap*) the bird's-foot trefoil genus. [Latinized Gr *lōtos*]
□ **lot'us-eat'er** *n* an indolent person who enjoys the luxuries of life. **Lot'us-eat'ers** or **Lotophagi** /lō-tof'ə-jī/ *n pl* (*Gr myth*) a people who ate the fruit of the lotus, among whom Odysseus lived for a time. **lot'us-eat'ing** *adj*. **Lo'tus-land** *n* the country of the Lotus-eaters. **lotus position** *n* a seated position used in yoga, cross-legged, with each foot resting on the opposite thigh.

louche /loosh/ *adj* shady, sinister, shifty or disreputable; ambiguous; orig squinting. [Fr *loucher* to squint]
■ **louche'ly** *adv*.

loud /lowd/ *adj* making a great sound; noisy; obtrusive; flashy or showy in a vulgar way. [OE *hlūd*; Ger *laut*; L *inclytus, inclutus*, Gr *klytos* renowned]
■ **loud** or **loud'ly** *adv*. **loud'en** *vt* and *vi* to make or grow louder. **loud'ish** *adj*. **loud'ness** *n*.
□ **loudhail'er** *n* a portable megaphone with microphone and amplifier. **loud'-lunged** *adj*. **loud'mouth** *n* (*inf*) someone who talks too much or offensively; a boaster. **loud'mouthed** *adj*. **loud'speak'er** *n* an electroacoustic device which amplifies sound. **loud'-voiced** *adj*.
■ **out loud** audibly.

Lou Gehrig's disease /loo ger'igz di-zēz'/ *n* amyotrophic lateral sclerosis, a progressive degenerative disease of the nervous system. [Lou *Gehrig* (1903–41), US baseball player who suffered from it]

lough /lohh/ *n* the Irish form of **loch**.

louis /loo'i/ *n* (*pl* **lou'is** /-iz/) a French gold coin superseded in 1795 by the 20-franc piece.
□ **lou'is-d'or**' *n* (*pl* **louis-d'or** /loo'i-dôr'/) a louis; a 20-franc piece. **Lou'is-Quatorze**' /-kä-törz'/ *adj* characteristic of the reign (1643–1715) of Louis XIV, eg in architecture and decoration. **Lou'is-Quinze**' /-kēz'/ *adj* characteristic of the reign of Louis XV (1715–74). **Lou'is-Seize**' /-sez'/ *adj* characteristic of the reign of Louis XVI (1774–92). **Lou'is-Treize**' /-trez'/ *adj* characteristic of the reign of Louis XIII (1610–43).

loun or **lound** see **lown**[2].

lounder /loon'/ or /lown'dər/ (*Scot*) *vt* to beat, to bethump. ◆ *n* a heavy blow.
■ **loun'dering** *n* a beating.

lounge /lownj/ *vi* to lie in a relaxed way; to idle. ◆ *vt* to idle (away). ◆ *n* a sitting room in a private house; a room in a public building for sitting or waiting, often providing refreshment facilities; (also **lounge'-bar**) a more expensive and luxurious bar in a public house; an act, spell or state of lounging; an idle stroll; a resort of loungers; a kind of sofa, *esp* with a back and one raised end. [Origin doubtful]

■ **loung'er** *n* someone who lounges; any long loose garment for wearing indoors; an extending chair or light couch for relaxing on. **loung'ey** *adj* (*inf*) relating to or reminiscent of a cocktail lounge or lounge music (qv below). **loung'ing** *n* and *adj*. **loung'ingly** *adv*. □ **lounge'core** *n* another name for easy listening music. **lounge lizard** *n* a person who indolently spends time at social events and gatherings. **lounge music** *n* easy listening music of a kind often used as background music in cocktail lounges, etc. **lounge suit** *n* a man's matching jacket and trousers for (formal) everyday wear.

loup[1] /lowp/ (*Scot*) *n* a leap. ◆ *vi* (*pat* **loup'it**; *pap* **loup'en** or **loup'it**) to leap; to dance; to flee; to burst. ◆ *vt* to leap over. [ON *hlaup*; cf **lope**[1] and **leap**[1]]
□ **loup'ing-ill** *n* a disease causing sheep to spring up in walking, due to a virus transmitted by ticks, one of several diseases in sheep known as **staggers**. **loup'ing-on'-stane** *n* a stone to mount a horse from. **loup'-the-dyke** *adj* runaway; flighty; wayward.

loup[2] a variant (*Walter Scott*) of **loop**[1] and (*Spenser*) of **loop**[2].

loupe /loop/ *n* a jeweller's and watchmaker's small magnifying glass, worn in the eye socket. [Fr]

lour or **lower** /lowr or low'ər/ *vi* to look sullen or threatening; to scowl. ◆ *n* a scowl or glare; a gloomy threatening appearance. [ME *louren*; cf Du *loeren*]
■ **lour'ing** or **lower'ing** *n* and *adj*. **lour'ingly** or **lower'ingly** *adv*. **lour'y** or **lower'y** *adj*.

loure /loor/ *n* an old slow dance, or its tune, *usu* in 6–4 time, sometimes included in suites. [Fr, bagpipe]

lourie or **loerie** /low'ri/ (*S Afr*) *n* a turaco. [Afrik, from Malay *lūrī*; see **lory**]

louse /lows/ *n* a wingless parasitic insect (genus *Pediculus*), with a flat body and short legs; extended to similar animals related and unrelated (see **bird-louse** under **bird**, **fish louse** under **fish**[1], etc; *pl* **lice** /līs/); a person worthy of contempt (*inf*; *pl* **lous'es**). ◆ *vt* /lowz/ to remove lice from; to spoil, make a mess of (with *up*; *inf*). [OE *lūs*, pl *lȳs*; Ger *Laus*]
■ **lou'ser** *n* (*Irish inf*) a contemptible person. **lou'sily** /-zi-/ *adv*. **lous'iness** *n*. **lou'sing** *n*. **lousy** /low'zi/ *adj* infested with lice; swarming or full (with *with*; *inf*); inferior, bad or unsatisfactory (*inf*). □ **louse'wort** *n* any plant of the genus *Pedicularis*, marsh-growing scrophulariaceous herbs popularly supposed to cause grazing animals to become lousy.

lout[1] (*obs* **lowt**) /lowt/ *n* an ill-mannered or aggressive man or youth; a bumpkin. ◆ *vt* (*Shakesp*) to treat with contempt, to flout. ◆ *vi* to behave loutishly. [Perh connected with **lout**[2]]
■ **lout'ish** *adj* ill-mannered and coarse; clownish. **lout'ishly** *adv*. **lout'ishness** *n*.

lout[2] (*obs* **lowt**) /lowt/ (*archaic*) *vi* to bow; to stoop. ◆ *n* a bow. [OE *lūtan* to stoop]

louvar /loo'vär/ *n* a large fish (*Luvarus imperialis*) found in temperate regions. [Origin uncertain; perh Ital dialect *lùvaru*, perh ult from L *ruber* red]

louvre or **louver** /loo'vər/ *n* a louvre-board; a turret-like structure on a roof for the escape of smoke or for ventilation; an opening or shutter with louvre-boards; a dovecote (*obs*). [OFr *lover, lovier*; origin obscure]
■ **lou'vred** or **lou'vered** *adj*.
□ **lou'vre-board** or **lou'ver-board** *n* a sloping slat placed horizontally or vertically across an opening. **lou'vre-** (or **lou'ver-)door** or **louvre-** (or **lou'ver-)win'dow** *n* a door or open window crossed by a series of sloping boards.

lovage /luv'ij/ *n* an umbelliferous salad plant (*Levisticum officinale*) of S Europe related to Angelica; a liquor made from its roots and seeds; any plant of the related genus *Ligusticum*, including *Scottish lovage*. [OFr *luvesche*, from LL *levisticum*, L *ligusticum*, literally, Ligurian]

lovat /luv'ət/ *n* a greyish- or bluish-green colour, usu in tweed or woollen cloth; cloth or wool of this colour (also **lov'at-green'**). ◆ *adj* of this colour. [From *Lovat*, near Inverness, Scotland]

love /luv/ *n* fondness; charity; an affection for something that gives pleasure; strong liking; devoted attachment to another person; sexual attachment; a love affair; the object of affection; a term of address indicating endearment or affection (often spelled **luv** to represent *dialect* or *inf* use); the god of love, Cupid, Eros, etc (*myth*); a kindness, a favour done (*Shakesp*); the mere pleasure of playing, without stakes; in some games, no score. ◆ *vt* to be fond of; to regard with pleasure and affection; to delight in with exclusive affection; to regard with benevolence. ◆ *vi* to feel love and affection. [OE *lufu*, love; Ger *Liebe*; cf L *libet, lubet* it pleases]
■ **lovabil'ity** or **loveabil'ity** *n*. **lov'able** or **love'able** /luv'ə-bl/ *adj* worthy of love; amiable; attracting affection. **lov'ableness** or

love'ableness *n*. **love'less** *adj*. **love'lessly** *adv*. **love'lessness** *n*. **love'lihead** *n* (*rare*) loveliness. **love'lily** *adv* (*rare*). **love'liness** *n*. **love'ly** *adj* exciting admiration; attractive; extremely beautiful; delightful (*inf*); loving, amorous (*Shakesp*). ◆ *adv* delightfully, very well (*inf*); lovingly (*Spenser*); beautifully (*obs*). ◆ *n* (*inf*) a beautiful woman, *esp* a showgirl or model. **lov'er** *n* someone who loves, *esp* someone in a sexual relationship with another person; one of the partners in a love affair, a paramour; someone who is fond of anything; a friend (*Shakesp*). ◆ *combining form* denoting someone with a keen interest in, eg *animal-lover, bird-lover*. **lov'ered** *adj* (*Shakesp*) having a love. **lov'erless** *adj*. **lov'erly** *adj* (*archaic*) like a lover. **love'some** *adj* (*archaic*) lovely; loving. **love'worthy** *adj* worthy of being loved. **lov'ey** *n* (*inf*) a term of endearment. **lov'ing** *n* and *adj*. **lov'ingly** *adv*. **lov'ingness** *n*.
□ **love affair** *n* a romantic sexual relationship, *esp* a short-lived one. **love apple** *n* the tomato. **love'-arrow** *n* a hair-like crystal of rutile enclosed in quartz (*mineralogy*); a calcareous dart protruded by a snail, supposed to have a sexual function. **love'bird** *n* a small African parrot (genus *Agapornis*), strongly attached to its mate; extended to other kinds of bird; either of the (*esp* romantically demonstrative) partners in a sexual relationship (*facetious*). **love'bite** *n* a temporary red patch on the skin caused by a sucking kiss. **love'-bro'ker** *n* (*Shakesp*) a go-between in love affairs. **love'-charm** *n* a magic spell intended to induce someone to fall in love, *esp* in the form of a philtre. **love child** *n* an illegitimate child. **love'-day** *n* (*Shakesp*) a day for settling disputes. **love'-drug** *n* Indian hemp. **love'-favour** *n* something given to be worn as a token of love. **love feast** *n* the agape, or a religious feast in imitation of it. **love'-feat** *n* an act of courtship. **love game** *n* (*tennis*) a game in which the loser has not scored (possibly from Fr *l'œuf* egg, cf **duck**[1] in cricket). **love handles** *n pl* an affectionate term for the deposit of fat sometimes found on either side of the back just below the waist. **love-hate relationship** *n* a relationship which alternates between emotional extremes, or in which both emotions exist concurrently. **love'-in** *n* a gathering devoted to sexual activity, of idealistic rather than orgiastic nature. **love'-in-a-mist'** *n* a fennel-flower (*Nigella damascena*); a West Indian passion flower. **love'-in-i'dleness** *n* the pansy. **love'-juice** *n* a concoction dropped in the eye to induce someone to fall in love. **love'-knot** or **lover's knot** *n* an intricate knot, used as a token of love. **love letter** *n* a letter to one's lover expressing feelings of affection. **love'-lies-bleed'ing** *n* a kind of amaranth with a drooping red spike. **love life** *n* a state of events in, or area of life concerning, romance or sexual attachments. **love'light** *n* a lustre in the eye expressing love. **love'lock** *n* a long or prominent lock of hair, *esp* one hanging at the ear, worn by men of fashion in Elizabethan and Jacobean times. **love'lorn** *adj* forsaken by one's love; pining for love. **love'lornness** *n*. **love'maker** *n*. **love'making** *n* sexual play and *usu* intercourse; amorous courtship. **love match** *n* a marriage for love, not money, status, etc. **love nest** *n* a place where lovers meet or live, *esp* when illicitly. **love potion** *n* a philtre. **love rat** *n* (*inf*) an unfaithful partner in a relationship (*usu* a man). **lover's knot** see **love-knot** above. **lovers' lane** *n* a quiet path or road frequented by lovers. **lovers' rock** *n* a type of reggae with a slow beat. **love seat** *n* an armchair for two. **love'-shaft** *n* a dart of love from Cupid's bow. **love'sick** *adj* sad, pining for love; languishing with love. **love'sickness** *n*. **love'-song** *n* a song expressing or relating to love. **love'-story** *n* a story with romantic love as its subject. **love'struck** or **love'-stricken** *adj* affected by love for someone; infatuated. **love'-suit** *n* (*Shakesp*) courtship. **love'-token** *n* a gift in evidence of love. **lovey-dovey** /luv'i-duv'i/ *adj* (*inf*) sentimentally and (over-)demonstratively affectionate. **loving cup** *n* a cup passed round at the end of a feast for all to drink from. **loving kindness** *n* (*Bible*) kindness full of love; tender regard; mercy.
■ **fall in love** to become in love (with). **for the love of it** for the sake of it; for the pleasure of it. **for the love of Mike** (*inf*) for any sake. **in love** (**with**) romantically and sexually attracted, devoted (to). **loved up** (*inf*) experiencing blissful or exaggeratedly benevolent feelings through being under the influence of a drug, *esp* ecstasy; in love; in an amatory mood. **make love to** to have sexual intercourse with; to make romantic or sexual overtures or advances to, to woo (*old*). **not for love or money** under no circumstances. **of all loves** (*Shakesp*) for any sake, by all means. **play for love** to play without stakes. **there's no love lost between them** they have no liking for each other.

Lovelace /luv'lās/ *n* a well-mannered libertine. [From *Lovelace*, in Samuel Richardson's novel *Clarissa*]

lover[1], etc see under **love**.

lover[2] an obsolete form of **louvre** or **louver**.

low[1] /lō/ *adj* (**lower** /lō'ər/; **lowest** /lō'ist/ or **low'ermost**) occupying a position that is far down or not much raised; of no great upward extension; not reaching a high level; depressed; not tall; (of type or blocks) below the level of the forme surface (*printing*); reaching far down; (of clothes) cut so as to expose the neck and chest; quiet and soft, not loud; of deep pitch, as sounds produced by slow vibrations are; produced with part of the tongue low in the mouth (*phonetics*);

nearly level or not much raised, in shallow relief; expressed in measurement by a small number; of numbers, small; of small value, intensity, quantity or rank; having little vitality, badly nourished; scanty, deficient; attributing lowness; for stakes of no great value; dejected; debased; base; mean; vulgar; humble; socially depressed; little advanced or backward in organization or culture; (of latitude) near the equator; (of dates) comparatively recent (*archaic*); attaching little value to priesthood, sacraments, etc. ◆ *n* that which is low or lowest; an area of low barometric pressure; a low or minimum level; low gear. ◆ *adv* in or to a low position, state or manner; humbly; with a low voice or sound; at low pitch; at a low price; late (*archaic*); in small quantity or to a small degree. [ON *lāgr*, Du *laag* low; related to OE *licgan* to lie]

■ **low'er** *vt* to make lower; to let or put down; to lessen; to dilute (*obs*). ◆ *vi* to become lower or less. ◆ *n* (*Scot*) (an examination at) the lower grade (qv below). **low'ering** *n* the act of bringing low, reducing or letting down. ◆ *adj* letting down; sinking; degrading. **low'ermost** *adj* lowest. **low'ish** *adj*. **low'lihead** *n* (*archaic*) humility. **low'lily** /-li-li/ *adv*. **low'liness** *n*. **low'ly** *adj* humble; modest; low in stature or in organization. ◆ *adv* in a low manner. **low'ness** *n*.

❑ **low-al'cohol** *adj* (of a drink) containing less alcohol by volume than is standard. **low'balling** *n* (*inf*) the business practice of tendering an unrealistically low price in order to secure a contract. **low'-born** *adj* of humble birth. **low'boy** *n* a Low-Churchman (*obs*); a short-legged dressing-table with drawers (*US*). **low'-bred** *adj* ill-bred; unmannerly. **low'brow** *n* and *adj* (a person who is) not intellectual or having no pretensions to intellect. **low'-cal'** or **lo'-cal'** *adj* (*inf*) low in calories. **Low Church** *adj* of a party within the Church of England setting little value on sacerdotal claims, ecclesiastical constitutions, ordinances and forms, holding evangelical views of theology, *opp* to *High Church*. **Low-Church'ism** *n*. **Low-Church'man** *n*. **low comedy** *n* comedy of farcical situation, slapstick or low life. **low'-cost'** *adj* cheap. **low'-country** *adj* lowland (**the Low Countries** Holland and Belgium). **low-cut'** *adj* (of a garment) with a low neck-line, revealing much of the chest. **low-down** *adj* (*inf*) base; dishonourable. ◆ *n* (*inf*) information, *esp* of a confidential or damaging nature. **low-down'er** *n* (*obs US*) a poor white person. **Low Dutch** *n* (*obs*) Low German including Dutch. **low'er-brack'et** *adj* in a low grouping in a list. **low'er-case** *adj* (*printing*) small as distinguished from capital, *orig* because kept in a lower case. **lower chamber** see **lower house** below. **low'er-class** *adj* relating to people of low social class. **lower criticism** see under **critic**. **lower deck** *n* the deck immediately above the hold; ship's crew (as opposed to officers). **low'er-deck** *adj* of or relating to the lower deck. **lower grade** *n* a former educational qualification awarded in Scotland; an examination or pass at this grade. **lower house** or **chamber** *n* the larger, more representative, of two legislative chambers. **lower regions** *n pl* Hades, hell. **lowest** (or **least**) **common denominator** and **lowest** (or **least**) **common multiple** see under **denominate** and **multiple** respectively. **low-fat'** *adj* containing only a small proportion of fat. **low frequency, low-gear, Low German** see under **frequent, gear** and **German** respectively. **low-hanging fruit** *n* (*inf*) something that can be easily acquired or achieved. **low'-key'** *adj* (in painting or photography) in mostly dark tones or colours, with few if any highlights; undramatic, understated, restrained; (of a person) not easily excited, showing no visible reaction. **low'land** *n* land low in relation to higher land (also *adj*). **low'lander** *n* (also with *cap*) a native of lowlands, *esp* the **Lowlands** of Scotland. **Low Latin** see under **Latin**. **low-level language** *n* a computer-programming language using easily remembered words or letters, each instruction translating into one machine code instruction (cf **high-level language**). **low level waste** *n* (*nuclear eng*) radioactive waste which, because of its low activity, does not require shielding during normal handling or transport. **low life** *n* sordid social circumstances; people of low social class; (also **low'life**) the criminal fraternity or a member of it; (also **low'life**) anyone considered dishonest or disreputable. **low'-life** *adj*. **low'-lifer** *n*. **low'light** *n* a dull or unenjoyable part of something; (*usu* in *pl*) a portion of hair artificially darkened to enhance the natural colour of the hair (also *vt*). **low'-lived** /-livd/ *adj* vulgar; shabby. **low'-loader** *n* a low trailer or wagon without sides, used for very heavy loads. **Low Mass** *n* mass celebrated without music and incense. **low'-mind'ed** *adj* having crude or vulgar motives or interests; vulgar. **low'-mind'edness** *n*. **low'-necked** *adj* (of a dress, blouse, etc) cut low in the neck and away from the shoulders, décolleté. **low-noise converter** *n* (*TV*) an aerial component that receives, magnifies and transmits by wire a satellite signal. **low'-paid'** *adj* (of a worker) receiving or (of a job) rewarded by low wages. **low'-pitched** *adj* of sound, low in pitch; (of a roof) gentle in slope; having a low ceiling. **low'-press'ure** *adj* employing or exerting a low degree of pressure (ie less than 50lb (about 22.7kg) to the sq in), said of steam and steam-engines; having low barometric pressure. **low profile** *n* a manner or attitude revealing very little of one's feelings, intentions, activities, etc. **low-pro'file** *adj* (of people) having such a manner or attitude; (of a tyre) wide in proportion to its height (*motoring*). **low relief** same as

bas-relief. low'-rent *adj* costing relatively little to rent; of inferior status (*inf*). **low'-rise** *adj* (of buildings) having only a few storeys, *opp* to *high-rise*. ◆ *n* a building of this kind. **low side window** *n* a narrow window (or lower part of a window) near the ground, sometimes found in old churches, *esp* in the chancel. **low'-slung'** *adj* (of a vehicle, etc) with body close to the ground; generally, hanging low; (of a building) not tall. **low'-spir'ited** *adj* downcast or depressed; not lively; sad. **low'-spir'itedness** *n*. **Low Sunday** *n* the first Sunday after Easter, so called in contrast to the great festival whose octave it ends. **low'-tar'** *adj* (of cigarettes) made of tobacco with a low tar content. **low technology** or **low tech** *n* simple, unsophisticated technology used in the production of basic commodities (also (with *hyphen* or **lo'-tech**) *adj*). **low-temperature physics** *n sing* the study of physical phenomena at temperatures near absolute zero. **low'-ten'sion** *adj* using, generating or operating at a low voltage. **low'-thought'ed** *adj* (*Milton*) having the thoughts directed to base or vulgar pursuits. **low tide** or **low water** *n* the lowest point of the ebbing tide. **low toby** see under **toby**. **Lowveld** /lō'felt/ or -*velt*/ *n* (also without *cap*) the lower altitude areas of the eastern Transvaal in South Africa. **low'-wat'er mark** *n* the lowest line reached by the tide; anything marking the point of greatest degradation, decline, etc (*fig*). **low wines** *n pl* the weak spirit produced from the first distillation of substances containing alcohol.

■ **an all-time low** the lowest recorded level. **in low water** short of money. **lay low** to overthrow, fell or kill. **lie low** see under **lie**[2]. **the lowest of the low** the most contemptible person or people.

low[2] /lō/ *vi* to make the noise of cattle. ◆ *n* the sound made by cattle. [OE *hlōwan*; Du *loeien*]

■ **low'ing** *n*.

low[3] /lō/ (*archaic*, except in place names) *n* a hill; a tumulus. [OE *hlǣw*; cf **law**[3]]

low[4] or **lowe** /low/ (*Scot*) *n* a flame. ◆ *vi* to blaze. [ON *logi*; cf Ger *Lohe*]

❑ **low-bell** /low'*, lō*' or *loo'bel*/ *n* (*dialect*) a small bell; a bell used by night along with a light, to frighten birds into a net.

lowan /lō'ən/ same as **mallee-bird** (see under **mallee**[1]) or **mound-bird** (see under **mound**[1]).

lower[1] /lowr/, **lowering** and **lowery** see **lour**.

lower[2] /lō'ər/ see under **low**[1].

lown[1] and **lowne** /lown/ *n* variants of **loon**[1].

lown[2] or **loun** /lown/, **lownd** or **lound** /lownd/ (*Scot*) *adj* sheltered; calm; quiet. ◆ *adv* quietly. ◆ *n* calm; quiet; shelter. ◆ *vi* to calm. [ON *logn* (noun)]

Lowrie /low'ri/ (*Scot*) *n* a nickname for the fox (also **Low'rie-tod** or **Tod-low'rie**). [*Laurence*]

lowse /lows/ (*Scot*) *adj* loose. ◆ *vt* (*pat* and *pap* **lows'it**) /lows or lowz/ to loose; to unyoke, set free; to redeem. ◆ *vi* to unyoke the horses; to knock off work. [See **loose**]

lowt see **lout**[1,2].

lox[1] /loks/ *n* liquid oxygen, used as a rocket propellant (also **lox'ygen**).

lox[2] /loks/ *n* a kind of smoked salmon. [Yiddish *laks*, from MHGer *lahs* salmon]

loxodrome /lok'sə-drōm/ *n* a line on the surface of a sphere which makes equal oblique angles with all meridians, a rhumb line (also called **loxodromic curve, line** or **spiral**). [Gr *loxos* oblique, and *dromos* a course]

■ **loxodromic** /-drom'ik/ or **loxodrom'ical** *adj*. **loxodrom'ics** or **loxod'romy** *n* the art of sailing on rhumb lines.

loxygen see **lox**[1].

loy /loi/ (*Irish*) *n* a long, narrow spade with a footrest on one side of the handle.

Loya Jirga see **jirga**.

loyal /loi'əl/ *adj* faithful; true as a lover; firm in allegiance; personally devoted to a sovereign (or would-be sovereign), government, leader, etc; expressing or manifesting loyalty; legitimate (*Shakesp*). [Fr, from L *lēgālis*, from *lēx, lēgis* law]

■ **loy'alism** *n*. **loy'alist** *n* a loyal adherent, *esp* of a sovereign or of an established government; (also with *cap*) in Northern Ireland, a supporter of the British government; (also with *cap*) in British history, a partisan of the Stuarts; (also with *cap*) in the American war of Independence, a person siding with the British. **loy'ally** *adv*.

❑ **loyal toast** *n* a toast to the sovereign at a formal dinner.

loyalty /loi'əl-ti/ *n* the condition of being loyal; (in *pl*) feelings of being loyal to a person or organization, etc. [Fr, as **loyal**]

❑ **loyalty card** *n* a machine-readable plastic card issued by certain retailers, enabling customers to accumulate points or credits to be redeemed for goods or cash.

lozell see **losel**.

■ words derived from main entry word; ❑ compound words; ■ idioms and phrasal verbs

lozenge /*loz'inj*/ *n* a diamond-shaped parallelogram or rhombus (*geom*); a small sweet, sometimes medicated, *orig* diamond-shaped; a diamond-shaped shield for the arms of a widow, spinster, or deceased person (*heraldry*). [Fr *losange* (of unknown origin)]
■ **loz'en** *n* (*Scot*) a windowpane. **loz'enged** *adj* divided into lozenges. **loz'engy** *adj* (*heraldry*) divided into lozenge-shaped compartments.
❑ **loz'enge-shaped** *adj*.

LP /*el-pē'*/ *n* a long-playing record.

LP *abbrev*: Labour Party; Lord or Lady Provost; low pressure.

LPG *abbrev*: liquefied petroleum gas.

L-plate see under **L** (*abbrev*).

lpm (*comput*) *abbrev*: lines per minute.

LPO *abbrev*: London Philharmonic Orchestra.

L'pool *abbrev*: Liverpool.

LPS *abbrev*: Lord Privy Seal.

LQTS (*med*) *abbrev*: long QT syndrome.

Lr (*chem*) *symbol*: lawrencium.

lr *abbrev*: lira (the former Italian unit of currency; also **Lr**).

LRAM *abbrev*: Licentiate of the Royal Academy of Music.

LRCP *abbrev*: Licentiate of the Royal College of Physicians (**Edin**, of Edinburgh; **Lond**, of London; **Irel**, of Ireland).

LRCS *abbrev*: Licentiate of the Royal College of Surgeons (**Ed**, of Edinburgh; **Eng**, of England; **Irel**, of Ireland).

LRP *abbrev*: lead replacement petrol.

LS *abbrev*: Lesotho (IVR); Linnaean Society of London; (also **ls**) *loco sigilli* (*L*), in the place of the seal.

LSA (*old*) *abbrev*: Licentiate of the Society of Apothecaries.

LSC *abbrev*: Learning and Skills Council; Legal Services Commission.

LSD *abbrev*: lysergic acid diethylamide (see under **lysis**).

LSD, £sd or **lsd** *abbrev*: librae, solidi, denarii (*L*), pounds, shillings and pence.

LSE *abbrev*: London School of Economics and Political Science.

LSI *abbrev*: large-scale integration.

LSO *abbrev*: London Symphony Orchestra.

LT *abbrev*: Lithuania (IVR); low tension.

Lt *abbrev*: Lieutenant.

LTA *abbrev*: Lawn Tennis Association.

Lt Cdr *abbrev*: Lieutenant Commander.

Lt Col. *abbrev*: Lieutenant Colonel.

Ltd *abbrev*: (used at the end of the names of limited liability companies) limited.

Lt Gen. *abbrev*: Lieutenant General.

Lt Gov. *abbrev*: Lieutenant Governor.

LTh *abbrev*: Licentiate in Theology.

LTOM (*commerce*) *abbrev*: London Traded Options Market.

Lu (*chem*) *symbol*: lutetium.

lu (*phys*) *abbrev*: lumen.

luau /*loo-ow'*/ *n* a Hawaiian dish made of coconut, taro, octopus, etc; a Hawaiian feast or party. [Hawaiian *lu'au*]

Lubavitch /*lub'ə-vich*/ *n pl* a sect of Hasidic orthodox Jews. [*Lubavitch*, a village in Belarus, where it was founded]
■ **Lub'avitcher** *adj*.

lubber /*lub'ər*/ or **lubbard** /*lub'ərd*/ *n* an awkward, big, clumsy person; a lazy, sturdy person. ◆ *adj* lubberly. [Origin doubtful]
■ **lubb'erlike** *adj*. **lubb'erly** *adj* and *adv*.
❑ **lubber fiend** *n* (*folklore*) a benevolent goblin or other creature who may secretly help with domestic work, Lob-lie-by-the-fire. **lubber hole** or **lubber's hole** *n* (*naut*) a hole in a mast platform saving climbing round the rim. **lubber line** or **lubber's line** *n* (*naut*) a line on the compass bowl marking the position of the ship's head.

lube /*loob*/ (chiefly *N Am* and *Aust*) a short form of **lubricant** and **lubricate**.

lubfish /*lub'fish*/ *n* a kind of stockfish. [**lob**]

lubra /*loo'brə*/ (*Aust*; *offensive*) *n* an Aboriginal woman. [From an Aboriginal language]

lubricate /*loo'* or *lū'bri-kāt*/ *vt* to make smooth or slippery; to cover or supply with oil or other material to overcome friction; to supply with alcoholic drink (*inf*); to bribe. ◆ *vi* to act as a lubricant. [L *lūbricus* slippery]
■ **lu'bric** or **lu'brical** *adj* (*archaic*) lubricious. **lu'bricant** *adj* lubricating. ◆ *n* a substance used to reduce friction. **lubrica'tion** *n*. **lu'bricative** *adj*. **lu'bricātor** *n*. **lubricious** /*-brish'əs*/ or **lu'bricous**

/*-kəs*/ *adj* slippery (*rare*); lewd (often *literary*). **lubric'iously** or **lu'bricously** *adv*. **lubricity** /*-bris'i-ti*/ *n* slipperiness; smoothness; instability; lewdness. **lubritō'rium** *n* (chiefly *US*) a place in a garage or service station where motor vehicles are lubricated.
❑ **lubricated water** *n* water with certain additives which make it flow more smoothly.

Lucan /*loo'* or *lū'kən*/ *adj* of or relating to Luke or Luke's gospel.

lucarne /*loo-* or *lū-kärn'*/ *n* a dormer window, *esp* in a church spire. [Fr (of unknown origin)]

luce /*loos* or *lūs*/ *n* a freshwater fish, the pike. [OFr *lus*, from LL *lūcius*]

lucent /*loo'* or *lū'sənt*/ *adj* shining; bright. [L *lūcēns*, *-entis*, prp of *lūcēre* to shine, from *lūx*, *lūcis* light]
■ **lu'cency** *n*.

lucerne /*loo-* or *lū-sûrn'*/ *n* purple medick, a plant resembling clover, also called (*esp US*) **alfalfa**, valuable as fodder for cattle, etc (also **lucern'** (*Browning* **lu'zern**); formerly often **la lucerne**). [Fr *luzerne*]

luces see **lux**.

lucid /*loo'* or *lū'sid*/ *adj* shining; transparent; easily understood; intellectually bright; not confused, sane. [L *lūcidus*, from *lūx*, *lūcis* light]
■ **lucid'ity** or **lu'cidness** *n*. **lu'cidly** *adv*.
❑ **lucid intervals** *n pl* times of sanity in madness, of quietness in fever, turmoil, etc.

Lucifer /*loo'* or *lū'si-fər*/ *n* the planet Venus as morning star; Satan; (*without cap*) a match of wood tipped with a combustible substance to be ignited by friction (also **lucifer-match'**; *archaic*). [L *lūcifer* light-bringer, from *lūx*, *lūcis* light, and *ferre* to bring]
■ **lucif'erase** *n* an oxidizing enzyme in the luminous organs of certain animals that acts on luciferin to produce luminosity. **Lucifē'rian** *adj* relating to Lucifer. **lucif'erin** *n* a protein-like substance in the luminous organs of certain animals, *esp* glow-worms and fireflies. **lucif'erous** *adj* light-bringing; light-giving.

lucifugous /*loo-* or *lū-sif'ū-gəs*/ *adj* shunning or avoiding light. [L *lūx*, *lūcis* light, and *fugere* to flee]

lucigen /*loo'* or *lū'si-jən*/ *n* a lamp burning oil mixed with air in a spray. [L *lūx*, *lūcis* light, and root of L *gignere*, *genitum* to beget]

Lucina /*loo-* or *lū-sī'na*/ *n* the Roman goddess of childbirth, Juno; also Diana; hence, the moon; a midwife (*archaic*). [L *Lūcīna*, thought by the Romans to be from *lūx*, *lūcis* light, as if the bringer to light]

Lucite® /*lū'sīt*/ *n* a kind of solid, transparent plastic, often used instead of glass.

luck /*luk*/ *n* fortune; good fortune; an object with which a family's fortune is supposed to be bound up. [Prob LGer or Du *luk*; cf Ger *Glück* prosperity]
■ **luck'ily** *adv* in a lucky way; I'm glad to say, fortunately. **luck'iness** *n*. **luck'less** *adj* without good luck; unhappy. **luck'lessly** *adv*. **luck'lessness** *n*. **luck'y** *adj* having, attended by, portending or bringing good luck.
❑ **luck'-penny** *n* a small sum returned for luck to the customer by a seller; a coin carried for luck. **lucky bag** *n* a bag sold without its contents being disclosed; a lucky dip; a receptacle for lost property on board a man-of-war (*naut*). **lucky charm** *n* an object which is supposed to bring good fortune. **lucky dip** *n* a tub or container in which to dip and draw a prize. **luck'y-piece** *n* a coin; the illegitimate child of a prosperous father (*inf*). **lucky stone** *n* a stone with a natural hole through it (carried for good fortune). **lucky strike** *n* a stroke of luck.
■ **down on one's luck** (*inf*) see under **down**[1]. **get lucky** (*inf*) to have a stroke of luck; to succeed in initiating a sexual relationship. **I should be so lucky** an ironic expression meaning loosely, 'that kind of luck does not happen to me'. **luck into** or **upon** (*inf*) to get or come across something by chance. **luck out** (*N Am*) to have a run or instance of good luck. **no such luck** (*inf*) unfortunately not. **push one's luck** (*inf*) to try to make too much of an advantage, risking total failure. **touch lucky** (*inf*) to have good luck. **tough luck** (*inf*) an expression of real or affected sympathy for someone's predicament. **try one's luck** (**at**) to attempt something. **worse luck** (*inf*) unfortunately.

lucken /*luk'ən*/ (*Scot*) *adj* closed. [OE *locen*, pap of *lūcan* to lock]
❑ **luck'enbooth** *n* a booth or shop, *esp* of the type found in Edinburgh in the 18c (**Luckenbooth brooch** a *usu* silver and heart-shaped brooch, *orig* sold at such a booth). **luck'engow'an** *n* the globe-flower.

lucky[1] see under **luck**.

lucky[2] or **luckie** (prefixed or vocative, **Lucky**) /*luk'i*/ (*Scot*) *n* an elderly woman; a woman who keeps an alehouse. [Perh from adj **lucky** (see under **luck**)]
❑ **luck'ie-dad** *n* a grandfather.

lucky[3] /*luk'i*/ (*sl*) *n* departure.
■ **cut** or **make one's lucky** (*archaic*) to bolt.

lucre /loo´ or lū´kər/ n sordid gain; riches. [L lucrum gain]
■ **lu´crative** /-krə-tiv/ adj profitable. **lu´cratively** adv. **lu´crativeness** n.

luctation /luk-tā´shən/ (obs) n struggle. [L luctātiō, -ōnis]

luculent /loo´ or lū´kū-lənt/ adj bright; clear; convincing. [L lūculentus, from lūx light]
■ **lu´culently** adv.

Lucullan /loo- or lū-kul´ən/ adj in the style of the Roman statesman Lucullus, famous for his banquets (also **Lucullē´an**, **Lucull´ian** or **Lucull´ic**).

lucuma /loo´kū-mə/ n a tree of the Lucuma genus of sapotaceous trees with edible fruit, mostly found in S America. [Quechua]

lucumo /loo´ or lū´kū-mō/ n (pl **lu´cumos** or (L) **lucumōn´es** /-ēz/) an Etruscan prince and priest. [L lucumō, from Etruscan]

Lucy Stoner /loo´si stō´nər/ (US) n a woman who keeps her maiden name after marriage. [From Lucy Stone, an American suffragist (1818–93)]

lud /lud/ n a form of **lord** (used when addressing a judge or facetiously).
■ **lud´ship** n.

Luddite /lud´īt/ n one of a band of protesters against unemployment who destroyed machinery in English factories about 1812–18; hence, any opponent of technological innovation, etc. ◆ adj of or relating to Luddites. [Said to be from Ned Ludd, who had smashed stocking-frames (machines on which stockings were made) at a slightly earlier date]
■ **Ludd´ism** n. **Ludd´itism** n.

luderick /loo´də-rik/ n an Australian fish (Girella tricuspidata; also called **blackfish**). [From an Aboriginal language]

ludic /loo´dik/ adj playful, esp spontaneously and aimlessly. [Fr ludique, from L ludus play]
■ **lu´dically** adv.

ludicrous /loo´ or lū´di-krəs/ adj ridiculous, absurd; intended to excite, or exciting, laughter; laughable; sportive (obs); humorous (obs). [L lūdicrus, from lūdere to play]
■ **lu´dicrously** adv. **lu´dicrousness** n.

ludo /loo´ or lū´dō/ n (pl **lud´os**) a game in which counters are moved on a board according to the numbers shown on thrown dice. [L lūdō I play]

lues /loo´ or lū´ēz/ n orig a pestilence; now syphilis (**lues venerea**). [L luēs]
■ **luetic** /-et´ik/ adj (an etymologically unjustifiable formation).

luff /luf/ n the forward edge of a fore-and-aft sail; the windward side of a ship; the act of sailing a ship close to the wind; the after part of a ship's bow where the planks begin to curve in towards the cutwater (also **loof**). ◆ vi to turn a ship towards the wind. ◆ vt to turn nearer to the wind; to move (the jib of a crane) in and out. [ME luff, lof(f), from OFr lof ; poss from a conjectured MDu form loef (modern Du loef)]
❑ **luffing crane** or **luffing-jib crane** n a jib crane with the jib hinged at its lower end to the crane structure so as to allow alteration of its radius of action.

luffa see **loofah**.

luffer-board /luf´ər-bōrd or -börd/ same as **louvre-board** under **louvre**.

Luftwaffe /lŏŏft´vä-fə/ (Ger) n air force.

lug[1] /lug/ vt (**lugg´ing**; **lugged**) to pull; to drag heavily; to carry (something heavy); of sailing ships, to carry (too much sail). ◆ vi to pull. [Cf Swed lugga to pull by the hair; perh connected with **lug**[2]]
■ **lugg´able** adj (esp of computers) portable, but with some difficulty (also n).
■ **lug in** to introduce without any apparent connection or relevance.

lug[2] /lug/ n the sideflap of a cap; the ear (inf; chiefly Scot); an ear-like projection or appendage; a handle; a loop; a box for carrying fruit or vegetables; a stupid or clumsy man; a chimney-corner (Scot). [Perh connected with **lug**[1]]
■ **lugged** /lugd/ adj having lugs or a lug. **lugg´ie** n (Scot) a hooped dish with one long stave.
❑ **lug´-chair** n an armchair with side headrests. **lug´hole** n (inf) (the hole in) the ear.

lug[3] /lug/ or **lugsail** /lug´sāl or lug´sl/ n a square sail bent upon a yard that hangs obliquely to the mast. [Origin uncertain]
■ **lug´ger** n a small vessel with lugsails.

lug[4] /lug/ or **lugworm** /lug´wûrm/ n a sluggish worm found in the sand on the seashore, often used for bait. [Origin doubtful]

lug[5] /lug/ n a pole or stick (dialect); a perch or rod of land (Spenser). [Origin obscure]

luge /loozh or lüzh/ n a light toboggan ridden lying on one's back. ◆ vi to ride on such a toboggan. [Swiss Fr]
■ **lug´er** n. **lug´ing** or **luge´ing** n and adj.

Luger® /loo´gər/ n a type of pistol.

luggage /lug´ij/ n the suitcases and other baggage of a traveller. [Ety as for **lug**[1]]
❑ **lugg´age-carrier** n a structure fixed to a bicycle, motor car, etc, for carrying luggage. **lugg´age-van** n a railway wagon for luggage.

lugger see under **lug**[3].

luggie see under **lug**[2].

lugsail see **lug**[3].

lugubrious /loo-goo´bri-əs or -gū´/ adj mournful; dismal. [L lūgubris, from lūgēre to mourn]
■ **lugu´briously** adv. **lugu´briousness** n.

lugworm see **lug**[4].

Luing cattle /ling kat´l/ n a breed of hardy beef cattle. [Luing, an island off W Scotland]

luit /lüt or lit/, also **luiten** /lüt´ən/ (Scot) pat and pap of **let**[1].

lukewarm /lūk´wörm/ adj moderately warm; tepid; half-hearted. [ME luek, luke ; doubtful whether related to **lew**[1], or to Du leuk]
■ **luke** adj (dialect) lukewarm. **luke´warmish** adj. **luke´warmly** adv. **luke´warmness** or **luke´warmth** n.

lulibub early form of **lollipop**.

lull /lul/ vt to soothe; to compose; to quiet. ◆ vi to become calm; to subside. ◆ n an interval of calm; a calming influence. [Imit]

lullaby /lul´ə-bī/ n a song to lull children to sleep, a cradle-song. ◆ vt to lull to sleep. [Ety as for **lull** and **bye**[2]; cf Swed lulla]

lulu /loo´loo/ (sl) n an outstandingly bad or impressive thing or person. [Origin obscure]

lulz /lulz/ (sl) n pl amusement derived from mischievous or provocative behaviour on the Internet. [Altered plural form of **lol** (in sense of laughing out loud)]

lum /lum/ (Scot) n a chimney; a chimney-pot hat (also **lum hat**). [Origin obscure; OFr lum light, and Welsh llumon chimney, have been suggested]
❑ **lum´-head** n the top of a chimney.

luma /loo´ma/ n (pl **lu´ma** or **lu´mas**) an Armenian monetary unit, $\frac{1}{100}$ of a dram. [Armenian]

lumbago /lum-bā´gō/ n (pl **lumbā´gos**) rheumatic pain in the muscles or fibrous tissues in the lumbar region. [L lumbāgō lumbago, from lumbus loin]
■ **lumbaginous** /-baj´i-nəs/ adj.

lumbang /loom-bäng´/ n the candlenut tree or other species of Aleurites, whose nuts yield **lumbang´-oil**. [Tagálog]

lumbar /lum´bər/ adj of or relating to the section of the spine between the lowest rib and the pelvis. [L lumbus loin]
❑ **lumbar puncture** n the process of inserting a needle into the lower part of the spinal cord to take a specimen of cerebrospinal fluid, inject drugs, etc.

lumber[1] /lum´bər/ n furniture stored away out of use; anything cumbersome or useless; timber, esp sawn or split for use (N Am). ◆ vt to fill with lumber; to heap together in confusion; to burden with something, eg a task or responsibility, that is unwanted or troublesome (inf); to cut the timber from. ◆ vi to work as a lumberjack. [Perhaps from **lumber**[4] or from **lumber**[2] influenced by **lumber**[4]]
■ **lum´berer** n a lumberjack. **lum´bering** n felling, sawing and removal of timber.
❑ **lum´ber-camp** n a lumberman's camp. **lum´berjack** or **lum´berman** n someone employed in the felling, sawing, etc of timber. **lum´berjacket** n a man's jacket, usu in bold-patterned heavy material. **lum´ber-mill** n a sawmill. **lumber room** n a room for storing things not in use. **lum´ber-yard** n a timber-yard.

lumber[2] /lum´bər/ vi to move heavily and clumsily; to rumble. [ME lomeren, perh a frequentative formed from lome, a variant of **lame**[1]; but cf dialect Swed lomra to resound]
■ **lum´berer** n. **lum´bering** adj. **lum´berly** or **lum´bersome** adj. **lum´bersomeness** n.

lumber[3] /lum´bər/ (sl) n flirtation, sexual play; a casual sexual partner. ◆ vt to have a casual sexual relationship with (someone). [Origin unknown]

lumber[4] /lum´bər/ (sl) n pawn (archaic); a pawnshop (archaic); prison. ◆ vt (archaic) to pawn; to imprison. [See **Lombard**]
■ **lum´berer** n (obs) a pawnbroker.
❑ **lum´ber-pie´** n a pie of meat or fish, with eggs.
■ **in lumber** (sl) in trouble; in prison.

lumbricus /lum-brī´kəs/ n a worm of the very common genus of earthworms Lumbricus, giving its name to the family **Lumbricidae** /-bris´i-dē/ to which all British earthworms belong. [L lumbrīcus]
■ **lum´brical** (or /-brī´/) adj wormlike. ◆ n (for **lumbrical muscle**) one of certain muscles of the hand and foot used in flexing the digits (also **lumbricā´lis**). **lumbriciform** /-bris´/ or **lum´bricoid** (or /-brī´/) adj wormlike.

lumen /loo' or lū'men/ n (pl **lu'mina** or **lu'mens**) a derived SI unit, the unit of luminous flux (symbol **lm**), equal to the light emitted in one second in a solid angle of one steradian from a point that is a radiation source of uniform intensity of one candela (abbrev **lu**); the cavity of a tubular organ (anat); the space within the cell wall (bot). [L lūmen, -inis light, from lūcēre to shine]
■ **lu'menal** or **lu'minal** adj of a lumen.

luminaire /lū-mi-ner'/ n the British Standards Institution term for a light fitting. [Fr]

luminous /lū' or loo'mi-nǝs/ adj giving light; shining; lighted; clear; lucid; (of colours) very bright and garish. [L lūmen, -inis light, from lūcēre to shine]
■ **lu'minance** n luminousness; the measure of brightness of a surface, measured in candela cm^2 of the surface radiating normally; the brightness of a television screen or visual display unit, adjustable to suit the operator. **lu'minant** adj giving light. ◆ n a means of lighting. **lu'minarism** n. **lu'minarist** n a person who paints luminously, or with skill in the creation of light and shade; an Impressionist or plein-airist (qv). **lu'minary** n a source of light, esp one of the heavenly bodies; someone who illustrates any subject or instructs mankind; a famous or prominent member of a group. ◆ adj (rare) providing light or enlightenment. **luminā'tion** n a lighting up. **lu'mine** /-in/ vt (obs) to illumine. **luminesce'** vi to show luminescence. **luminescence** /-es'ǝns/ n emission of light otherwise than by incandescence and so at a relatively cool temperature; the light so emitted. **luminesc'ent** adj. **luminif'erous** adj giving, yielding, or being the medium of, light. **lu'minist** n a luminarist. **luminosity** /-os'i-ti/ n luminousness; the measure of the quantity of light actually emitted by a star, irrespective of its distance. **lu'minously** adv. **lu'minousness** n.
□ **luminance signal** n a signal controlling the luminance of a colour TV picture, ie its image brightness, as distinct from its chrominance. **luminous energy** n energy emitted in the form of light. **luminous flux** n a measure of the rate of flow of luminous energy. **luminous intensity** n a measure of the amount of light radiated in a given direction from a point source. **luminous paint** n a paint that glows in the dark, those that glow continuously having radioactive additives.

lumme or **lummy** /lum'i/ (inf) interj expressing surprise or concern. [(Lord) love me]

lummox /lum'ǝks/ (inf) n a stupid, clumsy person. [Origin unknown]

lummy[1] /lum'i/ (sl; Dickens) adj excellent.

lummy[2] see **lumme**.

lump /lump/ n a shapeless mass; a bulge or protuberance; a swelling; a feeling as if of a swelling or tightening in the throat; a considerable quantity; the total as a whole; the gross; an inert, dull, good-natured or fair-sized person; a lumpfish. ◆ vt to throw into a confused mass; to consider everything together; to include under one heading, esp regardless; to endure willy-nilly; to put up with regardless; to be lumpish about; to dislike. ◆ vi to be lumpish; to gather or collect in a lump; to walk or move heavily. [Origin doubtful; found in various Gmc languages]
■ **lumpec'tomy** n the surgical removal of a lump, caused by cancer, in the breast, esp as opposed to removal of the entire breast. **lump'er** n someone who works on the lump (see **the lump** below); a docker; a militiaman (dialect); someone inclined to lumping in classification, opp to hair-splitter. **lump'ily** adv. **lump'iness** n. **lump'ing** adj in a lump; heavy; bulky. **lump'ish** adj like a lump; heavy; gross; dull; sullen. **lump'ishly** adv. **lump'ishness** n. **lump'kin** n a lout. **lump'y** adj full of lumps; like a lump.
□ **lump'fish** or **lump'sucker** n a sea fish (genus Cyclopterus), clumsy and with excrescences on its skin, with pectoral fins transformed into a sucker. **lump sugar** n loaf sugar broken into small pieces or cut in cubes. **lump sum** n a single sum of money in lieu of several. **lumpy jaw** n actinomycosis affecting the jaw in cattle.
■ **in the lump** in gross. **like it or lump it** enjoy it or put up with it. **take** or **get one's lumps** (inf) to be reprimanded or scolded. **the lump** the system of using self-employed workmen for a particular job, esp in order to evade tax and national insurance payments.

lumpen /lum'pǝn/ adj relating to a dispossessed and/or degraded section of a social class, as in **lumpen proletariat** (also as one word), the poorest down-and-outs; stupid, boorish. ◆ n pl the lumpen proletariat. [From Ger Lumpen a rag]
■ **lump'enly** adv.

luna /loo'nǝ/ n a N American moth (Actias luna), with crescent-shaped markings on its blue-green, yellow and black wings (also **luna moth**). [L luna moon]

lunacy /loo'nǝ-si/ n a form of insanity once believed to come with changes of the moon; insanity generally; extreme folly. [Ety as for **lunar**]
■ **lunatic** /loo'nǝ-tik/ adj affected with lunacy. ◆ n a person so affected; a madman or madwoman.

□ **lunatic asylum** n a former, now offensive, name for a psychiatric hospital. **lunatic fringe** n the more nonsensical, extreme-minded, or eccentric members of a community or of a movement.

lunar /loo'nǝr/ adj belonging to the moon; measured by the moon's revolutions; caused by the moon; for use on the moon; like the moon; of silver (old chem). ◆ n a lunar distance. [L lūna the moon, from lūcēre to shine]
■ **luna'rian** n (archaic) an inhabitant of the moon; a person who studies the moon. **lu'narist** n someone who thinks the moon affects the weather. **lun'arnaut** or **lun'anaut** n an astronaut who travels or has travelled to the moon. **lu'nary** n the moonwort fern; the plant honesty. ◆ adj lunar. **lu'nate** or **lu'nated** adj crescent-shaped. **luna'tion** n a synodic month. **lune** /loon or lūn/ n anything in the shape of a half-moon; a lunule; a fit of lunacy (Shakesp). **lunette'** n anything crescent-shaped; a crescent-shaped ornament; a semicircular or crescent-shaped space where a vault intersects a wall or another vault, often occupied by a window or by decoration; an arched opening in a vault; a detached bastion (fortif); a small horseshoe; a watchglass flattened more than usual in the centre; in the Roman Catholic Church, a moon-shaped case for the consecrated host. **lunisō'lar** adj relating to the moon and sun jointly (**lunisolar calendar** and **lunisolar year** a calendar or year divided according to the changes of the moon, but made to agree in average length with the solar year). **luniti'dal** adj relating to the moon and its influence on the tide (**lunitidal interval** the time interval between the moon's transit and the next high tide at a particular place). **lu'nula** n a lunule (obs); a crescent-like appearance, esp the whitish area at the base of a nail; a Bronze Age crescent-shaped gold ornament forming part of a necklace. **lu'nūlar** adj. **lu'nūlate** or **lu'nulated** adj shaped like a small crescent (bot); having crescent-shaped markings. **lu'nule** n anything shaped like a small crescent; a geometrical figure bounded by two arcs of circles.
□ **lunar caustic** n fused crystals of silver nitrate, applied to ulcers, etc. **lunar cycle** same as **Metonic cycle** (see **Metonic**). **lunar distances** n pl a method of finding longitude by comparison of the observed angular distance of the moon from a star at a known local time, with the tabulated angular distance at a certain Greenwich time. **Lunar Excursion Module** n (sometimes without caps) a module for use in the last stage of the journey to land on the moon (abbrev **LEM** or **lem**). **lunar month** see under **month**. **lunar theory** n the a priori deduction of the moon's motions from the principles of gravitation. **lunar year** see under **year**.

lunatic see under **lunacy**.

lunch /lunch or lunsh/ n a midday meal; formerly, a snack at any time of day (US); a light repast between breakfast and midday meal (archaic); a thick slice, a lump (dialect). ◆ vi to eat lunch. ◆ vt to provide lunch for. [Short form of **luncheon**, from ME none(s)chench noon drink]
■ **lunch'eon** n (esp a formal) lunch. ◆ vi (archaic) to lunch (also vt). **luncheonette'** n (orig US) a restaurant serving snacks and light meals. **lunch'er** n.
□ **lunch box** or **lunch'box** n a box or container in which one carries, esp to work, sandwiches, etc for lunch; a man's genitalia (sl). **lunch'eon-bar** n a counter where luncheons are served. **lunch'eon-basket** n a basket for carrying lunch, with or without cutlery, etc. **luncheon meat** n a type of pre-cooked meat containing preservatives, usu served cold. **luncheon** (or **lunch**) **voucher** n a ticket or voucher given by employer to employee to be used to pay for the latter's lunch. **lunch hour** or **lunch'time** n the time of, or time allotted to, lunch; an interval allowed for lunch. **lunch'-table** n.
■ **out to lunch** (inf; orig US) slightly crazy, in a world of his or her own.

lung /lung/ n a respiratory organ in animals that breathe atmospheric air; an open space in a town (fig). [OE lungen]
■ **lunged** /lungd/ adj. **lung'ful** n. **lung'less** adj.
□ **lung'-book** n a breathing organ in spiders and scorpions, constructed like the leaves of a book. **lung'fish** n any of certain species of S America, Africa and Australia, of the subclass Dipnoi, able to breathe atmospheric air using 'lungs' or modified air-bladders, the Australian Neoceratodus having only a single such 'lung'. **lung'-grown** adj having an adhesion of the lung to the pleura. **lung'worm** n any of various parasitic nematode worms that infest the lungs of vertebrates, esp domestic animals. **lung'wort** n a genus (Pulmonaria) of the borage family with spotted leaves, once thought good for lung diseases; a lichen (Lobaria pulmonaria) on tree trunks, used as a domestic remedy for lung diseases.
■ **iron lung** see under **iron**.

lunge[1] /lunj/ n a sudden thrust as in fencing; a forward plunge; in gymnastics, a rapid movement forwards or sideways with one leg bent at the knee and the other leg stretched out behind. ◆ vi (prp **lunge'ing** or **lung'ing**) to make a lunge; to plunge forward. ◆ vt to thrust with a lunge. [Fr allonger to lengthen, from L ad to, and longus long]

lunge² or **longe** /*lunj*/ *n* a long rope used in horse-training; training with a lunge; a training-ground for horses. ◆ *vt* to train or cause to go with a lunge. [Fr *longe*, from L *longus* long]
□ **lunge** (or **longe** or **lunging**) **whip** *n* a whip used with a lunge.

lungi /*loon'gē*/ *n* a long cloth used as loincloth, sash, turban, etc. [Hindi and Pers *lungī*]

lungie¹ /*lung'i*/ (*Scot*) *n* the guillemot. [Norw dialect *lomgivie*]

lungie² /*lung'i*/ or **lunyie** /*lun'yi*/ *n* Scots form of **loin**.

lunisolar, lunitidal, etc see under **lunar**.

lunk see **lunkhead**.

lunker /*lung'kər*/ (*inf, esp US*) *n* a particularly large specimen of an animal, *esp* a fish. [Origin unknown]

lunkhead /*lungk'hed*/ (*inf, esp US*) *n* a fool, blockhead (sometimes shortened to **lunk**). [Perh a form of **lump**, and **head**]

lunt /*lunt*/ (*Scot*) *n* a slow match or means of setting on fire; a sudden flame, blaze; smoke. ◆ *vt* to kindle; to smoke. ◆ *vi* to blaze up; to send up smoke; to smoke tobacco. [Du *lont* a match; cf Ger *Lunte*]

lunula, lunulate, lunule, etc see under **lunar**.

lunyie see **lungie²**.

Lupercal /*lū'* or *loo'pər-kal* or *-kl*/ *n* the grotto, or the festival (15 February) of *Lupercus*, Roman god of fertility and flocks (also (*pl*) **Lupercā'lia**). [Perh L *lupus* wolf, and *arcēre* to ward off]
■ **Lupercā'lian** *adj*.

lupin or (*esp US*) **lupine** /*loo'* or *lū'pin*/ *n* a plant of the papilionaceous genus (*Lupinus*), with flowers on long spikes; its seed. [L *lupīnus*]

lupine¹ /*loo'* or *lū'pīn*/ *adj* of a wolf; like a wolf; wolfish. [L *lupīnus*, from *lupus* a wolf]

lupine² see **lupin**.

luppen /*lup'n*/ (*Scot*) *pap* of **leap¹**.

lupulin /*loo'pū-lin*/ *n* a yellow powder composed of glands from hop flowers and bracts, used as a sedative. [L *lupus* hop-plant]
■ **lu'puline** or **lupulinic** /*-lin'ik*/ *adj*.

lupus /*loo'* or *lū'pəs*/ *n* a chronic tuberculosis of the skin, often affecting the nose, strictly **lupus vulgaris** (*med*); (with *cap*) a constellation in the southern hemisphere (*astron*). [L *lupus* a wolf]
■ **lu'poid** or **lu'pous** *adj*.
□ **lupus erythematosus** *n* (*med*) a disease of the connective tissue.

lur see **lure²**.

lurch¹ /*lûrch*/ *vi* to roll or pitch suddenly forward or to one side. ◆ *n* a sudden roll or pitch. [Origin obscure]

lurch² /*lûrch*/ *n* an old game, probably like backgammon; in various games, a situation in which one side fails to score at all, or is left far behind; a discomfiture. ◆ *vt* to defeat by a lurch; to outdo so as to deprive of all chance (*Shakesp*); to leave in the lurch. [OFr *lourche*]
■ **leave someone in the lurch** to leave someone in a difficult situation without help.

lurch³ /*lûrch*/ *n* (*archaic* or *dialect*) wait, ambush. ◆ *vt* (*archaic*) to forestall; to defraud, to overreach; to filch. [Connection with **lurk** difficult; influenced appar by **lurch²**]
■ **lurch'er** *n* someone who lurches (*archaic* or *dialect*); a glutton (*obs*); a dog with a distinct cross of greyhound, *esp* a cross of greyhound and collie.

lurdan, lurdane or **lurden** /*lûr'dən*/ (*archaic*) *n* a dull, heavy, stupid or sluggish person (also *adj*). [OFr *lourdin* dull, from *lourd* heavy]

lure¹ /*loor* or *lūr*/ *n* any enticement; bait; a decoy; a brightly-coloured artificial bait (*angling*); a bunch of feathers used to recall a hawk (*falconry*). ◆ *vt* to entice; to decoy. [OFr *loerre* (Fr *leurre*), from MHGer *luoder* (Ger *Luder*) bait]

lure² or **lur** /*loor*/ *n* a long curved Bronze Age trumpet of a style still used in Scandinavian countries for calling cattle, etc. [ON *lúthr*; Dan and Norw *lur*]

Lurex® /*lū'reks*/ *n* (fabric made from) a plastic-coated aluminium thread.

Lurgi /*loor'gi*/ *adj* relating to a German plant that enables coal gas to be made from low-grade coal.

lurgy or **lurgi** /*lûr'gi*/ (*esp facetious*) *n* a non-specific disease. [Popularized by BBC Radio's *The Goon Show* (1949–60)]

lurid /*loo'* or *lū'rid*/ *adj* glaringly bright; melodramatically sensational; dingily reddish-yellow or yellowish-brown (*bot*); gloomily threatening; pale or wan; ghastly; brimstony. [L *lūridus*]
■ **lu'ridly** *adv*. **lu'ridness** *n*.

lurk /*lûrk*/ *vi* to lie in wait; to be concealed; to skulk; to linger around furtively; to use the Internet only to read, and not to send, messages (*comput sl*). ◆ *n* a prowl; a lurking-place; a dodge or swindle (*esp Aust sl*). [Perh frequentative from **lour**]

■ **lurk'er** *n*. **lurk'ing** *n* and *adj*.
□ **lurk'ing-place** *n*.

lurry /*lur'i*/ (*Milton*) *n* any gabbled formula; confusion. [**liripipe**]

lurve /*lûrv*/ (*inf*) *n* love as sentimentalized by films and pop songs. [Representing a pronunciation of **love** associated with this meaning]

Lusatian /*loo-sā'shən*/ *adj* of or belonging to *Lusatia*, a former region in eastern Germany between the Elbe and the Oder rivers. ◆ *n* an inhabitant of the region; the language spoken there, a form of West Slavic.

luscious /*lush'əs*/ *adj* exceedingly sweet; delightful, pleasurable; (*esp* of musical sound or literary style) too rich, cloying, fulsome; attractive and voluptuous. [Origin unknown; **delicious**, influenced by **lush¹**, has been suggested]
■ **lusc'iously** *adv*. **lusc'iousness** *n*.

lush¹ /*lush*/ *adj* rich, juicy and succulent; luxuriant; luxurious; attractive; excellent (*sl*). [Perh a form of **lash²**]
■ **lush'ly** *adv*. **lush'ness** *n*.

lush² /*lush*/ (*sl, esp N Am*) *n* a drinker or drunkard; alcohol; a drink; a drinking bout. ◆ *vt* (*archaic*) to ply with alcohol. ◆ *vt* and *vi* to overindulge in alcohol. [Perh from **lush¹**]
■ **lush'er** *n*. **lush'y** *adj* tipsy.
□ **lush'-house** *n* (*archaic*) a disreputable public house.

Lusitanian /*lū-* or *loo-si-tā'ni-ən*/ *n* and *adj* Portuguese. [*Lusitania*, a province of the Roman Empire approximating to modern Portugal]
□ **Lusita'no-Amer'ican** *n* and *adj* (a) Brazilian of Portuguese descent.

lusk /*lusk*/ (*obs*) *n* a lazy fellow. ◆ *adj* lazy. ◆ *vi* to skulk; to lie about lazily. [Origin obscure]
■ **lusk'ish** *adj*. **lusk'ishness** *n*.

Luso- /*loo-sō-, -sə-, lū-*/ *pfx* denoting Portuguese. [See **Lusitanian**]
■ **Lu'sophile** *n* a lover of Portugal.

lust /*lust*/ *n* strong sexual desire; passionate desire; eagerness to possess; longing; appetite; relish (*rare*); pleasure (*Spenser* and *Shakesp*). ◆ *vi* to desire eagerly (with *after* or *for*); to have strong sexual desire; to have depraved desires. [OE *lust* pleasure]
■ **lust'er** *n*. **lust'ful** *adj* having lust; inciting lust; sensual. **lust'fully** *adv*. **lust'fulness** *n*. **lust'ick** or **lust'ique** *adj* (for Du *lustig*; *obs*) lusty, healthy, vigorous. **lust'ihead** (*archaic*), **lust'ihood** (*archaic*) or **lust'iness** *n*. **lust'ily** *adv*. **lust'less** *adj* (*Spenser*) listless, feeble. **lust'y** *adj* vigorous; healthy; stout; bulky; lustful (*Milton*); pleasing, pleasant (*obs*).
□ **lust'-breathed** /*-brēdh'id*/ *adj* (*Shakesp*) animated by lust. **lust'-di'eted** *adj* (*Shakesp*) pampered by lust.

lustrate, etc see under **lustre²**.

lustre¹ or (*US*) **luster** /*lus'tər*/ *n* characteristic surface appearance in reflected light; sheen; gloss; brightness; splendour; renown, distinction (*fig*); a pendant of cut glass used as an ornament on a vase, chandelier, etc; a vase, chandelier, etc ornamented with these; a dress material with cotton warp and woollen weft, and highly finished surface; a metallic pottery glaze. ◆ *vt* to impart a lustre to. ◆ *vi* to become lustrous. [Fr, from L *lūstrāre* to shine on]
■ **lus'treless** *adj*. **lus'tring** *n*. **lus'trous** *adj* bright; shining; luminous. **lus'trously** *adv*. **lus'trousness** *n*.
□ **lus'treware** *n* pottery, etc with a metallic glaze.

lustre² /*lus'tər*/ or **lustrum** /*lus'trəm*/ *n* (*pl* **lus'tres**, **lus'tra** or **lus'trums**) a ceremonial purification of the Roman people made every five years, after the taking of the census; a period of five years. [L *lūstrum*, prob from *luere* to wash or purify]
■ **lus'tral** *adj*. **lus'trate** *vt* to purify by sacrifice; to perambulate (*obs*). **lustra'tion** *n* purification by sacrifice; an act of purifying.

lustring /*lus'tring*/ *n* a glossy silk cloth (also **lus'trine** or **lutestring** /*loot'* or *lūt'string*/). [Fr *lustrine*, from Ital *lustrino*]

lustrum see **lustre²**.

lusty see under **lust**.

lusus naturae /*loo'səs na-tū'rē* or *loo'sŭs na-too'rī*/ (*L*) *n* a freak of nature.

lute¹ /*loot* or *lūt*/ *n* an old stringed instrument shaped like half a pear. ◆ *vi* to play on the lute. ◆ *vt* and *vi* to sound as if on a lute. [OFr *lut* (Fr *luth*); like Ger *Laute*, from Ar *al* the, and *'ūd* wood, the lute]
■ **lut'anist**, **lut'enist**, **lut'er** or **lut'ist** *n* a player on the lute. **luthier** /*lūt'i-ər*/ *n* a maker of lutes, guitars, and other stringed instruments.
□ **lute'string** *n* a string of a lute (see also **lustring**).

lute² /*loot* or *lūt*/ *n* clay, cement or other material used as a protective covering, an airtight stopping, a waterproof seal, etc; a rubber packing-ring for a jar. ◆ *vt* to coat or close with lute. [L *lutum* mud, from *luere* to wash]
■ **lut'ing** *n*.

lute³ /*loot* or *lūt*/ *n* a straight-edge for scraping off excess clay in a brick mould. [Du *loet*]

luteal see under **lutein**.

lutecium same as **lutetium**.

lutein /lū̄'/ or /loo'tē-in/ n a yellow pigment (a xanthophyll) found in egg yolk. [L *lūteus* yellow, *lūteum* egg yolk, and *lūtum* weld]
■ **luteal** /loo'ti-əl/ adj relating to (the formation of) the corpus luteum. **luteinīzā'tion** or **-s-** n the process of stimulation to the ovary, whereby ovulation occurs and a corpus luteum is formed. **lu'teinize** or **-ise** vt and vi. **lutē'olin** n the yellow pigment of weld or dyer's weed. **lutē'olous** adj yellowish. **lu'teous** /-i-əs/ adj golden-yellow. **lutescent** /-es'ənt/ adj yellowish.
❑ **luteinizing hormone** n a hormone that stimulates ovulation and the formation of the corpus luteum (qv) in females, and the production of androgen in males. **luteotrophic hormone** another name for **prolactin**.

lutenist see under **lute¹**.

lutestring see **lustring** and under **lute¹**.

Lutetian /lū-tē'shən/ adj Parisian. [L *Lutetia Parīsiōrum*, the mud town of the Parisii, Paris, from *lutum* mud]

lutetium /lū- or loo-tē'shi-əm/ n a metallic element (symbol **Lu**; atomic no 71), a member of the rare-earth group. [L *Lutetia* Paris; named in honour of Georges Urbain (1872–1938), Parisian chemist who first separated it from ytterbium]

Lutheran /loo'thə-rən/ adj relating to Martin *Luther*, the great German Protestant reformer (1483–1546), or to his doctrines. ◆ n a follower of Luther.
■ **Lu'theranism** or **Lu'therism** n. **Lu'theranize** or **-ise** vt. **Lu'therist** n.

luthern /loo'/ or /lū'thərn/ n a dormer window. [Prob a variant of **lucarne**]

luthier see under **lute¹**.

Lutine bell /loo-tēn'/ or /loo'ten bel/ n a bell recovered from the frigate *Lutine*, and rung at Lloyd's of London before certain important announcements.

lutten see **let¹**.

lutz /lŭts/ n in figure skating, a jump (with rotation) from the back outer edge of one skate to the back outer edge of the other. [Poss Gustave *Lussi* of Switzerland (1898–1993) the first exponent]

luv /luv/ (inf) n love, esp as a form of address. [Respelling of **love**]
■ **luvv'ie** or **luvv'y** n an actor or other member of the entertainment industry, esp when regarded as excessively pretentious or affected. **luvv'iedom** n.

lux /luks/ n (pl **lux**, **luxes** or **luces** /loo'sēs/) a derived SI unit, the unit of illuminance (symbol **lx**), equal to one lumen per square metre. [L *lūx* light]
❑ **lux'meter** n an instrument for measuring illumination.

luxate /luk'sāt/ (med) vt to put out of joint; to displace. [L *luxāre*, *-ātum*, from *luxus*, from Gr *loxos* slanting]
■ **luxā'tion** n a dislocation.

luxe /lūks, luks/ or (Fr) /lüks/ n luxury (see also **de luxe**). [Fr, from L *luxus* a dislocation, extravagance or luxury]

Luxembourg /luk'səm-bûrg/ adj of or relating to the Grand Duchy of *Luxembourg* in W Europe, or its inhabitants.
■ **Lux'embourger** n a native or citizen of Luxembourg.

luxmeter see under **lux**.

lux mundi /luks mun'dī or looks moon'dē/ (L) n light of the world.

luxulyanite, **luxulianite** or **luxullianite** /luk'sū'lyə-nīt or -soo' or -sul'yə/ n a tourmaline granite found at *Luxulyan*, Cornwall.

luxury /luk'shə-ri, also lug'zhə-ri/ n abundant provision of means of comfort, ease and pleasure; indulgence, esp in costly pleasures; anything delightful, often expensive, but not necessary; a dainty; wantonness (*Shakesp*). ◆ adj relating to or providing luxury. [OFr *luxurie*, from L *luxuria* luxury, from *luxus* excess]
■ **luxuriance** /lug-zhoo'ri-əns, -zū', -zhū' or luk-, etc/ or **luxu'riancy** n growth in rich abundance or excess; exuberance; overgrowth. **luxu'riant** adj exuberant in growth; overabundant; profuse; ornate; luxurious (*non-standard*). **luxu'riantly** adv. **luxu'riate** vi to be luxuriant, grow profusely; to live luxuriously; to enjoy luxury; to enjoy or revel in indulgence. **luxuriā'tion** n. **luxu'rious** adj of luxury; enjoying or indulging in luxury; providing or aiming to provide luxury; provided with luxuries; softening by pleasure; luxuriant (*Milton*); lustful (*Shakesp*). **luxu'riously** adv. **luxu'riousness** n. **luxurist** /luk'shə-rist or -sū-/ n someone given to luxury.
❑ **luxury goods** n pl (econ) goods on which a consumer spends a greater share of his or her income as that income rises.

luzern see **lucerne**.

Luzula /loo' or lū'zū-lə/ n the woodrush genus, with flat usu hairy leaves. [Old Ital *luzziola* (Mod *lucciola*) firefly, glow-worm, from its shining capsules]

LV abbrev : Latvia (IVR); luncheon voucher.

Lv (chem) symbol : livermorium.

LVO abbrev : Lieutenant of the (Royal) Victorian Order.

LW (radio) abbrev : long wave.

Lw (chem) symbol : the former symbol for lawrencium, now **Lr**.

lwei /lə-wā'/ n (pl **lwei'**) an Angolan monetary unit, $\frac{1}{100}$ of a kwanza. [Of Bantu origin]

LWM or **lwm** abbrev : low-water mark.

LWR abbrev : light-water reactor.

LWT abbrev : London Weekend Television.

LX /el-eks'/ (theatre) abbrev : electrical or electricals; technical staff who work on lighting and sound.

lx symbol : lux (SI unit).

LXX symbol : Septuagint.

lyam /lī'əm/, **lime** or **lyme** /līm/, or **leam** /lēm/ (obs or dialect) n a leash; a lyam-hound. [OFr *liem* (Fr *lien*), from L *ligāmen*, from *ligāre* to tie]
❑ **ly'am-hound**, **lime'-hound** or **lyme'-hound** n a bloodhound.

lyart see **liard**.

lyase /lī-āz'/ n an enzyme that assists in the dissolution of a molecule by forming a double bond. [Gr *lysis* dissolution, and **-ase**]

Lycaena /lī-sē'nə/ n a genus of butterflies giving its name to the family **Lycae'nidae**, usu small and blue or coppery. [Gr *lykaina* she-wolf]
■ **lycae'nid** n.

lycanthropy /lī- or li-kan'thrə-pi/ n the power of changing oneself into a wolf; a kind of madness, in which the patient has fantasies of being a wolf. [Gr *lykos* a wolf, and *anthrōpos* a man]
■ **lycanthrope** /lī'kan-thrōp or -kan'/ or **lycan'thropist** n a wolf-man or werewolf; a person suffering from lycanthropy. **lycanthropic** /-throp'/ adj.

lycée /lē'sā/ n a state secondary school in France. [Fr, lyceum]

lyceum /lī-sē'əm/ n (pl **lyce'ums**) (with cap) a gymnasium and grove beside the temple of Apollo at Athens, in whose walks Aristotle taught; (with cap and the) Aristotelian philosophy and those who follow it; a college; a place or building devoted to literary studies, lectures, etc; an organization for instruction by lectures (US); a lycée. [L *Lycēum*, from Gr *Lykeion*, from *Lykeios*, an epithet of Apollo (perh wolf-slayer, perh the Lycian)]

lychee, **litchi**, **lichee** or **lichi** /lī'chē/ or **leechee** /lē'chē/ n a Chinese fruit, a nut or berry with a fleshy aril; the tree (*Litchi chinensis*, family Sapindaceae) that bears it. [Chin *lìzhī*]

lychgate see under **lich²**.

Lychnic /lik'nik/ n the first part of the vespers of the Greek Orthodox Church. [Gr *lychnos* a lamp]
■ **Lychnap'sia** n (Gr *haptein* to touch or light) a series of seven prayers in the vespers of the Greek Orthodox Church. **lych'noscope** n a low side window (named on the theory that it was intended to let lepers see the altar lights).

lychnis /lik'nis/ n a plant of the campion genus *Lychnis* of the pink family. [Gr *lychnis* rose campion]

lycopene /lī'kə-pēn/ n a red carotenoid pigment found in tomatoes, extracted and used as an antioxidant. [Mod L *Lycopersicon* the tomato genus]

lycopod /lī'kə-pod/ n a club moss, any plant of the genus *Lycopodium* or of the Lycopodiales. [Gr *lykos* a wolf, and *pous, podos* a foot]
■ **Lycopōdiā'ceae** n pl a homosporous family of Lycopodiales. **Lycopōdiā'lēs**, **Lycopōdī'nae** or **Lycopodin'eae** n pl one of the main branches of the Pteridophytes, usu with dichotomously branched stems and axillary sporangia, commonly in cones. **Lycopō'dium** n the typical genus of Lycopodiaceae, club moss, or stag's horn; (without cap) a powder of the spores of Lycopodium.

Lycosa /lī-kō'sə/ n a genus of hunting spiders, including the true tarantula, typical of the family **Lycosidae** /-kos'i-dē/ or wolf-spiders. [Gr *lykos* a wolf, also a kind of spider]

Lycra® /lī'krə/ n (a fabric made from) a lightweight, synthetic, elastomeric fibre.

lyddite /lid'īt/ n a powerful explosive made in Kent, composed mainly of picric acid. [Tested at *Lydd*]

Lydford law /lid'fərd lö/ n the same kind of law as that called Jeddart or Jethart justice. [*Lydford* in Devon]

Lydian /lid'i-ən/ adj relating to *Lydia* in Asia Minor; (of music) soft and slow. ◆ n a native of Lydia; the language of ancient Lydia, apparently related to Hittite. [Gr *Lȳdiā* Lydia]
❑ **Lydian mode** n (in ancient Greek music) a mode of two tetrachords with a semitone between the two highest notes in each and a whole tone between the tetrachords (eg *c d e f* ; *g a b c* ; but reckoned

downwards by the Greeks); (in old church music) an authentic mode, extending from f to f, with f for its final. **Lydian stone** n touchstone.

lye[1] /lī/ n a strong alkaline solution; a liquid used for washing; a solution obtained by leaching. [OE *lēah*, *lēag*; Ger *Lauge*; related to L *lavāre* to wash]

lye[2] /lī/ n a short side-branch of a railway. [See **lie**[2]]

lyfull see **lifeful** under **life**.

lying see **lie**[1,2].

lykewake, **likewake** /līk'wāk/, **likewalk** or **lykewalk** /-wök/ (Scot; Eng **lichwake** /lich'/) n a watch over the dead, often involving festivities. [OE *līc*; Ger *Leiche* a corpse, and **wake**[1]]

lym /lim/ n a conjectural Shakespearean form of **lyme** (see **lyam**).

Lymantriidae /lī-man-trī'i-dē/ n pl the tussock moths, a family related to the eggers. [Gr *lȳmantēr* destroyer]

lyme and **lyme-hound** see **lyam**.

Lyme disease /līm di-zēz'/ n a viral disease transmitted to humans by ticks, affecting the joints, heart and nervous system. [First discovered in *Lyme*, Connecticut, USA]

lyme-grass /līm'gräs/ n a coarse sand-binding grass, *Elymus arenarius* or any other of the *Elymus* genus. [Origin unknown]

Lymeswold® /līmz'wöld/ n a kind of mild blue soft English cheese, marketed from 1982 to 1992. [Fanciful name, perhaps based on *Wymeswold* in Leicestershire]

lymiter (*Spenser*) same as **limiter** (see under **limit**).

Lymnaea a non-standard form of **Limnaea**.

lymph /limf/ n a colourless or faintly yellowish fluid collected into the lymphatic vessels from the tissues in animal bodies, of a rather saltish taste, and with an alkaline reaction; a vaccine; pure water (*archaic*). [L *lympha* water; *lymphāticus* mad]
■ **lymphadeni'tis** n (Gr *adēn* gland) inflammation of the lymph glands. **lymphadenop'athy** n a disease of the lymph nodes. **lymphangial** /-anj'əl/ adj (Gr *angeion* vessel) relating to the lymphatic vessels. **lymphan'giogram**, **lymphangiog'raphy** n same as **lymphogram**, **lymphography** (see below). **lymphangitis** /-an-jī'tis/ n inflammation of a lymphatic vessel. **lymphat'ic** adj relating to lymph; inclined to be sluggish and flabby, *orig* considered as the result of an excess of lymph; mad (*obs*). ◆ n a vessel that conveys lymph. **lymphat'ically** adv. **lymph'oblast** n (Gr *blastos* a shoot or bud) an abnormal cell, the production of which is linked to **lymphoblast'ic leukaemia**. **lymph'ocyte** /-ō-sīt/ n a small white blood cell, one of many present in lymphoid tissues, circulating in blood and lymph and involved in antigen-specific immune reactions. **lymphog'raphy** n radiography of the lymph glands and lymphatic system, recorded on a **lymph'ogram**; the description of the lymphatic system (*rare* or *obs*). **lymph'oid** adj of, carrying, or like lymph; relating to the lymphatic system. **lymph'okine** n (Gr *kinein* to move; *immunol*) any of a number of substances secreted by lymphocytes activated by contact with an antigen and thought to play a part in cell-mediated immunity. **lymphō'ma** n a tumour consisting of lymphoid tissue. **lymphotroph'ic** adj (of a virus) preferentially infecting lymphocytes. ❑ **lymphatic drainage** n a method of massage that encourages the flow of lymph, helping to eliminate waste products from the body (see also **manual lymphatic drainage** under **manual**). **lymphatic system** n the network of vessels that conveys lymph to the venous system. **lymph gland** or **node** n any of the small masses of tissue sited along the lymphatic vessels, in which lymph is purified, and lymphocytes are formed. **lymphoid tissue** n (*immunol*) body tissue, eg lymph nodes, spleen, thymus and adenoids, in which the predominant cells are lymphocytes.

lymphad /lim'fad/ n a kind of large rowing boat (*esp* formerly) much used in the Scottish Highlands. [Gaelic *longfhada*]

lymphangial, **lymphatic**, **lymphocyte**, etc see under **lymph**.

lynage (*Spenser*) same as **lineage** (see under **line**[1]).

lyncean see under **lynx**.

lynch /linch or linsh/ vt to judge and put to death without the usual forms of law. [Thought to be after Captain William *Lynch* (1742–1820) of Virginia who set up and presided over tribunals outside the regular law]
■ **lynch'er** n. **lynch'ing** n.
❑ **lynch'-law** n. **lynch mob** n a group of incensed or angry people who are intent on lynching someone.

lynchet see **linch**.

lynchpin a variant of **linchpin**.

lyne (*Spenser*) same as **line**[2] (linen).

lynx /lingks/ n an animal (*Felis lynx*) of the cat family, high at the haunches, with long legs, a short tail and tufted ears (pl **lynx'es**); (with *cap*) a constellation in the northern hemisphere. [L, from Gr *lynx*, *lynkos*]

■ **lyncean** /lin-sē'ən/ adj lynx-like; sharp-sighted.
❑ **lynx'-eyed** adj.

lyomerous /lī-om'ə-rəs/ adj relating to the **Lyom'erī**, soft-bodied fishes. [Gr *lyein* to loosen, and *meros* part]

Lyon /lī'ən/ n the chief herald of Scotland (also **Lord Lyon**, **Lyon King of arms** or **Ly'on-at-arms**). [From the heraldic *lion* of Scotland]
❑ **Lyon Court** n the court over which the Lyon presides, having jurisdiction in questions of coat-armour and precedency.

Lyonnaise /lī- or lē-ō-nez'/ (also without *cap*) adj of food, cooked or served with (*usu* fried) onions. [Fr, *à la Lyonnaise* in the style of Lyon or the Lyonnais region]

lyophil /lī'ō-fil/, **lyophile** /lī'ō-fīl/ or **lyophilic** /-fīl'ik/ adj (of a colloid) readily dispersed in a suitable medium. [Gr *lyē* separation, *phileein* to love]
■ **lyophiliza'tion** or **-s-** n freeze-drying. **lyoph'ilize** or **-ise** vt to dry by freezing. **ly'ophobe** /-fōb/ or **lyophobic** /-fōb'/ adj (Gr *phobeein* to fear) (of a colloid) not readily dispersed.

lyre /līr/ n a musical instrument like the harp, used *esp* in ancient Greece as an accompaniment to poetry, consisting of a convex resonating box with a pair of curved arms connected by a crossbar, from which the strings were stretched over a bridge to a tailpiece. [L *lyra*, from Gr *lyrā*]
■ **Ly'ra** n (*astron*) one of the northern constellations. **ly'rate** or **ly'rated** adj lyre-shaped; having the terminal lobe much larger than the lateral ones (*bot*). **ly'ra-way** or **ly'ra-wise** adv according to lute tablature. **lyric** /lir'/ adj (of poems or their authors) expressing individual or private emotions; (of a singing voice) having a light quality; relating to the lyre; intended or suitable to be sung, *orig* to the lyre. ◆ n a lyric poem; a song; (in pl) the words of a popular song; a composer of lyric poetry (*obs*). **lyrical** /lir'/ adj lyric; song-like; expressive or imaginative; effusive. **lyr'ically** adv. **lyricism** /lir'i-sizm/ n a lyrical expression; lyrical quality. **lyr'icist** n the writer of the words of a song, musical, opera, etc; a lyric poet. **lyr'icon** n an electronic wind instrument like a large flute (but played like a clarinet), used with a synthesizer. **lyriform** /lī'/ adj shaped like a lyre. **lyr'ism** /lī'r' or lir'/ n lyricism; singing. **lyrist** /lī'r' or lir'/ n a player on the lyre or harp; /lir'/ a lyric poet.
❑ **ly'ra-vi'ol** or **lyra viol** n an obsolete instrument like a viola da gamba adapted for playing from lute tablature. **lyre'bird** n either of two Australian passerine ground-dwelling birds of the genus *Menura* about the size of a pheasant, the tail feathers of the male arranged, in display, in the form of a lyre. **lyre guitar** n a form of lyre with a fingerboard, at its greatest popularity in the late 18c and early 19c. **lyriform organs** n pl (*zool*) patches of well-innervated chitin on the legs and other parts of spiders, believed to act as mechanoreceptors.
■ **wax lyrical** to become increasingly expressive or effusive in praise of something.

lyse see under **lysis**.

Lysenkoism /li-sen'kō-i-zm/ n the teaching of the Soviet geneticist TD *Lysenko* (1898–1976) that acquired characteristics are inheritable.

lysergic acid, **lysin**, etc see under **lysis**.

lysis /lī'sis/ n breaking down, eg of a cell (*biol*); the action of a lysin; the gradual abatement of a disease, as distinguished from *crisis*. [Gr *lysis* dissolution, from *lyein* to loose]
■ **lyse** /līz/ vi and vt to undergo or cause to undergo lysis. **-lyse** or **-lyze** /-līz/ v *combining form* to break down or divide into parts. **lysigenic** /lī- or lī-si-jen'ik/, **lysigenet'ic** or **lysigenous** /-sij'i-nəs/ adj caused by the breaking down of cells. **lysim'eter** n an instrument for measuring percolation of water through the soil. **lysin** /lī'sin/ n a substance that causes breakdown of cells. **lysine** /lī'sēn/ n an essential amino acid, a product of protein hydrolysis. **-lysis** /-lis-is/ n *combining form* denoting the action of breaking down or dividing into parts. **ly'sogeny** n (*biol*) that part of the life cycle of a temperate phage in which it replicates in synchrony with its host (cf **lytic cycle** below). **ly'sol** n a solution of cresol in soap, a poisonous disinfectant (a trademark in some countries). **lysosō'mal** adj. **ly'sosome** n (Gr *soma* a body) any of the tiny particles present in most cells, containing enzymes that play a part in intracellular digestion. **ly'sozyme** /-zīm/ n a bacteriolytic enzyme present in some plants, animal secretions (eg tears), egg white, etc. **-lyst** /-list/ or **-lyte** /-līt/ n *combining form* denoting something that can be broken down or divided into parts. **lytic** /lit'ik/ adj of, relating to, resulting from or causing lysis. **-lytic** or **-lytical** /-lit-/ adj *combining form* denoting something that can be broken down or divided into parts. **lyt'ically** adv.
❑ **lysergic acid** /lī-sûr'jik/ n a substance, $C_{16}H_{16}O_2N_2$, derived from ergot, causing (in the form of lysergic acid diethylamide, **LSD** and **ly'sergide**) a schizophrenic condition, with hallucinations and thought processes outside the normal range. **lytic cycle** n (*biol*) that part of the life cycle of a temperate phage in which it replicates

uncontrollably, destroying its host and eventually releasing many copies into the medium (cf **lysogeny** above).

lyssa /lis'ə/ (*pathol*) *n* rabies. [Gr, madness, rabies]

lyte a form of **light**[3] or **lite**[2].

-lyte see under **lysis**.

lythe[1] (*Spenser*) a form of **lithe**[1].

lythe[2] /līdh/ (*Scot*) *n* the pollack, a common fish of the cod family.

Lythrum /lith'rəm/ (*bot*) *n* the purple loosestrife genus, giving its name to a family of archichlamydeous dicotyledons, **Lythrā'ceae**,

commonly hexamerous, heterostyled, with epicalyx. [Latinized from Gr *lythron* gore, from the colour of its flowers]

■ **lythraceous** /lith-rā'shəs or lī-/ *adj*.

lytic, -lytic and **-lytical** see under **lysis**.

lytta /lit'ə/ (*zool*) *n* a cartilaginous or fibrous band on the undersurface of the tongue in carnivores, *esp* the dog, in which it was once thought to cause lyssa, or rabies. [Gr, Attic form of *lyssa* (see **lyssa**)]

-lyze see under **lysis**.

Mm

M or **m** /em/ *n* the thirteenth letter in the modern English alphabet, twelfth in the Roman, its sound a bilabial nasal; a unit of measurement (**em**) (*printing*); anything shaped like the letter M.
□ **M1** *n* a Garand rifle (qv). **M'-roof** *n* a roof formed by the junction of two simple roofs, resembling the letter M in cross-section. **M'-theory** *n* (*phys*) a variation of string theory (qv under **string**) that posits an eleven-dimensional universe.

M or **M.** *abbrev* : maiden over(s) (*cricket*); Malta (IVR); Master; medium; mega-; Member (of); *mille* (*L*), a thousand; million(s); money; *Monsieur* (*Fr*), Mr (*pl* **MM**); Motorway (followed by a number).
□ **M'-way** *n* a written contraction of **motorway** (see under **motor**).

M *symbol* : (as a Roman numeral) 1000; followed by a number, used to designate the seven categories of money supply in the UK (see **M0**, **M1**, etc, below; *econ*): meta- or meso- (*chem*).
□ **M0** *n* all notes and coins in current general circulation plus banks' till money and balances with the Bank of England. **M1** *n* all notes and coins in current general circulation plus all instantly-withdrawable bank deposits. **M2** *n* all notes and coins in current general circulation plus non-interest-bearing bank deposits, building society deposits, and National Savings accounts. **M3** *n* M1 plus all privately-held bank deposits and certificates of deposit. **M3c** *n* M3 plus all foreign currency bank deposits. **M4** *n* M1 plus most privately-held bank deposits and holdings of money market instruments. **M5** *n* M4 plus building society deposits.

M̄ *symbol* : (Roman numeral) 1000 000.

M' see **Mac¹**.

m or **m.** *abbrev* : male; mark or marks (former German currency); married; masculine; mass; *meridiem* (*L*), noon; metre(s); mile(s); mille- ; milli-; million(s); (**m**) mobile, *esp* referring to services delivered to mobile phones, as in *m-banking*, *m-ticket*; month(s).

m *symbol* : metre (SI unit).

m' /m or mə/ a short form of **my** as in *m'lud* (see under **lud**).

'm /m/ a short form of **am**; a contraction of **madam**.

MA *abbrev* : Massachusetts (US state); Master of Arts; Morocco (IVR).

ma /mä/ *n* a childish contraction for **mamma¹**.

maa /mä/ *vi* (of a goat) to bleat. [*Imit*]

ma'am /mäm, mam, məm/ *n* a contraction of **madam**, the pronunciation /mäm/ being used as a form of address to female royalty (also (*inf*) **marm** /mäm/ or **mum**).

maar /mär/ (*geol*) *n* a crater that has been formed by a single explosion and so does not lie in a cone of lava. [*Ger*]

Maastricht /mä'strihht/ *n* the political philosophy aimed at social and political integration within the European Union. [From the treaty signed at *Maastricht* in the Netherlands in 1992, which established certain principles of integration]

maatjes or **matjes** /mä'tyəs/ *n* young herring before it has spawned, cured in brine, sugar, and spices, and served as an hors d'œuvre. [Dan *maatjes* (*haring*) maiden herring]

MAB (*immunol*) *abbrev* : monoclonal antibody.

Mab /mab/ (*folklore*) *n* the name of a female fairy believed to be the bringer of dreams; the queen of the fairies.

mabela /mə-bel'ə/ (*S Afr*) *n* ground sorghum, used for making porridge and beer. [Zulu *amabele* sorghum]

Mabinogion /ma-bi-nog'i-on or -nö'gi/ *n* a collective title for four tales in the *Red Book of Hergest*, a 14c Welsh manuscript; extended to refer to the whole collection in Lady Charlotte Guest's edition and translation of 1838. [Welsh, juvenilities]

MAC /mak/ *abbrev* : Migration Authorization Code, used to change between broadband Internet providers; Multiplex Analogue Components, designating a method of encoding television signals.

Mac¹, also written **Mc** and **M'** /mak, mək/ a Gaelic prefix in names, meaning *son* (*of*). [Gaelic and Ir *mac* son; Welsh *mab*, OWelsh *map*]

Mac² /mak/ *n* (*esp US*) an informal term of address used to a man whose name is not known. [**Mac¹**]

Mac- see **Mc-**.

mac see **mackintosh**.

macabre /ma-, mə-kä'br', ma-, mə-kä'bər/ *adj* gruesome, ghastly; resembling the dance of death (qv). [Fr *macabre*, formerly also *macabré*, perh a corruption of *Maccabee* in reference to Bible, 2 Maccabees 14.43–6, said to have been represented in medieval drama, or from Heb *meqabēr* grave-digger]
■ **macaberesque** /-bər-esk'/ *adj*.

macaco /mə-kä'kō/ *n* (*pl* **maca'cos**) any of various kinds of lemur. [Fr *mococo*]

macadamia /ma-kə-dā'mi-ə or -dē'/ *n* a tree of the *orig* Australian *Macadamia* genus of evergreen trees (family Proteaceae). [John *Macadam* (1827–65), Scottish-born Australian chemist]
□ **macadamia nut** *n* (also **Queensland nut**) the edible nut of two species of macadamia, *Macadamia tetraphylla* and *Macadamia integrifolia*; the tree bearing this nut.

macadamize or **-ise** /mə-kad'ə-mīz/ *vt* to cover (a road) with small broken stones, so as to form a smooth, hard surface. [John Loudon *McAdam* (1756–1836), Scottish engineer]
■ **macad'am** *n* a macadamized road surface; material for macadamizing. **macadamīzā'tion** or **-s-** *n*.

macahuba see **macaw-tree**.

macallum /mə-kal'əm/ (*Scot*) *n* a dish of vanilla ice cream topped with raspberry sauce. [From the surname]

Macanese /ma-kə-nēz'/ *n* a member of the Portuguese-Chinese population of Macau, a Special Administrative Region of China, formerly a Portuguese colony. ◆ *adj* relating to Macau or its people.

macaque /mə-käk'/ *n* a monkey of the genus *Macaca*, to which the rhesus and the Barbary ape belong. [Fr, from Port *macaco* a monkey]

macarize or **-ise** /mak'ə-rīz/ *vt* to declare to be happy or blessed. [Gr *makar* happy]
■ **mac'arism** *n* a beatitude.

macaroni /ma-kə-rō'ni/ *n* (*pl* **macarō'nis** or **macarō'nies**) pasta in the form of short thin tubes; a medley; something fanciful and extravagant; in the 18c, a dandy; a rockhopper or crested penguin. [Neapolitan dialect *maccaroni* (Ital *maccheroni*), *pl* of *maccarone*, prob from *maccare* to crush]
■ **macaronic** /-ron'ik/ *adj* used of poetry in which vernacular words are given Latin inflections and intermixed with genuine Latin for comic effect; written or including lines in more than one language. ◆ *n* (often in *pl*) macaronic poetry. **macaron'ically** *adv*.
□ **macaroni cheese** *n* macaroni served with a cheese sauce.

macaroon /ma-kə-roon'/ *n* a sweet biscuit made with egg white and ground almonds or coconut. [Fr *macaron*, from Ital *maccarone* (see **macaroni**)]

macassar oil /mə-kas'ər oil/ *n* an oil obtained *esp* from the seeds of the sapindaceous tree *Schleichera trijuga*, or from ylang-ylang flowers, formerly used as a hair oil (also **macass'ar**). [*Macassar* (now Ujung Pandang) in Indonesia]

macaw /mə-kö'/ *n* any of the large, long-tailed, brightly-coloured tropical American parrots of the genus *Ara* or *Anodorhynchus*. [Port *macao*]

macaw-tree /mə-kö'trē/ or **macaw-palm** /-päm/ *n* a S American palm (genus *Acrocomia*) whose nuts yield a violet-scented oil (also **maco'ya** or **macahuba** /mä-kä-oo'ba/). [Sp *macoya*, from Arawak; Port *macauba*, from Tupí]

Macc. (*Bible*) *abbrev* : (the Apocryphal Books of) Maccabees.

Maccabaean or **Maccabean** /ma-kə-bē'ən/ *adj* relating to Judas *Maccabaeus*, or to his family the Hasmonaeans or **Macc'abees**, who freed the Jews from the persecution of Antiochus Epiphanes, king of Syria, c.166BC (1 Maccabees, 2 Maccabees).

■ words derived from main entry word; □ compound words; ■ idioms and phrasal verbs

macchia /mak'kyə/ n pl Italian form of **maquis** (a thicket).

macchiato /ma-ki-ä'tō/ n (pl **macchia'tos**) an espresso coffee with a small amount of frothy steamed milk. [Ital caffè macchiato, literally, stained coffee]

Mace® /mās/ n a type of tear gas (also **Chemical Mace**). ◆ vt (also without cap) to spray, attack or disable with Mace.

mace¹ /mās/ n a heavy, usu ornamented, staff carried as a mark of authority; a mace-bearer; a metal or metal-headed war-club, often spiked; a billiard cue (obs); a mallet used by a currier in dressing leather. [OFr mace (Fr masse), from hypothetical L matea, whence L dimin mateola a kind of tool]
■ **mā'cer** n a mace-bearer; (in Scotland) an usher in a law court. ◻ **mace'-bearer** n a person who carries a mace in a procession or ceremony.

mace² /mās/ n a spice which is ground from the dried layer immediately within a nutmeg drupe and outside shell and kernel. [ME macis (mistakenly supposed to be a plural), from Fr; of uncertain origin]
◻ **mace'-ale** n ale flavoured with mace.

macédoine /ma-sā-dwän', -sə-/ n a mixture of (usu diced) vegetables or fruit in syrup or jelly; a mixture or medley. [Fr, literally, Macedonia]

Macedonian /ma-sə-dō'ni-ən/ adj of or relating to the republic of Macedonia in S Europe, its language or its inhabitants; of or relating to the ancient region of Macedonia, corresponding to parts of modern-day Greece and Bulgaria as well as modern Macedonia. ◆ n a native or citizen of Macedonia; the language of Macedonia.

maceranduba same as **massaranduba**.

macerate /mas'ə-rāt/ vt to steep or soak; to soften, break up, or separate into pulp, by steeping; to emaciate, esp by fasting; to mortify. ◆ vi to break up or become soft by soaking; to become emaciated, waste away. [L mācerāre, -ātum to steep]
■ **macerā'tion** n. **mac'erātor** n a person who macerates by fasting; a paper-pulping machine.

MacFarlane's buat see under **bowat**.

MacGuffin or **McGuffin** /mə-guf'in/ n the element of a film, book, etc that drives, or provides an excuse for, the action, of supreme importance to the main characters but largely ignored by the audience or reader. [Coined by Sir Alfred Hitchcock (1899–1980), film-maker]

machair /mahh'ər/ n a low-lying sandy beach or boggy links affording some pasturage. [Gaelic]

Machairodus /ma-kī'rə-dəs/ or **Machaerodus** /-kē'/ n the prehistoric sabre-toothed tiger. [Gr machaira a sword, and odous, odontos a tooth]
■ **machair'odont** n and adj.

machan /mə- or ma-chän'/ (Ind) n a raised platform, esp built in a tree, to watch for game. [Hindi macān]

macher /mahh'ər/ n an influential or overbearing person. [Yiddish, from Ger, doer]

machete /mə-shet'i or -chet'i or -chā'ti/ n a heavy knife or cutlass used in Central and S America as a tool and a weapon. [Sp]

Machiavellian /mak-i-ə-vel'yən or -i-ən/ adj ruled by (esp political) expediency rather than morality; crafty, perfidious in conduct or action. ◆ n a follower of the political principles described by Niccolò Machiavelli, Florentine statesman and writer (1469–1527); any cunning and unprincipled politician.
■ **Machiavell'ianism** or **Machiavell'ism** n the political principles described by Machiavelli, or conduct based on them; cunning statesmanship.

machicolation /ma-chik-ō-lā'shən/ (fortif) n a space between the corbels supporting a parapet, or an opening in the floor of a projecting gallery, for dropping missiles, molten lead, etc, on an attacking enemy; a structure with such openings; the provision of such openings or structures. [Fr mâchicoulis]
■ **machic'olate** vt to provide or build with machicolations. **machic'olated** adj.

machinate /mash' or mak'i-nāt/ vi to form a plot or scheme, esp for doing harm. [L māchinārī, -ātus, from māchina, from Gr mēchanē contrivance]
■ **machinā'tion** n the action of machinating; (often in pl) an intrigue or plot. **mach'inātor** n a person who machinates.

machine /mə-shēn'/ n any artificial means or contrivance; any instrument for the conversion of motion; an engine; an engine-powered vehicle, esp a motorcycle; a person incapable of independent action; a person who acts with tireless efficiency; (in classical drama) a pulley-like device used for the entrance of an actor representing a god; a supernatural occurrence which furthers the action of a poem; an organized system of people or institutions; orig a political party organization (also **party machine**; US). ◆ vt to use

machinery for; to print, sew or make with a machine. [Fr, from L māchina, from Gr mēchanē, related to mēchos contrivance]
■ **machin'able** or **machine'able** adj. **machinabil'ity** n. **machin'ery** n machines in general; the working parts of a machine; combined means for keeping anything in action, or for producing a desired result; supernatural occurrences within a poem. **machin'ist** n a person who builds, operates or repairs machines.
◻ **machine code** n (comput) a programming language in which each instruction can be executed by the computer without any intermediate translation. **machine'gun** n an automatic rapid-firing gun on a stable but portable mounting. ◆ vt (**machine'gunning**; **machine'gunned**) to shoot at with a machinegun. ◆ adj with the speed or rhythm of a machinegun. **machine'-gunner** n. **machine head** n the part of a stringed musical instrument containing the tuning pegs. **machine hour method** n (business) a method of calculating depreciation by dividing the cost of a machine by the estimated number of hours of its useful life, and applying the resultant rate to the actual running hours in each year. **machine intelligence** n artificial intelligence. **machine language** n instructions for processing data, put into a form that can be directly understood and obeyed by a specific computer. **machine'-made** adj made by a machine. **machine'man** n a person who oversees the working of a machine. **machine'-pistol** n a small submachine-gun. **machine'-readable** adj (of data) in a form that can be directly processed by a computer. **machine'-ruler** n a machine for ruling lines on paper. **machine screw** n a screw, usu not more than $\frac{1}{4}$ inch in diameter, with a machine-cut thread, used with a nut, or in tapped holes in metal parts. **machine'-shop** n a workshop where metal, etc, is machined to shape. **machine tool** n a power-driven machine, such as a lathe, drill, press, etc, for shaping metal, wood, or plastic material. **machine'-tooled** adj. **machine translation** n (comput) the automatic production of text in one natural language from that in another. **machine'-washable** adj (of a textile article) that may be washed in a domestic washing machine (also n). **machine'-work** n work done by a machine. **machining allowance** n (engineering) the material provided beyond the finished contours on a casting, forging, or roughly prepared component, which is subsequently removed in machining to size.

machinima /mə-shin'ə-mə or -mä, also -shēn'/ n and adj (of) a genre of animated films based on, and using the technology contained in, commercially available computer games. [Prob **machine** and **cinema**]

machismo see under **macho**.

Mach number /mak, mähh num'bər/ n the ratio of the air speed (ie speed in relation to the air) of an aircraft to the velocity of sound under the given conditions; the speed of sound. [Ernst Mach (1838–1916), Austrian physicist and philosopher]
■ **mach'meter** n an instrument for measuring Mach number.

macho /mach'ō/ adj aggressively male; ostentatiously virile. ◆ n (pl **mach'os**) a man of this type; machismo. [Sp macho male, from L masculus]
■ **machismo** /ma-chiz'mō, -chēz', -kiz', -kēz'/ n the cult of male virility and masculine pride.

machree /mə-hhrē'/ (Anglo-Irish) n an affectionate form of address, my dear, my love. [Ir mo chroidhe of my heart, from mo my, and genitive of croi heart]

Machtpolitik /mahht'po-li-tēk/ (Ger) n power politics, esp the doctrine that a state should use force to attain its ends.

machzor see **mahzor**.

macintosh see **mackintosh**.

mack¹ /mak/ n a mackintosh.

mack² /mak/ (sl) n a pimp. [Short form of obsolete **mackerel**]

Mackem /mak'əm/ n a native of Sunderland or Wearside; the dialect of this area. ◆ adj of or relating to this area, its people, dialect, accent or culture.

mackerel /mak'(ə)rəl/ n an edible bluish-green N Atlantic fish (genus Scomber) with a silvery underside and wavy cross-streaks on its back; a pimp (obs). [OFr makerel (Fr maquereau)]
◻ **mackerel breeze** n a strong breeze that ruffles the surface of the sea and so favours mackerel fishing. **mackerel guide** n the common garfish, which visits the coasts just before the mackerel. **mackerel midge** n a small rockling. **mackerel shark** n the porbeagle.

mackinaw /mak'i-nö/ n a kind of blanket formerly distributed by the US government to Native Americans; a short heavy woollen coat, usu double-breasted and belted; a flat-bottomed lake-boat. [Mackinaw, an island between Lakes Huron and Michigan]

mackintosh or **macintosh** /mak'in-tosh/ n (short form **mac** or **mack** /mak/) a kind of waterproof rubberized cloth; a coat made with this material; any waterproof coat or raincoat. See also **McIntosh red**. [Charles Macintosh (1766–1843), a Scottish chemist, the patentee]

mackle /mak'l/ n a blur or other imperfection in printing, caused by a double impression, wrinkling, etc. ◆ vt to print imperfectly, blur. [See **macle**]

macle /mak'l/ n a dark spot in a crystal; chiastolite; a twin crystal. [Fr macle, from L macula spot]
■ **macled** /mak'ld/ adj (of a crystal or mineral) spotted.

Macleaya /mə-klē'ə or -klä'ə/ n a herbaceous Asiatic plant with pinnate leaves and cream-coloured, plume-like flowers. [Alexander Macleay (died 1848), British entomologist and statesman]

Macmillanite /mək-mil'ə-nīt/ n a Cameronian or Reformed Presbyterian. [Rev John Macmillan (1670–1753), one of the founders of the church]

Mâcon /mä-kõ'/ n a heavy red or white burgundy from the Mâcon district of central France.

macon /mā'kn/ n smoked, salted mutton. [mutton and bacon]

maconochie /mə-kon'ə-hhi/ (milit) n tinned meat and vegetable stew; any tinned food. [Packer's name]

macoya see **macaw-tree**.

macramé or **macrami** /mə-krä'mi/ n a fringe or trimming of knotted thread; ornamental knotted threadwork. [Appar from Turk maqrama towel]

macro see under **macro-**.

macro- /ma-krō- or -kro-/ combining form denoting long, great, sometimes interchanging with mega-. [Gr makros long, also great]
■ **mac'ro** n (pl **mac'ros**) (comput) a single instruction that brings a set of instructions into operation. **macro-axis** /mak'rō-aks'is/ n (crystallog) the longer lateral axis. **macrō'bian** adj (Gr bios life) long-lived. **macrobiō'ta** n pl the larger organisms in the soil. **macrobiote** /-bī'ōt/ n a long-living organism. **macrobiotic** /-bī-ot'ik/ adj prolonging life; long-lived; (of a seed) able to remain alive in a dormant state for years; relating to longevity or to macrobiotics. **macrobiot'ics** n sing the art or science of prolonging life; a cult partly concerned with diet, foods regarded as pure being vegetable substances grown and prepared without chemicals or processing. **macrocar'pa** n an evergreen conifer of New Zealand, Cupressus macrocarpa, planted esp for ornamentation and as a windbreak. **macrocephalic** /-si-fal'ik/ or **macrocephalous** /-sef'ə-ləs/ adj. **macrocephaly** /-sef'ə-li/ n (Gr kephalē head) largeness, or abnormal largeness, of the head. **mac'rocode** n (comput) a macroinstruction. **mac'rocopy** n an enlarged copy of printed material for use by people with weak sight. **mac'rocosm** /-kozm/ n (Gr kosmos world) a large and complex structure considered a whole, of which smaller similar structures contained within it are microcosms; the whole universe. **macrocos'mic** adj. **macrocos'mically** adv. **mac'rocycle** n a macrocyclic organic molecule or compound. **macrocy'clic** adj being or having a ring structure with a large number of atoms. **mac'rocyte** /-sīt/ n (Gr kytos a vessel, container) an abnormally large red blood cell associated with some forms of anaemia. **macrodactyl** /-dak'til/ n an animal with long fingers or toes. **macrodactylic** /-til'ik/ adj. **macrodactylous** /-dak'til-əs/ adj (Gr daktylos finger, toe) long-fingered; long-toed. **macrodac'tyly** n the condition of being macrodactylous. **macrodiag'onal** n (crystallog) the longer lateral axis. **mac'rodome** n (crystallog) a dome parallel to the macrodiagonal. **macroeconom'ic** adj. **macroeconomics** /-ēk-ən-om'iks, -ek'-/ n sing the study of economics on a large scale or of large economic units such as national income, international trade, etc. **macroevolu'tion** n major evolutionary developments over a long period of time, such as have given rise to the taxonomic groups above the species level. **macroevolu'tionary** adj. **mac'rofauna** and **mac'roflora** n collective terms for animals and plants respectively that are visible to the naked eye. **mac'rofossil** n a fossil large enough to be seen with the naked eye. **macrogamete** /-gam'ēt/ n the larger and apparently female gamete. **macroglob'ūlin** n any globulin with a molecular weight above about 400 000. **mac'roinstruction** n (comput) an instruction written in a programming language, usu in assembly language, which generates and is replaced by a series of microinstructions. **Macrolepidop'tera** n pl the larger butterflies and moths. **mac'rolide** n any of a class of antibiotics used to treat bacterial infections. **macrol'ogy** n much talk with little to say. **mac'ro-marketing** n marketing set in the context of the whole of a country's economy and social needs (cf **micromarketing**). **macromolec'ular** adj. **macromol'ecule** n a large molecule, esp one formed from a number of simpler molecules. **macronu'trient** n any substance required in large amounts by living organisms. **mac'rophage** /-fāj/ n any of the large phagocytic cells sited in the walls of blood vessels and found in connective tissue, usu immobile but stimulated into mobility by inflammation. **macrophotog'raphy** n close-up photography producing images larger than life-size. **macropin'akoid** and **mac'roprism** n (crystallog) a pinakoid and prism parallel to the macrodiagonal. **mac'ropod** n an animal of the **Macropod'idae** /-ē/ (Gr pous, podos foot), the family of marsupials comprising the kangaroos and related animals. **macrop'terous** adj (Gr pteron a wing) long-winged; long-finned. **macroscop'ic** adj visible to the naked eye, opp to microscopic; concerned with larger units. **macroscop'ically** adv. **macrosporan'gium** n (pl **-ia**) same as **megasporangium** (see under **mega-**). **mac'rospore** n same as **megaspore** (see under **mega-**). **Macrozā'mia** n (Gr zamia loss) a genus of Australian cycads; (without cap) a plant of this genus. **Macrura** /mak-roo'rə/ n pl (Gr ourā tail) a group of decapod crustaceans including lobsters, shrimps, prawns, etc. **macru'ral** or **macru'rous** adj long-tailed.

macron /mak'ron or -rən, or mā'kron or -krən/ n a straight line placed over a vowel to show it is long (as in ē), opp to breve. [Gr makros]

mactation /mak-tā'shən/ n killing or slaughter, esp of a sacrificial victim. [L mactātiō, -ōnis]

macula /mak'ū-lə/ n (pl **maculae** /-lē/) a spot, eg on the skin, the sun or a mineral. [L macula a spot]
■ **mac'ular** adj spotted; patchy; relating to the macula lutea. **mac'ulate** vt to spot or stain; to defile. ◆ adj /-lit/ spotted, stained; defiled. **maculā'tion** n the act of spotting or staining; a spot. **mac'ulāture** n an impression taken to remove remaining ink from an engraved plate before re-inking. **mac'ule** n a macula; a mackle. **mac'ulose** adj spotted.
❑ **macula lutea** /loo'ti-ə/ n (L luteus yellow) the yellow spot (qv).

macumba /ma-kŭm'ba/ n a religious cult in Brazil combining elements of Christianity and voodoo. [Port]

MAD /mad/ abbrev: magnetic anomaly detection, a technique for detecting submarines by checking underwater levels of magnetism; mutual assured destruction, a theory of nuclear deterrence.

mad /mad/ adj (**madd'er**; **madd'est**) mentally disordered or deranged; insane; resulting from or caused by madness; extremely and recklessly foolish; (often with about or for) extremely enthusiastic; infatuated; violently affected by pain, strong emotion, appetite, etc; furious with anger (inf; orig US); extravagantly playful or exuberant; rabid. ◆ vt (Shakesp) to drive mad. ◆ vi (archaic) to be mad; to act madly or irrationally. [OE gemǣd(e)d; OSax gimēd foolish]
■ **madd'en** vt to make mad; to enrage. ◆ vi to go mad; to act as if mad. **madd'ening** adj driving to madness; making very angry; extremely annoying. **madd'eningly** adv. **madd'ing** adj (archaic) distracted, acting madly. **madd'ingly** adv (archaic). **mad'ling** n (archaic) a mad person. **mad'ly** adv insanely, irrationally; frantically; extremely (inf). **mad'ness** n.
❑ **mad'brain** or **mad'brained** adj (Shakesp) mentally disordered; rash; hot-headed. **mad'-bred** adj (Shakesp) bred in madness or heat of passion. **mad'cap** n a person who acts madly; a wild, rash, or hot-headed person; an exuberantly playful person. ◆ adj fond of wild and reckless or extravagantly playful behaviour. **mad cow disease** n bovine spongiform encephalopathy (see under **bovine**). **mad'-doctor** n (obs) a person who studied and treated mental illness. **Mad Hatter** n a character in Lewis Carroll's Alice in Wonderland given to irrational behaviour and logic-chopping (see also **hatter** under **hat**). **mad'house** n a place characterized by noise, confusion, and unpredictable behaviour; a mental hospital (obs). **mad'man** or **mad'woman** n a man or woman who is insane; a foolish and reckless man or woman. **mad'wort** n a plant believed to cure canine madness (Alyssum, Asperugo, etc).
■ **go mad** to go insane; to become very angry (inf). **like mad** with great speed or energy, furiously. **mad as a hatter** see under **hat**.

Madagascan /ma-də-gas'kən/ adj of or relating to the island of Madagascar in the Indian Ocean, or to its inhabitants, or the Malagasy language. ◆ n a native or inhabitant of Madagascar.
❑ **Madagascar jasmine** same as **stephanotis**.

madam /mad'əm/ n (pl **mad'ams**; in the second sense, **Mesdames** /mā-däm'/) a courteous form of address to a woman, esp an elderly or married one, or any female customer in a shop, restaurant, etc; (with cap) the form of address to a woman in a formal letter; a woman of social rank or station; prefixed to an official title, as Madam Chairman, etc; the female head of a household (archaic); a formidable woman; a capricious or autocratic woman; a general term of reproach for a woman; a precocious young girl; a concubine (obs); the woman in charge of a brothel; (with cap) prefixed to a name instead of Mrs or Miss (in USA to distinguish mother-in-law from daughter-in-law; obs). ◆ vt to address as madam. [Fr ma my, and dame lady, from L mea domina]
■ **madame** /ma-däm', mad'əm/ n (usu with cap) (pl **mesdames** /mā-däm', -dam'/) used instead of Mrs as a title for a Frenchwoman or French-speaking woman; extended to any woman in an artistic profession, or one regarded as exotic, such as a palm-reader.

mad-apple /mad'a-pl/ n an aubergine; the Dead Sea apple (see under **apple**); a gallnut produced by the Asiatic gall wasp (Cynips insana). [From some form of Mod L melongēna, Ital melanzana; mālum insānum, transl as mad apple]

madarosis /ma-də-rō'sis/ (pathol) n abnormal loss of hair, esp of the eyebrows or eyelashes. [Gr madarōsis, from madaros bald, madaein to fall off]

madder /mad'ər/ n a herbaceous plant (Rubia tinctorum) whose root produces a red dye; any other species of Rubia. [OE mæddre, mædere; ON mathra, Du mede, later meed, mee]
□ **madd'er-lake** n a pigment mixed with either oil or water, made from madder root.
■ **field madder** a minute, lilac-flowered plant (Sherardia arvensis) of the same family.

maddock /mad'ək/ (dialect) n same as **mattock**.

made /mād/ pat and pap of **make**.
□ **made dish** n a dish composed of various ingredients, often recooked. **made ground** n ground formed by artificial filling in. **made man** or **woman** n a man or woman whose prosperity is assured. **made man** or **guy** n (sl) a man who has been initiated into the higher ranks of the Mafia. **made road** n a road with a surface constructed of tarmac, etc, not merely formed by traffic; a road with a metalled as opposed to a gravel surface. **made'up'py** or **made'-up'py** adj (sl) artificially invented. **made wine** n wine fermented from the juice of imported grapes.
■ **be** or **have it made** (inf) to have one's prosperity assured. **made for** ideally suited to or for. **made to measure** or **order** made to individual requirements. **made up** put together, finished; parcelled up; dressed for a part, disguised; wearing cosmetic make-up; meretricious; artificial, invented, fictional; highly delighted, chuffed (inf); consummate (Shakesp).

madefy /mad'i-fī/ (archaic) vt to moisten or make wet. [L madefacere, -factum, from madēre to be wet]
■ **madefac'tion** n.

Madeira /mə-dē'rə or -dā'/ n a rich fortified white wine produced in Madeira.
□ **Madeira cake** n a plain, rich sponge cake.

madeleine /mad-len' or mad'ə-lān/ n a small, plain sponge cake, often baked in the shape of a shell. [Fr, prob named after Madeleine Paulmier, 19c French pastry cook]

Madelenian same as **Magdalenian**.

mademoiselle /mad-mwa-zel'/ n a form of address to, or (with cap) a title for, an unmarried Frenchwoman or French-speaking woman, Miss (pl **Mesdemoiselles** /mād-/); a French governess or teacher. [Fr ma my, and demoiselle; see **damsel**]

maderize or **-ise** /mad'ə-rīz/ vi (of white wine) to become rusty in colour and flat in taste, as a result of absorbing too much oxygen during maturation. [Fr madériser, from the colour of Madeira wine]
■ **maderizā'tion** or **-s-** n.

madge¹ /maj/ n a lead hammer. [Woman's name]

madge² /maj/ n the barn owl; the magpie. [Appar from the woman's name]

madid /mad'id/ adj wet, dank. [L madidus, from madēre to be wet; related to Gr madaein]

madison /mad'i-sən/ n a high-speed track cycling event in which teams of two riders are in continuous relay with each other. [Madison Square Gardens, New York City, where first staged]

Madison Avenue /mad'i-sn av'ə-nū/ n the US advertising and public-relations industries; the characteristic methods or attitudes of these. [From the street which is their centre in New York City]

Madonna /mə-don'ə/ n the Virgin Mary, esp as represented in works of art; as a form of address, my lady (Shakesp). [Ital, literally, my lady, from L mea domina]
■ **madonn'aish** adj. **madonn'awise** adv after the fashion of the Madonna, esp in the arrangement of a woman's hair.
□ **Madonn'a-lily** n the white Mediterranean lily (Lilium candidum), which produces trumpet-shaped flowers.

madoqua /mad'ō-kwə/ n a very small Ethiopian antelope. [Amharic midaqua]

madras /mə-dräs'/ n a large, usu brightly-coloured headscarf, formerly exported from Madras (now Chennai) in SE India; a fine cotton or silk fabric, often with a woven stripe; sunn; a kind of medium-hot curry.

madrasa, madrassa, madrasah, madrassah /ma-dras'a/ or **medresa**, etc /mə-dres'ə/ n a Muslim college; a mosque school. [Ar madrasah]

madrepore /mad'ri-pōr, -pör/ n a coral (genus Madrepora) of the common reef-building type, occurring esp in tropical seas. [Ital madrepora from madre mother, from L māter, and Gr pōros a soft stone, stalactite, etc, or L porus a pore]
■ **madreporic** /-por'ik/ or **madreporit'ic** adj. **mad'reporite** or **madreporic plate** n in echinoderms, a perforated plate serving as opening to the stone canal.

madrigal /mad'ri-gəl/ n an unaccompanied song in several parts in counterpoint (music); a lyrical poem suitable for such treatment. [Ital madrigale, prob from LL mātricālis primitive, simple (from L mātrix, see **matrix**), altered under the influence of Ital mandria a herd, from L mandra, from Gr mandrā a stall, stable, sty, etc]
■ **madrigā'lian** adj. **mad'rigalist** n.

madrilène /mad'ri-len or -lēn/ n cold consommé flavoured with tomato juice. [Fr, from Sp madrileño of Madrid]

Madrileño /ma-dri-len'yō/ n (pl **Madrileñ'os**) a native or citizen of Madrid, the capital of Spain. [Sp madrileño from Madrid]

madroño /ma-drō'nyō/ n (pl **madrō'ños**) an evergreen tree of the genus Arbutus of N California, with thick, shiny leaves and edible berries (also **madrō'ña** /-nyə/ or **madro'ne**). [Sp madroño]

madzoon see **matzoon**.

mae see **mo¹**.

Maecenas /mī- or mē-sē'nas/ n a rich patron of art or literature. [After a Roman knight who befriended Virgil and Horace]

maelid /mē'lid/ (myth) n an apple nymph. [Gr mēlon apple, soft-skinned fruit]

maelstrom /māl'strom/ n a particularly powerful whirlpool; (with cap) a well-known whirlpool off the coast of Norway; a confused or disordered state of affairs; any resistless overpowering influence for destruction. [Du (now maalstroom), a whirlpool]

maenad /mē'nad/ n a female follower of Bacchus, a bacchante (Gr myth); a woman beside herself with frenzy. [Gr mainas, -ados raving, from mainesthai to be mad]
■ **maenad'ic** adj bacchanalian; furious.

Maeonian /mē-ō'ni-ən/ n and adj (a) Lydian. [Gr Maionia an old name for Lydia]
■ **Maeonides** /mē-on'i-dēz/ n Homer, as a supposed native of Lydia.

maerl /mä'ûrl/ n (a mass of) calcified red seaweed. [Breton]

maestoso /mä-e-stō'sō, mī-stō'sō/ (music) adj and adv with dignity or majesty. ◆ n (pl **maesto'sos**) a movement to be performed in this way. [Ital]

maestro /mī'strō, mä-es'trō/ n (pl **maestros** /mī'strōz/ or **maestri** /mä-es'trē/) a master, esp an eminent musical composer or conductor; (**Maestro**®) a European system of electronic funds transfer at point of sale (EFTPOS). [Ital]

Mae West /mā west/ n an airman's inflatable life jacket, used in World War II. [From its supposed resemblance, when inflated, to the figure of the American film star of that name (1892–1980)]

MAFF /maf/ abbrev: Ministry of Agriculture, Fisheries and Food (now replaced by **DEFRA**).

Maffia see **Mafia**.

maffick /maf'ik/ vi to celebrate exuberantly and boisterously. [By back-formation from Mafeking (now Mafikeng), South Africa, treated jocularly as a gerund or participle, from the scenes in the streets of London on the news of the relief of the town (1900)]
■ **maff'icker** n. **maff'icking** n.

maffled /maf'ld/ (inf) adj mentally confused, baffled.
■ **maff'lin** or **maff'ling** n a simpleton.

Mafia or **Maffia** /mä'fē-ə/ n a spirit of opposition to the law in Sicily, hence a preference for private and unofficial rather than legal justice; a secret criminal society originating in Sicily, controlling many illegal activities, eg gambling, narcotics, etc, in many parts of the world, and particularly active in the USA (also called **Cosa Nostra**); (also without cap) any group considered to be like the Mafia in the criminal and unscrupulous use of power, fear, etc to gain its ends. [Sicilian Ital mafia]
■ **Mafioso** /-fē-ō'sō, -zō/ n (pl **Mafiosi** /-sē, -zē/) a member of the Mafia (also without cap and as adj).

mafic /maf'ik/ (mineralogy) n a mnemonic term for the ferromagnesian and other non-felsic minerals present in an igneous rock. [magnesian, felsic]

ma foi /ma fwa'/ (Fr) interj my goodness (literally, upon my faith).

mag¹ /mag/ (inf) n short form of **magazine** (periodical publication).

mag² /mag/ (dialect) vi to chatter. ◆ vt to tease; (Walter Scott **magg**) to steal. ◆ n chatter; the magpie; the long-tailed titmouse. [From the name Margaret]
■ **mags** or **maggs** n pl (perh same as **mag³**; Scot) a gratuity; the free allowance granted to some workers, esp drinks for brewery employees.
□ **mags'man** n a street swindler.

mag³ /mag/ or **meg** /meg/ (archaic sl) n a halfpenny (also **maik** (now Scot) or **make** /māk/).

mag. /mag/ abbrev: magnesium; magnetic; magnetism; magnitude.

magalogue or **magalog** /mag'ə-log/ (inf) n a large mail-order catalogue in the form of a magazine. [*magazine* and cata*log(ue)*]

magazine /ma-gə-zēn', mag'ə-/ n a periodical publication containing articles, stories, etc, by various people, and often aimed at a specific group of readers; a television or radio programme containing a variety of news and factual reports; *orig* a storehouse; a place for military stores; a ship's powder-room; a metal container for additional cartridges in some automatic firearms; a similar device for feeding photographic slides or film into a projector. [Fr *magasin* store, from Ital *magazzino*, from Ar *makhāzin*, pl of *makhzan* a storehouse]
❑ **magazine'-gun** or **-rifle** n a gun or rifle from which a succession of shots can be fired without reloading.

Magdalen or **Magdalene** /mag'də-lən, -lēn or (in the name of the Oxford and Cambridge colleges) *mōd'lin*/ n (without *cap*) a repentant prostitute; an institution for receiving such persons (*abbrev* for *Magdalene hospital* or *asylum*). [Mary *Magdalene*, ie of Magdala (Bible, Luke 8.2), on the assumption that she was the woman in Luke 7.37–50]

Magdalenian /mag-də-lē'ni-ən/ or **Madelenian** /mad-/ (*archaeol*) *adj* belonging to an upper Palaeolithic culture that succeeded the Solutrean and preceded the Azilian. ◆ n the Magdalenian culture. [La *Madeleine*, a cave in the Dordogne region of France]

Magdeburg hemispheres /mag'de-bûrg hem'i-sfērz/ n pl two hemispherical cups held together by atmospheric pressure when the air is pumped out from between them. [Invented at *Magdeburg* in Germany]

mage /māj/ see under **magus**.

Magellanic clouds /ma-jə-lan'ik klowdz, or -gə-/ n pl two galaxies in the southern hemisphere, appearing to the naked eye like detached portions of the Milky Way, the nearest galaxies to the earth. [Ferdinand *Magellan* (c.1480–1521), Portuguese navigator]

Magen David /mä-gän' dä-vēd'/ n the Star of David (also **Mogen David** /mō'gən dō'vid/). [Heb, shield of David]

magenta /mə-jen'tə/ n the dyestuff fuchsine; its colour, a reddish purple. ◆ *adj* reddish-purple. [From its discovery about the time of the battle of *Magenta* in N Italy (1859)]

magg see under **mag**[2].

maggie /mag'i/ (*dialect*) n a magpie.

maggot /mag'ət/ n a legless grub, *esp* of a fly; a fad or whim; a whimsical or improvised tune (*obs*). [Poss a modification of ME *maddok*, *mathek*, dimin, see **mawk**]
■ **maggotorium** /-tō', -tö'/ n a place where maggots are bred for sale to fishermen. **magg'oty** *adj* full of maggots; crotchety; very drunk (*sl*).

maggot-pie see **magpie**.

maggs see **mag**[2].

Maghreb or **Maghrib** /mag'rəb/ n the countries of NW Africa collectively, sometimes including Libya (also *adj*). [Ar, the West]

magi and **magian** see **magus**.

magic /maj'ik/ n the art of producing marvellous results by compelling the aid of spirits, or by using the secret forces of nature, such as the power supposed to reside in certain objects as 'givers of life'; enchantment; sorcery; the art of producing illusions by sleight of hand; a secret or mysterious power over the imagination or will. ◆ *vt* (**mag'icking; mag'icked**) to affect or produce by, or as if by, magic. ◆ *adj* relating to, used in, or done by, magic; causing wonderful or startling results; marvellous, exciting (*inf*). [Gr *magikē* (*technē*) magic (art). See **magus**]
■ **mag'ical** *adj* relating to magic; wonderful, enchanting. **mag'ically** *adv*. **magician** /mə-jish'ən/ n a person skilled in magic; a wizard or sorcerer; an enchanter; a conjuror; a wonder-worker.
❑ **magic bullet** n (*inf*) a drug, etc, that is capable of destroying bacteria, cancer cells, etc without adversely affecting the host. **magic carpet** n one that, in fairy stories, can transport people magically through the air. **magic circle** n any privileged group to which many aspire but few are admitted (*inf*); see also **magic square** below. **magic eye** n a miniature cathode-ray tube in a radio receiver which helps in tuning the receiver by indicating, by means of varying areas of luminescence and shadow, the accuracy of the tuning; a lightbeam focused on a photoelectric cell which activates an automatic door, security alarm, etc, when broken. **magic lantern** n an apparatus for projecting pictures on slides onto a screen. **Magic Marker**® n (also without *cap* or **magi-marker**) a thick fibre-tip pen used for writing on display boards, etc. **magic mushroom** n any of various mushrooms, eg *Psilocybe mexicana*, which contain a hallucinogen. **magic number** n any number having particular significance in a specific context. **magic pyramid** n a puzzle resembling a Rubik's Cube (qv), but in the shape of a tetrahedron with similarly shaped pieces. **magic (or magical) realism** n a style of art, literature or cinema in which fantastical or surreal events or images are presented in a realistic or everyday context. **magic (or magical) realist** n. **magic square**,

circle, **cube**, **cylinder** or **sphere** n a figure filled with rows of numbers so arranged that the sums of all the rows will be the same, perpendicularly, horizontally or diagonally (as the square formed from the three rows 2, 7, 6; 9, 5, 1; 4, 3, 8).
■ **black magic** the black art, magic by means of evil spirits. **natural magic** the art of working wonders by a superior knowledge of the powers of nature; the power of investing a work of art with an atmosphere of imagination; sleight of hand. **sympathetic magic** magic aiming at the production of effects by mimicry, such as bringing rain by libations, or injuring a person by melting or sticking pins in his or her image. **white magic** magic without the aid of the Devil.

magilp see **megilp**.

Maginot-minded /mä'zhē-nō-mīn'did/ *adj* over-concerned with the defensive (*milit*); static in ideas. [From the abortive French *Maginot* Line fortifications (1929–35) along the German border, named after war minister André *Maginot* (1877–1932)]

magister /mə-jis'tər/ n a person licensed to teach in a medieval university; still used in the degree titles of *Magister Artium*, etc. [L *magister* master]
■ **magisterial** /maj-is-tē'ri-əl/ *adj* relating or suitable to, or in the manner of, a teacher, master artist, or magistrate; of the rank of a magistrate; authoritative; dictatorial; of a magistery. **magistē'rially** *adv*. **magistē'rialness** n. **magistē'rium** n the philosopher's stone; teaching authority or function. **magistery** /maj'is-tə-ri/ n in alchemy, a transmuting agent, such as the philosopher's stone; a product of transmutation; a precipitate; any sovereign remedy; magisterium. **magistral** /mə-jis'trəl, maj'is-/ *adj* of or relating to a master; masterly; authoritative; specially prescribed for a particular case as a medicine; effectual; guiding or determining the other positions (*fortif*). ◆ n (*obs*) a magistral medicine; a magistral line (*fortif*). **magistrand** /maj'/ n (at Scottish universities, now only at St Andrews and Aberdeen) an arts student ready to proceed to graduation.
❑ **Magister Artium** /mə-jis'tər är'shi-əm/ n Master of Arts.

magistrate /maj'i-strāt/ n a person with the power of putting the law in force, *esp* a justice of the peace, a provost, or a bailie. [Ety as for **magister**]
■ **mag'istracy** /-trə-si/ n the office or rank of a magistrate; magistrates in general; a body of magistrates. **magistratic** /-trat'ik/ or **mag'istral** *adj*. **mag'istrature** n.
❑ **magistrates' court** n an inferior court composed of justices of the peace or district judges with both criminal and civil jurisdiction.

Maglemosian /mag-li-mō'zi-ən/ (*archaeol*) *adj* of or designating a culture represented by finds at *Maglemose* in Denmark, transitional between Palaeolithic and Neolithic. ◆ n the Maglemosian culture.

maglev /mag'lev/ *adj* of a railway, train, carriage, etc, operating by *magnetic levitation* (qv); relating to this form of transport.

magma /mag'mə/ n (pl **mag'mata** /-mə-tə/ or **mag'mas**) a pasty or doughy mass of organic or mineral material; molten or pasty rock material; a glassy base of a rock. [Gr *magma*, *-atos* a thick ointment]
■ **magmatic** /-mat'ik/ *adj*. **mag'matism** n.

Magna Carta or **Magna Charta** /mag'nə kär'tə/ n the Great Charter obtained from King John in 1215, the basis of English political and personal liberty (*hist*); any document establishing rights. [L]

magna cum laude /mag'nə kum lö'dē, mag'nä kŭm low'de/ (L) with great distinction; used as the mark of the second level of excellence in N American universities (L *laus*, *laudis* praise).

magnalium /mag-nā'li-əm/ n a light, strong, easily-worked and rust-resisting alloy of *magnesium* and *aluminium*, used in aircraft construction, etc.

magnanimity /mag-nə-nim'i-ti/ n greatness of soul; that quality of mind which raises a person above all that is mean or unjust; generosity. [L *magnanimitās*, from *magnus* great, and *animus* mind]
■ **magnanimous** /-nan'-/ *adj*. **magnan'imously** *adv*.

magnate /mag'nāt, -nit/ n a person of rank or wealth, or of power; a noble. [L *magnās*, *-ātis*, from *magnus* great]

magnes /mag'nēz/ (*archaic*) n lodestone (also (*Spenser*) **mag'nesstone**). [L and Gr *magnēs*]

magnesium /mag-nē'z(h)i-əm, -z(h)yəm, -shi-əm, -shyəm/ n a bright silver-white metallic element (symbol **Mg**; atomic no 12), burning with a dazzling white light. [*Magnesia*, in Thessaly, eastern Greece]
■ **magnē'sia** n an imagined substance sought by the alchemists (*obs*); manganese (*obs*); a light white powder, oxide of magnesium; basic magnesium carbonate, used as a medicine. **magnē'sian** *adj* belonging to, containing, or resembling magnesia. **magnesite** /mag'nəs-īt/ n native magnesium carbonate.
❑ **Magnesian Limestone** n dolomite rock; a division of the Permian of England.

magnet /mag'nit/ n the lodestone (**natural magnet**); a bar or piece of metal, *esp* iron, to which the property of attracting other substances containing iron or some other metals has been imparted and which,

when suspended, will point approximately north to south; anyone or anything that attracts (*fig*). [Through OFr or L, from Gr *magnētis* (*lithos*) Magnesian (stone), from *Magnēsiā*, in Lydia or Thessaly] ■ **mag'netar** *n* (for 'magnetic star'; cf **pulsar** under **pulsate**) a dense neutron star with a magnetic field 10^{14} times stronger than that of the earth. **magnetic** /*mag-net'ik*/ or **magnet'ical** *adj* relating to magnets or to magnetism; having, or capable of acquiring, the properties of a magnet; attractive; strongly affecting others by personality; hypnotic. **magnet'ically** *adv*. **magnetician** /*-ish'ən*/ *n* a magnetist. **magnet'ics** *n sing* the science of magnetism. **mag'netism** *n* the cause of the attractive power of the magnet; the phenomena connected with magnets; the science that deals with the properties of magnets; attraction; influence of personality. **mag'netist** *n* a scientist specializing in magnetism. **mag'netite** *n* magnetic iron ore (Fe_3O_4), called lodestone when polar. **magnetīz'able** or **-s-** *adj*. **magnetīzā'tion** or **-s-** *n*. **mag'netize** or **-ise** *vt* to make magnetic; to attract as if by a magnet; to hypnotize (*archaic*); to convert (a school) into a magnet school (*US*). **mag'netīzer** or **-s-** *n*. **magneto** /*mag-nē'tō*/ *n* (*pl* **magnē'tos**) short form of **magneto-electric machine**, a small generator with a permanent magnet, used for ignition in an internal-combustion engine, etc. **mag'neton** *n* a natural unit of magnetic moment. **mag'netron** *n* a two-electrode valve in which the flow of electrons from a large central cathode to a cylindrical anode is controlled by crossed electric and magnetic fields, used to give high-powered microwave radiation. **magnon** /*mag'non*/ *n* a quantum of spin wave energy in magnetic material.
❑ **magnet** (**high**) **school** *n* in the USA, a school that, in addition to providing a general education, specializes in teaching a particular subject such as science, languages or performing arts. **magnetic battery** *n* several magnets placed with their like poles together, so as to act with great force. **magnetic board** *n* a white enamelled metal board upon which material for display is mounted by means of magnetic strips. **magnetic bottle** *n* the containment of a plasma during thermonuclear experiments by applying a specific pattern of magnetic fields. **magnetic bubble memory** or **store** *n* (*comput*) same as **bubble memory** (see under **bubble**). **magnetic card** *n* a piece of plastic or cardboard with a magnetizable surface on which data can be stored. **magnetic chuck** *n* a chuck having a surface in which alternate steel elements, separated by insulating material, are polarized by electromagnets, allowing light flat work to be held securely. **magnetic confinement** *n* (*nuclear eng*) in fusion research, the use of shaped magnetic fields to confine a plasma. **magnetic curves** *n pl* the curves formed by iron-filings around the poles of a magnet. **magnetic dip** or **inclination** *n* the angle between the horizontal and the line of the earth's magnetic field. **magnetic disk** or **disc** *n* (*comput*) a flat, circular sheet of material coated with a magnetic oxide, used to store programs and data. **magnetic diskette** *n* (*comput*) same as **floppy disk** (see under **flop¹**). **magnetic drum** *n* a storage device used in early computers, consisting of a rotating cylinder with a magnetic coating. **magnetic equator** *n* the line round the earth where the magnetic needle remains horizontal. **magnetic field** *n* the space over which magnetic force is felt. **magnetic fluid** *n* a hypothetical fluid formerly assumed to explain the phenomena of magnetism. **magnetic flux** *n* the surface integral of the product of the permeability of the medium and the magnetic field intensity perpendicular to the surface. **magnetic flux density** *n* the product of the field intensity and the permeability of the medium. **magnetic forming** *n* use of magnetic fields to shape metal. **magnetic induction** *n* induced magnetization in magnetic material; magnetic flux density. **magnetic ink** *n* ink with magnetic quality, used eg in printing cheques that are to be sorted by machine. **magnetic ink character recognition** *n* the reading by a computer of numbers printed in magnetic ink (*abbrev* **MICR**). **magnetic lens** *n* the counterpart of an optical lens, in which a magnet or system of magnets is used to produce a field which acts on a beam of electrons in a similar way to a glass lens on light rays. **magnetic levitation** *n* suspension of eg a train above a track by means of a magnetic field. **magnetic media** *n* a collective term for all forms of magnetic recording media, such as magnetic disks, tape, etc. **magnetic meridian** *n* the vertical plane through the magnetic needle. **magnetic mine** *n* a mine sunk to the sea-bottom, detonated by a pivoted magnetic needle when a ship approaches. **magnetic mirror** *n* (*nuclear eng*) a device based on the principle, used in mirror machines, that ions moving in a magnetic field towards a region of considerably higher magnetic field strength are reflected. **magnetic moment** *n* a measure of the magnetic strength of a permanent magnet, a current-carrying coil, a moving charge or individual atom in a magnetic field. **magnetic monopole** see **monopole**. **magnetic needle** *n* the light bar in the mariner's compass which, because it is magnetized, always points to the north. **magnetic north** *n* the direction indicated by the magnetic needle. **magnetic poles** *n pl* two nearly opposite points on the earth's surface, where the dip of the needle is 90°. **magnetic resonance imaging** *n* a medical imaging technique using the magnetic resonances of protons in the body tissue (*abbrev* **MRI**). **magnetic storm** *n* a disturbance in the

magnetism of the earth. **magnetic stripe** *n* (also **mag'-stripe**) a horizontal stripe on the back of a credit card, etc, which is read electronically to identify the card. **magnetic tape** *n* flexible plastic tape, coated on one side with magnetic material, used to register for later reproduction television images, or sound, or computer data. **magnetic therapy** *n* a therapeutic treatment using the properties of magnetic fields, eg to increase the permeability of cell walls and to accelerate the healing of fractures. **magnetic variation** *n* the angular difference between true north and magnetic north at a particular location.
■ **animal magnetism** Mesmer's name for hypnotism; the power to hypnotize; according to Christian Science, the false belief that mortal mind exists (and has power to transfer thoughts); sexual power of attraction due entirely to physical attributes. **artificial magnet** a magnet made by rubbing with other magnets. **bar magnet** a magnet in the form of a bar. **horse-shoe magnet** a magnet bent like a horseshoe. **permanent magnet** a magnet that keeps its magnetism after the force which magnetized it has been removed. **personal magnetism** the power of a personality to make itself felt and to exercise influence. **terrestrial magnetism** the magnetic properties possessed by the earth as a whole.

magneto- /*mag-nē-tō-*/ *combining form* denoting: magnetic; relating to magnetism; magneto-electric. [**magnet**]
■ **magneto-elas'tic** *adj* (of a material) that increases in elasticity when exposed to a magnetic field. **magnē'to-elec'tric** or **-elec'trical** *adj* relating to or operated by magneto-electricity. **magnē'to-electric'ity** *n* electricity produced by the action of magnets; the science concerned with this. **magnē'toencephalog'raphy** *n* the measuring of the weak magnetic signals produced by the brain. **magnē'tograph** *n* an instrument for recording the variations of the magnetic elements. **magnē'tohydrodynam'ic** *adj*. **magnē'tohydrodynam'ics** *n sing* a branch of mathematical physics dealing with interactions between an electricity-conducting fluid (such as an ionized gas) and a magnetic field; the practical application of such interactions to producing magnetohydrodynamic power by means of a **magnetohydrodynamic generator**. **magnetometer** /*mag-ni-tom'i-tər*/ *n* an instrument for measuring the strength or direction of a magnetic field, *esp* the earth's. **magnetom'etry** *n*. **magnētomō'tive** *adj* producing a magnetic flux. **magnēto-op'tical** *adj*. **magnēto-op'tics** *n sing* the study of the influence of magnetism on light (**magneto-optical effect** see **Kerr effect**). **magnetoresist'ive** *adj* (of a metal or semiconductor) exhibiting a change in electrical resistance when subjected to a magnetic field. **magnet'osphere** *n* that region surrounding the earth within which the behaviour of charged particles is influenced by the earth's magnetic field; any similar region surrounding another body. **magnetospher'ic** *adj*. **magnētostric'tion** (or /*-net'*/) *n* (*phys*) the phenomenon of elastic deformation of certain ferromagnetic materials, eg nickel, on the application of magnetizing force. **magnē'totail** *n* the tail-like region of a planet's magnetosphere, formed by the action of the solar wind.

magnifiable see under **magnify**.

magnific /*mag-nif'ik*/ or **magnifical** /*-i-kl*/ (*archaic*) *adj* magnificent; exalted; pompous. [L *magnificus*; cf **magnify**]
■ **magnif'ically** *adv*. **magnif'ico** *n* (*pl* **magnif'icoes**) (Ital, magnificent) a Venetian noble; a grandee.

Magnificat /*mag-nif'i-kat*/ *n* the song of the Virgin Mary (Bible, Luke 1.46–55) beginning in the Vulgate with this word; a song of praise or thanksgiving, a paean. [L '(my soul) doth magnify', 3rd pers sing pr indic of *magnificāre*]

magnification see under **magnify**.

magnificence /*mag-nif'i-səns*/ *n* the quality of being magnificent; well-judged liberality (*archaic*). [L *magnificēns, -entis*, literally, doing great things]
■ **magnif'icent** *adj* great in deeds or in show; noble; displaying greatness of size or extent; very fine, excellent (*inf*); pompous. **magnif'icently** *adv*.

magnifico see under **magnific**.

magnify /*mag'ni-fī*/ *vt* (**mag'nifying**; **mag'nified**) to make great or greater; to enlarge; to cause to appear greater; to exaggerate; to praise highly. ◆ *vi* (*archaic sl*) to signify. [L *magnificāre*, from *magnus* great, and *facere* to make]
■ **mag'nifiable** *adj* that may be magnified. **magnification** /*-fi-kā'shən*/ *n* the act, power or degree of magnifying; state of being magnified; enlarged appearance, state or copy; extolling. **mag'nifier** /*-fī-ər*/ *n* a person who, or instrument that, magnifies or enlarges, *esp* a pocket-lens (**magnifying glass**); a person who extols.

magniloquent /*mag-nil'ə-kwənt*/ *adj* speaking in a grand or pompous style; bombastic. [L *magnus* great, and *loquēns, -entis*, prp of *loquī* to speak]
■ **magnil'oquence** *n*. **magnil'oquently** *adv*.

magnitude /mag'ni-tūd/ n greatness; size; extent; importance; a measure of the intensity of a star's brightness (*astron*; see also **of the first magnitude** below). [L *magnitūdō*, from *magnus* great].
■ **absolute magnitude** see under **absolute**. **of the first magnitude** (of a star) of the first degree of brightness (*astron*); of a very important, significant or catastrophic kind (*fig*).

magnolia /mag-nō'li-ə, -lyə/ n any tree of the N American and Asiatic genus *Magnolia*, with beautiful foliage, and large solitary flowers, giving name to the family **Magnolia'ceae**, with a petaloid perianth and spirally arranged stamens and carpels; a light pinkish-white or purplish-white colour. ◆ *adj* of this colour. [Pierre *Magnol* (1638–1715), French botanist]
■ **magnolia'ceous** *adj*.

Magnox® /mag'noks/ (also without *cap*) n a material consisting of any of various magnesium-based alloys containing a small amount of aluminium, from which containers for the fuel of certain nuclear reactors are made. ◆ *adj* denoting a container or reactor using this material. [*magnesium no oxidation*]

magnum /mag'nəm/ n (pl **mag'nums**) a two-quart bottle or other container; as a bottle-size of champagne or other wine, the equivalent of two ordinary bottles, containing *usu* $1\frac{1}{2}$ litres; two quarts of alcohol. [L *magnum* (neuter) big]

magnum opus /mag'nəm ō'pəs, mag'nŭm op'ŭs/ (*L*) n a great work, *esp* of literature or learning; a writer's greatest achievement or the culmination of his or her efforts.

Magnus effect /mag'nəs i-fekt'/ or **Magnus force** /förs/ n the force which acts on a cylinder rotating in a stream of fluid flowing in a direction perpendicular to the cylinder's axis, the force thrusting in a direction perpendicular to both the axis and the direction of the flow. [HG *Magnus* (1802–70), German scientist]

Magog see **Gog and Magog**.

magot /mag'ət, mä-gō'/ n the Barbary ape; a small grotesque figure, in Chinese or Japanese workmanship. [Fr]

magot-pie see **magpie**.

magpie /mag'pī/ n the pie (*Pica pica*), a black-and-white chattering bird of the same type as the crow (also (*Shakesp*) **mag'ot-pie** or **magg'ot-pie**); extended to other black-and-white or pied birds (in Australia, a piping crow); a chattering person; an Anglican bishop (*obs*); a hit on the penultimate outermost division of a target (*shooting*); a person who hoards or steals objects (*fig*); a halfpenny (*obs sl*). [*Mag* or *Magot*, short form of *Margaret*, and **pie**³]
❑ **magpie lark** n a ground-dwelling black-and-white Australian bird (*Grallina cyanoleuca*). **magpie moth** n the moth of the gooseberry caterpillar.

magsman see under **mag²**.

maguey /mag'wā, mä-gā'i/ n agave. [Sp]

magus /mā'gəs/ n (pl **ma'gi** /-jī/) (in ancient Persia) a priest or member of a priestly class; an Eastern magician; a magician; (with *cap*) any of the Three Wise Men from the East who brought gifts to the infant Christ. [L, from Gr *magos*, from OPers *magus*]
■ **mage** /māj/ n a magus or sorcerer. **mage'ship** n. **mā'gian** *adj* relating to the magi or to a sorcerer. ◆ *n* a magus; a sorcerer. **mā'gianism** or **mā'gism** n the philosophy or teaching of the magi.

Magyar /mag'yär, mod'yor/ n a member of the majority ethnic group of Hungary; the Finno-Ugric language of Hungary. ◆ *adj* of the Magyars or their language; (without *cap*; of a garment) cut with the sleeves in a piece with the rest. [Magyar]
■ **Mag'yarism** n Hungarian nationalism. **Mag'yarize** or **-ise** *vt* and *vi* to make or become Magyar.

Mahabharata /mə-hä-bä'rə-tə/ n one of the great Sanskrit epics of ancient India, which describes the war between the descendants of Bharata. [Sans]

Mahadeva /mə-hä-dā'və/ n Siva. [Sans *mahat* great, and *deva* god]

maharaja or **maharajah** /mä-hä-rä'jä, mə-hä-rä'jə/ (*hist*) n a great Indian prince, *esp* a ruler of a state. [Hindi, from Sans *mahat* great, and *rājan* king]
■ **maharani** or **maharanee** /-rä'nē/ n (Sans *rānī* queen) the wife or widow of a maharaja; a woman with the rank of a maharaja in her own right.

maharishi /mä-hä-rē'shi/ n a leading instructor in the Hindu faith. [Sans *mahat* great, and *rishi* sage]

mahatma /mə-hät'mä, -hat'mə/ n a religious sage; an adept; a wise and holy leader. [Sans *mahātman* high-souled]

Mahayana /mä-hə-yä'nə/ n the most widespread form of Buddhism, practised *esp* in China, Japan, Tibet and the Himalayas, that seeks enlightenment for all humanity, embraces many methods for attaining it, and recognizes many texts as scripture (cf **Hinayana**). ◆ *adj* relating to or characteristic of this form of Buddhism. [Sans, literally, great vehicle]
■ **Mahaya'nist** n.

maha yoga /mä'hə yō'gə/ n a form of yoga practised with a master that incorporates all eight classical yogas (also called **siddha yoga**). [Sans *mahat* great]

Mahdi /mä'dē/ n (also **Meh'di**) the great leader of the faithful Muslims, who is to appear in the last days; a title of various insurrectionary leaders, *esp* one who overthrew the Egyptian power in Sudan in 1884–5. [Ar *mahdīy*]
■ **Mah'diism** or **Mah'dism** n. **Mah'diist** or **Mah'dist** n and *adj*.

Mahican see **Mohican**.

mahi-mahi /mä-hē-mä'hē/ n the dolphinfish, *esp* its flesh prepared as food. [Hawaiian, from *mahi* strong]

mah-jong or **mah-jongg** /mä-jong'/ n an old Chinese table game for four, played with small painted bricks or 'tiles'. [Chin, literally, sparrows, perh in allusion to the chattering sound of the tiles during play]

mahlstick see **maulstick**.

mahmal /mä'mäl/ n the empty litter sent to Mecca in the hadj. [Ar]

mahoe /mä'hō-i/ n a small, bushy white-barked tree of New Zealand. [Maori]

mahogany /mə-hog'ə-ni/ n a tropical American tree (*Swietenia mahogoni*) of the family Meliaceae; its wood, valued for furniture-making; the colour of the wood, a dark reddish-brown; a dining table (*inf*); gin and treacle (*obs sl* or *dialect*); brandy and water (*obs sl*). ◆ *adj* made of or like mahogany; dark reddish-brown. [Origin unknown]

Mahommedan and **Mahometan** see **Mohammedan**.

mahonia /mə-hō'ni-ə/ n a plant of the pinnate-leaved *Mahonia* genus (or section of *Berberis*) of the barberry family. [Bernard *McMahon* (died 1816), Irish-American gardener and botanist]

Mahoun /mə-hown', -hoon'/ or **Mahound** /-hownd', -hoond', also *mä'/* n Mohammed, imagined in the Middle Ages to be a pagan god (*archaic*); /mə-hoon'/ the Devil (*Scot*). [Short form of *Mahomet*]

mahout /mä-howt'/ n the keeper and driver of an elephant. [Hindi *mahāut, mahāwat*]

Mahratta see **Maratha**.

mahseer or **mahsir** /mä'sēr/ n a large freshwater fish (species *Barbus*) of N India. [Hindi *mahāsir*]

mahua or **mahwa** /mä'(h)wä/ n (also **mowa** or **mowra**) a kind of butter-tree (*Bassia*, or *Illipe*, *latifolia*) with edible flowers; an alcohol distilled from its flowers. [Hindi *mahūā*]
❑ **mahua butter** n a fat obtained from the seeds of the mahua.

mahzor or **machzor** /mahh-zōr', mähh'zōr/ n (pl **mahzorim** or **machzorim** /-ēm'/) the Jewish prayer-book used for festivals and other special occasions. [Heb *mahzor* a cycle]

maid /mād/ n an unmarried woman, *esp* one who is young (*archaic* and *poetic*); a virgin (*archaic*); a spinster; a female servant; a young skate. ◆ *vi* to work as a maidservant. [Short for **maiden**]
■ **maid'hood** n. **maid'ish** *adj*. **maid'less** *adj* without a maid.
❑ **maid'-child** n (*Shakesp*) a girl. **maid'-pale** *adj* (*Shakesp*) pale, like a sick girl. **maid'servant** n a female servant.
■ **maid of all work** or **maid'-of-all'-work** (*archaic*) a maid who does general housework. **maid of honour** see under **honour**. **old maid** a spinster; an extremely fussy or excessively cautious person; a card game in which players match pairs of cards from a pack of 51, the loser being left with the unmatched card.

maidan /mī-dän'/ n an open plain; an open space near a town, used as a sports ground or parade ground in India, Pakistan, etc. [Urdu, from Pers *maidān*]

maiden /mā'dn/ n a maid; a corn-maiden (*Scot*); a washing dolly; a clothes-horse; a horse that has never won a race; (*usu* with *cap*) a Scottish beheading machine similar to a guillotine (*hist*); a maiden over (*cricket*); a one-year-old tree (*hortic*). ◆ *adj* unmarried; virgin; female; relating to a virgin or young woman; consisting of maidens; unpolluted (*fig*); fresh; new; unused; in the original or initial state; grown from a seed; that has never been captured, climbed, trodden, penetrated, pruned, etc; (of a horse) that has never won a race; first. [OE *mægden*]
■ **maid'enhead** /-hed/ n (ME sfx -*hēd*(e) -hood) virginity; the first attempt, experience, or use of anything (*obs*); the hymen. **maid'enhood** n the state or time of being a maiden; maidenhead. **maid'enish** *adj* (*derog*) like a maiden. **maid'enlike** *adj* and *adv*. **maid'enliness** n. **maid'enly** *adj* maidenlike; becoming a maiden; gentle; modest. ◆ *adv* in the manner of a maiden.
❑ **maiden assize** n (*legal hist*) an assize at which no criminal cases were heard. **maiden aunt** n an unmarried aunt. **maiden battle** n a first contest. **maiden castle** n a common (though largely unexplained) name for a prehistoric earthwork; a castle that has never been captured. **maiden century** n (*cricket*) a batsman's or batswoman's first century. **maiden fortress** n a fortress that has never been

captured. **maid'enhair** *n* a fern (genus *Adiantum*) with fine footstalks; extended to species of spleenwort (**maid'enhair-spleenwort**). **maid'enhair-tree** *n* the ginkgo. **maiden herring** same as **maatjes**. **maid'en-meek** *adj* (*literary*) meek as a maiden. **maiden name** *n* the surname of a married woman before marriage. **maiden over** *n* (*cricket*) an over in which no runs are scored by the batsmen. **maiden pink** *n* a wild species of pink, *Dianthus deltoides*. **maiden speech** *n* a person's first speech, *esp* that of an MP in Parliament. **maiden stakes** *n sing* (in horse-racing) the prize in a race (**maiden race**) between horses that have not previously won a race. **maid'en-tongued** *adj* (*Shakesp*) soft-spoken, like a girl. **maiden voyage** *n* the first voyage of a ship, etc. **maid'enweed** *n* mayweed. **maid'en-widowed** *adj* (*Shakesp*) widowed while still a virgin.

maidism /mā'i-di-zm/ (*pathol*) *n* pellagra (attributed to a maize diet). [**maize**¹]

maieutic /mī- or mā-ū'tik/ *adj* (of the Socratic method of inquiry) bringing out latent thoughts and ideas. [Gr *maieutikos*, from *maia* good woman, a midwife; Socrates, son of a midwife, called himself a midwife to men's thoughts]
■ **maieut'ics** *n sing* the Socratic method.

maigre /mā'gər, meg'r'/ *adj* (of food) containing no animal flesh and so able to be eaten on a fast-day; relating to a fast-day or to a fast. ◆ *adv* (*obs*) without using animal flesh. ◆ *n* (also **meagre** /mē'gər/) a large Mediterranean food-fish (*Sciaena aquila*); any of various fishes of the family Sciaenidae, noted for making a croaking or drumming sound. [Fr *maigre* lean, from L *macer*]

maik /māk/ *n* same as **mag**³ or **make**³.

maiko /mī'kō/ *n* (*pl* **mai'ko** or **maik'os**) an apprentice geisha. [Jap]

mail¹ /māl/ *n* post, the postal system; correspondence; a batch of letters, parcels, etc; the person or method of transport by which mail is conveyed; a bag for carrying letters, parcels, etc; the contents of such a bag; a travelling bag (*obs*). ◆ *vt* to post; to send by post. [OFr *male* a trunk, a mail, from OHGer *malha, malaha* a sack]
■ **mail'able** *adj* capable of being sent by mail. **mail'er** *n* a special container for items sent by post; a promotional leaflet sent by post; a person who dispatches letters, periodicals, etc, by post; a program that sends electronic mail (*comput*). **mail'gram** *n* (*US*) a message sent electronically to a post office and then delivered to the addressee by ordinary mail. ◆ *vt* to send a mailgram to. **mail'ing** *n* a batch of items sent by post.
❑ **mail'bag** or (*esp N Am*) **mail'sack** *n* a bag in which mail is carried. **mail'-boat** *n* a boat that carries the public mail. **mail bomb** *n* a massive amount of electronic mail sent to a computer with the aim of filling up space in the computer's memory, and so causing it to stop functioning. **mail'box** *n* a letter-box (*esp N Am*); a file for storing electronic mail (*comput*). **mail'-cart, -coach, -car, -carriage, -drag** or **-gig** *n* a cart, etc, formerly used to carry the public mail; a small hand-cart, with long handles, for the conveyance of children. **mail'-catcher** *n* an apparatus for catching mail-bags thrown from a moving train. **mail drop** *n* a receptacle for mail (*N Am*); a delivery of mail, circulars, etc. **mail'-in** *n* (*esp N Am*) circulation of surveys, etc, by post. **mailing list** *n* a list of, or computer file containing, the names and addresses of those to whom advertising material, information, etc, is to be posted. **mailing machine** *n* any of various machines used in an office to seal, address, frank, etc, outgoing mail. **mail'man** or **mail'-carrier** *n* (*N Am*) a postman. **mail'merge** *n* (a computer program for) the producing of a series of letters addressed to individuals by merging a file of names with a file containing the text of the letter (also *vi*). **mail order** *n* an order for goods to be sent by post. **mail'-order** *adj*. **mail'-out** *n* a bulk sending of mail, a mailshot. **mail'-plane, mail'-train** or **mail'van** *n* an aeroplane, train or van that carries the public mail. **mail'room** *n* a room in an office, etc, for dealing with incoming and outgoing mail. **mail'shot** *n* an item of unsolicited, *usu* advertising, material sent by post (also *vt*).

mail² /māl/ *n* defensive armour for the body, formed of overlapping or meshed steel rings; armour generally; the protective shell or scales of an animal. ◆ *vt* to clothe in mail. [Fr *maille*, from L *macula* a spot or a mesh]
■ **mailed** *adj* covered in or protected by mail.
❑ **mail'-clad** *adj* (*Walter Scott*) wearing a coat of mail. **mailed fist** *n* (*fig*) physical or military force.

mail³ /māl/ (*Scot*; now chiefly *law*) *n* payment; rent. [Late OE *māl*, from ON *māl* speech, agreement; cf OE *mǣl*]
■ **mail'er** *n* a person who pays rent, *esp* a tenant farmer; a cottar. **mail'ing** *n* a rented farm; rent paid for this (*obs*).

mail⁴ or **maile** /māl/ (*obs*) *n* a halfpenny. [Anglo-Fr *mayle*, from assumed LL *metallea*; see **medal**]

mail⁵ /māl/ (*Scot*) *n* a spot, *esp* one caused by iron oxide on cloth. ◆ *vt* to spot or stain. [OE *māl*; see **mole**²]

mail⁶ /māl/ *vt* to wrap up (*obs*); to confine (a bird) in a handkerchief, etc, to tame or silence it (*falconry*). [Ety doubtful, poss as for **mail**¹]

maillot /mä'yō/ *n* tights worn by a ballet-dancer, gymnast, etc; a one-piece close-fitting swimsuit; a jersey. [Fr, literally, swaddling-clothes]

maim /mām/ *vt* to disable; to mutilate; to lame or cripple; to make defective. ◆ *n* (*archaic*) serious bodily injury; an injury, a disability; the loss of any essential part. ◆ *adj* (*obs*) maimed, crippled. [OFr *mahaing*]
■ **maimed** *adj*. **maimedness** /mām'd', mā'mid-nis/ *n*. **maim'ing** *n*.

main¹ /mān/ *adj* great; extensive; important; chief, principal; first in importance or extent; leading; general; strong (*Milton*); sheer (as in *main force*). ◆ *n* strength, *esp* in the phrase *might and main*; the principal part; the mainland; the high sea; a great expanse (*Shakesp* and *Milton*); a principal pipe or conductor in a branching system distributing water, gas, electricity, etc; (in *pl*) the water, gas or electricity supply available through such a system; that which is essential; the most part; purpose (*obs*). ◆ *adv* (*Scot* or *dialect*) exceedingly. [Partly OE *mægen* strength, partly ON *meginn* strong; influence of OFr *maine, magne*, (from L *magnus*) great, is questioned]
■ **main'ly** *adv* chiefly, principally; much (*obs* or *dialect*).
❑ **main'boom** *n* the spar that extends the foot of a fore-and-aft mainsail. **main'brace** *n* the brace attached to the mainyard (see also **splice**). **main chance** see under **chance**. **main clause** *n* (*grammar*) same as **principal clause** (see under **principal**). **main course** *n* the mainsail on square-rigged ships; the principal course of any meal. **main'-deck** *n* the principal deck of a ship. **main'door** *n* a door giving independent access to a house, distinguished from one opening into a common passage; a ground-floor house in a tenement building or villa-block, entered from the front by a door of its own (*Scot*). **main drag** see under **drag**. **main'frame** *n* a large, powerful computer, often with many simultaneous users, as opposed to a minicomputer or microcomputer. ◆ *adj* (of a computer) that is a mainframe. **main'land** /-lənd, -land/ *n* the principal or larger land, as opposed to neighbouring islands. **main'lander** *n*. **main line** *n* a railway line between important centres; a principal route, course, etc; an important vein (*sl*). **main'line** *adj* of or situated on a major route. ◆ *vi* and *vt* (*sl*) to take (a narcotic) intravenously; to consume (something) voraciously or at speed. **main'liner** *n*. **main'lining** *n*. **main'mast** /-məst, -mäst/ *n* the principal mast, usually second from the prow. **main memory** *n* (*comput*) same as **main store** below. **main plane** *n* the wings of an aeroplane considered as a unit. **main purpose rule** *n* (*law*) a rule presuming that an exemption clause in a contract, etc, is not intended to defeat the main object of that contract. **main'sail** /-sl, -sāl/ *n* the principal sail, generally attached to the mainmast. **main sequence** *n* (*astron*) the principal sequence of stars on the Hertzsprung-Russell diagram, running diagonally from upper left (high temperature, high luminosity) to lower right (low temperature, low luminosity) and containing about 90% of all known stars. **main'sheet** *n* the sheet or rope attached to the lower corner of the mainsail. **main'spring** *n* the spring that gives motion to any piece of machinery, *esp* that of a watch or a clock; principal motive, motivating influence (*fig*). **main'stay** *n* a rope stretching forward and down from the top of the mainmast; chief support. **main store** *n* the part of a computer's memory holding data and programs before, during, and after processing or execution. **main stream** *n* a river with tributaries; the chief direction or trend in any historical development, including that of an art. **main'stream** *adj* relating to the main stream (*lit* and *fig*); (of cigarette smoke) that which is drawn into a smoker's mouth or lungs; (of swing) coming in the line of development between early and modern (*jazz*); in accordance with what is normal or standard. ◆ *vt* (*esp N Am*) to make mainstream; to integrate (children with disabilities) into classes of able-bodied children (*educ*). **main'streaming** *n*. **Main Street** *adj* (*US*; also without *cap*) relating to the most mediocre or materialistic aspects of town or city life. **main'streeting** *n* (*Can*) electioneering or canvassing of support by a political candidate in the main streets of town, etc. **main'top** *n* a platform on the top of the lower mainmast. **maintop-gall'ant-mast** *n* the mast above the maintopmast. **maintop'mast** *n* the mast next above the lower mainmast. **maintop'sail** *n* the sail above the mainsail, in square-rigged ships. **main'yard** *n* the lower yard on the mainmast.
■ **in the main** for the most part; on the whole. **might and main** utmost strength. **Spanish Main** see under **Spanish**.

main² /mān/ (*obs*) *n* a banker's shovel for coins. [OFr *main*, from L *manus* hand]

main³ /mān/ *n* in games of chance, a number (5 to 9) called before throwing the dice; a game of chance; a cockfighting match; a set of cocks engaged in a match; a match in some other sports, *esp* bowling (now *dialect*). [Perh same as **main**²]

main⁴ /mān/ (*dialect*; *Shakesp*) *vt* to lame, maim.

Maine Coon /mān koon/ *n* a large domestic cat with a long tail. [*Maine*, the US state]

mainor, mainour /mā'nər/ or **manner** /man'ər/ (archaic or hist) n act or fact, esp of theft; that which is stolen. [Anglo-Fr meinoure, mainoure, mainoevere ; see **manoeuvre**]

■ **in** or **with the manner** in the act; in possession of the thing stolen.

mainpernor see under **mainprise**.

mainprise /mān'prīz/ (legal hist) n suretyship, esp for the appearance of a prisoner. [Anglo-Fr mainprise, mainpernour, from main hand, and prendre to take]

■ **mainpernor** /-pûr'nər/ n a person who gives mainprise.

mains /mānz/ (Scot) n pl a home farm. [**demesne** and **domain**]

maintain /mān-tān', mən-, men-/ vt to observe or practise; to keep in existence or in any state; to preserve from capture, loss or deterioration; to uphold; to carry on; to keep up; to support; to make good; to support by argument; to affirm; to defend; to support in an action in which one is not oneself concerned (law). [Fr maintenir, from L manū (ablative) tenēre to hold in the hand]

■ **maintainabil'ity** n. **maintain'able** adj. **maintained'** adj financially supported, eg (of a school, etc) from public funds. **maintain'er** n. **maintenance** /mān'tən-əns/ n the act of maintaining, supporting or defending; continuance; the means of support; defence, protection; (formerly illegal) outside interference in a lawsuit, etc in favour of one of the parties (law). ◆ vt to keep in working order.

❑ **main'tenance-man** n a man keeping machines, etc in working order.

■ **cap of maintenance** (hist) a cap formerly worn by or carried before a person of high office or rank. **maintain capital intact** (econ) to make good that part of a company's or country's capital goods consumed in production.

maiolica see **majolica**.

mair /mār/ Scots form of **more**.

maire /mer/ (Fr) n mayor.

maise /māz/ same as **mease**[1].

maison de ville /me-zõ də vēl'/ (Fr) n a town house or residence in town.

maisonnette or **maisonette** /mā-zə-net', -sə-/ n a small house or flat. [Fr maisonnette]

maister /mā'stər/ (obs or Scot) same as **master**.

■ **mais'terdome** n (obs). **mais'tring** n (obs). **mais'try** n (obs).

Mai Tai /mī tī/ n a cocktail containing rum, triple sec, grenadine and lime juice. [Tahitian maitai good]

maître de ballet /metr' də ba-le'/ n (also fem **maîtresse de ballet**) a person who trains dancers and takes rehearsals (formerly acting also as choreographer). [Fr, ballet-master]

maître d'hôtel /metr' dō-tel'/, also (inf) **maître d'** /metr' dē'/ n a house-steward or major domo; the manager of a hotel; a head waiter. See also **à la maître d'hôtel**.

maize[1] /māz/ n a tall cereal grass (Zea mays) grown esp in America, producing large ears (corncobs) of yellow kernels which are eaten as a vegetable or dried and ground into meal (also called **Indian corn** or **mealies**); the yellow colour of maize kernels. [Sp maíz, from Taino mahís]

■ **water maize** a giant perennial water lily (Victoria regia) native to tropical America.

maize[2] /māz/ same as **mease**[1].

Maj abbrev : Major.

majesty /maj'i-sti/ n the greatness and glory of God; grandeur; dignity; elevation of manner or style; royal state; a title of monarchs (His, Her or Your, Majesty ; Their or Your Majesties); a representation of God (sometimes Christ) enthroned; the canopy of a hearse. [Fr majesté, from L mājestās, -ātis, from mājor, mājus, compar of magnus great]

■ **majestic** /mə-jes'tik/ or **majes'tical** adj having or exhibiting majesty; stately; sublime. **majes'tically** adv in a majestic manner. **majes'ticalness** or **majes'ticness** n (obs) majesty.

Majlis /mäj-lis'/ n (also **Mejlis'**) the Iranian parliament; (also without cap) an assembly or council in various N African and Middle-Eastern countries. [Pers majlis]

majolica /mə-jol'i-kə, -yol'/ or **maiolica** /-yol'/ n tin-glazed, often highly decorated earthenware, produced esp in Italy in the 16c. [Ital maiolica from Majorca, from where it perh originated]

❑ **majol'icaware** n.

major /mā'jər/ adj greater, or great, in number, quantity, size, value or importance; (in boys' schools) senior; greater (than minor) by a semitone (music); involving a major third (see below; music). ◆ n a person of full legal age (in UK, before 1970, 21 years; from 1970, 18 years); an officer in rank between a captain and lieutenant-colonel; by courtesy, a sergeant-major; an officer in charge of a military band; anything that is major opposed to minor; (in pl) the major sports leagues (US); (a student taking) a main subject of study at a university

or college (N Am, Aust and NZ); a film company, record label, etc with a large distribution network; a kind of wig (obs). ◆ vi to specialize in a particular subject at college (with in ; N Am, Aust and NZ); to strut around with a self-important air (Walter Scott); to specialize in a particular product, etc (with in or on). ◆ vt to channel or concentrate (one's activities, efforts, etc) in a particular direction. [L mājor, compar of magnus great]

■ **majorat** /mä-zhō-rä/ n (Fr) primogeniture. **majorette'** n a member of a group of girls who march in parades, etc, wearing decorative, military-style uniforms, and usu twirling batons or playing instruments. **majorett'ing** n the practice of performing as majorettes. **majority** /mə-jor'i-ti/ n the greater number; the greater part, the bulk; the difference between the greater and the lesser number; pre-eminence; full age (see n above); (the party with) the winning margin or votes in an election; the office or rank of major. ◆ adj of the majority. **ma'jorly** adv (sl) extremely. **ma'jorship** n.

❑ **major axis** n (maths) (in conic sections) the axis passing through the foci. **major-dō'mō** n (pl **major-dō'mōs**) (Sp mayordomo, from Med L mājor domūs) an official who has the general management in a large household; a general steward. **major-gen'eral** n an officer in the army next in rank below a lieutenant-general. **major-gen'eralcy** or **major-gen'eralship** n the office or rank of major-general. **major histocompatibility complex** n (immunol) the collection of genes coding for the major histocompatibility antigens, which are involved in determining acceptance or rejection of transplanted organs (abbrev **MHC**). **majority carrier** n (electronics) in a semiconductor, the type of carrier (electrons or holes) that carries most of the measured current. **majority rule** n government by members, or by a body including members, of the largest ethnic group(s) in a country, as opposed to a political system which excludes them. **majority verdict** n the verdict reached by the majority in a jury, as distinct from a unanimous verdict. **major key, mode** or **scale** n (music) a key, mode or scale with its third a major third above the tonic. **major orders** n pl in the Roman Catholic Church, the higher degrees of holy orders, ie bishop, priest and deacon. **major piece** n (chess) a queen or rook. **major planet** n a planet of the solar system, as opposed to an asteroid. **major premise** n (logic) the premise in which the major term occurs. **major suit** n (bridge) spades or hearts, valued more highly than diamonds or clubs. **major term** n (logic) the term which is the predicate of the conclusion. **major third** n (music) an interval of four semitones. **major tone** n an interval of vibration ratio 8:9.

■ **go over to** or **join the majority** to die. **in the majority** forming the larger group or number.

Majorcan /mə-yör'kən or -jör'/ or **Mallorcan** /-yör' or -lör'/ adj of or relating to the Mediterranean island of Majorca or its inhabitants. ◆ n a native or inhabitant of Majorca.

majoritaire /mä-zho-rē-ter'/ (Fr) n a member of a majority section of a political party, esp of a socialist one.

majority see under **major**.

Major Mitchell /mā'jər mich'əl/ (Aust) n a cockatoo, Caeatua leadbeateri, with pink and white plumage. ◆ vi (facetious) to follow a zigzag route; to become lost. [Major Sir Thomas Mitchell (1792–1855), surveyor and explorer]

majuscule /maj'ə-skūl, mə-jus'kūl/ (palaeog) n a large letter whether capital or uncial. ◆ adj written or printed in large letters. [L (littera) mājuscula somewhat larger (letter)]

■ **majus'cular** adj.

mak /māk/ Scots form of **make**[1].

■ **makar** n see **maker** under **make**[1].

Makah /mə-kä'/ n (a member of) a tribe of Native Americans, mainly living in Washington state; the Wakashan language of the Makah. ◆ adj of or relating to the Makah or their language.

Makaton /mak'ə-ton/ n a simplified sign language used with young children and people with learning disabilities. [From the names of its developers, Margaret Walker, Kathy Johnston and Tony Cornforth]

make[1] /māk/ vt (**māk'ing**; **māde**) to fashion, frame, construct, compose or form; to create; to bring into being; to produce; to conclude, contract; to bring about; to perform; to force; to cause; to result in; to cause to be; to convert or turn; to appoint; to render; to represent as doing or being; to reckon; to get as result or solution; to occasion; to bring into any state or condition; to establish; (in the navy) to promote; to prepare; to shut (as a door) (Shakesp); to shuffle (cards); to declare as trumps (cards); to win a trick (cards); to obtain, gain or earn; to score; to constitute; to amount to; to count for; to turn out; to be capable of turning or developing into or serving as; to arrive in sight of; to reach, succeed in reaching; to accomplish, achieve; to attempt, offer or start; to be occupied with; to do; to cause or assure the success of; to persuade (esp a woman) to have sexual intercourse with one (sl); to have sexual intercourse with (sl). ◆ vi to behave (as if), esp in order to deceive; to proceed; to tend, to result; to contribute; to flow; to versify (archaic); to be in condition for making; to matter (as it *maksna*, it does not matter; *Scot*). ◆ *n* form or shape; structure, texture; build; formation; manufacture; brand; type; making; character or disposition; quantity made; establishment of an electric circuit or contact; trump declaration (*cards*). [OE *macian*; Ger *machen*]

■ **mak'able** or **make'able** *adj*. **māk'er** *n* a person who makes; (with *cap*) the Creator; (*esp* in Scots form, **makar** /*mak'*, *mäk'ər*/) a poet (*archaic*); the declarer (*bridge*); a jack in cards (*obs*); a caulker's tool. **māk'ing** *n* the act of forming (often in combination, as in *bread-making*, *cabinetmaking*, etc); structure; form; (in *pl*) gains; (in *pl*) materials or qualities from which something can be made; (in *pl*) materials used to prepare cigarettes, heroin, etc (*sl*).

□ **make'-and-break'** *n* the making and breaking of an electrical circuit; a device which causes this to happen. **make'bate** *n* (*archaic*) a mischief-maker. **make'-believe** *vi* see **make believe** below. ◆ *n* feigning (also **make'-belief**). ◆ *adj* feigned. **make'-do** *adj* makeshift. **make'-or-break'** *adj* see **make or break** below. **make'over** *n* a complete change in the style of a person's dress, appearance, etc, *esp* one following professional advice; a complete reorganization of a company under new management; an act of refurbishing a property, vehicle, etc. **make'-peace** *n* (*Shakesp*) a peace-maker. **make'-ready** *n* preparation of a letterpress sheet for printing, so as to obtain evenness of impression. **make'shift** *n* a temporary expedient or substitute. ◆ *adj* of the nature of or characterized by a temporary expedient. **make'under** *n* (*inf*) a complete change of dress, appearance, etc to make a person seem less glamorous. **make'-up** *n* (also without hyphen) the way anything is arranged, composed, or constituted, or the ingredients in its constitution; one's character, temperament, or mental qualities; cosmetics for self-beautification, worn *esp* by women, and by actors as an aid to impersonation; the effect produced thereby; the arrangement of composed types into columns or pages (*printing*). **make'-weight** *n* something which is thrown into a scale to make up the weight; a person or thing of little value added to compensate for a deficiency. **man'bag** *n* a bag for small articles carried by men. **man crush** *n* (*sl*) a heterosexual man's feeling of admiration for another man. **man-man'ager** *n* a person regarded in a terms of ability to direct the work of others (as in *a good man-manager*).

■ **be the making of** to ensure the success of. **have the makings of** to have all the necessary ability and inclination to become. **in the making** in the process of being formed, developed, etc, or of becoming. **make account of** see under **account**. **make a face** to grimace, contort the features. **make a figure** to be conspicuous. **make a fool of** see under **fool**[1]. **make after** to follow or pursue. **make against** to militate or tell against. **make a (good) meal**, **dinner**, etc to dine, etc (plentifully or heartily). **make allowances for** see under **allow**. **make a meal of** see under **meal**[1]. **make amends** to render compensation or satisfaction. **make an ass of oneself** to behave like a fool. **make a night** (or **day**) **of it** to extend an, *esp* enjoyable, activity through the whole night (or day). **make as if** or (*N Am*) **make like** or **as though** to act as if, to pretend that. **make at** to make a hostile movement against. **make away** (**with**) to put out of the way, get rid of, destroy, kill (see also **make off** or **away with** below). **make believe** to pretend, feign; to play at believing. **make bold** see under **bold**. **make certain** (**of**) to find out; to put beyond doubt; to secure. **make do** (**with**) to manage (with the *usu* inferior or inadequate means available). **make down** to refashion so as to fit a smaller person; to turn down the sheets and blankets of (*Scot*). **make eyes at** see under **eye**[1]. **make for** to set out for, seek to reach; to favour. **make free with** see under **free**. **make friends** to become friendly; to acquire friends. **make good**, **make light of**, **make little of**, **make love to**, **make merry** see under **good**, etc. **make head or tail of** to find any sense in. **make it** to reach an objective; to succeed in a purpose; to become a success (*inf*); to have one's way sexually (with) (*sl*). **make much of** to treat with fondness, to cherish, to foster; to turn to great account; to find much sense in, succeed in understanding. **make no doubt** to have no doubt, to be confident. **make nothing of** to regard as being of little importance; to have no hesitation or difficulty in (doing); to be totally unable to understand. **make of** to construct from (as material); to understand by; to make much of, to pet (*obs and Scot*); to esteem (*obs*). **make off** to decamp. **make off** or **away with** to run away with. **make on** (*Shakesp*) to make much of. **make one's way** to proceed; to succeed. **make or break** or **make or mar** to be the crucial test that brings success or failure to (**make'-or-break'** *adj*). **make or meddle with** to have to do with, interfere with. **make out** to descry, to see; to discern; to decipher; to comprehend, understand; to prove; to seek to make it appear; to draw up; to achieve (*obs*); to fill up; to make do, get along somehow; to succeed; to engage in lovemaking (with) (chiefly *N Am*; *sl*). **make over** to remake or reconstruct; to make a complete change in a person's style of dress, appearance, etc; to transfer (**make'over** *n*). **make sail** to increase the quantity of sail; to set sail. **make someone's day** see under **day**. **make sure** (**of**) to ascertain; to put beyond doubt or risk; to secure; to feel certain; to betroth (*obs*). **make the best of** to turn to the best advantage; to take in the best spirit. **make the most of** to use to the best advantage. **make up** to

fabricate; to feign; to collect; to put together; to parcel; to put into shape; to arrange; to settle (an argument); to become friends again (after a quarrel, etc); to constitute; to repair; to complete, supplement; to adjust one's appearance (as an actor for a part); to apply cosmetics to the face; to put type, etc into columns and pages; to set out and balance (accounts); to make good; to compensate; to decide (*Shakesp*). **make up one's mind** to come to a decision. **make up to** to make friendly, adulatory, or amorous approaches to; to compensate. **make way** see under **way**[1]. **make with** (*inf*; *orig N Am*) to start using, doing, etc (something), to bring on or into operation. **meet one's maker** to meet God, to die. **of one's own making** entirely the result of one's own decisions and actions. **on the make** (*inf*) bent on self-advancement or promotion, or on finding a sexual partner. **put the make on** (*sl*) to make sexual advances to.

make² /*māk*/ *n* same as **mag**[3].

make³ or (*Scot*) **maik** /*māk*/ (*obs* or *dialect*) *n* a mate or consort; an equal. [OE (*ge*)*mæcca*; see **match**[1]]
■ **make'less** *adj* without a mate; matchless.

makhani /*muk'ə-ni* or *mə-kä'ni*/ (*Ind cookery*) *adj* cooked in butter or cream. [Hindi, from *makkam* butter]

makimono /*mä-ki-mō'nō*/ *n* (*pl* **makimō'nos**) a long, painted scroll, often with narrative text, designed to be unrolled from right to left. [Jap, from *maki* roll, scroll, and *mono* thing]

Makkah or **Makah** /*mak'ə* or *-ä*/ *n* the Arabic name for **Mecca**.

mako¹ /*mä'kō*/ *n* (*pl* **ma'kos**) any of several sharks of the genus *Isurus* (also **mako shark**). [Maori]

mako² /*mä'kō*/ or **mako-mako** /*mä'kō-mä'kō*/ *n* (*pl* **ma'kos** or **ma'ko-ma'kos**) a small, evergreen tree of New Zealand with red berries that turn purple as they ripen (also called **wineberry**). [Maori]

makunouchi /*ma-kə-noo'chi*/ *n* the highest division in sumo wrestling; a top bout in this. [Jap]

MAL *abbrev*: Malaysia (IVR).

Mal. (*Bible*) *abbrev*: (the Book of) Malachi.

mal /*mal*/ (*Fr*) *n* pain, sickness.
□ **mal de mer** /*də mer*/ *n* seasickness. **mal du pays** /*dü pā-ē*/ *n* homesickness, nostalgia. **mal du siècle** /*dü syekl'*/ *n* depression about the state of the world (used by Sainte-Beuve (1833) and current in the 20c).
■ **grand mal** see under **grand**[2]. **petit mal** see under **petit**.

mal- /*mal-*/ *pfx* bad, badly; wrong, wrongly. [Fr, from L *male* badly]

Malabar-rat /*mal'ə-bär-rat'*/ *n* the bandicoot rat. [*Malabar* in India]

malabsorption /*mal-əb-sörp'shən*/ *n* poor absorption of one or more nutrients by the small intestine, a symptom of coeliac disease, cystic fibrosis, etc. [**mal-**]

Malacca-cane /*mə-lak'ə-kān*/ *n* a brown walking-stick made from the stem of a rattan. [*Malacca*, state in SW Malaysia, a centre of the trade]

malachite /*mal'ə-kīt*/ *n* a green mineral, basic copper carbonate. [Gr *malachē* mallow, as of the colour of a mallow leaf]

malacia /*ma-lā'shi-ə*/ (*med*) *n* pathological softening of tissue; abnormal appetite or food craving. [Gr *malakia* softness]

malacology /*ma-lə-kol'ə-ji*/ *n* the study of molluscs. [Gr *malakos* soft, and *logos* discourse]
■ **malacological** /-*kə-loj'*/ *adj*. **malacol'ogist** *n*.

malacophilous /*ma-lə-kof'i-ləs*/ (*bot*) *adj* pollinated by snails. [Gr *malakos* soft, and *phileein* to love]
■ **malacoph'ily** *n* pollination by snails.

Malacopterygii /*mal-ə-kop-tə-rij'i-ī*/ *n pl* a soft-finned suborder of bony fishes, including herrings and salmon. [Gr *malakos* soft, and *pteryx*, *pterygos* a wing or fin]
■ **malacopteryg'ian** *adj* and *n*.

Malacostraca /*ma-lə-kos'trə-kə*/ *n pl* the best-known class of crustaceans, including crabs, lobsters, shrimps, prawns, etc. [Gr *malakos* soft, and *ostrakon* a shell]
■ **malacos'tracan** *adj* and *n*. **malacos'tracous** *adj*.

maladaptation /*mal-a-dap-tā'shən*/ *n* faulty adaptation. [**mal-**]
■ **maladap'ted** *adj*. **maladap'tive** *adj*.

maladdress /*mal-ə-dres'*/ *n* awkwardness; clumsiness; tactlessness. [Fr *maladresse*]

maladjusted /*mal-ə-jus'tid*/ *adj* poorly or inadequately adjusted, *esp* to one's environment or circumstances; psychologically incapable of dealing with day-to-day situations. [**mal-**]
■ **maladjust'ment** *n*.

maladministration /*mal-əd-mi-ni-strā'shən*/ *n* bad management, *esp* of public affairs. [**mal-**]
■ **maladmin'ister** *vt*.

maladroit /mal'ə-droit, -droit'/ adj not dexterous; unskilful; clumsy; tactless. [Fr]
■ **maladroit'ly** adv. **maladroit'ness** n.

malady /mal'ə-di/ n illness; disease, whether of the body or the mind; a faulty condition. [Fr maladie, from malade sick, from L male habitus in ill condition, from male badly, and habitus, pap of habēre to have or hold]

mala fide /mā'lə fī'dē, mal'ä fē'dä/ (L) adv and adj in bad faith, treacherously.

Malaga /mal'ə-gə/ n a sweet dessert wine made from partially-dried grapes, from Málaga, in S Spain.

Malagasy /ma-lə-gas'i/, also (archaic) **Malagash** /-gash' or mal'/ adj of or relating to Madagascar, its inhabitants, or their language. ◆ n a native or inhabitant of Madagascar; the Austronesian language of Madagascar.

malagueña /ma-lə-gā'nyə/ n a Spanish dance or folk tune resembling the fandango. [Sp, belonging to the city of Málaga]

malaguetta /ma-lə-get'ə/ n grains of Paradise (also **malaguetta pepper**). [Origin obscure]

malaise /ma-lāz'/ n uneasiness, discomfort; a feeling of debility or of impending sickness; a general air of depression or despondency. [Fr malaise]

malakatoone same as **melocoton**.

malamute or **malemute** /mä'lə-mūt/ n (one of) a breed of powerful dogs with a double coat of hair, widely distributed in the Arctic regions and used esp for drawing sledges (also **Alaskan malamute** or **malemute**). [Inupiaq (Inuit language of W Alaska) malimiut]

malander, **mallander** or **mallender** /mal'ən-dər/ n an eruption of the skin behind a horse's knee (often in pl). [Fr malandre, from L malandria (sing or pl)]

malapert /mal'ə-pûrt/ (archaic) adj bold; forward; saucy; impudent. ◆ n a saucy or impudent person. [OFr, unskilful, from mal (L malus) bad, and appert for espert (L expertus; see **expert**) but understood in English as if from Fr apert open, outspoken, from L apertus open]
■ **mal'apertly** adv. **mal'apertness** n.

malapportionment /ma-lə-pōr'shən-mənt/ (US) n unequal or unfair apportioning of members to a legislative body. [**mal-**]

malappropriate /ma-lə-prō'pri-āt/ vt to misuse or misappropriate. [**mal-**]
■ **malappropriā'tion** n.

malapropism /mal'ə-pro-pi-zm/ n the misapplication of words without mispronunciation, from Mrs Malaprop in Sheridan's play, The Rivals, who uses words malapropos; a word so used.

malapropos /mal'a-prō-pō, mal-ə-prō-pō'/ adj out of place; unsuitable; inapt, inappropriate. ◆ adv inappropriately; untimely. ◆ n something untimely or inappropriate. [**mal-**]

malar /mā'lər/ adj of or relating to the cheek. ◆ n the cheekbone. [L māla the cheek, from mandere to chew]

malaria /mə-lā'ri-ə/ n a fever once attributed to bad air, actually due to a protozoan parasite transmitted by mosquitoes (med); poisonous air rising from marshes, once believed to produce fever; miasma. [Ital mala aria, from L malus bad, and āēr, āeris air]
■ **malā'rial**, **malā'rian** or **malā'rious** adj. **malārio'logist** n. **malārio'logy** n the study of malaria.

malarkey or **malarky** /mə-lär'ki/ (inf; orig US) n absurd talk; nonsense.

malassimilation /mal-ə-si-mi-lā'shən/ n imperfect assimilation or nutrition. [**mal-**]

malate see under **malic**.

Malathion® /ma-lə-thī'on/ n a phosphorus-containing insecticide used chiefly in the house and garden. [From diethyl maleate and **thio-**]

Malawian /mə-lä'wē-ən/ adj of or relating to the African country of Malawi or its inhabitants. ◆ n a native or inhabitant of Malawi.

malax /mal'aks/ or **malaxate** /-ak-sāt/ vt to soften by kneading, rubbing or mixing with a more liquid substance. [LL malaxāre to soften]
■ **mal'axage** n. **malaxā'tion** n specif the action of a wasp, etc chewing prey before feeding on it; a kneading movement in massage. **mal'axātor** n a kneading or grinding machine.

Malay /mə-lā'/ or **Malayan** /mə-lä'ən/ n a member of a people inhabiting Malaysia, Singapore and Indonesia (formerly known as the Malay Archipelago); the Austronesian language of the Malays. ◆ adj of the Malays, their language, or the countries inhabited by them. [Malay malāyu]
■ **Malay'sian** /-si-ən, -zhən or -shən/ adj relating to the Malay Archipelago or esp to Malaysia. ◆ n a native or inhabitant of Malaysia.

Malayalam or **Malayaalam** /ma-lə-yä'ləm/ n the Dravidian language of Kerala in SW India (also adj).

Malbec /mal'bek/ n a variety of grape orig grown near Malbec in SW France, used to produce red wine (also called in France **Cot** /kot/); a red wine produced from this grape.

malconformation /mal-kon-fōr-mä'shən/ n disproportionate or imperfect formation. [**mal-**]

malcontent /mal-kən-tent', mal'-kən-tent/ adj discontented or dissatisfied, esp in political matters. ◆ n /mal'-/ a discontented or disaffected person. [OFr malcontent]
■ **malcontent'ed** adj. **malcontent'edly** adv. **malcontent'edness** n.

mal del pinto see pinta[1].

mal de mer see under **mal**.

maldeployment /mal-di-ploi'mənt/ n inefficient use of personnel or other resources. [**mal-**]

maldistribution /mal-di-stri-bū'shən/ n uneven, unfair or inefficient distribution. [**mal-**]

Maldivian /möl-div'i-ən/ adj of or relating to the Maldives, an archipelago in the Indian Ocean, its inhabitants, or their language. ◆ n a native or inhabitant of the Maldives; another name for **Dhivehi**.

male[1] /māl/ adj masculine; of or relating to the sex that begets (not bears) young, or produces relatively small gametes; staminate (bot); adapted to fit into a corresponding hollow part (machinery). ◆ n a member of the male sex; apparently, a father (Shakesp). [OFr male, from L masculus male, from mās a male]
■ **male'ness** n.
❑ **male chauvinism** n. **male chauvinist** or **male chauvinist pig** n (inf; derog) a man who believes in the superiority of men over women and behaves accordingly (abbrev **MCP**). **male'-fern** n an elegant woodland fern formerly thought to be the male of the lady fern. **male menopause** n a critical period of change affecting late middle-aged men, often marked by decline in sexual power, loss of energy and decisiveness, etc. **male orchis** n the early purple orchis (cf **Orchis**). **male order** n (archit) the Doric order. **male pattern baldness** n the form of alopecia commonly affecting adult males. **male rhymes** n pl those in which stressed final syllables correspond. **male screw** see under **screw**.

male[2] /māl/ (Spenser) n same as **mail**[2].

maleate see under **malic**.

Malebolge /mä-lā-bol'jä/ n the eighth circle of Dante's Hell; a place characterized by filth or iniquity (fig). [Ital male bolge bad holes or pits, literally pockets]

malediction /ma-li-dik'shən/ n cursing; a calling down of evil, a curse. [L maledīcere, -dictum, from male ill, and dīcere to speak]
■ **maledicent** /-dī'sənt/ adj cursing. **mal'edict** /-dikt/ adj (archaic) accursed. ◆ vt and vi to curse. **maledic'tive** adj. **maledic'tory** adj.

malefactor /mal'i-fak-tər/ n an evil-doer; a criminal. [L malefacere to do evil]
■ **malefac'tion** n evil-doing; a crime, an offence (Shakesp). **malefac'tory** adj (rare). **malefic** /ma-lef'ik/ adj doing mischief; producing evil, baleful. **malef'ically** adv. **mal'efice** /-i-fis/ n (archaic) an evil deed; enchantment, sorcery. **maleficence** /-ef'i-səns/ n. **malef'icent** or **maleficial** /mal-i-fish'l/ adj (obs) hurtful; doing wrong.

maleffect /mal-i-fekt/ n an adverse effect. [**mal-**]

maleic see under **malic**.

malemute see **malamute**.

malengine /mal-en'jin/ (Spenser) n evil stratagem; deceit. [OFr malengin, from L malus, -um bad, and ingenium ingenuity]

malentendu /ma-lä-tä-dü'/ (Fr) n a misunderstanding.

malevolent /mə-lev'ə-lənt/ adj wishing evil; ill-disposed towards others; rejoicing in another's misfortune. [L malevolēns, -entis ill disposed, wishing evil]
■ **malev'olence** n. **malev'olently** adv.

malfeasance /mal-fē'zəns/ n evil-doing, wrongdoing (rare); an illegal deed, esp by an official (law). [Fr malfaisance, from L male ill, and facere to do]
■ **malfea'sant** adj and n.

malformation /mal-fōr-mä'shən/ n (a) faulty structure; (a) deformity. [**mal-**]
■ **malformed'** adj.

malfunction /mal-fungk'shən/ n the act or fact of working imperfectly. ◆ vi to work or function imperfectly. [**mal-**]
■ **malfunc'tioning** n.

malgrado /mal-grä'dō/ (obs) prep in spite of. [Ital]

malgre same as **maugre**.

malgré /mal-grā'/ (Fr) prep in spite of.

■ **malgré lui**, **moi**, etc in spite of his, my, etc efforts; willy-nilly. **malgré tout** /*too*/ nevertheless, all things considered.

mali or **mallee** /*mä'lē*/ *n* a member of the gardener caste in India, etc. [Hindi *mālī*]

Malian /*mä'li-ən*/ *adj* of or relating to the Republic of *Mali* in W Africa or its inhabitants. ◆ *n* a native or citizen of Mali.

Malibu board /*mal'i-boo bōrd*/ *n* a long, light surfing board equipped with fins. [*Malibu*, California]

malic /*mä'lik*, *mal'ik*/ *adj* obtained from apple juice, *esp* applied to an acid (HOOCCH₂CH(OH)COOH) found in unripe fruits. [L *mālum* an apple; Gr *mēlon*]

■ **ma'late** *n* a salt or ester of malic acid. **maleate** /*mal'i-āt*/ *n* a salt or ester of maleic acid. **maleic** /*mə-lē'ik*/ *adj*. **malonate** /*mal'ə-nāt*/ *n* a salt or ester of malonic acid.

❏ **maleic acid** *n* an acid (HOOCCHCHCOOH), isomeric with fumaric acid, obtained from malic acid (also called **cis-butenediō'ic acid**). **maleic hydrazide** *n* a chemical used in retarding plant growth. **malonic acid** /*ma-lon'ik*/ *n* a white crystalline acid, CH₂(COOH)₂ (also called **propanediō'ic acid**).

malice /*mal'is*/ *n* ill-will; spite; disposition or intention to harm another or others; a playfully mischievous attitude of mind. ◆ *vt* (*obs*) to have ill-will against; to wish to injure (*pap in Spenser* **mal'ist**). [Fr, from L *malitia*, from *malus* bad]

■ **malicious** /*mə-lish'əs*/ *adj* bearing ill-will or spite; motivated by hatred or ill-will; mischievous. **mali'ciously** *adv*. **mali'ciousness** *n*.
❏ **malice aforethought** *n* (*law*) the predetermination to commit a crime *esp* against a person, ie serious injury or murder.

malicho /*mal'i-chō*, *-kō*/ (*Shakesp*) *n* mischief. [Conjectured to represent Sp *malhecho* mischief]

malign /*mə-līn'*/ *adj* baleful; injurious; malignant. ◆ *vt* to speak evil of, *esp* falsely and rancorously, to defame; to regard with malice or hatred (*obs*); to grudge (*obs*). [Fr *malin*, fem *maligne*, from L *malignus* for *maligenus* of evil disposition, from *malus* bad, and *gen-* root of *genus*]
■ **malign'er** *n*. **malignity** /*mə-lig'ni-ti*/ *n* state or quality of being malign; a malicious act; great hatred, virulence; deadly quality. **malign'ly** *adv*. **malign'ment** *n*.

malignant /*mə-lig'nənt*/ *adj* disposed to do harm; baleful; actuated by great hatred; (also with *cap*) Royalist or Cavalier (*hist*); rebellious, disaffected (*obs*); tending to cause death, spreading or deteriorating rapidly, *esp* of a tumour) cancerous (*pathol*). ◆ *n* (*hist*; *usu* with *cap*) a Royalist or Cavalier. [L *malignāns*, *-antis*, prp of *malignāre* to act maliciously]
■ **malig'nance** *n*. **malig'nancy** *n*. **malig'nantly** *adv*.

malik /*mal'ik*/ or **melik** /*mel'ik*/ (*Ind*) *n* the head of a village; an owner; an employer. [Ar *mālik*]

Malines /*mə-lēn'*/ same as **Mechlin**.

malinger /*mə-ling'gər*/ *vi* to feign sickness in order to avoid duty or work. [Fr *malingre* sickly]
■ **maling'erer** *n*. **maling'ery** *n* feigned sickness.

Malinke /*mə-lin'ki*/ *n* a W African people living mainly in Senegal, Mali and Guinea; the language of this people. ◆ *adj* of or relating to the Malinke or their language.

malism /*mä'li-zm*/ *n* belief in the predominance of evil in the world. [L *malus* bad]

malison /*mal'i-zn*, *-sn*/ (*poetic*) *n* a curse, *opp* to *benison*. [OFr *maleison*; a doublet of **malediction**]

malist (*Spenser*) see under **malice**.

malkin, also **mawkin** /*mö'kin*/ *n* a dirty or lewd woman (*Shakesp*); a cat (*dialect*); a mop (*dialect*); a scarecrow (*dialect*); a hare (*Scot*). [Dimin of *Matilda* or *Maud*]

mall /*mal*, (*esp N Am*) *möl*/ *n* a public walk; a level shaded walk (from a former alley of the kind in London); a pedestrian shopping area or street, *esp* (*orig N Am*) an enclosed centre, often outside a town, with connected aisles of shops, restaurants, etc (*Brit* also **shopping mall**); a maul or heavy wooden hammer (*obs*); (a mallet used in) the old game of pall-mall (*hist*); a pall-mall alley (*hist*). ◆ *vt* to maul or beat. [See **maul** and **pall-mall**]
❏ **mall rat** *n* (*US sl*) a young person who spends a lot of leisure time in shopping malls.

mallam /*mal'əm*/ *n* an African scribe, teacher or learned man. [Hausa]

mallander see **malander**.

mallard /*mal'ərd*/ *n* a kind of wild duck common in the northern hemisphere, of which the male has a shiny green head. [OFr *mallart*, *malart*; origin obscure]

malleable /*mal'i-ə-bəl*/ *adj* able to be beaten, rolled, etc into a new shape (also *fig*). [L *malleus* a hammer]
■ **malleabil'ity** *n*. **mall'eableness** *n*. **mall'eably** *adv*.

malleate /*mal'i-āt*/ *vt* to hammer; to beat thin. [Ety as for **malleable**]

■ **malleā'tion** *n* hammering; a hammer-mark. **malleiform** /*mal'ē-i-förm*/ *adj* hammer-shaped. **malleus** /*mal'i-əs*/ *n* (*pl* **mallei** /*mal'ē-ī*/) any of the small bones of the middle ear in mammals.

mallecho an editorial emendation of **malicho**.

mallee[1] /*mal'ē*/ *n* any of many small trees of the genus *Eucalyptus*, *esp E. dumosa*; a mass of such trees (also **mallee scrub**); an arid area where mallee forms the predominant vegetation. [From an Aboriginal language]
❏ **mall'ee-bird**, **-fowl** or **-hen** *n* an Australian mound-bird. **mallee gate** *n* a makeshift gate.

mallee[2] same as **mali**.

malleiform see under **malleate**.

mallemuck /*mal'i-muk*/ *n* the fulmar or similar bird. [Du *mallemok*, from *mal* foolish, and *mok* gull; Ger *Mallemuck*]

mallender see **malander**.

malleolus /*mə-lē'ə-ləs*/ *n* a rounded bony projection on either side of the ankle. [L *malleolus*, dimin of *malleus* hammer]
■ **mallē'olar** (or /*mal'i-*/) *adj*.

mallet /*mal'it*/ *n* a hammer with a large, *esp* wooden head; a soft-headed stick used to beat a gong, etc (*music*); a long-handled hammer for playing croquet or polo. [Fr *maillet*, dimin of *mail* a mall]

malleus see under **malleate**.

malling jug /*mö'ling jug*/ *n* a type of tin-glazed jug produced in late 16c England. [West *Malling* in Kent, where first found]

Mallophaga /*ma-lof'ə-gə*/ *n pl* an order of wingless parasitic insects, bird-lice or biting-lice. [Gr *mallos* a flock of wool, and *phagein* to eat]
■ **malloph'agous** *adj*.

Mallorcan see **Majorcan**.

mallow /*mal'ō*/ *n* any plant of the genus *Malva*, from its emollient properties or its soft downy leaves; extended to other genera of Malvaceae; a mauve colour. [OE *m(e)alwe*, from L *malva*; Gr *malachē*, from *malassein* to soften]

malm /*mäm*/ *n* (also **malm'stone**) calcareous loam; earth of this kind, formerly used for making brick; an artificial mixture of clay and chalk. [OE *m(e)alm* (*-stān*) a soft (stone)]

malmag /*mal'mag*/ *n* a nocturnal lemuroid monkey of the East Indies, the tarsier. [Philippine word]

malmsey /*mäm'zi*/ *n* (also **malvasia** /*mäl-vä-sē'ə*/, **malvesie** /*mäl'və-zi*/ or **malvoisie** /*mäl-voi'zi*/) a sort of grape; a strong, sweet wine, first made in Greece and exported from *Monembasia*. [LL *malmasia*; cf OFr *malvesie*, Fr *malvoisie*, Ital *malvasia*, Sp *malvasia*]

malnourishment /*mal-nur'ish-mənt*/ *n* the state of suffering from malnutrition. [**mal-**]
■ **malnour'ished** *adj*.

malnutrition /*mal-nū-trish'ən*/ *n* inadequate or faulty nutrition. [**mal-**]

malocclusion /*mal-ə-kloo'zhən*/ (*dentistry*) *n* imperfect positioning of the upper and lower teeth when the jaw is closed. [**mal-**]

malodour /*mal-ō'dər*/ *n* an unpleasant or offensive smell. [**mal-**]
■ **malo'dorous** *adj*. **malo'dorousness** *n*.

malo-lactic /*mal-* or *mä-lə-lak'tik*/ *adj* concerning or involving the conversion of malic acid to lactic acid in the fermentation of wine.

malonate, **malonic acid** see under **malic**.

maloti /*ma-lō'ti*/ plural of **loti**.

Malpighia /*mal-pig'i-ə*/ *n* the Barbados cherry genus of tropical American trees, shrubs, and lianes, giving name to the family **Malpighiā'ceae** of the order Geraniales.
■ **Malpigh'ian** *adj* applied to several structures, *esp* in the kidney, investigated by Marcello *Malpighi* (1628–94), Italian anatomist.

malposition /*mal-pə-zish'ən*/ (*chiefly med*) *n* a wrong position, misplacement. [**mal-**]

malpractice /*mal-prak'tis* or *mal'*/ *n* an evil or improper practice; professional misconduct; treatment falling short of reasonable skill or care; the illegal attempt of a person in a position of trust to benefit at the expense of others. [**mal-**]
■ **malpractitioner** /*-tish'ən-ər*/ *n*.

malpresentation /*mal-pre-zən-tā'shən*/ *n* abnormal positioning of a fetus in childbirth. [**mal-**]

mal soigné /*mal swa-nyä'*/ (*Fr*) *adj* badly groomed, unkempt.

malstick see **maulstick**.

malt /*mölt*/ *n* barley or other grain steeped in water, allowed to sprout, and dried in a kiln, used in brewing beer, etc; malt liquor, *esp* malt whisky; a malted milk drink (*US*). ◆ *vt* to make into malt; to treat or combine with malt. ◆ *vi* to become malt; to drink malt liquor (*facetious*). ◆ *adj* containing or made with malt. [OE *m(e)alt*; cf Ger *Malz*]

■ **malt'ase** *n* an enzyme that produces grape-sugar from maltose. **malt'ed** *adj* containing or made with malt. **malt'ing** *n* a building where malt is made. **malt'ose** *n* a hard, white crystalline sugar, formed by the action of malt or diastase on starch. **malt'ster** *n* a person who makes or deals in malt. **malt'y** *adj*.
□ **malt'-dust** *n* grain-sprouts produced and screened off in malt-making. **malted milk** *n* (a drink made from) a powdered mixture of malted grains and dehydrated milk. **malt'-extract** *n* a liquid extract obtained from malt and used as a flavouring in food. **malt'-floor** *n* a perforated floor in the chamber of a malt-kiln, through which heat rises. **malt'-horse** *n* a heavy horse of a kind formerly used by brewers; a dull, stupid person (*Shakesp*). **malt'-house** *n* a malting. **malting floor** *n* a large store floor on which soaked grain is spread to germinate. **malt'-kiln** *n* a kiln in which sprouted grain is allowed to dry. **malt liquor** *n* any alcoholic drink, such as beer or porter, formed from malt. **malt'man** *n* a maltster. **malt'-mill** *n* a mill for grinding malt after drying in a kiln. **malt tea** *n* the liquid infusion of the mash in brewing. **malt vinegar** *n* a strong-flavoured vinegar produced from malt liquor. **malt whisky** *n* a whisky that is distilled entirely from malted barley. **malt'worm** *n* (*Shakesp*) a lover of malted liquors, a tippler.
■ **single malt** a whisky that is the product of one distillate of malted barley, etc, not a blend of several.

Malta /mol'/ or /möl'tə/ *adj* of or relating to the Mediterranean island of *Malta*. [L *Melita*, from Gr *Melitē*]
■ **Maltese** /-tēz'/ *adj* of Malta, its people or their language. ◆ *n* a native or inhabitant of Malta (*pl* **Maltese'**); the official language of Malta, Semitic with a strong Italian infusion.
□ **Malta fever** *n* undulant fever, once common in Malta (see also **brucellosis**). **Maltese cross** *n* the badge of the knights of Malta, a cross with four equal arms expanding from the centre, *usu* each with two points; (**maltese cross**) a mechanism providing intermittent frame-by-frame movement in a motion picture film projector (see **Geneva movement** under **Genevan**). **Maltese dog** *n* a very small spaniel with long silky hair.

maltalent /mal'ta-lənt/ (*Spenser*) *n* ill-will. [Fr *mal* ill, and *talent* disposition; see **talent**[1]]

Maltese see under **Malta**.

maltha /mal'thə/ *n* a thick mineral pitch; an ancient cement; mineral tar. [L, from Gr]

Malthusian /mal-thū'zi-ən/ *adj* relating to Thomas Robert *Malthus* (1766–1834), or to his teaching that the increase of population tends to outstrip that of the means of living and that sexual restraint should therefore be exercised. ◆ *n* a disciple of Malthus.
■ **Malthūs'ianism** *n*.

maltreat /mal-trēt'/ *vt* to use roughly or unkindly. [Fr *maltraiter*, from L *male* ill, and *tractāre* to treat]
■ **maltreat'er** *n*. **maltreat'ment** *n*.

malva /mal'və/ *n* a plant of the mallow genus *Malva*, giving name to the family **Malvā'ceae**, including hollyhock, cotton, etc, related to the lime family. [L; cf **mallow**]
■ **malvā'ceous** *adj*.

malvasia same as **malmsey**.

malversation /mal-vər-sā'shən/ *n* dishonest or unethical conduct in office, such as bribery, extortion or embezzlement; corrupt administration (of funds). [Fr, from L *male* badly, and *versārī*, *-ātus* to occupy oneself]

malvesie or **malvoisie** same as **malmsey**.

mal vu /mal vü/ (*Fr*) *adj* looked upon with disapproval.

malware /mal'wār/ (*comput*) *n* any software (eg a virus or Trojan) that is designed to cause damage to a computer system. [From *mal*icious *soft*ware]

Mam /mam/ *n* (a member of) a Native American people of Guatemala; the Mayan language of this people. [Sp *mame*, from a native name]

mam /mam/ (*dialect*) *n* mother.

mama see **mamma**[1].

mamaguy /mä'mə-gī/ (*W Indies*) *vt* to deceive or tease, either playfully or by flattery and lies. ◆ *n* an instance of this. [Sp *mamar el gallo*, literally, to feed the cock]

mamba /mam'bə/ *n* a large, deadly African snake (genus *Dendroaspis*), black or green. [Zulu *imamba* large snake]

mambo /mam'bō/ *n* (*pl* **mam'bos**) a voodoo priestess; a Latin American dance or dance tune of Haitian origin, resembling the rumba. ◆ *vi* to dance the mambo. [Am Sp, prob from Haitian]

mamee see **mammee**.

mamelon /mam'ə-lən/ *n* a rounded hill or protuberance. [Fr, nipple]

mameluco /ma-me-loo'kō/ *n* (*pl* **mamelu'cos**) in Brazil, a person of mixed European and S American parentage. [Port; cf **Mameluke**]

Mameluke /mam'ə-look/ (*hist*) *n* a member of a military force originally of Circassian slaves, forming the ruling class of Egypt from the mid-13c to the early 19c; a slave in a Muslim country, *esp* white. [Ar *mamlûk* a purchased slave, from *malaka* to possess]

mamey see **mammee**.

mamilla or (*N Am*) **mammilla** /ma-mil'ə/ *n* (*pl* **mamill'ae** or (*N Am*) **mammill'ae** /-ē/) the nipple of the mammary gland; any nipple-shaped protuberance. [L *mam(m)illa*, dimin of *mamma* breast]
■ **mam'illar** or **mam'illary** *adj* relating to the breast; nipple-shaped; studded with rounded projections. **mam'illate** or **mam'illated** *adj* having mamillae; nipple-shaped. **mamillā'tion** *n*. **mamill'iform** *adj*. **mammillā'ria** *n* (*pl* **mammilla'rias**) a plant belonging to the *Mammillaria* genus of flowering cactus, with nipple-shaped tubercles in rows.

mamma[1] or **mama** /mä-mä'** or (*US*) **mä'mə/ *n* mother (formerly considered genteel, now used chiefly by young children); a woman, *esp* a mature woman (chiefly *US*; *sl*). [Repetition of *ma*, a child's natural utterance]
■ **mammy** /mam'i/ *n* a child's word for mother; a black nursemaid of white children (*old US*).
□ **mamm'y-wagon** *n* in W Africa, an open-sided bus.

mamma[2] /mam'ə/ *n* (*pl* **mamm'ae** /-ē/) the milk gland; the breast. [L *mamma* breast]
■ **mamm'ary** *adj* of the nature of, or relating to, the mammae or breasts. ◆ *n* a breast. **mamm'ate** *adj* having breasts. **mammec'tomy** *n* a mastectomy. **mamm'ifer** *n* a mammal. **mammif'erous** *adj* having mammae. **mamm'iform** *adj* having the form of a breast. **mammilla** and **mammillaria** *n* see under **mamilla**. **mammogen'ic** *adj* (of hormones) promoting growth of the duct and alveolar systems of the milk gland. **mamm'ogram** or **mamm'ograph** *n* an X-ray photograph of the breast. **mammog'raphy** *n* radiological examination of the breast. **mamm'oplasty** *n* plastic surgery to change the shape of the breasts, as by the use of silicone implants, etc.

mammal /mam'əl/ *n* a member of the **Mammalia** /mə-mā'li-ə/, a class of vertebrates that maintain a constant body temperature and suckle their young, which are usually born alive. [L *mammālis* of the breast, from *mamma* the breast]
■ **mammā'lian** *adj*. **mammalif'erous** *adj* (*geol*) bearing remains of mammals. **mammalog'ical** *adj*. **mammalogist** /-al'ə-jist/ *n*. **mammal'ogy** *n* the scientific study of mammals.

mammary and **mammate** see under **mamma**[2].

mammatus /mə-mä'təs/ (*meteorol*) *adj* (of a cloud formation) having a pattern of sagging pouches hanging down from its base. ◆ *n* (*pl* **mamma'tus**) such a pattern. [L *mammātus* having protuberances, from *mamma* breast]

mammectomy see under **mamma**[2].

mammee, **mamee** or **mamey** /ma-mē'/ *n* a fruit (also **mammee apple**) of the West Indies and surrounding regions, having a sweet taste and aromatic odour; the tree producing it (*Mammea americana*, family Guttiferae). [Sp *mamey*, from Haitian]
□ **mammee'-sapo'ta** *n* the marmalade tree or its fruit.

mammer /mam'ər/ (*Shakesp*) *vi* to hesitate, to stand muttering and in doubt. [Prob imit]

mammet /mam'it/, **maumet**, **mawmet** /mö'mit/ or **mommet** /mom'it/ *n* an idol; a puppet, a figure dressed up (*Shakesp*). [*Mohammed*; cf **Mahoun** or **Mahound**]
■ **mamm'etry**, **maum'etry** or **maw'metry** *n* idolatry; idols collectively; Islam (*archaic*; *derog*).

mammifer and **mammiform** see under **mamma**[2].

mammilla see **mamilla**.

mammock /mam'ək/ (*archaic* or *dialect*) *n* a broken or torn piece, a shred (also **mumm'ock**). ◆ *vt* (*Shakesp*) to tear to pieces, to mangle. [Origin obscure]

mammogenic, **mammography**, etc see under **mamma**[2].

mammon /mam'ən/ *n* riches regarded as the root of evil; (with *cap*) the god of riches. [LL *mam(m)ōna*, from Gr *mam(m)ōnās*, from Aramaic *māmōn* riches]
■ **mamm'onish** *adj* devoted to gaining wealth. **mamm'onism** *n* devotion to gain. **mamm'onist** or **mamm'onite** *n* a person devoted to riches; a worldling. **mammonist'ic** *adj*.

mammoplasty see under **mamma**[2].

mammoth /mam'əth/ *n* an extinct species of elephant of the Pleistocene epoch, with a thick, hairy coat and long upcurving tusks. ◆ *adj* resembling the mammoth in size; gigantic. [Former Russ *mammot* (now *mamant* or *mamont*)]
□ **mamm'oth-tree** *n* the sequoia.

mammy and **mammy-wagon** see under **mamma**[1].

mamselle /mam-zel'/ *n* a contraction of **mademoiselle**.

■ words derived from main entry word; □ compound words; ■ idioms and phrasal verbs

mamzer /mam'zər/ or **momzer** /mom'zər/ n (pl **mam'zers** or **mom'zers**, **mam'zerim** or **mom'zerim**) an illegitimate child, a child of an unrecognized marriage (*Judaism*); a detestable or untrustworthy person (often as a term of abuse; *US sl*). [Yiddish, from Heb *mamzēr*]

MAN *abbrev* : metropolitan area network.

man[1] /man/ n (pl **men**) a human being; (*usu with cap*) mankind, the human genus (also in combination denoting a particular species of this); an adult human male; a male attendant or servant; a workman or male employee; a vassal; a follower; an uncommissioned soldier; a person possessing a distinctively manly character; a husband or male sexual partner; a piece used in playing chess, draughts, etc; a male member of a team, group, etc; a cairn or rock pillar; a hill with such a man; a ship, as in *man-of-war*; a word of familiar address; (*usu in pl*; with *cap*) in the Scottish Highlands, any of a group of men of strict religious belief, regarded as spiritual leaders in a parish (*hist*). ◆ *adj* and combining form male. ◆ *interj* expressing surprise, admiration, etc. ◆ *vt* (**mann'ing**; **manned** /mand/) to provide with a man or men; to provide with a (human) worker, operator, etc; to strengthen or put manhood into; to accustom (a hawk) to being handled, *esp* by strangers (*falconry*). [OE *mann*; Ger *Mann*, Du *man*]
■ **man'dom** n (*rare*) humanity, man collectively. **man'ful** *adj* having the good qualities of a man; manly; bold; courageous; vigorous; steadfast; noble-minded. **man'fully** *adv*. **man'fulness** n. **man'hood** n the state of being a man; manly quality; human nature; men collectively. **mankind'** n the human race, the mass of human beings; /man'kīnd/ human males collectively. ◆ *adj* (*Shakesp*) man-like, viragoish. **man'less** *adj*. **man'-like** *adj* having the appearance or qualities of a human being or of an adult human male. ◆ *adv* in the manner of a man; in a way that might be expected of a man; manfully. **man'liness** n. **man'ly** *adj* (**man'lier**; **man'liest**) befitting a man; brave; dignified; noble; relating to manhood; not childish or womanish. **manned** /mand/ *adj* provided with men, operators, etc. **mann'ish** *adj* (of a child or woman) resembling or behaving like an adult male (*usu derog*); masculine. **mann'ishly** *adv*. **mann'ishness** n.
◻ **man-about-town'** n a fashionable, sophisticated man. **man-and-dog'** *adj* (of an enterprise, organization, etc) extremely small-scale, minimally-staffed. **man-at-arms'** n a soldier, *esp* mounted and heavily-armed. **man'bag** n a bag for small articles carried by men. **man'-body** n (*Scot*) a man. **man boobs** n pl (*sl*) deposits of fat around a man's nipples, derogatively likened to female breasts. **man'-child** n (pl **men'-children**) (*literary*) a male child; a boy. **man crush** n (*sl*) a heterosexual man's feeling of admiration for another man. **man'-day** n (pl **man'-days**) a day's work by one person. **man'-eater** n a cannibal; a tiger or other animal that has acquired the habit of eating humans; a shark that eats human flesh; a woman given to acquiring and dispatching male admirers (*inf*). **man'-eating** *adj*. **man'-entered** *adj* (*Shakesp*) passed from boyhood into manhood. **man flu** n (*facetious*) a heavy cold (from the idea that men tend to exaggerate the seriousness of the condition). **Man Friday** n (pl **Man Fridays**) a factotum or servile attendant (from Robinson Crusoe's man). **man'handle** *vt* to move by manpower; to handle or treat roughly (*orig sl*). **man'hole** n a hole large enough to admit a person, *esp* to a sewer, cable-duct, etc. **manhood suffrage** n right to vote accorded to male citizens. **man'-hour** n (pl **man'-hours**) an hour's work by one person. **man'hunt** n an organized search for a person, *esp* one mounted by police, etc, for a criminal. **man in the moon** n a supposed likeness of a man's face seen on the surface of the moon; the fanciful character of children's rhymes, etc, derived from this. **man in the street** n the ordinary, everyday man; Tom, Dick, or Harry. **man-jack'** or **man jack** n individual man (as *every man-jack*). **man-machine interface** n (*comput*) the device or method by which a user communicates with a computer, eg a keyboard or mouse. **man'-made** *adj* made by man; humanly made or originated; (of fibre, fabric, etc) artificial, synthetic. **man-man'agement** n the organization of the work of members of staff. **man-man'ager** n a person regarded in a terms of ability to direct the work of others (as in *a good man-manager*). **man'-mark** *vt* (in football, hockey, etc) to mark (a particular opponent) closely. **man-mill'iner** n (*literary*) a male milliner; a man with frivolous interests or concerns (*archaic; derog*). **man-mind'ed** *adj* having the mind or qualities of a man. **man of business** n (*esp Scot*) an agent or a lawyer. **man of God** n a holy man; a clergyman (also **man of the cloth**). **man of his hands** n a man of prowess. **man of law** n a lawyer. **man of letters** n a scholar; a writer. **man of skill** n (*Scots law*) an expert witness or a professionally qualified person appointed by the court to provide a written report on a technical issue in a case. **man of straw** n a person of no substance (*esp* financially); one nominally, but not really, responsible; a sham opponent or argument set up for the sake of disputation. **man of the cloth** see **man of God** above. **man of the match** n the outstanding player in a sports match (also *fig*). **man of the moment** n the man (most capable of) dealing with the present situation. **man of the world** n a man with experience of the pains and (*esp* sexual) pleasures of life. **man-of-war'** or **man-o'-war'** n

(pl **men-of-war'** or **men-o'-war'**) a warship; a soldier (*archaic* or *facetious*); (in full **man-of-war bird**) the frigate bird; (see also **Portuguese man-of-war** under **Portuguese**). **man'-of-war's-man** n a man who serves on board a warship. **man'-orchid** n an orchid (*Aceras anthropophora*) whose flowers have a human-like shape. **man'pack** n a package of supplies or equipment designed to be carried by one person. **man'power** n the agency or energy of people in doing work; the rate at which a person can work; available resources in population or in able-bodied people. **Manpower Services Commission** n the former name for the **Training Agency** (see under **train**[1]). **man'-queller** n (*Shakesp*) a man-killer, a murderer. **man'rider** or **manriding train** n the formal name for a paddy train (qv). **man'riding** *adj* used of equipment on oil rigs that is used by personnel and is built to a higher standard of safety than material-handling systems. **man'rope** n (*naut*) a rope railing on a gangway or ladder. **man'-servant** n (pl **men'-servants**) a male servant. **man'shift** n the work done by one person in one shift or work period. **man'-size** or **man'-sized** *adj* suitable for, or requiring, a man; very big (*inf*). **man'slaughter** n the killing of a man; unlawful homicide without malice aforethought (*law*). **man'-slayer** n a person who kills a man. **man'-stealer** n a person who steals people, *esp* to make slaves of them. **man'trap** n a trap for catching trespassers; any source of potential danger; a woman who takes a mischievous pleasure in attracting and acquiring men (*inf*). **man'-watching** n the study of body language. **man'-week** or **man'-year** n (pl **man'-weeks** or **man'-years**) a week's or year's work by one person. **men'folk** or **men'folks** n pl male people, *esp* a woman's male relatives. **men's movement** n a movement begun in the USA in opposition to the women's movement (qv under **woman**), aiming to uphold the traditional role of men in society. **mens'wear** n clothing for men.
■ **as one man** all together; unanimously. **be one's own man** to be independent, not answerable to anyone else. **be someone's man** to be exactly the person someone is seeking for a particular purpose. **make a man of** to help a young man to acquire the characteristics associated with a mature adult. **man alive** an exclamation of surprise. **man and boy** from childhood to adulthood. **man to man** one man to another as individuals in fight or talk; frank(ly) and confidential(ly). **man up** (*inf*) to accept responsibility in the manner of a mature person. **men in grey suits** unseen establishment figures holding the ultimate power in an organization, political party, etc. **old man of the sea** see under **old**. **our man in…** a company or government representative in, or journalist covering, a particular area. **separate** (or **sort out**) **the men from the boys** to serve as a test of ability, calibre, courage, etc. **the Man of Sin** (*relig*) the Antichrist. **to a man** without exception.

man[2] see **mun**[1].

mana /mä'nə/ (*anthrop*) n personal authority or prestige. [Maori]

manacle /man'ə-kl/ n a handcuff. ◆ *vt* to handcuff; to shackle. [OFr *manicle*, from L *manicula*, dimin of *manica* sleeve, glove, handcuff, from *manus* hand]

manage /man'ij/ *vt* to control; to administer, be at the head of; to deal tactfully with; to handle; to wield; to conduct; to husband, use sparingly (*archaic*); to contrive successfully; to have time for; to cope with; to manipulate; to contrive; to bring about; to train (a horse, etc) by exercise. ◆ *vi* to conduct affairs; to get on, contrive to succeed. ◆ n (*archaic*) (a) manège. [Ital *maneggio*, from L *manus* the hand]
■ **manageabil'ity** n the quality of being manageable. **man'ageable** *adj* that can be managed; governable. **man'ageableness** n. **man'ageably** *adv*. **man'agement** n the art or act of managing; the manner of directing or of using anything; administration; skilful treatment; a body of managers. **man'ager** n a person who manages; in an industrial firm or business, a person who deals with administration and with the design and marketing, etc of the product, as opposed to its actual construction; a person who organizes other people's activities; a person legally appointed to manage a business, property, etc as receiver; a person of either House of Parliament appointed to deal with business involving both Houses; a program or system that manages a peripheral (*comput*); a party leader (*US*). **man'ageress** n a female manager (not *usu* used in official titles). **manage'rial** *adj* of or relating to a manager, or to management. **manage'rialism** n the adoption of business methods and management structures in the running of public services, etc. **manage'rialist** n and *adj*. **manage'rially** *adv*. **man'agership** n. **man'aging** *adj* handling; controlling; administering; contriving.
◻ **managed currency** n a currency whose circulation and exchange rate is controlled by government. **managed fund** n a unit-linked insurance or savings plan, etc, invested by professional managers. **management accountant** n an accountant employed within a company to produce financial analysis for use in decision-making. **management accounting** n cost-accounting to facilitate the management of a business. **management buy-in** n the purchase of a controlling share in a company by an outside management with support from banks, etc. **management buyout** n the purchase, by its management, of the majority of the shares in a company, *esp* when an

outside takeover is imminent. **management company** _n_ a company that manages a unit trust, group of properties, etc. **management consultant** _n_ a specialist who advises firms on the most efficient procedures applicable to particular businesses or industries. **management consulting** or **management consultancy** _n_. **management information system** _n_ (_comput_) a computerized system providing information for managerial decision-making. **managing director** _n_ a director in overall charge of an organization, often carrying out the decisions of a board of directors (_abbrev_ **MD**).

manakin /man'ə-kin/ _n_ a small passerine bird (family Pipridae) of tropical Central and S America, related to the Cotinga family; a manikin (_non-standard_). [See **manikin**]

mañana /man-yä'nə, män-yä'nä/ (_Sp_) _n_ and _adv_ tomorrow; (at) an unspecified time in the future.

manat /man'at/ _n_ (_pl_ **man'at**) the standard monetary unit of Azerbaijan (100 gopik) and Turkmenistan (100 tenge).

manatee or **manati** /ma-nə-tē'/ _n_ a large aquatic herbivorous mammal (_Manatus_ or _Trichechus_) of the warm parts of the Atlantic and the rivers of Brazil. [Sp _manatí_, from Carib _manatoui_; not connected with L _manus_ hand]

Manc /mangk/ (_inf_) _n_ and _adj_ a short form of **Mancunian**.

mancala /man-kä'lə/ _n_ any of several varieties of board game played in Africa and S Asia, using a board with rows of holes containing the pieces to be captured. [Ar _mangala_, from _nagala_ to move]

mancando /mang-kan'dō/ (_music_) _adj_ and _adv_ fading away. [Ital, lacking]

manche /mänsh/ (_heraldry_) _n_ a sleeve. [Fr]

Manchego /man-chä'gō/ _n_ a hard cheese made in the Spanish region of _La Mancha_.

Manchester /man'chis-tər, -chəs- or -ches-/ _adj_ belonging to or made in _Manchester_, or similar to goods made in Manchester, applied _esp_ to cotton cloths.
□ **Manchester school** _n_ the followers of Bright and Cobden, advocates of free trade and of individual freedom of action. **Manchester terrier** _n_ an English breed of small short-haired black-and-tan dog.

manchet /man'chit/ _n_ the finest grade of wheat bread (_obs_); a round loaf or roll of this (_archaic_ or _dialect_); a charge representing a loaf of manchet (_heraldry_). [Origin obscure]

manchineel /man-chi-nēl'/ _n_ a tropical American tree (genus _Hippomane_) of the spurge family, with poisonous latex. [Sp _manzanilla_, dimin of _manzana_ apple]

Manchu or **Manchoo** /man-choo' or man'/ _n_ a member of the Mongoloid race from which the NE Chinese region of Manchuria took its name, and which governed China from the 17c until 1912; the Altaic language of this people. ◆ _adj_ of or relating to the Manchus, their language, or to Manchuria. [Manchu, pure]
■ **Manchur'ian** _adj_.

mancipation /man-si-pā'shən/ (_Roman hist_) _n_ a legal transfer by actual or symbolic sale. [L _mancipātiō, -ōnis_, from _manus_ hand, and _capere_ to take]
■ **man'cipate** _vt_. **man'cipatory** /-pə-tə-ri/ _adj_.

manciple /man'si-pl/ _n_ a steward; a purveyor, _esp_ of a college or an inn of court. [OFr, from L _manceps, -cipis_ a purchaser; see above]

Mancunian /man(g)-kū'ni-ən/ _adj_ belonging to or relating to Manchester. ◆ _n_ a person born or living in Manchester. [Doubtful L _Mancunium_ (prob an error for _Mamucium_), a Roman station in Manchester]

mancus /mang'kəs/ (_hist_) _n_ (_pl_ **manc'uses**) a medieval coin or unit of account, equal to thirty pence. [OE _mancus_]

-mancy /-man-si, -mən-si/ _combining form_ denoting divination (by a specified method). [Gr _manteiā_]
■ **-mantic** _adj combining form_.

mand (_Spenser_) same as **manned** (see under **man¹**).

Mandaean or **Mandean** /man-dē'ən/ _n_ and _adj_ (a member) of an ancient S Babylonian sect, surviving in Iraq, their religion a corrupt Gnosticism, with many Jewish and Parsee elements (also called **Mendaites**, **Nasoraeans**, **Sabians**, or **Christians of St John**); (in, of, or relating to) the Aramaic dialect of their sacred books. [Mandaean _mandayyā_ knowledge, gnosis]

mandala /mun'də-lə, man' or man-dä'lə/ _n_ in Buddhism and Hinduism, a pictorial symbol of the universe, _usu_ a circle enclosing images of deities or geometric designs, often arranged in fours, used as an aid to religious meditation; in Jungian psychology, a symbol of the self, the wholeness or symmetry of the image corresponding to the degree of harmony in the self. [Sans _maṇḍala_]

mandamus /man-dā'məs/ (_law_) _n_ (_pl_ **mandā'muses**) a writ or command issued by a higher court to a lower. [L _mandāmus_ we command]

mandarin /man'də-rin, -rēn/ _n_ a member of any of nine ranks of officials under the Chinese Empire (_hist_); a statuette of a seated Chinese figure, often with a movable head (a **nodding mandarin**); (with _cap_) the most widely spoken form of Chinese, the official language of China; a high-ranking official or bureaucrat; a person of standing in the literary world, often one who tends to be reactionary or pedantic; (also **man'darine** or **mandarin orange**) a small kind of orange (of Chinese origin); its colour; the tree yielding this fruit; a liqueur. ◆ _adj_ relating to a mandarin or mandarins; (of style or language) formal and ornate. [Port _mandarim_, from Malay (from Hindi) _mantrī_ counsellor, from Sans _mantra_ counsel]
■ **man'darinate** _n_ the rank or office of a mandarin; mandarins as a group.
□ **mandarin collar** or **neck** _n_ a high, narrow, stand-up collar, the front ends of which do not quite meet. **mandarin duck** _n_ a crested Asiatic duck (_Aix galericulata_).

mandate /man'dāt/ _n_ a charge, instruction; a command from a superior official or judge to a subordinate, ordering him how to act, _esp_ from the Pope to a legate, etc; legal authorization given to a person, eg a Member of Parliament to act on behalf of another; a rescript of the Pope; permission to govern according to declared policies, regarded as officially granted by an electorate to a particular political party or leader upon the decisive outcome of an election; the power conferred upon a state by the League of Nations in 1919 to govern a region elsewhere; (also with _cap_) any of the regions governed in this way (also **mandated territory**). ◆ _vt_ /-dāt'/ to assign by mandate; to invest with authority. [L _mandātum_, from _mandāre_, from _manus_ hand, and _dare_ give]
■ **man'datary** or **man'datory** /-də-tə-ri/ _n_ the holder of a mandate; a mandate. **mandā'tor** _n_ the giver of a mandate. **man'datorily** _adv_. **man'datory** _adj_ containing a mandate or command; of the nature of a mandate; bestowed by mandate; compulsory; allowing no option.

Mande /man'dā/ _n_ (a member of) a large group of peoples of W Africa; the group of languages spoken by these peoples, belonging to the Niger-Congo family. ◆ _adj_ of or relating to these peoples or this group of languages.

Mandean see **Mandaean**.

Mandelbrot set /man'dəl-brot set/ _n_ a set of points in a highly iterated and diminishing function which produce a convoluted fractal boundary when plotted on a graph. [Benoit B _Mandelbrot_ (1924–2010), Polish-born mathematician]

mandible /man'di-bl/ _n_ a jaw or jawbone, _esp_ the lower; either part of a bird's bill; an organ performing the functions of a jaw in the lower animals, such as one of the first pair of mouth appendages in insects or crustaceans. [L _mandibula_, from _mandere_ to chew]
■ **mandib'ular** _adj_ relating to the jaw or jawbone. **mandib'ulate** or **mandib'ulated** _adj_.

mandilion see **mandylion**.

Mandingo /man-ding'gō/ _adj_ and _n_ (_pl_ **Manding'o**, **Manding'oes** or **Manding'os**) a former name for **Mande**.

mandioc, mandioca, mandiocca see **manioc**.

Man. Dir. _abbrev_: Managing Director.

mandir /mun'dər/ or **mandira** /mun'də-rä/ _n_ a Hindu or Jain temple. [Hindi]

mandolin or **mandoline** /man'də-lin, -lēn/ _n_ a round-backed instrument like a lute, sustained notes being played by repeated plucking; (_usu_ **mandoline**) a kitchen utensil with a blade for slicing vegetables, etc. [Ital _mandola_, _mandora_, dimin _mandolino_]
■ **mandō'la** _n_ a large tenor or bass mandolin. **mandolin'ist** _n_ a mandolin player. **mandō'ra** _n_ an early type of mandolin.

mandorla /man'dör-lə/ _n_ an oval panel, or a work of art filling one; the vesica piscis. [Ital, almond]

mandrake /man'drāk/ or (_Shakesp_) **mandragora** /-drag'ə-rə/ _n_ a poisonous plant (genus _Mandragora_) of the potato family, formerly thought to have magical powers because of the human-like shape of its forked root; extended to various other plants, such as white bryony. [L _mandragora_, from Gr _mandragorās_]

mandrel or **mandril** /man'drəl/ _n_ a bar of iron fitted to a turning-lathe on which articles to be turned are fixed; the axle of a circular saw; a miner's pick. [Fr _mandrin_]

mandrill /man'dril/ _n_ a large W African baboon with a red and blue muzzle and hindquarters. [Prob **man¹** and **drill³**]

manducate /man'dū-kāt/ (_formal_) _vt_ to chew or eat. [L _mandūcāre_, from _mandere_ to chew]
■ **man'ducable** _adj_. **manducā'tion** _n_. **man'ducatory** /-kə-tə-ri/ _adj_.

mandylion or **mandilion** /man-dil'i-ən/ n a loose outer garment worn eg by soldiers over their armour (hist); (with cap) the name given to a cloth supposedly bearing the imprint of Christ's face, known in Orthodox Christianity as the Image of Edessa (modern Urfa in Turkey) from where it was taken to Constantinople in 944 and finally lost in the sack of 1204. [MFr mandillon cloak, and Late Gr mandylion cloth; cf ult L mantel(l)um napkin or cloak, and L mantele, mantelium napkin]

mane /mān/ n long hair on the back of the neck and neighbouring parts of a horse, lion, etc; a long bushy head of hair. [OE manu; ON mön; Ger Mähne]
■ **maned** adj. **mane'less** adj.
□ **mane'-sheet** n a covering for the upper part of a horse's head.

-mane /-mān/ combining form an enthusiast or devotee (of a specified thing). [Gr maniā]

manège /ma-nezh'/ n the managing of horses; the art of horsemanship or of training horses; the actions and paces learned by an individual horse; a riding school. ◆ vt to train (a horse). [Fr; cf **manage**]

maneh same as **mina¹**.

manes /mä'nāz or mä'nēz/ (Roman myth) n pl the spirits of the dead. [L mānēs]

manet /man'et/ (pl **manent**) (L) as a stage direction, (he or she) remains on stage.

maneuver US spelling of **manoeuvre**.

manful see under **man¹**.

mang /mang/ (archaic sl) vi and vt to speak or talk (in). [Perh a corruption of **mag²**]

manga /mang'ga/ n a type of adult comic book popular in Japan. [Jap]

mangabeira /mang-ga-bā'rə/ n a Brazilian apocynaceous rubber tree (Hancornia speciosa). [Port, from Tupí mangaba]

mangabey /mang'gə-bā/ n the white-eyelid monkey, any species of the mainly W African genus Cercocebus, esp the sooty mangabey. [From a district in Madagascar, where, however, they are not found]

mangal /mang-gäl'/ n a brazier. [Turk]

mangalsutra /mang-gəl-soo'trə/ n a bead necklace worn by a married Hindu woman whose husband is living. [Sans]

manganese /mang-gə-nēz', mang'/ n a hard brittle greyish-white metallic element (symbol **Mn**; atomic no 25); (orig and commercially) its dioxide (black manganese) or other ore. [Fr manganèse, from Ital manganese, from L magnēsia]
■ **mang'anate** n a salt of manganic acid. **manganic** /-gan'ik/ adj of manganese of higher valency. **manganif'erous** adj containing manganese. **Mang'anin**® n an alloy of copper with manganese and some nickel. **mang'anite** n a salt of manganous acid (chem); a grey ore, hydrated oxide of manganese (mineralogy). **mang'anous** adj of manganese of lower valency.
□ **manganese bronze** n a bronze or brass with a little manganese. **manganese nodule** n a small irregular concretion, found on deep ocean-floor sediment, containing high concentrations of manganese and other metals. **manganese spar** n rhodochrosite. **manganese steel** n a very hard, shock-resistant steel containing a higher than usual percentage of manganese. **manganic acid** n a hypothetical acid existing only in solution.

mange see under **mangy**.

mangel-wurzel /mang'gl-wûr'zl/ or **mangold-wurzel** /man'gold-/ n a variety of beet cultivated as cattle food (also **mang'el** or **mang'old**). [Ger Mangold beet, and Wurzel root]

manger /mān'jər/ n a trough from which horses and cattle take food. [OFr mangeoire, from L mandūcāre to chew, eat]
■ **dog in the manger** see under **dog¹**.

mangetout /mäzh-too'/ n a type of pea cooked and eaten together with its pod (also **mangetout pea**, **snow pea** or **sugar pea**). [Fr, literally, eat-all]

mangey see **mangy**.

mangle¹ /mang'gl/ vt to hack, tear, or crush into a misshapen state; to mutilate or disfigure; to bungle (fig); to distort; to spoil. [Anglo-Fr mangler, mahangler, prob a frequentative of OFr mahaigner to maim, from mahaing a hurt]
■ **mang'ler** n.

mangle² /mang'gl/ n a rolling-press for smoothing linen; a similar (usu hand-turned) device with rollers for squeezing the water out of wet washing. ◆ vt to smooth with a mangle, to calender; to squeeze the water out of with a mangle. [Du mangel, from Gr manganon; cf **mangonel**]
■ **mang'ler** n.

mango /mang'gō/ n (pl **mang'oes** or **mang'os**) a tropical tree of the cashew-nut family (Mangifera indica), orig of S Asia; its yellowish-red fleshy fruit; a green musk-melon pickled. [Port manga, from Malay manggā, from Tamil mān-kāy mango-fruit]
■ **wild mango** an African tree of the family Simarubaceae with edible fruit, oil-giving seeds, and termite-resistant wood.

mangold and **mangold-wurzel** see **mangel-wurzel**.

mangonel /mang'gə-nel/ (hist) n a medieval war engine for throwing stones, etc. [OFr, from LL mangonum, from Gr manganon]

mangosteen /mang'gə-stēn/ n a tree, Garcinia mangostana, or its orange-shaped fruit, with thick, dark-brown rind and juicy rose-coloured flesh (also **mang'ostan**). [Malay mangustan]

mangouste see **mongoose**.

mangrove /mang'grōv/ n a tree, esp a species of Rhizophora, that grows in muddy swamps covered at high tide or on tropical coasts and estuary shores. [Origin obscure]

mangy, mangey /mān'ji/ or **maungy** /mön'ji/ (dialect) adj scabby; affected with mange; shabby, seedy; mean, cowardly. [Fr mangé eaten, pap of manger, from L mandūcāre to chew]
■ **mange** /mānj/ n (back-formation) inflammation of the skin of animals caused by mites. **mang'ily** adv. **mang'iness** n.

manhandle see under **man¹**.

Manhattan /man-hat'ən/ n a cocktail consisting of vermouth, whisky, Angostura bitters, and sometimes curaçao or maraschino. [Manhattan, New York]

manhole, **manhood**, **man-hour** and **manhunt** see under **man¹**.

mani /mä'ni/ n a stone prayer wall in a Tibetan Buddhist temple, usu carved with sacred images or texts (also **mani wall**). [Tibetan máni, from Sans maṇi precious stone]

mania /mā'ni-ə/ n a mental illness characterized by euphoria, excessively rapid speech and violent, destructive actions (psychiatry); the elated phase of manic-depressive psychosis (psychiatry); excessive or unreasonable desire; a craze. ◆ combining form an abnormal and obsessive desire or inclination, or, more loosely, an extreme enthusiasm, for a specified thing. [L, from Gr maniā]
■ **mā'niac** n a person affected with (a) mania; a madman; a keen enthusiast. ◆ adj affected by or relating to (a) mania; raving mad. ◆ combining form forming nouns and adjectives. **maniacal** /mə-nī'ə-kl/ adj. **mani'acally** adv. **manic** /man'ik/ adj of or affected by mania; ludicrously busy or energetic (inf). **man'ically** adv.
□ **man'ic-depress'ive** n a person suffering from manic-depressive psychosis (also adj). **manic-depressive psychosis** n a form of mental illness characterized by phases of depression and elation, either alone or alternately, with lucid intervals.

Manichean or **Manichaean** /ma-ni-kē'ən/ adj relating to, following, or designating the beliefs of Mani or Manichaeus, a native of Ecbatana (c.216–c.276AD), who taught that everything sprang from two chief principles, light and darkness, or good and evil. ◆ n (also **Man'ichee**) a believer in Manicheanism.
■ **Maniche'anism**, **Man'icheism**, **Manichae'anism** or **Man'ichaeism** n any belief in radical dualism.

manicotti /ma-ni-kot'i/ n pl large tubular pasta shapes, often stuffed with cheese, tomato, etc. [Ital, little sleeves, from manica sleeve]

manicure /man'i-kūr/ n the care of hands and nails; professional treatment for the hands and nails; a manicurist. ◆ vt to apply manicure to. [L manus hand, and cūra care]
■ **man'icurist** n someone who practises manicure.

manifest /man'i-fest/ adj that may be easily seen by the eye or perceived by the mind; in Freudian psychoanalysis, applied to those parts of a dream remembered on waking, opp to latent. ◆ vt to make clear or easily seen; to put beyond doubt; to reveal or declare. ◆ n the act of showing something publicly; (the form of) an apparition, ghost, etc; an open or public statement; a list or invoice of the cargo of a ship or aeroplane, used by customs officials and overseas agents; a list of passengers carried by an aeroplane. [L manifestus, prob from manus the hand, and festus pap of obs fendere to strike, to dash against (as in offendere)]
■ **manifest'able** or **manifest'ible** adj that can be manifested or clearly shown. **manifestā'tion** n an act of disclosing what is dark or secret; that by which something is manifested; an appearance of an apparition, ghost, etc; display; a mass-meeting, public procession or demonstration. **manifest'ative** adj. **man'ifestly** adv obviously, undoubtedly. **man'ifestness** n the state of being manifest.

manifesto /ma-ni-fes'tō/ n (pl **manifest'os** or **manifest'oes**) a public written declaration of the intentions, opinions, or motives of a leader, party, or body or of a sovereign. ◆ vi (rare) to issue a manifesto. [Ital; see **manifest**]

manifold /man'i-fold/ adj various in kind or quality; many in number; having many features; performing several functions. ◆ n a pipe with several lateral outlets to others, as in the exhaust system of the internal-combustion engine; an aggregate (maths); a topological space or surface that is related in a particular way to Euclidean space (*maths*); a carbon copy; the manyplies (*dialect*; also in *pl*). ◆ *vt* to multiply; to make simultaneous copies of. [**many** and **-fold**]

■ **man'ifolder** *n*. **man'ifoldly** *adv*. **man'ifoldness** *n*.

❑ **man'ifold-paper** *n* thin paper for making copies. **man'ifold-writer** *n* a copying apparatus.

maniform /man'i-förm/ *adj* having the form of a hand. [L *manus* the hand, and *förma* a shape]

manihoc see **manioc**.

Manihot /man'i-hot/ *n* a tropical American genus of the spurge family, including manioc. [**manioc**]

manikin or **mannikin** /man'i-kin/ *n* a dwarf; an anatomical model of a human body used for teaching purposes, as in art and medicine; a mannequin; a bird of the weaver finch family found chiefly in S Asia and N Australia; a manakin (*non-standard*). [Du *manneken*, a double dimin of *man*; Eng **man**[1]]

manila or **manilla** /mə-nil'ə/ *n* a cheroot or small cigar made in *Manila*; the fibre of the abaca plant; strong brownish paper *orig* made from abaca plant fibre.

❑ **Manila** (or **Manilla**) **hemp** *n* abaca plant fibre.

manilla /mə-nil'ə/ *n* a horseshoe-shaped ring used *esp* for ceremonial exchanges in parts of W Africa. [Sp, from LL *manilia* a bracelet, from L *manus* the hand, or L *monīlia* (pl of *monīle*) necklace, influenced by *manus*]

manille /mə-nil'/ *n* in the card games ombre and quadrille, the highest card but one. [Sp *malilla*]

manioc /man'i-ok/ *n* (also **man'dioc**, **mandio'ca**, **mandio'cca** and **man'ihoc**) a plant of the *Manihot* genus, cassava; meal obtained from the root of this plant. [Tupí *mandioca*]

maniple /man'i-pl/ *n* a company of foot soldiers in the Roman army (*hist*); (in the Western Christian Church) a clerical vestment used during the sacrament, a narrow strip worn on the left arm. [L *manipulāre*, from *manus* the hand, and *plēre* to fill]

■ **manipular** /mə-nip'ū-lər/ *adj*.

maniplies same as **manyplies**.

manipular see under **maniple** and **manipulate**.

manipulate /mə-nip'ū-lāt/ *vt* to work with the hands; to handle or manage; to treat by manipulation; to give a false appearance to, change the character, etc, of; to turn to one's own purpose or advantage; to move, edit or alter text, data files, etc (*comput*). [LL *manipulāre*, *-ātum*; see **maniple**]

■ **manipulabil'ity** *n*. **manip'ulable** or **manip'ulatable** *adj* capable of being manipulated. **manip'ular**, **manip'ulative** or **manip'ulatory** *adj* tending or attempting to manipulate. **manipulā'tion** *n* the act of manipulating; techniques, practised by osteopaths, chiropractors, etc, in which the hands are used to treat parts of the body, eg joints or soft tissues. **manip'ulatively** *adv*. **manip'ulātor** *n* a person who manipulates; a mechanical device for handling small, remote, or radioactive objects. See also **master-slave manipulator** under **master**.

Manis /mā'nis/ *n* the pangolin or scaly anteater. [Appar intended as sing of **manes**]

manitou /man'i-too/ *n* a spirit or sacred object among certain Native American tribes (also **manito** /-tō/). [Algonquin]

manjack /man'jak/ *n* a West Indian boraginaceous tree (*Cordia macrophylla*); its fruit.

man-jack, **mankind** see under **man**[1].

mankini /man-kē'ni/ *n* a man's one-piece swimsuit covering the crotch and shoulders and little else. [**man**[1] and **bikini**]

manky /mang'ki/ (*sl*; *orig Scot* and *dialect*) *adj* (**man'kier**; **man'kiest**) filthy, dirty, rotten. [Obs Scot *mank* defective, from OFr *manc*]

manly, **man-made**, **man-management** see under **man**[1].

manna /man'ə/ *n* the food miraculously provided for the Israelites in the wilderness (*Bible*); delicious food for body or mind; anything advantageous happening to one as by divine intervention or fate; a sugary substance exuded from the **mann'a-ash** (*Fraxinus ornus*) or **mann'a-larch** (**Briançon manna**), and other trees, from a species of tamarisk, from *Alhagi*, etc; edible fragments of the **mann'a-lichen** (*Lecanora*); float-grass seeds; honeydew. [Heb *mān hū* what is it?, or from *man* a gift]

■ **manniferous** *adj*. **mann'ite** or **mann'itol** *n* a sweet alcohol, $C_6H_8(OH)_6$, obtained from manna, from seaweeds of the genus *Laminaria*, etc. **mann'ose** *n* a sugar, $C_6H_{12}O_6$, obtained by oxidizing mannitol.

❑ **mann'a-croup** /-kroop'/ or **mann'a-groats** *n* (Russ *krupa*) grains of manna-grass. **mann'a-dew** *n* manna imagined to be solidified dew. **mann'a-grass** *n* an aquatic grass (genus *Glyceria*) with edible seeds, float grass.

mannequin /man'i-kin/ *n* a dummy figure, as used for display in shop windows, etc; a person, *usu* a woman, employed to wear and display clothes. [Fr, from Du; see **manikin**]

manner[1] /man'ər/ *n* the way in which anything is done; method; fashion; personal style of acting or bearing; custom; style of writing or of thought; sort (of; formerly often with omission of following *of*); style; (in *pl*) morals (*archaic*); (in *pl*) social conduct; (in *pl*) good or polite behaviour. [Fr *manière*, from *main*, from L *manus* the hand]

■ **mann'ered** *adj* having manners (*esp* in combination, as *well-* or *ill-mannered*); affected with mannerism; artificial; stilted. **mann'erism** *n* a constant sameness of manner; stiltedness; a marked peculiarity or trick of style or manner, *esp* in literary composition; manner or style becoming wearisome by its sameness; (*usu* with *cap*) a late-16c style of painting and architecture, *esp* in Italy, characterized by distortion of the human figure, bright harsh colours, etc. **mann'erist** *n* a person inclined to mannerism; (*usu* with *cap*) an artist working in the style of Mannerism. ◆ *adj* relating to mannerism or mannerists; (*usu* with *cap*) in the style of Mannerism. **manneris'tic** *adj*. **manneris'tically** *adv*. **mann'erless** *adj*. **mann'erliness** *n*. **mann'erly** *adj* showing good manners; well-behaved; not rude. ◆ *adv* with good manners; civilly; respectfully; without rudeness.

■ **all manner of** all kinds of. **by no manner of means** under no circumstances; in no way whatever. **in a manner** in a certain way. **make one's manners** (*archaic*) to salute a person on meeting by a bow, curtsy, etc. **shark's manners** (*inf*) rapacity. **to the manner born** accustomed to something (as if) from birth; naturally suited to a particular thing.

manner[2] /man'ər/ *n* see **mainor**.

manniferous see under **manna**.

mannikin see **manikin**.

manning, **mannish** see **man**[1].

mannite, **mannitol**, **mannose** see under **manna**.

mano /mä'nō/ *n* (pl **man'os**) (in Mexico, SW USA, etc) a stone roller for grinding maize or other grain by hand on a metate (qv). [Sp, hand, from L *manus*]

mano a mano /mä'nō a mä'nō/ (*Sp*) hand to hand, in single combat.

manoao /mä'nō-ow/ *n* (pl **ma'noaos**) a shrub of the heath group. [Maori]

manoeuvre or (*N Am*) **maneuver** /mə-noo'vər or -nū'/ *n* a piece of skilful management; a stratagem; a skilful and clever movement in military or naval tactics; any movement skilfully or cleverly executed; (*usu* in *pl*) a large-scale battle-training exercise of armed forces. ◆ *vi* and *vt* to perform a manoeuvre; to manage skilfully; to change the position of troops or ships; to effect or gain by manoeuvres. [Fr *manœuvre*, from L *manū* by hand, and *opera* work; cf **manure**]

■ **manoeuvrabil'ity** or (*N Am*) **maneuverabil'ity** *n*. **manoeu'vrable** or (*N Am*) **maneu'verable** *adj*. **manoeu'vrer** or (*N Am*) **maneu'verer** *n*.

manometer /ma-nom'i-tər/ *n* an instrument for measuring and comparing the pressure of fluids. [Gr *manos* rare, thin, and *metron* measure]

■ **manometric** /man-ō-met'rik/ or **manomet'rical** *adj*. **manom'etry** *n*.

ma non troppo /ma non trop'ō/ (*music*) *adv* but not too much (see also **troppo**). [Ital]

manor /man'ər/ *n* the land belonging to a nobleman, or the part of this formerly reserved for his own use, including the manor-house; the district over which the court of the lord of the manor had authority (*hist*); a tract of land in N America for which a fee-farm rent was paid (*hist*); an area or base of operation, *esp* a police district (*sl*). [OFr *manoir*, from L *manēre*, *mānsum* to stay]

■ **manorial** /ma-nö'ri-əl/ *adj* relating to or resembling a manor.

❑ **man'or-house** or **man'or-seat** *n* the house or seat belonging to a manor.

manpower see under **man**[1].

manqué /mä-kā'/ (*Fr*) *adj* having had ambition or potential, but without it being fulfilled (placed after the noun, as in *poet manqué*).

manred /man'red/ (*obs*) *n* (also (*Scot*) **man'rent**) homage; a body of vassals. [OE *mannrǣden*; **man**[1] and sfx *-rǣden*, expressing mode or state]

mansard-roof /man'särd-roof/ *n* a roof having its angle divided to slope more steeply in the lower part than in the upper (also **man'sard**). [François *Mansard* or *Mansart* (1598–1666), French architect]

manse /mans/ *n* an ecclesiastical residence, *esp* that of a parish minister of the Church of Scotland. [LL *mansus*, *mansa* a dwelling, from *manēre*, *mānsum* to remain]

■ **son of the manse** a minister's son.

■ words derived from main entry word; ❑ compound words; ■ idioms and phrasal verbs

mansion /man'shən/ *n* a large house; a manor-house; a house (*astrol*); (in *pl*) a large block of flats; abode, stay (*obs*); a resting place on a journey (*obs*); a dwelling-place (*archaic*; often in *pl*); an apartment or separate lodging in a building (*obs*). [OFr, from L *mānsiō*, *-ōnis*, from *manēre*, *mānsum* to remain, to stay]
■ **man'sionary** (*Shakesp* **man'sonry**) *n* residence; mansions.
❑ **man'sion-house** *n* a mansion, a large house.
■ **the Mansion House** the official residence of the Lord Mayor of London.

manslaughter see under **man**[1].

mansonry see under **mansion**.

mansuete /man'swēt/ (*archaic*) *adj* gentle; mild; tame. [L *mānsuētus*, from *manus* hand, and *suēscere* to accustom]
■ **man'suetude** /-swi-tūd/ *n*.

mansworn /man'swōrn, -swörn/ (*archaic*) *adj* perjured. [OE *mānswerian*, from *mān* evil, and *swerian* to swear]

manta /man'tə/ *n* a blanket; a cloak; a horse-cloth; a mantlet (*fortif*); (with *cap*) a type of gigantic fish with winglike fins and a whiplike tail; a giant ray or sea-vampire (also called **manta ray**). [Sp]

manteau or **manto** /man'tō/ (*hist*) *n* (*pl* **man'teaus** /-tōz/, **man'teaux** /-tō, -tōz/, **man'toes** or **man'tos**) a woman's loose gown of the 17c–18c. [Fr *manteau*, from L *mantellum*]

manteel /man-tēl'/ (*obs*) *n* a soldier's cloak; a woman's cape. [Fr *mantille*, from Sp *mantilla*]

mantel /man'tl/ *n* a manteltree; a mantelpiece; a mantelshelf. [**mantle**]
■ **man'telet** *n* a mantlet.
❑ **mantel clock** *n* a clock designed to sit on a mantelpiece, often being wound and adjusted from the front. **man'telpiece** *n* the ornamental structure over and in front of a fireplace; a mantelshelf. **man'telshelf** *n* the ornamental shelf over a fireplace. **man'teltree** *n* the lintel or arch of a fireplace.

mantelet see under **mantel** and **mantle**.

mantic /man'tik/ *adj* relating to divination; prophetic. See also **-mancy**. [Gr *mantikos*, from *mantis* a prophet]

manticore /man'ti-kör/ or **manticora** /-kö'rə/ *n* a fabulous animal with the body of a lion, tail of a scorpion, porcupine quills, and a human head. [L *manticora*, from Gr *mantichōrās*, a wrong reading for *martichorās*, from Pers *mardkhora* man-eater]

mantid see under **mantis**.

mantilla /man-til'ə/ *n* a small cloak; a kind of veil covering the head and the shoulders. [Sp, dimin of *manta*]

mantis /man'tis/ *n* (*pl* **man'tises** or **man'tes** /-tēz/) an insect of the genus *Mantis* or related genera, which carry their large spiny forelegs in the attitude of prayer (also called **praying insect** or **praying mantis**). [Gr *mantis*, *-eōs* prophet]
■ **man'tid** *n* any member of the *Mantis* genus.
❑ **mantis shrimp** *n* a stomatopod crustacean with claws like those of the mantis.

mantissa /man-tis'ə/ *n* the fractional part of a logarithm (*maths*); the significant digits of a floating-point number (*comput*). [L, make-weight]

mantle /man'tl/ *n* the status, role, authority, etc of a person as assumed by or passed on to another (in allusion to Elijah in Bible, 1 Kings 19.19 ff); a fold of the external skin of a mollusc or a brachiopod secreting the substance forming shell (*zool*); the back and folded wings of a bird; a scum on a liquid (*archaic*); a hood or network of fire-resistant material that becomes incandescent when exposed to a flame; the part of the earth immediately beneath the crust, constituting the greater part of the earth's bulk, and presumed to consist of solid heavy rock; a cloak or loose outer garment (*archaic*); a covering (*esp poetic*). ◆ *vt* to cover (*esp poetic*); to obscure; to form a scum on (*archaic*); to suffuse with colour (*literary*); to disguise. ◆ *vi* to spread or extend like a mantle; to develop a scum or crust (*archaic*); to froth or bubble; to be suffused with colour, to blush (*literary*); (of a hawk) to stretch the wings over the legs (*falconry*). [Partly through OE *mentel*, partly through OFr *mantel* (Fr *manteau*), from L *mantel(l)um*]
■ **man'tlet** or **man'telet** *n* a small cloak for women, worn *esp* in the 19c; a movable shield or screen (*fortif*). **man'tling** *n* cloth suitable for mantles; the drapery of a coat of arms (*heraldry*).
❑ **mantle rock** *n* loose rock at the earth's surface.

manto see **manteau**.

Mantoux test /man'too test/ (*med*) *n* a test for the existence of tuberculosis in humans by the injection of tuberculin into the skin. [Charles *Mantoux* (1877–1947), French physician]

mantra /man'trə/, also **mantram** /-trəm/ *n* a Vedic hymn (*Hinduism*); a sacred text used as an incantation; extended to music having a mystical effect; a word, phrase, etc, chanted or repeated inwardly in meditation (*Hinduism* and *Buddhism*). [Sans, instrument of thought]

mantrap see under **man**[1].

mantua /man'tū-ə/ *n* a woman's loose outer gown, worn in the 17c–18c (also (*Scot*) **mant'y**). [*manteau*, confused with *Mantua*, in Italy]
❑ **man'tua-maker** *n* a dressmaker.

Mantuan /man'tū-ən/ *adj* of or relating to *Mantua* in Italy. ◆ *n* a native or inhabitant of Mantua, *esp* Virgil; also the name of the Latin pastoral poet Baptista *Mantuanus* (1448–1516).

manty see **mantua**.

manual /man'ū-əl/ *adj* of the hand or hands; done, worked, or used by the hand(s), as opposed to automatic, computer-operated, etc; working with the hands. ◆ *n* a handbook or handy compendium of a large subject or treatise; an instruction book for a piece of machinery, etc; drill in the use of weapons, etc (*milit*); an old office-book like the modern Roman Catholic *Rituale*; an organ key or keyboard played by hand not foot; a primary feather. [L *manuālis*, from *manus* the hand]
■ **man'ually** *adv*.
❑ **manual alphabet** *n* sign language. **manual exercise** *n* (*milit*) drill in handling arms. **manual lymphatic drainage** *n* a massage therapy involving rhythmic manual techniques which improve drainage throughout the lymphatic system, used *esp* to reduce oedema (*abbrev* **MLD**).

manubrium /mə-nū'bri-əm/ *n* (*pl* **manū'bria** or **manū'briums**) any handle-like structure; the presternum or anterior part of the breastbone in mammals (*anat*); the pendent oral part of a jellyfish, etc. [L *manūbrium* a handle]
■ **manū'brial** *adj*.

manufacture /ma-nū-fak'chər/ *vt* to make, *orig* by hand, now *usu* by machinery and on a large scale; to fabricate, concoct or invent; to produce unintelligently in quantity. ◆ *vi* to be occupied in manufacture. ◆ *n* the practice, act or process of manufacturing; anything manufactured. [Fr, from L *manū* (ablative) by hand, and *factūra* a making, from *facere*, *factum* to make]
■ **manufact'ory** *n* a factory or place where goods are manufactured. **manufact'urable** *adj*. **manufact'ural** *adj*. **manufact'urer** *n* a person or business engaged in manufacturing; a director or manager of a firm that manufactures goods; a person who makes, concocts or invents; a factory worker (*obs*). **manufact'uring** *adj* and *n* (relating to or engaged in) manufacture.

manuka /mä'nū-kä, mə-noo'kə/ *n* an Australian and New Zealand tree (genus *Leptospermum*) of the myrtle family, with hard, close-grained wood, and aromatic leaves formerly used as a substitute for tea. [Maori]
❑ **manuka honey** *n* honey made from the nectar of manuka flowers, thought to have medicinal qualities.

manul /mä'nūl/ *n* another name for **Pallas's cat**. [Mongolian]

manumea /ma-nə-mä'ə/ *n* a Samoan pigeon with a notched lower mandible. [Samoan]

manumit /ma-nū-mit'/ *vt* (**manumitt'ing**; **manumitt'ed**) to release from slavery; to set free. [L *manūmittere* or *manū mittere* or *ēmittere* to send from one's hand or control, from *manus* the hand, and *mittere*, *missum* to send]
■ **manumission** /-mish'ən/ *n*. **manumitt'er** *n*.

manure /mə-nūr'/, formerly /man'ūr/ *n* any substance, *esp* dung, added to soil to make it more fertile. ◆ *vt* to cover or enrich (soil) with any fertilizing substance; to hold or occupy (*obs*); to manage (*obs*); to cultivate (*obs*). [Anglo-Fr *maynoverer* (Fr *manœuvrer*) in the *obs* sense of the verb; see **manoeuvre**]
■ **manūr'ance** *n* (*archaic*) cultivation. **manūr'er** *n*. **manūr'ial** *adj*. **manūr'ing** *n*.

manus /mä'nəs, mä'nūs/ *n* the hand or corresponding part of a vertebrate. [L]

manuscript /man'ū-skript/ *adj* written by hand or typed, not printed. ◆ *n* a book or document written by hand before the invention of printing; copy for a printer, handwritten or typed; handwritten form. [L *manū* (ablative) by hand, and *scrībere*, *scrīptum* to write]

Manx /mangks/ *n* the language of the Isle of *Man*, belonging to the Gadhelic branch of Celtic; (with *the*) the people of the Isle of Man. ◆ *adj* of or relating to the Isle of Man, its inhabitants or language.
❑ **Manx cat** *n* a breed of cat with only a rudimentary tail. **Manx'man** or **Manx'woman** *n*. **Manx shearwater** *n* a shearwater (*Puffinus puffinus*) with slender wings and black-and-white plumage.

many /men'i/ *adj* (*compar* **more** /mōr, mör/; *superl* **most** /mōst/) consisting of a great number; numerous. ◆ *n* and pronoun many people; a great number (*usu* with omission of *of*); company, retinue (*Spenser*; *perh* for **meinie**). [OE *manig*]
■ **man'yfold** *adj* (*cf* **manifold**) many in number. ◆ *adv* many times over.
❑ **man'y-coloured** *adj* having many colours. **man'y-eyed** *adj* having many eyes. **many-fold'ed** *adj* (*Spenser*) having many layers; having many folds. **many-head'ed** *adj* having many heads; consisting of many. **man'y-root** *n* the ruellia plant, a member of the acanthus

family. **many-sid'ed** adj having many qualities or aspects; having wide interests or varied abilities. **many-sid'edness** n. **many-tongued'** adj.

■ **have one too many** to drink to excess. **many a** many (with singular noun and verb). **many-headed beast** or **monster** the people, the irrational mob (a translation of Horace's *belua multorum capitum*). **the many** the crowd, ordinary people in general.

manyatta or **manyata** /man-yat'ə/ n a small Masai settlement or encampment. [Masai]

manyplies /men'i-plīz/ n sing and n pl the third stomach of a ruminant, the *omasum* or *psalterium* (also **man'iplies** and (*dialect*) **moniplies** or **monyplies** /mon', mun'/). [**many** and **ply¹**]

manzanilla /man-zə-nil'ə, -nē'yə/ n a very dry, light sherry. [Sp; also meaning camomile; same root as **manchineel**]

manzanita /man-zə-nē'tə/ n a Californian species of bearberry. [Sp, dimin of *manzana* apple]

manzello /man-zel'ō/ n (pl **manzell'os**) a musical instrument like the soprano saxophone. [Origin uncertain]

MAOI abbrev : monoamine-oxidase inhibitor.

Maoist /mow'ist/ n and adj (an adherent) of the Chinese type of communism as expounded by Mao Zedong.
■ **Mao'ism** n.
❏ **Mao'-jacket** or **Mao'-suit** n a high-collared, usu cotton jacket or suit in the style of those worn by Mao Zedong and his followers, common dress in modern China.

Maori /mow'ri, mä'ō-ri/ n (pl **Mao'ris** or **Mao'ri**) a member of the aboriginal people of New Zealand; the language of this people. ◆ adj of the Maoris or their language. [Maori]
❏ **Maori bug** n (NZ) a large wingless cockroach (*Platyzosteria novae-zelandiae*). **Maori chief** n a brightly-coloured fish of New Zealand. **Mao'ridom** n the Maori world or culture. **Maori hen** n the weka. **Mao'riland** n (archaic) New Zealand. **Maori oven** n (NZ) an open-air hollow filled with heated stones on which food is cooked. **Maori side-step** n (rugby) the action of running directly at, rather than swerving to avoid, an oncoming tackler. **Maoritanga** /mow-ri-tän'gə/ n Maori traditions and culture; the fact or state of being Maori.

maormor /mär'mör, -mör/ a non-standard form of **mormaor**.

map /map/ n a representation in outline of the surface features of the earth, the moon, etc, or of part of it, usu on a plane surface; a similar plan of the stars in the sky; a representation, scheme or example of the layout or state of anything; a person's face (sl). ◆ vt (**mapp'ing**; **mapped**) to make a map of; to place (the elements of a set) in one-to-one correspondence with the elements of another set (maths); to link (an item of data) with a location in a processor's memory (comput). [L *mappa* a napkin, a painted cloth, orig Punic]
■ **map'less** adj. **mapp'able** adj. **mapp'er** n. **mapp'ery** n (Shakesp) perh working with or making maps, planning out. **mapp'ist** n. **map'wise** adv in the manner of a map.
❏ **map'-measurer** n an instrument for measuring distances on a map. **map'-mounter** n a person who mounts maps, or backs them with cloth and fixes them on rollers, etc. **map'-pin** n a pin with a coloured head used to mark points on a map. **map projection** see **projection** under **project**. **map'-reader** n. **map'-reading** n the interpretation of what one sees on a geographical map.
■ **gene mapping** (biol) the determination of the positions and relative distances of genes on chromosomes either by means of linkage (qv under **link¹**) or by the arrangement of DNA sequences in a gene or cluster of genes. **map out** to plan, divide up, and apportion; to lay out a plan of. **off the map** out of existence, esp in the phrase *wipe off the map*; negligible; (of a location) remote from main thoroughfares, etc. **on the map** to be taken into account. **put on the map** to bring to public attention, to make well-known.

maple /mā'pl/ n any tree of the genus *Acer*, from the sap of some species of which sugar and syrup can be made; its timber. ◆ adj of maple. [OE *mapul* maple]
❏ **maple candy** n (N Am) a brittle confection made from maple sugar. **maple leaf** n the emblem of Canada; (with cap) a one-ounce Canadian gold coin depicting a maple leaf on the reverse. **maple sugar** n. **maple syrup** n.

mappemond /map'ə-mōnd, map-mōnd'/ n a map of the world (hist); the world itself (obs). [LL *mappa mundī*]

mapstick see **mopstick** under **mop¹**.

maquette /ma-ket'/ n a small model of something to be made on a larger scale, esp a model in clay or wax of a piece of sculpture. [Fr]

maqui /ma-kē'/ n a Chilean evergreen shrub (*Aristotelia maqui*, family Elaeocarpaceae) whose berry yields a medicinal wine. [Araucanian (S American language)]

maquiladora /mak-i-la-dō'rə/ n a factory or assembly plant owned by a US company in Mexico, operating under a free-trade agreement to

allow duty-free export of finished products for sale in the USA. [Mex Sp, from Sp *maquillar* to make up]

maquillage /ma-kē-yäzh'/ n (the art of using) cosmetics, make-up. [Fr]

maquis /ma-kē', ma'kē or mä'kē/ n sing and n pl a thicket formation of shrubs, as in Corsica and on Mediterranean shores (bot); (often with cap) French guerrilla resistance forces (1940–45), or a member of one. [Fr, from Ital *macchia*, from L *macula* mesh]
■ **maquisard** /mä-kē-zär/ n (often with cap) a member of the maquis.

MAR /mär/ (comput) abbrev : memory address register.

Mar. abbrev : March.

mar /mär/ vt (**marr'ing**; **marred** or (Spenser) **mard**) to spoil; to impair; to injure; to damage; to disfigure; to interfere with (obs). [OE *merran*]
■ **mar'dy** n (dialect) a spoilt child; a timid or petulant crybaby. ◆ adj (dialect) behaving like a spoilt child; petulant. ◆ vt (dialect) to behave like a mardy.
❏ **mar'plot** n (archaic) someone who defeats or mars a plot by unwarranted interference. **mar'prelate** vi and adj (to inveigh) after the manner of Martin *Marprelate*, the name assumed by the author of certain anti-episcopal tracts, 1588–9. **mar'sport** n (archaic) a spoilsport. **mar'text** n (rare) an ignorant preacher.

mara /mə-rä'/ n a hare-like S American rodent, the so-called Patagonian hare or *Dolichotis*.

marabou /mar'ə-boo/ or **marabout** /-boot/ n an adjutant bird, esp an African species; its feathers; a plume or trimming of its feathers; a feather necklet; a very white raw silk. [Ety as for **marabout¹**]

marabout¹ /mar'ə-boot/ n a Muslim hermit, esp in N Africa; a practitioner of the occult, a type of witch doctor; a Muslim shrine. [Fr, from Ar *murābit* hermit]

marabout² see **marabou**.

marabunta /ma-rə-bun'tə/ (W Indies) n any of various social wasps; a bad-tempered woman (sl). [Perh from W African dialect]

maraca /mə-rak'ə/ n a hand-held percussion instrument, usu one of a pair, consisting of a gourd or substitute filled with dried beans, beads, etc. [Carib]

marae /mə-rī'/ n a Maori meeting-place, traditionally an open courtyard. [Maori]

maraging /mä'rā-jing/ (metallurgy) n a process by which a metal alloy is slowly cooled in the air, becoming very strong and resistant to corrosion. [From *martensite* and *aging*]

marah /mä'rä/ n bitterness; something bitter. [Heb]

maranatha /ma-rə-nä'thə/ see **anathema maranatha** under **anathema**.

Maranta /mə-ran'tə/ n the arrowroot genus of monocotyledons giving name to the family **Marantä'ceae**, related to the banana and ginger families. [Bartolommeo *Maranta*, 16c Italian herbalist]

marari /mä-rä'rē/ (NZ) n the butterfish. [Maori]

maraschino /ma-rə-skē'nō, -shē'nō/ n (pl **maraschi'nos**) a liqueur distilled from a cherry grown in the Croatian region of Dalmatia. [Ital, from *marasca*, *amarasca* a sour cherry, from L *amārus* bitter]
❏ **maraschino cherry** n a cherry preserved in real or imitation maraschino and used for decorating cocktails, cakes, etc.

marasmus /mə-raz'məs/ (med) n a wasting away of the body, associated esp with malnutrition in infants. [Latinized, from Gr *marasmos*, from *marainein* to decay]
■ **maras'mic** adj. **Maras'mius** n a common genus of toadstools, including the fairy-ring champignon, drying up in sunshine but recovering in damp.

Maratha or **Mahratta** /mə-rä'tə/ n a member of a once dominant people of SW India. [Hindi *maratha*, from Sans *mahārāṣṭra* great kingdom]
■ **Marathi** /mə-rät'ē/ n their Sanskritic language.

marathon /mar'ə-thon, -thən/ n a long-distance foot-race (usu 26 miles 385 yards, 42.195km), commemorating the tradition that a Greek ran from Marathon to Athens with news of victory after a battle in 490BC; a long-distance race in other sports, eg swimming; any long, severe test of endurance. ◆ adj relating to running marathons; of great length in time, distance, etc; displaying powers of endurance and stamina. [*Marathōn*, town in Greece, about 22 miles from Athens]
■ **mar'athoner** n. **Marathōn'ian** adj and n.

Marattia /mə-rat'i-ə/ n a genus of ferns giving name to the **Marattia'ceae**, a tropical family of very large primitive eusporangiate ferns. [GF *Maratti* (died 1777), Italian botanist]

maraud /mə-röd'/ vi to wander in search of plunder. ◆ vt to plunder or raid. ◆ n (archaic) raiding; plundering. [Fr *maraud* rogue; origin obscure]
■ **maraud'er** n. **maraud'ing** adj and n.

■ words derived from main entry word; ❏ compound words; ■ idioms and phrasal verbs

maravedi /ma-rə-vā'di/ (hist) n an obsolete Spanish copper coin of little value. [Sp maravedí, from Ar Murābitīn the dynasty of the Almoravides (11c and 12c)]

marble /mär'bl/ n a hard, granular crystalline limestone taking a high polish and smooth finish; any rock of similar appearance taking a high polish; a slab, work of art, tombstone, tomb, or other object made of marble; a little hard ball (orig of marble) used in children's games; marbling; anything hard, cold, polished, white, or otherwise like marble (fig); (in pl) any of several games played with little (now usu glass) marbles; (in pl) one's wits or senses (sl). ◆ adj composed or made of marble; shining like marble; unyielding; hard; insensible; marbled. ◆ vt to stain, vein or print to resemble marble. [OFr marbre, from L marmor; cf Gr marmaros, from marmairein to sparkle] ■ mar'bled adj irregularly mottled and streaked like some kinds of marble; made from marble; furnished with marble. mar'bler n. mar'bling n a marbled appearance or colouring; the act of veining or painting in imitation of marble. mar'bly adj like marble. ❑ marble-breast'ed or marble-heart'ed adj (literary) hard-hearted, cruel, uncaring. marble cake n a sponge cake made by lightly mixing more than one shade of base mixture, having a marbled appearance when cut. marble-con'stant adj (literary) constant or firm as marble, immovable. mar'ble-cutter n a person who hews marble; a machine for cutting marble. mar'bled-white n a butterfly of the Satyridae. mar'ble-edged adj (of a book) having the edges marbled. mar'ble-paper n paper coloured in imitation of variegated marble. ■ Elgin marbles a collection of marble sculptures obtained chiefly from the Parthenon by Lord Elgin and purchased by the British Museum in 1816. have or lose (all) one's marbles (sl) have or lose one's wits.

Marburg disease same as **green monkey disease** (see **green monkey** under **green**[1]).

MARC /märk/ abbrev: machine readable cataloguing, a standardized system used by libraries to produce bibliographic records that can be read by computer.

marc /märk/ or (Fr) mär/ n grapeskins and other refuse from wine-making; brandy made from this (also **marc brandy**); any fruit refuse, eg from the making of cooking oil. [Fr]

Marcan /mär'kən/ adj of the evangelist St Mark or his gospel.

marcantant /mär'kən-tant/ (Shakesp) n a merchant. [Ital mercatante]

marcasite /mär'kə-sīt/ n sulphide of iron in orthorhombic crystals (in the gem trade it can be pyrite, polished steel, etc). [LL marcasīta, from Ar marqashīt(h)ā; origin unknown]

marcato /mär-kä'tō/ (music) adj (superl **marcatis'simo**) marked; emphatic; strongly accented. ◆ adv performed with a strong accent or emphasis. [Ital, from marcare to mark]

Marcel or **marcel** /mär-sel'/ n (in full **Marcel wave**) an artificial wave in hair, produced by styling with a hot iron, etc; a hairstyle with such waves. ◆ vt to style (hair) with marcel waves. [Marcel Grateau (1852–1936), French hairdresser] ■ marcelled' adj.

marcella /mär-sel'ə/ n a type of cotton or linen fabric, in twill weave. [Anglicization of Marseilles]

marcescent /mär-ses'ənt/ adj (of a part of a plant) withering without falling off. [L marcēscēns, -entis, prp of marcēscere, from marcēre to fade] ■ marcesc'ence n. marcesc'ible adj.

Marcgravia /märk-grä'vi-ə/ n a tropical American genus of climbing epiphytic shrubs, with pitcher-like bracts developed as nectaries, visited by hummingbirds, giving name to the family **Marcgraviā'ceae**, related to the tea family. [Georg Markgraf (1610–44), German traveller]

March /märch/ n the third month of the year. [L Martius (mēnsis) the month dedicated to Mars] ❑ **March beer** n a particularly strong beer traditionally brewed in March. **March hare** n a hare gambolling in the breeding season, proverbially mad because of its antics.

march[1] /märch/ vi to walk in a markedly rhythmical military manner, or in a grave, stately or resolute manner; to advance steadily or irresistibly. ◆ vt to cause to march; to force to go. ◆ n a marching movement; an act of marching; the distance covered by marching, esp for a specified amount of time; regular advance; a piece of music written for marching to, or similar in character and rhythm, usu with a trio; a move made by a chess piece. [Fr marcher to walk, prob from L marcus a hammer] ■ march'er n. ❑ **marching orders** n pl orders to march; dismissal from employment, etc (inf). **marching regiment** n one without permanent quarters. **march past** n the march of a body of troops, etc in front of the person who reviews it.

■ **forced march** a march necessarily carried out at great speed. **on the march** marching; advancing. **rogue's march** music played in derision of a person expelled. **steal a march on** to gain an advantage over, esp in a sly or secret manner.

march[2] /märch/ n (usu in pl) a boundary; a border; (in pl; also with cap) a border district. ◆ vi to have a common boundary. [Fr marche; of Gmc origin; cf **mark**[1], OE mearc] ■ **march'er** n an inhabitant or lord of a border district (also adj). ❑ **march'-dyke** or **march'-dike** n a boundary wall, usu of turf. **march'lands** n pl a border area between countries. **march'man** n a person living on or near a border. **march'-stone** n a boundary stone. **march'-treason** n (hist) an offence against the laws of the marches, eg raiding the neighbouring country in time of peace. ■ **Lord marcher** (hist) a lord who had royal prerogative in, and jurisdiction over, lands in the marches. **riding the marches** the old ceremony of riding round the bounds of a town, etc.

marchantia /mär-kan'shi-ə, -ti-ə/ n a liverwort of the Marchantia genus, with a flat, lobed and branched thallus, growing in damp places, giving name to the family **Marchantiā'ceae**. [Nicolas Marchant (died 1678), French botanist]

Märchen /mer'hhən/ (Ger) n (pl **Mär'chen**) a story or fable, a folk tale.

marchesa /mär-kā'za/ n (pl **marche'se** /-zē/) an Italian marchioness. [Ital; cf **marchioness**] ■ **marchese** /mär-kā'ze/ n (pl **marche'si** /-zē/) an Italian marquess.

marchioness /mär'shə-nes, -nis/ n the wife or widow of a marquis or marquess; a woman who holds a marquisate in her own right; a size of roofing slate 22 × 11in (55.88 × 27.94cm). [LL marchiōnissa, fem of marchiō, -ōnis a lord of the marches]

marchpane /märch'pān/ n until the 19c, same as **marzipan**. [Ital marzapane]

Marcionite /mär'shə-nīt/ n a follower of Marcion of Sinope (died 165AD), who, partly under Gnostic influences, constructed an ethico-dualistic philosophy of religion. ◆ adj of or relating to Marcion or the Marcionites. ■ **Mar'cionist** n. **Mar'cionītism** n.

Marcobrunner /mär'kō-brün-ər/ n a fine white German wine produced in Erbach, near Wiesbaden. [From the nearby Markbrunnen fountain]

Marconi® /mär-kō'ni/ adj relating to the Italian physicist Guglielmo Marconi (1874–1937), or his system of wireless telegraphy. ◆ vt and vi (without cap) to communicate by wireless telegraphy. ■ **marcō'nigram** n a message so transmitted. **marcō'nigraph** vt and vi.

Marco Polo sheep /mär'kō pō'lō shēp/ n a type of Asian wild sheep with large horns. [Marco Polo (1254–1324), Venetian explorer]

mard and **mardy** see **mar**.

Mardi Gras /mär-dē grä'/ (Fr) n Shrove Tuesday celebrated with a carnival in many places, famously Rio de Janeiro. [Fr, literally, Fat Tuesday]

mare[1] /mär/ n the female of the horse. [OE mere, fem of mearh a horse; cognate with Ger Mähre, ON merr, and Welsh march a horse] ❑ **mare's'-nest** n a supposedly worthwhile discovery that turns out to have no real value; a disordered place or situation. **mare's'-tail** n a tall marsh plant of the genus Hippuris; also applied to the horsetail; (in pl) long straight strands of grey cirrus cloud.

mare[2] /mä'rē/ or -ri, mar'e or -i/ n (pl **maria** /mä'ri-ə, ma'ri-a/) any of various darkish level areas on either the Moon or Mars. [L, sea] ❑ **mare clausum** /klō'səm, klow'sŭm/ n (L) a closed sea; a sea within the jurisdiction of one state. **mare liberum** /lib'ə-rəm, lē'be-rŭm/ n (L) a sea open to free navigation by ships of any nation.

mare[3] /mär/ n a folkloric evil spirit that terrifies or suffocates the sleeping person (Shakesp); a calamitous experience (sl). [Shortened from **nightmare** (under **night**)]

Marek's disease /mä'reks di-zēz'/ n a viral cancerous disease causing paralysis in poultry. [Jószef Marek (1868–1952), Hungarian veterinary surgeon]

maremma /mä-rem'ə/ n (pl **marem'me** /mē/) seaside marshland; an Italian sheepdog. [Ital, from L maritima seaside]

Marengo /mə-ren'gō/ adj (of meat) sautéed in oil and cooked with tomatoes, mushrooms, garlic and wine. [Named in honour of Napoleon's victory at the battle of Marengo in N Italy (1800)]

mareschal /mär'shl/ (archaic) n same as **marshal**.

Mareva injunction /mə-rē'və in-jungk'shən/ (law) n a court order freezing assets to prevent them being taken out of a country. [After the first company to be granted such an injunction]

Marfan syndrome /mär'fan sin'drōm/ n a genetic disorder that affects the connective tissue in the body, usu leading to extreme tallness and cardiovascular and optical defects. [ABJ *Marfan* (1858–1942), French paediatrician]

marg see **margarine**.

marg. *abbrev* : margin; marginal.

margarin /*mär'gə-rin*/ *n* a mixture of palmitin and stearin once thought a compound; a glyceryl ester of margaric acid. [Gr *margarītēs* a pearl] ■ **margaric** /-*gar'*/ or **margarit'ic** *adj* pearl-like. **margarite** /*mär'gə-rīt*/ *n* a pearly-lustred mineral sometimes regarded as a lime-alumina mica. **margaritif'erous** *adj* pearl-bearing. ◻ **margaric** or **margaritic acid** *n* an acid intermediate between palmitic and stearic.

margarine /*mär-jə-rēn'*, -*gə-*/ (contraction **marg** /*märg*/ or **marge** /*märj*/) *n* a butter-like substance made from vegetable oils and fats, etc. [Ety as for **margarin**]

margarita /*mär-gə-rē'tə*/ *n* a cocktail of tequila, lime or lemon juice, and orange-flavoured liqueur. [From the Sp name *Margarita*]

margay /*mär'gā*/ *n* a spotted S American tiger-cat. [Fr (or Sp), from Tupí *mbaracaià*]

marge[1] /*märj*/ (*poetic*) *n* margin, brink. [Fr, from L *margō*, -*inis*]

marge[2] see **margarine**.

margherita /*mär-gə-rē'tə*/ *n* a pizza topping of mozzarella cheese, tomato and basil. [Named in honour of *Margherita* of Savoy (1851–1926), queen of Italy]

margin /*mär'jin*/ or (*poetic and archaic*) **margent** /*mär'jənt*/ *n* an edge or border; (the width of) the blank edge on the page of a book or sheet of paper, or the rule (if any) separating it from the rest of the page; an amount (eg of time or money) allowed above what is strictly needed; in commodity futures markets, a proportion of money outstanding which is deposited with the broker; difference between selling and buying price, profit; an upper or lower limit; an amount by which one thing exceeds another. ◆ *vt* to provide with a margin or margins; to write in the margin. [L *margō*, *marginis* ; cf **mark**[1] and **march**[2]] ■ **mar'ginal** *adj* relating to a margin; in or on the margin; minor, subordinate or insignificant, not central, principal or mainstream; barely sufficient; not very relevant. ◆ *n* anything in or on a margin, *esp* a marginal constituency. **margina'lia** *n pl* notes written in a margin. **mar'ginalism** *n* an economic theory that the value of a product depends on its value to the final consumer. **mar'ginalist** *n*. **marginal'ity** *n*. **marginaliza'tion** or **-s-** *n*. **mar'ginalize** or **-ise** *vt* to write notes in the margin of; to push to the edges of anything, *esp* of consciousness, society, etc in order to reduce effectiveness. **mar'ginally** *adv*. **mar'ginate** *vt* to provide with a margin. ◆ *adj* (*bot* or *biol*) having a well-marked border (also **mar'ginated**). **margina'tion** *n*. **mar'gined** *adj*. ◻ **marginal constituency**, **seat** or **ward** *n* a constituency, seat or ward held with a small majority and not providing a safe seat for any of the political parties. **marginal cost** or **revenue** *n* (*econ*) the increase in a firm's total costs or revenue caused by producing one more unit of output. **marginal firm** *n* one whose profits are equivalent to the normal expected returns from the capital invested in them. **marginal land** *n* less fertile land which will be brought under cultivation only if economic conditions justify it. **marginal tax rate** *n* (*finance*) the percentage of each pound of extra income paid in tax. **mar'ginal-unit** *n* (*econ*) the last unit to be added to, or the first removed from, any supply. **margin call** *n* (*stock exchange*) a demand from a broker to increase the amount of money held on deposit. **margin index** *n* a form of thumb-index using coloured blocks rather than indentations in a book's margins.

margosa /*mär-gō'sə*/ *n* the tree that yields nim-oil. [Port *amargosa* (fem) bitter]

margrave /*mär'grāv*/ *n* a German nobleman of rank equivalent to an English marquess. [MDu *markgraaf* (Du *markgraaf* ; Ger *Markgraf*), from *mark* a border, and *grave* (now *graaf*) a count; cf Ger *Graf*, OE *gerēfa*, Eng **reeve**[1] and **sheriff**] ■ **mar'gravate** or **margrä'viate** *n* the jurisdiction or position of a margrave. **margravine** /*mär'grə-vēn*/ *n* a noblewoman of this rank; the wife or widow of a margrave.

marguerite /*mär-gə-rēt'*/ *n* the ox-eye daisy or other single chrysanthemum. [Fr, daisy, from Gr *margarītēs* pearl]

maria see **mare**[2].

mariachi /*ma-ri-ä'chi*/ *adj* designating a form of Mexican dance music played traditionally by strolling musicians. ◆ *n* (pl **maria'chis**) any of a group of musicians playing mariachi music. [Mex Sp]

mariage blanc /*ma-ri-azh blä'*/ (*Fr*) *n* an unconsummated marriage. [Fr, literally, white marriage]

mariage de convenance /*ma-ri-azh də kõ-və-näs'*/ (*Fr*) same as **marriage of convenance** (see under **marriage**).

marialite /*mä'ri-ə-līt*/ *n* a variety of scapolite rich in sodium, chlorine, and silica, poor in calcium. [*Maria* Rose vom Rath, mineralogist's wife]

Marian[1] /*mä'ri-ən*/ *adj* relating to the Virgin *Mary* or to Queen *Mary* (Tudor or Stuart). ◆ *n* a devotee, follower, or defender of (either) Mary; an English Roman Catholic of Mary Tudor's time. [L *Marīa*] ■ **Mariol'ater** *n* a person who practises Mariolatry. **Mariol'atrous** *adj*. **Mariol'atry**, also **Maryol'atry** *n* (Gr *latreiā* worship) excessive worship of the Virgin Mary, the veneration duly paid to her being properly hyperdulia (qv under **dulia**). **Mariol'ogist** *n*. **Mariol'ogy**, also **Maryol'ogy** *n* the study of the nature of, and doctrines and traditions concerning, the Virgin Mary.

Marian[2] /*mar'i-ən*, *mä'ri-ən*/ *adj* relating to the Roman general Gaius *Marius* (157–86BC).

mari complaisant /*ma-rē kõ-ple-zā'*/ (*Fr*) *n* a husband tolerant of his wife's infidelity. [Fr, literally, obliging husband]

mariculture /*mar'i-kul-chər*/ *n* the cultivation of plants and animals of the sea in their own environment. [L *mare* sea]

marid /*mar'id*, *mä-rēd'*/ *n* a member of the most powerful class of jinn. [Ar *mārid*, *marīd*, from *marada* to rebel]

Marie biscuit /*mə-rē' bis'kit*/ *n* a type of plain biscuit, *usu* thin with decorative indentations. [From the female personal name *Marie*]

Marie-Jeanne /*ma-rē-zhan'*/ *n* a bottle-size for wine, equivalent to three ordinary bottles (*usu* $2\frac{1}{4}$ litres).

Marie Rose /*mar'i rōz*/ *n* a seafood dressing made from mayonnaise and tomato sauce.

marigold /*mar'i-gōld*/ *n* a composite plant (genus *Calendula*) or its orange-yellow flower; extended to other yellow flowers (see under **corn**[1], **marsh**). [From the Virgin *Mary*, and **gold**[2]] ■ **African** and **French marigold** Mexican composites (genus *Tagetes*).

marigraph /*mar'i-gräf*/ *n* an instrument for recording tide levels. [L *mare* sea, and Gr *graphein* to write] ■ **mar'igram** *n* a record produced by this.

marijuana or **marihuana** /*ma-rə-(hh)wä'nə*/ *n* the hemp plant (*Cannabis sativa*); its dried flowers and leaves smoked as an intoxicant. [Am Sp]

Marilyn /*mar'ə-lin*/ *n* any British hill that has a reascent of 500 feet on all sides. [Appar coined facetiously from *Marilyn* Monroe (1926–62), US actress; cf **Munro**]

marimba /*mə-rim'bə*/ *n* an instrument resembling a xylophone, originally from Africa and now used *esp* in Latin American and jazz music (also **marim'baphone**). [African origin]

marina see under **marine**.

marinade /*ma-ri-nād'*/ *n* an alcoholic mixture or pickle in which fish, meat, etc is steeped before cooking, to improve the flavour or tenderize; ingredients steeped in this way. ◆ *vt* to steep in a marinade (also **mar'inate**). [Ety as for **marine**]

marine /*mə-rēn'*/ *adj* of, in, near, concerned with or belonging to the sea; done or used at sea; inhabiting, found in or obtained from the sea. ◆ *n* a soldier serving on board ship; a naval or mercantile shipping fleet; nautical service; naval affairs; a seascape. [Fr, from L *marīnus*, from *mare* sea] ■ **marina** /*mə-rē'nə*/ *n* a berthing area for yachts, etc, prepared with every kind of facility for a sailing holiday. **marinara** /*ma-ri-när'ə*/ *n* a seafood sauce served with pasta dishes. ◆ *adj* (of pasta) served with this sauce. **mar'iner** *n* (*esp literary*) a sailor. ◻ **marine acid** *n* hydrochloric acid. **marine boiler** *n* a steamship boiler. **marine engine** *n* a ship's engine. **marine glue** see under **glue**. **marine insurance** *n* insurance of ships or cargoes. **marine soap** *n* a coconut-oil soap, for washing with sea-water. **marine store** *n* a place where old ships' materials are bought and sold. **marine stores** *n pl* old ships' materials; supplies for ships. **marine trumpet** *n* the tromba marina. ■ **tell that to the marines** (*inf*) a phrase expressing disbelief and ridicule, from the sailor's contempt for the marine's ignorance of seamanship.

marinera /*ma-ri-ner'a*/ *n* a Peruvian folk dance danced in pairs; the music for this. [Sp *marinero*, -*nera* marine]

marinière /*ma-ri-ni-yer'*/ *adj* (*esp* of mussels) cooked in white wine with onions and herbs. [Fr *à la marinière* in the manner of the bargeman's wife]

Marinist /*mə-rē'nist*/ *n* a follower or imitator of the Italian poet Giambattista *Marini* (1569–1625). ■ **Marin'ism** *n* the poetic style of Marini, characterized by strained conceits.

Mariolatry, **Mariology**, etc see under **Marian**[1].

■ words derived from main entry word; ◻ compound words; ■ idioms and phrasal verbs

marionberry /mar'i-ən-ber-i/ n a hybrid fruit, a cross between a loganberry and a wild blackberry. [*Marion* County, Oregon, where it was developed]

marionette /mar-i-ə-net'/ n a puppet with jointed limbs moved by strings. [Fr, dimin of the name *Marion*, itself a dimin of *Marie* Mary]

Mariotte's law see **Boyle's law** under **law**[1].

mariposa /ma-ri-pō'zə/ n any of various plants of the *Calochortus* genus, with white, yellow or blue tulip-like flowers, native to N America (also **mariposa lily** or **tulip**). [Sp, butterfly]

marischal a Scots spelling of **marshal**.

marish /mar'ish/ (*obs*) n and adj same as **marsh**.

Marist /mar'ist/ n a member of a congregation within the Roman Catholic church emphasizing teaching, preaching and foreign missions. ◆ adj devoted to the Virgin Mary. [Fr *Mariste*]

maritage /mar'i-tij/ (*hist*) n the feudal superior's right to arrange the marriage of a vassal's heiress or heir, or to exact a fine in lieu of this; the fine exacted. [LL *marītāgium*]

marital /mar'i-təl, mə-rī'təl/ adj relating to a husband, or to a marriage; of the nature of a marriage. [L *marītālis*, from *marītus* a husband] ■ **mar'itally** (or /mə-rī'/) adv.

maritime /mar'i-tīm/ adj relating to the sea; relating to seafaring or sea-trade; having a sea-coast; situated near the sea; living on the shore, littoral; having a navy and sea-trade; (of a climate) having little seasonal variation in temperature. [L *maritimus*, from *mare* sea]

marivaudage /mä-rē-vō-däzh'/ n preciosity in literary style or expression. [Fr, from Pierre de *Marivaux* (1688–1763), French novelist and dramatist]

marjoram /mär'jə-rəm/ n an aromatic labiate plant (genus *Origanum*) used *esp* as a seasoning. [OFr *majorane*; origin doubtful]

mark[1] /märk/ n a visible indication or sign; a symbol; a distinctive badge or device; a brand; a set, group, or class, marked with the same brand; a type, model, issue, etc (*usu* numbered, as in *mark 1*); a rubber stamp; a token; a substitute for a signature, eg an X; a distinguishing characteristic; an impression or trace; a discoloured spot, streak, smear, or other local (*usu* small) modification of appearance; note; distinction; noteworthiness; a point awarded for merit; a footprint; a fair catch, formerly claimed by making an impression on the ground with one's heel (*rugby*); the starting-line in a race; a groove indicative of youth in a horse's incisor (as in *mark of mouth*); a tag on a lead-line indicating so many fathoms, feet, etc; the amount of departure (positive or negative), using equal intervals of time, from a space (a neutral or no-signal state) in accordance with a code (*telecom*); a suitable victim (of trickery, theft, etc) (*sl*); that which exactly suits one (*sl*); a boundary (*archaic*); a limit (*archaic*); a standard; a territory, *esp* a border territory (*archaic*); a tract of common land belonging to a village community (*hist*); a stone, post, etc, marking a boundary; an object indicating position or serving as a guide; an object to be aimed at, striven for, or attained, such as a butt, a goal, the jack at bowls, the pit of the stomach in boxing; a hawk's quarry (*obs*). ◆ vt to make a mark on; to indicate; to record; to put marks on (a child's, student's, etc, written work) to show where it is correct or incorrect (also *vi*); to make emphatic, distinct, or prominent; to characterize in a specified, distinct way; to impress or stamp with a sign; to take note of; to regard; (in football, hockey, etc) to remain close to (one's opponent) in order to try and prevent him or her from obtaining or passing the ball (also *vi*). ◆ vi to take particular notice; to become stained. [OE (Mercian) *merc* (WSax *mearc*) a boundary, a limit; Ger *Mark*, Gothic *marka*]

■ **marked** adj having visible marks; indicated; noticeable; prominent; emphatic; watched and suspected; destined (with *for*); doomed. **markedly** /mär'kid-li/ adv noticeably. **markedness** /mär'kid-nes/ n. **mark'er** n a person or tool that marks; something that marks a position, such as a stationary light or a flare; a person who marks the score at games, eg at billiards; a counter or other device for scoring; a bookmark; a marker pen (*N Am*); a recorder of attendances; a kind of school monitor; a memorial tablet (*US*); the soldier who forms the pivot round which a body of soldiers wheels when marching; a biomarker (qv). **mark'ing** n the act of making or giving a mark or marks; (*esp* in *pl*) disposition or pattern of marks. ◻ **mark'-down** see **mark down** below. **marker pen** n a thick, *usu* fibre-tipped pen for writing on display boards, etc. **marking gauge** n a carpenter's tool for scoring a line parallel to the edge of a piece of wood. **mark'ing-ink** n indelible ink, used for marking clothes. **mark'ing-nut** n the fruit of an East Indian tree (genus *Semecarpus*) of the cashew family, yielding a black juice used in marking clothes. **mark'man** n one of the community owning a mark; a marksman. **marks'man** or **marks'woman** n a person who is good at hitting a target; a person who shoots well. **marks'manship** n skill as a marksman or markswoman. **mark/space ratio** n (*telecom*) the ratio of the time occupied by a mark to that occupied by the space between marks in a telecommunication channel or recording system using

pulsed signals. **mark'-to-mark'et** adj (of an accounting system) valuing assets according to their market price. **mark'-up** n a price increase; the difference between the wholesale and retail price of an item for sale; the action of marking up (*printing, comput*). **mark'-white** n (*Spenser*) the centre of a target.

■ **a mark on** (*archaic sl*) (a person having) a preference for (a specified thing). **beside the mark** see under **beside**. **(God) bless** or **save the mark** (*archaic*) a phrase expressing ironical astonishment or scorn, from its use in archery. **make** (or **leave**) **one's mark** to make a notable impression; to gain great influence. **mark down** to set down in writing; to label at a lower price or to lower the price of (**mark'-down** n); to give (a student) a lower mark than is deserved; to note the position of; to destine for one's own. **mark off** to lay down the boundary lines of; to mark graduations on; to mark (on a list) as attended to or disposed of. **mark of the Beast** see under **beast**. **mark out** to lay out the plan or outlines of; to destine. **mark someone's card** to give someone the information he or she wants; to correct someone under a false impression, *esp* swiftly and with force, to put someone right. **mark time** to move the feet alternately in the same manner as in marching, but without moving forward; to merely keep things going without progressing. **mark up** to raise the price of; to prepare or correct (text) for a printer (*printing*); to add codes (to text) for interpretation by a computer (*comput*). **off the mark** off target; well away from the start in a race. **on your marks** (or **mark**) said before a race begins, to prepare the runners for the starting command or signal. **pass the mark** to pass on the badge of demerit to the next offender (as formerly in some schools). **soft mark** (*inf*) an easy dupe or victim; a person who is easy to cope with or manoeuvre. **up to the mark** satisfactory, up to standard; fit and well. **wide of the mark** (well) off target.

mark[2] /märk/ n a former unit of currency in Germany (in 1924 officially named the Reichsmark; in 1948 the Deutsche Mark or Deutschmark), Finland (the *markka*, *pl* *markkaa*, *orig* equivalent to a franc), and various other countries; a weight of 8 ounces for gold and silver (*obs*); its value in money at 20 pennies to an ounce = 13s 4d (*obs*). [OE *marc*, of doubtful origin]

market /mär'kit/ n a periodic gathering of people for the purposes of buying and selling; a building, square or other public place used for such meetings; a shop (*orig US*); a region or type of clientele in which there is a demand for certain goods; buying and selling; opportunity for buying and selling; demand; the state of being on sale; bargain; sale; rate of sale; value. ◆ adj relating to buying and selling; relating to a market or markets. ◆ vi to deal at a market; to buy and sell; to shop (chiefly *US*). ◆ vt to put on the market, to sell; to advertise, promote. [Late OE *market*, from ONFr *market* (Fr *marché*, Ital *mercato*), from L *mercātus* trade, a market, from *merx* merchandise]

■ **marketabil'ity** or **mar'ketableness** n. **mar'ketable** adj fit for the market; saleable. **marketeer'** n a person who buys or sells, *esp* at a market; (*esp* with *cap*) a British person who supported Britain's entry into the Common Market; a specialist in the techniques of marketing goods and services; see also **black-marketeer** under **black**. **mar'keter** n a person who goes to, or buys or sells at, a market; a person whose job is to promote and sell an organization's products or services. **mar'keting** n the business process of managing the flow of goods, services or processes from the producer to the user or customer, involving assessment of sales of the product, etc, and responsibility for its promotion, distribution and development; shopping (chiefly *US*). **marketizā'tion** or **-s-** n (*econ*) conversion into or adoption of a market economy. **mar'ketize** or **-ise** vt.

◻ **mar'ket-bell** n a bell to give notice of the time of market (*Shakesp*); the bell rung to signal the end of the day's trading on the New York Stock Exchange. **market cross** n a cross or similar structure set up where a market was formerly held. **mar'ket-day** n the fixed day of the week on which a market is held in a particular town, etc. **market economy** n an economy in which prices are determined by competition on the open market without government intervention. **market forces** n pl the combined influences of supply and demand which determine the price and quantity of a product traded. **market-gar'den** n a piece of land on which fruit and vegetables are grown for public sale. **market-gar'dener** n. **market-gar'dening** n. **mar'ket-hall** or **mar'ket-house** n a building in which a market is held. **marketing mix** n the combination of variables (product, price, promotion and place) that determines the demand for a product. **market leader** n a company that sells more goods of a specified type than any other company; a brand of goods selling more than any other of its kind. **mar'ket-led** adj determined by commercial demand. **market maker** n since 1986, a broker-dealer on the Stock Exchange. **mar'ket-making** n. **mar'ket-man** or **mar'ket-woman** n a person who sells, buys or works in a market. **market overt** n (*law*) the sale of goods in open or public view. **mar'ketplace** n the market-square of a town, etc; the world of commercial transactions. **market-price'** or **market-val'ue** n the current price a commodity, etc will fetch at sale. **market profile** n a description of the significant features, such as age and income, of members of a particular market. **market research** n research to determine consumers' opinions about a product or service, by conducting interviews, analysing sales figures, etc. **market researcher** n. **market share** n the percentage of the total market sales of a product attributable to a firm in a given period. **market square** n the open space in a town where markets are or were formerly held. **mar'ket-town** n a town having the privilege of holding a regular public market.

■ **go to market** (*Aust inf*) to become very angry and violent. **in the market for** wanting to buy. **on the market** available for buying.

markhor /mär'kör/ n a wild goat (*Capra falconeri*) of the mountains of Asia. [Pers *mārkhōr*]

markka /mär'kä/ n (pl **mar'kkaa** or **mar'kkas**) a former unit of currency in Finland, replaced by the euro. [Cf **mark²**]

Markov chain /mär'kof chän/ n a series of events, the probability of each of which depends on the probability of that immediately preceding it. [AA *Markov* (1856–1922), Russian mathematician]

marksman and **markswoman** see under **mark¹**.

marl¹ /märl/ n a calcareous clay often used as fertilizer; the ground (*poetic*). ◆ vt to cover or fertilize with marl. [OFr *marle* (Fr *marne*), from LL *margila*, a dimin of L *marga* marl]
■ **mar'ly** *adj* like marl; containing large amounts of marl.
❑ **marl'-pit** n a pit where marl is dug. **marl'stone** n (*geol*) a Middle Lias series of argillaceous limestones with ironstones, etc.

marl² /märl/ vt to bind with marline. [Du *marlen*, appar a frequentative of *marren* to bind]

marl³ or **marle** /märl/ an obsolete form of **marvel**.

marl⁴ /märl/ a dialect form of **marble**. *adj* mottled.
■ **marled** *adj* marbled. **marl'ing** n. **marl'y** or **mirl'y** *adj* marbled.

marlin /mär'lin/ n a large oceanic fish of the genus *Makaira*, related to the swordfishes. [**marline-spike**]

marline /mär'lin/ n a small rope for winding round a larger one to keep it from wearing (also **mar'lin**). [Du *marling*, verbal noun from *marlen* (see **marl²**), or *marlijn*, from *marren* and *lijn* rope (cf **moor²** and **line²**)]
❑ **mar'line-spike** n a spike for separating the strands of a rope in splicing (also **mar'linspike**).

marls see **meril**.

marly see under **marl¹,⁴**.

marm see **ma'am**.

marmalade /mär'mə-lād/ n a jam or preserve made from the pulp and sometimes rind of citrus fruit, *esp* oranges, originally of quinces. ◆ adj (of a cat) having a coat marked with orange and brown streaks. [Fr *marmelade*, from Port *marmelada*, from *marmelo* a quince, from L *melimēlum*, from Gr *melimēlon* a sweet apple, from *meli* honey, and *mēlon* an apple]
❑ **marmalade tree** n a tropical American sapotaceous tree (*Vitellaria*, or *Lucuma*, *mammosa*) cultivated for its fruit, the **marmalade plum**.

marmarosis /mär-mə-rō'sis/ n conversion of limestone into marble. [Gr *marmaros* crystalline rock, from *marmairein* to sparkle]
■ **mar'marize** or **-ise** vt.

marmelize or **-ise** /mär'mə-līz/ (*joc sl*) vt to thrash, defeat heavily, destroy, etc.

marmem alloy /mär'məm al'oi/ n an alloy which, under the influence of temperature changes, can be changed from one condition to another and back again. [*mar*tensite, *mem*ory, because the alloy 'remembers' its former condition]

Marmite® /mär'mīt/ n a spread for bread, etc made from yeast and vegetable extracts. [Ety as for **marmite**]

marmite /mär'mīt, mär-mēt'/ n a lidded metal or earthenware cooking pot, *esp* for soup. [Fr, pot or kettle, from OFr, hypocrite (because of its contents being concealed)]

marmoreal /mär-mō'ri-əl, -mö'/ adj of or like marble. [L *marmor* marble, from Gr *marmaros*; see **marmarosis**]
■ **marmor'eally** *adv*.

marmose /mär'mōs/ n a small S American opossum. [Fr, appar from *marmouset*; see **marmoset**]

marmoset /mär'mə-zet/ n a very small S American monkey with a long hairy tail and furry tufts on its ears. [Fr *marmouset* grotesque figure]

marmot /mär'mət/ n a genus of stout burrowing rodents (*Marmota* or *Cynomys*), in N America called the woodchuck. [Ital *marmotto*, from Romansch *murmont*, from L *mūs*, *mūris* mouse, and *mōns*, *montis* mountain]

marocain /mar'ə-kān/ n a dress material finished with a grain surface like morocco leather. [Fr *maroquin* morocco-leather; cf **maroquin**]

maron see **camaron**.

Maronian /ma-rō'ni-ən/ adj relating to the poet Virgil, Virgilian. [Publius Vergilius *Marō* (-*ōnis*)]

Maronite /mar'ə-nīt/ n a member of a former Monothelite sect, now Uniats, living around Lebanon (also adj). [St *Marōn*, about 400AD, or John *Marōn*, a patriarch of the sect in the 7c]

maroon¹ /mə-roon'/ n a brownish crimson; a detonating firework, *esp* one used as a distress signal. ◆ adj of the colour maroon. [Fr *marron* a chestnut, from Ital *marrone* a chestnut]

maroon² /mə-roon'/ vt to put and leave ashore on a desolate island; to isolate uncomfortably (*lit* or *fig*). ◆ n a fugitive slave, or a descendant of the same; a marooned person. [Fr *marron*, from Sp *cimarrón* wild]
■ **maroon'er** n. **maroon'ing** n.

maroquin /ma-rə-kēn', mar'ə-k(w)in/ n goat-leather; morocco leather. [Fr; cf **marocain**]

maror /mä-rör', -rör/ n a dish of bitter herbs (*esp* horseradish) eaten during the Jewish Passover, symbolizing the bitterness of the Egyptian oppression of the Israelites. [Heb]

marplot and **marprelate** see under **mar**.

Marq *abbrev*: Marquis.

marque¹ /märk/ n a brand or make, *esp* of car. [Fr]

marque² /märk/ n reprisals (*obs*); a privateer. [Fr]
■ **letter-of-marque'** or **letters-of-marque'** a privateer's licence to commit acts of hostility.

marquee /mär-kē'/ n a large tent used for parties, exhibitions, etc; an entrance canopy (chiefly N Am). [From **marquise**, as if pl]
❑ **marquee player** n (N Am) an outstanding player in a professional sports team.

Marquesan /mär-kā'zən or -sən/ n a native or inhabitant of the *Marquesas* Islands; the Polynesian language of the Marquesans. ◆ adj of or relating to the Marquesans or their language.

marquess /mär'kwis/ n in the UK, a title of nobility next below that of a duke (see also **marchioness**). [Ety as for **marquis**]
■ **mar'quessate** n the rank or position of a marquess.

marquetry or **marqueterie** /mär'ki-tri/ n work, *esp* in furniture, inlaid with pieces of varicoloured wood, ivory, metal, etc. [Fr *marqueterie*, from *marqueter* to inlay, from *marque* a mark]

marquis /mär'kwis, mar-kē'/ n (pl **mar'quis** or **mar'quises**) a variant spelling of **marquess**, used *esp* by holders of pre-Union title; a title of nobility ranking next above a count in various European countries. [OFr *marchis*, assimilated later to Fr *marquis*, from LL *marchēnsis* a prefect of the marches]
■ **mar'quisate** n the rank or position of a marquis; the domain of a marquis. **marquise** /mär-kēz'/ n in various European countries, a marchioness; a style of parasol about 1850 (*hist*); an entrance canopy; a marquee; a ring set with gems arranged to form a pointed oval; a gem cut into the shape of a pointed oval; a chilled dessert halfway between a mousse and a parfait, often flavoured with chocolate. **mar'quisette** n a woven clothing fabric, used also for curtains and mosquito nets.

marram or **marrum** /mar'əm/ n a seaside grass (*Ammophila*, or *Psamma*, *arenaria*), frequently used to counter sand-erosion. [ON *marr* sea, *halmr* haulm, stem]

Marrano /mə-rä'nō/ n (pl **Marra'nos**) a medieval Spanish or Portuguese Jew converted to Christianity, *esp* overtly practising Christianity to avoid persecution but secretly adhering to Judaism. [Sp, literally, pig, the meat of which is forbidden to Jews]

marrels see **meril**.

marri /mar'i/ n a W Australian tree (*Eucalyptus calophylla*), cultivated for its ornamental flowers. [From an Aboriginal language]

marriage /mar'ij/ n the ceremony, act or contract by which two people become married to each other; the union of a couple living together in a legal partnership; a declaration of king and queen in bezique, etc; a close union (*fig*). [OFr *mariage*; see **marry¹**]
■ **marriageabil'ity** n. **marr'iageable** *adj* suitable for marriage. **marr'iageableness** n.
❑ **marr'iage-bed** n the bed of a married couple; sexual intercourse within marriage (*euphem*); the rights and obligations of marriage. **marr'iage-bone** n a wishbone. **marr'iage-broker** n a person who, in certain cultures, arranges a marriage contract for a fee. **marriage bureau** n an introduction agency for matching single people wishing to marry; a business agency designed to match entrepreneurs with potential investors (*fig*). **marr'iage-contract** n a formal agreement to be married; an agreement concerning property rights between people about to marry. **marr'iage-favour** n a knot or decoration worn at a marriage. **marriage guidance** n help and advice given to people with marital problems. **marr'iage-licence** n a licence to marry without proclamation of banns in a church. **marr'iage-lines** n pl a certificate of marriage. **marriage of convenience** n a marriage (or *fig*, a close business union, etc) for reasons of expediency rather than affection.

■ words derived from main entry word; ❑ compound words; ■ idioms and phrasal verbs

marriage partner n one's husband or wife. **marr'iage-portion** n a dowry. **marr'iage-ring** n a wedding ring. **marr'iage-settlement** n an arrangement of property, etc before marriage, by which something is secured to the wife or her children if the husband dies.

marron /mar'ən/ n a freshwater crayfish of W Australia, *Cherax tenuimanus*. [From an Aboriginal language]

marrons glacés /ma-rɔ̃ gla-sä'/ (*Fr*) n pl chestnuts poached in syrup and coated with a sugar glaze.

marrow[1] /mar'ō/ n the soft tissue in the hollow parts of the bones (also **bone marrow**); pith or pulp of plants (*obs*); a vegetable marrow (see under **vegetable**); the essence or best part of anything; the inner meaning or purpose. [OE (Anglian) *merg, mærh* (WSax *mearg*); Ger *Mark*]
■ **marr'owish** adj of the nature of, or resembling, marrow. **marr'owless** adj having no marrow. **marr'owy** adj full of marrow; strong; forcible; pithy.
□ **marr'ow-bone** n a bone containing marrow; (in *pl*) the knees or the bones of the knees. **marr'owfat** n a rich kind of pea, also called **Dutch admiral pea**. **marr'ow-men** n pl (*hist*) those who in the Church of Scotland supported the teaching of *The Marrow of Modern Divinity* (1645) after its republication in 1718. **marr'ow-squash** n (*US*) vegetable marrow.
■ **spinal marrow** the spinal cord. **to the marrow** to the core.

marrow[2] /mar'ō/ (*N Eng*) n a mate; a companion; a match, equal, like; one of a pair. ◆ vi to be a marrow. ◆ vt to be a marrow to; to couple. [Origin unknown]
■ **marr'owless** adj.

marrowsky /ma-row'ski/ n a spoonerism. ◆ vi to utter a spoonerism. [Said to be from the name of a Polish count]

marrum see **marram**.

marry[1] /mar'i/ vt to take for husband or wife; to give in marriage; to unite in matrimony; to unite, join, put together (sometimes with *up*; fig). ◆ vi to take a husband or a wife. [Fr *marier*, from L *maritāre* to marry, *maritus* a husband, from *mās, maris* a male]
■ **marr'ied** adj. **marr'ier** n a person who marries; the sort of person likely to take a husband or wife. **marr'ying** n and adj.
■ **marry into** to become a member of (a family) by marriage; to acquire by marriage. **marry off** to find a spouse for or succeed in marrying (eg one's son or daughter).

marry[2] /mar'i/ (*archaic*) interj indeed!, forsooth! [By *Mary*]
■ **marry come up** an exclamation of defiant protest.

Mars /märz/ n the Roman god of war, identified with the Greek Ares; the planet next after the earth in terms of distance from the sun; iron (*alchemy*). [L *Mārs, Mārtis*]
□ **mars'quake** n a violent tremor on Mars, equivalent to an earthquake.

Marsala /mär-sä'lə/ (*Ital* mär-sä'lä) n a sweet, fortified wine from *Marsala* in Sicily.

Marsanne /mär-san'/ n a variety of grape *orig* grown near *Marsanne* in S France, used to produce white wine.

Marseillaise /mär-sə-lāz', -sā-ez'/ n the French national anthem, *orig* a revolutionary hymn composed by Rouget de Lisle in 1792, sung by the volunteers of *Marseilles* as they entered Paris, 30 July, and when they marched to the storming of the Tuileries.

marsh /märsh/ n a tract of wet land; a morass, swamp, or fen. ◆ adj inhabiting or found in marshes. [OE *mersc, merisc*, orig adj; see **mere**[2]]
■ **marsh'iness** n. **marsh'y** adj (**marsh'ier**; **marsh'iest**) of the nature of a marsh; covered with marshes.
□ **marsh fern** n a tall pale-green fern (*Thelypteris palustris*) growing in marshy woodlands and fens of Eurasia and N America. **marsh-fe'ver** n malaria. **marsh'-gas** n methane. **marsh-harr'ier** n a European harrier hawk frequenting marshes. **marsh hawk** n a common N American hawk with a white patch on its rump (also **hen harrier**). **marsh'land** n marshy country. **marsh'lander** n a person who inhabits marshland. **marsh'locks** n a marsh-growing species of cinquefoil (*Potentilla* or *Comarum*; also **marsh-cinq'uefoil**). **marsh-mall'ow** n a maritime marsh-growing plant (*Althaea officinalis*) very similar to the hollyhock. **marsh'mallow** n a spongy, jellylike sweet, *orig* made from marsh-mallow root, now from sugar, egg white, gelatin, etc; an excessively soft, sweet or sentimental person or thing. **marsh'-man** n an inhabitant of a marsh. **marsh marigold** n the kingcup (*Caltha palustris*), a marsh plant of the buttercup family with flowers like big buttercups. **marsh'-robin** n the chewink (qv). **marsh-sam'phire** n a plant of the genus *Salicornia*, glasswort. **marsh tit** n the grey tit (*Poecile palustris*). **marsh warbler** n a small brown-and-white Eurasian warbler with a pale stripe over the eyes. **marsh'wort** n a small umbelliferous marsh plant related to celery.

marshal /mär'shl/ n an officer in a royal household, *orig* the king's farrier, later having responsibility for military arrangements, the

regulation of ceremonies, preservation of order, points of etiquette, etc; any official with similar functions; a lawcourt officer with responsibility for prisoners; a prison-keeper; (at Oxford University) a proctor's attendant or bulldog; the chief officer who regulated combats in the lists (*hist*); (in France and the French colonies) an officer of the highest military rank; a civil officer appointed to execute the process of the courts (*US*); the chief officer of a police or fire brigade (*US*); a farrier (*obs*). ◆ vt (**mar'shalling**; **mar'shalled**) to arrange in order; to usher; to combine in or with one coat of arms. ◆ vi to come together in order. [OFr *mareschal* (Fr *maréchal*), from OHGer *marah* a horse, and *schalh* (Ger *Schalk*) a servant]
■ **mar'shalcy** n the rank, office or department of a marshal; *esp* (in the form **Mar'shalsea**) until 1842 a prison in Southwark, under the marshal of the royal household. **mar'shaller** n. **mar'shalling** n. **mar'shalship** n.
□ **marshalling yard** n a place where railway wagons are sorted out and made up into trains.
■ **air-marshal**, etc see under **air**. **field marshal** see under **field**. **marshal of the Royal Air Force** an officer of supreme rank in the Royal Air Force, ranking with an admiral of the fleet or a field marshal.

Marshallese /mär-shə-lēz'/ adj of or relating to the republic of the *Marshall Islands* in the central Pacific, its language or its inhabitants. ◆ n a native or citizen of the Marshall Islands.

Marsilea or **Marsilia** /mär-sil'i-ə/ n a genus of aquatic leptosporangiate ferns, with four-lobed leaves and bean-like stalked sporocarps, giving name to a family **Marsileā'ceae**. [LF *Marsigli* (1658–1730), Italian naturalist]

Marsipobranchii /mär-sip-ō-brang'ki-ī/ n pl the Cyclostomata (see **cyclostome**). [Gr *marsipos* pouch, and *branchia* gills]
■ **mar'sipobranch** n. **marsipobranch'iate** adj.

marsport see under **mar**.

marsquake see under **Mars**.

marsupium /mär-sū'pi-əm/ (*zool*) n a pouch. [L *marsūpium*, from Gr *marsip(p)ion, marsyp(p)ion* a pouch]
■ **marsū'pial** adj relating to a pouch or to the Marsupialia; of the nature of a pouch; of the Marsupialia. ◆ n a member of the Marsupialia. **Marsupiā'lia** n pl an order of mammals coextensive with the subclass Metatheria, animals whose young are born in a very imperfect state and are usually carried in a pouch by the female.

mart[1] /märt/ n a place of trade, a market. ◆ vi (*Shakesp*) to deal or trade. ◆ vt (*Shakesp*) to sell or trade in. [Du *markt* mart; cf **market**]

mart[2] /märt/ (*Scot* and *N Eng*) n a cow or ox fattened, killed (*usu* about Martinmas), and salted for winter use. [Gaelic *mart* cow, ox]

martagon /mär'tə-gən/ n a purple Eurasian lily with petals curling backwards, the Turk's cap lily. [Turk *martagān* a kind of turban]

martel /mär'tl/ (*hist*) n a medieval hammer-like weapon with a pointed head. ◆ vi (pat **mar'telled**) (*Spenser*) to hammer. [OFr *martel*]

martellato /mär-tel-lä'tō/ (*music*) adj and adv played with a hammering touch, or with short quick detached strokes of the bow. [Ital, hammered]

martello /mär-tel'ō/ n (pl **martell'os**) (in full **martello tower**) a circular fort for coastal defence. [Cape *Mortella* in Corsica, where one resisted for some time a British cannonade in 1794]

marten /mär'tən/ n an animal (eg the pine marten) closely related to the weasel, or other species of *Mustela*; its fur. [Fr *martre*, from the Gmc root seen in Ger *Marder*, and OE *mearth* marten]

Martenot see **Ondes Martenot**.

martensite /mär'tin-zīt/ n a constituent of rapidly cooled steel consisting of a solid solution of carbon in iron and resulting from the decomposition of austenite at low temperatures. [Adolph *Martens* (died 1914), German metallurgist]
■ **martensitic** /-zit'ik/ adj.

martext see under **mar**.

martial /mär'shl/ adj belonging or relating to Mars, the god of war, or to the planet Mars; of or relating to war, or to the armed forces; military; warlike. [Fr *martial*, from L *mārtiālis*, from *Mārs*]
■ **mar'tialism** n. **mar'tialist** n (*rare*) a soldier. **mar'tially** adv. **mar'tialness** n.
□ **martial art** n (*usu* in *pl*) any of various combative sports or methods of self-defence (*usu* of oriental origin) including karate and kung fu. **martial artist** n a practitioner of martial arts. **martial law** n the exercise of military power by a government, etc in time of emergency (war, riot, etc) with the temporary suspension of ordinary administration and policing.

Martian /mär'shən/ adj of Mars (god or planet); of war or battle (*Spenser*). ◆ n (*sci-fi*) an imagined inhabitant of Mars. [L *Mārtius*, from *Mārs*]

martin /mär'tin/ or (*obs*) **martinet** /-ti-net/ *n* a bird of the genus *Delichon* or related genera, similar to a swallow but with a shorter tail. [The name *Martin*]

martinet[1] /mär-ti-net', mär'/ *n* a strict disciplinarian; a system of drill drawn up by *Martinet*, a French general in the reign of Louis XIV (*obs*).
■ **martinet'ish** *adj*. **martinet'ism** *n*.

martinet[2] see **martin**.

martingale /mär'tin-gāl/ *n* a strap passing between a horse's forelegs, fastened to the girth and to the bit, noseband or reins, to keep its head down; a short spar under the bowsprit (*naut*); (in gambling) the policy of doubling the stake on losing. [Fr, perh from a kind of breeches worn at *Martigues* in Provence]

Martini[1] or **Martini-Henry** /mär-tē'nē-hen'ri/ *n* a 19c rifle with an action designed by Frederic *Martini* and barrel by H *Henry*, a gunsmith.

Martini[®2] /mär-tē'nē/ *n* a type of vermouth made by the firm of *Martini* and Rossi; (without *cap*) a cocktail of vermouth, gin, bitters, etc, *perh* named after its inventor.

Martinmas /mär'tin-məs/ *n* (also (*obs*) **Mar'tlemas**) the *mass* or feast of St *Martin*, 11 November; in Scotland, one of the term days (now fixed as 28 November) on which rents, annuities, etc are payable.

martlet /märt'lit/ *n* the martin; a representation of a martin or swallow without feet, used as a bearing, a crest, or a mark of cadency for a fourth son (*heraldry*). [Fr *martinet*, dimin of *martin* martin]

martyr /mär'tər/ *n* a person bearing witness to his or her religious beliefs by refusing to renounce them in death; a person who suffers for his or her beliefs; a person who suffers, or pretends to suffer, greatly from any cause, a victim. ◆ *vt* to make a martyr of, *esp* by putting to death; to torture. [OE, from L, from Gr, a witness]
■ **mar'tyrdom** *n* the state of being a martyr; the sufferings or death of a martyr; torment generally. **martyrium** /mär-tēr'i-əm/ *n* (*pl* **martyria**) (*L*) same as **martyry** below. **martyrīzā'tion** or **-s-** *n*. **mar'tyrize** or **-ise** *vt* to offer as a sacrifice; to cause to suffer martyrdom; to martyr. **martyrolog'ical** *adj*. **martyrol'ogist** *n*. **martyrol'ogy** *n* a history of martyrs; a discourse on martyrdom; an official list of martyrs. **mar'tyry** *n* a shrine, chapel or monument erected in memory of a martyr.

marvel /mär'vl/ *n* a wonder; anything astonishing or wonderful; astonishment (*archaic*). ◆ *vi* (**mar'velling**; **mar'velled**) to wonder; to feel astonishment. ◆ *vt* (*obs*) to wonder at. [Fr *merveille*, from L *mīrābilis* wonderful, from *mīrārī* to wonder]
■ **mar'vellous** *adj* astonishing; almost or altogether beyond belief; improbable; very good, extremely pleasing (*inf*). **mar'vellously** *adv*. **mar'vellousness** *n*.
❏ **marvel of Peru** /pə-roo'/ *n* a showy garden flower (*Mirabilis jalapa*, family Nyctaginaceae) from tropical America, open and scented in the evening.

marver /mär'vər/ *n* a slab of marble, cast iron, etc, on which molten glass is manually rolled during blowing. ◆ *vt* and *vi* to roll (glass) on a marver. [Fr *marbre* marble]

Marxian /märk'si-ən/ *adj* of or relating to Karl *Marx* (1818–83) or his economic and political theories, the basis of modern communism. ◆ *n* a follower of Marx, a Marxist.
■ **Marx'ianism** *n* Marxism. **Marx'ism** *n*. **Marx'ist** *n* and *adj*.
❏ **Marx'ism-Len'inism** *n* a variant of Marxism formulated by Lenin (see also **Leninism**). **Marxist literary theory** *n* an approach to literary criticism which emphasizes the effect of the struggle to control the material side of life on the production of art.

marxisant /märk-si-zä'/ (*Fr*) *adj* of Marxist sympathies.

Mary /mā'ri/ (*obs Aust derog sl*; also without *cap*) *n* a woman, *esp* an Aboriginal woman. [Pidgin, from the woman's name]

marybud /mā'ri-bud/ *n* a marigold bud.

Mary Jane /mā'ri jān/ (*N Am sl*) *n* marijuana. [Assumed transl of **marijuana**]

Maryolatry, **Maryology**, etc see under **Marian**[1].

marzipan /mär'zi-pan or -pan'/ *n* a sweet almond paste used in cakes and confectionery, formerly called **marchpane**. [Ger, from Ital *marzapane*]

Mas see **Mass**.

mas /mas/ *n* a house or farm in the south of France. [Provençal]

mas. or **masc.** *abbrev*: masculine.

-mas /-məs/ *combining form* denoting a church festival or feast-day, as in *Candlemas*, *Christmas*, *Martinmas*, etc. [Ety as for **mass**[2]]

masa /mas'ə/ *n* in Mexican cooking, a dough made from **masa harina**, ground, dried maize, used to make tamales, etc. [Sp, dough, from L *massa* a lump]

Masai /mä'sī/ *n* (*pl* **Masai** or **Masais**) (a member of) an African people of the highlands of Kenya and Tanzania; the language of this people. ◆ *adj* of the Masai or their language.

masala /mə-sä'lə/ *n* any of various mixtures of ground spices used in Indian cookery; a dish using this. [Hindi, mixture]

masc. see **mas**.

mascara /ma-skä'rə/ *n* colouring for the eyelashes, a cosmetic. [See ety for **mask**[1]]

mascaron /mas'kə-ron/ (*archit*) *n* a grotesque face on a keystone, doorknocker, etc. [See ety for **mask**[1]]

mascarpone /mas-kär-pō'nā/ *n* a soft Italian cream cheese. [Ital]

mascle /mas'kl/ *n* a lozenge-shaped, perforated bearing (*heraldry*); a lozenge-shaped plate for scale armour. [Appar OFr *mascle*, from LL *mascula*, from L *macula* mesh, influenced by OHGer *masca* mesh]
■ **mas'cled** *adj*. **mas'cūly** *adj*.

mascon /mas'kon/ *n* any of several mass concentrations of dense material, of uncertain origin, lying beneath the moon's surface. [*mass concentration*]

mascot /mas'kət/ *n* a talisman; a supposed bringer of good luck. [Fr *mascotte*]

masculine /mä'skū- or mas'kū-lin, -lin/ *adj* male (*rare*); characteristic of, peculiar to, or appropriate to, a man or the male sex; mannish; of the grammatical gender to which words denoting males belong. ◆ *n* the male sex or nature; a male; a word of masculine gender. [Fr, from L *masculīnus*, from *masculus* male, from *mās* a male]
■ **mas'culinely** *adv*. **mas'culineness** *n*. **mas'culinist** *n* and *adj* (a person) upholding men's rights or privileges (coined in supposed imitation of *feminist*). **masculin'ity** *n*. **masculinīzā'tion** or **-s-** *n*. **mas'culinize** or **-ise** *vt* to cause to develop a masculine character or appearance. ◆ *vi* to develop such character or appearance.
❏ **masculine ending** *n* (*prosody*) a stressed syllable at the end of a line. **masculine rhyme** *n* a rhyme on a final stressed syllable; in French, one without a final mute e.

masculy see under **mascle**.

maser or **MASER** /mā'zər/ *n* a device used to amplify long-range radar and radio astronomy signals (very small when not amplified) while generating little unwanted noise within itself. [*M*icrowave *a*mplification by *s*timulated *e*mission of *r*adiation]
■ **mase** *vi* (back-formation) to act as a maser by generating and amplifying microwaves.

MASH /mash/ (*US*) *n* mobile army surgical hospital.

mash[1] /mash/ *n* (in brewing and distilling) a mixture of crushed malt and hot water; a mixture, eg of bran with meal or turnips, beaten and stirred as a food for animals; any material beaten or crushed into a soft or pulpy state; mashed potatoes (*inf*); a crushed condition; a muddle, hash, or bungle. ◆ *vt* to make into a mash; to pound down or crush; to infuse (*dialect*; also *vi*). [OE *masc*(*-wyrt*) mash(*-wort*)]
■ **mashed** *adj* (*sl*) rendered incapable by drink or drugs. **mash'er** *n*. **mash'ing** *n*. **mash'y** *adj* produced by mashing; like a mash.
❏ **mash'man** *n* a worker in a brewery or a distillery who helps to make the mash. **mash'-tub**, **mash'-tun**, **mash'-vat** or **mash'ing-tub** *n* a vessel in which the mash is mixed in a brewery or distillery. **mash'-up** *n* (*music*) a recording in which a sample of one piece of music is recorded over the instrumental or rhythm track of another piece, *usu* of a different genre; a digital media file which may contain combinations of text, graphics, audio, video and animation (*comput*).

mash[2] /mash/ (*archaic sl*) *vt* to flirt with; to treat as a sweetheart, court. ◆ *vi* to flirt. ◆ *n* a person who mashes or is mashed; a masher; the action of mashing; an infatuation or crush. [Ety doubtful]
■ **mash'er** *n* a man who dresses showily to attract attention, a dandy; a flirt.
■ **mashed on** in love with.

mashallah /mä-shä'lä/ *interj* (among Muslims) what God will. [Ar *mā shā'llāh*]

mashie or **mashy** /mash'i/ *n* an old-fashioned golf club used for shots of medium length and loft, corresponding to a number five iron. [Perh Fr *massue* club]
❏ **mashie-nib'lick** *n* an old-fashioned golf club between mashie and niblick, corresponding to a number seven iron.

mashlam, **mashlin**, etc see **maslin**.

Mashona see **Shona**.

mashua /mash'ū-ə/ *n* a tuber plant, *Tropaeslum tuberosum*, grown in the Andes.

masjid /mus'jid/ *n* a mosque. [Ar]

Mas-John see under **Mass**.

mask[1] /mäsk/ *n* a covering for the face, or the upper part of it, for concealment, disguise, protection, amusement or ceremonial purposes; a disingenuous or hypocritical expression or posture, a false face; a grotesque representation of a face worn in ancient or Japanese, etc drama, or used as an architectural ornament, etc; a fox's (or other animal's) face or head; a mould of a face; a masque; a cosmetic face pack; a disguise, pretence, or concealment (*fig*); any means of screening or disguising; a screen to cover part of a light-sensitive surface (*photog*); a screen used to cover parts of a surface onto the exposed parts of which an integrated circuit is to be etched. ◆ *vt* to cover the face of with a mask; to hide, cloak, screen or disguise; to coat (food) with a sauce, etc, before serving. ◆ *vi* to masquerade; to be disguised in any way. [Fr *masque*, from Sp *máscara* or Ital *maschera*, of doubtful origin, appar connected in some way with LL *mascus*, *masca* a ghost, and with Ar *maskharah* a jester, man in masquerade] ■ **masked** *adj* wearing a mask; concealed; personate (*bot*). **mask'er** *n* a person who wears a mask; a masquerader; a device that produces a noise to mask a different auditory stimulus, used eg by tinnitus sufferers. ❑ **masked ball** *n* a ball at which the dancers wear masks. **masking agent** *n* a chemical that conceals the presence of another substance, *esp* one taken by an athlete to avoid testing positive for an illegal drug. **masking tape** *n* adhesive paper tape used in painting, decorating, etc to cover areas to be left unpainted.

mask² /*mäsk*/ (*Scot*) *vt* to steep or infuse. ◆ *vi* to be infusing. [See **mash¹**]

maskalonge, maskallonge, maskinonge and **maskanonge** see **muskellunge**.

maskirovka /*ma-ski-rov'kə*/ *n* the use or practice of deception as a military stratagem; camouflage. [Russ, camouflage, from *maska* disguise, mask]

maslin /*mas'lin*/ *n* a mixed grain, *esp* rye and wheat (also (*Scot*) **mash'lan, mash'lim, mash'lin, mash'loch** /-*lohh*/ or **mash'lum**). [OFr *mesteillon*, from LL *mistilio̅, -o̅nis*, from L *mistus* mixed, from *misce̅re* to mix]

masochism /*maz'* or *mas'ə-ki-zm*/ *n* pleasure, *esp* sexual pleasure, in being dominated or treated cruelly; morbid gratification in suffering pain, physical or mental. [Sacher-*Masoch* (1836–95), Austrian novelist who described it] ■ **mas'ochist** *n*. **masochist'ic** *adj*. **masochist'ically** *adv*.

mason /*mā'sn*/ *n* a person who cuts, prepares and lays stones; a builder in stone; a member of the society of freemasons. ◆ *vt* to build or repair in stone, brick, etc. [OFr *masson* (Fr *maçon*), from LL *maciō̅, -ō̅nis*, prob Gmc; cf MHGer *mezzo* a mason, whence Ger *Steinmetz* a stonemason; OHGer *meizan* to hew, whence Ger *Meissel* a chisel] ■ **masonic** /*mə-son'ik*/ *adj* relating to freemasonry. **mā'sonried** *adj* constructed of masonry. **mā'sonry** *n* the art, skill, or practice of a mason; the work of a mason; building work in stone; freemasonry. ◆ *adj* consisting of stone-work. ❑ **mason bee** *n* a small bee (*Osmia rufa*) that builds its nest in logs, old walls, etc. **mason's mark** *n* a device carved on stones by a mason to identify his share in the work. **mason wasp** *n* a solitary wasp (genus *Odynerus*) that builds its nest in sand or in old walls. ■ **master mason** see under **master**.

Mason-Dixon Line /*mā'sn-dik'sn līn*/ *n* the boundary between Pennsylvania and Maryland following a line surveyed between 1763 and 1767 by Charles *Mason* and Jeremiah *Dixon*, later thought of as separating the free Northern states from the slave states of the South.

Masonite® /*mā'sə-nīt*/ (*N Am, Aust* and *NZ*) *n* a kind of dark brown hardboard. [William H *Mason* (died 1940), its US inventor]

mason jar /*mā'sn jär*/ (*US*; also with *cap*) *n* an airtight glass jar for preserving food. [JL *Mason*, the patentee]

masoolah, massoola or **masula** /*mä-soo'lə*/ (*hist*) *n* a tall, many-oared Indian surf-boat. [Origin obscure]

Masora or **Masorah** /*mä-sö'rə, -sö'*/ *n* a collection of critical notes on the text of the Old Testament (also **Masso'ra, Masso'rah** or **Maso'reth**). [Heb *māsoreth*, Mod *māsōrāh*] ■ **Mas'orete** or **Mass'orete** /-*rēt*/ *n* a compiler of the Masora. **Masoretic** or **Massoretic** /-*ret'ik*/ *adj*.

masque /*mäsk*/ *n* a masked person; a company of maskers; a masquerade or masked ball; a form of courtly spectacle in vogue in the 16c and 17c, in which masked performers danced and acted, developing into a form of drama with scenery and music; a literary composition for the purpose; a mask (*obs*). [Ety as for **mask¹**] ■ **masqu'er** *n* a masker.

masquerade /*mä-skə-rād'*/ *n* an assembly of people wearing masks, costumes, *esp* at a ball; disguise; pretence. ◆ *vi* to wear a mask; to take part in a masquerade; to go in disguise; to pretend to be (with *as*). [Fr *mascarade* ; see **mask¹**] ■ **masquera'der** *n*.

Mass, Mas /*mäs*/, **Mess** or **Mes** /*mes*/ (*obs*) *n* shortened form of **master**.

❑ **Mas'-John, Mass'-John, Mes'-John** or **Mess'-John** *n* (*obs*) a contemptuous name for a Scottish parish minister.

Mass. *abbrev* : Massachusetts (US state).

mass¹ /*mas*/ *n* a lump of matter; matter, material (*obs*); a quantity; a collected or coherent body of matter; an unbroken expanse; the aggregate, total; the main body; the greater part; the principal part; the quantity of matter in any body, measured by its resistance to change of motion and the force of gravity exerted upon it; (in *pl* with *the*) the ordinary people, the people as a whole; (in *pl*) a large quantity or number (*inf*). ◆ *adj* relating to a mass, or to large numbers or quantities, or to ordinary people as a whole. ◆ *vt* to form into a mass; to bring together in masses. ◆ *vi* to assemble or come together in a mass or masses. [Fr *masse*, from L *massa* a lump, prob from Gr *māza* a barley cake, from *massein* to knead] ■ **mass'iness** *n*. **massive** /*mas'iv*/ *adj* bulky; weighty; giving an impression of weight; not separated into parts or elements; without crystalline form; great in quantity; on a very large scale, or of great size or power (*fig*); popular, great, successful (*sl*). ◆ *n* (*sl*) a gang, *esp* a street gang. **mass'ively** *adv*. **mass'iveness** *n*. **mass'y** *adj* massive, made up of masses. ❑ **mass defect** *n* the difference between the sum of the masses of the neutrons and protons in a nucleus and the mass of the nucleus itself. **mass-energy equivalence** *n* (*phys*) the fundamental principle that mass and energy are equivalent and interconvertible shown by the **mass-energy equation** $E=mc^2$. **mass market** *n* the market for mass-produced goods. **mass-mar'ket** *vt*. **mass-mar'keting** *n*. **mass media, mass medium** see under **medium**. **mass meeting** *n* a large meeting for a public protest or discussion. **mass noun** *n* a noun that denotes something that cannot be counted or made plural. **mass number** *n* the atomic weight of an isotope, the number of nucleons in the nucleus. **mass observation** *n* the study of the habits, opinions, etc of the general body of a community. **mass-produce'** *vt* to produce in great quantity by a standardized process. **mass-produced'** *adj*. **mass producer** *n*. **mass production** *n*. **mass radiography** *n* the X-raying of large numbers of people by means of mobile units. **mass spectrograph** *n* a vacuum system in which positive rays of various charged atoms are deflected through electric and magnetic fields so as to indicate the charge-to-mass ratios on a photographic plate, thus measuring the atomic masses of isotopes with precision. **mass spectrometer** *n* an instrument like the mass spectrograph that detects the charged particles electrically instead of photographically. **mass spectrometry** *n*. **mass transit** *n* (*US*) public transport. **mass-transit** *adj*. ■ **in mass** as a body; all together. **in the mass** in the aggregate; as a whole; indiscriminately. **law of mass action** (*chem*) the law stating that the rate of chemical change is proportional to the product of the concentrations of the reacting substances.

mass² (often with *cap*) /*mas* or *mäs*/ *n* the celebration of the Lord's Supper or Eucharist in Roman Catholic and some Protestant churches; the religious service for it; a musical setting of certain parts of the Roman Catholic liturgy; a church service (*Shakesp*). [OE *mæsse*, from LL *missa*, from L *mittere* to send away, perh from the phrase at the close of service, *ite, missa est* (*ecclesia*) go, (the congregation) is dismissed] ❑ **mass'-bell** *n* a sacring bell. **mass'-book** *n* the Roman Catholic missal or service-book. **mass'priest** *n* formerly, a Roman Catholic secular priest, as distinct from one living under a rule; later, a priest retained in chantries, etc to say masses for the dead; a Roman Catholic priest generally (*derog*).

massa /*mas'ə*/ (*esp Southern US*) *n* a corruption of **master**.

massacre /*mas'ə-kər*/ (*Spenser* sometimes *ma-sak'ər*)/ *n* indiscriminate slaughter, *esp* with cruelty; carnage. ◆ *vt* to kill with violence and cruelty; to slaughter. [Fr; origin doubtful]

massage /*mas'äzh*, *mə-säzh'*/ *n* a (system of) treatment using stroking, pressing, tapping, kneading, friction, etc to relieve both physical and mental pain by easing tension, removing blockages, etc; manipulation, alteration of the appearance of something (*esp* data of any kind) to show it in a more favourable light. ◆ *vt* to subject to massage; to present in a favourable light by devious means. [Fr, from Gr *massein* to knead] ■ **mass'ager, massa'gist, masseur** /-*sær'*, -*sûr'*/ or (*fem*) **masseuse** /-*sœz'*/ *n* a practitioner of massage. ❑ **massage parlour** *n* an establishment providing massages; an establishment providing highly specialized massage, a brothel (*euphem*).

massaranduba, also **masseranduba** or **maceranduba** /*mas-ə-ran-doo'bə*/ *n* the Brazilian milk-tree (*Mimusops elata*). [Port *maçaranduba*, from Tupí name]

massasauger /*ma-sə-sö'gər*/ *n* a small grey or brownish rattlesnake (*Sistrurus catenatus*) found in swampy regions of the USA. [*Missisauga* River, where first found]

massé /mas'ā/ n (in snooker, etc) a stroke made with the cue vertical or nearly so, so as to achieve a sharp swerve in the cue ball. [Fr]

masseter /ma-sē'tər/ n a muscle that raises the under-jaw. [Gr masētēr (not massētēr) chewer, from masaesthai to chew]

masseur and **masseuse** see under **massage**.

massicot /mas'i-kot/ n yellow lead monoxide. [Fr]

massif /ma-sēf', mas'if/ n a central mountain mass; an orographic fault-block. [Fr]

massive, massy, etc see under **mass**[1].

massoola see **masoolah**.

Massora, Massorah and **Massorete** see **Masora**.

mast[1] /mäst/ n a long upright pole, esp one for carrying the sails of a ship. ◆ vt to supply with a mast or masts. [OE mæst ; Ger Mast]
■ **mast'ed** adj. **mast'less** adj.
□ **mast'head** n the top of a mast; the name of a newspaper or periodical in the typographical form in which it normally appears, or a similar block of information regularly used as a heading. ◆ vt to raise to the masthead; to punish by sending to the masthead. **mast'house** n the place where masts are made or stored.
■ **before the mast** as a common sailor (ie with quarters in the forecastle, forward of the mast).

mast[2] /mäst/ n the fruit of the oak, beech, chestnut, and other forest trees, on which pigs feed; nuts, acorns. [OE mæst ; Ger Mast, whence mästen to feed]
■ **mast'ful** adj. **mast'less** adj. **mast'y** adj of the nature of mast; as if well fed on mast.
□ **mast cell** n a cell in connective tissue thought to produce histamine and other agents controlling the release of acid in the stomach. **mast'-fed** adj.

MASTA /mas'tə/ abbrev : Medical Advisory Service for Travellers Abroad.

mastaba /mas'tə-bə/ n an ancient Egyptian tomb with sloping sides and a flat roof, having an outer chamber in which offerings were made, connecting with an inner one containing the image of the dead person, with a shaft descending to the actual grave. [Ar mastabah a bench]

mastectomy /ma-stek'tə-mi/ (med) n surgical removal of a breast. [Gr mastos breast, and ektomē excision]
■ **radical mastectomy** the surgical removal of a breast together with some pectoral muscles and lymph nodes of the armpit.

master /mä'stər/ n a person (esp male) who commands or controls; a lord or owner; a leader or ruler; a teacher; an employer; the commander of a merchant ship; formerly, the navigator or sailing master of a ship-of-war; a person eminently skilled in anything, esp art; a person who has complete knowledge of an art, science, etc; a workman who has set up on his own account, or is qualified to do so; (with cap) formerly prefixed to a name or designation as Mr is now, now only of a boy in this use; (usu with cap) a title of prestige or office, eg a degree conferred by universities, such as Master of Arts, etc, an official of the Supreme Court, the designation of the heir apparent to certain Scottish titles, or of his son, the head of certain university colleges, of a lodge of freemasons, etc; a husband (dialect); an original (film, record, etc) from which copies are made; a master-card. ◆ adj chief; controlling; predominant; of a master; of the rank of a master; original. ◆ vt to become master of; to overcome; to gain control over; to acquire a thorough knowledge of; to become skilful in; to rule as master; to temper, to season; to treat with lye (tanning); to make a master copy of (a sound recording). ◆ vi (archaic; also vt with it) to act the master or be a schoolmaster. [Partly OE mægester, partly OFr maistre (Fr maître), both from L magister, from root of magnus great]
■ **mas'terate** n the degree, title or rank of master. **mas'terdom** n power of control; masterfulness. **mas'terful** adj exercising the authority, skill or power of a master; imperious; masterly (rare). **mas'terfully** adv. **mas'terfulness** n. **mas'terhood** n. **mas'tering** n the action of the verb master ; lye. **mas'terless** adj without a master or owner; ungoverned; unsubdued; beyond control. **mas'terliness** n. **mas'terly** adj like a master; with the skill of a master; overbearing (obs). ◆ adv with the skill of a master. **mas'tership** n the condition, authority, status, office, or term of office of a master; rule or power; superiority. **mas'tery** n the power or authority of a master; upper hand; control; supreme skill or knowledge.
□ **master aircrew** n an RAF rank equivalent to warrant officer. **master-at-arms'** n (pl **masters-at-arms**) in the navy, a petty officer with police duties; in the mercantile marine, a ship's chief police officer. **master-build'er** n a chief builder; a person who directs or employs others. **Mas'terCard**® a credit card issued by a group of banks, replacing the former Access card. **mas'ter-card** n the card that commands a suit or is the highest of all those remaining to be played. **mas'ter-class** n the dominant class in a society; a lesson, esp in music, given to talented students by a renowned expert; any performance displaying consummate skill. **mas'ter-clock** n one that

regulates other clocks electrically. **mas'ter-hand** n the hand of a master; a person highly skilled. **mas'ter-joint** n (geol) a joint of the most marked system of those by which a rock is intersected. **mas'ter-key** n a key that opens many (different) locks, esp all the locks in a certain building; a clue able to guide one out of many difficulties (fig). **masterly inactivity** n the position or part of a neutral or a Fabian combatant, carried out with diplomatic skill, so as to preserve a predominant influence without risking anything. **master-mar'iner** n the captain of a merchant-vessel or fishing-vessel. **master mason** n a freemason who has attained the third degree. **mas'termind** n a mind, or a person having a mind, of very great ability; the person conceiving or directing a project, esp a criminal enterprise. ◆ vt to originate, think out, and direct. **master page** n a word-processing template which automatically inserts repeated elements in each page of a document. **mas'terpiece**, also **mas'terwork** n a piece of work worthy of a master; one's greatest achievement. **master race** n a group of people who believe themselves to be fitted and entitled by their superior qualities to rule the world. **master sergeant** n (in the US Army, Air Force and Marine Corps) a senior non-commissioned officer. **mas'tersinger** n a Meistersinger (qv). **mas'terstroke** n a stroke or performance worthy of a master; superior performance; an effective, well-timed act. **mas'ter-switch** n a switch for controlling the effect of a number of other switches or contactors. **mas'ter-wheel** n the wheel in a machine which imparts motion to other parts. **mas'terwort** n a plant (Peucedanum, or Imperatoria, ostruthium) related to the parsnip, once used as a pot-herb and in medicine; applied also to Astrantia, etc.
■ **little masters** a 16c–17c group of followers of the German painter and engraver Albrecht Dürer, notable for fine work on wood and copper. **master of ceremonies** see under **ceremony**. **master of the horse** the Roman Magister Equitum, an official appointed by the dictator to act next under himself; an equerry, esp a high official of the British royal court. **Master of the King's** or **Queen's Musick** an honorary title conferred by the British sovereign usu on a distinguished British composer. **Master of the Rolls** in England, the head of the civil division of the Court of Appeal, appointed by the Crown on the advice of the Prime Minister. **Master of the Temple** the preacher of the Temple Church in London. **master-slave manipulator** a manipulator, esp one used to handle, from behind a protective screen, radioactive material. **masters of the schools** at Oxford University, the conductors of the first examination (Responsions) for the degree of BA. **old masters** a term applied collectively to the great European painters, esp of the 16c and 17c. **passed master** one who has passed as a master; a qualified or accomplished master, a thorough proficient (also **past master**).

mastic or **mastich** /mas'tik/ n a pale yellow gum resin from certain Mediterranean trees, used for varnish or cement; a tree exuding mastic, esp the lentisk (Pistachia lentiscus, cashew-nut family); a bituminous or oily cement of various kinds. [Fr mastic, from LL mastichum, from Gr mastichē]

masticate /mas'ti-kāt/ vt to chew; to knead mechanically, as in rubber manufacture. [L masticāre, -ātum ; cf Gr mastax jaw, mastichaein to grind the teeth]
■ **mas'ticable** adj that may be chewed. **mastica'tion** n. **mas'ticātor** n a person who masticates; a tooth or jaw (facetious); a machine for grinding; a machine for kneading india-rubber. **mas'ticatory** /-kə-tə-ri/ adj chewing; adapted for chewing. ◆n a substance chewed to increase the saliva.

masticot same as **massicot**.

mastiff /mas'tif/ n a thick-set, powerful breed of dog, often used as a guard dog. [OFr mastin, appar from L mansuētus tame; perh confused with OFr mestif mongrel]

Mastigophora /ma-sti-gof'ə-rə/ (zool) n pl the flagellates in a wide sense. [Gr mastīx, -īgos whip, and phoreein to carry]
■ **mastigoph'oran** n and adj. **mastigophoric** /-gə-for'ik/ or **mastigoph'orous** adj of the Mastigophora; whip-carrying.

mastitis /ma-stī'tis/ n inflammation of the breast or udder. [Gr mastos breast, and **-itis**]

mastodon /mas'tə-don/ n an animal of the Mastodon genus of extinct mammals resembling elephants, so named from the teatlike prominences of the molar teeth of some species. [Gr mastos breast, and odous, odontos a tooth]
■ **mastodon'tic** adj.

mastodynia /ma-stō-dī'ni-ə/ (med) n pain in the breasts. [Gr mastos breast, and odynē pain]

mastoid /mas'toid/ adj like a nipple or a teat. ◆ n a prominence on the temporal bone behind the ear (also **mastoid bone** or **process**); mastoiditis (inf). [Gr mastoeidēs like a breast]
■ **mastoid'al** adj. **mastoidī'tis** n inflammation of the air cells of the mastoid processes.

masturbate /mas'tər-bāt/ vi and vt to stimulate, *esp* by oneself, (the sexual organs) by manipulation, etc so as to produce orgasm. [L *masturbārī*]
■ **masturbā'tion** n. **mas'turbātor** n. **masturbāt'ory** adj.

masty see under **mast²**.

masu /mas'oo or mä'soo/ n a Japanese salmon (*Oncorhynchus masou*). [Jap]

masula see **masoolah**.

masurium /mə-soo'ri-əm, -sū'/ n a name proposed for element no 43 when its discovery was prematurely claimed (see **technetium**). [*Masurenland*, in E Prussia, now in N Poland]

mat¹ /mat/ n a piece of fabric or material of any of various types and thicknesses, laid on the ground for any of various purposes, eg covering part of the floor, standing or lying on, wiping one's shoes on at a threshold, absorbing shock on landing or falling in gymnastics, wrestling, etc; a rug; a smaller piece of cloth, cork or other material for placing under a vase, dish, or other object to prevent damage to the surface it stands on; a sack of matting used to cover a chest of tea, coffee, etc; a certain weight held by such a sack; a closely-interwoven or tangled mass, *esp* of hair or vegetation, or of brushwood protecting a riverbank; a web of rope yarn. ◆ vt (**matt'ing; matt'ed**) to cover with mats; to interweave; to tangle closely. ◆ vi to become tangled in a mass. [OE *matt*(e), *meatte*, from L *matta* a mat; perh of Punic origin]
■ **matt'ed** adj tangled. **matt'ing** n mat-making; becoming matted; covering with mats; material used as mats.
❑ **mat'grass** or **mat'weed** n a small, tufted, rushlike moorland grass (*Nardus stricta*); marram.
■ **on the mat** on the carpet (*fig*).

mat² /mat/ adj (of a surface) dull, lustreless or roughened to eliminate gloss (also **matt** or **matte**). ◆ n a dull uniform finish or surface; a border of dull gold or of white or colour round a picture; a punch for roughening a surface. ◆ vt to produce a dull surface on; to frost (glass). [Fr *mat*; Ger *matt* dull; cf **checkmate; amate², mate²**]

mat. abbrev : matinée; matrix.

matachin /ma-tə-chēn' or -shēn'/ n (pl **matachi'ni**) a masked sword-dancer or sword dance (*hist*); any of a group of native Mexican ritual dancers. [Fr (obs) *matachin* and Sp *matachín*, perh from Ar *mutawajjihīn* masked]
■ **matachi'na** n a female matachin.

matador /mat'ə-dör/ or **matadore** /mat'ə-dör/ n (usu **matador**) the man who kills the bull in bullfights; one of the three chief cards in the games ombre and quadrille; (usu **matadore**) a form of dominoes. [Sp, from *matar* to kill, from L *mactāre* to kill, to honour by sacrifice, from *mactus* honoured]
■ **matadō'ra** n a female matador.

matai /mat'ī/ n a coniferous tree of New Zealand (*Podocarpus spicatus*); the pale timber of this tree. [Maori]

matamata /ma-tə- or mä-tə-mä'tə/ n a S American river-turtle. [Port, from Tupí *matamatá*]

matatu /mə-tä'too/ (E Afr) n a truck or similiar vehicle that transports fare-paying passengers. [Swahili, from *tatu* three, perh referring to the original standard fare]

match¹ /mach/ n that which tallies or exactly agrees with another thing; an equal; a person who can stand up to or get the better of someone else; a condition of exact agreement, compatibility or close resemblance, *esp* in colours; equality in contest; a compact (*obs*); a formal contest or game; a pairing; a marriage; a person to be gained in marriage. ◆ vi to be exactly or nearly alike; to correspond; to form a union; to compete or encounter (*esp* on equal terms). ◆ vt and vi to be equal to; to be a counterpart to; to be compatible with, or exactly like, in colour, etc; to be able to compete with; to find an equal or counterpart to; to pit or set against another in contest or as equal; to treat as equal; to fit in with; to suit; to join in marriage; to make the impedances of (two circuits) equal, so as to produce maximum transfer of energy (*electronics*). [OE *gemæcca*; cf **make³**]
■ **match'able** adj. **matched** adj. **match'er** n. **match'ing** adj. **match'less** adj having no match or equal; superior to all; peerless; not matching (*Spenser*). **match'lessly** adv. **match'lessness** n.
❑ **match'board** n one of a number of boards with a tongue cut along one edge and a groove in the opposite edge, fitted one into the next to make a wall-facing, etc. **match'boarding** n. **matched sample** n a group of people of the same age, sex, income, etc, as another group, used as a sample to test products. **match'-joint** n the junction of matchboards. **match'maker** n a person who attempts to arrange marriages by bringing suitable partners together; a person who arranges boxing matches. **match'making** n. **match play** or **match'play** n scoring in golf according to holes won and lost rather than the overall total of strokes taken. **match point** n (in tennis, etc) the stage at which another point wins the match; the point that wins the match; a unit of scoring in bridge tournaments. **match'up** n

(chiefly N Am) a contest or comparison between two people or things, *esp* in sport.
■ **to match** in accordance or co-ordination, *esp* in colour.

match² /mach/ n a short stick of wood or other material tipped with an easily ignited material; a piece of inflammable material which easily takes or carries fire; a piece of treated cord, readily inflammable but slow-burning, for firing a gun, an explosive, etc. [OFr *mesche* (Fr *mèche*); origin obscure]
❑ **match'book** n a small cardboard folder holding matches and having an abrasive strip against which they may be struck. **match'box** n a box for holding matches. **match'-cord** n (*obs*) a piece of rope used as a slow-match. **match'lock** n the lock of a musket containing a match for firing it; a musket so fired. **match'-maker** n. **match'stick** n the wooden shaft of a match. ◆ adj very thin, like a matchstick; (of figures in a drawing, etc) having limbs suggested by single lines. **match'wood** n touchwood; wood suitable for matches; splinters.

matchmaker see under **match¹**.

match-maker see under **match²**.

mate¹ /māt/ n a companion; an equal; a fellow worker, occupant, etc (often in combination, as *workmate*, *flatmate*, etc); a friendly or ironic form of address; a husband or wife; an animal with which another is paired to produce young; one of a pair; a ship's officer under the captain or master; in the navy, formerly a rank to which a warrant officer might be promoted; an assistant or deputy (as *plumber's mate*). ◆ vt to be equal to, to rival (*archaic*); to marry; to cause (*esp* animals) to copulate; to couple; to fit. ◆ vi to claim equality (*archaic*); to marry; (*esp* of animals) to copulate; to consort (*archaic*). [Prob MLGer *mate* or earlier Du *maet* (now *maat*); cf OE *gemetta* a messmate, and **meat**]
■ **mate'less** adj without a mate or companion. **mate'ship** n (*esp Aust*) the bond between close friends. **mā'tily** adv. **mā'tiness** or **mā'teyness** n. **māt'y** or **māte'y** adj (**māt'ier; māt'iest**) (*inf*) friendly and familiar, *esp* in a studied or overdone manner. ◆ n a friendly or ironic form of address *esp* to a man.
❑ **mate's rates** n pl (*inf*) a reduced price available only to friends. **mating type** n (*bot*) a group of individuals within a species which cannot breed among themselves but which are able to breed with individuals of other such groups.

mate² /māt/ adj (*archaic*) checkmated; confounded; baffled; exhausted; daunted. ◆ vt to checkmate; to subdue (*archaic*); to baffle (*archaic*); to confound (*archaic*). ◆ n and interj checkmate. [OFr *mat* checkmated; see **checkmate**, and **mat²**]

mate³ or **maté** /mat'ā or mä'tā/ n a S American species of holly (*Ilex paraguayensis*); an infusion of its leaves and green shoots, Paraguay tea. [Sp *mate*, from Quechua *mati* a gourd (in which it is made)]

matelassé /mat-lä-sä'/, also **matelasse** or **matellasse** /mat-läs'/ n and adj (a jacquard fabric) having a raised pattern as if quilted. [Fr, from *matelas* a mattress]

matelot see **matlo**.

matelote /mat'ə-lōt/ n a fish stew cooked in wine, onions, herbs, etc; a sort of hornpipe. [Fr, from *matelot* a sailor]

mater /mā'/ or /mä'ter/ n mother (*sl, esp public school*); either of the two membranes of the brain, outer and inner, separated by the arachnoid, the *dura mater*, or *dura*, and *pia mater*, or *pia*. [L *māter*; cf Gr *mētēr*; **mother¹**]
❑ **mater dolorosa** /mā'tər dol-ə-rō'sə or mä'ter do-lō-rō'sa/ n (L, sorrowful mother) the grieving Virgin Mary, *esp* as depicted in art.

materfamilias /mā'/ or /mā'tər-fa-mil'i-as/ n (pl strictly **matresfamil'ias** /-träs-/, sometimes **materfamil'iases**) the mother of a family or household. [L *mater* a mother, and *familiās*, old genitive of *familia* a household]

material /mə-tē'ri-əl/ adj relating to matter; consisting of matter; being the substance of the thing (*Shakesp*); pithy, matterful (*Shakesp*); corporeal, not spiritual; bodily; physical; gross, lacking spirituality; relating to subject matter; relevant; of serious importance, *esp* of legal importance; relating to matter as opposed to form (*philos*). ◆ n that out of which anything is or may be made; a fabric; that which may be made use of for any purpose; a person who is suitable for a specified occupation, training, etc; (in *pl*) equipment, implements, etc needed for a task or activity. [L *māteriālis*, from *māteria* matter]
■ **matē'rialism** n the doctrine that denies the independent existence of spirit, and maintains that there is but one substance, matter; the explanation of history as the working out of economic conditions; blindness to, or denial of, the spiritual; excessive devotion to bodily wants or financial success. **matē'rialist** n and adj. **materialist'ic** or **materialist'ical** adj. **materialist'ically** adv. **materializā'tion** or **-s-** n. **matē'rialize** or **-ise** vt to render material; to cause to assume bodily form; to reduce to or regard as matter; to render materialistic. ◆ vi to take bodily form; to become actual; to take shape, develop; to turn up, put in an appearance, arrive (*inf*). **matē'rially** adv in material manner; in respect of matter or material conditions, or material cause; in a

considerable or important degree. **matē'rialness** or **materiality** /-al'i-ti/ n.

❑ **material alteration** n (law) a deliberate alteration (of date, amount, etc) to a bill of exchange, etc. **material distinction** n the distinction between individuals of the same species. **material evidence** n evidence tending to prove or to disprove the matter under judgement. **material fact** n any fact known to a potential insurant which might influence the provision of an insurance contract and which he or she is therefore obliged to disclose. **material fallacy** n (philos) a fallacy in the matter or thought, rather than in the logical form.

■ **dialectical materialism** Karl Marx's view of history as a conflict between two opposing forces, thesis and antithesis, which is resolved by the forming of a new force, synthesis, present conditions being due to a class struggle between the capitalists, whose aim is private profit, and the workers, who resist exploitation.

materia medica /mə-tē'ri-ə med'i-kə/ n substances used in medicine; the science of their properties and use. [LL, medical material]

materiel or **matériel** /ma-tē-ri-el', -tā-, or -ryel'/ n material; equipment; the baggage and munitions of an army. [Fr]

maternal /mə-tûr'nəl/ adj of a mother; motherly; on the mother's side; of the nature, or in the person, of a mother. [Fr maternel (Ital maternale) and maternité, from L māternus, from māter mother]

■ **mater'nalism** n. **maternalis'tic** adj. **mater'nally** adv. **mater'nity** n the fact of being in the relation of mother; motherhood; motherliness; maternal nature; a maternity hospital or ward. ◆ adj of or for women at or near the time of childbirth.

❑ **maternal immunity** n passive immunity acquired by the newborn baby or animal from its mother. **maternity leave** n paid absence from work to which a pregnant woman is entitled before and following childbirth. **maternity rights** n pl the statutory rights of women employees relating to pregnancy, such as the right to maternity leave, to return to work after giving birth, etc.

matey see under **mate**[1].

matfellon or **matfelon** /mat'fe-lən/ n the greater knapweed. [OFr matefelon; cf **mate**[2] and **felon**[2]]

matgrass see under **mat**[1].

math[1] see **mathematics** under **mathematic**.

math[2] /math/ (dialect) n a mowing. [OE mǣth]

math. abbrev : mathematics.

mathematic /ma-thə-mat'ik/ or **mathematical** adj relating to, or done by, mathematics; very accurate. [Gr mathēmatikē (epistēmē) (skill, knowledge) relating to learning, from mathēma, from root of manthanein to learn]

■ **mathemat'ically** adv. **mathematician** /-mə-tish'ən/ n a specialist or expert in mathematics. **mathemat'icism** n the belief that everything can be described or explained ultimately in mathematical terms. **mathemat'icized** or **-s-** adj. **mathemat'ics** n sing or n pl (inf short form **maths**, or N Am **math**) the science of magnitude and number, the relations of figures and forms, and of quantities expressed as symbols. **mathematiza'tion** or **-s-** n. **math'ematize** or **-ise** vi and vt to explain, formulate or treat (something) in mathematical terms (also **mathemat'icize** or **-ise**). **math'ematized** or **-s-** adj.

❑ **mathematical logic** same as **symbolic logic** (see under **symbol**).

mathesis /mə-thē'sis/ or (obs) math'i-sis/ n mental discipline, esp mathematical. [Gr mathēsis]

maths see **mathematics** under **mathematic**.

Mathurin /math'ū-rin/ or **Mathurine** /-rēn/ n a Trinitarian canon. [Perh from their house near St Mathurin's chapel in Paris]

matico /mă-tē'kō/ n (pl **mati'cos**) a Peruvian pepper shrub, used as a styptic. [Sp, dimin of Mateo Matthew]

Matilda /mə-til'də/ (Aust) n a swag. [Female personal name]

■ **walk** or **waltz Matilda** to travel around carrying one's swag.

matily see under **mate**[1].

matin /mat'in/ n morning (Shakesp); a morning song (Milton); (in pl; often with cap) one of the hours of the Divine Office, held between midnight and daybreak, now replaced by the Office of Readings (RC); (in pl) the daily morning service of the Church of England. ◆ adj of the morning; of matins. [Fr matines (fem pl), from L mātūtīnus belonging to the morning, from Mātūta goddess of morning, prob related to mātūrus early]

■ **mat'inal** adj.

matinée or **matinee** /mat'i-nā or mat-(ə-)nā'/ n a performance of a play, concert, or showing of a film held in the daytime, usu the afternoon; a woman's dress for morning wear. [Fr, a pre-dinner gathering or entertainment, from matin morning]

❑ **matinée coat** or **jacket** n a baby's coat or jacket made of wool or similar material. **matinée idol** n a handsome actor or filmstar, popular esp among women.

matiness see under **mate**[1].

matjes see **maatjes**.

matlo or **matlow** /mat'lō/ (sl) n (pl **mat'los** or **mat'lows** /-lōz/) a seaman, a sailor (also **matelot** /mat'lō/). [Fr matelot]

matooke or **matoke** /ma-tō'kā/ n in Uganda, plantain used as a staple food. [Bantu]

matrass /mat'rəs/ n a long-necked chemical flask; a hard-glass tube closed at one end. [Fr matras]

matriarch /mā'tri-ärk/ n the female head of a family, tribe or community; an elderly woman who dominates her family or associates; an elderly and much respected woman of great dignity. [Formed on the analogy of **patriarch**, from L māter mother]

■ **matriar'chal** adj. **matriar'chalism** n a condition of a society with matriarchal customs; the theory of such a society. **matriar'chate** n the position of a matriarch; a matriarchal condition or community. **ma'triarchy** n government by a mother or by mothers; an order of society in which descent is reckoned through the female line, or in which a woman is head of the family or the community.

matric see **matriculation** under **matriculate**.

matrice /mā'tris or mat'ris/ n same as **matrix**.

matrices see **matrix**.

matricide /mā'tri- or mat'ri-sīd/ n a murderer of his or her own mother; the murder of one's own mother. [L mātricīda, mātricīdium, from māter mother, and caedere to kill]

■ **matrici'dal** adj.

matriclinic, matriclinous, etc see **matroclinic.**

matricula /mə-trik'ū-lə/ n a register of members, students, etc. [LL mātrīcula a register, dimin of L mātrīx]

■ **matric'ular** adj relating to a register; contributed to the federal fund (as formerly by German states).

matriculate /mə-trik'ū-lāt/ vt to admit to membership by entering one's name in a register, esp in a college or university. ◆ vi to become a member of a college, university, etc, by being enrolled. ◆ n a person admitted to membership in a society. [Ety as for **matricula**]

■ **matriculā'tion** n the act of matriculating; the state of being matriculated; an entrance examination (familiarly **matric'**). **matric'ulātor** n. **matriculā'tory** adj.

matrifocal /ma-tri-fō'kəl/ (esp anthrop) adj centred on the mother; (of societies, families, etc) in which authority and responsibility rest with the mother. [L māter a mother, and focus a hearth]

■ **matrifocal'ity** n.

matrilineal /ma-tri-lin'i-əl/ or **matrilinear** /-ər/ adj (of descent or kinship) reckoned through the mother or through females alone. [L māter a mother, and līnea a line]

■ **matrilin'eally** adv. **mat'riliny** (or /-lī'ni/) n.

matrilocal /ma-tri-lō'kl/ adj (of a form of marriage) in which the husband goes to live with the wife's group. [L māter mother, and locālis, from locus place]

■ **matrilocal'ity** n.

matrimony /mat'ri-mə-ni/ n the state of being married, wedlock; the marriage ceremony; a card game of chance in which one of the winning combinations is that of king and queen; the combination of king and queen in that and various other games. [L mātrimōnium, from māter, mātris mother]

■ **matrimonial** /-mō'ni-əl/ adj relating to marriage. **matrimo'nially** adv.

matrix /mā'triks or mat'riks/ n (pl **ma'trices** /-tris-ēz or -iz/ or **ma'trixes**) the womb (obs); the place in which anything is developed or formed; that in which anything is embedded, such as ground-mass, gangue, intercellular substance, cementing material; the bed on which a thing rests, such as the cutis under a nail, the hollow in a slab to receive a monumental brass; a mould, eg for casting printing type; a rectangular array of quantities or symbols (maths); any rectangular arrangement of data in rows and columns; a table published by the Bank of England, giving recommended levels of Third World debt provision for individual institutions (finance). [L mātrīx, -īcis a breeding animal, later, the womb, from māter mother]

■ **matric** /māt' or mat'/ adj of, relating to, or having the properties of a matrix.

❑ **matric potential** n (bot) that component of the water potential of plants and soils that is due to the interaction of the water with colloids and to capillary forces. **matrix printer** n a printer attached to a computer which prints characters as a series of dots by firing pins against an inked ribbon (also **dot matrix printer**).

matroclinic /ma-trō-klin'ik/ or **matroclinous** /-klī'nəs/ adj (also **matriclin'ic** or **matriclī'nous**) inherited from the mother; more like the mother than the father. [L māter (or Doric Gr mātēr) mother, and Gr klīnein to lean]

■ **matroclī'ny** (also **matriclī'ny**) n.

matron /mā'trən/ n a usu married, and middle-aged to elderly, woman of dignified appearance and dependable personality; a woman in charge of domestic arrangements in a school or other institution; the former title of the senior nursing officer in charge of the nursing staff in a hospital, now **senior nursing officer**; a prison wardress (*US*); a married woman. [Fr *matrone*, from L *mātrōna*, from *māter* mother]
  ■ **mā'tronage** or **mā'tronhood** n the state of being a matron; a body of matrons. **mā'tronal** adj matronly; motherly; grave. **mā'tronize** or **-ise** vt to render matronly; to act as matron to; to chaperon. ◆ vi to become a matron or matronly. **ma'tron-like** adj. **mā'tronly** adj (of a woman) plump or portly with the onset of middle age, or dignified and imposing; belonging, or suitable, to a matron. **mā'tronship** n.
  ◻ **matron of honour** see under **honour**.

matronymic see **metronymic**.

matross /mə-tros'/ (*obs*) n a gunner's assistant in artillery. [Du *matroos*, appar from Fr *matelot* a sailor]

matryoshka /ma-tri-osh'kə/ n (pl **matryosh'ki**) a hollow wooden doll containing a series of smaller dolls, fitting one within the other (also **matryoshka doll**). [Russ, dimin of *mat'* mother]

matsuri /mat-soo'ri/ n a Shinto festival or public ceremony held at a shrine. [Jap]

Matt. (*Bible*) *abbrev* : (the Gospel according to St) Matthew.

matt see **mat²**.

mattamore /ma-tə-mōr', -mör' or mat'ə-/ n a subterranean chamber. [Fr *matamore*, from Ar *matmūrah*]

matte¹ /mat/ n a product of the smelting of sulphide ores (also called **regulus** and **coarse metal**). [Fr]

matte² /mat/ adj see **mat²**.

matte³ /mat/ (*cinematog*) n a kind of mask used to block out areas of the image, allowing a different image to be superimposed; an image produced in this way. [Fr]

matted see under **mat¹**.

matter /mat'ər/ n that which occupies space, and with which we become acquainted by our bodily senses; that out of which anything is made, material; the subject or material of thought, speech, writing, dispute, etc; substance as distinct from form (*philos*); good sense (*Shakesp*); anything engaging the attention; whatever has physical existence, as distinct from mind (*philos*); an affair, thing, concern, subject or question; a thing or substance of the kind specified, such as *printed matter*, *vegetable matter* ; cause or ground, as in *matter of concern* ; a thing of consequence; something that is amiss, as in *what is the matter?* ; that with which a court is concerned, something to be tried or proved; (with *neg*) importance, significance or consequence; an approximate amount, eg of money, as in *a matter of a few pounds* ; material for work, type set up, copy, etc (*printing*); pus (*med*). ◆ vi to be of importance, significance or consequence; to form or discharge pus (*med*). ◆ vt (*obs*) to mind or concern oneself about. [OFr *matiere*, from L *māteria* matter]
  ■ **matt'erful** adj (*archaic*) full of matter, pithy. **matt'erless** adj (now chiefly *dialect*). **matt'ery** adj purulent; containing, discharging, or covered with pus.
  ◻ **matter-of-fact'** adj adhering to literal, actual or pedestrian fact; not fanciful; prosaic. **matter-of-fact'ly** adv. **matter-of-fact'ness** n.
  ■ **a matter of course** a thing occurring routinely, in natural time and order. **a matter of form** a (mere) official procedure or conventional etiquette. **a matter of opinion** see under **opinion**. **as a matter of fact** see under **fact**. **for that matter** as for that; indeed. **no matter** it does not matter; it makes no difference. **the matter** (**with**) (the thing that is) amiss (with).

Matthaean /ma-thē'ən/ adj of the evangelist St Matthew or his gospel.

mattie /mat'i/ (*Scot*) n a young herring with undeveloped roe. [Du *maatjes* (*haring*), from LGer *mädeken* maiden]

matting see under **mat¹**.

mattins same as **matins** (pl of **matin**).

mattock /mat'ək/ n a kind of pickaxe for loosening soil, with a cutting end instead of a point. [OE *mattuc*]

mattoid /mat'oid/ n a person on the borderline between sanity and insanity. [Ital *mattoide*, from *matto* mad]

mattress /mat'ris/ n a more or less resilient large, oblong pad for sleeping or lying on, *usu* forming part of a bed; a mass of brushwood, etc, used to form a foundation for roads, etc, or for the walls of embankments, etc. [OFr *materas* (Fr *matelas*), from Ar *matrah* a place where anything is thrown]

maturate /mat'ū-rāt/ vt to make mature; to cause to suppurate (*med*). ◆ vi to become mature; to suppurate fully (*med*). [L *matūrāre*, -*ātum* to bring to ripeness or maturity]
  ■ **matura'tion** n a bringing or a coming to maturity; the process of suppurating fully; the final stage in the production of a germ-cell, at

which the reduction division occurs. **maturā'tional** adj. **matur'ative** (or /mat'/) adj promoting ripening; causing suppuration.

mature /mə-tūr', -chûr' or (*N Am*) -tūr'/ adj fully developed; having the mental, emotional and social development appropriate to an adult; perfected; ripe; well-thought-out; (of a bill, bond, or insurance policy) due for payment or conversion; in due time (*Milton*); suppurating. ◆ vt to bring to ripeness, full development or perfection; to bring to a head; to cause to suppurate. ◆ vi to come to or approach ripeness, full development, or perfection; to become due for payment or conversion (*finance*). [L *matūrus* ripe]
  ■ **matur'able** adj capable of being matured. **mature'ly** adv. **mature'ness** n. **matur'ity** n ripeness; full development; the time of becoming due or convertible (*finance*).
  ◻ **mature student** n a person who enters higher education later in life than is usual.

matutinal /ma-tū-tī'nl or mə-tū'ti-nl/, also **matutine** /mat'ū-tīn/ adj relating to the morning; happening early in the day. [L *mātūtīnālis*, *mātūtīnus* ; see **matin**]

matweed see under **mat¹**.

maty see under **mate¹**.

matzo, also **matzoh**, **matza** or **matzah** /mat'sə or -sō/ n (pl (with verb sing or pl) **mat'zoth** /-sōt or -sōth/, **mat'zos**, **mat'zot**, **mat'zas** or **mat'zahs**) unleavened bread, now *usu* in the form of large, square crackers, eaten during Passover, etc; a wafer or cracker of this. [Yiddish *matse* ; from Heb]
  ◻ **matzo ball** n a kind of dumpling made from ground matzo. **matzo meal** n matzo ground into meal.

matzoon /mät-soon'/ or **madzoon** /mäd-zoon'/ n a food similar to yoghurt made from fermented milk. [Armenian *madzun*]

mauby /mō' or mö'bi/ n a drink made from the bitter-tasting bark of a Caribbean tree. [Carib *mabi* drink made from sweet potatoes]

maud /möd/ n a Scottish shepherd's woollen plaid. [Origin unknown]

maudlin /möd'lin/ adj weeping (*archaic*); foolishly lachrymose, *esp* when in a fuddled, half-drunk state; weakly sentimental. [ME *Maudelein*, through OFr and L from Gr *Magdalēnē*, (woman) of Magdala, from the assumption that Mary Magdalene was the penitent woman in Bible, Luke 7.38]
  ■ **maud'linism** n the tearful stage of drunkenness.

maugre or **maulgre** /mö'gər, also -gri and mö(l)-grē'/ (*archaic*) prep in spite of, notwithstanding; a curse upon (*Spenser* ; with dative). ◆ adv out of spite, motivated by ill-will. ◆ n (*obs*) ill-will, spite. ◆ vt (now *Scot*) to show ill-will towards; to spite. [OFr *maugré*, *malgré* discontent, sorrow (Fr *malgré* in spite of), from L *male grātum*, from *male* badly, and *grātum* agreeable]

maul /möl/ vt to beat with a maul or heavy stick; to handle roughly, batter or maltreat; to injure by pawing or clawing; to split with a maul (*US*). ◆ vi to thrust forward in a close mass, *esp* in rugby. ◆ n a war-club or mace (*obs*); a heavy wooden hammer or beetle, a mall; a struggle for the ball when it is being held above the ground (*rugby*). [Fr *mail*, from L *malleus* hammer]
  ■ **maul'ers** n pl (*sl*) hands.

Maulana /mö-lä'nä/ n a scholar of Arabic and Persian, a learned Muslim man. [Ar *mawlana*]

maulgre see **maugre**.

maulstick /möl'stik/ n a stick with a pad on the end, used by painters to steady the hand holding the brush (also **mahl'stick** or **mal'stick**). [Du *maalstok*, from *malen* to paint, and *stok* stick, assimilated to **stick**]

maulvi /möl'vi/ n a teacher of Islamic law, a learned man. [Urdu *mulvī*, from Ar *maulawiyy*]

maumet and **maumetry** see **mammet** and **mammetry**.

maun /mön, män or mun/ (*Scot*) vt must. [See **mun¹**]
  ■ **maunna** /mön'ə or mun'ə/ must not.

maund¹ /mönd/ (*Shakesp*) n a basket. [OE *mand*]

maund² /mönd/ n a measure of weight in India and W Asia, its value varying in different places from about 25 to 85 pounds avoirdupois (*approx* 11.3 to 38.6kg). [Hindi and Pers *man*]

maund³ /mönd/ (*obs sl*) vt and vi to beg. [Poss Fr *mendier* to beg, from L *mendicāre*]
  ■ **maund'er** n a beggar. ◆ vi to beg.

maunder¹ /mön'dər/ vi to grumble; to mutter; to talk in a rambling, inconclusive way, to drivel; to wander about or behave in a listless, aimless way. [Perh *maunder* (obs) to beg, from L *mendicāre* to beg]
  ■ **maun'derer** n. **maun'dering** n drivelling talk.

maunder² see under **maund³**.

maundy /mön'di/ n the religious ceremony of washing the feet of the poor, in commemoration of Christ's washing the disciples' feet (Bible,

John 13), formerly practised by some monarchs. [Fr *mandé*, from L *mandātum* command (Bible, John 13.34)]

□ **maundy money** *n* the dole given away on **Maundy Thursday**, the day before Good Friday, by the royal almoner, *usu* a silver penny for each year of the sovereign's age, the small silver coins specially minted since 1662.

maungy see **mangy**.

maunna see under **maun**.

Mauretanian /mö-ri-tā'nyən/ *adj* of or relating to *Mauretania*, an ancient country in N Africa, corresponding to parts of present-day Algeria and Morocco. ◆ *n* a native or inhabitant of Mauretania.

Maurist /mö'rist/ *n* a member of the reformed Benedictine Congregation of St *Maur* settled from 1618 at the abbey of St *Maur*-sur-Loire, near Saumur, notable for its great scholarship. ◆ *adj* of or relating to the Maurists.

Mauritanian /mö-ri-tā'nyən/ *adj* of or relating to the NW African country of *Mauritania* or its people. ◆ *n* a native or inhabitant of Mauritania.

Mauritian /mo- or mö-rish'ən/ *adj* of the island of *Mauritius* (named after Maurice (1567–1625), Prince of Orange) or its people.

□ **Mauritius hemp** *n* the fibre of an amaryllidaceous plant, *Furcraea gigantea*.

Mauser /mow'zər/ *n* (any of) a series of German rifles, *esp* a magazine rifle of 1897. [PP von *Mauser* (1838–1914), German firearms inventor]

mausoleum /mö-sə-lē'əm/ *n* (pl **mausolē'a** or **mausolē'ums**) a magnificent tomb or monument; a gloomy or spiritless place (*fig*). [L *mausōlēum*, from Gr *Mausōleion*, the magnificent tomb of *Mausōlos* (died 353BC), satrap of Caria, erected by his widow Artemisia at Halicarnassus]

■ **mausolē'an** *adj* relating to a mausoleum; grand, stately, imposing (*poetic*).

mauther or **mawther** /mö'dhər/ (*dialect, esp E Anglia*) *n* (also, *esp vocatively*, **mawr** or **mor**) a girl; a big awkward girl. [Origin obscure]

mauvais /mo-ve'/ or (*fem*) **mauvaise** /-vez'/ (*Fr*) *adj* bad, worthless. □ **mauvaise honte** /mo-vez ɔt/ *n* false modesty, bashfulness. **mauvais goût** /goo/ *n* bad taste, lack of taste. **mauvais moment** /mo-mä/ *n* a bad, unpleasant moment (also **mauvais quart d'heure** /kär dær/ a brief but unpleasant experience, (literally) a bad quarter of an hour). **mauvais sujet** /sü-zhä/ *n* a worthless person. **mauvais ton** /tɔ̃/ *n* bad style, bad form.

mauve /mōv or möv/ *n* a purple aniline dye; its colour, that of mallow flowers, a light bluish purple. ◆ *adj* of the colour of mauve. [Fr, from L *malva* mallow]

■ **mauv'in, mauv'ine, mauve'in** or **mauve'ine** *n* mauve dye.

maven same as **mavin**.

maverick /mav'(ə-)rik/ (*orig US*) *n* a stray animal without an owner's brand, *esp* a calf; a person who does not conform, a determined individualist; anything dishonestly obtained; (with *cap*) a type of air-to-ground anti-tank missile, guided by a laser or TV camera. ◆ *adj* that is, or is characteristic of, a maverick. ◆ *vt* to seize without legal claim. [Samuel *Maverick* (1803–70), Texas cattle-raiser]

mavin or **maven** /mā'vin/ (*US sl*) *n* an expert, a pundit. [Yiddish, from Heb *mevin* understanding]

mavis /mā'vis/ *n* the song thrush (see **thrush**[1]). [Fr *mauvis*]

mavourneen /mə-voor'nēn/ (*Irish*) *n* and interj my dear one. [Ir *mo mhurnín*]

maw[1] /mö/ *n* the jaws or gullet of a voracious animal or (*facetious*) person; an insatiable gulf or ever-open mouth (*fig*); the stomach, *esp* (and now only) that of an animal; inclination, appetite (*Milton*); the craw of a bird (*obs*); the fourth stomach in ruminants; any other internal organ (now *rare*). [OE *maga*; Ger *Magen*]

□ **maw'bound** *adj* (of cattle) constipated by impaction of the rumen. **maw'-worm** *n* (now *rare*) a worm infesting the stomach or intestines.

maw[2] /mö/ (*chiefly Scot*) *n* a seagull. [ON *mār*]

maw[3] /mö/ (*hist*) *n* an old card game played with a pack of 36. [Origin unknown]

mawk /mök/ (now *dialect*) *n* a maggot. [ON *mathkr* maggot]

■ **mawk'y** *adj* (**mawk'ier; mawk'iest**) maggoty; mawkish.

mawkin see **malkin**.

mawkish /mö'kish/ *adj* insipid; sickly; weakly sentimental, maudlin; loathsome, disgusting; squeamish; maggoty (*obs*). [Ety as for **mawk**, in obs sense above]

■ **mawk'ishly** *adv*. **mawk'ishness** *n*.

Mawlawi see **Mevlevi**.

Mawlid /mow'lid/ *n* a Muslim festival celebrating the birthday of the prophet Mohammed. [Ar, birthday]

mawmet and **mawmetry** see **mammet**.

mawpus see **mopus**[1].

mawr and **mawther** see **mauther**.

mawseed /mö'sēd/ *n* poppy seed, *esp* as used for cage-bird food. [Ger dialect *Mahsaat*, from *Mah* poppy, and *saat* seed]

max /maks/ (*obs*) *n* gin. [Origin obscure]

max. *abbrev* : maximum.

■ **max out** (*sl*) to exhaust the limit of (a credit card, mobile-phone account, etc).

maxi /mak'si/ *adj* (*inf*) or *combining form* signifying very, or extra, large or long, as in *maxi-coat, skirt* or *dress*, an ankle-length coat, skirt, etc. ◆ *n* a maxi garment; a large size of racing yacht. [*maximum*]

□ **max'i-single** *n* a gramophone record longer than an ordinary single.

maxilla /mak-sil'ə/ *n* (pl **maxill'ae** /-ē/) a jawbone, *esp* the upper; (in arthropods) an appendage with masticatory function, just behind the mouth, modified in connection with feeding. [L *maxilla* jawbone]

■ **maxill'ary** (or /maks'/) *adj* of or relating to a jaw or maxilla. ◆ *n* a bone forming the posterior part of the upper jaw. **maxill'iped** /-ped/ or **maxill'ipede** /-pēd/ *n* (in crustaceans) a jaw-foot, an appendage behind the mouth, adapted to help in passing food to the mouth. **maxillofā'cial** *adj* (*esp* of surgery) of or relating to the jawbone and face. **maxill'ūla** (*pl* **maxill'ūlae** /-lē/) (in crustaceans) a maxilla of the first pair.

Maxim /mak'sim/ *n* short for **Max'im-gun**, an automatic machine-gun invented by Hiram *Maxim* (1840–1916).

maxim /mak'sim/ *n* a general principle, serving as a rule or guide; a pithy saying; a proverb. [Fr *maxime*, from L *maxima* (*sententia*, or some other word) greatest (opinion, etc), fem superl of *magnus* great]

■ **max'imist** *n* (also **maxim-mong'er**) a habitual maker of maxims.

maxima see **maximum**.

maxima cum laude /mak'si-ma kum lö'dē or kŭm low'de/ (*L*) with distinction, with the greatest praise (of attainment of high standard in degree examinations).

maximal, etc see under **maximum**.

maximin /mak'si-min/ *n* the highest value in a set of minimum values (*maths*); in games theory, the strategy of making all decisions in such a way as to maximize the chances of incurring the minimal potential loss. Cf **minimax**. [*maximum* and *minimum*]

maximum /mak'si-məm/ *adj* greatest. ◆ *n* (pl **max'ima** or **max'imums**) the greatest possible number, quantity, or degree; the highest point reached; the value of a variable when it ceases to increase and begins to decrease, *opp* to *minimum* (*maths*). [L, superl neuter of *magnus* great]

■ **max'imal** *adj* of the highest or maximum value. **max'imalist** *n* a person who makes the fullest demands; a Bolshevik; one who demands the maximum programme. **max'imally** *adv*. **maxima'phily** *n* the study and collection of maximum cards (see below). **maximīzā'tion** or **-s-** *n*. **max'imize** or **-ise** *vt* to raise to the highest degree. ◆ *vi* to give greatest scope to a doctrine. **max'imizer** or **-s-** *n*. □ **maximum and minimum thermometer** *n* a thermometer that shows the highest and lowest temperatures that have occurred since last adjustment. **maximum card** *n* a picture postcard bearing a stamp depicting the same or a similar image and related postmark on the picture side. **maximum permissible concentration** *n* (*radiol*) the recommended upper limit for the dose which may be received during a specified period by a person exposed to ionizing radiation (also **permissible dose**).

maxixe /mä-shē'shä/ *n* a Brazilian dance resembling the tango; the music for this. [Port]

maxwell /maks'wəl/ (*phys*) *n* the CGS unit of magnetic flux, equal to 10^{-8} weber. [James Clerk-*Maxwell* (1831–79), Scottish physicist]

□ **Maxwell's demon** *n* (*phys* and *chem*) an imaginary creature who, by opening and closing a tiny door between two volumes of gas, suggests the possibility of concentrating slower molecules in one volume and faster in the other, thus breaking the second law of thermodynamics. **Maxwell's equations** *n pl* (*phys*) the mathematical formulations of the laws of Gauss, Faraday and Ampère from which the theory of electromagnetic waves can be derived.

May /mā/ *n* the fifth month of the year; the early or carefree part of life; (without *cap*) may blossom. ◆ *vi* (also without *cap*) to gather may on Mayday; to participate in May sports. [OFr *Mai*, from L *Māius* (*mēnsis*), prob month sacred to *Māia*, mother of Mercury]

■ **may'ing** *n* the observance of Mayday customs.

□ **may apple** *n* an American plant, *Podophyllum*; the egg-shaped fruit of this. **may beetle** or **may bug** *n* the cockchafer. **may'-bird** *n* the whimbrel; the bobolink. **may bloom** or **may blossom** *n* the hawthorn flower. **May'day** *n* the first day of May, given to sports and to socialist and labour demonstrations (see also **mayday**). ◆ *adj*

happening on or appropriate to Mayday. **May-dew'** *n* the dew of May, *esp* that of the morning of the first day of May, said to whiten linen and beautify faces. **may'-duke** *n* a variety of sour cherry. **May'fair** *n* the West End of London, at one time scene of a fair in May. **may'flower** *n* the hawthorn or other flower that blooms in May. **may'fly** *n* a short-lived plectopterous insect (genus *Ephemera*) that appears in May; the caddis fly. **May'-game** *n* sport appropriate to Mayday; frolic generally. **May-la'dy** *n* the Queen of the May. **May laws** *n pl* (*hist*) Prussian laws passed in three successive Mays (1873–75), restricting the power of the Church. **may'-lily** *n* the lily of the valley. **May-lord'** *n* a youth directing May-games; one enjoying transitory dignity. **May meetings** *n pl* (*hist*) meetings of various religious and philanthropic societies held in London during the 19c. **May-morn'** or **-morn'ing** *n* any morning in May, *esp* the first; youthful freshness as of May (*Shakesp*). **may'pole** *n* a pole erected for dancing round on Mayday. **May queen** *n* a young woman crowned with flowers as queen on Mayday. **May'time** *n* the season of May. **may tree** *n* the hawthorn.
■ **May-September** (or **May-December**) **marriage**, **romance**, etc a marriage, romance, etc between a young woman and a much older man.

may¹ /mā/ *auxiliary v* (infinitive and participles obsolete; 2nd pers sing (*archaic*) **mayst** or **may'est**; 3rd pers **may**; *pat* **might** /mīt/ or (*obs* or *dialect*) **mought** /mowt/ (also used instead of *may* to make a possibility more remote, a question more tentative, or to make requests or administer rebukes); 2nd pers sing (*archaic*) **might'est** or **mightst**) expressing ability, possibility or contingency, permission or competence, probability, concession, purpose or result, a wish, or uncertainty (used with infinitive without *to*). [OE *mæg*, prt (old pat) of *magan* to be able, pat *mihte*; cognate with Gothic *magan*, Ger *mögen*]
■ **may'hap** (or **/-hap'/**) *adv* (*archaic*) perhaps.
■ **be that as it may** in spite of that. **come what may** whatever transpires. **may** (or **might**) **as well** used to make suggestions or to indicate frustration or despair. **may I add** or **it may be added** used to introduce an additional point. **may I ask** (*usu ironic*) used before or after a question. **that's as may be** that may be so.

may² /mā/ (*archaic* and *poetic*) *n* a maid. [Prob OE *mæg* a kinswoman]

Maya /mī'ə/ *n* a S American people of Central America and S Mexico who developed a remarkable pre-Columbian civilization; the language of this people; a member of this people (also **May'an**). ◆ *adj* (also **May'an**) of or relating to the Mayas.
■ **Mayol'ogist** *n*. **Mayol'ogy** *n*.

maya /mä'yə/ *n* illusion; the world of phenomena (*philos*). [Sans *māyā*]

maybe /mā'bē/ *adv* perhaps, possibly. ◆ *n* a possibility; a possible selection, appointee, etc. [*may be*, from **may**]

Mayday see under **May**.

mayday /mā'dā/ *n* the international radiotelephonic distress signal for ships and aircraft. [Fr (infinitive) *m'aider* (pronounced /mā-dā/) help me]

mayest see **may¹**.

mayflower and **mayfly** see under **May**.

mayhap see under **may¹**.

mayhem /mā'hem/ or /mā'əm/ *n* maiming; malicious damage (*law* and *US*); havoc, chaos (*inf*; *non-standard*). [Ety as for **maim**]

mayn't /mā'ənt/ contraction of **may not**.

Mayologist, etc see under **Maya**.

mayonnaise /mā-ə-nāz'/ or /mā'/ *n* a cold sauce consisting of a seasoned mixture of egg yolk, vegetable oil and lemon juice or vinegar (often shortened to **mayo**); any cold dish of which it is an ingredient, such as *shrimp mayonnaise*. [Fr, perh from *mahonnais* of Mahon, port in Minorca]

mayor /mā'(ə)r/ *n* the chief magistrate of a city or borough in England, Ireland, etc, whether man or woman; the head of a municipal corporation. [Fr *maire*, from L *mājor*, compar of *magnus* great]
■ **may'oral** *adj*. **may'oralty** or **may'orship** *n* the office of a mayor. **may'oress** *n* a mayor's wife, or other woman who performs her social and ceremonial functions.
■ **Lord Mayor** the chief magistrate of certain English, Welsh, Irish and Australian cities and boroughs. **Mayor of the Palace** (*hist*) in Merovingian France, the king's major-domo or prime minister, the real ruler.

maypole see under **May**.

mayst see **may¹**.

mayster /mā'ster/, **maysterdome**, etc Spenserian forms of **master**, **masterdom**, etc.

mayweed /mā'wēd/ *n* stinking camomile (*Anthemis cotula*); corn feverfew (*Matricaria inodora*), a scentless mayweed; applied to various similar plants. [OE *mægtha* mayweed, and **weed¹**]

mazard or **mazzard** /maz'ərd/ *n* a head or skull (*Shakesp*); a wild European cherry. [Prob **mazer**]

mazarine¹ /ma-zə-rēn'/ *n* a rich blue colour; a blue gown or fabric. ◆ *adj* of this colour; made of mazarine.
■ **mazarinade'** *n* (*hist*) a satire or pamphlet against Cardinal *Mazarin* (1602–61).
❑ **Mazarin** or **Mazarine Bible** *n* the first printed Bible, printed by Gutenberg and Fust about 1450, of which the Cardinal had twenty-five copies. **mazarine hood** *n* a hood of a form said to have been worn by the Duchesse de *Mazarin*.

mazarine² /ma-zə-rēn'/ *n* (also **mazarine dish** or **plate**) a 17c deep, *usu* metal, plate; a cooking and serving dish set inside a larger dish. [Origin uncertain]

Mazdaism /maz'dä-i-zm/ or **Mazdeism** /maz'dē-i-zm/ *n* the religion of the ancient Persians; Zoroastrianism. [See ety for **Ormuzd**]
■ **Maz'daist** *n* and *adj* (a) Zoroastrian. **Mazdē'an** *adj*.

maze¹ /māz/ *n* a labyrinth; a set of intricate windings; any confusingly elaborate and complicated system, etc; *orig* bewilderment (now *dialect*). ◆ *vt* to bewilder; to confuse. [Prob from a lost OE word; the compound *āmasod* amazed, occurs]
■ **maze'ful** *adj* (*Spenser*). **maze'ment** *n*. **mā'zily** *adv*. **mā'ziness** *n*. **mā'zy** *adj* winding or convoluted as a maze; confused, dizzy (*dialect*).

maze² /māz/ see **mease¹**.

mazeltov or **mazel tov** /maz'əl-tov, -tof, -töv, also mä'zəl-/ *interj* a Jewish expression conveying congratulations or best wishes. [Yiddish, from Heb]

mazer /mā'zər/ *n* a hard wood, probably maple; a type of drinking bowl made *esp* and *orig* of maple wood (*hist*). [OFr *masere*, of Gmc origin; cf OHGer *masar*, ON *mösurr* a maple-tree]

mazhbi /maz'bi/ *n* a Sikh of low caste. [Hindi, from Ar *mazhab* religion or sect]

mazout see **mazut**.

mazuma /mə-zoo'mə/ (*sl*) *n* money. [Yiddish]

mazurka /mə-zoor'kə or -zûr'/ *n* a lively Polish dance; the music for it, in triple time. [Pol, Masurian woman]

mazut or **mazout** /mə-zoot'/ *n* petroleum residue after distillation. [Russ *mazat'* to daub or smear]

mazzard see **mazard**.

MB *abbrev*: Manitoba (Canadian province); mark of the Beast; *Medicinae Baccalaureus* (*L*), Bachelor of Medicine; megabyte (also **Mb**).

mb or **mbar** *abbrev*: millibar.

MBA *abbrev*: Master of Business Administration.

mbaqanga /m-bə-kang'gə/ (*S Afr*) *n* a type of black African urban music, originating in Soweto. [Origin uncertain; perh related to Zulu *umbaqanga* porridge, mixture]

MBE *abbrev*: Member of (the Order of) the British Empire.

MBFR *abbrev*: Mutual Balanced Force Reduction.

MBI *abbrev*: management buy-in.

mbira /m-bē'rə/ *n* an African musical instrument played with the thumbs, consisting of several tuned metal strips attached at one end to a soundboard. [Shona]

MBM *abbrev*: meat and bone meal.

MBO *abbrev*: management buyout.

MBSc *abbrev*: Master of Business Science.

MBT *abbrev*: main battle tank.

mbyte *abbrev*: megabyte.

MC /em-sē'/ *n* a master of ceremonies (see under **ceremony**); (*esp* in hip-hop culture) a performer who introduces and embellishes electronic dance music. ◆ *vt* and *vi* (**MC'ing**; **MCed'**) to act as the MC (of).

MC *abbrev*: *Medium Coeli* (*L*), midheaven (*astrol*); Member of Congress; Member of Council; Military Cross; Monaco (IVR).

Mc see **Mac¹**.

Mc- or **Mac-** /mək-/ (*inf*) *pfx* implying that a thing is considered inferior or unworthy, as in a *McJob*. [Alluding to the *McDonald's* restaurant chain]

MCA *abbrev*: Medicines Control Agency; monetary compensatory amounts.

MCB *abbrev*: miniature circuit breaker.

MCC *abbrev*: Marylebone Cricket Club.

McCarthyism /mə-kär'thi-i-zm/ *n* the hunting down and removal from public employment of all suspected of Communism. [Joseph *McCarthy* (1909–57), US senator]

---

fāte; fär; mē; fûr; mīne; mōte; för; mūte; pŭt; dhen (then); *el'ə-mənt* (element) ◆ For other sounds see detailed chart of pronunciation

■ **McCar'thyite** *adj* of or relating to this kind of purge or any purge of dissident factions in a political party, etc. ♦ *n* a practitioner or advocate of McCarthyism.

McCoy see **the real Mackay** under **real¹**.

mcg *abbrev*: microgram (not in official use).

McGuffin see **MacGuffin**.

MCh *abbrev*: *Magister Chirurgiae* (*L*), Master of Surgery.

MCI *abbrev*: mild cognitive impairment, a slight impairment of memory that may be a precursor of dementia.

MCIJ *abbrev*: Member of the Chartered Institute of Journalists.

McIntosh red /mak'in-tosh red/ *n* a red-skinned variety of eating apple. [John *McIntosh* (1777–c.1845), Canadian farmer]

McJob /mək-job'/ (*sl*) *n* an unskilled low-paid job. [*McDonald's*, a chain of fast-food restaurants]

MCLIP *abbrev*: Member of the Chartered Institute of Library and Information Professionals.

McMansion /mək-man'shən/ *n* (*sl*) a large, luxurious house, designed without originality or taste. [*McDonald's*, the chain of fast-food restaurants, alluding to their uniformity]

MCMI *abbrev*: Member of the Chartered Management Institute.

McNaghten rules /mək-nö'tən roolz/ (*Eng law*) *n pl* rules dating from *Regina* vs *McNaghten* (1843), under which mental abnormality relieves from criminal responsibility only if the person was unaware of his or her actions or of committing a crime.

MCom *abbrev*: Master of Commerce.

MCP *abbrev*: male chauvinist pig (see under **male¹**).

MCPS *abbrev*: Mechanical-Copyright Protection Society.

MCR *abbrev*: middle common (or combination) room (see under **middle**).

Mc/s *abbrev*: megacycles per second.

McTimoney chiropractic /mək-tim'ə-ni kī-rə-prak'tik/ *n* a form of chiropractic in which gentle manipulation is typically used. [John *McTimoney* (1914–80), British chiropractor]

MD *abbrev*: Managing Director; Maryland (US state; also **Md.**); *Medicinae Doctor* (*L*), Doctor of Medicine; mentally deficient; Moldova (IVR).

Md (*chem*) *symbol*: mendelevium.

MDC *abbrev*: Movement for Democratic Change.

MDF *abbrev*: medium density fibreboard.

MDI (*comput*) *abbrev*: Multiple Document Interface.

Mdlle or **Mlle** *abbrev*: *Mademoiselle* (*Fr*), Miss.

Mdm. *abbrev*: Madame.

MDMA *abbrev*: methylene-dioxymethamphetamine (see **ecstasy**).

mdr-TB *abbrev*: multi-drug-resistant tuberculosis.

MDS *abbrev*: Master of Dental Surgery.

MDSc *abbrev*: Master of Dental Science.

ME *abbrev*: Maine (US state; also **Me.**); Methodist Episcopal; Middle East; Middle English; Mining or Mechanical Engineer; Most Excellent; myalgic encephalomyelitis (see under **myalgia**).

Me *abbrev*: Maître.

me¹ /mē or mi/ *pronoun* the form of **I** used for the objective (accusative and dative) case. [OE *mē*]
□ **me generation** *n* the generation either of the 1970s, typically self-absorbed, or of the 1980s, typically greedy and materialistic. **me-too'** *adj* denoting a person or product that imitates another in an attempt to cash in on its success.

me² an anglicized spelling of **mi**.

meacock /mē'kok/ (*Shakesp*) *adj* timorous, effeminate, cowardly. ♦ *n* a milksop. [Origin unknown]

mea culpa /mē'ə kul'pə or mā'ä kŭl'pä/ (*L*) (by) my own fault, I am to blame (an acknowledgement of one's guilt or mistake).

mead¹ /mēd/ *n* an alcoholic drink made by fermenting honey and water, *usu* with the addition of spices, etc. [OE *meodu*; Ger *Met*, Welsh *medd*]

mead² /mēd/ (*poetic*) *n* a meadow. [OE *mæd*; see **meadow**]

meadow /med'ō/ *n* a tract of grassland, *esp* used for hay; a rich pasture-ground, *esp* beside a stream. [OE *mæd*, in oblique cases *mædwe*, from *māwan* to mow; Ger *Matte*]
■ **mead'owy** *adj*.
□ **meadow-brown'** *n* a butterfly of the Satyridae. **meadow fescue** *n* a Eurasian fescue valuable as pasture and fodder. **meadow foxtail** *n* a perennial grass (*Alopecurus pratensis*), common in Europe and N Asia, and introduced into N America. **mead'ow-grass** *n* any grass of the genus *Poa* (**floating meadow-grass** manna-grass, float grass). **meadow lark** *n* (*US*) a name for various species of birds of the genus

Sturnella (family Icteridae). **meadow mouse** *n* a vole. **meadow mushroom** *n* the common edible mushroom (*Agaricus campestris*), the field mushroom. **meadow pipit** *n* *Anthus pratensis*, a common brown-and-white European songbird. **mead'ow-rue** *n* a genus (*Thalictrum*) of the buttercup family with rue-like leaves. **meadow saffron** *n* (also **naked lady**) the autumn crocus (*Colchicum autumnale*). **meadow-sax'ifrage** *n* a saxifrage (*Saxifraga granulata*) that grows on banks and dry meadows; applied also to umbelliferous plants of the genera *Seseli* and *Silaus*.

meadowsweet /med'ō-swēt/ *n* the rosaceous plant queen-of-the-meadows (*Spiraea ulmaria*), a tall fragrant plant growing *esp* in watery meadows. [Earlier *mead-sweet*, which may be from **mead¹** or from **mead²**, as the obsolete *meadwort* is in OE *meduwyrt*]

meagre /mē'gər/ *adj* scanty, insubstantial, inadequate; poor in quality; lacking richness or fertility, barren; having little flesh; lean, thin; without strength, weak; jejune, lacking fullness or imagination; maigre. ♦ *n* the maigre. [Fr *maigre*, from L *macer, macra, -rum* lean; cf Ger *mager*]
■ **mea'grely** *adv*. **mea'greness** *n*.

meal¹ /mēl/ *n* the food taken at one time; the act or occasion of taking food, such as a breakfast, dinner or supper. [OE *mæl* measure, time, portion of time; Du *maal*, Ger *Mahl*]
■ **meal'er** *n* a person who takes meals at a boarding house, lodging elsewhere.
□ **meals on wheels** *n* a welfare service taking cooked, *usu* hot, meals to old people in need of such help. **meal ticket** *n* a ticket that can be exchanged for a meal (*esp* at reduced price); a person or thing that one depends on for one's expenses or income (*inf*); someone who can be depended upon. **meal'-tide** (*Scot* meltith /mel'tith/ a meal) *n* (*archaic*) mealtime. **meal'time** *n* the time at which a meal is regularly taken.
■ **make a meal of** to consume as a meal; to enjoy to the full; to treat or perform in an unnecessarily laborious or meticulous way.

meal² /mēl/ *n* grain (now *usu* not wheat) or pulses ground to powder; in Scotland and Ireland, *specif* oatmeal; maize flour (*US*); other material in powder form; a powdery surface-covering (chiefly *bot*). ♦ *vt* to cover with meal; to add oatmeal to, *esp* to thicken (*Scot*); to grind into meal. ♦ *vi* (chiefly *Scot*) to yield or be plentiful in meal. [OE *melu, melo*; Ger *Mehl*, Du *meel* meal]
■ **meal'iness** *n*. **meal'y** or (*Scot*) **meal'ie** *adj* like meal in texture, powdery, floury; containing oatmeal (*Scot*); covered with, or as if with, meal; having a powdery surface; speckled, flecked; whitish, pale.
□ **meal'-ark** *n* (*Scot*) a large chest for holding oatmeal. **mealie pudding** *n* (*Scot*) a white pudding. **meal'-man** or **meal'-monger** *n* (*obs*) a dealer in meal. **Meal Monday** *n* the second Monday in February, a St Andrews (and formerly, Edinburgh) University holiday, *orig* to allow the students to go home and replenish their stock of meal. **meal moth** *n* a small moth (*Pyralis farinalis*) whose larvae are a serious pest of stored grain. **meal'-poke** *n* (*Scot*) a bag for oatmeal, formerly *esp* one carried by a beggar. **meal'-tree** *n* the wayfaring tree, from its mealy leaves and shoots. **meal'worm** *n* the larva of a beetle (genus *Tenebrio*) frequently found in granaries and flour-stores. **mealy bug** *n* a hothouse pest, a coccus insect with a white powdery appearance. **meal'y-mouthed** /-mowdhd/ *adj* smooth-tongued; over-squeamish, *esp* in choice of words. **mealy-mouth'edness** *n*.

meal³ /mēl/ (*Shakesp*) *vt* (in *pap* **meal'd**) to stain or spot. [OE *mælan*]

mealie, also **mealy** /mē'li/ *n* (*esp S Afr*) an ear of maize; (*esp* in *pl*) maize. [S Afr Du *milie* millet]
□ **mealie meal** *n* finely ground maize. **mealie pap** *n* porridge made with ground maize.

mean¹ /mēn/ *vt* (**mean'ing**; **meant** /ment/) to have in mind as signification; to intend, to purpose; to destine, to design; to signify. ♦ *vi* (with *well* or *ill*) to have good, or bad, intentions or disposition; (with *much, little*, etc) to be of much, little, etc importance (with *to*). [OE *mǽnan*; Ger *meinen* to think]
■ **mean'ing** *n* that which is in the mind or thoughts; signification; the sense intended; purpose. ♦ *adj* significant. **mean'ingful** *adj* having a valid meaning; full of significance, expressive; capable of interpretation (*logic*). **mean'ingfully** *adv*. **mean'ingless** *adj* senseless, without meaning; expressionless (*poetic; rare*); without significance, pointless. **mean'inglessly** *adv*. **mean'inglessness** *n*. **mean'ingly** *adv* significantly, expressively; intentionally (*archaic*).

mean² /mēn/ *adj* low in rank or birth; base; sordid; low in worth or estimation; of little value or importance; poor, humble; low; inconsiderable; despicable; shabby; paltry; small-minded; ungenerous; stingy; malicious, bad-tempered; out of sorts, uncomfortable (*US*); skilful, excellent (*sl*). [OE *gemǽne*; Ger *gemein*; L *commūnis* common]
■ **mean'ie** or **mean'y** *n* (*inf*) an ungenerous, ungracious, small-minded, or malicious person. **mean'ly** *adv*. **mean'ness** *n*.
□ **mean'-born** *adj* (*archaic*). **mean-spir'ited** *adj*. **mean-spir'itedness** *n*.
■ **no mean** formidable; not easily performed.

mean³ /mēn/ adj intermediate; average; moderate (obs). ◆ n that which is between or intermediate; an average amount or value; a middle state or position; an intermediate term in a progression; meantime (Spenser); a middle or intermediate part (music; obs); an instrument or medium; a mediator or intercessor (obs). [OFr meien (Fr moyen), from L mediānus, from medius middle]

■ **means** n sing or n pl that by whose instrumentality anything is caused or made to happen; a way to an end; (as pl) pecuniary resources; (as pl) what is required for comfortable living. **mean'time** or **mean'while** n the intervening time. ◆ adv in the intervening time; at the same time.

□ **mean free path** n the average distance travelled by a molecule, atom, etc, between collisions. **mean lethal dose** n (radiol) the single dose of whole body irradiation which will cause death, within a certain period, to 50% of those receiving it (abbrev **MLD**). **mean sea level** see **sea level** under **sea**. **means test** n the test of private resources, determining or limiting a claim to a concession or allowance. **means'-test** vt. **mean sun** n an imaginary sun moving uniformly in the equator, its position giving **mean time** or **mean solar time** (coinciding with true sun time four times a year). **mean'-tone** n (music) an interval of mean value between a major and a minor second, formerly used in a system of temperament.

■ **a means to an end** a method designed solely to achieve a goal, without regard for the value of the method itself. **arithmetic** (or **arithmetical**) **mean** the sum of a number of quantities divided by their number. **by all means** certainly. **by any means** in any way. **by means** (Spenser) because. **by means of** with the help or use of. **by no means** or **not by any means** certainly not. **geometric** (or **geometrical**) **mean** the nth root of the product of n quantities. **golden mean** the middle course between two extremes; a wise moderation. **harmonic mean** the reciprocal of the arithmetical mean of the reciprocals of two quantities. **in the mean** (Spenser) in the meantime. **quadratic mean** the square root of the arithmetical mean of the squares of the given quantities.

mean⁴, **meane**, **mein** or **mene** /mēn/ (Shakesp and Scot) vt and vi to lament, to moan; to complain. [OE mænan]

meander /mi-an'dər/ vi (of a river, etc) to wind about in a circuitous course; to form an intricate pattern; to wander listlessly or randomly, to ramble (perh influenced by **maunder¹**). ◆ n a sinuosity or turning, esp of a river (usu in pl); a winding course; a maze (obs); an intricate fret pattern, esp the Greek key pattern (art); perplexity (obs). [L Maeander, from Gr Maiandros a winding river in Asia Minor]

■ **mean'dered** adj formed into or covered with mazy passages or patterns. **mean'dering**, **mean'drian** (obs) or **mean'drous** adj winding, circuitous.

meane see **mean⁴**.

means see under **mean³**.

meant /ment/ pat and pap of **mean¹**.

meany see under **mean²**.

meare /mēr/ Spenser's spelling of **mere¹,⁴**.
■ **mear'd** vt (Spenser) pat of **mere⁴**.

mease¹ /mēz/, **maze**, **maize** or **maise** /māz/ (dialect) n a measure of five 'hundreds' of herrings, varying from 500 to 630. [OFr meise receptacle for herrings; ON meiss box, basket; OHGer meisa]

mease² /mēz/ (Scot) vt to assuage; to mitigate. [OFr amesir, from L ad to, and mītis mild]

measles /mē'zəlz/ n pl (but usu sing in construction) an infectious fever accompanied by eruptions of small red spots on the skin; a disease of pigs and cattle, caused by larval tapeworms; a blister or a disease of trees (obs). [ME maseles; cf Du mazelen measles, OHGer masala blister; Ger Masern measles]

■ **mea'sle** n a tapeworm larva. ◆ vt (archaic) to infect with measles. ◆ vi (archaic) to contract measles. **mea'sled** adj measly. **mea'sliness** n. **mea'sly** adj (**mea'slier**; **mea'sliest**) infected with measles, or with tapeworm larvae; spotty; paltry, miserable (inf).
■ **German measles** rubella.

measure /mezh'ər/ n the ascertainment of extent by comparison with a standard; a system of expressing the result of such ascertainment; the amount ascertained by comparison with a standard; that by which extent is ascertained or expressed; size; a standard or unit; a quantity by which another can be divided without remainder; an instrument for finding the extent of anything, esp a graduated rod or tape for length, or a vessel of known content for capacity; the quantity contained in a vessel of known capacity, formerly often a bushel; adequacy or due amount; some amount or degree, a portion; proportion; moderation; restraint; limit (Milton); extent; that which is meted out to one; treatment; a means to an end; an enactment or bill; rhythm; a unit of verse, one foot or two feet; metre; strict time; a bar of music; a strain; a dance, esp a slow and stately one; the width of a page or column, usually in ems (printing); (in pl) a series of beds or strata (geol). ◆ vt to ascertain or show the dimensions or amount of (often with out or up);

to mark out or lay off (often with off or out); to be a unit of measurement of; to mete out or distribute (with out); to proportion; to pit; to traverse; to sing or utter in measure (Spenser). ◆ vi to be of the stated size; to take measurements. [OFr mesure, from L mēnsūra a measure, from mētīrī, mēnsum to measure]

■ **meas'urable** adj substantial enough, or not too large, to be measured or computed; moderate; in small quantity or extent. **meas'urableness** or **measurabil'ity** n. **meas'urably** adv. **meas'ured** adj determined by measure; mensurable; rhythmical; with slow, heavy, steady rhythm; considered, calculated, deliberate; restrained. **meas'uredly** adv. **meas'ureless** adj boundless. **meas'urement** n the act of measuring; a standard system of measuring; the quantity found by measuring. **meas'urer** n. **meas'uring** n and adj.

□ **measured block** n (printing) a block of text of a fixed number of lines. **measurement goods** n pl light goods carried for charges according to bulk, not weight. **measuring cup**, **jug** or **spoon** n a cup, jug or spoon with graduations, or of a specific size, for measuring goods by volume. **meas'uring-rod** or **meas'uring-tape** n a graduated rod or tape for making linear measurements. **meas'uring-wheel** n a wheel with a perimeter of a standard length, used to make lateral measurements by recording the number of revolutions made as it is moved along the ground, etc. **measuring-worm'** n a looper caterpillar.

■ **above measure**, **beyond measure** or (archaic) **out of all measure** to an exceedingly great degree. **be the** (or **a**) **measure of** to be the (or a) standard by which to judge the quality, etc of. **for good measure** as something extra or above the minimum necessary. **get** or **have someone's measure** to realize or know the nature of someone's character and abilities, esp having been previously deceived. **hard measures** harsh treatment. **in a** (or **some**) **measure** to some degree. **made to measure** see under **made**. **measure one's length** to fall or be thrown down at full length. **measure strength** to engage in a contest. **measure swords** to compare lengths of swords before a duel; to fight (archaic). **measure up** (often with to) to reach a certain, or a required, standard; to be adequate. **out of all measure** see **above measure** above. **short measure** less than the due and professed amount. **take measures** to adopt means to gain an end. **take someone's measure** to estimate someone's character and abilities. **tread a measure** to go through a dance. **within measurable distance of** getting dangerously close to (something usu calamitous). **within measure** moderately. **without measure** immoderately.

meat /mēt/ n the edible part of anything, such as lobster meat, crab meat, etc; the flesh of animals used as food (sometimes beef, mutton, pork, veal, etc, as opposed to poultry or fish); game, etc, hunted for food; food for thought; substance, pith (fig); anything eaten as food (archaic); a meal (obs); the centre of the blade of a cricket bat, etc. [OE mete]

■ **meat'ily** adv. **meat'iness** n. **meat'less** adj without food (archaic); not containing meat. **meat'y** adj (**meat'ier**; **meat'iest**) full of meat; full of useful content or substance; fleshy, brawny; flesh-like in taste or smell; pithy.

□ **meat'-axe** or (N Am) **meat'-ax** n a cleaver. **meat'ball** n a ball of minced meat; a dull-witted person (N Am sl). **meat'-eater** n a person who eats meat; a carnivore. **meat'-fly** n a blowfly; a flesh-fly. **meat'-free** adj (of food) containing no animal products. **meat'head** n (US sl) a stupid person. **meat jelly** n jelly formed from the solidified juices of cooked meat. **meat loaf** n a loaf-shaped mass of chopped or minced meat, cooked and usually eaten cold. **meat'-man** n a seller of butcher's meat. **meat market** n a place where meat is bought and sold; a cattle market (qv). **meat'-offering** n a Jewish sacrificial offering of fine flour or first-fruits with oil and frankincense. **meat packer** n (US). **meat packing** n (US) the slaughter and processing of animals, esp cattle, for sale as meat. **meat paste** n a spread made of ground meat. **meat pie** n a pie containing meat, esp a small one for individual consumption. **meat plate** n a large, esp oval, plate on which meat is served. **meat rack** n (sl) a place where young male homosexual prostitutes gather. **meat safe** n a ventilated cupboard for storing meat. **meat'-salesman** n a person who sells meat, esp to retail butchers. **meat'screen** n a metal screen behind roasting meat, to throw back the fire's heat upon it. **meat'space** n (comput sl) the physical world, as opposed to cyberspace. **meat-tea'** n a high tea at which meat is eaten. **meat'-tub** n a pickling-tub. **meat wagon** n (sl, esp US) a police van for transporting prisoners; an ambulance; a hearse.

■ **easy meat** see under **easy**. **meat and drink** (fig) a source of sustenance, invigoration or pleasure. **meat and potatoes** (N Am sl) the basic or essential parts of anything.

meath or **meathe** /mēdh/ n an obsolete form of **mead¹**.

meatus /mi-ā'təs/ (anat) n (pl **mea'tuses**) an opening of a passage or canal. [L meātus (pl -ūs), from meāre to go, pass]
■ **mea'tal** adj.

meawes a Spenserian spelling of **mews** (pl of **mew²**).

---

meazel see **mesel**.

mebos /mā'bos/ (*S Afr*) *n* salted or sugared dried apricots. [Perh from Jap *umeboshi* a kind of plum]

Mecca /mek'ə/ *n* the birthplace of Mohammed, a place of pilgrimage for Muslims; a place heavily visited by, or with a special attraction for, a particular person or group, eg St Andrews as a Mecca for golfers.

Meccano® /mi-kä'nō/ *n* (a set of) small metal plates, rods, nuts and bolts, etc with which models can be constructed.

mech. *abbrev* : mechanical; mechanics.

mechanic /mi-kan'ik/ *n* a skilled worker, *esp* one specializing in making and repairing machinery; a person whose job is the repairing of motor vehicles; an air-mechanic; a person working at a manual trade, an artisan (*archaic*); a term of contempt for a person of a low social class (*obs*); (also **card mechanic**) a card-sharper (*US* and *Aust sl*). ◆ *adj* mechanical. [Gr *mēchanikos*, from *mēchanē* a contrivance] ■ **mechan'ical** *adj* relating to machines or mechanics; relating to dynamics; dynamical; worked or done by machinery or by mechanism; acting or done by physical, not chemical, means; machinelike; of the nature of a machine or mechanism; without intelligence or conscious will; performed simply by force of habit; reflex; skilled in practical matters (*obs*); manual (*archaic*); having a manual trade (*archaic*); technical (*obs*); mechanistic (*philos*). ◆ *n* (*Shakesp*) a manual worker, an artisan. **mechan'ically** *adv*. **mechan'icalness** *n*. **mechan'icals** *n pl* (*inf*) the mechanical parts of anything. **mechanician** /mek-ən-ish'ən/ *n* a machine-maker; a person skilled in constructing machines and tools. **mechan'ics** *n sing* dynamics, the science of the action of forces on bodies, including kinetics and statics; the art or science of machine-construction; the details of making or creating by manual or other process (also *n pl*); the system on which something works (also *n pl*). ◆ *n pl* routine procedure or procedures. **mech'anism** *n* a group of moving parts that interact to perform a function in a machine, etc; the arrangement and action by which a result is produced; a philosophy that regards the phenomena of life as explainable by mechanical forces; the means adopted unconsciously towards a subconscious end (*psychol*). **mech'anist** *n* a mechanician; a believer in philosophical mechanism. **mechanist'ic** *adj*. **mechanist'ically** *adv*. **mechaniza'tion** or **-s-** *n*. **mech'anize** or **-ise** *vt* to make mechanical; to adapt to mechanical working; to provide with armoured armed vehicles. **mech'anizer** *n*. **mechanomorph'ism** *n* the philosophy of mechanism; anthropomorphism applied to machines.
□ **mechanical advantage** *n* the ratio of the resistance in a machine to the force applied by it. **mechanical drawing** *n* instrument-aided drawing, eg of a machine, an architectural construction, etc. **mechanical engineer** *n*. **mechanical engineering** *n* the branch of engineering concerned with the design and construction of machines or mechanical devices. **mechanical powers** *n pl* the elementary forms or parts of machines, divided into three *primary* forms (the lever, inclined plane and pulley) and three *secondary* forms (the wheel and axle, the wedge and the screw). **mechanical tissue** *n* any tissue that gives a plant the power to resist stresses. **mechanics' institute** *n* (*hist*) an institution founded in England in 1823 to provide educational classes, libraries, etc, for its members (*orig* manual workers). **mechanorecept'or** *n* (*med*) a sense organ specialized to respond to mechanical stimuli such as pressure or deformation.

mechatronics /me-kə-tron'iks/ *n sing* the combined use or study of mechanical engineering and electronics in design and manufacture. [*mechanical and electronics*]
■ **mechatron'ic** *adj*.

Mechitharist see **Mekhitarist**.

Mechlin /mek'/ or /mehh'lin/ *n* (also **Mechlin lace**) a kind of bobbin lace produced at *Mechlin* or *Malines*, in Belgium, in which the motifs are outlined with thick, glossy thread.

MEcon *abbrev* : Master of Economics.

meconic /mi-kon'ik/ *adj* denoting an acid obtained from poppies. [Gr *mēkōn* the poppy]
■ **meconate** /mek'ən-āt or mēk'/ *n* a salt of meconic acid. **mec'onin** *n* a white, fusible, neutral substance ($C_{10}H_{10}O_4$) existing in opium. **mecō'nium** *n* (L, poppy-juice) the first faeces of a newborn child, or of a newly emerged insect image; opium. **meconops'is** *n* (*pl* **meconops'ēs**) (Gr *opsis* appearance) a plant of the *Meconopsis* genus of largely Asiatic blue poppies.

Mecoptera /mē-kop'tə-rə/ *n pl* an order of insects linking the Hymenoptera with the Trichoptera; the scorpion-flies. [Gr *mēkos* length, and *pteron* wing]

MEd *abbrev* : Master of Education.

Med /med/ *n* (*inf*) the Mediterranean Sea, or the region surrounding it.

med. *abbrev* : medical; medicine; medieval; medium; *medius, -dia, -dium* (L), middle.

medacca or **medaka** /mə-dä'kə/ *n* a small Japanese freshwater fish (*Oryzias latipes*), often kept in aquariums or ornamental ponds. [Jap *medaka*]

medaewart /med'ē-wärt/ (*Spenser*) *n* meadowsweet. [OE *meduwyrt* ; see **meadowsweet**]

médaillon /mā-dä-yõ'/ (*Fr*) *n* a small, round or oval cut of meat, fish, etc. [Literally, medallion]

medal /med'l/ *n* a piece of metal *usu* in the form of a coin bearing some design or inscription, struck or cast *usu* in commemoration of an event or as a reward of merit. ◆ *vt* (**med'alling** or (*N Am*) **med'aling**; **med'alled** or (*N Am*) **med'aled**) to decorate with a medal. ◆ *vi* to win a medal in a sporting competition. [Fr *médaille*, from Ital *medaglia*; through LL from L *metallum* metal]
■ **med'alet** *n* a small medal, *esp* one bearing a representation of one or more saints, worn by Roman Catholics. **medallic** /mi-dal'ik/ *adj*. **med'allist** or (*N Am*) **med'alist** *n* a person with expert knowledge of medals, or a collector of medals; a designer or maker of medals; a person who has gained a medal, eg as a prize in sports, or for bravery.
□ **medal play** or **med'alplay** *n* scoring in golf according to the overall number of strokes taken, rather than holes won and lost.

medallion /mi-dal'i-ən or -yən/ *n* a large medal, *esp* worn as jewellery on a chain; a bas-relief of a round (sometimes a square) form; a round ornament, panel, tablet, or design of similar form; a médaillon. ◆ *vt* (*rare*) to ornament or decorate with medallions; to make in the form of a medallion. [Fr *médaillon*]

Medau /mā'dow/ *n* a form of rhythmical exercise, mainly for women, using eg balls, hoops and clubs, developed by Hinrich *Medau* (1890–1974).

meddle /med'l/ *vi* to interfere unnecessarily and ill-advisedly (with *with* or *in*); to tamper (with *with*); to concern oneself (with *with* ; *archaic*); to engage in fight (*Shakesp*). ◆ *vt* and *vi* (*archaic*) to mix. [OFr *medler*, a variant of *mesler* (Fr *méler*), from LL *misculāre*, from L *miscēre* to mix]
■ **medd'ler** *n*. **medd'lesome** *adj* given to meddling. **medd'lesomely** *adv*. **medd'lesomeness** *n*. **medd'ling** *n* and *adj*.

Mede see under **Median**.

medevac /med'i-vak/ *n* the transport, *usu* by helicopter, of military or civilian casualties to hospital; a helicopter or other aircraft used for this. ◆ *vt* (**med'evacing**; **med'evaced**) to transport (a casualty) to a hospital. [*med*ical *evac*uation]

medfly see **Mediterranean fruit fly** under **mediterranean**.

media[1] see **medium**.

media[2] /mē'di-ə/ *n* (*pl* **mē'diae** /-ē/) a voiced consonantal stop, or a letter representing it, *p*, *b* or *d* (*phonetics*); the middle coat of a blood vessel layer in the wall of a blood vessel (*biol*); a middle primary vein of an insect's wing. [L *media* (*littera, tunica* or *vena*) middle (letter, coat or vein), fem of *medius* middle]

mediacy see under **mediate**.

mediaeval see **medieval**.

mediagenic see under **medium**.

medial /mē'di-əl/ *adj* intermediate; (of a consonant) occurring between two vowels (*phonetics*); median; relating to a mean or average. ◆ *n* (*phonetics*; *obs*) a media. [LL *mediālis*, from L *medius* middle]
■ **me'dially** *adv*.

Median /mē'di-ən/ (*hist*) *adj* of or relating to *Media*, an ancient kingdom NW of Persia (corresponding to modern NW Iran), its people, or their Indo-European language (also *n*). [Gr *Mēdos* a Mede]
■ **Mede** *n* one of the people of Media, fused as a nation with the Persians about 500BC. **Me'dic** *adj*. **Me'dism** *n* the adoption of Persian interests, ie treachery to a Greek. **Me'dize** or **-ise** *vi* to become Median, or like the Medians; to favour the Persians (called *Medes* by the Greeks). ◆ *vt* to make Median.
■ **law of the Medes and Persians** a law that cannot be changed, 'which altereth not' (Bible, Daniel 6.12).

median /mē'di-ən/ *adj* in the middle, running through the middle; situated in the straight line or plane (*median line* or *plane*) that divides anything longitudinally into symmetrical halves. ◆ *n* a straight line joining an angular point of a triangle with the middle point of the opposite side; a middle nervure of an insect's wing; in a series of values, the value middle in position (not *usu* in magnitude) (*stats*); a median strip (*N Am, Aust* and *NZ*). [L *mediānus*, from *medius* middle]
■ **me'dianly** *adv*.
□ **median strip** *n* (*N Am, Aust* and *NZ*) the central, often raised, strip separating opposing lanes of traffic on a motorway or dual carriageway.

mediant /mē'di-ənt/ (*music*) *n* the third tone of a scale, about midway between tonic and dominant. [LL *mediāns, -antis*, prp of *mediāre* to be in the middle]

■ words derived from main entry word; □ compound words; ■ idioms and phrasal verbs

mediastinum /mē-di-ə-stī'nəm/ (anat) n (pl **mediastī'na**) a membranous septum, or a cavity, between two principal portions of an organ, esp the folds of the pleura and the space between the right and left lungs. [Neuter of LL mediastīnus median (in classical L mediastinus is a drudge), from medius middle]
■ **mediastī'nal** adj.

mediate /mē'di-ət/ adj middle; intervening; indirect; related or acting through something intervening. ◆ vi /-āt/ to interpose between parties as a friend of each; to act as intermediary; to intercede; to be or act as a medium; to hold a mediate position. ◆ vt to bring about, end, promote, obtain, or communicate by friendly intervention, or by intercession, or through an intermediary; to be the medium or intermediary of; to transmit, convey, pass on. [LL mediāre, -ātum to be in the middle, from L medius middle]
■ **mē'diacy** n mediateness. **mē'diately** adv. **mē'diateness** n the state of being mediate. **mediā'tion** n the act of mediating or coming between; (an) intercession. **mē'diative** /-ə-tiv/ adj. **mediatīzā'tion** or **-s-** n. **mē'diatize** or **-ise** vt to cause to act in a subordinate position or through an agent; to reduce from immediate to mediate vassal (of the empire) without loss of dignity; to annex, or to subordinate, as a smaller state to a larger neighbouring one. **mē'diātor** n a person who mediates between parties in dispute. **mediatō'rial** adj. **mediatō'rially** adv. **mē'diatorship** n. **mē'diatory** adj. **mē'diātress** or **mediā'trix** n (pl **mē'diātresses** or **mediātrices** /-trī'sēz/) (archaic) a female mediator.

Medibank /med'i-bank/ n (in Australia) a former government-run medical insurance scheme, now supplementary to **Medicare**. [Medical bank]

medic¹ /med'ik/ adj (poetic) medical. ◆ n a physician (rare); a medical student (inf). [L medicus]
■ **medicas'ter** n (archaic) a quack.

medic² see **medick**.

medicable see under **medicate**.

Medicaid /med'i-kād/ (also without cap) n a US scheme providing assistance with medical expenses for people with low incomes. [Medical aid]

medical /med'i-kl/ adj of or relating to the science or practice of medicine; relating to treatments using drugs, etc, as distinct from surgery. ◆ n a medical examination to ascertain the state of a person's physical health; a medical student (inf). [LL medicālis, from L medicus a physician, from medērī to heal]
■ **medicaliza'tion** or **-s-** n. **med'icalize** or **-ise** vt to consider, describe or treat in medical terms. **med'ically** adv.
❑ **medical certificate** n a certificate from a doctor stating that a person is, or has been, unfit for work, etc, or that a person has, or has not, passed a medical examination. **medical jurisprudence** n forensic medicine. **medical officer** n a doctor in charge of medical treatment, etc, in an armed service or other organization (abbrev **MO**). **Medical Officer of Health** n formerly, a public officer in charge of medical services in a town, etc (abbrev **MOH**). **medical practitioner** n a doctor or surgeon.

medicament /me-dik'ə-mənt or med'i-kə-mənt/ n a substance used in curative treatment, esp externally. ◆ vt to treat with medicaments. [L medicāmentum, from medicāre]
■ **medicamental** /-ment'l/ or **medicament'ary** adj relating to medicaments. **medicament'ally** adv.

Medicare /med'i-kār/ (also without cap) n (in the USA) a scheme providing medical insurance for people aged 65 and over, and for certain categories of disabled people; (in Australia) the system providing universal medical insurance. [Medical care]

medicaster see under **medic¹**.

medicate /med'i-kāt/ vt to treat with medicine; to impregnate with anything medicinal; to drug, doctor, tamper with. [L medicāre, -ātum to heal, from medicus]
■ **med'icable** adj that may be healed. **med'icated** adj. **medicā'tion** n medical treatment; a medicine, drug, etc. **med'icative** adj.

Medicean /me-di-sē'ən/ adj relating to the Medici, a distinguished Florentine family which attained to sovereign power in the 15c.

medicine /med'(i-)sin or -sən/ n any substance used (esp internally) for the treatment or prevention of disease; a drug; the art or science of prevention, diagnosis, and cure (esp non-surgically) of disease; the practice or profession of a physician; remedial punishment; in primitive or tribal societies, a supernatural, esp curative, power; a thing possessing this, a charm; a physician (Shakesp). ◆ vt to treat or cure by medicine. [L medicīna, from medicus]
■ **medicinable** /med'sin-ə-bl/ adj having a healing power. **medicinal** /med-is'i-nl or sometimes med-i-sī'nl (in Shakesp, etc, med'si-nl) (Milton **med'cinal**) adj used in medicine; curative; relating to medicine; like medicine. ◆ n a medicinal substance. **medic'inally** adv. **mediciner** /med'sin-ər or med-is'i-nər/ n (archaic) a physician.

❑ **medicinal leech** n a freshwater leech (Hirudo medicinalis) formerly used for bloodletting. **medicine ball** n a heavy ball tossed and caught for exercise. **medicine bottle** n. **medicine chest** or **cabinet** n a small chest or a cabinet for keeping a selected set of medicines. **med'icine-dropper** n. **medicine man** or **woman** n (in primitive or tribal societies) a person believed to heal by supernatural agency, a shaman.
■ **a dose** or **taste of one's own medicine** harsh or unpleasant treatment given, often in revenge, to someone used to giving such treatment to others. **take one's medicine** to accept with stoicism an unpleasant but deserved punishment.

medick or **medic** /med'ik/ n any plant of the genus Medicago including lucerne, distinguished from clover by its spiral or sickle-shaped pods and short racemes. [L mēdica, from Gr Mēdikē (poā) Median (herb), ie lucerne]

medico /med'i-kō/ (sl) n (pl **med'icos**) a medical practitioner or student. [Ital medico, or Sp médico, from L medicus a physician]

medico- /me-di-kō-/ combining form relating to medicine or medical matters.
■ **medico-chirur'gical** adj relating to both medicine and surgery. **medico-le'gal** adj relating to the application of medicine to questions of law.

medieval or **mediaeval** /me-di-ē'vl/ or (US) mē-d(ē-)ē'vl/ adj of the Middle Ages; old-fashioned or primitive (inf). [L medius middle, and aevum age]
■ **medie'valism** or **mediae'valism** n the spirit of the Middle Ages; devotion to medieval ideals; a practice, etc, revived or surviving from the Middle Ages. **medie'valist** or **mediae'valist** n a person versed in the history, art, etc, of the Middle Ages; a devotee or follower of medieval practices. **medie'vally** or **mediae'vally** adv.

medina /mə-dē'nə/ n in N African cities, the ancient, native quarter. [Ar, town]

medio- /mē-di-ō-/ combining form denoting middle. [L medius middle]

mediocre /mē-di-ō'kər or mē'/ adj middling or average in quality, performance, etc; rather inferior. [Fr médiocre, from L mediocris, from medius middle]
■ **medioc'racy** /-ok'/ n government or rule by mediocre people. **medioc'rity** /-ok'/ n the state of being mediocre; average or inferior quality, etc; a mediocre person.

Medism see under **Median**.

meditate /med'i-tāt/ vi to consider thoughtfully (with about, on or upon); to engage in contemplation, esp religious. ◆ vt to consider deeply, reflect upon; to turn over in the mind; to intend. [L meditārī, prob cognate with L medērī to heal]
■ **med'itated** adj. **meditā'tion** n the act of meditating; deep thought; serious continuous contemplation, esp on a religious or spiritual theme; a meditative discourse; a meditative treatment of a literary or musical theme; the achievement through thought control of a tranquil state and total relaxation of mind and body. **med'itative** adj. **med'itatively** adv. **med'itativeness** n. **med'itātor** n.
■ **meditate the muse** (Latinism, after Milton) to give one's mind to composing poetry.

mediterranean /med-i-tə-rā'ni-ən/ adj situated in the middle of earth or land; landlocked; (with cap) of the **Mediterranean Sea** and the area surrounding it (so called from being in the middle of the land of the Old World) or its shores; (of physical type) slight in build, and of dark complexion. ◆ n (with cap) the Mediterranean Sea or the area surrounding it; a native or inhabitant of one of the countries bordering the Mediterranean Sea. [L mediterrāneus, from medius middle, and terra earth]
❑ **Mediterranean fever** n Malta or undulant fever. **Mediterranean fruit fly** n a small black-and-white two-winged fly, orig native to Africa but now widely distributed, the larvae of which feed on ripening fruit (often shortened to **med'fly**). **Mediterranean race** n a long-headed dark race of white people, of medium stature, inhabiting S Europe and N Africa.

medium /mē'di-əm/ n (pl **mē'dia** or **mē'diums**) an intermediate or middle position or condition; the middle place or degree; a middle course; a mean (obs); (in pl, **mediums**) medium-dated securities; any intervening means, instrument or agency; instrumentality; a substance through which any effect is transmitted; that through which communication is maintained; a channel (eg newspapers, radio, television) through which information, etc is transmitted to the public (pl **media**) (also **mass medium**, pl **mass media**); any material, eg magnetic disk, paper tape, on which data is recorded (comput; pl usu **media**); an enveloping substance or element in which a thing exists or lives; environment; the substance, eg oil or water, with which a pigment is mixed to make paint, the vehicle by which it is applied to a surface; a nutritive substance on which a culture (of bacteria, tissue, etc) may be fed; in spiritualism, the person through whom spirits are said to communicate with the material world (pl **mediums**); a person of supernormal sensibility (pl **mediums**). ◆ adj intermediate or moderate, coming midway between two opposing degrees or extremes; between fast and slow, long and short, etc; mean, average (*obs*); of a standard size of paper between demy and royal, now 18in by 23in. [L *medium*, neuter of *medius* middle]

■ **mediage'nic** *adj* able to communicate well or present a good image in the media, *esp* television. **mediumis'tic** *adj* of or relating to spiritualistic mediums.

□ **Media Mail** *n* a service offering the delivery of printed matter, film, etc by post at special charges. **me'dium-dated** *adj* (of securities) redeemable in five to fifteen years' time. **medium frequency** see under **frequent**. **me'dium-term** *adj* intermediate between short-term and long-term. **me'dium-wave** *adj*. **medium waves** *n pl* (*radio*) electromagnetic waves of between 200 and 1000 metres. ■ **circulating medium** money passing from hand to hand, as coin, banknotes, etc.

medius /mē'di-əs/ *n* the middle finger. [L *medius* middle]

Medize see under **Median**.

Medjidie /me-jē'di-ā/ *n* a Turkish order of knighthood founded by Sultan Abdul *Majīd*.

medlar /med'lar/ *n* a small tree (*Mespilus*, or *Pyrus*, *germanica*) related to the apple; its fruit. [OFr *medler*, *mesler*, from L *mespilum*, from Gr *mespilon*]

medle an old spelling (*Shakesp* and *Spenser*) of **meddle**.

medley /med'li/ *n* a mingled and confused mass; a miscellany; a song or piece of music made up of sections from various sources; a cloth woven from yarn of different colours; a mêlée, a fight (*obs*). ◆ *adj* of or relating to a medley. [OFr *medler*, *mesler* to mix]

□ **medley relay** *n* a race in which each team member runs a different distance or (in swimming) uses a different stroke.

Médoc /mā-dok'/ *n* a French wine produced in the district of *Médoc*, department of Gironde.

medresseh see **madrasa**.

meds /medz/ (*inf*) *n pl* medicines.

medulla /me-dul'ə/ *n* (pl **medull'ae** /-ē/ or **medull'as**) the inner portion of an organ, hair, or tissue; bone marrow; pith; a loose or spongy mass of hyphae. [L *medulla* marrow]

■ **medullar** or **medull'ary** *adj* consisting of, or resembling, marrow or pith. **medull'ate** *adj* having medulla. **med'ullated** *adj* provided with a medullary sheath.

□ **medulla oblonga'ta** (or /-ā'tə/) *n* that part of the brain that tapers off into the spinal cord. **medullary ray** *n* (*bot*) a band of cells (appearing as a ray in cross-section) cutting radially through wood and bast. **medullary sheath** *n* a thin layer surrounding the pith (*bot*); a whitish fatty membrane which surrounds the axons of the central nervous system in vertebrates and acts as an insulating coat (*anat*).

Medusa /me-dū'zə or -sə/ *n* one of the three Gorgons, whose head, with snakes for hair, turned beholders into stone, but was cut off by Perseus, and placed in Athena's aegis (*Gr myth*); (without *cap*; pl **medū'sae** /-zē/ or **medū'sas**) a jellyfish; (without *cap*) an individual of the free-swimming sexual generation of jellyfishes and Hydrozoa. [L *Medūsa*, from Gr *Medousa*, the Gorgon *Medusa* (literally, ruler)]

■ **medū'san** *adj* of or relating to a medusa or medusae. ◆ *n* a medusa. **medū'siform** *adj* like a jellyfish. **medū'soid** *adj* like a medusa. ◆ *n* a sexual hydrozoan that remains attached to the parent hydroid colony.

meed /mēd/ *n* wages (*archaic*); reward; what is bestowed for merit; measure, portion. [OE *mēd*; Ger *Miete*]

meek /mēk/ *adj* having a mild and gentle temperament; submissive. [ON *mjūkr*; early Mod Du *muik* soft]

■ **meek'en** *vt* to render meek. ◆ *vi* to become meek. **meek'ly** *adv*. **meek'ness** *n* the state or quality of being meek.

meer[1] /mēr/, an alternative spelling of **mere**[1,2,3].

■ **meered** or **mered** *adj* (*Shakesp*) (poss) set up as a *mere* or division, dividing; (according to some) sole, or entire.

meer[2] see **mir**[2].

meerkat, also **meercat** /mēr'kat/ *n* a mongoose-like S African carnivore (*Cynictis penicillata*), related to the ichneumon; the suricate; a ground-squirrel; a lemur; a monkey (*obs*). [Du *meerkat* monkey, as if 'overseas cat', from *meer* sea, and *kat* cat, but perh really an Asian word]

meerschaum /mēr'shəm or -showm/ *n* a fine light whitish clay, sepiolite, once supposed to be a petrified sea-scum; a tobacco pipe made of it. [Ger, from *Meer* sea, and *Schaum* foam]

meet[1] /mēt/ *vt* (pap and pat **met**) to come face to face with; to come into the company of; to become acquainted with, be introduced to; to encounter in conflict or battle (*archaic*); to find or come across in passing (now *dialect*); to come into contact with, join; to encounter or experience as treatment or response; to match or oppose adequately, to refute, eg an argument; to be suitable to or satisfy, eg a demand or requirement; to be sufficient in payment for; (in *imperative*) as a

request to receive or welcome a person on introduction; to cause to meet, bring into contact; to await the arrival of, keep an appointment with. ◆ *vi* to come together from different points; to assemble; to come into contact; to have an encounter; to balance, come out correct. ◆ *n* a meeting of participants in a fox hunt; a gathering for a sports competition or race; a covert pre-arranged meeting between criminals, *esp* drug dealers, or between police and an informant (*sl*); an intersection (*maths*). [OE *mētan* to meet, from *mōt*, *gemōt* meeting]

■ **meet'ing** *n* a coming face to face for friendly or hostile ends; an interview; an assembly; an organized assembly for the transaction of business; a sporting event, *esp* athletics or horse-racing; an assembly for religious worship, *esp* (in England) of Dissenters; a place of meeting; a junction.

□ **meet'ing-house** *n* a house or building where people, *esp* Quakers, meet for public worship.

■ **give the** (or **a**) **meeting** (*archaic*) to appoint or come to a rendezvous, for a duel or other purpose. **meet halfway** to make concessions to, or come to a compromise with. **meet in with** or **wi'** (*Scot*) to meet with, come across. **meet the ear**, or **eye** to be readily apparent. **meet up** (**with**) to meet, by chance or arrangement. **meet with** to come to or agree with, *esp* unexpectedly; to meet or come together with, *usu* for a purpose (*orig US*); to undergo, chance to experience; to obviate (as an objection) (*Bacon*). **well met** an old complimentary greeting.

meet[2] /mēt/ (*archaic* or *formal*) *adj* fitting; qualified; even, quits (*Shakesp*). ◆ *adv* (*Shakesp*) fittingly. [Prob from an OE (Anglian) form answering to WSax *gemǣte*, from *metan* to measure]

■ **meet'ly** *adv*. **meet'ness** *n*.

mefloquine /mef'lō-kwin/ *n* an antimalarial drug.

meg[1] see **mag**[3].

meg[2] /meg/ (*comput*) *n* short form of **megabyte**.

mega /meg'ə/ (*sl*) *adj* enormous, huge; very good or great. ◆ *adv* to a great extent, extremely. [From combining form **mega-**]

mega- /me-gə-/ (before a vowel **meg-** /meg-/), **megal-** /me-gəl-/ or **megalo-** /me-gə-lō-, -lo- or -lə-/ *combining form* meaning very big, unusually large, on a very large scale; in names of units, denoting a million times (10^6). [Gr *megas*, fem *megalē*, neuter *mega* big]

■ **meg'abar** *n* a unit of pressure equal to a million bars. **meg'abit** (*comput*) (loosely) one million bits. **meg'abuck** *n* (*N Am sl*) a million dollars; (in *pl*) very large sums of money. **meg'abyte** *n* (loosely) a million bytes; 2^{20} bytes. **megacephalous** /-sef'ə-ləs/ *adj* (Gr *kephalē* head) large-headed. **Megacheiroptera** /-kīr-op'tər-ə/ *n pl* the fruit bats. **megacity** /meg'ə-sit-i/ *n* a city of over a million inhabitants; a very large city. **meg'acurie** *n* a million curies. **meg'acycle** *n* a million cycles; a million cycles per second. **meg'adeath** *n* death of a million people, a unit in estimating casualties in nuclear war. **meg'adose** *n* a dose of drug, etc, far exceeding the normal amount taken. **meg'adyne** *n* a million dynes. **megafar'ad** *n* a million farads. **meg'afauna** (or /-fö'nə/) and **meg'aflora** (also /-flö'rə/) *n* large animals and plants respectively, visible to the naked eye. **meg'aflop** *n* (*comput*) a unit of processing speed equal to one million floating-point operations per second; a complete failure (*sl*). **meg'afog** *n* a fog signal with megaphones pointing in several directions. **megagam'ete** *n* a macrogamete. **meg'agauss** *n* a million gauss. **meg'aherbivore** *n* a herbivore weighing over 1000kg, eg an elephant or rhinoceros. **meg'ahertz** *n* a million hertz. **meg'ajoule** *n* a million joules. **meg'alith** *n* (Gr *lithos* stone; *archaeol*) a huge stone, as in prehistoric monuments. **megalith'ic** *adj* (*archaeol*) constructed with, or characterized by the use of, huge stones. **meg'aloblast** *n* an abnormally large nucleated red blood cell found in the bone marrow of people suffering from a **megaloblas'tic anae'mia** such as pernicious anaemia. **megalomā'nia** *n* the delusion that one is great or powerful; (loosely) a lust for power; a passion for possessions on a grandiose scale. **megalomā'niac** *n* and *adj*. **megalomaniacal** /-mə-nī'ə-kl/ *adj*. **megalop'olis** *n* a wide-spreading, thickly-populated urban area; an enormous city. **megalopol'itan** *n* and *adj*. **meg'alosaur** or **megalosau'rus** *n* (pl **meg'alosaurs** or **megalosau'ri** /-ē/) (Gr *sauros* a lizard) a gigantic lizard-hipped Jurassic and Cretaceous dinosaur (genus *Megalosaurus*), carnivorous in habits. **megalosau'rian** *adj*. **megamega-** *combining form* (*obs*) same as **tera-**. **meg'a-merger** *n* a merger of two or more very large organizations. **meg'anewton** *n* a million newtons. **meg'aparsec** *n* a million parsecs. **meg'apixel** *n* a million pixels. **meg'apode** *n* (Gr *pous*, *podos* foot) a mound-bird. **meg'arad** *n* a million rads. **meg'ascope** *n* (Gr *skopeein* to view) an instrument for projecting an enlarged image. **megascopic** /-skop'ik/ *adj* enlarged; visible to the naked eye. **megasporangium** /-spor-an'ji-əm/ *n* (pl **megasporan'gia**) a sporangium producing only megaspores. **meg'aspore** *n* the larger of two forms of spore; a spore giving rise to a female gametophyte. **megasporophyll** /-spor'ə-fil/ *n* a sporophyll that carries or subtends only megasporangia. **meg'astar** *n* an exceptionally famous superstar. **meg'astore** n (inf) a very large shop, esp any of the very large chain stores. **meg'astructure** n a very large building or construction. **megatechnol'ogy** n rapidly advancing high technology in eg microelectronics. **Megathē'rium** n (Gr thērion wild beast) a genus of gigantic extinct S American ground-sloths. **meg'aton** /-tun/ n one million tons; a unit of explosive power equalling a million tons of TNT (**megaton bomb** a bomb of this force). **meg'atonnage** n the total explosive capacity in megatons. **meg'avertebrate** n an extremely large vertebrate, eg an elephant. **meg'avitamin** adj consisting of or relating to large doses of vitamins. **meg'avolt** n a million volts. **meg'awatt** n a million watts (**megawatt days per tonne** the unit of energy output from reactor fuel (day = 24 hours)). **meg'ohm** n a million ohms.

Megaera /mə-jē'rə or me-gī'ra/ (Gr myth) n one of the Furies. [L, from Gr Megaira]

megafarad...to...**megaparsec** see under **mega-**.

megaphone /meg'ə-fōn/ n a funnel-shaped device for directing or magnifying sound, esp that of the voice. ◆ vt and vi to communicate by megaphone. [**mega-**, and Gr phōnē voice]
■ **megaphon'ic** adj.
□ **megaphone diplomacy** n diplomatic communication which is unsubtle or indirect, as when conducted through media announcements rather than direct approach.

megapixel...to...**megarad** see under **mega-**.

megaron /me'gə-ron/ n the central hall of an ancient Greek, esp Mycenaean, house. [Gr]

megascope...to...**megasporophyll** see under **mega-**.

megass or **megasse** /mə-gäs'/ same as **bagasse**.

megastar...to...**megawatt** see under **mega-**.

Megger® /meg'ə/ n an instrument that generates a high voltage to test the resistance of electrical insulation. [Perh from **megohm**]

megillah /mə-gil'ə/ n (pl **megill'ahs** or **megill'oth** /-lot/) a scroll containing a book of the Old Testament, esp the Book of Esther, to be read on certain feast-days (Judaism); a lengthy or tedious account, a screed (US sl). [Heb, roll, scroll]

megilp or **magilp** /mə-gilp'/ n an oil-painting medium consisting of linseed oil and mastic varnish or turpentine. [Origin unknown]

megohm see under **mega-**.

megrim[1] /mē'grim/ n vertigo, dizziness (also in pl; now rare); a whim, a caprice (archaic and Scot); migraine (obs); (in pl) depression, doldrums (now esp N Am). [OE, from Fr migraine ; see **migraine**]

megrim[2] /mē'grim/ n the scaldfish. [Origin uncertain]

meh /me/ (sl) interj expressing indifference or boredom. ◆ adj mediocre; (of a person) unmoved.

Mehdi see **Mahdi**.

mehndi /men'di/ n the art, esp in India, of painting intricate designs on the hands, feet and body with henna. [Hindi, henna, from Sans mehaghni turmeric]

meibomian /mī-bō'mi-ən/ adj of or relating to the sebaceous glands of the eyelid. [H Meibom (1638–1700), German anatomist]

Meiji /mā'ji/ n a period in Japanese history (1868–1912), following the overthrow of the shoguns, in which power was restored to the emperor. [Jap, literally, enlightened rule]

mein see **mean**[4].

meinie, meiney, meiny or (Scot) **menyie** /mā'ni/ n a retinue, a household (Shakesp); a herd (obs); a collection (Scot); a crowd, a rabble (Scot). [OFr mesnie, from L mānsio, -ōnis a dwelling]

meint see **ming**[1].

meiny see **meinie**.

meiofauna /mī'ə-fö-nə or -fö'nə/ n pl animals less than 1mm and more than 0.1mm across. [Gr meion less, and **fauna**]
■ **meiofau'nal** adj.

meionite /mī'ə-nīt/ n a scapolite with less sodium and silica than marialite. [Gr meiōn less, from the short vertical axis of its crystal]

meiosis /mī-ō'sis/ n (pl **meiō'ses**) understatement as a figure of speech, litotes (rhetoric); cell division by which the chromosomes are reduced from the diploid to the haploid number during the formation of gametes (biol). [Gr meiōsis diminution]
■ **meiotic** /-ot'ik/ adj. **meiot'ically** adv.

meishi /mā'shi/ n in Japan, a calling or business card. [Jap]

Meissen china, porcelain or **ware** same as **Dresden china**, etc.

Meissner effect /mīs'nər i-fekt'/ (phys) n an effect by which, by cooling a superconducting material below its critical temperature, its magnetic flux is expelled or excluded, depending on whether a magnetic field is applied before or after the cooling. [Fritz W Meissner (1882–1974), German physicist]

meister /mī'stər/ n an expert in a particular activity or field of knowledge. [Ger Meister master]

Meistersinger /mī'stər-zing-ər or -sing-/ n (pl **Meistersinger** or **Meistersingers**) any of the burgher poets and musicians of Germany in the 14c–16c, the successors of the Minnesingers. [Ger, master-singer]

meith /mēth/ (Scot) n a landmark; a boundary. [Prob ON mith a fishing-bank found by landmarks]

meitnerium /mīt-nē'ri-əm/ n an artificially produced radioactive transuranic element (symbol **Mt**; atomic no 109), formerly called **unnilennium**. [Lise Meitner (1878–1968), Austrian physicist]

Mejlis same as **Majlis**.

me judice /mē joo'di-sē or mā yoo'di-ke/ (L) I being judge, in my opinion.

Mekhitarist or **Mechitharist** /me-ki-tä'rist or -hhi-/ n an Armenian Uniat monk of a congregation founded by Mekhitar (1676–1749) at Constantinople in 1701, since 1717 with headquarters near Venice (also adj).

mekometer /mə-kom'ə-tər/ n a device for accurate measurement of distances by means of a light beam. [Gr mēkos length]

mel /mel/ (esp pharm) n honey. [L]

mela /mā' or mē'lə/ n a Hindu festival or fair. [Hindi, from Sans melā assembly]

melaconite /me-lak'ə-nīt/ n tenorite. [Gr melās black, and konis dust]

melaleuca /me-lə-loo'kə or -lū'/ n any Australian tree or shrub of the genus Melaleuca, having a black trunk and white branches. [Gr melās, -anos black, and leukos white]

melamine /mel'ə-mēn/ n a white crystalline organic substance used in forming **melamine resins**, thermosetting plastics used as adhesives, coatings, etc. [Ger Melamin]

melampode /me-lam'pōd or mel'am-/ (Spenser) n the black hellebore. [Gr melampodion]

melanaemia /me-lə-nē'mi-ə/ n the presence of melanin in the blood. [Gr melās, -anos black, and haima blood]

melancholy /mel'ən-ko-li or -kə-, formerly me-lang'ko-li/ n prolonged depression of spirits; dejection; melancholia; indulgence in thoughts of pleasing sadness; wistful pensiveness; black bile, considered one of the four chief bodily humours (obs); an excess of black bile, or the mental condition or temperament supposed to result from this (obs); surliness (obs). ◆ adj prone to, affected by, expressive of, or causing, melancholy; depressed; pensive; deplorable. [Gr melancholiā, from melās, -anos black, and cholē bile]
■ **melanchō'lia** n (pl **melanchō'liae** /-ī/) a mental state characterized by dejection and misery. **melanchō'liac** n a sufferer from melancholia (also adj). **melanchol'ic** /-kol'ik/ adj affected with, or caused by, melancholy or melancholia; dejected; mournful. ◆ n a melancholiac. **melanchol'ically** adv. **melanchō'lious** adj.

Melanesian /me-lə-nē'zi-ən, -zyən or -zh(y)ən/ adj of or relating to Melanesia, a group of Pacific islands lying NE of Australia. ◆ n a native or inhabitant of these islands; any of the languages spoken in Melanesia. [Gr melās, -anos black, and nēsos an island]
■ **Neo-Melanesian** see under **neo-**.

mélange or **melange** /mā-läzh'/ n a mixture; a medley. [Fr]

melanin /mel'ə-nin/ n the dark pigment in skin, hair, etc. [Gr melās, -anos black]
■ **melanic** /mi-lan'ik/ adj black or dark in pigmentation. **mel'anism** n the biological condition of having dark skin, plumage, etc; more than normal development of dark colouring matter. **melanist'ic** adj. **mel'anite** n a black garnet. **melano** /mi-lä'nō or mel'ə-nō/ n (pl **melanos**) an abnormally dark person or animal (formed on the analogy of albino). **mel'anocyte** /-sīt, also -lan'/ n an epidermal cell that can produce melanin. **mel'anoid** adj resembling melanin or melanosis. **melanō'ma** n (pl **melanō'mata** or **melanō'mas**) any skin tumour consisting of melanin-pigmented cells; (also **malignant melanoma**) a malignant tumour consisting of melanin-pigmented cells, which usually develops from a mole and metastasizes rapidly. **mel'anophore** /-för/ n a chromatophore containing melanin. **melanō'sis** n a condition of skin or body characterized by abnormally large deposits of melanin; a discoloration caused by this. **melanot'ic** or **mel'anous** adj dark-complexioned. **melanotrop'in** n a hormone secreted by the pituitary gland which stimulates the production of melanin by melanocytes. **melanū'ria** n the presence of a dark pigment in the urine. **melanū'ric** adj. **melaphyre** /mel'ə-fīr/ n (formed on analogy with porphyry) orig a dark porphyritic rock; applied very loosely to an altered basalt.

melanochroi /me-lə-nok'rō-ī or -nō-krō'ī/ n pl one of the racial types proposed by TH Huxley (1825–95), having dark hair and white skin. [Gr melās, -anos black, and either ōchros pale, or chroā skin]
■ **melanochrō'ic** or **melanochroous** /-ok'rō-əs/ adj.

melanterite /mi-lan'tə-rīt/ n native copperas. [Gr *melantēriā* a black pigment]

Melastomaceae /me-lə-stō-mā'si-ē or -mā'shi-ē/ n pl a tropical family of plants related to the myrtles, very abundant in S America, characterized by the leaf-veins diverging from the base and meeting at the tip, named from the Old World genus *Melastoma* /mi-las'tō-mə/. [Gr *melās* black, and *stoma* mouth, from the staining effect of its fruit on the lips]
■ **melastomā'ceous** adj.

melatonin /me-lə-tō'nin/ n a hormone secreted by the pineal gland during the hours of darkness that induces sleepiness and is thought to have useful application, eg in the treatment of jet lag. [Ety as for **melanin**, and sero*tonin*]

melba /mel'bə/ adj applied to several foods named after the Australian opera singer Dame Nellie *Melba* (1861–1931), such as **melba toast**, very thin crisp toast, and **melba sauce** a sauce for puddings, made from raspberries.
■ **do a Melba** (*old Aust sl*) to make repeated farewell performances; to return from retirement. **peach Melba** see under **peach**[1].

meld[1] /meld/ (*orig US*) vt and vi to merge, blend, combine. ◆ n a blending or merging. [Poss **melt**[1] and **weld**[1]]

meld[2] /meld/ (*cards*) vt and vi to declare or show (a card or combination of cards) to claim a score. ◆ n the act of melding; a card or combination of cards with which to meld. [OE *meldan*, or Ger *melden*]

melder /mel'dər/ (*Scot*) n the quantity of meal ground at one time. [ON *meldr*]

mêlée /mel'ā/ n a fight in which the combatants become intermingled; a confused, noisy conflict; an affray; a muddled collection or group. [Fr *méler* to mix; cf **meddle** and **mell**[1]]

Melia /mē'li-ə/ n a genus of trees including the nim or margosa, giving name to the family **Meliā'ceae** (mahogany, *Cedrela*, etc). [Gr *meliā* ash tree (from a resemblance in leaves)]
■ **meliā'ceous** /-shəs/ adj.

Meliboean /me-li-bē'ən/ adj of poetry, written for two alternating voices. [*Meliboeus*, one of the singers in Virgil's first eclogue]

melic[1] /mel'ik/ adj to be sung; lyric; strophic. [Gr *melikos*, from *melos* song]

melic[2] or **melick** /mel'ik/ n a grass (genus *Melica*) of the fescue family (also **mel'ic-grass**). [Origin obscure]

melicotton see **melocoton**.

melik see **malik**.

melilite /mel'i-līt/ n a tetragonal mineral, calcium aluminium magnesium silicate, often honey-yellow. [Gr *meli* honey, and *lithos* stone]

melilot /mel'i-lot/ n a genus (*Melilotus*) of clover-like plants with racemes of white or yellow flowers and a peculiar sweet odour. [Gr *melilōtos*, from *meli* honey, and *lōtos* lotus]

melinite /mel'i-nīt/ n an explosive made from picric acid. [Fr *mélinite*, from Gr *mēlinos* quince yellow, from *mēlon* quince]

meliorate /mē'li-ə-rāt/ vt and vi to improve. [LL *meliōrāre*, *-ātum*, from L *melior* better]
■ **meliorā'tion** n. **mē'liorātive** adj causing improvement; (of a word or sense) complimentary, favourable, *opp* to *pejorative*. **mē'liorātor** n. **mē'liorism** n the doctrine that the world can be improved through human endeavour (cf **optimism** and **pessimism**). **mē'liorist** n and adj. **meliorist'ic** adj. **meliority** /-or'i-ti/ n a better state or condition.

meliphagous /me-lif'ə-gəs/ adj (*esp* of birds) feeding upon honey. [Gr *meli* honey, and *phagein* (aorist) to eat]

melisma /me-liz'mə/ n (pl **melis'mata** or **melis'mas**) a song; a tune; a melodic embellishment. [Gr *melisma*, *-matos* a song, tune]
■ **melismatic** /-mat'ik/ adj florid in melody, *esp* where one syllable is sung to a number of notes.

melittin /mə-lit'in/ n a toxic polypeptide found in bee venom, responsible for the pain of the sting. [Gr *melitta* bee, and **-in** (1)]

mell[1] /mel/ (now *archaic*, *Scot* and *dialect*) vt and vi to mix, mingle. ◆ vi (*usu* with *with*) to have to do, to associate; to have sexual intercourse (*obs*); to join in fight; to be concerned; to meddle. [OFr *meller*; cf **meddle** and **medley**]

mell[2] /mel/ n a Scot and N Eng form of **mall** or **maul**.

mellay /mel'ā/ n another form of **mêlée**.

melliferous /me-lif'ə-rəs/ adj producing or forming honey. [L *mel*, *mellis* honey]
■ **mellificā'tion** n honey-making. **mellif'luence** n (L *fluere* to flow) a flow of sweetness; a smooth, sweet flow. **mellif'luent** or **mellif'luous** adj flowing with honey or sweetness; (of sounds) sweetly smooth. **mellif'luently** or **mellif'luously** adv. **mellif'luousness** n. **mell'ite** n

honey-stone. **mellit'ic** adj. **melliv'orous** adj (L *vorāre* to devour) eating honey.

Mellotron® /mel'ə-tron/ n an electronic musical instrument in which prerecorded sounds are played by pressing individual keys. [Coined from *mellow* and *electronic*]

mellow /mel'ō/ adj soft to the touch, palate, ear, etc; genial *esp* through age or experience; soft and ripe; well matured; slightly, but genially, drunk; relaxed. ◆ vt to soften by ripeness or age; to mature. ◆ vi to become soft; to be matured, ripened; to become gentler and more tolerant. [Prob OE *melu* meal, influenced by *mearu* soft, tender]
■ **mell'owly** adv. **mell'owness** n. **mell'owy** adj mellow.
□ **mell'ophone** n a valved brass instrument resembling the French horn, but less rich in tone. **mell'owspeak** n a bland non-assertive form of language associated with New Age philosophy.
■ **mellow out** (*sl*) to become relaxed or calm (*esp* under the influence of drugs).

melocoton or **melocotoon** /mel-ō-kot-ōn' or -oon'/ (*obs*) n a large kind of peach (also **malakatoone'** or **melicott'on**). [Sp *melocotón*, from Ital *melocotogna* quince, peach, from LL *mēlum cotōneum*, from Gr *mēlon Kydōnion* Cydonian (Cretan) apple, quince]

melodeon or **melodion** /mi-lō'di-ən/ n a small reed organ; a harmonium or type of accordion. [Ety as for **melody**]

melodica /mi-lod'i-kə/ n a small wind instrument with a mouthpiece at one end and a keyboard. [From *melodeon* and *harmonica*]

melodrama /mel'ō-drä-mə or -drä'mə/, also (now *rare*) **melodrame** /-dräm/ n a kind of romantic and sensational drama, crude, sentimental, and conventional, involving poetic justice and happy endings; a film or play that is excessively sensational, emotional, etc; a play with musical accompaniment to the action and spoken dialogue, with or without songs (*obs*); excessively dramatic behaviour. [Gr *melos* a song, and *drāma* action]
■ **melodramat'ic** /-drə-mat'ik/ adj of the nature of melodrama; overstrained; sensational. **melodramat'ically** adv. **melodramat'ics** n pl melodramatic behaviour. **melodramatist** /-dram'ə-tist/ n a writer of melodramas. **melodram'atize** or **-ise** vt to make melodramatic.

melody /mel'ə-di/ n an air or tune; music; an agreeable succession of single musical sounds, as distinguished from *harmony*. [Fr, through LL, from Gr *melōidiā*]
■ **melodic** /mi-lod'ik/ adj. **melod'ically** adv. **melod'ics** n sing the branch of music concerned with melody. **melō'dious** adj full of melody; pleasant to listen to. **melō'diously** adv. **melō'diousness** n. **mel'odist** n. **mel'odize** or **-ise** vi to make music; to perform a melody. ◆ vt to add a melody to; to make melodious.
□ **melodic minor** n a minor scale with major sixth and seventh ascending and minor sixth and seventh descending.

melomania /me-lō-mā'ni-ə/ n a craze for music. [Gr *melos* song, and *maniā* madness]
■ **melomā'niac** n. **melomanic** /-man'/ adj.

melon /mel'ən/ n any of several juicy, edible gourds; the plant bearing it; profits to be divided among stockholders, etc, *usu* in **cut the melon** (N Am *inf*). [Fr, from L *mēlō*, *-ōnis*, from Gr *mēlon* an apple]
□ **mel'on-pear** n a fruit, the pepino.

meloxicam /me-lok'si-kam/ n a non-steroidal anti-inflammatory drug used to relieve some symptoms of arthritis.

Melpomene /mel-pom'i-nē/ (Gr *myth*) n the Muse of tragedy. [Gr *Melpomenē*, literally, songstress]

melt[1] /melt/ vi (pat **melt'ed** or *archaic* **mōlt**; pap **melt'ed** or (*archaic*) **mōlt'en**, **ymōlt'en** or **ymōlt**') to change from a solid into a liquid state, *esp* by heat; to fuse; to dissolve; to stream with liquid; to lose distinct form; to blend; to shade off; to become imperceptible; to disperse, be dissipated, disappear (sometimes with *away*); to soften emotionally. ◆ vt to cause to melt in any sense. ◆ n the act of melting; the state of being melted; molten material; the quantity melted; a dish with melted cheese. [OE *meltan* (intransitive strong verb), and *mæltan*, *meltan* (causative weak verb, WSax *mieltan*); ON *melta* to digest, to malt, Gr *meldein*]
■ **melt'able** adj. **melt'er** n. **melt'ing** n and adj. **melt'ingly** adv. **melt'ingness** n. **melt'y** adj liable to melt. **mōlt'en** adj melted; made of melted metal. **mōlt'enly** adv.
□ **melt'down** n the process in which, due to a failure of the cooling system, the radioactive fuel in a nuclear reactor overheats, melts through its insulation, and is released into the environment; an unforeseen and disastrous failure, with possible wide-reaching effects, such as a crash on the stock market. **melt'ing-point** n the temperature at which a given solid begins to become liquid. **melt'ing-pot** n a container for melting things in; a place characterized by the intermixing of several races or cultures; a state of dissolution preparatory to shaping anew (see also **in the melting-pot** below). **melting temperature** n (*biol*) the temperature at which half the molecules in a nucleic acid solution have undergone thermal

denaturation, ie DNA dissociated into single strands. **melt'-water** *n* water running off melting ice or snow.

■ **in the melting-pot** in the process of changing and forming something new. **melt down** to turn metal into a molten state; (of fuel in a nuclear reactor) to overheat, causing radioactivity to escape. **melt in the mouth** (of food) to be delicious. **molten salt reactor** one in which uranium is dissolved in a molten mixture of fluoride salts. **molten sea** see under **sea**.

melt² see **milt**.

meltemi /mel-tem'ē/ *n* a seasonal wind of the E Mediterranean. [Gr, from Turk *meltem*]

meltith /mel'tith/ (*Scot*) *n* a meal; a cow's yield at one milking. [**mealtide**]

melton /mel'tən/ *n* a strong cloth for overcoats. [*Melton* Mowbray, in Leicestershire]

Mem. *abbrev*: Member.

mem /mem/ *n* the thirteenth letter of the Hebrew alphabet. [Heb]

mem. *abbrev*: member (also **Mem.**); *memento* (*L*), remember; memorandum; memorial.

member /mem'bər/ *n* a person who belongs to a society, club, political party, etc; a representative in a legislative body; an animal or plant that is part of a group; a distinct part of a whole, *esp* a limb of an animal; the penis (*euphem*); a clause (*grammar*). [Fr *membre*, from L *membrum*]

■ **mem'bered** *adj* having limbs. **mem'berless** *adj*. **mem'bership** *n* the state of being a member of or belonging to a society, etc; the members of a body, organization, etc regarded as a whole. **mem'bral** *adj* relating to the limbs rather than the trunk.

❑ **member of parliament** *n* (in UK) a member of the House of Commons (*abbrev* **MP**); a member of a legislative assembly in various countries.

membrane /mem'brān or -brin/ *n* a thin flexible solid sheet or film; a thin sheetlike structure, *usu* fibrous, connecting other structures or covering or lining a part or organ (*biol*); a skin of parchment. [L *membrāna*, from *membrum*]

■ **membranaceous** /-brə-nā'shəs/, **membrān'eous** (*rare*) or **mem'branous** /-brə-nəs/ *adj* like or of the nature of a membrane; thin, translucent, and papery (*bot*).

❑ **membrane bone** *n* one formed directly from connective tissue without passing through a stage of cartilage.

membrum virile /mem'brəm vi-rī'lē or -brŭm wi-rē'le/ (*L*) *n* the penis.

meme /mēm/ *n* a practice, belief, or other cultural feature that is passed on other than by genetic means (*biol*); an idea or question that is disseminated via the Internet and changes in form during the course of being passed on. [Gr *mimema*, something imitated, after **gene**]

■ **memetic** /mē-met'ik/ *adj*.

memento /mi-men'tō/ *n* (pl **memen'tos** or **-toes**) something kept or given as a reminder; a fit of reverie (*obs*). [L, imperative of *meminisse* to remember]

❑ **memento mori** /mō'rī or mo'rē/ *n* (*L*) remember that you must die; anything (eg a skull) to remind one of mortality.

Memnon /mem'non/ *n* an Ethiopian king who fought for the Trojans; a statue of Amenhotep, or Amenoph(is), III at Thebes in Egypt, thought by the Greeks to be of Memnon and to give out a musical sound at sunrise in salutation of his mother Eos (the Dawn). [Gr *Memnōn*]

■ **Memnōn'ian** *adj*.

memo /mem'ō/ *n* (pl **mem'os**) a contraction of **memorandum**.

memoir /mem'wär or -wör/ *n* (*usu* in *pl*) a written record set down as material for history or biography; a biographical sketch; a record of a study of some subject investigated by the writer; (in *pl*) the transactions of a society. [Fr *mémoire*, from L *memoria* memory, from *memor* mindful]

■ **mem'oirism** *n* the act or art of writing memoirs. **mem'oirist** *n* a writer of memoirs.

memorabilia, **memorable**, etc see under **memory**.

memorandum /me-mə-ran'dəm/ *n* (pl **memoran'dums** or **memoran'da**) something to be remembered; a note to assist the memory; a brief note of some transaction (*law*); a summary of the state of a question (*diplomacy*). [L, a thing to be remembered, neuter gerundive of *memorāre* to remember]

❑ **memoran'dum-book** *n* a book for keeping notes or memoranda. **memorandum of association** *n* a legal document required for registering a company under the Companies Act, stating the powers and objectives of the company with respect to the outside world. **memorandum of understanding** *n* a document outlining the broad details of a proposed business agreement as a precursor to a legal contract.

memory /mem'ə-ri/ *n* the power or process of retaining and reproducing mental or sensory impressions; an impression so reproduced; a having or keeping in the mind; time within which past things can be remembered; commemoration; a religious service in commemoration; remembrance; (of computers) a place for storing binary data. [L *memoria* memory]

■ **memorabil'ia** *n pl* (from *L*) things worth remembering; noteworthy points; objects associated with a (*usu* famous) person or event, by which the memory of that person or event is kept alive. **memorabil'ity** *n*. **mem'orable** *adj* deserving to be remembered; remarkable; easily remembered. **mem'orableness** *n*. **mem'orably** *adv*. **mem'orative** *adj* (*obs*) relating to memory; aiding the memory. **memorial** /-ōr' or -ör'/ *adj* serving or intended to preserve the memory of anything; done in remembrance of a person, event, etc; relating to memory; remembered (*obs*). ◆ *n* something which serves to keep in remembrance; a monument; a donation to charity in memory of someone who has died (*US*); a memorandum (*obs*); a written statement of facts; a record; memory (*obs*); (in *pl*) historical or biographical records. **memor'ialist** *n* a person who writes, signs or presents a memorial. **memor'ialize** or **-ise** *vt* to present a memorial to; to commemorate; to petition by a memorial. **memor'iter** *adv* (*L*) from memory; by heart. **mem'orizable** or **-s-** *adj*. **memoriza'tion** or **-s-** *n*. **mem'orize** or **-ise** *vt* to commit to memory; to cause to be remembered (*Shakesp*); to record, celebrate (*archaic*). **mem'orizer** or **-s-** *n*.

❑ **Memorial Day** *n* a day (Monday nearest 30 May) kept in honour of US servicemen killed in war (*orig* known as *Decoration Day* and kept, in most parts of the USA on 30 May, in honour of men killed in the US Civil War, 1861–65). **memoria technica** *n* (*L*) artificial memory; a mnemonic device. **memory bank** *n* (*comput*) a set of memory chips. **memory board** or **card** *n* an expansion card providing additional memory for a microcomputer. **memory foam** *n* a dense polyurethane foam that moulds under pressure or heat, used in some mattresses, pillows, etc. **memory lane** *n* (*inf*) an imaginary place where one retains fond memories of past events. **memory leak** *n* (*comput*) an informal term for the situation in which a program fails to release all the memory taken to execute a procedure. **memory manager** *n* the part of an operating system or other program that controls access to a computer's memory. **memory mapping** *n* a technique whereby a computer treats peripherals as part of main memory. **memory-res'ident** *adj* (of a computer program) able to be temporarily removed from and recalled to a screen while remaining in a computer's memory. **memory span** *n* (*psychol*) the capacity of a person's short-term memory, typically about seven items. **Memory Stick®** *n* (*comput*) a type of flash drive (qv under **flash**). **memory trace** *n* (*psychol*) a hypothetical change in the cells of the brain caused by the taking-in of information, etc.

■ **a memory like a sieve** see under **sieve**. **in living memory** within the memory of people still alive. **in memor'iam** to the memory of; in memory.

Memphian /mem'fi-ən/ *adj* relating to *Memphis*, an ancient capital of Egypt (also **Mem'phite** /-fīt/ or **Memphitic** /-fit'/).

MEMS /memz/ *abbrev*: microelectromechanical systems.

memsahib /mem'sä-ib/ *n* in colonial India, (a title of address for) a married European woman. [**ma'am** and **sahib**]

men plural of **man¹**.

❑ **menfolk**, **menfolks**, **menswear**, etc see under **man¹**.

menace /men'is or -as/ *n* a threat or threatening; a show of an intention to do harm; a threatening danger; a troublesome person or thing (*sl*). ◆ *vt* to threaten. ◆ *vi* to act in a threatening manner. [Fr, from L *mināciae* (pl) threats, from *minae* overhanging parts, threats]

■ **men'acer** *n*. **men'acing** *adj*. **men'acingly** *adv*.

menadione /me-nə-dī'ōn/ *n* vitamin K₃. [*methyl naphthoquinone*, and *-dione*, suffix denoting a compound containing two carbonyl groups]

menage obsolete form of **manage**.

ménage /mā-näzh'/ *n* a household; the management of a house; a benefit society (*Scot*); an arrangement for selling on instalment (*Scot*). [Fr, from L *mānsiō* dwelling]

❑ **ménage à trois** /a trwä/ *n* a household composed of three people having sexual relations, *esp* a husband and wife and the lover of one of them.

menagerie /mi-naj'ə-ri/ *n* a collection of wild animals in cages for exhibition; the place where these are kept; an unusual or outlandish assortment of people (*fig*). [Fr *ménagerie*, from *ménage* household]

menaquinone /me-nə-kwin'ōn/ *n* a form of vitamin K produced by bacteria in the intestine. [From *methyl-naphthoquinone*]

menarche /mə-när'kē/ *n* the first menstruation. [Gr *mēn* month, and *archē* beginning]

■ **menar'cheal** *adj*.

Mencap /men'kap/ *abbrev*: Royal Society for Mentally Handicapped Children and Adults.

mend /mend/ vt to remove a fault from; to repair; to make better; to correct; to improve; to improve upon; to supplement (obs). ◆ vi to grow better; to reform. ◆ n a repair; a repaired place, eg on a garment; an act of mending; (in pl) amends (archaic). [Shortened from **amend**] ■ **mend'able** adj. **mend'er** n. **mend'ing** n the act of repairing; a repair; things requiring to be mended, esp clothes by sewing. ■ **mend one's pace** (archaic) to go quicker. **mend one's ways** to reform one's behaviour. **on the mend** improving, recovering.

mendacious /men-dā'shəs/ adj lying; inclined to be untruthful. [L mendāx, -ācis, connected with mentīrī to lie] ■ **mendā'ciously** adv. **mendacity** /-das'i-ti/ n lying; a lie.

mendelevium /men-de-lē'vi-əm or -lā'-/ n an artificially produced radioactive transuranic element (symbol **Md**; atomic no 101). [DI Mendeleev (1834–1907), Russian scientist who developed the periodic table of elements]

Mendelian /men-dē'li-ən/ adj relating to or associated with the Austrian-German biologist Gregor Mendel (1822–84), or his teaching on heredity by genes. ◆ n a believer in Mendel's theory. ■ **Men'delism** /-də-lizm/ n.

mendicant /men'di-kənt/ adj begging; (of a friar) depending on alms. ◆ n a beggar; a friar who depends on alms (hist). [L mendīcāns, -antis, prp of mendīcāre to beg, from mendīcus a beggar] ■ **men'dicancy** or **mendicity** /-dis'i-ti/ n the condition of being a beggar; the act of begging.

mene see **mean**[4].

meneer /mə-nā'ər or mə-nēr'/ (S Afr) n same as **mynheer**.

Menevian /me-nē'vi-ən/ (geol) adj and n Middle Cambrian. [LL Menevia St David's, in Dyfed, Wales]

meng and **menge** see **ming**[1].

menhaden /men-hā'dən/ n an oily fish (Brevoortia tyrannus) of the herring family, found off the east coast of N America. [From an Algonquian name]

menhir /men'hēr/ n a prehistoric megalith or standing stone. [Breton men stone, and hir long]

menial /mē'ni-əl/ adj of or relating to a train of servants or work of a humiliating or servile nature; servile. ◆ n a domestic servant; someone performing servile work; a person of servile disposition. [Anglo-Fr menial; cf **meinie**] ■ **mē'nially** adv.

Ménière's disease /mān-yerz' or -ē-erz' di-zēz' or **syndrome** /sin'drōm/ n a disorder characterized by attacks of dizziness, buzzing noises in the ears, and progressive deafness, due to chronic disease of the labyrinth of the ear. [P Ménière (1799–1862), French physician]

meninx /mē'ningks/ n (pl **meninges** /men-in'jēz/) any of three membranes that envelop the brain and spinal cord. [Gr mēninx, -ingos a membrane] ■ **mening'eal** adj. **meningiō'ma** n (pl **meningiō'mas** or **meningiō'mata**) a tumour of the meninges of the brain and, more rarely, of the spinal cord. **meningitic** /-jit'ik/ adj. **meningitis** /-jī'-/ n inflammation of the meninges. **meningocele** /men-ing'gō-sēl/ n (Gr kēlē tumour) protrusion of the meninges through the skull. **meningococcal** /men-ing-go-kok'l/ or **meningococcic** /-kok'sik/ adj caused by a meningococcus. **meningococc'us** (pl **meningococci** /-kok'ī/) n a coccus which causes epidemic cerebrospinal meningitis.

Menippean /me-ni-pē'ən/ adj relating to, or in imitation or emulation of, the Greek satirist Menippos (3c BC) of Gadara, esp humorously detailed or erudite.

meniscus /me-nis'kəs/ n (pl **menis'ci** /-kī, -sī or -kē/ or **menis'cuses**) a crescent-shaped figure; a crescentic fibrous cartilage in a joint; a convexo-concave lens; a liquid surface curved by capillarity. [Gr mēniskos, dimin of mēnē the moon] ■ **meniscec'tomy** n (Gr ektomē cutting out) surgical removal of a meniscus cartilage. **menis'coid** adj (bot) hourglass-shaped. ▫ **meniscus telescope** n a compact telescope in which the spherical aberration of a concave mirror is corrected by a meniscus lens.

menispermum /me-ni-spûr'məm/ n any plant of the moonseed genus Menispermum, esp M. canadense, giving name to a family **Menispermā'ceae** related to the buttercup family. [Gr mēnē moon, and sperma seed] ■ **menispermā'ceous** adj.

Mennonite /men'ə-nīt/ n a member of a Protestant sect, originating in Holland and Switzerland and now found esp in the USA, believing in baptism on confession of faith, pacifism, etc. ◆ adj of or relating to the Mennonites. [Menno Simons (died 1559), chief founder] ■ **Menn'onitism** n.

meno /mā'nō/ (music) adv less. [Ital]

menology /mē-nol'ə-ji/ n a register or calendar of Saints' days, esp of the Greek Church. [Late Gr mēnologion, from mēn month, and logos account]

Menominee or **Menomini** /mi-nom'i-nē/ n (pl **Menom'inee** or **Menom'inees**) a member of a Native American people of Michigan and Wisconsin; the Algonquian language of this people; (without cap) a small whitefish found in the northern USA and Canada (also **menominee whitefish**). ◆ adj of or relating to the Menominee or their language. [Ojibwa]

meno mosso /mā'nō mos'sō/ (music) adv not so fast. [Ital]

menopause /men'ə-pöz or -ō-/ n the ending of menstruation, change of life. [Gr mēn month, and pausis cessation] ■ **menopaus'al** adj of, relating to or experiencing the menopause; suffering from strange moods or behaviour in middle age (inf). ■ **male menopause** see under **male**[1].

menopome /men'ə-pōm/ n the hellbender, so called from its persistent gill-aperture. [Gr menein to remain, and pōma lid]

menorah /mə-nō'rə or -nō'rə/ (also with cap) n a candelabrum with a varying number of branches, usu seven, used in Jewish religious ceremony. [Heb menōrāh]

menorrhagia /me-nə-rā'ji-ə/ (med) n excessive flow of blood during menstruation. [Gr mēn month, and -rragia, from rhēgnynai to break, burst]

menorrhoea or (US) **menorrhea** /me-nə-rē'ə/ n the normal flow of the menses. [Gr mēn month, and rhoiā flow]

Mensa /men'sə/ n one of the southern constellations, the Table; an international organization, founded in the UK in 1946, open to people with a high IQ rating. [L mēnsa table]

mensal[1] /men'səl/ adj monthly (also **men'sual**). [L mensis month]

mensal[2] /men'səl/ adj belonging to the table. [L mēnsa table]

mensch /mensh/ (US sl) n an honest, decent, morally-principled person. [Yiddish, a person]

mense /mens/ (Scot) n propriety; an ornament; credit. ◆ vt to grace or set off (something). [ON mennska humanity; cf OE menniscu humanity, mennisc human] ■ **mense'ful** adj decorous; respectable; gracious; generous. **mense'less** adj graceless, uncivil.

menses /men'sēz/ n pl the discharge of blood and other substances from the uterus during menstruation; the fact of menstruating, menstruation. [L mēnsēs, pl of mēnsis month]

mensh /mensh/ n an informal short form of **mention**.

Menshevik /men'shə-vik/ (hist) n a moderate or minority socialist in revolutionary Russia, opp to Bolshevik. [Russ menshye smaller, and agent sfx (-v)ik]

mens rea /menz rē'ə or mens rā'ə/ (law) n a wrongful purpose; criminal intent; knowledge of the unlawfulness of an act. [New L, guilty mind]

mens sana in corpore sano /menz sä'nä in kör'pö-rā sä'nō/ (L) a healthy mind in a healthy body.

menstruum /men'strü-əm/ n (pl **men'strua** or **men'struums**) (orig in alchemy) a solvent, esp one used in the preparation of drugs. [L neuter of mēnstruus monthly, from mēnsis] ■ **men'strual** adj monthly; relating to menstruation, or to the menses. **men'struate** vi to discharge the menses, have a period. **menstruā'tion** n the monthly discharge through the vagina of blood and other substances from the uterus in non-pregnant adult females. **men'struous** adj. ▫ **menstrual cycle** n the repeating cycle of changes in the reproductive system of some primates.

mensual see **mensal**[1].

Mensur /men-zoor'/ (Ger) n (pl **Mensur'en**) a fencing contest between students at some universities, where it is fashionable to sport a duelling scar. [Ger, measurement (from the measured distance of the participants), from L mēnsūra]

mensurable /men'sh(y)ə-rə-bl or -sū-/ adj measurable; having a fixed relative time-value for each note (music). [L mēnsūrāre to measure] ■ **mensurabil'ity** n. **mens'ural** adj relating to measure; measurable (music). **mensurā'tion** n the act or art of finding by measurement and calculation the length, area, volume, etc of bodies. **men'surātive** adj.

menswear see under **man**[1].

ment see **ming**[1].

-ment /-mənt/ n sfx denoting: a process, action, result or means, as in imprisonment, realignment; a state or condition, as in contentment. [L -mentum]

mental[1] /men'tl/ adj of or relating to the mind; done in the mind, esp in the mind alone, without outward expression; suffering from, provided for, or involved in the care of, disease or disturbance of the mind; mentally unbalanced (sl); ridiculous (sl). [Fr, from L mēns, mentis the mind] ■ **men'talism** n the process of mental action; the theory that the physical world exists and is explicable only as an aspect of the mind, idealism (*philos*). **men'talist** *n* an adherent of the theory of mentalism; a crazy person (*sl*). Also *adj*. **mentalis'tic** *adj*. **mentality** /-*tal'*i-ti/ *n* mind; mental endowment; a type of mind; a way of thinking. **men'tally** *adv*. **menta'tion** *n* mental activity. **menticide** /*men'*ti-sīd/ *n* the systematic reduction of a person's mind by psychological or other pressure to a point where views formerly repugnant will be accepted.

☐ **mental age** *n* the age in years, etc, at which an average child would have reached the same stage of mental development as the individual under consideration. **mental block** *n* a psychological barrier preventing the development of a thought process. **mental cruelty** *n* conduct in marriage, not involving physical cruelty or violence, that wounds feelings or personal dignity, offering grounds for separation or divorce. **mental deficiency** *n* mental retardation. **mental home** or **hospital** *n* (*old*) a home or hospital for people with mental illness. **mentally handicapped** *adj* having impaired intellectual ability, either congenitally or as a result of brain damage. **mental patient** *n* (*old*) a person being treated in a mental home or hospital. **mental retardation** *n* retarded development of learning ability, whether arising from innate defect or from some other cause. **mental set** *n* (*behaviourism*) the tendency to consider new problems, etc, in the same way as old ones; a mindset.

■ **go mental** (*sl*) to become mentally unbalanced, go mad; to become extremely angry.

mental[2] see under **mentum**.

mentee see under **mentor**.

menthol /*men'*thol/ *n* a camphor obtained from oil of peppermint, used as a decongestant and local analgesic. [L *mentha* mint]
■ **men'tholated** *adj* containing menthol.

menticide see under **mental**[1].

mention /*men'*shən/ *n* a brief reference, *esp* to a person's merit; the occurrence or introduction of a name or reference. ◆ *vt* to make reference briefly; to remark; to name. [L *mentiō, -ōnis*]
■ **men'tionable** *adj* fit to be mentioned; worth mentioning.
■ **don't mention it** apologies or thanks are not necessary. **honourable mention** an award of distinction not entitling to a prize. **not to mention** to say nothing of, a parenthetical rhetorical pretence of refraining from saying all one might say (and is about to say).

mento /*men'*tō/ *n* (*pl* **men'tōs**) a traditional Jamaican form of song or ballad, having a strong rhythm and often accompanying a dance. [Origin unknown]

mentonnière /men-to-ni-er'/ (*hist*) *n* a piece of armour covering the chin and throat. [Fr, from *menton* chin, from L *mentum*]

mentor /*men'*tor or -tör/ *n* a wise counsellor; a tutor; a trainer; a more senior or experienced colleague appointed to help and advise a junior employee. ◆ *vt* to act as a mentor to. [Gr *Mentōr*, the tutor by whom (or Athena in his form) Telemachus, son of Odysseus, was guided]
■ **mentee'** *n* (*non-standard*) a person under the direction of a mentor, *esp* in business. **mentorial** /-*tör'* or -*tör'*i-əl/ *adj*. **men'toring** *n*. **men'torship** *n*.

mentum /*men'*təm/ (*anat*) *n* the chin; the central part of the labium in insects. [L *mentum* the chin]
■ **men'tal** *adj* of or relating to the chin.

menu /*men'*ū/ *n* in a restaurant, etc, a list of dishes that may be ordered; the card listing these; a list of subjects, options (*fig*); *specif* a list of possible options or facilities displayed on a computer screen by software, and from which selection can be made via a keyboard or a mouse. [Fr, from L *minūtus* small]
☐ **men'u-bar** *n* (*comput*) a bar in a window used in selecting commands. **men'u-driven** *adj* (of computer software) offering the user lists of options for movement through the program.

menuisier /mə-nwē-zyā'/ (*Fr*) *n* a joiner.

menyie see **meinie**.

meo periculo /mē'ō pe-rik'ū-lō or mā'ō pe-rē'kŭ-lō/ (*L*) at my own risk.

meow /mi-ow'/ or **myow**/ same as **miaow**.

MEP *abbrev* : Member of the European Parliament.

mepacrine /*mep'*ə-krēn/ *n* a bitter yellow powder derived from acridine dye compounds, formerly used against malaria (also **atabrin** or **atebrin**). [*methyl*, *pa*ludism and a*cridine*]

meperidine /me-per'i-dēn or -din/ *n* pethidine. [*methyl* and pi*peridine*]

Mephistopheles /me-fi-stof'i-lēz/ *n* the Devil in the *Faust* story (short form **Mephis'tō**; also **Mephistoph'ilis**, **Mephostoph'ilus**, etc). [Ety unknown; prob influenced by Gr *mē* not, and *phōs, phōtos* light, or *philos* loving]
■ **Mephistophelē'an**, **Mephistophē'lian** or **Mephistophelic** /-*fel'*/ *adj* cynical, scoffing, fiendish.

mephitis /me-fī'tis/ *n* a poisonous exhalation; a foul stink. [L *mephītis*]

■ **mephitic** /-*fit'*/ or **mephitical** /me-fit'i-kl/ *adj*. **meph'itism** /-*it-izm*/ *n* mephitic poisoning.

meprobamate /me-prō-bam'āt/ *n* a drug formerly used as a muscle relaxant and as a sedative, but no longer recommended. [*methyl, propyl* and car*bamate*]

meranti /mi-ran'ti/ *n* the wood of any of the *Shorea* genus of trees of Malaysia. [Malay]

merbromin /mûr-brō'min/ *n* a green iridescent crystalline compound that forms a red solution in water, used as an antiseptic.

Merc /mûrk/ (*inf*) *n* a Mercedes® car. [Short form]

merc see **mercenary**.

Mercalli scale /mər-kal'i skäl/ *n* a scale of intensity used to measure earthquake shocks, graded from 1 (very weak) to 12 (catastrophic). [Giuseppe *Mercalli* (1850–1914), Italian geologist who devised it]

mercantile /*mûr'*kən-tīl/ *adj* relating to merchants; having to do with trade; of or relating to mercantilism; commercial; mercenary. [Fr, from Ital *mercantile*, from L *mercārī*; cf **merchant**]
■ **mer'cantilism** *n* the business of merchants; advocacy of the mercantile system. **mer'cantilist** *n* and *adj*.
☐ **mercantile agency** *n* an agency supplying information about the financial status of companies and individuals. **mercantile law** *n* the law relating to the dealings of merchants with each other. **mercantile marine** *n* the ships and crews of any country employed in commerce. **mercantile system** *n* an old economic strategy based on the theory that a nation's interests are best served by accumulating reserves of bullion, etc through the development of overseas trade and the restricting of imports, the impetus of much 17c and 18c colonization by European powers.

mercaptan /mər-kap'tan/ *n* a substance analogous to an alcohol, with sulphur instead of oxygen. [L *mercūrium captāns* laying hold of mercury, from the readiness with which it forms mercury mercaptide]
■ **mercap'tide** *n* a compound in which a metal takes the place of a hydrogen atom of a mercaptan.

mercat /mer'kət/ (*Scot*) *n* same as **market** (*n*).

Mercator /mər-kä'tər or mer-kä'tör/ *n* a Latin translation of the name of the Flemish-born German cartographer Gerhard Kremer (literally, shopkeeper, 1512–94).
☐ **Mercator's projection** *n* a representation of the surface of the globe in which the meridians are parallel straight lines, the parallels straight lines at right angles to these, their distances such that everywhere degrees of latitude and longitude have the same ratio to each other as on the globe itself.

mercenary /*mûr'*si-nə-ri/ *adj* hired for money; motivated by the hope of reward; too strongly influenced by desire of gain; sold or done for money. ◆ *n* a person who is hired; a soldier hired into foreign service (*inf* short form **merc** /mûrk/). [L *mercēnārius*, from *mercēs* hire]
■ **mer'cenarily** *adv*. **mer'cenariness** *n*. **mer'cenarism** *n* the state of being a mercenary.

mercer /*mûr'*sər/ *n* a dealer in textiles, *esp* expensive ones; a dealer in small wares. [Fr *mercier*]
■ **mer'cery** *n* the trade of a mercer; the goods of a mercer.

mercerize or **-ise** /*mûr'*sə-rīz/ *vt* to treat (cotton fabric or thread) under tension with caustic soda, so as to cause swelling and increase the strength and dye absorption. [John *Mercer* (1791–1866), inventor of the process]
■ **mercerīzā'tion** or **-s-** *n*. **mer'cerizer** or **-s-** *n*.

merchandise /*mûr'*chən-dīz or -dīs/ *n* goods bought and sold for gain; trade (*Bible* and *Shakesp*); dealing. [ME *marchandise*, from OFr]
■ **mer'chandizable** or **-s-** *adj*. **mer'chandize** or **-ise** *vt* to traffic in (*Shakesp*); to buy and sell; to plan the advertising or supplying of, or the selling campaign for (a product). ◆ *vi* to be engaged in the selling of a product. **mer'chandizer** or **-s-** *n* a person who is responsible for supplying a product. **mer'chandizing** or **-s-** *n* the selling of a product; the creation and selling of products, eg dolls and costumes, associated with a particular (*esp* children's) cinema film or television programme; such products.

merchant /*mûr'*chənt/ *n* a trader, *esp* wholesale; a shopkeeper (now *esp US*); a supercargo (*obs*); a merchantman; a person who specializes or indulges in a particular, *usu* undesirable, activity, eg *con merchant*, *speed merchant* (*sl*). ◆ *adj* commercial. ◆ *vi* to trade. ◆ *vt* to trade in. [Fr *marchand*]
■ **mer'chantable** *adj* fit or ready for sale; marketable. **mer'chanting** *n*. **mer'chantlike** *adj* and *adv* (*Shakesp*) like a merchant. **mer'chantry** *n* the business of a merchant; merchants collectively.
☐ **merchant bank** see under **bank**[1]. **merchant bar** *n* a bar of **merchant iron**, bar-iron made of repiled and rerolled wrought iron. **merchant navy** or **service** *n* the mercantile marine. **merchant of death** *n* arms manufacturers and dealers, *esp* those trading unscrupulously on the international market. **merchant prince**

n a merchant of great wealth, power, and consequence. **merchant ship** *n* a ship that carries merchandise. **merchant tailor** *n* a tailor who supplies the cloth for the clothes that he makes.

■ **speed merchant** see under **speed**.

merchet /*mûr'chit*/ (*hist*) *n* a fine paid to a lord for the marriage of a daughter. [Anglo-Fr *merchet*; see **market**]

merchild see under **mermaid**.

Mercosur /*mûr'kə-soor*/ *n* a free trade agreement between Argentina, Brazil, Paraguay, and Uruguay. [Sp, short for *Mercado Común del Cono Sur* common market of the southern cone]

mercury /*mûr'kū-ri*/ *n* a silvery metallic element (symbol **Hg**; atomic no 80), liquid at ordinary temperatures (also called **quicksilver**); the column of mercury in a thermometer or barometer; a plant (**dog's-mer'cury** *Mercurialis perennis*) of the spurge family; the plant good-King-Henry; a preparation of mercury; a messenger; a common title for newspapers; mercurial character (*obs*); (with *cap*) the Roman god of merchandise, theft, and eloquence, messenger of the gods, identified with the Greek Hermes; (with *cap*) the planet nearest the sun. [L *Mercūrius*, prob from *merx, mercis* merchandise]

■ **mer'curate** *vt* to mercurialize or treat with mercury; to convert into a compound with mercury. **mercurā'tion** *n*. **mercū'rial** *adj* containing mercury; of or like mercury; caused by mercury; (with *cap*) of or relating to Mercury the god or the planet; (sometimes with *cap*) having the qualities attributed to persons born under the planet, eloquent, etc; active, sprightly, often changing. ◆ *n* a drug containing mercury; the plant mercury (*obs*); (sometimes with *cap*) a person born under the planet (*obs*). **mercū'rialism** *n* a morbid condition due to mercury. **mercū'rialist** *n* (*obs*) a believer in the medical use of mercury; a mercurial person. **mercū'rialize** or **-ise** *vt* to treat with mercury or a drug containing mercury (*med*); to make mercurial. **mercū'rially** *adv*. **mercū'rialness** or **mercurial'ity** *n*. **mercū'ric** *adj* containing bivalent mercury. **mer'curize** or **-ise** *vt* same as **mercurate** above. **mer'curous** *adj* containing univalent mercury. ▫ **mercuric chloride** *n* a soluble toxic substance (HgCl$_2$), used as a pesticide. **mercury** (or **mercury tilt**) **switch** *n* a quiet electric switch activated by the movement of mercury in a phial over the contacts. **mercury vapour light** or **lamp** *n* a bright greenish-blue light, high in ultraviolet rays, produced by an electric discharge through mercury vapour.

mercy /*mûr'si*/ *n* forbearance towards someone in one's power; a good thing regarded as derived from God; a happy chance (*inf*); a forgiving disposition; clemency; compassion for the unfortunate. ◆ *interj* (short for *God have mercy*) an expression of thanks (now *obs*); (also **mercy on us**) an expression of surprise. [Fr *merci* grace, from L *mercēs, -ēdis* the price paid, wages, later favour]

■ **mer'ciable** *adj* (*Spenser*) merciful. **mer'ciful** *adj* full of, or exercising, mercy. **mer'cifully** *adv* luckily, thankfully; in a merciful way. **mer'cifulness** *n*. **mer'cify** *vt* (*Spenser*, in *pap* **mer'cifide**) to deal mercifully with; to pity. **mer'ciless** *adj* without mercy; unfeeling; cruel. **mer'cilessly** *adv*. **mer'cilessness** *n*. ▫ **mercy flight** *n* an aircraft flight taking a seriously ill or injured person to hospital when other means of transport are impracticable or unavailable. **mercy killing** *n* killing, *esp* painlessly, to prevent chronic unrelenting suffering. **mer'cy-seat** *n* the seat or place of mercy; the covering of the Jewish Ark of the Covenant; the throne of God.

■ **at the mercy of** wholly in the power of. **for mercy** (*obs*) or **for mercy's sake** an earnest conjuration in the form of an appeal to pity. **leave** (**a person**) **to someone's tender mercies** or **mercy** (*ironic*) to leave (a person) exposed to unpleasant treatment at someone's hands. **sisters of mercy** members of female religious communities who tend the sick, etc.

mere[1] /*mēr*/ *adj* only what is said and nothing else, nothing more, nothing better; absolute (*obs*); unmixed (*obs*); pure (*obs*). ◆ *adv* (*obs*) absolutely. [L *merus* unmixed]

■ **mered** and **meered** *adj* see under **meer**[1]. **mere'ly** *adv* simply; only; without being more or better; purely (*obs*); entirely (*obs*). **mer'est** *adj* slightest.

mere[2] or (*obs*) **meer** /*mēr*/ *n* a pool or lake. [OE *mere* sea, lake, pool; Ger *Meer*, Du *meer*, L *mare* the sea]

▫ **mere swine** *n* (*obs*) a porpoise; a dolphin.

mere[3] or **meri** /*mer'i*/ *n* a war-club. [Maori]

mere[4] /*mēr*/ (*dialect*) *n* a boundary. ◆ *vt* to bound; to mark off. [OE *gemǣre*]

▫ **meres'man** *n* (*dialect*) a man appointed to ascertain boundaries. **mere'stone** *n* (*dialect*) a boundary stone.

merel and **merell** same as **meril**.

merengue /*mə-reng'gä*/ *n* a Haitian or Dominican dance with a shuffling step. [Haitian *méringue* or Sp Am *merengue*]

mereology /*mē-ri-ol'ə-ji*/ *n* the formal study of the relationship between the parts of a system and the whole. [Gr *meros* part, and **-ology**]

■ **mereolog'ical** *adj*.

meretricious /*me-ri-trish'əs*/ *adj* (*orig*) of the nature of or relating to prostitution or characteristic of a prostitute; superficially attractive but of no real value or merit; flashy; gaudy; insincere. [L *meretrīx, -īcis* a prostitute, from *merēre* to earn]

■ **meretric'iously** *adv*. **meretric'iousness** *n*.

merfolk see under **mermaid**.

merganser /*mûr-gan'sər*/ *n* any bird of the genus *Mergus* (goosander, smew, etc). [L *mergus* a diving bird, and *ānser* a goose]

merge /*mûrj*/ *vt* to cause to be swallowed up or absorbed in something greater or superior; to cause to coalesce, combine, or amalgamate; to dip or plunge (*archaic*). ◆ *vi* to be swallowed up, or lost; to coalesce; to lose identity in something else; to combine or amalgamate. [L *mergere, mersum*]

■ **mer'gence** *n*. **mer'ger** *n* the act of merging or combining, *esp* the combining of commercial companies into one; a sinking of an estate, title, etc, in one of larger extent or of higher value (*law*).

merguez /*mûr-gez'*/ *n* a spicy N African sausage. [Fr, from Ar *mirqāz*]

meri see **mere**[3].

mericarp /*mer'i-kärp*/ *n* a separating one-seeded part of a schizocarp, *esp* half of a cremocarp. [Gr *meros* a part, and *karpos* fruit]

meridian /*mə-rid'i-ən*/ *n* an imaginary great circle through the poles of the earth, the heavens, or any spherical body or figure, or its representation on a map; *specif*, that cutting the observer's horizon at the north and south points, which the sun crosses at local noon; (in Chinese medicine) any of several lines or pathways through the body along which life energy flows; culmination or highest point, as of success, splendour, power, etc; midday; a midday dram or nap (*Scot*). ◆ *adj* on the meridian; relating to a meridian or the sun or other body on the meridian; at culmination or highest point; of or at midday. [L *merīdiānus, merīdiōnālis*, from *merīdiēs* (for *medīdiēs*) midday, from *medius* middle, and *diēs* day]

■ **merid'ional** *adj* relating to the meridian; in the direction of a meridian; midday; culminating; southern; characteristic of the south. ◆ *n* a southerner, *esp* in France. **meridional'ity** *n*. **merid'ionally** *adv*. ▫ **meridian altitude** *n* the arc of a meridian between a heavenly body and the horizon. **meridian circle** *n* a telescope mounted to revolve in the plane of the meridian. **meridian passage** *n* the transit or passage of a heavenly body across the observer's meridian.

■ **magnetic meridian** see under **magnet**. **prime** (or **first**) **meridian** the meridian from which longitudes are measured east or west, *specif* that through Greenwich.

meril, **merel** or **merell** /*mer'əl*/ *n* a counter used in the game of merils; (in *pl*) a rustic game played by two people with counters on a figure marked on the ground, a board, etc, consisting of three squares, one within another, the object to get three counters in a row at the intersection of the lines joining the corners and the mid-points of the sides (also **marls**, **marr'els**, **mor'als**, **morr'is** or **mir'acles**). [OFr *merel* counter]

■ **fivepenny morris** the game as played with five pieces each. **ninepenny morris** or **nine men's morris** the game as played with nine pieces each; the figure cut in the ground for the game (*Shakesp*).

merimake /*mer'i-māk*/ (*Spenser*) *n* merrymaking; sport.

meringue /*mə-rang'*/ *n* a crisp, baked mixture of beaten egg whites and sugar, used as a pie topping or forming individual cakes or moulds; a small light cake or mould of this, *usu* filled. [Fr; origin obscure; perh Gallicized form of *Meiringen*, Switzerland]

merino /*mə-rē'nō*/ *n* (*pl* **meri'nos**) a sheep of a fine-woolled Spanish breed (also **merino sheep**); a fine dress fabric, *orig* of merino wool; a fine woollen yarn, now mixed with cotton; knitted goods made of this; waste from fine worsted clothes; a free (ie non-convict) early immigrant in Australia, or descendant of such, *esp* in *pure merino* (*Aust*). ◆ *adj* belonging to the merino sheep or its wool; made of merino. [Sp, a merino sheep, also a governor, from L *mājōrīnus* greater, also (LL) a headman, from L *mājor* greater]

merism /*mer'i-zm*/ (*biol*) *n* repetition of parts. [Gr *meros* part]

■ **merist'ic** *adj*.

meristem /*mer'i-stem*/ *n* the formative tissue of plants, distinguished from the permanent tissues by the power its cells have of dividing and forming new cells. [Gr *meristos* divisible, *merizein* to divide, from *meros* a part]

■ **meristematic** /*-sti-mat'ik*/ *adj*. ▫ **meristem culture** *n* the aseptic culture on a suitable medium of excised shoot apical meristems (also **shoot tip culture**).

merit /*mer'it*/ *n* excellence that deserves honour or reward; worth; value; desert; that which one deserves, whether reward or punishment (*archaic*); (in *pl*, *esp* in *law*) the intrinsic right or wrong. ◆ *vt* to earn; to have a right to claim as a reward; to deserve. ◆ *vi* (*obs*) to acquire merit. [L *meritum*, from *merēre, -itum* to obtain as a lot, to deserve]

■ **meritoc'racy** *n* the class of people who are in prominent positions because of their ability, real or apparent; government by this class.

■ words derived from main entry word; ▫ compound words; ■ idioms and phrasal verbs

mer'itōcrat *n*. **meritōcrat'ic** *adj*. **meritorious** /-tōr'/ or -tör'/ *adj* possessing merit or desert; deserving of reward, honour, or praise. **meritor'iously** *adv*. **meritor'iousness** *n*.

■ **order of merit** arrangement in which the best is placed first, the next best second, and so on; (*caps*) a strictly limited British order, instituted in 1902, awarded for eminence in any field (*abbrev* **OM**).

merk /merk/ *n* the old Scots mark or 13s 4d Scots, 13⅓d sterling. [**mark**²]

merkin /mûr'kin/ *n* a hairpiece for the pubic area. [Origin uncertain]

merle¹ or **merl** /mûrl/ (*archaic* or *literary Scot*) *n* the blackbird. [Fr, from L *merula*]

merle² /mûrl/ *adj* and *n* (a dog, *usu* a collie) with bluish-grey fur flecked or streaked with black (also **blue merle**). [Cf **marl**⁴, **marly** and **mirly**]

merlin /mûr'lin/ *n* a species of small falcon, *Falco columbarius*. [Anglo-Fr *merilun*, from OFr *esmerillon*]

merling /mûr'ling/ (*obs*) *n* the whiting. [OFr *merlanke*, from L *merula* a sea carp]

merlon /mûr'lən/ (*fortif*) *n* the part of a parapet between embrasures. [Fr *merlon*, from Ital *merlone*, from *merlo* battlement]

Merlot /mer-lō'/ *n* a grape variety used to produce red wine, often blended as eg in claret; a light-bodied red wine produced solely from this grape. [Fr, literally, small blackbird; cf **merle**¹]

mermaid /mûr'mād/ *n* a mythical creature with a woman's upper body and a fish's tail (also **mer'maid'en**). [OE *mere* lake, sea, and *mægden* maid]

❑ **mer'child**, **mer'man** *n* similar creatures with the upper body of a child and man respectively. **mer'folk** or **mer'people** *n pl* such creatures collectively. **mermaid's glove** *n* the largest kind of British sponge. **mermaid's purse** *n* the egg case of skate, etc.

meroblastic /me-rō-blas'tik/ (*zool*) *adj* undergoing or involving cleavage in part of the egg surface only, due to a large amount of yolk elsewhere. [Gr *meros* part, and *blastos* a shoot, bud]

■ **meroblast'ically** *adv*.

merogenesis /me-rō-jen'i-sis/ (*biol*) *n* segmentation. [Gr *meros* part, and *genesis* production]

■ **merogenetic** /-ji-net'ik/ *adj*.

merogony /me-rog'ə-ni/ *n* the production of an embryo from a fertilized fragment of an ovum without a nucleus. [Gr *meros* part, and *gonē* birth]

meroistic /me-rō-is'tik/ (*zool*) *adj* (of an ovary) producing yolk-forming cells as well as ova. [Gr *meros* part, and *ōion* egg]

merome /mer'ōm/ *n* a merosome. [Gr *meros* part]

meronym /mer'ə-nim/ or -ō-/ (*semantics*) *n* a word whose relation to another in meaning is that of part to whole, eg *whisker* in relation to *cat*. [Gr *meros* part, and *onyma* name]

■ **meron'ymy** *n*.

Merops /mer'ops/ *n* the bee-eater genus. [Gr *merops* bee-eater]

■ **merop'idan** *n* a bird of the bee-eater family (**Merop'idae**).

merosome /mer'ō-sōm/ *n* one of the serial segments of which a body is composed, such as the ring of a worm, a metamere, a somite. [Gr *meros* part, and *sōma* body]

Merovingian /me-rō-vin'ji-ən/ *adj* relating to the first dynasty of Frankish kings in Gaul, founded by Clovis. ◆*n* a member of this family. [L *Merovingi*, from Meravaeus or *Merovech*, king of the Salian Franks (448–457), grandfather of Clovis]

merozoite /me-rō-zō'īt/ (*zool*) *n* a young trophozoite resulting from the division of a schizont. [Gr *meros* part, and *zōion* animal]

merpeople see under **mermaid**.

merry¹ /mer'i/ *adj* (**merr'ier**; **merr'iest**) sportive; cheerful; noisily gay; causing laughter; pleasant (*obs*); enlivened by drink, tipsily cheerful; lively; used as an intensifier of *hell*, as in *play merry hell with*. [OE *myr(i)ge*]

■ **merr'ily** *adv*. **merr'iment** *n* gaiety with laughter and noise; mirth; hilarity. **merr'iness** *n*.

❑ **merry-an'drew** *n* a quack's assistant (*hist*); a buffoon; a clown. **merry England** *n* an idealistically jovial picture of life in England in the past, *esp* in Elizabethan times (as used *orig*, eg by Spenser, the phrase meant 'fair, pleasant England'). **merr'y-go-round** *n* a revolving ring of wooden horses, etc for riding at a funfair; a roundabout; a whirl of activity, etc (*fig*); any activity inclined to circularity (*fig*). **merr'y-make** *n* (*archaic*) a merrymaking. ◆ *vi* to make merry. **merr'ymaker** *n*. **merr'ymaking** *n* a merry entertainment; festivity, revelry. **merr'yman** *n* (*obs*) a zany; a jester. **merry men** *n pl* an outlaw's companions; followers, assistants (*facetious*). **merr'y-night** *n* (*dialect*) a village festival or dance. **merr'ythought** *n* a fowl's furcula or wishbone.

■ **make merry** to be festive; to indulge in lively enjoyment; to turn to ridicule (with *with* or *over*). **the merry monarch** Charles II.

merry² /mer'i/ *n* a gean. [Fr *merise*]

mersalyl /mər-sal'il/ *n* a sodium salt ($C_{13}H_{16}NO_6HgNa$), used as a diuretic. [*mercury* and *salicyl*]

merse /mûrs/ (*Scot*) *n* low flat marshland, *usu* by a river or estuary. [Scot form of **marsh**]

Mersey beat /mûr'zē or -zi bēt/ *n* popular music in the style of the Beatles and other Liverpool groups during the 1960s (also **Mersey sound**). [From the river *Mersey*, on which Liverpool stands]

mersion /mûr'shən/ (*obs*) *n* dipping, *esp* in baptism. [L *mersiō*, *-ōnis*; cf **merge**]

Merulius /mə-roo'li-əs/ *n* the dry rot fungus genus.

merum sal /mer'əm or mer'ŭm sal/ (*L*) pure salt, genuine Attic wit.

merveilleux /mer-ve-yə'/ or (*fem*) **merveilleuse** /mer-ve-yœz'/ (*Fr*) *adj* marvellous. ◆ *n* a fantastic extremist in fashion in France during the Republican government of 1795–99, aping classical modes.

merycism /mer'i-si-zm/ *n* regurgitation of undigested food, in humans a symptom of disease. [Gr *mērykismos*]

Mes see **Mass**.

mes- see **meso-**.

mesa /mā'sə/ *n* a flat-topped hill with steep sides, *esp* in SW USA. [Sp, from L *mēnsa* table]

❑ **mesa transistor** *n* (*electronics*) a transistor constructed by etching down the semiconductor wafer in steps so that the base and emitter regions appear as plateaux above the collector.

mesail /mes'āl/ or **mezail** /mez-/ *n* a visor, *esp* one made in two parts. [Fr *mézail*]

mesal see **mesial**.

mésalliance /mā-zal-yãs'/ (*Fr*) *n* an unsuitable marriage; marriage with someone of lower social rank.

mesaraic /me-sə-rā'ik/ *adj* mesenteric. [Gr *mesaraikos*, from *mesos* middle, and *araiā* flank, belly]

mesarch /mes'ärk/ *adj* having the protoxylem surrounded by xylem formed later (*bot*); originating in a moderately moist habitat (*ecology*). [Gr *mesos* middle, and *archē* beginning]

❑ **mesarch succession** *n* an ecological succession originating in a mesic habitat.

mesaticephalic /mes-ə-ti-se-fal'ik/ or **mesaticephalous** /-sef'ə-ləs/ (*med*) *adj* intermediate between dolichocephalic and brachycephalic. [Gr *mesatos* midmost, and *kephalē* head]

■ **mesaticeph'aly** *n*.

mescal /mes-kal'/ *n* the peyote cactus, genus *Lophophora*, found in Mexico and the southwestern USA, the dried tubercles (**mescal buttons**) of which are chewed or drunk in infusion as an intoxicant; an alcoholic spirit distilled from the fermented juice of the agave. [Sp *mescal*, *mezcal*, from Nahuatl *mexcalli*]

■ **mescalin** or **mescaline** /mes'kəl-in or -īn/ *n* the principal alkaloid ($C_{11}H_{17}NO_3$) in mescal, producing hallucinations and schizophrenia. **mescal'ism** *n* the habitual use of mescal as an intoxicant; peyotism.

mesclun /mes'kloon/ or **mesclum** /mes'kloom/ *n* a mixed green salad of young leaves and shoots, eg of rocket, chicory, fennel, etc. [Fr, from Niçois *mesclumo* mixture]

Mesdames see **madam**.

Mesdemoiselles see **mademoiselle**.

mese /mes'ē/ (*Gr music*) *n* the middle string of the lyre; its note; the keynote. [Gr *mesē* (*chordē*) middle (string)]

mesel or **meazel** /mē'zl/ (*obs*) *n* a leper; leprosy (*Shakesp*). ◆ *adj* leprous. [OFr *mesel*, from L *misellus*, dimin of *miser* wretched]

■ **mes'eled** *adj*.

mesembrianthemum or conventionally **mesembryanthemum** /miz-em-bri-an'thi-məm/ *n* any of a genus (*Mesembrianthemum*) of succulent plants (family Aizoaceae), mostly S African (also called **ice-plant**, **Livingstone daisy**). [Gr *mesēmbriā* midday, from *mesos* middle, *hēmerā* day, and *anthemon* a flower; some are open only about midday]

mesencephalon /me-sen-sef'ə-lon/ *n* the mid-brain. [Gr *mesos* middle, and **encephalon**]

■ **mesencephalic** /-si-fal'ik/ *adj*.

mesenchyme /mes'en-kīm/ (*zool*) *n* mesodermal tissue, comprising cells which migrate from ectoderm, endoderm or mesothelium into the blastocoel, which differentiates into connective tissue and muscle. [Gr *mesenchyma*, from *enchyma* infusion]

■ **mesenchymal** /-en'kim-əl/ *adj*.

mesentery /mes'ən-tə-ri or mez'-/ *n* a fold of the peritoneum, keeping the intestines in place (*anat*); (in coelenterates) a vertical inward fold of the body-wall (*zool*). [Gr *mesos* middle, and *enteron* intestines]

■ **mesenterial** /-tē'ri-əl/ or **mesenteric** /-ter'ik/ *adj*. **mesenteron** /-en'tər-on/ *n* the mid-gut.

meseta /mə-sā'tə/ n a plateau, *specif* that of central Spain. [Sp, dimin of *mesa*; see **mesa**]

mesh /mesh/ n the opening between the threads of a net; the threads and knots surrounding such an opening; a network; a trap; the engagement of geared wheels, etc; a measure of the number of openings of a mesh. ◆ vt to catch in a net; to provide or make with meshes; to entwine; to co-ordinate or harmonize. ◆ vi (of gear-teeth, etc) to become engaged; to work in conjunction, to harmonize (often with *with*); to become entangled. [Perh MDu *maesche*; cf OE *max* net; Ger *Masche*]
■ **mesh'ing** n. **mesh'y** adj formed like network.
❑ **mesh'-work** n a network, a web.
■ **in mesh** (of gear-teeth, etc) engaged.

meshuga, **meshugga** or **meshugge** /mi-shŭg'ə/ (*sl*) adj mad; crazy. [Yiddish, from Heb]
■ **meshu'gaas** or **mishe'gaas** /-gäs/ n madness, foolishness. **meshugg'enah** or **meshugg'eneh** n a crazy person.

mesial /mē'zi-əl/ adj middle; facing towards the centre of the curve formed by the upper or lower teeth (*dentistry*); in or towards the median plane or line (also **mē'sal** or **mē'sian**). [Gr *mesos* middle]
■ **mē'sally** or **mē'sially** adv.

mesic[1] see under **meson**.

mesic[2] /mes' or mez'ik, mē'zik or -sik/ adj relating to, or adapted to life with, a moderate supply of moisture. [Gr *mesos* middle]

Mes-John see under **Mass**.

mesmerize or **-ise** /mez'mə-rīz/ vt to hypnotize; to fascinate; dominate the will or fix the attention on.
■ **mesmeric** /-mer'ik/ or **mesmer'ical** adj. **mesmer'ically** adv. **mes'merism** n hypnotism as expounded, with some fanciful notions, from 1775 by Friedrich Anton or Franz *Mesmer*, a German physician (1734–1815); hypnotic influence. **mesmerīzā'tion** or **-s-** n. **mes'merizer** or **-s-**, or **mes'merist** n. **mes'merizing** or **-s-** adj.

mesne /mēn/ (*law*) adj intermediate. [Law Fr *mesne* middle; cf **mean**[3]]
❑ **mesne lord** n a feudal lord holding land from a superior lord. **mesne profits** n pl profits wrongfully obtained by another during the rightful owner's absence.

meso- /me-sō- or me-zō-, also mē-, -so- or -zo-/, or (before a vowel) **mes-** /mes-, mez-, mēs- or mēz-/ *combining form* denoting middle. [Gr *mesos* middle]
■ **Mesoamer'ica** n Central America, between N Mexico and Panama. **Mesoamer'ican** adj and n (also without *cap*). **mes'oblast** n (Gr *blastos* shoot) the middle germinal layer; the mesoderm. **mesoblas'tic** adj. **mes'ocarp** n (Gr *karpos* fruit) the middle layer of a pericarp. **mesocephalic** /-si-fal'ik/ or **-cephalous** /-sef'ə-ləs/ adj having a medium skull, with a breadth of *approx* 75 to 80 per cent of its length. **mesoceph'alism** or **mesoceph'aly** n. **mes'oderm** n (Gr *derma* skin) the layer of embryonic cells between the ectoderm and the endoderm in a gastrula. **mesoderm'al** adj. **mesogas'tric** adj. **mesogas'trium** n (pl **mesogas'tria**) the region of the abdomen between the epigastrium and the hypogastrium. **mesogloea** /-glē'ə/ n (Gr *gloia* glue) in coelenterates and sponges, a structureless gelatinous layer between ectoderm and endoderm. **mesohipp'us** n one of the prehistoric group of three-toed ungulate mammals probably related to the modern horse. **mes'olite** n (Gr *lithos* stone) a zeolite intermediate in composition between natrolite and scolecite. **Mesolith'ic** adj intermediate between Palaeolithic and Neolithic. **mesom'erism** n (*chem*) resonance; a type of tautomerism. **mes'omorph** /-mörf/ n (Gr *morphē* form) a person of muscular bodily type, thought to correspond to a characteristically aggressive and extroverted personality type (see **ectomorph** under **ecto-** and **endomorph** under **endo-**). **mesomor'phic** or **mesomor'phous** adj relating to a mesomorph; relating to an intermediate state of matter between solid and liquid (*chem*). **mes'omorphy** n. **mes'opause** n the upper boundary of the mesosphere, the coldest region of the atmosphere. **mesopelagic** /-pi-laj'ik/ adj (Gr *pelagos* sea) relating to the intermediate regions between the surface and depths of the ocean. **mes'ophyll** n (Gr *phyllon* leaf) the spongy tissue within a leaf. **mes'ophyte** /-fīt/ n (Gr *phyton* plant) a plant intermediate between a xerophyte and a hydrophyte. **mesophytic** /-fit'ik/ adj. **mes'oscaphe** /-skäf/ n (Gr *skaphos* ship) a submersible observation chamber for use at less great depths than the bathyscaphe. **mes'osphere** n the region of the earth's atmosphere above the stratosphere and below the thermosphere. **mesospher'ic** /-sfer'ik/ adj. **mesothē'lial** adj. **mesothēliō'ma** n (from **epithelium** and **-oma**) a malignant tumour of the lining of the chest or abdomen, often caused by asbestos dust. **mesothē'lium** n (pl **mesothē'lia**) the cell tissue that forms the lining of the chest and abdomen in vertebrates and lines the body-cavity in vertebrate embryos. **mesother'apy** n (*med*) the treatment of a specific area of the body by injecting a substance into the mesoderm. **mesothoracic** /-thō- or -thō-ras'ik/ adj. **mesothor'ax** n the middle one of the three segments of an insect's thorax. **Mesozō'a** n pl (Gr *zōion* animal)

minute animals once thought intermediate between Protozoa and Metazoa, *prob* Metazoa reduced by parasitism. **Mesozō'ic** adj (Gr *zōē* life; *geol*) of or belonging to the middle era of the Phanerozoic eon, between 250 and 65 million years ago (also *n*).

meson /mē'zon or mes'on/ n a short-lived subatomic particle of smaller mass than a proton (η-mesons, π-mesons (also called **pī'ons**), and κ-mesons, k-mesons (also called **kā'ons**)). [Gr *meson* neuter of *mesos* middle]
■ **mes'ic** or **meson'ic** adj. **mes'otron** n (after **electron**; *obs*) formerly a meson.
❑ **mesic** or **mesonic atom** n a nucleus with an orbital meson.

mesonephric duct same as **Wolffian duct** (see under **Wolffian**).

mesophyll...to...**Mesozoic** see under **meso-**.

mesprise or **mesprize** see **misprise**[1,2].

mesquin /me-skē'/ or (*fem*) **mesquine** /-skēn'/ (Fr) adj mean, ungracious.
■ **mesquinerie** /-kēn-ə-rē/ n meanness.

mesquite or **mesquit** /me-skēt' or mes'kēt/ n a leguminous tree or shrub (genus *Prosopis*) of N America, with nutritious pods; the wood of this used as fuel in barbecuing. [Mex Sp *mezquite*, from Nahuatl *mizquitl*]

Mess and **Mess-John** see **Mass**.

mess[1] /mes/ n a mixture disagreeable to the sight or taste; a medley; (a person in a state of) disorder or confusion; embarrassment; a bungle; a dish of food, a course or meal (*archaic*); a set of usually four people served together at a banquet (*archaic*); a set of four (Shakesp); a number of people who take their meals together, *esp* in the armed forces; a place where such a group take their meals together; a cow's yield at one milking (*dialect*); a quantity of anything, *esp* of a specified food (*archaic* or *N Am dialect*); a take or haul of fish (US); a dish of soft, pulpy or sloppy food; liquid, pulpy or smeary dirt; excrement, *esp* of an animal (*inf*). ◆ vt to make a mess of (*usu* with *up*); to subject to a violent physical attack (with *up*) (US *inf*); to muddle; to make dirty or messy; to supply with a meal or food (*milit*). ◆ vi to make a mess; to play or trifle (with *with*); to meddle, involve oneself (with *with* or *in*) (*inf*; *esp* US); to tangle or come into conflict (with *with*) (*inf*; *esp* US); to eat a meal, to dine (*archaic*); to eat at a common table; to belong to a mess. [OFr *mes* (Fr *mets*) a dish, from L *mittere*, *missum* to send, in LL to place]
■ **mess'ily** adv. **mess'iness** n. **mess'y** adj (**mess'ier**; **mess'iest**) confused, untidy (also *fig*); involving, or causing, dirt or mess; bungling.
❑ **mess deck** n (*naut*) the crew's living-quarters on board ship; the crew's dining-hall (US). **mess jacket** n a waist-length jacket worn by officers at a formal mess dinner. **mess kit** n formal evening wear for officers; a soldier's eating utensils (also **mess gear**). **mess'mate** n a member of the same mess; a commensal. **mess'-room** n. **mess'-tin** n a soldier's utensil serving as plate, cup and cooking vessel. **mess'-up** n a mess, muddle, bungle or confusion.
■ **mess about** or **around** (*inf*) to potter about; to behave in a foolish or annoying way; to meddle or interfere (with *with*); to treat badly or inconsiderately; to upset, put into a state of disorder or confusion; to have an adulterous or otherwise illicit sexual relationship (often with *with*). **mess of pottage** a material advantage accepted in exchange for something of higher worth, as by Esau (Bible, Genesis 25.29 ff). **mess or mell** (Scot) to associate, have to do. **mess up** (*inf*; *esp* US) to make a mess of things, fail in some endeavour; to confuse psychologically (*inf*, *esp* US). **no messing** (*sl*) without a shadow of doubt.

mess[2] /mes/ n an obsolete form of **mass**[2].

message /mes'ij/ n any communication sent from one person to another; an errand; an official communication of a president, governor, etc, to a legislature or council; the teaching that a poet, sage, prophet, has to communicate to the world; an amount of digital information transmitted as a whole between a terminal and a computer, or between computers on a network (*comput*); (*usu* in pl) domestic shopping, a journey for the purpose, or the goods bought (Scot). ◆ vt to send as a message; to send a message to; to transmit as by signalling. ◆ vi (Dickens) to carry a message. [Fr, from LL *missāticum*, from L *mittere*, *missum* to send]
■ **mess'aging** n any form of electronic communication in which a message is sent directly to its destination, eg by mobile phone. **mess'enger** /-ən-jər/ n a person who brings a message; a person employed to carry messages and perform errands; a forerunner; a light scudding cloud preceding a storm; a small object sent along a line, as a paper up a kite string; the secretary-bird; a rope or chain connecting a cable with the capstan for heaving up the anchor; an officer who executes the summonses and other writs of the Court of Session and Court of Justiciary (*usu* called **mess'enger-at-arms**; Scots law). ◆ vt to send by messenger.

◻ **message board** *n* a bulletin board (qv). **message box** *n* a box that appears on the screen of a computer conveying information, eg about an error. **mess'age-boy** or **mess'age-girl** *n* an errand boy or girl. **mess'age-stick** *n* (*Aust*) a carved stick carried as identification by an Aboriginal messenger. **message switching** *n* (*comput*) a communication system in which data is transmitted between computers on a network as a whole and not split into packets (see **packet switching** under **pack¹**). **message unit** *n* (*US*) a unit used in charging timed, eg long-distance, telephone calls. **messenger RNA** *n* (*biochem*) a short-lived, transient form of RNA which serves to carry genetic information from the DNA of the genes to the ribosomes where the requisite proteins are made (*abbrev* **m-RNA**). **mess'enger-wire** *n* a wire supporting an overhead cable.

■ **get the message** (*sl*) to understand. **king's** or **queen's messenger** an officer who carries official dispatches. **shoot** (or **kill**) **the messenger** to attack the bearer of bad news rather than the source of it.

messan /mes'ən/ (*Scot*) *n* a lapdog; a cur. [Perh Gaelic *measan*]

Messeigneurs see **Monseigneur**.

Messerschmitt /mes'ər-shmit/ *n* a German fighter aircraft used by the Luftwaffe in World War II, *esp* the ME-109. [Willy *Messerschmitt* (1898–1978), aircraft designer]

Messiah /mə-sī'ə/ *n* (also **Messī'as**) the expected deliverer of the Jews; by Christians, applied to Jesus; (also without *cap*) a hoped-for deliverer, saviour, or champion generally. [Gr *Messiās*, from Aramaic *m'shīhā*, Heb *māshīah* anointed, from *māshah* to anoint]

■ **Messī'ahship** *n*. **Messianic** /mes-i-an'ik/ *adj* of or relating to a Messiah; (also without *cap*) inspired, or as though inspired, by a Messiah. **Messī'anism** *n* belief in a Messiah. **Messī'anist** *n*.

Messidor /me-si-dör'/ *n* the tenth month of the French revolutionary calendar, roughly 19 June to 18 July. [Fr, from L *messis* harvest, and Gr *dōron* a gift]

Messier catalogue /me'syā kat'ə-log/ (*astron*) *n* a listing of 108 galaxies, star clusters and nebulae compiled in 1770 and still widely used, designating objects M1, M2, etc. [Charles *Messier*, French astronomer, compiler of the list]

Messieurs see **Monsieur**.

Messrs /mes'ərs/ *abbrev* : *Messieurs* (*Fr*), Sirs, Gentlemen; used as pl of **Mr**.

messuage /mes'wij/ (*law*) *n* a dwelling and offices with the adjoining lands appropriated to the household; a mansion-house and grounds. [Anglo-Fr; poss orig a misreading of *mesnage*; cf **ménage**]

mestee /me-stē'/ or **mustee** /mu-stē'/ *n* the offspring of a white person and a quadroon. [Sp *mestizo*, from a LL derivative of L *mixtus* mixed]

■ **mestizo** /mes-tē'zō, -thō/ or *fem* **mesti'za** *n* (*pl* **mesti'zos** or **mesti'zas**) a person of mixed (*esp* Spanish and Native American) parentage.

mesto /mes'tō/ (*music*) *adj* sad. [Ital]

Met /met/ *abbrev* : Meteorological; Metropolitan.

met¹ *pat* and *pap* of **meet¹**.

met² /met/ *n* short form of **meteorology**.

◻ **met'cast** *n* a weather forecast. **met man** *n* a weather forecaster. **Met Office** *n* the Meteorological Office.

met. or **metaph.** *abbrev* : metaphor; metaphorical; metaphysics.

meta- /me-tə-/ or (before a vowel) often **met-** /met-/ *combining form* signifying: among, with; after, later; often implies change, as in *metamorphose* ; beyond, above, as in *metamathematics* ; position beyond, as in *metacarpal*. In chemistry, **meta-** indicates (1) a derivative of, or an isomer or polymer of, the substance named, or (2) an acid or hydroxide derived from the **ortho-** form of the substance by loss of water molecules, or (3) a benzene substitution product in which the substituted atoms or groups are attached to two carbon atoms which are themselves separated by one carbon atom (in this sense commonly represented by **m**). [Gr *meta* among, with, beside, after]

■ **metacarp'al** *adj* (also *n*). **metacarp'us** *n* (*pl* **metacarp'i** /-ī/) (Gr *karpos* wrist) the part of the hand (or its bones) between the wrist and the fingers, or the corresponding part of an animal, eg the foreleg of a horse between 'knee' and fetlock. **met'acentre** *n* (Gr *kentron* point) the point of intersection of a vertical line through the centre of gravity of a body floating in equilibrium and that through the centre of gravity of the displaced liquid when the body is slightly displaced. **metacen'tric** *adj*. **metachromat'ic** *adj* (Gr *chroma* colour) of dyes, capable of staining cells so that they turn a different colour to that of the dye; of cells, taking a colour different to that of the dye with which they are stained; of or relating to metachromatism. **metachrō'matism** *n* change in colour. **metachrosis** /-krō'sis/ *n* (Gr *chrōsis* colouring) ability to change colour in animals. **metacognition** /-kog-nish'ən/ *n* (*psychol*) awareness and understanding of one's own thought

processes, enabling one to learn effectively. **met'adata** *n pl* information about information already supplied, eg details about a site on the Internet. **met'afiction** *n* fiction which self-consciously comments on its status as fiction. **metafic'tional** *adj*. **met'afile** *n* (*comput*) graphical information capable of being transferred between systems or software. **metagalac'tic** *adj*. **metagal'axy** *n* the whole universe considered as a system of galaxies; any system of galaxies. **metagen'esis** *n* (Gr *genesis* generation; *biol*) alternation of generations. **metagenet'ic** *adj*. **metagnathous** /met-ag'nə-thəs/ *adj* (Gr *gnathos* jaw) (of birds) having crossed mandibles; (of insects) having biting jaws in the larvae, sucking in the adult state. **met'alanguage** *n* a language or a system of symbols used to discuss another language or symbolic system. **metal'dehyde** *n* a polymer of acetaldehyde. **metalinguis'tic** *adj* of or relating to (a) metalanguage or to metalinguistics. **metalinguis'tically** *adv*. **metalinguis'tics** *n sing* the study of the relation between a language and other features of behaviour in a particular culture, of language structure in relation to meaning, of expression or gesture accompanying spoken language, etc. **metamatē'rial** *n* (*phys*) an artificially created material having properties not found in nature. **metamathemat'ics** *n sing* the logical analysis of formal mathematics, its concepts, terminology, use of symbols, etc. **met'amer** *n* (Gr *meros* a part; *chem*) a compound metameric with another. **met'amere** /-mēr/ *n* (*zool*) a segment, merosome, or somite. **metamer'ic** *adj* (of chemical compounds) having the same molecular weight, but different structures and chemical properties; of or relating to a metamere or metameres. **metamer'ically** *adv*. **metam'erism** *n* a particular form of isomerism in which different groups are attached to the same central atom (*chem*); segmentation of an animal along the primary axis, producing a series of homologous parts (*zool*). **met'aphase** *n* the stage of mitosis at which the chromosomes are attached to the spindle but have not yet segregated. **metaphos'phate** *n* a salt of metaphosphoric acid. **metaphosphor'ic** *adj* applied to an acid (HPO_3) containing a molecule less of water than orthophosphoric acid. **metapsychic** /met-ə-sī'kik/ or **metapsych'ical** *adj* (from **psychic** on the analogy of **metaphysics**). **metapsych'ics** *n sing* the study of psychic phenomena beyond the limits of ordinary or orthodox psychology; psychical research. **metapsycholog'ical** *adj*. **metapsychol'ogy** *n* theories and theorizing on psychological matters, such as the nature of the mind, which cannot be verified or falsified by experiment or reasoning. **metasequoi'a** *n* a conifer (*Metasequoia glyptostroboides*) discovered as a fossil and since found existing in China. **metasil'icate** /-i-kāt/ *n* a salt of metasilicic acid. **metasilic'ic** /-is'ik/ *adj* applied to an acid (H_2SiO_3). **metasōmat'ic** *adj*. **metasōm'atism** *n* (Gr *sōma*, *-atos* body; *geol*) metamorphism by chemical changes in minerals. **metastabil'ity** *n* a state which appears to be chemically stable, often because of the slowness with which equilibrium is attained, eg that of a supersaturated solution; a metastable state. **metastable** /met'ə-stā-bl/ *adj* having metastability (**metastable state** an excited state, *esp* of an atom which has, however, insufficient energy to emit radiation). **metatarsal** /-tär'sl/ *adj* (also *n*). **metatar'sus** *n* (Gr *tarsos* the flat of the foot) that part of the foot, or its bones, between the tarsus and the toes, or the corresponding part of an animal. **met'atheory** *n* philosophical discussion of a particular theory; investigation of the properties of a formal language (*logic*). **Metatheria** /-thē'ri-ə/ *n pl* (Gr *thērion* a wild beast) the marsupials. **metathē'rian** *adj* of or relating to the marsupials (also *n*). **metathoracic** /-thō-ras'ik/ *adj*. **metathorax** /-thō'raks/ *n* the third and last segment of an insect's thorax. **Metazoa** /met-ə-zō'ə/ *n pl* (*sing* **metazō'on**) (Gr *zōion* animal; also without *cap*) many-celled animals, *opp* to *Protozoa*. **metazō'an** *adj* and *n*. **metazō'ic** *adj*. **metempiric** /met-em-pir'ik/ or **metempir'ical** *adj* beyond the scope of experience; of or relating to metempiricism. **metempir'icism** /-i-sizm/ *n* the study of the existence of things beyond the scope of experience (also **metempirics**). **metempir'icist** *n*.

metabasis /me-tab'ə-sis/ *n* a transition. [Gr *metabasis*, from *meta* (see **meta-**), and *bainein* to go]

■ **metabatic** /met-ə-bat'ik/ *adj*.

metabolism /me-tab'ə-li-zm/ *n* the sum total of the chemical changes in living organisms, *esp* with regard to their influence on the generation of energy, the processing of waste products, etc; these changes as they affect a specific substance in an organism; metamorphosis. [Gr *metabolē* change]

■ **Metab'ola** *n pl* in some classifications, insects that undergo metamorphosis. **metabolic** /-bol'ik/ *adj* relating to an organism's metabolism; exhibiting metamorphosis. **metabol'ically** *adv*. **metab'olite** *n* a product of or a substance necessary for metabolism. **metab'olizable** or **-s-** *adj*. **metab'olize** or **-ise** *vt* and *vi* to subject to, or be changed by, metabolism. **metab'olome** *n* the complete set of metabolites in an organism. **metabonō'mic** *adj*. **metabonō'mics** *n sing* the study of metabolic responses to external stimuli. **metabotrop'ic** *adj* (*biochem*) denoting a neurotransmitter receptor which affects cell activity by means other than direct regulation of the cell's ion channels (cf **ionotropic** under **ion**).

❑ **metabolic syndrome** *n* a collection of symptoms, including excess weight, high blood pressure and high blood sugar, believed to increase the risk of heart disease, stroke and diabetes.

metacarpal...to...**metachromatism** see under **meta-**.

metachronism /me-tak'ro-ni-zm/ *n* (an example of) the error of dating an event too late, *opp* to **prochronism**. [Gr *metachronios, metachronos* anachronistic, out of date, from *meta* (see **meta-**), and *chronos* time]

metachrosis...to...**metagalaxy** see under **meta-**.

metage /mē'tij/ *n* official weighing of coal, grain, etc; the charge for such weighing. [**mete¹**]

metagenesis, metagenetic and **metagnathous** see under **meta-**.

metagrobolize or **-ise** /me-tə-grob'ə-līz/ or **metagrabolize** or **-ise** /-grab'/ *vt* to mystify; to puzzle out. [Obs Fr *metagraboulizer* (Rabelais)]

métairie /mā-te-rē'/ *n* a piece of land cultivated under the system of *métayage* (see under **métayer**). [Fr; see **métayer**]

metal /met'l/ *n* any of numerous opaque elementary substances, possessing a peculiar lustre, fusibility, conductivity for heat and electricity, readiness to form positive ions, eg gold; an alloy; that which behaves chemically like a true metal; courage or spirit (now spelt **mettle**); intrinsic quality; heavy metal music (*inf*); the collective guns or firepower of a warship (*obs*); or, or argent, as a tincture (*heraldry*); molten material for glass-making; country-rock (*mining*); broken stones used for macadamized roads or as ballast for railways; (in *pl*) the rails of a railroad. ◆ *adj* made of metal. ◆ *vt* (**met'alling** or (*N Am*) **met'aling**; **met'alled** or (*N Am*) **met'aled**) to provide or cover with metal. [OFr, from L *metallum*, from Gr *metallon* a mine]
■ **met'alled** *adj* covered with metal, as a road. **metallic** /mi-tal'ik/ *adj* relating to, or like, metal; consisting of metal; (of a colour, etc) having the lustre characteristic of metals; (of a sound) like the sound produced by metal when struck. **metall'ically** *adv*. **met'alliding** *n* a high-temperature electrolytic technique for creating metal alloys on the surface of metals. **metallif'erous** *adj* bearing or yielding metal. **met'alline** *adj* of, like, consisting of, or mixed with, metal. **met'alling** *n* road metal, broken stones. **met'allist** or (*N Am*) **met'alist** *n* a worker in metals. **metalliza'tion** or **-s-** *n*. **met'allize** or **-ise** or (*N Am*) **met'alize** *vt* to make metallic; to deposit thin metal films on glass or plastic. **met'alloid** *n* a non-metal; an element resembling a metal in some respects, such as selenium or tellurium. ◆ *adj* (also **metalloid'al**) relating to, or of the nature of, the metalloids. **met'ally** *adj* suggestive of metal.
❑ **metal detector** *n* an electronic device for detecting the presence of metallic objects. **metal fatigue** *n* a failure caused in metal by continuous varied stresses on it. **met'almark** *n* any butterfly of the family Riodinidae, whose wing-markings have a metallic appearance. **metalorgan'ic** same as **metallo-organic** (see under **metallo-**). **met'alware** *n*. **met'alwork** *n*. **met'alworker** *n*. **met'alworking** *n*.

metalanguage and **metaldehyde** see under **meta-**.

metalepsis /me-tə-lep'sis/ (*rhetoric*) *n* metonymy, *esp* of a double, complicated, or indirect kind. [Gr *metalēpsis* substitution]
■ **metalep'tic** or **metalep'tical** *adj*.

metalinguistics see under **meta-**.

metall. or **metal.** *abbrev*: metallurgical; metallurgy.

metallic...to...**metallize** see under **metal**.

metallo- /me-ta-lō- or me-ta-lo-/ *combining form* denoting metal. [See **metal**]
■ **metallogenet'ic** *adj* (*geol*) relating to metallogeny. **metallogēn'ic** (or /-jen'/) *adj* (*geol*) (of an element) occurring as an ore or a naturally occurring metal, as opposed to in rocks. **metallog'eny** *n* (from Fr, from Gr *genesis* origin; *geol*) (the study of) the origin and distribution of mineral deposits, *esp* with regard to petrological, etc, features. **metallog'rapher** *n*. **metallograph'ic** *adj*. **metallograph'ically** *adv*. **metallog'raphy** *n* the study of the structure and constitution of metals.
❑ **metallo-organ'ic** *adj* (*chem*) (of a molecule) containing a metal atom and a carbon atom, although not necessarily directly bound together. **metall'ophone** *n* an instrument like a xylophone with metal bars, the hammers being operated by hand or by means of a keyboard. **metallopro'tein** *n* (*biol*) a conjugated protein in which the prosthetic group is a metal. **metallopro'teinase** *n* (*biol*) any of a group of enzymes that, in the presence of a metallic cofactor, destroy connective tissues and are active in the spread of tumours.

metalloid see under **metal**.

metallurgy /met'ə-lûr-ji or me-tal'ər-ji/ *n* art and science applied to metals, including extraction from ores, refining, alloying, shaping, treating, and the study of structure, constitution and properties. [Gr *metallourgeein* to mine, from *metallon* a mine, and *ergon* work]

■ **metallur'gic** or **metallur'gical** *adj* relating to metallurgy. **metallur'gically** *adv*. **met'allurgist** *n* (or, now more *usu* /-al'/).

metally see under **metal**.

metamaterial...to...**metamerism** see under **meta-**.

metamorphosis /me-tə-mör'fə-sis/ or /met-ə-mör-fō'sis/ *n* (pl **metamor'phoses** /-sēz/ or /-fō'sēz/) a change of shape, transformation; the transformation of a human being to an animal, a stone, tree, etc (*folklore*); the marked change which some living beings undergo in the course of growth, as caterpillar to butterfly, tadpole to frog. [Gr *metamorphōsis*, from *meta* (see **meta-**), and *morphē* form]
■ **metamor'phic** *adj* showing or relating to change of form; formed by alteration of existing rocks by heat, pressure, or other processes in the earth's crust (*geol*). **metamor'phism** *n* transformation of rocks in the earth's crust (**contact metamorphism**, by contact with or neighbourhood of igneous material, or **regional metamorphism**, owing to general conditions over a wide region). **metamor'phist** *n* a person who believes that Christ's body merged into the Deity at the Ascension. **metamor'phose** /-fōz/ or /-fōs/ *vt* to transform; to subject to metamorphism or metamorphosis; to develop in another form. ◆ *vi* to undergo metamorphosis.
❑ **metamorphic technique** *n* a form of therapy using massage on specific areas of the feet, hands, or head which are believed to relate to the body's prenatal experiences (also called **prenatal therapy**).

metanoia /me-tə-noi'ə/ *n* repentance; a fundamental change in character, way of life, etc; a spiritual conversion. [Gr *metanoia* a change of mind or heart, repentance]

metaphase see under **meta-**.

metaphor /met'ə-fər or -för/ *n* a figure of speech by which a thing is spoken of as being that which it only resembles, as when a ferocious person is called a tiger. [Gr *metaphorā*, from *meta* (see **meta-**), and *pherein* to carry]
■ **metaphoric** /-for'ik/ or **metaphor'ical** *adj*. **metaphor'ically** *adv*. **met'aphorist** *n*.
❑ **mixed metaphor** *n* an expression in which two or more metaphors are incongruously joined, such as *to take arms against a sea of troubles*.

metaphosphate and **metaphosphoric** see under **meta-**.

metaphrase /met'ə-frāz/ *n* (also **metaphrasis** /-af'rə-sis/) a turning of prose into verse, or verse into prose; a rendering in a different style or form; an altered wording; a word-for-word translation. ◆ *vt* to translate word-for-word; to alter the wording of. [Gr *metaphrasis*, from *meta* (see **meta-**), and *phrasis* a speaking]
■ **met'aphrast** /-frast/ *n* a person who produces a metaphrase. **metaphrast'ic** *adj*.

metaphysics /me-tə-fiz'iks/ *n sing* the branch of philosophy which investigates the first principles of nature and thought; ontology or the science of being; loosely and vaguely applied to anything abstruse, abstract, philosophical, subtle, transcendental, occult, supernatural or magical. [Orig applied to those writings of Aristotle which in the accepted order came after (Gr *meta*) those dealing with natural science (*ta physika*, from *physis* nature)]
■ **metaphys'ic** *n* metaphysics; philosophical groundwork. ◆ *adj* metaphysical. **metaphys'ical** *adj* relating to metaphysics; abstract; beyond nature or the physical; supernatural; fanciful; addicted to far-fetched conceits (applied by Johnson to Donne, Cowley and others). **metaphys'ically** *adv*. **metaphysician** /-ish'ən/ *n* a person skilled in metaphysics.

metaplasia /me-tə-plā'si-ə/ *n* tissue transformation, such as of cartilage into bone. [Gr *metaplasis, metaplasmos* a moulding afresh, from *meta* (see **meta-**), and *plassein* to form]
■ **metaplasis** /-ap'lə-sis/ *n* metaplasia; the period of maturity in the life cycle. **met'aplasm** /-plazm/ *n* cell-contents other than protoplasm; a change in a word by addition, dropping or exchange of parts. **metaplast'ic** *adj*.

metaplot see **metapelet**.

metapsychic...to...**metastable** see under **meta-**.

metastasis /me-tas'tə-sis/ *n* (pl **metas'tasēs**) transfer of disease from its original site to another part of the body (*pathol*); a secondary tumour distant from the original site of disease (*pathol*); removal from one place to another; transition; transformation; paramorphic change in rocks; metabolism (*rare*). [Gr *metastasis* change of place, from *meta* (see **meta-**), and *stasis* a standing]
■ **metas'tasize** or **-ise** *vi* (of a tumour, etc) to pass to another part of the body. **metastatic** /-stat'ik/ *adj*.

metatarsal and **metatarsus** see under **meta-**.

metate /mə-tä'tē or -tä'tā/ *n* (in Mexico, SW USA, etc) a stone with a concave surface, used in conjunction with a mano (qv) to grind maize or other grain. [Mex Sp, from Nahuatl *metlatl*]

Metatheria and **metatherian** see under **meta-**.

metathesis /me-tath'ə-sis/ n (pl **metath'esēs**) transposition or exchange of places, esp between the sounds or letters of a word; double decomposition (chem). [Gr, from metatithenai to transpose, from meta (see **meta-**), and tithenai to place]
■ **metath'esize** or **-ise** vt to transpose (by metathesis). **metathetic** /met-ə-thet'ik/ or **metathet'ical** adj.

metathoracic and **metathorax** see under **meta-**.

métayer /mā-tā-yā'/ or mā'/ n a tenant farmer who gives a fixed proportion of the crops, rather than money, in payment for rent. [Fr, from LL medietārius, from L medietās half, from medius middle]
■ **métayage** /-yäzh'/ or mā'/ n this system.

Metazoa, etc see under **meta-**.

metcast see under **met²**.

mete¹ /mēt/ vt (pat **mēt'ed** or (Spenser) **mott**) (with out) to measure; to apportion. ◆ n measure. [OE metan; Ger messen]
❑ **mete'stick**, **mete'wand** or **mete'yard** n a measuring-rod.

mete² /mēt/ n a boundary or limit. [L mēta a goal or boundary]

metempiric, etc see under **meta-**.

metempsychosis /met-emp-si-kō'sis/ n (pl **metempsychō'sēs**) the passing of the soul after death into some other body. [Gr metempsȳchōsis, from meta (see **meta-**), en in, and psȳchē soul]
■ **metempsychō'sist** n.

meteor /mē'tyər, -ti-ər or -ti-ör/ n orig, any atmospheric phenomenon (now rare); a luminous appearance; one of countless small bodies travelling through space, seen when they enter the earth's atmosphere as aerolites, fireballs or shooting stars; anything brilliant or dazzling but short-lived (fig). [Gr ta meteōra things on high, from meta and the root of aeirein to lift]
■ **meteoric** /mē-ti-or'ik/ adj above the earth's surface; atmospheric; influenced by weather; of or relating to meteors in any sense; of the nature of a meteor; transiently flashing like a meteor; remarkably rapid (fig). **meteor'ically** adv in the manner of a meteor. **me'teorist** n an expert on meteors. **me'teorite** n a meteor that has fallen to earth as a lump of stone or metal. **meteorit'ic**, **meteorit'ical** or **me'teorital** /-īt-l/ adj. **meteorit'icist** n. **meteorit'ics** n sing the science or study of meteors. **me'teorogram** n a meteorograph record. **me'teorograph** n an instrument by which several meteorological elements are recorded in combination. **me'teoroid** n a meteor that has not reached the earth's atmosphere. **meteoroid'al** adj. **me'teorolite** n (Gr lithos stone) a meteoric stone. **meteorolog'ic** or **meteorolog'ical** adj. **meteorolog'ically** adv. **meteorol'ogist** n. **meteorol'ogy** n the study of weather and climate. **me'teorous** adj (or, esp in poetry /mē-tē'ər-əs/) like a meteor, meteoric.
❑ **meteor crater** n a crater formed by the fall of a meteor. **meteoric iron** n iron as found in meteorites. **meteoric stones** n pl aerolites. **Meteorological Office** n a government department issuing weather forecasts, etc. **meteorological satellite** n a satellite used for weather observation and forecasting, carrying television cameras to transmit cloud-formation changes and radiometers to measure terrestrial and solar radiation. **meteor** (or **meteoric**) **shower** or **storm** n the profusion of meteors visible as the earth passes through a meteor swarm. **meteor streams** n pl streams of dust revolving about the sun, whose intersection by the earth causes meteor showers. **meteor swarm** n a number of meteoroids travelling on parallel courses.

meteor. or **meteorol.** abbrev : meteorology.

meteorism /mē'tyə-ri-zm or -ti-ə-/ (med) n excessive accumulation of gas in the intestines; tympanites. [Medical L meteōrismus, from Gr meteōrismos raising, or being raised, up, from meteōrizein to lift; cf **meteor**]

meter¹ /mē'tər/ n a measurer; an apparatus for measuring, esp the quantity of a fluid, or of electricity, used; a gauge or indicator; a parking meter. ◆ vt to measure by a meter. [**mete¹**]
❑ **meter maid** or **man** n (facetious) a traffic warden.

meter² US spelling of **metre¹,²**.

-meter /-mi-tər or -mē-/ combining form denoting: an instrument for measuring; a line of poetry with a specified number of feet, as in pentameter. [Gr metron measure]
■ **-metric** /-met-rik/ or **-metrical** adj combining form. **-metrically** adv combining form. **-metry** /-mi-tri/ combining form signifying: measuring; the science of measuring.

meth /meth/ n an informal short form of **methadone** or **methamphetamine**.

methadone /meth'ə-dōn/ (pharm) n a synthetic addictive drug similar to morphine, used in the treatment of drug addiction (also **meth'adon** /-don/). [dimethylamino-, diphenyl and heptanone]

methamphetamine /meth-am-fet'ə-mēn/ or **methylamphetamine** /mē-thil-/ n a methyl derivative of amphetamine with rapid and long-lasting action, illicitly used as a stimulant to the central nervous system.

methanal /meth'ə-nal/ n formaldehyde.

methane /mē'thān or meth'ān/ n an odourless, colourless, inflammable gas (CH₄), the simplest hydrocarbon, produced by decomposition of vegetable matter in wet conditions (also called **marsh-gas**, **fire damp**). [**methyl**]
■ **methan'ogen** n (biol) a micro-organism that produces methane.
❑ **methanoic** /meth-ə-nō'ik/ **acid** n formic acid. **methanom'eter** n (mining) an instrument for detecting the presence of methane in mines.

methanol /meth'ə-nol/ n methyl alcohol, wood spirit, used as a solvent and antifreeze. [**methane** and **-ol²**]

methaqualone /me-thə-kwā'lōn/ n a hypnotic drug (C₁₆H₁₄N₂O), formerly prescribed as a sedative.

Methedrine® /meth'ə-drēn/ n a former proprietary name for an amphetamine, methylamphetamine hydrochloride, a soft drug, but used by drug addicts.

metheglin /me-theg'lin/ n a spiced or medicated mead, traditionally associated with Wales. [Welsh meddyglyn, from meddyg medicinal (from L medicus physician), and llyn liquor]

methicillin /me-thi-sil'in/ n a semi-synthetic antibiotic drug used to treat infections by penicillin-resistant staphylococcal bacteria. [methyl and penicillin]

methinks /mē-thingks'/ (archaic or joc) or (obs) **methinketh** /-thing'kəth/ or **methink** /-thingk'/ (archaic or humorous) vt (impers; pat **methought** /mi-thöt'/) it seems to me; I think. [OE mē thyncth it seems to me; thyncan to seem, has been confused with thencan to think; cf Ger dünken to seem, denken to think]

methionine /me-thī'o-nēn/ (chem) n an essential sulphur-bearing amino acid.

method /meth'əd/ n the mode or rule used in carrying out a task or accomplishing an aim; orderly procedure; manner; orderly arrangement; methodicalness; classification; a system or rule; manner of performance; an instruction book systematically arranged (archaic). [Gr methodos, from meta after, and hodos a way]
■ **methodic** /mi-thod'ik/ or **method'ical** adj carried out or arranged in a systematic and orderly way; disposed in a just and natural manner; observing method, inclined to be systematic; formal. **method'ically** adv. **method'icalness** n. **Meth'odism** n (Christianity) the principles and practice of the Methodists. **meth'odist** n a person who observes method; (with cap) a follower of John and Charles Wesley, a name given first to a group of students at Oxford 'for the regularity of their lives as well as studies'; a member of the Methodist Church, a nonconformist denomination founded in 1795 on John Wesley's doctrines. ◆ adj of or relating to Methodism. **Methodist'ic** or **Methodist'ical** adj resembling the Methodists, esp as viewed by opponents; strict in religious matters. **Methodist'ically** adv. **meth'odize** or **-ise** vt to reduce to a system or method; to arrange in an orderly way. **meth'odizer** or **-s-** n. **methodolog'ical** adj. **methodolog'ically** adv. **methodol'ogist** n. **methodol'ogy** n a system of methods and rules applicable to research or work in a given science or art; evaluation of subjects taught, and the principles and techniques of teaching them. **Meth'ody** n a disrespectful nickname for a Methodist.
❑ **method acting** n acting as a personal living of a part, contrasted with mere technical performance (also called **the method**).

methomania /me-thō-mā'ni-ə/ n an intermittent morbid craving for alcohol. [Gr methē strong drink, and maniā madness]

methotrexate /me-thō-trek'sāt/ n a drug (C₂₀H₂₂N₈O₅) used in the treatment of cancer and arthritis and in bone marrow transplantation.

methought see **methinks**.

methoxamine hydrochloride /me-thok'sə-mēn hī-drō-klö'rīd/ n a drug formerly prescribed to slow down the action of the heart.

meths /meths/ n sing short form of **methylated spirit** (see under **methyl**).

Methuselah /mi-thū'zə-lə or -thoo'/ n a patriarch said to have lived 969 years (Bible, Genesis 5.27); any very old person; (without cap) a very large wine bottle (holding about 6½ quarts); (without cap) as a bottle-size of champagne, the equivalent of eight ordinary bottles.

methyl /mē'thīl or meth'il/ (chem) n the radical (CH₃) of wood (or methyl) alcohol (CH₃OH). [Gr methy wine, and hȳlē wood]
■ **meth'ylate** vt to mix or impregnate with methyl alcohol; to introduce the radical CH₃ into. ◆ n a methyl alcohol derivative; a compound with a methyl group. **methylā'tion** n. **meth'ylene** n the hypothetical compound CH₂. **methyl'ic** adj.
❑ **methyl alcohol** n methanol (CH₃OH). **methylamine** /-ə-mēn'/ n an inflammable gas (CH₃NH₂), obtainable from herring brine (see also **dimethylamine** under **dimethyl** and **trimethylamine** under **trimethyl**). **methylaminobenzene** n another name for **toluidine**. **methylamphetamine** n see **methamphetamine**. **methylated spirit** or **spirits** n alcohol made undrinkable (and therefore exempt

from tax) with methyl alcohol, and *usu* other things, used as a fuel in lamps, etc. **methyl chloride** *n* a refrigerant and local anaesthetic. **methyldo'pa** *n* an antihypertensive drug ($C_{10}H_{13}NO_4$). **methylene blue** *n* a blue dye used to indicate pH value. **methyl group** *n* (*chem*) the monovalent radical CH_3. **methylmer'cury** *n* a toxic organic compound of mercury. **methylphen'idate** *n* a compound that stimulates the central nervous system, used in treating attention deficit disorder. **methyl-propyl ether** *n* an inhalation anaesthetic. **methyltestos'terone** /-ōn/ *n* a synthetic androgen with similar actions and functions to those of testosterone. **methyl violet** *n* an antiseptic dye used as a stain in microscopy and formerly used as a disinfectant, a mixture of the hydrochlorides of tetra-, penta-, and hexamethylpararosaniline; crystal violet.

METI *abbrev* : Ministry of Economy, Trade and Industry (in Japan).

metic /met'ik/ (*hist*) *n* (in ancient Greece) a resident alien in a city, subject to a special tax. [Gr *metoikos*, from *meta* indicating change, and *oikos* a house]

metical /met'i-kəl/ *n* the standard monetary unit of Mozambique (100 centavos). [Port *metical*, from Ar *mithqāl* a measure of weight]

meticulous /me-tik' yə-ləs/ or -yŭ-/ *adj* scrupulously careful; overcareful; timid (*obs*). [L *meticulōsus* frightened, from *metus* fear] ■ **metic'ulously** *adv*. **metic'ulousness** *n*.

métier /mā'tyā/ *n* one's calling or business; that in which one is specially skilled. [Fr, from L *ministerium*]

metif /mā'tēf/ (also with *cap*) *n* the offspring of a white person and a quadroon. [Fr; cf **mestizo**]

Metis /mē'tis/ *n* a Greek personification of prudence. [Gr *mētis*]

Métis /mā-tēs'/ (also without *cap*) *n* (pl **Métis** /-tēs' or -tēz'/) (also *fem* **Métisse**) in Canada, a person of mixed white (*esp* French-Canadian) and Native Canadian parentage; (without *cap*) any person of mixed descent. [Fr; cf **mestizo**]

metol /mē'tol/ *n* p-methylaminophenol sulphate, the basis of a rapid developer for photographic negatives. [*Metol*, trademark, arbitrarily named by the inventor]

Metonic /mi-ton'ik/ *adj* of or relating to the Athenian astronomer *Metōn* or his cycle (**Metonic cycle** beginning on 27 June, 432BC) of 19 years after which the moon's phases recur on the same days of the year.

metonym /met'ə-nim/ *n* the name of a single aspect of or adjunct to a thing used as a way of referring to the whole thing itself, such as 'the ring' to mean 'boxing'. [Gr *metōnymiā*, from *meta*, indicating change, and *onyma* a name] ■ **metonym'ic** or **metonym'ical** *adj*. **metonym'ically** *adv*. **metonymy** /mi-ton'i-mi/ *n* the use of metonyms.

me-too see under **me**[1].

metope[1] /met'ə-pē or met'ōp/ (*archit*) *n* the slab, plain or sculptured, between the triglyphs of a Doric frieze. [Gr *metopē*, from *meta* and *opē* an opening for a beam-end]

metope[2] /met'ōp/ *n* the face, forehead or frontal surface generally. [Gr *metōpon* forehead, literally between the eyes, from *meta* and *ōps* eye] ■ **metopic** /mit-op'ik/ *adj*. **metopism** /met'ə-pizm/ *n* the condition of having a persistent metopic or frontal suture. **metoposcop'ic** or **metoposcop'ical** *adj*. **metopos'copist** *n*. **metoposcopy** /met-ə-pos'kə-pi/ *n* (Gr *skopeein* to look) the study of character from the physiognomy.

metopon /mi-tō'pon/ *n* a pain-relieving drug derived from opium but less habit-forming than morphine.

metopryl /met'ō-pril/ *n* an anaesthetic related to ether, but more powerful and having less disturbing after-effects.

metre[1] or (*US*) **meter** /mē'tər/ *n* a base SI unit, the unit of length (symbol **m**), *orig* intended to be one ten-millionth of the distance from pole to equator; later the distance between two marks on a platinum-iridium bar kept in Paris; currently defined as the length of the path travelled by light in a vacuum during a time interval of a specific fraction of a second; by British Act of Parliament (1963) 1 yard equals 0.9144 metre. [Fr *mètre*, from Gr *metron* measure] ■ **metric** /met'rik/ *adj* relating to the metre, or to the metric system. **met'rically** *adv*. **met'ricate** *vt* and *vi* to convert or change to the metric system. **metrica'tion** *n*. ❏ **me'tre-kil'ogram-sec'ond** *adj* relating to a system of scientific units for length, mass and time (*abbrev* **MKS**), now largely superseded by the SI. **me'tre-kil'ogram-sec'ond-am'pere** *adj* relating to the Giorgi system of scientific units for length, mass, time and current (*abbrev* **MKSA**). **metric hundredweight** see under **hundred**. **metric system** *n* the SI or any decimal system of weights and measures. **metric ton** see under **tonne**.

metre[2] or (*US*) **meter** /mē'tər/ *n* the regulated succession of groups of syllables (long and short, stressed and unstressed) in which poetry is usually written; verse, or poetry generally; a scheme of versification,

the character of a stanza as consisting of a given number of lines composed of feet of a given number, arrangement, and kind; musical time. ◆ *vt* and *vi* to versify. [OE *mēter* and OFr *metre*, both from L *metrum*, from Gr *metron* measurement, metre; and partly directly] ■ **metred** /mē'tərd/ *adj* rhythmical. **metric** /met'rik/ or **met'rical** *adj* relating to metre; in metre; consisting of verses. **met'rically** *adv*. **metrician** /me-trish'ən/ *n* a metricist. **met'ricist** /-sist/ *n* a person skilled in metres; someone who writes in metre. **met'ricize** or **-ise** /-sīz/ *vt* to analyse the metre of. **met'rics** *n sing* the art or science of versification (also **met'ric**). **metrifica'tion** *n* metrical structure; the act of writing verse. **met'rifier** *n* a versifier. **met'rist** *n* a person skilled in the use of metre; a person who studies metre. **metromā'nia** *n* a mania for writing verse.

■ **common metre** a quatrain in eights and sixes, of four and of three iambic feet alternately (also **service metre**, from its use in the metrical psalms, etc, and **ballad metre**, from its use in old ballads). **long metre** an octosyllabic quatrain, the four lines with four feet each. **short metre** the quatrain in sixes, with the third line octosyllabic.

metric[1] /met'rik/ *adj* quantitative. [Gr *metron* measure] ■ **met'rical** *adj* relating to measurement. **met'rically** *adv*. **met'rics** *n sing* the theory of measurement. **metrologic** /-loj'ik/ or **metrolog'ical** *adj*. **metrol'ogist** *n*. **metrol'ogy** *n* the science of weights and measures, or of weighing and measuring.

metric[2] see under **metre**[1].

metric[3] see under **metre**[2].

-metric and **-metrically** see under **-meter**.

metricate see under **metre**[1].

metri causa /met'rē kow'zə/ or **metri gratia** /grä'ti-ä or grä'shi-ə/ (*L*) for the sake of the metre; for metrical harmony.

metrician...to...metrist see under **metre**[2].

métro /mā'trō/ *n* (pl **mét'ros**) (often with *cap*) an urban railway system, running wholly or partly underground, *esp* and *orig* the Paris subway (also **metro** or **Metro**). [Fr *métro*. Abbrev of *chemin de fer métropolitain* metropolitan railway]

metro- or (before a vowel) **metr-** /mē-tr(ō)-, me-, mə-/ *combining form* signifying the uterus. [Gr *metra* womb] ■ **metritis** /mə-trī'tis/ *n* inflammation of the uterus. **metrorrhagia** /mē-trō-rā'ji-ə or me-/ *n* (Gr *-rragia*, from *rhēgnynai* to break, burst) bleeding from the uterus between menstrual periods.

metrology see under **metric**[1].

metromania see under **metre**[2].

metronidazole /me-trə-nī'də-zōl/ *n* a synthetic antibiotic drug used to treat trichomoniasis and other vaginal infections. [*methyl*, n*itro*- and im*idazole*]

metronome /met'rə-nōm/ *n* an instrument with an inverted pendulum that can be set to beat so many times a minute, the loud ticking giving the right speed of performance for a piece of music. [Gr *metron* measure, and *nomos* law] ■ **metronomic** /-nom'ik/ *adj*.

metronymic /met-rə-nim'ik/ or **matronymic** /mat-/ *adj* derived from the name of one's mother or other female ancestor; indicating the mother; using such a system of naming. ◆ *n* a name so derived (cf **patronymic**). [Gr *mētēr*, -*tros* mother, and *onyma* name]

metroplex /met'rō-pleks/ (*esp US*) *n* a large urban or metropolitan area, *esp* that formed by more than one city and the adjoining suburbs. [*metropolitan* and com*plex*]

metropolis /mə-trop'ə-lis/ *n* (pl **metrop'olises**) the capital of a country, county, etc; the chief cathedral city of a country, such as Canterbury of England, or chief see of a province; the mother city of an ancient Greek colony; the mother country or state of a colony; a chief centre, seat or focus; the main habitat of a particular species (*biol*). [Gr *mētropolis*, from *mētēr* mother, and *polis* city] ■ **metropolitan** /met-rə-pol'i-tən/ *adj* of a metropolis; of or comprising a city and its suburbs; of the mother church. ◆ *n* the bishop of a metropolis, presiding over the other bishops of a province, in the Eastern Orthodox churches, a person ranking between an archbishop and a patriarch, in the Roman Catholic Church and the Church of England, an archbishop; an inhabitant of a metropolis. **metropol'itanate** *n*. **metropol'itanism** *n*. **metropol'itanize** or **-ise** *vt* to make into or like a metropolis. **metropolit'ical** *adj*. ❏ **metropolitan area network** *n* a computer network operating over a city or community (*abbrev* **MAN**). **metropolitan county** or **district** *n* a county or district in a heavily-populated industrial area of England, the district running more, and the county fewer, public services than other districts or counties.

metrorrhagia see under **metro-**.

metrosexual /me-trō-sek'sū-əl or -shoo-əl/ (*inf*) *n* a heterosexual man who takes a keen interest in traditionally non-male activities such as fashion and personal grooming. ◆ *adj* of or relating to such a person. [Blend of **metropolitan** and **heterosexual**]

metrostyle /*met'*rə-stīl/ *n* a device for regulating speed in a player piano. [Gr *metron* measure, and *stȳlos* a pillar]

-metry see under **-meter**.

mettle /*met'*l/ *n* temperament; ardent temperament; spirit; sprightliness; courage. ◆ *adj* (*Scot*) mettlesome. [**metal**]

■ **mett'led** or **mett'lesome** *adj* high-spirited; ardent; (of horses) lively. **mett'lesomeness** *n*.

■ **put** (**someone**) **on his** or **her mettle** to rouse (a person) to his or her best efforts.

meu /mū/ *n* the plant baldmoney or spignel. [L *mēum*, from Gr *mēon*]

meum et tuum /mē'əm et tū'əm or me'ŭm et too'ŭm/ (*L*) mine and thine.

meunière /mə-nyer' or mø-nyer'/ *adj* (of food, *esp* fish) lightly coated in flour and fried in butter, then served in butter, lemon juice and herbs, *esp* parsley. [Fr *à la meunière* in the manner of the miller's wife (from the coating of flour)]

meuse[1], **muse** or **mews** /mūs or mūz/ *n* a way of escape through a hedge, etc. ◆ *vi* to pass through a meuse. [OFr *muce* a place for hiding things]

meuse[2] see under **mew**[3].

MeV *abbrev* : mega-electronvolt(s).

meve /mēv/ an obsolete form of **move** (*v*).

Mevlevi /mev-lə-vī'/ or **Mawlawi** /mow-lä-wī'/ *n* (pl **Mevlevīs'** or **Mawlawīs'**) (a member of) an order of Sufis *orig* from Turkey, practising ritual dancing as an aid to religious meditation (also called **whirling dervish**). [Turk *Mevlevi* or Pers *Mawlāwīya*, from *mawlānāa*, literally, our master, title given to a Sufi master]

mew[1] /mū/ *vi* (*esp* of a cat, kitten, or gull) to make a thin, high-pitched cry. ◆ *n* this sound. ◆ *interj* (*obs*) expressing derision. [Imit]

mew[2] /mū/ *n* a gull. [OE *mæw*; Du *meeuw*, ON *mār*, Ger *Möwe*]

mew[3] /mū/ *vt* to shed, moult or cast; to change, as the covering or dress; to confine, as in a cage. ◆ *vi* to shed antlers or feathers; to moult. ◆ *n* the process of moulting; a cage for hawks, *esp* while mewing; a coop; a place of confinement; a retreat; a hiding-place. [OFr *muer*, from L *mūtāre* to change]

■ **mews** or **meuse** /mūz or mūs/ *n* (*orig pl* of **mew**, now commonly as *sing* with new *pl* **mews'es**) a street or yard of stabling (often converted into dwelling-houses or garages), so called from the king's mews at Charing Cross when hawks were succeeded by horses.

mewl /mūl/ *vi* to mew; to cry feebly, as a child. [Imit]

■ **mewl'er** *n*.

mews[1] see under **mew**[3].

mews[2] see **meuse**[1].

MEX *abbrev* : Mexico (IVR).

Mex. *abbrev* : Mexican; Mexico.

Mexican /mek'si-kən/ *adj* of or relating to the republic of *Mexico* in Central America, or its people or the Nahuatl language. ◆ *n* a native or citizen of Mexico; an Aztec; the Nahuatl language; a Mexican dollar; a coarse cotton cloth. [Sp *Mexicano*, now *Mejicano*]

❑ **Mexican hog** *n* the peccary. **Mexican orange blossom** *n* an ornamental evergreen plant (*Choisya ternata*) with fragrant white flowers. **Mexican standoff** *n* (*US inf*) an impasse or stalemate. **Mexican tea** *n* a kind of goosefoot, used as an anthelminthic. **Mexican wave** *n* the wavelike effect (popularized during the 1986 World Cup in Mexico) produced when different groups of spectators stand up with hands raised and sit down again in a progressive movement around a stadium.

meynt see **ming**[1].

MEZ *abbrev* : *Mitteleuropäische Zeit* (*Ger*), Central European Time.

mezail see **mesail**.

meze, **mezze** or **mézé** /mä'zā/ *n* a type of appetizer or hors d'œuvre served in Greece, Turkey, Lebanon, etc, *esp* with an aperitif before dinner. [Turk *meze* a snack, an appetizer]

mezereon /me-zē'ri-ən/, also **mezereum** /-əm/ *n* a European shrub (*Daphne mezereum*) whose flowers appear in early spring; its extremely acrid bark, or the bark of related species, used in medicine. [Ar and Pers *māzaryūn*]

mezuza or **mezuzah** /mə-zŭz'ə/ *n* (pl **mezu'zahs** or **mezuzoth** /-zŭ-zōt'/) a parchment scroll containing scriptural texts that is placed in a case and fixed to the doorpost by some Jewish families as a sign of their faith. [Heb, literally, doorpost]

mezzaluna /met-sə-loo'nə/ *n* a kitchen implement with a curved blade and a handle at each end, used for chopping herbs, vegetables, etc. [Ital, literally, half-moon]

mezzanine /mez'ə-nēn/ *n* an entresol (also **mezzanine floor**; *archit*); a small low window in an attic, etc (also **mezzanine window**; *archit*); a room below the stage; the first balcony in a theatre, the circle (*N Am*). ◆ *adj* of or relating to a mezzanine. [Fr, from Ital *mezzanino*, from *mezzano*, from L *mediānus*, from *medius* middle]

❑ **mezzanine finance** *n* finance *usu* for the takeover of a large company, consisting of an unsecured, high-interest loan, sometimes with a share option for the lender.

mezza voce /met'sə vō'chä or med'zä/ (*music*) *adv* with medium volume or tone. ◆ *adj* played or sung in this style. ◆ *n* singing in this style. [Ital]

mezze see **meze**.

mezzo /met'sō/ *n* (pl **mez'zos**) a mezzo-soprano. ◆ *adj* (*music*) moderately. [Ital, literally, half]

mezzo-forte /met'sō- or med'zō-för'tā/ (*music*) *adv* moderately loudly. ◆ *adj* moderately loud. [Ital]

Mezzogiorno /met-sō-jör'nō/ *n* southern Italy, including Sardinia and Sicily. [Ital, literally, midday]

mezzo-piano /met'sō- or med'zō-pyä'nō, also -pē-ä'nō/ (*music*) *adv* moderately softly. ◆ *adj* moderately soft. [Ital]

mezzo-relievo or **mezzo-rilievo** /met'sō- or med'zō-ril-yä'vō/ *n* (pl **mez'zo-relie'vos** or **-rilie'vos**) a degree of sculptural relief halfway between high and low relief; a carving or sculpture in this form. [Ital]

mezzo-soprano /met'sō- or med'zō-sō-prä'nō/ *n* (pl **mezzo-sopra'nos**) a voice between soprano and contralto; low soprano; a part for such a voice; a person possessing such a voice. [Ital *mezzo* middle, and *soprano*]

mezzotint /met'sō- or med'zō-tint/ *n* (also **mezzotinto** /-tin'tō/ (pl **mezzotin'tos**)) a method of copperplate engraving giving an even gradation of tones by roughening a plate and removing the burr for lights; an impression from a plate so produced. ◆ *vt* to engrave using this method. [Ital *mezzotinto*, from *mezzo* middle, half, and *tinto* tint, from L *tingere, tinctum* to dye]

■ **mez'zotinter** *n*.

MF *abbrev* : machine-finished; medium frequency; Middle French; multi-frequency.

mf (*music*) *abbrev* : mezzo-forte.

MFA *abbrev* : Multi-Fibre Arrangement.

mfd *abbrev* : manufactured.

MFH *abbrev* : Master of Foxhounds.

mfrs *abbrev* : manufacturers.

MFS *abbrev* : Marfan syndrome (qv).

mft *abbrev* : *mistura* (for classical L *mixtura*) *fiat*, let a mixture be made.

mfv *abbrev* : motor fleet vehicle.

MG *abbrev* : machine-gun; Morris Garages.

Mg (*chem*) *symbol* : magnesium.

mg *abbrev* : milligram(s).

mganga /m-gang'gə/ *n* in E Africa, a native doctor, a witch doctor. [Swahili]

MGB (*hist*) *abbrev* : *Ministerstvo Gosudarstvennoi Bezopasnosti* (*Russ*), the Ministry for State Security, the Soviet secret police from 1946 until replaced by the KGB in 1954.

MGL *abbrev* : Mongolia (IVR).

Mgr *abbrev* : Manager; Monseigneur; Monsignor.

MHA *abbrev* : Member of the House of Assembly.

MHC *abbrev* : major histocompatibility complex.

MHD *abbrev* : magnetic hydrodynamic.

MHG *abbrev* : Middle High German.

mho /mō/ *n* (pl **mhos**) formerly a unit of electric conductance, that of a body with a resistance of one ohm (now **siemens**). [**ohm** spelt backwards]

mhorr or **mohr** /mör/ *n* a W African gazelle. [Ar]

MHR *abbrev* : Member of the House of Representatives.

MHRA *abbrev* : Medicines and Healthcare Products Regulatory Agency; Modern Humanities Research Association.

MHz *abbrev* : megahertz.

MI *abbrev* : Michigan (US state); Military Intelligence.

❑ **MI5** *n* Security Service. **MI6** *n* Secret Intelligence Service (initials based on wartime Military Intelligence departments).

mi /mē/ (*music*) *n* the third note of the scale in sol-fa notation (also anglicized in spelling as **me**). [See **Aretinian**]

mi. *abbrev* : mile.

MIA (*milit*) *abbrev* : missing in action.

mia-mia /mī'ə-mī'ə/ n an Aboriginal dwelling hut. [From an Aboriginal language]

miaow /mi-ow'/ or /myow'/ n the characteristic cry of a cat. ♦ vi to make this sound. ♦ interj (inf) said in response to a catty or spiteful remark.

miarolitic /mi-ə-rō-lit'ik/ (geol) adj having irregular cavities into which the constituent minerals of the rock project with perfectly terminated crystals. [Ital miarolo, local name of a granite]

miasma /mi- or mī-az'mə/, also **miasm** /mī'a-zm/ n (pl **mias'mata**, **mias'mas** or **mi'asms**) foul vapours, eg from rotting matter; unwholesome air; any unwholesome atmosphere (lit and fig). [Gr miasma, -atos pollution, from miainein to stain, pollute]
■ **mias'mal**, **miasmat'ic**, **mias'matous**, **mias'mic** or **mias'mous** adj.

miaul /mi-öl' or mi-owl'/ vi to cry as a cat, to miaow. ♦ n a miaow. [Fr miauler ; imit]

mibuna /mi-boo'nə/ n a Japanese vegetable of the cabbage family, closely related to mizuna. [Jap]

Mic. (Bible) abbrev : (the Book of) Micah.

mic /mīk/ n a microphone.

mic. abbrev : mica.

mica /mī'kə/ n (pl **mi'cas**) a rock-forming mineral (muscovite, biotite, lepidolite, etc) with perfect basal cleavage, the laminae flexible and elastic, and usu transparent, of various colours, used as an electric insulator and as a substitute for glass. [L mīca a crumb; use prob infl by association with mǐcāre to glitter]
■ **micaceous** /-kā'shəs/ adj. **mi'cate** vt to furnish with mica.
❑ **mi'ca-schist** or **mi'ca-slate** n a metamorphic rock consisting of alternate folia of mica and quartz.

Micawberish /mi-kö'bə-rish/ adj like Wilkins Micawber in Dickens's David Copperfield, jaunty and improvident, always 'waiting for something to turn up'.
■ **Micaw'berism** n.

mice /mīs/ plural of **mouse**.

micelle /mi-sel'/ or **micella** /mi-sel'ə/ (chem) n a group of molecular chains, a structural unit found in colloids; a hypothetical unit of living matter. [Dimin of L mīca crumb, grain]
■ **micell'ar** adj.

Mich. abbrev : Michaelmas; Michigan (US state).

Michaelmas /mik'əl-məs/ n the festival of St Michael, 29 September, a quarter day in England, Wales and Ireland. [mass²]
❑ **Michaelmas-dai'sy** n a wild aster; any of several garden plants of the Aster genus with clusters of small purple, pink, blue, etc, flowers. **Michaelmas term** n the autumn term at Oxford and Cambridge and some other universities, or at the Inns of Court.

miche /mich/ (dialect) vi to mouch, skulk, slink; to loaf; to play truant. ♦ vt to pilfer. [Poss same as **mooch**]
■ **mich'er** n. **mich'ing** n and adj.

Michelin star /mish'ələn stär/ n a symbol denoting merit, used in the classification of restaurants by the Michelin travel guidebooks.

Michurinism /mē-choo'ri-ni-zm/ n Lysenkoism. [IV Michurin (1855–1935), Russian horticulturalist]

mick /mik/, **mickey** or **micky** /mik'i/ n an Irishman (offensive sl); a Roman Catholic (offensive sl; chiefly Aust); a small bottle or flask containing alcohol (chiefly Can); a wild young bull (Aust). [Michael]
■ **mick'ey** adj (US sl) (of music, a band, etc) Mickey Mouse. **mickey**, **Mickey** or **Mickey Finn** n (sl) a doped drink; that which is added to the drink, usu a stupefying drug or a strong laxative. ♦ vt to drug someone's drink; to trick someone.
❑ **Mickey Mouse** n an animated cartoon character created by Walt Disney, 1928. ♦ adj (sl) simple, easy, often derisively so; unimportant, insignificant; (of music, a band, etc) trite, corny. **mick'ey-taking** n (sl) making fun of other people.
■ **take the mick, mickey, micky,** or (rare) **mike** (or **a mike**) **out of**, also **take** (or **extract**) **the michael** (perh with different origin; sl) to annoy; to make fun of.

mickery /mik'ə-ri/ (Aust) n a well or waterhole, esp in a dry riverbed. [From an Aboriginal language]

mickle /mik'l/ (archaic), also (Scot) **muckle** /muk'l/ adj much; great. ♦ n a great quantity. ♦ adv much. [OE micel, mycel]
■ **many a little** (or **pickle**) **makes a mickle** (often absurdly **many a mickle makes a muckle**) every little helps.

micky see **mick**.

Micmac /mik'mak/ n a Native Canadian people of E Canada; a member of it; the Algonquian language of this people.

mico /mē'kō/ n (pl **mi'cos**) a marmoset, esp the black-tailed. [Port, from Carib meku monkey]

MICR abbrev : magnetic ink character recognition.

micra see **micron**.

micro /mī'krō/ (inf) n (pl **mi'cros**) short for **microprocessor**, **microcomputer** or **microwave** (**oven**).

micro- or before a vowel sometimes **micr-** /mī-krō-, -krə- or -kr-/ combining form denoting: (1) (a) abnormally, comparatively or extremely small; (b) using, or used in, or prepared for, microscopy; (c) dealing with minute quantities, objects or values; (d) dealing with a small area; (e) magnifying, amplifying; (f) reducing, or reduced, to minute size; (2) in names of units, denoting a millionth part (10⁻⁶), as in microampere and microbar. [Gr mikros little]

microaerophile /mī-krō-ā'rō-fīl/ n an organism that thrives in an environment that is low in oxygen. [**micro-** (1c)]
■ **microaerophilic** /-fīl'ik/ adj.

microanalysis /mī-krō-ə-nal'i-sis/ n chemical analysis of minute quantities. [**micro-** (1c)]
■ **microanalyt'ical** adj.

microanatomy /mī-krō-ə-nat'ə-mi/ n the study of the anatomical structures of microscopic tissues. [**micro-** (1c)]

microarray /mī'krō-ə-rā/ n a small membrane or glass slide containing samples of biological material arranged in a regular pattern, used as a tool in genetic analysis. [**micro-** (1b)]

microbalance /mī'krō-bal-əns/ n a balance for measuring very small weights. [**micro-** (1c)]

microbarograph /mī-krō-bar'ō-grāf/ n a barograph that records minute variations of atmospheric pressure. [**micro-** (1c)]

microbe /mī'krōb/ n a microscopic organism, esp a bacterium. [Fr, from Gr mikros little, and bios life]
■ **micrō'bial**, **micrō'bian** or **micrō'bic** adj. **micrō'bicide** /-bi-sīd/ n a substance that kills microbes. **microbiolog'ical** adj. **microbiolog'ically** adv. **mīcrobiol'ogist** n. **mīcrobiol'ogy** n the biology of micro-organisms, such as bacteria, viruses or fungi. **mi'crobiota** n pl the smallest soil organisms.
■ **microbiological mining** (also called **bī'omining**) the use of natural or genetically-engineered bacteria to enhance or induce acid leaching of metals from ores (bacterial leaching); the use of bacteria to recover useful or toxic metals from natural drainage waters, mine drainage, or waste water from tips (bacterial recovery).

microbiome n /mī-krō-bī'ōm the community of microscopic organisms that lives inside a human body. [**micro-** (1c)]

microblogging /mī'krō-blog-ing/ n the posting of very short entries on a blog. [**micro-** (1a)]
■ **micrō'blog** n.

microbrewery /mī-krō-broo'ə-ri/ n a small, independent brewery, usu supplying a single town or area. [**micro-** (1a)]
■ **mī'crobrew** n a beer produced by a microbrewery.

microbrowser /mī'krō-browz-ər/ n a simplified form of web browser designed for use on mobile phones. [**micro-** (1f)]

microburst /mī'krō-bûrst/ n a sudden, violent downward rush of air usu associated with thunderstorms. [**micro-** (1d)]

microbus /mī'krō-bus/ n a minibus. [**micro-** (1a)]

microcapsule /mī'krō-kap-sūl/ n an extremely small, thin-walled capsule of plastic or wax, formed around liquid, powder, etc, which, when fractured, releases its contents to fulfil some purpose. [**micro-** (1a)]
■ **microencapsulā'tion** n.

microcar /mī'krō-kär/ n a very compact, small-engined car designed for use in large cities, esp in Japan. [**micro-** (1a)]

microcard /mī'krō-kärd/ n a card reproducing some 200 or more pages of a book in microscopic print for later reading by enlargement. [**micro-** (1f)]

microcassette /mī'krō-kə-set/ n a tiny cassette using very thin recording tape. [**micro-** (1f)]

microcephalous /mī-krō-sef'ə-ləs/, also **microcephalic** /-si-fal'ik/ adj abnormally small-headed. [Gr mikros little, and kephalē head]
■ **microceph'al** n an abnormally small-headed person. **microceph'aly** n abnormal smallness of head.

Microcheiroptera or (US) **Microchiroptera** /mī-krō-kī-rop'tə-rə/ n pl bats other than fruit-bats (which are large); microbats. [**micro-** (1a) and **chiroptera** (see **chiropteran** under **chiro-**)]

microchemistry /mī-krō-kem'i-stri/ n chemistry dealing with very small quantities. [**micro-** (1c)]

microchip /mī'krō-chip/ n a chip (qv) of silicon, etc. ♦ vt to implant (a domestic pet) with a microchip for purposes of identification. [**micro-** (1f)]

Microchiroptera see **Microcheiroptera**.

■ words derived from main entry word; ❑ compound words; ■ idioms and phrasal verbs

microcircuit /mī'krō-sûr-kit/ n an electronic circuit with components formed in one unit of semiconductor crystal. [**micro-** (1f)]
■ **microcir'cuitry** n.

microcirculation /mī-krō-sûr-kū-lā'shən/ n the circulation of blood or lymph in the finest blood vessels or capillaries of the circulatory and lymphatic systems. [**micro-** (1a)]

microclimate /mī'krō-klī-mit/ or -māt/ n the climate of a small area, esp if different from that of the surrounding area. [**micro-** (1d)]
■ **microclimat'ic** adj. **microclimat'ically** adv. **microclimatol'ogy** n the study of a microclimate or microclimates.

microcline /mī'krō-klīn/ n an anorthic potash-feldspar with its cleavage angle differing very slightly from a right angle. [Gr mikros little, and klīnein to slant]

micrococcus /mī-krō-kok'əs/ n (pl **micrococci** /-kok'sī/) a rounded bacillus. [**micro-** (1a) and Gr kokkos a grain]
■ **micrococc'al** adj.

microcode /mī'krō-kōd/ (comput) n a microinstruction or a sequence of microinstructions. [**micro-** (1c)]

microcomponent /mī-krō-kəm-pō'nənt/ n a minute component of eg a microcircuit. [**micro-** (1a)]

microcomputer /mī-krō-kəm-pū'ter/ n an old name for a small computer containing a microprocessor, often used as the control unit for some instrument, tool, etc, or as a personal computer; the microprocessor itself. [**micro-** (1f)]
■ **microcomput'ing** n.

microcopying /mī-krō-kop'ē-ing/ n copying on microfilm. [**micro-** (1f)]
■ **mī'crocopy** n and vt.

microcosm /mī'krō-ko-zm/ n a little universe or world; an object, situation, etc contained within another and displaying all its characteristics on a smaller scale, a miniature version; man, who was regarded by ancient philosophers as a model or epitome of the universe. [Gr mikros small, and kosmos world]
■ **microcos'mic** or **microcos'mical** adj relating to the, or a, microcosm.
□ **microcosmic salt** n sodium ammonium hydrogen phosphate, used as a blowpipe flux (orig obtained from human urine).
■ **in microcosm** on a small scale, as an exact copy or representative model of a larger group, etc.

microcrack /mī'krō-krak/ n a microscopic crack or fracture. ♦ vi and vt to form, or cause to form, microcracks. [**micro-** (1a)]
■ **mī'crocracking** n.

microcredit /mī'krō-kre-dit/ n the provision by banks of small business loans to borrowers with low income or no collateral. [**micro-** (1a)]

microcrystalline /mī-krə-kris'tə-līn/ or -lin/ adj having a crystalline structure visible only under the microscope. [**micro-** (1a)]

microcyte /mī'krə-sīt/ n a small red blood corpuscle. [**micro-** (1a), and Gr kytos a container (used as if = cell)]
■ **microcytic** /-sit'ik/ adj.

microdermabrasion /mī-krō-dûr-mə-brā'zhən/ n a gentler version of dermabrasion, involving the scrubbing but not the peeling of facial skin. [**micro-** (1a)]

microdetector /mī-krō-di-tek'tər/ n an instrument for detecting minute amounts of changes. [**micro-** (1c)]
■ **microdetec'tion** n.

microdissection /mī-krō-di-sek'shən/ or -dī-/ n dissection under the microscope. [**micro-** (1b)]

microdot /mī'krə-dot/ n a photograph of usu secret material reduced to the size of a large dot; a small pill containing concentrated LSD (sl). [**micro-** (1f)]

micro drive /mī'krō drīv/ n formerly, a device used on some microcomputers for writing and reading data to and from a continuous loop of tape held in a cartridge; now a very small hard disk drive. [**micro-** (1f)]

microeconomics /mī-krō-ē-kə-nom'iks/ or -e-/ n sing that branch of economics dealing with individual households, firms, industries, commodities, etc. ♦ n pl economic methods, principles, etc applicable to an individual firm, etc. [**micro-** (1d)]
■ **microeconom'ic** adj.

microelectronics /mī-krō-ē-lek-tron'iks/ or -e-/ n sing the technology of electronic systems involving microminiaturization, microcircuits or other microelectronic devices. [**micro-** (1f)]
■ **microelectron'ic** adj.

microencapsulation see under **microcapsule**.

microengineering /mī-krō-en-ji-nē'ring/ n engineering on a small scale, often using microelectronics. [**micro-** (1f)]

microenvironment /mī-krō-en-vī'rə-mənt/ (ecology) n the environment of small areas in contrast to large areas, with particular reference to the conditions experienced by individual organisms and their parts (eg leaves, etc). [**micro-** (1c)]

microevolution /mī-krō-ē-və-loo'shən or -e-/ n evolutionary change taking place over a relatively short period within a species or subspecies as a result of the repeated selection of certain characteristics. [**micro-** (1c)]

microfabrication /mī'-krō-fab-ri-kā'shən/ n fabrication on a small scale, esp of electronic devices. [**micro-** (1f)]

microfarad /mī'krō-far-ad/ n one millionth of a farad. [**micro-** (2)]

microfauna /mī'krō-fö-nə/ or -fö'nə/ n extremely small animals collectively, usu those invisible to the naked eye. [**micro-** (1a,b)]

microfelsitic /mī-krə-fel-sit'ik/ adj of the cryptocrystalline texture of a quartz-felsite groundmass. [**micro-** (1a)]

microfibre /mī-krō-fī'bər/ n a cloth of tightly woven synthetic fibre. [**micro-** (1a)]

microfiche /mī'krə-fēsh/ n (pl **mī'crofiche** /-fēsh/ or **mī'crofiches**) a sheet of microfilm suitable for filing. ♦ vt to record or store on microfiche. [**micro-** (1f), and Fr fiche slip of paper, etc]
□ **microfiche reader** n an optical device which illuminates frames of microfiche and projects an enlarged image onto a screen to be read by the user.

microfilament /mī-krō-fil'ə-mənt/ n a very thin filament present in large numbers in muscle and the cytoplasm of other cells. [**micro-** (1a)]

microfilaria /mī-krō-fi-lā'ri-ə/ n (pl **microfilā'riae** /-ri-ē/) the early larval stage of certain parasitic Nematoda. [**micro-** (1a)]

microfiling /mī'krō-fī-ling/ n the process of microfilming the contents of a file. [**micro-** (1f)]

microfilm /mī'krə-film/ n a photographic film for preserving a microscopic record of a document, which can be enlarged in projection. ♦ vt to record on microfilm. [**micro-** (1f)]
□ **microfilm reader** n an optical device that magnifies each page of microfilm and presents the image in an enlarged form on a screen to be read by the user.

microfinance /mī'krō-fī-nans/ n the provision of financial services on a small scale to individuals in developing countries. [**micro-** (1a)]

microfloppy /mī'krō-flop-i/ n a small (usu 3.5in) magnetic floppy disk. [**micro-** (1f)]

microflora /mī'krō-flö-rə/ n extremely small plants collectively, usu those invisible to the naked eye. [**micro-** (1a,b)]

microfluidic /mī-krō-floo-id'ik/ adj relating to minute quantities of fluids. [**micro-** (1c)]
■ **microfluid'ics** n sing the study of the behaviour and manipulation of minute quantities of fluids.

microform /mī'krə-förm/ n any of the media of reproduction by microphotography, such as microfiche, microfilm, videotape, etc. [**micro-** (1f)]

microfossil /mī'krō-fos-l or -il/ n a fossil that may only be examined by means of a microscope. [**micro-** (1a,b)]

microfracture /mī'krō-frak-chər/ n an extremely small fracture in a bone or rock. [**micro-** (1c)]
□ **microfracture surgery** n knee surgery in which microfractures are made in the bone in order to stimulate the growth of cartilage.

microgamete /mī-krə-gam'ēt or -ga-mēt'/ n the smaller, generally the male, gamete. [**micro-** (1a)]

microgeneration /mī-krō-je-nə-rā'shən/ n the generation of energy on a small scale by individuals for their own use, eg using solar panels. [**micro-** (1a)]

microgram /mī'krə-gram/ n a micrograph, a photograph or drawing of an object under a microscope; a message typed and photographically reduced for sending by air, enlarged on receipt and printed on a card; the card concerned. [**micro-** (1f)]

microgranite /mī-krə-gran'it/ n a completely but minutely crystalline rock of the composition of granite. [**micro-** (1a)]
■ **microgranit'ic** adj.

micrograph /mī'krə-gräf/ n a pantograph instrument for minute writing or drawing; a minute picture; a drawing or photograph of a minute object as seen through a microscope. [**micro-** (1f) and Gr graphein to write]
■ **micrographer** /mī-krog'rə-fər/ n a person who draws or describes microscopic objects. **micrographic** /mī-krə-graf'ik/ adj relating to micrography; minutely written or delineated; showing intergrowth of crystalline constituents on a microscopic scale (geol). **microg'raphy** n study with the microscope; the description of microscopic objects.

microgravity /mī-krō-grav'i-ti/ n the state or condition of having little or no gravity (also adj). [**micro-** (1c)]

microgroove /mī'krə-groov/ n the fine groove of long-playing gramophone records. [**micro-** (1a)]

microhabitat /mī-krō-hab'i-tat/ (biol) n a small area having environmental conditions differing from those of the surrounding area. [**micro-** (1d)]

microinjection /mī-krō-in-jek'shən/ n injection, eg into a single cell, performed under a microscope. [**micro-** (1a)]
■ **microinject'** vt.

microinstruction /mī'krō-in-struk-shən/ (comput) n a single, simple command encoding any of the individual steps, (eg add, compare) to be carried out by a computer. [**micro-** (1a)]

microkeratome /mī-krō-ker'ə-tōm/ n a tool used in eye surgery to make incisions of a predetermined depth in the cornea. [**micro-** (1c) and Gr keras, -atos horn, and tomē a cutting]

microkernel /mī'krō-kûr-nl/ (comput) n the smallest possible collection of processor-specific operating-system functions. [**micro-** (1a)]

microlending same as **microcredit**.

Microlepidoptera /mī-krō-le-pi-dop'tə-rə/ n pl small moths of various kinds. [**micro-** (1a)]

microlight /mī'krə-līt/ n a very light, usu single-seat, aircraft having either fixed or flexible wings. ◆ adj designating such an aircraft; very light in weight. [**micro-** (1a)]
■ **mī'crolighting** n the activity or sport of flying microlight aircraft.

microlite /mī'krə-līt/ n a mineral composed of calcium, tantalum and oxygen, occurring in very small crystals; an incipient crystal, detected under the microscope by polarized light. [**micro-** (1a) and Gr lithos a stone]
■ **mī'crolith** n a microlite; a very small stone implement of the Stone Age, usu used with a haft. **microlith'ic** adj. **microlitic** /-lit'ik/ adj.

micrology /mī-krol'ə-ji/ n the study of microscopic objects; the study or discussion of trivialities. [Gr mikros little, and logos discourse]
■ **micrologic** /-loj'/ or **microlog'ical** adj. **microlog'ically** adv. **microl'ogist** n.

micromanagement /mī'krō-man-ij-mənt/ n management of an organization or enterprise involving close and detailed supervision of its execution. [**micro-** (1c)]
■ **mī'cromanage** vi and vt. **mi'cromanager** n.

micromanipulation /mī-krō-mə-ni-pū-lā'shən/ n the technique of using delicate instruments, such as **microneedles** and **micropipettes**, to work on cells, bacteria, etc, under high magnifications, or of working with extremely small quantities in microchemistry. [**micro-** (1b,c)]

micromarketing /mī-krō-mär'kə-ting/ n marketing set in the context of individual business firms (cf **macro-marketing** under **macro-**). [**micro-** (1d)]

micromesh /mī'krō-mesh/ adj and n (having or made of) a very fine mesh, eg of hosiery. [**micro-** (1a)]

micrometeorite /mī-krō-mē'tē-ə-rīt or -tyə-rīt/ n a particle of meteoric dust too small to be consumed by friction in the atmosphere. [**micro-** (1a)]

micrometeorology /mī-krō-mē-tē-ə-rol'ə-ji/ n the study of atmospheric conditions over a small area, and usu to a very limited height above the ground. [**micro-** (1d)]

micrometer[1] /mī-krom'i-tər/ n an instrument, often attached to a microscope or telescope, for measuring very small distances or angles; (also **micrometer gauge** or **micrometer calliper** or **callipers**) an instrument which measures small widths, lengths, etc, to a high degree of accuracy. [**micro-** (1c)]
■ **micrometric** /mī-krə-met'rik/ or **micromet'rical** adj. **microm'etry** n measuring with a micrometer.

micrometer[2] see **micrometre**.

micrometre or (US) **micrometer** /mī'krə-mē-tər/ n one millionth of a metre (denoted by μ). [**micro-** (2)]

micromicro- (obs) combining form denoting a millionth of a millionth part, as in **micromicrocurie** (used in measuring the quantity of a radioactive substance present in stable material), **micromicrofarad**, etc (now **pico-**). [**micro-** (2)]

micromillimetre /mī-krə-mil'i-mē-tər/ n one millionth of a millimetre (now **nan'omètre**; obs); one thousandth of a millimetre (non-standard). [**micro-** (2)]

micro-mini /mī'krō-min-i/ adj extremely small, micro-miniature. ◆ n a very short miniskirt. [**micro-** (1a)]

microminiature /mī-krō-min'i-(ə-)chər/ adj made on an extremely small scale. [**micro-** (1f)]
■ **mīcrominiaturizā'tion** or **-s-** n reduction to extremely small size of scientific or technical equipment or any part of it. **mīcromin'iaturize** or **-ise** vt.

micron or **mikron** /mī'kron/ n (pl **mī'crons** or **mī'krons**, **mī'cra** or **mī'kra**) the former name for the micrometre. [Gr mikron, neuter of mikros little]

microneedle /mī'krō-nē-dl/ n a very fine needle used in micromanipulation (qv). [**micro-** (1b,c)]

Micronesian /mī-krə-nē'zhən, -z(h)yən or -zi-ən/ adj of or relating to Micronesia, a group of small islands in the Pacific, north of New Guinea. ◆ n a native or inhabitant of any of these islands; the group of Austronesian languages spoken there. [Gr mikros little, and nēsos an island]

micronutrient /mī-krə-nū'tri-ənt/ n a nutritive substance required in minute quantities by a living organism (also adj). [**micro-** (1a)]

micro-organism /mī-krō-ör'gə-ni-zm/ n a microscopic (or ultramicroscopic) organism. [**micro-** (1a)]

micropalaeontology /mī-krə-pa-li-on-tol'ə-ji or -pā-/ n a branch of palaeontology dealing with microfossils. [**micro-** (1a)]
■ **micropalaeontol'ogist** n.

micropegmatite /mī-krə-peg'mə-tīt/ n a micrographic intergrowth of quartz and feldspar. [**micro-** (1a)]
■ **micropegmatitic** /-tit'ik/ adj.

microphagous /mī-krof'ə-gəs/ adj (of an animal) feeding on minute particles of food. [**micro-** (1c)]

microphone /mī'krə-fōn/ n an instrument for intensifying sounds; a sensitive instrument (short form **mike** /mīk/), similar to a telephone transmitter, for picking up sound waves to be broadcast or amplified and translating them, eg by means of a diaphragm and carbon granules, into a fluctuating electric current. [Gr mikros small, and phōnē voice]
■ **microphonic** /-fon'ik/ adj.

microphotograph /mī-krə-fōt'ə-gräf/ n strictly, a photograph reduced to microscopic size; loosely, a photomicrograph, or photograph of an object as magnified by the microscope. [**micro-** (1f)]
■ **microphotographer** /-og'rə-fər/ n. **microphotographic** /-ə-graf'ik/ adj. **microphotog'raphy** n.

microphyll /mī'krō-fil/ n a relatively small leaf type, as found in club mosses and quillworts. [Gr mikros little, and phyllon leaf]
■ **microphyllous** /-fil'əs/ adj.

microphysics /mī-krə-fiz'iks/ n sing physics dealing with subatomic particles. [**micro-** (1c)]
■ **microphys'ical** adj.

microphyte /mī'krō-fīt/ n a microscopic plant. [**micro-** (1b)]
■ **microphyt'ic** adj.

micropipette /mī-krō-pi-pet'/ n a fine pipette used in micromanipulation (qv). [**micro-** (1b,c)]

micropolis /mī-krop'ə-lis/ n a small city. [**micro-** (1a)]

micropore /mī'krō-pōr/ n a very fine pore or opening in some material. [**micro-** (1a)]
■ **microporos'ity** n. **micropor'ous** adj.
❏ **microporous coatings** n pl stains or clear coatings, intended for use on timbers, that allow a surface to breathe.

microprint /mī'krō-print/ n a microphotograph of eg printed text, reproduced on paper, card, etc. [**micro-** (1f)]
■ **mī'croprinted** adj. **mī'croprinting** n.

microprism /mī'krō-pri-zm/ n a tiny prism used as a focusing aid on a single-lens reflex camera, which produces a shimmering image until an object viewed through it is in focus. [**micro-** (1a)]

microprobe /mī'krō-prōb/ n a device that produces a very thin electron beam by means of which the chemical make-up of various compounds may be examined. [**micro-** (1b)]

microprocessor /mī-krō-prō'se-sər/ n an integrated circuit on a silicon chip, or a number of these, acting as the central processing unit of a computer. [**micro-** (1f)]
■ **microprō'cessing** n.

microprogram /mī-krō-prō'gram/ (comput) n a series of microinstructions. [**micro-** (1a)]

micropropagation /mī-krō-pro-pə-gā'shən/ n propagation by growing new plants from single cells of the parent plant. [**micro-** (1c)]

micropsia /mī-krop'si-ə/ (med) n a condition of the eyes in which objects look smaller than usual. [Gr mikros little, and opsis appearance]

micropterous /mī-krop'tə-rəs/ (zool) adj with reduced fins or hind-wings. [Gr mikros little, and pteron wing]

micropump /mī'krō-pump/ n a miniature pump surgically inserted under the skin to administer medication at regular intervals. [**micro-** (1a)]

micropyle /mī'krə-pīl/ n the orifice in the coats of the ovule leading to the apex of the nucellus, through which the pollen tube commonly enters (*bot*); an opening by which a spermatozoon may enter an ovum (*zool*). [Gr *mikros* little, and *pylē* gate]

■ **micropy'lar** *adj*.

microraptor /*mī'krō-rap-tər*/ *n* a small Cretaceous dinosaur with long feathers on its legs and tail. [Mod L, from Gr *mikros* little, and **raptor**]

microreader /*mī'krō-rē-dər*/ *n* a device that produces an enlarged image of a microphotograph or microfilm. [**micro-** (1e)]

microsatellite /*mī-krō-sat'ə-līt*/ *n* any of various repetitive genomic DNA sequences that vary in length between individuals, used to study genetic diseases. [**micro-** (1c)]

microscale /*mī'krō-skāl*/ *adj* extremely small-scale. [**micro-** (1a)]

microscooter /*mī'krō-skoo-tər*/ *n* a small lightweight foot-propelled metal scooter used *esp* by children. [**micro-** (1a)]

microscope /*mī'krə-skōp*/ *n* an instrument for magnifying minute objects. [Gr *mikros* little, and *skopeein* to look at]

■ **microscopic** /*-skop'ik*/ or **microscop'ical** *adj* relating to a microscope or to microscopy; magnifying; able to see minute objects; invisible or hardly visible without the aid of a microscope; minute. **microscop'ically** *adv*. **microscopist** /*mī-kros'kop-ist* or *mī-krə-skō'pist*/ *n*. **micros'copy** *n*.

■ **acoustic microscope** one in which ultrasonic waves passed through the specimen are scanned by a laser beam. **come under the microscope** to be subjected to minute examination. **compound microscope** and **simple microscope** microscopes with respectively two lenses and a single lens. **electron**, **proton** and **ultraviolet microscope** one using a beam of electrons, protons, or ultraviolet rays respectively. **phase-contrast** (or **phase-difference**) **microscope** see under **phase**[1]. **reflecting microscope** see under **reflect**.

microsecond /*mī'krō-sek-ənd*/ *n* one millionth of a second. [**micro-** (2)]

microseism /*mī'krə-sī-zm*/ *n* a slight earth-movement detectable only instrumentally. [Gr *mikros* little, and *seismos* earthquake]

■ **microseis'mic** or **microseis'mical** *adj*. **microseis'mograph** *n* an instrument for recording microseisms and distant earthquakes. **microseismom'eter** *n* an instrument for measuring microseisms. **microseismom'etry** *n*.

microsite /*mī'krō-sīt*/ *n* a self-contained set of pages within a larger website, *usu* dealing with a particular topic. [**micro-** (1a)]

microskirt same as **micro-mini** (*n*).

microsleep /*mī'krō-slēp*/ *n* an episode lasting a few seconds during which external stimuli are not perceived, associated with narcolepsy or sleep deprivation. [**micro-** (1a)]

microsome /*mī'krə-sōm*/ *n* a minute granule or drop in cytoplasm. [Gr *mikros* little, and *sōma* body]

■ **microsō'mal** *adj*.

microspore /*mī'krə-spör*/ *n* the smaller of two forms of spore; a spore giving rise to a male gametophyte. [**micro-** (1a)]

■ **microsporangium** /*-spör-an'ji-əm*/ *n* (*pl* **microsporan'gia**) a sporangium producing only microspores. **microsporophyll** /*-spör'ə-fil*/ *n* a sporophyll that carries or subtends only microsporangia.

microstructure /*mī-krō-struk'chər* or *mī'-*/ *n* structure, *esp* of metals and alloys, as revealed by the microscope. [**micro-** (1a,b)]

microsurgery /*mī-krō-sûr'jə-ri*/ *n* surgery performed on cells or other very small body structures, requiring the use of a microscope. [**micro-** (1b)]

■ **microsur'geon** *n*. **microsur'gical** *adj*.

microswitch /*mī'krō-swich*/ *n* a minute electronic switch, activated by very slight movement or pressure. [**micro-** (1a)]

microtechnology /*mī-krō-tek-nol'ə-ji*/ *n* technology that makes use of microelectronics. [**micro-** (1f)]

microtome /*mī'krə-tōm*/ *n* an instrument for cutting thin sections of objects for microscopic examination. [Gr *mikros* little, and *tomē* a cut]

■ **microtomic** /*-tom'ik*/ or **microtom'ical** *adj*. **microtomist** /*-krot'ə-mist*/ *n*. **microt'omy** *n*.

microtone /*mī'krə-tōn*/ (*music*) *n* an interval less than a semitone. [**micro-** (1a)]

■ **microtō'nal** *adj*. **microtonal'ity** *n*. **microtō'nally** *adv*.

microtubule /*mī-krō-tū'būl*/ *n* any of the relatively rigid structures in the cytoplasm of many plant and animal cells. [**micro-** (1a)]

■ **microtū'bular** *adj*.

microtunnelling /*mī-krō-tun'ə-ling*/ *n* a technique used in laying underground pipes, etc, in which miniature boring machines excavate the required channel without breaking or damaging the road surface. [**micro-** (1a)]

microwave /*mī'krō-wāv*/ *n* in radio communication, a wave having a very short wavelength; now *usu* a wave in the radiation spectrum between normal radio waves and infrared; a microwave oven. ◆ *adj* of, relating to or denoting microwaves; relating to or appropriate for a

microwave oven. ◆ *vt* to cook or defrost in a microwave oven. ◆ *vi* to undergo microwaving. [**micro-** (1a)]

■ **microwav'able** or **microwave'able** *adj* suitable for cooking, defrosting, etc in a microwave oven.

❑ **microwave background** *n* (*astron*) a background of microwave radiation, discovered in 1963, thought to be a relic of the Big Bang (also **cosmic background radiation**). **microwave oven** *n* an oven in which food is cooked or defrosted by the heat produced by microwaves passing through it.

microwire /*mī'krō-wīr*/ *n* a very strong, very fine filament of metal or other material. [**micro-** (1a)]

microwriter /*mī'krō-rī-tər*/ *n* a hand-held five- or six-key device by means of which text can be generated on a printer or VDU. [**micro-** (1a)]

micrurgy /*mī'krûr-ji*/ *n* micromanipulation. [**micro-** (1b,c) and Gr *-ourgos* (as in *metallourgos* working a mine), from *ergon* work]

Micrurus see **Elaps**.

micturition /*mik-tū-rish'ən*/ (*med*) *n* the frequent desire to pass urine; the act of urinating. [L *micturīre*, *-ītum*, desiderative of *mingere*, *mi(n)ctum* to pass urine, *mi(n)ctiō*, *-ōnis* urination]

■ **mic'tion** *n* (*obs*) passing urine. **mic'turate** *vi* (*irregularly formed*) to urinate.

mid[1] /*mid*/ *adj* middle; situated between extremes; uttered with the tongue in a position between high and low (*phonetics*). ◆ *n* (*archaic* and *dialect*) the middle. [OE *midd*; cf Ger *Mitte*, L *medius*, Gr *mesos*]

■ **midd'est** *adj* (*Spenser*) middle; middlemost. **mid'most** *adj* middlemost. ◆ *n* the very middle. ◆ *adv* in the very middle. ◆ *prep* in the very middle of. **midst** *n* middle. ◆ *adv* in the middle. ◆ *prep* (also **'midst** as if for **amidst**) amidst (ME *middes*, from genitive of *mid*, with excrescent *t*, cf **whilst**; *perh* partly a *superl*).

❑ **mid-age'** *n* (*Shakesp*) middle age. **midair'** *n* a region somewhat above the ground; the midst of a course through the air. ◆ *adj* taking place in midair. **mid-Atlan'tic** *adj* (of an accent, style, etc) having a blend of both British and N American characteristics; of or relating to states in the middle of the Atlantic coast of the USA. **mid'band** *adj* (*telecom*) operating across a range of frequencies between those used by broadband and narrowband systems. **mid'brain** *n* the part of the brain derived from the second brain vesicle of the embryo. **mid'day** *n* noon. ◆ *adj* of, at, or relating to, noon. **Mideast'** *n* (chiefly *US*) the Middle East. **mid'field** *n* the middle area of a football, etc pitch, not close to either team's goal; the players who operate in this area, acting as links between a team's defending and attacking players. **mid'fielder** *n* a player in the midfield. **mid'-gut** *n* (*biol*) that part of the alimentary canal formed from the original gastrula cavity and lined with endoderm; also, the small intestine. **mid'-heaven** *n* the middle of the sky or of heaven; the meridian. **mid'-hour** *n* the middle time; an intervening hour. **mid'iron** *n* a golf club used for long approach shots. **mid'land** *adj* in the middle of, or surrounded by, land; distant from the coast; inland; *specif* (*esp* with *cap*) relating to or designating the central parts of England. ◆ *n* the interior of a country; (in *pl*; *esp* with *cap*) the central parts of England. **mid'lander** *n*. **mid-leg** *n* the middle of the leg. ◆ *adv* as high or deep as the middle of the leg. **mid-Lent'** *n* the middle of Lent; the fourth Sunday in Lent. **mid-life crisis** *n* the feeling of panic, pointlessness, etc sometimes experienced at middle age by those who are concerned that they are no longer young. **midlitt'oral** *n* that part of the seashore that lies between high and low neap tidemarks (also *adj*). **mid-mor'ning** *n*. **midnoon'** *n* noon. **mid-o'cean** *n* the middle of the ocean. **mid-ocean ridge** *n* (*geol*) a major, largely submarine, mountain range where two plates are being pulled apart and new volcanic lithosphere is being created. **mid-off'** *n* (*cricket*) a fielder, or a fielding position, behind the bowler on the offside. **mid-on'** *n* (*cricket*) a fielder, or a fielding position, behind the bowler on the onside. **mid'-point** *n* a point lying halfway between two other points (whether in time or space); a point lying at the centre of an area. **mid'rib** *n* (*bot*) the rib along the middle of a leaf. **mid-sea'** *n* the open sea. **mid-seas'on** *n* (also *adj*). **mid'section** *n* the middle part; the midriff. **mid'ship** *adj* in the middle of a ship. **mid'shipman** *n* formerly, the title of a young officer (*orig* quartered *amidships*) entering the navy, later a junior ranking below a sub-lieutenant but above a naval cadet, now, since 1957, only a shore ranking used during training (shortened informally to **mid** or **midd'y**). **mid'shipmate** *n* (*humorous*) a midshipman. **mid'ships** *adv* amidships. **mid'size** *adj* middle-sized, medium. **mid-sky'** *n* the middle of the sky. **midstream'** *n* the middle of the stream. ◆ *adv* in the middle of the stream. **mid'summer** (also /*-sum'*/) *n* the middle of the summer; the summer solstice, occurring about 21 June in the northern hemisphere. **Midsummer day** or **Midsummer's Day** *n* 24 June, a quarter day in England, Wales and Ireland. **midsummer madness** *n* temporary madness or erratic behaviour attributed to the hot sun of midsummer. **mid'summer-men** *n* (*sing* or *pl*) roseroot. **midsummer moon** *n* the month during which midsummer occurs, associated with midsummer madness. **mid'term** *n* the middle of an academic term, term of office, etc; an examination held in the middle of an academic term (*N Am*). ◆ *adj* relating to, or occurring at or around, the middle of term. **mid'town** *adj* and *n* (*N Am*) (in or toward) the middle part of town. **mid-Victo'rian** *adj* of or characteristic of the middle part of Queen Victoria's reign (1837–1901). ◆ *n* a person living in this period. **mid'way** *n* the middle of the way or distance (*obs*); a middle course (*archaic*); a central avenue in a fair or exhibition, or the sideshows, stalls, etc, set up there (*N Am*). ◆ *adj* in the middle of the way or distance. ◆ *adv* halfway. ◆ *prep* halfway along or across. **mid'-week** *n* the middle of the week; (with *cap*) among Quakers, Wednesday (cf Ger *Mittwoch*). ◆ *adj* in the middle of the week. **Mid'west** *n* Middle West. **Midwest'ern** *adj*. **Midwest'erner** *n*. **mid-wick'et** *n* (*cricket*) a fielder, or a fielding position, on the legside, about midway between mid-on and square leg. **mid-win'ter** *n* the middle of winter; the winter solstice, occurring about 21 December in the northern hemisphere. **mid'-year** *adj* and *n* (in) the middle of the (academic) year. ■ **in midstream** in the middle of a sentence, activity, etc.

mid² short for **midshipman** (see under **mid¹**).

mid- /mid-/ *combining form* denoting the middle part of; of or in the middle of. [From **mid¹** (adj); not always hyphenated]

'mid or **mid** short form of **amid**.

MIDAS /mī'dəs/ *abbrev* : Missile Defence Alarm System, from 1958 to 1966.

Midas /mī'dəs/ (*Gr myth*) *n* a king of Phrygia whose touch turned all to gold, and to whom Apollo gave ass's ears; (without *cap*) a kind of tamarin with gold-coloured hair on the feet and hands. ❑ **Midas's ear** *n* a shell of the genus *Auricula*. **Midas touch** *n* the ability to make money easily.

midband...to...midday see under **mid¹**.

midden /mid'ən/ (*archaic, Scot* and *dialect*) *n* a dunghill; a refuse-heap or compost heap; a mess, a clutter (*fig*); a kitchen midden (*archaeol*). [Scand, as Dan *mödding*, from *mög* dung; cf **muck**] ❑ **midd'en-cock** *n* an ordinary, farmyard cock (as opposed to a gamecock). **midd'enstead** *n* the site of a midden.

middle /mid'l/ *adj* equally distant (in measurement or in number of steps) from the extremes; avoiding extremes, done as a compromise; intermediate; intervening; of that voice which is intermediate between active and passive, reflexive or expressing an action in some way affecting the agent (*grammar*); (with *cap*) belonging to or happening in the part of a time, period or series between those called early or late, as in *the Middle Triassic*; (with *cap*) (of languages) between Old and Modern as in *Middle English, Middle High German*, etc. ◆ *vt* to place in the middle; to fold in the middle (*naut*); to hit (the ball) with the middle of the bat (*cricket*). ◆ *n* the middle point, part or position; midst; the central portion, waist; the middle voice (*grammar*); the middle term (*logic*); a middle article. [OE *middel* (adj); Du *middel*, Ger *Mittel*; see **mid¹**] ■ **midd'lemost** *adj* nearest the middle. ❑ **middle-age'** *n*. **middle-aged'** /-ājd'/ *adj* between youth and old age, variously reckoned to suit the reckoner. **middle-age** (or **middle-aged**) **spread** *n* a thickening of the body, *esp* the waist, attributable to the onset of middle-age. **Middle Ages** *n pl* the time between the fall of the W Roman Empire and the Renaissance (5c–15c). **Middle America** *n* the middle-class in the USA, *esp* the conservative elements of it; the countries lying between the USA and Colombia, sometimes including the West Indies. **Middle-Amer'ican** *n* and *adj*. **middle article** *n* a newspaper article of literary or general rather than topical interest. **midd'le-brack'et** *adj* in a midway grouping in a list. **midd'lebreaker** *n* (*US*) a lister. **midd'lebrow** *n* and *adj* (a person who is) midway between highbrow and lowbrow. **middle C** *n* the C in the middle of the piano keyboard; the first line below the treble or above the bass stave. **middle class** *n* the section of society which comes between the aristocracy and the working class. **midd'le-class** *adj*. **middle common room** or (*Cambridge University*) **middle combination room** *n* in some universities, a common room for the use of postgraduate and mature students (cf **junior common room, senior common room**; *abbrev* **MCR**). **middle distance** *n* (in a picture) the middle ground; a race distance of 800m or 1500m (*athletics*). **midd'le-distance** *adj* (in athletics) of or denoting a race of 800m or 1500m, or an athlete who takes part in such a race. **middle ear** *n* the part of the ear containing the malleus, incus and stapes. **midd'le-earth** *n* the earth, considered as placed between the upper and lower regions. **Middle East** *n* formerly, the countries from Iran to Burma (now Myanmar); now generally used of an area including the Arabic-speaking countries around the eastern end of the Mediterranean Sea and in the Arabian Peninsula, sometimes along with Greece, Turkey, Cyprus, Iran and the greater part of N Africa. **Middle-East'ern** *adj*. **Middle-East'erner** *n*. **middle eight** *n* an eight-bar section occurring two-thirds of the way through a conventionally structured pop song and acting as a foil to the rest of the piece. **Middle England** *n* the English middle classes outside London, regarded as politically and socially conservative. **Middle Englander** *n*. **Middle English** see under **English**. **middle finger salute** *n* (*sl*) an offensive gesture expressing anger, frustration, etc, in which the middle finger is extended upwards from a closed fist. **middle game** *n* the part of a chess game between the opening and the end game. **middle ground** *n* the part of a picture between the foreground and background; a compromise position. **midd'le-income** *adj* having, or relating to those who have, an average income which makes them neither rich nor poor. **Middle Kingdom** *n* China (*old*); the 11th to 13th dynasties in ancient Egypt (21c–17c BC). **midd'leman** *n* a person occupying a middle position; an intermediary, *esp* between producer and consumer; in Ireland, a person renting land in large tracts, and subletting it in smaller portions (*hist*). **middle management** *n* the junior managerial executives and senior supervisory personnel in a firm. **middle name** *n* any name between a person's first name and surname; the notable quality or characteristic of a specified thing or person (*facetious*). **middle-of-the-road'** *adj* midway between extremes; (*esp* of music) designed to appeal to a wide spectrum of tastes; unexciting, mediocre. **middle passage** *n* (*hist*) the voyage across the Atlantic from Africa to the West Indies on board a slave-ship. **middle price** *n* (of a stock market share) a price midway between the buying (offer) price and the selling (bid) price, as often shown in newspapers. **middle school** *n* a school for children between the ages of about 9 and 13; in some secondary schools, an administrative unit *usu* comprising the third and fourth forms. **midd'le-sized** *adj* of average size. **Middle States** *n pl* those states *orig* constituting the middle of the USA, ie New York, New Jersey, Pennsylvania and Delaware. **midd'le-stitching** *n* monk's seam. **middle term** *n* (*logic*) that term of a syllogism which appears in both premises but not in the conclusion. **midd'leware** *n* (*comput*) software that allows two otherwise incompatible programs or networks to operate together. **middle watch** *n* that from midnight to 4am. **midd'leweight** *n* a weight category variously applied in boxing, wrestling and weightlifting; a sportsperson of the specified weight for the category (eg in professional boxing above welterweight, **junior middleweight, light middleweight** or **super welterweight** (maximum 70kg/154lb), **midd'leweight** (maximum 73kg/160lb), and **super middleweight** (maximum 76kg/168lb)). **Middle West** *n* the region of the USA between the Appalachians and the Rockies, the Mississippi basin as far south as Kansas, Missouri, and the Ohio River. **Middle Western** *adj*. **Middle Westerner** *n*. **midd'le-world** *n* middle-earth. ■ **in the middle of** occupied with, engaged in (doing something); during; while.

middling /mid'ling/ *adj* indifferent; mediocre; fairly good; moderate (*inf*); intermediate (*obs*). ◆ *adv* (*inf*) fairly; fairly well. ◆ *n* (*usu* in *pl*) goods of a middle quality, size or price; the coarser part of ground wheat; partially concentrated ore. [Orig Scot, from **mid¹** and **-ling²**] ■ **midd'lingly** *adv*. ■ **fair to middling** fairly good.

Middx *abbrev* : Middlesex.

middy¹ /mid'i/ *n* an informal short form of **midshipman**; (also **middy blouse**) a loose blouse worn, *esp* formerly, by women and *esp* children, having a collar with a broad flap at the back in the style of a sailor's uniform.

middy² /mid'i/ *n* (*Aust inf*) a measure of beer, varying in amount from one place to another; the glass containing it. [Ety doubtful]

midfield, etc see under **mid¹**.

Midgard /mid'gärd/ (*Norse myth*) *n* the abode of men, middle-earth. [ON *mithgarthr* mid-yard]

midge /mij/ *n* a small gnat-like fly, *esp* of the family Chironomidae; a very small person. [OE *mycg, mycge* ; Ger *Mücke*] ■ **midg'et** *n* something very small of its kind; a very small person. **midg'y** *adj* (*inf*) infested with midges. ◆ *n* (*Scot*) a midge (also **midg'ie**).

MIDI *abbrev* : Musical Instrument Digital Interface, a standard protocol for communication between computers and musical instruments.

Midi /mē-dē'/ *n* the south (of France). [Fr *midi* midday; *midinette* is said to be from *midi* and *dînette* snack] ■ **midinette** /-net'/ *n* a young female worker, *esp* a shop assistant, in the Paris fashion or millinery business (apparently much seen in cafés at lunchtime).

midi /mid'i/ *n* short for **midi-coat, midi-skirt**, etc, or **midi-system** (see under **midi-**).

midi- /mi-di-/ *combining form* denoting something of middle size, length, etc. [**mid¹**; cf **mini-**] ■ **mid'i-coat, mid'i-skirt**, etc *n* a coat, skirt, etc, reaching to about mid-calf. **mid'i-system** *n* a (*usu* one-piece) music system, resembling a medium-sized stack system, ie with CD, tape deck, etc, stacked vertically.

midland, **midmost**, etc see under **mid**[1].

midnight /mid'nīt/ *n* the middle of the night; twelve o'clock at night; pitch darkness (*fig*). ◆ *adj* of or at midnight; dark as midnight. [**mid-** and **night**]
■ **mid'nightly** *adj* and *adv* (occurring) every midnight.
□ **midnight blue** *n* very dark, blackish blue. **midnight feast** *n* a secret feast held during the night, *esp* by children. **midnight sun** *n* the sun visible at midnight during summer in the polar regions.
■ **burn the midnight oil** see under **burn**[1].

mid-ocean...to...**midpoint** see under **mid**[1].

Midrash /mid'rash/ *n* the Hebrew exposition of the Old Testament, divided into *Haggada* and *Halachah*. [Heb, exposition]
■ **Midrashim** /mid-rä'shēm/ *n pl* commentaries on individual books or sections of the Old Testament.

midrib see under **mid**[1].

midriff /mid'rif/ *n* the diaphragm, the division in the middle of the body between the abdomen and the thorax, or stomach and chest; (loosely) the area of the body, or of clothing, from below the breast down to the waist. [OE *midd* middle, and *hrif* belly]

mid-sea...to...**mid-wicket** see under **mid**[1].

midwife /mid'wīf/ *n* (pl **midwives** /mid'wīvz/) a woman, or occasionally a man, who assists women in childbirth. ◆ *vt* (**mid'wīfing** or **mid'wīving**, **-wīfed** or **-wīved**) (also **mid'wive** /-wīv/) to assist in the birth of (a child) (also *fig*). [OE *mid* with (Ger *mit*, Gr *meta*), and *wīf* woman]
■ **mid'wifery** /-wif-ə-ri, -wif-ri, -if-ri or -wīf'ri/ *n* the art or practice of a midwife; assistance at childbirth; obstetrics.
□ **midwife toad** *n* either of two species of small European toad (*Alytes obstetricians* and *Alytes cisternasi*), so called because the males bear the fertilized eggs on their backs until they hatch.

mid-winter and **mid-year** see under **mid**[1].

mien /mēn/ *n* an air or look, manner, bearing (*literary*); a facial expression (*obs*). [Perh **demean**[2], influenced by Fr *mine*, of unknown origin]

mieve /mēv/ (*Spenser*) *vt* same as **move**.

mifepristone /mi-fep'ri-stōn/ *n* a synthetic compound that inhibits the action of progesterone, used in pill form to induce abortion in early pregnancy.

miff /mif/ (*inf*) *n* a slight feeling or fit of resentment; a minor quarrel, a tiff. ◆ *vt* to put in a bad mood, annoy or offend. ◆ *vi* to take offence; (of a plant) to wither away or fade (with *off*). [Cf Ger *muffen* to sulk]
■ **miffed** *adj*. **miff'ily** *adv*. **miff'iness** *n*. **miff'y** *adj* (also (*obs*) **mift'y**) quick to take offence, touchy; (of a plant) liable to wither away or fade.

MiG or **mig** /mig/ (*aeronautics*) *abbrev* : *Mi*koyan and *G*urevich (Soviet aircraft designers).

MIGA *abbrev* : Multilateral Investment Guarantee Agency.

might[1] /mīt/ *pat* of **may**[1].
■ **mightst** and **mightest** *auxiliary v* see under **may**[1].
□ **might'-have-been** *n* a person who, or thing that, might have been, or might have come to something.

might[2] /mīt/ *n* power; ability; strength; energy or intensity of purpose or feeling. [OE]
■ **might'ful** *adj* (*Shakesp*) mighty; powerful. **might'ily** *adv*. **might'iness** *n* the state of being mighty; power; greatness; great amount; a title of prestige; excellency. **might'y** *adj* having greater power; strong; valiant; very great; important; exhibiting might; wonderful. ◆ *adv* (now *inf*, *usu* with a tinge of irony except in *US*) very.
■ **might and main** utmost strength.

mightn't /mī'tənt/ a contraction of **might not**.

migmatite /mig'mə-tīt/ *n* a rock composed of two types of rock that have intermingled but are still distinguishable. [Gr *migma*, *-atos* mixture, and **-ite** (3)]

mignon /mē-nyõ'/ or (*fem*) **mignonne** /mē-nyon'/ (*Fr*) *adj* small and dainty.

mignonette /min-yə-net'/ *n* any of various plants of the *Reseda* genus, including a fragrant garden annual with green flowers; a fine kind of lace. [Fr *mignonnette*, fem dimin of *mignon* daintily small, a darling]

migraine (from 18c) /mē'grān or mī'/ or **megrim** (from 14c) /mē'grim/ *n* a severe throbbing pain affecting only one half of the head or face and *usu* accompanied by nausea; a condition marked by recurring migraines; (for the following meanings, **megrim**) vertigo; (in *pl*) lowness of spirits; a caprice (*archaic*). [Fr *migraine*, from Gr *hēmikrāniā*, from *hēmi* half, and *krānion* skull]

migrate /mī-grāt'/ *vi* to pass from one place to another; to change one's place of abode to another country, etc; to change habitat according to the season; to move (as parasites, phagocytes, etc) to another part of the body; to pass in a stream (as ions or particles). ◆ *vt*

(*comput*) to move (software, etc) from one system to another. [L *migrāre*, *-ātum*; cf *meāre* to go]
■ **mi'grant** *n* a person or animal that migrates or is migrating (also *adj*). **migrā'tion** *n* a change of abode; a removal from one country or climate to another, *esp* in a large number; a number moving together in this way. **migrā'tional** *adj*. **migrā'tionist** *n* a person who emigrates; a person who explains facts by a theory of migration. **migrā'tor** *n*. **mi'gratory** /-grə-tə-ri/ *adj* migrating, or accustomed to migration; wandering.
□ **migrant worker** *n* a person, *esp* an agricultural worker, who moves from place to place, or to another country, in search of work.

mihrab /mē-räb' or mēhh'/ *n* a niche or slab in a mosque marking the direction of Mecca. [Ar *mihrāb*]

mikado /mi-kä'dō/ (*hist*) *n* (pl **mika'dos**) a title given by foreigners to the Emperor of Japan. [Jap, exalted gate]

Mike or **mike** /mīk/ *n* (in international radio communication) a code word for the letter *m*.

mike[1] /mīk/ *n* short form of **microphone** or **microscope**. ◆ *vt* to attach a microphone to the clothing (*usu* with *up*).

mike[2] /mīk/ (*sl*) *vi* to loiter idly. ◆ *n* a period of doing this. [Origin unknown]

mike[3] variant of **mick**.

mikron see **micron**.

mikvah or **mikveh** /mik-va' or mik'və/ (*Judaism*) *n* a bath used for ritual purification. [Heb]

mil /mil/ *n* a unit ($\frac{1}{1000}$in) in measuring the diameter of wire; a proposed coin worth $\frac{1}{1000}$ of a pound; a former Cypriot coin of this value; (in pharmacy) a millilitre; (in the building trade, etc) a millimetre; a unit of angular measurement, used *esp* with artillery, equal to $\frac{1}{6400}$ of a circle or 0.05625°. [L *mīlle* a thousand]

mil. or **milit.** *abbrev* : military.

milady or **miladi** /mi-lā'di/ *n* a term of address used for an aristocratic or rich English lady, eg by household staff. [Fr modification of **my lady**]

milage see under **mile**.

Milanese /mi-lə-nēz'/ *adj* of or relating to *Milan*, its people, or the dialect of Italian spoken there. ◆ *n* a native or inhabitant of Milan.
□ **Milanese silk** *n* a finely-knitted lightweight silk or similar fabric.

Milankovitch theory /mi-lang'kə-vich thē'ə-ri/ (*meteorol*) *n* the theory that large oscillations in climate are related to changes in solar radiation received by the Earth. [Milutin *Milankovitch* (1879–1958), Serbian climatologist]

milch /milch or milsh/ *adj* giving milk. [OE *milce* (found in the compound *thri-milce* May, when cows can be milked three times a day); cf **milk**]
□ **milch'-cow** *n* a cow yielding milk or kept for milking; a ready source of gain or money (*fig*).

mild /mīld/ *adj* gentle in temper and disposition; not sharp or bitter; acting gently; gently and pleasantly affecting the senses; soft; calm. ◆ *n* mild ale. [OE *milde* mild; cf Ger *mild*, ON *mildr*, gracious, etc]
■ **mild'en** *vt* to make mild. ◆ *vi* to become mild. **mild'ly** *adv*. **mild'ness** *n*.
□ **mild ale** *n* formerly, new ale, without the taste that comes from keeping; now ale with less hop flavouring than pale ale. **mild-spok'en** *adj* having a mild manner of speech. **mild steel** *n* steel containing very little carbon.
■ **put it mildly** to understate the case.

mildew /mil'dū/ *n* a disease on plants, caused by the growth of minute fungi (*Erysiphe, Oidium*, etc); a similar appearance on other things or of another kind; a fungus causing the disease; honeydew (*obs*). ◆ *vt* to taint with mildew. [OE *meledēaw, mildēaw*, from a lost word for honey, and *dēaw* dew; influenced by *melu* meal]
■ **mil'dewed** *adj*. **mil'dewy** *adj*.

mile /mīl/ *n* (also called **statute mile**) a unit of linear measure, 1760yd or 5280ft (1.61km); a race of this distance; *orig*, a Roman unit of length, 1000 (double) paces (*mīlle passūs* or *passuum*; about 1611 English yards); (often in *pl*) a great distance or length (*inf*). [OE *mīl*, from L *mīlia*, pl of *mīlle* (*passuum*) a thousand (paces)]
■ **mīl'age** or **mile'age** *n* the total number of miles covered by a motor vehicle, etc; (also **milage** or **mileage allowance**) travelling allowance at so much a mile; miles travelled per gallon of fuel; use, benefit (*inf*; *fig*). **mī'ler** *n* a runner of a mile race. **miles** *adv* at a great distance; very much (*inf*).
□ **mile'-castle** *n* any of a series of small forts placed at mile intervals along a Roman wall. **mile-high club** *n* (*sl*) the set of people who have had sexual intercourse aboard an aeroplane in flight. **mileom'eter** or **mīlom'eter** *n* an instrument that records the number of miles that a vehicle, etc has travelled. **mile'post** or **mile'stone** *n* a post or stone

marker showing distance in miles; a stage or reckoning-point; an important event, stage, etc (*fig*).

■ **a mile a minute** uttering one's words with great speed. **geographical mile** one minute of longitude measured along the equator, a distance of 6087.025ft (1.855km). **go the extra mile** to do more than what is expected or required (from Bible, Matthew 5.41). **Irish mile** (*obs*) 2240 yards. **nautical mile** one minute of latitude measured along a meridian, a distance of 6082.66ft; formerly in British practice, 6080ft (1.8532km) (also called **Admiralty measured mile**); in official international use, 6076.1033ft (1.852km) (also called **international nautical mile**). **run a mile** to be too scared or intimidated to do something. **Scots mile** (*obs*) about 1976 yards.

miles gloriosus /*mē'lāz glö-rē-ō'səs, mī'lēs, glō-* or *-sŭs*/ (*L*) *n* (pl **milites gloriosi** /*mē'lē-tāz glör-ē-ō'sē, mī'li-tēz, glör-* or *-sī*/) a vainglorious soldier, used as a stock character in Roman and later comedy. [The eponymous hero of a play by Plautus]

Milesian[1] /*mī-* or *mi-lē'zyən* or *-zh(y)ən*/ *adj* of or relating to *Miletus*, an Ionian Greek city in Asia Minor. ◆ *n* a native or citizen of Miletus. [Gr *Mīlēsios*, from *Mīlētos*]
◻ **Milesian tales** *n pl* witty self-indulgent tales, from a lost book so called, by Aristides 'of Miletus' (2c BC).

Milesian[2] /*mī-* or *mi-lē'sh(y)ən* or *-zh(y)ən*/ *adj* of or relating to *Milesius* or *Miledh*, a mythical king of Spain, or his sons and their followers who seized Ireland; Irish. ◆ *n* (*usu joc*) an Irishman.

MILF or **milf** /*milf*/ (*vulgar sl*) a sexually attractive middle-aged woman. [From 'mother I'd like to fuck']

milfoil /*mil'foil*/ *n* yarrow, or any other species of *Achillea*; extended to other plants with finely divided leaves, such as **water milfoil** (genus *Myriophyllum*, family Haloragidaceae). [OFr, from L *millefolium*, from *mille* a thousand, and *folium* a leaf]

milia see **milium**.

miliary /*mil'i-ə-ri*/ *adj* of or like millet-seed; characterized by small skin eruptions resembling millet-seed (*med*). [L *miliārius*, from *milium* millet]
■ **miliaria** /*mil-i-ā'ri-ə*/ *n* (*med*) prickly heat.

Milice /*mē-lēs'*/ (*Fr*) *n* the government militia in Vichy France. [Fr, militia]
■ **Milicien** /*mil-is-yē*/ *n* (pl **Miliciens** /*-yē*/) a member of this.

milieu /*mē-lyœ'*/ *n* (pl **milieus'** or **milieux'** /*-yø*/) environment, setting, medium, element. [Fr, middle]

milit. *abbrev*: military.

militant /*mil'i-tənt*/ *adj* fighting; engaged in warfare; actively contending; combative; using violence; militaristic; strenuously active in support of a particular cause. ◆ *n* a person who takes active part in a struggle; someone who seeks to advance a cause by violence; a strenuously active supporter of a particular cause; (with *cap*) a member of **Militant Tendency**, an extreme left-wing organization, formerly within the British Labour Party. [Fr, from L *mīlitānt-* prp stem of *mīlitāre*, *-ātum* to serve as a soldier]
■ **mil'itancy** *n*. **mil'itantly** *adv*. **mil'itate** *vi* to have weight, tell (*esp* with *against*); to fight for a cause; to contend; to serve as a soldier (*archaic*).
■ **church militant** see under **church**.

militaria /*mi-li-tā'ri-ə*/ *n pl* weapons, uniforms, and other things connected with wars past and present. [**military**, and noun sfx *-ia*; or L, things military, neuter pl of *mīlitāris* military]

militarize, etc see under **military**.

military /*mil'i-tə-ri*/ *adj* of, relating to or characteristic of soldiers, armies, or warfare; warlike. ◆ *n* soldiery; the army; a soldier (*obs*). [Fr *militaire*, from L *mīlitāris* military, from *mīles*, *-itis* a soldier]
■ **mil'itar** *adj* (*obs*) military. **mil'itarily** *adv*. **mil'itarism** *n* an excess of the military spirit; domination by an army, or military class or ideals; belief in the merits of such domination; a tendency to overvalue military power or to view things from the soldier's point of view. **mil'itarist** *n* a soldier (*Shakesp*); a person who studies military science; a person imbued with militarism. **militarist'ic** *adj*. **militarist'ically** *adv*. **militarīzā'tion** or **-s-** *n*. **mil'itarize** or **-ise** *vt* to reduce or convert to a military model or method; to make militaristic; to subject to military domination.
◻ **military academy** *n* a training college for army officer cadets. **military band** *n* a band of brasses, woodwinds, and percussion. **military cross** *n* a decoration awarded for gallantry since 1914, *orig* to army officers (below major) and warrant officers, but later to other ranks as well (*abbrev* **MC**). **military honours** see under **honour**. **military-industrial complex** *n* the armed forces of a country, together with the industries producing military equipment, regarded as a powerful economic and political force. **military medal** *n* a medal for bravery in action awarded between 1916 and 1993 to non-commissioned and warrant officers and serving men (*abbrev* **MM**). **military police** *n* a body of men and women functioning as a police

force within the army (*abbrev* **MP**). **military policeman**, **policewoman** *n*.

militia /*mi-lish'ə*/ *n* a body of men enrolled and drilled as soldiers, but only liable to home service (transformed in 1908 into the Special Reserve; again called militia, 1921); the National Guard and its reserve (*US*); any military force made up of civilians, of varying size and standard of training, often hastily established in time of emergency; a general levy; a territorial force; troops of the second line. [L *mīlitia* military service or force, from *mīles*, *-itis* a soldier]
◻ **milit'iaman** *n*.

milium /*mil'i-əm*/ *n* (pl **mil'ia**) a whitish pimple formed on the skin, *usu* by a clogged sebaceous gland. [L, millet]

milk /*milk*/ *n* a white liquid secreted by female mammals for the nourishment of their young; a milklike juice or preparation; lactation. ◆ *vt* to squeeze or draw milk from; to supply with milk; to extract money, venom, etc from; to extract; to manipulate or exploit, as if milking a cow. ◆ *vi* to yield milk. [OE (Mercian) *milc* (WSax *meolc*) milk; Ger *Milch* milk; L *mulgēre*, Gr *amelgein*, to milk]
■ **milk'en** *adj* (*rare*) of or like milk. **milk'er** *n* a person who milks cows, etc; a machine for milking cows; a cow that gives milk. **milk'ily** *adv*. **milk'iness** *n* cloudiness; mildness. **milk'ing** *n* the act or art of milking (*lit* or *fig*); the amount of milk drawn at one time. ◆ *adj* relating to or used for milking. **milk'less** *adj*. **milk'like** *adj*. **milk'y** *adj* made of, full of, like, or yielding, milk; clouded; soft; gentle; weak, spineless.
◻ **milk-and-wa'ter** *adj* insipid; wishy-washy. **milk bar** *n* a shop selling milk, milk shakes, etc for drinking on the premises. **milk cap** *n* any fungus of the large and mainly inedible genus *Lactarius*, so called because of a milky fluid that it exudes when bruised. **milk chocolate** *n* eating chocolate made from cocoa, cocoa butter, sugar, and condensed or dried milk. **milk'-cow** *n* a milch-cow. **milk-denti'tion** *n* the first set of teeth. **milk'en-way** *n* (*Bacon*) the Milky Way. **milk fever** *n* a fever accompanying the secretion of milk shortly after childbirth; in cows, a condition that may occur (without fever) after calving, characterized by low sugar and calcium levels in the blood, paralysis and unconsciousness. **milk'fish** *n* a large silvery fish (*Chanos chanos*) of the Pacific and Indian Oceans, widely used as food and often bred in fish farms; a percoid fish (*Parascorpis typus*) of the coastal water of southern Africa. **milk float** *n* a small, open-sided vehicle used to deliver milk on a milk round. **milk'-gland** *n* a mammary gland. **milk glass** *n* a *usu* white, but sometimes coloured, opaque glass. **milk gravy** *n* (*N Am*) creamy gravy made with milk. **milk'-house** *n* a place for keeping milk. **milking machine** *n* a machine for milking cows. **milking parlour** see under **parlour**. **milking stool** *n* a stool on which the milker sits. **milk'ing-time** *n*. **milk'-kinship** *n* the bond arising from fostering. **milk leg** *n* the painful swelling of a woman's leg due to thrombosis of the femoral veins after childbirth, white-leg. **milk-liv'ered** *adj* (*Shakesp*) white-livered, cowardly. **milk loaf** *n* a loaf of a sweetish kind of bread, made with milk rather than water. **milk'maid** *n* a woman or girl who milks cows, or works in a dairy. **milk'man** *n* a man who sells or delivers milk. **milk'-molar** *n* a grinding milk tooth, shed and superseded by a premolar. **milk pan** *n* a saucepan with a pouring lip on one or each side, used for heating milk, etc. **milk porridge** *n* porridge made with milk instead of water. **milk pudding** *n* rice, tapioca, etc, cooked with milk. **milk punch** *n* a drink made of milk, rum or whisky, sugar, and nutmeg. **milk round** *n* a milkman's normal morning route; a periodic series of visits as in the yearly recruitment of undergraduates by large companies. **milk run** *n* a milkman's morning round; a routine flight (*orig US Air Force sl*); any routine or uneventful journey or enterprise (*sl*). **milk shake** *n* a drink made from cold milk shaken up with a flavouring and sometimes ice cream; a stimulating drench containing sodium bicarbonate given to a racehorse before a race (*sl*). **milk sickness** *n* trembles; the acute trembling, vomiting and weakness occurring in humans as a result of the consumption of meat or dairy products of cattle afflicted with trembles. **milk snake** *n* *Lampropeltis doliata*, a non-venomous N American snake of the Colubridae family, popularly believed to milk sleeping cattle. **milk'sop** *n* a piece of bread sopped or soaked in milk; a soft, unadventurous, effeminate man. **milk stout** *n* stout sweetened with lactose. **milk sugar** *n* lactose. **milk thistle** *n* lady's thistle (*Silybum marianum*), with white-veined leaves. **milk tooth** *n* one of the first or deciduous set of teeth. **milk train** *n* a local, early morning train service; a slow train stopping at small, local stations; an early morning flight or patrol (*RAF sl*). **milk'-tree** *n* a tree yielding a milklike nourishing juice, such as the cowtree of Venezuela, or the massaranduba of N Brazil. **milk vetch** *n* a plant of the genus *Astragalus*, cultivated as fodder and supposed to increase yield of milk. **milk'-walk** *n* a milkman's round. **milk'-warm** *adj* warm as new milk. **milk'weed** *n* a plant of the genus *Asclepias*, from its milky juice; any of various plants with milky juice (**milkweed butterfly** the monarch butterfly). **milk'-white** *adj*. **milk'wood** *n* any of various trees producing latex. **milk'wort** *n* a plant (producing *Polygala*) supposed by some to promote the production of milk in women. **Milky Way** *n* the Galaxy.

■ words derived from main entry word; ◻ compound words; ■ idioms and phrasal verbs

■ **cry over spilt milk** see under **cry. in milk** (of an animal) lactating. **milk and honey** abundance, plenty; luxury. **milk of human kindness** (*Shakesp*) compassionate nature. **milk of lime** or **milk of magnesia** a suspension of calcium hydroxide or magnesium hydroxide in water. **milk of sulphur** precipitated sulphur.

milko /mil'kō/ (*Aust sl*) *n* a milkman. [From the cry 'Milk-Oh!']

mill[1] /mil/ *n* a machine for grinding by crushing between hard, rough surfaces, or for more or less similar operations; a building or factory where corn, wheat, etc, is ground, or manufacture of some kind is carried on, such as spinning and weaving, paper-making, sawing of timber; a place or institution that mass-produces anything, *esp* in an impersonal or factory-like manner (*fig*); a snuffbox (also **mull**), *orig* one with grinding apparatus (*Scot*); a boxing match (*old sl*). ◆ *vt* to grind; to press, stamp, roll, cut into bars, full, furrow the edges of, or otherwise treat in a mill; to froth up; to beat severely with the fists (*old sl*); to turn over in the mind, to mull (with *over*). ◆ *vi* to move round in a curve; to practise the business of a miller; to box (*old sl*); (often with *about* or *around*) (of a crowd) to move in an aimless or confused manner. [OE *myln*, from LL *molīna*, from L *mola* a mill, from *molere* to grind]

■ **mill'able** *adj.* **milled** *adj* prepared by a grinding-mill or a coining-press; transversely grooved on the edge (as a coin or screw-head); treated by machinery, *esp* smoothed by calendering rollers in a paper mill. **mill'er** *n* a person who owns or works a mill; a milling machine. **mill'ing** *n* the business of a miller; the act of passing anything through a mill; the act of fulling cloth; the process of turning and ridging the edge of a screw-head or coin; a gruelling; aimless or confused movement of a crowd. **milloc'racy** *n* (*hist*) a governing class of mill owners, or their rule. **mill'ocrat** *n*. ▫ **mill'board** *n* stout pasteboard, used *esp* in binding books. **mill'dam** *n* the dam of a millpond; a millpond; a millrace or tail-race (*Scot*). **miller's dog** same as **tope**[3]. **miller's thumb** the bullhead. **mill'-eye** *n* the opening by which meal comes from a mill. **mill girl** *n*. **mill'hand** *n* a worker in a mill. **mill'-head** *n* (*mining*) ore accepted for processing after removal of waste rock and detritus. **mill'-horse** *n* a horse that turns a mill. **milling cutter** *n* a hardened steel disc or cylinder with teeth on the periphery and faces, used in a milling machine for grooving, slotting, etc. **milling grade** *n* (*mining*) ore sufficiently rich, in eg metal, to repay the cost of processing. **milling machine** *n* a machine-tool for shaping metal, with rotating cutters. **mill owner** *n*. **mill'pond** *n* a pond to hold water for driving a mill (proverbially smooth); the Atlantic Ocean (*facetious*). **mill'race** *n* the current of water that turns a millwheel, or the channel in which it runs. **mill'rind** *n* an iron support fitted across the hole in an upper millstone. **mill'run** *n* a millrace; a test of the quality or mineral content of ore or rock by milling it. **mill'scale** *n* scale formed on iron or steel during heating for forging. **mill-six'pence** *n* (*Shakesp*) a milled sixpence. **mill'stone** *n* either of the two stones used in a mill for grinding corn; a very heavy burden (*fig*). **millstone grit** *n* a hard, gritty sandstone suitable for millstones; (with *cap*) a series of grits, sandstones, shales, underlying the British Coal Measures. **mill'stream** *n* the stream of water that turns a millwheel. **mill'tail** *n* a tailrace. **mill'-tooth** *n* a molar. **mill'wheel** *n* a water wheel used for driving a mill. **mill'work** *n* the machinery of a mill; the planning and putting up of machinery in mills. **mill'worker** *n*. **mill'wright** *n* a wright or mechanic who builds and repairs mills. ■ **gastric mill** in Malacostraca, a digestive organ, sometimes known as the stomach, provided with muscles and ossicles for the trituration of food. **go** or **put through the mill** to undergo or subject to probationary hardships, suffering or experience, or severe handling. **run-of-the-mill** see under **run. see through a millstone** to see far into or through difficult questions.

mill[2] /mil/ *n* the thousandth part of a US dollar (not coined); a mil. [L *mille* a thousand]

mill[3] /mil/ (*sl*) *vt* and *vi* to rob; to steal.

mille /mēl/ (*Fr*) *n* thousand. ■ **millefeuille** or **millefeuilles** /mēl-fœy'/ *n* (Fr *feuille* leaf) a layered cake made with puff-pastry, cream, etc. **millefleurs** /mēl-flœr/ *n* (Fr *fleur* flower) a perfume prepared from many kinds of flowers; (also **mille fleurs**) a pattern of small, scattered flowers, used as a background in tapestry, on porcelain, etc.

millefiori /mē-le-fē-ō'rē/ *n* an ornamental glass-making technique, in which variously coloured rods are fused together and cut into transverse sections, often for embedding in clear glass; glass produced in this way (also **millefiori glass**). [Ital, thousand flowers]

millenary /mi-len'ə-ri or -lēn', also mil'ə-nə-ri/ *n* a thousand; a thousand years; a thousandth anniversary; a signatory of the Millenary Petition (*hist*); a believer in the millennium. ◆ *adj* consisting of a thousand, or a thousand years; relating to the millennium or to belief in it. [L *mīllēnārius* of a thousand, from *mīlle* thousand] ■ **millenā'rian** *adj* relating to the millennium. ◆ *n* a believer in the millennium. **millenā'rianism** *n.* **mill'enarism** *n.*

▫ **Millenary Petition** *n* (*hist*) a petition of Puritan tendency, signed by nearly a thousand clergymen, presented to James I of England on his arrival in London in 1603.

millennium /mi-len'i-əm/ *n* (pl **millenn'ia** or **millenn'iums**) a thousand years; a thousandth anniversary, millenary; the thousand years after the second coming of Christ; (*usu ironic*) a coming golden age. [L *mīlle* a thousand, and *annus* a year] ■ **millenn'ial** *adj.* ◆ *n* a member of the generation born in the early 1980s in whose lives the Internet has always been important. **millenn'ialist** *n* a believer in the millennium. **millenn'ianism** *n.* **millenn'iarism** *n.* ▫ **millennium bug** *n* a deficiency in computer programs due to using year codes with only two digits, which was prophesied to cause chaos at the change of century in the year 2000.

millepede see **millipede**.

millepore /mil'i-pōr or -pör/ *n* a hydrozoan coral with many pores or polyp-cells. [L *mīlle* a thousand, and *porus*, from Gr *poros* a passage]

miller see under **mill**[1].

Millerian /mi-lē'ri-ən/ *adj* relating to WH *Miller* (1801–80), mineralogist, or to the crystallographic notation used by him, by which a plane is represented by indices (**Miller** or **crystal indices**) which are the reciprocals of its intercepts on the axes (expressed as fractions of the parameters). ■ **mill'erite** *n* native nickel sulphide, crystallizing in needles, named in honour of WH Miller.

millesimal /mi-les'i-məl/ *adj* thousandth; consisting of thousandth parts. ◆ *n* a thousandth part. [L *mīllēsimus*, from *mīlle* a thousand] ■ **milles'imally** *adv.*

millet /mil'it/ *n* a food-grain (*Panicum miliaceum*); extended to other species and genera (*Setaria, Panicum*, etc). [Fr *millet*, from L *milium*] ▫ **mill'et-grass** *n* a tall, panicled woodland grass (*Milium effusum*). **mill'et-seed** *n* millet. ◆ *adj* of the size or appearance of seeds of millet; miliary.

milli- /mi-li-/ *combining form* in names of units, denoting a thousandth part (10^{-3}). [L *mīlle* a thousand] ■ **mill'iampere, mill'iare** /-är/, **mill'ibar, mill'ilitre**, etc, *n* a thousandth part of an *ampere, are, bar, litre*, etc. **millimicro-** *combining form* (*obs*) same as **nano-. millimilli-** *combining form* (*obs*) same as **micro-.**

Millian /mil'i-ən/ *adj* of or relating to the philosopher John Stuart *Mill* (1806–73), his theories or his followers. ◆ *n* a follower of John Stuart Mill.

milliard /mil'yärd/ *n* a thousand million. [Fr, from L *mīlle* a thousand]

milliary /mil'i-ə-ri/ *adj* relating to a Roman mile. ◆ *n* a Roman milestone. [L *mīlliārius*]

millibar /mil'i-bär/ *n* a unit of atmospheric pressure, a thousandth of a bar (*abbrev* **mb**). [**milli-**]

millième /mēl-yem'/ *n* a coin representing one-thousandth of the basic unit of currency, as in Egypt (also in Tunisia **millime** /mē-lēm'/). [Fr, from L *mīlle* a thousand]

milligram or **milligramme** /mil'i-gram/ *n* a unit of mass, a thousandth of a gram (*abbrev* **mg**). [**milli-**]

millilitre /mil'i-lē-tər/ *n* a unit of volume, a thousandth of a litre (*abbrev* **ml**). [**milli-**]

millimetre /mil'i-mē-tər/ *n* a unit of length, a thousandth of a metre (*abbrev* **mm**). [**milli-**]

millimole /mil'i-mōl/ (*chem*) *n* a thousandth of a mole (*abbrev* **mmol**). [**milli-** and **mole**[4]]

milliner /mil'i-nər/ *n* a person who makes or sells women's headgear, trimmings, etc; *orig* a dealer in goods made in *Milan*, or 'fancy goods'. [*Milaner* a trader in Milan wares, esp silks and ribbons] ■ **mill'inery** *n* the articles made or sold by milliners; the industry of making them. ■ **horse-milliner** see under **horse. man-milliner** see under **man**[1].

million /mil'yən or -i-ən/ *n* a thousand thousands (10^6); (loosely; *esp* in *pl*) a very great number (*inf*); a million pounds, dollars, etc; (in *pl*) the guppy. ◆ *adj* being a million in number. [Fr, from LL *mīlliō, -ōnis*, from L *mīlle* a thousand] ■ **millionaire** /-ār'/ *n* (also *fem* **millionair'ess**) a person with resources worth (more or less) a million pounds, dollars, etc. **mill'ionary** *adj* relating to, or consisting of, millions. **mill'ionfold** *adj* and *adv* (*usu* preceded by *a* or a numeral). **mill'ionth** *adj* and *n*. ■ **look like a million dollars** (*inf*) to appear very beautiful. **one in a million** a rare or exceptional person or thing. **the million** the mass of people generally, the multitude.

millipede or **millepede** /mil'i-pēd/, also **milliped** or **milleped** /-ped/ *n* any myriapod of the class Chilognatha, vegetarian cylindrical animals with many joints, most of which bear two pairs of legs; a woodlouse (*rare*). [L *mīllepeda* a woodlouse, from *mīlle* a thousand, and *pēs, pēdis* a foot]

milliprobe /mil'i-prōb/ *n* an instrument for analysing small quantities, *esp* a spectrometer. [**milli-**]

millirem /mil'i-rem/ *n* a unit of radiation dosage, a thousandth of a rem. [**milli-**]

millisecond /mil'i-sek-ənd/ *n* a thousandth of a second (*abbrev* **ms**). [**milli-**]

millisievert /mil'i-sē-vert/ *n* a unit of radiation dosage, a thousandth of a sievert (*abbrev* **msv**). [**milli-**]

mill-mountain /mil'mown'tən/ *n* purging flax (see under **flax**). [Origin unknown]

Mills-and-Boon /milz'ənd-boon'/ *adj* conforming to a highly unrealistic romantic ideal, as in the fiction published by *Mills and Boon*.

Mills bomb /milz bom/ or **grenade** /gri-nād'/ *n* a type of grenade, invented by the English engineer Sir William *Mills* (1856–1932), used by the British forces in both World Wars.

MILNET /mil'net/ *n* a long-distance US *mil*itary communications *net*work.

milo /mī'lō/ *n* (*pl* **mī'los**) any of several drought-resistant varieties of sorghum, *orig* from Africa but introduced elsewhere, cultivated as a grain and fodder crop (also **milo maize**). [Sotho *maili*]

milometer see **mileometer** under **mile**.

milord /mi-lörd'/ or (*rare*) **milor** *n* a term of address used for an aristocratic or rich Englishman, eg by household staff. [Fr modification of *my lord*]

Milquetoast /milk'tōst/ (also without *cap*) *n* a very timid, unassertive person. [Comic-strip character Caspar *Milquetoast* created in the 1920s by the American cartoonist HT Webster]

milreis /mil'rās/ *n* (*pl* **mil'reis**) a former unit of currency in Portugal and Brazil worth 1000 reis. [Port, thousand reis]

milsey /mil'si/ (*Scot*) *n* a milk-strainer. [**milk**, and either **sye** or **sile**]

milt /milt/ or **melt** /melt/ *n* the spleen (also, in Jewish cookery, **miltz** /milts/); the soft roe of male fishes. ◆ *vt* (of fishes) to impregnate. [OE *milte*, Ger *Milz* spleen]
■ **milt'er** *n* a male fish, *esp* in the breeding season.

miltonia /mil-tō'ni-ə/ *n* a plant of the *Miltonia* genus of tropical American orchids with brightly-coloured flowers. [Charles Fitzwilliam, Viscount *Milton* (1786–1857), English statesman and horticulturalist]

Miltonic /mil-ton'ik/ *adj* relating to John *Milton* (1608–74), English poet; relating to or in the characteristic style of his poetry.
■ **Miltonian** /-tōn'i-ən/ *adj* and *n*. **Mil'tonism** /-tən-izm/ *n*.
❑ **Miltonic sonnet** see under **sonnet**.

Miltown® /mil'town/ *n* a proprietary name for meprobamate.

miltz see **milt**.

Milvus /mil'vəs/ *n* the kite genus of birds of prey. [L *milvus* a kite]
■ **mil'vine** *adj*.

mim /mim/ (*Scot* and *dialect*) *adj* demure, prim. [Imit]
❑ **mim-mou'd** /-mood/ *adj* demurely spoken.

mimbar /mim'bär/ or **minbar** /min'/ *n* a mosque pulpit. [Ar *minbar*]

MIME /mīm/ *abbrev*: Multipurpose Internet Mail Extensions, an Internet standard for transmission of email.

mime /mīm/ *n* a play without dialogue, relying solely on movement, expression, etc; an actor in such a play (also **mime artist**); (in ancient Greek and Roman theatre) a farcical play making great use of flamboyant gesture and facial expression; an actor in such a farce; acting without words; a mimic; a buffoon. ◆ *vt* and *vi* to act as a mime; to move the mouth in time to recorded singing, giving the illusion of a live performance; to make the movements involved in the performing of a specific activity, eg as a clue in guessing-games; to mimic. [Gr *mīmos* a mime, *mīmēsis* imitation, *mīmētēs* an imitator]
■ **mīm'er** *n*. **mimesis** /mim- or mīm-ē'sis/ *n* imitation or representation in art; the rhetorical use of a person's supposed or imaginable words; simulation of one disease by another (*med*); mimicry (*biol*). **mime'ster** *n*. **mimet'ic** or **mimet'ical** /mim- or mīm-/ *adj* imitative; mimic; of, relating to or displaying mimicry, mimesis or miming. **mimet'ically** *adv*. **mimetite** /mim'i- or mīm'i-/ *n* a mineral, lead arsenate and chloride (from its resemblance to pyromorphite). **mimic** /mim'ik/ *n* a person who imitates, *esp* someone who performs in ludicrous imitation of others' speech and gestures; a mime-actor (*obs*); an unsuccessful imitator or imitation; a plant or animal exemplifying mimicry. ◆ *adj* miming (*obs*); imitative; mock or sham. ◆ *vt* (**mim'icking; mim'icked**) to imitate, *esp* in ridicule or so as to incur ridicule; to ape; to produce an imitation of; to resemble deceptively. **mimical** /mim'/ *adj* (*obs*). **mim'icker** *n*. **mimicry** /mim'/ *n* the skill, practice or act of mimicking; the adoption by one species of the colour, habits, sound or structure of another species, either for

camouflage or to deceive a third species into confusing them (*biol* and *zool*). **mīmog'rapher** *n* a writer of mimes. **mīmog'raphy** *n*. **Mī'mus** *n* the mockingbird genus.

mimeograph /mim'i-ō-gräf/ *n* an apparatus on which handwritten or typescript sheets can be reproduced from a stencil; a copy so produced. ◆ *vt* to produce a copy or copies of (something) in this way. [*Mimeograph*, formerly a trademark]

mimer...to...**mimetite** see under **mime**.

mimic¹, mimicker, mimicry see under **mime**.

mimic² and **mimmick** see **minnick**.

miminy-piminy /mim'i-ni-pim'i-ni/ same as **niminy-piminy**.

mimivirus /mim'i-vī-rəs/ *n* a virus found in amoebae, much larger and having a more complex genetic structure than any other known virus. [From *mimi*cking microbe, because it was mistaken for a bacterium when first discovered]

mimographer, etc see under **mime**.

mimosa /mi-mō'zə/ *n* (*pl* **mimō'sas** or **mimō'sae** /-sī/) a plant of the sensitive plant genus *Mimosa, esp* that having clusters of yellow flowers; popularly extended to *Acacia* and other genera of the **Mimosā'ceae** /mim- or mīm-/, a regular-flowered family of Leguminosae; Buck's fizz (chiefly *US*). [Gr *mīmos* a mimic, the movement of the leaf when touched seen as an imitation of a cowering animal]
■ **mimosā'ceous** /mim- or mīm-/ *adj*.

mimsy or **mimsey** /mim'zi/ (*orig dialect*) *adj* prim, demure; prudish. [**mim**; influenced by Lewis Carroll's invented word *mimsy*]

mimulus /mim'ū-ləs/ *n* a plant of the musk and monkey flower genus *Mimulus* of the figwort family. [Gr *mīmos* a mime, with L dimin sfx *-ulus*, from the grinning corolla]

Mimus see under **mime**.

MIN *abbrev*: Mobile Identification Number, a multi-digit identification number for a mobile phone.

Min. *abbrev*: Minister; Ministry.

min. *abbrev*: minimum; minute(s).

mina¹ /mī'nə/, also **maneh** /mä'ne/ or **mna** /mnä/ *n* (*pl* **mī'nas** or **mī'nae** /-ē/, **man'ehs** or **mnas**) a Greek weight, or sum of money, equivalent to 100 drachmas; a weight of money valued at fifty, or sometimes sixty, shekels (*Bible*). [L *mina*, from Gr *mnā*; cf Heb *māneh*]

mina² see **myna**.

minacious /mi-nā'shəs/ *adj* threatening. [L *mināx, -ācis*, from *minārī* to threaten]
■ **minacity** /-as'-/ *n*.

Minamata disease /mi-nə-mä'tə di-zēz'/ *n* a disease caused by eating fish contaminated with industrial waste containing mercury compounds, and characterized by a *usu* permanent condition involving impairment of speech and sight, muscular weakness, paralysis, etc, and sometimes coma or death. [*Minamata*, town in Japan where the disease was first recognized]

minar /mi-när'/ *n* a tower. [Ar *manār, manārat* lighthouse, from *nār* fire]
■ **min'aret** (or /-ret'/) *n* a mosque tower, from which the call to prayer is given. **minaret'ed** *adj*.

minatory /min'ə-tə-ri or mī'nə-/ *adj* threatening. [L *minārī, -ātus* to threaten]

minauderie /mē-nō-də-rē'/ *n* a display of affectation. [Fr]

minbar see **mimbar**.

mince /mins/ *vt* (**minc'ing; minced** /minst/) to cut into small pieces; to chop finely; to diminish, or suppress a part of, in speaking; to pronounce affectedly. ◆ *vi* to walk with affected nicety, *usu* with quick short steps; to speak affectedly. ◆ *n* minced meat; mincemeat. [OFr *mincier, minchier*, from L *minūtus*; cf **minute²**]
■ **minc'er** *n* a person who minces; a machine for mincing meat, etc. **minc'ing** *adj* not speaking frankly or openly; speaking or walking with affected nicety *esp* in an ostentatiously camp manner. **minc'ingly** *adv*.
❑ **minced collops** see under **collop**. **mince'meat** *n* meat chopped small; hence anything thoroughly broken or cut to pieces; a chopped, spiced mixture of dried fruit, peel, suet and other ingredients, *usu* steeped in brandy. **mince pie** *n* a pie made with mincemeat, *esp* in the latter sense.
■ **make mincemeat of** to destroy utterly (*esp fig*). **mince matters** or **words** to speak of things with affected delicacy, or to soften an account unduly.

minceur /mē-sœr'/ (*Fr*) *adj* (of food or cooking) lean, low-fat.

MIND /mīnd/ *n* a British mental health charity.

mind /mīnd/ *n* the state of thought and feeling; wits, right senses, sanity; consciousness; intellect; that which thinks, knows, feels, and wills;

inclination; attention; direction of the will; soul; personality; a thinking or directing person; memory; commemoration (*archaic* or *RC*); record, mention (*obs*); thought; judgement; opinion; purpose (*Shakesp* and *Milton*). ◆ *vt* to attend to; to tend, have care or oversight of; to be careful about; to beware of; to remind (*archaic* and *Scot*); to bring to mind (*Spenser*); to remember (*Scot*); (*reflexive*) to remember (with *of*; *archaic*); to purpose (*Shakesp*); to have a mind to (*dialect*); to apply oneself to; to be troubled by, object to, dislike; to notice (*obs* or *dialect*). ◆ *vi* to attend; to care; to look out, take heed; to be troubled, object; to remember (with *of*; *dialect*). ◆ *interj* be careful, watch out. [OE *gemynd*, from *munan* to think; Dan *minde* memorial, L *mēns* the mind]

■ **mind'ed** *adj* inclined; disposed. ◆ *combining form* denoting having a mind of a specified kind or inclination. **-mindedness** *combining form* denoting inclination. **mind'er** *n* a person who minds a machine, child, etc; a bodyguard, *orig* and *esp* of a criminal (*sl*); an aide or adviser employed by a public figure, *esp* to manage publicity (*inf*); a child left to be minded (*archaic*); a short wooden stick used by a child to propel a hoop. **mind'ful** *adj* bearing in mind; taking thought or care; attentive; observant; having memory (*archaic*); inclined (*obs*). **mind'fully** *adv*. **mind'fulness** *n* a method of reducing stress by developing awareness of one's own mental condition and focusing the attention on the present. **mind'ing** *n* (*Scot*) a memory, something recalled; a *usu* small gift, to mark an occasion or in remembrance of the giver. **mind'less** *adj* without mind; senseless; without reason; unmindful. **mind'lessly** *adv*. **mind'lessness** *n*.

❑ **mind'-altering** *adj* (of a drug) causing violent changes of mood and behaviour. **mind'-bender** *n* a brainteaser, a puzzle. **mind'-bending** *adj* mind-boggling; forcing the mind to unwonted effort, teasing the brain; permanently inclining the mind towards certain beliefs, etc. **mind'-blowing** *adj* (of a drug) producing a state of ecstasy; (of an experience, etc) producing a similar state, exhilarating; astonishing. **mind'-blowingly** *adv*. **mind-bod'y** *adj* relating to or designating the connection between the mind and the physical body. **mind'-boggling** *adj* astonishing; incomprehensible. **mind'-bogglingly** *adv*. **mind'-cure** or **mind'-healing** *n* the cure or healing of mental or physical illness through the mind or by the supposed influence of another's mind. **mind'-curer** or **-healer** *n*. **mind'-expanding** *adj* (of a drug) causing heightened perception, psychedelic. **mind'fuck** *n* (*vulgar sl*) an exhilarating experience; a sense or state of euphoria. **mind mapping** *n* a technique for stimulating and organizing one's thoughts by writing down key concepts and linking them with lines to show the relationships between them. **mind'-numbing** *adj* (*inf*) causing extreme boredom. **mind'-numblingly** *adv*. **mind'-reader** *n* a thought-reader, a psychic. **mind'-reading** *n*. **mind'set** *n* (a fixed) attitude or habit of mind. **mind's eye** *n* visual imagination, mental view, contemplation. **mind-your-own-bus'iness** *n* a Mediterranean plant (*Helxine soleirolii*) of the nettle family, having small, roundish leaves and producing tiny flowers (also called **baby's-tears**).

■ **absence of mind** inattention to what is going on owing to absorption of the mind in other things. **bear in mind** see under **bear**[1]. **blow one's** or **someone's mind** see under **blow**[1]. **break one's mind** (*obs*) to make known, confide or divulge one's thoughts. **cast one's mind back** to think about, try to recall past events, etc. **change one's mind** to come to a new resolution or opinion. **cross someone's mind** see under **cross**. **do you mind?** an interjection expressing annoyance or disagreement; (also **would you mind?**) do you object? **have a good** or (*archaic*) **great mind (to)** to wish or to be inclined strongly (to). **have a mind of one's own** to be strong-willed and independent, unwilling to be persuaded or dissuaded by others. **have half a mind (to)** to be somewhat inclined (to). **if you don't mind** if you have no objection. **in** (or of) **two minds** wavering, undecided. **know one's own mind** to be sure of one's intentions and opinions; to be self-assured. **make up one's mind** to come to a decision. **mind one's p's and q's** to be watchfully accurate and punctilious. **mind out** (often with *for*) to beware (of), look out (for). **mind you** an expression used to introduce a qualification added to something already said. **mind your eye** (*sl*) look out. **mind your own business** this is not your concern. **month's mind** a commemoration by masses one month after death or burial; a strong desire or inclination. **never mind** do not concern yourself or be upset; it does not matter; you are not to be told. **of one** (or **a**, or the same) **mind** in accord, agreed. **of two minds** uncertain what to think or do. **on one's mind** in one's thoughts, *esp* as a cause of concern. **out of mind** forgotten; out of one's thoughts. **out of one's mind** mad. **piece of one's mind** see under **piece**. **presence of mind** a state of mental calmness in which all the powers of the mind are on the alert and ready for action. **put in mind (of)** to remind (of). **put out of one's mind** to think no more about, forget about. **set one's mind on** to be determined to have or attain. **set** or **put one's mind to** to focus one's attention on. **speak one's mind** to say plainly what one thinks. **take someone's mind off** to distract someone from. **time out of mind** from time immemorial. **to my,** etc **mind** to my, etc thinking, in my, etc opinion; to my, etc liking.

year's mind a commemorative service on the anniversary of a death or burial.

Mindel /*min'dl*/ (*geol*) *n* the second stage of glaciation in the Alps (also *adj*). [*Mindel*, a tributary of the Danube, in Bavaria]
■ **Mindelian** /-*dē'li-ən*/ *adj*.

Mindererus spirit /*min-də-rē'rəs*/ *n* ammonium acetate solution, a diaphoretic. [Latinized name of the German physician RM *Minderer* (c.1570–1621)]

mine[1] /*mīn*/ *pronoun* genitive of **I**, used predicatively or absolutely, belonging to me; my people; that which belongs to me; (adjectivally, *esp* before a vowel or *h*, or after its noun) my (*archaic* and *poetic*). [OE *mīn*]

mine[2] /*mīn*/ *n* a place from which minerals, *esp* coal or precious metals, are dug (not *usu* a source of building-stone, and legally distinguished from a quarry by being artificially lighted); a cavity in the earth (*archaic*); a burrowing animal's gallery, such as an insect's in a leaf; an excavation dug under a position to give secret ingress, to subvert it, or to blow it up (*milit*); an explosive charge placed in this; a submerged or floating charge of explosives in a metal case to destroy ships; a landmine; a rich source (*fig*). ◆ *vt* to excavate, tunnel, make passages in or under; to obtain by excavation; to exploit (a natural resource) without, or at a faster rate than, replenishing it; to work as a miner; to bring down or blow up by a mine; to cover (an area) with explosive mines; to lay explosive mines in or under. ◆ *vi* to dig or work a mine or mines; to tunnel; to burrow; to lay mines; to proceed secretly or insidiously (*fig*). [Fr *mine* (noun), *miner* (verb), of doubtful origin]

■ **min'able** or **mine'able** *adj*. **mi'ner** *n* a person who works in a mine; a soldier who lays mines; an insect or other animal that makes galleries in the earth, leaves, etc; a honeyeater of the genus *Manorina* (*Aust*). **min'ing** *n* and *adj*. **min'y** *adj* relating to mines; like a mine. ❑ **mine'-captain** *n* the overseer of a mine. **mine detection** *n*. **mine detector** *n* an electromagnetic apparatus for detecting explosive mines. **mine dump** *n* (*S Afr*) a large mound of mining residue. **mine'field** *n* an area laid with explosive mines; an enterprise, etc containing many potential hazards or traps (*fig*). **mine'hunter** *n* a ship equipped for locating undersea mines. **mine'layer** *n* a ship or aircraft for laying mines. **mine owner** *n*. **miner's anaemia** *n* ankylostomiasis. **miner's inch** *n* the amount of water that will flow in twenty-four hours through an opening of one square inch at a pressure of six inches of water. **miner's lamp** *n* a lamp carried by a miner, *usu* attached to a helmet or cap. **miner's phthisis** *n* phthisis caused by breathing dusty air in mines. **miner's right** *n* (*Aust* and *NZ*) a licence to prospect for gold, minerals, etc. **miner's worm** *n* the hookworm that causes ankylostomiasis. **mine'shaft** *n* a well-like excavation or passage into a mine. **mine'stone** *n* ore, *esp* ironstone. **mine'sweeper** *n* a ship which drags the water to remove undersea mines. **mine'sweeping** *n*. **mine'-thrower** *n* (a *transl* of Ger *Minenwerfer* /*mē'nən-ver-fər*/, in soldiers' slang **minnie** /*min'i*/) a trench-mortar. **mine worker** *n* a miner. **mining bee** *n* a bee that builds its nest in long underground tunnels.

mine[3] /*mīn*/ (*Shakesp, Merry Wives of Windsor* I.3) *n perh* for **mind** (disposition), or **mien**.

mineola see **minneola**.

mineral /*min'ə-rəl*/ *n* any of various classes of inorganic substances, *esp* solid, naturally occurring and crystalline in form; a substance obtained by mining; ore; a substance neither animal nor vegetable; a mine (*Shakesp*); a poison (*Shakesp*); a mineral water (in a wide sense). ◆ *adj* relating to minerals; having the nature of minerals; (*esp* of water) impregnated with minerals; of inorganic substance or nature. [Fr *minéral*, from *miner* to mine; cf **mine**[2]]

■ **min'eralist** *n* a person with a specialist knowledge of minerals, a mineralogist. **mineraliza'tion** or **-s-** *n*. **min'eralize** or **-ise** *vt* to make into a mineral; to give the properties of a mineral to; to go looking for and examining minerals. **mineralīz'er** or **-s-** *n* a person who, or that which, mineralizes; an element, eg sulphur, that combines with a metal to form an ore; a gas or vapour that promotes the crystallizing out of minerals from an igneous magma. **mineralog'ical** *adj* relating to mineralogy. **mineralog'ically** *adv*. **mineral'ogist** *n* a person skilled or trained in mineralogy. **mineralogize** or **-ise** /-*al'*/ *vi* to collect or study minerals. **mineral'ogy** *n* the science of minerals. ❑ **mineral alkali** *n* (*obs*) sodium carbonate. **mineral caoutchouc** *n* elaterite. **mineral coal** *n* coal in the ordinary sense, distinguished from charcoal. **mineral jelly** *n* a soft yellow substance resembling soft soap, obtained from the less volatile residue of petroleum. **mineral kingdom** *n* that department of nature which comprises substances that are neither animal nor vegetable. **mineral oil** *n* any oil of mineral origin. **mineral pitch** *n* natural asphalt. **mineral processing** *n* the crushing and sizing of ore into waste and value by chemical, electrical, magnetic, physicochemical methods and gravity. **mineral spirits** *n pl* (*N Am*) white spirit. **mineral spring** or **well** *n* a spring of mineral water. **mineral tallow** *n* a soft yellowish natural hydrocarbon.

mineral tar *n* pissasphalt. **mineral water** *n* spring water impregnated with minerals; an artificial imitation of this; a usually effervescent non-alcoholic beverage. **mineral wax** *n* ozokerite. **mineral wool** *n* a mass of fibres formed by blowing steam through molten slag.

mineralocorticoid /*min-ə-ra-lō-kör'ti-koid*/ (*biochem*) *n* any of a group of hormones that regulate the balance of fluids and salts in the body. [**mineral** and **corticoid**]

Minerva /*mi-nûr'və*/ (*Roman myth*) *n* the Roman goddess of intelligence and skill, identified with the Greek Athene. [L]

Minervois /*mi-nûr-vwä'*/ *n* a wine made at *Minervois* in SW France.

minestrone /*mi-ni-strō'ni*/ *n* a thick, mixed-vegetable soup containing pasta or rice. [Ital]

minette /*mi-net'*/ *n* an intrusive rock of orthoclase and biotite in a close-grained groundmass. [Fr]

minever see **miniver**.

Ming /*ming*/ *n* a Chinese dynasty (1368–1644). ◆ *adj* of this dynasty, its time, or *esp* its pottery and other art.

ming[1] /*ming*/, **meng** /*meng*/ or **menge** /*menj*/ (*archaic*) *vt* and *vi* (pat and pap **minged** or **menged** (older forms **meint**, **meynt** /*ment, mänt*/, **ment**)) to mix; to unite, couple; to work up. [OE *mengan*; Ger *mengen*]

ming[2] /*ming*/ (*orig Scot*) *n* an unpleasant smell, a stink. *vi* to look or smell unpleasant. [Origin unknown]
  ■ **ming'er** *n* (*derog inf*) an unattractive or undesirable person or thing. **ming'ing** or **ming'in'** *adj* having an unpleasant smell, stinking; dirty or unpleasant.

minge /*minj*/ (*vulgar sl*; *orig dialect*) *n* the female genitalia; a woman, or women collectively, regarded as a sexual object or objects. [Dialect word; from Romany *minchi*]

mingle /*ming'gl*/ *vt* and *vi* to mix, blend, combine. ◆ *n* a mixture; a medley. [Frequentative of **ming**[1]]
  ■ **ming'lement** *n*. **ming'ler** *n*. **ming'ling** *n*. **ming'lingly** *adv*.
  ❑ **ming'le-mangle** *n* a confused mixture, a jumble. ◆ *adj* jumbled. ◆ *vt* to confuse, jumble together.

mingy /*min'ji*/ (*inf*) *adj* (**ming'ier**; **ming'iest**) niggardly, stingy, meagre. [Perh a portmanteau word from **mangy** or **mean**[2] and **stingy**[2]]
  ■ **min'giness** *n*.

mini /*min'i*/ *n* short for **minidress**, **minicomputer** or **miniskirt**; something small of its type; (**Mini**®) a type of small car. ◆ *adj* (*inf*) small, miniature.

mini- /*mi-ni-*/ *combining form* used to signify small. [Contraction of **miniature**]
  ■ **min'ibar** *n* a small refrigerator in a hotel room, stocked with drinks and light snacks. **min'ibike** *n* a lightweight motorcycle, *esp* for use off the public road. **min'ibreak** *n* a short holiday, eg a weekend or long weekend break. **min'ibudget** or **min'i-budget** *n* a supplementary budget, produced *esp* in times of fiscal emergency. **mini-buff'et** *n* a snack bar on a train. **minibus** *n* see separate entry. **min'icab** *n* an unlicensed taxicab that must be ordered by phone rather than hailed in the street. **min'icabbing** *n*. **min'icam** *n* a portable, shoulder-held TV camera, as used in news reporting. **min'i-car** *n*. **min'icomputer** *n* an obsolete type of computer, lying in capability between a mainframe and a microcomputer. **Min'iDisc**® *n* a small compact disc. **min'idish** *n* a small satellite dish used to receive digital television. **min'idisk** *n* a compact magnetic disk, used *esp* for recording sound in a computer. **min'idress** *n* a dress with a hemline well above the knees. **min'ifloppy** *n* a 5.25in floppy disk (*orig* distinguished from an 8in disk; cf **microfloppy**). **mini flyweight** *n* see **flyweight** under **fly**. **mini-lacrosse** see under **lacrosse**. **min'imart** *n* (*N Am*) a small supermarket, convenience store. **min'i-me** *n* (*inf*) someone who dresses and acts exactly like a taller or older person; a servile assistant. **minimō'to** *n* (*pl* **minimō'tos**) a miniature motorcycle designed for use off the public road (also (*esp N Am*) **pocket bike**). **mini-mo'torway** *n* one with two lanes. **min'ipill** *n* a low-dose oral contraceptive containing no oestrogen. **min'irugby**, **min'ivolley**, etc *n* a simplified version of rugby, volleyball, etc played with a reduced number of players on each side. **min'iseries** *n* a short series of television programmes broadcast *usu* over consecutive days. **min'iskirt** *n* a skirt whose hemline is well above the knees. **min'i-skis** *n pl* short, slightly thick, skis for learners. **min'i-sub** or **mini-sub'marine** *n* a small submarine used for underwater exploration, etc. **Min'itrack**® *n* a system for tracking an earth satellite or a rocket by radio signals from it to a series of ground stations. **min'ivan** *n* a small van with removable seats, used to transport goods or passengers.

miniate see under **minium**.

miniature /*min'i-(ə-)chər, min'yə-tūr* or *-tyər*/ *n* a small or reduced copy, type or breed of anything; a small-scale version of anything; manuscript illumination; a painting on a very small scale, on ivory, vellum, etc; the art of painting in this manner; a chess problem with few pieces or moves; rubrication (*obs*). ◆ *adj* on a small scale; minute;

applied to cameras taking 35mm film. ◆ *vt* to represent on a small scale. [Ital *miniatura*, from L *minium* red lead; meaning affected by association with L *minor*, *minimus*, etc, and their derivatives]
  ■ **min'iaturist** *n* a person who paints or makes miniatures. **miniaturizā'tion** or **-s-** *n*. **min'iaturize** or **-ise** *vt* to make very small; to make something on a small scale.
  ❑ **in miniature** on a small or reduced scale.

minibar...to...**mini-buffet** see under **mini-**.

minibus /*min'i-bus*/ *n* a small bus for ten to fifteen passengers; a light passenger horse-drawn vehicle (*obs*). [L *minor* less, *minimus* least, and **omnibus**]

minicab...to...**minidress** see under **mini-**.

Minié ball or **bullet** /*min'i-ā böl* or *būl'it*/ *n* a cone-shaped bullet containing powder in its base, designed to expand when fired from a **Minié rifle**. [CE *Minié* (1814–79), French officer, the inventor]

minifloppy see under **mini-**.

minify /*min'i-fī*/ *vt* (**min'ifying**; **min'ified**) to diminish, in appearance or reality. [Ill-formed (after **magnify**) from L *minor* less]
  ■ **minificā'tion** *n*.

minikin /*min'i-kin*/ *n* a diminutive or undersized person or thing; a small sort of pin (now *dialect*); a little darling (*archaic* and *dialect*); a thin length of gut used for the treble string of a lute (*obs*). ◆ *adj* diminutive; dainty; affected; mincing. [Obs Du *minneken*, dimin of *minne* love; cf **Minnesinger**]

minim /*min'im*/ *n* orig a least part; a note, formerly the shortest, equal to two crotchets (*music*); (in apothecaries' measure) one-sixtieth of a fluid drachm; (in apothecaries' weight) a grain; a short downstroke in handwriting; a diminutive creature (*Milton*); a friar, sister, or lay member of any of three orders founded by St Francis of Paula (1416–1507), so called as if humbler than even the Friars Minor. ◆ *adj* (*obs*) extremely minute. [Ety as for **minimum**]
  ❑ **minim rest** *n* a rest of the duration of a minim.

minima see **minimum**.

minimal /*min'ə-məl*/ *adj* of least, or least possible, size, amount or degree; of the nature of a minimum; negligible; (of art, etc) minimalist. [Ety as for **minimum**]
  ■ **min'imalism** *n*. **min'imalist** *n* a Menshevik; a person advocating a policy of the least possible action, intervention, etc; a practitioner of minimal art (qv below). ◆ *adj* of or relating to minimalism or minimalists. **min'imally** *adv* in a minimal way or to a minimal extent. ❑ **minimal art** *n* art whose practitioners reject such traditional elements as composition and interrelationship between parts of the whole. **minimal invasive therapy** *n* (*surg*) an operating procedure that does not necessitate stitching or scarring, eg gallstone removal by endoscopy and laser treatment.

minimart see under **mini-**.

minimax /*min'i-maks*/ *n* the lowest value in a set of maximum values (*maths*); (in game theory, eg chess) a strategy designed to minimize one's maximum possible loss; the theory (in a game for two players) that minimizing one's maximum loss equates with maximizing one's minimum gain. ◆ *vt* to minimize the maximum possible extent of (one's loss). [*minimum* and *maximum*]

miniment /*min'i-mənt*/ *n* an obsolete form of **muniment**.

minimoto and **mini-motorway** see under **mini-**.

minimum /*min'i-məm*/ *n* (*pl* **min'imums** or **min'ima**) the least quantity or degree, or the smallest possible; the lowest point or value reached or allowed; a value of a variable at which it ceases to diminish and begins to increase, opp to maximum (*maths*). ◆ *adj* smallest or lowest possible (obtained, recorded, etc). [L *minimus* smallest]
  ■ **min'imism** *n* inclination to reduce a dogma to the least possible. **min'imist** *n*. **minimizā'tion** or **-s-** *n*. **min'imize** or **-ise** *vt* to reduce to the smallest possible amount; to make as light or insignificant as possible; to estimate at the lowest possible; to lessen or diminish; to belittle. **min'imizer** or **-s-** *n*. **min'imus** *n* a being of the smallest size (*Shakesp*); in boys' schools, youngest of the surname.
  ❑ **minimizing glass** *n* a diminishing glass. **minimum lending rate** *n* (from 1972 to 1981) the minimum rate of interest charged by the Bank of England to the discount market. **minimum wage** *n* the lowest wage permitted by law. **minimum weight** same as **mini flyweight** (see **flyweight** under **fly**).

minion /*min'yən*/ *n* a darling, a favourite, *esp* of a prince; a flatterer; a servile dependant; an old type size, *approx* 7-point, between nonpareil and brevier, giving about 10½ lines to the inch (*printing*). [Fr *mignon*, *mignonne*]

minipill and **minirugby** see under **mini-**.

miniscule a non-standard spelling of **minuscule**.

miniseries see under **mini-**.

minish /*min'ish*/ (*archaic*) *vt* to make little or less; to diminish. [Fr *menuiser* to cut small (in carpentry, etc), from L *minūtia* smallness]

---

miniskirt and **mini-skis** see under **mini-**.

minister /min'i-stər/ n a member of the clergy in certain denominations of the Christian church; a person who officiates at the altar; the head, or assistant to the head, of certain religious orders; the responsible head of a department of state affairs; a diplomatic representative of a government in a foreign state, *esp* one ranking below an ambassador; a person who administers or proffers anything, in service or kindness; a person transacting business for another, an agent; a servant (*archaic*). ◆ *vi* to give attentive service (to); to perform duties at a Christian service, to act as an ecclesiastical minister; to supply or do things needful; to conduce or contribute (to). ◆ *vt* (*archaic*) to furnish, supply. [L *minister*, from *minor* less]
■ **ministė'rial** *adj* of or relating to a minister or ministry (in any sense); on the government side; administrative; executive; instrumental; conducive. **ministė'rialist** *adj* and *n* (of) a supporter of the government in office. **ministė'rially** *adv*. **min'istering** *adj* attending and serving. **ministė'rium** *n* (*pl* **ministė'ria**) the body of the ordained Lutheran ministers in a district. **min'istership** *n*. **min'istrant** *adj* administering; attendant. ◆ *n* an attendant. **ministrā'tion** *n* the act of ministering or performing service; (*usu pl*) help or service given; the office or service of a minister. **min'istrative** /-trə-tiv or -trā-tiv/ *adj* serving to aid or assist; ministering. **min'istress** *n* a woman who ministers. **min'istry** *n* the act of ministering; service; the office or duties of a minister; the clergy; the clerical profession; the body of ministers who manage the business of the country; a department of government, or the building it occupies; a term of office as minister.
❑ **Minister of State** *n* an additional, *usu* non-Cabinet, minister in (but ranking below the head of) a large government department. **Minister of the Crown** *n* a government minister in the Cabinet. **Minister without Portfolio** *n* a government minister, a member of the Cabinet having no specific department.

minisode /min'i-sōd/ *n* a heavily abridged version of a television programme, *esp* broadcast via the Internet. [*mini* episode]

mini-sub, mini-submarine see under **mini-**.

Minitel /min'i-tel or min'ē-/ *n* (in France) a public videotext system providing banking and mail order services, electronic messaging, etc.

Minitrack® see under **mini-**.

minium /min'i-əm/ *n* vermilion; red lead; its colour. [L *minium* red-lead, also cinnabar]
■ **min'iate** *adj* of the colour of minium. ◆ *vt* to paint with minium; to illuminate. **miniā'tion** *n*.

minivan see under **mini-**.

miniver or **minever** /min'i-vər/ *n* white fur, *orig* a mixed or variegated fur; the ermine in winter coat. [OFr *menu* small, from L *minūtus*, and *vair* fur, from L *varius* particoloured]

minivet /min'i-vət/ *n* a brightly-coloured shrike-like bird (*Pericrocotus* of several species) of India, etc. [Ety unknown]

minivolley see under **mini-**.

mink /mingk/ *n* a small animal (of several species) of the weasel family; its fur; a coat or jacket made from its fur. [Perh from Swed *mänk*]

minke /ming'kə/ *n* the lesser rorqual (also **minke whale**). [*Meincke*, a Norwegian whaler who harpooned one by accident]

Minkstone /mingk'stōn/ *n* a cast concrete with a very smooth finish. [Manufacturer's name]

min min /min min/ (*Aust*) *n* a will-o'-the-wisp. [From an Aboriginal language]

Minn. *abbrev* : Minnesota (US state).

minneola or **mineola** /mi-ni-ō'lə/ *n* a variety of citrus fruit developed from a tangerine and a grapefruit and resembling an orange, grown in the USA and elsewhere. [Poss *Mineola* in Texas]

Minnesinger /min'i-sing-ər or -zing-ər/ *n* any of a 12c–14c school of German amatory lyric poets, often themselves noblemen, composing love-lyrics (**Minn'esang**) to be sung at aristocratic courts. [Ger *Minne* courtly love, and *Singer* singer]

minnick /min'ik/, **minnock** /-ək/, **mimic** or **mimmick** /mim'ik/ (*dialect*) *n* an affected person. ◆ *vi* to be over-dainty in eating; to behave with affected primness.

minnie[1] /min'i/ (*Scot*; *childish*) *n* mother.

minnie[2] see **mine-thrower** under **mine**[2].

minnock see **minnick**.

minnow /min'ō/ *n* a very small freshwater fish (*Phoxinus phoxinus*) closely related to chub and dace; loosely extended to other small fish; a small, unimportant person or thing (*fig*). [Prob an OE form related to extant *myne*]

mino /mē'nō/ *n* (*pl* **mi'nos**) a raincoat of hemp, etc. [Jap]

Minoan /mī- or mi-nō'ən/ *adj* relating to or designating prehistoric Crete and its culture, from around 3000BC to 1100BC. ◆ *n* a member of this culture, a prehistoric Cretan; the language of the Minoans. [Gr *Mīnōs*, a legendary king of Crete]

minor /mī'nər/ *adj* lesser; inferior in importance, degree, bulk, etc; inconsiderable; lower; smaller (than major) by a semitone (*music*); in boys' schools, junior (placed after a surname); (of change-ringing) using six bells; (with *cap*) Minorite. ◆ *n* a person under the legal age of majority; the minor term, or minor premise (*logic*); (with *cap*) a Minorite or Minoress; anything that is minor opposed to major; a subsidiary subject studied at college or university (*N Am*); a student of such a subject; (in *pl*) the minor leagues in baseball, etc (*N Am*). ◆ *vi* (*N Am*; with *in*) to study as a minor, subsidiary subject at college or university. [L *minor* less; cf **minus**]
■ **minoritaire** /mē-nor-ē-ter/ *n* (*Fr*) a member of a minority section of a political (*esp* Socialist) party. **Mī'norite** *adj* relating to or designating a Franciscan order observing the strict rule of St Francis. ◆ *n* a member of such an order (also *fem* **Mī'noress**). **minority** /min- or mīn-or'i-ti/ *n* the condition or fact of being little or less; the state or time of being under age (also **mī'norship**); the smaller number; less than half; the party, social group, section of the population, etc of smaller numbers; the number by which it falls short of the other party, *opp* to *majority*. ◆ *adj* of the minority.
❑ **minor axis** *n* (in conics) that perpendicular to the major axis. **minor canon** see under **canon**[2]. **minority carrier** *n* (*electronics*) in a semiconductor, the type of carrier electrons or holes which carries the lesser degree of measured current. **minority group** *n* a section of the population with a common interest, characteristic, etc which is not common to most people. **minority report** *n* a report issued by a minority group of committee members to state their official position when they disagree with the majority. **minor key, mode** or **scale** *n* a key, mode or scale with its third a minor third above the tonic. **minor orders** *n pl* the lower degrees of holy orders, ie porter, exorcist, lector and acolyte. **minor piece** *n* (*chess*) a bishop or knight. **minor planet** *n* an asteroid. **minor poet** *n* a genuine but not great poet. **minor premise** *n* (*logic*) that in which the minor term occurs. **minor prophets** *n pl* the twelve from Hosea to Malachi in the Old Testament. **minor suit** *n* (*bridge*) clubs or diamonds. **minor term** *n* (*logic*) the term which is the subject of the conclusion. **minor third** *n* (*music*) an interval of three semitones. **minor tone** *n* an interval with a vibration ratio of 9:10.
■ **in a minority of one** alone.

Minorca /mi-nör'kə/ *n* a Mediterranean variety of poultry with glossy, *esp* black, plumage. [From the island of *Minorca* (Sp *Menorca*)]

Minoress, Minorite, minority, etc see under **minor**.

Minotaur /min'ə- or mī'nə-tör/ (*myth*) *n* the bull-headed monster in the Cretan Labyrinth, offspring of Pasiphae, wife of Minos. [Gr *Mīnōtauros*, from *Mīnōs* Minos, and *tauros* bull]
❑ **minotaur beetle** *n* a dung-beetle (*Typhaeus typhoeus*) with three thoracic horns.

minoxidil /mi-nok'si-dil/ *n* a synthetic drug used as a vasodilator and externally to stimulate the regrowth of hair in cases of baldness.

minshuku /min-shoo'koo/ *n* a Japanese guesthouse. [Jap]

minster /min'stər/ *n* an abbey church or priory church; often applied to a cathedral or great church without any monastic connection; a monastery (*obs*). [OE *mynster*, from L *monastērium* a monastery]

minstrel /min'strəl/ *n orig* a professional entertainer; now *esp* a medieval musician, itinerant or attached to a noble household, who sang or recited his own or others' poems, accompanying himself on a stringed instrument (*hist*); a poet, singer or musician (*poetic*); one of a troupe of entertainers, *orig* in 19c USA, performing in blackface and playing banjos, etc. [OFr *menestrel*, from LL *ministeriālis*, from L *minister* attendant]
■ **min'strelsy** /-si/ *n* the art or occupation of a minstrel; music (*archaic*); a company or body of minstrels; a collection of minstrels' poems or songs.

MINT /mint/ *abbrev*: Mexico, Indonesia, Nigeria and Turkey.

mint[1] /mint/ *n* any plant of the aromatic labiate genus *Mentha*, such as spearmint, peppermint or pennyroyal; any labiate (*US*); a sweet flavoured with mint or a synthetic substitute. [OE *minte*, from L *mentha*, from Gr *minthē, mintha*]
■ **mint'y** *adj* (**mint'ier**; **mint'iest**) smelling or tasting of mint; homosexual, effeminate (*sl*).
❑ **mint julep** see **julep**. **mint sauce** *n* chopped spearmint or other mint mixed with vinegar and sugar, used *esp* as a sauce for roast lamb; money (with pun on **mint**[2]; *sl*).

mint[2] /mint/ *n* a place where money is coined, *esp* officially; a source or place of fabrication (*lit* and *fig*); a vast sum of money. ◆ *vt* to coin; to invent; to stamp. ◆ *adj* in mint condition. [OE *mynet* money, from L *monēta*; see **money**]
■ **mint'age** *n* coining; coinage; stamp; duty for coining. **mint'ed** *adj* (*sl*) wealthy. **mint'er** *n*.

❑ **mint condition** or **state** *n* the condition of a newly-minted coin; perfect condition, as if unused. **mint'-man** *n* (*obs*) a person skilled in coining or coinage. **mint mark** *n* a mark showing where a coin was minted. **mint master** *n* a person supervising coinage at a mint; an inventor or coiner (*obs*). **mint'-new** *adj* in mint condition.

mint[3] /*mint*/ (*Scot* and *dialect*) *vt* and *vi* (often with *at*) to purpose; to attempt; to aim a blow (at); to make a threatening movement (towards); to venture; to aspire (to); to hint. ◆ *n* an attempt; aim; a threatening gesture; an incipient movement. [OE *myntan* to mean]

minuend /*min'ū-end*/ (*maths*) *n* the number from which another is to be subtracted. [L *minuendus* (*numerus*), from *minuere* to lessen]

minuet /*mi-nū-et'*/ *n* a slow, graceful dance in triple measure, invented in Poitou about the middle of the 17c and fashionable in 18c Europe; the music for, or as for, such a dance; the standard third movement in the classical sonata, symphony, etc. [Fr *menuet*, from *menu* small, from L *minūtus* small]

minus /*mī'nas*/ *prep* diminished by (*maths*); deficient in respect of, deprived of, without (*inf*). ◆ *adj* negative, less than zero; (of a student's grade) slightly below the letter specified. ◆ *n* a deficiency or subtraction; a negative quantity or term; the sign (also **minus sign**) of subtraction or negativity (−), *opp* to **plus**. [L *minus*, neuter of *minor* less]
❑ **minus strain** *n* (*bot*) one of two strains in heterothallism.

minuscule /*min'a-skūl* or *mi-nus'kūl*/ *n* a small, cursive script, originated by the monks in the 7c–9c (cf **majuscule**; *palaeog*); a manuscript written in it; a lower-case letter (*printing*). ◆ *adj* written or printed in minuscule; very small; very unimportant. [L (*littera*) *minuscula* smallish (letter)]
■ **minus'cular** *adj*.

minute[1] /*min'it*/ *n* the sixtieth part of an hour; the sixtieth part of an angular degree; an indefinitely small space of time; a particular moment; a brief jotting or note; (in *pl*) a brief summary of the proceedings of a meeting; a minute's walk, or the distance travelled in a minute. ◆ *vt* to make a brief jotting or note of; to record in the minutes. [Same word as **minute**[2]]
■ **minutely** /*min'it-li*/ *adj* (*Shakesp*) happening once a minute.
❑ **min'ute-bell** *n* a bell sounded every minute, in mourning. **minute book** *n* a book of minutes or short notes. **min'ute-drop** *n* a drop falling at a minute's interval. **min'ute-glass** *n* a sand-glass that runs for a minute. **minute gun** *n* a gun discharged every minute, as a signal of distress or mourning. **minute hand** *n* the hand that indicates the minutes on a clock or watch. **min'ute-jack** *n* (*Shakesp*) a timeserver, or a flighty, unstable person. **min'uteman** *n* (often *cap*) a man ready to turn out at a minute's warning, *orig* a militiaman in the American War of Independence (*hist*); a member of an armed right-wing organization in the USA, formed to take prompt action against Communist activities; a three-stage intercontinental ballistic missile. **minute steak** *n* a small, thin piece of steak that can be cooked quickly. **min'ute-watch** *n* a watch that marks minutes. **min'ute-while** *n* (*Shakesp*) a minute's time.
◼ **up to the minute** right up to date.

minute[2] /*mi-* or *mī-nūt'*/ *adj* extremely small; relating to the very small; exact, detailed. [L *minūtus*, pap of *minuere* to lessen]
■ **minute'ly** *adv*. **minute'ness** *n*.

minutia /*mi-nū'shi-a*/ *n* (*pl* **minū'tiae** /*-ē* or *-ī*/) (*usu* in *pl*) a minute particular or detail. [L *minūtia* smallness]
■ **minū'tiose** /*-shi-ōs*/ *adj*.

minx /*mingks*/ *n* (*old*) a cheeky or playful young girl; a disreputable woman. [Poss from **minikin**; or LGer *minsk*, *minske* a wench or jade, cognate with Ger *Mensch* man, human being]

miny see under **mine**[2].

minyan /*min'yan* or *min-yan'*/ (*Heb*) *n* (*pl* **minyanim** or **minyans**) the minimum number of people required by Jewish law to be present for a religious service to be held, ie ten male adults. [Heb, number]

Miocene /*mī'ō-sēn*/ (*geol*) *adj* of or belonging to an epoch of the Tertiary period, between 23 and 5 million years ago, and having a smaller proportion of fossil molluscs of living species than the Pliocene (also *n*). [Gr *meiōn* smaller, and *kainos* recent]

miombo /*mi-om'bō*/ *n* (*pl* **miom'bos**) an area of deciduous woodland occurring in parts of E Africa. [Swahili]

miosis or **myosis** /*mī-ō'sis*/ *n* abnormal contraction of the pupil of the eye. [Gr *myein* to close, blink]
■ **miot'ic** *adj* and *n*.

MIPS or **mips** /*mips*/ (*comput*) *abbrev*: millions of instructions per second.

MIR *abbrev*: mortgage interest relief.

mir[1] /*mēr*/ *n* (*pl* **mirs** or **mir'i**) a peasant farming commune in pre-Revolutionary Russia. [Russ, world]

mir[2] or **meer** /*mēr*/ (also with *cap*) *n* a Muslim ruler or commander, an ameer. [Hindi and Pers *mīr*, from Ar *amīr* ruler]

Mira /*mī'ra*/ *n* a variable star in the constellation Cetus. [L *mīra* (fem) wonderful]

mirabelle /*mir'a-bel*/ *n* a European species of plum-tree; the small, yellow, firm-fleshed fruit of this; a colourless liqueur distilled from this fruit (also **mirabelle brandy**). [Fr]

mirabile dictu /*mi-rä'bi-lā dik'too*/ (L) wonderful to tell.

mirabile visu /*mi-rä'bi-lā vē'soo*/ (L) wonderful to see.

mirable /*mī'ra-bl*/ *adj* (*Shakesp*) wonderful. [L *mīrābilis* wonderful]
■ **mirabil'ia** /*mir-* or *mīr-*/ *n pl* (*rare*) wonders. **Mirabilis** /*mir-* or *mīr-ab'il-is*/ *n* the marvel of Peru genus; (without *cap*) short form of **aqua mirabilis** (*obs*). **mirab'ilite** *n* (*mineralogy*) a hydrated form of sodium sulphate.

miracidium /*mī-ra-sid'i-am*/ (*zool*) *n* (*pl* **miracid'ia**) the ciliated first-stage larva of a trematode. [LL *miracidion*, from Gr *meirax* boy, girl]

miracle /*mir'a-kl*/ *n* an event or act which breaks a law of nature, *esp* one attributed to a deity or supernatural force; a marvel, a wonder; a miracle play. [Fr, from L *mīrāculum*, from *mīrārī*, *-ātus* to wonder at]
■ **miraculous** /*-ak'ū-las*/ *adj* of the nature of a miracle; done by supernatural power; very wonderful or remarkable; able to perform miracles. **mirac'ulously** *adv*. **mirac'ulousness** *n*.
❑ **miracle berry** or **fruit** *n* a tasteless African red berry which becomes sweet-tasting when mixed with a sour substance. **mir'acle-monger** *n* (*archaic*) a person who pretends to work miracles. **miracle play** *n* a medieval religious drama based on the legends of the saints or of the Virgin Mary; a mystery play (see **mystery**[1]). **miracle rice** *n* a hybrid, high-yield rice developed for use in Asia, etc.

miracles see **meril**.

mirador /*mi-ra-dör'*/ (*archit*) *n* a belvedere or watchtower. [Sp]

mirage /*mi-räzh'*/ *n* an optical illusion, appearing as a floating and shimmering image, like water, on the horizon, caused by the varying refractive index of surface layers of hot and cold air; something illusory (*fig*). [Fr *mirer* to look at, from L *mīrārī* to wonder at]

Miranda /*mi-ran'da*/ *adj* (in US law) relating to the rights (**Miranda rights**) enjoyed by a person who is arrested on suspicion of having committed a crime. [From a decision of the US Supreme Court in 1966 involving the case of Ernesto *Miranda*]
■ **miran'dize** or **-ise** *vt* to inform (a person being arrested) of the Miranda rights.

MIRAS or **Miras** /*mī'ras*/ *abbrev*: mortgage interest relief at source, abolished in 2000.

mirbane /*mûr'bān*/ *n* an apparently meaningless word, used in **essence** (or **oil**) **of mirbane**, a name for nitrobenzene as used in perfumery.

mire /*mīr*/ *n* deep mud; a marshy area, a bog; any problematical or ineluctable situation. ◆ *vt* to plunge and fix in mire; to soil with mud; to swamp, bog down. ◆ *vi* to sink in mud. [ON *mȳrr* bog]
■ **mir'iness** *n*. **mir'y** *adj* consisting of mire; covered with mire.
❑ **mire'-drum** *n* the bittern. **mire'-snipe** *n* the common snipe.

mirepoix /*mēr-pwa'*/ *n* sautéed, diced vegetables used for making sauces, or as a base for braised meat or fish, etc. [Duc de Lévis-Mirepoix, 18c French general, whose cook is said to have created the dish]

mirific /*mī-rif'ik*/ or **mirifical** /*-i-kal*/ *adj* wonder-working; marvellous. [L *mīrificus*, from *mīrus* wonderful, and *facere* to do]
■ **mirif'ically** *adv*.

mirin /*mir'in*/ *n* a sweet rice wine used in Japanese cookery. [Jap]

miriti /*mi-ri-tē'* or *mir'i-ti*/ *n* any palm of the genus *Mauritia*. [Tupí]

mirk, etc same as **murk**, etc.

mirliton /*mûr'li-tan* or *mēr-lē-tõ'*/ *n* a toy reed pipe; a small almond tart made with puff-pastry; the chayote fruit (chiefly *US*). [Fr]

mirly see under **marl**[4].

mirror /*mir'ar*/ *n* a surface, *orig* of polished metal, now *usu* of glass backed with metallic film, which reflects an image in front of it; such a surface set in a frame for mounting on a wall, holding in the hand, etc, *esp* to view oneself; any reflecting surface; a faithful representation of something (*fig*); a model or example, good or bad. ◆ *vt* (**mirr'oring**; **mirr'ored**) to reflect an image of in, or as if in, a mirror; to represent faithfully; to provide with a mirror or mirrors. [OFr *mireor*, *mirour*, from L *mīrārī*, *-ātus* to wonder at]
■ **mirr'orwise** *adj* and *adv* with interchange of left and right sides.
❑ **mirror ball** *n* a large revolving ball covered with small reflecting glass tiles, used in discos, etc. **mirror carp** *n* an ornamental variety of carp with a smooth shiny body. **mirror finish** *n* a highly-polished finish on a metal. **mirror glass** *n* a reflecting glass used, or as used, in a mirror. **mirror image** *n* an image with right and left reversed as in a mirror. **mirror machine** *n* a fusion machine using the magnetic mirror

principle to trap high-energy ions in a plasma. **mirror neuron** *n* (*anat*) a neuron that transmits impulses both when an action is performed and when the same action is observed. **mirror nuclides** *n pl* pairs of nuclides, one containing the same number of protons as the other has neutrons. **mirror site** *n* (*comput*) a website whose content is identical to that of another site, but having a different address in order to allow local users to access the site more easily. **mirror symmetry** *n* the symmetry of an object and its reflected image. **mirror writer** *n* a person who writes mirrorwise. **mirror writing** *n* writing which is like ordinary writing as seen in a mirror, ie in reverse.

mirth /*mûrth*/ *n* merriness; pleasure; delight; noisy gaiety; jollity; laughter. [OE *myrgth*, from *myrige* merry]
  ■ **mirth'ful** *adj* full of mirth; causing mirth; merry; jovial. **mirth'fully** *adv.* **mirth'fulness** *n.* **mirth'less** *adj.* **mirth'lessly** *adv.* **mirth'lessness** *n.*

MIRV /*mûrv*/ *n* a missile containing many thermonuclear warheads, able to attack separate targets; any of the warheads in such a missile.
  ◆ *vt* (*milit sl*; without *caps*) to provide with such missiles or warheads. [*M*ultiple *I*ndependently *T*argeted *R*e-entry *V*ehicle]

miry see under **mire**.

Mirza /*mûr'zə* or *mēr'zə*/ *n* as a Persian title (after a name), Prince; (before a name) official or learned man. [Pers *mirzā*, *mīrzā*]

MIS (*comput*) *abbrev* : Management Information System.

mis /*mis*/ (*Spenser*) *vi* to do amiss; to fail. [**miss**[1]]

mis- /*mis*-/ *pfx* denoting: wrongly, badly, as in *misbehave*, *mislead*, etc; wrong, bad, as in *misdeed*; lack, absence, as in *mistrust*. [OE *mis*-; ON *mis*-, Gothic *missa*-, Ger *miss*-; cf **miss**[1]]

misacceptation /*mis-ak-sep-tā'shən*/ (*obs*) *n* misinterpretation. [**mis-**]

misadventure /*mis-əd-ven'chər*/ *n* bad luck; mishap; accidental killing. [ME, from OFr *mesaventure*]
  ■ **misadvent'ured** *adj* (*Shakesp*) unfortunate. **misadvent'urer** *n.* **misadvent'urous** *adj.*

misadvertence /*mis-əd-vûr'təns*/ (*literary*) *n* inadvertence. [**mis-**]

misadvise /*mis-əd-vīz'*/ *vt* to advise badly or wrongly. [**mis-**]
  ■ **misadvised'** *adj.* **misadvī'sedly** *adv.* **misadvīs'edness** *n.*

misaim /*mis-ām'*/ *vt* to aim badly. [**mis-**]

misalign /*mis-ə-līn'*/ *vt* to align wrongly. [**mis-**]
  ■ **misalign'ment** *n.*

misallege /*mis-ə-lej'*/ (*obs*) *vt* to allege wrongly. [**mis-**]

misalliance /*mis-ə-lī'əns*/ *n* an unsuitable alliance, *esp* in marriage. [Fr *mésalliance*]
  ■ **misallied'** *adj.* **misally** /*mis-ə-lī'*/ *vt* (**misally'ing**; **misallied'**).

misallot /*mis-ə-lot'*/ *vt* to allot wrongly. [**mis-**]
  ■ **misallot'ment** *n.*

misandry /*mis-an'dri* or *mis'ən-dri*/ *n* hatred of men. [Gr *misandria*, from *misandros* hating men]
  ■ **mis'andrist** *n.* **mis'androus** *adj.*

misanthrope /*miz'* or *mis'ən-thrōp*/ or **misanthropist** /*miz-* or *mis-an'thrə-pist*/ *n* a hater of mankind, someone who distrusts everyone else. [Gr *mīsanthrōpos*, from *mīseein* to hate, and *anthrōpos* a man]
  ■ **misanthropic** /*mis-ən-throp'ik* or *miz-*/ or **misanthrop'ical** *adj* having a hatred or distrust of mankind. **misanthrop'ically** *adv.* **misan'thropos** *n* (*Shakesp*) a misanthrope. **misan'thropy** *n* hatred or distrust of mankind.

misapply /*mis-ə-plī'*/ *vt* to apply wrongly; to use for a wrong purpose. [**mis-**]
  ■ **misapplica'tion** /*-ap-*/ *n.*

misappreciate /*mis-ə-prē'shi-āt*/ *vt* to fail to appreciate rightly or fully. [**mis-**]
  ■ **misapprecia'tion** *n.* **misappre'ciative** *adj.*

misapprehend /*mis-ap-ri-hend'*/ *vt* to misunderstand; to take or understand in a wrong sense. [**mis-**]
  ■ **misapprehen'sion** *n.* **misapprehen'sive** *adj.* **misapprehen'sively** *adv* by or with misapprehension or mistake. **misapprehen'siveness** *n.*

misappropriate /*mis-ə-prō'pri-āt*/ *vt* to put to a wrong use; to take dishonestly for oneself. [**mis-**]
  ■ **misappropria'tion** *n.*

misarrange /*mis-ə-rānj'*/ *vt* to arrange wrongly; to put in wrong order. [**mis-**]
  ■ **misarrange'ment** *n.*

misarray /*mis-ə-rā'*/ (*Walter Scott*) *n* disarray. [**mis-**]

misassign /*mis-ə-sīn'*/ *vt* to assign wrongly. [**mis-**]

misaunter /*mi-sön'tər*/ (now *N Eng dialect*) *n* a misadventure or mishap. [OFr *mesaventure*; cf **aunter**]

misavised /*mis-ə-vī'zid*/ (*Spenser*) *adj* ill-advised. [**mis-**]

misbecome /*mis-bi-kum'*/ (*archaic*) *vt* to be unbecoming or unsuitable to. [**mis-**]
  ■ **misbecom'ing** *adj.* **misbecom'ingness** *n.*

misbegot /*mis-bi-got'*/ or **misbegotten** /*-got'n*/ *adj* unlawfully begotten, illegitimate (*Shakesp*); monstrous; illegally obtained; ill-conceived. [**mis-** and *pap* of **beget**]

misbehave /*mis-bi-hāv'*/ *vt* (reflexive) and *vi* to behave badly or improperly. [**mis-**]
  ■ **misbehaved'** *adj* (*Shakesp*) badly behaved; ill-bred. **misbehav'iour** *n.*

misbelief /*mis-bə-lēf'*/ *n* belief in a false doctrine or notion. [**mis-**]
  ■ **misbelieve** /*mis-bi-lēv'*/ *vt* to believe wrongly or falsely. **misbeliev'er** *n.* **misbeliev'ing** *adj.*

misbeseem /*mis-bi-sēm'*/ (*archaic*) *vt* to be unsuited or unsuitable to. [**mis-**]

misbestow /*mis-bi-stō'*/ *vt* to bestow improperly, or on the wrong person. [**mis-**]
  ■ **misbestow'al** *n.*

misborn /*mis'börn* or *mis-börn'*/ *adj* abortive (*obs*); deformed from birth (*obs*); born illegitimately and so of low social rank (*literary*). [**mis-**]
  ■ **misbirth'** *n* (*archaic*) an abortion.

misc. *abbrev* : miscellaneous.

miscalculate /*mis-kal'kyə-lāt*/ *vt* and *vi* to calculate wrongly. [**mis-**]
  ■ **miscalcula'tion** *n.*

miscall /*mis-köl'*/ *vt* to call by a wrong name; (in games) to make a bad or inaccurate call; to call by a bad name, to abuse or revile verbally (*Spenser*; now mainly *Scot* and *dialect*; also **misca'**). [**mis-**]

miscanthus /*mis-kan'thəs*/ *n* any of several hardy, ornamental, perennial grasses (family Gramineae) of China and Japan. [Gr *mischos* stalk, and *anthos* flower]

miscarriage /*mis-kar'ij* or *mis'ka-rij*/ *n* the act of giving birth spontaneously to a fetus too premature to survive, *usu* before the 28th week of pregnancy; any act or instance of miscarrying; failure; failure to reach the intended result or destination; misconduct, a misdeed (*obs*). [**mis-**]
  ■ **miscarr'y** *vi* to give birth to an unviable fetus; to be born as an unviable fetus; to be unsuccessful; to fail to attain the intended or complete effect; (of mail, etc) to fail to reach the intended destination. ◆ *vt* (*obs*) to lead astray.
  ❑ **miscarriage of justice** *n* failure of the courts to do justice.

miscast /*mis-käst'*/ *vt* (*usu* in *passive*) to cast (an actor or actress) in an unsuitable role; to cast an unsuitable actor or actress in (a role, play, film, etc); to miscalculate (*obs*; also *vi*). [**mis-**]

miscegenation /*mi-si-ji-nā'shən* or *-se-*/ *n* mixing of race; interbreeding, intermarriage or sexual intercourse between different races. [L *miscēre* to mix, and *genus* race]
  ■ **miscegen** /*mis'i-jən*/, **misc'egene** /*-jēn*/ or **misc'egine** /*-jin* or *-jīn*/ *n* an individual of mixed race. **misc'egenate** *vi* to practise miscegenation. ◆ *vt* to produce by miscegenation. ◆ *adj* (*rare*) of mixed race. **miscegenā'tionist**, **misc'egenātor** or **miscegenist** /*mis-ej'in-ist*/ *n* a person who favours or practises miscegenation.

miscellaneous /*mis-ə-lā'ni-əs*/ *adj* mixed or mingled; consisting of several kinds; (of a person) with a many-sided personality, multi-talented, etc (*literary*). [L *miscellāneus*, from *miscēre* to mix]
  ■ **miscellanarian** /*-ən-ā'ri-ən*/ *n* (*obs*) a writer of miscellanies. **miscellā'nea** *n pl* (*L*) a miscellany. **miscellān'eously** *adv.* **miscellān'eousness** *n.* **miscellanist** /*mis-el'ən-ist* or (*esp N Am*) *mis'əl-*/ *n* a writer of miscellanies. **miscellany** /*mis-el'* or (*esp N Am*) *mis'əl-*/ *n* a mixture of various kinds; a collection of writings on different subjects or by different authors.

mischallenge /*mis-chal'ənj* or *-inj*/ (*Spenser*) *n* an unjust challenge. [**mis-**]

mischance /*mis-chäns'*/ *n* bad luck; mishap. ◆ *vi* to chance wrongly, happen unfortunately; to meet with bad luck. [ME, from OFr *meschance*]
  ■ **mischance'ful** *adj* (*archaic*). **mischan'cy** *adj* (*chiefly Scot*) unlucky; dangerous.

mischanter /*mis-chän'tər*/ or **mishanter** /*mi-shän'*/ (*Scot* and *N Eng*) *n* an unlucky chance, misfortune. [**aunter**; perh influenced by *obs mischant*, *meschant*, from OFr *mescheant* (Fr *méchant*) unlucky, wicked]

mischarge /*mis-chärj'*/ *vt* to charge wrongly. ◆ *n* a mistake in charging. [**mis-**]

mischief /*mis'chif* or *-chēf*/ *n* petty misdeeds or annoyance; pestering playfulness; a mischievous person; an unfavourable consequence; evil; injury; damage, hurt; the troublesome fact; a source of harm; the Devil (*inf*). ◆ *vt* (*archaic*) to cause mischief; to suffer mischief.

[OFr *meschef*, from *mes-* (from L *minus* less), and *chef* (from L *caput* the head)]

■ **mischievous** /mis'chiv-əs (Spenser usu -chēv')/ adj causing mischief; prone to mischief; injurious. **mis'chievously** adv. **mis'chievousness** n.

❑ **mis'chief-maker** n someone who stirs up trouble. **mis'chief-making** n and adj.

mischmetal /mish'me-tl/ n an alloy of cerium with rare-earth metals and iron, used to produce the spark in cigarette and other lighters. [Ger *mischen* to mix, and **metal**]

miscible /mis'i-bl/ adj (esp of liquids) that may be mixed. [L *miscēre* to mix]

■ **miscibil'ity** n.

misclassify /mis-klas'i-fī/ vt to classify wrongly. [**mis-**]

■ **misclassifica'tion** n.

miscolour or (N Am) **miscolor** /mis-kul'ər/ vt to colour falsely; to give a wrong meaning to; to misrepresent. [**mis-**]

miscommunication /mis-kə-mū-ni-kā'shən/ n an instance of communicating inadequately. [**mis-**]

miscomprehend /mis-kom-pri-hend'/ vt to misunderstand. [**mis-**]

■ **miscomprehen'sion** n.

miscompute /mis-kəm-pūt'/ vt to compute or calculate wrongly. [**mis-**]

■ **miscomputa'tion** /-kom-/ n wrong computation; miscalculation.

misconceit /mis-kən-sēt'/ (Spenser) n misconception. ◆ vt to have a wrong conception of. [**mis-**]

misconceive /mis-kən-sēv'/ vt and vi to conceive wrongly or inadequately; to mistake; to suspect (obs). [**mis-**]

■ **misconceiv'er** n. **misconcep'tion** n.

misconduct /mis-kon'dukt/ n bad conduct; wrong or poor management; adultery; improper behaviour, not necessarily morally reprehensible, such as would lead any reasonable employer to dismiss an employee (law). [**mis-**]

■ **misconduct** /-kən-dukt'/ vt.

misconjecture /mis-kən-jek'chər/ n a wrong conjecture or guess. ◆ vt and vi to guess or conjecture wrongly. [**mis-**]

misconster /mis-kon'stər/ obsolete form of **misconstrue**.

misconstruction /mis-kən-struk'shən/ n wrong construction, construing or interpretation; faulty construction. [**mis-**]

■ **misconstruct'** vt.

misconstrue /mis-kən-stroo'** or -kon'stroo/ vt to construe or to interpret wrongly. [**mis-**]

miscontent /mis-kən-tent'/ (archaic) n, adj and vt discontent. [**mis-**]

■ **miscontent'ed** adj. **miscontent'ment** n.

miscopy /mis-kop'i/ vt to copy wrongly or imperfectly. ◆ n an error in copying. [**mis-**]

miscorrect /mis-kə-rekt'/ vt to alter or mark wrongly in would-be correction. [**mis-**]

■ **miscorrec'tion** n.

miscounsel /mis-kown'sl/ vt to advise wrongly. [**mis-**]

miscount /mis-kownt'/ vt and vi to count wrongly, to miscalculate; to misjudge. ◆ n a miscalculation. [**mis-**]

miscreant /mis'kri-ənt/ n orig a misbeliever, a heretic or infidel; a vile wretch, a detestable scoundrel. ◆ adj unbelieving (archaic); villainous, scoundrelly, wicked. [OFr *mescreant*, from *mes-* (from L *minus* less), and L *crēdēns, -entis*, prp of *crēdere* to believe]

■ **mis'creance, miscreancy** or **mis'creaunce** n (Spenser) false religious belief.

miscreated /mis-krē-ā'tid/ or (poetic) **miscreate** /mis-krē-āt'/ adj created imperfectly or improperly; deformed. [**mis-**]

■ **miscrea'tion** n. **miscrea'tive** adj that creates imperfectly or improperly. **miscrea'tor** n.

miscreaunce see under **miscreant**.

miscredit /mis-kred'it/ (archaic) vt to disbelieve. [**mis-**]

miscreed /mis-krēd'/ (poetic) n a false creed. [**mis-**]

miscue /mis-kū'/ n a stroke spoiled by the slipping off of the cue (snooker, etc); a mistake; a wrong cue (in any sense). ◆ vt to hit (a snooker ball) wrongly. ◆ vi to make a faulty stroke (snooker, etc); to answer the wrong cue, or to miss one's cue (theatre); to make a mistake. [**mis-**, or **miss¹**]

misdate /mis-dāt'/ vt to date wrongly. ◆ n a wrong date. [**mis-**]

misdeal /mis-dēl'/ n a wrong deal, as at cards. ◆ vt and vi (pat and pap **misdealt** /-delt'/) to deal wrongly; to divide improperly. [**mis-**]

misdeed /mis-dēd'/ n a wrongdoing, a bad or wicked deed. [OE *misdǣd*]

misdeem /mis-dēm'/ (archaic) vt and vi (pap **misdeemed'** or (Spenser) **misdempt'**) to think badly (of); to judge wrongly; to have a mistaken opinion (of); to suspect. [**mis-**]

■ **misdeem'ful** adj (dialect). **misdeem'ing** adj misjudging; suspicious; deceiving (Spenser). ◆ n misjudgement; suspicion.

misdemean /mis-di-mēn'/ vt (reflexive) and vi to misbehave. [**mis-** and **demean²**]

■ **misdemean'ant** n a person guilty of petty crime or misconduct. **misdemean'our** or (N Am) **misdemean'or** n bad conduct; a misdeed; (in UK formerly) a legal offence of less gravity than a felony.

misdempt see **misdeem**.

misdescribe /mis-dis-krīb'/ vt to describe wrongly. [**mis-**]

■ **misdescrip'tion** n.

misdesert /mis-di-zûrt'/ (Spenser) n undeservedness. [**mis-**]

misdevotion /mis-di-vō'shən/ n misdirected devotion. [**mis-**]

misdiagnose /mis-dī'əg-nōz or -nōz'/ vt to diagnose wrongly. [**mis-**]

■ **misdiagnō'sis** n.

misdial /mis-dī'əl or -dīl'/ vi and vt to dial (a telephone number) incorrectly. [**mis-**]

misdid see **misdo**.

misdiet /mis-dī'ət/ (Spenser) n improper feeding. [**mis-**]

misdight /mis-dīt'/ (Spenser) adj badly prepared or provided; in miserable circumstances. [**mis-**]

misdirect /mis-di-rekt'/ or -dī-/ vt to direct wrongly; (of a judge) to inform (a jury) incorrectly; to use (funds, etc) wrongly. [**mis-**]

■ **misdirec'tion** n.

misdo /mis-doo'/ vt (pat **misdid'**; pap **misdone'**; old infinitive (Spenser) **misdonne'**) to do wrongly or badly; to injure (obs); to kill (obs). ◆ vi to act wrongly or badly. [**mis-**]

■ **misdo'er** n. **misdo'ing** n.

misdoubt /mis-dowt'/ (archaic and dialect) vt to have a doubt, suspicion, misgiving, or foreboding of or about; to suspect. ◆ n suspicion; hesitation; misgiving. [**mis-**]

■ **misdoubt'ful** adj (Spenser).

misdraw /mis-drö'/ vt to draw or draft badly. [**mis-**]

■ **misdraw'ing** n.

misdread /mis-dred'/ (Shakesp) n dread of evil to come. [**mis-**]

mise /mēz or mīz/ n expenditure, outlay (obs); in Wales and the county palatine of Chester, a payment to a new king, prince, Lord of the Marches, or earl, to secure certain privileges (hist); the issue in a writ of right (law); the adjustment of a dispute by agreement (hist); a stake in gambling; the layout of cards. [OFr *mise* placing or setting, from L *mittere, missum*]

❑ **mise en place** /mē-zā-plas'/ n the preparation, such as laying tables and setting out the required ingredients and utensils, carried out in a restaurant before a meal is served. **mise en scène** /mē-zā-sen/ n the act, result, or art, of setting a stage or film scene or arranging a pictorial representation; a style of direction in the cinema which uses a relatively static camera with subjects in full shot, and very little cutting within a scene (cf **montage**); setting, physical surroundings.

misease /mis-ēz'/ (archaic) n distress; uneasiness. [OFr *mesaise*]

miseducation /mis-ed-ū-kā'shən/ n improper or damaging education. [**mis-**]

■ **mised'ucate** vt.

misemploy /mis-im-ploi'/ vt to employ wrongly or badly; to misuse. [**mis-**]

■ **misemploy'ment** n.

misentreat /mis-in-trēt'/ (obs) vt to ill-treat. [**mis-** and **entreat** (to treat)]

misentry /mis-en'tri/ n a wrong entry. [**mis-**]

miser¹ /mī'zər/ n a person who lives miserably in order to hoard wealth; a tight-fisted or niggardly person; a wretch (Spenser and Shakesp). ◆ adj like a miser. [L *miser* wretched]

■ **mi'serliness** n. **mi'serly** adj.

miser² /mī'zər/ n a well-boring instrument. [Origin doubtful]

miserable /miz'(ə-)rə-bl/ adj wretched; exceedingly or habitually unhappy; causing misery; extremely poor or mean; contemptible. ◆ n a wretch; very weak tea (rare). [Fr *misérable*, from L *miserābilis*, from *miser*]

■ **mis'erabilist** or **mis'erablist** n and adj (of or relating to) a singer, songwriter, etc whose material emphasizes the depressing aspects of life. **mis'erableness** n. **mis'erably** adv.

misère /mē-zer'** or mi-zār'/ (cards) n an undertaking to take no tricks. [Fr, misery]

Miserere /mi-ze-rē'ri or mi-se-rā're/ n Psalm 50 of the Vulgate (51 in the Authorized Version), from its first word; a musical setting of this; (without cap) a misericord in a church stall. [L, 2nd pers sing imperative of *miserērī* to have mercy, to pity, from *miser* wretched]

misericord or **misericorde** /mi-zer'i-körd or miz'ə-ri-, also -körd'/ n a bracket on a turn-up seat in a choirstall, allowing the user some support when standing, often intricately carved; mercy, forgiveness, pity (obs); a room in a monastery where some relaxation of rule was allowed; a relaxation of monastic rule; a narrow-bladed dagger for killing a wounded enemy. [OFr misericorde, from L misericordia, from misericors, -cordis tender-hearted, in relation to the obs sense]

miserly see under **miser**[1].

misery /miz'ə-ri/ n wretchedness; extreme pain; miserable conditions; misère (cards); avarice (Shakesp); a very unhappy experience; a doleful person (inf). [OFr, from L miseria]
❑ **misery index** n an estimate of the economic difficulty being experienced by a particular country, etc, usu calculated from the current rates of inflation and unemployment. **misery memoir** n the autobiography of a person who has known pain and suffering and wants the reader to endure a similar experience.
■ **put someone out of his** or **her misery** to release someone from mental or physical suffering.

misesteem /mis-e-stēm'/ n disrespect. ◆ vt to value wrongly. [**mis-**]

misestimate /mis-es'ti-māt/ vt to estimate wrongly. [**mis-**]

misfaith /mis-fāth'/ (archaic) n distrust. [**mis-**]

misfall /mis-föl'/ (obs) vt (pat **misfell**'; pap **misfall'en** (Spenser **misfalne**')) to befall unluckily. [**mis-**]

misfare /mis-fār'/ (Spenser) n misfortune. ◆ vi to fare badly. [OE misfaran]
■ **misfar'ing** n (Spenser) wrongdoing.

misfeasance /mis-fē'zəns/ (law) n the doing of a lawful act in a wrongful manner, as distinguished from malfeasance. [OFr mesfaisance, from pfx mes- (from L minus less), and faisance, from faire, from L facere to do]
■ **misfeas'or** n.

misfeature /mis-fē'chər/ n a bad or distorted feature, trait or aspect; deformity. [**mis-**]
■ **misfeat'ured** adj having bad or distorted features, etc. **misfeat'uring** adj distorting the features, disfiguring.

misfeed /mis-fēd'/ vt (pap and pat **misfed**') to feed (eg a machine) incorrectly (with paper, materials, etc). [**mis-**]

misfeign /mis-fān'/ (Spenser) vi to feign with bad intent. [**mis-**]

misfield /mis-fēld'/ (cricket) vi and vt to field badly or ineffectively. ◆ n /mis'/ a mistake or failure in fielding. [**mis-**]

misfile /mis-fīl'/ vt to file (information) under the wrong headings, etc. [**mis-**]

misfire /mis-fīr'/ vi to fail to go off, explode or ignite, at all or at the right time; to fail to have the effect intended (fig). ◆ n a failure to fire, or to achieve the desired effect. [**miss**[1], and **fire**]

misfit /mis'fit/ n a person who cannot adjust to his or her social environment, job, etc; a bad fit; a thing that fits badly or not at all. ◆ vt and vi /mis-fit'/ to fit badly. [**mis-**]

misform /mis-förm'/ vt to form or shape badly or improperly. [**mis-**]
■ **misformā'tion** n.

misfortune /mis-för'tūn/ n ill-fortune; an unfortunate accident; calamity; an illegitimate child, or the having of one (inf). [**mis-**]
■ **misfor'tuned** adj (archaic) unfortunate.

misgive /mis-giv'/ vt (pat **misgave**'; pap **misgiv'en**) to suggest apprehensions to, fill with forebodings; to give erroneously. ◆ vi to have apprehensive forebodings; to fail (Scot). [**mis-**]
■ **misgiv'ing** n (usu pl) a feeling that all is not well; mistrust.

misgo /mis-gō'/ (obs or dialect) vi (pat **miswent** (supplied from miswend); pap **misgone** /mis-gon'/ or (obs, now non-standard) **miswent**') to go the wrong way or go astray. [**mis-**]

misgotten /mis-got'n/ (Spenser) adj ill-gotten; misbegotten. [**mis-**]

misgovern /mis-guv'ərn/ vt to govern badly or unjustly. [**mis-**]
■ **misgov'ernaunce** n (Spenser) mismanagement. **misgov'ernment** n. **misgov'ernor** n.

misgraft /mis-gräft'/ vt to graft unsuitably. [**mis-**]
■ **misgraff** /mis-gräf'/ adj (Shakesp) badly grafted or matched.

misgrowth /mis-grōth'/ n an irregular growth; an excrescence; a sport of nature. [**mis-**]

misguggle /mis-gug'l/ or **mishguggle** /mish-/ (Scot) vt to bungle, mar. [**mis-**]

misguide /mis-gīd'/ vt to guide wrongly; to lead into error; to ill-treat (Scot). ◆ n (obs) misbehaviour. [**mis-**]
■ **misguid'ance** n. **misguid'ed** adj erring; misdirected; ill-judged. **misguid'edly** adv. **misguid'er** n.

mishallowed /mis-hal'ōd/ (archaic) adj consecrated to evil. [**mis-**]

mishandle /mis-han'dl/ vt to handle wrongly, unskilfully or roughly; to maltreat. [**mis-**]

mishanter same as **mischanter**.

mishap /mis'hap or mis-hap'/ n (a piece of) bad luck; unlucky accident; misfortune. ◆ vi (obs) to happen unfortunately. [**mis-**]
■ **mishapp'en** vi (Spenser) to happen unfortunately.

mishapt a Spenserian form of **misshaped**.

mishear /mis-hēr'/ vt and vi (pat and pap **misheard** /-hûrd'/) to hear wrongly. [**mis-**]

mishegaas see under **meshuga**.

mishguggle see **misguggle**.

mishit /mis-hit'/ vt (pat and pap **mishit**') to hit (a ball) faultily. ◆ n /mis'hit/ a faulty hit. [**mis-**]

mishmash /mish'mash/ n a hotchpotch, medley. [Reduplication of **mash**[1]; cf Ger Mischmasch, from mischen, from L miscere to mix]

mishmee or **mishmi** /mish'mē/ n the bitter rootstock of an Assamese gold-thread plant (Coptis teeta), with tonic properties. [Said to be Assamese mishmītīta]

Mishnah or **Mishna** /mish'nä/ n (pl **Mishnayōth** /nay-ōt'/) the Jewish oral law, finally redacted 220AD and forming the first section of the Talmud. [Heb mishnāh, from shānāh to repeat, teach, learn]
■ **Mishnā'ic** or **Mish'nic** adj.

misidentify /mis-ī-den'ti-fī/ vt to identify incorrectly. [**mis-**]
■ **misidentificā'tion** n.

misimprove /mis-im-proov'/ vt to turn to bad use; to make worse by would-be improvement. [**mis-**]
■ **misimprove'ment** n.

misinform /mis-in-förm'/ vt to inform or tell incorrectly or misleadingly. [**mis-**]
■ **misinform'ant** n. **misinformā'tion** n. **misinform'er** n.

misinstruct /mis-in-strukt'/ vt to instruct wrongly. [**mis-**]
■ **misinstruc'tion** n wrong instruction.

misintelligence /mis-in-tel'i-jəns/ n wrong or false information; misunderstanding; lack of intelligence. [**mis-**]

misintend /mis-in-tend'/ (obs) vt to intend or aim in malice. [**mis-**]

misinterpret /mis-in-tûr'prit/ vt to interpret wrongly; to explain wrongly. [**mis-**]
■ **misinterpretā'tion** n. **misinter'preter** n.

misjoin /mis-join'/ vt to join improperly or unsuitably. [**mis-**]
■ **misjoin'der** n (law) an incorrect union of parties or of causes of action in a suit.

misjudge /mis-juj'/ vt and vi to judge wrongly. [**mis-**]
■ **misjudg'ement** or **misjudg'ment** n.

misken /mis-ken'/ (Scot) vt to be, or to appear, ignorant of; to fail or refuse to recognize. [**mis-**]

miskey /mis-kē'/ vt to key (data on a computer, etc keyboard) incorrectly. [**mis-**]

miskick /mis-kik'/ vt to kick (a ball) with the wrong part of the foot. ◆ n /mis'kik/ an instance of this. [**mis-**]

Miskito /mis-kē'tō/ n a Native American people living in Nicaragua and Honduras; the language of this people. ◆ adj of or relating to the Miskito or their language. [Miskito]

misknow /mis-nō'/ vt to misapprehend, misunderstand. [**mis-**]
■ **misknowledge** /mis-nol'ij/ n.

mislay /mis-lā'/ vt (pap and pat **mislaid**') to lay in a place not remembered; to lose; to lay or place wrongly. [**mis-** and **lay**[1]]

mislead /mis-lēd'/ vt (pap and pat **misled**') to lead into error; to direct, inform or advise wrongly; to cause to go wrong. [**mis-**]
■ **mislead'er** n. **mislead'ing** adj deceptive. **mislead'ingly** adv.

misleared /mis-lērd'/ (Scot and N Eng dialect) adj mistaught; unmannerly; ill-conditioned. [**mis-**, and **leared**, pap of **lear**[1]]

misleeke /mis-lēk'/ (Spenser) vi for **mislike**.

misletoe a former spelling of **mistletoe**.

mislight /mis-līt'/ (poetic) vt to lead astray by a light. [**mis-**]

mislike /mis-līk'/ (archaic) vt to dislike; to displease. ◆ vi to disapprove. ◆ n dislike; disapprobation. [**mis-**]
■ **mislīk'er** n. **mislīk'ing** n.

mislippen /mis-lip'n/ (Scot and N Eng dialect) vt to distrust; to suspect; to disappoint, deceive; to neglect, overlook. [**mis-**]

mislive /mis-liv'/ (obs) vi to live a bad life. [**mis-**]

misluck /mis-luk'/ (esp Scot) n bad luck, misfortune. ◆ vi to meet with bad luck, to fail. [**mis-**]

mismake /mis-māk'/ (now Scot) vt to make or shape badly; to trouble or disturb. [**mis-**]
■ **mismade'** adj.

mismanage /mis-man'ij/ vt to manage badly or wrongly. [**mis-**]
■ **misman'agement** n.

mismanners /mis-man'ərz/ (obs) n pl bad manners. [**mis-**]

mismarry /mis-mar'i/ vt and vi to marry unsuitably. [**mis-**]
■ **mismarr'iage** n.

mismatch /mis-mach'/ vt to match unsuitably or badly. ◆ n /mis'/ a bad match. [**mis-**]
■ **mismatch'ment** n.

mismate /mis-māt'/ vt and vi to mate unsuitably. [**mis-**]
■ **mismat'ed** adj.

mismeasure /mis-mezh'ər/ vt to measure wrongly. [**mis-**]
■ **mismeas'urement** n.

mismetre /mis-mē'tər/ vt to spoil the metre of (a poem). [**mis-**]

misname /mis-nām'/ vt to give or call by an unsuitable or wrong name. [**mis-**]

misnomer /mis-nō'mər/ n a wrong or unsuitable name or term; (a) misnaming. ◆ vt to misname. [OFr from mes- (from L minus less), and nommer, from L nōmināre to name]

miso /mē'sō/ n (pl **mi'sos**) a paste, used for flavouring, prepared from soya beans and fermented in brine. [Jap]

miso- /mi-sō- or mī-sō-/ combining form signifying a hater of, hating. [Gr mīseein to hate]
■ **mis'oclere** /-klēr/ adj (Gr kleros clergy; rare) hating the clergy. **misogamist** /-og'ə-mist/ n (Gr gamos marriage) a hater of marriage. **misog'amy** n. **misogynist** /-oj'i-nist/ or -og'/ n (Gr gynē a woman) a woman-hater. **misogynist'ic**, **misogynist'ical** or **misog'ynous** adj. **misog'yny** n. **misol'ogist** n. **misology** /-ol'ə-ji/ n (Gr logos reason) hatred of reason, reasoning, or knowledge. **misoneism** /-nē'izm/ n (Gr neos new) hatred of novelty. **misoné'ist** n. **misonéist'ic** adj.

misobserve /mis-əb-zûrv'/ vt and vi to fail to observe; to observe incorrectly. [**mis-**]
■ **misobserv'ance** n.

misocapnic...to...**misoneistic** see under **miso-**.

misoprostol /mī-sō-pros'tol/ n a synthetic form of prostaglandin used chiefly in treating and preventing gastric ulcers, esp those caused by anti-inflammatory drugs.

misorder /mis-ör'dər/ n and vt disorder. [**mis-**]

misperceive /mis-pər-sēv'/ vt to perceive incorrectly, misunderstand. [**mis-**]
■ **mispercep'tion** n.

mispersuasion /mis-pər-swā'zhən/ (rare) n a wrong persuasion or notion; a false opinion. [**mis-**]
■ **mispersuade'** vt.

mispickel /mis'pi-kəl/ n arsenical pyrites, a mineral composed of iron, arsenic, and sulphur. [Ger]

misplace /mis-plās'/ vt to mislay; to set on, or attach to, a wrong or inappropriate object (fig); to indulge in unsuitable circumstances (fig); to put in a wrong place. [**mis-**]
■ **misplace'ment** n.
❏ **misplaced modifier** see **misrelated participle** under **misrelate**.

misplay /mis'plā/ n a wrong play, as in sport or games. ◆ vt and vi /mis-plā'/ to make a wrong play. [**mis-**]

misplead /mis-plēd'/ vt and vi to plead wrongly. [**mis-**]
■ **misplead'ing** n an error in pleading.

misplease /mis-plēz'/ (obs) vt to displease. [**mis-**]

mispoint /mis-point'/ vt to punctuate wrongly. [**mis-**]

mispraise /mis-prāz'/ vt to praise wrongly; to reproach. [**mis-**]

misprint /mis-print'/ vt to print wrongly. ◆ vi to make footprints in unusual positions. ◆ n (usu /mis'print/) a mistake in printing. [**mis-**]

misprise[1] or **misprize** /mis-prīz'/ vt to scorn; to slight; to undervalue. ◆ n (Spenser **mesprise'**, **mesprize'** or **misprize'**) scorn; slighting; failure to value. [OFr mespriser, from pfx mes- (from L minus less), and LL pretiāre, from L pretium price, value]

misprise[2] or **misprize** /mis-prīz'/ vt to mistake. [OFr mespris, pap of mesprendre to commit an offence; cf **misprision[1]**]
■ **mesprize'** n (Spenser) error. **misprised'** adj mistaken.

misprision[1] /mis-prizh'ən/ n the overlooking or deliberate concealing of the crime of another (law); any serious offence or failure of duty (positive or negative, according to whether it is maladministration or mere neglect); a mistake. [OFr mes- (from L minus less), and LL prēnsiō, -ōnis, from L praehendere to take]
■ **misprision of felony**, **treason**, etc knowledge of and failure to give information about a crime, treason, etc.

misprision[2] /mis-prizh'ən/ (archaic) n failure to appreciate the true value, nature or extent of something. [**misprise[1]**, after the model of **misprision[1]**]

mispronounce /mis-prə-nowns'/ vt to pronounce incorrectly. [**mis-**]
■ **mispronunciation** /-nun-si-ā'shən/ n (a) wrong or improper pronunciation.

misproportion /mis-prə-pör'shən/ n lack of due proportion. [**mis-**]
■ **mispropor'tioned** adj.

misproud /mis-prowd'/ (archaic) adj unduly proud. [**mis-**]

mispunctuate /mis-pungk'tū-āt or -pungk'choo-/ vt and vi to punctuate wrongly. [**mis-**]
■ **mispunctuā'tion** n.

misquote /mis-kwōt'/ vt to quote wrongly. ◆ n /mis'/ something quoted wrongly. [**mis-**]
■ **misquotā'tion** n.

misrate /mis-rāt'/ vt to value wrongly. [**mis-**]

misread /mis-rēd'/ vt (pat and pap **misread** /-red'/) to read wrongly; to misconstrue. [**mis-**]
■ **misread'ing** n.

misreckon /mis-rek'n/ vt and vi to reckon or compute wrongly, to miscalculate. [**mis-**]
■ **misreck'oning** n.

misregard /mis-ri-gärd'/ (Spenser) n inattention. [**mis-**]

misrelate /mis-ri-lāt'/ vt to relate incorrectly. [**mis-**]
■ **misrelā'tion** n.
❏ **misrelated participle** n a participle which the grammatical structure of the sentence insists on attaching to a word it is not intended to qualify (eg Lost in thought, the bus passed me without stopping; also called **misplaced modifier**).

misremember /mis-ri-mem'bər/ vt and vi to remember wrongly or imperfectly; to forget (Scot and dialect). [**mis-**]

misreport /mis-ri-pört'/ vt to report falsely, misleadingly or wrongly; to speak ill of (Shakesp). ◆ n false reporting or report; bad repute (obs). [**mis-**]

misrepresent /mis-re-pri-zent'/ vt to represent falsely; to give a misleading interpretation to the words or deeds of; to be an unrepresentative representative of. [**mis-**]
■ **misrepresentā'tion** n. **misrepresent'ative** adj.

misroute /mis-root'/ vt to route (eg a telephone call, traffic) wrongly. [**mis-**]

misrule /mis-rool'/ n disorder; bad or disorderly government. ◆ vt and vi to govern badly. [**mis-**]
■ **Lord of Misrule** a leader of Christmas revels (hist); a promoter of anti-establishment or anti-traditionalist views or activities.

Miss /mis/ n (pl **Miss'es**; either 'the Miss Hepburns' or 'the Misses Hepburn' may be said, the latter being more formal) a title prefixed to the name of an unmarried (formerly, and now dialect and US non-standard, also a married) woman or girl (orig less respectful than Mrs); also prefixed to a representational title, esp in beauty contests, eg Miss World; (without the name) an eldest daughter, young lady of the house (obs); vocatively used alone in (usu mock) severity, or to address a waitress, female teacher, etc; (without cap) a schoolgirl, or a girl or woman with the faults attributed to schoolgirls; a person between a child and a woman, esp in reference to clothing size; a kept mistress (obs). [Shortened form of **mistress**]
■ **miss'hood** n. **miss'ish** adj schoolgirlish; having the faults attributed to schoolgirls, ie sentimental, insipid, namby-pamby, squeamish, silly, etc. **miss'ishness** n. **miss'y** n a (usu disparaging) form of address used to a little girl. ◆ adj missish.

Miss. abbrev : Mississippi (US state).

miss[1] /mis/ vt (or vi archaic, with of) to fail to hit, reach, find, meet, touch, catch, get, have, take advantage of, attend, observe or see; to avoid (a specified danger); to fail (to do; archaic); to leave out, omit; to discover the absence of; to feel the loss or absence of; to think of (an absent person or thing) longingly, or (a former time) nostalgically; to do without (Shakesp). ◆ vi to fail to hit or obtain; to fail; to go wrong (obs); to miss fire. ◆ n the fact or condition or an act or occasion of missing; failure to hit the mark; loss; (the source of or reason for) a feeling of loss or absence; wrongdoing (Shakesp). [OE missan; Du missen to miss]
■ **miss'able** adj. **miss'ing** adj not to be found; not in the expected place; lacking; of unascertained fate (milit). **miss'ingly** adv (Shakesp) with a sense of loss.
❏ **missing link** n a hypothetical extinct creature thought to be intermediate between man and the anthropoid apes; any one thing required to complete a series.
■ **give (something) a miss** to allow an opponent to score by intentionally missing (billiards); to leave out, omit or avoid something. **go missing** to disappear, esp unexpectedly and inexplicably; to be mislaid. **miss fire** to fail to go off or explode (cf **misfire**). **miss oneself** (Scot) to miss out on an enjoyable experience. **miss one's tip** (sl) to fail in one's plan or attempt. **miss out** to omit; (also with on) to fail to experience or benefit (from). **miss stays** (naut) to fail in going about from one tack to another. **miss the bus** or **boat** (inf) to lose one's opportunity. **near miss** see under **near**.

■ words derived from main entry word; ❏ compound words; ■ idioms and phrasal verbs

miss² see **Miss**.

missa /mis'ə or -a/ (L) n (RC; also with cap) the Mass.
□ **missa** (or **Missa**) **solemnis** /sol-em'nis/ n High Mass.

missal /mis'l/ (RC) n a book containing the complete service for mass throughout the year. [LL missāle, from missa mass]

missay /mis-sā'/ (archaic) vt and vi (pat and pap **missaid** /-sed'/) to say or speak amiss, wrongly, falsely, or in vain; to slander; to revile. [**mis-**]
■ **missay'ing** n.

missee /mis-sē'/ vt and vi to see wrongly. [**mis-**]

misseem /mis-sēm'/ (Spenser) vt to be unbecoming to. [**mis-**]
■ **misseem'ing** adj unbecoming. ◆ n false appearance.

missel /mis'l or miz'l/ n the mistle-thrush; mistletoe (obs). [OE mistel, mistil mistletoe]
□ **miss'el-bird** or **miss'el-thrush** n a mistle-thrush.

missell /mis-sel'/ (finance) vt to sell an inappropriate financial product, eg a personal pension. [**mis-**]
■ **missell'ing** n.

missel-tree /mis'l-trē/ n a melastomaceous tree (Bellucia aubletii) of northern S America, with edible berries.

missend /mis-send'/ vt (pap and pat **missent'**) to send by mistake; to send to the wrong person or place. [**mis-**]

misset /mis-set'/ vt to set or place wrongly or unfitly; to put in a bad mood (Scot). [**mis-**]

misshape /mis-shāp'/ vt to shape badly or wrongly; to deform. ◆ n deformity; a misshapen item. [**mis-**]
■ **misshap'en** or **misshaped'** (Spenser **mishapt**) adj badly-shaped, deformed. **misshap'enly** adv. **misshap'enness** n.

missheathed /mis-shē'dh(i)d/ (Shakesp) adj wrongly sheathed. [**mis-**]

missile /mis'īl or (N Am) mis'l/ n a weapon or object for throwing by hand or shooting from a bow, gun, or other instrument, esp a rocket-launched weapon, often nuclear. ◆ adj capable of being thrown or projected; relating to a missile. [L missilis, from mittere, missum to throw]
■ **miss'ilery** or **miss'ilry** /-īl-ri or -l-ri/ n missiles collectively; (the study of) their design, manufacture and use.

missing see under **miss¹**.

missiology /mi-si-ol'ə-ji/ n the study of religious missions. [Irregularly formed from **mission** and **-logy**]

mission /mish'ən/ n an act of sending, esp to perform some function; a flight with a specific purpose, such as a bombing raid or a task assigned to an astronaut or astronauts; the errand or purpose for which one is sent; that for which one has been or seems to have been sent into the world, vocation; a sending out of people on a political or diplomatic errand, for the spreading of a religion, etc; an organization that sends out missionaries; its activities; a station or establishment of missionaries; any particular field of missionary enterprise; the body of people sent on a mission; an embassy; a settlement for religious, charitable, medical, or philanthropic work in a district; a religious organization or district not fully developed as a parish; a series of special religious services conducted by a missioner. ◆ adj of a mission or missions, esp characteristic of the old Spanish missions in California. ◆ vt (rare) to commission. [L missiō, -ōnis, from mittere to send]
■ **miss'ionarize** or **-ise** vt and vi to act as missionary (to, among, or in); to do missionary work. **miss'ionary** n a person sent on a mission, esp religious. ◆ adj relating to a mission or missions. **miss'ioner** n a missionary; a person in charge of parochial missions. **miss'ionize** or **-ise** vt and vi to do missionary work (upon, in, or among).
□ **mission architecture** n the style of the old Spanish missions in California, etc. **missionary-bish'op** n one having jurisdiction in an unconverted country, or in districts not yet formed into dioceses. **missionary position** n in sexual intercourse, the face-to-face position with the male on top. **missionary selling** n approaches made by manufacturers to develop goodwill with new contacts who are not the intended final purchasers of a particular product, and to increase sales. **mission creep** n the tendency for a military operation to exceed its initial purposes, drawing in more personnel and resources and pursuing more complex and wide-reaching objectives. **Mission Indian** n a member of any of the Native American tribes converted by early Spanish Catholic missionaries in California, etc. **mission statement** n a succinct statement of its aims and principles formulated by a business or other organization for the supposed benefit of its members and customers.

missis or **missus** /mis'iz or -is/ (inf) n lady of the house; wife; a term of address to a woman (usu by an unacquainted man). [**mistress**]

missive /mis'iv/ n that which is sent, as a letter; a messenger (Shakesp); a missile (obs); (in pl) letters sent between two parties in which one

makes an offer and the other accepts it (Scots law). ◆ adj sent; missile (obs). [LL missīvus, from L mittere, missum to send]
■ **letter missive** a missive, esp from a sovereign or authority to a particular person or body, such as one giving congé d'élire.

misspeak /mis-spēk'/ vt and vi (pat **misspoke'**; pap **misspok'en**) to speak wrongly. [**mis-**]

misspell /mis-spel'/ vt and vi (pat and pap **misspelt'** or **misspelled'**) to spell wrongly. [**mis-**]
■ **misspell'ing** n a wrong spelling.

misspend /mis-spend'/ vt (pap and pat **misspent'**) to spend badly; to waste or squander. [**mis-**]

misstate /mis-stāt'/ vt to state wrongly or falsely. [**mis-**]
■ **misstate'ment** n.

misstep /mis-step'/ vi to make a false step; to make a mistake. ◆ n a mistake in conduct, etc. [**mis-**]

missuit /mis-soot'/ or -sūt'/ vt to be unbecoming to. [**mis-**]

missummation /mis-sum-ā'shən/ n wrong addition. [**mis-**]

missus see **missis**.

mist /mist/ n watery vapour seen in the atmosphere; cloud in contact with the ground; thin fog; rain in very fine drops; a fine spray of any liquid; a suspension of liquid in a gas; condensed vapour on a surface; a dimness or dim appearance; anything that dims or darkens the sight or the judgement. ◆ vt to obscure or veil with, or as if with, mist; to apply a fine spray of water to (an indoor plant). ◆ vi to become misty or veiled; to form a mist or vapour-cloud. [OE mist darkness, dimness; Icel mistr, Du mist]
■ **mist'er** n a spray gun with a fine nozzle, used to apply moisture to the foliage of indoor plants. **mist'ful** adj misty. **mist'ily** adv. **mist'iness** n. **mist'ing** n mist; the action of the verb mist. ◆ adj misty; hazy; dimming. **mist'y** adj (**mist'ier**; **mist'iest**) full of, covered with, obscured by, mist; like mist; dim; obscure; clouded; vague; not perspicuous; (of eyes) tearful.
□ **mist'-flower** n a N American hemp agrimony, with clusters of blue or violet flowers. **mist net** n a net made of very fine threads used to trap birds. **mist'-net** vt to trap in such a net.
■ **mist up** or **over** (of a surface) to become covered with condensed vapour. **Scotch mist** a thick wetting mist; a drizzle.

mistake /mi-stāk'/ vt (pat **mistook'**; pap **mistak'en** (also **mista'en**)) to understand wrongly; to take for another thing or person (with for); to be wrong about; to think wrongly; to remove wrongfully (obs); (appar) to take or come upon to one's loss (Spenser); to believe wrongly to be (Spenser). ◆ vi to err in opinion or judgement; to do amiss. ◆ n the act of taking or understanding something wrongly; something understood or taken wrongly; an error; /mis'/ a faulty shot (cinematog). [ME mistaken, from ON mistaka to take wrongly, from mis- wrongly, and taka to take]
■ **mistak'able** adj. **mistak'ably** adv. **mistak'en** adj understood wrongly; guilty of making a mistake; under a misapprehension; erroneous; incorrect; ill-judged. **mistak'enly** adv. **mistak'enness** n. **mistak'er** n. **mistak'ing** n (Shakesp) a mistake.
□ **mistaken identity** n an error in identifying someone.
■ **and no mistake** (inf) assuredly. **be mistaken** to make or have made a mistake; to be misunderstood. **by mistake** accidentally. **mistake one's man** to think too lightly of the man one has to deal with. **mistake one's way** to take the wrong road.

misteach /mis-tēch'/ vt (pat and pap **mistaught** /mis-töt'/) to teach wrongly. [**mis-**]

mistell /mis-tel'/ vt (pap and pat **mistold'**) to count, narrate or inform, wrongly. [**mis-**]

mistemper /mis-tem'pər/ (obs) n and vt disorder. [**mis-**]
■ **mistem'pered** adj tempered or mixed badly (Shakesp); mixed or prepared for an evil purpose (Shakesp).

Mister /mis'tər/ n a title prefixed to a man's name, and to certain designations (as Mr Justice, Mr Speaker), written **Mr**; (without cap) an untitled man; (without cap) sir (inf). [**master**]
■ **mis'ter** vt to address as 'mister'.

mister¹ see under **mist**.

mister² /mis'tər/ n craft, trade, profession (obs); manner, kind (Spenser; without of as in what mister man, orig meaning 'man of what class', hence 'what kind of man'); need, necessity (Scot). ◆ vi (Spenser) to be necessary; to have need. ◆ vt to need. [OFr mestier (Fr métier) trade, from L ministerium service]
■ **mis'tery** n see **mystery²**.

misterm /mis-tûrm'/ vt to name wrongly or unsuitably. [**mis-**]

mistery see **mystery²**.

misthink /mis-thingk'/ vt (pat and pap **misthought** /mis-thöt'/) to think badly of (Shakesp); to think wrongly. ◆ vi (obs) to have wicked or mistaken thoughts. [**mis-**]
■ **misthought'** n a wrong notion.

mistico /mis'ti-kō/ n (pl **mis'ticos**) a small Mediterranean ship, between a xebec and a felucca in size. [Sp *místico*, prob from Ar]

mistigris /mis'ti-gris or -grē/ n a variation of poker in which a joker or blank card can be given any value; the card so used. [Fr *mistigri* jack of clubs]

mistime /mis-tīm'/ vt to time wrongly. [**mis-**]
■ **mistimed'** adj inopportune.

mistitle /mis-tī'tl/ vt to call by a wrong or unsuitable title. [**mis-**]

mistle same as **mizzle**[1] or **missel**.

mistle-thrush /mis'l-thrush/ n a large European thrush fond of mistletoe berries (also **miss'el-thrush**). [See ety for **mistletoe**, and **thrush**[2]]

mistletoe /mis'l-tō or miz'/ n a hemiparasitic evergreen shrubby plant (*Viscum album*) with white, viscous berries, growing on the apple, apricot, etc (very rarely on the oak); extended to other species of its genus or family (Loranthaceae). [OE *misteltān*, from *mistel, mistil* mistletoe, and *tān* twig; see **missel**]

mistold /mis-tōld'/ pat of **mistell**.

mistook /mi-stŭk'/ pat of **mistake**.

mistral /mis'tral or mi-sträl'/ n a violent cold dry north-east wind in S France. [Fr, from Provençal *mistral*, from L *magistrālis* masterful, *magister* master]

mistranslate /mis-tranz-lāt' or -trans-/ vt and vi to translate incorrectly. [**mis-**]
■ **mistranslā'tion** n.

mistrayned /mis-trānd'/ (*Spenser*) adj drawn away, misled. [**mis-**; see **train**[1]]

mistreading /mis-tred'ing/ (*Shakesp*) n a false step, misdeed. [**mis-**]

mistreat /mis-trēt'/ vt to treat badly or cruelly. [**mis-**]
■ **mistreat'ment** n.

mistress /mis'tris/ n (fem of **master**) a woman employer of servants or head of a house or family; a woman (or anything personified as a woman) having power of ownership; a woman teacher, *esp* in a school; a woman well-skilled in anything; a woman loved and courted by a man (*archaic*); a woman involved in an established sexual relationship with a married man, sometimes supported by him financially; *vocatively* madam (*archaic* and *dialect*); the jack at bowls (*Shakesp*); (with *cap*) a title corresponding to the modern form **Mrs**, once prefixed to the name of any woman or girl (*archaic* or *dialect*). ◆ adj (*literary*) principal; leading; ruling. ◆ vt to make a mistress of, pay court to as a mistress; to address as mistress; to become or be mistress of or over; (with *it*) to play the mistress. [OFr *maistresse* (Fr *maîtresse*), from LL *magistrissa*, fem from L *magister* master]
■ **mis'tressless** adj. **mis'tressly** adj. **mis'tress-ship** n.
❑ **Mistress of the Robes** see under **robe**[1].

mistrial /mis-trī'əl or mis'trī-əl/ n a trial void because of error; an inconclusive trial (*US*). [**mis-**]

mistrust /mis-trust'/ n distrust. ◆ vt to distrust; to suspect. ◆ vi to be suspicious. [**mis-**]
■ **mistrust'ful** adj. **mistrust'fully** adv. **mistrust'fulness** n. **mistrust'ingly** adv. **mistrust'less** adj.

mistryst /mis-trīst'/ (*Scot*) vt to disappoint by not keeping an engagement. [**mis-**]
■ **mistryst'ed** adj disturbed, put out.

mistune /mis-tūn'/ vt to tune wrongly or falsely; to put out of tune. [**mis-**]

misunderstand /mis-un-dər-stand'/ vt and vi (pap and pat **misunderstood'**) to take in a wrong sense; to fail to appreciate the true nature, motives, etc of. [**mis-**]
■ **misunderstand'ing** n a mistake as to the meaning of something; a slight disagreement. **misunderstood'** adj.

misuse /mis-ūs'/ n improper use; application to a bad purpose; evil usage or behaviour (*Shakesp*). ◆ vt /mis-ūz'/ (pat *Spenser* **misust** /-ūst'/) to use for a wrong purpose or in a wrong way; to treat badly or wrongly; to speak badly of (*Shakesp*); to deceive (*Shakesp*). [**mis-**]
■ **misus'age** n misconduct, evil practice (*Spenser*); bad or unfair treatment; wrong use. **misus'er** n.

misventure /mis-ven'chər/ n a misadventure. [**mis-**]
■ **misvent'urous** adj.

miswandred /mis-won'dərd/ (*Spenser*) adj strayed, gone astray. [**mis-**]

misween /mis-wēn'/ (*Spenser*) vt and vi to judge wrongly, have a wrong opinion of. [**mis-**]

miswend /mis-wend'/ (*Spenser*) vi (pat and pap **miswent'**; see **misgo**) to go astray or amiss; to come to grief, miscarry.

misword /mis-wûrd'/ n (*dialect*) an angry or harsh word. ◆ vt to word incorrectly. [**mis-**]
■ **misword'ing** n.

misworship /mis-wûr'ship/ vt to worship wrongly. ◆ n worship of a wrong object. [**mis-**]

miswrite /mis-rīt'/ vt to write incorrectly. [**mis-**]

misyoke /mis-yōk'/ vt to yoke or marry unsuitably. [**mis-**]

MIT abbrev : Massachusetts Institute of Technology.

mitch /mich/ (dialect) vi to play truant, esp from school. [Perh from OFr *muchier, mucier* to hide, lurk]

mite[1] /mīt/ n any of various tiny arachnids of the order Acarida, many of which carry disease, smaller than ticks and, unlike them, not always parasitic in habits. [OE *mīte*]
■ **mīticīd'al** adj. **mit'icide** n (L *caedere* to kill) a poison or other agent that destroys mites. **mīt'y** adj infested with mites.

mite[2] /mīt/ n a diminutive person; a small child; a very small amount; a small contribution proportionate to one's means; a minute portion or fragment; a jot as in *a mite late* (*inf*); *orig* an old Flemish coin of very small value; used to translate the Gr *lepton* (Mark 12.42) of which two make a *kodrantēs* or 'farthing' (*Bible*). [MDu *mīte* (Du *mijt*); perh ult the same as **mite**[1]]

miter see **mitre**[1,2].

mither see **moider**.

Mithras /mith'ras/ or **Mithra** /-rä/ n the ancient Persian god of light, whose worship became popular in the Roman Empire. [L and Gr *Mithrās*, from OPers *Mithra*]
■ **Mithraeum** /-rē'əm/ n (pl **Mithrae'a**) a grotto or temple sacred to Mithras. **Mithrā'ic** adj. **Mithrā'icism** or **Mith'raism** /-rä-izm/ n belief in or worship of Mithras. **Mith'raist** n.

mithridate /mith'ri-dāt/ n an antidote to poison. [*Mithridates*, king of Pontus (reigned c.120–63BC), who was said to have acquired immunity to poisons by taking gradually increased doses of it]
■ **mithridat'ic** or **mithradat'ic** adj antidotal; (with *cap*) relating to Mithridates, *esp* to his wars against Rome (also **Mithradat'ic**). **mith'ridatism** /-dāt-izm/ n immunity to a poison acquired by taking gradually increased doses of it. **mithrid'atize** or **-ise** vt.
❑ **mithridate mustard** n field penny-cress (*Thlaspi arvense*). **mithridate pepperwort** n field cress (*Lepidium campestre*).

miticidal and **miticide** see under **mite**[1].

mitigate /mit'i-gāt/ vt to mollify, appease; to make more easily borne; to lessen the severity, violence or evil of; to temper. [L *mītigāre, -ātum*, from *mītis* mild]
■ **mit'igable** adj. **mit'igant** adj mitigating. **mit'igāting** adj. **mitigā'tion** n. **mit'igātive** n and adj. **mit'igātor** n. **mit'igātory** adj.

mitochondrion /mi- or mī-tō-kon'dri-ən/ n (pl **mitochon'dria**) an energy-producing body, threadlike to spherical in shape, present in cytoplasm. [Gr *mitos* thread, and *chondros* cartilage]
■ **mitochon'drial** adj.

mitosis /mī- or mi-tō'sis/ n (pl **mitō'ses** /-sēz/) an elaborate process of cell division involving the arrangement of chromosomes in definite figures; karyokinesis. [Gr *mitos* fibre]
■ **mit'ogen** n (Gr *gennaein* to engender) a substance that causes cells to divide. **mitogenet'ic** or **mitogen'ic** adj. **mitotic** /-tot'ik/ adj. **mitot'ically** adv.
❑ **mitotic index** n the proportion in any tissue of dividing cells, *usu* expressed as per thousand cells.

mitraille /mē'trī-y' or -trī'y'/ n small shot or projectiles sent in a shower, esp from a mitrailleuse. [Fr]
■ **mitrailleur** /-yœr'/ n a machine-gunner; a mitrailleuse. **mitrailleuse** /-yœz'/ n a machine-gun (*orig* one having a number of barrels) that discharges a stream of small missiles.

mitre[1] or (*N Am*) **miter** /mī'tər/ n a high, pointed headdress, cleft crosswise on top and with two ribbons hanging from the back, worn by archbishops and bishops, and by some abbots in the Western Church; episcopal office or status (*fig*); *esp* in ancient Greece, a woman's headband; a belt or girdle (*Pope*, following *Homer*); an oriental hat or turban (*obs*); a gastropod of the genus *Mitra* or its conical shell (**mitre shell**). ◆ vt to adorn with a mitre. [Fr, from Gr *mitrā* fillet]
■ **mī'tral** adj of or like a mitre; of the mitral valve. **mit'riform** /mīt'/ or mit'/ adj mitre-shaped.
❑ **mitral valve** n a mitre-shaped valve of the heart. **mi'tre-wort** n bishop's cap.

mitre[2] or (*N Am*) **miter** /mī'tər/ n a joint (also **mi'tre-joint**) in which each piece is cut at an angle of 45° to its side, giving a right angle between the pieces; sometimes applied to any joint where the plane of junction bisects the angle; an angle of 45°; a gusset, a tapered insertion (*needlework*). ◆ vt to join with a mitre; to turn a corner in, by cutting out a triangular piece and joining (*needlework*). ◆ vi to meet in a mitre. [Prob same as **mitre**[1]]
❑ **mitre box** n a box with narrow slots to guide a saw when cutting a mitre. **mitre fold** n (in origami) a fold in which two corners are turned

down at equal angles to meet each other in the centre. **mitre wheel** *n* a bevel-wheel having its face inclined 45° to its axis.

mitt /mit/ *n* a mitten; a hand (*sl*); a padded leather glove worn by a baseball player; a thick, roughly-shaped glove designed to absorb, protect, etc (as *bath mitt*, *oven mitt*, etc). [Abbrev of **mitten**]

Mittel-Europa or **Mitteleuropa** /mit-əl-yoo-rō'pə/ *n* Central Europe. [Ger]
■ **Mittel-Europe'an** or **Mitteleurope'an** *adj* and *n*.

mitten /mit'n/ *n* a kind of glove with one undivided section covering the fingers and one the thumb; a glove covering the hand and wrist, but only the base of the fingers and thumb; a boxing glove (*sl*); dismissal (*sl*); (in *pl*) handcuffs (*sl*). [OFr *mitaine*; origin obscure]
■ **mitt'ened** *adj* covered with a mitten or mittens.
□ **mitten crab** *n* a burrowing crab (*Eriocheir sinensis*) with hairy claws, originally native to China but introduced elsewhere.
■ **frozen mitten** (*obs sl*) a chilly reception, the cold shoulder. **get the mitten** (*obs sl*) to be dismissed, *esp* as a suitor.

mittimus /mit'i-məs/ *n* a warrant granted for sending to prison a person charged with a crime (*law*); a writ by which a record is transferred out of one court to another (*law*); dismissal, discharge (*inf*); a nickname for a magistrate. [L, we send, from *mittere* to send]

Mitty see **Walter Mitty**.

mitumba /mi-tŭm'bə/ (*E Afr*) *n* second-hand clothes imported from developed countries (also *adj*). [Swahili, bale of cloth]

mity see under **mite**[1].

mitzvah /mits'və or mits-vä'/ *n* (*pl* **mitzvoth** /-vōt'/ or **mitzvahs**) a good deed. [Heb, literally, commandment]

miurus /mī-ū'rəs/ *n* (*prosody*) a hexameter with a short penultimate syllable. [Latinized from Gr *meiouros* curtailed, from *meiōn* less, and *ourā* a tail]

mix /miks/ *vt* (pat and pap **mixed** or **mixt**) to combine so that the parts of one thing, or the things of one sort, are diffused among those of another; to prepare or compound in such a way; to blend; to mingle; to join, combine; to piece together two lengths of film invisibly (*cinematog*); to combine and adjust (separate sound elements) for one recording (*music*, *broadcasting*, etc); to play (two records) one after the other with an overlap in which the beats match (*broadcasting*); to confound (*Milton*); to associate (*archaic*); to interbreed, cross; to involve. ◆ *vi* to become, or to be capable of becoming, mixed; to be joined or combined; to associate; to have social intercourse. ◆ *n* a mixing, mingling; a mixture, *esp* a standard mixture; a formula giving constituents and proportions; a jumble, a mess; the sound produced by mixing (*music*, *broadcasting*, etc); a version of a musical recording that has been mixed in a particular way. [L *miscēre*, *mixtus* to mix; exact relation to OE *miscian*, Ger *mischen*, uncertain]
■ **mix'able** *adj*. **mixed** /mikst/ *adj* mingled; promiscuous; of or for both sexes; miscellaneous; confused; not select; combining characters of two or more kinds; between front and back (*phonetics*). **mix'edly** (or /mikst'li/) *adv*. **mix'edness** (or /mikst'/) *n*. **mix'er** *n* a person who mixes; that by which or in which things are mixed; a person who is easily sociable in all sorts of company; a person who mixes drinks; a soft drink for adding to an alcoholic one; a troublemaker (*sl*); a device by means of which two or more input signals are combined to give a single output signal (*electronics*); a person who uses such a device (*inf*). **mixol'ogist** *n* (*US inf*) a maker of cocktails. **mixt** *adj* same as **mixed** above. **mix'ter-max'ter**, **mix'tie-max'tie**, **mix'ty-max'ty** or **mix'y-max'y** *n* (*Scot*) a confused jumble. ◆ *adj* and *adv* in a confused jumble. **mixtion** /miks'chən/ *n* a mixture of amber, mastic and asphaltum used as a mordant for gold-leaf; a mixture (*obs*). **mix'ture** /-chər/ *n* an act of mixing; the state of being mixed; the product of mixing; a product of mixing in which the ingredients retain their properties, as distinguished from a *compound* (*chem*); (in an organ) a compound-stop giving harmonics; a mixture of petrol vapour and air (*motoring*). **mix'y** *adj* mixed.
□ **mixed-abil'ity** *adj* of classes, etc accommodating members who differ in (*esp* academic) ability. **mixed bag** *n* any assortment of diverse people, things, characteristics, etc. **mixed blessing** *n* something which has both advantages and disadvantages. **mixed bud** *n* (*bot*) one containing young foliage leaves and also the rudiments of flowers or inflorescences. **mixed chalice** *n* the chalice prepared for the Eucharist, containing wine mixed with water. **mixed crystal** *n* a crystal formed from two or more distinct compounds. **mixed doubles** *n pl* a match in tennis, badminton, etc with a male and a female player as partners on each side. **mixed economy** *n* a national economy of which parts are state-owned and other parts privately-owned. **mixed farming** *n* farming of both crops and livestock. **mixed foursome** *n* a golf match with a male and female player as partners on each side. **mixed grill** see under **grill**[1]. **mixed language** *n* one which contains elements (eg vocabulary, syntax) from two or more separate languages. **mixed marriage** *n* one between people of different religions or races. **mixed martial arts** *n sing* a full combat sport with minimal rules. **mixed-me'dia** *adj* (of a work in the arts) combining traditional forms, eg acting, dance, painting, and electronic media, eg tape recording. **mixed metaphor** see under **metaphor**. **mixed number** *n* one consisting of an integer and a fraction, eg $2\frac{1}{2}$. **mixed train** *n* a railway train made up partly of passenger carriages and partly of goods wagons. **mixed-up'** *adj* psychologically or socially confused, bewildered, and badly-adjusted. **mix-in'** *n* (*US*) a fight. **mixing valve** *n* one which mixes hot and cold water (as in a **mixer tap**). **mix tape** *n* a compilation of recorded music by various artists. **mix'-up** *n* confusion; a confused jumble. **mix zone** *n* an area where two bodies, substances, etc are brought together; an area where reporters may interview athletes immediately after a sporting event.
■ **mix and match** to make a selection from a complementary range (**mix-and-match'** *adj*). **mixed up in** (or **with**) entangled in. **mix it** (*sl*) to fight forcefully; to cause trouble. **mix up** to confuse.

mixen /mik'sn/ *n* a dunghill. [OE *mixen*, from *mix*, *meox*, dung]

mixo- /mik-sō-/ *combining form* denoting mixed. [Gr *mīxis* mixing, *misgein* to mix]
■ **mixobarbar'ic** *adj* part barbaric, part Greek. **mixolyd'ian** *adj* (also with *cap*) (in ancient Greek music) the same as **hyperdorian** (see under **hyper-**); (in old church music) applied to an authentic mode extending from g to g, with g for its final. **mixotroph'ic** *adj* (*biol*) combining different modes of nutrition.

Mixtec /mē'stek/ *n* a Native American people of S Mexico; the language of this people. ◆ *adj* of or relating to the Mixtec or their language. [Nahuatl]

mixter-maxter, etc see under **mix**.

miz or **mizz** /miz/ (*inf*) *n* and *adj* short form of **misery** or **miserable**.

mizuna /mi-zoo'nə/ *n* a Japanese vegetable of the cabbage family that grows in large rosettes of feathery leaves. [Jap]

mizzen or **mizen** /miz'n/ *n* in a three-masted vessel, the hindmost of the fore-and-aft sails; the spanker or driver. ◆ *adj* belonging to the mizzen; nearest the stern. [Fr *misaine* foresail, foremast, from Ital *mezzana* mizzensail, from LL *mediānus* middle, from L *medius* middle; the development of meaning is puzzling]
□ **mizz'encourse** *n*. **mizz'enmast** *n*. **mizz'ensail** *n*.

mizzle[1] /miz'l/ *vi* to rain in small drops. ◆ *n* fine rain. [Cf LGer *miseln* mist]
■ **mizz'ling** *n*. **mizz'ly** *adj*.

mizzle[2] /miz'l/ (*sl*) *vi* to decamp. [Origin obscure]

mizzle[3] /miz'l/ *vt* to confuse. [Origin obscure]

mizzonite /miz'ə-nīt/ *n* a scapolite richer in sodium than meionite. [Gr *meizōn* greater, from its longer vertical axis]

MJ *abbrev*: megajoule(s).

Mjöllnir or **Mjölnir** /myœl'nir/ *n* Thor's terrible hammer. [ON]

MK *abbrev*: Macedonia (IVR); mark (of cars).

Mk *abbrev*: Mark (German currency); markka (Finnish currency).

MKS or **mks** *abbrev*: metre-kilogram-second (unit or system).

MKSA *abbrev*: metre-kilogram-second-ampere (unit or system).

mkt *abbrev*: market.

ml *abbrev*: mile(s); millilitre(s).

MLA *abbrev*: Member of the Legislative Assembly; Modern Language Association (*US*).

MLC *abbrev*: Meat and Livestock Commission; Member of the Legislative Council.

MLD *abbrev*: manual lymphatic drainage; mean lethal dose (*radiol*); minimum lethal dose.

m-learning /em'lûr-ning/ *n* (the provision of) learning via mobile electronic devices.

MLF *abbrev*: multilateral (nuclear) force.

MLitt *abbrev*: *Magister Litterarum* (*L*), Master of Letters, or of Literature.

Mlle *abbrev*: *Mademoiselle* (*Fr*), Miss (*pl* **Mlles**).

MLR *abbrev*: minimum lending rate.

MLRS *abbrev*: multiple launch rocket system.

MLSO *abbrev*: Medical Laboratory Scientific Officer.

MM *abbrev*: *Messieurs* (*Fr*), Gentlemen, Sirs; Military Medal.

mm *abbrev*: millimetre(s).

MMC *abbrev*: Monopolies and Mergers Commission (now replaced by **CC**).

Mme *abbrev*: *Madame* (*Fr*), Mrs (*pl* **Mmes**).

mmf *abbrev*: magnetomotive force.

MMI (*comput*) *abbrev*: man-machine interface.

MMM or **3M** *abbrev*: Minnesota Mining and Manufacturing Company.

mmol *abbrev*: millimole.

MMORPG *abbrev* : Massive Multiplayer Online Role-Playing Game.

MMR *abbrev* : measles, mumps and rubella (vaccine).

MMS *abbrev* : Multimedia Messaging Service.

MMus *abbrev* : Master of Music.

MN *abbrev* : Merchant Navy; Minnesota (US state).

Mn (*chem*) *symbol* : manganese.

MNA *abbrev* : Member of the National Assembly (in Quebec).

mna see **mina**[1].

MND *abbrev* : motor neurone disease.

mneme /nē'mē/ (*psychol*) *n* a person's capacity for retaining the after-effects of a particular experience or stimulation. [Gr *mnēmē* memory]

■ **mne'mic** *adj* relating to the mneme. **mne'mon** *n* a hypothetical unit of memory. **mnemonic** /ni-mon'ik/ *n* a device, eg a short verse, to help memory; (in *pl*, treated as *sing*) the art of assisting memory; a memorizing aid or an abbreviation for an operation, particularly in assembly language (*comput*). ◆ *adj* relating to the mneme; relating to mnemonics. **mnemon'ical** *adj*. **mnemon'ically** *adv*. **mne'monist** *n* a teacher or practitioner of mnemonics; someone from whose memory nothing is erased. **Mnemosyne** /nē-mos'i-nē or -moz'/ *n* (*myth*) the Greek Goddess of memory, mother of the Muses. **mnemotechnic** /nē-mō-tek'nik/ *n* and *adj* (a) mnemonic. **mnemotech'nics** *n pl* mnemonics. **mnemotech'nist** *n*.

MNR *abbrev* : marine nature reserve.

MO *abbrev* : magneto-optical (*comput*); Medical Officer; Missouri (US state; also **Mo.**); modus operandi; money order.

Mo (*chem*) *symbol* : molybdenum.

mo[1] /mō/ (*archaic*) *adv* and *adj* more; (also (*obs*) **moe**, (*Scot*) **mae** /mā/) more (in number, not quantity). [OE *mā* (adv); cf **more**, **most**]

mo[2] see **moment**.

mo. *abbrev* : month.

-mo /-mō/ *sfx* the final syllable of certain Latin ordinal numbers, used in composition with English cardinal numbers to denote the number of leaves in a gathering of a book (see **twelvemo** under **twelve** and **sixteenmo** under **sixteen**).

moa /mō'ə/ *n* a gigantic extinct bird (genus *Dinornis* and related genera) of New Zealand, resembling an ostrich. [Maori]

Moabite /mō'ə-bīt/ *n* one of the people of the ancient kingdom of *Moab*, east of the lower Jordan and the Dead Sea. ◆ *adj* of or relating to Moab.

❑ **Moabite stone** *n* a basalt slab found (1868) at Dibon in Moab, with a long inscription in Hebrew-Phoenician letters, about the revolt of Mesha, king of Moab, against Israel (9c BC; Bible, 2 Kings 3).

moan /mōn/ *n* a low murmur of pain; a sound like a murmur of pain; a lament; a complaint; a grumble (*inf*); a grumbler (*inf*); lamentation. ◆ *vt* to lament; to bemoan; to utter with moans; to condole with (*obs*). ◆ *vi* to make or utter a moan; to grumble (*inf*). [Unrecorded OE *mān* (noun) answering to the verb *mænan*]

■ **moan'er** *n*. **moan'ful** *adj* expressing sorrow; lamentable. **moan'fully** *adv*.

❑ **moaning minnie** *n* a person given to complaining (*inf*); a mortar used by German forces in World War II, producing a shrieking noise when fired (*wartime sl*); an air-raid siren (*wartime sl*).

moat /mōt/ *n* a deep trench round a castle or fortified place, sometimes filled with water; a mote-hill. ◆ *vt* to surround with a moat. [OFr *mote* mound]

■ **moat'ed** *adj*.

mob[1] /mob/ *n* a disorderly crowd; a riotous assembly; the mobile or fickle common people; the rabble; a gang; a large herd or flock (*Aust* and *NZ*). ◆ *adj* of or relating to the mob or a mob. ◆ *vt* (**mobb'ing**; **mobbed**) to attack in a disorderly crowd; to crowd around, *esp* with curiosity or admiration; to crowd into (a shop, etc) (*US*); to drive by mob action. ◆ *vt* and *vi* to form into a mob. [L *mōbile* (*vulgus*) fickle (multitude), from *movere* to move]

■ **mobbed** *adj* (*inf*) crowded. **mobb'ing** *n* (*animal behaviour*) a form of harassment directed at predators by potential prey. **mobb'ish** *adj*. **mobile** /mō'bi-li/ *n* (17c) the mob. **moboc'racy** *n* (*sl*) rule or ascendancy exercised by the mob. **mob'ocrat** *n*. **mobocrat'ic** *adj*. **mobs'man** *n* a member of a mob; a swell-mobsman (qv). **mob'ster** *n* (*US*) gangster.

❑ **mob-hand'ed** *adj* in large numbers; constituting a large group. **mob law** *n* lynch-law; the will of the mob. **Mob'speak** *n* (*inf*) the terminology and style of language used by organized criminals in the USA.

■ **the mob** or **the Mob** (*US sl*) the Mafia; organized crime in general.

mob[2] /mob/ (*obs*) *n* a loose woman; a négligé dress; a mob cap. ◆ *vt* (**mobb'ing**; **mobb'ed**) to muffle the head of. [Perh *Mab*, for *Mabel*; but cf ODu *mop* ; Mod Du *mopmuts* a woman's nightcap]

■ **mobbed** *adj* in déshabillé; muffled up.

❑ **mob cap** *n* (*hist*) a woman's indoor morning cap with puffy crown, a broad band, and frills.

■ **mob it** (*obs*) to go unobtrusively to an unfashionable part of the theatre.

mobble see **moble**.

mobby or **mobbie** /mob'i/ *n* a frothy beverage made from a fermented liquid of boiled tree bark, added to sugar syrup (*W Indies*); fruit juice for brandy-making, or brandy made from it (*old US*). [Carib *mabi*]

mobile[1] /mō'bīl, -bēl or -bil/ *adj* movable; able to move about; easily or speedily moved; not fixed; changing rapidly; (of a liquid) characterized by great fluidity. ◆ *n* (with *great*, *principal*, etc) translations of primum mobile (*obs*); a moving or movable body or part; an artistic structure, *orig* consisting of dangling forms, now sometimes having a base, in which movement is caused by air currents; short for **mobile phone**, **police**, **library**, etc. ◆ *combining form* denoting a vehicle specially designed for transporting a specific object or person, as in *Popemobile*, etc. [Fr, from L *mōbilis*, from *movēre* to move]

■ **mobility** /mō-bil'i-ti/ *n* quality or power of being mobile; freedom or ease of movement; description of the drift of ions (including electrons and holes in semiconductors) under applied electric fields, additional to thermal agitation (*electronics*); the mob (*sl*). **mō'bilizable** or **-s-** *adj*. **mōbilization** or **-s-** /mō- or mo-bil-i-zā'shən or -ī-/ *n* the act or action of mobilizing; a form of manipulation that includes traction of tissues and rotation of joints. **mō'bilize** or **-ise** *vt* to make movable, mobile, or readily available; to put in readiness for service in war; to call (eg troops) into active service. ◆ *vi* to make armed forces ready for war; to undergo mobilization. **mo'bilizer** or **-s-** *n*.

❑ **mobile home** *n* a caravan or other mobile structure with sleeping, cooking, etc facilities. **mobile phone** *n* a portable telephone operating by means of a cellular radio system. **mobile police** *n* police patrolling in vehicles. **mobile shop**, **library**, etc *n* a shop, library, etc set up in a motor vehicle and driven to customers' homes or neighbourhoods. **mobility allowance** *n* money paid by the government to disabled people to compensate for their travel costs.

■ **upwardly mobile** see under **up**.

mobile[2] see under **mob**[1].

Möbius strip /mō'bē- or mœb'ē-əs strip/ (*maths*) *n* the one-sided surface formed by joining together the two ends of a long rectangular strip, one end being twisted through 180 degrees before the join is made. [August F *Möbius* (1790–1868), German mathematician]

moble or **mobble** /mob'l/ (*obs*) *vt* to muffle, as in a mob. [Frequentative of **mob**[2]]

■ **mob'led** *adj* (*Shakesp*) muffled; other suggestions are, richly endowed (cf Fr *meublé*), set in motion, violently agitated (L *mōbilis*), or that there is no meaning at all.

moblog /mō'blog or mob'log/ *n* a weblog (qv under **web**) in which material, *esp* in the form of digital images, is recorded by means of a mobile phone or other portable device. [From *mobile* web*log*]

MOBO /mō'bō/ *abbrev* : Music of Black Origin; an annual award given to musicians considered to excel in this genre.

mobocracy, **mobster**, etc see under **mob**[1].

moby or **mobey** /mō'bi/ (*sl*) *n* a mobile version of a device, *esp* a telephone. [Short form of **mobile**]

MOC *abbrev* : Mozambique (ie Moçambique ; IVR).

moccasin or **mocassin** /mok'ə-sin/ *n* a heelless Native American shoe of deerskin or other soft leather; a shoe or slipper more or less resembling it; a venomous N American pit-viper. [Algonquian]

❑ **moccasin flower** *n* a lady's-slipper orchid. **moccasin telegraph** *n* (*Can sl*) the grapevine, gossip.

moch /mohh/ (*Scot*) *n* misty and humid weather. [Origin uncertain; ult related to **muggy**]

■ **moch'ie** or **moch'y** *adj* mouldy, damp; (of weather) humid and misty, muggy. **moch'iness** *n*.

Mocha /mok'ə or mō'kə/ *n* (also without *cap*) a fine coffee; *esp* a coffee, or coffee and chocolate, flavour; a deep brown colour; a soft leather used for gloves, made from sheepskin or goatskin. [Coffee first brought from *Mocha*, port on the Red Sea]

❑ **Mocha stone** *n* a moss agate or similar stone (first brought from Mocha).

mochell (*Spenser*) see **much**.

mock /mok/ *vt* to deride; to scoff at derisively; to make fun of; to mimic in ridicule; to simulate; to defy, tantalize, disappoint, deceive, disparage, or make a fool of as if in mockery (*fig*). ◆ *vi* to jeer; to scoff; to speak or behave insincerely or disparagingly. ◆ *n* ridicule; a bringing into ridicule; a scoff; a mockery; a thing mocked; (*esp* in *pl*) a practice examination taken at school as a preparation for a public

examination. ◆ adj sham; false; resembling, or accepted as a substitute for, the true or real thing. [OFr mocquer; origin uncertain]
■ **mock'able** adj worthy of derision. **mock'age** n (obs). **mock'er** n. **mock'ery** n derision; ridicule; a subject of ridicule; mimicry; imitation, esp a contemptible or insulting imitation; false show; insulting or ludicrous futility. **mock'ing** n and adj. **mock'ingly** adv.
❑ **mock-hero'ic** adj in exaggerated imitation of the heroic style. ◆ n a mock-heroic composition; (in pl) mock-heroic verses; (in pl) sham heroic utterances or behaviour. **mock-hero'ical** adj. **mock-hero'ically** adv. **mock'ingbird** n any of several American birds (genus Mimus) of the thrush family, that mimic other birds' songs and other sounds, esp Mimus polyglottos of the USA and Mexico. **mock'ingthrush** n a thrasher. **mock-mod'est** adj. **mock-mod'esty** n sham modesty. **mock moon** n a paraselene, or bright spot in the moon's halo, 22° to the right or left of the moon, due to refraction from ice crystals floating vertically. **mock orange** n a tall shrub (Philadelphus, commonly called syringa) of the saxifrage family with strong-scented flowers; a kind of cherry laurel (US). **mock privet** n a shrub (genus Phillyrea) related to privet. **mock sun** n a parhelion or spot in the sun's halo. **mock turtle soup** n an imitation of turtle soup, made of calf's head or veal. **mock'-up** n a full-size dummy model; a rough layout of a printed text, package, etc showing size, colour, etc.
■ **mocks the pauses** (Shakesp, Antony and Cleopatra V.1) perh throws away the opportunities given by the pauses. **put the mockers on** (sl) to put an end to, put paid to.

mockado /mok-ä'dō/ (obs) n (pl **mocka'does**) a cloth of Flemish origin imitating velvet and usu of wool, popular in the 16c–17c; trumpery. [Prob Ital mocaiardo haircloth]

mockernut /mok'ər-nut/ n a kind of hickory nut (Carya tomentosa) with a kernel difficult to extract.

mockney /mok'ni/ n a pseudo-cockney manner of speech affected by people wishing to acquire the street credibility associated with an accent more proletarian than their own (also adj). [mock cockney]

mocktail /mok'tāl/ n a cocktail containing no alcohol. [From mock cocktail]

mockumentary /mok-ū-men't(ə-)ri/ (inf) n a humorous film, TV programme, etc that parodies the form and style of a serious documentary. [From mock documentary]

mocock /mō-kok'/ or **mocuck** /mō-kuk'/ n a Native American birch-bark box or basket. [Orig Algonquian]

mocuddum see **muqaddam**.

MOD abbrev: Ministry of Defence.

Mod[1] /mod, mŏd or mōd/ (also without cap) n a Highland Gaelic literary and musical festival, held annually. [Gaelic mòd, from ON mōt; cf **moot**]

Mod[2] /mod/ n a member of a teenage faction, orig in the 1960s, distinguished by special dress (typically neat), etc, from their rivals, the Rockers.

mod[1] /mod/ (sl) vt and vi (**modd'ing**; **modd'ed**) to modify (a machine, computer software, etc) to perform a function not intended by the original manufacturer. [Shortened from **modify**]
■ **modd'er** n. **modd'ing** n.

mod[2] see **moderator** under **moderate**.

mod. abbrev: moderate; moderato (music); (also **Mod**) modern.

modafinil /mə-daf'i-nil/ n a stimulant drug that enhances wakefulness and vigilance, used in the treatment of narcolepsy.

mod con /mod kon/ n a modern convenience, any item of up-to-date plumbing, heating, etc.

mode /mōd/ n a way or manner of acting, doing, happening or existing; kind; form; manifestation; state of being (philos); a method of operation as provided by the software (comput); that which exists only as a quality of substance (philos); a mood (grammar); character as necessary, contingent, possible or impossible (logic); a mood (logic); actual percentage of mineral composition (petrology); the value of greatest frequency (stats); modality; fashion; that which is fashionable; fashionableness; a model of fashion (obs); alamode, or a garment made of it; openwork between the solid parts of lace; the method of dividing the octave according to the position of its steps and half steps (music); in old music, the method of time-division of notes (perfect into three, imperfect into two, major, division of large into longs, minor of long into breves). [L modus; partly through Fr mode]
■ **modal** /mōd'l/ adj relating to mode. ◆ n a modal auxiliary. **mod'alism** n the doctrine first set forth by Sabellius that the Father, the Son, and the Holy Spirit are not three distinct personalities but only three different modes of manifestation. **mod'alist** n a person who holds this theory. **modalist'ic** adj. **modality** /mōd-al'i-ti/ n fact or condition of being modal; mode; method, terms, style; any of the primary methods of sensation; classification of propositions as to whether true, false, necessary, possible or impossible (logic); the

quality of being limited by a condition (law; obs). **mod'ally** adv. **modish** /mōd'ish/ adj fashionable; affectedly, foolishly or absurdly fashionable. **mod'ishly** adv. **mod'ishness** n. **mod'ist** n a follower of the current fashion. **modiste** /mō-dēst/ n (Fr) a professedly fashionable dressmaker or milliner.
❑ **modal auxiliary** or **modal verb** n in English, any of the verbs can, could, may, might, will, would, shall, should, must and ought, and sometimes need, dare and used to, which modify the sense of a main verb and express concepts such as politeness, certainty and obligation. **mode dispersion** n (telecom) in optical fibre communications, distortion of individual signals, caused by different modes of propagation of the light inside the fibre. **mode'-locking** n (phys) a technique for producing laser pulses of very short duration.
■ **Greek modes** (music) a set of modes (named Aeolian, Locrian, Ionian, Dorian, Phrygian, Lydian, Mixolydian, etc) each consisting of two disjunct tetrachords with a whole tone (diazeuctic tone) between them, or two conjunct tetrachords with a whole tone above (where the prefix hyper- is used) or below them (where the prefix hypo- is used). **Gregorian, medieval** or **ecclesiastical modes** a set of modes that have the same names as Greek modes but do not correspond to them (see **authentic** and **plagal**). **major mode** (music) a modern mode consisting of two steps, a half step, three steps, and a half step. **minor mode** (music) a modern mode consisting of a step, a half step, two steps, a half step, and two steps.

model /mod'l/ n an imitation of something on a smaller scale; a person or thing closely resembling another; a preliminary solid representation, generally small, or in plastic material, to be followed in construction; something to be copied; a pattern; an architect's plan or design (obs); a person who poses for an artist, photographer, etc; a person who exhibits clothes to potential buyers by wearing them; a pattern or standard of excellence, often one to be copied or aspired to; an article of standard design or a copy of one; structural type; a medal (obs); a close covering or mould (Shakesp). ◆ adj of the nature of a model; set up for imitation; completely suitable for imitation, exemplary. ◆ vt (**mod'elling** or (N Am) **mod'eling**; **mod'elled** or (N Am) **mod'eled**) to form after a model; to shape; to make a model or copy of; to form in some plastic material; (of a mannequin) to display (a garment) by wearing it. ◆ vi to practise modelling. [OFr modelle, from Ital modello, dimin of modo, from L modus a measure]
■ **mod'eller** or (N Am) **mod'eler** n. **mod'elling** or (N Am) **mod'eling** n the act or art of making a model of something; a branch of sculpture; rendering of solid form; working as a model; the practice of adopting characteristics of people worthy of imitation (psychol).
❑ **Model T** n a four-cylinder motor car designed and mass-produced by the Ford Motor Company in the USA in the early 20c.

modello /mə-del'ō/ (Ital) n (pl **modell'i** or **modell'os**) an artist's detailed sketch or sculptural model for a larger work. [Ital; cf **model**]

modem /mō'dəm/ or /-dem/ (comput) n an electronic device which converts digital data from a computer into analogue signals that can be sent to another computer over a telephone system. ◆ vt to transmit or receive by means of a modem. [modulator and demodulator]

modena /mod'i-nə/ n a shade of crimson. [Modena in Italy]

moder /mō'dər/ n a layer of humus intermediate between mor and mull. [Ger, decay]

moderate /mod'ə-rāt/ vt to keep within measure or bounds; to regulate; to reduce in intensity; to make temperate or reasonable; to pacify; to preside as moderator over or at; to slow down (neutrons) in a nuclear reactor; to decide as an arbitrator (obs). ◆ vi to become less violent or intense; to preside or act as a moderator. ◆ adj /-rit/ kept within measure or bounds; not excessive or extreme; temperate; of middle rate, average. ◆ n a person who holds moderate views esp on political issues; a member of a faction in the Scottish Church in the 18c and early 19c, broad in matters of doctrine and discipline, opposed to Evangelicalism and popular rights. [L moderārī, -ātus, from modus a measure]
■ **mod'erately** adv. **mod'erateness** n. **modera'tion** n an act of moderating; the state of being moderated or moderate; freedom from excess; self-restraint; the process of slowing down neutrons in a nuclear reactor; (in pl) the first public examination for BA at Oxford (inf **Mods** or **mods**). **mod'eratism** n moderate opinions in religion or politics. **mod'erātor** n a person who, or that which, moderates; a president, esp in Nonconformist church assemblies and courts; formerly, an officer at Oxford and Cambridge who superintended degree examinations; either of two examiners presiding over the Mathematical Tripos at Cambridge; a moderations examiner at Oxford; a person appointed to standardize the marking, etc of school public examinations; a person who monitors the content of an Internet bulletin board or chat room (often shortened to **mod**); an oil-lamp with regulated flow of oil; material such as water, heavy water or graphite used to slow down neutrons in a nuclear reactor. **mod'erātorship** n. **mod'erātrix** n (obs) a female moderator.

❑ **moderate breeze** *n* (*meteorol*) a wind of force 4 on the Beaufort scale, reaching speeds of 13 to 18mph. **moderate gale** *n* a near gale (see under **near**).
■ **moderate (in) a call** (of a presbytery) to act with the congregation in calling the minister it has chosen.

moderato /mo-də-rä'tō/ (*music*) *adj* and *adv* at a moderate speed. ◆ *n* (*pl* **modera'tos**) a movement or passage to be played at this speed. [Ital]

modern /mod'ərn/ *adj* of or characteristic of present or recent time; not ancient or medieval; (in education) mainly or wholly concerned with subjects other than Greek and Latin; of a style of type with contrasting thick and thin strokes, serifs at right-angles, curves thickened in the centre (*printing*); everyday, commonplace (*Shakesp*); (with *cap*) (of a language) of or near the form now spoken and written, distinguished from *Old* and *Middle*. ◆ *n* a person living in modern times, *esp* distinguished from the ancient Greeks and Romans; a modernist; a modern printing type. [LL *modernus*, from *modo* just now, orig ablative of *modus*]
■ **moderne** /mə-dûrn'/ *adj* art deco. **mod'ernism** *n* modern usage, expression, or trait; modern spirit or character; a tendency to adjust Christian dogma to the results of science and criticism; (with *cap*) an early-20c movement in the arts characterized by the use of unconventional subject matter, experimental techniques, etc. **mod'ernist** *n* an admirer of modern ideas, ways, literature, studies, etc; a person who favours modernism; (with *cap*) a practitioner of Modernism. ◆ *adj* of or relating to modernism or modernists. **modernis'tic** *adj*. **modern'ity** *n*. **moderniza'tion** or **-s-** *n*. **mod'ernize** or **-ise** *vt* to adapt to the present time, conditions, needs, language or spelling. ◆ *vi* to adopt modern ways. **mod'ernizer** or **-s-** *n*. **mod'ernly** *adv*. **mod'ernness** *n*.
❑ **modern dance** *n* a style of dance more expressive and less stylized than classical ballet. **Modern Greats** see under **great**. **modern jazz** *n* a style of jazz which evolved in the early 1940s, characterized by greater rhythmic and harmonic complexity than previously. **modern pentathlon** see under **pentathlon**.

modest /mod'ist/ *adj* unpretentious; unobtrusive; unassuming; diffident; restrained by a sense of propriety; decent; chaste; of thoughts or language, etc, pure and delicate; not excessive or extreme; moderate. [L *modestus*, from *modus* a measure]
■ **mod'estly** *adv*. **mod'esty** *n* the quality or fact of being modest; a veil-like covering for the part of a woman's breast revealed by the low neckline of a dress.

modi see **modus**.

modicum /mod'i-kəm/ *n* (*pl* **mod'icums**) a small quantity; a small person (*obs*); (disrespectfully) a woman (*obs*). [L neuter of *modicus* moderate, from *modus*]

modify /mod'i-fī/ *vt* (**mod'ifying**; **mod'ified**) to moderate; to change the form or quality of; to alter slightly; to vary; to differentiate; (of a word or phrase) to limit or qualify the sense of (*grammar*); to determine the mode of (*philos*); to subject to an umlaut (*philology*); to assess, decree, or award (a payment) (*Scots law*). [Fr *modifier*, from L *modificāre, -ātum*, from *modus* a measure, and *facere* to make]
■ **mod'ifiable** *adj*. **modification** /-fi-kā'shən/ *n* the act of modifying or state of being modified; the result of alteration or change; changed shape or condition; a change due to environment, lasting only as long as the operative conditions (*biol*). **mod'ificative** or **mod'ificatory** *adj* tending to modify; causing change of form or condition. **mod'ified** /-fīd/ *adj* altered by modification; homologous but developed in a different direction (*biol*). **mod'ifier** /-fī-ər/ *n* a person who modifies; a modifying agent; a modifying diacritic, *esp* an umlaut (*philology*).

modillion /mo-dil'yən/ (*archit*) *n* an ornamental bracket under a Corinthian or other cornice. [Ital *modiglione*, from L *modulus*, from *modus* a measure]

modiolus /mo-dī'ə-ləs/ *n* (*pl* **modī'oli** /-lī/) the axis of the cochlea of the ear; (with *cap*, also **Modī'ola**) the horse mussel genus. [L *modiolus* nave of a wheel, water wheel bucket, drinking vessel, etc, dimin of *modus*]
■ **modī'olar** *adj*.

modish, modist and **modiste** see under **mode**.

modius /mō'di-əs or mod'i-ŭs/ *n* (*pl* **mod'dii** /-ī/) a Roman dry measure, roughly equivalent to a peck; a cylindrical headdress of the gods. [L *modius*]

modiwort a Scots form of **mouldwarp**.

mods see **moderation** under **moderate**.

modulate /mod'yŭ-lāt/ *vt* to regulate, adjust; to inflect; to soften; to vary the pitch or frequency of; to impress characteristics of signal wave on (carrier wave) (*radio*); to vary the velocity of electrons in an electron beam. ◆ *vi* to pass from one state to another; to pass from one key into another using a logical progression of chords that links the two keys (*music*). [L *modulārī, -ātus* to regulate; cf **module**]

■ **modulabil'ity** *n* the capability of being modulated. **mod'ular** *adj* of or relating to mode or modulation, or to a module. **modular'ity** *n*. **mod'ularized** or **-s-** *adj* consisting of modules; produced in the form of modules; divided into modules. **modulā'tion** *n*. **mod'ulātor** *n* a person who, or that which, modulates; any device for effecting modulation (*radio*); a chart used in the tonic sol-fa notation on which modulations are shown.

module /mod'ūl/ *n* a small measure or quantity; a unit of size, used in standardized planning of buildings and design of components; a self-contained unit forming part of a spacecraft or other structure; a standard unit or part of machinery, etc in a system; a set course forming a unit in an educational scheme; an assembly within a geometrical framework of electronic units functioning as a system; a component part of a program, complete in itself and with its own function (*comput*); a measure, often the semidiameter of a column, for regulating proportions of other parts (*archit*); a model, image (*Shakesp*). [L *modulus*, dimin of *modus* a measure]
■ **mod'ular** *adj*. **modular'ity** *n*. **moduleriza'tion** or **-s-** *n*. **mod'ularize** or **-ise** *vt* (of a college, university, etc) to adopt a teaching system based on modules. **mod'ulo** *adv* (*maths*) with respect to a (specified) modulus. **mod'ulus** *n* (*pl* **moduli** /mod'ū-lī/) a constant multiplier or coefficient (*maths*); a quantity used as a divisor to produce classes of quantities, each class distinguished by its members yielding the same remainders (*maths*); the positive square root of the sum of the squares of the real and imaginary parts of a complex number (*maths*); a quantity expressing the relation between a force and the effect produced.
❑ **modular construction** *n* (*comput*) the construction of hardware and software using interchangeable modules.

modus /mō'dəs or mod'ŭs/ *n* (*pl* **mō'dī**) manner, mode; the way in which anything works; a fixed payment instead of tithes. [L *modus* manner]
❑ **modus operandi** /op-ər-an'dī or -an'dē/ *n* mode of operation, way of working. **modus vivendi** /vi-ven'dī or -dē (also wē-wen'dē)/ *n* way of life or living; an arrangement or compromise by means of which those who differ may get on together for a time; such an arrangement between states or between a state and the Pope.

moe /mō/ see **mo¹** and **mow³**.

moellon /mō'ə-lon/ *n* rubble in mason-work. [Fr]

Moeso-gothic /mē-sō-goth'ik/ *adj* relating to the *Goths* who settled in *Moesia* (corresponding to modern Bulgaria and Serbia) in the 4c and 5c. ◆ *n* their language.

mofette /mō-fet'/ *n* an opening in the earth giving out carbon dioxide with some nitrogen and oxygen, the last stage of volcanic activity. [Fr, from Ital *mofeta*, perh L *mephītis* foul exhalation]

mofo see **motherfucker** under **mother**.

mofussil /mō-fus'l/ *n* (in India, Pakistan, etc) all areas outside the capital or great towns; rural as opposed to urban areas collectively. ◆ *adj* provincial; rural. [Hindustani *mufassil*, from Ar *mufassal* distinct, separate, pap of *fassala* to separate]

mog see **moggy**.

Mogadon® /mog'ə-don/ *n* a proprietary name for nitrazepam, a drug used to treat insomnia.

Mogen David see **Magen David**.

moggan /mog'ən/ (*Scot*) *n* a footless stocking. [Origin unknown]

moggy, moggie /mog'i/ or **mog** /mog/ *n* a cat (*sl*); a pet name for a cow, etc (*dialect*). [Perh *Maggie*]

Mogul /mō'g(ə)l/ *n* a Mongol or Mongolian, *esp* one of the followers of Baber, the conqueror of India (1483–1530) (also **Mughal**); a name applied to the best quality of playing-cards; (without *cap*) an influential person, a magnate; a steam locomotive having two leading wheels, six driving wheels, and no trailing wheels. ◆ *adj* relating to the Mogul Empire. [Pers *Mughul*, properly a Mongol]
■ **Great Mogul** the title formerly used by Europeans to refer to the Emperors of Delhi.

mogul /mō'g(ə)l/ *n* a mound of hard snow forming an obstacle on a ski slope; (in *pl*) a skiing discipline or event that involves skiing down a run which includes moguls. [Poss from Norw dialect *muge* heap]
■ **moguled** /mō'gəld/ *adj* (of a ski run) having moguls.

MOH *abbrev*: Medical Officer of Health, abolished in the UK in 1974; Ministry of Health.

mohair /mō'hār/ *n* the long, white, fine silken hair of the Angora goat; other hair as a substitute for it; cloth or yarn made from this, *usu* mixed with wool. [Ar *mukhayyar*; influenced by **hair**]

Mohammedan /mō-ham'i-dən/, **Mahommedan** /mə-hom'/, **Mahometan** /mə-hom'it-ən/, **Muhammadan** /moo-ham'a-dən/ or **Muhammedan** /-i-dən/ *adj* relating to Mohammed (formerly popularly rendered as Mahomet) or to his religion, Islam. ◆ *n* a

---

■ words derived from main entry word; ❑ compound words; ■ idioms and phrasal verbs

follower of Mohammed; a person who professes Islam, a Muslim. See also **Mahoun** and **mammet**. —This word and its derivatives are felt to be offensive by many Muslims, who prefer **Muslim**, **Islam**, **Islamic**, etc. [Ar *Muhammad*, the great prophet of Arabia (c.570–632); literally, praised]

■ **Mohamm'edanism**, **Mohamm'edism**, etc, *n* Islam, the religion of Mohammed, contained in the Koran. **Mohamm'edanize** or **-ise**, etc, *vt* and *vi* to convert to, or conform to, Islam.

Moharram see **Muharram**.

Mohawk /*mō'hök*/ *n* a Native American of an Iroquois people formerly living in upper New York State; the Iroquoian language of this people; a Mohock; (often without *cap*) a skating movement consisting of a stroke on the edge of one skate followed by a stroke in the opposite direction on the same edge of the other skate; a Mohican hairstyle (chiefly *N Am*). ◆ *adj* of or relating to the Mohawks or their language. [From an Algonquian name]

mohel /*mō'(h)el, moi'hel* or *-hel'*, also Heb *mō-hel'*/ *n* an official Jewish circumciser. [Heb]

Mohican /*mō-hē'kən*/ or **Mohegan** /*-gən*/ *n* a Native American of a people formerly living chiefly in the upper Hudson valley, or the Algonquian language spoken by them (also **Mahi'can**); a hairstyle in which the head is shaved except for a central strip from the nape to the brow, based on a Mohican style but now *esp* associated with punk fashion, in which the hair is spiked into a (*usu* brightly-coloured) crest. ◆ *adj* of the Mohicans or their language. [Algonquian]

Moho, Mohorovicic or **Mohorovicician discontinuity** /*mō'hō, mō-hō-rō'və-chich* or *mō-hō-rō'və-chi-chi-ən dis-kon-ti-nū'i-ti*/ *n* the boundary between the rocks of the earth's crust and the different rock of the mantle. [A *Mohorovičić* (1857–1936), Croatian geologist, who deduced a difference of rock nature from the behaviour of earthquake shocks]

Mohock /*mō'hok*/ *n* one of a band of aristocratic ruffians of early-18c London. [**Mohawk**]

mohr same as **mhorr**.

Mohs scale /*mōz skāl*/ *n* a scale of numbers from 1 to 10 (1 representing talc, 10 representing diamond) in terms of which the relative hardness of solids can be expressed. [F *Mohs* (1773–1839), German mineralogist]

mohur /*mō'hər*/ *n* a former Persian and Indian gold coin, in India equivalent to fifteen rupees. [Pers *mohr*]

moi /*mwa*/ *pronoun* me, often used facetiously in mock affectation, eg in the form of a question to express surprise at an allegation against one. [Fr]

moider /*moi'dər*/, **moither** /*-dhər*/ or **mither** /*mī'dhər*/ (*dialect*) *vt* to confuse; to stupefy, overcome; to pester, hassle. ◆ *vi* to work hard; to wander in thoughts or mind. [Dialect word; origin obscure]

moidore /*moi'dōr* or *-dör*/ *n* a former gold coin of Portugal. [Port *moeda d'ouro*, literally, money of gold, from L *monēta, dē, aurum*]

moiety /*moi'ə-ti*/ *n* half; either of two parts or divisions; a small share (*Shakesp*). [OFr *moite*, from L *medietās, -tātis* middle point, later half, from *medius* middle]

moil /*moil*/ (*archaic*) *vt* to wet; to bedaub; to defile. ◆ *vi* (*dialect*) to toil; to drudge; to move around in an agitated or confused state. ◆ *n* (*dialect* and *archaic*) a spot; a defilement; labour; trouble; turmoil. [OFr *moillier* (Fr *mouiller*) to wet, from L *mollis* soft]

■ **moil'er** *n*.

moineau /*moi'nō*/ *n* (*hist*) a small flat bastion to protect a fortification while being erected. [Fr]

Moira or **Moera** /*moi'ra*/ *n* (*pl* **Moirai** or **Moerae** /*-rī*/) any of the three Fates, goddesses controlling Man's destiny (*Gr myth*); fate, destiny. [Gr *Moira*]

moire /*mwär*, also *mwör, mōr* or *moir*/ *n* *orig* watered mohair; now watered silk or other fabric with a watered appearance (also **moire antique**). [Fr, from English **mohair**]

■ **moiré** /*mwär'ā* or *moi'ri*/ *adj* watered. ◆ *n* a watered appearance on a cloth or metal surface; sometimes for moire, the material.

□ **moiré effect** or **pattern** *n* an optical effect, a shifting wavy pattern seen when two surfaces covered with regular lines are superimposed.

moiser /*moi'sər*/ (*Yiddish*) *n* an informer.

moist /*moist*/ *adj* damp; humid; rainy; watery; (of eyes) tearful; juicy (*Shakesp*). ◆ *vt* (*Shakesp*) to moisten. [OFr *moiste* (Fr *moite*), perh from L *mustum* juice of grapes, new wine, perh L *mūcidus* mouldy]

■ **moisten** /*mois'n*/ *vt* to make moist; to wet slightly. ◆ *vi* to become moist. **moist'ify** *vt* (*joc*) to make moist. **moist'ly** *adv*. **moist'ness** *n*. **moist'ure** *n* moistness; that which makes slightly wet; liquid, *esp* in a small quantity. **moist'ureless** *adj*. **moist'urize** or **-ise** *vt* to add or restore moisture to. ◆ *vi* to apply moisturizer. **moist'urizer** or **-s-** *n* that which moisturizes, *esp* a cream that restores moisture to the skin.

moit see **mote**[1].

moither see **moider**.

MOJ *abbrev* : Ministry of Justice.

mojito /*mə-hē'tō*/ *n* (*pl* **moji'tos**) a Cuban cocktail containing rum, sugar, mint leaves, lime juice, ice and soda water. [Sp, little sauce]

mojo /*mō'jō*/ (*US sl*) *n* (*pl* **mo'jos** or **mo'joes**) magic; a magic spell or charm. [Prob W African in origin]

mokaddam see **muqaddam**.

moke /*mōk*/ (*sl*) *n* a donkey; a worn-out or inferior horse (*obs Aust* and *NZ*); a variety performer on several instruments; a black person (*US sl*; *offensive*). [Origin unknown]

moki /*mō'ki*/ *n* a New Zealand sea fish belonging either to the species *Latridopsis ciliaris* or *Chironemus spectabilis* (**red moki**); formerly, the blue cod, *Parapercis colias*. [Maori]

moko /*mō'kō*/ *n* (*pl* **mō'kos**) a system of tattooing practised by the Maoris; a Maori tattoo. [Maori]

mol *symbol* : mole (SI unit).

mola[1] /*mō'lə*/ *n* (*pl* **mo'las**) a brightly-coloured appliqué or embroidered panel made by Cuna women of Panama, used to decorate clothing. [Cuna]

mola[2] /*mō'lə*/ *n* the sunfish. [L, millstone]

molal see under **mole**[4].

molar[1] /*mō'lər*/ *adj* used for grinding; designating or relating to a grinding tooth; denoting a pregnancy in which a hydatidiform mole (*qv* under **hydatid**) develops in place of the placenta. ◆ *n* a grinding tooth, or back tooth. [L *molāris*, from *mola* a millstone, from *molere* to grind]

molar[2] and **molarity** see under **mole**[4].

Molasse /*mō-läs'*/ *n* a series of Oligocene or Miocene sandstones and sandy marls in Switzerland, France, and Germany. [Fr]

molasses /*mō-* or *mə-las'iz*/ *n sing* a thick, *usu* dark, treacle that is drained from sugar during refining; treacle (*N Am*). [Port *melaço* (Fr *mélasse*), from LL *mellāceum*, from *mel, mellis* honey]

mold see **mould**[1,2,3] and **mole**[2].

Moldovan /*mol-dō'vən*/ *adj* of or relating to the Republic of *Moldova* in E Europe, its inhabitants, or their language. ◆ *n* a native or citizen of Moldova; the official language of Moldova, a form of Romanian.

moldwarp same as **mouldwarp**.

mole[1] /*mōl*/ *n* a small insectivorous animal (genus *Talpa*) with very small eyes and soft fur, that burrows in the ground and casts up little heaps of loose earth; extended to related or similar animals; a person who works in darkness or underground; a spy who successfully infiltrates a rival organization, *esp* one not engaging in espionage until firmly established and trusted; a person with bad eyesight (*fig*); a boring machine which makes a tunnel, eg for a pipeline. [ME *molle, mulle*; cf Du *mol*, LGer *mol, mul*; poss shortened from **mouldwarp**]

□ **mole'cast** *n* a molehill. **mole'catcher** *n* a person whose business it is to catch moles. **mole cricket** *n* a burrowing insect (genus *Gryllotalpa*) of the cricket family, with forelegs like a mole's. **mole drainer** *n* (*agric*) a pointed cylinder on the lower edge of a blade, which is drawn longitudinally through soil to form a drainage channel (**mole drain**). **mole'-eyed** *adj* having eyes like those of a mole; seeing imperfectly. **mole'hill** *n* a little hill or heap of earth cast up by a mole. **mole hunt** *n*. **mole hunter** *n*. **mole plough** *n* a mole drainer. **mole rat** *n* a name for several burrowing rodents (*Spalax, Cryptomys, Bathyergus*, etc). **mole salamander** *n* the axolotl. **mole'skin** *n* the skin or fur of a mole; a superior kind of fustian, double-twilled, cropped before dyeing; (in *pl*) clothes, *esp* trousers, made of this fustian. **mole spade** *n* a small spade used by molecatchers.

■ **make a mountain out of a molehill** to magnify, overdramatize, etc a trifling matter. **mole out** to seek, or elicit, bit by bit, as if by burrowing.

mole[2] /*mōl*/ *n* (also (*Spenser*) **mōld**) a small spot or raised mark on the skin, often pigmented and hairy; a spot caused by iron on linen (*obs* except in Scots form **mail** and in **iron-mole** (see **iron mould** under **iron**)). [OE *māl*]

mole[3] /*mōl*/ *n* an abnormal fleshy mass of tissue formed in the uterus; see also **hydatidiform mole** under **hydatid**. [L *mola* millstone]

mole[4] /*mōl*/ *n* a base SI unit, the unit of amount of substance (symbol **mol**), defined as the amount of substance that contains as many (specified) entities (eg atoms, molecules, ions, photons) as there are atoms in 12 grams of carbon-12; formerly defined as equal to gram-molecule (*abbrev* **mol** /*mōl*/). [Ger, from *Molekül* molecule; both words (Ger and Eng) ult from L *mōlēs* mass]

■ **mol'al** *adj* of, relating to, or containing, a mole. **molal'ity** *n* the concentration of a solution expressed as the number of moles of dissolved substance per thousand grams of solvent. **mol'ar** *adj* of or relating to a mole; per mole; per unit amount of substance; of or relating to molecules; of or relating to mass or masses or to large masses (L *mōlēs* mass). **molar'ity** *n* the concentration of a solution expressed as the number of moles of dissolved substance per litre of solution.

❑ **mole'-electronics** *n sing* (also **molecular electronics**) the technique of growing solid-state crystals so as to form transistors, etc, for microminiaturization.

mole⁵ /mōl/ *n* a massive breakwater, causeway or masonry pier; a harbour protected by any of these; an ancient Roman mausoleum. [Fr *môle*, from L *mōlēs* mass]

mole⁶ /mō'li or -lā/ *n* in Mexican cooking, a sauce made mainly with chilli and chocolate, served with meat dishes. [Am Sp; see **guacamole**]

Molech see **Moloch**.

molecule /mol'i-kūl/ *n* the smallest particle of any substance that retains the properties of that substance, *usu* consisting of a limited group of atoms; a gram-molecule. [Fr *molécule*, from L *mōlēs* mass]
■ **molecular** /mol-ek'ū-lər/ *adj*. **molecularity** /mol-ek-ū-lar'i-ti/ *n*. **molec'ularly** *adv*.
❑ **molecular biology** *n* study of the molecules of the substances involved in the processes of life. **molecular electronics** see under **mole⁴**. **molecular formula** *n* a formula showing the number of atoms of each element in a molecule, eg benzene, C_6H_6. **molecular gastronomy** *n* cooking in which much is made of the appliance of scientific knowledge. **molecular genetics** *n sing* (*biol*) the study and manipulation of the molecular basis of heredity. **molecular sieve** *n* a crystalline substance allowing the passage of molecules below a certain size, used in separating mixtures. **molecular weight** *n* a former term for relative molecular mass (*qv* under **relate**).

molehill...to...**moleskin** see under **mole¹**.

molendinar /mo-len'di-nər/ (*pedantically facetious*) *adj* relating to a mill or a miller. ✦*n* a molar tooth. [LL *molendīnum* a mill, from L *molere* to grind]
■ **molen'dinary** *adj* (*pedantically facetious*) relating to a mill. ✦*n* a mill.

molest /mə- or mō-lest'/ *vt* to interfere with in a troublesome or hostile way; to touch, interfere with or attack sexually; to vex; to annoy. ✦*n* annoyance. [Fr *molester*, from L *molestāre*, from *molestus* troublesome]
■ **molestā'tion** /mo- or mō-/ *n*. **molest'er** *n*. **molest'ful** *adj*.

moline /mō'līn or -līn'/ (*heraldry*) *adj* like the rind of a millstone, applied to a cross with each arm ending in two outward curving branches. ✦*n* a moline cross. [L *mola* a mill]

molinet /mol'i-net/ *n* a stick used to whip drinking chocolate in the 18c. [Fr *moulinet*, dimin of *moulin* mill]

Molinism¹ /mol'i-ni-zm/ *n* the doctrine of the 16c Spanish Jesuit Luis de *Molina*, reconciling predestination and free will by God's foreknowledge, the efficacy of grace depending on the co-operation of the will.
■ **Mol'inist** *n*.

Molinism² /mol'i-ni-zm/ *n* a form of religious quietism originated by the Spanish priest Miguel de *Molinos* (1627–96), striving towards the extinction of the will and a complete withdrawal from the senses.
■ **Mol'inist** *n*.

moll /mol/ *n* a gangster's girlfriend; a prostitute (*archaic*). [*Moll*, an old familiar form of *Mary*]

mollah and **molla** see **mullah¹**.

mollie /mol'i/ same as **mallemaroking**.

mollify /mol'i-fī/ *vt* (**moll'ifying**; **moll'ified**) to soften; to assuage; to cause to abate; to appease. ✦*vi* to become soft; to relax in severity or opposition. [Fr *mollifier*, from L *mollificāre*, from *mollis* soft, and *facere* to make]
■ **mollification** /-fi-kā'shən/ *n*. **moll'ifier** *n*.

mollities /mo-lish'i-ēz/ (*archaic*) *n* softness, softening (*med*). [L *mollitiēs*, from *mollis* soft]
■ **mollitious** /-ish'əs/ *adj* luxurious.

mollusc or (*N Am*) also **mollusk** /mol'əsk/ *n* an animal belonging to the large phylum of invertebrates, **Mollusca** /-us'kə/, having no segments or limbs, and *usu* a mantle or fold of skin that secretes a shell (eg lamellibranchs, gastropods, cephalopods, and some smaller groups); a lazy or sluggish person (*facetious*). [L *molluscus* softish, from *mollis* soft]
■ **mollus'can** *adj* (*N Am* also **mollus'kan**) or **mollus'cous** of or belonging to the Mollusca; like a mollusc. **mollus'cicidal** *adj*. **mollus'cicide** /-ki-sīd/ *n* an agent for destroying molluscs, eg snails responsible for spread of disease. **mollus'coid** *n* a member of a now abandoned division of invertebrates of the **Molluscoid'ea**, Polyzoa and brachiopods. ✦*adj* of the Molluscoidea; like a mollusc.

Mollweide's projection /mol'vī-dəz prə-jek'shən/ *n* an equal-area representation of the surface of the globe in which the parallels of latitude are straight lines (closer together nearer the poles) and the meridians (apart from the central one) are curved, the curvature increasing toward the marginal meridians. [K *Mollweide* (died 1825), German mathematician and astronomer]

molly¹ /mol'i/ *n* any of various brightly-coloured tropical fish of the genus *Poecilia*. [Comte FN *Mollien* (1758–1850), French statesman]

molly² /mol'i/ *n* a milksop. [*Molly*, dimin of *Mary*]
■ **moll'ycoddle** *n* an effeminate man. ✦*vt* to coddle.
❑ **Molly Maguire** *n* any member of an Irish society formed in 1843 to resist government evictions, who disguised themselves as women; a member of a Pennsylvanian secret society formed to resist oppressive conditions in the mines, and crushed in 1877.

mollymawk /mol'i-mök/ (*NZ inf*) same as **mallemuck**.

Mollywood /mol'i-wŭd/ *n* the Malayalam-language film industry. [Modelled on **Bollywood**]

Moloch /mō'lok/ *n* a Semitic god to whom children were sacrificed (also **Mo'lech**; *Bible*); any cause to which dreadful sacrifice is made or destruction due; (*without cap*) an exceedingly spiny, harmless Australian lizard. [Gr and L *Moloch*, from Heb *Mōlek*]
■ **mo'lochize** or **-ise** *vt* to sacrifice (as to Moloch).

Molossian /mo-los'i-ən/ *adj* of *Molossia* or *Molossis* in the Epirus region of ancient Greece, famous in ancient times for its great mastiff dogs.
■ **moloss'us** *n* (*pl* **moloss'ī**) a metrical foot of three long syllables.

Molotov cocktail /mol'ə-tov kok'tāl, also -tof/ *n* a crude form of hand-grenade consisting of a bottle containing an inflammable liquid, eg petrol, and a wick to be ignited just before the missile is thrown; a petrol bomb. [VM *Molotov* (1890–1986), Russian statesman]

molt¹ see **moult**.

molt² see **melt¹**.

molten /mōl'tən/ see under **melt¹**.

molto /mol'tō/ (*music*) *adv* very; much. [Ital]

Molucca bean /mo-luk'ə bēn/ *n* nicker nut or bonduc.

mol wt *abbrev* : molecular weight.

moly /mō'li/ *n* a magic herb given by Hermes to Odysseus as a countercharm against the spells of Circe (*Gr myth*); a species of wild onion, *Allium moly*. [Gr *mōly*]

molybdenum /mo-lib'di-nəm, also -dē/ *n* a silvery-white metallic element (symbol **Mo**; atomic no 42). [Latinized neuter, from Gr *molybdaina* a lump of lead, a leadlike substance, from *molybdos* lead]
■ **molyb'date** *n* a salt of molybdic acid. **molybdén'ite** (or /-ib'dən-īt/) *n* a mineral, molybdenum disulphide. **molybdenō'sis** *n* a disease of cattle and sheep, characterized by chronic diarrhoea and emaciation, caused by an excess of molybdenum in the diet. **molyb'dic** *adj* of molybdenum of higher valency. **molybdō'sis** *n* lead-poisoning. **molyb'dous** *adj* of molybdenum of lower valency.
❑ **molybdic acid** *n* H_2MoO_4.

mom /mom/ (*N Am inf*) *n* mother (also **momm'a** or **momm'y**). [See **mamma¹**]
❑ **mom and pop** *n* (*chiefly N Am*) a small, privately owned business. **mom-and-pop** *adj*.

MOMA or **MoMA** /mō'mə/ *abbrev* : Museum of Modern Art (New York and elsewhere).

mome¹ /mōm/ (*obs*) *n* a buffoon; a carper. [**Momus**]

mome² /mōm/ (*Spenser*) *n* a blockhead. [Origin obscure]

moment /mō'mənt/ *n* a point of time; a time so short that it may be considered as a point; a very short time (*inf abbrev* **mo**); a second; a precise instant; the present, or the right, instant; moving cause or motive (*Shakesp*); importance, consequence; an infinitesimal change in a varying quantity (*maths*; *obs*); a stage or turning point; an element or factor (as in *psychological moment*, rightly used); a measure of turning effect (the **moment of a force** about a point is the product of the force and the perpendicular on its line of action from the point). [L *mōmentum*, for *movimentum*, from *movēre*, *mōtum* to move]
■ **momentān'eous** *adj* momentary; instantaneous. **mo'mentany** *adj* (*Shakesp*) momentary. **mo'mentarily** (or /-ter'ə-lē/) *adv* for a moment; every moment; at any moment (*N Am*). **mo'mentariness** *n*. **mo'mentary** *adj* lasting for a moment; short-lived. **mo'mently** *adv* every moment; for a moment. ✦*adj* occurring every moment; of a moment. **momentous** /-ment'/ *adj* of great consequence. **moment'ously** *adv*. **moment'ousness** *n*.
❑ **moment of inertia** *n* (*phys*) a quantity representing the resistance of a body to a force that causes it to rotate about its axis. **moment of truth** *n* the climax of a bullfight; a moment when, suddenly and dramatically, one is face to face with stark reality, often a testing moment (*fig*).

momentum /mō-men'təm/ n (pl **moment'a**) the quantity of motion in a body measured by the product of mass and velocity; force of motion gained in movement, impetus (inf). [Ety as for **moment**]

MOMI /mō'mi/ abbrev : Museum of the Moving Image (in London).

momma and **mommy** see **mom**.

mommet see **mammet**.

Momus /mō'məs/ (Gr myth) n the god of ridicule. [Latinized from Gr mōmos blame, reproach, personified]

momzer see **mamzer**.

Mon /mōn/ n a member of a people inhabiting parts of Myanmar (Burma) and W Thailand; the language of this people. ◆ adj of or relating to the Mon or their language. [Mon]
□ **Mon-Khmer'** adj of a group of Austroasiatic languages that includes Mon and Khmer.

Mon. abbrev : Monday; Monmouthshire (a former county, now mostly incorporated into modern Gwent).

mon /mon/ n (pl **mon**) a Japanese family badge or crest. [Jap]

mon- see **mono-**.

mona /mō'nə/ n a W African monkey, Cercopithecus mona. [Ital, Sp, or Port mona monkey]

monachism /mon'ə-ki-zm/ n monasticism. [Gr monachos solitary, from monos single, alone]
■ **mon'achal** adj. **mon'achist** adj. **Mon'achus** n the monk seal genus.

monacid /mon-as'id/ or **monoacid** /mo-nō-as'id/ adj having one replaceable hydrogen atom; capable of replacing one hydrogen atom of an acid. [**mono-**]

monact /mon'akt/ (zool) adj (of a sponge) having single-rayed spicules. [Gr monos single, alone, and aktis, -īnos a ray]
■ **monact'inal** /-i-nəl/ or **-ī'nəl/ adj. **monact'ine** /-in/ adj.

monad /mon'ad/ n the number one, a unit (hist); an ultimate unit of being, material and psychical; a spirit; God; a hypothetical primitive living organism or unit of organic life; a flagellate of the genus Monas or other related genera; a univalent element, atom, or radical. [Gr monas, -ados a unit, from monos single, alone]
■ **monad'ic** or **monad'ical** adj. **monad'iform** adj like a monad. **mon'adism** or **monadol'ogy** n a theory or doctrine of monads, esp Leibniz's. **mon'as** n a monad; (with cap) a genus of flagellates.

monadelphous /mo-nə-del'fəs/ (bot) adj (of stamens) united by the filaments in one bundle; (of a flower or plant) having all the stamens united in this way. [Gr monos single, alone, and adelphos brother]
■ **Monadel'phia** n pl in Linnaeus's system, a class of plants with stamens united in one bundle.

monadic...to...**monadism** see under **monad**.

monadnock /mə-nad'nok/ n an isolated hill of hard rock that has resisted the erosion suffered by the land around it. [Mount Monadnock, New Hampshire, USA]

monadology see under **monad**.

monal see **monaul**.

monandrous /mo-nan'drəs/ adj having or allowing one husband or male mate (at a time); having one stamen or one antheridium (bot). [Gr monos single, alone, and anēr, andros a man, male]
■ **Monan'dria** n pl in Linnaeus's system, a class of plants with one stamen. **monan'dry** n the condition or practice of being monandrous.

monarch¹ /mon'ərk/ n a sole hereditary head of a state, whether titular or ruling; a large butterfly (Danaus plexippus) with orange and black wings. [Gr monarchēs, from monos single, alone, and archein to rule]
■ **monarchal** /-ärk'əl/, **monarch'ial**, **monarch'ic** or **monarch'ical** adj. **Monarch'ian** n a Christian who denied the personal independent subsistence of Christ (dynamic when regarding the divinity of Christ as only a power (dynamis) communicated to him, modalistic when regarding Christ as the Father who had assumed flesh, a mere modus of the Godhead). **Monarch'ianism** n. **Monarchianis'tic** adj. **monarch'ically** adv. **mon'archism** n the principles of monarchy; love of or support for monarchy. **mon'archist** n an advocate of monarchy; a believer in monarchy; a Monarchian. ◆ adj advocating or believing in a monarchy. **monarchist'ic** adj. **mon'archize** or **-ise** vt to rule over as a monarch; to convert into a monarchy. ◆ vi (also vt with it) to play the monarch. **Monarch'o** n (Shakesp) a foppish fantastic megalomaniac (from a crazy Italian seen around the court of Elizabeth I). **mon'archy** n a kind of government of which there is a monarch; a state with monarchical government; the territory of a monarch.

monarch² /mon'ärk/ (bot) adj having one xylem strand. [Gr monos single, alone, and archē origin]

monarda /mə-när'də/ n a plant of the Monarda genus of N American aromatic herbs of the mint (Labiatae) family. [N Monardes (died 1588), Spanish botanist]

monas see under **monad**.

monastery /mon'ə-st(ə-)ri/ n a house for a community of monks, or (sometimes) nuns. [Late Gr monastērion, from monastēs a monk, from monos single, alone]
■ **monaste'rial**, **monastic** /-as'tik/ or **monas'tical** adj relating to monasteries, monks, or nuns; recluse; solitary. **monas'tic** n a monk. **monas'tically** adv. **monas'ticism** /-sizm/ n the monastic life or system of living.

Monastral® **pigment** /mo-nas'trəl pig'mənt/ n any of several blue or green phthalocyanine pigments.

monatomic /mon-ə-tom'ik/ (chem) adj consisting of one atom; having one replaceable atom or group; univalent. [**mono-**]

monaul or **monal** /mon'öl/ n a Himalayan pheasant (genus Lophophorus), the male of which has a brilliantly-coloured shimmering plumage. [Nepali munāl]

monaural /mon-ö'rəl/ adj having or using only one ear; relating to one ear; (of a radio broadcast, etc) giving the effect of sound from a single direction, not stereophonic. [**mono-**]
■ **monau'rally** adv.

monaxial /mon-ak'si-əl/ adj having only one axis. [**mono-**]
■ **monax'on** adj monaxial. ◆ n a monaxonic sponge or spicule. **monaxon'ic** adj. **Monaxon'ida** n pl an order of sponges with monaxon spicules only.

monazite /mon'ə-zīt/ (mineralogy) n a phosphate of cerium, lanthanum, neodymium, praseodymium, and usu thorium, a source of thorium itself. [Gr monazein to be solitary, on account of its rarity]

monchiquite /mon'shi-kīt/ n a fine-grained lamprophyric rock, composed of olivine and augite with little or no feldspar, in an analcite groundmass. [Serra de Monchique, in SW Portugal]

mondain /mɔ̃-dɛ̃'/ or (fem) **mondaine** /mɔ̃-den'/ (Fr) adj worldly, fashionable. ◆ n a person who lives in fashionable society.

Monday /mun'dā/ or -di/ n the second day of the week and first day of the working week, dedicated in ancient times to the moon. [OE mōnandæg, from mōnan, genitive of mōna moon, and dæg day, transl of LL diēs lūnae moon's day]
■ **Mon'dayish** adj having the Monday morning feeling (see below). **Mon'days** adv on Mondays.
□ **Monday Club** n a right-wing group of Conservatives formed in 1961, orig holding discussions over Monday lunch. **Monday morning feeling** n the tiredness and disinclination to work felt at the prospect, after the weekend, of another week's work ahead.
■ **black Monday, Handsel Monday, Meal Monday, Plough Monday** see under **black**, etc. **Cyber Monday** see separate entry.

mondegreen /mon'də-grēn/ n a phrase, often humorous or nonsensical, that results from mishearing the lyric of a song. [Coined in 1954 by Sylvia Wright after she had mistaken the phrase laid him on the green for Lady Mondegreen]

mondial /mon'di-əl/ adj of the whole world, worldwide. [Fr, from L mundus world]

mondo /mon'dō/ (sl; orig US) adv extremely, absolutely. [Ital, world, erroneously taken as an adverb in phrases such as mondo bizarro, etc]

monecious same as **monoecious**.

Monegasque /mo-nə-gask'/ adj of or relating to the Principality of Monaco on the Mediterranean Riviera, or its inhabitants. ◆ n a native or citizen of Monaco. [Fr monégasque, from Provençal mounegasc]

Monel metal® /mō-nel' met'l/ n a nickel-base alloy with high strength and resistance to corrosion.

moner /mō'nər/ or **moneron** /mo-nē'ron/ n (pl **monēr'a**) the name given by German biologist Ernst Haeckel (1834–1919) to his hypothetical simplest protozoan, the organism on which his version of the evolution theory is based. [Gr monērēs single]

monergism /mon'ər-ji-zm/ (theol) n the doctrine that regeneration is entirely the work of the Holy Spirit, the natural will being incapable of co-operation. [Gr monos single, alone, and ergon work]

monetary /mon'- or mun'i-tə-ri/ adj of or relating to money; consisting of money. [L monēta (see **money**)]
■ **monetar'ily** adv. **mon'etarism** n. **mon'etarist** n a person who advocates an economic policy based chiefly on the control of a country's money supply (also adj). **monetīzā'tion, monetarīzā'tion** or **-s-** n. **mon'etize, mon'etarize** or **-ise** vt to give the character of money to, to coin as money; to adapt to using money.
□ **monetary unit** n the principal unit of currency of a state.

moneth /munth/ (Spenser) same as **month**.

money /mun'i/ n (pl **mon'eys** or **mon'ies**; see below) coin, pieces of stamped metal used as a trading medium; any currency used in the same way; wealth. [OFr moneie (Fr monnaie), from L monēta money, a mint, Monēta (the reminder) being a surname of Juno, in whose temple at Rome money was coined]

■ **mon'eyed** or **mon'ied** *adj* having money; materially rich, well-off; consisting in money. **mon'eyer** *n* a person who coins money legally (*archaic*); a capitalist (*obs*). **mon'eyless** *adj* having no money. **mon'eys** or **mon'ies** *n pl* (*archaic* and *law*) sums of money; money. ❑ **money bag** *n* a bag for or of money. **mon'eybags** *n sing* (*inf*) a rich person. **money belt** *n* a belt with a pocket in it for holding money. **money bill** *n* a bill introduced into parliament or congress for raising revenue or otherwise dealing with money. **mon'ey-bound** *adj* unable to move for lack of money. **money box** *n* a box for collecting or saving money, *usu* with a slit for insertion. **money broker** *n* a person who carries out transactions in money for others. **mon'eychanger** *n* a person who exchanges one currency for another. **money clip** *n* a clip for holding (*esp* folded) banknotes together. **mon'ey-grubber** *n* a sordid accumulator of wealth. **mon'ey-grubbing** *n* and *adj*. **mon'eylender** *n* a professional lender of money at interest, *esp* an individual or small company arranging domestic loans at higher-than-commercial interest rates. **mon'eylending** *n*. **mon'eymaker** *n* a person who acquires wealth; anything that brings profit; a person who earns money. **mon'eymaking** *n* the act of gaining wealth. ◆ *adj* lucrative, profitable. **mon'eyman** *n* a person employed or specializing in finance. **money market** *n* (the dealers in) the market for short-term loans for business, etc. **money of account** *n* a monetary unit (not represented by current coins) used in keeping accounts. **money order** *n* an order for money deposited at one post office, and payable at another. **mon'ey-scrivener** *n* (*old*) a person who does financial business for clients. **money shot** *n* (in pornography) a shot which shows a man ejaculating. **money spider** *n* a very small spider supposed to bring luck in money. **mon'ey-spinner** *n* any scheme that brings in much money; a successful speculator; a money spider. **mon'ey-spinning** *adj* and *n*. **money supply** *n* the amount of money available to a country's economy. **mon'ey's-worth** *n* something as good as money; full value. **mon'ey-taker** *n* a person who receives payments of money, *esp* at an entrance door; someone who can be bribed. **money wages** *n pl* income in relation to money paid rather than its purchasing power. **mon'eywort** *n* a round-leaved loosestrife, creeping Jenny. ■ **a (good) run for one's money** (*inf*) fierce competition; enjoyment from an activity. **for my** (or **our**) **money** if I (or we) were to choose, express an opinion, etc. **hard money** coin. **in the money** among the prize-winners (*racing*, etc); well-off; of an option or warrant, having an intrinsic value, the market price of the underlying shares being above the stipulated price (*finance*). **made of money** extremely wealthy. **make money** to acquire wealth; to make a profit. **money down** money paid on the spot. **money for jam, old rope**, etc money obtained without effort. **money talks** the wealthy have much influence. **on the money** (*US sl*) spot-on, exact, just right. **pots of money** a large amount of money. **put money into** to invest in. **put money on** to place a bet on. **put one's money where one's mouth is** to support one's stated opinion by betting money; to give practical (*esp* financial) rather than merely hypothetical support. **ready money** money paid for a thing at the time at which it is bought; money ready for immediate payment.

mong[1] /*mung*/ (now *dialect*) *n* a mixture; a crowd. [OE *gemang*] ❑ **mong'corn** or **mung'corn** *n* maslin.

mong[2] /*mong*/ (*offensive sl*) *n* a foolish or inept person. [Short form of **Mongol** (in its offensive sense)]

mong[3] /*mung*/ (*Aust sl*) *n* a mongrel.

'mong and **'mongst** aphetic for **among** and **amongst**.

monger /*mung'gər*/ *n* (chiefly as a *combining form*) a dealer (except in a few instances, such as *ironmonger*), a person who traffics in a petty, or discreditable way, or in unpleasant subjects, eg a *gossipmonger*. [OE *mangere*, from L *mangō, -ōnis* a furbisher, slave-dealer, from Gr *manganeuein* to use trickery] ■ **mong'ering** or **mong'ery** *n*.

mongo /*mong'gō*/ *n* (pl **mon'go** or **mon'gos**) a Mongolian monetary unit, $\frac{1}{100}$ of a tugrik. [Mongolian, literally, silver]

Mongol /*mong'gol*/ *n* a member of Genghis Khan's clan, or of the various populations under him (*hist*); one of the people of Mongolia, a republic in east central Asia; their language; a member of a broad-headed, yellow-skinned, straight-haired, small-nosed human race, often with an epicanthic fold of skin (otherwise called **Tungus**); (often without *cap*) the old (no longer preferred, by some considered *offensive*) term for a person affected by Down's syndrome. ◆ *adj* Mongolian. [Said to be from Mongol *mong* brave] ■ **Mongolian** /*mong-gō'li-ən*/ *adj* of or relating to Mongolia, the Mongols, or their language. ◆ *n* a native or citizen of Mongolia; the language of Mongolia; a Mongoloid. **Mongolic** /*-gol'ik*/ *adj* Mongolian; of Mongolian type; of the division of the Ural-Altaic languages to which Mongolian, Buriat, and Kalmuck belong. **Mong'olism** *n* (often without *cap*) an old (no longer preferred usage) term for **Down's syndrome**. **Mong'olize** or **-ise** *vt* to make

Mongolian. **Mong'oloid** *adj* of Mongolian race or type; (often without *cap*) affected with Down's syndrome (no longer preferred usage). ◆ *n* a person of Mongolian race or type; (often without *cap*) an old term for a person affected by Down's syndrome (no longer preferred usage). ❑ **Mongoloid eye** *n* an eye with an epicanthic fold.

mongoose /*mong'* or *mung'goos*/ *n* (pl **mong'ooses**) (also **mung'oose** or (Fr) **mangouste'**) an Indian animal of the civet family, a great slayer of snakes and rats; any other species of the genus *Herpestes*, including the ichneumon; a Madagascan lemur. [Marathi *mangūs*]

mongrel /*mung'grəl*/ *n* an animal, *esp* a dog, of a mixed breed; a person, thing or word of mixed or indefinite origin or nature (*usu derog*); that which is neither one thing nor another. ◆ *adj* mixed in breed; ill-defined. [Prob from root of OE *mengan* to mix] ■ **mong'relism** *n*. **mongrelīzā'tion** or **-s-** *n*. **mong'relize** or **-ise** *vt*. **mong'relly** *adj*.

monial /*mō'ni-əl*/ *n* a mullion. [OFr, of unknown origin]

monicker or **moniker** /*mon'i-kər*/ (*sl*; *orig tramps' sl*) *n* an alias, nickname or real name. [Shelta *munik* name] ■ **mon'ickered** or **mon'ikered** *adj*.

monied and **monies** see under **money**.

monilia /*mo-nil'i-ə*/ *n* a fungus of the *Monilia* genus, having conidia in branched chains. [L *monīle* a necklace] ■ **moniliasis** /*-ī'ə-sis*/ *n* a disease of the mouth and digestive tract in birds, animals, and man (**thrush**[2]), caused by fungi of the genus *Monilia*. **monil'iform** *adj* (*biol*) like a string of beads.

moniment /*mon'i-mənt*/ see **monument**.

moniplies /*mun'* or *mon'i-plīz*/ see **manyplies**.

monism /*mon'i-zm*/ *n* a philosophical theory that all being may ultimately be referred to one category; thus *idealism*, *pantheism* and *materialism* are monisms, as opposed to the dualism of matter and spirit. [Gr *monos* single, alone] ■ **mon'ist** *n*. **monist'ic** or **monist'ical** *adj*.

monition /*mo-nish'ən*/ *n* a reminding or admonishing; warning; notice; a summons to appear and answer (*law*). [L *monēre, -itum* to warn, remind] ■ **mon'itive** *adj* conveying admonition. **mon'itory** *adj* giving admonition or warning.

monitor /*mon'i-tər*/ *n* a person employed to supervise; a senior pupil who assists in school discipline, or any other pupil with a special responsibility; a person who admonishes; an adviser; a detector for radioactivity; an instrument used in a production process to keep a variable quantity within prescribed limits by transmitting a controlling signal; a screen in a television studio showing the picture being transmitted; the screen in any set of audiovisual equipment; an apparatus for testing transmission in electrical communication; a low iron-clad with revolving gun-turrets (from an American ship so named, the first of its kind, 1862; *hist*); a genus (*Varanus*) of very large lizards of Africa, Asia, and Australia (from a belief that they give warning of the presence of a crocodile); a backboard (*obs*); a screen or visual display unit (*comput*). ◆ *vt* to act as monitor to; to check (eg the body and clothing of people working with radioactive materials) for radioactivity; to track, or to control (an aeroplane, guided missile, etc); to watch, check, supervise. ◆ *vi* (*radio*) to tap onto a communication circuit, *usu* in order to ascertain that the transmission is that desired; to listen to foreign broadcasts in order to obtain news, code messages, etc. [Ety as for **monition**] ■ **monitorial** /*-ōr'* or *-ör'*/ *adj* relating to a monitor. **monito'rially** *adv*. **mon'itorship** *n*. **mon'itress** *n* a female monitor.

monk /*mungk*/ *n* a man (other than a friar, but loosely often applied to a friar also) of a religious community living together under vows; a hermit (*obs*); a bullfinch; an inky blotch or overinked place in print; touchwood for firing mines (*obs*). [OE *munuc*, from L *monachus*, from Gr *monachos*, from *monos* alone] ■ **monk'ery** *n* (*derog*) monasticism; behaviour of monks; monks collectively. **monk'hood** *n* the state or character of a monk. **monk'ish** *adj* (*derog*) relating to a monk; like a monk; monastic. **monk'ishly** *adv*. **monk'ishness** *n*. ❑ **monk'fish** *n* the angelfish (shark); any of several types of angler-fish. **monk's cloth** *n* a type of heavy cotton cloth. **monk seal** *n* a seal (*Monachus albiventer*) of the Black Sea, Mediterranean, and NW Africa, dark grey above, light underneath. **monks'hood** *n* wolfsbane, a poisonous ranunculaceous plant (genus *Aconitum*) with a large hoodlike posterior sepal. **monk's rhubarb** *n* patience-dock. **monk's seam** *n* (*naut*) a strong seam formed by overlapping two pieces and stitching on each side and down the middle (also **middle-stitching**).

monkey /*mung'ki*/ *n* (pl **monk'eys**) any mammal of the Primates except man and (*usu*) the anthropoid apes; an ape; a term of contempt, or of playful endearment, for a mischievous or badly-behaved child or person; a lackey (*inf*); the falling weight of a pile-driver; a large hammer for driving bolts; 500 pounds, or dollars (*sl*); anger (*sl*); an oppressive burden or habit, *specif* a drug addiction (*US sl*); any of various kinds of container, *esp* for alcohol; a sheep (*obs Aust sl*); a type of cannon (*obs*). ◆ *vi* (often with *around*) to meddle with anything, to fool. ◆ *vt* to mimic, ape. [Perh from MLGer *moneke*, connected with Sp and Port *mono* monkey]

■ **monk'eyish** *adj.* **monk'eyism** *n* monkey-like behaviour.

❑ **monkey bag** *n* a small money bag, hung round the neck. **monkey block** *n* a small swivel-block, used to guide running rigging. **monkey board** *n* a footboard behind a vehicle; a high-level platform on an oil-derrick. **monkey boat** *n* a narrow, half-decked riverboat. **monkey bread** *n* the baobab tree or its fruit. **monkey business** *n* underhand dealings; mischievous behaviour. **monkey engine** *n* a pile-driving engine. **monkey flower** *n* a species of *Mimulus*. **monk'ey-gaff** *n* (*naut*) a small gaff above the spanker gaff for the flag. **monk'ey-gland** *n* ape's testicle, grafted experimentally on man (1920–30s) to effect rejuvenescence. **monk'ey-grass** *n* a coarse fibre from the leaf-stalks of *Attalea funifera*, used for brooms, etc. **monkey hammer** *n* a drop-press with a ram, which is raised and let drop freely. **monkey jacket** *n* a short close-fitting jacket. **monkey jar** *n* a water monkey. **monkey nut** *n* the peanut or ground-nut (genus *Arachis*). **monkey pod** *n* the rain tree. **monkey pot** *n* the round-lidded outer shell of the sapucaia nut. **monkey pump** *n* a straw let through a gimlet-hole for sucking alcohol from a cask. **monkey puzzle** *n* a coniferous tree (*Araucaria araucana*) with close-set prickly leaves (also called **Chile pine**). **monkey rail** *n* a light rail above the quarter-rail on a ship. **monkey rope** *n* a forest creeper or liana; a rope round a sailor's waist for working in a dangerous place. **monkey run** *n* a favourite place of parade and striking up of acquaintance. **monkey shine** *n* (*US sl*) a monkeyish trick. **monkey suit** *n* (*sl*) a man's evening suit. **monkey's wedding** *n* (*S Afr inf*) simultaneous sunshine and light rain. **monkey tail** *n* a vertical scroll at the end of a hand-rail. **monkey tricks** *n* mischief, pranks. **monkey wheel** *n* a tackle-block over which a hoisting-rope runs. **monkey wrench** *n* a wrench with a movable jaw, an adjustable spanner.

■ **have a monkey on one's back** (*inf*) to be addicted to drugs; to be burdened with a long-term problem. **have** or **get one's monkey up** (*sl*) to be angry. **make a monkey (out) of** to make a fool of. **not to give a monkey's** (*vulgar sl*) not to care, or be interested, at all. **suck the monkey** (*sl*) to drink from a cask through an inserted tube; to drink rum, etc from a coconut.

monkfish and **monkshood** see under **monk**.

Mon-Khmer see under **Mon**.

mono¹ /*mon'ō*/ (*inf*) *n* (pl **mon'os**) a monaural gramophone record; monaural reproduction; a monophonic ringtone. ◆ *adj* monaural.

mono² /*mon'ō*/ (*inf*) *n* short form of **infectious mononucleosis** (see under **infect**).

mono- /*mo-nō-*/ or (before a vowel) **mon-** /*mon-*/ *combining form* denoting single. [Gr *monos* single, alone]

monoacid same as **monacid**.

monoamine /*mo-nō-am'ēn*/ or -*in*, also -*ā'mēn*/ *n* an amine containing only one amino group. [**mono-**]

❑ **monoamine oxidase** *n* an enzyme involved in the inactivation of certain neurotransmitters. **monoamine-oxidase inhibitor** *n* one of a class of drugs that allow the build-up of serotonin in the brain, used to treat severe depression (*abbrev* **MAOI**).

monobasic /*mo-nō-bā'sik*/ (*chem*) *adj* capable of reacting with one equivalent of an acid; (of an acid) having one replaceable hydrogen atom. [**mono-**]

monoblepsis /*mo-nō-blep'sis*/ *n* a condition in which vision is more distinct when one eye only is used. [Gr *monos* single, and *blepsis* sight]

monobloc /*mon'ō-blok*/ *adj* made from a single piece of material. [Fr, from **mono-** and *bloc* block]

monobrow /*mon'ō-brow*/ *n* a unibrow. [**mono-**]

monocardian /*mo-nō-kär'di-ən*/ *adj* having an undivided heart. [Gr *monos* single, alone, and *kardiā* heart]

monocarpellary /*mo-nō-kär'pə-lə-ri* or -*pel'ə-*/ (*bot*) *adj* of or with only one carpel. [**mono-**]

monocarpic /*mo-nō-kär'pik*/ (*bot*) *adj* fruiting once only. [Gr *monos* single, alone, and *karpos* fruit]

■ **monocarp'** *n* a monocarpic plant. **monocarp'ous** *adj* monocarpic; having only one ovary; producing one fruit.

monoceros /*mo-nos'ə-ros*/ *n* a one-horned animal; the unicorn; *perh* the swordfish, or the narwhal (*Spenser*). [Gr *monokerōs*, from *monos* single, alone, and *keras* a horn]

■ **monoc'erous** *adj.*

monochasium /*mo-nō-kā'zi-əm*/ *n* (pl **monocha'sia**) a cymose inflorescence in which each axis in turn produces one branch. [Gr *monos* single, alone; appar on the analogy of **dichasium**, as if that were from Gr *di-* twice, and *chasis* separation]

■ **monocha'sial** *adj.*

monochlamydeous /*mon-ō-klə-mid'i-əs*/ (*bot*) *adj* having a one-whorled perianth. [**mono-**]

■ **Monochlamyd'eae** *n pl* a division of the Archichlamydeae or Choripetalae, usually with the perianth in one whorl.

monochord /*mon'ō-körd*/ *n* an acoustic instrument with one string, soundboard and bridge, *esp* one with a movable bridge and a graduated soundboard for use in the analysis of sounds; a similar instrument with more than one string and bridge; a clavichord; a tromba marina. [**mono-**]

monochroic /*mo-nō-krō'ik*/ *adj* of one colour. [Gr *monochroos*, from *monos* single, alone, and *chrōs* colour]

monochromatic /*mon-ō-krō-mat'ik*/ *adj* of one colour or wavelength only; completely colour-blind; done in monochrome. [Gr *monochrōmatos*, from *monos* single, alone, and *chrōma*, -*atos* colour]

■ **monochro'masy** *n* colour blindness in which objects are seen in shades of a single colour. **monochro'mat** or **monochro'mate** *n* a person who sees all colours as different shades of a single colour. **monochromat'ically** *adv.* **monochro'matism** *n* monochromasy. **monochro'mator** *n* a device capable of isolating and transmitting monochromatic or nearly monochromatic light. **mon'ochrome** *n* representation in one colour; a picture in one colour; black and white; monochromy. ◆ *adj* (of visual reproduction) using or having one colour; dull, monotonous. **monochro'mic** *adj.* **monochro'mist** *n* a person who practises monochrome. ◆ *adj* done, reproduced, etc in a single colour or hue; black and white. **mon'ochromy** or /-*ok'rə-mē*/ *n* the art of monochrome.

monocle /*mon'ə-kl*/ *n* a single eyeglass. [Fr *monocle*, from Gr *monos* single, alone, and L *oculus* eye]

■ **mon'ocled** *adj* wearing a monocle.

monocline /*mon'ō-klīn*/ (*geol*) *n* a fold in strata followed by resumption of the original direction. [Gr *monos* single, alone, and *klīnein* to cause to slope]

■ **monoclīn'al** *adj.*

monoclinic /*mon'ō-kli-nik*/ (*crystallog*) *adj* referable to three unequal axes, two intersecting each other obliquely and at right angles to the third. [Gr *monos* single, alone, and *klīnein* to incline]

monoclinous /*mon'ō-klī-nəs* or -*klī'*/ (*bot*) *adj* hermaphrodite. [Gr *monos* single, alone, and *klīnē* bed]

monoclonal /*mo-nō-klō'nəl*/ *adj* (of an antibody) derived from a single cell clone that can reproduce itself in vast quantities in the laboratory, having applications in the diagnosis and treatment of cancers, infections, etc. [**mono-**]

mono-compound /*mo-nō-kom'pownd*/ (*chem*) *n* a compound containing one atom or group of that which is indicated. [**mono-**]

monocoque /*mo-nō-kok'* or -*kōk'*/ *n* a fuselage or nacelle in which all, or nearly all, structural loads are carried by the skin (*aeronautics*); a motor vehicle structure in which body and chassis are a single unit, with all parts receiving stress (*motoring*); the hull of a boat made in one piece (*naut*). [Fr, literally, single shell]

monocotyledon /*mon-ō-ko-ti-lē'dən*/ *n* (often shortened to **monocot**) a plant of the class **Monocotylē'dones** /-*ēz*/ or **Monocot'ylae**, one of the two great divisions of angiosperms, the embryos with one cotyledon, leaves commonly parallel-veined, the parts of the flower *usu* in threes, the vascular bundles scattered and (with exceptions) without cambium. [**mono-**]

■ **monocotylē'donous** *adj.*

monocracy /*mo-nok'rə-si*/ *n* government by one person. [Gr *monos* single, alone, and *kratos* power]

■ **mon'ocrat** /-*ō-krat*/ *n.* **monocrat'ic** *adj.*

monocrystal /*mon'ō-kris-təl*/ *n* a single crystal. [**mono-**]

■ **monocrys'talline** *adj.*

monocular /*mon-ok'ū-lər*/, also **monoculous** /-*ləs*/ *adj* of, for, or with, one eye; one-eyed. [Gr *monos* single, alone, and L *oculus* an eye]

■ **monoc'ularly** *adv.*

monoculture /*mon'ō-kul-chər*/ *n* the growing of one kind of crop only, or a large area over which it is grown; a single, shared culture (eg ethnic, social, religious). [**mono-**]

■ **monocul'tural** *adj* of or relating to (a) monoculture.

monocycle /*mon'ō-sī-kl*/ *n* a unicycle. [**mono-**]

monocyclic /*mo-nō-sīk'lik*/ (*bot*) *adj* having one whorl or ring; having only one cycle. [**mono-**]

monocyte /mon'ō-sīt/ (anat) n a large phagocytic leucocyte with a single oval or kidney-shaped nucleus and clear cytoplasm. [Gr *monos* single, and *kytos* vessel]

monodactylous /mo-nō-dak'ti-ləs/ adj one-toed or one-fingered. [Gr *monos* single, alone, and *daktylos* finger, toe]
■ **monodact'yly** n the condition of having only one toe or finger on each foot or hand.

Monodelphia /mo-nō-del'fi-ə/ n pl one of the three primary divisions of mammals, the placental mammals or Eutheria. [Gr *monos* single, alone, and *delphys* womb]
■ **monodel'phian, monodel'phic** or **monodel'phous** adj.

monodic and **monodist** see under **monody**.

monodisperse /mo-nō-di-spûrs'/ adj (of a colloidal system) having particles all of effectively the same size. [**mono-**]

Monodon /mon'ō-don/ n the narwhal. [Gr *monos* single, alone, and *odous, odontos* tooth, tusk]
■ **mon'odont** adj one-tusked; of the Monodon.

monodrama /mon'ō-drä-mə/ n a dramatic piece for a single performer. [**mono-**]
■ **monodramatic** /-drə-mat'ik/ adj.

monody /mon'ə-di/ n (in Greek tragedy) a mournful ode or poem performed by a single mourner; any poem lamenting a death; a song for one voice; a composition in which one part or voice carries the melody, the others accompanying (*music*). [Gr *monōidiā*, from *monos* single, alone, and *ōidē* song]
■ **monodic** /-od'-/ or **monod'ical** adj. **mon'odist** n a person who writes monodies.

monoecious /mo-nē'shəs/ (*biol*) adj hermaphrodite; having separate male and female flowers on the same plant. [Gr *monos* single, alone, and *oikos* a house]
■ **Monoe'cia** n pl in the Linnaean system, a class of monoecious plants. **monoecism** /-ē'sizm/ n.

monofil /mon'ō-fil/ n a single strand of synthetic fibre; a fishing-line so constituted (also **monofil'ament**). [Gr *monos* single, alone, and L *fīlum* a thread]

monogamy /mo-nog'ə-mi/ n the rule, custom or condition of marriage to one wife or husband at a time, or (now rarely) in life; the practice, custom or condition of having no more than one mate (*zool*) or, loosely, one sexual partner, at a time. [Gr *monos* single, alone, and *gamos* marriage]
■ **monogamic** /mon-ō-gam'ik/ or **monogamous** /-og'əm-/ adj. **monog'amist** n. **monog'amously** adv.

monogenesis /mo-nō-jen'i-sis/ n development of offspring from a parent like itself; asexual reproduction; community of origin. [**mono-**]
■ **monogenet'ic** adj. **monogen'ic** adj of or relating to monogenism; of or determined by a single gene. **monogenism** /-oj'ən-izm/ n the doctrine of the common descent of all living things, or of any particular group (*esp* mankind) from one ancestor or pair. **monog'enist** n. **monogenist'ic** adj. **monog'enous** adj. **monog'eny** n descent from one common ancestor or pair; asexual reproduction.

monoglot /mon'ō-glot/ adj able to speak only one language; monolingual; using or written in only one language. ◆ n a person who speaks only one language; a book written in only one language. [Gr *monos* single, and *glōtta* tongue]

monogony /mo-nog'ə-ni/ n asexual reproduction. [Gr *monos* single, alone, and *gonos* begetting]

monogram /mon'ə-gram/ n a figure consisting of several letters interwoven or written into one. ◆ vt (**mon'ogramming; mon'ogrammed**) to mark with such a figure. [Gr *monos* single, alone, and *gramma, grammatos* a letter]
■ **monogrammatic** /-grə-mat'ik/ adj.

monograph /mon'ə-gräf/ n a treatise, book or paper written on one particular subject or any branch of it; a systematic account. ◆ vt to write a monograph on. [Gr *monos* single, alone, and *graphein* to write]
■ **monographer** /mon-og'rə-fər/ or **monog'raphist** n a writer of monographs. **monographic** /-graf'-/ or **monograph'ical** adj relating to a monograph or a monogram; drawn in lines without colours. **monog'raphy** n (*rare*) a monograph.

monogyny /mo-noj'i-ni/ or /-nog'-/ n the custom, practice or condition of having only one wife; marriage with one wife; the habit of mating with one female. [Gr *monos* single, alone, and *gynē* woman]
■ **Monogynia** /mon-ō-jin'i-ə/ n pl in various Linnaean classes of plants, an order having one style. **monogyn'ian** adj (*bot*) belonging to the Monogynia order. **monog'ynous** adj having one wife; practising monogyny; mating with one female; having one style; monogynian.

monohull /mon'ō-hul/ n a vessel with one hull, as opposed to a catamaran or trimaran. [**mono-**]

monohybrid /mo-nō-hī'brid/ n a cross between parents differing in one heritable character. [**mono-**]

monohydrate /mo-nō-hī'drāt/ n a hydrate containing one molecule of water per molecule of the compound. [**mono-**]

monohydric /mo-nō-hī'drik/ adj containing one hydroxyl group. [**mono-**]

monokini /mo-nō-kē'ni/ n a woman's topless beach garment consisting of the lower half of a bikini; a garment similar to a swimsuit, with open sides. [**mono-**, and facetious formation from **bikini**, as if *bi*- signified two]

monolatry /mo-nol'ə-tri/ n the worship of one god without excluding belief in others. [Gr *monos* single, alone, and *latreiā* worship]
■ **monol'ater** n. **monol'atrist** n. **monol'atrous** adj.

monolayer /mon'ō-lā-ər/ n a monomolecular layer. [**mono-**]
❑ **monolayer culture** n (*biol*) a tissue culture technique in which thin sheets of cells are grown, on glass or plastic, in a nutrient medium.

monolingual /mo-nō-ling'gwəl/ adj expressed in one language; speaking only one language. ◆ n a monolingual person. [Gr *monos* single, and L *lingua* tongue]
■ **monoling'ualism** n. **monoling'uist** n.

monolith /mon'ə-lith/ n a single block of stone forming a pillar or column; anything resembling a monolith in uniformity, massiveness or intractability. [Gr *monos* single, alone, and *lithos* a stone]
■ **monolith'ic** adj relating to or resembling a monolith; (of a state, an organization, etc) massive, and undifferentiated throughout; intractable for this reason.
❑ **monolithic integrated circuit** see under **integrate**.

monologue or (*US*) **monolog** /mon'ə-log/ n a soliloquy or speech by one person, or a composition intended to be spoken by one person; a tedious, loud or opinionated speech that blocks conversation (*inf*). [Gr *monos* single, alone, and *logos* speech]
■ **monologic** /-loj'-/ or **monolog'ical** adj. **monol'ogist** n a person who talks in or performs a monologue (also **mon'ologuist**). **monologize** or **-ise** /mon-ol'ə-jīz/ vi to indulge in this (also **monol'oguize** or **-ise** /-gīz/). **monol'ogy** n the habit of doing so.

monomachy /mo-nom'ə-ki/ n (also **monomā'chia**) single combat; a duel. [Gr *monos* single, alone, and *machē* a fight]

monomania /mo-nō-mā'ni-ə/ n mental illness in which the mind is consumed by a single idea; obsessive enthusiasm for a single subject or activity. [Gr *monos* single, alone, and *maniā* madness]
■ **monomā'niac** n a person affected with monomania. **monomā'niac** or **monomaniacal** /-mə-nī'ə-kl/ adj.

monomark /mon'ō-märk/ n a particular combination of letters, figures, etc as a mark of identification. [**mono-**]

monomer /mon'ə- or mō'nə-mər/ (*chem*) n a small molecule, capable of linking up with identical molecules to produce polymers, or with similar molecules to make copolymers. [Gr *monos* single, alone, and *meros* part]
■ **monomer'ic** adj.

monometallic /mon-ō-mi-tal'ik/ adj involving or using only one metal (as a standard of currency). [**mono-**]
■ **monometallism** /-met'əl-izm/ n. **monomet'allist** n.

monometer /mo-nom'i-tər/ (*prosody*) adj consisting of one measure. ◆ n a verse of one measure. [**mono-** and **meter**[1]]
■ **monomet'ric** or **monomet'rical** adj.

monomial /mo-nō'mi-əl/ n and adj (an algebraic expression) consisting of one term only; (a name) consisting of one word. [Ill-formed from Gr *monos* single, alone, and L *nōmen* name]

monomode /mon'ō-mōd/ adj designating a very fine optical fibre (less than 10 micrometres in diameter) used in telecommunications, in which the diameter of the inner core is comparable with the wavelength of light thus, as there is only one mode of light propagation, eliminating mode dispersion. [**mono-**]

monomolecular /mon-ō-mo-lek'ū-lər or -mə-lek'yə-/ adj (of a film or layer) one molecule in thickness. [**mono-**]

monomorphic /mo-nō-mör'fik/ (*biol*) adj existing in one form only. [Gr *monos* single, alone, and *morphē* form]
■ **monomor'phism** n. **monomor'phous** adj.

monomyarian /mon-ō-mī-ā'ri-ən/ adj having one adductor muscle. [Gr *monos* single, alone, and *mȳs, myos* muscle]

mononuclear /mo-nō-nū'kli-ər/ adj (of a cell) having a single nucleus; monocyclic. [**mono-**]
■ **mononucleosis** /mon-ō-nūk-li-ō'sis/ n (*med*) the presence in the blood of an abnormally large number of a type of leucocyte (see also **infectious mononucleosis** under **infect**).

monopetalous /mo-nō-pet'ə-ləs/ (*bot*) adj having petals united. [**mono-**]

monophagous /mo-nof'ə-gəs/ adj feeding only on one kind of food. [Gr monos single, alone, and phagein (aorist) to eat]
■ **monoph'agy** /-ji/ n feeding on one food; eating alone.

monophasic /mo-nō-fā'zik/ adj (of electric current) single-phase (also called **mon'ophase**); having one period of rest and one of activity during the 24 hours (biol). [**mono-**]

monophobia /mo-nō-fō'bi-ə/ n morbid fear of being alone. [**mono-**]
■ **monophō'bic** adj and n.

monophonic /mo-nō-fon'ik/ adj homophonic; monaural, opp to stereophonic. [Gr monos single, alone, and phōnē voice, sound]
■ **monoph'ony** n.

monophthong /mon'of-thong/ n a simple vowel sound. [Gr monophthongos, from monos single, alone, and phthongos sound, vowel]
■ **monophthongal** /-thong'gəl/ adj. **mon'ophthongize** or **-ise** /-gīz/ vt to turn into a monophthong.

monophyletic /mon-ō-fī-let'ik/ or /-fī-/ adj derived from a single stock or ancestral line. [Gr monos single, alone, and phȳletikos relating to a tribesman, from phȳlē tribe]

monophyodont /mo-nō-fī'ō-dont/ adj having only one set of teeth. ◆ n an animal with only one set of teeth. [Gr monophyēs of simple nature, from monos single, and odous, odontos tooth]

Monophysite /mō-nof'i-zīt or -sīt/ (Christianity) n a person who holds that Christ had only one nature, principally divine but with human form and attributes. [Gr monos single, alone, and physis nature]
■ **Monophysitic** /-sit'ik or -zit'ik/ adj. **Monoph'ysitism** n. —All words also without cap.

monopitch /mon'ō-pich/ (archit) adj (of a roof) forming a single, uniform slope. [**mono-**]

Monoplacophora /mon-ō-pla-kof'ə-rə/ n pl a very primitive limpet-like class of molluscs, believed, until the discovery (1952) of the living Neopilina off the W coast of Mexico, to have been extinct since early Silurian times. [Gr monos single, alone, plax, plakos plate, and phoros bearing, from the single piece of shell]

monoplane /mon'ə-plān/ n an aeroplane or glider with one set of planes or wings. [**mono-**]

monoplegia /mo-nō-plē'ji-ə/ (med) n paralysis limited to a single part of the body, or to one limb or muscle. [Gr monos single, alone, and plēgē stroke]
■ **monoplē'gic** adj and n.

monoploid /mon'ə-ploid/ adj haploid (qv). [**mono-**]

monopode /mon'ə-pōd/, now also **monopod** /mon'ə-pod/ n a one-footed person, esp a member of an imaginary race described in Pliny as each having a single foot large enough to be used by its owner as a sunshade; a one-footed support, platform stand, etc, eg for a camera. ◆ adj one-footed. [L monopodius, -um, from Gr monos single, alone, and pous, podos foot]
■ **monopo'dial** adj relating to or of the nature of a monopodium. **monopo'dially** adv. **monopo'dium** n (pl **monopo'dia**) (bot) a stem involved in **monopodial growth**, a pattern of growth in which a shoot continues to grow indefinitely and bears lateral shoots which behave similarly (cf **sympodial growth**).

monopole /mon'ō-pōl/ (phys) n (usu **magnetic monopole**) a particle, thought to exist, that has a single magnetic charge. [**mono-**]

monopoly /mo-nop'ə-li/ n sole power, or privilege, of dealing in anything; a business having such power or privilege; exclusive command or possession; something of which one has such a sole power, privilege, command, or possession; (**Monopoly**®) a board game for two or more players, their object being the acquisition of property. [L monopōlium, from Gr monopōlion, from monos single, alone, and pōleein to sell]
■ **monop'olism** n. **monopolis'tic** adj. **monopolis'tically** adv. **monopolīzā'tion** or **-s-** n. **monop'olize** or **-ise** vt to have a monopoly of; to keep to oneself, excluding all others; to engross. **monop'olizer, -s-** or **monop'olist** n.
❑ **Monopolies and Mergers Commission** n a former body set up to investigate monopolies, etc. **monopolistic competition** n (econ) imperfect competition (qv). **Monopoly money** n (inf) large sums of money treated lightly as though of no real consequence or value, like the sham notes exchanged in Monopoly.

monoprionidian /mon-ō-prī-ə-nid'i-ən/ adj (of graptolites) serrated on one side. [Gr monos single, alone, and priōn a saw]

monopropellant /mon-ō-prə-pel'ənt/ n a single propellant that produces propulsive energy as a result of a chemical reaction, usu induced by the presence of a catalyst. [**mono-**]

monopsony /mo-nop'sə-ni/ n a situation where only one buyer exists for the product of several sellers, or where one of several buyers is large enough to exert undue influence over the price of a product.

[Gr monos single, alone, and opsonia a purchase, from opsonein to buy]
■ **monop'sonist** n. **monopsonis'tic** adj.

monopteros /mo-nop'tə-ros/ or **monopteron** /-ron/ n a circular Greek temple with one ring of columns. [Gr monos single, alone, and pteron a wing]
■ **monop'teral** adj.

monoptote /mon'op-tōt/ n a word with only one case form. [Gr monoptōtos, from monos single, alone, and ptōtos fallen; cf ptōsis case (see **case**²)]

monopulse /mon'ō-puls/ n a type of radar system used in many gun-control and missile guidance systems, involving the transmission of a single pulse. [**mono-**]

monorail /mon'ō-rāl/ n a railway with carriages running astride of, or suspended from, one rail (also adj). [**mono-**]

monorchid /mon-ör'kid/ adj having only one testicle. [Faultily formed from Gr monorchis, from monos single, alone, and orchis, -eōs testicle]
■ **monorch'idism** or **monorch'ism** n.

monorhine /mon'ō-rīn/ adj having one nostril (also **monorhin'al**). [Gr monos single, alone, and rhīs, rhīnos nose]

monorhyme /mon'ə-rīm/ n a series or tirade of lines all rhyming together (also adj). [**mono-**]
■ **mon'orhymed** adj.

monosaccharide /mo-nō-sak'ə-rīd/ n a simple sugar that cannot be hydrolysed. [**mono-**]

monosemy /mon'ō-sē-mi/ (linguistics) n the fact of having only one meaning. [**mono-**, and Gr sēma a sign]
■ **mon'osemous** adj.

monosepalous /mo-nō-sep'ə-ləs/ (bot) adj having the sepals all united. [**mono-**]

monosis see monosy.

monoski /mon'ō-skē/ n a ski on which both feet are placed. ◆ vi to use a monoski. [**mono-**]
■ **mon'oskier** n. **mon'oskiing** n.

monosodium glutamate /mo-nō-sō'di-əm gloo'tə-māt/ n a white crystalline salt which brings out the flavour of meat (glutamate, a salt of glutamic acid), widely used as an additive in the food industry (abbrev **MSG**).

monosome /mon'ə-sōm/ n the unpaired accessory or X-chromosome. [Gr monos single, alone, and soma body]
■ **monosō'mic** adj. **mono'somy** n a condition in which one of a pair of diploid chromosomes is missing.

monostable /mo-nō-stā'bl/ (electronics) adj (of a circuit or system) fully stable in one state only but metastable in another state to which it can be driven for a fixed period by an input pulse. [**mono-**]

monostich /mon'ə-stik/ n a poem of one line. [Gr monos single, alone, and stichos row, line]
■ **monostichous** /-os'tik-əs/ adj in one line; in one row.

monostrophic /mo-nə-strof'ik/ (prosody) adj not divided into strophe, antistrophe, and epode; having the same strophic or stanzaic structure throughout. [Gr monostrophikos, from monos single, alone, and strophē a strophe]
■ **monostroph'ics** n pl monostrophic verses.

monostyle /mon'ō-stīl/ (archit) adj consisting of a single shaft. [Gr monos single, alone, and stȳlos a pillar]
■ **monostyl'ar** adj.

monosy /mon'o-si/ (biol) n separation of parts normally fused (also **mono'sis**). [Gr monōsis solitariness, from monos single, alone]

monosyllable /mo-nə-sil'ə-bl/ n a word of one syllable. [**mono-**]
■ **monosyllabic** /-ab'ik/ adj having only one syllable; terse or laconic. **monosyllab'ically** adv. **monosyll'abism** n.

monosymmetric /mo-nō-si-met'rik/ or **monosymmetrical** /-ri-kəl/ adj having only one plane of symmetry. [**mono-**]

monotelephone /mo-nō-tel'i-fōn/ n a telephone that transmits sounds of one pitch only. [**mono-**]

monothalamous /mo-nō-thal'ə-məs/, also **monothalamic** /-tha-lam'ik/ adj single-chambered; with only one cavity; (of fruit) formed from a single flower. [Gr monos single, alone, and thalamos a chamber]

monothecal /mo-nō-thē'kl/ adj having only one theca (also **monothe'cous**). [Gr monos single, alone, and thēkē case]

monotheism /mon'ə-thē-i-zm/ n the belief in only one God. [Gr monos single, alone, and theos God]
■ **mon'otheist** n. **monotheist'ic** or **monotheist'ical** adj. **monotheist'ically** adv.

Monotheletism /mo-nō-thel'i-ti-zm/ n the doctrine that Christ had only one will, opp to Ditheletism (also **Monothelism** /mon-oth'əl-izm/ or **Monothel'itism**). [Gr monos single, alone, and thelētēs a willer, from thelein to will]
■ **Monoth'elēte** or **Monoth'elite** n. **Monothelet'ic** or **Monothelet'ical** adj. —All words also without cap.

monotint /mon'ə-tint/ n (a) drawing or painting in a single tint. [**mono-**]

monotocous /mo-not'ə-kəs/ adj producing only one offspring at any one time; fruiting once only. [Gr monos single, alone, and tokos birth, offspring]

monotone /mon'ə-tōn/ n a single, unvaried tone or utterance; a succession of sounds having the same pitch; continued or extended sameness; sameness in colour. ◆ adj in monotone; monotonic (maths). ◆ vt and vi to sing, declaim, speak or utter, in a monotone. [Gr monos single, alone, and tonos a tone]
■ **monotonic** /-ton'ik/ adj in monotone; (of a function or sequence) having the property of either never increasing or never decreasing (maths). **monotonous** /mon-ot'ə-nəs/ adj uttered in one unvaried tone; marked by dull uniformity. **monot'onously** adv. **monot'onousness** n. **monot'ony** n dull uniformity of tone or sound; absence of modulation in speaking or reading; tedious sameness or lack of variety (fig).

monotreme /mon'ō-trēm/ n and adj (relating to) a member of the **Monotremata** /mon-ō-trē'mə-tə/, the lowest order of Mammalia, having a single opening for the genital and digestive organs. [Gr monos single, alone, and trēma, -atos a hole]
■ **monotre'matous** adj.

monotroch /mon'ō-trok/ (Walter Scott; facetious) n a wheelbarrow. [Gr monos single, alone, and trochos wheel]

Monotropa /mo-not'rə-pə/ n a genus of plants related to wintergreen, including the bird's-nest and Indian pipe, nourished by a fungal mycorrhiza in humus. [Gr monotropos solitary, from monos single, alone, and tropos turn]

monotype /mon'ə-tīp/ n a sole type, a species forming a genus by itself (biol); a single print made from a picture painted on a metal or glass plate (graphics); (**Monotype**®) the name of a machine that casts and sets type, letter by letter (printing). ◆ adj (biol) forming a genus by itself. [**mono-**]
■ **monotypic** /-tip'ik/ adj.

monounsaturated /mon-ō-un-sat'ū-rā-tid or -sach'ə-/ adj containing only one double or triple bond per molecule (cf **polyunsaturated**). [**mono-**]

monovalent /mo-nō-vā'lənt or mo-nov'ə-lənt/ (chem) adj univalent. [**mono-**]
■ **monova'lence** or **monova'lency** n.

monoxide /mo-nok'sīd/ (chem) n an oxide with one oxygen atom in the molecule. [**mono-**]

monoxylon /mo-nok'si-lon/ n a canoe made from one log. [Gr, from monos single, alone, and xylon wood]
■ **monox'ylous** adj.

monozygotic /mon-ō-zī-got'ik/ (biol) adj developed from one zygote. [**mono-**]
❏ **monozygotic twins** n pl twins developed from a single zygote, identical twins.

Monroe doctrine /mən-rō' dok'trin/ n the principle of non-intervention of European powers in the affairs of independent countries in the American continents. [President Monroe's message to the US Congress, December 1823]
■ **Monroeism** /mən-rō'izm/ n advocacy or support of this principle. **Monroe'ist** n.

Monseigneur /mɔ̃-sen-yœr'/ n (pl **Messeigneurs** /me-sen-yœr/) my lord; a title in France given to a person of high birth or rank, esp to bishops, etc (abbrev **Mgr**); (the title of) the Dauphin (hist). [Fr mon seigneur my lord, from L meum seniōrem (accusative) my elder]

Monsieur /mə-syø'/ n (pl **Messieurs** /mes-yø/, written **MM**; Eng /mes'ərz/, written **Messrs**) sir; a title of courtesy in France = Mr in English (printed **M** or in full); the eldest brother of the king of France (hist); (without cap) a Frenchman generally, formerly esp one of high rank. [Fr mon sieur my lord; cf **Monseigneur**]
❏ **Monsieur de Paris** n (euphem) the public executioner at the time of the French Revolution.

Monsignor /mon-sēn'yər (Ital mon-sēn-yōr')/ or **Monsignore** /-yō'rä/ n (pl **Monsignors** /-sēn'/ or **Monsigno'ri** /-rē/) a title conferred on prelates and on dignitaries of the papal household (abbrev **Monsig** or **Msgr**). [Ital from Fr]

monsoon /mon-soon'/ n a seasonal wind of the Indian Ocean, the **wet monsoon** from the SW between April and October, and the **dry monsoon** from the NE the rest of the year; a similar wind elsewhere; in N and W India, the rains accompanying the SW monsoon; an extremely heavy fall of rain, a violent storm (inf). [Port monção, from Malay mūsim, from Ar mausim a time, a season]
■ **monsoon'al** adj.
■ **break of the monsoon** the first onset of the monsoon rain.

mons pubis /monz pū'bis/ (anat) n (pl **montes pubis** /mon'tēz/) the mound of subcutaneous fatty tissue just above the genitals in humans. [L, hill of the pubis]

monster /mon'stər/ n an extraordinary, grotesque or gigantic animal, as told of in fables and folklore; an abnormally formed animal or plant; anything gigantic or abnormally large; anything of abhorrent appearance or behaviour; anything deviating from the usual course of nature; a prodigy (obs). ◆ adj gigantic, abnormally large. ◆ vt (sl) to subject to bullying or harsh criticism. [Fr monstre, from L mōnstrum an evil omen, a monster, from monēre, monitum to warn]
■ **monstrosity** /-stros'i-ti/ (obs **monstruos'ity**) n the state or fact of being monstrous; marked abnormality; an ugly or abnormally formed animal, plant, part or object; anything outrageously constructed. **mon'strous** (obs **mon'struous**) adj horrible, hideous; outrageous; preposterous; enormous, abnormally large; deviating from the usual course of nature, unnatural; miraculous (obs). ◆ adv (archaic and US) exceedingly. **mon'strously** adv. **mon'strousness** n.

monstera /mon-stē'rə/ n any plant of the Monstera genus of tropical American evergreen plants of the family Araceae, that have shining green perforated leaves and can be grown to a height of 20ft as hothouse or indoor plants, esp Monstera deliciosa (having aerial roots) and Monstera pertusa (the 'Swiss cheese plant'). [New L, perh because the leaves were thought freakish]

monstrance /mon'strəns/ n the ornamental receptacle in which the consecrated host is exposed in Roman Catholic churches for the adoration of the people. [OFr, from L mōnstrāre to show]

monstre sacré /mɔ̃-str' sa-krä'/ n a person (esp in the world of theatre or cinema) whose appeal to the public is increased by his or her eccentricity. [Fr, sacred monster]

monstrosity, monstrous, etc see under **monster**.

mons veneris /monz ven'ə-ris/ n (pl **montes veneris** /mon'tēz/) the mons pubis on the female human body. [L, hill of Venus]

Mont. abbrev: Montana (US state); Montgomeryshire (former county, now part of Powys).

montage /mon'täzh or mɔ̃-täzh'/ n (the act or process of making) a composite photograph or picture; the setting-up, assemblage or superimposition of photographic or cinematic images; a picture made partly by sticking objects on the canvas; editing of a cinema film; a style of direction in the cinema which uses frequent cutting and changes in camera position to actively create the action (cf **mise en scène**); a cinematic scene in which an extended period of time is condensed into a few minutes of film time by presenting fragments of the events occurring in that period. ◆ vt to make into, or set in, a montage. [Fr, from monter to mount]

Montagnard /mɔ̃-tä-nyär'/ n a member of the Mountain or extreme democratic wing of the French Legislative Assembly (1 October 1791 to 21 September 1792), so called because they sat on the topmost benches. [Fr, mountain-dweller]

Montagu's harrier /mon'tə-gūz har'i-ər/ n a bird of prey (Circus pygargus), with long wings and tail, native to Europe. [George Montagu (1751–1815), British naturalist]

montane /mon'tān/ adj mountainous; mountain-dwelling. [L montānus, from mōns, montis a mountain]

Montanism /mon'tə-ni-zm/ n a 2c heresy founded by the prophet and 'Paraclete' Montānus of Phrygia, an ascetic reaction in favour of the old discipline and severity.
■ **Mon'tanist** n and adj. **Montanist'ic** adj.

montant /mon'tənt/ n a vertical member in panelling or framing; (in fencing) apparently an upward blow (also, as if Sp, **montant'o**; Shakesp). [Fr, from monter to rise]

montan wax /mon'tən waks/ (chem) n a bituminous wax extracted under high temperature and pressure from lignite, used in candles and some polishes. [L montanus of a mountain]

montaria /mon-tä-rē'ə/ n (in Brazil) a light canoe made of one log. [Port]

montbretia /mon- or mont-brē'shyə/ n a plant of the Montbretia genus of S African iridaceous plants; a plant (genus Crocosmia) of the iris family bearing bright orange-coloured flowers; a plant of the genus Tritonia. [Coquebert de Montbret (1780–1801), French botanist]

mont-de-piété /mɔ̃-də-pyä-tā'/ (Fr) or **monte di pietà** /mon'tä dē pyä-tä'/ (Ital) n (pl **monts-de-piété** /mɔ̃-/ or **monti di pietà** /mon'tē/) a state pawnshop. [Fund (literally, mount) of pity or piety]

monte /mon'tä or -ti/ n a shrubby tract, a forest; a Spanish-American gambling card game. [Sp, mountain, scrub, cards remaining after a deal, from L mōns, montis a mountain]
■ **three-card monte** a Mexican three-card trick.

Monte Carlo method /mon'ti kär'lō meth'əd/ (maths) n a statistical procedure in which mathematical operations are performed on random numbers. [The casino at Monte Carlo and the various numerical systems tried there to win at roulette]

monteith /mən- or mon-tēth'/ n a large 17c or 18c bowl, usu of silver, fluted and scalloped, for cooling punch-glasses (said to be named from 'a fantastical Scot' who wore his cloak so scalloped); a cotton handkerchief with white spots on a coloured background (from Glasgow manufacturers).

montelimar /mon-tel'i-mär or mɔ̃-tā-lē-mär'/ n a type of nougat, orig made in Montélimar, SE France.

montem /mon'tem/ n a former custom of Eton boys to go every third Whit-Tuesday to a hillock on the Bath road and exact 'salt-money' from passers-by, for the university expenses of the senior scholar or school captain. [L ad montem to the hill]

Montenegrin /mon-ti-nē'grin/ n a native or inhabitant of the Yugoslav republic of Montenegro. ◆ adj of, relating to or denoting Montenegro or the Montenegrins.

Montepulciano /mon-ti-pûl-si-ä'nō or -chi-ä'nō/ n a grape variety grown esp in Italy, used to produce red wine; Montepulciano d'Abruzzo, a wine made from this grape.

Monterey Jack /mon'tə-rā jak/ n a mild cheese orig made in Monterey, California.

montero /mon-tā'rō/ n (pl monte'ros) a huntsman; a Spanish horseman's helmet-like cap with a flap (also montero-cap'). [Sp montero a huntsman, from monte, from L mōns, montis a mountain]

Montessorian /mon-te-sō'ri-ən or -sö'/ adj relating to Dr Maria Montessori or her method (c.1900) of nursery education, insisting on spontaneity and freedom from restraint.

Montezuma's revenge /mon-tə-zoo'məz ri-venj'/ (inf) n diarrhoea, esp caused by travelling in Mexico and/or eating Mexican food. [Montezuma II, 15c Mexican ruler]

montgolfier /mon-gol'fi-ər or mont-/ n a hot-air balloon. [The brothers Montgolfier, of Annonay, France, who sent up the first in 1783]

month /munth/ n one of the twelve conventional divisions of the year, or its length, a **calendar month**; such a length of time, loosely taken as four weeks or 30 days; the length of time taken by the moon to revolve once around the earth (29.53 days), a **lunar month**. [OE mōnath, from mōna moon]

■ **month'ling** n (archaic) a month-old child. **month'ly** adj performed in a month; done, recurring, or appearing once a month. ◆ n a monthly publication; a monthly rose; (pl) the menses (inf). ◆ adv once a month; in every month.

◻ **monthly nurse** n a nurse attending a woman in the first month after childbirth. **monthly rose** n a rose supposed to bloom every month. **month's mind** see under **mind**.

■ **a month of Sundays** see under **Sunday**. **anomalistic month** the interval between the moon's perigee passages = 27.5545 days. **sidereal** or **stellar month** the time in which the moon passes round the ecliptic to the same point among the stars = 27.3217 days. **solar month** one-twelfth of a solar year. **synodic month** the period of the moon's phases = 29.5306 days. **tropical** or **periodic month** the time from the moon's passing the equinox until it reaches it again = 27.3216 days.

monticellite /mon-ti-sel'īt/ n an orthorhombic calcium-magnesium silicate. [Teodoro Monticelli (1759–1845), Italian mineralogist]

monticle see **monticule**.

monticolous /mon-tik'ə-las/ adj mountain-dwelling. [L monticola a mountain-dweller, from mōns, montis mountain, and colere to inhabit]

monticule /mon'ti-kūl/ n (also **mon'ticle** or **montic'ulus**) a little elevation, hill, mound; a secondary volcanic cone. [L monticulus, dimin of mōns mountain]

■ **montic'ulate** or **montic'ulous** adj having small projections.

Montilla /mon-til'ə or -tē'yə/ n a sherry-like white wine produced in the region of Montilla in S Spain.

montmorillonite /mont-mə-ril'ə-nīt/ (mineralogy) n a hydrated silicate of aluminium, one of the important clay minerals and the chief constituent of bentonite and fuller's earth. [Montmorillon, in France]

montre /mɔ̃tr'/ n the visible pipes of an organ, usu the open diapason. [Fr, sample, show]

monture /mon'tūr or mɔ̃-tür'/ n a mounting, setting or frame. [Fr]

monty see **the full monty** under **full¹**.

monument /mon'ū-mənt/ (obs **moniment** /mon'i-/) n anything that preserves the memory of a person or an event, such as a building, pillar, tomb, tablet, statue, etc; any structure, natural or artificial, considered as an object of beauty or of interest as a relic of the past; a historic document or record (sometimes confused with **muniment**); a

stone, post, river, etc marking a boundary (US); a relic, indication or trace; a notable or enduring example; a warning token or admonition (Spenser); a prodigy (Shakesp). ◆ vt to commemorate by or on a monument. [L monumentum, monimentum, from monēre to remind]

■ **monumental** /-ment'əl/ adj, of, relating to, or of the nature of a monument, tomb, memento or token; memorial; massive and lasting; vast; impressive; amazing; very large. **monumental'ity** n. **monument'ally** adv.

mony /mun'i or mon'i/ a Scots form of **many**.

monyplies /mun'i-plīz/ see **manyplies**.

monzonite /mon'zə-nīt/ n a coarse-grained intermediate igneous rock. [Monte Monzoni in the Dolomite Mountains]

■ **monzonit'ic** adj.

moo /moo/ vi (of cattle) to low. ◆ n a cow's low. [Imit]

◻ **moo'-cow** n (childish) a cow. **moo'-juice** n (facetious) cow's milk.

moobs /moobz/ n pl (sl) man boobs (qv under **man¹**).

mooch or **mouch** /mooch/ vi to play truant (dialect); to go blackberrying (dialect); to slouch about; to skulk; to loiter, wander (about); to sponge, cadge. ◆ vt to pilfer; to beg, cadge (orig US). ◆ n the act of mooching; a scrounger (N Am). [Perh OFr muchier to hide; cf **miche**]

■ **mooch'er** or **mouch'er** n.

mood¹ /mood/ n temporary state of the emotions or of attitude; state of gloom or sullenness; atmosphere; anger, heat of temper (obs). [OE mōd mind; cf Ger Mut courage]

■ **mood'ily** adv. **mood'iness** n sullenness. **mood'y** adj (**mood'ier**; **mood'iest**) indulging in moods; sullen; angry (obs); faked, pretended (prison sl). ◆ n (usu pl, as **the moodies**, inf) a fit of being moody. ◆ n (sl) insidious, flattering talk; lies, deception. ◆ vt (sl) to persuade by flattery and cajolery.

◻ **mood'y-mad** adj (Shakesp) mad with anger.

mood² /mood/ n a form of the verb expressing the mode or manner of an action or of a state of being (grammar); the form of the syllogism as determined by the quantity and quality of its three constituent propositions (logic); (in medieval music) mode in the sense of relative time value. [**mode**]

Moog synthesizer® /mōg or moog sin'thə-sī-zər/ n an electronic musical instrument with a keyboard, that can produce a wide range of sounds. [Developed by Robert Moog (1934–2005), American engineer]

mooi /mō'i/ (S Afr) adj fine, a general word of commendation. [Afrik, from Du]

mook /mŏŏk/ n a book produced in a magazine format, esp in Japan. [magazine and book]

mooktar /mook'tär/ n same as **mukhtar**.

mool /mool/ a Scot and N Eng form of **mould³**.

moola or **moolah¹** /moo'lə/ (sl) n money. [Origin uncertain]

moolah² see **mullah¹**.

mooli /moo'li/ n a long white carrot-shaped root of Asia and E Africa, tasting similar to a radish. [Sans]

mooly see **muley**.

Moon /moon/ n a system of printing for the blind, using large, embossed characters (**Moon type**) designed to be read from left to right and right to left in alternate rows. [William Moon (1818–94), British inventor]

moon /moon/ n (often with cap) the earth's natural satellite, illuminated to varying degrees by the sun depending on its position; its appearance to an observer on earth, in respect of its degree of illumination (full moon, half moon, etc); a natural satellite of any planet; a month (literary); anything in the shape of a moon or crescent; a crescent-shaped outwork (fortif). ◆ vt to decorate with moons or crescents. ◆ vi to wander about listlessly or gaze vacantly at anything (usu with around or about); to present one's bare buttocks to public view, esp through a vehicle window (sl). [OE mōna; cf Ger Mond, L mēnsis, Gr men]

■ **mooned** adj marked with the figure of a moon. **moon'er** n a person who moons or moons about. **moon'ish** adj like the moon; variable; inconstant. **moon'less** adj without moonlight; (of a planet) having no moon. **moon'let** n a small planetary satellite, whether natural or man-made. **moon'y** adj of or relating to the moon; moon-like; crescent-shaped; bearing a crescent; round and shining; moonlit; inclined to moon, dreamy; fatuous; tipsy (sl). ◆ n a noodle.

◻ **moon'-ball** n (tennis) a high arcing shot. ◆ vi to hit such a shot. **moon'beam** n a ray of sunlight reflected from the moon. **moon'blind** adj affected with mooneye; blinded by the moon; nightblind; dim-sighted, purblind (now dialect). **moon blindness** n nyctalopia; mooneye (see below). **moon boot** n a bulky padded boot with a quilted fabric covering, for wearing in snow, reminiscent of an astronaut's boot. **moon'bow** n a rainbow cast by the moon.

moon'cake *n* a round cake with a lotus seed or sweet bean paste filling, *orig* eaten as part of the Chinese moon festival. **moon'calf** *n* a false conception or fleshy mass formed in the womb; a monster (*obs*); a deformed creature (*obs*); a dolt, fool. **moon daisy** *n* the ox-eye daisy. **moon'eye** *n* a disease affecting horses' eyes; a N American freshwater shad-like fish of the genus *Hiodon, esp H. tergisus.* **moon'-eyed** *adj* affected with mooneye, moonblind; round- or wide-eyed; drunk (*US sl*). **moon'face** *n* a full, round face. **moon'-faced** *adj.* **moon'fish** *n* the opah or other silvery disc-shaped fish. **moon flask** *n* a type of Chinese porcelain vase with a wide, circular body and a short, narrow neck. **moon'flower** *n* the ox-eye daisy; a night-blooming plant of the Convolvulaceae, *Calonyction aculeatum*, or any of several related plants. **moon gate** *n* a circular opening in a wall serving as a gateway, *esp* in Chinese architecture. **moon god** or **moon goddess** *n* a god or goddess representing or associated with the moon. **moon knife** *n* a leather-worker's crescent-shaped knife. **moon'light** *n* the light of the moon, sunlight reflected from the moon's surface; smuggled alcoholic spirit. ◆ *adj* lit by the moon; occurring in moonlight. ◆ *vi* to work outside one's normal working hours, *esp* when the income from this is not declared for tax assessment. **moon'lighter** *n* a person who moonlights; in Ireland about 1800, a person who committed violent offences against farmers and farms, in protest against the introduction of the land-tenure system (*hist*); a moonshiner. **moonlight flit** or **flitting** *n* a hasty removal by night, *esp* without paying due rent. **moon'lighting** *n.* **moon'lit** *adj* lit or illumined by the moon. **moon'-loved** *adj* (*poetic*) loved by the moon. **moon'-madness** *n* (*archaic*) lunacy, once thought to be connected with the moon's changes. **moon'phase** *n* the current phase of the moon, as indicated eg on a watch or calendar. **moon pool** *n* (*oil*) the open shaft let through the hull of a deep-sea drilling vessel to accommodate the vertical pipe-line connected to the oil-well. **moon'quake** *n* a tremor of the moon's surface. **moon'-raised** *adj* (*Walter Scott*) excited or maddened by the moon. **moon'raker** *n* a moonsail; a Wiltshireman. **moon'raking** *n* the following of crazy fancies. **moon rat** *n* a ratlike nocturnal mammal of SE Asia (*Echinosorex gymnurus*). **moon'rise** *n* the rising of the moon, or the time when this occurs. **moon'rock** *n* rock from the moon's surface; a synthetic narcotic drug combining heroin and crack (*sl*). **moon'roof** *n* a transparent roof section on a motor vehicle, *usu* opening or removable, a sunroof. **moon'sail** *n* a small sail, sometimes carried above the sky-scraper. **moon'scape** *n* the physical appearance of the surface of the moon, or a representation of it; a desolate landscape resembling this (*fig*). **moon'seed** *n* a plant (genus *Menispermum*) with lunate seeds. **moon'set** *n* the setting of the moon, or the time when this occurs. **moon'shine** *n* moonlight; show without reality (*fig*); nonsense (*inf*); a month (*Shakesp*); spirits illicitly distilled or smuggled (chiefly *N Am*). ◆ *adj* lit by the moon; made of moonlight, bodiless (*fig*). **moon'shiner** *n* (chiefly *N Am*) a smuggler or illicit distiller of spirits. **moon'shiny** *adj* lit by the moon; visionary, unreal. **moon'shot** *n* an act, or the process, of launching an object or vehicle to orbit, or land on, the moon. **moon'stone** *n* an opalescent orthoclase feldspar, *perh* sometimes selenite (its appearance once thought to change with the waxing and waning of the moon). **moon'strike** *n* the act or process of landing a spacecraft on the surface of the moon. **moon'struck** *adj* (also **moon'-stricken**) behaving as if mentally affected by the moon, lunatic, crazed. **moon'walk** *n* an astronaut's walk on the surface of the moon; a style of dancing resembling weightless movement. ◆ *vi* to perform a moonwalk. **moon'walker** *n.* **moon'wort** *n* a eusporangiate fern (*Botrychium lunaria*) with lunate pinnae; any other plant of the genus *Botrychium*; the plant honesty (from its silvery septum). ■ **eggs in moonshine** an old dish, fried eggs with onions and various flavourings. **many moons ago** (*inf*) a very long time ago. **over the moon** (*inf*) delighted.

moong bean same as **mung bean**.

Moonie /moo'ni/ (*inf, often derog*) *n* (pl **Moon'ies**) a member of the Unification Church, a sect founded in 1954 by Sun Myung Moon.

moonshee see **munshi**.

moop see **moup**.

Moor /moor or mör/ *n* a member of the mixed Arab and Berber people of Morocco and the Barbary coast; one of the Arab and Berber conquerors and occupants of Spain from 711 to 1492; a Mauretanian; formerly in India, a Muslim; a black person (*old*). [Fr *More, Maure*, from L *Maurus*, doubtfully connected with Byzantine Gr *mauros* black] ■ **Moor'ery** *n* a Moorish quarter. **Moor'ess** *n* a female Moor. **Moor'ish** *adj.* ❑ **Moorish Idol** *n* a tropical marine fish (*Zanclus canescens*).

moor¹ /moor/ or (*Scot*) **muir** /mür, mär or mūr/ *n* a wide expanse of uncultivated ground, *esp* upland, often covered with heath, and having a poor, peaty soil; a heath. [OE *mōr*]

■ **moor'ish** or **moor'y** *adj* resembling a moor; sterile; marshy; boggy. ❑ **moor'-band** *n* a hard ferruginous layer formed under moorland soil (also **moor'-band pan** or **moor'-pan**). **moor'burn** or **muir'burn** *n* (*Scot*) the seasonal burning of heather, etc on moorland to promote new growth. **moor'buzzard** *n* the marsh-harrier. **moor'cock** or **moor'fowl** *n* red, or black, grouse. **moor grass** *n* any of a variety of grasses found in moorland areas. **moor'hen** *n* the waterhen; a female moorfowl. **moor'ill** *n* (*Scot*) a cattle disease of moorland districts, marked by haemoglobin in the urine. **moor'land** *n* a tract of moor; moorish country. ◆ *adj* of moorland. **moor'log** *n* a deposit of decayed woody material under a marsh, etc. **moor'man** *n* an inhabitant of a moor. **moor'-pout** or (*Scot*) **muir'-pout** /-powt/, **moor'-poot** or (*Scot*) **muir'-poot** /-poot/ *n* a young grouse.

moor² /moor/ *vt* to fasten (a ship or boat) by cable or anchor. ◆ *vi* to make fast a ship, boat, etc; to be made fast. [Prob from an unrecorded OE word answering to MDu *mâren*] ■ **moor'age** *n* condition of being moored; act of mooring; a fee paid for mooring; a place for mooring. **moor'ing** *n* act of mooring; that which serves to moor or confine a ship; (in *pl*) the place or condition of a ship so moored; anything providing security or stability. ❑ **mooring mast** *n.*

Moore's law see under **law¹**.

moorva see **murva**.

moose /moos/ *n* (pl **moose**) the American elk; a member of an American secret fraternity, the Loyal Order of Moose. [Algonquian *mus, moos*] ❑ **moose'yard** *n* an area where the moose tread down the snow and spend the winter.

moot /moot/ *n orig* a meeting; a deliberative or administrative assembly or court (*hist*); its meeting-place; discussion; a law student's discussion of a hypothetical case. ◆ *vt* to argue, dispute; to propose for discussion. ◆ *vi* to dispute, plead. ◆ *adj* debatable. [OE (*ge*)*mōt* (noun), *mōtian* (verb), related to *mētan* to meet] ■ **moot'able** *adj.* **moot'er** *n.* **moot'ing** *n.* ❑ **moot case** *n* a case for discussion; a case about which there may be difference of opinion. **moot court** *n* a meeting for discussion of hypothetical cases, *esp* a mock court. **moot hall** or **moot house** *n* a town hall or council chamber; a hall for moot courts. **moot'-hill** *n* a hill used for meetings on which the moot was held (often confused with **mote-hill** (see under **motte²**)). **moot'man** *n* a law student who argues in moots. **moot point** *n* an undecided or disputed point.

moove an old spelling of **move**.

mop¹ /mop/ *n* a bunch of rags or lengths of yarn, or a piece of sponge on the end of a stick or pole, used for washing, removing dust, soaking up liquid, etc; any similar instrument, such as one for cleansing a wound, polishing, etc; a thick or bushy head of hair; an act of mopping; a hiring fair (*prob* from the custom of carrying a badge of occupation; *dialect*). ◆ *vt* (**mopp'ing**; **mopped**) to wipe, dab, soak up, or remove with, or as if with, a mop; to clear away or dispose of as residue. [Poss from OFr *mappe*, from L *mappa* a napkin; or poss from the name *Mabel*] ■ **mopp'er** *n.* **mopp'y** *adj* (*old sl*) drunk. **mop'sy** *n* a dowdy; a slattern; a term of endearment (*obs*). ❑ **mop'board** *n* (*US*) skirting-board. **mop'head** *n* (a person with) a shaggy unkempt head of hair. **mop-head'ed** *adj* having a shaggy, unkempt head of hair. **mop'stick** *n* the handle of a mop; a hand-rail nearly circular in section; (also **map'stick**) a rod for raising a piano damper. **mop'-up** *n* an action of mopping up. ■ **mops and brooms** half-drunk; out of sorts. **mop up** to clear away or clean up with a mop; to clear away, dispose of; to absorb (eg surplus credit); to capture or kill (enemy stragglers) after a victory, etc. **Mrs Mop** or **Mopp** a cleaner, charwoman.

mop² /mop/ *n* a grimace. ◆ *vi* to grimace, *esp* in the phrase *mop and mow*. [Cf Du *moppen* to pout]

mopane or **mopani** /mo-pä'ni/ *n* a small S African tree of the Leguminosae, growing in areas of low rainfall, with rough bark and racemes of small green flowers. [Tswana]

mope /mōp/ *vi* to move aimlessly and listlessly; to be listless or depressed. ◆ *vt* (*archaic*) to make spiritless or listless. ◆ *n* a listless or depressed person; (*esp* in *pl*) moping, low spirits. [Origin obscure] ■ **mop'er** *n.* **mop'ery** *n* low spirits; a minor or imagined violation of the law (*US sl*). **mop'ey** or **mop'y** *adj.* **mop'ingly** *adv.* **mop'ish** *adj* dull; spiritless, listless. **mop'ishly** or **mop'ily** *adv.* **mop'ishness** or **mop'iness** *n.* **mop'us** *n* (now *dialect*) a person who mopes.

moped /mō'ped/ *n* a lightweight motorcycle, *usu* with a two-stroke 50cc engine. [*motor-assisted ped*al cycle]

mopey see under **mope**.

mopoke /mō'pōk/ *n* (also **mope'hawk** or **more'pork**) the owl, *Ninox novaeseelandiae*, of Australia and New Zealand; the tawny frogmouth

---

■ words derived from main entry word; ❑ compound words; ■ idioms and phrasal verbs

(to which the owl's call is wrongly attributed; *Aust*); a dull-witted or boring person (*Aust sl*). [Imit of the cry of the owl]

Mopp see **Mrs Mop** under **mop**[1].

mopper, etc see under **mop**[1].

moppet /*mop'it*/ *n* (a term of endearment for) a little girl or child; a doll-like woman; a rag doll (*archaic*); a small woolly breed of dog (*rare*). [Dimin of **mop**[1]]

mopus[1] /*mop'əs*/ or **mawpus** /*mö'pəs*/ (*old sl*) *n* a small coin.

mopus[2] see under **mope**.

mopy see under **mope**.

moquette /*mō-ket'*/ *n* a carpet and soft-furnishing material with a loose velvety pile, the back made of thick canvas, etc. [Fr]

MOR *abbrev* : middle-of-the-road (music), *esp* in broadcasting.

Mor. *abbrev* : Morocco.

mor[1] /*mör* or *mōr*/ *n* a layer of humus formed by slow decomposition in acid conditions (cf **moder**, **mull**[4]). [Dan]

mor[2] see **mauther**.

mora[1] /*mō'rə* or *mö'*/ *n* delay, *esp* unjustifiable (*law*); the duration of a short syllable or half that of a long (*prosody*). [L, delay]

mora[2] or **morra** /*mor'ə*/ *n* the game of guessing how many fingers are held up. [Ital *mora*]

moraceous see under **Morus**.

moraine /*mo-rān'*/ *n* a ridgelike mass of earth, rock and stones at one time carried and finally deposited by a glacier; a garden imitation of this. [Fr]
■ **morain'al** or **morain'ic** *adj*.

moral /*mor'əl*/ *adj* of or relating to character or conduct considered as good or evil; ethical; adhering to or directed towards what is right; virtuous, *esp* in matters of sex; capable of knowing right and wrong; subject to moral law; having an effect on the mind or will; supported by evidence of reason or probability, *opp* to *demonstrative* ; (eg of a victory) real or effective, if not apparent; moralizing (*Shakesp*). ♦ *n* (in *pl*) writings on ethics; the doctrine or practice of the duties of life; moral philosophy or ethics; principles and conduct, *esp* sexual; (in *sing*) the practical lesson that can be drawn from anything; an exposition of such lesson by way of conclusion; a symbol (*Shakesp*); morality (in this sense sometimes pronounced /*mor-äl'*/ after Ger *Moral* or Fr *morale*); /*mor-äl'*/ confidence, morale (now *rare*); a certainty (*sl*, now *esp Aust*); an exact counterpart (*archaic sl*). ♦ *vt* and *vi* (*archaic*) to moralize. [L *mōrālis*, from *mōs*, *mōris* manner, custom, (*esp* in *pl*) morals]
■ **mor'alism** *n* a moral maxim; moral counsel; morality as distinct from religion. **mor'alist** *n* a person who teaches morals, or who practises moral duties; a moral as distinguished from a religious man; someone who takes pride in his or her morality. **moralist'ic** *adj*. **moralist'ically** *adv*. **morality** /*mor-al'i-ti*/ *n* the quality of being moral; that which renders an action right or wrong; the practice of moral duties apart from religion; virtue; the doctrine of actions as right or wrong; ethics; a medieval allegorical drama in which virtues and vices appear as characters (also **morality play**). **moralizā'tion** or **-s-** *n* act of moralizing, explanation in a moral sense. **mor'alize** or **-ise** *vt* to apply to a moral purpose; to explain in a moral sense; to make moral. ♦ *vi* to speak or write on moral subjects; to make moral reflections or pronouncements, or speak in an admonitory tone about moral standards. **mor'alizer** or **-s-** *n*. **mor'aller** *n* (*Shakesp*) a moralist. **mor'ally** *adv* in a moral manner; in respect of morals; to all intents and purposes, practically.
❑ **moral agent** *n* a person who acts under a knowledge of right and wrong. **moral certainty** *n* a likelihood great enough to be acted on, although not capable of being certainly proved. **moral courage** *n* the power to face disapprobation and ridicule. **moral defeat** *n* a success so qualified as to count as a defeat, or to point towards defeat. **moral faculty** *n* moral sense. **moral hazard** *n* (*econ*) the risk that people will behave imprudently when they will not be penalized for failure. **moral imagination** *n* (*esp US*) in business ethics, the ability to create new solutions to ethical problems. **moral law** *n* a law or rules for life and conduct, founded on what is right and wrong; the law of conscience; that part of the Old Testament which relates to moral principles, *esp* the ten commandments. **moral majority** *n* the majority of a society that is presumed to favour a strict moral code. **moral philosophy** *n* ethics. **Moral Rearmament** *n* a movement succeeding the Oxford Group in 1938, advocating absolute private and public morality (*abbrev* **MRA**). **moral rights** *n pl* rights that the creator of a published work has in relation to the work (since 1988 legally enforceable). **moral sense** *n* that power of the mind which knows or judges actions to be right or wrong, and determines conduct accordingly; tropological interpretation of eg the Bible, seeking to establish some secondary meaning. **moral support** *n* encouragement shown by approval rather than by active help. **moral theology** *n*

ethics treated with reference to a divine source. **moral victory** *n* a defeat in appearance, but in some important sense a real victory.

morale /*mor-äl'*/ *n* condition or degree of confidence, optimism, strength of purpose, etc, in a person or group; morality (*archaic*). [Fr, fem of *moral* moral; in later sense modification of **moral** to suggest Fr form and pronunciation]
❑ **morale'-booster** *n* a person, activity, etc which increases one's morale.

morality...to...**moralizer** see under **moral**.

morall *n* a word used in Shakespeare's *Midsummer Night's Dream* (V.1.205), emended by editors to **mural**, but possibly a misprint for **wall**.

moraller and **morally** see under **moral**.

morals see **meril**.

morass /*mə-ras'*/ *n* an area of soft, wet ground; a marsh; a dangerous or confused situation (*fig*). [Du *moeras*, from OFr *maresc*, influenced by Du *moer* moor]
■ **morass'y** *adj*.
❑ **morass ore** *n* bog-iron ore.

morat /*mö'rət*/ *n* a drink made of honey and mulberry juice. [LL *mōrātum*, from *mōrum* mulberry]

moratorium /*mo-rə-tö'ri-əm* or *-tö'*/ *n* (*pl* **morator'ia** or **morator'iums**) an emergency measure authorizing the suspension of payments of debts for a given time; the period thus declared; a temporary ban on, or decreed cessation of, any activity. [Neuter of LL *mōrātōrius*, adj from *mora* delay]
■ **moratory** /*mor'ə-tə-ri*/ *adj* delaying; deferring.

Moravian[1] /*mə-rā'vi-ən*/ *adj* of or relating to *Moravia*, part of the Czech Republic, or to its inhabitants. ♦ *n* a native or inhabitant of Moravia; a Czech dialect spoken in Moravia; a member of the *Unitas Fratrum* or *United Brethren*, a small body of Protestants of extraordinary missionary energy, founded in the 15c. [L *Moravia* Moravia, from *Morava* the river March]
■ **Morā'vianism** *n*.

Moravian[2] /*mo-* or *mə-rā'vi-ən*/ *adj* of the old province or the modern district of *Moray* in NE Scotland. ♦ *n* a native or inhabitant of Moray. [LL *Moravia*, from Gaelic *Muireibh* Moray]

moray, or (formerly) **murray**, **murrey** or **murry** /*mö'rā*, *mō-rā'*, *mur'i* or *mu-rā'*/ *n* any of several mainly tropical eels of the family Muraenidae (also **moray eel**). [Port *moreia*, from L *mūraena*, from Gr (*s*)*mȳraina*, fem of (*s*)*mȳros* eel]

morbid /*mör'bid*/ *adj* inclined to dwell on unwholesome or horrible thoughts; unwholesome; relating to, or of the nature of, disease (*med*); sickly. [L *morbidus*, from *morbus* disease]
■ **morbid'ity** *n* unwholesomeness; sickliness; ratio of incidence of an illness (*med*). **mor'bidly** *adv*. **mor'bidness** *n*.
❑ **morbid anatomy** *n* the science or study of diseased organs and tissues.

morbidezza /*mör-bi-det'sə*/ *n* the delicate or sensual rendering of flesh-tints in painting; delicacy, softness (*esp music*). [Ital]

morbiferous and **morbific** see under **morbus**.

morbilli /*mör-bil'ī*/ (*med*) *n pl* measles. [LL dimin of L *morbus* disease]
■ **morbill'iform** *adj*. **morbill'ivī'rus** *n* a virus, different species of which are responsible for human measles, canine distemper, diseases specific to seals and goats, etc. **morbill'ous** *adj*.

morbus /*mör'bəs*/ (*L*) *n* disease (used in phrases). [L]
■ **morbif'erous** *adj* disease-bringing. **morbi'fic** *adj* disease-causing.
❑ **morbus gallicus** *n* literally, the French disease, ie syphilis.

morceau /*mör'sō*/ *n* (*pl* **mor'ceaux** /*-sō*/) a morsel; a fragment; a piece of music; a short literary composition. [Fr; see **morsel**]
❑ **morceau de salon** /*də sä-lõ*/ *n* (*music*) a drawing-room piece.

morcha /*mör'chə*/ *n* in India, an organized hostile rally or demonstration. [Hindi, entrenchment]

mordacious /*mör-dā'shəs*/ *adj* given to biting; biting in quality (*lit* or *fig*). [L *mordēre* to bite]
■ **mordā'ciously** *adv*. **mordacity** /*-das'i-ti*/ *n*. **mordancy** /*mör'dən-si*/ *n*. **mor'dant** *adj* biting; incisive; serving to fix dyes, paints or gold-leaf. ♦ *n* a corroding substance; any substance that combines with and fixes a dyestuff in material that cannot be dyed directly; a substance used to cause paint or gold-leaf to adhere to a surface. ♦ *vt* to treat with a mordant. **mor'dantly** *adv*.

mordent /*mör'dənt*/ (*music*) *n* a grace note in which the principal note is preceded in performance by itself and the note below (**lower mordent**) or itself and the note above (**upper** or **inverted mordent**); the character indicating it; sometimes extended to other graces. [Ger, from Ital *mordente*]

Mordvin /mörd'vin/ n (pl **Mordvin** or **Mordvins**) a native or inhabitant of the Russian region of *Mordvinia*; the Finno-Ugric language spoken there. ◆ *adj* of or relating to the Mordvin or their language.

more[1] /mör/ *adj* (superl **most** /mōst/) (serving as *compar* of **many** and **much**) in greater number or quantity; greater in size or importance (now *rare*); additional; other besides. ◆ *adv* (superl **most** /mōst/) to a greater degree; rather; again; longer; further; moreover. ◆ *n* a greater thing; something further or in addition. [OE *māra* greater; as an adv **more** has superseded **mo**[1]]
 ■ **mo'rish** or **more'ish** *adj* (*inf*) such that one wants more.
 ■ **any more** anything additional; further. **more and more** continually increasing. **more by token** (*dialect*) in proof of this, besides. **more or less** about; roughly; in round numbers. **no more** nothing in addition; never again; no longer in existence; dead.

more[2] /mör or mör/ n a root; a stump; a plant (*Spenser*). [OE *moru*, *more* carrot, parsnip; Ger *Möhre*]

more[3] /mō'rē, mō'rē or mō're/ (L) *adv* in the manner.
 ■ **more majorum** /ma-jōr'am, -jör'am or mă-yör'ŭm/ after the manner of our or their ancestors. **more suo** /sū' or soo'ō/ in his or her own way, in characteristic fashion.

moreen /mo-rēn'/ n a stout corded fabric, woollen, cotton, or both, often watered. [Poss connected with **moire**]

moreish see under **more**[1].

morel[1] /mo-rel'/ n any edible discomycete fungus of the genus *Morchella*. [Fr *morille*; cf OHGer *morhila* (Ger *Morchel*) a mushroom; **more**[2]]

morel[2] /mo-rel'/ n a nightshade, *esp* black nightshade; (also /mor'al/) a dark-coloured horse (*obs*). ◆ *adj* blackish. [LL *morellus* blackish, perh from L *mōrum* a mulberry, perh Late Gr *mauros* black]

morel[3] see **morello**.

morello /ma-rel'ō/ or **morel** /mo-rel', mor'al/ n (pl **morel'os**) a dark-red cherry, much used in cooking and for cherry brandy (also **morello cherry**). [Poss from Ital *morello* dark-coloured (see **morel**[2]); poss from Flem *marelle*, from Ital *amarella*, a dimin from L *amārus* bitter]

morendo /mo-ren'dō/ (*music*) *adj* and *adv* dying away, in speed and tone. [Ital, dying]

moreover /mör-ō'var/ *adv* more over or beyond what has been said; further; besides; also. [**more**[1] and **over**]

morepork see **mopoke**.

mores /mō', mö'rēz or mö'rās/ n pl customs, manners. [L *mōs*, *mōris* custom]

Moresco /mo-res'kō/ n (pl **Mores'coes**) a Moorish dance or morris dance (Ital *Moresca*); a Moor or Morisco. ◆ *adj* Moorish. [Ital, Moorish]

Moresque /mo-resk'/ *adj* (*esp* of architecture, design, etc) in the Moorish manner. ◆ *n* an arabesque. [Fr, from Ital *Moresco*]

Moreton Bay /mör'tan bā/ n the first settlement in Queensland.
 □ **Moreton Bay chestnut** n an Australian papilionaceous tree (*Castanospermum australe*); its chestnut-like seed. **Moreton Bay fig** n an Australian fig tree (*Ficus macrophilla*).

Morgan /mör'gan/ n any horse of an American breed developed in Vermont by Justin *Morgan* in the late 18c, light and sturdy for farm work, but also bred for trotting races.

morganatic /mör-ga-nat'ik/ *adj* of or relating to a marriage between people of unequal rank (latterly only where one is of a reigning or mediatized house), the marriage being valid, the children legitimate, but unable to inherit the higher rank, the lower-born spouse not being granted the other's title. [LL *morganātica*, a gift from a bridegroom to his bride; cf Ger *Morgengabe*, OE *morgengifu* a morning gift]
 ■ **morganat'ically** *adv*.

morganite /mör'ga-nīt/ (*mineralogy*) n a pink or rose-coloured variety of beryl, obtained chiefly from California and Madagascar, used as a gemstone. [J Pierpont *Morgan* (1837–1913), US financier]

morgay /mör'gā/ n the small spotted dogfish or bounce. [Cornish and Welsh *morgi*, from mör sea, and *ci* dog]

morgen /mör'gan/ n a unit of land-measurement (in the Netherlands, South Africa, and parts of the USA, a little over two acres; formerly in Norway, Denmark and Prussia, about two-thirds of an acre). [Du and Ger; perh *morgen* morning, hence a morning's ploughing]

morgenstern /mör'gan-stûrn/ or -shtern/ n a morning star (weapon). [Ger]

Morglay /mör'glā/ n the name of the sword wielded by Sir Bevis of Hampton in a medieval English romance; hence, a sword. [Cf **claymore**]

morgue[1] /mörg/ n a place where dead bodies are laid out for identification, or kept prior to burial or cremation; a gloomy or depressing place (*fig*); a place, as in a newspaper office, where miscellaneous material for reference is kept. [Fr]

morgue[2] /mörg/ n haughtiness, arrogance. [Fr]

MORI /mor'i/ *abbrev* : Market & Opinion Research International.

moria /mö'ri-a/ n folly. [Gr *mōriā*]

moribund /mor'i-bund/ *adj* about to die; in a stagnant or dying state. [L *moribundus*, from *morī* to die]
 ■ **moribund'ity** n.

moriche /mo-rē'chā/ n the miriti palm. [Carib]

Moringa /mo-ring'ga/ n the horse-radish tree genus, constituting a family **Moringā'ceae**, apparently linking the poppies with the Leguminosae. [Perh Sinhalese *murungā*]

morion[1] or **morrion** /mö'ri-an or mor'i-/ (*hist*) n an open helmet, without visor or beaver (also **murr'en**, **murr'ion** or (*Spenser*) **murr'in**). [Fr, prob from Sp *morrión*, from *morra* crown of the head]

morion[2] /mor'i-an/ n black quartz, used as a gemstone. [Fr]

Morisco /mo-ris'kō/ n (pl **Moris'cos** or **Moris'coes**) a Moor, *esp* a Christianized Moor in Spain after the fall of Granada in 1492; the Moorish language (*obs*); (without *cap*) a morris dance or dancer; an arabesque. ◆ *adj* Moorish. [Sp, from *Moro* Moor, from L *Maurus*; cf **Moor**]
 ■ **Morisk'** n and *adj* (*obs*).

morish see under **more**[1].

Morisonian /mo-ri-sō'ni-an/ n a member of the Evangelical Union, formed in 1843 by the Rev James *Morison* (1816–93), after his separation from the United Secession Church, incorporated with the Congregational Union of Scotland in 1896.
 ■ **Morisō'nianism** n.

morkin /mör'kin/ n an animal that has died by accident. [Anglo-Fr *mortekine*, from L *morticīna* (fem adj) carrion, from *mors* death]
 ■ **mor'ling** or **mort'ling** n a sheep that has died as a result of disease; its wool.

mormaor /mör-mā'ar/ (*hist*) n a high-ranking or chief steward. [Gaelic *mormaer*, now *mòrmhaor*, from *mòr* great, and *maor* steward]

Mormon /mör'man/ n a member of a religious sect with headquarters since 1847 in Salt Lake City, Utah, polygamous until 1890, calling itself *The Church of Jesus Christ of Latter-day Saints*, founded in 1830 by Joseph Smith, whose *Book of Mormon* was given out as translated from the golden plates of *Mormon*, a prophet. ◆ *adj* of the Mormons.
 ■ **Mor'monism** n. **Mor'monite** n.

Mormops /mör'mops/ n a genus of repulsive-looking American leaf-nosed bats. [Gr *mormō* a bugbear, and *ōps* face]

morn /mörn/ (*poetic* and *dialect*) n the first part of the day; morning. [ME *morwen*, from OE *morgen*; Ger *Morgen*]
 ■ **the morn** (*Scot*) tomorrow. **the morn's morn** or **morning** (*Scot*) tomorrow morning. **the morn's nicht** (*Scot*) tomorrow night.

mornay /mör'nā/ or **mornay sauce** /sös/ n a cream sauce with cheese flavouring. ◆ *adj* (placed after the name of a food) served with this sauce. [Origin uncertain; perh Philippe de *Mornay* (1549–1623), French Huguenot leader]

morne[1] /mörn/ n the blunt head of a jousting-lance. [Fr *morner* (pap *morné*) to blunt]
 ■ **morné** /mör-nā'/ *adj* (of a lion rampant) without teeth or claws. **morned** *adj* (*heraldry*) blunted.

morne[2] /mörn/ (*archaic*) *adj* dismal, gloomy, sombre. [Fr]

morning /mör'ning/ n the first part of the day, *usu* regarded as the period from dawn to noon or the midday-meal; dawn, sunrise; the early part of anything; an early dram (chiefly *Scot*); a light meal before recognized breakfast (*dialect*). ◆ *adj* of the morning; taking place or being in the morning. [Contraction of ME *morwening*; cf **morn**]
 ■ **morn'ings** *adv* (*inf* or *dialect*) in the morning.
 □ **morning-af'ter pill** n a contraceptive pill taken within a specified time after intercourse. **morning coat** n a cutaway coat worn as part of morning dress. **morning dress** n the style of dress conventionally appropriate for men to wear to formal social functions in the early part of the day, including morning coat, striped trousers and usually a top hat (cf **evening dress**). **morning gift** n a gift made by the husband to the wife on the morning after marriage. **morning glory** n a plant of the genus *Ipomoea* (*esp Ipomoea purpurea*) or *Convolvulus*, with showy flowers of various colours; a racehorse which runs faster in morning training than in the actual race (*sl*). **morning gown** n a gown for wearing in the morning. **morn'ing-land** n the east. **morning prayer** n prayer in the morning; lauds (*RC*); matins (*C of E*). **morning room** n a sitting room for use in the morning. **morning sickness** n nausea and vomiting in the morning, experienced during the early stages of pregnancy. **morning star** n a planet, *esp* Venus, when it rises before the sun; a precursor; a medieval weapon, a spiky ball attached directly or by a chain to a handle. **morn'ingtide** n the morning time; early part. **morning watch** n the watch between 4am and 8am.
 ■ **the morning after** (*inf*) the unpleasant after-effects of a night of excessive drinking, etc.

■ words derived from main entry word; □ compound words; ■ idioms and phrasal verbs

Moro /mō'rō/ n (pl **Moro** or **Moros**) a member of any of the tribes of Muslim Malays in the Philippine Islands. [Sp, literally, Moor, from L *Maurus*]

Moroccan /mə-rok'ən/ adj of or relating to *Morocco* in N Africa or its inhabitants. ◆ n a native or inhabitant of Morocco.

morocco /mə-rok'ō/ n (pl **morocc'os**) a fine goatskin leather tanned with sumac, first brought from *Morocco* (also **morocco leather**); a sheepskin leather imitation of it; a very strong ale, anciently brewed in Westmorland. ◆ adj consisting of morocco.
■ **French morocco** an inferior kind of Levant morocco, with small grain. **Levant morocco** a fine quality of morocco, with large grain. **Persian morocco** a morocco finished on the grain side.

moron /mō'ron/ n a somewhat feeble-minded person; a former category of mental impairment, describing a person with an IQ of 50–69, ie one who remains throughout life at the mental age of eight to twelve. [Gr *mōros* foolish]
■ **moron'ic** adj. **moron'ically** adv.

morose /mə-rōs'/ adj sour-tempered, *esp* when habitually so; gloomy, sullen; severe. [L *mōrōsus* peevish, from *mōs*, *mōris* manner]
■ **morose'ly** adv. **morose'ness** n. **morosity** /-os'i-ti/ n (obs).

morph¹ /mörf/ n a variant form of an animal, etc (zool, etc); a shape, image or expression produced by morphing (comput, cinematog, TV). ◆ vt (comput, cinematog, TV) to transform or animate (a shape, image, etc) by using computer graphics. ◆ vi to change into something else by the use of computer graphics (comput, cinematog, TV); to change seamlessly (inf). [Gr *morphē* form]
■ **morph'ing** n (comput, cinematog, TV).

morph² see under **morphic**.

-morph /-mörf/, **morph-** /mörf-/ or **morpho-** /mör-fō-/ combining form denoting (something) of a specified form, shape or structure. [Gr *morphē* form]
■ **-morphic** adj combining form. **-morphism** n combining form. **-morphy** n combining form.

morphallaxis, **morpheme**, etc see under **morphic**.

Morpheus /mör'fūs, -fyəs or -fi-əs/ n the Greek god of dreams, son of Hypnos (sleep). [Gr *Morpheus*, literally, moulder, shaper, from *morphē* shape]
■ **morphē'an** (also /mör'/) or **morphet'ic** adj (irregularly formed).

morphew /mör'fū/ n a skin eruption. [Ital *morfea*]

morphia see **morphine**.

morphic /mör'fik/ adj relating to form, morphological. [Gr *morphē* form]
■ **morph** n (back-formation from **morpheme**; *linguistics*) the whole or a part of a spoken or written word corresponding to or representing one or more morphemes. **morphallax'is** n (pl **morphallax'es** /-ēz/) (Gr *allaxis* change) regeneration in a changed form. **morpheme** /mör'fēm/ n a simple linguistic unit that has meaning, and cannot be divided into smaller units. **morphēm'ic** adj. **morphēm'ically** adv. **morphēm'ics** n sing the study of morphemes. **morphogenesis** /-fə-jen'i-sis/ n the origin and development of a part, organ or organism. **morphogenet'ic** or **morphogen'ic** adj. **morphogeny** /-foj'i-ni/ n morphogenesis. **morphographer** /-fog'rə-fər/ n. **morphog'raphy** n descriptive morphology. **morphophōn'ēme** n (either or any of) two or more phonemes which form variant morphs representing one morpheme (as in wife, wives). **morphophonēm'ic** adj. **morphophonēm'ics** n sing. **morphō'sis** n morphogenesis. **morphot'ic** adj relating to morphosis. **morphotrop'ic** adj. **morphot'ropy** n (chem) the effect on crystalline form of the addition or substitution of an element or radical.

morphine /mör'fēn/ or **morphia** /mör'fi-ə/ n the principal alkaloid in opium, a hypnotic drug used extensively for pain-relief. [Gr *Morpheus* god of dreams]
■ **mor'phinism** n the effect of morphine on the system; the habit of taking morphine. **morphinomā'nia** n habitual craving for morphine. **morphinomā'niac** n.

morpho /mör'fō/ n (pl **morph'os**) a butterfly of the tropical American genus *Morpho*, of gigantic size and brilliant colouring, often bright blue. [Gr *Morphō*, a name of Aphrodite]

morpho- see **-morph**.

morphogenesis, etc, **morphographer**, etc see under **morphic**.

morpholine /mör'fə-lēn/ n an organic compound, C_4H_9NO, formerly used to coat fruit. [Ger *Morpholin*, from *Morphin* morphine]

morphology /mör-fol'ə-ji/ n the science of the development of shape or form, *esp* that of the outer form, inner structure, and development of living organisms and their parts; the science of the external forms of rocks and land-features; the study of the forms of words. [Gr *morphē* form, and *logos* word]
■ **morpholog'ic** or **morpholog'ical** adj. **morpholog'ically** adv. **morphol'ogist** n.

morphophoneme, etc see under **morphic**.

morra see **mora²**.

morrhua /mor'oo-ə/ n an old generic, now specific, name of the cod (*Gadus morrhua*). [LL *morua*]

morrice an obsolete form of **morris¹**.

morrion see **morion¹**.

morris¹ or (obs) **morrice** /mor'is/ n a morris dance (qv); a tune for such a dance. ◆ vi to perform such a dance. [**Moorish**]
❑ **morr'is-pike** n (Shakesp) a Moorish pike.

morris² see **meril**.

Morris chair /mor'is chār/ n a kind of armchair with an adjustable, reclining back and removable cushions. [William *Morris* (1834–96), English designer and architect]

morris dance /mor'is däns/ n a type of English folk dance, *perh* of Moorish origin, which came to be associated with May games, with (latterly) Maid Marian, Robin Hood, the hobby-horse, and other characters, who had bells attached to their clothes (also **morr'is** or **morr'ice**). [See **morris¹**]
■ **morris dancer** n. **morris dancing** n.

Morrison shelter /mor'i-sən shel'tər/ n a kind of portable, steel air-raid shelter for indoor use, developed during World War II. [Herbert S *Morrison*, Home Secretary 1940–5, who recommended their use]

Morris-tube /mor'is-tūb/ n a small-bore rifle-barrel inserted in the breech of a larger, for short-range practice. [R *Morris* (died 1891), the inventor]

morro /mor'ō/ n (pl **morr'os**) a rounded hill or headland. [Sp]

morrow /mor'ō/ (archaic or poetic) n the day following the present; tomorrow; the next following day; the time immediately after any event. [ME *morwe* for *morwen*; cf **morn**]

morsal see under **morsure**.

Morse /mörs/ n (a method of) signalling by a code in which each letter is represented by a combination of dashes and dots or long and short light-flashes, sound signals, etc, invented by Samuel FB *Morse* (1791–1872). ◆ adj of or relating to this signalling code.

morse¹ /mörs/ n the walrus. [Lappish *morsa*, or Finn *mursu*]

morse² /mörs/ n the fastening of a cope. [L *morsus* a bite, catch]

morsel /mör'səl/ n a bite or mouthful; a small piece of food; a choice piece of food, a dainty; a small piece of anything; a small person. ◆ vt to divide into morsels; to apportion in small amounts. [OFr *morsel* (Fr *morceau*, Ital *morsello*), dimin from L *morsus*, from *mordēre*, *morsum* to bite]

morsing-horn /mör'sing-hörn/ n the small horn that used to hold the fine powder for priming. [Fr *amorcer* to prime (a gun)]

morsure /mör'sūr/ n a bite. [L *morsus* bite]
■ **mors'al** adj.

mort¹ /mört/ n death (obs); a flourish sounded at the death of a buck, etc in hunting; a sheep that has died a natural death (cf **morling** or **mortling** under **morkin**); a dead body. [Fr *mort* death, dead]
❑ **mort'bell** n a funeral bell. **mort'cloth** n a pall. **mort'-head** n a death's-head. **mort'-safe** n (hist) a heavy grating used to guard a corpse against resurrectionists. **mort'-stone** n a wayside stone on which the bearers lay the bier for a rest.

mort² /mört/ (dialect) n a great deal. [Origin obscure]

mort³ /mört/ (sl) n a woman; a loose woman. [Origin obscure]

mort⁴ /mört/ n a salmon, three years old. [Origin obscure]

mortadella /mör-tə-del'ə/ n (pl **mortadelle** /del'i/) Italian pork sausage, flavoured with myrtle, spices, etc. [Ital, poss from Latin *murtus* myrtle]

mortal /mör'tl/ adj liable to death, certain to die at some future time; causing death; deadly; fatal; punishable with death; (of a sin) incurring the penalty of spiritual death, *opp* to *venial*; to the death; implacable; human; very great (inf); tediously long (inf); without exception (inf); very drunk (sl). ◆ n a human being. ◆ adv (dialect or inf) extremely; thoroughly. [L *mortālis*, from *morī* to die]
■ **mortality** /-tal'i-ti/ n the condition of being mortal; death; frequency or number of deaths, *esp* in proportion to population; the human race, nature or estate. **mor'talize** or **-ise** vt to make mortal. **mor'tally** adv.
❑ **mor'tal-star'ing** adj (Shakesp) having a deadly look.
■ **bill of mortality** see under **bill¹**.

mortar /mör'tər/ n a vessel in which substances are pounded with a pestle; a short piece of artillery for throwing a heavy shell, a bomb, a lifeline, etc; a mixture of cement, sand and water with which bricks, etc are bonded. ◆ vt to join or plaster with mortar; to bombard with a mortar. [OE *mortere*, from L *mortārium* a mortar, matter pounded]
❑ **mor'tarboard** n a square board, with a handle beneath, for holding mortar; a square-topped college cap.

mortgage /mör'gij/ n a conditional conveyance of, or lien upon, land or other property as security for the performance of some condition (*usu* the repayment of a loan to purchase the property itself), becoming void on the performance of the condition; the act of conveying, or the deed effecting it; a loan advanced by a building society, bank, etc, on the security of one's property; an individual (*usu* monthly) repayment of such a loan, or the amount repaid. ◆ *vt* to subject (a property) to a mortgage; to pledge as security for a debt. [OFr, from *mort* dead, and *gage* a pledge]

■ **mort'gageable** *adj.* **mortgagee'** *n* a person to whom a mortgage is made or given, ie the lender; someone who gives or grants a mortgage. **mort'gagor** /-jər/ *n* a person who mortgages his or her property, ie the borrower (also sometimes **mort'gager**).

❑ **mortgage rate** *n* the level of interest charged for a loan on a property.

mortice see **mortise**.

mortician /mör-tish'ən/ (chiefly *N Am*) *n* an undertaker. [L *mors, mortis* death]

mortify /mör'ti-fī/ *vt* (**mor'tifying**; **mor'tified**) to vex in a humiliating or embarrassing way; to subdue (physical desires, etc) by self-discipline and penance; to dispose of by mortification (*Scots law*; *obs*); to kill (*obs*); to destroy the vital functions of; to deaden. ◆ *vi* to lose vitality; to become gangrenous; to be subdued; to practise asceticism. [Fr *mortifier*, from LL *mortificāre* to cause death to, from *mors, mortis* death, and *facere* to make]

■ **mortif'ic** *adj* death-bringing; deadly. **mortification** /mör-ti-fi-kā'shən/ *n* the act of mortifying or state of being mortified; the death of part of the body; a subduing of the passions and appetites by a severe or strict manner of living; humiliation; chagrin; that which mortifies or vexes; a bequest to some charitable institution (*Scots law*; *obs*). **mor'tified** *adj.* **mor'tifier** *n.* **mor'tifying** *adj and n.* **mor'tifyingly** *adv.*

mortise or **mortice** /mör'tis/ *n* a hole made in wood, stone, etc to receive a tenon; a recess cut into a printing-plate for the insertion of type, etc (*printing*). ◆ *vt* to cut a mortise in; to join by a mortise and tenon. [Fr *mortaise*; ety unknown]

■ **mor'tiser** or **mor'ticer** *n.*

❑ **mortise lock** or **mortice lock** *n* a lock whose mechanism is covered by being sunk into the edge of a door, etc.

mortling see under **morkin**.

mortmain /mört'mān/ (*law*; *hist*) *n* the legal status of property which is transferred inalienably to an ecclesiastical or other body, said to be a dead hand, ie one that can never part with it again. [Fr *morte* (fem) dead, and *main*, from L *manus* hand]

■ **statutes of mortmain** acts of parliament restricting or forbidding the giving of property to religious houses.

Morton's fork /mör'tənz förk'/ or **crutch** /kruch/ *n* a casuistic device for trapping everyone alike, so called from the practice of the 15c Archbishop of Canterbury and statesman John *Morton*, of exacting loans not only from the rich who could patently afford it, but also from the apparently poor, who were presumed to be saving money.

mortuary /mör'tū-ə-ri/ or /-chə-ri/ *n* a place for the temporary storage of dead bodies; a payment to the parish priest on the death of a parishioner or to a bishop or archdeacon on the death of a priest. ◆ *adj* connected with death or burial. [L *mortuārius* (adj), from *mortuus* dead, and *morī* to die]

morula /mö'rū-lə/ *n* (pl **mor'ulas** or **mor'ulae** /-lē/) a solid spherical mass of cells resulting from the cleavage of an ovum; framboesia. [L *mōrum* a mulberry]

■ **mor'ular** *adj.*

Morus /mö'rəs/ *n* the mulberry genus, giving name to the family **Morā'ceae**, including fig, breadfruit and Ceará (a type of Brazilian) rubber. [L *mōrus* a mulberry tree; cf Gr *moreā*]

■ **morā'ceous** *adj.*

morwong /mör'wong/ or /mö'wong/ *n* an Australasian food-fish. [From an Aboriginal language]

MOS *abbrev*: metal oxide semiconductor.

mos *abbrev*: months.

Mosaic /mō-zā'ik/ *adj* of or relating to *Moses*, the great Jewish lawgiver.

■ **Mō'saism** *n.*

❑ **Mosaic Law** *n* the law of the Jews given by Moses at Mount Sinai.

mosaic /mō-zā'ik/ *n* the fitting together in a design of small pieces of coloured marble, glass, etc; a piece of work of this kind; anything of similar appearance, or composed by the piecing together of different things; a leaf mosaic; leaf mosaic disease (or **mosaic disease**); a hybrid with the parental characters side by side and not blended. ◆ *adj* relating to, or composed of, mosaic. [Fr *mosaïque*, from LL *mosaicum*, *mūsaicum*, from *mūsa*, from Gr *mousa* a muse; cf LL *mūsaeum* or *mūsīvum* (*opus*) mosaic (work)]

■ **mosa'ically** *adv.* **mosa'icism** /-i-sizm/ *n* the presence side by side of patches of tissue of unlike constitution. **mosa'icist** /-i-sist/ *n* a worker in mosaic.

❑ **mosaic gold** *n* an alloy of copper and zinc, ormolu; a stannic sulphide. **mosaic map** *n* a composite photographic map made from aerial photographs.

Mosasaurus /mō-sə-sö'rəs/ *n* a gigantic Cretaceous fossil pythonomorph reptile. [L *Mosa*, the Maas, near which the first was found, and Gr *sauros* a lizard]

mosbolletjie /mos-bol'ə-ki/ (*S Afr*) *n* a sweet bun made of dough leavened with grape must. [S Afr Du *most* must, and *bolletjie* bun, roll]

moschatel /mo-skə-tel'/ *n* a small plant (*Adoxa moschatellina*), constituting in itself the Adoxaceae (by some included in the honeysuckle family), with pale-green flowers and a supposed musky smell. [Fr *moscatelle*, from Ital *moschatella*, from *moscato* musk]

moschiferous /mo-skif'ə-rəs/ *adj* producing musk. [LL *moschus*, from Gr *moschos* musk, and L *ferre* to bring]

Moscow Mule /mos'kō mūl/ *n* a cocktail containing vodka, ginger ale and lemon juice. [*Moscow*, in Russia]

mose /mōz/ *vi* a word found only in the phrase **mose in the chine** (*Shakesp, Taming of the Shrew* III.2.48), meaning to have glanders. [Supposed to be for *mourn in the chine*, perh from Fr *morve d'eschine* glanders, running from the spine: the morbid matter of glanders was thought to come from the spine. Another suggestion is that *mose* is for *pose* catarrh, turned into a verb]

Moselle or **Mosel** /mō-zel'/ *n* a German white wine from the district of the river *Moselle* (Ger *Mosel*), with an aromatic flavour.

Moses basket /mō'zəz bä'skit/ *n* a portable cot for babies in the form of a basket with handles. [Story of Moses in the bulrushes, from Bible, Exodus 2.3]

mosey /mō'zi/ (*sl*) *vi* to move along slowly, saunter (*usu* with *along*); to jog; to make off; to hurry. [Origin uncertain]

mosh /mosh/ (*sl*) *vi* to dance energetically to loud rock music in a crowded space. [Origin uncertain; perh from *squash* and *mash*]

■ **mosh'er** *n.* **mosh'ing** *n.*

❑ **mosh pit** *n* a space, *esp* at the front of an auditorium, where moshing takes place.

moshav /mō-shäv'/ *n* (pl **moshavim** /-shə-vēm'/) an agricultural settlement in Israel; (also **moshav ovdim** /ōv-dēm'/ (pl **moshvei** /mosh-vā'/ **ovdim**)) a joint association of privately-owned farms, on which machinery and marketing are usually operated communally. [Heb, dwelling]

❑ **moshav shitufi** /shi-too-fē'/ *n* (pl **moshavim shitufim**) an Israeli agricultural association in which land and all resources are held in common, but the family unit is preserved, with its own house and garden.

mosher, moshing see under **mosh**.

moskonfyt /mo-skon'fät/ (*S Afr*) *n* a thick syrup made from grapes. [Afrik *mos* must, and *konfyt* jam]

Moslem /moz'lem/ or /-ləm/ same as **Muslim**.

moslings /moz'lingz/ *n pl* the thin shavings taken off by the currier in dressing skins. [Perh *morsellings*, as if dimin of **morsel**]

mosque /mosk/ *n* a Muslim place of worship. [Fr *mosquée*, from Ital *moschea*, from Ar *masjid* (in N Africa pronounced /mas'gid/), from *sajada* (*sagada*) to pray]

mosquito /mo-skē'tō/ *n* (pl **mosqui'toes** or **-os**) loosely, any small biting or stinging insect; any of several long-legged insects of the family Culicidae, the females of which have their mouth-parts adapted for bloodsucking and can therefore transmit disease, including malaria. [Sp, dimin of *mosca* a fly, from L *musca*]

❑ **mosquito canopy**, **curtain** or **net** *n* an arrangement of fine-meshed netting, *esp* over or round a bed, to keep out mosquitoes. **mosquito fish** *n* the topminnow. **mosquito hawk** *n* the nighthawk or goatsucker.

moss /mos/ *n* a bog (now chiefly *Scot*); boggy ground or soil; any of the Musci, a class of Bryophyta, small plants with simply constructed leaves, and no woody material, attached by rhizoids, the zygote growing into a small spore-bearing capsule that grows parasitically on the parent plant; a mass of such plants; a mosslike growth, covering or excrescence; loosely extended to plants of similar appearance to true mosses; a moss rose. ◆ *vt* to cover with moss; to clear of moss. ◆ *vi* to gather moss. [OE *mōs* bog; Du *mos*, Ger *Moos* moss, bog]

■ **moss'iness** *n.* **moss'like** *adj.* **moss'y** *adj* (**moss'ier**; **moss'iest**) overgrown or abounding with moss; like moss; boggy.

❑ **moss agate** *n* chalcedony with moss-like inclusions of chlorite, manganese oxide, etc. **moss'back** *n* (*N Am*) a person with antiquated views. **moss'backed** *adj.* **moss'bluiter** /-blüt'ər or -blit'ər/ *n* (*Scot*) the bittern. **moss'-cheeper** *n* (*Scot*) the titlark. **moss'-crop** *n* (*Scot*) cotton grass. **moss'-flow** *n* (*Scot*) a watery bog. **moss green** *n* a muted yellowy-green. **moss'-grown** *adj* covered with moss. **moss hag** or **moss hagg** *n* (*Scot*) a pit or slough in a bog. **moss'land** *n* wet, peaty land. **moss'-litter** *n* a loose mass of lumps of peaty material. **moss'plant** *n* a plant of moss; the sexual generation in the life history of a moss, on which the asexual generation is parasitic. **moss rose** *n* a variety of rose having a mosslike growth on and below the calyx. **moss stitch** *n* a knitting stitch alternating plain and purl stitches along each row and in succeeding rows, producing a mosslike texture. **moss'trooper** *n* (*hist*) one of the freebooters that used to frequent the Border between Scotland and England in the 17c. **moss'trooping** *n* and *adj*.

■ **club moss** see under **club** and **lycopod**. **Iceland moss** see under **Iceland**.

Mossad /mos'ad/ *n* the Israeli state intelligence service (since 1951), established *orig* in 1937 as *Mossad le Alujeh Beth*, the Committee for Illegal Immigration, to oversee illegal Jewish immigration into Palestine.

Mössbauer effect /mæs'bow-ər i-fekt'/ (*nuclear phys*) *n* an effect that occurs when an atomic nucleus emits a gamma-ray photon and must recoil to conserve linear momentum, used in the study of crystal structure. [Rudolf Ludwig *Mössbauer* (1929–2011), German physicist]

mossbunker /mos'bung-kər/ *n* the menhaden, an oily fish of the herring family. [Du *mars-banker* the scad or horse-mackerel]

mossie¹ /mos'i/ or **mozzie** /moz'i/ (*inf*) *n* short for **mosquito**.

mossie² /mos'i/ (*S Afr*) *n* (also **Cape sparrow**) a common South African sparrow, *Passer melanurus*, the male of which has a black head and curved white mark at the eye. [Afrik, from Du *mosje*, dimin of *mos* sparrow]

mosso /mos'ō/ (*music*) *adv* with movement, animatedly. [Ital, pap of *muovere* to move]

most /mōst/ *adj* (*superl* of **more¹**) the majority of; in greatest quantity or number. ◆ *adv* in the highest or greatest degree (used to form superlative of adjectives and adverbs); used as an intensifier; almost (*US dialect*; *perh* aphetic). ◆ *n* the greatest number or quantity. [The Northumbrian form *māst* (Scot *maist*) may have occurred in OE beside the ordinary form *mǣst*; or the vowel may come from analogy with the compar; cf Ger *meist*]

■ **most'ly** *adv* for the most part; usually. **most'what** *adv* (*Spenser*) for the most part, mostly.

■ **at most** or **at the most** at the maximum. **for the most part** chiefly; in the main. **make the most of** see under **make¹**. **the mostest** (*facetious*) the most, the ultimate.

-most /-mōst/ *sfx* indicating superlative, eg *hindmost*, *farthermost*. [OE superl sfx *-mæst*, *-mest*]

MOT /em-ō-tē'/ *n* a compulsory annual check made by order of the Ministry of Transport (now the Department for Transport) on vehicles over three years old (also **MOT test**). ◆ *vt* (*pap* and *pat* **MOT'd**) to give an MOT to.

mot¹ /mot/ (*obs*) *n* a motto; a hunter's horn-call. [Fr, from L *muttum* a murmur]

mot² /mō/ (*Fr*) *n* a word; a pithy or witty saying.

■ **le mot juste** /lə mō zhüst/ the word which fits the context exactly.

mot³ /mot/ (*Irish sl*) *n* a girl or young woman, *esp* a girlfriend. [Origin obscure]

mot⁴ see **motte¹**.

mot⁵ see **mote²**.

mote¹ /mōt/ *n* a particle of dust; a speck; a seed or other foreign particle in wool or cotton (*Yorks* **moit**); a stain or blemish; anything very small. [OE *mot*; Du *mot*]

■ **mōt'ed**, **mote'y** or (*Scot*) **motty** /mot'i/ *adj* containing a mote or motes.

❑ **mote spoon** *n* a perforated spoon formerly used to remove tea leaves from a teacup or teapot spout, or for straining other liquids.

mote² /mōt/ (*archaic*) *vt* (3rd pers sing prt **mote**; *pat* (*Spenser*) **mote** or **mot** /mot/, in *pl* **mot'en**; but see also **must¹**) may; must. [OE *mōt* may, pat *mōste*; confused with **mought**; Ger *muss* must]

■ **so mote I thee** so may I prosper (see **thee²**).

mote³ see **motte²**.

motel /mō-tel'/ *n* a hotel for motorists with rooms that are *usu* accessible from a parking area; a hotel with accommodation and servicing facilities for cars. [*motor hotel*]

■ **motel'ier** *n* the owner or manager of a motel.

moten see **mote²**.

motet or **motett** /mō-tet'/ (*music*) *n* a polyphonic choral composition, *usu* unaccompanied, with a biblical or similar prose text; loosely, an anthem or church cantata. [Fr *motet*, dimin of *mot*; cf **mot²**]

■ **motett'ist** *n*.

motey see under **mote¹**.

moth /moth/ *n* the cloth-eating larva of the clothes moth; the imago of the same kind; any member of the Heterocera, a popular and unscientific division of the Lepidoptera, broadly distinguished from butterflies by having duller colouring, a thicker body, antennae not clubbed, wings not tilted over the back in rest, and by the habit of flying by night; that which eats away at anything gradually and silently; any of various kinds of insect vermin (*obs*); a fragile, frivolous creature, readily dazzled into destruction (*fig*); a light aeroplane. [OE *moththe*, *mohthe*; Ger *Motte*]

■ **mothed** /motht/ *adj* moth-eaten. **moth'y** *adj* (**moth'ier**; **moth'iest**) full of moths; moth-eaten.

❑ **moth'ball** *n* a ball of naphthalene, or a similar substance, for keeping away clothes moths. ◆ *vt* to lay up in mothballs; to spray with a plastic and lay up (a ship, etc); to lay aside temporarily, postpone work on, keep in readiness for eventual use. **moth'-eat** *vt* (back-formation) to prey upon, as a moth eats a garment. **moth'-eaten** *adj* eaten or damaged by the larvae of moths (also *fig*). **moth'-flower** *n* a flower pollinated by moths. **moth'-hunter** *n* a goatsucker. **moth'proof** *adj* (of clothes, etc) chemically rendered resistant to moths (also *vt*).

■ **(put) in mothballs** (to put) temporarily in abeyance.

mother¹ /mudh'ər/ *n* a female parent; that which has produced or nurtured anything; a protective or nurturing quality; the female head of a religious house or other establishment; a matron; a familiar term of address to, or prefix to the name of, an old woman; extended to a female ancestor, stepmother, mother-in-law or foster-mother; an apparatus for chicken-rearing; the womb (*obs*); hysteria (*obs*); see also **motherfucker** below. ◆ *adj* received by birth, as it were from one's mother; being a mother; acting the part of a mother; originating; used to generate others. ◆ *vt* to give birth to; to acknowledge, adopt or treat as a son or daughter; to foster; to behave (too) protectively towards, as, or as if as, a mother; to attribute the maternity or authorship of (with *on* or *upon*); to find a mother for. [OE *mōdor*; Du *moeder*, ON *mōthir*, Ger *Mutter*, Ir and Gaelic *mathair*, L *māter*, Gr *mētēr*, Sans *mātr*]

■ **moth'erhood** *n* the state of being a mother. **moth'ering** *n* a rural English custom of visiting the mother church or one's parents on mid-Lent Sunday (**Mothering Sunday**). **moth'erless** *adj* without a mother. **moth'erliness** *n*. **moth'erly** *adj* relating to, or befitting, a mother; like a mother.

❑ **moth'erboard** *n* a printed circuit board in a computer which holds the principal components, with slots on its buses for the attachment of adapter cards. **Mother Carey's chicken** or **goose** *n* the storm petrel, or similar bird. **mother cell** *n* (*biol*) a cell that gives rise to others by division, a stem cell. **mother church** *n* the church from which others have sprung; a principal church. **mother city** *n* one from which another was founded as a colony. **mother country** or **moth'erland** *n* the country of one's birth; the home country of colonists, etc settled elsewhere. **moth'ercraft** *n* knowledge and skill required for the care of a child. **mother figure** *n* an older woman who symbolizes for one the qualities and authority of one's mother. **moth'erfucker** *n* (*taboo sl*, *esp US*) an extremely objectionable, unpleasant, etc person or thing (sometimes shortened to **moth'er**, **mutha** /mudh'ə/ or **mō'fō**). **moth'erfucking** *adj* (*taboo sl*, *esp US*) objectionable; often used as an intensifier or meaningless qualification. **mother hen** *n* a hen that has chicks; a person who clucks and fusses over others. **Mother Hubbard** *n* a woman's loose flowing gown, named after the heroine of a nursery rhyme. **moth'er-in-law** *n* (*pl* **moth'ers-in-law**) the mother of one's husband or wife; a stepmother (*obs*). **moth'er-in-law's tongue** *n* a houseplant with swordlike leaves, *Sansevieria*. **moth'erland** see **mother country** above. **mother liquor** or **mother lye** *n* mother water. **mother lode** *n* (*mining*) the main lode of any system. **moth'er-na'ked** *adj* completely naked, as at birth. **Mother of God** *n* the Virgin Mary. **mother-of-mill'ions** *n* ivy-leaved toadflax. **mother-of-pearl'** *n* the nacreous internal layer of the shells in some molluscs (also *adj*). **moth'er-of-thousands** *n* a perennial creeping plant with ivy-shaped leaves. **moth'er-right** *n* (*archaic*) succession in the female line; matriarchy. **Mother's Day** *n* a day for honouring mothers, as, in the USA, the second Sunday in May; also used for Mothering Sunday. **mother's help** *n* a person employed to help a mother with domestic duties, *esp* the supervision of children. **moth'ership** *n* a ship having charge of torpedo-boats or small craft; a ship which provides a number of other, *usu* smaller, ships with services, supplies, etc. **Mother Shipton** /ship'tən/ *n* a type of moth whose wing-markings resemble the profile of an old woman. **mother's mark** or **mother spot** *n* a birthmark. **mothers' meeting** *n* a periodical meeting of mothers connected with a church. **mother's** (or **mothers'**) **ruin** *n* (*sl*) gin. **mother superior** *n* the head of a convent or any community of nuns. **mother-to-be'** *n* (*pl* **mothers-to-be'**) a woman who is pregnant, *esp* with her first child. **mother tongue** *n* native language; a language from which another has its origin. **mother water** *n* residual liquid, still containing certain chemical substances, left after others have been crystallized or precipitated from it. **mother wit** *n* native wit; common sense. **moth'erwort** *n* the labiate plant *Leonurus cardiaca*, or any of several related plants formerly used in the treatment of disorders of the uterus.

■ **be mother** (*facetious*) to pour the tea. **every mother's son** every man without exception. **fits of the mother** (*obs*) hysteria. **the mother and father** (or **father and mother**) (**of**) (*inf*) the biggest, greatest (*usu fig*), as in *the mother and father of an argument* (or *all arguments*).

mother² /*mudh'ər*/ n dregs; scum; a slimy mass of bacteria that oxidizes alcohol into acetic acid (in full, **mother of vinegar**). ◆ *vi* to become mothery. [Poss the same as **mother¹**; or poss from Du *modder* mud; cf **mud**]
■ **moth'ery** *adj* like or containing mother.

mothering and **motherly** see under **mother¹**.

motif /*mō-tēf'*/ n a dominant or recurrent theme or subject in a musical, literary or other artistic work; a shape or design repeated in a pattern (*music*); an ornament added to a woman's garment, often symbolic; a design, symbol, etc on a manufactured article, whether decorative or identifying the manufacturer. [Fr *motif*; see **motive**]

motile /*mō'tīl*/ or (*N Am*) -*til*/ *adj* capable of moving spontaneously as a whole; characterized by motion; imagining most readily in terms of muscular action (*psychol*). ◆ *n* (*psychol*) a person whose imagery naturally takes the form of feelings of action. [L *mōtus* movement]
■ **motility** /-*til'i-ti*/ n.

motion /*mō'shən*/ n the act, state or manner of changing place; a single movement; change of posture; power of moving or of being moved; agitation; a natural impulse; a working in the mind; a feeling, an emotion (*obs*); a prompting, an instigation (*obs*); a formal proposal put before a meeting; an application to a court, during a case before it, for an order or rule that something be done, *esp* something incidental to the progress of the cause rather than its issue (*law*); evacuation of the bowels; a piece of mechanism; progression of a part (*music*); a puppet show (*obs*); a puppet (*Shakesp*); (*usu in pl*) faeces. ◆ *vt* to direct or indicate by a gesture; to move, propose; to make a movement indicating as one's intention (*obs*); to give motion to. ◆ *vi* to offer a proposal. [Fr *motion*, from L *mōtiō, -ōnis*, from *movēre, mōtum* to move]
■ **mō'tional** *adj*. **mō'tionist** n (*Milton*) a person who is good at making suggestions or recommendations. **mō'tionless** *adj* without motion. **mō'tionlessly** *adv*.
❑ **motion capture** n (in film) a technique in which the movements of actors are recorded as the basis of those of computer-generated characters. **motion-man** n (*obs*) a puppeteer. **motion picture** n (chiefly *US*) a cinema film. **motion sickness** same as **travel sickness** (see under **travel**).
■ **angular motion** change of angle between a standard direction and a line joining the moving object and a fixed point. **go through the motions** to make a half-hearted attempt; to pretend. **laws of motion** Newton's three laws: (1) every body continues in its state of rest, or of uniform motion in a straight line, except so far as it may be compelled by force to change that state; (2) change of motion is proportional to force applied, and takes place in the direction of the straight line in which the force acts; (3) to every action there is always an equal and contrary reaction.

motive /*mō'tiv*/ n an incitement of the will; a consideration or emotion that excites to action; a motif; a moving part of the body (*Shakesp*). ◆ *adj* causing motion; having the power to cause motion; concerned with the initiation of action; moving (*obs*). ◆ *vt* to motivate. [LL *mōtīvus* (adj), from L *movēre, mōtum* to move]
■ **mo'tivate** *vt* to provide with a motive; to induce; to give an incentive. **motivā'tion** n motivating force, incentive. **motivā'tional** *adj* relating to motivation. **motivā'tionally** *adv*. **mo'tivator** n. **mo'tiveless** *adj*. **mo'tivelessly** *adv*. **mo'tivelessness** n. **motiv'ic** *adj* of, having or concerning a musical motif. **motiv'ity** n the power of moving or of producing motion.
❑ **motivated art** n art produced under the influence of hallucinogenic drugs. **motivation** or **motivational research** n research into motivation, *esp* into consumer reaction, carried out scientifically. **motive power** n the energy or source of the energy by which anything is operated.

motley /*mot'li*/ *adj* multicoloured; variegated; made of, or dressed in, motley; jester-like; made up of various elements or types, heterogeneous. ◆ *n* a variegated garment or outfit, *esp* that formerly worn by a jester; a cloth of mixed colours (*obs*); a patchwork (*obs*); a jester (*Shakesp*). [Poss from OE *mot* a speck]
❑ **mot'ley-mind'ed** *adj* (*Shakesp*) having heterogeneous and inconsistent thoughts or intentions.

motmot /*mot'mot*/ n a tropical American bird (*Momotus* and related genera), related to rollers and kingfishers, that nibbles its tail feathers into a racket shape. [Said to be a Mexican name]

motocross /*mō'tə-kros*/ n a form of scrambling, motorcycle racing round a very rough circuit. [**motor**]

motoneuron /*mō-tə-nū'ron*/ n a motor neuron.

moto perpetuo /*mō'tō per-pet'oo-ō*/ (*Ital*) n (pl **mo'to perpet'ui** /-*oo-ī*/) perpetual motion; a piece of music that goes swiftly without stop from beginning to end.

motor /*mō'tər*/ n that which gives motion; a machine whereby some source of energy is used to give motion or perform work, *esp* an internal-combustion engine or a machine for converting electrical into mechanical energy; a motor car; a muscle, or a nerve, concerned in bodily movement; a mover. ◆ *adj* giving or transmitting motion; driven by a motor; of, for, with, or relating to, motor vehicles; concerned with the transmission of impulses; initiating bodily movement; relating to muscular movement or the sense of muscular movement. ◆ *vt* and *vi* to convey, traverse or travel by a motor vehicle. ◆ *vi* to put on speed, to move fast (*inf*). [L *mōtor*, from *movēre* to move]
■ **mo'torable** *adj* (*old*) (of roads) able to be used by motor vehicles. **moto'rial** *adj* motory. **mo'torist** n a person who drives a motor car, *esp* for pleasure. **moto'rium** n that part of the nervous system concerned in movement. **motorizā'tion** or **-s-** n. **mo'torize** or **-ise** *vt* to provide with, or adapt to the use of, a motor or motors; to interpret or imagine in terms of motor sensation. **mo'tory** *adj* causing, conveying or imparting motion; motor.
❑ **motor areas** n pl (*anat* and *zool*) nerve centres in the brain concerned with the initiation and co-ordination of movement. **mo'torbandit** n a robber who uses a motor car. **mo'torbicycle**, **mo'torbike**, **mo'torboat**, **motor bus**, **motor car**, **mo'torcoach**, **mo'torcycle**, **mo'tor-launch**, **motor lorry**, **mo'tor-ship**, etc n a bicycle, etc driven by a motor. **motorcade** /*mō'tər-kād*/ n (after **cavalcade**) a procession of motor cars, *esp* ones carrying a head of state and his or her entourage. **motor caravan** n a motor vehicle with living, sleeping, etc facilities, like a caravan. **mo'torcycling** n. **mo'torcyclist** n. **motor drive** n (*photog*) a battery-driven motor for fast winding of film between exposures. **mo'tor-driven** *adj* driven by a motor. **motor generator** n an electrical generator driven by an electric motor, whereby one voltage, frequency or number of phases, ie those of the motor, can be used to produce a different voltage, frequency or number of phases, ie those of the generator. **mo'torhome** n a van-like vehicle of varying size fully equipped to be a travelling home, a motor caravan. **mo'tor-jet** n a reciprocating engine with a fan for jet propulsion. **motor lodge** n a motel. **mo'torman** n a man who controls a motor, *esp* that of a tram-car or electric train. **mo'tormouth** n (*sl*) a non-stop talker. **motor neuron** or **neurone** n (*anat*) a neuron conveying a voluntary or motor impulse. **motor neurone disease** n a disease in which progressive damage to motor neurones leads to muscle weakness and degeneration. **motor scooter** n a small motorcycle, *usu* with an engine of under 225cc. **mo'torsport** n any sport which involves motor-powered vehicles, *esp* cars or motorcycles (also *adj*). **motor-trac'tion** n the conveyance of loads, including passengers, by motor vehicles. **motor-trac'tor** n an internal-combustion engine for hauling loads, *esp* for drawing agricultural implements. **mo'torway** n a trunk road for fast-moving motor vehicles, with separate carriageways for vehicles travelling in opposite directions, and limited access and exit points. **motorway madness** n (*inf*) reckless driving in bad conditions on motorways, *esp* in fog.

motorail /*mō'tō-rāl*/ n a system of carrying cars and passengers by train on certain routes. [**motor**]

motorbike...to...**motorway** see under **motor**.

motoscafo /*mō-tō-skä'fō*/ (*Ital*) n (pl **motoscafi** /-*fē*/) a motorboat.

Motown® /*mō'town*/ n a type of music that blends rhythm and blues and pop with gospel rhythms. [Motown Record Company in Detroit, Michigan (nicknamed *Motown*, for *motor town*), a major car-manufacturing centre]

motser /*mot'sər*/ or **motza** /*mot'zə*/ (*Aust inf*) n a large amount of money, *esp* the proceeds from a gambling win.

mott /*mot*/ (*Spenser*) pat of **mete¹**.

motte¹, **mott** or **mot** /*mot*/ (*SW US*) n a clump of trees, *esp* on a prairie. [Mex Sp *mata*]

motte² /*mot*/ or **mote** /*mōt*/ (*archaic*) n a mound, *esp* with a castle, a tumulus. [OFr *mote* (Fr *motte*); often confused with **moot** or **moot-hill**]
❑ **mote'-hill** n. **motte and bailey** n (*hist*) a type of fortification commonly built by the Normans, with a keep built on a mound surrounded by a walled bailey.

mottle /*mot'l*/ *vt* to variegate blotchily. ◆ *n* a blotched appearance, condition or surface; yarns of two colours folded together. [Prob from **motley**]
■ **mott'led** *adj*. **mott'ling** n.
❑ **mott'le-faced** *adj*.

motto /*mot'ō*/ n (pl **mott'oes** or **mott'os** /-*ōz*/) a short sentence or phrase adopted as representative of a person, family, etc, or accompanying a coat of arms; a passage prefixed to a book or chapter anticipating its subject; a scrap of verse or prose enclosed in a cracker or sweet wrapper; a recurring phrase (*music*). [Ital, from L *muttum* a murmur]

■ **mott'o'd** or **mott'oed** *adj*.

motty see under **mote**[1].

Motu /mō'too/ *n* (pl **Motu** or **Motus**) a member of a group of aboriginal people of Papua New Guinea; their language, of the Malayo-Polynesian family. ◆ *adj* of or relating to the Motu or their language.

motu /mō'too/ *n* (pl **motu** or **motus**) a small reef island in the S Pacific. [Maori]

motuca /mō-too'kə/ or **mutuca** /moo-too'kə/ *n* a large Brazilian biting fly of the family Tabanidae. [Tupí *mutuca* (Port *motuca*)]

motu proprio /mō'tū prō'pri-ō or mō'too pro'pri-ō/ (*L*) of his or her own accord without consultation.

motza see **motser**.

MOU *abbrev*: memorandum of understanding.

mou' or **mou** /moo/ *n* a Scots form of **mouth**.

mouch, **moucher**, etc same as **mooch**, etc.

moucharaby /moo-shar'ə-bi/ *n* a balcony enclosed with latticework. [Fr, from Ar *mashrabiyyah*]

mouchard /moo-shär'/ (*Fr*) *n* a police spy.

mouchoir /moo-shwär'/ (*Fr*) *n* a pocket-handkerchief.

moudiewart, **moudiwart**, **moudiewort** and **moudiwort** Scots forms of **mouldwarp**.

moue /moo/ (*Fr*) *n* a grimace of discontent, pout.

moufflon, **mouflon** or **muflon** /moo'flon/ *n* (pl **moufflon**, etc or **moufflons**, etc) a wild sheep of the mountains of Corsica, etc; extended to large big-horned wild sheep of other kinds. [Fr *mouflon*, from LL *mufrō, -ōnis*]

mought /mōt/ or *mowt*, also (*Spenser*) *möt/* (*obs* or *dialect*) pat of **may**. See also **mote**[2].

mouillé /moo'yā/ (*phonetics*) *adj* (of *l* and *n*) sounded in a liquid manner, palatalized (as *gl* in 'seraglio', or *ñ* in 'señor'). [Fr, moistened]

moujik /moo-zhik'/ or /moo'zhik/ *n* same as **muzhik**.

mould[1] or (*N Am*) **mold** /mōld/ *n* a woolly growth on bread, cheese, or other vegetable or animal matter; any one of various small fungi (such as *Mucor*, *Penicillium*, etc) of different classes, forming such growths. ◆ *vi* to become mouldy. ◆ *vt* to cause or allow to become mouldy. [ME *mowle*; cf ON *mygla*]

■ **mould'iness** *n*. **mould'y** *adj* (**mould'ier**; **mould'iest**) overgrown with mould; like mould; stale; musty; miserable, lousy (*inf*).

mould[2] or (*N Am*) **mold** /mōld/ *n* a template; the matrix in which a cast is made; a formed surface from which an impression is taken; the foundation on which certain manufactured articles are built up; a thing formed in a mould, *esp* a jelly or blancmange; nature, character; a form, model or pattern; that which is or may be moulded; a set of mouldings (*archit*); a wire tray used to make paper by hand. ◆ *vt* to knead; to mix (*obs*); to shape; to model; to form in a mould. [OFr *modle*, *molle* (Fr *moule*), from L *modulus* a measure]

■ **mould'able** *adj*. **mould'er** *n*. **mould'ing** *n* the process of shaping, *esp* any soft substance; anything formed by or in a mould; an ornamental edging or band projecting from a wall or other surface, such as a fillet, astragal or bead; a strip of wood that can be applied for the purpose.

□ **mould'-candle** *n* a candle made in a mould, not dipped. **mould-fac'ing** *n* a fine powder or wash applied to the face of a mould to ensure a smooth casting. **moulding board** *n* a baker's board for kneading dough. **mould'-loft** *n* a room in which the several parts of a ship's hull are laid off to full size from the construction drawings. **mould'-made** *adj* (of paper) made on a machine, but having a deckle-edge like that of handmade paper.

mould[3] or (*N Am*) **mold** /mōld/ *n* soil rich in decayed matter; loose soft earth; earth, considered as the material of which the body is formed or to which it returns; the earth of the grave; the ground, the land, the world (*obs* or *archaic*); (in *pl*) clods, *esp* in allusion to the grave (*Scot* **mouls** or **mools** /moolz/). ◆ *vt* to cover with soil. ◆ *vi* (*obs*) to moulder. [OE *molde*; Ger dialect *molt*, *molten*, Gothic *mulda*]

■ **mould'er** *vi* to crumble to mould; to turn to dust; to waste away gradually. ◆ *vt* to turn to dust. **mould'y** *adj* like, or of the nature of, mould.

□ **mould'board** *n* the curved plate in a plough which turns over the soil.

mouldwarp /mōld'wörp/ (*archaic* and *dialect*) *n* (also (*Scot*) **mowdiewart**, **mowdiwort** /mow'di-wûrt/, **moudiewart**, **moudiewort** /moo'di-wûrt/) a mole (the animal). [OE *molde* mould, earth, and *weorpan* to throw; cf OHGer *multwurf* (Ger *Maulwurf*), Dan *muldvarp*]

moulin /moo'lĩ/ *n* a shaft in a glacier worn by water running down a crack. [Fr *moulin* mill, and dimin *moulinet*, from LL *molīnum*]

moulinet /moo-li-net'/ or /moo'/ *n* a machine for bending a crossbow. **Moulinette**® /moo-li-net'/ or **Mouli**® /moo'li/ *n* a hand-operated, rotary device for puréeing food.

moult or (*N Am*) **molt** /mōlt/ *vi* to shed feathers or another covering; to be shed. ◆ *vt* to shed. ◆ *n* the act, process, condition or time of moulting. [OE (*bi*)*mūtian* to exchange, from L *mūtāre*; the *l*, introduced in spelling on analogy with *fault*, etc, afterwards sounded]

■ **moult'en** *adj* (*Shakesp*) having moulted. **moult'ing** *n*.

mound[1] /mownd/ *n* a bank of earth or stone raised as a protection; a hillock; a heap; a boundary-fence or hedge (*obs*). ◆ *vt* to enclose with a fence or an embankment (*obs*); to fortify with an embankment; to heap in a mound. [Origin obscure; OE *mund* means guardianship]

□ **mound'-bird** *n* the megapode, a bird of the Australian family Megapodidae, gallinaceous birds that build large mounds as incubators. **Mound Builder** *n* a member of any of the prehistoric Native American peoples who built great earthworks in SE USA. **mound'-builder** *n* a mound-bird.

mound[2] /mownd/ (*esp heraldry*) *n* a sovereign's orb. [Fr *monde*, from L *mundus* the world]

mounseer /mown'sēr/ or *-sēr'/* (*archaic* or *derisive*) *n* an illiterate or exaggeratedly anglicized pronunciation of **Monsieur**; a Frenchman.

mount[1] /mownt/ *vt* to climb, ascend; to get up on; to cover or copulate with; to cause to rise, to lift, raise, erect; to place on anything high; to put on horseback, etc; to provide with an animal, bicycle, etc to ride on; to fix in a setting, on a support, stand or backing; to provide with accessories; to put in position and state of readiness for use or exhibition; to stage; to be armed with; to carry, wear, or put on; to put into operation, carry out. ◆ *vi* to go up; to climb; to get up on horseback, a bicycle, etc; to extend upward; to extend backward in time; to rise in level or amount (*esp* with *up*); to amount (*obs*). ◆ *n* a rise; an act of mounting; manner of mounting; a step to mount by; a signal for mounting; a horse, etc that is ridden; that upon which a thing is placed or in which it is set for fixing, strengthening, embellishing, *esp* the card surrounding a picture; the slide, cover glass, etc used in mounting an object for the microscope. [Fr *monter* to go up, from L *mōns, montis* mountain]

■ **mount'able** *adj*. **mount'ed** *adj* on horseback; equipped with horses; set on high; raised on steps, generally three, as a cross (*heraldry*); set up; set. ◆ *combining form* set in or with a specified material, as *silver-mounted*. **mount'er** *n*. **mount'ing** *n* an act of mounting; anything upon which a thing has been mounted.

□ **mounting block** *n* a block or stone to enable one to mount a horse. ■ **have the mount** to ride (a particular horse) in a race. **mount guard** see under **guard**.

mount[2] /mownt/ *n* a mountain (*archaic* except as **Mount**, as pfx to a name); a small hill or mound, natural or artificial; a fleshy protuberance on the hand (*palmistry*). [OE *munt* and OFr *mont*, both from L *mōns, montis* mountain]

mountain /mown'tin/ *n* a high steep hill; a wine made from mountain grapes; (in Ireland) wild pasture land; a large quantity or excess, *esp* of agricultural, dairy, etc products bought up by an economic community to prevent a fall in prices; (with *cap*) the extreme party in the French Revolution (see **Montagnard**). ◆ *adj* of a mountain; growing, dwelling, etc on or among mountains. [OFr *montaigne*, from L *mōns, montis* mountain. In some compounds *mountain* is used like Ger *Berg*, as if = mine]

■ **mount'ained** *adj*. **mountaineer'** *n* a climber of mountains; an inhabitant of a mountainous area; a member of the Mountain (*hist*). ◆ *vi* to climb mountains. **mountaineer'ing** *n* mountain climbing. **mount'ainous** *adj* full of, or characterized by, mountains; large as a mountain; huge.

□ **mountain ash** *n* the rowan tree; any of several eucalyptus trees, *esp Eucalyptus regnans* (*Aust*). **mountain avens** see **avens**. **mountain beaver** *n* the sewellel. **mountain bicycle** or **bike** *n* a bicycle with a strong, heavy frame and wide tyres designed for use over rough terrain. **mountain biker** *n*. **mountain biking** *n*. **mountain blue** *n* blue basic carbonate of copper, azurite. **mount'ainboarder** *n*. **mount'ainboarding** *n* the sport of riding a **mount'ainboard**, a narrow board mounted on wheels and fitted with a steering mechanism, down mountain tracks or other types of rugged terrain. **mountain bramble** *n* the cloudberry. **mountain cat** *n* a catamount, a wildcat. **mountain chain** *n* a range of mountains forming a long line. **mountain cork** *n* a matted mass of a fibrous amphibole with a cork-like texture. **mountain devil** *n* a moloch. **mountain dew** *n* (*inf*) whisky, *esp* illicitly-distilled. **mount'ain-everlast'ing** *n* the cat's-foot (*Antennaria dioica*), a small woolly composite plant of the hills and seashore. **mountain flax** *n* any of various small herbs of the genus *Phormium* or *Linum*; amianthus. **mountain goat** *n* a white goatlike animal of the Rocky Mountains (genus *Oreamnus*); any of various wild goats of mountainous regions. **mountain hare** *n* a small species of hare, grey in summer, *usu* white in winter. **mount'ain-high** or **mount'ains-high** *adv* and *adj* high as a mountain, overwhelmingly high. **mountain laurel** *n* an ericaceous shrub of N America (genus *Kalmia*). **mountain leather** *n* a matted mass of a fibrous amphibole with a leathery texture. **Mountain Limestone** *n* the lowest division of the Carboniferous division of Palaeozoic rock in England, the Carboniferous Limestone. **mountain lion** *n* the puma or cougar. **mountain marrow** *n* lithomarge. **mountain meal** *n* bergmehl. **mountain railway** or (*N Am*) **mountain railroad** *n* a light narrow-gauge railway for mountainous regions, *usu* a rack railway. **mountain range** *n* a series of adjoining mountains. **mountain ringlet** *n Erebia epiphron*, a rare alpine butterfly. **mountain sheep** the bighorn, a large wild sheep of the Rocky Mountains, with large horns. **mountain sickness** *n* sickness brought on by breathing rarefied air. **mount'ainside** *n* the slope of a mountain. **mountain soap** *n* a greasy kind of halloysite. **Mountain Standard Time** or **Mountain Time** *n* one of the standard times used in N America, being 7 hours behind Greenwich Mean Time (*abbrev* **MST** or **MT**). **mountain tallow** *n* hatchettite. **mountain tea** *n* the American evergreen plant *Gaultheria procumbens* (also called **wintergreen**). **mount'ain-top** *n.* **mountain wood** *n* a fibrous wood-like asbestos.

■ **make a mountain out of a molehill** see under **mole**[1]. **Old Man of the Mountain** a popular name for the chief of the *Hashshāshīn* (see **assassin**).

mountant /mown'tənt/ *n* an adhesive paste for mounting photographs, etc; any substance in which specimens are suspended on a microscope slide. ◆ *adj* (*Shakesp*) rising on high. [Fr *montant*, prp of *monter* to mount]

mountebank /mown'ti-bangk/ *n* a buffoon; a charlatan; a quack seller of remedies, etc (*obs*). ◆ *vt* to gain or bring about by mountebankery. ◆ *vi* (or *vt* with *it*) to act as a mountebank. [Ital *montimbanco*, *montambanco*, from *montare* to mount, *in* on, and *banco* bench]

■ **moun'tebankery**, **moun'tebanking** or **moun'tebankism** *n*.

mountenance /mown'tə-nəns/ or **mountenaunce** /-näns/ (*Spenser*) *n* amount; distance. [Appar OFr *montance*, assimilated to **maintenance**; cf **mount**[1] and **mountant**]

Mountie or **Mounty** /mown'ti/ (*inf*) *n* a member of the Royal Canadian *Mount*ed Police.

moup or **moop** /moop/ (*Scot*) *vt* to nibble, munch; to mumble. ◆ *vi* to nibble or munch (with *at* or *on*); to consort or live (with *with*). [Origin obscure]

mourn /mörn/ or (*rare*) *moorn* /moorn/ *vi* to grieve for a death or other loss; to be sorrowful; to wear mourning; to murmur sorrowfully (*literary*). ◆ *vt* to grieve for; to utter in a sorrowful manner (*poetic*). [OE *murnan*; OHGer *mornēn* to grieve]

■ **mourn'er** *n* a person who mourns a death, etc; a person who attends a funeral, *esp* a relative of the deceased; a person hired to lament or weep for the dead; a penitent at a revival meeting (*US*). **mourn'ful** *adj* causing, suggesting, or expressing sorrow; feeling grief. **mourn'fully** *adv*. **mourn'fulness** *n*. **mourn'ing** *n* the act of expressing grief; the dress of mourners, or other tokens of mourning (also *Scot* in *pl*); the period during which one is officially mourning a death. ◆ *adj* grieving, lamenting; suitable for, or concerned with, mourning. **mourn'ingly** *adv*.

❑ **mourning band** *n* a band of black material worn round the sleeve or (*hist*) the hat, to signify that one is in mourning. **mourning border** *n* a black margin used on notepaper, etc, by those in mourning; a dirty edge on a fingernail (*inf*). **mourn'ing-bride** *n* the sweet scabious (*Scabiosa atropurpurea*), a Mediterranean plant with a dome-like flower-head. **mourning cloak** *n* an undertaker's cloak, formerly worn at a funeral; a large butterfly, the Camberwell beauty (*US*). **mourning coach** *n* a closed carriage formerly used for carrying mourners to a funeral. **mourning dove** *n* a N American pigeon (*Zenaidura macroura*) with a plaintive-sounding cry. **mourning piece** *n* a picture intended to be a memorial of the dead. **mourning ring** *n* a ring worn in memory of a dead person. **mourn'ing-stuff** *n* any lustreless black dress fabric, such as crape, cashmere, etc, for making mourning clothes.

■ **half-mourning** see under **half**. **in mourning** wearing black (in China, white) in token of mourning; (of a ship) painted blue; having black eyes (*sl*).

mournival /mör'ni-vəl/ *n* in the card game gleek, a set of four aces, kings, etc. [Fr *mornifle*]

mousaka same as **moussaka**.

mouse /mows/ *n* (pl **mice** /mīs/) any of several small rodents of the genus *Mus*, often found in houses and fields; extended to various voles and other animals more or less like the mouse, such as the *flitter-mouse* or *shrew-mouse*; a device, *usu* linked to a computer, which is moved by hand over a flat surface thereby causing the cursor to move correspondingly on screen (*comput*); a small lead weight used in inserting a sash cord into a window frame; a term of endearment (*obs*); a muscle (*obs*); part of a hindleg of beef, next to the round (also **mouse'-buttock** or **mouse'piece**; *dialect*); a match for firing a

cannon or mine (*obs*); a knot or knob to prevent slipping (also **mous'ing**; *naut*); a black eye, or discoloured swelling (*sl*); a timid, shy, colourless person. ◆ *vi* /mowz/ to hunt for mice or as if for mice; to prowl. ◆ *vt* to treat or to tear as a cat does a mouse; to paw or handle amorously (*archaic*); to secure with a mouse (*naut*). [OE *mūs*, pl *mȳs*; Ger *Maus*, L *mūs*, Gr *mȳs* mouse, muscle]

■ **mouse'kin** (*archaic*) or **mous'ie** *n* a young or little mouse. **mouser** /mow'zer/ or *mow'sər*/ *n* a cat good at catching mice; a prying person (*archaic*). **mousery** /mows'ər-i/ *n* a place where mice habitually gather. **mousey** or **mousy** /mows'i/ *adj* (**mous'ier**; **mous'iest**) like a mouse in colour or smell; full of or infested with mice; noiseless, stealthy; (of hair) of a dull light-brown or greyish-brown colour; (of a person) shy or unassertive. **mous'ily** *adv*. **mous'iness** *n*. **mousing** /mow'zing or mow'sing/ *n* and *adj*. **mousle** /mowz'l/ *vt* to pull about roughly or disrespectfully.

❑ **mouse'bird** *n* any of several small African birds (genera *Colius* and *Urocolius*) with a long tail and crested head. **mouse'-colour** *n* the grey colour of a mouse. **mouse'-colour** or **mouse'-coloured** *adj*. **mouse'-deer** *n* a chevrotain. **mouse'-dun** *adj* mouse-coloured. **mouse'-ear** *n* a name of several plants with soft leaves shaped like a mouse's ear, *esp* forget-me-not. **mouse-ear chickweed** *n* any plant of the genus *Cerastium*, related to chickweed. **mouse-eared bat** *n* a kind of bat, *Myotis myotis*, found chiefly in continental Europe and W Asia. **mouse hare** *n* a pika. **mouse hole** *n* a hole made or used by mice; a small hole or opening. **mouse'-hunt** *n* (*Shakesp*) a mouser. **mouse'mat** or **mouse'pad** *n* a small flat piece of fabric backed with foam rubber, used as a surface on which to move a computer mouse. **mouse'-milking** *n* (*US sl*) the pursuit of any project requiring considerable time and money put into it, but yielding little profit. **mouseover** see **rollover** under **roll**. **mouse potato** *n* (*sl*) a person who spends a great deal of time using a computer, *esp* for leisure (on the analogy of *couch potato* under **couch**[1]). **mouse'-sight** *n* myopia. **mouse'tail** *n* a small ranunculaceous plant (genus *Myosurus*) with a spike of seed vessels very like the tail of a mouse. **mouse'trap** *n* a trap for mice; any cheese of indifferent quality; Cheddar cheese. ◆ *vt* (*N Am inf*) to trick or ensnare by means of a stratagem.

mousmee or **mousmé** /moos'mā/ *n* a Japanese girl, *esp* a waitress. [Jap *musume*]

mousquetaire /moo-skə-tār'/ *n* a musketeer; a woman's cloak trimmed with ribbons, with large buttons, fashionable about 1855; a broad turnover linen collar worn a few years earlier. [Fr]

❑ **mousquetaire glove** *n* a woman's glove, long-armed, loose at the top, and without a lengthwise slit.

moussaka or **mousaka** /mŭ-sä'kə/ *n* a dish traditionally eaten in Greece, Turkey and the Balkans, consisting of alternate layers of minced lamb, aubergines and tomatoes, *usu* covered with béchamel sauce and cheese. [Mod Gr *mousakâs*, from Turk *musakka*]

mousse /moos/ *n* a light dish, either sweet or savoury, made with cream, eggs, flavouring, etc whisked separately and then folded together, *usu* eaten cold; a cosmetic preparation dispensed from an aerosol as a foam, used *esp* to style hair; a foamlike mixture of oil and sea water, produced by an oil spill and difficult to disperse. ◆ *vt* to style (hair) using mousse. [Fr, moss]

mousseline /moos'(ə-)lēn or moos-lēn'/ *n* fine French muslin; a very thin glassware; a claret glass made of it; a kind of mousse with whipped cream added; a dish made with mousseline sauce. [Fr]

❑ **mousseline-de-laine** /-də-len'/ *n* an all-wool type of muslin. **mousseline-de-soie** /-də-swä'/ *n* a silk muslin. **mousseline sauce** *n* a kind of sauce hollandaise made light by adding whipped cream or egg white.

moust see **must**[5].

moustache /mə-, mu- or mŭ-stäsh', or mus'tash/ *n* (also in *pl*) the unshaved hair on a man's upper lip. See also **mustachio**. [Fr *moustache*, from Ital *mostaccio*, from Doric Gr *mystax, -akos* the upper lip, mouth]

■ **moustached'** *adj*. **moustach'ial** *adj*.

❑ **moustache cup** *n* a cup with the top partly covered, formerly used to keep the moustache from getting wet.

■ **old moustache** an old soldier.

Mousterian /moo-stē'ri-ən/ *adj* of an early Palaeolithic culture between Acheulean and Aurignacian. [Le *Moustier*, a cave on the Vézère which has yielded implements of this age]

mousy see **mousey** under **mouse**.

moutan /moo'tan/ *n* a tree peony. [Chin *mŭdān*]

mouter /moo'tər/ a Scots form of **multure**.

mouth /mowth/ *n* (pl **mouths** /mowdhz/) the opening in the head of an animal or human by which it eats and utters sound; any opening or entrance, eg of a bottle, river, cave, etc; a person thought of as a consumer of food; a speaker; a spokesman or spokeswoman; cry, voice, utterance; a wry face, a grimace; backchat, insolence or boastful talk; the responsiveness of a horse to the bit. ◆ *vt* /mowdh/ to utter with exaggerated, affectedly pompous, or self-conscious action of the mouth; to form (words) silently by moving the lips; to utter or pronounce (*archaic*); to declaim or spout; to take in the mouth; to feel, mumble or mangle with the mouth; to train to the bit. ◆ *vi* to declaim, rant (also *vt* with *it*); to join mouths, to kiss (*Shakesp*); to grimace; (of a river, etc) to debouch. [OE *mūth*; Ger *Mund*, Du *mond*]

■ **mouthable** /*mowdh'ə-bl*/ *adj* lending itself to recitation or oratory. **-mouthed** /*-mowdhd*/ *combining form* having a mouth of a specified type, as *wide-mouthed*; using language of a specified type, as *foul-mouthed*. **mouther** /*mowdh'ər*/ *n* a person who mouths. **mouthful** /*mowth'fəl*/ *n* (*pl* **mouth'fuls**) as much food, etc as fills the mouth; a small quantity of food or drink; a big word; a momentous utterance (*sl*); an outburst of strong language. **mouth'less** *adj*. **mouthy** /*mowdh'i* or *mowth'i*/ *adj* (**mouth'ier**; **mouth'iest**) ranting; inclined to backchat, cheeky (*inf*); affectedly over-emphatic.

❑ **mouthbreather** /*mowth'brē-dhər*/ *n* a person who habitually breathes through the mouth. **mouth'breeder** or **mouth'brooder** *n* a cichlid fish that carries its young in its mouth for protection. **mouth'feel** *n* the sensory perception of a particular food while chewed, etc in the mouth. **mouth-filling** /*mowth'/* *adj* full-sounding. **mouth'-friend** *n* (*Shakesp*) a person who only professes friendship. **mouth harp** *n* a mouth organ. **mouth'-honour** *n* (*Shakesp*) insincere civility. **mouth'-made** *adj* (*Shakesp*) insincere. **mouth music** *n* music (*usu* accompanying dance) sung, not played on or accompanied by instrument(s). **mouth organ** *n* a small musical instrument encasing metallic reeds, played by the mouth, a harmonicon or harmonica; Pan-pipes. **mouth'parts** *n pl* any of the limblike parts adapted for feeding that surround the mouth of an arthropod. **mouth'piece** *n* the piece of a musical instrument, tobacco pipe, mask, etc held to or in the mouth; a cigarette holder; a gumshield; a spokesman or spokeswoman. **mouth-to-mouth'** *adj* designating a method of artificial respiration in which a person breathes air directly into the patient's mouth to inflate the lungs. **mouth'wash** *n* an antiseptic solution for cleansing the mouth and for gargling with; rubbish, nonsense (*inf*). **mouth'watering** *adj* causing the release of saliva in the mouth, highly appetizing (also *fig*).

■ **be all mouth** (*sl*) to be unable to support one's boastful talk with action. **by word of mouth** see under **word**. **down in the mouth** see under **down**[1]. **have a big mouth** (*inf*) to (habitually) talk indiscreetly, loudly, or too much. **keep one's mouth shut** (*inf*) not to divulge a secret, etc. **make a poor mouth** to profess poverty. **mouth off** (*sl, esp US*) to express one's opinions forcefully and loudly, sound off; to boast, brag. **shoot one's mouth off** (*sl*) to talk freely, inaccurately, tactlessly, etc. **shut** or **stop the mouth of** to silence. **watch one's mouth** (*inf*) to be careful not to be indiscreet.

mouton /*moo'tən*/ *n* a sheepskin which has been processed, sheared and dyed to resemble the fur of another animal. [Fr *mouton* a sheep]

mouvementé /*moov-mä-tā'*/ (*Fr*) *adj* full of movement, lively.

move /*moov*/ *vt* to cause to change place or posture; to set in motion; to impel; to excite to action; to cause (the bowels) to be evacuated; to persuade; to instigate; to arouse; to provoke; to provoke to anger (*obs*; now *move to anger* or *move anger in*); to touch the feelings or sentiments of; to propose formally before those present at a meeting; to recommend; to sell (*inf*). ◆ *vi* to go from one place to another; to change place or posture; to walk, to carry oneself; to change residence; to make a motion as in an assembly; to bow or salute on meeting (*archaic*); to begin to act; to take action; to become active or exciting (*inf*); to travel fast (*inf*); to hurry up (*inf*); to be sold (*inf*); to go about one's activities, live one's life, pass one's time; in chess, draughts, etc, to transfer a piece in one's turn to another square; (of the bowels) to be evacuated. ◆ *n* an act of moving; a beginning of movement; a proceeding or step, a manoeuvre; the changing of one's residence or business premises; play in turn, as at chess; (in chess, draughts, etc) one's turn to play; advantage depending on whose turn it is to play; the manner in which a chess piece or other playing-piece is or can be moved. [Anglo-Fr *mover*, OFr *movoir* (Fr *mouvoir*), from L *movēre* to move. The obsolete **meve**, **mieve** represent those forms in Fr with accented root-syllable, such as *meuvent* (3rd pers pl)]

■ **movabil'ity** or **moveabil'ity** *n*. **movable** or (*esp law*) **moveable** /*moov'ə-bl*/ *adj* mobile; changeable; not fixed; other than heritable (*Scots law*). ◆ *n* (*esp in pl*) a portable piece of furniture; a piece of movable or moveable property (*Scots law*). **mov'ableness** or **move'ableness** *n*. **mov'ably** or **move'ably** *adv*. **move'less** *adj* motionless, immobile; immovable. **move'lessly** *adv*. **move'lessness** *n*. **move'ment** *n* an act or manner of moving; change of position; an action or gesture; activity; impulse; an evacuation of the bowels, or the matter evacuated; motion of the mind, emotion; the moving parts in a mechanism, *esp* the wheelwork of a clock or watch; melodic progression; accentual character (*prosody*); tempo or pace; a main division of an extended musical composition, with its own more or less independent structure; the suggestion of motion conveyed by a work of art; a general tendency or current of thought, opinion, taste or

action, whether organized and consciously propagated or a mere drift. **mov'er** *n*. **mov'ing** *adj* causing motion; changing position; affecting the feelings, sentiments or sympathies; pathetic. **mov'ingly** *adv*. ❑ **movable feast** see under **feast**. **movement chart** *n* a chart plotting the movements of staff and documents within an office, intended to improve efficiency. **movement therapist** *n* a specialist in **movement therapy**, a physical therapy for the mentally or physically disabled aimed at developing or improving voluntary body movements. **moving average** *n* a sequence of values derived from an earlier sequence from which a mean was taken of each successive group of values with a constant number of members. **mov'ing-coil** *adj* of, or relating to, electrical equipment that incorporates a coil of wire so placed within a magnetic field as either to vibrate when current is passed through it, or to generate a current when vibrated. **moving map** *n* a map used on board a ship or aircraft that adjusts to keep the position of the moving vessel always in correspondence with a fixed centre point on the map. **moving pavement** or **walkway** *n* (in an airport, etc) a moving strip set into the floor that carries pedestrians along as though on a conveyor belt. **moving pictures** *n pl* the cinema; cinema films in general. **moving staircase** *n* an escalator. ■ **get a move on** to hurry up; to make progress. **know a move or two** to be sharp or streetwise. **make a move** to take a step, perform a manoeuvre; to prepare to depart. **make a move on** or **put the moves on** (*sl, esp US*) to make sexual advances to. **move heaven and earth** see under **heaven**. **move house** to move to a new place of residence; to move one's possessions to one's new home. **move in** to occupy new premises, etc. **move in on** (*inf*) to advance towards, close in on; to take steps towards controlling or usurping. **move out** to vacate premises. **move over** or **up** to move so as to make room for someone, etc. **movers and shakers** the people with power and influence. **on the move** changing or about to change one's place; travelling; progressing.

movie /*moo'vē*/ (*inf*) *n* a motion picture, a cinema film; a showing of such; (in *pl*; *usu* with *the*) motion pictures in general, or the industry that produces them. ◆ *adj* of, for or relating to (a showing of) a cinema film, or the film industry itself. [*Moving* picture and **-ie**] ■ **movieo'ke** *n* (modelled on **karaoke**) the entertainment of providing the voice parts to muted film scenes that are displayed on a screen. ❑ **mov'iegoer** *n*. **mov'ieland** *n* the world of film-making. **mov'iemaker** *n*. **movie theatre** or **house** *n* (*N Am*) a cinema.

Moviola® /*moo-vē-ō'lə*/ *n* a brand of upright film-editing machine (also used generically) combining image and soundtrack facilities, largely superseded by the more flexible multi-track desk-type machine. [**movie** and **Pianola**®]

MOW *abbrev*: Movement for the Ordination of Women (now known as **WATCH**).

mow[1] /*mō*/ *vt* (**mow'ing**; **mowed** /*mōd*/; **mowed** or **mown** /*mōn*/) to cut down, or cut the grass on, with a scythe or now *esp* a grass-cutting machine; to cut down in great numbers (*esp* with *down*) (also *fig*). [OE *māwan*; Ger *mähen*; L *metere* to reap] ■ **mowed** or **mown** *adj*. **mow'er** *n* a person who mows grass, etc; a machine with revolving blades for mowing grass. **mow'ing** *n* the act of cutting grass, etc; land from which grass is cut; (in *pl*) loose grass following mowing. ❑ **mowing machine** *n*.

mow[2] /*mow* or *mō*/ *n* a pile of hay, corn in sheaves, pease, etc, *esp* in a barn; a place in a barn for such a heap. ◆ *vt* (**mow'ing**; **mowed** /*mowd*/) to heap in a mow. [OE *mūga* heap; ON *mūgi* swath, crowd, mob] ■ **mow'burn** *vi* to heat and ferment in the mow. **mow'burnt** *adj*.

mow[3] /*mow*, also *mō*/, also (*obs*) **moe** /*mō*/ *n* a wry face. ◆ *vi* to make grimaces. [OFr *moue*, *moe* (Fr *moue*), or MDu *mouwe*, both meaning grimace] ■ **nae mows** /*nā mowz*/ (*Scot*) no laughing matter.

mowa /*mow'ə*/ same as **mahua**.

mowdiewart, **mowdiwart**, **mowdiewort** and **mowdiwort** Scots forms of **mouldwarp**.

mown see under **mow**[1].

mowra /*mow'rə*/ same as **mahua**.

MOX /*moks*/ *n* a form of nuclear fuel consisting of a mixture of uranium and plutonium oxides. [*mixed oxide*]

moxa /*mok'sə*/ *n* the leaf down of any of several wormwoods (*esp Artemisia moxa*), or sunflower pith, cotton wool, or other material, *usu* formed into a cone or stick and in Chinese medicine burned over acupuncture points, used as a counter-irritant, for cauterization, and in the relief of chronic, eg arthritic, pain. [Jap *mogusa*] ■ **moxibustion** /*-bust'yən*/ *n* (modelled on *combustion*) the cauterization of a wound by moxa; the burning of a herbal moxa as a counter-irritant; the use of a moxa in acupuncture.

moxie /mok'si/ (*N Am sl*) *n* courage, daring; energy, vigour. [*Moxie*®, a soft drink]

moy /moi/ (*Shakesp*) *n* supposed by Pistol (misunderstanding a Frenchman's *moi* me) to be the name of a coin, or possibly a measure (Fr *muid*, from L *modius*) of corn.

moya /moi'ä/ *n* volcanic mud. [Prob Am Sp]

Moygashel® /moi-gash'əl or -gə-shel'/ *n* a type of fine linen manufactured in Northern Ireland. [*Moygashel*, Co. Tyrone]

moyity (*Spenser*) same as **moiety**.

moyl or **moyle** /moil/ (*obs*) *n* a mule. [OFr *mul, mule*]

moyle (*Spenser*) same as **moil**.

moz or **mozz** /moz/ (*Aust sl*) *n* a curse or jinx. [Heb *mazzāl* luck]
 ■ **mozz'le** *n* luck, *esp* bad luck.

Mozambican or **Mozambiquan** /mō-zam-bē'kən/ *adj* of or relating to the republic of *Mozambique* in SE Africa, or its inhabitants. ◆ *n* a native or inhabitant of Mozambique.

Mozarab /mō-zar'ab/ *n* a privileged Christian Spaniard under Moorish rule. [Sp *Mozárabe*, from Ar *musta'rib* would-be Arab]
 ■ **Mozar'abic** *adj*.

Mozartian or **Mozartean** /mō-tsär'ti-ən/ *adj* of or like (the style, etc of) Wolfgang Amadeus *Mozart* (1756–91), Austrian composer.

moze /mōz/ (*textiles*) *vt* to gig, raise a nap on. [Origin obscure]

mozetta /mō-tset'ə/ *n* a short cape to which a hood may be attached, worn by popes, cardinals, bishops and abbots (also **mozzett'a**). [Ital, dimin from *mozzo* docked]

mozz see **moz**.

mozzarella /mot-sə-rel'ə/ *n* a mild, white Italian cheese with a springy texture, *orig* (and still occasionally) made from buffalo's milk. [Ital]

mozzie see **mossie**[1].

mozzle see under **moz**.

MP *abbrev*: Member of Parliament; Metropolitan Police; Military Police(man); mounted police; Municipal Police (*N Am*).

mp *abbrev*: melting-point (also **m.p.**); mezzo-piano (*music*).

MPAA *abbrev*: Motion Picture Association of America.

MPC *abbrev*: monetary policy committee (of the Bank of England); multimedia personal computer.

MPEG /em'peg/ (*comput*) *abbrev*: Moving Picture Experts Group, a standard for coding audio-visual information (also **MPG**).

mpg *abbrev*: miles per gallon.

mph *abbrev*: miles per hour.

MPharm *abbrev*: Master of Pharmacy.

MPhil *abbrev*: Master of Philosophy.

mpret /(ə)m-pret' or -bret'/ *n* a former title of the ruler of Albania. [Albanian, from L *imperātor* emperor]

MPS *abbrev*: Member of the Philological Society.

MP3 *abbrev*: MPEG-1 Layer 3, a compressed file format that allows fast downloading of audio data from the Internet.
 ❑ **MP3 player** *n* a device for storing and playing audio data that has been recorded using the MP3 format.

MPV *abbrev*: multipurpose vehicle.

MR *abbrev*: Master of the Rolls; Mauritian rupee; motivation(al) research (investigative study of consumer reaction).

Mr /mis'tər/ *n* (pl sometimes **Messrs** /mes'ərz/) the normal form of title prefixed to a man's name, whether full name or surname only, or sometimes to an office held by a man. [Abbrev of **Mister**]
 ❑ **Mr Right** *n* (*inf*) the ideal mate or marriage partner sought by a woman.

MRA *abbrev*: Moral Rearmament.

MRAM /em'ram/ (*comput*) *abbrev*: magnetoresistive random access memory.

MRBM *abbrev*: medium-range ballistic missile.

MRC *abbrev*: Medical Research Council.

MRCA *abbrev*: multirole combat aircraft.

MRCGP *abbrev*: Member of the Royal College of General Practitioners.

MRCP *abbrev*: Member of the Royal College of Physicians.

MRCSLT *abbrev*: Member of the Royal College of Speech and Language Therapists.

MRCVS *abbrev*: Member of the Royal College of Veterinary Surgeons.

MRE (*milit*) *abbrev*: Meal(s) Ready to Eat.

MRes *abbrev*: Master of Research.

MRG *abbrev*: Minority Rights Group.

MRI *abbrev*: magnetic resonance imaging.

mridangam, mridamgam /mri-däng'gəm/, **mridanga** /mri-däng'gə/ or **mridang** /mri-däng'/ *n* a two-headed Indian drum, one of the heads being larger than the other. [Sans *mridaṃíga*]

MRM *abbrev*: mechanically-recovered meat.

mRNA (*genetics*) *abbrev*: messenger RNA.

M-roof see under **M** (*n*).

MRPharmS *abbrev*: Member of the Royal Pharmaceutical Society.

M(R)RP *abbrev*: manufacturer's (recommended) retail price.

Mrs /mis'iz/ *n* the normal form of title prefixed to a married woman's name, whether her full name with her own or her husband's given name, or her surname only. [Abbrev of **Mistress**]

MRSA *abbrev*: methicillin-resistant Staphylococcus aureus, a bacterium that is resistant to most antibiotics.

MS *abbrev*: manuscript (*pl* **MSS**); Master of Surgery; Mauritius (IVR); Mississippi (US state); multiple sclerosis.

Ms /miz or məz/ *n* a title substituted for **Mrs** or **Miss** before the name of a woman, to avoid distinguishing between the married and the unmarried.

ms *abbrev*: manuscript; millisecond; (also **M/S**) months.

MSA *abbrev*: motorway service area.

msb (*comput*) *abbrev*: most significant bit.

MSc *abbrev*: Master of Science.

MSDOS® or **MS-DOS**® /em-es-dos'/ (*comput*) *abbrev*: Microsoft disk operating system.

MSF *abbrev*: Médecins sans Frontières.

MSG *abbrev*: monosodium glutamate.

Msgr *abbrev*: Monsignor.

msl *abbrev*: mean sea-level.

MSM *abbrev*: methyl sulphonyl methane, an anti-inflammatory agent.

MSP *abbrev*: Member of the Scottish Parliament.

MSS or **mss** *abbrev*: manuscripts.

MST *abbrev*: Mountain Standard Time.

msv *abbrev*: millisievert(s).

MSW *abbrev*: magnetic surface wave (*radar*); Medical Social Worker.

MT *abbrev*: mean time; Mechanical Transport; Montana (US state); Mountain Time.

Mt *abbrev*: metical (currency of Mozambique); Mount.

Mt (*chem*) *symbol*: meitnerium.

MTB *abbrev*: motor torpedo-boat.

MTBE *abbrev*: methyl tertiary-butyl ether, used as a petrol additive to reduce toxic emissions.

MTBF (*electronics*, etc) *abbrev*: mean time between failures.

MTD (*radar*) *abbrev*: moving target detector.

MTech *abbrev*: Master of Technology.

mth *abbrev*: month.

Mts *abbrev*: Mountains.

MTV *abbrev*: Music Television, a subscription television network specializing in music videos.

mu /mū, moo or mü/ *n* the Greek letter M, μ, equivalent to M or m; as a numeral, μ' = 40, ‚μ = 40000; used as a symbol for **micron** and **micro-** (2). [Gr *mȳ*]
 ❑ **mu-** (or *l-*)**meson** *n* a subatomic particle, classed formerly as the lightest type of meson, now as the heaviest type of lepton, having unit negative charge, now largely superseded by **muon**.

mucate and **mucedinous** see under **mucus**.

much /much/ *adj* (*compar* **more**; *superl* **most**) a great quantity of; great (*obs*); many (*Shakesp*). ◆ *adv* in a great degree; to a great extent; in nearly the same way; by far; (in old ironical use) like the modern slang 'not much', I don't think. ◆ *n* a great deal; anything of importance or worth. —Also in unshortened archaic form **much'el**, also (*Spenser*) **much'ell** or **moch'ell** and (*Scot* and *N Eng*) **mick'le** or **muck'le**. [ME *muche, muchel*, from OE *micel, mycel*]
 ■ **much'ly** *adv* (*archaic* and *joc*). **much'ness** *n* (*archaic*) greatness; magnitude.
 ■ **a bit much** too much to put up with, unreasonable. **as much as** or **much as** although, even though. **make much of** see under **make**[1]. **much about it** something like what it usually is. **much of a muchness** just about the same value or amount. **not much of a** rather poor specimen of a. **not up to much** (*inf*) not very good. **too much for** more than a match for. **too much of a good thing** more than can be tolerated.

muchacha /moo-cha'chə/ *n* a young woman or female servant. [Sp, fem of **muchacho**]

muchacho /moo-cha'chō/ n (pl **mucha'chos**) a young man or male servant. [Sp]

mucic acid, **mucid**, **muciferous** and **mucigen** see under **mucus**.

mucilage /mū'si-lij/ n a gluey mixture of carbohydrates in plants; any sticky substance; gum used as an adhesive. [LL *mucilago* mouldy juice, from *mucēre* to be mouldy]
■ **mucilaginous** /-laj'/ adj. **mucilag'inousness** n.

mucin see under **mucus**.

muck /muk/ n dung; manure; wet or clinging filth; anything contemptible or worthless; dirt, debris, rubble; gold (*poetic* and *archaic*); rubbishy reading matter; a mess. ◆ vt to clear of muck (with *out*); to manure with muck; to make dirty (with *up*); to make a mess of, to bungle (with *up*; **muck'-up** n); to treat inconsiderately (with *about* or *around*). ◆ vi (*usu* with *about* or *around*; *inf*) to potter; to act the fool. [Prob Scand; cf ON *myki*, Dan *mög* dung]
■ **muck'er** n a person who mucks; a money-grubber (*obs*); a mess; a mishap, disaster (*orig* a fall in the mire); a coarse, unrefined person; a best friend, mate, sidekick; a young townsman, not a student (*old US*). ◆ vt to hoard (*obs*); to squander; to vitiate. ◆ vi to come to grief; to make a muddle of anything. **muck'iness** n. **muck'y** adj (**muck'ier**; **muck'iest** nasty, filthy; of the nature of muck; like muck.
□ **muck-a-muck** see **high-muck-a-muck**. **muck'heap** or **muck'-midden** n a dunghill. **muck'-rake** n a rake for manure. ◆ vi to seek out and expose scandals or supposed scandals, whether for worthy or unworthy motives. **muck'-raker** n. **muck'-raking** n. **muck'spread** vi to spread manure. **muck'spreader** n an agricultural machine for spreading manure. **muck'spreading** n. **muck'sweat** n (*Brit*) profuse sweat. **muck'-worm** n a worm or grub that lives in muck; a person who acquires money by mean devices; a miser.
■ **Lady** or **Lord Muck** (*facetious*) a title or name applied to a woman or man assuming aristocratic airs. **make a muck of** (*inf*) to make dirty; to bungle, mismanage. **muck in** (**with**) (*inf*) to share with; to help, participate (in).

Mucker /muk'ər/ n a nickname for a member of a Königsberg sect (1835) of dualistic theosophists; (without *cap*) /muk'ər/ a fanatical reformer; a hypocrite. [Ger]

muckle /muk'l/ a Scottish form of **mickle**.

muckluck, **mukluk** or **mucluc** /muk'luk/ n an Inuit sealskin boot. [Inuit]

mucoid see under **mucus**.

mucor /mū'kər/ n a mould of the *Mucor* genus of zygomycete fungi, including some of the commonest moulds, giving name to an order or family **Mūcorā'les** or **Mūcorin'eae**. [L, mould]

mucosa and **mucosity** see under **mucus**.

mucous see under **mucus**.

mucro /mū'krō/ (*biol*) n (pl **mūcro'nes** /-nēz/ or **mū'cros**) a short stiff sharp point forming an abrupt end. [L *mūcrō*, *-ōnis* a sharp point]
■ **mu'cronate** /-krən-āt/ or **mu'cronated** /-id/ adj.

mucus /mū'kəs/ n the slimy fluid secreted by various membranes in the body, which it moistens and protects. [L *mūcus* nose mucus; cf *mungere* to wipe away]
■ **mu'cate** n a salt of mucic acid. **mucedinous** /-sed'/ or /-sēd'/ adj mouldy, mildewy. **mu'cid** adj mouldy, musty. **muciferous** /-sif'/ adj secreting or conveying mucus. **mu'cigen** /-si-jen/ n a substance secreted by the cells of mucous membrane, converted into mucin. **mu'cin** /mū'sin/ n any one of a class of albuminous substances in mucus. **mu'cinous** adj. **mucoid** /mū'koid/ adj like mucus. **mucopolysacch'aride** n (*chem*) a complex polysaccharide composed of amino sugars linked into repeating units. **mucopū'rulent** adj of mucus and pus. **mucosa** /mū-kō'sə/ n (pl **mucō'sae** /-sē/) a mucous membrane. **mucō'sal** adj. **mucosanguin'eous** adj consisting of mucus and blood. **mucos'ity** n. **mu'cous** adj like mucus; slimy; viscous; producing mucus. **mucoviscidō'sis** n cystic fibrosis. **mu'cūlent** adj like mucus.
□ **mucic acid** n a colourless crystalline acid obtained from lactose. **mucous membrane** n a lining of various tubular cavities of the body, eg the nose, with glands secreting mucus.

MUD (*comput*) abbrev : Multi-User Dungeon or Dimension, a class of interactive computer games on the Internet.

mud /mud/ n wet soft earth; a mixture of earthy or clayey particles with water; a similar mixture with certain added chemicals used as a lubricant in drilling gas- or oil-wells; something worthless or contemptible; vilification, abuse, slander, thought of as sticking or clinging like mud. ◆ vt to bury in mud; to clog with mud; to plaster with mud; to make dirty; to make turbid; to supply with mud. ◆ vi to hide in the mud. [Cf OLGer *mudde*, Du *modder*]
■ **mudd'er** n (*sl*) a racehorse that responds well to muddy conditions. **mudd'ily** adv. **mudd'iness** n. **mudd'y** adj (**mudd'ier**; **mudd'iest**) foul with mud; containing mud; covered with mud; of the nature of mud; like mud; mud-coloured; cloudy, murky; confused, befuddled;

stupid. ◆ vt and vi (**mudd'ying**; **mudd'ied**) to make or become muddy.
□ **mud'bath** n a bath in mud, *esp* as a medical treatment; an outdoor event taking place in muddy conditions (*inf*). **mud'boat** n a board or sled for travel over mud-flats or swamps; a boat for carrying away dredged mud. **mud'cat** n (*US*) a name given to several species of catfish. **mud'-clerk** n (*obs US*) an assistant purser. **mud'-cone** n a cone formed by a mud volcano. **mud dauber** n a wasp of the family Sphecidae that deposits its eggs in individual cells constructed of mud. **muddy-head'ed** adj confused, muddled. **muddy-mett'led** adj (*Shakesp*) spiritless. **mud engineer** n a person overseeing the use and supply of drilling mud on a gas- or oil-well. **mud'fish** n a fish that burrows in mud, *esp* a lungfish. **mud'flap** n a flap fixed behind the wheels of a vehicle to prevent mud, etc, being thrown up behind. **mud'flat** n a muddy stretch of land, *esp* near a river mouth, submerged at high water. **mud'flow** n a flow of mud down a slope. **mud'guard** n (on a bicycle, etc) a curved hood fixed over a wheel to catch mud-splashes thrown up by it. **mud hen** n any of a variety of water birds, such as rails, coots or gallinules, that inhabit marshy places. **mud'hole** n a hole with mud in it; an opening for removing sediment from a boiler, etc. **mud'hook** n (*sl*) an anchor. **mud'hopper** n a mudskipper. **mud'lark** n a name for various birds that frequent mud; a person who searches the banks of tidal rivers for scrap metal, ropes, etc, to sell; a street urchin (*archaic sl*); a mudder (*Aust sl*). ◆ vi to work or play in mud. **mud lava** n a stream of mud from a volcano. **mudlogg'er** n a person who looks for traces of oil, gas, etc in mud excavated from a borehole. **mudlogg'ing** n. **mud'-lump** n a raised area of mud, often giving off gases, as in the Mississippi delta. **mud minnow** n a small fish (genus *Umbra*) related to the pikes. **mud'pack** n a cosmetic paste for cleansing the skin, containing fuller's earth. **mud pie** n a small, moulded mass of mud made to play with by children; an insult or calumny hurled at someone; a rich dessert of chocolate and coffee mousse on a pastry base (*N Am*). **mud pump** n a pump used in drilling deep holes (eg oil wells) that forces thixotropic mud to the bottom of the hole and flushes out rock chips. **mud'puppy** n (*US*) the axolotl; an aquatic salamander (genus *Necturus*) of N America that retains certain larval features, including external gills. **mud'scow** n a flat mud-boat. **mud'skipper** n a goby found in Africa, Japan, etc, able to remain out of water and skip about on bare mud using its fins. **mud'slide** n a slippage of a mass of mud down a hillside, etc. **mud'slinger** n. **mud'slinging** n vilification or malicious slander intended to discredit another. **mud'stone** n an argillaceous rock not distinctly fissile. **mud turtle** n a freshwater turtle of the genus *Kinosternon*, found in N and Central America. **mud volcano** n a vent that emits gas and mud, often forming a conical mound. **mud'wort** n a small mud-growing scrophulaceous plant (*Limosella aquatica*). **mud wrestling** n competitive wrestling in an arena with a floor of wet mud.
■ **clear as mud** not at all clear. **his**, **her**, etc, **name is mud** he, she, etc, is very much out of favour. **mud in your eye** good health (used as a toast). **muddy the waters** to confuse a situation by introducing complications. **throw**, **fling** or **sling mud at** to insult, to slander.

muddle /mud'l/ vt to confuse; to mix up, fail to distinguish between (with *up*); to bungle; to make (eg water) muddy; to mix, stir (drinks, etc; *US*). ◆ vi to potter about; to blunder; to wallow, dabble, or grub about in mud (*archaic*). ◆ n confusion, mess; mental confusion, bewilderment. [Frequentative of **mud**]
■ **mudd'ler** n. **mudd'lingly** adv. **mudd'ly** adj.
□ **mudd'le-brained** adj mentally confused, muddled. **mudd'le-head** n a blockhead. **muddle-head'ed** adj. **muddle-head'edly** adv. **muddle-head'edness** n.
■ **muddle along** or **through** to progress slowly and haphazardly. **muddle away** to squander or fritter away confusedly.

mudéjar /moo-dhā'hhar/ (*Sp*; also with *cap*) n (pl **mudé'jares** /-ās/) a Spanish Moor, *esp* one permitted to remain in Spain after the Christian reconquest. ◆ adj of a style of architecture characteristic of the mudéjares. [Ar *mudajjan*, literally, one allowed to remain]

mudge[1] /muj/ (*inf* and *dialect*) n mud, sludge. [Perh from **mud** and **sludge**]

mudge[2] /muj/ (*inf*) vt to blur, confuse. ◆ vi to equivocate, prevaricate. [Orig used in *fudge and mudge*, poss from **muddle** and **fudge**[2]]
■ **mud'ger** n.

mudir /moo-dēr'/ n a local governor, *esp* in Egypt. [Ar *mudīr*]
■ **mudir'ieh** or **mudir'ia** n a mudir's province or office.

mudra /mə-drä'/ or /moo'drə/ n any of the symbolic hand gestures in Hindu religious ceremonies and classical Indian dance; a posture in which the body is held in yoga, an asana. [Sans, literally, sign, token]

mueddin see **muezzin**.

Muenster same as **Munster**.

muesli /moo'/ or /mū'zli/ n a dish of rolled oats, nuts, fruit, etc eaten *esp* as a breakfast cereal. [Swiss Ger]

muezzin /moo-ez'in/ n the Muslim official who calls the faithful to prayer (also **muedd'in**). [Ar mu'adhdhin]

muff[1] /muf/ n a cylinder of fur or thick fabric for keeping the hands warm; a similar contrivance for keeping the feet, ears, etc warm; a mitt (obs); the female genitals (vulgar sl). [Prob from Du mof; cf Ger Muff a muff]

■ **muffettee'** n (obs) a muffler; a woollen cuff.

muff[2] /muf/ (inf) vt to perform awkwardly; to bungle; to miss. ◆ vi to act clumsily, esp in letting a ball slip out of the hands. ◆ n a person who is awkward or unskilful, esp in sport; a duffer; a bungler, esp in sports; an unpractical person; a man lacking male vigour and strength (derog); someone who lacks savoir-faire; a failure, esp to hold a ball. [Poss **muff**[1]]

■ **muff'ish** adj.

muffettee see under **muff**[1].

muffin /muf'in/ n a savoury, round, breadlike cake, eaten hot, with butter; a sweet cup-shaped cake made with eggs and baking powder (orig N Am); a small plate; a man accompanying or chaperoning a young woman (sl); a poor ball-player. [Origin unknown]

■ **muffineer'** n a dish for keeping muffins hot; a castor for sprinkling salt or sugar on muffins.

◻ **muff'in-bell** n a bell rung by a muffin man. **muff'in-cap** n a round flat cap for men. **muff'in-fight** or **-worry** n (inf) a tea-party. **muffin man** n an itinerant muffin-seller. **muffin pan** n (N Am) a baking tray with cup-shaped indentations for making muffins. **muffin top** n (sl) a roll of fatty flesh that spills out over the top of a pair of low-cut trousers.

muffle[1] /muf'l/ vt to envelop, for warmth, concealment, stifling of sound, etc; to blindfold (archaic); to deaden or dull the sound of. ◆ n a boxing glove (obs); a means of muffling; a receptacle, oven, or compartment in which things can be heated in a furnace without contact with the fuel and its products; (a kiln containing) an inner chamber in which to fire painted porcelain, enamel, etc; a muffled state; a muffled sound. [Appar Fr moufle mitten]

■ **muff'led** adj. **muff'ler** n a scarf for the throat; any means of muffling; someone who muffles; a silencer fitted to the exhaust of a motor vehicle (N Am).

◻ **muffler shop** n (N Am) a garage specializing in fitting and repairing mufflers.

muffle[2] /muf'l/ n the thick naked upper lip and nose of an animal, eg a ruminant. [Fr mufle]

muflon see **moufflon**.

MUFTI abbrev : Minimum Use of Force Tactical Intervention.

Mufti /muf'ti/ n (pl **Muf'tis**) an expounder of Muslim law. [Ar muftī, from 'aftā to make a legal decision]

■ **Muf'tat** or **Muf'tiat** n a religious judicial board.

mufti /muf'ti/ n the civilian dress of someone who wears a uniform when on duty; plain clothes; a civilian. [Prob from **Mufti**]

mug[1] /mug/ n a cup with more or less vertical sides; its contents. [Poss Scand; cf Norw mugga, Swed mugg]

■ **mug'ful** /-fəl/ n (pl **mug'fuls**). **mugg'er** n a hawker of earthenware.

◻ **mug'-house** n (obs) an alehouse. **mug'-hunter** n (games) a pot-hunter.

mug[2] /mug/ (inf) n the face; the mouth. ◆ vi (**mugg'ing**; **mugged**) (theatre) to grimace. [Poss from the grotesque face on a drinking-mug]

◻ **mug'shot** or **mug shot** n (inf) a photograph of a person's face, esp one taken for police records.

mug[3] /mug/ (inf) n a simpleton; an easy dupe. [Poss from **mug**[2]]

■ **a mug's game** something only fools would do.

mug[4] /mug/ (inf) n a sap or swot; an exam. ◆ vt and vi (often with up) to study hard; to swot up. [Origin unknown]

mug[5] /mug/ (inf) vt and vi to attack from behind, seizing by the throat; to attack suddenly with the intention of robbing. [Perh **mug**[2]]

■ **mugg'ee** n the victim, or intended victim, of a mugger. **mugg'er** n. **mugg'ing** n.

mug[6] /mug/ n a woolly-faced sheep. [Cf **mug**[2]]

mugearite /moo-gē'rīt/ n a dark finely crystalline basic igneous rock composed mainly of oligoclase, orthoclase, and olivine, with iron oxides, developed at Mugeary in Skye.

mugger[1] /mug'ər/ n a broad-snouted Indian crocodile. [Hindi magar]

mugger[2] see under **mug**[1,5].

muggins /mug'inz/ n a fool, sucker, esp used facetiously to refer to oneself as such; a children's card game; a form of dominoes. [Ety doubtful]

muggle /mug'l/ (inf) n a person who does not have magic powers; an inept or unskilled person. [Popularized by British author JK Rowling (born 1965)]

Muggletonian /mu-gl-tō'ni-ən/ n a member of a sect founded by John Reeve and Lodowick Muggleton (1609–98), who claimed to be the two witnesses in the Bible in Revelation 11.3–6.

muggy /mug'i/ adj (**mugg'ier**; **mugg'iest**) foggy; (of weather) close and damp; (of straw, etc) wet or mouldy. [Perh ON mugga mist]

■ **mugg'iness** n dampness; a muggy condition. **mugg'ish** adj.

Mughal see **Mogul**.

mugwort /mug'wûrt/ n a common British wormwood. [OE mucgwyrt, literally, midge-wort]

mugwump /mug'wump/ (N Am) n a Native American chief; a person of great importance, or one who thinks himself or herself to be so; someone who keeps politically aloof. [Algonquian mugquomp a great chief]

■ **mug'wumpery** n.

Muhammedan see **Mohammedan**.

Muharram, Muharrem /moo-hur'um/ or **Moharram** /mō-hur'um/ n the first month of the Muslim year; a great fast in commemoration of the Israelites' flight from Egypt, and of Hasan and Hosain (grandsons of Mohammed), held during its first ten days; a public procession during the fast. [Ar, sacred]

muid /mü-ē'/ n an old French measure of capacity; a hogshead; a dry measure for corn, etc; /mä'id/ a sack of 3 bushels (S Afr). [Fr, from L modius; cf Du mud]

muil see **mule**[2].

muir, muirburn, etc see **moor**[1].

muist see **must**[5].

mujahideen, mujahedeen, mujahidin or **mujahedin** /moo-jə-hə-dēn'/ n pl Islamic fundamentalist freedom fighters. [Ar mujāhidīn fighters]

mujik see **muzhik**.

mukhabarat /mü-hhä-bə-rät'/ n a secret police force in some Middle Eastern countries. [Ar mukhābarāt]

mukhtar /mook'tär/ n an Indian lawyer; a chief local government official in Turkey. [Ar mukhtār chosen]

mukluk see **muckluck**.

mulatto /mü-lat'ō/ (old) n (pl **mulatt'os** or **mulatt'oes**) (also fem **mulatt'a** or **mulatt'ress**) the offspring of a black person and a person of European descent (also adj). [Sp mulato, dimin of mulo mule; Fr mulâtre]

mulberry /mul'b(ə-)ri/ n the edible blackberry-like fruit of any tree of the genus Morus (family Moraceae); the tree bearing it, with leaves on which silkworms feed; extended to various fruits or plants more or less similar superficially or really; the colour of the fruit, dark purple. ◆ adj mulberry-coloured. [Prob OHGer mulberi (Mod Ger Maulbeere), from L mōrum; cf Morus and **berry**[1]]

◻ **mul'berry-faced** adj having a face blotched with purple. **mulberry fig** n the true sycamore (sycomore), a fig tree with leaves like those of mulberry. **Mulberry harbour** n a preconstructed harbour (codename Mulberry) towed across the English Channel for the 1944 landings in Normandy in World War II.

mulch /mulch/ or **mulsh** /mulsh/ n loose material, strawy dung, etc, laid on the soil around plants, to protect roots, keep down weeds and retain moisture, sometimes with a nutritional function. ◆ vt to cover with mulch. ◆ adj soft. [Cf Ger dialect molsch soft, beginning to decay; OE melsc]

Mulciber /mul'si-bər/ n another name of Vulcan, the Roman god of fire and metalworking. [L]

■ **Mulcibē'rian** adj.

mulct /mulkt/ n a fine; a penalty. ◆ vt (pap **mulct'ed** or **mulct**) to fine; to swindle; to deprive (with of). [L mulcta a fine]

mule[1] /mūl/ n the offspring of a donkey (esp male) and a horse (esp female), widely used as a beast of burden; a hybrid; a cross between a canary and another finch; a cotton-spinning machine; an obstinate person; a coin with obverse and reverse designs struck from dies of two different issues; a person who smuggles drugs into a country for a dealer (sl). ◆ adj hybrid. [OE mūl, from L mūlus was superseded by OFr; mul (masc; in Mod Fr the dimin mulet is used), mule (fem), from L mūlus, mūla]

■ **muleteer** /mūl-i-tēr'/ n a mule-driver. **mul'ish** adj like a mule; obstinate. **mul'ishly** adv. **mul'ishness** n.

◻ **mule deer** n a long-eared, black-tailed deer of N America.

mule[2] /mūl/ or (Scot) **muil** /mül/ n a backless slipper or shoe. [Fr mule]

mulesing /mülz'ing/ (Aust) n the practice of removing wool-bearing skin from around the tail of (esp merino) sheep to prevent blowfly infestation. [JHW Mules (1876–1946), Australian sheep farmer]

muleta /mü-let'ə/ n a small cape fixed to a stick used by a matador in a bullfight. [Sp, small mule]

muley, **mulley** or **mooly** /moo'ⁱ or mū'li/ adj hornless. ◆ n a hornless cow; any cow. [Gaelic maol or Welsh moel bald]

mulga /mul'gə/ n any of several acacias, esp Acacia aneura, typically found in arid regions of Australia; (with the) the outback. [From an Aboriginal language]
❑ **mulga wire** n (Aust) the bush telegraph.

muliebrity /mū-li-eb'ri-ti/ n womanhood, femininity. [L muliebritās, -tātis, from mulier a woman]

mull¹ /mul/ vi and vt (usu with over) to cogitate, ponder, turn over in the mind. [Origin obscure]

mull² /mul/ vt to warm, spice and sweeten (wine, ale, etc). [Origin obscure]
■ **mulled** adj. **mull'er** n.

mull³ /mul/ (Scot) n a promontory. [Prob Gaelic maol or ON mūli snout; cf Ger Maul]

mull⁴ /mul/ vt to crumble. ◆ n a layer of humus formed by rapid decompostion, through the actions of a rich soil fauna, in near-neutral or alkaline conditions (cf **moder**, **mor¹**). [Cf OE myl dust]

mull⁵ /mul/ n a soft muslin (also **mul'mul** or **mul'mull**). [Hindustani malmal]

mull⁶ /mul/ (Scot) n a snuffbox. [See **mill¹**]

mull⁷ /mul/ n a muddle. ◆ vt to bungle. [Ety doubtful]

mull⁸ /mul/ (Shakesp) vt to **dull**, stupefy. [Origin obscure; perh from the mulling of wine]

mullah¹, **moolah**, **mollah** or **molla** /mul'ə, moo'lə, mŭl'ə or mol'ə/ n a Muslim learned in Islamic theology and law; a Muslim schoolmaster or teacher; a title of respect for a person whose work lies in advising on or expounding the law, etc; a fanatical preacher of war on the infidel. [Pers, Turk and Hindi mullā, from Ar maulā]

mullah² see **muller²**.

mullarky same as **malarkey**.

mullein /mul'in/ n a tall, stiff, yellow-flowered woolly plant (genus Verbascum) of the Scrophulariaceae, popularly known as **hag'-taper**, **Adam's flannel**, **Aaron's rod** or **shepherd's club**. [Anglo-Fr moleine]

muller¹ /mul'ər/ n a flat heavy stone or iron pulverizing tool. [Perh OFr moloir, from moldre (Fr moudre) to grind]

muller² /mŭl'ər/ or **mullah** /mŭl'ə/ (sl) vt to beat severely; to murder; to inflict a severe defeat on. [Origin unknown]
■ **mull'ered** or **mull'ahed** adj intoxicated.

Müllerian mimicry /moo-lē'ri-ən mim'i-kri/ n mimicry in which two or more inedible species resemble one another as a protective device. [Johanna FT Müller (1821–97), German zoologist]

mullet¹ /mul'it/ n a nearly cylindrical food-fish of the family Mullidae (**red mullet**) or Mugilidae (**grey mullet**). [OFr mulet, dimin from L mullus red mullet]

mullet² /mul'it/ (heraldry) n a five-pointed star, the cadency mark of a son. [OFr molette rowel of a spur, from L mola a millstone]

mullet³ /mul'it/ n a hairstyle that is short at the front, long at the back, and ridiculous all round. [Perh from dialect mullethead a fool]

mulley see **muley**.

mulligan /mul'i-gən/ (inf) n a stew made from various scraps of food (chiefly N Am); a free extra shot sometimes allowed to a player to recover from an errant shot (golf). [Perh from the surname]

mulligatawny /mul-i-gə-tö'ni/ n a curry-soup originating in India. [Tamil milagu-tannīr pepper-water]

mullion /mul'yən/ (archit) n an upright division between the panes or casements of a window. [Poss by metathesis from older, synonymous monial, from OFr]
■ **mull'ioned** adj.

mullock /mul'ək/ (Aust) n rubbish, esp mining refuse. [From obs or dialect mull dust; cf OE myl]
■ **poke mullock at** to mock, ridicule.

mulloway /mul'ə-wā/ n a large Australian food-fish, Sciaena antarctica. [Origin unknown]

mulmul and **mulmull** see **mull⁵**.

mulse /muls/ (obs) n a drink of honey and wine, or honey and water. [L mulsum, from mulsus mixed with honey]

mulsh same as **mulch**.

multangular...to...**multarticulate** see under **multi-**.

multeity /mul-tē'i-ti/ n manifoldness, very great numerousness. [L multus much, many, and -eity as in haecceity]

multi- /mul-ti-/ or sometimes before a vowel **mult-** /mult-/ combining form denoting much, many. [L multus much]

■ **multang'ular** adj having many angles. **multan'imous** (L animus mind) having a many-sided mind. **multartic'ulate** or **multiartic'ulate** adj many-jointed. **multi-acc'ess** adj (comput) denoting a system which allows several users to have apparently simultaneous access to a computer. **multi-auth'or** or **multi-auth'ored** adj denoting a text which has been written by several individuals. **multicam'erate** adj (L camera chamber) having many chambers or cells. **multicap'itate** adj (L caput, -itis head) many-headed. **multicast'ing** n (telecom) transmission of a message in a local area network from one node to all others. **multicau'line** adj (L caulis stem) having many stems. **multicell'ular** adj having, or made up of, many cells. **multicen'tral** or **multicen'tric** adj having or proceeding from many centres. **multichann'el** adj having or employing several communications channels. **multicipital** /mul-ti-sip'i-təl/ adj (L caput, -itis head) having many heads, multicapitate. **multicolour** /mul'ti-kul-ər/ n diversity or plurality of colour. ◆adj many-coloured. **mul'ticoloured** adj. **multicos'tate** adj (L costa rib) many-ribbed. **multicul'tural** adj (of a society) made up of many distinct cultural groups. **multicul'turalism** n the policy of accommodating any number of distinct cultures within the one society without prejudice or discrimination. **multicul'turalist** n and adj. **multicul'turally** adv. **multicus'pid** adj having more than two cusps. ◆n a multicuspid tooth. **multicus'pidate** adj. **mul'ticycle** n (obs) a velocipede with more than three wheels; one intended to carry several people. **multiden'tate** adj (L dēns, dentis tooth) many-toothed. **multidentic'ulate** adj having many denticulations or fine teeth. **multidigitate** /-dij'i-tāt/ adj (L digitus finger) many-fingered. **multidimen'sional** adj of more than three dimensions (maths); having several aspects or dimensions. **multidirec'tional** adj extending in a number of directions. **multidisciplin'ary** adj involving a combination of several (academic) disciplines, methods, etc. **multieth'nic** adj composed of or relating to more than one ethnic group. **mul'tifaced** adj many-faced. **multifac'eted** adj (of a gem) having many facets; having many aspects, characteristics, etc. **multifact'orial** adj involving or caused by many different factors. **multi-faith'** adj made up of representatives of many distinct religions. **mul'tifid** or **multif'idous** adj cleft into many lobes. **mul'tifil** or **multifil'ament** n a multiple strand of synthetic fibre. **multifil'ament** adj composed of many filaments. **multiflor'a** n an E Asian climbing rose (Rosa multiflora) having clusters of small flowers. **multiflo'rous** adj many-flowered. **mul'tifoil** adj having more than five foils or arcuate divisions. ◆n a multifoil ornament. **multifo'liate** adj (L folium leaf) with many leaves. **multifo'liolate** adj (bot) with many leaflets. **mul'tiform** adj having many forms, polymorphic. ◆n that which is multiform. **multiform'ity** n. **mul'tigrade** adj of or relating to a motor oil with a viscosity such as to match the properties of several grades of motor oil. **mul'tigrain** adj (of bread or breakfast cereal) containing more than one type of cereal grain. **multigrav'ida** n (pl **multigrav'idae** /-dē/ or **multigrav'idas**) (L gravida pregnant) a pregnant woman who has had one or more previous pregnancies. **mul'tigym** n an apparatus incorporating weights and levers in a variety of arrangements, enabling one to exercise and tone up one set of muscles at a time. **mul'tihull** n a sailing vessel with two or more hulls. **multiju'gate** or **multiju'gous** adj (L jugum yoke; bot) consisting of many pairs of leaflets. **multilat'eral** adj (L latus, lateris side) many-sided; with several parties or participants. **multilat'erally** adv. **multilat'eralism** n. **multilat'eralist** n and adj (a person) favouring multilateral action, esp in abandoning or reducing production of nuclear weapons. **multilineal** /-lin'/ or **multilin'ear** adj having many lines. **multilingual** /-ling'gwəl/ adj (L lingua tongue) in many languages; speaking several languages; (of a country, state or society) in which several languages are spoken. **multilin'gualism** n the ability to speak several languages. **multilin'guist** n a person who is multilingual. **multilo'bate** or **mul'tilobed** adj many-lobed. **multilobular** /-lob'ū-lər/ or **multilob'ulate** adj having many lobules. **multiloca'tional** adj existing or operating in several locations. **multiloc'ular** /-lok'ū-lər/ or **multiloc'ulate** adj many-chambered. **multil'oquence** n much speaking. **multil'oquous** adj. **multil'oquy** n. **multimē'dia** n the use of a combination of different media of communication (in eg entertainment or education); simultaneous presentation of several visual and/or sound entertainments; the integrated presentation of data in a variety of forms, eg text, graphics and sound (comput). ◆ adj of or relating to multimedia. **mul'timeter** n an instrument allowing simultaneous measurement of several values. **multimillionaire'** n a person who is a millionaire several times over. **mul'timode** adj designating an optical fibre with a core diameter sufficiently larger than the wavelength of light to allow propagation of light energy in a large number of different modes. **multinat'ional** n a large business company which operates in several countries. ◆ adj of this type of company; multiracial (S Afr). **multinō'mial** adj (maths) consisting of more than two terms; relating to multinomials. ◆n a multinomial expression. **multinom'inal** adj having many names. **multinū'clear**, **multinū'cleate** or **multinū'cleated** adj having several nuclei. **multinū'cleolate** adj having several nucleoli. **multi-own'ership** n ownership of property on the principle of time-sharing (qv). **mul'tipack** n a pack containing several items for sale at a lower unit price. **multipa'ra** n (pl **multipa'rae** /-rē/ or **multipa'ras**) (L parēre to bring forth) a woman who has given birth for the second or subsequent time, or is about to do so, as distinct from a primipara. **multipar'ity** n the condition of being a multipara; the condition of being multiparous. **multip'arous** adj relating to a multipara; producing more than one at birth (zool); giving rise to several lateral axes (bot). **multipar'tite** adj (L partītus divided) divided into many parts; much cut up into segments. **multipar'ty** adj (of a state, etc) having a political system based on the existence of more than one party; made up of many parties or members of several parties. **multipar'tyism** n. **mul'tiped** n (L pēs, pedis foot) a many-footed animal; (also **multipede** /-pēd/) a woodlouse (obs). **mul'tiphase** adj polyphase. **mul'tiplane** n an aeroplane with more than one pair of wings. **multi-ply** /mul'ti-plī/ n plywood of more than three thicknesses. **multipo'lar** adj having several poles or axons. **multipolar'ity** n. **multip'otent** adj (L potēns, -entis powerful; Shakesp) having the power to do many things. **multipres'ence** n the power of being in many places at once. **multipres'ent** adj. **multipro'cessing** n (comput) see **multitasking** below. **multipro'cessor** n (comput) a linked set of central processors that allows parallel processing. **multipro'gramming** n (comput) a technique of handling several programs simultaneously by interleaving their execution through time-sharing. **multipur'pose** adj. **multirā'cial** adj embracing, or consisting of, many races. **multirā'cialism** n the policy of recognizing the rights of all in a multiracial society. **multirā'cially** adv. **multiram'ified** adj (L rāmus branch, and facere to make) having many branches. **mul'tirole** adj. **mul'tiscreen** adj designating a technique of cinema projection in which the screen is divided into several frames each showing separate images; (of a cinema) having more than one screen and auditorium. **multisep'tate** adj (biol) having many septa. **multisē'rial** or **multisē'riate** adj in many rows. **mul'tiskill** vt to train (employees) in several skills. **multiskill'ing** n in technologically advanced industries, the training of employees in a variety of skills. **multisonant** /mul-tis'ən-ənt/ adj (L sonāns, -antis, prp of sonāre to sound) having many sounds; sounding much. **multispī'ral** adj having many coils. **mul'ti-stage** adj in a series of distinct parts; (of a rocket) consisting of a number of parts that fall off in series at predetermined places on its course. **mul'tistorey** or (esp N Am) **mul'tistory** adj having a (large) number of levels or floors. ◆ n a multistorey car park. **mul'tistrike** adj and n (designating) an ink ribbon for use on an electronic typewriter or printer which is struck by keys at different points vertically, often used to produce bold print. **multisulc'ate** adj (L sulcus furrow) having many furrows. **multitask'** vi. **multitask'ing** n the performance of several concurrent tasks by one person; the action of running several processes or jobs simultaneously on a system (also **multipro'cessing**; comput). ◆ adj of or relating to a computer system capable of doing this. **multithread'ing** n (comput) a programming system that enables actions to be carried out simultaneously. **mul'ti-track** adj (of a recording) made up of several different tracks blended together. ◆ n a system for making such recordings. ◆ vt to record using a multi-track system. **multituber'culate** or **multituber'culated** adj (of eg teeth) having many tubercles. **multiu'ser** adj (of a computer or computer game) able to be used by several people at once. **multivā'lence** (or /-tiv'ə-/) or **multivā'lency** (or /-tiv'ə-/) n. **multivā'lent** (or /-tiv'ə-/) adj (chem) having a valency greater than one. **multivār'iate** adj consisting of, or concerned with, many variables. **multivār'ious** adj differing widely. **mul'tiverse** n (esp in science fiction) a hypothetical set of several universes existing in parallel to each other. **multiver'sity** n a large university made up of several campuses. **multivibrā'tor** n an electronic oscillating device using two transistors, the output of one providing the input of the other. **multiv'ious** adj (L via way) going many ways. **mul'ti-vision** n (telecom) a form of visual presentation involving groups of slide projectors showing a complex series of images, with accompanying sound. **multivit'amin** n a pill containing several vitamins. **multiv'ocal** adj (L vōx, vōcis voice) having many meanings. ◆ n a word of many meanings. **multivoltine** /-vol'tīn/ adj (Ital volta turn, winding) of silkworm moths, having several annual broods. **mul'ti-wall** adj made of three or more layers of special paper. **multocular** /mul-tok'ū-lər/ adj (L oculus eye) having many eyes; (of a microscope) enabling several people to observe an object at once. **multungulate** /mul-tung'gū-lāt/ adj (L ungula hoof) having the hoof divided into more than two parts. ◆ n a multungulate mammal.

multi-access...to...**multi-faith** see under **multi-**.

multifarious /mul-ti-fā'ri-əs/ adj having great diversity; made up of many parts; manifold; in many rows or ranks (bot). [L multifārius; poss from fārī to speak]

■ **multifa'riously** adv. **multifa'riousness** n the state of being multifarious; multiplied variety; the fault of improperly joining in one bill distinct and independent matters, and thereby confounding them (law; obs).

multifid...to...**multiplane** see under **multi-**.

multiple /mul'ti-pl/ adj consisting of many elements or components, esp of the same kind; manifold; compound; multiplied or repeated; allowing many messages to be sent over the same wire (telegraphy). ◆ n a quantity which contains another quantity an exact number of times; an object for display, claimed to be art but designed for reproduction in numbers industrially; a multiple shop or store. [Fr, from LL multiplus, from root of L plēre to fill]

■ **mul'tiplet** n (phys) an optical spectrum line having several components; a group of elementary particles whose members differ only in electric charge. **multiply** /mul'ti-pli/ adv.

□ **multiple-choice'** adj (of an examination question) accompanied by several possible answers from which the correct answer is to be chosen. **multiple cinema** n a cinema which has been converted into two or more separate cinemas. **multiple fruit** n a single fruit formed from several flowers in combination, such as a pineapple, fig or mulberry. **multiple personality** n (psychiatry) a disorder in which the subject's personality fragments into a number of distinct personalities. **multiple sclerosis** n a chronic progressive disease in which there is a patchy deterioration of the myelin forming a sheath for the nerve fibres, resulting in various forms of paralysis throughout the body (abbrev **MS**). **multiple shop** or **store** n any of a series of shops belonging to the same firm, often dispersed about the country. **multiple star** n a group of stars so close as to seem one.

■ **common multiple** a number or quantity that can be divided by each of several others without a remainder. **least common multiple** the smallest number that forms a common multiple.

multiplepoinding /mul-ti-pl-poin'ding/ (Scots law) n a process by which a person who has funds claimed by more than one, in order not to have to pay more than once, brings them all into court so that one of them may establish his or her right.

multiplex /mul'ti-pleks/ adj multiple; having many elements; of or denoting a multiplex (telecom). ◆ n a system enabling two or more signals to be sent simultaneously on one communications channel (telecom); a cinema divided up into several small cinemas, a multiple cinema; a multiple (obs). ◆ vt (telecom) to incorporate in a multiplex system. [L multiplex, from plicāre to fold]

■ **mul'tiplexer** n. **mul'tiplexor** n a device enabling a computer to transmit data to many terminals by switching quickly from one user's data to another's.

multiply[1] /mul'ti-plī/ vt (**mul'tiplying**; **mul'tiplied**) to increase the number of; to accumulate; to magnify (obs); to reproduce; to obtain the product of (maths). ◆ vi to become more numerous; to be augmented; to reproduce; to perform the mathematical process of multiplication. [Fr multiplier, from L multiplicāre, from plicāre to fold]

■ **mul'tipliable** or **mul'tiplicable** (or /-plik'/) adj. **mul'tiplicand** (or /-kand'/) n a quantity to be multiplied by another (the multiplier). **mul'tiplicate** (or /-tip'/) adj consisting of more than one; in many folds. ◆ n the condition of being in many copies; any of these copies. **multiplicā'tion** n the act of multiplying or increasing in number; increase of number of parts by branching (bot); the rule or operation by which quantities are multiplied. **mul'tiplicative** (or /-plik'ə-tiv/) adj tending or having power to multiply; indicating how many times (grammar). **mul'tiplicātor** n (maths) a multiplier. **multiplicity** /-plis'i-ti/ n the state of being manifold; a great number. **mul'tiplier** n a person who multiplies; a quantity by which another is multiplied; a device or instrument for intensifying some effect (phys); a geared fishing-reel for drawing in the line quickly.

□ **multiplication constant** n (phys) the ratio of the average number of neutrons produced by fission in one neutron lifetime to the total number of neutrons absorbed or leaking out in the same interval. **multiplication table** n a tabular arrangement giving the products of pairs of numbers usu up to 12. **multiplying glass** n (obs) a magnifying glass; a faceted glass for multiplying reflexions.

■ **multiply words** to say much; to be wordy.

multiply[2] /mul'ti-pli/ see under **multiple**.

multi-ply...to...**multirole** see under **multi-**.

multiscience /mul-tish'əns or -tis'i-əns/ n knowledge of many things. [LL adj multiscius, from L scientia knowledge]

multiscreen...to...**multituberculate** see under **multi-**.

multitude /mul'ti-tūd/ n the state of being many; a great number or (rare) quantity; a crowd; the mob. [L multitūdō, -inis, from multus much]

■ **multitud'inary** adj (rare). **multitud'inous** adj. **multitud'inously** adv. **multitud'inousness** n.

multiuser...to...**multocular** see under **multi-**.

multum /mul'təm/ n an adulterant in brewing. [Prob neuter of L multus much]

multum in parvo /mul'təm or mŭl'tŭm in pär'vō, also -wō/ (L) much in little, a large amount in a small space.

multum non multa /mul'təm non mul'tə or nōn mŭl'ta/ (L) much, not many things.

multungulate see under **multi-**.

multure /mul'tyər/, or (Scot) **mouter** /moo'tər/ n a fee, generally in kind, for grinding grain; the right to such a fee. ◆ vt and vi to take multure (for). [OFr molture, moulture, from L molitūra a grinding]
■ **mul'turer** or (Scot) **mou'terer** n a person who receives multures; a miller; a person who pays multures.

mum¹ /mum/ or **mummy** /mum'i/ (inf) n mother, used esp by a child to address or refer to its mother. [Cf **mamma**¹]
■ **mum'sy** adj (**mum'sier**; **mum'siest**) (inf) maternal; homely, comfy; old-fashioned.
❑ **mummy porn** n (derog inf) a type of erotic fiction considered to appeal to women.

mum² /mum/ adj silent. ◆ n silence. ◆ interj not a word. ◆ vi (**mumm'ing**; **mummed**) (also **mumm**) to act in a mime; to act in a mummers' play; to masquerade. [An inarticulate sound with closing of the lips; partly OFr momer to mum, momeur mummer; cf Du mommen to mask]
■ **mumm'er** n an actor in a folk-play, usu at Christmas (hist); a masquerader; an actor (facetious). **mumm'ery** n mumming; great show without reality; foolish ceremonial. **mumm'ing** n.
❑ **mum'-bud'get** n and interj (obs) mum. **mum'chance** n a silent game with cards or dice (obs); a fool (dialect). ◆ adj silent. **Mumm'erset** n an imitation West Country accent used by actors.
■ **mum's the word** complete silence or secrecy is demanded, or promised.

mum³ /mum/ see **ma'am**.

mum⁴ /mum/ (esp N Am) n a short form of **chrysanthemum**.

mum⁵ /mum/ (obs) n a wheat-malt beer, sometimes with oat and bean meal. [Ger Mumme]

mumble /mum'bl/ vt and vi to say, utter or speak indistinctly, softly or perfunctorily; to mouth with the lips, or as if with toothless gums. ◆ n the sound of something mumbled. [Frequentative from **mum**²]
■ **mum'blement** n (Carlyle) mumbling speech. **mum'bler** n. **mum'bling** n and adj. **mum'blingly** adv.
❑ **mum'ble-news** n (Shakesp) a tale-bearer.

mumbo-jumbo /mum-bō-jum'bō/ n (pl **mum'bo-jum'bos**) empty or foolish ritual; baffling jargon, professional gobbledegook; (with cap) a god or bugbear of W Africa; any object of foolish worship or fear. [Said to be from Mama Dyanbo, a Mandingo god]

mumchance ...to... **mummery** see under **mum**².

mummied and **mummify** see **mummy**¹.

mummock /mum'ək/ see **mammock**.

mummy¹ /mum'i/ n an embalmed or otherwise preserved dead body, esp as prepared for burial by the ancient Egyptians; the substance of such a body, formerly used medicinally; dead flesh; anything pounded to a formless mass; a bituminous drug or pigment. ◆ vt (**mumm'ying**; **mumm'ied**) to mummify. [OFr mumie, from LL mumia, from Ar and Pers mūmiyā, from Pers mūm wax]
■ **mumm'ia** n mummy as a drug. **mummificā'tion** n. **mumm'iform** adj. **mumm'ify** vt to make into a mummy.
❑ **mumm'y-case** n a case for wrapping a mummy; **mumm'y-cloth** n cloth for wrapping a mummy; a similar fabric used as a basis for embroidery; a fabric like crape with cotton or silk warp and woollen weft. **mumm'y-wheat** n a variety of wheat, alleged (incredibly) to descend from grains found in Egyptian mummy-cases.

mummy² see **mum**¹.

mump /mump/ vt to mumble or mutter (dialect and Scot); to mumble or munch (dialect); to obtain by, or visit for the purpose of, begging or sponging (dialect); to cheat (obs). ◆ vi (dialect and Scot) to mumble; to sponge; to sulk; to grumble, complain (Scot); to mope; to grimace; to be silent (archaic); to play the beggar. [Cf **mum**² and Du mompen to cheat]
■ **mump'er** n a person who mumps; a beggar (old sl). **mump'ish** adj having mumps; dull; sullen. **mump'ishly** adv. **mump'ishness** n.
❑ **mump'ing-day** n St Thomas's Day, 21 December, when the poor used to go around begging corn, money, etc.

mumps /mumps/ n sing a bout of gloomy silence (old); an acute infectious disease characterized by a painful swelling of the parotid gland. ◆ n pl the swellings thus caused, protruding on either side of the face. [Suggesting the shape of the face when munching; cf **mump**]

mumpsimus /mump'si-məs/ n a view or opinion stubbornly held, even when shown to be misguided; a person holding such a view, or one adhering stubbornly to old ways. [An ignorant priest's blunder (in an old story) for L sūmpsimus, we have received, in the mass]

mumsy see under **mum**¹.

mun¹ /mun/ (dialect) vt (3rd pers **mun**) must (also **maun** or **man**). —The verb is used in the present indicative only. [ON mon, mun, or man (infinitive monu, munu), a preterite-present verb]

mun² /mun/ n a dialect form of **man**¹.

munch /munch or munsh/ vt and vi to chew with a steady, deliberate action of the jaws, and often with a crunching noise. [Prob imit]
■ **munch'er** n. **munch'ies** n pl (sl) small snacks, nibbles; (with the) an alcohol- or drug-induced craving for food.

Munchausen or **Munchhausen** /mün'chow-zn/ n an exaggerated, fantastical story, or its teller. ◆ adj used to describe a syndrome in which a person feigns injury or illness in order to obtain hospital treatment. [Baron Münchausen, hero of a series of improbable adventure stories by RE Raspe (1737–94)]
❑ **Munchausen (syndrome) by proxy** n a disorder in which a person inflicts injury on or causes illness in another in order to receive attention.

munchkin /munch'kin/ n (N Am sl) a low-level employee, an underling; a child. [Name of a fictional tiny people in LF Baum's Wizard of Oz (1900)]

Munda /mün'də/ n any member of a group of peoples of eastern India; (also called **Kolarian**) their group of languages, a division of the Austroasiatic family of languages. ◆ adj of the Mundas or their languages.

mundane /mun-dān'/ adj ordinary, banal; worldly; earthly; cosmic. [L mundānus, from mundus the world]
■ **mundane'ly** adv. **mundane'ness** or **mundanity** /-dan'i-ti/ n.

mundic /mun'dik/ n iron pyrites. [From Cornish]

mundify /mun'di-fī/ vt (**mun'difying**; **mund'ified**) to cleanse, purify. [LL mundificāre, from L mundus clean, and facere to make]
■ **mundificā'tion** n. **mundif'icative** adj.

mung bean /mung or mung bēn/ n a leguminous Asian plant, Phaseolus aureus, or its seeds, grown for forage and as a source of bean sprouts. [Hindi mūng]

mungcorn see under **mong**¹.

munge /munj/ (comput sl) vt to alter (data) so as to render it useless or incapable of automatic manipulation. [Origin uncertain]

mungo /mung'gō/ n (pl **mun'gos**) the waste produced in a woollen mill from hard spun or felted cloth, or from tearing up old clothes, used in making cheap cloth. [Origin obscure]

mungoose same as **mongoose**.

Munich /mū'nik or -nihh/ n a buying off or appeasing by granting concessions. [From the pact signed at Munich (1938), in which Britain, France and Italy agreed to yield the Czech Sudetenland to Hitler]
■ **Mu'nichism** n.

municipal /mū-nis'i-pl/ adj relating to home affairs; relating to (the government of) a borough, town or city. [L mūnicipālis, from mūniceps, -ipis, an inhabitant of a mūnicipium, a free town, from mūnia official duties, and capere to take]
■ **munic'ipalism** n concern for the interests of one's municipality; belief in municipal control. **municipality** /-pal'i-ti/ n a self-governing town or district; its governing body; a district governed like a city; (in France and other European countries) an area representing the smallest administrative unit, governed jointly by a mayor and an elected council, a commune. **municipalizā'tion** or **-s-** n. **munic'ipalize** or **-ise** vt to make into a municipality; to bring under municipal control or ownership. **munic'ipally** adv.

munificence /mū-nif'i-səns/ n magnificent generosity in giving; bountifulness. [L mūnificentia, from mūnus a present, and facere to make]
■ **munif'icent** adj. **munif'icently** adv.

munify /mū'ni-fī/ vt (**mu'nifying**; **mu'nified**) to fortify. [Irregularly formed from L mūnīre to fortify, and facere to make]
■ **munificence** /-nif'i-əns/ n (Spenser) defence, fortification.

muniment /mū'ni-mənt/ n (usu in pl) a record fortifying or making good a claim, esp a title deed to land; (in pl) furnishings, equipment, things provided; a means of defence. [L mūnīmentum fortification, later, title deed]

munition /mū-nish'ən/ vt to supply with munitions. ◆ n (usu in pl) fortification; defence; material used in war; weapons; military stores. [L mūnīre, -ītum to fortify; mūnīmentum fortification, later, title-deeds, from moenia walls]
■ **munite'** vt (Bacon) to fortify, strengthen. **munitioneer'** or **muni'tioner** n (also **muni'tion-worker**) a worker engaged in making munitions. **munitionette'** n (obs inf) a female munition-worker.

munnion /mun'yən/ same as **mullion**.

Munro /mun-rō'/ n (pl **Munros'**) a designation orig of Scottish (now also English, Irish and Welsh) mountains over 3000 feet. [Orig list made by Sir HT Munro (1856–1919), Scottish mountaineer]
❑ **Munro'-bagger** n a person whose aim is to climb every designated Munro. **Munro'-bagging** n.

Munsell scale /mun'sl skāl/ (printing) n a system for describing colours according to three attributes: hue, value and chroma (strength of colour). [AH *Munsell* (1858–1918), US inventor]

munshi or **moonshee** /moon'shē/ (Ind) n a secretary; an interpreter; a language teacher. [Hindi *munshī*, from Ar *munshi'*]

Munster or **Muenster** /mŭn'stər/ n a semi-soft, cow's milk cheese of *Munster* in NE France, often flavoured with caraway or aniseed.

munt see **muntu**.

munter /mun'tər/ (derog sl) n an unattractive person, esp a woman. [Origin uncertain]

muntin /mun'tin/ or **munting** /mun'ting/ n the vertical framing piece between door panels. [**montant**]

muntjak or **muntjac** /munt'jak/ n a small SE Asian deer, the male of which has tusks and small antlers. [Malay name]

muntu /mŭn'tŭ/ (S Afr sl; derog) n a black African (also **munt**). [Bantu *uMuntu* person]

Muntz metal /munts met'l/ n alpha-beta brass, 60% copper and 40% zinc. [GF *Muntz* (1794–1857), English metallurgist]

muon /moo' or mŭ'on/ (phys) n a subatomic particle, a type of lepton. ■ **mŭon'ic** adj. **muonium** /mŭ-ōn'i-əm/ n an isotope of hydrogen. ❑ **muonic atom** /mū-on'ik/ n a nucleus with an orbital muon.

muppet /mup'it/ (sl) n a foolish or stupid person. [From the puppet characters in *The Muppet Show*, US television series created by Jim Henson (1936–90)]

muqaddam, **mokaddam** or **mocuddum** /mō- or moo-kud'um/ n (in India, etc) a leader, a headman. [Ar]

MUR abbrev : Mauritian Rupee (also **MR**).

muraena or **murena** /mū-rē'nə/ n a favourite food-fish of the Romans, a moray, of the genus **Muraena**, giving name to a family of eels, **Murae'nidae**. [L *mūraena*; see **moray**]

murage see under **mure**.

mural /mū'rəl/ adj of, on, attached to, or of the nature of, a wall. ◆ n a mural decoration, esp a painting; a wall (in Shakespeare, only a conjectural emendation (obs); see **morall**). [L *mūrālis*, from *mūrus* a wall]
■ **mur'alist** n a person who paints or designs murals. ❑ **mural circle** n a large graduated circle, fixed to a wall, for measuring arcs of the meridian. **mural crown** n an embattled crown given among the ancient Romans to the first soldier to mount the wall of a besieged city. **mural painting** n a painting executed, esp in distemper colours, on the wall of a building.

murder /mŭr'dər/, also (now dialect) **murther** /-dhər/ n the act of intentionally and unlawfully killing a person; excessive or reprehensible slaughter that is not legally murder; torture, excessive toil or hardship (hyperbole); a collective term for a number of crows. ◆ vt to kill (usu a person) unlawfully with malice aforethought; to slaughter; to torture (hyperbole); to beat, defeat utterly (inf); to destroy (inf); to spoil by performing badly (inf); to consume voraciously (inf). [OE *morthor*, from *morth* death; Ger *Mord*, Gothic *maurthr*; cf L *mors, mortis* death]
■ **murderee'** n the victim, or intended victim, of a murderer. **mur'derer** (obs or dialect **mur'therer**) n (also fem **mur'deress**) a person who murders, or is guilty of murder; a small cannon (also **mur'dering-piece** obs). **mur'derous** adj. **mur'derously** adv. **mur'derousness** n.
■ **cry** or **scream blue murder** see under **blue**[1]. **get away with murder** to do as one pleases yet escape punishment or censure. **murder will out** murder cannot remain hidden; the truth will come to light.

mure /mūr/ n (Shakesp) a wall. ◆ vt to wall in or up; to confine; to close. [Fr *mur* and L *mūrus* a wall]
■ **mur'age** n (hist) a tax for the building or upkeep of town walls. **mur'iform** adj (bot) with cells arranged like bricks in a wall.

murena see **muraena**.

murex /mū'reks/ n (pl **mu'rexes** or **mu'rices** /-ri-sēz/) a gastropod mollusc of the *Murex* genus, yielding Tyrian purple dye. [L *mūrex, -icis*]

murgeon /mŭr'jən/ (Scot) n a grimace. ◆ vt and vi to mock with grimaces. [Origin obscure]

muriate /mū'ri-āt/ n (archaic) a chloride. [L *muria* brine]
■ **mur'iated** adj impregnated or combined with chlorine or a chloride. **muriatic** /-at'ik/ adj briny; hydrochloric (not in scientific use).

muricate /mū'ri-kət or -kāt/ (bot) adj rough or warty with short sharp points (also **mur'icated**). [L *mūricātus*, from *mūrex, -icis* a murex, a sharp stone]

murices see **murex**.

Muridae /mū'ri-dē/ n pl the mouse family. [L *mūs, mūris* a mouse]

murine /mū'rīn or -rin/ adj mouselike; belonging to the mouse family or subfamily. ◆ n a murine animal. [L *mūrīnus*, from *mūs, mūris* mouse]
❑ **murine typhus** n a mild form of typhus endemic among rats and passed to humans by fleas.

murk or **mirk** /mŭrk/, also (Scot) **mirk**/ n darkness (lit and fig). ◆ adj dark; gloomy; obscure. [OE *mirce* (noun and adj), ON *myrkr*, Dan and Swed *mörk*; the forms with *i* are chiefly due to Spenser and Scottish influence]
■ **murk'ily** adv. **murk'iness** n. **murk'ish** adj. **murk'some** adj. **murk'y** adj dark; obscure; gloomy; suspiciously unrevealed.

murl /mŭrl/ (Scot) vt and vi to crumble. [Origin obscure]
■ **murl'y** adj.

murlain, **murlan** or **murlin** /mŭr'lən/ (Scot) n a round, narrow-mouthed basket. [Gaelic *mùrlan*]

murmur /mŭr'mər/ n a low, indistinct sound, like that of running water; an abnormal rustling sound from the heart, lungs, etc; a muttered or subdued grumble or complaint; rumour (Shakesp). ◆ vi to utter a murmur; to grumble. ◆ vt to say or utter in a murmur. [Fr *murmure*, from L *murmur*; cf Gr *mormȳrein* to surge]
■ **murmurā'tion** n murmuring; a doubtful word for a flock of starlings. **mur'murer** n. **mur'muring** n and adj. **mur'muringly** adv. **mur'murous** adj. **mur'murously** adv.
❑ **murmur vowel** n (phonetics) a weak vowel, a schwa.

murphy /mŭr'fi/ (inf) n (pl **mur'phies**) a potato. [From the common Ir name *Murphy*]
❑ **Murphy's game** n a confidence trick whereby an envelope stuffed with paper is surreptitiously substituted for one full of money. **Murphy's law** n that one of Sod's laws by which if something can go wrong, it will.

murra or **murrha** /mur'ə/ n an unidentified precious material for vases, etc, first brought to Rome by Pompey (61BC) from the East, conjectured to be agate. [L *murra*; Gr *morria* (pl)]
■ **murrhine**, **murrine** /mur'īn or -in/ or **myrrhine** /mir'īn or -in/ adj.

murrain /mur'in or -ən/ n a pestilence (obs); now only a cattle-plague, esp foot-and-mouth disease. ◆ adj affected with murrain; confounded. ◆ adv confoundedly. [OFr *morine* pestilence, carcass]
■ **murr'ained** adj.

murram /mur'əm/ n a tough, clayey gravel used as road metal in tropical Africa. [Native name]

murray see **moray**.

murre /mŭr/ n a guillemot; a razorbill. [Origin obscure]
■ **murrelet** /mŭr'lit/ n a name for various small birds related to the guillemot.

murren (Shakesp and Milton) same as **murrain**.

murrey[1] /mur'i/ n and adj mulberry-colour, dark purplish-red. [OFr *moré*, from L *mōrum* mulberry]

murrey[2] see **moray**.

murrha, **murrhine** and **murrine** see **murra**.

murrin (Spenser) same as **murrain**.

murrion (Shakesp) same as **murrain**.

murry same as **moray**.

murther and **murtherer** obsolete or dialect forms of **murder** and **murderer**.

murva or **moorva** /moor'və/ n bowstring-hemp. [Sans *mūrvā*]

mus. abbrev : music; musical; museum.

Musa /mū'zə/ n the banana genus, giving name to a family **Musā'ceae**, order **Musā'les**, of (mostly) gigantic treelike herbs. [Latinized from Ar *mauz*]
■ **musā'ceous** adj.

Musak see **Muzak**®.

musang /mū- or moo-sang'/ n a paradoxure, or related animal. [Malay *mūsang*]

MusB abbrev : Bachelor of Music.

Musca /mus'kə/ n the house-fly genus; a small constellation in the south, between the Crux and the Chamaeleon. [L *musca* a fly]
■ **muscatō'rium** n (Gr church) a flabellum. **muscid** /mus'id/ adj of the house-fly family **Muscidae** /mus'i-dē/. ◆ n a member of the family. ❑ **muscae volitantes** /mus'ē vol-i-tan'tēz or mŭs'kī wo-li-tan'tās/ n (L fluttering flies) ocular spectra like floating black spots before the eyes.

muscadel see **muscatel**.

Muscadet /mus'kə-dā or mŭ-skă-de'/ n a variety of white grape grown esp in the lower Loire valley region of France; a typically light dry white wine made from this grape. [Fr; cf **muscatel**]

muscadin /mŭ-ska-de͂'/ (hist) n a Parisian fop or dandy; a middle-class moderate in the French Revolution. [Fr]

muscadine /*mus'kə-dīn* or -*dīn*/ *n* a variety of grape grown mainly in SE USA; an archaic form of **muscatel** (wine, grape or pear). [Perh Provençal *muscat*, fem *muscade*]

muscardine /*mus'kär-din*, -*dēn* or -*dīn*/ *n* a silkworm disease caused by a fungus (genus *Botrytis*). [Fr]

muscarine /*mus'kə-rin*/ *n* an alkaloid poison found in certain fungi. [L *muscarius*, from *musca* a fly]
■ **muscarin'ic** *adj* of, like, or producing effects similar to muscarine.

muscat /*mus'kat*/ *n* muscatel wine; a musky variety of grape or its vine. [Provençal *muscat*]

muscatel /*mus-kə-tel'* or *mus'*/ or **muscadel** /*mus-kə-del'* or *mus'*/ *n* a rich spicy wine, of various kinds; a grape of musky smell or taste; the vine producing it; a raisin from the muscatel grape; a variety of pear. [OFr *muscatel*, *muscadel*, from Provençal *muscat* musky]

muscatorium see under **Musca**.

Muschelkalk /*mŭsh'əl-kälk*/ (*geol*) *n* the middle member of the Trias system in Germany, largely shelly limestone. [Ger *Muschel* shell, and *Kalk* lime]

Musci /*mus'ī*/ *n pl* mosses, one of the two great divisions of the Bryophyta, the other being the Hepaticae or liverworts. [L *muscus* moss]
■ **mus'coid** /-*koid*/ or **mus'cose** *adj* mosslike. **muscology** /-*kol'ə-ji*/ *n* bryology.

muscid see under **Musca**.

muscle¹ /*mus'l*/ *n* a contractile structure by which bodily movement is effected; the tissue forming it; bodily strength; power, strength of other kinds (financial, political, etc) (*inf*). ◆ *vi* to force one's way, thrust. [Fr *muscle*, or directly from L *mūsculus*, dimin of *mūs* a mouse, muscle]
■ **muscled** /*mus'ld*/ *adj* having muscles. **musc'ling** *n* delineation of muscles, as in a picture. **musc'ly** *adj* muscular. **muscular** /*mus'kū-lər*/ *adj* relating to a muscle; consisting of muscles; having big or strong muscles; brawny; strong; vigorous. **muscularity** /-*lar'i-ti*/ *n*. **mus'cularly** *adv*. **musculā'tion** *n* muscular action; musculature. **mus'culature** *n* provision, disposition and system of muscles. **mus'culous** *adj* (*obs*) muscular.
□ **musc'le-bound** *adj* having the muscles stiff and enlarged by over-exercise. **muscle car** *n* a large motor car with an extremely powerful engine. **musc'leman** *n* a man of extravagant physical development, *esp* one employed to intimidate people. **musc'le-reading** *n* interpretation of slight involuntary muscular movements. **muscle** or **muscular sense** *n* kinaesthesis. **muscle shirt** *n* a tight-fitting, *usu* sleeveless, shirt with no buttons or collar. **muscular Christianity** *n* a vigorous combination of Christian living with devotion to athletic enjoyments. **muscular dystrophy** /*dis'trə-fi*/ *n* any of the forms of a hereditary disease in which muscles suffer progressive deterioration. **musculoskel'etal** *adj* relating to muscles and skeleton.
■ **muscle in** (*inf*) to force one's way in (*lit* and *fig*); to grab a share. **muscle out** (*inf*) to drive out by (threat of) violence.

muscle² see **mussel**.

muscology, **muscoid** and **muscose** see under **Musci**.

muscone same as **muskone** (see under **musk**).

muscovado /*mu-skə-vä'dō*/ *n* (pl **muscova'dos**) sugar in its unrefined state after evaporating the cane juice and draining off the molasses. [Sp *mascabado*]

Muscovy /*mus'kə-vi*/ *n* an old Russian principality having Moscow as its capital (*hist*); extended to Russia in general (*archaic*). [*Moscovia*, Latinized from Russ *Moskva* Moscow]
■ **Muscovian** /-*kō'vi-ən*/ *n* (*obs*) a Muscovite. ◆ *adj* Muscovite. **Mus'covite** *n* a citizen of Moscow or, generally, a Russian. ◆ *adj* of Muscovy (*hist*); Russian (*archaic*). **mus'covite** *n* (*mineralogy*) common white mica, first obtained in Russia, a silicate of aluminium and potassium; the mica in the form of thin transparent plates, formerly used as a kind of glass (also **Muscovy glass**). **Muscovitic** /-*vit'ik*/ *adj*.
□ **muscovy duck** see **musk duck** under **musk**.

muscular see under **muscle¹**.

MusD *abbrev* : Doctor of Music.

Muse /*mūz*/ (*Gr myth*) *n* any of the nine goddesses of the liberal arts, daughters of Zeus and Mnemosyne (**Calliope** of epic poetry; **Clio** of history; **Erato** of love poetry; **Euterpe** of music and lyric poetry; **Melpomene** of tragedy; **Polyhymnia** of sacred lyrics; **Terpsichore** of dancing; **Thalia** of comedy; **Urania** of astronomy); an inspiring goddess more vaguely imagined; poetic character; poetry or art; an inspired poet (*Milton*). [Fr, from L *Mūsa*, from Gr *Mousa*]

muse¹ /*mūz*/ *vi* to reflect in silence; to be mentally abstracted or absorbed in thought; to meditate or ponder (with *on*); to look or gaze in contemplation (with *on*). ◆ *vt* to say musingly; to meditate on (*obs*); to wonder at (*Shakesp*). ◆ *n* deep thought; contemplation; a state or instance of mental abstraction or absorption. [Fr *muser* to loiter, in OFr to muse; perh orig to hold the muzzle (OFr *muse*) in the air, as a dog that has lost the scent; perh influenced by **Muse**]

■ **mused** *adj* bemused, muzzy, fuddled. **muse'ful** *adj* meditative. **muse'fully** *adv*. **mus'er** *n*. **mus'ing** *n* and *adj*. **mus'ingly** *adv*.

muse² see **meuse¹**.

museologist and **museology** see under **museum**.

muset same as **musit**.

musette /*mū-zet'*/ *n* an old type of French bagpipe; a simple pastoral melody or gavotte trio *orig* composed for, or in imitation of, the bagpipe; a dance for such a melody; a small (*esp* army) knapsack (*US*). [Fr, dimin of *muse* a bagpipe]

museum /*mū-zē'əm*/ *n* (pl **musē'ums**) *orig* a temple, home or resort of the Muses; a place of study; a resort of the learned; an institution or repository for the collection, exhibition and study of objects of artistic, scientific, historic or educational interest; an art gallery (*US*); a collection of curiosities. [L *mūsēum*, from Gr *mouseion*; see **Muse**]
■ **museolog'ical** *adj*. **museol'ogist** *n*. **museol'ogy** *n* the study of museums and their organization.
□ **museum beetle** *n* a small beetle of the genus *Anthrenus* whose larvae and adults are destructive to hides, fur, zoological collections, etc. **museum piece** *n* a specimen so fine as to be suitable for exhibition in a museum, or (*facetiously*) so old-fashioned as to be unsuitable for anything else.

mush¹ /*mush*/ *n* meal, *esp* cornmeal, boiled in water or milk until thick; anything pulpy; sloppy sentimentality (*inf*); rubbish; background noise from a wireless receiver; a person's face (*sl*); an umbrella (*sl*; see also **mushroom**). ◆ *vt* to reduce to mush; to crush the spirit of, wear out (*dialect*). [Prob **mash¹**]
■ **mush'ily** *adv*. **mush'iness** *n*. **mush'y** *adj* (**mush'ier**; **mush'iest**).
□ **mush'mouth** *n* (*US sl*) a person who slurs or mumbles in speaking. **mush'-mouthed** *adj* (*US sl*) speaking indistinctly or slurringly; tongue-tied.

mush² /*mush*/ (*Scot*) *vt* to notch or scallop the edges of. [Perh Fr *moucher* to trim]

mush³ /*mush*/ (*N Am*) *vi* to travel on foot with dogs over snow. ◆ *n* a journey of this kind. ◆ *interj* a command to dogs to start moving or move faster. [Prob Fr *marcher* to walk]
■ **mush'er** *n*.

musha /*mush'ə*/ (*Irish*) *interj* expressing surprise. [Ir *maiseadh*]

mushroom /*mush'room*/ *n* an edible fungus of rapid growth with a stem and umbrella-shaped cap, *esp Agaricus*, or *Psalliota*, *campestris* or *field mushroom*; any edible fungus; any fungus of umbrella shape whether edible or not; any fungus; an object shaped like a mushroom, eg a wooden one for use in darning; a hat with drooping brim; an umbrella (*sl*); a pinkish-brown colour, like that of the field mushroom; anything of rapid growth and decay (*fig*); someone who rises suddenly from a low condition (*fig*); an upstart. ◆ *adj* of or like a mushroom in appearance, rapidity of growth, etc; of a pinkish-brown colour. ◆ *vi* to expand like a mushroom cap; to gather mushrooms; to increase or spread with remarkable or disconcerting rapidity. [OFr *mousseron*, perh *mousse* moss, which may be of Germanic origin]
■ **mush'roomer** *n*.
□ **mush'room-anchor** *n* an anchor with a mushroom-shaped head. **mushroom cloud** *n* a mushroom-shaped cloud, *esp* one resulting from a nuclear explosion. **mushroom pink** *n* a dusky brownish-pink.

music /*mū'zik*/ *n* the art of expression in sound, in melody, and harmony, including both composition and execution; (the art of) instrumental performance, as distinct from singing; the science underlying it; a musical composition (*obs*); the performance of musical compositions; compositions collectively; a connected series of (pleasing) sounds; pleasing sound generally; melody or harmony; sound of a definite pitch, not mere noise; a band of musicians (*archaic*); musical instruments (*obs* or *dialect*); written or printed representation of tones, expression, etc, or of what is to be played or sung; sheets or books of parts or scores collectively; harmonious character; fun (*US*). ◆ *adj* of or for music. ◆ *vi* (*prp* **mu'sicking**) (*rare*) to perform music. [Fr *musique*, from L *mūsica*, from Gr *mousikē* (*technē*) musical (art), from *Mousa* a Muse]
■ **mu'sical** *adj* relating to, of, with, or producing, music; pleasing to the ear; of definite pitch (unlike mere noise); melodious; having skill in, or aptitude or taste for, music. ◆ *n* a musical person, party or performance, *esp* a theatrical performance or film in which singing and *usu* dancing play an important part, a successor to musical comedy with a less frivolous plot. **musicale** /*mū-zi-käl'*/ *n* (Fr *soirée musicale*) a social gathering with music, or the programme of music for it. **musicality** /-*al'i-ti*/ *n*. **mu'sically** *adv*. **mu'sicalness** *n*. **musician** /*mū-zish'ən*/ *n* a person skilled in music; a performer or composer of music, *esp* professional. **musi'cianer** or **mu'sicker** *n* (*obs* or *dialect*). **musi'cianly** *adj* characteristic of, or becoming, a musician. **musi'cianship** *n*. **musicolog'ical** *adj*. **musicol'ogist** *n*. **musicol'ogy** *n* academic study of music in its historical, scientific and other aspects. **musicother'apy** *n* music therapy.

□ **musical box** *n* a toy that plays tunes automatically, by means of projections from a revolving barrel twitching a comb. **musical chairs** *n sing* the game of prancing round a diminishing row of chairs and securing one when the music stops; a series of interrelated shifts and changes involving a number of people (*facetious*). **musical comedy** *n* a light dramatic entertainment with sentimental songs and situations held together by a minimum of plot. **musical director** *n* the conductor of an orchestra in a theatre, etc. **musical flame** *n* a flame that gives a musical tone when surrounded by an open tube. **musical glasses** see **harmonica** under **harmony**. **musical sand** *n* sand of nearly uniform size of grain that gives out a definite note when walked on. **music box** *n* a barrel organ (*obs*); a musical box; a piano (*joc*). **music case** or **music folio** *n* a case or portfolio for carrying sheet music. **music centre** *n* a unit consisting of an amplifier, a CD and/or record player, cassette player and radio, with loudspeakers. **mu'sic-demy** *n* a size of writing paper, $20\frac{3}{4}$in $\times$ $14\frac{3}{8}$in. **music drama** *n* a term used by Wagner to describe opera in which the musical, dramatic and visual elements are given equal emphasis. **music hall** *n orig* and still sometimes a concert hall, now *usu* a hall for variety entertainments; variety entertainment or vaudeville performed there, consisting of a series of turns by different artists, interspersed with interludes of song, dance, etc. **mu'sic-hall** *adj*. **music holder** *n* a music-case; a clip, rack or desk for holding music during performance. **music house** *n* a concert hall; a firm dealing in music or musical instruments. **music master, mistress** or **teacher** *n* a teacher of music. **music paper** *n* paper ruled for writing music. **music pen** *n* a five-channelled pen for drawing the stave. **music rack** *n* a rack attached to a musical instrument for holding the player's music. **music roll** *n* a case for carrying music rolled up; a roll of perforated paper for mechanical piano-playing. **music room** *n* a room in which music is performed; a room beside the stage in which the musicians were stationed (*obs*). **mu'sic-seller** *n* a dealer in printed music. **mu'sic-shell** *n* a volute shell with markings like music. **music stand** *n* a light adjustable frame for holding music during performance. **music stool** *n* a piano stool. **music synthesizer** *n* (*comput*) an output device generating sounds similar to musical notes in response to digital signals. **music theatre** *n* a form of musical composition given a partly-staged presentation, developed *esp* in the USA in the 1950s. **music therapist** *n* a specialist in the use of **music therapy**, the controlled use of music in the treatment, education, etc of those with physical or mental disabilities or disorders.

■ **early music** medieval and Renaissance music (also sometimes extended to baroque). **face the music** see under **face**. **music of the spheres** see under **sphere**. **music to one's ears** anything that one is very glad to hear. **rough music** uproar; charivari.

musimon /*mū'si*- or *mus'i-mon*/ or **musmon** /*mus'mon*/ *n* the moufflon. [L *mus(i)mō*, *-ōnis*]

musique concrète /*mū-zēk kɔ̃-kret'*/ (*Fr*) *n* a kind of mid-20c music, made up of odds and ends of recorded sound variously handled.

musit /*mū'zit*/ (*Shakesp*) *n* a gap in a fence or thicket through which an animal passes. [**meuse¹**]

musive /*mū'siv*/ (*obs*) *adj* same as **mosaic**.

musk /*musk*/ *n* a strong-smelling substance, used in perfumery, obtained chiefly from the male musk deer; a similar substance secreted by other animals, eg the civet; a synthetic reproduction of either substance, for use in perfumery; the odour of either substance, or of its synthetic substitute; the musk deer; a species of *Mimulus*, said once to have smelt of musk. ◆ *adj* (used *attrib* with the names of many animals and plants) supposed to smell of musk. ◆ *vt* to perfume with musk. [Fr *musc*, from L *muscus*, Gr *moschos*, prob from Pers *mushk*, perh from Sans *muṣka* a testicle (for which the gland has been mistaken)]

■ **musked** /*muskt*/ *adj* smelling or tasting like musk. **musk'ily** *adv*. **musk'iness** *n*. **mus'kone** or **mus'cone** *n* a macrocyclic ketone that gives musk its distinctive smell and is synthesized for use as an ingredient in perfumes. **musk'y** *adj* (**musk'ier**; **musk'iest**) having the odour of musk.

□ **musk'-bag, -cod, -pod, -pouch** or **-sac** *n* a musk gland. **musk'-bag** or **musk'-ball** *n* a bag or ball containing musk, as a perfuming sachet. **musk beetle** *n* a longicorn beetle that smells of attar of roses. **musk'-cat** *n* a musk-yielding animal, *usu* the musk deer, *prob* confused with the civet cat; a scented effeminate dandy; a courtesan. **musk'-cavy** *n* the hog-rat. **musk deer** *n* a hornless deer (*Moschus moschiferus*) of Asia, the chief source of musk. **musk duck** *n* (also by confusion **muscovy duck**) a large musky-smelling S American duck (*Cairina moschata*). **musk gland** *n* a skin pit in some animals producing musk. **musk'-mallow** *n* a species of mallow with a faint odour of musk. **musk melon** *n* any of various common varieties of melon, including the honeydew (the name *appar* transferred from a musky-scented kind). **musk orchid** *n* a small musk-scented European orchid (*Herminium monorchis*). **musk ox** *n* a long-haired ruminant (*Ovibos moschatus*) of N Canada and Greenland, exhaling a strong musky smell. **musk pear** *n* a fragrant variety of pear. **musk'-plant** *n* a plant, *Mimulus moschatus*. **musk'-plum** *n* a fragrant kind of plum.

musk'rat *n* the musquash; a musk shrew; its fur. **musk rose** *n* a fragrant species of rose, with white flowers. **musk'-sheep** *n* the musk-ox. **musk shrew** *n* the desman; a musky-smelling Indian shrew. **musk thistle** *n* a thistle (*Carduus nutans*) with large drooping scented heads. **musk turtle** *n* any of a group of small American turtles of the genus *Sternotherus*, *esp S. odoratus* which has a particularly musky smell.

muskeg /*mu-skeg*/ (chiefly *Can*) *n* a swamp, bog or marsh. [Cree word]

muskellunge /*mus'kə-lunj*/ *n* a large N American freshwater fish (*Esox masquinongy*) of the pike family (also **maskallonge**, **maskalonge** /*mas'kə-lonj*/, **maskinonge** or **maskanonge** /*mas'kə-nonj*/). [Algonquian]

musket /*mus'kit*/ *n* a military firearm, *esp* of a long-barrelled smooth-bore kind fired from the shoulder, a popular infantry weapon between the 16c and 18c; a male sparrowhawk. [OFr *mousquet* musket, formerly a hawk, from Ital *moschetto*, perh from L *musca* a fly]

■ **musketeer'** *n* a soldier armed with a musket. **musketoon'** or **musquetoon'** *n* a short musket; a soldier armed with one. **mus'ketry** *n* muskets collectively; practice with, or the art of using, small arms; fire of muskets; a body of troops armed with muskets.

□ **mus'ket-proof** *adj* capable of resisting the force of a musket-ball. **mus'ket-rest** *n* a forked support for the heavy 16c musket. **mus'ket-shot** *n* shot for or from a musket; the discharge of a musket; the range of a musket.

muskle see **mussel**.

muskone, muskrat and **musky** see under **musk**.

Muslim /*muz'*, *mūz'* or *mus'lim*/ *n* a follower of the Islamic religion. ◆ *adj* of or relating to the followers of Islam. [Ar *muslim*, pl *muslimīn*, from *salma* to submit (to God); cf **Mussulman** and **Islam**]

■ **Mus'limism** or **Mos'lemism** *n*.

muslin /*muz'lin*/ *n* a fine soft plain-woven cotton fabric, of gauzy appearance; cotton cloth for shirts, etc (*US*); women collectively (*obs sl*; *derog*); sails, canvas (*naut sl*); a collector's name for several different moths. ◆ *adj* made of muslin. [Fr *mousseline*, from Ital *mussolino*, from Ital *Mussolo*, the town of Mosul in Mesopotamia]

■ **mus'lined** *adj* clothed with muslin. **muslinet'** *n* a coarse kind of muslin.

□ **mus'lin-kale** *n* (*Scot*) thin broth made without meat.

musmon see **musimon**.

muso /*mū'zō*/ (*sl*) *n* (*pl* **mū'sos**) a musician, a music enthusiast (*esp Aust*); a pop musician who concentrates excessively on technical details (*derog*). [**music**]

musquash /*mus'kwosh*/ *n* a large aquatic N American animal related to the voles, very destructive to dams and waterways (also **muskrat**); its fur. [Algonquian]

musquetoon see under **musket**.

musrol /*muz'rōl*/ (*obs*) *n* the nose-band of a bridle. [Fr *muserolle*, from Ital *museruola*, from *muso* muzzle]

muss or **musse** /*mus*/ (now *N Am* and *dialect*) *n* a scramble (*Shakesp*); a disturbance, a row (*obs*); confusion, disorder; confused conflict (*archaic*); a mess. ◆ *vt* and *vi* to disarrange; to mess (often with *up*). [Perh different words; cf **mess¹**]

■ **muss'iness** *n*. **muss'y** *adj* disordered.

mussel /*mus'l*/ (formerly also **muscle** /*mus'l*/ or **muskle** /*mus'kl*/) *n* an edible marine lamellibranch shellfish of the family Mytilidae with a brownish-black elongated oval shell; a freshwater lamellibranch of the Unionidae with a slightly flatter shell; the shell of any of these; a mussel-plum. [OE *mūs(c)le*; cf Ger *Muschel*, Fr *moule*; all from L *mūsculus*, dimin of *mūs* mouse]

■ **muss'elled** *adj* poisoned by eating infected mussels.

□ **muss'el-plum** *n* a dark-purple plum resembling a mussel-shell. **muss'el-scalp'** (*Scot* **muss'el-scaup**) *n* a bed of mussels. **muss'el-shell** *n*.

mussitation /*mu-si-tā'shən*/ *n* low muttering; a speaking movement of the mouth but without sound. [L *mussitāre*, frequentative of *mussāre* to mutter]

■ **muss'itate** *vt* (*obs*) to mutter.

Mussulman or **Musulman** /*mus'l-mən*/ or *-män'*/ (*archaic*) *n* (*pl* **Muss'ulmans** or (*non-standard* or *facetious*) **Muss'ulmen**) a Muslim. [Pers *musulmān*, from Ar *muslim*, *moslim* Muslim]

■ **Muss'ulwoman** *n* (*non-standard* or *facetious*) a female Muslim.

mussy see under **muss**.

must¹ /*must*/ *auxiliary v* (used only in the present (orig past) indicative: 3rd pers sing **must**; *pat* **must** (often replaced by **had to**)) (taking *infinitive* without *to*) used to express compulsion, necessity or obligation, with ellipsis of the verb (as in *I must away*), resolute intention, likelihood or conviction, or inevitability. ◆ *n* an essential, a necessity; a thing that should not be missed or neglected. [Orig *pat* of **mote²**, from OE *mōste*, *pat* of *mōt*; cf Ger *müssen*]

■ words derived from main entry word; □ compound words; ■ idioms and phrasal verbs

❏ **must'-have**, **must'-see**, etc *n* and *adj* (something) that one must have, see, etc in order to be in fashion.
■ **must needs** see under **need**.

must² /*must*/ *n* new wine; unfermented, or only partially fermented, grape juice or other juice or pulp for fermentation; the process of fermentation. [OE *must*, from L *mustum (vīnum)* new (wine)]
■ **must'y** *adj*.

must³ /*must*/ *n* a smell of dampness or staleness, mustiness; mould. [Appar a back-formation from **musty²**]

must⁴ or **musth** /*must*/ *n* a dangerous frenzy in some male animals, such as elephants. ◆*adj* in such a state. [Pers and Hindi *mast* intoxicated]
■ **must'y** *adj* in a frenzy.

must⁵, **muist** or **moust** /*müst* or *müst*/ (*obs Scot*) *n* musk; hair-powder. ◆*vt* to powder. [OFr *must*, a form of *musc*; see **musk**]

mustache US spelling of **moustache**.

mustachio /*mə-stä'shi-ō*/ *n* (pl **mustach'ios**) (often in *pl*) a large, elegantly curling moustache. [Sp *mostacho*, Ital *mostaccio*]
■ **mustach'ioed** *adj*.

mustang /*mus'tang*/ *n* the feralized horse of the American prairies. [Sp *mestengo*, now *mesteño*, belonging to the *mesta* or graziers' union, combined with *mostrenco* homeless, stray]

mustard /*mus'tərd*/ *n* any of various species of plants of the *Sinapis* section of plants of the genus *Brassica*, typically having yellow flowers and slender seed pods; their (powdered) seeds; a pungent condiment prepared from the seeds; the brownish-yellow colour of the condiment. ◆*adj* of a brownish-yellow colour. [OFr *mo(u)starde* (Fr *moutarde*), from L *mustum* **must²** (because the condiment was prepared with must)]
❏ **mustard and cress** *n* a salad of seedlings of white mustard and garden cress. **mustard gas** *n* the vapour from a poisonous blistering liquid, $(CH_2ClCH_2)_2S$, obtained from ethylene and sulphur chloride (also called **dichlorodiethyl sulphide**). **mustard oil** *n* a volatile oil obtained from black mustard seeds. **mustard plaster** *n* a counter-irritant skin application made from black and white mustard flour, deprived of their fixed oil. **mustard tree** *n* a name given to a shrub *Salvadora persica* (family Salvadoraceae, *prob* related to Oleaceae) on the theory that it is the plant referred to in the New Testament, which others think is only black mustard which has grown tall, as it does in the Middle East.
■ **black mustard** an annual herb (*Brassica nigra*), whose strongly-flavoured seeds are used in cookery. **cut the mustard** (*inf*) reach a required standard, make the grade; make a favourable impression on. **French mustard** the condiment prepared for the table by adding salt, sugar, vinegar, etc. **garlic mustard** see under **garlic**. **hedge-mustard** see under **hedge**. **keen as mustard** (*inf*) intensely enthusiastic. **Sarepta mustard** an annual herb (*Brassica juncea*), whose seeds and oil are used in cookery (also **brown mustard**). **white mustard** an annual herb (*Brassica alba*) of the Mediterranean region, whose seeds are used in cookery. **wild mustard** charlock, a common cornfield weed with yellowy flowers.

mustee same as **mestee**.

Mustela /*mu-stē'lə*/ *n* the marten genus, giving name to the family **Muste'lidae** (otters, badgers and weasels) and the subfamily **Mustelī'nae** (weasels and martens). [L *mustēla* weasel]
■ **mus'teline** /*-təl-īn*/ *adj* and *n*.

muster /*mus'tər*/ *n* an assembly or gathering, *esp* of troops for inspection or duties; a gathering together, round-up; inspection; an assembly; a register; a round-up of livestock (*Aust* and *NZ*); (*perh orig* a misunderstanding) a company of peacocks; an example (*archaic*); a commercial sample; a display, demonstration (*obs*). ◆*vt* and *vi* to assemble; to enrol; to number; to show forth (*obs*). ◆*vt* to summon up (often with *up*); to round up (livestock; *Aust* and *NZ*). ◆*vi* to pass muster. [OFr *mostre, moustre, monstre*, from L *mōnstrum*, from *monēre* to warn]
■ **must'erer** *n* (*Aust* and *NZ*) a person who musters (livestock).
❏ **muster book** *n* (*Shakesp*) a book in which military forces or a ship's crew are registered. **mus'ter-file** *n* (*Shakesp*) a muster roll. **mus'ter-master** *n* (*hist*) a person in charge of the muster roll. **muster roll** *n* a register of the officers and men in each company, troop, regiment, ship's crew, etc; roll-call (*naut*).
■ **muster in** (*US*) to enrol, receive as recruits. **muster out** (*US*) to discharge from service. **pass muster** to bear examination, appear adequate.

musth see **must⁴**.

mustn't /*mus'nt*/ contraction of **must not**.

musty¹ see under **must²,⁴**.

musty² /*mus'ti*/ *adj* (**must'ier; must'iest**) mouldy; spoiled by damp; stale in smell or taste; deteriorated from disuse.
■ **mus'tily** *adv*. **mus'tiness** *n*.

Musulman same as **Mussulman**.

mutable /*mū'tə-bl*/ *adj* that may be changed; subject to change; variable; inconstant, fickle. [L *mūtābilis* changeable]
■ **mutabil'ity** or **mū'tableness** *n*. **mū'tably** *adv*.

mutagen /*mū'tə-jən*/ (*biol*) *n* a substance that causes mutations. [*mutation* and **-gen**]
■ **mutagen'esis** *n* the origin or induction of a mutation. **mutagenic** /*-jen'ik*/ *adj*. **mutagenic'ity** *n* the condition of being mutagenic. **mū'tagenize** or **-ise** *vt* to treat with mutagens.

mutandum /*mū-tan'dəm*/ (*biol*) *n* (pl **mutan'da**) something to be altered.

mutant /*mū'tənt*/ (*biol*) *adj* (of a gene, animal or organism) suffering, or resulting from, mutation. ◆*n* a form resulting from mutation. [L *mūtans, -antis*, pres p of *mūtāre* to change]

mutate /*mū-tāt'*/ *vt* and *vi* to cause or undergo mutation. [L *mūtātio*, from *mūtāre, -ātum* to change, **mutate** being a back-formation from **mutation**]
■ **muta'tion** *n* change, *esp* biological or genetic; in German orthography, another name for the umlaut; (in Celtic languages) an alteration to the sound of an initial consonant caused by a preceding word; (in old music) a change of syllable for the same note in passing to another hexachord; a change in the genetic material that can be transmitted to offspring (cf **somatic mutation** under **soma¹**) (*biol*). **muta'tional** *adj*. **muta'tionally** *adv*. **muta'tionist** *n* a believer in evolution by mutation. **mu'tative** or **mu'tatory** *adj* changing; mutable. **mū'ton** *n* the smallest element of a gene capable of giving rise to a new form by mutation.
❏ **mutation mink** *n* a much valued shade of mink produced by selective breeding. **mutation rate** *n* the frequency, per gamete, of gene mutations in a given species per unit time (*esp* generation time). **mutation stop** *n* an organ stop whose tones differ from those the keys indicate by an interval other than a whole number of octaves.

mutatis mutandis /*mū-tā'tis mū-tan'dis* or *moo-tä'tēs moo-tan'dēs*/ (L) *adv* with necessary changes.

mutato nomine /*mū-tā'tō nom'i-nē* or *moo-tä'tō nō'mi-ne*/ (L) the name being changed.

mutch /*much*/ (*Scot*) *n* a woman's close-fitting linen cap. [MDu *mutse*; Du *muts*, Ger *Mütze*]

mutchkin /*much'kin*/ (*hist*) *n* a Scottish liquid measure, three-quarters of an imperial pint, or a quarter of an old Scottish pint. [Obs Du *mudseken*]

mute¹ /*mūt*/ *adj* physically or psychologically unable to speak; silent; refusing to plead (*law*); without vocal utterance, unspoken; unpronounced or faintly pronounced; pronounced by stoppage of the breath passage, plosive (*phonetics*). ◆*n* a person who is unable to speak; a silent person; a person who refuses to plead (*law*); a hired funeral attendant; a servant in an oriental household who is unable to speak; an actor with no words to speak; a stop-consonant, a plosive (*phonetics*); a clip, pad, or other device for subduing the sound of a musical instrument. ◆*vt* to deaden or muffle the sound of (eg a musical instrument) with a mute; to silence. [L *mūtus*]
■ **mut'ed** *adj* (of eg sound or colour) softened, not loud, harsh or bright. **mute'ly** *adv*. **mute'ness** *n*. **mut'ism** *n* inability or unwillingness to speak.
❏ **mute button** *n* a device on a telephone which when depressed allows the user to make comments inaudible to the person on the other end of the line. **mute swan** *n* the common swan (*Cygnus olor*). ■ **mute of malice** (*law*) refusing to plead.

mute² /*mūt*/ (now *dialect*) *vi* (of birds) to defecate. ◆*n* (*obs*) birds' faeces; an act of muting. [OFr *mutir, esmeutir*; prob Gmc]

mutessarif /*moo-təs-ä'rif*/ *n* the head of a Turkish sanjak. [Turk *mutesarif*, from Ar *mutasarrif*]
■ **mutessa'rifat** *n* his office or jurisdiction.

mutha see **motherfucker** under **mother**.

muti /*moo'ti*/ (*S Afr*) *n* traditional medicine, *esp* associated with witchcraft or witch doctors. [Zulu *umuthi* tree]

muticous /*mū'ti-kəs*/ (*bot*) *adj* awnless; spineless; pointless. [L *muticus* awnless]

mutilate /*mū'ti-lāt*/ *vt* to injure by cutting off a limb, to maim; to remove a material part of; to damage or spoil beyond recognition; to deform by slitting, boring, or removing a part. ◆*adj* mutilated. [L *mutilāre, -ātum*, from *mutilus* maimed]
■ **mutilā'tion** *n*. **mu'tilātor** *n*.

mutiny /*mū'ti-nē*/ *n* insurrection against constituted authority, *esp* naval or military; revolt, tumult, strife. ◆*vi* (**mu'tinying; mu'tinied**) to rise against authority, *esp* in military or naval service. [Fr *mutin* riotous, from L *movēre, mōtum* to move]
■ **mutine** /*mū'tin*/ *n* mutiny (*obs*); a mutineer, rebel (*Shakesp*). ◆*vi* (*Shakesp* and *Milton*) to mutiny, rebel. **mutineer'** *n* a person who mutinies or takes part in a mutiny. ◆*vi* to mutiny. **mu'tinous** *adj* ready or inclined to mutiny; rebellious, unsubmissive; of the nature of, or expressing, mutiny. **mu'tinously** *adv*. **mu'tinousness** *n*.

❑ **Mutiny Act** *n* an act regulating the government of the army, passed annually by the British parliament from 1689 to 1879, when it was superseded.

muton see under **mutate**.

mutoscope /*mū'tə-skōp*/ *n* an early form of cinematograph. [L *mūtāre* to change, and Gr *skopeein* to look at]

mutt /*mut*/ (*sl; orig US*) *n* a dog, *esp* a mongrel; a blockhead. [Perh for **muttonhead**]

mutter /*mut'ər*/ *vi* to utter words in a low, indistinct voice; to murmur, *esp* in hostility, mutiny, or menace; to grumble; (of thunder) to rumble faintly. ◆ *vt* to utter indistinctly. ◆ *n* a murmuring (*Milton*); indistinct utterance; low rumbling; subdued grumbling. [Prob imit, like dialect Ger *muttern*; L *muttīre*]
　■ **muttera'tion** *n* (*Richardson*) complaining. **mutt'erer** *n*. **mutt'ering** *n* and *adj*. **mutt'eringly** *adv*.

mutton /*mut'n*/ *n* sheep's flesh as food; a sheep (*obs* or *joc*); women as food for lust, hence a prostitute (*obs sl*); an em (*printing*). [OFr *moton* (Fr *mouton*) a sheep, from LL *multō, -ōnis*; perh of Celtic origin]
　■ **mutt'ony** *adj*.
　❑ **mutton bird** *n* an Australasian shearwater, *esp* the short-tailed, said by some to taste like mutton. **mutton chop** *n* a piece of mutton cut from the rib. ◆ *adj* (of whiskers) shaped like a mutton chop, ie broad and rounded on the cheek, tapering to meet the hairline. **mutton cloth** *n* a plain-knitted cloth (*usu* cotton) of loose texture. **mutt'ondum'mies** *n pl* (*sl*) white plimsolls. **mutt'on-fist** *n* a coarse, big hand; a printer's index-hand. **mutton ham** *n* a salted leg of mutton. **mutt'onhead** *n* a heavy, stupid person. **mutt'onheaded** *adj* stupid. **mutton suet** *n* the fat surrounding the kidneys and loins of sheep.
　■ **mutton dressed as lamb** (*inf*) an older woman who dresses or makes herself up in a style more suitable to a young one. **return to our muttons** (*inf*) return to the subject of discussion (a playful translation of the judge's 'Revenons à nos moutons' in the old French farce of *Maître Pathelin*, in which the witnesses wander from the matter in dispute, some sheep).

mutual /*mū'tū-əl* or *-choo-əl*/ *adj* interchanged; reciprocal; given and received; common, joint, shared by two or more (*Shakesp*; now regarded by many as incorrect); (of a financial institution, eg a building society or an insurance company) owned by its customers. ◆ *n* a financial institution owned by its customers. [Fr *mutuel*, from L *mutuus*, from *mūtāre* to change]
　■ **mu'tualism** *n* symbiosis; the theory that mutual dependence is necessary for the welfare of the individual and society; practice based on this. **mu'tualist** *n* and *adj*. **mutualis'tic** *adj*. **mutuality** /*-al'i-ti*/ *n*. **mutualizā'tion** or **-s-** *n*. **mu'tualize** or **-ise** *vt* to put upon a mutual footing. **mu'tually** *adv*.
　❑ **mutual admiration society** *n* (*facetious*) a group of people or circle of friends lavish in their praise of each other. **mutual friend** *n* (*Dickens*) a common friend. **mutual funds** *n pl* (*US*) unit trusts. **mutual improvement society** *n* a society whose members meet to hear lectures, read essays, hold debates, etc, in order to stimulate each other to improve in knowledge and in public speaking. **mutual inductance** *n* (*electronics*) the generation of electromotile force in one system of conductors by a variation of current in another system linked to the first by magnetic flux. **mutual inductor** *n* (*electronics*) a component consisting of two coils designed to have a definite mutual inductance. **mutual mistake** *n* (*law*) the situation arising when parties to a contract are at cross-purposes as to its subject or terms. **mutual wall** *n* a wall equally belonging to each of two houses.

mutuca see **motuca**.

mutuel /*mū'chūl*/ *n* shortened form of **pari-mutuel**.

mutule /*mū'tūl*/ *n* a kind of square, flat bracket, in Doric architecture, above each triglyph and each metope, with guttae. [L *mūtulus* a mutule, modillion]

mutuum /*mū'tū-əm*/ (*hist*) *n* a bailment consisting of a loan of goods for consumption, such as corn, coal, etc, to be returned in goods of the same amount. [L neuter of *mūtuus* lent]

mutuus consensus /*mū'tū-əs kon-sen'səs* or *moo'tū-ŭs kŏn-sān'sŭs*/ (*L*) *n* mutual consent.

muu-muu /*moo'moo*/ *n* a simple loose dress worn chiefly in Hawaii. [Hawaiian *mu'u mu'u*]

mux /*muks*/ (*US* and *dialect*) *vt* to spoil, botch. ◆ *n* a mess. [Origin obscure]

Muzak® /*mū'zak*/ *n* continuous background music played in restaurants, shops, etc (also (*non-standard*) **Musak**).
　■ **mū'zaky** *adj*.

muzhik, **moujik** or **mujik** /*moo-zhik'* or *moo'zhik*/ (*hist*) *n* a Russian peasant. [Russ *muzhik*]

muzzle /*muz'l*/ *n* the projecting jaws and nose of an animal; a strap or a cage for the mouth to prevent biting; the extreme end of a gun, etc. ◆ *vt* to put a muzzle on; to keep from hurting; to gag or silence. ◆ *vt*

and *vi* (of an animal) to touch, thrust or investigate with the muzzle. [OFr *musel* (Fr *museau*), from LL *mūsellum*, dimin of *mūsum* or *mūsus* beak]
　■ **muzz'ler** *n* a person who applies a muzzle; a blow on the mouth; a muzzle-loader; a direct headwind (*naut*).
　❑ **muzz'le-bag** *n* a canvas bag fixed to the muzzle of a gun at sea, to keep out water. **muzz'le-load'er** *n* a firearm loaded through the muzzle, *opp* to *breech-loader*. **muzz'le-load'ing** *adj*. **muzzle velocity** *n* the velocity of a projectile the moment it leaves the muzzle of a gun.

muzzy /*muz'i*/ *adj* (**muzz'ier**; **muzz'iest**) dazed, bewildered; tipsy; blurred; hazy. [Origin unknown]
　■ **muzz** *vt* (back-formation) to make muzzy. ◆ *n* a muddle or blur. **muzz'ily** *adv*. **muzz'iness** *n*.

MV *symbol*: megavolt(s).

Mv *abbrev*: mendelevium (now **Md**).

mv *abbrev*: merchant vessel; motor vessel; muzzle velocity.

MVD *abbrev*: *Ministerstvo Vnutrennikh Del*, the Soviet Ministry of Internal Affairs.

MVDS *abbrev*: multipoint (or microwave) video distribution system.

MVO *abbrev*: Member of the (Royal) Victorian Order.

MVP (*N Am*) *abbrev*: most valuable player.

mvule /*(ə)m-voo'lā*/ *n* a huge tropical African timber tree (*Chlorophora excelsa*) of the mulberry family. [Swahili]

MW *abbrev*: Malawi (IVR); medium wave; megawatt.

mwah /*mwä*/ *interj* an exclamation intended to convey the sound of a kiss. [Imit]

M-way see under **M** (*abbrev*).

MWF *abbrev*: Medical Women's Federation.

MWGM (*Freemasonry*) *abbrev*: Most Worshipful (or Worthy) Grand Master.

MX (*US*) *abbrev*: missile experimental.

Mx *abbrev*: Middlesex.

mx *abbrev*: maxwell (unit measuring magnetic flux).

MY *abbrev*: motor yacht.

my /*mī* (sometimes *mi*)/ *possessive adj* (used *attrib* only) of or belonging to me; sometimes used in addressing others, eg formally, *my lord*, *my lady* or affectionately, patronizingly, etc, eg *my dear, my friend*; used in interjection, eg *my God!* ◆ *interj* expressing surprise (perh for *my word* or *my God*). [**mine**[1], from OE *mīn* (genitive) of me]

MYA *abbrev*: Myanmar (IVR).

Mya /*mī'ə*/ *n* a genus of lamellibranch molluscs, the gapers, including the American soft or long clam. [Gr *mӯs* or *myax* a mussel]

myal see under **myalism**.

myalgia /*mī-al'ji-ə*/ *n* pain in a muscle. [Gr *mӯs* muscle, and *algos* pain]
　■ **myal'gic** *adj*.
　❑ **myalgic encephalomyelitis** /*en-sef-ə-lō-mī-ə-lī'tis*/ *n* chronic fatigue syndrome.

myalism /*mī'ə-li-zm*/ *n* a form of witchcraft of African origin, practised in the West Indies. [Prob W African; cf Hausa *maye*]
　■ **my'al** *adj*.

myall[1] /*mī'öl*/ *n* an Australian aborigine living traditionally. ◆ *adj* wild; unaccustomed to white society. [From an Aboriginal language]

myall[2] /*mī'öl*/ *n* an Australian acacia of various species with hard, scented wood; the wood of such a tree. [Aboriginal word *maiāl*]

myasthenia /*mī-əs-thē'ni-ə*/ *n* muscular weakness or debility. [Gr *mys* muscle, and **asthenia**]
　■ **myasthenic** /*-then'ik*/ *adj*.
　❑ **myasthenia gravis** /*grä'vis*/ *n* a chronic progressive disease in which the (*esp* facial) muscles become fatigued, with progressive muscular paralysis.

myc- see **myco-**.

mycelium /*mī-sē'li-əm*/ *n* (*pl* **myce'lia**) the white threadlike mass of filaments forming the vegetative part of a fungus. [Gr *mykēs* a mushroom]
　■ **myce'lial** *adj*.

Mycenaean /*mī-sē-nē'ən*/ *adj* of the ancient city state of *Mycēnae* (Gr *Mykēnai*) in Argolis, Agamemnon's kingdom, or its culture culminating in the Bronze Age. ◆ *n* an inhabitant of Mycenae.

Mycetes /*mī-sē'tēz*/ *n* the howler genus of S American monkeys. [Gr *mykētēs* bellower]

mycetes /*mī-sē'tēz*/ *n pl* fungi. [Gr *mykēs, -ētos*, pl *mykētes* a mushroom]

myco- /*mī-kō-*/ or (before a vowel) **myc-** /*mīk-*/, also **myceto-** /*mī-sē-tō-, -o-*/ or **mycet-** /*mī-sēt-*/ *combining form* denoting: fungus; mushroom. [Gr *mykēs, -ētos*, pl *mykētes* a mushroom]

■ **mycetol'ogy** n mycology. **mycetō'ma** n Madura foot, a disease of foot and leg in India, caused by a fungus. **Mycetozō'a** n pl the Myxomycetes or slime-fungi (when classed as animals). **mycetozō'an** n and adj. **mycobactē'rium** n (pl **mycobactē'ria**) any of several Gram-positive parasitic or saprophytic bacteria, eg those causing leprosy and tuberculosis. **mycodomatium** /-dō-mā'shyəm or -shi-əm/ n (pl **mycodomā'tia**) (Gr domation a chamber) a fungus-gall. **mycologic** /mī-kə-loj'ik/ or **mycolog'ical** adj. **mycologist** /-kol'/ n. **mycol'ogy** n the study of fungi. **mycophagist** /mī-kof'ə-jist/ n (Gr phagein to eat) a toadstool-eater. **mycoph'agy** n. **mycoplasma** /-plaz'mə/ n (pl **mycoplas'mas** or **mycoplas'mata**) a member of the Mycoplasma, a genus of pathogenic agents, the smallest free-living organisms known, including Mycoplasma pneumoniae which causes atypical pneumonia. **mycorrhiza** or **mycorhiza** /mī-kō-rī'zə/ n (pl **mycorrhī'zae** or **mycorhī'zae** /-zē/) (Gr rhiza root) a fungal mycelium investing or penetrating the underground parts of a higher plant and supplying it with material from humus instead of root hairs. **mycorrhī'zal** or **mycorhī'zal** adj. **mycosis** /-kō'sis/ n (pl **mycō'ses** /-sēz/) a disease due to growth of a fungus. **mycotic** /-kot'ik/ adj. **mycotoxicosis** /-tok-si-kō'sis/ n poisoning caused by a mycotoxin. **mycotoxin** /-tok'sin/ n any poisonous substance produced by a fungus. **mycotrophic** /-trof'ik/ adj (Gr trophē food) (of a plant) living in symbiosis with a fungus.

mydriasis /mi-drī'ə-sis/ n abnormal dilatation of the pupil of the eye. [Gr mydriāsis]
■ **mydriatic** /mid-ri-at'ik/ adj and n (a drug) causing the pupil to dilate.

myel- /mī-əl-/ or **myelo-** /mī-ə-lō-, -lo- or -lə-/ combining form denoting bone marrow or the spinal cord. [Gr myelos marrow]
■ **my'elin** n the substance forming the medullary sheath of nerve-fibres. **my'elinated** adj having a myelin sheath. **myelin'ic** adj. **myelī'tis** n inflammation of the spinal cord; inflammation of the bone marrow. **my'eloblast** n an immature cell of bone marrow, found in the circulating blood only in diseased conditions. **myeloblas'tic** adj. **myelogenous** /-oj'i-nəs/ adj producing bone marrow. **my'eloid** adj like, relating to, or of the nature of, marrow; relating to the spinal cord. **myeloma** /-lō'mə/ n (pl **myelō'mas** or **myelō'mata**) a tumour of the bone marrow, or composed of cells normally present in bone marrow. **my'elon** n the spinal cord.

mygale /mig'ə-lē/ n an American bird-catching spider of the genus Mygale. [Gr mygalē a fieldmouse, a shrew, from mȳs mouse, and galeē weasel]

myiasis /mī'i-ə-sis or mī-i-ā'sis/ n disease caused by presence of flies or their larvae. [Gr myia fly]

Mylar® /mī'lär/ n a strong plastic film, used in making audio tapes, packaging, etc.

mylodon /mī'lə-don/, also **mylodont** /mī'lə-dont/ n a sloth of the Mylodon genus of gigantic Pleistocene ground-sloths with a short, broad skull. ◆ adj of or relating to this genus. [Gr mylē a mill, and odous, odontos a tooth]

mylohyoid /mī-lō-hī'oid/ (anat) adj relating to or near the jawbone and the hyoid bone. ◆ n a muscle so placed. [Gr mylē a mill]

mylonite /mī'lə-nīt/ n a hard, compact, often streaky granular rock produced by crushing. [Gr mylōn a mill]
■ **mylonitic** /-it'ik/ adj. **mylonītīzā'tion** or **-s-** n. **my'lonitize** or **-ise** vt to turn into mylonite.

myna, **mynah** or **mina** /mī'nə/ n any of various related sturnoid Asiatic birds of which the species Gracula religiosa, black with white spots on the wings, can be taught to imitate human speech. [Hindi mainā]

mynheer /mīn-hār' or mə-nār'/ n my lord (archaic); Dutch for Mr or sir; a Dutchman or Afrikaaner. [Du mijn my, and heer lord]

myo- /mī-ō- or -o-/ combining form denoting muscle. [Gr mȳs, myos muscle]
■ **my'oblast** n a cell producing muscle-tissue. **myoblast'ic** adj. **myocar'dial** or **myocar'diac** adj of or relating to the myocardium (**myocardial infarction** destruction of the myocardium due to interruption of blood supply to the area). **myocardiop'athy** n any non-inflammatory disease of the myocardium. **myocardī'tis** n inflammation of the myocardium. **myocar'dium** n (pl **myocar'dia**) the muscular substance of the heart. **myoelec'tric** adj of apparatus, etc which uses the small electric currents produced within the body which normally cause muscular contraction and relaxation. **myofī'bril** n one of the elongated contractile filaments of protein that make up cells in striated muscle. **my'ogen** n an albumin, soluble in water, found in muscle. **myogen'ic** adj (of contraction) arising spontaneously in a muscle, independent of nervous stimuli. **myoglō'bin** n a protein that stores oxygen in muscle. **my'ogram** n a myographic record. **my'ograph** n an instrument for recording muscular contractions. **myograph'ic** or **myograph'ical** adj. **myog'raphist** n. **myog'raphy** n. **my'oid** adj like muscle. **myolog'ical** adj. **myol'ogist** n. **myol'ogy** n the study of muscles. **myō'ma** n a tumour composed of muscular

tissue. **myop'athy** n disease of the muscles or muscle tissue. **my'osin** n a protein that contributes to the process of contraction in muscles. **myosī'tis** n (irregularly formed) inflammation of a muscle. **my'ostatin** n a blood protein that limits muscle growth. **my'otome** n muscles which are controlled by the nerves from one segment of the spinal cord; a surgical instrument for dissecting muscle. **myotō'nia** n muscle-stiffness. **myoton'ic** adj (**myotonic dystrophy** a muscle-wasting disease that causes myotonia, as well as the usual symptoms of weakness and wasting). **my'otube** n a cylindrical cell that develops from a myoblast, representing a stage in the development of muscle fibres.

myomancy /mī'ō-man-si/ n divination by observing the way in which mice move when released from a cage. [Gr mȳs a mouse, and manteiā divination]
■ **myoman'tic** adj.

myopia /mī-ō'pi-ə/ n short-sightedness (also fig). [Gr myōps short-sighted, from myein to shut, and ōps the eye]
■ **my'ope** /-ōp/ or **my'ops** /-ops/ n a short-sighted person. **myopic** /-op'/ adj short-sighted (also fig). ◆ n a short-sighted person. **myop'ically** adv.

myosin see under **myo-**.

myosis see **miosis**.

myositis see under **myo-**.

myosotis /mī-o-sō'tis/ or **myosote** /mī'ə-sōt/ n a plant of the genus Myosotis, the forget-me-not genus of the borage family. [Gr myosōtis mouse-ear, from its furry leaves, from mȳs, myos a mouse, and ous, ōtos an ear]

myotube see under **myo-**.

myrbane same as **mirbane**.

myria- /mi-ri-ə-/ combining form denoting: ten thousand; a very large number, as in myriad and myriapod.

myriad /mir'i-əd/ n any immense number. ◆ adj numberless. [Gr mȳrias, -ados ten thousand]
■ **myr'iadfold** adj and n (or adv). **myr'iadth** n and adj.

myriapod /mir'i-ə-pod/ n a member of the **Myriapoda** /-ap'ə-də/, a class of crawling arthropods with many legs, such as the centipedes and millipedes (also **myr'iopod**). [Gr mȳriopous, -podos many-footed, from mȳrios numberless, and pous, podos a foot]

Myrica /mi-rī'kə/ n orig the tamarisk; the sweet-gale or bog myrtle genus, of the family **Myricā'ceae**. [Gr myrīkē (myrĭkē) tamarisk]

myringa /mi-ring'gə/ (anat) n the eardrum. [LL miringa, from Gr mēninx membrane]
■ **myringitis** /-in-jī'tis/ n inflammation of the eardrum. **myringoscope** /-ing'gə-skōp/ n an instrument for viewing the eardrum. **myringotomy** /-ing-got'əm-i/ n incision of the eardrum.

myriorama /mi-ri-ō-rä'mə/ n a picture composed of interchangeable parts that can be variously combined. [Gr mȳrios numberless, and horāma a view]

myrioscope /mir'i-ə-skōp/ n a variety of kaleidoscope. [Gr mȳrios numberless, and skopeein to view]

Myristica /mī-ris'ti-kə or mir-is'/ n the nutmeg genus of plants, giving name to the family **Myristicā'ceae**. [Gr mȳrizein to anoint]
■ **myris'tic** adj. **myristicivorous** /-is-ti-siv'ə-rəs/ adj feeding upon nutmegs.
□ **myristic acid** n a fatty acid ($C_{13}H_{27}COOH$) obtained from nutmegs.

myrmecoid /mûr'mi-koid/ adj antlike. [Gr myrmēkoeidēs like an ant]
myrmecology /mûr-mi-kol'ə-ji/ n the study of ants. [Gr myrmēx, -ēkos ant]
■ **myrmecolog'ic** or **myrmecolog'ical** adj. **myrmecol'ogist** n. **myrmecoph'agous** adj feeding on ants; of the antbear genus **Myrmecoph'aga**. **myr'mecophile** n. **myrmecoph'ilous** adj having a symbiotic relation with ants. **myrmecoph'ily** n.

Myrmidon /mûr'mi-dən/ n one of a tribe of warriors who accompanied Achilles to Troy (Gr myth); (without cap) a member of any ruffianly band under a daring leader; someone who carries out another's orders without fear or pity. [Gr Myrmidones (pl)]
■ **myrmidō'nian** adj.
□ **myrmidons of the law** n pl (facetious) policemen, bailiffs, etc.

myrobalan /mi- or mī-rob'ə-lən/ n the astringent fruit of certain Indian mountain species of the genus Terminalia (Combretaceae), used medicinally, and in ink, dyeing and tanning; the cherry plum. [Gr mȳrobalanos bito, from myron an unguent, and balanos an acorn]
■ **emblic myrobalan** see under **emblic**.

myrrh /mûr/ n a bitter, aromatic, transparent gum, exuded from the bark of a tree of the genus Commiphora, used medicinally and in perfume and incense; sweet cicely. [OE myrra, from L myrrha, from Gr myrrā; of Semitic origin; cf Ar murr]
■ **myrrh'ic** adj. **myrrh'ol** n the volatile oil of myrrh.

myrrhine see under **murra**.

myrtle /mûr'tl/ n any of various evergreen shrubs of the genus *Myrtus*, with beautiful and fragrant leaves; extended to various other plants, some near related, others not, eg a kind of beech in Australia (see also under **bog**, **wax**[1]). [OFr *myrtil*, dimin of *myrte*, from L *myrtus*, from Gr *myrtos*]
❑ **myr'tle-wax** n wax from the candleberry.

Myrtus /mûr'təs/ n the myrtle genus, giving name to the family **Myrtā'ceae**. [L, from Gr *myrtos*]
■ **myrtā'ceous** adj.

myself /mī-self'/ or /mi-self'/ pronoun (used in apposition with *I* or *me*, for emphasis or clarification) in person; (used reflexively) me. [**me**[1] and **self**]

mysophobia /mī-sō-fō'bi-ə/ n morbid fear of contamination. [Gr *mysos* defilement, and *phobos* fear]

mystagogue /mis'tə-gog or -gōg/ n an initiator into religious mysteries (also **mystagō'gus**). [Gr *mystēs* an initiate, and *agōgos* a leader]
■ **mystagog'ic** /-goj'/ or -gog'/ or **mystagog'ical** adj. **mys'tagogy** /-goj- or -gog-/ n.

mystery[1] /mis't(ə-)ri/ n (pl **mys'teries**) a secret doctrine; (usu in pl) in ancient religious, etc rites, known only to the initiated, such as the *Eleusinian mysteries*; (in pl) the secrets of freemasonry, etc; a phenomenon, circumstance or happening that cannot be explained; someone or something inscrutable, an enigma; enigmatic quality; something obscure, abstruse or arcane; a tale of suspense that baffles and intrigues; a truth divinely imparted (*relig*); a sacrament (*relig*); (also **mystery play**) a play depicting the life of Christ; a shiftless, drifting girl (*sl*). [L *mystērium*, from Gr *mystērion*, from *mystēs* an initiate, from *myeein* to initiate, from *myein* to close the eyes]
■ **mystē'rious** adj containing mystery; having an air of mystery; obscure, strange; secret; incomprehensible. **mystē'riously** adv. **mystē'riousness** n.
❑ **mys'tery-man** n a conjurer; a medicine man. **mys'tery-monger** n a dealer in mysteries. **mystery ship** n a Q-boat. **mystery shopper** n an undercover researcher who poses as a customer in order to evaluate shops, restaurants, etc. **mystery tour** n an excursion to a destination which remains secret until the journey's end.

mystery[2] or **mistery** /mis'tə-ri/ n office, service, duty (*obs*); craft, art, trade (*archaic*); skill (*Shakesp*); a trade guild (*hist*). [LL *misterium*, from L *ministerium*, from *minister* servant; confused with *mystērium* and prob with **maistry**, **mastery**]

mystic /mis'tik/ adj (also **mystical**) relating to mystery, the mysteries, or mysticism; mysterious; sacredly obscure or secret; involving a sacred or a secret meaning hidden from the eyes of the ordinary person, only revealed to a spiritually enlightened mind; allegorical. ◆ n a person who seeks or attains direct communion with God or the divine in elevated religious feeling or ecstasy. [L *mysticus*, from Gr *mystikos*, from *mystēs* an initiate; cf **mystery**[1]]
■ **mys'tically** adv. **mys'ticalness** n. **mys'ticism** /-sizm/ n the habit or tendency of religious thought and feeling of those who seek direct communion with God or the divine; fogginess and unreality of thought (with suggestion of **mist**).
❑ **mystic recitation** n the recitation of parts of the Greek liturgy in an inaudible voice.

mystify /mis'ti-fī/ vt (**mys'tifying**; **mys'tified**) to make mysterious, obscure, or secret; to involve in mystery; to bewilder; to puzzle; to hoax. [Fr *mystifier*]
■ **mystifica'tion** n. **mys'tifier** n someone who or that which mystifies; a hoaxer. **mys'tifying** adj. **mys'tifyingly** adv.

mystique /mi-stēk'/ n incommunicable spirit, gift or quality; the secret of an art as known to its inspired practitioners; a sense or aura of mystery, remoteness from the ordinary, and power or skill surrounding a person, activity, etc. [Fr]

myth /mith/ or (*archaic*) mīth/ n an ancient traditional story of gods or heroes, *esp* one offering an explanation of some fact or phenomenon; a story with a veiled meaning; mythical matter; a figment; a commonly-held belief that is untrue, or without foundation. [Gr *mȳthos* talk, story, myth]
■ **myth'ic** or **myth'ical** adj relating to myths; fabulous; fictitious, untrue. **myth'ically** adv. **myth'icism** /-sizm/ n theory that explains miraculous stories as myth. **myth'icist** n. **myth'icize** or **-ise** /-i-siz/ vt to make the subject of myth; to explain as myth. **myth'icizer** or **-s-** n. **myth'ism** n mythicism. **myth'ist** n a maker of myths; a mythicist. **myth'ize** or **-ise** vt to mythicize. **mythogen'esis** n the production or origination of myths. **mythog'rapher** n a writer or narrator of myths. **mythog'raphy** n representation of myths in art; collection or description of myths. **mythol'oger** or **mytholō'gian** n a mythologist. **mytholog'ic** or **mytholog'ical** adj relating to mythology, fabulous. **mytholog'ically** adv. **mythol'ogist** n. **mythol'ogization** or **-s-** n. **mythol'ogize** or **-ise** vt to interpret or explain the mythological character of; to turn into myth; to create myths. **mythol'ogizer** or **-s-** n. **mythol'ogy** n a body of myths; the scientific study of myths; symbolical meaning (*obs*). **myth'omane** n and adj (a) mythomaniac. **mythomā'nia** n (*psychiatry*) lying or exaggerating to an abnormal extent. **mythomā'niac** n and adj. **mythopoe'ia** /mith-ə-pē'ə/ n the creation or formation of myths. **mythopoeic** /mith-ō-pē'ik/ or **mythopoetic** /-pō-et'ik/ adj (Gr *poieein* to make) myth-making. **mythopoe'ist** n a myth-maker. **mythopō'et** n a myth-maker; a writer of poems on mythical subjects. **mythus** /mīth'əs/ (L) or **mythos** /mīth'os/ (Gr) n myth; mythology; theme, scheme of events; the characteristic or current attitudes of a culture or group, expressed symbolically (through poetry, art, drama, etc).
❑ **mythical theory** n the theory of DF Strauss (1808–74) and his school, that the Gospels are mainly a collection of myths, developed during the first two centuries, from the imagination of the followers of Jesus.
■ **comparative mythology** the science that investigates myths and seeks to relate those of different peoples.

Mytilus /mit'i-ləs/ n the common mussel genus, giving name to the family **Mytilidae** /mī-til'i-dē/. [L *mȳtilus*, *mītulus*, *mūtulus*]
■ **mytil'iform** adj. **myt'iloid** adj.

myxoedema or (*esp N Am*) **myxedema** /mik-sē-dē'mə/ n a diseased condition due to a deficiency of thyroid secretion, characterized by loss of hair, increased thickness and dryness of the skin, increase in weight, slowing of mental processes, and diminution of metabolism. [Gr *myxa* mucus, and *oidēma* swelling]
■ **myxoede'matous** or (*esp N Am*) **myxede'matous** adj. **myxoede'mic** or (*esp N Am*) **myxede'mic** adj.

myxoma /mik-sō'mə/ n (pl **myxō'mata**) a tumour of jellylike or mucous substance that usually forms just beneath the skin. [Gr *myxa* mucus]
■ **myxomatō'sis** n a contagious virus disease of rabbits. **myxō'matous** adj.

myxomycete /mik-sō-mī-sēt'/ n any of the Myxomycetes class of very simple plants or slime-fungi, by some classed as animals (phylum Mycetozoa), consisting of a naked mass of protoplasm with many nuclei, living on dead or decaying plant matter. [Gr *myxa* mucus, and *mykētes*, pl of *mykēs* a mushroom]

Myxophyta /mik-sō-fī'tə/ n pl the Cyanophyta. [Gr *myxa* slime, and *phyton* plant]

myxovirus /mik'sō-vī-rəs/ n any of a group of related viruses causing influenza, mumps, etc. [Gr *myxa* mucus, and **virus**]

mzee /əm-zā'/ n (in E Africa) an old person. [Swahili]

MZM abbrev : metical (Mozambique currency).

mzungu /əm-zŭng'goo/ n (in E Africa) a white person. [Swahili]

■ words derived from main entry word; ❑ compound words; ■ idioms and phrasal verbs

Nn

N or **n** /en/ n the fourteenth letter in the modern English alphabet, thirteenth in the Roman, its sound an alveolar nasal, or before *g* or *k* a velar nasal (as in *sing, sink*); an indefinite number, *esp* in a series (*maths*), often (*inf*) implicitly a large number; a unit of measurement (**en**) = half an em (*printing*); anything shaped like the letter N.
▪ **n**ᵗʰ or **nth** adj.
❏ **n'-type** adj (ie 'negative-type') of a semiconductor, having an excess of conduction electrons over mobile holes (see **hole**¹).
▪ **to the n**ᵗʰ (or **nth**) to any power; hence (*inf*) to an unlimited degree.

N or **N.** abbrev : knight (in chess; also **Kt**); naira (Nigerian currency); National; Nationalist; navy; New; ngultrum (Bhutanese currency); Norse; North; Northern; Norway (IVR); nuclear.
❏ **n-bomb** n (*US sl.*) a use of the word 'nigger', considered offensive.
the N-word n (*euphem*) nigger.

N symbol : (as a medieval Roman numeral) 90; newton (SI unit); nitrogen (*chem*).

Ñ symbol : (medieval Roman numeral) 90 000.

n or **n.** abbrev : name; nano-; neuter; neutron; new; nominative; noon; note; noun; number.

'n' an informal shortening of **and**¹.

NA abbrev : Netherlands Antilles (IVR); North America.

Na (*chem*) symbol : sodium. [Formerly called *natrium*]

na /nä/ (*Scot*) adv a Scots form of **no**¹; /ni or nä/ an enclitic form of **not**, as in hasna (= has not).

n/a abbrev : not applicable; not available.

NAACP (*US*) abbrev : National Association for the Advancement of Colored People.

Naafi or **NAAFI** /nä'fi/ n an organization for providing canteens for servicemen and servicewomen; one of the canteens. [From the initials of Navy, Army, and Air Force Institute(s)]

naam or **nam** /näm/ (*hist ; law*) n distraint. [OE *näm*, related to *niman* to take]

naan see **nan**¹.

naartje see **nartjie**.

nab¹ /nab/ (*inf*) vt (**nabb'ing**; **nabbed**) to seize, snatch; to catch in the act of doing wrong; to arrest. [Origin obscure; cf **nap**⁴]
▪ **nabb'er** n.

nab² /nab/ n a hilltop; a promontory; a projection; the keeper of a door-lock. [ON *nabbr* or *nabbi*]

nab³ /nab/ (*obs sl*) n the head; a hat.

Nabataean /na-bə-tē'ən/ or **Nabathaean** /-thē'/ n and adj (a member) of an ancient powerful Arab people who lived around Petra. [Gr *Nabat(h)aios*]

nabk /nabk or nubk/ n the Christ's-thorn. [Ar *nebq*]

nabla /nab'lə/ (*maths*) n in Cartesian co-ordinates, the symbol ∇, an inverted delta, also called **del**, representing the vector operator $\mathbf{i}\partial/\partial x + \mathbf{j}\partial/\partial y + \mathbf{k}\partial/\partial z$. [Gr *nabla* nebel (qv), from the shape]

nabob /nä'bob/ n a European who has amassed a fortune in the East (*archaic*); (in Europe) any person of great wealth, an important person; a nawab (*obs*). [Hindi *nawwāb*; see **nawab**]

nabs /nabz/ (*sl*) n a person, *esp* in such phrases as **his nabs**, himself. [Cf **nob**², **nib**²]

NACAB abbrev : National Association of Citizens' Advice Bureaux.

nacarat /nak'ə-rat/ n a bright orange-red; a fabric so coloured. [Fr]

nacelle /nə-sel'/ n a streamlined structure on an aircraft housing an engine, etc; the car of a balloon, airship, etc; a little boat (*obs*). [Fr, from LL *nāvicella*, from L *nāvis* ship]

NACFB abbrev : National Association of Commercial Finance Brokers.

nach see **nautch**.

nache /näch/ n the rump. [See **aitchbone**]

nacho /nach'ō/ n (pl **nach'os**) (*usu* in *pl*) a tortilla chip, *usu* topped with cheese or beans and flavoured with chilli, jalapeño peppers, etc. [Am Sp]

Nachschlag /nähh'shlähh/ (*music*) n a grace note whose time is taken off the preceding note. [Ger, from *nach* after, and *Schlag* stroke]

nachtmaal /nähht'mäl/ older form of **nagmaal**.

nacket /nak'it/ or **nocket** /nok'it/ n a snack, light lunch. [Origin obscure]

NACODS /nä'kodz/ abbrev : National Association of Colliery Overmen, Deputies and Shotfirers.

nacre /nä'kər/ n mother-of-pearl or a shellfish yielding it. [Fr; prob of Eastern origin]
▪ **na'cred** adj. **nä'creous** adj (also **nä'crous**). **nä'crite** n a clay mineral, identical in composition to kaolinite but differing in optical characteristics and atomic structure.

NACRO /nak'rō/ abbrev : National Association for the Care and Resettlement of Offenders.

NAD abbrev : nicotinamide adenine dinucleotide, a coenzyme.

nada /nä'də/ n nothing; nothingness. [Sp]

Na-Dene /nä-dēn', nä-dä'ni or nä-dä-nä'/ n a group of Native American languages comprising Athabascan, Haida, Tlingit and Eyak.

nadir /nä'dēr, nad'ēr or -dər/ n the point of the heavens diametrically opposite to the zenith; the lowest point of anything, *esp* an emotional state. [Fr, from Ar *nadīr* (*nazīr*) opposite to]

nads /nadz/ (*sl*) n pl the testicles. [Aphetic for **gonads**]

nae /nä/ adj a Scots form of **no**². ◆ adv same as **no**¹, *esp* with a comparative.
❏ **nae'body** n nobody. **nae'thing** n nothing.

naevus or (*US*) **nevus** /nē'vəs/, also (*obs*) **naeve** /nēv/ n (pl **naevi** or (*US*) **nevi** /nē'vī, nī'vē/ or **naeves**) a birthmark; a pigmented spot or an overgrowth of small blood vessels in the skin. [L]
▪ **nae'void** adj.

naff /naf/ (*sl*) adj inferior, worthless, *esp* in style or taste; vulgar, socially crass. ◆ n an incompetent. [Origin disputed; suggested derivations are: *naf*, back-slang for *fan(ny)* the female genitalia; *naff* navel or nothing; *naffy* (**Naafi**) generally contemptuous, specif 'shirking'; the phrase *not available for fucking or fornication*]
▪ **naff'ing** adj and adv used as an offensive qualification. **naff'ly** adv. **naff'ness** n.
▪ **naff all** nothing at all. **naff off** an offensive injunction to go away.

NAFTA /naf'tə/ abbrev : North American Free Trade Agreement.

nag¹ /nag/ n a horse, *esp* a small one; a riding horse, or an inferior horse (*inf*); a jade (*Shakesp*). [ME *nagge*; origin obscure; cf MDu *negge, negghe* (Mod Du *neg, negge*)]

nag² /nag/ vt or vi (**nagg'ing**; **nagged**) to find fault with, urge (to do something), cause pain to, or worry, constantly; (with *at*) to worry or annoy continually. ◆ n (also **nagg'er**) a person who persistently scolds or annoys another. [Cf Norw *nage* to grow, rankle, and Swed *nagga* to gnaw]
▪ **nagg'ing** n and adj. **nagg'y** adj.

naga /nä'gə/ n a snake, *esp* the cobra (*Ind*); a divine snake (*Hindu myth*). [Sans *nāga*]

nagana /nä-gä'nə/ n a disease of horses and cattle caused by a trypanosome transmitted by tsetse flies (also **ngana** /əng-gä'nə/). [Zulu *nakane*]

nagapie /nahh'ə-pi/ (*S Afr*) n the bushbaby or nocturnal lemur. [Afrik, literally, 'night-ape' (see **bushbaby**), from Du *nacht* night, and *aap* monkey]

nagari /nä'gə-rē/ n devanagari, the script in which Sanskrit, Hindi and other Indian languages are written; the group of alphabets to which devanagari belongs. [Sans *nāgarī* town-script, from *nāgaran* town (perh referring to a particular town); addition of *deva-* to form *devanagari* was a later development]

nagmaal /näk' or nähh'mäl/ (*S Afr*) *n* a Dutch Reformed Church Sacrament, the Lord's Supper. [Earlier *nachtmaal* night meal; from Du]

nagor /nā'gör/ *n* a W African antelope (*Redunca redunca*). [Fr, arbitrarily formed by French naturalist Georges Louis Leclerc, Comte de Buffon, from earlier *nanguer*]

Nah. *abbrev*: (*Bible*) Nahum.

nah /na/ *interj* a dialect form of **no¹**.

Nahal /na-häl'/ *n* an organization of young soldiers in Israel; (without *cap*) an agricultural settlement established and manned by such soldiers, *esp* in border areas. [Heb]

NAHT *abbrev*: National Association of Head Teachers.

Nahuatl /nä'wä-tl/ *n* a member of a group of native peoples of S Mexico and Central America, including the Aztecs; the language of these peoples, Aztec. ◆ *adj* of or relating to the Nahuatls or their language.

NAI *abbrev*: non-accidental injury.

Naia see **Naja**.

naiad /nī'ad or nā'əd/ *n* (pl **nai'adēs** or **nai'ads**) a river or spring nymph; the aquatic larva of the dragonfly, mayfly, stonefly or damselfly; an aquatic plant with narrow leaves and small flowers. [Gr *nāias, -ados,* pl *-ades,* from *naein* to flow]
■ **Nai'as** *n* a genus of water plants, giving name to a family **Naiadā'ceae**, related to or including the pondweeds.

naiant /nā'ənt/ (*heraldry*) *adj* swimming horizontally. [Prob from an Anglo-Fr form of OFr *noiant*, prp, from L *natāre* to swim]

naif or **naïf** /nä-ēf'/ *adj* naive.

naik /nä'ik/ *n* a lord or governor; a corporal of Indian infantry. [Urdu *nā'ik*, from Sans *nāyaka* leader]

nail /nāl/ *n* a horny plate at the end of a finger or toe, *usu* distinguished from a claw in being flattened; a claw; a small *usu* metal spike with a head, used for fastening wood, etc; a nail-shaped excrescence, *esp* one at the tip of a bird's bill; a measure of length (5.5cm or 2¼in). ◆ *vt* to fix with a nail; to pin down or hold fast (also *fig*); to fasten, pierce (*rare* or *obs*), or stud (*rare*) with nails; to expose as a lie (*inf*); to cause the downfall of (*inf*); to catch or secure (*inf*); to have sexual intercourse with (*vulgar sl*). [OE *nægel*; Ger *Nagel*]
■ **nailed** *adj* having nails; fastened with nails. **nail'er** *n* (*hist*) a maker of nails. **nail'ery** *n* (*hist*) a place where nails were made. **nail'ing** *n* making nails; fastening with nails. **nail'less** *adj.*
□ **nail bar** *n* an establishment which provides cosmetic treatments for the nails. **nail'-bed** *n* that portion of the true skin on which a fingernail or toenail rests. **nail'-biter** *n.* **nail'-biting** *n* chewing off the ends of one's fingernails. ◆ *adj* (of an event or experience) which induces nail-biting (as a sign of anxiety, excitement or tension). **nail bomb** *n* an explosive device packed with long nails. **nail'brush** *n* a brush for cleaning the fingernails or toenails. **nail enamel** *n* nail varnish. **nail file** *n* a file for trimming fingernails or toenails. **nail gun** *n* an electric tool used to put in nails. **nail'-head** *n* the head of a nail; an ornament shaped like one. ◆ *adj* /nāl'hed'/ (also **nail'-head'ed**) having a head suggesting that of a nail; having nail-head ornaments. **nail'-head-spar'** *n* calcite crystallized in a scalenohedron terminated by a rhombohedron. **nail'-hole** *n* a hole made by or for a nail; a notch for opening a pocket-knife. **nail polish** *n* nail varnish. **nail punch** or **set** *n* a tool for punching the head of a nail below or flush with the surface. **nail'-rod** *n* a strip of iron to be made into nails; iron in that form; strong coarse tobacco (*Aust*); a stick of liquorice. **nail scissors** *n pl* small scissors designed *esp* for trimming the fingernails and toenails. **nail set** see **nail punch** above. **nail varnish** *n* varnish for fingernails or toenails.
■ **a nail in one's** (or **the**) **coffin** any event, experience, etc which has the effect of shortening one's life; a contributory factor in the downfall of someone or something. **hard as nails** in excellent physical condition; physically or mentally tough; callous, unsympathetic, unsentimental. **hit the nail on the head** to touch the exact point. **nail a lie to the counter** to expose it and put it out of currency, from the old custom of shopkeepers with counterfeit coins. **nail down** to fasten (something) down with nails; to force (someone) to make a binding promise or to give his or her consent (*inf*); to fix or establish (something) definitely. **nailed on** (*horse-racing sl*) (of a horse) considered to be a near-certainty to win a race. **nail one's colours to the mast** see under **colour**. **nail up** to close or fasten with or as if with nails. **on the nail** on the spot, without delay, as payment.

nain /nān/ (*Scot*) *adj* own. [*mine ain* my own]
■ **nainsel''** or **nainsell'** *n* own self; a Highlander (from the Highlander's formerly alleged habit of referring to himself or herself as *her nainsel'*).

nainsook /nān'sŭk/ *n* a kind of muslin like jaconet. [Hindi *nainsukh*, from *nain* eye, and *sukh* pleasure]

Nair or **Nayar** /nī'ər/ *n* a people of Kerala who were formerly a noble and military caste of the Malabar coast and who practised a peculiar system of polyandry and matriliny.

naira /nī'rə/ *n* (pl **nai'ra** or **nai'ras**) the standard monetary unit of Nigeria (100 kobo).

NAIRU /nī'roo/ (*econ*) *abbrev*: non-accelerating inflation rate of unemployment.

naissant /nā'sənt/ *adj* nascent; rising or coming forth (*heraldry*). [Fr, prp of *naître*, from L *nāscī, nātus* to be born]

naive or **naïve** /nī- or nä-ēv'/ *adj* (also **naif** or **naïf'**) overtrusting and unworldly; with natural or unaffected simplicity, *esp* in thought, manners or speech; artless; ingenuous; simplistic. [Fr *naif*, fem *naive*, from L *nātīvus* native, from *nāscī, natus* to be born]
■ **naive'ly** or **naïve'ly** *adv.* **naive'ness** or **naïve'ness** *n.* **naiveté**, **naïveté** /nä-ēv'i-tā/, **naivety** or **naïvety** /nä-ēv'ti or nī-/ *n* excessive trustingness; natural simplicity and unreservedness of thought, manner or speech; ingenuousness. **naiv'ist** *adj.*
□ **naive painting** *n* primitive painting.

Naja /nā'jə or -yə/ *n* the cobra genus (also **Naia**). [Appar Linnaeus's misreading of **naga**, or of Sinhalese *naiā, nayā*]

naked /nā'kid/ *adj* without clothes; uncovered; bare; exposed; open to view; unconcealed; undisguised, blatant or flagrant; evident; unarmed; defenceless; unprovided; devoid (of); without ornament; without confirmation, supporting evidence, etc; simple; artless; without the usual covering; lacking some element (eg financial backing) necessary to complete or make valid a contract, etc (*commerce* and *finance*). [OE *nacod*; Ger *nackt*]
■ **na'kedly** *adv.* **na'kedness** *n.*
□ **naked bed** *n* (*obs*) a bed in which one is (*orig*) entirely naked, (later) without ordinary day clothes. **naked eye** *n* the eye unassisted by any kind of optical instrument (eg a telescope). **naked lady** or **ladies** *n* the meadow saffron; the autumn crocus (also **naked boys**). **naked-light mine** *n* (*mining*) a non-fiery mine, where safety lamps are not required.

naker /nā'kər/ (*hist*) *n* one of a pair of small, medieval kettledrums. [OFr *nacre*, from Ar *naqāra*]

nakfa /nak'fə/ *n* the standard monetary unit of Eritrea (100 cents). [*Nakfa*, town in Eritrea]

nala, **nalla** and **nallah** same as **nulla**.

nalidixic acid /na-li-dik'sik as'id/ *n* a synthetic compound used to treat infections of the urinary tract. [From *naphthalene, di-* and *carboxylic*]

naloxone /na-lok'sōn/ *n* a potent drug ($C_{19}H_{21}NO_4$) used as an antidote for various narcotics, *esp* morphine. [*N-*allylnoroxymorph*one*]

naltrexone /nal-trek'sōn/ (*med*) *n* an opioid drug prescribed to counteract alcoholism and drug addiction.

NAM *abbrev*: Namibia (IVR).

Nam /näm/ (*US*) *n* a contraction of **Vietnam**, *esp* referring to the war there in the 1960s and 1970s.

nam¹ *pat* of **nim²**.

nam² see **naam**.

namaste /nä'mə-sti/ or **namaskar** /nä-mə-skär'/ *n* (in India) a traditional form of greeting, a slight bow with the palms pressed together before the chest or face. [Sans *namas* obeisance, salutation, bow, and *te*, dative of *tuam* you, or *kara* doing]

namby-pamby /nam'bi-pam'bi/ (*derog*) *adj* lacking strength of character or (masculine) vigour, feeble; (of writing, etc) prettily or sentimentally childish. ◆ *n* (pl **nam'by-pam'bies**) namby-pamby writing or talk; a namby-pamby person. [Nickname given to Ambrose Philips (1674–1749), whose simple odes to children were despised by 18c Tories]
■ **nam'by-pam'bical** *adj.* **nam'by-pam'biness** *n.* **nam'by-pam'byish** *adj.* **nam'by-pam'byism** *n.*

name /nām/ *n* that by which a person or a thing is known or called; a designation; reputation; fame; a celebrity; family or clan; seeming or pretension without reality; authority; behalf; assumed character (of); (often with *cap*) a member of an underwriting syndicate in Lloyds insurance market. ◆ *adj* famous, well-known (as in a *name brand* or *product*). ◆ *vt* to give a name to; to mention the name of; to designate; to speak of or call by name; to state or specify; to utter (with cognate object); to mention for a post or office; to nominate; (of the Speaker) to mention (an MP) formally by name in the House of Commons as guilty of disorderly conduct; to make known the name of (someone implicated in a crime, an accomplice, etc) to the police, etc. [OE *nama*; Ger *Name*; L *nōmen*]
■ **nam'able** or **name'able** *adj* capable, or worthy, of being named. **named** *adj.* **name'less** *adj* not having a name; anonymous; undistinguished; indescribable; unspeakable; illegitimate. **name'lessly** *adv.* **name'lessness** *n.* **name'ly** *adj* (*Scot*)

famous (for). ◆ *adv* that is to say; by name; especially (*obs*). **nam'er** *n*. **name'worthy** *adj* worth naming; distinguished. **nam'ing** *n*.

□ **name brand** *n* a make of an article bearing a manufacturer's distinguishing name. **name'-calling** *n* verbal abuse. **name'check** *n* a mention of a person or thing by name. ◆ *vt* to mention by name. **name'-child** *n* a person called after one. **name day** *n* the feast-day of the saint whose name one was given; the day when a ticket bearing the buyer's name, etc is given to the seller, ticket day (*stock exchange*); the day on which a name is bestowed. **name'-drop** *vi*. **name'-dropper** *n*. **name'-dropping** *n* trying to impress others by casual mention of important or well-known persons as if they were one's friends. **name part** *n* the part that gives title to a play, title-role. **name'plate** *n* an attached plate bearing the name of occupant, owner, manufacturer, etc; a masthead (*press*; *US*). **name'sake** *n* a person bearing the same name as another. **name'-son** *n* a male name-child. **name'tape** *n* a short piece of cloth tape attached to a garment, etc, marked with the owner's name.

■ **call names** to abuse verbally. **in all but name** in reality, essentially, although not formally or ostensibly; virtually. **in name** fictitiously, as an empty title. **in the name of** on behalf of; for the sake of; by the authority of. **make a name for oneself** or **make one's name** to become famous. **name after** (or *N Am* **name for**) to give (a child) the same name as another person, in honour of that person. **name and shame** (*inf*) to make an announcement exposing the alleged perpetrator of a misdemeanour to public opprobrium. **name names** to give specific names, *esp* so as to accuse or blame the people thus named. **name the day** to fix a day, *esp* for a marriage. **no names, no pack-drill** (*inf*) mention no names, then no one gets into trouble. **proper name** a name given to a particular person, place or thing. **take a name in vain** to use a name lightly or profanely. **the name of the game** (*inf*) the thing that is important or essential; the central trend or theme, what it's all about (*usu derog*). **to one's name** belonging to one. **you name it** this applies to whatever you mention, want, etc.

Namibian /nə-*mib'i-ən*/ *adj* of or relating to the Republic of *Namibia* in SW Africa, or its inhabitants. ◆ *n* a native or citizen of Namibia.

namma hole same as **gnamma hole**.

nam pla /*nam plä*/ *n* the usual name in Thai cookery for **nouc mam**. [Thai]

nan¹ or **naan** /*nän*/ *n* a type of slightly leavened bread, as baked in Indian and Pakistani cookery. [Hindi]

nan² see **nanny**.

nana¹ see **nanny**.

nana² /*nä'nə*/ (*sl*) *n* an idiot, fool; the head, as in *off one's nana* (*Aust*). [Prob ba*nana*]

Nancy /*nan'si*/ (*derog sl*; also without *cap*) *n* (pl **Nan'cies**) an effeminate young man; a male homosexual. ◆ *adj* effeminate. —Also **Nance**, **Nan'cy-boy** or **Miss Nan'cy** (also without *cap*). [From the girl's name]

Nancy-pretty /*nan'si-prit-i*/ *n* the plant *Saxifraga umbrosa*, London Pride. [Prob for *none so pretty*]

NAND /*nand*/ (*comput*) *n* a logic circuit that has two or more inputs and one output, the output signal being 1 if any of its inputs is 0, and 0 if all its inputs are 1. [*not and*]

nandine /*nan'din*/ *n* a W African palm civet. [Prob a native name]

N and Q *abbrev* : Notes and Queries.

nandrolone /*nan'drə-lōn*/ *n* an androgenic anabolic steroid that is illegally used as a performance-enhancing drug by some athletes. [Altered from **nor-**, **andro-** and chem sfx -*one*]

nandu, nandoo or **nhandu** /*nan'doo*/ *n* the rhea, or S American ostrich. [Tupí *nandú*]

nanism /*nā-ni-zm*/ or /*nan'i-*/ *n* the condition of being dwarfed. [Gr *nānos, nannos* dwarf]

■ **naniza'tion** or **-s-** *n* artificial dwarfing.

nanite /*nan'īt*/ same as **nanomachine** (see under **nano-**).

nankeen /*nan'kēn*/ or /-*kēn'*/, also **nankin** /*nan'kin*/ or /-*kin'*/ *n* a buff-coloured cotton cloth first made at *Nanking* in China; a buff colour; (in *pl*) clothes, *esp* trousers, made of nankeen.

nannoplankton see **nano-**.

nanny /*nan'i*/ *n* (pl **nann'ies**) a she-goat (also **nanny goat**); a children's nurse, *esp* specially trained; a pet name for a grandmother (also **nan**, **nan'a** or **nann'a**). ◆ *adj* (*derog*) of institutions, the state, etc) protective to an intrusive extent. ◆ *vt* (**nann'ying**; **nann'ied**) to nurse; to overprotect; to supervise to the point of meddlesomeness. [From the woman's name]

■ **nann'yish** *adj* overprotective.

□ **nanny state** *n* the state regarded as overprotective and authoritarian in its institutions.

nannygai /*nan'i-gī*/ *n* a large edible marine fish, *Centroberyx affinis*, found off the SE coast of Australia (also **nann'yghai** or **nenn'igai**). [Aboriginal name]

nano- /*na-* or *nā-nō-*/ *combining form* denoting: 10^{-9}, as in *nanogram* and *nanosecond*; of microscopic size, as in *nanocomputer*. [Gr *nānos* a dwarf]

■ **nan'obot** *n* a microscopically small robot. **nan'ocomputer** *n* a computer using parts of microscopic size. **nan'ocomputing** *n*. **nanoelectron'ics** *n sing* the application of nanotechnology to electronic systems. **nan'omachine** *n* (also called **nä'nite**) a microscopically small machine or device, perhaps only a few atoms wide, manufactured using nanotechnology. **nan'omaterial** *n* any material whose particles are of dimensions of less than a nanometre. **nan'ometre** *n* one millionth of a millimetre. **nan'oparticle** *n* a particle with dimensions of about 5–40 nanometres. **nan'oplankton** or **nann'oplankton** *n* very small forms of plankton. **nan'opore** *n* a microscopic pore or opening, *specif* one between 10^{-7}m and 10^{-9}m. **nanopor'ous** *adj*. **nan'opublishing** *n* the publication of specialist information to a small group of people on the Internet rather than by traditional publishing methods. **nan'oscale** *adj* smaller than microscale, involving measurements in nanometres. **nanotechnol'ogy** or **nanotech'** *n* the manufacture and measuring of objects of tiny dimensions (also *adj*). **nan'otube** *n* a molecule of a fullerene that is cylindrical rather than ball-shaped. **nan'owire** *n* a wire whose diameter is measured in nanometres.

Nansen passport /*nan'sən päs'pört*/ *n* a passport that the League of Nations issued after World War I to stateless people. [F *Nansen* (1861–1930), Norwegian explorer, high commissioner for refugees with the League of Nations, 1920–22]

Nantz /*nants*/ (*archaic*) *n* brandy. [*Nantes* in France]

NAO *abbrev* : National Audit Office.

naos /*nā'os*/ *n* a temple; the inner cell of a temple. [Gr *nāos* temple]

Nap. *abbrev* : Napoleon.

nap¹ /*nap*/ *vi* (**napp'ing**; **napped**) to take a short or casual sleep. ◆ *n* a short or casual sleep. [OE *hnappian*]

■ **catch someone napping** (*inf*) to detect someone in error that might have been avoided; to catch someone unprepared or off his or her guard.

nap² /*nap*/ *n* a woolly surface on cloth, now (distinguished from *pile*) such a surface raised by a finishing process, not made in the weaving; the woolly surface removed in the process; a cloth with such a surface; a downy covering or surface on anything; bedding or a bedroll (*Aust inf*). ◆ *vt* (**napp'ing**; **napped**) to raise a nap on; to remove nap from. [ME *noppe*; appar from MDu or MLGer *noppe*]

■ **nap'less** *adj* without nap, threadbare. **napp'iness** *n*. **napp'y** *adj* downy; shaggy; frizzy (*US inf*).

nap³ /*nap*/ *n* the card game napoleon; a call of five in that game; the winning of five tricks; a racing tip that professes to be a certainty, one that one may 'go nap' on. ◆ *vt* (**napp'ing**; **napped**) to name (a particular horse) as certain to win.

□ **nap hand** *n* a series of five wins; a situation in which a risk seems worth taking.

■ **go nap** to undertake to win all five tricks; to score five times; to risk on a single attempt.

nap⁴ /*nap*/ *vt* (**napp'ing**; **napped**) to seize; to steal. [Cf Swed *nappa*, Dan and Norw *nappe* to catch or snatch; relation to **nab¹** uncertain]

napa or **nappa** /*nap'ə*/ *n* a soft leather made (*orig* at *Napa* in California) by a special tawing process, from sheepskin or goatskin.

napalm /*nā'päm*/ or /*nap'äm*/ *n* a petroleum jelly, highly inflammable, used in bombs and flame-throwers. ◆ *vt* to attack or destroy with napalm bombs. [*naphthenate palmi*tate]

nape /*nāp*/ *n* the back of the neck. [Origin uncertain]

Naperian see **Napierian**.

napery /*nā'pə-ri*/ (*archaic* or *Scot*) *n* household linen, *esp* for the table. [OFr *naperie*, from LL *napāria*, from *napa* a cloth, from L *mappa* a napkin]

naphtha /*naf'thə* (sometimes *nap'tə*)/ *n* a vague name for the liquid inflammable distillates from coal tar, petroleum, wood, etc, *esp* the lighter and more volatile ones; petroleum (*old*). [Gr *naphtha*]

■ **naph'thalene** *n* an unpleasant-smelling hydrocarbon consisting of two benzene rings ($C_{10}H_8$) obtained by distillation of coal tar, crystallizing in plates, used for killing moths, etc. **naphthalic** /*naf-thal'ik*/ *adj* relating to or derived from naphthalene. **naph'thalize** or **-ise** *vt* to treat with naphtha. **naph'thene** *n* any of the cycloalkanes, many of which occur in petroleum. **naphthe'nic** *adj*. **naph'thol** *n* a hydroxyl derivative of naphthalene ($C_{10}H_7OH$), of two kinds. **naphthyl'amine** (or /-*mēn'*/) *n* an amino-derivative of naphthalene ($C_{10}H_7NH_2$), of two kinds, used in dyeing.

Napierian or **Naperian** /nā-pē'ri-ən/ adj relating to the Scottish mathematician John *Napier* (1550–1617), or to his system of logarithms; now applied to natural logarithms, logarithms to the base e, the limit of $(1 + 1/m)^m$ when m approaches infinity, Napier's own base being a quantity depending on e^{-1}.
❏ **Napier's bones** (or **rods**) n pl an invention of Napier's for multiplying and dividing mechanically by means of rods.

napiform /nā'pi-förm/ adj turnip-shaped. [L *nāpus* a turnip]

napkin /nap'kin/ n a small square of linen, paper, etc, used at table for wiping the mouth and hands, protecting clothing, etc; a baby's nappy; a handkerchief (*Scot* or *obs*). [Dimin of Fr *nappe*, from L *mappa*]
❏ **napkin ring** n a ring in which a table napkin is rolled.

Naples yellow /nā'plz yel'ō/ n a light-yellow pigment, lead antimonate, *orig* an Italian secret.

NAPM (*US*) abbrev : National Association of Purchasing Management (now known as **ISM**).

NAPO abbrev : National Association of Probation Officers.

napoleon /nə-pō'lyən/ or /-li-ən/ n a twenty-franc gold coin issued by *Napoleon* I; a French modification of the game of euchre, each player receiving five cards and playing as an individual (commonly **nap**); a small, rich iced cake with layers of puff pastry filled with cream, custard or jam; (with *cap*) used generically in reference to *Napoleon* I (1769–1821), Emperor of the French, to denote a person of paramount power and frightening ruthlessness.
■ **Napoleonic** /-i-on'ik/ adj relating to Napoleon I or Napoleon III (1808–73). **Napol'eonism** n. **napol'eonite** n an orbicular diorite found in Corsica, Napoleon I's native island.

napoo /nä-poo'/ (*World War I sl*) adj and interj no more; good for nothing; dead. ◆ vt to kill. [Fr *il n'y en a plus* there is no more]

nappa see **napa**.

nappe /nap/ n a sheet of rock brought far forward by recumbent folding or thrusting (*geol*); a sheet (*maths*); one of the two sheets on either side of the vertex forming a cone (*maths*); a sheet of water flowing over a weir or similar structure. [Fr *nappe* tablecloth, from L *mappa*]

napper /nap'ər/ (*sl*) n the head.

nappy[1] /nap'i/ n (pl **napp'ies**) a pad of disposable material or a folded square of towelling, muslin, etc placed between a baby's legs and kept in place by a fastening at the waist, for absorbing urine and faeces. [A short form of **napkin**]
❏ **nappy rash** n an irritation of the skin on a baby's buttocks or genital area, *usu* caused by wet nappies.

nappy[2] /nap'i/ adj (of liquor, *esp* beer) having a head, frothy; heady, strong; tipsy; (of a horse) nervous, jumpy, excitable. ◆ n strong ale. [Perh from **nappy** shaggy; see under **nap**[2]]

napron /nā'prən/ n an earlier form of **apron**.

naras see **narras**.

narc /närk/ or **narco** /när'kō/ (*US sl*) n (pl **narcs** or **nar'cos**) a narcotics agent. [**narcotic**]

narceine or **narceen** /när'sēn/ n a narcotic alkaloid in opium, $C_{23}H_{27}O_8N$. [Fr *narcéine*, from Gr *narkē* numbness]

narcissus /när-sis'əs/ n (pl **narciss'uses** or **narciss'ī**) a plant of the daffodil genus *Narcissus* of the Amaryllis family, *esp Narcissus poeticus* (the poet's narcissus). [L, from Gr *Narkissos* a youth who pined away for love of his own image, and was transformed into the flower; the connection with *narkē* numbness (with reference to this plant's supposed effects on the body) seems to be fanciful]
■ **nar'cissism** n self-admiration; sensual gratification found in one's own body, whether as a normal stage of development or a pathological condition. **nar'cissist** n and adj. **narcissis'tic** adj.

narco see **narc**.

narco- /när-kō-/ or **narc-** /närk-/ combining form denoting: using drugs; of or relating to the illicit production of drugs (as in *narcoterrorism*); numbness or torpor. [Gr *narkē* numbness or torpor]
■ **narcoanal'ysis** n hypnoanalysis when narcotics are used in producing the hypnotic state. **narcocathar'sis** n narcoanalysis. **narcohypno'sis** n the use of narcotics to produce hypnosis. **narcosyn'thesis** n the bringing out of repressed emotions by narcotics so that they become freely accepted into the self. **narcoterr'orism** n crime carried out to support or protect an illegal trade in drugs. **narcother'apy** n the treatment of disturbed mental states by prolonged drug-induced sleep.

narcolepsy /när'kō-lep-si/ (*pathol*) n a condition marked by short attacks of irresistible drowsiness. [Gr *narkē* numbness, and *lēpsis* seizure]
■ **narcolep'tic** adj.

narcosis /när-kō'sis/ n (pl **narco'ses** /-sēz/) drowsiness, unconsciousness or other effects to the central nervous system produced by a narcotic. [Gr *narkōsis*, from *narkē* numbness or torpor]

narcotic /när-kot'ik/ adj producing torpor, sleep, or deadness; affecting the central nervous system so as to produce dizziness, euphoria, loss of memory and of neuromuscular co-ordination, and eventually unconsciousness; of or relating to narcotic drugs, or the users of such drugs. ◆ n anything having a narcotic effect, eg alcohol, an inert gas, or *esp* a drug. [Gr *narkōtikos*, from *narkē* numbness or torpor]
■ **narcot'ically** adv. **nar'cotine** /-kə-tēn/ n one of the alkaloids in opium. **nar'cotism** n the influence of narcotics. **nar'cotist** n. **narcotiza'tion** or **-s-** n. **nar'cotize** or **-ise** vt to subject to the influence of a narcotic.

nard /närd/ n spikenard; a name for matweed (*Nardus stricta*); any of several aromatic plants formerly used in medicine. ◆ vt to anoint with nard. [L *nardus*, from Gr *nardos*]

nardoo /när-doo'/ n an Australian clover-like fern of the genus *Marsilea*; its spore-forming, multicellular body, ground into flour and used as a food by Aborigines. [From an Aboriginal language]

nare /när/ n (*archaic*) a nostril, *esp* a hawk's. [L *nāris*, pl *nārēs*, nostril]
■ **nar'ēs** n pl (L; *anat*) the nostrils. **nar'ial** or **nar'ine** /-īn/ adj of or relating to the nostrils. **nar'icorn** n a horny termination of a bird's nostril.

narghile, **nargile**, **nargileh** or **narguileh** /när'gi-lä/ or /-li/ n a hookah (also **narghilly**, **narghily**, **nargilly**, **nargily**). [Pers *nārgīleh*, from *nārgīl* a coconut (from which it used to be made)]

narial, **naricorn**, **narine** see under **nare**.

nark /närk/ (*sl*) n an informer; a police spy, as in *copper's nark*; a policeman; a person who curries favour, a pick-thank; an annoying, obstructive person, a spoilsport (*esp Aust* and *NZ*); a persistent fault-finder or complainer; an annoying, unpleasant or baffling circumstance; an expert. ◆ vi to grumble. ◆ vt and vi to watch; to spy; to annoy or irritate; to tease. [Romany *nāk* nose]
■ **narked** adj annoyed. **nark'y** adj irritable.
■ **nark at** to fret with persistent criticism. **nark it!** stop it!

narks see **nitrogen narcosis** under **nitrogen**.

narquois /när-kwä'/ (*Fr*) adj mocking, malicious.

narras or **naras** /nar'əs/ n the edible melon-like fruit of a SW African long-rooted thorny cucurbitaceous shrub (*Acanthosicyos horrida*). [Khoikhoi *qnaras*]

narrate /nə- or na-rāt'/ vt to tell of (a series of events); to give a running commentary on (a film, etc). ◆ vi to recount or relate events. [L *narrāre*, *-ātum*, prob from *gnārus* knowing]
■ **narrāt'able** adj. **narra'tion** n the act of telling; that which is told; an orderly account of a series of events; the third part of a speech, comprising the exposition of the question (*rhetoric*). **narrative** /nar'ə-tiv/ n that which is narrated, a story; a written or spoken account of a series of events in the order in which they occur; that part of a literary work which relates events and action (as opposed to eg dialogue); the art, practice or technique of narration. ◆ adj narrating; giving an account of any occurrence; inclined to narration; telling a story. **narr'atively** adv. **narrā'tor** n. **narr'atory** adj like narrative; consisting of narrative.
❏ **narrative verdict** n (*Eng law*) a verdict in the form of a statement setting out the facts that have been ascertained about a case.

narre /när/ (*Spenser*) adv an old comparative of **nigh**.

narrow[1] /nar'ō/ adj of little breadth; of small extent from side to side; closely confining; limited; contracted in mind or outlook; bigoted; not liberal; parsimonious (*inf* or *dialect*); with little to spare; close; strict; precise; detailed, thorough; strict; keen; (of money) denoting the more liquid kinds (ie coins and notes), eg in hand, or readily withdrawn from a bank account, etc, *opp* to *broad*; (of a vowel) tense, *opp* to *broad* (*phonetics*); (of a phonetic transcription) with a different symbol for each phoneme and diacritical marks to show different varieties of these phonemes, *opp* to *broad* (*phonetics*); (of animal foodstuffs) relatively rich in protein as compared to fat and carbohydrate. ◆ n a narrow part or place; (*usu* in *pl*) a narrow passage, channel or strait. ◆ adv narrowly. ◆ vt to make narrow; to contract or confine. ◆ vi to become narrow; to reduce the number of stitches in knitting. [OE *nearu*]
■ **narr'owing** n the act of making less in breadth; the state of being contracted; the part of anything which is made narrower. ◆ adj becoming narrower. **narr'owly** adv barely; with close attention; in a narrow or restricted manner. **narr'owness** n.
❏ **narr'owband** adj broadcasting across a narrow range of frequencies. **narr'owboat** n a canal-boat, *esp* one of 7ft (2.1m) or less in width, and 72ft (about 22m) in length. **narr'owcast** vt. **narr'owcasting** n cable television; broadcasting to a limited, often targeted, audience; the production and distribution of material on video tapes, cassettes, etc. **narrow circumstances** n pl poverty, pennilessness. **narrow escape** n an escape only just managed. **narrow gauge** n a narrow-gauge railway. **narr'ow-gauge'** adj (of a railway) less than 4ft 8½in (about 1.4m) in gauge. **narr'ow-mind'ed**

adj of a narrow or illiberal mind; bigoted, prejudiced. **narr'ow-mind'edly** *adv.* **narr'ow-mind'edness** *n.* **narrow seas** *n pl* the seas between Great Britain and the Continent and Great Britain and Ireland. **narrow squeak** *n* a narrow escape.

narrow² see **nary** under **nary**.

narthex /när'theks/ *n* a western portico or vestibule in an early Christian or Oriental church or basilica, to which women and catechumens were admitted; a vestibule between the church porch and the nave; (with *cap*) a former genus of umbelliferous plants, now included in the genus *Ferula*. [Gr *narthēx* giant fennel, a cane or stalk, a casket or a narthex]

nartjie (*orig* **naartje**) /när'chi/ (*Afrik*) *n* a small sweet orange like the mandarin. [Prob connected with **orange**]

narwhal /när'wəl/ *n* a kind of whale (*Monodon monoceros*) with one large projecting spiral tusk (occasionally two tusks) in the male. [Dan *narhval*; ON *nāhvalr*, may be from *nār* corpse, and *hvalr* whale, from its pallid colour]

nary /nā'ri/ (*N Am* and *dialect*) *adv* never, not. [A variant of *ne'er a* never a]

■ **nary a** never a, not one (also **narrow a** /nar'ō/).

NAS *abbrev*: National Academy of Sciences (*US*); Noise Abatement Society.

nas /naz or nāz/ (*obs*) for **ne has** (*Spenser*) has not, and **ne was** was not.

NASA /na'sə/ *abbrev*: National Aeronautics and Space Administration (in the USA).

nasal /nā'zl/ *adj* of or relating to the nose; affected by, or sounded through, the nose. ◆*n* a sound uttered through the nose; a letter representing such a sound; a paired bone that forms the bridge of the nose; the nosepiece in a helmet. [L *nāsus* the nose]

■ **Nasalis** /naz-ā'lis/ *n* the proboscis monkey genus. **nasality** /nā-zal'i-ti/ *n.* **nasalization** or **-s-** /nā-zə-lī-zā'shən/ *n.* **na'salize** or **-ise** *vi* and *vt* to render (eg a sound) nasal. **na'sally** *adv.* **nasion** /nā'zi-on/ *n* the median point of the nasofrontal suture.

nasard /naz'ərd/ *n* an organ mutation stop. [Fr]

Nascar® /naz'kär/ *n* a form of motor racing using specially modified cars, popular in the USA. [Acronym from *National Association for Stock Car Auto Racing*]

nascent /nā'sənt or nas'ənt/ *adj* coming into being; beginning to develop; (of an atom or substance, *esp* hydrogen) at the moment of its formation and therefore with a higher reactivity than usual. [L *nāscēns*, *-entis*, prp of *nāscī*, *nātus* to be born]

■ **nasc'ence** (*rare*) or **nasc'ency** *n.*

NASDAQ® /naz'dak/ (*US*) *abbrev*: National Association of Securities Dealers Automated Quotation System, an electronic virtual stock exchange, popular with technology companies.

naseberry /nāz'bə-ri or -ber-i/ *n* the sapodilla plum; the tree bearing it. —Also **neesberry** /nēz'/ and **nisberry** /niz'/. [Sp *néspera*, *níspero* medlar tree, from L *mespilus* medlar; cf **medlar**]

nashgab /nash'gab/, also **gabnash** /gab'nash/ (*Scot*) *n* prattle; chatter; a pert chatterer.

nashi same as **Asian pear** (see under **Asian**).

Nasik /nä'sik/ *adj* of the district of *Nasik* in the Indian city of Mumbai, *esp* referring to an elaborate form of magic square devised there.

nasion see under **nasal**.

Naskhi see **Neskhi**.

naso- /nā-zō-/ *combining form* denoting: nose; of the nose (and something else). [L *nāsus* nose]

■ **nasofront'al** *adj* relating to the nose and the frontal bone. **nasogas'tric** *adj* relating to the nose and stomach, such as a **nasogastric tube** one which is passed into the stomach through the nose. **nasolac'rymal** *adj* relating to the nose and tears, eg in reference to the duct that carries tears from the eye and the nose. **nasophar'ynx** *n* that part of the pharynx above the soft palate.

nastalik or **nasta'liq** /na-stə-lēk'/ *n* Persian cursive script, having long horizontal strokes and rounded characters. [Ar, from *naskhi* cursive script, and *talik* hanging]

nastic /nā'stik or nas'/ *adj* (of plant movements) not related to the direction of the stimulus. [Gr *nastos* close-pressed]

nasturtium /na-stûr'shəm/ *n* (with *cap*) the watercress genus of the Cruciferae family; (in popular use) the Indian cress (*Tropaeolum majus*), a garden climber, with bright orange, yellow or red flowers and edible leaves. [L *nāsus* nose, and *torquēre* to twist (from its pungency)]

nasty /näs'ti/ *adj* disgustingly foul; nauseous; filthy; obscene or indecent; (of eg a video) containing scenes which are either highly pornographic or extremely violent, or both; threatening; threatening danger; spiteful; ill-natured; difficult to deal with; awkward;

unpleasant; (of eg a wound) sore; objectionable; very good (*esp US sl*). ◆*n* (*inf*) something or someone unpleasant or intractable; an obscene or sadistic film, as in *video nasty*. [Perh for earlier *nasky* (cf Swed dialect *naskug*, *nasket*); or perh connected with Du *nestig* dirty]

■ **nas'tily** *adv.* **nas'tiness** *n.*

■ **a nasty piece** (or **bit**) **of work** a person very objectionable in character and conduct.

-nasty /-na-sti/ *combining form* denoting nastic pressure or movement (in the direction specific in the first element) as in *epinasty* and *hyponasty*. [Gr *nastos* pressed close]

nasute /nā'zūt, -sūt or -zūt', -sūt'/ *adj* keen-scented; critically discriminating; beaked. ◆*n* a beaked soldier white ant. [L *nāsūtus*, from *nāsus* nose]

NASUWT *abbrev*: National Association of Schoolmasters (and) Union of Women Teachers.

Nat. /nat/ *abbrev*: National; Nationalist.

nat /nat/ (*inf*: often with *cap*) *n* a nationalist.

nat. *abbrev*: national; native; natural; *natus* (*L*), born.

natal¹ /nā'tl/ *adj* of or connected with birth; native. [L *nātālis*, from *nāscī*, *nātus* to be born]

■ **natalitial** /nat- or nāt-ə-lish'l/ *adj* relating to a birthday. **natality** /nə- or nā-tal'i-ti/ *n* birth; birth rate.

□ **natal therapy** *n* (in psychoanalysis) the treatment of rebirthing (qv).

natal² see under **nates**.

natale solum /na-tā'lē sō'ləm or nä-tä'le sol'ŭm/ (*L*) native soil.

natalitial, natality see under **natal¹**.

natant /nā'tənt/ (*formal*) *adj* floating; swimming. [L *natāns*, *-antis*, prp of *natāre*, frequentative of *nāre* to swim]

■ **natation** /nat- or nāt-ā'shən/ *n* swimming. **nātato'rial** or **nā'tatory** *adj* relating to swimming; having the habit of swimming; adapted or used for swimming. **nātato'rium** (*pl* **nātato'riums** or **nātato'ria**) *n* (*US*) a swimming-pool.

natch¹ /nach/ (*sl*) *adv* of course, short for **naturally**.

natch² /nach/ (*dialect*) *n* the rump. [See **aitchbone**]

natch³ see **nautch**.

nates /nā'tēz/ *n pl* (*anat*) the buttocks. [L *natis*, pl *natēs*]

■ **na'tal** *adj.* **na'tiform** *adj.*

NATFHE /nat'fē/ *abbrev*: National Association of Teachers in Further and Higher Education (now replaced by **UCU**).

natheless, nathelesse see **nathless**.

nathemore /nā-thə-mōr' or -mör'/ or **nathemo** /-mō'/ (*Spenser*) *adv* not or never the more. [OE *nā thȳ mā* never the more (cf **nathless**)]

nathless, natheless, nathelesse or **naythles** /näth', nath', näth', nādh', nadh', nädh'(ə)-les or (as *Spenser*) -les'/ (*archaic*) *adv* and *prep* notwithstanding. [OE *nā* never, *thȳ* by that (instrumental case), and *læs* less]

natiform see under **nates**.

nation¹ /nā'shən/ *n* a body of people marked off by common descent, language, culture, or historical tradition whether or not bound by the defined territorial limits of a state; the people of a state; a Native American tribe or federation of tribes; a set of people, animals, etc; a great number; an old division of students in universities; (in *pl*) the heathens or Gentiles. [L *nātiō*, *-ōnis*, from *nāscī*, *nātus* to be born]

■ **national** /nash'nəl or -ə-nəl/ *adj* relating to a nation or nations; belonging or peculiar to, characteristic of, or controlled by, a nation; public; general; attached to one's own country; nationalistic. ◆*n* a member or fellow member of a nation; a national (as opposed to a local) newspaper; (with *cap*) the Grand National. **nat'ionalism** *n.* **nat'ionalist** *n* a person who favours or strives after the unity, independence, interests or domination of a nation; a member of a political party specially so called, eg the Irish Nationalist party who aimed at Home Rule; an advocate of nationalization. ◆*adj* of or relating to nationalists or nationalism. **nationalist'ic** *adj.* **nationalist'ically** *adv.* **nationality** /-al'it-i/ *n* membership of, or the fact or state of belonging to, a particular nation; nationhood; a national group (often one of several) forming a political state; a group or set having the character of a nation; national character. **nationalīzā'tion** or **-s-** *n.* **nat'ionalize** or **-ise** *vt* to make national; to make the property of the nation; to bring under national management; to naturalize; to make a nation of. **nat'ionally** *adv.* **nationhood** /nā'/ *n* the state or fact of being a nation. **nationless** /nā'/ *adj* without nationality or nations. **na'tionwide** *adj* covering the whole nation (also *adv*).

□ **national anthem** (or *rare* **air**) *n* an official song or hymn of a nation, sung or played on ceremonial occasions. **National Assembly** *n* an assembly of elected representatives, part of the legislature of various countries; the French legislative assembly from 1789 to 1791. **National Assistance** *n* (formerly in Britain) a weekly allowance paid by the state to people on low incomes. **national bank** *n* a central bank; (in the USA) a commercial bank chartered by the Federal government and a member of the Federal Reserve System. **national call** n (formerly **trunk call**) a long-distance telephone call within the country, not international. **national church** n a church established by law in a country. **national code** n (Aust) Australian rules football. **National Convention** n a convention held every four years by a political party to choose its candidate for the forthcoming presidential elections (US); the sovereign assembly in France from 21 September 1792 to 26 October 1795. **National Curriculum** n the curriculum taught in all schools in England and Wales from 1989, divided into core subjects (English, mathematics and science) and foundation subjects (technology and design, history, geography, music, art, physical education and a foreign language), with testing at regular intervals to assess each child's performance in comparison with nationally set attainment targets, under the control of the **National Curriculum Council**. **national debt** n money borrowed by the government of a country and not yet paid back. **National Front** n (in Britain) an extreme right-wing political party with racist and fascist policies, now largely superseded by its offshoot the British National Party. **national grid** n the grid (qv) of power-lines in, or of lines on maps of, Great Britain. **National Guard** n a force which took part in the French Revolution, first formed in 1789; an organized military force in individual States, also subject to the call of the federal army (US). **National Health Service** n in Britain, the system under which medical, dental, etc treatment is available free, or at a nominal charge, to all, paid for out of public taxation. **National Hunt** n (also without caps) horse-racing over jumps, opp to flat racing. **national income** n the total money earned (from wages, interest, rents, etc) by the residents of a nation. **national insurance** n a system of compulsory insurance paid for by weekly contributions by employee and employer, and yielding benefits to the sick, retired, unemployed, etc. **National Lottery** n in Britain, a state-controlled lottery established in 1994. **national park** n an area owned by or for the nation, set apart for the preservation and enjoyment of what is beautiful or interesting. **National Savings Bank** n a bank, run by the government, with which money may be deposited to accumulate interest. **national school** n (in England, formerly) a school established by the **National Society** (established in 1811) to promote elementary education among poor people. **national service** n compulsory service in the armed forces. **National Socialism** n Nazism, the policies of the National Socialist Party. **National Socialist (German Workers') Party** n an extreme nationalistic fascist party in Germany, led by Adolf Hitler, which ruled Germany from 1933 to 1945. **national treasure** n someone or something regarded as a cultural asset to a nation. **National Trust** n a charitable body concerned with the preservation of historic monuments and buildings, and areas of natural beauty, in England, Wales and Northern Ireland (the **National Trust for Scotland** performs a similar function in Scotland). **National Vocational Qualification** n a qualification awarded in the workplace by the NCVQ for competence in job skills (abbrev **NVQ**). **nation state** n an independent state with a population largely of common descent, language or culture.

nation² /nāˈshən/ (US dialect) n, adj, adv and interj damnation.

native /nāˈtiv/ adj belonging naturally; innate; inherent; natural; in a natural state; unsophisticated; occurring in a natural station; occurring naturally as a mineral (not manufactured), or naturally uncombined (as an element); belonging by birth; having a right by birth; born or originating in the place; being the place of birth or origin; belonging to the people originally or at the time of discovery inhabiting the country, esp when they are not regarded as fully civilized; connected by birth; born in slavery or bondage (obs); applied to Australian plants and animals which have been given the same name as a different plant or animal found elsewhere, eg the native bear (the koala); (of an oyster) raised in a (British) artificial bed; denoting software, data, etc that is specifically designed for the system on which it is run (comput). ◆ n someone born in any place; someone born and for a long time resident in a place; someone born under a particular planet or sign; a member of a native race; a member of a non-white race, esp in a colonized country (derog inf; no longer common); (in South Africa) a black person (now considered offensive and no longer in official use); a person of non-Aboriginal descent born in Australia; an indigenous species, variety, or breed, or an individual of it; a native oyster; a person born in slavery or bondage (obs). [L nātīvus, from nāscī, nātus to be born]
■ naˈtively adv. naˈtiveness n. naˈtivism n the belief that the mind possesses some ideas or forms of thought that are inborn and not derived from sensation; the tendency to favour the natives of a country in preference to immigrants; the policy of protecting native culture from the threat of external influences. naˈtivist n and adj. nativisˈtic adj. nativity /nə-tivˈi-ti/ n the state or fact of being born; the time, place and manner of birth; nationality by birth; the fact or status of being native; (often with cap) the birth of Christ, hence the festival

commemorating it, Christmas, or a picture representing it; a horoscope; slavery or bondage by birth (obs).
❑ **Native American** n a member of the indigenous peoples of America. **Naˈtive-American** adj. **native bear** n the koala. **naˈtive-born** adj born in the country; having a (specified) status by virtue of birth (Scot; obs). **Native Canadian** n a Native American of Canada. **Naˈtive-Canadian** adj. **native cat** n a marsupial cat, a carnivorous, cat-sized white-spotted animal of the genus Dasyurus, with a pointed snout. **native companion** see **brolga**. **native land** n the land to which one belongs by birth. **native language** n the language one acquires first, usu that of one's native land. **native rock** n unquarried rock. **native speaker** n someone who speaks the language in question as his or her native language. **native title** n (Aust law) the rights of indigenous peoples to ownership of their traditional lands. **nativity play** n a play performed by children at Christmas-time representing events at the birth of Christ.
■ **go native** see under **go**¹. **one's native heath** one's homeland, one's own locality.

NATO or **Nato** /nāˈtō/ abbrev : North Atlantic Treaty Organization.

natrium see under **natron**.

natrolite /nāˈtrə- or natˈrə-līt/ n a common fibrous zeolite, hydrated sodium aluminium silicate. [**natron** and Gr lithos stone]

natron /nāˈtrən/ n a hydrated carbonate of sodium found on some lake borders. [Ar natrūn, from Gr nitron]
■ **naˈtrium** n (obs or New L) sodium.

NATS /nats/ abbrev : National Air Traffic Services.

natter /natˈər/ (inf) vi to rattle on in talk, esp grumblingly; to chatter, talk much about little; to be peevish (N Eng dialect). ◆ n a casual chatter or gossip. [Origin obscure]
■ **nattˈered** or **nattˈery** adj peevish. **nattˈerer** n.

natterjack /natˈər-jak/ n a European toad (Bufo calamita) with a yellow stripe down the back. [Origin unknown]

nattier blue /nāˈtyā blooˈ/ n a soft azure. [JM Nattier (1685–1766), French painter]

natty /natˈi/ (inf) adj dapper; spruce; clever, ingenious, deft. [Poss connected with **neat**¹]
■ **nattˈily** adv. **nattˈiness** n.

natura /nə-tūˈrə or na-tooˈra/ (L) n nature.
❑ **natura naturans** /natˈūr-əns or na-tooˈräns/ n creative nature. **natura naturata** /na-tūr-āˈtə or na-too-räˈta/ n created nature.

natural /nachˈ(ə-)rəl/ adj relating to, produced by or according to nature, to the natural world or human nature; provided by or based on nature; not miraculous or supernatural; not the work of humans, not artificial; not interfered with by humans; inborn, innate, inherent; having the feelings that may be expected to come by nature, kindly; normal; happening in the usual course; spontaneous; not far-fetched; not acquired; without affectation; not fictitious; physical, esp as opposed to spiritual or intellectual; lifelike, like nature; based on an innate moral sense, innate reason or instinct rather than revelation; related by actual birth (not adoption, etc); hence (now rare) legitimate; (now usu) illegitimate; natural-born, or having the status of the natural-born; in a state of nature, unregenerate; (of classification) according to ancestral relationships (biol); according to the usual diatonic scale, not sharp or flat (music); of a buff colour, like undyed or unbleached fabric; (of a playing card) not being a joker or a wild card; (of a sequence of cards) containing no wild cards. ◆ n someone having a natural aptitude (for), or being an obvious choice (for); a thing assured by its very nature of success, a certainty; a tone that is neither sharp nor flat (music); a character (♮) cancelling a preceding sharp or flat (music); a white key in keyboard musical instruments; a buff colour; two cards making 21 dealt to a player as his or her first hand in pontoon; an idiot (obs). [L nātūrālis, from nātūra nature]
■ **natˈuralism** n the following of nature; a close following of nature without idealization (esp in art); the theory that this should be the aim of art and literature, esp the form of realism advocated or practised by Emile Zola; a world-view that rejects the supernatural and spiritual and explains the world in terms of natural influences and forces, and cause and effect; any religious or moral system based on this; the belief that natural religion is of itself sufficient; deism; any action based on natural desires and instincts. **natˈuralist** n someone who studies nature, more particularly zoology and botany, esp zoology, and esp in the field; a dealer in live animals and articles of use and interest to students of nature, often a taxidermist; a believer in naturalism. **naturalistˈic** adj relating to or in accordance with nature, natural history or naturalism. **naturalistˈically** adv. **naturalizāˈtion** or **-s-** n. **natˈuralize** or **-ise** vt to grant the privileges of natural-born citizens to; to cause (an introduced species of plant, animal, etc) to adapt to a different climate or to different conditions of life; to adopt into the language; to admit among accepted institutions, usages, etc; to make natural or easy; to explain naturalistically. ◆ vi to acquire citizenship in another country; to study natural history in the field; (of a plant,

animal, etc) to adapt to a new environment. **nat'urally** *adv* in a natural manner; by nature; according to nature or one's own nature; in a lifelike manner; normally; in the ordinary course; of course. **nat'uralness** *n*.

❑ **natural abundance** *n* (*phys*) same as **abundance**. **natural background** *n* the radiation due to natural radioactivity and to cosmic rays, enhanced by contamination and fallout. **nat'ural-born** *adj* native. **natural childbirth** *n* childbirth with as little medical intervention, *esp* as little anaesthesia, etc as possible, relying on the mother doing special breathing and relaxation exercises. **natural classification** see **natural system** below. **natural cycle IVF** *n* IVF (qv) in which the woman is allowed to ovulate naturally rather than being given drugs to stimulate ovulation. **natural death** *n* death owing to disease or old age, not violence or accident. **natural frequency** *n* the frequency at which an object or system will vibrate freely in the absence of external forces (*phys*); the frequency at which resonance occurs in a circuit (*elec*). **natural gas** *n* gases issuing from the earth, whether from natural fissures or bored wells, applied particularly to the hydrocarbon gases associated with the production of petroleum and used as domestic or industrial fuel in place of town gas (see also **North Sea gas** under **north**). **natural historian** *n*. **natural history** *n orig* the description of all that is in nature, now used of the sciences that deal with the earth and its productions, ie botany, zoology and mineralogy, *esp* field zoology. **natural immunity** *n* that level of immunity with which a person is born (cf **acquired immunity**). **natural killer cell** *n* a naturally occurring lymphoid cell which attacks and destroys tumour cells and some virally infected cells in the absence of prior immunization and without evident antigen specificity. **natural language** *n* a language which has evolved naturally, *opp* to *artificial language*. **natural law** *n* a law of nature; the sense of right and wrong which arises from the constitution of the human mind, as distinguished from the results of revelation or legislation. **natural logarithm** *n* one to the base *e*. **natural magic** see under **magic**. **natural numbers** *n pl* the whole numbers 1, 2, 3 and upwards, sometimes also including 0. **natural order** *n* (in botany) a category now usually called a family. **natural philosopher** *n*. **natural philosophy** *n* the science of the physical properties of bodies; physics, or physics and dynamics. **natural radioactivity** *n* radioactivity that is found in nature. **natural religion** see **natural theology** below. **natural resources** *n pl* features, properties, etc of the land such as minerals, an abundance of water, timber, etc that occur naturally and can be exploited by human beings. **natural scale** *n* a scale of music written without sharps or flats. **natural science** *n* the science of nature, as distinguished from mental and moral science and from mathematics. **natural selection** *n* evolution by the survival of the fittest with inheritance of their fitness by the next generation. **natural system** or **natural classification** *n* a classification of plants and animals according to presumed relationship by descent, distinguished in botany from the artificial system of Linnaeus. **natural theology** or **natural religion** *n* religion derived from reasoned facts, not revelation. **natural therapy** *n* treatment based on the ability of the body to heal itself. **natural virtues** *n pl* those virtues (*esp* justice, prudence, temperance and fortitude) of which people are capable. **natural wastage** *n* (reduction of staff by) non-replacement of those who leave, eg through retirement. **natural year** see under **year**.

nature /nā'chər/ *n* (often with *cap*) the power that creates and regulates the world; all the natural phenomena created by this power, including plants, animals, landscape, etc as distinct from people; the power of growth; the established order of things; the cosmos; the external world, *esp* as untouched by humans; the qualities of anything which make it what it is, governing its character and behaviour; essence; being; constitution; kind or order; naturalness; normal feeling; disposition or temperament; kindliness; conformity to truth or reality; inborn mind, character, instinct or disposition; vital power of humans or animals (*obs*); the normal biological functions or needs of a body; the course of life; nakedness; a primitive undomesticated condition or community; the countryside, *esp* when unspoilt or picturesque; the strength or substance of anything; that which an individual inherits, determining in parts its structure, character and behaviour, as distinguished from *nurture*, or what is learnt from experience, environment or training. [Fr, from L *nātūra*, from *nāscī*, *nātus* to be born]

■ **na'tured** *adj* having a certain temper or disposition (*esp* in compounds, as in *good-natured*). **na'turing** *adj* creative. **na'turism** *n* communal nudity or nudity practised openly, sometimes in the belief that it encourages self-respect, respect for others and a feeling of being in harmony with nature; nature-worship. **na'turist** *n* and *adj*. **naturist'ic** *adj*. **nat'uropath** *n* a person who practises naturopathy. **naturopath'ic** *adj*. **nāturop'athy** (also /*nat*-/) *n* the promotion of health and natural healing by a system of diet, exercise, manipulation, care and hydrotherapy; the philosophy of the system.

❑ **nature cure** *n* the practice of or treatment by naturopathy. **na'ture-god** *n* a deity personifying some force of physical nature. **nature**

knowledge see **nature study** below. **na'ture-myth** *n* a myth symbolizing natural phenomena. **nature printing** *n* printing from plates that have been impressed with some natural object. **nature reserve** *n* an area of land specially managed and protected to preserve its flora and fauna. **nature strip** *n* (*Aust*) a strip of grass, etc bordering a road or footpath or dividing two carriageways. **nature study** or **nature knowledge** *n* a (school) discipline intended to cultivate the powers of seeing and enjoying nature by observation of natural objects, eg plants, animals, etc. **nature trail** *n* a path through the countryside, *usu* with signposts to draw attention to interesting natural features. **na'ture-worship** *n* worship of the powers of nature; naturism.

■ **against nature** immoral or unnatural. **debt of nature** death. **ease** (or **relieve**) **nature** to evacuate the bowels. **from nature** (*art* and *sculpt*) using objects taken from nature as models. **in** (or **of**) **the nature of** of the same sort as, that amounts to.

naturopath, **naturopathy** see under **nature**.

NAU *abbrev* : Nauru (IVR).

naught /nöt/ *n* nothing (*archaic*); a zero (*esp N Am*); wickedness, evil (*obs*). ◆ *adj* (*archaic*) good for nothing; worthless; bad; immoral; hurtful; foiled; ruined. ◆ *adv* ill; not at all. [OE *nāht*, *nāwiht*, from *nā* never, and *wiht* whit]

■ **be naught** (*obs*) keep out of the way; efface yourself; go to the devil. **bring to naught** (*archaic*) to frustrate, baffle. **come to naught** (*archaic*) to come to nothing, fail. **set at naught** (*archaic*) to treat as of no account, despise.

naughty /nö'ti/ *adj* bad; badly-behaved (now chiefly applied to children, or used playfully in feigned censure); verging on the indecorous; titillating; worthless (*obs*); wicked (*Shakesp*). ◆ *n* (*Aust* and *NZ inf*) an act of sexual intercourse. [**naught**]

■ **naught'ily** *adv*. **naught'iness** *n*.

❑ **naughty nineties** *n pl* (*joc*) the 1890s, renowned for gaiety and high living. **naughty step** *n* a place where a child who has misbehaved is sent as a punishment (also *fig*).

naumachy /nö'mə-ki/ or **naumachia** /nö-mā'ki-ə/ *n* (pl **nau'machies**, **naumā'chiae** /-ki-ē/ or **naumā'chias**) a mock sea battle, performed as a spectacle among the ancient Romans; a place for this. [Gr *naumachiā*, from *naus* a ship, and *machē* a fight]

naunt /nänt/ (*archaic*) *n* aunt. [For *mine aunt*]

nauplius /nö'pli-əs/ *n* (pl **nau'plii** /-pli-ī/) a larval form in many Crustacea, with one eye and three pairs of appendages. [L, a kind of shellfish, from Gr *Nauplios* a son of Poseidon, from *naus* a ship, and *pleein* to sail]

■ **nau'pliiform** /-plē-i-/ *adj*. **nau'plioid** *adj*.

Nauruan /nä-oo'roo-ən or now'roo-ən/ *adj* of or relating to the Republic of *Nauru* in the W Pacific, its language or its inhabitants. ◆ *n* a native or inhabitant of Nauru; the language of Nauru.

nausea /nö'si-ə, -zi-ə or -zhə/ *n* a feeling of sickness and inclination to vomit; sickening disgust or loathing; (*orig*) seasickness. [L, from Gr *nausiā* seasickness, from *naus* a ship]

■ **nau'seant** *adj* producing nausea. ◆ *n* a substance having this quality. **nau'seate** *vt* to cause to feel sick; to loathe; to strike with disgust. ◆ *vi* to feel nausea or disgust. **nau'seāting** *adj* causing nausea or (*fig*) disgust. **nau'seātingly** *adv*. **nau'seātive** *adj* (*obs*) inclined to or causing nausea. **nau'seous** /-shəs, -shi-əs or -si-əs/ *adj* affected by nausea; producing nausea; disgusting; loathsome. **nau'seously** *adv*. **nau'seousness** *n*.

naut. *abbrev* : nautical.

nautch /nöch/, **nach** or **natch** /näch/ *n* (in India) a performance given by professional dancing women known as **nautch'-girls**. [Hindi *nāch* dance]

nautical /nö'ti-k(ə)l/ *adj* of or relating to ships, to sailors, or to navigation (also (*rare*) **nau'tic**). [L *nauticus*, from Gr *nautikos*, from *nautēs* sailor, from *naus* a ship]

■ **nau'tically** *adv*. **nau'tics** *n sing* the science of navigation. ◆ *n pl* water sports.

❑ **Nautical Almanac** *n* a periodical book of astronomical tables specially useful to sailors. **nautical mile** see under **mile**.

nautilus /nö'ti-ləs/ *n* (pl **nau'tiluses** or **nau'tilī**) a tetrabranchiate cephalopod of the genus *Nautilus* (*esp* **pearly nautilus**) of southern seas, with a chambered external shell; a Mediterranean dibranchiate cephalopod with a paperlike shell (**paper nautilus** or argonaut) wrongly believed by Aristotle to use its arms as sails. [L, from Gr *nautilos* a sailor, a paper nautilus, from *naus* ship]

■ **nau'tiloid** *n* a mollusc of the subclass **Nautiloid'ea**, to which the nautilus and several extinct species belong.

NAV *abbrev* : net asset value.

nav. *abbrev* : naval; navigable; navigation; navigator.

Navaho see **Navajo**.

navaid /nav'ād/ n any of the electronic devices designed to aid navigation in a ship or aircraft. [Formed from *navigational* aid]

Navajo or **Navaho** /nav'ə-hō/ n (pl **Nav'ajos** or **Nav'ahos**) a Native American people of Utah, Arizona and New Mexico; a member of this people; their Athabascan language. [Sp *Navajó*, name of a particular pueblo]

naval /nā'vl/ adj relating to warships or a navy; serving in a navy; nautical (*obs*). [L *nāvālis*, from *nāvis* a ship]
■ **nav'alism** n the cult of naval supremacy or sea power.
□ **naval architect** n. **naval architecture** n the designing of ships. **Naval Brigade** n a body of seamen organized to serve on land. **naval crown** n (*hist*) a garland awarded to a Roman who had distinguished himself in a sea fight. **naval officer** n an officer in the navy; a custom-house officer of high rank (*US*).

Navaratra /na-və-rä'trə/ or **Navaratri** /-tri/ n a nine-day Hindu festival in honour of Durga. [Sans, period of nine nights, from *nava* nine, and *rātri* night]

navarch /nā'värk/ n an admiral in ancient Greece. [Gr *nauarchos*, from *naus* ship, and *archē* rule]
■ **nav'archy** n the office of navarch; a fleet.

navarho /nav'ə-rō/ n a low-frequency, long-range radio navigation system for aircraft. [*navigation, aid, rho* (ρ), a navigational symbol for distance]

navarin /nav'ə-rin/ or /nav-a-rē'/ n a stew of mutton or lamb, with turnip and other root vegetables. [Fr]

nave¹ /nāv/ n (*archit*) the middle or main body of a basilica, rising above the aisles; the main part of a church, generally west of the crossing, including or excluding its aisles. [L *nāvis* a ship]

nave² /nāv/ n the hub or central part of a wheel, through which the axle passes; the navel (*Shakesp*). [OE *nafu*; cf Du *naaf* and Ger *Nabe*]

navel /nā'vl/ n the umbilicus or depression in the centre of the abdomen; a central point; a nombril (*heraldry*). [OE *nafela*, dimin of *nafu* nave of a wheel]
□ **na'vel-gazing** n (*inf*) worthless, unproductive self-analysis, *esp* when direct action is required. **navel orange** n a variety of orange with a navel-like depression, and a smaller orange enclosed. **na'vel-string** n the umbilical cord. **na'velwort** n pennywort (genus *Cotyledon*).
■ **contemplate one's navel** (*joc*) to spend time navel-gazing.

navette /na-vet'/ n (in jewel-cutting) a pointed oval shape; a jewel cut in this shape. [Fr, shuttle, dimin of *nef* ship]

navew /nā'vū/ n a rape or coleseed with a carrot-shaped root; a wild Swedish turnip. [Fr *naveau*, dimin from L *nāpus*]

navicert /nav'i-* or nā'vi-sûrt/ n a certificate detailing a ship's cargo, issued to a neutral ship in time of war. [*navigational cert*ificate]

navicula /na-vik'ū-lə/ n an incense-boat; a plant of the *Navicula* genus of diatoms. [L *nāvicula*, dimin of *nāvis* a ship]
■ **navic'ular** adj boat-shaped; relating to the navicular bone. ◆ n the navicular bone.
□ **navicular bone** n a boat-shaped bone on the thumb side of the wrist joint, the scaphoid bone; a corresponding bone in the ankle joint. **navicular disease** n inflammation of the navicular bone in horses.

navigate /nav'i-gāt/ vi to conduct or manage a ship, aircraft, motor vehicle, etc in sailing, flying or moving along; to find one's way and keep one's course, *esp* by water or air; to sail; to give directions about the correct route to the driver of a vehicle. ◆ vt to direct the course of; to sail, fly, etc over, on or through. [L *nāvigāre, -ātum*, from *nāvis* a ship, and *agere* to drive]
■ **navigability** /-gə-bil'i-ti/ n. **nav'igable** adj (of a river, channel, etc) deep enough and wide enough to be passed by ships, etc; dirigible. **nav'igableness** n. **nav'igably** adv. **naviga'tion** n the act, science or art of conducting ships or aircraft, *esp* the finding of position and determination of course by astronomical observations and mathematical computations; travel or traffic by water or air (*esp N Am*); a voyage (*archaic*); shipping generally; a navigable route; a canal or artificial waterway. **naviga'tional** adj relating to navigation. **nav'igator** n a person who navigates or sails; a person who directs the course of a ship, etc; a person (*usu* co-driver) who describes the route to, and directs, the driver in a car rally or race; an explorer by sea; a navvy; an instrumental or other aid to navigation.
□ **navigational system** n any system of obtaining bearings and/or ranges for navigational purposes by radio techniques. **navigation bar** n (*comput*) the area along the border of a web page that displays hyperlinks to other parts of the website. **navigation light** n one of a set of lights shown by a ship or aircraft at night, indicating direction of travel.

navvy /nav'i/ (*inf*) n a labourer, *orig* a labourer on a navigation or canal; a machine for digging out earth, etc (see **steam navvy** under

steam). ◆ vi (**navv'ying**; **navv'ied**) to work as a navvy, or like a navvy. ◆ vt to excavate. [**navigator**]

navy /nā'vi/ n (often with *cap*) the whole of a nation's ships-of-war, with the crews and supporting crews; (often with *cap*) the officers and men belonging to a nation's warships; navy blue; a fleet of ships (*archaic* or *poetic*). ◆ adj of, used by or such as is supplied to the navy. [OFr *navie*, from L *nāvis* a ship]
□ **navy blue** n and adj very dark blue as used in naval dress. **navy list** n a list of officers and ships of a navy. **navy yard** n (*US*) a government dockyard.

naw /nö/ interj a dialect form of **no¹**.

nawab /nə-wäb'* or *-wöb'/ (*hist*) n a deputy or viceroy in the Mogul empire; a Muslim prince or noble; an honorary title bestowed by the Indian government; a nabob (*rare*). [Hindi *nawwāb*, from Ar *nawwāb*, respectful pl of *nā'ib* deputy]

Naxalite /näk'sə-līt/ n a member of any of various militant Maoist groups in India. [*Naxalbari* in W Bengal, site of a peasants' uprising in 1967]

nay /nā/ (*archaic* or *dialect*) adv no (for former distinction between *nay* and *no* see **no¹**); not only so, but; yet more; in point of fact. ◆ n a denial; a vote against. [ME *nay, nai*, from ON *nei*; Dan *nei*; cognate with **no¹**]
■ **nay'ward** n (*Shakesp*) the negative side.
□ **nay'say** n a refusal. ◆ vt to refuse; to deny, to contradict. **nay'sayer** n someone who refuses to do or agree to something, *esp* to support ideas or proposals. **nay'saying** adj and n.

Nayar see **Nair**.

NAYPIC or **Naypic** abbrev: (until 1995) National Association of Young People in Care.

naythles see **nathless**.

nayword /nā'wûrd/ n a catchword or watchword (*Shakesp*); a proverbial reproach, a byword (*Shakesp* **ayword**). [Origin obscure]

Nazarene /naz'ə-rēn/, also **Nazarean** /-rē'ən/ n an inhabitant of Nazareth, in Galilee; (with *the*) Jesus Christ; a follower of Jesus of Nazareth, *orig* used of Christians in contempt; an early Jewish Christian; any of a group of German painters who, in the early 19c, tried to restore the quality of religious art.

Nazarite /naz'ə-rīt/ n a Jewish ascetic under a vow (see Bible, Numbers 6; also **Naz'irite**); a Nazarene. [Heb *nāzar* to consecrate]
■ **Nazaritic** /-it'ik/ adj. **Naz'aritism** /-īt-izm/ n.

naze /nāz/ n a headland or cape. [OE *næs*; cf **ness**]

Nazi /nä'tsē/ n a member of the National Socialist German Workers' Party, founded in 1919 and achieving power in 1933 under the leadership of Adolf Hitler; a Hitlerite; any person with extreme racist and authoritarian opinions (*derog*). ◆ adj of or relating to the Nazis or Nazism. [Ger, short form of *Nationalsozialist* National Socialist]
■ **Nazifica'tion** n. **Naz'ify** vt and vi. **Naz'ism** or **Naz'iism** n.

nazir /nä'zir/ n formerly, an Indian court official who served summonses, etc; an official of various kinds. [Ar *nāzir* overseer]

Nazirite see **Nazarite**.

NB abbrev: Nebraska (US state; term not in official use); New Brunswick (Canadian province); North Britain or North British; *nota bene* (L), note well or take notice (also **nb**).

Nb (*chem*) symbol: niobium.

nb (*cricket*) abbrev: no-ball.

NBA abbrev: National Basketball Association (*N Am*); National Boxing Association (*US*); Net Book Agreement, a former agreement within the book trade that net books could not be sold at less than the price fixed by the publisher.

NBC abbrev: National Broadcasting Company (*US*); nuclear, biological and chemical (warfare, weapons, etc).
□ **NBC suit** n a suit that protects the wearer against the physical effects of nuclear, biological and chemical weapons.

NC abbrev: National Curriculum; network computer; North Carolina (US state); numerical control.

nc abbrev: no charge.

NCAA abbrev: National Collegiate Athletic Association (in the USA).

NCC abbrev: National Consumer Council; formerly, National Curriculum Council; formerly, Nature Conservancy Council.

NCCL abbrev: National Council for Civil Liberties (now known as Liberty).

NCEA (*NZ*) abbrev: National Certificate of Educational Achievement.

NCIS /en'sis/ abbrev: National Criminal Intelligence Service (now replaced by **SOCA**).

NCO abbrev: non-commissioned officer.

NCP abbrev: National Car Parks.

NCSC *abbrev*: National Care Standards Commission.

NCT *abbrev*: National Childbirth Trust.

NCVO *abbrev*: National Council for Voluntary Organizations.

NCVQ *abbrev*: National Council for Vocational Qualifications (now replaced by **QCA**).

ND *abbrev*: North Dakota (US state).

Nd (*chem*) *symbol*: neodymium.

nd *abbrev*: no date, not dated.

N.Dak. *abbrev*: North Dakota (US state).

NDP *abbrev*: National Democratic Party (in Canada and Egypt).

Ndrangheta or **'Ndrangheta** /ən-dran-get'ə/ *n* a secret criminal organization in Calabria, controlling crime and other illegal activities. [Ital]

NE *abbrev*: Nebraska (US state); New England; north-east; north-eastern.

Ne (*chem*) *symbol*: neon.

ne /nē or ni/ (*obs*) *adv* not. ◆ *conj* nor. [OE *ne*]

né /nā/ *adj* (of a man) born, used in giving the original name of a titled man. [Fr]

neafe or **neaffe** (*Shakesp*) see **nieve**.

neal /nēl/ *vt* and *vi* an apheretic form of **anneal**.

Neanderthal or **Neandertal** /ni-an'dər-täl/ *adj* of a Palaeolithic species of man whose remains were first found in 1857 in a cave in the *Neanderthal*, a valley in W Germany; primitive (*inf*); extremely old-fashioned and reactionary (*inf*). ◆ *n* (also **Nean'derthaler**, **Nean'dertaler**, **Neanderthal man**) a member of the Neanderthal species; a primitive or reactionary person (*inf*). ■ **Nean'derthaloid** *adj*. —All words also without *cap*.

neanic /nē-an'ik/ (*zool*) *adj* relating to the adolescent period in the life history of an individual. [Gr *neanikos* youthful]

neap /nēp/ *adj* (of tides) of smallest range, of least difference between high and low points. ◆ *n* a neap tide, occurring after the first and third quarters of the moon. ◆ *vi* (*archaic*) to tend towards the neap. [OE *nēp*, appar meaning helpless; *nēpflōd* neap tide] ■ **neaped** *adj* left aground between spring tides.

Neapolitan /nē-ə-pol'i-tən/ *adj* of the city or the former kingdom of Naples. ◆ *n* a native, citizen or inhabitant of Naples; (without *cap*) a small rectangular chocolate. [L *Neāpolitānus*, from Gr *Neāpolis* new town, from *neos, -ā, -on* new, and *polis* city] ▫ **Neapolitan ice cream** *n* ice cream made in layers of different colours and flavours. **Neapolitan sixth** *n* (*music*) a chord of the subdominant with its minor third and minor sixth. **Neapolitan violet** *n* a scented double variety of sweet violet.

near /nēr/ *adv* (**near'er**; **near'est**) to or at no great distance; (*orig* as *compar* of **nigh**) nigher, more closely, to or at a shorter distance; close; closely; nearly; almost; narrowly; thriftily, parsimoniously (*archaic*). ◆ *prep* close to (**near'er** and **near'est** are also used as prepositions). ◆ *adj* (**near'er**; **near'est**) nigh; not far away in place or time; close in relationship, friendship, imitation, approximation or in any relation; close, narrow, so as barely to escape; (eg of a road) short, direct; stingy, parsimonious (*inf*); (of horses, vehicles, roads, etc) left, left-hand. ◆ *vt* and *vi* to approach; to come nearer. [OE *nēar*, compar of *nēah* nigh (adv), and ON *nær*, compar (but also used as positive) of *nā* nigh; cf Ger *näher*] ■ **near'ly** *adv* at or within a short distance; closely; intimately; scrutinizingly, parsimoniously; almost; approximately but rather less. **near'ness** *n*. ▫ **near beer** *n* (*N Am inf*) any of several beers containing 0.5 per cent alcohol or less. **near'-begaun** or **near'-gaun** *adj* (*Scot*) niggardly. **near'by** *adj* neighbouring. ◆ *adv* (*usu* **nearby'**) close at hand. ◆ *prep* (also **near by**) close to. **near cut** *n* (*old*) a short cut. **near-death experience** an experience or sensation, when seemingly on the point of death, of being outside one's own body as an external observer of oneself. **near-earth object** *n* a large celestial object, such as an asteroid, whose orbit may possibly bring it into collision with the earth (*abbrev* **NEO**). **Near East** *n* formerly, an area including the Balkans and Turkey, and sometimes also the countries to the west of Iran; now synonymous with **Middle East** (see under **middle**). **near gale** *n* (*meteorol*) a wind of force 7 on the Beaufort scale, reaching speeds of 32 to 38mph. **near-gaun** see **near-begaun** above. **near'-hand** *adj* (*Scot*) near. ◆ *adv* nearly. **near'-legged** *adj* (*Shakesp*) (of horses) walking so that the legs interfere. **nearly man** *n* (*inf*) one who narrowly fails to achieve expected success. **near miss** *n* (*lit* and *fig*) a miss that is almost a hit; a narrowly avoided collision. **near point** *n* the nearest point the eye can focus. **near'side** *n* the side of a vehicle nearer to the kerb eg when it is being driven, in Britain the left side; the left side of a horse or other animal, or of a team of horses. ◆ *adj* on the nearside. **near-sight'ed** *adj* short-sighted. **near-sight'edly** *adv*. **near-sight'edness** *n*.

■ **a near thing** a narrow escape. **near as a touch**, **as ninepence** or **as dammit** (*inf*) very nearly. **nearest and dearest** one's closest family and friends.

near- /nēr-/ *combining form* denoting almost, as in **near'-white** of a colour closely resembling white, and **near'-silk'** artificial silk.

Nearctic /nē-ärk'tik/ *adj* of the New World part of the Holarctic region, including the part of N America to the north of the Tropic of Cancer, and Greenland. [Gr *neos* new, and *arktikos* northern, from *arktos* bear, the Great Bear]

neat[1] /nēt/ *adj* elegant; trim; tidy; finished, adroit; deft; well and concisely put; ingenious, effective, economical in effort or method; good, excellent (chiefly *N Am*); clean (*obs*); unmixed; undiluted; undiminished, net; clear, shining (*Spenser*). ◆ *adv* neatly. [Fr *net* clean, tidy, from L *nitidus* shining, bright, from *nitēre* to shine] ■ **neat'en** *vt* to make neat, tidy. **neat'ly** *adv*. **neat'ness** *n*. ▫ **neat-hand'ed** *adj* dexterous.

neat[2] /nēt/ (*archaic* or *dialect*) *n* (pl **neat**) an ox, cow, bull, etc. [OE *nēat* cattle, a beast, from *nēotan, nīotan* to use; cf Scot **nowt**[1] from ON *naut*] ▫ **neat'-cattle** *n pl*. **neat'-herd** *n*. **neat'-house** *n*. **neat's-foot oil** *n* an oil obtained from the feet of oxen. **neat's leather** *n* leather made of the hides of neat. **neat'-stall** *n*.

neath or **'neath** /nēth/ (*dialect* and *poetic*) *prep* beneath. [Apheretic for **aneath** or **beneath**]

NEB *abbrev*: New English Bible.

Neb. *abbrev*: Nebraska (US state).

neb /neb/ (*Scot and N Eng dialect*) *n* a beak or bill; the mouth (*obs*); the nose; a nib; the sharp point of anything. ◆ *vi* (**nebb'ing**; **nebbed**) to bill. ◆ *vt* to put a neb on. [OE *nebb* beak, face; cognate with Du *neb* beak] ■ **nebbed** /nebd/ *adj* having a neb.

nebbich /neb'ihh/, **nebbish** or **nebish** /neb'ish/ *n* (also **nebbishe** or **nebbisher** /neb'ish-ər/) a colourless, insignificant, incompetent person, a perpetual victim (also *adj*). [Yiddish]

Nebbiolo /neb-ē-ō'lō/ *n* (pl **Nebbiō'los**) a type of black grape grown *esp* in N Italy; a red wine produced from this grape. [From Ital *nebbia* fog, perh from the foggy weather in which it is often harvested]

nebbish see **nebbich**.

nebbuk, **nebek**, **nebeck** /neb'ək/ same as **nabk**.

nebel /nē'bəl/ *n* a Hebrew instrument, *appar* a harp. [Heb *nēbel*]

nebish see **nebbich**.

neb-neb /neb'neb/ *n* bablah pods. [Prob an African word]

Nebr. *abbrev*: Nebraska (US state).

nebris /neb'ris/ *n* a fawn-skin worn by Bacchus and his votaries. [Gr *nebris*]

nebuchadnezzar /neb-ū-kə(d)-nez'ər/ (also with *cap*) *n* a large bottle, *esp* of champagne, the equivalent of 20 ordinary bottles. [*Nebuchadnezzar*, king of Babylon in Bible, 2 Kings 24–25, following the tradition of calling bottle-sizes after well-known Old Testament figures]

nebula /neb'ū-lə/ *n* (pl **neb'ulae** /-lē/ or **neb'ulas**) a faint, misty appearance in the heavens produced either by a group of stars too distant to be seen singly, or by diffused gaseous matter; a little cloudiness; a slight opacity of the cornea; a liquid for spraying. [L *nebula* mist; cf Gr *nephelē* cloud, mist] ■ **neb'ular** *adj* relating to nebulae; like or of the nature of a nebula. **nebule** /neb'ūl/ *n* wavy moulding. **neb'ulé** /-lā/ or **neb'uly** *adj* (*heraldry*) wavy. **nebu'lium** *n* an element formerly assumed in order to explain certain lines in the spectra of gaseous nebulae, lines now known to be due to states of oxygen, and also nitrogen, not possible under earthly conditions. **nebulīzā'tion** or **-s-** *n*. **neb'ulize** or **-ise** *vt* to reduce to spray. **neb'ulīzer** or **-s-** *n* a device with a mouthpiece or face mask through which a drug is administered as a fine mist; an atomizer. **nebulos'ity** *n*. **neb'ulous** *adj* hazy, vague, formless (*lit* and *fig*); cloudlike; like, or the nature of, or surrounded by a nebula. **neb'ulously** *adv*. **neb'ulousness** *n*. **nebuly** see **nebulé** above. ▫ **nebular hypothesis** or **nebular theory** *n* the theory of Pierre-Simon Laplace that the solar system was formed by the contraction and breaking up of a rotating nebula.

NEC *abbrev*: National Executive Committee; National Exhibition Centre (Birmingham).

nécessaire /nā-se-ser'/ (*Fr*) *n* a dressing-case, workbox.

necessary /nes'ə-s(ə)-ri or nes'i-, also -se-/ *adj* that must be; that cannot be otherwise; unavoidable, inevitable; predestined; indispensable; (of a proposition) always true, and such that a denial leads to inevitable self-contradiction (*logic*); enforced (*archaic*); (of an agent) not free. ◆ *n* that which cannot be left out or done without, eg food (used chiefly in *pl*); a toilet (*obs* or *dialect*); money (*inf*). [L *necessārius*]

■ **necessā'rian** *n* and *adj*. **necessā'rianism** *n* see **necessitarianism** under **necessity**. **nec'essarily** (or /nes-is-e'rǝ-li/) *adv* as a necessary consequence; inevitably; (loosely) for certain. **nec'essariness** *n*.
❑ **necessary truths** *n pl* such as cannot but be true.

necessity /ni- or nǝ-ses'i-ti/ *n* a state or quality of being necessary; that which is necessary or unavoidable; unavoidable compulsion; compulsion as a law of nature, governing all human action; great need; poverty. [L *necessitās, -ātis*]

■ **necessitā'rian** or **necessā'rian** *n* and *adj*. **necessitā'rianism** or **necessā'rianism** *n* the philosophical theory that human actions are determined by precursory circumstances and cannot be willed. **necess'itate** *vt* to make necessary; to render unavoidable; to compel. **necessitā'tion** *n*. **necess'itied** *adj* (*Shakesp*) forced into a state of subjection or submissiveness as a result of poverty. **necess'itous** *adj* in necessity; very poor; destitute. **necess'itously** *adv*. **necess'itousness** *n*.
■ **natural necessity** the condition of being necessary according to the laws of nature, **logical** or **mathematical** according to those of human intelligence, **moral** according to those of moral law. **of necessity** necessarily. **works of necessity** work so necessary as to be allowable on the Sabbath.

neck /nek/ *n* the part connecting head and trunk (often in allusion to the halter or the yoke; *fig*); the flesh of that part regarded as food; anything resembling that part; the part connecting the head and body of anything, eg a violin; the plain lower part of the capital of a column (*archit*); any narrow connecting part, eg an isthmus; anything narrow and throatlike, such as the upper part of a bottle; (in mosses and ferns) the upper tubular part of the archegonium (*bot*); a plug of igneous or fragmental rock filling a volcanic vent; a col; the part of a garment on or nearest the neck; the length of a horse's head and neck, used to measure its lead in a race; impudence, audacity (*sl*). ◆ *vt* to strike, pull, or chop the neck of, *esp* so as to kill; to catch or fasten by the neck; to kiss amorously (*inf*); to make a neck on; to drink (*sl*). ◆ *vi* (*inf*) to kiss amorously. [OE *hnecca*; cf OHGer *hnac*, also Olr *cnocc* hill]
■ **neck'atee** *n* (*obs*) a neckerchief. **necked** *adj* having a neck. **neck'ing** *n* the neck of a column (*archit*); a moulding between the capital and shaft of a column, a gorgerin (*archit*); embracing, petting (*inf*). **neck'let** *n* a simple form of necklace; a pendant strung for the neck; a small boa or fur for the neck.
❑ **neck'band** *n* the part of a shirt, etc encircling the neck; a band worn on the neck. **neck'beef** *n* the coarse flesh of the neck of cattle; inferior stuff. **neck'-bone** *n* a cervical vertebra. **neck'cloth** *n* a piece of folded cloth worn round the neck by men as a band or cravat, with the ends hanging down, often made of lace. **neck'erchief** *n* an ornamental cloth, a kerchief for the neck. **neck'gear** *n* apparel for the neck. **neck'-herr'ing** *n* (*obs*) a heavy blow on the neck. **necking party** *n* (*inf*) a petting party. **neck'lace** /-lis or -lǝs/ *n* a lace, chain, or string of beads or precious stones worn around the neck; (in South Africa) the punishment of having a petrol-soaked tyre placed round the neck or shoulders and set alight, traditionally used by black people on those thought to be government sympathizers (also called **neck'lacing**). ◆ *vt* (in South Africa) to kill with a necklace. **neck'line** *n* the edge of a garment at the neck. **neck'-moulding** *n* a moulding where the capital of a column joins the shaft. **neck'piece** *n* a piece of cloth, etc forming, covering, or bordering a neck. **neck'-sweet'bread** *n* the thymus gland of veal or lamb. **neck'tie** *n* (*esp N Am*) a band of fabric tied round the neck under the collar and *usu* hanging down in front, a tie; a hangman's noose (*US sl*). **necktie party** *n* (*US sl*) a lynching. **neck'verse** *n* the test of ability to read for those who claimed benefit of clergy (qv), *usu* Psalm 51.1, success giving the privilege of being branded on the hand instead of hanging. **neck'wear** *n* clothing for the neck, such as ties or scarves. **neck'weed** *n* hemp, source of the hangman's rope (*old sl*); a kind of speedwell, from its reputed medicinal virtue (*US*).
■ **get it in the neck** (*inf*) to be severely dealt with or hard hit. **harden the neck** to grow more obstinate. **neck and crop** completely; bodily; in a heap; summarily and unceremoniously. **neck and neck** exactly equal; side by side. **neck of the woods** (*inf*) a particular area, part of the country. **neck or nothing** risking everything. **save one's neck** to escape narrowly with one's life or reputation. **stick one's neck out** to put oneself at risk, expose oneself to trouble, danger or contradiction. **talk through the back of one's neck** to talk wildly or absurdly wide of the truth. **tread on the neck of** to oppress or tyrannize over. **up to one's neck** (*inf*) deeply involved, *esp* in a troublesome situation.

necro- /nek-rō- or -rǝ/ *combining form* denoting dead or a dead body. [Gr *nekros* dead body, dead]
■ **necrōbiō'sis** *n* the natural degeneration and death of a cell in living tissue. **necrobiot'ic** *adj*. **necrog'rapher** *n* an obituary writer. **necrol'ater** *n*. **necrol'atry** *n* worship of, or morbid or sentimental reverence for, the dead or dead bodies. **necrōlog'ic** or **necrōlog'ical** *adj*. **necrol'ogist** *n*. **necrol'ogy** *n* (*formal*) an obituary list.

nec'rōmancer *n* a practitioner of necromancy; a sorcerer. **nec'rōmancy** *n* the art of revealing future events by calling up and questioning the spirits of the dead; enchantment; sorcery. **necrōman'tic** or **necrōman'tical** *adj*. **necrōman'tically** *adv*. **necroph'agous** *adj* feeding on carrion. **nec'rophile** /-fīl/ *n* someone who is morbidly attracted to, and *esp* has sexual intercourse with, corpses (also **nec'rophil** /-fil/). **necrophilia** /-fil'/ *n* necrophilism. **necrophiliac** /-fil'i-ak/ or **necrophilic** /-fil'ik/ *adj*. **necroph'ilism** or **necroph'ily** *n* a morbid (*esp* sexual) attraction towards dead bodies. **necroph'ilous** *adj*. **nec'rophōbe** *n*. **necrōphō'bia** *n* a morbid horror of corpses. **necrōphō'bic** *adj*. **necroph'orous** *adj* carrying away and burying dead bodies, as do burying beetles. **necrop'olis** *n* (*pl* **necrop'olises** /-lis-ǝz/ or **necrop'oleis** /-līs/) a cemetery or burial site. **nec'ropsy** (or /-rop'/) *n* a post-mortem examination. **necrōscop'ic** or **necrōscop'ical** *adj*. **necros'copy** *n* a post-mortem examination, autopsy. **necrot'omy** *n* dissection of a dead body; the surgical excision of necrosed bone from a living body.

necrosis /ne-krō'sis/ *n* death of part of the living body, *esp* of a concentrated area of cells owing to an interruption of the blood supply, etc, eg as a symptom of gangrene. [Gr *nekros* dead body]
■ **necrose** /nek-rōs'/ *vt* and *vi* to affect with or undergo necrosis. **necrot'ic** *adj*. **nec'rōtize** or **-ise** *vt* and *vi* to necrose.
❑ **nec'rōtizing fasciitis** see **fasciitis** under **fascia**.

nectar /nek'tǝr/ *n* the name given by Homer, Hesiod, Pindar, etc to the beverage of the gods, giving life and beauty; the honey of the glands of plants; any delicious drink; a drink made from concentrated fruit juice or fruit purée, water and sugar; anything very sweet or pleasant. [Gr *nektar*; ety doubtful]
■ **nectā'real**, **nectā'rean**, **nectā'reous** or **nec'tarous** *adj* of or like nectar. **nec'tared** *adj* imbued with nectar; mingled or filled with, or containing much, nectar. **nectā'reousness** *n*. **nectā'rial** *adj* of the nature of a nectary. **nectarif'erous** *adj* (*bot*) producing nectar. **nec'tarine** /-ēn or -in/ *n* (a tree bearing) a variety of peach with a smooth skin. ◆ *adj* /-in/ sweet as nectar. **nectarous** see **nectareal** above. **nec'tary** *n* (in plants) a glandular organ that secretes nectar.
❑ **nec'tar-guide** *n* a marking that guides insects to the nectary of a flower.

nectocalyx /nek-tō-kā'liks/ *n* (*pl* **nectocā'lyces** /-li-sēz/) a hydrozoan swimming-bell. [Gr *nēktos* swimming, and *kalyx* shell, flower-cup]

ned /ned/ (chiefly *Scot*; *sl*) *n* a young hooligan, a disruptive adolescent; a member of a teenage gang. [Poss the familiar form of *Edward*; see also **Ted**]

NEDC *abbrev*: (until 1992) National Economic Development Council (also (*inf*) **Neddy** /ned'i/).

neddy /ned'i/ *n* a donkey; a fool (*inf*); a racehorse (*Aust sl*). [From *Edward*]

née /nā/ *adj* (of a woman) born, used in stating a woman's maiden name. [Fr, fem pap of *naître* to be born]

need /nēd/ *n* lack of something which one cannot well do without; necessity; a state that requires relief, such as extreme poverty or distress; lack of the means of living. ◆ *vt* to have occasion for; to want; to require; (used before the infinitive with *to*, or in negative, interrogative, conditional, etc sentences without *to*) to require or be obliged (to do something); (used before a verbal noun) to require (to be dealt with in a particular way). ◆ *vi* (*archaic*) to be necessary. [OE *nēd, nīed, nȳd*; Du *nood*, OGer *Noth* (modern *Not*)]
■ **needcess'ity** *n* a dialectal or non-standard combination of **need** and **necessity**. **need'er** *n*. **need'ful** *adj* full of need; having need; needy; necessary; requisite. **need'fully** *adv*. **need'fulness** *n*. **need'ily** *adv*. **need'iness** *n*. **need'less** *adj* not needed; unnecessary; having no need (*Shakesp*). **need'lessly** *adv*. **need'lessness** *n*. **need'ly** *adv* (*Shakesp*) necessarily. **need'ment** *n* (*Spenser*) something needed. **needs** *adv* of necessity; indispensably. **need'y** *adj* very poor; craving affection or attention; necessary (*Shakesp*); (with *the*) people living in poverty. **need'y-hood** *n* (*Herrick*).
❑ **need'-be** *n* a necessity. **need'fire** *n* fire produced by friction, to which a certain virtue is superstitiously attached; a beacon.
■ **had need** (*archaic*) ought to. **must needs** or **needs must** (often *ironic*) must inevitably. **the needful** ready money (*sl*); whatever is requisite, *usu* in **do the needful** (*inf*).

needle /nē'dl/ *n* a small, sharp instrument with a hole for thread in the blunt end, for sewing; any similar slender, pointed instrument, as for knitting, etching, playing gramophone records, suturing, dissection, (hooked) for crochet; the suspended magnet of a compass or galvanometer; a pointer on a dial; the pointed end of a hypodermic syringe; a hypodermic injection (*inf*); anything sharp and pointed; a pinnacle of rock; an obelisk; a long slender crystal; a strong beam passed through a wall as a temporary support; a long, narrow, stiff leaf; a feeling of irritation (*sl*); dislike, enmity (*sl*). ◆ *adj* (of a contest) involving intense rivalry and acutely critical. ◆ *vt* to sew; to pierce; to penetrate; to thread; to pass through; to underpin with needles; to irritate, goad, heckle (*inf*); to add alcohol to (an already alcoholic drink) (*US sl*). ◆ *vi* to pass out and in; to sew. [OE *nǣdl*; Ger *Nadel*; cognate with Ger *nähen* to sew; L *nēre* to spin]

■ **need'leful** *n* as much thread as will serve for one threading of a needle. **need'ler** *n* a needlemaker. **need'ly** *adj* like needles.

❑ **needle bank** see **needle exchange** below. **need'le-bath** *n* a shower-bath with very fine strong jets. **need'le-book** *n* a needle-case in book form. **need'le-case** *n* a case for holding needles. **need'lecord** *n* a cotton material with closer ribs and flatter pile than corduroy. **need'lecraft** *n* the art of needlework; lace made with a needle; embroidery on canvas, done with woollen yarns, used on chair covers, etc. **needle exchange** or **needle bank** *n* a place where drug users may exchange old hypodermic syringes for new ones, *usu* free of charge, to help prevent the spread of disease or infection. **need'lefish** *n* a pipefish; a garpike. **need'le-furze** *n* the petty whin. **need'le-gun** *n* a gun in which the cartridge is exploded by the impact of a spike. **needle paper** *n* acid-free black paper used for wrapping needles. **need'lepoint** *n* the point of a needle; a very sharp point; point-lace made with a needle; embroidery on canvas, done with woollen yarns, used on chair covers, etc. **need'le-point'ed** *adj* pointed like a needle, round in section; (eg of a fish-hook) without a barb. **needle roller-bearing** *n* a roller-bearing without a cage, in which long rollers of small diameter are used, located endwise by a lip on the inner or outer race. **need'lestick** *adj* (of injuries) caused by medical staff pulling off a dirty or bloody hypodermic needle from a syringe and pricking their fingers with it by accident. **needle time** *n* the amount of time allowed to a radio channel for the broadcasting of recorded music. **need'le-tin** *n* cassiterite in slender crystals. **needle valve** *n* a cone-shaped valve, ending in a point, used to control the flow of a fluid. **need'lewoman** *n* a woman who does needlework; a seamstress. **need'lework** *n* work done with a needle; the business of a seamstress.

▪ **get the needle** (*inf*) to be irritated. **give the needle to** (*inf*) to irritate. **look for a needle in a haystack** (or (*rare*) **bottle of hay**) to engage in a hopeless search.

neeld /nēld/ or **neele** /nēl/ obsolete forms of **needle**.

neem, neemb, neem tree see **nim³**.

neep /nēp/ (*Scot*) *n* a turnip. [OE *nǣp*, from L *nāpus*]

ne'er /nār/ *adv* contraction of **never**.

❑ **ne'er'-do-well** (*Scot* **-weel**) *adj* and *n* (a) good-for-nothing.

Ne'erday /ner'/ or /nār'dā/ (chiefly *Scot*) *n* New Year's Day; (without *cap*) a gift on New Year's Day.

neesberry see **naseberry**.

NEET or (*sometimes*) **Neet** *n* and *adj* (a person who is) *not* in employment, education or training.

neeze or **neese** /nēz/ *vi* and *n* (to) sneeze. [Cf ON *hnjōsa*, and **sneeze**]

NEF *abbrev*: National Energy Foundation.

nef /nef/ *n* an ornamental stand or holder for a knife, fork, etc or for a table napkin, often in the shape of a ship; a church nave (*obs*). [Fr *nef* ship, nave, from L *nāvis*]

nefandous /ni-fan'dɔs/ *adj* abominable. [L *nefandus* unspeakable, from *ne-* not, and *fandus* to be spoken, from *fārī* to speak]

nefarious /ni-fā'ri-ɔs/ *adj* extremely wicked; villainous. [L *nefārius*, *nefāstus*, from *nefās* wrong, crime, from *ne-* not, and *fās* divine law, prob from *fārī* to speak]

■ **nefa'riously** *adv*. **nefa'riousness** *n*. **nefast** /ni-fast'/ *adj* abominable.

neg. *abbrev*: negative; negatively; negotiable.

nega- /ne-gɔ-/ *combining form* denoting a reduced or non-existent amount, as in *nega-demand, nega-mile*. [**negative**, after **mega-**]

negate /ni-gāt'/ *vt* to deny; to nullify; to imply the non-existence of; to make ineffective. [L *negāre, -ātum* to deny]

■ **negation** /-gā'shɔn/ *n* the act of saying no; denial; a negative proposition (*logic*); something that is the opposite (of a positive quality, state, etc); a thing characterized by the absence of qualities. **nega'tionist** *n* someone who merely denies, without offering any positive assertion. **negative** /neg'ɔ-tiv/ *adj* denying; expressing denial, refusal, or prohibition, *opp* to *affirmative*; denying the connection between a subject and a predicate (*logic*); lacking a positive quality; failing to affirm; opposite, contrary to, neutralizing, etc that which is regarded as positive; censorious (*US*); defeatist, pessimistic; obstructive, unconstructive; less than nothing (*maths*); reckoned or measured in the opposite direction to that chosen as positive (*maths*); at relatively lower potential (*elec*); of, having, or producing negative electricity (qv below; *elec*); having dark for light and light for dark (*optics* and *photog*); in complementary colours (*optics* and *photog*); acid (*chem*); laevorotatory (*optics*); having the index of refraction for the extraordinary ray less than for the ordinary in double refraction (*optics*); in a direction away from the source of stimulus (*biol*). ◆ *n* a

word or statement by which something is denied; a word or grammatical form that expresses denial or opposition; a negative proposition or term; the right or act of saying no, or of refusing assent; the side of a question or the decision which denies what is affirmed; an image in which the lights and shades are reversed; a photographic film or plate bearing such an image; a quantity less than nothing (*maths*); a negative quantity or quality. ◆ *vt* to prove the contrary of; to reject by vote; to veto; to reject by veto; to deny; to neutralize. **neg'atively** *adv*. **neg'ativeness** *n*. **neg'ativism** *n* a tendency to deny and criticize, without offering any positive assertions; a tendency to do the opposite of what one is asked to do. **neg'ativist** *n* and *adj*. **negativis'tic** *adj*. **negativ'ity** *n* the fact of being negative. **negā'tor** *n* one who negates; a word or particle that expresses negation. **neg'atory** *adj* expressing denial. **negatron** /neg'ɔ-tron/ *n* a negative electron, *opp* to *positron*.

❑ **negative angle** *n* one generated by a straight line moving clockwise. **negative cash flow** *n* a cash flow in which more money goes out of a business than comes into it. **negative electricity** *n* electricity arising from the excess of electrons. **negative equity** *n* the situation, caused by a fall in house prices, in which a person owns property that is worth less than the value of his or her mortgage. **negative feedback** *n* the return of part of an output signal back to the input, as a way of increasing the quality of amplified sound. **negative income tax** see under **income**. **negative interest** *n* money charged on or deducted from interest on bank deposits, etc. **negative ion therapy** *n* the use of negatively charged ions by breathing negatively ionized air or by direct application of the ions, to treat or prevent a wide range of medical conditions. **negative pole** *n* that pole of a magnet which turns to the south when the magnet swings freely. **negative proton** *n* an antiproton. **negative reinforcement** *n* (*behaviourism*) in conditioning situations, a stimulus, *usu* aversive, that increases the probability of escape or avoidance behaviour. **negative sign** *n* the sign ($-$, read *minus*) of subtraction.

neglect /ni-glekt'/ *vt* to treat carelessly; to pass by without notice, to disregard; to omit by carelessness; to fail to give proper care and attention to. ◆ *n* disregard; slight; lack of (proper) care or attention, negligence; omission; uncared-for state. [L *neglegere, neglectum*, from *neg-* or *nec-* not, and *legere* to gather]

■ **neglect'able** *adj* (*rare*) negligible. **neglect'edness** *n*. **neglect'er** *n*. **neglect'ful** *adj* careless; habitually neglecting or omitting to do things; slighting. **neglect'fully** *adv*. **neglect'fulness** *n*. **neglect'ingly** *adv* carelessly; heedlessly. **neglection** /-glek'shɔn/ *n* (*Shakesp*) negligence. **neglect'ive** *adj* (now *rare*) neglectful.

negligee /neg'li-zhā/ *n* (also **neg'ligé**) a woman's loose decorative nightdress or dressing-gown of flimsy material; a loose gown worn by women in the 18c; a necklace, *usu* of red coral. [Fr *négligée* (fem), neglected]

■ **négligé** /nā-glē-zhā'/ or *ne'* / *n* casual or informal dress. ◆ *adj* casually or informally dressed; carelessly or unceremoniously dressed; careless.

negligence /neg'li-jɔns/ *n* the fact or quality of being negligent; lack of proper care; habitual neglect; an act of carelessness or neglect (*archaic*), a slight; carelessness about dress, manner, etc; omission of duty, *esp* such care for the interests of others as the law may require. [L *negligentia* for *neglegentia*, from *neglegere* to neglect]

■ **neg'ligent** *adj* neglecting; careless; inattentive, *esp* to duties or responsibilities; disregarding ceremony or fashion. **neg'ligently** *adv*. **negligibil'ity** *n*. **neg'ligible** *adj* (sometimes **neg'ligeable**) as may be ignored because very little or very unimportant. **neg'ligibly** *adv*.

négociant /nā-gō-sē-ã'/ (*Fr*) *n* a merchant, *esp* a wine merchant.

negotiate /ni-gō'shi-āt/ *vi* to confer for the purpose of mutual arrangement; to bargain; to traffic. ◆ *vt* to arrange for by agreement; to manage; to transfer or exchange for value; to pass safely over, round, through, etc (eg a hazard); to cope with successfully (*inf*). [L *negōtiārī, -ātus*, from *negōtium* business, from *neg-* not, and *ōtium* leisure]

■ **negotiabil'ity** *n*. **nego'tiable** *adj* that can be negotiated; not fixed; (of bonds, etc) legally transferable. **nego'tiant** /-shi-ɔnt/ *n* a person, organization or state, etc involved in negotiations. **negotia'tion** *n*. **nego'tiator** *n*. **nego'tiatress** /-shyɔ-/ or **negotiatrix** /ni-gō'shyɔ-triks or ni-gō-shi-ā'triks/ *n* (*archaic*) a female negotiator.

Negress see under **Negro**.

Negrillo /ni-gril'ō/ *n* (pl **Negrill'os**) a member of any of a number of short-statured black African peoples. [Sp, dimin of *negro* black]

Negrito /ni-grē'tō/ *n* (pl **Negri'tos**) a member of any of a number of short-statured black peoples of SE Asia. [Sp, dimin of *negro* black]

negritude see under **Negro**.

Negro /nē'grō/ *n* (pl **Ne'groes**) (now *usu* considered to be *offensive* or *derog*; formerly also without *cap*) a member of any of the dark-skinned peoples of Africa or a person racially descended from one of them. ◆ *adj* of or relating to black people; black or darkly coloured (*zool*). [Sp *negro*, from L *niger, nigra, nigrum* black]

■ **Ne'gress** *n* (*usu* considered to be *offensive* or *derog*; formerly also without *cap*) a black woman or girl. **nē'gritude** *n* (translation of Fr *négritude*, apparently invented by the poet Aimé Césaire) the essential quality shared by all black people (also **nigritude**); Black identity, *esp* when viewed in a positive or empowering way. **ne'groid** *adj* (also with *cap*) typical of black or African peoples; having physical characteristics associated with black people. ◆ *n* a negroid person. **negroid'al** *adj*. **ne'grōism** *n* any peculiarity of speech among black people, *esp* in the Southern USA; devotion to the causes of the Black civil rights movement (*old*; sometimes *derog*). **ne'grophil** or **ne'grophile** *n* a person who has sympathy for the plight of black people, *esp* one who actively supports the movement for greater political and social freedoms for oppressed blacks. **negrophilism** /*ni-grof'*/ *n*. **negroph'ilist** *n* and *adj*. **ne'grophobe** *n* someone who dislikes black people. **negropho'bia** *n*.
◻ **ne'gro-corn** *n* (*W Indies*) durra. **ne'grohead** *n* tobacco soaked in molasses and pressed into cakes, so called from its blackness; an inferior rubber. **Negro pepper** see under **pepper**. **Negro spiritual** *n* an African-American religious song.

negroni /*nā-grō'nē*/ *n* a cocktail made with gin, vermouth, and Campari. [Poss from Camillo *Negroni*, Italian count credited with its invention in the early 20c]

Negus /*nē'gəs*/ (*hist*) *n* the king of Ethiopia. [Amharic]

negus /*nē'gəs*/ *n* a drink of port or sherry mixed with hot water, sweetened and spiced. [Said to be from Colonel *Negus* (died 1732), its first maker]

Neh. (*Bible*) *abbrev*: (the Book of) Nehemiah.

neif see **nieve**.

neigh /*nā*/ *vi* to utter the cry of a horse, or a similar cry. ◆ *vt* to utter or say with such a cry. ◆ *n* the cry of a horse. [OE *hnǣgan*]

neighbour or (*N Am*) **neighbor** /*nā'bər*/ *n* a person who lives near or next door to another; a person or thing that is near another; a fellow human being; one of a pair (*Scot*). ◆ *adj* (*archaic* and *US*) neighbouring. ◆ *vt* and *vi* to live or be near. ◆ *vi* to associate with one's neighbours. [OE *nēahgebūr*, from *nēah* near, and *gebūr* or *būr* a farmer]
■ **neigh'bourhood** or (*N Am*) **neigh'borhood** *n* the state of being neighbours, kindly feeling; a set of neighbours; a district, locality, *esp* with reference to its inhabitants as a community; a district; a region lying near; a near position; nearness; all the points that surround a given point in a specified degree of closeness (*maths*). **neigh'bouring** or (*N Am*) **neigh'boring** *adj* being near; adjoining. **neigh'bourless** or (*N Am*) **neigh'borless** *adj*. **neigh'bourliness** or (*N Am*) **neigh'borliness** *n*. **neigh'bourly** or (*N Am*) **neigh'borly** *adj* like or befitting a neighbour; friendly; social. ◆ *adv* in a neighbourly manner. ◻ **neighbourhood law centre** see **law centre** under **law[1]**. **neighbourhood watch** *n* a scheme under which local householders agree to keep a general watch on each other's property and the local streets, to try to prevent crime. **neigh'bour-stained** *adj* (*Shakesp*) stained with neighbours' blood.
■ **good neighbours** the fairies. **in the neighbourhood of** approximately, somewhere about.

neist /*nēst*/ a dialectal form of **nighest** (*superl* of **nigh**; *obs*) or **next**.

neither /*nī'*/ or /*nē'dhər*/ *adj* and pronoun not either, not one nor the other (of two); not any one (of more than two) (*archaic*; current usage of this sense is disputed). ◆ *conj* not either; and not; nor yet. ◆ *adv* not at all; in no case; either (a disputed usage). [OE *nāther*, *nāwther*, abbrev of *nāhwæther*, from *nā* never, and *hwæther* whether; the vowel assimilated to **either**]

neive see **nieve**.

nek /*nek*/ (*S Afr*) *n* a col. [Du, neck]

nekton /*nek'ton*/ *n* the assemblage of actively swimming organisms in a sea, lake, etc. [Gr *nēkton* (neuter), swimming]

NEL *abbrev*: National Engineering Laboratory.

nelis or **nelies** /*nel'is*/ *n* (*pl* **nel'is** or **nel'ies**) a variety of pear that does not ripen until winter. [Fr *nélis*]

nellie[1] or **nelly** /*nel'i*/ (*inf*) *n* life (in the slang phrase *not on your nellie* or *nelly*). [Said to be from *Nellie Duff*, rhyming with *puff*]

nellie[2] or **nelly** /*nel'i*/ (*sl*) *n* a weak or foolish person; an effeminate man (*offens*); (**nelly**) a large petrel. [From the woman's name]

nelson /*nel'sən*/ *n* a wrestling hold in which the arms are passed under both the opponent's arms from behind, and the hands joined so that pressure can be exerted with the palms on the back of his or her neck (also **full nelson**). [From the proper name]
■ **half nelson** this hold applied on one side only, ie with one arm under one of the opponent's arms; a disabling restraint (*fig*).

nelumbium /*ni-lum'bi-əm*/ or **nelumbo** /*-bō*/ *n* (*pl* **nelum'biums** or **nelum'bos**) a plant of the *Nelumbo* genus of water lilies including the Egyptian bean of Pythagoras, and the sacred lotus. [Prob Tamil]

Nemathelminthes /*nem-ə-thel-min'thēz*/ *n pl* according to some, a phylum of worms with unsegmented, cylindrical bodies, including nematodes, Nematomorpha and Acanthocephala (divided by others into separate phyla). [Gr *nēma*, *-atos* a thread, and *helmins*, *-minthos* worm]
■ **nemathel'minth** *n sing*. **nemathelmin'thic** *adj*.

nematic /*nə-mat'ik*/ (*chem*) *adj* being in or having a mesomorphic phase in which the atoms or molecules are arranged in parallel lines, but not in the parallel planes typical of a smectic substance. [Gr *nēma*, genitive *nēmatos* a thread]

nematoblast same as **cnidoblast** (see under **cnida**).

nematocyst /*nem'ə-tō-sist* or *nə-mat'ō-*/ *n* a stinging organ in jellyfishes, etc, a sac from which a stinging thread can be everted. [Gr *nēma*, *-atos* a thread, and *kystis* a bladder]
■ **nematocys'tic** *adj*.

nematode /*nem'ə-tōd*/ *n* a parasitic worm with an unsegmented, cylindrical body, a roundworm or threadworm (also *adj*). [Gr *nēma*, *-atos* thread, and *eidos* form]
■ **nematocide** /*-at'ə-sīd*/ *n* a substance that kills nematodes. **Nematōd'a** or **Nematoid'ea** *n pl* the class of nematodes. **nematodirī'asis** *n* (Gr *-īasis*, as in *psoriasis*, etc) a disease of young lambs caused by nematodirus larvae. **nematodī'rus** *n* (Gr *deirē* neck) a worm of the *Nematodīrus* genus of parasitic nematode worms found in the intestines of mammals. **nem'atoid** *adj*. **Nematoidea** see **Nematoda** above. **nematol'ogist** *n*. **nematol'ogy** *n* the study of nematodes.

Nematomorpha /*nem-ə-tō-mör'fə*/ *n pl* the hairworms. [Gr *nēma*, *-atos* thread, and *morphē* form]

nematophore /*nem'ə-tō-för* or *-för*/ *n* a mouthless type of hydrozoan polyp that engulfs food by pseudopodia. [Gr *nēma*, *-atos* thread, and *phoros* carrying]

Nembutal[®] /*nem'bū-təl*/ *n* a proprietary name for sodium pentobarbitone, used as a sedative, hypnotic and antispasmodic.

nem. con. *abbrev*: *nemine contradicente* (qv).

nem. diss. *abbrev*: *nemine dissentiente* (qv).

Nemean /*ne-mē'ən, nem'i-ən* or *nē'mi-ən*/ *adj* of *Nemea* (Gr *Nemeā*), the valley of Argolis, famous for its games held in the second and fourth years of each Olympiad, and for the lion killed by Hercules.

Nemertinea /*ne-mər-tin'i-ə*/ *n pl* a phylum of wormlike animals, mostly marine, ciliated, often brightly coloured with a protrusile proboscis, the ribbonworm (also **Nemer'tea**). [Gr *Nēmertēs*, one of the nereids]
■ **nemer'tean, nemer'tine** and **nemer'tian** *n* and *adj*.

nemesia /*ne-mē'zh(y)ə, -sh(y)ə* or *-si-ə*/ *n* a plant of the S African genus *Nemesia* of the figwort family, including some brightly-coloured garden flowers. [Gr *nemesion* a kind of catchfly]

Nemesis /*nem'i-sis*/ (Gr *myth*) *n* (*pl* **Nem'eses** /*-sēz*/) the Greek goddess of retribution; (without *cap*) retributive justice; something that cannot be achieved; a rival or opponent who cannot be beaten. [Gr *nemesis* retribution, from *nemein* to deal out or dispense]

nemine contradicente /*nem'ə-nē kon-trə-di-sen'tē* or *nā'mi-ne kon-trä-dē-ken'te*/ (L) without opposition; no one speaking in opposition (*abbrev* **nem. con.**).

nemine dissentiente /*nem'ə-nē di-sen-shi-en'tē* or *nā'mi-ne di-sen-ti-en'te*/ (L) no one dissenting (*abbrev* **nem. diss.**).

nemn /*nem*/ (*obs*) *vt* to name. [OE *nemnan*]

nemophila /*ne-mof'i-lə*/ *n* a plant of the N American genus *Nemophila* (family Hydrophyllaceae), favourite garden annuals, *esp* one with blue, white-centred flowers. [Gr *nemos* a glade, wooded pasture, and *phileein* to love]

nemoral /*nem'ə-rəl*/ *adj* of a wood or grove. [L *nemus*, *-oris* a grove]
■ **nem'orous** *adj*.

nempt /*nemt*/ (*Spenser*) *adj* named, called. [Pap of **nemn**]

NEMS /*nemz*/ *abbrev*: nanoelectromechanical systems.

nene /*nā'nā*/ *n* the Hawaiian goose, a rare bird of Hawaii, having grey-brown plumage, a black face and partially webbed feet. [Hawaiian]

nennigai see **nannygai**.

nenuphar /*nen'ū-fär*/ *n* a water lily, *esp* the common white or yellow; (with *cap*) same as **Nuphar**. [LL *nenuphar*, from Ar and Pers *nīnūfar*, *nīlūfar*, from Sans *nīlotpala*, from *nīla* blue, and *utpala* lotus]

NEO *abbrev*: near-earth object.

Neo /*nē'ō* or *nā'ō*/ *n* an artificial language launched by an Italian, Arturo Alfandari, in 1961.

neo- /*nē-ō-, nē-ə-* or *nē-o-*/ *combining form* denoting new, young, revived in a new form. [Gr *neos* new]
■ **Neo-Cath'olic** *adj* and *n* of, or a member of the school of, liberal Catholicism that followed Lamennais, Lacordaire and Montalembert

about 1830; Anglo-Catholic with extreme leanings towards Rome. **Neo-Chris'tian** *adj* and *n* of, or a believer in, a liberalized and rationalized Christianity. **Neo-Christian'ity** *n*. **neoclass'ic** or **neoclass'ical** *adj* belonging to a revival of the classical style, *esp* in art and architecture, *usu* in reference to one such major revival in the late 18c and early 19c. **neoclass'icism** /-*i*-sizm/ *n*. **neoclass'icist** *n*. **neocolōn'ialism** *n* the quasi-colonialism practised by strong powers in dominating weaker, though politically independent, states by means of economic pressure. **neocolō'nialist** *n* and *adj*. **neoconser'vatism** *n* a policy of reacting to liberalism by adopting more traditional attitudes. **neoconser'vative** *n* and *adj*. **neocor'tex** *n* the upper and most recently evolved part of the cerebral cortex, dealing with higher brain functions such as sight. **neocor'tical** *adj*. **Neo-Darwin'ian** or **Neo-Dar'winist** *n* and *adj*. **Neo-Dar'winism** *n* the modern version of Darwin's theory of evolution by natural selection, incorporating the discoveries of Mendelian and population genetics. **Neofascism** /-*fash*'izm/ *n* a movement attempting to reinstate the policies of fascism. **Neofasc'ist** *n* and *adj*. **neogenesis** /-*jen*'*ə*-sis/ *n* (*biol*, etc) regeneration of tissue. **neogenetic** /-*et*'*ik*/ *adj*. **Neo-Goth'ic** *n* and *adj* revived Gothic of the 19c. **neogrammā'rian** *n* a philologist of the 19c German school that introduced scientific exactitude into the study of sound change. **Neohell'enism** *n* the modern Hellenism inspired by the ancient; the devotion to ancient Greek ideals in literature and art, *esp* in the Italian Renaissance. **Neo-Impress'ionism** *n* a style of painting which aimed at producing greater luminosity of colour by applying pure unmixed colours in small dots. **Neo-Impress'ionist** *n* and *adj*. **Neo-Kant'ian** *n* and *adj*. **Neo-Kant'ianism** *n* the philosophy of Kant as taught by his successors. **Neo-Lamarck'ian** *n* and *adj*. **Neo-Lamarck'ism** *n* a modern adaptation of Lamarckism. **Neo-Lat'in** *n* and *adj* Romance, ie Italian, Rhaeto-Romanic, French, Provençal, Spanish, Portuguese and Romanian. **neolib'eral** *adj* and *n*. **neolib'eralism** *n* a political system that favours free-market economics within a liberal democracy. **Neo-Malthus'ianism** *n* the doctrine of the necessity for birth control to control population. **Neo-Melanē'sian** *n* a creole language based on English, developed in Melanesia. **neo-Naz'i** *n* a member or supporter of any of a number of modern movements espousing the principles of National Socialism or the like. **neo-Naz'ism** *n*. **neopā'gan** *n* and *adj*. **neopā'ganism** *n* a revival of paganism, or its spirit. **neopā'ganize** or **-ise** *vt* and *vi*. **Neo-Plas'ticism** (or **neoplasticism**) *n* a style of abstract painting in which geometrical patterns are formed of patches of flat colour enclosed by intersecting vertical and horizontal lines. **Neoplatonic** /-*plə*-*ton*'*ik*/ *adj*. **Neoplā'tonism** *n* a combination of Platonism with Oriental elements, developed by Plotinus, Porphyry, Proclus, etc. **Neoplā'tonist** *n* and *adj*. **Neopythagorē'an** *n* and *adj*. **Neopythagorē'anism** *n* a revived Pythagoreanism of Alexandria beginning in 1c BC. **neorē'alism** *n* a modern form of realism in the arts and literature; *specif*, a cinematic movement, or a style of cinematography, originating in post-war Italy, characterized by socio-political content, and the use of mise en scène (qv) and often non-professional actors to achieve a starkly realistic depiction of lower-class life. **neorē'alist** *n* and *adj*. **neorealist'ic** *adj*. **neotox'in** *n* any harmful substance, eg in the environment, causing illness or allergy. **Neotrop'ical** *adj* (*biol*) belonging to the tropics of the New World, tropical America. **neovī'talism** *n* the theory or belief that complete causal explanation of vital phenomena cannot be reached without invoking some extra-material concept. **neovī'talist** *n* and *adj*.

neoblast /*nē*'*ə*-blast/ (*zool*) *n* (in many of the lower animals, such as Annelida (worms)) any of the large amoeboid cells that play an important part in regeneration. [**neo-** and Gr *blastos* a shoot or bud]

Neo-Catholic etc see under **neo-**.

Neoceratodus /*nē*-*ə*-*se*-*rə*-*tō*'*dəs*/ *n* the name of the genus of Australian lungfish to which the barramunda belongs, now used in preference to *Ceratodus*. [**neo-** and **ceratodus**]

Neo-Christian...to...**neocolonialist** see under **neo-**.

Neocomian /*nē*-*ə*-*kō*'*mi*-*ən*/ (*geol*) *n* and *adj* Lower Cretaceous. [L *Neocōmium* Neuchâtel, from Gr *kōme* a village]

neocon /*nē*'*ō*-kon/ (*US inf*) *n* a neoconservative (also *adj*).

neoconservatism...to...**Neo-Darwinism** see under **neo-**.

neodymium /*nē*-*ə*-*dim*'*i*-*əm*/ *n* a silvery-grey toxic metallic element (symbol **Nd**; atomic no 60) isolated, along with praseodymium, from the once-supposed element didymium. [**neo-** and **didymium**]

Neofascism, etc see under **neo-**.

Neogaea /*nē*-*ə*-*jē*'*ə*/ (*biol*) *n* the Neotropical region. [**neo-** and Gr *gaia* the earth]
■ **Neogae'an** *adj*.

Neogene /*nē*'*ə*-jēn/ (*geol*) *adj* of or belonging to the later Tertiary period, the Miocene and Pliocene epochs (also *n*). [Gr *neogenēs* new-born]

neogenesis...to...**neoliberalism** see under **neo-**.

Neolithic /*nē*-*ə*-*lith*'*ik*/ *adj* of or relating to the later, more advanced, Stone Age. ◆ *n* the Neolithic period. [**neo-** and Gr *lithos* a stone]
■ **ne'olith** *n* a Neolithic artefact.

neologism /*nē*-*ol*'*ə*-ji-zm/ or **neology** /*nē*-*ol*'*ə*-ji/ *n* a new word, phrase or doctrine; a new use of an established word; the practice of coining or introducing neologisms; (*usu* **neology**) new doctrines, *esp* German rationalism (*theol*). [**neo-** and Gr *logos* a word]
■ **neolō'gian** *n*. **neologic** or **neological** /-*loj*'/ *adj*. **neolog'ically** *adv*. **neol'ogist** *n*. **neologis'tic** or **neologis'tical** *adj*. **neol'ogize** or **-ise** *vi* to introduce new words, coin neologisms.

Neo-Malthusianism, **Neo-Melanesian** see under **neo-**.

neomycin /*nē*-*ə*-*mī*'sin/ (*pharm*) *n* an antibiotic used to treat skin and eye infections. [**neo-**, Gr *mykēs* fungus, and **-in**]

neon /*nē*'on/ *n* a gaseous element (symbol **Ne**; atomic no 10) found in the atmosphere by Sir William Ramsay (1852–1916). [Neuter of Gr *neos* new]
❏ **neon lamp** or **light** *n* an electric discharge lamp containing neon, giving a red glow, used eg for advertising signs; (loosely) one of a variety of tubular fluorescent lamps giving light of various colours. **neon lighting** *n*. **neon tetra** *n* a small iridescently coloured Amazonian freshwater fish.

neonatal /*nē*-*ə*-*nā*'*t*(*ə*)*l*/ *adj* relating to the newly born. [New L *neonātus*, from Gr *neos* new, and L *nātus* born]
■ **ne'onate** *n* a newly born child. ◆ *adj* newly born. **neonatol'ogy** *n* the care and treatment of the newly born.

neo-Nazi, etc see under **neo-**.

neonomianism /*nē*-*ə*-*nō*'*mi*-*ə*-ni-zm/ (*theol*) *n* the doctrine that the gospel is a new law and that faith has abrogated the old moral obedience. [**neo-** and Gr *nomos* law]
■ **neonō'mian** *n*.

neopaganism, etc see under **neo-**.

neophile /*nē*'*ə*-fīl/ *n* someone who loves novelty and new things; someone who is obsessive about keeping up to date with fashion, trends, etc. [**neo-** and **-phile**]
■ **neophil'ia** *n*. **neophil'iac** *n*.

neophobia /*nē*-*ə*-*fō*'*bi*-*ə*/ *n* a dread or hatred of novelty. [Gr *neos* new, and *phobos* fear]
■ **nē'ophobe** *n*. **neophō'bic** *adj*.

neophyte /*nē*'*ə*-fīt/ *n* a new convert; a person newly baptized; a newly ordained priest; a novice in a religious order; a tiro or beginner. [Gr *neophytos* newly planted, from *neos* new, and *phyein* to produce]
■ **neophytic** /-*fit*'*ik*/ *adj*.

neopilina /*nē*-*ō*-*pi*-*lī*'*nə*/ *n* a mollusc of the genus *Neopilina* of the class Monoplacophora (qv). [**neo-** and *Pilina*, a Palaeolithic genus of similar appearance]

neoplasia /*nē*-*ə*-*plā*'*zi*-*ə*/ (*pathol*) *n* the formation or presence of a morbid growth of tissue. [**neo-** and Gr *plāsis* moulding]

neoplasm /*nē*'*ə*-pla-zm/ (*pathol*) *n* a morbid new growth of tissue. [**neo-** and Gr *plasma* something moulded]
■ **neoplas'tic** *adj*.

Neo-Plasticism, **Neoplatonism**, etc see under **neo-**.

Neoprene® /*nē*'*ə*-prēn/ *n* an oil-resisting and heat-resisting synthetic rubber made by polymerizing chloroprene. [**neo-** and **chloroprene**]

Neopythagoreanism, **neorealism**, etc see under **neo-**.

neostigmine /*nē*-*ə*-*stig*'mēn/ *n* a synthetic compound used as a drug in treating myasthenia gravis. [**neo-** and *physiostigmine*]

neoteny /*nē*-*ot*'*ə*-ni/ or **neoteinia** /*nē*-*ō*-*tī*'*ni*-*ə*/ (*biol*) *n* prolonged retention of larval or immature characteristics or features in the adult form. [**neo-** and Gr *teinein* to stretch]
■ **neotenic** /*nē*-*ō*-*ten*'*ik*/ *adj*. **neot'enous** *adj*.

neoteric /*nē*-*ō*-*ter*'*ik*/ or **neoterical** /-*i*-*kəl*/ *adj* of recent origin, modern. ◆ *n* a modern writer or philosopher. [Gr *neōterikos*, from *neōteros*, compar of *neos* new]
■ **neoter'ically** *adv*. **neot'erism** *n* the introduction of new things, *esp* new words. **neot'erist** *n*. **neoterize** or **-ise** /*nē*-*ot*'*ə*-*rīz*/ *vi*.

Neotropical, **neovitalism**, etc see under **neo-**.

Neozoic /*nē*-*ō*-*zō*'*ik*/ (*geol*) *adj* of or belonging to the period between the Mesozoic and the present age (also *n*). [**neo-** and Gr *zōikos* of animals]

NEP *abbrev* : Nepal (IVR).

nep /nep/ or **nip** /nip/ (now *dialect*) *n* catmint. [L *nepeta*]

Nepalese /*nep*-*ə*-*lēz*'/ *adj* of or relating to the Kingdom of *Nepal* in central Asia, or its people. ◆ *n* (*pl* **Nepalese'**) a native or citizen of Nepal.

Nepali /*nə*- or *ni*-*pö*'*lē* or -*pä*'/ *n* (*pl* **Nepal'i** or **Nepal'is**) the official language of Nepal, belonging to the Indic branch of Indo-European languages; a native or citizen of Nepal. ◆ *adj* of Nepal, its people or its language.

nepenthe /ni-pen'thē/ *n* a drink or drug causing sorrow to be forgotten (*poetic*); the plant yielding it. [Gr *nepenthēs, -es*, from pfx *nē-* not, and *penthos* grief]
■ **nepen'thean** *adj*. **Nepen'thes** /-thēz/ *n* nepenthe; the pitcher plant genus, constituting a family **Nepenthā'ceae** related to the family Sarraceniaceae and the sundews.

neper /nē' or nā'pər/ *n* a unit for expressing the ratio of two currents, two voltages, etc, the number of nepers being equal to the natural logarithm of the ratio (cf **decibel** and **bel**[1]). [John *Napier*; see **Napierian**]

nepeta /nep'ə-tə/ *n* catmint. [L]

nepheline /nef'ə-lēn/ *n* a rock-forming mineral, silicate of sodium, potassium and aluminium, colourless, *usu* crystallizing in hexagonal prisms (also **neph'elite**). [Gr *nephelē* a cloud (from the clouding effect of acid on it)]
■ **neph'elinite** *n* a basalt-like rock compound of nepheline and pyroxene, with no feldspar or olivine. ❑ **neph'eline-bas'alt** *n* a basalt with nepheline instead of (or in addition to) feldspar.

nephelometer /ne-fə-lom'i-tər/ *n* an instrument for measuring cloudiness, *esp* in liquids. [Gr *nephelē* cloud, and *metron* measure]
■ **nephelomet'ric** *adj*. **nephelom'etry** *n*.

nephew /nef'ū or nev'ū/ *n* the son of one's brother or sister; extended to the same relation by marriage; a grandson or descendant (*obs*); a pope's or priest's son (*euphem*). [(O)Fr *neveu*, from L *nepōs, nepōtis* grandson; cf OE *nefa*, Ger *Neffe* nephew]

nepho- /nef-o- or -ō-/ *combining form* denoting cloud. [Gr *nephos* cloud]
■ **neph'ogram** *n* a photograph of a cloud. **neph'ograph** /-gräf/ *n* an instrument for photographing clouds in order to determine their position. **nephologic** /-ə-loj'/ or **nepholog'ical** *adj*. **nephol'ogist** *n*. **nephology** /nef-ol'ə-ji/ *n* the study of clouds in meteorology. **neph'oscope** *n* an apparatus which determines the direction and velocity of movement of clouds.

nephro- or **nephr-** /nef-r(o)- or -r(ō)-/ *combining form* denoting kidney. [Gr *nephros* a kidney]
■ **nephralgia** /nef-ral'ji-ə/ or **nephral'gy** *n* pain in the kidneys. **nephrec'tomy** *n* surgical removal of a kidney. **neph'ric** *adj*. **nephrid'ium** *n* (in invertebrates and lower chordates) an organ serving the function of a kidney. **neph'rite** *n* the mineral jade, in the narrower sense, an old charm against kidney disease. **nephrit'ic** *n* (*obs*) a medicine for the kidneys. ◆ *adj* (also **nephrit'ical**) relating to the kidneys, or nephritis, or jade. **nephrī'tis** *n* inflammation of the kidneys. **neph'roid** *adj* kidney-shaped. **nephrolepis** *n* see separate entry. **nephrolog'ical** /-loj'/ *adj*. **nephrol'ogist** *n*. **nephrol'ogy** *n* the science concerned with the structure, functions and diseases of the kidneys. **neph'ron** *n* one of over a million functional units in the vertebrate kidney, responsible for reabsorption of water and nutrients and for the filtration of waste products from the blood. **nephrop'athy** *n* (Gr *pathos* suffering) disease of the kidneys. **neph'ropexy** *n* (Gr *pēxis* fixing) fixation of a floating kidney. **nephroptō'sis** *n* (Gr *ptōsis* fall) floating kidney. **nephrō'sis** *n* a disease of the kidney characterized by non-inflammatory degeneration of the tubules. **nephrot'ic** *adj*. **nephrot'omy** *n* incision into the kidney.

nephrolepis /nef-rə-lē'pis/ *n* any fern of the genus *Nephrolepis* with pinnate fronds and kidney-shaped indusia, some being grown as house plants. [Gr *nephros* a kidney, and *lepis* scale]

Nephrops /nef'rops/ *n* a genus of crustaceans, the Norway lobster. [New L, from Gr *nephros* kidney, and *ōps* eye]

nepionic /nep-i- or nē-pi-on'ik/ (*biol*) *adj* relating to the embryonic period in the life history of an individual. [Gr *nēpios* infant]

nepit see **nit**[4].

ne plus ultra /nē plus ul'trə or nā plŭs ŭl'trā/ (L) nothing further; the uttermost point or extreme perfection of anything.

nepotism /nep'ə-ti-zm/ *n* undue favouritism to one's relations and close friends, *orig* by a pope. [L *nepōs, nepōtis* a grandson]
■ **nepotic** /ni-pot'ik/ or **nepotis'tic** *adj*. **nep'otist** *n*.

Neptune /nep'tūn/ *n* the Roman sea god, identified with the Greek Poseidon; a remote planet of the solar system, discovered in 1846. [L *Neptūnus*]
■ **Neptū'nian** *adj* relating to Neptune or to the sea; formed by water (*geol*). ◆ *n* an imagined inhabitant of Neptune; a Neptunist. **Nep'tūnist** *n* a believer in the origin of rocks generally as chemical precipitates from the sea, *opp* to *Plutonist* or *Vulcanist*. **neptū'nium** *n* an artificially produced radioactive transuranic metallic element (symbol Np; atomic no 93) named as next after uranium, as Neptune is next after Uranus.

❑ **neptunium series** *n* a series formed by the decay of artificial radio-elements, the first member being plutonium-241 and the last bismuth-209, neptunium-237 being the longest-lived.

NERC /nûrk/ *abbrev* : Natural Environment Research Council.

nerd or **nurd** /nûrd/ (*sl*) *n* a clumsy, foolish, socially inept, feeble, unathletic, irritating or unprepossessing person, although often (eg in computers) knowledgeable. [Perh after a character invented by Dr Seuss (1904–91), US children's author]
■ **ner'dish** or **ner'dy** *adj*.

nereid /nē'rē-id/ *n* (*pl* **ner'eids** or (in sea-nymph sense) **nereides** /nē'rē-ə-dēz/) a sea nymph, daughter of the sea god *Nereus* (Gr *myth*); a marine polychaete worm (genus *Nereis*, or related genus) superficially like a long myriapod; (with *cap*) the smaller of the two satellites of the planet Neptune, the other being Triton. [Gr *nērēïs* or *nēreis*, from *Nēreus*]

nerine /ni-rī'nē/ *n* any plant of the S African genus *Nerine*, related to the amaryllis, with scarlet or rose-coloured flowers, *incl* the Guernsey lily. [L *nērinē* a nereid]

Nerita /ni-rī'tə/ *n* a round-shelled genus of gastropods of warm seas. [Gr *nēreitēs, nērītēs* a sea snail (of various kinds)]
■ **nerite** /nē'rīt/ *n* a sea snail of the genus *Nerita* or its family **Nerit'idae**. **neritic** /nē-rit'ik/ *adj* belonging to the shallow waters near land. **Neritina** /ner-it-ī'nə/ *n* a brackish and freshwater genus related to *Nerita*.

Nerium /nē'ri-əm/ *n* the oleander genus. [Latinized from Gr *nērion*]

nerk /nûrk/ (*sl*) *n* an irritating fool or idiot. [Poss **nerd** and **berk**]

nerka /nûr'kə/ *n* the sockeye salmon. [Origin unknown]

Nernst /nārnst/ *adj* invented by or due to the German chemist and physicist Walter *Nernst* (1864–1941), applied *esp* to an electric lamp with a filament or rod of rare-earth oxides whose conductivity is greatly increased by heating.

nero-antico /nā-rō-an-tē'kō/ *n* a deep-black marble found in Roman ruins. [Ital, ancient black]

neroli /ner'ə-lē/ *n* an oil distilled from orange flowers (also **neroli oil**). [Said to be named from its discoverer, an Italian princess]

Neronian /nē-rō'ni-ən/ *adj* relating to *Nero*, Roman emperor from 54 to 68AD; excessively cruel and tyrannical. [L *Nerō, -ōnis*]
■ **Neronic** /-ron'ik/ *adj*.

nerve /nûrv/ *n* a cord consisting of bundles of fibres that conveys impulses of sensation or movement between the brain or other centre and some part of the body (*anat*); self-possession; cool courage; impudent assurance, audacity (*inf*); (in *pl*) nervousness, anxiety; (in *pl*) a disordered nervous system, *esp* when unable to deal successfully with emotional stress or tension; a sore or sensitive spot or point; a sinew (now chiefly *fig*); a bowstring (*poetic*); strength; a leaf-vein or rib (*bot*); a nervure in an insect's wing (*zool*); a vault rib (*archit*). ◆ *vt* to give strength, resolution, or courage to (oneself, etc). [L *nervus* sinew; cf Gr *neuron*]
■ **nerv'al** *adj* of the nerves. **ner'vate** *adj* (of a leaf) having veins; nerved. **nervā'tion** or **nerv'ature** *n* disposition of nerves, *esp* in leaves; venation. **nerved** *adj* supplied with nerves. **nerve'less** *adj* without nerves or nervures; without strength; inert; slack, flabby; unnerved; without nervousness, calm. **nerve'lessly** *adv*. **nerve'lessness** *n*. **nerve'let** *n* a little nerve; a tendril. **nerv'er** *n* someone who or something which nerves. **nerv'ily** *adv*. **nerv'ine** /-ēn or -īn/ *adj* acting on the nerves; quieting nervous excitement. ◆ *n* a substance, esp a herbal remedy, that soothes nervous excitement. **nerv'iness** *n*. **nerv'ous** *adj* relating to the nerves; having the nerves easily excited or weak, agitated and apprehensive (often with *of*); caused by such a temperament or nervousness (such as *nervous energy*); in a jumpy state; shy; timid; having nerve; sinewy; strong, vigorous, showing strength and vigour. **nerv'ously** *adv*. **nerv'ousness** *n*. **nerv'ūlar** *adj*. **nerv'ūle** *n* a small branch of a nervure. **nervūrā'tion** *n*. **nerv'ure** *n* a leaf-vein; a chitinous strut or rib supporting and strengthening an insect's wing (*zool*); a rib of a groined vault (*archit*). **nerv'y** *adj* nervous; jumpily excited or excitable; calling for nerve or courage; cool; impudent or audacious (*N Am inf*).
❑ **nerve agent** *n* a nerve gas or similar substance. **nerve block** *n* local anaesthesia produced by injecting an anaesthetic into the nerve or nerves supplying that part of the body. **nerve cell** *n* any cell forming part of the nervous system; a neuron. **nerve centre** *n* an aggregation of nerve cells from which nerves branch out; (in an organization) the centre from which control is exercised (*fig*). **nerve cord** *n* a cord of nerve tissue that runs the length of an animal's body. **nerve end** or **ending** *n* the free end of a nerve, generally with accessory parts forming an end organ. **nerve fibre** *n* an axon. **nerve gas** *n* any of a number of gases, prepared for use in war, having a deadly effect on the nervous system, *esp* on nerves controlling respiration. **nerve** or **nervous impulse** *n* the electrical impulse passing along a nerve fibre when it has been stimulated. **nerve net** *n* a network of neurons in

invertebrates forming a simple nervous system. **nerve¹-racking** or **nerve¹-wracking** adj distressfully straining the nerves. **nervous breakdown** n a loose term indicating nervous debility following prolonged mental or physical fatigue; a euphemism for any mental illness. **nervous impulse** see **nerve impulse** above. **nervous system** n the brain, spinal cord and nerves collectively. **nervous wreck** n (inf) a very timid, anxious and jumpy person, esp when unable to deal successfully with stress or tension.

■ **bundle of nerves** (inf) a very timid, anxious person. **get on one's nerves** (inf) to become oppressively irritating. **live on one's nerves** to be (constantly) in a tense or nervous state; to be of an excitable temperament. **lose one's nerve** to lose confidence in one's ability; to become suddenly afraid. **war of nerves** see under **war¹**.

NES abbrev: National Eczema Society.

nescience /nesh'(i-)əns, nes'i-əns or -yəns/ (formal) n lack of knowledge; ignorance. [L nescientia, from nescīre to be ignorant, from ne- not, and scīre to know]

■ **nesc'ient** adj.

nesh /nesh/ (dialect) adj soft, crumbly; tender; delicate in one's health; susceptible to cold; cowardly, afraid; lacking energy. [OE hnesce]

■ **nesh'ness** n.

Nesiot /nē'si-ot/ (anthrop) n an Indonesian. [Gr nēsiōtēs an islander, from nēsos an island]

Neskhi, **Neski** /nes'ki/ or **Naskhi** /nas'ki/ n Arabic cursive handwriting. [Ar naskhī]

ness /nes/ n a headland. [OE næs, næss]

-ness /-nəs/ sfx forming nouns from adjectives and participles denoting state or condition, or an example of this (such as happiness, barrenness, kindness). [OE -nes]

nest /nest/ n a structure prepared by animals for egg-laying, brooding and nursing, or as a shelter; a place of retreat, resort, residence, or lodgement; a den; a comfortable residence; an edible receptacle in which food is served, such as a meringue nest; a group of machine-guns in a position fortified or screened by sandbags or anything similar; a place where anything (esp anything undesirable) teems, prevails or is fostered; the occupants of a nest, eg a brood, a swarm, a gang, etc; a set of things (eg boxes or tables) fitting one within another; a set of buildings, eg factories, divided into blocks and units; an accumulation; a tangled mass. ♦ vi to build or occupy a nest; to go bird-nesting. ♦ vt and vi to lodge or settle; to fit or place together or within another. ♦ vt to group (words derived from the same root) together under one headword in a dictionary; to embed (a subroutine or block of data) within a larger one (comput). [OE nest; Ger Nest, L nīdus]

■ **nest'er** n someone who builds a farm or homestead on land used for grazing cattle (US hist; derog); a creature that builds a nest. **nest'ful** n. **nest'ing** n. **nest'like** adj.

❑ **nest** or **nesting box** n a box set up for birds to nest in. **nest egg** n an egg, real or sham, left or put in a nest to encourage laying; something laid up as the beginning of an accumulation; money saved. **nest'ing-place** n.

■ **feather one's nest** see under **feather**.

nestle /nes'l/ vi to lie or press close or snug as in a nest; to settle comfortably or half hidden; to nest (archaic). ♦ vt to cherish, as a bird does her young; to push or thrust close; to provide a nesting-place for. [OE nestlian, from nest a nest]

■ **nestling** /nes'ling or nest'l/ n a young bird in the nest; any young person or animal.

Nestor /nes'tör or -tər/ n an old king of Pylos, a Greek hero at Troy remarkable for eloquence, wisdom and long life; an old counsellor; an old man; the kea parrot genus.

Nestorian /ne-stö'ri-ən or -stö'/ adj relating to Nestorius, patriarch of Constantinople (428–431), or to his teaching, that the divinity and humanity of Christ were not united in a single self-conscious personality. ♦ n a follower of Nestorius.

■ **Nestō'rianism** n.

net¹ /net/ n an open fabric, knotted into meshes; a piece, bag, screen or structure of such fabric used for catching fish, butterflies, etc, carrying parcels, stopping balls, dividing a tennis court, retaining hair or excluding pests; a network; machine-made lace of various kinds; a snare; a plan to trap or catch someone or something; a difficulty; a let (tennis); (usu in pl) a practice pitch surrounded by nets (cricket); a practice session on such a pitch (cricket); the shape of a three-dimensional figure when laid out flat (maths); (with cap and the) the Internet. ♦ adj of or like net or network; (often with cap) of or relating to the Internet. ♦ vt (nett'ing; nett'ed) to form into a net or network; to mark or cover with a net or network; to set with nets; to fish with nets; to form by knotting threads into meshes; to take with a net; to capture; (also vi) to send (eg a ball) into the net (sport). ♦ vi to form a net or network. [OE net, nett; Du net, Ger Netz]

■ **net'ful** n enough to fill a net. **nett'ed** adj made into a net; reticulated; caught in a net; covered with a net. **nett'ing** n the act or process of forming a net or network; a piece of network; any network of ropes or wire. **nett'y** adj like a net.

❑ **net'ball** n a team game in which the ball is thrown into a net hung from a pole. **net'book** n a portable computer smaller than a laptop. **Net'café** n an Internet café (qv). **net cord** n a string supporting a lawn tennis net; a shot in which the tennis-player strikes the net cord with the ball. **net'-fish** n any fish, like the herring, usu caught in nets (cf **trawl-fish** and **line-fish**). **net'-fish'ery** n a place for net-fishing; the business of net-fishing. **net'-fishing** n fishing with nets. **net game** or **net'-play** n (in tennis, etc) play near the net. **net'-minder** n (ice-hockey) a goal-tender. **net'-player** n (in tennis, etc) one who plays from near the net. **net practice** n cricket practice within nets. **net'roots** n pl (US inf) ordinary people who use the Internet as a medium for social and political campaigning. **Net'speak** n (inf) the style of language characteristically used on the Internet, disregarding many of the conventions of traditional grammar and making frequent use of abbreviations and acronyms. **nett'ing-need'le** n a kind of shuttle used in netting. **net'-veined** adj (eg of a leaf or an insect's wing) having veins that branch and meet in a network. **net'-winged** adj having net-veined wings. **net'work** n any structure in the form of a net; a system of lines, eg railway lines, resembling a net; a system of units, as eg buildings, agencies, groups of people, constituting a widely-spread organization and having a common purpose; a group of people with a common interest, esp of those who meet socially, who share information, swap contacts, etc; an arrangement of electrical components; a system of stations connected for broadcasting the same programme (radio and TV); a system of computer terminals and other peripheral devices that can pass information to one another. ♦ vt to broadcast on radio or TV stations throughout the country, as opposed to a single station covering only one region; to link (computer terminals and other peripheral devices) to enable them to operate interactively. ♦ vi to form business or professional contacts with people met on a social basis. **network computer** n a simple computer that relies on a server, accessed over a network to provide many of the functions normally found in a PC. **net'worker** n an employee who works from home on a personal computer linked to the computer network in his or her company's offices; a person who develops business and professional contacts through informal social meetings. **net'working** n.

■ **dance in a net** to act in imagined concealment.

net² or **nett** /net/ adj clear of all charges or deductions, opp to gross; (of weight) not including that of packaging; lowest, subject to no further deductions; (of eg a result) final or conclusive; clean (obs); bright (obs); unmixed, pure (obs); neat, trim (rare). ♦ vt (nett'ing; nett'ed) to gain or produce as clear profit. [neat¹]

❑ **net assets** n pl the total value of the assets of a company minus liabilities, used as an indication of the accounting value of the owners' interest or equity (also **net asset value**). **Net Book Agreement** see **NBA**. **net dividend** n the dividend paid to shareholders, excluding any tax credit. **net realizable value** n the amount expected to be received from the sale of an asset after deducting all the expenses incurred in the sale.

nete /nē'tē/ (Gr music) n the highest string or note of the lyre. [Gr nētē or neatē (chordē), literally, lowest (string)]

Neth. abbrev: the Netherlands.

netheless /nedh'(ə-)les/ adv (Spenser) for **nathless**.

nether /nedh'ər/ adj lower. [OE neothera, adj, from nither, adv, from the root ni- down; Ger nieder low]

■ **neth'erlings** n pl (Dickens) stockings. **neth'ermore** adj (rare) lower. **neth'ermost** adj lowest. **neth'erward** or **neth'erwards** adv (rare) downwards.

❑ **neth'erstock** n (obs) a stocking. **neth'erworld** n hell (also **nether regions**).

Netherlander /nedh'ər-lan-dər/ n an inhabitant of the Netherlands; formerly, a person from any of the Low Countries, incl Belgium.

■ **Netherland'ic** or **Neth'erlandish** adj Dutch.

Nethinim /neth'i-nim/ n pl the old Jewish temple servants. [Heb nethīnīm]

netiquette /net'i-ket/ (comput) n agreed standards for polite online behaviour. [**net¹** and **etiquette**]

netizen /net'i-zən/ (inf) n a competent and enthusiastic user of the Internet. [**net¹** and **citizen**]

netsuke /net'skē or -skā, net'sŭ-ke/ n a small Japanese carved ornament, once used to fasten small objects (eg a purse or pouch for tobacco, medicines, etc) to a sash. [Jap ne root or bottom, and tsuke, from tsukeru to attach]

nett see **net²**.

nettle¹ /net'l/ n any of various common weeds (genus *Urtica*) with stinging hairs; any of several similar plants, such as hemp-nettle. ◆ vt to sting (obs); to annoy. [OE *netele*; Ger *Nessel*]
■ **nett'lelike** adj. **nett'lesome** adj irritable; causing irritation. **nett'ly** adj.
❏ **nett'le-cell** n a nematocyst. **nett'le-cloth** n cloth of nettle-fibre; thick japanned cotton. **nett'le-fish** n a jellyfish. **nettle rash** n urticaria, a rash of itchy red or white weals, usu the symptom of an allergy (also called **hives**). **nett'le-tree** n a tree of the elm family (genus *Celtis*), with nettle-shaped leaves, edible drupes, and wood good for turning; a tropical and Australian tree (genus *Laportea*) of the nettle family, with virulently stinging leaves.
■ **dead-nettle** see under **dead**. **grasp the nettle** to set about an unpleasant task, duty, etc with firmness and resolution. **hemp-nettle** see under **hemp**.

nettle² same as **knittle**.

netty, **network**, etc see under **net**¹.

neuk /nūk or nŭk/ n a Scots form of **nook**.

neume or **neum** /nūm/ (medieval music) n a succession of notes sung to one syllable; a sign giving a rough indication of rise or fall of pitch. [OFr, from Gr *pneuma* breath]

neur- /nūr-/ or **neuro-** /nū-rō-/ combining form denoting: a nerve cell, a nerve fibre, nerve tissue, or the nervous system (esp the brain and spinal cord); the nerves and some other system, as in *neurovascular* and *neuromuscular*; an area of research, etc associated with the nervous system, as in *neuroanatomist*, *neurobiologist* and *neurophysiology*. [Gr *neuron* a nerve]
■ **neuralgia** /nū-ral'ji-ə/ n (Gr *algos* pain) paroxysmal intermittent pain along the course of a nerve; pain of a purely nervous character. **neural'gic** adj. **neuramin'idase** n (immunol) an enzyme found on the surface of several viruses, which destroys the glycosidic link between **neuraminic acid** and sugars on the surface of host cells, making the cells more likely to clump together. **neurasthenia** /nū-ras-thē'ni-ə/ n (Gr *astheneia* weakness) nervous debility. **neurasthē'niac** n a neurasthenic. **neurasthenic** /-then'ik or -thēn'ik/ adj and n (a person) suffering from neurasthenia. **neurā'tion** n nervation. **neurec'tomy** n the surgical excision of part of a nerve. **neurilemm'a** or **neurolemm'a** n (Gr *eilēma* covering) the external sheath of a nerve fibre. **neuril'ity** n the essential character of nerve. **neur'ine** /-ēn, -in or -īn/ n a very poisonous ptomaine formed in putrefying flesh. **neur'ism** n a supposed 'nerve-force' acting in evolution (cf **bathmism**). **neur'ite** n an axon or dendrite. **neuroanatom'ical** adj. **neuroanat'omist** n. **neuroanat'omy** n the study of the structure of the nervous system; the nerve structure of an organism. **neurobiolog'ical** adj. **neurobiol'ogist** n. **neurobiol'ogy** n the branch of biology dealing with the anatomy and physiology of the nervous system. **neur'oblast** n an embryonic nerve cell. **neuroblastō'ma** n (pl **neuroblastō'mas** or **neuroblastō'mata** /-mə-tə/) a malignant tumour composed of primitive nerve cells, arising in the adrenal gland or in connection with the sympathetic nervous system, and most commonly affecting children. **neurocanal'** n (embryol) a cavity in the embryonic nervous system which develops into the central canal of the spinal cord and ventricles in the brain. **neur'ochip** n a microchip used in neural networks. **neur'ocomputer** n a computer that uses neural networks to mimic the action of the human brain (also **neural computer**). **neurocomput'ing** n. **neurodegenerā'tion** n degeneration of nerve cells. **neurodegen'erative** adj. **neuroen'docrine** adj relating to the nervous and endocrine systems, and to their interaction. **neuroendocrinol'ogy** n the study of the interaction of the nervous and endocrine systems. **neuroethol'ogy** n the description of features of animal behaviour in terms of the mechanisms of the nervous system. **neurofibril** /-fī'bril/ n one of a large number of fine fibres present in the cytoplasm of a nerve cell. **neurofib'rillar** or **neurofibrill'ary** adj. **neurofibrō'ma** n (pl **neurofibrō'mas** or **neurofibrō'mata** /-mə-tə/) a fibroma of the peripheral nerves. **neurofibromatō'sis** n a condition characterized by the formation of neurofibromas and areas of dark pigmentation on the skin. **neurogen'esis** n the development and growth of nerves. **neurogen'ic** adj caused or stimulated by the nervous system, opp to *myogenic*. **neurog'lia** n (Gr *glia* glue) the supporting tissue of the brain and spinal cord, etc. **neur'ogram** n same as **engram**. **neurohor'mone** n a hormone formed in the nervous system. **neurohypnol'ogy** or **neurypnol'ogy** n old names for the science of hypnotism. **neurohypophy'sis** n (pl **neurohypophy'ses** /-sēz/) the posterior lobe of the pituitary gland (cf **adenohypophysis** under **aden-**). **neurolemma** see **neurilemma** above. **neuroleptanalgē'sia** n the administration of a tranquillizer and an analgesic at the same time to induce a sleeplike state, eg for minor surgery. **neuroleptanalgē'sic** adj. **neurolep'tic** n and adj (a drug) able to reduce nervous tension. **neur'olinguist** n. **neurolinguis'tic** adj. **neurolinguistic programming** n a system of alternative therapy that aims to programme the brain to improve self-awareness and the ability to

formulate and pursue goals. **neurolinguis'tics** n sing the branch of linguistics which deals with the processing and storage of language in the brain. **neurolog'ical** adj. **neurolog'ically** adv. **neurol'ogist** n. **neurol'ogy** n orig the study of the nervous system; that branch of medicine concerned with the diagnosis and treatment of diseases of the nervous system. **neurol'ysis** n breaking down of nerve tissue, or exhaustion of a nerve. **neurō'ma** n (pl **neurō'mas** or **neurō'mata**) a tumour consisting of nerve tissue. **neuromus'cular** adj relating to both nerves and muscles. **neur'opath** n (Gr *pathos* suffering) someone whose nervous system is diseased or in disorder. **neuropath'ic** or **neuropath'ical** adj. **neuropathist** /nūr-op'ə-thist/ n a specialist in nervous diseases. **neuropathogen'esis** n (the cause or origin of) the development of a disease or disorder of the nervous system. **neuropatholog'ical** adj. **neuropathol'ogist** n. **neuropathol'ogy** n the pathology of the nervous system. **neurop'athy** n nervous disease generally. **neuropep'tide** n any of several peptides found in brain tissue, classified as neurotransmitters and, in some cases, hormones. **neuropharmacol'ogist** n. **neuropharmacol'ogy** n the scientific study of the effects of drugs on the nervous system. **neurophysiolog'ical** adj. **neurophysiol'ogist** n. **neurophysiol'ogy** n the physiology of the nervous system. **neur'opil** n (Gr *pilos* hair; *zool*) (in vertebrates) a network of axons, dendrites and synapses within the central nervous system. **neur'oplasm** n the protoplasm of a nerve cell. **neuropsychiat'ric** adj. **neuropsychi'atrist** n. **neuropsychi'atry** n the branch of medicine dealing with diseases involving the mind and nervous system. **neuropsychol'ogist** n. **neuropsychol'ogy** n the study of the relationship between the brain and nervous system and behaviour. **neuroradiol'ogy** n the branch of radiology dealing with the diagnosis of diseases of the nervous system. **neur'oscience** n any or all of the scientific disciplines studying the nervous system and/or the mind and mental behaviour. **neurosci'entist** n. **neurosur'geon** n. **neurosur'gery** n surgery performed on the brain, spinal cord or other parts of the nervous system. **neurosur'gical** adj. **neurot'omist** n. **neurotomy** /-ot'ə-mi/ n the surgical cutting of a nerve. **neurotox'ic** adj. **neurotoxic'ity** n the degree to which a substance is poisonous to nerve tissue; the state caused by exposure to a neurotoxin. **neurotox'in** n a substance poisonous to nerve tissue. **neurotransmitt'er** n a chemical released from a nerve fibre by means of which an impulse passes to a muscle or another nerve. **neurotroph'ic** adj of or relating to the nutrition of the nervous system, or to nutritional changes influenced by the nervous system. **neurotroph'in** n any of a group of proteins that are important in the survival or growth of certain classes of embryonic neurons. **neurot'rophy** n nutrition of the nervous system; the influence of the nervous system on nutrition. **neurotrop'ic** adj having a special affinity for or growing in nerve cells. **neurovas'cular** adj relating to or affecting both nerves and blood vessels. **neurypnology** n see **neurohypnology** above.

neural /nū'rəl/ adj of or relating to the nerves or the central nervous system; dorsal, opp to *haemal*. [Gr *neuron* nerve]
■ **neur'ally** adv.
❏ **neural arch** n the arch of a vertebra protecting the spinal cord. **neural computer** same as **neurocomputer** (see under **neur-**). **neural computing** n computing using neurocomputers. **neural network** or **neural net** n a computer system modelled on the human brain, which 'learns' by trial and error rather than being programmed. **neural plate** n the part of the ectoderm of an embryo which develops into the neural tube. **neural tube** n the channel formed by the closing of the edges of a fold in the ectoderm of an embryo, later developing into the spinal cord and cerebral hemispheres.

neuralgia...to...**neurite** see under **neur-**.

neuritis /nū-rī'tis/ n inflammation of a nerve or nerves, in some cases with defective functioning of the affected part. [Gr *neuron* nerve, and **-itis**]
■ **neuritic** /-it'ik/ adj relating to, of the nature of or having neuritis. ◆ n someone suffering from neuritis.

neuro- see **neur-**.

neuroanatomist...to...**neuromuscular** see under **neur-**.

neuron /nū'ron/ or **neurone** /nū'rōn/ n a cell with the specialized function of transmitting nerve impulses, a nerve cell. [Gr *neuron* nerve]
■ **neurō'nal** or **neuron'ic** adj.

neuropath...to...**neuropsychology** see under **neur-**.

Neuroptera /nū-rop'tə-rə/ n pl a former order of insects, now placed in a superorder, **Neuropteroidea** /nū-rop-tə-roi'di-ə/, the insects generally having four net-veined wings, incl alder-flies, snake flies, lacewings, etc. [Gr *neuron* a nerve, *pteron* a wing, and *eidos* form]
■ **neurop'teran** n (pl **neurop'terans** or **neurop'tera**) any insect of the order Neuroptera (also adj). **neurop'terist** n a person who studies the Neuropteroidea. **neurop'terous** adj.

neuroradiology, **neuroscience**, etc see under **neur-**.

■ words derived from main entry word; ❏ compound words; ■ idioms and phrasal verbs

neurosis /nū-rō'sis/ *n* (*pl* **neurō'ses** /-sēz/) *orig* nervous activity distinguished from or associated with mental activity; functional derangement resulting from a disordered nervous system, *esp* without lesion of parts; mental disturbance characterized by a state of unconscious conflict, *usu* accompanied by anxiety and obsessional fears (also called **psychoneurosis**); loosely, obsession. [Gr *neuron* nerve, and **-osis**]
■ **neurotic** /-ot'ik/ *adj* of the nature of, characterized by or affected by neurosis; loosely, obsessive; hypersensitive. ◆ *n* a person suffering from neurosis; a drug used for treating nerve diseases (*archaic*). **neurot'ically** *adv*. **neurot'icism** /-i-sizm/ *n*.

neurosurgeon...to...**neurypnology** see under **neur-**.

neuston /nū'ston/ *n* minute organisms that float or swim on the surface of water. [Gr, neuter of *neustos* swimming]

neut. *abbrev* : neuter; neutral.

neuter /nū'tər/ *adj* neither one thing nor another; neutral; neither masculine nor feminine (*grammar*); neither active nor passive (*grammar*); intransitive (*grammar*); sexless; apparently sexless; sexually undeveloped; castrated; without an androecium or gynaeceum, or without a functional one (*bot*). ◆ *n* a neutral; a neuter word, plant or animal; *esp* a worker bee, ant, etc; a castrated cat. ◆ *vt* to castrate. [L *neuter* neither, from *ne* not, and *uter* either]

neutral /nū'trəl/ *adj* indifferent; taking no part on either side; not siding with either party; relating to neither party; not involved in a war or dispute; belonging to neither, *esp* of two adjoining countries; of no decided character; having no decided colour; indistinct in sound; with no noticeable smell; belonging to neither of two opposites, such as acid and alkaline or electrical positive and negative; not magnetized; (of a vowel) pronounced with the tongue in a relaxed, central position, as the vowel at the beginning of *around* (*phonetics*); neuter; (of eg a force or gear) without transmission of motion. ◆ *n* a person or nation that takes no part in a contest, a war, etc; a citizen or ship belonging to a neutral state; an electric conductor ordinarily at zero potential; a position of gear in which no power is transmitted; a neuter. [L *neutrālis*, from *neuter* neither]
■ **neutralino** /-lē'nō/ *n* (*particle phys*) a hypothetical particle that might be responsible for dark matter. **neu'tralism** *n* the policy of not entering into alliance with other nations or taking sides ideologically. **neu'tralist** *n* someone who takes or favours a neutral position (also *adj*). **neutralis'tic** *adj*. **neutrality** /-tral'i-ti/ *n* the fact or state of being neutral; those who are neutral. **neutralīzā'tion** or **-s-** *n*. **neu'tralize** or **-ise** *vt* to declare neutral, to grant neutrality to (eg a State); to make neutral chemically or electrically; to make inert; to make ineffective; to counteract; to nullify. ◆ *vi* to become neutral or neutralized. **neu'tralizer** or **-s-** *n*. **neu'trally** *adv*.
❑ **neutral axis** *n* (*engineering*) (in a beam subjected to bending) the line of zero stress. **neutral monism** *n* the philosophical theory that mind and matter are made up of the same elements differently arranged, none of which can be classified as mental or physical. **neutral spirits** *n pl* (*N Am*) non-flavoured alcohol of 1901 proof or higher, used for blending with other alcoholic liquors. **neutral zone** *n* the area between the attacking and defending zones in the middle of an ice-hockey rink; the area between the two lines of scrimmage in American football.

neutron /nū'tron/ (*phys*) *n* an uncharged particle of about the same mass as the proton. [L *neuter* neither]
■ **neutrett'o** *n* (*pl* **neutrett'os**) a name suggested for a neutral meson; a type of neutrino. **neutrino** /-trē'nō/ *n* (*pl* **neutri'nos**) an uncharged particle with zero mass when at rest.
❑ **neutron bomb** *n* a type of nuclear bomb which destroys life by immediate intense radiation, without blast and heat effects to destroy buildings, etc. **neutron number** *n* the number of neutrons in the nucleus of an atom. **neutron poison** *n* non-fissile material which absorbs neutrons and is used for the control of nuclear reactors (also **nuclear poison**). **neutron radiography** *n* radiography using a beam of neutrons. **neutron source** *n* a source of neutrons, eg a nuclear reactor or a chemical or accelerator source. **neutron star** *n* a heavenly body of very small size and very great density, an almost burnt-out and collapsed star, whose existence can be inferred from its gravitational effects.

neutrophil /nū'trō-fil/ *adj* (of a cell, etc) stainable with a neutral dye. ◆ *n* a neutrophil cell, etc; a leucocyte with granular cytoplasm and a lobular nucleus. [Ger, from L *neuter* (see **neuter**) and Gr *philos* (see **phil-** and **-phil**)]
■ **neutrophilic** /-fil'ik/ *adj*.

Nev. *abbrev* : Nevada (US state).

névé /nā'vā/ *n* firm, the granular snow, not yet compacted into ice, lying on the surface at the upper end of a glacier; a field of granular snow. [Fr, from L *nix, nivis* snow]

nevel /nev'əl/ (*Scot*) *vt* (**nev'elling**; **nev'elled**) to pound with the nieves or fists. [**nieve**]

never /nev'ər/ *adv* not ever; at no time; in no degree; not. ◆ *interj* (*inf*) surely not! [OE *næfre*, from *ne* not, and *æfre* ever]
❑ **nev'er-end'ing** *adj*. **nev'er-fad'ing** *adj*. **nev'er-fail'ing** *adj*. **nev'ermore** *adv* at no future time. **nev-er-nev'er** *n* the hire-purchase system (*inf*); (sometimes with *cap*) a remote, thinly peopled or desolate area (also **never** (or **never-never**) **land** or **country**; sometimes with *caps*). **never-never land** *n* (also with *caps*) an imaginary place, imaginary conditions, too fortunate ever to exist in reality. **nevertheless'** *adv* notwithstanding; in spite of that. **nevertuemore'** *adv* (*obs*) none the more. **nev'er-was'** *n* someone who never was of any account.
■ **never a** *no*. **never so** (*archaic*) ever so. **well I never!** or **I never did!** I never heard anything so surprising, shocking, etc.

nevus see **naevus**.

new /nū/ *adj* very recently made or produced; young; fresh; not much used; having lately become, happened or begun to be; recent, modern; (in place names) more recently founded and discovered than and named after, as in *New York* and *New Orleans*; not before seen or known; only lately discovered or experienced; other than the former or preceding, different; additional; strange, unaccustomed; lately begun; beginning afresh; renewed; reformed or regenerated; restored or resumed; (of crops) harvested early; not of an ancient family; fresh from anything; uncultivated or only recently cultivated. ◆ *n* that which is new; newness. ◆ *adv* (often joined by hyphen to an adjective) newly; anew. ◆ *vt* (*archaic*) to renew. ◆ *vi* (*archaic*) to be renewed. [OE *nīwe, nēowe*; Ger *neu*, Ir *nuadh*, L *novus*, Gr *neos*]
■ **new'bie** *n* (*inf*) a new arrival on a specific scene, eg on the Internet. **new'ie** *n* (*inf*) something new. **new'ish** *adj* somewhat new; nearly new. **new'ishly** *adv*. **new'ishness** *n*. **new'ly** *adv* very lately; afresh; in a new or different way. **new'ness** *n*.
❑ **New Age** *n* (also without *caps*) a cultural trend that emerged in the late 1980s, concerned with the union of mind, body and spirit, expressed through popular interest in a variety of beliefs and disciplines, including mysticism, meditation, astrology and holistic medicine; (also **New Age music**) a dreamy style of music of the late 1980s, *usu* using synthesizers. **New-Age'** *adj*. **New Ageism** *n* (also without *caps*) the New-Age movement. **New Ager** *n* (also without *caps*) someone involved or interested in the New-Age movement. **New-Age Traveller** *n* a member of an itinerant group of people adopting an alternative lifestyle and New-Age principles. **new Australian** *n* an immigrant to Australia. **new birth** *n* renewal, *esp* spiritual. **new blood** *n* (a person with) fresh talent; (a person exercising) a revitalizing influence. **new'-blown** *adj* just come into bloom. **new'born** *adj* newly born. ◆ *n* a newborn baby. **new broom** *n* (*fig*) see **new brooms sweep clean** under **broom**. **new chum** *n* (*inf*) a newly-arrived and inexperienced immigrant to Australia or New Zealand; a beginner, novice (*Aust sl*). **New Church** or **New Jerusalem Church** *n* the Swedenborgian Church. **new'come** *adj* recently arrived. **new'comer** *n* someone who has lately come; a beginner. **new'-Commonwealth** *adj* of or belonging to members of the Commonwealth who joined after World War II. **new'-create** *vt* (*Shakesp*) to create anew. **new critic** *n* a practitioner of new criticism. **new criticism** *n* literary criticism that concentrates on the text and rejects historical and biographical background information as unnecessary to an understanding of the work. **New Deal** *n* Franklin D Roosevelt's policies for prosperity and social improvement in the United States, 1933–40; a UK government initiative on employment launched in 1998; (without *caps*) any new arrangements or conditions considered better than previous ones. **New Economic Policy** *n* the Soviet economic programme from 1921 to 1928, which allowed some private ownership of business. **new economy** *n* the part of the economy based on computer, communications and information technologies (cf **old economy**). **new'-economy** *adj*. **New Englander** *n* a native or citizen of any of the New England states (Connecticut, Maine, New Hampshire, Rhode Island, Vermont and Massachusetts). **New English Bible** *n* a translation of the Bible and Apocrypha supervised by a committee formed of representatives from all the major British Christian denominations, first published in 1970. **new Europe** *n* the countries of eastern Europe, *esp* those that joined the EU in or after 2004. **new'-fallen** *adj* newly fallen. **newfangled** see separate entry. **new'-fash'ioned** *adj* made in a new way or fashion; lately come into fashion. **new'-fledged** *adj* having just got feathers. **new for old** *n* the basis for a house contents insurance policy claim that disregards any deterioration due to use or time. **new'-found** *adj* newly discovered or devised. **New Jersey tea** *n* redroot. **New Jerusalem** *n* the heavenly city; heaven. **New Jerusalem Church** see **New Church** above. **New Kingdom** *n* the 18th to 20th dynasties in ancient Egypt (16c–11c BC). **New Labour** *n* the part of the British Labour Party that gained control in the 1990s and seeks to apply a less extreme form of socialism in a market economy. **new lad** *n* a young man who, unlike the new man (qv below), unashamedly pursues a lifestyle characterized by hedonism, materialism, macho attitudes and interests, and open defiance of political correctness. **new'-laid** *adj*

newly laid. **New Latin** *n* the form of Latin in (*esp* legal) use since the Renaissance. **New Learning** *n* the new studies of the Renaissance. **New Left** *n* an extreme left-wing movement among students, etc in the 1960s. **New Light** *n* a member of a relatively more advanced or liberal religious school, applied *esp* to the party within the 18c Scottish Secession Church which adopted voluntaryist views of the relations of Church and State, also sometimes to the Socinianizing party in the Church of Scotland in the 18c, etc. **new look** *n* a change in women's fashions (1947), notably to longer and fuller skirts; a radical modification in the appearance of something. **new'ly-wed** *n* and *adj* (a person who is) recently married. **new'-made** *adj* recently made. **new man** *n* a reformed character; a fitter, healthier man; (sometimes with *caps*) a man who is prepared to show his feelings and who has adopted modern ideas *esp* with regard to health, the environment and sharing family responsibilities. **new'-marr'ied** *adj* newly married. **new maths** *n* a method of teaching mathematics which is more concerned with basic structures and concepts than numerical drills. **new'-mod'el** *vt* to model or form anew. **New Model Army** *n* the Parliamentary army as remodelled by Cromwell in 1645. **new moon** *n* the moment when the moon is directly in line between the earth and sun, and therefore invisible; the time when the waxing moon becomes visible; the narrow waxing crescent itself. **new'-mown** *adj* newly mown. **new'-old'** *adj* old but renewed; having both new and old qualities at the same time. **new penny** see under **penny**. **new poor** *n pl* those who have come to think themselves poor by loss of advantages. **New Red Sandstone** *n* (*geol*) an old name for the Permian and Trias. **new rich** *n pl* the recently enriched; parvenus. **New Right** *n* a conservative movement, prominent in the 1980s, which differs from the traditional Right in holding more staunchly right-wing or moralistic views, eg favouring the diminution or abolition of the welfare state and the restitution of capital punishment, and opposing abortion. **new'-risen** *adj* having newly risen. **New Romantic** *n* a member of a youth movement characterized by flamboyant epicene styles, prevalent in the 1980s (also *adj*). **new'-sad** *adj* (*Shakesp*) recently made sad. **New'speak** *n* a type of English described by George Orwell in his book *Nineteen Eighty-four* (1949), developed by reducing vocabulary to such a point, and forming new words of such ugliness and so little emotive value, that literature and even thought will be impossible; (also without *cap*) any type of language considered similar in style, etc (*esp derog*). **new star** *n* a nova. **New Style** see **style**. **New Testament** *n* the second part of the Christian Bible, consisting of writings about Christ and the Apostles after his death, and documents from the very first years of the Christian Church (*abbrev* **NT**). **new town** *n* a town planned and built by the government to aid housing conditions in nearby large cities, stimulate development, etc. **new variant Creutzfeldt-Jakob disease** see **Creutzfeldt-Jakob disease**. **New Wave** *n* a movement in French cinema in the late 1950s and 1960s which abandoned the linear narrative and experimented with untypical framing and fluid camera movements (also called **Nouvelle Vague**); a slightly later movement in jazz aiming at freedom from set patterns and styles; (also without *caps*) any similar new movement or grouping in the arts, media, music, etc. **New-Wave'** *adj*. **new woman** *n* a name applied, *esp* by scoffers, in the late 19c to such women as actively sought freedom and equality with men. **New World** *n* North, Central and South America. **new world order** *n* an aspiration to peaceful coexistence in the world. **New Year** *n* the first few days of the year. **New Year's Day** *n* the first day of the year. **New Year's Eve** *n* the last day of the year, 31 December. **New Zealander** *n* a native or citizen of New Zealand. ■ **of new** (*archaic*) anew; of late. **what's new?** (*inf*) tell me your news; there's nothing new about that!

Newcastle disease /nū'kǎ-səl di-zēz'/ *n* an acute, highly contagious viral disease of chickens and other domestic and wild birds, first recorded at *Newcastle* upon Tyne in 1926 (also called **fowl-pest**).

newel /nū'əl/ *n* the upright column around which the steps of a circular staircase wind; an upright post at the end or corner of a stair handrail (also **newel post**). [OFr *noual* (Fr *noyau*) fruit-stone, from LL *nucālis* nutlike, from L *nux, nucis* a nut]
■ **new'elled** *adj*.

newell /nū'əl/ (*Spenser*) *n* a new thing. [A combination of **novel** and **new**]

newfangled /nū-fang'gld/, earlier **newfangle** /-gl/ *adj* newly but superfluously devised; excessively or ostentatiously modern; unduly fond of new things. [ME *newefangel*, from *newe* (OE *nīwe*) new, and *fangel* ready to catch, from *fang-*, the stem of OE *fōn* to take]
■ **newfang'ledly** *adv*. **newfang'ledness** or **newfang'leness** *n*.

Newfie /nū'fi/ (*inf, esp Can*) *n* a person born or living in Newfoundland in Canada; a somewhat stupid or backward person (*derog*).

Newfoundland /nū-fownd'lənd or nū'fənd-land/ *adj* of the Canadian province of *Newfoundland*. ◆ *n* a very large, intelligent breed of dog from Newfoundland, *orig* and *esp* black, a strong swimmer.

Newgate /nū'gāt/ *n* a famous prison in London, *orig* housed in the *new gate* of the city, the latest building demolished in 1902–3.
□ **Newgate Calendar** *n* a record of Newgate prisoners, with their crimes.

newmarket /nū-mär'kit or nū'/ *n* a card game in which the stakes go to those who succeed in playing out cards whose duplicates lie on the table; a close-fitting coat, *orig* a riding coat, for men or women. [*Newmarket*, town in Suffolk famous for horse-racing]

news /nūz/ *n* (*orig pl*) information on recent events and current affairs; a report of a recent event; (preceded by *the*) a presentation of news on the television or radio; tidings; newly received information; something one had not heard before; a subject, person, place, etc considered suitable material for newspaper readers or for radio and television bulletins; newspaper; newsprint. ◆ *vt* to report. [Late ME *newes*; Fr *nouvelles*]
■ **news'iness** *n*. **news'less** *adj*. **news'worthiness** *n*. **news'worthy** *adj* sufficiently interesting to be told as news. **news'y** (*inf*) *adj* full of news or gossip. ◆ *n* (*US*) a newsagent; a newsboy or newsgirl.
□ **news agency** *n* an organization which collects material for newspapers, magazines, etc. **news'agent** *n* a shop owner or shop that sells newspapers. **news'boy** or **news'girl** *n* a boy or girl who delivers or sells newspapers. **news'cast** *n* a news broadcast or telecast. **news'caster** *n* a person who presents newscasts or telecasts; a machine which gives a changing display of news headlines, etc. **news'casting** *n*. **news conference** *n* a press conference. **news'dealer** *n* (*US*) a newsagent. **news desk** *n* the department of a newspaper office or broadcasting studio that gathers and reports news. **news fiction** see **faction**[2]. **news'flash** *n* a brief preliminary dispatch about news just becoming known. **news'girl** see **newsboy** above. **news'group** *n* (*comput*) a group that exchanges views and information by means of the Internet. **news'hawk** or **news'hound** *n* (*joc*) a reporter in search of news for eg a newspaper. **news'letter** *n* a sheet of news supplied to members of a particular group or locality; *orig* a written or printed letter containing news sent by an agent to subscribers, the predecessor of the newspaper. **news magazine** or **news'magazine** *n* a magazine, or radio or television broadcast, which discusses and comments on the news as well as reporting it. **news'man** or **news'woman** *n* a bringer, collector or writer of news; a seller of newspapers. **news'monger** *n* (*old*) a person who deals in news; a person who spends much time in hearing and telling news, a gossip. **news'paper** *n* a collection of folded printed sheets of paper published periodically (*usu* daily or weekly) for circulating news, etc; the paper on which such a publication is printed. **news'paperdom** *n*. **news'paperism** *n*. **news'paperman** or **news'paperwoman** *n* a journalist. **news'print** *n* inexpensive paper for printing newspapers on; loosely, ink used for printing newspapers. **news'reader** *n* a person who reads news on radio or television. **news'reel** *n* a film showing, or a programme commenting on, news items. **news'room** *n* a reading-room with newspapers, eg in a library; a room, etc where news is made ready for a newspaper, newscast, etc. **news'-sheet** *n* a printed sheet of news, *esp* an early form of newspaper. **news'-stand** *n* a street stall for the sale of newspapers. **news'-theatre** *n* (*old*) a cinema showing chiefly newsreels. **news'trade** *n* the business of newsagents. **news'-value** *n* interest to the general public as news. **news'vendor** *n* a street seller of newspapers. **news'wire** *n* a teleprinter which transmits news stories as they occur and up-to-the minute stock market results, etc. **newswoman** see **newsman** above. **news'-writer** *n* a reporter or writer of news.

newt /nūt/ *n* a tailed amphibian (genus *Triturus, Molge* or *Triton*) of the salamander family, the word being formed with initial *n*, borrowed from the article **an**[1], and **ewt**, a form of archaic or dialect **evet** or **eft**[1]. [OE *efeta, efete*]

newton /nū'tən/ *n* a derived SI unit, the unit of force (symbol **N**), equal to the force which, acting on a mass of one kilogram, produces an acceleration of one metre per second per second.
■ **Newtonian** /nū-tō'ni-ən/, also **Newtonic** /-ton'ik/ *adj* relating to, according to, formed or discovered by, Sir Isaac *Newton* (1642–1727).
□ **Newtonian mechanics** *n sing* the theory of mechanics dealing with the relationships between force and motion for large objects, based on Newton's laws of motion (also called **classical mechanics**). **Newtonian telescope** *n* a form of reflecting telescope. **Newton's cradle** *n* a sophisticated toy consisting of five metal balls hanging in a frame, caused to hit against one another at speeds which vary. **Newton's gravitational constant** see **gravitation** under **gravity**. **Newton's laws of motion** *n pl* the three laws first stated by Newton (1687) describing the effect of force on the movement of a body. **Newton's rings** *n pl* (*optics*) circular concentric interference fringes seen surrounding the point of contact of a convex lens and a plane surface.

New Zealand flax see **flax-bush** under **flax**.

■ words derived from main entry word; □ compound words; ■ idioms and phrasal verbs

next /nekst/ adj (orig superl of **nigh**) nearest in place, in kinship or other relation; nearest following (or preceding if explicitly stated) in time or order. ◆ adv nearest; immediately after; on the first occasion that follows; in the following place. ◆ n the next thing or person. ◆ prep (archaic or dialect) nearest to. [OE nēhst (nīehst), superl of nēh (nēah) near; Ger nächst]

■ **next'ly** adv. **next'ness** n (rare).

❑ **next best** adj next lowest in degree after the best (also n). **next biggest**, **next dearest**, etc adj next lowest (or highest, depending on context) in degree after the previous one mentioned (also n). **next'-door** adj dwelling in, occupying or belonging to the next house, shop, etc; at or in the next house; neighbouring; see also **next door** below. ◆ n the people or household living next door. **next friend** n a person appointed or permitted by a court of law to act on behalf of a minor or other person under legal disability. **next Saturday**, etc n (on) the first Saturday, etc after the present day; (in Scotland often) (on) the Saturday, etc of next week.

■ **next door** at or in the next house (often with to); near, bordering on, very nearly (with to). **next of kin** see under **kin**[1]. **next to** adjacent to; almost; thoroughly acquainted with (old US sl). **next to nothing** almost nothing at all.

nexus /nek'səs/ n (pl **nex'us**) a bond; a linked group. [L nexus, pl -ūs, from nectere to bind]

NF abbrev : National Front; Newfoundland (Canadian province); no funds (also **N/F**); Norman French; Northern French.

NFER abbrev : National Foundation for Educational Research.

NFL (US) abbrev : National Football League.

NFS abbrev : National Fire Service (from 1941 to 1948); not for sale.

NFT abbrev : National Film Theatre.

NFTS abbrev : National Film and Television School.

NFU abbrev : National Farmers' Union.

NFWI abbrev : National Federation of Women's Institutes.

NG abbrev : National Guard (in the USA).

ng abbrev : no good.

ngaio /nī'ō/ n (pl **ngai'os**) a New Zealand tree with white wood. [Maori]

ngana see **nagana**.

NGC abbrev : New General Catalogue, a catalogue listing all the galaxies, clusters and nebulae known in 1888.

NGO abbrev : non-governmental organization.

Ngoni see **Nguni**.

NGR abbrev : Nigeria (IVR).

ngultrum /əng-gul'trəm/ n the standard monetary unit of Bhutan (100 chetrum).

Nguni /əng-goo'ni/ n (pl **Ngu'ni** or **Ngu'nis**) a member of a group of Bantu-speaking peoples living in southern and eastern Africa, incl the Zulu, Xhosa, Ndebele and Swazi; the languages spoken by these people. —Also **Ngoni** /əng-gō'ni/.

ngwee /(ə)ng-gwē'/ n (pl **ngwee'**) a Zambian monetary unit, $\frac{1}{100}$ of a kwacha, or a coin of this value. [Native word, bright]

NH abbrev : New Hampshire (US state).

nhandu see **nandu**.

NHBC abbrev : National House-Building Council.

NHI abbrev : National Health Insurance.

NHS abbrev : National Health Service.

NI abbrev : National Insurance; Northern Ireland; North Island (of New Zealand).

Ni (chem) symbol : nickel.

niacin /nī'ə-sin/ n nicotinic acid.

niaiserie /nye-zə-rē' or nyez-rē'/ (Fr) n simplicity, foolishness.

nib[1] /nib/ n something small and pointed; the writing point of a pen, esp a fountain pen; a bird's bill; a peak; a projecting point or spike; a timber carriage pole; a handle on a scythe's shaft (dialect); (in pl) crushed coffee or cocoa beans; (in pl) included particles in varnish, wool, etc. ◆ vt (**nibb'ing**; **nibbed**) to provide with a nib; to point; to mend the nib of; to reduce to nibs. [Ety as for **neb**]

■ **nibbed** adj having a nib; (eg of nuts) roughly crushed.

nib[2] /nib/ (sl) n a person of the upper classes; a person of importance or appearance of importance. [Cf **nabs** and **nob**[2]]

■ **his nibs** or **her nibs** a mock title used for an important or self-important person, himself or herself; his or her mightiness.

nibble[1] /nib'l/ vt to bite gently or by small bites; to eat a little at a time. ◆ vi to bite gently; to show signs of cautious acceptance of or interest in eg an offer, or of gradual yielding, eg to temptation (with at); to find fault. ◆ n the act of nibbling; a little bit; (in pl) small items of savoury food eaten at parties, as snacks or appetizers, etc. [Origin obscure; cf LGer nibbelen, Du knibbelen]

■ **nibb'ler** n. **nibb'ling** n. **nibb'lingly** adv.

nibble[2] see **nybble**.

Nibelung /nē'bə-lŭng/ n (pl **Ni'belungen**) one of a supernatural race of dwarfs in Germanic mythology, guardians of a treasure wrested from them by Siegfried, the hero of the Nibelungenlied, an epic of c.1190–1210 (in the Nibelungenlied, the name Nibelungen is applied first to Siegfried's followers and subjects, and then to the Burgundians). [Ger]

niblick /nib'lik/ n an old-fashioned golf club for lofted shots, corresponding to a number eight or nine iron. [Origin uncertain]

NIC abbrev : National Insurance Contributions; Newly Industrialized Country; Nicaragua (IVR).

nicad /nī'kad/ n a battery, usu rechargeable, with a nickel anode and cadmium cathode (also adj).

NICAM or **Nicam** /nī'kam/ n near-instantaneous companded audio multiplexing, a system by which digital stereo sound signals are transmitted along with the standard TV signal, to allow the viewer to receive sound of CD quality.

Nicaraguan /ni-kə-rag'ū-ən or -rag'wən/ adj of or relating to the Republic of Nicaragua in Central America, or its inhabitants. ◆ n a native or citizen of Nicaragua.

niccolite /nik'ə-līt/ n a hexagonal mineral, nickel arsenide (also called **kupfernickel**). [See **nickel**]

NICE /nīs/ abbrev : National Institute for Clinical Excellence, a body within the NHS that provides advice on the use of medicines, surgical procedures, etc.

nice /nīs/ adj agreeable, delightful, respectable, good in any way, satisfactory (often used as a vague commendation); (of a person) good-natured, friendly, kind; bad, badly done, careless (ironic); forming or observing very small differences; calling for very fine discrimination; done with great care and exactness, accurate; delicate; dainty; fastidious; hard to please; over-particular; foolishly simple (obs); wanton (Shakesp); coy (Milton); critical, hazardous (archaic); easily injured (obs). [OFr nice foolish, simple, from L nescius ignorant, from ne not, and scīre to know]

■ **nice'ish** or **nic'ish** adj somewhat nice. **nice'ly** adv. **nice'ness** n the quality of being nice. **nicety** /nīs'i-ti/ n critical subtlety; a matter of delicate discrimination or adjustment; the quality of being nice; degree of precision; fineness of perception or feeling; exactness of treatment; delicate management; a refinement (often in pl); fastidiousness; a delicacy; coyness (Spenser and Shakesp). **nicish** see **niceish** above.

■ **nice and** (used almost adverbially) commendably, pleasantly. **to a nicety** with great exactness.

Nicene /nī'sēn/ adj relating to the town of Nicaea, in Bithynia, Asia Minor, where an ecumenical council in 325AD dealt with the theological controversy surrounding Arius of Alexandria, and where another in 787AD condemned the Iconoclasts.

■ **Nicaean** /nī-sē'ən/ n and adj.

❑ **Nicene Creed** n the Christian creed based on the results of the first Nicene Council.

niche /nēsh or nich/ n a recess in a wall; a situation, place or condition appropriate for a person or thing; an area of habitat providing the conditions necessary for an organism or species to survive (ecology); the position or status of an organism or species within its community or ecosystem, dependent upon its behaviour and relationship with other organisms or species in that community (ecology); a small, specialized group identified as a market for a particular range of products or services (commerce; also adj); a place in the market not subject to the normal pressures of competition (commerce). ◆ vt to place in a niche; to ensconce (oneself). [Fr, from Ital nicchia niche, of doubtful origin]

■ **niched** adj placed in a niche.

❑ **niche advertising** n advertising aimed at a niche market. **niche market** n a specialized but profitable market for a product. **niche marketing** n the marketing of a product aimed at a niche market.

nicher see **nicker**[2].

Nichrome® /nī'krōm/ n trademark for a nickel-chromium alloy with high electrical resistance and ability to withstand high temperatures.

Nick /nik/ n the Devil, esp in the phrase Old Nick (also (Scot) **Nickie-ben'**). [Appar for Nicholas]

nick[1] /nik/ n a notch; a small cut; (usu preceded by the) a prison or police station (inf); the line formed where floor and wall meet in a squash, etc court; a score for keeping an account (archaic); the precise moment of time; the precise point aimed at; (at the old dice game of hazard) a throw answering to a main; a hidden bottom in a beer tankard, the outer base being hollow (obs). ◆ vt to notch; to cut (usu slightly); to snip; to cut off; to cut in notches (eg the hair of a fool; Shakesp); to catch (sl); to arrest (sl); to steal (sl); to rob; to make a cut in (a horse's tail muscle), so that the tail is carried higher; to defraud; to mark by cutting, carve out; to score, eg on a tally; to tally with (*obs*); to hit with precision; to hit off (*obs*); to catch in the nick of time; to cheat at hazard, defeat by throwing a nick; at hazard, to throw the nick of. ◆ *vi* (of breeding animals) to mate well; (*usu* with *off* or *out*) to leave. ◆ *adj* (*inf*) able to be stolen. [Poss connected with **nock** or **notch**]

■ **nick'er** *n* someone who or something which nicks; any of a band of early 18c London rioters who made a practice of smashing windows by throwing copper coins at them.

◻ **nick'stick** *n* (*archaic*) a tally. **nick translation** *n* a method of radioactively labelling a DNA molecule.

■ **in good nick** (*inf*) in good health or condition. **in the nick of time** just in time; at the critical moment. **out of all nick** (*Shakesp*) out of all reckoning, exceedingly.

nick² /nik/ (*archaic*) *vt* to deny, in the phrase *to nick with nay*. [Origin unknown; poss OE *ne ic* not I]

nick³ /nik/ *n* an informal short form of **nickname**, *esp* one used on the Internet.

nickar see **nicker⁴**.

nickel /nik'l/ *n* a white magnetic very malleable and ductile metallic element (symbol **Ni**; atomic no 28) largely used in alloys; a five-cent piece (of copper and nickel; *N Am inf*). ◆ *adj* of nickel. ◆ *vt* (**nick'elling** or *N Am* **nick'eling**; **nick'elled** or *N Am* **nick'eled**) to plate with nickel. [Ger *Kupfernickel* niccolite, from *Kupfer* copper, and *Nickel* a mischievous sprite, goblin, because the ore looked like copper ore but yielded no copper]

■ **nick'elic** *adj* of trivalent nickel. **nickelif'erous** *adj* containing nickel. **nick'eline** *n* (*obs*) niccolite. **nick'elize** or **-ise** *vt* to plate with nickel. **nick'elous** *adj* of bivalent nickel.

◻ **nickel-and-dime'** (*N Am*) *adj* involving only a small amount of money; worth only a small amount of effort, concern, etc. ◆ *vt* to harass financially by charging a multitude of small costs. **nick'elback** *n* an additional defensive back brought into the game when the offensive team is likely to pass the football (*American football*). **nick'el-bloom** or **nick'el-ochre** *n* earthy annabergite. **nick'el-plat'ing** *n* the plating of metals with nickel. **nickel silver** *n* an alloy of nickel, copper and zinc, German silver. **nickel steel** *n* a steel containing some nickel.

nickelodeon /nik-ə-lō'di-ən/ (*US*; *old*) *n* formerly, a cinema to which admission cost five cents; an old form of jukebox; a Pianola operated by inserting a five-cent coin. [**nickel** and **odeon**]

nicker¹ /nik'ər/ (*sl*) *n* a pound sterling. [Origin unknown]

nicker² /nik'ər/, also **nicher** /nihh'ər/ (chiefly *Scot* and *N Eng*) *vi* to neigh; to snigger. ◆ *n* a neigh; a snigger; a loud laugh.

nicker³ /nik'ər/ (*archaic*) *n* a water monster or water demon. [OE *nicor*]

nicker⁴ /nik'ər/ *n* a clay marble (also **knicker**); the round seed of a *Caesalpinia* (or *Guilandina* if this is considered a separate genus), used for playing marbles (also **nick'ar**). [Cf Du *knikker*, North Ger *Knicker*]

nick-nack, etc same as **knick-knack**, etc.

nickname /nik'nām/ *n* a name given in jocular or fond familiarity, or in contempt. ◆ *vt* to give a nickname to. [ME *neke-name*, for *eke-name*, an additional (descriptive) name, with *n* from the indefinite article; see **eke¹** and **name**]

nickpoint see **knickpoint**.

nickum /nik'əm/ (*Scot*) *n* a mischievous boy.

nickumpoop see **nincompoop**.

nicky-tam /nik-i-tam'/ (*Scot*) *n* a piece of string, etc worn below the knee to keep the bottom of the trouser-leg lifted clear in dirty work or to exclude dust, etc.

nicol /nik'l/ *n* a crystal of calcium carbonate cut and cemented in such a way as to transmit only the extraordinary ray, used for polarizing light (also **Nicol** or **Nicol's prism**). [William *Nicol* (c.1768–1851), Scottish physicist]

nicompoop see **nincompoop**.

nicotian /ni-kō'sh(y)ən/ *adj* of tobacco. ◆ *n* a tobacco smoker. [Ety as for **nicotine**]

■ **nicotiana** /-shi-ä'nə or -ä'nə/ *n* any plant of the tobacco genus *Nicotiana*, of the family Solanaceae. ◆ *n pl* the literature of tobacco.

nicotine /nik'ə-tēn/ *n* a poisonous narcotic alkaloid of the pyrimidine series ($C_{10}H_{14}N_2$) obtained from tobacco leaves. [Jean *Nicot* de Villemain (1530–1600), French ambassador to Portugal who sent powdered tobacco back to Catherine de Medici]

■ **nicotinamide** /-tin'/ *n* a member of the vitamin B complex, deficiency of which can lead to the development of the disease pellagra. **nic'otined** *adj*. **nicotinic** /-tin'ik/ *adj*. **nic'otinism** *n* a morbid state induced by excessive use of tobacco.

◻ **nicotinamide adenine dinucleotide** see **NAD**. **nicotine patch** *n* a patch impregnated with nicotine and put on the skin to allow gradual absorption into the bloodstream. **nicotine replacement therapy** *n* a treatment to help people stop smoking, in which small quantities of nicotine are administered by patches, chewing gum, etc, until the craving for cigarettes is cured. **nicotinic acid** *n* niacin, a white crystalline substance, a member of the vitamin B complex, deficiency of which is connected with the development of the disease pellagra.

nicrosilal /ni-krō'si-ləl/ *n* a cast-iron alloy containing nickel, chromium, and silicon, used in high-temperature work.

nictate /nik'tāt/ *vi* to wink or blink (also **nic'titate**). [L *nictāre*, *-ātum* and its LL frequentative *nictitāre*, *-ātum* to wink]

■ **nicta'tion** or **nictita'tion** *n*.

◻ **nictitating membrane** *n* the third eyelid, developed in birds, reptiles and some mammals, a thin movable membrane that passes over the eye.

NICU /nik'ū/ (*med*; *US*) *abbrev* : neonatal intensive care unit.

nid /nid/ or **nide** /nīd/ (*archaic*) *n* a pheasant's nest or brood. [L *nīdus* nest]

nidal, nidation, etc see under **nidus**.

niddering, nidderling see **nithing**.

niddle-noddle /nid'l-nod'l/ *adj* and *adv* with nodding head. ◆ *vi* to noddle the head; to waggle. [**nod**]

■ **nid'-nod'** *vt* and *vi* to keep nodding.

nide see **nid**.

nidering, niderling see **nithing**.

nidget /nij'it/ (*archaic* or *non-standard*) *n* an idiot. [**idiot** with *n* from the indefinite article]

nidi plural of **nidus**.

nidicolous /ni-dik'ə-ləs/ *adj* (of young birds) staying for longer than average in the nest. [L *nīdus* a nest, and *colere* to inhabit]

nidificate see **nidify**.

nidifugous /ni-dif'ū-gəs/ *adj* (of young birds) leaving the nest soon after hatching. [L *nīdus* nest, and *fugere* to flee]

nidify /nid'i-fī/ *vi* (**nid'ifying**; **nid'ified**) to build a nest (also **nidificate** /nid'i-fi-kāt/). [L *nīdus* nest, and *facere* to make]

■ **nidifica'tion** *n*.

niding see **nithing**.

nidor /nī'dör/ *n* a strong smell or fume, *esp* of animal substances cooking or burning. [L *nīdor*, *-ōris*]

■ **nī'dorous** *adj*.

nidus /nī'dəs/ *n* (pl **nī'dī**) a nest or breeding-place; a place where anything is originated, harboured, developed or fostered; a place of lodgement or deposit; a point of infection (*med*); a nerve centre. [L *nīdus* a nest]

■ **nī'dal** *adj* relating to a nest or nidus. **nīdament'al** *adj* nest-forming; (of glands) secreting material for the formation of a nest or of an egg-covering. **nīdament'um** *n* an egg capsule. **nīdā'tion** *n* renewal of the lining of the uterus (*obs*); the process by which the blastocyst becomes attached to the wall of the uterus, implantation. **nīdūlā'tion** /nid-/ *n* nest-building.

nie an obsolete spelling of **nigh**.

niece /nēs/ *n* a brother's or sister's daughter; extended to a similar relation by marriage; *orig* a granddaughter, or any female descendant; euphemistically, a pope's or priest's daughter. [OFr, from LL *neptia*, from L *neptis*]

nief see **nieve**.

niello /ni-el'ō/ *n* (pl **niell'i** /-ē/ or **niell'os**) a method of ornamenting metal by engraving, and filling up the lines with a black compound; a piece of work so produced; an impression taken from the engraved surface before filling up; the compound used in niello-work, sulphur with silver, lead or copper. ◆ *vt* (**niell'oing**; **niell'oed**) to decorate with niello. [Ital *niello*, from LL *nigellum* a black enamel, from L *nigellus*, dimin of *niger* black]

■ **niellāted** /nē'/ *adj*. **niell'ist** *n*.

nielsbohrium /nēlz-bö'ri-əm/ *n* a former name for **bohrium**.

Niersteiner /nēr's(h)tī-nər/ *n* a Rhine wine, named after *Nierstein*, near Mainz.

NIESR *abbrev* : National Institute of Economic and Social Research.

Nietzschean /nē'chi-ən/ *adj* of or relating to Friedrich *Nietzsche* (1844–1900) or his philosophy. ◆ *n* a follower of Nietzsche.

■ **Nietzsch'eanism** *n*.

nieve, neive /nēv/, **neif** or **nief** (*Shakesp* **neafe** or **neaffe**) /nēf/ (*archaic* and *dialect*) *n* the fist. [ME *nefe*, from ON *hnefi*, *nefi*; cf Swed *näfve* fist]

■ **nieve'ful** *n* a closed handful.

❑ **nie'vie-nick'-nack** or **nie'vie-nie'vie-nick'-nack** n a Scottish children's pastime, a way of assigning by lot, by guessing which hand contains something, the holder repeating a rhyme.

nife /nī'fī/ n the earth's hypothetical core of nickel and iron. [Chemical symbols *Ni* nickel, and *Fe* iron]

nifedipine /nī-fed'i-pēn/ n a synthetic drug that prevents the absorption of calcium by the heart muscles, used in treating angina pectoris and high blood pressure. [**nitro-**, *-fe-* (from **phenyl**), **di-** and **pyridine**]

niff /nif/ (*sl*) n a stink. ◆ *vi* to smell bad.
■ **niff'y** adj.

niffer /nif'ər/ (*Scot*) vt to barter. ◆ *vi* to haggle. ◆ *n* an exchange; the dice game hazard. [Poss **nieve**]

niffnaff /nif'-naf'/ (*dialect*) n a trifle; a diminutive person. ◆ *vi* to trifle.
■ **niff-naff'y** or **niff'y-naff'y** adj fastidious.

Niflheim /niv'l-hām/ (*Norse myth*) n a region of mist, ruled over by Hel. [ON *Niflheimr*, from *nifl* mist, and *heimr* home]

nifty /nif'ti/ (*sl*) adj fine; spruce; sharp, neat; smart; quick; agile; stylish.
■ **nift'ily** adv. **nift'iness** n.

nigella /nī-jel'ə/ n any plant of the genus of ranunculaceous plants *Nigella*, with finely dissected leaves, and whitish, blue or yellow flowers, often almost concealed by their leafy involucres, one variety, *Nigella damascena*, being otherwise known as love-in-a-mist, devil-in-a-bush, and ragged lady. [Fem of L *nigellus* blackish, from *niger* black, from the plant's black seeds]

niger /nī'jər/ (*obs*) (*offensive, often taboo*) n a black person. [L *niger* black]
❑ **niger oil** n an oil obtained from the black seeds (**niger seeds**) of an E African composite plant, *Guizotia abyssinica*, also cultivated in India.

Nigerian /nī-jē'ri-ən/ adj of or relating to the republic of *Nigeria* in W Africa, or its inhabitants. ◆ *n* a native or citizen of Nigeria.

Nigerien /nē-zhā'ri-ən/ adj of or relating to the Republic of *Niger* in W Africa, or its inhabitants. ◆ *n* a native or citizen of Niger.

niggard /nig'ərd/ n a person who begrudges spending or giving away; a false bottom or side in a fire-grate. ◆ *adj* mean, stingy. ◆ *vt* and *vi* (*Shakesp*) to treat or behave as a niggard. [Origin obscure]
■ **nigg'ardise** or **nigg'ardize** /-īz/ n (*archaic*) niggardliness, meanness. **nigg'ardliness** n meanness, stinginess. **nigg'ardly** adj stingy; meagre. ◆ *adv* stingily; grudgingly.

nigger /nig'ər/ (*offensive, often taboo*) n a black person, or a member of any very dark-skinned race; a black insect larva of various kinds. ◆ *adj* dark-skinned; blackish-brown. ◆ *vt* to exhaust by overcropping; to char; to blacken. [Fr *nègre*, from Sp *negro*; see **Negro**]
■ **nigg'erdom** n black people collectively. **nigg'erish** adj. **nigg'erism** n an idiom or expression (regarded as) characteristic of black people; African blood. **nigg'erling** n a little black person. **nigg'ery** adj.
❑ **nigg'erhead** n a nodule, boulder or boss of dark-coloured rock; an American river mussel (genus *Quadrula*), a source of mother-of-pearl; negrohead tobacco; a tussock in a swamp (*US*).
■ **nigger in the woodpile** a hidden evil influence. **work like a nigger** to work extremely hard.

niggle /nig'l/ vi to trifle, potter; to busy oneself with petty criticism of detail; to move in a fidgety or ineffective way; to gnaw; to criticize in a petty way. ◆ *vt* to worry, irritate or nag; to work, make or perform with excessive detail; to make a fool of. ◆ *n* a minor criticism; a slight worry; small cramped handwriting. [Cf Norw *nigle*]
■ **nigg'ler** n. **nigg'ling** n fussiness, esp over minor detail; petty criticism. ◆ *adj* overelaborate; petty; fussy; cramped; (faintly but) persistently annoying. **nigg'lingly** adv. **nigg'ly** adj.

nigh /nī/ adj (*obs*) near. ◆ *adv* (*poetic, dialect* or *archaic*) nearly; near. ◆ *prep* (*poetic, dialect* or *archaic*) near to. ◆ *vt* and *vi* (*obs*) to approach, draw near; to touch. [OE *nēah, nēh*; Du *na*, Ger *nahe*]
■ **nigh'-hand** adv and prep (*obs*) near hand; almost, nearly. **nigh'ly** adv (*obs*) almost; closely; sparingly (*Spenser*). **nigh'ness** n (*obs*).
■ **nigh on** almost, nearly.

night /nīt/ n the end of the day, evening; (the period of) time from sunset to sunrise; the dark part of the 24-hour day; darkness; obscurity; ignorance, evil, affliction or sorrow (*fig*); death (*euphem*); the activity or experience of a night; a night set apart for some purpose, eg receiving visitors. ◆ *adj* belonging to night; occurring or done in the night; working or on duty at night. [OE *niht*; Ger *Nacht*, L *nox*, Gr *nyx*]
■ **night'ed** adj benighted; darkened; clouded (*Shakesp*). **nightie** n see **nighty** below. **night'less** adj having no night. **night'long** adj and adv lasting all night. **night'ly** adj done or happening by night or every night; dark as night (*Shakesp*). ◆ *adv* by night; every night. **nights** adv (*orig genitive* of n; *inf*) at or by night. **night'ward** adj occurring towards night. **night'y** or **night'ie** n (*inf*) a nightgown.
❑ **night air** n the air at night; a peculiarly unwholesome gas, formerly imagined by some to circulate at night. **night'-ape** n a bushbaby.

night'-attire n garments worn in bed. **night'-bell** n a doorbell for use at night, *esp* at a hotel. **night'bird** n a bird that flies or sings at night; a person who is active or about at night. **night'-blind** adj. **night'-blindness** n inability to see in a dim light, nyctalopia. **night'-blooming cereus** n a cereus with flowers that open at night. **night'-brawler** n a person who causes disturbances in the night. **night'cap** n a cap worn at night in bed; a drink, *esp* an alcoholic or hot one, taken before going to bed; the last event of the day, *esp* the second of a pair of consecutive baseball games or the last horse race of the day (*esp N Am inf*). **night'-cart** n (*hist*) a cart used to remove the contents of outside lavatories before daylight. **night'-cellar** n (*archaic*) a disreputable resort or tavern, open at night. **night'-chair** n a nightstool. **night'-churr** n the nightjar, so called from its cry. **night'class** n a class at night school. **night'clothes** n pl garments worn in bed. **night'-cloud** n stratus. **night'club** n a club for drinking, dancing, etc, open between evening and morning. **night'clubber** n. **night'clubbing** n. **night crawler** n a large earthworm which comes to the surface at night, used as bait for fishing. **night'-crow** n (*Shakesp*) an undefined bird of ill omen that cries in the night. **night'-dog** n (*Shakesp*) a dog that hunts in the night. **night'dress** n clothes, *esp* a woman's or child's loose dresslike garment, for sleeping in; a nightgown. **night duty** n work or duty done at night. **night'fall** n the onset or beginning of the night; the close of the day; evening. **night'faring** adj travelling by night. **night fighter** n a fighter plane equipped for interception at night. **night'fire** n a fire burning in the night; a will-o'-the-wisp. **night'-fish'ery** n a mode or place of fishing by night. **night'-flower** n a flower that opens by night. **night'-flow'ering** adj. **night'-fly** n a moth or fly that is active at night. **night'-fly'ing** adj flying by night (also n). **night'-foe** n someone who attacks by night. **night'-foss'icker** n (*Aust*) someone who rummages around at night for gold, etc in a mine or other working. **night'-foun'dered** adj (*Milton*) lost in the night. **night'-fowl** n a night-bird. **night'gear** n nightclothes. **night'-glass** n a small hand-held telescope with concentrating lenses for use at night. **night'gown** n a loose robe for sleeping in, for men or women; a dressing-gown (*obs*). **night'-hag** n a witch supposed to be about at night. **night'hawk** n an American nightjar, genus *Chordeiles*; a European nightjar; a person more active at night. **night heron** n a heron of nocturnal habit, of various kinds. **night'-house** n (*obs*) a tavern open during the night. **night'-hunter** n someone who hunts, poaches or prowls about the streets for prey by night. **night'jar** n any European nocturnal bird of the family Caprimulgidae, related to the swift family. **night latch** n a door-lock worked by a key from outside and a knob from inside. **night letter** n (*N Am*) formerly, a telegram sent overnight, and so at a cheaper rate. **night'life** n activity in the form of entertainments at night. **night'-light** n a lamp or candle that gives a subdued light all night; the faint light of the night; the light of phosphorescent sea animals. **night'-line** n a fishing-line set overnight. **night'-man** n a night-watchman, nightworker or scavenger by night. **night'mare** n (OE *mære*, ME *mare* the nightmare incubus; cf OHGer *mara* incubus, ON *mara* nightmare) an unpleasant dream; a horrifying or difficult experience; a dream accompanied by pressure on the breast and a feeling of powerlessness to move or speak, personified as an incubus or evil spirit. **night'marish** n **night'mary** adj. **night'marishly** adv. **night'marishness** n. **night nurse** n a nurse on duty during the night. **night out** n a festive night away from home, work and responsibilities; a domestic, or other, servant's night off work. **night owl** n an exclusively nocturnal owl; a person who sits up very late, or one who is habitually more active, alert, etc at night than during the day (*inf*). **night'-pal'sy** n (*archaic*) a numbness of the legs occurring on waking in the morning and passing off quickly. **night'piece** n a picture or literary or musical description of a night-scene; a painting to be seen by artificial light. **night-por'ter** n a porter in attendance during the night. **night'-rail** n (*hist*) a loose wrap or dressing-jacket. **night'-rav'en** n (*Shakesp*) a bird that cries at night, supposed to be of ill omen. **night'-rest** n the repose of the night. **night'rider** n (*US*) a member of a secret band of *usu* white men who carried out lynchings, etc of black people and black sympathizers, *esp* in the Southern USA after the Civil War; a member of the Ku Klux Klan. **night'-robe** n a nightgown; a dressing-gown. **night'-rule** n (*Shakesp*) a revel at night. **night safe** n a safe in the outside wall of a bank, in which customers can deposit money when the bank is closed. **night school** n classes held at night for people who have left school, *esp* for those at work during the day. **night-sea'son** n the night-time. **night shift** n a gang or group of workers that takes its turn at night; the period for which it is on duty; a nightdress (*archaic*). **night'shirt** n a shirt for sleeping in. **night'-shriek** n a cry in the night. **night'side** n the dark, mysterious or gloomy side of anything. **night'-sight** n power of vision by night; a sighting device on a camera, rifle, etc to enable it to be used at night. **night'-soil** n the contents of outside lavatories, cesspools, etc generally carried away at night and sometimes used for fertilizer. **night'-spell** n a charm against harm by night. **night'spot** n (*inf*) a nightclub. **night'stand** n a bedside table. **night starvation** n hunger pangs experienced in the middle of the night. **night'-steed**

n (*myth*) one of the horses in the chariot of Night. **night'stick** *n* (*N Am*) a truncheon. **night'-stool** *n* a close-stool (qv under **close¹**) for use in a bedroom. **night table** *n* (*N Am*) a bedside table. **night'-ta'per** *n* a night-light burning slowly. **night terror** or **terrors** *n* the sudden starting from sleep in fright. **night'-tide** *n* night-time; a floodtide in the night. **night'-time** *n* the time when it is night. **night'-tripp'ing** *adj* (*Shakesp*) tripping about in the night. **night vision** *n* the ability to see in the dark. **night'-wak'ing** *adj* remaining awake in the night. **night'-walk** *n* a walk in the night. **night'-walk'er** *n* (*archaic*) a sleepwalker; a person who walks about at night, *usu* for bad purposes, *esp* a prostitute. **night'-war'bling** *adj* singing in the night. **night'-watch** *n* a watch or guard at night; a person who is on guard at night; the time of watch at night. **night'-watch'man** *n* a person who is on watch at night, *esp* on industrial premises and building sites; a relatively unskilled batsman who is sent in to bat towards the end of the day's play in order to prevent a more skilled batsman from having to go in (*cricket*). **night'wear** *n* clothes worn at bedtime and while sleeping. **night'-work** *n* work done at night. **night'-worker** *n*.
■ **make a night of it** to spend the night, or a large part of it, in amusement or celebration. **night-night** (*inf* or *childish*) goodnight. **of a night** or **of nights** in the course of a night; some time at night. **something of the night** a suggestion of evil or menace.

nightingale¹ /nī'ting-gāl/ *n* a small bird of the thrush family (genus *Luscinia*), celebrated for the rich love-song of the male, heard chiefly at night; a person with a beautiful singing voice. [OE *nihtegale*, from *niht* night, and *galan* to sing, Ger *Nachtigall*]

nightingale² /nī'ting-gāl/ *n* a flannel scarf with sleeves, a garment formerly worn by hospital patients when sitting up in bed. [Florence *Nightingale* (1820–1910), English nurse in the Crimean war]

nightjar...to...**night-season** see under **night**.

nightshade /nīt'shād/ *n* a name given to various plants, *esp* of the Solanaceae family and chiefly poisonous or narcotic. [OE *nihtscada*, appar from *niht* night, and *scada* shade]
■ **black nightshade** a common plant of the nightshade family, *Solanum nigrum*, with poisonous leaves, white flowers and black berries. **deadly nightshade** the belladonna plant, all parts of which are poisonous. **enchanter's nightshade** see under **enchant**. **woody nightshade** bittersweet.

night shift...to...**night-worker** see under **night**.

nig-nog¹ /nig'nog/ (*sl*) *n* a fool; a raw recruit to the army or to a civilian service. [Origin uncertain]

nig-nog² /nig'nog/ (*offensive sl*) *n* a person of a dark-skinned race. [Reduplicated form of **nigger**]

nigrescence /nī- or ni-gres'əns/ (*rare*) *n* blackness; dark colouring or pigmentation; blackening. [L *niger* black]
■ **nigresc'ent** *adj* growing black or dark; blackish. **nigricant** /nig'ri-kənt/ *adj* black; blackish. **nig'rify** *vt* to blacken. **nig'ritude** *n* blackness; see also under **Negro**.

Nigritian /ni-grish'ən/ *n* and *adj* (an inhabitant) of *Nigritia* or Sudan, *esp* W Sudan. [L *niger* black]

nigritude see under **Negro** and **nigrescence**.

nigromancy /nig'rō-man-si/ *n* an old form of **necromancy**, the black art. [From association with L *niger* black]

nigrosine /nig'rō-sēn or -ro-sin/ or **nigrosin** /nig'rō-sin/ *n* a blackish coal-tar colour dye. [L *niger* black]

NIH (*US*) *abbrev*: National Institutes of Health.

nihil /ni- or nī'hil/ *n* nothing. [L]
■ **ni'hilism** /-hil- or -il-izm/ *n* belief in nothing; denial of all reality, or of all objective truth (*philos*); extreme scepticism; nothingness; (sometimes with *cap*) in tsarist Russia, a terrorist movement aiming at the overturn of all the existing institutions of society in order to build it up anew on different principles; terrorism or anarchy; complete destructiveness. **ni'hilist** *n*. **nihilist'ic** *adj*. **nihility** /-hil'/ *n* (*rare*) nothingness; a mere nothing.
■ **nihil ad rem** /ad rem/ (*L*) nothing to the point. **nihil obstat** /ob'stat/ (*RC*) nothing hinders, a book censor's form of permission to print.

nihonga /ni-hong'gə/ *n* a Japanese style of painting, using bright colours and traditional images. [Jap, literally, Japanese painting]

-nik /-nik/ *sfx* forming nouns denoting a person who does, practises, advocates, etc something, as in *beatnik, kibbutznik* or *peacenik*. [Russ suffix, influenced in meaning by Yiddish suffix denoting an agent]

nikab see **niqab**.

nikah /nē'kā/ (*Islam*) *n* a marriage contract or marriage ceremony. [Ar]

nikau or **nikau palm** /nik'ow (päm)/ *n* a Maori name for the palm tree *Rhopalostylis sapida*, native to New Zealand.

Nike /nī'kē/ *n* the Greek goddess of victory. [Gr *nīkē* victory]

nikethamide /ni-keth'a-mīd/ *n* a drug formerly used as a respiratory stimulant. [*nicotinic* acid, *diethyl*, and *amide*]

Nikkei index /nik'ā in'deks/ *n* the indicator of the relative prices of stocks and shares on the Tokyo Stock Exchange (also called **Nikkei average**). [From the title of the newspaper publishing it]

niks-nie see under **nix¹**.

nil /nil/ *n* nothing; zero. [L *nīl, nihil* nothing]

nil desperandum /nil de-spe-ran'dŭm/ (*L*) nothing is to be despaired of; never despair. [Horace, *Odes* I.7.27]

Nile blue /nīl bloo/ *n* a very pale greenish-blue colour.

Nile green /nīl grēn/ *n* a very pale green colour, thought of as the colour of the River *Nile*.

nilgai /nēl' or nil'gī/, **nilgau** or **nylghau** /-gow or -gö/ *n* (pl **nil'gai, nil'gais, nil'gau, nil'gaus, nyl'ghau** or **nyl'ghaus**) a large Indian antelope, the male slaty-grey, the female tawny. [Pers and Hindi *nīl* blue, and Hindi *gāī*, Pers *gāw* cow]

nill or **n'ill** /nil/ (*archaic*) *vt* (pat (*obs*) **nould, noulde** or **n'ould** /nŭd/, also **nilled**) to wish not to; to refuse. [OE *nylle*, from *ne* not, and *willan* to wish]

Nilometer /nī-lom'i-tər/ *n* a gauge for measuring the height of the River Nile. [Gr *neilometrion*]

Nilot /nī'lot/ or **Nilote** /-lōt/ *n* (pl **Nil'ot, Nil'ots, Nil'ote** or **Nilot'es** /-tēz/) an inhabitant of the banks of the Upper Nile; a member of any of several peoples in E Africa and Sudan; a person of the Upper Nile region. [Gr *Neilōtēs*]
■ **Nilotic** /-ot'ik/ *adj* of the Nile, the Nilots or the languages they speak.

nilpotent /nil'pō-tənt/ (*maths*) *adj* and *n* (of) a quantity which equals zero when multiplied by itself (cf **idempotent**). [L *nil* nothing, and **potent¹**]
■ **nil'potency** *n*.

nim¹ /nim/ *n* an old and widespread game, perhaps *orig* Chinese, in which two players take alternately from heaps or rows of objects (now *usu* matches). [Perh **nim²**]

nim² /nim/ *vt* (pat (*obs*) **nam** or (*archaic*) **nimmed**) to take (*obs*); to steal, pilfer (*archaic sl*). [OE *niman* to take]
■ **nimm'er** *n*.

nim³ /nēm/ *n* an Indian tree of the *Melia* genus, the fruit and seeds of which yield **nim'-oil**, an aromatic, medicinal oil (also **neem, neemb, neem tree** or **nimb**). [Hindi *nīm*]

nimbi see **nimbus**.

nimble /nim'bl/ *adj* light and quick in motion, agile; active; swift. [Appar OE *næmel, numol*, from *niman* to take; cf Ger *nehmen*]
■ **nim'bleness** or (*Spenser*) **nim'blesse** *n* quickness of motion either in body or mind. **nim'bly** *adv*.
□ **nim'ble-fing'ered** *adj* skilful with the fingers; thievish. **nim'ble-foot'ed** *adj* swift of foot. **nim'ble-witt'ed** *adj* quick-witted.

nimbus /nim'bəs/ *n* (pl **nim'bī** or **nim'buses**) a cloud or luminous mist encircling a god or goddess; a halo; a rain-cloud. [L]
■ **nimbed** /nimd/ *adj*. **nimbostratus** /-strā' or -stra'/ *n* (pl **nimbostra'ti** /-tī/) a low, dark-coloured layer of cloud, bringing rain. **nim'bused** *adj*.

NIMBY or **Nimby** /nim'bi/ (*sl*) *n* a person who is willing to have something occur so long as it does not affect him or her or take place in his or her locality. [From 'not in my back yard']
■ **nim'byism** *n*.

NiMH *abbrev*: nickel-metal hydride, denoting a type of rechargeable battery.

nimiety /ni-mī'i-ti/ *n* (*rare*) excess. [L *nimis* too much]
■ **nimious** /nim'i-əs/ *adj* (*Scots law*) excessive and vexatious.

niminy-piminy /nim'i-ni-pim'i-ni/ (*derog*) *adj* affectedly fine or delicate. ♦ *n* affected delicacy. [Imit]

nimonic /ni-mon'ik/ *adj* of alloys used in high-temperature work, eg gas turbine blades, chiefly nickel, with chromium, titanium and aluminium. [*nickel* and *Monel* metal]

Nimrod /nim'rod/ *n* any great hunter. [From the son of Cush in Bible, Genesis 10.8–10]

nincompoop /nin(g)'kəm-poop/ *n* a simpleton; an idiot, stupid person. —Shortened to **nin'com, nin'cum** and also **poop**; earlier forms **nic'ompoop** and **nick'umpoop**. [Origin unknown; probably not from L *nōn compos (mentis)* not in possession (of one's wits)]

nine /nīn/ *n* the cardinal number next above eight; a symbol representing that number (9, ix, etc); a set of nine things or people (such as a baseball team); a score of nine points, strokes, tricks, etc; an article of a size denoted by 9; a playing card with nine pips; (with *cap* and *the*) the nine Muses; the ninth hour after midnight or midday; the age of nine years. ◆ *adj* of the number nine; nine years old. [OE *nigon*; Du *negen*, L *novem*, Gr *ennea*, Sans *nava*]

■ **nine'fold** *adj* and *adv* having nine parts, in nine divisions; nine times as much. **ninth** /*nīnth*/ *adj* last of nine; next after the eighth; equal to one of nine equal parts. ◆ *n* a ninth part; a person or thing in ninth position; an octave and a second (*music*); a tone at that interval (*music*). **ninth'ly** *adv* in the ninth place, ninth in order.

❑ **nine-eleven** *n* (the day of) the destruction by terrorist action of the World Trade Center in New York City on 11 September 2001. **nine'-eyes** *n* a lamprey (from its seven pairs of gill-pouches); a butterfly (from its spots). **nine'-foot**, **nine'-inch**, **nine'-metre**, **nine'-mile**, etc *adj* measuring 9 feet, etc. **nine'-hole** *adj* (of a golf course) having nine holes, as opposed to the standard eighteen. **nine'holes** *n sing* a game in which a ball is to be bowled into nine holes in the ground or in a board; a difficulty, fix (*US*). **nine'pence** *n* the value of nine pennies; a coin of that value; a high standard of niceness, nimbleness, etc. **nine'penny** *adj* costing, offered at, or worth ninepence. ◆ *n* a ninepence. **nine'pin** *n* a bottle-shaped pin set up with eight others for the game of **nine'pins** in which players bowl a ball at them (see **skittle**). **nine'score** *n* and *adj* nine times twenty. **nine'-to-five** *adj* relating to an office job with regular hours, often considered dull and routine.

▨ **nine days' wonder** see under **wonder**. **ninepenny marl**, **ninepenny morris** or **nine men's morris** see under **meril**. **nine points of the law** satisfying the majority of the legal requirements that could be raised in objection or contention, hence, virtually assured, legitimate, valid, etc. **the nine worthies** see under **worthy**. **to the nines** to perfection, fully, elaborately.

nineteen /*nīn-tēn*/ or *nīn'tēn*/ *n* and adj nine and ten. [OE *nigontēne* (-*tiene*); see **nine** and **ten**]

■ **nine'teenth** (or /-*tēnth*'/) *n* and *adj*. **nineteenth'ly** *adv*.

❑ **nineteenth hole** *n* (*joc*) a golf clubhouse, *esp* the bar or restaurant. **nineteenth man** *n* the first substitute player in an Australian rules football team.

■ **nineteen to the dozen** (of speaking, done) in great quantity, not necessarily with equal quality.

ninety /*nīn'ti*/ *n* and adj nine times ten. [OE *nigontig* (*hundnigontig*)]

■ **nine'ties** *n pl* the numbers ninety to ninety-nine; the years so numbered in a life or a century; a range of temperature from ninety to just less than one hundred degrees. **nine'tieth** *adj* last of ninety; next after the eighty-ninth; equal to one of ninety equal parts. ◆ *n* a ninetieth part; a person or thing in ninetieth position.

■ **naughty nineties** see under **naughty**.

ninja /*nin'jə*/ (also with *cap*) *n* (pl **nin'ja** or **nin'jas**) one of a body of trained assassins and spies in feudal Japan, skilled in ninjitsu. [Jap]

■ **ninjit'su** or **ninjut'su** *n* a Japanese martial art, teaching stealth and camouflage.

ninny /*nin'i*/ *n* a simpleton (also (*archaic* or *dialect*) **nin'ny-hammer**). [Poss from **innocent**, or poss from Ital *ninno* child, Sp *niño*]

ninon /*nē'nõ*/ *n* a silk voile or other thin fabric. [Fr *Ninon*, a woman's name]

Nintendo® /*nin-ten'dō*/ *n* a video games console machine which allows computer games to be projected onto, and played using, a television screen. [The name of the manufacturer]

ninth see under **nine**.

Niobe /*nī'ō-bē*/ (*Gr myth*) *n* a daughter of Tantalus, turned into stone as she wept for her children, slain by Artemis and Apollo. [Gr *Niobē*]

■ **Niobē'an** *adj*.

niobium /*nī-ō'bi-əm*/ *n* a metallic element (symbol **Nb**; atomic no 41) discovered in the mineral tantalite and used in certain alloys (formerly called **columbium**). [**Niobe**, from the connection with tantalite]

■ **ni'obate** *n* a salt of niobic acid. **nio'bic** *adj* containing niobium in its pentavalent form (**niobic acid** hydrated niobium pentoxide). **ni'obite** *n* same as **columbite** (see under **Columbian**). **nīo'bous** *adj* containing niobium with a valency of less than five.

NIOSH /*nī'osh*/ *abbrev*: National Institute for Occupational Safety and Health (in the USA).

Nip see under **Nippon**.

nip¹ /*nip*/ *vt* (**nipp'ing**; **nipped** /*nipt*/) to pinch; to press between two surfaces; to remove or sever by pinching or biting (often with *off*); (eg of the cold or frost) to halt the growth or vigour of (eg vegetation); (*esp* of cold weather) to give a smarting or tingling feeling to; to concern closely and painfully (*obs*); to reprehend sharply (*obs*); to snatch (*esp US*); to steal (*inf*); to arrest (*sl*). ◆ *vi* to pinch; to smart; to go nimbly or quickly (*inf*). ◆ *n* an act or experience of nipping; the pinch of cold; a halt to the growth of vegetation caused eg by the cold or frost; a nipping quality; pungency or bite (*Scot*); a sharp reprehension (*obs*); a more or less gradual thinning out of a stratum (*mineralogy*); a simple fastening of a rope by twisting it round the object; a part of a rope fastened in this way (*naut*); a small piece,

such as might be nipped off; a cutpurse (*old sl*). [Prob related to Du *nijpen* to pinch]

■ **nipp'er** *n* a person or thing which nips; a chela or great claw, eg of a crab; a horse's incisor, *esp* of the middle four; a pickpocket or cutpurse (*sl*); a boy assistant to a costermonger, carter, etc; a little boy or (sometimes) girl (*inf*); (in *pl*) small pincers; (in *pl*) any of various pincer-like tools; (in *pl*) handcuffs (*inf*). ◆ *vt* to seize (two ropes) together. **nipp'ily** *adv*. **nipp'iness** *n*. **nipp'ingly** *adv*. **nipp'y** *adj* pungent, biting; nimble, quick (*inf*); niggardly; (*esp* of weather) very cold, frosty. ◆ *n* (with *cap*; *old*) a waitress, *esp* one in a Lyons teashop (also **Nipp'ie**).

❑ **nip'cheese** *n* a stingy person (*sl*); a purser (*obs naut*).

■ **nip and tuck** cosmetic surgery (*inf*); (*US*) at full speed; neck and neck. **nip in** to cut in. **nip in the bud** see under **bud¹**.

nip² /*nip*/ *n* (also (*US*) **nipp'er**) a small quantity of spirits. ◆ *vi* (**nipp'ing**; **nipped**) to take a nip. [Origin obscure]

■ **nipp'erkin** *n* (*archaic*) a small measure of alcoholic drink.

nip³ see **nep**.

nipa /*nē'*/ or */nī'pə*/ *n* (also with *cap*) a low-growing East Indian palm of brackish water (*Nipa fruticans*), with large feathery leaves used for thatching; an alcoholic drink made from it. [Malay *nīpah*]

nipperkin see under **nip²**.

nipple /*nip'l*/ *n* the rounded projecting point of the breast, the outlet of the milk ducts in women and female animals; a teat; a small projection with an orifice, *esp* for regulating flow or lubricating machinery; any nipple-like protuberance. ◆ *vt* to provide with a nipple. [A dimin of **neb** or **nib¹**]

❑ **nipp'le-shield** *n* a soft plastic shield worn over the nipple when breastfeeding by women whose nipples are particularly tender. **nipp'lewort** *n* a tall composite weed (*Lapsana communis*) with small yellow heads, once valued as a cure for sore nipples.

Nippon /*ni-pon'*/ *n* the Japanese name for Japan. [Jap *ni* sun, and *pon*, from *hon* origin]

■ **Nip** *n* (*offensive sl*) a Japanese person. **Nipponese'** *n* and *adj*.

nippy see under **nip¹**.

nipter /*nip'tər*/ *n* the ecclesiastical ceremony of washing the feet, the same as *maundy*. [Gr *niptēr* a basin, from *niptein* to wash]

niqab or **nikab** /*ni-käb'*/ *n* a veil covering the face, worn by Muslim women. [Ar]

niramiai /*ni-rä'mi-ī*/ (*sumo wrestling*) *n* a period (of minutes) spent stamping, thigh-slapping and glaring to intimidate an opponent before beginning to fight. [Jap]

NIREX /*nī'reks*/ *abbrev*: Nuclear Industry Radioactive Waste Executive.

nirl /*nirl*/ (*Scot*) *n* a lump; a crumb; a stunted person. ◆ *vt* to stunt; to shrink or shrivel; to pinch with cold. [Perh **knurl**; perh connected with Icel *nyrfill* niggard]

■ **nirled** or **nirl'it** *adj*. **nirl'y** or **nirl'ie** *adj* knotty; stumpy; stunted; niggardly.

nirvana /*nir-vä'nə* or *nûr-*/ *n* (also with *cap*) the cessation of individual existence, to which a Buddhist or Hindu aspires as the culmination of the meditative state; loosely, a blissful state. [Sans *nirvāna* a blowing out]

nis¹, **n'is** or **nys** /*nis* or *niz*/ (*obs*) a contraction for **ne is**, is not.

nis² or **nisse** /*nis*/ (*Scand folklore*) *n* (pl **niss'es**) a friendly goblin or other benevolent creature. [Dan and Swed *nisse*]

Nisan /*nī'san* or *nē-sän'*/ *n* the seventh civil, first ecclesiastical, month of the Jewish calendar (March to April), called Abib before the Babylonian captivity. [Heb *Nīsān*]

nisberry same as **naseberry**.

nisei /*nē'sā* or *nē-sā'*/ *n* an American or Canadian born of Japanese immigrant parents (cf **issei** and **sansei**). [Jap, second generation]

nisi /*nī'sī*/ (*law*) *adj* to take effect unless, after a time, some condition referred to is fulfilled. [The L conjunction *nisi* unless]

nisi prius /*nī'sī prī'əs* or *ni'si pri'ŭs*/ (*L*) unless previously, a name (from the first words of the writ) given to the jury sittings in civil cases.

nisse same as **nis²**.

Nissen hut /*nis'ən hut*/ *n* a semi-cylindrical corrugated-iron hut designed by Colonel PN *Nissen* (1871–1930).

nisus /*nī'səs*/ *n* effort; striving; impulse. [L *nīsus*, pl *-ūs*]

nit¹ /*nit*/ *n* the egg of a louse or similar insect; a young louse; a term of contempt (*Shakesp*, etc). [OE *hnitu*; Ger *Niss*]

■ **nitt'y** *adj* full of nits.

❑ **nit'-grass** *n* a rare grass (genus *Gastridium*) with nit-like flowers. **nit'-pick** *vi*. **nit'-picker** *n*. **nit'-picking** *n* (*inf*) petty criticism of minor details.

nit² /*nit*/ (*inf*) *n* a fool. [Poss from **nit¹**, or an abbrev of **nitwit**]

nit[3] /nit/ n a unit of luminance, one candela per square metre. [L *nitor* brightness]

nit[4] /nit/ (*comput*) n a unit of information equal to 1.44 bits (also **nep'it**). [Napierian di*git*]

nit[5] /nit/ (*Aust inf*) n watch, lookout, in the phrase *to keep nit*.

nite /nīt/ (*inf* and *non-standard*) n and adj night. [A spelling of *night* reflecting its pronunciation]

niter see **nitre**.

niterie or **nitery** /nī'tə-ri/ (*inf*) n a nightclub. [**night** and *-ery* as in **eatery**]

nithing /nī'dhing* or *nidh'ing/ (*hist*) n an infamous person; an abject coward; a traitor. ◆ adj cowardly; dastardly; niggardly. —Also, not standard, **niddering**, **nidering**, **nidderling**, **niderling** /nid'/ or **nī'ding**. [ON *nīthingr* (in OE as *nīthing*), from *nīth* contumely; Ger *Neiding*]

Nithsdale /niths'dāl/ n an 18c woman's riding hood. [From the Countess of *Nithsdale*, who contrived her husband's escape from the Tower of London in her clothes in 1716]

nitid /nit'id/ (*poetic*) adj shining, bright; merry. [L *nitidus*, from *nitēre* to shine]

Nitinol /nit'i-nol/ n an alloy of nickel and titanium, in particular one which, when shaped and then heated to fix that shape, will after reshaping or deformation return to the original shape on reheating. [The chemical symbols *Ni* and *Ti*, and the initial letters of the US Naval Ordnance Laboratory in Maryland where the alloy was discovered]

niton /nī'ton/ n a former name for radon. [L *nitēre* to shine]

nitraniline see under **nitro-**.

nitrate, **nitratine**, **nitration** see under **nitre**.

nitrazepam /nī-trā'zi-pam* or *-traz'i-/ n a hypnotic and tranquillizing drug taken for the relief of insomnia. [*Nitro-* and *-azepam* as in **diazepam**]

nitre or (*US*) **niter** /nī'tər/ n potassium nitrate or saltpetre (**cubic nitre** is sodium nitrate, or Chile saltpetre); sodium carbonate (*obs*); a supposed nitrous substance in the air, etc (*obs*). [Fr, from L *nitrum*, from Gr *nitron* sodium carbonate; prob of Eastern origin; cf Egyp *ntr(j)*, Heb *nether*, Ar *nitrún*]
■ **ni'trate** n a salt or ester of nitric acid; natural (potassium or sodium) or synthetic (calcium) nitrate, a fertilizer. ◆ vt /-trāt'/ to treat with nitric acid or a nitrate; to convert into a nitrate or nitro-compound. **nitratine** /nī'trə-tin/ n sodium nitrate as a mineral. **nitrā'tion** n. **ni'tric** adj of or containing nitrogen. **ni'tride** n a compound of nitrogen with a metal. ◆ vt to turn into a nitride; to harden the surface of by heating in ammonia gas. **ni'triding** n. **nitrificā'tion** n treatment with nitric acid; conversion into nitrates, *esp* by bacteria through the intermediate condition of nitrites. **ni'trify** vt and vi to subject to or suffer nitrification. **ni'trile** /-tril, -trēl* or *-trīl/ n any of a group of organic cyanides (general formula RC≡N). **ni'trite** n a salt or ester of nitrous acid. **ni'trous** adj of, like, derived from or containing nitrogen. **ni'try** adj (*obs*) applied to the air, as supposed to contain nitre. **ni'tryl** n nitroxyl (see under **nitro-**).
□ **nitric acid** n a colourless or pale yellow corrosive liquid (HNO_3), used in the production of fertilizers and explosives. **nitric anhydride** n a white crystalline solid (N_2O_5) which dissolves in water to produce nitric acid. **nitric oxide** n a colourless toxic gas (NO) produced by cellular metabolism and as an intermediate in the manufacture of nitric acid. **nitrous acid** n a pale-blue unstable solution (HNO_2) obtained by the action of an acid on nitrites. **nitrous anhydride** n a pale-blue liquid (N_2O_3) that reacts with water to form nitrous acid. **nitrous bacteria** n pl a type of nitrobacteria (qv). **nitrous oxide** n a colourless gas (N_2O) with a sweetish odour and taste, used as an anaesthetic, *esp* in dentistry (also **laughing gas**).

Nitrian /nit'ri-ən/ adj belonging to *Nitriae* (Nitriai), a region of ancient Egypt west of the Nile delta, including the Natron lakes and a great conglomeration of hermit settlements. [Gr *nitriā* a soda pit, from *nitron* soda]

nitric...to...**nitrite** see under **nitre**.

nitro /nī'trō/ n a short form of **nitroglycerine**.

nitro- /nī-trō-/ *combining form* indicating: of, made with or containing nitre, nitric acid or nitrogen; containing the group $-NO_2$. [Ety as for **nitre**]
■ **nitroan'iline** or **nitran'iline** n any nitro-derivative of aniline. **nitrobactē'ria** n pl bacteria that convert ammonium compounds into nitrites, and *esp* those that convert nitrites into nitrates. **nitroben'zene** n a yellow oily liquid ($C_6H_5NO_2$) obtained from benzene and nitric and concentrated sulphuric acid. **nitrocell'ulose** n cellulose nitrate, used as an explosive, and in lacquers, glues, etc. **nitro-com'pound** or **nitro-deriv'ative** n a compound in which one or more hydrogens of an aromatic or aliphatic compound are replaced by nitro-groups.

nitrocott'on n guncotton, an explosive made from cotton soaked in nitric and sulphuric acids. **nitroglyc'erine** n a compound produced by the action of nitric and sulphuric acids on glycerine that is both powerfully explosive and used medically as an arterial dilator. **ni'tro-group** n the radical NO_2. **nitrohydrochlor'ic** adj (**nitrohydrochloric acid** same as **aqua regia** (see under **aqua**)). **nitrom'eter** n an apparatus for estimating nitrogen or some of its compounds. **nitromē'thane** n a liquid (CH_3NO_2) obtained from chloroacetic acid and sodium nitrate and used as a solvent and as rocket-fuel. **nitromet'ric** adj. **nitropar'affin** n any of several compounds, derived from methane, in which a hydrogen atom is replaced by a nitro-group. **nitro'philous** adj (of plants) growing in a place where there is a good supply of nitrogen. **nitrosamine** /-sə-mēn* or *-sa'mēn/ n any of a class of neutral organic chemical compounds, many of which cause cancer. **nitrosā'tion** n conversion of ammonium salts into nitrites. **ni'tro-silk** n an artificial silk in which fibres of cellulose nitrate are made and then turned into cellulose. **nitrō'sō** adj of or containing a nitroso-group. **nitrō'sō-group** n the group NO. **ni'trosyl** adj nitroso. **nitrotol'uene** n a nitro-derivative of toluene. **nitrox'yl** n the group NO_2.

nitrogen /nī'trə-jən/ n a gaseous element (symbol **N**; atomic no 7) forming nearly four-fifths of common air, so called from its being an essential constituent of nitre. [Gr *nitron* sodium carbonate (but taken as if meaning nitre), and the root of *gennaein* to generate]
■ **nitrogenase** /nī-troj'ə-nāz/ n an enzyme complex that catalyses nitrogen fixation. **nitrogenizā'tion** or **-s-** n. **nitrogenize** or **-ise** /-troj'/ vt to combine or supply with nitrogen. **nitrog'enous** adj of or containing nitrogen.
□ **nitrogen cycle** n the sum total of the transformations undergone by nitrogen and nitrogenous compounds in nature, circulating between the atmosphere, soil and living organisms, from free nitrogen back to free nitrogen. **nitrogen dioxide** n a poisonous gas (NO_2) with a pungent smell. **nitrogen fixation** n the formation of compounds from free atmospheric nitrogen, either naturally (by lightning, ultraviolet radiation or the action of bacteria) or by an industrial process, eg to make fertilizers. **nitrogen monoxide** same as **nitric oxide** (see under **nitre**). **nitrogen mustard** n any of several compounds with a molecular structure resembling that of a mustard gas, used in cancer treatments. **nitrogen narcosis** n the intoxicating and anaesthetic effect of too much nitrogen in the brain, experienced by divers at considerable depths (also called **rapture of the deep** or **rapture of the depths** and (*sl*) **the narks**).

nitroglycerine...to...**nitroxyl** see under **nitro-**.

nitrous, **nitry**, **nitryl** see under **nitre**.

nitrox /nī'troks/ n a mixture of *nitr*ogen and *ox*ygen, used in underwater breathing apparatus.

nitty see under **nit**[1].

nitty-gritty /nit-i-grit'i/ (*inf*) n the basic or essential details, the fundamentals, *esp* in the phrase *get down to the nitty-gritty*. [Origin uncertain; perh from **grit**[1]]

nitwit /nit'wit/ n a blockhead, stupid person. [Poss Ger dialect *nit* not, and **wit**[1]]
■ **nit'witted** adj. **nitwitt'edness** n. **nitwitt'ery** n.

nival /nī'vəl/ adj growing among snow. [L *nix, nivis* snow]
■ **nivā'tion** n (*geol*) erosion caused by the action of snow. **niveous** /niv'i-əs/ adj (*literary*) snowy, white. **Nivôse** /nē-vōz'/ n the fourth month of the French revolutionary calendar, the month of snow, from about 21 December to 19 January.

nix[1] /niks/ (*sl*) n nothing; short for 'nothing doing, you'll get no support from me'; postal matter addressed wrongly (*old US, usu in pl*). ◆ vt to veto, reject or cancel. [Colloquial Ger and Du for Ger *nichts* nothing]
□ **nix-nie** or **niks-nie** /niks'nē/ n (*S Afr*) nothing at all.
■ **nix my dolly** (*obs sl*) never mind.

nix[2] /niks/ (*Ger myth*) n a usu malignant or spiteful water spirit (also fem **nix'ie** or **nix'y**). [Ger *Nix*, fem *Nixe*; cf **nicker**[3]]

nix[3] /niks/ interj a cry to give warning of the approach of a person in authority, eg a policeman or teacher.

nixer /nik'sər/ n (*Irish inf*) a job, *esp* a spare-time or irregular one, the earnings of which are not declared for tax purposes by the worker. [Origin uncertain; perh from *nix* nothing, or an *extra*]

nizam /ni-zäm'* or *nī-zam'/ n (also with *cap*) formerly, the title of the prince of Hyderabad in India (to 1950); a Turkish soldier. [Hindi *nizām* regulator]

NJ *abbrev* : New Jersey (US state).

NK *abbrev* : natural killer (see **natural killer cell** under **natural**).

NL *abbrev* : the Netherlands (IVR).

nl *abbrev* : *non licet* (*L*), it is not permitted; *non liquet* (*L*), it is not clear; *non lange* (*L*), not far.

NLC *abbrev* : National Lottery Commission (a UK regulatory body).

NLP *abbrev* : natural language processing; neurolinguistic programming.

NLRB (*US*) *abbrev* : National Labor Relations Board.

NM or **N.Mex.** *abbrev* : New Mexico (US state).

nm *abbrev* : nanometre; nautical mile.

NMC *abbrev* : Nursing and Midwifery Council.

NMD (*US*) *abbrev* : National Missile Defense.

n mile *abbrev* : (international) nautical mile.

NMR *abbrev* : nuclear magnetic resonance.

NMRI *abbrev* : nuclear magnetic resonance imaging.

NNE *abbrev* : north-north-east.

NNI *abbrev* : Noise and Number Index.

NNP *abbrev* : net national product.

NNW *abbrev* : north-north-west.

NO *abbrev* : natural order; New Orleans.

No (*chem*) *symbol* : nobelium.

no[1] /*nō*/ *adv* used as a sentence substitute to express a negative answer, refusal, disapproval, disbelief or to acknowledge a negative statement (formerly used *esp* in response to a question or statement containing a negative, in contradistinction to *nay*, used to express simple negation until superseded in this function by *no* in early 17c); not so; not; (with *compar*) in no degree, not at all. ◆ *n* (*pl* **noes** or **nos**) a denial; a refusal; a vote or voter for the negative. [OE *nā*, from *ne* not, and *ā* ever; cf **nay**]
❑ **no'-man** *n* someone ready to say 'no'. **no'-no** *n* (*pl* **no'-nos**, **no'-no's** or **no'-noes**) (*inf*) a failure, non-event; something which must not be done, said, etc; an impossibility, non-starter.
■ **no can do** see under **can**[1]. **no more** destroyed; dead; never again, not any longer. **not take no for an answer** to continue (with something) in spite of refusals. **the noes have it** no-votes or no-voters are in the majority.

no[2] /*nō*/ *adj* not any; not one; by no means properly called, certainly not, not at all. [OE *nān* none; see **none**]
❑ **no-account'** *adj* (*US inf*) worthless; insignificant. **no'-ball** *n* (*cricket*) a ball bowled in such a way that it is disallowed by the rules, and which counts as one run to the batting side. ◆ *vi* to bowl a no-ball. ◆ *vt* (of an umpire) to declare (a bowler) to have bowled a no-ball. **no-brain'er** *n* (*inf*) something entailing no great mental effort. **no-claims bonus** or **discount** *n* a reduction in the price of an insurance policy because no claims have been made on it. **no-fault'** *adj* (of insurance compensation payments) made without attachment to or admission of blame by any one person or party in particular. **no-fines'** *n* concrete from which the fine aggregate (ie sand) has been omitted. **no-fly zone** *n* an area in which (*esp* military) aircraft are not permitted to fly. **no-frills'** *adj* basic, not elaborate or fancy. **no-go area** see under **go**[1]. **no'-good** (*inf*) *adj* bad, worthless. ◆ *n* a bad, worthless person. **no-hitt'er** *n* (*baseball*) a game in which a pitcher does not allow an opponent to score a hit. **no-hope, no-hoper** see under **hope**[1]. **no'-man's-land** *n* a waste region to which no one has a recognized claim; neutral or disputed land, *esp* between entrenched hostile forces (also *fig*). **no'-meaning** *n* lack of meaning; something said that is deficient in meaning. **no-non'sense** *adj* sensible, tolerating no nonsense. **no one** or **no'-one** *n* and *pronoun* nobody. **no-score draw** *n* (*football*) a match in which neither team manages to score. **no'-show** *n* a person who does not arrive for something he or she has booked, eg a restaurant table or a flight; an instance of such non-arrival. **no-side'** *n* the end of a rugby match. **no-tech** *adj* (*inf*) not involving or using the most recent technology. **no-trump'** or **no-trumps'** *n* (*bridge*) a call for the playing of a hand without any trump suit. ◆ *adj* (no-trump) suitable for or relating to playing without a trump suit. **no-trump'er** *n* a no-trump call; a hand suitable for this; someone addicted to calling no-trumps. **no'way, no'ways** or **no'wise** *adv* in no way, manner, or degree (see also below). **no-win'** *adj* (of a situation) in which one is bound to lose or fail whatever one does.
■ **no dice** see under **dice**[1]. **no doubt** surely. **no end** and **no go** see under **end** and **go**[1]. **no joke** not a trifling matter. **no one** no single. **no time** a very short time. **no way** (*inf*) under no circumstances, absolutely not, an emphatic expression of disagreement or dissent.

no[3] /*nō*/ (*Scot*) *adv* not. [Perh from *nocht* ; see **not**[1] and **nought**]

no[4], **nō** or **noh** /*nō*/ *n* (*pl* **no** or **noh**) (often with *cap*) the traditional Japanese style of drama developed out of a religious dance (also **nō'gaku** /*-gä-koo*/ (*pl* **no'gaku**)). [Jap *nō*]

no. or **No.** *abbrev* : number.

n.o. (*cricket*) *abbrev* : not out.

Noachian /*nō-ā'ki-ən*/ *adj* of *Noah* or the time when he lived (also **Noachic** /*-ak'* or *-āk'*/).
❑ **Noah's ark** *n* a child's toy in imitation of the Ark with its occupants (Bible, Genesis 6–9).

nob[1] /*nob*/ *n* the head (*inf*); the jack of the suit turned up by the dealer in cribbage. [Perh **knob**]
■ **one for his nob** a point scored for holding the nob in cribbage; a blow on the head (*inf*).

nob[2] /*nob*/ (*inf*) *n* a person of wealth or *esp* high social rank. [Origin obscure; cf **nabs** and **nib**[2]]
■ **nobb'ily** *adv*. **nobb'iness** *n*. **nobb'y** *adj* smart.

nobble /*nob'l*/ (*sl*) *vt* to injure or drug (a racehorse) to prevent it from winning; to get hold of, *esp* dishonestly; to win over, persuade or dissuade, eg by bribery or coercion; to swindle; to prevent from doing something; to seize or grab; to arrest. [Perh **nab**[1]]
■ **nobb'ler** *n* (*sl*) a person who nobbles; a finishing stroke; a thimblerigger's assistant or accomplice; a dram of spirits.

nobbut /*nob'ət*/ (*dialect*) *adv* only. ◆ *prep* except. ◆ *conj* except that. [**no**[1,2] and **but**[1]]

nobelium /*nō-bel'i-əm* or *-bē'li-*/ *n* an artificially produced radioactive transuranic element (symbol **No**; atomic no 102). [First produced at the *Nobel* Institute, Stockholm]

Nobel prize /*nō-bel' prīz*/ *n* any of the annual prizes for work in physics, chemistry, medicine or physiology, literature, the promotion of peace, and economics instituted by Alfred B *Nobel* (1833–96), Swedish discoverer of dynamite.
■ **Nō'belist** *n* a Nobel laureate.
❑ **Nobel laureate** *n* a (past) winner of the Nobel prize in any category.

nobilesse see **noblesse**.

nobiliary see under **nobility**.

nobility /*nō-bil'i-ti*/ *n* the quality of being noble; high rank; dignity; excellence; greatness of mind or character; noble descent; (with *the*) nobles as a body, the aristocracy, peerage. [Ety as for **noble**]
■ **nobil'iary** *adj* of nobility. **nobil'itate** *vt* to ennoble. **nobilitā'tion** *n*.
❑ **nobiliary particle** *n* a preposition forming part of a title or certain names, eg Ger *von*, Fr *de*, Ital *di*.

noble /*nō'bl*/ *adj* illustrious; high in social rank or character; of high birth; impressive; stately; generous; excellent, worthy. ◆ *n* a person of high social title or rank; a peer; an obsolete gold coin worth *approx* one-third of a pound sterling (33p or 6 shillings 8d). [Fr *noble*, from L (g)*nōbilis*, from (g)*nōscere* to know]
■ **no'bleness** *n*. **no'bly** *adv*.
❑ **noble art** or **science** *n* (with *the*) boxing. **noble gas** *n* an inert gas. **no'bleman** *n* (*pl* **no'blemen**) a man who is noble or of high social rank; a peer. **noble metal** *n* one that does not readily tarnish on exposure to air, such as gold, silver, platinum (cf **base metal**). **no'ble-mind'ed** *adj*. **no'ble-mind'edness** *n*. **noble opal** *n* precious opal, a translucent or semi-transparent bluish- or yellowish-white variety with brilliant play of colours. **noble rot** *n* a mould which forms on over-ripe grapes and produces the characteristic richness of certain wines, eg Sauternes and Tokay. **noble savage** *n* a romantic and idealized view of primitive man. **noble science** see **noble art** above. **no'blewoman** *n* (*pl* **no'blewomen**) a woman who is noble or of high social rank; a peeress.
■ **most noble** an appellation formally prefixed to the title of a duke.

noblesse /*nō-bles'* or *nō'bles*/, also (*Spenser*) **nobilesse** /*nō'bi-les*/ *n* nobility; nobleness; nobles collectively. [Fr]
■ **noblesse oblige** /*ō-blēzh'*/ (*Fr*) rank imposes obligations.

nobody /*nō'bo-di* or *-bə-*/ *pronoun* no person; no one. ◆ *n* a person of no importance. [**no**[2] and **body**]
❑ **nobody's business** *n* (*inf*) a thing nobody could hope to deal with or nobody troubles about.
■ **like nobody's business** (*inf*) very energetically or intensively.

NOC *abbrev* : National Olympic Committee.

nocake /*nō'kāk*/ *n* meal made of parched maize. [Algonquian; cf Narragansett *nokehick*]

nocent /*nō'sənt*/ (*rare*) *adj* hurtful; guilty. ◆ *n* a person who is hurtful or guilty. [L *nocēns, -entis*, prp of *nocēre* to hurt]
■ **nō'cently** *adv*.

nochel see **notchel**.

nociceptive /*nō-si-sep'tiv*/ (*biol*) *adj* sensitive to pain; causing pain. [L *nocēre* to hurt, and *receptive*]
■ **nocicep'tor** *n* a sensory nerve-ending that sends signals that cause pain in response to certain stimuli.

nock /*nok*/ *n* a notch, or a part carrying a notch, *esp* on an arrow or a bow; the forward upper end of a sail that sets with a boom. ◆ *vt* to notch; to fit (an arrow) on the string of a bow. [Origin obscure, poss connected with Swed *nock* tip; appar not the same as **notch**]

nocket see **nacket**.

noct- /*nokt-*/ or **nocti-** /*nok-ti-*/ *combining form* denoting night. [L *nox, noct-*]

noctambulation /nok-tam-bū-lā'shən/ (*rare*) *n* sleepwalking. [L *nox*, *noctis* night, and *ambulāre*, *-ātum* to walk]
■ **noctam'bulism** *n*. **noctam'bulist** *n*.

noctilio /nok-til'i-ō/ *n* (*pl* **noctil'ios**) any member of the S American genus *Noctilio*, the hare-lipped bat. [L *nox*, *noctis* night, and the ending of *vespertiliō* bat]

noctiluca /nok-ti-loo'kə or -lū'/ *n* (*pl* **noctilu'cae** /-sē/) a member of the *Noctiluca* genus of phosphorescent marine flagellate infusorians, abundant around the British coasts. [L *noctilūca* the moon, a lantern, from *nox*, *noctis* night, and *lūcēre* to shine]

noctilucent /nok-ti-loo'sənt or -lū'/, also **noctilucous** /-kəs/ *adj* phosphorescent; glowing in the dark (*zool*); (of high-altitude dust- or ice-clouds) visible at night in latitudes greater than about 501, where they reflect light from the sun below the horizon (*meteorol*). [L *nox*, *noctis* night, and *lūcēre* to shine]
■ **noctilu'cence** *n*.

noctivagant /nok-tiv'ə-gənt/ *adj* wandering in the night. [L *nox*, *noctis* night, and *vagārī* to wander]
■ **noctivagā'tion** *n*. **noctiv'agous** *adj*.

Noctua /nok'tū-ə/ *n* a generic name sometimes used (without *cap*) as a general name for any member of the **Noctū'idae**, a large family (or group of families) of mostly nocturnal, strong-bodied moths, the owlet-moths. [L *noctua* an owl, from *nox*, *noctis* night]
■ **noc'tūid** *n* and *adj*.

noctuary /nok'tū-ə-ri/ *n* a record of the events or one's thoughts during the night. [L *nox*, *noctis* night, on the analogy of **diary**]

noctule /nok'tūl/ *n* the great bat, the largest British species. [Fr, from Ital *nottola*, from L *nox*, *noctis* night]

nocturn /nok'tûrn/ *n* (*RC*) any one of the three sections of the service of matins; a daily portion of the psalter used at nocturns (*obs*). [L *nocturnus*, from *nox*, *noctis* night]
■ **nocturn'al** *adj* belonging to night; happening, done, or active by night. ◆ *n* an astronomical instrument for finding the time at night; a person, animal or spirit active by night. **nocturn'ally** *adv*. **nocturne** /nok' or -tûrn'/ *n* a dreamy, romantic or pensive musical piece, generally for the piano, *esp* associated with the name of its inventor John Field (1782–1837) and Chopin, who developed it; a moonlight or night scene (*art*).

nocuous /nok'ū-əs/ (*rare*) *adj* hurtful, noxious. [L *nocuus*, from *nocēre* to hurt]
■ **noc'uously** *adv*. **noc'uousness** *n*.

nod /nod/ *vi* (**nodd'ing**; **nodd'ed**) to give a quick forward motion of the head, *esp* in assent, greeting or command; to let the head drop in weariness or dozing; to lean over as if about to fall; to bend or curve downwards, or hang from a curved support; to dance, dip or bob up and down; to make a careless mistake through inattention. ◆ *vt* to incline (the head); to move (the head) in assent, greeting or command; to signify or direct by a nod. ◆ *n* a quick bending forward of the head; a slight bow; a movement of the head as a gesture of assent, greeting or command; a nap; (often with *to*) an acknowledgement of influence or respect. [ME *nodde*, not known in OE]
■ **nodd'er** *n*. **nodd'ing** *n* and *adj*. **nodd'ingly** *adv*.
❑ **nodding acquaintance** *n* a slight acquaintance; someone with whom one is only slightly acquainted; superficial, incomplete knowledge or understanding. **nodding donkey** *n* (*inf*; *esp US*) a type of pump for pumping oil from land-based oil wells. **nodding duck** see under **duck**[1].
■ **Land of Nod** sleep (in punning allusion to the biblical land, Genesis 4.16). **nod off** (*inf*) to fall asleep. **nod through** in parliament, to allow to vote by proxy; to pass without discussion, a vote, etc. **on the nod** by general assent, ie without the formality of voting or without adequate scrutiny, etc; on credit (*sl*).

nodal, etc see under **node**.

nodder, **nodding** see **nod**.

noddle[1] /nod'l/ *n* the head or brain (*inf*); the back of the head (*obs*); the nape of the neck (*dialect*). [Origin obscure]

noddle[2] /nod'l/ *vt* and *vi* to nod slightly; to keep nodding. [From **nod**]

noddy[1] /nod'i/ *n* a simpleton, stupid person (*obs*); an oceanic bird (genus *Anous*) related to the terns, unaccustomed to man and therefore easily caught and so deemed stupid; a sequence in a filmed interview in which the interviewer is photographed nodding in acknowledgement of what the interviewee is saying (*inf*); an old game like cribbage; the jack in this and other games; an old form of cab with a door at the back. [Origin obscure; connection among meanings doubtful]
❑ **noddy suit** *n* (*milit sl*) an NBC suit.

noddy[2] /nod'i/ *n* an inverted pendulum with a spring, used to test oscillation. [Perh from **nod**]

node /nōd/ *n* a knot; a knob or lump; a swelling; a place, often swollen, where a leaf is attached to a stem; a point of intersection of two great circles of the celestial sphere, *esp* the orbit of a planet or the moon and the ecliptic (*astron*); a point at which a curve cuts itself, and through which more than one tangent to the curve can be drawn (*geom*); a similar point on a surface, where there is more than one tangent-plane (*geom*); a point of minimum displacement in a system of stationary waves (*phys*); the point in an electrical network where two or more conductors are connected (*elec eng*); a point of intersection or junction in any branching system; a complication in a story (*fig*); a nodus; a processing location, *esp* one attached to the Net (*comput*). [L *nōdus* knot; dimin *nōdulus*]
■ **nō'dal** *adj* of or like a node or nodes. **nōdal'ity** *n* knottedness; the state of being nodal. **nō'dalize** or **-ise** *vt* to make nodal. **nō'dally** *adv*. **nōd'āted** *adj* knotted. **nōdā'tion** *n* knottiness; a knotty place. **nodical** /nōd' or nod'/ *adj* relating to the nodes of a celestial body; from a node round to the same node again. **nodose** /nōd-ōs' or nōd'ōs/ *adj* having nodes, knots or swellings; knotty. **nodosity** /nō-dos'i-ti/ *n* knottiness; a knotty swelling. **nōd'ous** *adj* knotty. **nodular** /nod'ū-lər/ *adj* of or like a nodule; in the form of nodules; having nodules or little knots. **nod'ūlāted** *adj* having nodules. **nodūlā'tion** *n*. **nod'ūle** *n* a little rounded lump or swelling; a swelling on a root inhabited by symbiotic bacteria (*bot*); a nodus. **nod'ūled** *adj*. **nod'ūlose** or **nod'ūlous** *adj*. **nōd'us** *n* (*pl* **nōd'i** /-ī/) (*L*) a knotty point, difficulty, complication; a knotlike mass of tissue or cells, swelling or knoblike protuberance (*anat*); a swelling at the junction of nervures in an insect's wing.
❑ **node of Ranvier** /rä'vē-ā/ *n* a gap in the myelin sheath of a nerve fibre, named after LA *Ranvier* (1835–1922), French physician.

Noel or **Noël** /nō-el'/ *n* Christmas (also **Nowel** or **Nowell**; *obs* except in Christmas carols, on Christmas cards, etc); (without *cap*) a Christmas carol. [OFr (Fr *noël*; cf Sp *natal*, Ital *natale*), from L *natalis* belonging to a birthday]

noesis /nō-ē'sis/ *n* the activity of the intellect; purely intellectual apprehension or perception (*philos*). [Gr *noēsis*, from *noeein* to perceive or think]
■ **noemat'ical** *adj*. **noemat'ically** *adv*. **noetic** /nō-et'ik/ *adj* of or relating to the mind or intellect; purely intellectual.

Noetian /nō-ē'shən/ *n* a Patripassian or follower of *Noētus* of Smyrna (3c). ◆ *adj* of or relating to the Noetians.
■ **Noe'tianism** *n*.

nog[1], also **nogg** /nog/ *n* eggnog or a similar drink; Norwich strong ale (*obs*). [Origin unknown]

nog[2] /nog/ *n* a stump or snag; a wooden peg, pin or cog; a brick-sized piece of wood inserted in a wall to receive nails. ◆ *vt* (**nogg'ing**; **nogged**) to fix with nogs; to build with nogging. [Origin unknown]
■ **nogg'ing** *n* a brick or piece of rough timber filling between timbers in a partition or frame.

nogaku see **no**[4].

nogg see **nog**[1].

noggin /nog'in/ *n* a small mug or wooden cup; its contents, a measure of about a gill; (of beer, spirits, etc) (*inf*); the head (*inf*). [Origin unknown; Ir *noigín*, Gaelic *noigean*, are believed to be from English]

nogging see under **nog**[2].

noh see **no**[4].

nohow /nō'how/ (*inf*) *adv* not in any way, not at all; in no definable way. ◆ *adj* (also **no'howish**) out of sorts.

noils /noilz/ *n pl* short pieces of wool or other fibre separated from the longer fibres eg by combing. [Origin unknown]
■ **noil** *n* the wool or other fibre so separated.

noint or **'noint** an apheretic form of **anoint**.

noirish or **noir-ish** /nwä'rish/ *adj* redolent of some of the qualities of film noir (qv).

noise (*Spenser* **noyes**) /noiz/ *n* sound of any kind; an unmusical sound; (an) over-loud or disturbing sound; a din; (in *pl*) sounds made expressing sympathy, a reaction, feelings, etc without actual words; frequent or public talk; interference in the transference of heat, in an electrical current, etc; interference in a communication channel, as detected by hearing or (**visual noise**, eg snow on a television screen) sight; meaningless extra bits or words removed from data, or ignored, at the time of use (*comput*); a rumour (*obs*); a report (*Shakesp*); a band of musicians (*obs*). ◆ *vt* (*literary*; *usu* with *about* or *abroad*) to spread by rumour or word of mouth. ◆ *vi* (*rare*) to talk or call out loud. [OFr *noise* noise; perh from L *nausea* disgust, poss influenced by L *noxia*, in its (albeit disputed) meaning, disturbance or strife]
■ **noise'ful** *adj*. **noise'less** *adj*. **noise'lessly** *adv*. **noise'lessness** *n*. **nois'ily** *adv*. **nois'iness** *n*. **nois'y** *adj* making a loud noise or sound; accompanied by noise; clamorous; turbulent.
❑ **noise abatement climb procedure** *n* (*aeronautics*) the flying of a civil aircraft so that it climbs rapidly on take-off until reaching the built-

up area, where it maintains a positive rate of climb until the area is overflown or it reaches 5000ft. **noise control** n (acoustics) reduction of unwanted noise by various methods, eg absorption or isolation. **noise'maker** n (esp N Am) a device for making a loud noise at a football match, festivity, etc, such as a clapper. **noise pollution** n annoying or harmful (loud) noise.

■ **a big** or (rare) **a top noise** a person of great importance. **make a noise** to talk or complain a lot. **make a noise in the world** to achieve great notoriety. **noises off** (a stage direction indicating) sounds made off-stage to be heard by the audience.

noisette[1] /nwa-zet'/ n a small piece of meat (usu lamb) cut off the bone and rolled; a nutlike or nut-flavoured sweet. ◆ adj flavoured with or containing hazelnuts. [Fr, hazelnut]

noisette[2] /nwa-zet'/ n a hybrid between the China rose and the musk rose. [Philippe Noisette (1772–1849), French horticulturalist, who first grew it]

noisome /noi'səm/ adj harmful to health; disgusting or offensive to sight or smell. [noy]
■ **noi'somely** adv. **noi'someness** n.

noisy see under **noise**.

nole (Shakesp) see **noll**.

nolens volens /nō'lenz vō'lenz, nō'lāns vō' or wō'lāns/ (formal) adv willy-nilly. [L, unwilling, willing]

noli-me-tangere /nō-li-mē-tan'jə-ri/, also **noli me tangere** /nō-lē mā tang'ge-re/ n a warning against touching; lupus, etc of the face (archaic); a species of balsam, Impatiens noli-(me-)tangere, that ejects its ripe seeds at a light touch; a work of art showing Christ appearing to Mary Magdalene after the Resurrection. ◆ adj warning off. [Vulgate translation of Bible, John 20.17, from L nōlī (imperative of nōlle) be unwilling, do not, mē me, and tangere to touch]

noll, noul or **nowl** (Spenser **noule**, Shakesp **nole**) /nōl/ n the top of the head. [OE hnoll]

nolle prosequi /nol'e pros'ə-kwī/ (law) n an entry on a record to the effect that the plaintiff or prosecutor will proceed no further with (part of) the suit. [L, to not want to proceed]

Nollywood /nol'i-wŭd/ n the Nigerian film industry. [Modelled on **Bollywood**]

nolo contendere /nō'lō kon-ten'də-ri/ n a legal plea by which the accused does not admit guilt, but accepts conviction (eg when wishing to avoid lengthy legal proceedings), the charges being deniable if referred to in a separate case. [L, I do not wish to contend]

nolo episcopari /nō'lō e-pis-ko-pä'rī/ n refusal of a responsible position. [L, I do not wish to be a bishop]

nom /nɔ̃/ (Fr) n a name.
❑ **nom de guerre** /də ger'/ n an assumed name; a pseudonym. **nom de plume** see separate entry.

nom. or **nomin.** abbrev : nominal; nominative.

noma /nō'mə/ n a destructive ulceration of the cheek, esp that affecting hunger-weakened children. [L nomē ulcer, from Gr nomē ulcer, feeding, from nemein to feed, consume]

nomad or (rare) **nomade** /nō'mad/ or -məd, also nom'ad/ n a member of a wandering pastoral community; a rover, wanderer. ◆ adj of or relating to nomads. [Gr nomas, nomados, from nemein to drive to pasture]
■ **nomadic** /nōm- or nom-ad'ik/ adj. **nomad'ically** adv. **nom'adism** n. **nomadizā'tion** or **-s-** n. **nom'adize** or **-ise** vi to lead a nomadic or vagabond life. ◆ vt to make nomadic, force into a nomadic life. **nom'ady** n the state of living as or like a nomad.

nomarch, nomarchy see under **nome**.

nombles /num'blz/ a variant of **numbles** (see **umbles**).

nombril /nom'bril/ (heraldry) n a point a little below the centre of a shield. [Fr, navel]

nom de plume /nɔ̃ də plüm' or ploom', also nom/ n a pen-name, pseudonym. [Would-be Fr, from Fr nom name, de of, and plume pen]

nome /nōm/ n a province or department, esp in ancient Egypt or modern Greece. [Gr nomos]
■ **nomarch** /nom'ärk/ n the governor of a nome. **nom'archy** n a nome of modern Greece.

nomen /nō'men/ (L) n (pl **nō'mina**) a name, esp of the gens or clan, a Roman's second name, such as Gaius Julius Caesar.
❑ **nomen nudum** /nū'dəm or noo'düm/ n in biology, a mere name published without a description.

nomenclator /nō'mən-klā-tər/ n a person who bestows names, or draws up a classified scheme of names; a person who announces a list of names of people, esp (hist) in canvassing for a Roman election; a

book containing a list of words, a vocabulary (obs). [L nōmenclātor, from nōmen a name, and calāre to call]
■ **no'menclātive**, **nomenclatorial** /nō-men-klə-tō'ri-əl or -tō'/ or **nomenclā'tural** adj. **nomenclature** /nō-men'klə-chər or nō'mən-klā-chər/ n a system of names; terminology; a list of names; a vocabulary (obs); an act or instance of naming, esp within a particular system; (now considered loose) a name.

nomenklatura /no-men-klə'tū-rə/ (usu derog) n office-holders and managers in a communist regime (esp formerly in E Europe). [Russ]

nomic /nom'ik/ adj customary; (esp of spelling) conventional. [Gr nomikos, from nomos custom]

-nomic see under **-nomy**.

nomina plural of **nomen**.

nominal /nom'i-nəl/ adj relating to or of the nature of a name or noun; of names; by name; only in name; so-called, but not in reality; inconsiderable, small, minor, in comparison with the real value, hardly more than a matter of form; nominalistic (rare); according to plan (space flight). ◆ n (grammar) a noun or phrase, etc standing as a noun. [L nōminālis, from nōmen, -inis a name]
■ **nom'inalism** n the doctrine that the objects to which general terms refer are related to one another only by the terms. **nom'inalist** n and adj. **nominalist'ic** adj. **nominaliza'tion** or **-s-** n. **nom'inalize** or **-ise** vt to form a noun (eg from a verb). **nom'inally** adv in name only; theoretically; by name; as a noun.
❑ **nominal account** n an account concerned with revenue and expenses such as sales and purchases. **nominal par** see under **par**[1]. **nominal value** same as **nominal par** (see under **par**[1]).

nominate /nom'i-nāt/ vt to propose formally for election; to appoint; to name; to mention by name; to designate. ◆ adj (chiefly Scots law) nominated; elect. [L nōmināre, -ātum to name, from nōmen]
■ **nom'inable** adj namable; fit to be named. **nom'inately** adv by name. **nominā'tion** n the act or power of nominating; the state or privilege of being nominated; naming; (in horse breeding) the arranged mating of a mare with a stallion. **nominatival** /nom-in-ə-tī'vl or nom-nə-/ adj. **nominatī'vally** adv. **nominative** /nom'in-ə-tiv or nom'nə-tiv/ adj naming the subject (grammar); (in the case) in which the subject is expressed (grammar); (also /nom'in-ā-tiv/) nominated, appointed by nomination (not elected). ◆ n the nominative case; a word in the nominative case. **nom'inatively** adv. **nom'inātor** n a person who nominates.
❑ **nominative absolute** n (grammar) a nominative combined with a participle, but not connected with a finite verb or governed by any other word.

nominee /nom-i-nē'/ n a person who is nominated by another; a person who acts on behalf of another person, esp to keep that person's identity hidden; a person on whose life an annuity or lease depends; a person in whose name stocks and shares, etc are registered, but who is not the actual owner of them; a person to whom the holder of a copyhold estate surrenders his or her interest (obs). [L nōmināre, -ātum to nominate, with -ee as if from Fr]

nomism /nō'mi-zm or nom'i-zm/ n religious legalism; the view that moral conduct consists in the observance of a law. [Gr nomisma established custom, from nomos a law]
■ **nomist'ic** /nom-/ adj based on law or on a sacred book.

nomo- /nom-ə- or nō-mə-/ combining form denoting custom or law. [Gr nomos law]

nomocracy /nō- or no-mok'rə-si/ n government according to a code of laws. [Gr nomos law, and kratos power]

nomogeny /no- or nō-moj'ə-ni/ n the origination of life according to natural law, not miracle, opp to thaumatogeny. [Gr nomos law, and the root gen-, as in genesis origination]

nomography /no- or nō-mog'rə-fi/ n the art of making nomograms. [Gr nomos law, and graphein to write]
■ **nom'ogram** or **nom'ograph** n a chart or diagram of scaled lines or curves used to help in mathematical calculations, comprising three scales in which a line joining values on two determines a third (also called **isopleth**). **nomog'rapher** n. **nomograph'ic** or **nomograph'ical** adj. **nomograph'ically** adv.

nomology /no- or nō-mol'ə-ji/ n the science of law; the science of the laws of the mind; the science of the laws explaining or dealing with natural phenomena. [Gr nomos law, and logos discourse]
■ **nomological** /-ə-loj'/ adj. **nomol'ogist** n.

nomos /nom'os/ (Gr) n (pl **nomoi** /nō'moi/) a nome.

nomothete /nom'ō-thēt/ or (Gr) **nomothetes** /no-moth'i-tēz/ n a lawgiver; a legislator; (in ancient Athens) a member of a body charged with revision of the laws. [Gr nomothetēs, from nomos law, and the root the-, as in tithenai to set]
■ **nomothetic** /-thet'ik/ or **nomothet'ical** adj giving laws, legislative; of or relating to the formulation of general or universal laws, opp to idiographic.

-nomy /-nə-mi/ *combining form* denoting a science or field of knowledge, or the discipline of the study of these. [Gr -*nomia* administration, regulation]
■ **-nomic** *combining form* forming corresponding adjectives.

non /non *or* nōn/ (L) not.
■ **non compos mentis** /non kom'pos men'tis/ not of sound mind. **non licet** /non li'sit/ literally, it is not allowed; not permitted, unlawful (*law*). **non liquet** /non li'kwit/ literally, it is not clear; (of evidence, etc) unclear (*law*). **non multa, sed multum** /non mŭl'tä, sed mŭl'tŭm/ not many but much; not great in number but great in significance. **non obstante** /ob-stan'tē *or* ob-stan'te/ not hindering; notwithstanding. **non placet** /non plas'it/ literally, it does not please; a negative vote.

Words formed using the prefix **non-** are listed in the following entry or, if their meaning is self-evident, at the foot of the page; other words spelt with non- follow in the main word list. The words listed include the most common words with *non-*, but the prefix is living and many other words using it may be formed.

---

non- /non-/ *pfx* denoting not, absence of, reverse of (often when a form in *in-* or *un-* has a special meaning, or sometimes instead of *un-*); sometimes used of someone or something with pretensions, who or which is ludicrously unworthy of the name mentioned, eg *non-hero* and *non-event*. [L nōn not]

■ **non-abil'ity** *n* incapacity; inability. **non-accept'ance** *n* lack of acceptance; refusal to accept. **non-ac'cess** *n* (*law*) lack of opportunity for sexual intercourse. **non-accident'al** *adj* (**non-accidental injury** (*social work*) an injury such as a bruise, burn or fracture, *esp* to a child, which was not caused by an accident but was deliberately inflicted by another (older) person). **non-admiss'ion** *n* refusal of admission; failure to be admitted. **non-aggress'ion** *n* abstention from aggression (also *adj*). **non-aligned'** *adj* not aligned geometrically; not taking sides in international politics, *esp* not supporting either of the main international blocs, ie the former Warsaw Pact countries or the USA and the W European democracies. **non-align'ment** *n*. **non-appear'ance** *n* failure or neglect to appear, *esp* in a court of law. **non-atten'tion** *n* inattention. **non-attrib'utable** *adj* (of a press statement, etc) whose source is not able or permitted to be disclosed. **non-attrib'utably** *adv*. **non-bear'ing** *adj* (of a wall) bearing no load other than its own weight. **non-biolog'ical** *adj* not relating to biological forms; (of a washing powder) not containing enzymes. **non-Chris'tian** *n* a person who is not a Christian (also *adj*). **non-chromosō'mal** *adj* not found on a chromosome; not involving chromosomes. **non'-claim** *n* a failure to make a claim within the time limited by law. **non-class'ified** *adj* (of information) not classified secret. **non-cog'nizable** *adj* (*law*) (of an offence) that cannot be judicially investigated. **non-collē'giate** *adj* not belonging to a college or not having colleges (also *n*). **non-com'** *n* (*inf*) a non-commissioned officer. **non-com'batant** *n* anyone connected with an army who is there for some purpose other than that of fighting, such as a surgeon or a chaplain; a civilian in time of war. **non-comedogen'ic** *adj* (of cosmetics) not blocking the pores or causing spots or blackheads. **non-commiss'ioned** *adj* not having a commission, as an officer in the army below the rank of commissioned officer or warrant officer. **non-committ'al** *adj* not committing someone, or refraining from committing oneself, to any particular opinion or course of conduct; free from any declared preference or pledge; implying nothing, one way or the other, for or against. ◆ *n* a non-committal state or utterance. **non-committ'ally** *adv*. **non-commun'icant** *n* a person who does not take communion on any particular occasion or in general, *esp* formerly according to the rites of the Church of England; a person who has not yet communicated. **non-commun'ion** *n*. **non-compear'ance** *n* (*Scots law*) failure to appear in a court of law. **non-compound'er** *n* a person who does not compound or make composition; a Jacobite in favour of restoring James II unconditionally (*hist*). **non-con'** *n* (*inf*) a

Nonconformist (also *adj*). **non-concurr'ence** *n* refusal to concur. **non-concurr'ent** *adj*. **non-conduct'ing** *adj* not readily conducting, *esp* heat or electricity. **non-conduct'or** *n* a substance or object that does not readily conduct heat or electricity. **non-conform'ance** *n*. **nonconform'ing** *adj* not conforming, *esp* to an established church. **nonconform'ist** *n* a person who does not conform (*esp* a person who refused to conform or subscribe to the Act of Uniformity in 1662 making the Book of Common Prayer the only legal form of worship in England); *usu* applied in England (with *cap*) to a Protestant separated from the Church of England (also *adj*). **nonconform'ity** *n* lack of conformity, *esp* to the established church. **non'-content** *n* a person who is not content; (in the House of Lords) a person casting a negative vote. **non-conten'tious** *adj* not subject to contention. **non-contrib'utory** *adj* (of pensions) paid for entirely by the employer, with no contributions from the beneficiary; (of state benefit) not dependent on national insurance contributions paid by the beneficiary. **non-co-operā'tion** *or* **non-cooperā'tion** *n* failure or refusal to co-operate, *esp* (in India before 1947) with the government. **non-custō'dial** *adj* (of a legal sentence) not involving imprisonment. **non-dai'ry** *adj* (of foods) containing no dairy produce. **non-denominā'tional** *adj* not exclusively belonging to or according to the beliefs of any single denomination of the Christian church. **nondescript** *adj* see separate entry. **non-destruc'tive** *adj* having no destructive effect, *esp* of tests on products, substances or organisms (**non-destructive testing** the testing of structures, metals, etc for flaws without impairing their quality). **nondisjunc'tion** *n* (*biol*) the failure of one of a pair of homologous chromosomes to move towards its appropriate pole during meiosis. **non-divid'ing** *adj* (of a cell) not undergoing division. **non-dom'** *n* a person who chooses to live in a particular country (often for tax reasons) but is not domiciled there. **non-drip'** *adj* (of paint) thixotropic, of such a consistency that it does not drip when being applied. **non-effect'ive** *adj* (*milit*) having no effect; not efficient or serviceable; unfit or unavailable for service; relating to those who are unfit or unavailable. ◆ *n* a member of a force who is unfit or unavailable for active service. **non-effi'cient** *adj* not up to the standard required for service. ◆ *n* a soldier who has not yet undergone the full number of drills. **non-e'go** *n* (*philos*) the not-I, the object as opposed to the subject, whatever is not the conscious self. **non-elec'tive** *adj* not chosen by election. **non-elec'tric** *adj* (*obs*) conducting electricity. ◆ *n* (*obs*) a conductor. **non-elec'trolyte** *n* a substance, such as sugar, that gives a non-conducting solution. **non-en'try** *n* (Scots law; hist) a vassal's heir's failure to renew investiture; a payment that was due to the superior on such failure. **non-Euclid'ean** *adj* not according to Euclid's axioms and postulates. **non-event'** *n* an occasion of no significance. **non-exec'utive** *adj* (of eg directors) not employed by a company full-time, but brought in for advisory purposes (also *n*). **non-fat'** *adj* (of food) having had the fat removed. **non-feasance** *n* see separate entry. **non-ferr'ous** *adj* containing no iron; not iron; relating to metals other than iron. **non-fic'tion** *adj* (of a literary work) without any deliberately fictitious element, purely factual (**non-fiction novel** one whose material is entirely drawn from people and events in real life). ◆ *n* a branch of literature consisting of such works. **non-fic'tional** *adj*. **non-fig'urative** *adj* same as **non-representational** below. **non-flamm'able** *adj* not easily set on fire; not flammable (**non-flam film** acetate film). **non-for'feiting** *adj* (of a life insurance policy) not forfeited by reason of non-payment. **non-governmen'tal** *adj* not connected with or administered by the government. **non-gre'mial** *n* a non-resident member, *esp* of Cambridge University. ◆ *adj* applied to the examinations now called *local*. **non-he'ro** *n* a person whose status is in no way heroic. **non-Hodg'kin's lymphoma** *n* any form of cancer of the lymph nodes that is not Hodgkin's disease. **non-homol'ogous** *adj* (*biol*) not homologous; denoting pairing between regions of non-homologous chromosomes, sometimes involving short stretches of similar and *poss* repetitive sequences. **non-in'sulin-depend'ent** *adj* denoting a form of diabetes mellitus in which treatment with insulin is not required.

Some words formed with the prefix **non-**.

non-abrā'sive *adj*.	**non-bellig'erent** *adj and n*.	**non-consent'ing** *adj*.
non-absorb'ent *adj*.	**non-biolog'ical** *adj*.	**non-contā'gious** *adj*.
non-academ'ic *adj*.	**non-break'able** *adj*.	**non-controver'sial** *adj*.
non-access'ible *adj*.	**non-car'bonated** *adj*.	**non-conven'tional** *adj*.
non-addic'tive *adj*.	**non-Cath'olic** *adj*.	**non-core'** *adj*.
non-admin'istrative *adj*.	**non-clin'ical** *adj*.	**non-corrō'sive** *adj*.
non-alcohol'ic *adj*.	**non-combin'ing** *adj*.	**non-curr'ent** *adj*.
non-aller'gic *adj*.	**non-commer'cial** *adj*.	**non-deliv'ery** *n*.
non-arri'val *n*.	**non-commū'nicative** *adj*.	**non-democrat'ic** *adj*.
non-atten'dance *n*.	**non-compet'itive** *adj*.	**non-disciplin'ary** *adj*.
non-automat'ic *adj and n*.	**non-compli'ance** *n*.	**non-discrim'inating** *adj*.
non-believ'er *n*.	**non-comply'ing** *adj*.	**non-divis'ible** *adj*.
non-bellig'erency *n*.	**non-conclu'sive** *adj*.	**non-dom'iciled** *adj*.

■ words derived from main entry word; ◻ compound words; ▪ idioms and phrasal verbs

non-interven'tion n a policy of systematic abstention from interference in the affairs of other nations. **non-interven'tionist** n and adj. **non-intru'sion** n (in Scottish Church history) the principle that a patron should not force an unacceptable minister on an unwilling congregation. **non-intru'sionist** n and adj. **non-invā'sive** adj (of medical treatment) not involving surgery or the insertion of instruments, etc into the patient. **non-ion'ic** adj not forming ions (**non-ionic detergents** a series of detergents in which the molecules do not ionize in aqueous solution, unlike soap). **non-ion'izing radiation** n (phys; radiol) any radiation with a wavelength longer than about 100nm in the far ultraviolet which has insufficient energy to ionize matter. **non-i'ron** adj (of clothes or fabric) not needing ironing after washing. **non-iss'uable** adj not capable of being issued; which one cannot dispute or take issue with. **non'-iss'ue** n a matter not important enough to warrant discussion. **non-join'der** n (law) omission to join all the parties to an action or suit. **non-judgemen'tal** or **non-judgmen'tal** adj relating to or having an open attitude without implicit judgement, esp moral. **non-judgemen'tally** or **non-judgmen'tally** adv. **nonjur'ing** adj not swearing allegiance. **nonjur'or** n a person who refuses to swear allegiance, esp (with cap) a member of the clergy in England and Scotland who would not swear allegiance to William and Mary in 1689, holding themselves still bound by the oath they had taken to the deposed king, James II. **non-jur'y** adj not involving a jury in reaching a verdict. **non-lē'thal** adj (of eg aid to developing countries) not involving or including lethal or dangerous items, esp weapons. **non'-met'al** n an element that is not a metal (also adj). **non-metall'ic** adj not metallic; not of metal or like metal. **non-mor'al** adj unconcerned with morality; involving no moral considerations. **non-nat'ural** adj not natural; forced or strained. ◆n (usu in pl) in old medicine, anything not considered of the essence of human beings, but necessary to their wellbeing, such as air, food, sleep, rest, etc. **non-neg'ative** adj (maths) being positive or equal to zero. **non-negō'tiable** adj (of eg prices) not open to negotiation; (of bonds, etc) not transferable. **non-net'** adj (of a book) without a price fixed by the publisher, but with one which is determined by each bookseller selling that book. **non-nu'cleated** adj not nucleated. **non-objec'tive** adj (art) non-representational. **non-paramet'ric** adj (stats) not requiring assumptions about the form of a frequency distribution. **nonpareil** n and adj see separate entry. **nonpar'ous** adj not having given birth. **non-partic'ipating** adj not taking part; (of shares, etc) not giving the holder the right to a share in profits. **non-partisan'** (or /-pärt'/) adj not partisan; impartial. **non-par'ty** adj independent of party politics. **non-pathogen'ic** adj not causing disease. **non-pen'etrative** adj not involving penetration of one sexual partner by another. **non-perform'ance** n neglect or failure to perform. **non-persis'tent** adj (of eg insecticides and pesticides) decomposing rapidly after application and not lingering in the environment. **non'-per'son** n a person previously of political, etc eminence, now out of favour; a complete nonentity. **non-phys'ical** adj not relating to the body; not tangible; not sexual, platonic. **non-play'ing** adj (of eg the captain of a team) not taking an active part in the game(s). **nonplus** vt and n see separate entry. **nonpo'lar** adj without any permanent electric dipole moment. **non-prescrip'tion** adj (of medicines) able to be bought without a prescription. **non-prior'ity** adj without privilege of priority. **non-produc'tion** n. **non-produc'tive** adj not producing the goods, results, etc required; not directly concerned in production. **non-profess'ional** adj not professional or of a profession; not done in a professional capacity. **non-profi'cient** n a person who has made no progress in the art or study in which he or she is engaged. **non-prof'it** adj not involving or making a profit (**non-prof'it-making** not organized or engaged in with the purpose of making a profit for shareholders). **non-proliferā'tion** n lack of proliferation, esp a limit imposed on the proliferation of (usu nuclear) weapons. **non-provi'ded** adj (of an elementary school or education in England and Wales) maintained but not provided by the local education authority,

and managed by a committee in which the trustees form the majority. **non-quo'ta** adj not included in a quota. **non-regard'ance** n (Shakesp) lack of due regard. **non-renew'able** adj not able to be replenished; exhaustible. **non-representā'tional** adj (art) not aiming at the realistic depiction of objects. **non-res'idence** n the fact of not (permanently or for the moment) residing at a place, esp where one's official or social duties require one to reside or where one is entitled to reside. **non-res'ident** adj and n. **non-residen'tial** adj. **non-resist'ance** n the principle of not resisting violence by force, or of not resisting authority; passive submission. **non-resist'ant** or **non-resist'ing** adj. **non-restric'tive** adj (grammar) used of a relative clause that does not restrict the people or things to which its antecedent may refer. **non-return'** adj denoting a valve incorporating a device to prevent flow in one direction. **non-return'able** adj (of a bottle, jar or other container) on which a returnable deposit has not been paid; (of a deposit, etc) not repayable. **non-rig'id** adj (of an airship) having a balloon or gasbag with no internal framework to brace it, and no rigid keel. **non-sched'uled** adj not according to a schedule; (of an airline) operating between specified points but not to a specific schedule of flights. **non-sectā'rian** adj not involving religious sects; non-denominational. **nonsense** n see separate entry. **non-se'quence** n (geol) a break in the stratigraphical record, deduced generally on palaeontological evidence. **non-skid'** or **non-slip'** adj (of a surface) designed to reduce the chance of slipping to a minimum. **non-smo'ker** n a person who does not smoke; a railway compartment in which smoking is forbidden. **non-smok'ing** adj. **non-soci'ety** adj not belonging to a society, esp not a member of a trade union; employing people who are not members of a trade union. **non-spec'ialist** adj not devoting oneself to one particular subject, task, etc (also n). **non-specif'ic** adj not specific; (of a disease) not caused by any specific, identifiable, agent (**non-specific immunity** mechanisms that protect against non-microbial invasion of the body, incl physical barriers (eg skin, mucous membranes) and enzyme inhibitors). **non-stan'dard** adj not standard; (of language, vocabulary, etc) different from the usage of educated speakers, and (by some) not considered correct. **non-start'er** n a horse which, though entered for a race, does not run; a person, idea, etc with no chance at all of success. **non-stick'** adj (of eg a pan) treated so that food or other substance will not stick to it. **non-stop'** adj and adv uninterrupted(ly); without any stop or halt. **nonsuit** n and vt see separate entry. **non'-term** n (obs) a vacation between terms; a time of inactivity. **non-thing'** n something which does not exist; something trivial. **non'-U** adj consciously eschewed or avoided by the upper classes, hence socially unacceptable, opp to U. **non-u'nion** adj not attached to a trade union; not approved of by a union; employing, or produced by, non-union workers. **non-u'nionist** n. **non-u'sager** n (hist) a Nonjuror who rejected the usages. **non-u'ser** n omission to take advantage of a right (law); a person who does not take drugs (inf). **non-util'ity** adj not of the special kind made or sold for utility's sake. **non-ver'bal** adj (of communication) not using or involving words, but using eg gesture instead. **non-vi'olence** n (the ideal or practice of) refraining from violence on grounds of principle. **non-vi'olent** adj. **non-vol'atile** adj (comput) denoting a type of memory (**non-volatile memory**) that retains data even if the power is disconnected. **non-vo'ting** adj not voting; (of shares, etc) not giving the holder the right to vote on company decisions. **non-white'** n (a member of) a race other than the white race (also adj). **non-zē'ro** adj positive or negative in value; greater or less than zero.

nonage /non'ij or nō'nij/ (formal) n legal infancy, minority; a time of immaturity generally. [OFr nonage, from pfx non- (L nōn) and age age]
■ **non'aged** adj.

Some words formed with the prefix **non-**.

non-drink'er n.	**non-func'tional** adj.	**non-pay'ment** n.
non-drī'ver n.	**non-harmon'ic** adj.	**non-poi'sonous** adj.
non-econom'ic adj.	**non-hū'man** adj and n.	**non-rā'cial** adj.
non-elect' adj.	**non-infec'tious** adj.	**non-read'er** n.
non-elec'tion n.	**non-inflamm'able** adj.	**non-scientif'ic** adj.
non-essen'tial adj and n.	**non-involve'ment** n.	**non-sex'ist** adj.
non-eth'ical adj.	**non-lin'ear** adj.	**non-sol'uble** adj.
non-exis'tence n.	**non-marr'ying** adj.	**non-swimm'er** n.
non-exis'tent adj.	**non-mem'ber** n.	**non-tech'nical** adj.
non-fac'tual adj.	**non-nat'ural** adj.	**non-tox'ic** adj.
non-fā'tal adj.	**non-nū'clear** adj.	**non-tradi'tional** adj.
non-fatt'ening adj.	**non-obser'vance** n.	**non-vin'tage** adj.
non-flow'ering adj.	**non-opera'tional** adj.	**non-vol'atile** adj.
non-fulfil'ment n.	**non-pay'ing** adj.	**non-vot'er** n.

---

nonagenarian /nō-nə- or non-ə-ji-nā'ri-ən/ n a person who is ninety years old, or between ninety and a hundred (also adj). [L nōnāgēnārius relating to ninety, from nōnāgintā ninety]
- **nonagenary** /-jē'nə-ri/ adj (rare) of, containing, based on, ninety; nonagenarian (also n).

nonagesimal /nō-nə- or non-ə-jes'i-məl/ adj ninetieth. ◆ n the point of the ecliptic 90° from its intersection by the horizon. [L nōnāgēsimus ninetieth]

nonagon /non'ə-gon/ n a nine-sided geometrical figure. [L nōnus ninth, and Gr gōniā angle]
- **nonag'onal** adj.

nonane /nō'nān/ n a hydrocarbon (C₉H₂₀), ninth in the alkane series. [L nōnus ninth]
- ☐ **nonanoic acid** same as **pelargonic acid** (see under **pelargonium**).

nonary /nō'nə-ri/ adj (of a mathematical system) based on nine. [L nōnārius]

nonce¹ /nons/ n (almost confined to the phrase for the nonce, which in ME is sometimes a mere tag for rhyme's sake) the occasion; the moment, time being; the particular or express purpose (Shakesp). ◆ adj (of a word or expression) occurring, adopted or coined for a particular occasion only. [From for the nones, ie for then ones for the once, then being the dative (OE tham) of **the** and ones the genitive (OE ānes) of **one** substituted for the dative]

nonce² /nons/ (prison sl) n a sex offender, esp one convicted of assaulting children. [Ety uncertain]

nonchalance /non'shə-ləns/ n unconcern; coolness; indifference. [Fr, from non not, and chaloir to matter, interest, from L calēre to be warm]
- ■ **non'chalant** adj. **non'chalantly** adv.

non-come /non-kum' or -kom'/ (Shakesp) n one of Dogberry's blundering words, perh a confusion of nonplus and non compos mentis.

non compos mentis see under **non**.

nonconformist, nonconformity see under **non-**.

nondescript /non'di-skript/ adj not easily classified; not distinctive enough to be described, featureless (derog); neither one thing nor another; not described (obs). ◆ n a featureless person or thing, or one not easily described. [L nōn not, and dēscrībere, -scrīptum to describe]
- ■ **non'descriptly** adv. **non'descriptness** n.

none /nun/ or /non/ pronoun (pl or sing) not one; no person or people; not the thing in question; not any; no portion or amount. ◆ adj (separated from the noun; otherwise archaic; formerly esp before a vowel or h) no, not any. ◆ adv in no degree; by no means; not at all. [OE nān, from ne not, and ān one]
- ☐ **none'-so-prett'y** or **Nan'cy-prett'y** n the hardy perennial plant London Pride (Saxifraga umbrosa). **none'-spar'ing** adj (Shakesp) all-destroying. **nonetheless'** (or **none the less**) adv nevertheless.
- ■ **none other** (often with than) no other person. **none the** (followed by compar adj) in no way, to no degree. **none too** (inf) not very.

nonentity /non-en'ti-ti/ n a person or thing of no importance (derog); the state of not being; a thing which does not exist. [L nōn not, and entitās (see **entity**)]

Nones /nōnz/ n pl in the Roman calendar, the ninth day before the Ides (both days included), ie the 7th of March, May, July and October, and the 5th of the other months; (usu **none**) one of the hours of the Divine Office, orig held at the ninth hour of the day (3pm) (RC). [L nōnae, from nōnus ninth]

nonesuch or **nonsuch** /non' or nun'such/ n a unique, unparalleled or extraordinary thing (archaic); the plant black medick. [**none** and **such**]

nonet or (rare) **nonette** /nō-net'/ (music) n a composition for nine performers. [Ital nonetto]

nonetto /no-net'tō/ (Ital) n (pl **nonet'tos** or **nonet'ti** /-tē/) a nonet.

non-feasance /non-fē'zəns/ (law) n omission of something which ought to be or ought to have been done. [Pfx non- not, and OFr faisance doing, from faire, from L facere to do]

nong /nong/ (Aust and NZ sl) n a fool, idiot. [Origin uncertain]

noni /nō'ni/ n a small evergreen tropical plant (Morinda citrifolia); the fruit of this plant, whose juice is valued for its medicinal properties. [Tahitian]

nonillion /nō-nil'yən/ n a thousand raised to the tenth power (10³⁰); (esp formerly, in Britain) a million raised to the ninth power (10⁵⁴). ◆ adj being a nonillion in number. [Fr, from L nōnus ninth, and **million**]
- ■ **nonill'ionth** adj and n.

nonjuring, etc see under **non-**.

non licet, non liquet, non multa, sed multum see under **non**.

nonny /non'i/ n a meaningless word in old ballad refrain, etc, usu 'hey, nonny,' 'hey nonny nonny' or 'hey nonny no', once a cover for obscenity.

no-no see under **no¹**.

non obstante see under **non**.

nonpareil /non-pə-rel' or -rāl', also non'/ n a person or thing without equal; a fine variety of apple; a kind of confectionery; an old type size, approximately, and still used synonymously for six-point (printing). ◆ adj unequalled; matchless. [Fr non not, and pareil, from a LL dimin of L pār equal]

non placet see under **non**.

nonplus /non-plus'/ vt (**nonpluss'ing** (or US **nonplus'ing**); **nonplussed'** (or US **nonplused'**)) to perplex completely, make uncertain what to say or do. ◆ n a state in which no more can be done or said; great difficulty; perplexity. [L nōn not, and plūs more]
- ■ **nonplussed'** (or US **nonplused'**) adj.

nonsense /non'səns/ n anything which makes no sense; language without meaning; absurdity, foolishness; trifling; humbug; trivial things; something which is manifestly false; an absurd, illogical or unintelligible statement or action. ◆ interj expressing strong disagreement. [Pfx non- not, and **sense**]
- ■ **nonsensical** /-sens'/ adj without sense; absurd; (of a word, syllable, etc) consisting of an arbitrary group of sounds and having no meaning. **nonsensicality** /non-sens-i-kal'i-ti/ or **nonsens'icalness** n. **nonsens'ically** adv.
- ☐ **nonsense verse** n verse deliberately written to convey an absurd meaning, or without obvious meaning at all. **nonsense word** n a deliberately meaningless word.
- ■ **no-nonsense** see under **no²**.

non sequitur /non-sek'wi-tər/ n (the drawing of) a conclusion that does not follow logically from the foregoing premises; loosely, a remark, event or action that has no relation to what has gone before (abbrev **non seq.**). [L nōn not, and sequitur follows, 3rd pers sing present indicative of sequi to follow]

nonsuch see **nonesuch**.

nonsuit /non'sūt or -soot/ (law) n (in England) the stopping of a suit by voluntary withdrawal of the plaintiff, or by the judge when the plaintiff has failed to make out cause of action or to bring evidence. ◆ vt to subject (a plaintiff) to a nonsuit. [Anglo-Fr no(u)nsuy does not pursue]

nonuple /non'ū-pl or -oo-/ adj ninefold; having nine parts. [L nōnus ninth; nonuplus, not in L, formed on the analogy of duplus, quadruplus, etc]
- ■ **non'uplet** n a group of nine, esp a group of nine notes played in the time of six or eight.

nonylphenol /non-īl-fē'nol or non-il-, also nō-nīl-/ n a chemical used in detergents, emulsifiers, etc that mimics the effects of oestrogen and hence is believed to be involved in reducing fertility in men and male animals through the food chain. [**non**ane, **-yl** and **phenol**]

noob /noob/ (sl) n a beginner; a novice. [Short form of **newbie** (see under **new**)]

noodle¹ /noo'dl/ n a string- or ribbon-shaped strip of pasta or other unleavened dough. [Ger Nudel]

noodle² /noo'dl/ n a simpleton (inf); a blockhead (inf); the head (sl, esp N Am). [Cf **noddy¹** and **noddle¹**]
- ■ **nood'ledom** n (inf).

noodle³ /noo'dl/ (sl) vi to improvise on a musical instrument in a casual or desultory way, esp in jazz. [Ety uncertain]

Nook® /nŏŏk/ n the proprietary name of a type of e-reader.

nook /nŏŏk/ n a corner; a narrow place formed by an angle; a recess; a secluded retreat. [ME nok, noke; prob Scand; Gaelic and Ir niuc is prob from the Scot and N Eng form **neuk**]
- ■ **nook'y** adj.
- ☐ **nook'-shotten** adj (archaic) shot out into nooks and corners.
- ■ **every nook and cranny** (inf) everywhere.

nooky¹ see under **nook**.

nooky² or **nookie** /nŏŏk'i/ (sl) n sexual intercourse; a person, usu a woman, regarded as a sexual partner. [Ety uncertain]

noology /nō-ol'ə-ji/ n the science of the intellect. [Gr noos the mind, and logos discourse]
- ■ **nöogen'esis** n evolution of mind. **nöom'etry** n mind-measurement. **nö'osphere** n (in the philosophy of Teilhard de Chardin) the sphere of the mind, the collective memory and intelligence of the human race. **nöotrop'ics** n pl another name for cognitive enhancers or smart drugs.

noon /noon/ n the ninth hour of the day in Roman and ecclesiastical reckoning, 3pm; afterwards (when the church service called Nones was shifted to midday) midday; middle; greatest height, the culminating point. ◆ adj belonging to, or characteristic or typical of, midday; meridional. ◆ *vi* to rest at noon. [OE *nōn*, from L *nōna* (*hōra*) the ninth (hour)]

■ **noon'er** *n* (*US inf*) an activity undertaken during the lunch break; a brief, *esp* illicit, sexual encounter during the lunch break. **noon'ing** *n* (*esp US dialect*) (an interval for) a meal or rest about noon; midday. ❏ **noon'day** *n* midday; the time of greatest prosperity (*fig*). ◆ *adj* relating to midday; meridional. **noon'tide** or **noon'time** *n* (*literary*) the time of noon, midday. ◆ *adj* relating to noon; meridional.

no-one see under **no²**.

noop /noop/ (*Walter Scott*) *n* a knob, tip (of the elbow). [Cf **knop**]

noose /noos/ *n* a loop with running knot which draws tighter the more it is pulled, used for trapping or killing by hanging; a snare or bond generally, *esp* (*joc*) marriage. ◆ *vt* to tie or catch in a noose; to make a noose in or of. [Perh OFr *nous*, pl of *nou* (Fr *nœud*), from L *nōdus* knot]

■ **put one's head in a noose** to put oneself into a dangerous or vulnerable situation.

NOP *abbrev* : National Opinion Poll.

nopal /nō'pəl/ or /-päl/ *n* a Central American cactus of the genus *Nopalea*, used for rearing cochineal insects; broadly, the prickly pear (genus *Opuntia*). [Sp *nopal*, from Nahuatl *nopalli*]

nope /nōp/ (*sl*) *interj* an emphatic, *orig* N American form of **no¹**, pronounced with a snap of the mouth.

NOR /nör/ (*comput*) *n* a logic circuit that has two or more inputs and one output, the output signal being 1 if all its inputs are 0, and 0 if any of its inputs is 1 (also *adj*). [*not or*]

NOR *abbrev* : nucleolar-organizing region.

Nor *abbrev* : Norman (also **Norm**); North; Norway; Norwegian.

nor¹ /nör/ *conj* and not; neither, used *esp* in introducing the second part of a negative proposition, correlative to *neither*. [Appar from *nother*, a form of **neither**]

■ **nor ... nor ...** (*archaic*) neither ... nor ... **nor yet** and also not.

nor² /nör/ (*Scot* and *dialect*) *conj* than. [Origin obscure]

nor' /nör/ a short form of **north** (*esp* in combination).

nor- /nör-/ *pfx* denoting: an organic compound that is derived from another; a normal isomer. [*normal*]

noradrenalin /nör-ə-dren'ə-lin/ or **noradrenaline** /-lin or -lēn/ *n* a neurotransmitter hormone related to adrenalin, produced by the adrenal glands (also (*esp US*) **norepinephrine** /nör-ep-i-nef'rin or -rēn/).

Norbertine /nör'bər-tīn or -tin/ *n* and *adj* Premonstratensian. [From *Norbert*, the founder (1119)]

Nordic /nör'dik/ *adj* of a tall, blond, dolichocephalic type of (generally Germanic) peoples in NW Europe (loosely used by Nazis); of or relating to Finland or Scandinavia. ◆ *n* a member of a Nordic race. [Fr *nord* north]

❏ **Nordic skiing** *n* competitive skiing involving cross-country and jumping events. **Nordic walking** *n* a form of exercise that involves walking using poles like ski sticks to aid propulsion and exercise the upper body.

norepinephrine see **noradrenalin**.

norethisterone /nö-rə-this'tə-rōn/ *n* an oral progestogen.

Norfolk /nör'fək/ *adj* belonging to the English county of *Norfolk*. [OE *northfolc* north folk]

❏ **Norfolk capon** *n* a red herring. **Norfolk dumpling** or **Norfolk turkey** *n* a native or inhabitant of Norfolk. **Norfolk Island pine** *n* a tall Araucaria of Norfolk Island (in the Pacific, named after the ducal family of *Norfolk*). **Norfolk jacket** *n* a loose pleated man's jacket with a waistband.

nori /nö' or nö'ri/ *n* a seaweed of the genus *Porphyra* used as a foodstuff in the form of dried sheets (for wrapping sushi) or as a paste. [Jap]

noria /nö' or nö'ri-ə/ *n* an endless chain of buckets on a wheel for raising water from a stream into irrigation channels. [Sp *noria*, from Ar *nā'ūrah*]

norimon /nor'i-mon/ *n* a Japanese palanquin. [Jap *nori* to ride, and *mono* thing]

norite /nö'rīt/ *n* a type of rock, gabbro with a rhombic pyroxene. [**Norway**]

nork /nörk/ (*sl, orig Aust*) *n* a woman's breast. [Perh from Norco Co-operative Ltd, NSW butter manufacturers]

norland or **norlan'** /nör'lənd or nör'lən/ (*Scot* and *poetic*) *n* the north country. ◆ *adj* belonging to or coming from the north. [**north** and **land¹**]

Norm *abbrev* : Norman.

norm /nörm/ *n* a rule; a pattern; an authoritative standard; a type; the ordinary or most frequent value or state; an accepted standard of

behaviour within a society; an average standard of achievement, work required, production, etc. [L *norma* a rule]

■ **nor'ma** *n* a rule; a standard; a square for measuring right angles. **nor'mal** *adj* according to rule; not deviating from the standard; regular, typical, ordinary; well-adjusted mentally; functioning regularly; having an unbranched chain of carbon atoms (*chem*); (of a solution) having one gramme-equivalent of dissolved substance to a litre; perpendicular (*geom*). ◆ *n* a normal or usual value, state, instance or specimen; a perpendicular. **nor'malcy** *n* (*esp US*) normality, often of political, economic, etc conditions. **normal'ity** *n*. **normaliza'tion** or **-s-** *n* return to normality or the status quo. **nor'malize** or **-ise** *vt* to make normal; to bring within or cause to conform to normal standards, limits, etc; to heat (steel) in order to refine the crystal structure and to relieve internal stress. ◆ *vi* to become normal, regular. **nor'mally** *adv* in a normal manner; usually, as a rule; typically. **nor'mative** *adj* of or relating to a norm; establishing a standard; prescriptive. **nor'matively** *adv*. **nor'mativeness** *n*.

❏ **normal distribution** *n* (*stats*) a frequency distribution represented by a symmetrical, bell-shaped curve. **normal school** *n* in some countries, *esp* France and N Africa, a training college for teachers. **normal solution** see **normal** above and also **standard solution** under **standard**. **norm'-referenced** *adj*. **norm'-ref'erencing** *n* (*educ*) comparing a pupil's abilities with those of his or her peers.

norm. *abbrev* : normal.

Norma /nör'mə/ *n* the Rule, a small southern constellation. [L *norma* a rule]

normal, etc see under **norm**.

Norman /nör'mən/ *n* (pl **Nor'mans**) a native or inhabitant of Normandy; a member of a Scandinavian people that settled in N France about the beginning of the 10c, founded the Duchy of Normandy and conquered England in 1066; Norman French; Norman architecture. ◆ *adj* relating to the Normans or to Normandy. [OFr *Normanz*, *Normans*, nominative and accusative pl of *Normant* Northman, from Scand]

■ **Normanesque'** *adj*. **Nor'manism** *n*. **Nor'manize** or **-ise** *vt* and *vi* to make or become Norman in character.

❏ **Norman architecture** *n* a massive Romanesque style, prevalent in Normandy (10c–11c) and England (11c–12c), the churches with a semicircular apse and a great tower, deeply recessed doorways, small, round-headed windows and arches, and zigzag, billet, nail-head, and other characteristic ornaments. **Norman Conquest** *n* the conquest of England by Duke William of Normandy (1066). **Norman cross** *n* an elaborate memorial cross like a Gothic turret with pinnacles and with niches for figures. **Norman French** *n* the dialect of French spoken by the Normans, (after 1066) used by some members of society in England, and in lawcourts.

norman /nör'mən/ (*naut*) *n* a bar inserted in a windlass on which to fasten or veer a rope or cable.

normative, etc see under **norm**.

normotensive /nör-mō-ten'siv/ *adj* characterized by normal blood pressure; normalizing blood pressure. [L *norma* a rule, and *tensiō* pressure]

Norn¹ /nörn/ (*Norse myth*) *n* any of the three Fates: Urd, Verdande and Skuld (also (Latinized) **Norn'a**). [ON *norn*]

Norn² /nörn/ *n* the old Norse dialect of Orkney and Shetland (also *adj*). [ON *norrœna*]

norovirus /nö'rō-vī-rəs/ or **Norwalk virus** /nör'wök vī'rəs/ *n* a type of calicivirus which causes intestinal illness. [Identified after an outbreak of illness in *Norwalk*, Ohio, in 1972]

Norroy /nor'oi/ (*heraldry*) *n* an English king-of-arms whose jurisdiction lies north of the Trent (since 1943, **Norroy and Ulster**). [OFr *nord* north, and *roy* king]

Norse /nörs/ *adj* Norwegian; ancient Scandinavian. ◆ *n* the Norwegian language; the Germanic language of the ancient Scandinavians from which the modern Scandinavian languages are derived (also **Old Norse**). [Perh Du *noor(d)sch*; cf Icel *Norskr*; Norw *Norsk*]

■ **Norse'man** *n* a Scandinavian, a Viking.

■ **the Norse** the Norwegians or the Vikings.

norteño /nör-tā'nyō/, *fem* **norteña** /-nyə/ (*US*) *n* (pl **norteñ'os**, **norteñ'as**) (used by Americans of Latin American origin, Mexicans, etc) a North American, *esp* one of European origin. [Am Sp, northerner]

north /nörth/ *n* the point of the horizon or that pole of the earth or sky which at equinox is opposite the sun at noon in Europe or elsewhere on the same side of the equator, or towards the sun in the other hemisphere; the slightly different direction (**magnetic north**) in which a magnetic needle points; one of the four cardinal points of the compass; (often with *cap* and *the*) the north part of the Earth or of a region, country or town, eg the part of England lying north of the Humber; (with *cap* and *the*) the industrialized nations; (with *cap* and *the*) the part of the USA lying north of Maryland and the Ohio river, *esp* those states north of the Mason-Dixon line during the civil war; (*usu* with *cap*) in bridge, the player or position occupying the place designated 'north' on the table; the north wind (*poetic*). ◆ *adj* situated towards the north; forming the part that is towards the north; (of wind) blowing from the north; (of a pole of a magnet) *usu* turning to the north. ◆ *adv* towards the north. (with *of*) above, more than. ◆ *vi* (*archaic*) to turn or move north. [OE]

■ **norther** /*nörth'ər*/ *n* a north wind or gale, *esp* applied to a cold wind that blows in winter over Texas and the Gulf of Mexico. ◆ *vi* /*nördh'ər*/ to move or veer towards the north. **north'erliness** /-*dh*-/ *n*. **north'erly** /-*dh*-/ *adj* situated in the north; towards the north; (*esp* of the wind) coming from the north. ◆ *adv* on the north; towards the north; from the north. ◆ *n* a north wind. **northermost** see **northernmost** below. **north'ern** /-*dh*-/ *adj* situated in the north or further to the north; coming from the north; towards the north; connected with the north; living in the north; (with *cap*) of, from or relating to the North. ◆ *n* a northerner. **north'erner** /-*dh*-/ *n* (sometimes with *cap*) a native or inhabitant of the north, *esp* of the northern USA or the northern counties of England. **north'ernism** /-*dh*-/ *n* a form of expression or a characteristic peculiar to the north. **north'ernize** or **-ise** /-*dh*-/ *vt* to give a northern character to. **north'ernmost** /-*dh*-/ or **north'most** /-*th*-/, also (*obs*) **north'ermost** /-*dh*-/ *adj* situated furthest north. **north'ing** /-*th*-/ *n* motion, distance or tendency northward; the distance of a heavenly body from the equator northward; difference of latitude made by a ship in sailing; deviation towards the north. **northward**, **nor'ward** or **norward** /*nörth'wərd*, *nör'wərd* or *nor'əd*/ *adv* towards the north (also *adj* and *n*). **north'wardly** *adv* and *adj*. **north'wards** *adv* northward.

❑ **north'about** *adv* towards the north. **North Atlantic Drift** *n* the Gulf Stream. **north'bound** *adj* travelling in a northward direction. **north'-by-east'** *n* the direction midway between north and north-north-east. **north'-by-west'** *n* the direction midway between north and north-north-west. **north'-country** *adj* belonging to the northern part of the country, *esp* of England. **north-coun'tryman** *n*. **north-east'** or (*archaic* or *poetic*) **nor'-east'** (also /*nörth'* or *nör'*/) *n* the direction midway between north and east; the region lying in that direction; the wind blowing from that direction. ◆ *adj* and *adv* in or towards the north-east; (of a wind) from the north-east. **north-east'-by-east'** *n* the direction midway between north-east and east-north-east. **north-east'-by-north'** *n* the direction midway between north-east and north-north-east. **north-east'er** or **nor'-east'er** *n* a strong wind from the north-east. **north-east'erly** *adj* situated in the north-east; towards the north-east; (*esp* of the wind) coming from the north-east. ◆ *adv* on the north-east; towards the north-east; from the north-east. ◆ *n* a north-east wind. **north-east'ern** *adj* situated in the north-east or further to the north-east; coming from the north-east; towards the north-east; connected with the north-east; living in the north-east. **north-east'ward** *adv* towards the north-east (also *adj* and *n*). **north-east'wardly** *adv* and *adj*. **north-east'wards** *adv* north-eastward. **northern fern** *n* the hard fern (genus *Lomaria*). **northern hemisphere** *n* (also with *caps*) the hemisphere of the world which is north of the equator. **northern lights** *n pl* the aurora borealis. **North Germanic** see under **German**. **north'land** *n* the north (also *adj*). **north'lander** *n*. **North'man** *n* an ancient Scandinavian. **north'-north-east'** *n* the direction midway between north and north-east (also *adj* and *adv*). **north'-north-west'** *n* the direction midway between north and north-west (also *adj* and *adv*). **north polar** *adj*. **north pole** *n* the end of the earth's axis in the Arctic; its projection on the celestial sphere (*astron*); (*usu*) that pole of a magnet which when free points to the earth's north magnetic pole (logically the other end). **North Sea gas** and **North Sea oil** *n* natural gas and oil obtained from deposits below the North Sea. **north'-seeking** *adj* turning towards the earth's magnetic north pole. **North Star** *n* a star very near the north pole of the heavens, the Pole Star. **north water** *n* the space of open sea left by the winter pack of ice moving southward. **north-west'** or (*archaic* or *poetic*) **nor'-west'** (also /*nörth'* or *nör'*/) *n* the direction midway between north and west; the region lying in that direction; the wind blowing from that direction. ◆ *adj* and *adv* in or towards the north-west; (of a wind) from the north-west. **north-west'-by-north'** *n* the direction midway between north-west and north-north-west. **north-west'-by-west'** *n* the direction midway between north-west and west-north-west. **north-west'er** or **nor'-west'er** *n* a strong wind from the north-west (see also **nor'wester** below). **north-west'erly** *adj* situated in the north-west; towards the north-west; (*esp* of the wind) coming from the north-west. ◆ *adv* on the north-west; towards the north-west; from the north-west. ◆ *n* a north-west wind. **north'-west'ern** *adj* situated in the north-west or further to the north-west; coming from the north-west; towards the north-west; connected with the north-west; living in the north-west. **north-west'ward** *adv* towards the north-west (also *adj* and *n*). **north-west'wardly** *adv* and *adj*. **north-west'wards** *adv* north-westward. **nor'west'er** *n* a sou'wester; a drink of some strong liquor (see also **north-wester** above).

■ **North Atlantic Treaty Organization** a political alliance linking the United States and Canada to a group of European States, established by the **North Atlantic Treaty**, 4 April 1949 (*abbrev* **NATO** or **Nato**). **the North-east Passage** a passage for ships along the north coasts of Europe and Asia to the Pacific, first made by Baron Nordenskjöld in 1878–9. **the North-west Passage** a seaway from the Atlantic into the Pacific north of N America, first made (partly on the ice) by Sir Robert McClure, 1850–4.

Northants. /*nör-thants'*/ *abbrev* : Northamptonshire.

Northumb. /*nör-thum'*/ *abbrev* : Northumberland.

Northumbrian /*nör-thum'bri-ən*/ *n* a native of the modern Northumberland, or of the old kingdom of Northumbria (OE *Northhymbre, Northhymbraland*) which stretched from the Humber to the Forth, or of the modern region of Northumbria comprising Northumberland, Tyne and Wear, Co. Durham and Cleveland; the dialect of Old English spoken in Northumbria, later Northern English (*incl* Scots). ◆ *adj* of Northumberland or Northumbria.

Norueyses (*Spenser*) see under **Norway**.

Norwalk virus see **norovirus**.

norward, etc see **northward**, etc under **north**.

Norway /*nör'wā*/ *adj* Norwegian. ◆ *n* (pl (*Spenser*) **Norueyses**) (*obs*) a Norwegian.

❑ **Norway haddock** *n* the rosefish or bergylt. **Norway lobster** see under **lobster**. **Norway maple** *n* a Eurasian maple, *Acer platanoides* grown as a shade tree and for its yellow flowers. **Norway pine** *n* the red pine, *Pinus resinosa*; its wood. **Norway rat** *n* the brown rat. **Norway spruce** *n* the common European spruce *Picea excelsa* or *Picea abies*; its wood.

Norwegian /*nör-wē'jən*/ *adj* of or relating to the Kingdom of Norway in NW Europe, its people or its language. ◆ *n* a native or citizen of Norway; the language of Norway; a kind of fishing-boat used on the Great Lakes of America. [LL *Norvegia* Norway, from ON *Norvegr* (OE *Northweg*), from ON *northr* north, and *vegr* way]

■ **Norweyan** /-*wā'ən*/ *adj* (*Shakesp*) Norwegian.

❑ **Norwegian oven** or **nest** *n* a haybox.

nor'wester see under **north**.

Nos or **nos** *abbrev* : numbers.

nose /*nōz*/ *n* the projecting part of the face used in breathing, smelling, and to some extent in speaking; the power of smelling; flair, a faculty for tracking out, detecting, or recognizing (*fig*); scent, aroma, *esp* the bouquet of wine; a projecting forepart of anything; a projection; a beak; a nozzle; the projecting edge of a step, a moulding or a mullion; the withered remains of the flower on a gooseberry, apple, etc, opposite the stalk; the connecting part of a pair of spectacles; an informer (*sl*). ◆ *vt* and *vi* to proceed or cause to proceed gingerly, as if feeling with the nose. ◆ *vt* to smell; to examine by smelling or as if by smelling; to track out, detect or recognize (often with *out*); to touch, press or rub with the nose; to thrust the nose into; to come or be face to face with (*archaic*); to oppose rudely face to face (*archaic*); to provide with a nose (*archaic*); to remove the nose from (a gooseberry, etc); to pronounce with a nasal sound. ◆ *vi* to pry; to nuzzle; to move nose-first; to sniff (*archaic*); to taper away in a noselike form. [OE *nosu*; Ger *Nase*, L *nāsus*]

■ **nosed** *adj* having a nose (used *esp* in combination, as in *bottle-nosed, long-nosed*, etc). **nose'less** *adj*. **nos'er** *n* a blow on the nose; a bloody nose; a severe rebuff; a strong headwind; a prying person. **nos'ey** or **nos'y** *adj* long-nosed; large-nosed; prying (*inf*); bad-smelling; fragrant; sensitive to smells; nasal in sound. ◆ *n* (*inf*) a nickname for a person who pries. **nos'ily** *adv*. **nos'iness** *n* (*inf*) a tendency to pry. **nos'ing** *n* the act of using the nose to smell, track, touch, etc; the projecting rounded edge of the step of a stair, sill, moulding, etc.

❑ **nosy** see **nosey** above. **nose'bag** *n* a bag for food, hung on a horse's head; a picnicker's bag; food (*sl*). **nose'band** *n* the part of a horse's bridle coming over the nose, attached to the cheek-straps. **nose'bleed** *n* a bleeding from the nose; a name given to yarrow and various other plants (*obs* or *US*). **nose'bleeding** *n*. **nose candy** *n* (*N Am inf*) cocaine. **nose cone** *n* the front, *usu* conical, part of a spacecraft, etc. **nose'dive** *n* a headlong plunge. ◆ *vi* to plunge nose-first; to drop or decline sharply (*fig*). **nose'-flute** *n* a flute blown by the nose. **nosegay** see separate entry. **nose heaviness** *n* the state in which the forces acting upon an aircraft in flight are such that it tends to pitch downwards by the nose. **nose'-herb** *n* (*Shakesp*) a herb valued for its smell. **nose job** *n* (*inf*) cosmetic surgery on the nose. **nose'-leaf** *n* a membranous appendage on some bats' snouts. **nose'-led** *adj* led by the nose, ruled and fooled completely. **nose'-nippers** *n pl* a pince-nez. **nose'-painting** *n* reddening of the nose that often results from excessive drinking of alcohol. **nose'piece** *n* a nozzle; the end of a microscope tube carrying the objective; a nose-band; the part of a helmet formed to protect the nose. **nose rag** *n* (*sl*) a handkerchief. **nose'-ring** *n* an ornament worn in the septum of the nose or in either of its wings; a ring in the septum of the nose for controlling a bull, pig, etc. **nose tackle** n (American football) a defensive lineman who opposes the offensive centre. **nose wheel** n the single wheel at the front of a vehicle, etc, esp an aircraft. **Nosey Parker** n (inf; also without caps) a prying person.

■ **by a nose** by a very short distance or small margin. **cut off one's nose to spite one's face** to injure or disadvantage oneself through an act of revenge or anger towards another. **follow one's nose** to go straight forward, or take the obvious or instinctive course. **get up someone's nose** (inf) to annoy, irritate someone. **keep one's nose clean** (inf) to keep out of trouble, ie not to behave badly or dishonestly. **lead by the nose** see under **lead**¹. **look down one's nose at** to look at in a supercilious or condescending way. **make a long nose** see under **long**³. **nose out** to move forward slowly into traffic (in a vehicle). **nose to tail** (esp of vehicles in a queue) closely following one another. **nose to the grindstone** see under **grind**¹. **nose up** to direct or turn an aircraft nose upwards. **not see beyond** or **further than** (**the end of**) **one's nose** to see only what is immediately in front of one, ie not to see the long-term consequences of one's actions, etc. **on the nose** (in horse-race betting) to win only (not to come second or third); exactly (N Am inf); unsavoury, offensive (Aust inf). **put someone's nose out of joint** see under **join**. **rub someone's nose in it** (inf) to remind someone continually of something he or she has done wrong. **snap off someone's nose** to speak snappily. **through the nose** at a scandalously high price, exorbitantly. **thrust, poke** or **stick one's nose into** to meddle officiously with. **thumb one's nose** see under **thumb**. **turn up one's nose at** (inf) to refuse or receive contemptuously. **under one's** (**very**) **nose** (inf) in full view; close at hand. **with one's nose in the air** in a haughty, superior manner.

nosean /nō'zi-ən/ n a cubic mineral, aluminium sodium silicate and sulphate (also **nos'elite**). [KW Nose (died 1835), German mineralogist]

nosegay /nōz'gā/ n a bunch of fragrant flowers; a posy or bouquet. [**nose** (ie for the nose to smell) and **gay** (in obs sense of 'ornament')]

noselite see **nosean**.

nosey see under **nose**.

nosh /nosh/ (sl) vt and vi to eat. ◆ vi (esp US) to nibble, eat between meals. ◆ n food. [Yiddish]
■ **nosh'er** n. **nosh'ery** n (inf) a café or restaurant.
□ **nosh'-up** n (sl) a meal, esp a large one.

no-show, no-side see under **no**².

nosing see under **nose**.

nosocomial /no-sō-kō'mi-əl/ (formal) adj relating to a hospital. [Gr nosokomeion hospital, from nosos sickness, and komeein to tend]

nosode /nos'ōd/ n a homeopathic remedy consisting of a substance or substances discharged during an illness and used subsequently therapeutically. [Gr nosos disease, and eidos form]

nosography /no-sog'rə-fi/ n the description of diseases. [Gr nosos disease, and graphein to write]
■ **nosog'rapher** n. **nosographic** /nos-ə-graf'ik/ adj.

nosology /no-sol'ə-ji/ n the science of diseases; the branch of medicine which deals with the classification of diseases. [Gr nosos disease, and logos discourse]
■ **nosological** /-ə-loj'-/ adj. **nosol'ogist** n.

nosophobia /no-sə-fō'bi-ə/ n a morbid dread of contracting disease. [Gr nosos a disease, and phobos fear]

nostalgia /no-stal'j(i-)ə/ n homesickness; the desire to return to some earlier time in one's life, or a fond remembrance of that time, usu tinged with sadness at its having passed. [Gr nostos a return, and algos pain]
■ **nostal'gic** adj. **nostal'gically** adv.

nostalgie de la boue /no-stal-zhē də la boo'/ (Fr) literally, nostalgia for mud, craving for a debased or depraved physical life without civilized refinements or fastidiousness.

nostoc /nos'tok/ n an alga of the Nostoc genus of blue-green algae, beaded filaments forming gelatinous colonies on damp earth, etc, once thought to be derived from stars. [Appar coined by Paracelsus]

nostology /no-stol'ə-ji/ n the study of senility or the return to childish characteristics in old age. [Gr nostos return, and logos discourse]
■ **nostologic** /-ə-loj'-/ or **nostolog'ical** adj.

nostomania /no-stō-mā'ni-ə/ n an abnormal desire to go back to familiar places. [Gr nostos return, and **mania**]

nostopathy /no-stop'ə-thi/ n an abnormal fear of going back to familiar places. [Gr nostos return, and pathos suffering]

nostos /nos'tos/ (Gr) n a poem describing a return or a return journey.

Nostradamus /no-strə-dä'məs or -dā'/ n a person who professes to foretell the future. [From the French astrologer (1503–66)]
■ **nostradamic** /-dam'ik/ adj.

Nostratic /no-strat'ik/ n a hypothetical Eurasian language thought to be the common source of several major language families including the Indo-European and Semitic languages (also adj). [Ger nostratisch, from L nostrās, -ātis of our country]

nostril /nos'tril/ n either of the openings of the nose. [ME nosethirl, from OE nosthyr(e)l, from nosu nose, and thyrel opening; cf **drill**¹ and **thrill**]

nostrum /nos'trəm/ n any secret, quack or patent medicine; any favourite remedy or scheme. [L nostrum (neuter) our own, from nōs we]

nosy see under **nose**.

NOT /not/ (comput) n a logic circuit that has one input and one output, the output signal being 1 if its input is 0, and 0 if its input is 1. [**not**¹]

not¹ /not/ adv (also as enclitic form **-n't**) a word expressing denial, negation or refusal (used with verbs, and in place of a negative clause or predicate). ◆ interj (inf) used absolutely to deny a previous statement. [Same as **naught** and **nought**]
□ **not'-being** n the state or fact of not existing. **not'-I** n that which is not the conscious ego.
■ **not at all** don't mention it; it's a pleasure. **not but what** (archaic) all the same, nevertheless; not that. **not on** (inf) not possible; not morally, socially, etc acceptable. **not out** (cricket) still in; at the end of the innings without having been dismissed. **not that** though it is not the case that.

not² or **nott** /not/ adj with close-cut hair; polled. [OE hnot]
□ **not'-head'ed** adj. **not'-pat'ed** adj (Shakesp).

nota bene /nō'tə ben'i, bē'ni or not'ä ben'e/ (L) mark well, take notice (abbrev **NB**).

notabilia see under **notable**.

notable /nō'tə-bl/ adj worthy of being known or noted; remarkable; memorable; distinguished; noticeable; considerable; housewifely (archaic; sometimes with old pronunciation /not'/); capable, clever, industrious (archaic). ◆ n a person or thing worthy of note, esp in pl for people of distinction and political importance in France in pre-Revolution times. [L notābilis, from notāre to mark]
■ **notabil'ia** n pl (L) things worthy of notice; noteworthy sayings. **notabil'ity** n the fact of being notable; a notable person or thing. **no'tableness** n. **no'tably** adv.

notaeum /nō-tē'əm/ n the upper surface of a bird's body, opp to gastraeum. [Latinized from Gr nōtaion (neuter), adj, from nōtos or nōton the back]

notal see under **note**¹ and **notum**.

notandum /nō-tan'dəm/ n (pl **notan'da**) something to be specially noted or observed. [L, gerundive of notāre to note]

notaphily /nō-taf'i-li/ n the collecting of banknotes, cheques, etc as a hobby. [**note**¹ and **phil-**]
■ **notaph'ilic** adj. **notaph'ilism** n. **notaph'ilist** n.

notary /nō'tə-ri/ n an official authorized to certify deeds, contracts, copies of documents, affidavits, etc (generally **notary public**); anciently, a person who took notes or memoranda of others' acts. [L notārius]
■ **nota'rial** adj. **nota'rially** adv. **no'tarize** or **-ise** vt to attest to, authenticate (a document, etc) as a notary. **no'taryship** n.
■ **apostolical notary** the official who dispatches the orders of the Pope. **ecclesiastical notary** in the early church, a secretary who recorded the proceedings of councils, etc.

notation /nō-tā'shən/ n a system of specialized signs or symbols; the act of notating or writing down; annotation (rare). [L notātiō, -ōnis, from notāre, -ātum to mark]
■ **notate'** vt to write (music, etc) in notation. **nota'tional** adj.

notch /noch/ n a nick; a V-shaped indentation; a narrow pass; a step or level (inf). ◆ vt to make a nick in; to cut (hair, etc) unevenly (obs); to form, fix or remove by nicking; to fit arrow to bowstring (also **nock**); to record by a notch; to score, achieve (often with up). [Supposed to be from Fr oche (now hoche) with n from the indefinite article; not connected with **nock**]
■ **notched** adj nicked. **notch'er** n. **notch'ing** n a method of joining timbers, by fitting into a groove or grooves. **notch'y** adj having notches; (of a manual gearbox) not operating smoothly or easily.
□ **notch'back** n a car whose rear does not slope continuously from the roof to the bumper, but juts out from the bottom of the rear window (also adj). **notch'-board** n a board that receives the ends of the steps of a staircase.

notchel or **nochel** /noch'l/ (inf) n notice that one will not be responsible for another's debts. ◆ vt (**notch'elling** or N Am

notch'eling; **notch'elled** or N Am **notch'eled**) to repudiate the debts of (someone). [Origin unknown]

note[1] /nōt/ n a significant or distinguishing mark; a characteristic; that by which a person or thing is known; a significant tone or hint; a mark or sign calling attention; a written or printed symbol other than a letter; a stigma or mark of censure; an observation or remark; a comment attached to a text, explanatory, illustrative, critical, or recording textual variants; a brief written record, esp a jotting set down provisionally for use afterwards; an impression; a quality, hint or suggestion (of eg warning); a short statement or record; a bill or account (obs); a memorandum; a short informal letter; a formal, esp diplomatic, paper or letter; a small size of paper used for writing; a mark representing a sound (**whole note** a semibreve) (music); the sound or tone represented by the printed or written note; a key of a piano or other instrument; the song, cry or utterance of a bird or other animal; a tune (obs); music (poetic); a paper acknowledging a debt and promising payment, such as a note of hand or promissory note and esp a banknote; a voucher or receipt (obs); notice; attention; cognizance; distinction; reputation; eminence; importance; consequence; notability; intimation (Shakesp). ◆ vt to make a note of; to notice; to pay close attention to; to indicate, show; to mark; to stigmatize (obs); to mention, remark on; to record in writing or in musical notation; to add musical notation to; to set to music; to annotate; to denote. [Fr, from L nota a mark]

■ **nōt'al** adj. **nōt'ed** adj marked; well-known; celebrated; eminent; notorious. **nōt'edly** adv. **nōt'edness** n. **note'less** adj not attracting notice; unmusical. **note'let** n a short annotation or letter; a folded sheet of notepaper, usu with printed decoration, for short informal letters. **nōt'er** n a person who notes or observes; a person who makes notes, an annotator. **note'worthily** adv. **note'worthiness** n. **note'worthy** adj worthy of note or of notice.

❑ **note'book** n a book for keeping notes or memoranda; a small portable computer, orig one smaller than a laptop. **note'case** n a wallet for banknotes. **note of hand** n a promissory note. **note'-pad** n a block of paper for writing notes. **note'paper** n writing paper intended for letters. **note row** n (music) a tone row. **note'-shav'er** n (US) a person who discounts bills at an exorbitant rate; a usurer.

■ **note a bill** to record, with a notary public, one's refusal as a merchant to accept a bill of exchange. **of note** well-known, distinguished; significant, worthy of attention. **strike the right** (or **a false**) **note** to act or speak appropriately (or inappropriately). **take note** to observe carefully or closely (often with of).

note[2], **n'ote** or **no'te** /nōt/ (Spenser) vt wot not; (wrongly) could not. [OE nāt, for ne wāt; see **ne** and **wot**[2]]

nothing /nuth'ing/ n no thing; the non-existent; absence of anything; zero number or quantity; the figure representing it, a nought; a thing or person of no significance or value; an empty or trivial utterance; a low condition; a trifle; no difficulty or trouble. ◆ adv in no degree; not at all. ◆ adj (inf) worthless. [**no**[2] and **thing**]

■ **nothingā'rian** n a person who has no particular belief, esp in religion. **nothingā'rianism** n. **noth'ingism** n nothingness; triviality. **noth'ingness** n non-existence; the state of being nothing; worthlessness; insignificance; vacuity; a thing of no value.

❑ **noth'ing-gift** n (Shakesp) a gift of no value.

■ **be nothing to** not to be important to or concern (someone); not to be nearly as good as. **be nothing to do with** to be unconnected with; to be no concern of. **come to nothing** to have little or no result; to turn out a failure. **for nothing** for no good reason, in vain; free of charge. **have nothing on** (inf) to have no claim to superiority over; to have no information about (used esp by police of criminals); to have no engagement; to have no clothes on. **have nothing to do with** to avoid; to be unconnected with; to be no concern of. **like nothing on earth** (inf) grotesque, frightful. **make nothing of** see under **make**[1]. **next to nothing** almost nothing. **nothing but** only. **nothing doing** (inf) an emphatic refusal; an expression of failure. **nothing for it but** no alternative but. **nothing if not** primarily, above all; at the very least. **nothing less than** or **nothing short of** at least; downright. **nothing to it** or **nothing in it** having nothing in it worth while; easy. **stop** or **stick at nothing** to be ruthless or unscrupulous. **sweet nothings** (esp whispered) words of affection and endearment. **think nothing of** to regard as easy or unremarkable; not to balk or scruple at; to have a low opinion of. **to say nothing of** not to mention (see under **mention**).

Nothofagus /noth-ō-fā'gəs/ n a genus of timber trees of the southern hemisphere, related to beech. [Gr nothos spurious, and L fāgus beech]

notice /nō'tis/ n intimation; announcement; a formal announcement made by one of the parties to a contract of his or her intention to terminate that contract; information, esp about a future event; warning; a writing, placard, board, etc conveying an intimation or warning; time allowed for preparation; cognizance; observation; heed; mention; a dramatic or artistic review; civility or respectful treatment; a notion (obs). ◆ vt to mark or observe; to regard or attend to; to mention; to remark on, make observations about; to write or publish a notice of; to show sign of recognition of; to treat with civility. [Fr notice, from L nōtitia, from nōscere, nōtum to get to know]

■ **no'ticeable** adj that can be noticed, appreciable; worthy of notice; likely to be noticed. **no'ticeably** adv.

❑ **no'ticeboard** n a board for fixing notices on.

■ **at short notice** with notification only a little in advance. **give notice** to warn beforehand; to inform; to intimate, esp the termination of an agreement or (contract of) employment. **take notice** see under **take**.

notify /nō'ti-fī/ vt (**no'tifying**; **no'tified**) to make known; to declare; to give notice or information of. [Fr notifier, from L nōtificāre, -ātum, from nōtus known, and facere to make]

■ **no'tifiable** adj that must be made known; (of diseases) that must be reported to public health authorities. **notification** /-fi-kā'shən/ n the act of notifying; the notice given; the paper containing the notice. **not'ifier** n.

notion /nō'shən/ n a concept in the mind of the various marks or qualities of an object; an idea; a vague impression or understanding; an opinion, esp one not very well founded; a caprice, whim or inclination; a liking or fancy; a mind (Shakesp and Milton); any small, useful article ingeniously devised or invented (usu in pl); (in pl) items of haberdashery, such as buttons, ribbon and thread (N Am). [Fr, from L nōtiō, -ōnis, from nōscere, nōtum to get to know]

■ **no'tional** adj of the nature of a notion; having a full meaning of its own, not merely contributing to the meaning of a phrase (grammar); theoretical; hypothetical; ideal; fanciful; speculative, imaginary, unreal. **no'tionalist** n a theorist. **no'tionally** adv in notion or mental apprehension; in idea, not in reality. **no'tionist** n a person who holds ungrounded opinions.

❑ **notional income** n financial benefits, eg the use of a company car, that have a calculable cash value for taxation purposes.

notitia /nō-tish'i-ə/ n a roll, list or register; a catalogue of public functionaries, with their districts; a list of episcopal sees. [L nōtitia; cf **notice**]

notochord /nō'tō-körd/ (zool) n a skeletal rod formed of turgid vacuolated cells, foreshadowing the spinal column, found in lower vertebrates such as the lancelet. [Gr nōtos back, and chordē a string]

■ **notochord'al** adj.

Notodonta /nō-tō-don'tə/ n a genus of moths whose larvae have toothlike humps, giving name to the family **Notodont'idae**. [Gr nōtos back, and odous, odontos tooth]

■ **notodont'id** n a member of this family.

Notogaea /nō-tō-jē'ə/ n a zoological realm including Australia, the islands north of it, New Zealand and Polynesia. [Gr notos south, and gaia land]

■ **Notogae'an** or **Notogae'ic** adj.

notonectal /nō-tō-nek'təl/ adj swimming on the back, as do certain insects; of the water-boatman genus (**Notonec'ta**) or family (**Notonec'tidae**) of hemipterous insects. [Gr nōton the back, and nēktēs a swimmer]

notorious /nō-tō'ri-əs or -tō'/ adj publicly known (now only in a bad sense); infamous. [LL nōtōrius, from nōtus known]

■ **notorī'ety** n the state of being notorious; publicity; public exposure. **noto'riously** adv. **noto'riousness** n.

notornis /no-tör'nis/ n a bird of the Notornis genus of flightless rails, long thought extinct, but found surviving in New Zealand in 1948 (see also **takahe**). [Gr notos south, and ornis a bird]

Notoryctes /nō-tō-rik'tēz/ n a blind burrowing marsupial of S Australia, the marsupial mole. [Gr notos south, and oryktēs digger]

Nototherium /nō-tō-thē'ri-əm/ n a genus of Tertiary Australian fossil marsupials related to the wombat. [Gr notos south, and thērion a wild beast]

Nototrema /nō-tō-trē'mə/ n the pouch-toad, a S American genus of tree frogs, with a brood-pouch on the female's back. [Gr nōton the back, and trēma a hole]

notoungulate /nō-tō-ung'ū-lāt/ or **notungulate** /nō-tung'ū-lāt/ n any one of an extinct group of herbivorous, hoofed mammals common in S America between the Palaeocene and Pleistocene epochs (also adj). [Gr nōton the back, and L ungulatus hoofed]

notour /nō'tər/ (Scot; now only law) adj well-known, notorious. [LL nōtōrius]

Notre-Dame /not-rə-dam', nō-trə-dām' or (Fr) not-r'-däm'/ (Fr) n Our Lady.

no-trump see under **no**[2].

nott see **not**[2].

Notts. /nots/ abbrev: Nottinghamshire.

notum /nō'təm/ n the dorsal surface of the thorax in insects. [Latinized from Gr nōton back]

■ **nō'tal** adj of or relating to the back (of an insect).

■ words derived from main entry word; ❑ compound words; ■ idioms and phrasal verbs

notungulate see **notoungulate**.

Notus /nō'təs/ n the south or south-west wind. [L *notus*, from Gr *notos*]

notwithstanding /not-with-stan'ding or -widh-/ prep in spite of. ♦ conj in spite of the fact that, although. ♦ adv nevertheless, however, yet. [Orig a participial phrase in nominative absolute, corresponding to L *non obstante*]

nougat /noo'gä or nug'ət/ n a hard, chewy confection made of a sweet paste filled with chopped almonds, pistachio nuts, cherries, etc. [Fr (cf Sp *nogado* an almond cake), from L *nux, nucis* a nut]
■ **nougatine** /noo-gə-tēn'/ n a type of hard brown nougat.

nought /nöt/ n not anything; nothing; the figure 0. ♦ adv in no degree. ♦ adj same as **naught**. [Same as **naught**]
■ **noughties** n pl the years from 2000 to 2009.
■ **noughts and crosses** a game in which one player tries to make three noughts, the other three crosses, in a row in the spaces of crossed parallel lines. **set at nought** to despise, disregard, flout.

noul or (*Spenser*) **noule** /nōl/ n same as **noll**.

nould, noulde or **n'ould** (*obs*) pat of **nill**.

noumenon /noo' or now'mi-non or -mə-/ n (pl **nou'mena**) (in the philosophy of Kant) a thing in itself, an object regarded as having a status independent of its attributes; something whose existence is postulated but ultimately unknowable (eg God, the soul); a thing whose existence can be reasoned but never perceived. [Gr *nooumenon* (contraction for *noeomenon*), neuter of prp passive of *noeein* to think, from *noos* (*nous*) the mind]
■ **nou'menal** adj. **nou'menally** adv.

noun /nown/ (*grammar*) n a word used as the name of a person, animal, thing, place or quality, or a collection of these; formerly including the adjective. [Anglo-Fr *noun* (OFr *non*; Fr *nom*), from L *nōmen, nōminis* a name]
■ **noun'al** adj. **noun'y** adj having many nouns; having the nature or function of a noun.
□ **noun clause** or **noun phrase** n a clause or phrase equivalent to a noun.

nouns /nownz/ (*obs*) interj used as a mild oath, for *od's* (or *odd's*) *nouns* (see under **od²**).

noup /noop or nŭp/ (*obs Shetland; Walter Scott*) n a crag; a steep headland. [ON *gnúpr*]

nourice /nur'is/ (*obs*) n a nurse. [OFr *nurice*; see **nurse¹**]
□ **nour'ice-fee** n payment for a nurse.

nourish /nur'ish/ vt to feed; to provide with food; to support; to encourage the growth of in any way; to allow to grow; to bring up; to cherish (*fig*); to educate; to suckle (*obs*). [OFr *norir, nourir, -iss-* (Fr *nourrir*), from L *nūtrīre* to feed]
■ **nour'ishable** adj. **nour'isher** n. **nour'ishing** adj providing nourishment or much nourishment. **nour'ishingly** adv. **nour'ishment** n the act of nourishing; the state of being nourished; that which nourishes; nutriment.

nouriture or **nourriture** /nur'i-chər/ n nourishment; food; bringing up, nurture (*obs*). [See **nurture**]

noursle /nûr'sl/ (*Spenser*) vt (also **nousle, nousell** or **nuzzle**) to bring up; to foster. [A form of **nuzzle²** influenced by **nurse¹**]

nous /nows or noos/ n intellect; talent; common sense (*inf*). [Gr *nous*, contracted from *noos*]

nousell, nousle see **noursle**.

nousle see **nuzzle¹**.

nout see **nowt¹**.

nouveau /noo-vō'/ or (*fem*) **nouvelle** /-vel'/ (Fr) adj new.
■ **nouvelle** n a long short story.
□ **nouveau riche** /rēsh'/ n (pl **nouveaux riches** /rēsh'/) a person (or persons collectively) with newly acquired wealth, but without good taste or manners; an upstart. **nouveau-riche** adj. **nouveau roman** /rō-mä'/ n the anti-novel (qv). **nouvelle cuisine** see under **cuisine**. **Nouvelle Vague** /väg'/ n a movement in French cinema (beginning just before 1960) in which traditional narrative techniques and regard to box-office appeal were abandoned in favour of a freer, simpler, understated style and sometimes a dogmatically political content (also called **New Wave**). ♦ adj denoting a similar movement in other arts.
■ **art nouveau** see under **art¹**.

Nov. /nov/ abbrev: November.

nova /nō'və/ n (pl **no'vae** /-vē/ or **no'vas**) a star that suddenly increases in brightness for a number of days or years. [L *nova* (*stella*) new (star); fem of *novus* new]

novaculite /nō-vak'ū-līt/ n a hone-stone, a very hard fine-grained siliceous rock containing quartz. [L *novācula* razor]

novalia /nō-vā'li-ə/ (*Scots law; obs*) n pl wastelands newly reclaimed. [L *novālia*]

Novatian /nō-vā'shən/ adj of or relating to the antipope *Novatianus* (251AD), or his party or sect, who favoured severity against the lapsed.
■ **Nova'tianism** n. **Nova'tianist** n.

novation /nō-vā'shən/ n the substitution of a new obligation for the one existing (*law*); innovation. [L *novātiō, -ōnis*, from *novus* new]
■ **novate¹** vt and vi (back-formation).

novel /nov'l or nuv'l/ adj new and strange; of a new kind; felt to be new; new (*obs*). ♦ n a fictitious prose narrative or tale presenting a picture of real life, esp of the emotional crises in the life history of the people portrayed; (with *the*) such writing as a literary genre; a new constitution or decree of Justinian or some other Roman emperor, supplementary to the Codex (often in *pl*); that which is new (earlier /no-vel'/; *obs*); a piece of news (*obs*). [Partly through OFr *novelle* (Fr *nouvelle*), partly through Ital *novella*, partly direct, from L *novellus*, fem *novella*, from *novus* new]
■ **nov'eldom** n the world of fiction. **novelese** /-ēz'/ n (*derog*) the hackneyed style typical of poor novels. **novelette'** n a short novel, esp one that is feeble, trite and sentimental (*derog*); Schumann's name for a short piano piece in free form. **novelett'ish** adj. **novelett'ist** n. **nov'elish** adj savouring of a novel. **nov'elism** n innovation, novelty (*obs*); favouring of innovation; novel-writing. **nov'elist** n a novel-writer; an innovator (*obs*); a newsmonger or news-writer (*obs*). **novelist'ic** adj. **noveliza'tion** or **-s-** n. **nov'elize** or **-ise** vt to make new or novel; to turn into a novel or novels. ♦ vi to innovate; to write as a novelist. **nov'elizer** or **-s-** n. **novella** /nə-vel'ə/ n a short novel; /nov-el'la/ (*Ital*) a tale, short story (*pl* **novell'e** /-lā/); /nov-el'a/ (*L*) a Roman emperor's decree (*pl* **novell'ae** /-ē/). **nov'elty** n (*pl* **nov'elties**) newness; unusual appearance; anything new, strange or different from what was known or usual before; a small, *usu* cheap, manufactured article of unusual or gimmicky design.

November¹ /nō-vem'bər/ n the eleventh month of the year. [L *November*, from *novem* nine; in the original Roman calendar, November was the ninth month of a ten-month year]

November² or **november** /nō-vem'bər/ n (in international radio communication) a code word for the letter *n*.

novena /nō-vē'nə/ (*RC*) n a devotion of prayers or services on nine successive days, to obtain a particular request, through the intercession of the Virgin or some saint. [L *novēnus* nine each, from *novem* nine]

novenary /nov'ə-nə-ri or no-vē'nə-ri/ adj relating to the number nine. ♦ n a set of nine things. [L *novēnārius*, from *novem* nine]

novennial /nō-ven'yəl/ adj recurring every ninth year. [L *novennis*, from *novem* nine, and *annus* a year]

novercal /nō-vûr'kl/ adj relating to or befitting a stepmother. [L *novercālis*, from *noverca* a stepmother]

noverint /nō've-rint/ n a writ, beginning with the words *noverint universi*, let all men know. [L *nōverint*, 3rd person pl perfect subjunctive of *nōscere* to get to know]

Novial /nō'vi-əl or nō-vi-äl'/ n an artificial language devised by Otto Jespersen (1860–1943). [L *novus* new, and the initials of *international auxiliary language*]

novice /nov'is/ n someone new in anything; a beginner; a new convert or church member; an inmate of a religious house who has not yet taken the vows; a competitor that has not yet won a recognized prize; a racehorse that has not won a race in a season prior to the current season (*horse-racing*). [Fr, from L *novīcius*, from *novus* new]
■ **nov'icehood** n. **nov'iceship** n. **noviciate** or **novitiate** /-ish'i-āt/ n the state of being a novice, esp in a religious order; the period of being a novice, esp in a religious order; the novices' quarters in a religious house; a religious novice.

novity /nov'i-ti/ (*obs*) n innovation; newness. [L *novitās, -ātis*, from *novus* new]

Novocaine® /nō'və-kān/ n a proprietary name for procaine (qv).

novocentenary /nō-vō-sen-tē'nə-ri/ n a 900th anniversary. [L *novem* nine, and **centenary**]

novodamus /nō-vō-dā'məs/ (*Scots law*) n a charter or similar document containing a clause by which certain rights, privileges, etc are granted anew; the clause itself. [L (*de*) *novo damus* we grant anew]

novum /nō'vəm/ (*Shakesp*) n a dice game in which the chief throws were nine and five. [Poss L *novem* nine]

novus homo /nō'vəs hō'mō or nov'ŭs hom'ō/ (*L*) n a Roman magistrate whose ancestors had never held office; a new man.

now /now/ adv at the present time, or the time in question, or a very little before or after; immediately; in the present circumstances, as things are; nowadays; (in narrative) then; used meaninglessly or conversationally, or with the feeling of time lost or nearly lost, in remonstrance, admonition, warning, or taking up a new point. ♦ adj present. ♦ n the present time or the time in question. ♦ conj (often

followed by *that*) at this time when and because it is the fact; since at this time. ◆ *interj* expressing admonition, warning or (when repeated) reassurance. [OE *nū*; Ger *nun*, L *nunc*, Gr *nyn*]
■ **now'ness** *n* the quality of constantly being in or taking place at the present moment; a lively and up-to-date quality.
❑ **now'casting** *n* (*meteorol*) a system of rapid and very-short-range presenting of weather phenomena based on realtime processing of simultaneous observations from a network of remote sensing devices.
■ **as of now** from this time onwards. **for now** until later; for the time being. **just now** a moment ago; at this very moment. **now and then** or **now and again** sometimes; from time to time. **now ... now ...** at one time ... at another time ... **now of late** (*archaic*) lately. **now then!** an interjection expressing admonition or rebuke. **the now** (*Scot*) at present; presently; very lately.

nowadays /now'ə-dāz/ *adv* in these times (also *adj*). ◆ *n* the present time. [**now** and **days**, OE *dæges*, genitive of *dæg* day, to which the preposition **a** (OE *on*, which governed the dative) was later added]

noway, **noways** see under **no²**.

nowed /nowd/ (*heraldry*) *adj* knotted. [Fr *noué*]

Nowel, **Nowell** see **Noel**.

nowhere /nō'(h)wār/ *adv* in or to no place, not anywhere; out of the running. ◆ *n* a non-existent place. [**no²**, and **where**, **whence** or **whither¹**]
■ **no'whence** *adv* (*archaic*) from no place. **no'whither** *adv* (*archaic*) to no place; in no direction.
■ **from** or **out of nowhere** suddenly and inexplicably. **get nowhere** to make no progress. **in the middle of nowhere** isolated, remote from towns or cities. **nowhere near** not nearly.

nowise see under **no²**.

nowl /nōl/ (*Shakesp*) same as **noll**.

nown /nōn/ (*obs*) *adj* own. [Orig by wrong division of *mine own*, *thine own*]

nowt¹ or **nout** /nowt/ (*Scot*) *n* cattle. [ON *naut*; cognate with **neat²**, OE *nēat*]
❑ **nowt'-herd** *n*.

nowt² /nowt/ (*dialect* or *inf*) *n* nothing. [**naught**]

nowy /nō'i/ or /now'i/ (*heraldry*) *adj* having a convex curvature near the middle. [OFr *noé* (Fr *noué*), from L *nōdātus* knotted]

NOx *abbrev* : nitrogen oxide.

Nox /noks/ (also without *cap*) *n* nitrogen oxide, *esp* when regarded as emitted by cars, power stations, etc and as contributing towards pollution. [*nitrogen oxide*]
❑ **nox gases** *n pl*.

noxal /nok'sl/ *adj* relating to wrongful injury by an object or animal belonging to another. [LL *noxālis*, from *noxa* hurt]

noxious /nok'shəs/ *adj* poisonous; unwholesome; harmful. [L *noxius*, from *noxa* hurt, from *nocēre* to hurt]
■ **nox'iously** *adv*. **nox'iousness** *n*.

noy /noi/ *vt* (*Spenser*) to vex, hurt or annoy. ◆ *n* (*obs* or *dialect*) vexation, hurt or trouble. [Aphetic forms of **annoy**, etc; see also **noisome**]
■ **noy'ance** *n* (*Spenser* and *Shakesp*) annoyance. **noyes** /noiz/ *n* (*Spenser*) noise (see under **noise**). **noy'ous** *adj* (*Spenser*) vexatious; grievous; injurious. **noy'some** *adj* (*obs*) noisome; hurtful.

noyade /nwä-yäd'/ (*hist*) *n* execution by drowning, as carried out by the French revolutionist Jean Baptiste Carrier at Nantes in 1793–4. [Fr, from *noyer* to drown]

noyau /nwä-yō'/ *n* a liqueur made from brandy flavoured with bitter almonds or peach kernels. [Fr, fruit-stone, from L *nucālis* nutlike, from *nux*, *nucis* a nut]

nozzer /noz'ər/ (*naval sl*) *n* a raw recruit. [Origin uncertain]

nozzle /noz'l/ *n* a little nose; the snout; a projection; an outlet tube, or spout; an open end of a tube; (in some turbines) specially shaped passages for expanding steam, creating kinetic energy of flow with a minimum loss; (in oil engines) openings, controlled by the injection valve, through which fuel is sprayed into the cylinder. [Dimin of **nose**]

NP *abbrev* : new paragraph (also **np**); New Providence (the Bahamas); Notary Public.

Np (*chem*) *symbol* : neptunium.

np *abbrev* : *nisi prius* (qv); no place (of publication); noun phrase.

NPA *abbrev* : Newspaper Publishers' Association.

NPFA *abbrev* : National Playing Fields Association.

NPG *abbrev* : National Portrait Gallery.

NPL *abbrev* : National Physical Laboratory.

NPV *abbrev* : net present value.

NQT *abbrev* : newly qualified teacher.

nr *abbrev* : near.

NRA *abbrev* : National Rifle Association; National Rivers Authority (now replaced by **EA**).

NRPB *abbrev* : National Radiological Protection Board.

NRT *abbrev* : nicotine replacement therapy.

NRV *abbrev* : net realizable value.

NS *abbrev* : new series (also **ns**); New Style; Nova Scotia (Canadian province); Nuclear Ship.

Ns (*chem*) *symbol* : nielsbohrium.

ns *abbrev* : nanosecond(s); non-smoker (also **n/s**); not specified.

NSA (*US*) *abbrev* : National Security Agency.

NSAID *abbrev* : non-steroidal anti-inflammatory drug.

NS&I *abbrev* : National Savings and Investments.

NSB *abbrev* : National Savings Bank.

NSC *abbrev* : National Safety Council; National Security Council (*US*).

NSDAR same as **DAR**.

NSF *abbrev* : National Science Foundation; not sufficient funds (*finance*).

NSFnet *abbrev* : National Science Foundation network, a former computer network linking US universities, research establishments, etc.

NSIT *abbrev* : not safe in taxis (said of a male who is apt to make inappropriate sexual advances).

NSPCC *abbrev* : National Society for the Prevention of Cruelty to Children.

NSRA *abbrev* : National Small-bore Rifle Association.

NSU *abbrev* : non-specific urethritis.

NSW (*Aust*) *abbrev* : New South Wales.

NT *abbrev* : National Theatre (now known as **RNT**); National Trust; New Testament; Northern Territory (*Aust*); Northwest Territories (of Canada); no trumps (*cards*).

-n't shortened (enclitic) form of **not¹**.

NTA *abbrev* : National Training Award(s).

Nth *abbrev* : North.

nth see **N** (*n*).

NTP *abbrev* : normal temperature and pressure (also **ntp**).

NTS *abbrev* : National Trust for Scotland.

NTSC *abbrev* : National Television Standards Committee (in the USA).

nt wt *abbrev* : net weight.

NU *abbrev* : name unknown; Nunavut Territory (Canada).

Nu. *abbrev* : ngultrum (Bhutanese currency).

nu /nū or nü/ *n* the thirteenth letter (N, ν) of the Greek alphabet, corresponding to N, n; as a numeral ν' = 50, ,ν = 50 000. [Gr *nȳ*]

nu- /nū-/ *combining form* a version of **new** often used to denote genres of popular culture, as in *nu-metal, nu-disco*. [Phonetic respelling]

nuance /nū-äs', nwäs, nū-äns', nū'əns or nū'ans/ *n* a delicate or subtle degree or shade of difference. ◆ *vt* to give nuances to. [Fr, from L *nūbēs*, *nūbis* a cloud]
■ **nū'anced** *adj*.

nub¹ /nub/ *n* the point or gist; a small lump or chunk; a protuberance; a small bunch of fibres in yarn. See also **knub**. [Prob from **knub**]
■ **nubb'ly** or **nubb'y** *adj*.

nub² see **knub**.

nub³ /nub/ (*obs sl*) *n* the gallows. ◆ *vt* (**nubb'ing**; **nubbed**) to hang. [Origin unknown]
❑ **nubb'ing-cheat** *n* the gallows. **nubb'ing-cove** *n* a hangman.

nubbin /nub'in/ (*US*) *n* a small or underdeveloped ear of corn, fruit, etc. [Dimin of **nub¹**]

nubble¹ see under **knub**.

nubble² see **knubble**.

nubbly, **nubby** see under **nub¹**.

nubecula /nū-bek'ū-lə/ *n* (pl **nūbec'ulae** /-lē/) a cloudiness; (in *pl*) the Magellanic Clouds. [L *nūbēcula*, dimin of *nūbēs* cloud]

nubia /nū'bi-ə/ *n* a fleecy head-wrap formerly worn by women. [L *nūbēs* a cloud]

nubiferous /nū-bif'ə-rəs/ *adj* cloud-bringing. [L *nūbēs* a cloud, and *ferre* to bring]

nubigenous /nū-bij'i-nəs/ *adj* cloud-born. [L *nūbēs* a cloud, and *genus*, *generis* birth]

nubile /nū'bīl, -bil/ *adj* (*esp* of a woman) marriageable; sexually mature; sexually attractive. [L *nūbilis*, from *nūbere* to veil oneself, hence to marry]
■ **nubility** /-bil'i-ti/ *n*.

■ words derived from main entry word; ❑ compound words; ■ idioms and phrasal verbs

nubilous /nū'bi-ləs/ adj cloudy. [L nūbilus, from nūbēs a cloud]

Nubuck /nū'buk/ n leather made from cowhide but treated to resemble suede. [Prob **nu-** and **buck¹**]

nuc. abbrev : nuclear.

nucellus /nū-sel'əs/ n (pl nucell'i /-lī/) the mass of tissue within the integuments of a plant's ovule, containing the embryo-sac. [A modern dimin from L nux, nucis a nut; L has dimin nucella a little nut]
■ **nucell'ar** adj.

nucha /nū'kə/ (anat) n (pl nu'chae /-kē/) the nape of the neck. [LL nucha, from Ar nukhā' spinal marrow]
■ **nū'chal** adj.

nuciferous /nū-sif'ə-rəs/ (bot) adj nut-bearing. [L nux, nucis nut, and ferre to bear]

nucivorous /nū-siv'ə-rəs/ (zool) adj nut-eating. [L nux, nucis nut, and vorāre to devour]

nucleal /nū'kli-əl/ (rare) adj nuclear. [**nucleus**]

nuclear /nū'kli-ər/ adj of, or of the nature of, a nucleus; relating to the nucleus of an atom or the nuclei of atoms; relating to, derived from, or powered by the fission or fusion of atomic nuclei; possessing nuclear weapons. [**nucleus**]
■ **nuclearizā'tion** or **-s-** n. **nu'clearize** or **-ise** vt to make nuclear; to supply or fit with nuclear weapons.
◻ **nuclear binding energy** n the binding energy that holds together the constituent nucleons of the nucleus of an atom, always less than that of their constituent protons and neutrons. **nuclear charge** n a positive charge arising in the atomic nucleus because of protons, equal in number to the atomic number. **nuclear chemistry** n (chem) the study of reactions involving the transmutation of elements by spontaneous decay or particle bombardment. **nuclear disarmament** n a country's act of giving up its nuclear weapons. **nuclear energy** n a more exact term for **atomic energy**, energy released or absorbed during reactions taking place in atomic nuclei. **nuclear family** n the basic family unit consisting of the mother and father with their children. **nuclear fission** n spontaneous or induced splitting of an atomic nucleus. **nuclear-free zone** n an area in which the transport, storage, manufacture and deployment of nuclear weapons, and the transport or disposal of nuclear waste, are officially prohibited. **nuclear fuel** n material, such as uranium or plutonium, consumed to produce nuclear energy (also called **atomic fuel**). **nuclear fusion** n the creation of a new nucleus by merging two lighter ones, with the release of energy. **nuclear magnetic resonance** n resonance which can be produced in nuclei or most isotopes of the elements and which helps to identify the particular atoms involved, used in the practice of magnetic resonance imaging. **nuclear medicine** n the diagnosis and treatment of disease using radiation detectors or radioactive materials. **nuclear physics** n the science of forces and transformations within the nucleus of the atom. **nuclear power** n power obtained from a controlled nuclear reaction. **nuclear-pow'ered** adj. **nuclear reaction** n a process in which an atomic nucleus interacts with another nucleus or particle, producing changes in energy and nuclear structure. **nuclear reactor** n an assembly of fissile material with a moderator, in which a nuclear chain reaction is produced and maintained; the apparatus housing this. **nuclear sexing** n testing a person's sex by examining cells from inside the cheek which, in females, have a material near the nucleus that can be stained blue. **nuclear threshold** n the point in an armed conflict when nuclear weapons are resorted to. **nuclear umbrella** n protection provided by an alliance with a nuclear power. **nuclear warfare** n warfare using nuclear weapons. **nuclear waste** n radioactive waste. **nuclear weapon** n a bomb, missile, etc deriving its destructive force from the energy released by a nuclear reaction. **nuclear winter** n the period of lack of sunlight and resulting severe cold predicted by scientists as the aftermath of a nuclear war.

nuclease /nū'kle-āz/ n any of a number of enzymes inducing hydrolysis in nucleic acids. [**nucleus**]

nucleate /nū'kli-āt/ vt and vi to form into, or group around, a nucleus. ◆ vt to act, in a process of formation, as a nucleus for (eg crystals). [**nucleus**]
■ **nu'cleate** or **nu'cleated** adj having a nucleus. **nuclea'tion** n the action or process of nucleating; seeding clouds to control rainfall and fog formation. **nū'cleator** n.

nucleic acid see under **nucleus**.

nucleide see **nuclide**.

nuclein /nū'kli-in/ n a colourless amorphous substance of varying composition, obtained from cell nuclei. [**nucleus**]

nucleo- /nū-kli-ō- or -ə-/ combining form denoting: nucleus; nucleic acid; nuclear. [**nucleus**]
■ **nucleocap'sid** n (biol) a capsid of a virus containing nucleic acid. **nucleophil'ic** adj of, relating to or involving electron contribution to

covalent bonding. **nu'cleoplasm** n the protoplasm in the nucleus of a cell. **nucleopro'tein** n any of a group of compounds containing a protein molecule combined with a nuclein, important constituents of the nuclei of living cells. **nu'cleoside** n a deoxyribose or ribose sugar molecule to which a purine or pyrimidine base is covalently bound. **nu'cleosome** n a repeating unit of chromatin occurring along a strand of DNA. **nucleosyn'thesis** n the process in which atomic nuclei bind together to form chemical elements (eg in stars). **nu'cleotide** n a nucleoside with a phosphate group attached to the sugar, the individual components of a nucleic acid.

nucleolar, nucleolate, nucleolated see under **nucleolus**.

nucleolus /nū-klē-ō'ləs/ (biol) n (pl **nucleoli** /nū-klē-ō'lī/) a body (sometimes two bodies) with a cell nucleus, indispensable to growth (also **nu'cleole**). [**nucleus**]
■ **nucleo'lar** adj. **nu'cleolate** or **nu'cleolated** adj having a nucleus or nucleolus; (of a spore) containing one or more conspicuous oil-drops.
◻ **nucleolar-organizing region** n the region of the chromosomal DNA that codes for ribosomal RNA (abbrev **NOR**).

nucleon /nū'kli-on/ n a general name for a neutron or a proton. [**nucleus**]
■ **nucleon'ics** n sing nuclear physics, esp its practical applications.
◻ **nucleon number** n mass number.

nucleophilic...to...nucleotide see under **nucleo-**.

nucleus /nū'kli-əs/ n (pl **nuclei** /nū'kli-ī/) a central mass or kernel; that around which something may grow; a compartment within the interphase eukaryotic cell bounded by a double membrane and containing the genomic DNA (biol); the massive part of an atom, containing protons and neutrons and distinguished from the outlying electrons (phys); a stable group of atoms to which other atoms may be attached so as to form a series of compounds (chem); a core of flint from which pieces have been flaked off; the densest part of a comet's head or a nebula; a nut kernel (obs); a nucellus (obs). [L, from nux, nucis a nut]
◻ **nucleic acid** /nū-klē'ik or -klā'/ n a general term for a natural polymer (which can be single- or double-stranded) in which bases (purines or pyrimidines) are attached to a sugar phosphate backbone. **nucleus accumbens** /ə-kum'benz/ n (L accumbens lying down) a structure in the brain associated with feelings of pleasure and reward.

nuclide /nū'klīd/ n a species of atom of any element distinguished by the number of neutrons and protons in its nucleus, and its energy state (sometimes also **nu'cleide**). [**nucleus**]

nucule /nū'kūl/ n a nutlet. [L nucula, dimin of nux, nucis a nut]

nuddy /nud'i/ (inf) n (with the) a state of nudity. [Jocular pronunciation of nude]

nude /nūd/ adj naked; bare; without clothes; showing or involving naked or almost naked figures; undraped; flesh-coloured; (of eg contracts and agreements) made without a consideration (law). ◆ n a nude figure or figures; the condition of being naked; (with the) the representation of naked human figures as an art form; flesh-coloured fabric, used eg for stockings. [L nūdus naked]
■ **nudā'tion** n the act of making bare. **nude'ly** adv. **nude'ness** n. **nu'die** adj (sl) (esp of films, shows, magazines, etc) naked or featuring nudity (also n). **nu'dism** n the practice of going naked; (esp US) naturism. **nu'dist** n a person who goes naked, or approves of going naked; (esp US) a naturist. ◆ adj of, for or relating to nudists. **nu'dity** n (pl **nu'dities**) the state of being nude; a nude figure (rare); (in pl) naked parts usually covered.

nudge /nuj/ n a gentle poke or push, as with the elbow. ◆ vt to poke or push gently, esp to draw someone's attention to something, or as a reminder or encouragement; to push slowly and gently. [Origin obscure; perh connected with Norw nugge to rub, or with **knock** or **knuckle**]
■ **nudg'er** n.
■ **nudge, nudge** or **nudge, nudge, wink, wink** (inf) a phrase appended in mock or would-be confidentiality, to an implication of disreputable practice, or to a sexual innuendo.

nudibranch /nū'di-brangk/ n a shell-less marine gastropod, belonging to the **Nudibranch'ia**, with external, often branched gills on the back and the sides of the body (also adj). [Fr nudibranche, from L nūdus nude, and branchia gills]
■ **nudibranch'iate** adj of or belonging to members of the Nudibranchia. ◆ n a nudibranch.

nudicaudate /nū-di-kö'dāt/ adj (of eg rats) having a hairless tail. [L nūdus nude, and cauda tail]

nudicaul /nū'di-köl/ or **nudicaulous** /nū-di-kö'ləs/ adj having a leafless stem. [L nūdus nude, and caulis stem]

nudism, nudist, nudity see under **nude**.

nudnik /nud'nik/ (sl) n a tiring, dull or boring person. [Yiddish nudyen to bore, and **-nik**]

nuée ardente /nü-ā är-dāt'/ n a cloud of hot gas, ash, etc from a volcano, spreading horizontally. [Fr, burning cloud]

nuevo sol /nwā'vō sol/ see **sol³**.

nuff /nuf/ a slang or dialect form of **enough**.

nuffin /nuf'in/ a slang or dialect form of **nothing**.

nugae /nū'gē, -jē or noo'gī/ (L) n pl trifles.

nugatory /nū'gə-tə-ri/ adj trifling; worthless; inoperative; unavailing; futile. [L nūgātōrius, from nūgae trifles, trumpery]
■ **nu'gatoriness** n.

nuggar /nug'ər/ n a large boat used to carry cargo on the Nile. [Ar nuqqār]

nugget /nug'it/ n a lump, esp of gold; anything small but valuable (fig). [Origin unknown; there is a Swed dialect word nug a lump, block]
■ **nugg'ety** adj found in or full of nuggets; stocky, thickset (Aust).

NUI abbrev : National University of Ireland.

nuisance /nū'səns/ n something which annoys or hurts, esp if there is some legal remedy; that which is offensive to the senses; a person or thing that is troublesome or obtrusive in some way; hurt or injury (obs). [Fr, from L nocēre to hurt]
■ **nui'sancer** n (rare).
❑ **nuisance value** n the value or usefulness of someone's or something's capacity to cause problems when required.

NUJ abbrev : National Union of Journalists.

nuke /nūk/ (sl) n a nuclear weapon. ◆ vt to attack using nuclear weapons; to reheat or cook in a microwave oven. [Contraction of **nuclear**]

null¹ /nul/ adj of no legal force; void; invalid; having no significance; amounting to nothing, non-existent; (of a set) empty (maths); quantitively, or amounting to, zero (maths). ◆ n (obs) something with no value or meaning, a cipher or nought. ◆ vt to annul, nullify; to wipe out (obs). [L nūllus not any, from nē not, and ūllus any]
■ **null'ity** n the state of being null or void; something without legal force or validity; nothingness; lack of existence, force or efficacy. **null'ness** n.
❑ **null-modem cable** n (comput) a special cable used to link two PCs.
■ **decree of nullity** a decree that a marriage has never legally existed, eg because of a failure to publish the banns properly. **null and void** without legal force; not valid or binding.

null² /nul/ n a knurl; a kink. ◆ vi to kink. [**knurl**]
■ **null'ing** n knurling.

nulla, nullah, nala, nalla or **nallah** /nul'ə/ (Ind) n a ravine; a watercourse; a stream or drain. [Hindi nālā]

nulla-nulla /nul'ə-nul'ə/ n an Australian Aborigine's club (also **null'a**). [From an Aboriginal language]

nullifidian /nul-i-fid'i-ən/ adj having no faith, esp religious. ◆ n a person who has no faith. [L nūllus none, and fidēs faith]

nullify /nul'i-fī/ vt (**null'ifying**; **null'ified**) to make null; to annul; to make void or of no force. [Late L nūllificāre, from nūllus none, and facere to make]
■ **nullification** /-fi-kā'shən/ n a making void or of no effect, esp (US) of a contract by one of the parties, or of a law by one legislature which has been passed by another. **null'ifier** /-fī-ər/ n.

nullipara /nu-lip'ə-rə/ (obstetrics) n a woman who has never given birth to a child, esp if she is not a virgin. [L nūllus none, and parere to bring forth]
■ **nulliparity** /-i-par'i-ti/ n. **nullip'arous** adj.

nullipore /nul'i-pōr or -pör/ n a coralline seaweed. [L nūllus none, and porus a passage, pore]

nulli secundus /nul'ī si-kun'dəs or noo'lē se-kŭn'dŭs/ (L) second to none.

nullity, nullness see under **null¹**.

NUM abbrev : National Union of Mineworkers.

Num. or **Numb.** (Bible) abbrev : (the Book of) Numbers.

num. abbrev : number; numeral.

NUMAST /nū'mast/ abbrev : National Union of Marine, Aviation and Shipping Transport Officers.

numb /num/ adj having diminished power of sensation or motion; powerless to feel or act; stupefied; causing (Shakesp) or of the nature of (Milton) numbness. ◆ vt (**numbing** /num'ing/; **numbed** /numd/) to make numb; to deaden. [OE numen, pap of niman to take]
■ **numb'ingly** adv. **numb'ly** adv. **numb'ness** n.
❑ **numbskull** see **numskull**.

numbat /num'bat/ n a small Australian marsupial (Myrmecobius fasciatus) which feeds on termites. [From an Aboriginal language]

number /num'bər/ n that by which single things are counted or reckoned; quantity reckoned in units; a particular value or sum of single things or units; a representation in arithmetical symbols of such

a value or sum; a full complement; a specified or recognized, and often exclusive, set, class or group; the multitude (obs); some or many of the persons or things in question (often in pl); more than one; a total quantity or amount; numerousness; (in pl) numerical superiority; numerability; a numeral or series of numerals indicating a thing's place in a series, or one assigned to it for reference, as in a catalogue; a label or other object bearing such an indication; a person or thing marked or designated in such a way; an item; an issue of a periodical or serial publication; a self-contained portion of an opera or other composition; arithmetical faculty; (in pl) rhythm, verses, music; the property in words of expressing singular, dual, trial, etc and plural (grammar); a telephone number; a single item in a programme, esp of popular music and/or variety turns; an admired item of merchandise on show, usu of women's clothing (inf); a person or thing thought of with affection or familiarity, esp a girl (sl); (with cap, in pl) the fourth book of the Old Testament, in which an account of a census is given. ◆ vt to count; to count out in payment (Milton); to apportion; to have lived through; (also vi) to count as one of a group; (also vi) to mark with a number or assign a number to; (also vi) to amount to. [Fr nombre, from L numerus]
■ **num'berer** n. **num'berless** adj without number; more than can be counted. **num'berlessly** adv. **num'berlessness** n.
❑ **num'ber-cruncher** n (inf) a computer designed to carry out large quantities of complex numerical calculations; a person who operates such a computer, or carries out such calculations in his or her head. **num'ber-crunching** n. **numbered account** n a bank account identified only by a number, with the holder's name kept secret. **number eight** n in Rugby Union, the forward whose position is at the back of the scrum. **number line** n (maths) an infinite straight line on which the points correspond to the set of real numbers. **number nine** n (milit sl) a purgative pill. **number one** adj chief, most important. ◆ n the person or thing numbered one, the first in the numbered series; self, oneself (inf); the bestselling record or book at any particular time (inf); a lieutenant, first officer (under the rank of commander; naut sl); urine (sl or childish). **number plate** n the plaque on a motor vehicle showing its registration number. **numbers game, pool** or **racket** n (US) an illegal form of gambling in which players bet on the appearance of a chosen sequence of numbers in the financial pages of a newspaper, etc. **numbers man** n (US) someone who runs a numbers game. **number system** n (maths) any set of elements which has two binary operations called addition and multiplication, each of which is commutative and associative, and which is such that multiplication is distributive with respect to addition. **Number Ten** n (inf) 10 Downing Street, official residence of the British Prime Minister. **number theory** n the branch of mathematics studying integers and their properties. **number two** n second-in-command; faeces (sl or childish).
■ **any number of** many. **beyond** or **without number** too many to be counted. **by numbers** (of a procedure, etc) performed in simple stages with foolproof guidance provided (as if) in the form of a sequence of numbered instructions or steps. **do a number on** (sl) to defeat utterly; to cheat or take advantage of. **have** or **get someone's number** (inf) to size someone up. **his** (or **her**) **number is up** (inf) he (or she) is doomed, has not long to live. **in numbers** in large numbers. **number off** to call out numbers in sequence. **number of the beast** see **apocalyptic number** under **apocalypse**. **one's** (or **its**) **days are numbered** one's (or its) end is imminent. **play the numbers game** to rely on arithmetical calculations, or use of figures in general, to make a point.

numble-pie, numbles see **umbles**.

numdah /num'dä/ n an embroidered felt rug made in India. [Cf **numnah**]

numen /nū'men/ n (pl **nu'mina** /-min-ə/) a presiding deity. [L numen, -inis divinity]

numerable /nū'mə-rə-bl/ adj that may be numbered or counted. [L numerābilis, from numerus number]
■ **numerabil'ity** n. **nu'merably** adv.

numeraire /nū'mə-rär/ or (Fr) **numéraire** /nü-mā-rer'/ n a standard for currency exchange rates, etc. [Fr; see ety for **numerary**]

numeral /nū'mə-rəl/ adj relating to, consisting of, or expressing number. ◆ n a figure, mark or group of figures used to express a number, such as 1, 2, I, V, α, β, etc; a word used to denote a number (grammar); (in pl) a badge indicating regiment, year of curriculum, etc. [L numerālis, from numerus number]
■ **nu'merally** adv (rare) according to number.

numerary /nū'mə-rə-ri/ adj belonging to a certain number; contained within or counting as one of a body or a number, opp to supernumerary. [L numerārius, from numerus number]

numerate /nū'mə-rət/ adj having some understanding of mathematics and science; able to solve arithmetical problems. See also **innumerate**. ◆ vt /-āt/ to read off as numbers (from figures); orig to enumerate, to number. [L *numerātus*, pap of *numerāre* to number]

■ **nu'meracy** *n* the state of being numerate. **numerā'tion** *n* the act of numbering; the art of reading figures and expressing the value in numbers; a system or method of numbering. **nu'merātor** *n* a person who or thing which numbers; the upper number of a vulgar fraction, which expresses the number of fractional parts taken.

numeric /nū-mer'ik/ or **numerical** /-i-kl/ *adj* belonging to, expressed in, or consisting in, a number or numbers; in number independently of sign (*maths*); identical (*obs*; often with *same*). [L *numerus* number]

■ **numer'ically** *adv*.
❑ **numerical analysis** *n* the study of methods of approximation and their accuracy, etc. **numerical control** *n* automatic control of operation of machine tools by means of numerical data stored in computers. **numerical forecasting** *n* a method of weather forecasting based on a large number of observations at the earth's surface and throughout the atmosphere, and the calculation from these of the conditions which should follow in accordance with the known laws of physics. **numeric keypad** *n* a numbered pad forming a separate section on a computer keyboard, for inputting data or occasionally commands.

numerology /nū-mə-rol'ə-ji/ *n* the study of numbers as supposed to predict future events or influence people. [L *numerus* number, and **-logy**]

■ **numerolog'ical** *adj*. **numerol'ogist** *n*.

numero uno /noo'mə-rō oo'nō/ (*inf*) *n* number one, the most important person or thing, often oneself (also *adj*). [Ital]

numerous /nū'mə-rəs/ *adj* great in number or quantity; many; consisting of or relating to a large number; rhythmical. [L *numerōsus*, from *numerus* number]

■ **numeros'ity** *n* numerousness; condition in respect of number; harmonious flow. **nu'merously** *adv*. **nu'merousness** *n*.

numerus clausus /nū'mə-rəs klō'zəs or noo'me-rŭs klow'sŭs/ *n* a quota restricting the number of students (*esp* those of a particular race or creed) entering an academic institution. [L, literally, closed or restricted number]

numina see **numen**.

numinous /nū'mi-nəs/ *adj* relating to a divinity; suffused with, or arousing, deeply religious emotions, *esp* a sense of the presence of a divinity. ◆ *n* a divinity or deity, a numen. [L *nūmen*, *-inis* divinity]

■ **nu'minousness** *n*.

numismatic /nū-miz-mat'ik/ *adj* relating to money, coins or medals. [L *numisma*, from Gr *nomisma* current coin, from *nomizein* to use commonly, from *nomos* custom]

■ **numismat'ically** *adv*. **numismat'ics** *n sing* the study or collection of coins and medals (also **numismatol'ogy**). **numis'matist** *n*. **numismatol'ogist** *n*.

nummary /num'ə-ri/ *adj* relating to coins or money. [L *nummus* a coin]

■ **numm'ular** *adj* coin-shaped. **numm'ulary** *adj* nummary. **numm'ulāted** *adj* coin-shaped. **nummulā'tion** *n* the arrangement of blood corpuscles in rouleaux. **numm'uline** *adj* coin-shaped; nummulitic. **numm'ulite** *n* a large coin-shaped fossil foraminifer, forming limestones. **nummulitic** /-lit'ik/ *adj* relating to, composed of, or containing nummulites.

numnah /num'nə/ *n* a felt, or now *usu* sheepskin, cloth or pad placed under a saddle to prevent chafing. [Hindi *namdā*]

numpty /num(p)'ti/ (chiefly *Scot*) *n* an idiot. [Perh from obs *nump*]

numskull or **numbskull** /num'skul/ (*inf*) *n* a blockhead. [**numb** and **skull**[1]]

■ **num'skulled** *adj*.

nun[1] /nun/ *n* a female member of a contemplative religious order, *esp* one who has taken her final vows; a kind of pigeon with feathers on its head like a nun's hood; a blue tit; a male smew; a tussock moth (*Lymantria monacha*), a pest in pine forests. [OE *nunne*, from LL *nunna*, *nonna* a nun, an old maiden lady, *orig* mother; cf Gr *nannē* aunt, Sans *nanā* a child's word for mother]

■ **nun'hood** *n* the condition of a nun. **nunn'ery** *n* (*pl* **nunn'eries**) a house for nuns, a convent; nunship. **nunn'ish** *adj*. **nunn'ishness** *n*. **nun'ship** *n* the condition of a nun.

❑ **nun's-fidd'le** *n* an obsolete type of viol, a tromba marina. **nun's'-flesh** *n* an ascetic temperament. **nun's'-veil'ing** *n* a thin, soft, woollen dress material.

nun[2] /nun/ (*obs*) *n* a spinning top.

❑ **nun buoy** *n* a buoy that tapers conically each way.

nun[3] /noon/ *n* the fourteenth letter of the Hebrew alphabet. [Heb]

nunatak /nun'ə-tak/ *n* (*pl* **nu'nataks** or (*Swed*) **nu'nataker**) a point of rock appearing above the surface of land-ice. [Inuit]

nunc dimittis /nungk or nŭngk di-mit'is/ *n* (also with *caps*) the song of Simeon (from Bible, Luke 2.29–32) in the Roman Catholic Breviary and the Anglican evening service. [From the opening words, *nunc dīmittis* now lettest thou depart]

nunchaku /nun-chak'oo/ *n* a weapon consisting of two short thick sticks joined by a length of chain, used in some martial arts (also (*pl*; *esp US*) **nun'chucks**). [Jap]

nuncheon /nun'shən/ *n* a light meal; a lunch. [ME *noneschenche* noon-drink, from OE *nōn* noon, and *scenc* drink; cf **noon** and **skink**[3]]

nuncio /nun'si-ō/ *n* (*pl* **nun'cios**) an ambassador from the Pope; a messenger; a person who brings tidings. [Ital (now *nunzio*), from L *nūntius* a messenger, conjectured to be a contraction of *noventius*; cf *novus* new]

■ **nun'ciature** *n* a papal nuncio's office or term of office.

nuncle /nung'kl/ (*Shakesp*) *n* a contraction of **mine uncle**.

nuncupate /nung'kū-pāt/ (*law*) *vt* to utter as a vow; to declare (a will) orally. [L *nuncupāre* to call by name, prob from *nōmen* name, and *capere* to take]

■ **nuncūpā'tion** *n*. **nunc'ūpātive** *adj* (of a will) oral; designative. **nunc'ūpatory** /-pə-tə-ri/ *adj* (*obs*) nuncupative; dedicatory.

nundine /nun'dīn/ or *-din/ *n* the ancient Roman market-day, every eighth day (ninth by Roman reckoning, counting both days). [L *nūndinae* market-day, from *novem* nine, and *diēs* a day]

■ **nun'dinal** /-din-/ *adj* relating to a fair or market.

nunnation /nu-nā'shən/ *n* the addition of a final *n* in the declension of nouns. [As if L *nunnātiō*, from Ar *nūn* the letter 'n']

nunnery see under **nun**[1].

nuoc mam /nwok mäm/ *n* a spicy sauce made from raw fish. [Viet]

Nupe /noo'pā/ *n* (*pl* **Nu'pe** or **Nu'pes**) (a member of) a people living in west-central Nigeria; the language spoken by this people.

Nuphar /nū'fär/ *n* the yellow water lily genus. [Pers *nūfar*, reduced form of *nīnūfar*; see **nenuphar**]

nuptial /nup'shəl/ *adj* of or relating to marriage; relating to mating (*zool*). ◆ *n* (*usu* in *pl*) a marriage; a wedding ceremony. [L *nuptiālis*, from *nuptiae* marriage, from *nubere*, *nuptum* to marry]

■ **nuptiality** /-shi-al'i-ti/ *n* nuptial character or quality; marriage-rate; (in *pl*) wedding ceremonies and festivities.

nur, nurr see **knur**.

nuraghe /noo-rä'gā/ or **nurhag** /noo-räg'/ *n* (*pl* **nura'ghi** /-gē/ or **nurhags'**) a broch-like Sardinian round tower, *prob* of the Bronze Age. [Sardinian dialect]

■ **nuragh'ic** *adj* relating to, found in, etc nuraghi.

nurd see **nerd**.

nurdle /nûr'dl/ (*cricket*) *vi* to score runs by gently pushing or deflecting the ball with the bat rather than by hitting it hard.

nurl see **knurl**.

Nurofen® /nū'rə-fen/ *n* a proprietary painkiller containing ibuprofen.

nurse[1] /nûrs/ *n* a woman who suckles a child, *esp* another person's child, a wet nurse (*archaic*); a person who tends a child (*old*); a person who has the care of the sick, feeble or injured, *esp* one who is trained for the purpose; a person given the task of supervising a new or incompetent employee (*rare*); a worker bee, ant, etc that tends the young; a budding form in tunicates; someone who or that which feeds, rears, tends, saves, fosters or develops anything, or preserves it in any desired condition; a shrub or tree that protects a young plant (*hortic*); the state of being nursed, in the phrases *at nurse* or *out to nurse*. ◆ *vt* (also *vi*) to suckle (a baby); (also *vi*) to tend (eg an infant or a sick person); to bring up; to cherish; to manage or treat with care and economy; to play skilfully, manipulate carefully, or keep watchfully in touch with, in order to obtain or preserve the desired condition; to keep (the balls) together for a cannon or series of cannons (*billiards*); to hold, carry or cuddle (as a nurse does a child). [OFr *norrice* (Fr *nourrice*), from L *nūtrīx*, *-īcis*, from *nūtrīre* to nourish]

■ **nurse'like** *adj*. **nurse'ling** or **nurs'ling** *n* that which is nursed or fostered; an infant that is being suckled. **nurs'er** *n*. **nurs'ing** *n* the profession or practice of caring for the sick, feeble or injured (also *adj*). **nursling** see **nurseling** above.

❑ **nurse'-child** *n* a child in the care of a nurse; a foster-child. **nurse'maid** *n* a woman employed to take care of children; a person who guides or cares for another. ◆ *vt* to act as a nursemaid to. **nurse practitioner** *n* a registered nurse who takes on some of the tasks of primary health care usually performed by doctors, such as limited prescribing, plastering broken limbs, etc. **nurse'-tend** *vt* and *vi* to attend as a sick-nurse. **nurse'-tender** *n*. **nurse'-tending** *n*. **nurs'ing-bra** *n* a bra for women who are breastfeeding, with cups which (partially) unfasten. **nursing chair** *n* a low chair without arms, used when feeding a baby. **nurs'ing-fa'ther** *n* (*Bible*) a foster-father. **nursing home** *n* a private hospital or residence providing care, eg to the elderly or infirm. **nursing officer** *n* any of several grades of nurses having administrative duties.

■ **put** (**out**) **to nurse** to entrust to a nurse, *esp* a baby to a wet nurse, *usu* away from home; to put (an estate) under trustees.

nurse² /*nûrs*/ *n* a shark; a dogfish. [Earlier *nuss*, perh for (an) *huss*, *husk* a dogfish]

◻ **nurse'hound** *n* a European dogfish (*Scyliorhinus caniculus* or *S. stellaris*). **nurse shark** *n* any shark of the family Orectolobidae.

nursery /*nûr'sə-ri*/ *n* a room in a house set aside for children; a place providing residential or day care for young children; a place for nursing; a place where young animals are reared, or where the growth of anything is promoted; a place where plants are reared for sale or transplanting; nursing (*Shakesp*); a race for two-year-old horses (also called **nursery stakes**); a nursery cannon (*billiards*). ◆ *adj* relating to a nursery, or to early training. [**nurse¹**]

◻ **nursery cannon** *n* (*billiards*) a cannon (*esp* one of a series) with the three balls close together and being moved as little as possible. **nursery class** *n* a school class for children under five. **nurs'ery-gov'erness** *n* a governess for children who still require a nurse's care. **nurs'erymaid** *n* a woman employed in a nursery; a nursemaid. **nurs'eryman** *n* a man who owns or works in a nursery for plants. **nursery nurse** *n* a person trained in the care of young children, employed in a nursery. **nursery rhyme** *n* a traditional rhyme known to children. **nursery school** *n* a school for very young children (aged two to five). **nursery slopes** *n pl* slopes set apart for novice skiers.

nursing see under **nurse¹**.

nursle /*nûr'sl*/ a mistaken form of **nuzzle¹** or **nousle**.

nursling see under **nurse¹**.

nurture /*nûr'chər*/ *n* upbringing; rearing; training; whatever is derived from the individual's experience, training, environment, distinguished from *nature*, or what is inherited; anything that nourishes, *esp* food. ◆ *vt* to nourish; to bring up; to educate. [OFr *noriture* (Fr *nourriture*), from LL *nūtritūra*, from L *nūtrīre* to nourish]

■ **nur'turable** *adj*. **nur'tural** *adj*. **nur'turant** *adj*. **nur'turer** *n*.

NUS *abbrev* : National Union of Students.

NUT *abbrev* : National Union of Teachers.

nut /*nut*/ *n* popularly, any fruit with an edible seed in a hard shell; a hard dry indehiscent fruit formed from a syncarpous gynaeceum (*bot*); often the hazelnut, sometimes the walnut; the head (*inf*); a crazy person (also **nut'case**; *inf*); a person with an obsessive interest; a small, *usu* metal, hexagonal block with a hole in the middle, for screwing on the end of a bolt; a hard-headed person, one difficult to deal with, a tough; a young blood (also **knut** /*nut*/; *sl*); an en (*printing*); the ridge at the top of the fingerboard on a fiddle, etc (*music*); the mechanism for tightening or slackening a bow (*music*); a small lump of coal; a small, often ginger-flavoured biscuit or round cake; a coconut-shell drinking cup; (in *pl*) a source of joy (*inf*); (in *pl*) the testicles (*inf*). ◆ *vi* (**nutt'ing**; **nutt'ed**) to look for and gather nuts. ◆ *vt* (*inf*) to butt with the head. [OE *hnutu*; ON *hnot*, Du *noot*, Ger *Nuss*]

■ **nutā'rian** *n* (*rare*) a person who thinks nuts are the best kind of food. **nut'let** *n* a one-seeded portion of a fruit that divides as it matures, as in labiates; the stone of a drupe. **nut'like** *adj*. **nuts** (*inf*) *adj* crazy. ◆ *interj* expressing defiance, contempt, disappointment, etc. **nutt'er** *n* a crazy person (*inf*); a person who gathers nuts; nutbutter. **nutt'ery** *n* an area of nut-trees; a mental hospital (*sl*). **nutt'ily** *adv*. **nutt'iness** *n*. **nutt'ing** *n* the gathering of nuts. **nutt'y** *adj* containing many nuts; having the flavour of nuts; mentally unhinged (*sl*); foolishly amorous (*sl*).

◻ **nut'-brown** *adj* brown, like a ripe hazelnut. **nut'butter** *n* a butter-substitute or spread made from nuts. **nut'cracker** *n* a bird (genus *Nucifraga*) of the crow family which feeds on nuts and pine seeds; (*usu* in *pl*) an instrument for cracking nuts. ◆ *adj* like a pair of nutcrackers, eg toothless jaws. **nutcracker man** *n* a hominid whose bones were found in Tanzania in 1959, *orig* designated *Zinjanthropus* but later shown to be a species of *Australopithecus*. **nut cutlet** *n* a cutlet-shaped portion of a moist vegetable and nut mixture. **nut'gall** *n* a nutlike gall, produced by a gall wasp, chiefly on the oak. **nut'-grass** *n* any of various American sedges, *esp* one with edible tuberous roots. **nut'hatch** *n* any of various birds of the family Sittidae that hack at nuts and seek insects on the bark of trees like a creeper (also **nut'jobber** and **nut'pecker**). **nut'-hook** *n* a stick with a hook for pulling down nut-bearing boughs; a bailiff; a thief who uses a hook. **nut'house** *n* (*inf*) a mental hospital; a place where chaos and crazy behaviour reign. **nut'job** *n* (*sl*) a crazy person. **nutjobber** see **nuthatch** above. **nut'meal** *n* meal made from nuts. **nut oil** *n* an oil obtained from walnuts or other nuts. **nutpecker** see **nuthatch** above. **nut pine** *n* the stone pine or other species with large edible seeds. **nut'shell** *n* the hard covering of a nut. **nut'-tree** *n* any tree bearing nuts, *esp* the hazel. **nut'-wee'vil** *n* a weevil (genus *Balaninus*) whose larvae live on hazelnuts. **nut'wood** *n* (the wood of) any nut-bearing tree, *esp* the walnut. **nut'-wrench** *n* an instrument for turning nuts on screws.

■ **a tough** (or **hard**) **nut to crack** (*inf*) a difficult problem; a formidable opponent. **be nuts on** or **about** (*inf*) to be very fond of; to be fanatically enthusiastic about. **do one's nut** (*inf*) to become extremely angry, to rage. **in a nutshell** in a very small space; briefly, concisely. **not for nuts** (*inf*) not very well, incompetently. **nuts and bolts** (*inf*) the basic facts, the essential, practical details. **off one's nut** (*inf*) mentally unhinged, crazy.

nutant /*nū'tənt*/ *adj* nodding; drooping. [L *nūtāre* to nod]

■ **nutate'** *vi* to nod; to droop; to perform a nutation. **nutā'tion** *n* a nodding; a fluctuation in the precessional movement of the earth's pole about the pole of the ecliptic (*astron*); the sweeping out of a curve by the tip of a growing axis (*bot*); the periodic variation of the inclination of the axis of a spinning top (or gyroscope) to the vertical (*phys*). **nutā'tional** *adj*.

nutmeg /*nut'meg*/ *n* the aromatic kernel of an East Indian tree (genus *Myristica*), much used as a seasoning in cookery. ◆ *vt* (**nut'megging**; **nut'megged**) (*inf*; *sport*) to pass or kick the ball through the legs of (an opposing player). [ME *notemuge*, from *nut* and inferred OFr *mugue* musk, from L *muscus* musk]

■ **nut'megged** *adj*. **nut'meggy** *adj*.

NU tone (*telecom*) *abbrev* : number unobtainable tone.

nutraceutical /*nū-trə-sū'ti-kəl*/ *n* same as **functional food** (see under **function**). [*nutrition* and pharma*ceutical*]

nutria /*nū'tri-ə*/ *n* the coypu; its fur. [Sp *nutria* otter, from L *lutra*]

nutrient /*nū'tri-ənt*/ *n* any nourishing substance. ◆ *adj* feeding; nourishing. [L *nūtrīre* to nourish]

■ **nu'triment** *n* anything which nourishes; food. **nutrimental** /*-ment'l*/ *adj*. **nutri'tion** *n* the act or process of nourishing; food; the study of nutrients and the nutritional value of food. **nutri'tional** *adj*. **nutri'tionist** *n* an expert on foods and their nutritional values. **nutri'tious** *adj* nourishing. **nutri'tiously** *adv*. **nutri'tiousness** *n*. **nu'tritive** *adj* nourishing; of or concerned with nutrition. ◆ *n* a nutritious food. **nu'tritively** *adv*.

nutrigenomics /*nū-tri-jə-nom'iks*/ *n sing* the study of the combined effect of diet and genetic make-up on health. [From *nutri*tional *genomics*]

nutriment, etc, **nutrition**, etc, **nutritive**, etc see under **nutrient**.

nux vomica /*nuks vom'i-kə*/ *n* an East Indian tree (*Strychnos nux-vomica*; family Loganiaceae) whose orange berries contain seeds which yield strychnine and other poisonous alkaloid substances; the seed itself; a drug, *esp* a heart stimulant, made from it. [L *nux* a nut, and *vomere* to vomit]

nuzzer /*nuz'ər*/ *n* a present to a superior. [Hindi *nazr* gift]

nuzzle¹ /*nuz'l*/ *vt* and *vi* to poke, press, burrow, root, rub, sniff, caress or investigate with the nose. ◆ *vt* to thrust in (the nose or head). ◆ *vi* to snuggle; to go with the nose towards the ground. —Also **nousle** /*nuz'l*/ and (mistakenly) **nursle** /*nûr'sl*/. [Frequentative verb from **nose**]

nuzzle² /*nuz'l*/ *vt* to train; to bring up; to foster. [Origin obscure; confused with **nurse¹**; see **noursle**]

NV *abbrev* : Nevada (US state); new version.

NVALA or **NVLA** *abbrev* : National Viewers' and Listeners' Association (now known as Mediawatch-UK).

nvCJD *abbrev* : new variant Creutzfeldt-Jakob disease.

nvd *abbrev* : no value declared.

NVQ *abbrev* : National Vocational Qualification.

NW *abbrev* : north-west; north-western.

NWS *abbrev* : North Warning System, a system of radar stations in the Arctic regions of N America intended to detect possible attack by missiles or aircraft.

NWT *abbrev* : Northwest Territories (of Canada).

NY *abbrev* : New York (US city or state).

ny an obsolete spelling of **nigh**.

nyaff /*nyaf*/ (*Scot*) *n* a small or worthless person or thing. ◆ *vi* to yelp, yap; to talk frivolously or argue snappishly. [Perh imit of a small dog's bark]

nyala /*ən-yä'lə* or *nyä'lə*/ *n* (pl **nyal'a** or **nyal'as**) a large S African antelope. [Bantu (*i*)*nyala*]

Nyanja /*nyan'jə*/ *n* (pl **Nyan'ja** or **Nyan'jas**) (a member of) a people living around Lake Nyasa in Malawi; a group of Bantu languages spoken in southern Africa.

nyanza /*nyan'zə*, also *ni-* or *nī-an'zə*/ *n* a lake (*esp* in African proper names). [Bantu]

nyas /*nī'əs*/ *n* an old form of **eyas**.

■ words derived from main entry word; ◻ compound words; ■ idioms and phrasal verbs

nychthemeron /nik-thē'mə-ron/ n a complete day of 24 hours, a night and a day. [Gr *nychthēmeron*, from *nyx*, *nyktos* night, and *hēmerā* day]
■ **nychthē'meral** adj.

Nyctaginaceae /nik-tə-ji-nā'si-ē/ n pl a family of mainly tropical American plants, including bougainvillea, and the marvel of Peru, related to the goosefoots and the pinks. [Gr *nyx*, *nyktos* night]
■ **nyctaginā'ceous** adj.

nyctalopia /nik-tə-lō'pi-ə/ n properly, night-blindness, abnormal difficulty in seeing in a faint light; by confusion sometimes, day-blindness. [Gr *nyktalōps* night-blind, day-blind, from *nyx*, *nyktos* night, *alaos* blind, and *ōps* eye, face]
■ **nyctalōp'ic** adj. **nyc'talops** /-lops/ n (pl **nyctalō'pes**) a person with nyctalopia.

nyctanthous /nik-tan'thəs/ (bot) adj flowering at night. [Gr *nyx*, *nyktos* night, and *anthos* flower]

nyctinasty /nik'ti-nas-ti/ (bot) n sleep-movement in plants (eg the closing of petals), the joint effect of changes in light and temperature. [Gr *nyx*, *nyktos* night, and *nastos* pressed]
■ **nyctinas'tic** adj.

nyctitropism /nik-ti-tro'pi-zm/ n the assumption by plants of certain positions at night, *esp* ones different from daytime positions. [Gr *nyx*, *nyktos* night, and *tropos* turning]
■ **nyctitropic** /-trop'/ adj.

nyctophobia /nik-tō-fō'bi-ə/ n a morbid fear of the night or of darkness. [Gr *nyx*, *nyktos* night, and **phobia**]

nye[1] an obsolete spelling of **nigh**.

nye[2] /nī/ n a variant of **nid** or **nide**.

nying (obs) prp of **nie**, **ny** and **nye**[1].

nylghau see **nilgai**.

nylon /nī'lən/ or /-lon/ n any of numerous polymeric amides that can be formed into fibres, bristles or sheets; any material made from such filaments or fibres; a stocking made of such material. [Invented by the original manufacturers]

nymph /nimf/ n one of the divinities who lived in mountains, rivers, trees, etc (*myth*); a young and beautiful maiden (often *ironic*); an insect pupa (obs); an immature form of some insects, such as the dragonfly and mayfly, similar to the adult but with wings and sex organs undeveloped. [L *nympha*, from Gr *nymphē* a bride, a nymph]
■ **nymphae** /-ē/ n pl (anat) the labia minora. **Nymphaea** /-ē'ə/ n the white water lily genus, giving name to a family of dicotyledons **Nymphaeā'ceae**, related to the buttercup family. **nymphaeaceous** /-i-ā'shəs/ adj. **nymphae'um** n a temple, sanctuary or grotto of the nymphs. **nymph'al** adj. **nymph'alid** n a butterfly of the family **Nymphal'idae**, a brush-footed family with useless, reduced forelegs (also adj). **nymphē'an** adj. **nymph'et** or **nymphette'** n a young nymph; a sexually attractive and precocious young girl. **nymph'ic** or **nymph'ical** adj. **nymph'ish** adj. **nymph'like** adj. **nymph'ly** adj. **nymph'o** n (pl **nymph'os**) (inf) a nymphomaniac. **nymph'olepsy** n a species of ecstasy or frenzy said to have seized those who had seen a nymph (*folklore*); a yearning for the unattainable. **nymph'olept** n a person affected by nympholepsy. **nympholept'ic** adj. **nymphomā'nia** n morbid and uncontrollable sexual desire in women. **nymphomā'niac** n and adj. **nymphomaniacal** /-mə-nī'ə-kəl/ adj.

Nynorsk /nü'nörsk, nü' or nē'/ n one of the two official written varieties of Norwegian (the other being Bokmål), based on W Norwegian dialects and Old Norse. [Norw, literally, new Norwegian]

NYO abbrev : National Youth Orchestra.

NYOS abbrev : National Youth Orchestra of Scotland.

nys /nis or niz/ (Spenser) is not. [**ne** and **is**]

NYSE abbrev : New York Stock Exchange.

nyssa /nis'ə/ n a tree of the genus *Nyssa* (family Cornaceae) of small American and Asiatic trees with overlapping petals. [New L, perh from Gr *meta* post]

nystagmus /ni-stag'məs/ n a spasmodic, involuntary lateral oscillatory movement of the eyes, found in miners, etc. [Latinized from Gr *nystagmos*, from *nystazein* to nap]
■ **nystag'mic** or **nystag'moid** adj.

nystatin /nis'tə-tin/ n an antibiotic, produced by a strain of the bacterium *Streptomyces noursei*, used in treating fungal infections such as candidiasis. [New York *State* (where it originated), and **-in**]

NZ abbrev : New Zealand (also IVR).

NZPA abbrev : New Zealand Press Association.

Oo

abcdefghijklmnopqrstuvwxyz

Optima Designed by Hermann Zapf in 1958. Germany.

O[1] or **o** /ō/ n (pl **Oes, Os, O's**, **oes** or **o's** /ōz/) the fifteenth letter in the modern English alphabet, fourteenth in the Roman, derived from Greek *omicron* (O, o), with various sounds, as in note, not, for, work, son, do; one of the four blood types in the ABO blood group system; in a series of numbers, nought or nothing; (*usu* in *pl*) a spangle (*obs*); anything shaped like the letter O.

O[2] or **oh** /ō/ *interj* used in addressing or apostrophizing, marking the occurrence of a thought, reception of information, or expressing wonder, admiration, disapprobation, surprise, protest, pain, or other emotion. The form O is chiefly used in verse (*O for, O that*).
■ **Fifteen O's** fifteen meditations on Christ's Passion, each beginning with O, composed by St Bridget. **O's of Advent** seven anthems each beginning with O, sung on the days before Christmas Eve.

O or **O.** *abbrev*: Ohio (US state); old; ordinary; over(s) (*cricket*).
❑ **O grade** or **Ordinary grade** *n* in Scotland, (a pass in) a former examination generally taken at the end of the 4th year of secondary education (also *adj*, often with *hyphen*). **O level** or **Ordinary level** *n esp* in England and Wales, (a pass in) a former examination generally taken at the end of the 5th year of secondary education (also *adj*, often with *hyphen*).

O *symbol*: (as a medieval Roman numeral) 11; /ō/ oxygen (*chem*).

Ō *symbol*: (medieval Roman numeral) 11 000.

O' /ō/ *pfx* in Irish patronymics, descendant of. [Ir *ó*, *ua*, from OIr *au* descendant]

O- /ō-/ (*chem*) *pfx* signifying ortho-.

o' or **o** /ō, ə/ a shortened form of **of** and **on**.

-o /-ō/ (*sl* or *inf*) *sfx* used to form diminutives and abbreviations, eg *wino, aggro*.

o/a *abbrev*: on account of.

oaf /ōf/ n (pl **oafs** or (rarely) **oaves** /ōvz/) a lout; an idiot; a dolt; a changeling (*obs*). [ON *álfr* elf; cf **elf, ouphe**]
■ **oaf'ish** *adj* loutish; clumsy; idiotic, doltish. **oaf'ishly** *adv*. **oaf'ishness** *n*.

oak /ōk/ n a genus (*Quercus*) of trees of the beech family; their timber, much used for furniture, in building and in shipbuilding, etc; extended to various other trees, such as *poison oak, she-oak* (qqv); the leaves of the oak tree, *esp* when worn as a garland. ◆ *adj* made of oak. [OE *āc*; ON *eik*, Ger *Eiche*]
■ **oaked** *adj* (of wine) fermented in an oak barrel. **oak'en** *adj* (*old* or *poetic*) made of oak. **oak'ling** *n* a young oak. **oak'y** *adj* like oak, firm; having many oaks.
❑ **oak apple** *n* a gall caused by an insect on an oak. **Oak-apple Day** *n* 29 May, the anniversary of the Restoration in 1660, when country boys used to wear oak apples in commemoration of Charles II hiding in the branches of an oak (the Royal Oak) from Cromwell's troopers after the Battle of Worcester. **oak egg'er** *n* an egger moth whose caterpillars feed on oak. **oak'enshaw** *n* a little oak-wood. **oak fern** *n* a fern (*Thelypteris dryopteris*) of the polypody family (translation of Gr *dryopteris*, a name *perh* given to ferns growing on oak trees, transferred by Linnaeus to this species). **oak gall** *n* a gall on an oak tree caused by an insect of the Cynipidae family. **oak'-leaf** *n*. **oak-leaf cluster** *n* (*US*) a form of additional military decoration. **oak leather** *n* a fungus mycelium in the fissures of old oaks. **oak lump** *n* the lichen lungwort. **oak mast** *n* acorns collectively. **oak'-nut** *n* a gall on the oak. **oak tree** *n*. **oak wilt** *n* a serious fungal disease of oak trees, causing wilting and discoloration of foliage. **oak'-wood** *n*.
■ **sport one's oak** (*university sl*, chiefly *Oxford* and *Cambridge*) to keep one's outer door shut when one does not want visitors. **sudden oak death** see under **sudden**. **The Oaks** a classic English horse race (founded 1779) for three-year-old fillies, named after an estate near Epsom.

oaker (*Spenser*) same as **ochre**.

oakum /ō'kəm/ n old (*usu* tarred) ropes untwisted and teased out for caulking the seams of ships. [OE *ācumba* (*æcumbe*) from *ā-* away from, and the root of *cemban* to comb]

O&C *abbrev*: Oxford and Cambridge (Schools Examination Board) (now replaced by **OCR**).

O&M *abbrev*: organization and method(s).

OAP *abbrev*: old-age pensioner.

OAPEC /ō-ā'pek/ *abbrev*: Organization of Arab Petroleum Exporting Countries.

oar /ōr, ör/ n a light pole with a blade at one end for propelling a boat; a swimming organ; an oarsman or oarswoman; a pole for stirring. ◆ *vt* to propel by or as if by rowing. ◆ *vi* to row. [OE *ār*]
■ **oar'age** *n* oars collectively; rowing movement. **oared** *adj* provided with oars. **oar'less** *adj*. **oar'y** *adj* having the form or use of oars.
❑ **oar fish** *n* a ribbonfish (genus *Regalecus*). **oar'-footed** *adj* having swimming feet. **oar'-lap** *n* a rabbit with its ears standing out at right angles to the head. **oar'lock** *n* (*rare*) a rowlock. **oars'man** or **oars'woman** *n* a rower; a person skilled in rowing. **oars'manship** *n* skill in rowing. **oar'weed** see **ore**[2].
■ **lie** or **rest on one's oars** to abstain from rowing without removing the oars from the rowlocks; to rest, take it easy; to cease working. **put** or (**stick**) **one's oar in** to interpose when not asked.

OAS *abbrev*: *Organisation de l'Armée Secrète* (*Fr*), an organization of French settlers who opposed Algerian independence in the early 1960s; Organization of American States.

oas *abbrev*: on active service.

oasis /ō-ā'sis, rarely ō'ə-sis/ n (pl **oases** /-sēz/) a fertile spot or tract in a sandy desert; any place of rest or pleasure in the midst of toil and gloom; (**Oasis**®) a block of light permeable material used to hold cut flowers, etc in a flower arrangement. [Gr *oasis*, an Egyptian word; cf Coptic *ouahe*]

oast /ōst/ n a kiln to dry hops or malt. [OE *āst*]
❑ **oast house** *n* a building, *usu* with a conical roof, containing such kilns.

oat /ōt/ n (more often in *pl*) a well-known genus (*Avena*) of grasses, *esp Avena sativa*, whose seeds are much used as food; (in *pl*) its seeds; a musical pipe of oat-straw (*classical literature*); a shepherd's pipe (*literary* and *poetic*); pastoral song generally (*literary*). [OE *āte*, pl *ātan*]
■ **oat'en** *adj* consisting of an oat stem or straw; made of oatmeal. **oat'er** *n* (*N Am inf*) a Wild West film, a horse opera. **oat'y** *adj* like oats.
❑ **oat'cake** *n* a hard dry biscuit made with oatmeal. **oat grass** *n* a grass of *Avena* or similar genus used more as fodder than for the seed. **oat'meal** *n* meal made of oats; the pale variegated brown colour of oatmeal. ◆ *adj* of this colour.
■ **feel one's oats** (*inf*) to be lively and energetic or (*esp N Am*) assertive. **get one's oats** (*sl*) to have sexual intercourse. **off one's oats** (*inf*) without appetite, off one's food. **sow one's wild oats** to indulge in youthful dissipation or excesses. **wild oats** a wild species of oat (*Avena fatua*).

oath /ōth/ n (pl **oaths** /ōdhz/) a solemn appeal to a god or something holy or reverenced as witness or sanction of the truth of a statement; the form of words used; a more or less similar expression used lightly, exclamatorily, decoratively, or in imprecation; a swear-word; a curse. [OE *āth*; Ger *Eid*, ON *eithr*]
■ **oath'able** *adj* (*Shakesp*) capable of taking an oath.
❑ **oath'-breaking** *n* (*Shakesp*) perjury.
■ **on, under** or **upon oath** sworn to speak the truth; attested by oath. **take an oath** to pledge formally, have an oath administered to one.

oats see **oat**.

OAU *abbrev*: Organization of African Unity (now replaced by **AU**).

oaves see **oaf**.

■ words derived from main entry word; ❑ compound words; ■ idioms and phrasal verbs

OB *abbrev* : old boy; out of bounds; outside broadcast.

ob /*ob*/ *n* an objection (in the phrase **ob and sol** objection and solution). [From the marginal note *ob* in old books of controversial divinity]
◻ **ob-and-sol'er** *n* a disputant.

ob. *abbrev* : *obiit* (L), died; *obiter* (L), by the way.

oba /*ob'ə, ō'bə*/ *n* in W Africa, a chief or ruler. [Yoruba]

Obad. (*Bible*) *abbrev* : (the Book of) Obadiah.

Obamacare /*ō-bä'mə-kār*/ (*US inf*) *n* a name given to the Patient Protection and Affordable Care Act of 2010, which expanded access to healthcare in the USA. [Barack *Obama* (born 1961), US president under whom it was introduced]

obang /*ō'bang*/ *n* an old Japanese oblong gold coin. [Jap *ōban*]

obbligato /*o(b)-bli-gä'tō*/ or **obligato** /*o-bli-*/ (*music*) *n* (pl **obbliga'tos**, **obbliga'ti** /*-tē*/, **obliga'tos** or **obliga'ti**) a musical accompaniment of independent importance, *esp* that of a single instrument to a vocal piece. ◆ *adj* that cannot be done without, that must be used in performance. [Ital]

obcompressed /*ob'kəm-prest*/ (*bot*) *adj* flattened from front to back. [L pfx *ob-* towards; in New L, in the opposite direction, reversed]

obconic /*ob-kon'ik*/ or **obconical** /*-i-kəl*/ (*bot*) *adj* conical and attached by the point. [L pfx *ob-*, as in **obcompressed**]

obcordate /*ob-kör'dāt*/ (*bot*) *adj* (of eg a leaf) inversely heart-shaped and attached by the point. [L pfx *ob-*, as in **obcompressed**]

obdiplostemonous /*ob-di-plə-stē'mə-nəs* or *-plō-*/ (*bot*) *adj* having two whorls of stamens, the outer being situated opposite the petals. [L pfx *ob-*, as in **obcompressed**]

obdt *abbrev* : obedient.

obdurate /*ob'dū-rət*, sometimes (eg *Shakesp* and *Milton*) *-dū'*/ *adj* hardened in heart or in feelings; difficult to influence, *esp* in a moral sense; stubborn; hard. ◆ *vt* and *vi* /*-rāt*/ (*rare*) to make or become obdurate. [L *obdūrāre, -ātum*, from *ob-* (intens) against, and *dūrāre* to harden, from *dūrus* hard]
■ **ob'dūracy** (or /*ob-dū'rə-si*/) *n* the state of being obdurate; invincible hardness of heart. **ob'dūrately** (or /*-dū'*/) *adv*. **ob'dūrateness** (or /*-dū'*/) or **obdūrā'tion** *n*. **obdūre'** *vt* and *vi* (*obs*) to obdurate.

OBE *abbrev* : (Officer of the) Order of the British Empire.

obeah see **obi¹**.

obeche /*ō-bē'chē*/ *n* a large W African tree or its whitish wood. [Nigerian name]

obedience /*ō-bē'dyəns, -di-əns*/ *n* the act or practice of doing what one is told; the state of being obedient; willingness to obey commands; dutifulness; the collective body of people subject to any particular authority; a written instruction from the superior of an order to subordinate members; any official position under an abbot's jurisdiction; an obeisance (*archaic*). [L *obēdientia* ; see **obey**]
■ **obe'dient** *adj* obeying; ready to obey. **obediential** /*ō-bē-di-en'shl*/ *adj* relating to or of the nature of obedience. **obē'dientiary** /*-en'shə-ri*/ *n* someone subject to obedience; a person charged with an obedience in a monastery. **obe'diently** *adv*.
■ **canonical obedience** the obedience, as regulated by the canons, of an ecclesiastic to another of higher rank. **passive obedience** unresisting and unquestioning submission to authority, like that taught by some Anglican divines as due even to faithless and worthless monarchs.

obeisance /*ō-bā'səns*/ *n* a bow or act of reverence; an expression of respect; obedience (*obs*). [Fr *obeîssance*, from *obeîr*, from L root, as **obey**]
■ **obei'sant** *adj*.

obelisk /*ob'ə-lisk*/ *n* a tall, four-sided, tapering pillar, *usu* of one stone, topped with a pyramid; an obelus. [Gr *obeliskos*, dimin of *obelos* spit]
■ **obelisc'al** *adj* of, or of the nature of, an obelisk. **obelisc'oid** *adj* of the form of an obelisk; obeliscal.

obelus /*ob'i-ləs*/ *n* (pl **ob'eli** /*-lī*/) a sign (– or †) used in ancient manuscripts to mark suspected, corrupt or spurious words and passages; a dagger-sign (†) used in printing *esp* in referring to footnotes (**double obelus** ‡). [L *obelus*, from Gr *obelos* a spit]
■ **obelion** /*ō-bē'li-ən*/ *n* a point in the sagittal suture of the skull between the two parietal foramina. **ob'elize** or **-ise** *vt* to mark with an obelus; to condemn as spurious, doubtful, corrupt, etc.

Oberon /*ō'bə-rən* or *-ron*/ *n* king of the fairies, husband of Titania. [OFr *Auberon* ; prob Frankish]

obese /*ō-bēs'*/ *adj* abnormally fat. [L *obēsus*, from *ob-* completely, and *edere, ēsum* to eat]
■ **obese'ness** or **obesity** /*-bēs'* or *-bes'*/ *n*. **obe'sogen** *n* a substance that causes abnormal weight gain. **obesogen'ic** *adj* productive of obesity.

obey /*ō-bā'*/ *vi* to render obedience; to do what one is told; to be governed or controlled. ◆ *vt* to act as directed by; to comply with; to be controlled by. [Fr *obeîr*, from L *obēdīre*, from *oboedīre*, from *ob-* towards, and *audīre* to hear]
■ **obey'er** *n*.

obfuscate /*ob'fə-skāt* or *ob-fus'kāt*/ *vt* to darken; to obscure; to confuse or bewilder. [L *obfuscāre, -ātum*, from *ob-* (intens), and *fuscus* dark]
■ **ob'fuscated** *adj* (*inf*) drunk. **obfuscā'tion** *n*. **obfuscā'tory** *adj*.

ob-gyn or **ob/gyn** /*ō-bē-jē-wī-en'*/ (chiefly *US inf*) *n* the branch of medicine dealing with obstetrics and gynaecology; a medical practitioner specializing in this.

obi¹ /*ō'bi*/ or **obeah** (*obs* **obia**) /*ō'bi-ə*/ *n* witchcraft and poisoning practised in the West Indies, Guyana, etc; a fetish or charm. ◆ *vt* to bewitch. [Of W African origin]
■ **o'beahism, o'beism** or **o'biism** *n*.
◻ **o'bi-man** *n*. **o'bi-woman** *n*.

obi² /*ō'bi*/ *n* a broad sash worn with a Japanese kimono. [Jap *obi*, from *obiru* to wear]

obiit /*ob'i-it, ō'bi-it*/ (L) died.
■ **obiit sine prole** /*sīn'ē prō'lē* or *sin'e prō'le*/ died without issue.

obit /*ob'it* or *ō'bit*/ *n* short form of **obituary**; an anniversary or other commemoration of a death; date of death; funeral ceremonies; a religious office for a dead person; death (*obs*). [LL *obitus*, from *obīre, -itum* to go to meet, travel over, die, from *ob* in the way of, and *īre* to go]
■ **ob'ital** or **obit'ūal** *adj* relating to obits.

obiter /*ob'i-tər* or *-ter, ō'bi-tər*/ (L) *adv* by the way, cursorily.
◻ **obiter dictum** /*dik'təm, -tūm*/ *n* (pl **obiter dicta** /*dik'tə, -ta*/) (often in *pl*) something said by the way, a cursory remark; a comment made by a judge which, though carrying weight, does not bear directly on the case in hand and therefore need not influence the decision (*law*).

obituary /*ō-* or *ə-bit'ū-ə-ri*/ *n* an account of a deceased person; an announcement of someone's death; a collection of death-notices; in a newspaper often extended to include notices of births and marriages, etc; a register of deaths, *orig* in a monastery. ◆ *adj* relating to or recording the death of a person or persons. [Med L *obituārius*, from *obitus* ; see **obit**]
■ **obit'ūarist** *n* a writer of obituaries.

obj. *abbrev* : object; objective.

object /*ob'jekt* or *-jikt*/ *n* a material thing; that which is thought of or regarded as being outside, different from, or independent of, the mind, *opp* to *subject* ; that upon which attention, interest, or some emotion is fixed; a thing observed; an oddity or deplorable spectacle; that towards which action or desire is directed, an end; a thing presented or capable of being presented to the senses, *opp* to *eject* ; part of a sentence denoting that upon which the action of a transitive verb is directed, or standing in an analogous relation to a preposition (*grammar*); an entity, eg a picture or a piece of software, that can be individually manipulated (*comput*); interposition (*obs*); presentation to view or to the mind (*Shakesp*). ◆ *vt* /*əb-jekt'* or *ob-*/ to offer in opposition; to bring as an accusation; to put in front or in the way of anything or anybody (*archaic*); to present to sense or mind (*archaic*); to present, bring forward, or adduce (*archaic*); to impute (*obs*). ◆ *vi* to be opposed, feel or express disapproval (with *to, against*); to refuse assent. ◆ *adj* /*əb-jekt'* or *ob-*/ (*obs*) opposed, interposed or exposed. [L *objectus*, pap of *ob(j)icere*, or partly the noun *objectus, -ūs* (found in the ablative), or the frequentative verb *objectāre*, from *ob* in the way of, and *jacere* to throw]
■ **objectifica'tion** /*-jekt-*/ *n*. **object'ify** *vt* to make objective. **objec'tion** *n* the act of objecting; anything said or done in opposition; argument or reason against (with *to* or *against*); inclination to object, dislike, unwillingness. **objec'tionable** *adj* capable of being objected to; requiring to be disapproved of; distasteful. **objec'tionableness** *n*. **objec'tionably** *adv*. **objectival** /*ob-jekt-ī'vl*/ *adj* relating to or of the nature of an objective. **object'ivate** *vt* to render objective. **objectivā'tion** *n*. **object'ive** (also /*ob'*/) *adj* relating to or constituting an object; of the nature of, or belonging to, that which is presented to consciousness (*philos*); exterior to the mind, self-existent (*philos*); regarding or setting forth what is external, actual, practical, uncoloured by one's own sensations or emotions, *opp* to *subjective* ; existing or considered only in relation to mind, subjective (*scholastic philos*; *obs*); denoting the object (*grammar*); in the relation of object to a verb or preposition (*grammar*); objecting; (of lenses) nearest the object. ◆ *n* /*-jekt'*/ a goal or aim; the case of the grammatical object; a word in that case (*grammar*); an object-glass; the point to which the operations (*esp* of an army) are directed. **object'ively** *adv*. **object'iveness** *n*. **object'ivism** *n* a tendency to lay stress on what is objective; a theory that gives priority to the objective. **object'ivist** *n* and *adj*. **objectivist'ic** *adj*. **objectiv'ity** *n*. **objectivīzā'tion** or **-s-** *n*.

object'ivize or **-ise** vt to objectify. **ob'jectless** adj having no object; purposeless. **object'or** n.

❏ **object ball** n (snooker, etc) a ball that a player aims at striking with his own ball. **object code** n (comput) the translated version of a program which has been assembled or compiled (cf **source code**). **object finder** n a device in microscopes for locating an object in the field before examination by a higher power. **ob'ject-glass** n in an optical instrument, the lens or combination of lenses at the end next to the object. **objective danger** n (mountaineering) a danger such as a rockfall or avalanche that cannot be averted by the skill of the climber. **objective test** n a test or examination in which every question is set in such a way as to have only one right answer. **object language** n a language that is being investigated or described by another language; a language into which a program is translated by a compiler (comput). **object lesson** n a lesson in which a material object is before the class; a warning or instructive experience. **object of virtu** n an article valued for its antiquity or as an example of craftsmanship, etc. **object-oriented database** n a database built to handle data in the form of objects. **object-oriented programming** n (comput) programming in which units of data and their functional methods are treated as objects to be manipulated and placed in a hierarchy. **object program** n (comput) a program in machine language. **ob'ject-soul** n a vital principle attributed by the primitive mind to inanimate objects. ■ **no object** orig, not considered of importance, not the thing aimed at, esp in money no object; not constituting an obstacle or problem, as in distance, expense, etc no object.

objet /ob-zhā'/ (Fr) n an object.

❏ **objet d'art** /där'/ n (pl **objets** /-zhā'/ **d'art**) an article with artistic value. **objet de vertu** /də ver-tü'/ n (pl **objets de vertu**) a Gallicized (by the English) version of object of virtu (qv). **objet trouvé** /troo-vā'/ n (pl **objets trouvés** /-vā'/) a natural or man-made object displayed as a work of art.

objure /ob-joor'/ vt to swear. ♦ vt to bind by oath; to charge or entreat solemnly. [L objūrāre to bind by oath, from ob- down, and jūrāre to swear]

■ **objurā'tion** n the act of binding by oath; a solemn charge.

objurgate /ob'jər-gāt or -jûr'/ vt and vi to chide, scold. [L objurgāre, -ātum to rebuke, from ob- (intens), and jurgāre to chide]

■ **objurgā'tion** n. **objur'gative** or **objur'gatory** adj.

obl. abbrev : oblique; oblong.

oblanceolate /ob-län'si-ə-lāt/ (bot) adj (of eg a leaf) like a lance-head reversed, about three times as long as broad, tapering more gently towards base than apex. [Pfx ob-, as in **obcompressed**]

oblast /ob'läst/ n an administrative district in some republics of the former Soviet Union. [Russ]

oblate[1] /ob'lāt, ob-lāt'/ (obs) adj dedicated; offered up. ♦ n a dedicated person, esp one dedicated to monastic life but not professed, or to a religious life. [L oblātus offered up, used as pap of offerre to offer; see **offer**]

■ **oblā'tion** n an act of offering; a sacrifice; anything offered in worship, esp a Eucharistic offering; an offering generally. **oblā'tional** adj. **oblatory** /ob'lə-tə-ri/ adj.

oblate[2] /ob'lāt, ob-lāt', ō-blāt'/ adj flattened at opposite sides or poles, as a spheroid is, shaped like an orange, opp to **prolate**. [On the analogy of **prolate**; L pfx ob- against, or (New L) in the opposite direction]

■ **oblate'ness** n.

obligato see **obbligato**.

oblige /ə- or ō-blīj', formerly -blēj'/ vt to bind morally or legally; to constrain; to bind by some favour rendered, hence to do a favour to. ♦ vi (inf) to do something as a favour. [Fr obliger, from L obligāre, -ātum, from ob- down, and ligāre to bind]

■ **obligant** /ob'li-gənt/ n (Scots law) someone who binds himself or herself to another to pay or to perform something. **ob'ligate** /-li-gāt/ vt to bind by contract or duty; to bind by gratitude; to constrain (US and archaic). ♦ adj (biol) by necessity, without option. **obligation** /ob-li-gā'shən/ n the act of obliging; a moral or legal bond, tie, or binding power; an action, promise or requirement of such a kind that failure to perform or fulfil it contravenes the law; the thing to which one is bound; a debt of gratitude; a favour; a bond containing a penalty in case of failure (law). **obligā'tional** adj. **ob'ligātor** n. **obligatorily** /o-blig'ə-tər-i-li, ə-blig' or ob'lig-/ adv. **oblig'atoriness** (or /ob'lig-/) n. **oblig'atory** (or /ob'lig-/) adj binding; imposing duty; imposed as an obligation; obligate. **obligee** /ob-li-jē'/ n the person to whom another is bound by obligation (law); someone who is under an obligation for a favour. **oblige'ment** n a favour conferred. **oblīg'er** n. **oblīg'ing** adj prepared to confer favours; ready to do a good turn; courteous. **oblīg'ingly** adv. **oblīg'ingness** n. **obligor** /ob'li-gör/ n (law) the person who binds himself or herself to another.

❏ **obligate parasite** n (biol) one capable of living naturally only as a parasite (cf **facultative parasite**).

■ **holy day of obligation** (esp in the Roman Catholic Church) an important religious festival, on which attendance in church is obligatory.

oblique /ō- or ə-blēk'/ adj slanting; neither perpendicular nor parallel; not at right angles; not parallel to an axis; not straightforward; indirect; underhand; not a right angle (geom); having the axis not perpendicular to the plane of the base; skew; asymmetrical about the midrib (bot); of the monoclinic system (crystallog). ♦ n an oblique line, figure, muscle, etc; an oblique movement or advance, esp one about 45° from the original direction. ♦ vi to deviate from a direct line or from the perpendicular, to slant; to advance obliquely by facing half right or left and then advancing. ♦ vt (obs) to turn aslant. [L oblīquus]

■ **obliquation** /ob-li-kwā'shən/ n (obs) obliqueness. **oblique'ly** adv. **obliqueness** /-blēk'/ or **obliquity** /-blik'wi-ti/ n the state of being oblique; a slanting direction; crookedness of outlook, thinking or conduct, or an instance of it; irregularity (obs). **obliquid** /ob-lik'wid/ adj (Spenser) oblique. **obliq'uitous** adj.

❏ **oblique case** n (grammar) any case other than nominative and vocative. **oblique fracture** n (med) a fracture of a bone caused by an impact at an oblique angle. **oblique motion** n (music) upward or downward motion of one part while another remains stationary. **oblique narration** or **speech** n indirect speech (see **indirect**). **obliquity of the ecliptic** n (astron) the angle between the plane of the earth's orbit and that of the earth's equator.

obliterate /ə-blit'ə-rāt/ vt to blot out, so as not to be readily or clearly readable; to efface; to destroy completely; to close up and remove or destroy (a tubular part, etc; med and biol; also vi). [L oblitterāre, -ātum, from ob- over, and littera (lītera) a letter]

■ **oblit'erated** adj effaced; without defined margins. **obliterā'tion** n. **oblit'erative** adj. **oblit'erator** n.

oblivion /o- or ə-bliv'i-ən/ n forgetfulness; a state of having forgotten or of being unconscious; amnesty, pardon or forgiveness, as in act of oblivion (hist); a state of being forgotten. [L oblīviō, -ōnis, from the root of oblīvīscī to forget]

■ **obliv'ious** adj raptly or absent-mindedly unaware (with of or to); forgetful; apt to forget; causing, or associated with, forgetfulness (poetic); forgotten (obs). **obliv'iously** adv. **obliv'iousness** n. **obliviscence** /ob-li-vis'əns/ n forgetfulness; forgetting.

■ **act** or **bill of oblivion** (hist) an act or bill giving a general pardon for offences against the state.

oblong /ob'long/ adj long in one direction; (of a rectangular shape or figure) not square, having adjacent sides unequal, esp considerably so; (of eg a leaf) nearly elliptical, with sides nearly parallel, ends blunted, two to four times as long as broad (bot). ♦ n a rectangle with adjacent sides unequal; any oblong figure, whether angular or rounded. [L oblongus, from ob- (specific meaning obscure), and longus long]

obloquy /ob'lə-kwi/ n reproachful language; censure; calumny; slander; disgrace. [L obloquium, from ob against, and loquī to speak]

obmutescent /ob-mū-tes'ənt/ adj speechless; persistently silent. [L obmūtescens, -entis, prp of obmūtescere to become dumb, from ob- (intens), and mūtus dumb]

■ **obmutesc'ence** n.

obnoxious /əb- or ob-nok'shəs/ adj objectionable; offensive; noxious; hurtful (non-standard); exposed (rare); liable (to hurt, punishment, or censure; obs); subject to authority (obs). [L obnoxius, from ob exposed to, and noxa hurt]

■ **obnox'iously** adv. **obnox'iousness** n.

obnubilation /ob-nū-bi-lā'shən/ (literary) n clouding; darkening. [L obnūbilāre to cloud over, from L ob- over, and nūbilus cloudy]

■ **obnū'bilate** vt (obs).

obo /ō'bō/ n (pl **o'bos**) a vessel designed to carry oil and bulk ore, together or separately. [From oil bulk ore]

oboe /ō'bō or (archaic) ō'boi/ n a double-reed treble woodwind instrument; an organ stop of similar tone. [Ital oboe, from Fr hautbois; see **hautboy**]

■ **o'bôist** n a player on the oboe.

❏ **oboe d'amore** /ō'bō dä-mō'rä/ n (Ital, oboe of love) an old oboe a minor third lower. **oboe di caccia** /dē kat'cha/ n (Ital, oboe of the chase) an obsolete alto or tenor oboe.

obol /ob'əl/ n in ancient Greece, the sixth part of a drachma in weight or in money. [Gr obolos]

■ **ob'olary** adj (Lamb) extremely poor. **ob'olus** n (pl **ob'oli** /-ī/) (L) an obol; in the Middle Ages applied to various small coins, such as the English halfpenny.

obovate /ob-ō'vāt/ (bot) adj (of eg a leaf) egg-shaped in outline, with the narrow end next to the base. [Pfx ob-, as in **obcompressed**]

■ **obō'vātely** adv. **obō'void** adj (of a solid body, eg a fruit) egg-shaped, with the base as the narrower end.

obreption /ob-rep'shən/ (obs) n obtaining or seeking to obtain a gift, etc, by false statement, different both in sense and in etymology from

---

■ words derived from main entry word; ❏ compound words; ■ idioms and phrasal verbs

subreption (*law*); surprising by stealth. [L *obreptiō, -ōnis*, from *ob* in the way of, and *rēpere* to creep]
- **obreptitious** /-*tish'əs*/ *adj*.

obs *abbrev* : obscure; observation, as in *obs ward* (*med*); obsolete.

obs&gynae or **obs/gynae** /*obz ənd gī'ni*/ (*inf*) *n* the branch of medicine dealing with *obstetrics and gynaecology*.

obscene /*ob-* or *əb-sēn'*/ *adj* offensive to the senses or the sensibility; disgusting, repellent; indecent, *esp* in a sexual sense; (less strongly) offending against an accepted standard of morals or taste; (of publications, etc) tending to deprave or corrupt (*law*); filthy, loathsome (*archaic*); ill-omened (*obs*). [L *obscēnus*]
- **obscene'ly** *adv*. **obscene'ness** or **obscenity** /*-sen'* or *-sēn'*/ *n*.

obscure /*ob-* or *əb-skūr'*/ *adj* dark; not distinct; not easily understood; not clear, legible, or perspicuous; unknown; hidden; inconspicuous; lowly; not famous; living or enveloped in darkness. ◆ *n* darkness; an obscure place; indistinctness. ◆ *vt* to darken; to make dim; to hide; to make less plain; to make doubtful. ◆ *vi* (*obs*) to conceal oneself, hide; to darken. [Fr *obscur*, from L *obscūrus*, from *ob-* over, and the root seen in L *scūtum* shield, Gr *skeuē* covering]
- **ob'scurant** /*-ant* or *ob-skūr'ənt*/ *n* someone who tries hard to prevent enlightenment or reform. ◆ *adj* of or relating to obscurantism. **obscūrant'ism** (or /*-skūr'*/) *n* opposition to inquiry, reform or new knowledge. **obscūrant'ist** (or /*-skūr'*/) *n* an obscurant. ◆ *adj* obscurant. **obscūrā'tion** *n* the act of obscuring or state of being obscured. **obscūre'ly** *adv*. **obscūre'ment** *n* (*rare*). **obscūre'ness** *n*. **obscūr'er** *n*. **obscūr'ity** *n* the state or quality of being obscure; the state of being unknown or not famous; darkness; an obscure place, point or condition.

obsecrate /*ob'si-krāt*/ *vt* to beseech; to implore. [L *obsecrāre, -ātum* to entreat; from *ob* before, and *sacrāre*, from *sacer* sacred]
- **obsecrā'tion** *n* supplication; one of the clauses in the Litany beginning with by (*Christianity*).

obsequent /*ob'si-kwənt*/ *adj* (of a river) flowing in a contrary direction to the original slope of the land, parallel to the *consequent* and perpendicular to the *subsequent* streams. [L *ob* face to face with, and *sequēns, -entis*, prp of *sequī* to follow]

obsequies /*ob'si-kwiz*/ *n pl* (sing (*rare*) **ob'sequy** or (*Milton*) **obsequie**) funeral rites and solemnities. [LL *obsequiae*, a confusion of L *exsequiae* funeral rites, and *obsequium*; see **obsequious**[1]]
- **obsequial** /*-sē'kwi-əl*/ or **obsē'quious** *adj* (*Shakesp*).

obsequious[1] /*ob-* or *əb-sē'kwi-əs*/ *adj* servilely ingratiating; fawning; *orig* compliant, obedient, dutiful. [L *obsequiōsus* compliant, from *obsequium* compliance, from *ob-* towards, and *sequī* to follow]
- **obsē'quiously** *adv*. **obsē'quiousness** *n*.

obsequious[2] see under **obsequies**.

observe /*ob-* or *əb-zûrv'*/ *vt* to keep in view; to watch; to subject to systematic watching; to regard attentively; to watch critically and attentively in order to ascertain a fact; to ascertain by such watching; to notice; to pay attention to; to remark in words, to comment; to comply with; to act according to; to heed and to carry out in practice; to keep with ceremony; to celebrate; to keep (eg silence); to be deferential to or humour (*Shakesp*). ◆ *vi* to take observations; to make remarks. ◆ *n* (*Scot*) a remark. [Fr *observer*, from L *observāre, -ātum*, from *ob* towards, and *servāre* to keep]
- **observ'able** *adj* discernible, perceptible; worthy of note; notable; to be observed. ◆ *n* something that can be observed by the senses, with or without the help of instrument(s). **observ'ableness** *n*. **observ'ably** *adv*. **observ'ance** *n* the keeping of a law, rule or custom, or due performance of a duty or ceremony; the keeping of a festival, etc with ceremony or according to custom; a custom observed or to be observed; a rule of religious life; an order or company accepting it (*esp* the Observants), or their house; a deferential act or treatment; watchful heed (*Shakesp*); now rarely, observation. **observ'ancy** *n* observance; observation; a house of Observants. **observ'ant** *adj* observing; having powers of observing and noting; taking notice; keeping an observance; carefully attentive. ◆ *n* someone who complies strictly with a custom, etc; an obsequious attendant (*Shakesp*). **Observ'ant** or **Observ'antine** /*-ən-tin* or *-tēn*/ *n* a Franciscan friar of stricter rule. **observ'antly** *adv*. **observā'tion** *n* the act, or an act, of observing; the habit, practice, or faculty of seeing and noting; attention; the act of recognizing and noting phenomena as they occur in nature, as distinguished from *experiment*; a reading of an instrument; the result of such observing; watching; that which is observed; a remark; the fact of being observed; now rarely, observance. **observā'tional** *adj* consisting of or containing observations or remarks; derived from observation, as distinguished from *experiment*. **observā'tionally** *adv*. **observ'ative** *adj* observant; observational. **ob'servātor** *n* (now *rare* or *obs*) someone who observes in any sense; a remarker. **observ'atory** *n* a building or station for making astronomical and physical observations; a viewpoint; a spying-place. **observ'er** *n* a person who observes in any sense; a person whose function it is to take

observations; formerly, an airman who accompanied a pilot to observe, now a flying officer (qv); a member of the Royal Observer Corps, a uniformed civilian organization affiliated to the Royal Air Force; someone deputed to watch proceedings. **observ'ing** *adj* habitually taking notice; attentive. **observ'ingly** *adv*.
- **observation car** *n* a railway carriage designed to allow passengers to view scenery. **observation post** *n* a position (*esp* military) from which observations are made (and from which artillery fire is directed).

obsess /*ob-* or *əb-ses'*/ *vt* to occupy the thoughts of obstinately and persistently; to beset (*archaic*); to besiege (*obs*). ◆ *vi* (chiefly *US*, often with *about*) to be obsessive or excessively preoccupied about something. [L *obsidēre, obsessum* to besiege]
- **obsession** /*-sesh'ən*/ *n* a fixed idea; the morbid persistence of an idea in the mind, against one's will (*psychiatry*); persistent attack, *esp* of an evil spirit (*archaic*); the state of being molested in this way from outside, *opp* to *possession*, or control by an evil spirit from within (*archaic*); a siege (*obs*). **obsess'ional** *adj*. **obsess'ionally** *adv*. **obsess'ionist** *n* someone who is obsessed by a fixed idea. **obsess'ive** *adj* relating to or resulting from obsession; obsessing. ◆ *n* someone affected or characterized by obsessive behaviour. **obsess'ively** *adv*. **obsess'iveness** *n*.
- **obsessive-compul'sive** *adj* (*psychiatry*) denoting a form of neurosis in which the sufferer is driven to perform a particular act repeatedly.

obsidian /*ob-* or *əb-sid'i-ən*/ *n* a vitreous acid volcanic rock resembling bottle glass, a coarse green glass used in the making of bottles. [From *obsidiānus*, a false reading of L *obsiānus* (*lapis*), a stone found by one Obsius (wrongly Obsidius) in Ethiopia, according to Pliny]

obsidional /*ob-* or *əb-sid'i-ə-nəl*/ *adj* relating to a siege (also **obsid'ionary**). [L *obsidiō, -ōnis* a siege; see **obsess**]

obsign /*ob-sīn'*/ or **obsignate** /*ob-sig'nāt*/ *vt* to seal or confirm. [L *obsīgnāre* to seal up, from *ob-* over, and *sīgnāre* to mark, seal]
- **obsignā'tion** /*-sig-*/ *n*. **obsig'natory** *adj*.

obsolescent /*ob-sə-les'ənt*/ *adj* going out of use or out of date; in the process of disappearing or becoming useless; tending to become obsolete. [L *obsolescere, obsolētum*, perh from pfx *ob* in opposition, *solēre* to be accustomed, to use (to), and inchoative sfx *-scere*]
- **obsolesce** /*-les'*/ *vi* to be in the process of going out of use. **obsolesc'ence** *n*. **ob'solete** /*-lēt*/ *adj* gone out of use; antiquated; no longer functional or fully developed. ◆ *vt* (chiefly *US*) to cause to be or become obsolete. **ob'soletely** *adv*. **ob'soleteness** *n*. **obsolē'tion** *n* (*rare*). **ob'solētism** *n*.
- **planned obsolescence** the deterioration or the going out of date of a product according to a prearranged plan, *usu* involving its replacement; the deliberate inclusion in a product, eg a car, of features that lead to deterioration or out-of-dateness before the end of its useful life, to ensure future sales.

obstacle /*ob'stə-kl*/ *n* anything that stands in the way of or hinders progress. ◆ *adj* (*Shakesp*) stubborn. [Fr, from L *obstāculum*, from *ob* in the way of, and *stāre* to stand]
- **obstacle race** *n* a race in which competitors have to get over, get through, or otherwise negotiate a variety of physical obstacles.

obstetric /*əb-* or *ob-stet'rik*/ or **obstetrical** /*-ri-kəl*/ *adj* relating to the care of women during pregnancy and childbirth. [L *obstetrīcius* (the *-īc-* confused with sfx *-ic*), from *obstetrīx, -īcis* a midwife, from *ob* before, and *stāre* to stand]
- **obstet'rically** *adv*. **obstetrician** /*ob-sti-trish'ən*/ *n* a man or woman skilled in practising, or qualified to practise, obstetrics. **obstet'rics** *n sing* the branch of medicine and surgery that deals with pregnancy, childbirth and the care of the mother.

obstinate /*ob'sti-nət* or *-nit*/ *adj* blindly or excessively firm; unyielding; stubborn; not easily subdued or remedied. [L *obstināre, -ātum*, from *ob* in the way of, and *stanāre* (only in compounds), a form of *stāre* to stand]
- **ob'stinacy** /*-nə-si*/ or **ob'stinateness** *n*. **ob'stinately** *adv*.

obstipation /*ob-sti-pā'shən*/ (*pathol*) *n* severe constipation. [L *ob* against, and *stīpāre, -ātum* to press]

obstreperous /*əb-* or *ob-strep'ə-ras*/ *adj* noisy; unruly; making a loud noise; clamorous. [L *obstreperus*, from *ob* before, against, and *strepere* to make a noise]
- **obstrep'erate** *vt* (*Sterne*) to make an unruly noise. **obstrep'erously** *adv*. **obstrep'erousness** *n*.

obstriction /*ob-strik'shən*/ (*obs*) *n* obligation. [L *obstringere, obstrictum* to bind up]

obstropalous /*ob-strop'ə-ləs*/ and **obstropulous** /*ob-strop'ū-ləs*/ non-standard forms of **obstreperous**.

obstruct /*ob-strukt'* or *əb-*/ *vt* to block up; to hinder from passing or progressing; to shut off; to hamper. ◆ *vi* to be an obstruction; to practise obstruction. [L *obstruere*, *obstructum*, from *ob* in the way of, and *struere*, *structum* to pile up, build]

■ **obstruc'ter** *n* (rare). **obstruc'tion** *n* the act, or an act of obstructing; a state of being obstructed; that which hinders progress or action; an obstacle; the offence of obstructing another player (*sport*); opposition by delaying tactics, eg in a legislative assembly. **obstruc'tional** *adj*. **obstruc'tionally** *adv*. **obstruc'tionism** *n*. **obstruc'tionist** *n* someone, *esp* a politician in a legislative assembly, who practises obstruction (also *adj*). **obstruct'ive** *adj* tending to obstruct; hindering. ♦ *n* a hindrance; someone who hinders progress. **obstruct'ively** *adv*. **obstruct'iveness** *n*. **obstruct'or** *n*. **obstruent** /ob'strŭ-ənt/ *adj* obstructing; blocking up. ♦ *n* anything that obstructs, *esp* (*med*) in the passages of the body; an astringent drug (*med*); a stop or a fricative (*phonetics*).

❑ **obstruction lights** *n pl* (*aeronautics*) lights fixed to all structures near airports that constitute a danger to aircraft in flight.

obtain /ob-tān' or əb-/ *vt* to get; to procure by effort; to gain; to reach (*archaic*); to hold or occupy (*obs*). ♦ *vi* to be established; to continue in use; to hold good; to prevail or to succeed (*archaic*); to attain (*obs*). [Fr *obtenir*, from L *obtinēre* to occupy, from *ob* against, and *tenēre* to hold]

■ **obtainabil'ity** *n*. **obtain'able** *adj*. **obtain'er** *n*. **obtain'ment** *n*. **obtention** /-ten'shən/ *n* (rare) getting.

obtect /ob-tekt'/ or **obtected** /-tek'tid/ (*zool*) *adj* having wings and legs immovably pressed against the body in a hard chitinous case, as with many insect pupae. [L *obtegere*, *obtectum* to cover over, from *ob-* over, and *tegere* to cover]

obtemper /ob-tem'pər/, also **obtemperate** /-pə-rāt/ (Scots *law*) *vt* and *vi* to yield obedience (to). [L *obtemperāre*, *-ātum*, from *ob* before, and *temperāre* to restrain oneself]

obtend /ob-tend'/ (*obs*) *vt* to hold out in opposition; to put forward or allege. [L *obtendere* to stretch before, from *ob* in front of, and *tendere* to stretch]

obtention see under **obtain**.

obtest /ob-test'/ *vt* to call to witness; to adjure. ♦ *vi* (with *against* or *with*) to protest. [L *obtestārī* to call as a witness, from *ob* before, and *testis* a witness]

■ **obtesta'tion** *n*.

obtrude /əb- or ob-trood'/ *vt* to thrust forward or upon someone, unduly or in an unwelcome way. ♦ *vi* to be or become unpleasantly noticeable or prominent; to thrust oneself forward. [L *obtrūdere*, from *ob* against, and *trūdere*, *trūsum* to thrust]

■ **obtrud'er** *n*. **obtrud'ing** *n* and *adj*. **obtrusion** /-troo'zhən/ *n* an unwanted thrusting in, forward or upon. **obtrusive** /-troo'siv/ *adj* unduly prominent, protruding or projecting; tending to thrust oneself in or forward. **obtru'sively** *adv*. **obtru'siveness** *n*.

obtrusion, **obtrusive** see under **obtrude**.

obtund /əb- or ob-tund'/ (rare) *vt* to blunt or dull; to deaden. [L *obtundere* to strike upon, from *ob* against, and *tundere* to thump]

■ **obtund'ent** *adj* dulling. ♦ *n* an application to deaden irritation.

obturate /ob'tū-rāt/ *vt* to stop up. [L *obtūrāre*, *-ātum* to stop up; etymology obscure]

■ **obturā'tion** *n* stopping up; stopping of a hole to prevent the escape of gas (*gunnery*). **ob'turātor** *n* a structure or device that closes a cavity; the structures closing a large opening in the hip bone (*anat*).

obtuse /əb- or ob-tūs'/ *adj* blunt; not pointed; blunt or rounded at the tip (*bot*); greater than a right angle and less than 180° (*geom*); dull; dull-witted; insensitive. [L *obtūsus*, pap of *obtundere*; cf **obtund**]

■ **obtuse'ly** *adv*. **obtuse'ness** *n*. **obtus'ity** *n*.

❑ **obtuse'-ang'led** or **-ang'ular** *adj* having an angle greater than a right angle and less than 180°.

obumbrate /ob-um'brāt/ (rare) *vt* to overshadow. [L *obumbrāre*, *-ātum*, from *ob* in the way of, and *umbra* shadow]

■ **obumbrā'tion** *n*.

obvention /ob-ven'shən/ (*obs*) *n* any incidental occurrence or advantage, *esp* a fee. [L *obvenīre*, *-ventum* to come to meet, come by chance, from *ob* face to face with, and *venīre* to come]

obverse /ob'vûrs or ob-vûrs'/ *adj* turned towards one; complemental, constituting the opposite aspect of the same fact; having the base narrower than the apex (*bot*); obtained by obversion (*logic*). ♦ *n* /ob'vûrs/ the side of a coin bearing the head or principal symbol, often confused with *reverse* ; the face or side of anything normally presented to view; a counterpart or opposite aspect; a proposition obtained from another by obversion (*logic*). [L *obversus* turned against or towards, from *ob-* against, towards, and *vertere* to turn]

■ **obverse'ly** *adv*. **obver'sion** *n* the act of turning a thing towards one; (also called **permutation** and **equipollence**) a species of immediate inference where the contradictory of the original predicate is predicated of the original subject, the quality of the proposition being changed, eg to infer from *All A is B* that *No A is not B* (*logic*).

obvert' *vt* to turn in the direction of, or face to face with, something; to infer the obverse of (*logic*).

obviate /ob'vi-āt/ *vt* to prevent or dispose of in advance; to forestall; to meet on the way (*obs*). [L *obviāre*, *-ātum*, from *ob* in the way of, and *viāre*, *viātum* to go, from *via* a way]

■ **obviā'tion** *n*.

obvious /ob'vi-əs/ *adj* easily discovered or understood; clearly or plainly evident; not subtle; meeting one in the way (*obs*). [L *obvius*, from *ob via* ; see **obviate**]

■ **ob'viously** *adv*. **ob'viousness** *n*.

obvolute /ob'və-lūt or -loot/ or **obvoluted** /-lū'tid or -loo'tid/ (*bot*) *adj* arranged so that each leaf of a pair is folded lengthwise, enclosing one half of the other. [L *obvolūtus*, pap and *obvolvens*, *-entis*, prp of *obvolvere* to enwrap, from *ob* over, and *volvere*, *volūtum* to roll]

■ **obvolvent** /-vol'vənt/ *adj* (*archaic*) enwrapping; curved downward or inward (*zool*).

obvs /obvz/ (*sl*) *adv* obviously.

OC *abbrev* : Officer Commanding; Officer in Charge; (Officer of the) Order of Canada; original cover (*philately*).

oc *abbrev* : only child.

o/c *abbrev* : overcharge.

oca /ō'kə/ *n* a S American wood sorrel with edible tubers. [Sp, from Quechua]

ocarina /o-kə-rē'nə/ *n* a fluty-toned wind instrument, *orig* of terracotta, egg-shaped, with a long mouthpiece. [Ital, dimin of *oca* a goose]

OCCAM or **occam** /ok'əm/ (*comput*) *n* a programming language. [After William of *Occam* (see **Occamism**)]

Occamism or **Ockhamism** /ok'ə-mi-zm/ *n* the doctrine of the nominalist schoolman, William of *Occam* or *Ockham*, who died about 1349.

■ **Occ'amist** or **Ock'hamist** *n*.

❑ **Occam's** (or **Ockham's**) **razor** *n* the principle that entities are not to be multiplied beyond necessity.

occamy /ok'ə-mi/ *n* a silvery alloy. [**alchemy**]

occasion /ə-kā'zhən/ *n* a case, instance or time of something happening; a suitable time, moment or opportunity; a special time or season; a chance of bringing about something desired; an opportunity; an event which, although not the cause, determines the time at which another happens; a reason, pretext or excuse; requirement; need; (*usu* in *pl*) business; a special ceremony, celebration or event; formerly, in Scotland, a communion service; doing, occasioning, matter of responsibility (*Shakesp*); events or course of events (*Shakesp*); (in *pl*) necessary bodily functions (*obs*). ♦ *vt* to give occasion or rise to; to cause; to accustom (*obs*). [L *occāsiō*, *-ōnis* opportunity, from *ob*, in the way of, and *cadere*, *cāsum* to fall]

■ **occā'sional** *adj* happening or occurring infrequently, irregularly or now and then; produced on or for some special event or for special occasions; constituting the occasion; resulting from accident (*obs*). **occā'sionalism** *n* the Cartesian explanation of the apparent interaction of mind and matter by the direct intervention of God on the occasion of certain changes occurring in one or the other. **occā'sionalist** *n*. **occāsional'ity** *n*. **occā'sionally** *adv* now and then; on or for an occasion; casually (*obs*). **occā'sioner** *n*.

❑ **occasional cause** *n* the event which in the Cartesian philosophy is only the occasion, not the true cause; that by which the efficient cause comes into operation. **occasional conformist** *n* (*hist*) a Dissenter who qualified for office by conforming to the Church of England upon occasion. **occasional table** *n* a small portable *esp* ornamental table.

■ **occasioned by** caused by; necessitated by; (which was) a consequence of (*obs*). **on occasion** from time to time; in case of need; as opportunity offers. **rise to the occasion** see under **rise**. **take occasion** to take advantage of an opportunity (to).

Occident or **occident** /ok'si-dənt/ *n* the quarter of the sky where the sun, stars and planets set; the west, *opp* to *Orient*. [L *occidens*, *-entis* setting, prp of *occidere*, from *ob* towards, down, and *cadere* to fall]

■ **Occidental** or **occidental** /-dent'l/ *adj* western; characteristic of the West (*esp* Europe, America, the Western USA); (of a gem) relatively less precious (because the best stones were presumed to come from the East). ♦ *n* a westerner; a language invented by Edgar de Wahl (1922). **Occiden'talism** *n* the culture and ways of Occidental peoples. **Occiden'talist** *n* a person who studies Occidental languages; an Oriental who favours Western ideas, customs, etc. **occiden'talize** or **-ise** *vt* to cause to conform to Western ideas or customs. **occiden'tally** *adv*.

❑ **occidental topaz** *n* a semi-precious yellow quartz. **occidental turquoise** *n* odontolite.

occiput /ok'si-put/ (*anat*) *n* the back of the head or skull. [L *occiput*, from *ob* over, against, and *caput* head]

■ **occip'ital** *adj* relating to the back of the head. ♦ *n* the occipital bone. **occip'itally** *adv*.

❑ **occipital bone** *n* the bone at the back of the skull. **occipital lobe** *n* the posterior lobe in each cerebral hemisphere, dealing with the interpretation of vision.

Occitan /ok-si-tan'/ *n* another name for Langue d'Oc.

occlude /ə- or o-klood'/ *vt* to cut or shut off; to stop or cover (a passage, cavity or opening); to shut in or out; to bring together (the teeth or eyelids); (of eg a metal or other solid) to absorb or retain (eg a gas or liquid; *chem*). ◆ *vi* (*dentistry*; of the teeth) to bite or close together. [L *occlūdere*, *-clūsum*, from *ob* in the way of, and *claudere* to shut]

■ **occlu'dent** *adj* causing or resulting in occlusion; occluding. ◆ *n* that which occludes. **occlu'der** *n* (*med*, *ophthalmol*, etc) a device that occludes. **occlu'sal** /-səl/ *adj* (*dentistry*) relating to the occlusion of teeth. **occlu'sion** /-zhən/ *n* a closing of an opening, passage or cavity; the act of occluding or absorbing; the bite or mode of meeting of the teeth (*dentistry*); the formation or condition of an occluded front (*meteorol*). **occlu'sive** /-siv/ *adj* serving to close; characterized by occlusion. ◆ *n* (*phonetics*) a sound produced by closing the breath passage. **occlu'sor** *n* (*anat*) that which closes, *esp* a muscle for closing an opening.

❑ **occluded front** *n* (*meteorol*) an advancing cold front into which a mass of warm air has been driven obliquely, forming a bulge which narrows as the warm air is lifted up and the cold air flows in beneath.

occult /o-kult' or ok'ult/ *adj* hidden; secret; esoteric; unknown; beyond the range of sense or understanding; transcending the bounds of natural knowledge; mysterious; magical; supernatural; (of a line) faint or dotted or to be rubbed out later (*rare*); not discovered without test or experiment (*obs*). ◆ *n* (with *the*) occult practices or sciences. ◆ *vt* /o-kult'/ to hide or make disappear; to obscure, *esp* by occultation (*astron*). ◆ *vi* to become temporarily invisible; (of a heavenly body) to be hidden by occultation (*astron*). [L *occultus*, pap of *occulere* to hide, from *ob-* over, and the root of *celāre* to hide]

■ **occultā'tion** *n* a concealing, *esp* of one of the heavenly bodies by another; the state of being hidden. **occult'ed** *adj*. **occult'ing** *adj* (of a lighthouse, beacon, etc light) becoming temporarily invisible at regular intervals. **occ'ultism** *n* the doctrine or study of things hidden or mysterious, theosophy, etc. **occ'ultist** *n* someone who believes in occult things. **occult'ly** *adv*. **occult'ness** *n*.

❑ **occult sciences** *n pl* alchemy, astrology, magic, palmistry, etc.

occupance, etc, **occupation**, etc see under **occupy**.

occupy /ok'ū-pī/ *vt* (**occ'upying**; **occ'upied**) to take possession of; to capture; to hold; to keep possession of by being present in; to fill (a post, office); to take up (eg a space, time, etc); to tenant; to keep (often oneself) busy; to lay out in trade (*Bible*); to cohabit with (*obs*). ◆ *vi* (*obs*) to hold possession; to trade; to cohabit. [Fr *occuper*, from L *occupāre*, *-ātum*, from *ob* to, on, and *capere* to take; the *-y* is unexplained]

■ **occ'ūpance** (*rare*) or **occ'ūpancy** *n* the act or fact of occupying, or of taking or holding possession (*esp* of that which previously had no owner); possession; the time during which someone occupies a place or position; the proportion of, or extent to which, accommodation is used or occupied. **occ'ūpant** *n* someone who occupies property, a particular position, etc; someone who takes or has possession. **occ'ūpāte** *vt* (*obs*) to occupy. ◆ *adj* (*obs*) occupied. **occupā'tion** *n* one's habitual employment, profession, craft or trade; the act of occupying; possession; the state of being employed or occupied; the time during which a country, etc, is occupied by enemy forces; that which occupies or takes up one's attention. ◆ *adj* occupational. **occupā'tional** *adj* connected with habitual occupation. **occupā'tionally** *adv*. **occ'ūpātive** *adj* (*law*) held by tenure based on occupation. **occ'ūpier** /-pī-ər/ *n* a person who occupies; an occupant; someone who practises (*obs*); a dealer (*obs*).

❑ **occupational ailment**, **disease** or **injury** *n* a disease, injury, etc, to which workers engaged in a particular occupation are prone because of the conditions of that occupation. **occupational hazard** *n* a danger to which workers in a particular occupation are exposed. **occupational pension** *n* a pension paid by a person's employers, *usu* based on a personal pension scheme, as distinct from a state pension. **occupational psychologist** *n*. **occupational psychology** *n* the scientific study of human behaviour in the workplace, including personnel selection and stress management. **occupational therapist** *n*. **occupational therapy** *n* the treatment of a disease (including a mental disease) or an injury by a regulated course of suitable work. **occupation level** *n* in an archaeological site, any of several distinct layers of debris left by successive occupations, from which the site can be dated.

■ **army of occupation** troops stationed in the territory of a defeated enemy or subject country to keep order, to ensure compliance with the terms of a peace treaty, to prop up a weak or unpopular government, etc.

occur /ə- or o-kûr'/ *vi* (**occurr'ing**; **occurred'**) to be or be found; to happen; (with *to*) to come into the mind of; (of festivals) to fall on the same day; to meet (*obs*). [L *occurrere*, from *ob* in the way of, and *currere* to run]

■ **occurrence** /-kur'/ *n* the act or fact of occurring; anything that happens; an event, *esp* one unlooked-for or unplanned. **occurr'ent** *adj* occurring; happening; turning up; to be found; incidental. ◆ *n* someone or something that meets or comes in contact (*obs*); an occurrence or an item of news (*archaic*).

OCD *abbrev* : obsessive-compulsive disorder.

ocean /ō'shən/ *n* the vast expanse of salt water that covers the greater part of the surface of the globe; any one of its great divisions (Atlantic, Pacific, Indian, Arctic, Antarctic; also Southern (ie the belt of water round the earth between 40° and 66½° south) and German (ie the North Sea)); any immense expanse or vast quantity (*fig*). ◆ *adj* of or relating to the ocean generally. [OFr *occean*, from L *Ōceanus*, from Gr *Ōkeanos*, the river, or its god]

■ **oceanarium** /ō-shən-ā'ri-əm/ *n* (*pl* **oceanā'riums** or **oceanā'ria**) an enclosed part of the sea (also called **seaquarium**) or a large salt-water pond, in which dolphins, porpoises, etc, are kept and tamed. **oceanaut** /ō'shə-nöt/ *n* someone who lives for periods under the sea, in order to observe and explore. **Oceanian** /ō-shi-ä'ni-ən/ *adj* relating to *Oceania*, which includes Polynesia, Micronesia and Melanesia, with or without Australasia. ◆ *n* a native of Oceania, *esp* a Polynesian. **oceanic** /ō-shi-an'ik/ *adj* relating to the ocean; found or formed in the ocean or high seas, pelagic; wide like the ocean. **oceanicity** /-nis'/ *n* the extent to which the climate of a particular area is influenced by proximity to an ocean. **oceanid** /ō-sē'ən-id/ *n* (*pl* **ocē'anids** or **oceanides** /ō-sē-an'id-ēz/) (Gr *myth*) (with *cap*) a daughter of Oceanus; an ocean nymph. **oceanographer** /ō-shi-ən-og'rə-fər, or ō-shən- or ō-si-ən-/ *n*. **oceanographic** /ō-shi-an-ə-graf'ik, or ō-shən- or ō-si-an-/ or **oceanograph'ical** *adj*. **oceanog'raphy** *n* the scientific study and description of the ocean. **oceanolog'ical** *adj*. **oceanol'ogist** *n*. **oceanol'ogy** *n* oceanography.

❑ **ocean basin** *n* the depression in which the waters of an ocean are contained. **o'cean-going** *adj* sailing, or suitable for sailing, across the ocean. **o'cean-grey'hound** *n* a very fast steamer. **oceanic crust** *n* that part of the Earth's crust that is normally characteristic of oceans, consisting of *approx* 5km water, 1km sediments and 5km basaltic rocks. **oceanic islands** *n pl* islands far from the mainland. **ocean perch** *n* a scorpion-fish, *Sebastes marinus*, also known as the **bergylt**, **redfish** or **rosefish**. **o'cean-stream'** *n* (*Milton*) the river Oceanus (Okeanos), supposed to encircle the land of the world.

ocellus /ō-sel'əs/ *n* (*pl* **ocell'ī**) a simple eye or eye-spot, distinguished from a compound eye, in insects and other lower animals; an eyelike or ringed spot of colour. [L *ocellus*, dimin of *oculus* an eye]

■ **ocell'ar** *adj* of, or of the nature of, an ocellus or ocelli. **ocell'ate** (or /os'əl-āt/) or **oc'ellated** *adj* eyelike and ringed; having an eyelike spot or spots. **ocellation** /os-ə-lā'shən/ *n*.

ocelot /os'ə-lot or ō'sə-lot/ *n* an American cat (*Felis pardalis*), like a small leopard; its fur. [Nahuatl *ocelotl* jaguar]

■ **o'celoid** *adj* (*rare*).

OCF *abbrev* : Officiating Chaplain to the Forces.

och /ohh/ *interj* expressing impatience, or contemptuous dismissal, pshaw, tut (*Scot*); in Ireland and part of Scotland, expressing regret.

oche /ok'i/ (*darts*) *n* the line, groove or ridge behind which a player must stand to throw (also **hockey** or **hockey line**). [Ety uncertain; a connection with OE *oche* to lop (from OFr *ocher* to nick, cut a groove in), has been suggested; see also ety for **notch**]

ocher, **ocherous**, etc see **ochre**.

ochidore /ok'i-dōr or -dör/ *n* Charles Kingsley's name (not otherwise known) for a shore-crab.

ochlocracy /o-klok'rə-si/ *n* mob rule. [Gr *ochlokratiā*, from *ochlos* a crowd, and *kratos* power]

■ **och'locrat** /-lə-krat/ *n*. **ochlocrat'ic** or **ochlocrat'ical** *adj*. **ochlocrat'ically** *adv*. **ochlophobia** /ok-lə-fō'bi-ə/ *n* (Gr *phobos* fear) fear of crowds. **ochlophō'biac** *n*. **ochlophō'bic** *adj*.

ochone see **ohone**.

Ochotona /ok-ō-tō'nə/ (*zool*) *n* the pika genus. [Mongolian *ochodona*]

ochre or (*US*) **ocher** /ō'kər/ *n* a native pigment composed of fine clay and an iron oxide (limonite in yellow ochre, haematite in red); a paint manufactured from it, used for colouring walls, etc; a pale brownish-yellow colour; an earthy metallic oxide of various kinds; money, *esp* gold (*sl*). ◆ *vt* to mark or colour with ochre. ◆ *adj* of the colour of ochre. [Fr *ocre*, from L *ōchra*, from Gr *ōchrā*, from *ōchros* pale yellow]

■ **ochrā'ceous** or **ochreous** /ō'kri-əs/, **o'chroid** or **o'chrous** (sometimes **o'cherous**) or **o'chry** (also **o'chrey** or **o'chery**) *adj* consisting of, containing or resembling ochre. **ochroleu'cous** *adj* (Gr *leukos* white) yellowish-white.

■ **burnt ochre** a dark reddish-brown pigment made by heating ochre.

ochrea, etc see **ocrea**.

ochrous, **ochry**, etc see under **ochre**.

-ock /-ək/ sfx denoting a diminutive, as in hillock. [OE -oc or -uc]

ocker /ok'ər/ (Aust inf; also with cap) n an oafish uncultured Australian. ♦ adj boorish, uncultured; Australian. [A form of Oscar, esp after a character in a television programme]
■ **ock'erism** or **Ock'erism** n boorishness in Australians.

Ockhamism and **Ockham's razor** see **Occamism**.

o'clock see under **clock**[1].

ocotillo /ō-kō-tē'yō/ n (pl ocotill'os) a shrub, Fouquieria splendens, a native of Mexico and the south-western part of the United States, with spines and clusters of red flowers. [Am Sp, dimin of ocote, a type of tree, from Nahuatl ocotl]

OCR abbrev: optical character recognition, reader or reading (comput); Oxford Cambridge and RSA Examinations.

ocrea (commonly **ochrea**) /ok'ri-ə/ (bot) n (pl **oc'reae** or **och'reae** /-ē/) a sheath formed of two stipules united round a stem. [L ocrea a legging]
■ **oc'reāte** or **och'reate** adj.

Oct. abbrev: October.

oct abbrev: octavo.

oct- /okt-/ or **octa-** /ok-tə- or ok-ta-/, also **octo-** (qv) combining form denoting eight. [Gr okta-, combining form of oktō eight]
■ **octachord** /ok'tə-körd/ n (Gr chordē a gut string) an eight-stringed instrument; a diatonic series of eight tones. **octachord'al** adj. **octagon** /ok'tə-gon/ n (Gr gōniā an angle) a plane figure of eight sides and eight angles (also adj). **octagonal** /-ta'gən-əl/ adj. **octa'gonally** adv. **octahē'dral** adj. **octahē'drite** n (mineralogy) anatase, crystallizing in square bipyramids. **octahedron** /ok-tə-hē'drən/ n (pl **octahē'drons** or **octahē'dra**) (Gr hedrā a base) a solid bounded by eight plane faces. **octamerous** /ok-tam'/ adj (Gr meros a part) having parts in eights. **octameter** /ok-ta'mi-tər/ n (Gr metron a measure; prosody) a line of eight feet or measures. **Octan'dria** n pl (Gr anēr, andros a man) a Linnaean class of plants with eight stamens. **octan'drian** adj. **octandrous** /ok-tan'drəs/ adj (bot) having eight stamens. **octangular** /ok-tang'gū-lər/ adj having eight angles. **octapodic** /ok-tə-pod'ik/ adj. **octapody** /ok-ta'pə-di/ n (Gr pous, podos foot; prosody) a line of eight feet. **octastich** /ok'tə-stik/ n (Gr stichos row, line; prosody) a strophe of eight lines, also **octastichon** /ok-ta'sti-kon/. **octa'stichous** adj (bot) in eight rows. **octastroph'ic** adj (Gr strophē strophe; prosody) consisting of eight strophes. **octastyle**, also **octostyle** /ok'tə-stīl/ adj (Gr stȳlos a column; archit) having eight columns at the end. ♦ n a building or portico so designed. **octava'lent** adj (chem) having a valency of eight.

octa see **okta**.

octad /ok'tad/ n a set of eight things. [Gr oktas, -ados]
■ **octad'ic** adj.

octagon...to...**octahedron** see under **oct-**.

octal /ok'təl/ adj relating to or based on the number eight. ♦ n a numbering system using a base of eight. [Gr oktō eight]

octamerous...to...**octandrous** see under **oct-**.

octane /ok'tān/ n any of a group of eighteen isomeric hydrocarbons (C_8H_{18}), eighth in the alkane series. [Gr oktō eight, and sfx -ane, as in methane]
❑ **octane number** or **rating** n the percentage by volume of so-called iso-octane (see under **iso-**) in a mixture with normal heptane which has the same knocking characteristics as the motor fuel under test.

octangular see under **oct-**.

Octans /ok'tanz/ (astron) n a southern constellation containing the south celestial pole. [L octāns an eighth part]

octant /ok'tənt/ n an arc of one-eighth of the circumference of a circle; a sector of one-eighth of a circle; an angle-measuring instrument with such an arc; a division of space or of a solid figure or body divided into eight by three planes, usu at right angles; a position 45° distant from another position, esp of the moon from conjunction or opposition (astron). [L octāns, -antis an eighth]
■ **octantal** /-tant'əl/ adj.

octapla /ok'tə-plə/ n sing a book of eight (esp Biblical) parallel texts. [Gr oktaplā (contracted pl) eightfold]

octaploid, also **octoploid** /ok'tə-ploid/ adj eightfold; having eight times the haploid set of chromosomes (biol). ♦ n a cell, organism or form with eight sets of chromosomes. [Gr oktaploos eightfold, and eidos form]
■ **oc'taploidy** n the condition of being octaploid (also **oc'toploidy**).

octapody, etc see under **oct-**.

octaroon see **octoroon**.

octastich...to...**octavalent** see under **oct-**.

octave /ok'tiv, -tāv/ n a set of eight; the last day of eight beginning with a church festival; the eight days from a festival to its octave; an eighth, or an interval of twelve semitones (music); a note or sound an eighth above (or below) another (music); the range of notes or keys from any one to its octave (music); an organ stop sounding an octave higher than the basic pitch; a cask containing the eighth part of a pipe of wine; an eight-lined stanza; the first eight lines of a sonnet; the eighth of eight basic parrying positions (fencing). ♦ adj consisting of eight (esp lines); in octaves; sounding an octave higher (music). [Fr, from L octāvus eighth]
■ **octāv'al** adj relating to an octave; based on the number eight.
❑ **octave coupler** n (music) a device in an organ whereby, when a key is struck, a second note is produced an octave higher than the basic pitch. **oc'tave-flute'** n the piccolo, an octave above the ordinary flute.
■ **great octave** (music) the bass octave, conventionally represented by capital letters, from C, on the second line below the bass stave, up. **law of octaves** the relationship which arranges the elements in order of atomic weight and in groups of eight, with recurring similarity of properties. **small octave** the tenor octave, from the second space in the bass.

octavo /ok-tā'vō/ adj having eight leaves to the sheet; (conventionally) of a size so obtained, whether so folded or not. ♦ n (pl **octā'vōs**) a book printed on sheets so folded; (conventionally) a book of such a size; contracted **8vo**, usu meaning demy octavo $8\frac{1}{2} \times 5\frac{1}{2}$ in (146 × 228mm). [L in octāvō in the eighth, from octāvus eighth]

octennial /ok-ten'yəl, -i-əl/ adj happening every eighth year; lasting eight years. [L octennium eight years, from annus year]
■ **octenn'ially** adv.

octet, **octett** or **octette** /ok-tet'/ n a group of eight (lines of verse, electrons, musicians, etc); a composition for eight musicians; (**octet**) a stable group of eight electrons (chem). [On the analogy of **duet**, as Ital ottetto, Ger Oktett]

octillion /ok-til'yən/ n a thousand raised to the ninth power (10^{27}); (esp formerly, in Britain) a million raised to the eighth power (10^{48}). ♦ adj being an octillion in number. [Fr, from L octō eight, and **million**]
■ **octill'ionth** adj and n.

octingenary /ok-tin-jē'nə-ri/ or **octingentenary** /-jen-tē'nə-ri/ n an eight-hundredth anniversary. [L octingēnārius 800 each]

octo- /ok-tō-, -tə or -to-/, also **oct-** or **octa-** (qqv) combining form denoting eight. [Gr oktō, and L octō]
■ **octocentenary** /ok-tō-sen-tēn'ə-ri, -sin-ten'/ or **-sen'tin-/** n an eight-hundredth anniversary. **octofid** /ok'tə-fid/ adj (L findere to cleave; bot) cleft into eight segments. **Octogyn'ia** /-jin'/ n pl (bot) in various Linnaean classes, an order with eight pistils. **octogynous** /ok-toj'i-nəs/ adj (Gr gynē woman; bot) having eight pistils or styles. **octohe'dron** n an octahedron. **octopetalous** /ok-tə-pet'ə-ləs/ adj having eight petals. **octopod** /ok'tə-pod/ adj (Gr pous, podos foot) eight-footed or eight-armed. ♦ n an octopus or other member of the **Octopoda** /-to'/, an order of cephalopods with two gills. **octo'podous** /ok-tə-sep'ə-ləs/ adj (bot) having eight sepals. **octo'stichous** adj octastichous. **oc'tostyle** n and adj octastyle. **octosyllabic** /ok'tə-si-lab'ik/ adj consisting of eight syllables. ♦ n a line of eight syllables. **octosyllable** /-sil'ə-bl/ n a word or line of verse with eight syllables.

October /ok-tō'bər/ n the tenth month; strong ale brewed in that month (hist). [L octōber, from octō eight; in the original Roman calendar, October was the eighth month of a ten-month year]
■ **Octo'brist** n (hist) a member of a Russian moderate liberal party who made the tsar's manifesto of October 1905 their basis.

octocentenary see under **octo-**.

octodecimo /ok-tō-des'i-mō/ adj having eighteen leaves to the sheet; contracted **18mo**, often read eighteenmo. ♦ n (pl **octodec'imos**) a book with sheets so folded. [L octōdecim eighteen; cf **octavo**]

octofid see under **octo-**.

octogenarian /ok-tō-ji-nā'ri-ən/ n a person who is eighty years old, or between eighty and ninety (also adj). [L octōgēnārius relating to eighty, from octōgintā eighty]
■ **octogenary** /-jē'nə-ri/ adj (rare) of, containing, based on, eighty; octogenarian (also n).

octogynous...to...**octohedron** see under **octo-**.

octonary /ok'tə-nə-ri/ (rare) adj based on the number eight. ♦ n a set of eight; an eight-line stanza. [L octōnārius]
■ **octonarian** /ok-tə-nā'ri-ən/ adj (prosody) having eight feet. ♦ n a line of eight feet. **octonā'rius** n (pl **octonā'riī**) an octonarian.

octonocular /ok-tō-nok'ū-lər/ adj having eight eyes. [L octōnī eight at a time, and oculus eye]

octoploid same as **octaploid**.

octopod, etc see under **octo-**.

■ words derived from main entry word; ❑ compound words; ■ idioms and phrasal verbs

octopus /ok'tə-pəs, formerly ok-tō'/ n (pl **oc'topuses**, (archaic) **octō'podēs** (or /-top'/); **oc'topī** is wrong) any eight-armed cephalopod of the genus *Octopus*; a person or organization with widespread influence (fig). [Gr oktō eight, and pous a foot]
■ **oc'topoid** adj.

octopush /ok'tə-pŭsh/ (sport) n a kind of underwater hockey, in which a lead puck, called a squid, is used in place of a ball and pushers in place of sticks. [**octopus** and **push**]
■ **oc'topusher** n.

octoroon or **octaroon** /ok-tə-roon'/ (old) n the offspring of a quadroon and a person of European descent; someone who has one-eighth black blood. [Modelled on **quadroon**, from L octō eight]

octosepalous...to...**octosyllable** see under **octo-**.

octroi /ok'trwä or ok-trwa'/ n formerly, and still in some European countries, a commercial privilege, eg of exclusive trade; a toll or tax levied at the gates of a city on articles brought in; the place where, or officials to whom, it is paid; payment for passage of a car on a road. [Fr, from octroyer to grant, from some such LL form as auctōrizāre to authorize, from L auctor author]

OCTU abbrev : Officer Cadet Training unit.

octuor /ok'tū-ör/ n an octet. [L octo eight; modelled on quattuor four]

octuple /ok'tū-pl or -too'/ adj eightfold; having eight parts, members or divisions. ◆ vt or vi to multiply by eight. [L octuplus; cf **duple, double**]
■ **oc'tūplet** n a group of eight notes to be played in the time of six (music); one of eight (children or animals) born at one birth. **octūp'licate** adj eightfold; multiplied by eight. ◆ n one of eight corresponding things; eightfoldness.

ocular /ok'ū-lər/ adj relating to the eye or to vision; formed in, addressed to, or known by, the eye; received by actual sight; eyelike. ◆ n an eyepiece; an eye (facetious). [L oculus the eye]
■ **oc'ularist** n (Fr oculariste) a person who makes artificial eyes. **oc'ularly** adv. **oc'ulate** or **oc'ulated** adj having eyes, or spots like eyes. **oc'ulist** n a specialist in diseases and defects of the eye, an ophthalmologist. **oculus** /ok'ū-ləs/ n (pl **oc'ulī**) a round window.

oculo- /ok-ū-lō- or -lo-/ combining form of or relating to the eye or eyes. [L oculus the eye]
■ **oc'ulomō'tor** adj relating to or causing movements of the eye.

OD /ō-dē'/ (sl) n (pl **ODs** or **OD's**) an overdose (of drugs). ◆ vi (**OD'ing, OD'd**) to take an overdose.

OD abbrev : Officer of the Day; (also **O/D**) on demand; ordnance datum or data; (also **O/D**) overdraft or overdrawn.

od¹ /od or ōd/ n Reichenbach's arbitrary name for a force he supposed to manifest itself in light, magnetism, chemical action, hypnotism, etc.
■ **o'dic** adj. **o'dism** n belief in od. **odyle** or **od'yl** /od'il or ō'dil/ n (Gr hȳlē matter) od. **od'ylism** n.
□ **od'-force** n od.

od² or **odd** /od/ (archaic; also with cap) n and interj a form of **god**, used as a mild oath.
□ **odzooks'** same as **gadzooks** (see under **gad²**).
■ **od's bobs** God's body. **od's bodikins** God's body. **od's life** God's life. **od's nouns** /nownz/ God's wounds. **od's pitikins** /pit'i-kinz/ (Shakesp) God's pity. —All these phrases are also written without an apostrophe.

ODA abbrev : Overseas Development Administration (now replaced by **DFID**).

oda /ō'də/ n a room in a harem. [Turk; cf **odalisque**]

odal, odaller same as **udal, udaller**.

odalisque, odalisk /ō'də-lisk/ or **odalique** /-lik/ n a female slave in a harem. [Fr, from Turk ōdaliq, from ōdah a chamber]

odd¹ /od/ adj unpaired; left over; additional; extra; not one of a complete set; not exactly divisible by two, opp to even; one in excess of half the number; left over after a round number has been taken; (used after the number) slightly over, as in thirty odd; with something additional in lower denominations or lower powers of ten; strange; queer; occasional; casual; out-of-the-way; standing apart; not matching (Spenser); at variance (Shakesp). ◆ adv (Shakesp) oddly. ◆ n one stroke more than one's opponent (golf); a stroke allowed in handicap (golf); one trick above book (whist). [ON oddi point, a triangle, odd number; cf ON oddr, OE ord point]
■ **odd'ish** adj. **odd'ity** n the state of being odd or singular; strangeness; an odd quality or characteristic; a strange or odd person or thing. **odd'-like** adj (Scot) odd; odd-looking. **odd'ly** adv. **odd'ment** n something remaining over; one of a broken set (often in pl). **odd'ness** n. **odds** /odz/ n pl (sometimes treated as sing) inequality; difference in favour of one against another; more than an even wager; the amount or proportion by which the bet of one exceeds that of another; the chances or probability; advantage; dispute; scraps; miscellaneous pieces, as in odds and ends.

□ **odd'ball** n an eccentric person, a nonconformist in some respect. ◆ adj strange, peculiar; eccentric. **odd'-come-short** n (archaic) a short remnant; (in pl **odd'-come-shorts**) odds and ends. **odd'-come-short'ly** n (archaic) an early day, any time. **odd-e'ven** adj or n (Shakesp) of the time about midnight) appar neither one thing nor another. **Odd'fellow** n a member of a secret benevolent society called the Independent Order of Oddfellows. **odd'-job** adj. **odd-jobb'er** or **odd'-jobman** n. **odd-jobb'ing** n. **odd jobs** n pl occasional pieces of work such as small house repairs. **odd legs** n pl (engineering) callipers with two hinged legs, one curved distally and placed against an edge and the other with a scribing point. **odd'-look'ing** adj. **odd lot** n (stock exchange) a block of less than one hundred shares. **odd-lott'er** n someone who deals in odd lots. **odd'-man** n odd-jobman; an umpire; someone who has a casting vote; the singling out or elimination of one from a number for any purpose. **odds'man** n (Scot) an umpire or arbiter. **odds'-on'** adj (of a chance) better than even; in betting, a price that will result in a final return of less than double the original stake.
■ **at odds** at variance (with with). **give** or **lay odds** to offer a bet at favourable odds. **long odds** or **short odds** see **long³** and **short**. **make no odds** to make no significant difference. **odd man out** or **odd one out** a person who is left out when numbers are made up; a person who, whether through personal inclination or rejection by others, gets set apart from the group to which he or she belongs, because of eg a difference of interests, behaviour, etc. **odds and ends** miscellaneous pieces, perh orig meaning points and ends. **odds and sods** (inf) miscellaneous people, things, etc. **over the odds** (inf) more than expected, normal, necessary, etc. **shout the odds** (sl) to talk too much or too loudly. **take odds** to accept a bet; to offer a bet at unfavourable odds. **what's the odds?** what difference does it make?

odd² see **od²**.

ode /ōd/ n orig, a poem intended to be sung; an elaborate lyric, often of some length, generally addressed to somebody or something. [Fr ode, from Gr ōidē, contraction of aoidē, from aeidein to sing]
■ **o'dic** adj. **o'dist** n a writer of odes.

odea see **odeon**.

ODECA abbrev : Organización de Estados Centro-americanos (Sp), Organization of Central American States.

Odelsting or **Odelsthing** /ō'dəl-sting/ n the lower house of the Norwegian parliament. [Norw odel allodium, and ting (thing) court, parliament]

odeon /ō'di-ən, -dyən or -dē'/, also **odeum** /-əm/ n (pl **ō'deons** or **ō'dea**) in ancient Greece and Rome, a theatre for musical contests, etc; a concert hall. [Gr ōideion, L ōdēum]

ODI (cricket) abbrev : one-day international.

odic¹ see under **od¹**.

odic² see under **ode**.

Odin /ō'din/ n the Scandinavian equivalent of the Germanic god Woden. [ON Ōthenn]
■ **O'dinism** n the ancient worship of Odin; a modern revival of this. **O'dinist** n.

odism see under **od¹**.

odist see under **ode**.

odium /ō'di-əm/ n hatred; offensiveness; blame; reproach attaching to some act, etc (with of); the quality of provoking hate. [L odium]
■ **o'dious** adj hateful; denoting debt that is incurred by a government while pursuing a policy that is not in the interest of its citizens; offensive; repulsive; causing hatred. **o'diously** adv. **o'diousness** n.

odium theologicum /ō'di-əm thē-ə-loj'i-kəm, od'i-ŭm the-o-log'i-kŭm/ (L) n the hatred of theologians for each other's errors (or each other).

odograph /od'ə-gräf/ n a device for plotting automatically a course travelled; an odometer; a pedometer. [Gr hodos a way, and graphein to write]

odometer /o-dom'i-tər/ n an instrument for measuring the distance travelled by a wheeled vehicle (also **hodom'eter**). [Gr hodos a way, and metron a measure]
■ **odom'etry** or **hodom'etry** n.

Odonata /ō-do-nä'tə/ (zool) n pl the dragonfly order. [Ionic Gr odōn a tooth]
■ **odon'atist** or **odonatol'ogist** n someone who studies, or is an expert on, dragonflies. **odonatol'ogy** n.

odont- /o-dont-/ or **odonto-** /-don-tə-, -tō- or -to-/ combining form denoting tooth. [Gr odous, odontos a tooth]
■ **odontalgia** /-al'ji-ə/ or **odontal'gy** /-al'ji/ n (Gr algos pain) toothache. **odontal'gic** adj. **odon'tic** adj dental. **odont'ist** n (facetious) a dentist. **odont'oblast** n (Gr blastos a shoot) a dentine-forming cell. **odon'tocete** /-sēt/ n (Gr kētos whale) a toothed whale (also adj). **odontogenic** /-jen'ik/ adj. **odontogeny** /-oj'i-ni/ n the

origin and development of teeth. **odontogloss'um** *n* (Gr *glōssa* tongue) a plant of the genus *Odontoglossum*, of tropical American orchids. **odont'ograph** *n* an instrument for obtaining approximate curves for gear-teeth. **odontog'raphy** *n* a description or history of teeth. **odont'oid** *adj* toothlike (**odontoid peg** or **process** a projection from the second vertebra of the neck). **odont'olite** *n* (Gr *lithos* stone) bone-turquoise or occidental turquoise, a fossil bone or tooth coloured blue with phosphate of iron. **odontolog'ic** or **odontolog'ical** *adj*. **odontol'ogist** *n*. **odontol'ogy** *n* the science of the teeth. **odontō'ma** *n* (*pl* **odontō'mas** or **odontō'mata**) a tumour arising in connection with the teeth. **odontō'matous** *adj* relating to an odontoma. **odontopho'bia** *n* (*psychol*) fear of teeth. **odontophoral** /-*tof'ə-rəl*/ or **odontoph'oran** *adj* (Gr -*phoros* bearing). **odon'tophore** /-*tə-fōr* or -*för*/ *n* the rasping apparatus in molluscs, ie the radula, its support, or the whole apparatus. **odontoph'orous** *adj*. **Odontoph'orus** *n* a genus of American quails. **odontornithes** /-*ör-nī'thēz* or -*ör'ni-thēz*/ *n pl* (Gr *ornis*, *ornīthos* bird) fossil birds with teeth (not a natural class). **odontostom'atous** *adj* (Gr *stoma*, -*atos* mouth) having biting or toothed jaws.

odour or (*US*) **odor** /*ō'dər*/ *n* smell; savour (*fig*); repute (*fig*). [Anglo-Fr *odour*, from L *odor*, -*ōris*]

■ **o'dorant**, **o'dorate** or **odorif'erous** *adj* emitting a (*usu* strong) smell. **o'dorant** *n*. **odorif'erously** *adv*. **odorif'erousness** *n*. **odorim'etry** *n* the measurement of the strength and persistence of odours, olfactometry. **odorous** /*ō'də-rəs* (sometimes formerly *ōd-ō'rəs*)/ *adj* emitting an odour or scent; sweet-smelling; fragrant; bad-smelling (*inf*). **o'dorously** *adv*. **o'dorousness** *n*. **o'doured** *adj*. **o'dourless** *adj*.

■ **in bad odour** in bad repute or standing (with *with*); (similarly, but less commonly) **in good odour**. **the odour of sanctity** a fragrance after death alleged to be evidence of saintship; facetiously applied to the living who have denied themselves the sensual indulgence of washing; a sanctimonious manner.

ODPM *abbrev*: (from 2002 to 2006) Office of the Deputy Prime Minister.

odyl, **odyle** and **odylism** see under **od**[1].

Odyssey /*od'i-si*/ *n* a Greek epic poem, ascribed to Homer, describing the ten-year wanderings of *Odysseus* (Ulysses) on his way home from the Trojan war to Ithaca; (also without *cap*) a long wandering, or a tale of wandering. [Gr *Odysseia*]

■ **Odyssē'an** *adj*.

odzooks see under **od**[2].

OE *abbrev*: Old English.

Oe *symbol*: oersted.

oe same as **oy**.

OECD *abbrev*: Organization for Economic Co-operation and Development.

oecist /*ē'sist*/ or **oikist** /*oi'kist*/ (*hist*) *n* the founder of a colony. [Gr *oikistēs*, from *oikos* a house]

oecology, etc see **ecology**.

oecumenic, **oecumenical**, etc see **ecumenic**.

OED *abbrev*: Oxford English Dictionary.

oedema, also **edema** /*ē-dē'mə*/ *n* pathological accumulation of fluid in tissue spaces (*med*); dropsy; an unhealthy mass of swollen parenchyma (*bot*). [Gr *oidēma*, -*atos* swelling]

■ **oede'matose** or **oede'matous**, also **ede'matose** or **ede'matous** *adj*.

Oedipus /*ē'di-pəs* or -*də*-/ (*Gr myth*) *n* a king of Thebes who solved the Sphinx's riddle and unwittingly killed his father and married his mother. [Gr *Oidipous*, literally, Swell-foot]

■ **Oe'dipal** *adj*. **Oedipē'an** *adj*.

❑ **Oedipus complex** *n* (*psychol*) the attachment of a son to his mother with unconscious rivalry and hostility towards his father.

OEIC or **Oeic** /*oik*/ *abbrev*: open-ended investment company, a single-priced investment fund that is a hybrid of a unit and investment trust.

œil-de-bœuf /*æ-ē-də-bœf'*/ *n* (*pl* **œils-de-bœuf** /*æ-ē*-/) a small round window; an octagonal vestibule at the court of Versailles, hence one elsewhere. [Fr, ox-eye]

œillade /*æ-yäd'*, formerly *āl'yad*, *il'yad* or *il'i-ad*/ *n* (also (*Shakesp*) **ill'iad** or **el'iad** and (*old*) **eyliad** or **eyeliad** /*ī'li-ad*/) an ogle; a glance or wink (*Shakesp*). [Fr *œillade*, from *œil* eye]

OEM *abbrev*: original equipment manufacturer.

oen- or (*US*) **en-** /*ēn*-/ or **oeno-** or (*US*) **eno-** /*ē-nə*-, -*nō*- or -*no*/ *combining form* from wine (also **oin-** /*oin*-/ or **oino-**). [Gr *oinos* wine]

■ **oenan'thic** *adj* (Gr *anthos* flower) having or imparting the characteristic odour of wine. **oenolog'ical** *adj*. **oenol'ogist** *n*. **oenol'ogy** *n* the study of wines. **oe'nomancy** *n* divination from the appearance of wine poured out in libations. **oenomā'nia** *n*

dipsomania. **oen'omel** *n* (Gr *meli* honey) wine mixed with honey. **oenom'eter** *n* a hydrometer for measuring the alcoholic strength of wines. **oen'ophil** or **oenoph'ilist** *n* a connoisseur of wine, also (now *usu*) **oen'ophile** /-*fīl*/. **oenophil'ic** *adj*. **oenoph'ily** *n* love of and knowledge of wines.

Oenothera /*ē-nō-thē'rə*, sometimes *ē-noth'ə-rə*/ *n* the evening primrose genus of Onagraceae. [Gr *oinothēras*, perh a wrong reading for *onothēras*, a plant whose roots smelt of wine, perh oleander]

o'er /*ōr*, *ör* or (*Scot*) *owr*/ (*poetic*, *archaic* or *Scot*) *prep* and *adv* shortened form of **over**. For compounds, see **over-**.

oerlikon /*ûr'li-kon*/ (also with *cap*) *n* an aircraft or anti-aircraft cannon of Swiss origin. [*Oerlikon*, near Zürich]

oersted /*ûr'sted*/ (*phys*) *n* the CGS unit of magnetic field strength. [HC *Oersted* (1777–1851), Danish physicist]

Oes or **oes** /*ōz*/ a plural of **O** or **o** (see **O**[1]).

oesophagus or (*esp N Am*) **esophagus** /*ē*- or *e-sof'ə-gəs*/ *n* (*pl* **oesoph'agi** /-*gī*/) the gullet. [Gr *oisophagos* gullet; origin unknown; possibly connected with *phagein* to eat]

■ **oesophageal** /-*fə-jē'əl*/ *adj*. **oesoph'agoscope** /-*jə-skōp*/ *n* (Gr *skopeein* to look) an instrument for viewing or treating the oesophagus.

■ **peptic** or **reflux oesophagitis** heartburn.

oestrus /*ē'strəs*/, also **oestrum** /-*strəm*/ *n* a gadfly or bot; a vehement stimulus or frenzy; (in the following meanings and words, also, *esp US*, **estrus** /*es*-/) heat or sexual impulse, *esp* in female mammals; oestrous cycle. [L *oestrus*, from Gr *oistros*]

■ **oestradi'ol** *n* a natural oestrogen ($C_{18}H_{24}O_2$), also synthesized for use in cancer treatment and menstrual, etc disorders. **oes'tral** *adj*. **oes'triol** *n* an oestrogen produced by the ovaries. **oestrogen** /*ēs'trə-jən*/ *n* any one of the female sex-hormones; a substance found in plants, or synthesized, that has similar effects. **oestrogenic** /-*jen'*-/ *adj*. **oes'trone** *n* an oestrogen produced by the ovaries, weaker than oestradiol. **oes'trous** *adj*.

❑ **oestrous cycle** *n* the series of physiological changes from the beginning of one period of oestrus to the beginning of the next.

œuvre /*æ'vr'*/ (*Fr*) *n* (*pl* **œuvres** /*æ'vr'*/) work (of an artist, writer, etc).

OF *abbrev*: Oddfellow; Old French.

of /*ov*, *uv* or *əv*/ *prep* from; from among; out from; belonging to; among; proceeding or derived from; made from, having for material; having or characterized by; in the manner that characterizes; with respect to; owing to; with; over; concerning; during; by; on; in; specified as; constituted by; short of, to (in giving the time, eg *quarter of five*; *US*); measuring; aged; owning. [OE *of*; Du *af*, Ger *ab*, L *ab*, Gr *apo*]

ofay /*ō'fā* or *ō-fā'*/ (*US black derog sl*) *n* a white person (also *adj*). [Ety uncertain; possibly of African origin; *foe* in pig Latin also suggested, but unlikely]

Ofcom /*of'kom*/ *abbrev*: Office of Communications (a UK regulatory body).

OFDM *abbrev*: orthogonal frequency division multiplexing, a technique for transmitting large amounts of digital data over radio waves.

OFEX /*of'eks*/ *n* a share-trading facility for dealing in companies that are not quoted on the London Stock Exchange. [*off* and *exchange*]

off /*of*/ *adv* away; in or to a position that is not on something; in motion; out of continuity; out of connection, supply, activity, operation, or validity; to a finish, up; no longer available; in deterioration or diminution; into freedom. ◆ *combining form* used to signify a knockout competitive event, *esp* one held to decide a draw, as in *jump-off*, *play-off*, *swim-off*. ◆ *adj* most distant; on the opposite or farther side; on the offside of a cricket field; (of a horse or vehicle) right; out of condition or form; not devoted to the particular or usual activity (eg *off-day*, *off-season*). ◆ *prep* from; away from; removed from; opening out of; in or to a position or condition that is not on; disengaged from; disinclined to, not wanting; out to sea from; from a dish of; from a ball bowled by (*cricket*); with a handicap of (*golf*); not up to the usual standard of; not eating or drinking; not subject to or following. ◆ *n* the offside; (with *the*) the start, as in *ready for the off*. ◆ *vt* to put off; to take off; to kill (*US sl*). ◆ *vi* (or *vt* with *it*) to go off; to take off (with *with*; *inf*). ◆ *interj* away! depart! [Orig variant of **of**, distinguished from it by the 17c]

■ **off'ing** *n* the region some distance offshore; a place or time some way off. **off'ish** *adj* aloof in manner. **off'ishly** *adv*. **off'ishness** *n*. **off'-ward** or **off'-wards** *adv* off or away from, *esp* the shore.

❑ When compounds in this list can be used as both an adjective and adverb, the stress generally falls on the first syllable in adjectival use, but at the end of the word in adverbial use: **off-air** *adj* (of a recording, etc) received from a broadcast transmission; relating to, but not broadcast as part of, a radio or television programme. **off-and-on** *adj* occasional; intermittent. **off'-beam** *adj* mistaken, wrong-headed, misguided. **off'beat** *n* any of the *usu* unaccented beats in a musical bar. ◆ *adj* away from standard; unusual; eccentric. **off'-board** *adj* (*commerce*) of or relating to over-the-counter securities transactions. **off break** *n* (*cricket*) a ball that breaks from the offside towards the legside on pitching. **off-Broad'way** *adj* (of US theatres) not on Broadway, the centre of commercial theatre in New York; of or relating to the kind of theatre productions often presented in theatres not on Broadway, ie experimental, non-commercial, etc (**off-off-Broad'way** of or relating to very low-cost, often highly experimental theatre, *usu* presented in cafés, etc, and often considered the US equivalent of British fringe theatre). **off-cen'tre** *adj* not quite central. **off'-chance** or **off chance** *n* a remote chance (**on the off(-)chance** (with *that* or *of*) just in case, in the hope of (something happening)). **off-col'our** or **off-col'oured** *adj* (of eg a diamond) unsatisfactory in colour and so inferior; of mixed race (*offensive*); (**off-colour**) not completely healthy; (**off-colour**; of jokes, etc) smutty, blue (*inf*). **off'-come** *n* a subterfuge (*Scot*); a pretext (*Scot*); the manner of coming off, issue or success. **off'-comer** *n* (*inf*) a person living in a place, *esp* a rural area, in which he or she was not born, an incomer. **off'cut** *n* a small piece cut off or left over from a larger piece of some material (eg wood). **off'-cutter** *n* (*cricket*) a fast bowler's delivery that moves from off to leg after pitching. **off'-day** *n* see **off** (*adj*) above; a day when one is not at one's best or most brilliant. **off drive** *n* (*cricket*) a drive to the offside (also *vi* and *vt*). **off'-duty** *adj* not on duty. **off'-fore** *adj* and *n* (relating to) the right foreleg of a horse, *opp* to *near-fore*. **off'-grid** *adj* and *adv* not using one or more public utilities. **offhand'** *adv* extempore; at once; without hesitating. ◆ *adj* /*of'hand*/ without study; impromptu; free and easy; ungraciously curt or summary. **off'hand'ed** *adj*. **offhand'edly** *adv*. **offhand'edness** *n*. **offhand grinding** *n* (*engineering*) grinding in which the tool, eg a grinding wheel, is held in the hand and worked freely. **off'-job** *adj* outside normal work duties and conditions. **off'-job** (or **off'-the-job**) **training** *n* the part of a training course that a trainee follows away from the workplace at a college, etc, eg one day a week. **off-key'** *adj* and *adv* out of tune (*lit* and *fig*); conflicting, jarring, discordant. **off'-label** *adj* (*US*) (of a prescription drug) used to treat a condition for which the Food and Drug Administration has not approved it (also *adv*). **off'-licence** *n* a shop with a licence to sell alcoholic liquors for consumption off the premises only; such a licence. **off'-lim'its** *adj* prohibited, out of bounds. **off'line** or **off'-line** *adj* and *adv* (*comput*) not under the direct control of the central processing unit; not connected, switched off. **off'load** *vt* and *vi* (*orig S Afr*) to unload; to get rid of (something unwanted) by passing to someone else (with *onto*); to pass (the ball) to a teammate just as one is tackled (*rugby*). **off-mess'age** *adv* and *adj* (*politics*) not following the approved party line. **off-off-Broadway** see **off-Broadway** above. **off'peak** *adj* not at the time of highest demand; relating to times of the day when television or radio audiences are smaller, advertising rates for these times being lower, *opp* to *peak time*. **off'-piste** *adj* of or relating to skiing on new snow-surfaces, not on established tracks or runs. **off'-plan** *adj* relating to a home, etc bought before (completion of) building on the basis of plans seen, or to the buyer of such a property. **off'print** *n* a reprint of a single article from a periodical. **off'put** *n* (*Scot*) the act of putting off (in any sense). **off'-putter** *n*. **off'-putting** *n* an act of putting off. ◆ *adj* that puts off; disconcerting; causing disinclination or aversion. **off'-puttingly** *adv*. **off'-ramp** *n* (chiefly *N Am*) an exit road from a main thoroughfare. **off-reck'oning** *n* (*usu* in *pl*) a deduction; an account between army officers and governments concerning the men's clothes, etc (*obs*). **off'-road** *adj* of or relating to paths, tracks, etc, as opposed to roads; of or relating to vehicles, etc designed to operate away from roads. **off-road'er** *n* an off-road vehicle. **off-road'ing** *n* the practice of driving over rough terrain in specially designed vehicles, *esp* as a sport. **off'saddle** *vt* and *vi* to unsaddle. **off-sales'** *n* (*S Afr*) a shop where alcoholic drinks can be bought for consumption elsewhere. **off'scouring** *n* (*usu* in *pl*) matter scoured off; refuse; anything vile or despised. **off'scum** *n* scum, refuse. **off'season** *n*, *adj* and *adv* (of or at) a time (for eg a holiday) other than the most popular and busy. **off'set** *n* a thing set off against another as equivalent or compensation; a lateral shoot that strikes root and forms a new plant; a mountain spur; a side branch of anything; a sudden change of direction in a pipe; a reduction of thickness or the (*usu* sloping) ledge formed where part of a wall, buttress, bank, etc, is set back from the general face; a hillside terrace (*US*); a smudge on a newly printed sheet from another laid on it; offset printing; in surveying, a perpendicular from the main line to an outlying point; a small deviation of voltage or current (*elec*). ◆ *adj* set at an angle to the main alignment. ◆ *vt* /*of-set'*/ or /*of'set*/ to set off against something as an equivalent or compensation; to print using an offset process; to construct an offset in a wall, etc. ◆ *vi* to branch off; /*of'set*/ to make an effort. **offset'able** (or /*of'*/) *adj*. **offset printing**, **offset lithography** or **offset-litho printing** *n* a method of printing lithographs, etc, by first taking an impression from a plate on to a rubber cylinder and then transferring the impression to paper or metal, etc, using oil-based ink. **off-shake'** *vt* (*pap Spenser* **off-shakt'**) to shake off. **off'shoot** *n* a branch or derivative of anything. **offshore'** *adv* from the shore; at a

distance from the shore; abroad. ◆ *adj* /*of'shōr*/ or *-shör*/ placed or operating abroad; sited or operating outside the restrictions of British law and tax. ◆ *vt* and *vi* /*of'shōr*/ or *-shör*/ (of a business enterprise) to transfer (work, jobs, etc) to another country, *usu* one where workers can be paid a lower wage. **offshore purchase** *n* a purchase by one country in another. **off'side** *n* the far side; a horse's or vehicle's right, towards the middle of the road; that half of a cricket field on the opposite side to that on which the batsman stands when waiting to receive the ball, separated from the legside by an imaginary line drawn from wicket to wicket; /*of-sīd'*/ an instance of a player standing illegally between the ball and the opponents' goal (*football*, etc). ◆ *adj* and *adv* /*of-sīd'*/ on the offside; between the ball, or the last player who had it, and the opponents' goal; in American football, over the line of scrimmage or free-kick line when the ball is snapped. **offsīd'er** *n* (*Aust inf*) a subordinate or sidekick. **off'-site** *adj* and *adv* (working, happening, etc) away from a working site, etc. **off'-sorts** *n pl* wool set aside in sorting, or unsuitable for a given purpose. **off spin** *n* (*cricket*) spin imparted to a ball to cause an off break. **off'-spin** *adj*. **off spinner** *n* (*cricket*) someone who bowls off breaks. **off'spring** *n* a child or children; progeny; issue; ancestry (*obs*); source (*obs*). **off'-stage** *adj* and *adv* not on the stage as visible to the spectators. **off'-stream** *adj* and *adv* (of an industrial plant, etc) not in operation or production. **off'-street** *adj* (of parking) in a car park. **off'take** *n* the act of taking off in any sense; a take-off; that which is taken off; a channel, passage, or pipe for removing a fluid. **off-the-peg** see under **peg**. **off-the-shelf** see under **shelf**. **off'-white** *adj* not quite white, rather, yellowish or greyish white. ◆ *n* a colour, paint, etc, that is off-white.

■ **a bit off** (*inf*) (of behaviour, etc) unfair or unacceptable. **badly off** not well-off, poor. **be off** to go away quickly (as a command, also **be off with you**). **break off** and **come off** see under **break¹** and **come. from off** from a position on. **go off** and **go off with** see under **go¹**. **go off on one** (*sl*) to lose one's temper. **ill off** poor or ill provided. **in the offing** in sight or at hand; expected, or likely to take place, shortly. **make off** and **make off with** see under **make¹**. **off and on** occasionally, intermittently. **off beam** or **off the beam** see under **beam** or see **off-beam** above. **off duty** see under **duty**. **off line** same as **offline** above. **off one's oats**, **feed**, **head**, **rocker** or **trolley** see under **oat**, **feed¹**, **head**, **rock²** and **trolley¹**. **off the charts** see under **chart**. **off the cuff** see under **cuff¹**. **off the face** or **shoulder** (of a woman's hat, dress, etc) so as to reveal the face or shoulder. **off the grid** see under **grid** or **off-grid** above. **off the peg** see under **peg**. **off the wall** (*orig US*) see under **wall**. **off with** take off at once. **put off**, **show off** or **take off** see under **put¹**, **show** and **take**. **tell off** see under **tell¹**. **walk off** and **walk off with** see under **walk¹**. **well-off** rich, well-provided; fortunate.

off. *abbrev* : officer; official; officinal.

OFFA /*of'ə*/ (*educ*) *abbrev* : Office for Fair Access.

offal /*of'l*/ *n* waste or rejected parts, *esp* of a carcase; an edible part cut off in dressing a carcase, *esp* entrails, heart, liver, kidney, tongue, etc; anything worthless or unfit for use; refuse. [**off**, **fall¹**]

off-beam...to...**off-duty** see under **off**.

offend /*ə-*/ or *o-fend'*/ *vt* to displease; to make angry; to do harm to; to hurt the feelings of; to affront; to violate (a law); to cause to stumble or sin (*Bible*). ◆ *vi* to sin; to break the law; to cause anger; to be made to stumble or sin (*Bible*). [L *offendere*, *offensum*, from *ob* against, and *fendere*, *fensum* to strike (found in compounds); cf **defend**]
■ **offence'** (or *US* **offense**) *n* anger; displeasure; any cause of anger or displeasure; an injury; a transgression; a breach of law; a crime; a sin; affront; assault; those players in a team who assume the attacking role (*sport*); the attacking team, *esp* when in possession of the ball (*American football*); attacking play, position or style (*sport*); a stumbling (*Bible*). **offence'ful** *adj* (*Shakesp*) giving offence or displeasure; injurious. **offence'less** *adj* (*Milton*) unoffending; innocent. **offend'ed** *adj*. **offend'edly** *adv*. **offend'er** *n*. **offend'ing** *adj*. **offend'ress** *n* (*Shakesp*) a female offender. **offens'ive** *adj* causing offence, displeasure or injury; used in attack (*sport*, *milit*, etc); making the first attack. ◆ *n* the act or course of action of the attacking party; the posture of an attacker; a great and sustained effort to achieve an end, as in *peace offensive*. **offens'ively** *adv*. **offens'iveness** *n*.
■ **give offence** to cause displeasure. **take offence** to feel displeasure, be offended.

Offer /*of'ər*/ *abbrev* : Office of Electricity Regulation (now replaced by **Ofgem**).

offer /*of'ər*/ *vt* to present, *esp* as an act of devotion, homage, charity, etc; to express willingness; to hold out for acceptance or rejection; to lay before someone; to present to the mind; to propose to give, pay, sell or perform; to attempt (violence, resistance, etc); to make a show of attempting, make as if; to give the enemy an opportunity for (battle). ◆ *vi* to present itself; to be at hand; to incline or tend (*obs*); to make an offer, eg of marriage (*old*). ◆ *n* the act of offering; the state of being offered; the first advance; something which is offered; a proposal made; an attempt or essay; a knob on an antler. [L *offerre*, from *ob* towards, and *ferre* to bring]

■ **off'erable** *adj* that can be offered. **offeree'** *n* the person to whom something is offered. **off'erer** or (*law*) **off'eror** *n*. **off'ering** *n* the act of making an offer; something that is offered; a gift; a church collection; a sacrifice; (in *pl*) in the Church of England, certain dues payable at Easter; that which is offered on an altar (*Bible*). **off'ertory** *n* the act of offering; the thing offered; the verses or the anthem said or sung while the offerings of the congregation are being made; the money collected at a religious service; anciently, a linen or silken cloth used in various ceremonies connected with the administration of the Eucharist.

❑ **offer document** *n* a document that offers shares for sale to the public. **offer price** *n* (*stock exchange*) the price at which a dealer is willing to sell shares or other items to the market.

■ **offer up** in eg joinery, to position on a trial basis, in order to test for size and suitability before fixing. **on offer** being offered for sale, consumption, etc; for sale as a special offer. **special offer** *esp* in a shop, the offering of something for sale, or that which is offered, *usu* for a short time, at a bargain price.

offhand, etc see under **off**.

office /*of*'*is*/ *n orig* an act of kindness or attention; a service; (with *ill*, etc) a disservice; a function or duty; settled duty or employment; a position imposing certain duties or giving a right to exercise an employment; the possession of a post in the government; business; an act of worship; the order or form of a religious service, either public or private; that which a thing is designed or fitted to do; a place where business is carried on; a group of staff occupying such a place; a state department; the building in which it is housed; a doctor's consulting room (*N Am*); a cockpit in an aeroplane (*sl*); a euphemism for lavatory; a hint (*sl*); (in *pl*) the apartments of a house or the subsidiary buildings in which the domestic, etc, work is carried out. [Fr, from L *officium* a favour, duty or service]

■ **off'icer** *n* someone who holds an office; a person who performs some public duty; a person holding a commission in an army, navy or air force; someone who holds a similar post in any force or body organized on a similar plan; a policeman or policewoman; an office-bearer in a society. ◆ *vt* (of officers) to command or lead; to provide with officers. **official** /*ə-fish'əl*/ *adj* relating to an office; depending on the proper office or authority; done by authority; issued or authorized by a public authority or office; (of an explanation, etc) untrue but maintained in public, the truth being embarrassing or compromising; (of a drug) recognized in the pharmacopoeia (cf **officinal**). ◆ *n* a person who holds an office; a subordinate public officer; the deputy of a bishop, etc. **offic'ialdom** *n* officials as a body; the world of officials; officialism. **officialese'** *n* stilted, wordy and stereotyped English alleged to be characteristic of official letters and documents. **offic'ialism** *n* official position; excessive devotion to official routine and detail; the self-importance of a Jack-in-office. **officiality** /*ə-fish-i-al'i-ti*/ or **officialty** /*ə-fish'əl-ti*/ *n* (*rare*) the charge, office or jurisdiction of an official; the official headquarters of an ecclesiastical or other deliberative and governing body; officialism. **officially** /*ə-fish'ə-li*/ *adv*. **officiant** /*ə-fish'i-ənt*/ *n* someone who officiates at a religious service, someone who administers a sacrament. **offic'iate** *vi* to perform the duties of an office. **officia'tion** *n*. **offic'iator** *n*.

❑ **off'ice-bearer** *n* someone who holds office; someone who has an appointed duty to perform in connection with some company, society, church, etc. **office block** *n* a large building in which an office or variety of offices is housed. **off'ice-book** *n* a book of forms of church service. **office boy**, **office girl** *n* a boy or girl employed to do minor jobs in an office. **off'ice-holder** *n* someone who holds a government office; a civil servant, *usu* in administration (*US*). **office hours** *n pl* the time during which an office is open for business, typically 9am to 5pm Monday to Friday. **off'ice-hunter** *n* a self-seeking candidate for public employment. **office junior** *n* an employee who carries out general office duties under the direction of an office supervisor. **Office of Fair Trading** *n* a UK government agency set up in 1973 to protect traders and consumers against unfair trading practices (*abbrev* **OFT**). **officer of arms** *n* (also with *caps*) any of the thirteen officers of the College of Arms (qv). **officer of the day** *n* (*milit*) the officer in charge of camp or unit security on any particular day. **off'ice-seeker** *n* a candidate for office. **official list** *n* a list of the current prices of stocks and shares published daily by the London Stock Exchange. **official receiver** see under **receive**.

■ **last offices** rites for the dead; the preparation of a corpse for burial.

officinal /*o-* or *ə-fis'i-nəl* or *o-fi-sē'nəl*/ *adj* belonging to or used in a shop; used in medicine; (now **official**) recognized in the pharmacopoeia (*obs*); sold by pharmacists. [LL *officīnālis*, from L *officīna* a workshop, later a monastic storeroom, from *opus* work, and *facere* to do]

■ **offic'inally** *adv*.

officious /*ə-fish'əs*/ *adj* too forward in offering unwelcome or unwanted services; meddling; in diplomacy, informal, not official; obliging (*obs*); dutiful (*Shakesp*). [L *officiōsus*, from *officium*]

■ **offic'iously** *adv*. **offic'iousness** *n*.

offie or **offy** /*of'i*/ (*inf*) *n* an off-licence.

offing...to...**offtake** see under **off**.

Ofgas or **OFGAS** /*of'gas*/ *abbrev*: Office of Gas Supply (now replaced by **Ofgem**).

Ofgem or **OFGEM** /*of'jem*/ *abbrev*: Office of Gas and Electricity Markets (a UK regulatory body).

oflag /*of'läg* or *-lähh*/ *n* a German prisoner-of-war camp for officers. [Ger, short for *Offizierslager* officers' camp]

Oflot or **OFLOT** /*of'lot*/ *abbrev*: Office of the National Lottery (now replaced by **NLC**).

OFM *abbrev*: *Ordo* (or *Ordinis*) *Fratrum Minorum* (L), (of) the Order of Minor Friars, the Franciscans.

Ofqual or **OFQUAL** /*of'kwol*/ *abbrev*: Office of Qualifications and Examinations Regulation.

Ofsted or **OFSTED** /*of'sted*/ *abbrev*: Office for Standards in Education (an English regulatory body).

OFT *abbrev*: Office of Fair Trading.

oft /*oft* or *öft*/ *adv* (now mainly *poetic* or as *combining form* as in *oft-repeated*) often. [OE *oft*; Ger *oft*, Gothic *ufta*]

■ **oft'times** *adv* (*poetic*) often.

Oftel or **OFTEL** /*of'tel*/ *abbrev*: Office of Telecommunications (now replaced by **Ofcom**).

often /*of'n, öf'n, of'ən* or *of'tən*/ *adv* frequently; many times; in many cases. ◆ *adj* (*Bible*) frequent. [An extended form of **oft**]

■ **oft'enness** *n* (*rare*) frequency. **oft'entimes** *adv* (*archaic, literary* or *N Am*) many times; frequently.

■ **as often as not** in about half of the instances, quite frequently. **more often than not** in more than half the instances, frequently.

Ofwat or **OFWAT** /*of'wot*/ *abbrev*: Office of Water Services (a UK regulatory body).

og *abbrev*: own goal.

ogam /*og'əm*/ or **ogham** /*og'əm* or *ŏ'əm*/ *n* an ancient alphabet used in Celtic and Pictish inscriptions, its letters consisting of sets of parallel lines meeting or crossing a base line (the corner of the stone monument often serving as the base line); any of its twenty characters; an inscription in this alphabet. [OIr *ogam*, Mod Ir *ogham*]

■ **ogam'ic** (or /*og'*/), **oghamic** /*ə-gam'ik, og'ə-mik* or *ŏ'ə-mik*/ or **og'mic** *adj*.

ogdoad /*og'dō-ad*/ *n* a set of eight. [Gr *ogdoas, -ados*, from *oktō* eight]

ogee /*ō'jē* or *ō-jē'*/ *n* a moulding S-shaped in section (*archit*); an S-shaped curve. ◆ *adj* having S-shaped curves. [Fr *ogive*; see **ogive**]

■ **ogee'd** or **ogeed** *adj*.

Ogen melon /*ō'gen mel'ən*/ *n* a kind of melon, small and green-skinned. [From the kibbutz where the variety was developed]

oggin /*og'in*/ (*naval sl*) *n* the sea. [Said to be from earlier *hogwash* the sea]

ogham and **oghamic** see **ogam**.

ogive /*ō'jīv* or *ō-jīv'*/ (*archit*) *n* a diagonal rib of a vault; a pointed arch or window; a graph representing cumulative frequency (*stats*); something that has the form of an ogive, *esp* the nose of a rocket or missile. [Fr; origin doubtful, possibly from Ar *auj* summit]

■ **ogi'val** *adj*.

ogle /*ō'gl*/ *vt* to eye impertinently or lecherously; to eye greedily. ◆ *vi* to cast amorous glances; to stare impertinently. ◆ *n* an act of ogling. [Cf LGer *oegeln*, frequentative of *oegen* to look at; Ger *äugeln* to leer, *Auge* eye]

■ **o'gler** *n*. **o'gling** *n*.

ogmic see under **ogam**.

Ogpu /*og'poo* or *og-poo'*/ *n* the Russian secret police of 1922–34. [From the initials of *Obedinennoe Gosudarstvennoe Politicheskoe Upravlenie* Unified State Political Directorate]

ogre /*ō'gər*/, *fem* **ogress** /*ō'gres* or *-grəs*/ *n* a man-eating monster or giant of fairy tales; an ugly, cruel or bad-tempered person, or one whose sternness inspires fear. [Fr *ogre*, prob invented by Perrault]

■ **o'greish** or **o'grish** *adj*.

Ogygian /*ō-gij'i-ən* or *-jī'*/ *adj* relating to the mythical Attic king *Ogygēs*; prehistoric, primeval; very old; of Calypso's island, *Ogygia*.

❑ **Ogygian deluge** *n* a flood said to have occurred during the reign of Ogyges.

OH *abbrev*: Ohio (US state).

oh /*ō*/ *interj* denoting surprise, pain, sorrow, etc. [See **O²**]

■ words derived from main entry word; ❑ compound words; ■ idioms and phrasal verbs

OHG *abbrev* : Old High German.

ohm /ōm/ *n* a derived SI unit, the unit of electrical resistance (symbol Ω), equal to the resistance in a conductor in which a potential difference of one volt produces a current of one ampere; formerly defined as the resistance of a specified column of mercury under stated conditions. [Georg Simon *Ohm* (1787–1854), German electrician]
■ **ohm'age** *n* electrical resistance measured in ohms. **ohm'ic** *adj*. **ohm'ically** *adv*. **ohmmeter** /ōm'mēt-ər/ *n* an instrument for measuring electrical resistance.
□ **Ohm's law** *n* the law that strength of electric current is directly proportional to electromotive force and inversely to resistance.

OHMS *abbrev* : On Her (or His) Majesty's Service.

oho /ō-hō'/ *interj* expressing triumphant surprise or gratification.

-oholic and **-oholism** see **-aholic**.

ohone or **ochone** /ō-hōn' or -hhōn'/ (*Irish* and *Highland Scot*) *interj* expressing lamentation. [Ir and Gaelic *ochoin*]

OHP *abbrev* : overhead projector.

OHS *abbrev* : Office of Homeland Security (in the USA).

oi /oi/ *interj* used to attract attention, etc. [Imit]

-oid /-oid/ *n* and *adj* combining form denoting (something) that resembles or has the shape of, as in *anthropoid, asteroid, deltoid*. [Gr *-oeidēs*, from *eidos* shape, form]
■ **-oidal** *adj combining form*. **-oidally** *adv combining form*.

oidium /ō-id'i-əm/ (*bot*) *n* (pl **oid'ia** /-ə/) the conidial stage of the vine-mildew and other fungi. [Gr *ōion* an egg, with dimin sfx *-idion* Latinized]

oik /oik/ (*inf*) *n* a crass-witted, inferior person; a boor or lout; a cad; a chap, bloke (slightly *derog*). [Ety uncertain]

oikist see **oecist**.

oil /oil/ *n* any greasy, *usu* flammable liquid derived from animals, plants, mineral deposits or by artificial means, and used as a lubricant, fuel, foodstuff, etc; the juice from the fruit of the olive tree; any similar liquid obtained from parts of other plants; an oil painting; (in *pl*) paints or oil painting; (in *pl*) oilskins; news, information, *esp* in the *good oil* (*Aust inf*). ◆ *vt* to smear, lubricate or anoint with oil; to impregnate with oil; to turn (a solid fat) into oil. ◆ *vi* to take oil aboard as fuel; (of a solid fat) to turn into oil; to move ingratiatingly, stealthily, slily or cravenly, as in *oil out*, to extricate oneself dishonourably (*inf, esp old*). —See also **tall oil**. [OFr *oile* (Fr *huile*), from L *oleum*, from Gr *elaion*, from *elaiā* olive-tree, olive]
■ **oiled** *adj* smeared, treated, lubricated or impregnated with oil; preserved in oil; tipsy (*esp* in *well-oiled*; *sl*). **oil'er** *n* someone who or something that oils; an oilcan; (in *pl*) oilskins; a ship driven by oil; a ship that carries oil, a tanker; an oil well. **oil'ery** *n* the commodities, business or establishment of an oilman. **oil'ily** *adv*. **oil'iness** *n*. **oil'less** *adj*. **oil'y** *adj* consisting of, containing or having the qualities of oil; greasy; unctuous.
□ **oil bath** *n* a receptacle containing lubricating oil through which part of a machine passes. **oil beetle** *n* a beetle (of the genus *Meloe*) that emits a yellowish oily liquid from its legs when disturbed. **oil'-belt** *n* a belt of country yielding mineral oil. **oil'bird** *n* the guacharo. **oil'-burner** *n* a ship that uses oil as fuel; a lamp-burner for use with oil. **oil'-burning** *adj*. **oil'-cake** *n* a cattle food made of the residue of oilseeds when most of the oil has been pressed out. **oil'can** *n* a can for carrying oil or for applying lubricating oil. **oil'cloth** *n* a canvas coated with linseed oil paint; oilskin. **oil colour** *n* a colouring substance mixed with oil, an oil paint. **oil-control ring** *n* (*motoring*) same as **scraper ring** (see under **scrape**). **oil'-cup** *n* a small cup-like container, *usu* attached to machinery, for holding and dispensing lubricating oil. **oil drum** *n* a cylindrical metal barrel for oil. **oil engine** *n* an internal-combustion engine burning vapour from oil. **oil'field** *n* an area that produces mineral oil. **oil-filled cable** *n* (*elec eng*) cable with a central duct filled with oil, eliminating gaseous voids and consequent ionization. **oil'-fired** *adj* burning oil as fuel. **oil'-gas** *n* illuminating gas or heating gas made by destructive distillation of oil. **oil gauge** *n* an instrument for indicating the level of lubricating oil in an engine, etc. **oil gland** *n* the uropygial gland in birds, forming a secretion used in preening the feathers. **oil immersion** *n* a technique, used to extend the resolving power of a light microscope, in which a thin film of oil is placed between a special oil-immersion objective lens and the specimen. **oil length** *n* the ratio of drying oil to resin in eg a varnish (**long'-oil** having a high proportion, **short'-oil** a low proportion, of oil). **oil'man** *n* a man who deals in oils; a man who owns an oil well; a man involved in the operation of an oil well, oil rig, etc. **oil mill** *n* a grinding-mill for expressing oil from seeds, etc. **oil'nut** *n* the N American butternut, the buffalo-nut, or other oil-yielding nut. **oil paint** *n* an oil colour. **oil painting** *n* a picture painted in oil colours; the art of painting in oil colours. **oil palm** *n* a palm (*Elaeis guineensis*) whose fruit pulp yields palm oil. **oil pan** *n* the sump

in an internal-combustion engine. **oil paper** *n* paper that has been oiled, eg to make it waterproof. **oil platform** *n* a steel and/or concrete structure, either fixed or mobile, used in offshore drilling to support the rig and to keep stores, etc. **oil press** *n* a machine for expressing oils from seeds or pulp. **oil'-rich** *adj* having much oil. **oil rig** *n* the complete plant (machinery, structures, etc) required for oil-well drilling; (loosely) a mobile oil platform. **oil sand** *n* sand or sandstone occurring naturally impregnated with petroleum; tar sand. **oil'seed** *n* any seed that yields oil. **oilseed rape** *n* a plant with vivid yellow flowers, yielding vegetable oil. **oil shale** *n* a shale containing diffused hydrocarbons in a state suitable for distillation into mineral oils. **oil silk** *n* a transparent silk fabric impregnated with oxidized oil. **oil'skin** *n* cloth made waterproof by means of oil; a garment made of oilskin. **oil slick** *n* a patch of oil forming a film on the surface of water or (rarely) a road, etc. **oil'stone** *n* a whetstone used with oil. **oil string** same as **production string** (see under **produce**). **oil tanker** *n* a vessel constructed for carrying oil in bulk. **oil'-tree** *n* any of several trees or shrubs from which oil is obtained, that mentioned in Isaiah 41.19 in the Bible probably being the oleaster. **oil well** *n* a boring made on land or the seabed for extracting petroleum. **oily fish** *n* any fish whose meat is rich in fatty acids, including salmon and mackerel.
■ **long-oil** and **short-oil** see **oil length** above. **no oil painting** (*inf; facetious*) (facially) unattractive. **oil someone's palm** to bribe someone. **oil the wheels** to do something in order to make things go more smoothly, successfully, etc. **strike oil** to discover oil while boring for it; to find the way to success and riches.

OILC *abbrev* : Offshore Industry Liaison Committee, a UK trade union.

oillet /oi'lit/ *n* an obsolete form of **eyelet**.

oink /oingk/ *n* (the representation of) the noise made by a pig (also *interj*). ◆ *vi* to make such a noise.

oino- /oi-nō-, -nə- or -no-/ combining form occurring as an occasional variant for **oeno-** (see **oen-**).

ointment /oint'mənt/ *n* any greasy preparation for smoothing onto or rubbing into the skin for healing or cosmetic purposes; an unguent or lubricant; anything used in anointing. [Fr *oint*, pap of *oindre*, from L *unguere* to anoint]
■ **oint** *vt* (*Dryden*) to anoint.

Oireachtas /er'ək-thəs or er'əhh-təs/ *n* the legislature of the Republic of Ireland (President, Seanad, and Dáil). [Ir, assembly]

Oirish /oi'rish/ (*facetious*) *adj* portraying Irishness in a self-conscious, exaggerated or caricatured manner. [Sham-Irish pronunciation of *Irish*]
■ **Oi'rishness** *n*.

OIRT *abbrev* : *Organisation Internationale de Radiodiffusion et Télévision* (Fr), International Organization of Radio and Television (in E Europe) (now merged into **EBU**).

oiticica /oi-ti-sē'kə/ *n* any of several S American trees, *esp Licania rigida* and *Couepia grandiflora* (both rosaceous), whose nuts yield an oil used for quick-drying paints and varnishes. [Port, from Tupí *oity-cica*]

Ojibwa /ō-jib'wə/ *n* (pl **Ojib'wa** or **Ojib'was**) a member of a Native American people *orig* concentrated round Lakes Superior and Huron, also called **Chippewa** by Europeans; their language, of the Algonquian group. [Ojibwa, puckered, in reference to moccasin style]

ojime /ō'ji-mā/ *n* a carved bead through which pass the two cords attached to a Japanese inro or small container and which when slid down the cords serves to keep the inro closed. [Jap *o* string, and *shime* fastening]

OK or **okay** /ō-kā'/ (*inf*) *adj* all correct; all right; satisfactory. ◆ *adv* yes; all right, certainly. ◆ *interj* expressing agreement or approval; yes; certainly. ◆ *n* (pl **OKs**, **OK's** or **okays'**) approval; sanction; endorsement. ◆ *vt* (**OK'ing**, **OK''ing** or **okay'ing**; **OK'd'**, **OKed'** or **okayed'**) to mark or pass as right; to sanction. [Various explanations of the letters have been given; evidence suggests that *OK* became popular as an abbreviation of *oll korrekt*, a facetious misspelling of *all correct* current in the USA in the 1830s, and was then used as a slogan by Van Buren's party in the 1840 US presidential election (Van Buren was born at Kinderhook, near Albany in New York and was known as *Old Kinderhook*)]

OK *abbrev* : Oklahoma (US state).

Oka /ō'kə/ *n* a cured Canadian cheese. [After *Oka* in Quebec, where it is made by Trappist monks]

oka see **oke¹**.

okapi /ō-kä'pē/ *n* (pl **oka'pis**) an animal of Central Africa related to the giraffe. [Native name]

okay /ō-kā'/ (*inf*) *adj, adv, interj, n* and *vt* see **OK**.

oke¹ /ōk/ or **oka** /ō'kə/ *n* a Turkish weight of about 1.3kg or 2⅘lb. [Turk *ōqah*, apparently through Gr from L *uncia* ounce]

oke² /ōk/ (*inf*) *adv* a clipped form of **OK**.

❏ **okey-dokey** /ō-ki-dō'ki/ or **okey-doke** /-dōk'/ adj and adv (inf) OK.

okimono /ok-i- or ō-ki-mō'nō/ n a Japanese ornament or figurine. [Jap oku to put, and mono thing]

Okla. abbrev : Oklahoma (US state).

okra /ok'rə or ō'krə/ n (also known as **gumbo** and **lady's fingers**) a tropical plant, Hibiscus esculentus, of the mallow family, with edible pods; the pods themselves; a dish prepared with the pods. [From a W African name]

okta or **octa** /ok'tə/ (aeronautics and meteorol) n a unit equal to one-eighth of the sky area, used in specifying cloud cover for airfield weather condition reports. [Gr okta- eight]

-ol¹ /-ol/ (chem) sfx signifying the presence of a hydroxyl group, used esp in the names of alcohols, as eg phenol, ethanol, methanol, quinol. [Alcohol]

-ol² /-ol/ sfx denoting an oil or an oil-based substance, as in benzol. [L oleum oil]

OLAF /ō'laf/ abbrev : Office Européen de Lutte Anti-Fraude (Fr), European Anti-Fraud Office.

olanzapine /ə-lan'zə-pēn/ n an antipsychotic drug used to treat schizophrenia and other conditions.

Olbers' paradox /ol'bərz par'ə-doks/ (astron) n the apparent paradox, stated in 1826 and now explained by postulating a finite expanding universe, that the sky is dark at night although, as there are an infinite number of stars, it should be uniformly bright. [Heinrich Olbers (1758–1840), German astronomer and physicist, who first stated the paradox]

old /ōld/ adj (**old'er** or **eld'er** (qv); **old'est** or **eld'est**) advanced in years; having been long or relatively long in existence, use or possession; of a specified (or to-be-specified) age; of long standing; worn or worn-out; out of date; superseded or abandoned; former; old-fashioned; antique; ancient; early; belonging to later life; belonging to former times; denoting anyone or anything with whom or with which one was formerly associated, such as old school, etc; (of a language) of the earliest or earliest known stage; long practised or experienced; having the characteristics of age; familiar, accustomed; in plenty, in excess, or wonderful (esp in high old; inf); a general word of familiar or affectionate approbation or contempt (often good old or little old; inf); reckoned according to Old Style (see **style**). ◆ adv (Shakesp) of old. ◆ n an old person (archaic or, esp in pl, inf); olden times, eld. [OE ald (WSax eald); Du oud, Ger alt]

■ **olde** /ōld or ōld'i/ adj a facetious spelling of **old**, used to imply that something has a quaint charm. **old'en** vt and vi (rare) to age. ◆ adj former, old, past (now usu only in phrases in olden days/times). **old'ie** or (rarely) **old'y** n (inf) an old person; a film, song, etc produced or popularized, etc a considerable time ago. **old'ish** adj rather old. **old'ness** n. **old'ster** n a person who is growing old (inf); a midshipman of four years' standing, a master's mate.

❏ **old age** n the later part of life. **old-age pension** n a pension for someone who has reached old age, esp under a national system (first instituted in Britain in 1908; see also **retirement pension** under **retire**). **old-age pensioner** n. **old bachelor** n a rather elderly or confirmed bachelor. **Old Bailey** n the Central Criminal Court in London. **Old Believer** n (hist) in Russia, a dissenter from the Orthodox church, a Raskolnik. **Old Bill** n a soldier with a drooping moustache in World War I cartoons by Bruce Bairnsfather; the police (sl; sometimes with the). **old bird** n an astute, experienced person. **old boy** n one's father, husband, etc (inf); an old or oldish man, esp one in authority, or one who has some air of youthfulness; a former pupil; an affectionately familiar term of address to a male of any age (also **old bean**, **old chap**, **old fellow**, **old fruit**, **old man**, **old thing**; inf). **Old Boy network** n (also without caps) the members of a society (usu upper-class), closely interconnected, who share information and secure advantages for each other; this form of association. **Old Catholic** n a member of a body that broke away from the Roman Catholic Church on the question of papal infallibility. **old-clothes'man** n someone who deals in cast-off garments. **Old Contemptibles** n pl the British Expeditionary Force to France in 1914, from the then Kaiser's probably apocryphal reference to them as a contemptible little army. **old country** n the mother-country. **Old Dart** n (Aust sl) Great Britain. **old dear** n (sl) an old lady. **Old Dominion** n Virginia. **old economy** n the part of the economy based on traditional industries and the production of physical goods (cf **new economy** under **new**). **old'-economy** adj. **Old English** n see **English**; the form of black letter used by 16c English printers. **Old English sheepdog** n a large breed of dog with a long shaggy coat, usu white with large dark patches. **old-estab'lished** adj long established. **olde-worlde** /ōl-di-wûrld'i/ adj (inf) self-consciously imitative of the past or supposed past. **old Europe** n the countries of Western Europe. **old face** n (printing) the early roman type as used by Caslon. **oldfang'led** adj old-fashioned. **old fart** n (derog or facetious) a staid or curmudgeonly

old person. **old-fash'ioned** adj in the style of long ago; out of date; clinging to old things and old styles; with manners like those of a grown-up person (said of a child); (in **old-fashioned look**) quizzically disapproving or critical. ◆ n (N Am) a cocktail made from whisky, bitters, water and sugar. **old-fash'ionedness** n. **old fogey** or **old fogy** n a dull old person, or someone with old-fashioned notions. **old-fo'geyish** or **old-fo'gyish** adj like an old fogey. **Old French** n the French language until about 1400. **old gang** or **guard** n the old and conservative element in a party, etc. **old-gen'tlemanly** adj characteristic of an old gentleman. **old girl** n (inf) an old or oldish woman, esp one with an air of youthfulness; a former pupil; an affectionately familiar form of address to a female of any age. **Old Glory** n the US flag, the Stars and Stripes. **old gold** n a dull gold colour like tarnished gold, used esp in textile fabrics. **old'-growth** adj (of forest or woodland) ancient. **old guard** see **old gang** above. **old hand** n an experienced performer; an old convict. **Old Harry**, **Old Nick**, **Old One**, **Old Poker** or **Old Scratch** n the Devil. **old-hat'** adj out-of-date. **Old Hundred** or **Old Hundredth** n a famous tune set in England about the middle of the 16c to Kethe's version of Psalm 100, marked 'Old Hundredth' in Tate and Brady (1696). **old identity** n (Aust and NZ) a person who has been around a place for a long time. **Old Kingdom** n the 3rd to 6th dynasties in ancient Egypt (26c–22c BC). **old lady** n (inf) one's mother or wife; a noctuid moth (Mormo maura), with a dull pattern on its wings. **Old Light** (Scot **Auld Licht**) n a member of a relatively less advanced religious school, applied esp to the party in the Scottish Secession Church who continued to hold unchanged the principle of connection between Church and State. **old'-line** adj (N Am) conservative; traditional. **old-li'ner** n. **old maid** n a spinster, esp one who is likely to remain a spinster; a woman, or often a man, of the character supposed to be common among spinsters, ie fussy, prim, conventional, over-cautious, methodical; a simple game played by passing and matching cards; also the player left with the odd card. **old-maid'hood** or **old-maid'ism** n. **old-maid'ish** adj like the conventional old maid, prim. **old-maid'ishly** adv. **old man** n one's husband, father, or employer (inf); the captain of a ship; a familiar, friendly or encouraging term of address; unregenerate human nature; an adult male kangaroo; a plant, the southernwood. ◆ adj (Aust inf; also with hyphen) of exceptional size, intensity, etc. **old man of the sea** n a person or burden that one cannot shake off, from the old man in the Arabian Nights who, having been carried across a stream by Sinbad the Sailor, refused to get down off his back. **old man's beard** n a name for several plants including traveller's joy. **old master** n (often with caps) any great painter or painting of a period previous to the 19c (esp of the Renaissance). **old money** n wealth that has been in the same family for several generations; the possessors of such wealth. **old'-mon'ey** adj. **old moon** n the moon in its last waning quarter before its reappearance as a new moon. **Old Nick** see **Old Harry** above, and **Nick**. **Old Norse** see **Norse**. **Old Pretender** see under **pretend**. **Old Red Sandstone** n (geol) the lacustrine or continental equivalent of the (marine) Devonian, so called in contradistinction to the New Red Sandstone. **old rose** n any of several varieties of rose that existed before the development of hybrid tea roses; a deep soft pink. **old salt** n an experienced sailor. **old school** n those whose ways, thoughts or attitudes are such as prevailed in the past. **old'-school** adj. **old school tie** n a distinctive tie worn by old boys of a school; the emblem of (esp upper-class) loyalties shown by such people to each other. **old soldier** n an experienced person who knows how to make himself or herself comfortable, or how to turn things to his or her advantage; an empty bottle. **old song** n a mere trifle, a very small price. **old squaw** or **old'squaw** n (US) a kind of duck, the hareld. **old stager** n an experienced person, an old hand. **old story** n something one has heard before; something that happened long ago, or has happened often. **Old Style** n see **style**; a typeface in imitation of old face (printing). **old talk** n (W Indies) small talk. **old'-talk** vi (W Indies) to make small talk. **Old Testament** n the first part of the Christian Bible, containing writings about the history of the Hebrew people and books of prophecy (abbrev **OT**). **old'-time** adj of or relating to times long gone by; of long standing; old-fashioned. **old-tim'er** n an experienced person, a veteran; someone who has been where he or she is for a long time; an old-fashioned person; (esp as a form of address; US) an old person. **Old Tom** n (archaic) a kind of sweetened gin. **old wife** n an old woman; someone who has the character ascribed to old women; a cap for curing a smoking chimney (Scot); a kind of duck, the hareld; a fish of various kinds, sea-bream, filefish, alewife, menhaden, etc. **old woman** n one's wife or mother (inf); an old-womanish person. **old-wom'anish** adj like an old woman, esp fussy. **old'-world** adj belonging to earlier times; old-fashioned and quaint; (with cap) of the Old World. **Old World** n the eastern hemisphere.

■ **any old** see under **any**. **come the old soldier over someone** to impose on a person. **of old** long ago; in or of times long past; formerly. **the old sod** one's native country, esp used of Ireland, when also **the ould sod**.

OLE (*comput*) *abbrev*: Object Linking and Embedding.

olé /ō-lā'/ (*Sp*) *interj* an exclamation of approval, support or encouragement, sometimes used in English as an expression of triumph. [Ar *wa-llāh* by God]

-ole /-ōl/ *combining form* forming names of organic compounds, *esp* heterocyclic compounds. [L *oleum* oil]

Olea /ō'li-ə/ *n* the olive genus, giving name to the family **Oleā'ceae**, including ash, privet and jasmine. [L *olea* olive]
■ **oleā'ceous** *adj*.

oleaginous /ō-li-aj'i-nəs/ *adj* oily; producing oil; fawning or sycophantic (*facetious*). [L *oleāginus*, from *oleum* oil]
■ **oleag'inousness** *n*.

oleander /ō-li-an'dər/ *n* an evergreen shrub (*Nerium oleander*) of the Apocynaceae, with lance-shaped leathery leaves and beautiful red or white flowers, the rose-bay or rose-laurel. [LL *oleander*; derivation from *rhododendron*, influenced by *laurus* and *olea*, has been conjectured]

olearia /ō-li-ā'ri-ə/ *n* a plant of the *Olearia* genus of Australasian evergreen shrubs of the family Compositae, with white, yellow or mauve daisy-like flowers; a daisy-tree or bush (*inf*). [Johann Gottfried *Olearius* (1635–1711), German theologian and horticulturalist]

oleaster /ō-li-as'tər/ *n* properly the true wild olive; extended to the so-called wild olive, *Elaeagnus*. [L *oleāster*, from *olea* an olive-tree, from Gr *elaiā*]

oleate /ō'li-āt/ *n* a salt of oleic acid. [L *oleum* oil]
■ **olefiant** /ō-li-fī'ənt or ō-lē'fi-ənt/ *adj* oil-forming (as in **olefiant gas** ethylene). **o'lefin** or **-fine** /-fin or -fēn/ *n* any hydrocarbon of the ethylene series. **olefin'ic** *adj*. **olē'ic** (or /ō'li-ik/) *adj* relating to or derived from oil (as in **oleic acid** $C_{18}H_{34}O_2$). **oleif'erous** *adj* (of eg seeds) producing oil. **olein** /ō'li-in/ *n* a glycerine ester of oleic acid. **oleo** /ō'li-ō/ *n* (*pl* **o'leos**) short form of oleograph or oleomargarine; an oil-containing telescopic part of the landing gear of an aircraft, acting as a shock absorber on landing (also **oleo leg**). **o'leograph** *n* a print in oil colours to imitate an oil painting. **oleograph'ic** *adj*. **oleog'raphy** *n*. **oleophil'ic** *adj* having affinity for oils; wetted by oil in preference to water. **oles'tra** *n* a synthetic fat substitute that passes through the gastrointestinal tract without being digested or absorbed. **oleum** /ō'li-əm/ *n* a solution of sulphur trioxide in sulphuric acid (also **fuming sulphuric acid**).
□ **oleo leg** see **oleo** above. **oleomar'garine** *n* margarine (*US*); a yellow fatty substance obtained from beef tallow and used in the manufacture of margarine, soap, etc. **oleores'in** *n* a solution of a resin in an oil. **oleores'inous** *adj*.

olecranon /ō-li-krā'non or ō-lek'rə-non/ (*anat*) *n* a projection on the upper end of the ulna, at the elbow. [Gr *ōlekrānon*, from *ōlenē* elbow, and *krānion* head]
■ **olecrā'nal** (or /ō-lek'rə-nəl/) *adj*.

olefin, oleic, olein, etc see under **oleate**.

olent /ō'lənt/ *adj* having a smell. [L *olens, -entis*, prp of *olēre* to smell]

Olenus /ō'le-nəs/ *n* a typically Upper Cambrian genus of trilobites. [Gr *Ōlenos*, who was turned to stone]
■ **Olenell'us** *n* a similar Lower Cambrian genus.

oleo see under **oleate**.

oleraceous /o-lə-rā'shəs/ *adj* of the nature of a pot herb, for kitchen use. [L (*h*)*olerāceus*, from (*h*)*olus*, (*h*)*oleris* a pot herb or vegetable]

olestra and **oleum** see under **oleate**.

olfactory /ol-fak'tə-ri/ *adj* relating to, or used in, smelling. ◆ *n* an organ or nerve of smell. [L *olfacere* to smell, from *olēre* to smell, and *facere* to make]
■ **olfact'** *vt* (*facetious*) to smell. **olfact'ible** *adj*. **olfac'tion** *n*. **olfac'tive** *adj*. **olfactol'ogist** *n*. **olfactol'ogy** *n* the scientific study of smells and the sense of smell. **olfactom'eter** *n*. **olfactom'etry** *n* the measurement of the sharpness of the sense of smell; the measurement of odours, odorimetry. **olfactronics** /-tron'iks/ *n sing* (modelled on *electronics*) the precise measurement, analysis and detection of odours by means of electronic instruments.

olibanum /o-lib'ə-nəm/ *n* a gum resin flowing from incisions in species of *Boswellia*, *esp* species in E Africa and Arabia, frankincense. [LL, prob from Gr *libanos* frankincense]

olid /ol'id/ *adj* rank-smelling. [L *olidus*, from *olēre* to smell]

olig- /o-lig-/ or **oligo-** /o-li-gō-, -gə- or -go-/ *combining form* denoting little, few. [Gr *oligos* little, few]
■ **oligaemia** /ol-i-gē'mi-ə or -jē'mi-ə/ *n* abnormal deficiency of blood. **oligae'mic** *adj*. **ol'igarch** /-ärk/ *n* (Gr *archē* rule) a member of an oligarchy. **oligarch'al, oligarch'ic** or **oligarch'ical** *adj*. **oligarch'ically** *adv*. **ol'igarchy** /-är-ki/ *n* government by a small exclusive class; a state so governed; a small body of people who have the supreme power of a state in their hands. **oligist** /ol'i-jist/ *n* (Fr *fer oligiste*, from *fer* iron, and Gr *oligistos*, superlative of *oligos* little; as

containing less iron than magnetite; *mineralogy*) crystallized haematite. **Oligocene** /ol'i-gə-sēn/ *adj* (Gr *kainos* new; as having few fossil molluscs of living species; *geol*) of or belonging to an epoch of the Tertiary period, between 34 and 23 million years ago (also *n*). **oligochaete** /ol'i-gə-kēt/ *n* (Gr *chaitē* bristle) any worm of the **Oligochae'ta**, chaetopods in which the locomotor organs are reduced to bristles, eg earthworms, etc. **oligochrome** /ol'i-gə-krōm/ *adj* (Gr *chrōma* colour) painted in few colours (also *n*). **oligoclase** /ol'i-gə-klās or -klāz/ *n* (Gr *klāsis* cleavage, because thought to have a less perfect cleavage than albite; *mineralogy*) a soda-lime triclinic feldspar. **oligocythaemia** /ol-i-gō-sī-thē'mi-ə/ *n* (Gr *kytos* a vessel, and *haima* blood) a deficiency of red cells in the blood. **olig'omer** *n* a polymer made up of two, three or four monomer units. **oligom'erous** *adj* (Gr *meros* a part) having few parts; having fewer members than the other whorls of a flower. **oligonū'cleotide** *n* a nucleic acid with few nucleotides. **oligopep'tide** *n* a peptide composed of no more than ten amino acids. **oligop'olist** *n*. **oligopolist'ic** *adj*. **oligopoly** /ol-i-gop'ə-li/ *n* (Gr *pōleein* to sell) a situation in which there are few sellers of a particular product or service, and a small number of competitive firms control the market. **oligopsonist'ic** *adj*. **oligopsony** /ol-i-gop'sə-ni/ *n* (Gr *opsōnia* purchase of food) a situation in which a few large buyers purchase all or most of the output of a particular industry, each competitive buyer influencing the market. **oligosaccharide** /-sak'ə-rīd/ *n* a complex sugar containing between two and ten monosaccharide units linked together. **oligosperm'ia** *n* the condition of having an abnormally low number of sperm cells in the semen, a major cause of male infertility. **oligotrophic** /-trof'-/ *adj* (Gr *trophē* nourishment) (of a lake) having steep, rocky shores and scanty littoral vegetation, lacking in nutrients but rich in oxygen at all levels. **oligot'rophy** *n*. **oliguria** /o-li-gū'ri-ə/ *n* (Gr *ouron* urine; *med*) scantiness of urine secretion in proportion to liquid intake. **oligu'ric** *adj*.

olingo /ol-ing'gō/ *n* (*pl* **oling'os**) a nocturnal tree-dwelling animal of Central and South America. [Sp, from Quichean (native language in Guatemala) *ullimko* loud-yeller]
■ **olinguito** /ol-ing-gwē'tō/ *n* (*pl* **olingui'tos**) (Sp dimin sfx *-ito*) a small animal related to the olingo, living in the forests of Colombia and Ecuador.

olio /ō'li-ō/ *n* (*pl* **o'lios**) a savoury dish of different sorts of meat and vegetables; a mixture; a medley; a miscellany; a variety entertainment. [Sp *olla*, from L *ōlla* a pot; cf **olla**]

oliphant /ol'i-fənt/ *n* an obsolete form of **elephant**; an ancient ivory hunting-horn.

olitory /ol'i-tə-ri/ *adj* relating to kitchen vegetables. ◆ *n* a kitchen garden; a pot herb. [L (*h*)*olitor* gardener, from (*h*)*olus*, (*h*)*oleris* a pot herb or vegetable]

olive /ol'iv/ *n* a tree (*Olea europaea*) cultivated round the Mediterranean for its oily fruit; extended to many more or less similar trees; the small oval stoned fruit of the olive tree, yellowish-green when unripe, ripening to a shiny black, with bitter-tasting flesh; a colour like the unripe olive; a person of olive-coloured complexion; an olive-shaped or oval object of various kinds; the wood of an olive tree; peace, of which the olive-leaf or branch was the emblem; a gastropod mollusc (genus *Oliva*) of warm seas with an olive-shaped shell; a small rolled and stuffed piece of meat, as in *beef olive*. ◆ *adj* of a yellowish-green colour like the olive. [Fr, from L *olīva*]
■ **olivā'ceous** *adj* olive-coloured; olive-green. **ol'ivary** *adj* olive-shaped; of or relating to two masses of tissue (the **olivary bodies**) situated on the medulla oblongata. **olivenite** /ō-liv'ə-nīt or ol'iv-/ *n* a mineral, hydrated copper arsenate, often olive-coloured. **ol'ivet** *n* an olive-shaped button; an oval mock-pearl used in trade with primitive peoples in Africa. **olivine** /ol'iv-ēn/ *n* an orthorhombic rock-forming mineral, silicate of iron and magnesium, often olive-green, often found, altered (qv under **alter¹**), as serpentine.
□ **o'live-back** *n* a N American forest thrush (*Hylocichla ustulata*). **olive branch** *n* a branch of an olive tree as a symbol of peace; something which shows a desire for peace or reconciliation; a child (Psalm 128.3; *Prayer Book*). **olive drab** *n* the olive green of American military uniforms. **olive-drab'** *adj*. **olive green** *n* a dull dark yellowish green. **olive-green'** *adj*. **olive oil** *n* oil pressed from the fruit of the olive. **ol'ive-shell** *n* the shell of the mollusc Oliva. **ol'ive-yard** *n* a piece of ground on which olives are grown. **ol'ivine-rock** *n* dunite.

Oliver¹ /ol'i-vər/ *n* the comrade-in-arms of Roland (qv).

Oliver² see **Bath Oliver** under **Bath**.

oliver /ol'i-vər/ *n* a forge-hammer worked by foot. [Origin unknown]

Oliverian /ol-i-vē'ri-ən/ *n* an adherent of the Protector, *Oliver* Cromwell (1599–1658).

Olivetan /o-li-vē'tən/ *n* one of an order of Benedictine monks founded in 1313, the original house being at Monte *Oliveto*, near Siena.

olla /ol'ə, ō'la or ō'lyä/ *n* a jar or urn; an olio. [L *ōlla* and Sp *olla* pot]

❑ **olla-podrida** /ol'yä-pö-drē'dä/ n (Sp, rotten pot) a Spanish mixed stew or hash of meat and vegetables; any incongruous mixture or miscellaneous collection.

ollav or **ollamh** /ol'äv/ n a learned man among the ancient Irish. [Ir *ollamh*]

ollie /ol'i/ n in skateboarding and snowboarding, a jump into the air with the feet still touching the board, performed by pushing the tail of the board down with the back foot. [Perh from *Ollie*, nickname of Alan Gelfand (born 1963), US skateboarder]

olm /olm or ōlm/ n a blind, cave-dwelling, eel-like salamander of Europe (*Proteus anguinus*). [Ger]

Olmec /ol'mek/ n (pl **Olmec** or **Olmecs**) (a member of) a Native American people who lived in Mexico before the Mayas; the language spoken by this people. ◆ *adj* of or relating to the Olmec or their language.

ology /ol'ə-ji/ (*facetious*) n a science whose name ends in -(o)logy; any science.
■ **ol'ogist** n a scientist.

-ology a non-standard form of **-logy**.

oloroso /ō- or o-la-rō'sō or -zō/ n (pl **oloro'sos**) a golden-coloured medium-sweet sherry. [Sp, fragrant]

olpe /ol'pē/ n a Greek jug. [Gr *olpē*]

olykoek or **olycook** /ol'i-kook/ (*US*) n a kind of doughnut. [Du *oliekoek*, literally, oil-cake]

Olympus /ə-lim'pəs/ n the name of several mountains, *esp* of one in Thessaly, in Greek mythology the abode of the greater Greek gods; heaven. [Gr *Olympos*]
■ **Olym'pia** n a district in Elis, also the city of Pisa in it, where the Olympic games in honour of Olympian Zeus were celebrated. **Olym'piad** n in ancient Greece, a period of four years, being the interval from one celebration of the Olympic games to another, used in reckoning time (the traditional date of the first games being 776BC); in ancient Greece, a celebration of the Olympic games; a celebration of the modern Olympic games; (sometimes without *cap*) an international contest in bridge, chess, etc. **Olym'pian** n a dweller on Olympus, any of the greater gods, *esp* Zeus (*Gr myth*); a godlike person; a citizen or inhabitant of ancient Olympia; a competitor in the Olympic games. ◆ *adj* of Olympus; godlike; of Olympia (now *rare*). **Olym'pic** *adj* of Olympia; of Olympus (now *rare*); of the Olympic games. **Olym'pics** n pl the Olympic games, *esp* those of modern times; (sometimes without *cap*) an international contest in a non-athletic pastime.
❑ **Olympic games** n pl in ancient Greece, the games celebrated every four years at Olympia; the quadrennial international athletic contests held at various centres since 1896 (see also **paralympics**). **Olympic torch** n since 1936, a lighted torch brought from Olympia, Greece, to kindle the **Olympic flame**, which burns throughout the Olympic games.
■ **Winter Olympics** international contests in skiing, skating, and other winter sports, held every four years.

OM *abbrev*: Old Measurement; Order of Merit.

Om or **om** /ōm or om/ n a sacred syllable intoned as part of Hindu devotion and contemplation, symbolizing the Vedic scriptures, the three worlds (earth, atmosphere and air), and the Absolute. [Sans]

-oma /-ō-mə/ n combining form (pl **-ō'mas** or **-ō'mata**) denoting a tumour, abnormal growth, etc, as in *carcinoma, angioma, glioma*, etc. [Gr ending of nouns formed from verbs with infinitive -*oun*]

omadhaun /om'ə-dön/ (*Irish*) n a fool. [Ir *amadan*]

Omani /ō-mä'ni/ *adj* of or relating to the Sultanate of *Oman* in the Arabian Gulf, or its inhabitants. ◆ *n* a native or citizen of Oman.

omasum /ō-mā'səm/ n (pl **omā'sa**) a ruminant's third stomach, the psalterium or manyplies. [L *omāsum* ox tripe; a Gallic word]
■ **omā'sal** *adj*.

Omayyad see **Umayyad**.

ombre /om'bər, -brä or um'bər/ n a game played with a pack of forty cards, *usu* by three players, one against the others; the solo player. [Sp *hombre* a man, from L *homō, -inis*]

ombré /om'brä/ *adj* (of a fabric, etc) with colours or tones blending into each other to give a shaded or striped effect. [Fr, *pap* of *ombrer* to shade]

ombrella see **umbrella**.

ombro- /om-bro- or -brə-/ combining form denoting rain. [Gr *ombros* a rain-storm]
■ **ombrogenous** /-broj'in-əs/ *adj* thriving in, or dependent on, wet conditions. **ombrom'eter** n a rain gauge. **om'brophil** /-fil/ or **om'brophile** /-fīl/ n (Gr *philos* friend) a plant tolerant of much rain. **ombroph'ilous** *adj*. **om'brophobe** n (Gr *phobos* fear) a plant intolerant of much rain. **ombroph'obous** *adj*.

ombú or **ombu** /om-boo'/ n (pl **ombús'** or **ombus'**) a S American tree, a species of *Phytolacca*, that grows isolated in the pampas. [Sp, from Guaraní *umbú*]

Ombudsman /om'bŭdz-man or -mən/ n (pl **Om'budsmen**) (also without *cap*) *orig* in Sweden and Denmark a 'grievance man', an official who is appointed to investigate complaints against the Administration; in Britain officially 'Parliamentary Commissioner for Administration', an independent official who investigates complaints made by individuals against government departments; (often without *cap*) any official with a similar function. [Swed, representative]

OME *abbrev*: Office of Manpower Economics.

-ome /-ōm/ n combining form denoting a mass, as in *rhizome, biome*. [Gr -*ōma*]

omega /ō'mi-gə or -mä' or (*US*) -mē'/ n the last letter of the Greek alphabet, long o (Ω, ω); the conclusion; as a numeral ω' = 800, ,ω = 800 000; used as a symbol for **ohm**. [Late Gr *ō mega* great O (opposed to *omicron*); the earlier Gr name of the letter was ō]
❑ **omega fatty acid** n a fatty acid, found in unsaturated fat, belonging to one of two groups (**omega-3 fatty acids** and **omega-6 fatty acids**) regarded as beneficial in combating heart disease, depression, etc.

omelette or (*esp US*) **omelet** /om'lit or -lət/ n a savoury dish made of eggs beaten and fried in a pan (with or without cheese, herbs, ham or other addition). [Fr *omelette*, earlier *amelette*, apparently by change of suffix and metathesis from *alemelle* (*l'alemelle* for *la lemelle*) a thin plate, from L *lāmella, lāmina* a thin plate]

omen /ō'mən/ n a sign of some future event, either good or evil; threatening or prognosticating character; an event prognosticated (*Shakesp*). ◆ *vt* to portend. [L *ōmen, -inis*]
■ **o'mened** *adj* affording or attended by omens, *esp* as combining form, as in *ill-omened*.

omentum /ō-men'təm/ (*zool*) n (pl **omen'ta**) a fold of peritoneum proceeding from one of the abdominal viscera to another. [L *ōmentum*]
■ **omen'tal** *adj*.
■ **great omentum** the epiploon, a hanging flap of the peritoneum covering the intestines.

omeprazole /ō-mep'rə-zōl/ n a drug used in the treatment of gastric ulcers and heartburn.

omer /ō'mər/ n a Hebrew dry measure containing about $2\frac{1}{4}$ litres, $\frac{1}{10}$ epha; (with *cap*; *Judaism*) the seven-week period between the second day of Passover and the first day of Shavuoth, at the start of which an omer of grain or sheaf of corn is offered as a sacrifice. [Heb '*ōmer*]

omertà or **omerta** /ō-mer'tə/ n the Mafia code of honour requiring silence about criminal activities and stressing the disgrace of informing; a criminal conspiracy of silence. [Ital, dialect form of *umiltà* humility]

OMG *abbrev*: Oh my God!

omicron /ō-mī'kron, ō'mi- or om'i-/ n the fifteenth letter of the Greek alphabet, short o (O, o); as a numeral o' = 70, ,o = 70 000. [Late Gr *o mīcron* little O (opposed to *omega*); the earlier Greek name of the letter was *ou*]

ominous /om'i-nəs/ *adj* relating to, or containing, an omen; portending evil; inauspicious. [L *ōminōsus*, from *ōmen, -inis* an omen]
■ **om'inously** *adv*. **om'inousness** n.

omit /ə- or ō-mit'/ vt (**omitt'ing**; **omitt'ed**) to leave out; to fail (to do something, etc); to fail to use, perform; to disregard (*Shakesp*); to leave off, let go (*Shakesp*). [L *omittere, omissum*, from *ob-* in front, and *mittere, missum* to send]
■ **omiss'ible** *adj* that may be omitted. **omission** /-mish'n/ n the act of omitting; a thing omitted. **omiss'ive** *adj* omitting, of the nature of omission. **omiss'iveness** n. **omitt'ance** n (*Shakesp*) omission. **omitt'er** n.

omlah /om'lä/ n a staff of officials in India. [Ar '*umalā*]

ommateum /o-mə-tē'əm/ (*zool*) n (pl **ommate'a**) a compound eye. [Gr *omma, -atos* an eye]
■ **ommatid'ium** n (pl **ommatid'ia**) a simple element of a compound eye. **ommatophore** /-at'ə-fōr or -för/ n an eyestalk, as in snails.

omneity /om-nē'i-ti/ or **omniety** /om-nī'i-ti/ (*rare*) n allness, the condition of being all. [L *omnis* all]

omni- /om-ni/ combining form denoting all. [L *omnis* all]
■ **omniana** /-ä'nə or -ā'nə/ n pl miscellaneous collectable items about all sorts of things. **omnibenev'olence** n universal good will. **omnibenev'olent** *adj*. **omnicom'petence** n competence in all matters. **omnicom'petent** *adj*. **omnidirec'tional** *adj* acting in all directions. **omnidirectional'ity** n. **omnidirec'tionally** *adv*. **omnifa'rious** *adj* of all kinds. **omnifa'riously** *adv*. **omnifa'riousness** n. **omnif'erous** *adj* bearing or producing all kinds. **omnif'ic** *adj* all-creating. **omnif'icent** /-i-sənt/ *adj* all-creating. **omnif'icence** n. **om'niform** *adj* of, or capable of, every form. **omniform'ity** n. **om'nify**

vt (*rare*) to make universal. **omnigenous** /-nij'i-nəs/ *adj* of all kinds. **omnipar'ity** *n* general equality. **omnip'arous** *adj* producing all things. **omnipa'tient** *adj* enduring all things. **omnip'otence** or **omnip'otency** *n* unlimited power. **omnip'otent** *adj* all-powerful. **omnip'otently** *adv*. **omnipres'ence** *n* the quality of being present everywhere at the same time. **omnipres'ent** *adj*. **om'nirange** *n* a VHF radio navigation system in which transmitters on the ground allow a pilot to plot his or her exact position. **omnishambles** *n sing* (*sl*) a state of total confusion. **omniscience** /om-nis'i-əns, -nish'əns or -yəns/ *n* knowledge of all things. **omnisc'ient** *adj* all-knowing. **omnisc'iently** *adv*. **om'nivore** *n* an omnivorous person or animal. **omniv'orous** *adj* all-devouring; feeding on both animal and vegetable food (*zool*). **omniv'orously** *adv*. **omniv'orousness** *n*. **omniv'ory** *n* omnivorousness.

omnibus /om'ni-bəs/ *n* (*pl* **om'nibuses**) a large road vehicle for carrying a considerable number of passengers of the general public, etc (now *usu* in shortened form **bus**); an omnibus box; an omnibus book; an omnibus edition; a waiter's or waitress's assistant. ◆ *adj* widely comprehensive; of miscellaneous contents. [Literally, for all, dative pl of L *omnis*]
❑ **omnibus book** *n* a book containing reprints of several works or items, *usu* by a single author, or on a single subject, or of the same type. **omnibus box** *n* a theatre box with room for a number of people. **omnibus clause** *n* (eg *insurance*) one that covers many different cases. **omnibus edition** *n* (*TV* and *radio*) a programme comprising or edited from all the preceding week's editions of a particular series. **omnibus train** *n* one that stops at every station.

omnicompetence…to…**omnishambles** see under **omni-**.

omnium /om'ni-əm/ *n* a Stock Exchange term for the aggregate value of the different stocks in which a loan is funded; a cycling competition consisting of several different types of race, with points being awarded for performance in each. [L, of all; genitive pl of *omnis* all]
❑ **omnium-gath'erum** *n* (*inf*; *pseudo-L*) a miscellaneous collection.

omnivore, **omnivorous**, etc see under **omni-**.

omohyoid /ō-mō-hī'oid/ (*anat*) *adj* relating to the shoulder-blade and hyoid. ◆ *n* the muscle joining these. [Gr *ōmos* shoulder]

omophagia /ō-mə-fā'jyə or -ji-ə/ *n* the eating of raw flesh, *esp* as a religious observance (also **omophagy** /ō-mof'ə-ji/). [Gr *ōmophagiā*, from *ōmos* raw, and *phagein* to eat]
■ **omophagic** /-faj'ik/ or **omophagous** /-mof'ə-gəs/ *adj*.

omophorion /ō-mə-fō'ri-on or -fō'/ *n* an Eastern bishop's vestment like the pallium. [Gr *ōmophorion*, from *ōmos* shoulder, and *pherein* to carry]

omoplate /ō'mə-plāt/ *n* the shoulder-blade or scapula. [Gr *ōmoplatē*, from *ōmos* shoulder, and *platē* blade]

OMOV /ō'mov/ *abbrev* : one member one vote.

omphacite /om'fə-sīt/ (*mineralogy*) *n* a grass-green pyroxene. [Gr *omphax*, *-akos* an unripe grape]

omphalos /om'fə-los/ *n* the navel; a boss; a stone at Delphi believed to mark the centre of the world; a centre. [Gr *omphalos* navel]
■ **omphalic** /-fal'ik/ *adj*. **om'phaloid** *adj* navel-like. **om'phalomancy** *n* divination of the number of future children from the knots in the navel-string.

OMR (*comput*) *abbrev* : optical mark recognition.

omrah /om'rä/ *n* a Muslim lord. [Hindi *umrā*, orig pl of Ar *amīr*]

ON *abbrev* : Old Norse; Ontario (Canadian province).

on /on/ *prep* in contact with the upper, supporting, outer or presented surface of; to a position in contact with such a surface of; in or to a position or state of being supported by; having for basis, principle or condition; subject to; in a condition or process of; towards or to; directed towards; in the direction of; against; applied to; with action applied to; with inclination towards; close to, beside; exactly or very nearly at; at the time, date or occasion of; very little short of; just after; concerning, about; with respect to; by (in oaths and adjurations); at the risk of; assigned to; in addition to; at the expense of, or to the disadvantage of (*inf*); in (*obs*); (of gaining or taking) from (*Shakesp* and *Milton*); of (*obs* or *dialect*); (of marriage) to (*Scot*); (of waiting) for (*Scot*). ◆ *adv* in or into a position on something; towards something; in advance; on the way to being drunk (*sl*); forward; in continuance; in or into, or allowing connection, supply, activity, operation or validity; in progress; on the stage, the table, the fire, the programme, the menu, etc; not off. ◆ *interj* forward! proceed! ◆ *adj* relating to the onside of a cricket field; in a condition expressed by the adverb *on*; agreed upon; acceptable (*inf*); practicable, feasible (*inf*); willing to participate in an activity, bet, etc. ◆ *vi* to go on (*inf*); (with *with*) to put on (*inf*). [OE *on*; Du *aan*; ON *ā*; Ger *an*; Gr *ana*]
■ **onward** /on'wərd/ *adj* going on; advancing; advanced. ◆ *adv* (also **on'wards**) towards a place or time in advance or in front; forward; in continuation of forward movement. **on'wardly** *adv* (*rare*).

❑ When compounds in this list can be used as both an adjective and adverb, the stress generally falls on the first syllable in adjectival use, but at the end of the word in adverbial use: **on-and-off'** *adj* off-and-on, intermittent, occasional. **on'-board'** or **on'board** *adj* on, installed inside or carried aboard a vehicle or craft. **oncome** /on'kum or -kəm/ *n* (*Scot*) a coming on; a sudden fall of rain or snow; the beginning of an attack by an insidious disease. **on'coming** *n* an approach. ◆ *adj* advancing; approaching. **on'cost** *n* overhead expenses (see also **oncosts** below); an oncostman. ◆ *adj* paid by time; causing oncost or oncosts. **on'costman** *n* a mine worker paid by the day. **on'costs** *n pl* all items of expenditure that cannot be allocated to a specific job. **on'ding** *n* (*Scot*) onset, *esp* a sudden fall of rain or snow. **on drive** *n* (*cricket*) a drive to the onside. **on'-drive** *vi* and *vt*. **on'fall** *n* an attack or onslaught, *esp* (*Scot*) of illness; a fall of rain or snow (*Scot*). **on'flow** *n* a flowing on; an onward flow. **on'going** *n* a going on; a course of conduct; an event; (in *pl*) proceedings or behaviour, *esp* misbehaviour. **on'-going** *adj* currently in progress; continuing; which will not stop. **on'-job** *adj* combined with or in the course of normal work duties and conditions. **on'-job** (or **on'-the-job**) **training** *n* the part of a training course in which a trainee actually works on the job, *usu* at the workplace and under supervision. **on'-lend** *vt* to lend (money which has already been borrowed from another company, etc). **on'-licence** *n* a licence to sell alcoholic liquors for consumption on the premises. **on'line** or **on'-line** *adj* and *adv* (*comput*) attached to, and under the direct control of, the central processing unit; obtained from or by means of online equipment or data; connected to, or available through, the Internet or other computer network; taking place as part of, or relating to, a continuous (*esp* production) process. **onlī'ner** or **on-lī'ner** *n* (*inf*) a person who uses the Internet. **on'looker** *n* someone who is watching, a looker on, observer. **on'looking** *adj*. **on-mess'age** *adv* and *adj* (*politics*) following the approved party line. **on-off'** *adj* (of a switch, etc) which can be set to one of only two positions, either on or off; (of a relationship) not steady. **on'rush** *n* a rushing forward. **on'-screen** *adj* and *adv* as displayed or portrayed on a TV or computer screen. **on'set** *n* a violent attack; an assault; a storming; the beginning or outset. **on'setter** *n* (*archaic*) an assailant. **on'setting** *n* incitement. **onshore** /on'shōr or -shōr/ *adj* on or towards the land or shore. **on-shore'** *adv*. **onside'** *adj* and *adv* (*football*, etc) not offside. ◆ *n* /on'sīd/ (*cricket*) that half of the field on the side on which the batsman stands when waiting to receive the ball, the legside. **on'-site** *adj* and *adv* (working, happening, etc) on a site. **on'-stage** *adj* and *adv* on a part of the stage visible to the audience. **onstead** /on'sted/ *n* (*Scot*) a farmstead; a farmhouse with its offices; the offices alone. **on'-stream** *adj* and *adv* (of an industrial plant, etc) in or going into operation or production; passing through or along a pipe, system, etc (also *fig*). **on'to** *prep* to a place or position on (also **on to**); to the whole of (*maths*). ◆ *adj* (*maths*) describing a mapping of one set to a second set, involving every element of the latter. **on-trend'** *adj* fashionable.
■ **on and off** off and on, intermittently, occasionally. **on and on** (**and on**) used in phrases containing the particle *on* to emphasize duration, distance, etc. **on stream** same as **on-stream** above. **on to** see **onto** above; forward to; aware of, cognizant of (*inf*). **you're on!** (*inf*) I agree to your proposal, terms, etc.

-on /-ən or -on/ *n combining form* indicating: (1) an elementary particle; (2) a quantum component or molecular unit; (3) a chemical substance.

on- /on-/ a dialect form of the prefix **un-**.

onager /on'ə-jər/ *n* the wild ass of Central Asia; an ancient military engine for throwing great stones. [L, from Gr *onagros*, from *onos* an ass, and *agrios* wild]

Onagra /on'ə-grə/ (*bot*) *n* an old name for *Oenothera*, giving name to the family **Onagrā'ceae**. [Gr *onagrā*, the plant also known as *oinothēras*; see **Oenothera**]
■ **onagrā'ceous** *adj*.

onanism /ō'nə-ni-zm/ *n* masturbation; coitus interruptus. [After the biblical *Onan*, son of Judah; see Genesis 38.9]
■ **o'nanist** *n*. **onanist'ic** *adj*.

ONC *abbrev* : Ordinary National Certificate (a qualification now replaced by the BTEC National Certificate).

once /wons or wuns/ *adv* a single time; on one occasion; at a former time; at any time; at some time in the future (*rare*); firstly (*obs*); in short (*obs*). ◆ *n* one time. ◆ *adj* former. ◆ *conj* when once; as soon as. [OE *ānes*, orig genitive of *ān* one, used as adv]
■ **onc'er** *n* a d1 note (*sl*); someone who or something that does a particular thing only once; an MP who is considered likely to serve only one term (*Aust*); someone who goes to church once on Sunday (*church sl*).
❑ **once-accent'ed** *adj* (*music*) marked with one accent, applied to the octave beginning with middle C. **once'-errand** see **errand**. **once-for-all'** *adj* done, etc, once and for all. **once-o'ver** *n* a single comprehensive survey; a quick (sometimes casual) examination; a violent beating.

■ **all at once** suddenly; all at the same time, simultaneously. **at once** without delay; alike; at the same time. **for once** on one occasion only. **once again** or **once more** one more time, as before. **once and again** more than once; now and then. **once** (or **once and**) **for all** once only and not again. **once in a way** or **while** occasionally; rarely. **once or twice** a few times. **once upon a time** at a certain time in the past, the usual formula for beginning a fairy tale.

onchocerciasis /ong-kō-sər-kī'ə-sis/ n a disease of humans, also known as **river blindness**, common in tropical regions of America and Africa, caused by infestation by a filarial worm (*Onchocerca volvulus*), transmitted by various species of black fly, and characterized by subcutaneous nodules and very often blindness. [Gr *onkos* a hook, and *kerkos* a tail]

oncidium /on-sid'i-əm/ n an orchid of the tropical American genus *Oncidium*. [Gr *onkos* a hook]

onco- /ong-kō-, -kə- or -ko-/ *combining form* denoting a tumour. [Gr *onkos* bulk, mass or tumour]
■ **on'cogen** /-kə-jen/ n an agent causing oncogenesis. **on'cogene** /-kə-jēn/ n a gene, which may be carried by a virus, that affects the normal metabolism of a cell in such a way that it becomes cancerous. **oncogen'esis** n the formation of cancerous tumours. **oncogenet'icist** n someone who studies oncogenes. **oncogenic** /-kə-jen'/ adj of a virus, able to cause cancer, *esp* of one carrying an oncogene. **oncogenicity** /-is'i-ti/ n. **oncological** /-ə-loj'/ adj. **oncol'ogist** n. **oncol'ogy** n the study of tumours. **oncol'ysis** n the destruction of tumours. **oncolyt'ic** adj and n. **oncom'eter** n an instrument for measuring variations in the bulk of bodily organs. **On'coMouse**® n the name given to a strain of mouse, developed by Harvard University for research purposes, into which a human cancer gene has been introduced. **on'cornavirus** n an oncogenic RNA virus. **oncot'omy** n incision into a tumour.

oncome, oncoming see under **on**.

Oncorhynchus /ong-kə-ring'kəs/ n a N Pacific genus of salmon. [Gr *onkos* hook, and *rhynchos* beak]

oncost, oncostman see under **on**.

oncus see **onkus**.

OND *abbrev*: Ordinary National Diploma (a qualification now replaced by the BTEC National Diploma).

ondansetron /on-dan'si-tron/ n a drug used to treat vomiting and nausea, *esp* that resulting from chemotherapy or radiotherapy.

ondatra /on-dat'rə/ n the musquash. [Huron (Native American language)]

Ondes Martenot (or **ondes Martenot**) /5d mär-tə-nō'/ or **ondes musicales** /mü-zi-kal'/ (music) n pl an electronic musical instrument, an early form of synthesizer, with a keyboard and thermionic valve oscillators. [Fr, Martenot waves (or musical waves), from its French inventor, Maurice *Martenot* (1898–1980)]

ondine same as **undine**.

onding see under **on**.

on-dit /5-dē'/ n (pl **on-dits** /-dē'/ or -dēz'/) rumour; hearsay. [Fr]

one /won or wun/ n the number unity; a symbol representing that number (1, i, etc); an individual thing or person, identified by implied reference to a known noun, as in *two red pens and a blue one*; a joke, as in *the one about ...* (*inf*); a drink, as in *a quick one* (*inf*); a score of one point, stroke, trick, etc; an article of a size denoted by 1; the first hour after midnight or midday; the age of one year. ◆adj single; of unit number; undivided; the same; a certain; a single but not specified; only; an emphatic word for *a*, as in *That is one big problem* (*inf*); first; one year old. ◆*pronoun* somebody; anybody; I, me (*formal*). [OE *ān*; ON *einn*, Ger *ein*; L *ūnus*; Gr *oinē* ace]
■ **one'ness** n singleness; uniqueness; identity; unity; homogeneity or sameness. **oner, one-er** or **wunner** /wun'ər/ n (all meanings *inf* or *sl*) a person or thing truly unique or outstanding in any way; an expert; a single, uninterrupted action, process or operation (as in *in a oner*); a d1 note; a heavy blow; a big lie. **oneself** or **one's self** *pronoun* the emphatic and reflexive form of **one**.
❑ **one-ac'ter** n (*inf*) a one-act play. **one-and-thir'ty** n an old card game like vingt-et-un, with the aim of making the pips add up to 31 and no more. **one-armed bandit** see under **bandit**. **one'-day** adj (of an event, etc) lasting for one day. **one-dimen'sional** adj having only one dimension; without depth, shallow, superficial (*fig*). **one'-eyed** adj having only one eye. **one'fold** adj simple, single-minded. **one'-hand'ed** adj with, by or for one hand. **one'-horse** adj drawn by a single horse; (of a place) poor, mean, lacking amenities. **one-horse race** n a race, competition, etc, in which one particular competitor or participant is certain to win. **one'-ide'a'd** adj entirely possessed by one idea. **one'-legg'ed** adj. **one'-lin'er** n (*inf*) a short witty remark; a wisecrack, quip; a joke delivered in one sentence. **one'-man** adj of, for or done by one person (also **one'-person**; *fem* **one'-woman**). **one-man band** n a musician who carries and plays many instruments simultaneously; (also **one-man show**) an organization, activity, etc,

run very much by one person who refuses the help of others (*fig*). **one-man show** n a show performed by one person; a one-man band (*fig*) or the person running it. **one-na'tion** adj (of a country) socially integrated. **one-night'er** or **one-night stand** n a performance or performances, or anything similar, given on one single evening in one place by one or more people who then travel on to another place; a sexual relationship lasting only one night (*inf*). **one'-off** adj and n (something) made, intended, done, etc for one occasion only. **one'-one** adj one-to-one. **one-on-one** same as **one-to-one** below. **one-parent family** n a family in which, due to death, divorce, etc, the children are looked after by only one parent. **one'-piece** adj made in one piece. ◆n a garment, *esp* a swimsuit, made in one piece. **one'-shot** adj (intended to be) done, used, etc on only one occasion or for one particular purpose or project; one-off; not part of a serial. ◆n a thing that happens on one occasion only. **one-sid'ed** adj limited to one side; partial; biased; (of a competition, etc) with one person or side having a great advantage over the other; developed on one side only; turned to one side. **one-sid'edly** adv. **one-sid'edness** n. **one'-step** n a dance of US origin danced to quick march time; a piece of music for this dance. ◆vi to dance a one-step. **one'-stop** adj (of a store, etc) providing a variety of goods or services all at one source. **one'-time** adj former, past. **one'-to-one'** adj corresponding each one uniquely to one other; with one person meeting, opposing, playing, etc one other. **one'-track** adj incapable of dealing with more than one idea or activity at a time; obsessed with one idea to the exclusion of others. **one-trick pony** see under **pony**. **one-two'** n (*inf*) a blow with one fist followed by a blow with the other (*boxing*, etc; also *fig*); a movement in which a player passes the ball to another player, then runs forward to receive it again (*football*). **one-up'manship** n (title of humorous book by Stephen Potter, 1952) the art of being one up, ie scoring or maintaining an advantage over someone. **one'-way** adj proceeding, or permitting travel, or set apart for traffic, in one direction only; not requiring reciprocal action, etc; not reciprocated. **one-way glass** or **mirror** n a sheet of glass which can be looked through from one side but which appears from the other side to be a mirror. **one-world'er** n someone who subscribes to one-worldism. **one-world'ism** n a belief in the government of the world as a whole rather than as separate states and nations.
■ **all one** just the same; not important. **a** (or **the**) **one** (*inf*) a person special or remarkable in some way. **a one for** (*inf*) an enthusiast for. **at one** of one mind; reconciled (with *with*). **be made one** (*archaic*) to get married. **be one up on** to score an advantage over (another). **for one** as at least one, albeit possibly the only one, as in *I for one disagree*. **for one thing** as one reason for objection, there being potentially more. **in one** or **all in one** combined; as one unit, object, etc. **just one of those things** an unfortunate happening that must be accepted. **one and all** everyone without exception. **one another** see **another**. **one by one** singly in order. **one or two** a few.

-one /-ōn/ (*chem*) sfx denoting certain compounds, *esp* ketones.

oneiric or **oniric** /ō-nī'rik/ (*rare*) adj belonging to dreams. [Gr *oneiros* a dream]
■ **oneirocrit'ic** n (Gr *kritikos* judging) an interpreter of dreams. **oneirocrit'ical** adj. **oneirocrit'icism** n. **oneirodynia** /-ə-din'i-ə/ n (Gr *odynē* pain) troubled sleep; a nightmare. **oneirology** /on-ī-rol'ə-ji/ n (see **-logy**) the study of dreams. **oneir'omancer** n. **oneir'omancy** n (see **-mancy**) divination by dreams. **oneiros'copist** n (see **-scopy**) an interpreter of dreams. **oneiros'copy** n.

onely a Spenserian spelling of **only**.

oner see under **one**.

onerous /on'ə-rəs or ō'nə-rəs/ adj burdensome; oppressive. [L *onerōsus*, from *onus* a burden]
■ **on'erously** adv. **on'erousness** n.

onesie /won'zē/ n a soft, loose-fitting, one-piece garment worn by adults for sleeping or lounging. [From *Onesie*, trademark for a similar garment for infants]

oneyre or **oneyer** /ō'nər/ n a word found in the phrase **great oneyers** (*Shakesp, 1 Henry IV* II.i.74), *poss* meaning merely 'great ones'. [-*yer* explained as the suffix in *lawyer*, etc]

onfall...to...ongoing see under **on**.

onion /un'yən/ n a pungent edible bulb of the lily family; the plant yielding it (*Allium cepa*); applied also to some related species; in World War I, a flaming rocket used against aircraft; the head (*sl*). ◆vt to apply an onion to; to produce by means of an onion. [Fr *oignon*, from L *ūniō, -ōnis* union, a large pearl, an onion; see **union** under **Unio**]
■ **on'iony** adj.
❑ **onion dome** n a bulb-shaped dome having a sharp point, characteristic of Eastern Orthodox, *esp* Russian, church architecture. **onion fly** n an insect, *Delia antiqua*, whose larvae are a serious pest of onions. **on'ion-skin** n a very thin variety of paper.
■ **know one's onions** (*inf*) to know one's subject or job well. **off one's onion** (*sl*) off one's head.

---

oniric, etc see **oneiric**.

Oniscus /ə-nis'kəs/ n a genus of woodlice. [Gr *oniskos*, dimin of *onos* an ass]
■ **onis'coid** adj of the family of *Oniscus*; like a woodlouse.

onkus or **oncus** /ong'kəs/ (*Aust inf*) adj disordered; bad. [Ety unknown]

onliest see under **only**.

onlooker, etc see under **on**.

only /ōn'li/ adj single in number; without others of the same kind; without others worth considering. ◆ *adv* not more, other, or otherwise than; alone; merely; barely; just; pre-eminently (*obs*); singly (*rare*). ◆ *conj* but; except that. ◆ *prep* (*dialect*) except. [OE *ānlic* (adj), from *ān* one, and *-līc* like]
■ **onliest** /ōn'li-əst/ adj (*dialect*) only.
■ **if only** (as an expression of vain desire or regret) would that, I wish; if for no reason other than (to do something). **only too** very, extremely.

ono or **o.n.o.** abbrev : or near (or nearest) offer.

onocentaur /on-ə-sen'tör/ n a kind of centaur, half-man, half-ass. [Gr *onos* ass]

onomasiology /on-ə-mā-zi-ol'ə-ji/ n the study of the linguistic terms used to represent concepts; another name for **onomastics** (see under **onomastic**). [Gr *onomasia* term, and **-logy**]
■ **onomāsiolog'ical** adj.

onomastic /on-ə-mas'tik/ adj relating to a name, *esp* relating to the signature on a document written in another person's hand. [Gr *onomastikos, -on*, from *onoma* a name]
■ **onomas'tically** adv. **onomas'ticon** n a dictionary of proper names. **onomas'tics** n sing the study of the history of proper names.

onomatopoeia /on-ə-mat-ə-pē'ə/, also **onomatopoesis** /-pō-ē'sis/ or **onomatopoiesis** /-poi-ē'sis/ n the formation of a word in imitation of the sound of the thing meant; a word so formed; the use of words whose sounds help to suggest the meaning (*rhetoric*). [Gr *onomatopoiiā, -poiēsis*, from *onoma*, a name, and *poieein* to make]
■ **onomatopoeic** /-pē'ik/ or **onomatopoetic** /-pō-et'ik/ adj. **onomatopoe'ically** or **onomatopoet'ically** adv.

onrush see under **on**.

ONS abbrev : Office for National Statistics.

on-screen...to...**onside** see under **on**.

onslaught /on'slöt/ n an attack or onset; assault. [Prob Du *aanslag* or Ger *Anschlag*, refashioned as Eng]

onst /wunst/ adv a dialect form of **once**.

onstead...to...**onto** see under **on**.

ontogenesis /on-tə-jen'i-sis/ or **ontogeny** /on-toj'i-ni/ n the history of the individual development of an organized being, as distinguished from *phylogenesis*. [Gr *ōn, ontos*, prp of *einai* to be, and **genesis**]
■ **ontogenet'ic** or **ontogen'ic** adj. **ontogenet'ically** or **ontogen'ically** adv. **ontogenet'ics** n sing the study of ontogenesis.

ontology /on-tol'ə-ji/ n the science that deals with the principles of pure being; that part of metaphysics which deals with the nature and essence of things. [Gr *ōn, ontos*, prp of *einai* to be, and **-logy**]
■ **ontologic** /-tə-loj'ik/ or **ontolog'ical** adj. **ontolog'ically** adv. **ontol'ogist** n.

onus /ō'nəs/ n burden; responsibility. [L *onus, -eris* burden, weight]
▫ **onus probandi** /ō'nəs prō-ban'dī or o'nŭs pro-ban'dē/ n (*law*) the burden of proving.

onward, etc see under **on**.

onycha /on'i-kə/ n an ingredient in ancient Jewish incense; the nail-like operculum of a mollusc. [Ety as for **onyx**]
■ **onych'ia** n inflammation of the nail-bed. **on'ychite** n onyx marble. **onychī'tis** n inflammation of the soft parts about the nail. **onych'ium** n a pulvillus in insects. **onychocryptō'sis** n ingrowing toenail. **on'ychomancy** n divination by the fingernails. **onychophagist** /-kof'ə-jist/ n a nail-biter. **onychoph'agy** n. **Onychoph'ora** n pl (*zool*) the class of primitive arthropods to which *Peripatus* belongs. **onychoph'oran** n and adj.

onymous /on'i-məs/ adj bearing the author's name. [**anonymous**]

onyx /on'iks/ n an agate formed of alternate flat layers of chalcedony, white or yellow and black, brown or red, used for making cameos (*mineralogy*); onychite or onyx marble; a fingernail-like opacity in the cornea of the eye. [Gr *onyx, onychos* nail, claw, onyx]
▫ **onyx marble** n a banded travertine or stalagmite (also called **oriental alabaster**).

oo¹ or **oo'** /oo/ n Scots forms of **wool**.

oo² /oo/ pronoun a Scots form of **we**.
■ **oor** adj our.

oo- /ō-ə- or ō-o-/ combining form denoting egg. [Gr *ōion* egg]
■ **oocyst** /ō'ə-sist/ n (Gr *kystis* a bladder) in parasitic protozoa, a cyst surrounding a fertilized gamete. **oocyte** /ō'ə-sīt/ n (see **-cyte**) an ovum

before it matures and begins to divide. **oog'amous** adj. **oog'amously** adv. **oogamy** /ō-og'ə-mi/ n (see **-gamy** under **-gam-**) union of unlike gametes. **oogenesis** /ō-ə-jen'i-sis/ n (see **genesis**) the genesis and development of the ovum (also **oogeny** /ō-oj'i-ni/). **oogenet'ic** adj. **oogo'nial** adj. **oogonium** /ō-ə-gō'ni-əm/ n (pl **oogo'nia**) (Gr *gonos* offspring) the female reproductive organ in seaweeds and fungi; an immature female gamete that gives rise to oocytes. **oolite** /ō'ə-līt/ n (Gr *lithos* a stone; *geol*) a kind of limestone composed of grains like the eggs or roe of a fish; (with *cap*) stratigraphically the upper part of the Jurassic in Britain, consisting largely of oolites. **oolith** /ō'ə-lith/ n (Gr *lithos* a stone; *geol*) any of the tiny spherical grains of which oolite is composed. **oolitic** /ō-ə-lit'ik/ adj. **oolog'ical** adj. **ool'ogist** n. **oology** /ō-ol'ə-ji/ n (see **-logy**) the science or study of birds' eggs. **o'ophyte** /ō'ə-fīt/ n (see **-phyte** under **phyt-**) in ferns and mosses, the gametophyte. **oosphere** /ō'ə-sfēr/ n (Gr *sphaira* sphere) an unfertilized ovum. **oospore** /ō'ə-spōr/ or *-spör/ n (Gr *sporos* seed) a zygote, *esp* a resting zygote. **ootheca** /ō-ə-thē'kə/ n (pl **oothe'cae** /-kē/) n (Gr *thēkē* receptacle) a case containing the eggs of some insects. **ootid** /ō'ə-tid/ n an immature female gamete that develops into an ovum.

o/o abbrev : offers over (a specified sum).

oobit see **woubit**.

oocyst, **oocyte** see under **oo-**.

oodles /oo'dlz/ (*inf*) n sing or n pl abundance (also **ood'lins**). [Perh **huddle**]

oof /oof/ (old sl) n money (earlier **oof'tish**). [Yiddish, from Ger *auf (dem) Tische* on the table]
■ **oof'y** adj rich.

oogamous...to...**oogonium** see under **oo-**.

ooh /oo/ interj expressing pleasure, surprise, etc (also n and vi). [Imit]

ooidal /ō-oi'dl/ adj egg-shaped. [Gr *ōioeidēs*, from *ōion* and *eidos* form]

oolakan /oo'lə-kən/ same as **eulachon**.

oolite...to...**oology** see under **oo-**.

oolong or **oulong** /oo'long/ n a variety of black tea with the flavour of green. [Chin *wūlóng* black dragon]

oom /oom/ (*S Afr*) n uncle; used as term of respect for an elderly man. [Du]

oomiak, **oomiac**, or **oomiack** same as **umiak**.

oompah /oom'pä/ n a conventional representation of the deep sound made by a large brass musical instrument such as a tuba (also vi and vt).

oomph /ŭmf or oomf/ (*inf*) n vitality; enthusiasm; sex-appeal; personal magnetism. [Origin obscure]

oon /oon/ n a Scots form of **oven**.

oons /oonz/ (*archaic*) interj an oath. [From *God's wounds*]

oont /ŭnt/ n in India, a camel. [Hindi *ūṭ*]

OOP abbrev : object-oriented programming.

oop see **oup**.

oophoron /ō-of'ə-ron/ n (*zool*) an ovary. [Gr *ōiophoros, -on* egg-bearing]
■ **oophorec'tomize** or **-ise** vt. **oophorec'tomy** n (*surg*) removal of one or both ovaries, or of an ovarian tumour. **oophorī'tis** n inflammation of the ovary.

oophyte see under **oo-**.

oops /oops/ interj an exclamation drawing attention to or apologizing for, etc, a mistake.
▫ **oops'-a-daisy** a variant spelling of **ups-a-daisy**.

oor see under **oo²**.

oorial same as **urial**.

oorie same as **ourie**.

Oort cloud /ört klowd/ n a cloud of frozen comet nuclei orbiting the solar system. [Jan Hendrik *Oort* (1900–92), Dutch astronomer]

oose /oos/, **oosy** (both *Scot*) see **ooze²**.

oosphere...to...**ootid** see under **oo-**.

ooze¹ /ooz/ n gentle flow, as of water through sand or earth; slimy mud; a fine-grained, soft, deep-sea deposit, composed of shells and fragments of marine rhizopods, diatoms and other organisms; sap (*obs*); the liquor of a tan vat. ◆ vi to flow gently; to percolate, as a liquid through pores or small openings; to leak. ◆ vt to exude. [Partly OE *wōs* juice, partly OE *wāse* mud]
■ **ooz'ily** adv. **ooz'iness** n. **ooz'y** adj resembling ooze; slimy; oozing.

ooze² or **oose** /ooz/ (*Scot*) n fluff; nap. [Prob pl of **oo¹**]
■ **ooz'y** or **oos'y** adj.

OP abbrev : observation post (*milit*) or point; opposite prompt (*theatre*); Ordinis or Ordo Praedicatorum (L), (of) the order of Preachers, ie Dominicans; organophosphate.

op¹ /op/ (*inf*) n a military or surgical operation. [Short form of **operation**]

op² /op/ *abbrev* : operator; opposite; opus.

op³ or **o/p** *abbrev* : out of print.

opacity, opacous see under **opaque**.

opah /ō'pə/ *n* the kingfish (genus *Lampris*), a large sea-fish with laterally flattened body, constituting a family of uncertain affinities. [W African origin]

opal /ō'pl/ *n* amorphous silica with some water, *usu* milky white with fine play of colour, in some varieties precious and used as a gemstone; opal glass; the colouring of opal. ◆ *adj* of opal; like opal. [L *opalus*; Gr *opallios*, perh from Sans *upala* gem]
■ **o'paled** *adj*. **opalesc'ence** *n* a milky iridescence. **opalesc'ent** *adj*. **o'paline** /-ēn or -īn/ *adj* relating to, like or of opal. ◆ *n* opal glass; a photographic print fixed on plate glass. **o'palized** or **-s-** *adj* converted into opal; opalescent.
❑ **opal glass** *n* white or opalescent glass.

opaque /ō-pāk'/ *adj* shady; dark; dull; that cannot be seen through; impervious to light or to radiation of some particular kind; obscure, hard to understand; impervious to sense; doltish. ◆ *n* something, eg a space or medium, that is opaque; a substance used to block out areas of a negative (*photog*). ◆ *vt* to make opaque. [L *opācus*]
■ **opacity** /ō-pas'i-ti/ *n* opaqueness. **opacous** /ō-pā'kəs/ *adj* (*archaic*). **opaque'ly** *adv*. **opaque'ness** *n* the quality of being opaque; lack of transparency.

op art /op ärt/ *n* art using geometrical forms precisely executed and so arranged that movement of the observer's eye, or inability to focus, produces an illusion of movement in the painting. [*optical art*]

op cit *abbrev* : *opere citato* (*L*), in the work cited.

opcode /op'kōd/ *n* a code containing operation instructions for a microprocessor. [*operation*, and **code**]

OPCW *abbrev* : Organization for the Prohibition of Chemical Weapons.

ope /ōp/ (*poetic*) *adj*, vt and vi a short form of **open**.

OPEC /ō'pek/ *abbrev* : Organization of the Petroleum Exporting Countries.

op-ed /op'ed/ *n* and *adj* (being or relating to) a newspaper article printed *opposite* the *editorial* column, *usu* expressing the personal opinions of the writer.

opeidoscope /op-ī'də-skōp/ *n* an instrument for illustrating sound by means of light. [Gr *ops*, *opos* voice, *eidos* form, and **-scope**]

open /ō'pən/ *adj* not shut; allowing passage out or in; exposing the interior; unobstructed; free; unenclosed; exposed; uncovered; liable; generally accessible; available; ready to receive or transact business with members of the public; willing to receive or accept, amenable (with *to*); public; free to be discussed; obvious; unconcealed; undisguised; unfolded, spread out or expanded; unrestricted; not restricted to any class of people, as in *open championship*; (of a town) without military defences; not finally decided, concluded, settled or assigned; not dense in distribution or texture; widely spaced; loose; much interrupted by spaces or holes; showing a visible space between (*naut*); clear; unfrozen; not frosty; not hazy; free from trees; frank; unreserved; unstopped (*music*); without use of valve, crook or key (*music*); (of an organ pipe) not closed at the top; (of a vowel sound) low, with wide aperture for the breath; (of a consonant) without stopping of the breath stream; (of a syllable) ending with a vowel; of systems, etc, having a public specification (*comput*); permitting interoperability (*comput*). ◆ *vt* to make open; to make as an opening; to make an opening in; to clear; to expose to view; to expound; to declare open; to begin. ◆ *vi* to become open; to have an opening, aperture or passage; to serve as a passage; to begin to appear; to begin; to give tongue; to speak out. ◆ *n* a clear space; public view; open market; a competition or sporting event open to all competitors; an opening. [OE *open*; cf Du *open*, ON *opinn*, Ger *offen*; prob related to **up**]
■ **o'penable** *adj*. **o'pener** *n*. **o'pening** *n* the act of causing to be, or of becoming, open; an open place; an aperture; a gap; a street or road breaking the line of another; a beginning; a first stage; a preliminary statement of a case in court; the initial moves, or mode of beginning, in a game, etc; an event at which a new exhibition, shop, display, etc, is first opened to the public; the first performance of a play, etc; the two pages exposed together when a book is opened; an opportunity for action; a vacancy. ◆ *adj* occurring at the beginning (of something); initial; causing to become open. **o'penly** *adv*. **o'penness** *n*.
❑ **open access** *n* free and unlimited access, eg to a library or material on the Internet. **open-acc'ess** *adj*. **open adoption** *n* adoption of a child with continued contact with the true parents. **open aestivation** *n* (*bot*) aestivation without overlap or meeting of the edges of the perianth leaves. **open-air'** *adj* outdoor. **open-and-shut'** *adj* simple, obvious, easily decided. **open-armed'** *adj* cordially welcoming. **open book** *n* anything that can be read or interpreted without difficulty. **open borstal** *n* formerly, a borstal run on the same lines as an open

prison (qv below). **Open Brethren** *n pl* that section of the Plymouth Brethren whose members are allowed to associate fully with non-members. **open bundle** *n* (*bot*) a vascular bundle with cambium. **o'pen-cast** *n* (*mining*) an open excavation in the land surface (*also adj* and *adv*). **open-chain'** *adj* (*chem*) with atoms linked together like a chain with loose ends. **open cheque** *n* an uncrossed cheque which can be used to obtain cash on demand from a bank, etc. **open circuit** *n* an electrical circuit broken so that current cannot pass; in television, the customary system in which the showing is for general, not restricted, viewing. **open court** *n* a court proceeding in public. **open day** *n* a day on which an institution (*esp* a school) is open to the public, *usu* with organized exhibitions or events. **open diapason** *n* one of the chief foundation stops of an organ. **open door** *n* free and equal opportunity of trading for all; unrestricted admission or immigration. **open-door'** *adj*. **open economy** *n* one involved in overseas trade. **open-end'** or **open-end'ed** *adj* not closely defined, general and adaptable to suit various contingencies; (of a question, debate, etc) allowing free unguided answers or expressions of opinion; (of an investment trust) offering shares in unlimited numbers, redeemable on demand; (**open-end'ed**) without fixed limits. **open-end'edness** *n*. **o'pen-eyed** *adj* astonished; fully aware of what is involved; watchful (*Shakesp*). **o'pen-field** *adj* having the arable land in unenclosed strips held by different cultivators. **open fire** *n* an exposed fire on a domestic hearth. **open-hand'ed** *adj* with an open hand; generous; liberal. **open-hand'edly** *adv*. **open-hand'edness** *n*. **open harmony** *n* (*music*) chords not in close position. **open-heart'ed** *adj* with an open heart; frank; generous. **open-heart'edly** *adv*. **open-heart'edness** *n*. **o'pen-hearth** *adj* (*metallurgy*) making use of, or having, a shallow hearth of reverberating type. **open-heart surgery** *n* surgery performed on a heart that has been stopped and opened up while blood circulation is maintained by a heart-lung machine. **open house** *n* hospitality to all comers. **opening time** *n* the time when bars, public houses, etc, can begin selling alcoholic drinks. **open-jaw'** *adj* and *n* (of or relating to) a round-trip aircraft ticket or flight that allows the passenger to embark on the return flight at a different airport from the one to which he or she originally travelled. **open learning** *n* a system of learning based on individual study rather than formal classroom sessions, and using specially designed programmes of printed material, audio and video tapes, electronic media, etc. **open letter** *n* a letter addressed to one person but intended for public reading. **open market** *n* a market in which buyers and sellers compete without restriction. **open marriage** *n* a form of marriage that allows the partners social and sexual independence. **open-mic'** or **open-mike'** *adj* denoting an event, eg at a comedy club, at which members of the public are encouraged to perform. **open mind** *n* freedom from prejudice; readiness to receive and consider new ideas. **open-mind'ed** *adj*. **open-mind'edly** *adv*. **open-mind'edness** *n*. **open-mouthed'** *adj* gaping; expectant; greedy; clamorous; surprised, astonished. **open note** *n* (*music*) a note produced by an unstopped string, open pipe, or without a crook, etc; a printed or written note without a solid black head, a semibreve or minim (*US*). **open order** *n* spaced-out formation for drill, etc. **open-plan'** *adj* having few or no internal walls, partitions, etc. **open-plan house** *n* one whose rooms run from front to back with windows on both faces. **open primary** *n* (in US politics) a primary election in which all registered voters may participate. **open prison** *n* a prison without the usual close security, allowing prisoners considerably more freedom of movement than in conventional prisons. **open question** *n* a matter undecided; a question formed so as to elicit a full response or an opinion rather than a yes or no answer. **o'pen-reel** *adj* (of a tape recorder) reel-to-reel. **open sandwich** *n* one that has no bread, etc, on top. **open score** *n* (*music*) one with a separate stave for each part. **open sea** *n* unenclosed sea, clear of headlands. **open season** *n* a time of the year when one may kill certain game or fish (also *fig*). **open secret** *n* a matter known to many but not explicitly divulged. **open sesame** *n* a spell or other means of making barriers fly open (from the story of Ali Baba and the Forty Thieves in the *Arabian Nights*). **open shop** *n* a place of work not confined to union labour. **open side** *n* (*rugby*) the part of the field between the scrum, etc, and the farther touch-line. **open sights** *n pl* (*shooting*) in aiming, the eye unaided by the sights, *usu* in shooting at close range. **open skies** *n pl* the open air; reciprocal freedom for aerial inspection of military establishments; unrestricted use of *esp* commercial airports and airways. **open-source'** *adj* (*comput*) denoting a form of licensing by which software is made freely available for use and the source code can be extended or amended by third parties. **o'pen-stitch** (*Scot* **o'pen-steek**) *n* a kind of open-work stitching. **open system** *n* (*comput*) a network system complying with a set of international standards allowing general accessibility. **o'pen-top** or **o'pen-topped** *adj* (*esp* of a vehicle) without a roof or having an open top. **open town** *n* one without troops or military installations, and hence, according to international law, immune from attack of any kind. **open university** *n* (also with *caps*) a British university (founded in 1969) having no fixed entry qualifications, whose teaching is carried out by correspondence and

by radio and television, etc. **open verdict** *n* a verdict in a coroner's court that death has occurred, without specifying the cause; a verdict that a crime has been committed, without specifying the criminal. **o'pen-weave** *adj* and *n* (made of) a loosely woven fabric with visible spaces between the threads. **o'penwork** *n* any work showing openings through it, eg in embroidery. ♦ *adj* open-cast.
■ **open fire** to begin to shoot. **open out** to make or become more widely open; to expand; to disclose; to unpack; to develop; to bring into view; to open the throttle, accelerate. **open up** to open thoroughly or more thoroughly; to lay open; to disclose; to make available for traffic, colonization, etc; to accelerate; to begin firing; to become more communicative. **with open arms** cordially.

opepe /ō-pē'pē/ *n* a W African tree (*Sarcocephalus diderrichii*) yielding a hard yellowish wood used eg as a substitute for teak. [Yoruba]

opera[1] /op'(ə-)rə/ *n* musical drama; a company performing opera; an opera house. ♦ *adj* used in or for an opera. —See also **music drama, musical, musical comedy**. [Ital, from L *opera*; cf **operate**]
■ **operatic** /-at'ik/ *adj* relating to or resembling opera; (loosely) histrionic. **operat'ically** *adv*.
❑ **opera bouffe** or (*Fr*) **opéra bouffe** /o-pä-ra' boof'/ *n* funny or farcical opera. **opera buffa** /boof'ə or op'ä-ra boof'a/ *n* (*Ital*) comic opera, *esp* of the 18c, *opp* to *opera seria*. **opera cloak** *n* an elegant cloak for evening wear, *esp* in the auditorium of a theatre. **opéra comique** /kom-ēk'/ *n* (*Fr*) opera with some spoken dialogue, in the 18c having subjects less lofty than those of grand opera, in the 19c having no restriction as to subject (either comic or tragic). **op'era-dancer** *n* a dancer in ballets introduced into operas. **opera glass** or **glasses** *n* small binoculars used by audiences in the theatre. **opera hat** *n* a collapsible top hat. **opera house** *n* a theatre for opera. **opera seria** /sē'ri-ə or se'rya/ *n* (*Ital*) serious opera. **opera singer** *n*.
■ **comic opera** opéra comique; opera of an amusing nature; an absurd emotional situation. **grand opera** opera without dialogue, *esp* if the subject is very dramatic or emotional. **light opera** a lively and tuneful opera; an operetta (qv). **soap opera** see under **soap**.

opera[2] /op'ə-rə, sometimes ō'pə-/ plural of **opus**.

operate /op'ə-rāt/ *vi* to work; to exert strength; to produce any effect; to exert moral power; to be in activity, act, carry on business; to take effect upon the human system (*med*); to perform some surgical act upon the body with the hand or an instrument. ♦ *vt* to effect, bring about or cause to occur; to work; to conduct, run or carry on. [L *operārī*, *-ātus*, from *opera* work, effort, closely connected with *opus*, *operis* work]
■ **operabil'ity** *n*. **op'erable** *adj* capable of treatment by a surgical operation; able to be operated; practicable. **op'erand** *n* something on which an operation is performed, eg a quantity in mathematics or, in computing, the values on which program instructions operate. **op'erant** *adj* operative; active; effective; denoting behaviour that is spontaneous rather than responding to a stimulus (*psychol*). ♦ *n* an operator. **op'erāting** *adj*. **operā'tion** *n* (also (*inf, esp milit* or *surg*) **op**) the act or process of operating; something that is done or carried out; agency; influence; a method of working; an action or series of movements; a surgical procedure. **operā'tional** *adj* relating to operations; ready for action. **operā'tionalism** or **operā'tionism** *n* (*philos*) the theory that defines scientific concepts by means of the operations used to prove or determine them. **operā'tionalist** or **operā'tionist** *n* and *adj*. **operā'tionally** *adv*. **op'erative** *adj* having the power of operating or acting; exerting force; producing effects; efficacious. ♦ *n* a worker, *esp* one with special skills; a labourer. **op'eratively** *adv*. **op'erativeness** *n*. **op'erātor** *n* a person or thing that operates; someone responsible for the operation of a machine, instrument, or apparatus; someone employed to connect calls, etc, at a telephone exchange; someone who deals in stocks; the owner of a store, business, mine, etc (*US*); a symbol, signifying an operation to be performed (*maths*); a crooked or calculating person, a shark (*inf, esp US*); a sequence of DNA to which a repressor or an activator (a protein which increases the production of a gene product) can bind (*biol*).
❑ **operant conditioning** *n* (*psychol*) a learning procedure in which the subject's response to a stimulus is reinforced if the response is desired. **operating system** *n* (*comput*) a collection of programs that controls the activities of a computer system (also called **systems software**). **operating table** *n* the narrow table on which the patient lies during a surgical operation. **operating theatre** or **operating room** *n* a room in a hospital, etc equipped for the performing of surgical operations. **operational amplifier** *n* a very stable high-gain amplifier used in electronic circuits. **operational** or **operations research** research to discover how a weapon, tactic or strategy can be altered to give better results; similar research to promote maximum efficiency in industrial spheres. **operative words** *n pl* the words in a deed legally effecting the transaction (eg *devise and bequeath* in a will); (loosely; often in *sing*) the most significant word or words.

operculum /ō-pûr'kū-ləm/ *n* (pl **oper'cula**) a cover or lid (*bot*); the plate over the entrance of a shell (*zool*); the gill-cover of fishes; a coal-hole cover in a pavement. [L *operculum*, from *operīre* to cover]
■ **oper'cular** *adj* belonging to the operculum. **oper'culate** or **oper'culated** *adj* having an operculum.

opere citato /op'ə-rē sī-tā'tō or op'e-re ki-tä'tō/ (*L*) in the work cited (*abbrev* **op cit**).

operetta /o-pə-ret'ə/ *n* a short, light, often rather trivial, musical drama; often, *esp* formerly, light opera (see under **opera**[1]). [Ital, dimin of *opera*]
■ **operett'ist** *n* a composer of operettas.

operon /op'ə-ron/ (*biol*) *n* in bacteria, a set of functionally related genes that have a common promoter and are transcribed together. [*operate* and **-on** (2)]

operose /op'ə-rōs/ (*rare*) *adj* laborious; tedious. [L *operōsus*, from *opus*, *operis* work]
■ **op'erosely** *adv*. **op'eroseness** or **operosity** /-os'i-ti/ *n*.

ophi- /of-i-/ or **ophio-** /of-i-ō-, of-i-ə- or of-i-o-/ combining form signifying a snake. [Gr *ophis* snake]
■ **ophical'cite** *n* a marble containing green serpentine. **oph'icleide** /-klīd/ *n* (Fr *ophicléïde*, from Gr *kleis*, *kleidos* key) a keyed brass instrument developed from the serpent, a bass keybugle. **Ophid'ia** *n pl* (Gr *ophidion*, dimin of *ophis*) the snakes as an order or suborder of reptiles. **ophid'ian** *n* and *adj*. **ophidiā'rium** *n* (*rare*) a snake-house. **Ophiogloss'um** *n* (Gr *glōssa* tongue) the adder's-tongue genus, giving name to the **Ophioglossā'ceae**, a family of eusporangiate ferns. **ophiol'ater** *n* a person who worships snakes. **ophiol'atrous** *adj*. **ophiol'atry** *n* (see **-latry**) snake-worship. **oph'iolite** *n* serpentine (*obs*); a group of igneous rocks associated with deep-sea sediments; verd-antique. **ophiolit'ic** *adj*. **ophiolog'ic** or **ophiolog'ical** *adj*. **ophiol'ogist** *n*. **ophiol'ogy** *n* the study of snakes. **oph'iomorph** *n* (see **-morph**) a caecilian amphibian. **ophiomorph'ic** or **ophiomorph'ous** *adj* snakelike. **ophioph'agous** *adj* (see **-phagous** under **phag-**) snake-eating. **ophioph'ilist** *n* a snake-lover. **Oph'ism** *n* the creed or religion of the Ophites. **oph'ite** *n* a name given to various rocks mottled with green; at one time, serpentine-rock; later, a kind of diabase; (with *cap*) one of a Gnostic sect that reverenced snakes. **ophitic** /ə-fit'ik/ *adj* relating to ophite; having pyroxene crystals enclosing feldspar laths; (with *cap*) of the Ophites. **Oph'itism** *n*. **Ophiuchus** /-i-ook'əs or -ūk'/ *n* the Serpent-Bearer, a constellation between Aquila and Libra on the celestial equator. **ophiura** /-i-oo'rə or -ū'rə/ *n* (Gr *ourā* tail) a member of the *Ophiura* genus of brittlestars or sand-stars. **ophiu'ran** *n* and *adj*. **ophiu'rid** *n* and *adj*. **Ophiu'ridae** and **Ophiuroid'ea** *n pl* respectively a family and class of echinoderms like starfish with long, snaky, sharply differentiated arms, the brittlestars. **ophiu'roid** *n* and *adj*.

ophthalmo- or before a vowel often **ophthalm-** /of-thal-m(ō)-, -m(ə)- or -m(o)-/ combining form denoting eye. [Gr *ophthalmos* eye]
■ **ophthal'mia** *n* inflammation of the eye, *esp* of the conjunctiva. **ophthal'mic** *adj* relating to the eye (**ophthalmic optician** an optician qualified both to prescribe and to dispense spectacles, etc). **ophthal'mist** *n* an ophthalmologist. **ophthalmī'tis** *n* ophthalmia. **ophthalmolog'ical** *adj*. **ophthalmol'ogist** *n*. **ophthalmol'ogy** *n* the science of the eye, its structure, functions and diseases. **ophthalmom'eter** *n* an instrument for eye-measurements. **ophthalmom'etry** *n*. **ophthalmophō'bia** *n* the fear of being stared at. **ophthalmoplegia** /-plē'jyə/ *n* (see **-plegia**) paralysis of one or more of the muscles of the eye. **ophthalmoplegic** /-plēj'ik/ *adj*. **ophthal'moscope** *n* an instrument for examining the interior of the eye. **ophthalmoscop'ic** or **ophthalmoscop'ical** *adj*. **ophthalmoscop'ically** *adv*. **ophthalmos'copy** *n* examination of the interior of the eye with an ophthalmoscope.

opiate /ō'pi-āt or -ət/ *n* a drug containing opium or (loosely) a substance with similar addictive or narcotic properties (also **ō'pioid**); something that dulls sensation, physical or mental. ♦ *adj* containing or resembling opium (also **ō'pioid**); inducing sleep. ♦ *vt* /ō'pi-āt/ to treat with opium; to dull. [**opium**]
■ **o'piated** *adj*.

opificer /ə-pif'i-sər/ (*obs*) *n* an artificer. [L *opifex*, *-icis*, from *opus* work, and *facere* to make]

opine /ō-pīn'/ *vt* to suppose; to form or express as an opinion. [Fr *opiner*, from L *opīnārī* to think]
■ **opi'nable** *adj* capable of being thought.

opinicus /ə-pin'i-kəs/ (*heraldry*) *n* a composite beast, part lion, part dragon, with features of other animals. [Origin unknown]

opinion /ə-pin'yən/ *n* what seems to one to be probably true; judgement; estimation; favourable estimation; self-confidence (*Shakesp*); arrogance (*Shakesp*); reputation (*Shakesp*). [L *opīniō*, *-ōnis*]
■ **opin'ionāted**, **opin'ionātive** or **opin'ioned** *adj* unduly attached to and assertive of one's own opinions; stubborn. **opin'ionātedly** *adv*. **opin'ionātedness** *n*. **opin'ionately** (*obs*) and **opin'ionātively** *adv*.

opin'ionātiveness *n.* **opin'ionator** or (*rare*) **opin'ionist** *n* someone who holds or gives an opinion; an opinionated person.
☐ **opinion poll** *n* a test made of public opinion by questioning a representative sample of the population.
■ **a matter of opinion** a matter about which opinions differ. **be of the opinion that** to think or believe that.

opioid see **opiate**.

opisometer /op-i-som'i-tər/ *n* a map-measuring instrument with a wheel that traces a line on the map and then runs backward along a straight scale until the wheel reaches its original position on the screw that holds it. [Gr *opisō* backward, and **-meter**]

opistho- or before a vowel **opisth-** /ə-pis-thō- or -thə- or -tho-, or ə-pisth-/ *combining form* signifying behind. [Gr *opisthen* behind]
■ **opisthobranch** /ə-pis'thə-brangk/ *n* and *adj* (Gr *branchia* gills). **Opisthobranch'ia** *n pl* an order of gastropods having the gills behind the heart. **opisthocoelian** /-sē'li-ən/ *adj* (Gr *koilos* hollow) hollow or concave behind, as eg a vertebra is (also **opisthocoe'lous**). **opisthodomos** /op-is-thod'ə-mos/ *n* a rear-chamber in a Greek temple. **opisthogloss'al** *adj* (Gr *glōssa* tongue) having the tongue attached in front, free behind, as in frogs. **opisthog'nathous** *adj* (see **-gnathous** under **gnathic**) having receding jaws. **opis'thograph** *n* a manuscript or slab inscribed on the back as well as the front. **opisthograph'ic** *adj.* **opisthog'raphy** *n.* **opisthosō'ma** *n* (Gr *sōma* body) the abdomen of an arachnid. **opisthot'ic** *adj.* **opisthot'onos** *n* (Gr, drawn backwards, from *teinein* to stretch, pull tight) extreme arching backwards of the spine and neck as a result of spasm of the muscles in that region.

opium /ō'pi-əm/ *n* the dried narcotic juice of the white poppy; anything considered to have a stupefying or tranquillizing effect on people's minds, emotions, etc. [L *opium*, from Gr *opion*, dimin from *opos* sap]
■ **o'piumism** *n* (*pathol*) addiction to opium; the medical condition caused by the habitual use of opium.
☐ **opium den** *n* an establishment where opium can be smoked. **o'pium-eater** or **-smoker** *n* a person who habitually takes opium.

opobalsam /o-pə-böl'səm/ *n* balm of Gilead. [Gr *opobalsamon*, from *opos* juice, and *balsamon* balsam tree]

opodeldoc /o-pə-del'dok/ *n* a name given by Paracelsus to various local medical applications; soap liniment. [Derivation unknown, apparently Gr *opos* juice]

opopanax /ə-pop'ə-naks/ *n* a gum resin formerly used in medicine, obtained from the roots of a Persian (and S European) species of parsnip; a perfume obtained from the plant *Commiphora*. [Gr *opos* juice, and *panax* a panacea]

oporice /ə-por'i-sē/ *n* a former medicine prepared from quinces, pomegranates, etc. [Gr *opōrikē*, from *opōrā* late summer, summer fruits]

opossum /ə-pos'əm/ *n* (also (*Aust* and *US*) **possum** or (formerly) **'possum**) any member of the American genus *Didelphis*, or family Didelphidae, small marsupials, often pouchless, mainly arboreal, with prehensile tail; a phalanger (*Aust* and *NZ*); opossum-fur. [Native American]
☐ **opossum shrimp** *n* a shrimp-like crustacean of the order Mysidacea, the female of which carries her eggs and young in a brood pouch.

opotherapy /op-ə-ther'ə-pi/ *n* treatment by administration of extracts of animal organs, *esp* of ductless glands. [Gr *opos* juice, and **therapy**]

opp *abbrev* : oppose; opposed; opposite.

oppidan /op'i-dən/ *n* a town dweller; in university towns, someone who is not a member of the university, or a student not resident in a college; at Eton (and formerly elsewhere) a schoolboy who is not a foundationer or colleger. ◆ *adj* urban. [L *oppidānus*, from *oppidum* town]

oppignorate or **oppignerate** /o-pig'nə-rāt/ (*obs*) *vt* to pawn. [L *oppīgnorāre*, *oppīgnerāre*, from *ob* against, and *pīgnus*, *-oris* or *-eris* a pledge]
■ **oppignorā'tion** *n.*

oppilate /op'i-lāt/ (*pathol*) *vt* to block up, stop up. [L *oppīlāre*, *-ātum*, from *ob* in the way, and *pīlāre* to ram down]
■ **oppilā'tion** *n.* **opp'ilative** *adj.*

oppo /op'ō/ (*inf*) *n* (*pl* **opp'os**) opposite number (see under **opposite**). [Short form]

opponent /ə-pō'nənt/ *n* the person opposed to one in a contest, struggle, battle, etc; someone who opposes a course of action, belief, etc; an opponent muscle (*anat*). ◆ *adj* opposing; antagonistic (with *to* ; formerly with *with*); placed opposite or in front; (of a muscle) opposing one part (eg a digit) to another (*anat*). [L *oppōnens*, *-entis*, prp of *oppōnere*, from *ob* in the way of, and *pōnere* to place]
■ **oppo'nency** *n.*

opportune /op'ər-tūn or o-per-tūn', also (*Shakesp*) o-pör'tūn/ *adj* occurring at a fitting time; conveniently presented; timely; convenient; suitable; opportunist. [Fr *opportun*, from L *opportūnus*, from *ob* before, and *portus*, *-ūs* a harbour]
■ **opportune'ly** (or /op'/) *adv.* **opportune'ness** (or /op'/) *n.* **opportun'ism** (or /op'/) *n* the practice of regulating actions by favourable opportunities rather than consistent principles. **opportun'ist** (or /op'/) *n* someone who achieves success or advancement by adapting to the circumstances of the moment; a person without settled principles. ◆ *adj* (also **opportunist'ic**) characteristic of an opportunist. **opportun'ity** *n* an occasion offering a possibility; advantageous conditions; (*esp in pl*) a chance, opening or prospect; opportuneness (*rare*); fitness (*obs*).
☐ **opportunistic infection** *n* an infection to which normal people are resistant but which occurs in those whose immune system has been compromised by illness. **opportunistic species** *n* a species adapted to exploit temporary or local conditions. **opportunity cost** (*econ*) the cost of an investment (of money, resources, time, etc) in terms of its best alternative use. **opportunity shop** *n* (*Aust* and *NZ*) a charity shop (often shortened to **op shop**).

oppose /ə-pōz'/ *vt* to place in front or in the way (with *to*); to place or apply face to face or front to front; to set in contrast or balance; to set in conflict; to place as an obstacle; to face; to resist; to contend with. ◆ *vi* to make objection; to act in opposition. [Fr *opposer*, from L *ob* against, and Fr *poser* to place, from L *pausāre* to rest, stop; see **pose**[1]]
■ **opposabil'ity** *n.* **oppos'able** *adj* that may be opposed; capable of being placed with the front surface opposite (with *to*; as eg a thumb to other fingers). **oppose'less** *adj* (*Shakesp*) not to be opposed, irresistible. **oppos'er** *n.* **oppo'sing** *adj.*
■ **as opposed to** in contrast to; as distinct from.

opposite /op'ə-zit/ *adj* placed, or being, face to face, or at two extremities of a line; facing on the other side; directly contrary; diametrically opposed; opposed; corresponding; (of leaves) in pairs at each node, with the stem between (*bot*); (of floral parts) on the same radius (*bot*). ◆ *adv* in or to an opposite position or positions. ◆ *prep* in a position facing, opposing, contrary to, etc; as a leading performer in the same film or play as (another leading performer). ◆ *n* that which is opposed or contrary; an opponent; opposition (*Milton*). [Fr, from L *oppositus*, from *ob* against, and *pōnere*, *positum* to place]
■ **opp'ositely** *adv.* **opp'ositeness** *n.* **oppositive** /-poz'/ *adj* characterized by opposing; adversative; inclined to oppose.
☐ **opposite number** *n* (*inf*; short form **oppo**) someone who has a corresponding place in another organization, set, etc, one's counterpart; a person who is allotted to one as partner, opponent, etc; one's cohabiting or marriage partner; one's mate.
■ **be opposite with** (*Shakesp*) to be perverse and contradictory in dealing with.

opposition /op-ə-zish'ən/ *n* the act of opposing or of setting opposite; the state of being opposed or placed opposite; opposed or opposite position; an opposite; contrast; contradistinction; resistance; a difference of quantity or quality between two propositions having the same subject and predicate (*logic*); a body of opposers; (also with *cap*; with *the*) the parliamentary party that opposes the government or existing administration; the situation of a celestial body, as seen from the earth, when it is directly opposite to another, *esp* the sun (*astron*). ◆ *adj* of the parliamentary opposition. [L *oppositiō*, *-ōnis*, from L *oppōnere*, *oppositum* to place against or opposite]
■ **opposi'tional** *adj.* **opposi'tionist** *n* a member of the opposition.

oppress /ə-pres'/ *vt* to distress; to lie heavy upon; to treat with tyrannical cruelty or injustice; to load with heavy burdens, troubles, etc; to press against or upon; to crush (*obs*); to smother (*obs*); to overwhelm; to take by surprise (*obs*); to ravish (*obs*). [Fr *oppresser*, from LL *oppressāre*, frequentative of L *opprimere*, *oppressum*, from *ob* against, and *premere* to press]
■ **oppression** /ə-presh'ən/ *n* an act of oppressing; tyranny; a feeling of distress or of being weighed down; dullness of spirits; pressure (*Shakesp*). **oppress'ive** *adj* tending to oppress; tyrannical; heavy; burdensome; troubling; overpowering. **oppress'ively** *adv.* **oppress'iveness** *n.* **oppress'or** *n.*

opprobrium /ə-prō'bri-əm/ *n* disgrace, reproach or imputation of shameful conduct; anything that brings such reproach; infamy. [L *opprobrium*, from *ob* against, and *probrum* reproach]
■ **oppro'brious** *adj* reproachful, insulting or abusive; infamous; disgraceful (*archaic*). **oppro'briously** *adv.* **oppro'briousness** *n.*

oppugn /ə-pūn'/ *vt* to attack, *esp* by argument; to oppose; to call into question. [L *oppugnāre* to attack, from *ob* against, and *pugna* a fight]
■ **oppugnancy** /ə-pug'nən-si/ *n* (*Shakesp*) antagonism. **oppug'nant** *adj* opposing; hostile. ◆ *n* an opponent. **oppugner** /o-pūn'ər/ *n.*

OP's (*inf*) *abbrev* : other people's.

Ops *abbrev* : Operations; Operations officer; Operations room.

OPSI *abbrev* : Office of Public Sector Information.

■ words derived from main entry word; ☐ compound words; ■ idioms and phrasal verbs

opsimath /op'si-math/ n someone who learns late in life. [Gr *opsimathēs*, from *opse* late, and *mathē* learning]
■ **opsim'athy** n learning obtained late in life.

opsin /op'sin/ n a protein which forms part of the visual pigment rhodopsin. [Shortening of **rhodopsin**]

opsiometer /op-si-om'i-tər/ n an optometer. [Gr *opsis* sight, and **-meter**]

-opsis /-op-sis/ combining form denoting appearance of, or resemblance to, the thing specified, as in *meconopsis*; sight, as in *stereopsis*. [Gr *opsis* aspect, sight]

opsonium /op-sō'ni-əm/ n anything eaten with bread as a relish, *esp* fish. [Latinized from Gr *opsōnion*, from *opson* cooked food, relish]
■ **opsoma'nia** n any abnormal love for some special kind of food. **opsoma'niac** n. **opsonic** /op-son'ik/ adj relating to opsonin. **op'sonin** n a constituent of blood serum that makes bacteria more readily consumed by phagocytes. **op'sonize** or **-ise** vt to make (bacteria) more susceptible to consumption by phagocytes.

opt /opt/ vi where there is more than one possibility, to decide (to do), to choose or settle (with *for*); to make a choice, *esp* of nationality when territory is transferred. [L *optāre*, *-ātum* to choose, wish]
■ **opt'ant** n a person who opts; someone who has exercised a power of choosing, *esp* his or her nationality. **optative** /opt'ə-tiv or op-tā'tiv/ adj expressing a desire or wish; denoting a mood of verbs that expresses a wish (*grammar*). ◆ n (*grammar*) a mood of verbs, eg in Greek, expressing a wish; a verb in this mood. **op'tatively** (or /op-tā'/) adv. **op'ter** n.
❑ **opt'-out** n a decision or opportunity to opt out; a TV or radio programme broadcast by a regional station that has temporarily opted out of the main network transmission.
■ **opt in** to choose to take part. **opt out** to choose not to take part (with *of*); (of a school or hospital) to leave local-authority control.

opt. abbrev: optative; optic; optical; *optime* (*L*), very well indeed; optimum; optional.

Optic® /op'tik/ n a device attached to an inverted bottle for measuring alcoholic liquid dispensed.

optic /op'tik/ or **optical** /-ti-kl/ adj relating to sight, or to the eye, or to optics; (**optical**) constructed to help the sight; acting by means of light; amplifying radiation; visual. [Gr *optikos* optic, from *optos* seen]
■ **op'tic** n an eye (now mainly *facetious*); a lens, telescope, or microscope (*obs*). **op'tically** adv. **optician** /op-tish'ən/ n a person who makes or sells optical instruments, *esp* spectacles (see also **ophthalmic** under **ophthalmo-**); formerly, a person skilled in optics. **op'tics** n *sing* the science of light. **optoacous'tic** adj relating to or combining both vision and hearing. **optoelectron'ic** adj relating to optoelectronics; using both optical and electronic devices, etc. **optoelectron'ics** n *sing* the study or use of devices involving the interaction of electronic and light signals, or the conversion of one to the other (also **optron'ics**) **optol'ogist** n an optician. **optol'ogy** n. **optom'eter** n an instrument for testing vision. **optomet'ric** or **optomet'rical** adj. **optom'etrist** n an ophthalmic optician; a person qualified to practise optometry. **optom'etry** n the science of vision and eye-care; the science or procedure of examining the eyes and vision; the prescription and provision of spectacles, contact lenses, etc for the improvement of vision. **op'tophone** n an instrument that translates printed characters into arbitrary sounds, and so enables the blind to read ordinary type.
❑ **optical activity** n (*phys*) the ability of certain chemical compounds to rotate the plane of polarization of an already polarized beam of light in one direction or the other. **optical art** same as **op art**. **optical character reader** n (*comput*) a light-sensitive device for inputting data directly to a computer by means of optical character recognition (*abbrev* **OCR**). **optical character recognition** n (*comput*) the scanning, identification and encoding of printed characters by photoelectric means (*abbrev* **OCR**). **optical computing** n the technique of controlling the computer by pulses of light instead of by electronic means. **optical disk** n (*comput*) a disk that can be read from and often written to by a laser. **optical-electronic device** n (*phys*) an instrument used to locate weakly radiating sources by detecting their infrared emission. **optical fibre** n a thin strand of glass through which light waves may be transmitted, used eg in some communications systems, fibre optics, etc. **optical illusion** n something that has an appearance which deceives the eye; a misunderstanding caused by such a deceptive appearance. **optical maser** n laser. **optical microscope**, **telescope** n a microscope or telescope that operates by the direct perception of light from the object viewed, as opposed to an electron microscope or radio telescope. **optical pumping** n (*phys*) the act of stimulating a population inversion for a particular energy transition in a laser using an external light source of suitable frequency. **optical spectrum** n (*phys*) the visible radiation emitted from a source separated into its component frequencies. **optical splitter** n (*telecom*) a device for separating signals into two or more channels, eg optical fibres. **optical tweezers** n *pl* an

instrument used to manipulate microscopic objects by means of highly focused laser light. **optic axis** n the axis of the eye, a line through the middle of the pupil and the centre of the eye; the line which passes through the centre of curvature of a lens or mirror surface so that the rays are neither reflected nor refracted (also called **principal axis**); in a doubly refracting crystal, a direction in which no double refraction occurs. **optic disc** n the blind spot of the eye. **optic lobe** n the part of the mid-brain concerned with sight. **optic nerve** n the second cranial nerve, responsible for the sense of vision, which transmits information from the retina of the eye to the visual cortex of the brain. **optic thalamus** n (*anat*) an older name for **thalamus**.

optimal, etc see under **optimism**.

optimate /op'ti-māt/ n (pl (*L*) **optimā'tēs**) (*rare* in *sing*) a member of the aristocracy, *orig* in Rome. [L *optimās*, *-ātis*, from *optimus* best]

optime /op'ti-mi/ n at Cambridge University, one of those in the second (**senior optime**) or third (**junior optime**) rank of mathematical honours, after the wranglers. [L *optimē* (adv) very well, best]

optimism /op'ti-mi-zm/ n a disposition to take a bright, hopeful view of things, *opp* to *pessimism*; hopefulness or confidence generally; a belief that everything is ordered for the best; Leibniz's doctrine that the world is the best of all possible worlds (*philos*); the teaching or belief that good in the end will triumph over evil. [L *optimus* best]
■ **op'timal** adj optimum. **optimal'ity** n. **optimaliza'tion** or **-s-** n. **op'timalize** or **-ise** vt to bring to the most desirable or most efficient state. **op'timally** adv. **op'timist** n someone who maintains a hopeful, cheerful outlook; a supporter of the doctrine of optimism (*philos*). **optimist'ic** adj. **optimist'ically** adv. **optimiza'tion** or **-s-** n. **op'timize** or **-ise** vi to take the most hopeful view of anything. ◆ vt to make the most or best of; to make as efficient as possible, *esp* by analysing and planning processes; to prepare or revise (a computer system or program) so as to achieve the greatest possible efficiency. **op'timizer** or **-s-** n.

optimum /op'ti-məm/ n (pl **op'tima**) that point at which any condition is most favourable. ◆ adj (of conditions) best for the achievement of an aim or result; very best. [L, neuter of *optimus* best]

option /op'shən/ n an act of choosing; the power or right of choosing; a thing that is or may be chosen; an alternative for choice; a power (as of buying or selling at a fixed price) that may be exercised at will within a time-limit; a wish (*obs*). ◆ vt to have or grant an option on something. [L *optiō*, *-ōnis*, from *optāre* to choose]
■ **op'tional** adj left to choice; not compulsory; leaving to choice. **optional'ity** n. **op'tionally** adv.
❑ **option clause** n a clause in an insurance contract which gives the insurers an option to replace or reinstate the lost or damaged property as an alternative to paying its value.
■ **keep** or **leave one's options open** to refrain from committing oneself (to a course of action, etc). **local option** and **soft option** see **local**, **soft**.

optoelectronic, **optologist**, **optometry**, **optophone**, etc see under **optic**.

optronics see **optoelectronics** under **optic**.

opulent /op'ū-lənt/ adj wealthy; loaded with wealth; luxuriant; over-enriched. [L *opulentus*]
■ **op'ulence** n conspicuous wealth; luxury. **op'ulently** adv.

opulus /op'ū-ləs/ n the guelder-rose (*Viburnum opulus*). [L *opulus* a kind of maple]

opuntia /ō-pun'shi-ə/ n a plant of the prickly-pear genus (*Opuntia*) of the cactus family. [L *Opūntia* (*herba* plant) of *Opūs* (Gr *Opous*), a town of Locris where Pliny said it grew]

opus /ō'pəs, op'əs or op'ūs/ n (pl **o'puses** or **opera** /op'ə-rə/) a work, *esp* a musical composition, *esp* one numbered in order of publication, eg *opus* 6 (abbreviated *op* 6); used in naming various styles of Roman masonry. [L *opus*, *-eris* work]
❑ **opus Dei** /dā'ē/ n the work of God; liturgical worship; in Benedictine monastic practice, the primary duty of prayer; (with *caps*) an international Roman Catholic organization of lay people and priests. **opus latericium** /la-tə-rish'i-əm, -ik' or -te-rik'i-ŭm/ n a form of Graeco-Roman brickwork. **opus musivum** /moo-sī'vəm, mū- or moo-sē'wŭm/ n mosaic work. **opus operantis** /op-ə-ran'tis/ n the effect of a sacrament ascribed (as by Protestants) to the spiritual disposition of the recipient. **opus operatum** /op-ə-rā'təm or op-e-rä'tŭm/ n due celebration of a sacrament involving grace flowing from the sacramental act (the Roman Catholic view). **opus reticulatum** /ri-tik-yə-lā'təm or re-tik-ū-lä'tŭm/ n reticulated work.

opuscule /o-pus'kūl/ (*rare*) n a short work (also **opuscle** /ə-pus'l/ or **opus'culum** /-pus'kū-ləm/ (pl **opus'cula**)). [L dimin of *opus*]

OPW abbrev: Office of Public Works (in Ireland).

OR /ör/ (*comput*) n a logic circuit that has two or more inputs and one output, the output signal being 1 if any of its inputs is 1, and 0 if all of its inputs are 0. [**or**¹]

OR *abbrev* : operational or operations research; Oregon (US state; also **Or.**); other ranks (*milit*).

or[1] /ör/ *conj* used to link alternatives and possibilities where there are two, and the last two where there are several (*no home, clothes or food*); to introduce the second alternative where the first is introduced by *whether, either*; to offer a synonym (*the mountain lion or cougar*); between numbers to indicate a vague amount (*five or six*); (often **or rather**) to introduce qualifications or doubts (*We shall know tomorrow—or shall we?*); to mean 'because in that case' (*He can't be back or he would have telephoned*). [Contraction of ME *other*]

❑ **or else** *n* alternatively; because otherwise, because if not; used absolutely as a threat (*Do it or else!*).

or[2] /ör/ (*heraldry*) *n* the tincture gold or yellow, indicated in engraving and chiselling by dots. [Fr, from L *aurum* gold]

or[3] /ör/ (*archaic*) *conj* (or *adv*) and *prep* before (in time). [OE (Northumbrian) and ON *ār* early, with the sense of OE *ǣr* ere]

■ **or ever, or e'er**, or (by confusion) **or ere** (*poetic*) before ever, before even.

-or /-ər/ *sfx* (*esp* in words derived from Latin and legal terms) denoting a person or thing that performs an action or function, as in *actor, elevator*. —In most words indicating an agent either **-or** is standard or **-er** is standard, but in some both endings are acceptable. [L *-or* or *-ator*]

ora see **os**[2].

orach or **orache** /or'ich/ *n* an edible plant belonging to a genus (*Atriplex*) of the goosefoot family, sometimes used as spinach is. [OFr *arace* (Fr *arroche*), from L *atriplex*, from Gr *atraphaxys*]

oracle /or'ə-kl/ *n* a medium or agency of divine revelation; a response by or on behalf of a god; the place where such responses are given; the Jewish sanctuary; the word of God; a person with the reputation, or an air, of infallibility or great wisdom; an infallible indication; a wise, sententious or mysterious utterance; (**Oracle**®) the former teletext service of the Independent Broadcasting Authority. ◆ *vt* to utter as an oracle. ◆ *vi* to speak as an oracle. [L *ōrāculum*, from *ōrāre* to speak]

■ **oracular** /ə-rak'ū-lər/ or (now *rare*) **orac'ulous** *adj* of the nature of an oracle; like an oracle; seeming to claim the authority of an oracle; delivering oracles; prophetic; equivocal; ambiguous; obscure. **oracularity** /-lar'i-ti/, **orac'ularness** or **orac'ulousness** *n*. **orac'ularly** or **orac'ulously** *adv*.

■ **work the oracle** (*inf*) to achieve the desired result by manipulation, intrigue, wirepulling, favour, etc; to raise money.

oracy see under **oral**.

ora et labora /ö'ra or ö'rä et la-bö'ra or -bö'rä/ (L) pray and work.

oral /ö'rəl/ *adj* relating to the mouth; near the mouth; uttered by the mouth; (eg of an examination) spoken, not written; (of a method of teaching and communicating with the deaf) using lip-reading and vocal expression rather than sign language; (eg of poetry) passed on by word of mouth, *esp* from generation to generation; (eg of medicine) taken through the mouth; relating to the infant stage of development when satisfaction is obtained by sucking. ◆ *n* an oral examination. [L *ōs, ōris* the mouth]

■ **o'racy** *n* skill in self-expression and ability to communicate freely with others by word of mouth. **o'ralism** *n* the use of or belief in the oral method of teaching and communicating with the deaf. **o'ralist** *adj* and *n*. **oral'ity** *n* the state or quality of being oral; the preference for or tendency to choose the oral form of language. **o'rally** *adv*.

❑ **oral contraception** *n* inhibition of the normal process of ovulation and conception by taking orally, and according to a prescribed course, any of a variety of hormone-containing pills. **oral contraceptive** *n* a pill of this type. **oral history** *n* (the study of) information on events, etc of the past, obtained by interviewing people who participated in them. **oral hygiene, oral hygienist** *n* same as **dental hygiene** and **dental hygienist** respectively (see under **dental**). **Oral Law** *n* (*Judaism*) the Jewish religious law believed to have been passed down orally before being recorded in writing. **oral rehydration therapy** *n* the treatment of dehydration (caused by diarrhoea, etc) with drinks of a water, glucose and salt solution. **oral sex** *n* sexual relations involving the use of the mouth to stimulate the genitals of one's partner.

orang see **orang-utan**.

Orange /or'inj/ *adj* relating to the family of the princes of *Orange*, a former principality in S France from the 11c, passing by an heiress to the house of Nassau in 1531, the territory being ceded to France in 1713; favouring the cause of the Prince of Orange in Holland or in Great Britain and Ireland; of or favouring the Orangemen; extreme Protestant Irish Conservative.

■ **Or'angism** or **Or'angeism** *n*.

❑ **Or'angeman** *n* a member of a society revived and organized in Ireland in 1795 to uphold Protestant principles and supremacy.

orange /or'inj/ *n* a reddish-yellow fruit (hesperidium, a specialized type of berry) with tough skin, within which are juicy segments; the tree (*Citrus* genus of family Rutaceae) on which it grows; extended to various unrelated but superficially similar fruits and plants; a colour between red and yellow; an orange-flavoured drink. ◆ *adj* relating to an orange; orange-coloured. [Fr, ult from Ar *nāranj*; cf LL *arangia, aurantia, narancum*; Ital *arancia*, early *narancia*; Sp *naranja*; the loss of the *n* may be due to confusion with the indefinite article (*una, une*), the vowel changes to confusion with L *aurum*, Fr *or* gold]

■ **orangeade** /or-in-jād'/ *n* a drink made with orange juice. **or'angery** /-ri or -ər-i/ *n* a building for growing orange trees in a cool climate. **or'angey** /-ji/ *adj* somewhat orange in colour, flavour, etc. **or'angish** /-jish/ *adj*.

❑ **orange blossom** *n* the white blossom of the orange tree, often worn by brides; that of the mock orange, similarly used. **or'ange-coloured** *adj* orange blossom. **orange-flower water** *n* a solution of oil of neroli. **or'ange-grass** *n* a small American St John's-wort. **orange-lil'y** *n* a garden lily with large orange flowers. **orange peel** *n* the rind of an orange, often candied. **orange pekoe** *n* a type of high quality black tea made from very small leaves grown in India and Sri Lanka. **or'ange-root** *n* the plant golden-seal. **orange roughy** *n* an edible fish *esp* of SW Pacific waters. **orange squash** *n* a highly concentrated orange drink. **or'ange-squeezer** *n* an instrument for squeezing out the juice of oranges. **orange stick** *n* a thin stick, *esp* of orange-wood, used in manicure and make-up. **or'ange-taw'ny** *adj* and *n* (*Shakesp*) (of) a yellowish-brown or tan colour. **or'ange-tip** *n* a European butterfly (*Anthocaris caedamines*) with an orange patch near the tip of the forewing; a similarly marked American species (*Euchloe genutia*). **orange tree** *n*. **or'ange-wife** *n* (*Shakesp*) a woman who sells oranges. **or'ange-wood** *n* the wood of the orange tree.

■ **bitter, Seville**, or **sour orange** *Citrus aurantium* or its fruit, which is used to make marmalade. **sweet orange** *Citrus sinensis*, native of China and SE Asia, or any cultivated fruit derived from it.

orang-utan /o-, ə-, ö-rang'oo-tan, or -tan', also -ū-tan(')/ or **orang-outang** /-tang(')/, also **orang** /o-, ə-, ö-rang'/ *n* a reddish-brown, tree-dwelling anthropoid ape, found only in the forests of Sumatra and Borneo; a chimpanzee (*non-standard*). [Malay *ōranghūtan* man of the woods (said not to be applied by the Malays to the ape), from *ōrang* man, and *hūtan* wood or wild]

orant /ö'rənt or ö'/ *n* a worshipping figure in ancient Greek and early Christian art. [L *ōrans, -antis*, prp of *ōrāre* to pray]

ora pro nobis /ö'ra or ö'rä prō nō'bis or -bēs/ (L) pray for us.

orarian /ō- or ö-rä'ri-ən/ (*rare*) *adj* coastal. ◆ *n* a coast-dweller. [L *ōrārius*, from *ōra* shore]

orarium[1] /ō- or ö-rä'ri-əm/ *n* a handkerchief (*ancient hist*); a stole (*obs*); a scarf attached to a bishop's staff. [L *ōrārium*, from *ōs, ōris* mouth]

■ **ora'rion** *n* a Greek Church deacon's stole.

orarium[2] /ō- or ö-rä'ri-əm/ *n* a book of private devotions. [L *ōrāre* to pray]

oration /ö-rā'shən, ō- or ə-/ *n* a formal speech; a harangue. [L *ōrātiō, -ōnis*, from *ōrāre* to pray]

■ **orate'** *vi* (*esp facetious*) to harangue or hold forth.

orator /or'ə-tər/ *n* a public speaker; an eloquent person; a spokesman (*obs*); a petitioner (*obs*). [L *ōrātor, -ōris*, from *ōrāre* to pray]

■ **oratorial** /or-ə-tō'ri-əl or -tö'/ *adj* of an orator, oratory, or an oratory. **orato'rian** *adj* of an oratory; (with *cap*) of an Oratory. ◆ *n* a priest of an oratory; (with *cap*) a member of an Oratory. **oratorical** /-tor'/ *adj* characteristic of an orator; addicted to oratory; rhetorical; relating to or savouring of oratory. **orator'ically** *adv*. **or'atory** *n* the art of the orator; rhetoric; rhetorical utterances or expression; a place for private prayer; a lectern for praying at; a place of public speaking (*obs*); (with *cap*) one of various congregations in the Roman Catholic Church, *esp* the Fathers of the Oratory, established by St Philip Neri (1515–95); (with *cap*) a church of the Oratorians. **or'atress** or **oratrix** /or-ā'triks or or'ə-triks/ *n* a female orator.

oratorio /or-ə-tō'ri-ō or -tö'/ *n* (*pl* **orato'rios**) a story, *usu* biblical, set to music, with soloists, chorus, and full orchestra but without scenery, costumes or acting; the form of such a composition. [Ital *oratorio*, from L *ōrātōrium* an oratory, because they developed out of the singing at devotional meetings in church oratories]

■ **orato'rial** *adj*.

orb[1] /örb/ *n* a circle; a sphere; anything spherical; a celestial body; an eye or eyeball; the mound or globe of a monarch's regalia; the space within which the astrological influence of a planet operates; a sphere carrying a planet in its revolution; a cycle of time; an orbit; a world. ◆ *vt* to surround (*archaic*); to form into an orb. [L *orbis* a circle]

■ **orbed** *adj* in the form of an orb; circular. **orbic'ular** *adj* approximately circular or spherical; round; having the component minerals crystallized in spheroidal aggregates (*petrology*). **orbicula'ris** *n* (*pl* **orbicula'rēs**) a muscle surrounding an opening. **orbicular'ity** *n*. **orbic'ularly** *adv*. **orb'y** *adj* (*rare*) orbed.

orb² /örb/ (*obs*) *adj* bereaved, *esp* of children. ♦ *n* (*archit*; *obs*) an obscure term generally understood to mean a blind window or blank panel. [L *orbus* bereft]
■ **orb'ity** *n* (*obs*) bereavement, *esp* of children.

Orbilius /ör-bil'i-əs/ *n* a flogging schoolmaster (from the Roman poet Horace's teacher).

orbis terrarum /ör'bis te-rä'rəm/ *or* /te-rä'rŭm/ (*L*) the circle of lands, the whole world.

orbit /ör'bit/ *n* the path in which a celestial body moves round another (*astron*), or (*phys*) that in which an electron moves round the nucleus of an atom (also **or'bital**); a path in space round a celestial body; a regular course or beat, a sphere of action; (loosely) an orb; the hollow in which the eyeball rests (also (*anat*) **or'bita**); the skin round a bird's eye (*zool*). ♦ *vi* to move in or as though in orbit; to fly in a circle. ♦ *vt* (of a spacecraft, moon or other satellite) to travel round (a body) by a circular or elliptical path; (of an aircraft) to circle (a given point); to put into orbit. [L *orbita* a wheel-track, from *orbis* a ring or wheel]
■ **or'bital** *adj* of or relating to an orbit. ♦ *n* (*phys*) the orbit of an electron. **or'biter** *n* a spacecraft or satellite that orbits the earth or another planet without landing on it.
❑ **orbital engine** *n* an axial two-stroke engine with curved pistons in a circular cylinder block which rotates around a fixed shaft. **orbital road**, **motorway**, etc *n* one which goes round the outside of a town.

orc /örk/ *n* a killer whale or orca; a fierce sea-monster (*myth*); an ogre (*Tolkien*). [L *orca*]
■ **or'ca** *n* a black-and-white toothed whale of the killer-whale genus *Orcinus*.

Orcadian /ör-kā'di-ən/ *adj* of Orkney. ♦ *n* an inhabitant or a native of Orkney. [L *Orcadēs*, from Gr *Orkades* Orkney (Islands)]

orcein see under **orcinol**.

orch. *abbrev*: orchestra; orchestrated by.

orchard /ör'chərd/ *n* an enclosed garden of fruit trees. [OE *ort-geard*, prob from L *hortus* garden, and OE *geard*; see **yard²**. Some connect the first part with OE *wyrt*; see **wort¹**]
■ **or'charding** *n*. **or'chardist** *or* **or'chardman** *n* someone who grows and sells orchard fruits.
❑ **or'chard-grass** *n* (*US*) cock's-foot grass. **or'chard-house** *n* a glasshouse for cultivating fruits without artificial heat.

orchat /ör'chət/ *n* an obsolete form of the word **orchard**. [Partly *dialect*, partly due to confusion with Gr *orchatos* a row of trees]

orchel and **orchella** see **archil**.

orchestra /ör'ki-strə, formerly -kes'trə/ *n* a large company of musicians (strings, woodwind, brass, and percussion) playing together under a conductor; the part of a theatre or concert-room in which the instrumental musicians are placed; loosely applied to a small instrumental group, as in a restaurant; in the ancient Greek theatre, the place in front of the stage where the chorus danced. [Gr *orchēstrā*, from *orcheesthai* to dance]
■ **orchē'sis** *n* the art of dancing or rhythmical movement of the body, as in classical Greek dance. **orchesog'raphy** *n* notation of dancing. **orchestic** /-kes'tik/ *adj* relating to dancing. **orches'tics** *n sing* the art of dancing. **orchestral** /-kes'/ *adj* of or for an orchestra. **orches'tralist** *n* an orchestral composer. **orches'trally** *adv*. **or'chestrate** *vt* to compose or arrange (music) for performance by an orchestra; to organize so as to achieve the best or greatest overall effect (*fig*). ♦ *vi* to be in charge of orchestrating something. **orchestrā'tion** *n*. **or'chestrator** *n*. **orches'tric** *adj* orchestic; orchestral. **orchestrina** /-trē'nə/ *or* **orches'trion** *n* names given to various keyboard or barrel organ instruments designed to imitate an orchestra.
❑ **orchestra stalls** *n pl* front theatre seats, closest to the orchestra.

orchid /ör'kid/ *n* any plant or flower of the **Orchidā'ceae** or **Orchid'eae**, a family of monocotyledons, including many tropical epiphytes, with highly specialized, often showy, flowers, the upper petal (or labellum; by twisting actually the lower) serving as a landing-place for insects, the one fertile stamen (or two) united with the gynaeceum as a column (qv), the pollen in masses. [Gr *orchis*, *-ios* or *-eōs* a testicle (from the appearance of the root-tubers in Orchis and others); the *d* is a blunder, as if the genitive were *orchidos*]
■ **orchidā'ceous** *or* **orchid'eous** *adj*. **or'chidist** *n* a fancier or grower of orchids. **orchidol'ogist** *n*. **orchidol'ogy** *n* knowledge of orchids. **orchidomā'nia** *n* a craze for orchids. **orchidomā'niac** *n*. **Or'chis** *n* a genus of orchids, including several of the best-known British species; loosely applied to other genera; (without *cap*) a flower of any of these genera.
❑ **or'chid-house** *n* a place for growing orchids.

orchil and **orchilla** same as **archil**.

orchitis /ör-kī'tis/ *n* inflammation of a testicle. [Gr *orchis*, *-ios* or *-eōs* testicle]
■ **orchidec'tomy** *or* **orchiec'tomy** /-ki-ek'/ *n* excision of one or both testicles. **orchitic** /-kit'ik/ *adj*.

orcinol /ör'si-nol/ *n* a dihydric phenol obtained from archil and other lichens (also **or'cin** or **or'cine**). [See **archil**]
■ **orcein** /ör'si-in/ *n* a purple dyestuff obtained from orcinol.

ord /örd/ (*obs*) *n* a point, eg of a weapon; a beginning. [OE *ord*; cf **odd¹**]

ord. *abbrev*: ordained; order; ordinary; ordnance.

ordain /ör-dān'/ *vt* to arrange; to establish; to decree; to destine; to order; to assign, set apart; to appoint; to set apart for an office; to invest with ministerial functions; to admit to holy orders. [OFr *ordener* (Fr *ordonner*), from L *ordināre*, *-ātum*, from *ordō*, *-inis* order]
■ **ordain'able** *adj*. **ordain'er** *n*. **ordain'ment** *n*. **ordinee'** *n* a person who is being, or has just been, ordained.

ordeal /ör-dēl'/ *or* /-dē'əl/ *n* any severe trial or distressing or trying experience; an ancient form of referring a disputed question to the judgement of God, by lot, fire, water, etc (Latinized as **ordalium** /ör-dā'li-əm/). [OE *ordēl*, *ordāl* (WSax would be *ordǣl*), from pfx *or-* out, and *dǣl* deal, share; cf Du *oordeel*, Ger *Urteil*]
■ **ordā'lian** *adj*.
❑ **ordeal bean** *n* the Calabar-bean.

order /ör'dər/ *n* arrangement; sequence; disposition; proper arrangement; proper condition; the condition of normal or proper functioning; a regular or suitable arrangement; a method; a system; tidiness; a restrained or undisturbed condition; a form of procedure or ceremony; the accepted mode of proceeding at a meeting; a practice; grade, degree, rank or position, *esp* in a hierarchy; the degree of a curve or equation; a command; a written instruction to pay money; a customer's instruction to supply goods or perform work; the goods supplied; a pass for admission or other privilege; a class of society; a body of persons of the same rank, profession, etc; a fraternity, *esp* religious or knightly; a body modelled on a knightly order, to which members are admitted as an honour; the insignia of such a body; a group above a family but below a class (*biol*); one of the different ways in which the column and its entablature with their various parts are moulded and related to each other (*archit*); one of the successively recessed arches of an archway; due action towards some end, *esp* in the old phrase 'to take order'; the position of a weapon with butt on ground, muzzle close to the right side; equipment and uniform for a particular purpose, as in *battle order*; a portion or helping in a restaurant, etc (*N Am*); (in *pl*) the several degrees or grades of the Christian ministry. ♦ *vt* to arrange; to set in order; to put in the position of order (*milit*); to regulate; to command; to give an order for; to order to be (done, etc) (*US*); to conduct (*Shakesp*). ♦ *vi* to give commands; to request the supply of something, *esp* food. ♦ *interj* used in calling for order or to order. [Fr *ordre*, from L *ordō*, *-inis*]
■ **or'derer** *n*. **or'dering** *n* arrangement; management; the act or ceremony of ordaining eg priests or deacons. **or'derless** *adj* without order; disorderly. **or'derliness** *n*. **or'derly** *adj* in good order; regular; well-regulated; of good behaviour; quiet; being on duty; of or relating to orders (*milit*). ♦ *adv* regularly; methodically. ♦ *n* a private soldier with particular duties; formerly, a non-commissioned officer who carried official messages for his superior officer; a hospital attendant; a street cleaner.
❑ **order book** *n* a book for entering the orders of customers, the special orders of a commanding officer, or the motions to be put to the House of Commons; the amount of orders received and awaiting completion. **order form** *n* a printed form on which the details of a customer's order are written. **order in council** *n* an order by the sovereign with advice of the Privy Council. **orderly bin** *n* a street receptacle for refuse. **orderly officer** *n* the officer on duty for the day. **orderly room** *n* a room for regimental, company, etc, business. **order of battle** *n* arrangement of troops or ships in preparation for a fight. **order of magnitude** *n* the approximate size or number of something, *usu* measured in a scale from one value to ten times that value; (loosely) a rising scale in terms of size, quantity, etc. **order of the day** *n* business set down for the day; a proclamation by a dictator or military commander; something necessary, normal, prevalent, particularly popular, etc at a given time. **order paper** *n* a paper showing the order of business, *esp* in parliament.
■ **call to order** see **call¹**. **full orders** the priesthood. **holy orders** an institution, in the Roman and Greek Churches a sacrament, by which a person is specially set apart for the service of religion; the rank of an ordained minister of religion. **in order** with the purpose (with *to* or *that*); in accordance with rules of procedure at meetings; appropriate, suitable, likely; (also **in good**, **working**, etc **order**) operating, or able to operate, well or correctly; in the correct, desired, etc order. **in short order** (*US*) promptly. **in** or **of the order of** more or less of the size, quantity or proportion stated. **minor orders** in the Roman Catholic Church those of acolyte, exorcist, reader and doorkeeper, in the

Eastern Churches, reader. **on order** having been ordered but not yet supplied. **order about** or **around** to give orders to in a domineering fashion. **out of order** not in order; (of actions, behaviour, etc, or of people as acting or behaving in some way) outside normally acceptable standards, excessive or uncontrolled (*inf*). **sailing orders** written instructions given to the commander of a vessel before sailing. **sealed orders** instructions not to be opened until a specified time. **standing orders** see under **stand**. **take order** (*obs*) to take measures or steps. **take orders** to be ordained. **tall** or **large order** (*inf*) an *esp* unreasonably large request or difficult assignment. **to order** according to, and in fulfilment of, an order.

ordinaire /*ör'di-när*/ (*inf*) *n* vin ordinaire; table wine. [Fr]

ordinal /*or'di-nəl*/ *adj* indicating order of sequence; relating to an order. ◆ *n* an ordinal numeral (eg *first*, *second*, *third*, etc, distinguished from *cardinal*); a book of rules (*obs*); a service book; a book of forms of consecration and ordination. [LL *ordinālis*, from L *ordō*, *-inis* order]

ordinance /*ör'di-nəns*/ *n* that which is ordained by authority, fate, etc; regulation; a bye-law (*US*); artistic arrangement; planning; a decree; a religious practice enjoined by authority, *esp* a sacrament; a social class or order (*Shakesp*); preparation (*obs*); equipment (*obs*); ordnance (*obs*). [L *ordināre*, *-ātum*, from *ordō* order]
■ **or'dinand** *n* someone who is training to become a minister of the church; a candidate for ordination. **or'dinant** *adj* (*rare*) ordaining. ◆ *n* a person who ordains. **or'dinate** *n* a straight line parallel to an axis cutting off an abscissa; the y-co-ordinate in analytical geometry. ◆ *vt* to ordain; to co-ordinate or order. **ord'inately** *adv* in an ordered manner; restrainedly; with moderation. **ordinā'tion** *n* the act of ordaining; admission to the Christian ministry by the laying on of hands of a bishop or a presbytery; established order.

ordinary /*ör'di-nə-ri, ör'd(i)n-ri, örd'nə-ri*/, *Scot* **ordinar** /*örd'nər*/ *adj* according to the common order or type; usual; of the usual kind; customary; plain; undistinguished; commonplace; (of a judge or jurisdiction) by virtue of office, not by deputation; (of a judge in Scotland) of the Outer House of the Court of Session (**Lord Ordinary**); plain-looking (*inf*); of common rank. ◆ *n* something settled or customary; the common run, mass or course; an ungeared bicycle with one large and one small wheel, a penny-farthing; one of a class of armorial charges, figures of simple or geometrical form, conventional in character (*heraldry*); a reference book of heraldic charges; a rule or book that lays down the form of a religious service, *esp* the mass; an ordinary share; a judge acting in his own right by virtue of his office, eg an ecclesiastic such as a bishop or his deputy in ecclesiastical cases; a chaplain who attended those condemned to death, *esp* the chaplain of Newgate Prison (*hist*); a meal provided at a fixed charge; a place where such a meal is provided; the company partaking of it (*obs*); usual fare (*obs*). [L *ordinārius*, from *ordō*, *-inis* order]
■ **or'dinarily** *adv*. **or'dinariness** *n*.
□ **ordinary degree** same as **pass degree** (see under **pass**). **Ordinary grade** *n* see **O grade** under **O** (*abbrev*). **Ordinary level** *n* see **O level** under **O** (*abbrev*). **ordinary ray** *n* (*phys*) in double refraction, the ray that obeys the ordinary law of refraction. **ordinary seaman** *n* a seaman ranking below an able seaman. **ordinary shares** *n pl* shares in a company entitling the holder to the company's net profits as a dividend after preference shareholders have been paid (**preferred ordinary shares** have limited priority).
■ **in ordinary** in regular and customary attendance. **ordinary of the mass** the established sequence or fixed order for saying mass. **out of the ordinary** unusual.

ordinee see under **ordain**.

ordnance /*örd'nəns*/ *n* orig, any arrangement, disposition, or equipment; munitions; great guns, artillery; a department concerned with the supply and maintenance of artillery. [**ordinance**]
□ **ordnance datum** *n* the standard sea-level of the Ordnance Survey, now mean sea-level at Newlyn, Cornwall. **Ordnance Survey** *n* the preparation of maps of Great Britain and Northern Ireland by the *Ordnance Survey* (*Department*) (until 1889 under the Board of Ordnance).

ordonnance /*ör'də-nəns*/ *n* co-ordination, *esp* the proper disposition of figures in a picture, parts of a building, etc. [Fr; cf **ordinance**]

Ordovician /*ör-dō-vish'yən* or *-ən*/ (*geol*) *adj* of or belonging to a period of the Palaeozoic era, between 490 and 440 million years ago (also *n*). [L *Ordovicēs*, a British tribe of N Wales]

ordure /*ör'dyər*/ *n* dirt; dung; excrement; anything unclean (*fig*). [Fr, from OFr *ord* foul, from L *horridus* rough]
■ **or'durous** *adj*.

ore[1] /*ör* or *ör*/ *n* a solid, naturally-occurring mineral aggregate, of economic interest, from which one or more valuable constituents may be recovered by treatment; precious metal (*poetic*). [OE *ār* brass, influenced by *ōra* unwrought metal; cf L *aes*, *aeris* bronze]
□ **ore body** *n* a mass or vein of ore.

ore[2] /*ör*/ (*dialect*) *n* (also **ore'weed** or **oar'weed**) seaweed; tangle (genus *Laminaria*). [OE *wār*]

ore[3] or **o're** /*ör* or *ör*/ old spellings of **o'er**.
□ **ore-rested** *adj* a Shakespearean form of **overwrested**. **ore-wrought** or **ore-raught** *adj* Shakespearean forms of **over-reached** in the sense of overtook. —For other compounds see **over-**.

öre /*œ'rə*/ *n* (pl **öre**) a coin and monetary unit in Sweden, $\frac{1}{100}$ of a krona.

øre /*œ'rə*/ *n* (pl **øre**) a coin and monetary unit in Norway and Denmark, $\frac{1}{100}$ of a krone.

oread /*ō'* or *ō'ri-ad*/ (*myth*) *n* (pl **o'reads** or **orē'adēs**) a mountain nymph. [L *oreās*, *-adis*, from Gr *oreias*, *oreiados*, from *oros* a mountain]

orecchiette /*o-rə-kyet'i*/ *n* pasta in the form of small concave discs. [Ital, little ears]

orectic see under **orexis**.

Oreg. *abbrev*: Oregon (US state).

oregano /*ö-ri-gä'nō* or (*US*) *ö-reg'ə-nō*/ *n* (pl **oreganos**) the Mediterranean aromatic herb *Origanum vulgare* used in cooking; origanum. [Am Sp *orégano* wild marjoram, from L *orīganum*; see **origanum**]

oreide see under **oroide**.

oreography, etc see **orography**.

oreology, etc see **orology**.

Oreopithecus /*ō-* or *ö-rē-ō-pi-thē'kəs*, or *-pith'ə-kəs*/ *n* a hominid of which a complete skeleton was found in a Tuscan lignite mine. [Gr *oros* mountain, and *pithēkos* ape]

orepearch see **overperch** under **over-**.

oreweed see **ore**[2].

ore-wrought see under **ore**[3].

orexis /*o-rek'sis*/ *n* appetite. [Gr *orexis*]
■ **orec'tic** *adj*. **orex'in** *n* a hormone that stimulates the appetite and is thought to be important for sleep regulation (also **hypocretin**).

orf /*örf*/ *n* a viral infection of sheep, etc, communicable to man, characterized by the formation of vesicles and pustules on the skin and mucous membranes, *esp* on lips, nose and feet. [Dialect *hurf*; ON *hrūfa* scab]

orfe /*örf*/ *n* a golden-yellow semi-domesticated fish, a variety of id. [Ger *Orfe*, from Gr *orphōs* the great sea-perch]

organ /*ör'gən*/ *n* an instrument or means by which anything is done; a part of a body fitted for carrying on a natural or vital operation; the penis (*euphem*); a means of communicating information or opinions, eg a newspaper; a keyboard wind instrument consisting of a collection of pipes made to sound by means of compressed air; a system of pipes in such an organ, having an individual keyboard, a partial organ; a musical instrument in some way similar to a pipe-organ, including a pipeless organ; a barrel organ; a region of the brain thought to be concerned with some mental or moral quality; a bump marking its position and development; a musical instrument in general (*obs*). [L *organum*, from Gr *organon* instrument, tool, from *ergon* work]
■ **or'ganist** *n* someone who plays an organ. **organis'trum** *n* an early form of hurdy-gurdy. **organity** /*-gan'*/ *n* an organized whole. **or'ganon** *n* (pl **or'gana**) (Gr; *philos*, etc) a method of investigation. **or'ganum** *n* (pl **or'gana**) (*L*) an organon; in medieval music, a part in parallel motion to the canto fermo *usu* a fourth or fifth below or above.
□ **or'gan-bird** *n* the Australian magpie or pied butcherbird. **or'gan-builder** *n* someone who constructs organs. **or'gan-gallery** *n* a gallery in a church, etc, where an organ is placed. **or'gan-grinder** *n* a person who plays a hand-organ by a crank. **or'gan-harmo'nium** *n* a large harmonium. **organ of Corti** /*kör'ti*/ *n* the organ in the cochlea that contains the auditory receptors. **or'gan-pipe** *n* one of the sounding pipes of a pipe-organ. **organ-pipe coral** *n* a coral, *Tubipora*, with tubes arranged like organ-pipes. **or'gan-point** *n* a pedal point. **or'gan-screen** *n* an ornamented stone or wood screen in a church, etc, on which an organ is placed.

organdie or (*US*) **organdy** /*ör'gən-di*/ *n* fine translucent plain-woven cotton dress material with a stiff finish; fine muslin; book-muslin. [Fr *organdi*]

organelle /*ör-gə-nel'*/ (*biol*) *n* a specialized part of a cell, eg nucleus, mitochondrion, lysosome. [New L *organella*, dimin of L *organum* organ]

organic /*ör-gan'ik*/ *adj* relating to, derived from, like or of the nature of an organ (in any sense); of an organism, organum or organization; organized; inherent in organization; structural; formed as if by organic process (*art*); of design, etc, based on or inspired by, natural forms (*art*); belonging to the etymological structure of a word (*philology*); instrumental; mechanical;

containing or combined with carbon (*chem*); concerned with carbon compounds; (of crops, crop production, etc) produced without, or not involving, the use of fertilizers and pesticides not wholly of plant or animal origin; governed in its formation or development by inherent or natural factors rather than by a predetermined plan. ◆ *n* an organic substance. [Gr *organikos*, from *organon* instrument]

■ **organ'ical** *adj* (*obs*). **organ'ically** *adv*. **organicism** /*ör-gan'i-sizm*/ *n* the conception of nature, life or society as an organism; the theory that all disease is due to an organic lesion. **organ'icist** *n*. **organicist'ic** *adj*.

◻ **organic chemistry** *n* the chemistry of carbon compounds. **organic disease** *n* a disease accompanied by changes in the structures involved. **organic sensation** *n* sensation from internal organs, eg hunger. **organic vein** *n* (*obs*) the jugular vein.

organism /*ör'gə-ni-zm*/ *n* organic structure, or that which has it; that which acts as a unified whole; a living animal or plant. [**organize**]

■ **organis'mal** or **organis'mic** *adj* of or relating to an organism. **organis'mally** or **organis'mically** *adv*.

organize or **-ise** /*ör'gə-nīz*/ *vt* to form into an organic whole; to co-ordinate and prepare for activity; to arrange; to obtain (*inf*); to supply with organs. ◆ *vi* to be active in organization; to become organic. [OFr *organiser*, from Med L *organizāre*, from L *organum* organ]

■ **organizabil'ity** or **-s-** *n*. **organiz'able** or **-s-** *adj*. **organizā'tion** or **-s-** *n* the act of organizing; the state of being organized; the manner in which anything is organized; an organized system, body or society; a political party machine (*US*); the singing of the organum. **organizā'tional** or **-s-** *adj*. **organizā'tionally** or **-s-** *adv*. **or'ganized** or **-s-** *adj* having or consisting of parts acting in co-ordination; having the nature of a unified whole; organic. **or'ganizer** or **-s-** *n* someone who or something that organizes; part of an embryo that influences the development of the rest; (also **or'ganizer-bag** or **-purse**, etc) a container with separate divisions, pockets, etc in which the contents can be arranged for ease and speed of access; (also **personal organizer**) a small ring-binder with divisions in which information, diary, personal notes, etc, can be kept to hand; a desktop, laptop or pocket electronic device for the same purpose.

■ **organization and methods** the study and analysis of a company and its systems and procedures, in order to improve efficiency (*abbrev* **O and M**).

organo- /*ör'gə-nō-* or *-no-*/ *combining form* denoting organ; (also /*ör-gan'ō-*/) organic, as in organometallic compounds in which carbon atoms are linked directly with metal atoms, such as *organolead*, *organotin*, or in similar compounds in which the inorganic element is non-metallic, such as *organophosphorus*; (of a chemical compound) containing an organic radical, such as *organochlorine*; any one of a group of compounds of chlorine and carbon used in pest control. [L *organum*; see **organ**]

■ **organogeny** /*ör-gə-noj'i-ni*/ or **organogen'esis** *n* the development of living organs. **organogram** /*-gan'-*/ *n* a chart showing graded arrangement of personnel in an organization. **organog'raphy** *n* a description of the organs of plants or animals. **organolep'tic** *adj* (Gr root of *lambanein* to seize) affecting a bodily organ or sense; concerned with testing the effects of a substance on the senses, *esp* of taste and smell. **organometall'ic** /*-gan-*/ *adj* (*chem*) (of a molecule) containing a metal atom linked to a carbon atom; (loosely) metallo-organic. **organophos'phate** /*-gan-*/ *n* one of a group of chemical insecticides. **organotherapeutic** /*-pū'tik*/ *adj*. **organother'apy** *n* treatment of disease by administration of animal organs or extracts of them, *esp* of ductless gland extracts.

organon, organum see under **organ**.

organza /*ör-gan'zə*/ *n* a transparently thin material resembling organdie but made of silk or synthetic fibres. [Of uncertain origin]

organzine /*ör'gən-zēn*/ *n* a silk yarn of two or more threads put together with a slight twist; a fabric made of this yarn. [Fr *organsin*, from Ital *organzino*, possibly from *Urgenj* Turkestan]

orgasm /*ör'ga-zm*/ *n* the culmination of sexual excitement; immoderate excitement; turgescence of any organ (*obs*). ◆ *vi* to experience an orgasm. [Gr *orgasmos* swelling]

■ **orgas'mic** or **orgas'tic** *adj*. **orgas'mically** or **orgas'tically** *adv*.

orgeat /*ör'ji-at*, *-zhat* or *-zhä*/ *n* a syrup or drink made from almonds, sugar, etc, formerly from barley. [Fr *orge*, from L *hordeum* barley]

orgia, orgiast, orgic see **orgy**.

orgillous see **orgulous**.

orgone /*ör'gōn*/ *n* (also **orgone energy**) according to Wilhelm Reich, a vital force permeating the universe, which, concentrated in a specially made **orgone box**, could cure certain diseases. [*orgasm*, and sfx *-one* indicating chemical derivative]

orgue /*örg*/ (*obs*) *n* a row of stakes let down like a portcullis; a weapon with several barrels in a row. [Fr, organ]

orgulous /*ör'gū-ləs*/ or **orgillous** /*ör'gi-ləs*/ (*Shakesp*) *adj* haughty. [OFr *orguillus*; cf Fr *orgueil*, Ital *orgoglio* pride; prob of Germanic origin]

orgy /*ör'ji*/ *n* (also (properly *pl*) **or'gia**) a frantic unrestrained celebration; a riotous, licentious, or drunken revel; a bout of excessive or frenzied indulgence in some activity; (*usu* in *pl*) a secret rite, as in the worship of Bacchus; a religious or secret celebration in general (*obs*). [Fr *orgies*, from L, from Gr *orgia* (*pl*)]

■ **or'giast** *n* someone who takes part in orgies. **orgias'tic** or (*rare*) **or'gic** *adj*. **orgias'tically** *adv*.

oribi /*or'i-bi*/ *n* a small S African antelope, the palebuck. [Afrik, *appar* from a native language]

orichalc or (*Spenser*) **oricalche** /*or'i-kalk*/ *n* a gold-coloured alloy; brass. [Gr *oreichalkos*, from *oros* a mountain, and *chalkos* copper; sense influenced by association with L *aurum* gold]

■ **orichalceous** /*-kal'si-əs*/ *adj*.

oriel /*ö'* or *ö'ri-əl*/ *n* a small room or recess with a polygonal bay window, built out from a wall, resting on the ground or more *usu* supported on brackets or corbels; the window of an oriel (in full **oriel-win'dow**). [OFr *oriol* porch, recess or gallery]

■ **o'rielled** *adj*.

orient /*ö'* or *ö'ri-ənt*/ *adj* eastern (*usu* poetic); (of the sun, day, etc) rising (*archaic*); bright or pure in colour (*poetic*). ◆ *n* the part where the sun rises; sunrise; purity of lustre in a pearl; an orient pearl; (with *cap*) the East; (with *cap*) the countries of the East. ◆ *vt* (also /*-ent'*/) to set so as to face the east; to build (lengthwise) east and west; to place in a definite relation to the points of the compass or other fixed or known directions; to determine the position of, relatively to fixed or known directions; to acquaint (someone or oneself) with the present position relative to known points, or (*fig*) with the details of the situation. [L *oriens*, *-entis*, prp of *orīrī* to rise]

■ **o'riency** *n* (*rare*) orient quality. **oriental** or **Oriental** /*-ent'əl*/ *adj* eastern; relating to, in, or from the east; orient. ◆ *n* a native of E Asia (*offensive*); a person from the east of any place. **Orient'alism** *n* an eastern expression, custom, etc; scholarship in eastern languages and/or cultures. **Orient'alist** *n* an expert in eastern languages; an oriental. **orientality** /*-al'i-ti*/ *n*. **orient'alize** or **-ise** *vt* and *vi*. **orient'ally** *adv*. **o'rientāte** *vt* to orient. ◆ *vi* to face the east; to be oriented. **orientā'tion** *n* the act of orienting or orientating; the state of being oriented; determination or consciousness of relative direction; the assumption of definite direction in response to stimulus. **orientā'tional** *adj*. **o'rientātor** *n* an instrument for orientating. **o'riented** (or /*-ent'*/) or **o'rientated** *adj* directed (with *towards*); often used in combination as second element of *adj*, as in *child-oriented households*; normally aware of the elements of one's situation, ie time, place, persons (*psychiatry*; also *fig*). **orienteer'** *n* a person who takes part in orienteering. ◆ *vi* to take part in orienteering. **orienteer'ing** *n* the sport of making one's way quickly across difficult country with the help of map and compass.

◻ **oriental alabaster** *n* onyx marble. **oriental amethyst, emerald, topaz** *n* varieties of corundum resembling amethyst, emerald and topaz. **Oriental Region** *n* Southern Asia and its islands from the Persian Gulf to Wallace's Line. **oriental ruby** *n* the true ruby, a variety of corundum. **oriental turquoise** *n* true turquoise. **orientation behaviour** *n* the positioning of the body or of a behavioural sequence with respect to some aspect of the external environment. **orientation course** *n* a course giving information or training needed for a new situation or environment. **orientation table** *n* an indicator of tabular form for showing the direction of various objects, eg mountains.

orifice /*or'i-fis*/ *n* a mouth-like opening, *esp* small; an opening from the body or a body cavity. [Fr, from L *ōrificium*, from *ōs*, *ōris* mouth, and *facere* to make]

■ **or'ifex** *n* (*Shakesp*) an orifice. **orificial** /*-fish'əl*/ *adj*.

oriflamme /*or'i-flam*/ *n* a small banner of red silk split into several points, carried on a gilt staff, the ancient royal standard of France. [Fr, from LL *auriflamma*, from L *aurum* gold, and *flamma* a flame]

orig *abbrev*: origin; original; originally.

origami /*o-ri-gä'mi*/ *n* the *orig* Japanese art of folding paper so as to make figures shaped like animals, birds, etc. [Jap, paper-folding, from *ori* folding, and *kami* paper]

origanum /*o-rig'ə-nəm*/ *n* any of various aromatic herbs of the marjoram genus (*Origanum*) of labiates, or of other genus, used in cookery (see also **oregano**). [L *orīganum*, from Gr *orīganon*]

■ **or'igan** /*-gan*/ or **or'igane** /*-gän*/ *n* marjoram, *esp* wild marjoram.

Origenist /*or'i-jə-nist*/ *n* a follower of *Origen* (c.185–254AD) in his allegorical method of scriptural interpretation or his theology, *esp* his heresies, ie the subordination though eternal generation of the Logos, pre-existence of all men, and universal restoration, even of the Devil.

■ **Or'igenism** *n*. **Origenist'ic** *adj*.

origin /*or'i-jin*/ *n* the rising or first existence of anything; that from which anything first proceeds; the fixed starting-point or point from which measurement is made (*maths*); the place of attachment from which a muscle, etc arises, as distinct from its *insertion* (*anat*); source; derivation. [L *orīgō*, *-inis*, from *orīrī* to rise]

■ **orig'inal** *adj* relating to the origin or beginning; existing from or at the beginning; being such from the beginning; innate; standing as source in relation to something; not derived, copied, imitated or translated from anything else; originative; novel; originating or having the power to originate in oneself; creative; independent in invention; odd in character. ◆ *n* an origin; that which is not itself, or of which something else is, a copy, imitation or translation; a real person, place, etc, serving as model for one in fiction; an inhabitant, member, etc, from the beginning; a person of marked individuality or oddity; (in *pl*; *Milton*) original elements. **original'ity** *n*. **orig'inally** *adv*. **orig'inate** *vt* to give origin to; to bring into existence; to be the author, inventor or creator of. ◆ *vi* to have origin; to begin; (of a train or bus) to start its journey (from a certain point). **origina'tion** *n*. **orig'inative** *adj* having power to originate or bring into existence; originating. **orig'inator** *n*. ❑ **original equipment manufacturer** *n* (*comput*) a firm which makes basic computer hardware for other manufacturers to build into their own products (*abbrev* **OEM**). **original sin** *n* innate depravity and corruption believed to be transmitted to Adam's descendants because of his sin. **originating summons**, **application**, etc *n* (*law*) one which originates legal proceedings.

orillion /*o-ril' yən*/ (*fortif*) *n* a semicircular projection at the shoulder of a bastion intended to cover the guns and defenders on the flank. [Fr *orillon*, from *oreille* an ear, from L *auricula*, dimin of *auris* ear]

Orimulsion® /*o-ri-mul'shən*/ *n* an emulsion of bitumen, water and detergents, used as a fuel. [*Orinoco* in Venezuela, where the bitumen was originally obtained, and *emulsion*]

O-ring /*ō'ring*/ *n* a toroidal ring, *usu* of circular cross-section, used eg as an air or oil seal. [From its shape]

oriole /*ō'* or *ō'ri-ōl*/ *n* a golden-yellow bird (*Oriolus oriolus*, the **golden oriole** or **loriot**) with black wings, or other member of the genus or of the Old World family **Oriol'idae**, related to the crows; in America applied to birds of the Icteridae (see **Baltimore**). [OFr *oriol*, from L *aureolus* dimin of *aureus* golden, from *aurum* gold]

Orion /*ə-rī'ən*/ (*astron*) *n* a constellation containing seven very bright stars, three of which form **Orion's belt**. [*Ōriōn*, a giant hunter slain by Artemis]

orisha /*ə-rish'ə*/ *n* a minor god or spirit of a traditional West African religion and various cults of the West Indies and South America. [Yoruba]

orison /*or'i-zən*/ *n* a prayer. [OFr *orison* (Fr *oraison*), from L *ōrātiō*, *-ōnis*, from *ōrāre* to pray]

Oriya /*ō-* or *ō-rē'yə*/ *n* the language of Orissa in India, closely related to Bengali; a member of the people speaking it. ◆ *adj* of or relating to the Oriyas or their language.

orle /*örl*/ (*heraldry*) *n* a border within a shield at a short distance from the edge; a number of small charges set as a border. [OFr, border, from a dimin formed from L *ōra* border]

orleans /*ör'li-ənz*/ *n* a fabric of cotton warp and worsted weft. [*Orléans*, a city in France]

■ **Or'leanism** *n*. **Or'leanist** *n* a supporter of the family of the Duke of Orleans, brother of Louis XIV, as claimants to the throne of France (also *adj*).

orlistat /*ör'li-stat*/ *n* an orally administered drug that reduces the absorption of dietary fat by inhibiting the action of enzymes in the digestive system, used to treat obesity.

Orlon® /*ör'lon*/ *n* a type of acrylic fibre or crease-resistant fabric made from it.

orlop /*ör'lop*/ *n* (also **orlop deck**) the lowest deck in a ship, a covering to the hold. [Du *overloop* covering]

Ormazd see **Ormuzd**.

ormer /*ör'mər*/ *n* an ear-shaped shell, *esp* the edible *Haliotis tuberculata*, common in the Channel Islands, the ear-shell or sea-ear. [Channel Island Fr *ormer* (Fr *ormier*), from L *auris maris* sea-ear]

ormolu /*ör'mə-loo*/ *n* an alloy of copper, zinc, and sometimes tin; gilt or bronzed metallic ware; gold-leaf prepared for gilding bronze, etc. [Fr *or*, from L *aurum* gold, and Fr *moulu*, pap of *moudre* to grind, from L *molere* to grind]

Ormuzd or **Ormazd** /*ör'muzd*/ *n* a later form of the name **Ahura Mazda**, in early Zoroastrianism the creator and lord of the universe, later the good principle, *opp* to **Ahriman**. [Pers *Ahura Mazdá* the Wise Lord, or the Living God or Lord (*ahu* the living, life, or spirit, root *ah* to be), the Great Creator (*maz*, *dá*)]

ornament /*ör'nə-mənt*/ *n* anything meant to add grace or beauty or to bring credit; a trinket such as a china figure, vase, etc, intended for display; additional beauty or decoration; a mark of honour; (*usu* in *pl*) articles used in the services of the church

(*Prayer Book*). ◆ *vt* /*ör-nə-ment'* or *ör'nə-ment*/ to adorn; to furnish with ornaments. [Fr *ornement*, from L *ornāmentum*, from *ornāre* to adorn]

■ **ornament'al** *adj* serving to adorn; decorative, pleasantly striking in dress and general appearance. ◆ *n* a plant grown for ornament or beauty. **ornament'alism** *n*. **ornament'alist** *n*. **ornament'ally** *adv*. **ornamenta'tion** *n* the act or art of ornamenting; ornamental work. **ornament'er** or **ornament'ist** *n*.

ornate /*ör-nāt'* or *ör'nāt*/ *adj* decorated; much or elaborately ornamented. [L *ornāre*, *-ātum* to adorn]

■ **ornate'ly** (or /*ör'/*) *adv*. **ornate'ness** (or /*ör'/*) *n*.

ornery /*ör'nə-ri*/ (*N Am dialect* or *inf*) *adj* commonplace; inferior, poor, worthless; touchy, cantankerous; stubborn; low, mean, contemptible. [A variant of **ordinary**]

■ **or'neriness** *n*.

ornis /*ör'nis*/ *n* the birds collectively of a region, its avifauna. [Gr *ornis* bird]

ornithic /*ör-nith'ik*/ *adj* relating to birds. [Gr *ornithikos*, from *ornis*, *ornīthos* bird]

ornithichnite, **Ornithischia** see under **ornitho-**.

ornitho- or before a vowel **ornith-** /*ör-ni-th*(*ō*)-, *-th*(*ə*)- or *-th*(*o*)-/ *combining form* signifying bird. [Gr *ornis*, *ornīthos* a bird]

■ **ornithichnite** /*ör-ni-thik'nīt*/ *n* (Gr *ichnos* track) a fossil footprint of a bird. **Ornithischia** /*-this'ki-ə*/ *n pl* (Gr *ischion* hip joint) the order of bird-hipped dinosaurs, herbivorous and often heavily armoured. **ornithis'chian** *n* and *adj*. **Ornithodel'phia** *n pl* (Gr *delphys* womb) the Prototheria or Monotremata, from the ornithic character of the urogenital organs. **ornithodel'phian** *adj* of or relating to the Ornithodelphia (also *n*). **ornithodel'phic** or **ornithodel'phous** *adj* ornithodelphian. **Ornithogaea** /*-nī-thə-jē'ə*/ *n* (Gr *gaia* land) the New Zealand biological region. **ornithog'alum** *n* (Gr *ornithogalon* star-of-Bethlehem) a plant of a large genus (*Ornithogalum*) of herbs of the family Liliaceae. **ornitholog'ical** *adj*. **ornitholog'ically** *adv*. **ornithol'ogist** *n*. **ornithol'ogy** *n* the study of birds. **ornithomancy** /*ör-nī'thō-man-si* or *ör'nith-ō-*/ *n* (see **-mancy**) divination by means of birds, by observing their flight, etc. **ornithoman'tic** *adj*. **ornithomorph** /*ör-nī'thō-mörf* or *ör'nith-ō-mörf*/ *n* (see **-morph**) a figure or design in the form of a bird. **ornithomorph'ic** *adj*. **ornithoph'ilous** *adj* (see **-philous** under **phil-**) bird-pollinated. **ornithoph'ily** *n*. **ornithophō'bia** *n* fear of birds. **or'nithopod** *n* a member of the **Ornithop'oda**, a suborder of bipedal ornithischian dinosaurs. **ornithopter** /*-op'tər*/ *n* (Gr *pteron* wing) a flying machine with flapping wings. **ornithorhynchus** /*-ō-ring'kəs*/ *n* (Gr *rhynchos* snout) the duckbill, of the *Ornithorhynchus* genus. **ornithosaur** /*ör-nī'thə-sör*/ *n* (Gr *sauros* lizard) a pterodactyl. **ornithoscopy** /*-os'kə-pi*/ *n* (see **-scopy**) augury by observation of birds.

ornithoid /*ör'ni-thoid*/ *adj* birdlike. [Gr *ornis*, *ornīthos* bird, and *eidos* form]

ornithosis /*ör-ni-thō'sis*/ *n* the disease psittacosis. [Gr *ornis*, *ornīthos* bird, and **-osis**]

Orobanche /*o-rō-bang'kē*/ *n* the broomrape genus of dicotyledons, giving name to the family **Orobanchā'ceae**, root-parasites without green leaves. [Gr *orobanchē* dodder, also broomrape, from *orobos* bitter vetch, and *anchein* to strangle]

■ **orobanchā'ceous** *adj*.

orogenesis /*ō-* or *ō-* or *o-rō-jen'i-sis*/ (*geol*) *n* mountain-building, the processes that take place during an orogeny. [Gr *oros* mountain, and **genesis**]

■ **or'ogen** *n* an orogenic belt. **orogenet'ic** or **orogen'ic** *adj*. **orogeny** /*or-oj'ə-ni*, *ör-or* or *ör-*/ *n* a period of mountain-building, during which rocks are severely folded, metamorphosed, and uplifted; orogenesis. ❑ **orogenic belt** *n* a *usu* elongated region of the earth's crust that has been subjected to an orogeny.

orography /*o-rog'rə-fi*/ or **oreography** /*o-ri-og'*/ *n* the description of mountains. [Gr *oros*, *oreos* mountain, and **-graphy**]

■ **orograph'ic** or **oreograph'ic**, **orograph'ical** or **oreograph'ical** *adj*. **orograph'ically** or **oreograph'ically** *adv*.

oroide /*ō'* or *ō'rō-īd*/ *n* an alloy of copper and zinc or tin, etc, imitating gold. [Fr *or*, from L *aurum* gold, and Gr *eidos* form]

■ **o'rēide** *n* a similar or identical alloy.

orology /*o-rol'ə-ji*/ or **oreology** /*o-ri-ol'*/ *n* the scientific study of mountains. [Gr *oros*, *-eos* mountain, and **-logy**]

■ **orolog'ical** or **oreolog'ical** *adj*. **orol'ogist** or **oreol'ogist** *n*.

oropesa /*o-rō-pē'zə* or *-pā'sə*/ *n* a fish-shaped float used in marine minesweeping to support the sweeping wire. [From the name of a trawler]

oropharynx /*ō-* or *ō-rō-far'ingks*/ *n* the part of the pharynx between the soft palate and the epiglottis. [L *ōs*, *ōris* a mouth, and **pharynx**]

ororotund, etc see **orotund**.

■ words derived from main entry word; ❑ compound words; ■ idioms and phrasal verbs

orotund /ō'rə-tund, ō' or o'/, also **ororotund** /-ro-rə-tund/ adj (of a voice) full, round or sonorous; (of something said) pompous, grandiloquent. [L ōs, ōris mouth, and rotundus round]
■ **orotund'ity** or **ororotund'ity** n.

orphan /ör'fən/ n a child or animal deprived of father or mother, or (usu) both, through death; a machine, etc, that has been phased out or superseded; a short line at the end of a paragraph, a club-line (printing). ◆ vt to make an orphan. ◆ adj of, relating to or being an orphan. [Gr orphanos, related to L orbus bereaved]
■ **or'phanage** n a home for orphans; the state of being an orphan. **or'phanhood** or **or'phanism** n.
❑ **or'phan-asy'lum** n (archaic). **orphan disease** n any extremely rare disease.

orpharion /ör-fə-rī'ən or ör-fā'ri-ən/ n a large lute-like instrument with six to nine pairs of metal strings (also **orpheō'reon**). [Orpheus and Arīon, mythical musicians]

Orpheus /ör'fūs or -fi-əs/ (Gr myth) n a mythical Thracian musician and poet who could move inanimate objects by the music of his lyre, the founder or interpreter of the ancient mysteries.
■ **Orphe'an** adj relating to or associated with Orpheus; melodious. ◆ n a musician; (in pl) a name adopted by some amateur musical societies. **Or'phic** adj relating to the mysteries associated with Orpheus; esoteric. **Or'phism** n the system taught in the Orphic mysteries; an early 20c style of abstract art using brilliant colour (also **Orphic Cubism**).
❑ **Orpheus harmonica** n the panharmonicon.

orphrey /ör'fri/ n gold or other rich embroidery, esp bordering an ecclesiastical vestment. [OFr orfreis, from L auriphrygium Phrygian gold]

orpiment /ör'pi-mənt/ n a yellow mineral, arsenic trisulphide, used as a pigment. [OFr, from L auripigmentum, from aurum gold, and pigmentum paint]

orpine or **orpin** /ör'pin/ n a purple-flowered, broad-leaved stonecrop. [Fr orpin]

Orpington /ör'ping-tən/ n a breed of poultry (white, black or buff). [Orpington in W Kent]

ORR abbrev : Office of the Rail Regulator (a UK regulatory body).

orra /or'a or -ə/ (Scot) adj odd; not matched; left over; occasional; casual; supernumerary; worthless. [Origin unknown]
❑ **orra man** n a farm worker kept to do any odd job that may occur.

orrery /or'ə-ri/ n a clockwork model of the solar system. [From Charles Boyle, fourth Earl of Orrery (1676–1731) for whom one was made]

orris[1] /or'is/ n the Florentine or other iris; its dried rootstock (**orr'is-root**) smelling of violets, used in perfumery. [Perh **iris**]

orris[2] /or'is/ n a kind of gold or silver lace used esp in the 18c; upholsterers' galloon and gimp. [Perh OFr orfreis; see **orphrey**]

orseille /ör-sāl'/ same as **archil** or **orchil**. [Fr]
■ **orsellic** /-sel'/ adj.

ORT abbrev : oral rehydration therapy.

ortanique /ör'tə-nēk/ n a cross between the orange and the tangerine, or its fruit. [Portmanteau word: orange, tangerine, and unique]

orth- see **ortho-**.

orthian /ör'thi-ən/ (music) adj high-pitched. [Gr orthios]

orthicon /ör'thi-kon/ n a television camera tube more sensitive than the earlier iconoscope; a further development is the **image orthicon** (see under **image**). [**ortho-** and **iconoscope**]

ortho- /ör-thō- or -tho-/ sometimes before a vowel **orth-** /örth-/ combining form denoting: straight; upright; perpendicular; right; genuine; derived from an acid anhydride by combination with the largest number of water molecules (distinguished from meta-; chem); having substituted atoms or groups attached to two adjacent carbon atoms of the benzene ring (distinguished from meta- and para-, in this sense commonly represented by O-; chem). [Gr orthos straight, upright, right]
■ **or'tho** adj a contraction of **orthochromatic**. ◆ n (pl **or'thos**) an orthochromatic plate. **orthoax'is** n (pl **orthoax'es** /-ak'sēz/) (crystallog) the orthodiagonal. **orthobo'rate** n a salt of orthoboric acid (see **boric acid** under **borax**[1]). **orthocaine** /-kā'in or -kān/ n a white crystalline substance used as a local anaesthetic. **or'thocentre** n the point of intersection of the altitudes of a triangle. **Orthoceras** /ör-thos'ə-ras/ n (Gr keras horn) a genus of fossil cephalopods with a straight shell. **orthochromat'ic** adj (Gr chrōma colour) of or relating to a photographic emulsion sensitive to some but not all the colours of the visible spectrum (cf **panchromatic**). **or'thoclase** /-klās or -klāz/ n (Gr klasis fracture) common or potash feldspar, monoclinic, with cleavages at right angles. **or'tho-compound** n (chem). **or'tho-cousin** n the son or daughter of a father's brother or a mother's sister. **orthodiag'onal** n (in a monoclinic crystal) that lateral axis which is perpendicular to the vertical axis. **orthodontia** /-don'ti-ə/ or

orthodont'ics n (Gr odous, odontos tooth) rectification of crookedness in the teeth. **orthodont'ic** adj. **orthodont'ically** adv. **orthodont'ist** n. **or'thodox** adj (Gr doxa opinion) sound in doctrine; believing, or according to, the received or established doctrines or opinions, esp in religion; (with cap) of the Greek or Eastern Church (see **Eastern Church** under **east**). **or'thodoxly** adv. **or'thodoxy** n the state or quality of being orthodox. **orthodrom'ic** adj (Gr dromos a course or run; geog and naut) having great circles represented as straight lines; (of nerve fibres) conducting or able to conduct impulses in the normal direction. **orthod'romy** or **orthodrom'ics** n great-circle sailing, ie sailing by the most direct route. **orthoepic** /-ep'ik/ or **orthoep'ical** adj (Gr epos a word). **orthoep'ist** (or /ör'thō-ep-ist/) n. **orthō'epy** (or /ör'thō-ep-i/) n (the study of) correct pronunciation. **orthogen'esis** n (see **genesis**) the evolution of organisms systematically in definite directions and not accidentally in many directions; determinate variation. **orthogen'esist** n. **orthogenet'ic** adj relating to orthogenesis. **orthogenet'ically** adv. **orthogen'ic** adj orthogenetic; concerning the treatment of mentally and emotionally disturbed children. **orthogen'ics** n sing. **orthognath'ic** or **orthog'nathous** adj (Gr gnathos jaw) having a lower jaw that neither protrudes nor recedes. **orthog'nathism** n. **orthog'onal** adj (Gr gōniā angle) right-angled (**orthogonal projection** projection by lines perpendicular to the plane of projection). **orthogonal'ity** n. **orthog'onally** adv. **or'thograph** n a drawing in orthographic projection, esp of the elevation of a building. **orthog'rapher** n a person skilled in orthography; a speller. **orthograph'ic** or **orthograph'ical** adj relating or according to spelling; spelt correctly; in perspective projection, having the point of sight at infinity. **orthograph'ically** adv. **orthog'raphist** n an orthographer. **orthog'raphy** n (Gr orthographiā spelling or elevation; see **-graphy**) the art or practice of spelling words correctly; spelling; orthographic projection; apparently for orthographer (Shakesp). **orthokeratol'ogy** n a technique for improving the vision of people affected by myopia and astigmatism, in which the cornea is temporarily reshaped by a special contact lens which is then removed and re-used as necessary. **orthol'ogous** adj. **or'thologue** n a gene that shares a common ancestry with, and has a similar DNA configuration to, a gene in a different species (cf **paralogue**). **orthomorph'ic** adj (of a map) conformal. **orthopae'dic** or (N Am) **orthopē'dic**, also (rare) **orthopae'dical** or **orthopē'dical** adj. **orthopae'dically** or (N Am) **orthopē'dically** adv. **orthopaedics** or (N Am) **orthopēdics** /-pē'diks/, also **or'thopaedy** or **or'thopēdy**, formerly **orthopedī'a** (or /-pēd'ī/) n sing (Gr pais, paidos a child) the art or process of curing deformities arising from (orig childhood) disease or injury of bones. **orthopae'dist** or **orthopē'dist** n. **orthophos'phate** n an ordinary phosphate. **orthophosphor'ic** adj phosphoric. **or'thophyre** /-fīr/ n (orthoclase porphyry) a fine-grained syenitic rock with orthoclase crystals. **orthophyric** /-fir'ik/ adj. **orthopin'akoid** n in monoclinic crystals, a form consisting of two faces parallel to the orthodiagonal and the vertical axis. **orthopnoea** /-thōp-nē'ə/ n (Gr orthopnoia, from pneein to breathe) a condition in which one can only breathe when upright. **or'thopod** n (med sl) an orthopaedic surgeon. **or'thopraxis** or **or'thopraxy** n correct or orthodox practice esp in religion (see **praxis**). **or'thoprism** n in monoclinic crystals, a form parallel to the orthodiagonal. **orthopsychiat'ric** adj. **or'thopsychiatrist** n. **or'thopsychiatry** n the branch of psychiatry concerned with the prevention and correction of incipient mental illness. **Orthop'tera** n pl (see **-ptera** under **ptero-**) the cockroach order of insects with firm forewings serving as covers to the fanwise folded hind-wings. **orthop'teran** n and adj. **orthop'terist** or **orthopterol'ogist** n a person who studies the Orthoptera. **orthopterol'ogy** n. **orthop'teroid** adj. **orthop'teron** n (pl **orthop'tera**) any member of the Orthoptera. **orthop'terous** adj relating to the Orthoptera. **orthop'tic** adj (Gr optikos optic) relating to normal vision. **orthop'tics** n sing the treatment of defective eyesight by exercises and visual training. **orthop'tist** n. **orthorex'ia** n (med) a condition characterized by a morbid obsession with eating only foods considered healthy. **orthorhom'bic** adj (Gr rhombos rhomb; crystallog) referable to three unequal axes at right angles to each other. **orthoscop'ic** adj (Gr skopeein to look at) having or giving correct vision, true proportion, or a flat field of view. **orthosil'icate** n a salt of **orthosilicic** /-sil-is'ik/ **acid** H_4SiO_4. **orthō'sis** n (pl **orthō'ses**) a device that supports, corrects deformities in, or improves the movement of, the movable parts of the body. **orthostat'ic** adj (Gr orthostatos, from statos standing) standing erect; connected with the erect posture. **orthos'tichous** adj (Gr stichos a row) arranged in vertical rows. **orthos'tichy** n a straight row, eg of leaves vertically over one another on an axis. **orthot'ic** adj of or relating to orthotics. **orthot'ics** n sing the branch of medical science dealing with the rehabilitation of injured or weakened joints or muscles through artificial or mechanical support by orthoses. **or'thotist** n someone skilled in orthotics. **orthotonē'sis** n (Gr tonos accent; linguistics) accentuation of a proclitic or enclitic, opp to enclisis. **orthoton'ic** adj taking an accent in certain positions but not in others, also **or'thotone**. **orthotop'ic** adj

(Gr *topos* place; *med*) (of tissue, grafts, organ replacement, etc) done, put, occurring, etc at the normal place. **orthotrop'ic** *adj* (Gr *tropos* a turn) manifesting orthotropism; (of a material, such as wood) having elastic properties varying in different planes. **orthot'ropism** *n* growth in the direct line of stimulus, *esp* of gravity. **orthot'ropous** *adj* (of an ovule) straight, having the nucellus in direct continuation of the funicle. **orthot'ropy** *n* (of a material, such as wood) the state of being orthotropic.

orthros /ör'thros/ *n* one of the Greek canonical hours, corresponding in the Eastern Orthodox Church to the Western lauds. [Gr *orthros* dawn]

ortolan /ör'tə-lən/ *n* a kind of bunting, common in Europe and eaten as a delicacy. [Fr, from Ital *ortolano*, from L *hortulānus* belonging to gardens, from *hortulus*, dimin of *hortus* a garden]

orval /ör'vəl/ (*obs*) *n* a plant of the sage genus, the clary. [Cf Fr *orvale*]

Orvieto /ör-vyā'tō/ *n* a white wine from Orvieto in Italy.
- **Orvietan** /ör-vi-ē'tən/ *n* a supposed antidote to poison ascribed to an Orvieto man.

Orwellian /ör-wel'i-ən/ *adj* relating to or in the style of the English writer George *Orwell* (1903–50); characteristic of the dehumanized authoritarian society described in his novel *1984*. ◆ *n* a person who studies Orwell or his ideas.

oryctology /o-rik-tol'ə-ji/ (*obs*) *n* mineralogy; palaeontology. [Gr *oryktos* dug, quarried]

oryx /or'iks/ *n* an African antelope of the genus *Oryx*. [Gr *oryx*, *-ygos* a pick-axe or an oryx antelope]

Oryza /ö- or ö-rī'zə/ *n* a tropical genus of grasses, including rice. [Gr *oryza*]

orzo /ör'tsō/ *n* pasta in the form of small pieces like rice or barley. [Ital *orzo* barley]

OS *abbrev*: Old Style; operating system (*comput*); Ordinary Seaman; Ordnance Survey; outsize.

Os (*chem*) *symbol*: osmium.

os¹ /os/ (*anat*) *n* (pl **ossa** /os'ə/) a bone. [L]

os² /os/ (*anat* and *zool*) *n* (pl **ora** /ö'rə/) a mouth or mouthlike opening, *orig* used only in Latin names of particular structures. [L]

OSA *abbrev*: *Ordinis* or *Ordo Sancti Augustini* (L), (of) the Order of St Augustine.

Osage /ö-sāj' or ö'sāj/ *n* a Native American of a tribe living in Oklahoma, etc; the language of this people. ◆ *adj* of or relating to the Osage or their language. [Osage *Wazhazhe*]
- **Osage orange** *n* an ornamental tree (genus *Maclura*) of the mulberry family, often used for hedges, first found in the Osage country; its orange-like inedible fruit.

OSB *abbrev*: *Ordinis* or *Ordo Sancti Benedicti* (L), (of) the Order of St Benedict.

Oscan /os'kən/ *n* one of an ancient Italic people in S Italy; their Indo-European language, generally considered to be related to Latin. ◆ *adj* of or relating to the Oscans or their language.

Oscar®¹ /os'kər/ *n* a gold-plated statuette awarded by the American Academy of Motion Picture Arts and Sciences to a film writer, actor, director, etc, for the year's best performance in his or her particular line. [Name fortuitously given, possibly after an Academy employee's uncle]

Oscar² or **oscar** /os'kər/ *n* (in international radio communication) a code word for the letter *o*.

Oscar³ or **oscar** /os'kər/ (*obs Aust* and *NZ sl*) *n* cash. [Rhyming slang for *Oscar Asche* (1871–1936), Australian actor]

OSCE *abbrev*: Organization for Security and Co-operation in Europe.

oscheal /os'ki-əl/ (*med*) *adj* relating to the scrotum. [Gr *oscheon* scrotum]

oscillate /os'i-lāt/ *vi* to swing to and fro like a pendulum; to vibrate; to radiate electromagnetic waves; to vary between certain limits; to fluctuate. ◆ *vt* to cause to swing or vibrate. [L *ōscillāre*, *-ātum* to swing]
- **osc'illating** *adj*. **oscillā'tion** *n* a vibration. **osc'illātive** *adj* having a tendency to vibrate; vibratory. **osc'illātor** *n* someone who or something that oscillates; an apparatus for producing oscillations. **oscillatory** /os'il-ə-tə-ri/ *adj* swinging; moving as a pendulum does; vibratory. **oscill'ogram** *n* a record made by an oscillograph. **oscill'ograph** *n* an apparatus for producing a curve representing a number of electrical and mechanical phenomena which vary cyclically. **oscillograph'ic** *adj*. **oscillograph'ically** *adv*. **oscillog'raphy** *n*. **oscill'oscope** *n* an instrument that shows on a fluorescent screen the variation with time of the instantaneous values and waveforms of electrical quantities, including voltages translated from sounds or movements. **oscilloscopic** /-skop'ik/ *adj*.

Oscines /os'i-nēz/ *n pl* the songbirds, forming the main body of the order Passeriformes. [L *oscen*, *oscinis* a singing-bird]
- **osc'inine** or (faultily formed) **osc'ine** *adj*.

oscitancy /os'i-tən-si/ *n* yawning; sleepiness; stupidity. [L *ōscitāre* to yawn]
- **osc'itant** *adj*. **osc'itantly** *adv*. **osc'itate** *vi* to yawn. **oscitā'tion** *n* yawning; sleepiness.

osculant /os'kū-lənt/ *adj* kissing; adhering closely; intermediate between two genera, species, etc, linking (*biol*). [L *ōsculārī*, *-ātus* to kiss, from *ōsculum* a little mouth, a kiss, dimin of *ōs* mouth]
- **os'cular** *adj* relating to the mouth or osculum, or to kissing; osculating. **os'culāte** *vt* to kiss; to have three or more coincident points in common with (*maths*). ◆ *vi* to be in close contact; to form a connecting link. **osculā'tion** *n*. **os'culatory** *adj* of or relating to kissing or osculation. ◆ *n* a carved tablet kissed by the priest and (now rarely) by the people at mass. **os'cule** *n* a little mouth; a small mouthlike aperture. **os'culum** *n* (pl **os'cula**) an exhalant aperture in a sponge; a sucker on a tapeworm's head.
- **osculating orbit** *n* (*astron*) an ellipse whose elements represent the actual position and velocity of a comet at a given moment (the **epoch of osculation**).

-ose /-ōs or -ōz/ (*chem*) *sfx* denoting a carbohydrate. [From gluc*ose*]

oseltamivir /ō-sel-tam'i-vēr/ *n* an antiviral drug used to treat certain types of influenza.

OSF *abbrev*: *Ordinis* or *Ordo Sancti Francisci* (L), (of) the Order of St Francis.

OSHA *abbrev*: Occupational Safety and Health Administration (in the USA).

oshac /ō'shak/ *n* the ammoniac plant. [Ar *ushshaq*]

osier /ō'(zhy)ər, -zi-ər or -zyər/ *n* any willow whose twigs are used in making baskets, *esp Salix viminalis*. ◆ *adj* made of or like osiers. [Fr *osier* of unknown origin; there is a LL *ausāria* or *osāria* willow bed]
- **o'siered** *adj* covered or fringed with osiers; twisted like osiers. **o'siery** *n* osier-work.
- **o'sier-bed** *n* a place where osiers grow.

Osiris /ö-sī'ris/ *n* the greatest of Egyptian gods, son of Seb and Nut, or Heaven and Earth, husband of Isis, father of Horus. [Gr *Osīris*]
- **Osī'rian** *adj*.

-osis /-ö-sis/ *n combining form* denoting: (1) a condition or process; (2) a diseased condition. [L *-osis*, Gr *-ōsis*]

Osmanli /os-man'li/ *adj* of the dynasty of *Osmān*, who founded the Turkish empire in Asia, and reigned 1288–1326; of the Turkish empire; of the western branch of the Turks or their language. ◆ *n* a member of the dynasty; a Turk of Turkey. [Cf **Ottoman**]

osmate see under **osmium**.

osmeterium /os- or oz-mē-tē'ri-əm/ *n* (pl **osmetē'ria**) a forked process behind the head of certain caterpillars giving out a foul smell. [Gr *osmē* smell, stink, and sfx *-tērion*, denoting instrument]

osmiate, **osmic** see under **osmium**.

osmidrosis /os- or oz-mi-drō'sis/ *n* the secretion of ill-smelling sweat. [Gr *osmē* smell, and *hidrōs* sweat]

osmium /os' or oz'mi-əm/ *n* a hard, dense, grey metallic element (symbol **Os**; atomic no 76), whose tetroxide has a disagreeable smell. [Gr *osmē* smell]
- **os'mate** or **os'miate** *n* a salt of the hypothetical osmic acid. **os'mic** *adj* containing osmium in higher valency; relating to smells or to the sense of smell. **os'mious** or **os'mous** *adj* containing osmium in lower valency. **osmirid'ium** *n* iridosmine.
- **osmic acid** *n* strictly, a supposed acid H_2OsO_4; *usu* osmium tetroxide, an ill-smelling substance used as a stain for fats in optical microscopy and as a heavy metal deposit in electron microscopy.

osmosis /os- or oz-mō'sis/ *n* diffusion of liquids through a semipermeable membrane (*chem*); a gradual absorption or assimilation (*fig*). [Gr *ōsmos* = *ōthismos* impulse, from *ōtheein* to push]
- **osmom'eter** *n* an apparatus for measuring osmotic pressure. **osmomet'ric** *adj*. **osmom'etry** *n*. **osmoregulā'tion** *n* the process by which animals regulate the amount of water in their bodies and the concentration of various solutes and ions in their body fluids. **osmoreg'ulatory** /-lə-tər-i/ *adj*. **osmose'** *vi* and *vt* to undergo or cause to undergo osmosis. ◆ *n* /oz'/ (*archaic*) osmosis. **osmotic** /-mot'ik/ *adj*. **osmot'ically** *adv*.
- **osmotic pressure** *n* the pressure exerted by a dissolved substance in virtue of the motion of its molecules; a measure of this as the pressure which must be applied to a solution which is separated by a semipermeable membrane from a pure solvent in order to prevent the passage of the solvent through the membrane.

■ words derived from main entry word; □ compound words; ■ idioms and phrasal verbs

osmous see under **osmium**.

osmund /oz'mənd/ or **osmunda** /oz-mun'də/ n a fern of the royal-fern genus *Osmunda*, giving name to a family **Osmundā'ceae**. [Origin unknown]

osnaburg /oz'nə-bûrg/ n a coarse linen, *orig* brought from *Osnabrück* in Germany; a coarse cotton. ◆ *adj* made of osnaburg.

osp *abbrev*: *obiit sine prole* (L), died without issue.

osprey /os'pri or -prā/ n a bird of prey (*Pandion haliaetus*) that feeds on fish; an egret or other plume used in millinery, not from the osprey. [Supposed to be from L *ossifraga*, misapplied; see **ossifrage**]

OSS (*US*) *abbrev*: Office of Strategic Services, a forerunner of the **CIA**.

ossa see **os**[1].

osseous /os'i-əs/ *adj* bony; composed of, or like, bone; of the nature or structure of bone. [L *os, ossis* bone]

■ **ossā'rium** n an ossuary. **ossein** /os'i-in/ n the organic basis of bone. **osselet** /os'ə-let or os'let/ n a hard substance growing on the inside of a horse's knee. **oss'icle** n (*anat*) a little bone or bonelike plate. **ossic'ular** *adj*. **ossif'erous** *adj* yielding or containing bones. **ossif'ic** *adj* causing ossification. **ossificā'tion** n the process or state of being changed into a bony substance. **oss'ify** *vt* to make into bone or into a bonelike substance. ◆ *vi* to become bone; to become rigid, hardened, inflexible or set into a conventional pattern. **ossiv'orous** *adj* feeding on or consuming bones.

osseter /o-set'ər/ n a species of sturgeon. [Russ *osiotr*]

Ossi /os'i/ (*inf*) n (pl **Ossis**) a citizen of the former German Democratic Republic (East Germany) before reunification with the Federal Republic in 1990. See also **Wessi**. [Ger abbrev of *Ostdeutsch* East German]

ossia /ō-sē'a/ (*Ital*) *conj* or (giving an alternative in music).

Ossian /os(h)'i-ən/ n a legendary Gaelic poet whose poems James Macpherson (1736–96) professed to translate. [Gaelic *Oisin*]

■ **Ossianesque** /-esk'/ *adj* in the manner of Macpherson's Ossian. **Ossianic** /-an'ik/ *adj* relating to Ossian or to Macpherson's publications.

ossicle, etc see under **osseous**.

ossifrage /os'i-frāj/ n the lammergeier, a rare type of vulture; the osprey. [L *ossifraga*, probably the lammergeier, from *os, ossis* bone, and the root of *frangere* to break]

■ **ossifraga** /os-if'rə-gə/ n the giant fulmar.

ossify, ossivorous, etc see under **osseous**.

osso buco or **ossobuco** /os'sō boo'kō/ n an Italian dish of (*usu* veal) knuckle cooked with the bone and stewed in wine, herbs, etc. [Ital, hollow bone]

ossuary /os'ū-ə-ri/ n a place where bones are laid, eg a vault or charnel house; an urn for bones. [L *ossuārium*, from *os* bone]

OST *abbrev*: Office of Science and Technology; Original Soundtrack.

oste- see **osteo-**.

ostensible /o-sten'si-bl/ *adj* seeming, or outwardly apparent; pretended or professed; that may be shown (*obs*). [L *ostendere, ostensum* (*ostentum*) to show, and its frequentative *ostentāre*, from pfx *obs-* in front, and *tendere* to stretch]

■ **ostensibil'ity** n. **ostens'ibly** *adv*. **ostens'ive** *adj* of a clearly demonstrative nature (*logic*, etc); (of a definition) provided by pointing to examples of things to which the defined word or phrase properly applies; showing; deictic; ostensible. **ostens'ively** *adv*. **ostens'iveness** n. **osten'sory** n (*RC*) a monstrance. **ostent'** n appearance (*Shakesp*); portent (*rare*); ostentation (*rare*). **ostentā'tion** /-tən-/ n pretentious display intended to draw attention or admiration; boasting; the act of showing (*obs*). **ostentā'tious** *adj* given to show; fond of self-display; showy. **ostentā'tiously** *adv*. **ostentā'tiousness** n.

osteo- /o-sti-ō-, -ə- or -o-/ or **oste-** /o-sti-/ *combining form* signifying bone. [Gr *osteon* bone]

■ **osteal** /os'ti-əl/ *adj* relating to, composed of, or resembling bone; sounding like bone on percussion. **osteitis** /os-ti-ī'tis/ n inflammation of a bone. **osteoarthrit'ic** *adj*. **osteoarthrī'tis** n a form of arthritis in which the cartilages of the joint and the bone adjacent are worn away. **osteoarthrō'sis** n chronic non-inflammatory disease of the joints and the bone adjacent; osteoarthritis. **os'teoblast** n (see **-blast**) a bone-forming cell. **osteoblast'ic** *adj*. **osteochondrī'tis** or **osteochondrō'sis** n (Gr *chondros* cartilage) a disease in which abnormal growth of cartilage or bone leads to degeneration of the cartilage, usually in the joints. **osteoclasis** /os-ti-ok'lə-sis/ n (Gr *klasis* fracture) fracture of a bone for correction of a deformity; absorption and destruction of bone tissue by osteoclasts. **os'teoclast** n a surgical instrument for fracturing bone; a bone-destroying cell. **osteoclast'ic** *adj*. **osteocoll'a** n (Gr *kolla* glue) a calcareous incrustation on roots, etc, once thought able to unite broken bones. **os'teoderm** n (Gr *derma* skin) a bony dermal plate. **osteoderm'al, osteoderm'atous**,

osteoderm'ic or **osteoderm'ous** *adj*. **os'teogen** n a substance or layer from which bone is formed. **osteogen'esis** or **osteogeny** /-oj'/ n formation of bone (**osteogenesis imperfecta** the disease *brittle bones*, in which bones are abnormally liable to fracture). **osteogenet'ic, osteogen'ic** or **osteog'enous** *adj*. **Osteoglossidae** /-glos'i-dē/ n pl (Gr *glōssa* tongue) a family of bony fishes, including the arapaima. **osteog'raphy** n the description of bones. **ost'eoid** *adj* bonelike. **Osteol'epis** n (Gr *lepis* scale) an Old Red Sandstone fossil fish with bonelike scales. **osteolog'ical** *adj*. **osteolog'ically** *adv*. **osteol'ogist** n. **osteol'ogy** n the part of anatomy that deals with the study of bones and the skeleton. **osteō'ma** n a tumour composed of bone or bonelike tissue. **osteomalacia** /-mə-lā'shi-ə/ n (Gr *malakos* soft) softening of adult bones by absorption of their calcium salts, resulting from a deficiency of vitamin D (the equivalent to **rickets** in children). **osteomalā'cial** or **osteomalacic** /-las'ik/ *adj*. **osteomyelitis** /-mī-ə-lī'tis/ n (Gr *myelos* marrow) inflammation of bone and bone marrow. **os'teopath** /-path/ or **osteop'athist** /-ə-thist/ n a practitioner of osteopathy. **osteopathic** /ost-i-ə-path'ik/ *adj*. **osteopath'ically** *adv*. **osteop'athy** n a system of healing or treatment consisting largely of manipulation of the bones, and massage. **osteopē'nia** n (Gr *penia* poverty) a condition resulting in a reduction of bone density. **osteopetrō'sis** n a general name for a group of hereditary bone diseases, including *marble bone disease*, in which bone becomes abnormally dense. **os'teophyte** /-fīt/ n (see **-phyte** under **phyt-**) an abnormal bony outgrowth. **osteophytic** /-fit'ik/ *adj*. **osteoplast'ic** *adj*. **os'teoplasty** n plastic surgery of the bones, bone-grafting, etc. **osteoporō'sis** n (root as **pore**[1]) development of a porous structure in bone due to loss of calcium, resulting in brittleness. **osteoporotic** /-ot'ik/ *adj*. **osteosarcō'ma** n a malignant tumour derived from osteoblasts, composed of bone and sarcoma cells. **os'teotome** n (Gr *tomos* cutting; *surg*) an instrument for cutting bones. **osteot'omy** n the surgical cutting of a bone.

Ostiak see **Ostyak**.

ostinato /o-sti-nä'tō/ (*music*) n (pl **ostina'tos**) a ground-bass. [Ital; ety as for **obstinate**]

ostium /os'ti-əm/ n (pl **os'tia**) a mouth-like opening (*anat*); the mouth of a river (*obs*). [L *ostium*]

■ **os'tial** *adj*. **os'tiary** n a doorkeeper (*relig*); in the Roman Catholic Church, a member of the lowest of the minor orders; a river mouth (*obs*). **os'tiate** *adj* having an ostium or ostia. **os'tiolate** *adj* having an opening. **os'tiole** n a small opening.

OStJ *abbrev*: Officer of the Order of St John of Jerusalem.

ostler or (*obs and US*) **hostler** /os'lər or (*US*) hos'lər/ n a person who attends to horses at an inn (also *fem* **ost'leress**). [hosteler]

Ostmark /ost'märk/ n the standard monetary unit (100 pfennig) of East Germany prior to German unification. [Ger, east mark]

Ostmen /ōst'men/ (*hist*) n pl the Danish settlers in Ireland. [ON *Austmenn* Eastmen]

-ostomy the combining element is properly **-stomy**.

Ostpolitik /ost'po-li-tēk/ (*hist*) n the West German policy, initiated in the 1960s, of establishing normal trade and diplomatic relations with the E European communist countries; any similar policy. [Ger, Eastern policy]

ostracize or **-ise** /os'trə-sīz/ *vt* to exclude from society or from one's social group; in ancient Greece, to banish by popular vote, the voters writing on potsherds the name of the person they wanted banished. [Gr *ostrakon* a shell, tile or potsherd]

■ **os'tracism** /-sizm/ n expulsion from society; banishment by ostracizing.

ostracod /os'trə-kod/ n a member of the **Ostracō'da**, a class of minute crustacea with bivalve shells. [New L, from Gr *ostrakōdēs* having a shell, from *ostrakon* shell]

■ **ostracō'dan** or **ostracō'dous** *adj*.

ostracoderm /os'trə-kə-dûrm/ n any member (such as *Cephalaspis*) of a group of Silurian and Old Red Sandstone fishes or fish-like animals, generally cased in bony armour with undeveloped lower jaw, with flippers but not ordinary paired fins. [Gr *ostrakon* shell, and *derma* skin]

ostrakon or **ostracon** /os'trə-kon/ n (pl **os'traka** or **os'traca**) a potsherd or tile, *esp* one used in ostracism in Greece or for writing on in ancient Egypt. [Gr, shell]

■ **ostracean** /os-trā'shən/ or **ostrā'ceous** *adj* of the nature of an oyster. **Ostracion** /os-trā'shi-on/ n the coffer-fish genus.

Ostrea /os'tri-ə/ n the oyster genus. [L *ostrea*, from Gr *ostreon* oyster]

■ **ostreā'ceous** *adj*. **ostreicul'ture** /os-trē-i-/ n oyster culture, the artificial breeding of oysters for sale. **ostrēicul'turist** n. **os'treophage** /-fāj/ n (see **-phage** under **phag-**) an oyster-eater. **ostrephagous** /os-tri-of'ə-gəs/ *adj* oyster-eating. **ostreoph'agy** /-ə-ji/ n.

ostreger /os'tri-jər/ a variant of **austringer**, a keeper of goshawks.

ostreophagous, etc see under **Ostrea**.

ostrich /os'trich or -trij/ n the largest living bird (*Struthio camelus*), found in Africa, flightless but remarkable for its speed in running, and prized for its feathers; a person who refuses to face, or who ignores, unpleasant facts (from the ostrich's habit of burying its head when chased, in the belief, supposedly, that it cannot be seen). [OFr *ostruche* (Fr *autruche*), from L *avis* bird, and LL *struthiō*, from Gr *strouthiōn* an ostrich, and *strouthos* a bird]
■ **os'trichism** n the habit or policy of ignoring or refusing to face unpleasant facts. **os'trich-like** adj and adv (usu in reference to the supposed habit of hiding its head when in danger).

Ostrogoth /os'trə-goth/ n an eastern Goth, a member of the Germanic people who established their power in Italy in 493, and were overthrown in 555. [LL *Ostrogothī* eastern Goths]
■ **Os'trogothic** adj.

Ostyak or **Ostiak** /os'ti-ak/ n a member of a Ugrian people of Siberia; their language. ◆ adj of or relating to the Ostyaks or their language.

OT abbrev : occupational therapist; occupational therapy; Old Testament.

otaku /ō-tä'koo or -tak'oo/ (derog) n pl in Japan, socially inept young people with an obsessive interest in computer technology.

otalgia /ō-tal'ji-ə/ (med) n earache (also **otal'gy**). [Gr *ous*, *ōtos* ear, and *algē* pain]

otary /ō'tə-ri/ n (pl **o'taries**) any of the eared seals, including the sea-lions and fur seals, with well-developed external ears. [Gr *ōtaros* large-eared, from *ous*, *ōtos* ear]
■ **o'tarine** adj.

OTC abbrev : Officers' Training Corps; over-the-counter.

Otchipwe /ō-chip'wä/ n same as **Ojibwa**.

OTE abbrev : on-target earnings, the earnings of a salesman who achieves targeted sales; or the equivalent.

other /udh'ər/ adj second; alternate; different; different from or not the same as the one in question (often with *than*); not the same; remaining; additional; one of two; (probably) left (*Spenser*). ◆ pronoun (or n) other one; another; each other (*archaic* and *Scot*). ◆ adv otherwise (with *than*). [OE *ōther*; cf Ger *ander*, L *alter*]
■ **oth'erness** n. **oth'erwhere** adv (archaic and poetic) elsewhere. **oth'erwhile** or **oth'erwhiles** adv (archaic or poetic) at other times; sometimes. **oth'erwise** adv in another way or manner; by other causes; in other respects; under other conditions. ◆ adj different. ◆ conj else; under other conditions.
□ **oth'er-directed** adj (sociol) guided by standards set for one by external influences. **other ranks** n pl members of the armed services not holding commissions. **oth'erworld** n other world than; better than or beyond this (also adj). **oth'erworld'ish** adj. **otherworld'liness** n. **otherworld'ly** adj concerned with the world to come, or with the world of the imagination, to the exclusion of practical interests.
■ **every other** each alternate. **in other words** to put it in a different way. **or otherwise** or the opposite, as in *the efficiency or otherwise of the staff*. **other things being equal** associated circumstances being unchanged. **rather...than otherwise** rather than not. **someone**, **something**, **somewhere**, etc **or other** an undefined person, thing, place, etc. **the other** (inf) sexual relations. **the other day**, etc on an unspecified day, etc, not long past. **the other man** or **woman** (inf) a person who is having an affair with someone who is married or in a long-term relationship.

othergates /udh'ər-gāts/ (obs) adv in another way. ◆ adj (also **oth'erguess** or (in *Fielding*, *Goldsmith*, etc) **anoth'erguess**) of another kind. —Also spelt as separate words: **other gates**, **other guess**. [**other**, and genitive of **gate²**]

otic /ō'tik/ (med) adj of or relating to the ear. [Gr *ous*, *ōtos* ear]
■ **otī'tis** n inflammation of the ear.

otiose /ō'shi-ōs or -ti-/ adj (of a word, expression, etc in a particular context) superfluous, redundant; unoccupied; indolent; functionless; futile. [L *ōtiōsus*, from *ōtium* leisure]
■ **o'tiosely** adv. **otiosity** /-os'i-ti/ or **o'tioseness** n ease, idleness.

otitis see under **otic**.

oto- /o-tō-, ō-tə- or ō-tō-/ combining form relating to the ear. [Gr *ous*, *ōtos* ear]
■ **o'tocyst** /-sist/ n an auditory or equilibrial vesicle. **o'tolith** n (Gr *lithos* stone) a calcareous concretion in the ear of various animals, the movement of which helps the animal to maintain equilibrium; an ear-bone. **otolith'ic** adj. **otolog'ical** adj. **otol'ogist** n. **otol'ogy** n the branch of medicine concerned with the ear. **otorhinolaryngology** /-rī-nō-lar-ing-gol'ə-ji/ n (Gr *rhīs*, *rhīnos* nose, and *larynx*, -*yngos* larynx) the branch of medicine dealing with the ear, nose and larynx and their diseases (often shortened to **otolaryngol'ogy**) **otorrhoea** /ō-tə-rē'ə/ n (Gr *rhoiā* flow) a discharge from the ear. **otosclero'sis** n formation of spongy bone in the capsule of the labyrinth of the ear.

otosclerot'ic adj. **o'toscope** n an instrument for examining the ear. **otoscopic** /-skop'ik/ adj.

-otomy a non-standard form of **-tomy**.

otorhinolaryngology...to...**otoscope** see under **oto-**.

OTT (inf) abbrev : over-the-top (qv).

Ottamite see under **Ottoman**.

ottar /ot'ər/ see **attar**.

ottava /öt-tä'vä or ō-tä'və/ n an octave. [Ital; cf **octave**]
■ **ottavino** /-vē'nō/ n (pl **ottavin'os**) the piccolo.
□ **ottava rima** /rē'mä/ n an Italian stanza consisting of eight hendecasyllabic lines, rhyming *a b a b a b c c*.

otter /ot'ər/ n an aquatic fish-eating carnivore (*Lutra lutra*) of the weasel family with short smooth fur, a long slim body, stout tail and webbed feet; its brown short fur; a board travelling edge-up, manipulated on the principle of the kite, to carry the end of a fishing-line (or several hooked and baited lines) in a lake, or to keep open the mouth of a trawl (also **ott'er-board**); a device for severing the moorings of mines, a paravane. ◆ vt or vi to fish with an otter-board. [OE *otor*, related to **water**]
□ **otter hound** n a large, rough-haired breed of dog formerly used in otter-hunting. **ott'er-hunting** n. **otter shell** n a marine bivalve mollusc (genus *Lutraria*) that burrows in mud. **otter shrew** n a large otter-like aquatic W African insectivore (*Potamogale velox*). **ott'er-trawl** n a trawl with otter-boards. **ott'er-trawling** n.

otto /ot'ō/ see **attar**.

Ottoman /ot'ə-mən/ adj relating to the Turkish Empire or to the dynasty founded by *Othmān* or *Osmān*, or to his people, who overran the Near East and pushed into Europe in the 14c; Osmanli. ◆ n a Turk of Turkey; (the following meanings without *cap*) a low, stuffed seat without a back, sometimes in the form of a chest; a cushioned seat for several people sitting with their backs to one another; a variety of corded silk.
■ **Ott'amite** or **Ott'omite** n a Turk.

ottrelite /ot'ri-līt/ n a mineral like chlorite but harder. [*Ottrez* in the Ardennes region of Belgium, and Gr *lithos* stone]
□ **ott'relite-slate** n a clay-slate with minute plates of ottrelite.

OU abbrev : Open University; Oxford University.

ou¹ or **ow** /ŭ/ (Scot) interj expressing concession.
□ **ou ay** n why yes; O yes.

ou² /ō/ (S Afr inf) n (pl **ous** or **ouens** /ō'ənz/) a man. [Afrik]
□ **oubaas** /ō'bäs/ n (Afrik *baas* master) a boss. **ouma** /ō'mä/ n a grandmother. **oupa** /ō'pä/ n a grandfather.

ouabain or **wabain** /wä-bä'in/ n a poisonous compound obtained from apocynaceous seeds and wood (*Strophanthus*, etc). [French spelling, from Somali *wabayo* a tree that yields it]

ouakari see **uakari**.

ouananiche /wä-nə-nēsh'/ n a variety of salmon found in SE Canada. [Can Fr; from Algonquian]

oubaas see under **ou²**.

oubit /oo'bit/ see **woubit**.

oubliette /oo-bli-et'/ n a dungeon with no opening except in the roof; a secret pit in the floor of a dungeon into which a victim could be precipitated. [Fr, from *oublier* to forget]

ouch¹ /owch/ interj expressing pain. [Ger *autsch*]

ouch² /owch/ (archaic) n a brooch; a clasped ornament; the socket of a precious stone. [OFr *nouche*]

oucht /ohht/ (Scot) n anything. [Cf **aught**]

oud /ood/ n an Arab stringed instrument resembling a lute or mandolin. [Ar, as for **lute¹**]

Oudenarde /oo'də-närd/ n a tapestry representing foliage, etc, once made at *Oudenarde* in Belgium.

OUDS /owdz/ abbrev : Oxford University Dramatic Society.

oughly see **ouglie**.

ought¹ /öt/ vt pat of **owe**; now obs or dialect except as an auxiliary verb, taking an infinitive with *to*, and usu with time expressed by the tense of the infinitive, expressing duty or obligation, rightness or suitability, or probability. [OE *āhte*, pat of *āgan* to owe]
■ **ought'ness** n (archaic) rightness.

ought² /öt/ n a variant of **aught**; also a non-standard corruption of **naught**.
■ **oughtlings** /ohh'linz/ adv (Scot) at all.

ouglie or **oughly** old spellings of **ugly**.
□ **ough'ly-headed** adj (Milton).

ouguiya /oo-gē'yə/ n (pl **ougui'ya**) the standard monetary unit of Mauritania (5 khoums). [Fr, from Ar *'ūkiyya*; ult from L *uncia* ounce]

Ouija® /wē'jə or -ji/ (also without *cap*) *n* a board with signs and letters of the alphabet on it, used with a planchette in attempts to receive messages from the dead. [Fr *oui*, Ger *ja* yes]

ouistiti a French spelling of **wistiti**.

ouk or **oulk** /*ook*/ *n* Scots form of **week**.

oulakan or **oulachon** /*oo'lə-kən*/ see **eulachon**.

ould Scots or Irish form of **old**.

oulong same as **oolong**.

ouma see under **ou**².

ounce¹ /*owns*/ *n* $\frac{1}{16}$ of a pound avoirdupois; *orig* $\frac{1}{12}$ of the (legally obsolete) pound troy = 480 grains; a minute quantity. [OFr *unce*, from L *uncia* the twelfth part; cf **inch**¹]
■ **fluid ounce** the volume of an avoirdupois ounce of distilled water at 62° Fahrenheit, 0.0284 litre ($\frac{1}{20}$ pint); 0.0295 litre ($\frac{1}{16}$ US pint).

ounce² /*owns*/ *n* formerly a lynx; now generally the snow leopard, a big cat of Asia with markings similar to a leopard's; the jaguar; the cheetah; sometimes vaguely any moderate-sized wild beast of the cat tribe. [Fr *once*, perh for *lonce* (as if *l'once*), from Gr *lynx*]

oundy /*own'di*/ (*obs*) *adj* wavy; undé (*heraldry*). [Fr *ondé*; cf **undate**]

OUP *abbrev* : Oxford University Press.

oup or **oop** /*oop*/ (*Scot*) *vt* to bind round with thread or cord; to join. [Appar **whip**]

oupa see under **ou**².

ouphe or **ouph** /*owf* or *oof*/ (*Shakesp*) *n* same as **oaf**.

our /*owr*/ *possessive adj* or properly pronoun relating or belonging to us. [OE *ūre*, genitive of *wē* we]
■ **ourn** /*owrn*/ *pronoun* (*dialect*) ours. **ours** /*owrz*/ *pronoun* (the one or ones) belonging to us. **ourselves**' *pronoun* (*sing* **ourself**' used regally or, formerly, editorially) (used *reflexively*) us; (used emphatically for clarification in apposition to **we** or **us**) personally; our normal or usual selves, as in *we can relax and be ourselves*.

ourali /*oo-rä'lē*/ see **wourali**.

ourang-outang same as **orang-utan**.

ourari /*oo-rä'rē*/ see **wourali**.

ourebi same as **oribi**.

ourie, **oorie** or **owrie** /*oo'ri*/ (*Scot*) *adj* dingy; shabby; dreary; drooping; chill; inclined to shiver or shudder.

ouroboros or **uroboros** /*oo-rob'ə-ros* or *oo-rə-bor'əs*/ (*myth*) *n* a representation of a serpent with its tail in its mouth, symbolizing completion, totality, endlessness, etc. [Gr, literally 'tail-devouring', from *ourā* a tail, and *boraein* to eat]

ourology, **ouroscopy**, etc same as **urology**, etc (see under **uro-**¹).

-ous /*-əs*/ *sfx* forming adjectives denoting: character, quality or nature, as in *marvellous*; an element in its lower valency, as in *sulphurous* (*chem*). [L *-osus*]

ousel see **ouzel**.

oust /*owst*/ *vt* to eject or expel. [Anglo-Fr *ouster* (OFr *oster*; Fr *ôter*) to remove; of obscure origin]
■ **oust'er** *n* (*law*) ejection or dispossession.

out (see also **out-**) /*owt*/ *adv* (shading into *adj* predicatively), not within; forth; to, towards, or at the exterior or a position away from the inside or inner part or from anything thought of as enclosing, hiding or obscuring; from among others; from the mass; beyond bounds; away from the original or normal position or state; at or towards the far end, or a remote position; seawards; not within, or away from, one's dwelling, work premises, etc; in or into the open air; in or into a state of exclusion or removal; not in office; not in use or fashion; debarred, not to be considered; no longer in the game; no longer in as a batsman, dismissed; not batting; out of the contest and unable to resume in time; in the condition of having won; away from the mark; at fault; in error; not in form or good condition; at a loss; in or into a disconcerted, perplexed or disturbed state; in or into an unconscious state; not in harmony or amity; in distribution; in or onto the hands of others or the public; on loan; to or at an end; in an exhausted or extinguished state; completely; thoroughly; subjected to loss; in or to the field; in quest of or expressly aiming at something; in rebellion; on strike; in an exposed state; no longer in concealment or obscurity; in or into the state of having openly declared one's homosexuality; in or into the open; before the public; in or into society (*old*); on domestic service (*archaic*); in existence; at full length; in an expanded state; in bloom; in extension; loudly and clearly; forcibly; unreservedly. ◆*adj* external; outlying; remote; played away from home; outwards; not batting; exceeding the usual; in any condition expressed by the adverb *out*. ◆*n* a projection or outward bend (as in *outs and ins*); a way out, a way of escape; someone who is out; an instance of putting a player out (*baseball*); that which is outside; an omission in setting

type (*printing*); a paying out, *esp* (in *pl*) rates and taxes, etc (*dialect*); an outing (*dialect*); a disadvantage, drawback (*US*); permission to go out (*US*). ◆*prep* forth from (*inf* or *N Am*); outside of (now *rare*); without (*obs*). ◆*vt* to put out or throw out; to knock out; to make public the homosexuality of (a person in public life) without his or her permission (*inf*); to make public any facts about (a person in public life) that he or she does not wish to be revealed (*inf*). ◆*vi* to surface, be revealed, emerge publicly, as in *truth will out* ; to go out (*inf*); (with *with*) to bring out (*archaic* or *dialect*); (with *with*) to say suddenly or unexpectedly (*inf*). ◆*interj* expressing peremptory dismissal; announcing that a player is out, the ball not in court, etc; indicating that one has come to the end of one's transmission (*radio*); alas (*archaic*); shame (*usu out upon*; *archaic*). [OE *ūte*, *ūt*; Gothic *ut*, Ger *aus*, Sans *ud*]
■ **out'ed** *adj* having had private facts about oneself made public (*inf*); ejected. **out'er** *n* someone who makes public another person's homosexuality. **out'ing** *n* see separate entry. **out'ness** *n* the state of being out; externality to the perceiving mind, objectiveness. **out'ro** *n* (*pl* **out'ros**) the concluding section of a song, TV programme, etc. □ **out'-and-out** *adj* thoroughgoing; thorough-paced; utter; absolute; unqualified. ◆*adv* /*owt-ənd-owt'*/ finally and completely; definitely; unreservedly. **out-and-out'er** *n* (*inf*) any person or thing that is a complete or extreme type; a thorough-going partisan; a great lie. **out'-box** *n* (*comput*) a file for storing electronic mail that has been or is to be sent to another computer. **out-of-doors'** *adj* (also **out-of-door'**) open-air, outdoor (see under **out-**); outside of parliament. ◆*n* the open air. **out-of(-the)-bod'y** *adj* of or relating to an occurrence in which an individual has the experience of being outside his or her own body. **out-of-the-way'** *adj* uncommon, unusual; singular; secluded; remote. **out-of-town'** *adj* (of a retail outlet) situated away from a main commercial centre. **out-o'ver** /*owt-ō'vər*/ or **oot-owre** /*oot-owr'*/ *adv* and *prep* (*Scot*) out over; over. **out'-tray** *n* a shallow container for letters, etc, ready to be dispatched.
■ **at outs** (*US*) at odds. **from out** out from. **murder will out** see under **murder**. **on the outs** (with) (*inf*) on unfriendly terms (with); becoming unpopular, unfashionable, etc. **out and about** able to go out, convalescent; active out of doors. **out and away** (*old*) by far; beyond competition. **out at elbow** see **elbow**. **out for** abroad in quest of; aiming at obtaining or achieving; dismissed from batting with a score of. **out from under** out of a difficult situation. **out of** from within; from among; not in; not within; excluded from; from (a source, material, motive, condition, possession, language, etc); born of; beyond the bounds, range or scope of; deviating from, in disagreement with; away or distant from; without, destitute of; denuded of. **out of character** see under **character**. **out of course** (*rare*) out of order. **out of date** not abreast of the times; old-fashioned; obsolete; no longer valid; no longer current (**out-of-date'** *adj*). **out of doors** in or to the open air. **out of it** excluded from participation; without a chance; unable to behave normally or control oneself, usually because of drink or drugs (*sl*). **out of joint** see under **join**. **out of place** see under **place**. **out of pocket** see under **pocket**. **out of print** see under **print**. **out of sight** see under **sight**¹. **out of sorts** see under **sort**. **out of temper** see under **temper**. **out of the question** see under **question**. **out of the way** not in the way, not impeding or preventing progress. **out of this world** see under **world**. **out of time** see under **time**. **out of work** see under **work**. **out on one's feet** as good as knocked out; done for, but with a semblance of carrying on. **outs and ins** see **ins** and **outs** under **in**¹. **out there** in existence; unconventional, avant-garde (*inf*). **out to** aiming, working resolutely, to. **out to lunch** see under **lunch**. **out to out** in measurement from outside to outside; overall. **out upon** (*archaic*) shame on. **out with** let's do away with; not friendly with; see also **out** (*vi*) above. **out with it!** (*inf*) say what you have to say, and be quick about it, spit it out.

Words formed from the adverb **out** are listed in the entry above, and those formed using the prefix **out-** are listed in the following entry or, if their meaning is self-evident, at the foot of the page; other words spelt with **out-** follow in the main word list.

---

out- /*owt-*/ *pfx* (1) outside, not within, out-lying, eg *outhouse*, *outpatient*; (2) away from the inside or inner part (often *poetic*), eg *outspread, outpouring, outgoing, output*; (3) with prepositional force, meaning 'outside of', eg *outboard, outdoor*; (4) through, throughout, beyond, completely, eg *outwatch, outflank, outweary*; (5) indicating the fact of going beyond a norm, standard of comparison or limit, more than, more successfully than, farther than, longer than, etc, eg *outweigh, outmanoeuvre, outstep, outlast, out-Herod*. [See **out**]
■ **out-ask'** *vt* (*dialect*) to proclaim the banns of for the last time. **out'back** *n* the parts of Australia remote from the cities, the bush country (also *adj* and *adv*). **out'backer** *n*. **outbal'ance** *vt* to outweigh. **outbar'gain** *vt* to get the better of in a bargain. **outbid'** *vt* to make a higher bid than. **outblust'er** *vt* to exceed in blustering; to get the better

of by bluster; to deprive (of) by bluster. **out'board** adj (of an engine) designed to be attached to the outside of a ship or boat; towards or nearer the side of a ship or aircraft. ◆ adv outside, or towards the outside of a ship or aircraft. ◆ n an outboard engine; a boat equipped with an outboard engine. **out'bound** adj going out, departing. **out'bounds** n pl (Spenser) boundaries. **outbrag'** vt to surpass in bragging or boasting; to excel in beauty or splendour (Shakesp). **outbrave'** vt to excel in boldness or splendour (Shakesp); to outface. **out'break** n a breaking out of eg violence or illness; a disturbance. ◆ vi /-brāk'/ to burst forth. **outbreath'd** /-bretht'/ adj (Shakesp) out of breath. **outbreed'** vi and vt. **out'bred** adj resulting from outbreeding. **outbreed'ing** n breeding from parents not closely related; exogamy. **out'building** n a building such as a barn, stable, etc separate from, but used in connection with, a dwelling-house or a main building; an outhouse. **out'burst** n a bursting out; an eruption or explosion; a sudden violent expression of feeling. **outby** or **outbye** /owt-bī' or oot-bī'/ adv (Scot) out of doors; a little way off; outwards; towards the shaft (mining). ◆ adj /owt' or oot'/ outdoor; outlying. **out'cast** n someone who has been cast out or rejected by society or home and family; anything rejected, eliminated or cast out; a quarrel (Scot). ◆ adj rejected or cast out. **out'caste** n someone who is of no caste or has lost caste. ◆ vt /-käst'/ to put out of caste. **outclass'** vt to surpass so far as to seem in a different class, to be markedly better than. **outclassed'** adj. **out'come** n the issue; consequence; result. **outcraft'y** vt (Shakesp) to exceed in craft. **out'crop** n an exposed edge of rock or of a mineral vein at ground surface; a sudden emergence or occurrence. ◆ vi /-krop'/ to emerge from the ground in this way, to come to the surface. **outcross'** vt to breed (individuals of different strains but the same breed); to outbreed. ◆ n /owt'/ an outcrossed animal. **out'crossing** n. **out'cry** n a loud cry of protest, distress, etc; a confused noise; a widespread and public show of anger or disapproval; a public auction; public bargaining by a group. **outdare'** vt to surpass in daring; to defy. **outdate'** vt to put out of date. **outdāt'ed** adj outmoded, old-fashioned, obsolete. **outdāt'edness** n. **outdis'tance** vt to leave far behind; to outstrip. **outdo'** vt to surpass; to excel; to overcome. **out'door** adj outside the door or the house; in or for the open air; (of a person) preferring to be in the open air or fond of outdoor activities (**outdoor relief** (hist) help formerly given to a pauper not living in the workhouse). **outdoors'** adv out of the house; in or into the open air; abroad (archaic). ◆ n the world outside houses or other buildings, the open air. **outdoor'sy** adj (inf) of, characteristic of or suitable for or having a liking for the outdoors. **outdure'** vt (obs) to outlast. **outdwell'** vt (Shakesp) to stay beyond. **out'-dweller** n someone who dwells elsewhere, esp one who owns land in a parish but lives outside it. **out'edge** n the farthermost bound. **outface'** vt to stare down; to confront boldly; to contradict (obs); to force by confronting (with from; Shakesp); to maintain boldly or impudently to the face of (that; obs). **outfall** /owt'föl/ n the outlet of a river, drain, etc; the amount that flows out; a sortie (obs); a quarrel (dialect). **out'field** n arable land continually cropped without being manured, opp to infield (Scot); any open field at a distance from the farm steading; any undefined district or sphere; in cricket and baseball, the outer part of the field; the players who occupy it. **out'fielder** n a player positioned in the outfield. **out'fit** n a set of (esp selected and matching) clothes; the act of fitting out for an enterprise; complete equipment; expenses for fitting out; a company travelling or working together for any purpose, formerly esp in charge of cattle (US); any set of persons, a gang (inf); a business organization, etc (inf). ◆ vt to fit out, equip. ◆ vi to get an outfit. **out'fitter** n someone who makes or provides outfits; a person who deals in clothing, haberdashery, sporting equipment, etc. **out'fitting** n. **outflank'** vt to extend beyond or pass round the flank or side of; to circumvent. **out'fling** n a sharp retort or gibe. **out'flow** n a flowing out, a gush or outpouring; an outward current. **out'flush** n a sudden glow. **outfoot'** vt to outstrip; to outsail. **outfox'** vt to get the better of by cunning; to outwit. **outfrown'** vt to frown down. **outgas'** vt. **outgas'sing** n loss of, or removal of, occluded or adsorbed gas from a solid under vacuum conditions; also removal of gas from a liquid. **out'gate** n (Spenser and Scot and N Eng) an outlet; an exit. **outgen'eral** vt to get the better of by generalship; to prove a better general than. **out'giving** n a disbursement; an utterance; a declaration

of policy. **outglare'** vt to glare more than; to be more glaring than. **outgo'** vt (pat **outwent'**; pap **outgone'**) to outstrip; to surpass; to pass or live through; to overreach (obs). ◆ vi to go out; to come to an end. ◆ n /owt'/ (pl **out'goes**) that which goes out; expenditure, opp to income. **out'going** n the act or state of going out; extreme limit; expenditure. ◆ adj (of eg a tenant, office-bearer, etc) departing, leaving or retiring, opp to incoming; friendly, gregarious, extrovert. **out'goings** n pl expenditure. **outgross** /-grōs'/ vt (esp of a cinema film) to earn a higher gross revenue than. **outgrow'** vt to surpass in growth; to grow out of, grow too big for; to eliminate or become free from in course of growth. **out'growth** n that which grows out from anything; an excrescence; a product. **out'guard** n a guard at a distance, or at the farthest distance, from the main body. **outgun'** vt to defeat by means of superior weapons, forces, strength, etc. **out'gush** n a gushing outwards. ◆ vi /-gush'/ to pour out in profusion. **out'-half** n (rugby) a stand-off half. **out'haul** n (naut) a rope for hauling out the clew of a sail (also **out'hauler**). **out-Her'od** vt to outdo (the mystery-play character Herod) in violence (Shakesp, Hamlet III.2.13); to outdo, esp in what is bad. **outhire'** (Spenser **outhyre'**) vt to give out as if on hire. **out'house** n a building near to or up against a main building. **outjest'** vt to overcome by jesting (Shakesp); to excel in jesting. **out'jet** or **oot'** n a projection. **outjett'ing** or **outjutt'ing** n and adj. **outjock'ey** vt to outwit by trickery. **out'land** n (usu in pl) an outlying land or territory; a foreign land (archaic or poetic); land granted to tenants (hist). ◆ adj outlying; foreign (archaic). **out'lander** n a foreigner; an uitlander. **outland'ish** adj strange, bizarre; out-of-the-way; foreign (archaic). **outland'ishly** adv. **outland'ishness** n. **out'lash** n a sudden burst or stroke. **outlast'** vt to last longer than. **outlaunch'** (Spenser **outlaunce'**) vt to launch forth. **outlaw** n and vt see separate entry. **out'lay** n an expenditure of money, resources, etc; that which is laid out. ◆ vt /-lā'/ to lay out in view; to expend; to surpass in laying. **out'leap** n an act of leaping out; an excursion; an outburst. ◆ vt /-lēp'/ to leap beyond or over; to surpass in leaping. ◆ vi to leap out. **outlearn'** vt to excel in learning; to get beyond the study of; to elicit (Spenser). **out'let** n a vent or opening allowing the escape of something; a means of full or uninhibited expression; a market for a certain product, etc; a place where products or services are sold or distributed; a shop, etc selling a particular producer's products; an electrical power point (N Am) (**outlet village** or **mall** a shopping centre with shops selling brand- or designer-named products at reduced prices, usu outside a town). **outlie'** vt to surpass in telling lies (lie[1]); to lie beyond (lie[2]). ◆ vi (rare) to lie in the open; to camp; to lie stretched out. **out'lier** n a detached portion of anything lying some way off or out; an isolated remnant of rock surrounded by older rocks (geol); someone who lies in the open (rare); someone who lodges or lies apart from others or from a place with which he or she is connected; an outsider. **out'line** n the outer line; the line by which any figure or object appears to be bounded; a line representing this in a drawing, etc; a sketch showing only the main lines; a general statement without details; a statement of the main principles; a line representing a word in shorthand; a setline in fishing. ◆ vt to draw the exterior line of; to delineate or sketch. **outlinear** /owt-lin'i-ər/ adj like an outline. **outlive** /-liv'/ vt to live longer than; to survive; to live through; to live down. **out'lodging** n a lodging beyond bounds. **out'look** n a place for looking out from; a view or prospect; a prospect for the future; mental point of view; a vigilant watch. ◆ vt /owt-lūk'/ or (Shakesp) owt'/ to face courageously. ◆ vi to look out. **outlus'tre** vt (Shakesp) to outshine. **out'lying** adj remote from the centre or main part; lying out or beyond; lodging apart; on the exterior or frontier; detached. **outman'** vt to outdo in manliness; to outnumber in men. **outmanoeu'vre** vt to surpass in or by manoeuvring. **outman'tle** vt (archaic or poetic) to excel in dress or ornament. **out'marriage** n marriage to a partner outside one's own group, religion, etc. **outmeas'ure** vt to exceed in extent. **outmode'** vt to put out of fashion. **outmod'ed** adj outdated, old-fashioned or no longer current. **outmod'edness** n. **outmost** adj see **outermost** under **outer**. **outmove'** vt to move faster than; to get the better of by moving. **outname'** vt to surpass in notoriety. **outnight'** vt (Shakesp) to surpass in mentioning nights. **outnum'ber** vt to exceed in numbers. **outpace'** vt to walk or go faster than; to outstrip. **out-par'amour** vt (Shakesp) to

---

Some words formed with the prefix **out-**; the numbers in brackets refer to the numbered senses in the entry for **out-**.

outbar' vt (1).	**outdrink'** vt (5).	**outflush'** vi (5).
outbox' vt (5).	**outdrive'** vt (5).	**outfly'** vt and vi (5), (2).
outbreathe' vt and vi (2).	**outeat'** vt (5).	**outgive'** vt and vi (5), (2).
outburn' vt and vi (5), (4).	**outfight'** vt (5).	**out'goer** n (2).
outburst' vi (1).	**outfish'** vt (5).	**outguess'** vt (5).
outcompete' vt (5).	**outflash'** vt and vi (5), (2).	**outhit'** vt (5).
outcry' vt and vi (5), (2).	**outflow'** vi (2).	**outjump'** vt (5).
outdance' vt (5).	**out'flowing** n and adj (2).	**outmarch'** vt (4), (5).

■ words derived from main entry word; □ compound words; ▥ idioms and phrasal verbs exceed in addiction to mistresses. **out'-parish** *n* a parish associated with a town but beyond the boundary; an outlying parish. **out'part** *n* (*obs*) a part remote from the centre. **outpass'ion** *vt* to go beyond in passionateness. **out'-patient** *n* a non-resident patient attending a hospital (also *adj*). **outpeer'** *vt* (*Shakesp*) to surpass or excel. **out'-pension** *n* a pension granted to someone who is not resident in an institution. ◆ *vt* to grant an out-pension to. **out'-pensioner** *n* a non-resident pensioner. **outperform'** *vt* to outdo or surpass in a specific field of activity. **outperform'ance** *n*. **out'place** *vt*. **out'placement** *n* the process of finding new employment for workers, *esp* executives and middle management, by their employers as part of redundancy. **out'placer** *n* an agency that provides a service of outplacement. **outplay'** *vt* to play better than, and so defeat. **outpoint'** *vt* to score more points than. **out'port** *n* a port out of or remote from the chief port; a port away from the town or customs area; a remote fishing village (*Can*); a place of export. **out'-porter** *n* a porter who carries luggage to and from, and not merely in, the place of employment. **out'post** *n* a post or station beyond the main body of the army, etc; its occupants; a remote settlement or stronghold. **out'pouring** *n* a pouring out; a passionate or fluent and voluble utterance. **outpow'er** *vt* to surpass in power. **outpray'** *vt* to exceed in earnestness or length of prayer; to overcome in or by prayer. **outprice'** *vt* to offer a better price, financial return, etc, than. **outprize'** *vt* (*Shakesp*) to exceed in estimation. **out'put** *n* quantity produced or turned out; data in either printed or coded form after processing by a computer; punched tape or printout, etc by which processed data leaves a computer; a signal delivered by a telecommunications instrument or system. ◆ *vt* (of a computer, etc) to send out, supply, produce (data, etc) as output. **out'quarters** *n pl* quarters situated away from headquarters. **outrange'** *vt* to have a greater range than. **outrank'** *vt* to rank above. **outrate'** *vt* to offer a better rate of return than. **outreach'** *vt* to reach or extend beyond; to overreach; to stretch forth. ◆ *n* /*owt*'/ a reaching out; the extent or distance something can reach or stretch out; an organization's involvement in or contact with the surrounding community, *esp* that of a church for purposes of evangelism or that of community welfare organizations taking their services out to *esp* disadvantaged individuals and groups rather than expecting them to approach the welfare organizations. **outred'** or **outredd'en** *vt* to surpass in redness. **outreign'** *vt* to reign longer than; (*Spenser* **outraigne**) to reign to the end of. **outrelief'** *n* outdoor relief. **out'ride** *n* (*prosody*) an unaccented syllable or syllables added to a foot, *esp* in sprung rhythm. ◆ *vt* /-*rīd*'/ to ride beyond; to ride faster than; to ride safely through (a storm). **out'rider** *n* a person who rides beside a vehicle as a guard; a rider sent ahead as a scout, or to ensure a clear passage. **out'rigger** *n* a projecting spar for extending sails or any part of the rigging; a projecting device supported on a float, fixed to the side of a canoe, etc, to give stability; a projecting rowlock giving extra leverage to the oar; a boat having such a rowlock or rowlocks; a light racing-boat with projecting rowlocks; a projecting beam or framework attached to a building, ship or aircraft for any of various purposes; a projecting frame to support the controlling planes of an aeroplane; an extension from the splinter-bar of a carriage to take another horse. **out'right** *adj* out-and-out; utter, thoroughgoing; unmitigated; downright; total, absolute; direct. ◆ *adv* /-*rīt*'/ totally, completely, without qualification; directly, without concealment or circumlocution; straight ahead; unreservedly; undisguisedly; at once and completely. **out'run** *n* an outlying pasture or run. ◆ *vt* /-*run*'/ to go beyond in running; to exceed; to get the better of or to escape by running (**outrun** or **overrun the constable** to run into debt; to live beyond one's means). **out'runner** *n*. **outrush** *vi* to rush outwards. ◆ *n* /*owt*'/ a rushing out. **outsail'** *vt* to leave behind in sailing; to sail beyond. **outscorn'** *vt* (*Shakesp*) to face out with scorn. **outsell'** *vt* to be sold in larger quantities than; to fetch a higher price than; to exceed in value; to surpass in the number or amount of sales. **out'-sentry** *n* a sentry placed at a distance. **out'set** *n* a setting out; a beginning or start, *esp* in *at* or *from the outset*; an outward current. **out'setting** *n*. **out'settlement** *n* an outlying settlement. **outshine'** *vt* to shine more brightly than; to be better than. **outshoot'** *vt* to surpass in shooting; to extend beyond. ◆ *n* /*owt*'/ a thing that has developed from something else. **out'shot** *n* (*Scot*) a projection in a building or a recess made in

the wall of a room. **out'sight** *n* the power of seeing external things; /*owt*'*sīt* or *oot*'*sihht*/ outdoor possessions (*Scot*; also *adj*). **outsit'** *vt* to sit beyond the time of; to sit longer than. **out'size** *adj* over normal size, exceptionally large. ◆ *n* an exceptionally large size; anything, *esp* a garment, of exceptionally large size. **out'sized** *adj*. **out'skirts** *n pl* the outlying areas of a town, etc, suburbs; the fringes of a subject, etc. **outsleep'** *vt* to sleep longer than; to sleep through; to sleep to or beyond the time of. **outsmart'** *vt* (*inf*; *orig US*) to show more cleverness or cunning than, to outwit. **out'sole** *n* the outer sole of a boot or shoe which rests on the ground. **out'source** *vt* to obtain (goods or parts) from, or contract work with, an outside supplier. **out'sourcer** *n*. **out'sourcing** *n*. **outspend'** *vt* to spend more than or beyond the limits of. **outspent'** *adj* thoroughly tired out. **outspō'ken** *adj* speaking or spoken frankly, without circumlocution. **outspō'kenly** *adv*. **outspō'kenness** *n*. **outsport'** *vt* (*Shakesp*) to sport beyond the limits of. **outspread'** *vt* and *vi* to spread out or over. ◆ *adj* (or /*owt*'*spred*/) spread out. ◆ *n* (or /*owt*'*spred*/) an expanse. **outspread'ing** *adj*. **outspring'** *vi* (*literary*) to spring out. ◆ *n* /*owt*'/ outcome. **outstand'** *vt* to withstand; to stand or endure through or beyond (*archaic*). ◆ *vi* to stand out or project; to stand out (to sea); to stand over or remain. **outstand'ing** *adj* prominent; excellent; superior; unsettled; unpaid; still to be attended to or done. **outstand'ingly** *adv*. **outstare'** *vt* to stare down (*Shakesp*); to face the stare of boldly; to outdo in staring; to gaze at without being blinded. **out'station** *n* a subsidiary branch or post, *esp* in an outlying area or remote from headquarters; a place far from the source of services, at which Australian aborigines live in a traditional manner; an outlying post on an Australian sheep station. **outstay'** *vt* to stay beyond the limit of, as in *outstay one's welcome*; to stay longer than. ◆ *vt* to endure longer than. **outstep'** *vt* to step beyond, overstep. **outstrain'** *vt* to stretch out. **outstretch'** *vt* to stretch out; to reach forth; to spread out; to stretch to the end of; to stretch beyond. **outstretched'** *adj* extended, proffered. **outstrike** /*owt*-*strīk*'/ or *owt*'/ *vt* to outdo in striking. **outstrip'** *vt* to outrun; to leave behind; to surpass; to outdo in denuding oneself. **outsum'** *vt* to outnumber. **outswear'** *vt* to exceed in swearing; to overcome by swearing. **outsweet'en** *vt* to excel in sweetness. **outswell'** *vt* to swell more than (*Shakesp*); to overflow. **out'swing** *n* an outward swing or swerve. **out'swinger** *n* a ball bowled to swerve from leg to off (*cricket*); a ball kicked to swerve away from the goal or from the centre of the pitch. **out'swinging** *adj*. **outtake'** *vt* (*obs*) to take out; to except. ◆ *prep* (*obs*; also **outtak'en**) except. **out'-take** *n* (*film*) a sequence of film removed from the final edited version. **outtell'** *vt* (*archaic* or *poetic*) to tell forth; to tell to the end; to tell or count beyond. **outthink'** *vt* to surpass in thinking; to outwit. **outtongue'** *vt* (*Shakesp*) to speak louder than. **outtop'** *vt* to reach higher than; to excel. **out'turn** *n* the amount of anything turned out, produced or achieved, output. **outven'om** *vt* (*Shakesp*) to exceed in poisonousness. **outvill'ain** *vt* (*Shakesp*) to exceed in villainy. **outvoice'** *vt* (*Shakesp*) to exceed in clamour or noise; to drown the voice of. **outvote'** *vt* to defeat by a greater number of votes; to overrule by weight of opinion. **out'voter** *n* a voter not resident in the constituency. **out'-wall** *n* the outside wall of a building; external appearance (*Shakesp*). **out'wash** *n* (*geol*) material borne by melted water from a glacier, found deposited beyond the terminal moraine. **outwatch'** *vt* to watch longer than; to watch throughout the time of. **outwear'** *vt* to wear out; to spend or live through; to outlive or outgrow; to outlast. **outwea'ry** *vt* to tire out completely. **outweed'** *vt* (*Spenser*) to root out. **outweep'** *vt* to weep out or shed wholly; to surpass in weeping. **outweigh'** *vt* to exceed in weight or importance. **outwell'** *vt* and *vi* (*archaic* or *poetic*) to pour or well out. **outwent'** *vt* see **outgo** above. **outwick'** *vi* in curling, to strike the outside of another stone and so send it within a circle. **outwin'** *vt* (*Spenser*) to get out of. **outwind** /-*wīnd*'/ *vt* (*obs*) to unwind, extricate. **outwing'** *vt* to outstrip in flying; to fly beyond; to outflank. **outwit'** *vt* (**outwitt'ing**, **outwitt'ed**) to defeat by superior ingenuity; to surpass in wit or ingenuity. **outwith** /*owt*'*with*, *oot*'*with* or -*with*'/ *prep* (*Scot*) outside of. ◆ *adv* outwards. **out'work** *n* (often in *pl*) a defence work that lies outside the principal wall or line of fortification; outdoor work, field work; work done away from the shop or factory, etc. ◆ *vt* /-*wûrk*'/ (*pap* and *pat* **outwrought'**) (*Shakesp*) to surpass in work; to work out

---

Some words formed with the prefix **out-**; the numbers in brackets refer to the numbered senses in the entry for **out-**.

outmatch' *vt* (5).	**outroar'** (*Shakesp*) *vt* (2).	**outsprint'** *vt* (5).
outmigrā'tion *n* (2).	**outroot'** *vt* (2).	**outswim'** *vt* (5).
outpeep' *vi* (2).	**outscold'** (*Shakesp*) *vt* (5).	**outtalk'** *vt* (5).
outpour' *vt* and *vi* (2).	**outscore'** *vt* (5).	**outtrav'el** *vt* (4), (5).
outpour'er *n* (2).	**outsing'** *vt* (5).	**outval'ue** *vt* (5).
outpunch' *vt* (5).	**outsoar'** *vt* (5).	**outvie'** *vt* (5).
outrace' *vt* (5).	**outspeak'** *vt* and *vi* (2), (5).	**outwait'** *vt* (4), (5).
outri'val *vt* (5).	**outspeed'** *vt* (5).	**outwalk'** *vt* (4), (5).

---

or bring to an end; to finish. **out'worker** *n*. **outworn'** (or /*owt'*/) *adj* worn-out; obsolete. **outworth'** *vt* (*Shakesp*) to exceed in value. **outwrest'** *vt* (*Spenser*) to extort.

outage /*ow'tij*/ *n* the amount of a commodity lost in transport and storage; the amount of fuel used on a flight; stoppage of a mechanism due to failure of power; a period during which electricity fails or is cut off; a period when a reactor is working at a low level (*nuclear phys*). [**out**]

outdacious /*owt-dā'shəs*/ *adj* a non-standard corruption of **audacious**.

outer /*ow'tər*/ *adj* further out or without; external, *opp* to **inner**. ◆ *n* the outermost ring on a target, or a shot striking it (*archery*); (in an electrical distribution system) either of the conductors whose potential is above or below the earth's; an unsheltered part of the spectator enclosure at a sportsground (*Aust* and *NZ*). [OE *ūterra*]
■ **out'ermost** or **out'most** /*-məst* or *-mōst*/ *adj* (OE *ūtemest*, superlative) most or furthest out; most remote from the centre; most distant.
❑ **outer bar** *n* the junior barristers who plead outside the bar in court, as opposed to Queen's (or King's) Counsel and others who plead within the bar. **outer dead centre** *n* the position of the crank of a reciprocating engine or pump when the piston is at its nearest to the crankshaft (also **bottom dead centre**). **outer planet** *n* any of the planets in the solar system whose orbits lie outside the asteroid belt. **outer space** *n* space beyond the earth's atmosphere. **out'erwear** *n* (also **outer garments**) clothes such as jackets, suits, coats, etc worn over other clothes; clothes put on to go out of doors.
■ **on the outer** (*Aust* and *NZ*) excluded, out in the cold.

outher /*ö*/ or /*ow'dhər*/ an old, now dialect, form of **either**.

outing /*ow'ting*/ *n* an outdoor excursion; the act of making public another person's homosexuality or other personal information intended to be kept private; ejection; distance out. [**out**]
❑ **outing flannel** *n* (*US*) a type of flannelette.

outlaw /*owt'lö*/ *n* a person deprived of the protection of the law; (loosely) a bandit; an outcast; someone banished, exiled or on the run from the law; a wild, dangerous or unmanageable animal (*US*). ◆ *vt* to place beyond the law; to deprive of the benefit of the law; to ban, make illegal, proscribe. [OE *ūtlaga*, from ON *ūtlāgi*, from *ūt* out, and *lōg* law]
■ **out'lawry** *n* the act of putting someone out of the protection of the law; the state of being an outlaw.

outler /*oot'lər*/ (*Burns*) *adj* not housed. ◆ *n* a beast that is not housed; someone who is out of office. [Poss **outlier**]

outrage /*owt'rāj*/ *n* an atrocious act; gross offence to moral feelings; great anger or indignation; gross or violent injury; an act of wanton mischief; violation; rape; excess, undue divergence from a mean (*Spenser*); violence beyond measure (*Shakesp*); clamour (*Spenser*). ◆ *vt* to shock grossly; to treat with excessive abuse; to injure by violence, *esp* to violate, to ravish. [OFr *ultrage*, from *outre* beyond, from L *ultrā*; the word is not connected with **out** and **rage** but influenced by them]
■ **outrageous** /*owt-rā'jəs*/ *adj* iniquitous or disgraceful; shocking; monstrous; offensive or gross; furious; turbulent or violent; immoderate, wild or extravagant. **outrā'geously** *adv*. **outrā'geousness** *n*.

outrance /*oo-trās'*/ *n* the utmost extremity; the bitter end. [Fr, from *outre* beyond]
■ **à outrance** to the bitter end of a combat, in non-standard English use, **à l'outrance**.

outré /*oo'trā*/ *adj* beyond what is customary or proper; extravagant, fantastic. [Fr]

outrecuidance /*oo-tər-kwē'dəns* or *oot-r'-kwē-dãs'*/ (*Walter Scott*) *n* presumption or overweening. [Fr *outre* beyond, and OFr *cuider* to think or plume oneself, from L *cōgitāre*]

outremer /*oo-tr'-mer'*/ *n* the region beyond the sea; overseas. [Fr *outre* beyond, and *mer* sea]

outroop /*owt'roop*/ (*obs*) *n* an auction sale. [Du *uitroepen* to cry out, proclaim]
■ **out'rooper** *n* (*obs*) an auctioneer; the publicly appointed town crier of the City of London.

outrope /*owt'rōp*/ and **outroper** /*owt'rō-pər*/ same as **outroop** and **outrooper**.

outside /*owt'sīd* or *-sīd'*/ *n* the outer side; the farthest limit; the outer part or surface; the exterior; an outside passenger (*archaic*); (in *pl*) the top and bottom quires of a ream of paper. ◆ *adj* /*owt'sīd*/ on or from the outside; carried on the outside; exterior; superficial; external; extreme; (of a possibility) unlikely, remote; beyond the limit; not having membership; (of a criminal activity) carried out by a person or people not having contacts with someone near the victim; at a distance from a major centre of population (*Aust*);

of a position nearer or near the edge of the field (*rugby*, etc). ◆ *adv* /*owt-sīd'*/, sometimes *owt'*/ on or to the outside; not within; out of prison. ◆ *prep* /*owt'sīd* or *owt-sīd'*/ to or on the outside of; except for, apart from (*inf*); in a position nearer the edge of the field than (*rugby*, etc). [**out** and **side**[1]]
■ **outsi'der** *n* a person who is not a member of a particular company, profession, etc, a stranger, a layman; a person not considered fit to associate with; a person who is not an inmate; a person who is not participating; a racehorse, competitor, team, etc not included among the favourites in the betting; a person whose place in a game, at work, etc, is on the outside; (in *pl*) a pair of nippers for turning a key in a keyhole from the outside.
❑ **outside broadcast** *n* a broadcast not made from within a studio. **out'side-car** *n* an Irish jaunting car in which the passengers sit back to back. **outside chance** *n* a remote chance. **outside edge** see under **edge**. **outside half** *n* (*rugby*) a stand-off half. **outside left** *n* (*sport*) a forward player on the left wing. **outside novel** *n* the type of novel which deals with the author's thoughts and his or her relationship with the world. **outsi'der art** *n* art produced by a person who is not only not a trained artist but is also otherwise outside the mainstream. **outside right** *n* (*sport*) a forward player on the right wing.
■ **at the outside** at the most, etc. **get outside of** (*inf*) to eat or drink. **outside in** same as **inside out** (see under **inside**). **outside of** (*inf*, *esp US*) in or to a position external to; apart from, except.

outspan /*owt'span* or *-span'*/ (*S Afr*) *vt* and *vi* to unyoke (oxen) or unharness (a horse) from a vehicle. ◆ *n* /*owt'*/ a stopping-place. [Du *uitspannen*]

outspeckle /*oot-spek'l*/ (*obs Scot*) *n* a laughing stock, spectacle. [Perh connected with **kenspeckle**]

outward /*ow'twərd*/ *adj* toward the outside; on the outside; outer; external; exterior; appearing externally; apparent or seeming; formal; accidental or additional, not inherent; in a direction away from home or one's base; worldly, carnal (*theol*); dissolute (*dialect*). ◆ *adv* outwards; away from port; to a foreign port; superficially. ◆ *n* external appearance (*Shakesp*); the outside. [**out** and **-ward**]
■ **out'wardly** *adv* in outward appearance, apparently, superficially; externally; in an outward manner. **out'wardness** *n* externality; objectivity. **out'wards** *adv* in an outward direction, out.
❑ **Outward Bound**® *n* a scheme providing outdoor adventure training for young people. **outward-bound'** *adj* bound or heading in an outward direction or to a foreign port. **outward-sain'ted** *adj* (*literary*) appearing outwardly to be a saint.

ouvert /*oo-ver'*/, *fem* **ouverte** /*-vert'*/ (*Fr*) *adj* open.

ouvirandra /*oo-vi-ran'drə*/ *n* the lattice-leaf of Madagascar. [From the Malagasy name]

ouvrage /*oo-vräzh'*/ (*Fr*) *n* work.

ouvrier /*oo-vrē-ā'*/, *fem* **ouvrière** /*oo-vrē-er'*/ (*Fr*) *n* a worker or operative.

ouzel or **ousel** /*oo'zl*/ (*Shakesp* **woosel** or **woosell** /*woo'zl*/) *n* a blackbird (*archaic*); a water ouzel; apparently, a dark-complexioned person (*Shakesp*). [OE *ōsle*; cognate with Ger *Amsel*]
❑ **ou'zel-cock** *n*.
■ **ring ouzel** a blackish thrush with a broad white band on the throat. **water ouzel** the dipper.

ouzo /*oo'zō*/ *n* (*pl* **ou'zos**) an aniseed liqueur. [Mod Gr]

ova see **ovum**.

oval /*ō'vəl*/ *adj* strictly, egg-shaped, like an egg in the round or in section, rounded, longer than broad, broadest near one end; loosely, elliptical or ellipsoidal, or nearly so; rounded at both ends, about twice as long as broad, broadest in the middle (*bot*); relating to eggs (*obs*). ◆ *n* an oval figure or thing, eg an oval field; a cricket or football ground (*Aust*). [L *ōvum* egg; *ōvālis* is modern Latin]
■ **oval'ity** or **o'valness** *n*. **o'vally** *adv*.
❑ **oval window** same as **fenestra ovalis** (see under **fenestra**).

ovalbumin /*ō-val'bū-min* or *-bū'*/ *n* the albumin in egg whites. [L *ovum* egg, and **albumen**]

ovary /*ō'və-ri*/ *n* one of the two female reproductive glands; the part of the gynaeceum that contains the ovules (*bot*). [New L *ōvārium*, from L *ōvum* egg]
■ **ovā'rian** *adj* of or relating to the ovary. **ovariec'tomy** *n* (Gr *ektomē* a cutting out) surgical removal of one or both ovaries. **ovā'riole** *n* one of the egg-tubes forming an insect's ovary. **ovariot'omist** *n*. **ovariot'omy** *n* (see **-tomy**; *surg*) the cutting of an ovary; the removal of ovaries because of a tumour. **ovā'rious** *adj* (*rare*) consisting of eggs. **ovarī'tis** *n* inflammation of the ovary, oophoritis.

ovate[1] /*ō'vāt*/ *adj* egg-shaped; shaped in outline like an egg, broadest below the middle (*bot*). [L *ōvātus* egg-shaped]

ovate[2] /ov'āt/ n an Eisteddfodic graduate who is neither a bard nor a druid. [Welsh *ofydd* a philosopher or lord; fancifully identified with the unrelated Celtic word preserved in Gr as *ouāteis* (pl) Gaulish soothsayers]

ovate[3] see under **ovation**.

ovation /ō-vā'shən/ n an outburst of popular applause, an enthusiastic reception; in ancient Rome, a lesser triumph; rejoicing (*archaic*). [L *ovātiō, -ōnis*, from *ovāre* to exult]
■ **ovate**' vt (facetious back-formation) to receive with an ovation. **ovā'tional** adj. **ova'tor** n.
■ **standing ovation** see under **stand**.

oven /uv'ən/ n an arched cavity or closed compartment for baking, heating or drying; a small furnace. ♦ vt to cook in an oven. [OE *ofen*; Ger *Ofen*]
■ **ov'enable** adj (of dishes, plates, etc) made so as to withstand the heat of an oven without cracking; (of food) suitable for cooking in an oven.
□ **ov'enbird** n a name for various birds that build domed or oven-shaped nests, esp the S American genus *Furnarius*. **oven glove** n a type of thick reinforced glove worn when handling hot dishes. **ov'en-ready** adj (of food) prepared beforehand so as to be ready for cooking in the oven immediately after purchase. **ov'en-tit** n a dialect name for various birds, including the willow warbler; the ovenbird. **ov'enware** n dishes, such as casseroles, that will stand the heat of an oven. **ov'enwood** n brushwood.

over /ō'vər/ prep above in place, rank, power, authority, contention, preference, value, quantity, number, etc; in excess of; above and from one side of to the other; down from or beyond the edge of; from side to side or end to end of; along; throughout the extent of; during; until after; across; on or to the other side of; on, onto, about, or across the surface of; in discussion, contemplation, study of or occupation with; concerning; on account of; recovered from the effects of; in a sunk, submerged, or buried state beyond the level of, as in *over head and ears*. ♦ adv on the top; above; across; to or on the other side; from one person, party, condition, etc, to another; into a sleep; outwards so as to overhang or to fall from; down, away from an upright position; through, from beginning to end, *esp* in a cursory or exploratory way; throughout; into a reversed position; across the margin; again, in repetition; too much; in excess; left remaining; at an end. ♦ interj (*radio*) indicating that the speaker now expects a reply. ♦ adj (usu as pfx) upper or superior; surplus; excessive. ♦ n a series of (usu six) balls after which play changes from one end to the other (*cricket*); anything that is over; a surplus copy, etc; an excess, overplus. ♦ vt to go, leap or vault over. —Also, only as adv and prep **o'er** (now usu poetic), **ore** (obs), **o're** (obs), all pronounced /ōr or ȯr/, and in Scots **ower**, **owre** or **o'er**, pronounced /owr or ȯr/. [OE *ofer*; Ger *über*, L *super*, Gr *hyper*; cf **up**]
■ **overage** /ō'və-rij/ n surplus, excess (see also **over-age** under **over-**). **o'verly** adv (inf, orig US) excessively, too; casually (Scot); superciliously (obs). ♦ adj casual (Scot); supercilious, superior (obs).
□ **o'ver-and-un'der** n a double-barrelled gun having the barrels one on top of the other rather than side by side (also **under-and-o'ver**). **overby**' adv a little way over, esp in Scots forms **owerby, o'erby** /owr-bī'/. **over rate** n (cricket) the rate at which overs are bowled. **over-the-coun'ter** adj (of securities, etc) not listed on or traded through a stock exchange, but traded directly between buyers and sellers; (of drugs, etc) able to be bought or sold without prescription or licence. **over-the-top**' adj excessive, extreme, too much.
■ **all over** at an end; everywhere; at his, her or its most characteristic (*inf*); covered with, besmeared or bespattered with (*inf*). **all over again** again from the beginning, anew. **be all over** (**someone**) to make a fuss of, fawn on (someone). **over again** all over again. **over against** opposite. **over and above** in addition to; besides. **over and out** (*radio*) an expression used to announce the end of one's transmission. **over and over** (again) many times; repeatedly. **over head and ears** completely submerged. **over seas** to foreign lands. **over the hill** see under **hill**. **over the moon** see under **moon**. **over to you!** used

to transfer the initiative in speaking, etc, to another person. **put one over on** (*inf*) to gain an advantage over someone; to deceive someone.

> Words formed from the adverb or preposition **over** are listed in the entry above, and those formed using the prefix **over-** are listed in the following entry or, if their meaning is self-evident, at the foot of the page; other words spelt with *over-* follow in the main word list.

over- /ō-vər-/ pfx used with certain meanings of **over** prep, adv, or adj, as (1) above, across, across the surface; (2) beyond an understood limit; (3) down, away from the upright position; (4) upper or outer; (5) beyond what is usual or desirable; (6) completely; (7) (with neg) at all (as in *not over-generous*).

■ **overachieve**' vi to do better than predicted or expected. **overachieve'ment** n. **overachiev'er** n. **overact**' vt and vi to act or perform with exaggeration. **over-age** adj beyond the age limit specified for; too old (see also **overage** under **over**). **overall**' adv (also **over-all**') altogether; over the whole; everywhere (Spenser); above all (obs). ♦ adj /ō'/ including everything; everything being reckoned; all-round. ♦ n /ō'/ a protective loose coat worn over ordinary clothes for dirty work or (archaic) bad weather; (in pl) a one-piece protective work garment combining sleeved top and trousers, a boiler suit; dungarees (N Am); cavalryman's trousers. **o'veralled** adj. **overarch**' vt to arch over; to form an arch over. ♦ vi to hang over like an arch. ♦ n /ō'/ an overhead arch. **overarch'ing** adj forming an arch over something; denoting something that covers various issues, the interests of various affected groups, etc. **o'verarm** adj and adv with the arm raised above the shoulder. **overawe**' vt to daunt by arousing fear or reverence in. **overbal'ance** vt to cause to lose balance; to exceed in weight, value or importance. ♦ vi to lose balance, fall over. ♦ n excess of weight or value. **o'verbank** n a stage of a river where it flows over its banks. **overbear**' vt to bear down, overpower; to overwhelm; to overrule (objections or an objector). ♦ vi to be too productive. **overbear'ing** adj inclined to domineer; haughty and dogmatic; imperious. **overbear'ingly** adv. **overbear'ingness** n. **overbid**' vt and vi to outbid; to make a bid that is greater than or counts above; to bid more than the value of (something). ♦ n /ō'/ a higher bid; an unduly high bid. **overbidd'er** n. **overbidd'ing** n. **o'verbite** n (dentistry) the (amount of) extension of the upper incisors beyond the lower when the mouth is closed. **overblow**' vi to produce a harmonic instead of the fundamental tone, by increase of wind pressure (music); to blow over, be past its violence; to blow with too much violence. ♦ vt to blow away; to blow across; to overturn by blowing; to blow (an instrument) too strongly or deliberately so as to produce a harmonic (music); to cover with blossoms (poetic or literary). **overblown**' adj blown over or past; burnt by an excessive blast, in the Bessemer steel process; inflated to excess; more than full-blown; excessive. **overboard**' adv from on board, over the side of a ship or boat into the water (**go overboard about** or **for** (*inf*) to go to extremes of enthusiasm about or for; **throw overboard** to reject, jettison). **overbook**' vt and vi to make more reservations than the number of places (in a plane, ship, hotel, etc) actually available. **overbought**' adj (stock exchange) of a market in which excessive buying has caused too rapid a rise; see also **overbuy** below. **over-breathe**' vi (med) to hyperventilate. **over-breath'ing** n. **o'verbridge** n a bridge providing a superior crossing. ♦ vt /-brij'/ to span. **overbrow**' vt (archaic or poetic) to overhang like a brow. **overbuild**' vt to cover with buildings; to build above; to build in excess; to build too much upon or in. **overbulk**' vt (Shakesp) to oppress by bulk, or to dwarf by greater bulk. **overburd'en** (archaic **overburth'en**) vt to burden too heavily. ♦ n /ō'vər-/ an excessive burden; rock that must be removed to expose a vein or seam (mining); alluvial soil, etc, overlying a bed of clay or other substance to be dug, mined or quarried. **overburd'ensome** adj. **overburn**' vt to burn too much. ♦ vi to be too zealous. **overbus'y** adj too busy; officious. ♦ vt to occupy (oneself) too much. **overbuy**' vt (pat and pap **overbought**') to buy too much of; to buy for more expense than; to put (oneself) in the position of having bought too much; to buy too dear (Shakesp); see also **overbought** above. ♦ vi to buy too much. **overcall**' vt (bridge) to outbid; to bid above; to bid too

---

Some words formed with the prefix *over-*; the numbers in brackets refer to the numbered senses in the entry for **over-**.

overabound' vi (5).	**over-anx'ious** adj (5).	**overbrimmed**' (Walter Scott) adj (1).
overabound'ing adj (5).	**over-anx'iously** adv (5).	**overcare'ful** adj (5).
over-absorp'tion n (5).	**overbeat**' vt and vi (3).	**overcarr'y** vt (1, obs), (2), (5).
overabun'dance n (5).	**o'verblanket** n (4).	**overcau'tious** adj (5).
overabun'dant adj (5).	**overboil**' vt and vi (2), (5).	**overclad**' adj (1), (5).
overac'tive adj (5).	**overbold**' adj (5).	**overcol'our** vt (1), (5).
overactiv'ity n (5).	**overbold'ly** adv (5).	**over-con'fidence** n (5).
overambit'ious adj (5).	**overbound**' vt (1).	**over-con'fident** adj (5).
over-anxi'ety n (5).	**overbrim**' vi (2).	**over-cool**' vt (5).

high on; to rank as a higher bid than. ◆ *n* /ō'/ a higher bid than the opponent's preceding one. **overcan'opy** *vt* (*pap* **overcan'opied** (*Shakesp* **over-cann'oped**)) to cover as with a canopy. **overcapac'ity** *n* the state of having more workers, machinery, factory space, etc than is needed to meet the existing demand for one's product. **overcapitalizā'tion** or **-s-** *n*. **overcap'italize** or **-ise** *vt* to fix the capital to be invested in, or the capital value of, too high. **overcast'** *vt* to sew stitches over (a raw edge); to cover with stitches; to compute too high, overestimate; to recover, get over (*Scot*); to overthrow; to cast as a covering; to cast a covering over; to shade (*Spenser*). ◆ *vi* to grow dull or cloudy. ◆ *adj* clouded over. ◆ *n* /ō'/ a cloudy covering. **overcast'ing** *n*. **overcatch'** *vt* (*pap* **overcaught'**) (*obs* or *dialect*) to overtake. **o'vercharge** *n*. **o'vercheck** *n* a large prominent check pattern combined with a smaller; a cloth with such a pattern; a checkrein. **o'verclass** *n* (chiefly *US*) a social class consisting of highly affluent people who jealously defend their wealth and privilege. **overclock'** *vt* to modify (a computer component) so that it operates at a higher clock speed than was intended by the original manufacturer. **overcloud'** *vt* to cover over with clouds; to fill with gloom, sadness or anxiety. ◆ *vi* to become overclouded. **overcloy'** *vt* to surfeit. **overclub'** *vi* (*golf*) to hit a shot too far through using a club with insufficient loft. **o'vercoat** *n* an outdoor coat worn over one's indoor clothes, a topcoat. **o'vercoating** *n* cloth for overcoats. **overcome'** *vt* to get the better of; to conquer or subdue; to surmount; to come over; to cover, overspread (*archaic*). ◆ *vi* to be victorious. ◆ *n* (also (*Scot*) **o'ercome** or **owrecome**) /owr'kum/ a crossing over; a surplus, excess; a fit or sudden access of illness; a refrain, byword or recurring theme. **overcommit'** *vt* to make (someone) feel obliged to do more than they are capable of doing. **overcommit'ment** *n*. **overcom'pensate** *vt* to allow too much in compensation of. ◆ *vi* to go too far in trying to correct a fault that one (believes one) suffers from (with *for*; *psychol*). **overcompensā'tion** *n*. **overcompen'satory** *adj*. **overcook'** *vt* to cook (food) for too long; to apply excessive force or energy to (*inf*). **overcooked'** *adj*. **overcorrect'** *vt* to apply so great a correction to as to deviate in the opposite way; to correct beyond achromatism, so that the red rays come to a focus nearer the lens than the violet (*optics*). **overcorrec'tion** *n*. **overcount'** *vt* to outnumber; to reckon too high; to overreach. **o'vercrop** *vt* to take too much out of by cultivation. **overcrow'** (*archaic* or *literary*; *Spenser* **overcraw'**, *Shakesp* **orecrowe'**) *vt* to crow or triumph over. **overcrowd'** *vt* to crowd too many people, animals, etc into. **overcrow'ded** *adj*. **overcrow'ding** *n*. **overdat'ed** *adj* out of date. **over-deter'mined** *adj* too firmly resolved (to); too resolute or stubborn; having more than the necessary determining data or factors. **overdevel'op** *vt* to develop too far; to leave (a film) too long in the developer (*photog*). ◆ *vi* to become overdeveloped. **overdevel'opment** *n*. **overdiagno'sis** *n* (*med*) a tendency to diagnose a condition too readily. **overdight** /-dīt'/ *adj* (*Spenser*) dight or covered over; overspread. **overdo'** *vt* to do too much (**overdo it** or **things** to tire oneself out); to overact; to exaggerate; to carry too far; to harass or to fatigue; to cook too much; to use too much of; to excel. **overdo'er** *n*. **overdone'** *adj*. **overdo'sage** *n*. **o'verdose** *n* an excessive dose of drugs, medicine, etc. ◆ *vi* and *vt* (also /-dōs'/) to take or administer an overdose. **o'verdraft** *n* the overdrawing of a bank account; an arrangement with a bank allowing a customer to take more money from his or her account than is in it; the excess of the amount drawn over the sum against which it is drawn (see also **overdraught** below). **o'verdraught** /-dräft/ or (*US*) **o'verdraft** *n* a current of air passing over, or coming from above, a fire in a furnace, kiln, etc. **overdraw'** *vt* to exaggerate in drawing, etc; to exaggerate in telling, etc; to draw from (one's bank account) beyond one's credit. **overdress'** *vt* and *vi* to dress too ostentatiously or elaborately. ◆ *n* /ō'/ a dress that may be worn over a blouse, jumper, etc. **overdrive'** *vt* to work (someone, or oneself) too hard; to drive too hard; to outdrive. ◆ *n* /ō'/ a gearing device that transmits to the driving shaft a speed greater than engine crankshaft speed. **over-drowsed'** (*Wordsworth* **o'er-drows'ed**) *adj* overcome by drowsiness. **overdub'** *vt* to add (new sound) to a recording. ◆ *n* /ō'/ a new sound added to a recording. **overdue'** (or /ō'vər-/) *adj* behind

time for arrival; still unpaid after the time it is due. **overear'nest** *adj* too earnest; severe in manner (*Shakesp*). **overeat'** *vt* (often with *oneself*; also *vi*) to eat too much; *perh* to nibble all over, *perh* to surfeit on (*Shakesp*). **overegg'** *vt* to exceed acceptable limits in exaggeration or elaboration about, *esp* in the phrase *overegg the pudding*. **overes'timāte** *vt* to estimate or judge too highly. ◆ *n* /-mət/ an excessively high estimate. **overestimā'tion** *n*. **overexpose'** *vt* to give too much publicity to; to expose (a film) to too much light. **overexpo'sure** *n*. **over-ex'quisite** *adj* (*Milton*) excessively exact in imagining details. **overeye'** *vt* (*obs*) to survey, look upon; to watch. **o'verfall** *n* a rippling or race of water, *esp* caused by an uneven river- or seabed; a sudden increase of depth; a place or structure for overflow of surplus waters; a waterfall or cataract in a river. ◆ *vt* /-föl'/ to fall on or over; to assail. **overfar'** *adv* too far; to too great an extent (*Shakesp*). **overfin'ished** *adj* (of cattle and sheep) having too much finish (qv). **o'verflight** *n* a flight above and over. **o'verflour'ish** *vt* to cover with blossom, or with flourishes or ornament. **overflow'** *vt* (*pat* **overflowed'**; *pap* **overflowed'**, formerly **overflown'**) to flow over (a bank, rim, etc); to flow over the edge of; to flow over the surface of; to flood; to flow over and beyond; to cause to run over; (of eg people) to fill and then spread beyond (eg a room). ◆ *vi* to flow over an edge or limit; to abound (with *with*). ◆ *n* /ō'/ a flowing over; that which flows over (**overflow meeting** a supplementary meeting of those unable to find room in the main meeting); an excess number or quantity; the error that arises when a computer calculates a number which is too large for it to store (*comput*); a pipe or channel for spare water, etc; an inundation; a superabundance. **overflow'ing** *adj* flowing over; running over; overfull; overabounding (with *with*); exuberant. Also *n*. **overflow'ingly** *adv*. **overflush'** *adj* too flush. ◆ *n* /ō'/ superfluity. **overfly'** *vt* to outsoar; to fly over. **o'verfold** *n* a fold tilted over so that the dip on both sides of the axis is in the same direction. ◆ *vt* /-fōld'/ to fold over; to thrust into an overfold. **overfond'** *adj* too fond (with *of*); foolish to excess (*obs*). **overfond'ly** *adv*. **overfond'ness** *n*. **overfreight'** *vt* (*pap* **overfraught'**) to overload. ◆ *n* /ō'/ an excessive load. **overgall'** *vt* to blister or inflame all over, or greatly. **overgang'** (*Scot* and *N Eng*; *Scot* **o'ergang** /owr-gang'/) *vt* to dominate; to overspread; to exceed. **o'vergarment** *n* a garment worn on top of others. **overget'** *vt* to overtake (*obs*); to get over, recover from (*dialect* or *archaic*); to overcome, possess the mind of (*dialect* or *literary*). **overgive'** *vt* (*Spenser*) to give over or up. **overglaze'** *vt* to glaze over; to cover speciously. ◆ *n* /ō'/ an additional glaze given to porcelain, etc. ◆ *adj* /ō'/ applied to, or suitable for painting on, a glazed surface. **overgloom'** *vt* (*poetic*) to cover with gloom; to scowl over. **overgo'** *vt* (*pat* **overwent'**) (chiefly *dialect* or *archaic*) to exceed; to surpass; to overpower; to go over; to pass over, traverse; to spread over; to pass over, forbear to speak of. ◆ *vi* to go over; to pass on. **overgo'ing** *n* passing over; crossing, traversing; transgression. **overgrain'** *vt* and *vi* in painting, to grain over (a surface already grained). **overgrain'er** *n* a brush for overgraining. **overgrass'** *vt* to grass over, conceal with grass. **overgreen'** *vt* to cover with green or verdure; to conceal (*Shakesp*). **overground'** *adj* and *adv* above ground. **overgrow'** *vt* to grow beyond; to grow more than; to grow too great for; to rise above; to cover with growth. ◆ *vi* to grow beyond the normal or suitable size. **overgrown** /ō'vər-grōn or -grōn'/ *adj* grown beyond the natural size; covered over with uncontrolled vegetation, weeds, etc. **o'vergrowth** *n* excessive or abnormally great growth; excess or superfluity resulting from growth; that which grows over and covers anything; growth of a crystal around another (*crystallog*). **overhaile'** or **overhale'** *vt* to draw over (*Spenser*); to overtake, overpower (*obs*); to examine (*obs*). **o'verhair** *n* the long hair overlying the fur of many animals. **o'verhand** *adv* with hand above the object; palm downwards; with hand or arm raised above the shoulders or (in swimming) coming out of the water over the head; from below (*mineralogy*); with stitches passing through in one direction and back round the edges (*needlework*). ◆ *adj* done or performed overhand (**overhand knot** simplest of all knots, tied by passing the end over the standing part and through the bight). ◆ *vt* to sew overhand. **overhand'ed** *adj* and *adv* with hand above; with too many hands. **overhand'led** *adj* (*Shakesp*) handled or discussed too much. **overhang'** *vt* to hang over; to project

Some words formed with the prefix **over-**; the numbers in brackets refer to the numbered senses in the entry for **over-**.

overcov'er *vt* (6).	**overdye'** *vt* (1), (5).	**overexcite'** *vt* (5).
overcredu'lity *n* (5).	**overelab'orate** *adj* (5).	**overexert'** *vt* (5).
overcred'ulous *adj* (5).	**over-emo'tional** *adj* (5).	**overexer'tion** *n* (5).
overdar'ing *adj* (5).	**overem'phasis** *n* (5).	**overextend'** *vt* and *vi* (5).
overdepend'ence *n* (5).	**overem'phasize** or	**overfamil'iar** *adj* (5).
overdepend'ent *adj* (5).	**overem'phasise** *vt* (5).	**overfamiliar'ity** *n* (5).
overdiagnose' *vt* and *vi* (5).	**over-exact'** *adj* (5).	**overfed'** *adj* (5).
overdram'atize or **overdram'atise** *vt* (5).	**overexcitabil'ity** *n* (5).	**overfeed'** *vt* and *vi* (5).
overdust' *vt* (1).	**overexcit'able** *adj* (5).	**overfill'** *vt* and *vi* (5).

■ words derived from main entry word; ▫ compound words; ▪ idioms and phrasal verbs over; to impend over; to cover with hangings. ◆ *vi* to hang over, lean out beyond the vertical. ◆ *n* /ō'/ a projecting part; degree of projection. **overhaul'** *vt* to examine thoroughly and repair where necessary; to turn over for examination; to haul or draw over; to overtake or gain upon. ◆ *n* /ō'/ a thorough examination, *esp* with a view to repair; a hauling over. **overhead'** *adv* above one's head; aloft; in the zenith; in complete submergence; taking one with another, in the lump, on the average apiece (*Scot*). ◆ *adj* /ō'/ above one's head; located above; well above ground level; (of a projector) designed to sit on a speaker's desk and project transparencies on a screen behind him or her; all-round, general, average. ◆ *n* (*usu* in *pl*) the general expenses of a business, such as heating and lighting of premises, etc, as distinct from the direct cost of producing an article (also **overhead costs** or **charges**); a transparency viewed by means of an **overhead projector**; a shot played from above one's head (*tennis*, etc). **overhear'** *vt* to hear without being meant to hear, as an eavesdropper does; to hear by accident, as an unintentional or unnoticed listener does; to hear over again or in turn (*Shakesp*). **overheat'** *vt* to heat to excess; to overstimulate (the economy) with the risk of increasing inflation (*econ*). ◆ *vi* to become too hot; (of the economy) to become overstimulated. ◆ *vt* and *vi* to make or become agitated. ◆ *n* /ō'/ too great heat. **overheat'ing** *n*. **overhent'** *vt* (*pap* and *pat* **overhent'**) (*Spenser*) to overtake. **overhit'** *vt* to hit (a ball, etc) beyond the intended target (also *vi*); to go beyond (the right, fitting or intended level, point, etc). **overhold'** *vt* (*Shakesp*) to overvalue. **overhung'** *adj* overhanging; suspended from above; covered over with hangings or hanging vegetation, etc. **overindulge'** *vi* to indulge oneself to excess, *esp* in eating and drinking. ◆ *vt* to spoil (*esp* a child). **overindul'gence** *n*. **overindul'gent** *adj*. **overinform'** *vt* to give an excessive amount of information to; to animate too much. **overinsur'ance** *n*. **overinsure'** *vt* to insure for more than the real value. **overiss'ue** *vt* to issue in excess (eg banknotes or bills of exchange). ◆ *n* /ō'/ excessive issue. **overjoy'** *vt* (*rare*) to fill with great joy; to transport with delight or gladness. ◆ *n* /ō'/ (*rare*) joy to excess, transport. **overjoyed'** *adj*. **overjump'** *vt* to jump (too far) over; to jump farther than; to pass over. **overkest'** *vt* (*Spenser*) for **overcast** (*pat* and *pap*). **o'verkill** *n* something, eg power for destruction, in excess of what is necessary or desirable. **o'verking** *n* a king holding sovereignty over inferior kings. **o'verknee** *adj* reaching above the knee. **overla'bour** *vt* (*archaic*) to labour excessively over; to be too exact or meticulous with; to overwork. **overlade'** *vt* (*pap* **overla'den**) to overburden. **overlaid'** *adj* *pap* of **overlay**. **overlain'** *adj* *pap* of **overlie**. **o'verland** *adj* passing entirely or principally by land. ◆ *adv* (or /-land'/) by or over land. ◆ *vt* and *vi* (*Aust*) to drive (cattle) across country; to journey across country, *esp* a long way. **o'verlander** (or /-land'/) *n*. **overlap'** *vt* to extend over and beyond the edge of; to reach from beyond, across the edge, and partly rest on or cover; to coincide in part with; to ripple over (*poetic*). ◆ *vi* to have one part partly covering the other; to have something in common, to partly coincide; to advance down the flank outside the player with the ball (*football*, *rugby*, etc). ◆ *n* /ō'/ an overlapping part or situation; a disposition of strata where the upper beds extend beyond the boundary of the lower beds of the same series (*geol*). **overlard'** *vt* to smear over as with lard; to overload with fulsome expressions, eg of praise. **overlaunch'** *vt* (*shipbuilding*) to join by long splices or scarfs. **overlay'** *vt* (*pat* and *pap* **overlaid'**) to cover by laying or spreading something over; to cover to excess, encumber; by confusion, to overlie; to put an overlay or overlays on (*printing*); to lay or place as a covering (*rare*); to span (*Milton*). ◆ *n* /ō'/ a covering; anything laid on or over to alter the appearance; a piece of paper pasted on the impression-surface of a printing press, so as to increase the impression in a place where it is too faint; in artwork, a transparent sheet on which is drawn one element of the whole design, which is laid on top of another sheet or sheets to present the complete design; the process by which segments of a large program are brought from backing store for processing, with only those segments currently requiring processing being held in the main store (*comput*); a segment of a program transferred in this way (*comput*); (often **o'er'lay** or **owre'lay**) a large cravat (*Scot*). **overlay'ing** *n* a superficial covering; something that overlays; plating. **overleaf'** *adv* on the other side of the

leaf of a book. **overleap'** (*Scot* **owerloup'**) *vt* to leap over; to pass over without notice (**overleap oneself** to leap too far). **o'verleather** *n* (*Shakesp*) the upper part of a shoe. **overlend'** *vi* to lend too much. **overlent'** *adj*. **overlev'eraged** *adj* (of a business) having borrowed more money than it can repay (*finance*). **overlev'erage** *vi* and *vt*. **overlev'eraging** *n*. **overlie'** *vt* (**overly'ing**; **overlay'**; **overlain'**) to lie above or upon; to smother by lying on. **o'verlier** (or /-lī'/) *n*. **overlive** /-liv'/ *vt* to survive; to outlive; (*reflexive*) to outlast one's usefulness or time of vigour; (*reflexive*) to live too intensely, exhaust (oneself). ◆ *vi* to survive; to live too long; to live too fast, or so as to exhaust oneself prematurely; to live on too high a standard of luxury. **overload'** *vt* to load too heavily or fill too full. ◆ *n* /ō'/ an excessive load. **o'verlock** *vt* and *vi* to oversew (a fabric edge, hem, seam, etc) with an interlocking stitch to prevent fraying. **o'verlocker** *n* a person who or machine that does this. **o'verlocking** *n* the process of doing this, or the stitching produced. **overlook'** *vt* to look over; to see, or give a view of, from above; to view carefully; to oversee, superintend; to fail to notice or take into account; to allow (a misdemeanour, etc) to go unpunished; to slight; to bewitch by looking upon with the evil eye. ◆ *n* /ō'/ (chiefly *US*) a high place that gives a view of the area below; an oversight. **overlook'er** *n*. **o'verlord** *n* a supreme lord; a feudal superior; (with *cap*) the operational name for the Anglo-American invasion (1944) of Normandy in World War II. ◆ *vt* /-lörd'/ to be superior to. **o'verlordship** *n*. **overly** *adv* see under **over**. **overly'ing** *adj* lying on the top. **o'verman** *n* an overseer in mining, the man in charge of work below ground; Nietzsche's term for a superman. ◆ *vt* /-man'/ to supply (a ship) with too large a crew; to employ uneconomically large numbers of workers in (an industry, etc). **o'vermantel** *n* an ornamental structure, often with a mirror, set on a mantelshelf. **overmast'** *vt* (*naut*) to provide with too long or too heavy a mast or masts. **overmas'ter** *vt* to gain or have the mastery of; to overpower; to dominate. **overmatch'** *vt* (*esp US*) to be more than a match for; to match with a superior opponent; to defeat, overcome. ◆ *n* /ō'/ someone who is more than a match; a match in which one player, etc, is superior; an overmatching. **o'vermatter** *n* (*printing*) overset type matter, ie text that has been typeset but cannot be printed because of shortage of space. **overmeas'ure** (or /ō'/) *n* something given over the proper measure. ◆ *vt* /-mezh'/ to measure above the true value. **overmerr'y** *adj* extremely merry. **overmount'** *vt* to rise above; to excel in mounting. ◆ *vi* to mount too high. **o'vermuch** (or /-much'/) *adj* and *adv* too much. ◆ *n* an excessive amount. **overmultiplica'tion** *n*. **overmul'tiply** *vi* to become too numerous. **overmult'itude** *vt* (*Milton*) to outnumber. **overname'** *vt* (*Shakesp*) to repeat the names of. **overnet'** *vt* to cover with a net; to overfish with nets. **overnice'** *adj* too fastidious. **overnice'ly** *adv*. **overnice'ness** *n*. **o'vernight** *n* a stay lasting one night; the evening just past (*Shakesp*; now chiefly *US*). ◆ *vi* to spend the night. ◆ *adv* /-nīt'/ for the duration of the night, until the next morning during the night; in the course of the night; hence, extraordinarily quickly; on the evening of the day just past. ◆ *adj* done or occurring or existing overnight; sudden; for the time from evening until next morning (**overnight bag** or **case** a small case for carrying the clothes, toilet articles, etc, needed for an overnight stay). **o'vernighter** *n* a person staying overnight; an overnight bag. **overoff'ice** (*Shakesp* **o're-office**) *vt* appar, to lord it over by virtue of office, or perhaps to exercise one's office over. **overpage'** *adv* overleaf. **overpaint'** *vt* to put too much paint on; to depict with exaggeration; to cover (a painted area) with a new layer of paint. **overpart'** *vt* in acting, to assign too difficult a part to. **overpass'** *vt* to pass over; to pass by without notice; to exceed. ◆ *vi* to pass over; to elapse. ◆ *n* /ō'/ a road bridging another road or railway, canal, etc, a flyover. **overpast'** *adj* over; at an end. **overpay'** *vt* to pay too much; to be more than an ample reward for. **overpay'ment** *n*. **overped'al** *vi* to make excessive use of the sustaining pedal of a piano. **overpeer'** *vt* (partly from **peer¹**, partly **peer²**; *Shakesp*) to peer over or down upon; to look down on; to tower over; to excel. **overperch'** (*Shakesp* **orepearch'**) *vt* to fly up and perch on, fly over. **overpersuade'** *vt* to persuade (someone) against his or her inclination. **overpic'ture** *vt* to surpass pictorially; to cover with pictures. **overpitch'** *vt* to bowl (the ball) so that it bounces close enough to the batsman to be easily hit (*cricket*; also *vi*); to pitch too far, or beyond the best distance. **overpitched**' *adj* (of a roof) steeply pitched; (of a cricket ball) bowled so that it pitches too near the batsman. **overplaced**' (*Spenser* **overplast** /-plät'/) *adj* placed above. **overplay**' *vt* to overemphasize the importance or value of; to play better than (one's opponent); to try to gain more from (one's assets or advantages) than they can be expected to yield (**overplay one's hand** to overreach oneself in pressing one's advantage). ◆ *vt* and *vi* to exaggerate (an emotion, acting role, etc); to hit the ball beyond (the green) (*golf*). ◆ *n* /ō'/ an act or occasion of overplaying. **o'verplus** *n* that which is more than enough; surplus. ◆ *adj* surplus. **overply**' *vt* to ply beyond what can be borne or sustained. **overpoise**' *vt* to outweigh. ◆ *n* /ō'/ a weight sufficient to weigh another down. **overpost**' *vt* (*obs*) to hasten over quickly. **overpow'er** *vt* to overcome or reduce to helplessness, by force; to subdue; to overwhelm; to make (an engine, etc) too powerful. **overpow'ering** *adj* excessive in degree or amount; irresistible. **overpow'eringly** *adv*. **overpress**' *vt* to oppress; to burden too heavily; to press too much pressure on. **overpress'ure** *n* excessive pressure, *esp* of work. **overprice**' *vt* to ask too high a price for. **overpriced**' *adj*. **overprint**' *vt* to print too strongly or dark; to print too many copies of; to print over already printed matter (*esp* a postage stamp). ◆ *n* /ō'/ an offprint; something that is printed over an already printed surface, as on a postage stamp. **overprize**' *vt* to value too highly; to surpass in value (*obs*). **overproduce**' *vt* and *vi*. **overproduc'tion** *n* excessive production; production in excess of the demand. **overproof**' (or /ō'/) *adj* containing more alcohol than proof-spirit does. **overqual'ified** *adj* having qualifications and skills in excess of those required for a particular job, etc. **overrack**' *vt* to overstrain. **overrake**' *vt* to sweep over. **overrank**' *adj* too rank or luxurious. **overrate**' *vt* to give too high a value to, think too highly of. **overreach**' *vt* (*pat* and *pap* **overreached**' or (*archaic*) **overraught**') to reach or extend beyond; to overtake; to outwit or get the better of; (*reflexive*) to undo oneself by attempting too much, venturing too far, trying to be too clever, etc. ◆ *vi* to reach too far; (of a horse) to strike the hindfoot against the forefoot. ◆ *n* /ō'/ the act of overreaching; the injury thereby done. **overreact**' *vi* to react or respond with too much vehemence, or otherwise excessively. **overreac'tion** *n*. **overread** /-rēd'/ *vt* to read over. ◆ *adj* /-red'/ having read too much. **overreck'on** *vt* and *vi* to compute too highly. **overred**' *vt* (*Shakesp*) to cover with a red colour. **overren**' *vt* an archaic form of **overrun**. **override**' *vt* (*pat* **overrode**'; *pap* **overridd'en**) to pass over; to overlap; to set aside; to be valid against; to be more important than, prevail over; to injure or exhaust by too much riding; to ride over; to trample down on horseback; to slide or mount on the top or back of; to outride, overtake (*obs*). ◆ *n* /ō'/ an auxiliary (*esp* manual) control capable of temporarily prevailing over the operation of another (*esp* automatic) control. **o'verrider** *n* an attachment on the bumper of a motor vehicle to prevent another bumper becoming interlocked with it. **overrid'ing** *adj* dominant, stronger than anything else. **overruff**' *vt* and *vi* (*cards*) to trump with a higher trump. ◆ *n* /ō'/ an act of overruffing. **overrule**' *vt* to modify or to set aside by greater power; to prevail over the will of, against a previous decision of; to impose an overriding decision upon; to prevail over and set aside; to annul, declare invalid (*law*); to rule against; to disallow; to rule over (*obs*). ◆ *vi* to prevail. **overrul'er** *n*. **overrul'ing** *n* (*law*) the process by which a precedent is overruled and superseded by a statute or a superior court. ◆ *adj* dominating. **overrun**' *vt* (**overrunn'ing**; **overran**'; **overrun**') to spread over; to flow over; to grow over; to infest or swarm over; to infect widely; to spread over and take possession of; to run beyond; to exceed the limit of; to carry beyond a limit; to carry over into another line or page; to adjust the type of by overrunning (*printing*); to run over, across, through, all about; to run over, crush underfoot or under wheel; to outdo in running (*rare*); to escape from by running faster (*dialect*); (*reflexive*) to injure or exhaust oneself by too much running. ◆ *vi* to run over, overflow; to run beyond a limit; (of a vehicle engine) to slow down in response to a reverse torque transmitted through the gears from the wheels (**overrun the constable** see **outrun** under **out-**). ◆ *n* /ō'/ an act or occasion of overrunning; the extent of overrunning; an overrunning of type (*printing*); the overrunning of a vehicle engine

(**overrun brake** a brake fitted to a trailer that prevents it from travelling faster than the towing vehicle when reducing speed or going downhill). **overrunn'er** *n*. **oversail**' *vi* and *vt* (Fr *saillir* to project) to project (beyond). ◆ *n* /ō'/ projection. **overscore**' *vt* to score or draw lines across; to obliterate in this way. **overscutched** /-skucht' or -skuch'id/ *adj* (*Walter Scott*) worn-out (after *Shakesp, 2 Henry IV* III.2, where **overschutcht** is variously conjectured to mean overworn in service or whipped at the cart's tail). **o'versea** *adj* across, beyond or from beyond the sea. ◆ *adv* /-sē'/ (*rare*) overseas. **overseas**' *adv* in or to lands beyond the sea; abroad. ◆ *n* foreign lands. ◆ *adj* /ō'/ across or beyond the sea. **oversee**' *vt* to superintend; to overlook, disregard; to see without being meant to see; to see or look over. **overseen**' *adj* (*obs*) mistaken or ill-advised; drunk; versed (in). **o'verseer** /-sēr/ or -sē-ər/ *n* a person who oversees workmen, etc; a superintendent; formerly, an officer having care of the poor, and other duties; the manager of a plantation of slaves (*hist*); a critic or editor (*obs*). **oversell**' *vt* and *vi* (*pat* and *pap* **oversold**') to sell more of than is available; to exaggerate the merits of; to sell for too high a price; see also **oversold** below. **overset**' *vt* and *vi* to upset; to disorder; to set more type or copy than there is space available for (*printing*); to oppress, press hard (*obs*). **o'versew** (or /-sō'/) *vt* to sew (an edge or edges) overhand. **oversexed**' *adj* having unusually strong sexual urges. **overshade**' *vt* to throw a shade or shadow over; to darken. **overshad'ow** *vt* to throw a shadow over; to cast into the shade by surpassing, to outshine; to darken; to shelter or protect. **overshare**' *vi* to be unacceptably forthcoming with information about one's personal life. **overshar'ing** *n*. **overshine**' *vt* (*Shakesp*) to shine over or upon, illumine; to outshine. **o'vershoe** *n* a shoe, *esp* of waterproof material, worn over one's shoes to protect them. **over-shoe**' or **over-shoes**' *adv* deep enough to cover the shoes. **overshoot**' *vt* (*pap* and *pat* **overshot**') to shoot over or beyond (one's target); to pass beyond, exceed, fail to stop at (**overshoot oneself** to venture too far, to overreach oneself); (of a train or aircraft) to fail to come to a halt at (a station) or on (a runway); to shoot, dart, or fly across overhead; to surpass in shooting; to injure or exhaust by too much shooting; to shoot with colour over the surface of. ◆ *vi* to shoot or go too far. ◆ *n* /ō'/ an act or occasion of overshooting; the extent of overshooting. **overshot**' *adj* shot over; too much shot over; surpassed; overdone; in error by overshooting the mark; drunk (*obs sl*). ◆ *adj* /ō'/ having the upper jaw protruding beyond the lower; (of a water wheel) fed from above. **overshow'er** *vt* to shower over. **o'verside** *adj* acting or done over the side. ◆ *adv* /-sīd'/ over the side. ◆ *prep* (*Spenser* **over side**) over the side of. **o'versight** *n* a failure to notice; a mistake; an omission; supervision. **oversize**' *vt* to cover with size. ◆ *n* /ō'/ a large or larger size. ◆ *adj* (also **o'versized** (or /-sīzd'/)) very large, or larger than normal. **overskip**' *vt* to skip, leap or pass over; to overlook; to omit. **overslaugh** /ō'vər-slö/ *n* (Du *overslaan* to miss or skip over; *milit*) exemption from duty in turn when employed on something else; a sand-bar (*US*). ◆ *vt* /-slö'/ to remit or pass over by overslaugh; to pass over in favour of another (*US*); to hinder. **oversleep**' *vt* to indulge (oneself) in sleeping too long; to sleep beyond. ◆ *vi* to sleep too long. **overslip**' *vt* to slip by; to escape the notice of; to slip unnoticed from; to let slip. ◆ *vi* to slip by; to make a slip or error inadvertently. ◆ *n* /ō'/ (*obs*) an inadvertency; a close-fitting under-bodice. **o'versman** *n* an overseer (*archaic*); an umpire (*Scot*). **oversold**' *adj* (*stock exchange*) of a market in which excessive selling has caused too rapid a fall; see also **oversell** above. **o'versoul** *n* Emerson's term for the divine principle forming the spiritual unity of all being. **oversow**' *vt* to sow after something has been already sown; to sow over. **overspend**' *vt* to spend beyond (one's income, budget, etc); to exhaust or cripple (oneself) by spending. ◆ *vi* to spend too much. ◆ *n* an instance of overspending; the amount by which an allocated budget, etc, is overspent. **overspent**' *adj* excessively fatigued. **o'verspill** *n* something, or an amount, that is spilt over; a proportion of the population that leaves a district, displaced by changes in housing, etc; (in a public bar) beer, etc that overflows from a glass as it is being filled. **o'verspin** *n* the spinning of a flying ball in the same direction as if it were rolling on the ground. **overstaff**' *vt* to provide too many people as staff. **overstand**' *vt* (*archaic*) to out-stay. **overstare**' (*Shakesp* **ore-stare**') *vt* to outstare. **overstate**' *vt* to state too strongly; to

---

Some words formed with the prefix **over-**; the numbers in brackets refer to the numbered senses in the entry for **over-**.

overkeen' *adj* (5).	**overpeo'ple** *vt* (5).	**overproud**' *adj* (5).
overkeep' *vt* (5).	**overpop'ulate** *vt* (5).	**overrash**' *adj* (5).
overkind' *adj* (5).	**overpopula'tion** *n* (5).	**overrash'ly** *adv* (5).
overkind'ness *n* (5).	**overpraise**' *vt* (5).	**overrash'ness** *n* (5).
overleav'en *vt* (5).	**over-precise**' *adj* (5).	**over-refine**' *vt* (5).
overlong' *adj* and *adv* (5).	**overprepara'tion** *n* (5).	**over-refine'ment** *n* (5).
overloud' *adj* (5).	**overprepare**' *vi* and *vt* (5).	**overreli'ance** *n* (5).
overlus'ty (*Shakesp*) *adj* (5).	**overprepared**' *adj* (5).	**overreli'ant** *adj* (5).
overneat *adj* (5).	**overprotec'tive** *adj* (5).	**over-rev**' *vt* and *vi* (5).

■ words derived from main entry word; ◻ compound words; ▪ idioms and phrasal verbs exaggerate. **overstate'ment** n. **overstay'** vt to stay beyond (a time limit). **overstay'er** n an immigrant worker who stays beyond the time allowed by his or her work permit. **oversteer'** vi (of a motor-car) to exaggerate the degree of turning applied by the steering-wheel. ◆ n /ō'/ the tendency to do this. **overstep'** vt to step beyond; to exceed; to transgress. ◆ n /ō'/ (geol) the transgression of an overlapping stratum over the edges of underlying unconformable strata. **overstink'** vt (pat **overstunk'**; Shakesp **orestunck'**) to stink more than. **overstock'** vt to fill to excess. ◆ n /ō'/ an excessively large stock. **overstrain'** vt and vi to strain too much; to strain beyond the elastic limit. ◆ n /ō'/ too great strain. **overstrained'** adj strained to excess; exaggerated. **overstress'** vt and vi to stress too much. ◆ n /ō'/ too great stress. **overstretch'** vt to stretch to excess; to exaggerate. **overstride'** vt to stride across; to stand astride of. **overstrike'** vt (pat **overstruck'**; Spenser **overstrooke'**) to strike with a downward blow; to superimpose a new design on (a coin); to type on top of (a character already typed). ◆ n /ō'/ the act of printing one character on top of another. **overstrung'** adj too highly strung; (of a piano) having two sets of strings crossing obliquely to save space. **overstud'y** vt and vi to study too much. ◆ n /ō'/ too much study. **overstuff'** vt to stuff to excess; to cover (furniture) all over with upholstery. **oversubscribe'** vt to subscribe for (eg shares) beyond the number offered. **oversubscrip'tion** n. **oversupply'** vt to supply to excess. ◆ n /ō'/ an excessively large supply. **oversway'** vt (rare) to overrule; to bear down. **overswear'** vt (rare) to swear anew. **overswell'** vt and vi to overflow. **overswim'** vt to swim across. **overtake'** vt to draw level with and move past (something or someone travelling in the same direction); to catch up with; to manage to get done, put behind one; to catch; to come upon abruptly, as in overtaken by darkness or disaster; to take by surprise. **overtä'ken** adj (dialect) fuddled. **overtalk'** vt to talk over. **overtask'** vt to impose too many tasks on; to impose too heavy a task on. **overtax'** vt to tax excessively; to require too much of. **overteem'** vi to teem, breed or produce in excess. ◆ vt to exhaust or wear out by breeding. **overthink'** vi and vt to analyse (something) too much. **overthrow'** vt to throw over, overturn, upset; to ruin, subvert; to defeat utterly; to throw too far or too strongly. ◆ vi (obs) to be overturned; to throw too far. ◆ n /ō'/ the act of overthrowing or state of being overthrown; a return of the ball to the wicket that is missed by the fielders there (cricket); a run scored in consequence of this. **overthrow'er** n. **o'verthrust** (also **overthrust fault**) n (geol) a fault at a low angle from the horizontal in which the rocks on the upper side of the fault plane have moved upwards in relation to the rocks on the lower side of the fault plane. **overthwart'** vt (obs) to lie athwart; to cross. ◆ adj opposite, transverse; contrary, perverse. ◆ adv crosswise; opposite. ◆ prep across, on the other side of. **o'vertime** n time spent in working beyond the regular hours; work done in such time; pay for such work; a N American name for **extra time** (see under **extra¹**). ◆ adj and adv during, for or concerning such time. ◆ vt /ō-vər-tīm'/ to exceed the correct allowance of time for (a photographic exposure, etc). **overtime'ly** adj and adv (obs) too early, untimely. **o'vertimer** n a person who works overtime. **o'vertone** n a harmonic or upper partial (music); (in pl) a subtle meaning, additional to the main meaning, conveyed by a word or statement; (in pl) an implicit quality, or constant association. **overtop'** vt to rise over the top of; to be higher than; to surpass; to exceed. ◆ vi to rise too high. **overtow'er** vt to tower above. ◆ vi to soar too high. **overtrade'** vi to trade excessively or beyond capital; to buy in more than can be sold or paid for. ◆ vt to involve in trade in such a way. **overtrad'ing** n. **overtrain'** vt and vi to train so far as to do harm. ◆ vt to train too high. **o'vertrick** n (bridge) a trick in excess of the number specified in the contract. **overtrip'** vt (obs) to trip nimbly over. **overtrump'** vt to trump with a higher card than the trump already played. **overturn'** vt to throw down or over; to upset; to subvert. ◆ vi to be turned over or upside down. ◆ n /ō'/ an overturning; a turnover. **overturn'er** n. **overtype'** vt (comput) see **overwrite** below. **overuse** /-ūs'/ n excessive use (**overuse syndrome** a condition of muscular strain found among musicians, formerly known as **musicians' cramp**). ◆ vt /-ūz'/ to use too much. **overvaluä'tion** n. **overval'ue** vt to set too high a value on. ◆ n /ō'/ (old) an excessively high valuation. **overveil'** vt to veil over or cover.

o'verview n a general survey; an inspection (Shakesp). **o'verwash** n a washing over; material carried by glacier-streams over a frontal moraine (geol). ◆ adj of or relating to an overwash. **overwatch'** vt to watch over; to watch through; to overcome with long watching. **overwear'** vt (pat **overwore'**; pap **overworn'** see below) to wear out; to outwear, outlive. **overwear'y** vt to overcome with weariness, exhaust. ◆ adj excessively weary. **overweath'er** vt (Shakesp) to batter by violence of weather. **overween'** vi (archaic) to expect too much; to be presumptuous or arrogant. ◆ vt (reflexive) to think too highly of (oneself). **overween'ing** adj and n (of a person) arrogant, conceited; (of pride) inflated, excessive, immoderate. **overween'ingly** adv. **overween'ingness** n. **overweigh'** vt to be heavier than; to outweigh; to weigh down. **o'verweight** n weight beyond what is required or what is allowed; preponderance. ◆ adj /-wāt'/ above the weight required; above the ideal or desired weight; (of an investment fund) containing more than the optimum proportion of a certain type of asset. ◆ vt /-wāt'/ to weigh down; to put too heavy a burden on; to give too much weight or importance to. **over-weight'ed** adj not fairly balanced in presentation. **overwent'** vt and vi pat of **overgo**. **overwhelm'** vt to crush completely with something heavy or strong; to flow over; to bear down; to reduce to helplessness; to overpower; to affect overpoweringly; to defeat utterly, usu with superior numbers; to inundate or submerge, esp suddenly; to overhang (obs). **overwhel'ming** n and adj. **overwhel'mingly** adv. **overwhel'mingness** n. **overwind** /-wīnd'/ vt (pat and pap **overwound'**) to wind too far. **overwing'** vt to fly over; to outflank (obs). **overwin'ter** vi to pass the winter. ◆ vt and vi to keep (animals, plants, etc) alive or to stay alive through the winter. **overwise'** adj too wise; affectedly wise; wise in one's own estimation. **overwise'ly** adv. **o'verword** or (archaic) **o'erword** /ōr', ör'/ or (Scot) owr'/, also **owre'word** n the refrain of a song; a habitual saying. **overwork'** vt and vi (pat and pap **overworked'** or **overwrought'**) to work too hard. ◆ vt to make too much use of; to decorate the surface of. ◆ n excessive work; /ō'/ additional work. **overworn'** /-wōrn'/ or -wörn'/ adj worn-out; spoiled by use; threadbare; trite; out of date; spent or past. **overwound'** vt pat and pap of **overwind**. **overwrest'** vt to overstrain. **overwrest'le** vt (Spenser) to overcome by wrestling. **overwrite'** vt to write too much about; to write in a laboured manner; to cover over with writing or other writing; to superscribe; to exhaust by writing too much; (also **overtype'**) to type over and replace (existing characters) (comput). ◆ vi to write too much or in too contrived a manner. **overwrought'** adj (see also **overwork** above) worked too hard; too highly excited; with highly strained nerves; worked or embellished all over; overdone, too elaborate. **overyear'** vt (obs) to keep into a second or later year. ◆ adj (dialect) kept from one year to the next. ◆ adv (dialect) until next year.

overachieve...to...**overswim** see under **over-**.

overt /ō'vûrt or -vûrt'/ adj open to view, not concealed; public; evident. [Fr ouvert, pap of ouvrir to open]
■ **overt'ly** adv.
❑ **overt act** n something obviously done in execution of a criminal intent.
■ **market overt** open or public market.

overtake...to...**overtrump** see under **over-**.

overture /ō'vər-tūr/ n an instrumental prelude to an opera, oratorio, etc; a one-movement musical composition in similar style (sonata form); (usu in pl) an introductory proposition or opening move to negotiations, etc; an offer or proposal; an opening or opportunity; an opening or beginning; the method in the Presbyterian church of beginning legislation and maturing opinion by sending some proposition from the inferior courts to the General Assembly, and vice versa; also the proposal so sent; an opening up or disclosure (Shakesp); an open place (Spenser); an opening or aperture (obs). ◆ vt to lay a proposal before; to put forward as an overture. [OFr overture (Fr ouverture) opening]

overturn...to...**overyear** see under **over-**.

ovi- /o- or ō-vi-/ or **ovo-** /-vō- or -və-/ combining form denoting: egg; ovum. [L ōvum egg]

Some words formed with the prefix **over-**; the numbers in brackets refer to the numbered senses in the entry for **over-**.

overripe' adj (5).	**o'verskirt** n (4).	**oversubt'le** adj (5).
overri'pen vt and vi (5).	**o'versleeve** n (4).	**oversubt'lety** n (5).
overripe'ness n (5).	**overspec'ialize** or	**overte'dious** (Shakesp) adj (5).
overroast' vt (5).	**overspec'ialise** vi (5).	**overtire'** vt (5).
overscru'pulous adj (5).	**overspecializā'tion** or	**overtoil'** vt (5).
overscrup'ulousness n (5).	**overspecialisā'tion** n (5).	**overtrust'** vi (5).
oversen'sitive adj (5).	**overspread'** vt (1).	**overvi'olent** adj (5).
o'vershirt n (4).	**overstain'** vt (1).	**overwa'ter** vt (5).
oversimplificā'tion n (5).	**overstrew'** vt (1).	**overwrap'** vt (1), (5).
oversim'plify vt (5).	**overstrong'** adj (5).	**over-zeal'ous** adj (5).

■ **ovidū'cal** or **oviduc'tal** *adj*. **oviduct** /ō'vi-dukt/ *n* (see **duct**; *zool*) the tube by which the egg escapes from the ovary. **oviferous** /ō-vif'ə-rəs/ *adj* (L *ferre* to bear) egg-carrying. **oviform** /ō'vi-förm/ *adj* egg-shaped. **ovigerous** /ōv-ij'ə-rəs/ *adj* (L *gerere* to carry) egg-carrying. **ovipar'ity** /-par'i-ti/ *n*. **oviparous** /ō-vip'ə-rəs/ *adj* (L *parere* to bring forth) egg-laying. **ovip'arously** *adv*. **ovipos'it** *vi* to deposit eggs with an ovipositor. **oviposition** /-pə-zish'ən/ *n*. **ovipositor** /ō-vi-poz'i-tər/ *n* (L *positor*, from *pōnere* to place) an egg-laying organ in female insects and some female fishes. **oviraptor** /ō'vi-rap'tər/ *n* a small two-footed dinosaur with short forelimbs, thought to have fed on eggs. **ovisac** /ov'i-sak/ *n* (L *saccus*; see **sac**¹) a brood-pouch; an egg capsule. **ovo-lac'to** *adj* (of a vegetarian) having a diet excluding meat but permitting eggs and milk products. ◆ *n* (*pl* **ovo-lac'tos**) an ovo-lacto vegetarian. **ovotest'is** *n* (*pl* **ovotest'es** /-tēz/) an organ that produces both ova and spermatozoa. **ovoviviparity** /-par'i-ti/ *n*. **ovoviviparous** /ō-vō-vi-vip'ə-rəs or -vī-vip'/ *adj* (L *vīvus* living, and *parere* to bring forth) (of certain reptiles and fishes) producing eggs that are hatched in the body of the parent.

ovibos /ō'vi-bos or ov'i-bōs/ *n* the musk-ox. [L *ovis* sheep, and *bōs, bovis* ox]

■ **ovibō'vīne** *adj*.

ovicide /ō'vi-sīd/ (*facetious*) *n* sheep-killing. [L *ovis* sheep, and *caedere* to kill]

Ovidian /o- or ō-vid'i-ən/ *adj* of, like or relating to the Roman poet Ovid (43BC–17AD).

oviform¹ /ov'i-förm or ō'vi-/ *adj* like a sheep; ovine. [L *ovis* sheep, and **-form**]

■ **ovine** /ō'vīn/ *adj* of or relating to sheep; sheep-like.

oviform², **ovigerous** see under **ovi-**.

ovine see under **oviform**¹.

oviparous, **ovipositor** see under **ovi-**.

ovist /ō'vist/ *n* a believer in the doctrine that the ovum contains all future generations in germ. [L *ōvum* egg]

ovo- see **ovi-**.

ovoid /ō'void/ *adj* (of a solid or plane figure) egg-shaped; egg-shaped and attached by the broad end (*bot*). ◆ *n* an egg-shaped figure or body. [L *ōvum* egg, and **-oid**]

■ **ovoid'al** *adj* ovoid.

ovo-lacto see under **ovi-**.

ovolo /ō'və-lō/ (*archit*) *n* (*pl* **o'voli** /-lē/) a moulding with the rounded part composed of a quarter of a circle, or of an arc of an ellipse with the curve greatest at the top. [Ital dimin, from L *ōvum* egg]

ovotestis, **ovoviviparous** see under **ovi-**.

ovular see under **ovule**.

ovulate /ov'yū-lāt or -yə-/ *vi* to release ova from the ovary; to form ova. [From **ovule**]

■ **ovulā'tion** *n*. **ov'ulatory** /-lə-tər-i/ *adj*.

ovule /ov'ūl or ō'vūl/ *n* in flowering plants, the body containing the egg cell, which on fertilization becomes the seed, consisting of the nucellus and its integuments with the embryo-sac (megaspore); an unfertilized ovum (*zool*). [Med L *ōvulum*, dimin of *ōvum* egg]

■ **ov'ular** *adj* of or relating to an ovule. **ōvulif'erous** *adj* carrying ovules.

ovum /ō'vəm/ *n* (*pl* **o'va**) an egg; the egg cell, or female gamete (*biol*). [L *ōvum* egg]

ow¹ /ow/ *interj* expressive of pain. [Spontaneous utterance]

ow² same as **ou**¹.

owche /owch/ *n* same as **ouch**¹.

owe /ō/ *vt* (*pat* and *pap* **owed**) to be indebted for; to be under an obligation to repay or render; to feel as a debt or as due; to have to thank; to bear (a person a grudge); to concede or be bound to concede as a handicap; to own (*obs* or *dialect*). ◆ *vi* to be in debt. —The old *pat* **ought** and *pap* **own**, now differently used, are given separately; see also **owing**. [OE *āgan* to own, possess, present indicative *āh*, preterite *āhte*, *pap* *āgen*; ON *eiga*, OHGer *eigan* to possess]

owelty /ō'əl-ti/ (*law*; *obs*) *n* equality. [Anglo-Fr *owelté*, from L *aequālitās, -ātis*]

Owenite /ō'i-nīt/ *n* a disciple of Robert Owen (1771–1858), British social reformer, who proposed to establish society on a basis of socialistic co-operation; a follower of the ideas and leadership of David Owen, British politician and co-founder of the British Social Democratic Party (1981).

■ **Owenian** /ō-ēn'i-ən/ *adj*. **Ow'enism** *n*. **Ow'enist** *n*.

ower Scots form of **over** (*adv* and *prep*). For compounds see under **over-**.

owing /ō'ing/ *adj* due; to be paid; imputable. [**owe**]

■ **owing to** because of; in consequence of.

owl /owl/ *n* any member of the Strigiformes, nocturnal predacious birds with large broad heads, flat faces, large eyes surrounded by discs of feathers, short hooked beaks, silent flight, and howling or hooting cry; someone who sits up at night (also **night owl**); someone who sees badly or who avoids light; a solemn person; an owl-like breed of pigeon; a wiseacre; a dullard. ◆ *vi* to behave like an owl. ◆ *vt* (*hist*) to smuggle (*esp* wool or sheep from England to France). [OE *ūle*; Ger *Eule*, L *ulula*; imit]

■ **owl'er** *n* (*obs*) a smuggler (*esp* of wool or sheep). **owl'ery** *n* a place inhabited or frequented by owls; owlishness (*Carlyle*). **owl'et** *n* a young or small owl; an owl; a moth of the Noctuidae. **owl'ish** *adj* like an owl; solemn, *esp* if also bespectacled; wise; blinking; stupid. **owl'ishly** *adv*. **owl'ishness** *n*. **owl'-like** *adj*. **owl'y** *adj* owlish.

❑ **owl'-car** *n* (*old US*) a night tram-car. **owl'-eyed** *adj* having blinking eyes like an owl. **Owl'-glass**, **Owle'-glass**, **Howle'glass** or **Owl'spiegle** *n* Tyll Eulenspiegel, a mischievous clown hero of a folk tale popular in Germany from the 16c or earlier. **owl'-light** *n* (*poetic*) dusk, twilight. **owl'-moth** *n* a gigantic S American moth of the Noctuidae. **owl'-parr'ot** *n* the kakapo. **owl'-train** *n* (*old US*) a night train.

own¹ /ōn/ *vt* to possess, have belonging to one; to acknowledge as one's own; to confess; to allow to be true; to admit, concede; to acknowledge, recognize; to claim as one's own (*obs*); to dominate (an opponent) utterly (*sl*). ◆ *vi* to confess (with *to*). [OE *āgnian*, from *āgen* one's own; cf **own**²]

■ **own'er** *n* a possessor, proprietor; a captain of a warship (*sl*). **own'erless** *adj*. **own'ership** *n*.

❑ **own'er-dri'ver** *n* someone who drives his or her own vehicle. **own'er-occupa'tion** *n*. **own'er-occ'upied** *adj*. **own'er-occ'upier** *n* a person who owns the house in which he or she lives. **owner's equity** *n* the investment by an owner in his or her business, *usu* calculated as its current value minus any outstanding borrowing against it.

■ **own up** to confess (often with *to*).

own² /ōn/ *adj* and pronoun (preceded by *possessive adj* or *possessive case*) belonging to oneself and no-one else; often used with reflexive force (*my own, his own*, etc) serving instead of a genitive to *myself, himself*, etc; used with intensifying force (*her* (*very*) *own room*); used as an endearment (*my own* (*darling, dear*, etc)); used with a force similar to the emphatic *oneself*, etc (as in *he makes his own bed, his own worst enemy*). [OE *āgen*, *pap* of *āgan* to possess; cf **owe**]

❑ **own-brand'** or **own-la'bel** *adj* (of a commodity) carrying the trademark or label of the store that sells it (also *n*). **own goal** *n* a goal scored by mistake against one's own team (*football*, etc); a move that turns out to the disadvantage of the party making it.

■ **come into one's own** to take possession of one's rights; to have one's talents or merits realized. **get one's own back** to retaliate, get even. **hold one's own** see under **hold**¹. **of one's own** belonging to oneself and no-one else. **one's own** what belongs to oneself (as in *I may do what I like with my own*). **one's**, etc, **own man** or **woman** a free agent, not under another person's influence. **on one's own** on one's own account; on one's own initiative; by one's own efforts or resources; independently; set up in independence; alone, by oneself.

owre¹ Scots form of **over** (*adv* and *prep*). For compounds see under **over-**.

owre² /owr/ (*Spenser*) *n* same as **ore**¹.

owrie same as **ourie**.

owsen /ow'sən/ *n pl* Scots form of **oxen** (see **ox**).

owt /owt/ (*dialect*) *n* anything. [Variant of **aught**]

ox /oks/ *n* (*pl* **ox'en**) a general name for the male or female of common domestic cattle (bull and cow), *esp* a castrated male of the species; extended to other animals of bovine type. [OE *oxa*, *pl* *oxan*; Ger *Ochse*, Gothic *auhsa*, Sans *ukṣan*]

■ **ox'er** *n* *esp* in foxhunting, an ox-fence; in showjumping, an obstacle in the form of an ox-fence.

❑ **ox'-ant'elope** *n* any antelope of the hartebeest group. **ox'-bird** *n* the dunlin; the oxpecker; an African weaver bird; applied also to various other birds. **ox'blood** *n* a dark reddish-brown colour (also *adj*). **ox'-bot** *n* a warble-fly larva infesting cattle. **ox'-bow** /-bō/ *n* a collar for a yoked ox; a horseshoe-shaped bend in a river (forming an *ox-bow lake* when the neck is pierced and the bend cut off). **ox'-eye** *n* a wild chrysanthemum, *Chrysanthemum leucanthemum* (also called *Leucanthemum vulgare*), with a yellow disc and white rays (**ox-eye daisy**); sometimes (**yellow ox-eye**) the corn marigold; a name for various birds, *esp* the great titmouse; an elliptical dormer window. **ox'-eyed** *adj* having large, ox-like eyes. **ox'-fence** *n* a fence for confining cattle; a hedge with a rail and in many cases also a ditch. **ox'gang**, **ox'gate** or **ox'land** *n* (*obs*) a bovate or one-eighth of a carucate of ploughland, the share attributed to each ox in a team of eight (averaging about 13 acres). **ox'head** *n* the head of an ox; a blockhead. **ox'pecker** *n* an African genus (*Buphaga*) of birds related to starlings, that eat the parasites on cattle (also **beefeater** or **ox-bird**). **ox'tail** *n* the tail of an ox, *esp* as used for soup, stew, etc. **ox'-tongue** *n* the tongue of an ox, used as food; a composite plant (*Picris echioides*) of the daisy family, with yellow flowers and milky juice. **ox'-war'ble** *n* a swelling on the back of an ox; the fly whose larva produces it.

oxalis /*ok'sə-lis* or -*sal'is*/ *n* a plant of the wood-sorrel genus *Oxalis*, giving name to the family **Oxalidā'ceae**, closely related to the Geranium family. [Gr *oxalis*, from *oxys* sharp or acid]
  ■ **ox'alate** *n* a salt of oxalic acid. **oxalic** /-*sal'ik*/ *adj* applied to an acid (C₂H₂O₄) obtained from wood sorrel and other plants, used for cleaning metals and as a bleaching agent.

oxazine /*ok'sə-zēn*/ *n* any of several isomeric compounds having the formula C₄H₅NO, with the nitrogen, oxygen and carbon atoms arranged in a ring. [**oxy-²**, and **azine**]

Oxbridge /*oks'brij*/ *adj* and *n* (relating to) Oxford and Cambridge (universities), *esp* as typifying an upper-class-oriented kind of education, or as a road to unfair advantages, eg in obtaining jobs, or as the home of particular academic attitudes.

Oxfam /*oks'fam*/ *abbrev* : Oxford Committee for Famine Relief.

Oxford /*oks'fərd*/ *adj* belonging to the city, county or university of Oxford. ◆ *n* (without *cap*) a low-heeled laced shoe (also **Oxford shoe**); a light cotton or synthetic woven fabric (also **Oxford cloth**) used for men's shirts. [OE *Oxnaford*, literally, oxen's ford]
  ■ **Oxfordian** /-*förd'i-ən*/ *n* (*geol*) a division of the Upper Jurassic (also *adj*).
  □ **Oxford bags** *n pl* very wide trousers. **Oxford blue** *n* a dark blue (see also **blue¹**). **Oxford clay** *n* (*geol*) a dark blue or grey clay of the Oxfordian formation. **Oxford comma** *n* a comma used to separate the second-last item in a list from the last, *esp* when the last item is preceded by 'and' or 'or'. **Oxford English** *n* a form of standard English in which certain tendencies are (sometimes affectedly) exaggerated, widely believed to be spoken at Oxford. **Oxford groups** *n pl* informal circles of followers of Dr Frank Buchman, who exchanged religious experiences, and sought divine guidance individually (**the Oxford group** the name for his followers as a body from 1921 to 1938; see also **Moral Rearmament** under **moral**). **Oxford movement** see **Tractarianism** under **tract²**.

oxi- see **oxy-²**.

oxide /*ok'sīd*/ *n* a compound of oxygen and some other element or radical. [Fr *oxide* (now *oxyde*), formed from *oxygène* oxygen]
  ■ **ox'idant** *n* a substance acting as an oxidizer. **ox'idase** *n* any of a group of enzymes that promote oxidation in plant and animal cells. **ox'idate** /-*id-āt*/ *vt* to oxidize. **oxidā'tion** *n* oxidizing; the process of forming an insulating layer of silicon dioxide on a silicon chip (*comput*). **oxidā'tional** *adj*. **ox'idātive** *adj* involving or causing oxidization. **oxidīz'able** or **-s-** *adj*. **oxidizā'tion** or **-s-** *n*. **ox'idize** or **-ise** *vt* and *vi* to combine with oxygen; to deprive (an atom or ion) of electrons; to make or become rusty; to put a protective oxide coating on (a metal surface). ◆ *vi* to lose electrons. **oxidīz'er** or **-s-** *n* an oxidizing agent.
  □ **oxidā'tion-reduc'tion** same as **redox**. **oxidative stress** *n* (*pathol*) a condition of increased oxidant production in animal cells, characterized by the release of free radicals and resulting in cellular degeneration.

oxime /*ok'sēm*/ (*chem*) *n* any of a number of compounds obtained by the action of hydroxylamine on aldehydes or ketones that contain a bivalent group (= NOH) attached to a carbon atom. [*oxygen* and *im*ide]

oximeter /*ok-sim'i-tər*/ *n* a photoelectric instrument for measuring oxygen saturation of the blood. [*oxi-* and **-meter**]

oxlip /*ok'slip*/, also (*Shakesp*) **oxslip** /*oks'slip*/ *n orig* a hybrid between primrose and cowslip; now, a species of the genus *Primula* (*P. elatior*) like a large pale cowslip. [OE *oxanslyppe*, from *oxan*, genitive of *oxa* ox, and *slyppe* slime or a slimy dropping; cf **cowslip**]

Oxon *abbrev* : Oxfordshire; *Oxoniensis* (L), of Oxford.

Oxonian /*ok-sō'ni-ən*/ *adj* of or relating to Oxford or to its university. ◆ *n* an inhabitant, native, student or graduate of Oxford; a kind of shoe (*hist*). [L *Oxonia* Oxford, from OE *Oxnaford*]

oxonium /*ok-sō'ni-əm*/ (*chem*) *n* a univalent basic radical, H₃O, in which oxygen is tetravalent, forming organic derivatives, **oxonium salts**. [*oxygen* and *ammonium*]

oxslip see **oxlip**.

oxter /*ok'stər*/ (*Scot* and *Irish*) *n* the armpit. ◆ *vt* to take under the arm; to support by taking the arm. [OE *oxta*]

oxy-¹ /*ok-si-*/ *combining form* denoting sharp; pointed; acid. [Gr *oxys*]

oxy-² or (*old*) **oxi-** /*ok-si-*/ *combining form* denoting oxygen. [Gr *oxys* sharp]

  ■ **ox'yacet'ylene** *adj* and *n* (involving, using or by means of) a mixture of oxygen and acetylene, *esp* for cutting or welding metals at high temperatures. **ox'ya'cid**, **ox'ycom'pound**, **ox'y-salt**, etc *n* an acid, compound, salt, etc, containing oxygen; one in which an atom of hydrogen is replaced by a hydroxyl-group. **ox'y-bro'mide**, **-chlo'ride**, **-flu'oride**, **-hal'ide** or **-i'odide** *n* a compound of an element or radical with oxygen and a halogen (bromine, etc). **ox'y-cal'cium** *adj* involving or using a mixture of oxygen and calcium (**oxy-calcium light** limelight). **oxycō'done** *n* a powerful analgesic drug, synthesized from thebaine (often shortened to **ox'y**). **ox'yhaemoglo'bin** *n* a loose compound of oxygen and haemoglobin. **ox'y-hy'drogen** *adj* involving or using a mixture of oxygen and hydrogen. **oxytetracycline** /-*tet-rə-sīk'lēn*/ *n* a broad spectrum antibiotic used against a wide variety of infections.

oxygen /*ok'si-jən*/ *n* a gaseous element (symbol **O**; atomic number 8) without taste, colour or smell, forming part of the air, water, etc, and supporting life and combustion; something indispensable for existence. [Gr *oxys* sharp or acid, and the root of *gennaein* to generate, from the old belief that all acids contained oxygen]
  ■ **ox'ygenate** (or /*ok-sij'-*/) *vt* to oxidize; to impregnate or treat with oxygen. ◆ *n* a chemical containing oxygen used as a fuel additive to make combustion more efficient and thereby reduce the emission of pollutants. **oxygenā'tion** *n*. **ox'ygenator** *n* an apparatus performing functions of heart and lungs during an operation; something that supplies oxygen. **ox'ygenize** or **-ise** *vt* to oxygenate. **oxyg'enous** *adj*.
  □ **oxygen bar** *n* an establishment where patrons pay to experience the therapeutic effects of inhaling pure oxygen. **oxygen debt** *n* a depletion of the body's store of oxygen occurring during bursts of strenuous exercise, replaced after bodily activity returns to normal levels. **oxygen mask** *n* a masklike breathing apparatus through which oxygen is supplied in rarefied atmospheres to mountaineers, aircraft passengers, etc. **oxygen tent** *n* a tent-like enclosure in which there is a controllable flow of oxygen, erected round a patient to aid breathing.

oxymel /*ok'si-mel*/ *n* a mixture of vinegar and honey. [Gr *oxymeli*, from *oxys* sour, and *meli* honey]

oxymoron /*ok-si-mö'ron* or -*mö'*/ *n* a figure of speech by means of which contradictory terms are combined, so as to form an expressive phrase or epithet, such as *cruel kindness*, *falsely true*, etc. [Gr neuter of *oxymōros*, literally, pointedly foolish, from *oxys* sharp, and *mōros* foolish]
  ■ **oxymoron'ic** *adj*.

oxyntic /*ok-sin'tik*/ *adj* acid-secreting. [Gr *oxys* acid]

oxyrhynchus /*ok-si-ring'kəs*/ *n* an Egyptian fish, sacred to the goddess Hathor, represented on coins and sculptures. [Gr *oxyrrynchos*, from *oxys* sharp, and *rhynchos* a snout]

oxytocin /*ok-si-tō'sin*/ *n* a pituitary hormone that stimulates uterine muscle contraction and milk production, also produced synthetically for use in accelerating labour. [Gr *oxys* sharp, and *tokos* birth]
  ■ **oxytō'cic** *n* and *adj* (a drug) stimulating uterine muscle contraction.

oxytone /*ok'si-tōn*/ *adj* having the acute accent on the last syllable (*Gr grammar*); stressed on the final syllable. ◆ *n* a word so accented. [Gr *oxys* sharp, and *tonos* tone]
  ■ **oxytonic** /-*ton'ik*/ *adj*.

oy, **oye** or **oe** /*oi*, *ō-i* or *ō*/ (*Scot*) *n* a grandchild. [Gaelic *ogha*, *odha*]

oyer /*oi'ər*/ (*obs*) *n* a hearing in a lawcourt, an assize. [Anglo-Fr *oyer* (Fr *ouïr*), from L *audīre* to hear]
  ■ **oyer and terminer** /*tûr'min-ər'*/ a royal commission conferring power to hear and determine criminal causes (out of official use since 1972).

oyez or **oyes** /*ō-yā'*, -*yes'*, -*yez'or ō'*/ *interj* the call of a public crier or officer of a lawcourt for attention before making a proclamation. ◆ *n* /*oiz*/ (*Shakesp*) a proclamation. [OFr *oyez*, imperative of *oir* (Fr *ouïr*) to hear]

oyster /*oi'stər*/ *n* a bivalve shellfish (genus *Ostrea*) used as food; any of several similar related molluscs, such as the pearl oyster; an oyster-shaped piece of meat; a secretive person (*inf*); a source of advantage; the colour of an oyster, a pale greyish beige or pink. ◆ *adj* of this colour. ◆ *vi* to fish for oysters. [OFr *oistre* (Fr *huître*), from L *ostrea*, from Gr *ostreon* an oyster, from *osteon* a bone]
  □ **oys'ter-bank**, **-bed**, **-farm**, **-field**, **-park** *n* a place where oysters breed or are bred. **oys'ter-catcher** *n* a black-and-white wading bird, with red bill and feet, feeding on limpets and mussels (not oysters), also known as the **sea pie**. **oys'ter-fish'ery** *n* the business of catching oysters; a place where oysters are caught or farmed. **oys'ter-knife** *n* a knife for opening oysters. **oyster mushroom** *n* an edible fungus (*Pleurotus ostreatus* or related species) found *esp* in clusters on dead wood. **oys'ter-patt'y** *n* a small pie or pasty made from oysters. **oyster plant** *n* salsify, or a seaside boraginaceous plant (*Mertensia maritima*), both supposed to taste like oysters. **oys'ter-shell** *n* the shell of an

oyster. **oys'ter-tongs** *n pl* a tool for gathering oysters. **oys'ter-wench**, **-wife** or **-woman** *n* (all *obs*) a woman who sells oysters.

■ **the world is my** (*Shakesp* **world's mine**), **his**, etc, **oyster** the world lies before me, etc, ready to yield profit or success.

oystrige /oi'strij/ (*Spenser*) *n* for **ostrich**.

Oz /oz/ (*Aust sl*) *n* Australia (also *adj*).

oz or **oz.** *abbrev* : ounce (*pl* **oz** or **ozs**). [15c Ital *ōz*, abbrev of *onza*]

Ozacling® /oz'ə-kling/ (*printing*) *n* transparent adhesive film from which printed material can be cut for application to illustrations, etc.

ozaena /ō-zē'nə/ *n* a fetid discharge from the nostrils. [Gr *ozaina* a fetid polypus of the nose, from *ozein* to smell]

Ozalid® /oz'ə-lid/ *n* a method of duplicating printed matter onto chemically treated paper; a reproduction made by this process.

ozeki /ō-zē'ki/ *n* a champion sumo wrestler. [Jap *ōzeki*]

ozokerite /ō-zō'kə-rīt/ or /-kē'rīt/ or **ozocerite** /ō-zos'ə-rīt/ or /-zō-sē'/ *n* a waxy natural paraffin. [Gr *ozein* to smell, and *kēros* wax]

ozone /ō'zōn/ *n* an allotropic form (O_3) of oxygen present in the atmosphere, once regarded as health-giving, but toxic in concentrations such as may occur in industrial areas, having a pungent smell, formed when ultraviolet light or an electric spark acts on oxygen or air, and used in bleaching, sterilizing water, and purifying air; loosely, fresh bracing air; (see also **ozonosphere** below). [Gr *ozōn*, prp of *ozein* to smell]

■ **ozonā'tion** *n* ozonization. **ozonic** /ō-zon'ik/ *adj*. **ozonide** /ō-zōn'īd/ *n* an oily explosive organic compound, formed when ozone reacts with unsaturated molecules. **ozonif'erous** *adj* bringing or producing ozone. **ozonizā'tion** or **-s-** *n*. **ō'zonize** or **-ise** *vt* to turn into, charge with or treat with ozone. **ozoniz'er** or **-s-** *n* an apparatus for turning oxygen into ozone. **ozon'osphere** or **ozone layer** *n* a layer of the upper atmosphere where ozone is formed in quantity, protecting the earth from the sun's ultraviolet rays.

❑ **ō'zone-depleter** *n* something that causes ozone depletion. **ō'zone-depleting** *adj*. **ozone depletion** *n* damage to the ozone layer caused by compounds such as chlorofluorocarbons (CFCs). **ozone-friend'ly** *adj* (of certain aerosols, etc) not thought to be destructive of the ozone layer, being free of chlorofluorocarbons. **ozone hole** *n* a hole in the ozone layer, which allows ultraviolet rays into the earth's atmosphere. **ozone layer** see **ozonosphere** above.

ozs see **oz**.

Ozzie same as **Aussie**.

Pp

a b c d e f g h i j k l m n o p q r s t u v w x y z

Palatino Designed by Hermann Zapf in 1950. Germany.

P or **p** /pē/ *n* the sixteenth letter in the modern English alphabet, fifteenth in the Roman, corresponding to the Greek *pi* (Π, π), its sound a voiceless bilabial stop; anything shaped like the letter P. ◆ *combining form* much used in designating Inland Revenue forms, eg **P45** the form given to an employee changing jobs, carrying a statement of earnings to date in the current tax year, and deductions made from those earnings by the employer.

□ **P-Celt** or **P-Kelt** *n* a speaker of **P-Celtic** (see under **Celt**).
■ **mind one's p's and q's** see under **mind**.

P *abbrev* : parking; Pastor; pedal (*music*); peta-; Portugal (IVR); priest; Prince; probationary (or provisional) driver (*Aust*); pula.

□ **P'-plate** *n* (*Aust*) one of two plates attached to a car signifying that the driver is a licensed probationary or provisional driver (a **P'-plater**).

P *symbol* : (as a medieval Roman numeral) 400; (on road signs, etc) parking; pawn (in chess); phosphorus (*chem*); power (*phys*); pressure (*phys*).

P *symbol* : power.

P̄ *symbol* : (medieval Roman numeral) 400000.

p *abbrev* : page (*pl* **pp**); participle; pence; penny; peseta; peso; piano (*music*); pico-; positive; purl (*knitting*).

□ **p'-type** *adj* (ie 'positive type' of a semiconductor) having an excess of mobile holes over conduction electrons.

p- (*chem*) see under **para-**¹.

PA *abbrev* : Panama (IVR); Pennsylvania (US state; also **Pa.**); personal appearance; personal assistant; Press Association; public address (system); publicity agent; Publishers Association.

Pa *symbol* : pascal (SI unit); protactinium (*chem*).

pa¹ /pä/ *n* a childish or familiar word for father. [**papa**]

pa² or **pah** /pä/ *n* a Maori fort or settlement. [Maori]

pa. *abbrev* : past.

p.a. or **pa** *abbrev* : per annum.

paan see **pan**³.

pa'anga /pä-äng'gə/ *n* the standard monetary unit of Tonga (100 seniti). [Tongan, from a type of vine yielding disc-shaped seeds]

PABA /pa'bə/ *abbrev* : para-aminobenzoic acid.

pabouche /pə-boosh'/ *n* a slipper. [See **babouche**]

pabulum /pab'ū-ləm or -yə-/ *n* food of any kind, *esp* that of lower animals and of plants; provender; fuel; nourishment for the mind; entertainment or material that is mediocre, unsatisfying or worthless. [L *pābulum*, from *pāscere* to feed]
■ **pab'ular** *adj*. **pab'ulous** *adj*.

PABX *abbrev* : Private Automatic Branch Exchange.

PAC *abbrev* : Pan-Africanist Congress; Port Authorization Code, used to switch between mobile phone networks.

paca /pä'kə/ *n* the so-called spotted cavy of S America, related to the agouti. [Sp and Port, from Tupí *paca*]

pacable /pāk'ə-bl or pak'/ (*archaic*) *adj* capable of being appeased; willing to forgive. [L *pācāre* to appease, from *pāx, pācis* peace]
■ **pacation** /pə-kā'shən/ *n*.

PACE /pās/ *abbrev* : Police and Criminal Evidence Act.

Pace /pās/ *n* a dialect form of **Pasch**.

□ **pace egg** *n* an Easter egg, one hard-boiled and dyed. **pace'-egging** *n* begging for eggs, etc, at Easter; rolling pace eggs on the ground.

pace¹ /pās/ *n* a stride; a step; the space between the feet in walking, about 76 centimetres, or (among the Romans) the space between two successive positions of the same foot, *approx* 1.5 metres; gait; rate of walking, running, etc (of a person or animal); rate of speed in movement or work, often applied to fast living; a mode of stepping in horses in which the legs on the same side are lifted together; amble; a step of a stair, or the like; a pass or passage (*obs*). ◆ *vt* to traverse with measured steps; to measure by steps (often with *out*); to train to

perform paces; to set the pace for; to perform as a pace or paces. ◆ *vi* to walk; to walk slowly and with measured tread; to amble. [Fr *pas*, from L *passus* a step, from *pandere*, *passum* to stretch]
■ **paced** *adj* having a certain pace or gait. **pac'er** *n* a person who paces; one who sets the pace; a horse whose usual gait is a pace; a horse trained to pace in harness racing. **pac'ey** or **pac'y** *adj* (*inf*) fast; lively, smart.

□ **pace'-bowler** *n* (*cricket*) a bowler who delivers the ball fast. **pace'-bowling** *n*. **pace car** *n* a car that sets the pace in a warm-up lap of a motor race but does not take part in the race. **pace'maker** *n* a person who sets the pace in a race (also *fig*); a small mass of muscle cells in the heart which control the heartbeat electrically; an electronic device (in later models, with radioactive core) used to correct weak or irregular heart rhythms. **pace'man** *n* (*cricket*) a pace bowler. **pace'-setter** *n* a pacemaker, except in anatomical and electronic senses.
■ **go the pace** to go at a great speed; to live a fast life. **keep** or **hold pace with** to go as fast as; to keep up with. **make** or **set the pace** to regulate the speed for others by example. **pace oneself** to work in a slow, steady and controlled way in order to achieve one's goal without wasting resources. **put someone through his** or **her paces** to set someone to show what he or she can do, to test someone. **show one's paces** to show what one can do. **stand**, **stay** or **stick the pace** to keep up with the pace or speed that has been set.

pace² /pā'sē, pä'kā or pä'chā/ *prep* with or by the leave of (expressing disagreement courteously). [L, ablative of *pāx* peace]

pacha, **pachalic** see **pasha**.

pachak see **putchock**.

pachinko /pə-ching'kō/ *n* a form of pinball popular in Japan. [Jap *pachin* (onomatopoeic) representing trigger sound]

pachisi /pä-chē'sē or -zē/ *n* an Indian game like backgammon or ludo. [Hindi *pacīsī* of twenty-five, from the highest throw]

pachy- /pak-i-/ *combining form* signifying thick. [Gr *pachys* thick]
■ **pachycarp'ous** *adj* (Gr *karpos* fruit) having a thick pericarp. **pachydac'tyl** or **pachydac'tylous** *adj* (Gr *daktylos* digit) having thick digits. **pach'yderm** *n* (Gr *derma* skin) strictly, any animal of the old classification Pachydermata, but *usu* an elephant, rhinoceros, or hippopotamus; an insensitive person. **pachyderm'al** *adj*. **Pachyderm'ata** *n pl* in old classification, those ungulates that do not ruminate, ie elephant, horse, pig, etc. **pachyder'matous** *adj* thick-skinned; of the pachyderms; insensitive. **pachyderm'ia** *n* abnormal thickness of skin or mucous membrane. **pachyderm'ic** *adj*. **pachyderm'ous** *adj*. **pachym'eter** *n* an instrument for measuring small thicknesses. **pachysan'dra** *n* (Gr *anēr, andros* man) a shrubby evergreen plant of the box family.

pacify /pas'i-fī/ *vt* (**pac'ifying**; **pac'ified**) to appease; to calm; to bring peace to; to subdue. [Partly through Fr *pacifier*, from L *pācificus* pacific, from *pācificāre*, from *pāx, pācis* peace, and *facere* to make]
■ **pac'ifiable** *adj*. **pacif'ic** *adj* peacemaking; appeasing; inclining towards peace; peaceful; mild; tranquil; (with *cap*) of or relating to the ocean between Asia and America, so called by Magellan, the first European to sail on it, because he happened to cross it in peaceful weather conditions. ◆ *n* (with *cap*) the Pacific Ocean. **pacif'ical** *adj* pacific (rare except in **Letters pacifical**, translating Latin *literae pacificae*, letters recommending the bearer as one in peace and fellowship with the Church, also called **pacificae** /pa-sif'i-sē/ or **Letters of peace**). **pacif'ically** *adv*. **pacif'icate** *vt* to give peace to. **pacifica'tion** *n* peacemaking; conciliation; appeasement; a peace treaty. **pacif'icator** *n* a peacemaker. **pacif'icatory** /-ə-tə-ri/ *adj* tending to make peace. **pacif'icism** and **pacif'icist** less common forms of **pacifism** and **pacifist**. **pac'ifier** *n* a person or thing that pacifies; a baby's dummy or teething-ring (*esp N Am*). **pac'ifism** the beliefs and principles of pacifists. **pac'ifist** *n* a person who is opposed to war, or believes all war to be wrong.

□ **Pacific Rim** *n* the coastal regions around the Pacific Ocean; the countries of these regions. **Pacific Standard Time** or **Pacific Time** *n*

fāte; fär; mē; fûr; mīne; mōte; för; mūte; pŭt; dhen (then); *el'ə-mənt* (element) ● For other sounds see detailed chart of pronunciation one of the standard times used in N America, being 8 hours behind Greenwich Mean Time (*abbrev* **PST** or **PT**).

Pacinian corpuscle /pə-sin'i-ən kör'pu-sl/ *n* a nerve ending that is sensitive to pressure and vibration. [Filippo *Pacini* (1812–83), Italian anatomist]

pack[1] /pak/ *n* a bundle, *esp orig* one made to be carried on the back by a pedlar or pack animal; a backpack, rucksack; a collection, stock, or store; a bundle of some particular kind or quantity (eg of wool *approx* 109kg (240lb)); the quantity packed at a time or in a season; a complete set of playing-cards; a number of animals herding together or kept together for hunting; a shepherd's own sheep grazing along with his employer's as part payment (*Scot*); the forwards in a Rugby football team; the largest group of competitors during a race; a group of Cub Scouts in the Scout movement or of Brownies in the Guide movement; a worthless, disreputable or otherwise objectionable set of people; a gang, eg of thieves; a mass of pack ice; a sheet for folding round the body to allay inflammation, fever, etc; the use or application of such a sheet; a built support for a mine-roof; packing material; a cosmetic paste; a number of photographic plates or films exposed together; the act of packing or condition of being packed; mode of packing; a person of worthless or bad character (*obs*); a compact package, *esp* of something for sale; a number of similar products sold together; a parachute folded in its fabric container; a group (of eg submarines) acting together. ◆ *vt* to make into a bundled pack; to place compactly in a box, bag, or the like; to press together closely; to compress; to fill tightly or compactly; to fill with anything; to cram; to crowd; to envelop; to surround closely; to fill the spaces surrounding; to prepare (food) for preservation, transport and marketing; to send away, dismiss (*usu* with *off*); to form into a pack; to load with a pack; to carry in packs; to have the capacity to deliver, as in *pack a punch*; to carry or wear (a gun) (*inf*). ◆ *vi* to form into a pack; to settle or be driven into a firm mass; to form a scrum; to be capable of being put into a compact shape; to put one's belongings together in boxes, bags, etc, eg for a journey (often with *up*); to travel with a pack; to take oneself off, to depart in haste (*usu* with *off*); to plot, intrigue, arrange privately (*Shakesp*). [ME *packe*, *pakke*, appar from MFlem *pac* or Du or LGer *pak*]

■ **pack'age** *n* the act, manner or privilege of packing; a bundle, packet, or parcel; a case or other receptacle for packing goods in; a composite proposition, scheme, offer, etc in which various separate elements are all dealt with as essential parts of the whole (see also **package deal** below); a computer program in general form, to which the user adds any data applicable in a particular case. ◆ *vt* to put into a container or wrappings, or into a package. **pack'aged** *adj* (*lit* and *fig*). **pack'ager** *n* a specialist in the packaging of books, programs, etc. **pack'aging** *n* anything used to package goods; the total presentation of a product for sale, ie its design, wrapping, etc; the designing and complete production of eg illustrated books, programmes for television, etc for sale to a publisher, broadcasting company, etc. **pack'er** *n* a person who packs; someone who packs goods for sending out; an employer or employee in the business of preparing and preserving food; someone who transports goods by means of pack animals (*US*); a machine or device for packing. **pack'et** *n* a small package; a carton; a ship or vessel employed in carrying packets of letters, passengers, etc; a vessel plying regularly between one port and another (also **pack'et-boat**, **pack'et-ship**, etc); a large amount of money (*inf*); a small group; a cluster of bacteria; used as equivalent to a quantum (*fig*); a serious injury (*sl*); a block of coded data (*comput*; see **packet switching** below). ◆ *vt* to parcel up. **pack'ing** *n* the act of putting into packs or of tying up for carriage or storing; material for packing; anything used to fill an empty space or to make a joint watertight or airtight.

❑ **package deal** *n* a deal which embraces a number of matters and has to be accepted as a whole, the less favourable items along with the favourable. **package holiday** or **tour** *n* one in which all major elements, *esp* travel and accommodation, are pre-arranged by a tour company, to whom the holidaymaker pays a single fee. **pack animal** *n* an animal used to carry goods on its back. **pack'-cinch** /-sinsh/ *n* a wide girth for a pack animal. **pack'cloth** *n* a cloth in which goods are enclosed; packing-sheet. **pack'-drill** *n* a military punishment of marching about laden with full equipment. **packed file** *n* (*comput*) a file compressed to save space in transmission or on a disk. **packed lunch** *n* a lunch of sandwiches and other cold items prepared in advance and carried in a container. **pack'et-note** *n* a size of notepaper *approx* 14 × 23cm (*orig* $5\frac{1}{2}$ × 9in). **packet sniffer** *n* (*comput*) a tool used to capture and decode packets of data being transmitted over a network. **packet switching** *n* (*comput*) a system of communication in which packets of data are transmitted between computers of varying types and compatibility. **pack'frame** *n* a rigid support to which a load such as a pack may be strapped for carrying on the back. **pack'horse**, etc *n* a horse, etc used to carry goods on its back; a drudge. **pack ice** *n* a mass of large pieces of floating ice driven together by winds and currents. **packing box** *n* a box or framework

for packing goods in (also **packing case**); a stuffing box. **pack'ing-need'le** *n* a strong needle for sewing up packages. **pack'ing-paper** *n* a strong, thick kind of wrapping paper. **pack'ing-press** *n* a press for squeezing goods into a compact form for packing. **pack'ing-sheet** or **pack'sheet** *n* coarse cloth for packing goods. **pack'-load** *n* the load an animal can carry. **pack'man** *n* a pedlar or a man who carries a pack. **pack'mule** *n* a mule used for carrying burdens. **pack'-rat** *n* a kind of long-tailed rat, native to the western part of N America. **pack'saddle** *n* a saddle for packhorses, packmules, etc. **packsheet** see **packing-sheet** above. **pack shot** *n* (*advertising*) a close-up picture of the product being advertised. **pack'staff** *n* a staff for supporting a pedlar's pack when he or she rests (see also **pike**[2]). **pack'thread** *n* a coarse thread used to sew up packages. **pack'-train** *n* a line of loaded pack animals on the move. **pack'-twine** *n* thin twine for tying up parcels. **pack'way** *n* a narrow path fit for packhorses.

■ **pack it in** or **up** (*inf*) to stop or give up doing something. **pack up** (*inf*) to stop; to break down. **send someone packing** to dismiss someone summarily.

pack[2] /pak/ *vt* to fill up (a jury or meeting) with people of a particular kind for one's own purposes; (*esp* in *passive*) to bring into a plot as accomplice (*Shakesp*); to shuffle (cards), *esp* dishonestly (*obs*). ◆ *vi* (*Shakesp*) to make a secret or underhand arrangement. ◆ *n* (*obs*) such an arrangement. [Prob **pact**]

■ **pack cards with** (*Shakesp*, etc) to make a dishonest arrangement with.

pack[3] /pak/ (*Scot*) *adj* intimate, confidential. [Origin unknown]

package, **packer**, **packet** see under **pack**[1].

packfong a non-standard form of **paktong**.

paco /pä'kō/ *n* (*pl* **pa'cos**) an alpaca. [Sp, from Quechua *paco*]

pact /pakt/ *n* something which is agreed on; an agreement, *esp* informal or not legally enforceable. [L *pactum*, from *pacīscere*, *pactum* to contract]

■ **pac'tion** *n* (chiefly *Scot*) a pact. ◆ *vt* to agree. **pac'tional** *adj*.
■ **Warsaw Pact** see under **Warsaw**.

pactum /pak'təm or -tŭm/ (*L*) *n* a pact.

❑ **pactum illicitum** /i-lis'i-təm or i-lik'i-tŭm/ *n* an illegal compact. **pactum nudum** /nŭ'dəm or noo'dŭm/ *n* a pact in which a consideration is not given.

pacy see under **pace**[1].

pad[1] /pad/ *n* anything stuffed with a soft material, to prevent friction, pressure, or injury; for inking or for filling out, shaping, etc; a block of absorbent material that holds ink to be used on a stamping device; a soft saddle; a cushion; a number of sheets of paper or other soft material fastened together in a block; a guard shaped to protect different parts of the body in various sports, eg a leg-guard for cricketers; the fleshy, thick-skinned undersurface of the foot of many animals, such as the fox; the foot of an animal, *esp* of one traditionally hunted for sport; its footprint; a water-lily leaf (*N Am*); (*usu* in *pl*) thick watered ribbon used for watchguards; a rocket-launching platform; a bed, room, or home, *esp* one's own (*sl*); a device built into a road surface, operated by vehicles passing over it, controlling changes of traffic lights (**vehicle-actuated signals**) so as to give passage for a longer time to the greater stream of traffic. ◆ *vt* (**padd'ing**; **padd'ed**) to stuff, cover, or fill out with anything soft; to furnish with padding; to increase an amount due to be paid by adding false charges; to track by footprints; to impregnate, eg with a mordant. [Origin obscure; poss connected with **pod**[1]]

■ **padd'er** *n*. **padd'ing** *n* stuffing; matter of less value introduced into a book or article in order to make it of the length desired; the process of mordanting a fabric.
❑ **pad'-cloth** *n* a cloth covering a horse's loins. **padded cell** *n* a room with padded walls in a psychiatric hospital. **pad'-el'ephant** *n* a working elephant wearing a pad but no howdah. **pad'-saddle** *n* a treeless, padded saddle. **pad'saw** *n* a small sawblade with a detachable handle, used for cutting curves and awkward angles (also **keyhole saw**). **pad'-tree** *n* the wooden or metal frame to which harness-pads are attached.

pad[2] /pad/ *n* a path (*dialect*); a thief on the highroad (*usu* **footpad**; *archaic*); (contraction of **pad'-horse**) a horse for riding on the road; an easy-paced horse (*archaic* or *dialect*). ◆ *vi* (**padd'ing**; **padd'ed**) to walk on foot; to trudge along; to walk with a quiet or dull-sounding tread; to rob on foot (*archaic*). [Du *pad* a path]

❑ **pad'-nag** *n* (*archaic* or *dialect*) an ambling nag.
■ **pad the hoof** (*sl*) to walk, trudge. **stand pad** to beg by the roadside.

pad[3] same as **ped**[1].

padang /pad'ang/ (*Malay*) *n* a field, *esp* a playing field.

padauk or **padouk** /pə- or pä-dowk'/ *n* a timber tree of the red sanders genus. [Burmese]

paddle¹ /pad'l/ vi to wade about or dabble in a liquid or semi-liquid; to walk unsteadily or with short steps; to play or toy with the fingers (*archaic*); to trifle (*obs*); to make (land) bare of grass by constant trampling, etc (*dialect*). ◆ vt (*archaic*) to toy with or finger. ◆ n a spell of wading in shallow water. [Cf **pad²**, and LGer *paddeln* to tramp about]

■ **padd'ler** n someone who paddles; (in *pl*) a protective garment worn by children when paddling.

paddle² /pad'l/ n a small, long-handled spade; a short, broad, spoon-shaped oar, used for moving canoes; the blade of an oar; one of the boards of a paddle wheel or water wheel; a swimming animal's flipper; a paddle-shaped instrument for stirring, beating, etc; a small bat, as used in table-tennis (*N Am*). ◆ vi to use a paddle or progress by use of paddles; to row gently; to swim about like a duck. ◆ vt to propel by paddle; to strike or spank with a paddle or the like (*esp US*). [Origin obscure]

■ **padd'ler** n. **padd'ling** n the act of paddling; a flock of wild ducks on water.

❑ **padd'le-board** n one of the boards of a paddle wheel. **paddle boat** n a paddle steamer. **padd'le-box** n the covering of a paddle wheel. **padd'lefish** n a large freshwater fish of the Polyodontidae family with a long flattened snout. **padd'le-shaft** n the axle on which paddle wheels turn. **padd'le-staff** n a small spade or paddle. **paddle steamer** n a steamer propelled by paddle wheels. **paddle wheel** n a wheel-like framework with boards or paddles fitted across its edges, steam-driven to strike water and propel a ship, or turned by a stream to drive a mill, etc. **padd'le-wood** n the light, strong wood of a Guiana tree (genus *Aspidosperma*) of the dogbane family.

■ **paddle one's own canoe** to progress independently.

paddle³ /pad'l/, **padle** /pä'dl or pā'/ or **paidle** /pā'/ (*Scot*) n the lumpsucker (also (*masc*) **cock'-padd'le**, etc, (*fem*) **hen'-padd'le**, etc). [Origin unknown]

paddock¹ /pad'ək/ n an enclosed field under pasture, *orig* near a house or stable; (in horse-racing) the enclosed area where horses are paraded and mounted before a race; (in motor-racing) an area near the pits where cars may be worked on before races; any enclosed field (*Aust* and *NZ*). [Appar from earlier *parrock*, from OE *pearroc* park]

paddock² see **puddock**.

Paddy /pad'i/ n a familiar, often derogatory name for an Irishman; (without *cap*) a rage (*inf*); a paddy train (*mining sl*).

■ **Padd'yism** n a hibernicism.

❑ **Paddy's lantern** n the moon. **paddy train** n (*mining sl*) an underground colliery train for transporting miners from one point to another, pulled by a diesel- or electrically-powered locomotive, or by a rope-haulage system (properly **man'rider** or **manriding train**). **paddy wagon** n a black Maria. **padd'y-whack** n (*sl*) an Irishman, *esp* a big one; a rage; a slap, smack, blow, spanking, beating.

paddy² /pad'i/ n a rice field (also **paddy field**); growing rice; rice in the husk. [Malay *pādī* rice in the straw]

❑ **padd'y-bird** n the Java sparrow or ricebird.

paddymelon see **pademelon**.

padella /pə- or pa-del'ə/ n a shallow dish of fat with a wick used in illuminations. [Ital, a frying-pan, from L *patella*]

pademelon, paddymelon or **padymelon** /pad'i-mel-ən/ n any of several small wallabies. [From an Aboriginal language]

paderero /pad-ə-rā'rō/ same as **pederero**.

padishah /pä'di-shä/ n chief ruler; great king, a title of the Shah of Persia, and formerly of the Sultan of Turkey, the Great Mogul, or the (British) Emperor of India. [Pers *pad* master, and *shāh* king]

padle see **paddle³**.

padlock /pad'lok/ n a movable lock with a link turning on a hinge or pivot at one end, catching the bolt at the other (also *vt*). [Origin uncertain, poss dialect Eng *pad* a basket, and **lock¹**]

padma /pud'mə/ n the sacred lotus. [Sans]

padouk same as **padauk**.

padre /pä'drā/ n father, a title given to priests; an army chaplain; a parson. [Port (also Sp and Ital) *padre*, Ital *padrone*, from L *pater* father, *patrōnus* a patron]

■ **padro'ne** /-rō'ni/ n (pl **padrō'ni** /-nē/) a shipmaster (*archaic*); an innkeeper, café- or restaurant-owner; an employer, *esp* among Italian Americans; someone who hires out hand-organs, or who gets children to beg for him (*obs*).

pad thai /pad tī/ n a Thai-style dish of stir-fried rice noodles with seasoned shredded meat and vegetables, served with crushed peanuts. [Thai]

Paduan /pad'ū-ən/ adj of Padua (Ital *Padova*) in NE Italy. ◆ n a native of Padua; a counterfeit Roman bronze coin made at Padua in the 16c; the pavane.

paduasoy /pad'ū-ə-soi or pä'də-soi/ n a corded silk used in the 18c; a garment made of it. [Fr *pou-de-soie*, from *pou*, *pout*, *poult* (of unknown origin) *de soie* of silk; appar infl by *Padua*]

padymelon see **pademelon**.

paean, also **pean** /pē'ən/ n a lyric to Apollo or Artemis (or some other god); a song of praise, thanksgiving or triumph; exultation. [L *paeōn*, from Gr *paiōn*, *-ōnos*, from *Paiān*, *-ānos* the name of the physician of the gods in Homer, and later an epithet of Apollo]

■ **pae'on** or **paeon'ic** n (*prosody*) a foot of four syllables, any one long, three short. **paeon'ic** /-on'ik/ adj.

paed- or **ped-** /pēd-/ or **paedo-** or **pedo-** /pē-dō-/, also sometimes **paid-** /pīd-/ or **paido-** /pī-dō-/ combining form denoting child, boy. [Gr *pais*, *paidos* boy, child; *paideutēs* teacher]

■ **paedagog'ic** adj same as **pedagogic** (see under **pedagogue**). **paed'agogue** n same as **pedagogue**. **paed'erast**, etc n same as **pederast**, etc (see under **pederasty**). **paedeut'ic** or **paideut'ic** n (also n sing **paedeutics** or **paideutics**) educational method or theory. **paediat'ric** adj (Gr *iātrikos* medical) relating to the medical treatment of children. **paediatrician** /-ə-trish'ən/ n. **paediat'rics** n sing the treatment of children's diseases. **paedi'atrist** n. **paedi'atry** n. **paedobap'tism** n infant baptism. **paedobap'tist** n. **paedodont'ic** adj. **paedodont'ics** n sing the branch of dentistry concerned with care of children's teeth. **paedogen'esis** n reproduction by an animal in the larval state. **paedogenet'ic** adj. **paedolog'ical** adj. **paedol'ogist** n. **paedol'ogy** n the study of the growth and development of children. **paedomor'phic** adj of paedomorphism or paedomorphosis. **paedomorph'ism** n (Gr *morphē* form) retention of juvenile characters in the mature stage. **paedomor'phosis** n a phylogenetic change in which juvenile characteristics are retained in the adult. **paed'ophile** /-fīl/ n a person sexually attracted to children (*inf* short form **pae'do**). **paedophilia** /-fil'/ n sexual desire whose object is children. **paedophil'iac** or **paedophil'ic** adj and n. **paed'otribe** /-trīb/ n (Gr *paidotribēs*) in ancient Greece, a gymnastic teacher. **paedot'rophy** n (Gr *tropheiā* nursing) the art of rearing children.

paella /pī-el'ə or pä-el'ya/ n a stew containing saffron, chicken, rice, vegetables, seafood, etc. [Sp, from L *patella* pan]

paenula /pē'nū-lə/ n a Roman travelling cloak; a chasuble, *esp* in its older form. [L *paenula*]

paeon, paeonic see under **paean**.

paeony same as **peony**.

pagan /pā'gən/ n a person following any (*esp* polytheistic) pre-Christian religion; (with *cap*) a person following a polytheistic nature-worshipping religion; a person who is not a Christian, Jew or Muslim, regarded as uncultured or unenlightened, a heathen; more recently, someone who has no religion; a person who sets a high value on sensual pleasures. ◆ adj of or relating to pagans. [L *pāgānus* rustic, peasant, also civilian (because the Christians reckoned themselves soldiers of Christ), from *pāgus* a district]

■ **pā'ganish** adj heathenish. **pā'ganism** n. **pā'ganize** or **-ise** vt to render pagan or heathen; to convert to paganism.

PAGE abbrev: polyacrylamide gel electrophoresis.

page¹ /pāj/ n one side of a leaf of a book, etc (4 pages in a folio sheet, 8 in a quarto, 16 in an octavo, 24 in a duodecimo, 36 in an octodecimo); the type, illustrations, etc, arranged for printing one side of a leaf; a leaf of a book thought of as a single item; (in *pl*) writings, literature (*rhetoric*); an incident, episode, or whatever may be imagined as matter to fill a page; one of the blocks into which a computer memory can be divided for ease of reference. ◆ vt to number the pages of; to make up into pages (*printing*). [Fr, from L *pāgina* a page]

■ **paginal** /paj'/ adj. **paginate** /paj'/ vt to mark with consecutive numbers, to page. **pagina'tion** n the act of paging a book; the figures and marks that indicate the numbers of pages. **pā'ging** n the marking or numbering of the pages of a book.

❑ **page description language** n (*comput*) a language which interprets a stream of instructions, usually in plain ASCII, into a description of where each letter, drawing and half-tone is to be placed on the printed page. **page'-proof** n a proof of a book, etc made up into pages. **page-three'** adj shown on or appropriate for **page three**, the page on which, traditionally, certain popular newspapers print nude or semi-nude photographs of female models with well-developed figures. **page'-turner** n an exciting book, a thriller.

page² /pāj/ n a boy attendant; a boy employed as a messenger in hotels, clubs, etc; a messenger (boy or girl) in the US Congress, etc; a youth training for knighthood, receiving education and performing services at court or in a nobleman's household (*hist*); a contrivance for holding up a long skirt in walking (*hist*). ◆ vt to attend as a page; to seek or summon by sending a page around, by repeatedly calling aloud for *esp* using a public address system, or by means of a pager. [Fr *page*; of obscure origin]

■ **page'hood** *n* the condition of a page. **pā'ger** *n* an electronic device, *esp* portable, which pages a person, eg by means of a bleep, visual display, etc (cf **bleeper**).

❑ **page'boy** *n* a page; (also **pageboy hairstyle, haircut**) a hairstyle in which the hair hangs smoothly to about jaw level and is curled under at the ends.

pageant /paj'ənt or (*archaic*) pāj'/ *n* a dramatic performance, scene, or part (*archaic*); a movable stage or carriage for acting on (*obs*); a stage machine (*obs*); a spectacle, *esp* a magnificent procession or parade; a series of tableaux or dramatic scenes connected with local history or other topical matter, performed either on a fixed spot or in procession; a piece of empty show; display. ◆ *adj* of the nature of a puppet; specious. [Origin obscure; Anglo-L *pāgina* may be the classical word transferred from page to scene in a MS; or *pāgina* in the sense of slab may have come to mean boarding, framework]

■ **page'antry** *n* splendid display; pompous spectacle; a fleeting show.

Paget's disease /paj'its diz-ēz'/ *n* a chronic enlargement and weakening of bone tissue, *esp* in the elderly; a cancerous inflammation of the nipple associated with cancer of the breast. [Sir James *Paget* (1814–99), English surgeon]

paginal, paginate, etc see under **page**[1].

pagle see **paigle.**

pagoda /pə-gō'də/ or **pagod** /pag'od/, and formerly also pə-god' / *n* an Eastern temple, *esp* in the form of a many-storeyed tapering tower, each storey with a projecting roof; an ornamental building in imitation of this; an idol, a demigod (*obs*); a former Indian coin, bearing the figure of a pagoda. [Port *pagode*, from Pers *but-kadah* idol-house, or some other Eastern word]

❑ **pagoda sleeve** *n* a funnel-shaped outer sleeve turned back to show lining and inner sleeve. **pago'da-tree** *n* a name for various erect trees of pagoda-like form; a fabulous Indian tree that dropped pagodas (coins) when shaken.

pagri /pug'rē/ *n* (also **pugg'aree, pugg'ree** and **pugg'ery**) a turban; a light scarf worn round the hat to keep off the sun. [Hindi *pagrī*]

pagurian /pə-gū'ri-ən/, also **pagurid** /-rid or pag'/ *n* and *adj* (a crustacean) of the genus *Pagurus* or *Eupagurus*, the hermit crabs. [L *pagurus*, from Gr *pagouros* kind of crab]

pah[1] /pä/ *interj* an exclamation of disgust.

pah[2] see **pa**[2].

Pahari /pə-hä'ri/ *n* a group of Indo-European languages used in the region of the Himalayas, divided into **Eastern Pahari** (also called **Nepali**), **Central Pahari** and **Western Pahari**, composed of many dialects.

Pahlavi same as **Pehlevi.**

pahoehoe /pə-hō'ē-hō-ē/ *n* a hardened lava with a smooth undulating shiny surface. [Hawaiian]

paid /pād/ pat and pap of **pay**[1]. *adj* hired; satisfied (*obs*); drunk (*Shakesp*).

❑ **paid-up**[1] *adj* paid in full; having fulfilled financial obligations.

■ **put paid to** to finish; to destroy chances of success in.

paid- see **paed-.**

paideutic see **paedeutic** under **paed-.**

paidle see **paddle**[3].

paido- see **paed-.**

paigle or **pagle** /pā'gl/ (*archaic* and *dialect*) *n* the cowslip, sometimes also the oxlip. [Origin unknown]

paik /pāk/ (*Scot*) *vt* to thump, drub. ◆ *n* a blow; (in *pl*, with *his*, etc) a drubbing. [Origin unknown]

pail /pāl/ *n* an open cylindrical or conical container with a hooped handle, for holding or carrying liquids (also ice, coal, etc), a bucket; a pailful. [OE *pægel* a gill measure, appar combined with or influenced by OFr *paele* a pan, from L *patella* a pan, dimin of *patera*, from *patēre* to be open]

■ **pail'ful** *n* as much as fills a pail.

paillasse same as **palliasse.**

paillette /pal-yet' or pä-/ *n* a spangle. [Fr]

■ **paillon** /pal'yən or pä-yɔ̃/ *n* a piece of foil, to show through enamel, etc.

Pain /pān/ *abbrev*: Parents Against Injustice, an advice charity.

pain /pān/ *n* suffering; bodily suffering; (now only in *pl*) great care or trouble taken in doing anything; penalty; (in *pl*) the throes of childbirth; a tiresome or annoying person, task, etc (*inf*). ◆ *vt* to cause suffering to; to put to trouble (*archaic*; *esp reflexive*). [Fr *peine*, from L *poena* satisfaction, from Gr *poinē* penalty]

■ **pained** *adj* showing or expressing pain; suffering pain; distressed. **pain'ful** *adj* full of pain; causing pain; requiring labour, pain, or care; laborious, painstaking (*archaic*); distressing, irksome; (of a performance, etc) embarrassingly or irritatingly bad (*inf*). **pain'fully**

adv. **pain'fulness** *n*. **pain'less** *adj* without pain. **pain'lessly** *adv*. **pain'lessness** *n*.

❑ **pain barrier** *n* a level of extreme physical exertion beyond which resultant pain or discomfort begins to ease, *esp* in the phrase *go through the pain barrier*. **pain'killer** *n* anything that does away with pain, *esp* an analgesic; a nostrum claiming to end pain. **pain'killing** *adj*. **pains'taker** *n* someone who takes pains or care; a careful worker. **pains'taking** *adj* taking pains or care. ◆ *n* careful diligence. **pains'takingly** *adv*.

■ **be at pains** (**to**) or **take pains** (**to**) to put oneself to trouble, be assiduously careful (to). **for one's pains** (*usu ironic*) as a reward for or result of trouble taken. **pain in the neck, arse,** etc (*fig*) a feeling of acute discomfort; an exasperating circumstance; a thoroughly tiresome person, task, etc. **under** or **on pain of** under liability to the penalty of.

pain au chocolat /pɛ̃ ō shok-ō-lä'/ *n* a bread-roll, made with a large amount of butter and having a flaky consistency, with a chocolate paste filling. [Fr, chocolate bread]

painim /pā'nim/ see **paynim.**

paint /pānt/ *vt* to cover over with colouring matter; to represent in a coloured picture; to produce as a coloured picture; to apply with a brush; to apply anything to, with a brush; to describe or present as if by painting a picture (*fig*); to colour; to apply coloured cosmetics to; to adorn, diversify; to represent speciously or deceptively. ◆ *vi* to practise painting; to use coloured cosmetics on the face; to tipple (*sl*). ◆ *n* a colouring substance spread or for spreading on a surface; a cake of such matter; coloured cosmetics; a piebald horse (*US*). [OFr *peint*, pap of *peindre* to paint, from L *pingere* to paint]

■ **paint'able** *adj* suitable for painting. **paint'ed** *adj* covered with paint; ornamented with coloured figures; marked with bright colours; feigned. **paint'er** *n* someone who paints; an artist in painting; a person whose occupation is painting; a house-decorator; a vivid describer. **paint'erly** *adj* with the qualities of painting, as opposed to drawing, etc, ie with areas of colour rather than line or drawn detail; as if painted. **paint'iness** *n*. **paint'ing** *n* the act or employment of laying on colours; the act of representing objects by colours; a painted picture; vivid description in words. **paint'ress** *n* formerly, a woman artist who paints; a woman employed to paint pottery. **paint'ūre** *n* (*Dryden*) the art of painting; a picture. **paint'y** *adj* overloaded with paint, with the colours too glaringly used; smeared with paint; like paint, in smell, etc.

❑ **paint'ball** *n* (sometimes with *cap*) a type of war game where the ammunition used is paint fired from compressed-air guns; a paint-pellet as used in this. **paint'box** *n* a box in which different paints (for picture-painting) are kept in compartments. **paint'-bridge** *n* a platform used by theatrical scene-painters. **paint'brush** *n* a brush for putting on paint; the painted cup (see below). **painted cloth** *n* a hanging of cloth painted with figures, a substitute for tapestry, formerly common in taverns. **painted cup** *n* a scrophulariaceous plant (genus *Castilleja*) with brightly-coloured upper leaves. **painted grass** *n* striped canary-grass, gardener's garters. **painted lady** *n* the thistle butterfly, orange-red spotted with white and black; a painted woman (*derog*); the painted cup; a parti-coloured pink, sweetpea, or gladiolus, etc. **painted snipe** *n* a genus (*Rhynchaea*) of birds related to the snipes, the hen brightly-coloured. **painted woman** *n* (*derog*) a trollop. **painter's colic** *n* lead colic. **paint'er-stain'er** *n* a member of the London livery company of painters. **paint job** *n* (*inf*) an example or instance of painting, eg on a customized motor vehicle. **paint roller** *n* a roller used in house-painting, etc instead of a brush. **paint'-stripp'er** *n* a liquid containing a solvent or caustic ingredient, applied to a painted surface to remove the paint. **paint'work** *n* painted fixtures in a building; painted surfaces on a vehicle. **paint'works** *n sing* a paint-making factory.

■ **fresh as paint** very fresh and bright. **paint the lily** see under **lily. paint the town red** to enjoy a bout of unbridled revelry or celebration.

painter[1] /pān'tər/ (*naut*) *n* a rope for fastening a boat. [Origin obscure]

■ **lazy painter** a small painter for use in fine weather only.

painter[2] /pān'tər/ (*US*) *n* the cougar. [**panther**]

painter[3], **paintiness, painty,** etc see under **paint.**

paiock, paiocke, pajock or **pajocke** /perh pā'ok or pä'jok/ *n* an obscure word in Shakespeare (*Hamlet* III.2) conjectured to be a form of *peacock* (possibly a misprint for *pacock*; possibly = *pea-jock*).

pair[1] /pār/ *n* (*pl* **pairs** or (*inf*) **pair**) two things equal, or suited to each other, or growing, grouped or used together; a set of two equal, matching or similar things forming one instrument, garment, etc, such as a pair of scissors, tongs, or trousers; the other of two matching things; a set of similar things generally; a pack (of cards; *obs*); a flight of stairs; a couple; husband and wife; two people engaged to or in love with each other; a male and a female animal mated together; two people or things associated together; a partner; two horses harnessed together; two cards of the same designation; (in *pl* with *sing v*) another name for **Pelmanism**; two voters on opposite sides who have an agreement to abstain from voting; either of such a pair; a score of no runs in both innings of a two-innings match (*cricket*); a boat rowed by two; (in *pl*) a contest, etc in which competitors take part in partnerships of two. ◆ *vt* to couple; to sort out in pairs. ◆ *vi* to be joined in couples; to be a counterpart or counterparts; to mate; (of two opposing voters) to arrange to abstain, on a motion or for a period (also *vt*, usually *passive*). [Fr *paire* a couple, from L *paria*, neuter pl of *pār*, afterwards regarded as a fem sing meaning 'equal']

■ **paired** *adj* arranged in pairs; set by twos of a similar kind; mated. **pair'ing** *n*. **pair'wise** *adv* in pairs.

❑ **pair'-bond** *n* a continuing and exclusive relationship between a male and female. **pair'-bonding** *n*. **pair case** *n* a double casing for a (pocket) watch, *usu* consisting of an inner plain casing for the movement and an outer decorative one. **paired reading** *n* a teaching method in which a child and an adult read together until the child is confident enough to read on alone. **pair'-horse** *adj* (of a carriage) drawn by a pair of horses. **pair'ing-time** *n* the time when birds go together in pairs. **pair'-oar** *n* a boat rowed by two (also *adj*). **pair production** *n* (*electronics*) the production of a positron and an electron when a gamma-ray photon passes into the electrical field of an atom. **pair-roy'al** *n* three cards of the same denomination, *esp* in cribbage and in the obsolete game of post and pair; a throw of three dice all falling alike; a set of three (also **pairī'al**, **parī'al** and **prī'al**).

■ **king pair** see under **king**. **pair of colours** two flags carried by a regiment, one the national ensign, the other the flag of the regiment; hence, an ensigncy. **pair off** to arrange, set against each other, or set aside in pairs; to become associated in pairs; to become associated as romantic or sexual partners.

pair² or **paire** /*pār*/ *v* (*obs*) aphetic forms of **appair**.

pairial see **pair-royal** under **pair¹**.

pais /*pā*/ (*archaic*) *n* the people from whom a jury is drawn. [OFr]

paisa /*pī'sä*/ *n* (*pl* **paisa** or **paise** /*pī'sā*/) a monetary unit in India, Nepal and Pakistan, $\frac{1}{100}$ of a rupee; (also **poi'sha**) a monetary unit in Bangladesh, $\frac{1}{100}$ of a taka. [Hindi *paisā*]

paisano /*pī-zä'nō*/ *n* (*pl* **paisan'os**) among people of Spanish or Italian descent in America, a person from the same area or town; hence, a friend. [Sp, from Fr *paysan* peasant]

paisley /*pāz'li*/ *n* a woollen or other fabric with a pattern resembling Paisley pattern; an article made of this.

❑ **Paisley pattern** or **design** *n* a type of pattern whose most characteristic feature is an ornamental device known as a 'cone' (rather like a tree cone), used in the **Paisley shawl**, a shawl made in *Paisley*, Scotland in the 19c in the style of Kashmir shawls.

paitrick /*pā'trik*/ *n* a Scots form of **partridge**.

pajamas see **pyjamas**.

pajock, **pajocke** see **paiock**.

Pak *abbrev* : Pakistan; Pakistani.

pakapoo /*pak-ə-poo'*/ (*Aust* and *NZ*) *n* a Chinese version of lotto, in which betting tickets are filled up with Chinese characters. [Chin *bai' gē piaò* white pigeon ticket]

pak choi /*päk choi*/ *n* another name for **Chinese cabbage** (see under **china¹**). [Chin (Cantonese), white vegetable]

pakeha /*pä'kə-hä* or *pä'kē-hä*/ (*NZ*) *n* a white man; a non-Polynesian citizen. [Maori]

pakfong see **paktong**.

Pakhtu, **Pakhto**, **Pakhtun**, **Pakhtoon** see **Pashto**.

Pakistani /*pä-ki-stän'i*/ *adj* of or relating to the republic of *Pakistan* in Asia, its inhabitants or immigrants from Pakistan. ◆ *n* a native or citizen of Pakistan; an immigrant from, or a person whose parents, etc are immigrants from, Pakistan. ◆ *adj* of or relating to Pakistan or immigrants from Pakistan.

■ **Paki** /*pak'i*/ *n* (*Brit offensive sl*) a Pakistani (also *adj*).

pakka /*puk'ə*/ same as **pukka**.

pakora /*pə-kö'rə*/ *n* an Indian dish consisting of chopped vegetables, etc formed into balls, coated with batter and deep-fried. [Hindi]

paktong /*pak'tong*/ *n* nickel silver (also (*non-standard*) **pack'fong** or **pak'fong**). [Chin (Cantonese) *pak* white, and *t'ung* copper]

PAL /*pal*/ *abbrev* : phase alternation line, the colour-television system most commonly used in Europe.

pal /*pal*/ (*inf*) *n* a partner, mate; chum. ◆ *vi* (**pall'ing**; **palled** /*pald*/) to associate as a pal. [Romany]

■ **pally** /*pal'i*/ *adj*. **pal'sy** or **palsy-wal'sy** *adj* (*inf*) over-friendly; ingratiatingly intimate.

palabra /*pa-lä'brä*/ *n* a word; talk. [Sp]

■ **pocas** /*pö'käs*/ **palabras** few words.

palace /*pal'is*/ *n* the house of a king or a queen; a very large and splendid house; a bishop's official residence; a large public building; a large and *usu* showy place of entertainment or refreshment. [Fr *palais*,

from L *Palātium* the Roman emperor's residence on the *Palatine* Hill at Rome]

❑ **pal'ace-car** *n* a sumptuously furnished railway-car. **palace guard** *n* (one of) those responsible for the personal protection of a monarch; the group of intimates and advisers around a head of government, etc. **palace of culture** *n* in Russia, a cultural and recreational centre. **palace revolution** *n* a revolution within the seat of authority.

paladin /*pal'ə-din*/ (*hist*) *n* one of the twelve peers of Charlemagne's household; a knight errant, or paragon of knighthood. [Fr, from Ital *paladino*, from L *palātīnus* belonging to the palace; cf **palatine**]

palae- or **palaeo-**, also (*N Am*) **pale-** or **paleo-**, /*pal-i-* or *pal-i-ō-*/, also *pāl-*/ *combining form* meaning old; of or concerned with the very distant past. [Gr *palaios* old]

■ **Palaearc'tic** *adj* of the Old World part of the Holarctic region. **palaeanthrop'ic** or **palaeoanthrop'ic** *adj* (Gr *anthrōpos* man) of or relating to the earliest types of man. **palaeanthropolog'ical** or **palaeoanthropolog'ical** *adj* relating to the study of the earliest types of man. **palaeanthropol'ogist** or **palaeoanthropol'ogist** *n* a person who studies the earliest types of man. **palaeanthropol'ogy** or **palaeoanthropol'ogy** *n* the study of the earliest types of man. **Palaean'thropus** or **Palaeoan'thropus** (or /*-thrō'*/) *n* an extinct genus of man, including the Neanderthal and Heidelberg races. **palaeobiolog'ic** or **palaeobiolog'ical** *adj*. **palaebiol'ogist** or **palaeobiol'ogist** *n*. **palaebiol'ogy** or **palaeobiol'ogy** *n* the biological study of fossil plants and animals. **palaeobotan'ic** or **palaeobotan'ical** *adj*. **palaeobot'anist** *n*. **palaeobot'any** *n* the study of fossil plants. **Pal'aeocene** *adj* (*geol*) of or belonging to an epoch of the Tertiary period, between 65 and 55 million years ago (also *n*). **palaeoclī'mate** *n* the climate at any stage in the geological development of the earth. **palaeoclimat'ic** *adj* of or relating to a palaeoclimate. **palaeoclimatolog'ic** or **palaeoclimatolog'ical** *adj* of or relating to palaeoclimatology. **palaeoclimatol'ogist** *n*. **palaeoclimatol'ogy** *n* to study of palaeoclimates. **palaeocrys'tic** *adj* (Gr *krystallos* ice) consisting of ancient ice. **palaeoccurr'ent** *n* a current that existed at a particular stage in the geological development of the earth, as evinced by sedimentary rock formations. **palaeoecolog'ic** or **palaeoecolog'ical** *adj*. **palaeoecol'ogist** *n*. **palaeoecol'ogy** *n* (the study of) the ecology of fossil animals and plants. **palaeoenvi'ronment** *n* the environment in earlier ages. **palaeoenvironment'al** *adj*. **palaeoethnobot'any** *n* the study of ancient human plant use based on fossilized seeds and grains. **palaeoethnolog'ic** or **palaeoethnolog'ical** *adj*. **palaeoethnol'ogist** *n*. **palaeoethnol'ogy** *n* the science of early man. **palaeogaea** /*-jē'ə*/ *n* (Gr *gaia* earth) the Old World as a biological region. **Pal'aeogene** /*-jēn*/ *adj* (Gr *palai*(o)*genēs* born long ago; *geol*) of or belonging to the early Tertiary period, including the Palaeocene, Eocene and Oligocene epochs (also *n*). **palaeogeog'rapher** *n* a person who studies the geography of geological periods. **palaeogeograph'ic** or **palaeogeograph'ical** *adj*. **palaeogeog'raphy** *n* the study of the geography of geological periods. **palaeog'rapher** *n* (Gr *graphein* to write) an expert in or student of palaeography. **palaeograph'ic** or **palaeograph'ical** *adj*. **palaeog'raphist** *n*. **palaeog'raphy** *n* ancient modes of writing; the study of ancient modes of handwriting. **palae(o)ichthyolog'ic** or **palae(o)ichthyolog'ical** *adj*. **palae(o)ichthyol'ogist** *n*. **palae(o)ichthyol'ogy** *n* the study of ancient varieties of fish. **Pal'aeo-In'dian** *adj* and *n* (a member) of the earliest inhabitants of the Americas. **palaeolimnolog'ical** *adj*. **palaeolimnol'ogist** *n*. **palaeolimnol'ogy** *n* the scientific study of lakes of past ages. **pal'aeolith** *n* (Gr *lithos* stone) a Palaeolithic artefact. **Palaeolith'ic** *adj* of the earlier Stone Age. **palaeomag'netism** *n* a study of the magnetism of ancient rocks and fossils, and of bricks, pottery, etc made in past ages. **palaeontograph'ical** *adj*. **palaeontog'raphy** *n* descriptive palaeontology, the description of fossil remains. **palaeontolog'ical** *adj*. **palaeontol'ogist** *n*. **palaeontol'ogy** *n* (Gr *onta* neuter pl of prp of *einai* to be, and *logos* discourse) the study of fossils. **palaeopatholog'ic** or **palaeopatholog'ical** *adj*. **palaeopathol'ogist** *n*. **palaeopathol'ogy** *n* the pathological study of the ancient remains of animals and humans. **palaeopedolog'ical** *adj*. **palaeopedol'ogist** *n*. **palaeopedol'ogy** *n* the study of the soils of past geological ages. **palaeophȳtol'ogy** *n* palaeobotany. **Palaeosibē'rian** *adj* denoting four unrelated groups of languages spoken in NE Siberia. **Palaeothē'rium** *n* (Gr *thērion* a wild beast, from *thēr* animal, beast of prey) an odd-toed Eocene fossil ungulate with a tapir-like snout. **pal'aeotype** *n* a 19c phonetic adaptation of ordinary alphabetical type. **palaeotypic** /*-tip'ik*/ *adj*. **Palaeozo'ic** *adj* (Gr *zōē* life; *geol*) of or belonging to the oldest era of the Phanerozoic eon, between 540 and 250 million years ago (also *n*). **palaeozoolog'ical** *adj*. **palaeozool'ogist** *n*. **palaeozool'ogy** *n* the study of fossil animals.

palaestra /*pal-ēs'trə* or *-es'*/ (*ancient hist*) *n* a wrestling school; a gymnasium; wrestling; a training-ground. [L *palaestra*, from Gr *palaistrā*, from *palaiein* to wrestle]

■ **palaes'tral**, **palaes'tric** or **palaes'trical** *adj*.

palafitte /pal'ə-fīt/ n a prehistoric lake dwelling. [Ital *palafitta*, from *palo* (from L *pālus*) a stake, and *fitto*, pap of *figgere* (from L *figere*) to fix]

palagi /pə-lä'ji/ n a Samoan word for a person from outside the Pacific Islands, *esp* a European.

palagonite /pal-ag'ə-nīt/ n an altered basic vitreous lava. [*Palagonia* in Sicily]
  □ **palag'onite-tuff** n a tuff composed of fragments of palagonite.

palais /pal'ā/ (*old*) n (*pl* **palais** /-āz/) a dance-hall. [Shortened from *palais de danse*; from Fr, palace of dance]

palama /pal'ə-mə/ n (*pl* **pal'amae** /-mē/) the webbing of a water bird's foot. [Latinized from Gr *palamē* palm]
  ■ **pal'amate** adj.

palamino same as **palomino**.

palampore or **palempore** /pal'əm-pōr or -pör/ n a flowered chintz bedcover common in Asia. [From *Palampur*, N India, place of manufacture]

palanquin or **palankeen** /pal-ən-kēn'/ n a light litter for one passenger, a box borne on poles on men's shoulders. [Port *palanquim*; cf Hindi *palang* a bed, from Sans *palyaṅka* a bed]

palapa /pə-lap'ə/ n an open-sided, thatched structure offering protection from the sun. [Mex Sp, palm-tree covering]

palas /pal-äs' or -äsh'/ n the dhak tree. [Hindi *palās*]

palate /pal'it or -ət/ n the roof of the mouth, consisting of the *hard palate* in front and the *soft palate* behind; the prominent part of the lower lip that closes the tube of a personate corolla (*bot*); sense of taste; relish; mental liking; ability to appreciate the finer qualities of wine, etc (also *fig*). ◆ vt (*Shakesp*) to taste, to relish. [L *palātum*]
  ■ **palatabil'ity** n. **pal'atable** adj pleasant to the taste; acceptable to the mind or feelings. **pal'atableness** n. **pal'atably** adv. **pal'atal** adj relating to the palate; uttered by bringing the tongue to or near the hard palate (*phonetics*). ◆ n a sound so produced. **palataliza'tion** or **-s-** n. **pal'atalize** or **-ise** vt to make palatal. **pal'atine** adj relating to the palate. ◆ n a paired bone forming part of the roof of the mouth. **pal'atō-alvē'olar** (or /-ōl'/) adj (*phonetics*) produced by bringing the tongue to a position at or close to the hard palate and the roots of the upper teeth.
  ■ **cleft palate** a congenital defect of the palate, leaving a longitudinal fissure in the roof of the mouth.

palatial /pə-lā'shl/ adj of or like a palace, *esp* sumptuous and spacious. [See **palace**]

palatine[1] /pal'ə-tīn/ adj of the Palatine Hill or the palace of emperors there; of a palace; having royal privileges or jurisdiction; of a count or earl palatine (see below). ◆ n an officer of the palace; a noble invested with royal privileges and jurisdiction; a subject of a palatinate; a fur tippet (from the Princess Palatine of 1676); (with *cap*) one of the seven hills of Rome. [L *palātīnus*; cf **palace**]
  ■ **palat'inate** (or /pal'ət-/) n the office or rank of a palatine; the province of a palatine, *esp* an electorate of the ancient German Empire; an award made to a distinguished representative of Durham University at sports. ◆ adj (at Durham) light purple or lilac.
  ■ **count**, **earl**, etc, **palatine** a feudal lord with supreme judicial authority over a province. **county palatine** the province of such a lord.

palatine[2] see under **palate**.

Palauan /pə- or pä-low'ən/ adj of or relating to the Republic of *Palau* in the W Pacific, its people or its language. ◆ n a native or citizen of Palau.

palaver /pə-lä'vər/ n a conference, *esp orig* with African or other native tribespeople; a talk or discussion; idle copious talk; talk intended to deceive; a long, boring, complicated and seemingly pointless exercise; a fuss. ◆ vi to hold a palaver; to chatter idly. ◆ vt to flatter. [Port *palavra* word, from L *parabola* a parable, later a word, speech, from Gr *parabolē*; cf **parable**, **parabola**]
  ■ **palav'erer** n.

palay /pa-lā', pä-lī' or -lā'/ n the ivory-tree, a small S Indian tree (genus *Wrightia*) of the dogbane family, with hard white wood. [Tamil]

palazzo /pə-lat'sō/ n (*pl* **palazz'i** /-at'sē/) an Italian palace, often one converted into a museum; a house built in this style. [Ital from L *palātium*]
  □ **palazzo pants** n pl women's loose trousers with wide straight legs.

pale[1] /pāl/ adj whitish; (of a colour) not deep or vivid; not ruddy or fresh; wan; of a faint lustre, dim; lacking colour. ◆ vt to make pale. ◆ vi to turn pale; to become less impressive or significant. ◆ n paleness. [OFr *palle*, pale (Fr *pâle*), from L *pallidus* pale]
  ■ **pale'ly** adv. **pale'ness** n. **pāl'ish** adj somewhat pale. **pāl'y** adj (*archaic*) pale; palish.

□ **pale ale** n a light-coloured bitter ale. **pale'buck** n an antelope, the oribi. **pale'-dead** adj (*Shakesp*) lustreless. **pale'-eyed** adj (*Milton*) dim-eyed. **pale'face** n (attributed to Native Americans) a white person. **pale'-heart'ed** adj (*Shakesp*) dispirited. **pale'-vis'aged** adj (*Shakesp*).

pale[2] /pāl/ n a stake of wood driven into the ground for fencing; anything that encloses or fences in; a limit; the limit of what can be accepted as decent or tolerable (*fig*); an enclosure; a marked-off district; a broad stripe from top to bottom of a shield (*heraldry*). ◆ vt to enclose with stakes; to fence; to encircle, crown (*Shakesp*). [Fr *pal*, from L *pālus* a stake]
  ■ **pale'wise** adv (*heraldry*) vertically, like a pale. **palifica'tion** /pal- or pāl-/ n the act of strengthening with stakes. **pāl'iform** adj. **pāl'ing** n the act of fencing; wood or stakes for fencing; a fence of stakes connected by horizontal pieces; an upright stake or board in a fence. **pāl'y** adj (*heraldry*) divided by vertical lines.
  ■ **beyond the pale** intolerable; unacceptable. **English Pale** the district in Ireland within which only the English had power for centuries after the invasion in 1172. **Jewish Pale** the district of SW Russia in which only Jews were formerly allowed to live.

pale[3] /pāl/ (*dialect*) n a baker's peel; a cheese-scoop. ◆ vt to test by inserting a cheese-pale. [L *pāla* spade]

pale[4] see under **palea**.

pale- see **palae-**.

palea /pā'li-ə/ (*bot*) n (*pl* **pā'leae** /-ē/) the membranous inner bract (*inferior palea*) or bracteole (*superior palea*) of an individual grass-flower, above the glumes; a scale on a fern-leaf or stem; a scale on the receptacle of some composite plants. [L *palea* chaff]
  ■ **pale** /pāl/ n a grass palea. **paleā'ceous** adj chaffy. **palet** /pāl'it/ n a palea.

palely see under **pale**[1].

palempore see **palampore**.

paleness see under **pale**[1].

paleo-, etc see **palae-**.

Palestinian /pal-i-stin'i-ən or pal-ə-/ adj relating to the region of *Palestine* in SW Asia. ◆ n a native or inhabitant of Palestine; an Arab born in the region of Palestine, including areas under Israeli rule. [Cf **Philistine**]
  □ **Palestine soup** n artichoke soup, by a pun on *Jerusalem* (see **artichoke**).

palestra same as **palaestra**.

palet see under **palea**.

paletot /pal'tō/ n a loose overcoat. [Fr]

palette /pal'it/ n a little board, *usu* with a thumb hole, on which a painter mixes colours; the assortment or range of colours used by a particular artist or for any particular picture; a range or selection (*fig*); a plate against which one leans in working a drill; a small plate covering a joint in armour, *esp* at the armpit (*hist*). [Fr, from Ital *paletta*, from *pala* spade, from L *pāla* a spade]
  □ **palette knife** n a thin round-ended knife for mixing colours, cooking ingredients, etc.

palewise see under **pale**[2].

palfrey /pöl'fri/ (*archaic* or *poetic*) n a saddle-horse, *esp* for a lady (in Spenser's *Faerie Queene* applied to Una's ass). [OFr *palefrei*, from LL *paraverēdus*, prob from Gr *para* beside, LL *verēdus* a post-horse, appar a Celtic word; confused with L *frēnum* a bridle]
  ■ **palfrenier** /pal-frə-nēr'/ n a groom. **palfreyed** /pöl'/ adj riding on or supplied with a palfrey.

Pali /pä'lē/ n the sacred language of the Buddhists of India, etc, closely related to Sanskrit. [Sans *pāli* canon]

palification, **paliform** see under **pale**[2].

palilalia /pal-i-lā'li-ə/ n a speech abnormality characterized by the increasingly rapid repetition of words or phrases. [Mod L, from Gr *palin* again, and *lalia* speech]

Palilia /pə-lil'i-ə/ n pl (or *sing*) the festival of Pales (L *Palēs*), Roman goddess of flocks, held on 21 April, traditional date of the founding of Rome.

palillogy /pal-il'ə-ji/ n a repetition of a word or phrase. [Gr *palillogiā*, from *palin* again, and *logos* word, speech]

palimony /pal'i-mən-i/ (*inf*) n alimony or its equivalent demanded by one partner when the couple have been cohabiting without being married. [**pal** and **alimony**]

palimpsest /pal'imp-sest/ n a manuscript in which old writing has been rubbed out to make room for new; a monumental brass turned over for a new inscription. [Gr *palimpsēston*, from *palin* again, and *psāein* (contracted *psēn*) to rub]

palindrome /pal'in-drōm/ *n* a word, verse, or sentence that reads the same backward and forward. [Gr *palindromos* running back, from *palin* back, and *dromos* a running]
■ **palindromic** /-drom'- or -drōm'-/ or **palindrom'ical** *adj*. **pal'indromist** (or /pə-lin'-/) *n* an inventor of palindromes.

paling see under **pale**[2].

palingenesis /pal-in-jen'i-sis/ *n* (*pl* **palingen'eses** /-sēz/) a new birth; reincarnation; a second creation; regeneration; unmodified inheritance of ancestral characters; the reformation of a rock by refusion. —Also **palingenē'sia** or **palingen'esy**. [Gr *palin* again, and *genesis* birth]
■ **palingen'esist** *n*. **palingenet'ical** *adj*. **palingenet'ically** *adv*.

palinode /pal'i-nōd/ or (*obs*) **palinody** /-nō-di/ *n* a poem in which thoughts, feelings, etc expressed in an earlier poem are retracted; a recantation (*rare*). [Gr *palinōidia*, from *palin* back, and *ōidē* song]

palisade /pal-i-sād'/ *n* (also **palisā'do** (*pl* **palisā'does**)) a fence of stakes; a stake so used (*milit*); (in *pl*) a line of steep cliffs (*N Am*). ◆ *vt* to surround or defend with a palisade. [Fr *palissade* and Sp *palizada*, from L *pālus* a stake]
❑ **palisade tissue** *n* a tissue occurring in leaves, composed of cells placed closely together with their long axes perpendicular to the surface.

palisander /pal-i-san'dər/ *n* jacaranda or other rosewood. [Fr *palissandre*, from a name used in Guiana]

palish see under **pale**[1].

palki or **palkee** /päl'kē/ *n* a palanquin. [Hindi *pālkī*]

pall[1] /pöl/ *n* a covering of rich cloth; a rich cloth (*archaic*); a curtain, covering, or cloak, eg of smoke or darkness (*fig*); a corporal (*relig*); a frontal; a chalice-cover; a cloth spread over a coffin or tomb; a cloak, mantle, outer garment (*esp relig*); a pallium; a bearing representing a pallium (*heraldry*). ◆ *vt* to cover with, or as if with, a pall. [OE *pæll* a rich robe, from L *pallium*; see **pallium**]
❑ **pall'-bearer** *n* one of the mourners at a funeral who used to hold up the corners of the pall; one of those carrying (or walking beside) a coffin at a funeral.

pall[2] /pöl/ *vi* to become vapid, insipid, or wearisome; to lose relish; to lose strength (*obs*). ◆ *vt* to make vapid; to cloy; to daunt (*obs*); to weaken (*obs*); to pale (*obs*). [Prob from **appal**]

palla /pal'ə/ *n* (*pl* **pall'ae** /-ē/) a Roman woman's mantle. [L *palla*]

Palladian[1] /pə-lā'di-ən/ *adj* relating to *Pallas*, wisdom, or learning.

Palladian[2] /pə-lā'di-ən/ *adj* in the style of architecture introduced by Andrea *Palladio* (1518–80), modelled on Vitruvius.
■ **Pallā'dianism** *n*.

palladic, palladious see under **palladium**.

Palladium /pə-lā'di-əm/ *n* a statue of *Pallas*, on whose preservation the safety of Troy depended; anything of similar virtue; (without *cap*; *pl* **pallā'dia**) a safeguard. [L, from Gr *palladion*, from *Pallas*, *Pallados* Pallas]

palladium /pə-lā'di-əm/ *n* a metallic element (symbol **Pd**; atomic no 46) resembling platinum, remarkable for its capacity for occluding hydrogen. [Named by its discoverer, English chemist William Wollaston (1766–1828), after the newly discovered (1803) minor planet *Pallas*]
■ **palladic** /-lad'-/, **pallā'dious** or **pallā'dous** (or /pal'ə-/) *adj* containing palladium in smaller or greater proportion respectively.

pallae see **palla**.

pallah /pal'ə/ *n* the impala. [Tswana *phala*]

Pallas /pal'as/ *n* the Greek goddess **Athēnē** (also **Pall'as Athē'nē**); a minor planet discovered by German astronomer Heinrich Olbers in 1802.

Pallas's cat /pal'ə-siz kat/ *n* a wildcat of central Asia, *Felix manul* (also called **manul**). [Peter *Pallas* (1741–1811), German naturalist]

palled see **pal**.

pallescent /pə-les'ənt/ *adj* turning pale. [L *pallēscēns*, *-entis*, prp of *pallēscere* to turn pale]
■ **pallesc'ence** *n*.

pallet[1] /pal'it/ *n* a platform or tray for lifting and stacking goods, used with a fork-lift truck, and having a double base into which the fork can be thrust; a palette; a flat wooden tool with a handle, such as that used for shaping pottery; a flat brush for spreading gold-leaf; a tool for lettering book-bindings; (in a timepiece) the surface or part on which the teeth of the escape wheel act to give impulse to the pendulum or balance; a disc of a chain pump; a valve of an organ wind chest, regulated from the keyboard; a board for carrying newly moulded bricks; a piece of wood built into a wall for the nailing on of joiner-work. [**palette**]

■ **pall'eted** *adj* carried on a pallet or pallets. **palletiza'tion** or **-s-** *n* the adoption of pallets for moving goods; the packing of goods on pallets. **pall'etize** or **-ise** *vi* and *vt*. **pall'etizer** or **-s-** *n*.

pallet[2] /pal'it/ *n* a mattress, or couch, properly a mattress of straw; a small or poorly furnished bed. [Dialect Fr *paillet*, dimin of Fr *paille* straw, from L *palea* chaff]

pallia, pallial, palliament see **pallium**.

palliard /pal'yärd/ (*obs*) *n* a professional beggar, a vagabond; a rogue, libertine. [Fr *paillard*, from *paille* straw, from the vagabond's habit of sleeping on straw in barns, etc]

palliasse, also **paillasse** /pal-i-as', pal-yas' or pal'-/ *n* a straw mattress; an under-mattress. [Fr *paillasse*, from *paille* straw, from L *palea*]

palliate /pal'i-āt/ *vt* to soften by pleading something in favour; to mitigate; to alleviate; to excuse, extenuate; to cloak (*obs*); to disguise (*obs*). ◆ *adj* see under **pallium**. [L *palliāre*, *-ātum* to cloak, from *pallium* a cloak]
■ **palliā'tion** *n* the act of palliating. **pall'iative** /-ə-tiv/ *adj* serving to extenuate; mitigating; alleviating. ◆ *n* something which lessens pain, etc, or gives temporary relief. **pall'iatory** *adj*.
❑ **palliative care** *n* treatment of the terminally ill.

pallid /pal'id/ *adj* pale, wan; weak, insipid. [L *pallidus* pale]
■ **pallid'ity** *n*. **pall'idly** *adv*. **pall'idness** *n*.

palling see **pal**.

pallium /pal'i-əm/ *n* (*pl* **pall'ia**) a large, square mantle, worn in ancient Rome in imitation of the Greek himation; a white woollen vestment like a double Y, embroidered with crosses, worn by the Pope, and conferred by him upon archbishops; the mantle in molluscs, brachiopods, and birds (*zool*). [L]
■ **pall'ial** *adj* (*zool*). **pall'iament** *n* (*Shakesp*) a Roman consular candidate's robe. **pall'iate** *adj* having a pallium.

pall-mall /pal'mal'/ or /pel'mel'/ *n* an old game, in which a ball was driven through an iron ring with a mallet; an alley for the game (hence the street in London /pal'mal'/). [Obs Fr *pale-maille*, from *palmaille*, from Ital *pallamaglio*, from *palla* ball (cf OHGer *pallā*), and *maglio*, from L *malleus* a hammer; cf **ball**[1] and **pallone**]

pallone /päl-lō'nā/ *n* an Italian game in which a ball is struck with a gauntlet or armguard. [Ital, augmentative of *palla* ball]

pallor /pal'ər/ *n* paleness. [L *pallēre* to be pale]

pally see under **pal**.

palm[1] /päm/ *n* the inner surface of the hand between wrist and fingers; the corresponding part of a forefoot, or of a glove; the sole of the foot (*rare*); a handbreadth (7.5 or 10cm, ie 3 or 4 inches); the length of the hand from wrist to fingertip; a sailmaker's instrument used instead of a thimble; a flat expansion, as of an antler, or the inner surface of an anchor fluke; an act of palming; (also **palm'-play**) an old game in which a ball was struck with the palm. ◆ *vt* to touch or stroke with the palm; to hold in the palm; to take swiftly and unseen and conceal in the palm; to impose, pass off (*esp* with *off*, and *on* or *upon*); to bribe. [L *palma*; cf Gr *palamē* and OE *folm*]
■ **palmar** /pal'mər/ *adj* relating to the palm. **palmate** /pal'-/ or **pal'mated** *adj* hand-shaped; having lobes radiating from one centre (*bot*); webfooted (*zool*). **pal'mately** *adv*. **palmatifid** /pal-mat'i-fid/ *adj* (*bot*) shaped like the hand, with the divisions extending about halfway down. **palmā'tion** *n* palmate formation; a palmate structure or one of its parts or divisions. **palmatipart'ite** *adj* palmately divided rather more than halfway. **palmatisect** /pal-mat'i-sekt/ *adj* deeply cut in a palmate manner. **palmed** /pämd/ *adj* having a palm; held or concealed in the palm. **palm'ful** *n* as much as the palm will hold. **palmiped** /pal'mi-ped/ or **palmipede** /-pēd/ *n* a webfooted bird. ◆ *adj* webfooted. **palmist** /päm'ist/ *n* someone who tells a person's fortune from the lines on his or her palm. **palm'istry** *n*. **palmy** or **palmie** /päm'i/ *n* (*Scot*) a stroke of the tawse on the palm.
❑ **palm'corder** *n* a small hand-held camcorder. **palm'-grease** or **palm'-oil** *n* a bribe. **palm'top** *n* a small hand-held portable computer (also *adj*).
■ **grease someone's palm** to bribe someone. **in the palm of one's hand** in one's power; at one's command.

palm[2] /päm/ *n* any tree or shrub of the **Palmae** /pal'mē/, a large tropical and sub-tropical family of monocotyledons, sometimes climbers but *usu* branchless trees with a crown of pinnate or fan-shaped leaves; a leaf of this tree carried as a token of rejoicing or of victory; emblematically, pre-eminence, the prize; a branch of willow or other substitute in symbolic or ceremonial use. [OE *palm*, *palma*, *palme*, also directly from L *palma* palm tree, from the shape of its leaves; see **palm**[1]]
■ **palmaceous** /pal-mā'shəs/ *adj* of the palm family. **palmarian** /pal-mā'ri-ən/ or **palmary** /pal'mər-i/ *adj* worthy of the ceremonial palm; pre-eminent. **palmette** /pal-met'/ *n* (*Fr*) an ancient architectural ornament like a palm leaf. **palmett'o** /pal-/ *n* (*pl* **palmettos** or **palmettoes**) a name for several kinds of palm, notably Sabal and the

only European palm Chamaerops. **palmiet** /pal-mēt'/ n a S African aloe-like riverside plant of the rush family (*Prionum palmita*). **palmificā'tion** /pal-/ n artificial fertilization of dates by hanging a wild male flower cluster on a cultivated female tree. **palmitate** /pal'/ n a salt of **palmit'ic acid**, a fatty acid ($C_{15}H_{31}COOH$) obtained from palm oil, etc. **palmitin** /pal'/ n a white fat abundant in palm oil; a glycerine ester of palmitic acid. **palm'y** adj bearing palms; like a palm; flourishing.

❑ **pal'ma Christi** /pal'mə kris'ti/ n the castor-oil plant. **palm branch** n a palm leaf. **palm'-butt'er** n palm oil in a solid state. **palm'-cabb'age** n the bud of the cabbage palm. **palm cat** or **palm civet** n the paradoxure. **palm'-court'** adj suitable to a **palm court**, a large, palm-tree-decorated room or conservatory in a hotel, etc, in which, traditionally, light music is played by a small orchestra, a **palm-court orchestra**. **palm'-hon'ey** n evaporated sap of the Chilean *coquito-palm*. **palm'house** n a glass house for palms and other tropical plants. **palmitic acid** see palmitate above. **palm'-ker'nel** n the kernel of the oil palm, yielding **palm-kernel oil**. **palm oil** n an oil or fat obtained from the pulp of the fruit of palms, *esp* of the oil palm. **palm sugar** n jaggery. **Palm Sunday** n the Sunday before Easter, in commemoration of the strewing of palm branches when Christ entered Jerusalem. **palm tree** n. **palm'-tree justice** n justice without litigation and legal processes, from the old Arabic or Jewish idea of a wise man dispensing justice under a palm tree. **palm wine** n fermented palm sap.

palmar, **palmate**, etc see under **palm¹**.

palmer /pä'mər/ n a pilgrim carrying a palm-leaf in token of having been in the Holy Land; a palmer-worm; a bristly artificial fly. [**palm²**]
❑ **palm'er-worm'** n a hairy caterpillar of various kinds, *orig* one of wandering habits.

Palmerin /pal'mər-in/ n a knightly champion. [From *Palmerín*, a Spanish (or Portuguese) romance hero found as a child among *palm-trees*]

palmette, **palmetto**, **palmiet**, **palmitin**, etc see under **palm²**.

palmful see under **palm¹**.

palmipede, **palmist**, etc see under **palm¹**.

palmy see under **palm¹,²**.

palmyra /pal-mī'rə/ n an African and Asiatic palm (*Borassus flabellifer*) yielding toddy, jaggery, and **palmyra nuts**. [Port *palmeira* palm tree, confused with *Palmyra* in Syria]
❑ **palmyra wood** n properly, the wood of the palmyra palm; any palm timber.

palolo /pa-lō'lō/ n (pl **palo'los**) an edible seaworm that burrows in coral reefs, remarkable for its breeding swarms at a certain phase of the moon, the head remaining behind to regenerate (also **palolo worm**). [Samoan]

palomino /pal-ə-mē'nō/ n (pl **palomi'nos**) a horse of largely Arab blood, pale tan, yellow, or gold, with a white or silver mane and tail. [Am Sp, from Sp, like a dove]

palooka /pə-loo'kə/ (US sl) n a stupid or clumsy person, *esp* in sports. [Origin unknown]

paloverde /pal-ō-vûr'di/ n a thorny flowering tree (*Cercidium*) found in warm deserts of America. [Am Sp, green tree]

palp¹ /palp/ n a jointed sense-organ attached in pairs to the mouth-parts of insects and crustaceans (also **pal'pus**; pl **pal'pī**). [LL *palpus* a feeler (L, a stroking), from L *palpāre* to stroke]
▪ **pal'pal** adj. **pal'pate** adj (*zool*) of, relating to or possessing a palp or palps.

palp² /palp/ vt to feel, examine, or explore by touch; to speak fair (*obs*). [L *palpāre*, -*ātum* to touch softly, stroke, caress, flatter]
▪ **palpabil'ity** n. **palp'able** adj that can be touched or felt; perceptible; (of eg lies, etc) easily found out; obvious, gross. **palp'ableness** n. **palp'ably** adv. **palp'āte** vt to examine by touching or pressing (*esp med*). **palpā'tion** n the act of examining by means of touch.
❑ **palp'able-gross'** adj (*Shakesp*).

palpal see under **palp¹**.

palpate see under **palp¹,²**.

palpebral /palp'i-brəl/ adj of or relating to the eyelid. [L *palpebra* the eyelid]

palpi see **palp¹**.

palpitate /pal'pi-tāt/ vi to throb; to beat rapidly; to pulsate; to quiver. ◆ vt to cause to throb. [L *palpitāre*, -*ātum*, frequentative of *palpāre*; cf **palp¹,²**]
▪ **pal'pitant** adj palpitating. **palpitā'tion** n the act of palpitating; (often pl) abnormal awareness of heartbeat.

palpus see **palp¹**.

palsgrave /pölz'grāv/ n a count palatine. [Du *paltsgrave* (now *paltsgraaf*); cf Ger *Pfalzgraf*; see **palace** and **Graf**]
▪ **palsgravine** /pölz'grə-vēn/ n a countess palatine.

palstave /pöl'stāv/ or **palstaff** /-stäf/ n a Bronze Age axe, the flanges of the head joined by a cross ridge to engage the ends of the prongs of the kneed shaft. [Du *paalstav*, from ON *pālstafr*]

palsy¹ /pöl'zi/ n loss of control or of feeling, more or less complete, in the muscles of the body, *esp* when this results in involuntary trembling; paralysis. ◆ vt to affect with palsy; to deprive of action or energy; to paralyse. [From **paralysis**]
▪ **pal'sied** adj.

palsy² or **palsy-walsy** see under **pal**.

palter /pöl'tər/ vi to trifle in talk; to use trickery; to haggle; to equivocate. [Poss connected with **paltry**]
▪ **pal'terer** n.

paltry /pol'/ or /pöl'tri/ adj meagre, mean; of poor quality; trashy; worthless; not worth considering. [Cf Dan *pialter* rags, LG *paltrig* ragged]
▪ **pal'trily** adv. **pal'triness** n.

paludal /pal-ū'dl/ or /-oo'/, also (*rare*) /pal'/ adj relating to marshes; marshy; malarial. [L *palus*, *palūdis* a marsh; *palūster*, -*tris* marshy]
▪ **palu'dic** adj of marshes. **paludic'olous** adj (L *colere* to inhabit) marsh-dwelling; growing in marshes. **palu'dinal**, **pal'udine** or **palu'dinous** adj of marshes; marshy. **pal'udism** n malaria. **pal'udose** or **pal'udous** adj of marshes; marshy; inhabiting marshes; malarial. **Pal'udrine®** n a proprietary name for *proguanil hydrochloride*, a synthetic antimalarial drug. **palustral** /-us'trəl/, **palus'trian** or **palus'trine** /-trīn/ adj of marshes; inhabiting marshes.

paludament /pə-lū'də-mənt/ or /-oo'/ n a Roman general's or high military officer's cloak (also **paludament'um**). [L *palūdāmentum*]

palustral, etc see under **paludal**.

paly see under **pale¹,²**.

palynology /pal-i-nol'ə-ji/ n the study of spores and pollen grains. [Gr *palȳnein* to sprinkle]
▪ **palynolog'ical** adj. **palynol'ogist** n.

pam /pam/ n the jack of clubs, highest card in the game of loo; a game like nap, in which it is highest card. [Said to be from Fr *Pamphile*, from Gr *Pamphilos*, literally, beloved of all]

pam abbrev: pamphlet.

pampa /pam'pə/ n (usu in pl **pampas** /pam'pəz/ also used as sing /pam'pəs/) a vast treeless plain in southern S America. [Sp, from Quechua *pampa*, *bamba* plain]
▪ **pam'pean** adj. **pampero** /pam-pā'rō/ n (pl **pampe'ros**) a violent south-west wind on and from the pampas.
❑ **pampas grass** n a tall, ornamental, reed-like grass (*Gynerium*, or *Cortaderia*) with large thick silvery panicles.

pampelmoose, **pampelmouse** /pam'pl-moos/ see **pompelmoose**.

pamper /pam'pər/ vt to gratify to the full; to overindulge; to feed with fine food (*archaic*). [A frequentative from (obs) *pamp*, *pomp*; cf Ger dialect *pampen* to cram]
▪ **pam'peredness** n. **pam'perer** n.

pampero see under **pampa**.

pamphlet /pam'flit/ or /-flət/ n a small book stitched but not bound; a separately published treatise, *usu* controversial, on some subject of the day; a small booklet of information. [Anglo-L *panfletus*, possibly from a Latin erotic poem *Pamphilus* (from Gr *Pamphilos* beloved of all) very popular in the Middle Ages]
▪ **pamphleteer'** n a writer of (*esp* politically controversial or subversive) pamphlets. ◆ vi to write pamphlets. **pamphleteer'ing** n and adj.

PAMR abbrev: Public Access Mobile Radio.

Pamyat /pam'yat/ n a Russian anti-Semitic nationalist organization. [Russ, memory]

Pan /pan/ n the Greek god of pastures, flocks, and woods, worshipped in Arcadia, fond of music and represented with a goat's legs and feet, and sometimes horns and ears; later (from association with *pān* the whole) connected with pantheistic thought. [Gr *Pān*]
❑ **Pan'-pipes** or **Pan's pipes** n pl the syrinx, a musical instrument attributed to Pan, made of reeds of different lengths, fastened in a row.

pan¹ /pan/ n any broad, shallow container used in the home, in the arts or in industry; a saucepan; anything of similar shape, such as the upper part of the skull (**brain-pan**) or the patella (**knee-pan**); a lavatory bowl; a hollow in the ground, a basin, in which water collects in the rainy season, leaving a salt deposit on evaporation; a salt pan; a saltworks; the part of a firelock that holds the priming; a hard layer (**hard-pan**) in or under the soil; a small ice floe; a hollow metal drum as played in a steel band; a panful; the face (*sl*). ◆ vt (**pann'ing**; **panned**) to wash in a goldminer's pan; to obtain by evaporating in a pan; to yield; to obtain; to cook and serve in a pan; to review or criticize harshly (*inf*). ♦ *vi* to wash earth for gold; to yield gold (*usu* with *out*); to result, turn out (with *out*); to come to an end, be exhausted (with *out*); to cake; to enlarge or embellish in speech. [OE *panne*; a word common to the W Gmc languages, poss an early borrowing from L *patina*]

■ **pan'ful** *n* (*pl* **pan'fuls**). **pann'ikel** *n* (*obs*) a pannicle. **pann'ikin** *n* a small metal cup; a little pan or saucer; enough to fill a cup. **pann'ing** *n* washing for gold; the gold so obtained; harsh criticism (*inf*).

❑ **pan'cake** *n* a thin flat round cake of eggs, flour, sugar, and milk, fried in a pan; pancake make-up; an aircraft descent made in an emergency with the wheels up and landing flat on the belly of the aircraft (also *adj*). ♦ *vi* to descend or alight in such a way; (of a building) to collapse concertina-like. ♦ *vt* to cause to make a pancake (descent or landing). **pancake bell** *n* a church bell rung on Shrove Tuesday, taken as the signal for pancake-making. **Pancake Day** or **Tuesday** *n* Shrove Tuesday. **pancake ice** *n* polar sea ice in thin flat slabs, found as winter draws near. **pancake make-up** *n* cosmetic in cake form, moist, or moistened before application. **pan drop** *n* (*Scot*) a hard smooth peppermint sweet made in a revolving pan. **pan'-fry** *vt* to fry in a shallow pan. **pan'handle** *n* a strip of territory stretching out from the main body like the handle of a pan. ♦ *vi* and *vt* (*US*) to beg (from someone) *esp* on the street. **pan'handler** *n*. **pan loaf** *n* (*Scot*) a loaf baked in an individual tin, with a crust all round, *opp* to a *plain loaf*. **pan'stick** *n* foundation make-up like pancake make-up but in stick form.

■ **flash in the pan** a mere flash in the pan of a flintlock without discharge; a fitful show of beginning without accomplishing anything; a brief success.

pan² /*pan*/ *vt* and *vi* (**pann'ing**; **panned**) to move (a cinema, video or still television camera) about (or as if pivoting about) an axis while taking a picture so as to follow a particular object or to produce a panoramic effect; (in broadcasting or recording) to cause (sound) to appear to move by electronic means. [**panorama**]

pan³, **paan** /*pän*/ or **pawn** /*pön*/ *n* betel leaf; betel. [Hindi *pān*]

pan- /*pan-*/, **pant-** /*pant-*/ or **panto-** /*pan-tō-*/ *combining form* meaning all. [Gr *pās*, *pāsa*, *pān*, genitive *pantos*, *pāsēs*, *pantos*]

panacea /*pan-ə-sē'ə*/ *n* a cure for all things; a healing plant, of varying description (*obs*; *Spenser* **panachaea** /-*kē'ə*/). [Gr *panakeia*, from *akos* cure]

■ **panacē'an** *adj*.

panache /*pa-* or *pə-nash'* or *-näsh'*/ *n* swagger; grand manner, theatricality, sense of style; knightly splendour; a plume (*hist*). [Fr, from Ital *pennacchio*, from *penna* feather]

panada /*pə-nä'də*/ *n* a dish made by boiling bread to a pulp in water, and flavouring; a thick binding sauce of breadcrumbs or flour and seasoning. [Sp *pan* (L *pānis*) bread]

Panadol® /*pan'ə-dol*/ *n* a proprietary form of paracetamol.

panaesthesia or (*US*) **panesthesia** /*pa-nēs-thē'zi-ə*, *-zyə*, *-nes-* or *-nis-*/ *n* totality of perception; general awareness. [Gr *aisthēsis* perception]

■ **panaesthetism** /-*ēs'* or *-es'thi-tizm*/ *n*.

Pan-African /*pan-af'ri-kən*/ *adj* including or relating to all Africa, *esp* concerning policies of political unity among African states. [**pan-** and **African**]

■ **Pan-Af'ricanism** *n*.

Panagia same as **Panhagia**.

Pan Am /*pan-am'*/ *abbrev*: Pan-American (World Airways Incorporated).

Panama /*pan-ə-mä'* or *pan'*/ *adj* of or relating to the republic of *Panama* in Central America. ♦ *n* (without *cap*) a panama hat.

■ **Panamanian** /-*mä'ni-ən*/ *n* and *adj*.

❑ **panama hat** *n* a lightweight hand-plaited men's hat made, not in Panama but in Ecuador, of plaited strips of the leaves of a S American cyclanthaceous plant (*Carludovica palmata*); an imitation version of this.

Pan-American /*pan-ə-mer'i-kən*/ *adj* including all America or Americans, North and South. [**pan-** and **American**]

■ **Pan-Amer'icanism** *n*.

Pan-Anglican /*pan-ang'gli-kən*/ *adj* representing or including all who hold the doctrines and polity of the Anglican Church. [**pan-** and **Anglican**]

Pan-Arab /*pan-ar'əb*/ or **Pan-Arabic** /-*ar'əb-ik*/ *adj* of or relating to the policy of political unity between all Arab states. [**pan-** and **Arab**]

■ **Pan-Ar'abism** *n*.

panaritium /*pan-ə-rish'i-əm*/ *n* a whitlow. [LL *panāricium* for *parōnychium*, from Gr *parōnychiā*, from *para* beside, and *onyx*, *-ychos* nail]

panarthritis /*pan-är-thrī'tis*/ *n* inflammation involving all the structures of a joint. [**pan-** and **arthritis**]

panary /*pan'ə-ri*/ *adj* of or relating to bread. ♦ *n* a bread store. [L *pānārius*, from *pānis* bread]

panatella /*pan-ə-tel'ə*/ *n* a long, thin cigar. [Am Sp *panetela* a long, thin biscuit, from Ital, small loaf, from L *pānis* bread]

Panathenaea /*pan-ath-i-nē'ə*/ *n pl* the chief national festival of ancient Athens, the lesser festival being held annually, the greater one every fourth year. [Gr *Panathēnaia*]

■ **Panathenae'an** *adj*. **Panathenā'ic** *adj*.

panax /*pan'aks*/ or *pān'*/ *n* a tree or shrub of the genus *Polyscias*, related to, or included in, the genus *Panax*, of the Aralia family. [Gr *panax* a name for various healing plants; see **panacea**]

pancake see under **pan¹**.

pance see **pansy**.

pancetta /*pan-chet'ə*/ *n* an Italian variety of cured pork. [Ital, little belly]

Panchatantra /*pun-chä-tunt'rə*/ *n* the oldest extant Sanskrit collection of beast-fables, in five books. [Sans, five books]

panchax /*pan'chaks*/ *n* any of several kinds of brightly-coloured fish, genus *Aplocheilus*, native to Africa and SE Asia, often stocked in aquariums. [L, former generic name]

panchayat /*pun-chä'yət*/ *n* a village or town council. [Hindi *pañcāyat*, from Sans *pañca* five]

Panchen Lama /*pän'chən lä'mə*/ *n* a Tibetan religious leader second in importance to the Dalai Lama. [Tibetan *pandita chen-po* great scholar]

pancheon or **panchion** /*pan'shən*/ *n* a coarse earthenware pan. [Appar connected with **pan¹**; perh influenced by **puncheon²**]

panchromatic /*pan-krō-mat'ik*/ *adj* equally or suitably sensitive to all colours; rendering all colours in due intensity. [Gr *chrōma*, *-atos* colour]

■ **panchro'matism** *n*.

pancosmism /*pan-koz'mi-zm*/ (*philos*) *n* the theory that the material universe, within space and time, is all that exists. [**cosmism**]

■ **pancos'mic** *adj*.

pancratium /*pan-krā'shi-əm*/ *n* (in ancient Greece) a combination of boxing and wrestling. [Gr *pankration*, from *kratos* strength]

■ **pancrā'tian** *adj*. **pancrā'tiast** /-*shi-ast*/ *n* a competitor or victor in the pancratium. **pancratic** /-*krat'ik*/ *adj* of the pancratium; excelling all round in athletics or accomplishments; (of a lens) adjustable to different degrees of magnification. **pan'cratist** *n*.

pancreas /*pan(g)'kri-əs*/ *n* a large gland discharging into the duodenum and containing islands of endocrine gland tissue. [Gr *kreas*, *-atos* flesh]

■ **pancreatec'tomy** *n* surgical removal of all or part of the pancreas. **pancreat'ic** *adj*. **pan'creatin** *n* the pancreatic juice; a medicinal substance to aid the digestion, prepared from extracts of the pancreas of certain animals. **pancreatīt'is** *n* inflammation of the pancreas. **pancreozy'min** *n* a hormone that stimulates enzyme production by the pancreas.

❑ **pancreatic juice** *n* the alkaline secretion from the pancreas into the duodenum to aid the digestive process.

pand /*pand*/ (*Scot*) *n* the valance of a bed. [Cf OFr *pandre* to hang]

panda /*pan'də*/ *n* a raccoon-like animal (*Ailurus fulgens*) of the Himalayas (also called the **red** or **lesser panda**); (also, more correctly, **giant panda**) a similar but much larger herbivorous bear-like animal (*Ailuropoda melanoleuca*) of Tibet and China, apparently linking the red panda with the bears. [Said to be its name in Nepal]

❑ **panda car** *n* a police patrol car (formerly white with black or blue markings). **panda eyes** *n pl* (*inf*) dark-ringed eyes, produced by lack of sleep or by eye make-up that has been smudged or over-enthusiastically applied.

Pandaemonium see **Pandemonium**.

Pandanus /*pan-dā'nəs*/ *n* the screw pine, the typical genus of the **Pandanā'ceae**, a family of trees and bushes related to the bulrushes and bur-reeds. [Malay *pandan*]

■ **pandanā'ceous** *adj*.

pandar see **pander**.

pandation /*pan-dā'shən*/ (*archaic*) *n* warping. [L *pandātiō*, *-ōnis*, from *pandāre*, *-ātum* to bend]

Pandean /*pan-dē'ən*/ *adj* of the god Pan; of Pan-pipes. [Irregularly formed from *Pān*]

❑ **Pandean pipes** *n pl* Pan-pipes.

pandect /*pan'dekt*/ *n* a treatise covering the whole of any subject, *esp* the complete laws of a country; (in *pl*; with *cap*) the digest of Roman law made by command of the Emperor Justinian in the 6c.

[L *pandecta*, from Gr *pandektēs*, from *pās*, *pān* all, and *dechesthai* to receive]

■ **pandect'ist** *n*.

pandemic /pan-dem'ik/ *adj* affecting a whole people, epidemic over a wide area. ◆ *n* a pandemic disease. [Gr *pandēmios*, from *dēmos* people]

■ **pandemia** /-dē'mi-ə/ *n* a widespread epidemic. **pande'mian** *adj* vulgar; sensual.

Pandemonium or **Pandaemonium** /pan-di-mō'ni-əm/ *n* the capital of Hell in Milton's *Paradise Lost* ; (without *cap*) any very disorderly or noisy place or assembly; (without *cap*) tumultuous uproar. [Gr *pās*, *pān* all, and *daimōn* a spirit] The following also without *cap*:

■ **Pandemo'niac** *adj*. **Pandemoni'acal** *adj*. **Pandemo'nian** *adj*. **Pandemonic** /-mon'ik/ *adj*.

pander, also **pandar** /pan'dər/ *vi* to indulge, gratify (with *to*); to act as a pander; to minister to the passions. ◆ *vt* to play the pander for. ◆ *n* a person who procures for another the means of gratifying his or her base passions; a pimp. [*Pandarus*, in the story of Troilus and Cressida as told by Boccaccio (*Filostrato*), Chaucer, and Shakespeare]

■ **pan'deress** *n* a procuress. **pan'derism** *n* the employment or practices of a pander. **pan'derly** *adj* (*Shakesp*) acting as a pander. **pan'derous** *adj*.

pandermite /pan-dûr'mīt/ *n* a hydrogen calcium borate found in great quantities at *Panderma* (Bandirma) on the Sea of Marmara.

pandiculation /pan-dik-ū-lā'shən/ *n* the act of stretching and yawning. [L *pandiculārī*, *-ātus* to stretch oneself]

Pandion /pan-dī'on/ *n* the osprey genus. [Gr *Pandīōn*, father of Procne and Philomela]

pandit same as **pundit**.

P&L *abbrev* : profit and loss.

P&O or **P and O** *abbrev* : Peninsular and Oriental (Steam Navigation Company).

pandoor see **pandour**.

Pandora /pan-dō'rə or -dö'rə/ (*Gr myth*) *n* the first woman, made for Zeus so that he might through her punish man for the theft by Prometheus of heavenly fire, given a box which she disobediently opened to release all the ills of human life. [Gr *pās*, *pān* all, and *dōron* a gift]

❑ **Pandora's box** *n* any source of great and unexpected troubles.

pandora /pan-dō'rə or -dö'rə/ or **pandore** /pan-dōr' or -dör'/ *n* an ancient Eastern musical instrument like a long-necked lute with (commonly) three strings; a bandore. [Gr *pandoura* a 3-stringed instrument, fancifully connected with *Pān*, but probably an Eastern word; cf **bandore**, **banjo**, **mandolin**]

■ **pandū'ra** *n* a pandora; a Neapolitan instrument like a mandolin with eight metal wires, played with a quill. **pan'dūrate**, **pan'durated** or **pandū'riform** *adj* (*bot*) fiddle-shaped.

pandore /pan'dōr or -dör'/ *n* an esteemed variety of oysters formerly caught at Prestonpans on the Firth of Forth. [Said to be from the *doors* of the salt-*pans* where they were found]

pandour, also **pandoor** /pan'door/ *n* an 18th-century Croatian foot soldier in the Austrian service; a robber. [Fr, from Serbo-Croat *pàndūr*, from LL *banderius* follower of a banner]

pandowdy /pan-dow'di/ (*US*) *n* a deep-pan apple-pie or pudding richly spiced. [Origin unknown]

p and p or **p&p** *abbrev* : postage and packing.

pandura, **pandurate**, **panduriform** see under **pandora**.

pandy[1] /pan'di/ (*inf*) *n* a beating on the palm with a strap, formerly used as a school punishment. ◆ *vt* to slap. [L *pande* hold out, imperative of *pandere*]

pandy[2] /pan'di/ (*inf*; *hist*) *n* an insurgent sepoy in the Indian Mutiny. [Said to be from *Pande*, a common surname]

pane[1] /pān/ *n* a slab of window glass; a rectangular compartment; a panel; a flat side or face; a length of wall; the side of a quadrangle; a rectangular piece of ground; a piece of cloth (*obs*); a piece of cloth pieced together with others, or separated from others by slashing (*archaic*); a large sheet of stamps issued by the Post Office; half such a sheet separated from the other half by a gutter; a page of a book of stamps. ◆ *vt* to insert panes or panels in. [Fr *pan*, from L *pannus* a cloth, a rag]

■ **paned** /pānd/ *adj* made of panes or small squares; variegated.

pane[2] /pān/ same as **pean**[2].

pane[3] see **peen**.

paneer /pä-nēr'/ *n* a mild crumbly cheese used in Asian cookery. [Hindi *panīr*]

panegoism /pan-eg'ō-i-zm, -ēg'/ *n* solipsism. [Gr *egō* I]

panegyric /pan-i-jir'ik/ (or *US* sometimes *-jīr'*)/ *n* a eulogy, *esp* public and elaborate (on or upon); laudation. [Gr *panēgyrikos* fit for a national festival, from *pās*, *pān* all, and *agyris* (*agorā*) an assembly]

■ **panegyr'ic** or **panegyr'ical** *adj*. **panegyr'ically** *adv*. **panegyr'icon** *n* (in the Greek Church) a collection of sermons for festivals. **pan'egyrist** (or /-jir'* or *-ej'ər-/*) *n*. **pan'egyrize** or **-ise** (or /-ej'ər-/*) *vt* to write or pronounce a panegyric on; to praise highly. **pan'egyry** *n* a great assembly; a religious festival.

panel /pan'l/ *n* a bordered rectangular area; a thin flat piece sunk below the general surface of a door, shutter, wainscot, or the like, often with a raised border; a compartment; a rectangular piece of any material; a section of the bodywork of a vehicle; a rectangular division on a page, *esp* for the illustrations in children's comics; a board with dials, switches, etc for monitoring or controlling the operation of an electrical or other apparatus; a compartment or hurdle of a fence; a strip of material inserted in a dress; a cloth under a saddle (*obs*); a crude form of saddle; a slip of parchment; such a slip containing a list of names, *esp* of jurors; a jury; prior to the introduction of the national health service, a list of doctors available to treat those who paid into a national health insurance scheme; such a doctor's list of patients; an accused person or persons (in *sing*; *Scots law*); a thin board on which a picture is painted; a large long photograph; a group of people chosen for some purpose, such as to judge a competition, serve on a brains trust, or be the guessers in radio and television guessing games (**panel games**); a representative group of consumers or shops who report on their habits of buying or using products or services over a period of time. ◆ *vt* (**pan'elling**; **pan'elled**) to furnish with a panel or panels; to put on trial (*Scots law*). [OFr, from LL *pannellus*, from L *pannus* a cloth]

■ **pan'elling** *n* panel-work. **pan'ellist** *n* a member of a panel, *esp* in panel games.

❑ **panel beating** *n* the shaping of metal sheets for vehicle bodywork, etc. **panel beater** *n*. **panel doctor** *n* a doctor who was on the panel or had a panel. **panel heating** *n* indoor heating diffused from floors, walls, or ceilings. **panel pin** *n* a light, narrow-headed nail of small diameter used chiefly for fixing plywood or hardboard to supports. **panel saw** *n* a fine saw for cutting very thin wood at right angles to the grain. **panel show** *n* a television or radio programme in which panels of celebrities trade humorous remarks while ostensibly competing in a quiz. **panel system** *n* a system of office, etc design, in which partitions are used to create flexible work-areas within an open layout. **panel truck** *n* (*US*) a delivery-van. **panel van** *n* (*Aust* and *NZ*) a small van. **panel working** *n* a method of working a coalmine by dividing it into compartments.

panentheism /pan-en-thē'i-zm or pan-en'/ *n* the doctrine that the world is a part, though not the whole, of God's being. [**pan-** and Gr *en* in, and *theos* God]

■ **panenthē'ist** (or /*pan-en'*/) *n*.

panesthesia see **panaesthesia**.

panettone /pa-ne-tō'nā/ *n* (*pl* **panettōn'i** /-ē/) a light cake, *usu* made with sultanas and candied peel, traditionally eaten at Christmas in Italy. [Ital *panetto* a small loaf]

Pan-European /pan-ū-rə-pē'ən/ *adj* of, concerning or relating to all European countries, or to the movement for political and/or economic union in Europe. [**pan-** and **European**]

panful see under **pan**[1].

pang[1] /pang/ *n* a violent but *usu* brief pain; a painful emotion. ◆ *vt* to inflict a pang on. [Poss **prong**; *pronge* and *prange* have been found]

■ **pang'ing** *adj* (*Shakesp*) painful. **pang'less** *adj*.

pang[2] /pang/ (*Scot*) *vt* to stuff, cram. ◆ *adj* stuffed, crammed, crowded; tight. [Origin unknown]

■ **pang'-full'** or **pang'-fu''** *adj* filled full.

panga /pang'gə/ *n* a broad, heavy African knife used as a tool and as a weapon. [Swahili]

Pangaea or **Pangea** /pan-jē'ə/ *n* the postulated supercontinent that began to break up, forming the present continents of the earth. [**pan-** and Gr *gē* the earth]

pan-galactic /pan-gə-lak'tik/ *adj* of or relating to all the galaxies in the universe. [**pan-** and **galactic**]

pangamy /pan(g)'gə-mi/ *n* random mating. [Gr *gamos* marriage]

■ **pangamic** /pan-gam'ik/ *adj*.

pangenesis /pan-jen'i-sis/ *n* Darwin's theory that every cell of the body contributes gemmules to the germ-cells and so shares in the transmission of inherited characters. [Gr *genesis* production]

■ **pan'gen** or **pan'gene** /-jēn/ *n* a hypothetical unit of living matter. **pangenet'ic** *adj*.

Pan-German /pan-jûr'mən/ *adj* relating to or including all Germans. [**pan-** and **German**]

■ **Pan-Ger'manism** *n* a movement for a Greater Germany or union of all German peoples.

■ words derived from main entry word; ❑ compound words; ▪ idioms and phrasal verbs

Panglossian /pan-glos'i-ən/ or **Panglossic** /-ik/ adj taking an over-cheerful and optimistic view of the world as did Dr *Pangloss* in Voltaire's *Candide* (1759).

pangolin /pang-gō'lin/ or /pang'gə-lin/ n the scaly anteater, an edentate mammal (genus *Manis*; order Pholidota) of Asia and Africa. [Malay *peng-gōling* roller, from its habit of rolling up]

pangrammatist /pan-gram'ə-tist/ n someone who contrives verses or sentences containing all the letters of the alphabet. [Gr *gramma*, *-atos* letter]
■ **pan'gram** n a sentence containing all the letters of the alphabet, eg *the quick brown fox jumps over the lazy dog*.

Panhagia or **Panagia** /pan-hä'gi-ə or pan-ha'gi-ə/ adj all-holy, an epithet of the Virgin in the Eastern Church; a cut loaf elevated in her honour; a medallion of the Virgin worn by bishops. [Gr *hagios* holy]

panhandle, panhandler see under **pan**[1].

panharmonicon /pan-här-mon'i-kon/ n a mechanical musical instrument mimicking an orchestra. [**pan-** and **harmonicon** (see under **harmony**)]

panhellenic /pan-hel-ēn'ik or -en'/ adj relating to all Greece; including all Greeks; (with *cap*) of or relating to Panhellenism. [Gr *Hellēnikos* Greek, from *Hellas* Greece]
■ **panhellē'nion** or (L) **panhellē'nium** n a council representing all the sections of the Greeks. **Panhell'enism** /-ən-izm/ n a movement or aspiration for the political union of all Greek (or former Greek) territories. **Panhell'enist** n. **Panhellenis'tic** adj.

panic[1] /pan'ik/ n frantic or sudden fright; contagious fear; great terror, often without any visible reason or foundation; a state of terror about investments, impelling investors to rush and sell what they possess. ◆ adj relating or due to the god Pan; of the nature of a panic; inspired or caused by panic. ◆ vt (**pan'icking**; **pan'icked**) to throw into a panic. ◆ vi to be struck by panic. [Gr *pānikos* belonging to Pan; *pānikon* (*deima*) panic (fear), fear associated with the god Pan]
■ **pan'icky** adj inclined to, affected by, resulting from, or of the nature of, panic.
❑ **panic attack** n (*behaviourism*) an attack of intense terror and anxiety, lasting from several minutes to several hours. **pan'ic-bolt'** n an easily moved bolt for emergency exits. **panic button** n a button operating a distress or other emergency device or signal (also *fig*); a function on a website allowing a young user to alert authorities if they feel in danger from another user. **pan'ic-buy'** vi and vt to buy up stocks of a commodity which threatens to be in short supply (often precipitating a greater shortage than might otherwise have occurred). **pan'ic-buying** n. **pan'ic-mong'er** n someone who creates or fosters panics. **panic room** n a secure room within a building, designed as a refuge from threats such as severe weather, nuclear attack or disgruntled employees. **panic stations** n pl a state of panic or commotion. **pan'ic-strick'en** or **pan'ic-struck** adj struck with panic or sudden fear.

panic[2], also **panick** or **pannick** /pan'ik/ n any grass of the genus *Panicum* (see below), or of various closely related genera (also **pan'ic-grass'**); the edible grain of some species. [L *pānicum* Italian millet]
■ **pan'icle** n (*bot*) strictly, a branched raceme with each branch bearing a raceme of flowers, as in oat; loosely, a lax irregular inflorescence. **pan'icled**, **panic'ulate** or **panic'ūlated** adj furnished with, arranged in, or like, panicles. **panic'ūlately** adv. **Pan'icum** n a large genus of grasses having the one- or two-flowered spikelets in spikes, racemes or panicles.

panification /pan-i-fi-kā'shən/ n conversion into bread. [L *pānis* bread, and *facere* to make]

panim a Miltonic spelling of **paynim**.

panini /pa-nē'ni/ n pl (sometimes loosely used as *sing*, with pl **pani'nis**) grilled, Italian-style sandwiches; various types of Italian bread. [Pl of Ital *panino* little bread, roll]

Panionic /pan-ī-on'ik/ adj of or including all Ionians. [**pan-** and **Ionic**]

panisk or **panisc** /pan'isk/ n an inferior god, attendant on Pan. [Gr *Pāniskos*, dimin of *Pān*]

Pan-Islam /pan-iz'läm, -is'/ or -lam/ n the whole Muslim world; Pan-Islamism. [**pan-** and **Islam**]
■ **Pan-Islam'ic** adj. **Pan-Is'lamism** n an aspiration or movement for the union of all Muslims. **Pan-Is'lamist** n.

Panjabi same as **Punjabi**.

panjandrum /pan-jan'drəm/ n a figure of great power and self-importance, a burlesque potentate, from the Grand Panjandrum in a string of nonsense made up by Samuel Foote (1720–77), English wit, actor and dramatist (also **panjan'darum**).

panko /pan'kō/ n a type of breadcrumb used in Japanese cookery. [Jap *pan* bread, and *ko* flour]

panleucopenia /pan-lū-kō-pē'ni-ə/ n a viral disease of cats marked by a deficiency of white blood cells and causing fever, diarrhoea, and dehydration. [**pan-** and **leucopenia**]

panlogism /pan'lə-ji-zm/ n the theory that the universe is an outward manifestation of the Logos. [**Logos**]

panmixia /pan-mik'si-ə/ (*biol*) n random mating within a population, *esp* of a model system (also **panmix'is**). [Gr *mixis* mixing]
■ **panmic'tic** adj of, connected with or exhibiting panmixia.

panna cotta /pan'a kot'a/ n an Italian dessert made from cream. [Ital, literally, cooked cream]

pannage /pan'ij/ (*archaic*) n food picked up by swine in the woods, mast; the right to pasture swine in a forest. [OFr *pasnage*, from LL *pastiōnāticum*, from *pascere*, *pastum* to feed]

panne /pan/ n a fabric resembling velvet, with a long nap. [Fr]

panned see under **pan**[1,2].

pannelled /pan'ld/ vt (*pat*) conjectured to be a misprint for *spanielled*, ie followed or fawned on as by a spaniel (Shakesp, *Antony and Cleopatra* IV.12).

pannick see **panic**[2].

pannicle /pan'i-kl/ or **panniculus** /pə-nik'ū-ləs/ n a thin, sheet-like garment. [L *panniculus*, dimin of *pannus* a cloth]

pannier[1] /pan'yər or pan'i-ər/ n a provision-basket; a basket carried on one's back; one of a pair of baskets slung over a pack animal's back or over the rear wheel of a bicycle, motorcycle, etc; a sculptured basket (*archit*); a system of hoops formerly used for spreading out a woman's dress at the hips; the part spread out in this way; a piece of basketwork for protecting archers, or, when filled with gravel or sand, for forming and protecting dykes, embankments, etc; a covered basket of medicines and surgical instruments (*milit*); hence (blunderingly) an ambulance (*milit*). [Fr *panier*, from L *pānārium* a breadbasket, from *pānis* bread]
■ **pann'iered** adj.

pannier[2] /pan'yər or -i-ər/ n an informal name for a robed waiter in the Inns of Court. [Origin unknown]

pannikel an obsolete form of **pannicle**.

pannikell /pan'i-kel/ (*Spenser*) n the skull. [**pannicle**]

pannikin see under **pan**[1].

panning see under **pan**[1,2].

pannose /pan'ōs/ (*bot*) adj like felt. [L *pannōsus*, from *pannus* cloth]

pannus /pan'əs/ (*pathol*) n a layer of new connective tissue that forms over the synovial membrane of joints in rheumatoid arthritis, or over the cornea in trachoma. [L *pannus* cloth]

panocha /pä-nō'chə/ n a Mexican coarse sugar. [Sp]

panoistic /pan-ō-is'tik/ (*zool*) adj (of an ovary) producing ova only, not yolk-forming cells, *opp* to *meroistic*. [Gr *ōion* an egg]

panomphaean /pan-om-fē'ən/ adj all-oracular, an epithet of Zeus; applied (after Rabelais) to the word 'drink' (which is celebrated by all nations). [Gr *omphē* a divine voice]

panophobia /pan-ō-fō'bi-ə/ n a form of melancholia marked by groundless fears; a non-standard form of **pantophobia**. [Gr *Pān*, the god who inspired fears, and *phobos* fear]

panophthalmitis /pan-of-thal-mī'tis/ n inflammation of the whole eye (also **panophthal'mia**). [Gr *ophthalmos* eye]

panoply /pan'ə-pli/ n complete armour; a full suit of armour; a full or brilliant covering or array (also *fig*). [Gr *panopliā* full armour of a hoplite, from *pās*, *pān* all, and *hopla* (pl) arms]
■ **pan'oplied** adj in panoply.

panoptic /pan-op'tik/, also **panoptical** /-kl/ adj all-embracing; viewing all aspects. [Gr *panoptēs* all-seeing]

panopticon /pan-op'ti-kon/ n a prison in which all prisoners can be watched from one point; an exhibition room. [Gr *optikon* (neuter adj) for seeing]

panorama /pan-ə-rä'mə/ n a wide or complete view (*lit* and *fig*); a picture painted on the inside wall of a circular room, in such a way that all parts appear to be in perspective to a viewer at the centre; an extended picture unrolled bit by bit to give the impression of a sequence in time. [Gr *horāma* a view, from *horaein* to see]
■ **panoramic** /-ram'ik/ adj.
❑ **panorama head** n a swivel device fitted to the head of a camera tripod to permit the sideways swinging motion of the camera when taking panning shots. **panoramic camera** n one which takes very wide-angle views, generally by rotation about an axis and by exposing a roll of film through a vertical slit. **panoramic sight** n a gun sight that can be rotated, so enabling the user to fire in any direction.

panpharmacon /pan-fär'mə-kon/ n a universal remedy. [Gr *pharmakon* a drug]

Pan-pipes or **Pan's pipes** see under **Pan**.

Pan-Presbyterian /pan-prez-bi-tē'ri-ən/ adj of, including, or representing all Presbyterians. [**pan-** and **Presbyterian**]

panpsychism /pan-sī'ki-zm/ n the theory that all nature has a psychic side. [**pan-** and **psychism** (see under **psycho-**)]
■ **panpsych'ist** n. **panpsychist'ic** adj.

pansexual /pan-sek'sū-əl/ adj including all or many different forms of sexuality. [**pan-** and **sexual** (see under **sex**)]
■ **pansex'ualism** n the view that all mental activity is derived from sexual instinct. **pansex'ualist** n. **pansexual'ity** n.

Pan-Slav /pan-släv'/ adj of, including, or representing, all Slavs. [**pan-** and **Slav**]
■ **Pan-Slav'ic** adj. **Pan-Slav'ism** n a movement for the union of all Slav peoples. **Pan-Slav'ist** n. **Pan-Slavon'ic** adj.

pansophy /pan'sə-fi/ n universal knowledge. [Gr sophiā wisdom]
■ **pansophic** /-sof'ik/ or **pansoph'ical** adj. **pan'sophism** n. **pan'sophist** n.

panspermatism /pan-spûr'mə-ti-zm/, **panspermism** /-mi-zm/, **panspermy** /-mi/ or **panspermia** /-mi-ə/ n the theory that life could be diffused through the universe by means of germs carried by meteorites or that life was brought to earth by this means. [Gr sperma, -atos seed]
■ **panspermat'ic** or **pansper'mic** adj. **pansper'matist** or **pansper'mist** n.

panstick see under **pan¹**.

pansy /pan'zi/ n (also (obs; Spenser, etc) **pance**, **paunce** or **pawnce** /päns or pöns/) a name for various species of violet, esp the heart's-ease (Viola tricolor) and garden kinds derived from it, as well as other species with upturned side petals and large leafy stipules; a soft bluish purple; an effeminate or namby-pamby male (derog sl); a male homosexual (derog sl, often offensive). ◆ adj bluish-purple; effeminate (derog sl). [A fanciful use of Fr pensée thought, from penser to think, from L pēnsāre to weigh]
■ **pan'sied** adj.

pant¹ /pant/ vi to gasp for breath; to run gasping; to throb; to wish ardently, to long, to yearn (with for); (of ship's hulls, etc) to bulge and shrink successively. ◆ vt to gasp out (an utterance). ◆ n a gasping breath; a throb. [Appar related to OFr pantoisier to pant]
■ **pant'ing** n and adj. **pant'ingly** adv.

pant² /pänt/ (Scot and N Eng) n a public fountain; a puddle by a midden. [Origin obscure]

pant- see **pan-**.

pantable /pan'tə-bl/ same as **pantofle**.

pantagamy /pan-tag'ə-mi/ n a word that ought to mean universal bachelorhood, applied with unconscious irony to the universal marriage of the Perfectionists, in which every man in the community is the husband of every woman. [Gr gamos marriage, and agamiā bachelorhood]

pantagraph see **pantograph**.

Pantagruelism /pan-tə-groo'ə-li-zm or -tag'rŭ-/ n the theories and practice of Pantagruel as described by Rabelais (died 1553); burlesque ironical buffoonery as a cover for serious satire.
■ **Pantagruelian** /-el'i-ən/ adj and n. **Pantagruel'ion** n a magic herb, hemp. **Pantagru'elist** (or /-tag'rŭ-/) n.

pantaleon /pan-tal'i-on/ n a very large dulcimer invented about 1700 by Pantaleon Hebenstreit.

pantalets, also **pantalettes** /pan-tə-lets'/ n pl long frilled drawers, worn by women and children in the first half of the 19c; a detachable ruffle for these, or one simulating these; extended to various trouser-like garments for women. [Dimin of **pantaloons** (see **Pantaloon**)]
■ **pantalett'ed** adj.

Pantaloon /pan-tə-loon' or pan'/ n a character in Italian comedy, and afterwards in pantomime, a lean old man (orig a Venetian) more or less a dotard; (without cap; Shakesp) a feeble old man; (without cap; in pl) various kinds of trousers worn by or suggesting the stage pantaloon, such as the wide breeches of the Restoration, later combined breeches and stockings, later 18c trousers fastened below the calf or under the shoe, children's trousers resembling these, (usu **pants**) trousers generally or long woollen underpants. [Fr pantalon, from Ital pantalone, from St Pantaleone, a favourite saint of the Venetians]
■ **pan'talon** n a movement in a quadrille. **pantalooned'** adj. **pantaloon'ery** n buffoonery.

panta rhei /pan'ta rā'i/ (Gr) everything is in a state of flux.

pantechnicon /pan-tek'ni-kon/ n a furniture van (in full **pantech'nicon-van'**); orig a building in London intended for the sale of all kinds of artistic work, turned into a furniture-store; (loosely) a receptacle holding a large number of miscellaneous objects. [Gr technē art]

panter see **pantler**.

pantheism /pan'thē-i-zm/ n the doctrine that nature and the physical universe are constituents of the essence of God, that they are part of what God is; the worship of all gods (rare); belief in many or all gods. [Gr theos a god, and pantheion a Pantheon]
■ **pan'theist** n. **pantheist'ic** or **pantheist'ical** adj. **pantheol'ogist** n. **pantheol'ogy** n a synthesis of all religions and the knowledge of all gods. **Pantheon** /pan'thi-on or pan-thē'on/ n a temple of all the gods, esp the rotunda erected by Hadrian at Rome (c.119–125AD), now the church of Santa Maria Rotonda, a burial-place of great Italians; a building serving as a general burial-place or memorial of the great dead, as Sainte Geneviève at Paris; an 18c place of amusement in London (Oxford Street); (often without cap) all the gods collectively; a complete mythology.

panthenol /pan'thin-ol/ same as **pantothenol** (see under **pantothenic**).

pantheologist, etc, **Pantheon** see under **pantheism**.

panther /pan'thər/ n a leopard, esp a large one or a black one, formerly believed to be a different species; a puma (N Am). [Gr panthēr]
■ **pan'theress** n. **pan'therine** /-īn/ adj. **pan'therish** adj.
■ **Black Panther** see under **black**.

panti- /pan-ti-/ combining form denoting pants or panties.

panties see under **pants**.

pantihose /pan'ti-hōz/ same as **pantyhose** (see under **panty**).

pantile /pan'tīl/ n a roofing tile whose cross-section forms an ogee curve; a tile concave or convex in cross-section; a flat paving tile (obs). ◆ adj (obs sl) dissenting, since chapels were often roofed with these. [**pan¹** and **tile**]
■ **pan'tiled** adj. **pan'tiling** n.

pantine /pan'tēn/ (obs) n a pasteboard jumping jack, fashionable in the 18c. [Fr pantine, afterwards pantin]

pantisocracy /pan-ti-sok'rə-si or -tī-/ n a community (planned in the 18c by Coleridge and Southey) in which all should have equal power. [Gr pās, pantos all, isos equal, and krateein to rule]
■ **pantis'ocrat** n. **pantisocrat'ic** adj.

pantler /pant'lər/ (Shakesp) n the officer in a great family who had charge of the bread and other provisions (also **pant'er**). [Fr panetier, from L pānis bread]

panto see under **pantomime**.

panto- see **pan-**.

Pantocrator /pan-tok'rə-tər/ n the ruler of the universe, esp Christ enthroned, as in icons, etc. [Gr kratos power]

pantofle, **pantoffle** or **pantoufle** /pan'tof-l, -tof'l or -toof'l/, also **pantable** /pan'tə-bl/ n a slipper; a high chopin (hist); an overshoe (archaic). [Fr pantoufle]
■ **on one's pantables** on one's dignity or high horse, lofty in manner.

pantograph, also **pantagraph** /pan'tə-gräf/ n a jointed framework of rods, based on the geometry of a parallelogram, for copying drawings, plans, etc, on the same, or a different, scale; a similar framework for other purposes, such as for collecting a current from an overhead wire on electric locomotives, trams, etc. [Gr pās, pantos all, and graphein to write]
■ **pantographer** /-tog'rə-fər/ n. **pantographic** /-tō-graf'ik/ or **pantograph'ical** adj. **pantog'raphy** n. —Also **pan'tagrapher**, etc.
■ **laser pantography** a technique of tracing a circuit pattern onto a microchip by means of a laser beam.

pantomime /pan'tə-mīm/ n a Roman actor in mime (hist); a play or an entertainment in mime; a theatrical entertainment, usu about Christmas-time, developed out of this, no longer in mime, with showy scenery, topical allusions, songs and star attractions of the day, buffoonery and dancing, centred loosely on a nursery story, formerly ending with a transformation scene and a harlequinade; dumbshow, mime; a situation of fuss, farce or confusion (derog). ◆ adj of pantomime; pantomimic. ◆ vt to portray or communicate by exaggerated silent gestures or expressions. [L pantomīmus, from Gr pantomīmos imitator of all, from pās, pantos all, and mīmos an imitator]
■ **pan'to** n (pl **pan'tos**) an informal form of **pantomime** (also adj). **pantomimic** /-mim'ik/ or **pantomim'ical** adj. **pantomim'ically** adv. **pan'tomimist** n an actor in or writer of pantomime.
❑ **pantomime horse** n a character in a pantomime or other comic performance consisting of a horselike costume inhabited by two performers, one forming the head and front legs, the other the back and back legs.

panton /pan'tən/ (Scot) n a slipper. [Appar connected with **pantofle**]
❑ **pan'ton-shoe'** n a horseshoe for curing a narrow and hoof-bound heel.

Pantone® /pan'tōn/ *n* a colour standard system, used in printing, visual arts, etc, in which each shade of each colour has an internationally recognized number, enabling exact matching of colours (also *adj*). [**pan-** and **tone**¹]

pantophagy /pan-tof'ə-ji/ *n* omnivorousness. [Gr *phagein* to eat]
■ **pantoph'agist** *n*. **pantoph'agous** /-gəs/ *adj*.

pantopragmatic /pan-tə-prag-mat'ik/ *adj* meddling in everybody's business. ◆ *n* a universal busybody. [From an imaginary society portrayed by Thomas Love Peacock (1785–1866)]
■ **pantopragmat'ics** *n sing* the science of universal benevolent interference.

pantoscope /pan'tə-skōp/ *n* a panoramic camera; a very wide-angled photographic lens. [Gr *pās, pantos* all, and *skopeein* to look at]
■ **pantoscopic** /-skop'ik/ *adj* giving a wide range of vision; bifocal.

pantothenic /pan-tə-then'ik/ *adj* literally from all quarters; applied to an acid, a member of the vitamin B complex, so ubiquitous that the effects of its deficiency in people are not known. [Gr *pantothen* from everywhere]
■ **pantothen'ol** *n* a stable form of pantothenic acid (also **pan'thenol**).

pantoufle see **pantofle**.

pantoum /pan-toom'/, properly **pantun** /pan-toon'/ *n* a repetitive verse form, *orig* Malay, with quatrains rhyming *ab ab, bc bc*, etc, returning to rhyme *a* at the end. [Malay]

pantry /pan'tri/ *n* a small room or large walk-in cupboard where food is stored, a larder; a room in a large house where table linen is stored and cutlery, etc cleaned. [Fr *paneterie*, from LL *pānitāria*, from L *pānis* bread]
■ **pan'trymaid** *n*. **pan'tryman** *n*.

pants /pants/ *n pl* knickers or underpants; trousers (*esp N Am*). ◆ *n sing* (*sl*) nonsense; rubbish; anything considered worthless. [**pantaloons** (see **Pantaloon**)]
■ **pant'ies** *n pl* brief knickers for a girl or woman.
❑ **pants suit** or **pant'suit** *n* (*esp N Am*) a woman's suit of trousers and jacket.
■ (**be caught**) **with one's pants down** (*inf*) (to be caught) at an embarrassing and unsuitable moment, in a state of extreme unpreparedness. (**fly**) **by the seat of one's pants** (to get through a difficult or dangerous situation) by a combination of resourcefulness and sheer luck. **scare**, **bore**, etc **the pants off someone** (*sl*) to scare, bore, etc someone to a great degree.

pantun see **pantoum**.

panty /pan'ti/ *adj* and *combining form* denoting pants or panties. [See **pants**]
❑ **panty girdle** *n* a woman's foundation garment consisting of panties made of elasticated material. **pan'tyhose** or **pan'tihose** *n pl* (*esp N Am*) tights worn by women or girls with ordinary dress, ie not theatrical, etc. **panty line** *n* the outline of a person's underwear, sometimes visible beneath tight-fitting clothes; the limit on the upper thigh and *esp* the lower abdomen normally reached by a pair of briefs, the bikini line. **pan'ty-waist** *n* (*US*) an effeminate or cowardly man (from a child's garment of trousers and jacket buttoned together at the waist).

panzer /pan'tsər/ or (*Eng*) pan'zər/ (*hist*) *n* a German tank, used in World War II. [Ger, armoured troops]
❑ **panzer division** *n* a German armoured division.

paolo /pä'ō-lō/ *n* (*pl* **pa'oli** /-lē/) an obsolete papal silver coin. [Ital *Paolo* Paul, ie Pope Paul V]

pap¹ /pap/ *n* soft food for infants, such as bread boiled with milk; mediocre, stultifying or worthless entertainment, writing, etc; mash; pulp. ◆ *vt* to feed with pap. [Imit]
■ **papp'y** *adj*.
❑ **pap'-boat** *n* a boat-shaped container for pap. **pap'-meat** *n* soft food for infants. **pap'-spoon** *n*.

pap² /pap/ (*dialect*) *n* a nipple or breast; in place names, a round conical hill. [Appar Scand]

pap³ /pap/ (*sl*) *vt* (**papp'ing; papped**) to photograph (a famous person) as, or in the manner of, a paparazzo. ◆ *n* a paparazzo. [Short form of **paparazzo**]

pa p *abbrev*: past participle.

Papa or **papa** /pä'pə or pə-pä'/ *n* (in international radio communication) a code word for the letter *p*.

papa /pə-pä' or (*esp US*) pä'pə/ *n* father (*old pet name, joc or genteel*); /pä'pä/ a pope (*obs*); /pä'pä/ a priest of the Eastern Orthodox Church. [Partly through Fr *papa*, partly directly from LL *pāpa*, Gr *papās*, *pappās*, a child's word for father]

papacy /pā'pə-si/ *n* the office of pope; a pope's tenure of office; papal government. [LL *pāpātia*, from *pāpa* pope]

papain /pə-pā'in/ *n* a digestive enzyme in the juice of papaw (genus *Carica*) fruits and leaves, used for tenderizing meat. [Sp *papaya* papaw]

papal /pā'pl/ *adj* of or relating to the Pope or the papacy. [LL *pāpālis*, from *pāpa* pope]
■ **pa'pable** *adj* likely to, or qualified to, become pope. **pa'palism** *n* the papal system. **pa'palist** *n* a supporter of the Pope and of the papal system. **pa'palize** or **-ise** *vt* and *vi* to render or become papal or papalist. **pa'pally** *adv*.
❑ **papal cross** *n* a cross with three crossbars. **Papal knighthood** *n* a title of nobility conferred by the Pope. **Papal States** *n pl* States of the Church (see under **state**).

Papanicolaou smear /pap-ə-nik'ō-low (or *-nēk*') smēr/ or **Papanicolaou test** /test/ *n* a smear test for detecting cancer, *esp* of the womb, devised by George *Papanicolaou* (1883–1962), US anatomist (*abbrev* **Pap smear test** or **Pap test**).

papaprelatist /pā-pə-prel'ə-tist/ (*Walter Scott*) *n* a supporter of popish prelates.

paparazzo /pa-pə-rat'sō/ *n* (*pl* **paparazz'i** /-sē/) a photographer who specializes in spying on or harassing famous people in order to obtain photographs of them in unguarded moments, etc. [Ital, from the surname of a photographer in the film *La Dolce Vita* (1960) by Federico Fellini]

Papaver /pə-pā'vər/ *n* the poppy genus, giving name to the family **Papaverā'ceae**. [L *papāver* the poppy]
■ **papaveraceous** /pə-pav- or -pāv-ə-rā'shəs/ *adj* of the poppy family. **papaverine** /pə-pav'ə-rēn, -rīn or -pāv'/ *n* an alkaloid derived from poppy juice and used medicinally. **papaverous** /-pav'* or *-pāv'/ *adj* resembling or having the qualities of the poppy.

papaw¹ see **papaya**.

papaw² see **pawpaw**¹.

papaya /pə-pī'yə/ *n* the tree *Carica papaya*, or its large green-skinned edible fruit, native to S America but common in the tropics, the trunk, leaves, and fruit yielding papain, the leaves providing a powerful anthelmintic, an anti-worm preparation (also called **papaw**). [Sp *papayo* (tree), *papaya* (fruit) appar from Carib]

pape /pāp/ *n* a Scots form of **pope**¹.
■ **pāp'ish** *adj* popish. ◆ *n* (*dialect* and *non-standard*, by confusion with **papist**) a papist. **pāp'isher** *n*.

paper /pā'pər/ *n* a material made in thin sheets as an aqueous deposit from linen rags, esparto, wood pulp, or other form of cellulose, used for writing on, printing on, wrapping, and other purposes; extended to other materials of similar purpose or appearance, eg to papyrus, rice-paper, to the substance of which some wasps build their nests, to cardboard, and even to tinfoil ('silver paper'); a piece of paper; a written or printed document or instrument, note, receipt, bill, bond, deed, etc; (in *pl*) documents, *esp* for the purpose of personal identification, customs or passport controls, etc; a newspaper; an essay or literary contribution, *esp* one read before a society or submitted for a degree examination; a set of examination questions; free passes of admission to a theatre, etc, also the people so admitted; paper money; stocks and shares (*stock exchange sl*); wallpaper; a wrapping of paper; a quantity of anything wrapped in or attached to a paper. ◆ *adj* consisting or made of paper; papery; on paper. ◆ *vt* to cover with paper; to fold in paper; to treat in any way by means of any type of paper, eg to sandpaper, etc; to paste endpapers and fly-leaves to. [Anglo-Fr *papir*, OFr (Fr) *papier*, from L *papyrus*, from Gr *papȳros* papyrus]
■ **pa'perer** *n*. **pa'pering** *n* the operation of covering with paper; the paper so used. **pa'perless** *adj* using *esp* electronic means instead of paper for communication, recording, etc. **pa'pery** *adj* like paper.
❑ **pa'perback** *n* a book with a flexible paper cover (also *adj*). ◆ *vt* to publish in paperback form. **pa'perbark** *n* an Australian myrtaceous tree (*Melaleuca leucodendron*) with papery bark, the source of cajuput. **pa'per-birch'** *n* an American birch with papery bark. **pa'perboard** *n* a type of strong, thick cardboard; pasteboard. **pa'perbound** *n* a paperback (also *adj*). **pa'perboy** or **pa'pergirl** *n* a boy or girl who delivers newspapers. **pa'per-case** *n* a box for writing materials, etc. **paper chase** *n* the game of hare and hounds, in which some runners (*hares*) set off across country strewing paper by which others (*hounds*) track them; an investigation or process involving examination of many documents. **pa'per-cigar'** *n* (*obs*) a cigarette. **paper clip** *n* a clip of bent wire or the like, for holding papers together; a letter-clip. **pa'per-cloth** *n* a fabric prepared in the Pacific islands from the inner bark of the paper mulberry. **pa'per-coal** *n* a lignite that splits into thin layers. **pa'per-cred'it** *n* credit given to a person on the strength of their providing proof of being owed money by a third party. **pa'per-cutter** *n* a paperknife; a guillotine; a machine for cutting paper in sheets, for trimming the edges of books, etc. **pa'per-day** *n* (*law*) one of certain days in each term for hearing cases down in the paper or roll of business. **pa'per-enam'el** *n* an enamel for

cards and fine note-paper. **paper engineering** *n* the technique of making pop-up books, etc. **pa'per-faced** *adj* (*Shakesp*) having a thin face like a sheet of paper; faced with paper. **paper fastener** *n* a button with two blades that can be forced through papers and bent back to hold the sheets together. **pa'per-feeder** *n* an apparatus for delivering sheets of paper to a printing press, etc. **pa'per-file** *n* an appliance for filing papers. **pa'per-folder** *n* a folder (2nd sense). **pa'per-gauge** *n* a rule for measuring the typeface of matter to be printed, and the width of the margin. **pa'perhanger** *n* a professional hanger of wallpaper; a person who makes or deals in forged cheques (*US sl*). **pa'perhangings** *n pl* paper for covering walls. **pa'perknife** *n* a thin, flat blade for cutting open the leaves of books, other folded papers, or used as a letter-opener. **paper-mâch'é** *n* papier-mâché. **pa'per-maker** *n* a manufacturer of paper. **pa'per-making** *n*. **pa'per-mar'bler** *n* someone engaged in marbling paper. **paper mill** *n* a mill where paper is made. **paper money** *n* banknotes, pieces of paper stamped or marked by government or by a bank, as representing a certain value of money, which pass from hand to hand instead of the coin itself. **paper mulberry** *n* a tree (*Broussonetia papyrifera*) of E Asia and Polynesia, of the mulberry family, whose inner bark yields tapa cloth and paper-making material. **pa'per-mus'lin** *n* a glazed muslin. **paper nautilus** *n* the argonaut (see under **nautilus**). **pa'per-off'ice** *n* an office where state papers are kept. **paper profits** *n pl* the appreciation in value of a bond, share, etc. **pa'per-pulp** *n* pulpy material for making paper. **pa'per-push'er** *n* (*derog sl*) a clerk, *esp* in a humble or humdrum position. **pa'per-reed** *n* the papyrus. **paper round** or (*N Am*) **paper route** *n* (the job of making) a regular series of newspaper deliveries. **pa'per-rul'er** *n* a person who, or an instrument which, makes straight lines on paper. **pa'per-sail'or** *n* an argonaut. **pa'per-stain'er** *n* a person who prepares paperhangings; a poor author, scribbler (*derog inf*). **paper tape** *n* (*comput*) a paper data-recording tape, which records information by means of punched holes. **paper tape punch** *n* a machine that perforates paper tape. **paper tape reader** *n* a device that senses and translates the holes punched in a paper tape into machine-processable form. **pa'per-thin** *adj* very thin; flimsy. **paper tiger** *n* a person or organization that appears to be powerful but is in fact not. **paper trail** *n* a sequence of documents that can be followed, eg in a criminal investigation. **pa'perware** *n* items made of paper, eg books, manuals, packaging, etc. **pa'per-wash'ing** *n* (*photog*) water in which prints have been washed. **paper wasp** *n* a large wasp (*Polistes*) that builds a papery nest from wood pulp. **pa'perweight** *n* a small often decorative weight for keeping loose papers from being displaced. **pa'perwork** *n* clerical work; the keeping of records as part of a job; documents.

■ **on paper** planned, decreed, existing, etc in theory only; apparently, judging by statistics, but perhaps not in fact. **paper over** (**the cracks in**) to create the impression that there is or has been no dissent, error, or fault in (something doubtful). **paper the house** to fill a theatre by issuing free passes.

papeterie /*pap-ə-trē'*/ *n* a stationery-case. [Fr, stationery, paper-trade]

Paphian /*pā'fi-ən*/ *adj* relating to *Paphos* in Cyprus, sacred to Aphrodite; lascivious. ◆ *n* a native of Paphos; a votary of Aphrodite; a whore.

Papiamento /*pap-i-ə-men'tō*/ *n* a creole language derived from Spanish, spoken in the Dutch Antilles. [Sp *papia* talk]

papier collé /*pä-pyä kol-ā'*/ *n* scraps of paper and odds and ends pasted out in (*usu* abstract) artistic composition. [Fr, glued paper]

papier-mâché /*pap-yā-ma'shā* or (Fr) *pa-pyā-ma-shā'*/ *n* a material consisting of paper-pulp or of sheets of paper pasted together, often treated so as to resemble varnished or lacquered wood or plaster. ◆ *adj* of papier-mâché. [Would-be French, from Fr *papier* (see **paper**) and *mâché* chewed, from L *masticātus*]

Papilio /*pə-pil'i-ō*/ *n* the swallowtailed butterfly genus, giving name to the family **Papilionidae** /*-on'i-dē*/, in which all six legs are fully developed in both sexes; (without *cap*; *pl* **papil'ios**) a butterfly of this genus. [L *pāpiliō, -ōnis* butterfly]

■ **papiliona'ceous** *adj* of butterflies; butterfly-like; of a form of corolla somewhat butterfly-like, with a large posterior petal (*vexillum*), two side petals or wings (*alae*), and two anterior petals forming a keel (*carina*); of the **Papiliona'ceae**, a family of Leguminosae characterized by such a corolla, including pea, bean, clover, gorse, laburnum, etc.

papilla /*pə-pil'ə*/ *n* (*pl* **papill'ae** /*-ē*/) a small nipple-like protuberance; a minute elevation on the skin, *esp* of the fingertips and upper surface of the tongue, in which a nerve ends; a protuberance at the base of a hair, feather, tooth, etc; a minute conical protuberance on the surface of a petal. [L, dimin of *papula*]

■ **papill'ar** or **papill'ary** *adj* like, of the nature of, or having, papillae. **papill'ate**, **papillated** or **papillif'erous** /*pap-*/ *adj* having papillae. **papill'iform** *adj* in the form of a papilla. **papilli'tis** *n* inflammation of the head of the optic nerve. **papillo'ma** *n* a tumour formed by

hypertrophy of a papilla or papillae, such as a wart, etc. **papillōm'atous** *adj*. **pap'illōse** *adj* full of papillae, warty (also **papill'ous**). **papill'ūlate** *adj* finely papillose. **papill'ūle** *n* a very small papilla.

❑ **papillō'mavirus** *n* any of a genus of viruses that cause papillomas.

papillon /*pap-ē-yɔ̃'*/ *n* (a dog of) a breed of toy spaniel with erect ears. [Fr, butterfly]

papillose, **papillous** see under **papilla**.

papillote /*pap'il-ōt*, also *pap-ē-yot'*/ *n* a curlpaper for the hair; frilled paper used to decorate the bones of chops, etc (*cookery*); oiled or greased paper in which meat is cooked and served (*cookery*). [Fr, appar from *papillon* butterfly, from L *pāpiliō, -ōnis*]

papillule, etc see under **papilla**.

papish, **papisher** see under **pape**.

papist /*pā'pist*/ *n* a follower or advocate of the Pope; a Roman Catholic (*derog*). ◆ *adj* being a follower or advocate of the Pope; Roman Catholic (*derog*). [LL *pāpa* pope]

■ **pā'pism** *n* (often *derog*) popery. **pāpist'ic** or **papist'ical** *adj* relating to popery, or to the Church of Rome, its doctrines, etc. **pāpist'ically** *adv*. **pā'pistry** *n* popery.

papoose /*pə-poos'*/ *n* a Native American baby or young child; a pouch for carrying an infant on one's back (also **pappoose'**). [Narraganset *papoos*]

papovavirus /*pə-pō'və-vī-rəs*/ *n* any of a group of DNA-containing oncogenic viruses. [Composite coinage, and **virus**]

pappadom same as **poppadum**.

pappardelle /*pap-ər-del'i*/ *n* pasta in the form of long, thick ribbons. [Ital, from *pappare* to eat greedily]

pappus /*pap'əs*/ *n* a ring or parachute of fine hair or down, representing the calyx limb, which grows above the seed and helps in wind-dissemination in composites and some other plants (*bot*); the downy beginnings of a beard. [L *pappus*, from Gr *pappos* a grandfather, down, a pappus]

■ **papp'ōse** (or /*-ōs'*/) or **papp'ous** *adj*.

pappy[1] /*pap'i*/ (*US inf*) *n* father. [**papa**]

pappy[2] see under **pap**[1].

paprika /*pap'ri-kə* or *pa-prē'kə*/ *n* (a hot spice derived from) Hungarian red pepper, a species of *Capsicum*; a reddish-orange colour like that of the spice. [Hung]

Pap smear, **Pap test** see **Papanicolaou smear**.

Papuan /*pap'ū-ən*/ or **Papua New Guinean** /*pap'ū-ə nū gin'i-ən*/ *adj* of or relating to the island group of *Papua New Guinea* in the SW Pacific, or its inhabitants. ◆ *n* a native or inhabitant of Papua New Guinea; a group of languages spoken in Papua New Guinea and nearby islands. [Malay *papuwa* frizzled, referring to the hair of the inhabitants]

papula /*pap'ū-lə*/ or **papule** /*pap'ūl*/ *n* (*pl* **pap'ūlae** /*-lē*/ or **pap'ules**) a pimple; a papilla. [L *papula* a pimple]

■ **pap'ūlar** *adj*. **papūlā'tion** *n* the development of papules. **papūlif'erous** *adj*. **pap'ūlose** or **pap'ūlous** *adj*.

papyrus /*pə-pī'rəs*/ *n* (*pl* **papy'ri** /*-rī*/) the paper-reed (*Cyperus papyrus*, or related species), a tall plant of the sedge family, once common in Egypt; its pith cut in thin strips and pressed together as a writing material of ancient times; a manuscript on papyrus. [L *papȳrus*, from Gr *papȳros* ; prob Egyp]

■ **papyraceous** /*pap-i-rā'shəs*/ *adj* like paper, papery. **papyrologist** /*pap-i-rol'ə-jist*/ *n*. **papyrol'ogy** *n* the study of ancient papyri.

par[1] /*pär*/ *n* a state of equality; equal value; a norm or standard; the state or value of bills, shares, etc, when they sell at exactly the price marked on them, ie without *premium* or *discount*; equality of condition; the number of strokes that should be taken for a hole or a round by good play, two putts being allowed on each green (*golf*); a score of this number of strokes (also *vi* and *vt*). [L *pār* equal]

❑ **par contest** *n* (*bridge*) a competition in which points are awarded for the bidding of a prepared hand and for the playing of the hand in a directed contract. **par value** *n* value at par.

■ **above par** at a premium, or at more than the nominal value. **at par** at exactly the nominal value. **below par** at a discount, or at less than the nominal value; out of sorts, not particularly good in health, spirits, etc. **nominal par** the value with which a bill or share is marked, or by which it is known. **no par value** with no stated nominal value. **on a par with** equal to. **par for the course** a normal, average result or (*inf* ; *fig*) occurrence, state of affairs, etc. **par of exchange** the value of currency of one country expressed in that of another.

par[2] /*pär*/ *n* same as **parr**.

par[3] /*pär*/ or **para** /*par'ə*/ *n* informal short forms of **paragraph**.

par. *abbrev* : paragraph; parallel; parish.

Pará /*pä-rä'*/ *n* a city, state, and estuary of Brazil.

❑ **pará grass** *n* piassava. **pará nut** *n* Brazil nut. **pará rubber** *n* rubber produced from the tree *Hevea brasiliensis*.

para[1] /pär'ə/ *n* a small Turkish coin; $\frac{1}{40}$ of a piastre; $\frac{1}{100}$ of a Yugoslav dinar. [Turk *pārah*]

para[2] /par'ə/ *n* an informal short form of **paratrooper**.

para[3] see **par**[3].

para-[1] /par-ə-/ *pfx* denoting: beside; faulty; disordered; abnormal; false; a polymer of; a compound related to; closely resembling, or parallel to, as in *paramedic, paramilitary*; (in organic chemistry) having substituted atoms or groups attached to two opposite carbon atoms of the benzene ring, commonly represented by *p-*. [Gr *para* beside]
■ **paramed'ic** and **paramed'ical** *n* and *adj* (a person) helping doctors or supplementing medical work (see also under **para-**[2]).

para-[2] /par-ə-/ *combining form* denoting parachute.
■ **par'abrake** *n* a parachute used to help brake an aircraft when it has landed. **par'adoctor** *n* a doctor who parachutes to patients in remote areas. **par'adrop** *n* an airdrop (also *vt*). **par'afoil** *n* a form of steerable parachute, consisting of air-filled nylon cells. **par'aglider** *n* a glider with inflatable wings. **par'agliding** *n* the sport of drifting through the air to the ground while wearing a modified type of parachute, after having been towed into the air by, or jumping from, a plane. **par'akiting** *n* the sport of soaring suspended from a parachute which is being towed. **par'amedic** or **paramed'ico** *n* (*pl* **par'amedics** or **paramed'icos**) a paradoctor (see also under **para-**[1]). **par'amedic** or **paramed'ical** *adj*. **par'asailing** *n* a sport similar to paragliding, the participant wearing water-skis and a modified type of parachute, and being towed into the air by a motorboat. **par'ascending** *n* a sport similar to paragliding, the participant being towed into the wind behind a motor vehicle.

para-aminobenzoic acid /par-ə-a-mē'nō-ben-zō'ik as'id/ *n* a compound, $C_6H_4(NH_2)COOH$, found in most plants, but *esp* in yeast, and also in the liver, used in the production of dyes and pharmaceuticals.

para-aminosalicylic acid /par-ə-a-mē'nō-sal-i-sil'ik as'id/ *n* a drug formerly used along with streptomycin in the treatment of tuberculosis (*abbrev* **PAS**).

parabaptism /par-ə-bap'ti-zm/ *n* uncanonical baptism. [**para-**[1] and **baptism** (see under **baptize**)]

parabasis /pə-rab'ə-sis/ *n* (in classical Greek comedy) a speech in which the chorus comes forward and addresses the audience. [Gr, a going aside, from *para-* beside, beyond, and *basis* a going]

parabema /par-ə-bē'mə/ *n* (*pl* **parabe'mata**) (in Byzantine architecture) either the chapel of the prothesis or the diaconicon, when walled off from the bema. [Gr *para* beside, beyond, and *bēma* a step]
■ **parabemat'ic** *adj*.

paraben /par'ə-ben/ *n* any of several chemicals, used as preservatives, that are esters of **para-hydroxybenzoic acid** ($C_7H_6O_3$).

parabiosis /par-ə-bī-ō'sis/ *n* the physical union of two embryos or organisms, resulting in a functional connection, such as is the case with conjoined twins. [Gr *para* beside, and *biōsis* manner of life]
■ **parabio'tic** *adj*.
❑ **parabiotic twins** *n pl* conjoined twins.

parable /par'ə-bl/ *n* a comparison or similitude; a fable or story told to illustrate some doctrine or moral point; any such story told by Jesus Christ; a proverb (*archaic*); discourse (*archaic*). ◆ *vt* to represent by a parable. [Gr *parabolē* a placing alongside, comparison, parabola, etc, from *para* beside, beyond, and *ballein* to throw]

parabola /pə-rab'ə-lə/ *n* (*pl* **parab'olas**) a curve, one of the conic sections, the intersection of a cone and a plane parallel to its side, or the locus of a point equidistant from a fixed point (the *focus*) and a fixed straight line (the *directrix*), and having the equation with vertex as origin $y^2=4ax$; generalized to include any curve whose equation is $y^n=px^m$. [Ety as for **parable**]
■ **parab'ole** /-lē/ *n* (*rhetoric*) a comparison, simile, or metaphor. **parabol'ic** /par-ə-bol'ik/ or **parabol'ical** *adj* of or like a parable or a parabola or a parabole; expressed by a parable; belonging to, or of the form of, a parabola. **parabol'ically** *adv*. **parab'olist** *n*. **parab'olize** or **-ise** *vt* to set forth by parable; to treat as a parable; to shape like a parabola or paraboloid. **parab'oloid** *n* a surface or solid generated by the rotation of a parabola about its axis. **parab'oloid** or **paraboloid'al** *adj*.
❑ **parabolic geometry** *n* Euclidean geometry. **parabolic velocity** *n* (*astron*) the velocity which a body at a given point would require to describe a parabola about the centre of attraction.

parabolanus /par-ə-bō-lā'nəs/ *n* (in the early Eastern Church) a layman who tended the sick. [Gr *parabolos* venturesome, exposing oneself]

parabrake see under **para-**[2].

Paracelsian /par-ə-sel'si-ən/ *adj* of or relating to the famous German Swiss philosopher and physician, *Paracelsus* (1493–1541), or resembling his theories or practice. The name was coined for himself by Theophrastus Bombastus von Hohenheim, and apparently implied a claim to be greater than Celsus.

paracentesis /par-ə-sen-tē'sis/ (*surg*) *n* tapping of a body cavity to remove fluid or gas, etc. [Gr *parakentēsis*, from *para* beside, beyond, and *kenteein* to pierce]

paraceratherium /par-ə-ser-ə-thē'ri-əm/ *n* a gigantic Tertiary fossil rhinoceros of the genus *Paraceratherium* (also **Baluchitherium**, **indricotherium**). [Gr *thērion* a beast]

paracetamol /pa-rə-sē'tə-mol/ or *-set'ə-/ *n* a mild analgesic and antipyretic drug, often recommended instead of aspirin. [Gr *para* beside, beyond, and *acet*yl*amin*ophen*ol*]

parachronism /par-ak'rə-ni-zm/ *n* an error in dating, *esp* when anything is represented as later than it really was. [Gr *para* beside, beyond, and *chronos* time]

parachute /par'ə-shoot/ *n* a large fabric umbrella-like canopy, used where resistance to air is needed, *esp* one strapped to a person jumping from an aircraft, to give a slow descent, also one unfolded at the rear of an aircraft on landing, to assist braking (informal short form **chute**); any structure serving a similar purpose, such as a pappus or a patagium. ◆ *vi* to descend by parachute (also *fig*). ◆ *vt* to take and drop by parachute (also *fig*). [Fr *parachute*, from Ital *para*, imperative of *parare* to ward, from L *parāre* to prepare, and Fr *chute* fall]
■ **par'achutist** *n*.
❑ **parachute payment** *n* (*football*) a sum of money paid by the Premier League to a relegated team to compensate for the expected fall in income in the following season. **parachute troops** *n pl*.

paraclete /par'ə-klēt/ *n* an advocate or intercessor on behalf of another, *usu* applied (with *cap*) to the Holy Ghost (Bible, John 14.26). [Gr *paraklētos*, from *parakaleein* to call in, also to comfort, from *para* beside, beyond, and *kaleein* to call]

paracme /pər-ak'mē/ *n* the stage of decline or senescence after the culmination of development. [Gr *para* beside, beyond, and *akmē* a point]

paracrostic /par-ə-kros'tik/ *n* a poem whose initial letters reproduce its first verse. [**para-**[1] and **acrostic**]

paracusis /par-ə-kū'sis/ *n* disordered hearing. [Gr *para* beside, beyond, and *akousis* hearing]

paracyanogen /par-ə-sī-an'ə-jən/ *n* a polymer of cyanogen. [**para-**[1] and **cyanogen**]

parade /pə-rād'/ *n* show; display; ostentation; an assembling in order for exercise, inspection, etc; an area in which troops, etc assemble for this purpose; a procession; a public promenade; a row (of shops or houses); a parry (*fencing*). ◆ *vt* to show off; to thrust to the attention of others; to lead about and expose to public attention; to traverse (a square, etc) in parade; to marshal in military order for inspection, etc. ◆ *vi* to march up and down (as if) for show; to pass; to march, or drive, etc in procession or military order; to show off. [Fr, from Sp *parada*, from *parar* to halt, from L *parāre*, *-ātum* to prepare]
■ **parād'er** *n*.
❑ **parade ground** *n* a square, etc, for the parading of troops.

paradiddle /par'ə-did-l/ *n* a drum roll in which the principal beats are struck by the left and right sticks in succession. [Imit]

paradigm /par'ə-dīm/ *n* an example, exemplar; a set of the inflected forms of a word (*grammar*); a basic theory, a conceptual framework within which scientific theories are constructed. [Fr *paradigme*, from Gr *paradeigma*, from *paradeiknynai* to exhibit side by side, from *para* beside, beyond, and *deiknynai* to show]
■ **paradigmatic** /-dig-mat'ik/ or **paradigmat'ical** *adj* of, or in the form of, a paradigm. **paradigmat'ically** *adv*.
❑ **paradigm shift** *n* a radical change in one's way of thinking.

paradise /par'ə-dīs/ *n* the garden of Eden; heaven; the place (intermediate or final) where the blessed dead go; any place or state of bliss; a park or pleasure-ground *esp* in ancient Persia; a park in which foreign animals were kept; a parvis; a small private apartment (*archaic*). [Gr *paradeisos* a park, from OPers *pairidaēza* park]
■ **paradisaic** /par-ə-dis-ā'ik/, **paradisa'ical** *adj*, **paradisal** /-dī'səl/, **paradisean** /-dis'i-ən/, **paradisiac** /-dis'i-ak or -diz'i-ak/, **paradisiacal** /-dis'i'ə-kl/, **paradisic** /-dis'* or -diz'/, **paradisian** /-dis'* or -diz'/ or **paradisic** /-dis'* or -diz'/ *adj*.
❑ **paradise fish** *n* a Chinese freshwater fish (genus *Macropodus*), often kept for its beautiful colouring. **paradise flycatcher** *n* a tropical flycatcher (*Tersiphone*) with bright plumage and a long tail.
■ **bird of paradise** see under **bird**. **fool's paradise** see under **fool**[1].

paradoctor see under **para-**[2].

parador /par'ə-dör/ *n* (*pl* **paradores** /-dör'ās/) any of several types of (*usu* country) dwellings, eg castles, convents, etc converted for use as tourist accommodation in Spain. [Sp]

parados /par'ə-dos/ n earthworks protecting against a rear attack. [Fr, from L parāre to prepare, and dorsum back]

paradox /par'ə-doks/ n something which is contrary to received, conventional opinion; something which is apparently absurd but is or may be really true; a self-contradictory statement; the state of being any of these. [Gr paradoxos, -on contrary to opinion, from para beside, beyond, and doxa opinion]
■ **paradox'al** adj. **par'adoxer** n. **paradox'ical** adj. **paradox'ically** adv. **paradox'icalness** n. **Paradox'ides** /-i-dēz/ n a typically Middle Cambrian genus of trilobites, some very large (about two feet (60cm) long). **paradoxid'ian** adj. **par'adoxist** n. **paradoxol'ogy** n the utterance or maintaining of paradoxes. **par'adoxy** n the quality of being paradoxical.
□ **paradoxical sleep** n REM sleep.

paradoxure /par-ə-dok'sūr/ n a civet-like carnivore of S Asia and Malaysia, the palm cat of India. [Gr paradoxos paradoxical, from para beside, beyond, and ourā tail]
■ **paradoxū'rine** adj.

paradrop see under **para-²**.

paraenesis or **parenesis** /par-ēn'i-sis or -en'/ n exhortation. [Gr parainesis, from para, beside, beyond, and aineein to commend]
■ **paraenetic** /-net'ik/ or **paraenet'ical** adj.

paraesthesia or (US) **paresthesia** /par-ēs-thē'si-ə or -es-/ (med) n abnormal sensation in any part of the body. [Gr para beyond, and aisthēsis sensation]

paraffin /par'ə-fin/ n (also **par'affine**) orig paraffin wax, so named by its German discoverer, Karl von Reichenbach (1788–1869), from its having little chemical affinity for other bodies; generalized to mean any saturated hydrocarbon of the alkane series, gaseous, liquid, or solid, the general formula being C_nH_{2n+2} (now more commonly **alkane**); paraffin oil. ◆ vt to treat with paraffin. [L parum little, and affīnis having affinity]
■ **paraffin'ic**, **par'affinoid** or **par'affiny** adj.
□ **paraffin oil** n any of the mineral-burning oils associated with the manufacture of paraffin, mixtures of liquid paraffin and other hydrocarbons. **par'affin-scale'** n unrefined solid paraffin. **paraffin test** n a test using paraffin to detect trace elements left on the skin of someone who has been in contact with explosives, etc. **paraffin wax** n a white transparent crystalline substance consisting of a mixture of solid paraffins, produced by distillation of shale, coal, tar, wood, etc.
■ **liquid paraffin** a liquid form of petroleum jelly, used as a mild laxative.

paraffle or **parafle** /pə-rä'fl/ (Scot) n a pretentious display; a fuss. [Cf **paraph**]

parafoil see under **para-²**.

parage /par'ij/ n lineage (obs); high birth or rank; equality of birth or status, a state in which no homage or service is due (feudal law). [Fr]

paragenesis /par-ə-jen'i-sis/ or **paragenesia** /par-ə-jin-ē'zi-ə/ (geol) n the order in which minerals have developed in a given mass of rock; the development of minerals in such close contact that they become a joined mass. [**para-¹** and **genesis**]
■ **paragenet'ic** adj.

paraglider, **paragliding** see under **para-²**.

paraglossa /par-ə-glos'ə/ n (pl **paragloss'ae** /-ē/) either of two appendages of the ligula in insects. [Gr para beside, beyond, and glōssa tongue]
■ **paragloss'al** adj. **paragloss'ate** adj.

paragnathous /pər-ag'nə-thəs/ adj having equal mandibles. [Gr para beside, beyond, and gnathos jaw]
■ **parag'nathism** n.

paragnosis /pa-rəg-nō'sis/ (psychol) n knowledge of matters not susceptible to investigation by traditional scientific methods. [Gr para beside, beyond, and gnōsis knowing]

paragoge /par-ə-gō'jē or -gē/ or **paragogue** /par'ə-gog/ n an addition to the end of a word, such as t in against, amidst, amongst, whilst, or d in drownd (mistakenly for drown). [Gr paragōgē a leading part, addition, from para beside, beyond, and agein to lead]
■ **paragogic** /-goj'ik/ or **paragog'ical** adj.
□ **paragogic future** n the cohortative tense in Hebrew, a lengthened form of the imperfect or future, usu confined to the first person, giving the sense of 'let me' or 'let us'.

paragon /par'ə-gon or -gən/ n a model of perfection or supreme excellence; a match or equal (archaic); a mate (Spenser); a rival (archaic); (a) comparison (Spenser); emulation, competition (Spenser); a diamond of 100 carats or more; a black marble (obs); a camlet used in upholstery and dressmaking (obs); 20-point printing-type intermediate between great-primer and double-pica. ◆ vt (archaic or rare) to compare; to match; to surpass (Shakesp); to hold up as a paragon (Shakesp). [OFr paragon, from Ital paragone touchstone; origin obscure]

paragonite /par'ə-gən-īt or pər-ag'/ n a soda-mica, once mistaken for talc. [Gr paragōn misleading, from para beside, beyond, and agein to lead]

paragram /par'ə-gram/ n a play on words in which (esp initial) letters are changed. [Gr (skōmmata) para gramma (jokes) by letter]
■ **paragramm'atist** n a punster.

paragraph /par'ə-gräf/ n a distinct part of a discourse or writing marked by a sign (**paragraph mark**) or now usu by indenting or extra space between lines; a short passage, or a collection of sentences, with unity of content or purpose; a musical passage forming a unit; a short separate item of news or comment in a newspaper; a sign (in ancient manuscripts a short horizontal line, in the Middle Ages ¶, now ⁊ or z) marking off a paragraph. ◆ vt to form into paragraphs; to write or publish paragraphs about. [Gr paragraphos written alongside, from para beside, beyond, and graphein to write]
■ **par'agrapher** or **par'agraphist** n a person who writes paragraphs, news items esp for newspapers. **paragraphic** /-graf'/ or **paragraph'ical** adj. **paragraph'ically** adv.

paragraphia /par-ə-graf'i-ə/ n the writing of different words and letters to the ones intended, owing to disease or injury of the brain. [Gr para beside, beyond, and graphein to write]
■ **paragraphic** /-graf'ik/ adj.

Paraguayan /par-ə-gwī'ən or -gwā'/ n a native or inhabitant of Paraguay in S America. ◆ adj of or relating to Paraguay.
□ **Paraguay tea** n maté.

paraheliotropic /par-ə-hē-li-ō-trop'ik/ (bot) adj turning edgewise to the light. [Gr para beside, beyond, and hēlios the sun, with tropos a turn, from trepein to turn]
■ **paraheliotropism** /-ot'rə-pizm/ n.

parainfluenza virus /par-ə-in-floo-en'zə vī'rəs/ n any of a number of viruses causing influenza-like symptoms, esp in children.

parakeet or **parrakeet** /par'ə-kēt/ n a small long-tailed parrot of various kinds (also **paroquet**, **parroquet** /-ket/, or **paraquito** /pa-ra-kē'tō/ (pl **paraqui'tos**). [Sp periquito, Ital parrocchetto, or OFr paroquet (Fr perroquet); the origin and relations of these have not been determined]

parakiting see under **para-²**.

paralalia /par-ə-la' or -lā'li-ə/ n a form of speech disturbance, particularly that in which a different sound or syllable is produced from the one intended. [Gr para beside, beyond, and lalia speech]

paralanguage /par-ə-lang'gwij/ n elements of communication other than words, ie tone of voice, gesture, facial expression, etc. [**para-¹** and **language**]
■ **paralinguist'ic** adj. **paralinguist'ics** n sing the study of paralanguage.

paraldehyde /par-al'di-hīd/ n a polymer, $C_6H_{12}O_3$, of acetaldehyde (acetic aldehyde), a liquid with a characteristic smell, used to induce sleep. [**para-¹** and **aldehyde**]

paralegal /par-ə-lē'gl/ adj and n (of, concerning or being) a person who assists a professional lawyer. [**para-¹** and **legal**]

paraleipsis /par-ə-līp'sis/ or **paralipsis** /-lip'sis/ n (pl **paraleip'ses** or **paralip'ses**) a rhetorical figure by which one fixes attention on a subject by pretending to neglect it, as in 'I will not speak of his generosity', etc. [Gr paraleipsis, paraleipomenon (neuter pr participle passive), from paraleipein to leave aside, from para beside, beyond, and leipein to leave]
■ **paraleipom'enon** or **paralipom'enon** n (pl **paraleipom'ena** or **paralipom'ena** (esp in the Septuagint, etc) the Books of Chronicles) a thing left out, added in supplement.

paralexia /par-ə-lek'si-ə/ n a defect in the power of seeing and interpreting written language, with meaningless transposition of words and syllables. [Gr para beside, beyond, and lexis a word]

paralinguistic, **paralinguistics** see under **paralanguage**.

paralipsis, etc see **paraleipsis**.

parallax /par'ə-laks/ n an apparent change in the position of an object caused by change of position in the observer; (in astronomy) the apparent change (measured angularly) in the position of a heavenly body when viewed from different points, called the **daily** or **diurnal** or **geocentric parallax** when viewed from opposite points on the earth's surface, and the **annual** or **heliocentric parallax** when viewed from opposite points of the earth's orbit. [Gr parallaxis, from para beside, beyond, and allassein to change, from allos another]
■ **parallac'tic** or **parallac'tical** adj.
□ **parallactic motion** see **proper motion** under **proper**.

parallel /par'ə-lel/ adj (of lines, etc) extended in the same direction and equidistant in all parts; analogous, corresponding; alongside in time; exactly contemporary; (of an electrical circuit) arranged so that the current is split between parallel paths; having a constant interval (major and minor being reckoned alike; music); transferring more than one bit at a time (*comput*). ◆*adv* alongside and at an unvarying distance. ◆*n* a parallel line; a line of latitude; an analogue, or like, or equal; an analogy; a tracing or statement of resemblances; a besieger's trench parallel to the outline of the place besieged; a printer's reference mark of two vertical lines; parallel arrangement. ◆*vt* (**par'alleling**; **par'alleled**) to place so as to be parallel; to conform; to represent as parallel; to liken in detail; to find a parallel to; to match; to be or run parallel to. ◆*vi* to be or run parallel. [Gr *parallēlos*, as if *par' allēloin* beside each other]

■ **par'alleling** *n* a commercial practice whereby companies buy highly priced goods (eg perfume) in markets where prices are relatively low and sell them on in markets where prices are higher. **par'allelism** *n* the state or fact of being parallel; resemblance in corresponding details; a balanced construction of a verse or sentence, where one part repeats the form or meaning of the other; comparison; development along parallel lines; the theory or belief (in full **psychophysical parallelism**) that mind and matter do not interact but correspond. **par'allelist** *n* a person who draws a parallel or comparison; a believer in psychophysical parallelism. **parallelis'tic** *adj*. **par'allelize** or **-ise** *vt* to provide a parallel to. **par'allelly** *adv*. **par'allelwise** *adv*.
□ **parallel bars** *n pl* a pair of fixed bars used in gymnastics. **parallel cousin** *n* a first cousin. **parallel imports** *n pl* imports brought into a country through other than official channels, thus circumventing regulations, etc. **parallel importer** *n*. **parallel importing** *n*. **parallel motion** *n* a name given to any linkage by which circular motion may be changed into straight-line motion. **parallel port** *n* (*comput*) a connection point through which data may be sent and received using two or more wires simultaneously. **parallel processing** *n* (*comput*) the processing of several items of information at the same time using two or more processors. **parallel ruler** or **rulers** *n* rulers joined by two pivoted strips, for drawing parallel lines. **parallel slalom** *n* a slalom race in which two competitors ski down parallel courses. **parallel turn** *n* a skiing turn made by shifting the body while keeping the skis parallel. **par'allel-veined** *adj* (*bot*) having the main veins running side by side.
■ **in parallel** (of electrical apparatus) arranged in such a way that terminals of like polarity are connected together; (of electrical circuits) connected in such a way that any current flowing divides between them (cf **in series**); simultaneously (*fig*).

parallelepiped /par-ə-lel-ep'i-ped/ (or *-lel'-* or *-ə-pī'*)/ *n* a solid figure bounded by six parallelograms, opposite pairs being identical and parallel (also **parallelepip'edon** (*pl* **parallelepipeda**) and improperly **parallelopī'ped** or **parallelopī'pedon**. [Gr *parallēlepipedon*, from *parallēlos* and *epipedon* a plane surface, from *epi* on, and *pedon* ground]

parallelogram /par-ə-lel'ō-gram/ *n* a plane four-sided figure whose opposite sides are parallel. [Gr *parallēlogrammon*, from *grammē* a line]

■ **parallelogrammat'ic**, **parallelogrammat'ical**, **parallelogramm'ic** or **parallelogramm'ical** *adj*.
■ **parallelogram of forces** a figure in which the direction and amount of two component forces are represented by two sides of a parallelogram, those of their resultant by the diagonal.

paralogia /par-ə-loj'i-ə/ *n* impairment of reasoning power characterized by difficulty in expressing logical ideas in speech. [Gr *paralogismos*, from *para* beside, beyond, and *logismos*, from *logos* reason]

■ **paral'ogism** *n* false reasoning (also **paral'ogy**). **paral'ogize** or **-ise** *vi* to reason falsely.

paralogue /par'ə-log/ *n* a gene that has a similar DNA configuration to another gene in the same organism owing to the duplication of a common ancestral gene (cf **orthologue** under **ortho-**). [**parallel** and **homologue** (see under **homo-**)]

■ **paral'ogous** *adj*.

paralympics /pa-rə-lim'piks/ *n pl* a series of sporting events for people with physical and learning disabilities, running *parallel* to the traditional Olympic games.

■ **paralym'pian** *n* a competitor in paralympics. **paralymp'ic** *adj*.

paralysis /pə-ral'i-sis/ *n* a loss of power of motion, or sensation, in any part of the body, palsy; deprivation of the power of action. [Gr *paralysis* secret undoing, paralysis, from *lyein* to loosen]

■ **paralyse** or (*N Am*) **-yze** /par'ə-līz/ *vt* to afflict with paralysis; to deprive of the power of action; to bring to a standstill. **par'alyser** or (*N Am*) **par'alyzer** *n*. **paralytic** /par-ə-lit'ik/ *adj* of or relating to paralysis; afflicted with or inclined to paralysis; helplessly drunk (*inf*). ◆*n* someone who is affected with paralysis.
□ **paralysis agitans** /aj'i-tanz/ *n* Parkinson's disease. **paralysis time** *n* (*nuclear eng*) the time for which a radiation detector is rendered inoperative by an electronic switch in the control circuit.

paramagnetic /par-ə-mag-net'ik/ *adj* magnetic in the ordinary sense (said of bodies that when freely suspended between the poles of a

magnet place themselves parallel to the lines of force), *opp* to *diamagnetic*. [**para-**[1] and **magnetic** (see under **magnet**)]

■ **paramag'netism** *n*.

paramastoid /par-ə-mas'toid/ *adj* situated near the mastoid, paroccipital. ◆*n* a paramastoid process or projecting part. [**para-**[1] and **mastoid**]

paramatta or **parramatta** /par-ə-mat'ə/ *n* a fabric like that made from merino wool, made of worsted and cotton. [Appar from *Parramatta* in New South Wales]

Paramecium /par-ə-mē'si-əm or *-mē'shi-əm*/ *n* a genus of tiny animals including the slipper animalcule, a slipper-shaped infusorian; (without *cap*; *pl* **paramē'cia**) an animal of the genus. [Gr *paramēkēs* long-shaped, from *para* alongside, and *mēkos* length]

paramedic and **paramedical** see under **para-**[1] and **para-**[2].

paramenstruum /par-ə-men'strū-əm/ *n* the four days before and the four days after the onset of menstruation. [**para-**[1] and **menstruum**]

parament /par'ə-mənt/ (*obs*) *n* a rich decoration, hanging, or robe. [L *parāre* to prepare]

paramese /pa-ram'i-sē/ (*Gr music*) *n* the string or tone next above the mese. [Gr *paramesē*]

parameter /pə-ram'i-tər/ *n* a line or quantity which serves to determine a point, line, figure or quantity in a class of such things (*maths*); a constant quantity in the equation of a curve; in conic sections, a third proportional to any diameter and its conjugate diameter; the latus rectum of a parabola; the intercept upon an axis of a crystal face chosen for purpose of reference (the **parametral plane**); a quantity to which an arbitrary value may be given as a convenience in expressing performance or for use in calculations (*elec*); a variable; a variable which is given a series of arbitrary values in order that a family of curves of two other related variables may be drawn; any constant in learning or growth curves that differs with differing conditions (*psychol*); a boundary or limit to the scope of something. [Gr *para* beside, beyond, and *metron* measure]

■ **param'etral** or **parametric** /par-ə-met'rik/ or **paramet'rical** *adj*.
□ **parametric equalizer** *n* a device for boosting or cutting the frequency of audio signals.

paramilitary /pa-rə-mil'ə-t(ə)ri/ *adj* on military lines and intended to supplement the strictly military; organized as a military force, *esp* when engaged in active rebellion against the government, an occupying force, etc. ◆*n* a member of a paramilitary force. [**para-**[1] and **military**]

paramnesia /par-am-nē'zh(y)ə/ *n* a memory disorder in which words are remembered but not their proper meaning; the condition of believing that one remembers events and circumstances which have not previously occurred. [Gr *para* beside, beyond, and the root of *mimnēskein* to remind]

paramo /par'ə-mō/ *n* (*pl* **pa'ramos**) a bare windswept elevated plain in S America. [Sp *páramo*]

paramorph /par'ə-mörf/ (*mineralogy*) *n* a pseudomorph formed by a change in molecular structure without change of chemical composition. [Gr *para* beside, beyond, and *morphē* form]

■ **paramorph'ic** *adj*. **paramorph'ism** *n*.

paramount /par'ə-mownt/ *adj* superior to all others; supreme, *opp* to *paravail*. ◆*n* a paramount chief; a superior. [OFr *paramont*, *par* (L *per*) *à mont* (L *ad montem*); see **amount**]

■ **par'amouncy** or **par'amountcy** *n*. **par'amountly** *adv*.
□ **paramount chief** *n* a supreme chief.

paramour /par'ə-moor/ *n* a lover of either sex, formerly in an innocent, now *usu* in the illicit, sense. ◆*adv* (*obs*) by the way of love, as a lover, for love's sake, out of kindness. [Fr *par amour* by or with love, from L *per amōrem*]

paramyxovirus /par-ə-mik'sō-vī-rəs/ *n* any of a group of single-stranded ribonucleic acid viruses which includes the mumps and measles viruses. [**para-**[1] and **myxovirus**]

Paraná pine /pa-ra-nä' pīn/ *n* the tree *Araucaria brasiliana*, native to S Brazil; its wood. [*Paraná*, a river and state in Brazil]

paranephros /par-ə-nef'ros/ *n* the suprarenal gland, near the kidney. [Gr *para* beside, beyond, and *nephros* kidney]

■ **paraneph'ric** *adj*.

paranete /par-a-nē'tē/ (*Gr music*) *n* the string or tone next below the nete. [Gr *paranētē*]

parang /pär'ang/ *n* a heavy Malay knife. [Malay]

paranitroaniline /par-ə-nī-trō-an'i-lēn/ *n* a nitro-derivative of aniline, used in dyeing. [**para-**[1] and **nitroaniline** (see under **nitro-**)]

paranoia /par-ə-noi'ə/ or (*rare*) **paranoea** /-nē'ə/ *n* a form of mental disorder characterized by constant delusions, *esp* of grandeur, pride, persecution; intense (*esp* irrational) fear or suspicion. [Gr *paranoia*, from *para* beside, beyond, and *noos* mind]

■ **paranoi'ac** /-ak/ adj of, suffering from, paranoia. ◆ n a victim of paranoia (also **paranoe'ic** or **paranoic** /-no'ik/). **par'anoid** adj (also **paranoid'al**) affected by paranoia. ◆ n a person affected by paranoia.

paranormal /par-ə-nör'məl/ adj abnormal, esp psychologically; not explicable by the laws of nature or reason. ◆ n that which is paranormal; (with the) paranormal occurrences or phenomena. [**para-¹** and **normal**]

paranthelion /par-an-thē'li-on/ n (pl **paranthe'lia**) a diffuse whitish image of the sun, having the same altitude, at an angular distance of 90° to 140°. [Gr para beside, beyond, anti against, and hēlios the sun]

paranthropus /par-an'thrə-pəs/ n an extinct hominid ape usu included in the species Australopithecus robustus. [**para-¹** and Gr anthrōpos man]

paranymph /par'ə-nimf/ (ancient hist; Milton) n a friend who went with the bridegroom to fetch the bride, a groomsman or bridesmaid; someone who countenances and supports another. [Gr paranymphos, from para beside, beyond, and nymphē a bride]

paraparesis /pa-rə-pə-rē'sis/ (med) n weakness of muscles, esp in the legs, partial paralysis. [**para-¹** and **paresis**]
■ **paraparet'ic** adj.

parapenting /par'ə-pen-ting or -pãt-ing/ n a cross between hang-gliding and parachuting, a sport in which the participant jumps from a high place wearing a modified type of parachute, which is then used as a hang-glider. [**para-²** and Fr pent slope]

parapet /par'ə-pit or -pet/ n a bank or wall to protect soldiers from the fire of an enemy in front; a low wall along the side of a bridge, edge of a roof, etc. [Ital parapetto, from pfx para- (see **parachute**) and Ital petto, from L pectus the breast]
■ **par'apeted** adj having a parapet.

paraph /par'af/ n a mark or flourish under one's signature. ◆ vt to append a paraph to; to sign with initials. [Fr paraphe ; cf **paragraph**]

paraphasia /par-ə-fā'zhyə or -zi-ə/ n a form of aphasia in which one word is substituted for another. [**para-¹** and **aphasia**]
■ **paraphasic** /-fā'zik or -sik/ adj.

paraphernalia /par-ə-fər-nāl'yə or -i-ə/ n (usu sing) ornaments of dress of any kind; trappings; equipment; miscellaneous accessories; (as pl) formerly, property other than dower that remained under a married woman's own control, esp articles of jewellery, dress and personal belongings. [Late L paraphernālia (pl), from parapherna, from Gr para beside, beyond, and phernē a dowry, from pherein to bring]

paraphilia /par-ə-fil'i-ə/ n sexual perversion. [**para-¹** and Gr philia fondness, liking for]
■ **paraphiliac** /-fil'i-ak/ n a person who indulges in abnormal sexual practices (also adj).

paraphimosis /par-ə-fī-mō'sis/ n strangulation of the glans penis by constriction of the prepuce. [**para-¹** and **phimosis**]

paraphonia /par-ə-fō'ni-ə/ n (in Byzantine music) a melodic progression by fourths and fifths; a morbid change of voice; an alteration of the voice, as at puberty. [Gr para beside, beyond, and phōnē voice]
■ **paraphonic** /-fon'ik/ adj.

paraphrase /par'ə-frāz/ n (an) expression of the same thing in other words; an exercise in such expression; a verse rendering of a biblical passage for church singing, esp in the Church of Scotland. ◆ vt to express in other words. ◆ vi to make a paraphrase. [Gr paraphrasis, from para beside, beyond, and phrasis a speaking, from phrazein to speak]
■ **par'aphraser** or **par'aphrast** /-frast/ n a person who paraphrases. **paraphrast'ic** or **paraphrast'ical** adj. **paraphrast'ically** adv.

paraphraxia /par-ə-frak'si-ə/ or **paraphraxis** /-frak'sis/ n inability to perform purposive movements properly. [**para-¹** and Gr phraxis barricade]

paraphrenia /par-ə-frē'ni-ə/ n any mental disorder of the paranoid type. [**para-¹** and Gr phrēn mind]

paraphysis /pə-raf'i-sis/ n (pl **paraphyses** /-sēz/) a sterile filament among spore-bearing structures in lower plants. [Gr, a side-growth, from para beside, beyond, and physis growth]

parapineal /par-ə-pin'i-əl/ adj beside the pineal gland, usu applied to the pineal eye. [**para-¹** and **pineal**]

paraplegia /par-ə-plē'jyə or -plē'jə/ n paralysis of the lower part of the body. [Ionic Gr paraplēgiē a stroke on the side, from para beside, beyond, and plēgē a blow]
■ **paraplegic** /-plēj'ik or -plej'ik/ adj and n (a person) suffering from paraplegia.

parapodium /par-ə-pō'di-əm/ n (pl **parapō'dia**) one of the jointless lateral appendages of polychaete worms, etc; a swimming organ in some molluscs, a lateral expansion of the foot. [Gr para beside, beyond, and pous, podos a foot]
■ **parapō'dial** adj.

parapophysis /par-ə-pof'i-sis/ n (pl **parapoph'yses** /-sēz/) a ventral transverse process of a vertebra. [**para-¹** and **apophysis**]
■ **parapophysial** /par-ap-ō-fiz'i-əl/ adj.

parapsychism /par-ə-sī'ki-zm/ n panpsychistic parallelism. [**para-¹** and **psychism** (see under **psycho-**)]
■ **parapsy'chic** or **parapsy'chical** adj. **parapsycholog'ical** adj. **parapsycholog'ically** adv. **parapsychol'ogist** n. **parapsychol'ogy** n psychical research; the study of phenomena such as telepathy and clairvoyance which seem to suggest that the mind can gain knowledge by means other than the normal perceptual processes. **parapsychō'sis** n an abnormal psychosis.

paraquadrate /par-ə-kwod'rāt/ (anat) n the squamosal. [**para-¹** and **quadrate**]

Paraquat® /par'ə-kwot/ n a weedkiller very poisonous to human beings. [**para-¹** and quaternary, part of its formula]

paraquito /par-ə-kē'tō/ see **parakeet**.

para-red /par'ə-red'/ n an azo dye for cottons, derived from paranitroaniline. [**para-¹**]

pararhyme /par'ə-rīm/ n a form of rhyme in which the consonants, but not the vowel, of the last stressed syllable are identical in sound, as in sun and sin. [**para-¹** and **rhyme**]

pararosaniline /par-ə-roz-an'i-lēn/ n a base entering into various dyestuffs, such as magenta. [**para-¹** and **rosaniline**]

pararthria /par-är'thri-ə/ n disordered articulation of speech. [Gr para beside, beyond, and arthron a joint]

parasailing see under **para-²**.

parasang /par'ə-sang/ n an old Persian measure of length, reckoned at 30 stadia, or between 3 and 4 miles. [Gr parasangēs, from OPers (Mod Pers farsang)]

parascending see under **para-²**.

parascenium /par-ə-sē'ni-əm/ n (pl **parascē'nia**) (in the Greek theatre) a wing, side-scene. [Gr paraskēnion, from para beside, beyond, and skēnē tent, stage]

parasceve /par'ə-sēv or par-ə-sē'vē/ n preparation (obs); the eve of the Jewish Sabbath, Friday, the day of preparation (archaic); Good Friday (RC church). [LL parascēvē, from Gr paraskeuē preparation, from para beside, beyond, and skeuē equipment]

parascience /par'ə-sī-əns/ n the study of phenomena which cannot be investigated by rigorous traditional scientific method. [**para-¹** and **science**]

paraselene /par-ə-se-lē'nē/ n (pl **paraselē'nae** /-nē/) a mock moon, a bright patch on a lunar halo. [Gr para beside, beyond, and selēnē moon]

parasite /par'ə-sīt/ n an organism that lives in or on another living organism and derives subsistence from it without rendering it any service in return; in literary but not scientific use extended to an epiphyte; a hanger-on or sycophant; a person who lives at the expense of society or of others and contributes nothing. [Gr parasītos, from para beside, and sītos corn, bread, food]
■ **parasitaemia** /-ē'mi-ə/ n (Gr haima blood) the presence of parasites in the blood. **parasitic** /-sit'ik/ or **parasit'ical** adj of, of the nature of, caused by or like a parasite. **parasit'ically** adv. **parasit'icalness** n. **parasiticide** /-sit'i-sīd/ n that which destroys parasites. **par'asitism** /-sīt-izm/ n the act or practice of being a parasite. **par'asitize** or **-ise** vt to be a parasite on (another organism); to infect or infest with parasites. **par'asitoid** /-sīt-/ adj parasitic in one phase of the life history, thereafter independent (also n). **parasītol'ogist** n. **parasītol'ogy** n. **parasītō'sis** n infestation with parasites.

parasol /par'ə-sol or -sol'/ n a sunshade, rather similar to an umbrella; an aeroplane with its wings overhead. [Fr, from Ital parasole, from para, imperative of parare to ward, from L parāre to prepare, and sole, from L sōl, sōlis the sun]
❑ **parasol mushroom** n a tall white edible mushroom (Lepiota procera) resembling a parasol.

parasomnia /par-ə-som'ni-ə/ n any abnormal behaviour that occurs during sleep. [**para-¹** and **insomnia**]

parasphenoid /par-ə-sfē'noid/ adj alongside the sphenoid bone. ◆ n a bone of the skull, part of the cranial floor. [**para¹** and **sphenoid** (see under **sphene**)]

parastatal /par-ə-stā'tl/ adj indirectly controlled by the state. [**para-¹** and **statal** (see under **state**)]

parastichy /pər-as'ti-ki/ (bot) n a secondary helix joining leaf-bases on an axis, visible where the leaves are crowded together, eg the scales of a pine cone. [Gr para beside, beyond, and stichos a row]

parasuicide /par-ə-sū'i-sīd or -soo'/ n a deliberate harmful act against one's own person (such as taking an overdose of drugs) which appears to be an attempt at suicide but which was probably not intended to be successful; a person who performs such an act. [**para-¹** and **suicide**]

parasympathetic /par-ə-sim-pə-thet'ik/ see **sympathetic nervous system** under **sympathy**.

parasynthesis /par-ə-sin'thi-sis/ n derivation of words from compounds, eg *come-at-able*, where *come* and *at* are first compounded and then the derivative suffix *-able* added. [Gr]
■ **parasynthetic** /-thet'ik/ adj. **parasyn'theton** n (pl **parasyn'theta**) a word so formed.

parataxis /par-ə-tak'sis/ (grammar) n the arrangement of clauses or propositions without connectives. [Gr, from *para* beside, beyond, and *taxis* arrangement]
■ **paratac'tic** or **paratac'tical** adj. **paratac'tically** adv.

paratha /pə-rä'tə or -tä/ n a flat round cake of unleavened bread, traditionally eaten as an accompaniment to Indian food. [Hindi]

parathesis /pə-rath'i-sis/ n apposition (grammar); the compounding of words without change, as (L) *rēspūblica* from *rēs* and *pūblica* (philology). [Gr, placing alongside]

parathion /par-ə-thē'on/ n an insecticide containing phosphorus and sulphur, used chiefly in agriculture. [**para-**[1] and **thio-**]

parathyroid /par-ə-thī'roid/ (anat) adj beside the thyroid. ◆ n any of a number of small ductless glands apparently concerned with calcium metabolism. [**para-**[1] and **thyroid**]
❑ **parathyroid hormone** n a hormone secreted by a parathyroid gland that acts to raise the level of calcium in the blood (also **parathor'mone**).

paratonic /par-ə-ton'ik/ (bot) adj induced by external stimulus. [Gr *para* beside, beyond, and *tonos* a stretching]

paratroops /par'ə-troops/ n pl troops carried by air, to be dropped by parachute. [**para-**[2] and **troop**]
■ **par'atrooper** n.

paratyphoid /par-ə-tī'foid/ n a disease (of various types) resembling typhoid (also adj). [**para-**[1]]

paravail /par-ə-vāl'/ adj inferior; lowest (said of a feudal tenant); of least account, opp to *paramount*. [OFr *par aval* below, from L *per* through, *ad* to, and *vallem*, accusative of *vallis* valley]

paravane /par'ə-vān/ n a fish-shaped device with fins or vanes, sometimes called an 'otter', towed from the bow of a vessel to deflect mines along a wire and sever their moorings; an explosive device of similar design for attacking submerged submarines. [**para-**[1] and **vane**]

paravant or **paravaunt** /par-ə-vänt' or -vönt'/ (Spenser) adv in front, first, beforehand, pre-eminently. [OFr *paravant*, from *par* through, and *avant* before, from L *ab* from, and *ante* before]

par avion see under **avion**.

parawalker /par'ə-wö-kər/ n a metal structure like an external skeleton worn by a paraplegic to enable him or her to walk. [**para-**[1] and **walker** (see under **walk**[1])]

Parazoa /par-ə-zō'ə/ n pl a division of the animal kingdom, the sponges, co-ordinate with Protozoa and Metazoa (also without cap). [Gr *para* beside, beyond, and *zōion* animal]
■ **parazō'an** n and adj. **parazō'on** n (pl **parazō'a**) any member of the group Parazoa.

parboil /pär'boil/ vt orig to boil thoroughly; (now by confusion) to part-cook by boiling. [OFr *parbouillir*, from LL *perbullīre* to boil thoroughly; infl by confusion with **part**]

parbreak /pär'brāk/ (archaic) n an instance of vomiting. ◆ vt and vi /pär' or -brāk'/ (pap **parbreaked**) to vomit. [ME *brake* to vomit; cf Du *braken*; the prefix may be Fr *par-*]

parbuckle /pär'buk-l/ n a purchase made by making fast a rope in the middle and passing the ends under and then over a heavy object, eg a barrel, to be rolled up or down a sloping surface; a sling made by passing both ends of a rope through its bight. ◆ vt to hoist or lower by a parbuckle. [Earlier *parbunkel*, *parbuncle*; origin unknown]

Parca /pär'kə/ n (pl **Par'cae** /-sē/) any one of the Roman goddesses Nona, Decuma, and Morta, identified with the Greek Fates or Moirai. [L, prob connected with *parere* to produce, not *parcere* to spare]

parcel /pär'sl/ n a package, esp one wrapped in paper and tied with string; a continuous stretch of land; a little part; a portion; a quantity; a group; a set; a pack (derog); a lot; an item (archaic); a sum of money lost or won (inf). ◆ adv (archaic) partly. ◆ adj (archaic) in part. ◆ vt (par'celling; par'celled) to divide into portions (esp with *out*); to make up into parcels or a parcel (esp with *up*); possibly, to make up into a total, complete, round off, or to add up or detail, item by item (Shakesp, Antony and Cleopatra V.2); to cover with tarred canvas (naut). [Fr *parcelle* (Ital *particella*), from L *particula*, dimin of *pars*, *partis* a part]
■ **par'celwise** adv by parcels, piecemeal.
❑ **par'cel-bawd** n (Shakesp) someone partly a bawd. **parcel bomb** n a bomb wrapped in a parcel and designed to detonate when unwrapped. **par'cel-gilt'** adj partially gilded. **parcel post** n (also

formerly **parcels post**) a postal service for parcels. **parcel shelf** n a shelf behind the back seat of a motor vehicle.

parcener /pär'sən-ər/ n a coheir. [Anglo-Fr *parcener*, from LL *partōnārius*, from *pars* part]
■ **par'cenary** /-ə-ri/ n coheirship.

parch /pärch/ vt to make hot and very dry; to roast slightly; to scorch. ◆ vi to be scorched; to become very dry. [Origin unknown]
■ **parched** adj very dry; very thirsty (inf). **parch'edly** adv. **parch'edness** (or /pärcht'/) n.

Parcheesi® /pär-chē'zi/ n a board game adapted from pachisi (also **parche'si**).

parchment /pärch'mənt/ n the skin of a sheep, goat, or other animal prepared for writing on, etc; a piece of this material; a manuscript written on it; a thick, esp yellowish, fine-quality writing paper resembling it; a parchment-like membrane or skin. ◆ adj of parchment. [Fr *parchemin*, from L *pergamēna* (charta) Pergamene (paper), from Gr *Pergamos* Bergama, in Asia Minor]
■ **parch'mentize** or **-ise** vt to make like parchment, esp by treating with sulphuric acid. **parch'menty** adj like parchment.
❑ **parchment bark** n pittosporum. **parchment paper** n unsized paper made tough and transparent by dipping in sulphuric acid (also **vegetable parchment**).
■ **virgin parchment** a fine kind of parchment made from the skins of new-born lambs or kids.

parcimony an archaic spelling of **parsimony**.

parclose /pär'klōz/ n a screen or railing in a church enclosing an altar or temple, or separating a chapel or other portion from the main body of the church. [OFr *pap* (fem) of *parclore*, from L *per* through, and *claudere*, *clausum* to close]

pard[1] /pärd/ and **pardner** /pärd'nər/ (US) n slang forms of **partner**.

pard[2] /pärd/ n the leopard. [L *pardus* (masc), *pardalis* (fem), from Gr *pardos*, *pardalis*; prob of Eastern origin]
■ **pard'al** /-əl/, **pard'ale** /-ə or -āl/ (Spenser) or **pard'alis** n a leopard; a small leopard once supposed a different species. **pard'ed** adj spotted. **pard'ine** /-īn/ n.

pardi, **pardie**, **pardy** see **perdie**.

pardon /pär'dən/ vt to forgive; to allow to go unpunished; to excuse; to tolerate; to grant in remission, refrain from exacting or taking; to grant remission of sentence to (even if the condemned has been found innocent). ◆ vi to forgive; to grant pardon. ◆ n forgiveness, either of an offender or of his or her offence; remission of a penalty or punishment; forbearance; a warrant declaring that a pardon has been granted; a papal indulgence; a festival at which indulgences are granted (obs). [Fr *pardonner*, from LL *perdōnāre*, from L *per* through, away, and *dōnāre* to give]
■ **par'donable** adj that may be pardoned; excusable. **par'donableness** n. **par'donably** adv. **par'doner** n a person who pardons; a licensed seller of papal indulgences (hist). **par'doning** n and adj. **par'donless** adj unpardonable.
■ **I beg your pardon?** or **pardon?** what did you say? **pardon me** excuse me, used in apology and to soften a contradiction.

pare /pār/ vt to cut or shave off the outer surface or edge of; to trim; to remove by slicing or shaving; to diminish by small amounts (often with *down*). [Fr *parer*, from L *parāre* to prepare]
■ **par'er** n. **par'ing** n the act of trimming or cutting off; a piece which is pared off; the cutting off of the surface of grassland for cultivation.
❑ **paring chisel** n a long, thin chisel with bevelled edges.

parecious see **paroicous**.

paregoric /par-i-gor'ik/ adj soothing, lessening pain. ◆ n a medicine that soothes pain, esp an alcoholic solution of opium, benzoic acid, camphor, and oil of anise. [Gr *parēgorikos*, from *parēgoreein* to exhort, comfort, from *para* beside, beyond, and *agorā* marketplace]

pareira /pə-rā'rə/ n orig a tropical menispermaceous climbing plant (*Cissampelos pareira*) with many medicinal properties, native to India and the East Indies; its root (now called **false pareira**); a S American plant (*Chondrodendron tomentosum*) of the same family (also called **pareira brava** /brä'və/, ie wild), a source of curare; a tonic diuretic drug derived from the root of the latter. [Port *parreira* wallclimber]
■ **white pareira** (*Abuta rufescens*) another S American plant of the same family.

parella /pə-rel'ə/ n (also **parelle**) a crustaceous lichen (*Lecanora parella*) yielding archil; extended to others of similar use. [Fr *parelle*]

parencephalon /par-en-sef'ə-lon/ (anat) n a cerebral hemisphere. [Gr *para* beside, beyond, and *enkephalon* brain]

parenchyma /pə-reng'ki-mə/ n the ordinary soft thin-walled tissue of plants, not differentiated into conducting or mechanical tissue; soft spongy indeterminate tissue in animals. [Gr *para* beside, beyond, and *enchyma* infusion, inpouring]
■ **parenchym'atous** adj.

---

parenesis see **paraenesis**.

parent /pā'rənt/ n someone who begets or brings forth offspring; a father or a mother; a person who or thing which produces; that from which anything springs or branches; an author; a cause; (as a Gallicism) a relative. ◆ adj (of an organization, etc) which has established a branch or branches over which it usu retains some control. ◆ vt and vi to be or act as a parent (to). [Fr parent kinsman, from L parēns, -entis, old prp of parere to bring forth]
■ **pā'rentage** n descent from parents; extraction; rank or character derived from one's parents or ancestors; the relation of parents to their children; the state or fact of being a parent; parents collectively, or perh parent (Spenser). **parental** /pə-rent'əl/ adj. **parent'ally** adv. **pā'renthood** n the state of being a parent; the duty or feelings of a parent. **pā'renting** n the upbringing of and care for a child. **pā'rentless** adj without a parent.
❑ **parental leave** n a period of unpaid leave which may be taken by new parents of either sex in order to look after their child or make arrangements for its welfare. **parent company** n a company that holds the majority of the shares of another company or other companies. **pa'rentcraft** n the techniques of looking after babies and young children.

parenteral /pə- or pa-ren'tə-rəl/ adj not intestinal; (said of the administration of a drug) not by way of the alimentary tract. [Gr para beside, and **enteral**]
■ **paren'terally** adv.

parenthesis /pə-ren'thi-sis/ n (pl **paren'theses** /-sēz/) a word or passage of comment or explanation inserted in a sentence which is grammatically complete without it; a figure of speech consisting of the use of such insertion; a digression; an interval, space or interlude; (usu in pl) a round bracket () used to mark off a parenthesis. [Gr, from para beside, beyond, en in, and thesis a placing]
■ **parenth'esize** or **-ise** vt and vi. **parenthetic** /par-ən-thet'ik/ or **parenthet'ical** adj of the nature of a parenthesis; using or overusing parenthesis. **parenthet'ically** adv.

pareo see **pareu**.

Pareoean /par-ē-ē'ən/ adj of a race inhabiting S China, Myanmar (Burma), etc, otherwise called Southern Mongoloid (also n). [Gr para beside, and ēōs dawn]

parergon /par-ûr'gon/ n (pl **parer'ga**) a by-work, any work subsidiary to a person's principal employment. [Gr, from para beside, beyond, and ergon work]

paresis /par'i-sis/ or /pə-rē-sis/ (med) n a partial form of paralysis causing diminished activity of muscles but not diminishing sensation. [Gr, from parienai to relax]
■ **paretic** /-et'ik/ adj.
■ **general paresis** the manifestation of a syphilitic infection of long standing, consisting of progressive dementia and generalized paralysis.

paresthesia see **paraesthesia**.

pareu /pa-rā'ŭ/ or **pareo** /pa-rā'ō/ n a wraparound skirt worn by men and women in Polynesia. [Tahitian]

par excellence /pär ek-se-lãs' or ek'sə-ləns/ (Fr) adv as an example of excellence. ◆ adj superior to all others of the same sort. [Fr, literally, by excellence]

parfait /pär-fe' or -fã/ n a kind of frozen dessert containing whipped cream, fruit and eggs. [Fr, literally, perfect]

parfleche /pär-flesh'/ n a dried skin, usu of buffalo; an article made of it. [Can Fr]

pargana or **pergunnah** /pər-gun'ə or -ä/ n a division of an administrative district or zillah in India. [Hindi and Pers parganah]

pargasite /pär'gə-sīt/ n a green amphibole. [Pargas in Finland]

parget /pär'jit/ vt (**par'geting** or **par'getting**; **par'geted** or **par'getted**) to plaster over; to cover with ornamental plasterwork; to decorate the surface of; to bedaub. ◆ n plaster spread over a surface; cow-dung plaster for chimney flues; ornamental work in plaster; surface decoration. [Appar OFr parjeter to throw all over]
■ **parge** vt to plaster. **par'geter** or **par'getter** n. **par'geting** or **par'getting** n.
❑ **parge'-work** n.

parhelion /pär-hē'li-ən/ n (pl **parhē'lia**) a bright spot on the parhelic circle, the result of diffraction caused by the crystals in the atmosphere. [Irreg, from Gr parēlion, from para beside, beyond, and hēlios sun]
■ **parhelic** /-hē'lik or -he'lik/ or **parheliacal** /-hē-lī'ə-kl/ adj.
❑ **parhelic circle** n a band of luminosity parallel to the horizon, the result of diffraction caused by ice crystals in the atmosphere.

parhypate /pär-hip'ə-tē/ (Gr music) n the lowest note but one in a tetrachord, next above the hypate. [Gr para beside, beyond; see **hypate**]

pariah /pə-rī'ə, par'i-ə or pär'/ n a social outcast; a member of a caste in S India lower than the four Brahminical castes; a person of low or no caste; a pye-dog. [Tamil paraiyar]

parial see **pair-royal** under **pair¹**.

Parian /pā'ri-ən/ adj of the island of Paros in the Aegean Sea. ◆ n a native or inhabitant of Paros; a fine porcelain-like marble.
❑ **Parian marble** n a fine white marble found in Paros.

parietal /pə-rī'i-tl/ (anat) adj of a wall or walls; of, attached to, or having connection with the side, or the inside of the wall of a cavity, esp a plant ovary; relating to or near the parietal bone; residing, or relating to residence, within the walls of a college (US). ◆ n either of the two bones (**parietal bones**) which form part of the sides and top of the skull, between the frontal and the occipital. [L parietālis, from pariēs, parietis a wall]
❑ **parietal cells** n pl cells in the stomach lining that produce hydrochloric acid. **parietal lobe** n either of the divisions of the brain below the top of the skull.

pari-mutuel /par-ē-mü-tü-el'/ (Fr) n a totalizator, a betting-machine which automatically pools stakes and distributes winnings; the tote, a system of betting in which the winners receive a proportion of the total money staked, less the management charge. [Fr, literally, mutual bet]

pari passu /pä'rī pas'ū or par'ē pas'oo/ (L) with equal pace; together.

paripinnate /par-i-pin'it or -āt/ (bot) adj pinnate without a terminal leaflet. [L pār equal]

Paris /par'is/ adj of or originating in Paris, the capital of France.
■ **Parisian** /pə-riz'i-ən/ adj of or relating to Paris. ◆ n (also fem **Parisienne** /pə-riz-i-en' or -zyen/) a native or resident of Paris.
❑ **Paris doll** n (obs) a small figure dressed in the latest fashions, sent out by Paris modistes. **Paris green** n copper arsenite and acetate, a pigment and insecticide.

parischan, parischane see **parochin**.

parish /par'ish/ n a district having its own church, and its own minister or priest of the Established Church; a district assigned by a church to a minister or priest; a division of a county for administrative and local government purposes (not now in Scotland); (in Louisiana) a county; the people of a parish; a congregation or a denomination (US). ◆ adj belonging or relating to a parish; employed or supported by the parish; for the use of the parish. [Anglo-Fr paroche (Fr paroisse), from L parochia, from Gr paroikiā an ecclesiastical district, from para beside, and oikos a dwelling; altered by confusion with Gr parochos a purveyor]
■ **par'ishen** n see **parochin**. **parishioner** /pə-rish'ə-nər/ n a person who belongs to or is connected with a parish; a member of a parish church.
❑ **parish church** n the church of the establishment for a parish. **parish clerk** n the clerk or recording officer of a parish; the person who leads the responses in the service of the Church of England. **parish council** n a body elected to manage the affairs of a parish. **parish councillor** n. **parish minister** or **priest** n the minister or priest who has charge of a parish. **parish pump** n the symbol of petty local interests; parochialism. **par'ish-pump** adj. **parish register** n a book in which the baptisms, marriages, and burials in a parish are recorded. **parish top** n a spinning-top formerly kept for the amusement of the parish.
■ **on the parish** (hist) in receipt of poor relief, ie food, shelter, etc provided by the parish.

parison /par'i-sən/ n a lump of glass before it is moulded into its final shape. [Fr paraison, from parer to prepare, from L parāre]

parisyllabic /par-i-si-lab'ik/ adj (of a noun or verb) having the same number of syllables in (almost) all inflected forms. [L pār equal]

paritor /par'i-tər/ (Shakesp) n aphetic for **apparitor**.

parity¹ /par'i-ti/ n equality in status, esp in pay; parallelism; equivalence; a standard equivalence in currency; equality of price or value in different markets (commerce); (of two or more numbers) the property of being (both or all) odd or even (maths). [Fr parité, from L paritās, from pār equal]
❑ **parity check** n (comput) the addition of a redundant bit to a word to make the total number of 1's even or odd in order to detect simple bit errors. **parity law** n a law that a symmetry obtains in the natural world with no distinction between right and left, long held as basic, but shown in 1957 not to apply in the field of nuclear physics.

parity² /par'i-ti/ n the condition or fact of having borne children. [L parere to bring forth]

park /pärk/ n a piece of land in a town for public recreation; an enclosed piece of land in which animals are kept for hunting purposes; a tract of land surrounding a mansion, kept as a pleasure-ground, constituting a private estate; hence (with cap) often part of the name of a house, street, or district; (an area containing) a group of buildings housing related enterprises, eg a *science park*; a football, etc pitch (*inf*); a sports stadium (*N Am*); a piece of country kept in its natural condition as a nature-reserve or for public recreation; a paddock, grass field (*Scot*); a field (*Irish*); a level valley among mountains (*US*); a place occupied by artillery, wagons, etc (*milit*); a piece of ground where motor-cars or other vehicles may be left untended; an enclosed basin for oyster-culture; (in a vehicle with automatic transmission) a transmission setting in which movement is prevented. ◆ *vt* to place and leave (a vehicle) in a parking place or elsewhere; to deposit and leave, put (*inf*); to enclose in a park; to make a park of; to bring (eg artillery) together in a body; to register (securities) under some other name in order to hide their true ownership (*stock exchange sl*). ◆ *vi* to leave a vehicle in a car park, parking place, or elsewhere. [OFr *parc*, of Gmc origin; cf OE *pearruc*, *pearroc*]

■ **park′er** *n* a park-keeper (*obs*); a person who parks a vehicle. **park′ie** *n* an informal form of **park-keeper**. **park′ing** *n* the action of the verb park; a turf strip, sometimes with trees, along the middle of a street (*US*). **park′ish** *adj*. **park′like** *adj*. **park′ly** *adj*. **park′ward** or **park′wards** *adv*.
□ **park-and-ride′** *adj* (of a transport system) designed to encourage the maximum use of public transport within a city, etc by providing bus and train links from large car parks on the outskirts (also *n*). **parking lot** *n* (*N Am*) a car park. **parking meter** *n* a coin-operated meter that charges for motor-car parking-time. **parking place** *n* a place where one may temporarily stop and leave a vehicle. **parking ticket** *n* a notice of a fine, or summons to appear in court, for a parking offence. **park′-keeper** *n* a person employed to patrol a public park, keep order, etc. **park′land** or **park′lands** *n* parklike grassland dotted with trees. **park′-off′icer** *n* a park-keeper. **park′way** *n* a broad road adorned with turf and trees, often connecting the parks of a town.

parka /*pär′kə*/ *n orig* a fur shirt or coat with a hood, now a similar outer garment made of a windproof material (also **parkee** or **parki** /*pärk′ē*/). [Aleutian word]

parkie see under **park**.

parkin /*pär′kin*/ or **perkin** /*pûr′kin*/ (*Scot and N Eng*) *n* a biscuit or gingerbread made with oatmeal and treacle. [Ety unknown]

Parkinson's disease /*pär′kin-sənz diz-ēz′*/ *n* (also **Par′kinsonism**) shaking palsy, a disease characterized by rigidity of muscles, tremor of hands, etc, studied by James *Parkinson* (1755–1824).

Parkinson's law /*pär′kin-sənz lö*/ (*facetious*) *n* any one of the laws propounded by C Northcote *Parkinson* (1909–93), *esp* the law that in officialdom work expands so as to fill the time available for its completion.

parkish see under **park**.

parkleaves /*pärk′lēvz*/ *n* a woodland shrub with yellow flowers, once considered a panacea; tutsan. [Appar **park** and **leaf**]

Parkour /*pär-koor′*/ *n* same as **free running** (see under **free**). [Fr, from *parcours* route, itinerary]

parky /*pär′ki*/ (*inf*) *adj* chilly. [Origin unknown]

Parl. *abbrev* : Parliament; Parliamentary.

parlance /*pär′ləns*/ *n* a manner of speaking; an idiom; speaking (*archaic*); conversation (*archaic*). [OFr, from *parler* to speak; cf **parle**]

parlando /*pär-län′dō*/ (*music*) *adj* and *adv* in declamatory style; recitative. [Ital, speaking; cf **parle**]

parlay /*pär′lā*/ *vt* to bet (the original stake plus winnings), or lay out (an original investment plus earnings), in a later venture; to succeed in converting (an asset) into something more valuable; to exploit (a talent, characteristic, etc) to achieve personal success or fame. ◆ *n* a bet made with the stake and winnings from an earlier successful bet. [Fr *paroli*; from Neapolitan]

parle /*pärl*/ (*archaic*) *vi* to talk; to confer; to parley. ◆ *n* talk; speech; parleying. [Fr *parler* to speak, LL *parlāre*, from *parabolare*, from Gr *parabolē* a parable, a word]

parley[1] /*pär′li*/ *vi* to speak with another; to confer; to hold discussions with an enemy. ◆ *n* talk; a conference with an enemy; a conference. [OFr *parlee*, fem pap of *parler* to speak; cf **parle**]
■ **parleyvoo′** *n* (Fr *parlez-vous*? do you speak?; *sl*) French; a Frenchman. ◆ *vi* to speak French.

parley[2] see **parliament**.

parliament /*pär′lə-mənt*/ *n* an assemblage of the political representatives of a nation, often forming the supreme legislative body; (in France until the Revolution) one of certain superior and final courts of judicature, in which also the edicts of the king were registered before becoming law; a meeting for deliberation; gingerbread in the form of rectangular biscuits (also **par′liament-cake** or (*Scot*) **par′ley** or **par′ly**); a little-used term for a group of owls. [Fr *parlement*, from *parler* to speak]

■ **parliamentā′rian** *n* an adherent of Parliament in opposition to Charles I; a person who is skilled in the ways of parliament. ◆ *adj* (*hist*) on the side of parliament during the English Civil War. **parliamenta′rianism** or **parliament′arism** *n* the principles of parliamentary government; the parliamentary system. **parliamentarily** /*-ment′ər-i-li*/ *adv*. **parliament′ary** *adj* relating to parliament; enacted, enjoined, or done by parliament; according to the rules and practices of legislative bodies; (of language) civil, decorous; (in the Civil War) for Parliament against the Royalists. **parliamenting** /*-ment′ing*/ *n* acting as a member of parliament; debating.
□ **parliamentary agent** *n* a person employed by private individuals or societies for drafting bills or managing business to be brought before parliament. **parliamentary burgh** see under **burgh**. **parliamentary private secretary** *n* a Member of Parliament acting as an aide to a government minister (*abbrev* **PPS**). **parliamentary train** *n* a railway train which, by act of parliament (1844), ran daily with sufficient accommodation for passengers at a penny a mile. **par′liament-heel** *n* a slight careening of a ship. **par′liament-hinge′** *n* a hinge allowing a door to be laid back along the wall. **par′liament-house** *n* a building where parliament sits or has sat. **par′liament-man′** *n* a member of parliament; a parliamentarian.
■ **act of parliament** a statute that has passed through both the House of Commons and the House of Lords, and received the formal royal assent. (**Act of**) **Parliament clock** a type of wall clock (*usu* of mahogany, and with a large uncovered dial found *esp* in public houses) which became popular around 1797 in response to an act of parliament imposing a tax on all clocks and watches. **Parliamentary Commissioner for Administration** see **Ombudsman**.

parlour or (*esp N Am*) **parlor** /*pär′lər*/ *n* a simple unpretentious drawing room or dining room, or a smaller room of similar kind; a family sitting room or living room (*old*); a room where conversation is allowed in a monastery or nunnery; a private room for conversation or conference in a public building, office, etc; a more or less private room in an inn or public house; a shop fitted out like a room, or a room attached to a shop, *esp* for personal services to customers, or one providing a particular service or selling specified goods, such as a beauty parlour or an ice-cream parlour (*orig US*). ◆ *adj* used in or suitable for a parlour. [Anglo-Fr *parlur* (Fr *parloir*) from *parler* to speak]
□ **par′lour-board′er** *n* a pupil at a boarding school who enjoys particular privileges. **parlour car** or **parlor car** *n* (*US*) a luxuriously fitted railway saloon carriage. **parlour game** *n* an (*esp* informal) indoor game. **par′lour-maid** *n* a maidservant who waits at table. **parlour pink** *n* a rather tepid Socialist. **parlour tricks** *n pl* minor social accomplishments; performances intended to impress.
■ **beauty parlour** and **funeral parlour** see under **beauty** and **funeral**. **milking parlour** a special room or building in which cows are milked.

parlous /*pär′ləs*/ *adj* perilous. ◆ *adv* (*archaic* and *facetious*) extremely. [A form of **perilous** (see under **peril**)]

parly see **parliament**.

Parma see **Parma ham** and **Parma violet** under **Parmesan**.

parmacitie /*pär-mə-sit′i*/ *n* a Shakespearean form of **spermaceti**.

Parmesan /*pär-mi-zan′* or *pär′mi-zan*/ *adj* relating to *Parma* in N Italy. ◆ *n* (also **Parmesan cheese**) a hard dry cheese with a granular texture, often used grated on pasta dishes.
□ **Parma ham** *n* finely cured uncooked ham *usu* eaten thinly sliced as an hors d'œuvre. **Parma violet** *n* Neapolitan violet.

Parnassus /*pär-nas′əs*/ *n* a mountain in Greece, sacred to Apollo and the Muses; a collection of poems.
■ **Parnass′ian** *adj* of Parnassus; of the Muses; of a school of French poetry supposed to believe in art for art's sake (from the collections published as *le Parnasse contemporain*, 1866–76). ◆ *n* a poet; a member of the Parnassian school. **Parnass′ianism** *n*.
■ **grass of Parnassus** a white-flowered plant of wet moors (*Parnassia palustris*), of the saxifrage family.

Parnellism /*pär′nə-li-zm*/ *n* the principles and policy of Charles Stewart *Parnell* (1846–91) who sought to promote Home Rule for Ireland.
■ **Par′nellite** *n* a follower of Parnell (also *adj*).

paroccipital /*par-ok-sip′i-tl*/ (*anat*) *adj* near the occiput. [**para-**[1] and **occiput**]

parochial /*pə-rō′ki-əl*/ *adj* of or relating to a parish; (of sentiments, tastes, etc) restricted or confined within narrow limits; denominational (*US*). [L *parochiālis*, from *parochia*; see **parish**]
■ **parō′chialism** *n* a system of local government which makes the parish the unit; provincialism, narrowness of view. **parōchiality** /*-al′-*/ *n*. **parō′chialize** or **-ise** *vt* to make parochial; to form into parishes. ◆ *vi* to do parish work. **parō′chially** *adv*.
□ **parochial board** *n* (formerly, in Scotland) a board charged with poor relief.

parochin, parochine, parischan, parischane or **parishen** /*pä′ri-shin*/ (*Scot*) *n* a parish.

parody /par'ə-di/ n a burlesque or satirical imitation; an imitation so poor as to seem a deliberate mockery of the original. ◆ vt (**par'odying**; **par'odied**) to make a parody of. [Gr *parōidiā*, from *para* beside, and *ōidē* an ode]

■ **parod'ic** or **parod'ical** adj. **par'odist** n. **parodist'ic** adj.

paroemia /pə-rē'mi-ə/ n a proverb, adage. [Gr *paroimiā*, a proverb, from *paroimos* by the road, from *oimos* road]

■ **paroe'miac** adj. ◆ n (classical prosody) the anapaestic dimeter catalectic. **paroe'mial** adj. **paroemiog'rapher** n a writer or collector of proverbs. **paroemiog'raphy** n. **paroemiol'ogy** n the study of proverbs.

paroicous /pə-roi'kəs/ (bot) adj (of certain mosses) having the male and female reproductive organs beside or near each other (also **parecious** or **paroecious** /pə-rē'shəs/). [Gr *paroikos* dwelling beside, from *para* beside, and *oikos* a dwelling]

parol see **parole**.

parole /pə-rōl'/ n conditional release of a prisoner; the condition of having given one's word of honour, or privilege of having it accepted; word of honour (esp by a prisoner of war, to fulfil certain conditions; milit); officers' daily password in a camp or garrison (milit); word of mouth; (usu /pa-rol'/) language as manifested in the speech of individuals, opp to *langue* (linguistics). ◆ adj relating to parole; (usu **parol**, usu /par'/) given by word of mouth, opp to *documentary*, as in *parol evidence*. ◆ vt to put on parole; to release on parole. ◆ vi to give parole. [Fr *parole* word, from L *parabola* a parable, saying, from Gr; see **parable**]

■ **parolee'** n a prisoner who has been conditionally released.

paronomasia /par-on-o-mā'zi-ə/ n a play on words (also (obs) **paronom'asy** /-ə-si or -ə-zi/). [Gr *para* beside, and *onoma* name]

■ **paronomastic** /-mas'tik/ or **paronomas'tical** /-əl/ adj. **paronym** /par'o-nim/ n a word from the same root or having the same sound as another. **paron'ymous** adj. **paron'ymy** n.

paronychia /par-o-nik'i-ə/ n a whitlow (med); (with cap) the whitlow-wort genus of plants. [Gr *para* beside, and *onyx, onychos* nail]

■ **paronych'ial** adj.

paronymous, paronymy see under **paronomasia**.

paroquet see **parakeet**.

parotid /pə-rot'id/ or -rōt'/ adj near the ear. ◆ n the parotid gland, a salivary gland in front of the ear (also **parō'tis** (pl **parotides** /pə-rōt'i-dēz/)). [Gr *parōtis, -idos*, from *para* beside, and *ous, ōtos* ear]

■ **parot'ic** adj near or adjacent to the ear. **parotidī'tis** or **parotī'tis** n inflammation of the parotid gland, as in mumps.

parousia /pə-roo'zi-ə or -row'zi-ə/ (theol) n the second coming of Christ. [Gr *parousiā* presence, arrival]

paroxetine /pa-rok'sə-tēn/ n an antidepressant drug that prolongs the effect of serotonin in the brain by inhibiting its uptake.

paroxysm /par'ok-si-zm/ n a fit of acute pain; a sudden recurrence of symptoms; a fit of passion, laughter, coughing, etc; any sudden violent action. [Gr *paroxysmos*, from *para* beyond, and *oxys* sharp]

■ **paroxys'mal** adj.

paroxytone /par-ok'si-tōn/ adj (in ancient Greek) having the acute accent on the last syllable but one; having a heavy stress on the penultimate syllable. ◆ n a word so accented. [Gr *paroxytonos*, from *para* beside, *oxys* acute, and *tonos* tone]

parp /pärp/ (inf) vt and vi to sound (a car horn), to toot or blast (a car horn or trumpet, etc). ◆ n a toot or blast of a horn, etc. [Imit]

parpen /pär'pən/ n (also **par'pane, par'pend, par'pent, par'point, per'pend** and **per'pent**) a stone passing through a wall from face to face; a wall of such stones; a partition; a bridge parapet. [OFr *parpain*]

❑ **par'pen-stone** n. **par'pen-wall** n.

parquet /pär'kā, pär'kē or -ket'/ n a floor-covering of wooden blocks fitted in a pattern; the stalls of a theatre (US; **parquet circle** that part of the auditorium behind these). ◆ adj of parquetry. ◆ vt (pap **par'queted** /-kād, -kēd/ or **parquetted** /-ket'id/) to cover or floor with parquetry. [Fr *parquet*, dimin of *parc* an enclosure]

■ **par'quetry** /-ki-tri/ n flooring in parquet.

parr /pär/ n a young salmon up to two years of age, before it becomes a smolt; the young of several other kinds of fish. [Ety unknown]

parrakeet see **parakeet**.

parral see **parrel**.

parramatta see **paramatta**.

parrel or **parral** /par'əl/ n a band by which a yard is fastened to a mast. [Cf OFr *parail* rigging]

❑ **parrel truck** n a wooden ball strung on a parrel.

parrhesia /pa-rē'syə or -zyə/ n boldness of speech. [Gr *parrēsiā*, from *para* beside, beyond, and *rhēsis* speech]

parricide /par'i-sīd/ n the murder of a parent or near relative, or the murder of anyone to whom reverence is considered to be due; a

person who commits such a crime. [Fr, from L *parricīdium, pāricīdium* (the offence), *parricīda, pāricīda* (the offender), from *caedere* to slay; the connection with *pater*, father, is appar fanciful]

■ **parricīd'al** adj.

parritch /pär'ich or par'ich/ n a Scots form of **porridge**.

parrock /par'ək/ (dialect) n a small field or enclosure, esp one used for lambs; a paddock. ◆ vt to confine in a parrock. [OE *pearroc*]

parroquet see **parakeet**.

parrot /par'ət/ n one of a family of tropical and subtropical birds with brilliant plumage, a hooked bill, and zygodactyl feet, good imitators of human speech; an uncritical repeater of the words of others. ◆ vt (**parr'oting; parr'oted**) to repeat by rote; to teach to repeat by rote. ◆ vi (also vt with it) to talk like a parrot. [Poss Fr *Perrot*, dimin of *Pierre* Peter]

■ **parr'oter** n. **parr'otry** n unintelligent imitation. **parr'oty** adj like a parrot or parrot-coal.

❑ **parr'ot-beak, parr'ot-bill** or **parr'ot-jaw** n the New Zealand glory-pea, from the form of its flowers. **parr'ot-coal** n (Scot) cannel-coal (possibly from chattering as it burns). **parr'ot-cry'** n a catchphrase senselessly repeated from mouth to mouth. **parrot disease** or **fever** n psittacosis. **parr'ot-fashion** adv by rote. **parr'ot-fish** n a name applied to various fishes, esp of the wrasse family and the related Scaridae, from their colours or their powerful jaws. **parrot mouth** n a congenital malformation of the jaw that occurs in horses and other grazing animals preventing normal feeding. **parr'ot-wrasse'** n a parrot-fish, esp a Mediterranean species (*Scarus cretensis*) prized by the ancients.

parry /par'i/ vt (**parr'ying; parr'ied**) to ward or keep off; to turn aside, block or evade; to avert. ◆ n a turning aside of a blow or a thrust or of an attack of any kind, eg an argument or a gibe. [From Fr *parez*, imper of *parer* from L *parāre* to prepare, in LL to keep off]

parse /pärz, also pärs/ (grammar) vt to describe (a word) fully from point of view of classification, inflection, and syntax; to analyse (a sentence); to break down a string of characters, eg a program statement, into its component parts (comput). [L *pars (ōrātiōnis)* a part (of speech)]

■ **pars'er** n. **pars'ing** n.

parsec /pär'sek or sek'/ n the distance (about 3.26 light years) at which half the major axis of the earth's orbit subtends an angle of one second, a unit for measurement of distances of stars. [*parallax* and *second*]

Parsee or **Parsi** /pär'sē or -sē'/ n a descendant of the Zoroastrians who emigrated from Persia to India in the 8c; a Persian dialect dominant during the time of the Sassanidae. ◆ adj of or relating to the Parsees. [Pers *Pārsī*, from *Pārs* Persia]

■ **Par'seeism, Par'siism** (or /-sē'/) or **Par'sism** n the religion of the Parsees.

parsimony /pär'si-mən-i/ n sparingness or reluctance in the spending of money; praiseworthy economy in the use of means to achieve an end; avoidance of excess; frugality; niggardliness. [L *parsimōnia*, from *parcere, parsus* to spare]

■ **parsimonious** /pär'si-mō'ni-əs/ adj frugal; niggardly. **parsimō'niously** adv. **parsimō'niousness** n.

■ **law of parsimony** the principle of Occam's razor (see under **Occamism**).

parsing see under **parse**.

parsley /pärs'li/ n a bright-green umbelliferous herb (*Petroselinum crispum*) with finely divided, strongly scented leaves, used in cookery. [OE *petersilie*, modified by Fr *persil*, both from L *petroselīnum*, from Gr *petroselīnon*, from *petros* a rock, and *selīnon* parsley]

❑ **parsley fern** n a fern (*Cryptogramma crispa*) with bright-green crisped leaves similar in appearance to parsley.

parsley piert /pärs'li pērt/ or **parsley pert** /pûrt/ n a dwarf species of lady's-mantle (*Aphanes arvensis*), a weed of dry waste ground. [Prob Fr *perce-pierre*, literally, pierce-stone]

parsnip or (old) **parsnep** /pär'snip/ n an umbelliferous plant (*Pastinaca sativa* or *Peucedanum sativum*) or its edible carrot-like root. [L *pastināca*, from *pastinum* a dibble; prob affected by **neep**]

parson /pär'sn/ n the priest or incumbent of a parish; a rector; any minister of religion; a person who is licensed to preach. [OFr *persone*, from L *persōna* a person, prob in legal sense, or a mouthpiece]

■ **par'sonage** n the residence of a parson; orig the house, lands, tithes, etc, set apart for the support of the minister of a parish; tithes (*Walter Scott*). **parsonic** /-sōn'ik/ or **parson'ical** adj. **par'sonish** adj.

❑ **par'son-bird** n the tui. **parson's nose** n the piece of flesh at the tail end of a (cooked) fowl (also **pope's nose**).

part /pärt/ n something less than the whole; a portion; that which along with others makes up, has made up, or may at some time make up, a whole; a constituent; a component; a member or organ; an equal quantity; an equal or nearly equal division, constituent, etc, as in eg *three parts oil to one part vinegar* ; share; region; direction, hand, or side; participation; concern; interest; a role or duty; a side or party; a character taken by an actor in a play; the words and actions of a character in a play or in real life; a voice or instrument in orchestral, etc music; that which is performed by such a voice or instrument; a copy of the music for it; a constituent melody or succession of notes or harmony; a section of a work in literature (see also **partwork** below), or in music; a separately published portion or number (see also **partwork** below); an inflected form of a verb; the place where the hair is parted, a parting (*N Am*); a quantity which taken a certain number of times (when unspecified, less than the whole) will equal a larger quantity; (in *pl*) intellectual qualities, talents, or conduct. ◆ *adj* in part; partial. ◆ *adv* in part; partly. ◆ *vt* to divide; to separate; to break; to put or keep apart; to set in different directions; to distribute; to share; to leave, quit, depart (*Shakesp*). ◆ *vi* to become divided or separated; to separate; to go different ways; to depart; to come or burst apart; to relinquish (with *with*); to share (*Bible*). [OE and Fr *part*, from L *pars, partis*]

■ **part'ed** *adj* divided; separated; departed; assigned a part; endowed with parts or abilities (*Shakesp*); (of a leaf) deeply cleft (*bot*). **part'er** *n.* **partibil'ity** *n.* **part'ible** *adj* that may or must be parted or divided up (*esp* of inherited property); separable. **part'ing** *n* the action of the verb to part; a place of separation or division; a dividing line; a line of skin showing between sections of hair brushed in opposite directions on the head; leave-taking. ◆ *adj* separating; dividing; departing; leave-taking; of or at leave-taking. **part'ly** *adv* in part; in some degree.
❑ **part-exchange'** *n* a transaction in which an article is handed over as part of the payment for another article (*inf* short form **part-ex**; also *vt*, *adj* and *adv*). **part'ing-cup'** *n* a two-handled drinking cup. **parting shot** *n* a last, *usu* hostile, remark made on leaving; a Parthian shot. **part'-off** *n* (*W Indies*) a screen used to divide a room into two separate areas. **part'-own'er** *n* a joint owner. **part'-pay'ment** *n* payment in part. **part'-singing** *n*. **part'-song** *n* a melody with parts in harmony, *usu* unaccompanied. **part'-time'** *adj* and *adv* (done) for part of the usual working time only. ◆ *vi* to work part-time. **part'-tim'er** *n*. **part'-way** *adv* part of the way. **part'work** *n* one of a series of publications (*esp* magazines) issued at regular intervals, eventually forming a complete course or book. **part'-writing** *n* composition of music in parts.
■ **for my part** as far as concerns me. **for the most part** commonly; mostly. **in bad** or **ill part** unfavourably. **in good part** favourably; without taking offence. **in great part** to a great extent. **in part** partly; so far as part is concerned; not wholly but to some extent. **on the part of** so far as concerns; as done or performed by; in the actions of; on the side of. **part and parcel** essentially a part. **part brass rags** (*naut sl*) to quarrel. **part company** to separate. **parting of the ways** a point at which a fateful decision must be made. **part of speech** one of the various classes of words. **part way** some way, not all the way, approaching but not reaching, as eg *go part way towards an objective*. **take part in** to share or to assist in. **take part with** to take the side of. **take someone's part** to support or side with someone (in an argument, etc).

partake /pär- or pər-tāk'/ *vi* (**partā'king**; **partook'**; **partā'ken**) to take or have a part or share (*usu* with *of* or *in*); to take some, *esp* of food or drink; to have something of the nature or properties (of); to make common cause (*Shakesp*). ◆ *vt* to have a part in; to share; to have a share in the knowledge of; to give a share of (*Shakesp*); to inform (*Spenser*). [Back-formation from **partaker**, from **part** and **taker**]
■ **partā'ker** *n.* **partā'king** *n.*

partan /pär'tən/ (*Scot*) *n* any edible crab. [Gaelic]

parted see under **part**.

partenariat /pär-tə-nä'ri-at/ *n* a meeting between representatives of organizations from different countries with the aim of establishing mutually beneficial business arrangements. [Fr, partnership]

parter see under **part**.

parterre /pär-ter'/ *n* a formal arrangement of flower-beds; the pit of a theatre, *esp* the part under the galleries. [Fr, from L *per* along, and *terra* the ground]

parthenocarpy /pär-then-ō-kär'pi/ (*bot*) *n* the production of a fruit without a preliminary act of fertilization. [Gr *parthenos* a virgin, and *karpos* a fruit]
■ **parthenocar'pic** *adj*.

parthenogenesis /pär-thi-nō-jen'i-sis/ *n* reproduction by means of an unfertilized ovum. [Gr *parthenos* a virgin, and *genesis* production]
■ **parthenogenetic** /-ji-net'ik/ *adj*.

Parthenon /pär'thi-non/ *n* the temple of Athene *Parthenos*, on the Acropolis at Athens. [Gr *Parthenōn*, from *parthenos* a virgin]

Parthian /pär'thi-ən/ *adj* of *Parthia* in ancient Persia. ◆ *n* a native of Parthia.
❑ **Parthian shot** *n* a parting shot, from the Parthian habit of turning round in the saddle to discharge an arrow at a pursuer.

parti /par-tē'/ (*Fr*) *n* a group of people; a decision; a marriageable person considered as a match or catch.
❑ **parti pris** /prē'/ *n* bias, preconceived opinion.

partial /pär'shl/ *adj* relating to a part only; not total or entire; inclined to favour one person or party; having a preference or fondness (with *to*); of partiality (*Shakesp*); component; subordinate (*bot*). ◆ *n* (*acoustics*) a partial tone, one of the single-frequency tones which go together to form a sound actually heard. [Fr, from LL *partiālis*, from L *pars* a part]
■ **par'tialism** *n.* **par'tialist** *n* someone who is biased; someone who sees or knows only part; a particularist (*theol*). **partiality** /-shi-al'i-ti/ *n*. **par'tialize** or **-ise** *vt* (*Shakesp*) to bias. **par'tially** *adv*.
❑ **partial derivative** *n* (*maths*) a derivative obtained by letting only one of several independent variables vary. **partial fraction** *n* one of a number of fractions into which another fraction may be separated. **partial pressure** *n* the pressure exerted by any component in a mixture of gases. **partial product** *n* (*maths*) a quantity obtained by multiplying one part of a multiplicand and one part of a multiplier.
■ **partial out** (*stats*) to eliminate (a factor) so as to assess other factors when they are independent of its influence.

partibility, **partible** see under **part**.

particeps criminis /pär'ti-seps krim'i-nis or par'ti-keps krē'mi-nis/ (*law*) *n* someone who, though not present, helps in any way with the commission of a crime or who after the deed aids those who did it. [L, literally partner of the charge]

participate /pär-tis'i-pāt/ *vi* to have a share, or take part (in); to have some of the qualities (of). ◆ *vt* (*archaic*) to receive a part or share of. [L *participāre*, *-ātum*, from *pars, partis*, part and *capere* to take]
■ **partic'ipable** *adj* capable of being participated in or shared. **partic'ipant** *adj* participating; sharing. ◆ *n* a person, group, etc taking part. **partic'ipantly** *adv*. **partic'ipating** *adj* (of insurance) entitling policyholders to a share of the company's additional profits. **participā'tion** *n* the act of participating (as in **worker participation** the involvement of employees at all levels in the policy-making decisions of a company, etc). **partic'ipātive** *adj* capable of participating; participable. **partic'ipator** *n* someone who participates; a person who has a share in the capital or income of a company. **partic'ipatory** *adj* participable.

participle /pär'ti-sip-l/ (*grammar*) *n* a non-finite form of a verb used to form compound tenses (eg *broken* in the phrase *had broken*) and as an adjective (eg *burning* in the phrase *the burning bush*). [OFr (Fr *participe*), from L *participium*, from *pars, partis* a part, and *capere* to take]
■ **particip'ial** *adj*. **particip'ially** *adv*.
■ **past** or **perfect participle** a participle, usually passive in meaning, referring to past action. **present participle** a participle, active in meaning, referring to roughly contemporaneous action.

particle /pär'ti-kl/ *n* a little part; a very small portion; a clause of a document; a minute piece of anything, eg dust; a little hard piece; a material point (*mech*); a smallest amount; a short, *usu* indeclinable word, such as a preposition, a conjunction or an interjection; a prefix or suffix; a crumb of consecrated bread or a portion used in the communion of the laity (*RC*). [L *particula*, dimin of *pars, partis* a part]
■ **partic'ulate** *adj* having the form of, or relating to, particles. ◆ *n* a particulate substance.
❑ **particle accelerator** *n* a device by means of which the speed of atomic particles may be greatly accelerated. **particle beam weapon** *n* a weapon whose destructive force consists of a beam of high-energy subatomic particles. **par'ticleboard** *n* (*N Am*) same as **chipboard** (see under **chip**). **particle physics** *n sing* the study of fundamental particles and of fundamental interactions (also called **high-energy physics**). **particle size** *n* (*geol*) the general dimensions, eg average diameter or volume, of grains in a rock or sediment.

parti-coated, **parti-coloured** see under **party**.

particular /pər-tik'ū-lər/ *adj* relating to a part; predicating of part of the class denoted by the subject (*logic*); relating to a single person or thing; individual; special; worthy of special attention; detailed; markedly and discriminatingly or intimately attentive towards a person (*obs*); noteworthy; definite; concerned with or marking things single or distinct; minutely attentive and careful; fastidious in taste; particularist. ◆ *n* a distinct or minute part; a single point; a single instance; a detail; an item; personal relation (*Shakesp*); a favourite (*inf*); a favourite drink. [LL *particulāris*, from L *particula* ; cf **particle**]
■ **partic'ularism** *n* attention to one's own interest or party; a minute description; the doctrine that salvation is offered only to particular individuals, the elect, and not to the race (*theol*); attention to the interest of a federal state before that of the confederation; the policy of allowing much freedom in this way. **partic'ularist** *n* and *adj*.

particularist'ic *adj.* **particularity** /-*lar'i-ti*/ *n* the quality of being particular; minuteness of detail; a single instance or case; a detail; peculiarity; marked attention to a person (*obs*). **particulariza'tion** or **-s-** *n.* **partic'ularize** or **-ise** *vt* to render particular; to mention the particulars of; to enumerate in detail; to mention as a particular or particulars. ◆ *vi* to mention or attend to minute details. **partic'ularly** *adv* in a particular manner; individually; severally; in detail; in the manner of a particular proposition; intimately; notably; in a very high degree. **partic'ularness** *n.*
■ **in particular** especially; in detail; severally, individually (*obs*). **London particular** a Madeira wine formerly exported for the London market; hence, from its colour, a London fog (*inf*).

partie carrée /*par-tē kar-ā'*/ (*Fr*) *n* a party consisting of two men and two women.

partim /*pär'tim*/ (*L*) *adv* in part.

parting see under **part**.

partisan[1] or **partizan** /*pär-ti-zan'* or *pär'ti-zan*/ *n* an adherent, *esp* a blind or unreasoning adherent, of a party or a faction; a light irregular soldier who scours the country and forays; (in World War II) an irregular resister within the enemy occupation lines. ◆ *adj* of, relating to or characteristic of a partisan; biased. [Fr *partisan*, from a dialect form of Ital *partigiano*, from *parte* (L *pars, partis*) part]
■ **par'tisanship** (or /-*zan'*/) *n.*

partisan[2] /*pär'ti-zan*/ *n* a halberd-like weapon with twin axe-blades or spikes, common in the Middle Ages; a man armed with one. [Fr *partizane* (now *pertuisane*), from Ital *partesana*, of doubtful origin]

partita /*pär-tē'tə*/ (*music*) *n* (*pl* **parti'te** or **parti'tas**) (*esp* 18c) a suite; a set of variations. [Ital]

partite /*pär'tīt*/ *adj* divided; (*esp* of plant leaves) cut nearly to the base. [L *partītus*, pap of *partīrī* or *partīre* to divide, from *pars* part]

partition /*pär-tish'ən*/ *n* the act of dividing; the division of a country into politically autonomous states; the state of being divided; a separate part; that which divides; a wall between rooms; a barrier, septum or dissepiment (*bot*); a score (*music*). ◆ *vt* to divide into shares; to divide into parts by walls, septa, or anything similar. [See **partite**]
■ **parti'tioner** *n* a person who partitions property. **parti'tionist** *n* a person who favours the partition of a country. **parti'tionment** *n.* **par'titive** *adj* parting; dividing; distributive; indicating that a part is meant (*grammar*). ◆ *n* a partitive word (eg *some, most*). **par'titively** *adv.*
❑ **partition coefficient** *n* (*chem*) the ratio of the equilibrium concentrations of a substance dissolved in two immiscible solvents (also called **distribution coefficient**). **partition wall** *n* an internal wall.

Partitur /*pär-ti-toor'*/ (*Ger*) or **partitura** /*pär-ti-toor'a*/ (*Ital*) *n* a score in music. [L *partītus*; cf **partite**]

partizan see **partisan**[1].

Partlet /*pärt'lit*/ *n* a proper name for a hen, from Chaucer's *Pertelote* in the Nun's Priest's Tale; sometimes applied to a woman. [OFr *Pertelote*, a woman's name]

partlet /*pärt'lit*/ (*obs*) *n* orig a collar or ruff; a woman's covering for the upper breast, neck and shoulders, often finished with a ruff or frill; a kind of shirt. [Appar OFr *patelette* a band]

partly see under **part**.

partner /*pärt'nər*/ *n* a sharer; an associate; a person engaged with another or others in business; a person who plays on the same side with another in a game; a person who dances or goes to a formal dinner with another; a husband or wife; either member of a couple living together in a sexual relationship; an associate in commensalism or symbiosis (*biol*); (in *pl*; *naut*) a wooden framework round a hole in the deck, supporting a mast, etc. ◆ *vt* to join as a partner (*Shakesp*); to be the partner of. [Prob a form of **parcener**]
■ **part'nership** *n* the state of being a partner; a contract between individuals engaged in any business; a business run by partners.
■ **Partnership for Peace** a scheme set up in 1993 as a link between NATO and certain former Warsaw Pact countries (*abbrev* **PFP**).

parton /*pär'ton*/ (*phys*) *n* a hypothetical particle thought to be a constituent of nucleons. [**part** and *-on*, formed on the analogy of **neutron, proton**, etc]

partook /*pär-tŏk'*/ *pat* of **partake**.

partridge /*pär'trij*/ *n* (*pl* **par'tridge** or **par'tridges**) any member of a genus (*Perdix*) of game birds of the pheasant family; extended to many other birds, *esp* (in N America) the Virginian quail and the ruffed grouse, and (in S America) the tinamou. [Fr *perdrix*, from L *perdīx*, from Gr *perdīx*]
❑ **par'tridgeberry** *n* a N American trailing plant (*Mitchella repens*) of the madder family or its fruit; applied also to the checkerberry.

par'tridge-wood[1] *n* a hard variegated tropical American wood (genus *Andira*) of the Papilionaceae, used by American cabinetmakers; oak or other wood speckled owing to attack by a fungus.

parture /*pärt'yər*/ (*Spenser*) *n* departure. [Prob **part**]

parturient /*pär-tū'ri-ənt*/ *adj* of or related to childbirth; giving or about to give birth; bringing or about to bring about anything new. [L *parturīre*, desiderative from *parere* to bring forth]
■ **partūri'tion** *n* the act of giving birth.

part-way see under **part**.

party /*pär'ti*/ *n* a social gathering, *esp* one serving as a celebration; a small body of people associated together in any occupation or amusement; a detachment (*milit*); a company; a part (*obs*); a side in a battle, game, lawsuit, or other contest; a body of people united in favour of a political or other cause; the spirit of faction; a game (*obs*); a person concerned in any affair, as in *third party*; a person who enters into a contract, eg of marriage; a possible match in marriage; a person (*inf*). ◆ *adj* relating to a party; parted or divided (*heraldry*). ◆ *vi* (*inf*) to attend, hold or take part in parties or similar entertainments; to have a good time. [Fr *partie*, fem (and also *parti*, masc), pap of *partir*, from L *partīre, partīrī* to divide, from *pars* a part]
■ **par'tyism** *n* devotion to a (particular political) party.
❑ **par'ti-coat'ed** or **par'ty-coat'ed** *adj* having on a coat of various colours. **par'ti-col'oured** or **par'ty-col'oured** *adj* variegated. **party animal** *n* (*inf*) a person who likes to go to parties or generally have a good time. **par'ty-call'** *n* a social call on one's host or hostess after a party. **par'ty-cap'ital** *n* advantage or credit to one's party derived from some contingency. **par'tygoer** *n* a person on the way to a party, or who regularly goes to parties. **par'ty-gov'ernment** *n* government by the prevailing political party. **par'ty-ju'ry** *n* a jury half of natives and half of aliens. **party line** *n* a telephone exchange line shared by two or more subscribers; a boundary between properties; the policy rigidly laid down by the political party leaders. **party machine** see under **machine**. **party man** *n* a faithful member of a political party. **party piece** *n* an act or turn that one is known for performing to entertain others. **party plan selling** same as **party selling** below. **par'ty-political** *adj*. **party politics** *n sing* politics viewed from a party standpoint, or arranged to suit the views or interests of a party. **par'ty-pooper** *n* someone who spoils the enjoyment of others at a party or social occasion by their lack of enthusiasm, or by their inability or unwillingness to participate. **party popper** *n* a small device that makes a bang and ejects paper streamers when a string attached to it is pulled. **party sales** *n pl*. **party selling** *n* the selling of products by agents earning commission in the homes of customers who invite friends and neighbours as to a social gathering. **par'ty-size** *adj* (of an item of food, etc) smaller than the usual size, intended to be used as a snack at parties. **party spirit** *n* the unreasonable spirit of a party man; a festive atmosphere. **par'ty-spir'ited** *adj*. **par'ty-ver'dict** *n* a joint verdict. **party wall** *n* a wall between two adjoining properties or houses.
■ **bring to the party** to contribute, or have to offer. **the party's over** a favourable, enjoyable, carefree, etc situation has ended.

parulis /*pə-roo'lis*/ (*med*) *n* a gumboil. [Gr *para* beside, and *oulon* the gum]

parure /*pa-rür'*/ *n* a set of ornaments, etc. [Fr]

paruresis /*pär-ū'ri-sis*/ *n* difficulty in urinating in the presence of other people. [**para-**[1] (in sense of 'abnormal'), and **uresis**]

parvenu /*pär'və-nü* or *-nū*/ *n* an upstart; someone newly risen into wealth, notice, or power, *esp* if vulgar or exhibiting an inferiority complex. ◆ *adj* of or relating to a parvenu. [Fr pap of *parvenir*, from L *pervenīre* to arrive]

parvis /*pär'vis*/ or **parvise** /*pär'vēs*/ *n* an enclosed space, or sometimes a portico, at the front of a church; a room over a church porch (*non-standard*). [OFr *parevis*; same root as **paradise**]

parvovirus or **Parvo virus** /*pär'vō-vī-rəs*/ *n* any of a group of viruses which contain DNA and which are the causes of various animal (including canine) diseases. [L *parvus* little, and **virus**]

PAS see **para-aminosalicylic acid**.

pas /*pä*/ (*Fr*) *n* (*pl* **pas** /*pä*/) a step or dance *esp* in ballet; action; precedence. [Fr, from L *passus*; cf **pace**[1]]
❑ **pas d'armes** /*därm*/ *n* a joust, a tilt or a tourney. **pas de basque** /*də bask*/ *n* a ballet movement in which one leg is moved in a circle; a dance step, *esp* in jigs and reels, in which the weight is transferred from one foot to the other while the dancer remains on the spot. **pas de bourrée** /*də boo-rā*/ *n* a ballet movement in which one foot is swiftly placed behind or in front of the other. **pas de chat** /*də sha*/ *n* a ballet leap in which each foot is raised in turn to the opposite knee. **pas de deux, trois, quatre**, etc /*də do, trwä, kä-tr'*/ *n* a ballet sequence involving two, three, four, or more dancers. **pas redoublé** /*rə-doob-lā*/ *n* a quickstep. **pas seul** /*sœl*/ *n* a dance for one person, a solo dance.
■ **have the pas of someone** to take precedence over someone.

PASCAL /pas'kal, -kal', -käl or -käl'/ n a high-level computer programming language, designed in the 1960s and still widely used for general programming purposes. [Blaise *Pascal* (1623–62), French philosopher and scientist who devised a calculating machine]

pascal /pas'kal, -kal', -käl or -käl'/ n a derived SI unit, the unit of pressure or stress (symbol **Pa**), equal to one newton per square metre. [Ety as for **PASCAL**]
❑ **Pascal's triangle** n a group of numbers arranged to form a triangle in which each number is the sum of the two numbers to its right and left in the line above.

Pasch /pask/ or (*dialect*) **Pace** /pās/ n the Passover; Easter (*archaic*). [L *pascha*, from Gr *pascha*, from Heb *pesach* the Passover, from *pāsah* to pass over]
■ **pasch'al** adj.
❑ **paschal candle** n a large candle blessed and placed on the altar on the day before Easter. **paschal flower** same as **pasqueflower**. **paschal (full) moon** n the first full moon on or after the spring equinox, Easter being reckoned in the Roman Catholic Church as the first Sunday after the paschal moon. **paschal lamb** n the lamb slain and eaten at the Passover. **pasch'-egg** or (*dialect*) **pace'-egg** n an Easter egg. **Pasch of the Cross** n Good Friday.

pascual /pas'kū-əl/ adj growing on land used for grazing. [L *pascuum* pasture]

pasear /pä-sā-är'/ (*US sl* and *dialect*) vi to take a walk. ◆ n a walk. [Sp]
■ **paseo** /pä-sā'ō/ n a walk; a street or promenade.

pash[1] /pash/ (*sl*) n a contraction of **passion**; an adolescent infatuation. ◆ vi and vt to kiss or embrace passionately.

pash[2] /pash/ (*Shakesp*) vt to strike, to dash, to crush. ◆ vi to dash. ◆ n a blow. [Perh imit]

pash[3] /pash/ (*Shakesp*) n the head. [Origin unknown]

pasha /pash'ə or pä-shä'/ n a Turkish title (abolished 1934) given to governors and high military and naval officers (also **pacha**). [Turk *pasa*; cf **bashaw**]
■ **pash'alik** or **pach'alic** (or /pä-shä'lik/) n the jurisdiction of a pasha.

pashm /push'əm/ or **pashim** /push'ēm/ n the fine underfleece of Himalayan goats, used for making rugs, shawls, etc. [Pers, wool]
■ **pashmina** /push-mē'nə/ n a shawl made from pashm, or from cashmere and silk in imitation; pashm itself.

Pashto, Pushto /push'tō/, **Pashtu, Pushtoo** or **Pushtu** /-too/, **Pakhto** /puhh'tō/ or **Pakhtu** /-too/ n an official language of Afghanistan, also spoken in parts of Pakistan; a native speaker of this, a Pathan. ◆ adj of or relating to this language or people. [Pashto *Pashtō*, *Pakhtō*]
■ **Pash'tun, Push'tun, Pakh'tun** or **Pakh'toon**, etc n a member of a Pashto-speaking people in Pakistan and Afghanistan; (in *pl*) this people. ◆ adj of or relating to the Pashtuns.

pasigraphy /pə-sig'rə-fi/ n a system of ideographic writing. [Gr *pāsi* (dative pl) to or for all, and *graphein* to write]
■ **pasigraphic** /pas-i-graf'ik/ or **pasigraph'ical** adj.

paso doble /pas'ō or pä'sō dō'blä/ (*Sp*) n a march *usu* played at bullfights; a two-step; the music for this dance.

Pasok /pas'ok/ abbrev : *Panellinio Sosialistiko Kinima* (*Mod Gr*), Panhellenic Socialist Movement.

paspalum /pas'pä-ləm/ n any plant of an American and tropical genus (*Paspalum*) of pasture grasses, a common example being pampasgrass. [Gr *paspalos* millet]

paspy /pä'spi/ same as **passepied**.

pasqueflower /päsk'flowr/ n a species of anemone (*Anemone pulsatilla*) with bell-shaped purple flowers; extended to some other species. [Fr *passefleur*, appar from *passer* to surpass, modified after **Pasch**, as flowering about Easter]

Pasquil /pas'kwil/ or **Pasquin** /pas'kwin/ n the nickname (*perh* after somebody who lived near) of an ancient statue dug up in Rome in 1501, to which it became customary to attach lampoons and satires; an imaginary lampooner or satirist; a lampoon or satire. ◆ vt and vi to lampoon or satirize. [Ital *Pasquino*, *Pasquillo*]
■ **pas'quilant, pas'quiler** or **pasquina'der** n a lampooner. **pasquināde** n a lampoon. ◆ vt to lampoon.

pass /päs/ vi (pat and pap **passed** /päst/ or rarely **past**) to proceed; to go or be transferred from one place to another; to transfer the ball to another player (*football*, etc); to make one's way; to reach, extend, or have a course; to undergo change from one state to another; to be transmitted, communicated or transacted; to change ownership; to change; to shade off (*obs*); to be astir; to circulate; to be accepted or reputed or known; to go by; to go unheeded or neglected; to elapse, to go away; to disappear, come to an end, fade out; to die; to move over, through or onwards; to go or get through an obstacle, difficulty, test, ordeal, examination, etc; to get through an examination without honours; to be approved; to meet with acceptance; to be sanctioned; to be made law; to be talented; to come through; to be voided; to happen; to sit or serve (upon a jury); to adjudicate; to be pronounced; to care, reck (with *of* or *for*; *obs*); to surpass or beat everything (*obs*); to exceed bounds; to perform a pass (see *n* below); to abstain from making a call or declaration (*cards*); to choose not to answer a question in a quiz, etc. ◆ vt to go or get by, over, beyond, through, etc; to undergo, experience; to undergo successfully; to spend (time); to omit; to disregard; to exceed; to surpass; to cause or allow to pass; to transfer, transmit; to transfer (the ball) to another player (*football*, etc); to hand; to utter, pronounce; to circulate; to pledge (as one's word); to emit, discharge; to perform a pass with or upon; to perform as a pass; to esteem (*obs*). ◆ n a way by which one may pass or cross; a narrow passage, *esp* through or over a range of mountains or other difficult region; a narrow defile; an act of passing; the passing of an examination, *esp* without honours at degree level; currency (*obs*); reputation (*Shakesp*); event, issue, fulfilment, consummation; a state or condition (as in *pretty* or *sad pass*); a predicament, critical position; a passport; a written permission to go somewhere or do something, authorization, a permit; permission to be in a certain area (*S Afr hist*); a free ticket; a ticket or similar document paid for or received as a concession, allowing free or cheaper use of a facility, eg a *bus pass*; a thrust (*fencing*); transference of the ball to another team member (*football*, etc); transference in a juggling trick; an amorous advance (*inf*); an act of examining or reading data; a movement of the hand over anything, eg by a magician or mesmerist; perhaps trick, perhaps conduct (*Shakesp*, *Measure for Measure* V.1.368). ◆ *interj* expressing the decision not to answer a question in a quiz, etc. [Fr *pas* step, and *passer* to pass, from L *passus* a step]
■ **pass'able** adj that may be passed, travelled over, or navigated; that may bear inspection; that may be accepted or allowed to pass; tolerable. **pass'ableness** n. **pass'ably** adv. **pass'er** n. **passimeter** /pas-im'i-tər/ n an automatic ticket-issuing machine. **passing** /päs'ing/ adj going by, through, or away; transient, fleeting; happening now; incidental; casual; surpassing (*archaic*). ◆ adv (*archaic*) exceedingly; very. ◆ n the action of the verb to pass; a place of passing; a coming to an end; death; gold or silver thread with a silk core. **pass'less** adj having no pass; impassable.
❑ **pass-back'** n an act of passing (a ball, etc) to a member of one's own team nearer one's own goal. **pass band** n (*radio*) a frequency band in which there is negligible attenuation. **pass'book** n a book that passes between a trader and a customer, in which credit purchases are entered; a bank book; a booklet containing permission to be in a certain area, and other documents (*S Afr hist*). **pass'-check** n a passout ticket. **pass degree** n a university or college degree without honours. **passed pawn** n in chess, a pawn having no opposing pawn before it on its own or an adjacent file. **pass'er-by** n (*pl* **pass'ers-by**) someone who passes by or near. **passing bell** n a bell tolled immediately after a death, *orig* to invite prayers for the soul passing into eternity. **passing note** n (*music*) a note inserted to allow a smooth passage between other notes, but itself forming no essential part of the harmony; a note forming an unprepared discord in an unaccented place in the measure (also (*N Am*) **passing tone**). **passing shot** n (*tennis*) a shot hit past and beyond the reach of an opponent. **pass'key** n a key enabling one to enter a house; a key for opening several locks. **pass laws** n pl (*S Afr hist*) laws restricting the movements of black people. **pass'man** n (*archaic*) a person who gains a degree without honours; a prisoner who is permitted to leave his cell in order to carry out certain duties (*sl*). **pass'out** n and adj (a ticket, etc) entitling someone who goes out to return. **pass'word** n (*orig milit*) a secret word by which a friend may pass or enter (a camp, etc); a set of characters which a user inputs to a computer to gain access (*comput*).
■ **bring to pass** to bring about, cause to happen. **come to pass** to happen (appar *orig* a noun in these expressions). **in passing** while doing, talking about, etc something else. **make a pass at** to aim a short blow at, especially ineffectually (*inf*); to make an amorous advance to (*inf*). **pass as** or **for** to be mistaken for or accepted as. **pass away** to come to an end, go off; to die; to elapse. **pass by** to move, go beyond or past; to ignore or overlook. **pass off** to impose fraudulently, to palm off; to take its course satisfactorily; to disappear gradually. **pass on** to go forward; to proceed; to die; to transmit, hand on. **pass on** or **upon** to give judgement or sentence upon; to practise artfully, or impose, upon; to palm off. **pass out** to distribute; to die; to faint, become unconscious or dead drunk (*inf*); to go off; to complete military, etc training. **pass over** to overlook, to ignore; to die. **pass the time of day** to exchange any ordinary greeting of civility. **pass through** to undergo, experience. **pass up** to renounce, to have nothing to do with; to neglect (an opportunity).

pass. abbrev : passive.

passacaglia /pas-a-käl'ya/ (*music*) n a slow solemn old Spanish dance form, slower than the chaconne, in triple time, *usu* on a ground bass. [Italianized from Sp *pasacalle*, from *pasar* to pass, and *calle* street, appar because often played in the streets]

---

fāte; fär; mē; fûr; mīne; mōte; fōr; mūte; pŭt; dhen (then); el'ə-mənt (element) ◆ For other sounds see detailed chart of pronunciation

passade /pä-sād'/ *n* the motion of a horse to and fro over the same ground in dressage exercises. [Fr *passade*, Sp *pasada*, from L *passus* step]

■ **passado** /pä-sä'dō/ *n* (*pl* **passa'does** or **passa'dos**) (*obs*; *fencing*) a thrust with one foot advanced.

passage[1] /pas'ij/ *n* a means or way of passing; an alley; a corridor or lobby; a navigable channel or route; a crossing-place, ford, ferry, bridge, or mountain-pass; a duct or vessel in the body; an act of passing; transit; a crossing; migration; transition; lapse, course; transmission; evacuation of the bowels; the passing of a bill; a journey (now only by water or air, or *fig*); right of conveyance; possibility of passing; that which passes; traffic (*Shakesp*); an occurrence, incident, episode; transaction, interchange of communication or intercourse, dealings together; a continuous but indefinite portion of a book, piece of music, etc, of moderate length; a run, figure, or phrase in music; a stage in the maintenance or controlled development of micro-organisms under analysis, in which they are introduced into the host or culture, allowed to multiply, and extracted (*biol*); an old dicing game, the object to throw doublets above (passing) ten, with three dice. ◆ *vi* to make or perform a passage. ◆ *vt* (*biol*) to submit (a micro-organism) to a passage. [Fr *passage*, from L *passus* step]
□ **passage beds** *n pl* (*geol*) transitional strata. **pass'age-boat** *n* a boat plying regularly for passengers. **passage grave** *n* a burial chamber situated below ground and connected to the surface by a passage. **passage hawk** *n* a hawk caught while migrating, *esp* when immature. **pass'age-money** *n* fare. **pass'ageway** *n* a way of access; a corridor; an alley. **pass'agework** *n* music that allows a performer to display virtuosity.
■ **bird of passage** a migratory bird; a transient visitor (*fig*). **passage of arms** any armed struggle; an encounter, *esp* in words. **work one's passage** to earn one's passage at sea by unpaid labour on board (also *fig*).

passage[2] /pas-äzh' *or* pas'ij/ (*dressage*) *n* a slow sideways walk; a rhythmical trot with diagonal pairs of legs lifted high. ◆ *vi* to move at a passage. ◆ *vt* to cause (a horse) to move at a passage. [Fr *passager*, from *passéger*, from Ital *passeggiare* to walk, from L *passus* step]

passament see **passement**.

passamezzo see **passy-measure**.

passant /pas'ənt/ (*heraldry*) *adj* walking towards the dexter side, with dexter fore-paw raised. [Fr]

passata /pə-sä'tə/ *n* (*pl* **passatas**) an Italian sauce of puréed and sieved tomatoes. [Ital, passed (through a sieve)]

passé, *fem* **passée**, /pa-sā'/ (*Fr*) *adj* past one's best, faded; out of date, or nearly so; no longer fashionable.

passemeasure see **passy-measure**.

passement or **passment** /pas'mənt/ or **passament** /-ə-mənt/ *n* a decorative trimming of beads, braid, etc. ◆ *vt* to adorn with passement. [Fr]
■ **passementerie** /päs-mã-tə-rē/ *n* passement.

passenger /pas'in-jər/ *n* someone who travels in a private or public conveyance (as opposed to someone who drives or operates the vehicle, etc); someone carried along by others' efforts (*fig*); someone who passes (*obs*). ◆ *adj* of or for passengers. [OFr *passagier* (Fr *passager*), with inserted *n*, as in *messenger* or *nightingale*]
□ **pass'enger-mile** *n* one mile travelled by one passenger, as a measure of volume of traffic. **pass'enger-pigeon** *n* an extinct N American pigeon that flew in vast numbers in search of food.

passe-partout /päs-pär-too'/ *n* a means of passing anywhere; a master key; a card or something similar cut as a mount for a picture; a kind of simple picture frame, *usu* of pasteboard, the picture being fixed by strips pasted over the edges; adhesive tape or paper used in this way. [Fr, a master key, from *passer* to pass, *par* over, and *tout* all]

passepied /päs-pyä'/ *n* a dance of Breton origin like a slightly quicker minuet, popular in the 17c and 18c. [Fr, literally, pass-foot]

passer see under **pass**.

Passeres /pas'ə-rēz/ *n pl* an old order of birds (also called *Insessores*) comprising more than one-third of all the birds. [L *passer* a sparrow]
■ **Passerifor'mes** *n pl* the huge order of perching birds (sparrow-like in form) including amongst others all British songsters. **pass'erine** /-īn/ *adj* and *n*.

passible /pas'i-bl/ *adj* susceptible to or capable of suffering, or of feeling. [L *passibilis*, from *patī*, *passus* to suffer]
■ **passibil'ity** *n*. **pass'ibleness** *n*. **pass'ibly** *adv*.

passiflora /pas-i-flō'rə *or* -flö'rə/ *n* any plant of the passion flower genus, family **Passiflorā'ceae**. [L *passiō* passion, and *flōs*, *flōris* flower]

passim /pas'im/ (*L*) *adv* everywhere; throughout (*esp* a cited piece of writing); dispersedly.

passimeter, **passing** see under **pass**.

passion /pash'n/ *n* strong feeling or agitation of mind, *esp* rage, often sorrow; a fit of such feeling, *esp* rage; an expression or outburst of such feeling; ardent love; sexual desire; an enthusiastic interest or direction of the mind; the object of such a feeling; (*usu* with *cap*) the sufferings (*esp* on the Cross) and death of Christ; an account of this from one of the gospels; a musical setting of this; martyrdom; suffering; a painful bodily ailment (such as *iliac passion*); the fact, condition, or manner of being acted upon; passivity (*philos*); a passive quality. ◆ *vt* to imbue with passion. ◆ *vi* to exhibit passion. [OFr *passiun* and L *passiō*, *-ōnis*, from *patī*, *passus* to suffer]
■ **pass'ional** *adj* of or relating to the sufferings of a Christian martyr. **pass'ional** or **pass'ionary** *n* a book of the sufferings of saints and martyrs. **pass'ionate** *adj* moved by passion; showing strong and warm feeling; easily moved to passion; intense, fervid; compassionate (*Shakesp*); moving to compassion (*Spenser*). ◆ *vt* to express with passion; to imbue with passion, to impassion. **pass'ionately** *adv*. **pass'ionateness** *n*. **pass'ioned** *adj* moved by passion; expressing passion; expressed with passion. **Pass'ionist** *n* a member of a Roman Catholic congregation devoted to the commemoration of the Passion of Christ by missions, etc. **pass'ionless** *adj* free from or lacking passion, *esp* sexual desire; not easily excited to anger.
□ **passion flower** *n* any flower or plant of the genus *Passiflora*, consisting mostly of climbers of tropical and warm temperate America, from a fancied resemblance of parts of the flower to the crown of thorns, nails, and other emblems of Christ's Passion; the plant itself. **passion fruit** *n* any edible fruit of a passion flower, *esp* the granadilla. **Pass'ion-mū'sic** *n* music to which words describing the sufferings and death of Christ are set. **passion play** *n* a religious drama representing the sufferings and death of Christ. **Passion Sunday** *n* the fifth Sunday in Lent. **Pass'iontide** *n* the two weeks preceding Easter. **Passion week** *n* Holy week; the week before Holy week.

passive /pas'iv/ *adj* acted upon, not acting; inert; lethargic; not reacting; not actively resisting; suffering (*obs*); bearing no interest (*finance*); under a liability (*Scots law*); in or of which the subject is the person or thing that sustains, rather than performs, the action of the verb (*grammar*). ◆ *n* the passive voice (*grammar*); a passive verb (*grammar*); a passive person. [L *passīvus*, from *patī*, *passus* to suffer]
■ **pass'ivate** *vt* (*engineering*) to give (a metal) greater resistance to corrosion by coating the surface with eg oxides or phosphates. **pass'ively** *adv*. **pass'iveness** *n*. **pass'ivism** *n* passive resistance. **pass'ivist** *n* a passive resister. **passiv'ity** *n*.
□ **pass'ive-aggress'ive** *adj* (*psychol*) resisting the demands of others and seeking to manipulate them while avoiding direct confrontation. **passive immunity** *n* the short-term immunity acquired either artificially, through the administration of antibodies, or naturally, as in the very young who receive antibodies through the placenta or in colostrum. **passive obedience** *n* absolute submission to the ruling power; obedience to the 'divine right of kings'. **passive resistance** *n* deliberate refusal (on principle) to do what law or regulation orders, and submission to the consequent penalties. **passive resister** *n*. **passive smoking** *n* the involuntary inhalation of tobacco smoke that has been produced by others.

passless...to...**passman** see under **pass**.

passment see **passement**.

passout see under **pass**.

Passover /päs'ō-vər/ *n* an annual feast of the Jews, to commemorate the exodus of the Israelites from captivity in Egypt, so named from the destroying angel passing over the houses of the Israelites when he slew the first-born of the Egyptians. ◆ *adj* relating to the Passover.

passport /päs'pört *or* -pört/ *n* an official document issued by a government giving proof of the holder's identity and nationality, and permission to travel abroad with its protection; *orig* authorization to leave a port either to put to sea or to proceed inland; that which gives privilege of entry to anything (*fig*). [Fr *passeport*; cf **pass** and **port**[1]]

passus /pas'us/ *n* a section of a poem or story, a canto or fit. [L *passus*, plural *-ūs*, a step]

password see under **pass**.

passy-measure or **passemeasure** /pas'i-mezh'ər/ *n* an old dance, a pavan in quicker time (also called **passamezzo** /pas-sa-met'sō/ or **passy measures pavan**). [Ital *passemezzo*]

past /päst/ *adj* bygone; elapsed; ended; in time already passed; expressing action or being in time that has passed, preterite (*grammar*); just before the present; past one's best; having served a term of office. ◆ *n* time that has passed; things that have already happened; (one's) early life or bygone career, *esp* if marked by tragedy or scandal; the past tense; a verb or verbal form in the past tense. ◆ *prep* after; after the time of; beyond, in place, position, etc; beyond the possibility of. ◆ *adv* by; laid aside in store, for later use (*Scot*). ◆ *vt* and *vi* an unusual *pap* of **pass**. [An old pap of **pass**]

❑ **past master** *n* someone who has held the office of master (eg among freemasons); hence, someone thoroughly proficient (see also **passed master** under **master**). **past participle** see under **participle**. ■ **I**, etc **would not put it past him**, etc (*inf*) I, etc regard him, etc as (*esp* morally) capable of (some action disapproved of). **past it** (*inf*) or **past one's best** having decreased strength, ability, etc due to advancing age. **past praying for** beyond hope of redemption or recovery.

pasta /pä'stə or pas'tə/ *n* flour dough in fresh, processed (eg spaghetti, macaroni, shell shapes), and/or cooked form. [Ital, paste]

pastance /pas'təns/ (*archaic*) *n* a pastime. [Appar Fr *passe-temps* pastime]

paste /pāst/ *n* any soft plastic mass; dough for piecrust, etc; a doughy sweet; a smooth preparation of food suitable for spreading on bread; a glue whose main ingredients are flour and water; any of various adhesives, eg one for hanging wallpaper; material for making pottery; the basis of a person's character (*fig*); a fine kind of glass for making artificial gems. ◆ *adj* of paste. ◆ *vt* to fasten or cover with paste; to insert text, etc copied or cut from somewhere else (*comput*); to thrash (*inf*); to defeat utterly (*inf*). [OFr *paste* (Fr *pâte*), from LL *pasta*, from Gr *pasta* barley porridge (neuter pl of *pastos* sprinkled, salted), from *passein* to sprinkle]
■ **pāst'er** *n* someone who pastes; a slip of gummed paper. **pāst'iness** *n*. **pāst'ing** *n* (*sl*) a beating; a thorough defeat. **pāst'y** *adj* like paste in texture; (of a complexion) pale and unhealthy-looking.
❑ **paste'board** *n* a stiff board made of sheets of paper pasted together; a visiting card, playing card, or ticket (*sl*). ◆ *adj* of pasteboard; sham; trumpery. **paste'-down** *n* the outer leaf of an endpaper that is pasted down on the inside cover of a book; formerly, a paper used to line the inside cover of a book. **paste'-eel** *n* a nematoid worm found in paste. **paste'-grain** *n* an imitation of morocco leather, used in binding books and in making fancy goods. **paste'-up** *n* a draft of a printed page consisting of text, artwork, photographs, etc pasted onto a sheet, for photographing or as a plan for a printing plate; a collage. **past'y-faced'** *adj* having a pale and dull complexion.

pastel /pas'təl or -tel/ *n* a chalk-like crayon made from powdered pigments bound together with gum; a drawing made with pastels; the process or art of drawing with pastels; woad. ◆ *adj* in pastel; (of colour) soft, quiet. [Fr *pastel*, from Ital *pastello*, from L *pasta* paste]
■ **pastellist** /pas' or -tel'/ *n*.

paster see under **paste**.

pastern /pas'tərn/ *n* any rope, strap, etc used to tie up a horse by the leg, a hobble (*obs*); the part of a horse's foot from the fetlock to the hoof, where the shackle is fastened. [OFr *pasturon* (Fr *paturon*), from OFr *pasture* pasture, a tether for a horse; cf **pester**]

Pasteurian /pa-stûr'i-ən/ *adj* relating to Louis *Pasteur* (1822–95), French chemist and bacteriologist, or his methods.
■ **Pasteurell'a** *n* (*pl* **Pasteurellas** or **Pasteurellae** /-ē/) a genus of bacteria which cause various serious infectious diseases, including plague; (without *cap*) a bacterium of this genus. **Pasteurellō'sis** *n* (*pl* **Pasteurellō'sēs**) a disease caused by organisms of the genus *Pasteurella*. **pas'teurism** *n* Pasteur's method of inoculation with the attenuated virus of certain diseases, *esp* hydrophobia. **pasteurīzā'tion** or **-s-** *n* sterilization of milk, etc, by heating. **pas'teurize** or **-ise** *vt*. **pas'teurizer** or **-s-** *n* an apparatus for sterilizing milk, etc.

pastiche /pa-stēsh'/, also **pasticcio** /pa-stit'chō/ *n* (*pl* **pastich'es** or **pasticci** /-tit'chē/) a jumble; a pot-pourri; a composition (in literature, music, or painting) made up of bits of other works or imitations of another's style. [Fr (from Ital) and Ital, from Ital *pasta*, paste; see **paste**]
■ **pasticheur** /-ē-shær'/ *n* someone who makes pastiches.

pasties /pās'tiz/ *n pl* decorative nipple covers of a kind worn by striptease artists, etc. [From **paste**]

pastil /pas'til/ *n* same as **pastel** or **pastille**.

pastille /pas'til or pa-stēl'/ *n* a small (often medicated) sweet; a small cone of charcoal and aromatic substances, burned as incense, or for fumigation or fragrance; a paper tube containing a firework which causes a small wheel to rotate; the same as **pastel** (*art*). [Fr, from L *pastillus* a little loaf]

pastime /pä'stīm/ *n* that which serves to pass away the time; a hobby or recreation. [**pass** and **time**]

pastiness, pasting see under **paste**.

pastis /pas-tēs'/ *n* an alcoholic drink flavoured with aniseed. [Fr]

pastor /päs'tər/ *n* a person who has care of a flock or of a congregation; a shepherd; a member of the clergy; the rose-coloured starling (*Pastor roseus*), from its following sheep to feed on parasites. [L *pāstor*, from *pāscere*, *pāstum* to feed]
■ **pas'toral** *adj* relating to, depicting or evoking rural life, the countryside, etc, *esp orig* shepherds or shepherd life; of the nature of pastureland; of or relating to the pastor of a church and his or her obligations to the congregation; addressed to the clergy of a diocese by their bishop; relating to care and advice given by teachers to pupils beyond the basic teaching of their subject. ◆ *n* a poem, play, romance, opera, piece of music, or picture depicting the life of (*usu* idealized or conventionalized) shepherds, or rural life in general; such writing as a genre; a pastoral letter; a book on the care of souls; a pastoral staff. **pastorale** /pas-tə-räl' or päs-to-rä'lä/ *n* (*pl* **pastora'les** or **pastora'li** /-lē/) (*Ital*) a pastoral composition in music; a pastoral, rustic, or idyllic opera or cantata. **pas'toralism** *n* a way of life characterized by keeping sheep, cattle or other grazing animals; pastoral character, fashion, cult or mode of writing. **pas'toralist** *n*. **pas'torally** *adv*. **pas'torate** *n* the office of a pastor; a pastor's tenure of office; a body of pastors. **pas'torly** *adj* suitable for a pastor. **pas'torship** *n*.
❑ **pastoral address** or **letter** *n* an address or a letter by a pastor to his people, or by a bishop to his clergy. **pastoral charge** *n* position of a pastor; the church, etc, over which a pastor is placed; an address to a newly ordained minister. **pastoral epistles** *n pl* those in the Bible to Timothy and Titus. **pastoral staff** *n* a crosier, a tall staff forming part of a bishop's insignia, headed like a shepherd's crook. **pastoral theology** *n* that part of theology which deals with the duties of pastors in relation to the care of souls.

pastourelle /pä-stoo-rel'/ *n* a medieval poetic genre, *esp* Provençal and French, a dialogue between a knight and a shepherdess; a movement in a quadrille. [Fr, little shepherdess]

pastrami /pa-strä'mi/ *n* a smoked, highly seasoned (*esp* shoulder) cut of beef. [Yiddish, from Romanian *pastramă*, from *a păstra* to serve]

pastry /pā'stri/ *n* articles made of paste or dough collectively; the crust of pies, tarts, etc; a small cake; a place where pastry is made (*Shakesp*); the art or practice of making pastry (*obs*). [**paste**]
❑ **pas'trycook** *n* a maker or seller of pastry.

pasture /päs'chər/ *n* grazing; growing grass for grazing; grazing land; a grazing ground, piece of grazing land; feeding (*archaic*); food (*Spenser*). ◆ *vi* to graze. ◆ *vt* to put to graze; to graze on. [OFr *pasture* (Fr *pâture*), from L *pāstūra*, from *pāscere*, *pāstum* to feed]
■ **past'urable** *adj* fit for pasture. **past'urage** *n* the business of feeding or grazing cattle; pasture-land; grass for feeding; right of pasture. **past'ural** *adj* of pasture. **past'ureless** *adj*.
❑ **past'ure-land** *n* land suitable for pasture.
■ **put out to pasture** to release an animal into a pasture to graze; to force a person to retire from work.

pasty¹ /pas'ti or päs'ti/ *n* a (*usu* individual) meat and vegetable pie with an all-round crust, typically a pastry round folded in two around the filling, with the join crimped. [OFr *pastée*, from L *pasta*; see **paste**]

pasty² /pā'sti/ *adj* see under **paste**.

PAT *abbrev*: planned activities time (*educ*); Professional Association of Teachers.

Pat /pat/ *n* a nickname for an Irishman. [*Patrick*]

pat¹ /pat/ *n* a gentle stroke with a flat surface, such as the palm of the hand; such a stroke as a caress or mark of approbation; a sound as of such a stroke; a small soft mass, *esp* of butter, such as might be moulded by patting. ◆ *vt* (**patt'ing; patt'ed**) to strike (now only to strike gently) with the palm of the hand or other flat surface; to shape by patting. ◆ *vi* to tap; to make the sound of pats, eg with the feet. ◆ *adv* and *adj* hitting the mark precisely; at the right time or place; exactly to the purpose; with or ready for fluent or glib repetition; (of a hand in poker) not likely to be improved by drawing (*US*). [Prob imit]
■ **pat'ly** *adv* (*rare*) fitly, conveniently; glibly, fluently. **pat'ness** *n*.
❑ **pat'ball** *n* rounders; gentle hitting in other games.
■ **off pat** exactly memorized; pat. **pat on the back** a mark of encouragement or approbation. **stand pat** (in poker) to decide to play one's hand as it is; to refuse to change.

pat² see **pit³**.

pat³ /pat/ (*Scot*) *n* a pot.
❑ **pat'-lid'** *n*.

pa t *abbrev*: past tense.

pat. *abbrev*: patent; patented.

pataca /pə-tä'kə/ *n* the basic unit of currency in Macau and formerly in Timor (100 avos); a coin of one pataca in value. [Port]

patagium /pat-ə-jī'əm/ *n* (*pl* **patagi'a**) a bat's wing-membrane; the parachute of skin of a flying squirrel, etc; the fold of integument between the upper arm and the forearm of a bird; a paired scale on a moth's pronotum. [L *patagium*, from Gr *patageion* an edging]
■ **patagial** /pə-tä'ji-əl/ *adj*.

Patagonian /pat-ə-gō'ni-ən/ *n* a member of the native population of Patagonia; a giant. ◆ *adj* of Patagonia; gigantic. [Sp *patagón*, big foot (the tallness of the Patagonians was grossly exaggerated by travellers)]

patamar /pat'ə-mär/ n an Indian vessel with an arched keel and a great stem and stern rake. [Port, from Konkani *pātamāri*]

pataphysics or **'pataphysics** /pat'ə-fiz-iks/ n sing 'the science of imaginary solutions' invented by the French dramatist Alfred Jarry (1873–1907), writer of symbolic farce, from which is descended the theatre of the absurd. [Gr *ta epi ta metaphysika* (works) imposed on the metaphysics]

Patarin or **Patarine** /pat'ə-rin or -rēn/ (hist) n orig an adherent of a popular party in Milan opposed to marriage of priests (11c); later a nickname for Manichaeans, Cathars, and other heretics. [Said to be from *Pattaria*, a district in Milan]

Patavinity /pat-ə-vin'i-ti/ n the diction of the people of Padua, *esp* applied to the historian Livy; the use of dialect; provincialism generally. [L *patavīnitās*, from *Patavium* Padua]

patball see under **pat¹**.

patch¹ /pach/ n a piece put on or to be put on to mend a defect; a dressing, *esp* a plaster for a cut or sore; a pad for an injured eye; a piece of adhesive material impregnated with a medicinal drug and put on the skin so that the drug can be gradually absorbed (*med*); a cloth badge sewn onto a garment; a piece of ground or plot of land; an area or district, etc regularly visited, patrolled or traded in, etc; an overlay to obtain a stronger impression (*printing*); a small piece of black silk, etc, stuck by ladies on the face to bring out the complexion by contrast, common in the 17c and 18c; a similar piece of fabric worn as a political party badge; an imitation beauty spot; a smallish area differing in colour or otherwise from its surroundings; a period of time; a scrap or fragment; a scrap pieced together with others; a group of instructions added to a computer program to correct a mistake (*comput*). ◆ vt to mend with a patch; to put a patch on; to apply as a patch; to join in patchwork; to mend or construct hastily, clumsily, or temporarily (commonly with *up* or *together*); to resolve (an argument, settle (differences), sometimes only temporarily (*usu* with *up*); to construct as a patchwork; to mark with patches; to connect (a telephone call) using a patchboard (with *through*), to put through. [ME *pacche*; origin unknown; poss connected with **piece**]

■ **patch'able** adj. **patched** adj. **patch'er** n. **patch'ily** adv. **patch'ing** n and adj. **patch'y** adj covered with patches; diversified in patches; inharmonious, incongruous, irregular; incomplete.

❑ **patch'board** n (*telecom*, etc) a panel with multiple electric terminals into which wires may be plugged to form a variety of electric circuits. **patch box** n a fancy box for holding the patches worn on the face, generally having a mirror inside the lid. **patch pocket** n a simple pocket consisting of a piece of material sewn on all but one side onto the outside of a garment. **patch test** n a test for allergy in which allergenic substances are applied to areas of skin which are later examined for signs of irritation. **patch-up'** n a provisional repairing. **patch'work** n needlework formed of patches or pieces sewed together; an incongruous combination; work patched up or clumsily executed; a surface diversified in patches. **patchwork quilt** n a bedcover which may or may not be quilted, one side of which is made up of patchwork.

■ **hit** or **strike a bad patch** to experience a difficult time, to encounter unfavourable conditions, etc. **not a patch on** not fit to be compared with.

patch² /pach/ n a fool or jester (*archaic*); a stupid person (*dialect*); a bad-tempered or peevish person (*dialect*). [Perh from **patch¹**, from the patched coat; nickname of Cardinal Wolsey's fool, Sexton; perh Ital *pazzo* fool]

■ **patch'ery** n (*Shakesp*) knavery.

❑ **patch'cocke** or **patch'ocke** n (*Spenser*) perh a clown (reading and meaning doubtful; cf **paiock**).

patchouli or **patchouly** /pach'oo-lē/, also pə-choo'lē/ n a labiate shrub (*Pogostemon patchouly*) of SE Asia; an aromatic essential oil derived from its dried branches. [Tamil *pacculi*]

patchwork, **patchy** see under **patch¹**.

pate /pāt/ n (old or humorous) the crown of the head, *esp* when bald; the head; intelligence (*fig*). [Origin unknown]

■ **pāt'ed** adj having a pate.

pâté /pät'ā or pat'ā/ n orig a pie or pastry; now *usu* a paste made of blended meat, herbs, etc. [Fr]

❑ **pâté de foie gras** /də fwä grä/ n orig a pasty of fattened goose liver; now *usu* a paste made from the liver.

patella /pə-tel'ə/ n (pl **patell'as** or **patell'ae** /-ē/) the kneecap (*anat*); a little pan (*ancient hist*); a saucer-like apothecium (*bot*); (with *cap*) the limpet genus. [L, dimin of *patina* a pan]

■ **patell'ar** adj of the kneecap. **patell'ate** (or /pat'/) adj saucer-shaped; limpet-shaped. **patellec'tomy** n the surgical removal of the patella. **patell'iform** adj patellate.

❑ **patellar reflex** n the knee-jerk.

paten /pat'ən/ n a plate; a communion plate; a chalice-cover; a metal disc. [OFr *patene*, from L *patena*, *patina* a plate, from Gr *patanē*]

patent /pā'tənt/ or (*esp* in *letters patent* and *Patent Office*, and *US*) /pat'ənt/ adj lying open; conspicuous, obvious, evident; generally accessible; protected by a patent; spreading (*bot*); expanding; ingenious (*inf*). ◆ n an official document, open, and bearing a government seal, conferring an exclusive right or privilege, such as a title of nobility, or *esp* the sole right for a term of years to the proceeds of an invention; something invented and protected by a patent; a privilege; a certificate. ◆ vt to secure a patent for. [L *patēns*, *-entis*, prp of *patēre* to lie open]

■ **pā'tency** n openness; obviousness. **pā'tentable** adj. **pātentee'** n someone who holds a patent, or to whom a patent is granted. **pā'tently** adv openly, obviously. **pā'tentor** n a person, body, authority, etc that grants a patent.

❑ **patent agent** n someone who obtains patents on behalf of inventors. **patent leather** n finely varnished leather. **patent log** n a device for recording the speed of a vessel, consisting of a submerged rotator attached by line to a dial on the ship's rail. **patent medicine** n (strictly) a medicine protected by a patent; (loosely) any proprietary medicine, *esp* one liable to stamp duty, since made by secret process or for some other reason. **Patent Office** n an office for the granting of patents for inventions. **patent outside** or **inside** n a newspaper printed on the outside or inside only, sold to a publisher who fills the other side with his own material, such as local news, etc. **patent right** n the exclusive right reserved by a patent. **patent rolls** n pl the register of patents issued in Britain. **patent still** n a still performing several operations at once, and producing a purer spirit than a pot-still.

■ **nothing patent** (*sl*) not very good.

pater /pā'tər/ (*usu facetious*) n father. [L *pater*]

patera /pat'ə-rə/ n (pl **pat'erae** /-rē/) a round flat dish holding the wine used by the Romans in ritual sacrifices; a round flat ornament in bas-relief in friezes, etc, often applied loosely to rosettes and other flat ornaments (*archit*). [L, from *patēre* to lie open]

patercove /pat'ər-kōv/ n same as **patrico**.

paterero /pat-ə-rā'rō/ n (pl **patere'ros** or **patere'roes** /-rōz/) same as **pederero**.

paterfamilias /pā-tər-fə-mil'i-as or pat'ər-/ n (pl strictly **patresfamil'ias** /-trās-/, sometimes **paterfamil'iases**) the father or other male head of a family or household; any man regarded as exerting a paternal influence on others (often *facetious*). [L *pater* a father, and *familiās*, old genitive of *familia* a household]

paternal /pə-tûr'n(ə)l/ adj of a father; on the father's side; derived or inherited from the father; fatherly; showing the disposition or manner of a father. [L *pater* (Gr *patēr*) a father]

■ **pater'nalism** n a system or tendency in which well-meaning supervision and/or regulation, etc is apt to become unwelcome interference. **paternalis'tic** adj. **pater'nally** adv. **pater'nity** n the state or fact of being a father; fatherhood; the relation of a father to his children; origin on the father's side; origination or authorship.

❑ **paternity leave** n leave of absence from work often granted to a father-to-be so that he can be with his partner and assist her during and after the birth of a child. **paternity suit** n a lawsuit brought by a mother to establish that a certain man is the father of her child and is liable to pay financial support. **paternity test** n a medical test of blood, DNA, etc to establish whether or not a particular man is the father of a particular child.

paternoster /pa-tər-nos'tər or pā'/ n (with *cap*) the Lord's Prayer; a muttered formula or spell; a harangue; a large bead in a rosary, at which, in telling, the Lord's Prayer is repeated; a rosary; anything strung like a rosary, *esp* a fishing-line with hooks at intervals; an ornament shaped like beads, used in astragals, etc (*archit*); a lift for goods or passengers, consisting of a series of cars moving on a continuous belt, the floors remaining horizontal at the top and bottom of travel. [L *Pater noster* 'Our Father', the first words of the Lord's Prayer]

pater patriae /pā'tər pā'tri-ē or pat'er pat'ri-ī/ (L) n the father of his country.

Paterson's curse /pat'ər-sənz kûrs/ (*Aust*) n any of various naturalized orig European herbs regarded as harmful to livestock. [Ety doubtful]

pâte-sur-pâte /pät'sür-pät'/ n a type of decoration used on pottery, in which layers of slip are applied to a low relief. [Fr, paste-upon-paste]

path /päth/ n (pl **paths** /pädhz/) a way trodden out by the feet; a footpath; a way for pedestrians; a course, route or line along which anything moves; a course of action or conduct; the route to the location of a file in a directory or folder structure (*comput*). ◆ vi (*Shakesp*) to go. [OE *pæth*; Ger *Pfad*]

■ **path'less** adj without a path; untrodden.

❑ **path'-breaking** adj innovative. **path'finder** n a person who explores the route, a pioneer; a radar device used as an aircraft navigational aid; a radar device for guiding missiles into a target area.

path'name *n* a description of the location of a particular computer file in a directory structure. **path'way** *n* a path; (in neurology) the route of a sensory impression to the brain, or of a motor impulse from the brain to the musculature; the sequence of reactions by which one substance is metabolically converted to another (*biochem*).

path. or **pathol.** *abbrev* : pathological; pathology.

-path /-*path*/ *n combining form* a sufferer from a particular disorder, as in *psychopath*; a therapist for a particular disorder, as in *osteopath*. [Ety as for **pathos**]
■ **-pathetic** or **-pathic** *adj combining form*. **-pathist** *n combining form* denoting a therapist for a particular disorder. **-pathy** *n combining form* mental or emotional sensitivity or receptiveness; disease, disorder; therapy for a particular disorder.

Pathan /pə-*tan*' or pu-*tän*'/ *n* a member of a Pashto-speaking people of Afghanistan and NW Pakistan. ◆ *adj* of or relating to the Pathans. [Pashto *Pakhtun*]

pathetic, etc see under **pathos**.

-pathetic see under **-path**.

pathic see under **pathos**.

-pathic see under **-path**.

-pathist see under **-path**.

patho- /*path*-ō-/ *combining form* denoting disease or disorder, as in *pathology*. [Ety as for **pathos**]
■ **pathogen** /*path*'ō-jen/ *n* an organism or substance that causes disease. **pathogen'esis** or **pathogeny** /pə-*thoj*'ə-ni/ *n* (mode of) production or development of disease. **pathogenetic** /path-ō-ji-net'ik/ or **pathogenic** /-*jen*'ik/ *adj* producing disease. **pathogenicity** /-is'i-ti/ *n* the quality of producing or the ability to produce disease. **pathog'enous** *adj* same as **pathogenetic** above. **pathognomon'ic** /-og-nō-/ *adj* (Gr *gnōmōn* judge, index) indicative of a particular disease. **pathog'nomy** *n*. **pathog'raphy** *n* a description of or article on a disease; abnormality. **patholog'ic** *adj*. **patholog'ical** *adj* relating to pathology; relating to or caused by disease; (loosely) habitual or compulsive. **patholog'ically** *adv*. **pathol'ogist** *n* a person skilled in pathology, *usu* having as a duty the performing of post-mortems. **pathol'ogy** *n* the study of diseases or abnormalities or, more particularly, of the changes in tissues or organs that are associated with disease; a deviation from the normal, healthy state. **pathopho'bia** *n* (Gr *phobos* fear) morbid fear of disease. **pathophysiol'ogy** *n* the physiological disorder caused by a disease or injury.

pathos /*pā*'thos/ *n* the quality that arouses pity. [Gr *pathos* experience, feeling, pathos]
■ **pathetic** /pə-*thet*'ik/ *adj* affecting the emotions of pity, grief or sorrow; touching; sadly inadequate; contemptible, derisory (*inf*); relating to or affecting the passions or their expressions (*obs*); applied to the superior oblique muscle, which turns the eyeball downwards, and to the trochlear nerve connecting with it (*anat*). See also **-pathetic** under **-path**. ◆ *n* that which is pathetic; the style or manner designed to excite emotion; (in *pl*) attempts at pathetic expression. **pathet'ical** *adj*. **pathet'ically** *adv*. **pathic** /*path*'ik/ *adj* passive (and see also **-pathic** under **-path**). ◆ *n* a passive subject; a catamite. □ **pathetic fallacy** *n* (in literature, etc) the transference of human emotions to inanimate objects.

pathway see under **path**.

-pathy see under **-path**.

patible /pat'i-bl/ *adj* capable of suffering or being acted on; passible. [L *patibilis*, from *patī* to suffer]

patibulary /pə-*tib*'ū-lə-ri/ *adj* of or relating to a gibbet or gallows. [L *patibulum* a gibbet]

patience /*pā*'shəns/ *n* the quality of being able calmly to endure suffering, toil, delay, vexation, or any similar condition; sufferance; a card game of various kinds, generally for one person, the object being to fit the cards, as they turn up, into some scheme; a species of the dock plant (also **pa'tience-dock**'; *Rumex patientia*) used like spinach, or other species of dock; also applied to bistort. [Fr, from L *patientia*, from *patī* to bear]
■ **pa'tient** *adj* sustaining pain, delay, etc, calmly and without complaint; not easily provoked; persevering in long-continued or intricate work; expecting with calmness; long-suffering; enduring; susceptible (of an interpretation). ◆ *n* a person under medical or surgical treatment; a doctor's client; someone who bears or suffers (*obs*). ◆ *vt* (*Shakesp*) to make patient. **pa'tiently** *adv*.

patin obsolete form of **paten**.

patina /*pat*'i-nə/ *n* a film of basic copper carbonate that forms on exposed surfaces of copper or bronze; a similar film of oxide, etc, on other metals; a film or surface appearance that develops on other substances (wood, flint, etc) on long exposure or burial; a sheen

acquired from constant handling or contact (also *fig*); a shallow pan used in ancient Rome; a Eucharistic paten. [L *patina* a dish]
■ **pat'ināted** *adj*. **patinā'tion** *n*. **pat'ined** *adj*.

patine obsolete form of **paten**.

patio /*pa*'ti-ō or -tyō/ *n* (*pl* **pat'ios**) a courtyard; a paved area *usu* adjoining a house, where outdoor meals can be served, etc. [Sp, a courtyard]
□ **patio door** *n* a tall glazed door opening onto a patio.

pâtisserie or **patisserie** /pa-tē'sə-rē, also pə-tis'ə-ri/ *n* a shop which sells fancy cakes, etc; such cakes. [Fr]

patka /*pat*'kə/ *n* a scarf worn as a head-covering by Sikh men in place of a turban. [Pashto]

pat-lid see under **pat³**.

patly see under **pat¹**.

Patna rice /*pat*'nə rīs/ *n* a long-grained rice, *orig* grown at *Patna* in India, served with savoury dishes.

patness see under **pat¹**.

Pat. Off. *abbrev* : Patent Office.

patois /*pat*'wä/ *n* (*pl* **patois** /-wäz/) spoken regional dialect; (loosely) jargon. [Fr; origin disputed, some suggesting corruption of *patrois*, from LL *patriensis* a local inhabitant]

patonce /pə-*tons*'/ (*heraldry*) *adj* (of a cross) having four arms expanding in curves from the centre, with floriated ends. [Origin unknown]

patres conscripti /*pāt*', pat'rēz or -räs kon-skrip'tī or -tē/ (L) the conscript fathers, those enrolled as Roman senators.

patresfamilias see **paterfamilias**.

patrial /*pā*' or pa'tri-əl/ *adj* relating to one's native land; (of a word) denoting a native or inhabitant of the place from whose name the word was formed; relating to the legal right to enter and stay in the UK, or to one who has this right. ◆ *n* a patrial word; formerly, a citizen of the UK, a British colony or the British Commonwealth, who for certain reasons (eg because a parent was born in the UK) had a legal right to enter and stay in the UK. [Obs Fr, from L *patria* fatherland]
■ **pa'trialism** *n*. **patrial'ity** *n* the condition of being a patrial. **patrializā'tion** or **-s-** *n*. **pa'trialize** or **-ise** *vt*.

patria potestas /*pā*' or pa'tri-ə po-tes'täs/ (L) *n* the authority of a Roman father over his children.

patriarch /*pā*'tri-ärk/ *n* a man who governs his family by paternal right, a male head of a family; one of the early heads of families from Adam downwards to Abraham, Jacob, and his sons (*Bible*); a bishop ranking above primates and metropolitans; the head of certain Eastern Churches; a father or founder; a venerable old man; an oldest inhabitant; an old leader of any group; the most imposing and greatest of its kind. [Gr *patriarchēs*, from *patriā* family, from *patēr* father, and *archē* rule]
■ **patriarch'al** *adj* belonging or subject to a patriarch; like a patriarch; of the nature of a patriarch. **patriarch'alism** *n* the condition of tribal government by a patriarch. **pa'triarchate** *n* the province, dignity, office, term or residence of a church patriarch; patriarchy. **pa'triarchism** *n* government by a patriarch. **pa'triarchy** *n* a community of related families under the authority of a patriarch; the patriarchal system.
□ **patriarchal cross** *n* a cross with two horizontal bars.

patriation /pā-tri-ā'shən/ *n* the transferring of responsibility for the Canadian constitution (as enshrined in the British North America Act of 1867) from the British parliament to the Canadian parliament. [L *patria* fatherland]
■ **pāt'riate** *vt*.

Patrician see under **patrick**.

patrician /pə-*trish*'ən/ *n* a member or descendant by blood or adoption of one of the original families of citizens forming the Roman people, *opp* to *plebeian*; a nobleman of a new order nominated by the emperor in the later Roman Empire; an imperial Roman provincial administrator in Italy or Africa; a hereditary noble; an aristocrat. ◆ *adj* of or relating to the patricians; aristocratic. [L *patricius*, from *pater*, *patris* a father]
■ **patri'cianly** *adj*. **patriciate** /pə-*trish*'i-āt/ *n* the position of a patrician; the patrician order; patricians as a body.

patricide /*pat*'ri-sīd/ *n* the murder of one's own father; a person who murders his or her father. [Doubtful L *patricīda*, as if from *pater*, *patris* father, and *caedere* to kill; prob an error for *parricīda*; see **parricide**]
■ **patricī'dal** *adj*.

patrick /*pat*'rik/ *n* a 17c Irish halfpenny. [St *Patrick* (L *Patrīcius*), 5c Christianizer of Ireland]
■ **Patrician** /pə-*trish*'ən/ *adj* of St Patrick.
■ **St Patrick's cabbage** a saxifrage, London pride. **St Patrick's cross** a red saltire on a white background, representing Ireland.

patriclinic, **patriclinous**, etc see **patroclinic**.

patrico /pat'ri-kō/ (sl) n (pl **pat'ricoes**) a hedge-priest (also **pat'ercove**). [First part of word unexplained; see **cove²**]

patrifocal /pat'ri-fō-kəl/ (anthrop, etc) adj centred on the father; (of societies, families, etc) in which authority and responsibility rest with the father. [L pater, patris father, and focus a hearth]
■ **patrifocal'ity** n.

patrilineal /pat-ri-lin'i-əl/ or **patrilinear** /-ər/ adj traced through the father or through males alone. [L pater, patris father, and līnea line]
■ **patrilineage** /-lin'i-ij/ n. **patrilin'eally** adv. **pat'riliny** n patrilineal descent.

patrilocal /pat-ri-lō'kl/ adj (of a form of marriage) in which the wife goes to live with the husband's group. [L pater, patris father, and locālis, from locus place]

patrimony /pat'ri-mə-ni/ n an inheritance from a father or from ancestors; a church estate or revenue. [L patrimōnium a paternal estate, from pater, patris a father]
■ **patrimonial** /-mō'ni-əl/ adj. **patrimō'nially** adv.

patriot /pā'tri-ət or pat'ri-ət/ n a person who truly, though sometimes unquestioningly, loves and serves his or her country. ◆ adj devoted to one's country. [Gr patriōtēs fellow countryman, from patrios, from patēr a father]
■ **patriotic** /pat-ri-ot'ik or pāt-/ adj devoted to one's country; like a patriot; motivated by a love of one's country; for the public good (rare). **patriot'ically** adv. **pā'triotism** (or /pat'/) n.

Patripassian /pat-ri-pas'i-ən/ n a member of one of the earliest classes of anti-Trinitarian sectaries (2c), who denied the distinction of three persons in one God, maintaining that God the Father suffered along with, or in the person of, God the Son. ◆ adj of or relating to the Patripassians. [L pater, patris father, and patī, passus to suffer]
■ **Patripass'ianism** n.

patristic /pə-tris'tik/ or **patristical** /-əl/ adj relating to the fathers of the Christian Church. [Gr patēr, pat(e)ros a father]
■ **patris'ticism** /-sizm/ n the mode of thought, etc, of the fathers. **patris'tics** n sing the knowledge of the Christian fathers as a subject of academic study (sometimes **patrol'ogy**).
❑ **patristic similarity** n (bot) similarity due to common ancestry.

patroclinic /pat-rō-klin'ik/ or **patroclinous** /-klī'nəs/ adj (also **patriclin'ic** or **patriclī'nous**) inherited from the father; more like the father than the mother. [Gr patēr, pat(e)ros, L pater, patris father, and klinein to lean]
■ **patroclī'ny** (also **patriclī'ny**) n.

patrol /pə-trōl'/ vi (**patrōll'ing**; **patrōlled'**) to move systematically round or go the rounds of an area, for the purpose of watching, repressing, protecting, inspecting, etc; (of a police officer) to be on duty on a beat. ◆ vt to keep (an area) under surveillance by patrolling; to perambulate. ◆ n the act or service of patrolling; perambulation; a person or group of people patrolling an area; a body of aircraft, ships, etc having patrolling duties; a small detachment of soldiers, etc sent on reconnaissance or to make an attack, etc; one of the units of eight or so Scouts or Guides forming a troop. [OFr patrouiller to patrol, orig to paddle in the mud]
■ **patrol'er** n.
❑ **patrol car** n that used by police to patrol an area. **patrol'man** or fem **patrol'woman** n a police officer on duty on a beat (N Am); a police officer without rank (N Am); (also **patrol**) an employee of a motoring organization on patrol to help motorists in difficulties. **patrol'-wagon** n (N Am) a prison-van.

patrology see **patristics** under **patristic**.

patron /pā'trən/ n (also fem **pā'troness**) a protector; a person, group or organization, etc which gives support, encouragement and often financial aid; a (regular) customer; a habitual attender; an upholder; a proprietor of a restaurant, etc (also fem **patronne** /pa-tron'/); someone who has the right to appoint to any office, esp to a living in the church (C of E); (in ancient Rome) the former master of a freed slave, retaining certain rights; a Roman patrician who gave legal aid and other protection to his client in return for services; formerly, a person who accepted a dedication and gave the author a present; a guardian saint; a captain of a Mediterranean vessel; a slave-owner; a pattern (obs). [L patrōnus, from pater, patris father]
■ **patronage** /pat'/ n support given by a patron; protection (Spenser); guardianship of saints; the right of bestowing offices, privileges, or church benefices (C of E); habitual commercial dealings. ◆ vt (Shakesp) to countenance. **patronal** /pa-, pə-trō'nl/, pāt' or pat'rən-l/ adj. **patronize** or **-ise** /pat' or pāt'/ vt to act as a patron toward; to give encouragement to; to assume the condescending air of a patron toward; to give one's custom to or to frequent habitually. **pat'ronizer** or **-s-** n. **pat'ronizing** or **-s-** adj. **pat'ronizingly** or **-s-** adv. **pā'tronless** adj.
❑ **patron saint** n a saint regarded as the protector of a particular group, nation, etc.

patronymic /pat-rə-nim'ik/ adj derived from the name of a father or an ancestor. ◆ n a name so derived. [Gr patrōnymikos, from patēr a father, and onyma name]

patroon /pə-troon'/ n a captain of a ship; a coxswain of a longboat; a holder of a grant of land under the old Dutch government of New York or New Jersey. [Fr patron, Sp patrón, and Du patroon; cf **patron**]
■ **patroon'ship** n.

patsy /pat'si/ (sl, esp N Am) n an easy victim, a sucker; a scapegoat, fall guy. [Ety uncertain; perh from Ital pazzo fool or Yiddish Putz fool, simpleton]

patte /pat or pät/ n a narrow band keeping a belt or sash in its place. [Fr]

patté or **pattée** /pa-tā' or pat'i/ (heraldry) adj (of a cross) spreading towards the ends, or having the ends expanded in three clawlike divisions. [Fr, pawed]

patted see **pat¹**.

patten¹ /pat'n/ n a wooden shoe, a clog (hist); a wooden sole mounted on an iron ring to raise the shoe above the mud (hist); the base of a pillar (archit). ◆ vi (obs) to go on pattens. [OFr patin clog (now skate), perhaps from patte paw]
■ **patt'ened** adj with pattens.

patten² an old form of **paten**.

patter¹ /pat'ər/ vi to pat or strike often, as hailstones do; to make the sound of a succession of light pats; to run with short quick steps. ◆ n the sound of pattering. [Frequentative of **pat¹**]

patter² /pat'ər/ n glib talk, chatter, esp the insincere speech of salesmen, etc; the jargon of a particular group, place, etc. ◆ vi to talk or sing rapidly and glibly; to talk in this way, esp on the stage, as accompaniment to action or for comic effect. ◆ vt to repeat hurriedly, to gabble; to repeat the Lord's Prayer (obs); to gabble prayers (obs). [**paternoster**, with reference to the obs senses]
■ **patt'erer** n a street seller relying heavily on patter.
❑ **patt'er-song** n a comic song in which a great many words are sung or spoken very rapidly.
■ **patter flash** to talk the jargon of thieves.

pattern /pat'ərn/ n a person or thing to be copied; a model; a design or guide with help of which something is to be made (eg a set of dressmaker's paper templates); a model of an object to be cast, from which a mould is prepared; a sample; a typical example; a decorative design; a particular disposition of forms and colours; a design or figure repeated indefinitely; a coherent series of occurrences or features; the distribution of shot on a target. ◆ vt to make or be a pattern for (Shakesp); to match, parallel (Shakesp); to take as a pattern; to fashion after a pattern; to make a pattern on. [Fr patron patron, pattern; cf **patron**]
■ **patt'erned** adj.
❑ **patt'ern-maker** n a person who makes the patterns for moulders in foundry-work. **pattern race** n a horse-race open to all comers in a particular category, eg of a certain age or weight, usu contested by top-class horses, the object being to find the best. **patt'ern-shop** n the place in which patterns for a factory are prepared. **pattern therapy** n a system of therapy based on the healing properties of different shapes, eg pyramids. **patt'ern-wheel** n the count wheel in a clock.

patting see **pat¹**.

pattle /pat' or pär'l/ or **pettle** /pet'l/ (Scot) n a small long-handled spade for cleaning a plough. [Origin obscure; cf **paddle²**]

pattress /pat'ris/ n a metal or plastic box, housing the wiring, behind an electric socket, switch, etc (also **pattress box**); a plate or block fixed to a surface as a base for eg a ceiling rose. [L patera a shallow dish]

patty /pat'i/ n a little pie; a small flat cake of minced beef or other food. [Fr pâté; cf **pasty¹**]
❑ **patt'ypan** n a pan for baking patties. **patt'ypan squash** n (N Am) a round flattish variety of squash.

patulous /pat'ū-ləs/ (esp bot) adj spreading. [L patulus, from patēre to lie open]
■ **pat'ulin** n a toxic substance derived from the mould Penicillium patulum.

paua /pä'wə or pow'ə/ n (also **paw'a**) the New Zealand name for the abalone; its shell used as an ornament or decoration. [Maori]

pauciloquent /pö-sil'ə-kwənt/ adj of few words, speaking little. [L paucus little, and loquī to speak]

paucity /pö'sit-i/ n fewness; smallness of quantity; insufficiency, dearth. [L paucitās, -ātis, from paucus few]

paughty /pöhh'ti/ (Scot) adj haughty. [Origin unknown]

paul¹ same as **pawl**.

paul² /pöl/ n a paolo (qv).

pauldron /pöl'drən/ or **pouldron** /pōl'/ n a separable shoulder-plate in armour. [OFr *espalleron*, from *espalle* the shoulder]

Paulian /pö'li-ən/ or **Paulianist** /pö'li-ə-nist/ n a follower of Paul of Samosata, a 3c Monarchian Unitarian of Antioch (also *adj*).

Paulician /pö-lish'ən/ n a member of a 7c sect in Armenia and later in Thrace, with Marcionite and Adoptianist affinities (*perh* from Paul of Samosata, or the apostle, or one of their founders). ◆ *adj* of or relating to the Paulicians.

Pauli exclusion principle see **exclusion principle** under **exclude**.

Pauline /pö'līn/ adj of the apostle Paul. ◆ *n* a member of any religious order named after him; a scholar of St Paul's School, London. [L *Paulus, Paullus*, a Roman cognomen, meaning 'little']
■ **Paulinian** /-in'i-ən/ adj Pauline. **Paul'inism** n the teaching or theology of Paul. **Paul'inist** n. **Paulinist'ic** adj.

Paul Jones /pöl jōnz/ n a dance in the course of which each man takes a number of partners in succession, *perh* named after the Scottish-American seaman John Paul Jones (1747–92), who excelled in the capture of prizes.

paulo-post-future /pö'lō-pōst-fū'chər/ adj and n future perfect (*grammar*); future immediately after the present. [L *paulo* a little, *post* after, and *futūrum* future]

paulownia /pö-lō'ni-ə/ n any tree of the Chinese and Japanese genus *Paulownia*, of the figwort family, with showy flowers. [Named after the Russian princess Anna *Pavlovna* (1795–1865)]

Paul Pry /pöl prī/ n a person who pries into other people's business. [The eponymous character in John Poole's play (1825)]

Paul's-man /pölz'man/ n formerly, a lounger in the middle aisle of St Paul's, London.

paunce see **pansy**.

paunch /pönch or pönsh/ n the belly; a protuberant belly; the first and largest stomach of a ruminant; a rope mat to prevent chafing (*naut*). ◆ *vt* to eviscerate. [OFr *panche* (Fr *panse*), from L *pantex, panticis*]
■ **paunch'y** adj big-bellied.

pauper /pö'pər/ n a destitute person; a person not required to pay costs in a lawsuit; a person supported by charity or by some public provision (*hist*). [L, poor]
■ **pau'peress** n. **pau'perism** n the state of being a pauper. **pauperizā'tion** or **-s-** n. **pau'perize** or **-ise** vt to reduce to pauperism; to accustom to expect or depend on outside support.

paupiette /pō-pyet'/ n a thin piece of meat or fish rolled around a filling. [Fr, from L *pulpa* pulp]

pauropod /pö'rə-pod/ n a member of the **Pauropō'da**, a class of myriapods similar to centipedes. [Gr *pauros* small, and *pous, podos* a foot]

pause[1] /pöz/ n intermission; a temporary stop; a short break; cessation caused by doubt; hesitation; a mark for suspending the voice (*prosody*); a continuance of a note or rest beyond its time, or a mark indicating this (*music*); (also **pause button**) a control that causes a temporary stop in the playing of a DVD, video, etc. ◆ *vi* (*Shakesp vt* reflexive*) to make a pause. ◆ *vt* to cause to stop. [Fr, from L *pausa*, from Gr *pausis*, from *pauein* to cause to cease]
■ **paus'al** adj. **pause'ful** adj. **pause'fully** adv. **pause'less** adj. **pause'lessly** adv. **paus'er** n. **paus'ing** n and adj. **paus'ingly** adv.
■ **give pause** to cause to hesitate.

pause[2] /pöz/ (*dialect*) vt to kick. [Origin unknown]

pavage see under **pave**.

pavane /pa-vän'/ or **pavan** /pav'ən/ n (also **pav'en** or **pav'in**) a slow formal dance of Spanish origin, popular in Europe in the 16c and 17c; music for it, in 4–4 time. [Fr *pavane*, or Sp or Ital *pavana*, prob from L *pāvō, -ōnis* peacock]

pave /pāv/ vt to cover with slabs or other close-set pieces, so as to form a level surface for walking on; to cover with anything close-set; to be such a covering for. ◆ *n* (*US*) pavement. [Fr *paver*, prob a back-formation from *pavement*, from L *pavīmentum*, from *pavīre* to beat hard; cognate with Gr *paiein* to beat]
■ **pā'vage** n a charge, or right to levy a charge, for paving streets. **paved** adj. **pave'ment** n a paved surface, or that with which it is paved; a footway by the side of a street (sometimes even when unpaved); a paved road or its surface (*N Am*); a floor-like surface; an underlying bed, *esp* of fireclay under coal. ◆ *vt* to pave; to be a pavement for. **pā'ven** adj paved. **pā'ving** n and adj. **pā'viour** n (also **pā'ver** or (*N Am*) **pā'vior**) a person who lays paving-stones; a machine for tamping down paving-stones; a paving-stone.
□ **pavement artist** n a person who seeks a living by drawing coloured pictures on the pavement. **pavement epithelium** n epithelium in the form of a layer of flat cells. **pavement light** n a window of glass blocks in the pavement to light a cellar. **paving debate** n a parliamentary debate preliminary to the main debate. **pa'ving-stone** n a slab of stone or concrete used in a pavement, etc.

■ **on the pavement** homeless. **pave the way for** to prepare the way for; to make easier; to help to bring on.

pavé /pa-vā'/ (*Fr*) n a pavement; a setting of jewellery with the stones close together, covering the metal.

pavement, paven[1] see under **pave**.

paven[2] see **pavane**.

paver see **paviour** under **pave**.

pavid /pav'id/ adj timid. [L *pavidus* afraid, from *pavēre* to be frightened]

pavilion /pə-vil'yən/ n or **-i-ən**/ n a light building at a sports ground for players and spectators of a game; an exhibition building; an ornamental or showy building (often turreted or domed) for pleasure purposes; a tent, *esp* a large or luxurious one; a tent-like covering; a canopy (*obs*); a projecting section of a building, *usu* highly decorated and with a tent-like roof; a hospital block; (in gem-cutting) the undersurface of a brilliant, opposite to the crown; the bell of a horn; the outer ear; a flag or ensign (*obs*). ◆ *vt* to provide with pavilions; to cover, eg with a tent. [Fr *pavillon*, from L *pāpiliō, -ōnis* a butterfly, a tent]
□ **pavil'ion-roof** n a tent-like roof.
■ **Chinese pavilion** a set of bells hanging from a frame on a pole.

pavin see **pavane**.

paving see under **pave**.

pavior, paviour see under **pave**.

pavis or **pavise** /pav'is/ n a shield for the whole body. [OFr *pavais*, from Ital *pavese*, prob from *Pavia* in Italy]

pavlova /pav-lō'və/ n a type of sweet dish consisting of a meringue base topped with whipped cream and fruit (also with *cap*). [Named in honour of the Russian ballerina Anna *Pavlova* (1881–1931)]

Pavlovian /pav-lō'vi-ən/ (*psychol* and *physiol*) adj relating to the work of the Russian physiologist, Ivan *Pavlov* (1849–1936), on conditioned reflexes; (of reactions, responses, etc) automatic, unthinking.

Pavo /pā'vō/ n the peacock genus; a southern constellation. [L *pāvō, -ōnis* peacock]
■ **pavonazzo** /pa-və-nat'sō/ n a brightly-coloured marble. **pavone** /pə-vōn'/ n (*Spenser*) a peacock. **pavō'nian** or **pavonine** /pav'ən-īn/ adj.

paw[1] /pö/ n a clawed foot; a hand, or handwriting (*facetious* or *derog*). ◆ *vi* to draw the forefoot along the ground; to strike the ground with the forefoot; to strike out with the paw; to feel about or over anything, *esp* offensively. ◆ *vt* to scrape, feel, handle, or strike with the forefoot or hand; to handle indecently, coarsely, or clumsily. [OFr *poe, powe*, prob Gmc; cf Du *poot*, Ger *Pfote*]

paw[2] /pö/ (*obs*) interj pah. ◆ *adj* (also **paw'paw**) foul; obscene.

pawa see **paua**.

pawaw see **powwow**.

pawk /pök/ (*Scot*) n a trick. [Origin unknown]
■ **pawk'ily** adv. **pawk'iness** n. **pawk'y** adj drily or slyly humorous.

pawl /pöl/ n a catch engaging with the teeth of a ratchet wheel to prevent backward movement. [Origin obscure; poss connected with Du or Fr *pal*, L *pālus* stake]

pawn[1] /pön/ n something deposited as security for repayment or performance; the state of being pledged (as *in* or *at* pawn). ◆ *vt* to give as security for repayment of borrowed money, *esp* to a pawnbroker; to pledge or stake. [OFr *pan*; cf Du *pand*; connection with L *pannus*, cloth, very doubtful]
■ **pawnee**[1] n a person who takes anything in pawn. **pawn'er** n a person who gives a pawn or pledge as security for money borrowed.
□ **pawn'broker** n a broker who lends money on pawned articles. **pawn'broking** n. **pawn'shop** n a shop of a pawnbroker. **pawn'ticket** n a ticket marked with the name of the article, the amount advanced, etc, delivered to the pawner of anything.

pawn[2] /pön/ n in chess, any of sixteen pieces, eight on each side, of lowest rank, generally moving one square forward at a time or one square diagonally if taking an opposing piece; a humble tool or lightly valued agent (*fig*); an easily manipulated person. [OFr *paon* a foot soldier, from LL *pedō, -ōnis*, from L *pēs, pedis* the foot]

pawn[3] /pön/ n a gallery or covered walk. [Cf Du *pand*]

pawn[4], **pown** or **powin** /pown/ (chiefly *Scot*) n a peacock. [OFr *poun*, Fr *paon*, from L *pāvō, -ōnis*]

pawn[5] see **pan**[3].

pawnce see **pansy**.

Pawnee /pö'nē or -nē'/ n (pl **Pawnee** or **Pawnees**) a member of a Native American tribe, *orig* from Nebraska, etc, afterwards settling in Oklahoma; their language. ◆ *adj* of or relating to the Pawnee or their language.

pawnee[1] /pö'nē/ see under **brandy**.

pawnee[2], **pawner**, **pawnshop**, etc see under **pawn**[1].

pawpaw[1] /pö'pö/ or **papaw** /pə-pö'/ n a tree (*Asimina triloba*) of the custard apple family, or its fruit, native to N America; the papaya. [Prob variant of **papaya**]

pawpaw[2] see **paw**[2].

PAX *abbrev* : Private Automatic Exchange.

pax[1] /paks/ n peace; the kiss of peace; an osculatory. ◆ *interj* (*inf*) (let's call a) truce. [L *pāx* peace]
❑ **pax'-board** or **pax'-brede** n an osculatory.
■ **pax vobiscum** /vo-bis'kəm, vō-, or wō-bēs'kŭm/ peace be with you.

pax[2] /paks/ (*L*) n peace.

pax *abbrev* : passengers.

paxiuba /pä-shē-oo'bə/ n a Brazilian palm (*Iriartea exorrhiza*) with stilt-roots. [Port, from Tupí]

paxwax /paks'waks/ n the strong tendon in an animal's neck. [Orig *fax-wax*, from OE (Anglian) *fæx* hair, and *weaxan* to grow]

pay[1] /pā/ vt (**pay'ing**; **paid**, or in the nautical sense **payed** /pād/) to give what is due (in satisfaction of a debt, in exchange, in compensation or in remuneration, etc) to (the person, etc to whom it is owed); to give (money, etc) in satisfaction of a debt, in exchange, compensation, remuneration, etc; to settle or discharge (a claim, bill, debt, etc); to hand over money, etc, for; (of a sum of money, etc) to be or yield satisfactory remuneration or compensation for, or enough to discharge; to yield (a certain sum, profit, etc); to be profitable to, to benefit; to render, confer (attention, heed, court, a visit, etc); to satisfy, gratify (*obs*); to thrash (*Shakesp* and *dialect*); (of a rope) to allow or cause to run out (*naut*). ◆ *vi* to hand over money or other equivalent, or compensation, etc (with *for*); to afford to make payment, or constitute an equivalent or means of making payment (with *for*); to be worth one's trouble; to be profitable; to suffer or be punished (with *for*); to be the subject of payment. ◆ n satisfaction (*obs*); money given for service; salary, wages; receipt of wages, etc, service for wages, etc, hire or paid employment (*esp* for an evil purpose); payment or time of payment; remunerative yield of mineral. [Fr *payer*, from L *pācāre* to appease; cf *pāx* peace]
■ **paid** *adj* see separate entry. **pay'able** *adj* that may or should be paid; due; profitable. **payee'** n someone to whom money is paid. **pay'er** n. **pay'ing** n and *adj*. **pay'ment** n the act of paying; the discharge of a debt by money or its equivalent in value; that which is paid; recompense; reward; punishment.
❑ **pay and display** n a system of paying for parking in which a ticket is bought from a machine and displayed in the window of the parked vehicle. **pay-and-display'** *adj*. **pay-as-you-earn'** n a method of income tax collection in which the employer deducts tax from earnings before paying the employee (*abbrev* **PAYE**). **pay-as-you-go'** *adj* (of mobile phones) denoting that the user, the outright purchaser of the phone, pays only for calls made, using credit bought in advance; (of other services, eg the Internet) denoting that charges are made only when the service is used. **payback** see **pay back** below. **payback period** n (*econ*) the length of time a project will take to recover its initial outlay. **pay bed** n a bed, *specif* in a National Health Service hospital, available to a patient who pays for its use (**private pay bed** one available to a patient who pays for its use and for his or her own treatment; cf **amenity bed**). **pay'-bill** or **pay'-sheet** n a statement of money to be paid to workmen, etc. **pay'-box** or **pay'-desk** n a box or desk at which a customer pays. **payday** n a regular day for payment, eg of wages. **payday lender** n a company that provides payday loans (see below). **payday loan** n a short-term, high-interest loan, to be repaid on the borrower's next payday. **pay dirt** n gravel or sand containing enough gold to be worth working (also **pay gravel**); a source of riches. **pay envelope** n (*N Am*) pay packet. **pay'fone** same as **payphone** below. **paying guest** n (*euphem*) a lodger. **paylist** see **payroll** below. **pay'load** n that part of the cargo of an aeroplane or other conveyance for which revenue is obtained; the part of a rocket's equipment that is to fulfil the purpose of the rocket, such as a warhead, or apparatus for obtaining information. **pay'master** n the master who pays; the official in an organization, government, etc who pays out money. **Paymaster General** n the minister at the head of a department of the Treasury that makes payments on behalf of government departments; in the navy, an officer in charge of the bureau dealing with payments, clothing, etc (*US*); formerly also a similar officer in the army (*US*). **payment card** n a credit card. **pay'-off** n (time of) payment *esp* of a reward or punishment; outcome; a particularly useful or desirable result; dénouement. **pay'-office** n the place where payments are made. **pay-out** see **pay out** below. **pay packet** n an envelope containing a person's wages; wages. **pay-per-click** n a form of Internet advertising in which the advertiser pays according to the number of clicks made by users on the advertisement (also *adj*). **pay-per-view'** n a form of pay television (qv below) in which viewers use a smart card to gain access to the service (also *adj*). **pay'phone** n a coin- or card-operated public telephone. **pay'roll** n

the money for paying wages; (also **pay'list**) a list of people entitled to receive pay, with the amounts due to each; a computer program for calculating wages. **payroll giving** n contributions to charity which are deducted from one's wages and paid by one's employer directly to the charity concerned. **pay'slip** n a note to a worker (giving an analysis) of the sum paid in wages. **pay station** n (*US*) a telephone call-box. **pay television** or **pay TV** n satellite or cable television available to subscribers. **pay'wall** n an arrangement allowing access to a website only to users who have paid to subscribe to it.
■ **in the pay of** receiving payment from in return for services, used *esp* in a sinister sense. **pay back** to pay in return (a debt); to give tit for tat (**pay'back** n). **pay cash** to pay for something at the time of the transaction, ie not using credit terms. **pay down** to pay (eg a first instalment) in cash on the spot; to pay back debt. **pay for** to make amends for; to suffer for; to bear the expense of. **pay in** to contribute to a fund; to deposit money in a bank account. **pay off** to pay in full and discharge (a debt, an employee, etc); to take revenge upon; to requite; to fall away to leeward (*naut*); to yield good results, justify itself (see also **pay-off** above). **pay one's** (or **its**) **way** to have or bring enough to pay expenses; to compensate adequately for initial outlay. **pay out** to release (a rope, etc) gradually, to feed or run out; to disburse (**pay'-out** n); to punish deservedly. **pay round** to turn the ship's head. **pay the piper** see under **pipe**[1]. **pay through the nose** to pay more than the fair price, to pay dearly. **pay up** to pay in full; to pay arrears; to pay (for) in instalments; to accept the necessity and pay; to pay on demand.

pay[2] /pā/ (*naut*) vt (*pat* and *pap* **payed**) to smear (a wooden boat) with tar, etc as waterproofing. [OFr *peier*, from L *picāre* to pitch]

PAYE see **pay-as-you-earn** under **pay**[1].

PAYG *abbrev*: pay as you go.

paynim /pā'nim/ (*obs*) n (also **pai'nim** or (*Milton*) **pā'nim**) heathendom; a heathen; a non-Christian, *esp* a Muslim. ◆ *adj* heathen. [OFr *paienisme* paganism, from L *pāgānismus*, from *pāgānus* a pagan]
■ **pay'nimry** n heathendom.

pay-off, **pay-office** see under **pay**[1].

payola /pā-ō'lə/ n a secret payment or bribe to secure a favour, *esp* the promotion of a commercial product by a disc jockey; the practice of making or receiving payments of this kind. [Facetiously coined from **pay**[1] and Victrola, a make of gramophone, or pianola]

pay-out...to...**payroll** see under **pay**[1].

pays /pā-ē'/ (*Fr*) n country.
■ **les Pays Bas** /lā pā-ē bä/ the Low Countries, the Netherlands.

paysage /pā-ē-zäzh'/ n a landscape, a landscape painting (*obs* for a time then reborrowed). [Fr]
■ **paysagist** /pā'zə-jist/ n a landscape-painter.

paysd /pāzd/ (*Spenser*) for **peised** (*pat* and *pap* of **peise**) or **poised** (*pat* and *pap* of **poise**[1]).

payslip, **pay station**, **pay television** see under **pay**[1].

pazazz or **pazzazz** see **pizzazz**.

PB *abbrev*: Pharmacopoeia Britannica; Plymouth Brethren.

Pb (*chem*) *symbol*: lead. [L *plumbum*]

PBIT *abbrev*: profit before interest and tax.

pbuh *abbrev*: peace be upon him (always used by Muslims when mentioning the name of Mohammed).

PBX (*telecom*) *abbrev*: private branch exchange, a private telephone switching apparatus which routes calls between extensions and the public telephone network, and internally between extensions.

PC *abbrev*: personal computer; Police Constable; political correctness; politically correct; Privy Councillor.
❑ **PC card** n a card conforming to PCMCIA standards, used to add memory or devices to a laptop computer.

pc *abbrev*: per cent; personal computer; postcard.

PCAS *abbrev*: Polytechnics Central Admissions System (now replaced by **UCAS**).

PCB *abbrev*: polychlorinated biphenyl, any of several compounds with various industrial applications, regarded as environmental pollutants; printed circuit board.

PCC *abbrev*: parochial church council; Press Complaints Commission.

pce *abbrev*: piece.

PCI (*comput*) *abbrev*: Peripheral Component Interconnect, a local bus standard.

PCM *abbrev*: pulse code modulation.

pcm *abbrev*: per calendar month.

PCMCIA *abbrev*: Personal Computer Memory Card International Association.

PCN *abbrev*: personal communications network, a network for mobile telephone users.

PCP *abbrev*: pentachlorophenol, a water-insoluble fungicide widely regarded as an environmental pollutant; phencyclidine (qv); Pneumocystis carinii pneumonia, a major cause of death among AIDS patients.

PCR *abbrev*: politically correct retailing; polymerase chain reaction.

PCS *abbrev*: Principal Clerk of Session; Public and Commercial Services (Union).

PCT *abbrev*: primary-care trust (in the National Health Service).

pct (*esp N Am*) *abbrev*: per cent.

PCV *abbrev*: passenger-carrying vehicle.

PD (*US*) *abbrev*: Police Department.

Pd (*chem*) *symbol*: palladium.

pd *abbrev*: paid.

PDA *abbrev*: personal digital assistant.

PDF (*comput*) *abbrev*: portable document format, a file format that allows documents to be read by computers with different operating sytems.

PDI *abbrev*: pre-delivery inspection.

PDL (*comput*) *abbrev*: page description language.

pdq (*inf*) *abbrev*: pretty damn quick, hence as soon as possible.

PDSA *abbrev*: People's Dispensary for Sick Animals.

PE *abbrev*: Peru (IVR); physical education; potential energy; Prince Edward Island (Canadian province); Protestant Episcopal.

p/e *abbrev*: price-earnings ratio.

pea¹ /pē/ *n* (*pl* **peas**) the nutritious seed of the papilionaceous climbing plants *Pisum sativum* (garden pea) and *Pisum arvense* (field pea); the plant itself (also **pea'-plant**); extended to various similar seeds and plants (*esp* of the genus *Lathyrus*) and to various rounded objects, eg roe of salmon and some other fish, very small pieces of coal or small rounded stones. [Singular formed from **pease¹**, which was mistaken for a plural]
□ **pea'berry** *n* a small round coffee seed, growing singly. **pea'-brain** *n* (*inf*) a person of little intelligence. **pea'-brained** *adj* foolish. **peacod** see under **pease¹**. **pea'-crab** *n* a little round crab (genus *Pinnotheres*) that lives symbiotically in lamellibranch shells. **pea gravel** *n*. **pea'-green** (or /-grēn'/) *n* and *adj* yellowish green, like the colour of soup made from split peas; bright-green like fresh peas. **pea'-iron** *n* limonite in little round nodules. **pea'pod** *n* the seed case of a pea. **pea'-ri'fle** *n* a rifle throwing a very small bullet. **peas'cod** see **peasecod** under **pease¹**. **pea shingle** *n*. **pea'shooter** *n* a small tube for blowing peas through, used as a toy weapon. **pea soup**, **pea-souper**, **pea-soupy** see **pease-soup** under **pease¹**. **pea'-stone** *n* pisolite. **pea-straw** see **pease-straw** under **pease¹**. **pea'-trainer** *n* a structure for pea-plants to climb on. **pea-vin'er** *n* a machine that picks, washes and grades peas.
■ **Egyptian pea** the chickpea. **split peas** peas stripped of their covering, dried and halved. **Sturt's desert pea** see under **desert²**.

pea² /pē/ *n* an obsolete term for a **pea'fowl**, a male or female peacock. [OE *pēa* (*pāwa*), from L *pāvō*]
□ **pea'-chick** *n* a young peafowl. **pea'hen** *n* the female of the peacock.

peace /pēs/ *n* a state of quiet; freedom from disturbance; freedom from war; cessation of war; a treaty that ends a war; freedom from contention; ease of mind or conscience; tranquillity; quiet; stillness; silence. ◆ *vi* (*Shakesp*) to be silent. ◆ *interj* silence; be silent (*hist*). [OFr *pais* (Fr *paix*) from L *pāx*, *pācis* peace]
■ **peace'able** *adj* disposed to peace; peaceful. **peace'ableness** *n*. **peace'ably** *adv*. **peace'ful** *adj* enjoying peace; tending towards or favouring peace; inclined to peace; belonging to time of peace; consistent with peace; tranquil; calm; serene. **peace'fully** *adv*. **peace'fulness** *n*. **peace'less** *adj*. **peace'lessness** *n*. **peace'nik** *n* a pacifist, *esp* in a derogatory sense.
□ **peace'-breaker** *n* a person who breaks or disturbs the peace. **peace camp** *n* a camp set up by anti-war protesters close to a military establishment. **Peace Corps** *n* (in the USA and various other countries) a government agency that sends volunteers to developing countries to help with agricultural, technological and educational schemes. **peace dividend** *n* money left over from a government's defence budget as a result of negotiated arms reduction policies, available for peaceable (*esp* social) use; the fact of having such surplus money. **peace drug** or **pill** *n* (*inf*) a hallucinogen (PCP). **peace establishment** *n* the reduced military strength maintained in time of peace. **peace'keeper** *n*. **peace'keeping** *adj* (**peacekeeping force** a military force sent into an area with the task of preventing fighting between opposing factions). **peace'maker** *n* a person who makes or produces peace; a person who reconciles enemies; a revolver (*old facetious*). **peace'making** *n*. **peace'-monger** *n* a

peacemaker from the point of view of those who think him or her a sentimental busybody. **peace offering** *n* (among the Jews) a thank-offering to God; a gift offered towards reconciliation, propitiation, or deprecation. **peace officer** *n* an officer whose duty it is to preserve the peace; a police-officer. **peace'-part'ed** *adj* (*Shakesp*) dismissed from the world in peace. **peace'-par'ty** *n* a political party advocating the making or the preservation of peace. **peace pill** see **peace drug** above. **peace pipe** *n* the calumet. **peace process** *n* long-term negotiations leading to resolution of a conflict. **peace sign** *n* a sign made with the index and middle fingers in the form of a V, with palm turned outwards, indicating a wish for peace. **peace'time** *n* time when there is no war. ◆ *adj* of peacetime. **peace'-warrant** *n* a warrant of arrest issued by a Justice of the Peace.
■ **at peace** in a state of peace; not at war. **breach of the peace** see under **breach**. **hold one's peace** to remain silent. **in peace** in enjoyment of peace. **keep the peace** to refrain from disturbing the public peace; to refrain from, or to prevent, contention. **kiss of peace** see under **kiss**. **letter of peace** see **pacifical** under **pacify**. **make one's peace with** to reconcile or to be reconciled with. **make peace** to end a war. **peace of God** the protection from acts of private warfare formerly offered by the Church to consecrated persons and places, and on Sundays and holy days. **swear the peace** to take oath before a magistrate that a certain person ought to be put under bond to keep the peace. **the king's** or **queen's peace** see under **king**.

peach¹ /pēch/ *n* a sweet, juicy, velvety-skinned stone-fruit; the tree (*Prunus*, or *Amygdalus*, *persica*) bearing it, closely related to the almond; extended to other fruits and fruit trees, such as the quandong; peach brandy (*US*); anything regarded as a very choice example of its kind, *esp* a girl (*US* also **peacherino** /-ə-rē'nō/; *inf*); a yellow slightly tinged with red. ◆ *adj* of the peach; of the colour of a peach. [OFr *pesche* (Fr *pêche*, Ital *persica*, *pesca*), from L *Persicum* (*mālum*) the Persian (apple); its native country is unknown]
■ **peach'y** *adj* coloured or tasting somewhat of peach; very good, excellent (*inf*).
□ **peach'-bloom'** *n* the powdery bloom on a peach; a similar appearance on the face, on pottery, etc; a peach flower (also **peach blossom**); its pinkish colour; a moth with wings so coloured (*Thyatira batis*). ◆ *adj* of the colour of or resembling peach-bloom. **peach'-blow** *n* a pinkish glaze on porcelain, *esp* Chinese porcelain (also *adj*). **peach brandy** *n* a spirit distilled from the fermented juice of the peach. **peach'-coloured** *adj* of the colour of a ripe peach (yellowish, tinged with red) or of peach blossom (pink). **peach Melba** *n* a dish named in honour of the Australian soprano Dame Nellie *Melba*, consisting of peach halves served with ice cream and *usu* a raspberry sauce. **peach'-palm** *n* the pupunha, a S American palm (*Bactris* or *Guilielma*) with an edible fruit like a peach in appearance. **peach'-stone** *n*. **peach'-tree** *n*. **peach'-water** *n* a flavouring extract from peach-leaves. **peach'-wood** *n* the wood of the peach-tree; Nicaragua wood (genus *Caesalpinia*). **peach'-yell'ows** *n* a virus disease that turns peach-leaves yellow and kills the tree.

peach² /pēch/ *vt* (*Shakesp*) to accuse, inform against, betray. ◆ *vi* (with *on*) to betray one's accomplice; to become an informer. [Aphetic form of **appeach**]
■ **peach'er** *n*.

pea-chick see under **pea²**.

pea coat see **pea jacket**.

peacock /pē'kok/ *n* a genus (*Pavo*) of large birds of the pheasant kind, consisting of the common peacock (*Pavo cristatus*) and the Javan (*Pavo muticus*), noted for their showy plumage, *esp*, in the former, the deep iridescent greenish blue in the neck and tail-coverts; the male of either species; a vain person; peacock-blue (also *adj*); a peacock butterfly. ◆ *vt* to make like a peacock; to pick the best parts out of (*Aust*). ◆ *vi* to strut about or behave like a peacock; to acquire the choicest pieces of land (ie near water) (*Aust*). [**pea²** and **cock**]
■ **peacock'ery** *n* vain ostentation. **pea'cockish** *adj*. **pea'cock-like** *adj*. **pea'cocky** *adj*.
□ **pea'cock-blue** *n* the deep greenish-blue of the peacock's neck (also *adj*). **peacock butterfly** *n* a butterfly (*Inachis io*) with wingspots like those of the peacock's train. **peacock copper** *n* copper pyrites, from the colours of its tarnish. **pea'cock-fish** *n* a variegated Mediterranean wrasse. **pea'cock-flower** *n* a name for various species of *Poinciana* (flamboyant-tree, Barbados pride). **peacock ore** *n* bornite; copper pyrites. **pea'cock-pheas'ant** *n* an Asiatic genus (*Polyplectron*) related to the peacocks and Argus pheasants. **pea'cock-stone** *n* a jeweller's name for the cartilaginous ligament of some molluscs. **Peacock Throne** *n* the throne of the kings of Delhi, carried off to Persia in 1739.

pea-crab see under **pea¹**.

peafowl see **pea²**.

peag /pēg/ or **peak** /pēk/ *n* Native American shell money. [Massachuset *piak*]

peahen see under **pea²**.

pea jacket /pē' jak'it/ n a sailor's coarse thick overcoat (also **pea coat**). [Du *pĭe* (now *pij*) coat of coarse stuff, and **jacket** or **coat**]

peak¹ /pēk/ n a point; the pointed end or highest point of anything; the top of a mountain, *esp* when sharp; a summit; the highest point of a curve, etc on a graph; any point or period of maximum activity, intensity, performance, skill, etc; a sharp projection; the projecting front of a cap or (formerly) of a widow's hood; a projecting point of hair on the forehead; a pointed beard; the upper outer corner of a sail extended by a gaff or yard (*naut*); the upper end of a gaff (*naut*). ◆ *adj* maximum; of a maximum. ◆ *vi* to rise in a peak; to reach the height of one's powers, popularity, etc; (of prices, etc) to reach a highest point or level (sometimes with *out*). ◆ *vt* (*naut*) to tilt up. [Found from the 16c (*peked* in the 15c); appar connected with **pike²**]
■ **peaked** *adj* having a peak or peaks. **peak'y** *adj* having a peak or peaks; like a peak.
❑ **peak load** n the maximum instantaneous demand of electricity, or load on a power-station (cf **base-load** under **base¹**).
■ **off-peak** at, of or relating to a regular period of relatively low customer demand, eg for electricity or rail travel. **peak** (**viewing** or **listening**) **hours** or **time** the period in the day when the number of people watching television or listening to the radio is at its highest (for television *approx* 7.00–10.30pm).

peak² /pēk/ vi to droop, to look thin or sickly; to sneak or slink about (*Shakesp*); to mope (*obs*). [Origin unknown]
■ **peaked**, **peak'ing** or **peak'y** *adj* having a pinched or sickly look, sharp-featured.

peak³ see **peag**.

peal¹ /pēl/ n a loud sound; a number of loud sounds one after another; a set of bells tuned to each other; a chime or carillon; the changes rung upon a set of bells. ◆ *vi* to resound in peals; to appeal (*Spenser*). ◆ *vt* to give forth in peals; to assail with din (*Milton*). [Appar aphetic for **appeal**]

peal² or **peel** /pēl/ (*dialect*) n a grilse; a young sea-trout. [Origin unknown]

pean¹ US spelling of **paean**.

pean² /pēn/ n a heraldic fur, differing from ermine only in the ground being sable and the spots or. [Perh OFr *pene, panne*]

pean³ same as **peen**.

peanut /pē'nut/ n the edible seed of a S American plant (*Arachis*), developing in pods underground, the groundnut or monkey nut; the plant itself; (in *pl*) something very trifling or insignificant, *esp* a paltry sum of money, chickenfeed (*inf*). [**pea¹** and **nut**]
❑ **peanut butter** n a paste made from ground roasted peanuts. **peanut oil** n oil expressed from peanuts.

pear /pār/ n a fruit, a pome tapering towards the stalk and bulged at the end; the tree (*Pyrus communis*) of the apple genus which bears it; extended to various fruits (such as *alligator pear, anchovy-pear, prickly pear*, etc); (in gem-cutting) a pear-shaped brilliant. [OE *pere, peru*, from LL *pira*, from L *pirum* (wrongly *pyrum*) pear]
❑ **pear cider** n an alcoholic drink made from fermented pear juice. **pear drop** n a pear-shaped pendant; a sweet shaped and flavoured like a pear. **pear'monger** n a seller of pears. **pear'-push** or **pear'-switch** n an electric push-button in a hanging pear-shaped bob. **pear'-shaped** *adj* tapering towards one end and bulged at the other; in the shape of a pear; (of a vocal quality) mellow, resonant, non-nasal. **pear'-tree** n.
■ **go pear-shaped** (*inf*) to put on weight around the hips, waist or bottom; to go awry or out of kilter.

pearce a Spenserian spelling of **pierce**.

peare a Spenserian spelling of **peer¹**.

pearl¹ /pûrl/ n a typically round, milky-white concretion of nacre formed in certain species of oyster and other shellfish, around a foreign body or otherwise, prized as a gem; nacre, mother-of-pearl; a paragon or prized example; a lustrous globule; a granule; a tubercle of an antler burr; cataract of the eye; a five-point type (about 15 lines to the inch) (*printing*). ◆ *adj* made of or like pearl; granulated; (of an electric light bulb) made from frosted, rather than clear, glass as a precaution against glare. ◆ *vt* to set or adorn with pearls or pearly drops; to make pearly; to make into small round grains. ◆ *vi* to take a rounded form; to become like pearls; to fish for pearls. [Fr *perle*, prob from dimin of L *perna* leg, leg-of-mutton-shaped; cf Ital dialect *perna* pearl, Ital *pernocchia* pearl oyster]
■ **pearled** *adj*. **pearl'er** n a pearl-fisher or a pearl-fisher's boat. **pearlesc'ent** *adj* having a pearly sheen. **pearl'iness** n. **pearl'ing** n and *adj*. **pearl'ized** or **-s-** *adj* treated so as to give a pearly or lustrous surface. **pearl'y** *adj* like pearl, nacreous; rich in pearls. ◆ n (*pl* **pearl'ies**) (in *pl*) pearl buttons; (in *pl*) costermongers' clothes covered with pearl buttons; a costermonger, or a member of his family, wearing such clothes.

❑ **pearl ash** n partly purified potassium carbonate. **pearl barley** see under **barley¹**. **pearl button** n a mother-of-pearl button. **pearl disease** n bovine tuberculosis. **pearl diver** n someone who dives for pearls. **pearl'-essence** n a silvery preparation from fish scales used in making artificial pearls. **pearl'-eye** n cataract. **pearl'-eyed** *adj*. **pearl'-fisher** n someone who fishes for pearls. **pearl'-fishery** n. **pearl'-fishing** n. **pearl'-gray'** or **pearl'-grey'** n a pale grey (also *adj*). **pearl millet** n the bulrush millet or spiked millet (*Pennisetum typhoideum*), a grain much grown in India. **pearl mussel** n a freshwater mussel (*Unio margaritifera*) that yields pearls. **pearl onion** n a type of small onion often eaten pickled. **pearl oyster** n any oyster that produces pearls, *esp Avicula* (or *Meleagrina*) *margaritifera*. **pearl'-pow'der** n a cosmetic of basic bismuth nitrate or of bismuth oxychloride. **pearl'-sā'go** n sago in round granules. **pearl'-shell** n mother-of-pearl; a pearly or pearl-bearing shell. **pearl'-sheller** n. **pearl'-shelling** n. **pearl'-spar** n a pearly-lustred pale dolomite. **pearl'-stone** n perlite. **pearl'-tapiō'ca** n tapioca granulated and graded according to its size; a potato-starch imitation. **pearl'-white** n material made from fish scales, used in making artificial pearls; basic nitrate of bismuth, used in medicine and as a cosmetic; bismuth trichloride, used as a pigment; lithopone; calcium sulphate. **pearl'wort** n a member of a genus (*Sagina*) of small plants related to chickweed. **pearly gates** n pl (from the Bible, Revelation 21) entrance to heaven. **pearly king** or (*fem*) **pearly queen** n a costermonger whose costume is considered the most splendidly decorated with pearl buttons. **pearly nautilus** see **nautilus**. **pearly whites** n pl (*inf*) the teeth.
■ **cultured pearl** a true pearl formed by artificial means, eg by planting a piece of mother-of-pearl wrapped in oyster epidermis in the body of an oyster. **false**, **imitation** or **simulated pearl** an imitation pearl, eg a glass bulb coated with pearl essence.

pearl² /pûrl/ n a small loop on the edge of lace, ribbon, etc; (in knitting) purl. ◆ *vt* to purl. [Cf **purl¹**]
■ **pearl'ing** or **pearl'in** n (*Scot*) lace of silk or of thread; (in *pl*) edgings of such lace or clothes trimmed with it.
❑ **pearl'-edge** n an edging of small loops.

Pearl Harbour /pûrl här'bər/ n (*fig*) a sudden and devastating attack. ◆ *vt* (*rare*) to mount a surprise attack of great force against. [*Pearl Harbor*, US naval base near Honolulu, attacked by the Japanese Air Force on 7 December 1941]

pearlies see **pearly** under **pearl¹**.

pearlin see under **pearl²**.

pearlite /pûr'līt/ n a constituent of steel composed of alternate plates of ferrite and cementite. [**pearl¹**]
■ **pearlit'ic** *adj*.

pearly see under **pearl¹**.

pearmain /pār'mān or pə-mān'/ n a variety of apple. [Appar OFr *parmain, permain*]

pearst Spenserian spelling of **pierced** (see under **pierce**).

peart or (*obs*) **piert** /pērt/ (*dialect*) *adj* lively; saucy; in good health and spirits. [**pert**]
■ **peart'ly** *adv*.

peasant /pez'ənt/ n a member of a lowly class of smallholders (*hist*); a person who works on the land; a person who lives in the country, a rustic (*inf*); an ignorant or uncultured person (*derog*). ◆ *adj* of or relating to peasants, rustic, rural; rude. [OFr *paisant* (Fr *paysan*), from *pays*, from assumed L *pāgēnsis*, from *pāgus* a district]
■ **peas'antry** n peasants as a class; the condition or quality of a peasant. **peas'anty** *adj* in the style of a peasant.
❑ **peasant proprietor** n a peasant who owns and works his or her own farm. **Peasants' Revolt** n Wat Tyler's rising of 1381. **Peasants' War** n a popular insurrection in Germany, in 1525.

pease¹ /pēz/ n (*archaic*) a pea or pea-plant (*pl* **pease**; *old pl* **peason** /pēz'ən/), now almost wholly superseded by the new singular **pea** and plural **peas** (see **pea¹**) except in a collective sense. [ME *pēse*, pl *pēsen*, from OE *pise*, pl *pisan*, from LL *pisa*, L *pisum*, from Gr *pison* or *pisos*]
❑ **pease'-bann'ock** n a bannock made of pease-meal. **pease'-blossom** n. **pease'-brose** n brose made of pease-meal. **pease'cod**, **peas'cod** or **pea'cod** n the pod of the pea. **pease'cod-bell'ied** *adj* (of a doublet) peaked downwards in front. **pease'cod-cuirass'** n a cuirass shaped like the peasecod-bellied doublet. **pease'-meal**, **pease'-porr'idge** or **pease pudding** n meal, porridge, or pudding made from pease. **pease'-soup** or **pea soup** n soup made from pease; a thick yellow heavy-smelling fog (also **pea'-soup'er**; *inf*). **pea'-soup'y** *adj*. **pease'-straw** or **pea'-straw** n the stems and leaves of the pea-plant after the peas have been picked.

pease² see **peise**.

peaseweep /pēz'wēp/ see **peewit**.

peason the old plural of **pease¹**.

---

peat[1] /pēt/ n a shaped block dug from a bog and dried or to be dried for fuel; the generally brown or nearly black altered vegetable matter (chiefly bog moss) found in bogs, from which such blocks are cut. [From the 13c in SE Scotland in Anglo-L as *peta* a peat; poss of British origin; cf **piece**]

■ **peat'ary**, **peat'ery** or **pēt'ary** n same as **peat bank** below. **peat'y** adj like, of the nature of, abounding in, or composed of peat; smoky in flavour, like whiskies distilled using water from areas rich in peat, or in the production of which peat has been used as a fuel.

□ **peat bank**, **peat bed**, **peat bog**, **peat'land**, **peat moor** or **peat moss** n a region, bog, moor, etc, covered with peat; a place from which peat is dug. **peat'-caster** n a person who digs peats and throws them on the bank to dry. **peat'-casting** n. **peat'-creel** n a basket for carrying peats. **peat'-hag** or **peat'-hagg** n a hag in a peat bog (see **hag**[2]). **peat'-hole** n. **peat'man** n a carter or seller of peats. **peat'-reek** n the smoke of peat, believed by some to add a special flavour to whisky; highland whisky. **peat'-reek'er** n an ornamental apparatus for producing the smell of peat-smoke. **peat'-smoke'** n. **peat'-spade** n a spade having a side wing at right angles for cutting peat in rectangular blocks. **peat'-stack** n a stack of peats, drying or stored.

peat[2] /pēt/ (obs) n an endearment applied to a woman, girl, friend or favourite; an advocate favoured by a judge (Scot). [Origin obscure]

■ **peat'ship** n (Walter Scott).

peau de soie /pō-də-swä'/ n a type of smooth silk or rayon fabric. [Fr, literally skin of silk]

peavey or **peavy** /pē'vi/ (US) n a lumberman's spiked and hooked lever. [Joseph *Peavey*, its 19c inventor]

peaze see **peise**.

peba /pē'bə/ n a S American armadillo. [Tupí]

pebble /peb'l/ n a small roundish stone, esp worn down by water; transparent and colourless rock-crystal; a lens made of it; a semi-precious agate; a grained appearance on leather, as if pressed by pebbles; a large size of gunpowder. ◆ adj of pebble. ◆ vt to stone or pelt; to cover with pebbles; to impart pebble to (leather). [OE *papol*(-stān), a pebble(-stone)]

■ **pebb'led** adj. **pebb'ling** n. **pebb'ly** adj full of pebbles.

□ **pebble-bed reactor** n (nuclear eng) a reactor with a cylindrical core into which spherical fuel pellets are inserted at the top and removed at the base. **pebb'ledash** n a method of coating exterior walls with small pebbles set into the mortar; this coating. ◆ vt to treat or coat with pebbledash. **pebb'le-glasses** n pl (often facetious) spectacles with very thick lenses. **pebb'le-pow'der** n gunpowder in large cubical grains. **pebb'le-stone** n a pebble. **pebb'le-ware** n a fine pottery of mixed coloured clays.

pébrine /pā-brēn'/ n a destructive protozoan disease of silkworms. [Fr]

PEC, also sometimes **pec** /pek/ abbrev : photoelectric cell.

pec[1] /pek/ (inf) n (usu in pl) a pectoral muscle.

pec[2] see **PEC**.

pecan /pē'kən, -kan or pi-kan'/ n a N American hickory (also **pecan tree**); its edible smooth-shelled nut (also **pecan nut**). [Native American name; cf Cree *pakan*]

peccable /pek'ə-bl/ adj liable to sin. [L *peccāre*, -ātum to sin]

■ **peccabil'ity** n. **pecc'ancy** n sinfulness; transgression. **pecc'ant** adj sinning; offending; morbid, diseased or disease-producing (med). **pecc'antly** adv.

peccadillo /pek-ə-dil'ō/ n (pl **peccadill'os** or **peccadill'oes**) a trifling fault, a small misdemeanour. [Sp *pecadillo*, dimin of *pecado*, from L *peccātum* a sin]

peccancy, **peccant**, etc see under **peccable**.

peccary /pek'ə-ri/ n either of two species of pig-like S American animals. [Carib *pakira*]

peccavi /pek-ä'vē/ n (pl **pecca'vis**) an admission of guilt or sin. [L *peccavi* I have sinned]

pech or **pegh** /pehh/ (Scot) vi to pant. ◆ n a pant. [Imit]

Pecht or **Peght** /pehht/ (Scot) n a Pict. [OE (Anglian) *Pehtas* (WSax *Peohtas*) Picts]

peck[1] /pek/ vt to strike or pick up with the point of the beak or other sharp instrument; to make (a hole, etc), render or cause to be (damaged, pierced, etc) by a quick movement of the beak, etc; to eat sparingly or with affectation of daintiness, or (sl) to eat in general; to kiss in a quick or cursory manner or movement. ◆ vi to strike or feed with the beak or in a similar manner; to eat daintily or sparingly (with at); to nit-pick or quibble (with at); to nag or criticize (with at). ◆ n an act of pecking; a hole made by pecking; a quick or cursory kiss; food (sl). [Appar a form of **pick**[1]]

■ **peck'er** n that which pecks; a woodpecker; a kind of hoe; a part with an up-and-down movement in a telegraph instrument; spirit, resolve, humour (as if orig beak, nose, as in keep your pecker up ; inf);

the penis (sl, orig US). **peck'ing** n. **peck'ish** adj somewhat hungry (inf); irritable (US sl). **peck'ishness** n.

□ **peck'erwood** n (US) a woodpecker; a white person, esp one from the rural South (derog). **pecking order** or **peck order** n a social order among poultry (or other birds) according to which any bird may peck a less important bird but must submit to being pecked by a more important one; order of prestige or power in a human social group; order of importance or prevalence.

peck[2] /pek/ n formerly, a measure of capacity for dry goods, 2 gallons, or one quarter of a bushel; a measuring vessel holding this quantity; an indefinitely great amount (eg a peck of troubles). [ME *pekke*, *pek*, from OFr *pek* generally a horse's feed of oats; origin unknown]

peck[3] /pek/ vt (also Shakesp **pecke**) to pitch; to jerk. ◆ vi to incline; to stumble, esp of a horse by failing to put the foot down flat. [A form of **pitch**[1], cf **pick**[2]]

■ **peck'ing** n stone-throwing.

Pecksniffian /pek-snif'i-ən/ adj like, or of, the hypocrite *Pecksniff* in Dickens's novel *Martin Chuzzlewit*.

Pecora /pek'ə-rə/ n pl the Cotylophora, or ruminants other than camels and chevrotains. [L pl of *pecus*, *-oris* cattle]

pecorino /pek-ə-rē'nō/ n an Italian hard cheese made from ewes' milk. [Ital, of ewes, from *pecora* sheep]

pecten /pek'tən/ n (pl **pec'tines** /-tin-ēz/) a comb-like structure of various kinds, eg in a bird's or reptile's eye; the pubic bone; a tactile organ in scorpions; a member of the scallop genus (*Pecten*) of molluscs, with a ribbed shell. [L *pecten*, *-inis* a comb]

■ **pectinaceous** /-ā'shəs/ adj like the scallops. **pec'tinal** adj of a comb; comb-like; having bones like the teeth of a comb. **pec'tinate** or **pec'tinated** adj toothed like a comb; having narrow parallel segments or lobes; like the teeth of a comb. **pec'tinately** adv. **pectina'tion** n the state of being pectinated; a comb-like structure. **pectin'eal** adj of the pubic bone; comb-like. **pec'tinibranchiate** /-brangk-i-āt/ adj having comb-like gills.

pectic /pek'tik/ adj of, relating to, or derived from pectin. [Gr *pēktikos* congealing, from *pēgnynai* to fix]

■ **pec'tin** n a mixture of carbohydrates found in the cell walls of fruits, used for the setting of jams and jellies. **pectīzā'tion** or **-s-** n. **pec'tize** or **-ise** vt and vi to congeal. **pec'tōse** n a pectin-yielding substance contained in the fleshy pulp of unripe fruit.

□ **pectic acid** n an insoluble substance (of several varieties) formed by hydrolysis of pectins.

pectinaceous, **pectinal**, **pectinate**, etc, **pectination**, **pectineal**, **pectines**, etc see **pecten**.

pectization, **pectize** see under **pectic**.

pectolite /pek'tə-līt/ n a zeolite-like monoclinic acid, calcium sodium silicate. [Gr *pēktos* congealed, and *lithos* stone]

pectoral /pek'tə-rəl or pek-tö'rəl/ adj of, for, on, or near the breast or chest; coming from the heart or inner feeling (fig). ◆ n a pectoral fin; either of the two muscles (*pectoralis major* and *pectoralis minor*) situated on either side of the top half of the chest and responsible for certain arm and shoulder movements (inf short form **pec**); armour for the breast of a person or a horse; an ornament worn on the breast, esp the breastplate worn by the ancient Jewish high-priest, and the square of gold, embroidery, etc, formerly worn on the breast over the chasuble by bishops during mass; a chest protector; a medicine for the chest; a pectoral cross. [L *pectorālis*, from *pectus*, *pectoris* the breast]

■ **pec'torally** adv. **pectoril'oquy** n (L *loquī* to talk) the sound of a patient's voice heard through the stethoscope when applied to the chest in certain morbid conditions of the lungs.

□ **pectoral cross** n a gold cross worn on the breast by bishops, etc. **pectoral fins** n pl the anterior paired fins of fishes. **pectoral girdle** n the shoulder-girdle, consisting of shoulder-blade and collarbone (and coracoid in vertebrates other than mammals). **pectoral sandpiper** n a N American sandpiper, the male of which inflates its breast in courtship. **pectoral theology** n the theology of those who make much of experience and emotion as guides to a knowledge of divine truth.

pectose see under **pectic**.

peculate /pek'ū-lāt/ vt and vi to appropriate dishonestly for one's own use, pilfer, embezzle. [L *pecūlārī*, *-ātus*, from *pecūlium* private property, related to *pecūnia* money]

■ **pecula'tion** n. **pec'ulātor** n.

peculiar /pə- or pi-kū'lyər or -li-ər/ adj odd, strange; own; of one's own; belonging exclusively (to); privately owned; appropriated; preserved; characteristic; special (to); very particular; having eccentric or individual variations in relation to the general or predicted pattern, as in peculiar motion or velocity (astron); (of a star) having a variable magnetic field. ◆ n a parish or church exempt from the jurisdiction of the ordinary or bishop in whose diocese it is placed; anything exempt from ordinary jurisdiction; private property or right (obs); (usu with *cap*) one of the Peculiar People (see below); a type of unusual kind that has to be specially cast (*printing*). [L *peculium* private property]

■ **peculiarity** /-li-ar'i-ti/ *n* the quality of being peculiar or singular; that which is found in one and in no other; something which distinguishes anything from others; idiosyncrasy; individuality; oddity. **pecu'liarize** or **-ise** *vt* to set apart. **pecu'liarly** *adv*. **pecu'lium** *n* private property, *esp* that given by a father to a son, etc.

❑ **peculiar motion** see **proper motion** under **proper**. **Peculiar People** *n* the Jews, as God's chosen people (Deuteronomy 26.18, Titus 2.14); an Evangelical denomination, founded in 1838, believing in the divine inspiration of the Holy Scriptures, and practising believers' baptism, Holy Communion, and Divine healing.

pecuniary /pi-kū'nya-ri or -ni-a-ri/ *adj* relating to money; consisting of money. [L *pecūnia* money, from the root that appears in L *pecudēs* (pl) cattle, and **fee**]

■ **pecu'niarily** *adv*. **pecu'nious** *adj* (*rare*) rich.

ped[1] /ped/ (*dialect*) *n* a pannier or hamper (also **pad**). [Origin unknown]

ped[2] /ped/ *n* short for **pedestrian**.

ped[3] /ped/ *n* a naturally-formed unit or mass of soil, such as a crumb, block or aggregate. [Gr *pedon* ground]

ped-[1] see **paed-**.

ped-[2] see **pedi-**.

-ped /-ped/ or **-pede** /-pēd/ *combining form* denoting foot. [L *pēs, pedis* foot]

pedagogue /ped'a-gog/ *n* a teacher; a pedant. ◆ *vt* to teach. [Partly through Fr and L from Gr *paidagōgos* a slave who led a boy to school, from *pais, paidos* boy, and *agōgos* leader, from *agein* to lead]

■ **pedagogic** /-gog' or -goj'/ or **pedagog'ical** *adj*. **pedagog'ically** *adv*. **pedagog'ics** /-gog' or -goj'/ *n sing* the science and principles of teaching. **ped'agogism** /-gizm or -jizm/ or **ped'agoguism** *n* the spirit or system of pedagogy; teaching. **ped'agoguery** /-gog-a-ri/ *n* a school; schoolmastering; pedagoguishness. **ped'agoguish** *adj* like a pedagogue. **ped'agoguishness** *n*. **ped'agogy** /-gog-i or -goj-i/ *n* the science of teaching; instruction; training.

pedal /ped'l/ *n* a lever pressed by the foot; the lower and thicker part of a piece of straw; a plait made of these; a pedal point; a pedal-organ; a pedal-board. ◆ *vi* (**ped'alling** or (*US*) **ped'aling**; **ped'alled** or (*US*) **ped'aled**) to use a pedal or pedals; to advance by use of the pedals. ◆ *vt* to drive or operate by using the pedals. ◆ *adj* (also (*zool*) /pē'dl/) of the foot; of the feet of perpendiculars (*geom*); of, with, or relating to, a pedal or pedals. [L *pedālis*, from *pēs, pedis* foot]

■ **pedalier** /-ēr'/ *n* a pedal-board attached to a piano for the bass strings. **ped'aller** *n* a person who uses pedals. **ped'alling** *n*. **pedalo** /ped'a-lō/ *n* (*pl* **ped'aloes** or **ped'alos**) a small pedal-propelled boat used (*esp* on lakes) for pleasure.

❑ **ped'al-ac'tion** *n* the apparatus worked by the pedals of a musical instrument. **pedal bin** *n* a rubbish bin with a hinged lid opened by a pedal. **ped'al-board** or **ped'al-clavier'** *n* the keyboards or pedals of an organ or other instrument. **ped'al-bone** *n* a horse's coffin bone. **pedal cycle** *n*. **ped'al-organ** *n* the division of an organ played by means of pedals. **pedal point** *n* an organ point, a tone or tones (*usu* tonic and dominant) sustained normally in the bass, while other parts move independently. **pedal pushers** *n pl* formerly, women's knee-length breeches, gathered below the knee; now, any (*esp* tight-fitting) women's trousers reaching just below the knee. **pedal steel guitar** *n* an electric steel guitar on a fixed stand and fitted with foot pedals for adjusting pitch, creating glissando effects, etc.

Pedaliaceae /pi-dā-li-ā'si-ē/ *n pl* a family of tubifloral dicotyledons related to the bignonias. [Gr *pēdalion* a rudder, from the keeled fruit]

pedalier, pedaller, pedalo, etc see under **pedal**.

pedant /ped'nt/ *n* an over-educated person who parades his or her knowledge; a person who values academic learning too highly; a person fond of making over-fine distinctions, or one insisting on strict adherence to or interpretations of rules, etc; a schoolmaster (*Shakesp*). [Ital *pedante* (perh through Fr *pédant*); connection with **pedagogue** not clear]

■ **pedantic** /pid-ant'ik/ or **pedant'ical** *adj* schoolmasterly; of the character or in the manner of a pedant. **pedant'ically** *adv*. **pedant'icism** /-i-sizm/ *n* a pedant's expression. **pedant'icize** or **-ise** /-i-sīz/ *vt* to make pedantic, give pedantic form to. **ped'antism** *n* pedantry; pedanticism. **ped'antize** or **-ise** *vi* to play the pedant. ◆ *vt* to turn into a pedant. **pedantoc'racy** *n* government by pedants. **pedant'ocrat** *n*. **pedantocrat'ic** *adj*. **ped'antry** *n* the character or manner of a pedant; a pedantic expression; unduly rigorous formality.

pedate /ped'āt/ *adj* footed; footlike; palmately lobed with the outer lobes deeply cut, or ternately branching with the outer branches forked (*bot*). [L *pedātus* footed, from *pēs, pedis* foot]

■ **ped'ately** *adv*. **pedatifid** /pi-dat'i-fid/ *adj* divided in a pedate manner, but having the divisions connected at the base.

pedder /ped'ar/ or **pether** /pedh'ar/ (now *Scot*) *n* a pedlar (also (*Walter Scott*) **pedd'er-coffe** /prob -kōv/). [Appar from **ped**[1]]

peddle /ped'l/ *vi* to go from place to place or house to house selling (small goods); to trifle. ◆ *vt* to sell or offer as or like a pedlar; to deal in or sell (drugs) illegally, *usu* in small quantities; to promote (ideas, etc) enthusiastically and persistently. [Appar partly a back-formation from **pedlar**, partly from **piddle**]

■ **pedd'ler** *n* (*esp US*). **pedd'ling** *adj* unimportant. ◆ *n* the trade or tricks of a pedlar.

-pede see **-ped**.

pederasty /ped'a-rast-i/ *n* sexual relations, *specif* anal intercourse, between a man and a boy. [Gr *pais* boy, and *erastēs* lover]

■ **ped'erast** *n* a man who practises pederasty. **pederast'ic** *adj*.

pederero /ped-a-rā'rō/ *n* (*pl* **pedere'roes** or **pedere'ros**) an old gun for discharging stones, pieces of iron, etc, also for firing salutes (also **padere'ro, patere'ro, pedre'ro**, etc). [Sp *pedrero*, from L *petra* stone, from Gr *petrā*]

pedesis /pe-dē'sis/ *n* Brownian movement. [Gr *pēdēsis* jumping]

■ **pedetic** /pi-det'ik/ *adj*.

pedestal /ped'i-stl/ *n* the support of a column, statue, vase, washbasin, etc; (also called **axle-guard** or **pillow-block**) the fixed casting which holds the brasses in which a shaft turns. ◆ *vt* to place on a pedestal. [Fr *piédestal*, from Ital *piedistallo*, for *piè di stallo* foot of a stall, from *piè* foot (L *pēs, pedis*), *di* of (L *dē*), and *stallo* stall (see **stall**[1])]

■ **ped'estalled** *adj*.

❑ **pedestal desk** *n* a desk for which sets of drawers act as the side supports for the writing surface.

■ **put** or **set on a pedestal** to regard as worthy of a worshipping admiration, *esp* to attribute an unnatural degree of moral or sexual purity to.

pedestrian /pa- or pi-des'tri-an/ *n* a walker, someone travelling on foot; someone who practises feats of walking or running (*rare*). ◆ *adj* on foot; of or related to walking; not mounted on Pegasus, hence prosaic, uninspired; flat or commonplace. [L *pedester, -tris* (adj), from *pēs, pedis*]

■ **pedes'trianism** *n* walking, *esp* as an exercise or athletic performance; pedestrian quality (*fig*). **pedestrianizā'tion** or **-s-** *n*. **pedes'trianize** or **-ise** *vi* to walk. ◆ *vt* to convert (a street) to use by pedestrians only.

❑ **pedestrian crossing** *n* a part of a roadway (often controlled by traffic lights) marked for the use of pedestrians who wish to cross, and on which they have right of way. **pedestrian precinct** see under **precinct**.

pedetic see under **pedesis**.

pedi- /ped-i-/ or **ped-** /ped-/ *combining form* denoting foot. [L *pēs, pedis* foot]

pediatrics N American spelling of **paediatrics** (see under **paed-**).

pedicab /ped'i-kab/ *n* a light vehicle consisting of a tricycle with the addition of a seat, *usu* behind, covered by a half hood, for a passenger or passengers. [L *pēs, pedis* the foot, and **cab**[1]]

pedicel /ped'i-sel/ (*biol*) *n* the stalk of a single flower in an inflorescence; the stalk of a sedentary animal; the stalk of an animal organ, eg a crab's eye. [Botanists' dimin of L *pēs, pedis* the foot]

■ **pedicellā'ria** *n* (*pl* **pedicellā'riae**) a small stalked (or sessile) pincer-like calcareous structure on the surface of a starfish or sea-urchin. **ped'icellate** (or /-dis'/ or -sel'/) *adj* provided with a pedicel.

pedicle /ped'i-kl/ *n* a short stalk or pedicel (*bot*); a narrow stalk-like structure or short bony process (*zool*); in deer, a bony protrusion of the skull from which an antler grows. [L *pediculus* a little foot, from *pēs, pedis* foot]

■ **ped'icled** *adj*. **pedic'ūlate** *adj* stalked; belonging to the **Pediculā'tī**, the angler-fish order, whose pectoral fins have a wristlike articulation. **pedic'ulated** *adj*.

Pediculus /pi-dik'ū-las/ *n* the louse genus; (without *cap*; *pl* **pedic'ulī**) a louse. [L *pēdiculus*, dimin of *pēdis* a louse]

■ **pedic'ular** *adj* of lice; lousy. **Pediculā'ris** *n* the lousewort genus. **pediculā'tion** or **pediculō'sis** *n* lousiness. **pedicūl'icide** *n* a substance for killing lice. **pedic'ulous** *adj* lousy.

pedicure /ped'i-kūr/ *n* a treatment of corns, bunions and other minor ailments of the feet; a person who treats the feet. ◆ *vt* to apply foot-treatment to. [L *pēs, pedis* foot, and *cūra* care]

■ **ped'icurist** *n*.

pedigree /ped'i-grē/ *n* a line of ancestors; a scheme or record of ancestry; lineage; genealogy; distinguished and ancient lineage; derivation; descent; succession, series, set. ◆ *adj* of known descent, pure-bred, and of good stock. [Appar Fr *pied de grue* crane's-foot, from the arrowhead figure in a stemma]

■ **ped'igreed** *adj* having a pedigree.

---

pediment /*ped*'i-mənt/ *n* a triangular structure crowning the front of a Greek building, less steeply sloped than a gable (*archit*); a similar structure in later architecture, whether triangular or any other shape, over a portico, door, window or niche; a gently sloping surface, *usu* of bare rock beneath a thin sediment, formed by erosion of cliffs or steep slopes (*geol*). [Earlier *periment*, prob for **pyramid**]
■ **pedimental** /-*ment*'l/ *adj.* **ped**'**imented** *adj* furnished with a pediment; like a pediment.

pedipalp /*ped*'i-palp/ *n* the second paired appendage in Arachnida (also **pedipalp**'**us**); a whip scorpion. [L *pēs, pedis* foot, and *palpus* stroking, in LL a feeler]
■ **Pedipalp**'**ī** or **Pedipalp**'**ida** *n pl* the whip scorpions, an order of Arachnida with large pedipalps.

pedlar /*ped*'lər/ *n* a person who goes about with a small stock or selection of goods for sale (technically, someone who carries the goods personally, eg in a pack, distinguished from a *hawker*, who has a horse and cart, etc); a person who peddles. [Prob from **pedder**, with inserted *l*, as in **tinkler** from **tinker**]
■ **ped**'**lary** *n* the wares or occupation of a pedlar.

pedo- see **paed-**.

pedogenic /*ped*-ə-*jen*'ik/ *adj* involved in the natural formation of soil. [Gr *pedon* ground, and **-genic** (1)]

pedology[1] /*ped-ol*'ə-ji/ *n* the study of soils. [Gr *pedon* ground, and *logos* discourse]
■ **pedological** /-ə-*loj*'/ *adj.* **pedol**'**ogist** *n.*

pedology[2] N American spelling of **paedology** (see under **paed-**).

pedometer /*pid-om*'i-tər/ *n* an instrument for counting paces and so approximately measuring distance walked. [L *pēs, pedis* foot, and Gr *metron* measure]

pedrail /*ped*'rāl/ *n* a tractor with footlike pieces on the circumference of its wheels; one of the pieces. [L *pēs, pedis* foot, and **rail**[1]]

pedrero /*ped-rā*'rō/ see **pederero**.

pedro see **sancho-pedro**.

peduncle /*pi-dung*'kl/ *n* the stalk of an inflorescence or of a solitary flower; the stalk by which a sedentary animal (such as a barnacle) is attached to a substratum (such as a rock) (*zool*); any stalklike part in a body (*zool*); a narrow stalklike connecting part (eg between the thorax and abdomen of insects); a tract of white fibres in the brain; a narrow process of tissue linking a tumour to normal tissue. [Botanists' L *pedunculus*, from L *pēs, pedis* the foot]
■ **pedun**'**cular** *adj.* **pedun**'**culate** or **pedun**'**culated** *adj.*

pee[1] /*pē*/ or **pee-pee** /*pē*'pē/ (*inf*) *vi* to urinate (also *n*). [For **piss**]

pee[2] /*pē*/ *n* the sixteenth letter of the modern English alphabet (P or p).

peece an obsolete spelling of **piece**.

peek /*pēk*/ *n* a sly look, a peep. ◆ *vi* to peep. ◆ *vt* (*comput*) to read the contents of a single specified location of memory. [Origin obscure]
□ **peek**'**aboo**' *n* (also **peek**'**abo**') a child's peeping game. ◆ *adj* (of clothes) having openings intended to reveal areas of the body; (of a hairstyle) having one eye concealed by a fringe.

peel[1] /*pēl*/ *vt* to strip off the skin, bark, or other covering from; to strip (eg skin or other covering layer) off; to pill, pillage, plunder (*obs*). ◆ *vi* to come off like skin; to lose or shed the skin; to undress (*inf*; often with *off*). ◆ *n* rind, *esp* that of oranges, lemons, etc, in the natural state or candied; a cosmetic treatment in which a layer of facial skin is removed. [OE *pilian*, from L *pilāre* to deprive of hair, from *pilus* a hair; perh infl by Fr *peler* to skin; cf **pill**[2]]
■ **peeled** *adj* pillaged; bald; tonsured; stripped of skin, rind, or bark. **peel**'**er** *n* a person who peels; a plunderer; a plant that impoverishes the soil; an instrument or machine for peeling or decorticating. **peel**'**ing** *n* the act of stripping; a piece, strip, or shred stripped off; the removing of the layers of a paper overlay, to get a lighter impression (*printing*).
□ **peel-and-eat**' *n* (*Scot*) potatoes served in their jackets (also *adj*).
■ **pack and** (or **or**) **peel** to have dealings (with) (*Scott*). **peel off** to leave a flying formation by a particular manoeuvre (*aeronautics*); (of a ship) to veer away from a convoy; (of a person or group of persons) to veer off, separate from the mass.

peel[2] /*pēl*/ *n* a shovel, *esp* a baker's wooden shovel; an instrument for hanging up paper to dry; the blade of an oar (*US; archaic*). [OFr *pele*, from L *pāla* a spade]

peel[3] or **pele** /*pēl*/ *n* a palisaded enclosure (*hist*); a peel-house; a stake (*obs*). [Anglo-Fr *pel*, from L *pālus* stake]
□ **peel**'**-house** or **peel**'**-tower** *n* (also **pele**'**-house** or **pele**'**-tower**; also with *cap*) *orig* a fortified dwelling-house, *usu* entered by a ladder to the first floor, with a vaulted ground floor for cattle, common on the English/Scottish Borders (*hist*); now a loosely used term.

peel[4] /*pēl*/ (*croquet*) *vt* to cause (another player's ball) to go through the next hoop. [Walter *Peel* (*fl* 1868), British croquet player]

peel[5] same as **peal**[2].

peeler[1] /*pē*'lər/ *n* a policeman. [Sir Robert *Peel* who established the Irish police (1812–18) and improved the force in Britain (1828–30)]
■ **Peel**'**ite** *n* a follower of Peel in the reform of the Corn Laws in 1846.

peeler[2] see under **peel**[1].

peelgarlic see **pilgarlick**.

peel-house, peel-tower see under **peel**[3].

peelie-wally /*pē*'li-wal'i/ (*Scot*) *adj* pale, ill-looking, off-colour. [Thought to be reduplicated form of Scot *peelie* thin, emaciated; perh a connection with **wally**[2], in allusion to the paleness of china, or of dentures]

peeling see under **peel**[1].

peen, pean, pein, pene /*pēn*/ or **pane** /*pān*/ *n* the end of a hammer head opposite the hammering face. ◆ *vt* to strike or work (metal) with a peen; to fix (eg a rivet) by hammering into place (*usu* with *in* or *over*). [Origin uncertain; cf Norw *pen*, Ger *Pinne*, Fr *panne*]

peenge /*pēnj*/ or /*pēnzh*/ (*Scot*) *vi* to whine like a peevish child. [Perh based on **whinge**]

peeoy, pioy or **pioye** /*pē-ō*'i/ (*Scot*) *n* a home-made firework, a cone of damp gunpowder.

peep[1] /*pēp*/ *vi* to look through a narrow opening; to look out from concealment; to look slyly, surreptitiously, or cautiously; to be just showing; to begin to appear. ◆ *vt* to cause to project slightly from concealment; to direct as if to view. ◆ *n* a sly or cautious look; a beginning to appear; a speck of light or flame; a glimpse; a slit; an eye (*sl*). [Origin obscure]
■ **peep**'**er** *n* someone who peeps; a prying person; the eye (*inf*); any of various types of glass or lens (*sl*).
□ **peep**'**hole** *n* a hole through which one may look without being seen. **peeping Tom** *n* a man who furtively spies on other people, *esp* one who peeps in at windows; a voyeur. **Peep-o'-day Boys** *n pl* an Ulster Protestant society (1780–95) opposed to the Catholic *Defenders*. **peep of day** *n* the first appearance of light in the morning. **peep**'**show** *n* a small entertainment, film or series of pictures, *esp* of erotic or pornographic nature, viewed through a small hole, *usu* fitted with a magnifying glass. **peep sight** *n* a backsight with a small hole. **peep**'**-through** *adj* capable of being seen through. **peep**'**-toe** *n* a shoe cut away so as to show the toe (also *adj*).

peep[2] /*pēp*/ *vi* to cheep like a chicken. ◆ *n* a high feeble sound. [Imit; cf **pipe**[1], L *pīpāre*, Fr *pépier*, Ger *piepen, piepsen* to cheep, Gr *pīpos* a young bird]
■ **peep**'**er** *n* a young bird; a tree-frog (*US*).
■ **not a peep** (*inf*) no noise, not a sound.

peep[3] or **peepe** /*pēp*/ (*Shakesp*) *n* earlier forms of **pip**[4].

pee-pee see **pee**[1].

peeper see under **peep**[1,2].

peeps /*pēps*/ (*sl*) *n pl* a person's friends or entourage. [From **people**]

peepul see **pipal**.

peer[1] /*pēr*/ *n* (also *fem* **peer**'**ess**) an equal; a fellow; an antagonist (*Spenser*); a noble of the rank of baron upward; generally, a noble; a member of the House of Lords; one of Charlemagne's paladins; a member of any similar body. ◆ *vt* to equal; to confer a peerage on (*inf*). ◆ *vi* to rank as equal. ◆ *adj* relating to a peer group. [OFr (Fr *pair*), from L *pār, paris* equal]
■ **peer**'**age** *n* the rank or dignity of a peer; the body of peers; a book of the genealogy, etc, of the different peers. **peer**'**less** *adj* unequalled; matchless. **peer**'**lessly** *adv*. **peer**'**lessness** *n*.
□ **peer group** *n* a group of people equal in age, rank, merit, etc. **peer of the realm** *n* a noble entitled to a seat in the House of Lords. **peer pressure** *n* compulsion towards doing or obtaining the same things as others in one's peer group. **peer review** *n* an assessment of a piece of scientific or academic work by experts in the field. **peer-to-peer**' *adj* (*comput*) denoting a system in which the workload of a network is evenly distributed among the workstations (*abbrev* **P2P**).
■ **House of Peers** the House of Lords. **life peer** or **peeress** a person invested with a non-hereditary peerage, entitling them to the title of baron or baroness and a seat in the House of Lords. **spiritual peer** a bishop or archbishop qualified to sit in the House of Lords, as opposed to a **temporal peer** any other member.

peer[2] /*pēr*/ *vi* to look narrowly or closely; to look with strain, or with half-closed eyes; to peep; to appear. ◆ *vt* (*obs*) to protrude. [Origin unknown; perh partly ME *piren* (cf LGer *pīren*), infl by *pere*, aphetic form of **appear**, partly from *pere* itself]
■ **peer**'**y** *adj* inclined to peer; prying; sly.

peerage, peeress see under **peer**[1].

peerie[1] or **peery** /*pēr*'i/ (*Scot*) *n* a pear- or cone-shaped wooden peg-top. [Appar **pear**, pronounced *pēr* in Scot]

peerie[2] /*pēr*'i/ (*Orkney* and *Shetland*) *adj* small. [Origin uncertain]

peerless, etc see under **peer**[1].

peery see **peerie**¹.

peesweep /pēz'wēp/ see **peewit**.

peetweet /pēt'wēt/ (*US*) *n* the spotted sandpiper. [Imit]

peeve, peeved see under **peevish**.

peever /pē'vər/ (*Scot*) *n* a tile, slab, tin-lid, etc used in playing hopscotch.
■ **pee'vers** *n sing* hopscotch.

peevish /pē'vish/ *adj* irritable; fretful, complaining; wayward; perverse (*Shakesp*); vexatious (*obs*); foolish (*obs*). [Origin unknown]
■ **peeve** *vt* (back-formation) to irritate. ◆ *vi* to be fretful; to show fretfulness. ◆ *n* a fretful mood; a grievance, grouse or cause of annoyance. **peeved** *adj* (*inf*) annoyed. **peev'ishly** *adv*. **peev'ishness** *n*.

peewee¹ see **peewit, pewee**.

peewee² /pē'wē/ *adj* very small; for or involving young children. ◆ *n* a very small person or thing. [**wee**¹, with *pee* as a rhyming addition]

peewit or **pewit** /pē'wit/, also pū'it/ *n* (also (*Scot*) **pees'weep, pease'weep** and **pee'wee**) the lapwing; its cry. [Imit]

peg /peg/ *n* a pin (*esp* of wood); a fixture for hanging a hat or coat on; a pin for tuning a string (*music*); a small stake for securing tent ropes, or marking a position, boundary claim, etc; a pin for scoring, as in cribbage; a pin in a cup to show how far down one may drink; hence a drink measure, *esp* of brandy and soda; a degree or step; a set level applied to eg an exchange rate or a price (*econ*); a wooden or other pin used in shoemaking; a turtle harpoon; a clothes-peg; a cricket stump; a piton; a peg-top; a wooden leg (*inf*); a leg (*inf*); a poke or thrust (*dialect* or *sl*); a theme (*fig*). ◆ *vt* (**pegg'ing; pegged**) to fasten, mark, score, furnish, pierce, or strike with a peg or pegs; to insert or fix like a peg; to pin down; (*usu* with *as*) to classify, categorize; to score (as at cribbage); to keep from falling or rising by buying or selling at a fixed price (*stock exchange*); to hold (prices, pensions, etc) at a fixed level, or directly related to the cost of living; to stabilize; to drive (a coach, etc) (*obs sl*); to throw or target. ◆ *vi* (*usu* with *away*) to keep on working assiduously; to make one's way vigorously. [Cf LGer *pigge*, Du dialect *peg*, Dan *pig*]
■ **pegged** *adj*. **pegg'ing** *n*.
❑ **peg'board** *n* a board having holes into which pegs are placed, used for playing and scoring in games or for display or storage purposes. **peg'box** *n* part of the head of a musical instrument in which the pegs are inserted. **peg leg** *n* (*inf*) a simple wooden leg; a person with a wooden leg. **peg'-tank'ard** *n* a drinking vessel having each one's share marked off by a knob. **peg'-top** *n* a spinning top with a metal point, spun by winding a string round it and suddenly throwing it; (in *pl*) trousers narrowing at the ankles. ◆ *adj* shaped like a top.
■ **a peg too low** tipsy; depressed. **off the peg** of a garment, (bought) ready to wear from an already-existing stock; of an item, (bought) ready to use, not purpose-built; not adjusted to suit the circumstances, etc (*fig*) (**off'-the-peg** *adj*). **peg back** (in sport, *esp* racing) to gain an advantage over an opponent. **peg down** to restrict (someone) to an admission, following a certain course of action. **peg out** (in croquet) to finish by driving the ball against the peg; (in cribbage) to win by pegging the last hole before show of hands; to mark off with pegs; to become exhausted, be ruined, or die (*sl*). **round peg in a square hole** or **square peg in a round hole** a person who is unsuited to the particular position he or she occupies. **take down a peg (or two)** to bring down, deflate, humiliate or humble.

Pegasus /peg'ə-səs/ *n* the winged horse that sprang from Medusa's blood, by later writers associated with the Muses (*Gr myth*); hence, an embodiment of the power that raises a poet's imagination above the earth; (without *cap*) a member of a genus (*Pegasus*) of small fishes superficially like seahorses, of the coastal waters of Asia and Australia, with large, winglike, pectoral fins; one of the constellations in the northern sky. [L *Pēgasus*, from Gr *Pēgasos*]
■ **Pegasē'an** *adj*.

peggy /peg'i/ *n* a small warbler of various kinds, eg the whitethroat; a washerwoman's dolly; a size of roofing slate 25.4 × 35.6cm (10 × 14in). [Childish form of *Margaret*]

pegh see **pech**.

Peght see **Pecht**.

pegmatite /peg'mə-tīt/ *n* graphic granite, a granite with markings like Hebrew characters; a very coarsely crystallized granite, as in dykes and veins (*geol*); any very coarse-grained igneous rock occurring in this manner. [Gr *pēgma* a bond, framework, from the root of *pēgnynai* to fasten]
■ **pegmatitic** /-tit'ik/ *adj*.

peh /pā/ *n* the seventeenth letter of the Hebrew alphabet. [Heb]

Pehlevi /pā'le-vē/ or **Pahlavi** /pä'lä-vē/ *n* an ancient West-Iranian idiom of the Sassanid period (3c–7c AD), largely mixed with Semitic words; the characters used in writing it. ◆ *adj* spoken or written in Pehlevi. [Pers *Pahlavi* Parthian]

peignoir /pen'wär or pän'/ *n* a woman's dressing-gown, *esp* a fine lightweight one (*orig* one worn when combing the hair); (loosely) a morning gown. [Fr, from *peigner*, from L *pectināre* to comb]

pein see **peen**.

peinct /pānt/ an obsolete spelling of **paint**.

peine forte et dure /pen for-tā dür'/ (*Fr; hist*) *n* literally, strong and severe punishment, a kind of judicial torture involving pressing with weights.

peirastic /pī-ras'tik/ *adj* experimental; tentative. [Gr *peirastikos*, from *peira* a trial]
■ **peiras'tically** *adv*.

peise, peize, pease, peaze or **peyse** /pāz or pēz/ (*obs*) *n* weight; a weight; a balance; a blow (*Spenser*). ◆ *vt* to balance (*Spenser, Shakesp*); to poise (*Spenser*); to put weights on, weigh down (*Shakesp*). ◆ *vi* (*Spenser*) to press or settle downwards. [OFr *peis* weight, *peser* to weigh; cf **poise**¹]

peishwa, peishwah see **peshwa**.

pejorate /pē'jər-āt or pī'/ *vt* to make worse. [L *pējor* worse]
■ **pejorā'tion** *n* a making or becoming worse; deterioration. **pejor'ative** (or /pē'/) *adj* derogatory, disparaging, depreciating. ◆ *n* a derogatory word or suffix. **pejor'atively** (or /pē'/) *adv*.

pekan /pek'ən/ *n* the woodshock, a large N American marten with dark-brown fur. [Can Fr *pékan*, from Algonquin *pékane*]

peke /pēk/ (*inf*) *n* a Pekinese dog. [Short form]

Pekingese or **Pekinese** /pē-kin-ēz' or pē-king-/ *adj* of Peking (now *usu* Beijing), China. ◆ *n* a native or inhabitant of Peking; *esp* formerly, the chief dialect of Mandarin; a dwarf pug-dog of a breed brought from Peking.
❑ **Peking** or **Pekin duck** *n* a large white breed of duck, bred *esp* for food. **Peking man** *n* a type of fossil man first found (1929) SW of Peking, related to Java man.

pekoe /pēk'ō or pek'ō/ *n* a scented black tea. [Chin (Amoy) *pék-hô* white down]

pel /pel/ (*comput*) *n* an earlier, now less common, word for a pixel. [From picture el*ement*]

pela /pā'lä/ *n* white wax from a scale insect. [Chin *bái là* white wax]

pelage /pel'ij/ *n* an animal's coat of hair or wool. [Fr]

Pelagian /pi-lā'ji-ən/ *n* a follower of *Pelagius*, a 5c British monk, who denied original sin. ◆ *adj* of or relating to Pelagius or his followers.
■ **Pelā'gianism** *n*.

pelagic /pi-laj'ik/ *adj* oceanic; of, inhabiting, or carried out in, the deep or open sea; living in the surface waters or middle depths of the sea; (of sediments) deposited under deep-water conditions. [Gr *pelagos* sea]
■ **pelagian** /pi-lā'ji-ən/ *adj* pelagic. ◆ *n* a pelagic animal.

pelargonium /pel-ər-gō'ni-əm/ *n* any plant of a vast genus (*Pelargonium*) of the Geraniaceae family of plants, having clusters of red, pink or white flowers, often cultivated under the name of geranium. [Gr *pelargos* stork, the beaked capsules resembling a stork's head]
❑ **pelargonic acid** *n* an oily fatty acid, obtained *esp* from the leaves of plants of the *Pelargonium* genus (also called **nonanoic acid**).

Pelasgic /pe-las'jik or -laz'/ *adj* relating to the *Pelasgians* or *Pelasgi*, prehistoric inhabitants of Greece, of unknown origin (also **Pelas'gian**).
❑ **Pelasgian architecture** *n* cyclopean architecture.

Pele /pā'lā/ *n* the Hawaiian volcano goddess.
❑ **Pele's hair** *n* volcanic glass drawn out into threads as it flies through the air.

pele¹ see **peel**³.

pele² a Spenserian spelling of **peal**¹.

Pelecypoda /pel-e-sip'ə-də/ *n pl* the Lamellibranchs. [Gr *pelekys* axe, and *pous, podos* foot]
■ **pelec'ypod** *n*.

pelerine /pel'ə-rin or -rēn/ *n* a woman's tippet or cape, *esp* one with long pointed ends coming down in front. [Fr *pèlerine* tippet, pilgrim (fem); see **pilgrim**]

pelf /pelf/ (*derog*) *n* riches (in a bad sense); money. [OFr *pelfre* booty; cf **pilfer**]

pelham /pel'əm/ (often with *cap*) *n* on a horse's bridle, a type of bit, a combination of the curb and snaffle designs. [Perh the name *Pelham*]

pelican /pel'i-kən/ *n* a large tropical and subtropical waterfowl with an enormous pouched bill, fabled in the Middle Ages to wound its breast and feed its young with its blood; an alembic with beaks that lead back to the body, used for continuous distillation; a dentist's beaked instrument (*hist*); an old species of ordnance, or its shot. [LL *pelicānus*, from Gr *pelekan, -ānos* pelican; cf *pelekās, -āntos* a woodpecker, and *pelekys* an axe]

❑ **pel'ican-fish** *n* a deep-sea fish (genus *Eurypharynx*) with an enormous mouth and comparatively small body. **pel'ican-flower** *n* the goose-flower, an Aristolochia with a gigantic flower. **pel'ican's-foot** *n* a marine gastropod mollusc (*Aporrhais pespelicani*); its shell, which has a lip like a webbed foot.

■ **pelican in her piety** (*heraldry*) a pelican with wings indorsed, feeding her young with her blood.

pelican crossing /pel'i-kən kros'ing/ *n* a pedestrian-operated street crossing, having a set of lights including an amber flashing light which indicates that motorists may proceed only if the crossing is clear. [Adapted from *pedestrian light controlled crossing*]

pelisse /pe-lēs'/ (*hist*) *n orig* a fur-lined or fur garment, *esp* a military cloak; a lady's long mantle; a young child's overcoat. [Fr, from LL *pellicea* (*vestis*), from L *pellis* a skin]

pelite /pē'līt/ *n* any rock derived from clay or mud. [Gr *pēlos* clay, mud]

■ **pēlitic** /-lit'ik/ *adj*. **pē'loid** *n* any naturally produced medium used in medical practice as a cataplasm. **pēlol'ogy** *n*. **pēlother'apy** *n* treatment by mud baths and the like.

pell /pel/ (*obs*) *n* a skin or hide; a roll of parchment. [OFr *pel* (Fr *peau*), from L *pellis* a skin or hide]

pellach, pellack see **pellock**.

pellagra /pel-ag'rə or -āg'rə/ *n* a chronic disease marked by shrivelled skin, wasted body, mental illness and paralysis, caused by a dietary deficiency of nicotinic acid. [Gr *pella* skin, and *agrā* seizure; or Ital *pelle agra* rough skin]

■ **pellag'rin** *n* someone afflicted with pellagra. **pellag'rous** *adj* connected with, like, or afflicted with pellagra.

pellet /pel'it/ *n* a little ball; a small rounded boss; a small rounded mass of compressed iron ore, waste material, etc; a small pill; a ball of shot, *esp* a flat-ended ball for use in air rifles, etc; a mass of undigested refuse thrown up by a hawk or owl. ◆ *vt* to form into pellets (*Shakesp*); to form (eg seeds for easier planting) into a pellet by surrounding with an inert substance which breaks down with moisture; to hit, pelt or bombard with pellets. [OFr *pelote*, from L *pila* a ball]

■ **pell'etify, pell'etize** or **-ise** *vt* to form (*esp* solid waste material, iron ore, etc) into pellets. **pelletizā'tion** or **-s-** *n*.

pellicle /pel'i-kl/ *n* a thin skin or film; a film or scum on liquid; a protein covering that preserves the shape of single-cell organisms (*biol*). [L *pellicula*, dimin of *pellis* skin]

■ **pellic'ular** *adj*.

pellitory¹ /pel'i-tə-ri/ *n* a plant (*Parietaria officinalis*) of the nettle family, growing on old walls (called *pellitory of the wall*), or other member of the genus (cf **pellitory²**). [L (*herba*) *parietāria*, from *parietārius*, from *pariēs, parietis* a wall]

pellitory² /pel'i-tə-ri/ *n* a N African and S European plant (*Anacyclus pyrethrum*), known as *pellitory of Spain*, related to camomile; extended to various similar plants, such as yarrow and feverfew. Cf **pellitory¹**. [ME *peletre*, from L *pyrethrum*, from Gr *pyrethron* pellitory of Spain; see **Pyrethrum**]

pell-mell /pel'mel'/ *adv* confusedly; headlong; helter-skelter; vehemently. ◆ *adj* confusedly mingled; indiscriminate; headlong. ◆ *n* disorder; confused mingling; a hand-to-hand fight. [OFr *pesle-mesle* (Fr *pêle-mêle*), -*mesle* being from OFr *mesler* (Fr *mêler*) to mix, meddle, from LL *misculāre*, from L *miscēre*; and *pesle* a rhyming addition, perh infl by Fr *pelle* shovel]

pellock or **pellack** /pel'ək/ or **pellach** /pel'əhh/ (*Scot*) *n* a porpoise. [Origin unknown]

pellucid /pe-lū'sid or -loo'sid/ *adj* perfectly clear; transparent. [L *pellūcidus*, from *per* through, and *lūcidus* clear, from *lūcēre* to shine]

■ **pellucid'ity** *n*. **pellu'cidly** *adv*. **pellu'cidness** *n*.

pelma /pel'mə/ *n* the sole of the foot. [Gr *pelma, -atos* sole, stalk]

■ **pelmatic** /-mat'ik/ *adj*. **Pelmatozō'a** *n pl* a division of the Echinodermata, typically stalked, including crinoids and the fossil blastoids and cystoids.

Pelmanism /pel'mə-ni-zm/ *n* a system of mind training to improve the memory; (*usu without cap*) a card game in which the cards are spread out face down and must be turned up in matching pairs. [The *Pelman* Institute, London, founded 1898, which devised the system]

pelmet /pel'mit/ *n* a fringe, valance, or other device hiding a curtain rod. [Perh Fr *palmette*]

peloid, pelology see under **pelite**.

Pelopid /pel'ō-pid/ (*Gr myth*) *n* a descendant of *Pelops*, son of Tantalus, and grandfather of Agamemnon and Menelaus.

Peloponnesian /pel-ō-pə-nē'sh(y)ən, -zh(y)ən or -zyən/ *adj* of the *Peloponnesus* or Peloponnese, the southern peninsula of Greece. ◆ *n* a native of the Peloponnese. [Gr *Peloponnēsos* Peloponnese, from *Pelops* (see **Pelopid**), and *nēsos* an island]

❑ **Peloponnesian War** *n* a war between Athens and Sparta, 431–404BC.

peloria /pi-lō'ri-ə or -lö'ri-ə/ *n* regularity in a normally irregular flower (also **pelorism** /pel'ər-izm/ or **pel'ory**). [Gr *pelōr* a monster]

■ **peloric** /pi-lor'ik/, **pel'orized** or **-s-** *adj*.

pelorus /pe-lō'rəs or -lö'/ *n* a kind of compass from which bearings can be taken. [Perh *Pelorus* Hannibal's pilot]

pelory see **peloria**.

pelota /pel-ō'tə or -o'/ *n* any of various related games of Basque origin, popular in Spain, S France and Latin America, in which two players hurl a ball against a marked wall using a basket-like racket strapped to the wrist; the ball used. [Sp *pelota* ball]

pelotherapy see under **pelite**.

peloton /pel'ə-ton/ *n* the main body of riders in a cycle race. [Fr, small ball]

pelt¹ /pelt/ *vt* to hurl, or fire, in a persistent or rapid stream; to assail (formerly with repeated blows, now *usu*) with a torrent of missiles or blows, or of words, reproaches, pamphlets, etc; to drive by showers of missiles, etc; to shower. ◆ *vi* to shower blows or missiles; (of rain or hail, etc) to beat vigorously (sometimes with *down*); to speak angrily; to speed. ◆ *n* a blow; a pelting; a downpour, eg of rain; a storm of rage; a rapid pace. [Origin obscure]

■ **pelt'er** *n* someone who or that which pelts; a shower of missiles; a sharp storm of rain, of anger, etc. ◆ *vi* to go full pelt; to pelt (*dialect*). **pelt'ing** *n* and *adj*.

■ **full pelt** or **at full pelt** at full speed.

pelt² /pelt/ *n* a raw animal hide with the fur still on; a hawk's prey when killed, *esp* when torn. [Appar a back-formation from *peltry*, from OFr *pelleterie*, from L *pellis* a skin]

■ **pelt'ry** *n* the skins of animals with the fur on them; furs.

❑ **pelt'monger** *n* a dealer in skins.

pelta /pel'tə/ *n* a small light shield or buckler (*ancient hist*). [L, from Gr *peltē*]

■ **peltast** /pelt'ast/ *n* a light-armed Greek soldier with a pelta. **pelt'ate** *adj* (*bot*) having the stalk attached not to the edge but near the middle of the undersurface.

Peltier effect /pel'ti-ā i-fekt'/ (*phys*) *n* the generation or absorption of heat at a junction, within an electric circuit, of two metals. [From Jean *Peltier* (1785–1845), French physicist]

pelting¹ /pel'ting/ (*Shakesp*) *adj* paltry, contemptible. [Appar connected with **paltry**]

■ **pelt'ingly** *adv*.

pelting² see under **pelt¹**.

peltmonger see under **pelt²**.

Pelton wheel /pel'tən (h)wēl'/ *n* a water wheel with specially shaped cups around the circumference into which one or more jets of water are aimed at high speed, invented by Lester Allen *Pelton*, American engineer (1829–1908).

peltry see under **pelt²**.

pelvis /pel'vis/ (*anat*) *n* (*pl* **pel'vises** or **pel'ves** /-vēz/) the bony cavity at the lower end of the trunk, of which the part above the plane through the promontory of the sacrum and the pubic symphysis is the *false pelvis*, the part below the *true pelvis*; the bony frame enclosing it; the cavity of the kidney; the basal part of a crinoid cup. [L *pelvis* a basin]

■ **pel'vic** *adj*. **pel'viform** *adj* basin-shaped. **pelvim'eter** *n* an instrument for measuring the pelvis. **pelvim'etry** *n*.

❑ **pelvic fin** *n* a fish's paired fin homologous with a mammal's hindleg. **pelvic floor** *n* the muscular lower section of the abdomen which is attached to the pelvis. **pelvic girdle** or **arch** *n* the posterior limb-girdle of vertebrates, with which the hind-limbs articulate, consisting of the haunch-bones (ilium, pubis and ischium united), which articulate with the sacrum. **pelvic inflammatory disease** *n* a damaging inflammatory condition affecting a woman's pelvic organs, *esp* the Fallopian tubes, caused by a bacterial infection.

pelycosaur /pel'i-kə-sör/ *n* a spiny-backed reptile of the order **Pelycosauria**, belonging to the Carboniferous and Permian periods. [Gr *pelux, pelukos* axe, and *sauros* lizard]

pembroke /pem'brük/ *n* (in full **pembroke table**) a small four-legged table with hinged flaps. [Appar from *Pembroke*, in Wales]

PEME /pē'mē/ *abbrev* : Pulsed Electro Magnetic Energy, the basis of a technique used in magnetic therapy.

pemmican or **pemican** /pem'i-kən/ *n* a Native American preparation of lean meat, dried, pounded, and mixed with fat and other ingredients; a highly condensed, nutritious preparation of dried ingredients, used *esp* as emergency rations; highly condensed information or reading-matter (*fig*). [Cree *pimekan*]

pemoline /*pem'ə-lēn*/ *n* a white crystalline powder, $C_9H_8N_2O_2$, used as a stimulant of the central nervous system, *esp* in the treatment of fatigue, depression and memory loss.

pemphigus /*pem'fi-gəs*/ *n* a diseased condition of the skin with watery vesicles. [False Latin, from Gr *pemphix*, -*īgos* blister]
■ **pem'phigoid** *adj*. **pem'phigous** *adj*.

PEN /*pen*/ *abbrev* : (the International Association of) Poets, Playwrights, Editors, Essayists and Novelists; Protected Equity-linked Notes (*finance*).

Pen *abbrev* : Peninsula.

pen¹ /*pen*/ *n* an instrument used for writing (with ink or otherwise), formerly made of a quill, but now of other materials; a nib; a nib with a holder; writing; literary style; an author; a hand-held electronic device applied to a screen to enter data in a computer; see also **light pen** under **light¹** (*comput*); a large feather; a flight-feather; a quill; a cuttle-bone. ◆ *vt* (**penn'ing**; **penned**) to write, to commit to paper. [OFr *penne*, from L *penna* a feather]
■ **pen'ful** *n* as much ink as a pen can take at a dip; as much as the reservoir of a fountain pen can hold; what can be written with one dip of ink. **penned** *adj* written; quilled. **penn'er** *n* (*archaic*) a case for carrying pens.
□ **pen'-and-ink'** *n* writing materials; a pen drawing. ◆ *adj* writing; written; (of a drawing) executed with pen and ink. **pen'-case** *n* a receptacle for a pen or pens. **pen'craft** *n* penmanship; the art of composition. **pen'-driver** *n* a clerk. **pen'-feather** *n* a quill feather; a pin feather (*dialect*). **pen'-feathered** *adj*. **pen friend** or **pen pal** an otherwise unknown person (*usu* abroad) with whom one corresponds. **pen'-gun** *n* (*Scot*) a popgun made of a quill. **pen'holder** *n* a rod on which a nib may be fixed. **pen'knife** *n orig* a knife for making or mending pens; a small pocket knife with folding blade or blades. **pen'light** *n* a small pen-shaped electric torch (**penlight battery** a long, thin battery, as used in a penlight). **pen'man** *n* (also *fem* **pen'woman**) a person skilled in handwriting; a writer or author. **pen'manship** *n*. **pen name** a writer's assumed name. **pen'-pusher** *n* (*inf*) a clerk who does boring, routine writing. **pen'-wiper** *n* a piece of cloth, leather, etc, for wiping ink from pens.

pen² /*pen*/ *n* a small enclosure, *esp* for animals; a cattle farm (*W Indies*); an estate or plantation (*W Indies*); animals kept in, and enough to fill, a pen; a dam or weir; a covered dock, eg for servicing submarines. ◆ *vt* (**penn'ing; penned** or **pent**) to put or keep in a pen; to confine; to dam. [OE *penn* pen]
□ **pen'fold** *n* a fold for penning cattle or sheep; a pound.
■ **submarine pen** a dock for a submarine, *esp* if protected from attack from above by a deep covering of concrete.

pen³ /*pen*/ (*inf*) *n* a short form of *penitentiary*.

pen⁴ /*pen*/ *n* a female swan. [Origin unknown]

penal /*pē'nl*/ *adj* relating to, liable to, imposing, constituting, or used for, punishment; constituting a penalty; very severe. [L *poenālis*, from *poena*, from Gr *poinē* punishment]
■ **pēnalīzā'tion** or **-s-** *n*. **pē'nalize** or **-ise** *vt* to make (something) punishable; to impose a penalty or disadvantage on (eg someone guilty of an offence or lapse). **pē'nally** *adv*.
□ **penal code** *n* a codified system of law relating to crime and punishment. **penal laws** *n pl* laws imposing penalties, *esp* (*hist*) in matters of religion. **penal servitude** *n* hard labour in a prison under different conditions from ordinary imprisonment, substituted in 1853 for transportation, then abolished 1948. **penal settlement** *n* a settlement peopled by convicts.

penalty /*pen'l-ti*/ *n* punishment; suffering or loss imposed for breach of a law; a fine or loss agreed upon in case of non-fulfilment of some undertaking; a fine; a disadvantage imposed upon a competitor for breach of a rule of the game, for failing to attain what is aimed at, as a handicap, or for any other reason arising out of the rules; a kick, shot or stroke awarded or imposed as a result of a breach of the rules; a loss or suffering brought upon one by one's own actions or condition; a score for an opponent's failure to complete a contract or for the bidder's success when the call is doubled (*bridge*). [LL *poenālitās*; see ety for **penal**]
□ **penalty area** or **box** *n* (in association football) the area or box in front of the goal in which a foul by the defending team may result in a penalty kick being awarded against them. **penalty bench** or **box** *n* (in ice-hockey) an area or box beside the rink in which a player must stay for his or her allotted penalty period. **penalty corner** *n* (in hockey) a free stroke taken on the goal line. **penalty goal** *n* one scored by a penalty kick or shot. **penalty kick** *n* a free kick, or the privilege granted to a player to kick the ball as he or she pleases, because of some breach of the rules by the opposing side. **penalty killer** *n* (in ice hockey) a player who specializes at defending a powerplay. **penalty line** *n* the boundary of the penalty area. **penalty rate** *n* (*Aust*) a higher

than normal rate of payment, for work done outside normal hours or in unusual conditions. **penalty shoot-out** *n* an attempt to settle a tied football match by having each team take a series of penalty kicks. **penalty shot** *n*. **penalty spot** *n* (in football and hockey) a spot marked in front of the goal from which a penalty kick or shot is taken. **penalty try** *n* (*rugby*) a try awarded when only an offence by the defending side has prevented a try being scored.
■ **death penalty** punishment by putting to death. **under** (or **on**) **penalty of** with liability in case of infraction to the penalty of.

penance /*pen'əns*/ *n* an act of humiliation or punishment, either undertaken voluntarily or imposed by a priest to express or show evidence of sorrow for sin; the sacrament by which absolution is conveyed (involving contrition, confession, and satisfaction) (*RC* and *Orthodox church*); expiation; punishment (*Milton*); repentance (*obs*); hardship. ◆ *vt* to impose penance on. [OFr; cf *penitence*]

Penang-lawyer /*pi-nang' lö'yər*/ *n* a walking-stick made from the stem of a prickly dwarf palm (*Licuala acutifida*); misapplied to a Malacca cane. [*Penang*, its place of origin, and **lawyer**, or poss from Malay *pinang líyar* wild areca, or *pinang láyor* fire-dried areca]

penannular /*pen-an'ū-lər* or *pēn-*/ *adj* in the form of an almost complete ring. [L *paene* almost, and *annulāris* annular]

penates /*pe-nā'tēz* or *pe-nä'täs*/ *n pl* the household gods of a Roman family. [L *penātēs*, prob from the root found in *penus* provisions, storeroom, *penes* in the house of, and *penetrāre* to penetrate]

pence /*pens*/ *n* a plural of **penny**; a non-standard form of **penny**.

pencel see **pensil**.

penchant /*pã'shã*/ *n* a liking or inclination (with *for*); decided taste; bias. [Fr, prp of *pencher* to incline, from assumed LL *pendicāre*, from L *pendēre* to hang]

pencil /*pen'sl*/ *n* a writing or drawing instrument that leaves a streak of graphite, chalk, slate, or other solid matter, *esp* (*lead pencil*) one of graphite enclosed in wood and sharpened as required; a small stick of various materials shaped like a lead pencil, for medical, cosmetic, or other purpose; a fine paintbrush; a small tuft of hairs; the art of painting or drawing; a system of straight lines meeting in a point (*geom*); a set of rays of light diverging from or converging to a point (*optics*); a narrow beam of light (*phys*); something long, fine and narrow in shape. ◆ *vt* (**pen'cilling; pen'cilled**) to paint, draw, write, or mark with a pencil; (with *in*) to enter provisionally, eg in a diary; to note (something) allowing for or expecting later alteration (*fig*); to apply a pencil to. [OFr *pincel* (Fr *pinceau*), from L *pēnicillum* a painter's brush, dimin of *pēnis* a tail]
■ **pen'cilled** *adj* painted, drawn, written or marked with a pencil; marked as if with a pencil; showing fine concentric streaking; having pencils of rays; radiated; tufted. **pen'ciller** *n*. **pen'cilling** *n* the art or act of painting, writing, sketching, or marking with a pencil; marks made with a pencil; fine lines on flowers or feathers; a sketch; the marking of joints in brickwork with white painting.
□ **pen'cil-case** *n* a case for pencils; a metal case used to hold a movable piece of blacklead or the like, used as a pencil. **pen'cil-ce'dar** *n* juniper of various kinds suitable for lead pencils. **pen'cil-com'pass** *n* a compass having a pencil on one of its legs. **pen'cil-lead** *n* graphite for pencils; a stick of it for a metal pencil-case. **pencil moustache** *n* an extremely thin moustache. **pen'cil-ore** *n* radiating botryoidal graphite. **pen'cil-pusher** same as **pen-pusher** (see under **pen¹**). **pen'cil-sharpener** *n* an instrument for sharpening lead pencils, etc, by rotation against a blade or blades. **pen'cil-sketch** *n*. **pencil skirt** *n* a straight, close-fitting skirt. **pen'cil-stone** *n* a pyrophyllite used for making slate-pencils.

pencraft see under **pen¹**.

pend¹ /*pend*/ (*Scot*) *n* a vaulted passage; a vaulted entrance to a passageway. [L *pendēre* to hang]

pend² /*pend*/ *vi* to hang, as in a balance, to impend. [Fr *pendre* or L *pendēre* to hang; sometimes aphetic for **append** or for **depend**]
■ **pend'ing** *adj* hanging; impending; remaining undecided; not fully dealt with or completed. ◆ *prep* during; until, awaiting.

pend³ an old spelling of **penned**, from **pen¹** or **pen²**.

pendant or sometimes **pendent** /*pen'dənt*/ *n* anything hanging, *esp* for ornament; a hanging ornament *esp* one worn on a chain, etc around the neck; the hanging (*esp* decorated) end of a waistbelt; an earring; a lamp hanging from the roof; an ornament of wood or of stone hanging downwards from a roof; a pennant (*naut*); a pendant-post (see below); anything attached to another thing of the same kind, an appendix; a companion picture, poem, etc. [Fr *pendant*, prp of *pendre* to hang, from L *pendēns*, -*entis*, prp of *pendēre* to hang]
■ **pend'ency** *n* a state or quality of being pendent; droop. **pen'dent** *adj* (sometimes **pen'dant**) hanging; dangling; drooping; overhanging; not yet decided; grammatically incomplete, left in suspense. **pendentive** /-*dent'*/ *n* (*archit*) one of four spherical triangles formed by a dome springing from a square base; part of a groined vault resting

on one pier. **pen'dently** *adv.* **pen'dicle** *n* a pendant; a dependency or appendage; a thing attached to something else, such as a privilege to a post, or a small piece of land to a rented property. **pen'dicler** *n* the tenant of a pendicle.

❑ **pen'dant-post'** *n* a post placed against a wall, *usu* resting on a corbel or capital, with a tie beam or hammer beam fixed to its upper end.

pendente lite /pen-den'tē li'tē or pen-den'te li'te/ (*L*) *adv* during the process of litigation.

pendicle see under **pendant**.

pending see under **pend²**.

Pendolino® /pen-də-lē'nō/ *n* a type of tilting train (qv under **tilt**). [Ital, dimin of *pendolo* pendulum]

pendragon /pen-drag'ən/ *n* an ancient British supreme chief. [Welsh *pen* head, and *dragon* a dragon, dragon-standard]

■ **pendrag'onship** *n*.

pendulum /pen'dū-ləm/ *n* (*pl* **pen'dulums**) theoretically, a heavy material point suspended by a weightless thread, free to swing without friction (*simple pendulum*); any weight so hung from a fixed point as to swing freely (*compound pendulum*); the swinging weight which regulates the movement of a clock; anything that swings, passes or is free to swing or be passed to and fro; anything that undergoes obvious and regular shifts or reversals in direction, attitude, opinion, etc. [Neuter of L *pendulus* hanging, from *pendēre* to hang]

■ **pen'dular** *adj* relating to a pendulum. **pen'dulate** *vi* to swing, vibrate. **pen'duline** *adj* building a pendulous nest. **pendulos'ity** *n*. **pen'dulous** *adj* hanging loosely; swinging freely; drooping; dangling; overhanging; suspended from the top; floating in air or space. **pen'dulously** *adv*. **pen'dulousness** *n*.

❑ **pendulum arbitration** *n* (*business*) a process used to settle disputes, in which the arbitrator chooses one complete final offer, no adjustment of terms being allowed.

■ **compensation pendulum** a pendulum so constructed that its rod is not much altered in length by changes of temperature. **Foucault's pendulum** see separate entry.

pene see **peen**.

Peneian /pē-nē'ən/ *adj* relating to the river *Pēnēus* in the Vale of Tempe in Thessaly. [Gr *Pēnēios*, now Salambria]

penelopize or **-ise** /pi-nel'ə-pīz/ *vi* to act like *Penelope*, the wife of Odysseus, who in his long absence, undid her day's weaving work at night, to create work as an excuse with which to deter suitors. [Gr *Pēnelopē*]

peneplain /pē'ni-plān or -plān'/ *n* a land surface so worn down by denudation as to be almost a plain (also **pe'neplane**). [L *paene* almost, and **plain¹**]

penes see **penis**.

penetrate /pen'i-trāt/ *vt* to thrust or force a way into the inside of; to pierce into or through; to insert the penis into the vagina or anus of; to force entry within a country's borders or through an enemy's front line (*milit*); to gain access into and influence within (a country, organization, market, etc) for political, financial, etc, purposes; to permeate; to reach the mind or feelings of; to pierce with the eye or understanding, see into or through whether with the eye or intellect (*fig*); to understand. ◆ *vi* to reach the inside; to be understood. [L *penetrāre, -ātum*, from *penes* in the house, possession, or power of; formed on the model of *intrāre* to enter, from *intus* within; cf **penates**]

■ **penetrability** /-trə-bil'i-ti/ *n*. **pen'etrable** *adj*. **pen'etrableness** *n*. **pen'etrably** *adv* so as to be penetrated. **penetrā'lia** *n pl* (*pl* of L *penetral* or *penetrāle*) the inmost parts of a building; the most holy place in a temple; innermost mysteries. **penetrā'lian** *adj*. **pen'etrance** *n* (*genetics*) the frequency, expressed as a percentage, with which a gene exhibits an effect. **pen'etrancy** *n*. **pen'etrant** *adj* penetrating. ◆ *n* (*chem*) a substance which increases the penetration of a liquid into porous material or between contiguous surfaces, by lowering its surface tension. **pen'etrāting** *adj* piercing; loud and clear; having keen and deep insight; sharp; keen; discerning. **pen'etrātingly** *adv*. **penetrā'tion** *n* the act or power of penetrating or entering; acuteness; discernment; the space-penetrating power of a telescope; the sexual act of inserting the penis into the vagina or anus; the process and practices of espionage or infiltration within an organization, country, etc. **pen'etrātive** *adj* tending or able to penetrate; piercing; having keen and deep insight; reaching and affecting the mind; (of sexual intercourse) involving penetration. **pen'etrātively** *adv*. **pen'etrātiveness** *n*. **pen'etrātor** *n*. **penetrom'eter** *n* an instrument for measuring the hardness of a substance according to the depth of penetration of a needle driven into it.

❑ **penetration agent** *n* a person employed to penetrate and obtain information within an organization, country, etc.

penfold see under **pen²**, and cf **pinfold**.

penful see under **pen¹**.

penguin¹ /peng'gwin/ *n* (also **pin'guin**) any bird of the order Sphenisciformes, flightless seabirds of the southern hemisphere with modified flipper-like wings used for swimming, and black or bluish plumage except for the mainly white breast; a former name for the great auk; a training aeroplane that cannot fly (*sl*); a member of the Women's Royal Air Force, 'flappers who did not fly' (*old sl*). [According to some, Welsh *pen* head, and *gwyn* white, or the corresponding Breton words, though the great auk had a black head with two white patches: conjectures are *pin-wing*, and L *pinguis* fat]

■ **pen'guinery** or **pen'guinry** *n* a penguin rookery or breeding-place. ❑ **penguin suit** *n* (*inf*) a man's black dinner jacket and white shirt.

penguin² same as **pinguin²**.

penholder see under **pen¹**.

peni Spenserian spelling of **penny**.

penial see under **penis**.

penicillate /pen-i-sil'it, -āt or pen'/ *adj* tufted; forming a tuft; brush-shaped. [L *pēnicillus* paintbrush, dimin of *pēnis* tail]

■ **penicill'iform** *adj* paintbrush-shaped. **penicill'in** *n* a group of substances that stop the growth of bacteria, extracted from moulds, *esp* from *Penicillium notatum*, of the genus of fungi, **Penicill'ium** (**Ascomycetes**; see under **ascus**), which includes also the mould of jam, cheese, etc (*Penicillium glaucum*). **penicill'inase** *n* an enzyme, produced by certain bacteria, that inactivates the effect of some penicillins.

penie Spenserian spelling of **penny**.

penile see under **penis**.

penillion see under **pennill**.

peninsula /pen-in'sū-lə/ *n* a strip of land jutting out into water, a near-island. [L *paenīnsula*, from *paene* almost, and *īnsula* an island]

■ **penin'sular** *adj*. **peninsular'ity** *n*. **penin'sulate** *vt* to form into a peninsula.

❑ **peninsular unit** *n* (in estate agent, etc parlance) a kitchen unit projecting into the room, a breakfast bar. **Peninsular War** *n* the war in Spain and Portugal carried on by Great Britain against Napoleon's marshals (1808–14).

■ **the Peninsula** Spain and Portugal.

penis /pē'nis/ *n* (*pl* **pē'nises** or **pē'nes** /-nēz/) the external male organ used for copulation, and also (in mammals) for the excretion of urine. [L *pēnis*, orig a tail]

■ **pē'nial** or **pē'nile** *adj*.

❑ **penis envy** *n* (*psychol*) the Freudian concept of a woman's subconscious wish for male characteristics.

penistone /pen'i-stən/ *n* a cloth, a coarse frieze, formerly made at *Penistone* in Yorkshire.

penitent /pen'i-tənt/ *adj* suffering pain or sorrow for past sin and feeling a desire to reform; contrite; repentant; expressing sorrow for sin; undergoing penance; appropriate to penance. ◆ *n* a person who repents of his or her sin; someone who has confessed sin, and is undergoing penance; a member of one of various orders devoted to penitential exercises and work among criminals, etc (*RC*). [L *paenitēns, -entis*, prp of *paenitēre* to cause to repent, to repent]

■ **pen'itence** *n*. **pen'itency** *n* (*rare*). **penitential** /-ten'shl/ *adj* of the nature of, relating to or expressive of penitence. ◆ *n* a book of rules relating to penance; a penitent; (in *pl*) the behaviour or garb of a penitent; black clothes (*inf*). **peniten'tially** *adv*. **penitentiary** /-ten'shə-ri/ *adj* relating to penance; penitential; penal and reformatory. ◆ *n* a prison (*N Am*); a penitent; an officer who deals with cases of penitence and penance; a Roman Catholic office (under the **Grand Penitentiary**) at Rome dealing with cases of penance, dispensations, etc; a book for guidance in imposing penances; a place for the performance of penance (*obs*); an asylum for prostitutes (*archaic*); a reformatory prison or house of correction. **pen'itently** *adv*.

❑ **penitent form** *n* a seat for penitents at an evangelistic meeting. **penitential garment** *n* a rough garment worn for penance. **penitential psalms** *n pl* seven psalms (numbers 6, 32, 38, 51, 102, 130 and 143) suitable for singing by penitents.

penk same as **pink⁸**.

penknife, **penlight**, **penman**, etc see under **pen¹**.

Penn. *abbrev* : Pennsylvania (US state).

penna /pen'ə/ *n* (*pl* **penn'ae** /-ē/) (*ornithol*) a feather, *esp* one of the large feathers of the wings or tail. [L *penna* feather]

■ **pennaceous** /-ā'shəs/ *adj* featherlike. **penn'ate** *adj* pinnate; winged, feathered, or like a wing in shape. **penne** /pen/ *n* (*Spenser*) a pen; a pinion. **penned** *adj* feathered; quilled; winged. **penn'iform** *adj* feather-shaped.

pennal /pen'əl or pen-äl'/ *n* formerly, a name for a freshman at a German university. [Ger *Pennal*, from L *pennāle* pen-case]

■ **penn'alism** *n* a system of bullying new students once in vogue at German universities.

pennant[1] /pen'ənt or (naut) pen'ən/ n a line dangling from the masthead, etc, with a block for tackle, etc (naut); a long narrow flag; a signalling or identifying flag; a pennon; a flag awarded for victory in a game, championship, etc, esp in baseball (N Am). [A combination of **pendant** and **pennon**]

■ **broad pennant** a long swallowtailed flag flown by a commodore.

pennant[2] /pen'ənt/ n and adj literally, brook-head, a Welsh place name. [Welsh pen head, and nant brook]

❏ **pennant flag** n a Welsh or West Country stone used for paving (also **pennant grit**, **rock** or **stone**).

pennate see under **penna**.

pennatula /pen-at'ū-lə/ n (pl **pennat'ūlae** /-ē/ or **pennat'ūlas**) the sea pen, a soft coral (genus Pennatula). [Fem of L pennātulus winged, from penna feather]

■ **pennatulā'ceous** adj.

penne[1] /pen'i or -ā/ n pasta in the form of short thick tubes. [Ital, quills, from L penna feather]

penne[2] (Spenser) see under **penna**.

penneeck or **penneech** /pen-ēk'/ (Scott) n an old card game with a new trump for every trick.

penner see under **pen**[1].

pennied, **pennies** see **penny**.

penniform see under **penna**.

penniless see under **penny**.

pennill /pen'il, or in Welsh pen'ihl/ n (pl **penill'ion**) literally, a verse or stanza. [Welsh]

❏ **penill'ion-singing** n a form of Welsh verse-singing in which the singer improvises an independent melody and verse arrangement against an accompaniment (usu on the harp) consisting of a traditional Welsh melody repeated; a modern, modified form of penillion-singing involving one or more singers and allowing advance preparation.

pennine /pen'īn/ n a mineral of the chlorite group found in the Pennine Alps (between Switzerland and Italy), a hydrous silicate of aluminium, magnesium, and iron (also **penn'inite** /-in-īt/).

Pennisetum /pen-i-sē'təm/ (bot) n a genus, mainly African, of grasses with bristles around the spikelets, including bulrush millet or pearl millet. [L penna feather, and saeta bristle]

pennon /pen'ən/ n a medieval knight-bachelor's ensign; a flag or streamer attached to a lance; a flag; a long narrow flag or streamer; a pinion or wing (Milton). [OFr penon streamer, arrow-feather, prob from L penna feather]

■ **penn'oncelle**, **pen'oncelle**, **penn'oncel** or **pen'oncel** n a small flag like a pennon. **penn'oned** adj bearing a pennon.

penn'orth see **pennyworth** under **penny**.

penny /pen'i/ n (pl **pennies** /pen'iz/ (as material objects) or **pence** /pens/ (as units of value)) a coin, orig silver, later copper, then bronze from 1860, formerly worth $\frac{1}{12}$ of a shilling, or $\frac{1}{240}$ of a pound, now (orig **new penny**) equal to a hundredth part of d1; its value; applied to various more or less similar coins; a cent (N Am inf); a small sum; (in pl) money in general; a denarius (Bible); pound, in fourpenny, sixpenny, tenpenny nails, being of four, six, ten pound weight to the thousand. ◆ adj sold for a penny; costing a penny. [OE penig, oldest form pending; cf Ger Pfennig; Du penning; ON penningr]

■ **penn'ied** adj possessed of a penny. **penn'iless** adj without a penny; without money; poor. **penn'ilessness** n.

❏ **penny-a-line** n and vi. **penny-a-lin'er** n a hack writer of the worst, or worst-paid, kind. **penny-a-lin'erism** n a hack writer's verbal expression. **penny ante** n (orig US) a variety of the game of poker in which only modest stakes are allowed. **penn'y-an'te** adj of no great value or significance. **penny arcade** n an amusement arcade with slot machines orig operated by a penny. **penn'y-bank** n (obs) a savings-bank that takes pennies. **penny black** n the first adhesive postage stamp, issued by Britain in 1840. **penny-bun** or **penny-bun mushroom** n a cep, Boletus edulis. **penn'ycress** n a cruciferous plant of the genus Thlaspi, with round flat pods. **penn'y-dog'** n the tope or miller's dog, a kind of shark. **penny dreadful** see under **dread**. **penn'y-far'thing** n a penny and a farthing; an 'ordinary', an old-fashioned bicycle with a big wheel at the front and a little one at the back. **penn'y-fee** n wages in money; (without hyphen) a small wage (Scot). **penny gaff** n (sl) a low-class theatre. **penn'y-in-the-slot'** adj worked by putting a penny in a slot. **penn'yland** n (hist) land valued at a penny a year. **penny loafer** n (orig US) a style of casual shoe with a slot into which a coin could be placed. **penny mail** n (Scot) rent in money, not in kind; a small sum paid to a feudal lord. **penn'y-piece** n a penny. **penn'y-pig** n (Scot) a money box, properly of earthenware (pig). **penn'y-pinch** vi. **penn'y-pinch'ing** adj miserly, too concerned with saving money. **penn'y-plain'** adj plain, straightforward, unpretentious (from 19c children's paper cut-out figures for toy theatres, costing one penny if plain, twopence if coloured; hence, **penny-plain, twopence-coloured** used of any two basically similar

articles, one having a more attractive appearance). **penn'y-post** n a means of, or organization for, carrying a letter for a penny. **penn'y-rent'** n rent in money; income. **penny share** or **stock** n (stock exchange) a share or stock trading for less than d1 or $1, usu bought very speculatively. **penn'y-stone** or **-stane** n (Scot) a round flat stone used as a quoit. **penn'ystone-cast'** n a stone's throw for such a stone. **penn'y-wedd'ing** n (archaic) a wedding at which the guests each contribute a small sum towards the entertainment, etc, the surplus being presented as a gift to the bride and bridegroom. **penn'yweight** n a unit equal to twenty-four grains of troy weight (the weight of a silver penny), or $\frac{1}{20}$ of an ounce troy. **penny whistle** n a tin whistle or flageolet. **penn'y-wis'dom** n prudence in petty matters. **penny wise** adj careful at saving small sums, esp when careless in the saving of larger ones (**pound foolish**); niggardly on occasions when generosity is needed or expected. **penn'ywort** n a name given to various plants with round leaves, esp Hydrocotyle (an umbelliferous marsh-plant) and navelwort (genus Cotyledon). **penn'yworth** n a penny's worth of anything; the amount that can be got for a penny; an unsolicited remark expressing one's opinion (also **two pennyworth**, etc); a good bargain (also **penn'orth** /pen'ərth/; inf).

■ **a penny for your thoughts** (inf) what are you thinking (so deeply) about? **a pretty penny** a considerable sum of money. **in for a penny, in for a pound** there is no point in half measures. **in penny numbers** a very few, or a very little, at a time. **not a penny the worse** none the worse. **pennies from heaven** money obtained without effort and unexpectedly. **Peter's pence** Rome-scot, a tax or tribute of a silver penny paid to the Pope, in England perhaps from the time of Offa of Mercia and in Ireland from Henry II, then abolished under Henry VIII; a similar tax elsewhere; a voluntary contribution to the Pope in modern times. **spend a penny** see under **spend**. **the penny drops** now I (etc) understand. **turn an honest penny** to earn some money honestly. **two** (or **ten**) **a penny** in abundant supply and consequently of little value.

pennyroyal /pen-i-roi'əl/ n a species of mint (Mentha pulegium) once valued in medicine; a related plant, Hedeoma pulegioides (US). [ME puliol real, from Anglo-Fr puliol real, from L pūleium, pūlegium penny-royal, and regālis, -e royal]

pennyweight, **pennywort**, **pennyworth** see under **penny**.

pennywinkle same as **periwinkle**[2].

penology or **poenology** /pē-nol'ə-ji/ n the study of punishment in its relation to crime; the management of prisons. [Gr poinē punishment, and logos discourse]

■ **penological** /-nə-loj'/ adj. **penologist** /-nol'ə-jist/ n.

penoncel, **penoncelle** see under **pennon**.

pensée /pä-sā'/ (Fr) n thought.

pensel see **pensil**.

pensieroso /pen-sye-rō'sō/ (Ital) adj melancholy; thoughtful.

pensil, **pensel** or **pencel** /pen'sl/ n a small pennon. [Anglo-Fr pencel, dimin of penon pennon]

pensile /pen'sīl or -sil/ adj hanging; suspended; overhanging; (of birds) building a hanging nest. [L pēnsilis, from pendēre to hang]

■ **pen'sileness** or **pensility** /-sil'i-ti/ n.

pension /pen'shən/ n an allowance by the State of money to a person who has retired, has been disabled, has reached old age, been widowed, orphaned, etc; an allowance paid by an employer to a retired employee; a periodical payment, as tribute, wages, etc (obs); an allowance of money as a bribe for future services, as a mark of favour, or in reward of one's own or another's merit; /pä-syɔ̃/ a continental boarding house; board. ◆ vt to grant a pension to. [Fr, from L pēnsiō, -ōnis, from pendere, pēnsum to weigh, pay]

■ **pen'sionable** adj entitled, or entitling, to a pension. **pen'sionary** adj receiving a pension; of the nature of a pension. ◆ n a person who receives a pension; someone whose services are available to anyone paying the price, a hireling; the syndic or legal adviser of a Dutch town (hist). **pen'sioner** n a person who receives a pension; a dependant; a gentleman-at-arms (obs); someone who pays out of his or her own income for commons, chambers, etc, at Cambridge University, the equivalent of an Oxford commoner; a boarder, esp in a religious house (obs). **pen'sionless** adj.

❏ **pension fund** n a fund which invests contributions paid into it by working persons, to provide them with pensions on retirement, etc.

■ **Grand Pensionary** (hist) the president of the States General of Holland. **pension off** to dismiss, or allow to retire, with a pension; to dismiss or discard as no longer of value.

pensionnat /pä-syo-na'/ (Fr) n a boarding school.

pensive /pen'siv/ adj meditative; expressing thoughtfulness with sadness. [Fr pensif, -ive, from penser to think, from L pēnsāre to weigh, from pendere to weigh]

■ **pen'siv'd** adj (Shakesp) made pensive. **pen'sively** adv. **pen'siveness** n.

penstemon or **pentstemon** /pen-stē'mən or pent-/ n a plant of a mainly N American showy-flowered genus (*Penstemon* or *Pentstemon*) of the Scrophulariaceae family, with a sterile fifth stamen. [Gr *pente* five, and *stēmōn* warp, as if stamen]

penstock /pen'stok/ n a sluice; (in a hydroelectric or other plant) a valve-controlled water conduit. [**pen²** and **stock¹**]

pensum /pen'səm/ n a task; a school imposition (*US*). [L *pēnsum*]

Pent *abbrev*: Pentecost.

pent¹ *pat* and *pap* of **pen²**, to shut up.
□ **pent'-up** *adj* held in; repressed.

pent² /pent/ n a penthouse; a sloping or overhanging covering. [From **penthouse**, *appar infl by* Fr *pente* slope]
□ **pent'roof** n a roof that slopes one way only.

pent- /pent-/ or **penta-** /pen-tə-/ *combining form* denoting five. [Gr *pente* five]

pentachlorophenol /pen-tə-klo-rə-fē'nol/ n a widely used fungicidal and bactericidal compound, used *esp* as a wood preservative.

pentachord /pen'tə-körd/ (*music*) n a musical instrument with five strings; a diatonic series of five notes. [**penta-** and Gr *chordē* string]

pentacle /pen'tə-kl/ n a pentagram or similar figure (sometimes a hexagram) or amulet used as a defence against demons. [LL *pentaculum*, appar from Gr *pente*; according to some, OFr *pentacol*, from *pendre* to hang, *à* on, and *col* the neck]

Pentacrinus /pen-tak'rin-əs/ n a genus of fossil crinoids, in the form of a feathery five-rayed star on a long pentagonal stalk. [**penta-** and Gr *krinon* lily]
■ **pentac'rinoid** *adj* like or related to Pentacrinus. ◆ n a young form of some crinoids that resembles Pentacrinus.

pentact /pen'takt/ *adj* five-rayed. ◆ n a five-rayed sponge spicule. [**pent-** and Gr *aktīs, aktīnos* ray]
■ **pentactinal** /-ak'tin-əl or -ak-tī'nəl/ *adj*.

pentacyclic /pen-tə-sī'klik or -sik'lik/ *adj* having five whorls. [**penta-** and Gr *kyklos* wheel]

pentad /pen'tad/ n a set of five things; a period of five years or five days; an atom, element or radical with a combining power of five. [Gr *pentas, -ados*]
■ **pentad'ic** *adj*.

pentadactyl or **pentadactyle** /pen-tə-dak'til/ *adj* having five digits. ◆ n a creature with five digits on each limb; an animal with five digits. [**penta-** and Gr *daktylos* finger, toe]
■ **pentadactyl'ic** or **pentadac'tylous** *adj*. **pentadac'tylism** *n*. **pentadac'tyly** *n*.

pentadelphous /pen-tə-del'fəs/ *adj* having five bundles of stamens; united in five bundles. [**pent-** and Gr *adelphos* brother]

pentagon /pen'tə-gon/ n a rectilineal plane figure having five angles and five sides (*geom*); a fort with five bastions; (with *cap*) the headquarters of the US Department of Defense at Washington (from the shape of the building); the US Department of Defense. [Gr *pentagōnon*, from *pente* five, and *gōnia* angle]
■ **pentagonal** /pen-tag'ən-əl/ *adj*. **pentag'onally** *adv*.

pentagram /pen'tə-gram/ n a stellate pentagon or five-pointed star; such a figure used as a symbol in magic, mysticism, etc. [Gr *pentagrammon*, from *pente* five, and *gramma* a letter]

pentagraph a wrong form of **pantograph**.

Pentagynia /pen-tə-jin'i-ə/ (*obs*) n pl a Linnaean order of plants (in various classes) with five pistils. [**penta-** and Gr *gynē* a woman, in the sense of female]
■ **pentagyn'ian** or **pentagynous** /-aj'-/ *adj*.

pentahedron /pen-tə-hē'dron/ n (pl **pentahē'drons** or **pentahē'dra**) a five-faced solid figure. [**penta-** and Gr *hedrā* a seat]
■ **pentahē'dral** *adj*.

pentalogy /pen-tal'ə-ji/ n a pentad, *esp* of published works; a series of five related books. [**penta-** and **-logy**]

pentalpha /pen-tal'fə/ n a pentacle. [**pent-** and Gr *alpha* the letter alpha]

Pentameron /pen-tam'ə-rən/ n a famous collection of folk tales in Neapolitan dialect by Giambattista Basile (died 1632) supposed to be told during five days. [Ital *Pentamerone*, from Gr *pente* five, and *hēmerā* day]

pentamerous /pen-tam'ə-rəs/ *adj* having five parts or members; having parts in fives. [**penta-** and Gr *meros* a part]
■ **pentam'erism** *n*. **pentam'ery** *n*.

pentameter /pen-tam'ə-tər/ n a line of verse of five measures or feet (also *adj*). [Gr *pentametros*, from *pente* five, and *metron* a measure]
■ **elegiac pentameter** a verse of two penthemimers, the first admitting spondees instead of dactyls, the second dactyls only. **iambic pentameter** see under **iambus**.

pentamidine /pen-tam'i-dēn/ (*pharm*) n a drug first used to combat tropical diseases such as sleeping sickness, later found effective against pneumocystis carinii pneumonia. [*pent*ane, *amid*e and chem sfx *-ine*]

Pentandria /pen-tan'dri-ə/ (*obs*) n pl in Linnaeus's classification, a class of plants with five stamens. [**pent-** and Gr *anēr, andros* a man, male]
■ **pentan'drian** or **pentan'drous** *adj*.

pentane /pen'tān/ (*chem*) n a hydrocarbon (C_5H_{12}), fifth member of the alkane series. [**pent-**]
□ **pentanō'ic acid** n valeric acid, a colourless carboxylic acid used in making perfume.

pentangle /pen'tang-gl/ n a pentacle; a pentagon. [**pent-** and **angle¹**]
■ **pentang'ular** *adj*.

pentaploid /pen'tə-ploid/ *adj* fivefold; having five times the haploid number of chromosomes (*biol*). ◆ n a cell, organism, or form with five sets of chromosomes. [Gr *pentaploos* fivefold, and *eidos* form]
■ **pent'aploidy** n the condition of having five sets of chromosomes.

pentapody /pen-tap'ə-di/ n a measure of five feet. [**penta-** and Gr *pous, podos* a foot]
■ **pentapodic** /pent-ə-pod'ik/ *adj*.

pentapolis /pen-tap'ə-lis/ n a group of five cities, *esp* those of Cyrenaica, namely Cyrene, Berenice, Arsinoe, Ptolemais, and Apollonia. [**penta-** and Gr *polis* a city]
■ **pentapolitan** /pent-ə-pol'i-tən/ *adj*.

pentaprism /pen'tə-pri-zm/ (*photog*) n a five-sided prism that corrects lateral inversion by turning light through an angle of 90°, used on reflex cameras to allow eyelevel viewing. [**penta-** and **prism**]

pentarch¹ /pen'tärk/ *adj* (of roots) having five vascular strands. [**pent-** and Gr *archē* beginning]

pentarch² /pen'tärk/ n a ruler or governor in a pentarchy. [**pent-** and Gr *archē* rule]
■ **pentarchy** /pent'ärk-i/ n government by five persons; a group of five kings, rulers, states, or governments.

pentastich /pen'tə-stik/ n (pl **pentastichs** /-stiks/) a group of five lines of verse. [**pent-** and Gr *stichos* row, line]
■ **pentastichous** /pen-tas'ti-kəs/ *adj* five-ranked.

pentastyle /pen'tə-stīl/ *adj* having five columns in front. ◆ n a building or portico with five columns. [**penta-** and Gr *stȳlos* a pillar]

pentasyllabic /pen-tə-si-lab'ik/ *adj* five-syllabled. [**penta-** and **syllabic** (see under **syllable**)]

Pentateuch /pen'tə-tūk/ n the first five books of the Old Testament. [Gr *pentateuchos* five-volumed, from *penta* and *teuchos* a tool, (later) a book]
■ **pentateuch'al** *adj*.

pentathlon /pen-tath'lon/, also (*L*) **pentathlum** /-ləm/ n a sporting contest consisting of five exercises, *orig* wrestling, disc-throwing, spear-throwing, leaping, and running; a five-event athletic contest formerly held at the modern Olympic games. [Gr *pentathlon*, from *pente* five, and *athlon* contest]
■ **pentath'lete** n a competitor in a pentathlon.
■ **modern pentathlon** an Olympic event consisting of swimming, cross-country riding, running, fencing and pistol-shooting.

pentatomic /pen-tə-tom'ik/ (*chem*) *adj* having five atoms, *esp* five atoms of replaceable hydrogen; pentavalent. [**pent-** and Gr *atomos* atom]

pentatonic /pen-tə-ton'ik/ (*music*) *adj* consisting of five tones or notes, applied *esp* to a scale, a major scale with the fourth and seventh omitted. [**penta-** and Gr *tonos* tone]

pentavalent /pen-tə-vā'lənt or pen-tav'ə-lənt/ (*chem*) *adj* having a valency of five. [**penta-** and **-valent**]

pentazocine /pen-tā'zə-sēn/ n a pain-killing drug. [**pent-**, **azo-**, **oct-** and **-ine¹**]

penteconter /pen-ti-kon'tər/ n an ancient Greek ship with fifty oars. [Gr *pentēkontērēs*, from *pentēkonta* fifty]

Pentecost /pen'ti-kost/ n a Jewish festival held on the fiftieth day after the Passover (also called the **Feast of Weeks**, and **Shabuoth** or **Shavuot**); the Christian festival of Whitsuntide, seven weeks after Easter. [Gr *pentēkostē* (*hēmerā*), fiftieth (day)]
■ **Pentecost'al** *adj* of or relating to Pentecost; of or relating to any of several fundamentalist Christian groups placing great emphasis on the spiritual powers of the Holy Spirit. ◆ n a Pentecostalist; (in pl) offerings formerly made to the parish priest at Whitsuntide. **Pentecost'alist** n a member of a Pentecostal church.

Pentelic /pen-tel'ik/ or **Pentelican** /pen-tel'ik-ən/ *adj* of Mount Pentelicus near Athens, famous for the marble found there.

pentene see **pentylene**.

penteteric /pen-ti-ter'ik/ *adj* occurring every fourth (or by the old mode of reckoning, fifth) year. [Gr *pentetērikos*, from *etos* a year]

penthemimer /pen-thi-mim'ər/ (*prosody*) *n* a metrical group of $2\frac{1}{2}$ feet. [Gr *pente* five, *hēmi-* half, and *meros* a part]
■ **penthemim'eral** *adj*.

penthia /pen'thi-ə/ *n* (according to Spenser) another name for the unidentified plant astrophel.

penthouse /pent'hows/ *n* (*pl* **pent'houses** /-how-ziz/) *orig* a separate room or dwelling on a roof; now *usu* a flat on the top floor, or roof, of a (*usu* tall) building, *esp* a luxury flat; a shed or lean-to projecting from or adjoining a main building; (in real tennis) a roofed corridor surrounding the court; a protection from the weather over a door or a window; anything of similar form, eg an eyebrow. ◆ *vt* to provide or cover with, or as if with, a penthouse. [From Fr *appentis*, from LL *appendicium* an appendage]

pentice or **pentise** /pen'tis/ earlier forms of **penthouse**.

pentimento /pen-ti-men'tō/ (*art*) *n* (*pl* **pentimen'ti** /-tē/) the revealing of a (part of a) painting beneath another painted over it at a later time; such a part or painting revealed. [Ital, from *pentirsi* to repent]

pentito /pen-tē'tō/ *n* (*pl* **pentiti** /-tē'tē/) in Italy, a Mafia criminal who has become a police informer. [Ital, pap of *pentirsi* to repent]

Pentium® /pen'ti-əm/ *n* a brand of computer processing chip. [**pent-**, denoting the fifth version of the particular product line]

pentlandite /pent'lən-dīt/ *n* a native sulphide of iron and nickel. [Joseph Barclay *Pentland* (1797–1873), Irish traveller in S America]

pentobarbitone /pen-tə-bär'bi-tōn/, or (*US*) **pentobarbital** /-bär'bi-tal/ (*pharmacol*) *n* a barbiturate drug, $C_{11}H_{17}N_2O_3Na$, formerly prescribed as a sedative.

pentode /pen'tōd/ (*electronics*) *n* a thermionic tube with five electrodes. [Gr *pente* five, and *hodos* way]

pentomic /pen-tom'ik/ *adj* (of an army division) formed into five units, *esp* when using atomic weapons. [Gr *pente* five, and **atomic**]

pentose /pen'tōs/ (*chem*) *n* a sugar (of various kinds) with five carbon atoms. [Gr *pente* five]
■ **pent'osan** /-san/ or **pent'osane** /-sān/ *n* a carbohydrate that yields pentose on hydrolysis.

Pentothal® /pen'tō-thal/ *n* a registered trademark for thiopentone sodium (in *N Am* thiopental sodium), an intravenous anaesthetic, a sodium thiobarbiturate compound (also **Pentothal sodium**).

pentoxide /pen-tok'sīd/ (*chem*) *n* a compound having five atoms of oxygen combined with another element or radical. [Gr *pente* five, and **oxide**]

pentroof see under **pent²**.

pentstemon see **penstemon**.

pent-up see under **pent¹**.

pentyl /pen'tīl/ or /til/ *adj* of or relating to the amyl group (CO_5H_{11}), derived from pentane. [Gr *pente* five, and *hȳlē* matter]

pentylene /pen'ti-lēn/ or **pentene** /pen'tēn/ (*chem*) *n* amylene, an unsaturated hydrocarbon (C_5H_{10}) of the olefine series (in several isomers). [Gr *pente* five, and *hȳlē* matter]

penuche, **penuchi** same as **panocha**.

penuchle see **pinochle**.

penult /pi-nult'/ or /pē'nult/ or **penultima** /pi-nul'ti-mə/ *n* the last but one syllable. [L *paenultima* (*syllaba*, etc), from *paene* almost, and *ultimus* last]
■ **penult'imate** *adj* last but one. ◆ *n* the penult; the last but one.

penumbra /pe-num'brə/ *n* a partial or lighter shadow round the perfect or darker shadow produced by an eclipse or by a large unfocused light source shining on an opaque object; the less dark border of a sunspot or any similar spot; the part of a picture where the light and shade blend into each other. [L *paene* almost, and *umbra* shade]
■ **penum'bral** *adj*. **penum'brous** *adj*.

penury /pen'ū-ri/ *n* want, lack; great poverty. [L *pēnūria*]
■ **penū'rious** *adj* poverty-stricken; niggardly; miserly; lacking (*obs*); scanty (*obs*). **penū'riously** *adv*. **penū'riousness** *n*.

peon /pē'on/ *n* a day-labourer or farm worker, *esp* formerly in Spanish-speaking America, one working off a debt by bondage; in India /pūn/, a foot soldier (*hist*), a policeman (*hist*), or a messenger; in SE Asia, a minor office-worker. [Sp *peón* and Port *peão*, from LL *pedō*, *-ōnis* a foot soldier, from L *pēs*, *pedis* a foot]
■ **pē'onage** or **pē'onism** *n* agricultural servitude of the above kind.

peony or **paeony** /pē'ə-ni/, also (*obs*) **pioney** and **piony** /pī-/ *n* any plant of the genus *Paeonia*, of the buttercup family, perennial and deciduous shrubs having large showy crimson, pink, yellow or white globular flowers; its flower. [OE *peonie* and OFr (Northern) *pione* (Fr *pivoine*), from L *paeōnia*, from Gr *paiōniā*, from *Paiōn*, *Paiān* physician of the gods (see **paean**) from its use in medicine]

people /pē'pl/ *n* (in the following senses, used as a *sing* with a *pl* **peoples** or, often in the Bible, **people**) a set of persons; a nation; a community; a body of persons held together by a common origin, speech, culture, political union, or by a common leadership, headship, etc; transferred to a set of animals as if forming a nation; (in the following senses, used as a *pl*) the mass of the nation; general population; populace; the citizens; voters; subjects; followers; retainers; employees; servants; attendants; congregation; close relatives; members of one's household; parents; ancestors and descendants; inhabitants of a place; transferred to animal inhabitants; the persons associated with any business; laity; (approaching a *pronoun*) they, one, folks. ◆ *combining form* denoting belonging or relating to the general populace, as in *people power*, *people-oriented*. ◆ *vt* to stock with people or inhabitants; to inhabit; to occupy as if inhabiting. [OFr *poeple*, from L *populus*]
■ **peo'plehood** *n*.
❑ **people carrier** *n* a vehicle with seating capacity for eg a large family; a people mover. **people mover** *n* a car, carriage, etc, used to transport people at airports, etc, usually running on a fixed rail or track. **people person** *n* (*inf*) someone who enjoys or excels at working or dealing with others. **people power** *n* the power of ordinary people to influence political decisions by means of demonstrations, etc. **people's democracy** *n* a form of government in which the proletariat, represented by the Communist Party, holds power, seen ideologically as a transitional state on the way to full socialism. **people's front** same as **popular front** (see under **popular**). **people skills** *n pl* (*inf*) the ability to work or deal with others harmoniously. **People's Party** see **populist** under **popular**. **People's Republic** *n* a name adopted by some socialist or communist states.

PEP /pep/ *abbrev*: personal equity plan; political and economic planning.

pep /pep/ (*inf*) *n* vigour, go, spirit, life. ◆ *vt* to put pep into (*usu* with *up*). [**pepper**]
■ **pep'ful** *adj*. **pepp'y** *adj*.
❑ **pep pill** *n* a pill containing a stimulant drug. **pep talk** *n* a strongly-worded talk designed to arouse enthusiasm for a cause or course of action.

peperino /pep-ə-rē'nō/ *n* a dark tuff with many crystals and rock fragments, found in the Alban Hills. [Ital *peperino*, from L *piper* pepper]

peperomia /pe-pə-rō'mi-ə/ *n* any of a large genus (*Peperomia*) of subtropical herbaceous plants of the family Piperaceae, many grown as house plants for their ornamental foliage. [Gr *peperi* pepper, and *homoios* like, similar]

peperoni see **pepperoni**.

pepful see under **pep**.

pepino /pə-pē'nō/ *n* (also called **mel'on-pear**) a purple-striped pale yellow fruit with sweet flesh, oval (often elongated) in shape; the spiny-leaved S American plant (*Solanum muricatum*) that bears this fruit. [Sp, cucumber]

peplos /pep'los/ or **peplus** /pep'ləs/ *n* a draped outer robe worn *usu* by women in ancient Greece. [Gr *peplos*]
■ **pep'lum** *n* a peplos; an overskirt supposed to be like the peplos; hence, a short skirt-like section attached to the waistline of a dress, blouse or jacket.

pepo /pē'pō/ *n* (*pl* **pē'pos**) the type of fruit found in the melon and cucumber family, a large many-seeded berry formed from an inferior ovary, *usu* with hard epicarp. [L *pepō*, *-onis*, from Gr (*sikyos*) *pepōn* (a melon eaten) ripe, distinguished from a cucumber eaten unripe]

pepper /pep'ər/ *n* a pungent aromatic condiment consisting of the dried berries of the pepper plant, whole or ground (**black pepper**), or with the outer parts removed (**white pepper**); any plant of the genus **Piper**, *esp P. nigrum*, or of the family Piperaceae; a plant of the solanaceous genus *Capsicum* or one of its pods (**red**, **yellow** or **green pepper**; also called **sweet pepper**); cayenne (also **cayenne pepper**); extended to various similar condiments and the plants producing them. ◆ *vt* to sprinkle or flavour with pepper; to sprinkle; to pelt with shot, etc; to pelt thoroughly; to do for. ◆ *vi* to pelt; to shower liberally; to discharge shot, etc, in showers. [OE *pipor*, from L *piper*, from Gr *peperi*, from Sans *pippali*]
■ **pepp'erer** *n* a grocer (*obs*); someone who or that which peppers. **pepp'eriness** *n*. **pepp'ering** *n*. **pepp'ery** *adj* having the taste or qualities of pepper; pungent; hot, choleric, irritable.
❑ **pepper-and-salt'** *adj* mingled black and white; (of hair) flecked or streaked with grey. **pepper box** *n* a pepper pot; a turret or other object of similar shape. **pepp'er-cake** *n* a kind of spiced cake or gingerbread. **pepp'er-caster** or **-castor** *n* a pepper pot. **pepp'ercorn** *n* the dried berry of the pepper plant; something of little value. ◆ *adj* like a peppercorn (eg the small tight knots in which certain African peoples traditionally wear their hair); trivial, nominal, as in *peppercorn rent*. **pepp'ercorny** *adj*. **peppered moth** *n* a geometric moth that is white with black speckles but appears in a dark variety in polluted industrial areas. **pepp'er-gin'gerbread** *n* (*Shakesp*) hot-spiced gingerbread.

pepper grass *n* any cress of the genus *Lepidium*; pillwort (genus *Pilularia*). **pepp'ermill** *n* a small handmill in which peppercorns are ground. **pepp'ermint** *n* an aromatic and pungent species of mint (*Mentha piperita*); the essence distilled from it; a sweet flavoured with it. **peppermint cream** *n* a sweet creamy peppermint-flavoured substance; a sweet made of this. **pepp'ermint-drop** *n* a peppermint-flavoured, *usu* hard, sweet. **pepper pot** *n* a pot or bottle with a perforated top for sprinkling pepper; a West Indian dish of cassareep, flesh or dried fish, and vegetables, *esp* green okra and chillis. **pepp'er-shrike** *n* a tropical American songbird of the family Vireonidae. **pepper spray** *n* an aerosol spray containing irritants derived from cayenne pepper, used as a weapon of self-defence. **pepper tree** *n* an evergreen tree of the genus *Schinus*, chiefly native to tropical America, often grown for its ornamental appearance. **pepp'erwort** *n* a cress of the genus *Lepidium*, *esp* dittander (*L. latifolium*).
■ **Jamaica pepper** allspice. **long pepper** the fruit of *Piper longum*. **Negro pepper** the produce of *Xylopia* (family Anonaceae), also called **Ethiopian pepper**.

pepperidge /pep'ə-rij/ *n* the tupelo. [Origin unknown]

pepperoni or **peperoni** /pep-ə-rō'ni/ *n* a hard, spicy beef and pork sausage. [Ital *peperoni*, pl of *peperone* chilli, pepper, from L *piper* pepper]

peppy see under **pep**.

pepsin or **pepsine** /pep'sin/ *n* any of a group of digestive enzymes in the gastric juice of vertebrates, which breaks down proteins under acidic conditions; a preparation containing pepsin from a pig's or other stomach (*med*). [Gr *pepsis* digestion, from *peptein* to digest]
■ **pep'sinate** *vt* to treat with pepsin; to mix or combine with pepsin. **pep'sinogen** *n* a precursor found in granular form in the mucous membrane of the stomach which converts into pepsin in a slightly acid medium. **pep'tic** *adj* relating to or promoting digestion; having a good digestion; of or relating to pepsin or the digestive juices. **pepticity** /-tis'i-ti/ *n* eupepsy. **pep'tics** *n pl* (*joc*) the digestive organs. **pep'tidase** *n* an enzyme which breaks down peptides into their constituent amino acids. **pep'tide** *n* any of a number of substances formed from amino acids in which the amino group of one is joined to the carboxyl group of another. **peptidoglycan** /-tīd-ō-glī'kan/ *n* (Gr *glykys* sweet) a substance giving form and strength to the cell walls of certain bacteria. **peptizā'tion** or **-s-** *n*. **pept'ize** or **-ise** *vt* to bring into colloidal solution; to form into a sol from a gel. **pep'tōne** *n* a product of the action of enzymes on proteins, used eg as a bacteriological culture medium. **peptonizā'tion** or **-s-** *n*. **pep'tonize** or **-ise** *vt* to convert into peptones.
❏ **peptic ulcer** *n* an ulcer of the stomach, duodenum, etc. **peptide bond** *n* (*biochem*) the bond formed by condensation of the amino group and carboxyl group of a pair of amino acids, and thus found in the peptide chains of proteins. **peptide nucleic acid** *n* a compound analogous to DNA in which a synthetic peptide takes the place of the sugar in DNA.

Pepysian /pēp'si-ən/ *adj* relating to or associated with Samuel *Pepys* (1633–1703), his famous diary, or his library.

per¹ /pûr/ or /pər/ *prep* for each or a; (chiefly commercial) by; in the manner or direction of (*heraldry*). [L and OFr *per*]
■ **as per usual** (*inf*) as usual.

per² /pûr/ or /per/ (*L*) through, by means of, according to (also **as per**).
■ **per annum**, **diem** or **mensem** /an'əm or -ŭm, dī'əm or dē'em, or men'səm or men'sem/ yearly, daily or monthly. **per ardua ad astra** /är'dū-ə ad as'trə or är'dū-ä ad as'trä/ by steep and toilsome ways to the stars (the motto of the RAF). **per capita** /kap'i-tə or kap'i-tä/ or **per caput** /kap'ŭt/ (counting) by heads; for each person; all sharing alike. **per contra** /kon'trə or kon'trä/ on the contrary; as a contrast. **per curiam** /kū'ri-am or koo'ri-am/ (*law*) by a court. **per fas et nefas** /fas et nē'fas or fäs et ne'fäs/ through right and wrong. **per impossibile** /im-po-si'bi-lē or im-po-si'bi-le/ by an impossibility; if it were so, which it is not. **per incuriam** /in-kū'ri-am or in-koo'ri-am/ (*law*) through lack of care, a phrase designating a court decision that is given in ignorance of the relevant statute, and therefore not binding as a precedent. **per minas** /mī' or mē'näs/ (*law*) by means of threats, by menaces. **per procurationem** /prok-ū-rä-shi-ō'nem or prō-koo-rä-ti-ō'nem/ by the agency of another, by proxy. **per saltum** /sal'təm or sal'tŭm/ at a single leap; all at once. **per se** /sē or sā/ by himself, etc; essentially; in itself. **per stirpes** /stûr'pēz or stir'pās/ (of an inheritance) bequeathed in blocks to families who subdivide it equally among the members, rather than directly to individuals themselves (per capita).

per. *abbrev*: period; person.

per- /pûr- or pər-/ *combining form* denoting: (1) the highest degree of combination with oxygen or other element or radical (*chem*); (2) in words from Latin, through, beyond, or thoroughly, or indicating destruction.

peracute /pûr-ə-kūt'/ *adj* very sharp or violent. [L *peracūtus*, from *per-* thoroughly, and *acūtus* sharp]

peradventure /pûr-əd-ven'chər/ *adv* by adventure; by chance; perhaps. ◆ *n* (*obs*) uncertainty; question. [OFr *per* (or *par*) *aventure* by chance]

peraeon, **peraeopod** see **pereion**.

perai /pē-rī'/ see **piranha**.

perambulate /pər-am'byū-lāt/ *vt* to walk through, about, around, up and down, or over; to pass through for the purpose of surveying; to establish the boundary of (eg a parish) by ceremonially walking round it, to beat the bounds of; to patrol; to wheel in a pram. ◆ *vi* to walk about. [L *perambulāre, -ātum*, from *per* through, and *ambulāre* to walk]
■ **perambulā'tion** *n* the act of perambulating; a survey or inspection by travelling through; beating the bounds; the district within which a person has the right of inspection. **peram'bulātor** *n* a person who perambulates; a wheel for measuring distances on roads; a light hand-pushed carriage for a baby or young child (now *usu* **pram**). **peram'bulatory** *adj*.

per an. *abbrev*: per annum (see **per²**).

perborate /pər-bö'rāt/ *n* a salt consisting of an oxidized borate, used as a bleaching agent. [**per-** (1) and **borate** (see under **borax¹**)]

Perca see **perch²**.

percale /per-käl' or pər-käl'/ *n* a closely-woven French cambric. [Fr; cf Pers *purgālah* rag]
■ **percaline** /pûr-kə-lēn' or pûr'/ *n* a glossy cotton cloth.

percase /pər-kās'/ (*obs*) *adv* perchance; perhaps. [L *per* through, by, and *casus* a chance, a fall]

perce /pûrs/ (*Spenser*) same as **pierce**.
■ **perce'able** *adj* (*Spenser*) pierceable. **perce'ant** *adj* (*Keats*) piercing. **perc'en** *vt* (*infinitive*) to pierce.

perceive /pər-sēv'/ *vt* to become or be aware of through the senses; to get knowledge of by the mind; to see, see clearly; to understand; to discern; to view subjectively; to believe, suppose; to see partially, or be mistaken in (what one sees). [OFr *percever*, from L *percipere, perceptum*, from pfx *per-* thoroughly, and *capere* to take]
■ **perceiv'able** *adj*. **perceiv'ably** *adv* perceptibly. **perceiv'er** *n*. **perceiv'ing** *n* and *adj*.
❏ **perceived noise decibel** *n* a unit used to measure the amount of annoyance caused to people by noise.

per cent (sometimes written or printed with a point after it as if an abbreviation for *per centum*, but pronounced as a complete word /pər-sent'/) in the hundred; for each hundred or hundred pounds. *n* a percentage; one part in each hundred; (in *pl*, in combination) securities yielding a specified percentage (eg *three-percents*). [L *per centum*]
■ **percent'age** *n* rate per hundred; an allowance of so much for every hundred; a proportional part; commission (*inf*); profit, advantage (*inf*). **percent'al** or **percen'tile** *adj*. **percen'tile** *n* the value below which falls a specified percentage (eg 25, 50 or 75) of a large number of statistical units (eg scores in an examination); percentile rank.
❏ **percentile rank** *n* grading according to percentile group.
■ **play the percentages** (in sport, gambling, etc) to play, operate or proceed by means of unspectacular safe shots, moves, etc as opposed to spectacular but risky ones which may not succeed, on the assumption that this is more likely to lead to success in the long run.

percept /pûr'sept/ *n* an object perceived by the senses; the mental result of perceiving. [L *percipere, perceptum*; see **perceive**]
■ **perceptibil'ity** *n*. **percep'tible** *adj* that can be perceived; that may be known by the senses; discernible. **percep'tibly** *adv*. **percep'tion** *n* the act or power of perceiving; discernment; apprehension of any modification of consciousness; the combining of sensations into a recognition of an object; direct recognition; a percept; reception of a stimulus (*psychol* and *bot*). **percep'tional** *adj*. **percep'tive** *adj* able or quick to perceive; discerning; active or instrumental in perceiving. **percep'tiveness** *n*. **perceptiv'ity** *n*. **percep'tūal** *adj* of the nature of, or relating to, perception.

perch¹ /pûrch/ *n* a rod for a bird to alight, sit, or roost on; anything serving that purpose for a bird, a person, or anything else; a high seat; a pole serving as a navigation mark; a pole joining the fore and hind gear of some vehicles; a bar or frame for stretching cloth for examination; a bar for fixing leather for softening treatment; a peg or bar for hanging things on (*obs*); a pole (*obs* or *dialect* except in special uses); a rod or pole, a measure of 5$\frac{1}{2}$ yards (5.03 metres) or (*square perch*) 30$\frac{1}{4}$ square yards (25.3 square metres); a measure of stonework, 24$\frac{3}{4}$ or 25 cubic feet (0.7 cubic metres). ◆ *vi* to alight, sit or roost on a perch; to be set on high; to be balanced on a high or narrow footing; to settle. ◆ *vt* to place, as on a perch; to stretch, examine, or treat on a perch. [Fr *perche*, from L *pertica* a rod]
■ **perch'ed** *adj* (*Milton*) having perches. **perch'er** *n* a bird with feet adapted for perching. **perch'ery** *adj* (of eggs) laid by hens kept in a

modified deep litter system, where provision is made for the birds to roost as they would in the wild on branches, etc. **perch'ing** *n* examination of cloth on a perch; a process of leather-softening. ◆ *adj* with feet adapted for perching; insessorial.
❑ **perched block** *n* a block of rock carried by a glacier and left perched high up, often in an unstable position, when the ice recedes. **perching birds** *n pl* the Passeriformes.

perch² /*pûrch*/ *n* a spiny-finned freshwater fish of the genus **Perca** /*pûr'kə*/; extended to various similar or related fishes. [L *perca* (partly through Fr *perche*), from Gr *perkē* a perch, perh connected with *perknos* dusky]
■ **Percidae** /*pûr'si-dē*/ *n pl* the perch family. **per'ciform** or **per'cine** /*-sīn*/ *adj* of or like a perch. **per'coid** /*-koid*/ *n* and *adj* (a member) of the perch family.

perchance /*pər-chäns'*/ *adv* by chance; as it may happen; perhaps. [Anglo-Fr *par chance*]

perched, **percher**, **perchery** see under **perch¹**.

percheron /*per'shə-rɔ* or *pûr'shə-ron*/ *n* a draught horse of a breed originating in La *Perche* in S Normandy. [Fr]

perchloric /*pər-klō'rik*, *-klö'* or *-klor'ik*/ (*chem*) *adj* containing more oxygen than chloric acid, *esp* applied to an oily explosive acid, $HClO_4$. [**per-** (1)]
■ **perchlö'rate** *n* a salt of perchloric acid.

perchloroethylene /*pər-klö-rō-eth'i-lēn*/ *n* a liquid used as a solvent in dry-cleaning.

Percidae, **perciform**, **percine** see under **perch²**.

percipient /*pər-sip'i-ənt*/ *adj* perceiving; having the faculty of perception; observant, perceptive. ◆ *n* a person who perceives or can perceive; someone who receives impressions telepathically or by other means outside the range of the senses. [L *percipiēns, -entis*, prp of *percipere*; cf **perceive, percept**]
■ **percip'ience** or (*rare*) **percip'iency** *n*.

percoct /*pər-kokt'*/ *adj* well-cooked; overdone; hackneyed. [L *percoctus*, from *percoquere* to cook thoroughly]

percoid /*pûr'koid*/ see under **perch²**.

percolate /*pûr'kə-lāt*/ *vt* and *vi* to pass through pores, small openings, etc; to filter; to make (coffee) in a percolator. ◆ *vi* (*usu* with *through*) to spread or become known gradually. ◆ *n* a filtered liquid. [L *percōlāre, -ātum*, from *per* through, and *cōlāre* to strain]
■ **percolation** /*pûr-kō-lā'shən*/ *n*. **per'colātor** *n* an apparatus for percolating; a coffee pot inside which boiling water is made to pass repeatedly over coffee grounds laid on a filter.

percolin /*pûr'kə-lin*/ *n* a small, possibly mythical, bird, supposedly a cross between a partridge and a quail.

percurrent /*pər-kur'ənt*/ *adj* running through the whole length. [L *percurrere* to run through, *percursor* one who runs through]
■ **percursory** /*-kūr'*/ *adj* cursory.

percuss /*pər-kus'*/ *vt* to strike so as to shake; to strike or tap sharply; to tap for the purposes of diagnosis. [L *percussiō, -ōnis*, from *percutere, percussum*, from pfx *per-* thoroughly, and *quatere* to shake]
■ **percuss'ant**, also **percussed'** *adj* (*heraldry*) bent round and striking the side (eg of a lion's tail). **percussion** /*-kush'ən*/ *n* collectively, instruments played by striking, such as drums, cymbals, xylophones (*music*); striking; impact; tapping directly or indirectly upon the body to find the condition of an organ by the sound (*med*); massage by tapping; the striking or sounding of a discord, etc, as distinguished from preparation and resolution (*music*); a device for making an organ-pipe sound promptly by striking the reed (*music*). **percuss'ional** *adj*. **percuss'ionist** *n* a musician who plays percussion instruments. **percussive** /*-kus'*/ *adj*. **percuss'ively** *adv*. **percuss'or** *n* a percussion hammer. **percutient** /*-kū'shyent*/ *adj* striking or having the power to strike. ◆ *n* something that strikes or has the power to strike.
❑ **percussion bullet** *n* a bullet that explodes on striking. **percussion cap** *n* a metal case containing a substance which explodes when struck, formerly used for firing rifles, etc (see also **cap¹**); a small paper case of the same type, used to make children's toy guns sound realistic (*usu* **cap**). **percuss'ion-fuse** *n* a fuse in a projectile that acts on striking. **percussion hammer** *n* a small hammer for percussion in diagnosis. **percuss'ion-lock** *n* a gun lock in which a hammer strikes a percussion cap. **percuss'ion-pow'der** *n* powder that explodes on being struck, fulminating powder.
■ **bulb of percussion** see under **bulb**.

percutaneous /*pər-kū-tā'ni-əs*/ *adj* done or applied through the skin. [**per-** (2), and L *cutis* the skin]
■ **percutā'neously** *adv*.

percutient see under **percuss**.

perdendo /*per-den'dō*/ (*music*) *adj* and *adv* slowing and softening at the same time (also **perden'dosi** /*-sē*/). [Ital]

perdie or **perdy** /*pər-dē'*, sometimes *pûr'dē*/ (*Spenser, Shakesp*) *adv* assuredly (also **pardi'**, **pardie'** or **pardy'**). [OFr *par dé* by God]

perdition /*pər-dish'ən*/ *n* everlasting misery after death, damnation (*Christianity*); hell (*Christianity*); loss (*archaic*); ruin (*archaic*); utter loss or ruin (*archaic*). [L *perditiō, -ōnis* loss, from *perdere, perditum*, from pfx *per-* entirely, and *dare* to give, give up]
■ **perdi'tionable** *adj*.

perdu or **perdue** /*pər-dū'*/ *adj* lost to view; concealed; in a post of extreme danger (*obs*); on a forlorn hope or on a desperate enterprise (*obs*); reckless. ◆ *n* an outlying sentinel (*Shakesp*); someone lying in concealment or ambush; a person on a forlorn hope (*obs*). [Fr, pap of *perdre* to lose, from L *perdere* to destroy; see **perdition**]
■ **lie perdu** or **perdue** (*milit*) to lie in ambush, concealed and on the watch.

perduellion /*pər-dū-el'yən*/ (*archaic*) *n* treason. [L *perduelliō, -ōnis*]

perdurable /*pər-dūr'ə-bl* or (*Shakesp*) *pûr'*/ (*rare*) *adj* very durable, long continued; everlasting. [L *perdūrāre*, from *per* through, and *dūrāre* to last]
■ **perdūrabil'ity** *n*. **perdūr'ably** *adv* very durably; everlastingly. **perdūr'ance** *n*. **perdūrā'tion** *n*. **perdūre'** *vi* to endure.

perdy see **perdie**.

père /*per*/ (*Fr*) *n* father.
❑ **Père David's** /*dä' vidz*, *dä' vēdz* or *-vēdz'*/ *deer* *n* a breed of large grey deer discovered in China by Father A *David* (1826–1900), French missionary.

peregal /*per'i-gl*/ (*obs*) *adj* fully equal. ◆ *n* an equal. [OFr *paregal*, from L pfx *per-* thoroughly, and *aequālis* equal]

peregrine /*per'i-grin*/ *n* (in full **peregrine falcon**) a species of falcon (*Falco peregrinus*), so named because it was captured in flight and not taken from the nest; a foreign resident (*archaic*); a pilgrim or traveller in a foreign land (*archaic*). ◆ *adj* foreign (*archaic*); outlandish (*archaic*); making a pilgrimage or journey (*archaic*). [L *peregrīnus* foreign, from *peregre* abroad, from *per* through, and *ager* field]
■ **per'egrinate** *vi* to travel about; to live in a foreign country; to go on a pilgrimage. ◆ *vt* to traverse. ◆ *adj* foreign-looking. **peregrinā'tion** *n* travelling about; wandering; pilgrimage; a complete and systematic course or round; a sojourn abroad. **per'egrinātor** *n* someone who travels about. **per'egrinatory** *adj* of or relating to a peregrinator; wandering. **peregrin'ity** *n* foreignness; outlandishness.

pereion /*pə-rī'on* or *-rē'*/ *n* (*pl* **perei'a**) the thorax in Crustacea. [Faultily formed from Gr *peraioein* to transport, to carry across]
■ **perei'opod** *n* a crustacean's thoracic walking leg (also in etymologically correct forms **peraeon** and **peraeopod** /*-rē'*/).

pereira /*pə-rer'ə* or *-rā'rə*/ or **pereira bark** /*bärk*/ *n* a S American apocynaceous tree, the bark of which is used medicinally; the bark itself. [From Jonathan *Pereira* (1804–53), English pharmacologist]

peremptory /*pər-em'* or *pər-emp'tə-ri* or *per'əm-* or *per'əmp-tə-ri*/ *adj* dogmatic; imperious; arrogantly commanding; final; admitting no refusal or denial; definitely fixed (*law*); precluding debate or dispute (*Roman law*); utter (*obs*). [L *peremptōrius*, from *perimere, peremptum* to destroy, prevent, from pfx *per-* entirely, and *emere* to take, to buy]
■ **peremp'torily** (or **per'**) *adv*. **peremp'toriness** (or **per'**) *n*.

perennial /*pə-ren'yəl* or *-i-əl*/ *adj* lasting through the year; perpetual; never-failing; growing constantly; lasting more than two years (*bot*); (of insects) living more than one year. ◆ *n* a plant that lives more than two years. [L *perennis*, from *per* through, and *annus* a year]
■ **perenn'ate** *vi* to live perennially; to survive from season to season, *esp* through a period of inactivity. **perennā'tion** /*per-*/ *n*. **perennial'ity** *n* the quality of being perennial (also (*archaic*) **perenn'ity**). **perenn'ially** *adv*.

perennibranchiate /*pə-ren-i-brang'ki-ət* or *-āt*/ *adj* retaining the gills throughout life. [L *perennis* lasting through the years, and *branchiae* gills]
■ **perenn'ibranch** /*-brangk*/ *adj* and *n*.

perennity see **perenniality** under **perennial**.

perentie or **perenty** /*pə-ren'ti*/ *n* a large monitor lizard (*Varanus giganteus*) of arid regions of Australia. [From an Aboriginal language]

perestroika /*per-i-stroy'kə*/ (*Russ*) *n* reconstruction or restructuring, *specif* the restructuring of political and economic systems carried out in the former Soviet Union in the 1980s. [Russ]

perf. *abbrev* : perfect.

perfay /*pər-fā'*/ (*archaic*) *interj* by my faith. [OFr *par fei*]

perfect /*pûr'fekt* or *-fikt*/ *adj* done thoroughly or completely; completed; mature; complete; having all organs in a functional condition; having androecium and gynaeceum in the same flower (*bot*); completely skilled or versed; thoroughly known or acquired; exact; exactly conforming to definition or theory; without flaw, blemish or fault; having every moral excellence; sheer, utter; absolute;

completely contented (*Shakesp*); denoting completed action (*grammar*); certain, convinced (*Shakesp*); of the simpler kind of consonance (*music*); triple (*old music*; applied to time). ◆ *n* the perfect tense; a verb in the perfect tense. ◆ *vt* /pər-fekt'/ or /pûr'/ to make perfect; to finish; to teach fully, to make fully skilled in anything; to print the second side of (a sheet of paper). [ME *parfit*, from OFr *parfit*; assimilated to L *perfectus*, pap of *perficere*, from pfx *per-* thoroughly, and *facere* to do]

■ **perfecta'tion** *n* (*rare*). **perfect'er** (or /pûr'/) *n*. **perfect'i** /-ī/ *n pl* a body of Catharists in the 12c and 13c, living very strict lives. **perfectibil'ian** *n* a believer in the perfectibility of mankind. **perfect'ibilism** *n* the belief that man is capable of becoming perfect or of progressing indefinitely towards perfection. **perfect'ibilist** *n*. **perfectibil'ity** *n* capability of becoming perfect; perfectibilism. **perfect'ible** *adj* capable of becoming or being made perfect. **perfec'tion** *n* the state of being perfect; the process of making or becoming perfect; a quality in perfect degree; the highest state or degree; an embodiment of the perfect; loosely, a degree of excellence approaching the perfect. **perfec'tionate** *vt* to bring to perfection. **perfec'tionism** *n*. **perfec'tionist** *n* a person who claims to be perfect; a person who aims at or calls for nothing short of perfection; someone who holds some doctrine concerning perfection; someone who thinks that moral perfection can be attained in this life; (with *cap*) one of the Bible Communists or Free-lovers, a small American sect founded by JH Noyes (1811–86), which settled at Oneida in 1848, holding that the gospel if accepted secures freedom from sin. **perfectionist'ic** *adj* seeking to attain perfection; being a perfectionist. **perfect'ive** *adj* tending to make perfect; (of a verb aspect) denoting completed action (*grammar*). **perfect'ively** *adv*. **per'fectly** *adv*. **per'fectness** *n* the state or quality of being perfect; completeness. **perfect'o** *n* (*pl* **perfect'os**) (Sp, perfect) a large tapering cigar. **perfect'or** *n* someone who perfects; a machine for printing both sides at once.

◻ **perfect binding** *n* an unsewn bookbinding in which the backs of the gathered sections are sheared off and the leaves held in place by glue. **perfect cadence** *n* (*music*) one passing from the chord of the dominant to that of the tonic. **perfect competition** *n* (*econ*) free competition for the sale of a commodity. **perfect fifth** *n* (*music*) the interval between two sounds whose vibration frequencies are as 2 to 3. **perfect fluid** *n* an ideal fluid, incompressible, of uniform density, and offering no resistance to distorting forces. **perfect fourth** *n* (*music*) the interval between sounds whose vibration frequencies are as 3 to 4. **perfect game** *n* (*baseball*) a game in which a pitcher does not allow any batter to reach base. **perfect gas** same as **ideal gas** (see under **ideal**). **perfect insect** *n* the imago or completely developed form of an insect. **perfect interval** *n* (*music*) the fourth, fifth, or octave. **perfect market** *n* (*econ*) a market where there are many buyers and sellers, none of whom can influence prices individually. **perfect metals** *n pl* noble metals. **perfect number** *n* (*maths*) a number equal to the sum of its factors (including unity), as $6=1+2+3$ and $28=1+2+4+7+14$. **perfect pitch** *n* (*music*) the pitch of a note as determined by the number of vibrations per second; the ability to identify or remember a note accurately; a term often used for **absolute pitch** (see under **absolute**). **perfect square** *n* a square number (qv). **perfect storm** *n* a particularly violent storm caused by the simultaneous occurrence of various intense meteorological phenomena; the disastrous effect of a combination of adverse events. **perfect tense** *n* a tense signifying action completed in the past (eg *I have said*) or at the time spoken of (as in the **past perfect** or **pluperfect**, eg *I had said*, and the **future perfect**, eg *I shall have left by then*). **perfect year** see **year**.

■ **to perfection** perfectly.

perfecta /pər-fek'tə/ (*orig US*) *n* a form of bet in which the punter has to select, and place in the correct order, the two horses or dogs, etc which will come first and second in a race. [Am Sp (quiniela) *perfecta* perfect (quinella). cf **quinella** and **trifecta**]

perfervid /pər-fûr'vid/ (*poetic*) *adj* very fervid; ardent; eager. [L *perfervidus*, from *prae* before, and *fervidus* fervid]

■ **perfervidity** /pûr-fər-vid'i-ti/ *n*. **perfer'vidness** *n*. **perfer'vour** or **perfer'vor** *n*.

perfet /pûr'fet/ *adj* an older form (used by Milton) of **perfect**.

perficient /pər-fish'ənt/ *adj* effectual; actually achieving a result. [L *perficiēns, -entis*, prp of *perficere* to complete, from pfx *per-* thoroughly, and *facere* to do, make]

perfidious /pər-fid'i-əs/ *adj* faithless; unfaithful, deceitful, treacherous. [L *perfidiōsus*, from *perfidia* faithlessness, from pfx *per-*, implying destruction, and *fidēs* faith]

■ **perfid'iously** *adv*. **perfid'iousness** *n*. **perfidy** /pûr'fid-i/ *n*.

perfin /pûr'fin/ *n* a postage stamp into which the initials of an organization are perforated to prevent unofficial use. [*per*forated *in*itials]

perfluor- /pər-floor-/ or **perfluoro-** pər-floo-rō-/ *combining form* denoting (in a chemical compound) substitution of most or all of the hydrogen by fluorine. [**per-** (1) and **fluorine**]

■ **perfluorocar'bon** *n* an organic compound in which much of the hydrogen has been replaced by fluorine; any binary compound of carbon and fluorine, similar to a hydrocarbon.

perfoliate /pər-fō'li-āt/ (*bot*) *adj* (of a leaf) having the base joined around the stem, so as to appear pierced by the stem (*orig* said of the stem passing through the leaf, or of the plant). [**per-** (2), and L *folium* a leaf]

■ **perfolia'tion** *n*.

perforans /pûr'fə-rans/ (*anat*) *n* the long flexor muscle of the toes, or the deep flexor muscle of the fingers, whose tendons pass through those of the perforatus. [Ety as for **perforate**]

■ **perforatus** /pûr-fər-ā'tas/ *n* the short flexor of the toes or the superficial flexor of the fingers.

perforate /pûr'fə-rāt/ *vt* to bore through or into; to pierce or to make a hole through; to make a series of small holes in (paper, etc) to facilitate tearing; to penetrate; to pass through by a hole. ◆ *adj* (more usually **per'forated**) pierced by a hole or holes; having an aperture; dotted with pellucid dots (*bot*); pierced by rows of small holes for easy separation (eg of a sheet of postage stamps). [L *perforāre, -ātum*, from *per* through, and *forāre* to bore]

■ **per'forable** *adj*. **per'forant** *adj* perforating. **perforation** /pûr-fə-rā'shən/ *n* the act of making a hole; the formation of a hole or aperture; the condition of being perforated; a hole through or into anything; a series, or one of a series, of small holes, as for ease in tearing paper. **per'forative** *adj* having the power to pierce. **per'forator** *n* someone who bores; a boring instrument or organ.

perforce /pər-fōrs' or -fôrs'/ *adv* by force; of necessity. [OFr *par force*]

perform /pər-fôrm'/ *vt* to do; to carry out duly; to act in fulfilment of; to carry into effect; to fulfil; to bring about; to render; to execute; to go through duly; to act; to play in due form. ◆ *vi* to do what is to be done; to execute a function; to act, behave; to act a part; to play, sing or dance; to do feats, tricks, or other acts for an audience; to lose one's temper (*Aust inf*). [Anglo-Fr *parfourmer*, appar an altered form of *parfourner*, from OFr *parfournir*, from *par*, from L *per* through, and *fournir* to furnish]

■ **perform'able** *adj* capable of being performed; practicable. **perform'ance** *n* the act of performing; a carrying out of something; something done; a piece of work; manner or success in working; execution, *esp* as an exhibition or entertainment; an act or action; the power or capability of a machine (*esp* a motor vehicle) to perform; an instance of awkward, aggressive, embarrassing, etc, behaviour (*inf*). **perform'ative** *adj* of a statement or verb that itself constitutes the action described, eg *I confess my ignorance*. ◆ *n* such a statement, *opp* to *constative*. **perform'er** *n* a person who performs; someone who does or fulfils what is required; an executant; someone who takes part in a performance or performances; an entertainer. **perfor'ming** *adj* that performs; trained to perform tricks. ◆ *n* performance.

◻ **performance art** *n* a theatrical presentation in which several art forms, such as acting, music and photography, are combined. **performance artist** *n*. **performance poet** *n* a poet who produces poetry primarily for public performance rather than for publication in print. **performance poetry** *n* poetry written primarily for public performance by the poet. **performance test** *n* (*psychol*) a test, *usu* to assess a person's intelligence, done by observing his or her ability to manipulate eg blocks of different colours or shapes. **performing arts** *n pl* those for which an audience is usually present, eg drama, ballet, etc. **performing right** *n* the right to give a public performance of a piece of music, a play, etc.

perfume /pûr'fūm, formerly and still sometimes pər-fūm'/ *n* fragrance; sweet-smelling smoke or fumes from burning; a fragrant substance (*usu* a liquid) applied to the body to give a pleasant smell; any substance made or used for the sake of its pleasant smell. ◆ *vt* /pər-fūm'/ or pûr'fūm/ to scent. [Fr *parfum*, from L *per* through, and *fūmus* smoke]

■ **per'fumed** (or /pər-fūmd'/) *adj*. **per'fumeless** (or /-fūm'/) *adj*. **perfū'mer** *n* a person who fumigates; a maker or seller of perfumes. **perfū'mery** *n* perfumes in general; the art of preparing perfumes; the shop or place in a shop where perfumes are sold. **per'fūmy** *adj*.

perfunctory /pər-fungk'tə-ri/ *adj* done merely as a duty to be got through; done for form's sake, or in mere routine; acting without zeal or interest; merely formal; hasty and superficial. [L *perfunctōrius*, from *perfunctus*, pap of *perfungī* to execute, from pfx *per-* thoroughly, and *fungī* to do]

■ **perfunc'torily** *adv*. **perfunc'toriness** *n*.

perfuse /pər-fūz'/ *vt* to pour or diffuse through or over; to pass (a liquid) through an organ or tissue. [L *perfūsus* poured over, from *per* through, and *fundere, fūsus* to pour]

■ **perfusate** /-fūz'āt/ *n* that which is perfused. **perfusion** /-fū'zhən/ *n* the pouring on or diffusion through anything; treatment by continuous blood transfusion (med). **perfu'sionist** n the member of a surgical team administering this. **perfusive** /-fū'siv/ adj.

pergameneous /pûr'gə-mē'ni-əs/ adj parchment-like. [L pergamēna; see **parchment**]
■ **pergamentaceous** /-mən-tā'shəs/ adj parchment-like.

pergola /pûr'gə-lə/ n a framework for climbing plants, more open than a trellis, and usu passing overhead to form a canopied wall. [Ital, from L pergula a shed]

pergunnah see **pargana**.

perh abbrev : perhaps.

perhaps /pər-haps'/ adv it may be; possibly; as it may happen. [From the pl of **hap**[1], after the model of **peradventure**, **percase**, and **perchance**]

peri /pē'ri/ n (in Persian mythology) a beautiful but malevolent being with supernatural powers; a beautiful fairy. [Pers parī or perī a fairy]

peri- /per-i- or pə-ri-/ combining form denoting: (1) around; (2) (esp in astronomy) near. [Gr peri around]

periagua /per-i-ä'gwə/ see **piragua**.

periaktos /per-i-ak'tos/ n (in the ancient Greek theatre) a tall revolving prism at the side of the stage, projecting a variety of backdrops. [Gr, revolving]

perianth /per'i-anth/ (bot) n the calyx and corolla together, esp when not clearly distinguishable (also adj). [**peri-** (1), and Gr anthos flower]

periapsis /per-i-ap'sis/ (astron) n (pl **periap'ses** /-sēz/) the point of the orbit of a planet, comet, etc at which it is closest to the body around which it revolves. [**peri-** (2), and apsis (see under **apse**)]

periapt /per'i-apt/ (Shakesp) n an amulet. [Gr periapton something hung round, from peri around, and haptein to fasten]

periastron /per-i-as'tron/ (astron) n that stage in the orbit of a comet, a component of a binary star, etc when it is closest to the star around which it revolves. [**peri-** (2), and Gr astron star]

periblast /per'i-blast/ (biol) n in meroblastic eggs, the margin of the blastoderm merging with the surrounding yolk. [**peri-** (1), and Gr blastos a sprout]

periblem /per'i-blem/ (bot) n the layer of primary meristem from which the cortex is formed, covering the plerome. [Gr periblēma garment, mantle, from peri around, and ballein to throw]

peribolos /per-ib'o-los/, also **peribolus** /-ləs/ n (pl **perib'oloi** or **perib'oli**) a precinct; its enclosing wall. [Gr, from peri around, and ballein to throw]

pericardium /per-i-kär'di-əm/ (anat) n the sac round the heart. [Latinized from Gr perikardion, from peri around, and kardiā heart]
■ **pericar'diac**, **pericar'dial** or **pericar'dian** adj. **pericardi'tis** n inflammation of the pericardium.

pericarp /per'i-kärp/ (bot) n the wall of a fruit, derived from that of the ovary. [Gr perikarpion, from peri around, and karpos fruit]
■ **pericar'pial** adj.

pericentral /per-i-sen'trəl/ adj surrounding a centre or central body. [**peri-** (1), and Gr kentron point, centre]
■ **pericen'tric** adj.

perichaetium /per-i-kē'shyəm/ (bot) n a sheath or cluster of leaves around the archegonia (or the antheridia) in mosses and liverworts. [**peri-** (1), and Gr chaitē flowing hair]
■ **perichae'tial** /-shl/ adj.

perichondrium /per-i-kon'dri-əm/ (anat) n the fibrous membrane covering a cartilage. [**peri-** (1), and Gr chondros cartilage]
■ **perichon'drial** adj.

perichoresis /per-i-kor-ē'sis/ (theol) n circumincession. [Gr, rotation, from perichorein to rotate, from peri around, and chorein to make room]

perichylous /per-i-kī'ləs/ (bot) adj having water-storing tissue outside the green tissue. [**peri-** (1), and Gr chylos juice]

periclase /per'i-klāz or -klās/ (chem) n magnesium oxide occurring naturally in isometric crystals. [Gr pfx peri- very, and klasis fracture (from its perfect cleavage)]

Periclean /per-i-klē'ən/ adj of Pericles (c. 495–429BC) or the golden age of art and letters at Athens.

periclinal /per-i-klī'nəl/ adj sloping downwards in all directions from a point (geol); parallel to the outer surface (bot). [Gr periklinēs sloping on all sides, from peri around and klīnein to slope]
■ **per'icline** n a variety of albite which usually occurs as elongated crystals; a type of twinning in feldspars.

periclitate /pər-ik'li-tāt/ (archaic) vt to endanger. [L periclitārī, -ātus]

pericon /per-i-kōn'/ n (pl **pericones** /-kō'nāz/) an Argentinian folk dance performed by couples dancing in a ring. [Am Sp]

pericope /pər-ik'o-pē/ n an extract or passage, esp one for reading in church. [Gr perikopē, from peri around, and koptein to cut]

pericranium /per-i-krā'ni-əm/ n the membrane that surrounds the cranium; (loosely) the skull or brain. [Latinized from Gr perikrānion, from peri around, and krānion skull]
■ **pericrā'nial** adj. **per'icrāny** n (obs) pericranium.

periculous /pər-ik'ū-ləs/ (obs) adj dangerous. [L perīculum danger]

pericycle /per'i-sī-kl/ (bot) n the outermost layer of the stele of a plant. [Gr perikyklos all round, from peri around, and kyklos a circle]
■ **pericy'clic** adj.

pericynthion /per-i-sin'thi-ən/ n same as **perilune**. [**peri-** (2), and Cynthia, a name of the goddess of the moon]

periderm /per'i-dûrm/ n the horny cuticular covering of a hydroid colony; the cork cambium with the cork and tissues derived from it, forming a protective covering in plants. [**peri-** (1) and Gr derma skin]
■ **periderm'al** adj.

peridesmium /per-i-des'mi-əm/ (anat) n the areolar tissue around a ligament. [**peri-** (1) and Gr desmos a band]

peridial see under **peridium**.

peridinian /per-i-din'i-ən/ n a dinoflagellate. [Gr peridinein to whirl around]
■ **Peridin'ium** n a genus of dinoflagellates; (without cap; pl peridin'iums or peridin'ia) a member of the genus.

peridium /pər-id'i-əm/ n the outer coat of a fruiting body of a fungus. [Latinized from Gr pēridion, dimin of pērā a wallet]
■ **perid'ial** adj.

peridot /per'i-dot/ or **peridote** /-dōt/ n olivine; a green olivine used in jewellery. [Fr péridot ; origin unknown]
■ **peridot'ic** adj. **peridotite** /-dō'tīt/ n a coarse-grained igneous rock mainly composed of olivine, usu with other ferromagnesian minerals but little or no feldspar.

peridrome /per'i-drōm/ n the space between the cell and surrounding pillars in an ancient temple. [Gr peridromos running round, from peri around, and dromos a run]

periegesis /per-i-e-jē'sis/ n a description in the manner of a tour; a progress or journey through. [Gr periēgēsis, from peri around, and hēgeesthai to lead]

perigastric /per-i-gas'trik/ (physiol) adj surrounding the alimentary canal. [**peri-** (1) and Gr gastēr belly]
■ **perigastri'tis** n inflammation of the outer surface of the stomach.

perigee /per'i-jē/ (astron) n the point of the moon's, or any artificial satellite's, orbit at which it is nearest the earth, opp to apogee. [Gr perigeion, neuter of perigeios round or near the earth, from peri and gē earth]
■ **perigē'al** or **perigē'an** adj.

perigenesis /per-i-jen'i-sis/ n reproduction (according to the theory of Ernst Haeckel) by transmission not only of chemical material but of vibrations of plastidules. [**peri-** (1) and Gr genesis generation]

periglacial /per-i-glā'si-əl, -glās'yəl or -glās'shəl/ adj bordering a glacier; of, like or relating to a region bordering a glacier. [**peri-** (1) and L glaciālis icy, from glaciēs ice]

perigon /per'i-gən/ n an angle of 360° (also called a **round angle**). [**peri-** (1) and Gr gōniā angle]

perigone /per'i-gōn/ (bot) n an undifferentiated perianth; a covering of the seed in sedges. [**peri-** (1) and Gr gonē generative organ]
■ **perigo'nial** adj. **perigo'nium** n a cluster of leaves round moss antheridia.

Perigordian /per-i-gör'di-ən/ adj relating to the Palaeolithic epoch to which the Lascaux Cave paintings and other examples of primitive art belong. [Périgord region in SW France]

perigynous /pər-ij'i-nəs/ (bot) adj of a flower, having the perianth and stamens inserted on a flat or cup-shaped structure which arises below, and is not fused to, the ovary; of the perianth and stamens, so inserted. Cf **epigynous** and **hypogynous**. [**peri-** (1) and Gr gynē woman (used for female)]
■ **perig'yny** n.

perihelion /per-i-hē'li-ən/ n the point of the orbit of a planet or a comet at which it is nearest to the sun, opp to aphelion; culmination (fig). [**peri-** (2) and Gr hēlios the sun]

perihepatic /per-i-hi-pat'ik/ adj (physiol) surrounding the liver. [**peri-** (1) and Gr hēpar, hēpatos liver]
■ **perihepatitis** /-hep-ə-tī'tis/ n (med) inflammation of the peritoneum covering the liver.

perikaryon /per-i-kar'i-on/ n (pl **perikar'ya**) that part of a nerve cell which surrounds the nucleus. [**peri-** (1) and Gr karyon kernel]

peril /per'il/ n danger. ◆ vt (**per'illing**; **per'illed**) to expose to danger. [Fr péril, from L perīculum]
■ **per'ilous** adj dangerous. **per'ilously** adv. **per'ilousness** n.

---

perilune /per'i-lūn/ or -loon/ n (also **pericynthion**) the point in a spacecraft's orbit round the moon where it is closest to it, opp to apolune. [**peri-** (2) and Fr lune, from L luna moon]

perilymph /per'i-limf/ n the fluid surrounding the membranous labyrinth of the ear. [**peri-** (1) and **lymph**]

perimenopause /per-i-men'ə-pöz/ n the period immediately before the menopause during which a woman may experience menopausal symptoms. [**peri-** (1) and **menopause**]

perimeter /pər-im'i-tər/ n the circuit or boundary of any plane figure, or the sum of all its sides (geom); the boundary of a camp or fortified position; the outer edge of any area; an instrument for measuring the field of vision (ophthalmol). [Gr perimetros, from peri around, and metron measure]
■ **perimetric** /per-i-met'rik/, **perim'etral** or **perimet'rical** adj. **perim'etry** n (ophthalmol) measurement of the field of vision.

perimorph /per'i-mörf/ n one mineral enclosing another. [**peri-** (1) and Gr morphē form]
■ **perimorph'ic** adj. **perimorph'ous** adj.

perimysium /per-i-miz'i-əm/ (anat) n the connective tissue which surrounds and binds together muscle fibres. [**peri-** (1) and -mysium, from Gr mys muscle]

perinaeum see **perineum**.

perinatal /per-i-nā'tl/ adj relating to the period between the seventh month of pregnancy and the first month of the baby's life. [**peri-** (1) and **natal**[1]]
■ **perinatol'ogy** n the branch of medicine dealing with the perinatal period.

perinephrium /per-i-nef'ri-əm/ n the fatty tissue surrounding the kidney. [**peri-** (1) and Gr nephros kidney]
■ **perineph'ric** adj. **perinephrī'tis** n (med) inflammation of the perinephrium.

perineum or **perinaeum** /per-i-nē'əm/ (physiol) n the lower part of the body between the genital organs and the anus. [Latinized from Gr perinaion, from inein to empty out]
■ **perine'al** adj.

perineurium /per-i-nū'ri-əm/ (physiol) n the sheath of connective tissue surrounding a bundle of nerve fibres. [**peri-** (1) and Gr neuron nerve]
■ **perineu'ral** adj. **perineurī'tis** n (med) inflammation of the perineurium.

period /pē'ri-əd/ n a stretch of time; a long stretch, an age; one of the main divisions of geological time; a stage or phase in history, in a person's life and development, in a disease, or in any course of events; a time; a division of the school day, the time of one lesson; the end of a course; a recurring time; the menstrual discharge or the time when it occurs; the time in which anything runs its course; an interval of time at the end of which events recur in the same order; the time required for a complete oscillation, reciprocal of the frequency; the time of a complete revolution of a heavenly body about its primary; the difference between two successive values of a variable for which a function has the same value (maths); the recurring part of a circulating decimal (maths); a set of figures (usu three) in a large number marked off eg by commas; a series of chemical elements represented in a horizontal row of the periodic table; an end (rare); a goal (archaic); a complete sentence, esp one of elaborate construction; a division analogous to a sentence (music); (in pl) rounded rolling rhetoric; a mark (.) at the end of a sentence, a full stop (the word is sometimes added at the end of a sentence to emphasize the finality of the statement); a rhythmical division in Greek verse. ◆ adj (of eg architecture, furniture or a play) characteristic, representative, imitative of, belonging to or dealing with a past period. ◆ vt (Shakesp) to put an end to. [Fr période, from L periodus, from Gr periodos, from peri around, and hodos a way]
■ **periodic** /pēr-i-od'ik/ adj relating to a period or periods; of revolution in an orbit; having a period; recurring regularly in the same order; (loosely) occurring from time to time; characterized by or constructed in periods; relating to the periodic table; relating to periodicals (rare). **period'ical** adj periodic; published in numbers at more or less regular intervals; of, for, or in such publications. ◆ n a magazine or other publication that appears at stated intervals (not usu including newspapers). **period'icalist** n a person who writes in a periodical. **period'ically** adv at regular intervals; in a periodic manner; in a periodical publication; (loosely) from time to time. **periodicity** /-dis'/ n the fact or character of being periodic; frequency. **periodīzā'tion** or **-s-** n division into periods. **pē'riodize** or **-ise** vt.
□ **periodical cicada** n an American cicada whose nymphs reach adulthood after seventeen years (also **seventeen-year locust**). **periodic function** n (maths) one whose values recur in a cycle as the variable increases. **periodic law** n the principle that the properties of atoms are periodic functions of their atomic numbers. **periodic sentence** n a sentence constructed in such a way that it is not until the final clause that the requirements of sense and grammar are met. **periodic system** n the classification of chemical elements according to the periodic law. **periodic table** n a table of chemical elements in order of atomic number arranged in horizontal series and vertical groups, showing how similar properties recur at regular intervals. **periodic wind** n a wind which blows at or for a certain period, eg a trade wind, a monsoon, a land breeze, a sea-breeze. **period of grace** n a specific time allowed to both parties to a contract to fulfil any obligations arising from that contract. **period piece** n an object belonging to a past age esp with charm or value; a person ludicrously behind the times; a play, novel, etc, set in a past time.
■ **the period** the current age, or age in question.

periodate /pə-rī'ō-dāt/ n a salt or ester of periodic acid. [**per-** (1) and **iodine**]
□ **periodic acid** /per-ī-od'ik/ n an acid (H_5IO_6) containing more oxygen than iodic acid.

periodontal /per-i-ō-dont'əl/ adj (relating to tissues or regions) around a tooth. [**peri-** (1) and odous, odontos tooth]
■ **periodon'tia** /-shi-ə/, **periodon'tics** or **periodontol'ogy** n the branch of dentistry concerned with periodontal diseases. **periodon'tist** n. **periodontī'tis** n the inflammation of the tissues surrounding the teeth.

perionychium /per-i-o-nik'i-əm/ (anat) n the skin surrounding a fingernail or toenail. [**peri-** (1) and Gr onyx a nail]

Periophthalmus /per-i-of-thal'məs/ n a genus of fishes, related to gobies, with protruding mobile eyes and pectoral fins used as legs. [Latinized from Gr peri around, and ophthalmos eye]

periosteum /per-i-os'ti-əm/ n a tough fibrous membrane covering the nonarticular surface of bones (also **per'iost**). [Gr periosteon (neuter adj), from peri around, and osteon a bone]
■ **perios'teal** adj. **periostit'ic** adj. **periostī'tis** n inflammation of the periosteum.

periostracum /per-i-os'trə-kəm/ n the horny outer layer of a mollusc's shell. [Latinized from Gr peri around, and ostrakon shell]

periotic /per-i-ō'tik or -ot'ik/ adj around the inner ear. ◆ n a periotic bone. [**peri-** (1) and Gr ous, ōtos the ear]

peripatetic /per-i-pə-tet'ik/ adj walking about; itinerant (eg of a teacher who is employed to teach at more than one establishment, travelling from one to another); Aristotelian. ◆ n a pedestrian; an itinerant; an Aristotelian. [Gr peripatētikos, from peripatos a walk, from peri around, and pateein to walk; Aristotle is said to have taught in the walks of the Lyceum at Athens]
■ **peripatet'ical** adj. **peripatet'icism** /-i-sizm/ n the philosophy of Aristotle.

Peripatus /pə-rip'ə-təs/ n a genus of arthropods of the Onychophora phylum, showing affinities with worms; (without cap) a member of the genus. [Gr peripatos a walking about; cf **peripatetic**]

peripeteia or **peripetia** /per-i-pe-tī'ə/ n a sudden change of fortune, esp in drama (also **perip'ety**). [Gr peripeteia, from peri around, and pet- the root of piptein to fall]
■ **peripetei'an** or **peripeti'an** adj.

periphery /pə-rif'ə-ri/ n a line or surface acting as a boundary; the outside of anything; a surrounding region. [Gr periphereia, from peri around, and pherein to carry]
■ **periph'eral** adj of or relating to a periphery; not of primary importance, incidental, minor; auxiliary (comput). ◆ n a peripheral unit. **peripheral'ity** n. **peripheric** /per-i-fer'ik/ or **peripher'ical** adj (archaic).
□ **peripheral unit** or **device** n (in a computer system) any of the input (eg card reader), output (eg magnetic tape), and storage devices, which are connected to or controlled by the central processing unit. **periphery camera** same as **all-round camera** (see under **all**).

periphonic /per-i-fon'ik/ adj of or relating to a sound system with many speakers. [**peri-** (1) and Gr phōnē voice]

periphrasis /pə-rif'rə-sis/ n (pl **periph'rases** /-sēz/) the use of more words than is strictly necessary, circumlocution; roundabout expression. [Gr periphrasis, from peri around, and phrasis speech]
■ **periphrase** /per'i-frāz/ n (pl **periphrās'es**) periphrasis. ◆ vt to say with circumlocution. ◆ vi to use circumlocution. **periphrastic** /per-i-fras'tik/ or **periphras'tical** adj using periphrasis; using at least two words instead of a single inflected form, esp of a verb tense involving an auxiliary. **periphras'tically** adv.

periphyton /pə-rif'i-ton or pe-ri-fī'ton/ n aquatic organisms which are attached to, or cling to, stems and leaves of rooted plants, rocks, etc. [**peri-** (1) and Gr phytos, from phytein to grow]

periplast /per'i-plăst/ (zool) n intercellular substance; the ectoplasm of flagellates; a cuticle covering the ectoplasm. [**peri-** (1), and Gr plastos moulded]

---

periplus /per'i-plus/ n a circumnavigation; a narrative of a coasting voyage. [Gr *periploos*, contraction *-plous*, from *peri* around, and *ploos*, *plous* a voyage]

periproct /per'i-prokt/ (*zool*) n the region around the anus, *esp* in a sea urchin. [**peri-** (1) and Gr *prōktos* anus]

peripteral /pə-rip'tə-rəl/ (*archit*) adj having one row of columns all round. [Gr *peripteros*, from *peri* around, and *pteron* a wing]
■ **perip'tery** n a peripteral building; the turbulent air immediately adjacent to a flying or falling object.

perique /pə-rēk'/ n a strongly-flavoured tobacco from Louisiana. [Perh *Périque*, nickname of a grower]

perisarc /per'i-särk/ (*zool*) n (in some Hydrozoans) the chitinous layer covering the polyps, etc. [**peri-** (1) and Gr *sarx, sarkos* flesh]

periscian /pə-rish'i-ən/ n a person living inside the polar circle, whose shadow moves round in a complete circle on those days on which the sun does not set (also *adj*). [**peri-** (1) and Gr *skiā* a shadow]

periscope /per'i-skōp/ n a device (eg a tube with mirrors) by which an observer can look at something which is not in the direct line of sight (eg out of a submarine or over the heads of a crowd). [Gr *periskopeein* to look around]
■ **periscopic** /-skop'ik/ adj.

periselenium /per-i-si-lē'ni-əm/ (*astron*) n (in an elliptical orbit about the moon) that point which is closest to the moon. [**peri-** (2) and Gr *selēnē* moon]

perish /per'ish/ vi to pass away completely; to waste away; to decay; to lose life; to be destroyed; to be ruined or lost. ◆ vt to destroy; to ruin; to cause to decay; to distress with cold, hunger, etc. [OFr *perir*, prp *perissant*, from L *perīre, peritum* to perish, from pfx *per-*, and *īre* to go]
■ **perishabil'ity** n. **per'ishable** adj that may perish; subject to speedy decay. ◆ n that which is perishable; (in *pl*) food or other stuff liable to rapid deterioration. **per'ishableness** n. **per'ishably** adv. **per'ished** adj distressed by cold, hunger, etc (*inf* or *dialect*); (of materials such as rubber) weakened or injured by age or exposure. **per'isher** n (*inf*) a mischievous or annoying person. **per'ishing** adj and adv (*inf* or *dialect*) freezing cold; vaguely used as a pejorative. **per'ishingly** adv.
■ **do a perish** (*obs Aust inf*) almost to die of lack of food or drink.

perisperm /per'i-spûrm/ (*bot*) n nutritive tissue in a seed derived from the nucellus. [**peri-** (1) and Gr *sperma* seed]
■ **perisper'mal** adj. **perisper'mic** adj.

perispomenon /pe-ri-spō'mə-non/ adj having a circumflex accent on the last syllable. ◆ n a word carrying such an accent. [Gr, drawn round, circumflexed, from *peri* around, and *spaein* to pull, pluck]

perissodactyl /pə-ris-ō-dak'til/ (*zool*) adj having an odd number of toes. ◆ n an animal of the **Perissodac'tyla**, a division of ungulates with an odd number of toes, including the horse, tapir, rhinoceros, and some extinct species (distinguished from the *Artiodactyla*). [Gr *perissos* odd, and *daktylos* a finger, toe]
■ **perissodac'tylate** adj. **perissodactyl'ic** adj. **perissodac'tylous** adj.

perissosyllabic /pə-ris-ō-si-lab'ik/ adj having an additional syllable. [Gr *perissosyllabos*, from *perissos* excessive, and *syllabē* syllable]

peristalith /pə-ris'tə-lith/ n a stone circle. [Irregularly formed from Gr *peri* around, *histanai* to set up, and *lithos* a stone]

peristalsis /per-i-stal'sis/ n the waves of contraction that force onward the contents of the alimentary canal and other tubular organs. [Gr *peristaltikos*, from *peristellein* to wrap round, from *peri* around, and *stellein* to place]
■ **peristal'tic** adj. **peristal'tically** adv.

peristerite /pər-is'tər-īt/ n an albite feldspar with a pigeon-like play of colour. [Gr *peristerā* pigeon]

peristeronic /pə-ris-tə-ron'ik/ adj of pigeons; pigeon-fancying. [Gr *peristerōn, -ōnos* pigeon-house]

peristome /per'i-stōm/ n the area, or a structure, surrounding a mouth; the fringe of teeth around the mouth of a moss-capsule; the margin of a gastropod shell. [**peri-** (1), and Gr *stoma, -atos* mouth]
■ **peristōm'al** adj. **peristomat'ic** adj. **peristōm'ial** adj.

peristrephic /per-i-stref'ik/ adj moving round, revolving, rotatory. [Irregularly formed from Gr *peristrephein* to whirl, from *peri* around, and *strephein* to turn]

peristyle /per'i-stīl/ (*archit*) n a range of columns round a building or round a square; a court, square, etc, with columns all round. [L *peristȳl(i)um*, from Gr *peristȳlon*, from *peri* around, and *stȳlos* a column]
■ **peristy'lar** adj.

peritectic /per-i-tek'tik/ adj in the state between solid and liquid; melting. [**peri-** (1) and Gr *tektikos* able to melt]

perithecium /per-i-thē'si-əm/ or *-shi-əm*/ n (*pl* **perithe'cia**) a flask-shaped fruiting body in fungi. [**peri-** (1) and Gr *thēkē* case]
■ **perithe'cial** adj.

peritoneum or **peritonaeum** /per-i-tə-nē'əm/ (*zool*) n a serous membrane enclosing the viscera in the abdominal and pelvic cavities. [Gr *peritonaion*, from *peri* around, and *teinein* to stretch]
■ **peritonē'al** or **peritonae'al** adj. **peritonēos'copy** n (*med*) the visual examination of the peritoneal cavities by means of an endoscope inserted through an incision in the abdomen. **peritonitic** /-it'ik/ adj of peritonitis; suffering from peritonitis. **peritonī'tis** n (*med*) inflammation of the peritoneum.

peritrack /per'i-trak/ n a taxiway. [*perimeter track*]

peritrich /per-it'rik/ n (*pl* **perit'richa** /-kə/) a bacterium bearing a ring of cilia around the body. [**peri-** (2) and Gr *thrix, trichos* hair]
■ **perit'richous** adj of or relating to peritricha; bearing a ring of cilia around the body.

peritus /pe-rē'tŭs/ n (*pl* **periti** /-tē/) a theological expert acting as a consultant within the Roman Catholic Church. [LL, from L, skilled]

perityphlitis /per-i-ti-flī'tis/ n inflammation of some part near the caecum or blind-gut. [**peri-** (1) and Gr *typhlos* blind]

perivitelline /per-i-vi-tel'ēn/ (*biol*) adj surrounding the yolk of an egg. [**peri-** (1) and **vitelline**]

periwig /per'i-wig/ (*hist*) n a wig. ◆ vt (**per'iwigging**; **per'iwigged**) to dress with, or as if with, a wig. [Earlier *perwyke, perwig, perywig*, etc, from Fr *perruque*; see **peruke** and **wig**¹]
❑ **per'iwig-pā'ted** adj wearing a periwig.

periwinkle¹ /per'i-wing-kl/ n a creeping evergreen plant, growing in woods (*Vinca minor* and *Vinca major*; family **Apocynaceae**); the light blue colour of some of its flowers. ◆ adj of this colour. [ME *peruenke*, from OE *peruince*, from L *pervinca*]

periwinkle² /per'i-wing-kl/ n (also **penn'ywinkle, winkle**) an edible gastropod with a spiral shell (*Littorina littorea*) abundant between tidemarks, or any other member of the genus *Littorina*; extended to other kinds. [OE (pl) *pinewinclan* (or perh *winewinclan*), from *wincle* a whelk]

perjink /pər-jingk'/ (*Scot*) adj (also **perjink'ety**) prim; finical. [Origin unknown]
■ **perjink'ity** n a nicety.

perjure /pûr'jər/ vt to lie under oath to tell the truth, to forswear oneself (*reflexive*); to cause to swear falsely. ◆ vi to swear falsely. ◆ n (*Shakesp*) a perjured person. [OFr *parjurer*, from L *perjūrāre*, from *per-* neg pfx, and *jūrāre* to swear]
■ **per'jured** adj having sworn falsely; (eg of an oath) being sworn falsely. **per'jurer** n. **perjurious** /-joo'ri-əs/ or **per'jurous** adj (*archaic*) guilty of or involving perjury. **per'jury** n false swearing; the breaking of an oath; the crime committed by someone who, when giving evidence on oath or affirmation as a witness in a court of justice, gives evidence which he or she knows to be false (*law*).

perk¹ /pûrk/ vi (now *archaic*) to bear oneself with self-confidence or self-assertion; to cock up; to stick out; to thrust forward (also vt with *it*); to move with pert briskness; to sit upright; to cock or toss or hold up the head; to dress smartly, dress up. ◆ adj (*archaic*) brisk; self-confident in manner. [Origin uncertain]
■ **perk'ily** adv. **perk'iness** n. **perk'y** adj self-assertive; cocky; pert; in good spirits.
■ **perk up** to recover spirits or energy, *esp* in sickness; to jerk up, cock up; to decorate so as to look newer, more interesting, etc, to smarten up.

perk² /pûrk/ (*inf*) n short for **perquisite**.

perk³ /pûrk/ (*inf*) vt to percolate (coffee). ◆ n a coffee percolator.

perk⁴ /pûrk/ a Scot, N Eng and E Anglian form of **perch**¹.

perkin see **parkin**.

perky see under **perk**¹.

Perl or **PERL** /pûrl/ n a high-level computer programming language. [Acronym of *p*ractical *e*xtraction and *r*eport *l*anguage]

perlite /pûrl'īt/ n any acid volcanic glass with a perlitic structure; pearlite. [Fr *perle*, Ger *Perle* pearl]
■ **perlitic** /-it'ik/ adj showing little concentric spheroidal or spiral cracks between rectilineal ones.

perlocution /pûr-lə-kū'shən/ (*philos*) n the effect (eg frightening, comforting, persuading) produced when a particular word is uttered, regarded as an act (cf **illocution**). [**per-** (2) and **locution**]
■ **perlocū'tionary** adj.

perlous /pûr'ləs/ (*Spenser*) adj same as **perilous** (see under **peril**).

perlustrate /pər-lus'trāt/ (*archaic*) vt to traverse and inspect. [L *perlustrāre, -ātum*]
■ **perlustrā'tion** n.

perm[1] /pûrm/ (*inf*) *n* short form of **permanent wave**. ◆ *vt* (*inf*) to impart a permanent wave to (hair). [**permanent**]

perm[2] /pûrm/ (*inf*) *n* short form of **permutation**. ◆ *vt* to permute; to arrange a forecast according to some defined system of combination or permutation. [**permutation**]

permaculture /pûr'mə-kul-chə/ *n* a system of self-sustaining natural agriculture, requiring generous mulching, no artificial fertilizers, use of natural resources, and only minimal weeding. [*perman*ent agri*culture*]

permafrost /pûr'mə-frost/ *n* permanently frozen subsoil. [*perman*ent *frost*]

permalink /pûr'mə-link/ *n* a hyperlink designed to provide a permanent connection to a web page. [*perman*ent *link*]

permalloy /pûr'ma-loi/ *n* any of various alloys of iron and nickel, often containing other elements, eg copper, molybdenum or chromium, which has high magnetic permeability. [*perme*able *alloy*]

permanent /pûr'mə-nənt/ *adj* remaining, or intended to remain, indefinitely, not expected to change or vary, not temporary. [L *permanēns, -entis*, prp of *permanēre*, from *per* through, and *manēre* to continue]
  ■ **per'manence** *n* the fact or state of being permanent. **per'manency** *n* permanence; a thing that is permanent. **per'manently** *adv*.
  ❑ **permanent health insurance** *n* a type of insurance that provides an income in cases of prolonged absence from work because of illness or disability (*abbrev* **PHI**). **permanent magnet** see under **magnet**. **permanent marker** a marker pen designed to make indelible markings. **permanent press** *n* a process by which clothes can be made to retain pleats, trouser-creases, etc. **permanent set** *n* (*engineering*) the distortion or extension of a structure, etc, which remains after the elastic limit has been exceeded by stress, load, etc. **permanent teeth** *n* the adult teeth, which come after the milk teeth lost in childhood. **permanent wave** *n* a long-lasting artificial wave or curl in hair induced by chemical treatment, now usually contracted as **perm. permanent way** *n* the finished road of a railway.

permanganic /pûr-mang-gan'ik/ *adj* applied to an acid ($HMnO_4$) and its anhydride (Mn_2O_7) containing more oxygen than manganic acid and anhydride. [**per-** (1) and **manganese**]
  ■ **permanganate** /pər-mang'gə-nāt/ *n* a salt of permanganic acid, *esp* **potassium permanganate** ($KMnO_4$) which is used as an oxidizing and bleaching agent and as a disinfectant.

permatan /pûr'mə-tan/ (*inf*) *n* a complexion that appears to remain unnaturally bronzed throughout the year. [*perman*ent sun*tan*]
  ■ **per'matanned** *adj*.

permeate /pûr'mi-āt/ *vt* to pass through the pores of; to penetrate and fill the pores of; to pervade; to saturate. ◆ *vi* to diffuse. [L *permeāre*, from *per* through, and *meāre* to pass]
  ■ **permeabil'ity** *n* the ability of material to allow a gas or liquid to pass through it; (also **magnetic permeability**) the ability of a material to alter the magnetic field around it. **per'meable** *adj*. **per'meably** *adv*. **permeam'eter** *n* an instrument for measuring permeability, *esp* of magnetizing force and flux. **per'meance** *n* the act of permeating; the reciprocal of the reluctance of a magnetic circuit. **per'mease** *n* any enzyme which acts to assist the entry of certain sugars into cells. **permea'tion** *n*. **per'meative** *adj* having the power to permeate.
  ❑ **permeability coefficient** *n* (*geol*) a measure of the ability of a rock or soil to allow fluids to pass through it.

permethrin /pûr-mē'thrin/ *n* a garden pesticide, used against whitefly, etc.

Permian /pûr'mi-ən/ (*geol*) *adj* of or belonging to a period of the Palaeozoic era, between 300 and 250 million years ago (also *n*). [*Perm*, in Russia]
  ❑ **Permo-Carbonif'erous** *adj* Upper Carboniferous and Lower Permian (also *n*).

per mil or **per mill** *abbrev* : *per mille* (*L*), by the thousand, or in each thousand.

permis de séjour /per-mē' də sā-zhoor'/ (*Fr*) *n* permission to reside in a foreign country, given by the police of that country; the permit issued.

permissible, etc see under **permit**.

permit /pər-mit'/ *vt* (**permitt'ing**; **permitt'ed**) to allow; (*reflexive*) to indulge (in) (*archaic*); to leave, refer, submit (to) (*obs*). ◆ *vi* to allow. ◆ *n* /pûr'/ permission, *esp* in writing; an official document giving authorization; a licence. [L *permittere, -missum* to let pass through, from *per* through, and *mittere* to send]
  ■ **permissibil'ity** *n*. **permiss'ible** *adj* that may be permitted; allowable. **permiss'ibly** *adv*. **permission** /-mish'ən/ *n* an act of permitting; authorization, leave. **permiss'ive** *adj* granting permission or liberty; permitted, optional; lenient, indulgent; allowing much freedom in social conduct *esp* concerning sexual matters (as in **the permissive society**, said to have been ushered in in most (*esp* Western) countries by the sexually and socially liberating 1960s).

permiss'ively *adv*. **permiss'iveness** *n*. **permitt'ance** *n* (*rare*) permission. **permitt'er** *n*. **permittiv'ity** *n* (**absolute permittivity**) the ratio of the electric displacement in a medium to the electric field intensity producing it; (**relative permittivity**) the ratio of the electric displacement in a medium to that which would be produced in free space by the same field.
  ❑ **permissible dose** *n* (*radiol*) same as **maximum permissible concentration** (see under **maximum**). **permissive temperature** *n* (*biol*) the temperature at which a temperature-sensitive mutant will grow (cf **restrictive temperature**).

Permo-Carboniferous see under **Permian**.

permutate /pûr'mū-tāt/ or **permute** /pər-mūt'/ *vt* to interchange, transmute, change the order of; to subject to permutation. [L *permūtāre* to change thoroughly, from pfx *per-*, and *mūtāre* to change]
  ■ **permūtabil'ity** *n*. **permūt'able** *adj* interchangeable. **permutā'tion** *n* the arrangement of a set of things in every possible order (*maths*); transmutation; any one possible order of arrangement of a given number of things taken from a given number; immediate inference by obversion (*logic*); (*esp* in football pools) a forecast of a specified number of results from a larger number of matches based on some defined system of combination or permutation (often shortened to **perm**); any such system; barter (*obs*). **permutā'tional** *adj*.

pern /pûrn/ *n* a honey buzzard (genus *Pernis*). [Mistakenly used by French zoologist Georges Cuvier (1769–1832) for Gr *pternis* a kind of hawk]

pernancy /pûr'nən-si/ (*law*) *n* receiving. [Anglo-Fr *pernance* (OFr *prenance*)]

Pernettya /pər-net'i-ə/ *n* a genus (family Ericaceae) of evergreen shrubs with bright berries. [AJ *Pernetty* (1716–1801), French explorer]

pernicious[1] /pər-nish'əs/ *adj* destructive; highly injurious; malevolent. [L *perniciōsus*, from pfx *per-*, and *nex, necis* death by violence]
  ■ **perni'ciously** *adv*. **perni'ciousness** *n*.
  ❑ **pernicious anaemia** see under **anaemia**.

pernicious[2] /pər-nish'əs/ (*Milton*) *adj* swift, ready, prompt. [L *pernīx, -īcis* nimble]

pernickety /pər-nik'i-ti/ *adj* (of a person) over-particular about unimportant details, finical; (of a task) exacting minute care. [Scot; origin unknown]
  ■ **pernick'etiness** *n*.

pernoctate /pûr'nok-tāt/ *vi* (*usu facetious*) to pass or spend the night. [**per-** (2) and L *nox, noctis* night]
  ■ **pernocta'tion** *n* passing the night; a watch, vigil.

Pernod® /per'nō/ *n* an alcoholic drink made in France, flavoured with aniseed, *usu* mixed with water and drunk as an apéritif.

perogi see **pierogi**.

perone /per'o-nē/ *n* the fibula. [Gr *peronē*]
  ■ **peronē'al** *adj*. **peronē'us** *n* one of several fibular muscles.

Peronism /per'o-ni-zm or pə-rō'ni-zm/ *n* the political beliefs of Juan Perón (1895–1974), former president of Argentina.
  ■ **Peronis'mo** (*Sp*) Peronism. **Peronist** or (*Sp*) **Peronist'a** *n* a supporter or follower of Peronism.

peroration /per-ə-rā'shən, -ō- or -ö-/ *n* the conclusion of a speech, a summing up; a long formal speech (*inf*); a rhetorical performance. [L *perōrātiō, -ōnis*, from *per* through, and *ōrāre* to speak, from *ōs, ōris* the mouth]
  ■ **per'orate** *vi* to make a peroration; to harangue (*inf*).

perovskia /pə-rov'ski-ə/ *n* a genus of hardy deciduous shrubs of the Labiatae family, grown for their aromatic grey-green foliage and blue flowers. [Mod L, named after VA *Perovski*, Russian governor]

perovskite /pə-rov'skīt/ *n* a mineral form of calcium titanate ($CaTiO_3$), yellow, brown or almost black in colour, having the crystal form of certain high-temperature ceramic superconductors. [Count Lev Alekseevich *Perovski* (1792–1856), Russian statesman]

peroxide /pə-rok'sīd/ *n* an oxide with the highest proportion of oxygen; one that yields hydrogen peroxide on treatment with an acid; the bleach hydrogen peroxide, H_2O_2 (*inf*). ◆ *vt* to treat or bleach with hydrogen peroxide. ◆ *adj* (*inf*) bleached with hydrogen peroxide. [**per-** (1) and **oxide**]
  ■ **perox'idase** *n* an enzyme, found in many plants, bacteria and leucocytes, which acts as a catalyst in the oxidation of various substances by peroxides. **peroxidā'tion** *n*. **perox'idize** or **-ise** *vt* and *vi*. **perox'isome** *n* an organelle that contains enzymes.

perp /pûrp/ (*US inf*) *n* a perpetrator (of a crime).
  ❑ **perp walk** *n* an act by police of deliberately escorting a recently arrested criminal suspect in public for the benefit of the media.

perpend[1] /pûr'pənd/ same as **parpen**.

perpend[2] /pər-pend'/ *vt* to weigh in the mind, to consider carefully. [L *perpendere*, from pfx *per-*, and *pendere* to weigh]

perpendicular /pûr-pən-dik'ū-lər/ adj erect; vertical; upright; in the direction of gravity or at right angles to the plane of the horizon; at right angles (to a given line or surface; geom); in the Perpendicular style of architecture. ◆ n an instrument for determining the vertical line; a straight line or plane perpendicular to another line or surface; verticality or erectness; (in a ship) a vertical line from each end of the waterline; a meal or entertainment at which the guests do not sit (sl). [L perpendiculāris, from perpendiculum a plumb line, from pfx per-, and pendēre to hang]
■ **perpendicularity** /-lar'i-ti/ n the state of being perpendicular. **perpendic'ularly** adv.
❑ **Perpendicular style** n a late English style of Gothic architecture (late 14c to mid-16c) marked by vertical window-tracery, the depressed or four-centre arch, fan tracery vaulting, and panelled walls.

perpent /pûr'pənt/ same as **parpen**.

perpetrate /pûr'pi-trāt/ vt to commit or execute (esp an offence, a poem, or a pun). [L perpetrāre, -ātum, from pfx per-, and patrāre to achieve]
■ **per'petrable** adj. **perpetrā'tion** n. **per'petrātor** n.

perpetual /pər-pet'ū-əl/ adj never-ceasing; everlasting; not temporary; incessant; (of a sports trophy, etc) awarded every year; continuously blooming; perennial. ◆ adv perpetually. ◆ n a perennial; a continuously blooming hybrid rose. [L perpetuālis, from perpetuus continuous]
■ **perpet'ualism** n. **perpet'ualist** n a person who advocates the perpetual continuation of anything. **perpetuality** /-al'i-ti/ n. **perpet'ually** adv.
❑ **perpetual calendar** n a calendar by means of which it may be ascertained on which day of the week any given day has fallen or will fall; one which may be used for any year, or for more than a year. **perpetual check** n in chess, a situation in which one player's king is continually placed in check by the other player who may thereby claim a draw. **perpetual curate** n formerly in the Church of England, an incumbent of a parish who had no endowment of tithes, since 1868 called a vicar. **perpetual motion** n a hypothetical machine, or motion of such a machine, that should do work indefinitely without an external source of energy. **perpetual-mo'tionist** n a believer in the possibility of perpetual motion. **perpetual screw** n an endless screw.

perpetuate /pər-pet'ū-āt/ vt to cause to last for ever or for a very long time; to preserve from extinction or oblivion; to pass on, to cause to continue to be believed, known, etc. ◆ adj (archaic) perpetuated. [L perpetuāre, -ātum, from perpetuus perpetual]
■ **perpet'uable** adj. **perpet'uance** n perpetuation. **perpetuā'tion** n continuation or preservation for ever, or for a very long time; preservation from extinction or oblivion. **perpet'uātor** n.

perpetuity /pûr-pi-tū'i-ti/ n the state of being perpetual; endless time; duration for an indefinite period; something lasting for ever; the sum paid for a perpetual annuity; the annuity itself; an arrangement whereby property is tied up, or rendered inalienable, for all time or for a very long time. [L perpetuitās, -ātis, from perpetuus perpetual]

perpetuum mobile /pər-pet'ū-əm mō'bi-li or per-pet'ū-ūm mō-bi-le/ (L) n perpetual motion.

perplex /pər-pleks'/ vt to puzzle with difficulties or intricacies; to bewilder; to tease with suspense or doubt; to complicate; to interweave; to tangle. ◆ n (obs) a difficulty. [L perplexus entangled, from pfx per-, and plexus involved, pap of plectere]
■ **perplex'edly** adv. **perplex'edness** n. **perplex'ing** adj. **perplex'ingly** adv. **perplex'ity** n the state of being perplexed; confusion of mind arising from doubt, etc; embarrassment; doubt; intricacy; tangle.

per pro abbrev : per procurationem (L) (see under **per²**).

perquisite /pûr'kwi-zit/ n (often informally shortened to **perk**) an incidental benefit from one's employment; a casual profit; anything left over that a servant or other has by custom a right to keep; a tip expected on some occasions; property acquired otherwise than by inheritance (law; obs); emoluments; something regarded as falling to one by right. [L perquīsītum, from perquīrere to seek diligently, from pfx per-, and quaerere to ask]
■ **perquisition** /-zish'ən/ n a strict search; diligent inquiry. **perquis'itor** n the first purchaser of an estate.

perradius /pər-rā'di-əs/ n (pl **perradii** /-ī/) any one of the primary radii of a coelenterate. [**per-** (2) and **radius**]
■ **perra'dial** adj.

Perrier® /per'i-ā/ n (also **Perrier water**) a sparkling mineral water from a spring of that name in S France.

perrier /per'i-ər/ (obs) n a machine or gun firing stones. [OFr]

perron /per'ən or pe-rɔ̃'/ n a raised platform or terrace at an entrance door; an external flight of steps leading up to it. [Fr, from L petra stone]

perruque, perruquier see **peruke**.

perry /per'i/ n fermented pear juice. [OFr peré, from LL pēra (L pirum) pear]

Pers abbrev : Persian.

pers abbrev : person; personal.

persant or **persaunt** (Spenser) same as **perceant** (see under **perce**).

perscrutation /pûr-skroo-tā'shən/ n a thorough search. [**per-** (2) and L scrūtārī to search carefully]

perse¹ /pûrs/ adj dark blue or bluish-grey. ◆ n such a colour; a cloth of such colour. [OFr pers]

perse² /pûrs/ (pat and pap **perst**) a Spenserian form of **pierce**.

per se see under **per²**.

persecute /pûr'si-kūt/ vt to harass, afflict, hunt down, or put to death, esp for religious or political opinions. [L persequī, persecūtus, from pfx per-, and sequī to follow]
■ **persecū'tion** n. **per'secūtive** adj. **per'secūtor** n. **per'secūtory** adj.
❑ **persecution complex** n (psychiatry) a morbid fear that one is being plotted against by other people.

Perseid see under **Perseus**.

perseity /pər-sē'i-ti/ n an independent existence. [L per sē in itself]

perseline /pûr'si-lēn/ n a Spenserian form of **purslane**.

Perseus /pûr'sūs or -si-əs/ n a fabled Greek hero who slew the Gorgon Medusa, and rescued Andromeda from a sea monster (Gr myth); a constellation in the northern sky. [Gr Perseus]
■ **Per'seid** /-si-id/ n a meteor of a swarm whose radiant is in the constellation Perseus.

persevere /pûr-si-vēr', formerly (Shakesp) pər-sev'ər/ vi to continue steadfastly; to keep on striving; to continue (obs). [Fr persévérer, from L persevērāre, from persevērus very strict, from pfx per-, and sevērus strict]
■ **persevē'rance** (formerly /pər-sev'ər-əns/) n the act or state of persevering; continued application to anything which one has begun; persistence despite setbacks. **persev'erant** adj steadfast. **persev'erate** vi to recur or tend to recur (psychiatry); to repeat the same actions or thoughts. **perseveration** /pûr-sev-ər-ā'shən/ n meaningless repetition of an action, utterance, thought, etc; the tendency to experience difficulty in leaving one activity for another. **persev'erātor** n. **persevē'ring** adj. **persevē'ringly** adv.
❑ **perseverance of saints** n the Calvinistic doctrine that those who are effectually called by God cannot fall away so as to be finally lost.

Persian /pûr'shən, -shyən, -zhən or -zhyən/ adj of, from, or relating to Persia (now Iran), its inhabitants, or language. ◆ n a native or citizen of Persia; the language of Persia; a male figure serving as a column (archit); a Persian cat.
■ **Per'sianize** or **-ise** vt and vi. **Persic** /pûr'sik/ adj Persian. ◆ n the Persian language. **Per'sicize** or **-ise** /-sīz/ vt and vi to turn Persian; to assimilate to what is Persian. **Per'sism** n a Persian idiom. **Per'sist** n a person who has a scholarly knowledge of Persian language, culture, history, etc.
❑ **Persian berry** n a name given to the fruit of several buckthorns. **Persian blinds** n pl persiennes. **Persian carpet** n a rich, soft carpet of the kind woven in Persia. **Persian cat** n a kind of cat with long, silky hair and a bushy tail. **Persian Gulf** n the Arabian Gulf, the arm of the Arabian Sea which separates Iran (to the north) from (to the south) Saudi Arabia and the Arab States. **Persian lamb** n a lamb of the Karakul or Bukhara breed; its black, curly fur used to make coats, hats, etc. **Persian powder** n an insect-powder made from Pyrethrum. **Persian wheel** n a large undershot wheel for raising water.

persicaria /pûr-si-kā'ri-ə/ n (bot) a species of knotgrass with black-blotched leaves; extended to other species of Polygonum, by some made a separate genus. [LL persicāria peach tree, from the similarity in leaves]

persico or **persicot** /pûr'si-kō/ n a cordial flavoured with kernels of peaches and apricots. [Fr persico (now persicot), from Ital persico, from L persicum a peach]

persienne /per-si-en'/ n an Eastern cambric or muslin with a coloured printed pattern; (in pl) Persian blinds, outside shutters of thin movable slats in a frame. [Fr, Persian (fem)]

persiflage /pûr-si-fläzh' or pûr'/ n banter; flippancy. [Fr, from persifler to banter, from L per through, and Fr siffler, from L sībilāre to whistle, to hiss]
■ **persifleur** /-flûr'/ n a banterer.

persimmon /pər-sim'ən/ n a tree of the American or African genus Diospyros; its plum-like fruit. [From a Native American word]

Persism, Persist see under **Persian**.

persist /pər-sist'/ vi to continue steadfastly or obstinately, esp against opposition (often with in); to persevere; to insist; to continue to be, to remain (Milton); to continue to exist; to remain in the mind after the external cause is removed. ◆ *vt* to assert or repeat insistently. [L *persistere*, from *per*, and *sistere* to cause to stand, to stand, from *stāre* to stand]

■ **persis'tence** or **persis'tency** *n* the quality of being persistent; perseverance; obstinacy; duration, *esp* of an effect after the stimulus has been removed, eg of a cathode-ray tube. **persis'tent** *adj* persisting; pushing on, *esp* against opposition; tenacious; fixed; constant or constantly repeated; remaining after the usual time of falling off, withering, or disappearing (*zool*; *bot*); continuing to grow beyond the usual time; remaining relatively stable after release into the environment (*chem*). ◆ *n* a person or thing that is persistent. **persis'tently** *adv*. **persis'tingly** *adv*. **persis'tive** *adj* (*Shakesp*) persistent.

❑ **persistent cruelty** *n* (*law*; in matrimonial proceedings) behaviour likely to cause danger to the life or health of a spouse. **persistent vegetative state** *n* (*med*) an irreversible condition induced by lack of oxygen, in which the sufferer is still alive, but is incapable of any thought processes and any voluntary physical action (*abbrev* **PVS**).

person /pûr'sn/ *n* (*pl* in the sense of an individual human being, *usu* **people** /pē'pl/; in formal, technical, etc use **per'sons**) a living soul or self-conscious being; a character represented, as on the stage; a capacity in which one is acting; a personality; a human being, sometimes used contemptuously or patronizingly; an individual of a compound or colonial animal; the outward appearance, etc of a human being; bodily form; human figure (often including clothes); bodily presence or action; a personage (*obs*); a human being (**natural person**), or a corporation (**artificial person**) regarded as having rights and duties under the law; a hypostasis of the Godhead (*theol*); a form of inflection or use of a word as it, or its subject, relates to the person, persons, thing, or things speaking (**first person**), spoken to (**second person**), or spoken about (**third person**) (*grammar*). ◆ *combining form* used instead of **man**[1] to avoid illegal or unnecessary discrimination on grounds of sex, eg *barperson*, *chairperson*, *postperson*. [L *persōna* an actor's mask]

■ **per'sonable** *adj* of good appearance, attractive; easy to get on with, likeable. **per'sonableness** *n*. **per'sonage** *n* bodily frame or appearance; a person, *esp* an important or august one; a character in a play or story; recognized or imagined character or personality (*Spenser*, etc). **per'sonhood** *n*. **per'sonize** or **-ise** *vt* to personify.

❑ **Person Friday** a Man or Girl Friday (see **man** and **girl**). **per'sonpower** *n* manpower, applying to either sex. **per'son-to-per'son** *adj* (of a telephone call) personal; involving meeting or contact (also *adv*).

■ **in person** in actual bodily presence; by one's own act, not by an agent or representative. **on** or **about one's person** with one, worn or carried about one's body.

persona[1] /pər-sō'nə/ *n* (*pl* **perso'nae** /-nē* or *-nī/* or **perso'nas**) Jung's term for a person's system of adaptation to the world or manner assumed when dealing with it, involving the outermost part of the consciousness, the expression of the personality, masking one's inner thoughts and feelings, etc; social facade or public image; a Roman actor's mask; a character in fiction, *esp* drama; a speaker in a poem. [Ety as for **person**]

persona[2] /pər-sōn'ə or *-a/* (L) *n* person.

❑ **persona grata** /grä', grä'tə or *-a/* *n* a person who is acceptable, liked, or favoured, *esp* one who is diplomatically acceptable to a foreign government (also used as *adj*). **persona muta** /mū'tə or *moo'ta/* *n* a character in an opera who neither speaks nor sings. **persona non grata** *n* the opposite of **persona grata** above.

■ **dramatis personae** see under **drama**. **in propria persona** (*LL*) /in prō'pri-ə or *pro'pri-a/* in person.

personable, **personage** see under **person**.

personal /pûr'sə-nl/ *adj* of the nature of a person; of or relating to a person or personality; relating, referring, or pointing to a particular person or persons; aiming offensively at a particular person or persons; belonging or peculiar to a person; own; one's own; of private concern; relating to private concerns; bodily; in bodily presence; (of a telephone call) made to a particular person; by one's own action; indicating person (*grammar*); tailored to the needs of a particular person; done in person; *orig* not recoverable by an action for the restitution of the specific thing, but such as compensation might be claimed for, *opp* to *real* (*Eng law*); hence (now) passing at death not to the heir (as real property) but to the executor. ◆ *n* (*N Am*; often in *pl*) a personal ad (qv below). [L *persōna* an actor's mask, perh from Etruscan *phersu* masked figures, commonly associated (in spite of difference of quantity) with *personāre*, *-ātum*, from *per* and *sonāre* to sound; cf **parson**]

■ **personalia** /-ā'li-ə/ *n pl* notes, anecdotes, or particulars relating to persons. **per'sonalism** *n* the character of being personal; a theory or doctrine that attributes personality, or spiritual freedom and responsibility, as distinct from mere individuality, to human beings, *esp* that enunciated by French philosopher Emmanuel Mounier in

1936. **per'sonalist** *n* someone who writes personal notes; a believer in, or follower of, personalism. **personalis'tic** *adj*. **personalizā'tion** or **-s-** *n*. **per'sonalize** or **-ise** *vt* to apply to, or take as referring to, a definite person; to tailor to or cater for the desires of a particular person; to mark with a person's name, initials, monogram, etc; to give a mark or character to (something) so that it is identifiable as belonging to a certain person; to personify. **per'sonally** *adv* in a personal or direct manner; in person; individually; for my part (*inf*). **per'sonalty** *n* (*law*) personal estate, all the property which, when a person dies, goes to the executor or administrator, as distinguished from the realty, which goes to the heir-at-law.

❑ **personal ad** *n* a message or advertisement in a personal column. **personal allowance** *n* an amount, determined by the government, which is deducted from income before arriving at the taxable amount. **personal assistant** *n* someone who helps a particular individual such as an executive, *esp* performing secretarial or administrative work (*abbrev* **PA**). **personal chair** *n* a university chair created for the period of tenure of a particular person. **personal column** *n* a newpaper column containing personal messages, advertisements, etc. **personal communications network** see **PCN**. **personal computer** *n* a single-user microcomputer (*abbrev* **PC**). **personal digital assistant** *n* a hand-held computer containing a personal information manager (*abbrev* **PDA**). **personal dosimeter** *n* a sensitive tubular electroscope, charged by a generator and discharged by ionizing radiation, used by workers in areas of potential radiation hazard. **personal effects** *n pl* those belongings worn or carried about one's person; private or intimate possessions. **personal equation** see under **equal**. **personal equity plan** *n* (from 1987 to 1999) a financial investment scheme, offering certain tax benefits, that encouraged individuals to invest in British companies (*abbrev* **PEP**). **personal estate** or **property** *n* property other than land or buildings, passing at death to one's executor, not to one's heir-at-law, *opp* to *real estate* or *property*. **personal exception** *n* (*Scots law*; *obs*) a ground of objection which applies to an individual and prevents him from doing something which, but for his conduct or situation, he might do. **personal foul** *n* (*basketball*) a foul awarded against a player for illegal physical contact. **personal identification number** see **PIN**. **personal identity** *n* the continued sameness of the individual person, through all changes, as testified by consciousness. **personal information manager** *n* a computer program used to organize and hold details of appointments, addresses, etc. **personal organizer** see under **organize**. **personal pronoun** *n* (*grammar*) a pronoun which stands for a definite person or thing. **personal property** see **personal estate** above. **personal remark** *n* a remark, *esp* derogatory, made to, referring to, or aimed at a particular person or persons. **personal rights** *n pl* rights which belong to a person as a living, rational being. **personal security** *n* a pledge given by a person, as distinguished from the delivery of some object of value as security. **personal service** *n* delivery of a message or an order into a person's hands, as distinguished from delivery in any other indirect way; attention or service of the proprietor of a concern, rather than one of his employees or assistants. **personal shopper** *n* a person employed by a retail outlet to advise individual customers on their specific requirements and to give them practical help in selection and purchasing. **personal space** *n* the immediate environment for personal activity which an individual seeks to control, and in which intrusion is unwelcome; an individual's free time for leisure activities. **personal stereo** *n* a small lightweight cassette or CD player designed to be carried around (eg in one's pocket or attached to one's belt) and listened to through earphones. **personal trainer** *n* a person employed to direct a fitness exercise programme for an individual. **personal transaction** *n* something done by a person's own effort, not through the agency of another. **personal video recorder** *n* a device used to make digital recordings of television broadcasts on a hard disk (*abbrev* **PVR**). **personal watercraft** same as **jet ski** (see under **jet**[2]).

personality /pər-sə-nal'i-ti/ *n* the fact or state of being a person or of being personal; existence as a person; individuality; distinctive or well-marked character; a person *esp* a remarkable one; a celebrity; direct reference to, or an utterance aimed at, a particular person or persons, *esp* of a derogatory nature, a personal remark; personalty (*law*; *rare*); the integrated organization of all the psychological, intellectual, emotional, and physical characteristics of an individual, especially as they are presented to other people (*psychol*); the sum of such characteristics which make a person attractive socially. [**person**]

❑ **personality cult** *n* excessive adulation of the individual, *esp* someone in public life. **personality disorder** *n* (*psychiatry*) any of various types of mental illness in which a person tends to behave in ways which are harmful to her or himself or to others.

personalize, etc, **personally**, **personalty** see under **personal**.

personate /pûr'sə-nāt/ *vt* to assume the likeness or character of; to play the part of; to mimic; to pass oneself off as, to impersonate, *esp* with criminal intent; to represent in the form of a person; to symbolize.

♦ *adj* feigned (*archaic*); mask-like; (of a lipped corolla) closed by an upward bulge of the lower lip (*bot*). [**person**]
■ **per'sonāted** *adj* feigned. **per'sonāting** *n*. **personā'tion** *n*. **per'sonātive** *adj* dramatic; presenting or presented through persons. **per'sonātor** *n*.

personhood see under **person**.

personify /pər-son'i-fī/ *vt* (**person'ifying**; **person'ified**) to represent as a person; to ascribe personality to; to be the embodiment of; to personate (*rare*). [L *persōna* a person, and *facere* to make; see **persona**[2]]
■ **personificā'tion** *n*. **person'ifīer** *n*.

personize see under **person**.

personnel /pûr-sə-nel'/ *n pl* the persons employed in any service; (*loosely*) people in general; (*sing*) an office or department that deals with employees' appointments, records and welfare, etc (also **human resources**). [Fr, personal]
❑ **personnel carrier** *n* a military vehicle, often armoured, for carrying troops. **personnel monitoring** *n* monitoring for radioactive contamination of any part of an individual or their clothing.

perspective /pər-spek'tiv/ or formerly /pûr'/ *n* the art or science of drawing objects on a surface, so as to give the picture the same appearance to the eye as the objects themselves; appearance, or representation of appearance, of objects in space, with effect of distance, solidity, etc; correct proportion in all the parts; a way of regarding facts and their relative importance; point of view; a picture in perspective; a picture or model that seems confused except when viewed in the right direction, or in some other way gives a fantastic effect (*Shakesp*); a telescope, microscope, or other optical instrument (also **perspective glass**; *obs*); a peepshow (*obs*); optics (*obs*); a vista; a prospect of the future; inspection (*obs*). ♦ *adj* optical (*obs*); relating or according to perspective. [L (*ars*) *perspectīva* perspective (art), from *perspicere*, *perspectum*, from *per*, and *specere* to look]
■ **perspectī'val** *adj*. **perspec'tively** *adv*. **perspec'tivism** *n* the theory that things can only be known from an individual point of view at a particular time (*philos*); the use of subjective points of view in literature and art. **perspec'tivist** *n* an artist whose work emphasizes the effects of perspective; someone who studies the rules of perspective.
❑ **perspective plane** *n* the surface on which the picture of the objects to be represented in perspective is drawn.
■ **in** (or **out of**) **perspective** according to (or against) the laws of perspective; in correct (or incorrect) proportion; in (or not in) prospect (*obs*).

Perspex® /pûr'speks/ *n* a proprietary thermoplastic resin of exceptional transparency and freedom from colour, used for windscreens, etc.

perspicacious /pûr-spi-kā'shəs/ *adj* clear-minded, astute, perceptive, discerning; clear-sighted (*archaic*). [L *perspicāx*, *-ācis*; see **perspective**]
■ **perspicā'ciously** *adv*. **perspicacity** /-kas'i-ti/ *n*.

perspicuous /pər-spik'ū-əs/ *adj* expressed or expressing clearly; lucid. [L *perspicuus*; see **perspicacious**, **perspective**]
■ **perspicū'ity** *n*. **perspic'ūously** *adv*. **perspic'ūousness** *n*.

perspire /pər-spīr'/ *vi* to sweat; to exude. ♦ *vt* to exhale. [L *perspīrāre*, *-ātum*, from *per* through, and *spīrāre* to breathe]
■ **perspīr'able** *adj* capable of being perspired or of perspiring. **perspirate** /pûr'spir-āt/ *vi* (*rare*) to sweat. **perspiration** /-spir-ā'shən/ *n* the act of perspiring; sweat. **perspīr'atory** *adj*.

perst see **perse**[2].

perstringe /pər-strinj'/ (*obs*) *vt* to constrain; to touch on; to dull; to censure. [L *perstringere*, from pfx *per-* thoroughly, and *stringere* to bind]

persuade, also (*obs*) **perswade** /pər-swād'/ *vt* to induce by reasoning, advice, etc; to bring to any particular opinion; to cause to believe; to convince; to seek to induce (*obs*); to urge (*Shakesp*). ♦ *vi* to use persuasive methods; to plead (*obs*); to prevail (*obs*). [L *persuādēre*, *-suāsum*, from pfx *per-*, and *suādēre* to advise]
■ **persuād'able** *adj*. **persuād'er** *n* someone who or that which persuades; a gun (*sl*); a device used to fit metal type into a chase (*printing*). **persuasibility** /-swās-i-bil'i-ti/ *n*. **persuās'ible** *adj* capable of being persuaded. **persuasion** /-swā'zhən/ *n* the act, process, method, art, or power of persuading; an inducement; the state of being persuaded; settled opinion; a creed; a party adhering to a creed; a kind (*facetious*). **persuasive** /-swās'/ *adj* having the power to persuade; influencing the mind or passions. ♦ *n* that which persuades or wins over. **persuā'sively** *adv*. **persuā'siveness** *n*. **persuās'ory** *adj* persuasive.

persue[1] /pûr'sū/ (*Spenser*) *n* a track of blood. [Fr *percée* act of piercing, confused with **pursue**]

persue[2] an obsolete spelling of **pursue**.

persulphate /pər-sul'fāt/ *n* that sulphate of a metal which contains the relatively greater quantity of oxygen or of the acid radical; a salt of **persulphuric** /-fū'rik/ **acid** ($H_2S_2O_8$). [**per-** (1) and **sulphate**]

perswade obsolete spelling of **persuade**.

PERT or **pert** (*business*) *abbrev*: programme evaluation and review technique.

pert /pûrt/ *adj* forward; saucy; impertinent; presumingly free in speech; unconcealed; brisk; perky (*Shakesp*); jaunty; flourishing; adroit (*obs*); objectionable (*obs*); open (*obs*). ♦ *n* an impudent person. [Aphetic for **apert**; see also **peart**]
■ **pert'ly** *adv*. **pert'ness** *n*.

pertain /pər- or pûr-tān'/ *vi* to belong; to relate, be applicable (with *to*). [OFr *partenir*, from L *pertinēre*, from pfx *per-*, and *tenēre* to hold]
■ **per'tinence** or **per'tinency** /pûr'/ *n* the state of being pertinent; an appurtenance (*obs*). **per'tinent** *adj* relating or related; to the point; fitted for the matter on hand; fitting or appropriate; suitable; apposite. ♦ *n* (chiefly *Scot*) a minor property forming part of a heritable estate. **per'tinently** *adv*.

pertake an old spelling (*Spenser*, *Shakesp*) of **partake**.

perthite /pûr'thīt/ (*geol*) *n* a parallel intergrowth of orthoclase and albite. [*Perth*, Ontario, where it was found]
■ **perthitic** /-it'ik/ *adj*.

pertinacious /pûr-ti-nā'shəs/ *adj* thoroughly tenacious; holding obstinately to an opinion or a purpose; obstinate; unyielding. [L *pertināx*, *-ācis* holding fast, from pfx *per-*, and *tenāx* tenacious, from *tenēre* to hold]
■ **pertinā'ciously** *adv*. **pertinā'ciousness** or **pertinacity** /-nas'i-ti/ *n* the quality of being pertinacious or unyielding; obstinacy; resoluteness.

pertinence, **pertinent**, etc see under **pertain**.

perttaunt like an obscure phrase in Shakespeare (*Love's Labours Lost* V.2.67), possibly meaning like a *pair taunt* or *purtaunt*, a double pair-royal. [**pair**[1], and Fr *tant* so much, ie counting as much again as a pair-royal in post and pair]

perturb /pər-tûrb'/, also (*rare*) **perturbate** /pûr'tər-bāt/ *vt* to disturb greatly; to agitate. [L *perturbāre*, *-ātum*, from pfx *per-*, and *turbāre* to disturb, from *turba* a crowd]
■ **pertur'bable** *adj*. **pertur'bance** *n* perturbation. **pertur'bant** *n* anything that perturbs. ♦ *adj* perturbing. **perturbā'tion** *n* the act of perturbing or state of being perturbed; disquiet of mind; irregularity; the disturbance produced in the simple elliptic motion of one heavenly body around another by the action of a third body, or by the non-sphericity of the principal body (*astron*); disturbance in a system caused by an outside influence; a perturbing agent. **perturbā'tional** *adj*. **pertur'bative** *adj*. **per'turbātor** *n*. **pertur'batory** *adj* and *n*. **perturbed'** *adj*. **pertur'bedly** *adv*. **pertur'ber** *n*.
❑ **perturbation theory** *n* (*phys*) a mathematical method of determining the effect of small local changes on the behaviour of a system.

pertuse /pər-tūs'/ or (*rare*) **pertusate** /-tū'sāt or pûr'/ or **pertused** /-tūst'/ *adj* punched; pierced; slit. [L *pertundere*, *-tūsum*, from *per* through, and *tundere* to strike]
■ **pertusion** /-tū'zhən/ *n*.

pertussis /pər-tus'is/ (*med*) *n* whooping cough. [**per-** (2) and L *tussis* cough]
■ **pertuss'al** *adj*.

peruke /pər-ook'/, formerly /per'/ *n* a wig (also (*Fr*) **perruque** /per-ük/). [Fr *perruque*, from Ital *parrucca* (Sp *peluca*); connection with L *pilus* hair, very doubtful]
■ **perru'quier** /-ook'yər or -ük-yā/ *n* a wig-maker. **peruk'ed** *adj* wearing a peruke.

peruse /pər-ooz'/ *vt* to read attentively or critically; (*loosely*) to read; *orig* to use up, wear out; to pass in scrutiny, one by one or piece by piece (*Shakesp*); to examine in detail; to revise. [L pfx *per-* thoroughly, and *ūtī*, *ūsus* to use]
■ **perus'al** *n* the act of perusing; careful examination; scrutiny; study; reading. **perus'er** *n*.

Peruvian /pə-roo'vi-ən/ *adj* of or relating to *Peru*, a country of S America. ♦ *n* a native or inhabitant of Peru.
❑ **Peruvian bark** *n* cinchona bark.
■ **balsam of Peru** or **Peru balsam** a fragrant acrid black viscid liquid, containing esters of benzoic and cinnamic acids, obtained from a tropical American papilionaceous tree, *Myroxylon pereirae*. **marvel of Peru** see under **marvel**.

perv /pûrv/ (*sl*) *n* a (sexual) pervert; an act of perving (*Aust*); someone who pervs (*Aust*). ♦ *vi* (also **perve**) to behave as a perv; (with *at* or *on*) to look at lustfully or for sexual pleasure (*Aust*). [**pervert**]
■ **perv'y** *adj*.

---

pervade /pər-vād'/ vt to diffuse or extend through the whole of, to permeate; to pass through (rare). [L pervādere, from per through, and vādere to go]

■ **pervasion** /-vā'zhən/ n. **pervasive** /-vā'siv/ adj tending to pervade, or having the power to pervade. **perva'sively** adv. **perva'siveness** n.

perverse /pər-vûrs'/ adj turned aside from right or truth; obstinately determined when in the wrong; capricious and unreasonable in opposition; wrong-headed, stubborn; wayward; deliberately wicked; against the evidence or judge's direction on point of law (law); adverse (Milton). [Partly through Fr, from L pervertere, perversum, from pfx per- wrongly, and vertere to turn]

■ **perverse'ly** adv. **perverse'ness** n. **perversion** /-vûr'shən/ n the act or process of perverting; the condition of being perverted; the product of the process of perverting; a diverting from the true object; a turning from what is right or true; a distortion; a misapplication; a pathological deviation of sexual instinct; the formation of a mirror image (maths); the mirror image itself. **pervers'ity** n the state or quality of being perverse. **pervers'ive** adj tending to pervert. **pervert'** vt to cause to turn away from the right course; to misconstrue, to interpret wrongly; to corrupt; to cause to turn from truth or virtue; to divert, turn (Shakesp); to form a mirror image of (maths). ◆ vi to go wrong, or away from the right course. ◆ n /pûr'vûrt/ someone whose sexual instinct is perverted; a person who has abandoned the doctrine assumed to be true. **pervert'ed** adj. **pervert'er** n. **pervert'ible** adj.

perviate see under **pervious**.

pervious /pûr'vi-əs/ adj permeable; passable; penetrable; open (to new ideas etc). [L pervius, from per through, and via a way]

■ **per'viate** vt to make a way through, penetrate. **per'viously** adv. **per'viousness** n.

Pes abbrev: peseta.

pes /pāz or pez/ n (pl **pedes** /ped'āz or ped'ēz/) the human foot; an animal foot or footlike part. [L]

Pesach or **Pesah** /pā'sahh/ n the festival of Passover. [Heb]

pesade /pə-zäd', -sād' or -zād'/ n a dressage manoeuvre in which a horse rears up on its hindlegs. [Fr; from Ital]

■ **lance pesade** see **lance prisado**.

pesant, **pesaunt** old spellings of **peasant**.

pesante /pe-san'tā/ (music) adj and adv heavy; weighty. [Ital]

pescatarian /pes-kə-tā'ri-ən/ n a person who excludes meat from their diet but will eat fish. [Ital pesce fish; modelled on **vegetarian**]

peseta /pe-sā'ta or -ə/ n a former unit of currency in Spain, replaced by the euro. [Sp, dimin of pesa weight]

pesewa /pə-soo'a, -sā'wa or -ə/ n (pl **pesewa** or **pesewas**) a Ghanaian monetary unit, $\frac{1}{100}$ of a cedi.

Peshito or **Peshitto** /pe-shē'tō/ or **Peshitta** /-tə/ n a Syriac translation of the Bible (also adj). [Syriac p'shīt\t)tô, -tá the simple]

Peshmerga /pesh-mûr'gə/ n pl (usu with the) (members of) a militia force fighting for Kurdish independence. [Kurdish, those who face death]

peshwa /pā'shwa/ n the chief minister of the Mahrattas, later the real sovereign (also **peish'wa** or **peish'wah**). [Pers pēshwā chief]

pesky /pes'ki/ (inf) adj annoying, troublesome (used as a pejorative). [Perh **pest**]

■ **pes'kily** adv.

peso /pā'sō/ n (pl **pe'sos**) a standard monetary unit in the Philippines and some Central and S American countries, worth 100 centesimos in Uruguay and 100 centavos elsewhere; formerly, a Spanish five-peseta piece. [Sp, from L pēnsum weight]

pessary /pes'ə-ri/ n a surgical plug worn in the vagina to support the womb; a suppository inserted into the vagina. [Fr pessaire, from LL pessārium, from Gr pessos a pebble, pessary]

pessima, **pessimal** see **pessimum**.

pessimism /pes'i-mi-zm/ n a tendency to look on the dark side of things, opp to optimism; a depressing view of life; (loosely) despondency, hopelessness; the doctrine that the world is bad rather than good (philos); the worst state (obs). [L pessimus worst]

■ **pess'imist** n a person who believes that everything is tending to the worst; a person who looks too much on the dark side of things. **pessimis'tic** or **pessimis'tical** adj. **pessimis'tically** adv.

pessimum /pes'i-məm/ n (pl **pess'ima**) that point at which any condition is least favourable. ◆ adj (of conditions) worst, least favourable (also **pess'imal**). [L, neuter of pessimus worst]

pest /pest/ n any deadly epidemic disease; plague (now rare); anything destructive; any insect, fungus, etc that destroys cultivated plants; a troublesome person or thing. [Fr peste and pestilence, from L pestis, pestilentia]

■ **pest'ful** adj pestilential. **pestici'dal** adj relating to a pesticide. **pesticide** /pes'ti-sīd/ n a substance for killing pests. **pestif'erous** adj

bringing plague or pestilence; pestilential; noxious; pestilent; annoying; plague-stricken. **pestif'erously** adv. **pest'ilence** n any deadly epidemic disease; bubonic plague; any morally harmful influence. **pest'ilent** adj deadly; producing pestilence; hurtful to health and life; pernicious; mischievous; vexatious. **pestilential** /-len'shl/ adj of the nature of pestilence; producing or infested with pestilence; destructive; baneful; detestable; pestering. **pestilen'tially** adv. **pest'ilently** adv. **pestolog'ical** adj. **pestol'ogist** n. **pestol'ogy** n the study of agricultural pests and methods of combating them.
□ **pest'house** n (hist) a hospital for patients suffering from plague or any other infectious or contagious disease. **pest'ilence-stricken** adj.

Pestalozzian /pes-ta-lot'si-ən/ adj relating to or associated with Swiss educational reformer Johann Heinrich Pestalozzi (1746–1827) or his programme. ◆ n a follower of Pestalozzi.

pester /pes'tər/ vt to annoy persistently; to clog (obs); to huddle (Milton); to infest (archaic). ◆ n an annoyance. [Appar from OFr empestrer (Fr empêtrer), to entangle, from L in in, and LL pāstōrium a foot-shackle, from L pāstus, pap of pāscere to feed; cf **pastern**; influenced by **pest**]

■ **pes'terer** n. **pes'teringly** adv. **pes'terment** n. **pest'erous** adj.
□ **pester power** n the ability of children to influence their parents' behaviour by making frequent requests.

pesticide, **pestiferous**, **pestilence**, etc see under **pest**.

pestle /pes'l/, also pes'tl/ n an instrument for pounding or grinding, esp a small club-like kitchen utensil used in conjunction with a small bowl or mortar; a leg of an animal, esp as food (now dialect). ◆ vt to pound. ◆ vi to use a pestle. [OFr pestel, from L pistillum a pounder, from pīnsere, pistum to pound]

pesto /pes'tō/ n an Italian sauce made chiefly of basil and cheese, with pine nuts and olive oil, originating in Liguria. [Ital]

pestology see under **pest**.

PET abbrev: polyethylene terephthalate; positron emission tomography, a technique for imaging the internal structures of the body; potentially exempt transfer, a gift made during the donor's lifetime, tax-free provided the donor survives for seven years after making the gift.

Pet. (Bible) abbrev: (the Letters of) Peter.

pet[1] /pet/ n a tame animal kept for companionship or amusement; an indulged favourite; used as an endearment. ◆ adj kept as a pet; for or of pet animals; indulged; cherished; favourite. ◆ vt (**pett'ing**; **pett'ed**) to treat as a pet; to fondle; to pamper; to indulge. ◆ vi (inf) to indulge in amorous caressing. [Origin unknown; not from Gaelic]

■ **pett'ed** adj. **pett'er** n. **pett'ing** n.
□ **pet aversion** or **hate** n a chief object of dislike. **pet'-day** n (Scot) a day of sunshine in the middle of bad weather. **pet name** n a name used in familiar affection. **pet'-sit** vi to look after a pet in its owner's absence. **pet'-sitter** n. **petting party** n (inf) a gathering for the purpose of amorous caressing as an organized sport.

pet[2] /pet/ n a slighted and offended feeling; a slight or childish fit of aggrieved or resentful sulkiness; the sulks, huff. ◆ vi to be peevish, to sulk. [Origin unknown]

■ **pett'ed** adj in a pet; apt to be in a pet. **pett'edly** adv. **pett'edness** n. **pett'ish** adj peevish; sulky; inclined to sulk; of the nature of or expressive of sulkiness. **pett'ishly** adv. **pett'ishness** n.

PETA or **Peta** abbrev: People for the Ethical Treatment of Animals.

peta- /pe-tə-/ combining form denoting 10^{15}, as in petajoule and petametre. [Origin uncertain; prob Gr **penta-**]

■ **pet'aflop** n (comput) a unit of processing speed equal to 10^{15} floating-point operations per second. ◆ adj able to perform at this speed, as in petaflop computer.

petal /pet'l/ n one of the usu brightly-coloured leaflike parts of a flower, a corolla leaf. [Gr petalon a leaf]

■ **petalif'erous** or **pet'alous** adj having petals. **pet'aline** /-īn/ adj of or like a petal. **pet'alism** n a method of ostracism practised in ancient Syracuse, the name being written on an olive leaf. **pet'alled** adj having petals; also used as combining form, as in white-petalled. **pet'alody** n (Gr eidos form) transformation, esp of stamens, into petals. **pet'aloid** adj having the appearance of a petal. **petaloma'nia** n abnormal increase in number of petals. **petalous** adj see petaliferous above.

pétanque /pā-tãk'/ n the name in S France for the game, of Provençal origin, in which steel bowls are rolled or hurled towards a wooden marker ball, in other regions called **boules**. [Fr, from Provençal pèd tanco feet fixed (or together) as in the mandatory throwing position]

petar see **petard**.

petara /pi-tä'rə/ n a travelling box or basket for clothes (also **pita'ra** or **pita'rah**). [Hindi pitārāh, petārāh]

petard /pe-tär′ or -tärd′/ n a case containing an explosive, used for blowing in doors, etc (Shakesp **petar**′); a moving firework. [OFr, from *péter* to crack or explode, from L *pēdere* to break wind]
■ **hoist with one's own petard** see under **hoist**.

petary /pē′tə-ri/ n a peat bog. [Medieval L *petāria*, from root of **peat**[1]]

petasus /pet′ə-səs/ n a low broad hat worn by the Greeks in antiquity; either the broad petasus that Hermes is represented as wearing in early Greek art or, by association, the winged hat he wears in later art. [Latinized from Gr *petasos*]

petaurist /pe-tö′rist/ n a flying phalanger. [Gr *petauristēs* an acrobat]
■ **petaur**′**ine** adj.

petchary /pech′ə-ri/ n the grey kingbird. [Imit]

petcock /pet′kok/ n a small tap or valve for draining condensed steam from steam-engine cylinders, or for testing the water level in a boiler. [Poss obs *pet* to fart, or **petty**, and *cock* a tap]

petechia /pe-tē′ki-ə/ (med) n (pl **pete**′**chiae** /-ē/) a small red or purple spot on the skin, the result of a ruptured blood vessel. [Latinized from Ital *petecchia*]
■ **petech**′**ial** adj.

peter[1] /pē′tər/ vi to dwindle away to nothing, be dissipated or exhausted (with *out*). [Origin unknown; orig US mining slang]

peter[2] /pē′tər/ n the Blue Peter (flag); a call for trumps (*whist*); a high card followed by a low card, so played as a signal to one's partner (*bridge*). ◆ vi to signal that one has a short suit (*whist*); to play a high card followed by a low card (*bridge*).
□ **pe**′**ter-boat** n a kind of fishing-boat; a dredger's boat that goes equally well forward or astern. **pe**′**ter-man** n a fisherman (in allusion to the apostle). **Peter-see-me**′ n a Spanish wine (from a grape introduced by Pedro *Ximenes*). **Peter's pence** see under **penny**.

peter[3] /pē′tər/ (sl) n a safe; a prison cell; the penis; a till (*Aust*); the witness box (*Aust*).
□ **pe**′**terman** n a safe-blower.

Peterloo /pē-tər-loo′/ n a popular term for the incident at St Peter's Fields, Manchester, in 1819, in which a peaceable demonstration for reform was charged by cavalry, leaving 11 dead and 400 to 500 injured. [St *Peter*'s Fields and Water*loo*]

peterman see under **peter**[3].

peter-man see under **peter**[2].

Peter Pan /pē′tər pan/ n a character in JM Barrie's play of that name (1904), hence the type of person who never grows up, *esp* a youthful or immature man.
□ **Peter Pan collar** n a flat collar with rounded ends.

Peter principle /pē′tər prin′si-pl/ (*facetious*) n the theory that members of an organization, etc, are generally promoted to posts one stage above their level of competence. [Advanced by Laurence Peter (1919–90) and Raymond Hull in their book, *The Peter Principle* (1969)]

petersham /pē′tər-shəm/ n a heavy corded ribbon used for belts, hatbands, etc; a heavy greatcoat designed by Lord *Petersham*; rough-napped cloth, generally dark blue, of which it was made. [Lord *Petersham* (1790–1851), English army officer]

Peters' projection /pē′tərz prə-jek′shən/ n an equal-area map projection, one that shows accurately the relative sizes of continents, oceans, etc. [Arno *Peters* (1916–2002), German cartographer]

pether see **pedder**.

pethidine /peth′ə-dēn/ n a synthetic analgesic and hypnotic, acting like morphine, much used in childbirth (also called **meperidine** /mə-per′i-dēn or -din/). [Perh mixture of *piperidine* and *ethyl*]

pétillant /pā-tē-yä′/ (Fr) adj (of wine) slightly sparkling.

petiole /pet′i-ōl/ n a leaf-stalk (*bot*); a stalk-like structure, *esp* that of the abdomen in wasps, etc (*zool*). [L *petiolus* a little foot, a petiole]
■ **pet**′**iolar** adj of, or of the nature of, a petiole. **pet**′**iolate**, **pet**′**iolated** or **pet**′**ioled** adj stalked. **pet**′**iolule** /-ol-ūl/ n (*bot*) the stalk of a leaflet in a compound leaf.

petit /formerly *pet*′*it*, now *pet*′*i*, pə-tē′ or as Fr pə-tē/ adj a form of **petty**, in sense of insignificant, now obsolete except in legal and other French terms. [Fr]
■ **petite** /pə-tēt′/ adj applied to a woman, small-made (with a suggestion of neatness); a variant spelling of **petit**, applied to either sex (*obs*).
□ In the following compounds, the older borrowings tend to be the more highly anglicized, while newer ones retain French pronunciation: **petit battement** /bat-mä′/ n (*ballet*) a light tapping or beating with the foot. **petit bourgeois** /boor-zhwä′/ n a member of the lower middle class. **petit déjeuner** /dā-zhœ-nā/ n breakfast. **petite bourgeoisie** /boor-zhwä-zē/ n the lower middle class. **Petite Sirah** /si-rä/ n a grape *orig* cultivated in SE France, now widely grown in the Americas; a red wine made from this grape. **petit four** /för, för or foor/

n a small very fancy biscuit. **petit grain** /grān/ n dried unripe bitter oranges, or an oil distilled from them or their leaves and twigs. **petit jury** n (*law*) a jury of twelve people, in England now the only form of jury (also **petty jury**; see also **grand juror** under **grand**[1]). **petit maître** /me-tr′/ n a fop. **petit mal** /mal/ n a mild form of epilepsy without convulsions. **petit pain** /pē/ n a bread roll. **petit point** /point or pwē/ n tapestry work using small stitches diagonal to the canvas threads. **petits pois** /pə-tē pwä/ n pl small green peas.

petition /pə-tish′ən/ n a formal request to an authority; a written supplication signed by a number of people; a written application to a court of law; the thing asked for; a supplication; a prayer; a parliamentary bill (*obs*); an axiom or postulate (*obs*). ◆ vt to address a petition to; to ask for. [L *petītiō*, -*ōnis*, from *petere* to ask]
■ **peti**′**tionary** adj. **peti**′**tioner** n someone who petitions; (with *cap*) one of the party that petitioned Charles II in 1680 to summon Parliament, opp to *Abhorrer* (*hist*). **petit**′**ioning** n. **peti**′**tionist** n. **petitory** /pet′i-tə-ri/ adj petitioning.
□ **Petition of Right** n a parliamentary declaration, in the form of a petition of the rights of the people, assented to by Charles I in 1628.

petitio principii /pe-tish′i-ō prin-sip′i-ī or pe-tē′ti-ō prēn-kip′i-ē/ (*logic*) n a begging of the question. [L]

petitory see under **petition**.

Petrarchan /pe-trär′kən/ or **Petrarchian** /-ki-ən/ adj relating to or in the style of the Italian poet Francesco *Petrarca* or *Petrarch* (1304–74). ◆ n a follower or imitator of Petrarch.
■ **Petrarch**′**al** adj. **Petrarch**′**ianism** n. **Petrarch**′**ianist** n. **Petrarchism** /pe′trärk-izm or pe-trärk′izm/ n. **Pe**′**trarchist** (or /-trärk′/) n. **Petrarchize** or **-ise** /pe′trärk-īz or -trärk′/ vi to write in Petrarch's manner, to imitate Petrarch. —The older pronunciation of /pē′trärk/ gives alternative pronunciations for the above words.
□ **Petrarchan** (or **Petrarchian**) **sonnet** n see under **sonnet**.

petrary /pet′rə-ri/ n a contrivance for hurling stones. [LL *petrāria*, from L *petra*, from Gr *petrā* rock]

petre /pē′tər/ (*inf*) n short form of **saltpetre**.

petrel /pet′rəl/ n any bird of the family Procellariidae related to the albatrosses, shearwaters and fulmars, *esp* the **storm** (popularly **stormy**) **petrel** or Mother Carey's chicken or similar species, dusky seabirds, rarely landing except to lay their eggs, and including the smallest webfooted bird known. [L *Petrus* Peter, from the fact that it appears to walk on the water; see Bible, Matthew 14.29]

Petri dish /pē′tri, pä′tri or pet′ri dish/ (also without *cap*) n a shallow glass dish with an overlapping cover used for cultures of bacteria (also **Petri plate**). [JR *Petri* (1852–1922), German bacteriologist]

petrify /pet′ri-fī/ vt (**pet**′**rifying**; **pet**′**rified**) to frighten into immobility; to turn into stone; to fossilize by molecular replacement, preserving minute structure (*geol*); (loosely) to encrust with stony matter; to make hard like a stone. ◆ vi to become stone, or hard like stone. [L *petra*, from Gr *petrā* rock, and L *facere*, *factum* to make]
■ **petrifac**′**tion** n turning or being turned into stone; a petrified object; a fossil. **petrifac**′**tive** or **petrif**′**ic** adj petrifying. **petrifica**′**tion** n petrifaction.

Petrine /pē′trīn/ adj relating to or written by the Apostle *Peter*. [L *Petrinus*, from *Petrus*, Gr *Petros* Peter]
■ **Pē**′**trinism** /-trin-izm/ n the Tübingen theory of FC Baur (1792–1860) and his school, of a doctrinal trend in primitive Christianity towards Judaism, ascribed to Peter and his party in opposition to Paulinism.

petrissage /pā-trē-säzh′/ n massage by longitudinal rubbing and lateral squeezing. [Fr, from *pétrir* to knead]

petro-[1] /pet-rō-/ combining form signifying petroleum. [*petroleum*]
■ **petrōchem**′**ical** n and adj (of or relating to) any chemical obtained from petroleum. **petrōchem**′**istry** n. **pet**′**rocurr**′**ency**, **pet**′**romoney**, **pet**′**rodollars** and **pet**′**ropounds** n currency, etc, acquired by the oil-producing countries as profit from the sale of their oil to the consumer countries.

petro-[2] /pet-rō- or pi-tro-/ combining form signifying rock. [Gr *petrā* rock]
■ **pet**′**rodrome** n (Gr *dromos* a running) an African elephant shrew of the genus **Petrodromus**. **petrogen**′**esis** n (the study of) the origin, formation, etc, of rocks. **petrogenet**′**ic** adj. **pet**′**roglyph** n (Gr *glyphein* to carve) a rock-carving, *esp* prehistoric. **petrōglyph**′**ic** adj. **pet**′**roglyphy** n. **pet**′**rogram** n (Gr *gramma* a drawing) a picture on stone. **petrog**′**rapher** n. **petrograph**′**ic** or **petrograph**′**ical** adj (**petrographic province** (*geol*) a region characterized by a group of genetically related rocks). **petrograph**′**ically** adv. **petrog**′**raphy** n (Gr *graphein* to write) the systematic description and classification of rocks. **petrolog**′**ical** adj. **petrolog**′**ically** adv. **petrol**′**ogist** n. **petrol**′**ogy** n (Gr *logos* discourse) the science of the origin, chemical and mineral composition and structure, and alteration of rocks. **petrōphys**′**ical** adj. **petrōphys**′**icist** n. **petrōphys**′**ics** n sing (Gr

physikos natural) that branch of physics relating to the physical properties of rocks.

petrol /*pet'rəl*/ *n* formerly, petroleum; now a mixture of light volatile hydrocarbons obtained by the fractional distillation or cracking of petroleum, used as a fuel in motor-cars, aeroplanes, etc (also (*N Am*) **gasoline**); petrol blue. ◆ *vt* (**pet'rolling**; **pet'rolled**) to supply with petrol. [L *petra* rock, and *oleum* oil]
■ **pet'rolage** *n* treatment with petrol to stamp out mosquitoes. **petrolatum** /*-ā'təm*/ *n* petroleum jelly. **petroleous** /*pi-trō'li-əs*/ *adj* containing or rich in petroleum. **petroleum** /*pi-trō'li-əm*/ *n* a (*usu* liquid) mineral oil containing a mixture of hydrocarbons obtained from oil wells, and used to make petrol, paraffin, lubricating oil, fuel oil, etc. **pétroleur** /*pā-trol-œr'*/, *fem* **pétroleuse** /*-øz*/ *n* (*Fr*) a rioter who uses petroleum, as in the Paris uprising of 1871. **petrolic** /*pi-trol'ik*/ *adj* of petrol or petroleum. **petrolif'erous** /*pet-*/ *adj* yielding petroleum.
❑ **petrol blue** *n* a vibrant greenish-blue colour. **petrol bomb** *n* a petrol-filled bottle stopped with rags that are set alight just before the bottle is thrown. **petroleum coke** *n* almost pure carbon, the final by-product of the distillation of crude oil, used in refining, electrodes, as a fuel, etc. **petroleum ether** *n* a volatile mixture of hydrocarbons distilled from petroleum and used as a solvent. **petroleum jelly** *n* soft paraffin (*paraffinum molle*), a mixture of petroleum hydrocarbons used in emollients, as a lubricant, etc (see also **liquid paraffin** under **paraffin**). **pet'rolhead** *n* (*inf*) a motor vehicle enthusiast. **petrol lighter** *n* a cigarette lighter in which the striking of a spark ignites a petrol-soaked wick. **petrol pump** *n* a machine from which measured amounts of petrol are dispensed for use in motor vehicles. **petrol station** *n* a garage which sells petrol, a filling station.

petrology see under **petro-²**.

petronel /*pet'rə-nel*/ *n* a short large-calibre rifle carried by mounted soldiers in the 16c and 17c. [Fr *petrinal*, from L *pectus, pectoris* the chest, from where it was fired, or L *petra* stone, ie gun-flint]

petronella /*pe-trə-nel'ə*/ *n* a Scottish country dance. [Poss from the name *Petronella*]

petrous /*pet'rəs*/ *adj* stony; petrosal. [L *petrōsus*, from *petra*, from Gr *petrā* rock]
■ **petrosal** /*pi-trōs'əl*/ *adj* relating to the stony part of the temporal bone around the inner ear (also *n*).

pe-tsai cabbage /*pā-tsī' kab'ij*/ same as **Chinese cabbage** (see under **china¹**).

petted, etc see under **pet**¹,².

petter see under **pet**¹.

Petter engine /*pet'ər en'jin*/ *n* a kind of oil engine. [Makers' name]

pettichaps or **petty-chaps** /*pet'i-chaps*/ *n* the garden or other warbler. [N of England; appar **petty** and **chap³**]

petticoat /*pet'i-kōt*/ *n* a skirt, *esp* an underskirt, or a garment of which it forms part; any garment or drapery of similar form; *orig* a short or small coat; a woman (*inf*); any bell-shaped structure; the part of an archery target outside the scoring area. ◆ *adj* (*usu facetious*) feminine; female; of women. [**petty** and **coat**¹]
■ **pett'icoated** *adj*.
❑ **pett'icoat-breeches** *n pl* loose short breeches worn by men in the 17c. **petticoat government** *n* domination by women. **pett'icoat-tails'** *n* small *usu* triangular cakes of shortbread.

pettifogger /*pet'i-fog-ər*/ *n* a lawyer who deals, often deceptively and quibblingly, with trivial cases. [**petty**, and MLGer *voger* a person who does things]
■ **pett'ifog** *vi* to play the pettifogger. **pett'ifoggery** *n*. **pett'ifogging** *n* and *adj* paltry, trivial, cavilling (behaviour).

petting see under **pet**¹.

pettish, etc see under **pet**².

pettitoes /*pet'i-tōz*/ *n pl* pig's feet as food (formerly *appar* also other parts and of other animals); human feet (*Shakesp*). [Origin obscure, but early associated with **petty** and **toe**]

pettle¹ /*pet'l*/ (*Scot*) *vt* to indulge, pet. [Frequentative of **pet**¹]

pettle² /*pet'l*/ same as **pattle**.

petty /*pet'i*/ *adj* small; of little or less importance; minor; trifling; lower in rank, power, etc; inconsiderable, insignificant; contemptible; small-minded; spiteful. ◆ *n* a junior schoolboy. [Fr *petit*]
■ **pett'ily** *adv*. **pett'iness** *n*.
❑ **Petty Bag** *n* a former office of the Court of Chancery; a clerk of that office. **petty bourgeois, petty bourgeoisie** *n* variants of **petit bourgeois** and **petite bourgeoisie** under **petit**. **petty cash** *n* miscellaneous small sums of money received or paid; a sum of money kept for minor expenses which *usu* do not need to be referred to a higher authority. **petty-chaps** see **pettichaps**. **petty jury** see **petit jury** under **petit**. **petty larceny** see under **larceny**. **petty officer** *n* a naval officer ranking with a non-commissioned officer in the army. **Petty Sessions** *n pl* a court in which magistrates try trivial cases and

refer others to a higher court. **petty whin** *n* a low spiny papilionaceous shrub (*Genista anglica*) like a small whin.

petulant /*pet'ū-lənt*/ *adj* showing peevish impatience, irritation, or caprice; forward, impudent in manner; *orig* wanton, lascivious. [L *petulāns, -antis*, from assumed *petulāre*, dimin of *petere* to seek]
■ **pet'ulance** or **pet'ulancy** *n*. **pet'ulantly** *adv*.

Petunia /*pə-tū'nyə*/ or *pi-* or *-ni-ə*/ *n* a S American genus of ornamental plants closely related to tobacco; (*without cap*) a plant of this genus. [Tupí *petun* tobacco]

petuntse /*pe-tŭnt'si*/ *n* a feldspathic rock used in making Chinese porcelain (also **petuntze**). [Chin *báidūnzř* little white brick]

pew /*pū*/ *n* an enclosed compartment or fixed bench in a church; formerly a place for a preacher or reader; a box or stall in another building; a seat (*inf*). [OFr *puie* raised place, balcony, from L *podia*, pl of *podium*, from Gr *podion*, dimin of *pous, podos* foot]
❑ **pew'-chair** *n* an additional seat hinged to the end of a pew. **pew'-fellow** *n* an occupant of the same pew; hence, a companion. **pew'-holder** *n* a person who rents a pew. **pew'-opener** *n* an attendant who showed people to pews. **pew'-rent** *n* rent paid for the use of a pew.

pewee or **peewee** /*pē'wē*/ *n* a tyrant bird of N America. [Imit of its call]

pewit /*pē'wit* or *pū'it*/ same as **peewit**.

pewter /*pū'tər*/ *n* formerly an alloy of three to nine parts of tin and one of lead; now tin with a little copper, antimony, and/or bismuth; a container made of pewter, *esp* a beer tankard; the bluish-grey colour of pewter; prize-money (*sl*). ◆ *adj* made of pewter. [OFr *peutre*; cf Ital *peltro*, LGer *spialter*, Eng **spelter**]
■ **pew'terer** *n* someone who works in pewter.
❑ **pew'ter-mill** *n* a lapidary's pewter polishing-wheel for amethyst, agate, etc.

peyote /*pā-yō'tā*/ *n* a cactus of N Mexico and SW USA; (also called **mescal**) an intoxicant made from the tops of this cactus (**peyote buttons**). [Nahuatl *peyotl*]
■ **peyō'tism** *n* the taking of peyote, *esp* as part of a religious ceremony; a Native American religion in which peyote is taken sacramentally. **peyō'tist** *n*.

peyse see **peise**.

pezant an old spelling of **peasant**.

Peziza /*pe-zī'zə*/ *n* a genus of discomycete fungi with cup-like apothecia. [Gr *pezis* a puff-ball]
■ **pezi'zoid** *adj*.

PF *abbrev*: Patriotic Front; Procurator Fiscal.

Pf *abbrev*: pfennig.

pf (*music*) *abbrev*: pianoforte.

PFA *abbrev*: Professional Footballers' Association.

Pfc (*US*) *abbrev*: private first class.

PFD *abbrev*: personal flotation device.

pfennig /*(p)fen'ig* or *-ihh*/ *n* a former monetary unit of Germany, $\frac{1}{100}$ of a mark (also (*obs*) **pfenn'ing**).

PFI *abbrev*: Private Finance Initiative, a scheme whereby public works are financed commercially.

PFLP *abbrev*: Popular Front for the Liberation of Palestine.

PFP *abbrev*: Partnership for Peace.

PG *abbrev*: Parental Guidance (a certificate denoting a film in which some scenes may be unsuitable for young children); paying guest.

Pg *abbrev*: Portugal; Portuguese.

PGA® *abbrev*: Professional Golfers' Association.

PGCE *abbrev*: Postgraduate Certificate in Education.

PGD *abbrev*: preimplantation genetic diagnosis, a technique for screening embryos that have been fertilized in vitro before implantation in the uterus.

PGM *abbrev*: Past Grand Master.

pH /*pē-āch'*/ or **pH value** /*val'ū*/ *n* a number used to express degrees of acidity or alkalinity in solutions, formerly the logarithm to base 10 of the reciprocal of the concentration of hydrogen ions, but now related by formula to a standard solution of potassium hydrogen phthalate, which has value 4 at 15°C. [From Ger *Potenz* power, and *H* the symbol for hydrogen]

PHAB /*fab*/ *abbrev*: Physically Handicapped and Able Bodied.

Phacelia /*fə-sē'li-ə*/ (*bot*) *n* a chiefly American genus of annuals of the Hydrophyllaceae family; (*without cap*) any plant of the genus.

phacoid /*fak'* or *fāk'oid*/ or **phacoidal** /*fə-koi'dl*/ *adj* lentil-shaped; lens-shaped. [Gr *phakos* a lentil, and *eidos* form]
■ **phacolite** /*fak'ə-līt*/ *n* a zeolite often lenticular in shape. **phac'olith** *n* a small lenticular igneous intrusion, shaped by folding in an anticline.

Phaedra complex /fē'drə kom'pleks/ (*psychol*) *n* the difficult relationship which can arise between a new step-parent and the (*usu* teenage) son or daughter of the original marriage. [Greek story of *Phaedra* who fell in love with her stepson and committed suicide after being repulsed by him]

phaeic /fē'ik/ *adj* dusky. [Gr *phaios* dusky]
■ **phae'ism** *n* duskiness, incomplete melanism (in butterflies).

phaelonion see **phelonion**.

phaen- /fēn-/ or **phaeno-** /fē-no- or -nō-/ same as **phen-** or **pheno-**.

phaenogam /fē'nō-gam/ *n* a spermatophyte or phanerogam (also **phe'nogam**). [Gr *phainein* to show, and *gamos* marriage]
■ **Phaenogamae** /fē-nog'ə-mē/ *n pl.* **phaenogamic** /-nō-gam'ik/ or **phaenogamous** /-nog'ə-məs/ *adj*.

phaenology same as **phenology**.

phaenomenon same as **phenomenon**.

phaenotype same as **phenotype**.

phaeo- /fē-ō-/ *combining form* denoting dusky, as in **phaeomelanin** /fē-ō-mel'ə-nin/, a reddish-brown pigment in animals, including birds. [Gr *phaios* dusky]

Phaeophyceae /fē-ō-fish'i-ē/ *n pl* the brown seaweeds, one of the main divisions of algae, in which the chlorophyll is masked by a brown pigment. [Gr *phaios* dusky, and *phȳkos* seaweed]

Phaethon /fā'i-thon/ *n* the son of Helios, the Greek sun-god, who came to grief in driving his father's chariot (*Gr myth*); the tropicbird genus (as seeking to keep to the sun's course). [Gr *Phaethōn, -ontos*, literally, shining; cf *phaos, phōs* light]
■ **Phaethon'tic** *adj*.

phaeton /fā'i-tən or fā'tən/ *n* an open four-wheeled carriage for one or two horses. [From **Phaethon**]

phag- /fag-/ or **phago-** /fag-ō-/ *combining form* denoting feeding or eating, as in *phagocyte*. [Gr *phagein* to eat]
■ **-phaga** /-fag-ə/ *combining form* denoting (in zoological names) 'eaters'. **-phage** /-fāj/ or **-fäzh/ *combining form* denoting eater or destroyer. **-phagous** /-fəg-əs/ *combining form* denoting feeding on. **-phagus** /-fəg-əs/ *combining form* denoting one feeding in a particular way, or on a particular thing. **-phagy** /-fə-ji/ *combining form* denoting eating of a specified nature.

phage short for **bacteriophage**.

phagedaena or **phagedena** /faj- or fag-i-dē'nə/ (*med*) *n* hospital gangrene, rapidly spreading destructive ulceration, once common in hospitals. [Gr *phagedaina*, from *phagein* to eat]
■ **phagedae'nic** or **phagedē'nic** *adj*.

phagocyte /fag'ō-sīt/ *n* a white blood corpuscle that engulfs bacteria and other harmful particles. [Gr *phagein* to eat, and *kytos* a vessel]
■ **phagocytic** /-sit'/ or **phagocyt'ical** *adj*. **phag'ocytism** /-sīt-/ *n* the nature or function of a phagocyte. **phag'ocytose** /-sīt-ōs/ *vt* to subject to phagocytic action. **phagocytō'sis** *n* destruction by phagocytes.

phagophobia /fag-ō-fō'bi-ə/ *n* fear of or aversion to eating. [**phago-** and **phobia**]

-phagous, -phagus, -phagy see under **phag-**.

Phalaenopsis /fal'i-nop-sis/ (*bot*) *n* a genus of evergreen epiphytic orchids.

phalange, etc see under **phalanx**.

phalanger /fa-lan'jər/ *n* any one of a group of small arboreal Australasian marsupials, a possum. [Gr *phalangion* spider's web, from their webbed toes]

phalanstery /fal'ən-stə-ri/ *n* the set of buildings occupied by a phalange in the ideal social system of Fourierism (qv), a vast structure set in a square league of cultivated land. [Fr *phalanstère*, formed from Gr *phalanx* on the model of *monastère* monastery]
■ **phalansterian** /-stē'ri-ən/ *adj* of or relating to a phalanstery. **phalanstē'rianism** or **phal'ansterism** *n*. **phal'ansterist** *n*.

phalanx /fal'angks or fā'langks/ *n* (*pl* **phal'anxes** or **phalanges** /fal-an'jēz/) a solid formation of ancient Greek heavy-armed infantry; a solid formation of soldiers; a solid body of supporters or partisans; a solid body of people generally; a Fourierist community; a bone of a digit; the part of a finger or toe corresponding to it; a joint of an insect's leg; a bundle of stamens. [Gr *phalanx, -angos* a roller, phalanx, phalange, spider]
■ **phalangal** /fal-ang'gl/ *adj* phalangeal. **phalange** /fal'anj/ *n* (*pl* **phal'anges**) a phalanx (in biological senses); (also /-fal-äzh/) a socialistic community in Fourier's scheme, consisting of 1800 people living in a phalanstery; (with *cap*) the Falange (qv); (with *cap*) the Christian right-wing group in Lebanon, modelled on the Spanish Falange. **phalan'geal** *adj*. **phalangid** /fal-an'jid/ *n* a long-legged arachnid, a harvester spider. **phalan'gist** *n* a Spanish falangist; a member of the Lebanese Phalange.

phalarope /fal'ə-rōp/ *n* a wading bird (genus *Phalaropus*) with feet like those of a coot. [Gr *phalaris* a coot, and *pous* a foot]

phallus /fal'əs/ *n* (*pl* **phall'ī** or **phall'uses**) the penis; the erect penis as a symbol of generation in primitive religion; (with *cap*) the stinkhorn genus of fungi. [L, from Gr *phallos*]
■ **phall'ic** *adj* relating to or like the phallus; of or relating to the stage of psychosexual development in which the child's interest and gratification is concentrated on his or her genital organs (*psychol*). **phall'icism** /-sizm/ or **phall'ism** *n* worship of the generative power of nature. **phall'in** and **phalloid'in** *n* two of the poisons occurring in the fungus *Amanita phalloides*. **phallocen'tric** *adj* centred on the phallus; dominated by or expressive of male attitudes. **phallocentric'ity** *n*. **phallocen'trism** *n*. **phall'ocrat** *n* a person who supports or assumes the existence of a male-dominated society; a man who argues for his superiority over women because of his masculinity. **phallocrat'ic** *adj*. **phall'oid** *adj* like a phallus in shape.

Phanariot /fa-nar'i-ot/ *n* (also **Fanariot**) one of the Greeks inhabiting the *Fanar* quarter of Constantinople; one of a class of Greek officials, in Turkish history mostly diplomats, administrators and bankers, also hospodars of Wallachia and Moldavia. ◆ *adj* of or relating to the Phanariots. [Gr *phānarion* lighthouse, from that on the Golden Horn]

phanerogam /fan'ə-rō-gam/ (*biol*; *old*) *n* a spermatophyte. [Gr *phaneros* visible, and *gamos* marriage]
■ **Phanerogamae** /-og'ə-mē/ or **Phanerogamia** /-ō-gam'i-ə/ *n pl* a division of plants comprising all spermatophytes. **phanerogam'ic** *adj*. **phanerog'amous** *adj*.

phanerophyte /fan'ə-rə-fīt or fə-ner'ə-fīt/ (*biol*) *n* a tree or shrub with the perennating buds borne more than 25cm above soil level. [Gr *phaneros* visible, and *phyton* plant]

Phanerozoic /fan-ər-ə-zō'ik/ (*geol*) *adj* of or belonging to the eon from the start of the Cambrian period (540 million years ago) to the present (also *n*). [Gr *phaneros* visible, and *zōion* an animal]

phang an old spelling (*Shakesp*) of **fang**.

phantasiast see under **phantasy**.

phantasm /fan'tazm/ *n* (also **phantas'ma**) a vision; an illusion; an airy or insubstantial figure, an apparition, a spectre; a counterfeit; an impostor (*obs*). [Gr *phantasma*, from *phantazein* to make visible, from *phainein* to bring to light, from *phaein* to shine]
■ **phan'tasim** or **phan'tasime** *n* (*Shakesp*) a fantastic person. **phantas'mal** *adj*. **phantasmā'lian** *adj* (*rare*). **phantasmal'ity** *n*. **phantas'mally** *adv*. **phantas'mic** or **phantas'mical** *adj*. **phantasmogenet'ic** *adj* producing or causing phantasms. **phantasmogenet'ically** *adv*.

phantasmagoria /fan-taz-mə-gō'ri-ə or -gö'/ *n* a fantastic dreamlike series of illusive images or of real forms. [Name given to a show of optical illusions in 1802, from Fr *phantasmagorie*, from Gr *phantasma* an appearance, and perh *agorā* an assembly]
■ **phantasmago'rial** *adj* relating to or resembling a phantasmagoria. **phantasmagor'ic** or **phantasmagor'ical** *adj*.

phantasy, phantastic, phantastry same as **fantasy**, etc.
■ **phantā'siast** *n* one of those Docetae who believed Christ's body to have been a mere phantom (see **Docetism**).

phantom /fan'təm/ (*Spenser* **phantosme** /fan-tōm'/) *n* a deceitful appearance; an immaterial form, a spectre; a visionary experience, such as a dream; an unreal vision or appearance, an illusion. ◆ *adj* illusory; unreal; non-existent; spectral; imaginary; ghostly-looking; transparent and hardly visible. [OFr *fantosme*, from Gr *phantasma*]
■ **phantomat'ic**, **phan'tomish** or **phan'tomy** *adj* (all *archaic*) relating to a phantom.
□ **phantom circuit** *n* (as in telecommunications) an additional circuit which does not in fact exist, the extra performance being obtained by suitable arrangements of real circuits. **phantom limb** *n* the sensation experienced by an amputee of the amputated limb still being attached to the body. **phantom material** *n* (*radiol*) material producing absorption and backscatter of radiation similar to human tissue, hence used to study radiation doses, etc (also called **tissue equivalent material**). **phantom pain** *n* a sensation of pain in a phantom limb. **phantom pregnancy** *n* false pregnancy (qv). **phantom withdrawal** *n* (*inf*; *finance*) the apparently unauthorized and unexplained removal of money from bank accounts through automated teller machines.

phar or **pharm** *abbrev*: pharmaceutical (also **pharma**); pharmacopoeia; pharmacy.

Pharaoh /fā'rō/ *n* a title of the kings of ancient Egypt; faro (*obs*). [L and Gr *pharaō*, from Heb *par'ōh*, from Egyp *pr-'o* great house]
■ **pharaonic** /fā-rā-on'ik/ *adj*.
□ **Pharaoh** (or **Pharaoh's**) **ant** *n* a tiny yellow-brown tropical ant which has spread through many countries and infests heated buildings, eg hospitals, restaurants, blocks of flats. **Pharaoh's serpent** *n* the coiled ash of burning mercuric thiocyanate, a type of indoor firework. **Pharaonic circumcision** *n* the ancient practice of female

---

■ words derived from main entry word; □ compound words; ■ idioms and phrasal verbs

circumcision by the removal of the clitoris and labia majora and minora.

phare /fär/ *n* a lighthouse. [Fr; see **pharos**]

Pharisee /far'i-sē/ *n* a member of an ancient Jewish sect, a lay democratic party among the Jews, whose legalistic interpretation of the Mosaic law led to an obsessive concern with the mass of rules covering the details of everyday life; anyone more careful of the outward forms than of the spirit of religion, a formalist; a very self-righteous or hypocritical person. [OE *phariseus*, from LL *pharisaeus*, from Gr *pharisaios*, from Heb *pārūsh* separated]
■ **pharisa'ic** or **pharisa'ical** *adj* relating to or like the Pharisees; hypocritical. **pharisa'ically** *adv*. **pharisa'icalness** *n*. **phar'isaism** *n* (also **phar'iseeism**).

pharm, pharma see **phar**.

pharmaceutic /fär-mə-sū'tik (or -kū'tik)/ or **pharmaceutical** /-əl/ *adj* relating to the knowledge or art of preparing medicines. [Gr *pharmakeutikos*]
■ **pharmaceu'tical** *n* a chemical used in medicine. **pharmaceu'tically** *adv*. **pharmaceu'tics** *n sing* the science of preparing medicines. **pharmaceu'tist** *n*.

pharmacist see under **pharmacy**.

pharmaco- /fär-mə-kō-/ *combining form* indicating drugs. [Gr *pharmakon* a drug]
■ **pharmacodynam'ics** *n sing* the science of the action of drugs on the body. **pharmacogenom'ics** or **pharmacogenet'ics** *n sing* the study of the effect of an individual's genetic constitution on the body's response to drugs. **pharmacog'nosist** *n*. **pharmacognos'tic** *adj*. **pharmacog'nosy** *n* the study of drugs of plant origin. **pharmacokinet'ic** *adj*. **pharmacokinet'icist** *n*. **pharmacokinet'ics** *n sing* the study of the way the body deals with drugs. **pharmacol'ogical** *adj*. **pharmacol'ogically** *adv*. **pharmacol'ogist** *n*. **pharmacol'ogy** *n* the science of drugs. **pharmacop'olist** *n* (Gr *pōleein* to sell) a dealer in drugs. **pharmacother'apy** *n* treatment by drugs.

pharmacopoeia /fär-mə-kə-pē', -pey'ə or -pē'(y)ə/ *n* a book or list of drugs with directions for their preparation and details of their uses, side-effects and recommended dosages; a collection of drugs. [Gr *pharmakopoiiā*, from *pharmakon* a drug, and *poieein* to make]
■ **pharmacopoe'ial** *adj*. **pharmacopoe'ian** *adj*.

pharmacopolist, pharmacotherapy see under **pharmaco-**.

pharmacy /fär'mə-si/ *n* the art, practice or science of collecting, preparing, preserving, and dispensing medicines; a druggist's shop; a dispensary. [Gr *pharmakeiā* use of drugs, *pharmakon* a drug]
■ **phar'macist** /-sist/ *n* a druggist, a person skilled in pharmacy; someone legally qualified to sell drugs and poisons.

pharming[1] /fär'ming/ *n* the commercial production of substances from transgenic plants or animals for medical use. [Formed from **pharmaceutical** and **farming**]
■ **pharm** *vt* and *vi* (back-formation).

pharming[2] /fär'ming/ (*comput*) *n* the covert redirection of computer users from legitimate websites to counterfeit sites in order to gain confidential information about them. [By analogy with **phishing**]
■ **pharm** *vi* (back-formation).

pharos /fā'ros/ *n* a lighthouse or beacon. [From the famous lighthouse on the island of *Pharos* in the Bay of Alexandria]

pharynx /far'ingks/ (*anat*) *n* (*pl* **phar'ynges** /-in-jēz/ or **phar'ynxes**) the cleft or cavity forming the upper part of the gullet, lying behind the nose, mouth, and larynx. [Gr *pharynx, -ygos*, later *-yngos*]
■ **pharyngal** /fa-ring'gl/ or **pharyngeal** /fa-rin'ji-əl or -jē'əl/ *adj*. **pharyngitic** /far-in-jit'ik/ *adj* relating to pharyngitis. **pharyngitis** /far-in-jī'tis/ *n* inflammation of the mucous membrane of the pharynx. **pharyn'gology** *n* the study of the pharynx and its diseases. **pharyngoscope** /fa-ring'gə-skōp/ *n* an instrument for inspecting the pharynx. **pharyngoscopy** /far-ing-gos'kə-pi/ *n*. **pharyngot'omy** *n* the operation of making an incision into the pharynx.

phase[1] /fāz/ *n* (also **phasis** /fā'sis/) a stage in growth or development (*lit* and *fig*); the aspect or appearance of anything at any stage; the stage of advancement in a periodic change, measured from some standard point; the appearance at a given time of the illuminated surface exhibited by the moon or a planet; a homogenous part of a chemical system separated from other parts by distinct boundaries (*chem*); the sum of all those portions of a material system which are identical in chemical composition and physical state (*chem*); the particular state of a substance, as a solid, liquid, or gas (*chem*); a morph (*zool*); one of the circuits in an electrical system in which there are two or more alternating currents out of phase with each other by equal amounts (*elec*). ◆ *vt* to do by phases or stages. [Gr *phasis*, from *phaein* to shine]
■ **phased** *adj* adjusted to be in the same phase at the same time; by stages. **phase'less** *adj* unchanging. **phā'sic** (or /-sik/) *adj*. **phā'sing** *n*

a technique used to achieve a distorted sound from electronic instruments by introducing a phase shift in one copy of the sound signal and recombining this with the original.
❑ **phase-contrast** (or **phase-difference**) **microscope** *n* one in which phase differences due to the refractive index of cellular components are converted to differences of light intensity, of particular value in examining living unstained cells. **phase modulation** *n* the varying of the phase of a radiowave used as a technique for transmitting information.
■ **in** (or **out of**) **phase** in the same phase together (or in different phases). **phase in** (or **out**) to begin (or cease) gradually to use or make, etc. **primary phase** crude technical raw material.

phase[2] same as **faze**.

phaseolin /fə-sē'ə-lin/ *n* a protein found in kidney beans used to increase the protein content and nutritional value of other crops. [L *phaseolus* a kidney bean]

phasic, phasis[1] see **phase**[1].

phasis[2] see under **phatic**.

Phasma /faz'mə/ *n* the spectre insect (stick insect and leaf insect) genus. [Gr *phasma* a spectre]
■ **phas'mid** *n* a member of the **Phas'midae** or **Phasmat'idae**, the family to which the genus *Phasma* belongs, or of the (sub)order **Phasmatō'dea**.

phat /fat/ (*sl*) *adj* fine, excellent (*esp* of music); (of a woman) sexy. [Origin uncertain]

phatic /fat'ik/ *adj* using speech for social reasons, to communicate feelings rather than ideas. [Gr *phasis* utterance]
■ **phasis** /fā'sis/ *n*.

PHB *abbrev*: polyhydroxybutyrate.

PhD *abbrev*: *Philosophiae Doctor* (L), Doctor of Philosophy.

pheasant /fez'nt/ *n* (*pl* **pheasant** or **pheasants**) a richly-coloured, long-tailed (in the male form), gallinaceous bird (*Phasianus colchicus*), a half-wild game bird in Britain; extended to others of the same or related genus (such as *golden, silver, Argus*, or *Amherst's pheasant*) and to other birds; the tufted grouse (*US*); a francolin (*S Afr*); the lyrebird (*Aust*); also the coucal (*swamp pheasant*); the flesh of any of these birds as food. [Anglo-Fr *fesant*, from L *phāsiānus*, from Gr *phāsiānos* (*ornis*) (bird) from the river Phasis, in Colchis (ancient Asia)]
■ **pheas'antry** *n* an enclosure for rearing pheasants.
❑ **pheas'ant's-eye** *n* a ranunculaceous plant (genus *Adonis*) with deep-red dark-centred flowers.

pheazar /fē'zər/ (*Shakesp*) *n* perh one who feezes, *perh* for **vizier**.

pheer, pheere same as **fere**[1].

pheeze, pheese see **faze**.

phellem /fel'əm/ (*bot*) *n* cork. [Gr *phellos* cork]
■ **phell'oderm** *n* (Gr *derma* skin) a layer of secondary cortex formed by the phellogen on its inner side. **phellogen** /fel'ō-jen/ *n* a layer of meristem that forms cork on the outside, otherwise known as cork cambium. **phellogenetic** /-ji-net'ik/ *adj*. **phell'oid** *adj* cork-like and formed like cork, but not (or very slightly) suberized. **phelloplas'tic** *n* a model in cork. **phelloplas'tics** *n sing* the making of models in cork.

phelonion or **phaelonion** /fi-lō'ni-on/ *n* an Eastern vestment like a chasuble. [Late Gr *phailonion, phelonion*, dimin of *phailonēs*, *phelonēs*, for *phainolēs*, from L *paenula* a cloak]

phen- /fēn-/ or **pheno-** /fē-nō-/ *combining form* denoting: showing; visible; related to benzene (see **phene**). [Gr *phainein* to show]

phenacetin /fi-nas'i-tin/ *n* a drug, $C_{10}H_{13}NO_2$, formerly used as an antipyretic. [**acetic** and **phene**]

phenacite /fen'ə-sīt/ or **phenakite** /-kīt/ *n* a mineral, beryllium silicate, sometimes deceptively like quartz. [Gr *phenax* and *phenākistēs* a deceiver, and *skopeein* to look at]
■ **phen'akism** *n* deceit. **phenakist'oscope** *n* an instrument in which figures on a disc seen successively through a slit give the impression of motion.

phenanthrene /fi-nan'thrēn/ *n* a crystalline hydrocarbon ($C_{14}H_{10}$) found in coal tar and used in dyestuffs, explosives and drugs. [**phen-** and **anthracene**]

phenate see under **phene**.

phencyclidine /fen-sī'kli-dēn/ *n* an analgesic and anaesthetic drug, $C_{17}H_{25}N.HCl$, no longer in clinical use, but abused as a hallucinogen (*abbrev* **PCP**; also called (*inf*) **angel dust**). [**phen-**, *cyclo-*, and *piperidine*]

phene /fēn/ *n* an old name for benzene. [Gr *phainein* to show, because obtained in the manufacture of illuminating gas]
■ **phēn'ate** *n* a phenolate. **phēn'ic** (or /fen'/) *adj* of benzene or of phenyl.

phenetics /fi-net'iks/ (*biol*) *n sing* a system of classification of organisms based on observable similarities and differences irrespective of whether or not the organisms are related. [*phenotype* and *genetics*]
■ **phenet'ic** *adj*.

phengite /fen'jīt/, also **phengites** /-jī'tēz/ *n* a transparent stone used in ancient times for windows, *prob* selenite; sometimes applied to kinds of mica. [Gr *phengītēs*, from *phengos* light]

phengophobia /fen-gō-fō'bi-ə/ *n* fear of or aversion to daylight, photophobia. [Gr *phainein* to show, and **phobia**]

phenic see under **phene**.

Phenician same as **Phoenician**.

pheno- see **phen-**.

phenobarbitone /fē-nō-bär'bi-tōn/ *n* a sedative and hypnotic drug used to treat epilepsy (also (chiefly *US*) **phenobar'bital**).

phenocopy /fē'nō-kop-i/ *n* a copy of a genetic abnormality that is produced by the environment and cannot be inherited. [Gr *phanein* to show, and **copy**]

phenocryst /fē'nō-krist/ *n* a larger crystal in a porphyritic rock. [Gr *phainein* to show, and **crystal**]

phenogam, etc see **phaenogam**.

phenol /fē'nol/ *n* carbolic acid, a weak acid, C_6H_5OH, produced as hygroscopic needles from coal tar, a powerful disinfectant; extended to the class of aromatic compounds with one or more hydroxyl groups directly attached to the benzene nucleus, weak acids with reactions of alcohols. [See **phene**; **-ol[1]**]
■ **phēn'olate** *n* a salt of a phenol. **phenol'ic** *adj*. **phenolphthalein** /fē-nol-fthal'i-in or -thal'/ *n* a substance ($C_{20}H_{14}O_4$) derived from phenol and phthalic anhydride, brilliant red in alkalis, colourless in acids, used as an indicator. ❑ **phenolic resins** *n pl* a group of plastics made from a phenol and an aldehyde. **phenol red** *n* a red dye used to indicate pH and to test kidney function.

phenology or **phaenology** /fē-nol'ə-ji/ *n* the study of organisms as affected by climate, *esp* dates of seasonal phenomena, such as opening of flowers or arrival of migrants. [Gr *phainein* to show, and *logos* discourse]
■ **phenological** /-ə-loj'/ *adj*. **phenol'ogist** *n*.

phenolphthalein see under **phenol**.

phenom /fē-nom'/ (*sl*) *n* someone or something phenomenally good.

phenome /fē'nōm/ (*genetics*) *n* the complete set of phenotypes of an individual or group. [Modelled on **genome**]

phenomenon or now rarely **phaenomenon** /fi-nom'i-nən or -non/ *n* (*pl* **phenom'ena**, sometimes used as *sing* in non-standard English) anything directly apprehended by the senses or one of them; an event that may be observed; the appearance which anything makes to our consciousness, as distinguished from what it is in itself (*philos*); a feature of life, social existence, etc; (loosely) a remarkable or unusual person, thing, or appearance, a prodigy. [Gr *phainomenon*, pl -*a*, neuter prp passive of *phainein* to show]
■ **phenom'enal** *adj* very or unexpectedly large, good, etc; remarkable; relating to a phenomenon; of the nature of a phenomenon. **phenom'enalism** *n* the philosophical doctrine that phenomena are the only realities, or that knowledge can only comprehend phenomena (also called **externalism**). **phenom'enalist** *n*. **phenomenalist'ic** *adj*. **phenomenality** /-al'i-ti/ *n* the character of being phenomenal. **phenom'enalize** or **-ise** *vt* to represent as a phenomenon. **phenom'enally** *adv*. **phenom'enism** *n* phenomenalism. **phenom'enist** *n*. **phenom'enize** or **-ise** *vt* to bring into the world of experience. **phenomenolog'ical** *adj*. **phenomenol'ogist** *n*. **phenomenol'ogy** *n* the science of or a description of phenomena; the philosophy of Edmund Husserl (1859–1938), opposed to positivism, and concerned with describing personal experiences without seeking to arrive at metaphysical explanations of them.

phenothiazine /fē-nō-thī'ə-zēn or fen-ō-/ *n* a toxic, heterocyclic compound, $C_{12}H_9NS$, used as a veterinary anthelmintic; any of a number of derivatives of this, used as tranquillizers. [**pheno-**, **thio-**, **azo-** and *-ine*]

phenotype /fē'nō-tīp/ *n* the observable characteristics of an organism produced by the interaction of genes and environment; a group of individuals having the same characteristics of this kind. ◆ *vt* to categorize by phenotype. [Gr *phainein* to show, and **type**]
■ **phenotypic** or **phenotypical** /-tip'/ *adj*.

phentermine /fen'tər-mēn/ *n* an appetite-suppressing drug used (*esp* formerly) in treating obesity. [*phenyl*, *tertiary* and *butyla*mine]

phenyl /fē'nil/ *n* an organic radical, C_6H_5, found in benzene, phenol, etc. [**phene**, and Gr *hylē* material]
■ **phenyl'ic** *adj*.

❑ **phenylal'anin** or **phenylal'anine** *n* an essential amino acid present in most proteins. **phenylbutazone** /-būt'ə-zōn/ *n* an analgesic and antipyretic formerly used in the treatment of rheumatic disorders, also illegally used in horse-doping (also *inf* **bute**). **phenylethylamine** /-eth'il-ə-mēn/ *n* a compound related to amphetamine, found in the brain and in substances such as chocolate, that acts as a neurotransmitter. **phenylketonuria** /-kē-tō-nū'ri-ə/ *n* an inherited metabolic disorder in infants in which there is an inability to break down phenylalanine, later resulting in mental defect, unless a phenylalanine-free diet is given. **phenylketonū'ric** *n* a person who suffers from phenylketonuria (also *adj*). **phenylthiocar'bamide** *n* a crystalline compound used to test for the presence of a certain dominant gene (the compound tasting bitter to those who possess the gene).

pheon /fē'on/ (*heraldry*) *n* the barbed head of a dart or arrow, *esp* as a heraldic bearing. [Ety dubious]

Pherecratic /fer-e-krat'ik/ or **Pherecratean** /-krə-tē'ən/ *adj* of the Greek poet *Pherecratēs*. ◆ *n* a metre used by him, spondee, dactyl, spondee, with variations.

pheromone /fer'ə-mōn/ *n* a chemical substance secreted by an animal which influences the behaviour of others of its species, eg that secreted by the queen bee. [Gr *pherein* to bear, and **hormone**]
■ **pheromō'nal** *adj*.

phese see **faze**.

phew /fū/ *interj* an exclamation of relief, astonishment, petty vexation, unexpected difficulty, impatience, contempt, etc. [A half-formed whistle]

PHI *abbrev*: permanent health insurance.

phi /fī or fē/ *n* the twenty-first letter (Φ, φ) of the Greek alphabet, *orig* as aspirated *p* (as in *upheave*), now pronounced as *f* and transliterated *ph*; as a Greek numeral φ' = 500, ͵φ = 500 000. [Gr *phei*]

phial /fī'əl/ *n* a container for liquids, *esp* now a small bottle, *usu* for medicine. ◆ *vt* (**phi'alling**; **phi'alled**) to put or keep in a phial. [L *phiala*, from Gr *phialē* a broad shallow bowl]
■ **phi'aliform** *adj* saucer-shaped.

Phi Beta Kappa /fī' (or fē') bē'tə (or bā'tə) kap'ə/ *n* the oldest of the American college societies, membership of which is conferred on those of high academic distinction; a member of this society. [Gr Φ.Β.Κ., the initial letters of its motto, from *Philosophiā biou kybernētēs* Philosophy is the guide of life]

Phil *abbrev*: Philadelphia (US city); (the Letter to the) Philippians (*Bible*); philological; philology; philosophical; philosophy.

phil- /fil-/ or **philo-** /fil-ō-/ *combining form* denoting: loving; lover. [Gr *philos* friend, from *phileein* to love]
■ **-phil** /-fil/ or **-phile** /-fīl/ *sfx* lover of; loving. **-philia** or **-phily** *sfx* love of. **-philiac** or **-philic** (also, as *n sfx* lover of) or **-philous** *sfx* loving. **-philus** *sfx* (in biological names) lover of (*usu* a specified food).

philabeg see **filibeg**.

Philadelphian /fil-ə-del'fi-ən/ *adj* of the US city of Philadelphia, Pennsylvania; of a mystic sect emphasizing brotherly love, founded in London in 1652 under the influence of Jakob Böhme; of the ancient Greek city of Philadelphia or Philadelpheia (now Ala-shehr in modern Turkey). ◆ *n* a native or inhabitant of Philadelphia; a member of the Philadelphian sect. [**phil-**, and Gr *adelphos* a brother, *adelphē* a sister]
❑ **Philadelphia chromosome** *n* an abnormal small chromosome found in patients suffering from a certain form of leukaemia. **Philadelphia lawyer** *n* a very able, shrewd, or sharp lawyer.

Philadelphus /fil-ə-del'fəs/ *n* a genus of tall deciduous shrubs with showy flowers (family **Philadelphā'ceae**); (without *cap*) any shrub of this genus, *esp* the mock orange. [New L, from Gr *philadelphon* loving one's brother]

philamot see **filemot**.

philander /fi-lan'dər/ *vi* to womanize; to flirt or have casual affairs with women; to make love. ◆ *n* (with *cap*) a proper name for a lover in Greek literature; a lover; a man who seeks the company of women, or who follows women around; a male flirt; a philandering. [Gr *philandros* fond of men or of a husband, from *anēr*, *andros* a man, husband; misapplied as if meaning a loving man]
■ **philan'derer** *n* a man who enjoys and often has a reputation for philandering.

philanthropy /fi-lan'thrə-pi/ *n* love of mankind *esp* as shown by contributing (money, time, etc) to general welfare. [**phil-** and Gr *anthrōpos* a man]
■ **philanthrope** /fil'ən-thrōp/ or *usu* **philan'thropist** *n* someone who tries to benefit mankind. **philanthropic** /-throp'ik/ or **philanthrop'ical** *adj* doing good to others, benevolent. **philanthrop'ically** *adv*.

philately /fil-at'i-li/ *n* the study and collection of postage and revenue stamps, related labels, etc; stamp-collecting. [Fr *philatélie*, invented in 1864, from Gr *atelēs* tax-free, from *a-* (privative) and *telos* tax]

■ **philatelic** /fil-ə-tel'ik/ *adj.* **philat'elist** *n.*

-phile see under **phil-**.

Philem. (*Bible*) *abbrev*: (the Letter to) Philemon.

philharmonic /fil-är-mon'ik/, also *-här-* or *-ər-/ adj* fond of music. [**phil-**, and Gr *harmoniä* harmony]
□ **philharmonic pitch** *n* a musical pitch slightly higher than French pitch (439 vibrations a second for A).

philhellenic /fil-he-le'nik/ or *-len'ik/ adj* loving or having an enthusiasm for Greece, *esp* Greek culture; favouring the Greeks. [**phil-**, and Gr *Hellēn* a Greek]
■ **philhellene** /-hel'ēn/ or **philhellenist** /-hel'in-ist/ *n* a supporter of Greece, *esp* in the Greek War of Independence of 1821–32. **philhell'enism** *n.*

philhorse or **pilhorse** /fil'hörs or pil'hörs/ (*Shakesp*) *n* same as **fill-horse** (see under **fill**[2]) or **thill-horse** (see under **thill**[2]).

-philia, -philiac see under **phil-**.

philibeg same as **filibeg**.

-philic see under **phil-**.

Philippian /fi-lip'i-ən/ *n* a native of *Philippi* in Macedonia. ◆ *adj* relating to *Philippi* or its inhabitants.

Philippic /fi-lip'ik/ *n* one of the three orations of Demosthenes against Philip of Macedon; (without *cap*) any discourse full of invective. [Gr *philippikos, philippizein,* from *Philippos* Philip]
■ **Phil'ippize** or **-ise** *vi* to side with Philip; to utter an oracle inspired by Philip, or by bribery of the prevailing power.

philippina, philippine same as **philopena**.

Philippine /fil'i-pēn/ *adj* of or relating to the *Philippines* (see also **Filipino**).

Philistine /fil'i-stīn or (*US*) fil-is'tīn/ *n* in ancient times one of the inhabitants of SW Palestine, enemies of the Israelites; (also without *cap*) a person of material outlook, *usu* indifferent or hostile to culture; a name applied by German students to anyone not connected with the university (also **Philis'ter**; *Ger*); (without *cap*) an enemy (*sl*); (without *cap*) a bailiff (*sl*). [Gr *Philistinos, Palaistinos,* from Heb *P'lishtīm*]
■ **Philistē'an, Philis'tian** (both *Milton*) or **Phil'istine** *adj.* **phil'istine** *adj* (of a person) material in outlook, uncultured. **Phil'istinism** *n* (sometimes without *cap*). **Phil'istinize** or **-ise** /-tin-/ *vt.*

phillabeg, phillibeg same as **filibeg**.

Phillips curve /fil'ips kûrv/ (*econ*) *n* a curve joining the points on a graph which shows the relationship between the rate of inflation and the rate of unemployment. [AWH *Phillips* (1914–75), New Zealand economist]

phillipsite /fil'ip-sīt/ (*mineralogy*) *n* a zeolite, hydrated silicate of potassium, calcium, and aluminium, often cross-shaped by twinning. [W *Phillips* (1775–1828), English mineralogist]

Phillips screw® /fil'ips skroo/ *n* a type of screw with a recessed cross in the head designed to receive the protuberant cross-shaped tip of a **Phillips screwdriver**®. [*Phillips Screws*, original US manufacturing company]

phillumeny /fi-loo'mə-ni/ *n* the collecting of matchbox labels. [L *lūmen, -inis* light]
■ **phillu'menist** *n.*

Phillyrea /fi-lir'i-ə/ *n* the mock privet genus, Mediterranean shrubs related to olive and privet. [Gr *philyreā*]

philo- see **phil-**.

Philodendron /fil-ō-den'dron/ *n* a genus of tropical American climbing plants; (without *cap*) a plant of this genus. [Gr *philodendros* fond of trees]

philogyny /fi-loj'i-ni/ *n* love of women. [Gr *philogyniä,* from *gynē* a woman]
■ **philog'ynist** *n.* **philog'ynous** *adj.*

philology /fi-lol'ə-ji/ *n* the science of language, *esp* of its historical development, historical linguistics; the study of ancient literary and non-literary texts; the study of culture through ancient texts; *orig* the knowledge which enabled scholars to study and explain the languages of Greece and Rome. [Gr *philologiä,* from **phil-** and *logos* word]
■ **philol'oger, philologian** /-ə-lō'-/, **philol'ogist** or **phil'ologue** /-log/ *n* a person who studies or has knowledge of philology. **philologic** /-ə-loj'ik/ or **philolog'ical** *adj.* **philolog'ically** *adv.*
■ **comparative philology** the study of languages by comparing their history, forms, and relationships with each other.

Philomel /fil'ō-mel/ or **Philomela** /-mē'lə/ *n* the nightingale personified in Greek mythology (also (*obs*) **Phil'omene** /-mēn/).

[Gr *Philomēla,* daughter of Pandion, changed into a nightingale or swallow]

philomot see **filemot**.

philopena, philopoena or **philippina** /fi-li-pē'nə/ or **philippine** /fil'i-pēn/ *n* a game in which each of two people eats a twin kernel of a nut, and one pays a forfeit to the other on certain conditions; the nut itself; the gift made as a forfeit. [Appar from the Ger formula of claiming the gift, *Guten Morgen, Vielliebchen,* Good morning, well-beloved, confused with Gr *philos* friend, *poinē* penalty, and with Ger *Philippchen* little]

philoprogenitive /fil-ō-prō-jen'i-tiv/ *adj* having or relating to instinctive love of offspring; inclined to produce offspring. [**philo-**, and L *progeniēs* progeny]
■ **philoprogen'itiveness** *n.*

philosopher /fi-los'ə-fər/ *n* a lover of wisdom; a person who studies or is versed in or devoted to philosophy; formerly, a person who studies natural science or the occult; now mainly a metaphysician; someone who acts calmly and rationally in changing or trying situations. [Gr *philosophos,* from *sophiä* wisdom]
■ **philosophas'ter** *n* (see **-aster**) a superficial philosopher; someone who poses as a philosopher. **phil'osophe** /-sof, -zof or -zof'/ *n* a philosopher; a thinker of the type of the French Encyclopedists. **philos'opheress** or **philos'ophess** *n* (both *rare*). **philosophic** /-sof'/ or *-zof'/* or *usu* **philosophic'ical** *adj* relating or according to philosophy; skilled in or given to philosophy; befitting a philosopher; adopting or ready to adopt a rational approach, *esp* calmly uncomplaining in defeat or difficulty. **philosoph'ically** *adv.* **philos'ophism** *n* would-be philosophy. **philos'ophist** *n.* **philosophist'ic** or **philosophist'ical** *adj.* **philos'ophize** or **-ise** *vi* to reason like a philosopher; to form philosophical theories. ◆ *vt* to explain philosophically. **philos'ophizer** or **-s-** *n* a would-be philosopher. **philos'ophy** *n orig* the pursuit of wisdom and knowledge; investigation or contemplation of the nature of being; knowledge of the causes and laws of all things; the principles underlying any sphere of knowledge; reasoning; a particular philosophical system; calmness of temper, stoicism.
□ **philosopher's stone** *n* an imaginary stone or mineral compound, long sought after by alchemists as a means of transforming other metals into gold. **philosophical pitch** *n* a pitch used in acoustical calculations based on 512 vibrations for treble C.
■ **moral** and **natural philosophy** see under **moral** and **natural**.

-philous see under **phil-**.

philoxenia /fil-ok-sē'ni-ə/ *n* hospitality. [Gr, from *xenos* guest, stranger]

philtre or **philter** /fil'tər/ *n* a drink (or sometimes a spell) to excite love. [Fr *philtre,* from L *philtrum,* from Gr *philtron,* from *phileein* to love, and *-tron,* agent sfx]

philtrum /fil'trəm/ *n* the hollow that runs from the base of the nose to the upper lip. [Gr *philtron* love charm, dimple]

-philus, -phily see under **phil-**.

phimosis /fī-mō'sis/ (*med*) *n* narrowness or constriction of the foreskin, which prevents it from being drawn back over the glans penis. [Gr *phīmōsis* muzzling, from *phīmos* a muzzle]

phinnock same as **finnock**.

phishing /fish'ing/ (*comput*) *n* the practice of sending counterfeit email messages in an attempt to get the recipients to divulge confidential information, eg details of bank accounts. [Altered form of **fishing**]

phisnomy /fiz'nə-mi/ *n* an old form of **physiognomy**, in the sense of the face.

phiz /fiz/ or **phizog** /fiz-og'/ (*sl*) *n* the face. [**physiognomy**]

phlebitis /fli-bī'tis/ *n* inflammation of the wall of a vein. [Gr *phleps, phlebos* a vein]
■ **phlebog'raphy** same as **venography** (see under **vena**). **phlebolite** /fleb'ə-līt/ *n* (Gr *lithos* stone) a calcareous concretion found in a vein. **phlebot'omist** *n* a bloodletter; a technician trained to take blood for testing. **phlebot'omize** or **-ise** *vt* (Gr *tomē* a cut) to bleed; to perform phlebotomy on (a patient). **phlebot'omy** *n* bloodletting; surgical incision into a vein.

Phlegethontic /fleg-i-thon'tik/ *adj* of or like the *Phlegethon,* a fiery river of Hades. [Gr *phlegethōn, -ontos,* prp of *phlegethein,* from *phlegein* to burn]

phlegm /flem/ *n* the thick, slimy matter secreted by the mucous membrane of the respiratory organs, and discharged by coughing, regarded in old physiology as one (cold and moist) of the four humours or bodily fluids; the temperament supposed to be due to the predominance of this humour, sluggish indifference; calmness; one of the principles of old chemistry, a watery distilled liquid. [By later return to Greek spelling, from ME *fleem, fleme, flemme,* from OFr *flemme, fleume,* from L *phlegma,* from Gr *phlegma, -atos* flame, inflammation, phlegm (regarded as produced by heat), *phlegmasiä,* *phlegmonē* inflammation, from *phlegein* to burn] The following words are pronounced /*fleg*-/ unless indicated otherwise:

■ **phlegmagogic** /-*mä-goj'ik* or -*mä-gog'ik*/ *adj*. **phleg'magogue** /-*mä-gog*/ *n* a medicine expelling phlegm. **phlegmā'sia** *n* inflammation, *esp Phlegmasia alba dolens* white-leg. **phlegmat'ic** or **phlegmat'ical** *adj* generating, or having a great deal of, phlegm; of a calm, unemotional, unexcitable disposition. **phlegmat'ically** *adv*. **phleg'mon** *n* purulent inflammation. **phlegmon'ic**, **phleg'monoid** or **phleg'monous** *adj*. **phlegmy** /*flem'i*/ *adj*.

Phleum /*flē'əm*/ *n* a small genus of grasses, timothy grass. [Gr *phleōs* plume-grass]

phloem /*flō'əm*/ (*bot*) *n* a type of tissue in plants responsible for transporting metabolites, especially sugars. [Gr *phloos* bark]

phlogiston /*flo-jis'ton*, -*gis'ton* or -*tən*/ *n* an imaginary element, believed in the 18c to separate from every combustible body in burning. [Gr neuter of verbal *adj phlogistos* burnt, inflammable, from *phlogizein* to set on fire]

■ **phlogis'tic** *adj* of, like, or containing phlogiston (*chem*); combustible (*archaic*); inflammatory (*med*); fiery. **phlogis'ticate** *vt* to combine with phlogiston.

phlogopite /*flog'ə-pīt*/ *n* a magnesia mica, yellow or brown in colour. [Gr *phlogōpos* fiery-looking, from *phlox* flame, and *ōps* face]

Phlomis /*flō'mis*/ *n* a genus of labiate herbs and shrubs with whorls of white, yellow or purple flowers and wrinkled, often woolly, leaves; (without *cap*) a plant of this genus. [Gr *phlomis* mullein]

Phlox /*floks*/ *n* a Siberian and American genus of the Polemoniaceae family, well-known garden plants; (without *cap*; *pl* **phlox** or **phlox'es**) a plant of this genus, with clusters of white, red or bluish-purple flowers. [Gr *phlox* flame, wallflower, from *phlegein* to burn]

PHLS *abbrev* : Public Health Laboratory Service.

phlyctaena or **phlyctena** /*flik-tē'nə*/ (*med*) *n* (*pl* **phlyctae'nae** or **phlycte'nae** /-*nē*/) a small blister or vesicle. [Gr *phlyktaina* a blister, from *phlyein* to swell]

pho¹ /*fō*/ *n* (*pl* **phos**) a Vietnamese noodle soup. [Viet; perh a corruption of Fr *feu* fire]

pho² same as **foh**.

phobia /*fō'bi-ə*/ or (*rare*) **phobism** /*fō'bi-zm*/ *n* a fear, aversion or hatred, *esp* a morbid and irrational one. ◆ *combining form* denoting a fear or hatred of (a specified object, condition, etc). [Gr *phobos* fear]

■ **-phobe** *combining form* denoting someone who has a (specified) phobia. **phō'bic** *adj* like or relating to a phobia; suffering from a (specified) phobia. ◆ *n* someone afflicted with a phobia. **phō'bist** *n*.

Phoca /*fō'kə*/ *n* the common seal genus; (without *cap*; *pl* **pho'cas** or **pho'cae** /-*sē*/) a seal; (without *cap*) a scaly sea monster (*Spenser*). [L *phōca*, from Gr *phōkē* a seal]

■ **Phocidae** /*fō'si-dē*/ *n pl* the true seals, with backward-turned hind-flippers and no external ear. **pho'cine** /*fō'sīn*/ *adj* relating to seals; seal-like.

Phocaena /*fō-sē'nə*/ *n* the porpoise genus. [Gr *phōkaina*]

phocomelia /*fō-kō-mēl'i-ə*, -*mel'*/ or -*yə*/ *n* the condition of having one or more limbs like a seal's flippers, shortened and close to the body. [Gr *phōkē* seal, and *melos* limb]

phoebe /*fē'bi*/ *n* a N American flycatcher of the genus *Sayornis*. [Imit]

Phoebus /*fē'bəs*/ *n* Apollo, the Greek sun-god (*Gr myth*); the sun. [Latinized, from Gr *Phoibos, Phoibē; phoibos, -ē* bright, *phaein* to shine]

■ **Phoebe** /*fē'bē*/ *n* Apollo's sister Artemis, the moon goddess (*Gr myth*); the moon. **Phoebe'an** *adj*.

Phoenician /*fi-nish'ən* or -*yən*/ *adj* of ancient *Phoenicia*, on the coast of Syria, its people, colonies (including Carthage), language, and arts. ◆ *n* one of the people of Phoenicia; their Semitic language. [Gr *Phoinix, -īkos*]

phoenix /*fē'niks*/ *n* a legendary Arabian bird, worshipped in ancient Egypt, the only individual of its kind, that burned itself every 500 years or so and rose rejuvenated from its ashes; hence anything that rises from its own or its predecessor's ashes; a paragon; a southern constellation. [OE *fenix*, later assimilated to L *phoenīx*, from Gr *phoinix*]

■ **phoen'ixism** *n* (*stock exchange*) the practice of forming, *usu* with the same directors, workforce, premises, etc of a bankrupted company, a new company that is therefore able to continue the same trading debt-free.

phoh same as **foh**.

Pholas /*fō'ləs*/ *n* the piddock genus of rock-boring molluscs; (without *cap*; *pl* **pholades** /*fō'lə-dēz*/) a mollusc of this genus. [Gr *phōlas, -ados*, (adj) lurking in a hole, (noun) the date-shell]

pholidosis /*fo-li-dō'sis*/ (*zool*) *n* arrangement of scales, as in fishes and reptiles. [Gr *pholis, -idos* scale]

phon /*fon*/ *n* (*acoustics*) a unit of loudness, the number of phons of a particular sound being equal to the number of decibels of a pure tone (with a frequency of 1000 hertz) judged, or proved by measurement, to be of the same loudness. ◆ *combining form* /*fōn*-/ sound, voice. [From Gr *phōnē* sound]

■ **phonal** /*fōn'l*/ *adj* vocal. **phonasthenia** /*fō-nas-thē'ni-ə*/ *n* (Gr *astheneia* weakness) weakness of voice; difficulty in speaking. **phonautograph** /*fon-ö'tə-gräf*/ *n* an instrument for recording sound vibrations. **phonautographic** /-*graf'ik*/ *adj*. **phonautograph'ically** *adv*. **phonmeter** /*fon'mē-tər*/ or **phonometer** /*fə-nom'i-tər*/ *n* (Gr *metron* measure) an apparatus for estimating loudness levels in phons. **pho'non** *n* (*phys*) a quantum of vibrational energy in a crystal lattice, induced by heat.

phonate /*fə-, fō-* or *fo-nāt'*/ *vi* to utter vocal sound or sounds. [From Gr *phōnē* sound]

■ **phōnā'tion** *n* production of vocal sound. **phōn'atory** (or /*fō-nā'tər-i*/) *adj*.

phonautograph, etc see under **phon**.

phone¹ or **'phone** /*fōn*/ *n* short for **telephone**; (in *pl*) headphones (*inf*). ◆ *vt* and *vi* to telephone.

■ **phō'ner** *n* a person who telephones.

□ **phone call** *n*. **phone'card** *n* a card, bought from newsagents, tobacconists, post offices, etc, which can be used instead of cash to pay for phone calls from appropriate public phones (also *adj*). **phone hacking** *n* the practice of gaining unauthorized access to information stored on another person's phone. **phone'-in** *n* a radio or television programme in which phone calls are invited from listeners or viewers and are broadcast live, with discussion by an expert or panel, etc, in the studio. **phoner-in'** *n*. **phone sex** *n* the act of having a sexually explicit conversation by telephone; the provision of such conversation as a commercial service.

phone² /*fōn*/ (*phonetics*) *n* a single elementary speech sound. [Gr *phōnē* sound]

-phone /-*fōn*/ *combining form* used to signify speaking, or someone who speaks (a given language), as in *Francophone*; used to denote an instrument producing, reproducing or transmitting sound as in *microphone*. [Gr *phōnē* voice, sound]

■ **-phonic** *adj*.

phoneme /*fō'nēm*/ (*linguistics*) *n* the smallest significant unit of sound in a language; any of the speech sounds in a language that serve to make one word different from another. [Gr *phōnēma* an utterance, sound made]

■ **phonemat'ic** *adj* phonemic. **phonemat'ically** *adv*. **phonemic** /-*nēm'* or -*nem'*/ *adj*. **phonēm'ically** *adv*. **phonēm'icist** *n*. **phonemicizā'tion** or **-s-** *n*. **phonēm'icize** or **-ise** *vt* to analyse into phonemes; to treat as a phoneme. **phonēm'ics** *n sing* the science or study of the phonemes of a language; the phonemes of a language and the patterns and structures in which they occur.

phonendoscope /*fon-en'də-skōp*/ *n* a device which amplifies small sounds (*esp* in the human body). [**phon** and Gr *endō* within, and *skopeein* to view]

phoner, etc see under **phone¹**.

phonet. *abbrev* : phonetics.

phonetic /*fə-net'ik*/ *adj* of, concerning, according to, or representing the sounds of spoken language (also **phonet'ical**). [Gr *phōnētikos* relating to speech]

■ **phonet'ically** *adv* according to pronunciation. **phonetician** /*fō-ni-tish'ən*/ *n* someone who is expert in phonetics. **phonet'icism** *n* phonetic character or representation. **phonet'icist** *n* someone who advocates phonetic spelling. **phoneticizā'tion** or **-s-** or **phonetizā'tion** or **-s-** *n*. **phonet'icize** or **-ise**, or **phon'etize** or **-ise** *vt* to make phonetic; to represent phonetically. **phonet'ics** *n sing* that branch of linguistic science that deals with pronunciation and speech production. ◆ *n pl* phonetic representations. **pho'netism** *n* phonetic writing. **pho'netist** *n* a phonetician; an advocate or user of phonetic spelling.

□ **phonetic alphabet** *n* a list of symbols used in phonetic transcriptions; a system (used in voice communications) in which letters of the alphabet are identified by means of code words. **phonetic spelling** *n* the writing of a language by means of a separate symbol for every sound; an unconventional spelling system adopted as a guide to pronunciation.

phoney or (*esp US*) **phony** /*fō'ni*/ (*inf*) *adj* counterfeit, fake; unreal. ◆ *n* someone insincere, a fraud; something not genuine, a fake. ◆ *vt* to fake, counterfeit, achieve by faking. [Origin uncertain; perh from Ir *fáinne* a ring, from the old practice of tricking people into buying gilt rings which they believed to be genuine gold]

■ **phon'eyness** or (*esp US*) **phon'iness** *n*.

phonic /*fon'ik* or *fō'nik*/ *adj* relating to sounds, *esp* vocal sound; voiced. [Gr *phōnikos* relating to speech]

■ **phon'ically** (or /fŏ'nik-/) *adv.* **phon'ics** (or /fŏn'iks/) *n sing* the science of sound, or of spoken sounds; the phonic method.
❑ **Phonic Ear**® *n* a type of radio microphone system, for the benefit of the deaf, in which the teacher wears a transmitter and the student wears a receiver, either with a built-in or an individual hearing aid. **phonic method** *n* a method of teaching reading through the phonetic value of letters or groups of letters.

phoniness see under **phoney**.

phonmeter see under **phon**.

phono- /fŏ-nō-, fŏ-no- or fŏ-nə-/ *combining form* denoting voice or sound. [Gr *phōnē* sound, voice]
■ **phonocamptic** /fŏ-nə-kamp'tik/ *adj* (Gr *kamptein* to bend; *archaic*) reflecting sound, echoing; relating to echoes. **phonocamp'tics** *n sing* the branch of acoustics dealing with echoes. **phonocar'diogram** *n* a tracing of the sounds made by the heart, recorded by **phonocar'diograph**. **phō'nofiddle** *n* a one-stringed musical instrument which emits sounds through a metal amplifying horn. **phonogram** /fŏ'nə-gram/ *n* a character representing a sound; a phonographic record. **phonograph** /fŏ'nə-gräf/ *n* (Gr *graphein* to write) a character used in writing, etc to represent a sound; Edison's instrument for recording sounds on a cylinder and reproducing them; the ordinary word for any gramophone (*old US*). **phonographer** /fŏ-nog'rə-fər/ or **phonog'raphist** *n* a writer of phonographic shorthand. **phonographic** /fŏ-nə-graf'ik/ *adj* phonetic; of phonography; of or by means of the phonograph. **phonograph'ically** *adv*. **phonog'raphy** /fŏ-nog'rə-fi/ *n* the art of representing each spoken sound by a distinct character; Pitman's phonetic shorthand; the use of the phonograph. **phonolog'ical** *adj*. **phonol'ogist** *n*. **phonology** /fŏ-nol'ə-ji/ *n* (Gr *logos* discourse) phonetics; now generally (the study of) the system of sounds in a language, and sometimes the history of their changes. **phonopho'bia** *n* a morbid fear of noise, or of speaking aloud. **phonophore** /fŏ'nə-fōr or -fōr/ or **phonopore** /fŏ'nō-pōr or -pōr/ *n* (Gr *phoros* carrying, *poros* passage) a sound-conducting apparatus, of various kinds; a device for telephoning and telegraphing simultaneously by the same wire. **phonotac'tics** *n sing* (Gr *tassein* to arrange) (the study of) the order or arrangement of sounds and groups of sounds in a particular language. **phonotype** /fŏ'nə-tīp/ *n* (Gr *typos* impression) phonetic type. ◆ *vt* to print phonetically. **phonotyp'ic** /-tīp'ik/ or **phonotyp'ical** *adj*. **phō'notypist** (or /-tīp'ist/) *n*. **phō'notypy** /-tīp-i/ *n*.

phonog. *abbrev*: phonography.

phonogram...to...**phonography** see under **phono-**.

phonolite /fŏ'nə-līt/ *n* clinkstone, a fine-grained intermediate igneous rock that rings when struck by a hammer, composed of nepheline (or leucite), sanidine, and other minerals. [Gr *phōnē* and *lithos* a stone]
■ **phonolitic** /-lit'ik/ *adj*.

phonology, etc see under **phono-**.

phonometer, **phonon** see under **phon**.

phonophobia...to...**phonotypy** see under **phono-**.

phony see **phoney**.

phooey /foo'i/ *interj* an exclamation of contempt, scorn, disbelief, etc. [Perh connected with **phew**, or a similar exclamation, or perh from Yiddish *fooy*, Ger *pfui*]

-phore or **-phor** /-fōr or -fōr/ *combining form* used to denote 'carrier', as in *semaphore* and *chromatophore*. [Gr *phoros* bearing, from *pherein*]

phorminx /för'mingks/ (*music*) *n* (*pl* **phormin'ges** /-jēz/) a kind of cithara. [Gr]

Phormium /för'mi-əm/ *n* a New Zealand genus of the lily family, New Zealand flax or flax-lily; (without *cap*) a plant of this genus. [Latinized, from Gr *phormion* mat, faggot, kind of sage]

phosgene /fos'jēn/ *n* a poisonous gas, carbonyl chloride (COCl₂), *orig* prepared by passing carbon monoxide and chlorine over a charcoal catalyst. [Gr *phōs* light, and the root of *gignesthai* to be produced]

phosphate, etc, **phosphatide**, **phosphaturia** see under **phosphorus**.

phosphene /fos'fēn/ *n* light seen when the eyeball is pressed; a luminous pattern seen when the brain is stimulated electrically. [Gr *phōs* light, and *phainein* to show]

phosphide, **phosphine**, **phosphite**, **phosphor** see under **phosphorus**.

Phosphorus /fos'f(ə-)rəs/ or **Phosphor** /fos'fər/ *n* the morning-star. [L *phōsphorus*, from Gr *phōsphoros* light-bearer, from *phōs* light, and *phoros* bearing, from *pherein* to bear]

phosphorus /fos'fə-rəs/ *n* a waxy poisonous inflammable non-metallic element (symbol **P**; atomic no 15), giving out light in the dark. [L *phōsphorus*, from Gr *phōsphoros* light-bearer, from *phōs* light, and *phoros* bearing, from *pherein* to bear]

■ **phos'phatase** *n* an enzyme that catalyses the hydrolysis of phosphate esters. **phosphate** /fos'fāt/ *n* a salt of phosphoric acid. ◆ *vt* to treat or coat with a phosphate as a means of preventing corrosion. **phosphatic** /fos-fat'ik/ *adj* of the nature of or containing a phosphate. **phos'phatide** *n* a phospholipid. **phos'phatize** or **-ise** *vt* to phosphate. **phosphaturia** /fos-fat-ū'ri-ə/ *n* excess of phosphates in the urine. **phos'phide** /-fīd/ *n* a compound of phosphorus and another element. **phos'phine** /-fēn or -fīn/ *n* phosphuretted hydrogen gas (PH₃); extended to substances analogous to amines with phosphorus instead of nitrogen. **phos'phite** *n* a salt of phosphorous acid. **phosphocreatine** /-krē'ə-tin/ *n* a compound of phosphoric acid and creatine found in muscle, where it serves to store energy. **phospholip'ase** *n* same as **lecithinase** (see under **lecithin**). **phospholip'id** *n* a lipid which contains a phosphate group and *usu* also a nitrogenous group, a component of cell membranes. **phosphon'ic acid** same as **phosphorous acid** (see **phosphorous** below). **phosphōn'ium** *n* the radical PH₄, analogous to ammonium. **phosphopro'tein** *n* a protein that has been enzymically phosphorylated so that it contains a phosphate group and is an important functional modifier. **phos'phor** *n* phosphorus; a phosphorescent or fluorescent substance generally. **phos'phorate** *vt* to combine or impregnate with phosphorus; to make phosphorescent. **phosphoresce'** *vi* to shine in the dark like phosphorus. **phosphoresc'ence** *n*. **phosphoresc'ent** *adj*. **phos'phoret** (or /-et'/) *n* (*obs*) a phosphide. **phos'phoretted** (or /-et'/) *adj* see **phosphuretted** below. **phosphoric** /fos-for'ik/ *adj* of or like phosphorus; phosphorescent; containing phosphorus in higher valency (*chem*) (**phosphoric acid** orthophosphoric, H₃PO₄, metaphosphoric, HPO₃, or pyrophosphoric, H₄P₂O₇ acid; **phosphoric anhydride** P₂O₅). **phos'phorism** *n* (*obs*) phosphorescence; poisoning by phosphorus. **phos'phorite** *n* (*mineralogy*) impure massive apatite. **phos'phorize** or **-ise** *vt* to combine or impregnate with phosphorus; to make phosphorescent. **phos'phorous** *adj* phosphorescent; containing phosphorus in lower valency (*chem*) (**phosphorous acid** H₃PO₃; **phosphorous anhydride** P₂O₃). **phosphor'ylase** *n* an enzyme playing a part in phosphorylation. **phosphor'ylate** *vt*. **phosphoryla'tion** *n* the act or process of converting a protein or sugar into a compound of phosphorus. **phosphuret** /fos'fūr-et or -et'/ *n* (*obs*) a phosphide. **phos'phuretted** (or /-et'/) *adj* combined with phosphorus (**phosphuretted** or **phosphoretted hydrogen** phosphine).
❑ **phosphor bronze** *n* an alloy of copper, tin and phosphorus. **phossy jaw** *n* necrosis of the jawbone with fatty degeneration of the kidney, common among matchmakers when yellow phosphorus was used.

phot /fot or fŏt/ *n* the CGS unit of illumination, equal to 1 lumen per square centimetre. [Gr *phōs*, *phōtos* light]

phot. or **photog.** *abbrev*: photographic; photography.

phot- see **photo-²**.

photic /fŏ'tik/ *adj* of light; light-giving; sensitive to light; accessible to light (as eg the uppermost layer of sea). [Gr *phōs*, *phōtos* light]
■ **phōt'ics** *n sing* optics.

Photinia /fŏ-tin'i-ə/ *n* a genus of evergreen or deciduous trees and shrubs of the Rosaceae family, grown for their foliage, and the deciduous varieties for autumn colour and the fruits which succeed their small white flowers; (without *cap*) a plant of the genus.

photism /fŏ'ti-zm/ *n* a hallucinatory vision of light; a visual sensation that results from the experience of hearing, feeling, tasting, smelling or thinking something. [Gr *phōs*, *photos* light]

photo /fŏ'tō/ *n* (*pl* **phō'tos**) short form of **photograph**.
❑ **photo call** *n* an arranged opportunity for press photographers to take publicity photographs of eg a celebrity. **photo CD** *n* a compact disc storing photographs for display on a computer or television screen. **photo finish** *n* a race finish in which a special type of photography is used to show the winner, etc; a neck-and-neck finish to any contest. **photo opportunity** *n* an opportunity for press photographers to get good or interesting pictures of a celebrity, either arranged by the celebrity (*esp* for publicity purposes) or arising more or less by chance during an event attended by the celebrity (short form **photo op**). **photo sharing** *n* the practice of posting digital photographs on a website so that they can viewed by other users of the site. **photo-sharing** *adj*. **photo shoot** *n* (*inf*) a session in which a photographer takes pictures of a celebrity, etc. **photo story** *n* a series of photographs used to tell a story in the manner of strip cartoons.

photo-¹ /fŏ-tō-, fŏ-to- or fŏ-tə-/ *combining form* denoting: photographic; made by, or by the aid of, photographic means; representing **photo**, or **photographic** or **photographical** (see under **photography**). [**photograph** (see under **photography**)]
■ **pho'toblog** *n* a blog in the form of a series of photographs (also *vi*). **pho'tobomb** *vi* and *vt* (*inf*) to place oneself in the background of a photograph deliberately and without the knowledge of the

photo-   1166   photo-

photographer or subject. **pho'tocomposition** *n* (*printing*) filmsetting, the setting of copy by projecting images of letters successively on a sensitive material from which printing plates are made. **photocop'iable** *adj*. **pho'tocopier** *n* a machine which makes photocopies. **pho'tocopy** *n* a photographic reproduction of written matter, etc. ◆ *vt* to make a photocopy of. **pho'tocopying** *n*. **pho'to-engraving** or **pho'to-etching** *n* any process of engraving by aid of photography, *esp* from relief plates. **pho'to-essay** *n* an extensively illustrated article or book on a particular subject. **Pho'tofit**® *n* (also without *cap*) a method of making identification pictures using photographs of facial elements, an alternative to identikit (qv); such a picture. **photogen'ic** /-jen'ik, -jē'nik/ *adj* having the quality of photographing well, appearing attractive in photographs; (loosely) attractive, striking; photographic (*obs*). **photog'eny** /-toj'i-ni/ *n* (*obs*) photography. **photogeol'ogy** *n* the study of geology by means of aerial photographs. **photoglyph** /-glif/ *n* (Gr *glyphē* carving) a photographic engraving; a photogravure. **photoglyph'ic** *adj*. **photog'lyphy** *n*. **pho'togram** *n* a photograph; a type of picture produced by placing an object on or near photographic paper which is then exposed to light. **photogrammet'ric** *adj*. **photogramm'etrist** *n*. **photogramm'etry** *n* (*image technol*) the use of photographic records for precise measurement of distances or dimensions, eg aerial photography for surveying. **photogravure** /-fō-tō-grə-vūr'/ *n* (Fr *gravure* engraving) a method of photo-engraving in which the design etched on the metal surface is intaglio, not relief; a picture produced by this method. **photojour'nalism** *n* journalism in which written material is subordinate to photographs. **photojour'nalist** *n*. **photolith'ograph** *n* and *vt*. **photolithog'rapher** *n*. **photolithograph'ic** *adj*. **photolithog'raphy** *n* a process of lithographic printing from a photographically produced plate. **photomac'rograph** *n* a photograph of an object that is unmagnified or only slightly magnified. **photomacrograph'ic** *adj*. **photomacrog'raphy** *n*. **pho'tomap** *n* a map produced from or drawn on aerial photographs. **photomechan'ical** *adj* relating to mechanical printing from a photographically prepared plate. **photomechan'ically** *adv*. **photomicrograph** /-fō-tō-mī'krə-gräf/ *n* (see **micro-** and **graph**) an enlarged photograph of a microscopic object taken through a microscope. **photomicrographer** /-krog'rə-fər/ *n*. **photomicrographic** /-krə-graf'ik/ *adj*. **photomicrog'raphy** *n*. **photomon'tage** /-täzh/ *n* (the art of compiling) a picture made by cutting up photographs, etc, and arranging the parts so as to convey, without explicitly showing, a definite meaning. **photomosa'ic** *n* a picture made from several photographs, *esp* of an area. **pho'tonovel** *n* a novel in the form of a series of photographs with speech balloons. **pho'to-process** *n* any process by which a matrix for printing is got by photographic means. **photore'alism** *n* (*art*) an *esp* detailed, precise painting style (suggestive of and often worked from a photograph), giving an effect of (often exaggerated) realism. **photorealis'tic** *adj*. **pho'to-relief** *n* a plate or image in relief got by photographic means. **pho'tosetting** *n* photocomposition. **Pho'toshop**® *n* a computer program for editing digital images. ◆ *vt* (often without *cap*) to alter a digital image using this program. **Photostat**® /fō'tō-stat/ *n* (see **-stat**) a photographic apparatus for making facsimiles of manuscripts, drawings, etc, directly; a facsimile so made. ◆ *vt* and *vi* (without *cap*) to make a photographic facsimile. **phototelegraph** /fō'tō-tel'i-gräf/ *n* an instrument for transmitting drawings, photographs, etc, by telegraphy. **phototeleg'raphy** *n* (see also under **photo-**²). **phototype** /fō'tō-tīp/ *n* (Gr *typos* impression) a printing block on which the material is produced photographically; a print made from such a block; the process of making such a block. ◆ *vt* to reproduce by phototype. **phototype'setter** *n*. **phototype'setting** *n* the production of type images on a photographic medium by optical means and often using a computer connected to a device which enables publication with high-quality print. **phototypic** /-tip'ik/ *adj*. **phototypy** /fō'tō-tī-pi or fō-tot'i-pi/ *n*. **photoxylography** /fō-tō-zī-log'rə-fi/ *n* (see **xylo-** and **graph**) wood engraving after a photographic impression on a woodblock. **photozincograph** /fō'tō-zing'kə-gräf/ *n* a picture produced by photozincography. **photozincog'raphy** *n* the process of engraving on zinc by taking an impression by photography and etching with acids.

photo-² /fō-tō-, fō-to- or fō-tə-/ or **phot-** /fōt-/ *combining form* signifying light. [Gr *phōs*, *phōtos* light].

■ **photoac'tive** *adj* affected physically or chemically by light or other radiation. **photo-age'ing** *n* ageing (*esp* of the skin) caused by exposure to ultraviolet light. **photobiol'ogist** *n*. **photobiol'ogy** *n* a branch of biology dealing with the effects of light and other forms of radiant energy on organisms. **photocatal'ysis** *n* the promotion, acceleration or retardation of a chemical reaction by light. **photocatalyt'ic** *adj*. **photocath'ode** *n* a cathode that discharges electrons when exposed to light. **pho'tocell** *n* a photoelectric cell. **photochem'ical** *adj*. **photochem'ist** *n*. **photochem'istry** *n* the part of chemistry dealing with changes brought about by light, or other radiation, and with the production of radiation by chemical change. **photochromic** /-krōm'ik/ *adj* changing colour, and hence changing

the amount of light transmitted when the incident light increases, or decreases. ◆ *n* a photochromic material. **photochrom'ics** *n sing* the science and technology of photochromic materials. ◆ *n pl* photochromic materials. **photochrom'ism** *n*. **pho'tochromy** *n* a former process of colour photography. **photocoagulā'tion** *n* the medical use of a laser or other light source to harden or destroy tissue, *esp* in the eye. **photoconduct'ing** or **photoconduc'tive** *adj* relating to, or showing, photoconductivity. **photoconductiv'ity** *n* the property of varying conductivity under the influence of light. **photocurr'ent** *n* an electric current produced by light. **photodegra'dable** *adj* (of plastic) that will decompose after exposure to certain forms of light. **photodi'ode** *n* a two-electrode semiconductor device, used as an optical sensor. **photodissociā'tion** *n* (*chem*) dissociation produced by the absorption of radiant energy. **photodynam'ic** *adj* relating to a treatment for cancer in which an introduced drug is activated by a laser beam. **photoelas'tic** *adj* relating to or exhibiting photoelasticity. **photoelastic'ity** *n* the property of certain solids of exhibiting optical changes due to compression or other stresses. **photoelec'tric** *adj* relating to photoelectricity, or to photoelectrons (**photoelectric cell** any device in which incidence of light of suitable frequency causes an alteration in electrical state, *esp* by photo-emission, eg in order to activate a switch, etc). **photoelectric'ity** *n* the emission of electrons from the surface of certain materials by incidence of photons exceeding a certain energy. **photoelec'trode** *n* an electrode which can exhibit photoelectricity. **photoelec'tron** *n* an electron released from a surface by a photon. **photoelectron'ics** *n sing* the science dealing with the interactions of matter and photons, *esp* those involving the emission of electrons. **photo-emiss'ion** *n* the emission of electrons from the surface of a body after the incidence of photons. **photofiss'ion** *n* nuclear fission induced by gamma rays. **pho'toflood** or **photoflood lamp** *n* an incandescent lamp with a tungsten filament designed to run at a higher temperature but with a shorter life so that its emission spectrum more closely matches sunlight. **photogen** /fō'tə-jən/ *n* (see **-gen**) a light-producing organ in animals; a light paraffin oil (also **photogene**). **pho'togene** /-jēn/ *n* an after-image; a sensitive emulsion; a photograph (*obs*). **photogenic** /-jen'** or *-jēn'*/ *adj* producing light; produced by light; see also **photogenic** under **photo-**¹. **photoionizā'tion** or **-s-** *n* ionization produced by the action of electromagnetic radiation. **photokinesis** /-ki-nē'sis or -kī-/ *n* (Gr *kīnēsis* movement) movement occurring in response to variations in light intensity. **photoluminesce'** *vi* to produce photoluminescence. **photoluminesc'ence** *n* luminescence produced by exposure to photons. **photoluminesc'ent** *adj*. **pho'tolyse** *vt* to cause photolysis in. ◆ *vi* to undergo photolysis. **photolysis** /fō-tol'i-sis/ *n* (see **lysis**) decomposition or dissociation of a molecule as the result of the absorption of radiation (*chem*). **photolytic** /fō-tə-lit'ik/ *adj*. **photom'eter** *n* an instrument for measuring luminous intensity, *usu* by comparing two sources of light. **photomet'ric** *adj*. **photom'etry** *n* (the branch of physics dealing with) the measurement of luminous intensity. **photomul'tiplier** *n* a photocell with a series of dynodes which amplify the emission current by electron multiplication. **photonas'tic** /-nas-tik/ *adj*. **pho'tonasty** *n* (Gr *nastos* close-pressed; *biol*) a response in plants, etc to a change of intensity of light regardless of the direction of the light source. **photoneg'ative** *adj* tending to move away from light (*biol*); decreasing in conductivity when exposed to light (*phys*). **photope'riod** *n* the period during every 24 hours when an organism is exposed to daylight. **photoperiod'ic** *adj*. **photoperiodic'ity** *n*. **photope'riodism** *n* the physiological and behavioural reactions of organisms to changes in the length of the daylight period. **pho'tophil** *adj* (see **-phil** under **phil-**) light-loving; turning towards the light. ◆ *n* an organism that seeks the light. **photophil'ic** *adj*. **photophilous** /-tof'/ *adj*. **photoph'ily** *n*. **phō'tophobe** *n* and *adj*. **photopho'bia** *n* (see **phobia**) a fear of or aversion to light. **photophobic** /-fōb'ik/ *adj*. **pho'tophone** *n* (Gr *phōnē* voice) an obsolete apparatus that transmits sound by converting it to a light signal and then back to sound at a remote receiver, analogous to a modern fibre optics system. **photophonic** /-fon'ik/ *adj*. **photophony** /-tof'ə-ni/ *n*. **pho'tophore** /-fōr or -för/ *n* (see **-phore**; *zool*) a luminiferous organ. **photophoresis** /-fə-rē'sis/ *n* (Gr *phorēsis* a carrying) migration of suspended particles under the influence of light. **photop'ia** *n* vision in bright light, the eye's adjustment to daylight. **photop'ic** *adj*. **photopolarim'eter** *n* an instrument for measuring the polarization of light from planets or other distant objects. **photopol'ymer** *n* a light-sensitive polymer used in printing plates, microfilms, etc. **photopos'itive** *adj* tending to move towards light (*biol*); increasing in conductivity when exposed to light (*phys*). **photopsia** /fō-top'si-ə/ or **photopsy** /-top'si/ *n* (Gr *opsis* appearance) the appearance of flashes of light, owing to irritation of the retina. **photorecep'tor** *n* a nerve-ending receiving light stimuli. **photorefract'ive** *adj* of a material whose refractive index changes in response to light. **photoresist'** *adj* (of an organic material) that polymerizes on exposure to ultraviolet light and in that form resists attack by acids and solvents (also *n*). **photosens'itive** *adj* affected by light, visible or invisible. **photosensitiv'ity** *n*. **photosens'itize** or **-ise**

---

vt to make photosensitive by chemical or other means. **photosens'itizer** or **-s-** *n*. **pho'tosphere** *n* the luminous envelope of the sun's globe, the source of light. **photospheric** */-sfer'ik/ adj*. **photosynthesis** */-sin'thi-sis/ n* (*bot*) the use of light energy to drive chemical reactions, most notably the reduction of carbon dioxide to carbohydrates by the green pigment chlorophyll. **photosyn'thesize** *vi* and *vt*. **photosynthet'ic** *adj*. **phototac'tic** *adj*. **phototax'is** *n* (Gr *taxis* arrangement; *biol*) locomotory response or reaction of an organism or cell to the stimulus of light. **phototeleg'raphy** *n* telegraphy by means of light (see also under **photo-**[1]). **phototherapeut'ic** *adj*. **phototherapy** */fō'tō-ther'ə-pi/* or **phototherapeutics** */-pū'tiks/ n* (Gr *therapeuein* to tend) the treatment of disease by light. **phototransist'or** *n* a transistor that amplifies current in response to light. **phototrope** */-trōp/ n* a substance exhibiting phototropism. **phototroph'ic** *adj* (*biol*) using light to generate energy needed to absorb nutrients. **phototropic** */-trop'ik/ adj*. **phototropism** */fōt-ot'rəp-izm/ n* (see **-trope**) orientation in response to the stimulus of light (*bot*); reversible colour change on exposure to light (*chem*). **photot'ropy** *n* change of colour due to wavelength of incident light. **pho'totube** *n* an electron tube in which a cathode converts light into electric current. **photovoltaic** */-vol-tā'ik/ adj* producing an electromotive force across the junction between dissimilar materials when the junction is exposed to light or ultraviolet radiation, eg in a **photovoltaic cell**. **photovolta'ics** *n sing* the science and technology of photovoltaic devices and substances.

photog */fə-tog'/ n* an informal shortening of **photographer** (see under **photography**).

photography */fə-tog'rə-fi/ n* the art or process of producing permanent and visible images by the action of light, or other radiant energy, on chemically prepared surfaces. [Gr *phōs, phōtos* light, and *graphein* to draw]
■ **photograph** */fō'tə-gräf/ n* an image so produced. ◆ *vt* to make a picture of by means of photography. ◆ *vi* to take photographs; to be capable of being photographed. **photog'rapher** *n*. **photographic** */-graf'ik/* or **photograph'ical** *adj*. **photograph'ically** *adv*. **photog'raphist** *n* (*rare*).
❑ **photographic memory** *n* the ability to retain information or images in exact detail.

photon */fō'ton/ n* a quantum of light or other electromagnetic radiation. [Gr *phōs, phōtos* light, with *-on* after **electron**]
■ **photon'ic** *adj*. **photon'ics** *n sing* the study of the applications of photons, eg in communication technology.

phr *abbrev* : phrase.

phrase */frāz/ n* a manner of expression in language; an expression; a group of words (sometimes as in *Shakesp* a single word) generally not forming a clause but felt as expressing a single idea or constituting a single element in the sentence; a pithy expression; a catchword; an empty or high-sounding expression; fussy talk about one's feelings (*Scot*); a short group of notes felt to form a unit (*music*). ◆ *vt* to express in words; to style; to flatter or wheedle (*Scot*); to mark, bring out, or give effect to the phrases of (*music*). [Gr *phrasis*, from *phrazein* to speak]
■ **phras'al** *adj* consisting of, or of the nature of, a phrase. **phrase'less** *adj* incapable of being described. **phraseogram** */frā'zi-ə-gram/ n* a single sign, written without lifting the pen, for a whole phrase (*esp* in shorthand). **phra'seograph** *n* a phrase that is so written. **phraseolog'ic** or **phraseolog'ical** *adj*. **phraseolog'ically** *adv*. **phraseol'ogist** *n* a maker or collector of phrases. **phraseol'ogy** *n* style or manner of expression or arrangement of phrases; peculiarities of diction; a collection of phrases in a language. **phra'ser** *n* a mere maker or repeater of empty phrases. **phra'sing** *n* the wording of a speech or passage; the grouping and accentuation of the sounds in performing a melody (*music*). ◆ *adj* using phrases, *esp* (*Scot*) airing one's views or feelings or making flowery speeches. **phra'sy** *adj* inclined to use wordy phrases.
❑ **phrasal verb** *n* a phrase, consisting of a verb and an adverb or preposition, or both, having the function of a verb, eg *blow over, sift through, put up with*. **phrase book** *n* a book containing or explaining phrases used in a language. **phrase'man**, **phrase'maker** or **phrase'monger** *n* a user or maker of wordy or fine-sounding phrases.
■ **turn of phrase** an expression; one's manner of expression.

phratry */frā'tri/ n* a social division of a people, often exogamous. [Gr *phrātriā*; cf L *frāter*, Eng **brother**]

phreak */frēk/* (*inf*) *n* a person who hacks into a telephone system in order to make free calls. [Contraction of *phone freak*]
■ **phreak'ing** *n*.

phreatic */frē-at'ik/ adj* relating to underground water supplying, or probably able to supply, wells or springs, or to the soil or rocks containing it, or to wells; (of underground gases, etc) present in or causing volcanic eruptions. [Gr *phrear* well, and *phreātia* cistern]

■ **phreat'ophyte** *n* a deep-rooted plant drawing its water from the water table or just above it. **phreatophyt'ic** *adj*.

phrenesiac */fri-nē'zi-ak/* (*Walter Scott*) *adj* hypochondriac. [Ety as for **phrenesis**]

phrenesis */fri-nē'sis/ n* phrenitis; delirium; frenzy. [Gr *phrēn*, *phrenos* midriff (supposed seat of passions, mind and will)] For **phrenetic**, **phrenetical**, and **phrenetically** see **frenetic**.
■ **phren'ism** *n* a supposed 'mind-force' described by ED Cope as active in nature and evolution. **phrenit'ic** *adj* of or affected with phrenitis. **phreni'tis** *n* inflammation of the brain; brain fever.

phrenic */fren'ik/ adj* of or near the midriff; mental (*obs*). [Fr *phrénique*, from Gr *phrēn, phrenos* midriff]

phrenism, phrenitic, phrenitis see under **phrenesis**.

phrensical, phrensy old forms of **frenzical, frenzy**.

phrentick an old form of **frantic** (or **phrenetic** (see **frenetic**)).

phrontistery */fron'ti-stə-ri/ n* a thinking-place. [Gr *phrontistērion*, from *phrontistēs* a thinker, from *phroneein* to think; applied by Aristophanes to the school of Socrates]

Phrygian */frij'i-ən/ adj* relating to Phrygia in Asia Minor, or to its people. ◆ *n* a native of Phrygia; a Montanist; the language of the ancient Phrygians.
❑ **Phrygian cap** *n* an ancient type of conical cap with the top turned forward, which in the French Revolution came to symbolize liberty. **Phrygian mode** *n* (in ancient Greek music) a mode of two tetrachords with a semitone in the middle of each and a whole tone between the tetrachords (eg: *d e f g; a b c d*; but reckoned downwards by the Greeks); (in old Church music) an authentic mode extending from *e* to *e*, with *e* as its final.

phthalic */thal'ik/* or **fthal'ik/** (*chem*) *adj* applied to three acids, $C_6H_4(COOH)_2$, and an anhydride, derived from naphthalene. [**naphthalene**]
■ **phthal'ate** *n* a salt or ester of phthalic acid. **phthal'ein** */-i-in/ n* any one of a very important class of dye-yielding materials formed by the union of phenols with phthalic anhydride. **phthal'in** *n* a colourless crystalline compound obtained by reducing a phthalein. **phthalocy'anin** or **phthalocy'anine** *n* any of a group of green and blue organic colouring matters of great fastness and brilliance.

phthiriasis */thī-rī'ə-sis* or *fthī-rī'ə-sis/ n* infestation with lice. [Gr *phtheiriāsis*, from *phtheir* a louse]

phthisis */thī'sis*, also *fthī'* or *tī'/* (*med*; *old*) *n* a wasting disease; tuberculosis, *esp* of the lungs. [Gr *phthisis*, from *phthi*(n)*ein* to waste away]
■ **phthisic** */tiz'ik*, sometimes *thī'sik, fthī'sik* or *tī'sik/ n* phthisis; vaguely, a lung or throat disease. **phthis'ical** or **phthis'icky** *adj*.

phut */fut/ n* a dull sound *esp* of collapse, deflation, etc. ◆ *vi* to make, go, or land with a phut or phuts. [Hindi *phatnā* to split]
■ **go phut** to break, become unserviceable; to come to nothing.

pH value see **pH**.

phwoar */fwör/* (*inf*) *interj* an expression of appreciation of the attractiveness of another person (also **phwoah**, etc). [Imit]

phyco- */fī-kō-/ combining form* denoting seaweed. [Gr *phȳkos* seaweed]
■ **phycocyan** */sī'ən/* or **phycocy'anin** */-ə-nin/ n* (Gr *kyanos* dark blue) a blue pigment found in algae. **phycoerythrin** */-e-rith'rin/ n* (Gr *erythros* red) a red pigment found in algae. **phycolog'ical** *adj*. **phycologist** */-kol'ə-jist/ n*. **phycol'ogy** *n* the study of algae. **phycomycete** */-mī'sēt/ n* (Gr *mykēs* a fungus) a fungus of the class **Phycomycetes** */-mī-sē'tēz/*, showing affinities with the green seaweeds. **phycophaein** */-fē'in/ n* (Gr *phaios* grey) a brown pigment found in seaweeds. **phycoxan'thin** *n* (Gr *xanthos* yellow) a yellow pigment found in diatoms, brown seaweeds, etc.

phyla see **phylum**.

phylactery */fi-lak'tə-ri/ n* a slip of parchment inscribed with certain passages of Scripture, worn in a box on the left arm or forehead by Jewish men; a charm or amulet; a reminder; ostentatious display of religious forms; a case for relics; (in medieval art) a scroll at the mouth of a figure in a picture bearing the words he or she is supposed to speak. [Gr *phylaktērion*, from *phylax* a guard]
■ **phylacteric** */-ter'ik/* or **phylacter'ical** *adj*.

phyle */fī'lē/ n* a tribe or division of the people of a state in ancient Greece, at first on a kinship, later on a local, basis. [Gr *phȳlē*]

■ **phylarch** /fīˈlärk/ n the chief officer of a tribe; (in Athens) the commander of the cavalry of a tribe. **phyˈlarchy** n the office of phylarch.

phyletic /fīˈletˈik/ (biol) adj relating to a phylum; according to presumed evolutionary descent. [Gr phylētikos, from phȳlē]

phyllary /filˈə-ri/ (bot) n an involucral bract. [Gr phyllarion, dimin of phyllon leaf]

phyllite /filˈīt/ n a rock intermediate between clay-slate and mica-schist. [Gr phyllon a leaf]

phyllo see **filo**.

phylloclade /filˈō-klād/ (bot) n a flattened branch with the form and functions of a leaf. [Gr phyllon leaf, and klados shoot]

phyllode /filˈōd/ (bot) n a petiole with the appearance and function of a leaf-blade. [Gr phyllon leaf, and eidos form]
■ **phyllˈody** /-ō-di/ n transformation of flower parts into leaves. **phyllˈoid** adj leaf-like.

phyllomania /filˈō-māˈni-ə/ (bot) n excessive production of leaves, at the expense of flower or fruit production. [Gr phyllon leaf, and maniā madness]

phyllome /filˈōm/ (bot) n any leaf or homologue of a leaf. [Gr phyllōma foliage]

phyllophagous /fi-lofˈə-gəs/ adj leaf-eating. [Gr phyllon leaf, and phagein to eat]

phyllopod /filˈə-pod/ n a crustacean of the order **Phyllopoda** /-opˈə-də/, entomostracans with foliaceous legs. [Gr phyllon leaf, and pous, podos foot]

phylloquinone /filˈō-kwinˈōn or -ōnˈ/ n vitamin K₁, one of the fat-soluble vitamin K group, essential for normal blood coagulation. [Gr phyllon leaf, and **quinone**]

phyllotaxis /filˈō-takˈsis/ (bot) n the disposition of leaves on the stem (also **phyllˈotaxy**). [Gr phyllon a leaf, and taxis arrangement]
■ **phyllotactˈic** or **phyllotactˈical** adj.

Phyllotria see **Elodea**.

phylloxera /fil-ok-sēˈrə/ n an insect of the Phylloxera genus of insects, similar to greenfly, very destructive to vines. [Gr phyllon a leaf, and xēros dry]

phylogenesis /fīˈlō-jenˈi-sis/ or **phylogeny** /fīˈlojˈi-ni/ n evolutionary pedigree or genealogical history. [Gr phȳlon race, and genesis origin]
■ **phylogenetˈic** adj. **phylogenetˈically** adv. **phylogenetˈics** n sing the study of phylogenesis.

phylum /fīˈləm/ n (pl **phyˈla**) a main grouping of the animal kingdom, corresponding to a division in the plant kingdom; a group of languages thought to be related. [New L, from Gr phȳlon race]

phys abbrev: physician; physics; physiology.

physalia /fīˈsāˈli-ə/ n a member of the Physalia genus of large oceanic colonial hydrozoans with a floating bladder, including the Portuguese man-of-war. [Gr phȳsallis a bladder, from phȳsaein to blow]

physalis /fisˈə-lis or fīsˈ/ n a member of the Cape gooseberry genus Physalis, of the Solanaceae family, with persistent bladdery calyx; its edible yellow fruit. [Gr phȳsallis a bladder; cf **physalia**]

physeter /fī-sēˈtər/ n a sperm whale (old); a spouting whale (obs). [Gr phȳsētēr a blower, a whale, from phȳsaein to blow]

physharmonica /fis-här-monˈi-kə/ n an early form of harmonium. [Gr phȳsa bellows, and **harmonica**]

physi- /fizˈi-/ or **physio-** /fizˈi-ō-, -ə-, -o-/ combining form signifying nature. [Gr physis nature]

physiatrics /fiz-i-atˈriks/ (N Am) n sing physiotherapy. [**physi-**, and iātros physician]

physic /fizˈik/ n orig natural philosophy, physics (obs); the science, art, or practice of medicine (obs); a medicine (rare); anything healing or wholesome (fig). ◆ adj (obs) physical, natural; medicinal. ◆ vt (**physˈicking**; **physˈicked**) (obs) to give medicine to; to heal. [Gr physikos natural, from physis nature]
■ **physˈicism** /-sizm/ n belief in the material or physical as opposed to the spiritual. **physˈicky** adj like medicine.
❑ **physic garden** n orig a garden of medicinal plants; a botanic garden. **physic nut** n the purgative seed of the tropical American tree Jatropha curcas, of the spurge family.

physical /fizˈi-kl/ adj relating to the world of matter and energy, or its study, natural philosophy; material; materialistic (obs); bodily; requiring bodily effort; involving bodily contact; medical (rare); medicinal (obs); wholesome (Shakesp). ◆ n a physical examination of the body, eg to ascertain fitness; (usu in pl) commodities that can be bought and used. [**physic**]
■ **physˈicalism** n the theory that all phenomena are explicable in spatiotemporal terms and that all statements are either analytic or reducible to empirically verifiable assertions. **physˈicalist** n. **physicalˈity** n physical quality; preoccupation with the bodily. **physˈically** adv.
❑ **physical anthropology** n the anthropology of local human biological adaptation. **physical astronomy** n the study of the physical condition and chemical composition of the heavenly bodies. **physical chemistry** n the study of the dependence of physical properties on chemical composition, and of the physical changes accompanying chemical reactions. **physical education** n instruction in sport and gymnastics at school. **physical force** n force applied outwardly to the body, as distinguished from persuasion, etc. **physical geography** n the study of the earth's natural features, eg its mountain chains and ocean currents, etc. **physical jerks** n pl (inf) bodily exercises. **physical sciences** n pl those sciences (physics, geology, etc) concerned with non-living matter. **physical training** n instruction in sport and gymnastics in the armed services.
■ **get physical** (inf) to use physical force; to indulge in sexual contact.

physician /fi-zishˈn/ n a doctor; someone legally qualified to practise medicine; someone skilled in the use of physic or the art of healing; someone who makes use of medicines and treatment, distinguished from a surgeon who practises manual operations; a healer or healing influence (fig). [**physic**]
■ **physiˈciancy** n the post or office of physician. **physiˈcianer** n (rare) a physician. **physicˈianship** n.

physics /fizˈiks/ n sing orig natural science in general; now, the science of the properties (other than chemical) of matter and energy, and the forces and interrelationships between them. [**physic**]
■ **physˈicist** /-sist/ n an expert in or student of physics; a person who studies nature (obs); someone who believes the phenomena of life are purely physical. **physicochemˈical** adj relating to or involving both physics and chemistry; relating to physical chemistry (qv).

physio /fizˈi-ō/ (inf) n (pl **physˈios**) a physiotherapist; physiotherapy.

physiocracy /fiz-i-okˈrə-si/ n government, according to François Quesnay (1694–1774) and his followers, by a natural order inherent in society, land and its products being the only true source of wealth, direct taxation of land being the only proper source of revenue. [**physio-** and **-cracy**]
■ **physˈiocrat** /-ō-krat/ n someone who maintains these opinions. **physiocratˈic** adj.

physiognomy /fiz-i-onˈə-mi or -ogˈnə-mi/ n the art of judging character from appearance, esp from the face; the face as an index of the mind; the face (inf); the general appearance of anything; character, aspect. [Gr physiognōmiā, a shortened form of physiognōmoniā, from physis nature, and gnōmōn, -onos an interpreter]
■ **physiognomic** /-nomˈik/ or **physiognomˈical** adj of or relating to physiognomy. **physiognomˈically** adv. **physiognˈomist** n.

physiography /fiz-i-ogˈrə-fi/ n description of nature, descriptive science; physical geography. [**physio-** and **-graphy**]
■ **physiogˈrapher** n. **physiographic** /-ō-grafˈik/ or **physiographˈical** adj.

physiolatry /fiz-i-olˈə-tri/ n nature-worship. [**physio-** and **-latry**]
■ **physiolˈater** n a nature-worshipper.

physiologus /fi-zi-olˈə-gəs/ n a work containing descriptions of animals, a bestiary. [Gr physiologos a natural philosopher]

physiology /fiz-i-olˈə-ji/ n the science of the processes of life in animals and plants. [**physio-** and **-logy**]
■ **physiologic** /-ə-lojˈik/ or **physiologˈical** adj. **physiologˈically** adv. **physiolˈogist** n.
❑ **physiological saline** n a salt solution prepared to have the same osmotic pressure as bodily fluids.

physiotherapy /fiz-i-ō-therˈə-pi/ n treatment of disease by remedies such as massage, fresh air, physical exercise, etc, rather than by drugs (also **physiotherapeutics** /-pūˈtiks/). [**physio-** and Gr therapeiā treatment]
■ **physiotherapeutˈic** adj. **physiotherˈapist** n.

physique /fi-zēkˈ/ n bodily type, build, or constitution. [Fr]

physitheism /fizˈi-thē-i-zm/ n the ascription of physical form and attributes to deity; deification of the powers of nature. [**physi-** and Gr theos god]
■ **physitheisˈtic** adj.

physostigmine /fī-zō-stigˈmēn/ n a compound ($C_{15}H_{21}N_3O_2$) derived from the Calabar bean, formerly used to treat glaucoma. [Physostigma, the genus to which the Calabar bean belongs, and **-ine¹** (1)]

phyt- /fīt-/ or **phyto-** /fīˈtō-, -tə- or -to-/ combining form denoting plant. [Gr phyton plant]
■ **-phyte** combining form used to indicate a plant belonging to a particular habitat, or of a particular type. **-phytic** /-fitˈik/ adj combining form. **phytoalexˈin** n (Gr alexein to ward off) any

substance produced by a plant as a defence against disease. **phytobenthos** /-ben'thos/ n (Gr *benthos* depth) plants living at the bottom of water collectively. **phytochem'ical** n a chemical derived from a plant. ◆ adj of chemicals in plants. **phytochem'istry** n the chemistry of plant growth and metabolism and of plant products. **phy'tochrome** n a plant pigment which absorbs red or infrared rays and has an important role in controlling growth, flowering, germination, etc. **phytoestrogen** /fī-tō-ēs'trə-jən/ n a plant substance similar to a weak oestrogen. **phytoestrogen'ic** adj. **phytogen'esis** or **phytogeny** /-toj'i-ni/ n evolution of plants. **phytogenet'ic** or **phytogenet'ical** adj relating to phytogenesis. **phytogenic** /-jen'ik/ adj of vegetable origin. **phytogeog'rapher** n. **phytogeograph'ic** or **phytogeograph'ical** adj. **phytogeog'raphy** n the geography of plant distribution. **phytog'rapher** n a descriptive botanist. **phytograph'ic** adj. **phytog'raphy** n descriptive botany. **phytohor'mone** n a plant hormone, regulating growth, etc. **Phytolacc'a** n the pokeweed genus, giving name to the family **Phytolaccā'ceae**, related to the pinks and the goosefoots. **phytolog'ical** adj. **phytol'ogist** n a botanist. **phytol'ogy** n botany. **phy'ton** n the smallest part of a plant that when cut off may grow into a new plant. **phytonadione** /fī-tō-nə-dī'ōn/ n phylloquinone, vitamin K₁. **phytonū'trient** n any of various organic substances derived from plants that are believed to have health-giving properties. **phytopatholog'ical** adj. **phytopathol'ogist** n. **phytopathol'ogy** n (Gr *pathos* suffering) the study of plant diseases. **phytophagic** /-faj'ik/ or **phytophagous** /-tof'ə-gas/ adj (Gr *phagein* to eat) plant-eating. **phytoplank'ton** n (Gr *plankton* (neuter) wandering) vegetable plankton. **phytoremediā'tion** n the use of plants to decontaminate soil by absorbing pollutants such as heavy metals. **phyto'sis** n the presence of vegetable parasites or disease caused by them. **phytosterol** /-tos'tə-rol/ n (formed on the model of *cholesterol*) a substance very like cholesterol obtained from plants. **phytot'omist** n. **phytotomy** /-tot'ə-mi/ n (see **-tomy**) plant anatomy. **phytotox'ic** adj poisonous to plants; relating to a phytotoxin. **phytotoxic'ity** n harmfulness to plants. **phytotox'in** n a toxin produced by a plant; a substance toxic to plants. **phytotron** /fī'tō-tron/ n an apparatus that produces climates artificially for the study of plant growth.

PI abbrev : Private Investigator.

pi¹ /pī or pē/ n the sixteenth letter (Π, π) of the Greek alphabet, corresponding to the Roman P; as a numeral, π' = 80, ͵π = 80000; a symbol for the ratio of the circumference of a circle to the diameter, approx 3.14159 (maths). [Gr *pei, pī*]
□ **pi-** (or π-)**meson** n (also called **pion**) the source of the nuclear force holding protons and neutrons together (phys).

pi² /pī/ (inf) adj obtrusively religious, sanctimonious. ◆ n a pious or sanctimonious person or talk. [Short form of **pious**]
□ **pi'-jaw** n sermonizing; an admonition.

pi³ (printing) same as **pie²**.

PIA abbrev : Pakistan International Airlines; Personal Investment Authority (now replaced by **FSA**).

pia¹ /pē'ə/ n a tropical monocotyledonous plant (genus *Tacca*; family Taccaceae) with a rhizome yielding E India or Madagascar arrowroot. [Polynesian name]

pia² /pī'ə or pē'a/ (L) fem adj pious.
□ **pia desideria** /dez-i-dēr'i-ə or dā-sēd-er'i-a/ n pious regrets. **pia fraus** /fröz or frows/ n pious fraud.

piacevole /pyə-chä'vo-lā/ (music) adj and adv in a pleasant or playful manner. [Ital]

piacular /pī-ak'ū-lər/ adj expiatory; requiring expiation; atrociously bad. [L *piāculum* sacrifice, from *piāre* to expiate, from *pius* pious]
■ **piacularity** /-lar'i-ti/ n.

piaffe /pi-af'/ or pyaf/ (dressage) vi to perform a piaffer. [Fr *piaffer*]
■ **piaff'er** n a movement on the spot in which the horse's feet are lifted in the same succession as a trot, but more slowly (also called **Spanish-walk**).

pia mater /pī'ə mā'tər/ (anat) n the vascular membrane surrounding the brain and spinal cord; the brain (Shakesp). [L *pīa māter* tender mother, a medieval translation of Ar *umm raqīqah* thin mother]

piano /pē-an'ō, pyan'ō or pē-ä-nō/ n (pl **pian'os**) (in full **pian'oforte**) a large musical instrument, a shaped wooden case on legs, with a keyboard at which the player sits, the keys working small hammers to sound tautened wires inside; (pl **pian'os** or **pian'i**) a soft passage (music). ◆ adj and adv (music) soft, softly. [Ital *pianoforte*, from *piano* soft, from L *plānus* level, and *forte* loud, from L *fortis* strong]
■ **pianette** /pē-ə-net'/ n a small upright piano. **pianino** /pya-nē'nō or pē-ə-nē'nō/ n (pl **piani'nos**) orig an upright piano; a small upright piano. **pi'anism** n the technique of playing the piano. **pianissimo** /pya-nēs'si-mō or pē-ə-nis'i-mō/ adj and adv (music) very soft. ◆ n (pl **pianiss'imos**) a very soft passage. **pianississimo** /pya-nē-sis'i-mō or pē-ə-ni-sis'i-mō/ adj and adv (music) as soft or softly as possible. **pianist** /pē'ə-nist or pyan'ist (also pē-an'ist)/ n a person who plays the

piano, esp expertly (also (Fr) **pianiste** /pē-a-nēst'/ sometimes used as fem). **pianist'ic** adj of or relating to pianism or a pianist. **pianist'ically** adv. **pianoforte** n a piano (see above). ◆ adj and adv (music) soft, then loud. **Pianola**® /pya-nō'lə or pē-ə-/ n a mechanical, playerless piano with keys operated by air pressure, the sequence determined by the pattern of perforations in a removable paper roll (a **piano roll**). **piano'list** n.
□ **piano accordion** n a sophisticated type of accordion with a keyboard like that of a piano. **piano organ** n a piano like a barrel organ, played by mechanical means. **pian'o-play'er** n a pianist; a mechanical contrivance for playing the piano. **piano roll** n see **Pianola**® above. **pian'o-school** n a school where piano-playing is taught; a method or book of instruction for the piano. **piano stool** n a stool for a pianist, usu adjustable in height, and often hollow for storing sheet music. **piano wire** n wire used for piano strings, and for deep-sea soundings, etc.
■ **player piano** a Pianola.

piano nobile /pyä'nō nō'bi-lā/ (archit) n the main floor of a large house or villa, usu on the first floor. [Ital, noble storey]

piarist /pī'ə-rist/ n a member of a religious congregation for the education of the poor, founded in Rome in 1597 by Joseph Calasanza. [L *patrēs scholārum piārum* fathers of pious schools]

piassava /pē-ə-sä'və/ or **piassaba** /-ba/ n a coarse stiff fibre used for making brooms, etc, obtained from Brazilian palms, *Attalea* (coquilla) and *Leopoldinia* (chiquichiqui); the tree yielding it. [Port from Tupí]

piastre /pi-as'tər/ n a monetary unit in current or former use in several N African and Middle-Eastern countries, $\frac{1}{100}$ of a (Lebanese, Egyptian, Syrian, etc) pound; a coin of this value; a piece of eight. [Fr, from Ital *piastra* a leaf of metal; see **plaster**]

piazza /pē-at'sə, also pē-ad'zə or pē-az'ə/ n a place or square surrounded by buildings; a walk under a roof supported by pillars (non-standard); a veranda (US). [Ital, from L *platea*, from Gr *plateia* a street (fem of *platys* broad)]
■ **piazz'ian** adj.

pibroch /pē'brohh/ n the classical music of the bagpipe, free in rhythm and consisting of theme and variations. [Gaelic *piobaireachd* pipe-music, from *piobair* a piper, from *piob*, from Eng **pipe¹**]

PIBS (finance) abbrev : permanent interest-bearing share.

pic /pik/ (inf) n (pl **pics** or **pix**) a picture.

Pica /pī'kə/ n the magpie genus; (without cap) an unnatural craving for unsuitable food (med). [L *pīca* magpie]

pica¹ /pī'kə/ (printing) n an old type size, approximately, and still used synonymously for, 12-point, giving about 6 lines to the inch, much used in typewriters; a size of type giving ten characters or spaces to the inch. [Possibly used for printing *pies*; see **pie²**]
■ **small pica** 11-point.

pica² see **Pica**.

picador /pik'ə-dōr or -dör/ n a mounted bullfighter with a lance. [Sp, from *pica* a pike]

picamar /pik'ə-mär/ n a bitter oily liquid obtained from tar. [L *pix, picis* pitch, and *amārus* bitter]

picante /pi-kän'tā/ adj spicy (esp of food; also fig). [Sp, biting, pricking]

picaresque see under **picaroon**.

picarian /pi-kā'ri-ən/ adj belonging to an obsolete order (**Pica'riae** /-ē/) of birds incl the woodpeckers. ◆ n any member of the order. [L *pīcus* woodpecker]

picaroon /pik-ə-roon'/ n a person who lives by his or her wits; a cheat; a pirate. [Sp *picarón*, augmentative of *pícaro* rogue]
■ **picaresque** /-resk'/ adj relating the episodic adventures of a likeable rogue or vagabond; of or relating to Spanish novels of this type, much in vogue in the 17c.

picayune /pik-ə-ūn'/ adj (US inf) petty. ◆ n a small coin worth 6¼ cents, current in the USA before 1857; a five-cent piece, or other small coin; anything of little or no value (US inf). [Provençal *picaioun* an old Piedmontese copper coin]
■ **picayun'ish** adj.

piccadill /pik'ə-dil/, **piccadell** /-del/, **piccadillo** /-dil'ō/ (pl **piccadill'oes**), or **piccadilly** /-i/, also **pick-**, (obs) n a cut or vandyked edging, esp to a woman's collar; a wide high collar of the early 17c; a stiff support for a collar or ruff; (in the form **piccadilly**) a man's upright collar with the points turned over, first worn about 1870. [Cf Sp *picadillo* a kind of hash, or *pica* spear, hence wire support for a ruff]

piccalilli /pik-ə-lil'i/ n a pickle of various vegetable substances with mustard and spices. [Ety uncertain]

piccaninny or **pickaninny** /pik-ə-nin'i/ (now offensive) n a little child, esp a black child; an Aboriginal child (Aust). ◆ adj very little.

[Orig W Ind, from Port *pequenino*, dimin of *pequeno* little, or possibly Sp *pequeño niño* little child]
■ **picc'anin** *n* (*S Afr*) a piccaninny.

piccies see **piccy**.

piccolo /pik'ə-lō/ *n* (*pl* **picc'olos**) a small flute, an octave higher than the ordinary flute; an organ stop of similar tone. [Ital, little]

piccy /pik'i/ (*inf*) *n* (*pl* **picc'ies**) a picture, *esp* a photograph.

pice /pīs/ *n* (*pl* **pice**) a former unit of currency in India, $\frac{1}{4}$ of an anna. [Hindi *paisā*]
■ **new pice** $\frac{1}{100}$ of a rupee, a paisa (qv).

Picea /pis'i-ə or pī'si-ə/ *n* the spruce genus of conifers. [L *picea* pitch pine, from *pix* pitch]

piceous /pis'i-əs/ *adj* like pitch; inflammable; black; reddish-black. [L *piceus*, from *pix* pitch]
■ **picene** /pī'sēn/ *n* a hydrocarbon ($C_{22}H_{14}$) derived from tar.

pichiciego /pich-i-si-ā'gō/ *n* (*pl* **pichicie'gos**) a small burrowing S American armadillo. [Native American]

pichurim /pich'ŭ-rim/ *n* a S American tree (*Nectandra puchury*) of the laurel family; its aromatic kernel (also **pichurim bean**). [Port *pichurim*, from Tupí *puchury*]

picine see under **Picus**.

pick¹ /pik/ *n* a tool for breaking ground, rock, etc, with a head pointed at one end or both, and a handle of varying length fitted to the middle; a pointed hammer; an instrument of various kinds for picking; a plectrum; an act, opportunity, or right of choice; a portion picked; the best or choicest; dirt on a printing type; a manoeuvre in which an attacker who does not have the ball obstructs a defender from challenging the ball-carrier (*sport*; *N Am*); a diamond in cards, also a spade (*Scot and N Eng dialect*). ◆ *vt* to break up, dress or remove with a pick; to make with a pick or by plucking; to poke or pluck at, as with a sharp instrument or the nails; to pluck the strings of (a guitar, mandolin, etc); to clear, remove, or gather by single small movements; to detach, extract, or take separately and lift or remove; to pluck; to pull apart; to cull; to choose; to select, *esp* one by one or bit by bit; to peck, bite, or nibble; to eat in small quantities or delicately; to open (eg a lock) by a sharp instrument or other unapproved means; to rifle by stealth; to seek and find a pretext for (eg a quarrel). ◆ *vi* to use a pick; to eat in small or delicate mouthfuls; to pilfer. [Ety obscure; cf **peck¹**, **pike²**]
■ **picked** /pikt/ *adj* selected, hence the choicest or best; (of flowers or fruit) plucked; exquisite, refined, punctilious (*Shakesp*); having spines or prickles, sharp-pointed. **pick'edness** *n*. **pick'er** *n* a person who picks or gathers up; a tool or machine for picking; someone who removes defects from and finishes electrotype plates; a pilferer. **pick'ery** *n* (*Scots law*) pilfering. **pick'ing** *n* the action of the verb to pick; the quantity picked; that which is left to be picked; dabbing in stoneworking; the final finishing of woven fabrics by removing burs, etc; removing defects from electrotype plates; (in *pl*) odd gains or perquisites. **pick'y** *adj* (*inf*) fussy or choosy, *esp* excessively so; able to pick out or pick over dexterously.
□ **pick'-cheese** *n* the blue or the great titmouse; the fruit of the mallow. **picker-up'** *n* a person who or machine or device that picks things up. **pick'lock** *n* an instrument for picking or opening locks; a person who picks locks. **pick'-me-up** *n* a stimulating drink; a medicinal tonic; anything that revivifies. **pick''n'mix** or **pick'-and-mix'** *n* and *adj* (an assortment of loose sweets) chosen by the individual customer from a range of types available at a self-service counter; (a discriminatory selection) chosen to suit one's individual taste or needs (*fig*). **pick'off** *n* an electronic device that detects movement, used eg in an aircraft guidance system. **pick'pocket** *n* someone who picks or steals from other people's pockets. **pick'-purse** *n* someone who steals the purse or from the purse of another. **pick'-thank** *n* someone who seeks to ingratiate himself or herself by officious favours, or by tale-bearing. **pick'-tooth** *n* a toothpick. **pick'-up** *n* an act of picking up; reception; a stop to collect something or someone; a recovery; an improvement; something picked up; accelerating power; a device for picking up an electric current; (also **pick-up head**) a transducer, activated by a sapphire or diamond stylus following the groove on a gramophone record, which transforms the mechanical into electrical impulses; a transducer on an electric musical instrument; (also **pick-up truck**) a light motor vehicle with the front of a saloon car and the rear in the form of a small truck; a man's chance, informal acquaintance with a woman, or vice versa, *usu* implying a sexual relationship; the woman or man in such a relationship; a game, or a team, for which the captains pick their players alternately from a single group or squad. ◆ *adj* for picking up; picked up. **pick-your-own** *n* a method of selling fruit or vegetables by which private customers pick the produce they wish to buy at the place where it is grown; produce sold in this way. ◆ *adj* sold or operating by this system.

■ **pick a hole in someone's coat** to find fault with someone. **pick at** to find fault with; to nibble food without enthusiasm; to poke at and detach pieces from, using the fingernails, etc. **pick holes in** to find fault with. **pick oakum** to make oakum by untwisting old ropes. **pick off** to kill selectively, or one by one, by shooting with great accuracy, *usu* from a distance; to detach and remove. **pick on** to single out, *esp* for anything unpleasant; to nag at; to carp at. **pick one's way** to choose carefully where to put one's feet, as (or as if) on dirty or dangerous ground. **pick out** to make out, distinguish; to pluck out; to select from a number; to play (a tune, etc) uncertainly; to mark with spots of colour, etc. **pick over** to go over and select. **pick someone's brains** to make use of another's brains or ideas for one's own ends. **pick to pieces** to pull apart; to criticize adversely in detail. **pick up** to lift from the ground or floor; to improve gradually; to gain strength bit by bit; to answer a telephone; to take into a vehicle, or into one's company; to scrape acquaintance informally with, *esp* of a man with a woman; to acquire by chance; to gain; to come upon, make out, distinguish (eg a signal, a track, a comet, etc). **pick up on** (*inf*) to notice and react to; to point out an error. **pick up the pieces** to restore (*esp* emotional) matters to their former equilibrium after they have been brought to disarray or collapse.

pick² /pik/ a Scot and N Eng form of **pitch²**; also of **pitch¹** *esp* *vi* to throw the shuttle across the loom, and *n* a throw of the shuttle, or a weft thread; also a form of **pique¹**.
□ **pick'-and-pick'** *n* (*weaving*) a term indicating alternate picks of yarns of two different colours or kinds.

pickaback see **piggyback**.

pickadill, **pickadell**, **pickadillo**, **pickadilly** see **piccadill**.

pickaninny see **piccaninny**.

pickaxe /pik'aks/ *n* a picking tool, with a point at one end of the head and a cutting blade at the other, used in digging. [ME *pikois*, from OFr *picois* a mattock, *piquer* to pierce, *pic* a pick]

pickeer /pi-kēr'/ *vi* to forage (*obs*); to skirmish; to scout; to flirt (*obs*). [Ety uncertain]
■ **pickeer'er** *n*.

pickelhaube /pik-l-how'bə or pik'l/ *n* a German spiked helmet. [Ger]

pickerel /pik'ər-əl/ *n* a young pike; a pike, *esp* of smaller species (*US*). [**pike¹**]
□ **pick'erel-weed** *n* pondweed; Pontederia (*US*).

pickery see under **pick¹**.

picket, also **piquet** or **picquet** /pik'it/ *n* a person or group stationed to watch and dissuade those who go to work during a strike; a small outpost, patrol, or body of men set apart for some special duty; picket-duty; a pointed stake or peg driven into the ground, eg for fortification, tethering, military punishment or surveying; a surveyor's mark; the old military punishment of standing on one foot on a pointed stake. ◆ *vt* (**pick'eting**; **pick'eted**) to deal with as a picket or by means of pickets; to place pickets at or near; to post as a picket; to tether to a stake; to strengthen or surround with pickets; to peg down; to subject to the picket. ◆ *vi* to act as picket. [Fr *piquet*, dimin of *pic* a pickaxe]
■ **pick'eter** *n* a person who pickets in a labour dispute.
□ **pick'et-duty** *n*. **picket fence** *n* (*US*) a fence made of pales. **pick'et-guard** *n* a guard kept in readiness in case of alarm. **picket line** *n* a line of people acting as pickets in a labour dispute.
■ **picket out** (in a labour dispute) to close or bring to a standstill by picketing.

pickle¹ /pik'l/ *n* a liquid, *esp* brine or vinegar, in which food is preserved; an article of food preserved in such liquid; (in *pl*) preserved onions, cucumber, gherkins, etc, as a condiment; acid or other liquid used for cleansing or other treatment as part of a manufacturing process; a tricky situation, predicament or muddle (*inf*); a troublesome child (*inf*). ◆ *vt* to preserve with salt or vinegar, etc; to rub with salt or salt and vinegar, as an old naval punishment; to clean or treat with acid or other chemical. [ME *pekille*, *pykyl*, *pekkyll*, *pykulle*; cf Du *pekel*; Ger *Pökel*]
■ **pick'led** *adj* preserved in pickle; drunk (*inf*). **pick'ler** *n* someone who pickles; a container for pickling; an article suitable, or grown, for pickling.
□ **pick'le-herring** *n* a pickled herring; a merry-andrew, a clown (*obs*).

pickle² /pik'l/ or **puckle** /puk'l/ (*Scot*) *n* a small quantity; a grain of corn. [Origin unknown]

pickle³ /pik'l/ *vt* and *vi* to peck; to pick; to eat sparingly; to pilfer. [Dimin or frequentative of **pick¹**]

pickmaw /pik'mö/ (*Scot*) *n* the blackheaded gull. [Perh **pick²** (pitch), and **maw²**]

Pickwickian /pik-wik'i-ən/ *adj* relating to or resembling Mr *Pickwick*, the hero of Dickens's *Pickwick Papers* (1836–37). ◆ *n* a member of the Pickwick Club.

■ words derived from main entry word; □ compound words; ■ idioms and phrasal verbs

■ **in a Pickwickian sense** in a recondite or merely imaginary sense, a phrase by which a member of the Pickwick Club explained away unparliamentary language.

picky see under **pick**[1].

picnic /pik'nik/ *n* an excursion during which people eat a meal in the open air; the food eaten; *orig* a fashionable social entertainment, towards which each person contributed a share of the food; an undertaking that is mere child's play (often *ironically*). ◆ *adj* of or for a picnic; picnicking. ◆ *vi* (**pic'nicking**; **pic'nicked**) to have a picnic. [Fr *pique-nique*]
■ **pic'nicker** *n*. **pic'nicky** *adj*.
❑ **picnic races** *n pl* (*Aust* and *NZ*) rural horse races for amateurs.
■ **no picnic** something neither easy nor pleasant.

pico- /pē-kō- or pī-kō-/ *combining form* denoting 10^{-12}, as in *picocurie* and *picosecond*. [Sp *pico* a small quantity]

picornavirus /pi-kör'nə-vī-rəs/ *n* any of a group of viruses including the enteroviruses and rhinoviruses. [**pico-**, **RNA**, and **virus**]

picot /pē'kō/ *n* a loop in an ornamental edging; a raised knot in embroidery. ◆ *vt* to ornament with picots. [Fr *picot* point, prick]
■ **picoté** /pē-ko-tā/ *adj*.

picotee /pik-ə-tē'/ *n* a variety of carnation, *orig* speckled, now edged with a different colour. [Fr *picoté* prickled]

picotite /pik'ə-tīt/ (*mineralogy*) *n* a dark spinel containing iron, magnesium, and chromium. [From *Picot* Baron de la Pérouse (1744–1818), who described it]

picquet see **picket**.

picra /pik'rə/ *n* short for **hiera-picra**. [Gr *pikros* bitter]
■ **pic'rate** *n* a highly explosive salt of picric acid. **pic'ric** *adj*. **pic'rite** *n* (*mineralogy*) a coarse-grained igneous rock composed mainly of olivine with ferromagnesian minerals and usually some plagioclase. **picrocar'mine** *n* a stain for microscope work made from carmine, ammonia, water and picric acid. **picrotox'in** *n* a bitter poisonous principle in the seeds of *Cocculus indicus*.
❑ **picric acid** *n* $C_6H_2(NO_2)_3OH$ trinitrophenol, used as a yellow dyestuff and as the basis of high explosives (also called **2,4,6-trinitro-1-hydroxybenzene**).

Pict /pikt/ *n* one of an ancient people of obscure origins who lived in Britain, *esp* NE Scotland; (in Scottish folklore) one of a dwarfish race of underground dwellers, to whom (with the Romans, the Druids and Cromwell) ancient monuments are generally attributed; Steele's term for a painted woman. [L *Pictī* Picts; poss the same as *pictī*, pap of *pingere* to paint; cf **Pecht**]
■ **Pict'ish** *adj*. ◆ *n* the language of the Picts, of uncertain affiliations and origins.
❑ **Picts' house** *n* an earth-house (qv).

pictarnie /pik-tär'ni/ (*Scott*) *n* a tern. [Origin unknown]

pictograph /pik'tə-gräf/ *n* a picture used as a symbol for a word or phrase; a pictorial representation of values, statistics, etc. [L *pictus* painted, and Gr *graphein* to write, or *gramma* a letter, figure]
■ **pic'togram** *n* a pictograph; a graphic representation. **pictograph'ic** *adj*. **pictograph'ically** *adv*. **pictography** /pik-tog'rə-fi/ *n* picture-writing.

pictorial /pik-tō'ri-əl or -tö'/ *adj* of or relating to painting or drawing; of a painter (*obs*); of, by means of, like, or of the nature of a picture or pictures; vivid. ◆ *n* a periodical in which pictures are prominent. [L *pictor, -ōris* painter, from *pingere*, *pictum* to paint]
■ **picto'rially** *adv*. **pictorical** /-tor'i-kl/ *adj* (*rare*). **pictor'ically** *adv* (*rare*) in the manner of a painter.

picture /pik'chər/ *n* an imitative representation of an object on a surface; a photograph; a portrait; a tableau; a situation or outlook; a visible or visual image; a mental image; (an image on) a television screen; a person exactly like another as in *He's the picture of his father*; an impressive or attractive sight, like a painting, or worthy of being painted; a visible embodiment; a vivid verbal description; a cinema film; the art or act of painting; (in *pl*) a cinema show, or the building in which it is given. ◆ *vt* to depict or represent in a picture; to form a likeness of in the mind; to describe vividly in words. [L *pictūra*, from *pingere*, *pictum* to paint]
■ **pic'tural** *adj* relating to, illustrated by, or consisting of pictures. ◆ *n* (*Spenser*) a picture.
❑ **picture book** *n* a book of pictures; a highly illustrated children's book. **pic'ture-book** *adj* classically or stereotypically beautiful. **picture card** *n* (*cards*) a court card, a card bearing the representation of a king, queen or jack. **picture cord** *n* cord for hanging pictures. **picture frame** *n* a frame for surrounding a picture. **picture gallery** *n* a gallery, hall, or building where pictures are exhibited. **pic'ture-goer** *n* a frequent visitor to the cinema. **picture hat** *n* a lady's wide-brimmed hat, such as those that appear in portraits by Gainsborough. **picture house** or **picture palace** *n* a building for cinema shows. **Pic'turephone**® *n* a device which allows speakers on the telephone

to see each other. **pic'ture-play** *n* a story told in motion pictures. **picture postcard** *n* a postcard bearing a picture, traditionally a local view. **pic'ture-postcard** *adj* like a postcard in traditional or idealized prettiness. **picture ratio** see **aspect ratio** under **aspect**. **picture restorer** *n* a person who cleans and tries to restore old pictures. **picture rod**, **picture rail** or **picture moulding** *n* a rod or moulding on a wall from which pictures may be hung. **picture tube** *n* a cathode-ray tube in a television set. **picture window** *n* a *usu* large window designed to act as a frame to an attractive view. **pic'ture-wire** *n* wire for hanging pictures. **pic'ture-writing** *n* the use of pictures to express ideas or relate events.
■ **get the picture** (*inf*) to understand the situation. **in the picture** adequately briefed; having a share of attention. **put in the picture** give all the relevant information.

picturesque /pik-chə-resk'/ *adj* like a picture; such as would make a striking picture, implying some measure of beauty together with quaintness or immediate effectiveness; (of language) vivid and colourful, or (*facetious*) vulgar; having taste or feeling for the picturesque. [Ital *pittoresco*, from *pittura* a picture, from L *pictūra*]
■ **picturesque'ly** *adv*. **picturesque'ness** *n*.

PICU /pik'ū/ (*med; US*) *abbrev* : paediatric intensive care unit.

picul /pik'ul/ *n* a Chinese weight, about 60kg. [Malay *pikul* a man's load]

piculet /pik'ū-lit/ *n* a small tropical American woodpecker. [*Dimin* from *Picus*, the woodpecker genus]

Picus /pī'kəs/ *n* an ancient Italian god, a son of Saturn, turned into a woodpecker by Circe; the woodpecker genus. [L *Pīcus*]
■ **pī'cine** /-sīn/ *adj*.

PID (*med*) *abbrev* : pelvic inflammatory disease.

piddle /pid'l/ *vi* to urinate (*inf*); to deal in trifles; (*esp* with *about*) to trifle, mess about; to eat with little relish. ◆ *n* (*inf*) urine; an act of urination. [Origin obscure]
■ **pidd'ler** *n* a trifler. **pidd'ling** *adj* trifling, paltry.

piddock /pid'ək/ *n* the pholas. [Origin unknown]

pidgin /pij'in/ *n* a Chinese corruption of **business** (also **pidg'eon** or **pig'eon**); affair, concern (also **pidg'eon** or **pig'eon**; *inf*); any combination and distortion of two languages as a means of communication.
■ **pidginīzā'tion** or **-s-** *n*.
❑ **pidgin English** *n* a jargon, mainly English in vocabulary with Chinese arrangement, used in communication between Chinese and foreigners; any lingua franca consisting of English and another language.

pi-dog see **pye-dog**.

pie[1] /pī/ *n* a quantity of meat, fruit, or other food baked within or under a crust of prepared pastry; an easy thing (*inf*); a welcome luxury, prize, or spoil (*inf*). [Origin unknown; poss from **pie**[3], as a miscellaneous collector; the Gaelic *pighe* is from English]
❑ **pie chart**, **pie diagram** or **pie graph** *n* a circle divided into sections by radii so as to show relative numbers or quantities. **pie'-counter** *n* a counter at which pies are sold; the source of patronage, bribes, spoils of office (*US; archaic*). **pie'crust** *n* the pastry covering or enclosing a pie. **piecrust table** *n* a Chippendale table with a carved raised edge. **pie'dish** *n* a deep dish in which pies are made. **pie'-eyed** *adj* (*sl*) drunk. **pie'man** *n* someone who sells pies, *esp* in the street. **pie'-plant** *n* (*US dialect*) rhubarb. **pie'-shop** *n*.
■ **a finger in the pie** see under **finger**. **Périgord pie** a pie of partridge flavoured with truffles (*Périgord*, France, now contained in the departments of Dordogne and Lot-et-Garonne). **pie in the sky** some improbable future good promised without guarantee (from an early 20c song).

pie[2], **pye** or **pi** /pī/ *n* type confusedly mixed (*printing*); a mixed state; confusion. ◆ *vt* (**pie'ing** or **pye'ing**; **pied**) to reduce to pie. [Origin obscure; perh connected with **pie**[1], or **pie**[4]]

pie[3] /pī/ *n* a magpie; a chatterer. [Fr, from L *pīca*]

pie[4] or **pye** /pī/ *n* a book of rules for determining the Church office for the day. [LL *pīca*, poss the same as L *pīca* magpie (from the black-and-white appearance of the page)]
■ **by cock and pie** (*Shakesp*) an altered oath, *appar* by God and the pie.

pie[5] /pī/ *n* a former unit of currency in India, worth $\frac{1}{3}$ of a pice, or $\frac{1}{12}$ of an anna. [Marathi *pāī* a fourth]

piebald, also **pyebald** /pī'böld/ *adj* black and white in patches; loosely, of other colours in patches; motley; heterogeneous. ◆ *n* a piebald horse or other animal. [**pie**[3] and **bald**]

piece /pēs/ *n* a part or portion of anything, *esp* detached; a separate lump, mass or body of any material, considered as an object (in Scots without *of* following); a distance; a span of time; a single article; a definite quantity, eg of cloth or paper; a literary, dramatic, musical, or artistic composition; a production, a specimen of work; an example; an exemplification or embodiment; a sandwich or a little bread, buttered or not, *esp* as a lunch (*Scot*); a gun; a portion (*obs*); a wine cup (*obs*); a coin; a man in chess, draughts, or other game (in chess sometimes excluding pawns and the king); a person, now *usu* (disrespectfully) a woman. ◆ *vt* to enlarge by adding a piece; to patch; to combine. ◆ *vi* to have a between-meal snack (*US sl*). ◆ *combining form* consisting of a given number of separate parts, pieces, members, etc, as in *three-piece suite*. [OFr *piece*, from LL *pecia*, *petium* a fragment, a piece of land (thought to be of Celtic (Brythonic) origin); cf **patch**¹, **peat**², **petty**, and *Pit-* in place names]

■ **piece**'**less** *adj* not made of pieces. **piece**'**meal** *adv* (**meal**¹ in sense of 'measure') in pieces; to pieces; bit by bit. ◆ *adj* done bit by bit; fragmentary. ◆ *n* a small piece; bit by bit proceeding. ◆ *vt* to dismember. **piec**'**en** *vt* (*dialect*) to join (*esp* broken threads in spinning). **piec**'**ener** or **piec**'**er** *n* a person who is employed in a spinning-factory to join broken threads.

□ **piece goods** *n pl* textile fabrics made in standard lengths. **piece rate** *n* a fixed rate paid according to the amount of work done. **piece**'**work** *n* work paid for by the piece or quantity, not by time. **piece**'**worker** *n*

■ **all to pieces** or **to pieces** into a state of disintegration or collapse; through and through, thoroughly (*US*). **a piece** each. **a piece of** an instance of; a bit of, something of. **a piece of cake** see under **cake**. **a piece of one's mind** a frank outspoken reprimand. **a piece of piss** see under **piss**. **go to pieces** to break up entirely (*lit* and *fig*); to lose completely the ability to cope with the situation. **in pieces** in, or to, a broken-up state. **of a piece** as if of the same piece, the same in nature; homogeneous, uniform; in keeping, consistent (with *with*). **piece of eight** see under **eight**. **piece of goods** (*dialect*; *derog*) a woman. **piece of work** a task; a fuss, ado; a person (*usu* with *nasty*, etc). **piece out** to eke out. **piece together** to put together bit by bit. **piece up** to patch up; *perh* to incorporate in one's own share (*Shakesp*). **say one's piece** to contribute one's opinion. **the piece** (*Scot*) apiece. **to pieces** see **all to pieces** above.

pièce /*pyes*/ (*Fr*) *n* a piece, item; (a barrel of) about 220 litres (of wine). □ **pièce de résistance** /*də rä-zē-stäs*/ *n* the best item; the substantial course at dinner, the joint. **pièce d'occasion** /*do-ka-zyõ*/ *n* something (*usu* a literary or musical work) composed, prepared, or used for a special occasion.

piecemeal, piecen, piecener, piecer see under **piece**.

pied¹ /*pīd*/ *adj* variegated like a magpie; of various colours. [**pie**³]
■ **pied**'**ness** *n*.
□ **pied piper** *n* a charismatic person who entices others to follow a course of action, *usu* to their detriment (after the piper in Browning's poem *The Pied Piper of Hamelin* (1842), whose piping enticed away first the town's rats then its children). **pied wagtail** *n* a black-and-white wagtail.

pied² see **pie**².

pied-à-terre /*pyä-a-ter*'/ (*Fr*) *n* (*pl* **pieds-à-terre**) a dwelling kept for temporary, secondary, or occasional lodging.

piedmont /*pēd*'*mont*/ (*US*) *n* a mountain-foot region (also *adj*). [*Piedmont* in Italy, literally, mountain-foot]
■ **pied**'**montite** *n* a dark-red mineral, a hydrous silicate of calcium, aluminium, manganese and iron.

pied noir /*pyä nwär*'/ (*Fr*) *n* (*pl* **pieds noirs**) a N African (*esp* Algerian) person of French descent.

pie-dog see **pye-dog**.

piel'd /*pēld*/ (*Shakesp*) *adj* tonsured. [See **peel**¹]

Piemontese /*pē-mon-tēz*'/ *n* a breed of cattle *orig* from N Italy, bred for beef with a low fat content.

piend /*pēnd*/ *n* a salient angle. [Origin unknown]

pier /*pēr*/ *n* a mass of stone, ironwork, or woodwork projecting into the sea or other water, as a breakwater, landing stage, or promenade; a jetty or a wharf; the mass of stonework between the openings in the wall of a building; the support of an arch, bridge, etc; a masonry support for a telescope or the like; a buttress; a gate pillar. [ME *pēr*, LL *pēra*; origin doubtful]
■ **pier**'**age** *n* a toll paid for using a pier.
□ **pier glass** *n orig* a mirror hung between windows; a tall mirror. **pier**'**head** *n* the seaward end of a pier. **pier table** *n* a table fitted for the space between windows.

pierce /*pērs*/ *vt* to thrust or make a hole through; to enter, or force a way into; to touch or move deeply; to penetrate; to perforate; to make by perforating or penetrating. ◆ *vi* to penetrate. ◆ *n* a perforation; a stab; a prick. [OFr *percer*; of doubtful origin]
■ **pierce**'**able** *adj* capable of being pierced. **pierced**' *adj* perforated; penetrated. **pierc**'**er** *n* someone or that which pierces; any sharp instrument used for piercing; a sting; a keen eye (*archaic*). **pierc**'**ing** *adj* penetrating; very acute; keen, sharp. ◆ *n* a hole made in body

piercing (*qv*); the site of such a hole; studs or rings used in body piercing. **pierc**'**ingly** *adv*. **pierc**'**ingness** *n*.

Pierian /*pī-ē*'*ri-ən*/ *adj* of Pieria in Thessaly, the country of the Muses; of the Muses. [Gr *Pīeriā*]
■ **pierid** /*pī*'*ə-rid*/ *n* any butterfly of the Pieridae family. **Pierides** /*pī-er*'*i-dēz*/ *n pl* (*sing* **Pī**'**eris**) the nine Muses. **pieridine** /*pī-er*'*i-dīn*/ *adj* of the Pieridae (see below). **Pī**'**eris** *n* the cabbage-butterfly genus, typical of the family **Pier**'**idae** /*-dē*/; a genus of American and Asiatic shrubs, of the family Ericaceae.

pierogi, pirogi or **perogi** /*pə-rō*'*gi*/ *n* (*pl* **piero**'**gi**, etc or **pierog**'**ies**, etc) (*usu* in *pl*) a traditional Polish dish, a semicircular filled dumpling, *orig* savoury, now also sweet, boiled and then briefly sautéed and served with melted butter. [Pol *pierógi* dumplings]

Pierrot /*pē*'*ə-rō* or *pyer-ō*/ *n* a white-faced clown with loose long-sleeved garb; (*without cap*) formerly, a member of a group of entertainers in similar dress at seaside resorts, etc; an 18c women's low-cut basque, with sleeves. [Fr, dimin of *Pierre* Peter]
■ **pierrette** /*pē-ə-ret*'/ *n* a female performer in a pierrot group.

pierst (*Spenser*) short form of **pierced** (*pat* and *pap*).

piert same as **peart**; see also **parsley piert**.

Piesporter /*pēz*'*pör-tər*/ *n* a Moselle wine made in *Piesport*, Germany.

piet same as **pyot**.

pietà /*pyä-tä*'/ (*art*) *n* a representation of the Virgin with the dead Christ across her knees. [Ital, from L *pietās*, *-ātis* pity]

pietism, pietist, etc see under **piety**.

pietra dura /*pyä*'*trə doo*'*rə*/ *n* inlaid mosaic work with hard stones, such as jasper, agate, etc, or, strictly, with one type of stone only. [Ital, hard stone]
■ **pietre dure** /*pyä*'*tre dū*'*re*/ *n pl* (used as *sing*) this type of (*usu* relief) mosaic work done with a variety of semi-precious stones.

piety /*pī*'*i-ti*/ *n* the quality of being pious; dutifulness; devoutness; sense of duty towards parents, benefactors, etc; dutiful conduct; a conventional belief or attitude; pity (*obs*). [OFr *piete*, from L *pietās*, *-ātis*]
■ **pi**'**etism** *n* pious feeling; an exaggerated show of piety. **pi**'**etist** *n* someone marked by strong devotional feeling; a name first applied to a sect of German religious reformers of deep devotional feeling (end of 17c). **pietist**'**ic** or **pietist**'**ical** *adj*.

piezo- /*pē-zō-, pē-et-sō-, pī-i-zō-, pī-ē-zō-* or *-zo-*/ combining form denoting pressure. [Gr *piezein* to press]
■ **pi**'**ezo** *adj* short for **piezoelectric**. **piezochem**'**istry** *n* the chemistry of substances under high pressure. **piezoelec**'**tric** *adj*. **piezoelectri**'**city** *n* electricity developed in certain crystals by mechanical strain, and the effect of an electric field in producing expansion and contraction along different axes. **piezomagnet**'**ic** *adj*. **piezomag**'**netism** *n* magnetism developed in a similar way to piezoelectricity, using a magnetic instead of an electric field. **piezometer** /*-om*'*i-tər*/ *n* an instrument for measuring pressure or compressibility.

piffero /*pif*'*ə-rō*/ *n* (*pl* **piff**'**eros**) a fife; an Italian bagpipe; a crude oboe. [Ital, from OHGer *pfīfari* piper]
■ **pifferaro** /*-ä*'*rō*/ *n* (*pl* **pifferari** /*-rē*/) a piffero-player.

piffle /*pif*'*l*/ (*inf*) *n* nonsense; worthless talk. ◆ *vi* to trifle; to act ineffectually. [Origin unknown]
■ **piff**'**ler** *n*. **piff**'**ling** *adj* trivial, petty.

pig¹ /*pig*/ *n* any mammal of the family Suidae, omnivorous ungulates with thick, bristly skin, *esp* the domesticated *Sus scrofa*, a farm animal bred as food for humans; its flesh as food, *esp* that of the young animal; someone who is like the popular image of a pig, dirty, greedy, gluttonous, or cantankerous (also used mildly in reproach); an oblong mass of unforged metal, as first extracted from the ore; the mould into which it is run, *esp* one of the branches, the main channel being the *sow*; a device that is propelled through a pipeline or duct by pneumatic, hydraulic or gas pressure, for clearing, cleaning, tracking or scanning purposes, etc (*technol*); same as **go-devil** (see under **go**¹); a feast (*sl*); a policeman (*sl*); a segment of an orange (*sl*); something very difficult (*sl*). ◆ *vi* (**pigg**'**ing**) **pigged** to give birth to pigs; to live, herd, huddle, sleep, or feed like pigs; to eat greedily (*sl*). [ME *pigge*; cf Du *bigge* big]
■ **pigg**'**ery** *n* a place where pigs are kept; piggishness. **pigg**'**ie**, **pigg**'**y**, **pig**'**let** or **pig**'**ling** *n* a little pig. **pigg**'**ies** *n pl* a child's word for toes. **pigg**'**ing** *n* (*technol*) operating a pig or running a pig along a pipeline. ◆ *adj* (*sl*) expressing aversion, of something troublesome, unpleasant or difficult. **pigg**'**ish** *adj* like a pig; greedy; dirty; cantankerous; mean. **pigg**'**ishly** *adv*. **pigg**'**ishness** *n*. **pigg**'**y** *adj* like a pig.
□ **pig**'**-bed** *n* a pig's sleeping place; a mould of sand in which a pig of iron is cast. **pig**'**boat** *n* (*US naval sl*) a submarine. **pig**'**-deer** *n* the babiroussa. **pig**'**-eyed** *adj* having small, pinkish, dull eyes with heavy lids. **pig**'**-faced** *adj*. **pig**'**feed** *n* food for pigs. **pig**'**-fish** *n* (*US*) a name

---

for various kinds of grunt (*Haemulon*, etc); in Australia, a name for various wrasses. **piggyback** *adv*, etc see separate entry. **piggy bank** see under **pig²**. **pighead'ed** *adj* having a pig-like head; stupidly obstinate. **pighead'edly** *adv*. **pighead'edness** *n*. **pig'-herd** *n*. **pig'-ig'norant** *adj* (*inf*; *derog*) very ignorant. **pig'-in-the-midd'le** or **pigg'y-in-the-midd'le** *n* a children's game in which a person standing between two or more others tries to intercept a ball, etc, passing back and forth between them; a person caught between opposing viewpoints, strategies, etc (*fig*). **pig iron** *n* iron in pigs or rough bars. **pig'-jump** *vi* (*Aust*; of a horse) to jump from all four legs without bringing them together. **pig Latin** *n* a secret language or jargon made up by children, *esp* one in which an initial consonant is transposed to the end of the word, followed by *-ay*, so that eg *pig* becomes *igpay*. **pig'-lead** *n* lead in pigs. **pig'-lily** *n* (*S Afr*) the lily of the Nile. **pig'-man** *n* a man responsible for or expert in looking after pigs. **pig'meat** *n* bacon, ham or pork. **pig'nut** *n* the earthnut (genus *Conopodium*). **pig'pen** *n* a pigsty. **pig'-rat** *n* the bandicoot rat. **pig'sconce** *n* a pigheaded person; a blockhead. **pig sick** or **pig'-sick** *adj* (*inf*) extremely fed up or annoyed. **pig'skin** *n* the skin of a pig prepared as a strong leather; a saddle (*sl*); a football (*N Am sl*). **pig'-sticker** *n*. **pig'-sticking** *n* boar-hunting with spears. **pig'sty** *n* a pen for keeping pigs; a very dirty or untidy place (*inf*). **pig's'-wash** or **pig'wash** *n* swill. **pig's whisper** a low whisper (*dialect*); a very short space of time. **pig swill** or **pig'swill** *n* kitchen, etc, waste fed to pigs. **pig'tail** *n* the tail of a pig; the hair of the head plaited behind or at the side; a short length of rope or cable; a roll of twisted tobacco. **pig'weed** *n* goosefoot, amaranth, cow parsnip, or other plant eaten by pigs. **pig'-woman** *n* a woman who roasted pigs at fairs.
■ **a pig in a poke** see under **poke²**. **in pig** (of a sow) pregnant. **make a pig of oneself** (*inf*) to overindulge in food or drink. **make a pig's ear of** (**something**) (*inf*) to make a mess of something, to do something badly or clumsily. **on the pig's back** (*Irish*) in a position of prosperity and comfort. **pig it** (*inf*) to live in squalid or dirty surroundings. **pig out** to overeat, go on a binge. **pigs might fly** (*inf*; as an expression of scepticism) that is highly unlikely. **when pigs fly** (*inf*) never.

pig² /*pig*/ (*Scot*) *n* an earthenware crock, hot-water bottle, or other vessel; earthenware; a potsherd. [Origin unknown]
□ **piggy bank** *n* a money box made of pottery, shaped like a pig through false association with **pig¹**; a child's money box, whether or not pig-shaped. **pig'-man** or **-woman** *n* a dealer in earthenware articles.
■ **pigs and whistles** wrack and ruin.

pigeon¹ /*pij'ən* or *-in*/ *n* orig a young dove; a dove; any bird of the dove family; extended to various other birds (eg the *Cape pigeon*); a girl (*obs*); someone who is fleeced (*sl*); short for **stool pigeon** (see under **stool**). ◆ *vt* to gull or hoax. [OFr *pijon*, from L *pīpiō*, *-ōnis*, from *pīpīre* to cheep]
■ **pig'eonry** *n* a place for keeping pigeons.
□ **pig'eon-berry** *n* (*US*) pokeweed or its fruit. **pig'eon-breast'ed** or **-chested** *adj* having a narrow chest with the breastbone projecting. **pigeon breast** or **pigeon chest** *n*. **pig'eon-fancier** *n* someone who keeps and breeds pigeons for racing or exhibiting. **pig'eon-fancying** *n*. **pig'eon-flier** or **-flyer** *n* someone who sends out homing pigeons. **pig'eon-flying** *n*. **pig'eon-heart'ed** *adj* timid. **pig'eonhole** *n* a compartment for storing and classifying papers, for leaving letters, etc; a compartment of the mind or memory; a niche for a pigeon's nest; a hole of similar appearance; (in *pl*) the stocks; (in *pl*) an old outdoor game like bagatelle. ◆ *vt* to put into a pigeonhole; to classify methodically, or too rigidly; to lay aside and delay action on, or treat with neglect; to furnish with or make into pigeonholes. **pig'eonholer** *n*. **pig'eon-house** *n* a dovecot. **pig'eon-liv'ered** *adj* mild. **pigeon pair** *n* boy and girl twins or a boy and girl as sole children in a family. **pigeon pea** *n* dal. **pig'eon-post** *n* transmission of letters by pigeons. **pig'eon's-blood** *n* a dark red colour, ruby. **pigeon's milk** *n* partly digested food regurgitated by pigeons to feed their young; an imaginary liquid for which children are sent, eg on 1 April. **pig'eon-toed** *adj* having the toes more or less turned inward; (of birds) having all toes at one level. **pig'eon-wing** *n* a caper or leap in dancing.
■ **clay pigeon** see under **clay**.

pigeon² same as **pidgin**.

piggin /*pig'in*/ *n* a small pail or bowl constructed of staves and hoops, like a barrel, one stave usually prolonged as a handle; a vessel of various other kinds. [Poss from **pig²**]

pigging, **piggish**, **piggy**, etc see under **pig¹**.

piggyback /*pig'i-bak*/ or **pickaback** /*pik'ə-bak*/, also **pickback** /*pik'bak*/ or **pickapack** /*pik'ə-pak*/ *adv* (carried) on the back and shoulders of someone like a pack; on something, or as an addition to something. ◆ *adj* on the back like a pack; of or for a piggyback; (of a vehicle or plane) conveyed on top of another; of or relating to a surgical procedure that leaves the patient's own heart functioning along with a transplanted heart. ◆ *n* a ride on someone's back. ◆ *vt* to

carry by piggyback; to attach or append. [Connection with **pick²** (pitch), **pack¹** and **back¹** obscure]
□ **piggyback** or (**pickaback**) **plant** *n* a popular name for the perennial plant *Tolmiea menziesii*, which produces plantlets at the base of the leaf.

pight /*pīt*/ an old *pat* and *pap* (*Spenser*) of **pitch¹**, pitched, set; also a false archaism for the present tense. *adj* well-knit (*Spenser*); resolved (*Shakesp*).

pightle /*pī'tl*/ *n* a small enclosure; a croft. [Ety dubious]

pigmaean, **pigmean**, **pigmoid** see under **pygmy**.

pigment /*pig'mənt*/ *n* paint or dye; any substance used for colouring; that which gives colour to animal and vegetable tissues; piment (*Walter Scott*). [L *pīgmentum*, from *pingere* to paint]
■ **pigmental** /*-men'tl*/ or **pig'mentary** *adj*. **pigmentā'tion** *n* coloration or discoloration by pigments in the tissues. **pig'mented** *adj*.

pigmy same as **pygmy**.

pignorate or **pignerate** /*pig'nə-rāt*/ (*archaic*) *vt* to give or take in pledge or pawn. [L *pignus*, *-eris* or *-oris* a pledge]
■ **pignorā'tion** *n*.

pigsney, **pigsny** or **pigsnie** /*pigz'ni*/ *n* a term of endearment (sometimes contempt), *esp* to a woman (*archaic* or *dialect*); an eye (playfully; *obs*). [*pig's eye*, with prosthetic *n* (from *an eye*, *mine eye*)]

pi-jaw see **pi²**.

pika /*pī'kə*/ *n* the tailless hare (genus *Ochotona*), a small mammal of the order Lagomorpha, found in mountain regions. [Tungus *piika*]

pike¹ /*pīk*/ *n* a voracious freshwater fish (*Esox lucius*) with a pointed snout; extended to various other fishes. [**pike²**, from its sharp head]
□ **pike'minnow** *n* a large edible fish of the genus *Ptychocheilus*. **pike'-perch** *n* a percoid fish with pike-like jaws.

pike² /*pīk*/ *n* a weapon with a long shaft and a sharp head like a spear, formerly used by foot soldiers; a sharp point; a spiked staff; a sharp-pointed hill or summit; a pick (*dialect*). ◆ *vt* to kill or pierce with a pike; to pick (*dialect*). [OE *pīc* pick, spike; but also partly from Fr *pic* with the same meaning, and *pique* the weapon, and prob partly from Scand]
■ **piked** /*pīkt* or *pīk'id*/ *adj* spiked; ending in a point. **pīk'er** *n* someone who picks (*dialect*); a pilferer (*dialect*).
□ **pike'-head** *n* the head of a pike or spear. **pike'man** *n* a man armed with a pike; someone who wields a pick. **pike'staff** *n* the staff or shaft of a pike; a staff with a pike at the end.
■ **plain as a pikestaff** (*orig* **packstaff**) perfectly plain or clear.

pike³ /*pīk*/ *n* a turnpike; a toll; a main road (*US*). [Short for **turnpike**]
■ **pī'ker** *n* a tramp.
□ **pike'-keeper** or **pike'man** *n* a man in charge of a turnpike.

pike⁴ /*pīk*/ (*diving* and *gym*) *n* (also **piked position**) a posture in which the body is bent sharply at the hips with legs kept straight at the knees and toes pointed (also *adj*). ◆ *vi* to adopt this position. [Origin uncertain]
■ **piked** *adj*.

pike⁵ /*pīk*/ *vi* to renege on a commitment (*Aust* and *NZ inf*); to speed (*old inf*). ◆ *vt* (*obs*) to betake (oneself) quickly. [Perh orig *get oneself a pikestaff* (a pilgrim's spiked staff); perh Fr *piquer* to spur]
■ **pīk'er** *n* a person who bets, gambles, speculates, or does anything else in a very small way; a shirker or mean character (*sl*).

pikelet /*pī'klit*/ *n* a kind of teacake, or crumpet, or muffin (*dialect*); a drop scone (*Aust* and *NZ*). [Welsh *bara pyglyd* pitchy bread]

pikey /*pī'ki*/ (*derog sl*) *n* orig an itinerant person, a gypsy; a boorish and uneducated person, *esp* one engaged in a criminal or antisocial activity. ◆ *adj* characteristic of a pikey. [Perh shortened from **turnpike**]

pikul same as **picul**.

pila see **pilum**.

pilaff see **pilau**.

pilaster /*pi-las'tər*/ *n* a square column, partly built into and partly projecting from a wall. [Fr *pilastre*, from Ital *pilastro*, from L *pīla* a pillar]
■ **pilas'tered** *adj*.

Pilates /*pi-lä'tēz*/ *n* an exercise system intended to stretch the muscles, improve the posture, etc. [J *Pilates* (1880–1967), its German inventor]

pilau /*pi-low'* or *pē'low*/ *n* a highly spiced Asian dish of rice with a fowl or other meat, or fish, boiled together or separately (also **pillau'**, **pilaw'**, **pilaf'**, **pilaff'** (or /*pil'*/) or **pilow'**). [Pers *pilāw*, Turk *pilāw*, *pilāf*]

pilch /*pilch*/ (*archaic*) *n* an outer garment, *orig* a fur cloak, later a coarse leather or woollen cloak; a rug for a saddle; a light saddle; a flannel cloth for wrapping a child. [OE *pyl(e)ce*, from LL *pellicea*, from L *pellis* skin]
■ **pilch'er** *n* (*Shakesp*) a scabbard.

pilchard /pil'chərd/ n a European sea fish like the herring, but smaller, thicker, and rounder, common off Cornwall (earlier (Shakesp)) **pil'cher**. [Origin unknown; poss Scand (cf Norw *pilk* artificial bait); Ir *pilseir* is prob from English]

pilcorn /pil'körn/ n the naked oat, a variety in which the glume does not adhere to the grain. [For *pilled corn* (see **pill**²)]

pilcrow /pil'krō/ n a paragraph-mark. [Origin obscure]

pile¹ /pīl/ n a set of things fitted or resting one over another, or in a more or less regular figure; a heap of combustibles for cremating a dead body, or for the burnt-offering, or for burning to death; a set of weights fitting one within another; a stack of arms; a heap of shot; a set of wrought-iron bars placed together for welding and rolling into one; a series of alternate plates of two metals for generating an electric current; a set of coins placed vertically one upon another; a great amount of money, a fortune (*sl*); a large amount or supply (*inf*); a tall building; a nuclear reactor, *orig* the graphite blocks forming the moderator for the reactor (*obs*); the under iron for striking coins (*obs*); the reverse of a coin (*obs*). ◆ *vt* to lay in a pile or heap; to collect in a mass; to heap up or load in a heap or heaps; to accumulate; to weld and roll (several iron bars) into one. ◆ *vi* to come into piles; to accumulate; to go in crowds; to get in or out (with *in* or *out* ; *inf*). [Fr, from L *pīla* a pillar]
■ **pī'ler** n.
❑ **pile'-cap** n the top of a nuclear reactor; see also under **pile**². **pile'-up** n a large-scale collision, *esp* of motor vehicles.
■ **pile arms** to prop three muskets, *orig* with fixed bayonets, so that the butts remain firm, the muzzles close together pointing obliquely (also **stack arms**). **pile into** to collide with. **pile it on** (*inf*) to overdo or exaggerate something. **pile on** (or **up**) **the agony** (*inf*) to affect or exaggerate distress, pain, etc, eg in order to win sympathy; to add cruelly to another's pain, grief, etc. **pile up** to accumulate; to form a disorderly mass or heap; to become involved in a pile-up; to run ashore.

pile² /pīl/ n a large stake or cylinder driven into the earth to support foundations; an arrowhead; a Roman javelin; an inverted pyramidal figure (*heraldry*). ◆ *vt* to drive piles into; to support with or build on piles. [OE *pīl*, from L *pīlum* a javelin]
■ **pī'ling** n.
❑ **pile'-cap** n (*civil eng*) a reinforced concrete block cast around a set of piles to create a unified support; see also under **pile**¹. **pile'-driver** n a machine for driving in piles; (in games) a very heavy stroke, kick, etc. **pile'-driving** n and adj. **pile'-dwelling** n a dwelling built on piles, *esp* a lake dwelling. **pile shoe** n the iron or steel point fitted to the foot of a pile to give it strength to pierce the earth and so assist driving. **pile'work** n work or foundations made of piles. **pile'-worm** n a shipworm.

pile³ /pīl/ n the raised or fluffy surface of a fabric, carpet, etc; (as distinguished from *nap*) the raised surface of a fabric made not in finishing but in weaving, either by leaving loops (which may be cut) or by weaving two cloths face to face and cutting them apart; a covering of hair, *esp* soft, fine, or short hair; down; human body-hair; a single hair. [L *pilus* a hair]
■ **pī'leous** adj (*rare*) relating to or consisting of hair. **pīlif'erous** adj bearing hairs; ending in a hair-like point. **pil'iform** adj hair-like.

pile⁴ /pīl/ n (*usu* in *pl*) a haemorrhoid. [L *pila* a ball]
■ **pile'wort** n the lesser celandine (*Ranunculus ficaria*), once thought a remedy for piles.

pilea, pileate, pileated, pilei see **pileum**.

pileorhiza /pī-li-ō-rī'zə/ (*bot*) n a root cap. [L *pīleus* or *pīleum* (see **pileum**), Gr *rhiza* root]

pileous see under **pile**³.

piler see under **pile**¹.

pileum /pī'li-əm/ n (*pl* **pil'ea**) the top of a bird's head. [L *pīleum*, *pīleus*, for *pilleum*, *pilleus* a felt cap; cf Gr *pīlos* felt, a felt cap]
■ **pī'leate** or **pī'leated** adj cap-shaped; capped; crested. **pi'leus** n (*pl* **pilei** /pī'lī-ī/) a Roman felt cap; the expanded cap of a mushroom or toadstool, or other fungus.

pilfer /pil'fər/ vi and vt to steal in small quantities. [Prob connected with **pelf**]
■ **pil'ferage, pil'fering** or (*old*) **pil'fery** n petty theft. **pil'ferer** n. **pil'feringly** adv.

pilgrim /pil'grim/ n a person who travels *esp* a distance to visit a holy place; allegorically or spiritually, a person journeying through life as a stranger in this world; a wanderer, wayfarer (*archaic* and *poetic*); a Pilgrim Father; an original settler; a newcomer. ◆ adj of or relating to a pilgrim; like a pilgrim; consisting of pilgrims. [Assumed OFr *pelegrin* (Fr *pèlerin*), from L *peregrīnus* foreigner, stranger; see **peregrine**]
■ **pil'grimage** n the journeying of a pilgrim; a journey to a shrine or other holy place, or to a place venerated for its associations; the journey of life; a lifetime. ◆ adj visited by pilgrims. ◆ vi to go on a

pilgrimage; to wander. **pil'grimager** n (*derog*) a person who goes on a pilgrimage. **pil'grimer** n someone who goes on a pilgrimage. **pil'grimize** or **-ise** vi (or *vt* with *it*) to play the pilgrim.
❑ **pil'grim-bott'le** n a flat bottle with ears at the neck for a cord. **Pilgrim Fathers** n *pl* the Puritans who sailed for America in the *Mayflower*, and founded Plymouth, Massachusetts, in 1620. **pilgrim's shell** n a scallop shell (called a cockle) used as a sign that one had visited the shrine of St James of Compostela. **pilgrim's sign** n a badge, often a leaden brooch, obtained at the shrine and worn on the hat by a pilgrim.

pilhorse /pil'hörs/ see **philhorse**.

pili¹ /pē-lē'/ n the nut (also **pili'nut'**) of trees of the burseraceous genus *Canarium*. [Tagálog]

pili² see **pilus**.

piliferous, piliform see under **pile**³.

piling see under **pile**².

Pilipino /pil-i-pē'nō/ same as **Tagálog**.

pill¹ /pil/ n a little ball, flattened sphere or disc, etc of medicine for swallowing (see also **the pill** below); a ball, eg a cannonball, tennis-ball, or (in *pl*) billiards (*facetious*); anything disagreeable that must be accepted; a tiresome person; a doctor (*sl*; also in *pl*); (in *pl*) little balls that form on the surface of fabric during use, through rubbing, etc. ◆ *vt* to dose with pills; to form into pills; to blackball (*sl*). ◆ *vi* (of fabric) to (have a tendency to) develop pills on the surface. [L *pila*, perh through OFr *pile*, or from a syncopated form of the dimin *pilula*]
■ **pill'ing** n.
❑ **pill'box** n a box for holding pills; a small blockhouse (*milit*); a kind of one-horse carriage (*archaic*); a small round brimless hat. **pill bug** n a woodlouse that rolls itself into a ball. **pill'head** or **pill'-popper** n (*sl*) a regular, *usu* addicted, taker of sedative and/or stimulant pills, eg barbiturates and amphetamines. **pill'worm** n a millipede that curls up. **pill'wort** n a water fern (genus *Pilularia*) found at lake-margins, with pill-like sporocarps.
■ **on the pill** taking contraceptive pills regularly. **the pill** any of various contraceptive pills (see **oral contraception** under **oral**).

pill² /pil/ vt and vi to plunder (*archaic*); to peel (*dialect*); to make or become hairless (*obs*). ◆ n (*Spenser*) a husk or integument. [OE *pylian* and OFr *peler*, both from L *pilāre* to deprive of hair; cf **peel**¹]
■ **pill'age** n the act of plundering; plunder. ◆ *vt* and *vi* to plunder. **pill'ager** n.

pillar /pil'ər/ n a detached support, not necessarily cylindrical or of classical proportions (*archit*); a structure of similar form erected as a monument, ornament, object of worship, etc; a tall upright rock; a mass of coal or rock left in a mine to support the roof; anything in the form of a column; a supporting post; the post supporting a bicycle saddle; (in a car) a vertical column of bodywork, eg the door pillar separating the front and rear doors; a cylinder holding the plates of a watch or clock in position; a pillarbox; someone who, or anything that, sustains. [OFr *piler* (Fr *pilier*), from LL *pīlāre*, from L *pīla* a pillar]
■ **pill'arist** n (also **pill'ar-saint**) an ascetic living on the top of a pillar, a stylite.
❑ **pillar box** n a short hollow pillar for posting letters in. **pill'ar-box red** n the traditional bright-red colour of British pillar boxes (also *adj*). **pill'ar-root** n a supporting root descending from a branch.
■ **from pillar to post** from one state of difficulty to another; hither and thither. **Pillars of Islam** the five major Islamic duties, ie the statement of faith, prayer, fasting, almsgiving, and pilgrimage to Mecca.

pillau see **pilau**.

pillicock /pil'i-kok/ n the penis (allusively in *Shakesp*); a term of endearment to a boy. [Cf Norw dialect *pill*]

pillion /pil'yən or -i-ən/ n the passenger-seat of a motorcycle, or a baggage-carrier, usable as an extra seat; a pad or light saddle for a woman; a cushion behind a horseman for a second rider (*usu* a woman) or for a bag. ◆ *adv* on a pillion. ◆ *vt* to seat on or provide with a pillion. [Prob Ir *pillín*, Gaelic *pillin*, *pillean*, a pad, a packsaddle, from *peall* a skin or mat, from L *pellis* skin]
■ **pill'ionist** n (also **pill'ion-rider**) someone who rides pillion.
❑ **pill'ion-seat** n.

pilliwinks /pil'i-wingks/ n *pl* an instrument of torture for crushing the fingers. [Origin unknown]

pillock /pil'ək/ n (*sl*) a stupid or foolish person. [**pillicock** and dialect forms *pillick*, *pilluck*]

pillory /pil'ə-ri/ n (*hist*) a wooden frame, supported by an upright pillar or post, with holes through which the head and hands were put as a punishment, abolished in England in 1837. ◆ *vt* (**pill'orying**; **pill'oried**) to set in the pillory (*hist*); to hold up to criticism or ridicule. [OFr *pilori*; Provençal *espilori*; of uncertain origin]
■ **pill'orize** or **-ise** vt to pillory.

pillow /pil'ō/ n a cushion for a sleeper's head; any object used for the purpose; a cushion for lace-making; a support for part of a structure;

something resembling a pillow in shape or feel. ◆ *vt* to lay or rest for support; to serve as pillow for; to provide or prop with pillows. ◆ *vi* (*archaic*) to rest the head. [OE *pyle*, also *pylu*, from L *pulvīnus*]

■ **pill'owed** *adj* supported by or provided with a pillow. **pill'owy** *adj* like a pillow; round and swelling; soft.

❑ **pill'ow-bere** (*archaic*) or **pill'ow-beer** *n* (*archaic*) a pillowcase. **pillow-block** see under **pedestal**. **pill'owcase** or **pill'owslip** *n* a cover for a pillow. **pill'ow-cup** *n* a last cup before going to bed. **pill'ow-fight** *n*. **pill'ow-fighting** *n* the game of thumping one another with pillows. **pillow lace** *n* lace worked with bobbins on a padded cushion. **pillow lava** *n* lava showing pillow-structure. **pill'ow-structure** *n* (in lavas) separation into pillow-shaped blocks. **pillow talk** *n* talk between lovers in bed.

pill-popper, pillworm, pillwort see under **pill¹**.

pilniewinks see **pinnywinkle**.

Pilocarpus /pī-lō-kär'pəs/ *n* a genus of S American rutaceous shrubs, including jaborandi. [Gr *pīlos* felt, a felt cap, and *karpos* fruit]

■ **pilocar'pin** or **pilocar'pine** /-pēn/ *n* an alkaloid ($C_{11}H_{16}O_2N_2$) obtained from jaborandi leaves.

pilose /pī'lōs/ *adj* hairy; having scattered soft or moderately stiff hairs. [L *pilōsus*, from *pilus* hair]

■ **pilosity** /-los'i-ti/ *n*. **pī'lous** *adj* hairy.

pilot /pī'lət/ *n* a person who operates the controls of an aircraft, hovercraft, spacecraft, etc; someone who is qualified to act as pilot; a person who conducts ships in and out of a harbour, along a dangerous coast, etc; a steersman (*archaic*); a guide; a cowcatcher (*US*); a pilot film or broadcast. ◆ *adj* relating to pilot(s); acting as guide or control; trial (of eg a model on a smaller scale) serving to test the qualities or future possibilities of a machine, plant, etc, or (of a film or broadcast) to test public reaction so as to assess the probable popularity of a proposed radio or television series. ◆ *vt* to act as pilot to. [Fr *pilote*, from Ital *pilota*, appar for earlier *pedota*, which may be from Gr *pēdon* oar, in pl, rudder]

■ **pī'lotage** *n* piloting; a pilot's fee. **pī'lotless** *adj* without a pilot; (of an automatic aeroplane) not requiring a pilot.

❑ **pilot balloon** *n* a small balloon sent up to find how the wind blows. **pī'lot-boat** *n* a boat used by pilots on duty. **pilot burner, jet** or **light** *n* a small gas-burner kept alight to light another (see also **pilot lamp** below). **pilot cloth** *n* a coarse, stout cloth for overcoats. **pilot engine** *n* a locomotive sent before a train to clear its way, as a pilot. **pilot fish** *n* a carangoid fish that accompanies ships and sharks. **pilot flag** or **jack** *n* the flag hoisted at the fore by a vessel needing a pilot. **pilot house** *n* a shelter for steering-gear and pilot (also called **wheelhouse**). **pilot jacket** *n* a pea jacket. **pilot lamp** or **light** *n* a small electric light to show when current is on, or for some other purpose. **pi'lotman** *n* a railway employee assigned to guide trains across a section of single-track line. **pilot officer** *n* (in the Royal Air Force) an officer ranking with an army second lieutenant. **pi'lot-plant** *n* prototype machinery set up to begin a new process. **pilot project** or **scheme** *n* a scheme serving as a guide on a small scale to a full-scale scheme. **pilot whale** *n* any of several types of whale of the *Globicephala* genus, family Delphinidae.

pilotis /pi-lot'ē* or *pi-lo-tēz'/ (*archit*) *n pl* a series of slender columns or stilts used on the ground floor of a building to raise the main floor to first-floor level, and leaving open space below (eg for car parking). [Fr *pillars* stilts]

pilous see under **pilose**.

pilow see **pilau**.

Pils /pils/ or *pilz/ *n* a lager beer similar to Pilsener. [Short form]

Pilsener or **Pilsner** /pilz'* or *pils'nər/ (also without *cap*) *n* a light-coloured, flavoursome variety of lager, *orig* brewed in *Pilsen*, Czech Republic.

Piltdown man /pilt'down man/ *n* a once-supposed very early form of man represented by parts of a skull found at *Piltdown*, Sussex (1912), the skull being exposed as a fake in 1953 (see also **Eoanthropus**).

pilule /pil'ūl/ *n* a little pill (also **pil'ula**). [L *pilula*, dimin of *pila* ball]

■ **pil'ular** *adj*.

pilum /pī'ləm/ *n* (*pl* **pī'la**) the heavy javelin used by Roman foot soldiers. [L *pīlum*]

pilus /pī'ləs/ *n* (*pl* **pī'lī**) a hair. [L *pilus*]

PIM (*comput*) *abbrev*: personal information manager (see under **personal**).

piment /pi-ment'/ (*obs*) *n* spiced sweetened wine (also (*Walter Scott*) **pigment** /pig'mənt/). [OFr *piment*, Sp *pimiento*, from L *pīgmentum* paint]

■ **pimento** /pi-ment'ō/ *n* (*pl* **pimen'tos**) formerly, Cayenne pepper; now allspice or Jamaica pepper, the dried unripe fruits of a West Indian tree (*Pimenta officinalis*) of the myrtle family; the tree itself; its wood. **pimiento** /pi-mē-en'tō/ *n* (*pl* **pimien'tos**) the sweet, red, yellow or green pepper, capsicum.

pimp /pimp/ *n* a man who lives with, and sometimes solicits for, a prostitute and lives off her earnings, or one who solicits for a prostitute or brothel and is paid for his services; a person who procures gratifications for the lust of others, a pander. ◆ *vi* to act or live as a pimp; to pander. ◆ *vt* (*sl*) to decorate (a car, house, etc) in a flashy way. [Origin obscure, perh related to Fr *pimpant* well-dressed, smart, from OFr *pimper* to dress smartly]

■ **pimp'ing** *n*.

pimpernel /pim'pər-nel/ *n* burnet (*obs*); burnet saxifrage (genus *Pimpinella*) (*obs*); now, the poor man's weather glass (*Anagallis arvensis*), a plant of the primrose family, with scarlet (or blue, etc) flowers. [OFr *pimpernelle*, Mod Fr *pimprenelle*, and Ital *pimpinella* burnet; origin doubtful]

■ **Pimpinell'a** *n* the anise and burnet saxifrage genus of umbelliferous plants.

■ **bastard pimpernel** a small plant (*Centunculus minimus*) related to the scarlet pimpernel. **bog pimpernel** a small creeping plant (*Anagallis tenella*) of the primrose family, with pale pink flowers on slender stems. **water pimpernel** a water plant of the primrose family, brookweed. **yellow pimpernel** the wood loosestrife (*Lysimachia nemorum*).

Pimpinella see under **pimpernel**.

pimping¹ /pim'ping/ *adj* petty; puny; paltry; sickly. [Origin obscure]

pimping² see under **pimp**.

pimple /pim'pl/ *n* a small raised swelling on the skin; any small swelling, protuberance, or hill. [Origin uncertain]

■ **pim'pled** or **pim'ply** *adj* having pimples.

PIN /pin/ *abbrev*: personal identification number, a multi-digit number for use with a debit card and computerized cash dispenser to authorize access to information, withdrawal of cash, etc.

❑ **PIN pad** *n* a keypad into which a PIN is entered during a chip-and-PIN transaction.

■ **chip and PIN** see under **chip**.

pin /pin/ *n* a piece of wood or of metal used for fastening things together; a peg or nail; a sharp-pointed piece of wire with a rounded head for fastening clothes, etc; an ornamental elaboration of this; a cylindrical part inserted into something, such as the stem of a key, or part of a lock that a hollow-stemmed key fits; any of the metal projections on an electric plug; the projecting part of a dovetail joint; a peg aimed at in quoits; a peg in the centre of an archery target; the rod of a golf flag; a skittle or ninepin; a chess piece (*obs*); a tuning peg in a stringed instrument; a measuring peg in a drinking cup; a degree, stage, pitch; a leg (*inf*); a peak; the projecting bone of the hip; a hard spot or excrescence; a cask of $4\frac{1}{2}$ gallons; short for clothes-pin, rolling pin, tirling-pin, etc; an act of pinning or state of being pinned; anything of little value. ◆ *vt* (**pinn'ing**; **pinned**) to fasten with a pin; to fix, to fasten, to enclose; to hold down (*fig*); to make a small hole in; to insert chips of stone between the stones of; to attack an opponent's piece which is unable to move without exposing a more valuable piece to attack (*chess*). [OE *pinn*, prob from L *pinna* a feather, a pinnacle]

■ **pinn'er** *n* someone who pins; a pin-maker; a pinafore; a headdress with lappets flying loose; one of these lappets. **pinn'ing** *n* a fastening; a chip of stone, etc, inserted in a joint of masonry.

❑ **pin'ball** *n* a form of bagatelle; a scoring game, played on a slot machine, in which a ball runs down a sloping board set with pins or other targets. **pin'board** *n* a board for pinning notices, pictures, etc on. **pin'-butt'ock** *n* (*Shakesp, All's Well That Ends Well*) a sharp, pointed buttock. **pin'case** *n* (*obs*). **pin curl** *n* a lock of hair made to curl by winding it around one's finger, etc, and securing it with a hairpin. **pin'cushion** *n* a small pad for holding pins. **pin'down** *n* a discredited technique for controlling and disciplining disruptive children, *esp* teenagers, in residential care, involving solitary confinement and removal of clothing other than nightwear or underwear, and sometimes physical punishment and mental harassment (also *adj*). **pin'-dust** *n* brass filings, a product of pin-making. **pin'-eyed** *adj* (*bot*) long-styled, with the stigma like a pinhead in the throat of the corolla (*esp* of a *Primula*). **pin feather** *n* a young, unexpanded feather. **pin'-feathered** *adj*. **pin'-fire** *adj* (of a firearm) discharged by a pin driven into the fulminate. **pin'fish** *n* a spiny fish of various kinds. **pin'head** *n* the head of a pin; anything very small; a stupid person (*sl*). **pin'hole** *n* a hole for or made by a pin, or such as a pin might make. **pinhole camera** *n*. **pinhole glasses** *n pl* spectacles, consisting of a *usu* plastic opaque lens with many perforations, considered beneficial in improving a variety of visual defects by reducing the amount of light reaching the eye. **pinhole photography** *n* the taking of photographs by the use of a pinhole instead of a lens. **pin'hooker** *n* (*sl*) a speculator who buys up foals hoping to make a profit on them when selling them as yearlings for racing. **pin'-leg** *n* (*Scot*) a wooden leg. **pin'-maker** *n*. **pin'-making** *n*. **pin'-man** *n* a seller of pins; a matchstick drawing, in which the limbs and body are represented by single lines. **pin money** *n orig* money allotted by a man to his wife or female dependants for private expenses; extra money earned by a man or woman to spend on incidental or luxury items; a trifling amount of money. **pin'point** *n* the point of a pin; anything very sharp or minute. ◆ *vt* to place or define very exactly. **pin'prick** *n* the prick of a pin; a petty irritation, or something done to irritate. **pin'stripe** *n* a very narrow stripe in cloth; cloth with such stripes; a garment made of such cloth, *esp* a suit (*inf*). **pin'striped** *adj* (of fabric or garments) having pinstripes; (of a person) wearing a pinstriped suit (*inf*). **pin'table** *n* a pinball machine. **pin'tail** *n* a type of duck, *Anas acuta*, with a pointed tail; a sand grouse. **pin'tailed** *adj* having a long, narrow tail. **pin tuck** *n* a very narrow ornamental tuck. **pin'-up** *adj* (of a person) such as might have their portrait pinned up on a wall for admiration. ◆ *n* a person of such a kind; a portrait or photograph so pinned up for admiration. **pin'wheel** *n* a wheel with pins at right angles to its plane, to lift the hammer of a striking clock; a paper toy windmill; a revolving firework. **pin'worm** *n* a parasitic nematode.

■ **a merry pin** (*archaic*) a merry mood. **on pins and needles** in agitated expectancy. **pin and web** (*Shakesp*) a disease of the eye, *appar* cataract, characterized by a small excrescence like a pin-head, and a film (also **web and pin**). **pin down** to trap or hold fast; to force a commitment or definite expression of opinion from; to identify or define precisely. **pin it on** or **pin it onto (someone)** to blame it on (someone), prove (someone) responsible for something. **pin one's faith** or **hopes on** to count, rely or bank solely on. **pin on one's sleeve** (*obs*) to make entirely dependent on oneself, or at one's disposal. **pins and needles** a tingling feeling in one's arm, hand, leg or foot, due to impeded circulation (see also **on pins and needles** above).

piña /pē'nyə/ *n* the pineapple (*obs*); a fine cloth of pineapple-leaf fibre (also **pi'ña-cloth**). [Sp, pine cone, pineapple]

pinacoid see **pinakoid**.

piña colada /pē'nyə kə-lä'də, pē'nya kō-lä'dha/ or **pina colada** /pē'nə kə-lä'də/ *n* a drink made from pineapple juice, rum and coconut. [Sp, strained pineapple]

pinacotheca /pin-ə-kō-thē'kə/ *n* a picture gallery (also (*Ger*) **pinakoth'ek**). [Latinized from Gr *pinakothēkē*, from *pinax*, *-akos* a tablet, picture, and *thēkē* repository]

pinafore /pin'ə-för or -för/ *n* a loose protective or decorative garment worn, formerly *esp* by a child, over a dress; a pinafore dress. [**pin** and **afore**]

■ **pin'afored** *adj*.

❑ **pinafore dress** or **skirt** *n* a dress without sleeves or collar or a skirt with a bib, designed to be worn over a blouse or sweater.

pinakoid or **pinacoid** /pin'ə-koid/ *n* a crystal face, or a crystallographic form consisting of a pair of faces, parallel to two axes. [Gr *pinax*, *-akos*, slab, and *eidos* form]

■ **pinakoid'al** or **pinacoid'al** *adj*.

pinaster /pī- or pi-nas'tər/ *n* the cluster pine. [L *pīnāster*, from *pīnus* pine]

piñata /pin-yä'tə or pin-ya'ta/ *n* a hollow pottery or papier-mâché figure filled with sweets, gifts, etc and hung from a ceiling, to be smashed by blindfolded people with sticks at a Christmas or other party in Latin American countries. [Sp, literally, pot]

pince-nez /pēs'nā/ *n* (*pl* **pince'-nez** /-nāz or -nā/) a pair of eyeglasses without side-pieces, having a springed clip to hold them firmly on the nose. [Fr, pinch nose]

■ **pince'-nezed** /-nād/ *adj*.

pincer /pin'sər/ *n* a grasping claw or forceps-like organ; (in *pl*) a gripping tool with jaws and handles on a pivot, used for drawing out nails, squeezing, etc. ◆ *vt* to pinch with pincers. [OFr *pincer* to pinch]

❑ **pincer movement** *n* an advance that closes in on an enemy force from two sides simultaneously.

pinch /pinch/ or /pinsh/ *vt* to compress a small part of between fingers and thumb or between any two surfaces, to nip; to squeeze; to crush; to nip off; to bite (*obs*); to bring or render by squeezing or nipping; (of eg cold or hunger) to affect painfully or injuriously; to cause to show the effects of such pain or injury; to harass; to hamper; to restrict; to stint, be miserly or frugal with; to find fault with (*obs*); to steal (*inf*); to arrest (*inf*); to over-urge (*horse-racing*); to move along with a lever. ◆ *vi* to nip or squeeze; to be painfully tight; to encroach; to carp; to live sparingly; to narrow, taper off (*mining*). ◆ *n* an act or experience of pinching; a critical time of difficulty or hardship; an emergency; a pleat (*obs*); an upward curl of a hat-brim (*obs*); a place of narrowing, folding, difficulty, or steepness; a quantity taken up between the finger and thumb; hence, any small quantity; an iron bar used as a lever. [OFr *pincier*; prob Gmc]

■ **pinched** *adj* having the appearance of being tightly squeezed; hard pressed by want or cold; (of the face, or general appearance) haggard with cold, tiredness, hunger, etc; narrowed; straightened. **pinch'er** *n* someone who or something which pinches; (in *pl*) pincers (*dialect*). **pinch'ing** *n* and *adj*. **pinch'ingly** *adv*.

❑ **pinch'cock** *n* a clamp that stops the flow of liquid by pinching a tube. **pinch'commons** *n sing* a niggard with food. **pinch effect** *n* (*nuclear eng*) in a plasma carrying a large current, the constriction arising from the interaction of the current with its own magnetic field. **pinch'fist**, **pinch'gut** or **pinch'penny** *n* a niggard. **pinch'-hit** *vi* (*baseball*) to bat in place of another in an emergency (also *fig*). **pinch'-hitter** *n* a batter replacing another in an emergency or for tactical reasons (*baseball*; also *fig*); a player promoted in the batting order to score quickly (*cricket*). **pinch'point** *n* a constricted, awkward or congested point, eg in the traffic system.

■ **at a pinch** in a case of necessity or emergency. **feel the pinch** (*inf*) to be in financial difficulties, to find life, work, etc difficult because of lack of money. **know where the shoe pinches** to know by direct experience what the trouble or difficulty is. **take with a pinch of salt** see under **salt**[1].

pinchbeck /pinch'- or pinsh'bek/ *n* a yellow alloy of copper with much less zinc than ordinary brass, simulating gold, invented by Christopher Pinchbeck (c.1670–1732), English watchmaker. ◆ *adj* sham; in bad taste.

pindari or **pindaree** /pin-dä'rē/ *n* a mercenary freebooter troublesome in India until 1817. [Hindi *pindārī*]

Pindaric /pin-dar'ik/ *adj* after the manner or supposed manner of the Greek lyric poet *Pindar*. ◆ *n* a Pindaric ode; an irregular ode, according to the 17c conception of Pindar. [Gr *pindarikos*, from *Pindaros*]

■ **Pin'darism** *n* the manner or supposed manner of Pindar; 'intoxication of style' (*Matthew Arnold*). **Pin'darist** *n*. **Pin'darize** or **-ise** /-də-rīz/ *vt* and *vi*.

pinder /pin'dər/ *n* someone who impounds cattle (also **pinn'er**). [OE *pyndan* to shut up, from *pund*; cf **poind**, **pound**[2]]

pine[1] /pīn/ *n* any tree of the north temperate coniferous genus *Pinus*, with pairs or bundles of needle-leaves on short shoots and scale-leaves only on long shoots, represented in Britain by the **Scots pine** (*Pinus sylvestris*); extended to various more or less nearly related trees and to some plants only superficially similar; the timber of the pine; a pineapple plant or its fruit. ◆ *adj* of pines or pinewood. [OE *pīn*, from L *pīnus*]

■ **pī'nery** *n* a pine-house; a pine-forest. **pī'ny** (*non-standard* **pī'ney**) *adj* of, like, or abounding in pine trees.

❑ **pine'-barren** *n* a level sandy tract growing pine trees. **pine beauty**, **pine carpet** *n* kinds of moths whose larvae feed on pine trees. **pine'-beet'le** *n* any beetle that attacks pine trees, *esp* the **pine'-chāfer** (*Hylurgus piniperda*) which bores up through the leader. **pine cone** *n* the cone or strobilus of a pine tree. **pine'-finch** *n* an American finch like the goldfinch; a large grosbeak of pine forests. **pine'-house** *n* a house in which pineapples are grown. **pine kernel** see **pine nut** below. **pine marten** *n* a British species of marten, *Mustela martes*, now rare, dark brown, with yellowish throat, and partly arboreal in habit. **pine needle** *n* the acicular leaf of the pine tree. **pine nut** or **kernel** *n* the edible seed of a pine tree of various species. **pine tar** *n* a dark, oily substance obtained from pine wood, used in paints, etc, and medicines. **pine tree** *n*. **pine-tree money** *n* a silver money coined at Boston in the 17c bearing the figure of a pine tree. **pine'wood** *n* a wood of pine trees; pine timber. **pine'-wool** *n* a fibrous substance prepared from the leaves of the pine.

pine[2] /pīn/ *vi* to waste away, *esp* under pain or mental distress; to languish with longing; to long; to repine. ◆ *vt* to torment (*obs*); to consume, cause to wear away; to starve; to grieve for (*Milton*). ◆ *n* punishment, torture (*obs*); suffering (*archaic*); want, starvation (*Spenser*). [OE *pīnian* to torment, from L *poena* punishment]

pineal /pin'i-əl or pī'ni-əl/ *adj* shaped like a pine cone; connected with the pineal body. [L *pīnea* a pine cone, from *pīnus* pine]

■ **pinealec'tomy** *n* surgical removal of the pineal body.

❑ **pineal body** or **gland** *n* a small organ at the end of an upgrowth from the optic thalami of the brain, that releases melatonin into the bloodstream. **pineal eye** *n* a vestigial third eye in front of the pineal body, best developed in a New Zealand reptile, the tuatara.

pineapple /pī'na-pl/ *n* a large S American multiple fruit with tough spiny skin; the bromelaceous plant (*Ananas*) bearing it; a finial shaped like a pineapple or pine cone; a hand grenade (*inf*); a bomb (*inf*); a pine cone (*obs*). [From the fruit's resemblance to a pine cone]

❑ **pineapple weed** *n* the rayless mayweed (*Matricaria suaveolens*), which resembles the pineapple in smell.

pinene /pī'nēn/ *n* a colourless liquid hydrocarbon, the chief constituent of turpentine, eucalyptus oil, etc. [L *pinus* pine]

pinery, piney see under **pine**[1].

pinetum /pī-nē'təm/ *n* (*pl* **pine'ta**) a plantation of pine trees; a collection of pine trees for botanical or ornamental purposes. [L *pīnētum* pine grove, from *pīnus* pine]

pinfold /pin'fōld/ *n* a pound or enclosure for cattle. ◆ *vt* to impound. [OE *pundfald*, affected by *pyndan*; see **pound**[2], **fold**[2], and **pinder**]

■ words derived from main entry word; ❑ compound words; ■ idioms and phrasal verbs

ping /ping/ n a sharp ringing or whistling sound, eg of a bullet; a test to check the accessibility of nodes, users, etc on a network (*comput*). ◆ vi to make such a sound. ◆ vt to cause to make such a sound; to check with a ping; to send an electronic message to. [Imit]

■ **ping'er** n an acoustic transmitter for the study of ocean currents; (**Pinger**®) a domestic clockwork device set to give a warning signal at a chosen time; any of various devices sending out an acoustic signal for directional, timing, etc purposes.

❑ **Ping'-Pong**® n a trademark for table tennis. ◆ adj (without *cap*) moving backwards and forwards, to and fro (*fig*).

pingo /ping'gō/ n (pl **ping'os** or **ping'oes**) a large cone-shaped mound having a core of ice formed by the upward expansion of freezing water surrounded by permafrost. [Inuit]

Ping-Pong® see under **ping**.

pinguid /ping'gwid/ adj fat. [L *pinguis* fat]

■ **ping'uefy** /-gwi-fī/ vt and vi to fatten; to make or become greasy. **Pinguic'ula** n the butterwort genus. **pinguid'ity** or **ping'uitude** n fatness.

pinguin[1] same as **penguin**[1].

pinguin[2] /ping'gwin/, also **penguin** /peng'-/ n a West Indian plant, *Bromelia pinguin*; its fruit. [Perh L *pinguis* fat; confused with **penguin**[1]]

pinhead, **pinhole**, etc see under **pin**.

pinion[1] /pin'yən/ vt to confine by holding or binding the arms; to cut a pinion of; to confine the wings of. ◆ n a wing; the last joint of a wing; a flight-feather, *esp* the outermost. [OFr *pignon*, from L *pinna* (*penna*) wing]

pinion[2] /pin'yən/ n a small wheel with teeth or 'leaves', a small cog. [Fr *pignon*, from L *pinea* pine cone]

pinite /pin'īt/ or /pīn'-/ n a greyish-green or brown hydrous silicate of aluminium and potassium, *usu* amorphous. [Ger *Pinit*, from the *Pini* mine in Saxony]

pink[1] /pingk/ n a light red colour; any plant or flower of the caryophyllaceous genus *Dianthus*, including carnation and sweet william; extended to some other plants, such as **sea pink** (thrift), **Carolina pink** (see under **Carolina**), **Indian pink** (see under **Indian**); a scarlet hunting-coat or its colour; the person wearing it; a person who is something of a socialist but hardly a red (also *inf* **pink'o**; *pl* **pink'os** or **pink'oes**); the fine flower of excellence; the most perfect condition; the highest point, the extreme; an exquisite (*obs*). ◆ adj of the colour pink; slightly socialistic; slightly pornographic, somewhat blue (*film*, etc); relating to homosexuals. ◆ vt and vi to make or become pink. [Ety doubtful]

■ **pink'iness** n. **pink'ing** n the reddening of gemstones by heat. **pink'ish** adj somewhat pink. **pink'ishness** n. **pink'ness** n. **pink'y** adj slightly pink.

❑ **pink'-collar** adj of or relating to women as a section of the workforce. **pink elephants** see under **elephant**. **pink'-eye** n acute contagious conjunctivitis; an acute contagious infection in horses due to a filterable virus, the eye sometimes becoming somewhat red; a red discoloration in salt fish, etc. **pink'-eyed** adj having pink eyes (see also under **pink**[6]). **pink gin** n gin with Angostura bitters. **Pink Lady** n a cocktail typically made of gin, grenadine, cream, egg white and lemon juice. **pink noise** n noise of mid to low frequency. **pink pound** n the spending power attributed to homosexuals as a market sector. **pink'root** n Indian pink, or other species of *Spigelia*; its root, a vermifuge. **pink salmon** n a Pacific species of salmon, the humpback; its flesh as food. **pink slip** n (*US inf*) a notice of dismissal given to an employee. **pink-slip'** vt to dismiss from employment.

■ **in the pink** in perfect health or condition. **pink of perfection** the acme of perfection.

pink[2] /pingk/ vt to decorate by cutting small holes or scallops; to make a serrated edge on; to stab or pierce, *esp* with a sword or rapier. ◆ n a stab; an eyelet. [Cf LGer *pinken*, to peck]

■ **pinked** adj pierced or worked with small holes; with the edge serrated.

❑ **pinking iron** n (*archaic*) a tool for pinking or scalloping. **pinking shears** *n pl* scissors with serrated cutting edges.

pink[3] /pingk/ n (in an engine) a characteristic metallic knocking noise caused by detonation; a tinkling sound; a chaffinch's call; a chaffinch; a type of seabird (*obs*). ◆ vi (of an engine) to detonate or knock. [Imit]

pink[4] /pingk/ n a small sailing ship, *usu* with a narrow stern (also **pink'ie** or **pink'y**). [MDu *pin(c)ke*; Ger *Pinke*]

pink[5] /pingk/ n a yellow lake pigment (see **lake**[2]). [Prob different word from **pink**[1]]

■ **Dutch pink** a yellow lake obtained from quercitron bark; blood (*sl*).

pink[6] /pingk/ vi to wink; to blink; to peer; to peep. ◆ adj (*Shakesp*) blinking. [Du *pinken* to wink]

■ **pink'y** adj winking.

❑ **pink'-eyed** adj having small or half-shut eyes (see also under **pink**[1]).

pink[7] /pingk/ adj (*Shakesp*) small. ◆ n (*Scot*) anything small, such as a peep of light. [Du *pink* the little finger]

■ **pink'ie** or **pink'y** adj (*Scot*) small. ◆ n (*Scot, N Am*) the little finger.

pink[8] /pingk/ or **penk** /pengk/ n a minnow; a samlet. [Cf Ger dialect *Pinke*]

Pinkerton /ping'kər-tən/ (also without *cap*) n a private detective. [Allan *Pinkerton* (1819–84), American detective]

pinkie see under **pink**[4,7].

pinko see **pink**[1].

Pinkster /pingk'stər/ (*old US*) n Whitsuntide (also **Pinxter**). [Du *pinkster(en)*, MDu *pinxter*, ult, from Gr *pentēkostē* Pentecost]

pinky see under **pink**[1,4,6,7].

Pinna /pin'ə/ n a genus of molluscs related to the mussels, with triangular shells. [Gr]

pinna /pin'ə/ (*biol*) n (pl **pinn'ae** /-ē/) a leaflet of a pinnate leaf, or any similar expansion; a wing, fin, feather, or similar expansion; the outer ear, *esp* the upper part. [L *pinna* a feather, dimin *pinnula*]

■ **pinn'ate** or **pinn'ated** adj shaped like a feather; having a row of leaflets on each side of the rachis, or other expansions arranged in similar manner; (*usu* **pennate**) having wings, fins, or winglike tufts. **pinn'ately** adv. **pinnatifid** /pin-at'i-fid/ adj (of leaves) pinnately cut roughly halfway down. **pinnatipart'ite** adj (of leaves) pinnately cut rather more than halfway. **pinnat'iped** adj (of birds) with lobate feet. **pinnat'isect** adj (of leaves) pinnately cut nearly to the midrib. **pinn'iped** /-i-ped/ or **pinn'ipede** /-pēd/ n (see **-ped**) a member of the **Pinnipē'dia**, or paddle-footed Carnivora, ie seals, sea lions, and walruses. **pinn'ūlate** or **pinn'ulated** adj. **pinn'ūle**, also **pinn'ūla** n a lobe of a leaflet of a pinnate leaf; a branchlet of a crinoid arm.

pinnace /pin'is or -əs/ n a small vessel with oars and sails; a boat with eight oars; a warship's tender boat; loosely, a small boat; a whore (*fig*; *obs*). [Fr *pinasse*]

pinnacle /pin'ə-kl/ n a slender turret or spiry structure in architecture; a high pointed rock or mountain like a spire; the highest point. ◆ vt to be the pinnacle of; to set on a pinnacle; to raise as a pinnacle; to provide with pinnacles. [Fr *pinacle*, from LL *pinnāculum*, dimin from L *pinna* a feather]

■ **pinn'acled** adj.

pinnae...to...**pinnatisect** see **pinna**.

pinner /pin'ər/ see under **pin** and **pinder**.

pinnet /pin'it/ n a pinnacle (*Walter Scott*); a streamer (*Scot*). [Perh **pennant**[1], associated with L *pinna* pinnacle]

pinnie or **pinny** /pin'i/ n short for **pinafore**, *esp* applied to an apron or overall worn by a woman or child.

pinniewinkle see **pinnywinkle**.

pinniped, **pinnipede**, **Pinnipedia** see under **pinna**.

pinnock /pin'ək/ (*dialect*) n the hedge sparrow; the blue tit. [ME *pynnuc*]

pinnoed /pin'ōd/ (*Spenser*) adj pinioned. [Perh a misprint]

pinnula, **pinnulate**, **pinnule**, etc see under **pinna**.

pinny see **pinnie**.

pinnywinkle, **pinniewinkle** /pin'i-wing-kl/ and **pilniewinks** /pil'ni-wingks/ mistaken forms of **pilliwinks**.

pinochle, **pinocle** or **penuchle** /pē'nu-kl/ n a game like bezique; (in this game) a declaration of queen of spades and jack of diamonds. [Origin unknown]

pinocytosis /pī-nō-sī-tō'sis/ (*immunol*) n ingestion by cells of vesicles containing fluid from the environment. [From Gr *pinein* to drink, and **cyt-** and **-osis** (2)]

pinole /pē-nō'lā/ n parched Indian corn or other seeds ground and eaten with milk; a mixture of vanilla and aromatic substances in chocolate. [Sp from Aztec *pinolli*]

piñon /pin'yon or pēn'yōn/ (*US*) n an edible pine seed; the tree bearing it. [Sp]

Pinot /pē'nō/ (also without *cap*) n a variety of both black and white grape; a wine made from the Pinot grape, eg *Pinot Noir*. [Fr *pin* pine, from the similarity of the grape bunch to a pine cone in shape]

■ **pinotage** /pē'nō-täzh/ n a variety of grape grown mainly in South Africa, produced by crossing Pinot with another grape; a red wine made from this grape.

pinpoint see under **pin**.

pinscher see **Doberman**.

pint /pīnt/ n a measure of capacity equal to half a quart or 4 gills, in imperial measure (liquid or dry) about 0.568 litre or 20 fluid ounces, in US measure (liquid) 0.473 litre or 16 US fluid ounces, (dry) 0.551 litre; a pint of beer (*inf*). [Fr *pinte*; origin uncertain]

■ **pint'a** /pīn'tə/ n (*inf*) a pint of milk; generally, a drink.

❑ **pint'-pot** *n* a pot for holding a pint, *esp* a pewter pot for beer; a seller or drinker of beer. **pint'-size** or **-sized** *adj* (*inf*) very small, *usu* of a person. **pint'-stoup** *n* a vessel for holding a Scots pint (about 3 imperial pints).

pinta[1] /pin'tə/ *n* a contagious skin disease occurring in the tropics, characterized by loss of skin pigmentation, also called **mal del pinto** /mal del pin'tō/ (Sp, disease of the spotted person). [Sp, from LL *pinctus*, from L *pictus* painted]

pinta[2] see under **pint**.

pintable see under **pin**.

pintado /pin-tä'dō/ *n* (*pl* **pinta'dos**) a kind of petrel, the Cape pigeon; the guinea fowl; chintz (*obs*). [Port, painted]

pintail see under **pin**.

Pinteresque /pin-tə-resk'/ *adj* in the style of the characters, situations, etc, of the plays of Harold Pinter (1930–2008), English dramatist, marked *esp* by halting dialogue, uncertainty of identity, and air of menace.

pintle /pin'tl/ *n* a bolt or pin, *esp* one on which something turns; the plunger or needle of the injection valve of an oil engine, opened by oil pressure on an annular face, and closed by a spring; the penis (*archaic* or *dialect*). [OE *pintel*]

pinto /pin'tō/ (*US*) *adj* mottled; piebald. ◆ *n* (*pl* **pin'tos**) a piebald horse. [Sp, painted]
❑ **pinto bean** *n* a kind of bean resembling a kidney bean, mottled in colour.

pinxit /pingk'sit/ (*L*) (he or she) painted (this) (*abbrev* **pinx.**).

Pinxter see **Pinkster**.

piny[1] see under **pine**[1].

piny[2] /pī'ni/ (*obs* or *dialect*) *n* same as **peony**.

Pinyin /pin-yin'/ *n* an alphabetic system (using Roman letters) for the transcription of Chinese, *esp* Mandarin. [Chin *pīnyīn* phonetic, alphabetic (transcription)]

piolet /pyo-lā'/ or *pyō-lā'/ *n* an ice-axe; an early form of ski stick. [Fr, from Piedmontese dialect *piola*]

pion /pī'on/ *n* a *pi*-meson (see under **pi**[1]).
■ **pīon'ic** *adj*.

pioned /pī'ə-nid/ (*Shakesp*) *adj perh* trenched, excavated (cf **pioneer**); *perh* overgrown with wild orchids, said to be called **pionies** (peonies) at Stratford.

pioneer /pī-ə-nēr'/ *n* someone who is among the first in new fields of enterprise, exploration, colonization, research, etc; a pioneer species (qv below); a military artisan, employed in peacetime in painting and repairing barracks, and such work, in war in preparing the way for an army, and minor engineering works, such as trenching; an excavator; a labourer. ◆ *adj* of or relating to pioneers. ◆ *vt* to act as pioneer to; to prepare as a pioneer. [OFr *peonier* (Fr *pionnier*), from *pion* a foot soldier, from LL *pedō*, *pedōnis*, from L *pēs*, *pedis* a foot; cf **pawn**[2] and **peon**]
■ **pioneer'ing** *adj*. **pī'oner** or **py'oner** *n* (*Shakesp*) a military pioneer; an excavator. **pī'oning** (*Spenser* **py'onings**) *n* pioneer work; trenching.
❑ **pioneer species** *n* (*bot*) a species which tends to be among the first to occupy bare ground.

pioney and **piony** /pī'ə-ni/ *n* obsolete forms of **peony**.

pioted see under **pyot**.

piou-piou /pū-pū'/ *n* a French private soldier. [Fr slang; *perh pion*; see **peon**]

pious /pī'əs/ *adj* dutiful; showing, having, or resulting from piety; professing to be religious. [L *pius*]
■ **pi'ously** *adv*.
❑ **pious fraud** *n* a deception practised with a good end in view; a religious humbug (*inf*). **pious opinion** *n* a belief widely held but not made a matter of faith.

pioy, **pioye** same as **peeoy**.

pip[1] /pip/ *n* a small hard seed or fruitlet in a fleshy fruit; a pippin (*obs*). [Appar from **pippin**]
■ **pip'less** *adj*. **pipp'y** *adj*.

pip[2] /pip/ *n* a short, high-pitched signal analogous in sound to the word 'pip', *esp* as used in radio signals, the speaking clock, payphones, etc.
■ **the pips** (*inf*) the six pips broadcast by the BBC, made up of five short (counting down from 55 to 59 seconds) and one long (marking the start of the new minute and hour).

pip[3] /pip/ (*sl*) *vt* (**pipp'ing**; **pipped**) to defeat narrowly; to blackball; to pluck, plough, reject, or fail in an examination; to foil, thwart, get the better of; to hit with a bullet, etc; to wound; to kill. ◆ *vi* to die (*esp* with *out*; *archaic*). [Perh from **pip**[1]]

■ **pipped at the post** defeated at the point when success seemed certain, or at the last moment.

pip[4] /pip/, earlier **peep** or **peepe** (*Shakesp*) /pēp/ *n* a spot on dice, cards or dominoes; a star as a mark of rank (*inf*); a speck; (on a radar screen) indication, eg spot of light, of the presence of an object; a single blossom or corolla in a cluster (*bot*). [Ety uncertain]
■ **a pip** (or **peepe**) **out** one in excess of the total of pips aimed at in the old card game of one-and-thirty, hence, having overshot one's mark; tipsy.

pip[5] /pip/ *n* roup in poultry, etc; an ailment or distemper vaguely imagined; syphilis (*sl*); spleen, hump, disgust, offence (*inf*). ◆ *vt* to affect with the pip. [Appar from MDu *pippe*, from LL *pipīta*, from L *pītuīta* rheum]
■ **give someone the pip** (*inf*) to annoy or offend someone.

pip[6] /pip/ *vi* to chirp, as a young bird does. [Cf **peep**[2]]

pipa[1] /pē'pə/ *n* a S American toad of the genus *Pipa*, the female being noted for carrying her developing young on her back, the Surinam toad. [Suriname dialect]

pipa[2] /pē-pä'/ *n* a traditional Chinese pear-shaped lute. [Chin *pípá* loquat]

pipage see under **pipe**[1].

pipal, **pipul** or **peepul** /pē'pul/ or *-pəl/ *n* the bo tree. [Hindi *pīpul*]

pipe[1] /pīp/ *n* a metal or plastic tube for the conveyance of water, gas, etc; any tube, or tubular part or thing, natural or artificial; a musical wind instrument, or part of an instrument, consisting of or including a tube; any of an organ's upright metal or wooden tubes; (in *pl*) a bagpipe; the note of a bird; a voice, *esp* a high voice; (*usu* in *pl*) the windpipe; any of various hollow organs in an animal body; a pipe-like volcanic vent, a cylindrical mass of ore, etc; an entrance to a decoy; a tube with a bowl at one end for smoking; a fill of tobacco; the smoking of a fill of tobacco; a stick of eg pipeclay for curling hair or a wig (*Sterne*); a boatswain's whistle; the direction of the output of a program or command into another (*comput*). ◆ *vi* to play a musical pipe; to whistle (as the wind or a boatswain does); to speak or sing, *esp* in a high voice; to peep or sing, as a bird does; to weep; to become pipy. ◆ *vt* to play on a pipe; to lead or call by means of a pipe; (with *in*) to accompany or call ceremonially in with pipe music; to render, or cause to be, by playing a pipe; to propagate by piping (*hortic*); to force (icing, cream, etc) out through a nozzle in a thin strip as decoration; to ornament with piping; to supply with pipes; to convey by pipe; to transmit (television, radio signals) by electricity or along a wire. [OE *pīpe*, from L *pīpāre* to cheep; cf Du *pijp*, Ger *Pfeife*]
■ **pīp'age** *n* conveyance or distribution by pipe. **piped** /pīpt/ *adj* tubular or fistulous; transported by means of a pipe; transmitted simultaneously to many outlets from a central control location by means of an audio system, telephone or electricity line, etc. **pipe'ful** *n* (*pl* **pipe'fuls**) enough to fill a pipe. **pipe'less** *adj*. **pipe'like** *adj*. **pīp'er** *n* a player on a pipe, *esp* a bagpipe; a broken-winded horse; a young pigeon or other bird; a kind of gurnard; a pipe-smoker; a decoy dog; a kind of caddis-worm. **pīp'ing** *adj* playing a pipe; sounding like a pipe; producing a shrill sound, whistling; thin and high-pitched; characterized by pipe-playing, as opposed to martial music, as in the phrase *the piping times of peace*; hissing hot; very hot. ◆ *n* the action of the verb pipe in any sense; pipe-playing; a system of pipes; tubing; small cord used as trimming for clothes; strings and twists of icing ornamenting a cake; a slip or cutting from a joint of a stem (*hortic*); the action of hydraulicking. **pīp'y** *adj* pipelike; having pipes; piping.
❑ **pipe band** *n* a military or marching band of bagpipe players and drummers, led by a pipe major. **pipe bomb** *n* a crude bomb made of a length of pipe packed with explosives. **pipe'-case** *n* a case for a tobacco pipe. **pipe'clay** *n* a fine white, nearly pure, kaolin, free from iron, used for making tobacco pipes and fine earthenware, and for whitening military belts, etc. ◆ *vt* to whiten with pipeclay. **pipe'-cleaner** *n* a length of wire with tufts of fabric twisted into it, used to clean pipe-stems. **piped music** *n* continuous background music played in a restaurant, etc, or piped from a central studio to other buildings. **pipe dream** *n* a futile and unreal hope or fancy such as one has when relaxing while smoking a pipe (*orig* an opium-smoker's fantasy). **pipe'-dreamer** *n*. **pipe'fish** *n* a fish (of several species) of the seahorse family, a long thin fish covered with hard plates, the jaws forming a long tube. **pipe fitting** *n* any of the wide variety of pipe connecting-pieces used to make turns, junctions, and reductions in piping systems. **pipe'-key** *n* a key with a hollow barrel. **pipe'-layer** *n* someone who lays pipes for water, gas, etc; a political wirepuller (*old US sl*). **pipe'-laying** *n*. **pipeless organ** *n* a musical instrument, played like an organ, in which sounds, built up from whatever harmonics may be chosen, are produced by a loudspeaker. **pipe'-light** or **-lighter** *n* a spill for lighting a pipe. **pipe'line** *n* a long continuous line of piping to carry water from a reservoir, oil from an oilfield, etc; a line of piping to carry solid materials; any continuous line of communication, or supply, or of progress and development (*fig*); see also **in the pipeline** below. ◆ *adj* (*comput*) denoting a processor,

program, etc involving parallel processing of instructions which is overlapped to enable streams of instructions to be decoded and executed concurrently. ◆ *vt* to carry by pipeline; to carry out using a pipeline process (*comput*). **pipe'lining** *n*. **pipe major** *n* the chief of a band of bagpipers. **Pipe Office** *n* (*hist*) an office in the Court of Exchequer in which the Clerk of the Pipe made out the Pipe Roll. **pipe of peace** see **calumet**. **pipe'-opener** *n* (*inf*) a walk or spell of exercise in the fresh air; a practice game or trial run. **pipe organ** *n* a musical organ with pipes. **pipe rack** *n* a rack for storing tobacco pipes. **Pipe Roll** *n* (*hist*) the Great Roll of the Exchequer, containing yearly accounts of sheriffs, etc (possibly from its pipelike form). **pipe snake** *n* a tropical burrowing snake. **pipe'-stem** *n* the tube of a tobacco pipe. **pipe'stone** *n* a red argillaceous stone used by Native Americans for making tobacco pipes. **pipe'-stopp'le** or **-stapp'le** *n* (*Scot*) a tobacco pipe stem; anything very thin and brittle-looking. **pipe'-track** *n* the course of a pipe across country. **pipe'-tree** *n* (*obs*) the mock orange (**white pipe-tree**); the lilac (**blue pipe-tree**). **pipe'work** *n* a vein of ore in the form of a pipe; piping or pipes collectively, eg in an organ. **pipe'wort** *n* a rare rush-like water plant (*Eriocaulon septangulare*) of Ireland and the Hebrides, the only European representative of its family, Eriocaulaceae. **pipe'-wrench** *n* a wrench that grips a pipe when turned one way. **piping crow** *n* an Australian bird (genus *Gymnorhina*) called a magpie, really related to the shrikes. **piping hare** *n* a pika. ■ **boatswain's pipe** see **boatswain's whistle** under **whistle**. **drunk as a piper** very drunk. **in the pipeline** waiting to be considered or dealt with; in preparation. **pay the piper** to bear the expense (and so **call the tune** have control); to have to pay heavily. **pipe and tabor** a small recorder, fingered by the left hand, and a small drum beaten with the right, formerly in use in rustic jollities. **pipe down** to subside into silence; to stop talking or be quiet (*inf*); to dismiss (a ship's company) from muster (the final order of the day). **pipe one's eye, tune one's pipes** to weep. **pipe up** (*inf*) to interject, say something; to begin to speak. **piping hot** (of food, *usu* when served) very hot, literally so hot as to make a hissing or sizzling noise. **put that in your pipe and smoke it!** (*inf*; of some unwelcome home truth, etc) there! how do you like that?

pipe² /pīp/ *n* a cask or butt (of wine), of two hogsheads, varying according to the wine, ordinarily about 105 gallons in Britain, 126 US gallons; a Portuguese wooden cask or *pipa*, used for storage and as a measure of (*esp* port) wine, holding 500 litres (formerly 429 litres); the measure of a pipe. [OFr *pipe* cask, tube; cf **pipe¹**] □ **pipe'-wine** *n* (*Shakesp*) wine from the cask, not bottled.

pip emma /pip em'ə/ (*milit sl*) *adv* post meridiem, in the afternoon (cf **ack emma**). [Formerly signallers' names for the letters PM]

Piper /pīp'ər/ *n* the pepper genus, giving name to a family **Piperā'ceae** of dicotyledons. [L *piper* pepper]
■ **piperaceous** /-ā'shəs/ *adj*. **piper'azine** *n* (*piperidine* and **az-**) a cyclic crystalline nitrogen compound used in medicine, insecticides and anti-corrosion substances. **piperic** /pīp-er'ik/ *adj* applied to an acid ($C_{12}H_{10}O_4$) obtained from piperine. **piper'idine** *n* a heterocyclic reduction product of pyridine ($C_5H_{11}N$) with a peppery odour. **pip'erine** *n* an alkaloid ($C_{17}H_{19}O_3N$) found in pepper. **pip'eronal** (or /pi-per'/) *n* a phenolic aldehyde of very pleasant odour, used as a perfume and in flavourings, etc (also called **heliotropin**).

piper see under **pipe¹**.

pipette /pi-pet'/ *n* a tube for transferring and measuring fluids. ◆ *vt* to transfer or measure, using a pipette. [Fr, dimin of *pipe* pipe]

pipi¹ /pē'pē/ *n* a Brazilian Caesalpinia; its pods used in tanning. [Tupí *pipai*]

pipi² /pi'pē/ *n* any of various edible shellfishes of Australasia. [Maori]

piping see under **pipe¹**.

pipistrelle /pi-pi-strel'/ *n* a small reddish-brown bat, the commonest British bat. [Fr, from Ital *pipistrello*, a form of *vespertilio*, from L *vespertiliō* bat, from *vesper* evening]

pipit /pip'it/ *n* any member of a lark-like genus (*Anthus*) of birds related to wagtails. [Prob imit]

pipkin /pip'kin/ *n* a small pot, now only of earthenware; a piggin (*US* dialect). [Poss a dimin of **pipe²**]

pipped see **pip³**.

pippin /pip'in/ *n* an apple of various varieties; something or someone especially nice, attractive, good, etc (*old sl*); a fruit pip (*obs*). [OFr *pepin*]

pipping see **pip³**.

pippy see under **pip¹**.

pipsissewa /pip-sis'i-wə/ *n* a N American plant of the wintergreen family whose evergreen leaves yield a substance used as a diuretic. [From a Native American language]

pipsqueak /pip'skwēk/ (*sl*) *n* something or someone insignificant or contemptible; a German shell of the First World War; a two-stroke motorcycle. [**pip²** and **squeak**]

pipul same as **pipal**.

pipy see under **pipe¹**.

piquant /pē'kənt or -känt/ *adj* stinging; pleasantly pungent; appetizing; stimulating, provocative. [Fr, prp of *piquer* to prick]
■ **piq'uancy** *n*. **piq'uantly** *adv*.

pique¹ /pēk/ *n* animosity or ill-feeling; offence taken; a feeling of anger or vexation caused by wounded pride; resentment of a slight; dudgeon; point or punctilio (*obs*). ◆ *vt* to wound the pride of; to nettle; to arouse, stir, provoke; (*reflexive*) to pride (oneself; with *on, upon,* or (*Boswell*) *at*). [Fr *pique* a pike, pique, *piquer* to prick; cf **pike²**, **prick**]

pique² /pēk/ *n* (in piquet) the scoring of 30 points in one hand before the other side scores at all. ◆ *vt* to score a pique against. ◆ *vi* to score a pique. [Fr *pic*; see **piquet¹**]

pique³ /pēk/ (*Browning*) *n* for **peak¹**.

piqué /pē'kā/ *n* a stiff corded cotton fabric; inlaid work of gold or silver in point or strip (sometimes with mother-of-pearl) on tortoiseshell or ivory; (in snooker, etc) a shot with backspin, made with the cue vertical or nearly so (cf **massé**). ◆ *adj* made of piqué. [Fr, pap of *piquer* to prick]
□ **piqué work** *n* inlaying in piqué; needlework with a raised design made by stitching.

piquet¹ /pi-ket', -kā'/ *n* a game for two with 32 cards, with scoring for declarations and tricks. [Fr; origin unknown]

piquet² same as **picket**.

piquillo /pi-kēl'yō, -kē'ō/ *n* (*pl* **piquill'os**) a type of red pepper grown in N Spain. [Sp, literally, little beak]

Pir /pēr/ (also without *cap*) *n* a Muslim title of honour given to a holy man or religious leader. [Pers *pīr* old man, chief]

piracy see under **pirate**.

piragua /pi-ra'gwə or -rä'/ *n* a S American dugout canoe, or a craft with a single trunk as foundation, often a schooner-rigged barge (also **peria'gua** or (*Fr*) **pirogue** /pi-rōg'/). [Sp *piragua*, from Carib *piraqua*]

pirai see **piranha**.

Pirandellian /pir-an-del'i-ən/ *adj* relating to, or in the style of, the writings of the Italian dramatist and novelist Luigi *Pirandello* (1867–1936).

piranha /pi-rä'nə/, **piraña** /pē-rän'yə/, **piraya** /pē-rä'yə/, **perai** /pe-rī'/ or **pirai** /pē-/ *n* a ferocious S American river fish (*Serrasalmo* or *Pygocentrus*) of the Characinidae. [Port from Tupí *piranya, piraya*]

pirarucu /pē-rä-roo-koo'/ *n* the arapaima. [Port, from Tupí *pira* fish, and *urucú* red]

pirate /pī'rət or -rit/ *n* a person who, without authority, attempts to capture ships at sea; a robber or marauder operating at sea; a pirates' ship; a person who publishes a work without the authority of the owner of the copyright, or otherwise makes use of or takes over another person's work without legal sanction; a private bus, or its driver, plying on the recognized route of others; someone who, in ordinary life, shows the predatory spirit of the sea rovers; a person who runs an unlicensed radio station. ◆ *adj* operating illegally; (loosely) operating, produced, sold, etc separately from and in defiance of the official system. ◆ *vt* to rob as a pirate; to publish or reproduce without permission of the copyright owner, or otherwise usurp (someone else's work or ideas); to use, tap, operate, produce, etc (something) illegally. [L *pīrāta*, from Gr *peirātēs*, from *peiraein* to attempt]
■ **piracy** /pī'rə-si* or (*rare*) *pī'/ *n* the crime of a pirate; robbery on the high seas; unauthorized publication or reproduction; infringement of copyright. **piratic** /pī-rat'ik/ or **pirat'ical** *adj* pertaining to a pirate; practising piracy. **pirat'ically** *adv*.

piraya see **piranha**.

piri-piri¹ /pir'ē-pir'ē or pē'rē-pē'rē/ *n* a spicy sauce made with red chilli peppers (also *adj*). [Ety uncertain; perh from Swahili *pilipili* pepper]

piri-piri² /pir'ē-pir'ē or pē'rē-pē'rē/ *n* a New Zealand weed with prickly burrs (*Acaena sanguisorbae*) used medicinally and as a tea. [Maori]

pirl see **purl²**.

pirlicue or **purlicue** /pir' or pûr'li-kū/ (*Scot*) *n* a peroration; a résumé in conclusion. ◆ *vt* and *vi* to summarize in conclusion. [Origin uncertain]

pirn /pûrn/ or (*Scot*) *pirn/ *n* a reel, bobbin, or spool. [Origin unknown]
■ **wind someone a bonny pirn** to set a fine problem for someone, involve someone in difficulties.

pirnie /pir'ni/ (*Scot*) *adj* unevenly wrought; striped. ◆ *n* (*Scot*) a striped woollen nightcap. [Appar connected with **pirn**]
■ **pirn'it** *adj* (*Scot*) interwoven with different colours; striped.

pirog /pi-rog'/ n a large Russian pie, usu made with a yeast dough. [Russ]

pirogi see **pierogi**.

pirogue see **piragua**.

pirouette /pir-oo-et'/ n (in dancing) a spin performed on the tip or point of the toe or on the ball of the foot. ◆ vi to spin round thus. [Fr]
- **pirouett'er** n.

pirozhki /pē-rozh'kē/ or **piroshki** /pē-rosh'kē/ n pl small triangular pastries with meat, fish or vegetable fillings. [Russ, little pies]

pis aller /pē-za-lā' or pē-zal'ā/ (Fr) the last or worst shift, a makeshift.

Pisces /pī'sēz, pis'ēz, pis'kēz or pis'kās/ n pl the class of fishes (zool); the Fishes, a constellation giving its name to, and formerly coinciding with, a sign of the zodiac (astron); the twelfth sign of the zodiac, between Aquarius and Aries (astrol); a person born between 20 February and 20 March, under the sign of Pisces (astrol; pl **Pis'ces**). [L piscis a fish; pl piscēs]
- **piscary** /pisk'ə-ri/ n the right of fishing; a fishing pond. **piscā'tor** n an angler (also fem **piscā'trix**). **piscatorial** /pis-kə-tö'ri-əl or -tö'/ or **piscatory** /pis'kə-tə-ri/ adj relating to fishing or fishermen; fishing. **Piscean** /pīs'i-ən/ n and adj (relating to or characteristic of) a person born under the sign of Pisces. **piscine** /pis'īn/ adj of fishes; of the nature of a fish.

pisci- /pis-i-/ combining form denoting fish. [L piscis a fish]
- **piscicolous** /-ik'ə-ləs/ adj parasitic in or on fishes. **piscicul'tural** adj. **pis'ciculture** n the rearing of fish by artificial methods. **piscicul'turist** n. **piscifau'na** n the assemblage of fishes in a region, formation, etc. **pis'ciform** adj having the form of a fish. **pis'civore** n an animal that feeds on fish. **pisciv'orous** adj fish-eating, living on fishes.

piscina /pi-sē'nə or -sī'/ n (pl **pisci'nas** or **pisci'nae**) (also **piscine** /pis'ēn or -ēn'/) a fish pond; a swimming pool (as in Roman baths); a basin and drain in old churches, usu in a niche south of an altar, into which water used in washing the sacred vessels was emptied. [L piscīna, from piscis fish]

piscine¹ see under **Pisces**.

piscine² see **piscina**.

piscivorous see under **pisci-**.

pisco /pis'kō/ n an alcoholic spirit distilled from grape wine. [Pisco, port in Peru from where it was exported]
- **pisco sour** n a cocktail made with pisco, lemon juice, egg white and sugar syrup.

pisé /pē'zā/ n rammed earth or clay for walls or floors (also adj). [Fr]

pish¹ /pish/ (old) interj expression of impatience or contempt. ◆ n an utterance of the exclamation. ◆ vt to pooh-pooh. [Imit]

pish² /pish/ n and v a Scottish form of **piss**.
- **pished** adj.

pisheog or **pishogue** /pi-shōg'/ (Irish) n sorcery; superstitious nonsense. [Ir piseog]

pisiform /pī'si-förm or piz'i-förm/ adj pea-shaped. ◆ n a pea-shaped bone of the carpus. [L pisum pea, and förma shape]

pisky see **pixie**.

pismire /pis'mīr/ (archaic or dialect) n an ant or emmet. [piss, from the strong smell of the ant-hill, and ME mire (doubtful OE mīre) ant]

pisolite /pī'sə-līt or piz'ə-līt/ (geol) n a coarse oolite consisting of pea-shaped concretions (**pisoliths**). [Gr pisos pease, and lithos stone]
- **pisolitic** /-lit'ik/ adj.

piss /pis/ (vulgar) vi to urinate. ◆ vt to discharge as urine; to urinate on. ◆ n urine; an act of urination. [Fr pisser]
- **pissed** adj (sl) extremely drunk; annoyed, pissed off (N Am). **piss'er** n (sl) one who urinates; an annoying person or thing; a toilet; the penis.
- **piss artist** n (sl) someone who drinks heavily; a person who is all talk, a foolish show-off. **piss'head** n (sl) a heavy drinker, a habitual drunkard. **piss'-poor** adj (sl) of a contemptibly low standard. **piss'-pot** n (archaic) a chamberpot. **piss'-take** n (sl) an instance of mockery. **piss'-taker** n. **piss-'taking** n and adj. **piss'-up** n (sl) a drinking bout.
- **a piece of piss** (sl) an easy thing to do, a piece of cake. **on the piss** (sl) engaged in a bout of heavy drinking. **piss about** or **around** (sl) to behave in a foolish or time-wasting way; to inconvenience (someone). **piss down** (sl) to rain heavily. **pissed off** (sl) annoyed; fed up. **piss off** (sl) to go away (often as imperative). **piss (someone) off** (sl) to annoy or upset (someone). **take the piss (out of)** (sl) to mock, tease.

pissasphalt /pis'as-falt/ n a semi-liquid bitumen. [Gr pissa pitch, and asphaltos asphalt]

pissoir /pē-swär'/ n a public urinal. [Fr]

pistachio /pi-stach'i-ō, -stash' or -yō, or pi-stä'chi- or -stä'/ n (pl **pista'chios**) the almond-flavoured yellowish-green fruit-kernel of a small W Asiatic tree (Pistacia vera) of the same genus of the cashew family as the mastic tree; flavouring obtained from these nuts; light green colour (also adj). [Sp pistacho and Ital pistacchio, from LL pistāquium, from Gr pistakion, from Pers pistah]

pistareen /pi-stə-rēn'/ n an old Spanish two-real piece formerly used in the USA. [Prob **peseta**]

piste /pēst/ n a beaten track, esp a ski trail in the snow; a strip of ground used for some sporting activity, eg fencing. [Fr]

pistil /pis'til/ (bot) n the ovary of a flower, with its style and stigma. [L pistillum a pestle]
- **pis'tillary** adj. **pis'tillate** adj having a pistil but no (functional) stamens, female. **pis'tillode** n an abortive pistil.

pistol /pis'tl/ n a small handgun, held in one hand when fired. ◆ vt (**pis'tolling**; **pis'tolled**) to shoot with a pistol. [Through Fr and Ger from Czech]
- **pistoleer'** n (obs) someone who carries or uses a pistol.
- **pistol grip** n a handle (usu with a trigger mechanism) for a camera, etc, shaped like the butt of a pistol. **pis'tol-whip** vt to hit (someone) with a pistol.
- **hold a pistol to someone's head** (fig) to use threats to force someone to do what one wants.

pistole /pi-stōl'/ (hist) n any of numerous old gold coins of varying value, eg a Spanish coin of the 17c worth about 17 contemporary English shillings, or a Scots 12-pound piece of William III worth one contemporary English pound. [OFr pistole, earlier pistolet]
- **pis'tolet** n (hist) a pistol; a pistole; a gold coin of various kinds, of an average worth of 6s in the 16c.

pistoleer, pistolling, etc, **pistol-whip** see **pistol**.

piston /pis'tən/ n a cylindrical piece moving to and fro in a hollow cylinder, as in engines and pumps; a valve mechanism for altering the effective length of the tube in brass and other musical instruments; a push-key for combining a number of organ stops. [Fr, from Ital pistone, from pestare to pound, from L pinsere, pistum]
- **piston ring** n a split ring fitted in a circumferential groove around a piston rim forming a spring-loaded seal against the cylinder wall. **piston rod** n the rod to which the piston is fixed, and which moves up and down with it.

pit¹ /pit/ n a hole in the earth; a mine shaft; a mine, esp a coalmine; a place from where minerals are dug; a prison, esp a castle prison entered from above (archaic); a cavity in the ground or in a floor for any purpose, such as the reception of ashes or the inspection of the underside of motor cars, etc; a place beside the track where cars in a race can be refuelled and repaired; a hole for storing root-crops; a covered heap of potatoes, etc; a grave, esp one for many bodies; hell, or its lowest depths; a hole used as a trap for wild animals; an enclosure in which animals are kept in captivity (esp bears); an enclosure for cockfights or the like; orig the ground floor of a theatre, or its occupants, or the part of the ground floor behind the stalls, now usu the area in front of the stage reserved for the orchestra in a theatre (also **orchestra pit**); a bed (inf); a very dirty or untidy place (sl); part of a corn-exchange floor assigned to some particular business, now esp a securities or commodities trading floor (US); a noisy card game mimicking a US corn exchange; any hollow or depression, eg the pit of the stomach below the breastbone; an indentation left by smallpox; a minute depression in a surface; a hollow made by a raindrop; a thin place in a cell wall, affording communication with another cell (bot). ◆ vt (**pitt'ing**; **pitt'ed**) to mark with little hollows; to put into a pit; to set (eg cocks in a cockpit); to match (with against). ◆ vi to become marked with pits; to make a pit stop; to retain an impression for a time after pressing (med). [OE pytt, from L puteus a well]
- **pitt'ed** adj marked with small pits. **pitt'ing** n. **pitt'ite** n (old) someone who frequents the pit of a theatre.
- **pit brow** n (mining) the top of a shaft. **pit bull** or **pit bull terrier** n a large breed of bull terrier developed orig for dogfighting. **pit'-coal** n coal in the ordinary sense, not charcoal. **pit'-dwelling** n a primitive home made by roofing over a pit. **pit'fall** n a lightly covered hole as a trap; a hidden danger or unsuspected difficulty (fig). **pit'head** n (mining) the ground at the mouth of a pit, and the machinery, etc, on it. **pit'man** n a man who works in a coalpit or a sawpit, esp at sinking, repair, and inspection of shafts and at pumping in a mine; a rod connecting a rotary with a reciprocating part (US). **pit pony** n a pony employed for haulage in a coalmine. **pit'prop** n a (usu timber) support in the workings of a coalmine. **pit'-saw** n a saw used in a sawpit. **pit'-saw'yer** n a bottom-sawyer. **pit stop** n a stop a racing-car makes during a motor race when it goes into the pits for repairs or refuelling. **pit village** n a group of miners' houses near a pit; a cluster of pit-dwellings. **pit viper** n any member of an American group of snakes, including the rattlesnake, able to detect prey in the dark by means of a pit sensitive to body heat, located between eye and nose.
- **pit and gallows** a feudal baron's right to drown female and hang male felons. **the pits** (inf) the absolute worst place, conditions, thing, person, etc possible.

pit² /pit/ (*esp N Am*) *n* a fruit-stone. ◆ *vt* (**pitt'ing**; **pitt'ed**) to remove the stone from. [Appar Du *pit*]

pit³ /pit/ (*Scot*) *vt* (*pat* **pat** /pät/; *pap* **putten** /put'n/ or **pitt'en**) to put. [See **put¹**]

pita¹ /pē'tə/ *n* the fibre of various species of *Bromelia*, *Agave*, etc (also **pi'ta-flax** or **-hemp**). [Sp, from Quechua *pita* fine thread]

pita² see **pitta**.

pitahaya /pit-ə-hī'yə/ or **pitaya** /pi-tī'yə/ *n* a cactus of the genus *Hylocereus*, found in SW USA and Mexico; its edible brightly coloured fruit, containing translucent white flesh and small black seeds (also **dragon fruit**). [Sp]

Pitaka /pit'ə-kə/ *n* any one of the three divisions of the Buddhist canon. [Sans, basket]

pitapat or **pit-a-pat** /pit'ə-pat/, **pitty-pat** /pit'i-pat/ or **pit-pat** /pit'pat/ *adv* with a pattering or tapping noise; with a palpitating sensation. ◆ *adj* fluttering; pattering. ◆ *n* a light, quick step; a succession of light taps; a pattering noise; a palpitating sensation. ◆ *vi* (**pit-a-patt'ing**; **pit-a-patt'ed**) to step or tread quickly; to patter or tap lightly; to palpitate. [Imit]

pitara or **pitarah** see **petara**.

pitch¹ /pich/ *vt* (*pat* and *pap* **pitched**, or *obs* **pight** (qv)) to thrust or fix in the ground; to set up; to establish; to set or plant firmly; to set in position; to lay out for sale; to set, cover, stud, or face; to pave (a road) with stones set on end or on edge; to make a foundation of stones for; to set in array (*obs*); to pit in opposition; to determine or fix (*obs*); to establish the slope of; to set in a key, to give this or that musical pitch, emotional tone, or degree of moral exaltation, etc, to; to try to interest someone in buying or endorsing (a product); to fling, throw, or toss, *esp* in such a manner as to fall flat or in a definite position; to hit (a golf ball) so that it flies in a high arc and does not roll much on landing; to bowl (the ball) so as to strike the ground (at a particular spot) (*cricket*). ◆ *vi* to settle; to alight; to fix the choice (on); to encamp; to plunge forward; to oscillate about a transverse axis (*aeronautics*); (of a ship) to plunge and lift alternately at bow and stern; to slope down; to descend or fall away abruptly; to interlock; (of a cricket or golf ball) to bounce; to throw the ball to the batter (*baseball*). ◆ *n* a place set apart for playing or practising a game; the act or manner of pitching; a throw or cast; degree, *esp* of elevation or depression; highest point (*fig*; literal meaning is *archaic*); height; a descent; slope or degree of slope; ground between the wickets (*cricket*); the point where a ball alights; a shot in golf where the ball flies in a high arc and does not roll much on landing; a ball thrown to the batter (*baseball*); a station taken by a street trader, etc; a salesman's particular line of persuasive talk; a particular means of interesting someone in buying, endorsing, etc something; the degree of acuteness of a sound that makes it a high or low, etc, note, or the standard degree of acuteness assigned to a particular note (*music*); degree of intensity; distance between successive points or things, such as the centres of teeth in a wheel or a saw, characters in type or the threads of a screw; (of a propeller) the angle between the chord of the blade and the plane of rotation; the distance a propeller would advance in one revolution. [14c; ety uncertain]

■ **pitch'er** *n* a person who pitches; a paving-stone or sett; a baseball player who delivers the ball to the batter; one who pitches a stall; a cutting or stake intended to take root. **pitch'ing** *n* the action of the verb to pitch; a facing of stone; a foundation of stone for a road surface; a cobblestone surface of a road.

□ **pitch and putt** *n* (a game played on) a golf course with short holes, needing only a pitch from tee to green. **pitch and run** *n* a pitch shot played so that the ball runs on after pitching. **pitch-and-toss'** *n* a game in which coins are thrown at a mark, the player who throws nearest having the right of tossing all, and keeping those that come down heads up. **pitch bend** *n* the technique of modifying the pitch of a musical note; the facility to do this. **pitch circle** *n* in a toothed wheel, an imaginary circle along which the tooth pitch is measured and which would put the wheel in contact with another that meshed with it. **pitched battle** *n* a deliberate battle on chosen ground between duly arranged sides; a violent confrontation generally. **pitched roof** *n* a roof having two surfaces sloping downwards from a central ridge. **pitch'ed-roofed** or **pitch'-roofed** *adj*. **pitch'-farthing** *n* chuck-farthing. **pitch'fork** *n* a fork for tossing hay, etc; a tuning fork. ◆ *vt* to lift with a pitchfork; to throw suddenly into a position or situation. **pitching tool** *n* a blunt-edged chisel, used to knock off superfluous stone. **pitching wedge** *n* a lofted golf club for playing pitch shots. **pitch'man** *n* (also **pitch'person**; *fem* **pitch'woman**) a street or market trader (*N Am*); an advertising man, *esp* in the media; someone who delivers a strong sales pitch. **pitch'pipe** *n* a small pipe to pitch the voice or to tune strings, etc with. **pitch'-wheel** *n* a toothed wheel which operates with another of the same design.

■ **pitch and pay** (*Shakesp*) to pay ready money. **pitch in** (*inf*) to set to work briskly; to join in, co-operate. **pitch into** to rebuke or assail

vigorously; to throw oneself into (work, a task, etc). **pitch on** or **upon** to let one's choice fall on or upon. **pitch up** (*inf*) to arrive.

pitch² /pich/ *n* the black shining residue of distillation of tar, etc; extended to various bituminous and resinous substances, such as *Burgundy pitch*; resin from certain pine trees. ◆ *vt* to smear, cover, or caulk with pitch. [OE *pic*, from L *pix*, *picis*]

■ **pitch'iness** *n*. **pitch'y** *adj* like or characteristic of pitch; smeared with pitch; full of pitch; black.

□ **pitch-black'** *adj* black as pitch. **pitch-dark'** *adj* utterly dark. **pitch'pine** *n* a name for several American pines that yield pitch and timber (*Pinus palustris, Pinus rigida*, etc). **pitch'stone** *n* a volcanic glass of resinous lustre, *usu* acid. **pitch'-tree** *n* a tree yielding pitch, turpentine, or resin, *esp* silver fir, spruce, kauri pine, Amboina pine.

pitchblende /pich'blend/ *n* a black mineral composed of uranium oxides, a source of uranium and radium. [Ger *Pechblende*, **pitch²** and **blende**]

pitcher¹ /pich'ər/ *n* a vessel, *usu* of earthenware, for holding or pouring liquids; a cylindrical tinned milk-can (*Scot*); a jug or ewer (*N Am*); a modified leaf or part of a leaf in the form of a pitcher, serving to catch insects. [OFr *picher*, from LL *picārium* a goblet, from Gr *bīkos*, a wine vessel]

■ **pitch'erful** *n*.

□ **pitcher plant** *n* an insectivorous plant with pitchers, *esp* Nepenthes, also Sarracenia, Darlingtonia, etc.

■ (**little**) **pitchers have** (**long** or **big**) **ears** children tell tales; there may be listeners.

pitcher² see under **pitch¹**.

pitch-pole, also **pitch-poll** /pich'pōl/ *n* a somersault (*obs*); a type of harrow (*rare*). ◆ *vi* to go head over heels; to somersault; to flip over lengthways; (of a boat) to turn stern over bow. [**pitch¹** and **poll¹**]

pitchy see under **pitch²**.

piteous /pit'i-əs/ *adj* arousing or deserving pity; compassionate (*archaic*); paltry (*Milton*). [OFr *pitos, piteus*; cf *pity*]

■ **pit'eously** *adv*. **pit'eousness** *n*.

pitfall see under **pit¹**.

pith /pith/ *n* the soft tissue within the ring of vascular bundles in the stems of dicotyledonous plants; similar material elsewhere, as the white inner skin of an orange; the soft spongy interior of a feather; spinal marrow; the innermost, central or most important part; condensed substance, essence; mettle; vigour; substance, weight, significance; importance. ◆ *vt* to remove the pith of; to sever, pierce, or destroy the marrow or central nervous system of; to kill (animals) in this way. [OE *pitha*; Du *pit*, kernel]

■ **pith'ful** *adj*. **pith'ily** *adv*. **pith'iness** *n*. **pith'less** *adj*. **pith'like** *adj*. **pith'y** *adj* full of pith; forcible; strong; energetic; sententious and masterful.

□ **pith'ball** *n* a pellet of pith. **pith hat** or **helmet** *n* a sun helmet made of sola pith. **pith'-tree** *n* a tropical African papilionaceous tree (*Herminiera elaphroxylon*) whose very pithlike wood is used for floats, canoes, etc.

pithead see under **pit¹**.

Pithecanthropus /pith-ə-kan'thrə-pəs/ or /pith-i-kan-thrō'pəs/ *n* a fossil hominid discovered by Dutch palaeontologist Dr Eugene Dubois in Java in 1891–2, a former genus of primitive man, now included in the genus *Homo*. [Gr *pithēkos* ape, and *anthropos* man]

pithecoid /pi-thē'koid/ *adj* apelike. [Gr *pithēkos* ape, and *eidos* form]

pithos /pith'os/ *n* (*pl* **pithoi** /pith'oi/) a large Greek storage jar. [Gr]

pithy see under **pith**.

pitiable, etc, **pitied**, **pitier**, **pitiful**, **pitiless**, etc see **pity**.

pitman see under **pit¹**.

pit-mirk /pit-mûrk'/ (*Scot*) *adj* pitch-dark.

piton /pē'ton/ or Fr /pē-tɔ̃/ *n* an iron peg or stanchion to which a rope may be attached, used in mountaineering. [Fr]

Pitot tube /pē'tō tūb/ *n* a tube with openings at one end and one side, placed in a stream of liquid, an airstream, etc, to measure the velocity and pressure of flow, or speed of an aircraft, etc. [From its originator, Henri *Pitot* (1695–1771), French physicist]

pit-pat see **pitapat**.

Pitta /pit'ə/ *n* a genus of birds, the so-called ant thrushes of the Old World; (without *cap*) a bird of this genus. [Telugu *pitta*]

pitta or **pita** /pit'ə/ *n* (also **pitta bread** or **pita bread**) a type of slightly leavened bread, originating in the Middle East, *usu* made in the form of flat hollow ovals; one of these ovals. [Mod Gr, a cake]

pittance /pit'əns/ *n* a very small portion or quantity; a miserable wage; *orig* a special additional allowance of food or drink in a religious house, or a bequest to provide it; a dole. [OFr *pitance*, from L *pietās* pity]

pitted see under **pit¹,²**.

---

fāte; fär; mē; fûr; mīne; mōte; för; mūte; pŭt; dhen (then); *el'ə-mənt* (element) ◆ For other sounds see detailed chart of pronunciation

pitten see pit³.

pitter /pit'ər/ vi to make a sound like a grasshopper. [Imit]
□ **pitt'er-patt'er** /-pat'ər/ adv with a light pattering sound. ◆ vi to make or move with such a sound. ◆ n such a sound.

pittie-ward /pit'i-wərd/ (Shakesp) n poss little park (Merry Wives of Windsor III.1.5).

Pittite /pit'īt/ n a follower of William Pitt (1759–1806), British statesman. ◆ adj relating to Pitt or the Pittites.
■ **Pitt'ism** n.

pittite see under pit¹.

pittosporum /pi-tos'pə-rəm/ n an evergreen shrub native to Australasia and parts of Africa and Asia, with leathery leaves and purple, white or greenish-yellow flowers (also called **parchment bark**). [Mod L, from Gr pitta pitch, and sporos seed]

pitty-pat see pitapat.

pituita /pit-ū-ī'tə/ or **pituite** /pit'ū-īt/ (archaic) n phlegm, mucus. [L pītuīta]

pituitary /pi-tū'i-t(ə-)ri/ adj of or relating to the pituitary gland; of or relating to phlegm or mucus (archaic). ◆ n the pituitary gland. [L pītuīta phlegm]
■ **pitū'itrin** n a hormone produced by the pituitary gland.
□ **pituitary gland** or **body** n a ductless endocrine gland at the base of the brain affecting growth, once thought to produce mucus.

pituri /pit'(ch)ə-ri/ n an Australian solanaceous shrub, Duboisia hopwoodii; the narcotic obtained from its leaves. [From an Aboriginal language]

pity /pit'i/ n a feeling of sorrow for the sufferings and misfortunes of others, compassion; a cause or source of such a feeling; an unfortunate chance; a matter for regret. ◆ vt (**pit'ying**; **pit'ied**) to feel pity for; to feel grief at; to cause pity in (obs). [OFr pite (Fr pitié, Ital pietà), from L pietās, pietātis, from pius pious]
■ **pit'iable** adj to be pitied; miserable, contemptible. **pit'iableness** n. **pit'iably** adv. **pit'ier** n. **pit'iful** adj exciting pity; sad, wretched; despicable; feeling pity; compassionate. ◆ adv (Shakesp) pitifully. **pit'ifully** adv. **pit'ifulness** n. **pit'iless** adj without pity; merciless, cruel. **pit'ilessly** adv. **pit'ilessness** n. **pit'ying** adj. **pit'yingly** adv.
□ **pity party** n (inf) a period of indulgent self-pity.
■ **it pitieth me, you, them**, etc (Prayer Book) it causes pity in me, you, them, etc.

pityriasis /pit-i-rī'i-sis/ n (med) any of several skin diseases marked by the formation and flaking away of dry scales, esp pityriasis versicolor. [Gr pityron bran]
■ **pit'yroid** adj (archaic) bran-like. **pityrospor'um** n a yeastlike fungus which can cause pityriasis versicolor.

più /pyoo or pē'oo/ (Ital; music) adv more.
■ **più mosso** /mō'sō or mo'so/ quicker.

pium /pi-oom'/ n a small but very troublesome Brazilian biting fly. [Tupí]

piupiu /pē'oo-pē-oo/ n a skirt, traditionally made from strips of flax, worn by Maori men and women for dances, celebrations and ceremonial occasions. [Maori]

pivot /piv'ət/ n a pin or shaft on which anything turns; a soldier upon whom, or position on which, a body wheels; a centrally placed player who passes the ball to others (sport); a person or thing on whom or which anything depends or turns; the action of turning the body using one foot as a pivot. ◆ adj of the nature of a pivot; cardinal; serving as a pivot. ◆ vt to mount on a pivot. ◆ vi to turn on or as if on a pivot. [Fr pivot, perh related to Ital piva pipe, peg, pin]
■ **piv'otal** adj of, containing, or acting like a pivot; crucially important. **piv'otally** adv. **piv'oted** adj. **piv'oter** n someone who makes and fits pivots; a person who pivots. **piv'oting** n the pivot-work in machines.
□ **pivot bridge** n a swing bridge moving on a vertical pivot in the middle. **piv'ot-man** n a man on whom a body of soldiers turns; a man of cardinal importance in industry, etc.

pix¹ /piks/ n same as pyx.

pix² /piks/ (inf) n pl (sing pic) pictures, usu in the sense of photographs.

pixel /pik'səl/ (comput, image technol) n the smallest element with controllable colour and brightness in a video display, or in computer graphics. [pix² and element]
■ **pix'ellated** adj made up of pixels; displayed as enlarged pixels so as to distort or disguise.

pixie or **pixy** /pik'si/, also (SW Eng dialect) **pisky** /pis'ki/ n a small fairy. [Origin obscure; cf Swed pysk, pyske a small fairy]
□ **pixie hat** n a child's pointed hat. **pixie hood** n a child's pointed hood, usu tied under the chin. **pix'y-led** adj bewildered. **pix'y-ring** n a fairy ring. **pix'y-stool** n a toadstool or mushroom.

pixilated or **pixillated** /pik'si-lā-tid/ (esp US) adj bemused, bewildered; slightly crazy; intoxicated; pixellated. [Pixie and poss titillated]
■ **pixilā'tion** or **pixillā'tion** n (see also separate entry).

pixilation or **pixillation** /pik-si-lā'shən/ n a technique for making human figures and animals appear to be animated artificially, eg by the use of stop-frame camera methods, usu to create a whimsical effect (film, theatre, TV; from pixilated and animation); a video effect in which a picture is broken down into a comparatively small number of square elements (image technol; associated with **pixel**; see also under **pixilated**.

pixy see pixie.

pizazz see pizzazz.

pize /pīz/ n a term of imprecation, pox, pest. [Origin uncertain]

pizza /pēt'sə/ n a flat usu round slab of dough topped with tomato sauce, cheese and various chopped vegetables and/or meats, and baked. [Ital]
■ **pizzaiola** /pēt-sī-ō'lə/ adj having a rich sauce made with tomatoes. **pizzeria** /pēt-sə-rē'ə/ n a bakery or restaurant where pizzas are sold and/or made.

pizzazz, pizazz, pazzazz, or **pazazz** /pi- or pə-zaz'/ (inf) n a combination of flamboyance, panache and vigour, in behaviour, display or performance. [Onomatopoeic coinage by Diana Vreeland, US fashion editor (c.1903–89)]

pizzicato /pit-si-kä'tō/ (music) adj played by plucking the string (not arco or col arco, with the bow). ◆ adv by plucking. ◆ n (pl **pizzica'tos**) a tone so produced; a passage so played; the manner of playing by plucking. [Ital, twitched, from pizzicare to twitch]

pizzle /piz'l/ n the penis; the penis of a bull used as an instrument of punishment, in flogging. [LGer pesel or Flem pezel]

PJs or **pjs** /pē'jāz/ n pl (inf) pyjamas.

PK abbrev: Pakistan (IVR); psychokinesis.

Pk abbrev: Park (in place and street names).

pk abbrev: park; peak; peck.

PKU abbrev: phenylketonuria.

PL abbrev: Poet Laureate; Poland (IVR); programming language (comput); Public Library.

Pl abbrev: Place (in street names, etc).

pl abbrev: plural.

PLA abbrev: Port of London Authority; Pre-school Learning Alliance.

placable /plak' or plāk'ə-bl/ adj that may be appeased; easily appeased; relenting; willing to forgive, forgiving. [L plācābilis, from plācāre to appease]
■ **placabil'ity** n. **plac'ableness** n. **plac'ably** adv.

placard /plak'ärd/ n a written or printed notice stuck on a wall or otherwise publicly displayed; a notice written or printed on wood, cardboard or other stiff material, and carried, hung, etc, in a public place; an official permit or proclamation with a thin seal (obs); a placcat or placket (obs). ◆ vt (sometimes /plə-kärd'/) to publish or notify by placard; to post or set up as a placard; to put placards on or in. [OFr plackart, placard, etc, from plaquier to lay flat, plaster, from MFlem placken to plaster]

placate /plə-kāt', plā-kāt'/ vt to conciliate, appease. [L plācāre, to appease, related to placēre]
■ **placā'tion** n propitiation. **placatory** /plak' or plāk'ə-tə-ri, plə-kā'/ adj conciliatory.

placcat or **placcate** see placket.

place /plās/ n a portion of space; a portion of the earth's surface, or any surface; a position in space, or on the earth's surface, or in any system, order, or arrangement; a building, room, piece of ground, etc, assigned to some purpose (eg place of business, entertainment, worship); a particular locality; a town, village, etc; a dwelling or home; a mansion with its grounds; a battlefield (obs); a fortress, fortified town (obs); an open space in a town, a market-place or square; (with cap) used in street names esp for a row or group of houses, a short street or a circus; a seat or accommodation in a theatre, train, at table, etc; space occupied; room; the position held by anybody, employment, office, a situation, esp under government or in domestic service; due or proper position or dignity; that which is incumbent on one; precedence; position in a series; high rank; position attained in a competition or assigned by criticism; position among the first three in a race; stead; pitch reached by a bird of prey (obs except in pride of place, qv); (in reading-matter, narrative, conversation, etc) the point which the reader or speaker has reached when he stops or is interrupted; a topic, matter of discourse (obs); a passage in a book (obs). ◆ vt to put in any place; to assign to a place; to find a place, home, job, publisher, etc, for; to find a buyer for (usu a large quantity of stocks or shares; commerce); to propose, lay or put (with before); to induct; to appoint; to identify; to invest; to arrange (a loan, bet, etc); to put (trust, etc, in); to state the finishing positions of (the competitors, esp the first three) in a race or competition; to ascribe (with to; archaic). ◆ vi (esp US) to finish a race or competition (in a specified position); to finish a race in second (if otherwise unspecified) position (*horse-racing*). [Partly OE (Northumbrian) *plæce* marketplace, but mainly Fr *place*, both from L *platea*, from Gr *plateia* (*hodos*) broad (street)]

■ **placed** *adj* set in place or in a place; having a place; among the first three in a race; inducted to a position or office. **place'less** *adj* without place or office. **place'ment** *n* placing or setting; assigning to places; assigning to a job; a temporary job providing work experience, *esp* for someone on a training course. **plac'er** *n.* **plac'ing** *n* position, *esp* a finishing position in a race or competition; the process of finding an intermediary buyer for large numbers of (*usu* newly issued) shares, etc (*commerce*). □ **place card** *n* a card placed before each setting on the table at a banquet, formal dinner, etc, with the name of the person who is to sit there. **place'holder** *n* a symbol representing a missing term or quantity in a mathematical expression. **place'-hunter** *n* (*archaic*) someone who covets and strives after a public post. **place kick** *n* (in rugby, etc) a kick made when the ball has been placed on the ground for that purpose. **place'-kicker** *n.* **place'man** *n* (*pl* **place'men**) someone who has a place or office under a government, *esp* if gained by selfishness or ambition. **place mat** *n* a table mat set at a person's place setting. **place'-monger** *n* someone who traffics in appointments to places. **place name** *n* a geographical proper name. **place setting** *n* each person's set of crockery, cutlery and glassware as used at a dining table. **place value** *n* the value that a digit has because of the position that it occupies in a number. ■ **all over the place** scattered; in a muddle or mess, confused, disorganized (*inf*). **fall into place** to be resolved. **give place** (**to**) to make room (for); to be superseded (by). **go places** see under **go¹**. **have place** to have existence. **in place** in position; opportune. **in place of** instead of. **in the first place** firstly, originally. **know one's place** to show proper subservience. **lose one's place** to falter in following a text, etc, not know what point has been reached. **lose the place** (*inf*) to flounder, be at a loss, be all at sea; to lose one's temper. **out of place** out of due position; inappropriate, unseasonable. **put** or **keep someone in his** or **her place** to humble someone who is arrogant, presumptuous, etc, or keep him or her in subservience. **take one's place** to assume one's rightful position. **take place** to come to pass, to occur; to take precedence. **take someone's place** to act as substitute for, or successor to, someone. **take the place of** to be a substitute for.

placebo /plə-sē'bō/ *n* (*pl* **placē'bos** or **placē'boes**) a medicine given to humour or gratify a patient rather than to exercise any physically curative effect; a pharmacologically inactive substance administered as a drug either in the treatment of psychological illness or in the course of drug trials; vespers for the dead (*RC*); a sycophant (*obs*). [From the first words of the first antiphon of the office of vespers, *Placēbō Dominō* I shall please the Lord] □ **placebo effect** *n* a beneficial effect of a placebo, ascribed to the patient's belief in its efficacy.

placenta /plə-sen'tə/ *n* (*pl* **placen'tae** /-tē/ or **placen'tas**) in mammals, the flattened structure formed by the intimate union of the allantois and chorion with the uterine wall of the mother, serving for the respiration and nutrition of the growing young (*zool*); the part of the ovary of a flowering plant that bears the ovules (*bot*); any mass of tissue bearing sporangia or spores. [L *placenta* a flat cake, from Gr *plakoeis* (contraction of *plakous*) from *plax*, *plakos* anything flat] ■ **placen'tal** *adj.* ◆ *n* a placental mammal. **Placentalia** /plas-ən-tā'li-ə/ *n pl* Eutheria, the subclass of placental mammals. **placentā'tion** *n* the arrangement and mode of attachment of placentae or of placenta and fetus. **placent'iform** *adj* cake-shaped. **placentol'ogy** *n* the scientific study of placentae.

placer¹ /plas'ər or plās'ər/ *n* a superficial deposit from which gold or other mineral can be washed. [Sp *placer* sandbank, from *plaza* place] □ **plac'er-gold** *n.*

placer² see under **place**.

placet¹ /plā'set or pla'ket/ *n* a vote of assent in a governing body; permission given, *esp* by a sovereign, to publish and carry out an ecclesiastical order, such as a papal bull or edict (*hist*). [L *placet* it pleases, 3rd pers sing pr indic of *placēre* to please]

placet² a wrong form of **placit** (see **placitum**).

placid /plas'id/ *adj* displaying calmness of nature, not easily disturbed or angered. [L *placidus*, from *placēre* to please] ■ **placid'ity** or **plac'idness** *n.* **plac'idly** *adv.*

placing see under **place**.

placitum /plas'i-təm or plak'i-tŭm/ *n* (*pl* **plac'ita**) (also **plac'it** and wrongly **plac'et**) a decision of a court or an assembly; a plea or pleading. [L pap neuter of *placēre* to please] ■ **plac'itory** *adj* relating to pleas or pleading.

plack /plak/ *n* an old Scottish copper coin worth one-third of an English penny of the same period. [Prob Flem *placke*, an old Flemish coin, *orig* a flat disc] ■ **plack'less** *adj.*

placket /plak'it/ *n* (in armour) a breastplate or backplate, or a leather doublet with strips of steel (also (*obs*) **placc'ate** or (*Shakesp*) **placc'at**); an apron (*archaic*); a petticoat (*archaic*); the wearer of a petticoat, a woman (*archaic*); an opening in a skirt, shirt, etc for a pocket, or at the fastening; a piece of material sewn behind this; a pocket, *esp* in a skirt. [Origin obscure; perh a variant of **placard** breastplate] □ **plack'et-hole** *n* (*archaic*) a slit in a skirt.

placoderm /plak'ə-dûrm/ *adj* (of fossil fishes) covered with bony plates. ◆ *n* a fish so covered. [Gr *plax*, *plakos* anything flat, and *derma* skin]

placoid /plak'oid/ *adj* (of scales) plate-like; (of fish, eg sharks) having placoid scales, irregular plates of hard bone, not imbricated. [Gr *plax*, *plakos* anything flat and broad, and *eidos* form]

plafond /pla-fɔ̃'/ *n* a ceiling, *esp* decorated; a soffit; an earlier version of contract bridge. [Fr, ceiling, score above the line in bridge, from *plat* flat, and *fond* bottom]

plagal /plā'gl/ (*music*) *adj* of a Gregorian mode, having the final in the middle of the compass instead of at the bottom (cf **authentic**). [Gr *plagios*, sidewise, from *plagos* a side] □ **plagal cadence** *n* one in which the subdominant chord precedes the tonic.

plage /pläzh/ *n* a fashionable beach; a bright, highly disturbed area in the chromosphere, *usu* presaging, or associated with, a sunspot. [Fr]

plagiarize or **-ise** /plā'jə-rīz/ *vt* and *vi* to steal ideas or writings from another person and present them as one's own. [L *plagiārius* kidnapper, from *plaga* a net] ■ **plā'giarism** *n* the act or practice of plagiarizing. **plā'giarist** *n* a person who plagiarizes. **plā'giary** *n* (*archaic*) a plagiarist; plagiarism. ◆ *adj* (*obs*) practising or obtained by plagiarism.

plagio- /plā-ji-ō-, -ə-, -o-/ *combining form* meaning oblique. [Gr *plagios* oblique]

plagiocephaly /plā-ji-ō-sef'ə-li or -kef'/ (*med*) *n* a twisted condition of the head, the front of the skull being larger on one side, the back larger on the other.

plagioclase /plā'ji-ō-klās, -klāz or plaj'/ *n* a feldspar whose cleavages are not at right angles, eg albite, anorthite, or any mixture of them. [Gr *plagios* oblique, and *klasis* a fracture]

plagiostome /plā'ji-ō-stōm/ *n* any fish families of the **Plagiostomata** /-stō'mə-tə/ or **Plagiostomi** /-os'tə-mī/, the cross-mouthed fishes, sharks and rays, whose mouth is a transverse slit on the underside of the head. [Gr *plagios* crosswise, and *stoma*, *-atos* mouth] ■ **plagiostom'atous** or **plagios'tomous** *adj.*

plagiotropism /plā-ji-ot'rə-pi-zm/ *n* orienting at an angle to the direction of stimulus. [Gr *plagios* crosswise, and *tropos* a turning] ■ **plagiotropic** /plā-ji-ō-trop'ik/ *adj.* **plagiotrop'ically** *adv.* **plagiotropous** /-ot'rə-pəs/ *adj.*

plagium /plā'ji-əm/ *n* the crime of kidnapping. [L *plagium*, from *plaga* a net]

plague /plāg/ *n* a deadly epidemic or pestilence, *esp* a fever caused by a bacillus (*Bacillus pestis*) transmitted by rat-fleas from rats to man, characterized by buboes, or swellings of the lymphatic glands, by carbuncles and petechiae; murrain; a sudden abnormal infestation, such as *a plague of greenfly*; any troublesome thing or person; a nuisance or vexation (*inf*); a blow or wound (*obs*); an affliction regarded as a sign of divine displeasure. ◆ *vt* to infest with disease (*rare*); to pester or annoy. [OFr *plague*, from L *plāga* a blow; cf Gr *plēgē*] ■ **plague'some** *adj* (*inf*) troublesome, annoying. **pla'guily** *adv* confoundedly. **plaguy** (*archaic*) or **plaguey** /plā'gi/ *adj* of, or of the nature of, plague; vexatious; troublesome; confounded. ◆ *adv* (*Shakesp*) confoundedly. □ **plague'-pit** *n* a common grave for plague victims. **plague'-sore** *n* an ulcer due to plague. **plague'-spot** *n* a spot on the skin indicating plague; a place where disease is constantly present; an evil place. **plague'-stricken** *adj.* ■ **a plague on** may a curse rest on. **avoid like the plague** (*inf*) to keep well away from, shun absolutely. **what the** (or *Shakesp* **a**) **plague** what the devil.

plaice /plās/ *n* a flatfish of the family Pleuronectidae (*Pleuronectes platessa*), brown with orange spots, used as food; any of several related fish (*N Am*). [OFr *plaïs* (Fr *plie*), from LL *platessa* a flatfish, perh from Gr *platys* flat] □ **plaice'-mouth** *n* a mouth placed awry. ◆ *adj* wry-mouthed.

plaid /plād, plad/ *n* a long piece of woollen cloth, worn over the shoulder, *usu* in tartan as part of Highland dress, or checked as formerly worn by Lowland shepherds; cloth for it, tartan; a plaidman.

◆ *adj* like a plaid in pattern or colours. [Perh Gaelic *plaide* a blanket; but that may be from the Scot word]

■ **plaid'ed** *adj* wearing a plaid; made of plaid cloth. **plaid'ing** *n* a strong woollen twilled fabric.

❑ **plaid'man** *n* a Highlander. **plaid'-neuk** /-*nük*/ *n* a pocket at the end of a plaid.

Plaid Cymru /plīd kum'ri/ (*Welsh*) *n* the Welsh Nationalist party. [*Plaid* party; *Cymru* Wales]

plain¹ /plān/ *adj* flat; level; even; unobstructed; without obscurity; clear; obvious; simple; downright, utter; not ornate; unembellished; unvariegated; uncoloured; unruled; without pattern, striation, markings, etc; without gloss; uncurled; not twilled; (in knitting) denoting a straightforward stitch with the wool passed round the front of the needle (cf **purl¹**); not elaborate; without addition; not highly seasoned; deficient in beauty; ugly (*euphem*); without subtlety; candid; outspoken; straightforward; undistinguished; ordinary; other than a court card; other than trumps. ◆ *n* an extent of level land; the open country, *esp* as a field of battle or as a setting for pastoral or romantic literature (*poetic*). ◆ *adv* clearly; distinctly. ◆ *vt* (*Shakesp*) to make plain. [Fr, from L *plānus* plain]

■ **plain'ish** *adj*. **plain'ly** *adv*. **plain'ness** *n*.

❑ **plain bob** see **bob¹**. **plain'chant** *n* plainsong. **plain chocolate** *n* dark chocolate, made with some sugar added but without milk. **plain'clothes** *adj* wearing ordinary clothes, not uniform (eg of a policeman on detective work). **plain cook** *n* someone competent in plain cookery. **plain'-cook** *vi* to practise plain cookery. **plain cookery** *n* the cooking of ordinary simple traditional dishes. **plain'-darn** *vt* and *vi* to darn with the ordinary cross pattern. **plain dealer** *n* a person who is candid and outspoken. **plain dealing** *n*. **plain'-dealing** *adj*. **plain flour** *n* flour that is not mixed with a raising agent. **plain'-heart'ed** *adj* having a plain or honest heart; sincere. **plain'-heart'edness** *n*. **plain Jane** *n* (*derog inf*) a plain, dowdy girl. **plain'-Jane** *adj* ordinary, unremarkable; plain, *esp* of a garment. **plain language** *n* straightforward, understandable language. **plain loaf** *n* (*Scot*) a batch loaf (qv under **batch¹**). **plain sailing** *n* sailing in open, unrestricted waters (*naut*); an easy, straightforward task, affair, etc (*fig*); see also **plane sailing** under **plane¹**. **plains'man** *n* (*pl* **plains'men**) a dweller in a plain, *esp* in N America. **plain'song** *n* unmeasured, unaccompanied music sung in unison in ecclesiastical modes from early times, and still in use in Roman Catholic and some Anglican churches; a simple melody; that to which a descant can be added. ◆ *adj* (*Shakesp*) singing a simple theme. **plain speaking** *n* straightforwardness or bluntness of speech. **plain'-spoken** *adj* plain, rough, and sincere; frank, candid, *esp* if rather blunt. **plain'stanes** *n pl* (*Scot*) flagstones, pavement (also **plain'stones**). **plain text** *n* (*comput*) text that is readable and uncoded. **plain weave** *n* a weave in which the weft is passed alternately under and over the warp. **plain'work** *n* plain needlework, as distinguished from embroidery.

■ **plain as a pikestaff** see under **pike²**.

plain² /plān/ (*archaic*) *vt* and *vi* to complain; to lament. ◆ *n* a complaint. [OFr *plaigner* (Fr *plaindre*), from L *plangere* to beat the breast, lament]

■ **plain'ant** *n* a person who complains; a plaintiff. **plain'ful** *adj*. **plain'ing** *n* (*Shakesp*) complaint.

Plains /plānz/ (also without *cap*; *esp US*) *adj* of or from the Great Plains of N America.

❑ **Plains Indian** *n* a member of any of the Native American tribes originally inhabiting the Great Plains.

plaint /plānt/ *n* lamentation (*literary*); complaint (*archaic*); a mournful song; a statement of grievance, *esp* the exhibiting of an action in writing by a complainant in a court of law. [OFr *pleinte* (Fr *plainte*), from L *plangere*, *planctum* to beat the breast, lament]

■ **plaint'ful** *adj* (*archaic*) complaining. **plaint'less** *adj*.

plaintiff /plān'tif/ (*Eng law*) *n* formerly, a person who commences a suit against another (replaced by *claimant* in official use) (also (*Spenser*) *adj*). [OFr *plaintif* (masc *adj*) complaining]

plaintive /plān'tiv/ *adj* mournful; querulous. [OFr *plaintif*, *plaintive*, from L *plangere*; see **plaintiff** and **plaint**]

■ **plain'tively** *adv*. **plain'tiveness** *n*.

plaister /plā'stər/ (*obs* or *Scot*) *n* a form of **plaster**.

plait /plat or plāt or (now rare) plēt/ *n* a braid in which strands are passed over one another in turn; material so braided; a braided tress (in these senses sometimes spelt **plat**); a pleat (*obs* or *dialect*; in this sense pronounced /plēt/). ◆ *vt* to braid or intertwine (usu /plat/); to pleat (now rare; usu /plēt/). [OFr *pleit*, *ploit* (Fr *pli*), from L *plicāre*, *-itum* or *-ātum* to fold]

■ **plait'ed** *adj*. **plait'er** *n*. **plait'ing** *n*.

plan /plan/ *n* a figure or representation of anything projected on a plane or flat surface, *esp* that of a building or floor, as disposed on the ground; a large-scale detailed map of a small area; a scheme for accomplishing a purpose; an intended method; a scheme drawn up

beforehand; a scheme of arrangement; (in the Methodist churches) a quarterly programme of services with preachers for each church in the circuit. ◆ *vt* (**plann'ing**; **planned**) to make a plan of; to design; to lay plans for; to devise; to purpose. ◆ *vi* to make plans. [Fr, from L *plānus* flat]

■ **plan'less** *adj*. **planned** *adj* intended; in accordance with, or achieved by, a careful plan made beforehand. **plann'er** *n* a person who plans, *esp* the development of a town, etc; a calendar showing the whole year, etc, at a glance, used for forward planning. **plann'ing** *n* the act or practice of making plans, *esp* for the development of a town, etc.

❑ **planned economy** *n* one in which the government decides levels of production, prices and wages, etc. **planned obsolescence** see under **obsolescent**. **planning blight** see under **blight**. **planning permission** *n* permission from a local authority to erect or convert a building or to change the use to which a building or piece of land is put. **plan-position indicator** *n* (*radar*) an apparatus in which the position of reflecting objects is shown on the screen of a cathode-ray tube, as if on a plan (*abbrev* **PPI**).

planar, **planation** see under **plane¹**.

planarian /plə-nā'ri-ən/ *adj* and *n* turbellarian (see **Turbellaria**). [Mod L *Planāria*, genus name, from *plānārius* on level ground (taken as if meaning flat), from *plānus* flat]

planch /plansh/ *n* a slab; a plank (*obs*); a floor (*dialect*). ◆ *vt* (*obs*) to floor; to board. [Fr *planche*, from L *planca*]

■ **planch'ed** *adj* (*Shakesp*) boarded. **planchet** /plan'shit/ *n* a blank metal disc to be stamped as a coin. **planchette** /plä-shet or plan-shet'/ *n* a board mounted on two castors and a pencil-point, used as a medium for automatic writing and supposed spirit-messages.

Planck's constant /plangks kon'stənt/ (*phys*) *n* the constant (*h*), in the expression for the quantum of energy, equal to 6.626×10^{-34} Js (joule seconds). [Max *Planck* (1858–1947), German physicist]

Planck's law /plangks lö/ (*phys*) *n* the basis of quantum theory, that the energy of electromagnetic waves is confined in indivisible packets or quanta, each of which has to be radiated or absorbed as a whole, the magnitude being proportional to frequency. [Ety as for **Planck's constant**]

plane¹ /plān/ *n* a surface of which it is true that, if any two points on the surface be taken, the straight line joining them will lie entirely on the surface (*geom*); any flat or level material surface; one of the thin horizontal structures used as wings and tail to sustain or control aeroplanes in flight; short for aeroplane or airplane (also **'plane**); an act of planing or soaring; in mines, a main road for the transport of coal or other mineral; any grade of life or of development or level of thought or existence. ◆ *adj* having the character of a plane; relating to, lying in, or confined to a plane; level; smooth. ◆ *vt* to make plane or smooth (see also **plane²**). ◆ *vi* to travel by aeroplane; to soar; to volplane; (of a boat) to skim across the surface of the water. [L *plānum* a flat surface, neuter of *plānus* flat; cf **plain¹** and **plane²**]

■ **planar** /plān'ər/ *adj* relating to a plane; lying in a single plane, flat. **planation** /plə-nā'shən/ *n* making level. **planer** /plān'ər/ *n* someone who levels or makes plane; a smoothing instrument (see also **plane²**); a wooden block beaten with a mallet to level a forme of type (*printing*).

❑ **planar diode** *n* one with plane parallel electrodes. **plane chart** *n* a chart used in plane sailing, the lines of longitude and latitude being projected onto a plane surface, so being represented parallel. **plane'-polarized** or **-s-** *adj* (of light) consisting of vibrations in one plane only. **plane sailing** *n* the calculation of a ship's place in its course as if the earth were flat instead of spherical; see also **plain sailing** under **plain¹**. **plane table** *n* an instrument used in field-mapping, with a sighting-telescope for observing objects, whose angles may be noted on a paper on the table of the instrument; an inclined table on which ore is dressed. ◆ *vt* to survey with a plane table. **planing bottom** *n* (*aerodynamics*) the part of the undersurface of a flying-boat hull that provides hydrodynamic lift.

plane² /plān/ *n* a carpenter's tool for producing a smooth surface by paring off shavings; any similar smoothing or paring tool or machine. ◆ *vt* to smooth or remove with a plane (see also **plane¹**). [Fr *plane*, from LL *plāna*, from *plānāre* to smooth]

■ **plā'ner** *n* someone who uses a plane; a tool or machine for planing. ❑ **plā'ning-machine** *n* a machine for planing wood or metals.

plane³ /plān/ *n* any tree of the genus *Platanus*, *esp* the oriental plane (*P. orientalis*) and the N American plane or buttonwood (*P. occidentalis*), trees with palmatifid leaves shedding their bark in thin slabs; in Scotland, the sycamore or great maple (*Acer pseudoplatanus*). [Fr *plane*, from L *platanus*; see **platane**]

planer see under **plane¹,²**.

planet /plan'it/ *n* any of the large celestial bodies that revolve about the sun reflecting the sun's light and generating no heat or light of their own, these being Mercury, Venus, Earth, Mars, Jupiter, Saturn, Uranus and Neptune; a satellite of a planet (**secondary planet**); an astrological influence vaguely conceived; (in old astronomy) a heavenly body whose place among the fixed stars is not fixed (including sun and moon). [Fr *planète*, from Gr *planētēs* wanderer, from *planaein* to make to wander]

■ **planeta′rium** *n* (*pl* **planeta′ria**) a machine showing the motions and orbits of the planets, often by the projecting of their images onto a (domed) ceiling; a hall or building containing such a machine. **plan′etary** *adj* relating to the planets or a planet, or this planet; consisting of or produced by planets; under the influence of a planet (*astrol*); erratic; revolving in an orbit. **planetes′imal** *n* in one theory of the origin of the solar system, any of many very small units absorbed into the planets as these formed. **planetic** /*plan-et′ik*/ or **planet′ical** *adj*. **plan′etoid** *n* an asteroid; an artificial body put into orbit. **planetoi′dal** *adj*. **planetol′ogist** *n*. **planetol′ogy** *n* the science of the planets.

❑ **planetary gear** *n* a gearwheel that travels around a central gearwheel. **planetary nebula** *n* a ring-shaped nebula around a star, consisting of a shell of gas, illuminated by the star's short-wave radiation. **plan′et-strick′en** or **plan′et-struck** *adj* (*astrol*) affected by the influence of the planets, *esp* adversely; blasted.

■ **inferior planets** the planets within the earth's orbit (Mercury and Venus). **minor planet** a rocky object that orbits the sun but is smaller than a planet. **on another planet** (*inf*) not in touch with reality. **superior planets** the planets outside the earth's orbit.

planform /*plan′förm*/ *n* a representation of an object seen vertically from above projected on a plane or flat surface. [**plan**]

plangent /*plan′jənt*/ *adj* resounding, resonant; noisy, loud, ringing, clangorous; resounding mournfully. [L *plangēns*, *-entis*, prp of *plangere* to beat]

■ **plan′gency** *n*. **plan′gently** *adv*.

plani- /*plan-i-*/ *combining form* signifying plane (see **plane**[1]). [L *plānus* flat]

■ **planigraph** /*plan′i-grāf*/ *n* an instrument for reducing or enlarging drawings. **planimeter** /*plə-nim′i-tər*/ *n* an instrument for measuring the area of a plane figure. **planimetric** /*plān-* or *plan-i-met′rik*/ or **planimet′rical** *adj*. **planim′etry** *n* the mensuration of plane surfaces. **planisphere** /*plan′is-fēr*/ *n* a sphere projected on a plane; a map of the celestial sphere, which can be adjusted so as to show the area visible at any time. **planispher′ic** *adj*.

planish /*plan′ish*/ *vt* to polish (metal, etc); to flatten. [Obs Fr *planir*, *-issant*, from *plan* flat]

■ **plan′isher** *n* a person who or tool that planishes.

planisphere, etc see under **plani-**.

plank /*plangk*/ *n* a long piece of timber, thicker and *usu* narrower than a board; a special board on which fish, etc, is cooked and served (*N Am*); one of the principles or aims that form the platform or programme of a political party, etc. ◆ *vt* to cover with planks; to pay down or table (with *down*); to cook on a plank (*US*); to put down with a thump (often with *down*; *Scot* or *dialect*). [L *planca* a board]

■ **plank′ing** *n* the act of laying planks; a series of planks; work made up of planks.

❑ **plank bed** *n* a prison bed of wood without a mattress.

■ **walk the plank** to suffer the former maritime punishment of being forced to walk off the end of a plank projecting over the ship's side.

plankton /*plangk′tən*/ *n* the drifting organisms in oceans, lakes or rivers. [Neuter of Gr *planktos*, *-ē*, *-on* wandering]

■ **planktonic** /*-ton′ik*/ *adj*.

planned, **planner**, **planning** see **plan**.

plano- /*plān-ō-* or *plan-ō-*/ *combining form* signifying plane (see **plane**[1]). [L *plānus* flat]

■ **plano-concave** /*plā′nō-kon′kāv*/ *adj* plane on one side and concave on the other. **plano-conical** /*plā′nō-kon′i-kəl*/ *adj* plane on one side and conical on the other. **plano-convex** /*plā′nō-kon′veks*/ *adj* plane on one side and convex on the other. **planograph′ic** *adj* (of printing) using a flat printing surface. **planometer** /*plə-nom′ə-tər*/ *n* a flat device used as a gauge for flat surfaces. **Planor′bis** *n* a genus of pond-snails with flat spiral shells.

planoblast /*plan′ō-blāst*/ *n* a free-swimming medusa. [Gr *planos* wandering]

■ **planogam′ete** *n* a motile gamete.

plano-concave...to...**Planorbis** see under **plano-**.

plant /*plänt*/ *n* a vegetable organism, or part of one, ready for planting or lately planted; a slip, cutting, or scion; an offshoot; a young person; a sapling; a cudgel; any member of the vegetable kingdom, *esp* (*popularly*) one of the smaller kinds; growth; amount planted; the sole of the foot; mode of planting oneself, stand; something deposited beforehand for a purpose; equipment, machinery, apparatus, for an industrial activity; a factory; the buildings, equipment, etc of eg a school, university or other institution; a bedded oyster (*US*); a thief's hoard (*sl*); a spy, detective, picket or cordon of detectives, or police

trap (*inf*); an object, etc deployed so as to incriminate someone unjustly; a deceptive trick, put-up job (*inf*); a shot in which one pockets, or tries to pocket, a ball by causing it to be propelled by another ball which has been struck by the cue ball (*snooker*). ◆ *vt* to put into the ground for growth; to introduce; to insert; to fix; to place firmly; to set in position; to station, post; to found; to settle; to locate; to place or deliver (eg a blow or a dart); to leave in the lurch; to bury (*sl*); to hide (*inf*); to deploy (stolen goods, etc) in such a way as to incriminate someone; to interpose (a question or comment) as a snare or stumbling block; to place as a spy, etc (*inf*); to instil or implant; to furnish with plants; to colonize; to stock; to furnish or provide (with things disposed around); to salt (a mine) (*sl*). ◆ *vi* to plant trees, colonists, etc. [OE *plante* (noun), from L *planta* shoot, slip, cutting, and OE *plantian* (verb)]

■ **plant′able** *adj*. **plant′age** *n* (*Shakesp*) plants in general. **planta′tion** *n* a place planted, *esp* with trees; formerly a colony; an estate used for growing cotton, rubber, tea, sugar, or other product of warm countries; a large estate (*Southern US*); the act or process of introduction; the act of planting (*Milton*). **plant′er** *n* a person who plants or introduces; the owner or manager of a plantation; a pioneer colonist; a settler; an instrument for planting; an ornamental pot or other container for plants. **plant′ing** *n* the act of setting in the ground for growth; the art of forming plantations of trees; a plantation (*Scot*). **plant′less** *adj*. **plant′let** or **plant′ling** *n* a little plant. **plant′-like** *adj*. **plantoc′racy** *n* a ruling class of plantation owners and managers; government by this class. **plant′ule** *n* a plant embryo.

❑ **plant′-associa′tion** or **plant′-forma′tion** *n* an assemblage of plants growing together under similar conditions, as in a salt-marsh or a pine-wood. **plantation song** *n* a style of song formerly sung by the black workers on American plantations. **planter's punch** *n* a cocktail consisting of rum, lime or lemon juice and sugar. **plant hormones** see **growth substance** under **growth**. **plant′-house** *n* a structure for growing plants of warmer climates. **plant′ie-cruive** /*-kroov*/ *n* (*Orkney* and *Shetland*) a kitchen garden, an enclosure for cabbage. **plant′-lore** *n* folklore of plants. **plant louse** *n* (*pl* **plant lice**) an aphis or greenfly. **plant pot** *n* a pot for growing a plant in. **plants′man** or **plants′woman** *n* a person who has great knowledge of and experience in gardening.

■ **plant out** to transplant to open ground, from pot or frame; to dispose at intervals in planting.

planta /*plan′tə*, *-ta*/ *n* (*anat*) (also **planta pedis** /*ped′is*/) the sole of the foot. [L]

■ **plan′tar** *adj* of or relating to the sole of the foot. **plan′tigrade** *adj* (L *-gradus* walking; *zool*) walking fully on the soles of the feet. ◆ *n* an animal that walks on the soles of the feet.

plantage see under **plant**.

Plantagenet /*plan-taj′ə-nət*/ *n* the royal house or dynasty that reigned in England from 1154 to 1485 (see also **Angevin**); a member of that house or dynasty. ◆ *adj* of or relating to the Plantagenet house or dynasty. [L *planta* sprig, and *genista* broom, a sprig of broom reputedly being worn in the cap of Geoffrey, Count of Anjou, father of the founder of the house, Henry II]

plantain[1] /*plan′tin*, *-tān*/ *n* a musaceous plant; its fruit, a coarse green-skinned banana used as a staple food in tropical countries; (in India) a banana. [Origin doubtful]

❑ **plan′tain-eater** *n* an African bird (genus *Musophaga*) of the family Musophagidae, a touraco.

plantain[2] /*plan′tin*, *-tān*/ *n* any plant of the genus *Plantago* (eg waybread or ribgrass; family **Plantaginā′ceae**) that presses its leaves flat on the ground and has greenish flowers on a slim stem. [L *plantāgō*, *-inis*, from *planta* the sole of the foot]

■ **plantaginaceous** /*plan-taj-i-nā′shəs*/ *adj*.

❑ **plantain lily** *n* a plant of the *Hosta* genus with white, blue or lilac flowers.

plantain[3] /*plan′tin*, *-tān*/ (*obs*) *n* a platane or plane-tree. [Obs Fr *plantain*, from L *platanus*]

plantar see under **planta**.

plantation, **planter** see under **plant**.

plantigrade see under **planta**.

Plantin /*plan′tin*/ *n* the name of a family of typefaces based on 16c Flemish types. [Christophe *Plantin* (1514–89), Antwerp printer]

planting, etc...to...**plantule** see under **plant**.

planula /*plan′ū-lə*/ *n* (*pl* **plan′ulae** /*-lē*/) a free-swimming two-layered, often flattened larva of coelenterates, etc. [Dimin of L *plānus* flat]

■ **plan′ular** *adj*. **plan′uliform** *adj*. **plan′uloid** *adj*.

planuria /*plan-ū′ri-ə*/ *n* the discharge of urine through an abnormal passage (also **plan′ury**). [Gr *planos* wandering, and *ouron* urine]

planxty /*plangk′sti*/ *n* an Irish dance tune composed in honour of a patron. [Origin unknown; perh coined by the Irish harpist Turlough O'Carolan (1670–1738)]

---

fāte; fär; mē; fûr; mīne; mōte; för; mūte; pūt; dhen (then); *el′ə-mənt* (element) • For other sounds see detailed chart of pronunciation

plaque /*plăk* or *plak*/ *n* a plate, tablet, or slab hung on, applied to or inserted in a surface as an ornament, memorial, etc; a tablet worn as a badge of honour; a patch, such as a diseased area (*med*); a film composed of saliva and bacteria that forms on teeth (*dentistry*); an area in a bacterial or tissue culture where the cells have been destroyed by infection with a virus. [Fr; cf **plack**]
■ **plaquette**' *n* a small plaque.

plash[1] /*plash*/ *vt* to interweave (branches and twigs) by partly cutting through, bending and twining, so as to form a hedge, etc; to bend down; to break down; to make, mend, or treat (a hedge) by cutting, bending, and interweaving stems and branches. ◆ *n* a plashed branch; a plashed place. [OFr *plassier*, from L *plectere* to twist; cf **pleach**]
■ **plash'ing** *n*.

plash[2] /*plash*/ or (*Spenser*) **plesh** /*plesh*/ *n* a shallow pool; a puddle. [OE *plæsc*]
■ **plash'et** *n* a puddle. **plash'y** *adj*.

plash[3] /*plash*/ *n* a dash of water; a splashing sound; a sudden downpour (*esp Scot*). ◆ *vi* to dabble in water; to splash. ◆ *vt* to splash. [Cf MLGer *plaschen*, early Mod Du *plasschen*; perh connected with **plash**[2]]
■ **plash'y** *adj*.

plasm /*plazm*/ *n* a formative substance, protoplasm, used as a *combining form* as in *cytoplasm, germ plasm*; plasma; a mould or matrix (*obs*). [Gr *plasma, -atos* a thing moulded, from *plassein* to mould]
■ **plas'ma** *n* the liquid part of blood, lymph, or milk; a very hot ionized gas, having approximately equal numbers of positive ions and of electrons, highly conducting (*phys*); plasm; a bright-green chalcedony (*geol*); protoplasm. **plasmalemm'a** *n* a cell membrane, which in plants is situated under the cell wall. **plasmapherē'sis** *n* the process of taking only the plasma from a blood donor, the blood cells being separated from the plasma by a centrifuge and returned to the donor. **plas'masphere** *n* the inner region of the magnetosphere, lying above the ionosphere. **plasmat'ic**, **plasmat'ical** or **plas'mic** *adj* of or occurring in plasma; protoplasmic. **plas'mid** *n* a circular piece of DNA which can exist and reproduce autonomously in bacteria. **plas'min** *n* fibrinolysin, an enzyme that breaks down the fibrous protein (fibrin) in blood clots. **plasmin'ogen** /-*ə-jən*/ *n* the substance in blood plasma from which plasmin is formed. **plasmodesm** /*plaz'mō-dezm*/ or **plasmodesma** /-*dez'ma*/ *n* (*pl* **plasmodesma'ta**) (Gr *desmos* bond) a thread of protoplasm connecting cells. **plasmo'dial** *adj*. **plasmo'dium** *n* (*pl* **plasmo'dia**) a naked mass of protoplasm with many nuclei, as in myxomycetes; a parasitic sporozoan of the genus *Plasmodium* which causes malaria. **plasmog'amy** *n* fusion of cytoplasm only. **plas'molyse** or (*N Am*) **-yze** /-*līz*/ *vt*. **plasmolysis** /-*mol'i-sis*/ *n* (see **lysis**) removal of water from a cell by osmosis, with resultant shrinking. **plasmolytic** /-*mō-lit'ik*/ *adj*. **plas'mon** *n* the total of the genetic material in a cell. **plasmosō'ma** or **plas'mosome** *n* (*pl* **plasmosō'mata** or **plas'mosomes**) (see **-some**[2]) a nucleolus.
❑ **plasma cell** *n* a lymphocyte producing antibodies. **plasma membrane** *n* the boundary between a cell and its environment, consisting of a thin layer of lipid and protein molecules. **plasma screen** *n* a television or computer screen on which images are formed by passing an electric current through tiny plasma-filled bubbles.

plast or **plaste** /*plăst*/ (*Spenser*) *pat* and *pap* of **place**.

-plast /-*plast*/ *combining form* denoting a particle of living matter or an organized living cell. [Gr *plastos* formed]

plaster /*plă'stər*/ *n* a fabric coated with an adhesive substance for local application as a remedy, or with a pad for the protection of a cut, etc; (*esp formerly*) a curative substance spread on linen and applied locally; a pasty composition that sets hard, *esp* a mixture of slaked lime, sand, and sometimes hair, used for coating walls, etc; plaster of Paris; calcium sulphate, gypsum. ◆ *adj* made of plaster. ◆ *vt* to apply plaster, or a plaster, or a plaster cast to; to treat with plaster; to bedaub; to smear; to cover excessively, injudiciously, or meretriciously; to stick (with *on* or *over*); to reduce to plaster or a sticky mass; to damage by a heavy attack; to smooth (hair) down; to smooth (with *over*); to treat with gypsum; to attach with plaster. ◆ *vi* (with *over*) to smooth plaster over (cracks, etc). [OE *plaster* (in medical sense) and OFr *plastre* (builder's plaster) both from LL *plastrum*, from L *emplastrum*, from Gr *emplastron* for *emplaston*, from *en* on, and *plassein* to mould, apply as a plaster]
■ **plas'tered** *adj* daubed, treated, etc, with plaster; shattered; intoxicated (*inf*). **plas'terer** *n* a person who plasters, or someone who works in plaster. **plas'teriness** *n*. **plas'tering** *n*. **plas'tery** *adj* like plaster.
❑ **plas'terboard** *n* a slab of hardened plaster faced on both sides with paper or thin board, used to form or line interior walls. **plaster cast** *n* a copy obtained by pouring a mixture of plaster of Paris and water into a mould formed from the object; an immobilizing and protective covering of plaster of Paris for a broken limb, etc. **plaster of Paris** *n*

gypsum (*orig* found near *Paris*) partially dehydrated by heat, which dries into a hard substance when mixed with water. **plaster saint** *n* a virtuous person; someone who pretends hypocritically to be virtuous. **plas'terstone** *n* gypsum. **plas'terwork** *n*.

plastic /*plas'tik* or *pläs'tik*/ *n* a mouldable substance, *esp* now any of a large number of polymeric substances, most of them synthetic, mouldable at some stage under heat or pressure (see **thermoplastic** and **thermosetting** under **thermo-**), used to make domestic articles and many engineering products; a modeller or sculptor (*obs*); the art of modelling or of sculpture; short for **plastic money** (*inf*). ◆ *adj* having the power to take on different forms, mouldable; shaping, formative; of or relating to moulding or modelling; modifiable; capable of permanent reshaping without giving way; capable of or relating to metabolism and growth; made of plastic; unattractively synthetic or artificial. ◆ *combining form* denoting growing, forming, as in *neoplastic*. [Gr *plastikos* (adj) from *plassein*, to mould]
■ **plasticity** /-*tis'i-ti*/ *n* the state or quality of being plastic; the quality in a picture of appearing to be three-dimensional; the ability of a species to vary in size and appearance as adaptation to different climates and habitats, as in dogs (*biol*). **plas'ticize** or **-ise** /-*ti-sīz*/ *vt* and *vi* to make or become plastic. **plasticiz'er** or **-s-** *n* a substance that induces plasticity. **plas'ticky** *adj*. **plas'tics** *n sing* the scientific study, or industrial production, of plastic materials; plastic surgery; the art of modelling or sculpture. ◆ *adj* dealing with plastic materials (as in the plastics industry).
❑ **plastic art** *n* the art or any of the arts of shaping in three dimensions, such as ceramics, sculpture, modelling; art which is, or appears to be, three-dimensional. **plastic bag** *n* a bag made of polythene, etc in any of various sizes and qualities, *esp* one with handles used as a carrier. **plastic bomb** *n* a bomb made with a certain explosive chemical that can be moulded. **plastic bullet** *n* a four-inch cylinder of PVC fired for the purpose of riot control. **plastic clay** *n* clay from which earthenware and bricks are made. **plastic explosive** *n* an adhesive explosive material of jelly-like consistency. **plastic force** *n* the force or power of growth in animals and plants. **plastic money** *n* (*inf*) credit and debit cards. **plastic operation** *n* a surgical operation which restores a lost part, or repairs a deformed or disfigured part, of the body. **plastic surgeon** *n*. **plastic surgery** *n* the branch of surgery concerned with plastic operations. **plastic wood** *n* a filler that sets to resemble wood. **plastic wrap** *n* (*N Am*) clingfilm.

Plasticine® /*plas'ti-sēn*/ *n* a kind of modelling material that remains soft and can be reworked, used *esp* by children.

plastid /*plas'tid* or *pläs'tid*/ *n* a living cell (*obs*); a differentiated granule in protoplasm. [Gr *plastis, -idos* modeller (fem)]
■ **plast'idule** *n* Haeckel's hypothetical unit of living protoplasm.

plastilina /*plä-sti-lē'na*/ *n* a mixture of clay with oil, zinc oxide, wax, and sulphur for modelling. [Ital]

plastination /*plas-ti-nā'shən*/ *n* a method of preserving biological specimens by replacing perishable tissues with a plastic polymer. [**plastic** and **preservation**]
■ **plas'tinate** *vt* (back-formation).

plastique /*pla-stēk'*/ *n* graceful poses and movements in dancing; plastic explosive. [Fr, from Gr *plastikos* (see **plastic**)]

plastisol /*plas'ti-sol*/ *n* a suspension of powdered resin in liquid plasticizer, convertible by heat into a solid plastic and used in castings and linings. [**plastic** and **sol**[2]]

plastogamy /*pla-stog'ə-mi*/ *n* plasmogamy. [Gr *plastos* moulded, and *gamos* marriage]

plastron /*plas'tron*/ *n* a fencer's wadded breast-shield; the ventral section of the shell of a tortoise or turtle, or other animal; the front of a dress shirt; a separate ornamental front part of a woman's bodice; a steel breastplate worn under the hauberk (*hist*). [Fr *plastron*, from Ital *piastrone*, from *piastra* breastplate; cf **piastre**, **plaster**]
■ **plas'tral** *adj*.

-plasty /-*plas-ti*/ *combining form* signifying plastic surgery involving a bodily part, tissue or a specified process, as in *rhinoplasty*. [Gr *-plastia*; cf **-plast**]

plat[1] see **plait**.

plat[2] /*plat*/ *n* a plot of ground (*archaic*); a diagram or a plan (*obs* or *US*); a scheme (*obs*). ◆ *vt* (now *US*) to make a plan of, plot out. [**plot**[1], infl by **plat**[3]]

plat[3] /*plat*/ *n* a flat thing (*obs*); a flat surface, part, or side (*obs*); a mould-board (*dialect*); a flat place or region (*esp US*). [Appar Fr *plat*]

platane or **platan** /*plat'ən*/ *n* a plane tree, any tree of the genus **Plat'anus**, giving name to the family **Platana'ceae**, related to the witch-hazel family. [L *platanus*, from Gr *platanos*, from *platys* broad]
■ **platanā'ceous** *adj*.

platanna /*plə-tan'ə*/ *n* (also **platanna frog**) an African frog, *Xenopus laevis*, used in research, and formerly used in tests for pregnancy. [Afrikaans, from *plat-hander* flat-handed]

---

platband /plat'band/ n a fascia or flat moulding projecting less than its own breadth; a lintel or flat arch; an edging of turf or flowers. [Fr *platebande* flat band]

plat du jour /plä də zhoor'/ or (Fr) *pla dü zhoor'* / n (pl **plats du jour**) a dish on a restaurant menu specially recommended that day. [Fr]

plate /plāt/ n a shallow dish of any of various sizes according to purpose, eg *dessert plate*, *dinner plate*, *side plate* ; a plateful; a portion served on a plate; a sheet, slab, or lamina of metal or other hard material, *usu* flat or flattish; metal in the form of sheets; a broad piece of armour; a scute or separate portion of an animal's shell; a broad thin piece of a structure or mechanism; a plate-like section of the earth's crust, involved in plate tectonics (see below); a piece of metal, wood, etc, bearing or to bear an inscription to be affixed to anything; an engraved piece of metal for printing from; an impression printed from it, an engraving; an illustration in a book, *esp* a whole-page one separately printed and inserted; a mould from type, etc, for printing from, as an electrotype or stereotype; part of a denture fitting the mouth and carrying the teeth; the whole denture; a device worn in the mouth by some children in order to straighten the teeth; a film-coated sheet of glass or other material to photograph on; a plate rail (see below); a horizontal supporting timber in building; a five-sided white slab at the home base (*baseball*); a light racing horseshoe; a thermionic valve anode (*orig* flat); precious metal, *esp* silver (*hist*; Sp *plata* silver); a silver coin (*Shakesp*); wrought gold or silver; household utensils in gold or silver; table utensils generally; plated ware such as **Sheffield plate**, a silver-plated copper ware; a cup or other prize for a race or other contest; a race or contest for such a prize; a church collection; (in *pl*) the feet (*sl*; *orig* rhyming slang for *plates of meat*). ♦ *vt* to overlay with metal; to armour with metal; to cover with a thin film of another metal; to put (food) onto a plate in preparation for eating; to make a printing plate of. [OFr *plate*, fem (and for the dish *plat*, masc), flat, from Gr *platys* broad]

■ **pla'ted** *adj* covered with plates of metal; covered with a coating of another metal, *esp* gold or silver; armoured with hard scales or bone (*zool*). **plate'ful** *n* as much as a plate will hold. **plate'let** *n* a minute particle in blood, concerned in clotting. **plate'-like** *adj*. **plā'ter** *n* a person who or something which plates; a moderate horse entered for a minor, *esp* a selling, race. **plā'ting** *n*. **plā'ty** *adj* plate-like; separating into plates.

❑ **plate armour** *n* protective armour of metal plates. **plate'-basket** *n* a basket for forks, spoons, etc. **plate'-fleet** *n* (*hist*) ships that carried American silver to Spain. **plate glass** *n* a fine kind of glass used for mirrors and shop-windows, *orig* poured in a molten state on an iron plate. **plate'-glass** *adj* made with or consisting of plate glass; (of a building) having large plate-glass windows, appearing to be built entirely of plate glass; (hence) used of any very modern building or institution, *esp* British universities founded in the mid-20c. **plate'layer** *n* a person who lays, fixes, and attends to the rails of a railway. **plate'-leather** *n* a chamois leather for rubbing gold and silver. **plate'maker** *n* a person or machine that makes printing plates. **plate'man** *n* a man who has the care of silver plate in a hotel, club, etc. **plate'mark** *n* a hallmark. **plate'-powder** *n* a polishing powder for silver. **plate'-print'ing** *n* the process of printing from engraved plates. **plate'-proof** *n* a proof taken from a plate. **plate rack** *n* a frame for holding plates, etc, when not in use or when draining after washing. **plate rail** *n* on early railways, a flat rail with an outer flange. **plate'-room** *n* a room where silver-plated goods or printing plates are kept. **plate'-ship** *n* (*hist*) a ship bringing silver to Spain from the Americas. **plate tectonics** *n sing* (*geol*) the interacting movements of the rigid plates or sections that make up the earth's crust, floating on the semi-molten rock of the interior; the science or study of these movements; the study of the crust in terms of this theory. **plate'-warmer** *n* an apparatus for warming dinner plates or keeping them warm.

■ **half'-plate** (in photography) a size of plate measuring $4\frac{3}{4}$ by $6\frac{1}{2}$ inches ($4\frac{1}{4}$ by $5\frac{1}{2}$ in the USA). **hand** or **give** (**someone something**) **on a plate** (*fig*) to cause or allow (someone) to achieve or obtain (something) without the least effort. **on one's plate** (*fig*) in front of one, waiting to be dealt with. **quar'ter-plate** (in photography) a plate size $3\frac{1}{4}$ by $4\frac{1}{4}$ inches. **step up to the plate** to accept a burden or responsibility. **whole'-plate** (in photography) a plate size $6\frac{1}{2}$ by $8\frac{1}{2}$ inches.

plateasm /plat'i-azm/ n pronunciation with a wide mouth-opening, as in Doric Greek. [Gr *plateiasmos*, from *platys* broad]

plateau /plat'ō or pla-tō'/ n (pl **plateaux** /-tōz/ or **plateaus**) a large level tract of elevated land, a tableland; a temporary stable state reached in the course of upward progress; the part of a curve representing this; an ornamented tray, plate, or plaque; a lady's flat-topped hat. ♦ *vi* to reach a level, even out (sometimes with *out*). [Fr, from OFr *platel*, dimin of *plat*]

platen /plat'n/ n a flat part that in some printing presses pushes the paper against the forme; the roller of a typewriter; in a photocopier,

the glass surface on which a document to be copied is placed; the worktable of a machine tool. [Fr *platine*, from *plat* flat]

plateresque /plat-ə-resk'/ (*archit*) *adj* applied to a style resembling silversmith's work. [Sp *plateresco*, from *platero* silversmith, from *plata* silver]

platform /plat'förm/ n a raised floor for speakers, musicians, etc; a raised pavement alongside the track in a railway station giving access to trains; a position prepared for mounting a gun; any raised level surface; a terrace; a flooring; a plateau; a deck for a temporary or special purpose; a floating installation *usu* moored to the seabed, for drilling for oil, marine research, etc; flooring outside an inner entrance to some buses, trams, or sometimes railway carriages; a site; a platform shoe or boot; the thick heavy sole of such a shoe or boot; a basis; the publicly declared principles and intentions of a political party, taken as forming the basis of its policies; any situation giving one access to an audience, that one can exploit as an opportunity for promoting one's views; the people occupying the platform at a meeting, etc; public speaking or discussion (*fig*); a medium for discussion; a scheme of church government or of administrative policy; a scheme, device, plan of action (*Shakesp*); the hardware and/or software for a system (*comput*); a ground-plan (*obs*); a plane figure or surface (*obs*). ♦ *adj* on, relating to, admitting to, etc, a platform; (of shoes, boots, etc) having a very thick sole (a **platform sole**), giving extra height. ♦ *vt* to provide with a platform; to sketch, plan; to place on, or as if on, a platform. ♦ *vi* (*rare*) to speak or appear on a platform. [Fr *plateforme*, literally, flat form]

❑ **platform game** *n* a computer game in which players must move around a series of platforms, *usu* collecting objects and fighting enemies as they go.

platforming /plat'för-ming/ n a process for reforming low-grade petrol into high-grade, using a platinum catalyst. [**platinum** and **form**[1]]

plating see under **plate**.

platinum /plat'i-nəm/ n a steel-grey malleable and ductile metallic element (symbol Pt; atomic no 78), one of the precious metals, which is very valuable, very heavy and hard to fuse (older name **plat'ina**). ♦ *adj* made of platinum; similar in colour to platinum. [Sp *platina*, from *plata* silver]

■ **platinic** /plə-tin'ik/ *adj* of platinum, *esp* tetravalent. **platinif'erous** *adj* platinum-bearing. **plat'inize** or **-ise** *vt* to coat with platinum. **plat'inoid** *n* one of the metals, such as palladium, iridium, etc, with which platinum is always found associated; an alloy of copper, zinc, nickel, and tungsten resembling platinum. **plat'inotype** *n* (also with *cap*) an obsolete method of photography by reducing a compound of platinum; a photograph so produced. **plat'inous** *adj* of bivalent platinum.

❑ **platinum black** *n* platinum in the form of a velvety black powder. **platinum-blond'** *adj* (of hair) silvery blond. **platinum blonde** *n* a woman with hair of this colour. **platinum disc** *n* a platinum replica of a record, presented to the composer, performer, etc to commemorate achieving sales above a certain amount (for a UK album, 300000 copies). **platinum lamp** *n* an electric lamp with a platinum filament. **platinum metal** *n* any of the group of related metals comprising platinum and the platinoids. **platinum parachute** *n* (*inf*) a payment, even more extravagant than a golden parachute (qv under **golden**), offered to a senior member of a firm on his or her dismissal, in order to soften the fall back down to the real world.

■ **go platinum** (*inf*) (of a record) to sell in quantities sufficient to merit a platinum disc.

platitude /plat'i-tūd/ n flatness; a dull commonplace or truism; an empty remark made as if it were important. [Fr, from *plat* flat]

■ **platitudina'rian** *n* someone who indulges in platitudes. **plat'itudinize** or **-ise** *vi*. **platitud'inous** *adj*.

Platonic /plə-ton'ik/ *adj* of or relating to Plato, the Greek philosopher (c.427–347BC), or to his philosophy; (often without *cap*; of love) between soul and soul, *orig* between male friends, without sensual desire (a Renaissance interpretation of Plato's theory); (without *cap*; of friendship or love) affectionate, but not involving sexual relations; relating to or experiencing platonic love. ♦ *n* a Platonist; a platonic lover; (*usu* in *pl*) platonic love. [Gr *platōnikos*, from *Platōn*, *-ōnos* Plato]

■ **Platon'ical** *adj* (now *rare*). **platon'ically** *adv*. **Platon'icism** *n* the doctrine, practice, or profession of platonic love; Platonism (*obs*). **Plā'tonism** *n* the philosophy of Plato; Platonicism. **Plā'tonist** *n* a follower of Plato. **Platonize** or **-ise** /plā'tən-īz/ *vt* to render Platonic. ♦ *vi* to follow Plato.

❑ **Platonic solid** *n* any of the five regular polyhedrons (tetrahedron, hexahedron, octahedron, dodecahedron, and icosahedron). **Platonic year** see under **year**.

platoon /plə-toon'/ n a subdivision of a company (*milit*); a squad; a group of people acting together; *orig* a small body of soldiers in a hollow square formation, or such a body firing together; a volley (*archaic*). [Fr *peloton* ball, knot of men, from L *pīla* ball]

Plattdeutsch /plät'doich/ n and adj Low German. [Ger]

platted and **platting** same as **plaited** and **plaiting** (see under **plait**).

platteland /plä'tə-länt/ (S Afr) n rural districts. [Afrik]

platter /plat'ər/ n a large flat plate or dish; a gramophone record (old inf, esp US); one of the circular disks on a hard disk drive (comput). [Anglo-Fr plater, from plat a plate]

platy[1] see under **plate**.

platy[2] /plat'i/ n a small brightly-coloured viviparous Central American fish (genus Xiphophorus). [Shortening of former genus name Platypoecilus, from **platy-** and Gr poikilos variegated]

platy- /plat-i-/ combining form signifying flat or broad. [Gr platys, broad]

platycephalous /plat-i-sef'ə-ləs/ adj having the vault of the skull flattened (also **platycephalic** /-si-fal'ik/). [**platy-** and **-cephalous**]

Platyhelminthes /plat-i-hel-min'thēz/ n pl the flatworms, a phylum including planarians, tapeworms, and flukes. [**platy-** and Gr helmins, -inthos intestinal worm]

■ **platyhel'minth** n.

platypus /plat'i-pəs/ or -pŭs/ n (pl **plat'ypuses**) an aquatic burrowing and egg-laying Australian monotreme (genus Ornithorhynchus), one of the primitive forms of mammals, with broadly webbed feet and duck-like bill (also **duck-billed platypus**). [**platy-** and Gr pous, podos a foot]

platyrrhine /plat'i-rīn/ or **platyrrhinian** /plat-i-rin'i-ən/ adj broadnosed; belonging to the division of the monkeys found in S America, which have widely spaced nostrils. ◆ n a New World monkey; a broad-nosed person. [Gr platyrrīs, -īnos, from rhīs, rhīnos nose]

platysma /plat-iz'mə/ n a broad sheet of muscle in the neck. [Gr platysma a flat piece]

plaudit /plö'dit/ n (now usu in pl) an act of applause; praise bestowed, enthusiastic approval. [Shortened from L plaudite applaud, an actor's call for applause at the end of a play, pl imperative of plaudere, plausum to clap the hands]

■ **plaud'itory** adj.

plaudite /plö'di-ti or plow'di-te/ (L) imperative applaud; clap your hands.

plausible /plö'zi-bl/ adj likely, reasonable, seemingly true; seemingly worthy of approval or praise; fair-showing; specious; (of a person) smooth-tongued and ingratiating; that may be applauded (obs); acceptable (obs). [L plaudere to clap the hands]

■ **plausibil'ity** or **plaus'ibleness** n. **plaus'ibly** adv in a plausible manner; with applause, by acclamation (Shakesp); commendably, pleasantly (obs). **plausive** /plö'ziv/ adj plausible (Shakesp); pleasing (Shakesp); applauding.

plaustral /plö'strəl/ adj (facetious) of a wagon. [L plaustrum a wagon]

play /plā/ vi (**play'ing**; **played**) to engage in pleasurable activity; to perform acts not part of the immediate business of life but in mimicry or rehearsal or in display; to amuse oneself; to sport; to make sport; to trifle; to behave without seriousness; to behave amorously or sexually; to take part in a game; (with for) to compete on the side of; to proceed with the game, perform one's part in turn; to deliver a ball, etc, in the course of a game; to co-operate (inf); to perform on a musical instrument; to produce or emit music; (of music) to come forth; to act a part; to move about irregularly, lightly, or freely; to have some freedom of movement; to flicker, flutter, shimmer, pass through rapid alternations; to appear faintly and fleetingly (usu with round); to move in, discharge, or direct a succession, stream, or shower (eg of water, light, waves, or missiles); to contend with weapons (archaic); to operate (obs); to wield a weapon; to gamble; to have a holiday (Shakesp; also Scot); to be off work (N Eng). ◆ vt to perform; to ply, wield; to cause or allow to play; to set in opposition, pit; to send, let off, or discharge in succession or in a stream or shower; to give a limited freedom of movement to; hence, to manage; to allow (a fish) to tire itself by its struggles to get away; to engage in (a game or recreative mimicry); to proceed through (a game, part of a game, or an aggregate of games); to stake or risk in play; to gamble on (inf); to bring into operation in a game, as by striking (a ball), by throwing (a card) on the table, by moving (a chess piece); to compete against in a game or sport; to compete on the side of (with for); to act (eg comedy or a named play); to act the part of, in a play or in real life; to act or perform in (eg a circuit of theatres or halls or a town, etc); to pretend in fun; to perform music on; to perform (a tune, etc) on a musical instrument; to cause (a radio, stereo system, etc) to emit sound; to lead, bring, send, render, or cause to be by playing; (reflexive) to amuse (oneself; obs and Scot); (reflexive) to waste time, fool around (inf). ◆ n activity; operation; action of wielding; light fluctuating movement or change; some freedom of movement, as opposed to absolute tightness or tautness; scope; recreative activity; display of animals in courtship; amusement; fun; dalliance; a game (Shakesp); the playing of a game; manner of playing; procedure or policy in a

game; holiday (Shakesp and Scot); a fair or festival (dialect); being off work (N Eng); gambling; a drama or dramatic performance; manner of dealing, as in fair play (fig). [OE pleg(i)an, verb, plega, noun]

■ **play'able** adj capable (by nature or by the rules of the game) of being played, or of being played on. **play'er** n a person who plays; a person participating in or skilled at esp a game or sport; an actor; a trifler; an instrumental performer; a mechanism for playing a musical instrument; an apparatus for playing records, etc, as in record player, CD player; (in Northern Ireland) a terrorist, esp one who is young and unknown; anyone who has an interest in and who plays a part in, eg formulating a policy, taking a decision, etc (inf). **play'ful** adj full of fun, frolicsome, frisky; high-spirited, humorous. **play'fully** adv. **play'fulness** n. **play'let** n a short play. **play'some** adj playful.
❑ **play'-act** vi. **play'-acting** n performance of plays; pretence. **play action** n (American football) an attempt to disguise a passing play by simulating a running play. **play'-actor** or **play'-actress** n (usu derog) professional actor or actress. **play'back** n the act of reproducing a recording of sound or visual material, esp immediately after it is made; a device for doing this (see also **play back** below). **play'bill** n a bill announcing a play. **play'book** n a printed play or book of plays. **play'-box** n (old) a box for toys and other valued possessions, esp in a boarding school. **play'boy** n (rare) **play'girl** n a light-hearted irresponsible person, esp rich, leisured and pleasure-seeking; a child-actor (archaic). **Play'bus**® n a bus equipped with facilities for children's play, driven to districts where no adequate playgroup facilities are available. **play'-by-play'** n (N Am) a running commentary on a sporting event (also adj). **play date** n (chiefly N Am) an arrangement between adults for their children to meet to play together. **play'-day** n a holiday. **play'-debt** n a debt incurred in gambling. **played'-out** adj exhausted; used up; no longer good for anything. **player piano** see under **pianoforte**. **play'fellow** n a playmate. **playgirl** see **playboy** above. **play'-göer** n someone who habitually attends the theatre. **play'-going** n. **play'ground** n an outdoor area for playing in, esp one connected with a school; a place of recreation; a holiday region. **play'group** n an informal, sometimes voluntarily run group having morning or afternoon sessions attended by preschool children sometimes with their parents or carers, for creative and co-operative play. **play'house** n a theatre; a child's toy house, usu big enough for a child to enter. **playing card** n one of a pack (usu of fifty-two cards, divided into four suits) used in playing games. **playing field** n a grass-covered space set apart, marked out, and kept in order for games (**a level** or **flat playing field** (inf) fair competition). **play'leader** n a person trained to supervise and organize children's play in a playground, etc. **play'list** n those recordings selected to be broadcast regularly by a radio station. ◆ vt to include on a playlist. **play'maker** n (sport) a member of a team who is skilled at initiating moves that might lead to a score. **play'-mare** n (Scot) a hobby-horse, as in the old morris-dance. **play'mate** n a companion in play, esp child's play. **play'-off** n a game to decide a tie, a championship, promotion, etc; a game between the winners of other competitions; see also **play off** below. **play on** or **upon words** n a pun or other manipulation of words depending on their sound. **play'pen** n an enclosure within which a young child may safely play. **play'room** n a room for children to play in. **play'school** n a nursery school or playgroup. **play'slip** n a form on which a participant in a lottery draw indicates his or her chosen numbers. **play'-spell** n a time allowed for play. **play'suit** n a set of clothes for a child or woman, usu shorts and a top or one-piece, for sunbathing, relaxing, etc. **play'thing** n a toy; a person or thing treated as a toy. **play'time** n a time for play; (in schools) a set period for playing, usu out of doors. **play'-way** n the educational use of play. **play'-world** n an imaginary world feigned in play. **play'wright** or **play'-writer** n a dramatist.
■ **bring**, **call** or **come into play** to bring, call or come into exercise, operation or use. **hold in play** (or archaic **hold play**) to keep occupied, esp to gain time or detain. **in** (or **out of**) **play** (of a ball, etc) in (or not in) a position to be played. **make a play for** (inf) to try to get; to attempt to seduce. **make great play with** or **of** to make a lot of; to treat or talk of as very important. **make play** to keep things going, push on with the game. **play about** to behave irresponsibly, not seriously. **play along** (with with) to co-operate or agree with someone, usu temporarily. **play a part** (with in) to be instrumental in, help in doing something; to act a theatrical role. **play around** to play about; to have amorous affairs with men or women other than one's partner. **play at** to engage in the game of; to make a pretence of; to practise without seriousness. **play back** to play (a sound or video recording) that has just been made. **play ball** (inf) to co-operate. **play by ear** see under **ear**[1] (see also **play it by ear** below). **play catch-up** to make great efforts to become up to date or draw level in a competition. **play down** to treat (something) as not very important or probable, esp less so than it is. **play fair** (sometimes with with) to act honestly. **play false** (sometimes with with; archaic) to act dishonestly towards or betray someone. **play fast and loose** to act in a shifty, inconsistent, and reckless fashion. **play fine** (in billiards) to strike the object ball near the edge (as opposed to **play full**, to strike it nearer the middle than the

edge). **play for safety** to play safe. **play for time** to delay action or decision in the hope or belief that conditions will become more favourable later. **play hard to get** to make a show of unwillingness to co-operate with a view to strengthening one's position. **play havoc** or **hell with** to upset, disorganize; to damage. **play into the hands of** to act so as to give, *usu* unintentionally, an advantage to. **play it** (*inf*; *usu* followed by an *adj*) to behave in or manage a particular situation in a stated way, as in *play it cool*. **play it by ear** to improvise a plan of action to meet the situation as it develops (see also **play by ear** under **ear**[1]). **play it** (or **one's cards**) **close to the** (or **one's**) **chest** to be secretive about one's actions or intentions in a particular matter. **play off** to manipulate so as to counteract; to set (one person against another); to take part in a play-off; to play from the tee (*golf*); to have as a handicap (*golf*); to toss off (*Shakesp*); to bring off (eg a hoax). **play on** to strike the ball onto one's own wicket (*cricket*); (also **play upon**) to direct one's efforts to the exciting of, work upon (feelings, emotions, etc). **play out** to play to the end; to wear out, to exhaust; to act out. **play safe** to take no risks. **play the field** (*inf*) to spread one's interests, affections or efforts over a wide range of subjects, people, activities, etc, rather than concentrating on any single one. **play the game** to act strictly honourably. **play up** to strike up, begin the music; to redouble one's efforts, play more vigorously; to show up well in a crisis or emergency; to give (*esp* undue) prominence to, or to boost; to fool; to function faultily (*inf*); to behave unco-operatively (*inf*); (of an impaired part of the body) to give one trouble or pain (*inf*). **play upon** see **play on** above. **play up to** to act so as to afford opportunities to (another actor); to flatter. **play with** to play in the company of, or as partner or opponent to; to dally with; to stimulate (the genitals of), to masturbate (oneself or someone else).

playa /plä' or plä'(y)ə/ *n* a basin which becomes a shallow lake after heavy rainfall and dries out again in hot weather. [Sp]

Play-Doh® /plā'dō/ *n* a soft reusable modelling material for young children (loosely, and sometimes also of a home-made version, **play'dough**).

PlayStation® /plā'stā-shən/ *n* a computer games console used with a TV screen.

plaza /plä'zə/ *n* a public square or open, *usu* paved, area in a city or town; a shopping centre (*N Am*). [Sp]

PLC or **plc** *abbrev* : public limited company.

plea /plē/ *n* a lawsuit (*Scots law* and *hist*); a pleading; a prisoner's or defendant's answer to a charge or claim; a claim (*Shakesp*); an excuse; a pretext; an urgent entreaty. ◆ *vt* and *vi* to dispute in a lawcourt. [OFr *plai*, *plaid*, *plait*, from LL *placitum* a decision, from L *placēre*, *-itum* to please]
❑ **plea bargain** *n*. **plea'-bargain** *vi*. **plea bargaining** *n* the legal practice (*esp* in the USA) of arranging more lenient treatment by the court in exchange for the accused's admitting to the crime, turning State's evidence, etc.

pleach /plēch/ *vt* to intertwine the branches of (eg a hedge); to fold (the arms; *Shakesp*); to plash. [From form of OFr *pless(i)er*, from L *plectere*; see **plash**[1]]

plead /plēd/ *vi* (*pat* and *pap* **plead'ed**, also (*Spenser*, *Scot*, *US*, and *dialect*) **pled**) to carry on a plea or lawsuit; to argue in support of a cause against another; to put forward an allegation or answer in court; to implore, make an entreaty (with *with*). ◆ *vt* to maintain by argument; to allege in pleading; to put forward as a plea; to offer in excuse; to sue for (*archaic* and *Scot*). [OFr *plaidier*; cf **plea**]
■ **plead'able** *adj* capable of being pleaded. **plead'er** *n* a person who pleads; an advocate. **plead'ing** *adj* imploring. ◆ *n* the act of putting forward or conducting a plea; (in *pl*) the statements of the two parties in a lawsuit; entreaty. **plead'ingly** *adv*.
❑ **pleading diet** *n* (*Scots law*) a preliminary appearance in court of the accused person before a trial, at which the accused indicates whether he or she will plead guilty or not guilty, and lodges any special pleas, eg of insanity, etc.
■ **plead guilty** (or **not guilty**) to state that one is guilty (or innocent) of a crime with which one is charged. **special pleading** unfair or one-sided argument aiming rather at victory than at truth.

pleasance /plez'əns/ (*archaic* and *poetic*) *n* a pleasure ground or specialized part of a garden; pleasure; enjoyment; pleasantness; complaisance, pleasant behaviour (*obs*); that which gives pleasure. [OFr *plaisance*, from *plaisant*, prp of *plaisir*; cf **pleasant**]

pleasant /plez'ənt/ *adj* pleasing; agreeable; inoffensive; affable; good-humoured; cheerful; merry (*obs*); tipsy (*facetious*). [OFr *plaisant*, prp of *plaisir* to please]
■ **pleas'antly** *adv*. **pleas'antness** *n*. **pleas'antry** *n* (*pl* **pleas'antries**) an agreeable remark made for the sake of politeness; pleasantness, enjoyment (*obs*); jocularity; a facetious utterance or trick.

please /plēz/ *vt* to give pleasure to; to delight; to satisfy; to be the will or choice of (to do something). ◆ *vi* to give pleasure; to like, think fit, choose (*orig* impersonal with dative, eg *it pleases* (*to*) *me* ; later *me*

pleases ; then *I* please). ◆ *interj* used in making polite requests, or in politely accepting an offer, etc, as in *yes, please*. [OFr *plaisir* (Fr *plaire*), from L *placēre* to please]
■ **pleased** /plēzd/ *adj* grateful; delighted; willing, or inclined (to do something). **pleas'er** *n*. **pleas'ing** *adj* and *n*. **pleas'ingly** *adv*. **pleas'ingness** *n*.
❑ **pleaseman** /plēz'man or -mən/ *n* (*Shakesp*) an officious fellow, a pick-thank.
■ **if you please** if you like; a polite formula of request or acceptance (*old*); forsooth (*ironic*); certainly (*ironic*). **may it please you** or **so please you** deferential or polite formulas of address or request. **please**, also (now *rare*) **please to** a polite formula equivalent to **if you please** above, now felt as imperative, perhaps *orig* from the older **please it you** or **please it** (sometimes printed **pleaseth** in *Shakesp*) or **please you** may it please you. **pleased as Punch** delighted. **pleased with oneself** self-satisfied; conceited. **please yourself** do as you like.

pleasure /plezh'ər/ *n* agreeable emotions; gratification of the senses or of the mind; recreation; sensuality; dissipation; a source of gratification; what the will prefers; purpose; command. ◆ *vt* to give (*esp* sexual) pleasure to. ◆ *vi* (*archaic*; with *in*) to take pleasure in. [ME and OFr *plesir*]
■ **pleasurable** /plezh'ə-rə-bl/ *adj* able to give pleasure; delightful; gratifying; pleasure-seeking (*obs*). **pleas'urableness** *n*. **pleas'urably** *adv*. **pleas'ureful** *adj*. **pleas'ureless** *adj*. **pleas'urer** *n* a pleasure-seeker.
❑ **pleasure boat** *n* a boat used for pleasure or amusement. **pleas'ure-giving** *adj*. **pleasure ground** *n* ground laid out in an ornamental manner for pleasure and recreation. **pleasure house** *n* a house to which one retires for recreation or pleasure. **pleasure principle** *n* the principle that dominates the instincts, directing one's behaviour towards seeking pleasure and avoiding pain. **pleas'ure-seeker** *n* someone who seeks pleasure; a holiday-maker. **pleas'ure-seeking** *n*. **pleasure trip** *n* an excursion for pleasure.
■ **at pleasure** when, if or as one pleases.

pleat /plēt/ *n* any of several types of fold sewn or pressed into cloth; a plait or braid (*obs* or *dialect*). ◆ *vt* to make pleats in; to plait or intertwine (*obs* or *dialect*). [From **plait**]
■ **pleat'ed** *adj*. **pleat'er** *n*.

pleather /pledh'ər/ *n* a PVC fabric, used *esp* in clothing, that looks and feels like leather. [From *pla*stic and l*eather*]

pleb /pleb/ (*inf*) *n* a person of unpolished manners or vulgar tastes, a plebeian, a boor. [**plebeian**]
■ **plebb'y** *adj*. **plebifica'tion** *n*. **pleb'ify** *vt* to make plebeian or vulgar.

plebe /plēb/ (*US inf*) *n* a first-year cadet at a naval or military academy. [Perh from **plebeian**]

plebeian /plə- or pli-bē'ən/ (*Shakesp* also **plebean** /pleb'i-ən/) *adj* of the Roman plebs (*qv*); of the common people; low-born; undistinguished; vulgar-looking; vulgar, lacking taste or refinement. ◆ *n* a member of the plebs of ancient Rome; a commoner; a member of a despised social class; a boor, a vulgarian. [L *plēbēius*, from *plēbs*, *plēbis*]
■ **plebei'anism** *n*. **plebei'anize** or **-ise** *vt*.

plebiscite /pleb'i-sit or -sīt/ *n* a direct vote of the whole nation or of the people of a district on a special point; an ascertainment of general opinion on any matter; a law enacted by the plebs assembled in the *Concilia tributa* (*Roman hist*). [Partly through Fr *plébiscite*, from L *plēbiscītum*, from *plēbs* plebs, and *scītum* decree, from *scīscere* to vote for]
■ **plebisc'itary** *adj*.

plebs /plebz/ *n* one of the two divisions of the Roman people, *orig* the less privileged politically (see also **pleb** and **plebeian**). [L *plēbs*, *plēbis*]

Plecoptera /ple-kop'tər-ə/ *n pl* the stonefly order of insects, with hindwings folded fanwise. [Gr *plekein* plait, and *pteron* wing]
■ **plecop'terous** *adj*.

Plectognathi /plek-tog'nə-thī/ (*zool*) *n pl* an order of bony fishes including filefishes, globe fishes, coffer-fishes and sunfishes. [Gr *plektos* plaited, and *gnathos* a jaw]
■ **plectognathic** /-tə-gnath'ik/ or **plectog'nathous** /-nə-thəs/ *adj*.

Plectoptera /plek-top'tə-rə/ *n pl* a former name for the order of insects now known as Ephemeroptera. [Gr *plektos* twisted, and *pteron* a wing]
■ **plectop'terous** *adj*.

plectrum /plek'trəm/ *n* (*pl* **plec'trums** or **plec'tra**) a pointed device held in the fingers or on the thumb, with which the strings of eg a guitar are struck; the quill or other device for plucking the strings of the ancient Greek lyre or other musical instrument. —Also **plec'tre** /-tər/ or **plec'tron** (*pl* **plec'trons** or **plec'tra**). [L *plēctrum*, from Gr *plēktron*, from *plēssein* to strike]

pled /pled/ see **plead**.

pledge /plej/ *n* a solemn promise; *orig* something given as a security; a gage; a token or sign of assurance; a child, as a token of love or binding obligation; someone who becomes surety for another (*obs*); a hostage (*obs*); a friendly sentiment expressed by drinking; a state of being given, or held, as a security. ◆ *vt* to give as security; to bind by solemn promise; to vow; to give assurance of; to drink a toast in response to; to drink at the invitation of another; to drink to the health of. [OFr *plege* (Fr *pleige*), from LL *plevium, plivium*, prob Gmc]
■ **pledge'able** *adj*. **pledgee'** *n* the person to whom a thing is pledged. **pledger, pledgeor** or **pledgor** /plej'ər/ *n*.
■ **take** or **sign the pledge** to give a written promise to abstain from intoxicating liquor.

pledget /plej'it/ *n* a wad of lint, cotton, etc, used as dressing for a wound or sore; an oakum string used in caulking. [Origin unknown]

pledgor see under **pledge**.

-plegia /-plē-j(i-)ə/ *combining form* denoting paralysis of a specified kind, as in *paraplegia, quadriplegia*. [Gr *plēgē* stroke, from *plēssein* to strike]
■ **-plēgic** *adj* and *n combining form*.

Pleiad /plī'ad/ *n* any one of the seven daughters of Atlas and Pleione, changed into stars after his death (one 'lost' or invisible) (*Gr myth*); a brilliant group of seven, *esp* seven Alexandrian tragic poets or a group of 16c French poets (*usu* as in Fr, **Pléiade** /plā-ē-äd/) comprising Ronsard, Du Bellay, Baïf, Daurat, and others variously selected. [Gr *pleias, plēias, -ados*, pl *-ades*]
□ **Plei'ads** or **Pleiades** /plī'ə-dēz/ *n pl* a group of six stars visible to the naked eye and a multitude of telescopic stars in the shoulder of the constellation Taurus.

plein-air /ple-ner'/ *adj* open-air; attaching importance to painting in the open air. [Fr *en plein air* in the open air]
■ **plein-air'ist** *n* a plein-air painter.

pleio- or **plio-** /plī-ō-, -ə-, -o-/ or **pleo-** /plē-ō-, -ə-, -o-/ *combining form* signifying more. [Gr *pleiōn* or *pleōn*, compar of *polys* many, much]

Pleiocene /plī'ō-sēn/ *adj* and *n* same as **Pliocene**.

pleiochasium /plī-ō-kā'zi-əm/ *n* a cymose inflorescence in which each branch bears more than two lateral branches. [**pleio-** and Gr *chasis* separation; but cf **monochasium**]

pleiomerous /plī-om'ər-əs/ *adj* having more than the normal number of parts. [**pleio-** and Gr *meros* part]
■ **pleiom'ery** *n* the condition of having more than the normal number.

pleiotropic /plī-ō-trop'ik or -trō'pik/ *adj* (of a gene) having an effect simultaneously on more than one character in the offspring. [**pleio-** and Gr *tropos* turn]
■ **pleiot'ropism** *n*. **pleiot'ropy** *n*.

Pleistocene /plī'stə-sēn/ (*geol*) *adj* of or belonging to the earlier epoch of the Quaternary period, between 1.8 and 0.01 million years ago (also *n*). [Gr *pleistos* most (numerous), and *kainos* recent, from the proportion of fossil molluscs of living species]

plenary /plē'nə-ri/ *adj* full; entire; complete; absolute; unqualified; passing through all its stages, *opp* to *summary* (*law*); having full powers; (of an assembly, session, etc) to be attended by all members or delegates. [LL *plēnārius*, from L *plēnus* full, from *plēre* to fill]
■ **plē'narily** *adv*. **plē'narty** *n* the state of a benefice when occupied. □ **plenary indulgence** *n* in the Roman Catholic Church, full or complete remission of temporal penalties to a repentant sinner. **plenary inspiration** *n* inspiration which excludes any mixture of error. **plenary powers** *n pl* full powers to carry out some business or negotiations.

plenilune /plen'-, plēn'i-loon or -lūn/ *n* the full moon; time of full moon. [L *plēnilūnium*, from *plēnus* full, and *lūna* moon]
■ **plenilu'nar** *adj*.

plenipotence /pli-nip'ə-təns/ or **plenipotency** /pli-nip'ə-tən-si/ *n* complete power. [L *plēnus* full, and *potentia* power]
■ **plenip'otent** *adj* having full power. **plenipotential** /plen-i-pə-ten'shəl/ *adj*. **plenipoten'tiary** /-shə-ri or -shyə-ri/ *adj* having or conferring full powers; (of authority or power) absolute. ◆ *n* a person invested with full powers, *esp* a special ambassador or envoy to some foreign court (*archaic* short form **plen'ipo** (*pl* **plen'ipos** or **plen'ipoes**)).

plenish /plen'ish/ (*archaic* or *Scot*) *vt* to supply, stock; to provide (eg a house or farm) with necessary furniture, implements, stock, etc. [OFr *plenir, -iss-*, from L *plēnus* full]
■ **plen'ishing** *n* (*Scot*) furniture.

plenist see under **plenum**.

plenitude /plen'i-tūd/ *n* fullness; completeness; plentifulness; repletion. [L *plēnitūdō, -inis*, from *plēnus* full]
■ **plenitud'inous** *adj*.

pleno jure /plē'nō joor'ē or plā'nō yoor'e/ (*L*) *adv* with full authority.

plentitude a non-standard form of **plenitude**.

plenty /plen'ti/ *n* a full supply; all that can be needed; an abundance; a substantial number or amount. ◆ *adj* plentiful (*Shakesp*); in abundance. ◆ *adv* (*inf*) abundantly. [OFr *plente*, from L *plēnitās, -ātis*, from *plēnus* full]
■ **plenteous** /plen'tyəs/ *adj* (*literary*) fully sufficient; abundant; fruitful; well-provided; rich; producing or giving plentifully. **plen'teously** *adv*. **plen'teousness** *n*. **plen'tiful** *adj* copious; abundant; yielding abundance. **plen'tifully** *adv*. **plen'tifulness** *n*.
■ **horn of plenty** see **cornucopia**. **in plenty** abundant, as in *food in plenty*.

plenum /plē'nəm/ *n* a space completely filled with matter, *opp* to *vacuum*; (also **plenum chamber**) a sealed chamber containing pressurized air (*aeronautics*, etc); a full assembly. [L *plēnum* (*spatium*) full (space)]
■ **plē'nist** *n* someone who believes all space to be a plenum.
□ **plenum system** or **plenum ventilation** *n* (*archit*) an air-conditioning system in which the air propelled into a building is maintained at a higher pressure than that of the atmosphere.

pleo- see **pleio-**.

pleochroism /plē-ok'rō-i-zm/ *n* the property in some crystals of transmitting different colours in different directions. [Gr *chroā* colour]
■ **pleochroic** /plē-ō-krō'ik/ *adj*.

pleomorphic /plē-ō-mör'fik/, also **pleomorphous** /-fəs/ *adj* occurring in several different forms, polymorphic; changing form several different times during its life cycle (*biol*).
■ **pleomor'phism** or **plē'omorphy** *n*.

pleon /plē'ən/ *n* the abdomen of a crustacean, bearing the swimming legs. [Gr *pleōn* swimming, prp of *pleein*]
■ **ple'opod** *n* a swimming leg.

pleonasm /plē'ə-nazm/ *n* redundancy, *esp* of words; a redundant expression. [Gr *pleonasmos*, from *pleōn* more]
■ **plē'onast** *n* someone who is given to pleonasm. **ple'onaste** *n* (Fr *pléonaste*) a dark green to black magnesia-iron spinel (from its multitude of faces). **pleonas'tic** or **pleonas'tical** *adj*. **pleonas'tically** *adv*.

pleonexia /plē-ə-nek'si-ə/ *n* greed, avarice. [Gr]
■ **pleonec'tic** *adj*.

pleopod see under **pleon**.

pleroma /pli-rō'mə/ *n* fullness; abundance; (in Gnosticism) the divine being, including all aeons (qv) which emanate from it. [Gr *plērōma*, from *plērēs* full]
■ **pleromatic** /-mat'ik/ *adj*.

plerome /plē'rōm/ (*bot*) *n* the central part of the apical meristem, the part of the primary tissue from which growth takes place. [Gr *plērōma* filling]

plesh /plesh/ (*Spenser*) *n* a plash, a pool. [**plash**²]

plesiosaur /plē'si-ə-sör/ *n* a great Mesozoic fossil Sauropterygian reptile (genus *Plesiosaurus* or related genus) with a long neck, short tail, and four flippers. [Gr *plēsios* near, and *sauros* lizard]
■ **plesiosaur'ian** *adj*.

plessimeter, plessor, etc see **plexor**.

plethora /pleth'ə-rə, sometimes pli-thō'rə or -thö'/ *n* excessive fullness of blood; over-fullness or excess in any way; loosely, a large amount. [Gr *plēthōrā* fullness, from *pleos* full]
■ **plethoric** /pli-thor'ik (sometimes *pleth'ə-rik*)/ or **plethor'ical** *adj*. **plethor'ically** *adv*.

plethysmograph /ple-thiz'mə-gräf/ (*med*) *n* an apparatus for measuring variations in the size of parts of the body, eg when varying amounts of blood flow through them. [Gr *plēthysmos* enlargement, and *graphein* to write]

pleugh, also **pleuch** /ploo or ploohh/ *n* a Scots form of **plough**.

pleura /ploo'rə/ *n* (*pl* **pleu'rae** /-rē/) a delicate serous membrane that covers the lung and lines the cavity of the chest; a side-piece, *esp* a pleuron (see below). [Gr *pleurā* and *pleuron* rib, side]
■ **pleu'ral** *adj*. **pleurapoph'ysis** *n* (*pl* **pleurapoph'yses**) a lateral process of a vertebra, with the morphological character of a rib; a rib. **pleurisy** /ploo'ri-si/ *n* inflammation of the pleura. **pleurit'ic** *adj* (also **pleurit'ical**) of, affected with, or causing pleurisy. ◆ *n* a sufferer from pleurisy. **pleuri'tis** *n* pleurisy. **pleur'odont** *adj* and *n* (an animal, *esp* a reptile) with teeth attached to the inside of the jawbone, rather than rooted in it. **pleurodynia** /ploo-rō-din'i-ə/ *n* (Gr *odynē* pain) neuralgia of the muscles between the ribs. **pleu'ron** *n* (*pl* **pleu'ra**) the side-wall of a somite, *esp* of an insect's thorax. **pleuropneumo'nia** *n* pleurisy complicated with pneumonia; a contagious disease of cattle, caused by a virus, characterized by pleurisy and pneumonia. **pleurot'omy** *n* (*med*) incision into the pleura.
□ **pleu'risy-root** *n* an American asclepias plant (*Asclepias tuberosa*) reputed as a diaphoretic and expectorant.

Pleuronectes /ploo-rə-nek'tēz/ *n* the plaice genus, giving name to the family **Pleuronec'tidae**. [Gr *pleurā* side, and *nēktēs* a swimmer]

plexiform see under **plexus**.

plexiglass or (*US*) **Plexiglas**® /plek'si-glās/ *n* a type of light. [*pl*astic flexible *glass*]

plexor /plek'sər/ or **plessor** /ples'ər/ (*med*) *n* a percussion hammer. [Gr *plēxis* a stroke, *plēssein* to strike]
■ **plexim'eter** or **plessim'eter** *n* a small plate to receive the tap in examination by percussion. **pleximet'ric** or **plessimet'ric** *adj*. **plexim'etry** or **plessim'etry** *n*.

plexus /plek'səs/ *n* (*pl* **plex'uses** or **plex'us** (L *plexūs*)) a complex network of nerves, ganglia, blood vessels and lymphatic vessels anywhere in the body, such as the *solar plexus* behind the stomach, serving the viscera; any involved network. [L *plexus, -ūs* a weaving]
■ **plex'iform** *adj* in the form of a network; complex. **plex'ure** *n* an interweaving.

pliable /plī'ə-bl/ *adj* easily bent or folded; flexible; adaptable; easily persuaded; yielding to influence. [From Fr *plier* to fold]
■ **plīabil'ity** *n*. **plī'ableness** *n*. **plī'ably** *adv*.

pliant /plī'ənt/ *adj* bending easily; flexible; tractable; easily influenced; *perh* suitable, *perh* of compliant mood (*Shakesp*). [Prp of Fr *plier* to bend]
■ **plī'ancy** *n*. **plī'antly** *adv*. **plī'antness** *n*.

plica /plī'kə/ *n* (*pl* **plī'cae** /-sē/) a fold; plica Polonica. [L *plica* a fold]
■ **plī'cal** *adj*. **plī'cate** (or /*pli-kāt*'/) or **plī'cāted** (or /*pli-kā'ted*/) *adj* folded fanwise, pleated. **plī'cate** (also /*pli-kāt*'/) *vt* to pleat. **plī'cately** *adv*. **plīcā'tion** or **plicature** /plik'-/ *n* the act of folding; the state of being folded; a fold.
❑ **plica Polonica** *n* a matted condition of the hair, with an adhesive secretion, a parasitic fungus, and vermin, formerly prevalent in Poland.

plié /plē'ā/ *n* a movement in ballet, in which the knees are bent while the body remains upright. [Fr, bent]

plied, plier, plies see under **ply**[1,2].

pliers /plī'ərz/ *n pl* a tool like a pair of pincers, with serrated jaws for gripping small objects, and for bending and cutting wire. [From **ply**[1]]

plight[1] /plīt/ *n* a difficult or dangerous situation, an alarming predicament; a fold (*Spenser*); a plait, or mode of plaiting (*archaic*); condition, trim (*archaic*); good condition (*archaic*); mood (*archaic*); array (*Spenser*). ◆ *vt* (*pap* **plight'ed**, also (*Spenser*) **plight**) (*obs*) to plait, weave, fold, enfold. [Assimilated in spelling to **plight**[2], but derived from OFr *plite*, from L *plicāre, plicitum*; see **plait**]
■ **plight'ed** *adj* plaited; involved (*Shakesp*).

plight[2] /plīt/ *vt* (*pap* **plight'ed**, also **plight**) to pledge. ◆ *n* risk (*obs*); pledge (*archaic*); engagement (*archaic*); promise (*archaic*). [OE *pliht* risk; *plēon* to risk; cf Du *plicht*, Ger *Pflicht* an obligation]
■ **plight'er** *n*. **plight'ful** *adj* grievous.
■ **plight one's troth** to pledge oneself in marriage.

plim /plim/ (*dialect*) *vt* and *vi* to swell. [Perh connected with **plump**[1]]

plimsoll or **plimsole** /plim'səl, -sol or -sōl/ *n* a rubber-soled canvas shoe (the line where the sole joined the upper having been supposed to resemble the Plimsoll line).
❑ **Plimsoll line** or **mark** /-səl or -sol/ *n* a ship's load-line, or set of load-lines for different waters and conditions, required by the Merchant Shipping Act (1876) passed at the instance of Samuel *Plimsoll* (1824–98), English politician.

pling /pling/ (*comput sl*) *n* an exclamation mark.

plink /plingk/ *n* a short, relatively high-pitched, sound, as of the string of a musical instrument being plucked (also *vt* and *vi*). [Imit]
■ **plink'y** *adj*.

plinth /plinth/ *n* the square block under the base of a column; a block serving as a pedestal; a flat-faced projecting band at the bottom of a wall; any similar projecting base, eg in furniture. [L *plinthus*, Gr *plinthos* a brick, squared stone, plinth]

plio- see **pleio-**.

Pliocene /plī'ō-sēn/ (*geol*) *adj* of or belonging to an epoch of the Tertiary period, between 5 and 1.8 million years ago, and having a greater proportion of fossil molluscs of living species than the Miocene (also *n*). [Gr *pleiōn* greater, more numerous, and *kainos* recent]

Pliohippus /plī-ō-hip'əs/ *n* a Miocene and Pliocene genus of fossil horses. [Gr *hippos* horse]

pliosaur /plī'ə-sör/ *n* a fossil marine reptile similar to the plesiosaur, with a shorter neck, larger head, and more powerful jaws. [Gr *pleōn* more, and *saurus* lizard]

pliskie /plis'ki/ (*Scot*) *n* condition or plight; a mischievous trick. [Origin unknown]

plissé /plē-sā'/ (*Fr*) *adj* (of a fabric) chemically treated to produce a shirred or puckered effect. ◆ *n* fabric with such a finish.

PLO *abbrev* : Palestine Liberation Organization.

ploat see **plot**[2].

plod[1] /plod/ *vi* (**plodd'ing**; **plodd'ed**) to walk heavily and laboriously; to study or work on steadily and laboriously. ◆ *vt* to traverse or make (one's way) by slow and heavy walking. ◆ *n* a heavy walk; a thud. [Prob imit]
■ **plodd'er** *n* a person who keeps on plodding; a dull, heavy, laborious person; someone who gets on more by sheer toil than by inspiration. **plodd'ing** *adj* and *n*. **plodd'ingly** *adv*.

plod[2] /plod/ (*obs*) *vt* to plot. [**plot**[1], by confusion with **plod**[1]]

plod[3] /plod/ (*sl*) *n* a policeman; the police force. [From PC *Plod*, a character in children's stories by Enid Blyton; prob influenced by **plod**[1]]

-ploid /-ploid/ (*biol*) *adj combining form* indicating the possession of a certain number of chromosome sets, as in *haploid, diploid, triploid*, etc. [From the termination *-ploos* -fold, in Gr *haploos* onefold, *diploos* twofold, etc, and **-oid**]
■ **-ploidy** *n combining form*.

ploidy /ploi'di/ (*biol*) *n* the number of chromosome sets in a cell; the condition of having a certain number of chromosome sets. [From **-ploid**]

-ploitation /-ploit-ā-shən/ *n combining form* denoting the commercial exploitation of the specified thing in film and other media (eg *sexploitation*). [ex*ploitation*]

plong, plonge and **plongd** Spenserian spellings of **plunge** and **plunged**.

plonk[1] /plongk/ *vt* to put down, etc, so as to make a hollow or metallic sound, or heavily, or emphatically. ◆ *vi* to plump down, plonk oneself. ◆ *n* a plonking movement or the sound made by it. ◆ *interj* imitating this sound. ◆ *adv* with a plonk, as in *it landed plonk on the desk*. [Imit]
■ **plonk'er** *n* a large marble (also **plunk'er**); anything large, *esp* a smacking kiss (*inf*); a stupid person, a clot, an idiot (*sl*); the penis (*vulgar sl*). **plonk'ing** *adj* (*inf*) enormous (sometimes *adverbially* or *intensive* with *great*); relating to the practice of plonking. ◆ *n* the practice of uttering jejune or pedestrian remarks in a deliberate and portentous tone. **plonk'y** *adj* relating to or in the style of such a practice.

plonk[2] /plongk/ *n* (*orig Aust sl*) wine, *esp* of poor quality. [Ety doubtful; prob from Fr *blanc* white, from *vin blanc* white wine]

plook, plookie see **plouk**.

plop /plop/ *n* the sound of a small object falling vertically into water; the sound of the movement of small bodies of water; the sound of a cork coming out of a bottle, or of a bursting bubble. ◆ *adv* with a plop; plump. ◆ *vi* (**plopp'ing**; **plopped**) to make the sound of a plop; to drop or plump into water; to defecate (*inf*). ◆ *vt* to let drop with a plop. [Imit]

plosive /plō'siv or -ziv/ (*phonetics*) *adj* and *n* (a consonantal sound) accompanied by plosion.
■ **plo'sion** *n* (*phonetics*) the release of breath after stoppage in articulating certain consonantal sounds.

plot[1] /plot/ *n* a small piece of ground; a spot or small area on any surface (*obs*); a ground plan of a building, plan of a field, etc; the story or scheme of connected events running through a play, novel, etc; a secret scheme, *usu* made in combination with others, to bring about something, often illegal or evil, a conspiracy; a stratagem or secret contrivance. ◆ *vt* (**plott'ing**; **plott'ed**) to lay out in plots, dispose; to make a plan of; to create the plot of (a play, etc); to represent on or by a graph; to conspire or lay plans for. ◆ *vi* to conspire. [OE *plot* a patch of ground; influenced by (or partly from) Fr *complot* a conspiracy; cf **plat**[2]]
■ **plot'ful** *adj*. **plot'less** *adj*. **plott'er** *n*. **plott'ing** *n* and *adj*. **plott'ingly** *adv*.
❑ **plot'-proof** *adj* safe from any danger by plots. **plott'ing-paper** *n* paper ruled in squares for graph-drawing.
■ **lose the plot** (*inf*) to be at a loss, lose one's way; to lose one's temper; to become insane. **the plot thickens** the situation is becoming more complicated.

plot[2] /plot or plōt/ or **ploat** /plōt/ (*Scot and N Eng*) *vt* to dip or steep in very hot water; to burn, scald, scorch; to scald and pluck; to pluck, strip of feathers, hair, etc; to fleece (*fig*); to remove fluff, etc from (a garment) (*not Scot*). [Cf MDu and Flem *ploten* to pluck, but other roots may be involved]
■ **plott'ie** or **plott'y** *n* a spiced hot drink, such as mulled wine.

plotter[1] same as **plouter**.

plotter[2], **plotting** see under **plot**[1].

plottie, plotty see under **plot**[2].

plough or (*N Am* or *archaic*) **plow** /plow/ *n* an instrument for turning up the soil in ridges and furrows; a joiner's plane for making grooves; agriculture (*fig*); a plough-team; ploughed land; (with *cap*) the grouping formed by the seven brightest stars of the constellation of the Great Bear. ◆ *vt* to turn up with a plough; to make furrows or ridges in; to make with a plough; to put into or render with a plough (also *fig*); to tear, force, or cut a way through; to furrow; to wrinkle; to reject in an examination (*old inf*); to fail in (a subject) (*old inf*). ◆ *vi* to work with a plough; (with *through* or *into*) to crash, force one's way, move, drive, etc, violently or uncontrollably (through or into; see also **plough (one's way) through** below); to fail (*old inf*). [Late OE *plōh*, *plōg* a ploughland; cf ON *plógr*]

■ **plough'able** *adj*. **plough'er** *n*. **plough'ing** *n*. **plough'wise** *adv* and *adj* as in ploughing.

❑ **plough'boy** *n* a boy who drives or guides horses in ploughing. **plough'gate** *n* (*Scot hist*) an undetermined or variable unit of land, by later writers taken as about 50 English acres, but earlier much more; a quantity of land of the extent of 100 Scots acres. **plough'-iron** *n* the coulter, share, or other iron part of a plough. **plough'-jogger** *n* (*facetious*) a ploughman. **plough'land** *n* land suitable for tillage; as much land as could be tilled with one plough (with a proportionate amount of pasture), a carucate or eight oxgangs (*hist*). **plough'man** *n* (*pl* **plough'men**) a man who ploughs. **ploughman's lunch** *n* a cold meal of bread, cheese, cold meat, pickle, etc. **ploughman's spikenard** see under **spikenard**. **Plough Monday** *n* an old ploughmen's festival, the Monday after Twelfth Day, supposed to mark the resumption of work after the holidays. **plough'share** *n* (OE *scear* ploughshare, from *sceran* to shear, cut) the detachable part of a plough that cuts the undersurface of the sod from the ground; a bird's pygostyle (also **ploughshare bone**). **plough'-staff** *n* a tool for clearing a plough of earth, etc. **plough'-stilt** *n* a plough-handle. **plough'-tail** *n* the end of a plough where the handles are; farm labour (*fig*). **plough'-team** *n* the team of horses, oxen, etc (*usu* two), that pulls a simple plough. **plough'-tree** *n* a plough-handle. **plough'wright** *n* someone who makes and mends ploughs.

■ **plough a lonely furrow** to be separated from one's former friends and associates and go one's own way. **plough back** (*fig*) to reinvest (profits of a business) in that business. **plough in** to cover with earth by ploughing. **plough on** to make laborious progress. **plough (one's way) through** to work, read, eat, etc, steadily but slowly and laboriously through. **plough the sands** to work in vain or to no purpose. **put one's hand to the plough** to begin an undertaking.

plouk or **plook** /*plook*/ (*Scot*) *n* a small lump or knob; a pimple, spot. [Gaelic *pluc*]

■ **plouk'ie** or **plook'ie** *adj*.

plouter or **plowter** /*plow'tər*/, also **plotter** /*plot'ər*/ (*Scot*) *vi* to dabble in liquid; to potter. ◆ *n* a paddling or dabbling. [Prob imit]

plover /*pluv'ər*/ *n* a general name for birds of the family Charadriidae to which the lapwing and dotterel belong; extended to some related birds; a dupe (*old sl*); a prostitute (*old sl*). [Fr *pluvier*, from L *pluvia* rain; possibly from their restlessness before rain; cf Ger *Regenpfeifer*, literally, rain-piper]

■ **plov'ery** *adj* abounding in plovers.
❑ **plover's egg** *n* a lapwing's egg, or substitute.

plow /*plow*/ (chiefly *US*) same as **plough**.

plowter see **plouter**.

ploy /*ploi*/ *n* an employment, doings, affair, frolic, escapade, or engagement for amusement; a method or procedure used to achieve a particular result; a manoeuvre in a game, conversation, etc. [Prob **employ**]

PLP *abbrev* : Parliamentary Labour Party.

PLR *abbrev* : public lending right (see under **public**).

plu or **plu.** *abbrev* : plural.

pluck /*pluk*/ *vt* to pull off, out, or away; to pull forcibly; to snatch away; to rescue; (with *down*) to bring down, humble (*archaic*); to pull; to tug; to sound (a musical string) by pulling sharply with the nails or a plectrum, to pick; to shape (eyebrows) by removing some of the hairs; to twitch; to strip, *esp* of feathers; to despoil, rob, fleece; to fail, refuse a pass to, in an examination (*old sl*, from the custom of plucking a piece of silk at the back of the proctor's gown in protest); to swindle (*sl*). ◆ *vi* to make a pulling or snatching movement (with *at*). ◆ *n* a single act of plucking; the heart, liver, and lungs of an animal; hence, heart, courage, spirit. [OE *pluccian*; related to Du *plukken*, Ger *pflücken*]

■ **plucked** *adj* subjected to plucking; having pluck. **pluck'er** *n*. **pluck'ily** *adv*. **pluck'iness** *n*. **pluck'ing** *n* the action of the verb; a type of erosion caused by meltwater from a glacier freezing to ice on rocks around it, and plucking pieces from the rock as the ice moves. **pluck'y** *adj* having courageous spirit and pertinacity.

■ **pluck off** (*Shakesp*) to abate, come down the scale. **pluck up** to pull out by the roots; to summon up (*esp* courage); to gather strength or spirit.

pluff /*pluf*/ (*Scot* or *dialect*) *n* a puff; a mild explosion; a shot; a powder-puff. ◆ *vt* to puff; to shoot. ◆ *vi* to go off with a puff; (eg of a cake) to rise. [Imit]
■ **pluff'y** *adj* puffed up; fluffy.

plug /*plug*/ *n* any peg or bung stopping, or for stopping, a hole, *esp* preventing the escape of water from a sink; a stopper; a mechanism releasing the flow of water in a lavatory; filling for a tooth; volcanic rock stopping a vent; a device with metal pins for inserting into a socket to make an electrical connection; a piece of wood inserted in a wall to take nails; a fireplug; a spark plug; a plug-hat (*sl*); a blow or punch; a compressed cake of tobacco; a piece of it cut for chewing; a worn-out horse; a book that will not sell; a piece of favourable publicity, *esp* one incorporated in other material (*inf*); anything worn-out or useless; an instance of dogged plodding. ◆ *vt* (**plugg'ing**; **plugged**) to stop with a plug or as a plug; to insert a plug in; to insert as a plug; to shoot (*sl*); to punch with the fist (*sl*); to force into familiarity by persistent repetition, *esp* for advertising purposes (*inf*); to din into the ears of the public. ◆ *vi* (*inf*) to go on doggedly (often with *away*); (of a golf ball) to become embedded in wet ground or sand. [Appar Du *plug* a bung, a peg; cf Swed *plugg* a peg, Ger *Pflock*]

■ **plugg'er** *n* someone who plugs in any sense; that which plugs, *esp* a dentist's instrument. **plugg'ing** *n* the act of stopping with a plug, or punching (*sl*), or promoting (*sl*); material of which a plug is made.

❑ **plug'-and-play** *adj* (of a computer component) having an identifier that allows it to be configured automatically (also *n*). **plug gauge** *n* a gauge inserted into a hole to measure its diameter. **plug'-hat** *n* (*US*) a top hat. **plug'hole** *n* a hole through which water is let out of a sink, bath, etc. **plug'-in** *n* (*comput*) a module or program that is capable of extending an existing program in specific ways. ◆ *adj* (of a module or program) having such capabilities (*comput*); denoting an electrical apparatus that requires to be plugged in to the mains supply. **plug'-ug'ly** *n* (*US*) a street ruffian; a thug, tough. ◆ *adj* (*inf*) extremely ugly.

■ **go down the plughole** (*inf*) to fail, be wasted or lost. **plug in** to connect (an electrical apparatus, etc) with the electricity supply by inserting a plug into a socket. **pull the plug on** (*inf*) to end, put a stop to.

plum /*plum*/ *n* an oval drupe or stone-fruit with juicy, sweet-tasting yellowish flesh and typically a purple skin when ripe, or the tree producing it (*Prunus domestica* or related species) of the rose family; extended to various fruits and trees more or less similar (eg *sapodilla plum*, *coco-plum*, *date plum*); a raisin as a substitute for the true plum; plum-colour; a sugar-plum; a big stone embedded in concrete; something choice that may be extracted (sometimes in reminiscence of Jack Horner) or attained to, such as one of the best passages in a book, one of the prizes of a career, or a government office as a reward of services, etc; formerly, a sum of d100000; its possessor. ◆ *adj* plum-colour; choice, cushy. [OE *plūme*, from L *prūnum*; cf Gr *prou(m)non*]

■ **plumm'y** *adj* full of plums; plum-like; desirable, profitable; (of voice) unusually rich and resonant, or, loosely, affectedly drawling, *esp* as thought characteristic of upper-class speech; (of a person) with a plummy voice, loosely, upper-class.

❑ **plum'-bloss'om** *n*. **plum'-cake** *n* a cake containing raisins, currants, etc. **plum'-colour** *n* and *adj* deep reddish-purple. **plum'cot** *n* a hybrid between *plum* and *apricot*, developed by US horticulturalist Luther Burbank (1849–1926). **plumdamas** /*-dä'məs*/ *n* (*Scot*) a damson. **plum-duff** *n* a boiled flour pudding made with raisins. **plum'-porr'idge** *n* an antiquated dish, of porridge with plums, raisins, etc. **plum-pudd'ing** *n* an English national dish made of flour and suet, with raisins, currants, and various spices. **plum'-stone** *n*. **plum tomato** *n* a large somewhat plum-shaped Italian variety of tomato.

plumage /*ploom'ij*/ *n* a natural covering of feathers; feathers collectively. [Fr, from *plume*, from L *plūma* a feather, down]
■ **plum'aged** *adj*.

plumassier, **plumate** see under **plume**.

plumb /*plum*/ *n* a heavy mass, as of lead, hung on a string to show a vertical line, or for some other purpose; verticality; a sounding lead, a plummet. ◆ *adj* vertical; (of a cricket pitch) level, true; unquestionably in a leg-before-wicket position (*cricket sl*); sheer, thorough-going, out-and-out. ◆ *adv* vertically; precisely; utterly (*esp US*, now *archaic* or *dialect*). ◆ *vt* to test by a plumb line; to make vertical; to sound as by a plumb line; to pierce the depth of, fathom, by eye or understanding; to weight with lead; to seal with lead; to supply or fit (a building, etc) with plumbing; to connect (eg a bath, washing machine, etc) with the plumbing system, ready for use (*usu* with *in*). ◆ *vi* to hang vertically; to work as a plumber. [Fr *plomb* and its source L *plumbum* lead]

■ **plumbate** /*plum'bāt*/ *n* a salt of plumbic acid. **plumbeous** /*plum'bi-əs*/ *adj* leaden; lead-coloured; lead-glazed. **plumber** /*plum'ər*/ *n orig* a worker in lead; now someone who installs and mends pipes, cisterns, and other fittings for the supply of water and gas and for household drainage. **plumb'ery** *n* plumber-work; a plumber's workshop.

plumbic /plum'bik/ adj due to lead; of quadrivalent lead. **plumbiferous** /-bif'/ adj yielding or containing lead. **plumbing** /plum'ing/ n the operation of making plumb; the craft of working in lead; the work of a plumber; the system of pipes in a building for gas, water and drainage; (the design, style, working, etc of) lavatories (euphem); the urinary system or tract (facetious). **plum'bism** /-bizm/ n lead poisoning. **plumbisol'vency** or (non-standard) **plumbosol'vency** n. **plumbisol'vent** or **plumbosol'vent** adj able to dissolve lead. **plum'bite** /-bīt/ n a salt of the weak acid lead hydroxide. **plumb'less** adj incapable of being sounded. **plumbous** /plum'bəs/ adj of bivalent lead. **plumbum** /plum'bəm/ n (obs) lead. ▫ **plumb bob** n a weight at the end of a plumb line. **plumb'er-block** same as **plummer-block**. **plumber's snake** see **snake**. **plumb'er-work** n the work of a plumber. **plumbic acid** n an acid of which lead dioxide is the anhydride. **plumb line** n a line to which a bob is attached to show the vertical line; a vertical line; a plummet. **plumb rule** n a board with plumb line and bob, for testing the verticality of walls, etc.

plumbago[1] /plum-bā'gō/ n (pl **plumbā'gos**) (with cap) a Mediterranean and tropical genus of ornamental plants (some cultivated) giving name to the **Plumbaginaceae** /-baj-i-nā'si-ē/, a family of salt-steppe and seaside plants including sea pink and sea lavender, related to the primrose family; any plant of this genus. [L plumbāgō, Pliny's translation of the Greek name molybdaina lead, lead ore, the plant Plumbago (from its blue flowers)] ▪ **plumbaginaceous** /-baj-i-nā'shəs/ adj.

plumbago[2] /plum-bā'gō/ n (pl **plumbā'gos**) graphite. [L plumbāgō, -inis, from plumbum lead] ▪ **plumbaginous** /-baj'i-nəs/ adj.

plumbate, plumbeous, plumber, etc see under **plumb**.

plumber-block same as **plummer-block**.

plumbic, plumbiferous, plumbing, plumbum, etc see under **plumb**.

plumcot, plumdamas see under **plum**.

plume /ploom/ n a feather, esp a large showy one; the vane of a feather; a bunch or tuft of feathers; a feather, or anything similar, used as an ornament, symbol, crest, etc; a feather as a token of honour; the plumule of a seed; any feathery structure (obs); anything resembling a feather, such as a thin wisp of rising smoke, etc. ◆ vt to preen; (reflexive) to pride (oneself; with on or upon); to adorn with plumes; to set as a plume (Milton); to strip of feathers. [OFr, from L plūma a small soft feather] ▪ **plumassier** /ploo-mä-sēr'/ n a worker in feathers; a feather-seller. **plu'mate, plu'mose** or **plu'mous** adj feathered; feathery; plume-like. **plumed** adj feathered; adorned with a plume; plucked (obs). **plume'less** adj. **plume'let** n a plumule; a little tuft. **plu'mery** n plumes collectively. **plumigerous** /-ij'ə-rəs/ adj plumaged. **plu'miped** adj having feathered feet. **plu'mist** n a feather-dresser. **plu'my** adj covered or adorned with down or plume; like a plume. ▫ **plume'-bird** n a long-tailed bird of paradise. **plume'-grass** n a tall grass (genus Erianthus) related to sugar-cane, with great silky panicles, grown for ornament. **plume'-moth** n any moth of the families Pterophoridae and Orneodidae, with deeply cleft wings. **plume'-pluckt** adj (Shakesp) stripped of plumes, humbled. **plume poppy** n the popular name for any plant of the genus Macleaya, hardy, very tall flowering perennials of the Papaveraceae.

plummer-block /plum'ər-blok/ n a metal frame or case for holding the end of a revolving shaft. [Origin unknown]

plummet /plum'it/ vi to plunge headlong. ◆ vt to fathom, sound. ◆ n a leaden or other weight, esp on a plumb line, sounding-line, or fishing-line; a plumb rule. [OFr plomet, dimin of plomb lead; see **plumb**]

plummy see under **plum**.

plump[1] /plump/ adj somewhat fat and rounded; chubby; well filled out, full; (of a cheque) large, generous (inf). ◆ vt and vi to make or grow plump; to swell or round. [Appar the same word as Du plomp blunt, LGer plump] ▪ **plump'en** vi (rare). **plump'er** n a pad kept in the mouth to round the cheeks, used by actors. **plump'ish** adj. **plump'ly** adv. **plump'ness** n. **plump'y** or **plump'ie** adj (Shakesp) plump.

plump[2] /plump/ vi to fall or drop into liquid, esp vertically, passively, resoundingly, without much disturbance; to flop down; to rain suddenly and heavily (esp Scot); to come suddenly or with a burst; to give all one's votes without distribution; to choose or opt decisively or abruptly (with for). ◆ vt to plunge or souse; to fling down or let fall flat or heavily; to blurt; to strike or shoot (sl). ◆ n the sound or act of plumping; a sudden heavy fall of rain (esp Scot); a blow (sl). ◆ adj and adv with a plump; in a direct line; downright; in plain language; without hesitation, reserve, or qualification. [LGer plumpen or Du plompen, to plump into water; prob influenced by **plumb** and **plump**[1]]

▪ **plump'er** n a plump, fall or blow; an undistributed vote that could have been divided; someone who gives all his or her votes to one candidate or option; a downright lie (sl); anything very big of its kind, a whopper (sl). **plump'ly** adv.

plump[3] /plump/ (archaic or dialect) n a cluster; a clump (of trees, spearmen, waterfowl, etc). [Origin unknown]

plumula /ploom'ū-lə/ n (pl **plum'ulae** /-lē/) a plumule. [L plūmula, dimin of plūma a feather, down feather] ▪ **plumulā'ceous** or **plum'ular** adj. **Plumulā'ria** n a genus of Hydrozoa forming feathery colonies. **plumulā'rian** n and adj. **plum'ulate** adj downy. **plum'ule** n a little feather or plume; a down feather; the embryo shoot in a seed; a scent-giving scale on the forewing of some male butterflies. **plum'ulose** adj.

plumy see under **plume**.

plunder /plun'dər/ vt to carry off the goods or possessions of by force, to pillage; to carry off as booty; to carry off booty from. ◆ vi to pillage, carry off plunder. ◆ n pillage; booty; personal or household goods (US). [Ger plündern to pillage, from Plunder household stuff, now trash] ▪ **plun'derage** n the stealing of goods on board ship. **plun'derer** n. **plun'derous** adj.

plunge /plunj/ vt to put or thrust suddenly under the surface of a liquid, or into the midst of, the thick of, or the substance of anything; to immerse. ◆ vi to fling oneself or rush impetuously, esp into water, downhill, or into danger or discourse; to turn suddenly and steeply downward; to fire down on an enemy from a height; to gamble or squander recklessly; (of a ship) to pitch; to pitch suddenly forward and throw up the hindlegs. ◆ n an act of plunging. [OFr plonger, from L plumbum lead] ▪ **plung'er** n a person who plunges; part of a mechanism with a plunging movement, such as the solid piston of a force pump; a suction instrument for clearing blockages in pipes; a cavalryman (obs milit sl); a reckless gambler or squanderer. **plung'ing** adj and n. ▫ **plunge bath** n a bath large enough to immerse the whole body. **plunge-cut milling** n (engineering) milling without transverse movement of the workpiece relative to the cutter. **plunge pool** n a small swimming pool deep enough to immerse the body, esp used for its invigorating coolness after a sauna. **plunging fold** n (geol) a fold whose axis is not horizontal. **plunging neckline** n a low-cut neckline in a woman's dress, blouse, etc. ▪ **take the plunge** to commit oneself definitely after hesitation.

plunk /plungk/ vt to twang; to pluck the strings of (a banjo, etc); to plonk; to strike with a sudden blow (N Am inf). ◆ vi to plump. ◆ n a sound made by plucking the strings of a banjo, etc. ◆ adv with a plunk. [Imit] ▪ **plunk'er** n a large marble (also **plonk'er**).

plup or **plup.** abbrev : pluperfect.

pluperfect /ploo-pûr'fikt/ (grammar) adj denoting action that took place before the past actions being described, eg had entered, had been crying. ◆ n the pluperfect tense; a pluperfect verb or form. [L plūs quam perfectum (tempus) more than perfect (tense)]

plur or **plur.** abbrev : plural.

plural /ploor'l/ adj numbering more than one; more than onefold; expressing more than one, or, where dual is recognized, more than two (grammar). ◆ n (grammar) the plural number; a plural word form. [L plūrālis, from plūs, plūris more] ▪ **plur'alism** n a (condition of) society in which different ethnic, etc, groups preserve their own customs, or hold equal power; plurality; the holding by one person of more than one office at once, esp ecclesiastical livings; a system allowing this; a philosophy that recognizes more than one principle of being, opp to monism, or more than two, opp to monism and dualism. **plur'alist** n someone who holds more than one office at one time; a believer in pluralism. ◆ adj of or relating to pluralists. **pluralist'ic** adj. **plurality** /-al'i-ti/ n the state or fact of being plural; numerousness; a plural number; the greater number, more than half; a majority over any other, distinguished from majority, which is used for an absolute majority or majority over all others combined (US); the holding of more than one benefice at one time; a living held by a pluralist. **pluralīzā'tion** or **-s-** n. **plur'alize** or **-ise** vt to make plural. ◆ vi to hold two or more benefices or offices simultaneously. **plu'rally** adv. ▫ **plural society** n one in which pluralism is found. **plural vote** n the power of voting in more than one constituency, or more than once in one.

pluri- /ploor-i-/ combining form denoting: several; usu more than two. [L plūs, plūris more] ▪ **plurilit'eral** adj (Heb grammar) containing more letters than three. **pluriloc'ular** adj multilocular. **plurip'ara** n a multipara. **pluripo'tent** adj (zool) capable of forming many cell types. **pluripres'ence** n presence in more places than one at the same time. **plurise'rial** or **plurise'riate** /-ri-ət/ adj in several rows.

plurisie /ploor'i-si/ (Shakesp) n superabundance. [L plūs, plūris more; confused with **pleurisy**]

plus /plus/ (maths and inf) prep with the addition of. ◆ adj positive; additional; advantageous; having an adverse handicap (games); used postpositively to mean rather more than, as in 200 plus, of a grade higher than, as in alpha plus or (inf) unusually great, as in success plus. ◆ conj (inf) and also, in addition. ◆ n (pl **plus'es** or **pluss'es**) an addition; a surplus; a positive quality or term; an advantage (inf); the sign (also **plus sign**) of addition or positivity (+), opp to minus. ◆ vt and vi (**plus'ing** or **pluss'ing**; **plused** or **plussed**) to increase (in value). [L plūs more]
□ **plus'age** or **pluss'age** n an extra amount. **plus-one** n (inf) the person who accompanies one to an entertainment, etc. **plus-size** adj (of a garment) of exceptionally large size. **plus strain** n (bot) one of the two strains in heterothallism.
■ **plus or minus** (used in approximating) with the addition or subtraction of, with an error range of (so many).

plus fours /plus fōrz' or förz/ n pl baggy knickerbockers or a knickerbocker suit. [plus four; from the four additional inches of cloth required to create the overhang at the knee]

plush /plush/ n a fabric with a longer and more open pile than velvet; (in pl) footman's breeches. ◆ adj of plush; (also **plush'y**) luxurious, orig pretentiously so (inf). [Fr pluche for peluche, from L pilus hair; cf **pile³**]

plus twos /plus tooz/ n pl a shorter version of plus fours.

pluteus /ploo'ti-əs/ n a sea urchin or brittlestar larva, shaped like a many-legged easel. [L pluteus a shed, boarding, desk]
■ **plu'teal** adj.

Pluto /ploo'tō/ n the Greek god of the underworld (Gr myth); a dwarf planet beyond Neptune, discovered in 1930. [L Plūtō, -ōnis, from Gr Ploutōn, -ōnos Pluto]
■ **plu'toid** n (astron) any dwarf planet beyond Neptune. **plu'ton** n (geol) a mass of rock which has solidified below the earth's surface. **Pluto'nian** adj of Pluto; of the underworld. **Plutonic** /-ton'ik/ adj of Pluto; (also without cap) hypogene, deep-seated, relating to or formed under conditions of subterranean heat (geol); Plutonist. **Plutonism** /ploo'tən-izm/ n. **Plu'tonist** n and adj (obs geol) Vulcanist. **plutó'nium** n an artificially produced radioactive transuranic element (symbol **Pu**; atomic no 94), named as next after neptunium (93; Pluto being regarded at the time as the planet beyond Neptune), having many isotopes, the fissile isotope ²³⁹Pu being particularly important in the production of nuclear power.

pluto- /ploo-tō-, -tə-, -to-/ combining form denoting wealth. [Gr ploutos wealth]
■ **plutocracy** /ploo-tok'rə-si/ n government by the wealthy; a society governed by the wealthy; a ruling body or class of rich people. **plutocrat** /ploo'tə-krat/ n someone who is powerful because of his or her wealth. **plutocrat'ic** adj. **pluto-democ'racy** n a wealth-dominated democracy. **plutol'atry** n (see **-latry**) worship of wealth. **plutol'ogist** n. **plutol'ogy** or **pluton'omy** n political economy. **pluton'omist** n.

pluvial /ploo'vi-əl/ adj of or by rain; rainy. ◆ n (from Med L pluviāle a rain-cloak) a cope or ceremonial mantle (hist); a period of prolonged rainfall (geol). [L pluvia, rain]
■ **pluviom'eter** n a rain gauge. **pluviomet'ric** or **pluviomet'rical** adj. **plu'viose** or **plu'vious** adj rainy. **Pluviôse** /plü-vē-ōz/ n (Fr) the fifth month of the French Revolutionary calendar, the rainy month, about 20 January to 18 February.
□ **pluvius insurance** n insurance cover taken out eg by the organizer of a fête against loss of takings due to rain.

ply¹ /plī/ n (pl **plies**) a fold; a layer or thickness; a layer of hard rock or of hard or soft rocks in alternation (mineralogy); a bend or set; a strand; condition, esp good condition (Scot). ◆ vt and vi (**ply'ing**; **plied**) to bend or fold. [(O)Fr pli a fold, plier to fold, from L plicāre]
■ **pli'er** n someone who plies.
□ **ply'wood** n boarding made of thin layers of wood glued together, the grain of each at right angles to that of the next.

ply² /plī/ vt (**ply'ing**; **plied**) to work at steadily; to use or wield diligently or vigorously; to keep supplying or assailing (with); to importune; to row or sail over habitually. ◆ vi to work steadily; to make regular journeys over a route; to be in attendance for hire; to beat against the wind; to make one's way, direct one's course. [Aphetic, from **apply**]
■ **pli'er** n someone who plies; a trader (obs); a tout (obs).

Plymouth /plim'əth/ n a port in Devon; a port named after it in Massachusetts, with the supposed landing-place of the Pilgrims (Plymouth Rock).
■ **Plym'outhism** n. **Plym'outhist**, **Plym'outhite** or **Plymouth Brother** n one of the **Plymouth Brethren**, a religious sect, founded in Dublin c.1825, out of a reaction against High Church principles and against a dead formalism associated with unevangelical doctrine (its first congregation was established at Plymouth in 1831).
□ **Plymouth Rock** n an American breed of poultry; a nickname for a Plymouth Brother.

plyometrics /plī-ō-met'riks/ n sing a method of exercise involving repeated rapid stretching of the muscles. [Gr pleiōn more, and metron measure]
■ **plyomet'ric** adj.

plywood see under **ply¹**.

PM abbrev : Past Master; Postmaster; (also **pm**) post mortem (L), after death; Prime Minister; Provost-Marshal.

Pm (chem) symbol : promethium.

pm abbrev : (also **p.m.**) post meridiem (L), after noon; premium.

PMBX (telecom) abbrev : private manual branch exchange.

PMDD abbrev : premenstrual dysphoric disorder.

PMG abbrev : Paymaster General; Postmaster General.

PMO abbrev : Principal Medical Officer.

PMQs abbrev : Prime Minister's Questions.

Pmr abbrev : Paymaster.

PMRAFNS abbrev : Princess Mary's Royal Air Force Nursing Service.

PMS abbrev : premenstrual syndrome.

PMT abbrev : photomechanical transfer; premenstrual tension.

pn abbrev : promissory note.

PNA abbrev : Palestinian National Authority; peptide nucleic acid.

PND abbrev : postnatal depression.

PNdB abbrev : perceived noise decibel.

pneum- see **pneumo-**.

pneuma /nū'mə/ n breath; spirit, soul; a neume. [Gr pneuma, -atos breath, from pneein to breathe]
■ **pneumathode** /nū'mə-thōd/ n (Gr hodos a way) a respiratory opening in plants. **pneumatic** /-mat'ik/ adj relating to air or gases; containing or inflated with air; (of a woman's figure) full, generously proportioned, esp referring to a large bust (inf); worked or driven by compressed air; containing compressed air; with air-cavities (zool); spiritual. **pneumat'ical** adj (rare). **pneumat'ically** adv. **pneumaticity** /nū-mə-tis'i-ti/ n the condition of having air-spaces. **pneumat'ics** n sing the science of the mechanical properties of gases, pneumatology (also **pneumodynam'ics**).
□ **pneumatic trough** n a vessel with a perforated shelf, for filling gas-jars over a liquid.

pneumato- /nū-ma-, nū-mə- or nu-mə-tō-, -tə-, -to-/ combining form denoting breath or air (see also **pneumo-**). [Gr pneuma, -atos breath, from pneein to breathe]
■ **pneumatolog'ical** adj. **pneumatol'ogist** n. **pneumatol'ogy** n the theory of the existence of spirits or spiritual beings; psychology (archaic); the doctrine of the Holy Spirit (theol); pneumatics (archaic). **pneumatol'ysis** n (see **lysis**) the destructive action of the hot vapours of magma on igneous rock. **pneumatolyt'ic** adj. **pneumatom'eter** n an instrument for measuring the quantity of air breathed or the force of breathing. **pneu'matophore** (or /-mat'/) n an upward-growing respiratory root in swamp plants; a gas-filled float supporting a coelenterate.

pneumo- /nū-mō-, -mə-/, **pneum-** /nūm-/, **pneumon-** /nū-mon-, -mən-/ or **pneumono-** /nū-mə-nō-, -nə-/ combining form denoting: lung; (**pneumo-**, as a reduced form of **pneumato-**) air or breath. [Gr pneumōn, -onos lung, from pneein to breathe]
■ **pneumococc'us** n a bacterium in the respiratory tract which is a causative agent of pneumonia. **pneumoconiosis** /nū-mō-kō-ni-ō'sis/, **pneumokonio'sis** or **pneumonokonio'sis** n (Gr konia dust) any of various diseases caused by habitually inhaling mineral or metallic dust, as in coalmining. **pneumoconiot'ic** n a person suffering from pneumoconiosis. **pneumocys'tis** n any microorganism of the genus Pneumocystis (**pneumocystis carinii pneumonia** a potentially fatal infection which can affect people whose immune system is damaged by disease (eg AIDS) or drugs). **pneumodynam'ics** n sing same as **pneumatics** (see under **pneuma**). **pneumogas'tric** adj relating to the lungs and stomach. ◆ n the vagus. **pneumonec'tomy** n surgical removal of lung tissue. **pneumō'nia** n inflammation of the lung (**pneumonia blouse** (facetious) a low-necked blouse, once an object of disapproval). **pneumonic** /-mon'/ adj relating to the lungs. ◆ n a medicine for lung diseases. **pneumonī'tis** n inflammation of the alveoli; pneumonia. **pneumotho'rax** n (med) the existence, or introduction of, air between the lung and chest wall; lung collapse resulting from the escape of air from the lung into the chest cavity, a potential hazard of working in compressed air, eg deep-sea diving.

PNG abbrev : Papua New Guinea (also IVR); /ping/ portable network graphic, a format for graphics on the World Wide Web (comput).

■ words derived from main entry word; □ compound words; ■ idioms and phrasal verbs

Pnyx /pniks or niks/ n the meeting-place of the ancient Athenian assembly. [Gr pnyx, genitive pyknos, perh cognate with pyknos crowded]

PO abbrev : Petty Officer; Pilot Officer; Postal Order; Post Office.

Po (chem) symbol : polonium.

po[1] /pō/ (inf) n (pl **pos**) a shortening of **chamberpot** (see under **chamber**). [**pot**, prob from a euphemistic French pronunciation]

po[2] /pō/ (inf) adj a shortening of **po-faced**.

po abbrev : postal order.

po. abbrev : pole.

POA abbrev : Prison Officers' Association.

poa /pō'ə/ n any plant of the meadow-grass genus Poa. [Gr poā grass]
■ **poāˈceous** adj.

poach[1] /pōch/ vt to cook slowly in simmering liquid. [Appar Fr pocher to pocket, from poche, pouch, the white of an egg forming a pocket around the yolk]
■ **poachˈer** n someone who poaches eggs; a container with hollows for poaching eggs in.
□ **poached-egg flower** n Romneya; an annual, Limnanthes douglasii, with yellow and white flowers.

poach[2] /pōch/ vi to intrude on another person's land in order to pursue or kill game, or on another person's fishing to catch fish; to encroach on another's rights, profits, area of influence, etc, or on a partner's place or part in a game; to lurk around the opposing team's penalty area in the hope of scoring an opportunist goal (football); to seek an unfair advantage; (Shakesp **potche**) to thrust; to trample in mud; to become trampled and muddy. ◆ vt to take illegally on another's ground or in another's fishing; to seek or take game or fish illegally on; to take in unfair encroachment; to poke or thrust (dialect); to stir up (dialect); to trample into holes and mud. [A form of **poke**[1] or from OFr pocher to poke]
■ **poachˈer** n. **poachˈiness** n. **poachˈing** n. **poachˈy** adj spongy and sodden.

poaka /pō-ä'kə/ (Maori) n a New Zealand bird, one of the stilts.

poake a Shakespearean spelling of **poke**[2].

pocas palabras /pō'kǎs pa-lä'brǎs/ (Sp) n few words.

po'chaise /pō'shāz or posh'āz/ see **post-chaise** under **post**[3].

pochard /pō'chərd, poch'ərd/, **pockard** /pok'ərd/ or **poker** /pō'kər/ n a red-headed diving-duck (Nyroca or Aythya ferina), esp the male, the female being the dun-bird. [Origin obscure]

pochay /pō'shā/ see **post-chaise** under **post**[3].

pochette /po-shet'/ n a small bag, esp one carried by women; a pocket notecase or wallet. [Fr, dimin of poche pocket]

pochoir /posh'wär/ n a form of colour stencilling, by hand, onto a printed illustration. [Fr, stencil]

pock[1] /pok/ n a small elevation of the skin containing pus, as in smallpox; a pockmark. [OE poc a pustule; Ger Pocke, Du pok; see **pox**]
■ **pocked** adj. **pock'y** adj marked with pustules; infected with pox; confounded, damned (obs inf).
□ **pock'mark** or **pock'pit** n the mark, pit, or scar left by a pock, esp one caused by chickenpox or smallpox; similar pitting or scarring of any surface. **pock'marked** adj. **pock'pitted** adj.

pock[2] /pok/ n a Scots form of **poke**[2].
□ **pockman'tie** or **pockmank'y** n corrupt forms of **portmanteau**. **pock-pudding** /pok'pud'n/ n a fruit pudding cooked in a bag; a Scottish contemptuous name for a mere Englishman.

pockard see **pochard**.

pocket /pok'it/ n a little pouch or bag, esp one fitted in or attached to a garment or a snooker table or the cover of a book; a cavity; a rock cavity filled with ore, veinstone, etc; a portion of the atmosphere differing in pressure or other condition from its surroundings; a small isolated area or patch, as of military resistance, unemployment, etc; the innermost compartment of a pound-net; one's personal stock of money; a bag of wool, etc, containing about ½ sack; the area behind the offensive linemen (American football). ◆ adj for the pocket; of a small size. ◆ vt (**pock'eting**; **pock'eted**) to put in one's pocket or a pocket; to receive and keep for oneself, to accept (a cash prize payment, etc); to appropriate; to take stealthily; to conceal; to enclose; to hem in; to play into a pocket (snooker, etc). ◆ vi to form a pocket. [Anglo-Fr poket (Fr pochette, dimin of poche pocket]
■ **pock'etful** n (pl **pock'et-fuls**) as much as a pocket will hold. **pock'etless** adj.
□ **pocket battleship** n a small battleship, built to specifications limited by treaty, etc. **pocket bike** same as **minimoto** (see under **mini-**). **pock'etbook** n a notebook; a wallet for papers or money carried in the pocket; a small book for the pocket; a handbag (US). **pocket borough** see under **borough**. **pock'et-comb** n a hair-comb small

enough for carrying in the pocket. **pock'et-glass** n a small mirror for carrying in the pocket. **pocket gopher** n an American burrowing rodent, the pouched rat. **pock'et-handk'erchief** n a handkerchief for carrying in the pocket. **pock'et-hole** n the opening in a garment giving access to a pocket. **pocket knife** n a knife with one or more blades folding into the handle, for carrying in the pocket. **pocket money** n money carried for occasional expenses; an allowance, esp to a child. **pocket mouse** n a small rodent of the genus Perognathus, native to the N American desert. **pock'et-picking** n the act or practice of picking other people's pockets. **pock'et-piece** n a coin carried to bring luck. **pock'et-pis'tol** n a pistol for carrying in the pocket; a small travelling flask for liquor. **pock'et-sized** adj small enough for the pocket. **pocket veto** n (US) a President's indirect veto of a bill passed by Congress, done by delaying its signing until the legislative session is over.
■ **have deep pockets** to have access to extensive financial resources. **in one's pocket** under one's control or influence; very close to one. **in** (or **out of**) **pocket** with or without money; the richer or the poorer by a transaction (**out'-of-pock'et** adj of expenses, etc, paid in cash). **line one's pockets** to make or take money dishonestly from business entrusted to one. **pick a person's pocket** to steal from his or her pocket. **pocket an insult, affront**, etc to submit to or put up with it without protest. **pocket one's pride** to humble oneself to accept a situation.

pockmanky, pockmantie see under **pock**[2].

pocky, etc see under **pock**[1].

poco /pō'kō/ (Ital) adj little.
■ **pococuran'te** /-koo-ran'tā or -kū-ran'ti/ adj (Ital curante, prp of curare to care) uninterested; indifferent; nonchalant. ◆ n a habitually uninterested or indifferent person. **pococurantism** /-kū-rant'izm/ or **pococuranteism** /-kū-rant'i-izm/ n. **pococurant'ist** n.
■ **poco a poco** little by little.

poculiform /pok'ū-li-förm/ adj cup-shaped. [L pōculum cup]

pod[1] /pod/ n the fruit, or its shell, in peas, beans, and other leguminous plants, the legume; sometimes extended to the siliqua; an egg-case, eg of a locust; a silk cocoon; a musk-bag; a paunch; a groove along an auger or bit; the socket into which a bit, etc, fits; a protective housing for (external) engineering equipment, eg aircraft engines, nuclear reactor, space or submarine instruments, or for weapons carried externally, eg on an aircraft; a decompression compartment; a self-contained compartment, esp for meeting, observation or transportation. ◆ vt (**podd'ing; podd'ed**) to shell or hull. ◆ vi to form pods; to fill as pods. [Origin uncertain]
■ **podd'y** adj corpulent. ◆ n (Aust inf) a young animal, esp a calf or lamb.

pod[2] /pod/ n a school, esp of whales or seals; sometimes applied to groups of other animals, fish and birds. [Origin unknown]

pod[3] /pod/ (inf; photog) a short form of **tripod, monopod** (see **monopode**), etc.

pod abbrev : pay on delivery.

pod- /pod-/ combining form see **podo-**.

-pod /-pod/ or **-pode** /-pōd/ combining form denoting foot. [Gr pous, podos foot]

podagra /po-dag'rə, pod'ə-grə/ (med) n gout, properly in the feet. [Gr podagrā, from pous, podos foot, and agrā a catching]
■ **podag'ral** (or /pod'/), **podag'ric, podag'rical** or **podag'rous** (or /pod'/) adj gouty.

podal and **podargus** see under **podo-**.

podcast /pod'käst/ vt and vi to publish (sound files) on the Internet in a form in which they can be downloaded onto a digital audio player. ◆ n a set of files that is published and downloaded in this way. [iPod®, a brand of digital audio player, and **-cast**]
■ **pod'caster** n. **pod'casting** n.

podcatcher /pod'ka-chər/ n a program for downloading podcasts onto a digital audio player. [**podcast** and **catch**]
■ **pod'catching** n.

poddy see under **pod**[1].

-pode see **-pod**.

podestà /pō-də-stä' or po-dest-tä'/ (hist) n a governor, chief magistrate, or judge in an Italian town. [Ital podestà, from L potestās, -ātis power]

podex /pō'deks/ n the rump; the anal region. [L pōdex]

podge /poj/ or **pudge** /puj/ n a squat, fat and flabby person or thing; excess body fat (inf). [Origin obscure]
■ **podg'iness** n or **pudg'iness** n. **podg'y** or **pudg'y** adj.

podiatrist, podiatry and **podite** see under **podo-**.

podium /pō'di-əm/ n (pl **pō'dia**) a continuous pedestal, a stylobate (archit); a platform, dais; a wall enclosing an arena; a foot or hand (anat); a tube-foot. ◆ vi (inf) to win a place on the victors' podium by finishing in the leading places in a sporting competition. [Latinized from Gr *podion*, dimin of *pous, podos* foot]

■ **pō'dial** *adj.*

podley /*pod'li*/ (*Scot*) *n* a young coalfish. [**pollack**]

podo- /*pod-ō-, -ǝ-, -o-,* or *pōd-/* or **pod-** /*pod-* or *pōd-/* *combining form* denoting foot. [Gr *pous, podos* foot]

■ **pō'dal** or **pōdal'ic** *adj* of the feet. **podargus** /*pǝ-där'gǝs*/ *n* (Gr *podargos* swift-footed) a bird of the frogmouth genus *Podargus*. **podi'atrist** *n*. **podiatry** /*pod-ī'ǝ-tri*/ *n* (Gr *iātros* physician) treatment of disorders of the foot. **podite** /*pod'īt*/ *n* a walking leg of a crustacean. **podocarp** /*pō-dō-kärp*/ *n* (Gr *karpos* fruit) a yew tree of the eastern and southern genus *Podocarpus*. **podoconio'sis** *n* (*med*) endemic elephantiasis of the lower legs. **Podogona** /*-og'ǝ-nǝ*/ *n* (Gr *gonos* reproductive organ) the Ricinulei (qv). **podol'ogist** *n*. **podol'ogy** *n* the scientific study of the feet. **podophthalmous** /*-of-thal'mǝs*/ *adj* (Gr *ophthalmos* eye) having eyes on stalks, as do many higher crustaceans. **podophyll'in** *n* a cathartic resin obtained from the rhizomes of the Podophyllum genus. **Podophyllum** /*-ō-fil'ǝm, -of'i-lǝm*/ *n* (Gr *phyllon* leaf) a genus of the barberry family. **Podostemon** /*-ō-stē'mǝn*/ *n* (Gr *stēmōn* warp, as if stamen, from the stalk on which the stamens stand) the typical genus of a family of dicotyledons, **Podostemaceae** /*-mā'si-ē*/, growing in tropical waterfalls, the vegetative parts more like a thallus than an ordinary flowering plant. **Podura** /*-dū'rǝ*/ *n* (Gr *ourā* tail) a genus of springtails.

podsol or **podzol** /*pod-zol'* or *pod'*/ *n* any of a group of soils characterized by a greyish-white leached and infertile topsoil and a brown subsoil, typical of regions with a subpolar climate. [Russ, from *pod* under, and *zola* ash]

■ **podsol'ic** *adj*. **podsoliza'tion** or **-s-** or **podzoliza'tion** or **-s-** *n*.

Podunk /*pō'dungk*/ (*US*) *n* an imaginary, typical, dull, out-dated country town. ◆ *adj* dull and old-fashioned. [From either of two villages, near Worcester, Massachusetts, or Hartford, Connecticut]

Podura see under **podo-**.

poe-bird or **poy-bird** /*pō'i-bûrd*/ (*obs*) *n* the New Zealand parson-bird or tui. [Captain Cook's name, from Tahitian *poe* pearl beads, taken by him to mean earrings, on account of the side-tufts of the bird's neck]

poem /*pō'im* or *-ǝm*/ *n* a composition in verse; a composition of high beauty of thought or language and artistic form, typically, but not necessarily, in verse; anything supremely harmonious and satisfying. [Fr *poème*, from L *poēma*, from Gr *poiēma*, from *poieein* to make]

■ **poemat'ic** *adj*.

poenology same as **penology**.

poesy /*pō'i-zi*/ *n* poetry collectively or in the abstract; a poem (*obs*); a motto or posy (*obs*). ◆ *vi* (*Keats*) to utter poetry. [Fr *poésie*, from L *poēsis*, from Gr *poiēsis*, from *poieein* to make]

poet /*pō'it* or *-ǝt*/ *n* (also *fem* **pō'etess**) the author of a poem or (formerly) of any work of literary art; a verse-writer; someone skilled in making poetry; someone with a poetical imagination. [Fr *poète*, from L *poēta*, from Gr *poiētēs*, from *poieein* to make]

■ **pōetas'ter** *n* (see **-aster**) a petty poet; a writer of contemptible verses. **pōetas'tering** *n*. **pōetas'tery** or **pōetas'try** *n*. **poetic** /*pō-et'ik*/ or **poet'ical** *adj* of the nature or having the character of poetry; relating or suitable to a poet or to poetry; expressed in poetry; in the language of poetry; imaginative. ◆ *n* a writer of poetry (*obs*); poetics (qv below). **pōet'ically** *adv*. **poet'ics** *n sing* the branch of criticism that relates to poetry. **poet'icism** *n* a word or phrase that is typically, *usu* tritely, poetic. **poet'icize** or **-ise** *vt* and *vi* to make poetic; to write poetry about; to write, speak, or treat, poetically. **pōet'icule** *n* a petty poet. **pō'etize** or **-ise** *vi* to write as a poet. ◆ *vt* to make poetical; to record or celebrate in poetry. **pō'etresse** *n* (*Spenser*) a poetess. **pō'etry** *n* the art of the poet; the essential quality of a poem; poetical composition or writings collectively (rarely in *pl*); poetical quality. **pō'etship** *n*.

❑ **poetic justice** *n* ideal or fitting apportioning of reward and punishment. **poetic licence** *n* an allowable departure from strict fact, rule or logic for the sake of effect, as frequently occurs in poetry. **poet laureate** *n* formerly, a person who received a degree in grammar (ie poetry and rhetoric) at the English universities; now, (with cap) the poet appointed to a lifetime post in the Royal household, required to compose poems for state occasions, etc.

■ **poetry in motion** exceedingly beautiful, harmonious, rhythmical, etc, movement.

po-faced /*pō'fāst*/ (*inf*) *adj* (also shortened to **po**) stupidly solemn and narrow-minded; stolid, humourless. [Perh *pot-faced* or *poor-faced*]

poffle /*pof'l*/ (*Scot*) *n* a pendicle. [Origin obscure]

pogge /*pog*/ *n* the armed bullhead (*Agonus cataphractus*), a bony-plated fish. [Origin unknown]

pogo /*pō'gō*/ *vi* (*prp* **po'going**) to jump up and down on the spot to music, a popular punk form of dancing of the 1970s (also *n*). [**pogo stick**, from the movement]

pogo effect /*pō'gō i-fekt'*/ (*space flight*) *n* unstable, longitudinal oscillations induced in a launch system, mainly due to sloshing (qv) of fuel and engine vibration. [Poss **pogo stick**, from the movement]

pogonotomy /*pō-gō-not'ǝ-mi* or *-gǝ-/* *n* shaving. [Gr *pōgōn, pōgōnos* beard, and *tomē* a cutting]

pogo stick /*pō'gō stik*/ *n* a child's toy consisting of a stick with a handle and footholds, mounted on a strong spring, on which to stand and bounce along. [*Pogo*, a trademark]

pogrom /*pog'rǝm* or *pog-rom'*/ *n* an organized massacre, *orig* (late 19c) *esp* of Russian Jews. [Russ, destruction, devastation]

poh /*pō*/ *interj* expressing impatient contempt. [Cf **pooh**]

pohutukawa /*pǝ-hoo-tǝ-ka'wǝ*/ *n* the New Zealand Christmas tree which bears red blooms at Christmas-time, *Metrosideros excelsa*, of the family Myrtaceae. [Maori]

poi[1] /*poi*/ *n* a Hawaiian dish, a paste of fermented taro root. [Hawaiian]

poi[2] /*poi*/ *n* a light ball swung on a string in traditional Maori dancing. [Maori]

poignado or **poinado** /*poi-nä'dō*/ *n* (*pl* **poi(g)na'does**) obsolete forms of **poniard**.

poignant /*poin'yǝnt, -ǝnt*/ *adj* touching, moving, exciting pathos; stinging, pricking; sharp; acutely painful; penetrating; pungent; piquant. [OFr *poignant*, prp of *poindre*, from L *pungere* to sting]

■ **poign'ancy** *n*. **poign'antly** *adv*.

poikilitic /*poi-ki-lit'ik*/ *adj* mottled; having small crystals of one mineral irregularly scattered in larger crystals of another (*petrology*). [Gr *poikilos* variegated]

■ **poi'kilocyte** /*-ō-sīt*/ *n* an irregular red blood corpuscle. **poi'kilotherm** *n* a cold-blooded animal. **poikilotherm'al** or **poikilotherm'ic** *adj* having a variable blood-temperature, 'cold-blooded'. **poikilotherm'y** (or /*poi'*/) *n* cold-bloodedness.

poilu /*pwa-lü'*/ (*Fr*) *n* a French private soldier (nickname; meaning 'hairy').

poinado see **poignado**.

poinciana /*poin-si-ä'nǝ*/ *n* a tree of the tropical genus *Poinciana* of the Caesalpiniaceae. [De *Poinci*, 17c governor in French West Indies]

poind /*pēnd* or *pind*/ (*Scot*) *vt* to distrain; to impound. [OE *pyndan* to impound; cf **pound[2]**]

■ **poind'er** *n*. **poind'ing** *n*.

poinsettia /*poin-set'i-ǝ*/ *n* a spurge, *Euphorbia pulcherrima*, with petal-like bracts, *usu* scarlet, and small yellow flowers, *orig* from Mexico and Central America. [Joel Roberts Poinsett (1779–1851), US Minister to Mexico]

point[1] /*point*/ *n* a dot; a small mark used in Semitic alphabets to indicate a vowel, to differentiate a consonant, or for other purpose; a dot separating the integral and fractional parts of a decimal; a mark of punctuation; that which has position but no magnitude (*geom*); a whit (as in *no point*; *Shakesp*); a place or station, considered in relation to position only; a place or division in a scale, course, or cycle (as in *boiling point, dead point*); a moment of time, without duration; a precise moment; a state; a juncture; a critical moment; the verge; a culmination; a conclusion; resolution (*obs*); condition, case, plight (as in *in good point*; *obs*); any one of nine fixed positions on a shield (*heraldry*); the entry, or the first notes, of a subject, eg in a fugue (formerly marked by a dot; *obs*); a short strain or phrase of music, a call on an instrument, *esp* military, as in a *point of war* (*archaic*); a unit in scoring, judging, or measurement; a unit used in quoting changes of prices of stocks and securities; a percentage of the profits from a venture; a feature or character taken into account in judging; a distinctive mark or characteristic; a unit of measurement of type, approx $\frac{1}{72}$ inch; one of thirty-two divisions of the compass (**points of the compass**) or the angle between two successive divisions ($\frac{1}{8}$ of a right angle); a unit in rationing by coupon; (in piquet) the strongest suit held and called, or the score for holding it; a particular; a heading, clause, or item; a position forming a main element in the structure of an argument or discourse; a matter in debate, under attention, or to be taken into account; that which is relevant; that upon which one insists or takes a stand; the precise matter; the essential matter; that without which a story, joke, etc, is meaningless or ineffective; a clearly defined aim, object, or reason; use, value; a particular imparted as a hint; lace made with a needle (also **point'-lace**); loosely, lace; a piece of point-lace (*obs*); a sharp end; a tip, or free end; a thing, part, or mark with a sharp end; a piercing weapon or tool; an etching needle; the sharp end of a sword; (in *pl*) sword-fighting; a tine; a spike; a tapering piece in electrical apparatus, such as the end of a lightning conductor; (in *pl*) the pair of electrical contacts that complete the circuit in the distributor of an internal-combustion engine; a cape or headland; a horse's or other animal's extremity; a tagged lace formerly used for fastening clothes; a nib; a movable rail by means of which trains are transferred from one track to another; a tapering division of a backgammon board; a fielder, or a fielding position, on the offside fairly near the batsman on a line with the popping crease (*cricket*); a defence position (*lacrosse*); the leading party of an advanced guard; a position at the head of a herd or a body of troops; a socket for making a connection with electric wiring; pointedness; pungency; sting; the act or position of pointing; the vertical rising of a hawk, indicating the position of the prey; a feat (*obs*); pointe; $\frac{1}{100}$ part of a carat. ◆ *adj* (*phonetics*) articulated with the tip of the tongue. ◆ *vt* to insert points in; to mark with points; to mark off in groups of syllables for singing; to sharpen; to give point to; to prick in or turn over with the point of a spade; to show the position or direction of or draw attention to (now *usu* with *out*); to place in a certain direction, direct (with *at*); to indicate; to insert white hairs in (a fur); to rake out old mortar from, and insert new mortar in, the joints of; to ration by points. ◆ *vi* to have or take a position in a direction (with *at*, *to*, *toward*, etc); to indicate a direction or position by extending a finger, a stick, etc; of dogs, to indicate the position of game by an attitude; to hint; to aim. [Partly Fr *point* point, dot, stitch, lace, partly Fr *pointe*, sharp point, pungency, respectively from L *punctum* and LL *puncta*, from L *pungere*, *punctum* to prick]

■ **point'ed** *adj* having a sharp point; sharp; Gothic (*archit*); keen; telling; epigrammatic; precise; explicit; aimed at particular persons; (of a remark) having a marked personal application. **point'edly** *adv*. **point'edness** *n*. **point'er** *n* someone who points, in any sense; a rod for pointing to a blackboard, map, screen, etc; a symbol, eg an arrow, on a screen, moved by means of a mouse (*comput*); an index-hand; a hint, tip, suggestion, indication; a hyperlink (*comput*); a tool for clearing out old mortar from joints; a breed of dogs that point on discovering game; a horse ridden in point-to-point races (*horse-racing*); (in *pl*) two stars of the Great Bear nearly in a straight line with the Pole Star. **point'ing** *n* the action of the verb; the mortar between joints. **point'less** *adj*. **point'lessly** *adv*. **point'lessness** *n*. **point'y** *adj* having points, or pointed in shape.

❑ **point after** *n* (*American football*) a goal kick taken after a touchdown is scored. **point'-and-click'** *adj* of or relating to a computer interface in which the user moves a cursor on a screen by manipulating a mouse and clicks on a mouse button to select or activate a program, etc. **point'-and-shoot'** *adj* (of a camera) setting focus and exposure automatically. **point duty** *n* the duty of a policeman stationed at a particular point to regulate traffic. **pointed arch** *n* a lancet arch. **point guard** *n* (*basketball*) a player positioned away from the basket who directs attacking play. **pointing device** *n* (*comput*) any device such as a mouse or trackball used to move a pointer on a screen. **point'ing-stock** *n* a thing to be pointed at, a laughing stock. **point'-lace** see *n* above. **point man** *n* a soldier at the head of a body of troops or patrol; a person who takes the lead (*US*). **point mutation** *n* a genetic mutation converting one allele into another. **point of honour** see under **honour**. **point of no return** *n* that point on a flight from which one can only go on, for lack of fuel to return (also *fig*). **point of order** *n* a question raised during a formal meeting or debate, eg in Parliament, as to whether proceedings are according to the rules. **point of sale** *n* (in retailing) the place where a sale is made (*abbrev* **POS**). **point'-of-sale'** *adj* of, relating to, or occurring at the place where a sale is made. **point-of-sale terminal** *n* an electronic terminal used at retail outlets (eg supermarket checkouts) which records, and processes *esp* for stock-control purposes, sales-transaction information (*abbrev* **POS** or **POST**). **point of the compass** see *n* above. **point of view** *n* the position from which one looks at anything, literally or figuratively. **point set** *n* (*maths*) an aggregate. **points'man** *n* someone on point duty; someone in charge of rail points. **point source** *n* a source of radiation that is, or is considered as, a mathematical point. **point'-to-point'** *adj* from one fixed point to another; across country. ◆ *n* a cross-country race, a steeplechase. **point-to-poin'ter** *n* a horse ridden in a point-to-point. **poin'ty-head'ed** *adj* (*N Am inf*) intellectual; intelligent.

■ **at a point**, **at point** or **points** or **at all points** (*Shakesp*, etc) in readiness; resolved; completely; in all respects. **at the point of** on the verge of. **cardinal point** see under **cardinal**. **carry one's point** to gain what one contends for. **dead point** see under **dead**. **from point to point** (*obs*) from one detail to another. **give points to** to give odds to; to give an advantageous hint on any subject. **in point** apposite. **in point of** in the matter of. **in point of fact** as a matter of fact. **make a point of** to treat as essential, make a special object of. **not to put too fine a point on it** to speak bluntly. **on the point of** close upon; very near. **point for point** exactly in all particulars. **point out** to point to, show, bring someone's attention to. **point up** to emphasize. **potatoes and point** a feigned Irish dish, potatoes alone, with a herring, etc, to point at. **put upon points** to ration by points. **score points off someone** to advance at the expense of another; to outwit, get the better of someone in an argument or repartee. **stand upon points** to be punctilious. **stretch** (or **strain**) **a point** to go further (*esp* in concession) than strict rule allows. **to point** (*Spenser*, *Shakesp*) to the smallest detail. **to the point** apposite. **up to a point** partly, not wholly.

point² /*point*/ *vt* to appoint, determine, fix. [Aphetic for **appoint**]

point-blank /*point'blangk'*/ *adj* aimed directly at the mark without allowing for the downward curve of the trajectory; permitting such an aim, ie at very close range; direct; straightforward; blunt. ◆ *adv* with point-blank aim; directly; bluntly; flat. ◆ *n* a point-blank shot or range; reach (of jurisdiction) (*Shakesp*). [Appar from **point** (noun) and *blank*, from Fr *blanc* white, referring to the white centre of the target]

point d'appui /*pwɛ̃ da-pwē'*/ (*Fr*) *n* a point of support, a prop or fulcrum.

point-device or **point-devise** /*point'di-vīs'*/ *n* (*obs*) the point of perfection, in the phrase *at point device*. ◆ *adj* (*archaic*) fastidiously exact, *esp* in dress. ◆ *adv* with exactitude; down to the smallest detail. [Literally to the point arranged, or arranged to the point, from OFr *devis* devised]

pointe /*pwɛ̃t*/ (*Fr*; *ballet*) *n* the extreme tip of the toe, or the position of standing on it.

pointel /*poin'tl*/ *n* a sharp instrument, *esp* a style; a pistil (*obs*). [OFr]

pointillism /*pwan'ti-li-zm*/ or **pointillisme** /*pwɛ̃-tē-yē'zm'*/ *n* (in painting) the use of separate dots of pure colour instead of mixed pigments. [Fr *pointillisme* from *pointille*, dimin of *point* point]

■ **pointillé** /*pwɛ̃-tē-yā*/ *adj* ornamented with a pattern of dots made by a pointed tool. **poin'tillist** or **pointilliste** /*-tē-yēst*/ *n* and *adj*.

poise¹ /*poiz*/ *n* self-confidence; graceful carriage or balance of body; dignity and assurance of manner; balance; equilibrium; weight (*obs*); a weight, eg of a clock (*obs*); bias; momentum (*Spenser*); impact (*Shakesp*); suspense. ◆ *vt* to balance; to hold so as to get some notion of the weight; to carry or hold in equilibrium; to ponder, weigh in the mind (*rare*); to weigh (*obs*); to weight, weigh down (*obs*); to make stable, ballast (*obs*); to counterbalance (*obs*). ◆ *vi* to hang in suspense; to hover; to be ready. [OFr *poiser* (Fr *peser*), from L *pēnsāre*, frequentative of *pendere* to weigh, and OFr *pois*, from L *pēnsum* weight]

■ **poised** *adj* having or showing poise or composure; balanced. **pois'er** *n*.

poise² /*pwäz*/ *n* a CGS unit of viscosity, equal to 0.1 pascal seconds. [JLM *Poise*uille (1799–1869), French physician]

poisha see **paisa**.

poison /*poi'zn*/ *n* any substance which, taken into or formed in the body, destroys life or impairs health; any malignant influence; a substance that inhibits the activity of a catalyst (*chem*); a material that absorbs neutrons and so interferes with the working of a nuclear reactor. ◆ *vt* to administer poison to; to injure or kill with poison; to put poison on or in; to taint; to mar; to embitter; to corrupt; to infect. ◆ *adj* poisonous. [OFr *puison* poison, from L *pōtiō*, *-ōnis* a draught, from *pōtāre* to drink; cf **potion**]

■ **poi'sonable** *adj*. **poi'soner** *n*. **poi'sonous** *adj* having the quality or effect of poison; noxious; malicious; offensive (*inf*). **poi'sonously** *adv*. **poi'sonousness** *n*.

❑ **poisoned chalice** *n* an apparent gift or benefit that is likely to cause great trouble to the recipient. **poi'son-fang** *n* one of two large tubular teeth in the upper jaw of venomous snakes, through which poison passes from glands at their roots when the animal bites. **poison gas** *n* any injurious gas used in warfare. **poi'son-gland** *n* a gland that secretes poison. **poison ivy**, **poison oak** or **poison sumac** or **sumach** *n* names for various N American sumacs with ulcerating juice. **poi'son-nut** *n* nux vomica. **poison pen** *n* a writer of malicious anonymous letters. **poison pill** *n* (*inf*) any of various actions, such as merger, takeover or recapitalization, taken by a company to prevent or deter a threatened takeover bid; a clause or clauses in a company's articles of association put into effect by an unwanted takeover bid, and making such a takeover less attractive.

■ **what's your poison?** (*inf*) what would you like to drink?

poisson /*pwa-sɔ̃'*/ (*Fr*) *n* a fish.

❑ **poisson d'avril** /*dav-rēl*/ *n* an April fool.

Poisson's distribution /*pwä-sɔ̃z dis-tri-bū'shən*/ or **Poisson distribution** /*pwä-sɔ̃'*/ (*stats*) *n* a distribution that, as a limiting form of binomial distribution, is characterized by a small probability of a specific event occurring during observations over a continuous interval (eg of time or distance). [S Denis *Poisson* (1781–1840), French mathematician]

Poisson's ratio /*pwä-sɔ̃z rä'shi-ō*/ (*phys*) *n* one of the elastic constants of a material, defined as the ratio of the lateral contraction per unit breadth to the longitudinal extension per unit length when a piece of material is stretched. [Ety as for **Poisson's distribution**]

poitrel /*poi'trəl*/ *n* armour for a horse's breast. [OFr *poitral*, from L *pectorāle* a breastplate, from *pectus*, *-oris* the breast]

pokal /*pō-käl'*/ *n* an ornamental drinking vessel. [Ger, from Ital *boccale*, from Gr *baukalis* a vessel for cooling wine, etc]

poke¹ /*pōk*/ *vt* to thrust or push the end of anything against or into; to prod or jab; to cause to protrude; to thrust forward or endways; to make, put, render, or achieve by thrusting or groping; to stir up, incite;

---

fāte; fär; mē; fûr; mīne; mōte; för; mūte; pŭt; dhen (then); *el'ə-mənt* (element) ◆ For other sounds see detailed chart of pronunciation

to dress with a poking-stick (*obs*); (of a man) to have sexual intercourse with (*sl*); to store data in a single specified memory location; to seclude or confine in a poky place (*inf*). ◆ *vi* to thrust, make thrusts; to protrude; to feel about, grope; to potter; to stoop; to pry about; to live a dull or secluded life. ◆ *n* an act of poking. [ME *pōken*; appar of LGer origin]

■ **pō'ker** *n* someone who pokes; a rod for poking or stirring a fire; an instrument for doing poker work; a stiff person; a mace or mace-bearer (*facetious*); a poking-stick. **po'ker** or **pō'kerish** *adj* like a poker; stiff. **pō'kerishly** *adv*. **pokey** *adj* and *n* see **poky** below. **pō'king** *adj* pottering; petty; confined; stuffy; shabby. **pō'ky** or **pō'key** *adj* poking, confined; slow, lacking energy or speed (*inf*); powerful (*inf*). ◆ *n* (*pl* **pō'kies** or **pō'keys**) (*N Am*) jail.

❑ **poker work** *n* work done by burning a design into wood with a heated point. **pō'king-stick** *n* a small rod formerly used for adjusting the pleats of ruffs.

■ **better than a poke in the eye (with a burnt** or **sharp stick)** (*inf*) an expression of pleasure, *esp* qualified (*Aust*); generally, referring to something only moderately desirable. **by the holy poker** a facetious oath of unknown meaning, perhaps belonging to **poker²**. **poke fun at** to make the object of ridicule, taunt. **poke one's head** to stoop, hold the head forward. **poke one's nose** to pry. **red-hot poker** Kniphofia or Tritoma.

poke² /pōk/ *n* (now chiefly *dialect*; also *Scot* **pock**) a bag; a pouch; a pokeful; a pocket. [ME *poke*; affinities uncertain]

■ **poke'ful** *n* as much as a poke will hold.

■ **a pig in a poke** a thing bought unseen, or a commitment made to something unknown or unknowable.

poke³ /pōk/ *n* a projecting brim or front of a bonnet; a poke bonnet. [Perh from **poke¹**, or from **poke²**]

■ **poked** *adj*.

❑ **poke bonnet** *n* a bonnet with a projecting front formerly worn by women.

poke⁴ /pōk/ *n* a name for various American species of *Phytolacca* (also **poke'weed** and **poke'berry**); American or white hellebore (**Indian poke**). [Of Algonquian origin]

poker¹ /pō'kər/ *n* a card game in which players bet on their hands and the winning player takes the pool of staked money, first played in America about 1835. [Ety uncertain; poss from German or French]

❑ **poker face** *n* an inscrutable face, useful to a poker-player; its possessor. **po'ker-faced** *adj*. **poker machine** see **pokie**.

poker² /pō'kər/ *n* a bugbear. [Cf Dan *pokker*, Swed *pocker*]

■ **pō'kerish** *adj* causing terror; uncanny.

■ **Old Poker** see **Old Harry** under **old**.

poker³ see **pochard**.

poker⁴, etc see under **poke¹**.

pokerish see under **poker²**.

pokeweed see **poke⁴**.

pokey see under **poke¹**.

pokie /pō'ki/ (*orig Aust*) *n* (in full **poker machine**) a type of fruit machine.

poking, **poky** see under **poke¹**.

POL (*milit*) *abbrev*: petrol, oil and lubricants.

pol /pol/ (*inf*) *n* a pol*itician* or political activist.

Polabian /pō-lā'bi-ən/ *n* a member of a former W Slavonic people occupying the basin of the lower Elbe; their extinct language. ◆ *adj* of or relating to the Polabians or their language. [Slav *po* beside, and *Labe* the Elbe]

polacca /po-lak'ə/ *n* a three-masted Mediterranean vessel, with fore- and mainmasts each in one piece (also **polacre** /po-lä'kər/); a polonaise, or composition in the manner of a polonaise. [Ital *polacca*, *polacra* Polish (fem); Fr *polacre*: application to the vessel not explained]

Polack /pō'lak/ (*sl*; *usu derog*) *n* a Pole. ◆ *adj* Polish. [Pol *Polak*; Ger *Polack*]

Poland /pō'lənd/ *adj* of Poland in central Europe, Polish.

■ **Po'lander** *n* (*obs*) a Pole.

polar /pō'lər/ *adj* of, or relating to, a pole (see **pole¹**) or poles; belonging to the neighbourhood of a pole; referred to a pole; of the nature of, or analogous to, a pole; axial; having polarity; directly opposed; having a dipole (*chem*). ◆ *n* (*geom*) the locus of the harmonic conjugate of a fixed point or pole with respect to the points in which a transversal through it cuts a circle or other conic. [L *polāris*, from *polus*; see **pole¹**]

■ **polarim'eter** *n* an instrument for measuring the rotation of the plane of polarization of light, or the amount of polarization of light. **polarimetric** /pō-lə-ri-met'rik/ *adj*. **polarimetry** /pō-lə-rim'i-tri/ *n*. **Polaris** /pō-lä'ris/ *n* the Pole Star; a submarine-launched ballistic missile. **polariscope** /pō-lar'i-skōp/ *n* an instrument for showing

phenomena of polarized light. **polarity** /pō-lar'i-ti/ *n* the state of having two opposite poles; the condition of having properties different or opposite in opposite directions or at opposite ends; the tendency to develop differently in different directions along an axis, as a plant towards base and apex, some animals towards head and tail; particular relation to this or that pole or opposed property rather than the other; directedness (*fig*). **polarization** or **-s-** /pō-lə-rī-zā'shən/ *n* an act of polarizing; the state of being polarized; development of poles; loosely, polarity; the effect of deposition of products of electrolysis upon electrodes, resulting in an opposing electromotive force; the separation of the positive and negative charges of a molecule by an external agent (*chem*); the restriction (according to the wave theory) of the vibrations of light to one plane; opposedness or doubleness of aspect or tendency. **polarize** or **-ise** /pō'lə-rīz/ *vt* to subject to polarization; to give polarity to; to develop new qualities or meanings in (*fig*); to split into opposing camps (also *vi*). ◆ *vi* to acquire polarity. **po'larized** or **-s-** *adj*. **po'larizer** or **-s-** *n* a device for polarizing light. **polarograph'ic** *adj*. **polarog'raphy** *n* a technique for determining the concentration and nature of the ions in a solution by an electrolytic process in which the current through the cell is measured as a function of the applied voltage. **Po'laroid**® *adj* a trademark applied to photographic equipment, light-polarizing materials, etc. ◆ *n* a photograph taken using a Polaroid camera. **po'laron** *n* (*electronics*) a free electron trapped by polarization charges on surrounding molecules.

❑ **polar axis** *n* (*astron*) that diameter of a sphere which passes through the poles; in an equatorial telescope, the axis, parallel to the earth's axis, about which the whole instrument revolves in order to keep a celestial object in the field. **polar bear** *n* a large white bear found in the Arctic regions. **polar body** *n* (*biol*) one of two small cells detached from the ovum during the maturation divisions. **polar cap** *n* a polar icecap. **polar circle** *n* the Arctic or the Antarctic Circle. **polar co-ordinates** *n pl* (*maths*) co-ordinates defining a point by means of a radius vector and the angle which it makes with a fixed line through the origin. **polar distance** *n* angular distance from the pole. **polar equation** *n* (*maths*) an equation in terms of polar co-ordinates. **polar forces** *n pl* forces that act in pairs and in different directions, as in magnetism. **polarity therapy** *n* a system of treatment aimed at balancing the elements of the life-force within the body and improving its flow. **polarizing filter** *n* a filter that allows the passage of light which is polarized in one direction only, used in photography to reduce surface reflections. **polarized light microscopy** *n* the method of examining thin, transparent materials, *esp* from rock, using polarized light to reveal birefringence. **polar lights** *n pl* the aurora borealis or australis. **polar star** *n* a star near a pole of the heavens, *esp* Polaris. **polar wandering** *n* movement of the magnetic poles and of the poles of the earth's rotation through geological time.

polder /pōl'dər/ *n* a piece of low-lying reclaimed land; the first stage in its reclamation. ◆ *vt* to reclaim (land). [Du]

Pole /pōl/ *n* a native or citizen of *Poland*; a Polish-speaking inhabitant of Poland.

pole¹ /pōl/ *n* the end of an axis, *esp* of the earth, the celestial sphere, or any rotating sphere; either of the two points on a great or small circle on a sphere, in which its axis cuts the surface of the sphere; the point on a crystal face where the normal from the origin cuts the sphere of projection; the end of an elongated body; a differentiated end; either of the two points of a body in which the attractive or repulsive energy is concentrated, as in a magnet; an electric terminal or electrode; one end of the mitotic spindle, where the spindle fibres come together; a fixed point (*geom*); a point from which a pencil of rays radiates; a fixed point defining a polar; an opposite extreme (*fig*); the heavens (*poetic*, after Greek use). [L *polus*, from Gr *polos* pivot, axis, firmament]

❑ **pole piece** *n* an iron mass that concentrates and directs magnetic energy. **Pole Star** *n* Polaris, a star near the N pole of the heavens; a guide or director.

■ **poles apart** or **asunder** widely separated, very different.

pole² /pōl/ *n* a long rounded shaft, rod, or post, *usu* of wood; a small tree; a single shaft to which a pair of horses may be yoked; a measuring rod of definite length; hence a measure of length, $5\frac{1}{2}$ yards, of area, $30\frac{1}{4}$ square yards; the position next to the inner boundary-fence in a racecourse or on a racing circuit, etc (now *usu* **pole position**); the tail of certain animals. ◆ *vt* to propel, push, strike, or stir with a pole; to provide or support with poles. ◆ *vi* to use a pole. [OE *pāl* (Ger *Pfahl*), from L *pālus* a stake]

■ **pō'ler** *n* (*Aust*) one of a pair of bullocks harnessed to the pole; a shirker. **pō'ling** *n* supplying, propelling, or stirring with a pole or poles; the practice of burning green logs (poles) to produce reducing gases in the fire refining of copper; poles collectively.

❑ **pole'-clipt** *adj* (*Shakesp*) hedged in with poles. **pole dancer** *n* an erotic dancer performing on and around a fixed vertical pole. **pole dancing** *n*. **pole position** *n* the most advantageous position in any competition or race, etc (see also above). **pole vault** *n* an athletic event in which the competitor uses a pole to achieve great height in jumping over a crossbar. **pole'-vault** vi. **pole'-vaulter** n.

■ **pole on** (Aust sl) to impose on. **under bare poles** with all sails furled. **up the pole** (sl) in a predicament; drunk; crazed; pregnant; in favour (milit).

poleaxe or **poleax** /pōl'aks/ n a battle-axe, orig short-handled; a long-handled axe or halbert; a sailor's short-handled axe for cutting away rigging; a butcher's axe with a hammer-faced back. ◆ vt to strike or fell with or as if with a poleaxe (also fig). [Orig pollax, from **poll**[1] head, and **axe**, confused with **pole**[2]]

polecat /pōl'kat/ n a large relative of the weasel, which emits a stink, also called **fitchet** and **foumart** (Mustela putorius); a prostitute (Shakesp); a skunk (US). [ME polcat; poss Fr poule hen, and **cat**[1]]
□ **pole'cat-ferret** n the hybrid offspring of the ferret and polecat.

Pol Econ abbrev : Political Economy.

polemarch /pol'i-märk/ n a title of several officials in ancient Greek states, orig a military commander. [Gr polemarchos, from polemos war, and archē rule]

polemic /po-lem'ik/ adj given to disputing; controversial. ◆n a controversialist; a controversy; a hostile controversial writing or argument. [Gr polemikos, from polemos war]
■ **polem'ical** adj. **polem'ically** adv. **polem'icist** or **pol'emist** n someone who writes polemics or engages in controversy. **polem'ics** n sing the practice or art of controversy and debate. **pol'emize** or **-ise** vt.

polemonium /pol-i-mō'ni-əm/ n a plant of the Jacob's ladder genus Polemonium, giving name to the **Polemonia'ceae**, the phlox family. [Gr polemōnion St John's wort, or other plant]
■ **polemoniā'ceous** adj.

polenta /po-len'tə/ n an Italian dish of boiled cornmeal, usu grilled or fried and served with a rich sauce. [Ital, from L polenta peeled barley]

poley /pō'li/ (Aust) adj (of cattle) hornless (also n). [**poll**[1]]

poleyn /pō'lān/ n a piece of armour protecting the knee. [ME, from OFr polain]

polianite /pō'li-ə-nīt/ n a steel-grey mineral, manganese dioxide. [Gr poliainesthai to grow grey, from polios hoary]

Polianthes /pol-i-an'thēz/ n the tuberose genus of the amaryllid family. [Gr polios hoary, and anthos a flower]

police /pə-lēs'/ n a body of men and women employed to maintain order, etc; its members collectively; the system of regulations for the preservation of order and enforcement of law (archaic); the internal government of a state (archaic). ◆ adj of the police. ◆ vt to control as police; to provide with police; to guard or to put or keep in order. [Fr, from L polītīa, from Gr polīteiā, from polītēs a citizen, from polis a city]
□ **police burgh** see under **burgh**. **police constable** n a policeman or policewoman of ordinary rank. **police'-court** n a former name for a borough court. **police dog** n a dog trained to help the police. **police force** n a country's full complement of police; the body of police responsible for any individual area. **police inspector** n a superior officer of police who has charge of a department, next in rank to a superintendent. **police'-judge** or **police'-mag'istrate** n a judge or magistrate who formerly presided in a police-court. **police'man** n a man who is a member of a police force. **police'-manure** n (Scot) street sweepings used as manure. **Police Motu** n a former name for the Motu language. **police office** or **police station** n the headquarters of the police of a district, used also as a temporary place of confinement. **police officer** n a member of a police force, esp a constable. **police procedural** n a crime novel, film, etc which focuses on the procedures used by the police in their investigations into a crime. **police state** n a country in which secret police are employed to detect and stamp out any opposition to the government in power. **police trap** n a strategic means whereby the police keep motor traffic under scrutiny and detect offenders against the law; a concealed and concerted timing arrangement to enforce a speed limit. **police'woman** n a woman who is a member of a police force.

policy[1] /pol'i-si/ n a course of action, esp one based on some declared or respected principle; a system of administration guided more by interest than by principle; the art of government; statecraft; dexterity of management; a constitution (obs); prudence; cunning; in Scotland (sometimes in pl), the pleasure-grounds around a mansion. [OFr policie (Fr police), from L polītīa, from Gr polīteiā (see **police**); in Scot perh influenced by L polītus embellished]

policy[2] /pol'i-si/ n a document containing a contract of insurance; a kind of gambling by betting on the numbers to be drawn in a lottery (US). [Fr police policy, appar from LL apodissa a receipt, from Gr apodeixis proof]
□ **pol'icyholder** n a person who holds a contract of insurance. **pol'icy-shop** n a place where the game of policy is played.

polio /pō'li-ō/ n (pl **po'lios**) short form of **poliomyelitis**; a person who has or has had polio, esp someone paralysed by it (rare).
□ **pō'liovirus** n any of several enteroviruses causing poliomyelitis.

poliomyelitis /pōl-i-ō-mī-ə-lī'tis or pol-/ (med) n a viral infection, one form of which attacks the muscle-controlling nerves of the brain and spinal cord and causes paralysis, formerly called infantile paralysis. [Gr polios grey, and myelos marrow, and **-itis**]

poliorcetic /pol-i-ar-set'ik/ adj of or relating to the beleaguerment of towns or fortresses. [Gr poliorkētikos, from poliorkein to besiege, from polis city, and erkos an enclosure]
■ **poliorcet'ics** n sing siegecraft.

polis[1] /pol'is/ n an ancient Greek city state; a political system based on city states. [Gr, city]

polis[2] /pō'lis/ (Scot and Irish) n the police; a police officer. [Altered from **police**]

Polish /pō'lish/ adj of or relating to the Republic of Poland in NE Europe, its people, or its language. ◆ n the Slavonic language of the Poles.
□ **Polish notation** n a system of notation, orig developed in Poland, used in symbolic logic, in which parentheses are not necessary.

polish /pol'ish/ vt to make smooth and glossy by rubbing; to bring to a finished state; to impart culture and refinement to. ◆ vi to take a polish. ◆ n an act of polishing; gloss; refinement of manners; a substance applied to produce a polish. [OFr polir, polissant, from L polīre to polish]
■ **pol'ishable** adj. **pol'ished** adj cultured, refined; accomplished; (of rice) with the husk removed. **pol'isher** n. **pol'ishings** n pl particles removed by polishing. **pol'ishment** n.
□ **pol'ishing-paste** n. **pol'ishing-powder** n. **pol'ishing-slate** n a diatomaceous slaty stone used for polishing glass, marble, and metals.
■ **polish off** (inf) to finish off; to dispose of finally. **polish up** or **polish up on** to work at or study in order to improve.

Politburo or **Politbureau** /po-lit'bū-rō or pol'-/ n in the former Communist countries, the policy-making committee, effectively the most powerful organ of the Communist Party's executive (in the Soviet Union from 1952 to 1966, the name then being replaced by Presidium). [Russ politicheskoe political, and byuro bureau]

polite /pə- or po-līt'/ adj refined; cultivated; having courteous manners; glossy, polished (obs). [L polītus, pap of polīre to polish]
■ **polite'ly** adv. **polite'ness** n. **politesse** /pol-ē-tes'/ n (Fr) formal or superficial politeness.
□ **polite literature** n belles-lettres, ie poetry, essays, standard novels, etc, as distinguished from scientific treatises and the like.

politic /pol'i-tik/ adj in accordance with good policy; acting or proceeding from motives of policy; prudent; discreet; astutely contriving or intriguing; political (rare); constitutional (obs). [Gr polītikos, from polītēs a citizen]
■ **polit'ical** adj relating to policy or government; relating to parties differing in their views of government; interested or involved in politics; politic (obs). **polit'ically** adv. **politicas'ter** n (Milton; see also **-aster**) a petty politician. **politician** /-tish'ən/ n someone versed in the science of government; someone engaged in political life or statesmanship; someone interested in party politics; a politic person; someone who makes a profession or a game of politics; an intriguer (US; obs). ◆ adj (Milton) politic. **politicīzā'tion** or **-s-** n. **polit'icize** or **-ise** /-i-sīz/ vt to make political. ◆ vi to play the politician; to discuss politics. **pol'itick** vi. **pol'iticker** n. **pol'iticking** n engaging in political activity, such as seeking votes. **pol'iticly** adv. **pol'itics** n (sing) the art or science of government; (as sing) the management of a political party; (as sing or pl) political affairs or opinions; (as pl) manoeuvring and intriguing; (as pl) policy-making, as opposed to administration; (as pl) the civil rather than the military aspects of government. **politique** /pol-ē-tēk/ n (Fr) in French history, one of a moderate party between Huguenots and Catholics; a religious indifferentist; a temporizer.
□ **political animal** n in the original Aristotelian sense, a social animal, one which lives in communities; someone who is enthusiastic about or involved in politics; someone who enjoys politicking. **political correctness** n the avoidance of expressions or actions that may be understood to exclude or denigrate groups or minorities traditionally perceived as disadvantaged by eg race, sex, disability, class, political alignment or sexual inclination; the use of recommended alternative expressions intended to be non-discriminatory (abbrev **PC**). **political economy** n the science of the production, distribution, and consumption of wealth. **political geography** n that part of geography which deals with the division of the earth for purposes of government, eg states, colonies, counties, and the work of man, such as towns, canals, etc. **political prisoner** n someone imprisoned for his or her political beliefs, activities, etc. **political science** n the science or study of government, its principles, aims, methods, etc. **political status** n the status of a political prisoner. **political verse** n Byzantine and modern Greek accentual verse, esp iambic verse of fifteen syllables.

politico /pə-lit'i-kō/ (inf) n (pl **polit'icos** or **polit'icoes**) (usu derog) a politician, or a person who is interested in politics. [Ital or Sp]

politico- /pə-lit-i-kō-/ *combining form* used to form nouns or adjectives, denoting politics or political, as in *politico-economic*, *politico-industrial*. [Gr *polītikos*, from *polītēs* a citizen]
■ **polit'ico-econom'ic** *adj* of the science of political economy; of politics and economics.

politique see under **politic**.

polity /pol'i-ti/ *n* political organization; form of political organization, constitution; a body of people organized under a system of government. [Gr *polīteiā*]

polje /pol'yə/ *n* (*geol*) a large depression found in some limestone areas, due in part to subsidence following underground solution. [Serbo-Croat]

polka /pōl'kə *or* pol'kə/ *n* a Bohemian dance or a tune for it, in 2–4 time with accent on the third quaver, invented about 1830; applied to various things fashionable at the same time, *esp* a woman's jacket. ◆ *vi* (**pol'kaing**; **pol'kaed**) to dance a polka (also **polk**). [Perh Czech *půlka* half step; or from Pol *polka* a Polish woman]
❑ **polka dot** *n* any of a number of large dots in a pattern on fabric, etc. **pol'ka-dot'** *or* **pol'ka-dott'ed** *adj*.

Poll *or* **poll** /pol/ *n* a parrot. [*Poll*, a common name for a parrot; cf **Polly**]
❑ **poll'-parrot** *n*. ◆ *vt* and *vi* to parrot.

poll[1] /pōl/ *n* a register, *esp* of voters; (often *pl*) a voting; an aggregate of votes; the taking of a vote; a taking of public opinion by means of questioning (also **opinion poll**); the head; the hair of the head; the head and shoulders of a ling, a type of cod (*obs*); the blunt end of the head of a hammer, miner's pick, etc; a head as a unit in numbering, an individual; a number of individuals (*Shakesp*); a polled animal. ◆ *adj* polled; cut evenly (see also **deed poll** under **deed**[1]). ◆ *vt* to receive or take the votes of; to receive, take, or cast (a vote); to receive (a stated number of votes); to question (someone) in a poll; to subject to polling (*comput*); to cut the hair, horns, top (of a tree), or edge (of a deed) from; to tax excessively, practise extortion upon (*archaic*). ◆ *vi* to vote; to practise extortion (*archaic*). [Cf obs Du and LGer *polle* top of the head]
■ **polled** *adj* shorn; pollarded; deprived of horns; hornless. **poll'er** *n*. **poll'ing** *n* the action of the verb; a technique by which each of several terminals connected to the same central computer is periodically interrogated in turn by the computer to determine whether it has a message to transmit (*comput*). **poll'ster** *n* someone who carries out, or who puts his or her faith in, a public opinion poll.
❑ **poll'-axe** *n* a poleaxe. **polling booth** *n* the place, *esp* the partially enclosed cubicle, where a voter records his or her vote. **polling station** *n* the building where voters go to vote. **poll'-money** *or* **poll'-tax** *n* a tax of so much a head, ie on each person alike. **poll tax** *n* a tax levied equally on all adult members of a society, regardless of income; the community charge (*inf*).
■ **at the head of the poll** having the greatest number of votes at an election.

poll[2] /pol/ (*old Cambridge University sl*) *n* the body of students who did not seek or obtain honours; a pass degree. [Said to be from Gr *hoi polloi* the many]
❑ **poll'-degree'** *n*. **poll'man** *n*.

pollack, also **pollock** /pol'ək/ *n* a common fish of the cod family, with a long narrow jaw and no barbel; extended to the coalfish (*US*). [Ety obscure; connection with Gaelic *pollag* doubtful]

pollan /pol'ən/ *n* an Irish whitefish, *esp* that (*Coregonus pollan*) found in Lough Neagh, Northern Ireland. [Perh Ir *poll* lake; cf **powan**]

pollard /pol'ərd/ *n* a tree having the whole crown cut off, leaving it to send out new branches from the top of the stem; a hornless animal of horned kind; fine bran; flour or meal containing it; a base foreign coin bearing a head (*obs*). ◆ *adj* pollarded; awnless; bald. ◆ *vt* to make a pollard of. [**poll**[1]]

pollaxe same as **poleaxe**.

pollen /pol'ən/ *n* the fertilizing powder formed in the anthers of flowers. ◆ *vt* to cover or fertilize with pollen. [L *pollen*, *-inis* fine flour]
■ **polleno'sis** *n* hay fever. **poll'inate** *vt* to convey pollen to. **pollina'tion** *n*. **poll'inator** *n*. **pollin'ic** *adj* of or relating to pollen. **pollinif'erous** *adj* bearing or producing pollen. **pollin'ium** *n* (*pl* **pollin'ia**) an agglutinated mass of pollen grains.
❑ **pollen analysis** *n* use of pollen grains in peat bogs, etc, as a means of determining past vegetation and climates or the age of fossil remains. **pollen basket** *n* a hollow in a bee's hindleg in which pollen is carried. **pollen count** *n* the amount of pollen in the atmosphere, estimated from deposits on slides exposed to the air. **pollen grain** *n* a grain of pollen, the microspore in flowering plants. **pollen sac** *n* a cavity in an anther in which pollen is formed, the microsporangium of flowering plants. **pollen tube** *n* an outgrowth from a pollen grain by which the gametes are conveyed to the ovule.

pollent /pol'ənt/ *adj* strong. [L *pollēns*, *-entis*, prp of *pollēre* to be strong]

pollex /pol'eks/ *n* (*pl* **pollices** /pol'i-sēz/) the thumb, or its analogue in animals. [L *pollex*, *-icis*]
■ **poll'ical** *adj*.

pollice verso /pol'i-sē vûr'sō, pol'i-ke ver'sō *or* wer'sō/ (*L*) with the thumb turned up or outwards (now often assumed, *prob* wrongly, to mean downwards), the signal made by the spectators for the death of a Roman gladiator.

pollicie *or* **pollicy** (*Spenser*) same as **policy**[1].

pollicitation /pol-is-i-tā'shən/ *n* a promise; a promise which has not yet been accepted. [L *pollicitātiō*, *-ōnis*]

pollination, etc, **pollinic**, etc see under **pollen**.

polliwig, **polliwog** see **pollywog**.

pollman see under **poll**[2].

pollock same as **pollack**.

pollster, **poll tax**, etc see under **poll**[1].

pollusion /po-loo'zhən, -lū'/ (*Shakesp*) *n* Goodman Dull's blunder for **allusion** in *Love's Labours Lost* IV.2.44.

pollute /po-loot' *or* -lūt'/ *vt* to make dirty physically; to contaminate, make (any feature of the environment) offensive or harmful to human, animal, or plant life; to make unclean morally; to defile ceremonially, profane. ◆ *adj* defiled. [L *polluere*, *pollūtus*, from *pol-*, a form of *prō* or *per*, and *luere* to wash]
■ **pollu'tant** *n* and *adj* (a substance) causing pollution. **pollu'ted** *adj*. **pollu'tedly** *adv*. **pollu'tedness** *n*. **pollu'ter** *n*. **pollution** /po-loo'shən *or* -lū'/ *n*. **pollu'tive** *adj* causing pollution.

Pollux /pol'əks/ *n* the twin brother of Castor (*myth*); a star in the constellation of the Twins. [L for Gr *Polydeukēs*]

Polly /pol'i/ (*inf*) *n* a parrot. [From the personal name, a form of *Molly*; cf **Poll**]

polly /pol'i/ (*old inf*) *n* Apollinaris water (qv).

pollyanna /pol-i-an'ə/ (also with *cap*) *n* someone whose naive optimism may verge on the insufferable. [From *Pollyanna*, fictional creation of US author Eleanor Hodgman Porter (1868–1920)]
■ **pollyann'aish** *or* **pollyann'ish** *adj*. **pollyann'aism** *n* a pollyannaish observation.

pollywog *or* **polliwog** /pol'i-wog/ *or* **pollywig** *or* **polliwig** /-wig/ *n* a tadpole (also **porwigg'le**). [ME *pollwyggle*, from **poll**[1] and **wiggle**]

polo[1] /pō'lō/ *n* (*pl* **pō'los**) a game like hockey played on horseback using long-handled mallets (**polo sticks**) and a ball, of Oriental origin; a similar aquatic (**water polo**), bicycle (**bicycle polo**), or skating (**rink polo**) game; a jersey with a polo neck. [Balti (Tibetan dialect in Kashmir) *polo* polo ball; Tibetan *pulu*]
■ **po'loist** *n*.
❑ **polo neck** *n* a pullover collar fitting the neck closely and doubling over, as *orig* in the jersey worn by polo-players; a jersey with such a collar. **polo shirt** *n* a short-sleeved open-necked casual shirt, typically of a knitted cotton fabric, sometimes extended to a similar long-sleeved shirt.

polo[2] /pō'lō/ *n* (*pl* **pō'los**) a Spanish gypsy dance. [Sp, an Andalusian popular song]

poloidal /po-loi'dəl/ *adj* of eg a magnetic field, generated by an electric current flowing in a ring. [*pol*ar and tor*oidal*]

polonaise /pol-ə-nāz'/ *n* a Polish national dance or promenade of slow movement in 3–4 time; a musical form in the same rhythm; a woman's bodice and skirt in one piece, showing an underskirt; a similar child's garment once worn in Scotland. [Fr, Polish (fem)]

Polonia /po-lō'ni-ə/ *n* the medieval Latin name for Poland.
■ **Polo'nian** *adj* and *n*. **po'lonism** *n* a Polish idiom or characteristic. **polonium** /pol-ō'ni-əm/ *n* a radioactive element (symbol **Po**; atomic no 84) discovered by Polish-born physicist Marie Curie. **Polonization** *or* **-s-** /pō-lən-ī-zā'shən/ *n*. **po'lonize** *or* **-ise** *vt* and *vi* to make or become Polish. **polo'ny** *or* **polo'nie** *n* (*Scot*) a child's polonaise.

polony[1] /po-lō'ni/ *n* a dry sausage of partly cooked meat. [Prob *Bologna*, in Italy; perh *Polonia*]

polony[2] see under **Polonia**.

polt /pōlt/ *n* a hard blow (now *dialect*); a club (*obs*). ◆ *vt* (*dialect*) to beat. [Origin obscure]
❑ **polt'foot** *n* a club foot. ◆ *adj* club-footed. **polt'-footed** *adj*.

poltergeist /pōl' *or* pol'tər-gīst/ *n* a mysterious invisible force asserted to throw or move things about; a noisy ghost. [Ger *poltern* to make a racket, and *Geist* ghost]

poltroon (*Shakesp* **poultroone**) /pol-troon'/ *n* a despicable coward (also *adj*). [Fr *poltron*, from Ital *poltrone*, from *poltro* lazy]
■ **poltroon'ery** *n* lack of spirit.

■ words derived from main entry word; ❑ compound words; ■ idioms and phrasal verbs

poluphloisboiotatotic, **poluphloisboiotic** see **polyphloisbic** under **poly-**.

polverine /pol'və-rēn/ (obs) n glass-makers' potash. [Ital polverino, from L pulvis, pulveris dust]

poly /pol'i/ (inf) n (pl **pol'ys**) a polytechnic; polythene (also adj); a polyphonic ringtone.

poly- /pol-i-/ combining form denoting: many; several; much; a polymer, such as polyethylene (see below); affecting more than one part (med). [Gr polys, poleia, poly much]

■ **polyacid** /-as'id/ adj having several replaceable hydrogen atoms; capable of replacing several hydrogen atoms of an acid. **polyacrylamide** /-ə-kril'ə-mīd/ n the highly cross-linked polymer of acrylamide (**polyacrylamide gel electrophoresis** a technique for separating nucleic acids or proteins on the basis of charge, shape and/or size (abbrev **PAGE**)). **pol'yact**, **polyactī'nal** (or /-akt'in-əl/) or **polyact'ine** adj (Gr aktīs, -īnos ray) (of a marine animal) having many rays or tentacles. **Polyadel'phia** n pl (Gr adelphos brother) in Linnaeus's system, a class of plants with three or more bundles of stamens. **polyadel'phous** adj (of stamens) united in several bundles; having the stamens so united. **polyam'ide** n a polymeric amide, such as nylon. **polyam'ory** n the practice of having more than one sexual and emotional relationship at a time, with the full consent of all partners. **polyam'orous** adj. **Polyan'dria** n pl (Gr anēr, andros man, male) in Linnaeus's system, a class of plants with many stamens inserted in the receptacle. **polyan'drous** adj having or allowing several husbands or male mates (at a time); having a large and indefinite number of stamens or of antheridia (bot). **pol'yandry** (or /-an'/) n the condition or practice of being polyandrous; the social usage of some peoples in which a woman normally has several husbands. **polyan'iline** n a polymer of aniline that is an electrical conductor. **polyan'thus** n (pl **polyan'thuses**) (Gr anthos flower) a many-flowered supposed hybrid between cowslip and primrose; also applied to certain hybrid roses. **pol'yarch** /-ärk/ adj (Gr archē origin) having many xylem strands. **pol'yarchy** /-ärk-i/ n (Gr archein to rule) government by many persons. **polyatom'ic** adj (chem) having many atoms, or replaceable atoms or groups; multivalent. **polyax'ial** (L axis) or **polyax'on** adj (Gr axōn axis) having many axes or several axis cylinders. ◆ n a monaxonic sponge spicule. **polyaxon'ic** adj. **polybās'ic** adj capable of reacting with several equivalents of an acid; (of acids) having several replaceable hydrogen atoms. **polycar'bonate** n any of a range of strong thermoplastics. **polycarp'ic** adj (Gr karpos fruit) fruiting many times, or year after year. **polycarp'ous** adj polycarpic; having an apocarpous gynaeceum. **pol'ycarpy** n. **polycent'ric** adj multicentric. **Polychaeta** /-kē'tə/ n pl (Gr chaitē bristle) a class of marine chaetopods with numerous bristles. **pol'ychaete** /-kēt/ n any worm of the Polychaeta. **polychlor'inated** adj (**polychlorinated biphenyl** see **PCB**). **polychlor'oprene** n neoprene. **pol'ychrest** /-krest/ n (Gr polychrēstos from chrēstos useful) a thing, esp a medicine, useful in several ways. **polychroic** /-krō'ik/ adj pleochroic. **pol'ychroism** n. **polychromat'ic** adj polychrome; (of electromagnetic radiation) composed of several different wavelengths. **polychrom'ic** adj. **pol'ychrome** /-krōm/ adj (Gr chrōma colour) many-coloured. ◆ n a work of art (esp a statue) in several colours; varied colouring. **pol'ychromy** n the art of decorating in many colours. **pol'yclinic** n a general clinic or hospital. **polyclō'nal** adj of or involving many clones. **polycon'ic** adj relating to or composed of many cones. **pol'ycotton** adj and n (of) a fabric made from polyester and cotton. **polycotylē'don** n (bot) a plant with more than two cotyledons. **polycotylē'donous** adj. **polycrot'ic** adj (Gr krotos a beat) (of the pulse) having several beats to each heartbeat. **polyc'rotism** n. **pol'ycrystal** n an object composed of several or many variously orientated crystals. **polycrys'talline** adj. **pol'yculture** n the simultaneous production of several different crops and types of livestock in one region. **polycyclic** /-sī'klik/ adj (Gr kyklos wheel) having many circles, rings, whorls, turns, or circuits; containing more than one ring of atoms in the molecule. **polycyst'ic** adj containing many cysts. **polycythaemia** /-sī-thē'mi-ə/ n (-**cyte** cell, and Gr haima blood) an excess of red blood corpuscles. **polydac'tyl** adj having more than the normal number of fingers or toes (also n). **polydac'tylism** or **polydac'tyly** n. **polydac'tylous** adj. **polydē'monism** or **polydae'monism** n the belief in and worship of numerous supernatural powers. **polydip'sia** n (Gr dipsa thirst) excessive thirst. **polyelec'trolyte** n a polymer containing many electrolytic ions. **polyem'bryonate** adj. **polyembryonic** /-on'ik/ adj. **polyembryony** /-em'bri-ən-i/ n formation of more than one embryo from one ovule or from one fertilized ovum. **polyene** /pol'i-ēn/ n a hydrocarbon with many carbon-carbon double bonds. **polyes'ter** n any of a range of polymerized esters, some thermoplastic, some thermosetting, used in textiles. **polyeth'ylene** n see **polythene** below (**polyethylene glycol** a hydrophilic hydrocarbon that interacts with the membranes of cells and is used in lubricants and emulsifiers). **polygala** /pol-ig'ə-lə/ n (Gr polygalon milkwort, gala milk) any plant of the milkwort genus Polygala, giving name to the family

Polygala'ceae. **polygalaceous** /-lā'shəs/ adj. **pol'ygam** n (Gr gamos marriage) in Linnaeus's classification, a plant of the class **Polygā'mia**, having male, female, and hermaphrodite flowers. **polygamic** /-gam'ik/ adj. **polygamist** /pol-ig'/ n. **polyg'amous** adj. **polyg'amously** adv. **polygamy** /pol-ig'ə-mi/ n the rule, custom, or condition of marriage to more than one person at a time, or (now rarely) in life; sometimes used for polygyny; mating with more than one in the same breeding season (zool); occurrence of male, female, and hermaphrodite flowers on the same or on different plants (bot). **pol'ygene** /-jēn/ n any of a group of genes that control a single continuous character (eg height). **polygen'esis** n multiple origin, esp of mankind. **polygenet'ic** adj of polygenesis; springing from several sources; (of dyes) giving different colours with different mordants. **polygen'ic** adj polygenetic; forming more than one compound with a univalent element. **polyg'enism** n belief in multiple origin, esp of mankind. **polyg'enist** n. **polyg'enous** adj of multiple origin or composition. **polyg'eny** n polygenesis. **pol'yglot**, also **pol'yglott** adj (Gr polyglōttos, from glōtta tongue) able to speak many languages, multilingual; using or written in many languages. ◆ n a person who speaks many languages; a book written in many languages; a collection of versions in different languages of the same work, esp a Bible. **polyglott'al**, **polyglott'ic**, **polyglott'ous** adj. **pol'ygon** /-gon or -gən/ n (Gr polygōnon, from gōniā angle) a plane figure bounded by straight lines, esp more than four; an object in the form of a polygon, esp in the building of earthworks and fortifications. **polygona'ceous** adj. **polyg'onal** adj (**polygonal numbers** figurate numbers). **polyg'onally** adv. **polygon'atum** n (Gr polygonaton, from gony, -atos knee) the Solomon's seal genus Polygonatum, of the lily family. **polyg'onum** n (Gr polygonon) any plant of the knot-grass genus Polygonum, with swollen joints and sheathing stipules, of the dock family **Polygona'ceae**. **polyg'ony** n (Spenser) the plant bistort. **pol'ygraph** n an instrument which measures very small changes in body temperature, pulse rate, respiration, etc, and which is often used as a lie-detector; a copying, multiplying, or tracing apparatus; a copy. **polygraph'ic** adj. **polygraphy** /po-lig'rə-fi/ n voluminous writing; the use of the polygraph as a lie-detector. **Polygynia** /-jin'/ n pl (Gr gynē woman, female) in various Linnaean classes of plants, an order with more than twelve styles. **polygyn'ian** adj of the Polygynia. **polygynous** /-lij'/ or -lig'i-nəs/ adj having several wives; mating with several females; having several styles; polygynian. **polygyny** /-lij'/ or -lig'/ n the custom, practice, or condition of having a plurality of wives or styles; the habit of mating with more than one female. **polyhalite** /-hal'īt/ n (Gr hals salt) a triclinic mineral, sulphate of magnesium, potassium, and calcium. **polyhed'ral** adj. **polyhedric** /-hēd' or -hed'/ adj. **polyhēd'ron** (or /-hed'/) n (pl **polyhed'rons** or **polyhed'ra**) (Gr hedrā seat) a solid figure or body bounded by plane faces (esp more than six). **polyhis'tor** n (Gr polyistōr, from historeein to inquire, learn) a person of great and varied learning. **polyhistorian** /-tō'ri-ən or -tö'/ n. **polyhistoric** /-tor'ik/ adj. **polyhis'tory** /-tə-ri/ n. **polyhy'brid** n a cross between parents differing in several heritable characters. **polyhy'dric** adj having several hydroxyl groups, polyhydroxy. **polyhydrox'y** adj (chem) (of a compound) containing two or more hydroxyl groups per molecule. **polyhydroxybu'tyrate** n a natural polymer which can be used to manufacture fully biodegradable plastic (abbrev **PHB**). **Polyhymnia** /pol-i-him'ni-ə/ or **Polymnia** /pol-im'ni-ə/ n (Gr hymnos hymn, ode) the muse of the sublime lyric. **polyim'ide** n a polymer containing imide groups, used in heat-resistant materials. **polyi'soprene** n a rubber-like polymer of isoprene. **polylemm'a** n (Gr lēmma an assumption; logic) a form of argument in which the maintainer of a certain proposition is committed to accept one of several propositions all of which contradict his or her original contention. **polymas'tia**, **polymast'ism** or **pol'ymasty** n (Gr mastos breast) the presence of supernumerary breasts or nipples. **polymas'tic** adj. **pol'ymath** n (Gr polymathēs, from the root of manthanein to learn) a person whose knowledge covers a wide variety of subjects. **polymath'ic** adj. **polym'athy** n much and varied learning. **pol'ymer** n (Gr meros part; chem) any naturally occurring or synthetic substance built up from a series of smaller units (monomers), which may be simple or complex, esp one of those of higher molecular weight as produced by polymerization. **polymerase** /pol-im'ə-rās/ n any of several enzymes present in cell nuclei that promote the polymerization of DNA or RNA (**polymerase chain reaction** a powerful technique for amplifying DNA sequences without using genetic manipulation methods which need biological vectors (abbrev **PCR**)). **polymeric** /-mer'ik/ adj of, in a relation of, or manifesting polymerism. **polym'eride** n a polymer. **polym'erism** n. **polymerīzā'tion** or **-s-** n. **polym'erize** or **-ise** vt to combine to form a more complex molecule having the same empirical formula as the simpler ones combined; to cause to form a polymer; to make polymerous. ◆ vi to change into a polymer. **polym'erous** adj having many parts; having many parts in a whorl (bot). **polym'ery** n the condition of being polymerous. **Polymnia** n see **Polyhymnia** above. **polymethyl methacrylate** n the chemical name for any rigid glassy thermoplastic, such as Perspex, Lucite, etc. **pol'ymorph** n (Gr *polymorphos* many-formed, from *morphē* form) any one of several forms in which the same thing may occur; an organism occurring in several forms; a substance crystallizing in several systems. **polymorph'ic** *adj*. **polymorph'ism** *n*. **polymorphonū'clear** *adj* (of a leucocyte) having a nucleus divided into lobes and cytoplasm containing granules. **polymorph'ous** *adj*. **polymyositis** /-mī-ō-sī'tis/ *n* (see **myo-**) inflammation of several muscles at the same time. **polymyx'in** *n* an antibiotic derived from soil bacteria. **Polynē'sian** *adj* (Gr *nēsos* an island) of *Polynesia*, one of the three groups into which the Pacific islands are divided, its prevailing race of light-brown-skinned people, or their languages (a division of the Austronesian). ◆ *n* a native or inhabitant of Polynesia. **polyneuritis** /-nūr-ī'tis/ *n* simultaneous inflammation of several nerves. **polynō'mial** *adj* and *n* (*maths*) (an expression) consisting of a sum of terms each of which contains a constant and one or more variables raised to a power. **polynō'mialism** *n*. **polynucleotide** /pol-i-nū'kli-ə-tīd/ *n* a nucleic acid that is made up of a number of nucleotides. **polyō'ma** /-ō-/ *n* a small DNA virus which causes tumours in mice. **polyomino** /pol-i-om'in-ō/ *n* (*pl* **polyom'inos**) (on the false analogy of *domino*) a flat, many-sided shape made up of a number of identical squares placed edge to edge. **polyonym** /pol'i-ō-nim/ *n* (Gr *onyma* name) a name consisting of several words. **polyonym'ic** *adj* (of a name) of more than two words. **polyon'ymous** *adj* having many names. **polyon'ymy** *n* multiplicity of names for the same thing. **polypep'tide** *n* a peptide in which many amino acids are linked to form a chain. **polypet'alous** *adj* with free petals. **polyphagia** /-fā'ji-ə/ *n* (Gr *phagein* to eat) bulimia; the habit in animals, *esp* certain insects, of eating many different kinds of food. **polyphagous** /po-lif'ə-gəs/ *adj* (of an animal) eating many different kinds of food; given to eating excessive amounts of food, *esp* as the result of a pathological condition. **polyph'agy** /-ji/ *n* the character of being polyphagous. **polyphar'macy** *n* the (*esp* indiscriminate and excessive) use of many different drugs in treating a disease. **pol'yphase** *adj* having several alternating electric currents of equal frequency with uniformly spaced phase differences. **polyphasic** /-fāz'ik/ *adj* going through several phases of activity followed by rest in any twenty-four hours. **Polyphē'mian** or **Polyphē'mic** *adj*. **Polyphē'mus** *n* (*Gr myth*) the Cyclops blinded by Odysseus. **polyphē'nol** *n* a compound with two or more phenolic hydroxyl groups. **polyphiloprogenitive** /pol-i-fil-ō-prō-jen'i-tiv/ *adj* (of imagination or inventiveness) very fertile. **polyphloisbic** /pol-i-flois'bik/, **poluphloisboiotic** /pol-oo-flois-boi-ot'ik/ or **polyphloesboean** /pol-i-flēs-bē'ən/ *adj* (Gr *polyphloisbos*, from *phloisbos* din; the *oi* and *oe* from the genitive ending in Homer's phrase *polyphloisboio thalassēs* of the much-roaring sea) loud-roaring (also used by Thackeray in the quasi-superlative form **poluphloisboiotatot'ic**). **pol'yphon** /-fon/ or **pol'yphone** /-fōn/ *n* (Gr *phōnē* a voice) a lute-like musical instrument; a musical box playing tunes from perforated metal discs; (**pol'yphone**) a letter or symbol having more than one phonetic value, able to be pronounced or sounded in more than one way (*phonetics*). **polyphonic** /-fon'ik/ *adj* many-voiced; of polyphones; of polyphony. **pol'yphonist** *n* a contrapuntist. **polyph'ony** *n* composition of music in parts each with an independent melody of its own; the use of polyphones (*phonetics*). **polyphyletic** /-fī-let'ik/ or -fī-/ *adj* (Gr *phyletikos* relating to a tribesman, from *phylē* a tribe) of multiple origin; descended by convergent lines from several ancestral groups. **polyphyllous** /-fil'əs/ *adj* (Gr *phyllon* leaf; *bot*) having the perianth leaves free. **polyphy'odont** *adj* having more than two successive dentitions. **pol'ypill** *n* a pill containing several different types of medication. **Polyplacoph'ora** *n pl* (Gr *plax, plakos* a plate, slab) an order of molluscs, *incl* eg the chitons, bilaterally symmetrical, with a shell composed of eight transverse dorsal plates. **pol'yploid** *adj* (on the analogy of *haploid* and *diploid*) having more than twice the normal haploid number of chromosomes (also *n*). **pol'yploidy** *n* the polyploid condition. **pol'ypod** *n* an animal with many feet; a polypody. **Polypodium** /-pō'di-əm/ *n* (Gr *podion*, dimin of *pous* a foot) the typical genus of **Polypodiā'ceae**, the family with stalked sporangia and vertical annulus to which most ferns belong, so named from the many-footed appearance of the rhizome. **pol'ypody** *n* any fern of the genus *Polypodium*, *esp P. vulgare*. **Polyporus** /po-lip'ə-rəs/ *n* (Gr *poros* a pore) a large genus of pore fungi (qv under **pore¹**), often forming hoof-like and bracket-like growths on trees. **polyprop'ylene** *n* a polymer of propylene, similar in properties to polythene. **polyprō'todont** *n* (Gr *prōtos* first, and *odous, odontos* tooth) any member of the **Polyprotodont'ia**, the suborder of marsupials, including opossums, dasyures, etc, with many small incisors. **Polyp'terus** *n* (Gr *pteron* a fin) an African genus of Crossopterygian river fishes, with the dorsal fin represented by detached rays. **polyptych** /pol'ip-tik/ *n* (Gr *ptychos* a fold) a picture, altarpiece, etc, consisting of four or more panels hinged or folding together. **pol'yrhythm** *n* the simultaneous combination of different rhythms in a piece of music. **polyrhyth'mic** *adj*. **polysaccharide** /-sak'ə-rīd/ *n* a carbohydrate of a class including starch, etc, that hydrolyzes into more than one simple sugar. **polyse'mant** /-sē'/ or **pol'yseme** /-sēm/ *n*

(*linguistics*) a word with more than one meaning. **poly'semous** *adj* (*linguistics*). **pol'ysemy** *n* (*linguistics*). **polysep'alous** *adj* (*bot*) having the sepals separate from each other. **polysilox'ane** *n* any of a number of polymers which are the basis of silicone chemistry. **pol'ysome** *n* a group of ribosomes linked by a molecule of ribonucleic acid and functioning as a unit in the synthesis of proteins. **pol'ysomy** *n* a condition in which one or more extra chromosomes, *esp* sex chromosomes, are present in the cells of the body. **Polys'tichum** /-kəm/ *n* (Gr *stichos* a row) a genus of shield-ferns also known by the name *Aspidium*. **polysty'lar** or **pol'ystyle** *adj* (Gr *stylos* column) having many columns. **polysty'rene** *n* a polymer of styrene resistant to moisture and to chemicals, with many commercial and industrial applications. **polysulph'ide** *n* a sulphide whose molecules contain two or more sulphur atoms. **polysyllab'ic** or **polysyllab'ical** *adj*. **polysyllab'ically** *adv*. **polysyllab'icism** or **polysyll'abism** *n*. **polysyll'able** *n* a word of many, or of more than three, syllables. **polysyll'ogism** *n* a series of syllogisms, the conclusion of one serving as the premiss for the next. **polysyndeton** /-sin'di-tən/ *n* (Gr *syndeton* a conjunction; *rhetoric*) figurative repetition of connectives or conjunctions. **polysyn'thesis** *n*. **polysynthet'ic** or **polysynthet'ical** *adj* made up of many separate elements; built up of a number of small crystals in parallel growth (*crystallog*); combining many simple words of a sentence in one, as in the native languages of America (also called **incorporating**; *philology*). **polysynthet'ically** *adv*. **polysynthet'icism** /-i-sizm/ or **polysyn'thetism** *n* the character of being polysynthetic. **polytechnic** /-tek'nik/ *adj* (Gr *technikos*, from *technē* art) of many arts or technical subjects. ◆ *n* a college where such subjects were taught up to and including degree level, traditionally offering a wide variety of vocational courses on a full- or part-time basis (all now upgraded to university status). **polytech'nical** *adj*. **pol'ytene** /-tēn/ *adj* (L *taenia* band) (of abnormally large chromosomes) composed of many reduplicated strands, found in the fly genus *Drosophila*. **polytetrafluoreth'ylene** or **polytetrafluoroeth'ylene** *n* an inert plastic with non-adhesive surface properties. **polythal'amous** *adj* (Gr *thalamos* a chamber) having several cells or chambers. **pol'ytheism** /-thē-izm/ *n* (Gr *theos* a god) the doctrine of a plurality of gods. **pol'ytheist** *n*. **polytheist'ic** or **polytheist'ical** *adj*. **polytheist'ically** *adv*. **pol'ythene** or **polyethylene** *n* a generic name for certain thermoplastics, polymers of ethylene, manufactured in a range of qualities from light and rigid to thin and flexible, and used to make a variety of products *incl* domestic utensils, storage bags, carrier bags, etc. **polytocous** /pol-it'ə-kəs/ *adj* (Gr *tokos* birth) producing many or several at a birth or in a clutch. **polyto'nal** *adj*. **polytonal'ity** *n* use at the same time of two or more musical keys. **Pol'ytrack®** *n* an artificial surface for horse-racing. **Polytrichum** /po-lit'ri-kəm/ *n* (Gr *thrix, trichos* hair) a genus of tall hairy-capped mosses. **pol'ytunnel** *n* plastic sheeting stretched over rows of plants as protection from weather, etc. **polytypic** /-tip'ik/ *adj* having many types and representatives. **polyunsat'urate** *n* a polyunsaturated fat or oil. **polyunsat'urated** *adj* (*chem*) containing more than one carbon-carbon double bond in the molecule (**polyunsaturated fats** or **oils** glycerides of polyunsaturated fatty acids, less likely to increase blood cholesterol). **polyurethane** /-ū'rə-thān/ *n* any of a range of resins, both thermoplastic and thermosetting, used in the production of foamed materials, coatings, etc. **polyuria** /-ū'ri-ə/ *n* (*med*) excessive secretion of urine. **polyvalent** /po-li-vā'lənt or pol-iv'ə-lənt/ *adj* multivalent. **polyvi'nyl** *n* a vinyl polymer (**polyvinyl acetate** a colourless resin used in paints, adhesives, and as a coating for porous surfaces; **polyvinyl chloride** a vinyl plastic used as a rubber substitute for coating electric wires, cables, etc, and as a dress and furnishing fabric (*abbrev* **PVC**)). ◆ *adj* of, consisting of, containing or made of polyvinyl. **pol'ywater** *n* a supposed form of water, said to be a polymer, with properties different from those of ordinary water. **Polyzō'a** *n pl* (*sing* **polyzo'on**) (Gr *zōion* an animal) a phylum of aquatic animals, almost all colonial, with a cup-shaped body, U-shaped food-canal, and a wreath of tentacles about the mouth. **polyzo'an** *n* and *adj*. **polyzoarial** /-ā'ri-əl/ *adj*. **polyzoā'rium** or **polyzō'ary** *n* a polyzoan colony, or its supporting skeleton. **polyzō'ic** *adj* having many zooids; relating to the Polyzoa. **polyzo'nal** *adj* (Gr *zōnē* belt) composed of many zones or belts. **polyzō'oid** *adj* like or of the nature of a polyzoon.

polyacid...to...**polyethylene** see under **poly-**.

Polyfilla® /pol'i-fil-ə/ *n* a type of plaster used for domestic repairs such as filling cracks and holes.

polygala...to...**polyneuritis** see under **poly-**.

polynia /po-lin'i-ə/ or **polynya** /-lin'yə/ *n* open water amid sea ice, *esp* in Arctic waters. [Russ *polyn'ya*]

polynomial...to...**polyonymy** see under **poly-**.

polyp or (*obs*) **polype** /pol'ip/ *n* (*pl* **pol'yps** or **pol'ypes** /pol'ips/) an octopus or cuttlefish (*obs*); later extended to other animals with many arms or tentacles, *esp* coelenterates and Polyzoa; an individual of a colonial animal; a pedunculated tumour growing from mucous membrane (*pathol*). [L *polypus*, from Gr *polypous*, *-podos*, from *pous* foot]

■ **pol'ypary** *n* the common supporting structure of a colony of polyps. **pol'ypide** or **pol'ypite** *n* a polyp of a colonial animal. **polyp'idom** *n* (Gr *domos* house) a polypary. **pol'ypine** *adj*. **pol'ypoid** *adj* (*med*) like a polypus. **polypô'sis** *n* the presence or development of polyps. **pol'ypous** *adj* of the nature of a polyp. **polypus** /*pol'i-pəs*/ *n* (*pl* **po'lypî**) (Gr *polypous*, adapted into L as 2nd declension) a pedunculated tumour growing from the mucous membrane.

polypeptide…to…**polyzooid** see under **poly-**.

Pom see **pom**[1].

pom[1] or **Pom** /*pom*/ (*Aust and NZ inf*) *n* and *adj* short for **pommy**.

pom[2] /*pom*/ (*inf*) *n* a Pomeranian dog.

pomace /*pum'is*/ *n* crushed apples for cider-making, or the residue after pressing; anything crushed to pulp, *esp* after oil has been expressed. [Appar LL *pōmācium* cider, from L *pōmum* apple, etc]
□ **pom'ace-fly** *n* a fruit fly (genus *Drosophila*).

pomaceous see under **pome**.

pomade /*pom-äd'*/ *n* ointment for the hair, Latinized as **pomā'tum**. ◆ *vt* to anoint with pomade, put pomade on. [Fr *pommade*, from Ital *pomada*, *pomata* lipsalve, from L *pōmum* an apple]

Pomak /*pō-mäk'*/ *n* a Bulgarian Muslim. [Origin uncertain; poss from Bulg *pomagach* helper]

pomander /*po-* or *pō-man'dər*/ *n* a ball of perfumes, or a perforated globe or box in which this or a similarly perfumed preparation is kept or carried; an orange or other fruit studded with cloves to scent the air. [OFr *pomme d'ambre* apple of amber]

pomato /*po-mä'tō*, *-mä'tō*/ *n* (*pl* **poma'toes**) a tomato grafted on a potato. [Portmanteau word]

pomatum see **pomade**.

pombe /*pom'be* or *-bä*/ *n* any of various Central and E African alcoholic drinks. [Swahili]

pome /*pōm*/ *n* an apple (*rare*); any of the fruits of the apple family, eg apple, pear or quince, the enlarged fleshy receptacle enclosing a core formed from the carpels (*bot*); a king's globe or orb; a priest's hand-warming ball of hot water. [L *pōmum* a fruit, an apple]
■ **pomaceous** /*-ā'shəs*/ *adj* relating to, consisting of, or resembling apples; of the apple family or the apple section of the rose family. **pome'roy** or **pomroy** /*pom'* or *pum'roi*/ *n* an old variety of apple. **pom'iculture** *n* fruit-growing; pomology. **pomif'erous** *adj* bearing apples, pomes, or fruit generally. **pomolog'ical** *adj*. **pomol'ogist** *n*. **pomol'ogy** *n* the study of fruit-growing.
□ **pome'-cit'ron** *n* the citron. **pome'-water** or **pom'water** *n* (*Shakesp*) a sweet juicy apple.

pomegranate /*pom'ə-* or *pom'(i-)gra-nit*, formerly *pom-* or *pum-gran'it*/ *n* an Oriental fruit much cultivated in warm countries, with a thick leathery rind and numerous seeds with pulpy edible seed coats; the tree (*Punica granatum*; family Punicaceae) bearing it. [OFr *pome grenate*, from L *pōmum* an apple, and *grānātum* having many grains]

pomelo /*pum'* or *pom'il-ō*/ *n* (*pl* **pom'elos**) the grapefruit-like fruit of a tropical tree grown in Eastern countries; the tree that bears it; a grapefruit (*N Am*); a similar pear-shaped fruit or the tree that bears it, also called **shaddock**. [Ety uncertain]

Pomeranian /*pom-i-rā'ni-ən*/ *adj* of *Pomerania*, a region in N Central Poland. ◆ *n* a native of Pomerania; a spitz or Pomeranian dog, a cross from the Eskimo dog, with a sharp-pointed face and an abundant white, creamy, or black coat.

pomeroy see under **pome**.

pomfret[1] /*pum'* or *pom'frit*/ *n* a round flat liquorice sweet made in *Pontefract* (once pronounced /*pum'frit*/) in W Yorkshire (also **Pomfret cake** or **Pontefract cake**). [Anglo-Fr *Pontfret*, from L *pōns*, *pontis* bridge, and *fractus* broken]

pomfret[2] /*pom'frit*/ *n* any of several fishes, including a SE Asian fish valued as food. [Earlier *pamflet*, from Fr *pample*, from Port *pampo*]

pomiculture, **pomiferous** see under **pome**.

pommel /*pum'l*/ *n* a knob, *esp* on a sword-hilt; the high part of a saddle-bow; a heavy-headed ramming tool; either of two handles on top of a gymnastics horse (**pommel horse**); a ball-shaped finial. ◆ *vt* a less usual spelling of **pummel**. [OFr *pomel* (Fr *pommeau*), from L *pōmum* an apple]
■ **pomm'elled**, also (*heraldry*) **pommelé** /*pom'ə-li*/ or **pomm'etty** *adj* having a pommel.

pommy /*pom'i*/ (*Aust and NZ sl*, often *derog*) *n* (often shortened to **pom**) an immigrant from the British Isles; a British (*esp* English) person in general. ◆ *adj* British. [Origin obscure; perh from **pomegranate**, alluding to the colour of the immigrants' cheeks, or rhyming slang for *jimmygrant*, immigrant, or from the abbrev POME (Prisoner of Mother England) stamped on the shirts of early convict-settlers]

po-mo /*pō'mō'*/ *adj* an informal short form of **post-modern** (see under **post-**).

pomoerium /*pō-mē'ri-əm*/ *n* an open space around a town, within and beyond the walls. [L *pōmoerium*, appar for *postmoerium*, from *post* and *moiros*, old form of *mūrus* wall]

pomologist, etc see under **pome**.

Pomona /*pə-* or *pō-mō'nə*/ *n* the Roman goddess of fruits. [L *Pōmōna*, from *pōmum* fruit, apple]

pomp /*pomp*/ *n* great show or display; ceremony; ostentation; vanity or self-importance; consequential bearing; a procession. [Fr *pompe*, from L *pompa*, from Gr *pompē* a sending, escort, procession, from *pempein* to send]
■ **pomposity** /*-os'i-ti*/ *n* solemn affectation of dignity; a ridiculously pompous action, expression, or person. **pomp'ous** *adj* affectedly self-important or solemn; stately (*archaic*). **pomp'ously** *adv*. **pomp'ousness** *n*.

pompadour /*pom'pə-door* or *-dör*/ *n* a fashion of dressing women's hair by rolling it back from the forehead over a cushion (*hist*); a corsage with a low square neck (*hist*); a pattern for silk, with pink, blue, and gold leaves and flowers; a pink colour. ◆ *adj* in or relating to the style of hairdressing or dress described above, associated with Mme de Pompadour's time. [Marquise de *Pompadour* (1721–64)]

pompano /*pom'pə-nō*/ *n* (*pl* **pomp'ano** or **pomp'anos**) a general name for carangoid fishes (family Carangidae), *esp* edible American fishes of the genus *Trachynotus*. [Sp *pámpano* a fish of another family]

Pompeian /*pom-pē'ən* or *-pā'*/ *adj* relating to *Pompeii*, Italian city buried by an eruption of Mount Vesuvius in 79AD, excavated since 1755.
□ **Pompeian red** *n* a red colour like that on the walls of Pompeian houses.

pompelmoose /*pom'pəl-moos*/ *n* the shaddock, *esp* the grapefruit (also called **pam'pelmoose**, **pam'pelmouse**, **pom'pelmous**, **pom'pelmouse**, **pum'ple-nose**, **pom'pelo** (*pl* **pom'pelos**), or **pom'elo**). [Du *pompelmoes*; origin obscure]

Pompey /*pom'pi*/ (*sl*) *n* Portsmouth.

pompey /*pom'pi*/ (*Dickens*) *vt* to pamper.

pompholyx /*pom'fə-liks*/ *n* a vesicular eruption or eczema chiefly on the palms and soles (*med*); impure zinc oxide. [Gr *pompholyx*, *-ygos* bubble, slag, from *pomphos* a blister]
■ **pomphol'ygous** *adj*.

pompier-ladder /*pom'pi-ər-lad'ər* or *pɔ̃-pyā-*/ *n* a fireman's ladder, a pole with crossbars and hook. [Fr *pompier* fireman, from *pompe* pump]

pompion /*pum'pi-ən*/ see **pumpkin**.

pompom /*pom'pom*/, **pompon** /*pom'pon*/ or (*obs*) **pompoon** /*pom-poon'*/ *n* a jewelled hair ornament on a pin (*obs*); a fluffy or woolly ball, tuft, or tassel worn on a shoe, hat, etc. [Fr *pompon*]

pom-pom /*pom'pom*/ (*inf*) *n* an automatic quick-firing gun, *esp* a multi-barrelled anti-aircraft gun. [Imit]

pomposity, **pompous** see under **pomp**.

pomroy, **pomwater** see under **pome**.

'pon /*pon*/ aphetic for **upon**.

ponce /*pons*/ (*sl*) *n* a man who lives on the immoral earnings of a prostitute; a pimp; an obnoxious person; an effeminate, posturing man. ◆ *vi* to act as or like a pimp. ◆ *vt* to cadge. [Ety uncertain]
■ **pon'cy** or **pon'cey** *adj*.
■ **ponce about** *or* **around** to fool about; to act the ponce or in a showy manner.

ponceau[1] /*pon'sō* or (*Fr*) *pɔ̃-sō'*/ *n* and *adj* poppy colour. ◆ *n* (*pl* **ponceaux** /*-sōz'*/) a red dye. [Fr]

ponceau[2] /*pɔ̃-sō'*/ *n* a small bridge or culvert. [Fr]

poncho /*pon'chō*/ *n* (*pl* **pon'chos**) a S American cloak, a blanket with a hole for the head; a cyclist's waterproof cape of similar design; any similar garment. [Sp from Araucanian (S American language)]

pond[1] /*pond*/ *n* a small *usu* artificial lake; the stretch of water between locks in a canal; (also with *cap*) the Atlantic (*facetious*). ◆ *vt* to make into a pond. ◆ *vi* to collect into a pond. [ME *ponde*; cf **pound**[2]]
□ **pond'age** *n* the capacity of a pond.
□ **pond'-life** *n* animal life in ponds; despicable or worthless people (*inf*). **pond lily** *n* a water lily. **pond'-master** *n* the man in charge of a swimming-pond. **pond scum** *n* green algae forming a layer on stagnant water. **pond skater** *n* any long-legged aquatic insect of the Gerridae family. **pond snail** *n* a pond-dwelling snail, *esp Limnaea*. **pond'weed** *n* any plant of the genus *Potamogeton* (**Canadian pondweed** *Anacharis*).

pond[2] /*pond*/ *n* a unit of measurement equal to the gravitational force on a mass of one gram. [L *pondus*, *ponderis* a weight]

ponder /pon'dər/ vt to weigh in the mind; to think over; to consider; to weigh (obs). ◆ vi to think (often with on and over). [L ponderāre, and pondus, ponderis a weight]

■ **ponderabil'ity** n. **pon'derable** adj able to be weighed or measured; having sensible weight; appreciable. **pon'deral** adj relating to weight; ascertained by weight. **pon'derance** or **pon'derancy** n weight. **pon'derate** vt and vi (literary) to weigh; to ponder. **pondera'tion** n (literary) weighing or weighing up. **pon'derer** n. **pon'deringly** adv. **pon'derment** n. **ponderosity** /-os'i-ti/ n. **pon'derous** adj heavy; weighty; massive; unwieldy; lumbering; (of a speech, etc) solemnly laboured. **pon'derously** adv. **pon'derousness** n.

pondok /pon'dok/ or **pondokkie** /pon-dok'i/ (S Afr) n a crude dwelling, a hut, shack, etc. [Khoikoi pondok a hut, or perh Malay pondok a leaf shelter]

pone[1] /pōn/ (US) n maize bread; a maize loaf or cake. [Algonquian pone]

pone[2] /pō'ni or pōn/ (cards) n the player to the right of the dealer, who cuts the cards; sometimes the player to the left. [L pōne, imperative of ponere to place]

ponent /pō'nənt/ (Milton) adj western. [Ital ponente, setting (of the sun), from L pōnēns, -entis, prp of pōnere to put]

ponerology /pon-ə-rol'ə-ji/ (theol) n the doctrine of wickedness. [Gr ponēros bad, and logos discourse]

poney see **pony**.

pong[1] /pong/ (inf) vi to smell bad. ◆ n a bad smell. [Prob Romany pan to stink]

■ **pong'y** adj.

pong[2] /pong/ (theatre sl) vi to make impromptu additions to one's part in order to extend it, to gag.

ponga or **punga** /pong'ə/ n a tall tree fern of New Zealand (Cyathea dealbata), with large thick leaves. [Maori]

pongee /pun- or pon-jē'/ n a soft unbleached silk, made from cocoons of a wild silkworm; a fine cotton. [Perh Chin bĕnjí own loom]

pongo /pong'gō/ n (pl **pong'os** or (Aust) **pong'oes**) an anthropoid ape, orig probably the gorilla, but transferred to the orang-utan; a monkey; a soldier (milit sl); an Englishman (Aust inf). [Congo mpongi]

■ **pon'gid** /-jid/ adj and n.

pongy see under **pong**[1].

poniard /pon'yərd/ n a small dagger. ◆ vt to stab with a poniard. [Fr poignard, from poing, from L pugnus fist]

ponk /ponk/ vi and n a rare variant of **pong**[1].

pons /ponz/ (anat) n (pl **pon'tēs**) a connecting part, esp the pons Varolii, a mass of fibres joining the hemispheres of the brain. [L pōns, pontis a bridge]

■ **pon'tal**, **pon'tic**, **pon'tile** or **pon'tine** adj relating to the pons of the brain.

pons asinorum /ponz as-i-nōr'əm, -nōr' or pōns as-i-nōr'ŭm/ (L) n the asses' bridge (see under **ass**[1]); any severe test of a beginner.

pont /pont/ n in South Africa, a small ferry-boat guided across narrow stretches of water by a rope or cable. [OE punt shallow boat]

pontage /pont'ij/ n a toll paid on bridges; a tax for repairing bridges. [LL pontāgium, from L pōns, pontis a bridge]

pontal see under **pons**.

Pontederia /pont-e-dē'ri-ə/ (bot) n an American genus of monocotyledonous water- or bog-plants, called pickerel-weed, giving name to a family **Pontederiā'ceae**. [Giulio Pontedera (1688–1757), Italian botanist]

Pontefract cake see **pomfret**[1].

pontes see **pons**.

pontianac or **pontianak** /pont-i-ä'nak/ n the naturally occurring rubber-like substance, jelutong. [Pontianak, in Borneo]

Pontic /pon'tik/ adj of the ancient kingdom and Roman province of Pontus, or of the Pontus Euxinus or Black Sea. [Gr Pontikos, from pontos sea]

pontic see under **pons**.

ponticello /pon-ti-chel'ō/ n (pl **ponticell'os**) the bridge of a stringed instrument. [Ital, dimin of ponte bridge, from L pōns, pontis]

pontie see under **punty**.

pontifex /pon'ti-feks/ n (pl **pontifices** /-tif'i-sēz or -kās/) (in ancient Rome) a member of a college of priests that had control of matters of religion, their chief being Pontifex Maximus; a pontiff; a bridge-builder. [L pontifex, pontificis (partly through Fr pontife), which was supposed to be from pōns, pontis a bridge, and facere to make, but is possibly from an Oscan and Umbrian word puntis propitiatory offering]

■ **pon'tiff** n a pontifex; a high priest; a bishop, esp the Pope or sovereign pontiff (RC); an oracular person. **pontif'ic** or **pontif'ical** adj of or belonging to a pontiff; splendid; pompously dogmatic. **pontif'ical** n an office-book for bishops. **pontifical'ity** n. **pontif'ically** adv. **pontif'icals** n pl the formal clothes of a priest, bishop, or pope. **pontif'icate** /-kət/ n the dignity of a pontiff or high-priest; the office and dignity or reign of a pope. ◆ vi /-kāt/ to perform the duties of a pontiff; to behave, esp to speak, in a pompous, self-important way. **pon'tifice** /-fis/ n (Milton) bridgework, a bridge. **pon'tify** vi to play the pontiff.

□ **pontifical mass** n mass celebrated by a bishop while wearing his full vestments.

pontil, pontile[1] see **punty**.

pontile[2] see under **pons**.

pontine /pon'tīn, -tēn/ adj of or relating to bridges; see also under **pons**. [L pōns, pontis a bridge]

Pont-l'Évêque /pɔ̃-lā-vek'/ (Fr) n a soft Cheddar cheese originating in Pont-l'Évêque in NW France.

pontlevis /pont-lev'is, (Fr) pɔ̃-lə-vē' or -le-/ n a drawbridge. [Fr]

pontoon[1] /pon-toon'/ n (also **ponton** /pon'tən or pon-toon'/) a flat-bottomed boat, a ferry-boat, barge, or lighter; such a boat, or a float, used to support a bridge; a bridge of boats; a low vessel carrying plant, materials, and men for work at sea or on rivers; the floating gate of a dock; a boat-like float of a seaplane; a float. ◆ vt to cross by pontoon. [Fr ponton, from L pontō, -ōnis a punt, pontoon, from pōns a bridge]

■ **pontoneer'**, **pontonier'**, **pontonnier'** or **pontoon'er** n a builder of pontoon bridges.

□ **pontoon bridge** n a platform or roadway supported upon pontoons.

pontoon[2] /pon-toon'/ n a card game of chance, or the winning score of 21 points which is its object. [**vingt-et-un**]

ponty see **punty**.

pony, formerly also **poney** /pō'ni/ n any of several breeds of small horse, usu one less than 14.2 hands high; 25 pounds sterling (sl); a translation, crib or key (US sl); a small glass, esp of beer. ◆ vt and vi (sl) to pay or settle (with up); to prepare or translate by help of a crib. [Scot powny, powney, pownie, prob from OFr poulenet, dimin of poulain, from LL pullānus a foal, from L pullus a young animal]

□ **pony carriage** n. **pony engine** n a shunting engine. **pony express** n (in the USA) a former method of long-distance postal delivery employing relays of horses and riders. **po'nyskin** n the skin of a foal, esp from the Kyrgyz Steppes, used as a fur. **po'nytail** n a hair style in which the hair is gathered together at the back and hangs down like a pony's tail. **po'ny-trekking** n cross-country pony-riding in groups as a pastime.

■ **Jerusalem pony** an ass. **one-trick pony** (inf) a person who is very good at one thing but fails to achieve wider success.

Ponzi scheme /pon'zi skēm/ n a fraudulent scheme that promises unusually high profits to investors, who are paid using deposits from new investors. [C Ponzi (1882–1949), Italian-born confidence trickster]

ponzu /pon'zoo/ n a sauce made with rice vinegar, mirin, soy sauce and yuzu, used in Japanese cookery. [Jap]

poo /poo/ (sl) n and vi same as **poop**[3].

■ **in the poo** (Aust) in an awkward situation.

pooch /pooch/ (inf) n a dog, esp a mongrel.

pood /pood/ n a Russian weight, approx 36lb avoirdupois. [Russ pud]

poodle /poo'dl/ n a breed of domestic dog of various sizes, which has a curly coat (often clipped to a standard pattern); a lackey. [Ger Pudel; LGer pudeln to paddle, splash]

□ **pood'le-dog** n a poodle; an assiduous follower. **pood'le-faker** n (old-fashioned sl) a (usu young) man who sought the company of women, a ladies' man.

poof[1] /pŭf/, formerly **pouf**, **pouffe** /pŭf or poof/ or **puff** /puf/ (derog sl) n a male homosexual (also **poof'tah**, **poof'ter** or **poufter** /-tə or -tər/). [Fr pouffe puff]

■ **poof'y** adj effeminate.

poof[2] /pŭf/ interj an exclamation expressing suddenness, contempt, dismissal, etc.

poogye or **poogyee** /poo'gē/ n an Indian nose-flute. [Hindi pūgī]

pooh /poo or pŭ/ interj an exclamation of disdain, dismissal, or disgust (eg at an offensive smell). [Imit]

□ **pooh-pooh'**, **poo-poo'** vt to make light of; to ridicule, dismiss contemptuously.

Pooh-Bah /poo'bä/ n a person who holds many offices simultaneously; a person who affects superiority. [Character in Gilbert and Sullivan's The Mikado]

Pooh sticks /poo stiks/ n a game in which participants throw twigs, etc into running water upstream of a bridge, the winner being the person whose twig emerges first downstream of the bridge (also

Pooh'sticks). [A game played by Winnie the *Pooh* in the stories by AA Milne (1882–1956)]

pooja or **poojah** same as **puja**.

pook or **pouk** /*pook*/ (*Scot*) *vt* (*pat* and *pap* **pook'it** or **pouk'it**) to pluck; to pinch. [Origin unknown]

pooka /*poo'kə*/ *n* (in Irish folklore) a malevolent goblin or spirit, sometimes assuming an animal form, said to haunt bogs and marshes. [Ir *púca*]

pool[1] /*pool*/ *n* a small body of still water; a temporary or casual collection of water or other liquid; a puddle; a deep part of a stream; an underground accumulation (in the pores of sedimentary rock) of petroleum or gas; a swimming-pool. ◆ *vi* to collect into a pool; to accumulate. [OE *pōl*; Du *poel*, Ger *Pfuhl*; relation to Ir and Gaelic *poll*, and Welsh *pwll* undetermined]
■ **pool'side** *n* and *adj*.

pool[2] /*pool*/ *n* the stakes in certain games; the collective stakes of a number of people who combine in a betting arrangement; an organized arrangement for betting in this way; a group of people combining in this way; a game, or a set of players, at quadrille, etc; a game or contest of various kinds in which the winner receives the pool; any of various games played on a table smaller than a billiard table, each player trying to pocket a number of (*esp* coloured and numbered) balls; a common stock or fund; a combination of interest; a combine; an arrangement for eliminating competition; a group of people who may be called upon as required, eg, a group of typists; (in *pl*; often with *the*) a competition based on betting on the results of a number of football games. ◆ *vt* to put into a common fund or stock. ◆ *vi* to form a pool. [Fr *poule* a hen, also stakes (poss through an intermediate sense of plunder), but associated in English with **pool**[1]]
■ **scoop the pool** (*inf*; *gambling*) to win a substantial amount of money from collective stakes.

poon /*poon*/ *n* an Indian tree, *Calophyllum inophyllum*, or other species of the genus (family Guttiferae). [Sinhalese *pūna*]
□ **poon'-oil** *n* an oil expressed from its seeds. **poon'-wood** *n*.

poonac /*poo'nak*/ *n* coconut oil-cake. [Sinhalese *punakku*]

poonce see **punce**[2].

poontang /*poon'tang*/ (*US sl*) *n* sexual intercourse; the female genitals; a woman regarded as a sexual partner. [Fr *putain* a prostitute]

poop[1] /*poop*/ *n* the after part of a ship, the part towards the stern; a high deck at the stern. ◆ *vt* (of a wave) to break over the stern of; to ship (waves) over the stern. [Fr *poupe*, from L *puppis* the poop]
■ **pooped** *adj* having a poop.

poop[2] /*poop*/ (*inf*, *esp N Am*) *vt* to make out of breath; to exhaust. ◆ *vi* to become winded or exhausted; (often with *out*) to stop. [Orig unknown]

poop[3] /*poop*/ (*sl*) *n* faeces; defecation. ◆ *vi* to defecate.
□ **poop scoop** or **poop'er-scooper** *n* an implement for lifting and removing faeces (*esp* one used by dog-owners to remove faeces deposited by their pets on pavements, in parks, etc).

poop[4] /*poop*/ (*N Am inf*) *n* information; the facts. [Origin unknown]

poop[5] or **poupe** /*poop*/ (*obs*) *vt* (*pap* in *Shakesp* **poupt**) to befool; to cozen; to undo; to do for. [Cf Du *poep* clown]

poop[6] /*poop*/ *n* short for **nincompoop**.

poo-poo see under **pooh**.

poor /*poor*/ *adj* possessing little or nothing; without means (*esp* financial) of subsistence; needy; deficient; lacking; unproductive; scanty; mere; inferior; inadequate, shameful; sorry; spiritless; in a sorry condition; (in modest or ironical self-depreciation) humble; unfortunate, to be pitied (*esp* of the dead). [OFr *poure*, *povre* (Fr *pauvre*), from L *pauper* poor]
■ **poor'ish** *adj*. **poor'ly** *adv* in a poor manner; badly; inadequately; in a small way; meanly. ◆ *adj* unwell. **poor'ness** *n*.
□ **poor box** a money box for gifts for the poor. **Poor Clare** see under **Clare**. **poor'house** (or *Scot* **poor's'-house**, **puir's'-house**, **-hoose**) *n* (*hist*) a house established at the public expense for sheltering the poor, a workhouse. **poor-John**[1] *n* (*Shakesp*) salt hake. **poor law** *n* (often in *pl*) the law or laws relating to the support of the poor. **poor'-law** *adj*. **poor'-mouth** *vi* to claim poverty. ◆ *vt* to malign. **poor rate** *n* (*hist*) a rate or tax for the support of the poor. **poor relation** *n* any person or thing similar but inferior or subordinate to another. **poor relief** *n* money, food, etc for the poor. **poor's'-box** *n* a poor box. **poor'-spir'ited** *adj* lacking in spirit. **poor'-spir'itedness** *n*. **poor's'-roll** *n* (*Scots law*; *obs*) the list of poor litigants allowed to sue *in formā pauperis*. **poor white** *n* (*usu derog*) a member of a class of poor, improvident, and incompetent white people in the Southern states of the USA, South Africa and elsewhere, often called by the blacks *poor white trash*.

■ **poor man of mutton** (*Scot*) cold mutton broiled, *esp* the shoulder. **poor man's weather glass** the pimpernel, reputed to close its flowers before rain.

poori see **puri**.

poor-oot see **pour-out** under **pour**.

poort /*pōrt* or *poort*/ (*S Afr*) *n* a mountain pass. [Du, from L *porta* gate]

poortith /*poor'tith*/ (*Scot*) *n* poverty. [OFr *pouerteit*, *poverteit*, from L *paupertās*, *-ātis*]

poorwill /*poor'wil*/ *n* a NW American nightjar (genus *Phalaenoptilus*), smaller than the whippoorwill. [From its note]

poot see **pout**[3].

Pooter /*poo'tər*/ *n* a petit bourgeois, conventional and unimaginative. [Charles *Pooter* in *Diary of a Nobody* (1892), by G and W Grossmith]
■ **Poo'terish** *adj*. **Poo'terism** *n*.

pooter /*poo'tər*/ *n* an entomological collecting bottle into which small arthropods are introduced by suction. [Ety obscure]

pootle /*poo'tl*/ (*inf*) *vi* to move casually, idly or at a leisurely pace. [Poss alteration of **tootle**]

poove /*poov*/ (*sl*) *n* same as **poof**[1].
■ **poo'very** *n*. **poo'vy** *adj*.

POP *abbrev*: persistent organic pollutant; Point of Presence, a point of access to the Internet; Post Office Preferred (of sizes of envelopes, packets, etc).

pop[1] /*pop*/ *n* a mild explosive sound, like that of drawing a cork; a shot; an attempt (*inf*); a pistol (*sl*); ginger beer, champagne or other effervescing drink (*inf*); pawn, or an act of pawning (*inf*). ◆ *vi* (**popp'ing**; **popped**) to make a pop; to shoot; to burst with a pop; (of eyes) to protrude; to come, go, slip, or pass suddenly, unexpectedly or unobtrusively; to pitch or alight; to propose marriage (*sl*). ◆ *vt* to cause to make a pop or to burst with a pop; to shoot; to thrust or put suddenly or quickly; to pawn (*inf*); to swallow in pill form or inject (a drug) (*drug sl*); to open (eg a lock or secure container) by force (*inf*). ◆ *adv* with a pop; suddenly. [Imit]
■ **popp'er** *n* someone who pops; anything that makes a pop; a press-stud; a utensil for popping corn; (in *pl*) amyl nitrate or butyl nitrate inhaled from a crushed capsule (*drug sl*). **popp'it** or **popp'et** *n* one of *usu* a number of beads each having a small protrusion on one side and a hole on the other, by means of which they can be linked together.
□ **pop'corn** *n* maize burst open and swelled by heating; a kind of maize suitable for this. **pop'-eye** *n* a prominent or protruding eye. **pop'-eyed** *adj* having prominent or protruding eyes; open-eyed, agog (as from interest, excitement, etc). **pop'-fastener** *n* a press-stud. **pop'gun** *n* a tube for shooting pellets by compressed air; a contemptible gun. **pop'over** *n* a thin hollow cake or pudding made from batter. **popp'ing-crease** see under **crease**[1]. **pop'-shop** (*inf*) a pawnshop. **pop'sock** *n* a woman's nylon stocking reaching up to the knee. **pop'-top** *n* (*N Am*) a ring pull (qv under **ring**[1]). **pop'-under** *n* (*comput*) an additional window, *usu* containing an advertisement, that is activated when accessing a particular website but remains hidden until the main window is closed. **pop'-up** *adj* (of appliances, books, etc) having mechanisms or pages that rise or move quickly upwards; (of a menu) appearing when an option is selected (*comput*); (of a shop, restaurant, etc) opening quickly but temporarily. ◆ *n* (*comput*) an additional window, *usu* containing an advertisement, that appears on a computer screen when accessing a particular website. **pop'-visit** *n* a visit at an odd time, a casual visit. **pop'-weed** *n* bladderwort.
■ **a pop** (*inf*) each; apiece. **pop off** (*inf*) to make off; to die; to fall asleep. **pop one's clogs** see under **clog**. **pop the question** (*inf*) to make an offer of marriage. **take** or **have a pop at** (*inf*) to criticize or attack, *esp* in public; to try out.

pop[2] /*pop*/ (*inf*) *adj* popular. ◆ *n* currently popular music (also **pop music**), *esp* the type characterized by a strong rhythmic element and the use of electrical amplification.
■ **popp'ish** or **popp'y** *adj* of or like pop music.
□ **pop art** *n* art drawing deliberately on commonplace material of modern urbanized life. **pop artist** *n*. **pop concert** *n* a concert at which pop music is played. **pop culture** *n* commercial and leisure activity based on pop music. **pop festival** *n*. **pop group** *n* a (*usu* small) group of musicians who play pop music. **pop record** *n*. **pop singer** *n*. **pop song** *n*.
■ **top of the pops** (*old*) (of a recording) currently (among) the most popular in terms of sales; currently very much in favour (*fig*).

pop[3] see **poppa**, **poppet**[1], **poppycock**.

pop. *abbrev*: popular; popularly; population.

popadum see **poppadum**.

pope[1] /*pōp*/ *n* (often *cap*) the bishop of Rome, head of the Roman Catholic Church; formerly applied also to the patriarch of Alexandria and other bishops; any spiritual head; a person wielding, assuming, or thought to assume authority like that of the Pope; a parish priest in the Greek Orthodox Church; the head of the Coptic Church. [OE *pāpa*, from LL *pāpa*, from Gr *pappas* (late Gr *papās*), a child's word for father]

■ **pope'dom** *n* the office, dignity, or jurisdiction of the Pope; a pope's tenure of office. **pope'hood** or **pope'ship** *n* the condition of being pope. **pope'ling** *n* a little pope. **po'pery** *n* a hostile term for Roman Catholicism or whatever seems to savour of it. **po'pish** *adj* (*derog*) relating to the Pope or to popery. **po'pishly** *adv*.

□ **Pope Joan** *n* a mythical female pope; an old card game like newmarket. **pope's eye** *n* the gland surrounded with fat in the middle of the thigh of an ox or a sheep; a cut of steak (also called **popeseye steak**). **pope's head** *n* a long-handled brush. **pope's knights** *n pl* Roman Catholic priests, formerly called Sir. **pope's nose** *n* the parson's nose (qv).

■ **Black Pope** see under **black**.

pope² /pōp/ *n* the ruff, a European freshwater fish.

popera /pop'ə-rə/ (*inf*) *n* operatic music presented so as to appeal to a mass audience; popular music that imitates operatic forms or techniques. [**pop²** and **opera¹**]

poperin see **poppering**.

popery, popeship see under **pope¹**.

Popian /pō'pi-ən/ *adj* relating to or in the style of the poet Alexander Pope (1688–1744).

popinjay /pop'in-jā/ *n* a conceited person; a fop or coxcomb; a parrot; a figure of a parrot set up to be shot at (*hist*). [OFr *papegai*; cf LL *papagallus*; Late Gr *papagallos* (also *papagas*), a parrot; prob Eastern; influenced by **jay¹**]

popish, etc see under **pope¹**.

poplar /pop'lər/ *n* a genus (*Populus*) of rapidly growing trees of the willow family, including aspen, white poplar, black poplar (with its variety Lombardy poplar), cottonwood, etc; widespread in northern temperate regions; the tulip tree, tulip poplar (*US*). [OFr *poplier*, from L *pōpulus* poplar-tree]

poplin /pop'lin/ *n* a corded fabric with a silk warp and worsted weft; an imitation in cotton or other material. [Perh Fr *popeline*, from Ital *papalina* papal, from the papal town of Avignon, where it was made]
■ **poplinette'** *n* an imitation poplin.

popliteal /pop-lit'i-əl/ or often *pop-li-tē'əl/ adj* of the back of the knee (also **poplit'ic**). [L *poples, -itis*]

poppa /pop'ə/ (*inf, esp N Am*) *n* papa (short form **pop** or **pops**).

poppadum or **popadum** /pop'ə-dəm/ or *-dom/ n* a thin circle or strip of dough fried in oil, etc until crisp. —Also in several variant spellings. [Tamil, Malayalam *poppatam*]

popped, popper see **pop¹**.

Popperian /pop-ē'ri-ən/ *adj* of or relating to the theories, teachings, etc of the British philosopher Sir Karl *Popper* (1902–94). ♦ *n* a student or supporter of Popper's philosophy.

poppering /pop'ə-ring/ or **poperin** /-rin/ (*obs*) *n* a variety of pear (also **poppering pear** or (*Shakesp*) **pop'rin pear**). [*Poperinghe* in Belgium]

poppet¹ /pop'it/ *n* a darling (short form **pop**); a puppet (*obs*); a doll (*obs*); a timber support used in launching a ship; a lathe-head; a valve that lifts bodily (also **popp'et-valve**). [An earlier form of **puppet**]
□ **popp'et-head** *n* a framework with pulleys for ropes at the top of a mineshaft.

poppet² see under **pop¹**.

poppied see under **poppy¹**.

popping see under **pop¹**.

poppish see under **pop²**.

poppit see under **pop¹**.

popple /pop'l/ *vi* to flow tumblingly; to heave choppily; to bob up and down; to make the sound of rippling or bubbling, or of repeated shots. ♦ *n* a poppling movement or sound. [Imit; or a frequentative of **pop¹**]
■ **popp'ly** *adj*.

poppy¹ /pop'i/ *n* a cornfield plant (of several species) or its large scarlet flowers; any other species of the genus *Papaver*, such as the opium poppy, or of the related genera *Glaucium* (**horned poppy**; see under **horn**) or *Meconopsis* (see **Welsh poppy** below), etc; also extended to various unrelated plants. [OE *popig*, from L *papāver* poppy]
■ **popp'ied** *adj* covered or filled with poppies; soporific; affected by opium.
□ **Poppy Day** *n orig* Armistice Day (qv), later the Saturday nearest Armistice Day, or (later) Remembrance Sunday (qv under **remember**), when artificial poppies are sold for charity. **popp'y-head** *n* a capsule of the poppy; a finial in wood, *esp* at a pew end. **popp'y-oil** *n* a fixed oil from the seeds of the opium poppy. **poppy seed** *n*. **poppy water** *n* a soporific drink made from poppies.

■ **blue poppy** a blue Meconopsis of the northern temperate zone. **Flanders poppy** an emblem, from World War I, of the fallen British soldiers. **Welsh poppy** *Meconopsis cambrica*, which has pale-yellow flowers.

poppy² see under **pop²**.

poppycock /pop'i-kok/ (*inf*) *n* balderdash. [Du *pappekak*, literally, soft dung]

poprin see **poppering**.

pops see **poppa**.

Popsicle® /pop'si-kl/ (*N Am*) *n* an ice lolly.

popsy /pop'si/ (*old*) *n* term of endearment for a girl or young woman (also **pop'sy-wop'sy**); an attractive young woman (*inf*). [Prob dimin abbrev of **poppet**]

populace /pop'ū-ləs/ *n* the common people; those not distinguished by rank, education, office, etc. [Fr, from Ital *popolazzo*, from L *populus* people]

popular /pop'ū-lər/ *adj* of the people; pleasing to, enjoying the favour of or prevailing among the people; liked by one's associates; suited to the understanding or the means of ordinary people; seeking the favour of the common people (*obs*); democratic; plebeian (*obs*); vulgar (*obs*). ♦ *n* something popular, such as a popular or moderate-priced concert, (tabloid) newspaper, etc (short form **pop**; cf **pop²**). [L *populus* the people]
■ **popularity** /-lar'i-ti/ *n* the fact or state of being popular; seeking to gain favour with the people. **popularīzā'tion** or **-s-** *n*. **pop'ularize** or **-ise** *vt* to make popular; to democratize; to present in a manner suited to ordinary people; to spread among the people. **pop'ularīzer** or **-s-** *n*. **pop'ularly** *adv*. **pop'ulate** *vt* to people; to supply with inhabitants; to fill in (a cell etc) with data (*comput*); to devastate (*obs*). ♦ *vi* to multiply by propagation. ♦ *adj* /-lət, -lāt/ (*obs*) inhabited, peopled. **popula'tion** *n* the act of populating; the number of inhabitants; the number of inhabitants of a particular class; the plants or animals in a given area; a group of persons, objects or items considered statistically. **pop'ulism** *n*. **pop'ulist** *n* (in the USA) a member of the People's Party, founded in 1891, advocating public ownership of public services, graduated income tax, etc, or of a similar party elsewhere (*hist*); someone who believes in the right and ability of the common people to play a major part in governing themselves; a supporter, wooer or student of the common people. ♦ *adj* (of a political or social programme, cause, etc) appealing to the mass of the people. **pop'ulous** *adj* full of people; numerously inhabited; numerous (*Shakesp*); popular (*rare*). **pop'ulously** *adv*. **pop'ulousness** *n*.
□ **popular etymology** *n* folk etymology. **popular front** *n* an alliance of the more progressive or left-wing political parties in the state. **population explosion** see under **explode**. **population inversion** *n* (*phys*) the reversal of the normal ratio of populations of two different energy states, ie, that normally fewer and fewer atoms occupy states of successively higher energies.

poral see under **pore¹**.

porbeagle /pör'bē-gl/ *n* a N Atlantic and Mediterranean shark of the genus *Lamna*. [From Cornish dialect; origin unknown]

porcelain /pör'l/ or *pör's(ə-)lin* or *-s(ə-)lən/ n* a fine type of pottery, white, thin, transparent or semi-transparent, first made in China; objects made of this, china. ♦ *adj* of porcelain. [OFr *porcelaine*, from Ital *porcellana* cowrie]
■ **porcell'anite** *n* a jasper-like shale highly indurated by contact metamorphism. **porcell'anize** or **-ise** or **porc'elainize** or **-ise** *vt* to bake into porcelain or porcellanite. **porcell'anous** (or /pör', pör'/) *adj* like porcelain (also **porcellā'neous**, **porc'elainous** or **porcelai'neous**).
□ **porcelain cement** *n* cement for mending china. **porcelain clay** *n* kaolin.

porch /pörch or pörch/ *n* a building forming an enclosure or protection for a doorway; a portico or colonnade; a veranda (*N Am*); the Stoic school of philosophy (from the Painted Porch in the Agora of Athens where Zeno taught). [OFr *porche*, from L *porticus*, from *porta* a gate]

porchetta /pör-ket'ə/ *n* seasoned, boneless roast pork cut from a whole roast pig; roast suckling pig. [Ital, from *porco* pig]

porcine /pör'sīn/ *adj* of pigs; swinish. [L *porcīnus*, from *porcus* a swine]

porcini /pör-chē'ni/ (*chiefly N Am*) *n pl* ceps. [Ital, from *porcino* pig-like]

porcpisce /pör'pis/ (*Spenser*) *n* same as **porpoise**.

porcupine /pör'kū-pīn/ *n* a large spiny rodent of various kinds. [OFr *porc espin*, from L *porcus* a pig, and *spīna* a spine]
□ **porcupine fish** *n* a tropical sea fish covered in spines. **porcupine grass** *n* a coarse, hard, spiny, tussocky grass (genus *Triodia*) that covers vast areas in Australia, commonly called spinifex. **porcupine wood** *n* the wood of the coconut palm, from its spine-like markings.

pore¹ /pōr or pör/ n a minute passage or interstice, esp the opening of a sweat gland. [Fr, from L *porus*, from Gr *poros* a passage]
■ **por'al** adj of or relating to pores. **por'iness** n. **poromer'ic** adj (of eg synthetic leather) permeable to water vapour. **poroscope** /pōr' or pör'ə-skōp/ n an instrument for investigating porosity or for examining pores or fingerprints. **poroscopic** /-skop'ik/ adj. **poroscopy** /-os'kə-pi/ n. **porose** /-ōs' or pör', pör'/ adj. **porosity** /-os'i-ti/ n the quality or state of being porous; the ratio of the volume of pores to the total volume (of eg a rock); a thing or part that is porous. **por'ous** adj having many pores; permeable by fluids, etc; easily breached. **por'ousness** n. **por'y** adj.
◻ **pore fungus** n any fungus having the spore-bearing surface within small pores or tubes. **porous alloys** n pl alloys obtained by taking the constituents in powder form and pressing them together. **porous plaster** n a plaster for the body, with holes to prevent wrinkling.

pore² /pōr or pör/ vi to gaze with close and steady attention (usu with *over*, *on* or *upon*); to ponder. [Origin obscure]
■ **por'er** n.

porge /pörj or pörj/ vt in Jewish ritual, to cleanse (a slaughtered animal) ceremonially by removing the forbidden fat, sinews, etc. [Ladino (Jewish Spanish) *porgar* (Sp *purgar*), from L *pūrgāre* to purge]

porgy or **porgie** /pör'gi/ n a name given to many fishes, chiefly American species of sea bream. [Partly Sp and Port *pargo*, appar from L *pargus*, a kind of fish; partly from Native American names]

Porifera /po-rif'ə-rə/ n pl a phylum of animals, the sponges. [L *porus* a pore, and *ferre* to bear]
■ **por'ifer** n a member of the Porifera. **porif'eral** adj. **porif'eran** adj and n (a member) of the Porifera. **porif'erous** adj having pores.

poriness see under **pore¹**.

porism /pö' or pö'ri-zm/ n in ancient Greek geometry, a corollary; also a kind of proposition intermediate between a problem and a theorem, according to some a proposition affirming the possibility of finding such conditions as will render a certain problem capable of innumerable solutions. [Gr *porisma* a corollary, porism, from *poros* a way]
■ **porismat'ic** /pör-/ or **porismat'ical** adj. **poris'tic** or **poris'tical** adj.

pork /pörk or pörk/ n pig's flesh as food; a pig (obs); government money to be used for a pork barrel (US). [Fr *porc*, from L *porcus* a hog]
■ **pork'er** n a young pig; a pig fed to be slaughtered and used for pork; an overweight person (derog sl). **pork'ling** n a young pig. **pork'y** adj pig-like; fat.
◻ **pork barrel** n (US sl) (a bill or policy promoting spending of Federal or state money on) projects undertaken because of their appeal to the electorate rather than their meeting a real need; the money itself. **pork'-butch'er** n someone who kills pigs or sells pork. **pork-chop'** n a slice from a pig's rib. **pork pie** n a pie made of minced pork. **pork'-pie hat** n a hat with a low flat circular crown, shaped somewhat like a pie. **pork scratchings** n pl crisp pieces of fried pork fat or rind eaten as a snack.

porky¹ /pör'ki/ (inf) n (pl **por'kies**) a lie. [Rhyming slang *pork pie* lie]
porky² see under **pork**.

porlock /pör'lok/ (sl) vt to hinder by an irksome intrusion or interruption. [From the visitor from *Porlock* in Somerset who disastrously interrupted Coleridge as he wrote his dream-inspired poem *Kubla Khan*]
■ **a person from Porlock** someone who intrudes, someone who interrupts at an awkward moment.

porn /pörn/ or **porno** /pör'nō/ (inf) n short for **pornography**. ◆ adj short for **pornographic**.
◻ **porn shop** n a shop selling pornographic literature, etc. **porn squad** n the branch of the police force that enforces the law as regards obscene publications.

porn- /pörn-/ or **porno-** /pör-nō, -ə-, -o-/ combining form denoting obscene or obscenity. [Gr *pornē* a prostitute]
■ **pornifica'tion** n the spread of sexualized imagery and attitudes from pornography (into everyday life). **pornocracy** /pör-nok'rə-si/ n (see **-cracy**) the influence of courtesans esp over the papal court in the earlier half of the 10c. **pornog'rapher** n. **pornography** /pör-nog'rə-fi/ n (see **-graphy**) books, magazines, films, etc dealing with or depicting sexual acts, in a more or less explicit way, intended to arouse sexual excitement; description or portrayal of prostitutes and prostitution. **pornographic** /pör-nə-graf'ik/ adj. **pornograph'ically** adv. **pornotō'pia** n (by facetious analogy with *Utopia*) the perfect setting for the antics described in pornography. **pornotō'pian** adj.

porogamy /pör- or pör-og'ə-mi/ (bot) n the entry of the pollen tube through the micropyle, opp to *chalazogamy*. [Gr *poros* a pore, and **-gamy**]
■ **porogamic** /-ō-gam'ik/ adj.

poromeric, poroscope, etc, **porose**, etc see under **pore¹**.

porosis /pō-rō'sis or pö-/ (med) n (pl **poro'ses**) formation of callus, the knitting together of broken bones. [Gr *pōrōsis*, from *pōros* callus]

porosity, porous, etc see under **pore¹**.

porpentine /pör'pən-tīn/ (Shakesp) n same as **porcupine**.

porpess, porpesse see **porpoise**.

Porphyra /pör'fi-rə/ n a genus of seaweeds, with flat translucent red or purple fronds, also called **purple laver**. [Gr *porphyrā* purple (dye)]

porphyria /pör-fīr'i-ə/ n (pathol) any of various disorders of metabolism resulting in the excretion of an excessive quantity of porphyrins in the urine, some types characterized by skin photosensitivity. [Gr *porphyrā* purple (dye)]
■ **por'phyrin** /-fi-rin/ n any of a large group of red or purple crystalline pigments present in plant and animal tissues.

porphyrio /pör-fīr'i-ō/ n (pl **porphyr'ios**) any bird of the purple-coot genus *Porphyrio*. [Gr *porphyriōn* purple coot]

porphyrogenite /pör-fi-roj'ə-nīt/ n a Byzantine emperor's son born in the purple or porphyry room assigned to empresses; hence, a prince born with his father's accession; a person born into the nobility, or a position of high rank. [L *porphyrogenitus* for Gr *porphyrogennētos*, from *porphyros* purple, and *gennētos* born]
■ **porphyrogenitism** /-ō-jen'it-izm/ n the Byzantine principle of the first son born after his father's accession succeeding to the throne. **porphyrogen'iture** n.

porphyry /pör'fi-ri/ n a very hard, variegated rock of a purple and white colour, used in sculpture (*porfido rosso antico*); (loosely) an igneous rock with large crystals in a fine-grained groundmass (geol). [Gr *porphyrītēs*, from *porphyros* purple]
■ **por'phyrite** n an old-fashioned name for an altered andesite or fine-grained diorite; porphyry. **porphyritic** /-it'ik/ adj like, or of the nature of, porphyry; having large crystals scattered among small or in a fine-grained or glassy groundmass. **por'phyrous** adj purple.

porpoise /pör'pəs/ n (formerly also **por'pess**, **por'pesse** or (Spenser) **porc'pisce**) a short-snouted genus (*Phocaena*) of cetaceans related to the dolphin family, 1.2 to 2.5 metres (4 to 8 feet) long, gregarious in habits, yielding an oil and leather; extended to similar forms, esp (loosely) the dolphin. ◆ vi to move like a porpoise. [OFr *porpeis*, from L *porcus* a pig, and *piscis* a fish]

porporate /pör'pə-rət/ (Browning) adj clad in purple. [Ital *porporato*, from L *purpurātus*]

porraceous /por-ā'shəs/ adj leek-green. [L *porrāceus*, from *porrum* a leek]

porrect /po-rekt'/ vt to stretch forth; to present, hold out for acceptance. ◆ adj extended forward. [L *porrigere, porrectum* to stretch out]
■ **porrec'tion** n.

porrenger see **porringer**.

porridge /por'ij/ n a kind of food usu made by slowly stirring oatmeal or rolled oats in boiling water or milk (in Scotland traditionally treated as a pl); pottage (obs); jail, or a jail sentence, esp in the phrase **do porridge** to serve a jail sentence (sl). [**pottage** perh altered by influence of obs or dialect *porray* vegetable soup, from L *porrum* leek]
◻ **porr'idge-stick** n a stick for stirring porridge.

porrigo /por-ī'gō/ n (pl **porri'gos**) scalp disease of various kinds. [L *porrīgō, -inis* dandruff]
■ **porriginous** /-ij'/ adj.

porringer or **porrenger** /por'in-jər/ n a small dish, usu with a handle, for soup, porridge, etc; a headdress shaped like such a dish (Shakesp). [Earlier *poddinger*, related to *pottinger*; see **porridge**, **pottage**; for inserted n cf **passenger**, **messenger**]

port¹ /pōrt or pört/ n a harbour; a town with a harbour. [OE *port*, from L *portus, -ūs* related to *porta* a gate]
◻ **port admiral** n the admiral commanding at a naval port. **port charges** n pl harbour dues. **port of call** n a port where vessels can call for stores or repairs. **port of entry** n a port where merchandise is allowed by law entry to and exit from a country.

port² /pōrt or pört/ (naut) n the larboard or left side of a ship. ◆ adj left. ◆ vt and vi to turn left. [Ety doubtful]
■ **port the helm** in former helm orders, to turn the tiller to port, or the upper part of the wheel to starboard, and so the rudder, and the ship, to starboard; since 1933 **port** means turn the ship to port.

port³ /pōrt or pört/ n an opening in the side of a ship; a porthole or its cover; any socket on a computer by which data can pass to and from peripheral units (comput); part of a horse's bit curved for the tongue; a passageway for a ball or curling-stone; a gate or gateway (obs); a town gate, or its former position (now chiefly Scot); an outlet or inlet for a fluid. [Fr *porte* (perh also OE *port*), from L *porta* gate]
■ **port'age** n (Shakesp) an opening.

port⁴ /pōrt/ or /pört/ n (also **port wine**) a fortified wine (dark-red or tawny, sometimes white) of the Douro valley, shipped from *Oporto*, Portugal.
■ **port'y** adj of the nature, taste or colour of port.
❑ **port-wine stain** or **mark** n a deep-red, slightly raised (often extensive) birthmark. **port-wi'ny** n porty.

port⁵ /pōrt/ or /pört/ vt to carry or convey (*obs*); to hold in a slanting direction upward across the body (*milit*); to adapt (a program, etc) for another computer system. ◆ n bearing; demeanour; carriage of the body, deportment; imposing bearing; style of living; a retinue (*obs*); the position of a ported weapon. [Fr *port*, *porter*, from L *portāre* to carry]
■ **portabil'ity** n the quality of being portable; the ability of a program to be used on another computer system. **port'able** adj easily or conveniently carried or moved about; endurable (*Shakesp*); (of a computer program) easily adapted for use on a wide range of computers. ◆ n a portable article. **port'age** n an act of carrying; carriage; the price of carriage; a space, track, or journey, over which goods and boats have to be carried or dragged overland; a sailor's private venture in a voyage (*Shakesp*). ◆ vt to transport goods, boats, etc overland between waterways. **port'ance** n (*Spenser*; *Shakesp*) carriage, bearing. **port'ate** adj (*heraldry*) in a position as if being carried. **port'atile** adj portable. **port'ative** adj easily carried. ◆ n (*hist*) a portable organ (often *pair of portatives*).
❑ **port-cray'on** (or **porte-**) n (Fr *porte-crayon*) a handle for holding a crayon. **porte-bonheur** /*port'bon-œr'*/ n (Fr) a charm carried for luck. **porte'-monnaie'** /*-mon-e'*/ n (Fr) a purse or pocketbook. **port'-fire** n a slow-match or match-cord.

port⁶ /pōrt/ or /pört/ (*hist*) n a town with market privileges; a borough. [Connection with **port¹** and **port³** obscure]
❑ **port'man** n (*hist*) a burgess, *esp* one chosen to administer town affairs. **port'reeve** n (OE *portgerēfa*; *hist*) a mayor or principal magistrate.

port⁷ /pōrt/ or /pört/ n an instrumental tune; a bagpipe composition. [Gaelic]
❑ **port a beul** /bē'əl/ n mouth music.

port⁸ /pōrt/ or /pört/ (*Aust inf*) n a bag, a suitcase. [Short form of **portmanteau**]

porta /pōr'/ or /pör'tə/ (*zool*) n a gate-like structure, *esp* the transverse fissure of the liver. [L *porta* gate]
■ **por'tal** adj.
❑ **portal system** n the portal vein with its tributaries, etc. **portal vein** n the vein that conveys to the liver the venous blood from intestines, spleen, and stomach.

portability see under **port⁵**.

portable see under **port⁵**.

portage see under **port³,⁵**.

portague see under **Portuguese**.

Portakabin® /pōr'/ or /pör'tə-kab-in/ n a small *portable* building for use as a temporary office, etc.

portal¹ /pōr'/ or /pör't(ə)l/ n a gate or doorway, *esp* a great or magnificent one; any entrance; the arch over a gate (*archit*); the lesser of two gates; a website, often incorporating a search engine, that provides access to a wide range of other sites on the World Wide Web. [OFr *portal*, from LL *portāle*, from L *porta* a gate]

portal² see under **porta**.

Portaloo® /pōr'/ or /pör'tə-loo/ n a portable lavatory. [**loo¹**]

portamento /pör-/ or /pör-tə-men'tō/ (*music*) n (pl **portamen'ti** /-tē/) a continuous glide from one tone to another; sometimes applied to an execution between staccato and legato. [Ital]

portance see under **port⁵**.

portas see **portesse**.

portate, **portatile**, **portative**, **port-crayon** see under **port⁵**.

portcullis /pōrt-/ or /pört-kul'is/ n a grating that can be let down to close a gateway of a castle, fortress, etc; a lattice (*heraldry*); one of the pursuivants of the English College of Heralds; an Elizabethan silver halfpenny with a portcullis on the reverse. ◆ vt to obstruct, as with a portcullis. [OFr *porte coleïce* sliding gate]

port de bras /*por-də-bra'*/ (Fr) n the practice or technique of arm movements in ballet; a balletic figure illustrating this technique.

Porte /pōrt/ or /pört/ (*hist*) n the Turkish imperial government, so called from the Sublime Porte or High Gate, the chief office of the Ottoman government at Constantinople. [Fr *porte*, from L *porta* gate]

porte-bonheur, etc see under **port⁵**.

porte-cochère /pört-/ or /port-ko-sher'/ n a house entrance admitting a carriage. [Fr *porte*, from L *porta* gate, and Fr *cochère*, fem adj from *coche* coach]

portend /pōr-/ or /pör-tend'/ vt to betoken; to warn of as something to come; to presage. [L *portendere*, *portentum*, from *por-*, equivalent to *prō* or *per*, and *tendere* to stretch]
■ **portent** /pōr'/ or /pör'tent/ n that which portends or foreshows; the quality of being portentous, ominousness; an evil omen; a prodigy, a marvel. **portentous** /-tent'-/ adj ominous; prodigious, extraordinary; impressive or solemn; pompous, self-important. **portent'ously** adv. **portent'ousness** n.

porteous see **portesse**.

porter¹ /pōr'/ or /pör'tər/ n (also *fem* **port'eress** or **port'ress**) a doorkeeper or gatekeeper; a caretaker in a college, university, etc, or in a block of flats; a person at the door or entrance to an office block, factory, etc who greets visitors, takes messages, allows or monitors entrance, etc; someone who waits at the door to receive messages. [OFr *portier*, from LL *portārius*, from L *porta* a gate]
■ **port'erage** n the office or duty of a porter.
❑ **porter's lodge** n a house or an apartment near a gate for the use of the porter.

porter² /pōr'/ or /pör'tər/ n a person employed at a railway station, hotel, market, etc to carry passengers' luggage, parcels, etc; a person employed in a hospital to move patients, etc; an attendant on a train (*US*); a dark-brown malt liquor, *prob* from its popularity with London porters. [OFr *porteour* (Fr *porteur*), from L *portātor*, *-ōris*, from *portāre* to carry]
■ **port'erage** n carriage; the charge made by a porter for carrying goods. **port'erly** adv like a porter. ◆ adj (*obs*) of a porter; coarse.
❑ **porter'-house** n a house where porter is sold; a chop-house. **port'erhouse** or **por'terhouse-steak** n a choice cut of beefsteak next to the sirloin.

portesse /pōr'/, /pör'təs or -tes/ (*hist*) n a portable breviary (also **port'ess**, **port'as**, **port'hors**, **port'house**, **port'ous**, **port'hos** or **porteous** /pōr'/ or /pör'tyəs/). [OFr *portehors* (LL *porteforium*), from L *portāre* to carry, and *forīs* out of doors]
❑ **porteous roll** (*Scots law*; *obs*) a list of persons to be tried.

portfolio /pōrt-/ or /pört-fō'li-ō/ n (pl **portfo'lios**) a case or pair of boards for holding loose papers, drawings, etc; a collection of such papers, eg drawings or photographs put together as examples of a student's work; a list of securities held; the office of a cabinet minister with responsibility for a government department; the area of responsibility of such a minister. [Ital *portafogli(o)*, from L *portāre* to carry, and *folium* a leaf]

porthole /pōrt'/ or /pört'hōl/ n a hole or opening in a ship's side for light and air, or (formerly) for pointing a gun through. [**port³** and **hole¹**]

porthors, **porthos**, **porthouse** see **portesse**.

portico /pör'/ or /pör'ti-kō/ n (pl **por'ticos** or **por'ticoes**) a range of columns along the front or side of a building (*archit*); a colonnade; the Painted Porch (*philos*; see **porch** and **stoic**). [Ital, from L *porticus*, a porch]
■ **por'ticoed** adj provided with a portico.

portière /por-tyer'/ n a curtain hung over the door or doorway of a room; a portress, concierge. [Fr]

portigue see under **Portuguese**.

portion /pōr'/ or /pör'shən/ n a part; an allotted part; an amount of food served to one person; destiny; the part of an estate descending to an heir; a dowry. ◆ vt to divide into portions; to allot as a share; to provide with a portion. [OFr, from L *portiō*, *-ōnis*]
■ **por'tioned** adj. **por'tioner** n (*Scots law*) the holder of a small feu *orig* part of a greater; a portionist of a benefice (**heir'-por'tioner** see under **heir**). **por'tionist** n a postmaster of Merton College; one of two or more incumbents sharing a benefice. **por'tionless** adj having no portion, dowry, or property.

Portland /pōrt'/ or /pört'lənd/ adj belonging to or associated with the Isle of *Portland*, a peninsula of Dorset.
■ **Portlandian** /-land'i-ən/ n a group of sands and limestones, the middle group of the Upper or Portland Oolite (also *adj*).
❑ **Portland arrowroot** or **Portland sago** n a farina prepared in the Isle of Portland from wake-robin tubers. **Portland cement** n a cement made by burning a mixture of clay and chalk of the colour of Portland stone. **Portland sheep** n a breed of small, blackfaced sheep found in the Isle of Portland. **Portland stone** n an oolitic building-stone which is quarried in the Isle of Portland.

portland see **portlast**.

portlast /pōrt'/ or /pört'ləst/ (*obs naut*) n probably the gunwale (also **portoise** /-tiz/ and wrongly **port'land**). [Origin unknown]
■ **yards down a portlast** with yards down on or near the deck.

portly /pōrt'/ or /pört'li/ adj corpulent, stout; having a dignified appearance (*archaic*). [**port⁵**]
■ **port'liness** n.

portman see under **port⁶**.

■ words derived from main entry word; ❑ compound words; ■ idioms and phrasal verbs

portmanteau /pört- or pört-man'tō/ n (pl **portman'teaus** or **portman'teaux** /-tōz/) a large travelling bag that folds back flat from the middle (also (obs) **portman'tle** or **portman'tua**); a rack for hanging clothes (rare); Lewis Carroll's term for a blend, a word into which are packed the sense (and sound) of two words, eg slithy for lithe and slimy (also **portmanteau word**). ◆ adj combining or covering two or more things of the same kind. [Fr, from porter to carry, and manteau a cloak]

portobello /pör- or pör-tə-bel'ō/ n (pl **portobell'os**) a mature mushroom with an open cap.

portoise see **portlast**.

portolano /pör-tə-lä'nō/ n (pl **portola'nos** or **portola'ni** /-nē/) in the Middle Ages, a navigation manual giving sailing directions and illustrated with charts showing ports, coastal features, etc (also **portolan**, **portulan** or **portulan chart** /por'tə-lən or -tū-/). [Ital, navigation manual, harbour master]

portous see **portesse**.

portrait /pör', pör'trit or -trāt/ n a painting, photograph or other likeness of a real person; a vivid description in words; portraiture (rare). ◆ adj (of something rectangular in format) having the shorter sides at the top and bottom, opp to landscape (printing). ◆ vt (obs) to portray. [OFr po(u)rtrait, po(u)rtraire, from L prōtrahere, -tractum; see **protract**]

■ **por'traiture** n a likeness; the art or act of making portraits; a collection of portraits; verbal description. **portray** /pör- or pör-trā'/ vt to paint or draw the likeness of; to describe in words; to act the part of in a drama; to adorn with portraiture or representations (obs). **portray'al** n the act of portraying; a representation. **portray'er** n. □ **por'trait-bust** n. **por'trait-gallery** n. **por'trait-painter** n. **por'trait-painting** n.

portray, **portrayal** see under **portrait**.

portreeve see under **port**[6].

portress see **porter**[1].

Port Salut /pör sa-lü'/ n a mild cheese orig made at the Trappist monastery Le Port du Salut in Bayonne, France.

Portugaise /pör- or pör-tū-gāz'/ adj Portuguese; in a Portuguese style. [Fr]

■ **à la Portugaise** cooked with tomato or having a prevalent flavour of tomato; with a tomato-based sauce, often with onion, garlic and herbs.

Portuguese /pör-, pör-tū-gēz' or pör' or pör'/ adj of or relating to the Republic of Portugal in SW Europe, its people or its language. ◆ n (pl **Portuguese** (from which the vulgar sing **Portuguee'** or **-gee**')) a native or citizen of Portugal; the language of Portugal.

■ **portague** or **portigue** /pört' or pört'ə-gū/ n an old Portuguese gold coin of the 16c and 17c.

□ **Portuguese man-of-war** n any of several hydrozoans of the genus Physalia, having tentacles able to give a painful, sometimes deadly, sting.

portulaca /pör-, pör-tū-lā'kə or -lak'ə/ n any plant of the purslane genus Portulaca, giving name to the family **Portulacā'ceae**, mostly succulent herbs of dry places, related to the Caryophyllaceae. [L portulāca purslane]

porty see under **port**[4].

porwiggle see **pollywog**.

pory see under **pore**[1].

POS see **point of sale** under **point**[1].

pos[1] /poz/ (sl) adj short for **positive**.

pos[2] see **po**[1].

pos. abbrev : position; positive.

posada /pō-sä'də/ n a Spanish inn, or one in a Spanish-speaking country. [Sp, from posar to lodge]

posaune /pō-zow'nə/ n the trombone. [Ger]

pose[1] /pōz/ n an attitude; an assumed attitude; an affectation of a mental attitude; (in dominoes) the right to begin the game; a secret hoard (Scot). ◆ vi to assume or maintain a pose; to attitudinize; (with as) to pretend to be. ◆ vt to put in a suitable attitude; to posit; to assert; to claim; to put forward, propound. [Fr poser to place, from LL pausāre to cease, from L pausa pause, from Gr pausis; between Fr poser and L pōnere, positum, there has been confusion, which has influenced the derivatives of both words]

■ **pose'able** adj. **pos'er** n a person who poses esp (inf) someone who dresses or behaves, etc, so as to be noticed. **poseur** /pōz-œr'/ or (fem) **poseuse** /-œz'/ n (Fr) an attitudinizer; a person who adopts poses and affects opinions, etc, in order to impress others. **pos'ey** or (rare) **pos'y** adj (derog) affected, adopting poses for effect.

□ **pos'ing pouch** n a garment covering only the genitals, as worn by male artist's models.

pose[2] /pōz/ vt (archaic) to puzzle; to perplex by questions; to bring to a standstill. [Aphetic, for **oppose**, or **appose**[2], confused with it]

■ **pos'er** n someone who or something which poses; a difficult question. **pos'ing** n and adj. **pos'ingly** adv.

posé /pō-zā'/ (heraldry) adj standing still. [Fr, pap of poser; see **pose**[1]]

Poseidon /po- or pə-sī'dən or -dön/ (Gr myth) n the Greek sea god, identified with Neptune by the Romans. [Gr Poseidōn, -ōnos]

■ **Poseidōn'ian** adj.

poser see under **pose**[1,2].

poseur, poseuse see under **pose**[1].

posh[1] /posh/ (inf) adj smart, stylish, top-class; expensive, and therefore of the wealthy classes; superb. ◆ adv in a way associated with the upper classes, as talk posh. ◆ vt and vi (usu with up) to trim up, to polish. [Popularly supposed to be from 'port outward starboard home', the most desirable position of cabins when sailing to and from the East before the days of air-conditioning, but no evidence has been found to support this; poss linked with **posh**[2]]

■ **posh'ly** adv. **posh'ness** n.

posh[2] /posh/ (obs sl) n money, esp a small amount, a halfpenny; a dandy. [Appar from Romany posh half]

poshteen see **posteen**.

posigrade /poz'i-grād/ (aeronautics and astronautics) adj having or producing positive thrust; of or relating to a posigrade rocket. [Positive in contrast to retrograde]

□ **posigrade rocket** n a small propellant rocket that is fired to give forward acceleration when required, esp on a multi-stage rocket when jettisoning a redundant stage.

posit /poz'it/ vt (**pos'iting**; **pos'ited**) to set in place, dispose; to postulate, assume as true, definitely or for argument's sake. ◆ n a statement made on the assumption that it will be proved valid. [L pōnere, positum to lay down]

positif /poz'i-tif/ n a separate set of stops on an organ; the manual that controls such a set. [Fr]

position /pə-zish'ən/ n situation; place occupied; attitude, disposition, arrangement; state of affairs; a proposition or thesis; the ground taken in argument or in a dispute; a principle laid down; place in society; high standing; a post or appointment; occurrence in an open or closed syllable; situation of the left hand in playing the violin, etc (music); method of finding the value of an unknown quantity by assuming one or more values; the commitment of a dealer in commodities, currencies or securities (stock exchange). ◆ adj of or defining position. ◆ vt to set in place; to determine the position of, locate. [Fr, from L positiō, -ōnis, from pōnere, positum to place]

■ **posi'tional** adj. **posi'tioned** adj placed. **posi'tioner** n.

□ **position paper** n an official report stating the views and intentions of an organization with regard to a particular matter. **position ratio** n a ratio determining the position of a point in a range or of a ray in a pencil, ie that of the distances from two fixed points in the range, or of the sines of the angular distances from two fixed rays.

positive /poz'i-tiv/ adj definitely, formally or explicitly laid down; express; beyond possibility of doubt; absolute; expressing a quality simply without comparison (grammar); downright, out-and-out; fully convinced; over-confident in opinion; matter-of-fact; concrete; material; actual; characterized by the presence of some quality, not merely absence of its opposite; affirmative; feeling or expressing agreement to or approval of something; having a good or constructive attitude; having qualities worthy of approval; (of a bacteriological test) confirming the presence of the suspected organism, etc; greater than zero, or conventionally regarded as greater than zero, indicating such a quantity (maths); in the direction of increase, actual or conventional; in a direction towards the source of stimulus (biol); having the lights and shades not reversed (photog and optics); having a relatively high potential (elec); of, having or producing, positive electricity (see below); dextrorotatory (optics); having a greater index of refraction for the extraordinary than for the ordinary ray in double refraction; basic (chem). ◆ n that which is positive; reality; a positive quantity; a positive quality; the positive degree, or an adjective or adverb in it; an image in which lights and shades or colours, or both, are unchanged; a photographic plate with the lights and shades of the original; a positive organ (see below); a positif. [L positīvus fixed by agreement, from pōnere, positum to place]

■ **pos'itively** adv. **pos'itiveness** n the state or quality of being positive; certainty; confidence. **pos'itivism** n actual or absolute knowledge; certainty; assurance; positive philosophy (see below). **pos'itivist** n a believer in positivism. **positivist'ic** adj. **positiv'ity** n.

□ **positive action** same as **affirmative action** (see under **affirm**). **positive angle** n one generated by a straight line moving anticlockwise. **positive discrimination** see under **discriminate**. **positive electricity** n electricity developed, eg in glass by rubbing with silk, arising from deficiency of electrons. **positive feedback** *n* feedback in which the output of a system is used to increase the input. **positive organ** *n* a small supplementary church organ, *orig* portable and placed upon a stand. **positive philosophy** *n* the philosophical system originated by Auguste Comte (1798–1857), its foundation being the doctrine that man can have no knowledge of anything but phenomena, and that the knowledge of phenomena is relative, not absolute; also 20c developments of this (**logical positivism**) much concerned with determining whether or not statements are meaningful. **positive pole** *n* (of a magnet) that end (or pole) which turns to the north when the magnet swings freely. **positive rays** *n pl* canal-rays, a stream of positively electrified particles towards the cathode of a vacuum tube (**positive-ray analysis** the detection of gases, and determination of their molecular weights, by measuring the parabolas produced on a photographic plate by positive rays deflected in two directions at right angles to each other by a magnetic and an electric field). **positive reinforcement** *n* (*behaviourism*) the following of a response by a positive event or stimulus, thus increasing the likelihood of the response being repeated. **positive sign** *n* the sign (read *plus*) of addition. **positive vetting** *n* a method of screening individuals to ensure their suitability for highly responsible positions.

positron /*poz'i-tron*/ (*phys*) *n* (also **pos'iton**) a particle differing from the electron in having a positive charge; a *positive* elec*tron*.

■ **positronium** /-*trōn'i-əm*/ *n* a positron and an electron bound together as a short-lived unit, similar to a hydrogen atom.

❑ **positron emission tomography** (or **PET**) **scanner** *n* a device that uses gamma rays to monitor brain activity, by following the movement of a radioactive tracer substance injected into the bloodstream.

posnet /*pos'nit*/ *n* a small cooking pot with feet and a handle. [OFr *pocenet*]

posology /*po-* or *pə-sol'ə-ji*/ *n* the science of quantity; the science of dosage. [Gr *posos* how much, and *logos* a word, discourse]

■ **posological** /-*ə-loj'i-kl*/ *adj*.

poss[1] *adj* an informal short form of **possible**.

poss[2] /*pos*/ (*dialect*) *vt* to agitate (clothes) in washing them, with a stick, etc. [Perh imit modification of Fr *pousser* to push, from L *pulsāre* to beat]

■ **poss'er** *n* (*archaic*; also **poss'-stick**) a wooden stick, *usu* with a perforated metal plate on the bottom, for possing clothes in a washtub.

posse /*pos'i*/ *n* a force or body (of constables); any group temporarily established for some purpose; a gang or group of (*esp* young) friends (*sl*); power; possibility. [L *posse* to be able, and *comitātūs* of the county]

■ **in posse** (*law*) in potentiality; possibly. **posse comitatus** /*kom-i-tā'tas* or *-tā'toos*/ force of the county, men called out by the sheriff to aid in enforcing the law.

possess /*pə-zes'*/ *vt* to have or hold as owner, or as if owner; to have as a quality; to seize; to obtain; to attain (*Spenser*); to maintain; to control; to be master of; to occupy and dominate the mind of; to have sexual intercourse with (a woman); to put in possession (with *of*, formerly with *in*); to inhabit, occupy (*obs*); to inform, acquaint; to imbue; to impress with the notion or feeling; to prepossess (*obs*). [OFr *possesser*, from L *possidēre*, *possessum*]

■ **possess'able** *adj*. **possessed'** *adj* in possession; self-possessed; dominated by a spirit that has entered one, or some other irresistible influence. **possession** /*poz-esh'ən*/ *n* the act, state or fact of possessing or being possessed; a thing possessed; a subject foreign territory; control of the ball in football, etc. **possess'ional** *adj* relating to possession. **possess'ionary** *adj*. **possess'ionate** *adj* (*formal*) holding or allowed to hold possessions, *opp* to *mendicant*. ◆ *n* a possessionate monk. **possess'ioned** *adj*. **possess'ive** *adj* relating to or denoting possession; unwilling to share what one has with others; reluctant to allow another person to be independent of oneself, too inclined to dominate; genitive (*grammar*). ◆ *n* (*grammar*) a possessive adjective or pronoun; the possessive case or a word in it. **possess'ively** *adv*. **possess'iveness** *n* extreme attachment to one's possessions; desire to dominate another emotionally. **possess'or** *n*. **possess'orship** *n*. **possess'ory** *adj*.

❑ **possession order** *n* a court order granting possession of a property. ■ **what possesses him, her**, etc**?** what malign influence causes him, her, etc, to act so foolishly?, what has come over him or her? **writ of possession** (*law*) a process directing a sheriff to put a person in possession of property recovered in ejectment.

posset /*pos'it*/ *n* a drink, milk curdled with eg wine, ale or vinegar, formerly used as a remedy for colds, etc; a small amount of milk, etc, regurgitated by a baby after a feed. ◆ *vt* (*Shakesp*) to curdle. ◆ *vi* to make a posset; (of a baby) to regurgitate a little milk, etc, after feeding. [ME *poschot*, *possot*; origin unknown]

❑ **posset cup** *n* a large cup or covered bowl for posset.

possible /*pos'i-bl*/ *adj* capable of existing or happening; not contrary to the nature of things; that could be true, conceivable, contingent;

capable of being done or managed, achievable, practicable; such as one may tolerate, accept or get on with; potential, capable of development. ◆ *n* a possibility; something or someone that is potentially selectable; the highest possible score in shooting; one's best (*Gallicism*); (in *pl*) necessaries (*sl*). [L *possibilis*, from *posse* to be able]

■ **poss'ibilism** *n* the policy of confining efforts to what is immediately possible or practicable. **poss'ibilist** *n*. **possibil'ity** *n* the state of being possible; a candidate, etc capable of winning, being successful, etc; that which is possible; a contingency; (in *pl*) potential, promise for the future. **poss'ibly** *adv* perhaps; by any possible means, within the limits of possibility; conceivably, with reason.

possie or **pozzy** /*poz'i*/ (*Aust inf*) *n* a position. [Shortened forms of **position**]

Possum® or **possum** /*pos'əm*/ *n* any of a range of electronic services by means of which severely disabled people can perform tasks, eg operate household equipment or a word processor. [*patient-operated selector mechanism*]

possum[1] (formerly also **'possum**) /*pos'əm*/ *n* in America, an aphetic form of **opossum** (*inf*); applied also to the Australasian phalanger. ◆ *vi* (*Aust* and *US*) to play possum.

■ **play possum** to feign death, sleep, illness or ignorance; to dissemble. **stir the possum** (*Aust*) to liven things up.

possum[2] see **Possum**®.

POST *abbrev* : point-of-sale terminal (see under **point**[1]); power-on self-test (*comput*).

post[1] /*pōst*/ *n* a stout, stiff stake or pillar of timber or other material, *usu* fixed in an upright position; an upright member of a frame, a vertical timber supporting a horizontal one (often in compounds, as in *doorpost*, *goalpost*); an upright pole marking the beginning or end of a race track, a starting-post or winning post; the pin of a lock; the shaft of an earring, the part that passes through the hole in the earlobe; a solid thickish stratum (*geol*); a pillar of coal left in a mine as a support; a tavern doorpost, on which a score was chalked (*Shakesp*). ◆ *vt* to stick up on a post, hence on a board, door, wall, hoarding, etc; to announce, advertise or denounce by placard; to announce the name of in a published list; to make available online or on an Internet site; to placard as having failed in an examination, or failed to be classed; to announce (a ship) as overdue; to affix a bill or notice to. [OE *post*, from L *postis* a doorpost, from *pōnere* to place]

■ **post'er** *n*.

❑ **post hole** *n* (*archaeol*) a hole sunk in the ground to take a fence post, roof support, etc. **Post'-it**® or **Post-it note**® *n* a small piece of paper on which a note may be written, the adhesive on its back allowing it to be temporarily affixed to a variety of surfaces. **post mill** *n* a windmill pivoted on a post.

■ **between you and me and the** (**bed-, lamp-, gate-**, etc) **post** in confidence. **first past the post** having reached the winning post first, having won the race (see also **first-past-the-post** under **first**). **from pillar to post** see under **pillar**. **sheriff's post** (*hist*) a post at a sheriff's door (see under **sheriff**).

post[2] /*pōst*/ *n* an appointment; office, position or job; a fixed place or station, *esp* a place to which a soldier or body of soldiers is assigned for duty; a body of soldiers so stationed; (generally) one's place of duty, one's station; full rank as naval captain (see **post captain** below); a settlement or trading establishment, *esp* in a remote area; a bugle-call (*first* or *last post*) summoning soldiers to their quarters at night, or (*last post*) blown at funerals. ◆ *vt* to station somewhere on duty; to transfer (personnel, a military unit) to a new location; to appoint to a post; to send or appoint (to a ship) as full captain. [Ital *posto*, from L *positum*, from *ponere* to place]

■ **post'ing** *n*.

❑ **post captain** *n* formerly, a full captain in command of, or having commanded, a ship of more than twenty guns (a **post ship**), distinguished from a commander (called a captain by courtesy). **post exchange** see **PX**. **post'holder** *n* the holder of a position or job.

post[3] /*pōst*/ *n* an officially established system for the conveyance and delivery of mail; letters and parcels delivered by this system, mail; a collection or delivery of mail; a post office, or post-office letter box; an item published on the World Wide Web; a messenger carrying letters by stages or otherwise (*hist*); a public letter-carrier (*hist*); a postman (*obs* or *dialect*); a mail-coach (*hist*); a packet-boat (*obs*); a posthorse (*Shakesp*); a fixed place or stage on a road, for forwarding letters and change of horses (*hist*); a name often given to a newspaper; haste (*Shakesp*); a size of writing paper, double that of common notepaper (*orig* with watermark, a post horn). ◆ *vt* to put into a letter box, or hand over at a post office, for conveyance and delivery; to enter in a ledger, or (with *up*) update (a ledger), or transfer to another book or account (*bookkeeping*); to supply with news or the latest information; to publish on the World Wide Web; to shift or transfer (eg blame) to another (with *over* or *off*; *Shakesp*). ◆ *vi* to travel with posthorses or with speed; to move up and down in the saddle, in time with the horse's movements. ◆ *adv* with posthorses; with speed. [Fr *poste*, from Ital *posta*, from L *posita*, from *pōnere*, *positum* to place]

■ **post'er** *n* someone who travels post (*Shakesp*); a posthorse (*hist*); the person who posts a letter; see also **poster¹**. **post'ie** *n* (*Scot* and *Aust inf*) a postman. **post'ing** *n* and *adj*.

❑ **post'bag** *n* a mailbag; a term used collectively for letters received. **post'box** *n* a letter box. **post boy** *n* (*hist*) a boy who rides posthorses or who carries letters; a postilion. **post'bus** *n* a small bus used for delivering mail and for conveying passengers, *esp* in rural areas. **post'card** *n* a card for writing messages on, often with a picture on one side, designed for sending through the post without an envelope; such a card not issued by the post office, as distinct from a postal card (*qv* under **postal**) (*US*). ◆ *vt* to send a postcard to. **post chaise** (popularly **po''chay**, **po'chay** and **po''chaise**) *n* (*hist*) a carriage, *usu* four-wheeled, for two or four passengers, with a postilion, used in travelling with posthorses. **post-chaise'** *vi* to travel by post chaise. **post'code** *n* a code, often a combination of letters and numbers, specific to a particular section of housing, added to addresses to ease the task of sorting mail for delivery. ◆ *vt* to provide with or affix a postcode. **postcode lottery** *n* (*inf*) a situation in which the provision of services such as medical treatment or education, rather than being uniform everywhere, varies in quality according to where people live. **post day** *n* the day on which the post or mail arrives or departs. **post-free'** *adj* and *adv* without charge for postage; with postage prepaid. **posthaste'** *n* (from the old direction on letters, *haste*, *post*, *haste*) haste in travelling like that of a post. ◆ *adj* speedy; immediate. ◆ *adv* with utmost haste or speed. **post horn** *n* a postman's horn; a long straight brass horn blown by a coach guard. **post'horse** *n* a horse kept for posting. **post'house** *n* an inn, *orig* where horses were kept for posting; a post office. **post letter** *n* a letter in the custody of the post office. **post'man** *n* a man who delivers mail; a post or courier (*hist*). **postman's knock** *n* a party game in which players take turns to pretend to deliver a letter, and get a kiss from the 'recipient'. **post'mark** *n* the mark stamped upon an item of mail at a post office defacing the postage stamp or showing the date and place of despatch or of arrival. ◆ *vt* to mark an item of mail in this way. **post'master** *n* a person in charge of a local post office; someone who supplies posthorses (*hist*); (with *cap*) a portionist or scholar on the foundation of Merton College, Oxford. **postmaster general** *n* the minister at the head of a country's postal services; (with *caps*) this post in the UK, abolished in 1969. **post'mastership** *n*. **post'mistress** *n* a woman in charge of a local post office. **post office** *n* an office for receiving and transmitting letters by post, and other business; (with *caps*) a government department or national authority in charge of the conveyance of letters, etc in various countries. **post-office box** *n* one of a series of private numbered boxes or locations in a post office, where mail is kept until called for by the addressee. **Post Office Savings Bank** *n* the older name of the National Savings Bank. **post'-paid'** *adj* having the postage prepaid. **post'person** *n* a postman or postwoman. **post'rider** *n* (*hist*) the rider of a posthorse. **post road** *n* (*hist*) a road with stations for posthorses. **post time** *n* the time for the despatch or for the delivery of letters. **post town**, **post village** *n* a town or village with a post office. **post'woman** *n* a woman who delivers mail.

■ **general post** a game in which the players change places simultaneously. **keep posted** (*inf*) to supply with the latest news.

post⁴ /*pōst*/ *n* a stake in a game; a good or winning hand as in the old card game of **post and pair**, in which players vied on the goodness of their hand, a pair-royal (*qv* under **pair¹**) being best. ◆ *vt* to stake. [**post²**, or Ital *posta* a stake]

Words formed using the prefix **post-** are listed in the following entry or, if their meaning is self-evident, at the foot of the page; other words spelt with *post-* follow in the main word list.

---

post- /*pōst-*/ *pfx* meaning (1) after, as in *post-classical*, *post-primary*, *post-Reformation*, *postwar*, etc; (2) behind, as in *post-nasal*, *post-ocular* (*esp anat*). [L *post* after, behind]

■ **post-bell'um** *adj* after the war. **postcava** /*-kā'və*/ *n* (*anat*) the inferior vena cava, the vein carrying blood from the lower limbs and abdomen. **post-commun'ion** *n* the part of the Eucharistic office after the act of communion. ◆ *adj* succeeding communion. **post-consum'er** *adj* (of a consumer product) used and available for recycling. **postdate'** *vt* to date after the real time; to mark with a date (eg for payment) later than the time of signing. **post-dilu'vial** *adj* after the Flood; after the diluvial period (*obs geol*). **post-dilu'vian** *n* and *adj*. **post'doc** *n* (*inf*) (a person engaged in) postdoctoral research. **postdoc'toral** *adj* relating to academic work carried out after obtaining a doctorate. **post-ech'o** *n* (*pl* **post-ech'oes**) (*sound recording*) the unwanted effect of a faint repetition heard just after the actual sound on a tape recording,

caused by the transfer of material between surfaces of the wound tape (see also **pre-echo**). **post'-entry** *n* an additional entry of merchandise at a custom house; a subsequent insertion or entry (*bookkeeping*); a late entry in a race. **post-exil'ian** or **post-exil'ic** *adj* after the time of the Babylonian captivity of the Jews. **post'-existence** *n* existence in a subsequent life. **post'face** *n* something added by way of a concluding note at the end of a written work, *opp* to *preface* (*rare*). **postfem'inism** *n* a movement that regards the main principles of feminism as either achieved or misguided and seeks a new programme. **postfem'inist** *n* and *adj*. **post'fix** *n* a suffix (**postfix notation** a form of algebraic notation where the operator follows the operands). ◆ *vt* /*-fiks'*/ to add at the end; to suffix. **post-form'ing** *adj* see **post-forming sheet** under **sheet¹**. **post-glā'cial** *adj* occurring or formed after a glacial period. ◆ *n* a post-glacial period or deposit of material. **postgrad'uate** or (*inf*) **post'grad** *n* a student studying or researching for an advanced qualification after obtaining a first university degree. ◆ *adj* relating to such students or their work. **post-hypnot'ic** *adj* (**post-hypnotic suggestion** a suggestion made to a hypnotized subject, who does not act upon it until some time after emerging from the hypnotic trance). **Post-Impress'ionism** *n* (also without *caps*) a movement in painting succeeding Impressionism, at the end of the 19c, van Gogh, Gauguin, Matisse and Cézanne being among its exponents and its aim being subjective interpretation of things, as distinct from the objective representation typical of Impressionism. **Post-Impress'ionist** *n* and *adj*. **postindus'trial** *adj* (of a society, economy, etc) no longer dependent on heavy industry. **post-lin'gual** *adj* subsequent to the acquisition of language (**post-lingually deafened** having lost one's hearing, as distinct from being deaf since birth; see also **prelingual**). **post'lude** *n* (*music*) a concluding movement or voluntary, *opp* to *prelude*. **postmerid'ian** *adj* belonging to the afternoon or evening, the time of day after the sun has crossed the meridian. **post-millenā'rian** *n* a believer in post-millennialism. **post-millenn'ial** *adj*. **post-millenn'ialism** *n* the doctrine that the Second Advent will follow the millennium. **post-millenn'ialist** *n*. **post-mod'ern** *adj*. **post-mod'ernism** *n* a style (in any of the arts) following upon, and showing movement away from or reaction against, a style, theory, etc termed 'modernist'; returning to traditional materials and an earlier, *esp* classical, style, *esp* in reaction eg to international modern (*qv*) (*archit*). **post-mod'ernist** *adj* and *n*. **post-mor'tem** *adj* (L *mortem*, accusative of *mors*, *mortis* death) after death (as *adv phrase*, **post mortem**). ◆ *n* a post-mortem examination, an autopsy; an after-the-event discussion, *esp* of what went wrong, held after a game or other contest. **postna'tal** *adj* relating to or typical of the period after birth. **postnā'tī** (or /*-nä'tē*/) *n pl* those born after the event (understood as being) referred to (cf **antenati** under **antenatal**). **post-Ni'cene** *adj* after the Nicene council. **post-nup'tial** *n* after marriage. **post-obit** /*-ob'it* or *-ōb'it*/ *n* (L *obitum*, accusative of *obitus* death) taking effect after someone's death. ◆ *n* a borrower's bond securing payment on the death of someone from whom he or she has expectations. **post-op'erative** *adj* relating to the period just after a surgical operation (often shortened to **post'-op**). **post-orb'ital** *adj* behind the eye or eye socket. **postpar'tum** or **post-par'tum** *adj* after childbirth. **postpose'** *vt* (*grammar*) to place after in the syntax of a sentence, etc. **postposi'tion** *n* the position of a word after another that it modifies, to which it is syntactically related; such a word; placing or position after. **postposi'tional** *adj*. **postposi'tionally** *adv*. **postpos'itive** *adj* (*grammar*) used in postposition. **postpos'itively** *adv*. **postpran'dial** *adj* (L *prandium* a repast) following a meal, *esp* dinner. **post-produc'tion** *n* (*cinematog*, *TV*) the work of editing and dubbing a film that follows the shooting of it. **postscē'nium** *n* the part of the stage behind the scenery. **post'script** *n* (L *postscrīptum* something written after, *pap* of *postscrībere* to write after) a part added to a letter after the signature (*usu* introduced by the initials **PS**); a supplement added to the completed text of a book, etc; a talk following a news broadcast, etc; a comment or information provided additionally; (**PostScript®**) a page-description language in which commands and data are passed to the computer as a stream of ASCII characters determining the position and nature of all elements on the page, widely used in desktop publishing (*comput*). **post-struc'turalism** *n* a revision of the structuralist (*qv* under **structure**) view of literature, holding that language has no objectively identifiable or absolute meaning, and that therefore texts allow of any number of interpretations. **post-struc'turalist** *n* and *adj*. **post-synchronizā'tion** or **-s-** *n* (*cinematog*) the process of recording and adding a soundtrack to a film after it has been shot (*inf* short forms **post-synch'** and **post-synch'ing**). **post-synch'ronize** or **-ise** *vt*. **post-ten'sion** *vt* to stretch the reinforcing wires or rods in (pre-stressed concrete) after the concrete is set. **post-ten'sioned** *adj*. **Post-Ter'tiary** *adj* (*geol*) later than Tertiary, ie Pleistocene and Holocene (also *n*). **post-traumat'ic** *adj* (**post-traumatic stress disorder** the mental stress that can follow a traumatic experience, characterized by flashbacks, nightmares, anxiety, etc). **post-vin'tage** *adj* (**post-vintage thoroughbred** see under **thorough**). **postvi'ral** *adj* (**postviral syndrome** a condition, following a viral infection, characterized by periodic fatigue, diminished concentration, depression, dizziness, etc. See also **myalgic encephalomyelitis** under **myalgia**). **post-vocal'ic** *adj* (*phonetics*) after a vowel. **post-war'** *adj* (**post-war credit** a portion of income tax credited to an individual for repayment after World War II).

postage /pō'stij/ *n* money charged or paid (*esp* in advance in the form of a stamp) for conveyance by post; travel with posthorses (*obs*). [**post**³]
◻ **postage meter** *n* (*esp N Am*) a franking-machine. **postage stamp** *n* a small adhesive label, or a printed or embossed stamp, showing that a postal charge of the specified amount has been paid; an area of astonishing smallness (*facetious*).

postal /pō'stəl/ *adj* of, by or relating to, the mail service. ◆ *n* (*US*; in full **postal card**) a postcard issued by the post office with a printed stamp. [**post**³]
■ **pos'tally** *adv*.
◻ **postal ballot** *n* the submission of votes by post. **postal card** *n* (*US*) see *n* above. **postal code** *n* a postcode. **postal meter** *n* (*N Am*) a postage meter (qv). **postal note** *n* (*Aust* and *NZ*) a postal order. **postal order** *n* an order issued by the postmaster authorizing the holder to receive at a post office payment of the sum printed on it. **postal tube** *n* a cylinder for sending rolled-up papers by post. **postal union** *n* an association of the chief countries of the world for international postal purposes. **postal vote** *n* a vote submitted by post rather than placed directly into a ballot box.

postcava see under **post-**.

post chaise, **postcode** see under **post**³.

Postcomm /pōst'kom/ *n* Postal Services Commission, a UK regulatory body.

postdate...to...**postdoctoral** see under **post-**.

posteen /po-stēn'/ *n* an Afghan greatcoat, generally of sheepskin with the fleece on (also (*non-standard*) **poshteen**'). [Pers *postī* leather]

poster¹ /pō'stər/ *n* a large printed bill, notice, advertisement, picture or placard for displaying on a wall, etc. ◆ *vt* to stick bills or posters on; to advertise or publish by posters. [**post**¹]
■ **posteriza'tion** or **-s-** *n* (*image technol*) a video effect in which the picture is produced in a limited number of flat tones and colours. **po'sterize** or **-ise** ◆ *vt* (*N Am*) to make (a sporting opponent) appear slow or foolish through a display of technical brilliance.
◻ **poster boy** or **girl** *n* (a person considered as) an outstanding representative of a particular movement, cause, activity, etc such as might appear on a poster (also **poster child**). **poster colours** or **paints** *n pl* matt watercolours for designing posters and other reproduction work. **poster session** *n* a presentation of information or a short paper, *esp* at a conference, by means of wall-mounted posters and illustrations, the presenter being available to explain, discuss or elaborate on the material.

poster² see under **post**¹,³.

poste restante /pōst re-stät' or res'tänt/ *n* a department of a post office where letters are kept until called for. [Fr, remaining post]

posterior /po-stē'ri-ər/ *adj* coming after; later; positioned behind or at the back; on the side next to the axis (*bot*). ◆ *n* (*usu* in *pl*) one's descendants; posterity; (formerly in *pl*) one's rear parts, the buttocks (*inf*; *facetious*); (in *pl*) latter part (*Shakesp*; *facetious*). [L *posterior*, compar of *posterus*, following, later, coming after, from *post* after]
■ **posterior'ity** *n*. **postē'riorly** *adv*.

posterity /po-ster'i-ti/ *n* those coming after; succeeding generations; all one's descendants. [L *posteritās*, *-ātis* the future, future generations, from *posterus* next, following, later]

postern /pos'tərn or pō'stərn/ *n* a back door or gate; a small private door; a sallyport (qv under **sally**¹). ◆ *adj* (of a door, gate, etc) back; private. [OFr *posterne*, *posterle*, from L *posterula*, a dimin from *posterus* coming after]

postface, **postfeminism**, **postfix**, **postgraduate** see under **post-**.

posthaste see under **post**³.

post hoc /pōst hok/ (*L*) *adj* and *adv* after the event.

posthorse, **posthouse** see under **post**³.

posthumous /pos'tū-məs/ *adj* after death; (of a child) born after the father's death; (of a literary or musical composition) published after the author's or composer's death. [L *posthumus*, *postumus*, superl of *posterus* coming after, from *post* after; the *h* inserted from false association with *humāre* to bury]
■ **post'humously** *adv*.

postiche /po-stēsh'/ *adj* superfluously and inappropriately superadded to a finished work; counterfeit or false. ◆ *n* a superfluous and inappropriate addition; a hairpiece, a wig. [Fr, from Ital *appositizio* artificial, false, from LL (unattested) *appositicius* superadded, from L *appasitus*; see **apposite**]

posticous /po-stī'kəs/ (*bot*) *adj* posterior; outward, extrorse. [L *postīcus* hinder, from *post* after]

postie see under **post**³.

postil /pos'til/ *n* a marginal note, *esp* in the Bible; a commentary; a homily; a book of homilies. ◆ *vt* and *vi* to gloss. [OFr *postille* (Ital *postilla*), from LL *postilla*, possibly from L *post illa* (*verba*) after those (words)]
■ **pos'tillate** *vt* and *vi*. **postillā'tion** *n*. **pos'tillātor** or **pos'tiller** *n*.

postilion or **postillion** /pō- or po-stil'yen/ (*hist*) *n* a post boy; someone who guides posthorses, or horses pulling any sort of carriage, riding on one of them. [Fr *postillon*, from Ital *postiglione*, from *posta* post]

postillate, etc see under **postil**.

postindustrial see under **post-**.

postliminary /pōst-lim'i-nə-ri/ *adj* subsequent; sometimes erroneously used for **postliminiary** (see under **postliminy**). [Constructed on the analogy of **preliminary**; see **postliminous**]

postliminous /pōst-lim'i-nəs/ *adj* being by way of a supplement or appendix, postliminary (also (*non-standard*) **postlimin'ious**). [L *post* after, and *līmen* threshold]

postliminy /pōst-lim'i-ni/ *n* the right of returned exiles, prisoners, etc, to resume their former status; the right by which persons or things taken in war are restored to their former status. [L *postlīminium*, literally, return behind the threshold, from *post* behind, and *līmen*, *-inis* threshold]
■ **postlimin'iary** or **postlimin'ious** *adj*.

postlude see under **post-**.

postman, **postmark**, **postmaster** see under **post**³.

postmeridian see under **post-**.

post meridiem /pōst mə-rid'i-əm or me-rē'di-em/ (*L*) after noon (*abbrev* **pm**).

postnatal, **postpartum** see under **post-**.

postpone /pōst-pōn', pə-spōn'/ *vt* to put off to a future time; to defer; to delay; to subordinate (*obs*); to postpose (*grammar*). [L *postpōnere*, from *post* after, and *pōnere* to put]
■ **postpone'ment** or (*rare*) **postpō'nence** *n*. **postpō'ner** *n*.

postpose, etc, **postprandial**, **postscenium**, **postscript** see under **post-**.

postulancy, **postulant** see under **postulate**.

postulate /pos'tū-lāt/ *vt* to claim; to take for granted, assume; to assume as a possible or legitimate operation without preliminary construction (*geom*); to nominate, subject to sanction of ecclesiastical authority. ◆ *vi* to make demands. ◆ *n* /pos'tū-lət/ that which is postulated; a stipulation; an assumption; a fundamental principle; a position assumed as self-evident; an operation whose possibility is assumed (*geom*); an axiom (*geom*); a necessary condition; a person nominated to a benefice by the king, pending the Pope's consent (*Scot hist*). [L *postulāre*, *-ātum* to demand, from *poscere* to ask urgently]
■ **pos'tulancy** *n* the state or period of being a postulant. **pos'tulant** *n* a petitioner; a candidate, *esp* for holy orders or admission to a religious community. **postulā'tion** *n*. **postulā'tional** *adj*. **postulā'tionally** *adv*. **pos'tulator** *n* (*relig*; *RC*) the presenter of a case for beatification or canonization. **pos'tulatory** *adj* supplicatory; assuming or assumed as a postulate.

Some words formed with the prefix **post-**; the numbers in brackets refer to the numbered senses in the entry for **post-**.

postclass'ical *adj* (1).	**postmen'strual** *adj* (1).	**post-pri'mary** *adj* (1).
postco'ital *adj* (1).	**postna'sal** *adj* (2).	**post-Reforma'tion** *adj* (1).
postconsonan'tal *adj* (1).	**postoc'ular** *adj* (2).	**postsur'gical** *adj* (1).
postmenopau'sal *adj* (1).	**posto'ral** *adj* (2).	**post'-tax** *adj* (1).

■ words derived from main entry word; ◻ compound words; ■ idioms and phrasal verbs

postulatum /pos-tū-lā'təm/ or /pos-tū-lä'tŭm/ (L) n something postulated, a postulate. [Neuter pap of *postulāre*, *-ātum* to demand]

posture /pos'chər/ n the way one holds one's body in standing, sitting or walking; carriage, bearing; a particular position or attitude of the body; a pose or attitude adopted for effect; the relative disposition of parts of any object; a mental attitude adopted towards a particular issue, etc; a state of affairs. ◆ vi to assume a posture; to pose; to attitudinize. ◆ vt to place in a particular pose. [Fr, from L *positūra*, from *pōnere*, *positum* to place]

■ **pos'tural** adj. **pos'turer** and **pos'turist** n someone who attitudinizes; an acrobat.

❏ **postural integration** n a system of treatment aimed at restoring and/or improving the flow of the life-force through the body by using various techniques to realign the body's posture.

postviral see under **post-**.

posy[1] /pō'zi/ n a little bunch of flowers; a motto or sentiment, eg engraved inside a ring (*archaic*). [Alteration of **poesy**]

posy[2] see **posey** under **pose**[1].

pot[1] /pot/ n any of various *usu* deep and round domestic containers used as cooking utensils, or for preservation and storage; the contents or capacity of such a container; a chamberpot; a flowerpot or plantpot; a teapot; earthenware, or a handmade earthenware vessel; a vessel of fireclay used to contain the glass during melting (*glass-making*); a trophy, *esp* a cup (*inf*); a pocket, or a stroke in which the object ball enters a pocket (*snooker*, etc); (*usu* in *pl*) a large sum of money (*inf*); a large stake or bet (*inf*); an accumulated pool of bets in a gambling game; a heavily-backed horse; an important person (*usu* big *pot*; *inf*); a pot-belly (*inf*); a pot shot (*inf*); a simple helmet (*hist*); a wicker trap for lobsters, etc, a lobster pot; a size of paper (also **pott**) about 12 by 15 inches (30.5 by 38cm; so called from its original watermark). ◆ adj made of clay or earthenware. ◆ vt (**pott'ing**; **pott'ed**) to put into pots, for preserving, etc; to cook in a pot; to plant in a pot; to manufacture (pottery); to drain molasses from (sugar) during the refining process; to shoot (a creature) for the pot (ie as a meal), by a pot shot, or generally to bag, win, secure; to pocket (a snooker or billiard ball); to epitomize or summarize, *esp* simplistically; to encapsulate (an electronic component) in a protective insulating resin; to sit (a baby) on a chamberpot. ◆ vi to make pottery, *esp* by hand; to take a pot shot (with *at*); to tipple (*Shakesp*). [Late OE *pott*; cf Ger *Pott*; Swed *potta*; Dan *potte*; Fr *pot*; origin unknown]

■ **pot'ful** n (pl **pot'fuls**) as much as a pot will hold. **pott'able** adj (*snooker*, etc). **pott'ed** adj cooked or preserved in a pot; condensed, concentrated; abridged; (of music, etc) recorded for reproduction, canned (*inf*); intoxicated by drugs or alcohol (*N Am inf*).

❏ **pot'ale** n refuse from a grain distillery. **pot bank** n a pottery. **pot barley** n barley whose outer husk has been removed by millstones. **pot'-bellied** adj. **pot-bell'y** n (*inf*) a protuberant belly; a person who has a protuberant belly; (also **pot-bellied stove**) a wood- or coal-burning stove of bulbous design (*N Am*). **pot'boiler** n a work in art or literature produced merely with regard to saleability, to secure the necessaries of life; a producer of such works; a pebble heated up and used for boiling water (*archaeol*). **pot'boiling** n. **pot'-bound** adj (of a pot plant) having its roots cramped by too small a pot, without room for growth. **pot'boy** n a serving boy in a public house. **pot companion** n a comrade in drinking. **pot furnace** n a furnace, which may be variously fired, in which a number of pots for glassmaking are set. **pot'gun** n a mortar; a popgun. **pot'-hanger** n a device for hanging a pot or a pothook on. **pot hat** n a bowler hat; formerly, a top hat. **pot'-head** n a stupid person; see also **pothead** under **pot**[2]. **pot herb** n a vegetable, *esp* one used for flavouring, eg parsley. **pot holder** n a piece of thick padded material used to protect the hands when handling hot dishes, etc. **pot'hole** n a hole worn in rock in a stream bed by eddying detritus; a deep hole eroded in limestone, a pot (see **pot**[4]); a hole worn in a road surface. ◆ vi and vt to explore (limestone potholes). **pot'holer** n. **pot'holing** n. **pot'hook** n a hook for hanging a pot over a fire; a hooked stroke in writing. **pot'house** n (*old*) an alehouse. **pot'-hunter** n someone who hunts to get food; someone who shoots merely for the sake of a bag; someone who competes merely for the sake of prizes. **pot'-hunting** n. **pot'-lid** n the cover of a pot; (*Scot* **pat'-lid**) a curling-stone played exactly on the tee. **pot liquor** n a thin broth in which meat has been boiled. **pot luck** n (in the expression **take pot luck**) what may happen to be in the pot and so be available to make a meal, *esp* for the unexpected arrival; whatever happens to be available. **pot'man** n a pot companion; a pot boy. **pot metal** n an alloy of copper and lead; scraps of old iron pots, etc. **pot plant** n a plant grown in a pot. **pot roast** n a dish of braised meat, *esp* with added vegetables. **pot'-roast** vt to braise. **pot'sherd** /-shûrd/ n (*esp archaeol*) a fragment of pottery (also **pot'shard**, (*Spenser*) **pot'share**). **pot'shop** n a small public house. **pot shot** n a shot within easy range; a casual or random shot; a shot taken at a bird or animal with a view to one's next meal; a critical remark aimed at an easy or undeserving target. **pot'-sick** adj (of a plant) sickly from

growing in a pot. **pot stick** n a stick for stirring what is being cooked in a pot. **pot still** n a still in which heat is applied directly to the pot containing the wash (cf **patent still**). **pot'-still** adj made in a pot still. **pot'stone** n impure talc or steatite, a massive finely felted aggregate of talc, *usu* with mica and chlorite, from which cooking pots were fashioned in earlier times. **potting compost** n a compost mixture used for growing plants in pots. **potting shed** n a garden shed in which plants are grown in pots before being planted out in beds. **pot-val'iant** or **pot-val'orous** adj full of drink-inspired courage. **pot valour** n. **pot'-walloper** n see separate entry **pot-waller**.

■ **big pot** (*inf*) an important person. **go to pot** (*inf*) to go to ruin; to go to pieces (*orig* to supply the cooking pot, not the melting-pot). **keep the pot boiling** or **a-boiling** to procure the necessaries of life; to keep things going briskly without stopping. **pot of gold** the object of fairytale quests, traditionally to be dug up where the rainbow ends; any vainly sought source of wealth, etc. **pot on** to transfer (a plant) into a larger pot. **pot up** to put (a plant) into a pot. **put someone's pot on** (*Aust inf*) to inform on someone, give someone away; to undo or finish someone. **the pot calling the kettle black** castigation of another's faults by someone with the same shortcomings.

pot[2] /pot/ (*inf*) n the drug cannabis in any of its forms, *incl* marijuana and hashish. [Perh a shortening of Mexican Sp *potiguaya*]

❏ **pot'head** n a habitual taker of cannabis.

pot[3] /pot/ n short form of **potentiometer**.

pot[4] /pot/ (*dialect*) n a deep hole eg in limestone country, a pothole. [Perh same as **pot**[1], or from a Scandinavian source]

potable /pō'tə-bl/ adj fit to drink. ◆ n (*rare*) a beverage. [L *pōtābilis*, from *pōtāre* to drink]

potage /po'täzh/ n thick soup. [Fr]

potager /pot'ə-jər/ or /pot'ə-zhä/ n a vegetable garden or kitchen garden laid out in a decorative way, often incorporating flowers. [Fr, from **potage**]

potamic /pə-tam'ik/ adj of or relating to rivers. [Gr *potamos* a river]

■ **potamolog'ical** adj. **potamol'ogist** n. **potamol'ogy** n the scientific study of rivers.

potamogeton /pot-ə-mō-jē'ton/ or /-gē'ton/ n a plant of the pondweed genus (*Potamogeton*) of water plants, with floating and submerged leaves, which gives its name to a family of monocotyledons, **Potamogetonā'ceae**. [Gr *potamogeitōn* pondweed, from *potamos* river, and *geitōn* neighbour]

potash /pot'ash/ n (also, earlier, **pot'-ash** and **potass** /pə-tas', pot'as/) a powerful alkali, potassium carbonate, *orig* obtained in a crude state by leaching wood *ash* and evaporating the solution in *pots*; (in *pl*, *usu* **pot ashes** or **pot'-ashes**) the original name for the alkali in its crude form; potassium hydroxide (*caustic potash*); sometimes the monoxide or (vaguely) some other compound of potassium; potash water. ◆ adj containing or rich in potassium. ◆ vt to treat with potash. [Eng **pot** and **ash**[1], or the corresponding Du *pot-asschen* (modern *potas*)]

❏ **potash alum** n alum (qv). **potash water** or **potass water** n an aerated water containing potassium bicarbonate.

potass see **potash**.

potassa /pə-tas'ə/ (*chem*; now *rare*) n potash; potassium monoxide or potassium hydroxide; formerly used for potassium in compound names, eg *carbonate of potassa*. [New L, from **potass** (see **potash**)]

potassium /pə-tas'i-əm/ n a silvery alkaline metallic element (symbol **K**; atomic no 19) discovered by Davy in 1807 in potash, occurring naturally in compounds. [**potass** (see **potash**) or **potassa**]

■ **potass'ic** adj.

❏ **potassium-argon dating** n estimation of the date or prehistoric mineral formation from the proportion of potassium-40 to argon-40, the latter having developed from the former by radioactive decay and being trapped in the rock. **potassium carbonate** n a white deliquescent substance used in manufacturing glass and soap (see also **potash**). **potassium chlorate** n a soluble crystalline substance that is a powerful oxidizing agent and is used in manufacturing explosives, fireworks and matches. **potassium chloride** n a crystalline substance used as a fertilizer and in photographic processing. **potassium cyanide** n a poisonous soluble solid used *esp* in extracting gold and silver from their ores. **potassium hydrogen carbonate** n a white crystalline powder used in baking powder, carbonated soft drinks and as an antacid. **potassium hydrogen tartrate** n cream of tartar (qv). **potassium hydroxide** n a white deliquescent substance used in manufacturing liquid soaps, shampoos and detergents, caustic potash. **potassium iodide** n a crystalline solid used in photography, also added to table salt to prevent iodine deficiency. **potassium nitrate** n a crystalline oxidizing agent used as a meat preservative, fertilizer and in explosives. **potassium permanganate** n a purple crystalline oxidizing agent used as a disinfectant and in analytical chemistry. **potassium sorbate** n a substance used as an antifungal food perservative. **potassium sulphate** n a soluble substance used in glass-making and as a fertilizer.

potation /pə-tā'shən/ n the activity of drinking; a draught; liquor. [L pōtātiō, -ōnis, from pōtāre, -ātum to drink]

potato /pə-tā'tō/ n (pl **potā'toes**) orig the sweet potato, plant or tuber (see under **sweet**); now usu a S American plant, Solanum tuberosum, widely grown in temperate regions, or its tuber; someone who sits or lies about by the hour in vegetable-like inertia, as in couch potato, beach potato (sl). [Sp patata, from Haitian batata sweet potato]
□ **potato apple** n the small berry-like fruit of the potato plant. **potato blight** n a destructive disease of the potato caused by either of the parasitic fungi Alternaria solani (**early blight**) or Phytophthora infestans (**late blight**). **potato bogle** n (Scot) a scarecrow. **potato chips** n pl (usu simply **chips**) long thinly sliced pieces of potato fried in fat; potato crisps (esp N Am). **potato crisps** n pl (usu simply **crisps**) very thin crisp fried slices of potato, widely produced commercially. **potato disease** or **rot** n any of several bacterial or fungal diseases of potatoes. **potato finger** n (Shakesp) a fat finger. **potato pancake** n a pancake made from a batter containing grated potatoes. **potato pit** n a clamp of potatoes. **potato race** n any of various types of race involving the picking up, carrying or passing on of potatoes; a stopping-and-starting style of sprinting race. **potato ring** n an 18c Irish ceramic or metal (esp silver) ring for standing a bowl on. **potato scone** n a flat savoury griddle cake made from flour, milk and mashed potato. **potato spirit** n alcohol made from potatoes. **potato trap** n (sl) the mouth.
■ **hot potato** (sl) a controversial issue; a tricky problem or assignment that one would prefer not to touch. **small potatoes** (US) anything of no great worth. **the potato** or **the clean potato** (inf) the right thing.

potatory /pə-tā'tə-ri/ (rare) adj relating to (excessive) drinking. [L pōtātōrius, from pōtāre, -ātum to drink]

pot-au-feu /pot-ō-fö'/ (Fr) n (pl **pot-au-feu**) a large earthenware cooking pot or casserole; a stew, esp with boiled beef and vegetables, traditionally cooked in such a pot in France.

Potawatomi /pot-ə-wot'ə-mē/ n (pl **Potawatomi** or **Potawatomis**) (a member of) a tribe of Native Americans, originally from the Great Lakes region; the Algonquian language of the Potawatomi. ◆ adj of or relating to the Potawatomi or their language.

potch or **potche** /poch, pōch/ a variant of **poach²** in sense of thrust or trample.
■ **potch'er** n (paper-making) a machine for breaking and bleaching pulp.

pote /pōt/ vt and vi to poke, thrust, esp with the foot (obs except dialect); to crimp with a poting-stick (obs). [OE potian to thrust]
□ **po'ting-stick** n (obs) a poking-stick for ruffs, etc.

poteen or **potheen** /po-tyēn', -chēn' or -tēn'/ n Irish whiskey illicitly distilled. [Ir poitín, dimin of pota pot, from Eng **pot** or Fr pot]

potence¹ see under **potent¹**.

potence² /pō'təns/ n a gibbet (obs); a gibbet-shaped structure; (in watchmaking) a bracket for supporting the lower pivot; a revolving ladder in a dovecot; a right-angled military formation. [Med L potentia a crutch]

potencé /pō'tən-sā/ (heraldry) adj (of a cross) having limbs that terminate in a crossbar. ◆ n a figure in the shape of T. [Fr, from **potence²**]

potency see under **potent¹**.

potent¹ /pō'tənt/ adj powerful; mighty; strongly influential; cogent; (of a male) capable of erection, sexual intercourse, or ejaculation. ◆ n (Shakesp) a prince or potentate. [L potēns, -entis, prp of posse to be able]
■ **po'tency** or (more rarely) **po'tence** n the quality of being potent; power; potentiality; strength or effectiveness, eg of a drug; in a male, the ability to have sexual intercourse; (**potency**) a wielder of power, a potentate; (**potency**; of a point with respect to a circle) the rectangle between the segments into which a chord of the circle is divided at the point (geom). **pō'tentize** or **-ise** vt to make potent. **pō'tently** adv.

potent² /pō'tent/ (obs) n a crutch with a crosspiece fitting under the arm; a support. ◆ adj (heraldry) (of a cross) having limbs terminating in crossbars, potencé. [Fr potence a crutch, support]

potentate /pō'tən-tāt/ n a powerful ruler; a monarch. [L potentātus power, a ruler, from potens; see **potent¹**]

potential /pə-ten'shl/ adj latent; possible or likely, though as yet not tested or actual; expressing power, possibility, liberty, or obligation (grammar); powerful, efficacious. ◆ n the range of capabilities that a person or thing has; powers or resources not yet developed or made use of; anything that may be possible; a possibility; the potential or subjunctive mood, or a verb in it (grammar); the work done in bringing a unit of mass, electricity, etc from infinity to a point in a field of force, expressed as a function of that point (phys). [L potentiālis, from potentia power]
■ **potential'ity** n. **poten'tialize** or **-ise** vt and vi. **poten'tially** adv.

□ **potential barrier** n (phys) a place in a field of force where the potential is high and the passage of particles impeded. **potential difference** n (phys) a difference in the electrical states existing at two points, which causes a current to tend to flow between them. **potential divider** same as **voltage divider** (see under **volt¹**). **potential energy** n (phys) the power of doing work, possessed by a body in virtue of its position. **potential well** n (phys) an area of low potential in a field of force.

potentiary /pə-ten'shi-ə-ri/ (Thackeray) n a person invested with power or influence. [From **plenipotentiary**]

potentiate /pə-ten'shi-āt/ vt to give power to; to make (drugs or chemicals) more potent or effective by using them in combination; to stimulate or boost the activity of (biochem, physiol). [L potentia power]
■ **poten'tiated** adj. **potentia'tion** n.

potentilla /pō-tən-til'ə/ n a plant of the genus Potentilla of the rose family, including silverweed and barren strawberry, differing from Fragaria (strawberry) in having a dry receptacle. [LL, dimin of L potēns powerful, from its once esteemed medicinal virtues]

potentiometer /pə-ten-shi-om'i-tər/ n (short form **pot**) an instrument for measuring difference of electric potential; a rheostat. [L potentia and **-meter**]
■ **potentiomet'ric** adj. **potentiom'etry** n.

pothecary /poth'i-kə-ri/ n an aphetic form of **apothecary** (also **pot'icary**).

potheen see **poteen**.

pother /podh'ər (formerly pudh'ər)/, or **pudder** /pud'ər/ n a choking smoke or dust; fuss; commotion; turmoil. ◆ vt to fluster or perplex. ◆ vi to make a pother. [Origin unknown; appar not connected with **powder**]
■ **poth'ery** adj.

pothole, **pothook**, **pothouse** see under **pot¹**.

poticary see **pothecary**.

potiche /po-tēsh'/ n an Oriental vase rounded or polygonal in shape, narrowing at the neck. [Fr potiche, potichomanie]
■ **potichomania** /-shə-mā'ni-ə/ n a craze for imitating Oriental porcelain by lining glass vessels with paper designs, etc.

potin /po-tε̃'/ n an old alloy of copper, zinc, lead and tin. [Fr]

potion /pō'shən/ n a draught of liquid medicine, poison or some magic elixir. [Fr, from L pōtiō, -ōnis, from pōtāre to drink]

potlatch, also **potlach** /pot'lach/ n in NW USA, a Native American winter festival, the occasion for emulation in extravagant gift-giving and, in one tribe, even property-destruction; any feast or gift (inf). [Chinook, from Nootka patlatsch a gift]

potometer /pə-tom'ə-tər/ n an instrument for measuring the rate at which a plant takes in water. [Gr poton drink]

potoo /po-tō'/ or -too'/ n any of several birds of the genus Nyctibius of tropical America, related to the nightjar, short-legged and large-eyed, with a small downward-curving beak and protective grey, white and buff colouring. [Imit of its cry]

potoroo /pō-tə-roo'/ or pot-/ n a small marsupial related to the kangaroo, the rat-kangaroo. [From an Aboriginal language]

potpourri /pō-pür'i, pō'pə-ri/ or -rē'/ n orig a mixed stew, olla-podrida; a fragrant mixture of dried petals, leaves, spices, etc used to scent a room, etc; a selection of tunes strung together, a medley; a literary production composed of unconnected parts; a hotchpotch or miscellany. [Fr pot pot, pourri rotten (pap of pourrir, from L putrēre, rot) translating Sp olla podrida]

POTS (inf; comput) abbrev: Plain Old Telephone System.

potsherd see under **pot¹**.

potstone see under **pot¹**.

pott a variant spelling of **pot¹**, esp as a paper size.

pottage /pot'ij/ n a thick soup; soup; vegetables boiled with or without meat (archaic); oatmeal porridge (obs). [Fr potage food cooked in a pot, later, soup, from pot jug, pot]

potter¹ /pot'ər/ n a maker of pottery. [pot]
■ **pott'ery** n articles of baked clay collectively, esp earthenware vessels; a place where such goods are commercially manufactured; the work or art of the potter. ◆ adj made of clay or earthenware.
□ **potter's field** n a burial ground for strangers and paupers (from that bought with the money Judas received for betraying Jesus). **potter wasp** n a solitary wasp that builds clay nests for its eggs. **potter's wheel** n (a device incorporating) a horizontally revolving dish on which to shape clay vessels such as bowls, plates, jugs, etc.

potter² /pot'ər/ vi to busy oneself in a desultory way with trifling tasks; to progress in an unhurried manner, to dawdle (with along, etc). ◆ n pottering; diffuse talk. [Frequentative of **pote**]
■ **pott'erer** n. **pott'ering** n and adj. **pott'eringly** adv.

pottery see under **potter**[1].

pottingar /pot'in-gər/ (obs Scot) n a form of **apothecary**.

pottinger /pot'in-jər/ n a maker of pottage; a small bowl, a porringer. [Earlier pottager; for inserted n cf **messenger**, **passenger**, etc]

pottle /pot'l/ n half a gallon, or thereabouts (archaic); a pot containing this amount (archaic); a punnet or small, esp conical, basket for strawberries. [OFr potel, dimin of pot pot]
□ **pott'le-bodied** adj having a body shaped like a pottle. **pott'le-deep** adj to the bottom of the pottle-pot. **pott'le-pot** n (Shakesp) a half-gallon pot or drinking vessel.

potto /pot'ō/ n (pl **pott'os**) a W African loris (Perodicticus potto); also applied to the kinkajou. [Said to be a W African name]

Pott's disease /pots di-zēz'/ (pathol) n a weakening disease of the spine caused by tuberculous infection, often causing curvature of the back. [Named after Sir Percival(l) Pott (1714–88), English surgeon, who first described it]

Pott's fracture /pots frak'chər/ (pathol) n a fracture of the lower end of the fibula usu with dislocation of the ankle, sometimes with a fracture also of the malleolus of the tibia. [Ety as for **Pott's disease**]

potty[1] /pot'i/ (inf) adj crazy, dotty; (with about) madly keen on; trifling, petty. [Origin obscure]
■ **pott'iness** n.

potty[2] /pot'i/ (childish or facetious) n a chamberpot, esp one designed for children too young to use a full-size toilet. [Dimin of **pot**[1]]
□ **pott'y-chair** n a child's chair fitted with a potty. **pott'y-mouth** n (inf) a person who habitually uses bad language. **pott'y-mouthed** adj. **pott'y-train** vt to teach a young child to use a potty. **pott'y-training** n.

POTUS /pō'təs/ abbrev: President of the United States.

pot-waller /pot'wö-lər/ n in certain English boroughs, before the Reform Bill of 1832, someone who satisfied the test as a voter by boiling his pot on his own fireplace within the borough, sometimes in the open air before witnesses to establish a bogus claim (variously altered popularly to **pot'-wabbler**, **-wobbler**, **-walloner**, **-wall'oper**). [pot and OE w(e)allan to boil]
□ **pot'-wall'oping** adj.

pouch /powch or (Scot) pooch/ n a pocket, purse or bag; in marsupials such as the kangaroos, a pocket of skin on the belly, in which the young are carried until weaned; a fleshy fold in the cheek of hamsters and other rodents, for storing undigested food; a puffy bulge under the eye. ◆ vt to pocket; to form into a pouch; to tip. ◆ vi to form a pouch; to be like a pouch. [ONFr pouche (OFr poche); cf **poke**[2]]
■ **pouched** adj having a pouch. **pouch'ful** n (pl **pouch'fuls**). **pouch'y** adj baggy.
□ **pouched mouse** n a small marsupial, Phascogale; an American jumping rodent (genus Dipodomys) with cheekpouches opening outwards. **pouched rat** n any American burrowing rodent of the family Geomyidae, with outward-opening cheekpouches.

pouder and **poudre** obsolete spellings of **powder**.

pouf[1] or **pouffe** /poof/ n a large firmly stuffed drum-shaped or cube-shaped hassock for use as a low seat or footrest; a puffed or bouffant type of hairstyle fashionable in the 18c; a pad worn in the hair by 18c women to help shape such a hairstyle; in dressmaking, material gathered up into a bunch; a soft ottoman. ◆ vt to give a puffed shape to (clothing or hair). [Fr pouf]
■ **poufed** or **pouffed** adj.

pouf[2] and **pouffe** less common spellings of **poof**[1].

pouftah and **poufter** other spellings of **pooftah** and **poofter** (see **poof**[1]).

Poujadist /poo-zhä'dist/ n a follower of the French politician Pierre Poujade (1920–2003), antiparliamentarian champion of the small man and of tax reduction. [Fr Poujadiste]
■ **Poujad'ism** n.

pouk and **poukit** see **pook**.

pouke see **puck**[1].

poulaine /poo-lān'/ n a long, pointed shoe-toe. [OFr (à la) Poulaine (in the fashion of) Poland]

poulard /poo-lärd'/ n a fattened or spayed hen. [Fr poularde, from poule hen]

poulder and **pouldre** obsolete spellings of **powder**.

pouldron /pōl'drən/ see **pauldron**.

poule /pool/ n a hen, esp a chicken for boiling; a promiscuous young woman; a prostitute; a movement in a quadrille. [Fr]
□ **poule de luxe** /də lüks/ n (pl **poules** /pool/ **de luxe**) (sl, esp US) a prostitute.

poulp or **poulpe** /poolp/ n the octopus. [Fr poulpe, from L pōlypus, from Doric Gr pōlypos = polypous; see **polyp**]

poult /pōlt/ n a chicken; the young of the common domestic fowl or other farmyard or game bird. [Fr poulet, dimin of poule hen; see **pullet**]

poulterer /pōl' or pōl' tə-rər/ or (archaic) **poulter** /pōl'tər/ n a dealer in dead fowls and game. [ME poulter, from OFr pouletier, from poulet; see **poult**]
□ **poulters' measure** n a rhymed couplet in which the first line has 12 syllables and the second 14 (from the varying number of eggs formerly sold by poulterers as a dozen).

poultfoot same as **poltfoot** (see under **polt**).

poultice /pōl'tis/ n a hot semi-liquid mixture spread on a bandage and applied to the skin to reduce inflammation, formerly used as a treatment for boils. ◆ vt to put a poultice on. [L pultēs, pl of puls, pultis (Gr poltos) porridge]

poultroone see **poltroon**.

poultry /pōl' or pōl'tri/ n domestic or farmyard fowls collectively; the meat of such fowls. [OFr pouleterie, from pouletier poulterer]
□ **poult'ry-farm**, **poultry yard** n a farm or yard where poultry are bred or confined.

pounce[1] /powns/ vi to spring or swoop suddenly in an attempt to attack or seize (with on, upon); to seize or fix upon eagerly (with on, upon); to dart. ◆ vt to seize with the claws; to emboss by blows on the other side (hist; perh from a different source); to puncture or pink (obs); to ornament with small holes (hist). ◆ n an act of pouncing on one's prey, victim, etc; the claw or talon of a hawk or other bird of prey, esp the innermost, or any but the hind claw; a punch or thrust (now dialect); a puncture (obs). [ME; orig sense was talon; perh derived in some way from L punctiō, -ōnis, from pungere, punctum to prick; cf **puncheon**[1]]
■ **pounced** adj equipped with claws.

pounce[2] /powns/ n sandarach, cuttle-bone, or other fine powder formerly used for preparing a writing surface or absorbing ink; coloured powder shaken through perforations to mark a pattern on a surface beneath. ◆ vt to prepare with pounce; to trace, transfer or mark with pounce; to powder or sprinkle (obs). [Fr ponce pumice, from L pūmex, pūmicis]
□ **pounce bag** or **pounce box** n a perforated bag or box for sprinkling pounce. **pounce pot** n a container for pounce for preparing writing surfaces, etc.

pouncet-box /pown'sit-boks/ n a pomander (also shortened to **poun'cet**; Shakesp); sometimes used for **pounce box** (see under **pounce**[2]). [Prob for pounced-box, ie perforated box; see **pounce**[2]]

pounching (Spenser) for **punching** (prp of **punch**[1]).

pound[1] /pownd/ n (pl formerly **pound**, now **pounds** (except inf and in compounds and certain phrases)) a unit of money, orig the value of a pound weight of silver; the standard monetary unit of the UK, 100 pence, formerly 20 shillings (the pound sterling, written d, for libra); the pound scots (hist; at the time of the Union with England in 1707 worth 1s. 8d.); the unit of currency in some former British dependencies and certain other countries, including Egypt, Syria, Lebanon, and (formerly) Ireland, Australia, New Zealand, Cyprus, Malta, Sudan and Jamaica; a unit of weight of varying value, long used in western and central Europe, more or less answering to the Roman libra and represented by its symbol lb; in avoirdupois weight, 16 ounces avoirdupois, 7000 grains, or 0.45359237kg; formerly, in troy weight, 12 ounces troy, 5760 grains, or about 373.242 grams; a pound weight (Shakesp); the balance (Spenser). ◆ vt (sl) to bet on as almost a certainty. [OE pund, from L (libra) pondō (pound) by weight, pondō by weight, from pendere to weigh]
■ **pound'age** n a charge or tax made on each pound sterling or weight; a commission, or a share in profits, of so much a pound; bodyweight, esp if excessive. **pound'al** n (phys) the foot-pound-second unit of force, ie that required to give acceleration of one foot per second per second to a one-pound mass. **pound'er** n a specimen weighing a pound. ◆ combining form denoting something weighing or carrying so many pounds, a field gun designed to fire shot weighing so many pounds, or person who has, receives or pays, so many pounds sterling.
□ **pound cake** n a sweet rich cake containing a pound, or equal proportions, of each chief ingredient. **pound cost averaging** n (finance) a method of investing by paying regularly a fixed amount for eg units in a particular trust, regardless of the fluctuating market price of the units. **pound day** n a day on which gifts of one pound weight of various goods are invited for charity. **pound-fool'ish** adj neglecting the care of large sums in attending to little ones (ie being penny wise). **pound force** n the gravitational force of 1lb weight and mass; a unit of such force (abbrev **lbf**). **pound sign** n the sign d, representing the pound sterling; the hash sign (US). **pound weight** n as much as weighs a pound; a weight of one pound used in weighing.

---

fāte; fär; mē; fûr; mīne; mōte; för; mūte; pŭt; dhen (then); el'ə-mənt (element) • For other sounds see detailed chart of pronunciation

■ **pound of flesh** strict exaction of one's due in fulfilment of a bargain, etc, to the point of making the other party suffer beyond what is reasonable (from *Shakesp, Merchant of Venice*).

pound² /*pownd*/ *n* an enclosure in which to keep stray animals, distrained goods or vehicles removed by the police, etc; any confined place; a pond (now *Scot* and *dialect*); a level part of a canal between two locks; the last compartment of a pound net. ◆ *vt* to put in a pound; to enclose, confine. [OE *pund* (in compounds) enclosure]
■ **pound'age** *n* a charge for pounding stray cattle.
❑ **pound'-keeper** or **pound'-master** *n*. **pound net** *n* an arrangement of nets for trapping fish.

pound³ /*pownd*/ *vt* to beat into fine pieces or to a pulp; to grind to a powder, eg with a pestle; to beat or thump with the fists, etc, to batter; to keep treading (the streets, pavements, etc); to bruise; to lay on, shower (*Spenser*). ◆ *vi* (of the heart) to thump; (of feet, hooves, etc) to strike the ground resoundingly; to run with heavy steps; to struggle on. ◆ *n* the act or sound of pounding. [OE *pūnian* to beat; *-d* excrescent, as in **sound¹, bound²**]
■ **pound'er** *n*. **pound'ing** *n*.

poundage see under **pound¹,²**.

poundal see under **pound¹**.

poupe /*poop*/ and **poupt** /*poopt*/ (*Shakesp; pap*) see **poop⁵**.

pour /*pōr* or *pör*/ *vt* to cause or allow to flow in a stream; to send forth or emit in a stream; to serve (tea, wine, etc) by pouring; to recount (one's story) or rehearse (one's woes) volubly (with *forth, out*); to send downstream (*Spenser*); to spread out (*obs*); to drain (eg cooked potatoes; *Scot*). ◆ *vi* to stream; to rain heavily; to emanate or proceed in profusion; to pour out tea, coffee, etc; (of a container, eg a teapot) to allow liquid contents to run out duly. ◆ *n* a pouring; an amount poured at a time. [ME *pouren*; origin obscure]
■ **pour'able** *adj* that can be poured. **pour'er** *n*. **pourie** /*poor'i*/ *n* (*Scot*) a container with a spout; a cream jug; an oilcan. **pour'ing** *n* and *adj*.
❑ **pour'-out** or **poor'-oot** *n* (*Scot*) the scattering of coins to children as the bride and bridegroom depart after a wedding.
■ **it never rains but it pours** when things, *esp* troublesome things, start happening, they happen all at once. **pouring wet** raining hard. **pour oil on troubled waters** see under **water**.

pourboire /*pör-* or *pür-bwär'*/ *n* a gratuity, a tip. [Fr, from *pour* for, and *boire* to drink]

pourie see under **pour**.

pourparler /*pör- pür-pär'lā*/ *n* (*usu* in *pl*) an informal preliminary conference. [Fr]

pourpoint /*pör'* or *pür'point*/ *n* a medieval quilted doublet. [Fr]

poursew or **poursue, poursuit** or **poursuitt** Spenserian for **pursue** and **pursuit**.

pourtray (*pap* in *Spenser* **pour'trahed** (3 syllables), **pourtrayd, purtraid, purtrayd**) an archaic spelling of **portray**.
■ **pour'traict** *n* an obsolete spelling of **portrait**.

pousada /*poo-sä'də*/ *n* a traditional hotel in Portugal or a Portuguese-speaking country. [Port, from *pousar* to rest]

pousowdie see **powsowdy**.

pousse /*poos*/ (*Spenser*) *n* pease. [**pulse²**]

pousse-café /*poos-ka-fā'*/ *n* a cordial, liqueur, or combination of several in layers, served after coffee. [Fr, push-coffee]

poussette /*poo-set'*/ *n* a figure in country dancing in which couples hold both hands and move up or down the set, changing places with the next couple. ◆ *vi* to perform a poussette. [Fr, dimin of *pousse* push]

poussin /*poo-sĭ'*/ *n* a chicken reared for eating at four to six weeks old; a small whole poussin, served as an individual portion, roasted, or split and fried or grilled. [Fr]

pout¹ /*powt*/ *vi* to push out the lips, the lower lip or both lips in an expression either sulky or sexually alluring; to protrude. ◆ *vt* to cause (*esp* the lips) to protrude. ◆ *n* a pouting expression, or act of pouting; a protruding condition. [ME *powte*, of doubtful origin]
■ **pout'er** *n* someone who pouts; a variety of pigeon that can puff out its crop. **pout'ing** *n*. **pout'ingly** *adv*. **pout'y** *adj* inclined to pout, sulky.

pout² /*powt*/ *n* a fish of the cod family, the bib (also **whiting pout**). [OE (*ǣle-*)*pūte* (eel)pout, perh connected with **pout¹** with reference to the fish's inflatable membrane on the head]
■ **pout'ing** *n* the whiting pout.
■ **eel'pout** see under **eel**. **horn pout** or **horned pout** an American catfish (genus *Amiurus*).

pout³ or **poot** /*poot*/ *n* a Scots form of **poult**. ◆ *vi* to shoot at young partridges or young grouse.

pouther /*pŭdh'ər*/ a Scots form of **powder**.

poutine /*poo-, pŭ-tēn'* or *-tin'*/ *n* a Canadian dish consisting of potato chips covered in cheese curds and gravy. [Can Fr]

pout net /*powt net*/ (*Scot*) *n* a fishing-net of conical shape with a semicircular mouth, its flat edge being dragged or pushed along the stream bed. [Origin uncertain]

POV *abbrev* : point-of-view.

poverty /*pov'ər-ti*/ *n* the state of being poor; need, want of necessities; a lack or deficiency; meagreness or inadequacy; a band of pipers (*obs*). [OFr *poverte* (Fr *pauvreté*), from L *paupertās, -ātis*, from *pauper* poor]
❑ **poverty line** *n* the dividing line between incomes that are sufficient, and incomes that are insufficient, to purchase life's necessities. **pov'erty-stricken** *adj* suffering from poverty. **poverty trap** *n* a state of poverty from which there is no escape, any increase in income resulting in a diminution or withdrawal of low-income government benefits.

POW *abbrev* : prisoner of war.

pow¹ /*pow*/ (*inf*) *interj* imitative of impact, etc.

pow² /*pow*/ (*Scot*) *n* a head, a poll; a head of hair. [**poll¹**]

pow³ /*pow*/ (*Scot*) *n* a slow-moving stream, generally found in carse lands; a small creek at the mouth of a river or in an estuary, affording a landing-place for boats, *esp* on the Forth. [Scot *poll*]

powan /*pow'ən*, *pō'ən*/ *n* a Scottish species of whitefish (genus *Coregonus*) found in Loch Lomond and Loch Eck. [Scot form of **pollan**]

powder /*pow'dər*/ *n* any solid in the form of fine dust-like particles; (also **face powder**) a cosmetic in this form patted onto the skin to give it a soft smooth appearance; hair-powder (qv); gunpowder; dust (*obs*); powder snow (*skiing*); a dose of medicine in powder form. ◆ *vt* to reduce to powder, to pulverize; to sprinkle, daub or cover with powder; to sprinkle with salt or spices in preserving, to salt (*obs* or *dialect*); to sprinkle. ◆ *vi* to crumble into powder; to use powder for the hair or face. [OFr *poudre*, from L *pulvis, pulveris* dust]
■ **pow'dered** *adj* reduced to powder eg (of food) through dehydration and crushing; sprinkled, daubed or dusted with powder; salted. **pow'dery** *adj* of the nature of powder; covered with powder; dusty; friable.
❑ **powder blue** *n* a pale blue colour, *orig* produced from powdered smalt (qv). **powder box** *n* a box for face powder, hair-powder, etc. **powder burn** *n* a minor burn caused to skin in proximity to a gunpowder explosion. **powder closet** or **pow'dering-clos'et** *n* (*hist*) a small room in which hair was powdered. **powder compact** see **compact¹**. **powder down** *n* a kind of down on some birds that readily disintegrates in powder. **powdered sugar** *n* (*N Am*) very fine sugar produced by grinding granulated sugar. **powder flask** or **powder horn** *n* a flask (*orig* a horn) for carrying gunpowder. **pow'dering-gown** *n* a loose dressing-gown worn while the hair was being powdered. **pow'dering-tub** *n* a vessel in which meat is salted; a tub used in the treatment of venereal disease by sweating (*obs*). **powder keg** *n* a small barrel for gunpowder; a potentially explosive situation. **powder magazine** *n* a place where gunpowder is stored. **powder metallurgy** *n* the science and art of preparing metals for use by reducing them, as a stage in the process, to powder form. **powder mill** *n* a mill in which gunpowder is made. **powder monkey** *n* a boy carrying powder from the magazine to the gunners on a ship-of-war (*hist*); generally, someone who carries out blasting operations. **powder puff** *n* a pad of velvety or fluffy material for dusting powder onto the skin; an effeminate male homosexual (*sl*). **powder room** *n* a ship's powder magazine; a room for powdering the hair (also **pow'dering-room**); a ladies' cloakroom or toilet (*euphem*). **pow'der-skiing** *n* (the art of) skiing in powder snow such as that encountered off piste. **powder snow** *n* freshly fallen loose thick dry snow. **powdery mildew** *n* a plant disease affecting eg roses, caused by a parasitic fungus (family Erysiphaceae), whose spores appear as a powdery white covering on leaves and stems; any of the fungi that cause this disease.
■ **keep one's powder dry** to preserve one's energies so as to be able to act when the moment comes, play a waiting game; to observe all practical precautions. **powder one's nose** (*euphem*; of a woman) to go to the toilet.

Powellism /*pow'ə-li-zm*/ *n* the views on immigration and on various economic issues expressed by J Enoch *Powell*, British politician and scholar (1912–98).
■ **Pow'ellite** *n* and *adj*.

powellite /*pow'ə-lit* or *-līt*/ *n* a mineral, calcium molybdate. [John Wesley *Powell* (1834–1902), American geologist, etc]

powellize or **-ise** /*pow'ə-līz*/ *vt* to season and preserve (timber) by boiling in a saccharine solution. [W *Powell*, the inventor of the process]

■ words derived from main entry word; ❑ compound words; ■ idioms and phrasal verbs

power /pow'ər or powr/ n the skill, physical ability, opportunity or authority to do something; strength or energy; force or effectiveness; an individual faculty or skill; capacity for producing an effect; the moving force of anything; control or influence exercised over others; right to command, authority; political control; rule; governing office; permission to act; a paper giving authority to act; potentiality; a person or group wielding authority or strong influence; that in which such authority or influence resides; a state influential in international affairs; (a state having) military strength of a specified kind; an armed force (*archaic*); (often in *pl*) a spiritual agent; a being of the sixth order of the celestial hierarchy (*medieval theol*); a great deal or great many (now *dialect* or *inf*); a mark of subjection (Bible, 1 Corinthians 11.10; New English Bible 'a sign of authority'); the sound value of a letter; the rate at which a system absorbs energy from, or passes energy into, another system, *esp* the rate of doing mechanical work, measured in watts or other unit of work done per unit of time (*mech*, *phys*, etc); any of the forms of energy, or any of these as the driving force of a machine, etc; mechanical or electrical energy as distinct from manual effort; an instrument serving as a means of applying energy (see **mechanical powers** under **mechanic**); the product of a number of equal factors (as in 12 *to the power of* 4, or $12^4 = 12 \times 12 \times 12 \times 12$), generalized to include negative and fractional numbers (*maths*); the specified number of such factors, the index or exponent; the potency (*qv*) of a point with respect to a circle (*geom*); magnifying strength, or a lens possessing it (*optics*). ◆ *adj* concerned with power; (of eg a tool) worked, or assisted in working, by mechanical or electrical power; motor-driven; involving a high degree of physical strength and skill (*esp sport*, as in *power tennis*). ◆ *vt* (often with *up*) to equip with mechanical or electrical power. ◆ *vi* and *vt* (*inf*) to move or propel with great force, energy or speed. [OFr *poer* (Fr *pouvoir*), from LL *potēre* (for L *posse*) to be able]

■ **pow'ered** *adj* (often as *combining form*) equipped with mechanical, etc power, as in *nuclear-powered*. **pow'erful** *adj* having great power; mighty; forcible; efficacious; intense; impressive; noticeable; (of a smell) strong and *usu* disagreeable; great in quantity (*inf*). ◆ *adv* (*inf*) exceedingly. **pow'erfully** *adv*. **pow'erfulness** *n*. **pow'erless** *adj* without power, deprived of power; weak; impotent; helpless. **pow'erlessly** *adv*. **pow'erlessness** *n*.

❑ **pow'er-amplifier** or (*inf*) **pow'er-amp** *n* (*electronics*) the stage or element in an amplifer that regulates power output (also **power unit**). **pow'er-assisted** *adj* helped by or using mechanical power. **power base** *n* an area, body of people, etc providing the foundation of a person or organization's power. **power block** *n* a politically important and powerful group or body. **pow'erboat** *n* a boat propelled by a motor, a motorboat. **power breakfast**, **lunch** or **tea** *n* (*inf*) a high-level business or political discussion held over breakfast, lunch or tea. **power broker** *n* a highly influential person able to sway the decisions, policies, etc of various groups. **power cut** *n* an interruption of, or diminution in, the electrical supply in a particular area. **power dive** *n* a *usu* steep dive by an aeroplane, made faster by using the engine(s). **pow'er-dive** *vi* and *vt*. **pow'er-diving** *n*. **pow'er-dressed** *adj*. **power dressing** *n* the wearing, by businesswomen, of smart suits tailored on austerely masculine lines so as to give an impression of confident efficiency and have a daunting effect on colleagues, contacts, etc. **power drill**, **lathe**, **loom** or **press** *n* a drill, lathe, loom or press worked by electricity or other form of power such as water or steam. **pow'er-driven** *adj* worked by (*esp* mechanical or electrical) power. **power factor** *n* (*elec eng*) the ratio of the total power dissipated in an electric circuit to the total equivalent volt-amperes applied to that circuit. **pow'erhouse** *n* a place where power is generated, a power station; a remarkably forceful or energetic person (*inf*). **pow'erlifting** *n* the sport of weightlifting. **power line** *n* a cable or conductor supplying mains electricity, *esp* an overhead one supported on poles or pylons. **power lunch** see **power breakfast** above. **power nap** *n* a short restorative sleep or rest in the middle of the day taken by a person involved in a demanding activity. **power of attorney** see under **attorn**. **power-on self-test** *n* (*comput*) the checks carried out automatically by the BIOS software when a computer is first switched on (*abbrev* **POST**). **power pack** *n* a device for adjusting an electric current to the voltages required by a particular piece of electronic equipment. **power plant** *n* an industrial plant for generating power; the assemblage of parts generating motive power in a motor car, aeroplane, etc. **pow'erplay** *n* strong, attacking play designed to put pressure on the defence, with players and action concentrated in one small area (*team sport*); similarly concentrated pressure applied as a tactic in eg military, political or business encounters; (in ice hockey) a temporary numerical superiority created by an opponent's absence while serving a penalty; a period in a limited-overs cricket match during which there are special restrictions on where fielders may be positioned. **power point** *n* a wall socket at which an electrical appliance may be connected to the mains; formerly, a 15-amp socket as distinct from a 5-amp one; (**PowerPoint®**) a computer program for creating slides to be used in formal presentations. **power politics** *n sing* international politics in which the course taken by states depends upon their knowledge that they can back their decisions with force or other coercive action. **power series** *n* (*maths*) an infinite series of the form $\Sigma a_n x^n$, or $a_0 + a_1 x^1 + a_2 x^2 + a_3 x^3 ...$, ie whose terms are ascending integral powers of a variable multiplied by constants. **power set** *n* (*maths*) a set comprising all the subsets of a given set. **pow'er-sharing** *n* joint responsibility for shaping and executing policy held by all parties within an organization, etc. **power shovel** *n* a mobile excavating machine. **power station** *n* an electricity generating station. **power steering** *n* a steering system in a vehicle in which the rotating force exerted on the steering wheel is supplemented by engine power. **power structure** *n* the distribution and application of power within an organization or community. **power suit** *n* a tailored suit worn to project authority and confidence. **power take-off** *n* a device for transferring power from an engine to another piece of equipment. **pow'ertrain** *n* (*engineering*) (in a motor vehicle) the drive-transmitting sequence represented by the engine, transmission, and parts connecting gearbox to wheel. **power unit** *n* a power-amplifier (see above). **power user** *n* a computer user who is highly skilled and demands high quality and performance from software, etc. **power walking** *n* walking briskly as an aerobic exercise.

■ **in power** in office; in potentiality (*Spenser*). **in someone's power** at someone's mercy; within the limits of what someone can do. **the powers that be** the existing ruling authorities (Bible, Romans 13.1).

powin, **pown** see **pawn⁴**.

pownd Spenserian spelling of **pound³**.

powney, **pownie**, **powny** /pow'ni/ see etymology of **pony**.

powre Spenserian spelling of **pour**.

powsowdy or **pousowdie** /pow-sow'di/ (*Scot*) *n* any mixture of heterogeneous kinds of food. [Origin uncertain]

powter /pow'tər/ (*Scot*) *vi* to poke; to rummage. ◆ *vt* to poke; to get by groping. [Origin obscure]

powwaw /pow-wö'/ (*Shakesp*) *interj* pooh.

powwow /pow'wow/ or **pawaw** /pä-wö'/ *n* a conference, *orig* one between or with Native Americans; amongst Native Americans, a rite, often with feasting; a Native American shaman, a magician or medicine man. ◆ *vi* /pow-wow'/ to hold a powwow; to confer. [Algonquian *powwaw*, *powah* a priest, literally a dreamer]

pox /poks/ *n* (*usu* as *combining form*) any of several virus diseases causing a rash of pustules (as in *chickenpox*, *cowpox*); smallpox (*archaic*); syphilis (*inf*; also formerly, *great pox*, *French pox*, *Spanish pox*); sheep-pox. ◆ *vt* (*obs*) to infect with pox, ie, syphilis. [Pl of **pock¹**]
■ **pox'y** *adj* suffering from pox; spotty; dirty, diseased, rotten (*inf*); applied in irritation to anything unpleasant, contemptible or troublesome (*inf*).

❑ **pox'virus** *n* any one of a group of DNA-containing animal viruses, including those which cause smallpox, cowpox, myxomatosis and certain fibromata.

■ **a pox on** (or **of**), **a pox take**, etc (*archaic*) a plague on, curse (so-and-so, such-and-such), used as an imprecation.

poy-bird see **poe-bird**.

poynant /poi'nənt/ (*Spenser*, etc) *adj* same as **poignant**.

poynt an old spelling of **point**.

poyse an old spelling of **poise¹**.

poyson an old spelling of **poison**.

poz or **pozz** /poz/ *adj* an old slang shortening of **positive**.

Pozidriv® /poz'i-drīv/ *n* the proprietary name of a type of screwdriver with a cross-shaped tip.

pozzolana /pot-sə-lä'nə/ or **pozzuolana** /-swə-/ *n* a volcanic dust first found at *Pozzuoli*, near Naples, which forms with mortar a cement that will set in air or water.
■ **pozzola'nic** *adj*.

pozzy see **possie**.

PP *abbrev*: parish priest; past president; present pupil.

pp *abbrev*: pages; *per procurationem* (L), by proxy (also *per pro* (L), for and on behalf of); pianissimo (*music*); past participle.

PPA *abbrev*: Pre-school Playgroups Association (now known as **PLA**).

PPARC *abbrev*: Particle Physics and Astronomy Research Council (now replaced by the Science and Technology Facilities Council).

PPC *abbrev*: *pour prendre congé* (Fr), to take leave; prospective parliamentary candidate.

ppc *abbrev*: picture postcard.

PPE *abbrev*: Philosophy, Politics and Economics, as a university school or course of study.

PPI *abbrev*: Plan Position Indicator; proton pump inhibitor.

P-plate see under **P** (*abbrev*).

ppm *abbrev* : parts per million.

PPP *abbrev* : Private Patients' Plan; Public-Private Partnership.

ppp (*music*) *abbrev* : pianississimo.

PPS *abbrev* : Parliamentary Private Secretary; *post postscriptum* (*L*), an additional postscript.

PQ *abbrev* : Province of Quebec (Canada).

PR *abbrev* : press release; prize ring; proportional representation; public relations; Puerto Rico.

Pr (*chem*) *symbol* : praseodymium.

Pr. *abbrev* : priest; Prince; Provençal.

pr *abbrev* : pair; per; *per rectum* (*L; med*), through the rectum.

pr. *abbrev* : present; price.

praam same as **pram²**.

prabble /prab'l/ (*Shakesp*) *n* a spelling representing the Welsh pronunciation of **brabble**.

practic (also spelt **practick** or **practique**) /prak'tik/ (*archaic*) *adj* relating to, or of the nature of, practice or action; practising; in practice; skilled (*Spenser*); cunning (*Spenser*). ◆ *n* practice as opposed to theory; (*esp* in *pl*) practices, doings; practical experience; a brief record of legal decisions, used to establish precedent (*Scots legal hist*); a practical man. [Obs Fr *practique*, from L *practicus*, from Gr *praktikos* relating to action, from *prassein* to do]

practicable /prak'ti-kə-bl/ *adj* capable of being done, carried out or accomplished, feasible; capable of being used or followed, usable; (of a road, etc) passable; (of a stage window, light switch, etc) functioning, practical (qv). [Fr *practicable* and L *practicāre*, from *practicus*; see **practic**]

■ **practicabil'ity** or **prac'ticableness** *n*. **prac'ticably** *adv*.

practical /prak'ti-kl/ *adj* in, relating to, concerned with, well adapted to, or inclining to look to, actual practice, actual conditions, results, or utility; efficient in action; (potentially) effective in use; (of clothes, equipment, etc) plain, sensible or suitably tough for everyday use; workable; being such in effect if not in name; virtual; trained by experience, not professionally; practising, actually engaged in a specified profession (*a practical farmer*); (of a piece of stage equipment, *esp* electric lights, etc) capable of being operated on stage (*theatre*). ◆ *n* a practical examination or lesson, eg in a scientific subject; (*usu* in *pl*) a practical man (*old*). [An expansion of **practic** (adj)]

■ **prac'ticalism** *n* devotion to what is practical. **prac'ticalist** *n*. **practical'ity** *n* practicalness; a practical matter, a practical feature or aspect of an affair. **prac'tically** *adv* for all practical purposes, virtually; very nearly, as good as; in a practical way; by a practical method. **prac'ticalness** *n*.
□ **practical arts** *n pl* those that are materially useful, eg dressmaking, carpentry. **practical joke** *n* a trick played on someone, as distinct from a joke told. **practical politics** *n sing* proposals or measures that may be carried out at once or in the near future. **practical reason** or **reasoning** *n* (*philos*) reasoning that governs decisions to act or is employed in weighing up relative advantages or merits of various courses. **practical units** *n pl* an obsolete system of electrical units, in which the ohm, ampere and volt were defined by physical magnitudes.

practice /prak'tis/ *n* the process of doing something or carrying something out; the performance of an act; habitual action, a habit; a custom; a way of proceeding, generally; a normal method of legal procedure; repeated performance as a means of acquiring skill, eg in playing a musical instrument; skill so acquired; the exercise of a profession; a professional person's business, as a field of activity or a property; negotiation (*archaic*); scheming, plotting or trickery; the process of working upon someone's feelings; a compendious way of multiplying quantities involving several units, by means of aliquot parts (*maths*). [From **practise** (verb) with spelling by analogy with *advice, device*]

practician /prak-tish'ən/ (*old*) *n* a practiser or practitioner; a practical man. [Obs Fr *practicien*, from L *practica*, Gr *praktikē* a skill]

practicum /prak'ti-kəm/ (*N Am*) *n* a course of practical work undertaken to supplement academic studies. [Neuter of L *practicus* practical; cf Ger *Praktikum* a course of practical work]

practise /prak'tis/ formerly -tīz'/, also (*N Am*) **practice** *vt* to carry out in practice (eg what one preaches); to go in for, or make a habit of; to exercise (eg self-control); to live one's life in accordance with (a religion); to work at or follow (a profession, eg medicine or law); to exercise oneself in (an art, etc), on (a musical instrument) or in the performance of (a musical piece, song, speech, etc) in order to acquire or maintain skill; to train by practice, to drill; to frequent (*obs*); to work (some evil) against someone (with *on*, *upon*); to effect (*obs*); to contrive by some means (*Milton*); to plot (*Shakesp*); to attempt or proceed (to do something; *obs*). ◆ *vi* to follow a profession, eg

medicine or law, to be in practice; to exercise oneself in any art, eg instrumental music; to act habitually (*obs*); to scheme, plot or intrigue (with *against*; *obs*) to tamper with (with *upon*, *on*); to have dealings (with *with*; *obs*); to work upon (someone's feelings) unscrupulously (with *on*, *upon*) (*old*). [Med L *practizāre*, altered from *practicāre*, from L *practica*; see **practician**]

■ **prac'tisant** *n* (*obs*) a fellow conspirator. **prac'tised** *adj* skilled through practice. **prac'tiser** *n*. **prac'tising** *adj* actually engaged in a specified profession; actively following, and holding faithfully to, a particular religion, etc.

practitioner /prak-tish'ə-nər/ *n* someone who is in practice, *esp* in medicine; someone who practises or goes in for something specified. [Formed irregularly from **practician**]

practive /prak'tiv/ (*obs*) *adj* practical, active, concerned with practice. [Modelled on *active*]

practolol /prak'tə-lol/ *n* a drug formerly used to treat cardiac arrhythmia, but suspected of causing side effects including eye damage.

prad /prad/ (*sl*) *n* a horse. [Du *paard*, from LL *paraverēdus*; see **palfrey**]

Prader-Willi syndrome /prä'dər-vil'i sin'drōm/ *n* a rare genetic condition characterized mainly by a chronic appetite for food, leading to obesity, and also by mental handicap, growth and behavioural problems, etc (*abbrev* **PWS**). [Andrea *Prader* (1919–2001) and Heinrich *Willi* (1900–71), Swiss paediatricians who in 1956 first described the condition]

prae- see **pre-**.

praecava see **precava**.

praecoces /prē-kō'sēs or prī-kō'kāz/ *n pl* (*ornithol; old*) birds whose young are hatched with a covering of down and can leave the nest at once to seek food, *opp* to *altrices*. [L pl of *praecox*, -*cocis*; see **precocious**]

■ **praecocial** *adj* see **precocial**.

praecordial see **precordial**.

praedial or **predial** /prē'di-əl/ *adj* relating to, connected with, or derived from, the land; landed; rural; agrarian; attached to the land or a farm. ◆ *n* a praedial slave. [LL *praediālis*, from *praedium* an estate]

praefect see **prefect**.

praeludium /prē-lū'di-əm or prī-loo'di-ŭm/ (*L*) *n* (*pl* **praelu'dia**) a prelude. [L *prae* before, and *ludere* to play]

praemunire /prē-mū-nī'ri or prī-moo-nē're/ *n* a writ issued under statutes of Richard II, summoning a person accused of suing in a foreign court for matters cognizable by the law of England, used *esp* against papal claims, and later extended to various offences; an offence that could be so dealt with; the penalty for such an offence; a predicament or scrape (*usu humorous*). [From the words of the writ, *praemūnīre faciās* cause to warn, or see that thou warn, the word *praemūnīre*, properly to fortify in front, defend, being confused with *praemonēre* to forewarn]

praenomen /prē-nō'mən or prī-nō'men/ *n* (*pl* **praeno'mens** or **praenomina** /-nō'mi-nə/) the name prefixed to the family name in ancient Rome, as, eg, *Gaius* in Gaius Julius Caesar; the generic name of a plant or animal (*rare*). [L, from *prae* before, in front of, and *nōmen* name]

praepostor, **prepostor** /prē-pos'tər/ or **prepositor** /-poz'i-tər/ *n* the name used for a prefect in some English public schools. [L *praepositus*, pap of *praepōnere*, from *prae* in front, and *pōnere* to put]

Praeraphaelite see **Pre-Raphaelite**.

Praesepe /prī-sē'pi/ *n* a cluster of stars in the constellation Cancer.

praeses see **preses**.

praesidium see **presidium**.

praeter- see **preter-**.

praetor /prē'tər, -tör or prī'tor/ or (*esp N Am*) **pretor** /prē'tər/ *n* a magistrate of ancient Rome next in rank to the consuls. [L *praetor*, for *praeitor*, from *prae* in front of, before, and *īre*, *itum* to go]

■ **praeto'rial** *adj*. **praetorian** /-tō' or -tö'/ *adj*. ◆ *n* a former praetor or man of equivalent rank; a member of the emperor's bodyguard. **praeto'rium** *n* a general's tent; a governor's residence; a court or headquarters. **prae'torship** *n*.
□ **praetorian gate** *n* the gate of a Roman camp in front of the general's tent, and nearest to the enemy. **praetorian guard** *n* (*hist*) the bodyguard of the Roman Emperor.

pragmatic /prag-mat'ik/ *adj* concerned with what is practicable, expedient and convenient, or with practical consequences, rather than with theories and ideals; matter-of-fact, realistic; seeing historical events purely in terms of their practical lessons; relating to, or of the nature of, pragmatism (*philos*); relating to affairs of state; meddlesome, opinionated, pragmatical. ◆ *n* a busybody (*old*); an opinionated person (*old*); an edict (*hist*); a man of business (*obs*). [Gr *pragmatikos*, from *prāgma*, *-matos* deed; see **pragmatism**]

■ **pragmat'ical** *adj* interfering with the affairs of others, officious, meddlesome; self-important; opinionated, dogmatic; active (*obs*); practical, matter-of-fact, pragmatic (*obs*). **pragmatical'ity** *n*. **pragmat'ically** *adv*. **pragmat'icalness** *n*. **pragmat'ics** *n sing* the study of inherent practical usage, and social and behavioural aspects, of language; a study of linguistic sign systems and their use.

❑ **pragmatic sanction** *n* a special decree issued by a sovereign, such as that of the Emperor Charles VI, settling his dominions upon Maria Theresa.

pragmatism /prag'mə-ti-zm/ *n* pragmatic quality, realism, matter-of-factness; concern for the practicable rather than for theories and ideals; a humanistic philosophy, or philosophic method, that makes practical consequences the test of truth (*philos*); a treatment of history in terms of cause and effect and practical lessons (*old*). [Gr *prāgma*, *-matos* deed, from *prāssein* to do]

■ **prag'matist** *n* a pragmatic person; someone who advocates the practicable rather than the ideal course; a believer in philosophical or historical pragmatism. **pragmatiza'tion** or **-s-** *n*. **prag'matize** or **-ise** *vt* to interpret or represent as real; to rationalize (a myth). **prag'matizer** or **-s-** *n*.

prahu see **proa**.

Prairial /pre-ri-äl', pre-ryäl' or prā'ri-əl/ *n* the ninth month of the French revolutionary calendar, the month of meadows, about 20 May to 18 June. [Fr, from *prairie* meadow]

prairie /prā'ri/ *n* a treeless plain, flat or rolling, naturally grass-covered. [Fr, from LL *prātaria*, from L *prātum* a meadow]

■ **prai'ried** *adj*.

❑ **prairie chicken**, **fowl**, **grouse** or **hen** *n* an American genus (*Cupidonia* or *Tympanuchus*) of grouse; the sharp-tailed grouse (genus *Pedioecetes*) of the western USA. **prairie dog** *n* a gregarious burrowing and barking N American ground squirrel (genus *Cynomys*). **prairie oyster** *n* a raw egg with condiments; the testicle of a calf, cooked and eaten (*US*). **prairie schooner** *n* an emigrants' long covered wagon. **prairie turnip** *n* breadroot. **prairie value** *n* the value of land in its natural state before it has been improved by man. **prairie wolf** *n* the coyote.

praise /prāz/ *vt* to express admiration or approval of; to commend; to extol; to glorify or worship (one's god) with hymns, thanksgiving, etc; to assign a value to, appraise (*Shakesp*). ◆ *n* the expression of admiration or approval; commendation; glorification, worship; the musical part of worship; praise-deserving merit (*old*); (in ejaculatory expressions) substituted for God (*obs Scot inf*). [OFr *preiser*, from LL *preciāre* for L *pretiāre* to prize, from *pretium* price]

■ **praise'ful** *adj*. **praise'less** *adj*. **prais'er** *n*. **praise'worthily** *adv*. **praise'worthiness** *n*. **praise'worthy** *adj* worthy of praise; commendable. **prais'ing** *n* and *adj*. **prais'ingly** *adv*.

■ **sing the praises of** to commend enthusiastically.

praiseach /prash'ahh/ *n* a kind of oatmeal porridge, often with vegetables; a mess, a jumble of small pieces; wild mustard (*Brassica arvensis*). [Ir, from L *brassica* cabbage]

prajna /präj'nə/ *n* (in Buddhism) understanding of the truth achieved directly rather than through reasoning. [Sans]

Prakrit /prä'krit/ *n* a name for (any of) the Indo-Aryan dialects contemporary with Sanskrit, or for (any of) the later languages derived from them. [Sans *prākṛta* the natural, from *prakṛti* nature]

■ **Prakrit'ic** *adj*.

praline /prä' or prä'lēn/ *n* an almond or nut kernel with a brown coating of sugar, or a similar confection made with crushed nuts (also **prawlin** /prö'lin/). [Fr *praline*, from French soldier Marshal Duplessis-Praslin (1598–1675), whose cook invented it]

pralltriller /präl'tri-lər/ *n* (*music*) an upper or inverted mordent, a grace in which the principal note is preceded in performance by itself and the note above. [Ger]

pram[1] /pram/ *n* a small wheeled carriage for a baby, pushed by a person on foot; a milkman's hand cart. [Shortening of **perambulator**]

❑ **pram-face** *n* (*derog sl*) a young lower-class single mother.

■ **throw one's toys out of the pram** see under **toy**.

pram[2] or **praam** /präm/ *n* a flat-bottomed Dutch or Baltic lighter; a fishing-vessel, lighter or tender of the Dutch and Baltic coasts, generally flat-bottomed with a squared-off prow; a barge fitted as a floating battery. [Du *praam*, of Slavic origin]

prana /prä'nə/ *n* the breath of life; in Hindu religion, *esp* yoga, breath as the essential life force. [Sans]

■ **pranaya'ma** *n* (*yoga*) controlled breathing.

prance /präns/ *vi* (of a horse) to bound from the hind legs; to caper or dance along; to move with an exaggeratedly springing gait; to swagger, to parade ostentatiously; to ride a prancing horse. ◆ *vt* to

cause to prance. ◆ *n* an act of prancing; a prancing gait; swagger. [ME *praunce*; related to Dan *pransk* spirited (of a horse)]

■ **pranc'er** *n*. **pranc'ing** *adj* and *n*. **pranc'ingly** *adv*.

pranck, **prancke** see **prank**[3].

prandial /pran'di-əl/ (*esp facetious*) *adj* relating to dinner. [L *prandium* a morning or midday meal]

prang /prang/ (*orig RAF sl*) *n* a vehicle crash; a bombing-attack. ◆ *vt* to crash or smash (a vehicle or aircraft); to crash into (eg another car); to bomb (a target) or bomb (a place) heavily; to shoot down (an aircraft). [Prob imit]

prank[1] /prangk/ *n* a trick; a practical joke; a frolic; a malicious or mischievous trick; an evil deed (*obs*). ◆ *vi* to play pranks. [Origin uncertain]

■ **prank'ful**, **prank'ish**, **prank'some** and **prank'y** *adj*. **prank'ster** *n* someone given to playing pranks, a practical joker.

prank[2] /prangk/ (*archaic*) *vt* to dress or adorn showily; to bespangle or cover in colourful profusion; to place in a setting, like a jewel. ◆ *vi* (also *vt* with *it*) to make an ostentatious show. [Related to Du *pronken*, Ger *prunken* to show off; cf **prink**]

■ **prank'ing** *n* and *adj*. **prank'ingly** *adv*.

prank[3], **pranck** or **prancke** /prangk/ (*obs*) *vt* to pleat or fold; to set in order. [Origin uncertain]

prank[4] /prangk/ (*rare*) *n* prancing, capering. ◆ *vi* (also *vt* with *it*) to prance. [Poss connected with **prance**]

■ **prank'le** *vi* to prance lightly.

prase /prāz/ *n* a leek-green quartz. [Gr *prason* leek]

praseodymium /prā-zi-ə-dim'i-əm/ *n* a metallic element with green salts (symbol **Pr**; atomic no 59) isolated, along with neodymium, from the once-supposed element didymium. [Gr *prasios* leek-green, from *prason* leek, and **didymium**]

prat[1] or **pratt** /prat/ (*sl*) *n* the buttocks. ◆ *vt* (*Shakesp* punningly) to beat on the buttocks. [Origin uncertain]

■ **prat'fall** *n* a fall landing on the prat; a humiliating blunder or ignominious failure. ◆ *vi* to make a pratfall.

prat[2] /prat/ (*abusive sl*) *n* a fool, an ineffectual person. [Poss a use of **prat**[1]]

prate /prāt/ *vi* to talk foolishly or sententiously; to talk boastfully or insolently; to tattle; to be loquacious. ◆ *vt* to utter in a prating manner; to blab. ◆ *n* foolish or superfluous talk. [Cf LGer *praten*, Dan *prate*, Du *praaten*]

■ **pra'ter** *n*. **pra'ting** *n* and *adj*. **pra'tingly** *adv*.

pratie or **praty** /prā'ti/ *n* an Anglo-Irish form of **potato**.

pratincole /prat'ing-kōl/ *n* a bird related to the plovers, with swallow-like wings and tail. [L *prātum* meadow, and *incola* an inhabitant]

pratique /pra-tēk' or prat'ik/ *n* permission given to a ship to trade or deal in a port after quarantine or on showing a clean bill of health. [Fr, intercourse, from L *practica* practice, from Gr *prāssein* to do]

pratt see **prat**[1].

prattle /prat'l/ *vi* to talk idly and volubly, to chatter inconsequentially; (of a young child) to utter baby-talk. ◆ *vt* to utter in a prattling way. ◆ *n* empty talk. [Dimin and frequentative of **prate**]

■ **pratt'lement** *n* prattle. **pratt'ler** *n* someone who prattles; a little child (*old*).

❑ **pratt'lebox** *n* a prattler.

praty see **pratie**.

prau see **proa**.

praunce Spenser's form of **prance**.

pravastatin /prav'ə-stat-in/ *n* a statin drug used to lower the amount of cholesterol in the blood.

pravity /prav'i-ti/ (*rare*) *n* wickedness. [L *prāvitās*, *-ātis*]

prawle /pröl/ *n* Shakespeare's Welsh form of **brawl**[1].

prawlin see **praline**.

prawn /prön/ *n* a small edible shrimp-like crustacean (*Leander serratus* or any related species). ◆ *vi* to fish for prawns. [ME *prayne*, *prane*; origin unknown]

❑ **prawn cocktail** *n* a dish of prawns with salad, mayonnaise, etc, served as an appetizer or starter. **prawn cracker** *n* a light, deep-fried prawn-flavoured crisp traditionally eaten as an accompaniment to Chinese, etc food.

■ **come the raw prawn** (*Aust inf*) to make an attempt to deceive.

praxinoscope /prak'si-nə-skōp/ *n* an optical toy creating the illusion of motion by reflection of a sequence of pictures in a rotating box. [Irregularly formed from Gr *prāxis* doing, and **-scope**]

praxis /prak'sis/ *n* the practice or practical side of an art or science, as distinct from its theoretical side; customary or accepted practice; (an example or a collection of examples serving to provide) a practical exercise. [Gr *prāxis*, from *prāssein* to do]

Praxitelean /prak-si-tə-lē'ən/ or -tē'li-ən/ *adj* of, relating to, reminiscent of or in the style of *Praxiteles*, Greek sculptor (*fl* c.350BC).

pray /prā/ *vi* (**pray'ing**; **prayed**) to express one's desires to, or commune with, a god or some spiritual power (with *to*); to intercede with one's god on behalf of another person, etc (with *for*); to ask earnestly (often with *for*). ◆ *vt* to ask earnestly and reverently, in the course of worship; to hope earnestly or fervently; to supplicate; to beg or entreat; to say (a prayer); to render, get, put, or cause to be, by praying (*rare*). ◆ *interj* (often *ironic*) I ask you, may I ask. [OFr *priere*, from Med L *precāria*, from L *precārius* obtained by prayer, from *prex*, *precis* prayer]
■ **prayer** /prā'ər/ *n* someone who prays. **pray'ing** *n* and *adj*. **pray'ingly** *adv*.
❑ **praying insect** or **mantis** see **mantis**.
■ **pray against** in Parliament, to address a prayer to the Crown for the annulment of (an order or obligation). **pray in aid** (*law*; *Shakesp*) to call in, or call for, help.

prayer¹ /prār or prā'ər/ *n* the act of praying; entreaty; an address to a god or spiritual power in the form of a petition or offer of praise, penitence, etc; generally, the act of communing with one's god; the wish put forward or the words used; the thing prayed for; a form used or intended for use in praying; public worship; (in *pl*) (a time set aside for) worship in a family, school, etc; a petition to a public body, eg a legislature; in Parliament, a motion addressed to the Crown asking for the annulment of an order or regulation; the slightest of chances (*inf*). [OFr *preier* (Fr *prier*) to pray, from L *precārī*, from *prex*, *precis* a prayer]
■ **pray'erful** *adj* given to prayer, expressing one's earnest desires through prayer; in a spirit or mental attitude of prayer. **prayer'fully** *adv*. **prayer'fulness** *n*. **prayer'less** *adj* without or not using prayer. **prayer'lessly** *adv*. **prayer'lessness** *n*.
❑ **prayer bead** *n* one of the beads on a rosary; a jequirity bean. **prayer book** *n* a book containing prayers or forms of devotion, *esp* the Book of Common Prayer of the Church of England. **prayer flag** *n* in Tibetan Buddhism, a flag on which a prayer is inscribed. **prayer mat** same as **prayer rug** below. **prayer meeting** *n* a shorter and simpler form of public religious service, in which laymen often take part. **prayer rug** *n* a small carpet on which a Muslim kneels at prayer. **prayer shawl** same as **tallith**. **prayer wheel** *n* a drum wrapped with strips of paper inscribed with prayers deemed by Buddhists of Tibet to be proffered when the drum is turned.

prayer² see under **pray**.

pre /prē/ (*inf*) *prep* before, prior to. [From **pre-**]

pre- /prē-/ (as living prefix) or **prae-** /prē- or prī-/ (Latin spelling, more common formerly) *pfx* (1) before in time, beforehand, in advance, as in *prehistoric*, *pre-war*, *prewarn*; (2) in front, in front of, the anterior part of, as in *predentate*, *premandibular*, *presternum* (*esp anat*); (3) surpassingly, to the highest degree, as in *pre-eminent*, *prepotent*. [L *prae*, in front of, before]

> Words formed using the prefix **pre-** are listed as separate entries in the main word list or, if their meaning is self-evident, at the foot of the page.

preace /prēs/ (*Spenser*) same as **press**¹.

preach /prēch/ *vi* to deliver a sermon; to discourse earnestly; to give advice in a sententious, tedious, obtrusive or offensive manner. ◆ *vt* to set forth or expound in religious discourses; to deliver (a sermon); to proclaim or teach publicly; to advise, advocate, recommend or inculcate; to render or put by preaching. ◆ *n* (*inf*) a sermon. [Fr *prêcher*, from L *praedicāre*, -*ātum* to proclaim]
■ **preach'er** *n* someone who discourses publicly on religious matters; a minister or clergyman; an assiduous inculcator or advocate. **preach'ership** *n*. **preach'ify** *vi* (*inf*) to preach, *esp* tediously; to sermonize or moralize; to give advice wearisomely. **preach'ily** *adv*. **preach'iness** *n*. **preach'ing** *n* and *adj*. **preach'ment** *n* a sermon (*derog*); a sermon-like discourse; sermonizing. **preach'y** *adj* given to tedious moralizing; savouring of preaching.
❑ **preach'ing-cross** *n* a cross in an open place at which monks, etc, preached. **preaching friar** *n* a Dominican. **preach'ing-house** *n* a Methodist church.
■ **preach down** or **up** respectively, to decry or extol. **preaching with a view** preaching as a candidate in a vacant pastoral charge. **the Preacher** the authors or spokesman of the Book of Ecclesiastes in the Old Testament; the book itself.

pre-Adamite /prē-ad'ə-mīt/ *n* someone who lived, or a descendant of those who lived, or a believer in the existence of a human race, before *Adam*. ◆ *adj* of or relating to the pre-Adamites. [**pre-** (1)]
■ **pre-adamic** /-ə-dam'ik/ or **pre-adam'ical** *adj* existing before Adam. **pre-adamit'ic** or **pre-adamit'ical** *adj*.

preadaptation /prē-a-dap-tā'shən/ (*biol*) *n* the possession by organisms of features apparently functionless in their present environment that will have a function in aiding survival in a future one. [**pre-** (1)]
■ **preadapt'** *vt*. **preadap'ted** *adj*. **preadap'tive** *adj*.

preadmonish /prē-əd-mon'ish/ *vt* to forewarn. [**pre-** (1)]
■ **preadmoni'tion** *n*.

preamble /prē' or prē-am'bl/ *n* a preface; an introduction, *esp* that of an Act of Parliament, giving its reasons and purpose; (*Milton* **praeamble**) a prelude. ◆ *vt* and *vi* to make a preamble (to). [Fr *préambule*, from L *prae* in front of, and *ambulāre* to go]
■ **pream'būlary** or **pream'būlatory** *adj*. **pream'būlate** *vi* to go first (*obs*); to make a preamble.

preamplifier /prē-am'pli-fī-ər/ *n* (often shortened to **pre'amp**) an electronic device that boosts and clarifies the signal from eg a radio, record player, microphone, etc before it reaches the main amplifier. [**pre-** (1)]

prease or **preasse** (*Spenser*) same as **press**¹.

preaudience /prē-ö'di-əns/ *n* the right to be heard before another; precedence at the bar among lawyers. [**pre-** (1)]

Preb. *abbrev* : Prebend; Prebendary.

prebend /preb'ənd/ *n* the share of the revenues of a cathedral or collegiate church allowed to a clergyman who officiates in it at stated times. [LL *praebenda* an allowance, from L *praebēre* to allow, grant]
■ **prebendal** /pri-ben'dl/ *adj* (**prebendal stall** the cathedral stall, or the benefice, of a prebendary). **preb'endary** *n* a resident clergyman who enjoys a prebend, a canon; the honorary holder of a disendowed prebendal stall.

prebiotic /prē-bī-ot'ik/ *adj* relating to the time before the appearance of living things. ◆ *n* a substance that stimulates the growth of probiotics in the body. [**pre-** (1)]

preborn /prē-börn'/ *adj* being carried in the womb, unborn. [**pre-** (1)]

prebuttal /prē-but'l/ (*inf*) *n* a statement or campaign intended to counter an attack or criticism before it has been made. [**pre-** (1); modelled on *rebuttal*]

Precambrian /prē-kam'bri-ən/ (*geol*) *adj* of or belonging to the earliest geological time, between *approx* 4500 and 540 million years ago (also *n*). [**pre-** (1)]

pre-cancel /prē-kan'səl/ *vt* to cancel (a postage stamp), eg by applying a postmark before use (also *n*). [**pre-** (1)]

precancerous /prē-kan'sə-rəs/ *adj* (of tissue) showing structural alterations recognized as associated with the subsequent development of cancer. [**pre-** (1)]

precarious /pri-kā'ri-əs/ *adj* depending on chance; insecure; uncertain; dangerous, risky; depending upon the will of another; supplicating (*obs*). [L *precārius*, from *precārī* to pray]
■ **precā'riously** *adv*. **precā'riousness** *n*.

precast /prē-käst/ *adj* (of concrete blocks, etc) cast before being put in position. [**pre-** (1)]

precative /prek'ə-tiv/ *adj* supplicating; expressing entreaty (*grammar*). [L *precātīvus*, from *precārī* to pray]

precatory /prek'ə-tə-ri/ *adj* of the nature of, or expressing, a wish, request or recommendation. [L *precātōrius*, from *precārī* to pray]

precaution /pri-kö'shən/ *n* a measure taken beforehand to ensure a satisfactory result, to prevent an undesirable one, or to steer clear of danger; due circumspection or foresight; (in *pl*) the using of contraceptives (*inf*). ◆ *vt* (*obs*) to forewarn. [**pre-** (1)]
■ **precau'tional**, **precau'tionary** or **precau'tious** *adj*.

precava or **praecava** /prē-kā'və/ (*anat*) *n* the superior vena cava, the vein carrying blood from the head, arms and thorax. [**pre-** (2)]

precede /pri-sēd'/ *vt* to go before in position, time, rank or importance; to cause to be preceded, to preface or introduce. ◆ *vi* to be before in time or place. [Fr *précéder*, from L *praecēdere*, -*cēssum*, from *prae* before, and *cēdere* to go]
■ **precedence** /pres'i-dəns or prē'si-dəns, also pri-sē'dəns/ *n* the act of going before in time; the right of going before; priority; the fact of being before in rank; the place of honour; the foremost place in ceremony (also **precedency** /pres'i-dən-si, prē'si- or pri-sē'dən-si/). **precedent** /pres'i-dənt or prē'si-dənt/ *n* a previous incident, legal case, etc that is parallel to one under consideration; the measures taken or judgement given in such a case, serving as a basis for a decision in the present one; that which precedes; the original of a copy (*Shakesp*); a token (*Shakesp*); a model (*obs*). ◆ *adj* /pri-sē'dənt/ preceding. **precedented** /pres'-, prē'si-/ *adj* having a precedent; warranted by an example. **precedential** /pres-i-den'shl/ *adj* of the nature of a precedent. **prece'dently** *adv*. **prece'ding** *adj* going before in time, rank, etc; antecedent; previous; immediately before.
■ **take precedence over** or **of** to precede in ceremonial order.

preceese /prī-sēz'/ a Scots form of **precise**.

precentor /pri-sen'tər or prē-, also (Scot) pri-zen'tər/ (relig) n (also fem **precen'tress** or **precen'trix**) the leader of the singing of a church choir or congregation; in some English cathedrals, a member of the chapter who deputes this duty to a succentor. [LL praecentor, -ōris, from L prae before, and canere to sing]
■ **precen'torship** n.

precepit /pres'i-pit/ (Shakesp) n a precipice.

precept /prē'sept/ n a rule of action; an instruction in moral conduct, a principle, maxim or commandment; a practical instruction in a technique; a written order, writ or warrant from a magistrate or other authority to a subordinate official eg to convene a court or jury, hold an election, etc (law); a document granting possession or bestowing a privilege (Scot); an order to levy money under a local rating or taxation system; a command or mandate (old). ◆ vt to issue a precept to. [L praeceptum, neuter pap of praecipere to take beforehand, from prae before, and capere to take]
■ **preceptial** /pri-sep'shl/ adj (Shakesp) consisting of precepts. **precep'tive** adj containing or giving precepts; directing in moral conduct; didactic. **precep'tor**, fem **precep'tress** n someone who delivers precepts; a teacher; an instructor; a tutor (US); the head of a school; the head of a preceptory of Knights Templars. **precepto'rial** /prē-/ adj. **precep'torship** n. **precep'tory** /pri-/ adj giving precepts. ◆ n a community of Knights Templars (occasionally extended to a commandery of the Hospitallers); its estate or buildings.

preces /prē'sēz/ (church) n pl prayers, esp in preces and responses. [L, pl of prex, precis prayer]

precession /pri-sesh'ən/ n the fact or act of preceding; a progression or going forward (non-standard for **procession**; obs); the precession of the equinoxes (see below) or the analogous phenomenon in spinning tops and the like, whereby the wobble of the spinning object causes its axis of rotation to become cone-shaped. [LL praecessiō, -ōnis, from praecēdere ; see **precede**]
■ **precess** /-ses'/ vi (back-formation from **precession**; of a spinning-top, etc) to wobble. **precess'ional** adj.
■ **precession of the equinoxes** a slow westward motion of the equinoctial points along the ecliptic, caused by the greater attraction of the sun and moon on the excess of matter at the equator, such that the times at which the sun crosses the equator come at shorter intervals than they would otherwise do.

précieuse /prā-syœz'/ n a woman affecting a fastidious over-refinement. [Fr, from the literary women of 17c France who were extremely fastidious in their use of language]

precinct /prē'singkt/ n a space, esp an enclosed one, around a building (eg a cathedral, college, etc) or other object (also in pl); a district or division within certain boundaries; a district of jurisdiction or authority; a division for police or electoral purposes (US); a police station of such a division (US); (in pl) environs. [LL praecinctum, neuter pap of praecingere, from prae around, in front of, and cingere to gird]
■ **pedestrian precinct** a traffic-free area of a town, esp a shopping centre. **shopping precinct** a shopping centre, esp if traffic-free.

precious /presh'əs/ adj of great price or worth; cherished; very highly esteemed; (with a possessive) grand, fine, much-vaunted (ironic, as in sick of hearing about his precious children); egregious (ironic); too consciously refined, fastidious or dainty. ◆ adv extremely, confoundedly, as in precious little, few, etc (inf); preciously (Shakesp).

◆ n used as a term of endearment. [OFr precios (Fr précieux), from L pretiōsus, from pretium price]
■ **preciosity** /presh-i-os'i-ti or pres-/ n fastidious over-refinement. **prec'iously** adv. **prec'iousness** n.
❑ **precious metals** n pl gold, silver, platinum (also, rarely, mercury or others of high price). **precious stone** n a stone of value and beauty, esp with regard to its use in jewellery or ornamentation, a gem.

precipice /pres'i-pis/ n a high vertical or nearly vertical cliff or rock face; a perilous state of affairs; a headlong fall (obs). [L praecipitium a headlong fall, a precipice, from praeceps, praecipitis headlong, steep]
■ **prec'ipiced** adj.
❑ **precipice bond** n (finance; inf) a bond that yields a high fixed income, but whose capital value can decline sharply if the stock-market index falls.

precipitant /pri-sip'i-tənt/ adj falling headlong; rushing downwards or onwards at too great a velocity; impulsively hasty, precipitate. ◆ n (chem) a substance that causes the formation of a precipitate, a precipitating agent. [L praecipitans, prp of praecipitāre to throw headlong]
■ **precip'itance** or **precip'itancy** n the quality of being precipitate; a headlong fall; headlong haste or rashness; an impulsively hasty action. **precip'itantly** adv.

precipitate /pri-sip'i-tāt/ vt to hurl headlong; to force into hasty action; to pitch (oneself) over-enthusiastically into action, etc; to bring on suddenly or prematurely; to cause to come out of solution or suspension and settle as a solid deposit (chem); to cause (moisture, water vapour) to condense and fall as rain, hail, snow, etc (meteorol). ◆ vi to come out of solution or suspension and settle as a solid deposit (chem); (of moisture, water vapour) to condense and fall as rain, hail, snow, etc (meteorol); to rush in haste; to fall headlong (Shakesp). ◆ adj /pri-sip'i-tət/ falling, hurled or rushing headlong; sudden and hasty; without deliberation; rash. ◆ n /-tət/ a substance separated from solution or suspension, usu falling and settling at the bottom as a solid deposit; moisture deposited as rain, hail, snow, etc (meteorol). [L praecipitāre, -ātum to throw or cast headlong, from praeceps, -ipitis headlong, steep, from prae in front, and caput, -itis head]
■ **precip'itately** adv. **precipitā'tion** n the act of precipitating; a headlong fall or rush; a sheer drop (Shakesp); impulsive action; great hurry; rash haste; impulsiveness; rain, hail, snow and sometimes also dew (meteorol); the amount of rainfall, etc; the separation of suspended matter, the formation or sinking of a precipitate, or the precipitate itself (chem). **precip'itātive** adj. **precip'itātor** n someone who precipitates; a precipitating agent; an apparatus or tank for precipitation.

precipitin /pri-sip'i-tin/ (med) n an antibody which in contact with an antigen produces a precipitate. [Formed from **precipitate**]
■ **precipitinogen** /-tin'ə-jen/ n a soluble antigen that stimulates the formation of a precipitin. **precipitinogen'ic** adj.

precipitous /prə-sip'i-təs/ adj like a precipice; sheer; precipitate (rare). [Obs Fr précipiteux, from L praeceps headlong, steep; see **precipitate**]
■ **precip'itously** adv. **precip'itousness** n.

précis /prā'sē/ n (pl **précis** /-sēz/) an abstract, a summary. ◆ vt (**précising** /prā'sē-ing/; **précised** /prā'sēd/) to make a précis of. [Fr]

precise /pri-sīs'/ adj definite; exact; accurate; free from vagueness; very, identical; scrupulously exact; over-exact; prim; formal; scrupulous in observing the rules of religion (old); puritanical (hist).

Some words formed with the prefix **pre-**; the numbers in brackets refer to the numbered senses in the entry for **pre-**.

preacquaint' vt (1).	**preconstruct'** vt (1).	**prenego'tiate** vi and vt (1).
preacquaint'ance n (1).	**preconstruc'tion** n (1).	**prenegotia'tion** n (1).
preadoles'cence n (1).	**preconsume'** vt (1).	**preno'tify** vt (1).
preadoles'cent adj (1).	**precool'** vt (1).	**prenu'bile** adj (1).
preannounce' vt (1).	**precopula'tory** adj (1).	**preoc'ular** adj (2).
preappoint' vt (1).	**predawn'** n (1).	**preopera'tional** adj (1).
prearrange' vt (1).	**predefine'** vt (1).	**preop'erative** adj (1).
prearrange'ment n (1).	**predefini'tion** n (1).	**preo'ral** adj (2).
preassur'ance n (1).	**predesign'** vt (1).	**preor'der** vt (1).
pre-buy' vi and vt (1).	**predevel'op** vt and vi (1).	**pre-posi'tion** vt (2).
prechris'tian or **pre-Chris'tian** adj (1).	**predevel'opment** n (1).	**prepro'grammed** adj (1).
preclass'ical adj (1).	**predoom'** vt (1).	**prerecord'** vt (1).
preco'ital adj (1).	**pre-employ'** vt (1).	**prerecord'ed** adj (1).
precolo'nial adj (1).	**pre-engage'** vt (1).	**pre-Reforma'tion** adj (1).
pre-Colum'bian adj (1).	**pre-engage'ment** n (1).	**preregistra'tion** n and adj (1).
precompose' vt (1).	**pre'flight** adj (1).	**pretest'** vt (1).
precondemn' vt (1).	**preheat'** vt (1).	**pre-war'** adj and adv (1).
pre-con'quest n (1).	**pre-let'** vt (1).	**prewarm'** vt (1).
preconsonan'tal adj (1).	**premix'** vt (1).	**prewarn'** vt (1).

---

fāte; fär; mē; fûr; mīne; mōte; fôr; mūte; pŭt; dhen (then); el'ə-mənt (element) ● For other sounds see detailed chart of pronunciation

[Fr *précis, précise* from L *praecīsus*, pap of *praecīdere*, from *prae* around, and *caedere* to cut]

■ **precise'ly** *adv* in a precise manner; exactly; (as a rejoinder) quite, I agree entirely. **precise'ness** *n*. **precisian** /*pri-sizh'ən*/ *n* an over-precise person; a formalist; a Puritan (*hist*; *derog*). **preci'sianism** *n*. **preci'sianist** *n* a precisian. **preci'sion** *n* the quality of being precise; exactness; minute accuracy; mental separation or abstraction of ideas, etc (partly associated with **prescission** (see under **prescind**); *Berkeley*); reliability, reproducibility or repeatability (*stats*, etc); a precise definition (*obs*). ◆ *adj* operating, or carried out, with minute accuracy. **precis'ionist** *n* someone who insists on precision; a purist. **precisive** /*pri-sī'siv*/ *adj* dividing off, separating or abstracting mentally; relating to precision.

preclinical /*prē-klin'i-kəl*/ (*med*) *adj* taking place before, or without yet having gained, practical clinical experience with patients; of, relating to or occurring during the stage before the symptoms of a disease are recognizable; (of a drug) not yet having undergone clinical testing. [**pre-** (1)]

preclude /*pri-klood'*/ *vt* to rule out, eliminate or make impossible; to hinder by anticipation, counteract in advance, obviate; to prevent (with *from*); to shut out beforehand; to close beforehand. [L *praeclūdere, -clūsum*, from *claudere* to shut]
■ **preclusion** /*pri-kloo'zhən*/ *n*. **preclusive** /*-kloo'siv*/ *adj* tending to preclude; hindering beforehand. **preclu'sively** *adv*.

precocial or **praecocial** /*pri-, prē-kō'sh(y)əl*/ *adj* of or relating to birds whose young are hatched with a covering of down and can leave the nest at once to seek food (*ornithol*); premature, forward. [See **precocious**]

precocious /*pri-kō'shəs*/ *adj* early in developing or reaching some stage of development; (of a child) strikingly advanced or mature in mental development, speech, social behaviour, etc, sometimes irksomely so; (of a talent or aptitude) abundantly apparent at an early stage; (of plants) flowering or fruiting, or (of fruit) ripening, early; flowering before leaves appear; (of birds) precocial. [L *praecox, -ocis*, from *prae* before, and *coquere* to cook, ripen]
■ **precō'ciously** *adv*. **precō'ciousness** or **precocity** /*pri-kos'i-ti*/ *n* the state or quality of being precocious; early, if not over-early, development or maturity of mind.

precognition /*prē-kog-nish'ən*/ *n* foreknowledge; a written statement of evidence likely to be given by a witness in court (*Scots law*). [L *praecognitio, -ōnis* foreknowledge, and *praecognoscere* to know beforehand]
■ **precog'nitive** /*pri-*/ *adj*. **precognosce** /*prē-kog-nos'*/ *vt* to take a precognition of.

precognize or **-ise** /*prē'kəg-nīz, -kog'* or *-kog-nīz'*/ *vt* to know beforehand. [**pre-** (1)]
■ **precog'nizant** or **-s-** *adj* having foreknowledge.

precompetitive /*prē-kəm-pet'i-tiv*/ *adj* denoting a period of industrial or commercial development during which competitors work together. [**pre-** (1)]

preconceive /*prē-kən-sēv'*/ *vt* to conceive or form a notion of before having actual knowledge. [**pre-** (1)]
■ **preconceit'** *n* (*obs*) a preconceived notion. **preconcep'tion** *n* the act of preconceiving; an opinion formed in advance, without actual knowledge.

preconcert /*prē-kən-sûrt'*/ *vt* to settle beforehand. [**pre-** (1)]
■ **preconcert** /*-kon'*/ *n* a previous arrangement. **preconcert'edly** *adv*. **preconcert'edness** *n*.

precondition /*prē-kən-dish'ən*/ *n* a condition that must be satisfied beforehand, a prerequisite. ◆ *vt* to prepare beforehand. [**pre-** (1)]

preconize or **-ise** /*prē'kə-nīz*/ *vt* to proclaim; to summon publicly; (of the Pope) to proclaim and ratify the election of as bishop. [L *praecō, -ōnis* a crier, a herald]
■ **preconization** or **-s-** /*prē-kən-ī-zā'shən* or *-kon-i-*/ *n*.

preconscious /*prē-kon'shəs*/ *adj* (of memories, ideas, etc) currently absent from, but which can be readily recalled to, the conscious mind (*psychol*); having occurred, existed, etc before consciousness, or the conscious self, developed. [**pre-** (1)]
■ **precon'sciousness** *n*.

precontract /*prē-kən-trakt'*/ *vt* to contract beforehand; to betroth previously. [**pre-** (1)]
■ **precontract** /*-kon'*/ *n* a previous contract or betrothal.

precook /*prē-kook'*/ *vt* to cook beforehand. [**pre-** (1)]

precordial or **praecordial** /*prē-kör'di-əl*/ *adj* in front of the heart. [**pre-** (2), and L *cor, cordis* heart]

precritical /*prē-krit'i-kl*/ *adj* preceding a crisis or critical phase; prior to the development of the critical faculties. [**pre-** (1)]

precurrer /*prē-kur'ər*/ (*Shakesp*) *n* a forerunner. [L *praecurrere* to go before]

precurse /*pri-kûrs'*/ (*Shakesp*) *n* a prognostication or foretoken. [L *praecursus* a forerunning]

precursor /*prē-kûr'sər*/ *n* something that exists or goes in advance of another; an indication of the approach of an event; a forerunner, herald or harbinger; a predecessor; a substance from which the one in question is derived or manufactured (*chem*). [L *praecurrere, -cursum* to run or go before, precede]
■ **precur'sive** or **precur'sory** *adj*.

precut /*prē-kut'*/ *vt* to cut beforehand. ◆ *adj* /*prē'*/ cut in advance; prefabricated. [**pre-** (1)]

precycle /*prē-sī'kl*/ *vi* (of a consumer) to avoid unnecessary waste by preferring to buy products with minimal packaging. [**pre-** (1); modelled on **recycle**]

predacious or (*irreg*) **predaceous** /*pri-dā'shəs*/ *adj* living by prey; predatory. [Formed from **predatory**]
■ **predā'ciousness** or **predac'ity** *n*.

predate[1] /*prē-dāt'*/ *vt* to date before the true date; to antedate; to be earlier than. [**pre-** (1)]

predate[2] /*pri-dāt'*/ *vt* to eat, prey upon. ◆ *vi* to hunt prey. [L *praedātio, -ōnis* from *praedāri, -ātus*, predate being a back-formation from **predation**; see **predator**]
■ **preda'tion** *n* plundering, depredation; the killing and consuming of other animals for survival, the activity of preying. **pred'ative** *adj*.

predator /*pred'ə-tər*/ *n* an animal that preys on another; a predatory person, state or other body. [L *praedātor*, from *praedāri, -ātus* to plunder, from *praeda* booty]
■ **pred'atorily** *adv*. **pred'atoriness** *n*. **pred'atory** *adj* (of creatures) killing and feeding on others; (of people, states, etc) plundering or exploiting those that are weaker; relating to or characterized by plundering or preying; destructive, deleterious (*obs*).
❏ **predatory pricing** *n* the setting of prices at a level so low that competitors are forced out of the market.

predecease /*prē-di-sēs'*/ *vt* to die before (another person, or, unusually, an event). ◆ *n* (*rare*) a death that occurs before another person's. [**pre-** (1)]
■ **predeceased'** *adj* deceased at an earlier time.

predecessor /*prē'di-ses-ər* or (*N Am*) *pred'i-*/ *n* the person who preceded one in one's job or position; the previous version, model, etc of a particular thing, product, etc; (with reference to a day, week, etc) the one preceding the one in question; an ancestor. [L *praedēcessor*, from *prae* before, and *dēcessor* a retiring officer, from *dē* away, and *cēdere* to go, depart]

predella /*pri-del'ə*/ *n* the platform or uppermost step on which an altar stands; a board behind an altar, a retable; a painting or sculpture on the face of either of these; a painting in a compartment along the bottom of an altarpiece. [Ital, prob, from OHGer *pret* board]

predentate /*prē-den'tāt*/ *adj* having teeth in the forepart of the jaw only. [**pre-** (2)]

predesignate /*prē-dez'ig-nāt* or *-des'*/ *vt* to specify beforehand. ◆ *adj* designated in advance; having the quantification of the predicate distinctly expressed (*logic*). [**pre-** (1)]
■ **predesigna'tion** *n*. **predes'ignatory** *adj*.

predestine /*prē-des'tin* or *pri-*/ *vt* to destine or decree beforehand; to foreordain. [**pre-** (1)]
■ **predestina'rian** *adj* believing in or relating to the doctrine of predestination. ◆ *n* someone who holds the doctrine of predestination. **predestina'rianism** *n*. **predes'tinate** *vt* to determine beforehand; to preordain by an unchangeable purpose. ◆ *adj* /*-it*/ foreordained; fated. **predestina'tion** *n* the act of predestinating or fact of being predestined; the doctrine that whatever is to happen has been unalterably fixed by God from the beginning of time, *esp* with regard to which souls are to be saved and which damned (*theol*); fixed fate. **predes'tinative** *adj*. **predes'tinator** *n* someone who predestinates or foreordains; a predestinarian (*obs*). **predes'tiny** *n* irrevocably fixed fate.

predetermine /*prē-di-tûr'min*/ *vt* to determine or settle beforehand. [**pre-** (1)]
■ **predeter'minable** *adj*. **predeter'minate** /*-ət*/ *adj* determined beforehand. **predetermina'tion** *n*. **predeter'miner** *n* (*grammar*) a word or phrase preceding a determiner, such as *both*. **predeter'minism** *n* determinism.

predevote /*prē-di-vōt'*/ *adj* foreordained. [**pre-** (1)]

predial see **praedial**.

predicable /*pred'i-kə-bl*/ *adj* capable of being predicated or affirmed of something; attributable. ◆ *n* anything that can be predicated of another, or *esp* of many others; one of the five attributes, ie genus, species, difference, property and accident (*logic*). [L *praedicabilis*, from *praedicāre* to proclaim, and *-abilis* able]
■ **predicabil'ity** *n*.

predicament /pri-dik'ə-mənt/ n a difficult position, a plight or dilemma; a situation or set of circumstances generally; one of the classes or categories which include all predicables (*logic*). [LL *praedicāmentum* something predicated or asserted]
■ **predicamental** /-ment'l/ *adj*.

predicant /pred'i-kənt/ *adj* preaching; predicating. ◆ *n* a preacher; a preaching friar or Dominican; another spelling of **predikant**; an affirmer of anything. [L *praedicāns, -antis*, prp of *praedicāre* to proclaim; see **predicate**]

predicate /pred'i-kāt/ *vt* to affirm or assert; to state as a property or attribute of the subject of a proposition (*logic*); to imply, entail the existence of; to make (an expression) the predicate of a proposition; to base on certain grounds (with *on, upon; US*); to preach (*rare*); sometimes erroneously used for **predict**. ◆ *n* /-kət/ that which is predicated of the subject of a proposition, or the second term of a proposition, affirmed or denied by means of the copula (*logic*); the word or words in a sentence by which something is said about the subject (*grammar*). [L *praedicāre, -ātum* to proclaim, from *prae* forth, and *dicāre* (orig) to proclaim]
■ **predicā'tion** *n*. **predicative** /pri-dik'ə-tiv or pred'i-kā-tiv/ *adj* (of an adjective) contained within, *esp* normally, the predicate of a sentence (*grammar*); expressing predication or affirmation; affirming or asserting. **predic'atively** *adv*. **pred'icatory** *adj* affirmative.
□ **predicate calculus** see under **calculus**.

predict /pri-dikt'/ *vt* to foretell, *esp* on the basis of present knowledge. [L *praedictus*, pap of *praedīcere*, from *dīcere* to say]
■ **predic'table** *adj* capable of being predicted; easily foreseen, only to be expected; boringly consistent, lacking the capacity to surprise; unoriginal, trite. **predictabil'ity** or **predic'tableness** *n*. **predic'tably** *adv*. **prediction** /-shən/ *n* the act or art of predicting; something foretold. **predic'tive** *adj* foretelling, anticipating; prophetic. **predic'tively** *adv*. **predic'tor** *n* someone or something that predicts (also **predic'ter**); an anti-aircraft range-finding and radar device.

predigest /prē-dī-jest' or -di-/ *vt* to break down (food) by means that simulate the digestive process, to make it more easily digestible; to present (literature, complex subject matter, etc) in a simplified form, or simplistically, to make it more comprehensible. [**pre-** (1)]
■ **predigestion** /-jest'yən/ *n* preliminary digestion; hasty digestion (*obs*).

predikant /prä-di-känt'/ or **predicant** /pred'i-kant/ *n* a Dutch Reformed preacher, *esp* in South Africa. [Du, from L *praedicāns, -antis*; see **predicant, preach**]

predilection /prē-di-lek'shən or pred-i-/ *n* a favourable predisposition; a special liking or preference. [L *praedīligere* to prefer, from *prae* above others, and *dīligere, dīlectum* to love]
■ **predilect'** or **predilec'ted** *adj* (*rare*) chosen in preference; favoured.

predispose /prē-dis-pōz'/ *vt* (often with *to* or *towards*) to dispose or incline (someone) beforehand (eg to react in a certain way); to render favourable or conducive to something; to render (someone) liable or susceptible (eg to an illness; also without direct object). [**pre-** (1)]
■ **predispō'sing** *adj*. **predisposition** /-pə-zish'ən/ *n*. **predisposi'tional** *adj*.

prednisolone /pred-nis'ə-lōn/ *n* a synthetic corticosteroid drug similar to and derived from prednisone.

prednisone /pred'ni-zōn or -sōn/ *n* a drug similar to cortisone, used eg as an anti-inflammatory agent. [Perh from *pregnant*, *diene* and *cortisone*]

predominate /pri-dom'i-nāt/ *vi* to be dominant; to prevail; to be most prominent or noticeable; to be most numerous or abounding; to be superior in strength or authority; to have a commanding position. ◆ *vt* (*Shakesp*) to prevail over. [**pre-** (3)]
■ **predom'inance** or **predom'inancy** *n*. **predom'inant** *adj* preponderating; prevailing; most numerous or prominent; ruling; having superior power; ascendant; commanding in position or effect. **predom'inantly** *adv*. **predom'inate** /-nət/ *adj* (*rare*) predominant. **predominā'tion** *n*.

Pre-Dravidian /prē-drə-vid'i-ən/ *adj* belonging or relating to a dark, broad-nosed race of people with tightly curling hair, including Sakai, Veddas and Australian aborigines. ◆ *n* a person belonging to this race. [**pre-** (1)]

predy /*of unknown pronunciation*/ (*obs naut*) *adj* cleared for action. ◆ *vt* to make ready. [Origin uncertain; poss from make the ship *ready*]

pree /prē/ (*Scot*) *vt* to make a trial of, *esp* by tasting or by kissing. [**prieve** (see under **prief**)]

pre-echo /prē-ek'ō/ *n* (*pl* **pre-ech'oes**) the unwanted effect of a faint sound anticipating the actual sound on a tape recording, caused by the transfer of material between surfaces of the wound tape (*sound recording*; see also **post-echo** under **post-**); a foretaste. [**pre-** (1)]

pre-eclampsia /prē-i-klamp'si-ə/ (*med*) *n* a toxic condition occurring in late pregnancy, with eclamptic symptoms, eg high blood pressure, excessive weight gain, proteins in the urine, oedema, and sometimes severe headaches and visual disturbances. [**pre-** (1), and see **eclampsia**]

pre-elect /prē-i-lekt'/ *vt* to choose beforehand. [**pre-** (1)]
■ **pre-elec'tion** *n* election in anticipation; preference (*obs*). ◆ *adj* before election.

pre-embryo /prē-em'bri-ō/ (*biol*) *n* (*pl* **pre-em'bryos**) the name used for the formation that will become the human embryo, in the first fourteen days after fertilization. [**pre-** (1)]
■ **pre-embryon'ic** *adj*.

preemie, premie or **premy** /prē'mē/ (*inf*) *n* short for *prem*ature baby.

pre-eminent /prē-em'i-nənt/ *adj* supreme among the eminent; more important or influential than others; surpassing others in good or bad qualities; outstanding; extreme. [**pre-** (3)]
■ **prē-em'inence** *n*. **prē-em'inently** *adv*.

pre-emphasis /prē-em'fə-sis/ (*telecom*) *n* the process of increasing the strength of some frequency components of a signal to assist them to override noise or other distortion in the system. [**pre-** (1)]

pre-empt /prē-emt'/ or **-empt'**/ *vt* to secure as first comer; to secure by pre-emption; to take possession of, to appropriate; to forestall or thwart (a person or plan); to supplant or replace (a television programme, etc). ◆ *vi* (*bridge*) to make a pre-emptive bid. [L *prae* before, and *emptiō, -ōnis* a buying, from *emere* to buy, **pre-empt** being a back-formation from **pre-emption**]
■ **prē-empt'ible** *adj*. **prē-emp'tion** *n* the act or right of purchasing before others are offered the chance to do so; (also **pre-emption right**) the right of a citizen to purchase a certain amount of public land if certain conditions are fulfilled (*US*); a piece of land so obtained; a belligerent's right to seize neutral contraband at a fixed price; seizure; the act of attacking first to forestall hostile action. **prē-empt'ive** *adj* having the effect of pre-empting; (of an attack or strike) effectively destroying the enemy's weapons before they can be used (*milit*). **prē-empt'or** *n*.
□ **prē-emptive bid** *n* (*bridge*) an unusually high bid intended to deter others from bidding.

preen¹ /prēn/ *vt* (of a bird) to clean and arrange (the feathers), or to clean and arrange the feathers of (a part of the body); to groom (oneself) *esp* with evident vanity; to plume, pride or congratulate (oneself) (with *on*). ◆ *vi* to spend time preening oneself. [Appar **prune**² assimilated to **preen**²]
□ **preen gland** *n* a bird's uropygial gland, which secretes oil used in preening the feathers.

preen² /prēn/ (*Scot*) *n* a pin. ◆ *vt* to pin. [OE *prēon* pin, brooch]

pre-establish /prē-i-stab'lish/ *vt* to establish beforehand. [**pre-** (1)]
□ **pre-established harmony** see under **harmony**.

preeve /prēv/ *n* and *vt* an obsolete form of **proof** and **prove**.

pre-exilic /prē-eg-zil'ik or -ek-sil'/ *adj* (also **pre-exil'ian**) before the exile, used of Old Testament writings prior to the Jewish exile (c.586–538BC). [**pre-** (1)]

pre-exist /prē-ig-zist' or -eg-/ *vi* to exist beforehand, *esp* in a former life. ◆ *vt* to exist before. [**pre-** (1)]
■ **prē-exist'ence** *n* (*theol*) previous existence, *esp* of the soul before the generation of the body with which it is united in this world, or of Christ before his incarnation. **prē-exist'ent** *adj*.

pref. *abbrev* : preface; preference; preferred.

prefab /prē'fab/ (*inf*) *n* a prefabricated building, *esp* a house.

prefabricate /prē-fab'ri-kāt/ *vt* to make standardized parts of beforehand, for assembling later. [**pre-** (1)]
■ **prefab'ricated** *adj* composed of such parts. **prefabricā'tion** *n*. **prefab'ricātor** *n*.

preface /pref'is/ *n* something said by way of introduction or preliminary explanation; a statement, *usu* explanatory, placed at the beginning of a book, not regarded as forming (like the introduction) part of the composition; the ascription of glory, etc, in the liturgy of consecration of the Eucharist (*relig*); anything preliminary, introductory or immediately antecedent (with *to*). ◆ *vt* to precede or serve to introduce; to open or introduce; to provide with a preface; to say by way of preface (*obs* or *rare*); to front, place or be in front of (*rare*). ◆ *vi* (*old*) to make preliminary remarks. [Fr *préface*, from LL *prēfātia* for L *praefātiō*, from *prae* before, and *fārī, fātus* to speak]
■ **prefacial** /pri-fā'shl/ *adj* (*rare*). **prefatorial** /pref-ə-tō'ri-əl or -tō'/ *adj* serving as a preface or introduction. **prefato'rially** or **prefatorily** /pref'ə-tə-ri-li/ *adv*. **pref'atory** *adj* of or relating to a preface; serving as a preface or introduction; introductory.

prefade /prē-fād'/ *vt* deliberately to give (newly manufactured jeans, cloth, etc) a faded appearance by some artificial process; to adjust (sound) to a suitable level before fading in (*sound recording*). [**pre-** (1)]

prefard /pri-färd'/ a Spenserian form of **preferred** (*pat* of **prefer**).

prefatorial, etc see under **preface**.

prefect or (*esp hist*, RC and *old*) **praefect** /prē'fekt/ *n* a name given to any of various officials placed in authority over others; a commander or magistrate (*Roman hist*); a school pupil with some measure of authority over others, *esp* in the form of minor disciplinary powers; the administrative head of a department in France, of a province in Italy, or of any similar administrative district elsewhere; a senior teacher at a Jesuit school, or (also **prefect apostolic**) a church official in charge of a missionary district (*RC*). [OFr *prefect* (Fr *préfet*) and L *praefectus*, pap of *praeficere*, from *prae* above, superior to, and *facere* to make] ■ **prefectoral** /prē-fek'tar-əl/ or **prefectorial** /-tō'ri-əl or -tŏ'/ *adj*. **prē'fectship** *n*. **prefect'ural** *adj*. **prē'fecture** *n* the office, term of office, or district of a prefect; in Japan, any of 46 administrative districts headed by a governor; the house or office occupied by a prefect. □ **prefect of police** *n* the head of the Paris police.

prefer /pri-fûr'/ *vt* (**preferring** /pri-fûr'ing/; **preferred** /pri-fûrd'/) to hold in higher estimation; to like better (with *to*, or *rather than*; not with *than* alone); to choose or select rather or sooner than others; to advance or promote over the head of colleagues; to submit (a charge or accusation) to a court of law for consideration (*law*); to give priority to (particular creditors); to put forward, offer or present, for acceptance, etc (*archaic*); to set in front (*obs*). [Fr *préférer*, from L *praeferre*, from *prae* before, and *ferre* to bear] ■ **preferabil'ity** /pref-/ *n*. **pref'erable** (*obs* **preferrable** /pri-fûr'/) *adj* to be preferred; more desirable; having priority. **pref'erably** *adv* from choice; as is better or more desirable. **pref'erence** *n* the choice, favouring, liking of one rather than another, estimation of one above another; the state of being preferred; that which is preferred; priority; an advantage given to one over another; a card game resembling auction bridge. **preferential** /pref-ə-ren'shl/ *adj* having, giving, or allowing, a preference; discriminating in favour of someone or something; (of a ballot or voting) requiring the voter to put candidates in order of preference; see also **preference shares** below. **preferen'tialism** *n*. **preferen'tialist** *n* someone who favours a preferential tariff. **preferen'tially** *adv*. **prefer'ment** *n* advancement; promotion; a superior appointment or position, *esp* in the Church, enhancing one's social and financial status; the act of preferring. **preferr'er** *n*. □ **preference** (also **preferential**) **shares** or **stock** *n pl* shares or stock on which dividends must be paid before those on other kinds. **preferential tariff** or **duty** *n* a lower tariff or duty imposed on imports from some (eg developing) countries than on those from others. **preferred shares** *n pl* (*US*) same as **preference shares** above. ■ **in preference to** rather than.

prefigure /prē-fig'ər/ *vt* to imagine beforehand; to foreshadow or be a foretoken of. [**pre-** (1)] ■ **prefig'urate** /-ū-rət/ *adj* prefigured. ◆ *vt* to prefigure. **prefigūrā'tion** *n*. **prefig'urative** *adj*. **prefig'urement** /-ər-mənt/ *n*.

prefix /prē'fiks/ *n* an affix added at the beginning of a word; a title placed before a name, eg *Mrs*, *Sir*. ◆ *vt* /prē-fiks' or prē'fiks/ to put before, or at the beginning; to add as a prefix; to fix beforehand. [L *praefīgere*, from *prae* in front, and *fīgere* to fix] ■ **prefixion** /-fik'shən/ *n*. **prefix'ture** *n*.

prefloration /prē-flō-rā'shən, -flō- or -flə-/ (*bot*) *n* the manner in which the petals and sepals are folded in the flower-bud, aestivation. [**pre-** (1), and L *flōs, flōris* flower]

prefoliation /prē-fō-li-ā'shən/ (*bot*) *n* the manner in which the leaf is folded within the leaf bud, vernation. [**pre-** (1), and L *folium* leaf]

preform /prē- or pre-förm'/ *vt* to form beforehand (*Shakesp*); to determine the shape of beforehand. [**pre-** (1)] ■ **prēformā'tion** *n*. **prēformā'tionism** *n*. **prēformā'tionist** *n* a believer in the now exploded theory that the plant or animal (and therefore all its descendants) was already preformed in the germ (the ovum, according to the ovists, the sperm, according to the animalculists) and had only to be unfolded without formation of any new parts. **prēfor'mative** *adj*.

prefrontal /prē-fron'tl or -frun'tl/ (*anat*) *adj* in front of, or in the forepart of, the frontal bone, lobe, scale, etc; belonging or relating to such a part. ◆ *n* a bone or scale so situated. [**pre-** (1)]

prefulgent /prē-ful'jənt/ *adj* extremely bright. [**pre-** (3)]

preggers /preg'ərz/ (*inf*) *adj* pregnant.

pre-glacial /prē-glā'shl or -si-əl/ *adj* earlier than the glacial period. [**pre-** (1)]

pregnable /preg'nə-bl/ *adj* capable of being taken by assault or force; vulnerable. [Fr *prenable*, from *prendre* to take; see **impregnable**]

pregnant¹ /preg'nənt/ *adj* (of a woman or female animal) carrying a child or young in the womb; impregnated; fertilized (*obs*); heavily laden, swelling (*obs*); fertile, teeming, fruitful (*obs*); (of the mind or wit) inventive, productive; productive of results, momentous, significant for the future; loaded (eg with significance, menace, etc); full of meaning, significance or implications; pithy, witty, to the point (eg *Shakesp*); full of promise (*obs*); receptive, disposed, ready, apt, ready to act (*Shakesp*); conveying a compressed meaning beyond what the grammatical construction can strictly carry (*grammar*). [L *praegnāns, -antis*, from earlier *praegnās, -ātis*, thought to be from *prae* before, and the root of *gnāscī* to be born] ■ **preg'nancy** or (*obs*) **preg'nance** *n*. **preg'nantly** *adv*.

pregnant² /preg'nent/ (*archaic*) *adj* (of evidence, proof, reasons, arguments) weighty, cogent, convincing, obvious or clear. [OFr *preignant*, prp of *preindre*, from L *premere* to press]

pregustation /prē-gu-stā'shən/ *n* a foretaste. [**pre-** (1)]

prehallux /prē-hal'uks/ (*zool*) *n* a rudimentary innermost toe. [**pre-** (2)]

preheminence an obsolete spelling of **pre-eminence**.

prehend /pri-hend'/ *vt* to seize or grasp (*rare*); to apprehend without conscious perception (*philos*). [L *praehendere, -hēnsum* to seize] ■ **prehen'sible** *adj* (*rare*) capable of being grasped or apprehended. **prehen'sile** /-sīl/ *adj* (*zool*) capable of grasping. **prehensility** /prē-hen-sil'i-ti/ *n*. **prehension** /pri-hen'shən/ *n* the action of grasping (*zool*); intellectual or (*philos*) unconscious apprehension. **prehen'sive** *adj* prehensile, relating to grasping (*zool*); relating to (unconscious) apprehension. **prehen'sor** *n* someone or something that grasps or seizes. **prehen'sory** or **prehenso'rial** *adj* (*zool*) prehensile.

prehistoric /prē-hi-stor'ik/ or **prehistorical** /prē-hi-stor'i-kəl/ *adj* belonging or relating to a time before extant historical records; antiquated, completely out of date (*inf*); primitive (*inf*). [**pre-** (1)] ■ **prēhistō'rian** *n*. **prēhistor'ically** *adv*. **prēhis'tory** *n*.

prehnite /prā'nīt/ (*mineralogy*) *n* a zeolite-like mineral, an acid calcium aluminium silicate, *usu* a pale green. [Named after Colonel von *Prehn* (1733–85), who brought it from South Africa]

prehuman /prē-hū'mən/ *adj* at a stage of development before full humanity has been developed; earlier than the appearance of man. [**pre-** (1)]

preif or **preife** /prēf/ obsolete forms of **proof**.

pre-ignition /prē-ig-nish'ən/ *n* the premature ignition of the explosive mixture of fuel and air in an internal-combustion engine. [**pre-** (1)]

pre-industrial /prē-in-dus'tri-əl/ *adj* (of a society, economy, etc) having not yet undergone industrialization. [**pre-** (1)]

prejink /pri-jingk'/ same as **perjink**.

prejudge /prē-juj'/ *vt* to judge or decide upon before hearing the whole case, or all sides, etc; to condemn unheard. [Fr *préjuger*, from L *praeiudicāre*; see **prejudicate**] ■ **prejudge'ment** or **prejudg'ment** *n*.

prejudicate /pri-joo'di-kāt/ (*obs*) *vt* to spoil, prejudice; to influence or bias, to prejudice; to judge beforehand. ◆ *vi* to act in a prejudicial manner; to form an opinion beforehand. ◆ *adj* /-kət/ (of an opinion) preconceived; (of a person) biased; settled in advance (*rare*). [L *praejūdicāre, -ātum*, from *prae* before, and *judicāre* to judge] ■ **preju'dicant** /-kənt/ *adj* prejudging. **prejudicā'tion** *n*. **prejud'icative** *adj*.

prejudice /prej'ŭ-dis/ *n* a judgement or opinion formed prematurely or without due consideration of relevant issues; prepossession or bias in favour of or against anything; unthinking hostility; injury or harm; disadvantage; a prejudgement (*obs*); (*Spenser* **prejudize**) prognostication. ◆ *vt* to fill with prejudice; to prepossess or bias in favour or against something; to injure, harm or endanger; to prejudge, *esp* unfavourably (*obs*). [Fr *préjudice* injury, wrong, and L *praejūdicium* a previous judgement, harm, injury, from *prae* before, and *jūdicium* judgement] ■ **prej'udiced** *adj* having prejudice; biased. **prejudicial** /-dish'l/ *adj* injurious; detrimental; prejudiced (*obs*). **prejudic'ially** *adv*. ■ **without prejudice** a phrase used to require an understanding that nothing said at this stage is to detract from one's rights, to damage claims arising from future developments, or to constitute an admission of liability.

pre-judicial /prē-joo-dish'l/ (*law*) *adj* relating to matters to be decided before a case comes to court. [L *praejūdicium* a preliminary enquiry]

prelacy see under **prelate**.

prelapsarian /prē-lap-sā'ri-ən/ *adj* belonging or relating to the time before the Fall, man's first lapse in sin; innocent. [**pre-** (1), and L *lāpsus* a fall]

prelate /prel'it/ *n* a churchman of high rank; an abbot or prior or the superior of a religious order; a clergyman; a chief priest (*obs*). [Fr *prélat*, from L *praelātus*, from *prae* before, and *lātus* borne] ■ **prelacy** /prel'ə-si/ *n* the office or authority of a prelate; the order of bishops or the bishops collectively; church government by prelates; episcopacy. **prel'ateship** *n*. **prel'atess** *n* a female prelate. **prelatial** /pri-lā'shəl/ *adj* of a prelate. **prelatic** /pri-lat'ik/ or **prelat'ical** *adj* relating to prelates or prelacy; episcopal or episcopalian (*derog*).

■ words derived from main entry word; □ compound words; ■ idioms and phrasal verbs

prelat'ically *adv.* **prelā'tion** *n* preferment; promotion; eminence. **prel'atish** *adj* (*Milton*). **prel'atism** *n* (*usu derog*) episcopacy or episcopalianism; domination by prelates. **prel'atist** *n* an upholder of prelacy. **prel'atize** or **-ise** *vt* and *vi* to make or to become prelatical. **prel'ature** *n*. **prel'aty** *n* prelacy.

prelect /pri-lekt'/ *vi* to lecture. [L *praelegere, -lectum*, from *prae* in front, and *legere* to read]

■ **prelec'tion** *n*. **prelec'tor** *n* a public reader or lecturer.

prelibation /prē-lī-bā'shən/ *n* a foretaste; an offering of first-fruits. [L *praelībātiō, -ōnis*, from *prae* before, and *lībāre* to taste]

prelim /prē'lim or pri-lim'/ (*inf*) often in *pl*) *n* a preliminary or entrance examination; (in *pl*) the preliminary matter, ie titles, preface, contents list, introduction, of a printed book (*printing*).

preliminary /pri-lim'i-nə-ri or -in-ri/ *adj* introductory; preparatory; preceding or preparing for the main matter. ◆ *n* an introductory or preparatory measure, activity, statement, etc (often in *pl*); a preliminary or entrance examination. [L *prae* before, and *līmen, -inis* threshold]

■ **prelim'inarily** *adv.*

prelingual /prē-ling'gwəl/ *adj* before the use of language. [**pre-** (1)]
❑ **prelingually deaf** *n* deaf since before the acquisition of language, ie from birth (see also **post-lingual** under **post-**).

preliterate /prē-lit'ər-ət/ *adj* (of a society, culture, etc) having not yet developed a written language. [**pre-** (1)]

preload /prē-lōd'/ (*sl*) *vi* to drink alcohol before going on a night out. [**pre-** (1)]

■ **preload'ed** *adj* (*comput*) denoting software that is already installed on a personal computer at the time of purchase.

prelude /prel'ūd/ *n* an event that precedes and prepares the ground for one more momentous; anything done, said, performed, etc by way of an introduction or preliminary; a preliminary strain, passage or flourish, often improvised (*music*); an introduction to or first movement of a suite, or a movement preceding a fugue (*music*); an overture (*music*); an introductory voluntary (*music*); a short independent composition with a recurring motif, *esp* for the piano; a poetical composition of introductory nature or function. ◆ *vt* /prel'ūd or *esp* formerly pri-lūd' or -lood'/ to precede as a prelude, serve as prelude to; to introduce with a prelude; to perform as a prelude. ◆ *vi* to provide a prelude; to perform a prelude; to serve as a prelude. [Fr *prélude*, from LL *praelūdium*, from L *lūdere* to play]

■ **preludial** and **preludious** /pri-loo'- or -lū'/ *adj* (*rare*). **prelusive** /-loo'siv, lū'/ *adj* of the nature of a prelude; introductory. **prelu'sively** and **prelu'sorily** *adv.* **prelu'sory** /-sə-ri/ *adj* introductory.

preludio /pre-loo'di-ō/ (*Ital*) *n* (*pl* **prelu'di** /-dē/) a prelude.

prem /prem/ (*inf*) *n* a premature baby.

premandibular /prē-man-dib'ū-lər/ (*anat*) *adj* in front of the lower jaw. ◆ *n* a bone so placed in fishes, etc. [**pre-** (2)]

premarital /prē-mar'i-təl/ *adj* before marriage. [**pre-** (1)]

premature /prem'ə-tūr, prē'mə- or -tūr'/ *adj* occurring before the usual or expected time; unduly early; over-hasty; (of a human baby) born less than 37 weeks after conception, or (sometimes) having a birth weight of between 2½ and 5½ pounds irrespective of length of gestation; ripe before the due time. [L *praemātūrus*, from *prae* in advance, and *mātūrus* ripe]

■ **premature'ly** *adv.* **premature'ness** *n*. **prematur'ity** *n*.

premaxilla /prē-mak-sil'ə/ (*anat*) *n* (*pl* **premaxill'ae** /-ē/) a bone in front of the maxilla. [**pre-** (2)]

■ **premaxill'ary** (or /-mak'/) *adj*. ◆ *n* the premaxilla.

premed /prē-med'/ (*inf*) *adj* premedical. ◆ *n* premedication; (also **premed'ic**) a premedical student; premedical studies.

premedical /prē-med'i-kl/ *adj* of or relating to a course of study undertaken in preparation for professional medical training. [**pre-** (1)]

premedicate /prē-med'i-kāt/ *vt* to administer premedication to. [**pre-** (1)]

■ **premedica'tion** *n* drugs given to sedate and prepare a patient, *esp* for the administration of a general anaesthetic prior to surgery, etc.

premeditate /pri- or prē-med'i-tāt/ *vt* to plan or think out beforehand; to meditate upon beforehand. ◆ *vi* to deliberate beforehand. [L *praemeditārī, -ātus*, from *prae* before, and *meditārī* to meditate]

■ **premed'itated** *adj*. **premed'itatedly** *adv*. **premeditā'tion** *n*. **premed'itative** *adj*.

premenstrual /prē-men'stroo-əl or -strəl/ *adj* relating to or in the days immediately preceding menstruation. [**pre-** (1)]
❑ **premenstrual dysphoric disorder** *n* a severe form of premenstrual tension. **premenstrual tension** or **syndrome** *n* a condition characterized by a variety of symptoms, eg depression, nervous tension, headaches and pain in the breasts, caused by hormonal changes preceding menstruation (*abbrev* **PMT** or **PMS**).

premia see **premium**.

premie see **preemie**.

premier /prem'i-ər, -yər, also prē'mi-ər or (formerly) pri-mēr', or (in French context) prə-myā'/ *adj* prime or first; chief; leading, principal (as in *premier danseur* the principal male dancer of a ballet company, etc); most ancient, created earliest (as in *premier earl*) (*heraldry*, etc). ◆ *n* a person of chief rank or office; a prime minister or head of government; the Secretary of State (*obs*; *US*). [Fr *premier* (fem *première*), from L *prīmārius* of the first rank, from *prīmus* first]

■ **première** /prəm-yer' or prem'yər/ *n* the first performance of a play or showing of a film (also **premiere**); the principal female dancer of a ballet company, a prima ballerina (also **première danseuse** /dā-søz/); a leading lady in a theatrical company. ◆ *vt* (also **premiere, premier**) to give a first showing or performance of. ◆ *vi* to have or make a first showing or performance. **prem'iership** *n* the office of prime minister; a competition between sporting clubs, *esp* the most prestigious clubs in a sport, or victory in this.

premier cru /prə-myā krü'/ (*Fr*) *n* the best of the grands crus (qv under **grand²**).

premillenarian /prē-mi-lə-nā'ri-ən/ *n* a believer in the premillennial coming of Christ (also *adj*). [**pre-** (1)]

■ **premillena'rianism** *n*.

premillennial /prē-mi-len'yəl or -i-əl/ *adj* before the millennium. [**pre-** (1)]

■ **premillenn'ialism** *n* premillenarianism. **premillenn'ialist** *n*.

premise /prem'is/ *n* a proposition stated or assumed for the sake of argument, *esp* one of the two propositions in a syllogism from which the conclusion is drawn (also **prem'iss**; *logic*); (*usu* in *pl*) the matter set forth at the beginning of a deed (*law*); (in *pl*) the beginning of a deed setting forth its subject-matter (*law*); (in *pl*) the aforesaid (*property*; *law*); hence, a building and its adjuncts, *esp* a public house or place of business; a presupposition (also **prem'iss**); a condition stipulated beforehand (*Shakesp*); (in *pl*) antecedent happenings or circumstances (*Shakesp*). ◆ *vt* /pri-mīz' or prem'is/ to mention or state first, or by way of introduction; to prefix; to state or assume as a premise; to perform or administer as a preliminary (*med*). [Fr *prémisse* from L (*sententia*, etc) *praemissa* (a sentence, etc) put before, from *prae* before, and *mittere, missum* to send]

■ **premī'sed** *adj* (*Shakesp*) sent before due time.

premium /prē'mi-əm/ *n* (*pl* **pre'miums** or (*rare*) **pre'mia**) a sum regularly payable for insurance; an admission fee paid by someone entering an apprenticeship or profession; a sum added to a fixed wage, rate, etc, a bonus; excess over original price or par, *opp* to *discount*; anything offered as an incentive to buy; a reward, prize or bounty. ◆ *adj* of highest quality, and so costly. [L *praemium* prize, reward, from *prae* above, and *emere* to buy]
❑ **Premium Bond** or **Premium Savings Bond** *n* a Government bond, the holder of which gains no interest, but is eligible for a money prize allotted by a draw held at stated intervals.

■ **at a premium** in great demand; above par. **put a premium on** to attach particular value to, to esteem highly.

premolar /prē-mō'lər/ (*anat*) *adj* in front of the true molar teeth. ◆ *n* a tooth between the canine and molars (called molar or milk-molar in the milk dentition). [**pre-** (2)]

premonition /prē-mə-nish'ən or prem-/ *n* a feeling that something is going to happen before it actually does, a presentiment or intuition; a forewarning. [L *praemonēre* to give prior warning to, from *prae* before, and *monēre* to warn]

■ **premon'itive** or **premon'itory** *adj* conveying a warning or premonition. **premon'itor** *n* someone or something that gives warning beforehand. **premon'itorily** *adv*.

Premonstratensian /pri-mon-strə-ten'shən, -shyən or -si-ən/, also **Premonstrant** /-mon'strənt/ *adj* of an order of canons regular, the Norbertines or White Canons, founded by St Norbert in 1119 at *Prémontré* near Laon, or of a corresponding order of nuns. ◆ *n* a member of the order. [L *prātum mōnstrātum* the meadow pointed out, or (*locus*) *praemōnstrātus* (the place) foreshown (in a vision), ie *Prémontré*]

premorse /pri-mörs'/ *adj* ending abruptly, as if bitten off. [L *praemorsus* bitten in front, from *prae* in front, and *mordēre, morsum* to bite]

premosaic /prē-mō-zā'ik/ *adj* before the time of *Moses*. [**pre-** (1) and **Mosaic**]

premotion /prē-mō'shən/ *n* an (*esp* divine) impulse determining the will. [**pre-** (1)]

premove /prē-moov'/ *vt* to incite or prompt to action. [**pre-** (1)]

■ **premove'ment** *n*.

premy see **preemie**.

prenasal /prē-nā'zl/ (*anat*) *adj* in front of the nose. ◆ *n* a bone at the tip of the nose, as in pigs. [**pre-** (2)]

prenatal /prē-nā'tl/ *adj* before birth. [**pre-** (1)]

❑ **prenatal therapy** same as **metamorphic technique** (see under **metamorphosis**).

prenominate /pri-nom'i-nāt/ vt to name or state beforehand. ◆ adj /-nət or -nāt/ forenamed. [**pre-** (1)]

prenotion /prē-nō'shən/ n a preconception. [**pre-** (1)]

prent /prent/ (Scot) same as **print**.

prentice or **'prentice** /pren'tis/ aphetic for **apprentice**.
■ **pren'ticeship** or **'pren'ticeship** n.

prenuptial /prē-nup'shəl or -chəl/ adj before marriage. [**pre-** (1)]
❑ **prenuptial agreement** n an agreement made between two people before marriage relating to the disposition of their assets in the event of divorce (short form **pre'nup**).

prenzie adj in Shakesp (Measure for Measure III.1.95,98) variously explained as representing primsie, princely, Fr prenez garde, or connected with **prone²** (a homily), or a misprint.

preoccupy /prē-ok'ū-pī/ vt to engross or fill the mind of (someone) or dominate (someone's attention, thoughts, mind, etc) to the exclusion of other concerns; to prejudice, bias (obs); to occupy, fill or (obs) wear beforehand or before others. [**pre-** (1)]
■ **prēocc'upancy** n the circumstance of occupying before others; the condition of being preoccupied. **prēocc'upant** n a prior occupant. **prēocc'upate** vt (obs) to preoccupy; to anticipate. **prēoccupā'tion** n absorption, engrossment; abstraction, pensiveness; an enthusiasm, chief interest or obsession; prejudice (obs); the act or fact of occupying beforehand or before others. **prēocc'upied** adj lost in thought, abstracted; having one's attention wholly taken up, engrossed (with with); already occupied; (of a genus or species name) not available for adoption because it has already been applied to another group.

preon /prē'on/ (phys) n a hypothetical particle, a possible constituent of a quark. [**pre-** (1) and **-on** (1)]

preoption /prē-op'shən/ n (the right of) first choice. [**pre-** (1)]

preordain /prē-ör-dān'/ vt to ordain, appoint or determine beforehand. [**pre-** (1)]
■ **preordain'ment** n. **preor'dinance** n a rule previously established; that which is ordained beforehand. **preordinā'tion** n the act of preordaining.

pre-owned /prē-ōnd'/ (chiefly US) adj second-hand. [**pre-** (1)]

prep /prep/ (inf) n a preparatory school (also **prep school**); a pupil in a preparatory school; a preparatory race, ie a minor one that tests a horse's capabilities before the major one (horse-racing); preparation, homework (school sl). ◆ vt (**prepp'ing**; **prepped**) (orig N Am; med) to prepare (a patient) for an operation, etc.

prep. abbrev: preparation; preposition.

prepack /prē-pak'/ or **prepackage** /prē-pak'ij/ vt to pack (eg food) before offering for sale. [**pre-** (1)]
■ **prēpacked'** or **prēpack'aged** adj.

prepaid see **prepay**.

preparation, preparative, preparator see under **prepare**.

preparatory /pri-par'ə-t(ə-)ri/ adj introductory, preliminary, antecedent; serving to prepare; attending a preparatory school or undergoing preparatory instruction. ◆ adv preparatorily, previous or prior (with to). [LL praeparātōrius, from parāre to prepare]
■ **prepar'atorily** adv.
❑ **preparatory school** n a usu private school that prepares pupils for public school or other higher school; a private school that prepares young people for college (N Am).

prepare /pri-pār'/ vt to make or get ready; to equip or fit out; to bring into a suitable state for some purpose; to put into the necessary frame of mind, to brace mentally (for, or to do, something); to adapt, adjust, acclimatize in readiness (for, or to do, something); to train, eg for an examination; to learn, eg for examination purposes; to make a preliminary study of (work prescribed for a class); to provide, supply (archaic); to bring into a required state by subjecting to some technical process; to make, produce, mix or compound (eg a chemical) by some process; to cook and dress for serving (food, a meal); to think out beforehand (eg a plan, strategy); to draw up (a document, report, etc); to anticipate or lead up to (eg a discord by use of the dissonant note as a consonance in the preceding chord; music). ◆ vi to make oneself ready; to make preparations; to be under preparation (esp archaic). ◆ n (Shakesp) preparation. [Fr préparer, from L praeparāre, from prae before, and parāre to make ready]
■ **preparation** /prep-ə-rā'shən/ n the act or process of preparing; a preliminary measure or arrangement; the process or course of being prepared; the preliminary study of prescribed classwork, homework; readiness; something that has been prepared or made up, eg a medicine, ointment, application, etc; an anatomical or other specimen prepared for study or preservation; the day before the Sabbath or other Jewish feast-day; devotional exercises, prayers, etc preparing for or introducing an office, eg Holy Communion; the previous introduction,

as an integral part of a chord, of a note continued into a succeeding dissonance (music). **preparative** /pri-par'ə-tiv/ adj serving to prepare; preliminary. ◆ n something done, performed, administered, etc, to prepare the way; a preparation. **prepar'atively** adv. **prepar'ator** n (esp technical; old) someone who prepares medicines, scientific specimens, etc. **prepared** /pri-pārd'/ adj made ready, fit or suitable; already treated or processed, ready mixed or ready made; ready, willing, or not disinclined (to do something). **prepā'redly** /-rid-li/ adv. **prepā'redness** /-rid-nəs/ n. **prepā'rer** n.
❑ **prepared piano** n a piano that has been altered to give special effects, such as by placing objects on the strings.

prepay /prē-pā'/ vt (pap and pat **prepaid'**) to pay before or in advance. ◆ adj same as **pay-as-you-go** (see under **pay¹**). [**pre-** (1)]
■ **prepay'able** adj. **prepay'ment** n.

prepense /pri-pens'/ adj (esp law) premeditated; intentional, chiefly in the phrase **malice prepense** ie malice aforethought or intentional. ◆ vt (Spenser) to consider. [OFr purpense]
■ **prepense'ly** adv. **prepens'ive** adj (Fielding).

prepollence /pri-pol'əns/ n predominance. [LL praepollentia, from prae beyond, above, and pollēre to be strong]
■ **prepoll'ency** n. **prepoll'ent** adj.

prepollex /prē-pol'əks or -eks/ (zool) n (in some animals) a rudimentary innermost finger. [**pre-** (2)]

preponderate¹ /pri-pon'də-rāt/ vi to prevail or exceed in number, quantity, importance, influence, or force (with over); to weigh more; to turn the balance. ◆ vt (obs) to outweigh. [L praeponderāre, -ātum, from prae above, beyond, and ponderāre, -ātum to weigh, from pondus a weight]
■ **prepon'derance** or **prepon'derancy** n. **prepon'derant** adj. **prepon'derantly** or **prepon'derātingly** adv.

preponderate² /pri-pon'də-rāt/ (Fielding) vt and vi to ponder beforehand. [**pre-** (1)]

prepone /prē-pōn'/ vt to reschedule for an earlier time or date, to advance or bring forward. [**pre-** (1), on the model of **postpone**]

prepose /prē-pōz'/ (grammar, etc) vt to place or prefix (a word, etc) before another. [L praepōnere, -positum to place in front]

preposition¹ /prep-ə-zish'ən/ (grammar) n a word placed usu before a pronoun, noun or its equivalent to express position, movement, circumstance, etc relative to or affecting it; a prefix (obs). [L praepositiō, -ōnis, from praepōnere, -positum, from prae before, and pōnere to place]
■ **preposi'tional** adj. **preposi'tionally** adv.

preposition² /prē-pə-zish'ən/ (esp grammar) n position in front. [**pre-** (2)]

prepositive /pri-poz'i-tiv/ (grammar) adj placed before or prefixed to another word. [LL praepositīvus, from praepōnere, -positum to place in front]
■ **prepos'itively** adv.

prepositor see **praepostor**.

prepossess /prē-pə-zes'/ vt to bias or prejudice, esp favourably, to impress; to preoccupy; to fill (eg the mind) beforehand with some opinion or feeling; to possess or take beforehand (obs or law). [**pre-** (1)]
■ **prepossessed'** adj biased, prejudiced. **prepossess'ing** adj tending to prepossess; making a favourable impression; attractive, pleasing. **prepossess'ingly** adv. **prepossession** /-zesh'ən/ n bias, usu favourable; preoccupation; previous possession.

preposterous /pri-pos'tə-rəs/ adj utterly absurd; contrary to the order of nature or reason; literally inverted, having or putting the last first (rare). [L praeposterus reversed, from prae before, and posterus after]
■ **prepos'terously** adv. **prepos'terousness** n.

prepostor see **praepostor**.

prepotent /prē-pō'tənt/ adj powerful in a very high degree; prevailing over others or another in taking effect; having the ability to transmit an unusually high proportion of one's genetic characteristics to one's offspring (biol); taking precedence in effect. [**pre-** (3)]
■ **prepo'tence** or **prepo'tency** n.

preppy /prep'i/ (orig N Am inf) adj vaguely denoting the style and looks of those who (might wish to seem to) have attended a preparatory school (qv), ie expensively fashionable in a neatly groomed, respectably conservative way. ◆ n a present or former pupil of a preparatory school, or someone cultivating the appearance of one. [**prep school** (see **prep**)]
■ **prepp'ily** adv. **preppi'ness** n.

preprandial /prē-pran'di-əl/ adj before a meal, esp dinner. [**pre-** (1)]

prepress /prē'pres/ (publishing) n the preparation of an edited book, magazine, etc for printing, incl typesetting and page make-up (also adj). [**pre-** (1)]

■ words derived from main entry word; ❑ compound words; ■ idioms and phrasal verbs

pre-print /prē'print/ *n* part of a publication printed in advance. [**pre-** (1)]

preproduction /prē-prə-duk'shən/ *n* the work done on a film, broadcast, etc that precedes the making of it. [**pre-** (1)]

prepuberty /prē-pū'bər-ti/ *n* the period of childhood before, *esp* immediately before, puberty. [**pre-** (1)]
■ **prepu'bertal** *adj*.

prepubescent /prē-pū-bes'ənt/ *adj* prepubertal. [**pre-** (1)]

prepuce /prē'pūs/ (*anat*) *n* the loose skin of the penis, the foreskin; a similar fold of skin over the clitoris. [L *praepūtium*]
■ **preputial** /pri-pū'shyəl/ or *-shəl/ adj*.

prepunctual /prē-pungk'tū-əl/ *adj* more than punctual; coming before time. [**pre-** (3)]

pre-qualify /prē-kwol'i-fī/ *vi* to qualify beforehand (eg for a short list). [**pre-** (1)]
■ **prequalifica'tion** *n*.

prequel /prē'kwəl/ (*inf*) *n* a film or book produced as a follow-up to one that has proved a success, based on the same leading characters but showing what happened before the start of the original story. [**pre-** (1) and **sequel**]

Pre-Raphaelite or (as spelt by DG Rossetti) **Praeraphaelite** /prē-raf'(ā-)ə-līt/ *n* someone who seeks to return to the spirit and manner of painters before the time of *Raphael* (1483–1520); a member of a group (the Pre-Raphaelite Brotherhood, or 'PRB', 1848) of painters and others (DG Rossetti, W Holman Hunt, JE Millais, etc) who practised or advocated a truthful, almost rigid, adherence to natural forms and effects. ◆ *adj* of, relating to, reminiscent of or in the style of the Pre-Raphaelites. [**pre-** (1), *Raphael*, and **-ite**]
■ **Pre-Raph'aelism** or **Pre-Raph'aelitism** *n*. **Pre-Raphaelis'tic** or **Pre-Raphaelitis'tic** *adj*. **Pre-Raphaeli'tish** *adj*.

prerelease /prē-ri-lēs'/ *n* the release of a cinema film, record, etc before its official date of release; the exhibition of a film so released; anything so released. ◆ *adj* relating to the showing of film before its official public release. [**pre-** (1)]

prerequisite /prē-rek'wi-zit/ *n* a condition or requirement that must previously be satisfied. ◆ *adj* required as a condition of something else. [**pre-** (1)]

prerogative /pri-rog'ə-tiv/ *n* a privilege that is exclusive to a person, group, etc; a right arising out of one's rank, position or office; a faculty peculiar to the nature of any being, eg a human being; the right of voting first (*rare*). ◆ *adj* arising out of or held by prerogative; voting first. [L *praerogātīvus* asked first for his vote, from *prae* before others, and *rogāre, -ātum* to ask]
■ **prerog'atived** *adj* (*Shakesp*) having a prerogative. **prerog'atively** *adv*.
❑ **Prerogative Court** *n* formerly, a court having jurisdiction over testamentary matters.
■ **royal prerogative** the discretionary rights which a sovereign has by virtue of office, varying from country to country.

prerosion /prē-rō'zhən/ *n* corrosion of a crystal by a solvent forming new faces (*prerosion faces*) on the corners and edges. [L *praerōdere, -rōsum* to gnaw at the tip, from *prae* in front, and *rōdere* to gnaw]

prerupt /prē-rupt'/ *adj* broken off; abrupt. [L *praeruptus*, from *prae* in front, and *rumpere* to break]

Pres. *abbrev*: President.

pres. *abbrev*: present.

presa /prā'sä, -sə/ or *-zä/ n* (*pl* **pre'se** /-sā/ or *-zā/*) a symbol (X̶, ·S· or :S:) used to indicate the points at which successive voice or instrumental parts enter a round, canon, etc. [Ital, an act of taking up]

presage /pres'ij/ or *pri-sāj'/ vt* to portend; to forebode; to warn of as something to come; to forecast; to have a presentiment of; to point out, reveal (*Spenser*). ◆ *vi* to have or utter a foreboding. ◆ *n* /pres'ij/, formerly also *pri-sāj'/* an indication of the future; a prognostic; an omen; a foreboding; a presentiment. [L *praesāgium* a foreboding, from *prae* before, and *sāgus* prophetic]
■ **presage'ful** *adj*. **presage'ment** *n* (*obs*). **presa'ger** *n*.

presanctify /prē-sangk'ti-fī/ *vt* to consecrate beforehand. [**pre-** (1)]
■ **presanctifica'tion** *n*.

presbycousis, **presbycusis** /prez-/ or *pres-bi-koo'sis/*, **presbyacousis** or **presbyacusis** /-ə-koo'sis/ (*med*) *n* progressive loss of hearing with advancing old age. [Gr *presbys* old, and *akousis* hearing]

presbyopia /prez-bi-ō'pi-ə/ *n* difficulty in accommodating the eye to near vision, long-sightedness, a defect increasing with age (also **pres'byopy**). [Gr *presbys* old, and *ōps, ōpos* the eye]
■ **pres'byope** *n* someone suffering from presbyopia. **presbyopic** /-op'ik/ adj*.

presbyte /prez'bīt/ *n* in strict etymological sense, an old man, but used for a presbyopic person. [Gr *presbytēs* an old man]
■ **presbyt'ic** /-bit'/ adj*. **pres'bytism** *n*.

presbyter /prez'bi-tər/ *n* (in the Presbyterian Church) an elder; (in Episcopal churches) a minister or priest ranking between a bishop and a deacon; a member of a presbytery; a presbyterian (*obs*). [Gr *presbyteros*, compar of *presbys* old]
■ **presbyt'eral** *adj* of a presbyter or presbyters. **presbyt'erate** /-rət/ *n* the office of presbyter; a body of presbyters; the order of presbyters. **presbyterial** /-tē'ri-əl/ *adj* of a presbytery; of church government by elders. **presbytē'rially** *adv*. **pres'bytership** *n*. **pres'bytery** *n* a church court ranking next above the kirk session, consisting of the ministers and one ruling elder from each church within a certain district; the district so represented; the presbyterian system; part of a church reserved for the officiating priests, the eastern extremity; a priest's house (*RC*).

Presbyterian /pres-bi-tē'ri-ən/ *adj* of or belonging to any Protestant Church with a system of government by elders or presbyters developed as a result of the Reformation led by Calvin in Geneva and by John Knox in Scotland; (also without *cap*) of, relating to or maintaining this form of church government. ◆ *n* a member of such a church; (also without *cap*) an upholder of the Presbyterian system. [Church L *presbytērium* presbytery]
■ **Presbytē'rianism** *n* (also without *cap*) the form of church government by presbyters. **Presbytē'rianize** or **-ise** *vt* and *vi* (also without *cap*) to make or become Presbyterian; to move towards Presbyterianism.
■ **Reformed Presbyterian Church** the Cameronians (qv). **United Presbyterian Church** a religious body formed by the union of the Secession and Relief Churches in 1847, included in the United Free Church from 1900, and (except a minority) in the Church of Scotland from 1929.

preschool /prē-skool'/ or *prē'skool/ adj* before school; not yet at school. ◆ *n* a nursery school or kindergarten. [**pre-** (1)]
■ **prē'schooler** *n* a preschool child.

prescience /pres'i-əns, presh'-, -əns, -yəns or *prē'/ n* foreknowledge; foresight. [L *praesciēns, -entis*, prp of *praescīre*, from *prae* before, and *scīre* to know]
■ **pre'scient** *adj*. **pre'sciently** *adv*.

prescientific /prē-sī-ən-tif'ik/ *adj* of or relating to the time before the scientific age, before knowledge was systematized. [**pre-** (1)]

prescind /pri-sind'/ *vt* to cut off, cut short, separate; to abstract. ◆ *vi* to withdraw one's attention (*usu* with *from*). [L *praescindere* to cut off in front]
■ **prescind'ent** *adj*. **prescission** /pri-sish'ən/ *n*.

prescious /pre'shyəs/ or *prē'/ adj* prescient. [L *praescius*, from *praescīre*; cf **prescience**]

prescission see under **prescind**.

prescribe /pri-skrīb'/ *vt* to lay down as a rule or direction; to give as an order; to enjoin (*archaic*); to give instructions for the preparation and dispensing of (a medicine, etc) or for (a certain procedure, diet, etc), as a remedy (*med*); to limit, confine, set bounds to (*obs*); to claim as a prescriptive right (*law; obs*). ◆ *vi* to lay down rules; to give or make out a prescription (*med*); to make a claim on account of long possession (with *to, for*; *law*); to become unenforceable or invalid through time, to lapse (*law*). [L *praescrībere, -scrīptum* to write before, lay down in advance, object to, from *prae* before, in front, and *scrībere* to write]
■ **prescrib'er** *n*. **prescript** /prē'skript* formerly *-skript'/ n* (*archaic*) an ordinance or rule; a remedy or treatment prescribed. ◆ *adj* /prē'* or *-skript'/* (*rare*) prescribed. **prescriptibil'ity** /pri-/ *n*. **prescrip'tible** *adj* (*law*) subject to prescription. **prescrip'tion** *n* the act of prescribing or directing; a written direction for the preparation or dispensing of a medicine (**by** or **on prescription** (obtainable) on presentation of a doctor's prescription); the medicine itself; a written description from an optician stating the type of lenses necessary to correct one's vision; a formula or recipe; (also **positive prescription**) the creation or fortification of a legal right to land or buildings through unchallenged use or possession for a fixed period of time (*law*); (also **negative prescription**) the extinction of a legal right through failure to assert it by legal action within a fixed period of time (*law*). **prescrip'tive** *adj* prescribing, laying down rules; pronouncing on right and wrong usage (*linguistics*); (of a right, etc) consisting in, or acquired by, custom or long-continued use; customary. **prescrip'tively** *adv*. **prescrip'tiveness** *n*. **prescrip'tivism** *n* (recommendation of) the practice of laying down rules, *esp* on correct and incorrect usage in language; the contention that moral pronouncements have prescriptive force in the manner of imperatives, and no truth value (*philos*). **prescrip'tivist** *n*.

prescutum /prē-skū'təm/ *n* (*zool*) a tergal plate in front of the scutum of insects. [**pre-** (1)]

prese see **presa**.

preselect /prē-si-lekt'/ vt to select beforehand. [**pre-** (1)]
■ **preselec'tion** n. **preselec'tor** n a component of a radio receiver, improving reception.

pre-sell /prē-sel'/ vt to sell (something) before it has been produced. [**pre-** (1)]

presence /prez'əns/ n the state or circumstance of being present, opp to absence ; one's attendance at an event, etc; someone's company or immediate neighbourhood; the place where a great personage is; a presence chamber (obs); an assembly, esp of great persons (obs); the physical impression created by one's person; imposing, commanding or authoritative physical bearing; military or political representation or influence; a being felt to be present, esp in a supernatural way. [OFr, from L praesentia ; see **present¹**]
❑ **presence chamber** n the room in which a great personage receives company.
■ **in the presence of** in front of, or in the near vicinity of (someone). **presence of mind** the power of keeping one's wits about one; coolness and readiness in emergency, danger or surprise. **real presence** (theol) the true and substantial presence, according to the belief of Roman Catholics, Eastern Orthodox, etc, of the body and blood of Christ in the Eucharist.

pre-senile /prē-sē'nīl/ (med) adj belonging to or typical of the period of life preceding, esp just preceding, old age. [**pre-** (1)]
❑ **pre-senile dementia** n a condition similar to senile dementia that has its onset in middle age.

presension see under **presentient**.

present¹ /prez'ənt/ adj being here or in the place in question, opp to absent ; ready at hand; found or existing in the thing in question; now under view or consideration; now existing, not past or future; denoting a verb tense used to express an action happening or condition existing just now, or for making general statements (grammar); (of a verb or participle) in or of the present tense (grammar); immediate; (with to) having a place in, entering into (the thoughts, mind, etc; old); (of a person, the mind, etc) attentive to the matter in hand, not absent or abstracted (obs). ◆ n the present time; the present tense; a verb in the present tense; the present business or occasion; the present document or (in pl) writings (law, etc). [OFr, from L praesens, -sentis present]
■ **presentee'ism** n attendance at a place of work beyond the required hours, so as to be seen to be enthusiastic. **pres'ently** adv at present, now (obs or Scot and N Am); before long, in a while; directly, immediately; necessarily, inevitably, ipso facto (old); for the time being (obs); at once (obs). **pres'entness** n.
❑ **pres'ent-day** adj belonging to or found in the present time, contemporary. **present value** n the current value of a sum of money as opposed to its value in the future after having been invested.
■ **at present** at the present time, now. **for the present** as far as concerns the present time, for the moment; now, for the time being.

present² /pri-zent'/ vt to give, make a gift of (something to someone) or furnish (someone with something esp as a gift) esp formally or ceremonially; to deliver, convey or hand over; to introduce (one person to another, esp more distinguished, person); to introduce (someone) at court; to betake (oneself) to an appointed place to await instructions, interviews, etc; to bring (an actor or other performer) before the public, on stage, etc; to stage (a play), show (a film), etc; to introduce or compère (a television or radio show); to exhibit to view; to have as a characteristic; to pose or set (a problem, etc) or burden (someone with a problem, etc); to offer for consideration or acceptance (ideas, proposals, etc); to offer (a sight or other perceptual data) to the senses; to set out (written work, etc) in any manner; (of an idea, opportunity, etc) to suggest or offer (itself); to hand over (a cheque) for acceptance or (a bill) for payment; to assemble arguments for, and expound (a case); to depict, portray or represent; to bring before God's presence for dedication (Bible); to appoint (a clergyman to a benefice); to nominate (a scholar, etc to a foundation); to put forward (a candidate for examination, the award of a degree, etc); to bring (an offence, etc) to the notice of the authorities (old); to charge or bring up for trial (old); to symbolize (archaic); to represent the character of, act, impersonate (archaic); to apply; to offer the greetings of, 'remember' (someone to someone) (obs); to point, direct, aim, turn in some direction; to put on (eg a cheerful face) in public; to hold (a weapon) in the aiming position or vertically in front of the body in salute to a superior (**present arms** to hold (one's weapon) in the vertical saluting position; milit). ◆ vi (of the baby's head, shoulder or buttocks) to be in the position for emerging first (obstetrics); (of a patient) to report to a doctor (with certain signs and symptoms; med); (of chances, opportunities, etc) to offer, be available (rare); to make presentation to a living (relig). ◆ n the position of a weapon in presenting arms or in aiming (**at present** in the presenting-arms position). [OFr presenter, from L praesentāre, from praesēns present (in place or time)]

■ **presentabil'ity** n. **present'able** adj capable of being presented; fit to be presented; fit to be seen; passable. **present'ableness** n. **present'ably** adv. **presentation** /prez-ən-tā'shən/ n the act of presenting; the manner in which something is presented, laid out, explained or advertised; the expounding or unfolding of eg a case, argument, etc; the right of presenting; that which is presented; something performed for an audience, a play, show or other entertainment; an illustrated talk presenting information eg to a business audience; immediate cognition (psychol); representation; the position of a baby in the womb just before birth, ie whether head or buttocks downwards (obstetrics). ◆ adj that has been presented; of or for presentation. **presentā'tional** adj. **presentā'tionism** n (psychol) the doctrine of immediate cognition of objects. **presentā'tionist** n. **presentative** /pri-zent'ə-tiv/ adj subject to the right of presentation (relig); presenting an idea to the mind, (esp one that is not imitative); relating to immediate cognition (psychol). **presentee** /prez-ən-tē'/ n someone who is presented to a benefice. **presenter** /pri-zent'ər/ n. **present'ive** adj (linguistics) presenting a conception to the mind, not a mere relation. **present'iveness** n. **present'ment** n the act of presenting; a statement; a jury's statement to a court of matters within its knowledge; a representation; an image, delineation, picture; a theatrical representation or performance; a presentation to consciousness (psychol, philos).

present³ /prez'ənt/ n a gift; a percentage of the prize money given to a winning jockey (horse-racing). [OFr present, orig presence, hence gift (from the phrase mettre en présent à, to put into the presence of, hence to offer as a gift to)]

presential /pri-zen'shl/ (rare) adj relating to presence; having or implying actual presence; present; as if present; having presence of mind, alert; formed from the present tense (grammar). [Med L praesentiālis, from praesentia presence]
■ **presentiality** /-shi-al'i-ti/ n. **presen'tially** adv.

presentient /prē-sen'shyənt, -shənt or -shi-ənt/ adj having a presentiment. [**pre-** (1)]
■ **prēsen'sion** n.

presentiment /pri-zen'ti-mənt or -sen'/ n a premonition or foreboding, esp of evil. [**pre-** (1)]
■ **presentimental** /-men'tl/ adj.

presentive, presentment see under **present²**.

preserve /pri-zûrv'/ vt to keep safe from harm or loss; to keep safe from danger or death, to keep alive; to keep in existence; to retain; to maintain, keep up; to keep sound; to keep from or guard against decay; to freeze, dry, pickle, season, boil in sugar or otherwise treat (food) for keeping; to guard (game, or land, rivers, etc) against shooting or fishing by unauthorized persons. ◆ vi to preserve game, fish, ground, or water, etc. ◆ n a jam, pickle or other preserved form of fruit or vegetables; an area of land or stretch of water where game or fish are reared for private shooting or fishing; an area of work or activity regarded as restricted to certain people and forbidden to outsiders; (in pl) spectacles or goggles to protect the eyes from dust or strong light (old). [Fr préserver, from L prae before, and servāre to keep]
■ **preservabil'ity** n. **preserv'able** adj. **preservā'tion** /prez-/ n the process of preserving or of being preserved; repair. **preservā'tionist** n someone who is interested in preserving traditional and historic things. **preserv'ative** adj serving to preserve. ◆ n a preserving agent, eg a chemical added to food; a safeguard; a prophylactic medicine, etc. **preserv'atory** adj and n. **preserv'er** n.
❑ **preservation order** n a legally binding directive ordering the preservation of a building deemed to be historically important. **preserv'ing-pan** n a large pan usu with a hooped handle and a lip, in which jams, etc are made.
■ **well-preserved** (inf; of a person) not showing the signs of ageing one would expect in a person of such an age.

preses or **praeses** /prē'siz/ (chiefly Scot) n (pl **prē'ses** or **prae'ses** /-sēz/) a president or chairman. [L praeses, -idis, from praesidēre ; see **preside**]

preset /prē-set'/ vt (**presett'ing; preset'**) to adjust (a piece of electronic equipment, etc) so that it will operate at the required time; to set initially or preliminarily. ◆ n /prē'/ a device or control that presets. [**pre-** (1)]

pre-shrink /prē-shringk'/ vt to shrink (cloth) before it is made up into garments, etc. [**pre-** (1)]
■ **pre-shrunk'** adj.

preside /pri-zīd'/ vi to act as chairman, be in the chair; to be at the head of the table (at a meal); to be in charge or in a position of superintendence (with over); to be the guardian or tutelary god of a place (with over); to dominate (a place, scene, etc) like a presence (with over); to be at the organ or piano, orig as a kind of conductor. ◆ vt (rare) to be at the head of, to control. [Fr présider, from L praesidēre, from prae above (others), and sedēre to sit]
❑ **presiding officer** n a person in charge of a polling place.

president[1] /prez'i-dənt/ n the elected head of a republic; the head of a board, council, or department of government; someone who is chosen to preside over the meetings of a society, conference, etc; in the European Union, a member state that assumes a role analogous to this for a six-month period; the title of the head of certain colleges, universities and other institutions; the chairman of a company, a bank governor, or head of an organization generally (esp US); the celebrant at Holy Communion; a colonial or state governor (hist). ◆ adj (Milton) presiding, superintending. [Fr président, from L praesidēns, -ēntis, prp of praesidēre; see **preside**]
■ **pres'idency** n the office of a president, or his or her rank, term of office, jurisdiction or official place of residence; (with cap) the office of president of the Council of Ministers of the European Union, which is held in rotation by each member state for six months at a time; each of three main divisions of India (hist); a Mormon governing council. **pres'identess** n (old) a female president or the wife of a president. **presidential** /-den'shl/ adj of a president or presidency; presiding, superintending. **pres'identship** n.
■ **Lord President** the presiding judge of the Court of Session. **Lord President of the Council** a member of the House of Lords who presides over the privy council.

president[2] (Spenser, Shakesp, Milton) for **precedent** (see under **precede**).

presidial /pri-sid'i-əl/ adj relating to a garrison, a presidio or a president; provincial (Fr hist). [Fr présidial, from LL praesidiālis, from praeses, -idis governor, and praesidium garrison]

presidiary /pri-sid'i-ə-ri/ adj garrisoning, serving as a garrison; of a garrison. [L praesidiārius, from praesidium garrison]

presidio /pri-sid'i-ō or pre-sē'dhyō/ n (pl presid'ios) (in areas of Spanish control or settlement) a military post; a penal settlement. [Sp, from L praesidium garrison]

presidium /pri-sid'i-əm/ n (pl presid'iums or presid'ia) a standing committee in the former Soviet system (also **praesid'ium**). [L praesidium a garrison, from praesidēre to preside]

presignify /prē-sig'ni-fī/ vt to intimate beforehand. [**pre-** (1)]
■ **presignifica'tion** n.

press[1] /pres/, also (all obs) **preace**, **prease** and **preasse** /prēs/ vt to exert a pushing force upon; to squeeze; to compress; to clasp; to thrust (something into or against something else); to squeeze out, express (eg juice from fruit); to iron (clothes); to produce (a gramophone record) from a mould by a compressing process; to raise to the shoulders and then raise above the head (weightlifting); to flatten and dry (flowers, set) or otherwise shape and condense by the application of weight or other squeezing force; to imprint, stamp, print (obs); to put to death by application of heavy weights (hist); (of troubles, etc) to bear heavily on, oppress; to harass; to beset; to urge strongly or insistently; to importune; to insist on; to invite with persistent warmth; to offer urgently or abundantly (with upon); to present (eg a point) with earnestness, to impress on one's hearers; to lay stress upon; to hurry on with great speed, to expedite; to bring (charges) officially against someone (law); to throng, crowd (archaic). ◆ vi to exert pressure or to push with force (with on, against, etc); to crowd; to thrust oneself forward with violence (archaic); to be urgent in application, entreaty, or effort (with for); to strive (obs); to strive or strain too hard, with a resulting loss of ease and effectiveness (sport). ◆ n an act of pressing; pressure; an apparatus or machine for flattening, compressing or otherwise forcing into shape, or for extracting juice, etc, or for punching solid articles from soft metal, clay, etc; a printing machine, a printing press; (the practice or process of) printing; a printing organization; often extended to a publishing house; printing activities; newspapers and periodicals collectively; the journalistic profession; (with cap) a common name for a newspaper; (favourable or unfavourable) reception by newspapers and periodicals generally; a crowd, throng; the action of crowding or thronging; the thick of a fight; stress (archaic); urgency, hurry (archaic); a lift to shoulder level, then above the head (weightlifting); a cupboard or shelved closet or recess; a bookcase. [Fr presser, from L pressāre, frequentative of premere, pressum to press]
■ **pressed** adj under pressure, in a hurry; (with for) short of (time or money; inf). **press'er** n. **press'ful** n. **press'ing** n an article or articles, esp gramophone records, made from the same mould or press. ◆ adj urgent; importunate; crowding. **press'ingly** adv. **pression** /presh'ən/ n (rare) pressure; impress.
❑ **press agent** n an agent who arranges for newspaper advertising and publicity, esp for an actor or theatre. **press association** n an association of newspapers formed to act as a news agency for the members of the association, each supplying local news, etc to the association; (with caps) a British news agency formed as a press association in 1868. **press bed** n a bed enclosed in a cupboard, or folding up into it. **press book** n a book printed at a private press. **press box** n a structure or area set aside for the use of reporters at sports, shows, etc. **press button** n a push-button. **press'-button** adj.

press conference n a meeting of a public personage with the press for making an announcement or to answer questions. **press council** n a body set up to monitor and uphold standards in journalism. **press cutting** n a paragraph or article cut out of a newspaper or magazine. **pressed day** n the third day of a three days' visit. **pressed glass** n glass given shape and pattern by pressure in a mould. **press fastener** n a press stud. **press'fat** n (Bible) the vat for collecting the liquor from an olive press or winepress. **press gallery** n a reporters' gallery at a sports stadium, theatre, etc. **press'man** n an operator of a printing press; (and **press'woman**) a journalist or reporter. **press'mark** n a mark on a book to show its location in a library. **press office** n the department of an organization, government ministry, etc, responsible for releasing information concerning its activities to the press. **press officer** n. **press proof** n the last proof before printing. **press release** n an official statement or report supplied to the press. **press'room** n the room in which printing presses are housed and operated; a room for the use of journalists. **press stud** n a clothes-fastener consisting of complementary halves that interlock when pressed together. **press'-up** n a gymnastic exercise performed face down, raising and lowering the body on the arms while keeping the trunk and legs rigid. **press'work** n the operation of a printing press; printed matter; journalistic work.
■ **at press** or **in the press** in course of printing; about to be published. **be hard pressed** to be at a loss (to manage something), be in a jam. **go to press** to begin to print or to be printed. **liberty** or **freedom of the press** the right of publishing material without submitting it to a government authority for permission. **press ahead**, **forward** or **on** to continue, esp energetically, often in spite of difficulties or opposition. **press flesh** (or **the flesh**) (orig US; of politicians, etc) to go about shaking hands with people, esp potential supporters (**flesh'-pressing** n). **press of canvas** or **sail** as much sail as can be carried. **press the button** to put machinery into operation; to start things moving, esp in a momentous or irreversible way. **the press** printed matter generally, esp newspapers; journalists as a class.

press[2] /pres/ vt to carry off and force into service, esp in the navy (hist); to requisition, commandeer; to turn to use in an unsuitable or provisional way. ◆ n recruitment by force into service, impressment; authority for impressing. [**prest**[2]]
❑ **press gang** n a gang or body of sailors under an officer, empowered to impress men into the navy. **press'-gang** vt to force into service in the army or navy; to dragoon into participation in any enterprise (inf). **press money** n earnest-money (see **earnest**[2]).

pressie see **prezzie**.

pression see under **press**[1].

pressor /pres'ər/ (physiol) adj causing an increase in blood pressure. [LL, something or someone that presses, from premere, pressum to press]

pressure /presh'ər/ n the action of pressing or squeezing; the state of being pressed; impression, stamp (Shakesp); constraining force or influence; coercion, forceful persuasion; the need to perform a great deal at speed; tension, strain or stress; (usu in pl) a cause of anxiety; urgency; a strong demand; the force produced by pressing; a force exerted on a surface specif by a gas or liquid, measured as so much weight upon a unit of area; difference of electrical potential. ◆ vt to apply pressure to; to subject to pressure; to force by pressure, to pressurize, coerce (with into). [L pressura, from premere to press]
■ **pressuriza'tion** or **-s-** n. **press'urize** or **-ise** vt to adjust the pressure within (an enclosed compartment such as an aircraft cabin) so that nearly normal atmospheric pressure is constantly maintained; to subject to pressure; to force by pressure (into doing something), to coerce.
❑ **pressure altitude** n (aeronautics) the apparent altitude of the local ambient pressure related to the international standard atmosphere. **pressure cabin** n a pressurized cabin in an aircraft. **press'ure-cook** vt to cook in a pressure cooker. **pressure cooker** n a thick-walled pan with an airtight lid, in which food is cooked at speed by steam under high pressure. **pressure gradient** n (meteorol) the rate of change of the atmospheric pressure horizontally in a certain direction on the earth's surface as shown by isobars on a weather chart. **pressure group** n a number of people who join together to influence public opinion and government policy on some issue. **pressure helmet** n an airman's helmet for use with a pressure suit. **pressure point** n any of various points on the body on which pressure may be exerted to relieve pain, control bleeding, etc. **pressure ridge** n a ridge formed by lateral pressure in floating ice in polar waters. **pressure sore** n a bedsore. **pressure suit** n an automatically inflating suit worn by aircraft crew against pressure-cabin failure at very high altitudes. **pressure therapy** n the therapeutic use of pressure points. **pressure-tube reactor** n a nuclear reactor in which the fuel elements are contained in many separate tubes rather than in a single pressure vessel. **pressure vessel** n a nuclear containment vessel, usu of thick steel or prestressed concrete, capable of withstanding high pressure; a

vessel constructed to contain pressurized material. **pressure waistcoat** *n* a waistcoat worn by aircraft crew through which oxygen passes under pressure to the lungs to aid breathing at high altitudes. **pressurized water reactor** *n* a nuclear reactor using water-cooling at a pressure such that the boiling point of the water is above the highest temperature reached (see also **boiling-water reactor** under **boil**¹, **light-water reactor** under **light**²).

prest¹ /prest/ (*Spenser, Shakesp*) *adj* ready. [OFr *prest*, from L *praestō* at hand]

prest² /prest/ (*obs*) *vt* to lend; to pay in advance; to engage by paying earnest-money; to enlist; to impress for service. ◆ *n* a loan; payment in advance; enlistment money. [OFr *prester*, from L *praestāre* to offer, discharge]
■ **presta′tion** *n* payment or service required by custom or promise.

Prestel® /pres′tel/ *n* the viewdata (qv) system of British Telecom.

Prester John /pres′tər jon/ *n* the mythical medieval Christian priest-king of a vast empire conceived, during the crusades, to be in Central Asia, but according to a later tradition in Ethiopia. [OFr *prestre* (Fr *prêtre*) priest]

presternum /prē-stûr′nəm/ (*anat*) *n* the anterior part of the sternum. [**pre-** (2)]

prestidigitation /pres-ti-dij-i-tā′shən/ *n* sleight of hand. [Fr *prestidigitateur*, from *preste* nimble, and L *digitus* finger]
■ **prestidig′itātor** *n* a conjurer.

prestige /pre-stēzh′ or -stēj′/ *n* standing or ascendancy in people's minds owing to associations, station, success, etc; charm, magic, glamour (qv); a name or reputation to 'conjure' with (see next sense); *orig* a conjuring trick or illusion (*obs*). ◆ *adj* consisting in, or for the sake of, prestige; considered to have or give prestige; superior in quality, style, etc. [Fr, from L *praestigium* delusion, from *praestringere* to dazzle, blind; see also **prestriction**]
■ **prestigious** /-tij′əs/ *adj* having prestige, esteemed; lending or conferring prestige; deceitful, juggling, using legerdemain (*obs*).

prestigiator /pre-stij′i-ā-tər/ *n* a conjurer. [L *praestigium* delusion; see **prestige**]

presto /pres′tō/ (*music*) *adj* very quick. ◆ *n* (*pl* **pres′tos**) a presto movement or passage. ◆ *adv* quickly, quicker than *allegro*. ◆ *adv* or *interj* (also more *usu* **hey presto** as in conjuring tricks) at once. [Ital, from L *praestō* at hand]
■ **prestis′simo** *adv, n* (*pl* **prestis′simos**) and *adj* (*superl*).

pre-stressed /prē-strest′/ *adj* (of concrete) strengthened with stretched wires or rods rather than large steel bars as in reinforced concrete. [**pre-** (1)]

prestriction /pri-strik′shən/ (*obs, rare*) *n* blindness; blindfolding. [L *praestrictiō, -ōnis*, from *praestringere* to draw tight, bind, restrain, blind]

pre-stun /prē-stun′/ *vt* to stun (cattle) before slaughter, to lessen suffering. [**pre-** (1)]

presume /pri-zūm′ or -zoom′/ *vt* to suppose (something to be the case) though one has no proof; to take for granted; to assume provisionally; to be so bold as (to do something) *esp* without the proper right or knowledge, to make bold, dare or venture. ◆ *vi* to venture beyond what one has ground for; to act forwardly or without proper right, to take liberties; (with *on, upon*) to rely or count on, *esp* without justification, or to take unfair advantage of (eg someone's good nature). [L *praesūmere, -sūmptum*, from *prae* before, and *sūmere* to take, from *sub* under, and *emere* to buy]
■ **presūm′able** *adj* that may be presumed or supposed to be true. **presūm′ably** *adv* as one may reasonably suppose or expect, doubtless. **presūm′er** *n*. **presūm′ing** *adj* venturing without permission; unreasonably or impertinently bold. ◆ *conj* (often with *that*) making the presumption that. **presūm′ingly** *adv*. **presumption** /-zum′shən or -zump′shən/ *n* the act of presuming; supposition; strong probability; that which is taken for granted; an assumption or belief based on facts or probable evidence; confidence grounded on something not proved; a ground or reason for presuming; conduct going beyond proper limits, impertinent over-boldness; a presumption of fact or presumption of law (*law*). **presumptive** /-zump′tiv or -zum′tiv/ *adj* grounded on probable evidence; giving grounds for presuming (see also **heir presumptive** under **heir**); presuming (*obs*); used of embryonic tissue which will normally be differentiated into a particular organ or tissue (*biol*). **presump′tively** *adv*. **presumptuous** /-zump′tū-əs or -zum′-/ *adj* tending to presume, impertinently bold. **presump′tuously** *adv*. **presump′tuousness** *n*.
❑ **presumption of fact** *n* (*law*) an assumption of a fact from known facts. **presumption of law** *n* (*law*) a conclusion drawn by a court of law from evidence, either one that must be drawn failing proof to the contrary (**rebuttable presumption**) or one that cannot by rebutted by contrary evidence (**conclusive** or **irrebuttable presumption**).

presuppose /prē-sə-pōz′/ *vt* to assume or take for granted; to involve as a necessary antecedent, imply. [**pre-** (1)]
■ **presupposition** /prē-sup-ə-zish′ən/ *n* the act of assuming or presupposing; something taken for granted beforehand, an assumption.

presurmise /prē-sər-mīz′/ (*Shakesp*) *n* a surmise previously formed. [**pre-** (1)]

pret. *abbrev* : preterite.

prêt-à-porter /pre-ta-por-tā′ or -pör-/ (*Fr*) *n* and *adj* ready-to-wear (garments).

pre-tax /prē′taks/ *adj* before the deduction of tax. [**pre-** (1)]

pre-teen /prē-tēn′/ *n* (*usu* in *pl*) a child who is not yet, *esp* not quite yet, a teenager (also *adj*). [**pre-** (1)]

pretence or (*N Am*) **pretense** /pri-tens′/ *n* an act of pretending; make-believe; an act put on deliberately to mislead, a sham, a false show; a claim, *esp* an unjustified one (eg to expertise in something); an assertion, by implication false; a misleading declaration of intention (as in *under false pretences*); show or semblance; a trivial pretext; pretentiousness, show, affectation or ostentation; an aim, purpose or thing aimed at (*obs*). [Anglo-Fr *pretense*, from Med L *praetēnsus* for L *praetentus*, pap of *praetendere* to pretend]
■ **pretence′less** *adj* without a pretext.

pretend /pri-tend′/ *vt* to make believe; to feign or affect (to be or do something); to imply, assert or claim falsely; to claim to feel, profess falsely (eg friendship); to venture, attempt, undertake or be so bold as (to do something); to stretch forth, or in front (*Spenser*); to offer (*obs*); to purpose (*obs*); to indicate (*obs*). ◆ *vi* to feign; to make believe; to make claim (to eg expertise in something); to aspire (with *to*; *archaic*); to be a suitor (with *to*; *archaic*); to reach or go forward (*obs*). ◆ *adj* (*inf* or *childish*) imaginary, make-believe. [L *praetendere* to stretch forward, hold in front, allege, from *prae* before, and *tendere, tentum, tēnsum* to stretch]
■ **preten′dant** (or **-ent**) *n* a claimant; a suitor; a pretender. **preten′ded** *adj*. **preten′dedly** *adv*. **preten′der** *n* a claimant, *esp* to a throne; a candidate; a suitor (*obs*); someone who pretends. **preten′dership** *n*. **preten′dingly** *adv*.
■ **Old Pretender** and **Young Pretender** respectively the son and grandson of James II as claimants to the British throne.

pretension /pri-ten′shən/ *n* foolish vanity or pretence, self-importance or affectation, pretentiousness; a claim, by implication an unjustified one; an aspiration, eg to marriage; a pretext. [Med L *praetensio, -onis*, from L *praetendere*; see **pretend**]

pre-tension /prē-ten′shən/ *vt* to stretch (the reinforcing wires or rods in pre-stressed concrete) before the concrete is cast. [**pre-** (1)]
■ **pre-ten′sioned** *adj*. **pre-ten′sioner** *n* (also without *hyphen*) a device (*usu* used in conjunction with the traditional locking system) that causes a seat belt to tighten in the event of a sudden forward movement by the wearer.

pretentious /pri-ten′shəs/ *adj* pompous, self-important or foolishly grandiose; phoney or affected; showy, ostentatious; (of a claim) false (*rare*). [Formerly *pretensious*, from L *pretensio*; see **pretension**]
■ **preten′tiously** *adv*. **preten′tiousness** *n*.

preter- or (*esp* in obsolete words) **praeter-** /prē-tər-/ *pfx* signifying beyond, as in **preterhu′man** more than human. [L *praeter*]

preterite or **preterit** /pret′ə-rit/ *adj* denoting a verb tense used to express past action (*grammar*); past, belonging to the past. ◆ *n* (*grammar*) this tense of verbs, the past tense (also **preterite tense**); a word in this tense; a form of this tense. [L *praeteritus*, pap of *praeterīre* to go past, from *praeter* beyond, and *īre, itum* to go]
■ **pret′erist** *n* (*theol*) someone who holds the prophecies of the Apocalypse already fulfilled. **pret′eriteness** *n*. **preterition** /prē-tə-rish′ən/ *n* the act of passing over; omission of mention in a will; paraleipsis (*rhetoric*); the doctrine that God passes over the non-elect in electing to eternal life. **preteritive** /pri-ter′i-tiv/ *adj* (*grammar*) used only in the preterite.
❑ **preter′ito-pres′ent**, **-presen′tial** or **pret′erite-pres′ent** *adj* (*grammar*) used of verbs that have an original preterite still preterite in form but present in meaning such as the modal or modal auxiliary verbs. ◆ *n* a verb of this type.

preterm /prē-tûrm′/ *adj* and *adv* born prematurely. [**pre-** (1)]

pretermit /prē-tər-mit′/ (*rare*) *vt* (**prētermitt′ing**; **prētermitt′ed**) to pass by; to omit; to leave undone; to desist from for a time. [L *praetermittere, -missum*, from *mittere* to send]
■ **pretermission** /-mish′ən/ *n*.

preternatural /prē-tər-nach′ə-rəl/ *adj* out of the ordinary course of nature; abnormal; supernatural. [**preter-**]
■ **preternat′uralism** *n* preternatural character or event; belief in the preternatural. **preternat′urally** *adv*. **preternat′uralness** *n*.

preterperfect /prē-tər-pûr′fikt/ (*old grammar*) *n* perfect. [**preter-**]

■ **preterpluper'fect** *adj* pluperfect (*grammar*); beyond the more than perfect (*facetious*).

pretext /prē'tekst/ *n* an ostensible motive or reason, put forward as an excuse or to conceal the true one. [L *praetextus*, *-ūs* pretext, outward show, and *praetextum* pretext, from *prae* in front, and *texere* to weave]
■ **pre'texting** *n* assuming a false identity in order to obtain information.

pretor see **praetor**.

pretty /prit'i/ *adj* (*usu* of women and girls) facially attractive, *esp* in a feminine way; attractively small, neat, dainty or graceful; charming to look at, decorative; (of music, sound, etc) delicately melodious; superficially attractive or insipidly charming only, lacking striking beauty or distinction; tricky, clever; ingenious; grand, fine (*esp ironic*); commendable; neat; stalwart (*archaic* or *Scot*); considerable, substantial. ◆ *n* (*pl* **prett'ies**) a pretty thing or person; a knick-knack; the fairway of a golf course (*old*); the fluted part of a glass. ◆ *adv* fairly; rather; very, extremely; prettily (*inf* or *dialect*). ◆ *vt* (with *up*) to prettify. [OE *prættig* tricky, from *prætt* trickery; the origin of the word is uncertain]
■ **prettifica'tion** *n*. **prett'ify** *vt* to make pretty in an excessively ornamental or over-dainty way. **prett'ily** *adv* in a pretty manner; pleasingly; elegantly; neatly. **prett'iness** *n* the quality of being pretty; an instance of the quality; a prettyism. **prett'yish** *adj* somewhat pretty. **prett'yism** *n* trivial daintiness of style or an instance of it.
□ **pretty-prett'iness** *n*. **pretty-prett'y** *n* (*pl* **pretty-prett'ies**) (*inf*) a knick-knack. ◆ *adj* insipidly pretty, over-pretty or over-dainty. **prett'y-spoken** *adj* speaking or spoken prettily.
■ **a pretty penny** a large sum of money. **only pretty Fanny's way** only what must be expected and accepted of the person (coined by Irish poet Thomas Parnell). **pretty much** more or less. **pretty nearly** almost. **pretty well** almost, more or less. **sitting pretty** enjoying one's advantageous position; happily unaffected by problems besetting others.

pretzel /pret'səl/ *n* a glazed salted biscuit made in rope shape and twisted into a kind of loose knot. [Ger *Brezel*]

preux chevalier /prø shə-va-lyā'/ (*Fr*) *n* a valiant knight.

prevail /pri-vāl'/ *vi* to be victorious (with *over*, *against*); to win through; to have the upper hand, have the edge; to urge successfully, to persuade (with *on*, *upon*); to be usual or most usual; to predominate; to hold good, be in use, be customary; to gain strength (*obs*). ◆ *vt* (*obs*) to avail; to persuade. [L *praevalēre* to be superior or stronger, from *prae* above, beyond, and *valēre* to be strong]
■ **prevail'ing** *adj* very general or common; most common or frequent; predominant; currently popular; powerful, effective; controlling. **prevail'ingly** *adv*. **prevail'ment** *n* (*Shakesp*) the power of overcoming.
□ **prevailing wind** *n* the wind that blows most frequently in any particular region.

prevalent /prev'ə-lənt/ *adj* prevailing; widespread; common, frequent; widely practised or accepted; powerful; victorious (*obs*). [L *praevalēns*, *-ēntis*, prp of *praevalēre*; see **prevail**]
■ **prev'alence** or **prev'alency** *n*. **prev'alently** *adv*.

prevaricate /pri-var'i-kāt/ *vi* to avoid stating the truth or coming directly to the point; to quibble; to deviate (*obs*); to shift about from side to side (*obs*); to undertake an enterprise with the object of wrecking it (*obs*); to betray a client by collusion with his or her opponent (*law*). ◆ *vt* (*obs*) to pervert, transgress. [L *praevāricārī*, *-ātus* to walk straddlingly or crookedly, to act collusively, from *prae* above, beyond, and *vāricus* straddling, from *vārus* bent]
■ **prevarica'tion** *n*. **prevar'icātor** *n* someone who prevaricates; formerly in Cambridge University, a satirical orator at the ceremony of Commencement.

preve see **prove**.

prevene /pri-vēn'/ *vt* to precede (*rare*); to anticipate (*obs*). [L *praevenīre* to precede; see **prevent**]
■ **prevenancy** /prev'ən-ən-si/ *n* (*rare*) courteous anticipation of others' wishes. **prevē'nience** *n*. **prevē'nient** *adj* antecedent, preceding, anticipatory; predisposing; preventive (*obs*).

prevent /pri-vent'/ *vt* to stop (someone from doing something, or something from happening), to hinder; to stop the occurrence of, to make impossible, to avert; to thwart; to anticipate, forestall (*obs*); to balk (someone of his or her purpose), to debar or preclude (*obs*); to precede (*obs*); to be, go, or act earlier than (*obs*); to go faster than (*obs*); to satisfy in advance (*obs*); to meet or provide for in advance (*obs*). [L *praevenīre*, *-ventum* to come before, to anticipate, from *prae* before, and *venīre* to come]
■ **preventabil'ity** *n*. **preven'table** or **preven'tible** *adj*. **preven'ter** *n* someone or something that prevents or hinders; a supplementary rope or part (*naut*). **preven'tion** *n* the action of preventing; avoidance or preclusion of something by care and forethought; an anticipation

or premonition (*obs*); an obstruction (*obs*). **preven'tive** or (by irregular formation) **preven'tative** *adj* tending to prevent or hinder; prophylactic; concerned with the prevention of smuggling (*hist*). ◆ *n* that which prevents; a prophylactic. **preven'tively** *adv*. **preven'tiveness** *n*.
□ **preventive detention** *n* prolonged imprisonment, with corrective training, for persistent or dangerous offenders of 30 or over for periods of from 5 to 14 years.

preverb /prē'vûrb/ (*linguistics*) *n* a particle or prefix which precedes a verb or verb-root. [**pre-** (1)]
■ **prever'bal** *adj* occurring or standing before a verb; relating to the period of babyhood before the development of speech.

pre-vernal /prē-vûr'nl/ (*bot*) *adj* flowering before spring; coming early into flower or leaf. [**pre-** (1)]

preview or (*US*) **prevue** /prē'vū/ *n* a showing or viewing of a film, exhibition, etc, before it is open to the public; a public performance of a play before it officially opens; an advance showing to the public of excerpts from a film, a trailer (*N Am*); a hint or foretaste. ◆ *vt* /prē'vū/ to give or attend a preview of (an exhibition, play, etc); /prē-vū'/ to look at beforehand (*rare*); to foresee. ◆ *vi* (of an exhibition, play, etc) to be previewed. [**pre-** (1)]

previous /prē'vi-əs/ *adj* occurring before, earlier; already arranged, prior; former; premature, over-hasty (*facetious*). ◆ *n* (*police inf*) previous convictions. ◆ *adv* (with *to*) prior to, before. [L *praevius* leading the way, from *prae* before, and *via* a way]
■ **prē'viously** *adv*. **prē'viousness** *n*.
□ **previous examination** *n* the little go (qv) at Cambridge University. **previous question** *n* (in the House of Commons) a motion to end the present debate before a vote is taken; (in the House of Lords and US assemblies) a motion to vote without delay on the matter being debated; (in public meetings) a motion to pass on to the next business.

previse /pri- or prē-vīz'/ *vt* (*rare*, *literary*) to foresee; to forewarn. [L *praevidēre*, *-vīsum*, from *prae* before, and *vidēre* to see]
■ **prevision** /-vizh'ən/ *n* foresight; foreknowledge. ◆ *vt* to endow with prevision. **previsional** /-vizh'ə-nəl/ *adj*.

prevocalic /prē-vō-kal'ik/ *adj* occurring or standing before a vowel. [**pre-** (1)]

pre-wash /prē'wosh/ *n* a preliminary wash before the main wash, *esp* in a washing machine; a setting for this on an automatic washing machine. ◆ *vt* to give a preliminary wash to (a garment). [**pre-** (1)]

prewyn a Shakespearean form of **prune³**.

prex /preks/ (*US university sl*) *n* the president of a college (also **prex'y**).

prey /prā/ *n* the creature or creatures that a predatory beast hunts and kills as food; a victim or victims; a sufferer from (depression, fears, etc) (with *to*); booty, plunder (*archaic*, *rare*); that which is preserved from loss in battle, eg one's own life (*Bible*); depredation (*rare*); the act of seizing (*Spenser*, *Shakesp*). ◆ *vi* (with *on* or *upon*) to hunt and kill (another creature) as food, to attack as prey; to bully, exploit or terrorize as victims; to distress or afflict; to make depredations on; to take plunder from. ◆ *vt* (*Spenser*) to plunder. [OFr *preie* (Fr *proie*), from L *praeda* booty]
■ **prey'ful** *adj* (*Shakesp*) bent upon prey.
■ **beast of prey** and **bird of prey** see under **beast** and **bird** respectively.

prez /prez/ *n* an informal shortening of **president**.

prezzie or **pressie** /prez'i/ (*inf*) *n* a present or gift.

prial /prī'əl/ *n* same as **pair-royal** (see under **pair¹**).

Priapus /prī-ā'pəs/ *n* an ancient deity personifying male generative power, guardian of gardens, later regarded as the chief god of lasciviousness and sensuality. [Latinized from Gr *Priăpos*]
■ **Priapean** /prī-ə-pē'ən/ *adj*. **Priapic** /-ap'ik/ *adj* of or relating to Priapus; (without *cap*) of, relating to, exhibiting, etc a phallus; (without *cap*) excessively concerned or preoccupied with virility and male sexuality. **prī'apism** *n* persistent erection of the penis (*pathol*); licentiousness, lewdness.

pribble /prib'l/ *n* a modification of **prabble**, *usu* found with it in *pribble and prabble* (also **pribb'le-prabb'le**).

price /prīs/ (also *Spenser* **prise** /prīs or prīz/) *n* the amount, *usu* in money, for which a thing is sold or offered; that which one forgoes or suffers for the sake of or in gaining something; money offered for the capture or killing of anybody; (the size of) the sum, etc, by which one can be bribed; betting odds; preciousness, worth, value (*archaic*); (also **prize**) valuation (*Spenser*, *Shakesp*). ◆ *vt* to fix, state, or mark the price of; to ascertain the price of (*inf*); to pay the price of (*Spenser*); to prize, value (*Shakesp*). [OFr *pris* (Fr *prix*), from L *pretium* price; cf **praise**, **prize¹**]
■ **priced** *adj* having a price assigned; valued at such-and-such a price. **price'less** *adj* beyond price; invaluable; supremely and delectably absurd. **price'lessly** *adv*. **price'lessness** *n*. **pri'cer** *n*. **pri'cey** or **pri'cy** *adj* (**pri'cier**; **pri'ciest**) (*inf*) expensive. **pri'ciness** *n*.

❑ **Price Code** *n* a set of regulations used by the British government between 1973 and 1979 to control prices, as a measure against inflation. **Price Commission** *n* a body set up by the British government in 1973 (abolished in 1979) to control prices, as a measure against inflation. **price control** *n* the fixing by a government of maximum, or sometimes minimum, prices chargeable for goods or services. **price current** *n* (often in *pl*, **prices current**) a list of prevailing prices at any time; a list of prices paid for any class of goods, etc. **price'-cutting** *n* lowering of prices to secure custom. **price discrimination** *n* the practice of selling the same product at different prices in different markets. **price-earnings ratio** *n* the ratio of the market price of a common stock share to its earnings. **price'-fixing** *n* the establishing of the price of a commodity, etc by agreement between suppliers or by government price control, rather than by the operation of a free market. **price index** *n* an index number which relates current prices to those of a base period or base date, the latter *usu* being assigned the value of 100. **price leadership** *n* the establishment of the price of a commodity by the market leader. **price level** *n* the average of many prices of commodities. **price list** *n* a list of prices of goods offered for sale. **price ring** *n* a group of manufacturers who co-operate for the purpose of raising or maintaining the price of a commodity above the level that would be established by a free market, a cartel. **price support** *n* the maintenance by a government of price levels through subsidy, etc. **price tag** *n* a tag or label showing price; the cost of something, typically a project or undertaking. **price war** *n* a form of commercial competition in which firms competing in the same market successively lower their prices in order to secure a larger share of that market.

■ **above** or **beyond price** so valuable that no price can or would be enough. **at any price** no matter what the cost may be. **at a price** at a somewhat high price. **in great price** (*archaic*) in high estimation. **of price** (*archaic*) of great value. **price of money** the rate of discount in lending or borrowing capital. **price oneself out of the market** to charge more than customers or clients are willing to pay. **price on someone's head** a reward for someone's capture or slaughter. **what price...?** what about (this or that) now?, what are the chances of (this or that) happening now?, so much for (this or that); what do you think of? **without price** beyond price, priceless; without anything to pay.

prick /prik/ *vt* to pierce slightly with a fine point; to cause slight pain by doing this; (of eg the conscience) to cause pangs to; to pierce (a hole); to urge with, or as if with, a spur or goad; to incite; (*usu* with *up*; of an animal) to erect, cock, stick up (its ears); to insert (eg seedlings) in small holes (*usu* with *in*, *out*, etc); to indicate with a prick or dot, to tick off, hence to select; to trace (eg a pattern) with pricks; to write out in musical notation (*obs*); to pin (*obs*); to deck out (*obs*); to pick, poke or pluck out with a point (*obs*); to stick all over or stud (with something; *obs*); to pierce the skin of (a suspected witch) to find insensitive spots (*hist*). ✦ *vi* to pierce, make punctures; to have a sensation of pricking, to smart; (of the conscience) to cause one pangs; (of wine) to begin to turn sour; (of an animal's ears; with *up*) to stand erect; to ride with spurs, or quickly (*archaic*); to detect witches by the pricking method (*hist*). ✦ *n* the act, feeling, or stimulus of piercing or puncturing; a puncture; a mark or wound made by puncturing; the penis (*vulgar sl*); a term of abuse for a person one dislikes or thinks a fool (*vulgar sl*); a hare's footprint; anything sharp and piercing, such as a thorn, spine, goad (*obs* or *archaic*); a note in written music (*obs*); a graduation on a dial (*Shakesp*); a dot (*obs*); a point of space or time (*obs*); an hour-point on a clock (*Shakesp*); a point, peak, acme (*Spenser*); the centre of an archery target (*obs*); a mark or target (*obs*). [OE *prica* point; cf Du *prik*]

■ **prick'er** *n* a piercing instrument; a witch-finder; a light horseman; a priming wire. **prick'ing** *n* and *adj*.

❑ **prick'-eared** *adj* having erect or noticeable ears. **prick'-louse** or **prick'-me-dain'ty** *n* (*Scot*) an affected person. ✦ *adj* over-precise. **prick'-song** *n* (*Shakesp*) written music; descant. **prick spur** *n* a spur with one point. **prick'-teaser** same as **cockteaser** (see under **cock**[1]). **prick-the-gar'ter** *n* fast-and-loose. **prick'wood** *n* the spindle-tree; the dogwood.

■ **kick against the pricks** to react futilely against discipline or authority, to the extent of injuring oneself (*Bible*, Acts 9.5). **prick up one's ears** to begin to listen intently.

pricket /prik'it/ *n* a fallow deer buck in his second year, with straight unbranched antlers; a spike serving as a candlestick; a candlestick with such a spike. [**prick**]

prickle /prik'l/ *n* a sharp point growing from the epidermis of a plant or from the skin of an animal; a prickling sensation; a little prick. ✦ *vt* and *vi* to prick slightly. ✦ *vi* to have a prickly feeling. [OE *pricel*]

■ **prick'liness** *n*. **prick'ling** *n* and *adj*. **prick'ly** *adj* full of or covered with prickles; tingling as if prickled; easily annoyed, irritable, thin-skinned; potentially controversial.

❑ **prick'leback** *n* the stickleback. **prickly ash** *n* the toothache tree (genus *Xanthoxylum*). **prickly heat** *n* a skin disease, inflammation of the sweat glands with intense irritation. **prickly pear** *n* a cactaceous genus (*Opuntia*) with clusters of prickles; its pear-shaped fruit. **prickly**

poppy *n* a flowering plant of the poppy family with prickly leaves (genus *Argemone*).

pride /prīd/ *n* the state or feeling of being proud; excessive self-esteem; haughtiness; a proper sense of what is becoming to oneself and scorn of what is unworthy; self-respect, personal dignity; a feeling of pleasure or satisfaction on account of something worthily done by oneself or someone connected with one, one's family, possessions, etc; something of which one is proud; splendour; magnificence; beauty displayed; ostentation; exuberance; prime, flower; high spirit, mettle; a peacock's attitude of display; sexual excitement in a female animal (*Shakesp*); a company of lions; used in plant names, eg *pride of India*, *London pride*. ✦ *vt* to congratulate or pique (oneself) (with *on*); to make proud (*obs*). [OE *prȳde*, *prȳte*, from *prūd*, *prūt* proud]

■ **pride'ful** *adj*. **pride'fully** *adv*. **pride'fulness** *n*. **pride'less** *adj*.

■ **pride of place** the distinction of a position of special prominence or chief importance; the culmination of an eagle's or hawk's flight (see **place**). **take** (**a**) **pride in** to be proud of; to be conscientious about maintaining high standards in (one's work, etc).

pridian /prid'i-ən/ *adj* of or relating to yesterday. [L *prīdiānus*, from *prīdiē* the previous day, from *prius* before, and *diēs* day]

pried see **pry**[1].

prie-dieu /prē-dyø'/ *n* a praying-desk or chair for praying on. [Fr, pray-God]

prief or **priefe** /prēf/ (*Spenser* or *Scot*) *n* proof. [See ety of **proof**, **prove**]

■ **prieve** *vt* to prove; to test.

prier see under **pry**[1].

priest /prēst/ *n* (in the Roman Catholic and Orthodox churches) an ordained minister; (in the Anglican Church) a minister ranking between a deacon and a bishop; an official conductor of religious rites; a mediator between a god and worshippers; a club or mallet for killing fish. ✦ *vt* to ordain as priest. ✦ *vi* to act as priest. [OE *prēost*, from L *presbyter*, from Gr *presbyteros* an elder]

■ **priest'craft** *n* priestly policy directed to worldly ends. **pries'tess** *n* a female priest in non-Christian religions. **priest'hood** *n* the office or character of a priest; the priestly order. **priest'-like** *adj*. **priest'liness** *n*. **priest'ling** *n* a contemptible priest. **priest'ly** *adj* belonging to, characteristic of or befitting a priest or priests. **priest'ship** *n*.

❑ **priest'-king** *n* a king with priestly functions. **priest'-rid** or **-ridden** *adj* dominated by priests. **priest's** or **priest hole** *n* (*hist*) a secret room providing a hiding-place for a Roman Catholic priest in time of persecution or repression.

prieve see under **prief**.

prig[1] /prig/ *n* a precisian, a puritan; a person of precise morals without a sense of proportion; a sanctimonious person, certain of his or her blamelessness and critical of others' failings; a coxcomb (*obs*). [Origin uncertain]

■ **prigg'ery** *n*. **prigg'ish** *adj*. **prigg'ishly** *adv*. **prigg'ishness** *n*. **prigg'ism** *n*.

prig[2] /prig/ (*Scot*) *vi* (**prigg'ing**; **prigged**) to entreat; to importune; to haggle. [Origin uncertain]

■ **prig down** to seek to beat down (a price or the seller).

prig[3] /prig/ *n* a tinker (*obs sl*); a thief (*sl*; *Shakesp*). ✦ *vt* (**prigg'ing**; **prigged**) to filch. [Origin uncertain]

■ **prigg'er** *n* a thief. **prigg'ing** *n*. **prigg'ism** *n*.

prill /pril/ *vt* to turn into pellet form, eg by melting and letting the drops solidify in falling. ✦ *n* a pellet, or pelleted material, formed by prilling. [Cornish mining term, of uncertain origin]

prim[1] /prim/ *adj* (**primm'er**; **primm'est**) rigidly punctilious and precise; stiffly formal; over-demure; prudishly disapproving. ✦ *vt* (**primm'ing**; **primmed**) to deck or dress with great nicety; to set (the face) or purse (the lips, mouth) in a prim expression; to neaten. ✦ *vi* to look prim; to prim the mouth. [Late 17c cant]

■ **prim'ly** *adv*. **prim'ness** *n*.

prim[2] /prim/ *n* (*med inf*) a primigravida, as in **elderly prim** one of 25 and over.

prima /prē'mə/ or *-ma*/ (*Ital*) *adj* first. [Ital, feminine of *primo* first, from L *prīmus*]

❑ **prima ballerina** /bal-ə-rēn'ə/ or *ba-le-rē'na*/ or **prima ballerina assoluta** /as-so-loo'ta/ or *-ta*/ *n* (*pl* **prima ballerinas** or **prime** /-mā/ **ballerine** /-nā/ **assolute** /-tā/) the leading ballerina (Ital *assoluta* without rival). **prima donna** or **prima donna assoluta** /don'ə or don'na/ *n* (*pl* **prima donnas** or **prime donne** /-nā/ **assolute**) the leading female singer in an opera company (without rival); (**prima donna**) a person, *esp* a woman, who is temperamental, over-sensitive and hard to please.

primacy /prī'mə-si/ *n* the (condition of being in) the position or place that is first in rank or importance; the office or rank of a primate.

primaeval see **primeval**.

prima facie /prī'mə fā'shē, -shi-ē, prē'mä fak'i-ā/ (L) on the first view; at first sight; (of evidence) sufficient to support the bringing of a charge (*law*); (of a case) supported by prima facie evidence (*law*).

primage /prīm'ij/ n a payment, in addition to freight, made by shippers for loading, *orig* a gratuity to captain and crew, afterwards made to owners. [Anglo-L *primāgium*]

primal /prī'məl/ adj first; primitive; original; chief, fundamental. [Med L *prīmālis*, from L *prīmus* first]
■ **primal'ity** n. **pri'mally** adv.
❑ **primal therapy** or **primal scream therapy** n therapy in which patients are encouraged to scream as they re-experience the agonies of birth, the frustrations of infancy and the traumas of childhood (see also **rebirthing** under **rebirth**).

primaquine /prī'mə-kwēn/ n an antimalarial drug derived from quinoline.

primary /prī'mə-ri/ adj first; original; of the first order (eg in a system of successive branchings); first-formed; primitive; chief; elementary; fundamental; first-hand, direct; belonging to the first stages of education, elementary; (of an industry) involving extraction of raw materials; (of a feather) growing on the manus (*ornithol*); relating to primaries (*US*); (with *cap*) Palaeozoic (but *orig* applied to rocks supposed to be older than any fossiliferous strata; *geol*). ◆ n that which is highest in rank or importance, a planet in relation to its satellites; a primary coil; a primary feather; a primary school; a substance obtained directly, by extraction and purification, from natural, or crude technical, raw material (cf **intermediate**); a meeting of the voters of a political party in an electoral division to nominate candidates, or to elect delegates to a nominating convention representing a larger area (*US politics*); an election (also **primary election**) by local members of a party of candidates to be nominated for election, or of delegates to nominate them (*US politics*); (with *cap*) the Palaeozoic era (*geol*). [L *prīmārius*, from *prīmus* first]
■ **prī'marily** adv. **prī'mariness** n.
❑ **primary assembly** n in US politics, a primary. **primary battery** or **cell** n a battery or cell producing an electric current by irreversible chemical action. **primary care** n the first level of health care, as provided by a general practitioner or nurse. **primary coil** n one carrying an inducing current. **primary colours** n pl those from which all others can be derived by mixing, that is (for light) the three spectral colours red, green and blue, which, mixed equally, produce white light, or (for pigments) cyan, magenta and yellow, which, mixed equally produce black (*printing*), or (in general use) red, yellow and blue; also, all the colours of the spectrum, red, orange, yellow, green, blue, indigo, and violet. **primary meristem** n any of the three meristematic tissues in the developing plant embryo, from which epidermis, ground tissue and vascular bundles arise. **primary planet** n a planet distinguished from a satellite. **primary process** n (*psychiatry*) a thought process governed by the pleasure principle. **primary production** n (*ecology*) see **production** under **produce**. **primary school** n a school providing primary education, *usu* for children between five and eleven years. **primary stress** n (*linguistics*) the main stress in a word, the stress that falls on the most heavily accented syllable.

primate /prī'māt or -mit/ n a bishop or archbishop to whose see was formerly annexed the dignity of vicar of the holy see (*RC church*); an archbishop over a province (*C of E*); a member of the order **Primates** /prī-mā'tēz/ the highest order of mammals, including lemurs, monkeys, anthropoid apes and humans (*zool*). [LL *prīmās*, *-ātis*, from L *prīmus* first]
■ **primā'tal** adj. **pri'mateship** n. **primā'tial** /-shl/ and **primatic** /-mat'ik/ or **primat'ical** adj. **primatol'ogist** n. **primatol'ogy** n the study of the Primates.

primavera /prē-mə-vā'rə/ adj made with assorted sautéed spring vegetables. [Ital, literally, spring]

prime¹ /prīm/ adj first in order of time, rank or importance; primary; chief; main; of the highest quality; supremely typical; (of broadcasting time) commanding the highest audience figures; original; in sexual excitement (*Shakesp*); (of a number other than one) divisible by no whole number except unity and itself (*maths*); (of two or more numbers) relatively prime (see below) (with *to*; *maths*). ◆ n one of the hours of the Divine Office, *orig* held at the first hour of the day (6am) (*RC*); the time from the beginning of the artificial day to terce; the beginning; the spring; the world's youth; the new moon, or its first appearance (*obs*); the best part; the height of perfection; full health and strength; a prime number; a first subdivision or symbol marking it (') (*maths*, etc); a fundamental tone; an old card game, probably the same as **primero**; the first guard against sword thrusts, also the first and simplest thrust (*fencing*). [L *prīmus* first; partly through OE *prīm*, from L *prīma* (*hōra*) first (hour)]
■ **prime'ly** adv. **prime'ness** n. **prī'my** adj (*Shakesp*) in one's prime, blooming.

❑ **prime cost** see under **cost¹**. **prime meridian** n a meridian chosen to represent 0°, *esp* that passing through Greenwich, from which other lines of longitude are calculated. **prime minister** n the head of a parliamentary government; the chief minister of state. **prime mover** n in medieval astronomy, the primum mobile; a natural source of energy; a machine that transforms energy from such a source into motive power; the main cause or instigator of an action, project, etc. **prime number** n a number, other than one, divisible only by itself or unity. **prime rate** or **prime lending rate** n the lowest rate of interest charged by a bank at any given time, *usu* available only to large concerns with high credit ratings, forming the base figure on which other rates are calculated. **prime time** n (*radio* and *TV*) the peak period for viewing and listening during the day, having the highest rates. **prime'-time** adj. **prime vertical** n a great celestial circle passing through the east and west points of the horizon, and cutting the meridian at right angles at the zenith.
■ **prime of life** the period of one's life following youth, during which one is at one's most active, productive and successful. **relatively prime** (*maths*) having no common integral factor but unity.

prime² /prīm/ vt to charge, fill; to supply (a gun, firearm, bomb, etc) with powder or other means of igniting the charge; to lay a train of powder to; to bring into activity or working order by a preliminary charge (eg people by giving them liquor, a pump by pouring in water, an internal-combustion engine by injecting gas or oil); to coach or cram beforehand with information or instructions; to apply a primer to, preparatory to painting; to make up with cosmetics (*obs*). ◆ vi to prime a gun; (of a boiler) to send water with the steam into the cylinder; (of the tides) to recur at progressively shorter intervals. [Ety obscure]
■ **prī'mer** n someone or something that primes; a priming-wire; a detonator; a preparatory first coat of paint, etc; the particular type of paint used for this. **prī'ming** n the progressive shortening of the interval between tides as spring tide approaches; a detonating charge that fires a propellant charge; a tube for priming an internal-combustion engine; a priming-wire; a preparatory coat of paint.
❑ **prī'ming-iron** or **-wire** n a wire passed through the touch hole of a cannon to clear it and pierce the cartridge. **prī'ming-powder** n detonating powder; a train of powder.

primer /prī'mər or prim'ər/ or **primmer** /prim'er/ n a small prayer book or book of hours for lay people, used also for teaching reading; a first reading-book; an elementary introduction to any subject; /prim'ər/ printing type of two obsolete sizes, **long primer** (approx 10-point) and **great primer** (approx 18-point). [L *prīmārius* primary]

primero /pri-mā'rō/ n an old card game. [Sp *primera*]

primeur /prē-mœr'/ (Fr) n novelty; early fruit.

primeval or **primaeval** /prī-mē'vl/ adj belonging to the earth's beginnings; primitive; instinctive. [L *prīmaevus*, from *prīmus* first, and *aevum* an age]
■ **prime'vally** or **primae'vally** adv.

primigenial /prī-mi-jē'ni-əl/ adj (also (*non-standard*) **primoge'nial**) first or earliest formed or produced; original; primal. [L *prīmigenius*, from *prīmus* first, and *genus* kind]

primigravida /prī-mi-grav'i-də/ (*obstetrics*) n (pl **primigrav'idae** /-dē/ or **primigrav'idas**) a woman pregnant for the first time (see also **prim²**). [New L, from *primus* first, and feminine adj *gravida* pregnant]

primine /prī'min/ n (*bot*) the outer (or rarely the inner or first formed) coat of an ovule. [L *prīmus* first]

primipara /prī-mip'ə-rə/ (*obstetrics*) n (pl **primip'arae** /-rē/ or **primip'aras**) a woman who has given birth for the first time only, or is about to do so. [New L feminine, from L *primus* first, and *parere* to bear, bring forth]
■ **primipar'ity** n. **primip'arous** adj.

primitiae /prī-mish'i-ē/ n pl first-fruits (*relig*); the first year's revenue of a benefice (also (*Spenser*) **primi'tias**). [L *prīmitiae*, from *prīmus* first]
■ **primitial** /-mish'l/ adj of or relating to first-fruits; (loosely) primeval, original.

primitive /prim'i-tiv/ adj belonging to earliest times or the earlier stages of development; original; ancient; antiquated, old-fashioned; simple, rough, crude or rudimentary; not derivative (*philology*); fundamental; first formed, of early origin (*biol*); of the earliest formation (*old geol*); (of a culture or society) not advanced, lacking a written language and having only simple technical skills; simple, naive or unsophisticated in style and approach (*art*). ◆ n an unsophisticated person or thing; that from which other things are derived; a root word; (with *cap*) a Primitive Methodist; a painter or picture of pre-Renaissance date or manner; a modern painting or artist characterized by simplicity or naivety of approach to subject and technique. [L *prīmitīvus*, an extension of *prīmus* first]
■ **prim'itively** adv. **prim'itiveness** n. **prim'itivism** n approbation of primitive ways, primitive Christianity, primitive art, etc; Primitive Methodism. **prim'itivist** n.

❑ **Primitive Methodism** *n*. **Primitive Methodist** *n* a member of a religious body (Primitive Methodist Connection) founded in 1810, united with the Wesleyan Methodists and United Methodists in 1932. **primitive streak** *n* in developing mammals, birds and reptiles, a thickening of the upper layer of the blastoderm along the axis of the future embryo.

primo[1] /prē'mō/ (*Ital*) *adj* first. ◆ *n* (*pl* **pri'mos**) (*music*) the first or principal part in a duet or trio. [L *prīmus* first]

primo[2] /prī'mo or prē'mō/ *adv* in the first place. [L, ablative of *prīmus* first]

primogenial see **primigenial**.

primogenit /prī-mō-jen'it/ (*obs*) *adj* and *n* first-born. [L *prīmōgenitus*, from *prīmō* first (adv), and *genitus* born, or *genitor* begetter]
■ **primogen'ital**, **primogen'itary** and **primogen'itive** *adj*. **primogen'itive** *n* (*Shakesp*) primogeniture. **primogen'itor** *n* an earliest ancestor; a forefather; the founding ancestor of a people. **primogen'itrix** *n* a female ancestor. **primogen'iture** *n* the circumstance of being first-born; the principle or right of inheritance of the first-born child or (**male primogeniture**) son. **primogen'itureship** *n* (*rare*).

primordial /prī-mör'di-əl/ *adj* existing from the beginning, *esp* of the world; original; rudimentary; earliest formed; of an early stage in growth (*biol*). ◆ *n* the first principle or element. [L *prīmordium*, from *prīmus* first, and *ordīrī* to begin]
■ **primor'dialism** *n*. **primordiality** /-al'i-ti/ *n*. **primor'dially** *adv*. **primor'dium** *n* the primitive source; the first discernible rudiment.
❑ **primordial soup** *n* (*biol*) a solution of organic compounds believed to have composed the earth's lakes and oceans, from which cellular life developed.

primp /primp/ *vi* to dress in a fussy or affected manner; to preen, titivate. ◆ *vt* to tidy, smarten or titivate (oneself or one's hair, outfit, etc). [Connected with **prim**[1]]

primrose /prim'rōz/ *n* a plant (*Primula vulgaris*) or its pale yellow flower, common in spring in woods and meadows; extended to other plants of the genus *Primula*; formerly used for some other (and brighter) flower, also the daisy and (*US*) a kind of wild rose; a conventionalized flower, sometimes four-petalled (*heraldry*); the pale yellow colour of a primrose; the choicest (*Spenser*). ◆ *adj* pale yellow, like a primrose. ◆ *vi* to gather primroses. [OFr *primerose*, as if from L *prīma rosa*; perhaps really through ME and OFr *primerole*, from LL *prīmula*, from *prīmus* first]
■ **prim'rosed** *adj*. **prim'rosy** *adj*.
❑ **Primrose League** *n* an association for Conservative propaganda formed in 1883 in memory of Lord Beaconsfield, named from his supposed favourite flower. **primrose path** or **way** *n* (from *Shakesp*, *Hamlet* and *Macbeth*) the life of pleasure. **primrose peerless** *n* the two-flowered daffodil.
■ **evening primrose** see **evening** under **even**[2].

primsie /prim'zi/ (*Scot*) *adj* prim, demure. [**prim**[1]]

primula /prim'ū-lə/ *n* a plant of the *Primula* genus of flowers including the primrose, cowslip, oxlip, etc, from which is named the dicotyledonous family **Primulā'ceae**, including pimpernel, water violet, cyclamen, etc. [LL, little first one or firstling, from L *prīmus* first]
■ **primulā'ceous** *adj*. **prim'uline** /-lēn/ *n* a yellow coal-tar dye.

primum mobile /prī'məm mō'bi-le, mob'i-lē or prē'mŭm mō'bi-le/ *n* in medieval astronomy, the outermost of the revolving spheres of the universe, carrying the others round in 24 hours; any great source of motion. [L]

Primus® /prī'məs/ *n* (also **primus stove**) a portable cooking stove burning vaporized oil.

primus /prī'məs/ *adj esp* formerly in boys' public schools, appended to the surname of the oldest or most senior of several boys with the same surname. ◆ *n* (for *primus episcopus* first bishop) a presiding bishop in the Scottish Episcopal Church, without metropolitan authority. [L, first]
■ **primus inter pares** /prī'məs in'tər pär'ēz or prē'mŭs in'ter pär'ās/ first among equals (also, modernly, *fem* **prima** /-mə or -ma/ **inter pares**).

primy see under **prime**[1].

prin. *abbrev* : principal.

prince /prins/ *n* the son of a sovereign; a non-reigning male member of a royal or imperial family; a sovereign of a small territory; a title of nobility, as eg formerly in Germany (*Fürst*); a ruler, leader or chief (*obs*); a sovereign, a king or queen (*archaic*); anybody or anything that is first in merit or demerit, the most outstanding or notorious representative of a class, as in *the prince of gamblers*. ◆ *vt* (with *it*) to play the prince. [Fr, from L *princeps*, from *prīmus* first, and *capere* to take]
■ **prince'dom** *n* a principality; the estate, sovereignty or rank of a prince. **prince'hood** *n* the rank or quality of a prince. **prince'kin** *n* a little or young prince. **prince'let** or **prince'ling** *n* a

petty prince. **prince'like** *adj* like, characteristic of or befitting a prince. **prince'liness** *n*. **prince'ly** *adj* of or belonging to a prince or princess; of the rank of prince; princelike; befitting a prince; magnificent; sumptuous; lavish. ◆ *adv* in a princely manner. **prin'cified** *adj* ridiculously dignified.
❑ **Prince Albert** *n* a man's double-breasted frock-coat, worn especially in the early 20c; a type of body piercing in which a ring is inserted through the urethra and the head of the penis. **prince-bish'op** *n* a bishop ranking as prince or having the power of prince of his diocese. **Prince Charming** *n* the prince in the tale of Cinderella, symbolizing the romantic ideal of a handsome husband. **prince consort** *n* a prince who is husband of a reigning queen. **prince-impe'rial** *n* the eldest son of an emperor. **prince of darkness** or **prince of this world** *n* Satan. **Prince of Peace** *n* Christ; the Messiah. **Prince of Wales** *n* since 1301, a title *usu* conferred on the eldest son of the English, and later British, sovereign. **prince royal** *n* the eldest son of a sovereign. **Prince Rupert's drops** see under **drop**. **prince's feather** *n* a tall showy Amaranthus with spikes of rose-coloured flowers; London pride; any of various other plants. **prince's metal** *n* a gold-like alloy of copper and zinc, with more zinc than in brass, Prince Rupert being credited with its invention.

princess /prin'ses or prin-ses'/ *n* the wife or daughter of a prince; the daughter of a sovereign, or a non-reigning female member of a royal or imperial family; a title of nobility in some countries; an affectionate form of address to a woman or girl; a woman who is pre-eminent in her field or class; a desirable but remote or unattainable woman; a size of roofing slate, 24×14in (610×356mm). ◆ *adj* (also **princesse** *Fr*; /prin' or -ses'/) denoting a close-fitting style of dress with a flared skirt, composed of vertical panels extending from shoulder to hem (**princess dress** a dress in this style; **princess line** this style). [OFr *princesse*, feminine of *prince*]
■ **prin'cessly** *adv* like a princess.
❑ **princess royal** *n* a title which may be conferred on the eldest daughter of a sovereign.

principal /prin'si-pl/ *adj* highest in rank or importance; chief, main; constituting a capital sum or principal (*finance*). ◆ *n* the head of a college or university, or sometimes of a school; someone who takes a leading part; a leading actor or performer in a play, show, etc; the person who commits a crime, or someone who aids and abets him or her in doing it (*law*); a person for whom another becomes surety (*law*); a person who, being *sui juris*, employs someone else to do an act which he or she is competent himself to do (*law*); someone who fights a duel; the sum of money on which interest is paid; a main beam, rafter, girder or timber; a roof-truss; the structural framework of a roof; an organ stop similar to a diapason but *usu* sounding an octave higher than the basic pitch (*music*); a collective name for all the pipes of different pitches that produce the basic sound of an organ (*music*). [L *principālis*, from *princeps*, *-ipis* chief]
■ **principality** /-pal'i-ti/ *n* the status, rank or power of a prince; the condition of being a prince; the territory of a prince or one that he derives his title from; (in *pl*) one of the nine orders of angels in the Celestial hierarchy (*medieval theol*). **prin'cipally** *adv*. **prin'cipalness** *n*. **prin'cipalship** *n*.
❑ **principal axis** *n* a line through the centre of curvature of a lens. **principal boy** *n* (*theatre*) the role of the young male hero in pantomime, *usu* played by a woman. **principal clause** *n* (*grammar*) a clause which could function as an independent sentence, a main clause. **principal parts** *n pl* (*grammar*) those forms of a verb from which all other forms may be deduced, eg, in English, the infinitive, the past tense and the past participle.
■ **the Principality** Wales.

principate /prin'si-pāt/ *n* princehood; principality; the Roman Empire in its earlier form, preserving the appearance of a republican government. [L *principātus*, from the emperor's title *princeps* (*cīvitātis*) chief (of the city or state)]

principium /prin-sip'i-əm or pring-kip'i-ŭm/ *n* (*pl* **princip'ia**) a beginning; a first principle or element; the general's quarters in a Roman camp. [L *principium*]
■ **princip'ial** *adj* elementary.

principle /prin'si-pl/ *n* a source, root, origin; a fundamental or primary cause; a beginning (*obs*); essential nature; a theoretical basis or assumption from which to argue, etc; an instinct or natural tendency (as in *the pleasure principle*); a faculty of the mind; a source of action; a scientific law, *esp* as explaining a natural phenomenon or the way a machine works; a fundamental truth on which others are founded or from which they spring; a law or doctrine from which others are derived; a general rule that guides one's (moral) conduct; consistent regulation of behaviour according to moral law; the morality or moral aspect of eg a policy or course of action; a norm of procedure (as in *the principle of first come first served*); a component (*obs*); a constituent of a substance that gives it its distinctive character (*chem*); motive power or the source of it (*Milton*). ◆ *vt* (*obs*) to ground in principles; to impress a doctrine on. [L *principium* beginning, from *princeps*]

■ **prin**'**cipled** *adj* holding certain principles; having, or behaving in accordance with, good principles; invoking or founded on a principle. ◻ **principle of contradiction** *n* the logical principle that a thing cannot both be and not be. **principle of equivalence** *n* a statement of the theory of relativity, shown by an observer being unable to distinguish whether the laboratory is in a uniform gravitational field or in an accelerated frame of reference. **principle of least time** *n* a statement that the path of a ray, eg of light, from one point to another will be that taking the least time (also **Fermat's principle of least time**). **principle of relativity** *n* a universal law of nature stating that the laws of mechanics are not affected by a uniform rectilinear motion of the system of co-ordinates to which they are referred (see also **relativity** under **relate**). **principle of sufficient reason** see under **reason**. **principle of the excluded middle** *n* (*logic*) the principle that a thing must be either one thing or its contradictory.

■ **first principles** fundamental principles, not deduced from others. **in principle** so far as general character or theory is concerned without respect to details or particular application; broadly or basically; in theory. **on principle** on grounds of (moral) principle; for the sake of obeying or asserting a particular principle of morality or wisdom.

princox /*pring*'*koks* or *prin*'/, also **princock** /-*kok*/ (*Shakesp*) *n* a conceited fellow; a coxcomb; a jocular, grotesque or ironical endearment. [Origin obscure]

prink /*pringk*/ *vt* to titivate, groom or smarten (*usu* oneself; sometimes with *up*). ◆ *vi* to preen oneself. [Appar connected with **prank**[2]]

■ **prink about** to behave archly or flirtatiously.

print /*print*/ *n* an impression; a mould or stamp; printed state; printed characters or lettering; an edition; a printed copy; a printed picture; an engraving; a newspaper; a positive photograph made from a negative (or negative from positive); a fingerprint; a printed cloth, *esp* calico stamped with figures; a plaster-cast in low relief (*archit*); a moulded pat of butter; exactitude of plaiting, crimping, or setting (a ruff, hair, etc) (*archaic*); exactitude (*archaic*). ◆ *adj* printed (*obs*); of printed cotton. ◆ *vt* to place (characters, etc) on paper, etc, by means of types, plates or blocks or by other methods; to reproduce (text or pictures) by such means or methods; to cause to be so reproduced; to publish (a book, article, etc); to press (something) into a yielding surface, so as to leave an indented mark; to impress (a surface); to mark (a figure, design, etc) in or on a surface by pressure; to stamp a pattern on or transfer it to (eg a textile); to produce as a positive picture from a negative, or as a negative from a positive (*photog*); to write in separated, as opposed to joined-up, characters, in the manner of typography; to express in writing (*Shakesp*); to designate in print (*Milton*); to fix or impress (a scene, etc) indelibly (on the memory, etc). ◆ *vi* to practise the art of printing; to publish a book; to yield an impression or (*photog*) a positive, etc; to write in separated characters, in typographic style. [ME *print*, *prente*, etc, from OFr *preinte*, *priente*, from *preindre*, *priembre*, from L *premere* to press]

■ **printabil**'**ity** *n*. **print**'**able** *adj* capable of being printed; fit to print. **print**'**er** *n* someone or something that prints; someone who is employed in printing books, etc; any of a variety of devices for printing eg telegraph messages, photographs, the output from a computer, etc; a cotton cloth made for printing. **print**'**ery** *n* a printing house. **print**'**ing** *n* the act, art or business of the printer; the whole number of copies printed at one time; an impression; handwriting in which a space is left between each character. **print**'**less** *adj* receiving or leaving no impression.

◻ **printed circuit** *n* a wiring circuit, free of loose wiring, formed by printing the design of the wiring on copper foil bonded to a flat base and etching away the unprinted foil. **printed circuit board** *n* the combined circuit and supporting base. **printer's devil** see under **devil**. **printer's ink** *n* printing ink. **printer's mark** *n* an engraved device used by printers as a trademark. **printer's pie** *n* a jumble of indiscriminately mixed type (*printing*); any confused jumble. **print**'**head** or **print**'**ing-head** *n* the part or unit in a printer that does the work of reproducing characters on paper. **printing house** *n* an establishment where books, etc are printed. **printing ink** *n* ink used in printing, a *usu* thickish mixture of pigment (such as carbon black) with oil and sometimes varnish. **printing machine** *n* a printing press worked by power. **printing office** *n* a printing house (qv above). **printing paper** *n* a paper suitable for printing purposes. **printing press** *n* a machine by which impressions are taken in ink upon paper from types, plates, etc. **print**'**maker** *n* a worker who produces prints. **print**'**out** *n* the printed information or output from a computer, etc. **print run** *n* the number of copies of a book, newspaper, etc, printed at a time. **print**'**-seller** *n* a seller of prints or engravings. **print shop** *n* a print-seller's shop. **print**'**-through** *n* the degree to which matter printed on one side of paper, etc is visible from the other side (*printing*); in magnetic tape recordings, the transfer of a recording from one layer to another when the tape is wound on a spool. **print**'**works** *n* an establishment where cloth is printed.

■ **in print** (of a text, etc) existing in printed form; (of a book) printed and still available from a publisher; (of hair or a ruff, etc) in exact order, formally set, crimped, pleated or plaited (*obs*). **out of print** no longer in print; no longer available from a publisher. **print out** to print; to produce a printout.

prion[1] /*prī*'*on*/ *n* any petrel of the genus *Pachyptila*, blue-grey above and white below, feeding on the plankton of the southern oceans. [Gr *priōn* a saw]

prion[2] /*prī*'*on* or *prē*', also -*ōn*/ (*pathol*) *n* a transmittable or inheritable mutant or 'rogue' protein, postulated as the cause of certain diseases of the brain and nervous system in animals and humans, including BSE and scrapie. [Coined from **protein**]

prior[1] /*prī*'*ər*/ *adj* previous, earlier; (of an engagement) already arranged for the time in question; more important, pressing or urgent. ◆ *adv* (with *to*) before; up to the time of, until. ◆ *n* (*US inf*) an earlier criminal conviction. [L *prior*, -*ōris* former, previous, superior]

prior[2] /*prī*'*ər*/ *n* the deputy of the abbot in an abbey (*claustral prior*); the head of a priory of monks (*conventual prior*) or of a house of canons regular or of friars; in Italy, formerly, a magistrate. [L *prior*, -*ōris*, a superior or principal, from the adj (see **prior**[1])]

■ **prī**'**orate** *n* the rank or term of office of a prior or prioress; a priory or the community it comprises. **pri**'**oress** *n* an abbess's deputy; the head of a priory of nuns. **pri**'**orship** *n* the office or tenure of office of a prior. **prī**'**ory** *n* a convent of monks or nuns subject to an abbey.

■ **grand priory** a province of the Knights of St John, under a **grand prior**.

priority /*prī-or*'*i-ti*/ *n* the state of being first in time, place, or rank; preference; the privilege of preferential treatment; something that ought to be considered or dealt with in the earliest stage of proceedings. ◆ *adj* having, entitling to, or allowed to those who have, priority. [Med L *priōritās*, from *prior* former, previous, earlier, superior]

■ **prioritiza**'**tion** or **-s-** *n*. **prior**'**itize** or **-ise** *vt* and *vi* to arrange, deal with, etc in order of priority, importance or urgency; to accord priority or urgent status to.

■ **get one's priorities right** to give things appropriate attention in appropriate order.

prisage /*prī*'*zij*/ *n* the former right of the English kings to two tuns of wine from every ship importing twenty tuns or more. [OFr *prise* taking]

Priscianist /*prish*'*ə-nist* or -*yə-nist*/ *n* a grammarian. [*Priscianus*, Latin grammarian (*fl* 500AD)]

■ **break Priscian's head** to breach the rules of grammar.

prise[1] or **prize** /*prīz*/ *vt* to force (*esp* up, out or open) with a lever; to draw (eg information) laboriously (out of someone). ◆ *n* (a tool giving) purchase or leverage. [Fr *prise* hold, grip, a capture; see **prize**[2]]

prise[2] see **price**, and **prize**[1,2,4].

priser obsolete form of **prizer**; see under **prize**[1,4].

prism /*pri-zm*/ *n* a solid whose ends are similar, equal and parallel polygons, and whose sides are parallelograms (*geom*); an object of that shape, *esp* a triangular prism of glass or the like for resolving light into separate colours; a crystal form of three or more faces parallel to an axis (*crystallog*); (loosely) prismatic colours or spectrum. [Gr *prīsma*, -*atos* a piece sawn off, sawdust, a prism, from *prīein* to saw]

■ **prismat**'**ic** or **prismat**'**ical** *adj* resembling, belonging to or using a prism; built up of prisms (*crystallog*); (of colours or light) (as though) produced by means of a prism, hence clear and brilliant. **prismat**'**ically** *adv*. **pris**'**moid** *n* (*geom*) a figure like a prism, but with similar unequal ends. **pris**'**moidal** *adj*. **pris**'**my** *adj* prismatic in colour.

◻ **prismatic colours** *n pl* the seven colours into which a ray of white light is refracted by a prism, that is red, orange, yellow, green, blue, indigo and violet. **prismatic compass** *n* a surveying instrument which by means of a prism enables the compass reading to be taken as the object is sighted. **prismatic powder** *n* pebble-powder. **triangular**, **quadrilateral**, etc **prism** a prism whose ends are triangles, quadrilaterals, etc.

prison /*priz*'*n*/ *n* a public building for the confinement of convicted criminals and accused persons waiting to be tried, a jail; any place of confinement or situation of intolerable restriction; custody, imprisonment. ◆ *vt* (*poetic*) to shut in prison; to enclose; to restrain. [OFr *prisun*, from L *prensiō*, -*ōnis*, for *praehensiō* seizure, from *praehendere*, -*hensum* to seize]

■ **pris**'**oner** *n* someone under arrest or confined in prison; a captive, *esp* in war; anyone kept under restraint against his or her will. **pris**'**onment** *n* (*Shakesp*) imprisonment, confinement. **pris**'**onous** *adj* (*Dickens*).

◻ **prison bars** *n pl* the bars of a prison window, door, etc; whatever confines or restrains; (as *sing*) prisoners' base. **pris**'**on-breaker** *n* someone who escapes from prison. **pris**'**on-breaking** *n*. **prison camp** *n* an enclosed guarded camp where prisoners of war or political prisoners are kept. **prison crop** *n* hair cut very short. **prison door** *n*.

prisoner of conscience see under **conscience**. **prisoner of war** n a person captured during a war, *esp* a member of the armed forces, but also including militia, irregular troops and, under certain conditions, civilians. **prisoners'** (or **prisoner's**) **base** n a game in which those caught are held as prisoners (*appar* for *prison bars*). **prison house** n a prison or prison building. **prison officer** n the official title of a warder (still so called unofficially) in prison. **prison ship** n. **prison van** n a closed vehicle for transporting prisoners. **prison visitor** n someone who visits prisoners in jail as a voluntary service. **prison yard** n. ■ **take no prisoners** to be utterly ruthless in accomplishing one's ends. **take prisoner** to capture and hold as a prisoner.

prissy /pris'i/ adj insipidly prim, prudish or fussy; effeminate. [Probably **prim**[1] and **sissy**]
■ **priss'ily** adv. **priss'iness** n.

pristane /pris'tān/ (*chem*) n a saturated hydrocarbon oil found in the livers of some marine creatures, eg sharks. [Coined from Gr *pristis* sawfish, shark]

pristine /pris'tēn or -tīn/ adj original; former; belonging to the earliest time; pure, unspoilt, unchanged; fresh, clean, unused or untouched. [L *pristinus* former, early; cf *priscus* ancient]

prithee or **prythee** /pridh'ē or -i/ (*archaic*) interj (used in expressing requests, desires, etc) pray, please. [Contracted form of *I pray thee*]

prittle-prattle /prit'l-prat'l/ n empty talk. [Reduplication of **prattle**]

privacy /priv'ə-si or prī'və-si/ n seclusion; (one's right to) freedom from intrusion by the public; avoidance of notice, publicity or display; secrecy, concealment; a place of retreat or retirement (*rare*); a private matter (*rare*). [**private**]

privado /pri-vä'dō/ (*obs*) n (pl **priva'dos** or **priva'does**) a private friend, *esp* of a prince. [Sp, from L *prīvātus* private]

privat-dozent or **-docent** /prē-vät'dō-tsent/ n in German universities, a recognized teacher who is not a member of the salaried staff. [Ger, from L *prīvātus* private, and *docens, -entis* teaching, from *docēre* to teach]

private /prī'vət/ adj (of a person or individual) not in public office; (of a member of parliament) not holding government office; (of a soldier) not an officer or non-commissioned officer; peculiar to oneself, personal, individual; own; relating to personal affairs; set apart or divorced from matters of state; in an unofficial capacity; belonging to or concerning an individual person or company; (of industries, etc) owned and run by private individuals, not by the state; not coming under the state system of education, health care, social welfare, etc; paid for or paying individually by fee; independent; not open to or available for the use of the general public; not made known generally; confidential; retired from observation, secluded; of reserved personality, shunning publicity; alone (*old*); privy (*obs*). ◆ n privacy; a private person (*Shakesp, Milton*); (in pl) private parts; a private soldier; a secret message (*Shakesp*). [L *prīvātus*, pap of *prīvāre* to deprive, to separate]
■ **pri'vately** adv. **prī'vateness** n (*rare*). **privatiza'tion** or **-s-** n. **pri'vatize** or **-ise** vt to transfer from ownership by the state into private ownership; to denationalize. **pri'vatizer** or **-s-** n.
□ **private act** or **bill** n one that deals with the concerns of private persons. **private company** n a company whose shares may not be offered to the general public. **private detective** see **detective** under **detect**. **private enterprise** n an economic system in which individual private firms operate and compete freely. **private equity company** n (*commerce*) a private company that uses borrowed capital to fund takeovers. **private eye** n (*inf*) a private detective. **private first class** n a rank in the US Army between private and corporal. **private hotel** n a term of uncertain meaning, popularly understood to imply that the proprietors do not commit themselves to receiving chance travellers. **private house** n the dwelling-house of a private individual, as contrasted with a shop, office or public building. **private income** n private means (qv below). **private investigator** n (*esp N Am*) a private detective. **private judgement** n freedom to judge for oneself, eg (*relig*) unhindered by the interpretation of the church. **private law** n that part of law which deals with the rights and duties of persons as individuals in relation to each other. **private life** n personal, social and family relationships and activities, *esp* of someone much in the public eye. **private means** n income from investments, etc as opposed to salary or fees for work done. **private member's bill** n a bill introduced and sponsored by a private member in parliament. **private parts** n pl (*euphem*) the external sexual or excretory organs. **private patient** n in the UK, a patient whose treatment is not being paid for by the National Health Service. **private pay bed** see **pay bed** under **pay**[1]. **private practice** n in the UK, medical practice that does not come under the National Health Service. **private press** n a printing concern run by a private individual for recreation rather than profitmaking. **private school** n a school run independently by an individual or a group, *esp* for profit. **private secretary** n a secretary who looks after the personal and confidential affairs of a business person, etc; an aide

to a government minister or senior official. **private sector** n the part of a country's economy owned, operated, etc, by private individuals and firms, *opp* to *public sector*. **private treaty** n a method of selling property in which the selling price is negotiated directly by the buyer and seller. **private view** n a preview of an art exhibition, etc held for specially invited guests, before it is opened to the general public. **private wrong** n an injury done to an individual in his or her private capacity.
■ **in private** not in public; away from public view; secretly.

privateer /prī-və-tēr'/ n a private vessel commissioned to seize and plunder an enemy's ships in wartime; the commander or one of the crew of a privateer. ◆ vi to cruise in a privateer. [**private**]
■ **privateer'ing** n.
□ **privateers'man** n a crew member on a privateer.

privation /prī-vā'shən/ n the state of being deprived of something, *esp* of what is necessary for comfort; the absence of a quality (*logic*). [L *prīvātio, -ōnis*, from *prīvāre* to deprive]

privative /priv'ə-tiv/ adj causing privation; consisting in the absence or removal of something; (of an affix, etc) expressing absence or negation (*grammar*). ◆ n that which is privative or depends on the absence of something else; a term denoting the absence of a quality (*logic*); a privative affix or word (*grammar*). [L *prīvātīvus*, from *prīvāre* to deprive]
■ **priv'atively** adv.

privet /priv'it/ n a half-evergreen European shrub (*Ligustrum vulgare*) of the olive family, used for hedges; applied to other members of the genus *Ligustrum*. [Origin uncertain]

privilege /priv'(ə-)lij or -i-lij/ n an advantage, right or favour granted to or enjoyed by an individual, or a select few; freedom from burdens borne by others; advantages and power enjoyed by people of wealth and high social class; a happy advantage; (an opportunity that one interprets as) a special pleasure or honour, as in *a privilege to meet you*; a prerogative; a franchise, monopoly or patent granted to an individual or company; an option to purchase or sell securities (*US stock exchange*); a sacred and vital civil right; advantage yielded in a struggle (*Shakesp*); right of sanctuary (*Shakesp*). ◆ vt (*usu in passive*) to grant a privilege to; to exempt (with *from*); to authorize or license. [Fr *privilège*, from L *prīvilēgium*, from *prīvus* private, and *lēx, lēgis* a law]
■ **priv'ileged** adj enjoying a privilege or privileges; enjoying the advantages of wealth and class.
■ **breach of privilege** any interference with or slight done to the rights or privileges of a legislative body. **privilege of parliament** or **parliamentary privilege** special rights or privileges enjoyed by members of parliament, such as freedom of speech (not subject to slander laws), and freedom from arrest except on a criminal charge. **question of privilege** any question arising out of the rights of an assembly or of its members. **writ of privilege** an order for the release of a privileged person from custody.

privy /priv'i/ adj private; of or belonging to a particular person, own, personal; for private uses; secret; (of a place, etc) appropriate to withdrawal or retirement; (with *to*) sharing the knowledge of (something secret), apprised of, party to; familiar, intimate (*obs*). ◆ n a person having an interest in an action, contract, conveyance, etc (*law*); a lavatory, *esp* in its own shed or outhouse (*old*). [Fr *privé*, from L *prīvātus* private]
■ **priv'ily** adv (*literary*) privately; secretly. **priv'ity** n privacy (*archaic*); secrecy (*archaic*); something kept private or secret (*obs*); innermost thoughts or private counsels (*obs*); knowledge, shared with another, of something private or confidential; knowledge implying concurrence; any legally recognized relation between different interests.
□ **privy chamber** n a private apartment in a royal residence. **privy council** n *orig* the private council of a sovereign, advising in the administration of government; (with *caps*) now in the UK, a committee of advisors to the sovereign whose membership consists of all present and past members of the Cabinet and other eminent people, its functions being mainly formal or performed by committees, etc; (with *caps*) in certain countries of the British Commonwealth, a body of advisers to the governor-general, including eg cabinet ministers of the country concerned. **privy councillor** or **counsellor** n (also with *caps*). **privy purse** n (also with *caps*) an allowance for the private or personal use of the sovereign. **privy seal** see under **seal**[1].
■ **gentlemen of the privy chamber** officials in the royal household in attendance at court. **Lord Privy Seal** see under **seal**[1].

prix fixe /prē fēk's'/ (Fr) n fixed price.

prize[1] (*Spenser, Shakesp* **prise**) /prīz/ n a reward or symbol of success offered or won in competition by contest or chance, or granted in recognition of excellence; anything well worth striving for; a highly valued acquisition; privilege or advantage (*Shakesp*); esteem (*Spenser*); valuation, appraisal (*Shakesp*). ◆ adj awarded, worthy of, or constituting a prize; treasured; (ironically) perfect, great (as in *a prize fool*). ◆ vt to value; to value highly; to set a price on (*obs*); (*Spenser* pryse) to pay for. [A differentiated form of **price** and **praise**, from OFr *pris* (noun), and *prisier* (verb), from L *pretium* price]

■ **pri'zable** *adj* valuable. **prized** *adj* valued highly; treasured. **pri'zer** *n* (*rare*) an appraiser.

❑ **prize list** *n* a list of winners. **prize'man** or **prize'woman** *n* a winner of a prize, *esp* an academic prize. **prize'-winner** *n*. **prize'-winning** *adj*.

prize² (*Spenser, Shakesp* **prise**) /*prīz*/ *n* that which is taken by force, or in war, *esp* a ship; seizure (*obs*). ◆ *vt* to make a prize of. [Fr *prise* capture, thing captured, from L *praehensa*, feminine pap of *praehendere* to seize]

❑ **prize court** *n* a court for judging regarding prizes made on the high seas. **prize crew** *n* a crew put aboard a prize to bring her to port. **prize money** *n* share of the money or proceeds from any prizes taken from an enemy.

prize³ see **prise**¹.

prize⁴ (*Spenser* **prise**) /*prīz*/ *n* an athletic contest (*obs*); a match (*old*). [Possibly from **prize**¹]

■ **pri'zer** *n* a contestant in a prize or match.

❑ **prize'fight** *n* a public boxing match fought for money, *esp* in the 18c and 19c. **prize'fighter** *n* orig someone who fights in a prize; a professional boxer. **prize'fighting** *n*. **prize ring** *n* a ring for prizefighting; the practice itself.

■ **play one's** (or **a**) **prize** to engage in a match; to sustain one's part.

prn *abbrev : pro re nata* (L), as the need arises.

PRO *abbrev* : Public Record Office; public relations officer.

pro¹ /*prō*/ *adv* in favour. ◆ *prep* in favour of. ◆ *n* (*pl* **pros** /*prōz*/) someone who favours or votes for some proposal; a reason or argument in favour. [L *prō* for]

❑ **pro and con** *adv* (L *prō et contrā*) for and against. ◆ *vt* and *vi* (**pro'ing and conn'ing** or **pro-and-conn'ing**; **pro'd and conned**, **con'd** or **pro-and-conned'**) to consider or discuss for and against. ■ **pros and cons** reasons or arguments for and against.

pro² /*prō*/ *n* (*pl* **pros** /*prōz*/) (*inf*) a contraction of **professional** (golfer, cricketer, actor, etc; see under **profession**¹), of **probationary** (nurse, see under **probation**), and of **prostitute**. ◆ *adj* of or relating to a pro or pros.

❑ **pro'-am'** *adj* (of eg a golf tournament) involving both professionals and amateurs (also *n*). **pro-celeb'rity** *adj* (of eg a golf tournament) involving professionals and celebrities.

pro³ /*prō*/ (L) *prep* for.

❑ **pro-forma** /-*för'mə*/ *adj* as a matter of form (also *adv*); (of an account, etc) made out to show the market price of specified goods; with goods being paid for before dispatch. ◆ *n* (also **pro forma**) a pro-forma invoice; loosely, an official form or record for completion. ■ **pro aris et focis** /*är'ēz et fö'sēz* or *är'ēs et fö'kēs*/ for altars and firesides; for the sake of one's religion and one's home. **pro bono publico** /*bo'nō pub'li-kō* or *bö'nō pŭ'bli-kō*/ for the public good (often shortened to **pro bono**). **pro forma** /*för'mə* or *för'mä*/ as a matter of form. **pro hac vice** /*hak vī'sē, wē'ke* or *vē'ke*/ for this turn or occasion. **pro indiviso** /*in-di-vī'sō, -zō* or *in-dē-wē'sō, -vē'*/ as undivided; applied to rights which two or more persons hold in common (*law*). **pro memoria** /*mə-mör'i-ə, -mör'* or *me-mō'ri-ä*/ for a memorial. **pro patria** /*pä'tri-ə* or *pä'tri-ä*/ for one's country. **pro rata** /*rä'tə* or *rä'tä*/ in proportion. **pro re nata** /*rē nä'tə* or *rä nä'tä*/ for a special emergency, as the need arises or circumstances dictate. **pro tanto** /*tan'tō*/ for so much. **pro tempore** /*tem'pə-rē* or *tem'po-re*/ for the time being.

pro-¹ /*prō-*/ (L) *combining form* (1) occurring as an etymological element with the senses before (in place or time), forward, forth, publicly; as a living prefix (2) denoting instead of, in place of, acting on behalf of, as in *pro-chancellor* ; (3) denoting tending to cause; (4) denoting in favour of, supporting, backing, as in *pro-American, pro-European, pro-privatization, pro-conservation*. [L prep *prō*, earlier *prōd*, in combination sometimes *pro-*; cf **pro-**²]

■ **pro-choice'** *adj* (denoting the lobby) upholding or supporting the right of a woman to have an abortion. **pro-choi'cer** *n*. **pro-life'** *adj* (denoting the lobby) opposing abortion, euthanasia and experimentation on human embryos. **pro-li'fer** *n*. **pro-marketeer'** *n* a person in favour of Britan's entry into, or continued membership of, the European Single Market.

pro-² /*prō-*/ (Gr) *combining form* denoting before (in time or place); earlier than; in front of; the front part of; primitive; rudimentary. [Gr prep *pro* before; cf L *prō*, Eng **for, fore**]

proa /*prō'ə*/, **prau** /*prä'oo* or *prow*/ or **prahu** /*prä'oo* or *prä'hoo*/ *n* a Malay sailing-boat or rowing boat, *esp* a fast sailing-vessel with both ends alike, and a flat side with an outrigger kept to leeward. [Malay *prāŭ*]

proactive /*prō-ak'tiv*/ *adj* tending actively to instigate changes in anticipation of future developments, as opposed to merely reacting to events as they occur; ready to take the initiative, acting without being

prompted by others; (of a prior mental experience) tending to affect or inhibit a subsequent, *esp* learning, process (*psychol*). [**pro-**²]

■ **proac'tively** *adv*.

proairesis /*prō-ā'ri-sis* or *-ī'ri-sis*/ *n* the act of choosing. [Gr, choosing]

pro-am see under **pro**².

prob /*prob*/ (*inf*) *n* a problem.

prob. *abbrev* : probable.

probable /*prob'ə-bl*/ *adj* having more evidence for than against; giving ground for belief, likely to be correct; likely to happen; likely to have happened, likely to be the case; plausible; capable of being proved (*rare*). ◆ *n* a probable opinion; a person or thing likely to be selected; a candidate with a good chance of success; something that is a likelihood. [Fr, from L *probābilis*, from *probāre*, *-ātum* to prove]

■ **probabil'iorism** *n* the doctrine that in case of doubt one is constrained to choose the more probable opinion. **probabil'iorist** *n*. **prob'abilism** *n* the doctrine that in a disputed or doubtful case of law one should follow the opinion supported by a recognized Doctor of the Church (*RC theol*); the theoretical premise that knowledge, scientific rules, etc cannot be absolute but can suffice to represent probability (*philos*). **prob'abilist** *n*. **probabilis'tic** *adj*. **probabil'ity** *n* (*pl* **probabil'ities**) the quality of being probable, likelihood; the appearance of truth; that which is probable; the chance or likelihood of something happening; a measure of the likelihood of something occurring, expressed as a ratio of positive cases to total potential cases. **prob'ably** *adv*.

❑ **probability theory** *n* the branch of mathematics concerned with quantities that have random distribution and the likelihood of the occurrence of particular events. **probable cause** *n* (*law*) reasonable grounds for taking an action such as making an arrest or a search; (in Scotland) an entitlement to legal aid based on having a proveable case. **probable error** *n* a quantity assumed as the value of an error, such that the chances of the real error being greater are equal to those of its being less. **probable evidence** *n* evidence not conclusive, but carrying some degree of force.

■ **in all probability** quite probably.

proball /*prō'bl*/ (*Shakesp*) *adj* supposed to mean plausible. [Apparently a contracted form of **probable**]

proband /*prō'band*/ *n* a person with some distinctive characteristic (*esp* a physical or mental disorder) who serves as the starting-point for a genetic study of the transmission of this feature through his or her descendants. [L *probandus*, gerundive of *probāre* to test]

probang /*prō'bang*/ (*med*) *n* a slender flexible rod, tipped with a sponge or button, for passing down the throat and into the oesophagus, in order to apply medication or remove an obstruction. [Called *provang* by its inventor, the Welsh judge, Walter Rumsey (1584–1660); origin uncertain; probably influenced by **probe**]

probate /*prō'bāt* or *-bit*/ *n* the proof before a competent court that a written paper purporting to be the will of a person who has died is indeed his or her lawful act; the official copy of a will, with the certificate of its having been proved. ◆ *adj* relating to the establishment of wills and testaments. ◆ *vt* (*N Am*) to establish the validity of (a will) by probate; to place a probate on; to place a probation sentence on. [L *probāre*, *-ātum* to test, prove]

■ **probative** /*prō'bə-tiv*/ *adj* testing; affording proof. **prō'batory** *adj* testing.

❑ **Probate Court** *n* a court created in 1858 to exercise jurisdiction in matters touching the succession to personal estate in England. **probate duty** *n* (*hist*) a tax on property passing by will.

probation /*prō-bā'shən* or *prə-*/ *n* testing; proof; a preliminary time or condition appointed to allow suitability or unsuitability (eg of a new employee) to appear; noviciate; suspension of sentence, allowing liberty under supervision on condition of good behaviour (*esp* to young, or first, offenders); time of trial; moral trial. [L *probātiō*, *-ōnis*, from *probāre* to test]

■ **probā'tional** *adj* relating to, serving purpose of, probation or trial. **probā'tionary** *adj* probational; on probation. ◆ *n* a probationer. **probā'tioner** *n* someone who is on probation or trial; an offender under probation; a novice; someone licensed to preach, but not ordained to a pastorate (*esp Scot*). **probā'tionership** *n*.

❑ **probation officer** *n* a person appointed to advise and supervise offenders under probation.

probe /*prōb*/ *n* an instrument for exploring a wound, locating a bullet, etc; an act of probing; an exploratory bore; a prod; an investigation; any of various instruments of investigation in space research (eg a multi-stage rocket), electronics, etc; a pipelike device attached to an aircraft for making connection with a tanker aeroplane so as to refuel in flight; a device used in docking two space modules; a radioactive or otherwise labelled fragment of DNA or RNA used to find and identify nucleic acid sequences by hybridizing with them. ◆ *vt* to examine

with or as if with a probe; to examine searchingly. ◆ *vt* and *vi* to pierce. [L *proba* proof, later examination, from *probāre* to prove]
■ **pro'beable** *adj*. **pro'ber** *n* someone or something that probes.
◻ **probe scissors** *n pl* scissors used to open wounds, one blade having a button at the end.

probenecid /prō-ben'is-id/ *n* a drug that promotes excretion of uric acid, used in treating gout. [*propyl*, *benzene* and *acid*]

probiotics /prō-bī-ot'iks/ *n sing* treatment by the ingestion of bacteria that support the useful and harmless bacteria in the body against the harmful ones. [**pro-¹** (4), and **biotic**]
■ **probiot'ic** *adj* relating to probiotics; denoting (a substance containing) bacteria that are useful for the body. ◆ *n* a probiotic micro-organism.

probit /prō'bit/ (*stats*) *n* a unit for measuring probability in relation to an average frequency distribution. [*Probability un*it]

probity /prō'bi-ti or prob'/ *n* uprightness; moral integrity; honesty. [L *probitās*, *-ātis*, from *probus* good, honest]

problem /prob'ləm/ *n* a matter difficult to settle or solve; a source of perplexity; a question or puzzle propounded for solution; in chess, the question how to win in so many moves beginning with a hypothetical situation; a proposition in which something is required to be constructed, not merely proved as in a theorem (*geom*). ◆ *adj* presenting, posing or constituting a problem; difficult to deal with. [Gr *problēma*, *-atos*, from *pro* before, in front, and *ballein* to throw]
■ **problemat'ic** or **problemat'ical** *adj* of the nature of a problem; questionable; doubtful; (of a proposition) stating what is possible but not necessarily the case (*logic*). **problemat'ically** *adv*. **problemat'ics** *n pl* matters that are problematic or that raise questions. **prob'lematize** or **-ise** *vt* to perceive or treat (a subject) as a problem in need of a solution. **prob'lemist** *n* a person who composes or solves chess, etc problems.
◻ **problem child** *n* one whose character presents an exceptionally difficult problem to parents, teachers, etc. **problem novel** or **play** *n* one presenting or expounding a social or moral problem. **problem page** *n* a page or section in a magazine devoted to dealing with readers' personal problems. **problem-solving behaviour** *n* the use of various strategies to overcome difficulties in attaining a goal.
■ **have a problem with** to be troubled by; to object to or disagree with. **no problem** or **not a problem** that's easy; that's all right.

proboscis /prō-bos'is or prə-, also -bosk' or -bōs'/ *n* (*pl* **probosc'ises** or **probosc'ides** /-i-dēz/) a trunk or long snout; a trunk-like process such as the suctorial mouth-parts of some insects; a nose (*facetious*). [L, from Gr *proboskis* a trunk, from *pro* expressing motive, and *boskein* to feed]
■ **Proboscid'ea** *n pl* the elephant order of mammals. **proboscid'ean** or **proboscid'ian** *adj* and *n*.
◻ **proboscis monkey** *n* a very long-nosed monkey from Borneo (*Nasalis larvatus*).

probouleutic /prō-boo-lū'tik/ *adj* for preliminary deliberation. [Gr *probouleusis* preliminary deliberation]

Probus /prō'bəs or -biz/ *n* an association that provides regular gatherings for retired professional and business people. [*professional* and *business*]

procacity /prə-kas'i-ti/ *n* petulance. [L *procācitās*, *-ātis*, from *procāx* forward, insolent, shameless, from *procāre* to demand]
■ **procacious** /-kā'shəs/ *adj*.

procaine /prō'kān/ *n* a crystalline substance used as a local anaesthetic. [**pro-¹** (2) and **cocaine**]

procaryon, etc see **prokaryon**.

procathedral /prō-kə-thē'drəl/ *n* a church used temporarily as a cathedral. [**pro-¹** (2)]

proceed /prō-sēd' or prə-/ *vi* to go on; to continue; to advance; to pass on; to begin and go on; to act according to a method; to go from point to point; to advance to a higher degree (as in *proceed MA*) or more developed state; to prosper; to come forth; to result; to be descended; to take measures or action; to take legal action; to prosecute; to go on, be transacted, happen (*Shakesp*). ◆ *vt* to say in continuation. ◆ *n* /prō'sēd/ (*usu* in *pl*) outcome; money got from anything. [Fr *procéder*, from L *prōcēdere*, from *prō* before, and *cēdere*, *cessum* to go]
■ **procedural** /-sēd'yə-rəl/ *adj*. **procē'dure** *n* a mode of proceeding; a method of conducting business, *esp* in a law case or a meeting; a course of action; a step taken or an act performed. **proceed'er** *n*. **proceed'ing** *n* the action of moving forward; progress; advancement; a course of conduct; *perh* an advantage (*Shakesp*); a step; an operation; a transaction; (in *pl*) legal action; a record of the transactions of a society.

proceleusmatic /pros-e-lūs-mat'ik/ *adj* inciting, encouraging. ◆ *n* (*classical prosody*) a foot consisting of four short syllables. [Gr *prokeleusmatikos*, from *pro* before, and *keleuein* to urge, order]

Procellaria /pros-e-lā'ri-ə/ *n* the petrel genus. [L *procella* a storm]
■ **procella'rian** *adj*.

procephalic /prō-si-fal'ik/ *adj* of the forepart of the head. [Gr *pro* before, and *kephalē* head]

procerebrum /prō-ser'i-brəm or -se-rē'brəm/ *n* the forebrain; the prosencephalon. [L *prō* before, and *cerebrum* brain]
■ **procer'ebral** *adj*.

process¹ /prō'ses/ or (*esp N Am*) pros', also (*Milton*) prō-ses' / *n* a state of being in progress or being carried on; course; a narrative (*Shakesp*); a series of actions or events; a sequence of operations or changes undergone; a photo-process (*printing*); a writ by which a person or matter is brought into court (*law*); an action, suit, or the proceedings in it as a whole; progression; proceeding; an edict (*Shakesp*); a projection or projecting part, *esp* on a bone (*biol, anat*). ◆ *vt* to serve a summons on; to sue or prosecute; to subject to a special process; to produce or print photomechanically; to prepare (eg agricultural produce) for marketing by some special process, eg canning or bottling; to arrange (documents, etc) systematically; to examine and analyse; to test the suitability of (a person) for some purpose; (of a computer) to perform operations of adding, subtracting, etc, or other operations on (data supplied); to subject (data) to such operations. [Fr *procès*, from L *prōcessus*, *-ūs* advance; cf **proceed**]
■ **pro'cessed** *adj* produced by a special process, eg synthetically, photomechanically, etc; subjected to a certain process. **prō'cessor** *n* something or someone that processes; a device which processes data (*comput*); a central processing unit (*comput*). **process'ual** *adj* governed by or related to an established process; having a direct function (*N Am*).
◻ **process block** *n* a photomechanically made block for printing a picture. **process control** *n* direct automatic control of a physical industrial process by computer. **process engineering** *n* the branch of engineering concerned with industrial processes. **pro'cess-server** *n* a sheriff's officer.
■ **data processing** the handling and processing of information by computers. **in the process** (or **in process**) **of** in the course of (doing something, being made, etc).

process² see under **procession**.

procession /prō-sesh'ən or prə-/ *n* the act of proceeding; a file or train of people, vehicles, boats, etc moving forward together by way of ceremony, display, demonstration, etc; the movement of such a train; a litany sung in procession (*Christianity*). ◆ *vi* (*rare*) to go in procession. ◆ *vt* (*rare*) to go through or around in procession; to celebrate by a procession. [L *prōcessiō*, *-ōnis*; cf **proceed**]
■ **process** /prō-ses'/ *vi* (back-formation) to go in procession. **process'ional** *adj*. ◆ *n* (*Christianity*) a book of litanies, hymns, etc for processions; a hymn sung in procession. **process'ionalist** *n*. **process'ionary** *adj*. **process'ioner** *n* (*US*) a county officer who determines boundaries. **process'ioning** *n* going in procession; perambulation of boundaries (*US*).
◻ **processionary moth** *n* a European moth (*Thaumetopoea processionea*) whose caterpillars go out seeking food in great processions.
■ **Procession of the Holy Ghost** (*theol*) the emanation of the Holy Spirit from the Father (**single procession**), or from the Father and Son (**double procession**).

processor, **processual** see under **process¹**.

procès-verbal /pros-ā-vûr-bäl' or (*Fr*) pro-se-ver-bäl' / (*Fr*) *n* (*pl* **-verbaux** /ver-bō/) a written statement or report.

prochain or **prochein ami** or **amy** /pro-shen a-mē/ (*law*) *n* a next friend (qv). [OFr]

pro-chancellor /prō-chän'sə-lər/ *n* in certain British universities, the deputy to the vice-chancellor. [**pro-¹** (2)]

pro-choice, **pro-choicer** see under **pro-¹**.

prochronism /prō'krə-ni-zm/ *n* a dating of an event before the right time, *opp* to *metachronism*. [Gr *pro* before, and *chronos* time]

procidence /pros'i-dəns or pros'/ (*med*) *n* prolapse. [L *prōcidentia*, from *prō* forward, and *cadere* to fall]
■ **pro'cident** *adj*.

procinct /prō-singkt'/ (*Milton*) *n* preparedness. [L *prōcinctus*, *-ūs*, from *prō* beforehand, and *cingere*, *cinctum* to gird]

proclaim /prō-klām' or prə-/ *vt* to cry aloud; to publish abroad; to announce officially; to attest or indicate unmistakably; to denounce; to announce the accession of; to place under restrictions by proclamation. ◆ *n* a proclamation; a proclaiming. [Fr *proclamer*, from L *prōclāmāre*, *prōclāmāre*, from *prō* out, and *clāmāre* to cry]
■ **proclaim'ant** *n*. **proclaim'er** *n*. **proclamation** /prok-lə-mā'shən/ *n* the act of proclaiming; that which is proclaimed; an official notice given to the public; a proscription. **proclamatory** /-klam'ə-tə-ri/ *adj*.

proclitic /prō-klit'ik/ (*linguistics*) *adj* (of a word) transferring its stress to the following word, or lacking stress and forming a phonological unit with the following word. ◆ *n* a proclitic word. [A 19c coinage on the analogy of **enclitic**, from Gr *pro* forward, and *klīnein* to lean]

■ **pro'clisis** (or /*prok'*/) *n* pronunciation of a word as a proclitic.

proclivity /*prō-kliv'i-ti* or *prǝ-*/ *n* inclination; propensity. [L *prōclīvis*, from *prō* forward, and *clīvus* a slope]

■ **proclive** /*-klīv'*/ *adj* (*archaic*) inclined; prone; headlong.

procoelous /*prō-sē'lǝs*/ *adj* cupped in front. [Gr *pro* before, and *koilos* hollow]

proconsul /*prō-kon'sl*/ *n* a Roman magistrate with almost consular authority outside the city, *orig* one whose consulate had expired, often the governor of a province (*hist*); sometimes applied to a governor of a colony or dominion; a member of the genus *Proconsul* of prehistoric African anthropoid apes. [L *prōconsul*]

■ **procon'sular** /*-sū-lǝr*/ *adj*. **procon'sulate** /*-sū-lit* or *-lāt*/ *n*. **procon'sulship** *n* the office, or term of office, of a proconsul.

procrastinate /*prō-kras'ti-nāt*/ *vi* to defer action; to put off what should be done immediately. ◆ *vt* (*rare*) to put off until some future time, to defer. [L *procrāstināre, -ātum*, from *prō* onward, and *crāstinus* of tomorrow, from *crās* tomorrow]

■ **procrastinā'tion** *n* the act or habit of putting off, dilatoriness. **procras'tinative, procras'tinating** or **procras'tinatory** *adj*. **procras'tinativeness** *n*. **procras'tinator** *n*.

procreate /*prō'kri-āt*/ *vt* to engender; to beget; to generate. ◆ *vi* to produce offspring. [L *prōcreāre, -ātum*, from *prō* forth, and *creāre* to produce]

■ **prō'creant** /*-kri-ǝnt*/ *n* a generator. ◆ *adj* generating; connected with or useful in reproduction. **prōcreā'tion** *n*. **prōcreā'tional** *adj*. **prō'creātive** *adj* having the power to procreate; generative; productive. **prō'creātiveness** *n*. **prō'creātor** *n* a parent.

Procrustean /*prō-krus'ti-ǝn*/ *adj* taking violent measures to ensure conformity to a standard. [From *Procrustes*, a legendary Greek robber, who stretched or cut his captives' legs to make them fit a bed]

procrypsis /*prō-krip'sis*/ (*biol*) *n* protective coloration. [Gr *pro* before, and *krypsis* hiding, from *kryptein* to hide]

■ **procryp'tic** *adj*. **procryp'tically** *adv*.

proctal /*prok'tl*/ *adj* anal or rectal. [Gr *prōktos* anus]

procto- /*prok-tǝ-, -tō-* or *-to-*/ or (before a vowel) **proct-** /*prokt-*/ combining form denoting rectum or anus. [Gr *prōktos* anus]

■ **proctalgia** /*-al'ji-ǝ*/ *n* (see **-algia**) neuralgic pain in the rectum. **proctī'tis** *n* inflammation of the rectum. **proctodae'al** /*-tō-dē'ǝl* or *-tǝ-*/ *adj*. **proctodae'um** *n* (Gr *hodaios* on the way) the posterior part of the alimentary canal, formed embryonically by invagination of the ectoderm. **proctol'ogist** *n*. **proctol'ogy** *n* the medical study and treatment of the anus and rectum. **proc'toscope** *n* an instrument for examining the rectum. **proctos'copy** *n*.

proctor /*prok'tǝr*/ *n* an official in some English universities whose functions include enforcement of university regulations; an examination supervisor or invigilator at a university (*N Am*); a procurator or manager for another; an attorney in the ecclesiastical courts; a representative of the clergy in Convocation. [**procurator**]

■ **proc'torage** *n*. **procto'rial** /*-tōr'* or *-tör'i-ǝl*/ *adj*. **procto'rially** *adv*. **proc'torize** or **-ise** *vt* to exercise the power of a proctor against. **proc'torship** *n*.

■ **king's** or **queen's proctor** an official who intervenes in divorce cases in England if collusion or fraud is suspected.

procumbent /*prō-kum'bǝnt*/ *adj* lying or leaning forward; prone; prostrate; growing along the ground (*bot*). [L *prōcumbens, -entis*, prp of *prōcumbere*, from *prō* forward, and *cumbere* to lie down]

procurator /*prok'ū-rā-tǝr*/ *n* a financial agent in a Roman imperial province, sometimes administrator of part of it (*hist*); someone who manages affairs for another; someone authorized to act for another; an agent in a law court. [L *prōcūrātor, -ōris*; see **procure**]

■ **procuracy** /*prok'ū-rǝ-si*/ *n* the office of a procurator. **procurā'tion** *n* the management of another's affairs; the instrument giving authority for this; a sum paid by incumbents to the bishop or archdeacon on visitations; see also under **procure**. **procuratorial** /*-rǝ-tō'ri-ǝl* or *-tör'*/ *adj*. **proc'uratorship** *n*. **proc'uratory** /*-rǝ-tǝr-i*/ *n* authorization to act for another.

❑ **procurator fiscal** see under **fiscal**.

procure /*prō-kūr'* or *prǝ-*/ *vt* to contrive to obtain or bring about; to encompass (eg someone's downfall, etc); to obtain (prostitutes) for clients; to induce (*obs*); to induce to come, bring (*Shakesp*); to urge earnestly (*Spenser*). ◆ *vi* to pander, pimp. [Fr *procurer*, from L *prōcūrāre* to manage, from *prō* for, and *cūrāre, -ātum* to care for]

■ **procur'able** *adj* available, obtainable. **procurā'tion** *n* the process of procuring; see also under **procurator**. **procure'ment** *n* the act of procuring. **procur'er** *n* someone who procures; a pander. **procur'ess** *n* a female procurer, a bawd. **procur'ing** *n*.

procureur /*pro-kü-rœr'*/ (*Fr*) *n* a procurator.

❑ **procureur général** /*zhān-ā-ral*/ *n* in France, the public prosecutor-in-chief.

Procyon /*prō'si-ǝn*/ *n* a first-magnitude star in the constellation of the Lesser Dog; the raccoon genus, giving name to the family **Procyon'idae** (raccoons, coatis, etc). [Gr *Prokyōn* the star Procyon, rising before the Dogstar, from *pro* before, and *kyōn* a dog]

■ **procyon'id** *n* a member of the Procyonidae.

Prod /*prod*/, **Proddy** or **Proddie** /*prod'i*/ (*offensive sl*) *n* (*esp* in Ireland) a Protestant.

prod /*prod*/ *vt* (**prodd'ing**; **prodd'ed**) to prick; to poke, eg with a fingertip or the end of a stick; to stimulate into action. ◆ *n* an act of prodding; a sharp instrument such as a goad, awl or skewer; a reminder. [Origin uncertain; OE *prodbor* seems to mean auger]

■ **prodd'er** *n*.

prodigal /*prod'i-gl*/ *adj* wasteful of one's means; squandering; lavish. ◆ *n* a waster; a spendthrift; a wanderer returned (also **prodigal son**). ◆ *adv* (*Shakesp*) prodigally. [Obs Fr, from L *prōdigus*, from *prōdigere* to squander, from pfx *prōd-* (early form of *prō-*) away, forth, and *agere* to drive]

■ **prodigality** /*-gal'i-ti*/ *n* the state or quality of being prodigal; extravagance; profusion; great liberality. **prod'igalize** or **-ise** *vt* to spend lavishly, to waste. **prod'igally** *adv*.

prodigy /*prod'i-ji*/ *n* any person or thing that causes great wonder, *esp* a child of precocious genius or virtuosity; a wonder; a monster; a portent (*archaic*). [L *prōdigium* a prophetic sign, from pfx *prōd-* (earlier form of *prō-*) in advance, and prob the root of *adagium* (see **adage**)]

■ **prodigios'ity** *n*. **prodig'ious** *adj* astonishing; more than usually large in size or degree; monstrous; of the nature of a prodigy (*archaic*). **prodig'iously** *adv*. **prodig'iousness** *n*.

proditor /*prod'i-tǝr*/ *n* a traitor. [L *prōditor, -ōris*, from *prōdere, -itum* to betray, from *prō* forth, and *dare* to give]

■ **prodito'rious** /*-tör'i-ǝs* or *-tör'*/ or **prod'itory** *adj*.

prodrome /*prod'rōm*/ *n* (also **prod'romus** /*prod'rǝ-mǝs*/ (*pl* **prod'romi**)) an introductory treatise; a premonitory event; a sign of approaching disease. [Latinized from Gr *prodromos* forerunner, from *pro* before, and *dromos* a run]

■ **prod'romal** and **prodrom'ic** *adj*.

prodrug /*prō'drug*/ *n* a compound that is inactive in its original form but is converted by the metabolic processes of the body into an active drug. [**pro-²**]

produce /*prǝ-dūs'*/ *vt* to bring into being; to bring forth; to yield; to bring about; to make; to put (a play, show, etc) on the stage; to prepare (a programme) for broadcasting on radio or television; to be in charge of the recording of (a piece of music), making artistic decisions about the finished overall sound; to prepare for exhibition to the public; to bring forward or out; to extend. ◆ *vi* to yield; to create value. ◆ *n* /*prod'ūs*/ that which is produced; product; proceeds; crops; yield, *esp* of fields and gardens. [L *prōdūcere, -ductum*, from *prō* forward, and *dūcere* to lead]

■ **produce'ment** *n* (*Milton*) product. **produc'er** *n* someone who produces commodities; someone who produces a play, show, programme, recording, etc; someone who exercises general control over, but does not actually make, a cinema film (cf **director**); a furnace in which a mixed combustible gas is produced by passing air and steam through incandescent coke. **producibil'ity** *n*. **produc'ible** *adj* capable of being produced; capable of being generated or made; capable of being exhibited. **product** /*prod'ǝkt* or *-ukt*/ *n* a thing produced; a result; a work; an item made and offered for sale; offspring; a quantity obtained by multiplying (*maths*); a substance obtained from another by chemical change (*chem*). **productibil'ity** /*prǝ-dukt-*/ *n* the capability of being produced. **product'ile** *adj* capable of being drawn out in length. **produc'tion** *n* the act of producing or process of being produced; that which is produced; fruit; product; a work, *esp* of art; the staging of a play, show, etc; the staged performance itself; a bringing out; change in biomass expressed on an area basis; **primary production** being by green plants, **secondary production** by heterotrophic organisms (*ecology*); the creation of values (*econ*); extension; a document produced in court (*Scots law*). **produc'tional** *adj*. **produc'tive** *adj* having the power to produce; generative; that produces (with *of*); (of a cough) producing mucus (*med*); worthwhile; producing richly; fertile; efficient. **produc'tively** *adv*. **produc'tiveness** *n*. **productiv'ity** /*prod-* or *prōd-*/ *n* the rate or efficiency of work, *esp* in industrial production.

❑ **producer gas** *n* gas made in a producer, chiefly a mixture of hydrogen and carbon monoxide diluted with nitrogen. **producer** (or **producers'**) **goods** *n pl* goods, such as raw materials and tools, used in the production of consumer(s') goods. **production car, vehicle**, etc *n* one made in the routine course of production, as distinct from one made for a special purpose such as testing. **production line** *n* an assembly line. **production number** *n* an item in a musical show or film involving singing and dancing by a large number of performers. **production platform** *n* an oil platform (qv). **production string** *n* the smallest casing in an oil well, reaching from the producing zone to the well head (also **oil string**). **productivity deal** *n* an agreement whereby employees receive increased wages or salaries if they agree to improve their efficiency and increase their output. **product liability** *n* the responsibility of manufacturers or traders for making or selling a faulty product. **product life cycle** *n* the four stages in the economic evolution of a product, ie introduction, growth, maturity and decline. **product placement** *n* a disguised form of advertising whereby a particular product is included noticeably in a shot in a feature film, etc. ■ **make a production of** (or **out of**) (*inf*) to make an unnecessary fuss or commotion about (something).

proem /prō'em/ *n* an introduction; a prelude; a preface. [Fr *proème*, from L *prooemium*, from Gr *prooimion*, from *pro* before, and *oimē* a song, *oimos* a way]
■ **proemial** /prō-ē'mi-əl/ *adj*.

proembryo /prō-em'bri-ō/ (*bot*) *n* (*pl* **proem'bryos**) a group of cells formed in the dividing zygote, from which part the embryo arises. [**pro-²**]

proenzyme /prō-en'zīm/ *n* an enzyme in an inactive form which can be activated, often by another enzyme. [**pro-²**]

Prof. *abbrev* : professor.

prof /prof/ *n* a familiar contraction of **professor** (see under **profess**).

proface /prō-fās'/ (*Shakesp*) *interj* may it profit you, a phrase of welcome. [OFr *prou* profit, and *fasse*, 3rd pers sing present subjunctive of *faire* to do]

profane /prō-fān' *or* prə-/ *adj* not sacred; secular; showing contempt of sacred things; (of language) irreverent or blasphemous; uninitiated; unhallowed; ritually unclean or forbidden. ◆ *vt* to treat (something holy) with contempt or insult; to desecrate; to violate; to put to an unworthy use. [L *profānus* outside the temple, not sacred, unholy, from *prō* before, and *fānum* a temple]
■ **profanation** /prof-ə-nā'shən/ *n*. **profanatory** /prō-fan'ə-tər-i/ *adj*. **profane'ly** *adv*. **profane'ness** *n*. **profān'er** *n*. **profanity** /-fan'-/ *n* irreverence; that which is profane; profane language or conduct; a blasphemy or oath.

profectitious /prō-fek-tish'əs/ *adj* derived from a parent or ancestor. [LL *profectīcius*, from L *proficīscī*, *profectus* to proceed]

profess /prə-fes' *or* prō-/ *vt* to make open declaration of; to declare in strong terms; to claim, often insincerely, to have a feeling of; to pretend to; to claim to be expert in; to be professor of; to receive into a religious order by profession (*RC*). ◆ *vi* to enter publicly into a religious order; to pretend friendship (*Shakesp*); to be a professor. [L *professus*, pap of *profitērī*, from *prō* publicly, and *fatērī* to confess]
■ **professed'** *adj* openly declared; avowed; alleged; acknowledged; having made a profession (of a religious belief, etc). **profess'edly** *adv*. **profess'ing** *adj* avowed; pretending, soi-disant. **profession** /-fesh'ən/ *n* the act of professing; an open declaration; an avowal; a declaration of religious belief made upon entering a religious order; a pretence. **professor** /prə-fes'ər/ *n* someone who professes; someone who openly declares belief in certain doctrines; a university or college teacher of the highest grade, *esp* the head of a department (used as a title prefixed to the name); in N America, a university or college teacher of any grade (prefixed to the name), rising from *assistant professor*, *associate professor* to full *professor* (see also **associate professor** under **associate**); a title assumed by charlatans, quacks, dancing-masters, etc. **profess'orate** *n* professoriate. **profess'oress** *n* (*rare*) a female professor. **professorial** /prof-es-ō'ri-əl *or* prof-es-ö'ri-əl/ *adj*. **professo'rially** *adv*. **professo'riate** *n* the office or chair of a professor; his or her period of office; a body of professors. **profess'orship** *n*.

profession¹ /prə-fesh'ən/ *n* a non-manual occupation requiring some degree of learning or training; a calling, habitual employment; the collective body of people engaged in any profession. [L *professiō*, *-ōnis* from *professus*; see **profess**]
■ **profess'ional** *adj* of, belonging to or relating to a profession; engaged in a profession or in the profession in question; competing for money prizes or against those who sometimes do so; undertaken as a means of subsistence, *opp* to *amateur*; showing the skill, artistry, demeanour or standard of conduct appropriate in a member of a profession or of a particular profession; (of a foul, etc) deliberate, intended (to prevent the opposition from scoring) (*euphem; sport*). ◆ *n* someone who makes his or her living by an art that is also practised at an amateur level; someone who engages in sport for livelihood or gain or against those who do so (with various rules of interpretation for each sport), *opp* to *amateur*; a member of a profession; a person following a career; (in full, **professional examination**) any one of the successive examinations towards a degree in medicine (in Scottish universities). **profess'ionalism** *n* the status of professional; the competence or the correct demeanour of those who are highly trained

and disciplined; the outlook, aim, or restriction of the mere professional; the predominance of professionals in sport. **professionaliza'tion** *or* **-s-** *n*. **profess'ionalize** *or* **-ise** *vt* to give a professional character to; to give over to professionals. **profess'ionally** *adv*.
■ **the oldest profession** prostitution.

profession² see under **profess**.

proffer /prof'ər/ *vt* (**proff'ering**; **proff'ered**) to offer for acceptance, to tender or present; to offer to undertake. ◆ *n* an offer or tender; the act of proffering; an incipient act. [Anglo-Fr *proffrir*, from L *prō* forward, and *offerre* ; see **offer**]
■ **proff'erer** *n*.

proficient /prə- *or* prō-fish'ənt/ *adj* competent; well-skilled; thoroughly qualified. ◆ *n* a person who is making progress in learning (*Shakesp*); an adept; an expert. [L *prōficiens*, *-entis*, prp of *prōficere* to make progress]
■ **profi'cience** (now *rare* or *obs*) *or* **profi'ciency** *n*. **profi'ciently** *adv*.

profile /prō'fīl/ (formerly also *-fēl* and *-fil*) *n* an outline; a head or portrait in a side view; the outline of any object without foreshortening (*art*); a drawing of a vertical section of country, an engineering work, etc; a graph; a short biographical sketch, eg in a newspaper or magazine; an outline of the characteristic features (of eg a particular type of person); an outline of the course of an operation; one's manner, attitude or behaviour considered with regard to the extent to which it attracts attention to oneself and one's activities or reveals one's feelings, intentions, etc, or the extent of one's involvement, etc (as in *low*, *high*, etc *profile*); a public image, *esp* one created and controlled by design. ◆ *vt* to draw in profile; to make an outline of; to show in profile; to give a profile to; to shape the outline of; to write or give a profile of. [Ital *profilo*, from *profilare* to outline, from L *prō* forth, and *filāre* to spin or draw a line]
■ **pro'filer** *n*. **pro'filing** *n* the process of compiling a profile of a person's physical (eg DNA) or psychological characteristics. **pro'filist** *n* someone who draws profiles.

profit /prof'it/ *n* gain; the gain resulting from the use of capital; the excess of selling price over first cost; advantage; an increase in good or value; benefit; improvement. ◆ *vt* to benefit or be of advantage to. ◆ *vi* to gain advantage; to receive profit; to make progress, to improve (*Shakesp*); to be of advantage. [Fr, from L *prōfectus* progress, from *prōficere*, *prōfectum* to make progress]
■ **profitabil'ity** *n*. **prof'itable** *adj* yielding or bringing profit or gain; lucrative; productive. **prof'itableness** *n*. **prof'itably** *adv*. **profiteer'** (*derog*) a person who takes advantage of an emergency to make exorbitant profits. ◆ *vi* to act as a profiteer. **profiteer'ing** *n*. **prof'iter** *n*. **prof'iting** *n*. **prof'itless** *adj* without profit. **prof'itlessly** *adv*.
❑ **profit and loss account** *n* a financial statement recording revenue and expenses, balanced, *usu* annually, to show profits or losses. **profit centre** *n* a department or process in a business for which separate costs and revenue (and therefore profit) can be worked out. **profit margin** *n* the amount of profit a business has after deducting expenditure. **prof'it-orientated** *adj* whose chief aim is profit. **prof'it-sharing** *n* a voluntary agreement under which an employee receives a share, fixed beforehand, of the profits of a business. **prof'it-taker** *n*. **prof'it-taking** *n* the selling-off of shares, commodities, etc, in order to profit from a rise in the purchase price.
■ **with profits** denoting an insurance policy which attracts a bonus based on the company's profits during the year.

profiterole /prə-fit'ə-rōl/ *n* a small puff of choux pastry, *usu* filled with cream and covered with a chocolate sauce. [Fr; dimin of *profit* profit]

profligate /prof'li-git, -gət *or* -gāt/ *adj* debauched, having given oneself over to vice; dissolute; prodigal, rashly extravagant; overthrown, defeated (*obs*). ◆ *n* a person leading a profligate life; someone who is recklessly extravagant or wasteful. [L *prōfligātus*, pap of *prōfligāre*, from *prō* forward, and *flīgere* to dash]
■ **prof'ligacy** /-gə-si/ *n* the state or quality of being profligate; a life devoted to vice; abundance, profusion. **prof'ligately** *adv*.

profluent /prō'flū-ənt/ (*Milton*) *adj* flowing out or onwards. [L *prō* forth, and *fluere* to flow]
■ **pro'fluence** *n*.

Pr. of Man. (*Bible*) *abbrev* : (the Apocryphal Book of the) Prayer of Manasses.

pro-forma or **pro forma** see under **pro³**.

profound /prō- *or* prə-fownd'/ *adj* deep; deep-seated; far below the surface; far-reaching; intense; abstruse; intellectually deep; penetrating deeply into knowledge. ◆ *n* (*poetic*) the sea or ocean; an abyss or great depth. [Fr *profond*, from L *profundus*, from *prō* forward, and *fundus* bottom]
■ **profound'ly** *adv*. **profound'ness** *or* **profundity** /-fund'-/ *n* the state or quality of being profound; the depth of a place, of one's knowledge, etc; something which is profound.

profulgent /prə-ful'jənt or prō-ful'jənt/ adj shining out, radiant. [L prō forth, and fulgens, -entis, prp of fulgēre to shine]

profuse /prō- or prə-fūs'/ adj excessively liberal; lavish; extravagant; copious; overabundant. [L prōfūsus, pap of prōfundere, from prō forth, and fundere to pour]
■ **profuse'ly** adv. **profuse'ness** n. **profuser** /-fūz'ər/ n (Herrick) a prodigal or spendthrift. **profusion** /-fū'zhən/ n the state of being profuse; extravagance; prodigality.

prog[1] /prog/ (inf) n a radio or television programme.

prog[2] /prog/ vt (obs or dialect) to pierce; to prick; to poke. ♦ vi (obs or dialect) to poke about for anything; to forage for food; to beg. ♦ n a pointed instrument (now esp dialect); a thrust (dialect); provisions, esp for a journey (inf). [Origin unknown; perh several distinct words]

prog[3] /prog/ adj short form of **progressive**.
□ **prog rock** n (also **progressive rock**) a genre of rock music, popular esp in the 1970s, featuring complex and often lengthy compositions incorporating elements of classical music and jazz, with lyrics inspired by science fiction, fantasy and mythology.

prog[4] /prog/ (university sl) n a proctor. ♦ vt to proctorize.
■ **progg'ins** n a proctor.

progenitor /prō-jen'i-tər/ n a forefather; an ancestor; a parent (also fig); the founder of a family. [L prōgenitor and prōgeniēs, from prōgignere, from prō before, and gignere, genitum to beget]
■ **progen'itive** adj. **progenito'rial** /-tōr'i-əl or -tör'i-əl/ adj. **progen'itorship** n. **progen'itress** or **progen'itrix** n a female parent or ancestor. **progen'iture** n an act or instance of begetting. **progeny** /proj'ə-ni/ n offspring (also fig); descendants; race; lineage (Shakesp).

progeria /prō-jer'i-ə/ n a rare disease causing premature ageing in children. [Gr pro before, and gēras old age]

progesterone /prō-jes'tə-rōn/ n a female sex hormone that prepares the uterus for the fertilized ovum and maintains pregnancy. [progestin, sterol, and -one]
■ **proges'tin** n (**pro-**[2], gestation, and -in) any hormone concerned with changes before pregnancy, esp **proges'togen** any of a range of hormones of the progesterone type (several synthetic progestogens are used in oral contraceptives).

proggins see under **prog**[4].

proglottis /prō-glot'is/ or **proglottid** /'id/ n (pl **proglott'idēs**) a detachable tapeworm segment. [Gr pro before, and glōttis, -idos a pipe mouthpiece]

prognathous /prog'nə-thəs, also prog-nā'thəs or prōg-nā'thəs/ (zool) adj with a projecting jaw; (of a jaw) projecting (also **prognathic** /prog-nath'ik or prōg-nath'ik/). [Gr pro forward, and gnathos a jaw]
■ **prog'nathism** or /-nath'izm or -nāth'izm/) n.

Progne /prog'nē/ n a personification of the swallow, or sometimes of the nightingale (poetic); an American genus of swallows. [Philomela's sister, L Procnē (or Prognē, from Gr Proknē) transformed into a swallow or a nightingale]

prognosis /prog-nō'sis/ n (pl **prognōs'es** /-ēz/) a forecasting or forecast, esp of the course of a disease. [Gr prognōsis, from pro before, and gignōskein to know]
■ **prognostic** /prog-nost'ik or prəg-nost'ik/ n a foretelling, forecast or prediction; an indication of something to come, an omen; a symptom on which prognosis can be based (med). ♦ adj indicating what is to happen by signs or symptoms; of prognosis. **prognos'ticate** vt to foretell; to indicate the coming of. **prognostica'tion** n. **prognos'ticative** adj. **prognos'ticator** n a predictor or foreteller; a person who predicts coming events, future weather conditions, etc (obs).

prograde /prō'grād/ adj (of metamorphism) from a lower to a higher metamorphic level, or caused by a rise in temperature or pressure (geol); (of movement or rotation) in a forward direction, ie in the same direction as that of adjacent bodies (astron). ♦ vi (geog; of a coastline, etc) to advance seawards because of a build-up of sediment. [**pro-**[2] and contrast with retrograde]
■ **progradā'tion** n.

programme or (esp N Am, and comput) **program** /prō'gram/ n a paper, booklet, or the like, giving an outline of proceedings arranged for an entertainment, conference, course of study, etc, with relevant details; the items of such proceedings collectively; a plan of things to be done; a TV or radio presentation produced for broadcast singly or as one of a series; the sequence of actions to be performed by a computer in dealing with data of a certain kind; a sequence of encoded instructions to a computer to fulfil a task or series of actions; a course of instruction (by book or teaching machine) in which subject-matter is broken down into a logical sequence of short items of information, and a student can check immediately the suitability of his or her responses; a curriculum or course of study (esp US); a public notice (obs Scot). ♦ vt to provide with, enter in, etc a programme; to prepare a program for (a computer, etc); to create a certain pattern of

thought, reaction, etc in the mind of (fig). [Gr programma proclamation, from pro forth, and gramma a letter]
■ **programmabil'ity** n (comput). **programm'able** adj (comput) capable of being programmed to perform a task, calculation, etc automatically. ♦ n a programmable calculator. **programmatic** /-grə-mat'ik/ adj of a programme; of, or of the nature of, programme music. **programmat'ically** adv. **pro'grammed** adj. **pro'grammer** n a person who programs a computer; (also **programme picture**) a B-movie, a low-budget cinema film produced to accompany the main picture of a cinema show. **pro'gramming** n.
□ **programmable read-only memory** n (comput) a type of read-only memory which can be programmed after manufacture but is then fixed. **programmed learning** n learning by programme (qv above). **programme music** n music that is intended to depict a scene or tell a story. **programme picture** see **programmer** above. **programme trading** see **program trading** below. **programming language** n an artificial language with codes, symbols, rules, etc devised to enable people to instruct computers. **Programming Language 1** n a computer programming language which combines the best qualities of commercial- and scientific-oriented languages (abbrev **PL/1**). **program** or **programme trader** n. **program** or **programme trading** n the automatic buying or selling of securities, etc by computer when the price reaches pre-set limits.
■ **programme evaluation and review technique** a method of planning, monitoring and reviewing the progress, costs, etc of a complex project.

progress /prō'gres, sometimes (esp US) pro'/ n a forward movement; an advance; a continuation; an advance to something better or higher in development; a gain in proficiency; a course; movement from place to place; a procession; an official or state journey made by a dignitary, noble or other person of high rank; a circuit. ♦ vi /prə-gres'/, formerly prō'/ to go forward; to make progress; to go on, continue; to go on a state or official journey; to go. ♦ vt to traverse (obs); to cause (esp building or manufacturing work) to proceed steadily. [OFr progresse (now progrès), from L prōgressus, from prō forward, and gradī, gressus to step]
■ **progression** /prə-gresh'ən or prō-gresh'ən/ n motion onward; the act or state of moving onward; progress; movement by successive stages; a regular succession of chords (music); movements of the parts in harmony (music); a change from term to term according to some law (maths); a series of terms so related (see **arithmetic**, **geometry**, **harmony**). **progress'ional** adj. **progress'ionary** adj. **progress'ionism** n sympathy with or advocacy of progress; belief that social or other evolution is towards higher or better things. **progress'ionist** n a believer in progressionism; a progressive; a person who favours progress or reform. ♦ adj of or relating to progressionism or progressionists. **progress'ism** (or /prō' or pro'/) n progressionism. **progress'ist** (or /prō' or pro'/) n a person who advocates a progressive policy; a progressionist. **progress'ive** adj moving forward; making progress; modern, esp displaying or applying liberal or enlightened views or practices; of the nature of progress; advancing by successive stages; (of a disease, condition, etc) increasing steadily in severity or extent; (in games, eg **progressive whist**) played by several sets of players, some of whom move from one table to the next after each hand according to the rules of the game; (of a dance) involving moving on to a new partner at some point in the sequence of movements; advancing towards better and better or higher and higher; in favour of social and political progress or reform; (usu with cap) applied to a political party with progressive policies; (of taxation) in which the rate increases as the amount to be taxed increases; continuous (grammar). ♦ n someone who favours progress or reform; (usu with cap) a member of a party with 'progressive' in its title; the progressive aspect or tense (grammar); a verb in this; any of a sequence of printing proofs showing each colour separately and the cumulative effect of each colour upon the other(s). **progress'ively** adv. **progress'iveness** n. **progress'ivism** n. **progress'ivist** n.
□ **progress chaser** n an employee responsible for monitoring and expediting the progress of work. **progressive rock** see under **prog**[3].
■ **in progress** going on; in course of happening or being produced.

progymnasium /prō-jim-nā'zi-əm or (Ger) prō-gim-nä'zi-ŭm/ n in Germany, a gymnasium (qv) for pupils up to age 16 only, at which university entrance qualifications are not obtainable. [Ger]

prohibit /prō- or prə-hib'it/ vt to forbid; to prevent. [L prohibēre, prohibitum, from prō before, and habēre to have]
■ **prohib'iter** or **prohib'itor** n. **prohibition** /prō-hi-bi'shən or prō-i-bi'shən/ n the act of prohibiting, forbidding or interdicting; an interdict; the forbidding by law of the manufacture and sale of alcoholic drinks; (usu with cap) the period (1920–33) when the manufacture and sale of alcoholic drinks was prohibited in the USA. **prohibi'tionary** adj. **prohibi'tionism** n. **prohibi'tionist** n a person who favours prohibition, esp of the manufacture and sale of alcoholic drinks. **prohibitive** /-hib'/ adj tending to make impossible or preclude;

(of costs, charges, etc) unaffordably high. **prohib'itively** adv. **prohib'itiveness** n. prohibitor see **prohibiter** above. **prohib'itory** adj that prohibits or forbids; forbidding.

proign /proin/ an obsolete form of **prune**[2].

proin or **proine** /proin/ obsolete forms of **prune**[1,2,3].

proinsulin /prō-in'sū-lin/ n an inactive substance produced in the pancreas that is converted by enzymes into active insulin. [**pro-**[2]]

project /proj'ekt or prō'jekt/ n a scheme of something to be done; a proposal for an undertaking; an undertaking; an exercise usu involving study and/or experimentation followed by the construction of something and/or the preparation of a report (educ); a projection; a notion (Shakesp); speculative imagination (obs). ♦ vt /pra-jekt' or prō-jekt'/ to throw out or forward; to speak or sing in such a way as to aim (the voice) at the rear of the auditorium, etc (theatre, etc); to throw, kick or propel; to cause to jut out or stretch out; to scheme, plan or devise; to set out, set before the mind (Shakesp); to cast (eg a light, shadow or image) on a surface or into space; to throw an image of; to show outlined against a background; to predict or expect on the basis of past results or present trends; to derive a new figure from, so that each point on the new figure corresponds to a point of the original figure according to some rule, esp by a system of parallel, converging or diverging rays through the original points meeting a surface (geom); to externalize; to make objective. ♦ vi to jut out; to throw projecting powder on a metal which is to be transmuted (alchemy). [L prōjicere, prōjectum, from prō forth, and jacere to throw]
■ **projec'tile** adj caused by projection; impelling; capable of being thrown or thrust out or forward. ♦ n /prō-jek'tīl or pra-jek'tīl, also, less commonly, proj'ik-tīl or (US) -til/ n a body projected by force; a missile, esp one discharged by a gun. **projec'ting** n and adj. **projec'tion** /-shan/ n an act or method of projecting; the fact or state of being projected; planning; something which is projected; an instance of jutting out; something which juts out; the standing out of a figure; a figure obtained by projecting another (geom); a forecast; a method of representing geographical detail on a plane, or the representation so obtained (also **map projection**); a projected image; the reading of one's own emotions and experiences into a particular situation (psychol); a person's unconscious attributing to other people of certain attitudes towards himself or herself, usu as a defence against his or her own guilt, inferiority, etc (psychol); the throwing in of powdered philosopher's stone (projecting powder) to effect transmutation, hence transmutation itself in general (alchemy). **projec'tional** adj. **projec'tionist** n an operator of a film projector; an operator of certain television equipment; someone who projects or makes projections, esp in map-making. **projec'tive** adj projecting; of projection; derivable by projection (geom); unchanged by projection (geom). **projectivity** /proj-ak-tiv'i-ti/ n. **projectiza'tion** or **-s-** n the direction of aid to developing countries towards a specific project, without regard to wider issues or needs. **project'ment** n (rare) a design or plan. **projec'tor** n an apparatus for projecting, esp an image or a beam of light; someone who plans some enterprise; a promoter of speculative schemes for moneymaking; a straight line joining a point with its projection (geom). **projec'ture** n a jutting out.
❑ **projecting powder** or **powder of projection** n (alchemy) the philosopher's stone in powder form. **projection television** n optical presentation of a TV picture on a separate open screen. **projective geometry** n a branch of geometry dealing with **projective properties**, ie those properties of figures which remain unchanged when the figures are projected. **projective test** n (psychol) a test that uses one's responses to images, words, etc to reveal unconscious elements of personality. **project-manage** vt. **project manager** n a person responsible for planning and expediting a project.

projet de loi /pro-zhā da lwa'/ (Fr) n a legislative bill.

prokaryon /prō-kar'i-an/ (biol) n (also **procar'yon**) the cell of a blue-green alga, bacterium, etc, without a nucleus containing chromosomes but with its DNA lying freely in the cytoplasm (cf **eukaryon**). [**pro-**[2], and Gr karyon a kernel]
■ **prokar'yote** /-ōt/ or **prokar'yot** /-at/ n a (usu unicellular) organism with such a cell or cells (also adj). **prokaryot'ic** adj.

proke /prōk/ (dialect) vt and vi to poke. [Origin obscure]
■ **prōk'er** n a poker.

prolactin /prō-lak'tin/ n a hormone produced by the pituitary gland, which stimulates lactation and also acts as a contraceptive.

prolamine /prō'la-mēn/ or **prolamin** /prō'la-min/ n one of a group of alcohol-soluble proteins.

prolapse /prō-laps' or prō'laps/ (med) n (also **prolap'sus**) a falling down or out of place (usu of an organ, esp the womb). ♦ vi /-laps'/ to slip out of place. [L prōlābī, prōlapsus to slip forward, from prō forward, and lābī to slip]

prolate /prō'lāt or sometimes prō-lāt'/ adj (of eg a spheroid) drawn out along the polar diameter, opp to oblate; widespread. ♦ vt /prō-lāt'/

(obs) to lengthen out in utterance. [L prōlātus produced, from prō forward, and lātus, used as pap of ferre to carry]
■ **pro'lately** adv. **pro'lateness** n. **prolation** /prō-lā'shan/ n an utterance; the time-ratio of a semibreve to a minim (three minims to a semibreve in **great** or **perfect prolation**, two in **lesser** or **imperfect prolation**) (medieval music). **prolative** /prō-lā'tiv or prō'la-tiv/ adj (grammar) completing the predicate.

prole[1] /prōl/ (inf) n and adj proletarian.

prole[2] obsolete form of **prowl**.

proleg /prō'leg/ (zool) n an insect larva's abdominal leg, distinguished from a thoracic or 'true' leg. [**pro-**[1] (2) and **leg**]

prolegomena /prō-le-gom'i-na/ n pl (sing **prolegom'enon**) (sometimes used as sing) an introduction, esp to a treatise; an introductory study. [Gr prolegomenon, pl -a, neuter of prp passive of prolegein, from pro before, and legein to say]
■ **prolegom'enary** or **prolegom'enous** adj.

prolepsis /prō-lep'sis or prō-lēp'sis/ n (pl **prolep'sēs**) anticipation; the rhetorical figure of anticipation, ie the use of a word not literally applicable until a later time; a figure of speech by which objections are anticipated and answered. [Gr prolēpsis, from pro before, and lambanein to take]
■ **prolep'tic** or **prolep'tical** adj. **prolep'tically** adv.

proler obsolete form of **prowler**.

proletarian /prō-li-tā'ri-an/ adj of the poorest labouring class; of the proletariat; having little or no property. ♦ n a member of the poorest class; a member of the proletariat; a plant without reserves of food (bot). [L prōlētārius (in ancient Rome) a citizen of the sixth and lowest class, who served the state not with his property but with his offspring (prōlēs)]
■ **proletā'rianism** n the condition of the poorest classes. **proletarianizā'tion** or **-s-** n. **proletā'rianize** or **-ise** vt. **proletā'riat** or (esp formerly) **proletā'riate** n the poorest labouring class; the wage-earning class, esp those without capital. **pro'letary** /-ar-i/ n and adj proletarian.

prolicide /prō'li-sīd/ n the killing of offspring; the killing off of the human race. [L prōlēs offspring, and caedere to kill]
■ **prolicī'dal** adj.

pro-life, **pro-lifer** see under **pro-**[1].

proliferate /prō- or pra-lif'a-rāt/ vi to grow by multiplication of parts (cells, buds, shoots, etc) (biol); to reproduce by proliferation (biol); to reproduce abundantly (biol); to greatly increase in numbers rapidly. ♦ vt to produce by multiplication of parts; to cause to grow or increase rapidly. [L prōlēs offspring, and ferre to bear]
■ **proliferā'tion** n a great and rapid increase in numbers; growth by multiplication of cells (biol); production of vegetative shoots from a reproductive structure (biol); repeated production of new parts (biol); production of shoots that may become new plants (biol); production of abnormal or supernumerary parts (biol); a structure formed by proliferating (biol); the spread of nuclear weapons capability to countries not already possessing such weapons. **prolif'erative** or **prolif'erous** adj. **prolif'erously** adv.

prolific /prō- or pra-lif'ik/ adj reproductive; fertilizing; fertile; producing many offspring; (of an author, artist, etc) producing many works; fruitful; abundant. [L prōlēs offspring, and facere to make]
■ **prolif'icacy** /-a-si/ n. **prolif'ical** adj (rare or obs). **prolif'ically** adv. **prolificā'tion** n the production of young; development of a shoot by continued growth of a flower (bot). **prolificity** /-is'i-ti/ n. **prolif'icness** n.

proline /prō'lēn or -lin/ n an amino acid commonly occurring in proteins. [Ger Prolin, contracted from Pyrrolidin pyrrolidine]

prolix /prō'liks or prō-liks'/ adj long and wordy; long-winded; dwelling too long on particulars; long (obs or rare). [L prōlixus, from prō forward, and liquī to flow]
■ **prolixious** /prō-lik'shas/ adj (Shakesp) dilatory, tiresome or superfluous. **prolix'ity** n. **prolix'ly** adv. **prolix'ness** n.

proll /prōl/, **proller** /prō'lar/ obsolete forms of **prowl** and **prowler**.

prolly /prol'i/ (sl) adv probably. [Contraction]

prolocutor /prō-lok'ū-tar/ n (also fem **prōloc'utrix**) a spokesman; a chairman, esp of the lower house of Convocation in the Anglican Church. [L prōlocūtor, from prōloquī, -locūtus to speak out, from loquī to speak]
■ **prolocu'tion** /prō- or pro-/ n an introductory speech or saying. **prōloc'utorship** n.

PROLOG or **Prolog** /prō'log/ (comput) n a high-level programming language. [programming logic]

prologue or (N Am) **prolog** /prō'log/ n in a classical Greek play, the part before the entry of the chorus; an introduction to a poem, etc; a speech before a play; the speaker of a prologue; an introductory event or action. ◆ *vt* to introduce; to preface. [Fr, from L *prologus*, from Gr *prologos*, from *pro* before, and *logos* speech]

■ **pro'logize** or **-ise** /-*gīz* or -*jīz*/ *vi* to speak a prologue (also **pro'loguize** or **-ise**).

prolong /prō- or prə-*long*'/ *vt* to lengthen out; to postpone (*Spenser* and *Shakesp*). ◆ *vi* to lengthen out. [L *prōlongāre*, from *prō* forward, and *longus* long]

■ **prolongable** /prō-*long*'ə-bl/ *adj*. **prolongate** /prō'*long-gāt*/ *vt* to lengthen. **prolongation** /-*long-gā*'shən/ *n* a lengthening out; a piece added in continuation; a continuation. **prolonger** /-*long*'ər/ *n*.

prolonge /prō-*lonj*' or prō-*lōzh*/ (*milit*) *n* a rope for a gun-carriage. [Fr]

prolusion /pra-, prō-*loo*'zhən or -*lū*'/ *n* a preliminary performance, activity or display; an essay preparatory to a more solid treatise. [L *prōlūsiō*, -*ōnis*, from *prō* before, and *lūdere*, *lūsum* to play]

■ **prolu'sory** /-sə-ri/ *adj*.

PROM /prom/ (*comput*) *abbrev* : programmable read-only memory.

prom /prom/ *n* a contraction of **promenade**; a promenade concert; a school or college dance (*US*).

❑ **prom queen** *n* (*US*) a female student elected by her peers to preside over a school prom.

■ **the Proms** a series of promenade concerts held annually in London.

promachos /prom'ə-kos or prom'ə-hhos/ *n* a champion or defender; a tutelary god. [Gr]

pro-marketeer see under **pro-**[1].

promenade /prom-i-*näd*' or prom', also (*esp US*) *prom-i-nād*'/ *n* a walk, ride or drive, for pleasure, show or gentle exercise; (also /-*näd*'/) a processional sequence in a dance; a school or college dance, a prom (*US*); a place where people walk to and fro; a paved terrace on a sea front; an esplanade. ◆ *vi* to walk, ride or drive about, *esp* in a stately or leisurely manner; (also /-*näd*'/) to make a promenade in dancing. ◆ *vt* to lead about and exhibit; to walk, ride or drive about or through. [Fr, from *promener* to lead about (*se promener* to take a walk), from L *prōmināre* to drive forwards, from *prō* forward, and *mināre* to push, *mināri* to threaten]

■ **promenad'er** *n* someone who promenades; a member of the standing portion of the audience at a promenade concert.

❑ **promenade concert** *n* one in which part of the audience stands throughout and can move about. **promenade deck** *n* a deck on which passengers may walk about.

prometal /prō'me-tl/ *n* a kind of cast iron highly resistant to heat.

promethazine /prō-*meth*'ə-zēn/ *n* a drug used, generally in the form of its hydrochloride, as an antihistamine, to counteract travel sickness, and as a pre-operative sedative. [**propyl**, **methyl**, **azo-** and **-ine**[1]]

Promethean /prō-*mē*'thi-ən or -thyən/ *adj* relating or alluding to *Prometheus* who, according to Greek myth, stole fire from heaven, for which Zeus chained him to a rock to be tortured by a vulture; daringly innovative. ◆ *n* a glass tube containing sulphuric acid and an inflammable mixture brought together by pressing, an early kind of match.

■ **promē'thium** (formerly **promē'theum**) *n* a radioactive lanthanide element (symbol **Pm**; atomic no 61).

prominent /prom'i-nənt/ *adj* standing out; projecting; most easily seen; catching the eye or attention; in the public eye; important. [L *prōminens*, -*entis*, prp of *prōminēre* to jut forth, from *prō* forth, and *minae* projections, threats]

■ **prom'inence** *n* the state or quality of being prominent; a prominent point or thing; a projection. **prom'inency** *n* a prominence. **prom'inently** *adv*.

■ **solar prominence** a reddish cloud of incandescent gas shooting out from the sun, visible during a total eclipse.

promiscuous /pra- or prō-*mis*'kū-əs/ *adj* confusedly or indiscriminately mixed; collected together without order; indiscriminate (now *usu* referring to someone indulging in indiscriminate sexual intercourse); haphazard; belonging to a mixed set; far from choice (*old sl*); casual, accidental (*inf*). [L *prōmiscuus*, from *prō* (intensive), and *miscēre* to mix]

■ **promiscū'ity** /prom-/ *n* mixture without order or distinction; promiscuous sexual intercourse. **promis'cuously** *adv*.

promise /prom'is/ *n* an undertaking to do or keep from doing something; expectation, or that which raises expectation; a ground for hope of future excellence; fulfilment of what is promised (*rare*). ◆ *vt* to undertake by promise to do, give, etc; to betroth; to encourage to expect; to give reason to expect; to assure; to undertake to bestow. ◆ *vi* to make a promise or promises; to give rise to or reason for hopes or expectations; to act as sponsor (*rare*). [L *prōmissum* neuter pap of *promittere* to send forward, from *prō* forward, and *mittere* to send]

■ **promisee'** *n* the person to whom a promise is made. **prom'iseful** *adj*. **prom'iseless** *adj*. **prom'iser** *n*. **prom'ising** *adj* giving grounds for hope or expectation; likely to turn out well. **prom'isingly** *adv*. **prom'isor** *n* (*law*) the person making a promise. **promiss'ive** /prə-/ *adj* conveying a promise; of the nature of a promise. **promiss'or** *n* (*Roman law*) the maker of a promise. **prom'issorily** *adv*. **prom'issory** *adj* containing a promise of some undertaking to be fulfilled.

❑ **prom'ise-breach** *n* (*Shakesp*) the breaking of a promise. **prom'ise-breaker** *n* (*Shakesp*). **prom'ise-crammed** *adj* (*Shakesp*) fed to repletion with empty promises. **promised land** *n* the land promised by God to Abraham and his descendants, Canaan; heaven. **prom'ise-keeping** *n* (*Shakesp*). **promissory note** *n* a written promise to pay a sum of money on some future day or on demand.

■ **be promised** to have a previous engagement (*Shakesp*); to be betrothed (to another). **breach of promise** see under **breach**. **promises, promises** (*inf*) a sceptical response to an assurance of future action. **the Promise** the assurance of God to Abraham that his descendants would become the chosen people.

prommer /prom'ər/ (*inf*) *n* a (regular) attender of promenade concerts, *esp* a promenader.

promo /prō'mō/ (*inf*) *n* (*pl* **pro'mos**) a short form of **promotion**, *esp* in the sense of a promotional video recording (also *adj*).

promontory /prom'ən-tər-i or -tri/ *n* a headland or high cape; a projection, ridge or eminence (*anat*). ◆ *adj* standing out like a promontory. [LL *prōmontōrium* (L *prōmunturium*), assimilated to *mōns* mountain]

promote /pra-*mōt*' or prō-*mōt*'/ *vt* to raise (a person, *esp* an employee) to a higher grade; to further; to further the progress of; in chess, to raise (a pawn) to the rank of queen; to move to a higher division of a league (*sport*); to take steps for the passage or formation of; to set in motion (eg the office of a judge in a criminal suit) (*church law*; *obs*); to encourage the sales of by advertising; to help forward (*obs* or *dialect*). [L *prōmovēre*, -*mōtum*, from *prō* forward, and *movēre* to move]

■ **promotabil'ity** *n*. **promo'table** *adj* able to be promoted or suitable for promotion. **promō'ter** *n* a person who promotes; a person who takes part in the setting-up of companies; the organizer of a sporting event, *esp* a boxing match; a professional informer (*obs*); a DNA region in front of the coding sequence of a gene, involved in the initiation of transcription (*biol*); a substance that increases the efficiency of a catalyst (*chem*); a substance that encourages the formation or growth of tumour cells (*med*). **promō'tion** /-shən/ *n* the act of promoting; advancement in rank or in honour; encouragement; preferment; a venture, *esp* in show business; advertising in general, or an effort to publicize and increase the sales of a particular product. **promō'tional** *adj*. **promō'tive** *adj*. **promō'tor** *n* a person who presents candidates for graduation in Scottish universities.

■ **be on one's promotion** to have the right to or hope of promotion; to be on good behaviour with a view to promotion.

prompt /prompt or promt/ *adj* ready in action; performed at once; paid or due at once; ready for delivery; readily inclined (*Shakesp*). ◆ *adv* promptly, punctually, to the minute. ◆ *vt* to incite; to instigate; to move to action; to supply forgotten words to, *esp* in a theatrical performance; to help with words or facts when at a loss; to suggest to the mind. ◆ *n* a time limit for payment (*commerce*); an act of prompting; words provided by the prompter; a question, statement or fixed sequence of characters which appears on a computer screen, showing that the operator may proceed, or choose from set options. [L *promptus*, from *prōmere* to bring forward]

■ **prompt'er** *n* someone who prompts, *esp* actors. **prompt'ing** *n*. **prompt'itude** *n* promptness; readiness; quickness of decision and action. **prompt'ly** *adv*. **prompt'ness** *n*. **prompt'uary** *n* a repository; a reference book of facts. **prompt'ure** *n* (*Shakesp*) a suggestion; instigation.

❑ **prompt book** or **prompt copy** *n* a copy of a play for the prompter's use. **prompt box** *n* a box for the prompter in a theatre. **prompt neutron** *n* one released in a primary nuclear fission process with practically zero delay. **prompt'-note** *n* (*commerce*) a reminder note of the time-limit for a payment. **prompt side** *n* the side of the stage where the prompter is, *usu* to the actor's left in Britain, to the right in the USA.

promulgate /prom'əl-gāt or (*US*) pra-*mul*'gāt/ *vt* to proclaim or announce publicly; to make widely known; to put (eg a law) into effect by proclamation (also (*archaic*) **promulge** /prō-*mulj*'/). [L *prōmulgāre*, -*ātum*]

■ **promulgā'tion** *n*. **prom'ulgātor** *n*.

promuscis /prō-*mus*'is/ (*zool*) *n* a proboscis, *esp* of Hemiptera. [L *promuscis*, -*idis*, an altered form of *proboscis*]

■ **promusc'idate** *adj* like or having a promuscis.

promycelium /prō-mī-*sē*'li-əm/ (*bot*) *n* (*pl* **promyce'lia** /-li-ə/) a short germ-tube put out by some fungal spores, producing spores of different types. [**pro-**[2]]

pronaos /prō-nā'os/ n (pl **prona'oi**) the vestibule in front of a temple. [Gr *pronāos*, from *pro* before, and *nāos* a temple]

prone[1] /prōn/ adj with the face, ventral surface or palm of the hand downward; prostrate; directed downward; (loosely) lying or laid flat; descending steeply; disposed, inclined, naturally tending; willing; ready, eager (*Shakesp*); in *Measure for Measure* I.2, of uncertain meaning, but perhaps meaning passive, or with downcast eyes, or fervent (*Shakesp*). ◆ *combining form* liable to suffer a specified thing, as in *accident-prone*. [L *prōnus* bent forward]
■ **prōn'ate** vt and vi (*physiol*) to turn (the foot) sole inwards; to turn (the hand) palm downward or backward with radius and ulna crossed, *opp* to supinate. **prōnā'tion** n (*physiol*) the act of pronating. **prōnā'tor** n (*physiol*) the muscle of the forearm that pronates the hand. **prone'ly** adv. **prone'ness** n.

prone[2] /prōn/ (*obs*) n a place in a church where intimations are given out; hence, a homily. [Fr *prône*]
■ **proneur** /prō-nœr'/ n a flatterer.

pronephros /prō-nef'ros/ (*zool*) n in vertebrates, the anterior portion of the kidney, functional in the embryo but functionless and often absent in the adult. [**pro-**[2] and Gr *nephros* kidney]
■ **proneph'ric** adj.

prong /prong/ n a tine, tooth or spike of a fork or forked object; a tine, spur or projection, eg on an antler; a fork of any kind (now chiefly *dialect*); a fork of a stream or inlet (*US*). ◆ vt to stab with a prong; to furnish with prongs. [ME *prange*; origin obscure]
■ **pronged** adj having prongs.
□ **prong'buck** n the pronghorn (properly, the male). **prong'-hoe** n a hoe with prongs. **prong'horn** n an American antelope-like ruminant (*Antilocapra americana*), the only representative of the family Antilocapridae, with deciduous horns pronged in front. **prong'-horned** adj.

pronominal see under **pronoun**.

pronotum /prō-nō'təm/ n (pl **pronō'ta**) the back of an insect's prothorax. [**pro-**[2], and Gr *nōton* back]
■ **pronō'tal** adj.

pronoun /prō'nown/ n a word used instead of a noun, noun phrase, etc already known or understood from the context, or (eg *it*) as a dummy subject or object with little or no meaning. [**pro-**[1]]
■ **pronominal** /prə-nom'in-əl or prō-nom'in-əl/ adj belonging to, or of the nature of, a pronoun. **pronom'inally** adv.

pronounce /prə-nowns' or prō-nowns'/ vt to proclaim; to utter formally or rhetorically; to declare; to utter; to articulate. ◆ vi to pass judgement; to articulate one's words. ◆ n (*Milton*) pronouncement. [Fr *prononcer*, from L *prōnūntiāre*, from *prō* forth, and *nūntiāre* to announce, from *nūntius* a messenger]
■ **pronounce'able** adj capable of being pronounced. **pronounced'** adj marked with emphasis; marked, very noticeable. **pronoun'cedly** /-səd-li/ adv. **pronounce'ment** n a confident or authoritative assertion or declaration; the act of pronouncing. **pronoun'cer** n. **pronoun'cing** n and adj. **pronunciation** /prō-nun-si-ā'shən/ n a way of pronouncing; articulation.

pronto /pron'tō/ (*inf*) adv promptly, quickly. [Sp, from L *prōmptus* at hand]

pronucleus /pro-nū'kli-əs/ (*biol*) n the nucleus of a germ-cell after meiosis and before fertilization. [**pro-**[2]]
■ **pronū'clear** adj.

pronunciamento /prə- or prō-nun-si-ə-men'tō/ n (pl **pronunciamen'tos** or **pronunciamen'toes**) a manifesto; a formal proclamation. [Sp]

pronunciation see under **pronounce**.

pronuncio /prō-nun'shi-ō/ n (pl **pronun'cios**) a papal ambassador of lower diplomatic status than a nuncio. [**pro-**[1] (2)]

proo or **pruh** /proo/ (*Scot*) interj a call to a cow to come near, or to a horse to stop.

prooemium /prō-ē'mi-əm/, also **prooemion** /-on/ same as **proem**.

pro-oestrus /prō-ēs'trəs/ (*zool*) n in mammals, the coming-on of heat in the oestrus cycle. [**pro-**[2]]

proof /proof/ n (pl **proofs**) something which proves or establishes the truth of anything; the fact, act or process of proving or showing to be true; demonstration; evidence that convinces the mind and goes toward determining the decision of a court; an instrument of evidence in documentary form (*law*); the taking of evidence by a judge upon an issue framed in pleading (*Scots law*); a trial before a judge without a jury (*Scots law*); a checking operation (*maths*); a test; experience (*obs*); issue, outcome or upshot (*obs*); testing, *esp* of guns; ability to stand a test; invulnerability; impenetrability; armour of proof (see below); a standard strength of spirit (alcohol and water of relative density 12/13 at 51°F, ie 49.28 per cent of alcohol by weight); an impression taken for correction (*printing*); an early impression of an

engraving; a coin, intended for display, etc rather than circulation, struck from polished dies on polished blanks (also **proof coin**); the first print from a negative (*photog*). ◆ adj impervious; invulnerable; of standard strength (of alcohol). ◆ vt to make impervious, *esp* to water; to take a proof of; to test. ◆ *combining form* denoting (to make) able to withstand or resist, as in *waterproof, childproof, weatherproof*, etc. [OFr *prove* (Fr *preuve*); see the ety for **prove** for an explanation of the vowel in *obs* or *Scot* forms **preeve, prief, priefe**]
■ **proof'ing** n the process of making waterproof, gasproof, etc; material used for this purpose. **proof'less** adj lacking proof or evidence.
□ **proof'-charge** n a charge used to test the strength of a gun. **proof'-correct** vt (*printing*) to correct in proof. **proof'-correcting** or **proof correction** n. **proof'-house** n a building fitted out for proving firearms. **proof'-mark** n a mark stamped on a gun to show that it has stood the test. **proof'-puller** n (*printing*) a person who pulls proofs. **proof'read** vt and vi to read and correct (printed matter) in proof. **proof'reader** n a person who reads printed proofs to look for and correct errors. **proof'reading** n. **proof sheet** n an impression taken on a slip of paper for correction before the final printing. **proof spirit** n a standard mixture of alcohol and water. **proof text** n a passage of the Bible adduced in proof of a doctrine.
■ **armour of proof** (*hist*) armour that has been tested, or can be confidently relied on. **artist's proof** a first impression from an engraved plate or block. **burden of proof** see under **burden**[1]. **over** or **under proof** containing in 100 volumes enough alcohol for so many volumes more, or less, than 100. **proof before letters** a proof taken before the title is engraved on the plate.

prootic /prō-ot'ik/ (*anat*) adj in front of the ear. ◆ n an anterior bone of the auditory capsule. [**pro-**[2], and Gr *ous, ōtos* ear]

PROP /prop/ abbrev: Preservation of the Rights of Prisoners.

prop[1] /prop/ n a rigid support; a supplementary support; a stay; a strut; a timber supporting a mine roof; a supporter or upholder; a leg (*sl*); a boxer's extended arm (*sl*); either of the two forwards at the ends of the front row of the scrum (also **prop forward**; *rugby*); an act of propping in a horse (*horse-racing, orig Aust*). ◆ vt (**propp'ing; propped**) to hold up by means of something placed under or against (often with *up*); to support or sustain (often with *up*); to keep (a failing enterprise, etc) going (often with *up*); to hit straight or knock down (*sl*). ◆ vi (*horse-racing, orig Aust*) (of a horse) to stop suddenly. [ME *proppe*; cf Du *proppe* vine-prop, support]
■ **propp'ant** n (*mining*) a material, eg sand, used to keep open fissures in an oil-bearing sediment (see also **fracking**).
□ **prop forward** see n above. **prop'-root** n a root growing down from a trunk or branch, serving to prop up a tree.

prop[2] /prop/ n an informal short form of: propeller; (theatrical) property; (geometrical) proposition.
■ **props** n pl stage properties. ◆ n sing a person in charge of theatrical properties.
□ **prop-jet** n see separate entry. **prop shaft** see **propeller shaft** under **propel**.

prop[3] /prop/ (*sl*) n a tiepin; a brooch. [Du *prop*]

prop. abbrev: proper; properly; property; proposition; proprietor.

propaedeutic /prō-pē-dū'tik/ n (often in *pl*) a preliminary study. [Gr *propaideuein* to teach beforehand, from *pro* before, and *paideuein* to teach]
■ **propaedeut'ic** or **propaedeut'ical** adj.

propaganda /prop-ə-gan'də/ n the organized spreading of doctrine, true or false information, opinions, etc, *esp* to bring about change or reform; an association or scheme for doing this; the information, etc spread; (with *cap*) a Roman Catholic committee, founded in 1622, responsible for foreign missions and the training of missionaries. [L *congregatio de propaganda fide* congregation for propagating the faith, the full title of the Propaganda]
■ **propagan'dism** n the practice of propagating tenets or principles; zeal in spreading one's opinions; proselytism. **propagan'dist** n and adj. **propagandis'tic** adj. **propagan'dize** or **-ise** vt and vi.
□ **propaganda machine** n all the means employed in the process of spreading propaganda; the process itself.

propagate /prop'ə-gāt/ vt to increase by natural process; to multiply; to pass on; to transmit; to spread from one to another; to increase (*obs*). ◆ vi to multiply; to breed. [L *prōpāgāre, -ātum*, connected with *prōpāgō* a layer]
■ **prop'agable** adj. **propagā'tion** n. **prop'agātive** adj. **prop'agātor** n someone or something that propagates; a heated, covered box in which plants may be grown from seed or cuttings. **propage** /prō-päj'/ vt (*Congreve*) to beget or propagate. **prop'agule** or **prōpag'ulum** n a small plant outgrowth, eg a bud or a spore, which becomes detached from the parent and grows into a new plant (*bot*); any part of an organism from which a new individual can be produced (*biol*); the

minimum population of a species from which a new colony can be produced (*ecology*).

propale /prō-pāl'/ (*obs Scot*) *vt* to disclose. ◆ *vi* (*Walter Scott*) to make a display. [LL *prōpalāre*, from *prōpalam* openly, from *prō* forth, and *palam* openly]

propane /prō'pān/ *n* a hydrocarbon gas (C_3H_8), the third member of the alkane series. [**propionic acid**]

■ **propanol** /prō'pə-nol/ *n* propyl alcohol. **prō'panone** *n* acetone. ☐ **propanō'ic acid** same as **propionic acid**.

proparoxytone /prō-pa-rok'si-tōn/ *adj* (in ancient Greek) having the acute accent on the third last syllable; having heavy stress on the third last syllable. ◆ *n* a word accented or stressed in this way. [Gr *proparoxytonos*; see **paroxytone**]

propel /prə-pel'/ or /prō-pel'/ *vt* (**propell'ing**; **propelled'**) to drive forward; to cause to move. [L *prōpellere*, from *prō* forward, and *pellere* to drive]

■ **propell'ant** *n* something which propels; an explosive for propelling projectiles; the fuel used to propel a rocket, etc; the gas in an aerosol spray. **propell'ent** *adj* driving. ◆ *n* a driving agent; a motive. **propell'er** *n* someone who, or something which, propels; a driving mechanism; a shaft with spiral blades (**screw-propeller**) for driving a ship, aeroplane, etc; a steamer with a screw-propeller; a helical device for blowing air (**air-propeller, propeller fan**); an artificial bait which spins (*angling*). **propel'ment** *n* propulsion; a propelling mechanism. ☐ **propell'er-blade** *n*. **propell'er-head** *n* (*sl*) an obsessively studious or technologically-minded person. **propeller shaft** *n* the shaft of a propeller; the driving shaft between the gearbox and the rear axle in a motor vehicle (also **prop shaft**). **propelling pencil** *n* a pencil with a replaceable lead held in a casing that can be turned to push the lead forward as it is worn down.

propend /prə-pend'/ or /prō-pend'/ (*Shakesp*) *vi* to incline. [L *prōpendēre, -pensum* to hang forward]

■ **propend'ent** *adj* (*obs*) inclining or inclined. **propense** /-pens'/ *adj* (*obs*) inclined; sometimes used in the sense of *prepense*, deliberate, premeditated. **propense'ly** *adv*. **propense'ness, propen'sion** (*Shakesp*) or (*now usu*) **propens'ity** *n* inclination of mind; favourable inclination; a tendency to good or evil; disposition; a tendency to move in a certain direction. **propen'sive** *adj* (*obs*) inclined.

propene, propenoic acid see **propylene** under **propyl**.

propense, propensity, etc see under **propend**.

proper /prop'ər/ *adj* own; appropriate; peculiar; confined to one; in natural colouring (*heraldry*); strict; strictly applicable; strictly so-called (*usu* after *n*); thorough, out-and-out (*now* *inf*); actual, real; befitting; decorous, seemly; conforming strictly to convention; goodly; belonging to only one; comely; used only on a particular day or festival (*church*). ◆ *n* (*church*) a service, psalm, etc set apart for a particular day or occasion. ◆ *adv* (*inf*) very, exceedingly; properly. [Fr *propre*, from L *proprius* own]

■ **prop'erly** *adv* in a proper manner; strictly; entirely, extremely (*inf*). **prop'erness** *n*. ☐ **proper chant** *n* (*obs*) the key of C major. **proper-false'** *adj* (*Shakesp*) handsome and deceitful. **proper fraction** *n* a fraction that has a numerator of a lower value than the denominator. **proper motion** *n* a star's apparent motion relative to the celestial sphere, due partly to its own movement (**peculiar motion**), and partly to that of the solar system (**parallactic motion**). **proper noun** or **proper name** *n* the name of a particular person, animal, thing, place, etc, in English *usu* written with an initial capital letter, *opp* to *common noun*.

properdin /prō-pûr'din/ *n* a natural immunizing substance varyingly present in the blood, possibly with a bearing on resistance to malignant disease. [L *prō* for, and *perdere* to destroy]

properispomenon /prō-per-i-spom'ə-non/ *n* (*pl* **properispom'ena** /-nə/) (in ancient Greek) a word with the circumflex accent on the penultimate syllable (also *adj*). [Gr *properispōmenon*, neuter prp passive of *properispaein* to put a circumflex on the penultimate syllable (see **perispomenon**)]

property /prop'ər-ti/ *n* that which is proper to any person or thing; a quality that is always present; a characteristic; an essential detail (*Shakesp*); any quality; propriety, fitness (*obs*); that which is one's own; the condition of being one's own; a piece of land owned by somebody; the right of possessing, employing, etc; ownership; an asset, something which brings profit or income (see also **hot property** under **hot**[1]); an article required on the stage (often shortened to **prop**); a mere tool or cat's-paw (*obs*); individuality, personal identity (*Shakesp*). ◆ *vt* (*Shakesp*) to treat as a property; to appropriate. ◆ *adj* of the nature of a stage property. [OFr *properte*; see **propriety**]

■ **prop'ertied** *adj* imbued with properties (*Shakesp*); possessing property. ☐ **property band** *n* any of the various ranges of house values, on the basis of which sums payable under the Council Tax are calculable.

property man, master, mistress, etc *n* the person who has charge of stage properties. **property qualification** *n* a qualification (eg for office or voting) depending on possession of a certain amount of property. **property room** *n* the room in which stage properties are kept. **property tax** *n* a tax levied on property, at the rate of so much per cent on its value.

prophage /prō'fāj/ (*biol*) *n* a phage genome which replicates in synchrony with its host, into whose genome it is often integrated. [**pro-**[2]]

prophase /prō'fāz/ (*biol*) *n* the first stage of mitosis or meiosis during which chromosomes condense and become recognizably discrete. [**pro-**[2]]

prophecy /prof'i-si/ *n* an inspired or prophetic utterance; a prediction; the public interpretation of Scripture, or preaching (*obs*). [OFr *prophecie*, from L *prophētīa*, from Gr *prophēteia*, from *prophētēs* prophet]

prophesy /prof'i-sī/ *vi* (*pat* and *pap* **proph'esied**) to utter prophecies; to speak prophetically; to expound the Scriptures (*obs*); to preach (*obs*); to foretell the future. ◆ *vt* to foretell. [A variant of **prophecy**]

■ **proph'esier** *n*. **proph'esying** *n*.

prophet /prof'it/ *n* (also *fem* **proph'etess**) someone who speaks on behalf of a deity; someone who proclaims a divine message; an inspired teacher, preacher or poet; someone who speaks on behalf of a group, movement or doctrine; a foreteller, whether claiming to be inspired or not; a tipster (*sl*). [Fr *prophète*, from L *prophēta*, from Gr *prophētēs*, from *pro* for, and *phanai* to speak]

■ **proph'ethood** *n*. **prophetic** /prə-fet'ik/ or **prophet'ical** *adj*. **prophet'ically** *adv*. **prophet'icism** *n* prophetic quality. **proph'etism** *n* the actions of a prophet or prophets. **proph'etship** *n*. ☐ **prophet of doom** *n* a person who continually predicts unfortunate events, disasters, etc. **prophet's thumbmarks** *n pl* (*horse-racing*) indentations in a horse's skin.

■ **former prophets** the Old Testament books of Joshua, Judges, Samuel and Kings. **latter prophets** the Old Testament books from Isaiah to Malachi, divided into the major prophets and minor prophets; the prophets to whom these books are ascribed. **major prophets** the prophets whose books come before that of Hosea, ie Isaiah, Jeremiah and Ezekiel, as opposed to the **minor prophets**, the prophets from Hosea to Malachi. **school of the prophets** a school among the ancient Jews for training young men as teachers of the people. **the Prophet** Mohammed. **the prophets** one of the three divisions into which the Jewish scriptures are divided, consisting of the former and the latter prophets (qqv above).

prophylactic /pro-fi-lak'tik/ *adj* guarding against disease. ◆ *n* something that prevents disease; a condom (*usu* US). [Gr *prophylaktikos*, from *pro* before, and *phylax*, a guard; *prophylaxis* is not a Greek word]

■ **prophylax'is** *n* preventive treatment against diseases, etc.

prophyll /prō'fil/ (*bot*) *n* a bracteole. [**pro-**[2], and Gr *phyllon* leaf]

propine /prə-pīn'/ (*archaic*, chiefly *Scot*) *vt* to pledge in drinking; to present or offer. ◆ *n* a tip; a gift. [L *propīnāre*, from Gr *propīnein* to drink first, from *pro* before, and *pīnein* to drink]

propinquity /prə-ping'kwi-ti/ *n* nearness. [L *propinquitās, -ātis*, from *propinquus* near, from *prope* near]

propionic acid /prō-pi-on'ik as'id/ *n* one of the fatty acids, C_2H_5COOH; the first of the series that yields derivatives of a fatty character. [**pro-**[2], and Gr *pīon* fat]

■ **prō'pionate** *n* any ester or salt of propionic acid.

propitiate /prə-pish'i-āt/ *vt* to render favourable; to appease. [L *propitiāre, -ātum* to make favourable, from *propitius* well-disposed]

■ **propi'tiable** *adj*. **propitia'tion** *n* the act of propitiating; atonement; atoning sacrifice. **propi'tiātive** *adj*. **propi'tiātor** *n*. **propi'tiatorily** /-shi-ə-tər-i-li/ *adv*. **propi'tiatory** *adj* propitiating; expiatory. ◆ *n* the Jewish mercy-seat, the covering over the Ark of the Covenant; a propitiation (*archaic*). **propitious** /-pish'əs/ *adj* favourable; disposed to be gracious; of good omen. **propi'tiously** *adv*. **propi'tiousness** *n*.

prop-jet /prop'jet/ (*aeronautics*) *adj* and *n* (a jet aeroplane) having a turbine-driven propeller. [*propeller* and **jet**]

propodeon /prō-pod'i-on/ (*zool*) *n* in some Hymenoptera, the first abdominal segment, fused with the thorax and so in front of the waist (sometimes incorrectly Latinized as **propod'eum**). [**pro-**[2], and Gr *podeōn* a wineskin neck]

propolis /prop'ə-lis/ *n* bee-glue, a sticky resinous substance gathered by bees from trees to be used in building and protecting their hives, valued nutritionally and cosmetically for its rich bioflavonoid content. [Gr]

propone /prə-pōn'/ *vt* (now *Scot*) to put forward, propose, propound; to put before a court of law. [L *prōpōnere*, from *prō* forward, and *pōnere* to place]

■ **propōn'ent** *n* a propounder or proposer; a favourer or advocate. ◆ *adj* bringing forward, proposing; bringing an action.

proportion /prə-pōr'shən or -pör'/ *n* the relation of one thing to another in magnitude; appropriate relationship of parts to each other as regards size, quantity, etc; due relation; relation of rhythm or of harmony (*music*); adjustment in due ratio (*Shakesp*); ratio; the identity or equality of ratios (*maths*); the rule of three, the method of finding the value of a quantity that stands in the same ratio to a given quantity as two other quantities stand in relation to each other (*maths*); an equal or just share; a relative share, portion, inheritance, contribution, quota or fortune; a part or portion (*inf*); (in *pl*) dimensions; form, figure (*obs*). ◆ *vt* to adjust or fashion in due proportion; to regulate the proportions of; to be in due proportion to (*Shakesp*); to divide proportionally. [L *prōportiō*, *-ōnis*, from *prō* in comparison with, and *portiō* part, share]

■ **propor'tionable** *adj* that may be proportioned; having a due or definite relation. **propor'tionableness** *n*. **propor'tionably** *adv*. **propor'tional** *adj* relating to proportion; in proportion; having the same or a constant ratio (*maths*); proportionate, in suitable proportion. ◆ *n* (*maths*) a number or quantity in a proportion. **proportional'ity** *n* the state of being proportional; the weighing-up of good against evil (eg evil means of achieving good ends) or of the relative evilness of proposed actions, eg in consideration of the concept of a just war (*ethics*). **propor'tionally** *adv*. **propor'tionate** /-nət/ *adj* in fit or correct proportion; proportional. ◆ *vt* /-nāt/ to adjust in proportion. **propor'tionately** *adv*. **propor'tionateness** *n*. **propor'tioned** *adj*. **propor'tioning** *n* adjustment of proportions. **propor'tionless** *adj* badly proportioned. **propor'tionment** *n*.

❑ **proportional representation** *n* any of various systems which give or are intended to give parties in an elected body a representation as nearly as possible proportional to their voting strength.

■ **in proportion** (often with *to*) in a (given) ratio; having a correct or harmonious relation (with something); to a degree or extent which seems appropriate to the importance, etc of the matter in hand. **out of (all) proportion** not in proportion.

propose /prə-pōz'/ *vt* to offer for consideration or acceptance; to proffer; to offer; to suggest or put to someone as something to be done; to purpose or intend; to move formally; to nominate; to invite one's companions, etc to drink (a toast); to enunciate; to bring to one's own or another person's attention; to propound; to face (*Shakesp*); to imagine or suppose (*Shakesp*); to formulate as something to be exacted (*Shakesp*); to put forward or exhibit (*obs*). ◆ *vi* to form or put forward an intention or design; to offer, *esp* marriage; to converse (*Shakesp*). ◆ *n* a proposal (*obs*); talk, discourse (*Shakesp*). [Fr *proposer*, from pfx *pro-*, and *poser* to place; see **pose**[1]]

■ **propōs'able** *adj*. **propōs'al** *n* an act of proposing; an offer, *esp* of marriage; a tender (*US*); anything proposed; a plan. **propōs'er** *n*.

proposition /prop-ə-zish'ən/ *n* an act of propounding or (more rarely) proposing; the thing propounded or proposed; an offer (*Shakesp*); a question propounded (*Shakesp*); a statement of a judgement; a form of statement in which a predicate is affirmed or denied of a subject (*logic*); a premise, *esp* a major premise (*logic*); a statement of a problem or theorem for (or with) solution or demonstration (*maths*); enunciation of a subject in a fugue (*music*); a possibility, suggestion, course of action, etc, to be considered; any situation, thing or person considered as something to cope with, eg an enterprise, job, opponent, etc (*sl*, *orig US*); an invitation to sexual intercourse (*inf*). ◆ *vt* to make a proposition to (someone), *esp* to solicit (a woman) for sexual relations. [L *prōpositiō*, *-ōnis*, from *prō* before; see **position**]

■ **proposi'tional** *adj*.

❑ **propositional attitude** *n* (*philos*) the attitude adopted by a person towards a proposition. **propositional calculus** see under **calculus**.

propound /prə-pownd'/ *vt* to offer for consideration; to set forth as an aim or reward; to purpose (*Spenser*); to produce for probate (*law*; *obs*). [**propone**]

■ **propound'er** *n*.

proppant see under **prop**[1].

propraetor /prō-prē'tər, prō-prē'tör or prō-prī'tor/ *n* a magistrate of ancient Rome, who, after acting as praetor in Rome, was appointed to the government of a province. [L *prōpraetor*, from *prō praetōre* for the praetor]

■ **propraetorial** /-tō'ri-əl or -tö'ri-əl/ or **propraeto'rian** *adj*.

propranolol /pro- or prō-pran'ə-lol/ *n* a compound, $C_{16}H_{21}NO_2$, used in the form of its hydrochloride as a beta-blocker (qv) *esp* in the treatment of cardiac arrhythmia, angina and hypertension; (with *cap*) propranolol hydrochloride. [**propyl** and **propanol**]

proprietor /prə- or prō-prī'ə-tər/ *n* an owner (also *fem* **propri'etress** or **propri'etrix**). [LL *proprietārius*, from *proprius* own; **proprietor** has been formed irregularly; it is not a Latin word]

■ **proprī'etary** *adj* of the nature of property; legally made only by a person or body of persons having special rights, *esp* a patent or trademark; relating to or belonging to the legal owner; (of a company, etc) privately owned and run; owning property. ◆ *n* an owner; a body of owners; ownership; a proprietary or patented drug (*med*); a business secretly owned by or controlled by the CIA and used to provide cover for its agents and activities (*US*). **proprī'etorial** /-tō'ri-əl/ or -tö'ri-əl/ *adj*. **proprī'eto'rially** *adv*. **proprī'etorship** *n*.

propriety /prə- or prō-prī'ə-ti/ *n* conformity with good manners; conformity with convention in language and conduct; (in *pl*) the conventions of respectable behaviour; rightness, eg in the use of words; appropriateness; seemliness; decency; a character, quality or property (*obs*); particular nature, individuality (*Shakesp*); ownership (*obs*). [Fr *propriété*, from L *proprietās*, *-ātis*, from *proprius* own]

proprioceptive /prō-pri-ō-sep'tiv/ (*biol*) *adj* of, relating to, or made active by, stimuli signalling the relative positions of body parts. [L *proprius* own, after **receptive**]

■ **propriocep'tion** *n*. **propriocep'tor** *n* a sensory nerve-ending receptive of such stimuli.

❑ **proprioceptive sense** *n* the sense of muscular position.

proproctor /prō-prok'tər/ *n* a proctor's substitute or assistant. [**pro-**[1] (2)]

props /props/ (*sl*) *n pl* the respect that is due to a person, *esp* in the phrase *give props to*. [Contraction of *proper respects*]

proptosis /prop-tō'sis/ (*pathol*) *n* forward displacement, *esp* of the eye. [Gr *proptōsis*, from *pro* forward, and *ptōsis* fall]

propugnation /prō-pug-nā'shən/ (*Shakesp*) *n* defence. [L *prō* for, and *pugnāre* to fight]

propulsion /prə-pul'shən/ *n* the act of causing something to move forward; a force which causes forward movement. [L *prōpellere*, *prōpulsum* to push forward; see **propel**]

■ **propul'sive** *adj*. **propul'sor** *n* something which propels or provides propulsion. **propul'sory** *adj*.

propyl /prō'pil/ *n* the alcohol radical C_3H_7. [**propionic acid**, and Gr *hȳlē* matter]

■ **pro'pylamine** *n* an amine of propyl. **pro'pylene** or **pro'pene** *n* a gaseous hydrocarbon (C_3H_6). **propyl'ic** *adj*.

❑ **propenoic** /prō-pə-nō'ik/ **acid** *n* acrylic acid. **propyl alcohol** *n* propanol, an aliphatic alcohol, C_3H_7OH. **propylene glycol** *n* a colourless liquid derived from propylene used as a solvent and in antifreeze.

propylaeum /prop-i-lē'əm/ or **propylon** /prop'i-lon/ *n* (*pl* **propylae'a** or **prop'yla**) a gateway of architectural importance, leading into a temple, etc. [Gr *propylaion* (used in *pl*, -a) and *propylon*, from *pro* before, and *pylē* a gate]

■ **prop'ylite** *n* (*geol*) an andesite altered by solfataric action, *orig* applied to andesites of the beginning (or gateway) of the Tertiary period. **propylītīzā'tion** or **-s-** *n*. **prop'ylitize** or **-ise** *vt*.

pro rata see under **pro**[3].

prorate /prō-rāt' or prō'rāt/ (mainly *US*) *vt* to distribute proportionately. [**pro rata**]

■ **prorāt'able** *adj*. **prorā'tion** *n*.

prore /prōr or prör/ (*poetic*) *n* a prow; a ship. [Obs Fr, from L *prōra* prow, from Gr *prōira*]

prorector /prō-rek'tər/ *n* a university or college rector's substitute or assistant. [**pro-**[1] (2)]

prorogue /prə-rōg' or prō-rōg'/ *vt* to discontinue the meetings of for a time without dissolving; to prolong (*obs*); to postpone (*Shakesp*); *perh* to keep from exertion (*Shakesp*). [L *prōrogāre*, *-ātum*, from *prō* forward, and *rogāre* to ask]

■ **prō'rogāte** *vt* to prorogue; to extend by agreement, in order to make a particular action competent (*Scots law*); to confer jurisdiction by agreement of parties on a judge or court not otherwise having jurisdiction to decide the dispute (*Scots law*). **prōrogā'tion** *n*.

prosaic /prō-zā'ik/ or **prosaical** /prō-zā'ik-əl/ *adj* like prose; unpoetical; matter-of-fact; commonplace; dull; in or relating to prose (*rare*). [L *prosa* prose]

■ **prosā'ically** *adv*. **prosā'icalness** *n*. **prosā'icism** /-i-sizm/ *n* prosaism. **prosā'icness** *n* the quality of being prosaic. **prō'sāism** *n* a prose idiom; a prosaic phrase; prosaic character. **prō'sāist** *n* a writer of prose; a commonplace person. **prosateur** *n* see under **prose**.

prosauropod /prō-sör'ə-pod/ *n* a reptile-like dinosaur of the division *Prosauropoda* which lived in the Triassic period (also *adj*).

proscenium /prō-sē'ni-əm/ *n* the front part of the stage; the curtain and its framework, *esp* the arch that frames the more traditional type of stage (**proscenium arch**); the stage itself in an ancient theatre. [L, from Gr *proskēnion*, from *pro* before, and *skēnē* stage]

prosciutto /prə- or pro-shoo'tō/ n (pl **prosciu'tti** or **prosciu'ttos**) finely cured uncooked ham. [Ital, literally, pre-dried]

proscribe /prō-skrīb'/ vt to put on the list of those who may be put to death; to outlaw; to ostracize; to prohibit; to denounce. [L *prōscribere*, from *prō-* before, publicly, and *scrībere, scrīptum* to write]
■ **prōscrib'er** n. **prō'script** n a person who is proscribed. **prōscrip'tion** n. **prōscrip'tive** adj. **prōscrip'tively** adv.

prose /prōz/ n ordinary spoken and written language with words in direct straightforward arrangement without metrical structure; all writings not in verse; a passage of prose for translation from or, *usu*, into a foreign language, as an exercise; a composition in prose (*obs*, except as an exercise in Latin or Greek); a narrative (*obs*); a piece of dull, tedious speaking or writing; a familiar, gossipy talk (*inf*; *esp* formerly); (something having) prosaic character; a prosy talker. ◆ adj of or in prose; not poetical; plain; dull. ◆ vi to write prose; to speak or write tediously. ◆ vt to compose in prose; to turn into prose. [Fr, from L *prōsa*, from *prorsus* straightforward, from *prō* forward, and *vertere, versum* to turn]
■ **prosateur** /prō-za-tœr/ n (Fr) a prose-writer. **prō'ser** n. **prō'sify** vt to make (something) prosaic; to turn (something) into prose. ◆ vi to write prose. **prō'sily** adv. **prō'siness** n. **prō'sing** n speaking or writing in a dull or prosy way. **prō'sy** adj dull, tedious, humdrum; addicted to prosing.
❑ **prose'-man** (*Pope*) or **prose'man** n a writer of prose. **prose poem** n a prose work or passage having some of the characteristics of poetry. **prose'-writer** n.

prosecco /prō-sek'ō/ n an Italian sparkling white wine. [Ital]

prosector /prə- or prō-sek'tər/ n a person who dissects bodies to illustrate anatomical lectures; the official anatomist of a zoological society. [LL *prōsector*, from *prōsecāre, -sectum* to cut up, from *prō-* away, and *secāre* to cut]
■ **prosecto'rial** /-ōr'i-əl or -ör'i-əl/ adj. **prosec'torship** n.

prosecute /pros'i-kūt/ vt to pursue by law; to bring before a court; to carry on with, persevere with or pursue, in order to reach or accomplish; to engage in or practise; to follow up; to pursue or chase (*obs*). ◆ vi to carry on a legal prosecution. [L *prōsequī, -secūtus*, from *prō* onwards, and *sequī* to follow]
■ **pros'ecūtable** adj. **prosecū'tion** n the act of prosecuting in any sense; the prosecuting party in legal proceedings. **pros'ecūtor** n someone who prosecutes or pursues any plan or business; someone who carries on a civil or criminal suit. **prosecutorial** /pros-i-kū-tō'ri-el or -tö'ri-əl/ or **prosecū'tory** adj. **pros'ecūtrix** n (pl **pros'ecūtrixes** or **prosecutrices** /pros-i-kū-trī'sēz or pros-i-kū'tri-sēz/) a female prosecutor.
■ **director of public prosecutions** or **public prosecutor** a person appointed to conduct criminal prosecutions in the public interest (in the USA, **prosecuting attorney** or **district attorney**).

proselyte /pros'i-līt/ n someone who has changed from one religion or opinion to another; a convert, *esp* from paganism to Judaism. ◆ vt and vi (*US*) to proselytize. [Gr *prosēlytos* a newcomer, resident foreigner, from *pros* to, and the stem *elyth-* used to form aorist for *erchesthai* to go]
■ **pros'elytism** n being, becoming, or making a convert; conversion. **pros'elytize** or **-ise** vt to (attempt to) convert. ◆ vi to (attempt to) make proselytes. **pros'elytizer** or **-s-** n.
❑ **proselyte of the gate** n (*hist*) a heathen allowed to live in Palestine on making certain concessions to Judaism.

prosencephalon /pros-en-sef'ə-lon/ (*zool*) n the forebrain, comprising the cerebral hemispheres and olfactory processes. [Gr *pros* to, used as if equivalent to *pro* before, and *enkephalon* brain, from *en* in, and *kephalē* head]
■ **prosencephalic** /-si-fal'ik/ adj.

prosenchyma /pro-seng'ki-mə/ (*bot*) n a plant-tissue of long cells with pointed ends, conducting or supporting tissue. [Gr *pros* to, and *enchyma* an infusion, pouring in]
■ **prosenchymatous** /-kim'ə-təs/ adj.

proseuche /pro-sū'kē/ or **proseucha** /-kə/ n (pl **proseu'chae** /-kē/) a place of prayer, an oratory. [Gr *proseuchē* prayer, place of prayer, from *pros* to, and *euchē* prayer]

prosify see under **prose**.

prosimian /prō-sim'i-ən/ n a primate of the suborder **Prosimii**, eg the lemur, loris and tarsier (also adj). [**pro-²**, and L *simia* ape]

prosing see under **prose**.

prosit /prō'sit/ interj good luck to you, a salutation in drinking toasts. [L *prōsit*, 3rd pers sing present subjunctive of L *prōdesse* to be of use, from *prō(d)-* for, and *esse* to be]

proslambanomenos /pros-lam-ba-nom'e-nos/ (Gr *music*) n an additional note at the bottom of the scale. [Gr prp passive of *proslambanein* to take in addition, from pfx *pros-*, and *lambanein* to take]

proso /prō'sō/ or **proso millet** /mil'it/ n a name for one of the main varieties of millet, *Panicum miliaceum*, grown *esp* in Russia and China. [Russ]

prosocial /prō-sō'shəl/ adj in the interests of society as a whole. [**pro-¹** (4)]

prosody /pros'ə- or pros'ə-di/ n the study of versification; the study of rhythm, stress and intonation in speech. [L *prosōdia*, Gr *prosōidiā*, from *pros* to, and *ōidē* a song]
■ **prosodial** /pros-ō'di-əl or prəs-ō'di-əl/, **prosodic** /-od'ik/ or **prosod'ical** adj. **prosō'dian** or **pros'odist** n someone skilled in prosody. **prosod'ically** adv.

prosoma /prō-sō'mə or prə-/ same as **cephalothorax** (see under **cephal-**). [**pro-²** and **soma¹**]

prosopagnosia /pros-ō-pag-nō'si-ə or 'zi-ə/ (*psychiatry*) n the inability to recognize faces of persons well-known to the sufferer. [LL *prosopagnosia*, from Gr *prosōpon* face, *a-* without, and *gnōsis* knowledge]

prosopography /pros-ō-pog'rə-fi/ n a biographical sketch, a description of a person's appearance, character, life, etc; the compiling or study of such material. [Gr *prosōpon* face, person, and *graphein* to write]
■ **prosopograph'ical** adj.

prosopon /pros-ō-pon'/ n (*theol*) the outer appearance, personification or embodiment of one of the persons of the Trinity. [Gr *prosōpopoiiā*, from *prosōpon* face, person, and *poieein* to make]
■ **prosopopoeia** or **prosopopeia** /pros-ō-pō-pē'ə/ n (*rhetoric*) personification. **prosopopoe'ial** or **prosopope'ial** adj.

prospect /pros'pekt/ n an outlook; a direction of facing; a lookout or viewpoint (*Milton*); a wide view; a view, sight, field of view; a scene; a pictorial representation; a position for being observed (*Shakesp*); a survey or mental view; an outlook on the probable future; an expectation; (often *pl*) a chance of success or advancement; a wide street (also with *cap*; also Russ **Prospekt** /prəs-pyekt'/); a prospect-glass (*obs*); a probable customer (*esp US*); a person thought likely to succeed; a place thought likely to yield a valuable mineral (*mining*); a sample, or a test, or the yield of a test of a sample from such a place; a probable source of profit. ◆ vi /pros-pekt'/ to look around (*obs*); /prəs-pekt'/ or (N Am) pros'pekt/ to make a search, *esp* for chances of mining; to promise or yield results to the prospector. ◆ vt /-pekt'/ to face or view (*obs*); /-pekt'/ or pros'pekt/ to explore, search, survey or test for profitable minerals. [L *prōspectus*, from *prōspicere*, *prōspectum*, from *prō-* forward, and *specere* to look]
■ **prospect'ing** (or (N Am) /pros'/) n searching a district for minerals with a view to further operations. **prospec'tion** n looking to the future; foresight. **prospec'tive** adj probable or expected future; looking forward; yielding distant views; looking to the future. ◆ n prospect. **prospec'tively** adv. **prospec'tiveness** n. **prospectiv'ity** n (*geol*) the potential of an area to yield valuable minerals. **prospec'tor** (or (N Am) /pros'/) n someone who prospects for minerals. **prospec'tus** n (pl **prospec'tuses**) the outline of any plan submitted for public approval, particularly of a literary work or of a joint-stock concern; an account of the organization of a school, etc.
❑ **pros'pect-glass** n (*obs* or *dialect*) a telescope or field glass. **prospec'tive-glass** n (*obs*) a prospect-glass; a scrying crystal for seeing future or faraway events.

prosper /pros'pər/ vi to thrive; to get on; to experience favourable circumstances; to flourish; to turn out well. ◆ vt to cause to prosper. [L *prosperus* favourable]
■ **prosperity** /-per'i-ti/ n the state of being prosperous; success; good fortune. **pros'perous** adj thriving; affluent; successful. **pros'perously** adv. **pros'perousness** n.

prostacyclin /pro-stə-sī'klin/ n a prostaglandin which dilates blood vessels and inhibits blood clotting. [**prostaglandin** and **cyclic**]

prostaglandin /pro-stə-glan'din/ n any of a group of chemical substances secreted by various parts of the body into the bloodstream and found to have a wide range of effects on the body processes, eg on muscle contraction. [*prostate gland*, a major source of these]

prostanthera /pros-tan-thē'rə/ n any bush of the Australian labiate genus *Prostanthera*, with strongly scented leaves and red or white flowers. [Gr *prostithenai* to add, and L *anthera* anther]

prostate /pros'tāt/ n a gland in males at the neck of the bladder, which releases a liquid that forms part of semen (also **prostate gland**). [Gr *prostatēs*, someone who stands in front, the prostate, from *pro* before, and *sta* the root of *histanai* to set up]

■ **prostatec'tomy** /pros-tə-/ n surgical removal of (part of) the prostate gland. **prostatic** /pros-tat'ik/ adj. **pros'tatism** /-tət-izm/ n an illness or disorder associated with enlargement of the prostate. **prostatī'tis** n inflammation of the prostate gland.

prosthesis /pros'thə-sis (esp linguistics) or pros-thē'sis (esp med)/ n (pl **prostheses** /-sēz/) the fitting of artificial parts to the body (med); such an artificial part; prothesis, the addition of a sound or syllable to the beginning of a word, eg for ease of pronunciation (linguistics). [Gr prosthesis, adj prosthetikos, from pros to, and thesis putting]
■ **prosthetic** /-thet'ik/ adj relating to prosthesis; relating to a group or radical of different nature, such as a non-protein part of a protein molecule (chem). ◆ n an artificial part of the body. **prosthet'ics** n sing the surgery or dentistry involved in supplying artificial parts to the body. **pros'thetist** n.

prosthodontia /pros-thō-don'shi-ə or -ti-ə/ (dentistry) n the provision of false teeth (also **prosthodon'tics**). [Gr prosthesis addition, from pros to, thesis putting, and odous, odontos tooth]
■ **prosthodon'tist** n.

prostitute /pros'ti-tūt/ n a person (usu a woman) who accepts money in return for sexual intercourse; someone who offers their skills, efforts or reputation for unworthy ends. ◆ vt to devote to, or offer or sell for, an unworthy, evil or immoral use; to hire out for sexual intercourse; to degrade by publicity or commonness; to devote or offer as a religious act (obs). ◆ adj openly devoted to lewdness; given over (to evil); shamefully or ignobly mercenary; hackneyed, debased by commonness (obs). [L prōstituere, -ūtum to set up for sale, from prō before, and statuere to place]
■ **prostitū'tion** n the act or practice of prostituting; devotion to unworthy or shameful purposes. **pros'titūtor** n.

prostomium /prō-stō'mi-əm/ (zool) n the part of a worm's head in front of the mouth. [Gr pro before, and stoma mouth]
■ **prostō'mial** adj.

prostrate /pros'trāt/ adj prone; lying or bent with one's face on the ground; (loosely) lying at length, with the body stretched out; procumbent, trailing (bot); lying at someone's mercy; reduced to helplessness; completely exhausted. ◆ vt /pros-trāt' or pros'/ to throw forwards on the ground; to lay flat; to overthrow; to reduce to impotence or exhaustion; to bend in humble reverence (reflexive). [L prōstrātus, pap of prōsternere, from prō forwards, and sternere to spread]
■ **prostra'tion** n.

prostyle /prō'stīl/ (Gr archit) n a front portico without antae; a building with such a portico and no other. ◆ adj having a prostyle. [Gr prostȳlon, from pro before, and stȳlos a column]

prosumer /prō-sū'mər/ n a consumer who buys many newly introduced and high-quality products. [**professional** and **consumer**]

prosy see under **prose**.

prosyllogism /prō-sil'ə-ji-zm/ (logic) n a syllogism whose conclusion becomes the major premise of another. [Gr pro before, and syllogismos syllogism]

Prot. abbrev : Protestant.

prot- see **proto-**.

protactinium /prō-tak-tin'i-əm/ n a radioactive element (symbol **Pa**; atomic no 91) that yields actinium on disintegration. [Gr prōtos first, and **actinium**]

protagonist /prə- or prō-tag'ə-nist/ n orig the chief actor, character or combatant; now often applied to any (or in pl, all) of the main personages or participants in a story or event; (loosely) a champion or advocate. [Gr prōtos first, and agōnistēs a combatant or actor]

protamine /prō'tə-mēn/ n any of the simplest proteins, found esp in the sperm of certain fish. [**proto-** and **amine**]

protandry /prō-tan'dri/ n in a hermaphrodite organism, the maturation and loss of the male elements before the female elements develop (zool); in a flower, opening of the anthers before the stigmas can receive pollen, so preventing self-pollination (bot). Cf **protogyny**. [Gr prōtos first, and anēr, andros man, male]
■ **protan'drous** adj.

protanomaly /prō-tə-nom'ə-li/ (med) n a form of colour blindness in which there is a decreased response to red. [Gr protos first (red being the first primary colour), and anomalos abnormal]
■ **protanom'alous** adj.

protanopia /prō-tə-nop'i-ə/ (med) n a form of colour blindness in which red and green are confused because the retina does not respond to red. [Gr protos first (red being the first primary colour), and ops eye]
■ **prō'tanope** n a sufferer from protanopia. **prōtanop'ic** adj colour-blind to red.

pro tanto see under **pro³**.

protasis /prot'ə-sis/ n (pl **prot'asēs**) the conditional clause of a conditional sentence (cf **apodosis**); the first part of a dramatic composition, opp to epitasis. [Gr protasis proposition, premise, protasis, from pro before, and tasis a stretching]
■ **protatic** /prə-tat'ik/ adj.

protea /prō'ti-ə/ n a plant of the large South African genus Protea of shrubs or small trees, of the mainly Australian family **Proteā'ceae**, with big cone-shaped heads of flowers. [**proteus**, from the varied character of the family]
■ **proteā'ceous** adj.

Protean, protean see under **proteus**.

protease see under **protein**.

protect /prə-tekt' or prō-tekt'/ vt to shield from danger, injury, change, capture or loss; to defend; to strengthen; to seek to foster by import duties; to act as regent for (Shakesp); to screen off (eg machinery) for safety. [L prōtegere, -tectum, from prō- in front, and tegere to cover]
■ **protect'ant** n. **protect'ed** adj defended; strengthened; (of a species) recognized as being in danger of extinction and forbidden to be hunted or collected. **protect'ing** adj. **protect'ingly** adv. **protec'tion** n the act of protecting; the state of being protected; defence; that which protects; a guard; a pass or other document guaranteeing against molestation or interference; a condom or other barrier method used during sexual intercourse to prevent conception or infection; a fostering of home produce and manufactures by import duties; patronage; concubinage; control of another country's foreign relations, and sometimes internal affairs, without annexation; protection money (qv below) or the practice of extorting it (inf). **protec'tionism** n. **protec'tionist** n someone who favours the protection of trade by duties on imports. ◆ adj of or relating to protectionism or protectionists. **protec'tive** adj affording protection; intended to protect; defensive; sheltering. ◆ n that which protects; a condom (esp US). **protec'tively** adv. **protec'tiveness** n. **protec'tor** n someone who protects from injury or oppression; a protective device; a means of protection; a guard; a guardian; a regent; (usu with cap) the head of the state during the 17c English Commonwealth (hist). **protec'toral** adj of a protector or a regent. **protec'torāte** n the position, office, term of office or government of a protector; (with cap) the Commonwealth period (hist); guardianship; authority over a vassal state; the relation assumed by a state over a territory which it administers without annexation and without admitting the inhabitants to citizenship. **protectorial** /prō-tek-tōr'i-əl or -tōr'i-əl/ adj. **protec'torless** adj. **protec'torship** n. **protec'tory** n an institution for destitute or delinquent children. **protec'tress** or **protec'trix** n a female protector.
◻ **protected state** n a state under the protection of another state but less subject to the control of that state than a protectorate. **protection money** n money extorted from shopkeepers, businessmen, etc as a bribe for leaving their property, business, etc unharmed. **protective coloration** n similarity of animals' colour to that of their natural surroundings, which helps to prevent them from being seen by their enemies. **protective custody** n detention of a person ostensibly for his or her personal safety but often in fact from doubt as to his or her possible actions eg as an enemy of the state. **protective tariff** n an import tax designed to protect the home markets rather than raise revenue.
■ **cathodic protection** see under **cathode**.

protégé or (fem) **protégée** /prō'tə-zhā or pro'tə-zhā/ n someone under the protection or patronage of another person; a pupil; a ward. [Fr, from pap of protéger to protect, from L prōtegere]

proteiform see under **proteus**.

protein /prō'tēn or prō'tē-in/ n any member of a group of complex nitrogenous substances that are an important constituent of the bodies of plants and animals, eg compounds of carbon, hydrogen, oxygen, nitrogen, usu sulphur, often phosphorus, etc, their molecules consisting of one or several polypeptide chains, each of which is a linear polymer of several hundred amino acids. [Gr prōteios primary, from prōtos first]
■ **protease** /prō'tē-ās or -āz/ n any enzyme that splits up proteins. **proteid** /prō'tē-id/ n an archaic name for protein. **proteinaceous** /prō-tēn-ā'shəs/, **proteinic** /prō-tēn'ik/ or **protein'ous** adj. **proteinū'ria** n the presence of abnormally high levels of protein in the urine, esp as a symptom of kidney damage. **proteoclastic** /-klas'tik/ adj same as **proteolytic** below. **proteoglycan** /-glī'kan/ n a fibrous macromolecular protein found in cartilage. **pro'teolyse** /-ō-līz/ vt. **proteolysis** /-ol'i-sis/ n splitting of proteins by enzymes. **proteolytic** /-ō-lit'ik/ adj. **proteome** /prō'tē-ōm/ n the set of proteins expressed by a genome. **proteō'mic** adj. **proteō'mics** n sing the study of proteomes, esp their role in physiology and the action of drugs. **prō'teōse** n any of a number of substances formed from proteins by proteolysis.
◻ **protease inhibitor** n a compound that inhibits the action of protease in replicating viruses, used in treating AIDS. **protein structure** n the three-dimensional structure of a protein resulting from

the sequence of amino acids in the polypeptide chain, the binding of non-protein moieties, and the association with other protein subunits.

pro tem /prō tem/ short for **pro tempore** (L), for the time being.

protend /prō-tend'/ (archaic) vt to stretch forth; to hold out. [L prōtendere, -tentus (-tēnsus), from prō- forward, and tendere to stretch]
■ **protense'** n (Spenser) extension in time. **proten'sion** n duration. **proten'sity** n. **proten'sive** adj.

proteoclastic...to...**proteose** see under **protein**.

proterandry /pro- or prō-tə-ran'dri/ (bot and zool) n protandry. [Gr proteros earlier, and anēr, andros man, male]
■ **proteran'drous** adj.

proterogyny /pro- or prō-tə-roj'i-ni, also -rog'/ (bot and zool) n protogyny. [Gr proteros earlier, and gynē woman, female]
■ **proterog'ynous** adj.

Proterozoic /prot-ə- or prō-tə-rō-zō'ik/ (geol) adj of or belonging to the most recent eon of Precambrian time, between 2500 and 540 million years ago, orig **Lower Palaeozoic** (also n). [Gr proteros earlier, and zōē life]

protervity /prō-tûr'vi-ti/ n peevishness; perversity; wantonness. [L prōtervus or protervus]

protest /prə-test' or prō-test'/ vi to express or record dissent or objection; to make a solemn affirmation, profession or avowal. ◆ vt to make a protest against; to make a solemn declaration of; to declare; to declare the non-acceptance or non-payment of (a bill of exchange); to proclaim (Shakesp); to vow (Shakesp); to call to witness (Milton). ◆ n /prō'test/ a declaration of objection or dissent; an affirmation or avowal; the noting by a notary-public of an unpaid or unaccepted bill; a written declaration, usu by the master of a ship, stating the circumstances attending loss or injury of ship or cargo, etc. ◆ adj expressing, or used to express, dissent or objection. [Fr protester, from L prōtestārī, -ātus to bear witness in public, from prō before, and testārī, from testis a witness]
■ **Protestant** /prot'is-tənt/ n a member or adherent, or someone who shares the beliefs, of one of those churches founded by the Reformers (formerly by some confined to Anglicans or Lutherans, now disavowed by some Anglicans), or of any of the churches which have developed or separated from them; one of those who, in 1529, protested against an edict of Charles V and the Diet of Spires denouncing the Reformation; (without cap) an avowed lover (Herrick); (without cap; sometimes /prō-tes'tant/) someone who protests. ◆ adj /prot'is-tənt/ of, or relating to, Protestants or, more usu, Protestantism; (without cap; /prot'is-tənt or prō-tes'tant/) protesting. **Prot'estantism** n the Protestant form or forms of religion; the Protestant denominations; the state of being a Protestant. **Prot'estantize** or **-ise** vt. **protestation** /prot'is-, prō-tes-tā'shən/ n an avowal or solemn declaration; a declaration in pleading (law); a protest. **protest'er** or **protest'or** n someone who protests, esp (with cap; Scot hist) a Remonstrant or opponent of the Resolutioners. **protest'ingly** adv.
❑ **Protestant work ethic** n an attitude to life stressing the virtue of hard work over enjoyment, popularly associated with the Protestant denominations.
■ **under protest** unwillingly, having made a protest.

proteus /prō'tūs or prō'ti-əs/ n (pl **pro'teuses**) the olm, a member of a European genus (Proteus) of blind, cave-dwelling tailed amphibians; a member of a genus (Proteus) of rodlike bacteria found in the intestines and in decaying organic matter. [Gr Prōteus, an ancient Greek sea god who assumed many shapes to evade having to foretell the future]
■ **Protean** or **protean** /prō-tē'ən or prō'ti-ən/ adj readily assuming different shapes; variable; inconstant; versatile. **proteiform** /prō-tē'i-förm/ adj.

Protevangelium /prō-te-van-jel'i-əm/ n God's warning to the serpent (Bible, Genesis 3.15) that there would be enmity between its offspring and Eve's, and that her offspring would crush the serpent's head, seen as the earliest announcement of the gospel; a gospel attributed to James the Less; an inferred source of the canonical gospels. [Gr prōtos first, and L evangelium, from Gr euangelion gospel]

prothalamion /prō-thə-lā'mi-on/, also **prothalamium** /-əm/ n (pl **prothalā'mia**) a poem celebrating a coming marriage. [Appar coined by Spenser from Gr pro before, and thalamos a bride-chamber]

prothallus /prō-thal'əs/ or **prothallium** /prō-thal'i-əm/ n (pl **prothall'ī** or **prothall'ia**) the gametophyte or sexual generation in ferns and related plants, a small plate of tissue derived from a spore and bearing antheridia and archegonia; the homologous stage in gymnosperms. [Gr pro before, and thallos a young shoot]
■ **prothall'ial**, **prothall'ic** or **prothall'oid** adj.

prothesis /proth'i-sis/ n in the Greek Orthodox Church, the preliminary oblation of the Eucharistic elements before the liturgy; the table used for this; the chapel or northern apse where the table stands;

the development of an extra initial sound at the beginning of a word (linguistics). [Gr prothesis, from pro before, and the root of tithenai to place]
■ **prothetic** /prə-thet'ik or prō-thet'ik/ adj.

prothonotary /prō-thon'ə-tə-ri or prō-thō-nō'tə-ri/ or **protonotary** /prō-ton'ə-tə-ri or prō-tō-nō'tə-ri/ n a chief notary or clerk; a chief secretary of the chancery at Rome; a chief clerk or registrar of a court. [LL prōt(h)onotārius, from Gr prōtos first, and L notārius a clerk]
■ **prothonotā'rial** or **protonotā'rial** adj. **prothonotā'riat** or **protonotā'riat** n the college constituted by the twelve apostolical prothonotaries (bishops and senior members of the curia) in Rome.

prothorax /prō-thō'raks or prō-thō'raks/ (zool) n (pl **prothor'axes** or **prothor'aces** /-ə-sēz/) the anterior segment of the thorax of insects. [**pro-²**]
■ **prothoracic** /-ras'ik/ adj.

prothrombin /prō-throm'bin/ n a proteinlike substance present in blood plasma. [**pro-²** and **thrombin**]

prothyl, **prothyle** see **protyle**.

Protista /prō-tis'tə/ (biol) n pl a large group of unicellular organisms on the borderline between plants and animals; a term for a biological kingdom including Protozoa and Protophyta. [Gr prōtistos very first, from prōtos first]
■ **prō'tist** n any member of the Protista. **protist'ic** adj. **protistol'ogist** n. **protistol'ogy** n.

protium /prō'ti-əm or -shi-əm/ n ordinary hydrogen of atomic weight 1, as distinguished from deuterium and tritium. [Gr prōtos first]

Proto® /prō'tō/ (S Afr) n the name of a type of breathing apparatus used in mine rescues.
❑ **Proto** (or **proto**) **team** n a team of people trained to deal with underground rescues, etc.

proto- /prō-tō-/ or, before a vowel, **prot-** /prōt-/ combining form denoting: first; first of a series; first-formed; primitive; ancestral; a (specified) protolanguage (linguistics). [Gr prōtos first]

protoactinium /prō-tō-ak-tin'i-əm/ (chem) n a former variant of **protactinium**.

protoavis /prō-tō-ā'vis/ n a member of the genus Protoavis of the Triassic period, with a dinosaur-like tail and hind legs but certain anatomical features characteristic of modern birds. [**proto-**, and L avis bird]

Protochordata /prō-tō-kör-dā'tə/ (zool) n pl a division of the Chordata comprising the Cephalochordata, Hemichordata and Urochordata (ie all members of the Chordata except the vertebrates), marine animals distinguished by the absence of a cranium, of a vertebral column and of specialized anterior sense organs. [**proto-** and **Chordata** (see **chordate** under **chord²**)]
■ **prōtōchord'ate** n and adj.

Protococcus /prō-tō-kok'əs/ n a former genus of rounded unicellular algae, one of which (renamed Pleurococcus vulgaris) forms a green film common on trees, etc. [**proto-**, and Gr kokkos a berry]
■ **protococc'al** adj. **Protococcales** /-ā'lēz/ n pl the order of green algae to which Pleurococcus vulgaris belongs.

protocol /prō'tō-kol or -tə-/ n a body of diplomatic etiquette; the regulations, customs, etiquette, etc to be observed by any group or on any occasion; a set of rules governing the transmission of data between two computers which cannot communicate directly; an original note or minute, or the draft of a record, contract or transaction; a draft treaty; an official or formal account or record; a factual record of observations, eg in scientific experiments (chiefly US); a record of transfer of lands (US); an official formula. ◆ vi (**pro'tocolling**; **pro'tocolled**) to issue or form protocols. ◆ vt to make a protocol of (also **prō'tocolize** or **-ise**). [Fr protocole, from LL prōtocollum, from Late Gr prōtokollon, a glued-on descriptive first leaf of a manuscript, from Gr prōtos first, and kolla glue]
■ **prōtocol'ic** adj. **prō'tocolist** n a registrar or clerk.

protogalaxy /prō-tō-gal'ək-si/ n a large cloud of gas thought to be slowly condensing into stars, an early stage in the formation of a galaxy. [**proto-**]

protogine /prō'tō-jin or prō'tō-jēn/ n a gneissose granite with sericite, found in the Alps. [Gr prōtos first, and gīnesthai to come into being (as once thought to be the first-formed granite)]

protogyny /prō-toj'i-ni or -tog'/ n in a hermaphrodite organism, ripening of the female germ cells before the male (zool); in a flower, ripening of the stigmas before the stamens (bot). Cf **protandry**. [**proto-**, and Gr gynē woman, female]
■ **protog'ynous** adj.

proto-historic /prō-tō-hi-stor'ik/ adj belonging to the earliest age of history, just after the prehistoric and before the development of written records, etc. [**proto-**]
■ **proto-his'tory** n.

protohuman /prō-tō-hū'mən/ n a prehistoric primate, a supposed ancestor of modern man (also *adj*). [**proto-**]

protolanguage /prō'tō-lang-gwij/ n a hypothetical language (eg *Proto-Germanic, Proto-Indo-European*) regarded as the ancestor of other recorded or existing languages, and reconstructed by comparing these. [**proto-**]

protolithic /prō-tō-lith'ik/ adj of or relating to the earliest Stone Age. [**proto-**, and Gr *lithos* stone]

protomartyr /prō'tō-mär-tər/ n the first martyr in any cause, *esp* St Stephen. [Late Gr *prōtomartyr*]

protomorphic /prō-tō-mör'fik/ adj primordial; primitive. [**proto-**]

proton /prō'ton/ (*phys*) n an elementary particle of positive charge and unit atomic mass, the atom of the lightest isotope of hydrogen without its electron. [Gr, neuter of *prōtos* first]
■ **protonic** /prō-ton'ik/ adj.
❑ **proton beam** n a beam of protons produced by a proton accelerator. **proton pump inhibitor** n any of several short-term treatments for gastric and duodenal ulcers and for the eradication of the bacterium helicobacter pylori (*abbrev* **PPI**). **proton synchrotron** see **accelerator** under **accelerate**.

protonema /prō-tə-nē'mə/ (*bot*) n (*pl* **protonē'mata**) a branched filament produced by germination of a moss spore, giving rise to moss plants from buds. [**proto-**, and Gr *nēma* thread]
■ **protonē'mal** or **protonematal** /prō-tō-nem'ə-təl/ adj.

protonotary same as **prothonotary**.

proto-ore see **protore**.

protopathic /prō-tə-path'ik/ (*physiol*) adj of or relating to a certain type of nerve which is only affected by the coarser stimuli, eg pain; of or relating to this kind of reaction. [**proto-** and **pathic**]
■ **protop'athy** n.

Protophyta /prō-tof'i-tə/ (*biol*) n pl a group of unicellular plants. [**proto-**, and Gr *phyton* a plant]
■ **protophyte** /prō'tə-fīt/ n a member of the Protophyta. **protophytic** /prō-tō-fit'ik/ adj.

protoplasm /prō'tə-plazm/ n living material within a cell divided into discrete structures; the protein of which cells are composed. [**proto-**, and Gr *plasma* form, from *plassein* to form]
■ **protoplasm'ic**, **protoplas'mal** and **protoplasmat'ic** adj. **prō'toplast** n the person who, or thing which, was first formed; an original; the first parent; the living part of a plant cell excluding the cell wall, or isolated from the cell wall by some means such as the action of enzymes (*biol*). **protoplas'tic** adj.

protore /prō'tōr/ or '*tör*/ or **proto-ore** /prō'tō-ōr/ or '*ör*/ (*geol* and *mining*) n metalliferous material prior to the formation of ore by enrichment. [**proto-**]

protospatharius /prō-tə-spä-thā'ri-əs/ (*hist*) n the captain of the guards at Byzantium (also (*Fr*) **protospathaire** /prō-tō-spä-tār' or -*spä-thār*'/ or **protospataire**'). [Gr *prōtos* first, and *spathārios* a guardsman, from *spathē* a blade]

protostar /prō'tō-stär/ n a condensing mass of gas, a supposed early stage in the formation of a star. [**proto-**]

protostele /prō'tə-stēl or prō'tə-stēl-i/ (*bot*) n a stele in which the vascular tissue forms a solid core, with centrally placed xylem surrounded by phloem. [**proto-**]

protostome /prō'tō-stōm/ n a mollusc, arthropod or other invertebrate with a mouth developing directly from the blastopore. [**proto-**, and Gr *stoma* mouth]

Prototheria /prō-tə-thē'ri-ə/ (*zool*) n pl the monotremes. [**proto-**, and Gr *thēr* wild beast]
■ **protothē'rian** adj.

Prototracheata /prō-tə-trak-i-ā'tə/ (*zool*) n pl a former name for the class of primitive tracheate arthropods now called Onychophora. [**proto-**; see **trachea**]

prototrophic /prō-tō-trof'ik/ (*biol*) adj of bacteria, able to grow in its unsupplemented medium (*cf* **auxotroph**). [**proto-**, and Gr *trophē* food]
■ **prō'totroph** n a prototrophic organism. **prō'totrophy** n.

prototype /prō'tə-tīp/ n the first or original type or model from which anything is copied; an exemplar; a pattern; an ancestral form. ◆ vt to make, or use, a prototype of. [Fr, from Gr *prōtos* first, and *typos* a type]
■ **pro'totypal** or **prototypical** /-tip'i-kl/ adj.

protoxide /prō-tok'sīd/ (*chem*) n that oxide of a series which has the smallest number of oxygen atoms. [**proto-**]

protoxylem /prō-tə-zī'ləm/ (*bot*) n the first part of the xylem to be formed. [**proto-**]

Protozoa /prō-tō-zō'ə/ n pl the lowest and simplest of animals, unicellular forms or colonies multiplying by fission. [**proto-**, and Gr *zōion* an animal]

■ **protozō'al** or **protozō'an** adj. **protozō'an** or **protozō'on** n (*pl* **protozō'ans** and **protozō'a**) a member of the Protozoa. **protozō'ic** adj relating to the Protozoa; containing remains of the earliest life on Earth (variously applied) (*obs geol*). **protozoolog'ical** /-zō-ə-loj'i-kl/ adj. **protozool'ogist** n. **protozool'ogy** n. **protozoon** see **protozoan** above.

protract /prə- or prō-trakt'/ vt to draw out or lengthen in time; to prolong; to put off in time, postpone (*obs*); to lengthen out; to protrude; to draw to scale. [L *prōtrahere, -tractum,* from *prō* forth, and *trahere* to draw]
■ **protrac'ted** adj drawn out in time; prolonged; postponed (*obs*); lengthened out; drawn to scale. **protrac'tedly** adv. **protrac'tile** /-tīl or (*US*) -til/ or **protrac'tible** adj able to be thrust out. **protrac'tion** /-shən/ n the act of protracting or prolonging; the delaying of the termination of something; the plotting or laying down of the dimensions of anything on paper; a plan drawn to scale. **protrac'tive** adj drawing out in time; prolonging; delaying. **protrac'tor** n someone who, or something which, protracts; an instrument for measuring or drawing angles on paper; a muscle whose contraction draws a part of the body forward or away from the body (*anat*).

protreptic /prō-trep'tik/ adj exhorting or encouraging; didactic. ◆ n an exhortation. [Gr *protreptikos*, from *pro* forward, and *trepein* to turn, direct]
■ **protrep'tical** adj.

protrude /prə- or prō-trood'/ vt to thrust or push out or forward; to obtrude. ◆ vi to stick out or project. [L *prōtrūdere, -trūsum,* from *prō* forward, and *trūdere* to thrust]
■ **protrud'able**, **protrusible** /-troos'i-bl/ or **protru'sile** /-sīl or (*US*) -sil/ adj able to be protruded. **protru'dent** adj protruding, prominent. **protru'sion** /-zhən/ n the act of protruding; the state of being protruded; something which protrudes. **protru'sive** adj thrusting or impelling forward; protruding. **protru'sively** adv. **protru'siveness** n.

protuberance /prə- or prō-tū'bə-rəns/ n a bulging out; a swelling. [L *prōtūberāre, -ātum,* from *prō* forward, and *tūber* a swelling]
■ **protū'berant** adj. **protū'berantly** adv. **protū'berate** vi to bulge out. **protūberā'tion** n.

protyle /prō'tīl/ n a name proposed by Sir William Crookes in 1886 for a hypothetical primitive substance from which the chemical elements were thought to have possibly been formed (also **prothyle**, **prothyl** or **protyl** /-til/). [Gr *prōtos* first (though Crookes himself gave Gr *pro* before, as the etymon), and *hȳlē* matter]

proud /prowd/ adj having excessive self-esteem; arrogant; haughty; having a proper sense of self-respect; exultantly aware of the credit due to or reflected on oneself; having a glowing feeling of gratification (because of; with *of*); giving reason for pride or boasting; manifesting pride; having an appearance of pride, vigour, boldness and freedom; stately; high-spirited, fearless, untamable; swelling; sexually excited (*esp* of some female animals); of eg a nail-head, projecting or standing out from a plane surface. [OE *prūd, prūt* proud; perh from a LL word connected with L *prōdesse* to be of advantage]
■ **proud'ful** adj (*esp dialect*) proud. **proud'ish** adj somewhat proud. **proud'ly** adv. **proud'ness** n (*rare*) pride.
❑ **proud flesh** n a growth or excrescence of flesh in a wound, excessive granulation tissue. **proud-heart'ed** adj (*Shakesp*) having a proud spirit. **proud-mind'ed** adj (*Shakesp*) proud in mind. **proud'-pied** adj (*Shakesp*) gorgeously variegated. **proud-stom'ached** adj (*archaic*) haughty, arrogant.
■ **do someone proud** (*inf*) to provide lavish entertainment for someone; to honour someone, give someone cause for pride.

proul and **prouler** earlier forms of **prowl** and **prowler**.

Proustian /proos'ti-ən/ adj relating to or associated with the French novelist Marcel *Proust* (1871–1922), or to his novels or his style. ◆ n an admirer of Proust.

proustite /proos'tīt/ n a red silver ore, sulphide of arsenic and silver, also known as **ruby silver ore**. [JL *Proust* (1754–1826), French chemist, who distinguished it from pyrargyrite]

Prov. *abbrev*: Provence; (the Book of) Proverbs (*Bible*); Provincial; Provost.

provand, **provend** /prov'ənd/ or **proviant** /prov'i-ənt/ n an allowance of food; provender (*Shakesp*); provisions; fodder. [MLGer *provande*, Du *provande* or *proviand*, Ger *Proviant*, appar from LL *provenda* for L *praebenda*, from *praebēre* to allow]
■ **prov'ant** adj (*obs*) issued to soldiers, hence inferior.

prove /proov/ vt (*pap* **proved** or **prov'en**, see below) to establish or ascertain as truth by argument or otherwise; to demonstrate; to check by the opposite operation (eg division by multiplication) (*maths*); to obtain probate of (a will) (*law*); to experience or suffer; to test; to test the genuineness of; to ascertain; to cause or allow (dough) to rise. ◆ vi to try or test, *esp* by tasting; to turn out; to be shown afterwards; to become (*archaic*); to turn out well (*obs*); (of dough) to rise. —Also *(obs)* **preve**, with *pap* **prov'en** surviving as the usual past participle in N America (pronounced /proov'n/) and becoming more common in Britain (pronounced /proov'n/ or /prōv'n/), and retained *specif* in Scots law (pronounced /prŏv'n/) in the verdict **not proven**, declaring that the charges in a criminal trial have not been proved. [OFr *prover* (Fr *prouver*) from L *probāre*, from *probus* excellent; perh partly from OE *prōfian* to assume to be, from L *probāre*. Fr formerly had two forms of the verb (*preuver* and *prouver*), using respectively the vowels developed from the original L *o* in stressed and unstressed positions, and ME also has two forms, giving **preeve**, **prieve**, etc, whence Scot **pree**, as well as **prove**]

■ **prove'able** or **prov'able** *adj*. **prove'ably** or **prov'ably** *adv*. **prov'er** *n*. **prov'ing** *n* the action of the verb. ◆ *adj* testing, as in **proving ground** a place for testing scientifically (also *fig*) and **proving flight** a test flight.

■ **prove oneself** to do something which shows one's ability, courage, loyalty, etc. **the exception proves the rule** generally held to mean that the finding or making of an exception proves that the rule holds good for all cases that are not exceptions, but held by some to mean that the exception tests the rule, thereby proving its general validity.

provection /prō-vek'shən/ *(linguistics) n* the transferring of a letter from the end of one word to the beginning of the next, eg *a newt* from *an ewt*. [LL *provectio*, from L *pro-* forth, and *vehere, vectum* to carry]

proveditor /prō-ved'i-tər/, **proveditore** /prō-ved-i-tō're or prō-ved-i-tö're/, **provedor**, **provedore** or **providor** /prov-i-dōr' or prov-i-dör'/ *n* a high official, governor, inspector or commissioner, *esp* in the Republic of Venice *(hist)*; a purveyor. [Ital *provveditore* (formerly *proveditore*), Port *provedor*, Sp *proveedor*]

proven see **prove**.

provenance /prov'i-nəns/ *n* the source, *esp* of a work of art; a record of the owners and source of a work of art. [Fr, from L *prō-* forth, and *venīre* to come]

Provençal /prov-ä-säl'/ *adj* of or relating to *Provence*, in France, or to its inhabitants or language. ◆ *n* a native of Provence; the language of Provence, a form of Langue d'oc. [L *prōvinciālis*, from *prōvincia* province]

■ **Provençale** /prov-ä-säl'/ *adj* in cooking, prepared with oil and garlic and *usu* tomatoes.

Provence-rose /pro-vãs'rōz/ *n* the cabbage rose, *Rosa centifolia*, *orig* cultivated in Provence.

provend see **provand**.

provender /prov'in-dər or prov'ən-dər/ *n* food; dry food for animals, such as hay or corn, *esp* a mixture of meal and cut straw or hay. ◆ *vt* and *vi* to feed. [OFr *provendre* for *provende*, from LL *provenda*; see **provand**]

provenience /prō-vē'ni-əns/ *(chiefly US) n* provenance. [L *prōvenīre*; see **provenance**]

proventriculus /prō-ven-trik'ū-ləs/ *(zool) n* in birds, the anterior thin-walled part of the stomach, containing the gastric glands; in insects and crustaceans, the muscular thick-walled chamber of the gut. [**pro-²**, and L *ventriculus*, dimin of *venter* belly]

proverb /prov'ûrb/ *n* a short familiar saying expressing a supposed truth or moral lesson; a byword; a saying that requires explanation (*obs*, eg *Bible*); (in *pl*; with *cap*) a book of maxims in the Old Testament; a dramatic composition in which a proverb gives a name and character to the plot. ◆ *vt* to speak of proverbially; to make a byword of; to provide with a proverb. [Fr *proverbe*, from L *prōverbium*, from *prō-* publicly, and *verbum* a word]

■ **prover'bial** /prə-vûr'bi-əl/ *adj* like or of the nature of a proverb; expressed or mentioned in a proverb; notorious, well-known. **prover'bialism** *n* a saying in the form of, or like, a proverb. **prover'bialist** *n*. **prover'bialize** or **-ise** *vi* to speak in proverbs. **prover'bially** *adv*.

proviant see **provand**.

provide /prə-vīd' or prō-vīd'/ *vt* to supply; to afford or yield; to appoint or give a right to a benefice, *esp* before it is actually vacant; to stipulate; to make ready beforehand (*obs*); to prepare for future use (*obs*). ◆ *vi* to make provision, to procure supplies, means or whatever may be desirable or necessary; to take measures (for or against). [L *prōvidēre*, from *prō* before, and *vidēre* to see]

■ **provi'dable** *adj*. **provi'ded** or **provi'ding** *conj* (often with *that*) on condition; on these terms; with the understanding. **provi'der** *n*.

❑ **provided school** *n* formerly, in England and Wales, a school maintained by, and under the management of, the local authority.

providence /prov'i-dəns/ *n* foresight; prudent management and thrift; timely preparation; the foresight and benevolent care of God (*theol*); God, considered in this relation (*usu* with *cap*; *theol*); an instance of God's arranging or intervening in something for his purpose (*theol*); an

occurrence attributed to God's ordering or intervention (*theol*); a disaster (*US*). [L *prōvidens, -entis*, prp of *prōvidēre*, from *prō* before, and *vidēre* to see]

■ **prov'ident** *adj* seeing beforehand, and providing for the future; prudent; thrifty; frugal. **providential** /prov-i-den'shl/ *adj* affected by, or proceeding from, divine providence; fortunate; opportune; provident (*rare*). **providen'tially** *adv*. **prov'idently** *adv*.

❑ **provident society** same as **friendly society** (see under **friend**).

providor see **proveditor**.

province /prov'ins/ *n* a portion of an empire or a state marked off for purposes of government or in some way historically distinct; the district over which an archbishop has jurisdiction; a territorial division of the Jesuits, Templars and other religious orders; a faunal or floral area (*biol*); a region; a field of duty, activity or knowledge; a department; (in *pl*) all parts of the country except the capital (*esp* theatre and press). [Fr, from L *prōvincia* an official charge, hence a province]

■ **provincial** /prə-vin'shl/ *adj* relating to a province; belonging to a province or the provinces; local; showing the habits and manners of a person from a province or country district; unpolished, unsophisticated; narrow-minded. ◆ *n* an inhabitant of a province or country district; an unpolished or unsophisticated person; the superintendent of the heads of the religious houses in a province (*RC*). **provin'cialism** *n* a manner, mode of speech or turn of thought peculiar to a province or a country district; a local expression; the state or quality of being provincial; the ignorance and narrowness of interests shown by someone who gives his or her attention entirely to local affairs. **provin'cialist** *n*. **provinciality** /prə-vin-shi-al'i-ti/ *n*. **provin'cialize** or **-ise** *vt* to make provincial. **provin'cially** *adv*.

provincial rose /prə-vin'shl rōz/ *n* a rose, a variety of *Rosa gallica*, cultivated at *Provins* /pro-vẽs/ in Seine-et-Marne, France (also **province rose** or **Provins rose**); a shoe rosette (*Shakesp*).

provine /prə-vīn'/ *vt* and *vi* to propagate by layering. [Fr *provigner*, from OFr *provain*, from L *prōpāgō, -inis* a slip, layer]

provirus /prō-vī'rəs/ *(med) n* the form of a virus when it is integrated into the DNA of a host cell. [**pro-¹** (2)]

■ **provi'ral** *adj*.

provision /prə-vizh'ən/ *n* the act of providing; something that is provided or prepared; measures taken beforehand; a clause in a law or a deed; a stipulation; a rule for guidance; an appointment by the Pope to a benefice not yet vacant; preparation; previous agreement; a store or stock; (*usu* in *pl*) a store of food; (in *pl*) food. ◆ *vt* to supply with provisions or food. [Fr, from L *prōvīsiō, -ōnis*, from *prōvidēre*; see **provide**]

■ **provi'sional** *adj* provided for the occasion; to meet necessity; (of eg an arrangement) adopted on the understanding that it may be changed later; containing a provision; (with *cap*) relating to the Provisional IRA (Irish Republican Army), the militant group which in 1969 split from the main body of the IRA (which was thereafter known as the Official IRA). ◆ *n* (with *cap*) a member of the Provisional IRA (*inf* shortening **Prō'vō**). **provi'sionally** *adv*. **provi'sionary** *adj* (*rare*) provisional.

❑ **provisional judgement** *n* a judgement given as far as the available evidence admits, but subject to correction when more light is shed on the matter. **provisional order** *n* an order granted by a secretary of state, which, when confirmed by the legislature, has the force of an act of parliament. **provisional remedy** *n* a means of detaining in safety a person or property until a decision is made on some point in which they are concerned. **provision merchant** *n* a general dealer in articles of food.

proviso /prə-vī'zō or prō-vī'zō/ *n* (*pl* **provi'sos** or **provi'soes**) a provision or condition in a deed or other writing; the clause containing it; any condition. [From the L law phrase *prōvīsō quod* it being provided that]

■ **provi'sorily** /-zə-ri-li/ *adv*. **provi'sory** *adj* containing a proviso or condition; conditional; making provision for the time; temporary.

provisor /prə-vī'zər or prō-vī'zər/ *(obs* or *hist) n* someone who provides; a purveyor; a person to whom the Pope has granted the right to the next vacancy in a benefice. [L *prōvīsor, -ōris* provider]

■ **Statute of Provisors** an act of the English parliament passed in 1351 to prevent the Pope from exercising the power of creating provisors.

provitamin /prō-vit'ə-min or prō-vīt'ə-min/ *(physiol) n* a substance which is not a vitamin but which is readily transformed into a vitamin within an organism. [L *prō* before, and **vitamin**]

Provo see **Provisional** under **provision**.

provocable, etc see under **provoke**.

provoke /prə-vōk'/ *vt* to annoy or exasperate; to excite or call into action, stimulate; to incite or bring about; to excite with anger or sexual desire; to call up or evoke (feelings, desires, etc); to summon (*archaic*); to call out or challenge (*obs*). ◆ *vi* (*Dryden*) to appeal. [L *prōvocāre*, *-ātum*, from *prō-* forth, and *vocāre* to call]

■ **provocable** /*prov'ək-ə-bl* or *prə-vōk'ə-bl*/ *adj* (*esp* formerly) provokable. **prov'ocant** *n*. **provocateur** /*pro-vo-ka-tœr*/ *n* (*Fr*) someone who stirs up unrest and dissatisfaction for political ends (see also **agent provocateur**). **provocā'tion** *n* the act of provoking; something that provokes; any cause of anger. **provocative** /*-vok'ə-tiv*/ *adj* tending, or intended, to provoke or excite; exciting sexual desire, *esp* by design. ◆ *n* anything that provokes. **provoc'atively** *adv*. **provoc'ativeness** *n*. **prov'ocātor** *n*. **provoc'atory** *adj*. **provōk'able** *adj*. **provoke'ment** *n* (*Spenser*). **provōk'er** *n*. **provōk'ing** *adj* irritating; stimulating. **provōk'ingly** *adv*.

provolone /*pro-və-lō'nē*/ *n* a N Italian soft cheese. [Ital]

provost /*prov'əst*/ *n* the dignitary presiding over a cathedral or collegiate church; in certain colleges, the head; in Scotland, the chief councillor of a district council, formerly the chief magistrate of a burgh, corresponding to a mayor in England; an officer who arrests and keeps in custody (*Shakesp*). ◆ *adj* /*prə-vō'* or (*US*) *prō'vō*/ relating to military police, as in *provost officer*. [OE *profast* (*prafost*), OFr *provost* (Fr *prevôt*), from LL *prōpositus*, from *prō-* for *prae* at the head, and *positus* set]

■ **prov'ostry** *n* the position or authority of a provost. **prov'ostship** *n* the position of a provost.

❑ **provost guard** /*prō'vō*/ *n* (*US*) a detachment of soldiers acting as military police. **provost marshal** /*prə-vō*/ or (*US*) *prō'vō*/ *n* (in the army and air force) the head of military police, an officer with special powers for enforcing discipline and securing prisoners until trial; (in the navy) the officer (master-at-arms) having charge of prisoners. **provost-ser'geant** /*prə-vō'* or (*US*) *prō'vō-*/ *n* a sergeant of military police.

■ **Lady Provost** the wife (or other female relative, etc) of a Lord Provost, *esp* when supporting him in certain of his official duties. **Lord Provost** the title of the provost of Edinburgh, Glasgow, Perth, Aberdeen or Dundee.

prow[1] /*prow*, formerly sometimes *prō*/ *n* the front part of a ship; the nose of an aeroplane; a projecting front part; a ship (*poetic*). [Fr *proue*, or Port, Sp or Genoese *proa*, from L *prōra*, from Gr *prōira*]

prow[2] see under **prowess**.

prowess /*prow'is* or *prow'es*/ *n* bravery; valour; daring; accomplishment. [OFr *prou* (Fr *preux*); connected with L *prōd-* in *prōdesse* to be useful]

■ **prow** /*prow*/ *adj* (*archaic*) valiant. **prow'essed** *adj*.

prowl /*prowl*, formerly *prōl*/ *vi* to keep moving about, restlessly as if in search of something or stealthily (as if) in search of prey or plunder. ◆ *n* the act of prowling. [ME *prollen*; origin unknown]

■ **prowl'er** *n* one who prowls, *esp* loitering stealthily with a view to committing a crime. **prowl'ing** *n* and *adj*. **prowl'ingly** *adv*.

❑ **prowl car** *n* (chiefly *US*) a police patrol car.

■ **on the prowl** occupied in prowling.

prox. *abbrev*: proximo.

prox. acc. *abbrev*: proxime accessit (qv).

proxemics /*prok-sē'miks*/ *n sing* the study of the human use of physical space in non-verbal communication, *esp* the distances that people maintain between themselves and others while interacting. [**proximity**, on the model of **phonemics**, etc]

proximate /*prok'si-mət* or *-māt*/ *adj* nearest or next; without anything between, eg a cause and its effect; near and immediate; immediately before or after. [L *proximus* next, superl of *prope* near]

■ **prox'imal** *adj* (*biol*) at the near, inner or attached end, *opp* to *distal*. **prox'imally** *adv*. **prox'imately** *adv*. **proximā'tion** and **proxim'ity** *n* immediate nearness in time, place, relationship, etc.

❑ **proximate cause** *n* a cause which immediately precedes the effect. **proximate object** *n* (*philos*) an object or thing which must exist, or otherwise it would be logically impossible to have cognition of it. **proximity fuse** *n* a device for causing a missile or shell to explode when it comes near the target. **proximity talks** *n pl* a form of diplomatic negotiation in which the parties involved do not meet face to face but deal with independent mediators.

proxime accessit /*prok'si-mā ak-ses'it* or *a-kes'it*/ *n* (*pl* **proxime accessits**) the person next in order of merit to the winner. [L, he or she came closest]

proximo /*prok'si-mō*/ (*old commerce*) *adv* next month. [L *proximo* (*mense*) next (month)]

proxy /*prok'si*/ *n* the agency of someone who acts for another; someone who acts or votes for another; the writing by which he or she is authorized to do so; a substitute. [**procuracy**]

❑ **proxy server** *n* (*comput*) an intermediate server via which client devices can access other servers. **proxy-wedd'ed** *adj* (*Tennyson*) wedded by proxy.

proyn or **proyne** /*proin*/ obsolete forms of **prune**[1,2,3].

Prozac® /*prō'zak*/ *n* the proprietary name for **fluoxetine**.

prozymite /*proz'i-mīt*/ *n* a person who uses leavened bread in the Eucharist, *opp* to azymite. [Gr *prozymia* ferments]

PRP *abbrev*: performance-related pay; profit-related pay.

PRS *abbrev*: Performing Rights Society; President of the Royal Society.

PRT *abbrev*: petroleum revenue tax.

Pruce /*proos*/ (*obs*) *n* Prussia. ◆ *adj* Prussian. [Anglo-Fr *Prus*, *Pruz*, etc]

prude /*prood*/ *n* a person of priggish or affected modesty; someone who has or pretends to have extreme propriety. ◆ *adj* (*rare*) priggish or affectedly modest; claiming extreme propriety. [OFr *prode*, fem of *prou*, *prod* excellent; cf **prow** under **prowess**, **proud**]

■ **pru'dery** *n* the manners, opinions, etc of a prude. **pru'dish** *adj*. **pru'dishly** *adv*. **pru'dishness** *n*.

prudent /*proo'dənt*/ *adj* cautious and wise in conduct; discreet; characterized by, behaving with, showing, having or dictated by forethought. [L *prūdēns*, *prūdentis*, contraction of *prōvidēns*, prp of *prōvidēre* to foresee]

■ **pru'dence** *n* the quality of being prudent; wisdom applied to practice; attention to self-interest; caution. **prudential** /*prū-den'shl*/ *adj* having regard to considerations of prudence; relating to prudence; prudent; concerned with administration (*US*). ◆ *n* (*gen* in *pl*) a matter or consideration of prudence; a prudent maxim. **pruden'tialism** *n* a system based on prudence alone. **pruden'tialist** *n*. **prudentiality** /*prū-den-shi-al'i-ti*/ *n*. **pruden'tially** *adv*. **pru'dently** *adv*.

prudery see under **prude**.

prud'homme /*prü-dom'*/ *n* a discreet man (*obs*); a skilled workman (*obs*); in France, a member of a board for settling labour disputes. [OFr *prud* or *prod* (nominative *pros*) good, and *homme* man]

prudish, etc see under **prude**.

pruh see **proo**.

pruina /*proo-ī'nə*/ (*bot*) *n* a powdery bloom or waxy secretion. [L *pruīna* hoarfrost]

■ **pruinose** /*proo'i-nōs*/ *adj* covered with pruina; having a frosted look.

pruine a Shakespearean spelling of **prune**[3].

prune[1] /*proon*/ *vt* (formerly also **proin**, **proine**, **proyn** or **proyne**) to trim by lopping off superfluous parts; to remove anything superfluous from (*fig*); to remove by pruning. [OFr *proignier*; origin unknown]

■ **pru'ner** *n*. **pru'ning** *n* the act of pruning or trimming.

❑ **pruning bill** or **hook** *n* a hooked bill for pruning with. **pruning knife** *n* a large knife with a slightly hooked point for pruning. **pruning saw** *n* a saw with a *usu* tapering straight or curved blade, often attached or attachable to a long handle, for pruning trees, etc. **pruning shears** *n pl* shears for pruning shrubs, etc.

prune[2] /*proon*/ (*archaic*) *vt* to preen (formerly also **proin**, **proine**, **proyn**, **proyne** or **proign**). [Origin obscure]

prune[3] /*proon*/ *n* (formerly also **pruine**, **proin**, **proine**, **proyn**, **proyne** or (*Shakesp*) **prewyn**) a dried plum; a plum suitable for drying (*US*); a plum (*obs*); the dark purple colour of prune juice; a dud pilot (*RAF sl*); a despised or silly person (*inf*). ◆ *adj* of the colour of prune juice. [Fr, from L *prūna*, pl of *prūnum* (taken for a singular noun); cf Gr *prou(m)non* plum]

prunella[1] /*proo-nel'ə*/ *n* a sore throat; quinsy; (with *cap*; also **Brunell'a**) the self-heal genus of labiate plants, once reputed to cure prunella. [Latinized from Ger *Bräune* quinsy (from the brownness of the tongue), or LL *brūnus*, from general Germanic *brūn* brown]

prunella[2] /*proo-nel'ə*/ *n* a strong silk or woollen material, formerly used for academic and clerical gowns and women's shoes (also **prunelle'** and **prunell'o** (*pl* **prunell'os**)). ◆ *adj* made of prunella. [Appar Fr *prunelle* sloe, dimin of *prune* plum]

prunella[3] /*proo-nel'ə*/ *n* a bird of the genus *Prunella* (formerly *Accentor*), including the hedge sparrow. [L *prunum* a plum]

prunello[1] /*proo-nel'ō*/ *n* (*pl* **prunell'os**) a little prune; a kind of dried plum. [Obs Ital *prunella*, dimin of *pruna* (now *prugna*) plum]

prunello[2] see **prunella**[2].

prunt /*prunt*/ *n* a moulded glass ornament attached to a glass object such as a vase; a tool for making it. [Origin uncertain]

■ **prunt'ed** *adj*.

prunus /*proo'nəs*/ *n* a tree or shrub belonging to the genus *Prunus*, including the plum, apricot, peach, cherry, almond and sloe. [L, plum tree]

prurient /*proo'ri-ənt*/ *adj* having an unhealthy interest in sexual matters; arousing such interest; itching; causing itching (*bot*; *rare*). [L *prūriens*, *-entis*, prp of *prūrīre* to itch]

■ **pru'rience** or **pru'riency** *n*. **pru'riently** *adv*.

prurigo /proo-rī'gō/ (med) n (pl **prurī'gos**) an eruption on the skin, causing great itching. [L prūrīgō, -inis, from prūrīre to itch]
■ **pruriginous** /-rij'i-nəs/ adj.

pruritus /proo-rī'təs/ (med) n itching. [L prūrītus, from prūrīre to itch]
■ **pruritic** /-rit'ik/ adj.

prusik /prus'ik/ (mountaineering) n (in full, **prusik sling**; also cap) a type of rope sling attached to a climbing rope, which grips firmly when carrying weight but when unweighted can be moved up the rope. ◆ vi and vt (**prus'iking**; **prus'iked**) to climb or raise (oneself) up by means of two such slings. [Karl Prusik (1895–1961), Austrian climber]
□ **prusik knot** n (also cap) the type of knot by which a prusik sling is attached to a rope.

Prussian /prush'ən/ adj of or relating to Prussia, a former state of N Central Europe, now in Germany. ◆ n an inhabitant, native or citizen of Prussia.
■ **Pruss'ianism** n the spirit of Prussian nationality; arrogant militarism. **Pruss'ianize** or **-ise** vt and vi to make or become Prussian. **Pruss'ianizer** or **-s-** n. **prussiate** /prus'** or prush'i-āt/ n (chem) a cyanide; a ferricyanide; a ferrocyanide. **pruss'ic** (also sometimes /proos'ik/) adj relating to Prussian blue. **Prussifica'tion** n. **Pruss'ify** vt to Prussianize, assimilate to Prussian ways, etc.
□ **Prussian** (or **prussian**) **blue** n ferric ferrocyanide, a colour pigment, discovered in Berlin; the very dark blue colour of this. **prussic acid** n hydrocyanic acid, a deadly poison, first obtained from Prussian blue.
■ **Old Prussian** the extinct Baltic language of the former inhabitants of East and West Prussia.

pry[1] /prī/ vi (**prying**; **pried**) to peer or peep into something that is private (also fig); to examine things with impertinent curiosity. ◆ n an act of prying (rare); someone who pries (like Paul Pry, in John Poole's (1792–1879) comedy of that name). [ME prien; origin unknown]
■ **prī'er** (also **pry'er**) n someone who pries. **pry'ing** n and adj. **pry'ingly** adv.
■ **pry out** to investigate or find out by prying.

pry[2] /prī/ vt a form of **prise**[1].

prys and **pryse** old spellings of **price** and **prize**[1].

pryse /prīz/ (Walter Scott) n a horn-blast at the taking or killing of a deer. [OFr pris taken; cf **prize**[2]]

prytaneum /pri-ta-nē'əm/ (ancient hist) n (pl **prytanē'a**) the town hall of an ancient Greek city. [Latinized from Gr prytaneion, from prytanis a presiding magistrate]

pr'ythee or **prythee** /pridh'ē/ same as **prithee**.

Przewalski's horse (also found in various other spellings) /prə-she- or prə-zhi-val'skiz hörs/ n a wild horse discovered in Central Asia by Nikolai Przewalski (1839–88), Russian explorer.

PS abbrev: Pferdestärke (Ger), horsepower (now esp metric horsepower); (Royal) Pharmaceutical Society; Philological Society; Police Sergeant; postscript; private secretary; prompt side (theatre).

Ps. abbrev: Psalm or Psalms (also **Psa.**); (the Book of) Psalms (Bible).

PSA abbrev: pleasant Sunday afternoon; formerly, Property Services Agency; prostate-specific antigen, a protein whose presence in large quantities is an indication of prostate cancer; Public Services Authority.

psaligraphy /sa-lig'rə-fi/ n the art of paper-cutting to make pictures. [Gr psalis shears, and graphein to write]

psalm /säm/ n a devotional song or hymn, esp one of those included in the Old Testament **Book of Psalms**. [OE psalm, psealm, from LL psalmus, from Gr psalmos, music of or to a stringed instrument, from psallein to pluck]
■ **psalmist** /säm'ist/ n a composer of psalms, esp (with cap) David. **psalmodic** /sal-mod'ik/ or **psalmod'ical** adj relating to psalmody. **psalmodist** /sal'mə-dist or säm'ə-dist/ n a singer of psalms. **psalmodize** or **-ise** /sal'mə-dīz or säm'/ vi to practise psalmody. **psalmody** /sal' or säm'/ n (Gr psalmōidiā singing to the harp) the singing of psalms, esp in public worship; psalms collectively.
□ **psalm'-book** n a book containing psalms for purposes of worship. **psalm'-tune** n.

Psalter /söl'tər/ n the **Book of Psalms**, esp when printed separately from the rest of the Bible; (without cap) a book of psalms. [OE saltere, from L psaltērium, from Gr psaltērion a psaltery]
■ **psalterian** /söl-tē'ri-ən/ adj relating to a psalter; like a psaltery. **psal'tery** n an ancient and medieval stringed instrument like the zither, played by plucking; (with cap; rare) the Psalter. **psal'tress** n a woman who plays the psaltery.

psalterium /söl-tē'ri-əm/ n (pl **psaltē'ria**) the third division of a ruminant's stomach, the omasum or manyplies. [From the appearance of its lamellae, like a stringed instrument; see **psaltery**]

psammite /sam'īt/ (geol; rare) n any rock composed of sand-grains. [Gr psammos sand]
■ **psammitic** /sam-it'ik/ adj. **psamm'ophil** or **psamm'ophile** n a sand-loving plant. **psammoph'ilous** adj. **psammophyte** /sam'ō-fīt/ n (biol) a plant adapted to growing on sand. **psammophytic** /sam-ō-fit'ik/ adj.

p's and q's /pēz ən(d) kūz'/ n pl correct social manners and behaviour, esp in the phrase to mind one's p's and q's. [Various explanations have been given; among these are the supposed admonition to children learning to write not to confuse the letters p and q, and an alteration of p(l)ease and (than)k you's]

PSBR (econ) abbrev: Public Sector Borrowing Requirement.

psc (milit) abbrev: passed staff college.

pschent /ps'hhent, pskent or skent/ (ancient hist) n the crown of the Egyptian pharaohs. [Gr, from Egyp]

PSDR (econ) abbrev: Public Sector Debt Repayment.

psellism /sel'i-zm or psel'i-zm/ n a defect in articulation (also **psellis'mus**). [Gr psellismos, from psellos stammering]

psephism /sē'fi-zm or psē'fi-zm/ (ancient hist) n a decree of the Athenian assembly (from their voting with pebbles). [Gr psēphos a pebble]
■ **pse'phite** n (geol) a rock composed of pebbles, a conglomerate. **psephit'ic** adj. **psepholog'ical** adj. **psephol'ogist** n. **psephol'ogy** n the sociological and statistical study of election results and trends (also **psephoanal'ysis**).

pseud /sūd or sood/ (inf) n a pretentious person, esp intellectually. ◆ adj (also **pseud'o**) false, sham; pretentious. [**pseud-**]
■ **pseud'ery** n (inf) falseness; pretentiousness. **pseud'ish** adj false, spurious; pretentious.

pseud. abbrev: pseudonym.

pseud- /sūd- or sood-/ or **pseudo-** /sū-dō- or soo-dō-/ combining form denoting: sham, false, spurious; deceptively resembling; isomerous with or closely related to (chem); temporary, provisional. [Gr pseudēs false]
■ **pseudaesthē'sia** n imaginary feeling, eg in an amputated limb. **pseudax'is** n (bot) a sympodium. **pseudepig'rapha** n pl books ascribed to Old Testament characters, but not judged genuine by scholars. **pseudepigraph'ic, pseudepigraph'ical** or **pseudepig'raphous** adj. **pseudepig'raphy** n the ascription to books of false names of authors. **pseudimā'go** n (zool) a subimago. **pseu'doacid** n a substance that can exist in two tautomeric forms, one of which functions as an acid, eg nitromethane. **pseudo-archā'ic** adj sham antique; artificially archaistic; clumsily and inaccurately imitative of the old, eg in style. **pseudo-ar'chāism** n. **pseu'dobulb** n (bot) a swollen stem internode in some orchids. **pseu'docarp** n (bot) a fruit formed from other parts in addition to the gynaeceum. **pseudo-Christian'ity** n. **pseudoclass'icism** n. **pseu'docode** n (comput) instructions written in symbolic language which must be translated into an acceptable program language before they can be executed. **pseudocyesis** /-sī-ē'sis/ n (Gr kyēsis, from kyein to be pregnant; psychol) a psychosomatic condition marked by many of the symptoms of pregnancy. **pseudoephedrine** /-ef'i-drēn or -i-fed'rin/ n (chem) a naturally occurring isomer of ephedrine, used in the form of its hydrochloride as a bronchodilator. **pseudofolliculi'tis** n (med) a chronic disorder, esp of the neck, of men who shave, in which the tips of the shaved hairs cause the formation of papules. **pseu'dogene** n a copy of a gene that is defective and not transcribed. **pseudo-Goth'ic** adj and n sham or would-be Gothic. **pseu'dograph** n a writing falsely ascribed. **pseudog'raphy** n unsatisfactory spelling. **pseudohermaph'roditism** n (anat) a congenital condition in which a man has external genitalia resembling those of a woman, and vice versa. **pseudologia** /-lō'ji-ə/ n (Gr, falsehood; med) lying in speech or writing (**pseudologia fantastica** pathological lying, a psychiatric disorder in which the sufferer has an uncontrollable tendency to tell lies and create fantastic stories). **pseu'dologue** n a liar; a person suffering from pseudologia fantastica. **pseudol'ogy** n the art or science of lying. **pseu'domartyr** n a false martyr. **pseu'domembrane** n a false membrane. **pseudomō'nad** (or (esp US) /-dom'/) or **pseudomō'nas** n (pl **pseudomō'nads** (or /-dom'/) or **pseudomō'nadēs**) (bacteriol) a member of the genus Pseudomonas of schizomycetes, comprising short rod-shaped bacteria which are found in soil and in water. **pseu'domorph** n (geol) a portion of a mineral showing the outward form of another which it has replaced by molecular substitution or otherwise. **pseudomor'phic** or **pseudomor'phous** adj. **pseudomor'phism** n. **pseu'donym** n a fictitious name assumed eg by an author. **pseudonym'ity** n. **pseudon'ymous** adj. **pseudon'ymously** adv. **pseu'dopod** n a psychic projection from a medium (spiritualism); a footlike process of the body-wall, not a true leg but serving as one, as eg in caterpillars (zool); a pseudopodium. **pseudopō'dium** n (pl **pseudopō'dia**) (biol) a process protruding from the cell of a protozoan, etc, used for

movement or feeding. **pseudopreg'nancy** n same as **pseudocyesis** above. **pseudoran'dom** adj (comput) referring to a set of numbers generated by a computer and therefore not entirely random, but sufficiently so for most purposes. **pseu'doscope** n a kind of stereoscope that interchanges convex and concave in appearance. **pseudoscor'pion** n any member of the order **Pseudoscorpionid'ea** of arachnids, tiny carnivorous creatures resembling tailless scorpions, found under stones, bark, leaves, etc. **pseudosolu'tion** n (chem) a colloidal suspension. **pseudosymm'etry** n (crystallog) a deceptively close approach by a crystal to a higher degree of symmetry, eg when the axes of a tetragonal crystal are so close to being equal that on casual inspection the crystal appears to be cubic (**pseudocubic symmetry**) or when a crystal that is not quite hexagonal appears to be so (**pseudohexagonal symmetry**).

pshaw /pshö, shö or pshə/ interj expressing contempt or impatience. ◆ vi to say 'pshaw'. ◆ vt to say 'pshaw' at. [Spontaneous expression]

psi /psī, psē, sī or sē/ n the twenty-third letter (Ψ, ψ) of the Greek alphabet, equivalent to ps; as a Greek numeral ψ' = 700, ,ψ = 700000. [Gr psei]
■ **psi'on** n a psi particle. **psion'ic** adj. **psion'ics** n sing the use of the paranormal in the treatment of illness, etc.
❏ **psionic medicine** n psionics. **psi particle** n an elementary particle with a very long life, formed by an electron-positron collision. **psi phenomena** n pl the phenomena of parapsychology.

psi abbrev: pounds per square inch.

psilanthropism /sī-lan'thrə-pi-zm or psī-lan'thrə-pi-zm/ n the doctrine that Christ was a mere man. [Gr psílos bare, and anthrōpos man]
■ **psilanthropic** /-throp'ik/ adj. **psilan'thropist** n. **psilan'thropy** n.

psilocin /sī'lō-sin/ n a hallucinogenic drug found, like psilocybin, in the Mexican mushroom Psilocybe mexicana and other mushrooms. [**psilocybin**]

psilocybin /sī-lō-sī'bin/ n a hallucinogenic drug, obtained from the Mexican mushroom Psilocybe mexicana and other mushrooms. [Gr psílos bare, and kybē head]

psilomelane /sī-lom'ə-lān, sī-lō-mel'ān or psī-/ n (geol) an oxide of manganese, usu with barium, etc, occurring in smooth black botryoidal masses. [Gr psílos bare, and melās, -anos black]

Psilophyton /sī-lō-fī'ton or psī-lō-fī'ton/ n (palaeontol) a very simple Devonian fossil pteridophyte, from which is named the order **Psilophytales** /-fī-tā'lēz/, early landplants. [Gr psílos bare, and phyton plant]

psilosis /sī-lō'sis or psī-lō'sis/ n loss of hair (pathol); sprue (from the loss of epithelium) (obs pathol); deaspiration (Gr grammar). [Gr psīlōsis, from psílos bare]
■ **psilot'ic** adj relating to psilosis.

Psilotum /sī-lō'təm or psī-lō'təm/ (bot) n a genus of rootless pteridophytes from which is named the order **Psilotá'ceae**. [Gr psílōton the name of some plant, from psílos bare (because of the almost leafless stem)]

psion, etc see under **psi** (n).

PSIS abbrev: Permanent Secretaries Committee on the Intelligence Services.

Psittacus /sit'ə-kəs or psit'ə-kəs/ n the grey-parrot genus. [Gr psittakos parrot]
■ **psitt'acine** /-sīn/ adj of or like parrots. **psittacosaur** /(p)si-tak'ō-sör/ or **psittacosaur'us** n (Gr sauros lizard) a bipedal herbivorous dinosaur of the Mesozoic period. **psittacosis** /-kō'sis/ n a contagious bacterial disease of birds such as parrots and parakeets, and also chickens, ducks and pigeons, communicable to humans, with symptoms of fever, headache, nausea, etc.

PSL (econ) abbrev: private sector liquidity, one measure of the money supply.

PSNI abbrev: Police Service of Northern Ireland.

psoas /sō'əs or psō'əs/ n a muscle of the loins and pelvis (anat); the tenderloin. [Gr (pl) psoai, the accusative psoās being mistaken for a nominative singular]

psocid /sō'sid, sō'kid, psō'sid or psō'kid/ n any member of the family **Psocidae** or of the order Psocoptera (to which the Psocidae belong), tiny winged or wingless insects, eg booklice, barklice, etc, which feed on decaying animal or vegetable matter, fungi, lichens, etc. [From Psocus, a genus included in the family and order, from Gr psōchein to grind up]

Psocoptera /(p)sō-kop'tə-rə/ n pl the Corrodentia, an order of insects consisting of the booklice, barklice, etc. [Psocus a genus included in the order, and Gr pteron wing]

psora /sö'rə, sō'rə, psö'rə or psō'rə/ (obs med) n scabies, itch. [Gr psōrā, psōriāsis itch]

■ **psori'asis** n a skin disease in which red scaly papules and patches appear. **psoriat'ic** adj. **pso'ric** adj.
❏ **psoriatic arthropathy** or **psoriatic arthritis** n (med) any of various forms of arthritis occurring in people suffering from psoriasis.

psoralen /sö'rə-len or sō'rə-len/ (chem and med) n any of a number of naturally occurring chemicals, found eg in parsnips, celery and parsley, which make the skin more sensitive to ultraviolet light and which are used in the treatment of acne and psoriasis, and in some suntan lotions, but which because of their sensitizing effect are carcinogenic. [From Psoralea, a genus of leguminous plants which contain psoralens]

PSS (comput) abbrev: Packet Switching System.

PST abbrev: Pacific Standard Time.

pst or **psst** /pst/ interj used to attract someone's attention quietly or surreptitiously. [Imit]

PSTN abbrev: Public Switched Telephone Network.

PSV abbrev: public service vehicle.

PSW abbrev: psychiatric social worker.

psych or **psyche** /sīk/ (sl) vt to subject to psychoanalysis; to work out (a problem, the intentions of another person, etc) psychologically (often with out); to defeat or intimidate by psychological means (sometimes with out); to get (oneself or another person) psychologically prepared for some challenge, ordeal, etc (usu with up); to stimulate (usu with up). [**psychological**, **psychoanalysis**, etc]
❏ **psych'-up** n (sl) the act of psyching oneself or someone else up.

psychagogue see under **psycho-**.

psyche[1] /sī'kē/ n the soul, spirit or mind; the principle of mental and emotional life, conscious and unconscious; a butterfly (obs); a cheval-glass; (with cap) the personification of the soul, depicted as a young woman with butterfly wings, the beloved of Eros (Gr myth); (with cap) a genus of bombycid moths (the females wingless, sometimes legless); (with cap) one of the minor planets. [Gr psychē soul, butterfly, Psychē Psyche]
■ **psychoph'ily** n (bot) pollination by butterflies.

psyche[2] see **psych**.

psychedelic, **psychiatrist**, **psychic**, etc see under **psycho-**.

psycho /sī'kō/ (inf) n (pl **psy'chos**) a psychopath. ◆ adj psychopathic.

psycho- /sī-kō-, -kə-, -ko-/ or **psych-** /sīk-/ combining form denoting: soul or spirit; mind, mental; psychological. [Gr psychē soul, butterfly]
■ **psych'agogue** /-ə-gog/ n (Gr agōgos guide) the conductor of souls to the underworld (a title of Hermes); someone who calls up spirits; someone who guides the mind; a means of restoring consciousness. **psychasthenia** /sī-kəs-thē'ni-ə or -thə-nī'ə/ n (Gr astheneia weakness; obs) a severe functional mental disorder, characterized by fixed ideas, ruminative states and hypochondriacal conditions. **psychedelia** /sī-kə-dē'li-ə/ or (more correctly but less commonly) **psychodel'ia** n the production of, or the culture associated with, psychedelic experiences. ◆ n pl (objects, etc associated with) psychedelic experiences. **psychedel'ic** or (more correctly but less commonly) **psychodel'ic** (or /-dē'lik/) (Gr dēlos visible, clear) adj relating to a state of relaxation and pleasure, with heightened perception and increased mental powers generally; relating to drugs which cause, or are believed to cause, the taker to enter such a state; relating to visual effects and/or sound effects whose action on the mind is a little like that of psychedelic drugs; dazzling in pattern. **psychi'ater** n (Gr iātros physician; archaic) a psychiatrist. **psychiat'ric** or **psychiat'rical** adj. **psychi'atrist** n a person who is medically qualified to treat diseases of the mind. **psychi'atry** n. **psy'chic** adj (also **psy'chical**) relating to the psyche, soul or mind; spiritual; spiritualistic; beyond, or apparently beyond, the physical; sensitive to, in touch with, or apparently having powers or capabilities derived from, something that has not yet been explained physically, eg apparently prescient or telepathic (**psychical research** investigation of phenomena apparently implying a connection with another world; **psychic bid** (bridge) the bid of a suit in which one is not strong to deceive an opponent, or for some other reason; **psychic determinism** the Freudian theory that mental processes are always determined by motivations, conscious or unconscious; **psychic force** a power not physical or mechanical, supposed to cause certain so-called spiritualistic phenomena). ◆ n that which is of the mind or psyche; a spiritualistic medium. **psy'chically** adv. **psy'chicism** n psychical research. **psy'chicist** see **psychist** below. **psy'chics** n sing the science of psychology; psychical research. **psy'chism** n the doctrine of a universal soul. **psy'chist** n a psychologist (obs); a person interested in psychical research (also **psy'chicist**); a player who makes psychic bids (bridge). **psychoac'tive** adj of a drug, affecting the brain and influencing behaviour, heightening sensitivity, etc (also **psychotrop'ic**). **psychoan'alyse** or (N Am) **-yze** vt to subject to psychoanalysis. **psychoanal'ysis** n a method of investigation and psychotherapy whereby nervous diseases or mental ailments are traced to forgotten

---

■ words derived from main entry word; ❏ compound words; ▪ idioms and phrasal verbs hidden concepts in the patient's mind and treated by bringing these to light. **psychoan'alyst** n someone who practises psychoanalysis. **psychoanalyt'ic** or **psychoanalyt'ical** adj. **psych'obabble** n excessive or needless use of psychologists' jargon; needless, meaningless or mindless use of jargon generally, eg by those involved in some of the modern spiritual and therapeutic movements or organizations. **psychobiograph'ical** adj. **psychobiog'raphy** n a biography concerned mainly with the psychological development of its subject. **psychobiolog'ical** adj. **psychobiol'ogist** n. **psychobiol'ogy** n the study of the relationship between the functions of the body and the mind. **psychochem'ical** adj psychoactive. ◆ n a substance with psychoactive effect, esp a chemical intended as a weapon of war, specif a psychogas. **psychochem'istry** n the treatment of mental illness by drugs. **psychodelia** n see psychedelia above. **psychodelic** adj see psychedelic above. **psychodram'a** n a method of treatment of mental disorders in which the patient is led to objectify and understand his or her difficulty by spontaneously acting it out. **psychodramat'ic** adj. **psychodynam'ic** adj relating to mental and emotional forces, their source in past experience, and their effects. **psychodynam'ics** n sing the study of psychodynamic forces, etc. ◆ n pl psychodynamic forces. **psy'chogas** n a gas which makes a person's performance deteriorate very seriously without his or her being aware of it. **psychogen'esis** n (the study of) the origin or development of the mind (also **psychogenet'ics**); origination in the mind. **psychogenet'ic** or **psychogenet'ical** adj. **psychogen'ic** adj originating in the mind or in a mental condition. **psychogeriat'ric** adj. **psychogeriatric'ian** n. **psychogeriat'rics** n sing the study of the psychological problems of old age. **psychog'ony** n the origin or development of the mind or soul. **psych'ogram** n writing supposedly produced by a spirit or under the influence of a spirit. **psych'ograph** n an instrument by which a psychogram is obtained. **psychograph'ic** or **psychograph'ical** adj. **psychograph'ics** n sing the quantitive study of personalities and attitudes, used as a tool in marketing. **psychog'raphy** n writing supposedly produced by or under the influence of a spirit; psychological biography or delineation. **psychohistor'ian** n. **psychohistor'ical** adj. **psychohis'tory** n history studied from a psychological point of view. **psy'choid** n the hypothetical regulative principle directing the behaviour of an organism. **psychokinē'sis** n movement by psychic agency. **psychokinet'ic** adj. **psycholing'uist** n. **psycholinguis'tic** adj. **psycholinguis'tics** n sing the study of language development, language in relation to the mind, language in thought, etc. **psycholog'ic** or **psycholog'ical** adj (**psychological block** an inability to think about, remember, etc a particular subject, event, etc for psychological reasons; **psychological moment** strictly speaking, the psychological element or factor (Ger Moment); misunderstood by a French translator from German and applied to the moment of time when the mind could best be worked on; hence now often the very moment, the nick of time; **psychological operation** one carried out in **psychological warfare**, the use of propaganda to influence enemy opinion or morale). **psycholog'ically** adv. **psychol'ogism** n a doctrine depending on psychological conceptions; the view that all natural and social sciences should be based on psychology. **psychol'ogist** n a person who has studied and is qualified in psychology. **psychol'ogize** or **-ise** vi. **psychol'ogy** n the science of the mind; the study of mind and behaviour; attitudes, etc characteristic of an individual, type, etc, or animating specific conduct; subtle or cunning behaviour or actions, using (or supposedly using) a knowledge of a person's mind in order to achieve one's own ends. **psychom'eter** n someone who has the occult power of psychometry; an instrument for measuring reaction times, etc. **psychomet'ric** or **psychomet'rical** adj. **psychometrician** /-trish'ən/ or **psychom'etrist** n. **psychomet'rics** n sing the branch of psychology dealing with measurable factors. **psychom'etry** n psychometrics; the occult power of divining properties of things by mere contact. **psychomō'tor** adj relating to such mental action as induces muscular contraction. **psychoneuroimmunol'ogy** n the study of the effects of mental states and other psychological factors in the body's immune system. **psychoneurō'sis** n (pl **psychoneurō'sēs**) mental disease without any apparent anatomical lesion; a functional disorder of the mind in someone who is legally sane and shows insight into his or her condition. **psychoneurot'ic** n and adj. **psychonom'ic** adj. **psychonom'ics** n sing the study of the individual mind in relation to its environment. **psychopannychism** /-pan'ik-izm/ n (Gr pannychos all night long, from pās all, and nychios nightly) (belief in) the sleep of the soul from death to resurrection. **psychopann'ychist** n someone who holds this belief. **psy'chopath** /-path/ n someone who shows a pathological degree of specific emotional instability without specific mental disorder; someone suffering from a behavioural disorder resulting in inability to form personal relationships and in indifference to, or ignorance of, his or her obligations to society, often manifested by antisocial behaviour such as acts of violence, sexual perversion, etc. **psychopath'ic** adj relating to psychopathy or the behaviour or condition of a psychopath. ◆ n a psychopath. **psychop'athist** n

or **psychopathol'ogist** n. **psychopathol'ogy** n the branch of psychology that deals with the abnormal workings of the mind; an abnormal psychological condition. **psychop'athy** n any disorder of mental functions, insanity. **psychopharmacol'ogist** n. **psychopharmacol'ogy** n the study of the effects of drugs on the mind. **psychophily** n see under psyche[1]. **psychophys'ical** adj (**psychophysical parallelism** see **parallelism** under **parallel**). **psychophys'icist** n. **psychophys'ics** n sing the study of the relation between mental and physical processes. **psychophysiol'ogy** n experimental or physiological psychology. **psy'chopomp** n (Gr pompos guide) a conductor of souls to the other world. **psychoprophylax'is** n a method of training for childbirth aimed at enabling women to manage and control the pain of labour. **psychosex'ual** adj of or relating to the psychological aspects of sex, eg sexual fantasies. **psychō'sis** n (pl **psychō'sēs**) mental condition; a serious mental disorder characterized by eg illusions, delusions, hallucinations, mental confusion and a lack of insight on the part of the patient into his or her condition. **psychosō'cial** adj of or relating to matters both psychological and social. **psychosomat'ic** adj (Gr sōma body) of mind and body as a unit; concerned with or denoting physical diseases having a psychological origin. **psychosomat'ics** n sing the study of psychosomatic conditions. **psychosomimet'ic** adj of a drug, producing symptoms like those of mental illness; referring to (eg drug-induced) changes in behaviour and personality resembling those due to psychosis. **psychosur'gery** n brain surgery in the treatment of cases of mental disorder. **psychosyn'thesis** n the combining of the various individual elements of the mind or personality into an integrated whole by psychoanalysis or other mode of psychotherapy; specif, a form of psychotherapy created by Italian psychiatrist Roberto Assagioli (died 1974) emphasizing the importance of the individual's free will and employing techniques such as meditation adopted from eastern religions. **psychotech'nics** n sing the use of psychological theory in politics, economics, etc. **psychotherapeut'ics** or **psychother'apy** n the treatment of mental illness by hypnosis, psychoanalysis and similar psychological means. **psychother'apist** n. **psychot'ic** adj relating to psychosis. ◆ n a person who is suffering from a psychosis. **psychot'icism** n. **psychotomimet'ic** adj psychosomimetic. **psychotox'ic** adj harmful to the mind or personality. **psychotrop'ic** adj same as **psychoactive** above. ◆ n a psychotropic drug.

psychrometer /sī-krom'i-tər/ n orig a thermometer; now, a wet-and-dry-bulb hygrometer. [Gr psȳchros cold, and metron a measure]
■ **psychrometric** /sī-krō-met'rik/ or **psychromet'rical** adj. **psychrom'etry** n.

psychrophilic /sī-krō-fil'ik/ (bot) adj growing best at low temperatures. [Gr psȳchros cold, and phileein to love]

psylla /sil'ə/ n an insect of the genus Psylla; (also **psyll'id**) an insect of the homopterous family **Psyllidae** /-dē/ (which includes the genus Psylla), sap-sucking plant pests also known as **jumping plant lice**. [Gr psylla a flea]
❑ **psyllid yellows** n a disease of potato plants caused by psyllids, in which the leaves turn yellow and curl up.

psyllium /sil'i-əm/ n a flowering plant of the plantain family. [L, from Gr psylla flea (from the resemblance of its seeds to fleas)]

psyop /sī'op/ a contraction of **psychological operation** (see **psychologic** under **psycho-**).

psywar /sī'wör/ a contraction of **psychological warfare** (see **psychologic** under **psycho-**).

PT abbrev : Pacific Time; personal trainer, or training; physical therapy; physical training; postal telegraph; pupil teacher; purchase tax (hist).

Pt (chem) symbol : platinum.

pt abbrev : part; past; past tense; pint or pints; point; port; post-town.

PTA abbrev : Parent-Teacher Association; Passenger Transport Authority.

pta abbrev : peseta.

ptarmic /tär'mik or ptär'mik/ n a substance that causes sneezing. [Gr ptarmos a sneeze]

ptarmigan /tär'mi-gən/ n a mountain-dwelling species of grouse (Lagopus mutus), which turns white in winter, known outside the British Isles as the rock ptarmigan; extended to other species of Lagopus, such as the willow grouse, but not to Lagopus scoticus, the red grouse. [Gaelic tàrmachan; the initial pt- derives from an incorrect assumed connection with Gr ptarmos (see **ptarmic**)]

PTE abbrev : Passenger Transport Executive.

Pte (milit and commerce) abbrev : Private.

pter-, -ptera, etc see **ptero-**.

pteranodon /(p)te-ran'ə-don/ n a toothless flying reptile of the Cretaceous period with a hornlike crest. [Gr pteron wing, an- without, and odous, odontos tooth]

Pterichthys /(p)te-rik'this/ n a genus of Old Red Sandstone fish-like creatures with winglike appendages. [Gr *pteron* a wing, and *ichthys* a fish]

pteridology see under **Pteris**.

pteridophyte /(p)ter'i-dō-fīt/ (*bot*) n a vascular cryptogam or a member of the **Pteridophyta** /-of'i-ta/, one of the main divisions of the vegetable kingdom including ferns, lycopods and horsetails. [Gr *pteris*, *-idos* a fern, and *phyton* a plant]

pteridosperm /(p)ter'i-dō-spûrm/ n a fossil plant of a group resembling ferns, but having seeds. [Gr *pteris*, *-idos* fern, and *sperma* seed]

pterin /ter'in/ or /pter'in/ n any of a group of substances occurring as pigments in butterfly wings, important in biochemistry. [Gr *pteron* a wing]
□ **pteroic acid** /ter-ō'ik/ or /pter-ō'ik/ n the original folic acid found in spinach. **pteroylglutamic acid** /ter'ō-il-glū-tam'ik/ or /pter-ō'/ n the simplest folic acid, effective in correcting the anaemia in pernicious anaemia but ineffective against the concomitant neurological complications.

pterion /ter'i-on, tē'ri-on, pter'i-on/ or /ptē'ri-on/ n (*pl* **pter'ia**) in craniometry, the suture where the frontal, squamosal and parietal bones meet the wing of the sphenoid. [Gr dimin of *pteron* wing]

Pteris /ter'is, tē'ris, pter'is/ or /ptē'ris/ n a genus of ferns with spore-clusters continuous along the pinnule margin, *usu* taken to include bracken, which some separate as **Pterid'ium**. [Gr *pteris*, *-idos* or *-eōs* male-fern, from *pteron* a feather]
■ **pteridol'ogist** n. **pteridol'ogy** n the study of ferns. **pteridomā'nia** n a passion for ferns. **pteridoph'ilist** n a fern-lover.

ptero- /ter-ō-, pter-ō-, -ə-, -o-/ or **pter-** /ter-, pter-/ *combining form* denoting feather, wing. [Gr *pteron* wing]
■ **-ptera** *combining form* (*zool*) used to denote organisms having a specified type or number of wings or winglike parts. **-pteran** or **-pterous** *adj combining form*.

pterodactyl or (*rare*) **pterodactyle** /ter-ə-dak'til or pter-ə-dak'til/ n a fossil (Jurassic and Cretaceous) flying reptile with large and birdlike skull, long jaws, and a flying membrane attached to the long fourth digit of the forelimb. [Gr *pteron* wing, and *daktylos* finger]

pteroic acid see under **pterin**.

pteropod /ter'ə-pod or pter'ə-pod/ n any member of the **Pteropoda** /-op'ə-də/, a group of gastropods that swim by means of winglike expansions of the foot. [Gr *pteron* wing, and *pous*, *podos* foot]
□ **pteropod ooze** n a deep-sea deposit composed largely of pteropod shells.

pterosaur /ter'ə-sör or pter'ə-sör/ n a member of the **Pterosaur'ia**, an extinct order of flying reptiles, including the pterodactyls. [Gr *pteron* wing, and *sauros* lizard]
■ **pterosaur'ian** n and *adj*.

-pterous see under **ptero-**.

pteroylglutamic acid see under **pterin**.

pterygium /ter-ij'i-əm or pter-ij'i-əm/ n (*pl* **pteryg'ia**) a vertebrate limb (*zool*); a winglike growth (*biol*); a wing-shaped area of thickened conjunctiva which spreads over part of the cornea and sometimes over the eyeball (*med*). [Latinized from Gr *pterygion*, dimin of *pteryx*, *-ygos* wing]
■ **pteryg'ial** *adj* of or relating to a wing or fin. ◆ n a bone in a fin.

pterygoid /ter'i-goid or pter'i-goid/ *adj* (*anat*) winglike; of or near the pterygoid. ◆ n (in full, **pterygoid bone, plate** or **process**) in various vertebrates, a paired bone of the upper jaw behind the palatines, known in human anatomy as the pterygoid plates of the sphenoid bone. [Gr *pteryx*, *-ygos* wing]

Pterygotus /ter-i-gō'təs or pter-i-gō'təs/ n a genus of eurypterids, so named because of their broad swimming paddles. [Latinized from Gr *pterygōtos* winged]

pteryla /ter'i-lə or pter'i-lə/ (*zool*) n (*pl* **pter'ylae** /-lē/) a tract of skin bearing contour feathers in birds. [Gr *pteron* feather, and *hylē* forest]
■ **pterylograph'ic** or **pterylograph'ical** *adj*. **pterylograph'ically** *adv*. **pterylog'raphy** n a description of pterylae. **pterylō'sis** n arrangement of pterylae.

PTFE (*chem*) *abbrev*: polytetrafluoroethylene.

ptilosis /ti-lō'sis/ n plumage or mode of feathering. [Gr *ptilōsis*, from *ptilon* a down feather]

ptisan /tiz'n or tiz-an'/ n (also **tisane**) a medicinal drink made from barley; a decoction. [Gr *ptisanē* peeled barley, barley-gruel, from *ptissein* to winnow]

PTO *abbrev*: please turn over; Public Telecommunications Operator.

ptochocracy /tō-kok'rə-si or ptō-kok'rə-si/ n the rule of beggars or paupers, wholesale pauperization. [Gr *ptōchos* a beggar, and **-cracy**]

Ptolemaic /tol-i-mā'ik/ *adj* (also **Ptolemaean** /-mē'ən/) relating to or associated with the *Ptolemies*, Greek kings of Egypt (from Alexander the Great's general to Cleopatra's son), or to Ptolemy the astronomer (*fl* 150AD).
■ **Ptolemā'ist** n a believer in the **Ptolemaic system**, Ptolemy's form of the ancient Greek planetary theory, according to which the heavenly bodies revolve about the earth in motions compounded of eccentric circles and epicycles.

ptomaine /tō'mān, tō-mān', also (now *rare*) tō'mā-īn, tō'mā-ēn or tō'mā-in/ (*chem*) n a loosely used name for amino-compounds, some poisonous, formed from putrefying animal tissues, eg putrescine, cadaverine, neurine and choline. [Ital *ptomaina*, from Gr *ptōma* a corpse]
□ **ptomaine poisoning** n (*obs med* or loosely) food poisoning, formerly thought to be caused by ptomaines, few of which, it is now known, are poisonous if eaten.

ptosis /tō'sis or ptō'sis/ (*med*) n (*pl* **ptō'ses** /-sēz/) downward displacement; drooping of the upper eyelid. [Gr *ptōsis*, from *piptein* to fall]

PTSD (*med*) *abbrev*: post-traumatic stress disorder.

PTT *abbrev*: Post, Telegraph and Telephone/Telecommunications, designating the statutory body which exists in some countries with responsibility for the operation and regulation of all public services; formerly, Postes, Télégraphes et Téléphones (*Fr*); formerly, Postes, Télécommunications et Télédiffusion (*Fr*).

P2P *abbrev*: peer-to-peer.

Pty or **pty.** *abbrev*: proprietary.

ptyalin /tī'ə-lin or ptī'ə-lin/ n a ferment in saliva that turns starch into sugar. [Gr *ptyalon* spittle, from *ptyein* to spit]
■ **ptyalagogic** /-ə-goj'ik or -gog'ik/ *adj*. **ptyalagogue** /-al'ə-gog/ n (*med*) a sialagogue. **pty'alism** n (*med*) excessive flow of saliva. **pty'alize** or **-ise** *vt* to induce ptyalism in.

ptyxis /(p)tik'sis/ (*bot*) n the folding of each individual leaf in the bud, distinguished from *vernation*, the arrangement of the whole. [Gr *ptyxis*]

PU *abbrev*: pick-up.

Pu (*chem*) *symbol*: plutonium.

pu (*horse-racing*) *abbrev*: pulled up.

pub /pub/ (*inf*) n a public house.
■ **pubb'ing** n the practice of frequenting pubs.
□ **pub'cō** n (*pl* **pub'cōs**) a company that operates a chain of pubs. **pub'-crawl** n a progression from pub to pub, stopping for one or more drinks in each. ◆ *vi* to participate in such a progression.

Pub.Doc. *abbrev*: public document.

puberty /pū'bər-ti/ n the beginning of sexual maturity. [L *pūber* and *pūbēs*, *-eris* grown-up, downy, and *pūbēs*, *-is* grown-up youth, the pubes]
■ **pube** /pūb/ n (*vulgar sl*) a pubic hair. **pū'beral** or **pū'bertal** *adj*. **pūberulent** /-ber'ū-lənt/ or **pūber'ūlous** *adj* feebly or minutely pubescent. **pū'bes** /-bēz/ n (*anat*) the lower part of the hypogastric region; the hair which grows there at puberty. **pūbescence** /-es'əns/ n puberty; a soft downy covering, *esp* in plants, of appressed hairs (*bot*). **pūbes'cent** *adj*. **pū'bic** *adj* of the pubes or the pubis. **pūbiō-** (wrongly **pūbo-**) *combining form*. **pū'bis** n (*pl* **pū'bises**; **pū'bēs** is not possible, as pubis is a genitive singular, not a nominative singular) (for L *os pūbis* bone of the pubes; *anat*) a bone of the pelvis which in humans forms the anterior portion of the *os innominatum*.

public /pub'lik/ *adj* of or belonging to the people; relating to a community or a nation; general; common to, shared in by, or open to, all; generally known; in open view, unconcealed, not private; engaged in, or concerning, the affairs of the community; employed by the government, a local authority, etc; devoted or directed to the general good (now *rare* except in *public spirit*; cf **public-spirited** below); international; open to members of a university as a whole, not confined to a college; of a public house; (of eg housing) owned by a local authority, etc, not private. ◆ n the general body of mankind; the people, in any vague or indefinite sense or grouping; a part of the community regarded from a particular viewpoint, eg as an audience or a target for advertising; the people, the state, the nation (*obs*); public view, a public place, society, or the open, as in *in public*; a public house, a tavern (*archaic*). [L *pūblicus*, from *pop(u)lus* the people]
■ **pub'lican** n the keeper of an inn or public house; a tax farmer (*Roman hist*); a tax collector (*Roman hist*). **publicā'tion** n the act of publishing or making public; a proclamation; the act of sending out (a book, etc) for sale; something that is published, a book. **pub'licist** /-sist/ n someone who publicizes something; an advertising agent; someone who writes on or is skilled in public law, or on current

political topics (*rare*). **publicity** /*pub*-lis'i-ti/ *n* publicness, the state of being open to everyone's observation or knowledge; notoriety; acclaim; the process of making something known to the general public; advertising. **pub'licize** or **-ise** /-sīz/ *vt* to give publicity to; to make known to the general public, to advertise. **pub'licly** *adv*. **pub'licness** *n* (*rare*).

☐ **public act** see **public bill** below. **public address system** *n* a system that enables (large) groups of people to be addressed clearly, consisting of microphones, amplifiers and loudspeakers. **public art** *n* works of art put on display for the general public in public places as opposed to museums, etc; the provision of such works of art. **public bar** *n* a bar, *usu* less well furnished than a lounge bar, and *usu* serving drinks at lower prices. **public bill** or **act** *n* a parliamentary bill or act of legislation affecting the general public. **public company** or **public limited company** *n* a company whose shares can be offered for sale to the general public (*abbrev* **plc**). **public convenience** see **convenience** under **convenient**. **public corporation** *n* one owned by the government and run on business principles, being for the most part self-governing. **public data network** *n* (*comput*) a communications system for carrying digital data which is open to anyone who wishes to subscribe. **public defender** *n* (*US*) a defence lawyer engaged at public expense to represent those unable to pay legal fees. **public document** *n* any document, such as a statistical report or register, which is made public and which can be consulted by members of the public. **public domain** *n* the status of a published work which is not, or is no longer, subject to copyright. **public-domain'** *adj* (*comput*) available to the general public free of charge. **public enemy** *n* someone whose behaviour is considered to be a menace to a community in general. **public expenditure** *n* spending by government, local authorities, etc. **public funds** *n pl* government-funded debt. **public health** *n* the maintenance of the health of a community, eg by sanitation, hygienic food preparation, etc, and the measures to achieve this. **public health inspector** see **environmental health officer** under **environment**. **public holiday** *n* a general holiday. **public house** *n* a house open to the public (*obs*); a building chiefly used for selling alcoholic liquors to be consumed on the premises; an inn or tavern. **public image** see under **image**. **public inquiry** *n* an investigation held in public into various aspects (eg safety, environmental effect) of eg a proposed engineering or building project. **public-key'** *adj* (*comput*) of a system of cryptography in which encoding of messages to a particular recipient is done using a public (communal) key, and decoding is by a different (private) key known only to the recipient. **public lands** *n pl* lands belonging to a government, *esp* such as are open to sale, grant, etc. **public law** *n* the law governing relations between public authorities, such as the state, and the individual; sometimes used for international law which, however, may be either public or private. **public lecture** *n* a lecture open to the general public. **public lending right** *n* an author's right to payment when his or her books are borrowed from public libraries. **public liability** see under **liable**. **public limited company** see **public company** above. **public nuisance** *n* an illegal act harming the general community rather than an individual (*law*); an annoying, irritating person (*inf*). **public opinion** *n* the opinion of the general public on matters which affect the whole community. **public opinion poll** *n* a taking of public opinion based on the answers of scientifically selected elements in the community to questioning. **public orator** *n* an officer of English universities who is the voice of the Senate on all public occasions. **public ownership** *n* ownership by the state, eg of nationalized industry. **public prosecutor** *n* an official whose function is to prosecute people charged with offences. **public purse** *n* the nation's finances. **public relations** *n sing* the relations between a person, organization, etc and the public; the business of setting up and maintaining favourable relations; a department of government, an industrial firm, etc, dealing with this. **public-rela'tions** *adj*. **public school** *n* an endowed grammar school providing a liberal education for those who can afford it, eg Eton, Harrow, Rugby, Winchester, Westminster, Shrewsbury, Charterhouse, St Paul's, Merchant Taylors'; a school under the control of a publicly elected body and publicly funded (*US*). **pub'lic-school** *adj*. **public sector** *n* government-financed industry, social service, etc. **public servant** *n* a person employed by the government. **public speaking** *n* the making of formal speeches to a large audience; the art of making such speeches. **public spending** *n* spending by the government. **public-spir'ited** *adj* having feelings actuated by regard to the public interest; with a regard to the public interest. **public-spir'itedly** *adv*. **public transport** *n* buses, trains, etc for the use of the general public. **public trustee** *n* (also with *caps*) an official who is appointed to act as a trustee or executor where required. **public utility** *n* a service or supply provided in a town, etc, for the public, as gas, electricity, water or transport; a company providing such a service (*US*); (in *pl*) public utility shares. **public woman** *n* (*obs*) a prostitute. **public works** *n pl* building, etc operations financed by the state.

■ **go public** to become a public company; to make widely known something that has been private. **in public** openly, publicly.

publican, publication, publicity, etc see under **public**.

publish /*pub*'lish/ *vt* to issue to the public; to produce and offer for sale (*orig* any article, now books, newspapers, etc); to put into circulation; (*esp* in *passive*) to publish the work of (an author); to make public; to divulge; to announce; to proclaim. ◆ *vi* (of an author) to have one's work published; to publish a book, newspaper, material, etc. [Fr *publier*, from L *pūblicāre*, with *-ish* on the model of other verbs]
■ **pub'lishable** *adj*. **pub'lisher** *n* someone who publishes books; someone who attends to the issuing and distributing of a newspaper; someone who makes something public; a newspaper proprietor (*US*). **pub'lishing** *n* the business of producing and offering for sale books, newspapers, etc. **pub'lishment** *n* publication (*rare*); publication of banns (*old US*).

Puccinia /*puk*-sin'i-ə/ *n* a genus of rust-fungi, including the wheat-rust, parasitic in alternate generations on barberry and wheat or other grass. [Named after Tomaso *Puccini* (died 1735), Italian anatomist]
■ **pucciniā'ceous** *adj*.

puccoon /*pu-koon'*/ *n* bloodroot; extended to species of gromwell and other American plants yielding pigments. [Algonquian name]

puce /*pūs*/ *n* and *adj* brownish-purple or deep purplish-pink. [Fr *puce*, from L *pūlex, -icis* a flea]

pucelle /*pū-sel'*/ (*obs*) *n* a maid or virgin, *esp* (with *cap*) the Maid of Orleans, Joan of Arc (1412–31); a slut (also **puzzle**). [Fr, from LL *pūlicella*; origin doubtful]
■ **pū'celage** *n* (*obs*) virginity.

puck[1] /*puk*/ or **pouke** /*pūk*/ *n* a goblin or mischievous sprite; (with *cap*) Robin Goodfellow, a merry fairy in eg Shakespeare's *Midsummer Night's Dream*, etc (**Puck-hairy** in Ben Jonson's *Sad Shepherd*). [OE *pūca*; cf ON *pūki*, Ir *puca*, Welsh *pwca*]
■ **puck'ish** *adj* impish; full of mischief.

puck[2] /*puk*/ *n* a hard thick rubber disc used instead of a ball in ice hockey. [Origin unknown]

pucka see **pukka**.

pucker /*puk'ər*/ *vt* to wrinkle; to make gathers in (*needlework*). ◆ *vi* to become wrinkled, contracted or gathered. ◆ *n* a corrugation or wrinkle; a group of wrinkles, *esp* irregular ones; agitation, confusion (*inf*). [Cf **poke**[2]]
■ **puck'ery** *adj* astringent; tending to wrinkle.
■ **pucker up** (*sl*) to set one's lips into a position ready for kissing.

puckfist /*puk'fist* or *-fīst*/ *n* a puffball fungus; a braggart (*archaic*); a niggardly person (*obs*). [Appar **puck**[1] and the root of OE *fisting* breaking of wind]

puckish see under **puck**[1].

puckle see **pickle**[2].

pud[1] /*pŭd*/ (*inf*) *n* pudding.

pud[2] /*pud*/ (*inf*) *n* a paw, fist or hand (also **pudd'y**). [Cf **pad**[2], or Du *poot* paw]

pud[3] /*pood*/ same as **pood**.

pudden, puddening, etc see **pudding**.

pudder /*pud'ər*/ same as **pother**.

pudding /*pŭd'ing*/ *n* (also (now *inf* or *dialect*) **pudden** /*pŭd'n* or *pud'n*/) the dessert course of a meal; meat, fruit, etc cooked in a casing of suet dough; a soft kind of cooked dish, *usu* farinaceous, commonly with sugar, milk, eggs, etc; a skin or gut filled with seasoned minced meat and other materials (such as blood or oatmeal), a kind of sausage; stuffing for a cooked carcase (*Shakesp*); (*usu* in *pl*) entrails (*archaic*); a pad of rope, etc used as a fender on the bow of a boat or elsewhere (also **pudd'ening**); material gain (*archaic*); a fat, dull or heavy-witted person (*inf*). [ME *poding*; origin unknown; relation to LGer *pudde-wurst* black pudding, and to Fr *boudin* black pudding, is obscure]
■ **pudd'ingy** /-ing-i/ *adj* like a pudding, *esp* in being soft or stodgy.
☐ **pudding bag** *n* a bag for cooking a pudding in; a piece of good fortune. **pudding basin** or **bowl** *n* a nearly hemispherical container for cooking a pudding in. **pudd'ing-ba'sin** or **pudd'ing-bowl** *adj* (of a haircut) looking as if achieved by placing such a container over the head and merely cutting off protruding hair. **pudd'ing-faced** *adj* having a fat, round, smooth face. **pudd'ing-head'ed** *adj* (*inf*) stupid. **pudd'ing-pie** *n* a suet-dough pudding with meat baked in it; any of various kinds of pastry. **pudd'ing-pipe** *n* the long pulpy pod of the purging cassia tree. **pudd'ing-plate** *n* a shallow bowl-like plate, *usu* smaller than a soup plate. **pudd'ing-sleeve** *n* a large loose sleeve gathered in near the wrist. **pudd'ing-stone** *n* (*geol*) conglomerate. **pudd'ing-time** *n* (*obs*) dinner-time; the right moment.
■ **in the pudding club** (*sl*) pregnant.

puddle /*pud'l*/ *n* a small muddy pool; a non-porous mixture of clay and sand; a muddle (*inf*); a muddler (*inf*). ◆ *vt* to make muddy; to work into puddle, to stir and knead; to cover with puddle; to make watertight by means of clay; to convert from pig iron into wrought iron. ◆ *vi* to make a puddle or puddles, to cause a puddle or puddles to form; to mess about, *esp* in puddles or mud; to stir up a muddy mess. [Appar dimin of OE *pudd* ditch]

■ **pudd'ler** *n*. **pudd'ling** *n*. **pudd'ly** *adj* full of puddles.

puddock /pud'ək/ or **paddock** /pad'ək/ (*archaic and Scot*) *n* a toad or frog. [Dimin from late OE *pade*, *padde* toad; ON *padda*]

□ **padd'ock-stool** *n* a toadstool.

puddy see under **pud²**.

pudency /pū'dən-si/ *n* (*Shakesp*) shamefacedness, modesty. [L *pudēre* to make (or be) ashamed; *pudendum* something to be ashamed of; *pudīcus* chaste; *pudibundus* shamefaced]

■ **pudendal** /-den'dəl/ *adj* relating to the pudenda. **puden'dous** *adj* (*obs*) shameful. **puden'dum** *n* (*also* **puden'da** *pl*) the external genital organs, *esp* female. **pu'dent** *adj* (*rare*) modest. **pu'dibund** *adj* shamefaced; prudish. **pudibund'ity** *n*. **pu'dic** *adj* modest (*obs*); pudendal. **pudicity** /-dis'i-ti/ *n* (*rare*) modesty. **pu'dor** *n* (*obs*) sense of shame.

pudge and **pudgy** same as **podge** and **podgy**.

pudsey or **pudsy** /pud'zi/ same as **podgy** (see under **podge**).

pudu /poo'doo/ *n* a small S American deer, about 30cm (1ft) high, with spiky antlers. [Am Sp, from a S American language]

pueblo /pweb'lō/ *n* (*pl* **pueb'los**) a town or settlement (in Spanish-speaking countries); a communal habitation of the Native Americans of New Mexico, etc; (with *cap*) a Native American of the pueblos. [Sp, town, from L *populus* a people]

puer /pūr/ *n* and *vt* same as **pure** (in tanning).

puerile /pū'ər-īl or (*US*) -il/ *adj* relating to children (*rare*); childish; trifling; silly. [L *puerīlis*, from *puer* a child]

■ **puerilism** /pū'ər-il-izm/ *n* (*psychol*) reversion to a childlike state of mind. **puerility** /-il'i-ti/ *n* the quality of being puerile; something that is puerile; a childish expression; an instance of childishness or foolish triviality.

puerperal /pū-ûr'pə-rəl/ (*med*) *adj* relating to childbirth. [L *puerpera* a woman in labour, from *puer* a child, and *parere* to bear]

■ **puer'perally** *adv*. **puerpē'rium** *n* the time from onset of labour to return of the womb to its normal state.

□ **puerperal fever** *n orig* any fever occurring in connection with childbirth; now confined to endometritis or septicaemia caused by the introduction of bacteria into the genital tract. **puerperal psychosis** (or *archaic* **mania**) *n* a mental illness sometimes occurring after childbirth.

Puerto Rican /pwär', pwûr' or pwer'tō rē'kən/ *adj* of or from the Caribbean island of *Puerto Rico*. ◆ *n* a native or inhabitant of Puerto Rico.

puff /puf/ *vi* to blow in whiffs; to breathe out vehemently or pantingly; to snort scornfully (*obs*); to emit puffs; to issue in puffs; to make the sound of a puff; to go with puffs; to swell up (*esp* with *up*). ◆ *vt* to drive with a puff; to blow; to emit in puffs; to play (eg a wind instrument) or smoke (eg a pipe) with puffs; to inflate or swell (*esp* with *up*); to elate unduly; to extol, *esp* in disingenuous advertisement; to put out of breath. ◆ *n* a sudden, forcible breath, blast or emission; a gust or whiff; a cloud or quantity of vapour, dust, air, etc, emitted at one time; an inhalation of tobacco smoke; a sound of puffing; a downy pad for powdering (eg one's face); anything light and porous, or swollen and light; a biscuit or cake of puff pastry or the like; a part of a fabric gathered up so as to be left full in the middle (*needlework*); a quilted bedcover; ostentation; praise intended as, or serving as, advertisement; a homosexual (*sl*; see **poof¹**). [OE *pyffan*, or a related form; cf Ger *puffen*, etc]

■ **puffed** *adj* distended; inflated; (of eg a sleeve) gathered up into rounded ridges; out of breath. **puff'er** *n* someone who puffs; a steam-engine; a steamboat, *esp* in Scotland a small cargo-carrying boat used in coastal waters; someone employed to bid at an auction to incite others and so run up prices; a wheel-lock pistol; a puffer fish. **puff'ery** *n* advertisement disguised as honest praise; puffs collectively. **puff'ily** *adv*. **puff'iness** *n*. **puff'ing** *n*. **puff'ingly** *adv*. **puff'y** *adj* puffed out with air or any soft matter; swollen, engorged; bombastic; coming in puffs; puffing; short-winded.

□ **puff adder** *n* a thick, venomous African snake (*Bitis arietans* or related species) that distends its body when irritated. **puff'ball** *n* a gasteromycete fungus (*Lycoperdon*, etc) with ball-shaped fructification filled when ripe with a powdery mass of spores; a tight-waisted full skirt gathered in at the hem to an underskirt, so as to be shaped like a ball; any similar short or long ball-shaped skirt. **puff'bird** *n* any bird of a Central and S American family related to the barbets, with the habit of puffing out the head-feathers. **puff'-box** *n* a box for powder for the face or body and a puff. **puffer fish** *n* a globefish. **puff pastry** or *US* **puff paste** *n* pastry composed of thin flaky layers. **puff'-puff** *n* (*esp* formerly) a child's word for a railway engine or train.

■ **puffed out** quite out of breath; inflated, distended, expanded. **puffed up** swollen; inflated with pride, presumption, or the like.

puffin /puf'in/ *n* any of various seabirds (*esp* of the genus *Fratercula*) of the auk family, with brightly coloured parrot-like beaks, *esp* (in Britain) *Fratercula arctica*. [Origin obscure; a connection with **puff** is conjectured]

puffin crossing /puf'in kros'ing/ *n* a type of street crossing, a development of the pelican crossing, which has automatic detection of pedestrian requirements. [Adapted from *pedestrian user-friendly intelligent crossing*]

pug¹ /pug/ *n* a small short-haired dog with a wrinkled face, upturned nose, and short curled tail (also **pug dog**); a goblin or sprite (*obs*; in Ben Jonson, **Pug**, an inferior devil); a term of endearment (*obs*); a prostitute (*obs*); a senior servant (*archaic sl*); a monkey (*obs* or *dialect*); a fox (*archaic*); a pug nose; a pug-moth; a pug-engine. [A connection with **puck¹** is conjectured]

■ **pugg'ish** *adj* like a monkey or a pug-dog; snub-nosed. **pugg'y** *n* a term of endearment (*obs*); (also **pugg'ie**) a monkey (*Scot*); a fox (*archaic*). ◆ *adj* puggish.

□ **pug'-engine** *n* a shunting engine. **pug'-faced** *adj* monkey-faced. **pug'-moth** *n* a name for the smaller moths of the geometrid family Larentidae. **pug nose** *n* a short, thick nose with the tip turned up. **pug'-nosed** *adj*.

pug² /pug/ *n* clay, ground and worked with water. ◆ *vt* to beat; to grind with water and make plastic; to pack with pugging. [Origin unknown]

■ **pugg'ing** *n* beating or punching; the working of clay for making bricks, in a pug mill; clay, sawdust, plaster, etc, put between floors to deaden sound.

□ **pug mill** *n* a machine for mixing and tempering clay.

pug³ /pug/ (*Anglo-Ind*) *n* an animal's footprint. ◆ *vt* to track. [Hindustani *pag*]

pug⁴ /pug/ (*inf*) *n* a boxer. [Shortened from **pugilist** (see under **pugilism**)]

pug⁵ see under **pugging¹**.

puggaree, puggery same as **pagri**.

pugging¹ /pug'ing/ (*Shakesp*) *adj* thieving. [Origin unknown]

■ **pug** *vt* and *vi* (*dialect*) to tug.

pugging² see under **pug²**.

puggled /pug'ld/ (*Scot*) *adj* mentally or physically exhausted. [Perh Eng dialect *puggled* very drunk, or an alteration of Eng *buggered*]

■ **pugg'le** *vt*.

puggree see **pagri**.

puggy see under **pug¹**.

pugh an old spelling of **pooh**.

pugil /pū'jil/ *n orig* a small handful; now, as much as the thumb and two fingers can lift, a pinch. [L *pugillus*]

pugilism /pū'ji-li-zm/ *n* the art or practice of boxing; prize-fighting. [L *pugil* a boxer]

■ **pu'gilist** or (*obs*) **pu'gil** *n* a boxer. **pugilist'ic** or **pugilist'ical** *adj*. **pugilist'ically** *adv*.

pugnacious /pug-nā'shəs/ *adj* given to fighting; combative; quarrelsome. [L *pugnax*, *-ācis*, from *pugnāre* to fight]

■ **pugnā'ciously** *adv*. **pugnā'ciousness** or **pugnacity** /-nas'i-ti/ *n* inclination to fight; fondness for fighting; quarrelsomeness.

Pugwash conference /pug'wosh kon'f[ə-]rəns/ *n* any of a series of conferences held at intervals by scientists from many countries to discuss the dangers and difficulties into which the world is running. [Name of the village in Nova Scotia where the first conference was held in 1957]

puh a Shakespearean spelling of **pooh**.

puir /pür or pär/ (*Scot*) *adj* poor.

puisne (*Shakesp* **puisny**) /pū'ni/ *adj* an obsolete form of **puny**, surviving as applied to certain judges, meaning junior; petty, insignificant (*Shakesp*). ◆ *n* a puisne judge. [OFr, from *puis*, from L *posteā* after, and *né*, from L *nātus* born]

puissant or **puissaunt** /pū'is-ənt, pwis'ənt or (*poetic*) pū-is'ənt/ (*archaic*) *adj* powerful. [Fr *puissant*, appar formed as a prp from a vulgar L substitute for L *potēns*, *-entis*; see **potent¹**]

■ **puissance** (also **puissaunce**) /pū'is-əns, -öns', -äns', pwis'əns, etc/ *n* power (*archaic*); /usu pwēs'äs or pwēs'äns/ (a showjumping competition with very high jumps testing) the power of a horse. **puissantly** /-ənt-li/ *adv*.

puja /poo'jə/ (*Hinduism*) *n* (an act of) worship; reverential observance; a festival. [Sans *pūjā* worship]

■ **pujari** /poo-jär'i/ *n* a priest.

puke¹ /pūk/ *vt* and *vi* (*inf*) to vomit. ◆ *vt* (*archaic*) to cause to vomit. ◆ *n* vomit (*inf*); the act of vomiting; an emetic (*archaic*); a despicable person (*inf*). [Poss connected with Flem *spukken* and Ger *spucken*]

■ **pū'ker** *n* (*archaic*) an emetic. **pū'key** or **pū'ky** *adj* (*inf*) reminiscent of or resembling vomit; nauseous.

puke² /pūk/ (obs) n a fine woollen cloth; a colour between russet or purple and black. ◆ adj made of puke (Shakesp); of the colour puke. [MDu puuc the best woollen cloth]

pukeko /puk'ə-kō/ n (pl puk'ekos) a New Zealand wading bird with bright plumage. [Maori]

pukka, pucka or **pakka** /puk'ə/ (orig Anglo-Ind) adj thoroughly good; thorough; complete; solidly built; settled; durable; permanent; full-weight; straightforward; genuine; sure; high-class. [Hindustani pakkā cooked, ripe]
□ **pukka sahib** n a gentleman.

puku /poo'koo/ n an antelope (Adenota, or Kobus, vardoni) found in southern central Africa, esp in swampy areas and near rivers. [Zulu mpuku]

pul /pool/ n (pl **puls** or **puli** /poo'li/) an Afghan monetary unit, $\frac{1}{100}$ of an afghani. [Pashto, from Pers pūl copper coin]

pula /poo'lä/ n the standard monetary unit of Botswana (100 thebe). [Tswana, rain]

pulchritude /pul'kri-tūd/ (formal) n beauty. [L pulchritūdō, -inis, from pulcher beautiful]
■ **pulchritud'inous** adj.

puldron (obs) same as **pauldron**.

pule /pūl/ vt and vi to pipe; to whimper or whine. [Imit; cf Fr piauler]
■ **pū'ler** n. **pū'ling** n and adj. **pū'lingly** adv. **pū'ly** adj whining; sickly.

Pulex /pū'leks/ n the flea genus, giving name to the family **Pulicidae** /-lis'i-dē/. [L pūlex, -icis]
■ **pū'licide** /-sīd/ n (L caedere to kill) a poison or other agent which destroys fleas.

Pulitzer prize /pūl'it-sər or pū'lit-sər prīz/ n any of various annual prizes for American literature, journalism and music. [J Pulitzer (1847–1911), US newspaper publisher who instituted the prizes]

pulka /pul'kə/ n a Laplander's boat-shaped sledge (also **pulk** or **pulk'ha**). [Finnish pulkka, Lappish pulkke, bulkke]

pull /pul/ vt to pluck; to remove by plucking; to extract; to pick by hand; to strip, deprive of feathers, hair, etc; to draw or drag; to move, or try or tend to move, towards oneself or in the direction so thought of; to make, or cause to be, by pulling; to row; to transport by rowing; to move in a particular direction when driving (usu with out, over, etc); to stretch; to hold back (eg a blow in boxing, or a racehorse to prevent its winning; see also **pull up** below); to take as an impression or proof, orig by pulling the bar of a hand-press (printing); to hit (the ball) too much to the left for a right-handed player, or to the right for a left-handed player (golf); to hit (the ball) with a horizontal bat from waist height round onto the legside (cricket); to bring down; to take a drink of; to draw or fire (a weapon); to snatch or steal (sl); to arrest (sl); to raid (sl); to succeed in forming a (sexual) relationship with (sl); to attract (eg a crowd) (sl); to withdraw. ◆ vi to give a pull; to perform the action of pulling anything; to tear or pluck; to drag or draw; to strain at the bit; to exert oneself; to go with a pulling movement; to move in a particular direction, esp when in a motor vehicle (usu with away, out, over, etc); to row; to suck; to succeed in initiating a sexual relationship (sl). ◆ n an act, bout or spell of pulling; a pulling force; a row; a stiff ascent; a draught of liquor; a proof, a single impression (printing); advantage; influence; an apparatus for pulling; the quantity pulled at one time; resistance; a shot hit too far to the left for a right-handed player, or to the right for a left-handed player (golf); an attacking stroke played with a horizontal bat where the batsman hits the ball from waist height round onto the legside (cricket). [OE pullian to pluck or draw]
■ **pull'er** n.
□ **pull'back** n a hindrance; a drawback; a retreat or withdrawal; a device formerly used for making a skirt hang close and straight in front (see also **pull back** below). **pull'-down** adj able or intended to be pulled down in some way or by some means; (of a computer menu) able to be accessed by means of the cursor or a key, and displayed over the material already on screen. **pull'-in** n a stopping-place (also adj); a transport café (see also **pull in** below). **pull'-on** adj (of eg clothes) requiring only to be pulled on, without fastening. ◆ n a pull-on garment of any kind. **pull'-out** adj denoting a section of a magazine, etc that can be removed and kept separately (see also **pull out** below). **pull'over** n a jersey, jumper, or other body garment put on over the head. **pull'-tab** n a ring pull, a tongue of metal with a ring attached to it, which pulls to open a beer, etc can; in eg illustrations, esp in children's books, a piece of paper or card attached to a part of an illustration, which can be pulled to make (that part of) the illustration move or alter in some way. **pull technology** n (comput) the acquiring of information from a server on the Internet by request (cf **push technology** under **push¹**). **pull'-through** n a cord with a rag for cleaning a rifle barrel. **pull'-up** n an act of pulling up; a sudden stoppage; a suitable place (esp for lorry-drivers, etc) for pulling up; an

exercise in which one hangs from a bar by the hands, and pulls oneself up so that one's chin is level with the bar.
■ **on the pull** (sl) frequenting places such as nightclubs, pubs, etc with the intention of finding a sexual partner. **pull about** to distort; to treat roughly. **pull a face** to grimace. **pull a fast one on** (sl) to take advantage of by a trick. **pull ahead** to move into the lead. **pull apart** or **pull to pieces** to cause to break into pieces by pulling; to criticize harshly. **pull away** to move into the lead; to withdraw. **pull back** to retreat or withdraw (see also **pullback** above). **pull caps** (archaic) to scuffle. **pull devil, pull baker** (in an argument, competition, etc) do your best, both sides. **pull down** to take down or apart; to demolish; to bring down; to reduce in health or vigour; to cause to come down into some position by pulling or by some other means (see also **pull-down** above). **pull for** to row for; to support. **pull in** to draw in; to make tighter; to draw a motor vehicle into the side of the road, or drive into the car park of a café, etc and halt (see also **pull-in** above); to arrest; to earn; (of a train) to arrive at a station. **pull off** to carry through successfully. **pull oneself together** to regain one's self-control; to compose oneself, preparing to think or to act. **pull one's punches** see under **punch¹**. **pull one's weight** to give full effect to one's weight in rowing; to do one's full share of work, co-operate wholeheartedly. **pull out** to draw out; to drive a motor vehicle away from the side of the road or out of a line of traffic; (of a train) to leave a station; to abandon a place or situation which has become too difficult to cope with (inf; **pull'-out** n; see also above). **pull over** to draw over to the side of the road, either to stop or to allow other vehicles to pass. **pull rank** see under **rank¹**. **pull round** to bring, or come, back to good health or condition, or to consciousness. **pull someone's leg** see under **leg**. **pull the long bow** to lie or boast inordinately. **pull the rug from under (someone)** see under **rug¹**. **pull through** to bring or get to the end of something difficult or dangerous with some success (see also **pull-through** above). **pull together** to co-operate. **pull up** to pull out of the ground; to tighten the reins; to bring to a stop; to halt; (of a horse) to be brought to a halt by the jockey or (reflexive) to stop of its own volition (horse-racing); to take to task; to gain ground; to arrest. **pull up stakes** to prepare to leave a place.

pullet /pul'it/ n a young hen, esp from first laying to first moult. [Fr poulette, dimin of poule a hen, from LL pulla a hen, fem of L pullus a young animal]
□ **pull'et-sperm** n (orig the chalaza, once believed to be the male element in the egg; Shakesp, derog) eggs.

pulley /pul'i/ n (pl **pull'eys**) a wheel turning about an axis, and carrying a rope, chain or band on its rim, used for raising weights, changing direction of pull, transmission of power, etc; a block; a combination of pulleys or blocks; a frame on which clothes are hung to dry, suspended from a ceiling by pulleys (Scot). [ME poley, puly, from OFr polie, from LL polegia, supposed to be from a dimin of Gr polos axle]

Pullman /pul'mən/ or **Pullman car** /kär/ n a luxuriously furnished railway saloon or sleeping-car, first made by George M Pullman (1831–97) in America.

pullorum disease /pə-lōr'em diz-ēz or pə-lör'əm/ (vet) n a serious, often fatal, disease of young poultry caused by the bacterium Salmonella pullorum (formerly Bacterium pullorum). [L pullorum, genitive pl of pullus chicken]

pullulate /pul'ū-lāt/ vi to sprout; to sprout or breed abundantly; to teem; to increase rapidly. [L pullulāre, -ātum, from pullulus a young animal, sprout, from pullus]
■ **pullula'tion** n.

pulmo /pul'mō, pūl'mō/ (med) n (pl **pulmo'nes** /-nēz/) a lung. [L pulmō, -ōnis lung]
■ **pul'mobranch** /-brangk/ n (zool) a lung-book (qv). **pulmobranch'iate** /-mə-nä'ri-ə/ n the lungwort genus of the borage family. **pul'monary** /-mən-ər-i/ adj of the lungs or respiratory cavity; leading to or from the lungs; of the nature of lungs; having lungs; diseased or weak in the lungs. **Pulmonā'ta** n pl an air-breathing order or subclass of Gastropoda, including many land and freshwater snails. **pul'monate** n (zool) a member of the Pulmonata. ◆ adj having lungs, lung-sacs, lung-books or similar organs. **pulmonic** /-mon'ik/ adj of the lungs. ◆ n (obs) a sufferer from, or medication for, lung disease. **Pul'motor®** n an apparatus for forcing air and/or oxygen into, and air out of, the lungs.

pulp /pulp/ n any soft fleshy part of an animal, eg the tissue in the cavity of a tooth; the soft part of plants, esp of fruits; any soft structureless mass; the soft mass obtained from the breaking and grinding of rags, wood, etc before it is hardened into paper; crushed ore; nonsense; sentimentality; a cheap magazine printed on wood-pulp paper, or of a trashy and sentimental or sensational character (also **pulp magazine**); fiction of the type published in such a magazine; a film, etc of such a type. ◆ vt to reduce to pulp; to make pulpy; to deprive of pulp. ◆ vi to become pulp or like pulp. [L pulpa flesh, pulp]

■ **pulp'er** *n* a machine for reducing various materials to pulp. **pulp'ify** *vt*. **pulp'ily** *adv*. **pulp'iness** *n*. **pulp'ous** *adj*. **pulp'y** *adj*.

◻ **pulp'board** *n* a coarse cardboard made *usu* from a single layer of pulp. **pulp cavity** *n* the hollow of a tooth which contains pulp. **pulp'-engine** *n* a machine for making pulp for paper. **pulp'mill** *n* a machine or factory for pulping wood, roots or other material. **pulp novel** *n*. **pulp novelist** *n*. **pulp'stone** *n* a grindstone for pulping wood. **pulp'wood** *n* wood suitable for paper-making; a board of compressed wood pulp and adhesive.

pulpit /puˈlˈpit/ *n* a raised structure for preaching from; an auctioneer's desk or the like; preachers or preaching collectively; a position one can exploit as a means of promulgating one's views; a platform (*obs*); a safety railing at the bow of a yacht. ◆ *adj* belonging to the pulpit. [L *pulpitum* a stage]

■ **pul'pited** *adj*. **pulpiteer'** or **pul'piter** *n* someone who speaks from a pulpit, a preacher. **pul'pitry** *n* sermonizing. **pul'pitum** *n* (*archit*) a rood loft.

pulpous, pulpy, etc see under **pulp**.

pulque /pulˈkä/ or /pulˈkē/ *n* a fermented drink made in Mexico from agave sap. [Am Sp]

pulsar see under **pulsate**.

pulsate /pulˈsāt/ or /pul-sātˈ/ *vi* to beat, throb; to vibrate; to change repeatedly in force or intensity; to thrill with life or emotion. [L *pulsāre*, *-ātum* to beat, frequentative of *pellere*, *pulsum* to drive]

■ **pul'sar** /-sär/ *n* (for 'pulsating star', but see also **pulsating star** below) any of a number of interstellar sources of regularly pulsed radiation, first discovered in 1967, and thought to be rotating neutron stars. **pulsatance** /pulˈsə-təns or pul-sāˈtəns/ *n* (*phys*) the angular frequency of a periodic motion, frequency multiplied by 2π. **pul'satile** /-sə-tīl/ or (*US*) -til/ *adj* capable of pulsating; pulsatory; rhythmical; played by percussion (*music*). **Pulsatill'a** *n* pasqueflower (because it is beaten by the wind). **pulsā'tion** *n* a beating or throbbing; a motion of the heart or pulse; any measured beat; vibration. **pulsative** /pulˈsə-tiv or -sātˈiv/ *adj*. **pulsā'tor** (or /pulˈsə-tər/) *n* a machine, or part of a machine, that pulsates or imparts pulsation, eg for separating diamonds from earth, for regulating the rhythmical suction of a milking machine, or for pumping. **pulsatory** /pulˈsə-tə-ri or -sāˈtə-ri/ *adj* beating or throbbing.

◻ **pulsating current** *n* an electric current that changes periodically in intensity but not direction. **pulsating star** *n* a type of variable star of regularly fluctuating brightness, the fluctuations being caused by the expansion and contraction of the star.

pulse¹ /puls/ *n* the beating of the heart and the arteries; a beating or throbbing; a measured beat or throb; a vibration; a single variation, beat or impulse; a signal of very short duration (*radio*); a thrill (*fig*). ◆ *vi* (of eg the heart) to beat; to throb; to pulsate. ◆ *vt* to drive by pulsation; to produce, or cause to be emitted, in the form of pulses. [L *pulsus*, from *pellere, pulsum*; partly OFr *pouls, pous*, remodelled on Latin]

■ **pulsed** *adj*. **pulse'less** *adj*. **pulse'lessness** *n*. **puls'idge** *n* (*Shakesp*; used by Mistress Quickly in *2 Henry IV* II.4.23) pulse. **pulsif'ic** *adj* producing a single pulse. **pulsim'eter** *n* an instrument for measuring the strength or quickness of the pulse. **pulsom'eter** *n* a pulsimeter; a pump that draws in water by condensation of steam in two chambers alternately.

◻ **pulse code modulation** *n* a system of transmission in which the audio signals are sampled periodically, coded in digital form, and transmitted (*abbrev* **PCM**). **pulse diagnosis** *n* a diagnostic technique involving the palpation of pulses and assessment of their rate and rhythms, etc, specific pulse characteristics being considered indicative of specific organ conditions. **pulse dialling** *n* a telephone dialling system in which digits are transmitted as electrical pulses, the number of pulses corresponding to the value of each digit. **pulse'jet** or **puls'ojet** *n* in jet propulsion, an intermittent jet. **pulse modulation** *n* modulation in which pulses are varied to represent a signal. **pulse'-rate** *n* the number of beats of a pulse per minute. **pulse'-wave** *n* the expansion of the artery, moving from point to point, like a wave, as each beat of the heart sends the blood to the extremities.

■ **feel someone's pulse** to test or measure someone's heartbeat by feeling for the pulse eg at the neck or wrist; to explore a person's feelings or inclinations in a tentative way. **keep one's finger on the pulse** to keep in touch with current events, ideas, opinions, etc.

pulse² /puls/ *n sing* or *n pl* the seeds of leguminous plants as food collectively, beans, peas, lentils, etc; (any of) the plants yielding them. [L *puls, pultis* porridge; cf Gr *poltos* and **poultice**]

■ **pultā'ceous** *adj* macerated and softened.

pulsidge, pulsojet, etc see under **pulse¹**.

pultaceous see under **pulse²**.

pultrusion /pul-trooˈzhən/ *n* a process for producing reinforced plastic products in which strands of the reinforcing material are surrounded with liquid resin and then pulled through a *usu* heated die to shape and cure the resin. [**pull** and **extrusion**]

■ **pultrude'** *vt*.

pultun, pultan, pulton or **pultoon** /pulˈtun, pulˈtən, pulˈtün/ *n* an Indian infantry regiment. [Hindustani *pultan*, from **battalion**]

pulture see **puture**.

pulu /pooˈloo/ *n* a silky fibre from the Hawaiian tree-fern leaf-bases. [Hawaiian]

pulv. (*pharm*) *abbrev* : *pulvis* (L), powder.

pulver /pulˈvər/ *vt* (*obs*) to reduce to powder. [L *pulvis, pulveris* powder]

■ **pul'verable** *adj* (*rare*). **pulverā'tion** *n* (*rare*) pulverization. **pul'verine** *n* barilla ash. **pul'verizable** or **-s-** (or /-īzˈə-bl/) *adj*. **pulverīzā'tion** or **-s-** *n*. **pul'verize** or **-ise** *vt* to reduce to dust or fine powder; to defeat thoroughly, destroy, thrash (*fig*). ◆ *vi* to turn into dust or powder. **pul'verizer** or **-s-** *n* someone who pulverizes; a machine for pulverizing or for spraying. **pul'verous** *adj* dusty or powdery. **pulverulence** /-verˈū-ləns/ *n*. **pulver'ūlent** *adj* consisting of fine powder; powdery; dusty-looking; readily crumbling.

◻ **Pulver Wednesday** or **pulvering day** *n* (*obs*) Ash Wednesday.

pulvil /pulˈvil/ (*obs* or *hist*) *n* (also **pulvil'io, pulvill'io** or **pulville'**) perfumed powder; extended to snuff and other powders. ◆ *vt* (**pul'villing; pul'villed**) to powder or scent with pulvil. [Ital *polviglio*, from *polve* powder, from L *pulvis*]

■ **pul'vilized** or **-s-** *adj*.

pulvillar, etc see under **pulvinus**.

pulvinus /pul-vīˈnəs/ (*bot*) *n* (*pl* **pulvi'ni** /-nī/) a cushion-like swelling, *esp* one at the base of a leaf or leaflet, by whose changes of turgidity movements are effected. [L *pulvīnus* cushion, pillow; dimin *pulvillus*]

■ **pulvill'ar** *adj* of a pulvillus; cushion-like. **pulvill'iform** *adj*. **pulvill'us** *n* (*pl* **pulvill'i** /-ī/) a little cushion or pad (*esp obs med*); a pad between the claws of an insect's foot (*zool*). **pulvinar** /-vīˈnər, -närˈ/ *adj* cushion-like; of a pulvinus (*bot*). ◆ *n* a Roman cushioned seat (*hist*); a small pillow or pad (*obs med*); a knob on the optic thalamus (*anat*). **pul'vinate** /-vin-āt/ or **pul'vinated** *adj* (*esp biol*) cushion-like; pillowy; bulging. **pul'vinule** *n* (*bot*) the pulvinus of a leaflet.

pulwar /pulˈwär/ *n* a light keelless boat used on the Ganges. [Hindustani *palwār*]

puly see under **pule**.

pulza-oil /pulˈzə-oil/ *n* an oil obtained from physic-nut seeds. [Origin unknown]

puma /pūˈmə/ *n* (*pl* **pu'mas**) the cougar (*Felis concolor*), a large reddish-brown American cat (also called **mountain lion**). [Am Sp, from Quechua]

pumelo /pumˈi-lō/ same as **pomelo**.

pumice /pumˈis or (*esp Scot*) pūˈmis/ *n* an acid glassy lava so full of gas cavities that it floats in water; a frothy portion of any lava; a piece of such lava used for smoothing or cleaning. ◆ *vt* (also (*rare*) **pumicate** /pūˈmi-kāt/) to smooth or clean with pumice-stone. [OE *pumic(-stān)*, pumice(-stone); reintroduced, from OFr *pomis*; both from L *pūmex, -icis*]

■ **pumiceous** /-mishˈəs/ *adj*.

◻ **pum'ice-stone** *n*.

pumie or **pumy** /pumˈi/ (*Spenser*) *n* a pebble or stone (also **pumie stone, pumy stone**). [**pumice-stone**]

pummel /pumˈl/ *n* a less usual spelling of **pommel**. ◆ *vt* (**pumm'elling; pumm'elled**) to beat, pound or thump, *esp* with the fists. [**pommel**]

pump¹ /pump/ *n* a machine for raising and moving fluids (*orig esp* bilge-water in ships), or for compressing, rarefying, or transferring gases; a stroke of a pump; an act of pumping. ◆ *vt* to raise, force, compress, exhaust, empty, remove or inflate with a pump; to discharge by persistent effort; to fire (bullets, etc) rapidly and repeatedly; to move in the manner of a pump; to shake (someone's hand) vigorously up and down, as though working a pump-handle; to subject to, or elicit by, persistent questioning; to pump water on (*obs*); to put out of breath (*esp in passive*; often with *out*; *inf*). ◆ *vi* to work a pump; to work like a pump; (of mercury in a barometer) to rise and fall suddenly; to spurt; to propel or increase the speed of a sailing-boat by rapidly pulling the sails in and out (*naut*). [Ety uncertain]

■ **pumped** *adj* (*inf*; often with *up*) excited; enthused; stimulated. **pump'er** *n*.

◻ **pump'-action** *adj* denoting a repeating rifle or shotgun whose chamber is fed by a pump-like movement. **pumped storage** *n* in a hydroelectric system, the use of electricity at times of low demand to pump water up to a high storage reservoir, to be used to generate electricity at times of high demand. **pump gun** *n* a pump-action gun. **pump'-handle** *n* the lever that works a pump. **pump'-head** or **pump'hood** *n* a frame covering the upper wheel of a chain pump, serving to guide the water into the discharge-spout. **pump'-priming** *n* starting a pump working efficiently by introducing fluid to drive out the air; investing money in order to stimulate commerce, local support, etc. **pump room** *n* the room at a mineral spring in which the waters are drunk. **pump'-water** *n* water from a pump. **pump'-well** *n* a well from which water is obtained by pumping; the compartment in which a pump works.

■ **pump iron** (*inf*) to exercise with weights, to develop one's muscles. **pump up** to inflate; to increase.

pump² /*pump*/ *n* a light shoe without a fastening, worn *esp* for dancing. [Origin unknown]

■ **pumped** *adj* wearing pumps.

pumpernickel /*pŭm'* or *pum'pər-ni-kl*/ *n* a coarse dark rye bread. [Ger; orig a term of abuse ('Smelly Nick' or 'Farty Nick'), poss then applied to the bread because of its gas-creating effect on the digestive system]

pumpkin /*pump'kin, pum'kin*, or (*US*) *pung'kin*/ *n* a plant (*Cucurbita pepo*) of the gourd family, or its fruit (also (*obs*) **pomp'ion, pump'ion**). [OFr *pompon*, from L *pepō*, from Gr *pepōn* ripe; see **pepo**]

□ **pump'kinseed** *n* a freshwater sunfish of N America.

pumple-nose see **pompelmoose**.

pumy see **pumie**.

pun¹ /*pun*/ *vi* (**punn'ing**; **punned**) to play on words alike or nearly alike in sound but different in meaning. ◆ *n* a play on words. [A late-17c word; origin unknown; Ital *puntiglio* a fine point, has been conjectured (see **punctilio**), as has a connection with **pun²**]

■ **punn'ing** *n* and *adj*. **punn'ingly** *adv*. **pun'ster** *n* a person who makes puns.

pun² /*pun*/ *vt* (**punn'ing**; **punned**) to pound (*Shakesp*); to ram; to consolidate by ramming. [See **pound³**]

■ **punn'er** *n* a tool for punning, a ram.

puna /*poon'ə*/ *n* a bleak tableland in the Andes; a cold wind there; mountain sickness. [Am Sp, from Quechua]

punalua /*pŭ-nə-loo'ə*/ (*anthrop*) *n* a system of group marriage, sisters (by blood or tribal reckoning) having their husbands in common, or brothers their wives, or both. [Hawaiian]

■ **punalu'an** *adj*.

punani, punaani, punaany or **punany** /*poo-nä'ni*/ (*vulgar sl; orig W Indies*) *n* (*sing* or *pl*) the female genitalia; women collectively, regarded as sexual objects. [Perh from an African word]

punce¹ see **punch¹**.

punce² or **poonce** /*pŭns*/ (*Aust sl*) *n* an effeminate man. [Variant of **ponce**]

Punch /*punch* or *punsh*/ *n* a hook-nosed hunchback, chief character in the puppet show *Punch and Judy*; the name of a humorous illustrated weekly magazine, first published in 1841. [Shortened from **Punchinello**]

punch¹ /*punch* or *punsh*/ *vt* to strike with the fist (sometimes with *out*); to thump (sometimes with *out*); to prod; to poke; to drive (cattle; *US* and *Aust*); to kick (also **punce** /*puns*/; *dialect*); to stamp, pierce, perforate, indent, by a forward, downward, etc movement of a tool or part of a machine; to make, obtain or remove by such a movement (often with *out*); to press in vigorously (a key or button), or the key or button of; to record by pressing a key; to play a low shot with a short follow-through (*sport*). ◆ *vi* to perform an act of punching; to clock (*in* or *out*). ◆ *n* a vigorous blow, or attempted blow, with the fist; striking power; effective forcefulness; a tool or machine for punching; a die; a prop for a mine-roof; a low shot played with a short follow-through (*sport*). [**pounce¹**; or from **puncheon¹**; poss in some senses for **punish**]

■ **punch'er** *n* someone who punches; an instrument for punching; a cowpuncher or cattle drover (*US*); the driver of a team (*Aust*). **punch'y** *adj* vigorous, powerful; punch-drunk (*inf*).

□ **punch'-bag** or (*N Am*) **punch'ing-bag** *n* a large stuffed bag used for boxing practice; a person who is the target of another person's outbursts of anger (*fig*). **punch'-ball** *n* a suspended ball used for boxing practice; a game similar to baseball in which the ball is punched. **punch'board** *n* a cardboard frame divided into a number of compartments each concealing a slip of paper, some of which entitle the holder to a prize. **punch'-card** or **punched card** *n* a card with perforations representing data, formerly used in the operation of computers. **punch'-drunk** *adj* having a form of cerebral concussion from past blows in boxing, with results resembling drunkenness; dazed (*inf* short form **punch'y**). **punched tape** *n* (*comput*) same as **paper tape** (see under **paper**). **punching-bag** see **punch-bag** above. **punch'line** *n* the last line or conclusion of a joke, in which the point lies; the last part of a story, giving it meaning or an unexpected twist. **punch'-prop** *n* (*mining*) a short piece of wood used as a prop. **punch'-up** *n* a fight with fists.

■ **pull one's punches** to hold back one's blows; to be deliberately less hard-hitting in one's criticism than one might be.

punch² /*punch, punsh* or (*obs*) *pŭnsh*/ *n* a drink traditionally of spirits, water, sugar, lemon juice, and spice (but now with many variations). [Traditionally thought to be from Hindi *pāc* five, from Sans *pañca* (from the supposed five original ingredients), but there are difficulties with this, as the original pronunciation seems to have been /*pŭnsh*/ which would not be a reflex of *pāc*, and there could be anything from three to six ingredients; a connection with **puncheon²** has also been suggested]

□ **punch'bowl** *n* a large bowl for making punch in; a large bowl-shaped hollow in the ground. **punch'-ladle** *n* a ladle for filling glasses from a punchbowl.

punch³ /*punch* or *punsh*/ *adj* (*dialect*) short and thick. ◆ *n* a thick-set short man (*obs*); a short-legged draught horse, chestnut in colour, *orig* bred in Suffolk (also **Suffolk punch**). [Poss shortened from **puncheon²**, or from **Punchinello**, or a variant of **bunch**]

■ **punch'y** *adj*.

puncheon¹ /*pun'chn* or *pun'shn*/ *n* a dagger (*obs*); a tool for piercing or for stamping; a short supporting post; a split trunk with one face smoothed for flooring, etc. [OFr *poinson*, from L *pungere*, *punctum* to prick]

puncheon² /*pun'chn* or *pun'shn*/ *n* a cask; a liquid measure of from 70 to 120 gallons (*obs* or *hist*). [OFr *poinson* a cask; origin obscure]

Punchinello /*pun-chi-nel'ō* or *-shi-*/ *n* (*pl* **Punchinell'os** or **Punchinell'oes**) a hook-nosed character in an Italian puppet show; a buffoon, any grotesque personage. [Ital *Pulcinella* a Neapolitan buffoon, of doubtful origin]

punchy see under **punch**¹,³.

puncta see **punctum**.

punctate /*pungk'tāt*/ or **punctated** /*-tā'tid*/ (*biol* or *pathol*) *adj* dotted; pitted. [L *punctum* a point, puncture, from *pungere*, *punctum* to prick]

■ **punctā'tion** *n*. **punctā'tor** *n* someone who marks something with dots, *esp* applied to the Massoretes, who invented the Hebrew vowel points.

punctilio /*pungk-til'i-ō* or *pungk-til'yō*/ *n* (*pl* **punctil'ios**) a point in behaviour or ceremony requiring, or only observed by those having, fine or over-fine sensibilities with regard to etiquette; a point about which one is scrupulous; nicety or exact observance of etiquette. [Ital *puntiglio* and Sp *puntillo*, dimins of *punto*, from L *punctum* a point]

■ **punctil'ious** *adj* scrupulous and exact; attentive to etiquette and punctilios. **punctil'iously** *adv*. **punctil'iousness** *n*.

puncto /*pungk'tō*/, **puncto banco** see **punto**.

punctual /*pungk'tū-əl*/ *adj* exact in keeping time and appointments; done at the exact time; up to time; of the nature of a point; relating to a point or points (*maths*); of punctuation; precise, exact (*obs*); punctilious; relating to a point in time (*linguistics*). [LL *punctuālis*, from *punctum* a point]

■ **punc'tualist** *n* (*obs*; *rare*) an authority on or observer of punctilios. **punctuality** /*-al'i-ti*/ *n*. **punc'tually** *adv*.

punctuate /*pungk'tū-āt*/ *vt* to mark with points; to mark off (a piece of writing) with full stops, commas, question marks, etc; to intersperse; to emphasize. [LL *punctuāre*, *-ātum* to prick, from L *punctum* (see **punctum**)]

■ **punctuā'tion** *n* the act or art of dividing sentences by points or marks; in the theory of punctuated equilibrium, any of the bursts of rapid change that interrupt the long periods of stability (*biol*). **punctuā'tionist** *n* a believer in punctuated equilibrium. **punc'tuātive** *adj*. **punc'tuātor** *n*.

□ **punctuated equilibrium** or **equilibria** *n* (*biol*) (a theory which states that evolution happens in) short bursts of major change that interrupt long periods of stability. **punctuation mark** *n* any of the points or marks used in punctuating writing.

punctum /*pungk'təm*/ (*anat*) *n* (*pl* **punc'ta**) a point or dot; a minute aperture. [L *punctum*, from *pungere*, *punctum* to prick]

■ **punc'tūlate** or **punc'tūlated** *adj* minutely dotted or pitted. **punctūlā'tion** *n*. **punc'tūle** *n* a minute dot, pit or aperture.

□ **punctum caecum** /*pungk'təm sē'kəm* or *pŭngk'tŭm kī'kŭm*/ *n* (L, blind spot; *anat*) the point of the retina from which the optic nerve fibres radiate.

puncture /*pungk'chər*/ *n* an act of pricking; a small hole made with a sharp point; perforation of a pneumatic tyre, a flat tyre. ◆ *vt* to make a puncture in; to deflate (someone's pride, self-confidence, etc). ◆ *vi* to get a puncture. [L *punctūra*, from *pungere* to prick]

■ **punctūrā'tion** *n*. **punc'tured** *adj* perforated; pierced; marked with little holes; consisting of little holes. **punc'turer** *n*.

pundit /*pun'dit*/ *n* any learned person; an authority, now *usu* someone who considers himself or herself an authority; (also **pan'dit**) a Hindu learned in Sanskrit and in Hindu culture, philosophy and law. [Hindi *paṇḍit*, from Sans *paṇḍita*]

■ **pun'ditry** *n*.

pundonor /pŭn-dō-nōr'/ or /pŭn-dō-nör'/ n (pl **pundonor'es** /-ās/) a point of honour. [Sp, from *punto de honor*]

punga see **ponga**.

pungent /pun'jənt/ adj sharp; pricking or acrid in taste or smell; keenly touching the mind; painful; sarcastic; ending in a hard sharp point (*bot*). [L *pungens, -entis*, prp of *pungere* to prick]
 ■ **pun'gency** or (*poetic*) **pun'gence** n. **pun'gently** adv.

Punic /pū'nik/ adj of ancient Carthage; Carthaginian; faithless, treacherous, deceitful (as the Romans alleged the Carthaginians to be); purple (*obs*). ◆ n the Semitic language of ancient Carthage. [L *Pūnicus*, from *Poenī* the Carthaginians]
 ■ **Pu'nica** n the pomegranate genus, constituting the family **Punica'ceae** /-si-ē/ (related to the myrtle and loosestrife families). **punica'ceous** adj.
 ❑ **Punic apple** n (*obs*) the pomegranate. **Punic faith** n treachery.

punily see under **puny**.

punish /pun'ish/ vt to cause (someone) to suffer for an offence; to cause someone to suffer for (an offence); to handle, treat or beat severely (*inf*); to consume a large quantity of (*inf*). ◆ vi to inflict punishment. [Fr *punir, punissant*, from L *pūnīre* to punish, from *poena* penalty]
 ■ **punishabil'ity** n. **pun'ishable** adj. **pun'isher** n. **pun'ishing** adj causing suffering or retribution; severe, testing. **pun'ishingly** adv. **pun'ishment** n the act or method of punishing; a penalty imposed for an offence; in conditioning, the weakening of a response which is followed by an aversive or noxious stimulus, or by the withdrawal of a pleasant one (cf **negative reinforcement**); severe handling (*inf*).

punitive /pū'ni-tiv/ adj concerned with, inflicting, or intended to inflict, punishment. [L *pūnīre* to punish]
 ■ **punition** /-nish'ən/ n (*obs*) punishment. **pu'nitory** adj punitive.
 ❑ **punitive damages** see **exemplary damages** under **exemplar**.

Punjabi, also (less commonly) **Panjabi** and (formerly) **Punjabee** or **Punjaubee** /pun-jä'bē, -jö'/ n a native or inhabitant of the *Punjab* in India and Pakistan; the language of the Punjab. ◆ adj of the Punjab. [Hindi *Panjābī*]

punk[1] /pungk/ n a follower of punk rock, typically using cheap utility articles as clothes or decoration; anything or anyone worthless; nonsense; a foolish person; a homosexual, often a boy (*old sl*); a prostitute (*obs*). ◆ adj of, relating to or inspired by punk rock and its followers; rotten; worthless; miserable. [Origin unknown; poss from **punk**[2]]
 ■ **punk'ish** or **punk'y** adj. **punk'ishness** or **punk'iness** n.
 ❑ **punk rock** n a style of popular music of the late 1970s, fast and aggressive, with violent, often obscene or subversive lyrics.

punk[2] /pungk/ n touchwood; tinder; amadou, a preparation made from fungi to be used as tinder. [Poss **spunk**; or poss of Native American origin]

punka or **punkah** /pung'kə/ (*Ind*) n a fan; a palm-leaf fan; a large mechanical fan for cooling a room. [Hindi *pākhā* a fan]

punner see under **pun**[2].

punnet /pun'it/ n a small shallow basket for fruit such as strawberries. [Origin unknown]

punning, punster see under **pun**[1].

punt[1] /punt/ n a flat-bottomed boat with square ends, *esp* one propelled by means of a long pole pushed against the bottom of a river, etc. ◆ vt to propel by pushing a pole against the bottom; to transport by punt. ◆ vi to go in a punt; to go shooting in a punt; to propel a punt or boat with a pole. [OE *punt*, from L *pontō, -ōnis* punt, pontoon; cf **pontoon**[1]]
 ■ **punt'er** n.
 ❑ **punt'-fishing** n fishing from a punt. **punt'-gun** n a heavy large-bore gun used for shooting water fowl from a punt. **punt'-pole** n a pole for propelling a punt. **punts'man** n a sportsman who uses a punt.

punt[2] /punt/ n the act of kicking a dropped football before it touches the ground; *specif*, in American football, such a kick into the opposing team's territory, *usu* on the fourth down when it seems unlikely that the team in possession of the ball will gain the distance necessary to retain possession; the depression in the bottom of a glass container, a kick. ◆ vt to kick in this manner or for this reason; to knock. [Origin obscure]
 ■ **punt'er** n.

punt[3] /punt/ vi to stake against the bank (*gambling*); to back a horse (*horse-racing*). ◆ n a gamble or bet. [Fr *ponter*]
 ■ **punt'er** n someone who punts, a professional gambler; a customer or client (*inf*); an ordinary person (*inf*, sometimes *derog*).

punt[4] /pŭnt/ n a former unit of currency in the Republic of Ireland, replaced by the euro (also called **Irish pound**).

puntee see **punty**.

punto /pun'tō/, also **puncto** /pungk'tō/ (*obs*) n (pl **pun'tos** or **punc'tos**) a moment; a point or punctilio; a pass or thrust in fencing. [Sp and Ital *punto*, from L *punctum* a point]
 ❑ **punto banco** or **puncto banco** n (Ital *banco* bank) a gambling game similar to baccarat. **punto dritt'o** n (Ital *dritto* direct; *obs fencing*) a direct or straight hit. **punto river'so** or (*Shakesp*) **rever'so** n (Ital *riverso* reversed; *obs fencing*) a backhanded stroke.

punty, puntee, pontie, ponty /pun'ti/, **pontil** or **pontile** /pon'til/ n an iron rod used in holding and manipulating glassware during the process of making. [Prob Fr *pontil*, appar from Ital *pontello, puntello*, dimin of *punto* point]

puny /pū'ni/ adj (**pū'nier; pū'niest**) very small; stunted; feeble; inexperienced (*Shakesp*); puisne (*obs*). [**puisne**]
 ■ **pū'nily** adv. **pū'niness** n.

pup /pup/ n a short form of **puppy**. ◆ vt and vi (**pupp'ing; pupped**) to give birth to a pup or pups.
 ❑ **pup'fish** n either of two varieties of tiny fish of the family Cyprinidae, native to the warmer waters of the western USA. **pup tent** n a small tent, easily carried.
 ■ **buy a pup** to be swindled. **in pup** of a bitch, pregnant. **sell a pup** to inveigle someone into a specious bad bargain; to swindle.

pupa /pū'pə/ n (pl **pupae** /pū'pē/ or **pū'pas**) an insect in the *usu* passive stage between larva and imago (*zool*); an intermediate stage of development in some other invertebrates (*biol*). [L *pūpa* a girl, a doll]
 ■ **pū'pal** adj of a pupa. **pūpā'rial** adj. **pūpā'rium** n (pl **pūpā'ria**) the last larval skin separated but retained as a hard protective covering for the pupa; sometimes, the covering and the pupa. **pū'pate** vi to become a pupa. **pūpā'tion** n. **pūpigerous** /-pij'ə-rəs/ adj having a puparium. **pūpip'arous** adj having pupae developed within the body of the mother, giving birth to offspring already at the pupal stage.
 ❑ **pu'pa-case** n a puparium.

pupil[1] /pū'pl/ or /pū'pil/ n someone who is being taught, a student or schoolchild; any of the students or schoolchildren that, as a teacher, one is instructing or has instructed, as in *one of her pupils*; a boy up to the age of 14, or a girl up to 12 (*Roman* and *Scots law*); a ward (*law*). ◆ adj under age. [Fr *pupille*, from L *pūpillus, pūpilla*, dimins of *pūpus* boy, *pūpa* girl]
 ■ **pu'pillage** or **pu'pilage** n the state of being a pupil or student; the time during which one is a pupil or student (in *Shakesp*, etc, sometimes taken as two words, **pupil age**). **pu'pillar** or **pu'pilar** adj pupillary. **pupillar'ity** n the state or time of being legally a pupil. **pu'pillary** adj relating to a pupil or ward, or someone under academic discipline. **pu'pilship** n.
 ❑ **pupil teacher** n (*old*) a pupil who does some teaching, *esp* as part of his or her training for later entry into the profession.

pupil[2] /pū'pl/ or /pū'pil/ n the round opening in the eye through which the light passes; a central spot, *esp* within a spot. [L *pūpilla* pupil of the eye, *orig* the same as **pupil**[1], from the small image to be seen in the eye]
 ■ **pupilabil'ity** n an intentionally unintelligible word in Sterne's *Tristram Shandy*. **pu'pillar, pu'pilar, pu'pillary** or **pu'pilary** adj. **pu'pillate** adj (*zool*) having a central spot of another colour.

pupiparous see under **pupa**.

puppet /pup'it/ n a doll or image moved by strings, wires, rods or the hand; a marionette; a person, state, etc under the control of another. ◆ adj behaving like a puppet; controlled by others. [Earlier **poppet**; cf OFr *poupette*, dimin from L *pūpa*]
 ■ **puppeteer'** n a person who manipulates puppets. **pupp'etry** n play of, or with, puppets; puppets collectively; puppet-like action; puppet shows; anything like or associated with puppets; puppets' dress (*obs*).
 ❑ **puppet play** n a drama performed by puppets. **puppet show** n an exhibition of puppets; a puppet play. **pupp'et-valve** same as **poppet-valve** (see **poppet**[1]).

puppodum /pup'ə-dəm/ same as **poppadum**.

puppy /pup'i/ n a young dog, a whelp; a lapdog or toy dog (*obs*); a young seal; a young rat; a conceited young man; a puppet (*dialect*); (often in *pl*) a beloved object (*inf*). ◆ vt and vi to pup. [Appar Fr *poupée* a doll or puppet, from L *pūpa*]
 ■ **pupp'ydom** n. **pupp'yhood** n. **pupp'yish** adj. **pupp'yism** n conceit in men.
 ❑ **pupp'y-dog** n. **puppy fat** n temporary fatness in childhood or adolescence. **pupp'y-headed** adj (*Shakesp*) having the mind of a puppy. **puppy love** same as **calf-love** (see under **calf**[1]). **pupp'y-walker** n a person who brings up a puppy until it is ready for training as a working dog; an experienced policeman who introduces a new recruit to his or her beat (*sl*).

pupunha /poo-pŭn'yə/ n the peach-palm; its fruit. [Port, from Tupí]

pur[1] see **purr**.

pur[2] /pûr/ (*obs*) n the jack in the game of post and pair.

pur³ /pūr/ (*Fr*) *adj* pure.
  ■ **pur sang** /sä/ *n* pure blood; thoroughbred; total.

Purana /poo-rä'nə/ *n* any one of a class of sacred books of Hindu mythology, cosmology, etc, written in Sanskrit. [Sans *purāṇa*, from *purā* of old]
  ■ **Puranic** /-rän'ik/ *adj*.

Purbeck /pûr'bek/ *adj* of the Isle (really a peninsula) of *Purbeck*, in Dorset.
  ■ **Purbeck'ian** *adj* (*geol*) Upper Jurassic (also *n*).
  ❑ **Purbeck marble** or **stone** *n* a freshwater shelly limestone quarried in the Isle of Purbeck.

purblind /pûr'blīnd/ *adj* nearly blind; *orig* apparently wholly blind; dim-sighted, *esp* spiritually; dim-witted. [**pure** (or perh OFr intens pfx *pur-*), and **blind**]
  ■ **pur'blindly** *adv*. **pur'blindness** *n*.

purchase /pûr'chəs or -chis/ *vt* to buy; to obtain by effort, risking danger, etc; to seek to bring about (*obs*); to bring about (*obs*); to acquire; to get in any way other than by inheritance (*law*); to be amends for (with *out*) (*Shakesp*); to raise or move by a mechanical power. ◆ *vi* to strive (*Shakesp*); to make purchases; to accumulate possessions (*obs*). ◆ *n* the act of purchasing; that which is purchased; acquisition; prize, booty (*archaic*); seizure (*obs*); whatever one can do for oneself by expedients (*obs*); annual rent; a bargain (*obs*); a price (*obs*); any mechanical advantage in raising or moving bodies or apparatus; an advantageous hold, or means of exerting force advantageously. [OFr *porchacier* to seek eagerly, pursue, from *pur* (L *prō*) for, and *chacier* to chase]
  ■ **pur'chasable** *adj*. **pur'chaser** *n*.
  ❑ **purchase money** *n* the money paid, or to be paid, for anything. **purchase order** *n* a commercial document issued as a formal request for the provision of goods or services. **purchase system** *n* the system by which, before 1871, commissions in the British Army could be bought. **purchase tax** *n* formerly, a British form of sales tax levied on specified goods and at differential rates.
  ■ **not worth a day's**, etc **purchase** not likely to last a day, etc. **so many years' purchase** the value or price of a house, estate, etc equal to the amount of so many years' rent or income.

purdah /pûr'də/ *n esp* formerly, in Hindu and Muslim communities, the seclusion of women from the sight of strangers, by means of a screen or curtain in the home or by a veil worn in public; the screen, curtain, etc used for this; seclusion generally (*fig*). [Urdu and Pers *pardah* curtain]
  ■ **pur'dahed** *adj* (of a woman) secluded, in purdah.
  ❑ **purdah bus**, **carriage**, etc *n* one for women only, in which the occupants are screened by shutters or blinds.

Purdey® /pûr'di/ *n* a gun manufactured by the firm of James *Purdey* and Sons Ltd. ◆ *adj* denoting such guns, gun-mechanisms, etc.

purdonium /pûr-dō'ni-əm/ *n* a kind of coal scuttle introduced by a Mr *Purdon*.

pure /pūr/ *adj* clean; unsoiled; unmixed; not adulterated; free from guilt or defilement; chaste; free from bad taste, bad grammar, bad manners, insincerity, barbarism, etc; modest; mere; that and that only; utter, sheer; free (from any stated characteristics); (of a study) confined to that which belongs directly to it; non-empirical, involving an exercise of the mind alone, without involving the results of experimentation; excellent, fine (*obs*); homozygous, breeding true (*biol*); unconditional (*law*); free from ritual uncleanness. ◆ *n* purity; dog's faeces or any similar substance used by tanners (also **puer**; *hist*). ◆ *adv* purely; utterly, completely (*inf*); without mixture. ◆ *vt* to cleanse or refine; to treat with pure (also **puer**). [Fr *pur*, from L *pūrus* pure]
  ■ **pure'ly** *adv* chastely; unmixedly; unconditionally; wholly, entirely; merely; wonderfully, very much (*dialect*). **pure'ness** *n*. **purism** *n* see separate entry. **purity** *n* see separate entry.
  ❑ **pure'-blood**, **pure-blood'ed** or **pure'-bred** *adj* of unmixed race. **pure culture** *n* (*biol*) a culture containing a pure stock of one species of micro-organism. **pure mathematics** *n sing* mathematics treated without application to observed facts of nature or to practical life. **pure reason** *n* reason alone, without involvement of emotion, etc; in Kant, the power of grasping a priori forms of knowledge (*philos*). **pure science** *n* science considered apart from practical applications.

purée or **puree** /pū'rā/ *n* food material reduced to pulp eg by being processed in a liquidizer; a soup without solid pieces. ◆ *vt* to make a purée of. [Fr]

Purex /pūr'eks/ *n* a process for recovering plutonium and uranium from spent uranium fuel by using tributyl phosphate as a solvent. [*purification and extraction*]

purfle /pûr'fl/ *vt* to ornament the edge of, eg with embroidery or inlay. ◆ *n* a decorated border; a profile (*obs*). [OFr *pourfiler*, from L *prō* before, and *fīlum* a thread]
  ■ **pur'fling** *n* a purfle, *esp* around the edges of a violin.

purfled /pûr'fld/ (*Scot*) *adj* short-winded.
  ■ **pur'fly** *adj* (*Carlyle*).

purge /pûrj/ *vt* to purify; to remove impurities from; to clear of undesirable elements or persons; to remove as an impurity; to clarify; to clear from accusation; to expiate; to empty (the bowels); to make (someone) evacuate the bowels; to atone for or wipe out (*esp* a contempt of court; *law*). ◆ *vi* to become pure by clarifying; to empty the bowels; to empty the bowels frequently; to take a purgative. ◆ *n* the act of purging; an expulsion or massacre of people regarded as untrustworthy or otherwise undesirable; a purgative. [Fr *purger*, from L *pūrgāre, -ātum*, from earlier *pūrigāre*, from *pūrus* pure]
  ■ **purgation** /-gā'shən/ *n* a purging; a clearing away of impurities; the act of clearing from suspicion or imputation of guilt (*law*); a cleansing. **purgative** /pûrg'ə-tiv/ *adj* cleansing; having the power of emptying the intestines. ◆ *n* a medicine that empties the intestines. **pur'gatively** *adv*. **purgato'rial** or **purgato'rian** *adj* relating to purgatory. **pur'gatory** *adj* purging or cleansing; expiatory. ◆ *n* a place or state in which souls are after death purified from venial sins (*RC*); any kind or state of suffering for a time; intense discomfort (*inf*); a ravine (*US*); a swamp (*US*). **purger** /pûrj'ər/ *n*. **purging** /pûrj'/ *adj* cleansing; used in the names of certain plants that act as purgative medicines, as in *purging buckthorn*.

puri or **poori** /poo'ri/ *n* a small cake of unleavened Indian bread, deep-fried and served hot; a small round cake filled with a spicy vegetable mixture and deep-fried. [Hindi]

purify /pū'ri-fī/ *vt* (**pu'rifying**; **pu'rified**) to make pure; to cleanse from a foreign or harmful matter; to free from guilt, from ritual uncleanness, or from improprieties or barbarisms in language. ◆ *vi* to become pure. [Fr *purifier*, from L *pūrificāre*, from *pūrus* pure, and *facere* to make]
  ■ **purifica'tion** *n*. **pu'rificative** *adj*. **pu'rificator** *n* a cloth used during the celebration of Holy Communion to wipe the vessels and the hands and lips of the celebrant. **pu'rificatory** *adj* serving to purify or cleanse. **pu'rifier** *n*.
  ❑ **Purification of the Blessed Virgin Mary** *n* a feast observed in the Roman Catholic Church on 2 February, in commemoration of the purification of the Virgin Mary according to the Jewish ceremonial (Bible, Leviticus 12.1–4) 40 days after the birth of Christ.

Purim /pū'rim or poo-rēm'/ (*Judaism*) *n* the Feast of Lots held about 1 March, in which the Jews commemorate their deliverance from the plot of Haman, as related in the Bible, Book of Esther (see *esp* 3.7). [Heb *pūrīm* (sing *pūr*) lots; origin unknown]

purine /pūr'in or pūr'ēn/ or **purin** /pū'rin/ *n* a cyclic double-ring crystalline substance $C_5H_4N_4$, which with oxygen forms uric acid ($C_5H_4N_4O_3$), and with many derivatives; any of a number of these derivatives, cyclic diureides, such as adenine and guanine, *esp* one which is part of the nucleotide chains of DNA and RNA. [Contracted from L *pūrum ūricum (acidum)* pure uric (acid)]

purism /pū'ri-zm/ *n* fastidious, *esp* over-fastidious, insistence on purity (*esp* of language in vocabulary or idiom). [L *pūrus* pure]
  ■ **pūr'ist** *n* and *adj*. **pūris'tic** or **pūris'tical** *adj*. **pūris'tically** *adv*.

Puritan /pūr'i-tən/ *n* a person who in the time of Elizabeth I and the Stuarts wished to carry the reformation of the Church of England further by purifying it of ceremony; an opponent of the Church of England on account of its retention of much of the ritual and belief of the Roman Catholics; an opponent of the Royalists in the 17c; (the following meanings also without *cap*) a person of similar views to, or in sympathy with, those of the historical Puritans; a person strictly moral in conduct; slightingly, someone professing a too-strict morality; an advocate of purity in any sense. ◆ *adj* (also without *cap*) relating to the Puritans. [L *pūrus* pure]
  ■ **pūritanic** /-tan'ik/ or **puritan'ical** *adj* (*usu derog*). **pūritan'ically** *adv*. **pūr'itanism** *n*. **pūr'itanize** or **-ise** *vt* and *vi*.

purity /pūr'i-ti/ *n* the condition of being pure; freedom from mixture of any kind, or from sin, defilement or ritual uncleanness; chastity; sincerity; freedom from foreign or improper idioms or words. [L *pūritās, -ātis*, from *pūrus* pure]

Purkinje cell /pər-kin'ji sel/ *n* a branching nerve cell found in the cerebral cortex of the brain. [JE *Purkinje* (1787–1869), Bohemian physiologist]

purl¹ /pûrl/ *vt* to embroider or edge with gold or silver thread; to fringe (eg lace) with a wavy edging. ◆ *vt* and *vi* to knit with a purl stitch. ◆ *n* twisted gold or silver wire; a loop or twist, *esp* on an edge (also **pearl**); a succession of such loops, or a lace or braid having them; a fold, pleat or frilling; knitting with a purl stitch. ◆ *adj* (also **pearl**) denoting an inverted stitch made with the wool passed behind the needle (cf **plain¹**; *knitting*). [Origin uncertain; perhaps from different words; cf **pearl²**]

purl² /pûrl/ *vi* to flow with a murmuring sound; to flow in eddies; to curl or swirl. ◆ *n* a trickling brook (*obs*); a movement or murmuring eg of a stream among stones; an eddy or ripple (also **pirl**). [Cf Norw *purla* to babble, Swed dialect *porla* to purl, ripple]

■ **purl'ing** *n* and *adj*.

purl[3] /pûrl/ (except for first sense, *inf*) *vi* to spin round; to capsize; to go head over heels; to fall headlong or heavily. ◆ *vt* to throw headlong. ◆ *n* a heavy or headlong fall; an upset. [Connected with **purl**[1]]

■ **purl'er** *n* a headlong or heavy fall or throw, *esp* in the phrases *go* or *come a purler*.

purl[4] /pûrl/ *n* formerly, ale with wormwood; ale warmed and spiced. [Origin unknown]

purler[1] /pûrl'ər/ (*orig* and *esp Aust*) *n* something extremely good.

purler[2] see under **purl**[3].

purlicue same as **pirlicue**.

purlieu /pûr'lū/ *n* (frequently in *pl*) a person's usual haunts; (in *pl*) borders or outskirts; *orig* a tract of land regarded as part of a (*esp* royal) forest, later excluded but still subject to certain forest laws, eg regarding hunting. [Anglo-Fr *puralee* land by perambulation, from OFr *pur* (= L *prō*) for, and *allee* going; infl by Fr *lieu* place]

purlin or **purline** /pûr'lin/ (*building*) *n* a piece of timber stretching across the principal rafters to support the common or subsidiary rafters. [Origin obscure]

purloin /pər-loin'/ or /pûr'loin/ *vt* and *vi* to filch, steal. [Anglo-Fr *purloigner* to remove to a distance, from *pur-* (L *prō*) for, and *loin* (L *longē*) far]

■ **purloin'er** *n*.

purpie or **purpy** /pûr'pi/ (*obs Scot*) *n perh* purslane, *perh* brooklime. [Perh OFr *porpié*, from LL *pullipēs* colt's foot, purslane; perh from **purple**, from the colour of the brooklime's flower]

■ **water purpie** brooklime.

purple /pûr'pl/ *n* a mixture of blue and red; crimson (*hist*); the Tyrian crimson dye, obtained in ancient times from various shellfish (Murex, Purpura, Buccinum, etc) (*hist*); any shellfish from which the dye is obtained; a crimson cloth or garment worn in ancient times by kings and emperors (*hist*); the rank, power or position of king or emperor; the red robe of a cardinal; the cardinalate (from the red hat and robes); (with *the*) bishops; a purple pigment; a purple-red pigment in the rods of the mammalian eye and in parts of other eyes (**visual purple**); a purple flower (see **long-purples** under **long**[1]); (in *pl*) purpura; (in *pl*) swine-fever; (in *pl*) ear-cockle (see under **ear**[2]). ◆ *adj* of the colour purple; blood-red, bloody (*hist*); of writing, fine or over-ornate. ◆ *vt* to make purple. ◆ *vi* to become purple. [OE (Northumbrian) *purpl*(e) purple (*adj*), from *purpur* purple (noun), from L *purpura*, from Gr *porphyrā* purple fish]

■ **pur'plish** or **pur'ply** *adj* somewhat purple. ❑ **pur'ple-born** *adj* born in the purple (qv below). **pur'ple-coloured** *adj*. **purple emperor** *n* one of the largest of British butterflies and one of the most richly coloured (*Apatura iris*). **purple finch** *n* an American finch, the male of which has a red head and breast. **purple fish** *n* a shellfish yielding purple dye. **purple gallinule** *n* a bird of the rail family (genus *Porphyrio*) with purplish plumage. **purple heart** *n* (the purple-coloured wood of) a species of *Peltogyne* of the family Caesalpiniaceae (also **purple wood**); a mauve heart-shaped tablet of a stimulant drug of the amphetamine type; (with *caps*) a US decoration for wounds received on active service. **pur'ple-hued** *adj*. **pur'ple-in-grain** *adj* dyed fast in purple. **purple of Cassius** *n* a red or purple pigment discovered by Andreas Cassius (c.1683), made from stannous, stannic and gold chlorides in solution. **purple patch** *n* a passage of fine, or (often) over-ornate, writing (also **purple passage**); a time of good luck or success.

■ **born in the purple** born in the purple chamber of the Byzantine empresses (*hist*; see **porphyrogenite**); hence, of exalted birth.

purport /pûr-pōrt', pûr-pört', pûr'pərt, pùr'pōrt, pûr'pört/ *n* the meaning conveyed; substance, gist, tenor; outward appearance or guise, as conveying an impression (*Spenser*); purpose (*rare*). ◆ *vt* /pûr-pōrt', pûr-pört' or pûr'/ (of a document, etc) to give out as its meaning; to convey to the mind; to seem, claim or profess (to mean, be, etc); to mean or intend (*rare*). [OFr, from *pur* (Fr *pour*), from L *prō* for, and *porter*, from L *portāre* to carry]

■ **purport'edly** *adv*. **pur'portless** *adj*.

purpose /pûr'pəs/ *n* an idea or aim kept in the mind as the goal towards which one's efforts are directed; the power of seeking the goal desired; the act or fact of purposing; a desired goal; a useful function; a definite intention; determination; the intention of going (*Shakesp*); purport (*Shakesp*); conversation, conversational speech (*Spenser*); (in *pl*) a sort of conversational game involving questions and answers (*obs*). ◆ *vt* to intend. ◆ *vi* (*Spenser*) to converse or talk. [OFr *pourpos*, *propos*, from L *prōpositum* a thing intended, from *prō* forward, and *pōnere*, *positum* to place; cf **propose**]

■ **pur'posed** *adj* intentional; intended; set on a purpose; purposeful. **pur'poseful** *adj* directed towards a purpose; motivated by a sense

of purpose. **pur'posefully** *adv*. **pur'posefulness** *n*. **pur'poseless** *adj* without purpose; aimless; having no purpose in mind. **pur'poselessly** *adv*. **pur'poselessness** *n*. **pur'pose-like** *adj* (*Scot*) efficient-looking; purposeful. **pur'posely** *adv* intentionally. **pur'posive** *adj* directed towards an end; showing intention or resolution, purposeful. **pur'posiveness** *n*. ❑ **purpose-built'** *adj* specially made or designed to meet particular requirements.

■ **on purpose** (also *obs* **of purpose** and *old* **of set purpose**) intentionally. **to good** (or **some**) **purpose** with good effect. **to the purpose** to the point, relevant to the matter in question.

purpresture /pûr-pres'chər/ *n* encroachment on public property. [OFr *purpresture*, from *pur* (L *prō*) for, and *prendre*, from L *praehendere* to take]

Purpura /pûr'pū-rə/ *n* a genus of marine gastropods yielding a purple dye; (without *cap*) purples, an eruption of small purple spots, caused by extravasation of blood (*med*). [L *purpura*, from Gr *porphyrā* purple fish]

■ **pur'pure** *n* and *adj* (*obs* except *heraldry*) purple. **purpū'real** *adj* (*poetic*) purple. **purpū'ric** *adj* (*med*) relating to purpura. **pur'purin** *n* a purple colouring matter obtained from madder.

purpy see **purpie**.

purr or (*obs*) **pur** /pûr/ *vi* (of a cat) to utter a soft, low, vibrating sound when contented; (of a vehicle engine or other machinery) to make a sound similar to this; (of a person) to express pleasure or gratification. ◆ *vt* to express by purring; to say or utter in a tone vibrating with satisfaction. ◆ *n* an act or the sound of purring. [Imit]

■ **purr'ing** *n* and *adj*. **purr'ingly** *adv*.

purse /pûrs/ *n* a small bag for carrying money; a sum of money in a purse; a sum given as a present or offered as a prize; funds; formerly, a live coal flying out of the fire, regarded as a good omen; a woman's handbag (*N Am*); a purse-like receptacle or cavity (*obs med* or *biol*). ◆ *vt* to put into a purse or one's own purse, to pocket; to contract (one's lips) into a rounded, puckered shape, *esp* in order to express displeasure, etc; to contract or draw into folds or wrinkles. ◆ *vi* to pucker; to steal purses (*obs*). [OE *purs*, appar from LL *bursa*, from Gr *byrsa* a hide]

■ **purse'ful** *n* as much as a purse can hold; enough to fill a purse. **purs'er** *n* formerly, a naval paymaster; an officer in charge of cabins, stewards, etc. **purs'ership** *n*. ❑ **purse'-bearer** *n* a person who has charge of another person's money; a treasurer; a person who carries in a bag the Great Seal for the Lord Chancellor, or the royal commission for the Lord High Commissioner. **purse'-net** *n* a bag-shaped net that closes by a drawstring at the neck. **purse'-pride** *n*. **purse'-proud** *adj* proud of one's wealth; insolent from wealth. **purse'-seine** *n* a seine-net that can be drawn into the shape of a bag. **purse'-seiner** *n* a fishing-vessel equipped with such nets. **purse'-sharing** *n* the sharing-out of an individual fee or prize between all members of the recipient's firm or team. **purse'-snatcher** *n*. **purse'-snatching** *n*. **purse strings** *n pl* the strings fastening a purse (*usu fig*). **purse'-taking** *n* robbing.

■ **privy purse** an allowance for a sovereign's private expenses. **public purse** see under **public**.

pursew Spenser's usual spelling of **pursue**.

purslane /pûr'slin/ *n* (also **purslain**) a pot-herb and salad herb (*Portulaca oleracea*) of the family Portulacaceae; any member of the genus or the family. [OFr *porcelaine*, from L *porcilāca*, *portulāca*; see **portulaca**]

■ **sea purslane** a fleshy seaside sandwort (*Arenaria*, or *Honckenya*, *peploides*); any of various species of orach. **water purslane** a small-flowered prostrate lythraceous plant of wet places (*Lythrum portula*).

pursue /pər-sū' or pər-soo'/ *vt* to follow in order to overtake and capture or kill; to chase; to hunt; to follow with haste; to follow up; to follow the course of; to be engaged in; to carry on; to seek to obtain or attain; to proceed in accordance with; to proceed with; to harass or persecute, persist in opposing or seeking to injure; to prosecute or sue (*Scots law*). ◆ *vi* to follow; to go on or continue; to act as a prosecutor at law. [Anglo-Fr *pursuer*, *pursiwer*, from popular L *prosequere* or *-īre* or *persequere* or *-īre*, for L *prōsequī* and *persequī*, from *prō-* and *per-* (the prefixes being confused), and *sequī* to follow]

■ **pursu'able** *adj*. **pursu'al** or (more often) **pursu'ance** *n* pursuit; the act of carrying out or following (eg *in pursuance of this policy*). **pursu'ant** *adj* pursuing; in pursuance (with *to*; approaching an *adv*). **pursu'antly** *adv*. **pursu'er** *n* someone who pursues; a plaintiff (*Scots law*). **pursu'ing** *n* and *adj*. **pursu'ingly** *adv*.

pursuit /pər-sūt' or pər-soot'/ *n* the act of pursuing; an endeavour to attain; an occupation; employment; that which is pursued; a cycle race in which two riders start at opposite sides of a track and try to

overtake each other. [Anglo-Fr *purseute*, from the same root as **pursue**]
❑ **pursuit plane** *n* a type of military aeroplane used in pursuing enemy aeroplanes.

pursuivant /pûr'si-vənt, -swi-vənt/ *n* an attendant or follower; a state messenger with power to execute warrants; an officer ranking below a herald. [Fr *poursuivant*, prp of *poursuivre* to pursue]

pursy[1] /pûr'si/ *adj* puffy; fat; short-winded. [OFr *poulsif* broken-winded, from *poulser* (Fr *pousser*), from L *pulsāre* to drive]
■ **purs'iness** *n*.

pursy[2] /pûr'si/ *adj* pursed up; puckered. [**purse**]

purtenance /pûr'tə-nəns/ (*obs*) *n* something which pertains or belongs; the guts, *esp* of an animal. [Earlier form of **pertinence**]

purtraid, purtrayd see **pourtray**.

purty /pûr'ti/ (*dialect, esp US*) *adj* pretty.

purulent /pū'rū-lənt or pū'rŭ-lənt/ *adj* consisting of, of the nature of, forming, full of, characterized by, or like pus. [L *pūrulentus*, from *pūs*, *pūris* pus]
■ **pū'rulence** or **pū'rulency** *n*. **pū'rulently** *adv*.

purvey /pûr-vā'/ *vt* to provide or furnish; to supply. ◆ *vi* to provide meals or provisions as one's business. [Anglo-Fr *purveier*, from L *prōvidēre*; see **provide**]
■ **purvey'ance** *n* the act of purveying; preparation in advance (*Spenser*); furnishings, equipment (*Spenser*); a procuring of provisions; that which is supplied; the former royal prerogative of procuring provisions for the court at a fixed price, requisitioning horses, etc (*hist*). **purvey'or** *n* someone whose business is to provide food or meals; an official who formerly exacted provisions for the use of the royal household.

purview /pûr'vū/ *n* scope; range; a field of activity or view; competence; the body or enacting part of a statute distinguished from the preamble; enactment. [Anglo-Fr *purveu* provided, pap of *purveier*; see **purvey**]

pus /pus/ *n* a thick yellowish or greenish fluid formed by suppuration, consisting of serum, white blood cells, bacteria and debris of tissue. [L *pūs, pūris*; cf Gr *pyon*]

puschkinia /pŭsh-kin'i-ə/ *n* any plant of the genus *Puschkinia*, spring-flowering bulbous plants native to W Asia with bell-shaped flowers, including *Puschkinia scilloides*, the striped squill. [A Mussin-*Puschkin* (1760–1805), Russian scientist]

Puseyism /pū'zi-i-zm/ *n* Tractarianism, the High Church and Catholic principles of Dr EB *Pusey* (1800–82) and other Oxford divines, as set out in the 'Tracts for the Times' (1833–41).
■ **Pūseyist'ic** or **Pūseyist'ical** *adj*. **Pū'seyite** *n*.

push[1] /pŭsh/ *vt* to thrust or press against; to drive by pressure; to press or drive forward; to urge; to press hard; (of a plant) to produce (fruit, shoots, roots, etc); to advance or carry to a further point; to hit (the ball) too much to the right for a right-handed player, or to the left for a left-handed player (*golf*); to promote, or seek to promote, vigorously and persistently; to make efforts to promote the sale of; to effect by thrusting forward; to peddle (drugs); to come near, be approaching (an age or number); to insert (data) on to a stack (*comput*). ◆ *vi* to make a thrust; to butt (*obs*); to exert pressure; to make an effort; to press forward; to make one's way by exertion; to reach out; to be urgent and persistent; to play a push-stroke. ◆ *n* a thrust; an impulse; pressure; a help to advancement; enterprising or aggressive pertinacity; an effort; an onset; an offensive; a push-stroke; a shot hit too much to the right for a right-handed player, or to the left for a left-handed player (*golf*); a gang of roughs (*Aust*); a group of people sharing an interest or background (*Aust*); a company; (with *the*) dismissal or rejection (*inf*). [Fr *pousser*, from L *pulsāre*, frequentative of *pellere*, *pulsum* to beat]
■ **pushed** *adj* (*inf*) in a hurry; short of money. **push'er** *n* someone who pushes; a machine, or part of a machine, that pushes; a propeller placed behind the wing of an aircraft; an aeroplane propelled by such a propeller; a child's table implement, or a finger of bread, used for pushing food onto a fork or spoon; the stick used to propel the puck in the game of octopush (qv); a self-assertive person; someone who assiduously seeks social advancement; a drug dealer. **push'ful** *adj* energetically or aggressively enterprising. **push'fully** *adv*. **push'fulness** *n*. **push'iness** *n*. **push'ing** *adj* pressing forward eg in business; enterprising; self-assertive. **push'ingly** *adv*. **push'y** *adj* aggressive; self-assertive, *esp* obtrusively so.
❑ **push'back** *n* resistance to a proposed course of action. **push'-ball** *n* a game in which an enormous ball is pushed. **push'bike** *n* (also, *esp* formerly **push'-bicycle** or **push'-cycle**) a bicycle driven by pedals. **push'-button** *n* a knob, eg on a doorbell or a vending machine, which when pressed causes the bell, vending machine, etc to operate. ◆ *adj* operated by, or using, a push-button or push-buttons. **push-button civilization** *n* one in which the ordinary unskilled person has the benefits of technology at the pressing of a button.

push-button war *n* one carried on by guided missiles, released by push-button. **push'-cart** *n* (*US*) a street vendor's barrow. **push'chair** *n* a lightweight wheeled folding chair for conveying a baby or child. **push-cycle** see **pushbike** above. **push fit** *n* a joint (as between two pipes) made by pushing one part into another. **push'-off** *n* the act of pushing a boat off from the shore, etc, or, in swimming, of pushing oneself off the end of the pool in turning; a send-off. **push'-out** *n* the act of pushing (someone or something) out, eg of pushing an opponent out of the ring in some forms of wrestling. **push'over** *n* an easy thing; a person or side easily overcome; a person easily persuaded or won over. **push'-over try** *n* (*rugby*) one scored after the attacking side in a scrum has pushed the defenders back until the ball is able to be touched down behind the try-line. **push'pin** *n* a children's game in which pins are pushed one across another (*Shakesp*); a large-headed drawing pin, used *esp* to mark points on maps (*US*). **push'pit** *n* a safety railing at the stern of a yacht. **push'-pull** *adj* denoting any piece of apparatus in which two electrical or electronic devices act in opposition to each other, used eg of an amplifier in which two thermionic valves so acting serve to reduce distortion. **push-pull train** *n* one which can be pulled or pushed by the same locomotive. **push'rod** *n* in an internal-combustion engine, a metal rod that opens, and sometimes closes, the valves. **push'-start** *vt* to start (a motor-car) by pushing it while it is in gear. ◆ *n* the act of starting a car in this way. **push'-stroke** *n* a push instead of an ordinary hit or stroke at a ball; in snooker, etc, an illegal stroke in which the cue is still in contact, or comes into contact again, with the cue ball when the cue ball touches the object ball. **push technology** *n* (*comput*) the sending of unrequested messages to a client on the Internet (cf **pull technology** under **pull**). **push'-tug** *n* a tug for pushing, rather than pulling, barges. **push'-up** *n* a press-up (see under **press**[1]). **push-up bra** *n* a bra so engineered as to lift the breasts noticeably.
■ **at a push** when circumstances urgently require; if really necessary. **give** (or **get**) **the push** (*sl*) to dismiss or reject, or be dismissed or rejected. **push along** (*inf*) to leave, go on one's way. **push around** (*inf*) to bully. **push back** to postpone; (with *against*) to resist a proposed course of action. **push for** to make strenuous efforts to achieve. **push off** of a rower or a boat, to leave the bank, shore, etc; to depart (*inf*). **push on** to continue. **push one's fortune** to busy oneself in seeking a fortune. **push one's luck** see under **luck**. **push out** (of person, boat) to row or be rowed out towards open water. **push the boat out** (*inf*) see under **boat**. **push the bottle** (*inf*) to take one's liquor and pass the bottle round. **push through** to compel acceptance of. **push up the daisies** (*inf*) to be dead and buried. **when push comes to shove** when the time to act or make a decision comes.

push[2] /pŭsh/ (*Shakesp*) *interj* pish. ◆ *n* an exclamation of 'push'. [**pish**[1]]

Pushto, Pushtoo, Pushtu see **Pashto**.

pusillanimous /pū-si-lan'i-məs/ *adj* lacking firmness or determination; mean-spirited; cowardly. [L *pusillanimis*, from *pusillus* very little, and *animus* mind]
■ **pusillanim'ity** *n*. **pusillan'imously** *adv*.

pusle an obsolete spelling of **puzzle**[1] or **pucelle**.

puss[1] /pŭs/ *n* a familiar name for a cat; (in hunting or coursing) a hare; a playfully pejorative name for a child or a girl; a puss-moth. [Cf Du *poes* puss; Ir and Gaelic *pus* a cat]
■ **puss'y** *n* a dimin of **puss** (also **puss'y-cat**); anything soft and furry; a willow-catkin; the female pudenda (*sl*; this and other sexual senses *perh* a different word); sexual intercourse (*sl*); a woman considered as a sexual object (*derog sl*); a man considered as weak or ineffectual (*derog sl*).
❑ **puss'-gentleman** *n* (*obs*) a dandy. **puss in the corner** *n* a children's game in which the places are continually being changed, while the player who is out tries to secure one of the places while it is empty. **puss'-moth** *n* a thick-bodied hairy notodontid moth (*Dicranura*, or *Cerura*, *vinula*) whose caterpillar feeds on willow or poplar leaves. **puss'yfoot** *n* a prohibitionist (from *Pussyfoot*, nickname of William E Johnson (1862–1945), US revenue officer noted for his stealthy ways and his prohibitionist campaigns). ◆ *vi* to go stealthily; to act timidly, cautiously or non-committally. **puss'yfooter** *n*. **puss'y-whipped** *adj* (*vulgar sl*) bullied, henpecked. **pussy willow** *n* a common American willow, *Salix discolor* or other species with silky spring catkins.

puss[2] /pŭs/ (*sl*) *n* the face. [Ir *pus* a mouth]

pussel /pus'l/ or /puz'l/ (*Shakesp*) *n* a slut. [**pucelle**]

pusser /pus'ər/ (*Brit and Aust naval sl*) *adj* regulation, smart, genuine, official, formal, etc. ◆ *n* a supply officer. [**purser**]
❑ The possessive form **pusser's** is used in many compounds, eg **pusser's dagger** a seaman's knife, and often with a derogatory sense, as in **pusser's sneer** and **pusser's logic** a false economy.

pussy see under **puss**[1].

pustule /pŭs'tūl/ n a pimple containing pus; a pimple-like or warty spot or lump. [L *pustula*]

■ **pus'tulant** adj causing pustulation (also n). **pus'tular** or **pus'tulous** adj. **pus'tulate** vt, vi and adj. **pustula'tion** n.

put¹ /pŏŏt/ vt (**putting** /pŏŏt'ing/; **put**) to place, or cause to be, in such and such a position, state, predicament, relation, etc; to set; to place, lay or deposit; to apply; to append or affix; to connect; to add; to commit; to assign; to start (someone *on* eg a diet, a study or a track); to push or thrust; (also **putt**) to cast, throw or hurl (*esp* by a thrusting movement of the hand from the shoulder); to drive; to impel; to convey or transport; to force or constrain; to incite; to subject; to reduce; to convert; to render; to express; to assert; to propound; to submit to a vote; to impose; to impute; to call on, oblige, stake, venture or invest; to repose (eg trust, confidence). ◆ vi to thrust (*archaic* or *Scot* and *N Eng*); to proceed, make one's way (*naut*); to set out, esp hurriedly; to flow (*US*). ◆ n a push or thrust; (also **putt**) a throw, esp of a heavy object from the shoulder; on the Stock Exchange, an option of selling within a certain time certain securities or commodities, at a stipulated price (also **put option**). [Late OE *putian* (found in the verbal noun *putung* instigation); there were also *potian* and *pȳtan*, which may account for some of the dialect forms; cf Dan *putte*, Swed *putta*]

■ **putter** /pŏŏt'ər/ n someone who puts; someone who pushes or hauls trams in a coalmine (*hist*). **putt'ing** n putting the shot (qv below).

❑ **put'-and-take** n a gambling game played with a top on which are marked instructions to give to or take from a bank or pool of objects. **put'-down** n a snub; an action intended to assert one's superiority. **put'-in** n (*rugby*) the act of throwing the ball into a set scrum. **put'-off** n an excuse or evasion; a postponement. **put'-on** n a hoax. **put option** see **put** (n) above. **putt'er-on** n (*Shakesp*) an instigator. **putt'er-out** n (*obs*) someone who deposited money on going abroad, on condition of receiving a larger sum on his return, if he ever returned. **put'-through** n a transaction in which a broker arranges the buying and the selling of shares. **putt'ing-stone** n a heavy stone used in putting the shot. **put-up'** adj arranged beforehand in a false but deceptively plausible way.

■ **put about** to publish or circulate; to change the course of (*esp* a ship) or to change course; to distress (*Scot*). **put across** to carry out successfully, bring off; to perform so as to carry the audience with one. **put an end** (or **a stop**) **to** to cause to discontinue. **put away** to renounce; to divorce; to kill (*esp* an old or ill animal); to stow away, pack up or set aside; to put into the proper or desirable place; to imprison; to admit to a mental hospital (*inf*); to eat or drink (*inf*). **put back** to push backward; to delay; to repulse; to turn and sail back for port (*naut*); to reduce one's finances (*inf*). **put by** to set aside; to parry; to store up. **put case** see under **case²**. **put down** to crush or quell; to kill (*esp* an old or ill animal); to snub or humiliate; to degrade; to snub, silence or confute (*Shakesp*); to enter, write down on paper; to reckon; to attribute; to give up (*rare*); to surpass or outshine; to preserve, put in pickle (*dialect*); of an aeroplane, to land (often with *at*); to pay (a deposit); to put (a baby) to bed (*inf*); to drop (a catch) (*cricket*). **put for** to make an attempt to gain. **put forth** to extend; to propose; to publish; to exert; to display; to lend at interest; to set out from port; to produce or extrude. **put forward** to propose; to advance. **put in** to introduce; to insert; to lodge, deposit or hand in; to make a claim or application (for); to enter; to enter a harbour; to interpose; to perform towards completing a total; to spend, pass or fill up (time) with some occupation; to appoint. **put in an appearance** see under **appear**. **put in mind** to remind. **put it across someone** to defeat someone by ingenuity. **put it on** to pretend (to be ill, etc). **put it past someone** (*usu* with *not*) to judge it inconsistent with someone's character. **put off** to lay aside; to lay aside the character of; to palm off; to turn (someone) aside from what he or she wants or intends with evasions, excuses or unsatisfying substitutes; to divert, turn aside from a purpose; to postpone; to idle away, spend in vain; to disconcert; to cause aversion or disinclination in; to push from shore; to take off (*archaic*); to dismiss (*archaic*). **put on** to clothe oneself or someone else with; to assume (a character or quality), esp deceptively; to mislead or deceive; to superimpose; to impose; to affix, attach, apply; to add (eg weight, charges, etc); to stake or wager; to move forward; to move faster (*obs*); to set to work; to set in operation; to incite; to turn on the supply of; to score; to stage; see also **well put on** below. **put on to** to make aware of; to connect with by telephone. **put out** to expel; to dismiss from a game and innings; to send out; to stretch out; to extinguish; to place (money) at interest; to expand; to publish; to disconcert; to inconvenience; to offend; to dislocate; to exert; to produce; to place with others or at a distance; to go out to sea, leave port; to remove bodily or blind (an eye); to render unconscious (*sl*); (of a woman) to be willing to grant sexual favours (*sl*, *orig N Am*). **put over** to refer (*Shakesp*); to carry through successfully; to impress an audience, spectators, the public, favourably with; to impose, pass off. **put paid to** see under **paid**. **put the make on** see under **make¹**. **put through** to bring to an end; to accomplish; to put in telephonic communication; to cause to undergo or suffer; to process (*comput*).

putting the shot, **stone** or **weight** the act or sport of hurling a heavy stone or weight from the hand by a sudden thrust from the shoulder (see also **putt¹**). **put to** to apply; to add to; to connect with; to harness; to shut; to set to. **put to death** see under **death**. **put to it** to press hard; to distress. **put to rights** see under **right¹**. **put to sea** to begin a voyage. **put to the sword** see under **sword**. **put two and two together** to draw a conclusion from various facts. **put up** to accommodate with lodging; to take lodgings; to nominate or stand for election; to offer for sale; to present (eg a good game, a fight, or a defence, a prayer); to stake; to parcel up; to supply and pack (an order, a picnic, etc); to stow away, put aside; to sheathe; to settle beforehand; to compound; to endure tamely (*obs*); to start (a hare) from cover. **put-up job** a dishonest scheme prearranged *usu* by several people. **put upon** to take undue advantage of; to impose on. **put up to** to incite to; to make conversant with, to supply with useful information or tips about. **put up with** to endure. **stay put** to remain passively in the position assigned. **well put on** or (*Scot*) **well putten on** respectably dressed.

put² /pŭt/ see **putt¹,²,³**.

putamen /pū-tā'mən/ n (pl **putamina** /-tām'in-ə/) a fruit-stone (*bot*); the membrane within an eggshell (*zool*); the lateral part of the lenticular nucleus of the cerebrum (*anat*). [L *putāmen* clippings, waste, from *putāre* to prune]

putative /pū'tə-tiv/ adj supposed; reputed; commonly supposed to be. [L *putātīvus*, from *putāre*, -*ātum* to suppose]

■ **pū'tatively** adv.

❑ **putative marriage** n a marriage supposed invalid by canon law, but entered into in good faith by at least one of the parties.

putcher /pŭch'ər, puch'ər/ or **putcheon** /pŭch'ən or puch'ən/ n a conical wicker or wire trap for catching salmon. [Origin unknown]

putchock, **putchuk** or **pachak** /pu-chuk' or puch'ək/ n costus-root (see **costus**). [Hindustani *pachak* ; origin obscure]

puteal /pū'ti-əl/ n a wall round the top of a well. [L *puteal*, -*ālis*, from *puteus* a well]

puteli /put'e-lē/ n a flat-bottomed boat used on the Ganges. [Hindi *paṭelī*]

putid /pū'tid/ adj rotten; foul. [L *pūtidus*]

putlog /put'log/ or **putlock** /put'lok/ n a crosspiece in a scaffolding, the inner end resting in a hole left in the wall. [Origin obscure; **putlock** seems to be the older form]

putois /pü-twä'/ n a brush of polecat's hair, or of some substitute for it, for painting pottery. [Fr]

Putonghua /poo'tŭng-hwä/ n the official spoken language of China, based on the Beijing variety of Mandarin. [Chin, common speech]

put-put /put'put, put-put', pŭt'pŭt or pŭt-pŭt'/ n the noise of a small motor; a vehicle powered by such a motor. ◆ vi (**put'-putting**; **put'-putted**) to make such a noise; to move with such a noise. [Imit]

putrefy /pū'tri-fī/ vt (**pu'trefying**; **pu'trefied**) to cause to rot; to corrupt. ◆ vi to rot. [L *putrefacere*, *putrescere*, and *putridus*, from *puter*, *putris* rotten]

■ **putrefacient** /-fā'shənt/ adj causing putrefaction. **putrefaction** /-fak'shən/ n rotting. **putrefac'tive** adj. **putrefī'able** adj. **putrescence** /-tres'əns/ n incipient rottenness. **putresc'ent** adj. **putresc'ible** adj and n. **putresc'ine** /-ēn or -in/ n a substance, $H_2N(CH_2)_4NH_2$, formed during the putrefaction of flesh (also called **1,4-diaminobū'tane**). **pu'trid** adj rotten; disgusting; wretchedly bad (*inf*). **putrid'ity** or **pu'tridness** n. **pu'tridly** adv.

❑ **putrid fever** n (*obs med*) typhus.

putsch /pŭch/ n a sudden revolutionary outbreak; a coup d'état. [Swiss Ger dialect]

■ **putsch'ist** n a person who takes part in a putsch.

putt¹ /put/ vt (**putt'ing**; **putted**) to hurl (a shot, stone or weight) in the sport of putting the shot (also **put** /put or pŭt/ (see **put¹**); to hit (a golf ball) with a putter so that it rolls along the ground and towards, ideally into, the hole (also *archaic* **put** /put/). ◆ vi (*golf*) to make a putt or putts. ◆ vt and vi (*golf*) (in combination with a number) to take a given number of putts to put the ball in the hole, as in *he four-putted* (*at*) *the last hole*. ◆ n a throw (also **put** /put or pŭt/ (see **put¹**); a stroke made with a putter on, or sometimes near, a putting green (*golf*). [A Scottish form of **put¹**]

■ **putt'er** n someone who putts or can putt; a *usu* short-handled golf-club with an upright striking-face, used in putting. **putt'ing** n the exercise of hurling a heavy weight (also **putting the shot** (see under **put¹**); *Scot*); the act or art of making a putt (*golf*); a game played with putters and golf balls on a small course with several holes.

❑ **putt'ing-cleek** n an old-fashioned putter of cleek design, the blade long and narrow, running straight from the shaft. **putting green** n the turf, made firm and smooth for putting, round each of the holes of a golf course; a small golf course with several holes for practice or for putting as an informal game. **putt'ing-stone** see under **put**[1].

■ **putt out** to complete a hole in a round of golf by putting the ball into the hole.

putt[2] or **put** /put/ *n* an old card game like nap. [Perh **put**[1]]

putt[3] or **put** /put/ (*archaic*) *n* a greenhorn; a bumpkin. [17c slang; origin unknown]

puttanesca /pŭ-tə-nes'kə/ *n* a pasta sauce made with tomatoes, olives, capers and anchovies. [Ital, in some way connected with *puttana* (slang) a prostitute]

puttee /put'ē/ or **puttie** /put'i/ *n* a cloth strip wound round the leg from ankle to knee as a legging. [Hindi *pattī*]

putten see **pit**[3].

putter[1] /put'ər/ (*US*) original form of **potter**[2].

putter[2] see under **put**[1].

putter[3] see under **putt**[1].

putti plural of **putto**.

puttie see **puttee**.

puttier see under **putty**.

putto /pŭt'ō/ *n* (*pl* **putti** /pŭt'ē/) a plump, naked, very young boy, often winged, in Renaissance or Baroque art. [Ital]

puttock /put'ək/ *n* a kite (*Shakesp*); a buzzard; a kite-like person. [ME *puttok*, perh connected with OE *pyttel* kite]

putty /put'i/ *n* a fine cement of slaked lime and water (**plasterers' putty**); a cement of whiting and linseed oil (**glaziers'** or **painters' putty**); *orig* putty-powder (**polishers'** or **jewellers' putty**); a yellowish-grey colour; a weak-willed, easily manipulated person (*fig*). ◆ *vt* (**putt'ying**; **putt'ied**) to fix, coat or fill with putty. [Fr *potée* potful, putty-powder, from *pot*]

■ **putt'ier** *n* a glazier.

❑ **putt'y-coloured** *adj.* **putt'y-faced** *adj* having a putty-coloured face. **putt'y-knife** *n* a blunt, flexible tool for laying on putty. **putt'y-powder** *n* stannic oxide (often with lead oxide) used for polishing glass.

puture /pū'tyər/ or **pulture** /pul'tyər/ (*hist*) *n* the claim of foresters, etc to food for man, horse and dog within the bounds of a forest. [Anglo-Fr *puture*, and ONFr *pulture*, from LL *pu(l)tūra*, appar from L *puls, pultis* porridge]

putz[1] /puts/ (*N Am inf*) *n* a stupid person; the penis. [Yiddish, penis]

putz[2] /pŭts/ *n* (*pl* **putz'es**) (*US*) in Pennsylvanian Dutch homes, a representation of the Nativity traditionally placed under a Christmas tree. [Ger *putzen* to decorate]

puy /pwē/ *n* a small volcanic cone, eg in Auvergne. [Fr, hill, from L *podium* a height; cf **pew**, **podium**]

Puy lentil /pwē len'til/ *n* a small type of lentil with a mottled green and blue skin. [Le *Puy-en-Velay*, town in France where they are grown]

puzel, **puzzel** same as **pucelle**, **pussel**.

puzzle[1] /puz'l/ *vt* to perplex; to bewilder; to cause difficulty in solving or understanding to; to set a problem that causes difficulty to; to entangle, complicate; to solve by systematic or assiduous thinking (with *out*). ◆ *vi* to be bewildered; to work hard at solving something; to search about. ◆ *n* bewilderment; perplexity; anything that puzzles; a problem; a riddle or a toy designed to test skill or ingenuity. [Origin obscure]

■ **puzz'ledom** *n* (*rare*) bewilderment. **puzz'lement** *n* the state of being puzzled. **puzz'ler** *n*. **puzz'ling** *adj* posing; perplexing. **puzz'lingly** *adv.*

❑ **puzz'le-head** *n* someone who is puzzle-headed. **puzz'le-headed** *adj* having one's head full of confused notions. **puzz'le-head'edness** *n*. **puzz'le-monkey** *n* a monkey puzzle. **puzz'le-peg** *n* a piece of wood fastened under a dog's jaw so as to keep the dog's nose off the ground. **puzzle-prize book** *n* a book containing a puzzle, the successful solver of which is rewarded with a prize.

puzzle[2] see **pucelle**.

puzzolana /pŭt-sō-lä'nə/ *n* same as **pozzolana**.

PVA *abbrev*: polyvinyl acetate (see under **poly-**).

PVC *abbrev*: polyvinyl chloride (see under **poly-**).

PVFS *abbrev*: postviral fatigue syndrome (see under **post-**).

PVR *abbrev*: personal video recorder.

PVS *abbrev*: persistent (or permanent) vegetative state; postviral syndrome (see under **post-**).

Pvt. (*milit*) *abbrev*: Private.

PW *abbrev*: Policewoman.

pw *abbrev*: per week.

PWA (*US*) *abbrev*: person with AIDS.

PWD *abbrev*: Public Works Department.

pwn /pōn/ *vt* (*sl*) to dominate or humiliate (an opponent), *esp* in online gaming. [Perh orig a mistyping of **own**[1]]

PWR *abbrev*: pressurized water reactor.

PWS *abbrev*: Prader-Willi syndrome.

pwt *abbrev*: pennyweight.

PX /pē eks/ *n* a shop selling goods for US servicemen and their families overseas. [Abbrev of **post** and **exchange**]

pxt *abbrev*: *pinxit* (*L*), painted (this).

PY *abbrev*: Paraguay (IVR).

pya /pyä/ or /pē'ä/ *n* a monetary unit in Myanmar, $\frac{1}{100}$ of a kyat. [Burmese]

pyaemia /pī-ē'mi-ə/ (*med*) *n* infection of the blood with bacteria from a septic focus, with abscesses in different parts of the body (also **pye'mia**). [Gr *pyon* pus, and *haima* blood]

■ **pyae'mic** *adj.*

pyat see **pyot**.

pycnic same as **pyknic**.

pycnidium /pik-nid'i-əm/ (*bot*) *n* a roundish fructification formed by many species of fungi, containing fertile hyphae and asexual spores. [Gr *pyknos* thick, dense, and dimin sfx *-idion*, Latinized to *-idium*]

■ **pycnid'iospore** *n* an asexual fungal spore produced in a pycnidium.

pycnite /pik'nīt/ (*geol*) *n* a columnar variety of topaz. [Gr *pyknos* dense]

pycno- or **pykno-** /pik-nō-, pik-nə- or pik-no-/ *combining form* dense, close. [Gr *pyknos* dense]

■ **pycnoconid'ium** *n* (*bot*) a pycnidiospore. **pycnodysostosis** or **pyknodysostosis** /-dis-os-tō'sis/ *n* (Gr *dys* abnormal, *osteon* bone, and *-osis* diseased state; *med*) a rare inherited bone disease characterized by short stature and fragility and thickening of the bones. **pycnog'onid** *n* a member of the **Pycnogon'ida** (Gr *gony* knee) the sea spiders, a class of marine arthropods with more leg than body. **pycnog'onoid** *adj.* **pycnom'eter** or **pyknom'eter** *n* an instrument for determining specific gravities. **pyc'non** *n* in ancient Greek music, that part of the tetrachord (chromatic or enharmonic) where the smallest intervals fall; in medieval music, a semitone. **pycnōs'is** *n* (*biol*) the shrinkage of the stainable material of a nucleus into a deeply staining knot, *usu* a feature of cell degeneration. **pyc'nospore** *n* (*bot*) a pycnidiospore. **pyc'nostyle** *adj* (Gr *stylos* column; *archit*) (of ancient Greek temples and buildings of a similar style) with close-set columns, $1\frac{1}{2}$ diameters apart. ◆ *n* a pycnostyle building.

pye[1] see **pie**[4].

pye[2] see **pie**[2].

pyebald see **piebald**.

pye-dog /pī'dog/ *n* (in Asia) an ownerless or half-wild dog (also **pariah dog**, **pi'-dog** or **pie'-dog**). [Hindustani *pāhī* outsider]

pyeing see **pie**[2].

pyelitis /pī-ə-lī'tis/ (*med*) *n* inflammation of the pelvis of the kidney. [Gr *pyelos* a trough]

■ **pyelitic** /-lit'ik/ *adj.* **py'elogram** *n* an X-ray picture of the renal pelvis, the kidney and the ureter. **pyelography** /-log'rə-fi/ *n*. **pyelonephritic** /-rit'ik/ *adj.* **pyelonephritis** /-nef-rī'tis/ *n* inflammation of the kidney and the renal pelvis.

pyemia see **pyaemia**.

pyengadu /pyeng-gä-doo'/ *n* the ironwood (genus *Xylia* of the family Mimosaceae) of Myanmar, etc. [Burmese *pyengkadō*]

pyet see **pyot**.

pygal /pī'gəl/ (*zool*) *adj* belonging to the rump or posteriors of an animal. ◆ *n* the posterior median plate of the carapace of tortoises. [Gr *pȳgē* rump]

pygarg /pī'gärg/ *n* an animal mentioned in eg the Authorized Version of the Bible, *poss* the addax antelope (translated as 'white-rumped deer' in the New English Bible, and as 'ibex' in the New International Version). [Gr *pȳgē* rump, and *argos* white]

pygidium /pī-gid'i-əm or pī-jid'i-əm/ (*zool*) *n* in insects, the tergum of the last abdominal somite; the tail-shield of a trilobite. [Latinized from Gr *pȳgidion*, dimin of *pȳgē* rump]

■ **pygid'ial** *adj.*

pygmy or **pigmy** /pig'mi/ *n* a member of any of the unusually short-statured human races (Negritos, Negrillos and others); a dwarf; any person, animal or thing relatively diminutive or in some way insignificant; a person of low moral, etc stature; an anthropoid ape (*obs*); one of the ancient diminutive people who lived in underground houses, etc in whom some scholars see the historical origins of the fairies and elves of folklore; an elf; *orig* a member of a race of dwarfs said by Homer and other ancient writers to have lived in N Africa and to have fought and been destroyed by cranes (*myth*). ◆ *adj* dwarfish; (*esp* of a breed or species) diminutive; of the pygmies. [Gr *pygmaios* measuring a *pygmē* (13½ inches, the distance from elbow to knuckles)]

■ **pygmaean** or **pigmaean**, **pygmean** or **pigmean** /pig-mē'ən/ *adj*. **pyg'moid** or **pig'moid** *adj*.

❑ **pygmy chimpanzee** see **bonobo**. **pygmy goose** *n* any of three small ducks (not geese) of the genus *Nettapus*, found in Africa, S Asia and Australasia. **pygmy shrew** *n* a small shrew with a brown coat and pale underparts.

pygostyle /pī'gō-stīl/ (*zool*) *n* the bone of a bird's tail. [Gr *pȳgē* rump, and *stylos* a column]

pyinkado /pying'kə-dō/ *n* an Asian tree (*Xylia dolabriformis*); its durable wood, valued for construction work. [Burmese]

pyjamas /pi-jä'məz, formerly also pī-jä'məz/ or (*N Am*) **pajamas** /pə-jä'məz/ *n pl* light loose-fitting trousers and a jacket or top, worn *esp* for sleeping in; loose trousers tied round the waist, worn in the East. [Pers and Hindustani *pāējāmah*, from *pāē* leg, and *jāmah* clothing]

■ **pyja'ma'd** or **pyja'maed** *adj* wearing pyjamas.

❑ **pyjama jacket** *n*. **pyjama trousers** *n pl*.

pyknic /pik'nik/ *adj* (of a human physical type) characterized by short squat stature, small hands and feet, relatively short limbs, domed abdomen, short neck, and round face. [Gr *pyknos* thick]

pykno-, pyknodysostosis, pyknometer see **pycno-**.

pyknosome /pik'nə-sōm/ *n* same as **amplosome**.

pylon /pī'lon/ *n* (*pl* **py'lons**) a structure for supporting power cables; a guiding mark at an aerodrome; an external structure on an aeroplane for attaching an engine, etc; a gateway, gate-tower, gatehouse or building through which an entrance passes, *esp* the gateway of an Egyptian temple (*archit*); an artificial leg (*med*). [Gr *pylōn, -ōnos*, from *pylē* a gate]

pylorus /pī-lö'rəs, pī-lö'rəs, pi-lö'rəs or pi-lö'rəs/ (*anat*) *n* the opening from the stomach to the intestines. [L, from Gr *pylōros* a gatekeeper, the pylorus, from *pylē* an entrance, and *ōrā* care; cf *ouros* a guardian]

■ **pylor'ic** /-lor'/ *adj*.

pyne same as **pine²**.

pyoid /pī'oid/ (*med*) *adj* purulent. [Gr *pyon* pus]

■ **pyoderm'a** *n* (Gr *derma* skin) a skin infection in which pus is formed. **pyogenesis** /pī-ə-jen'i-sis/ *n* formation of pus. **pyogen'ic** *adj*. **pyorrhoea** /-rē'ə/ *n* (Gr *rhoiā* flow) discharge of pus; now, suppuration in the sockets of teeth. **pyorrhoe'al** or **pyorrhoe'ic** *adj*.

pyoner, pyonings see under **pioneer**.

pyorrhoea see under **pyoid**.

pyot, pyat, pyet or **piet** /pī'ət/ (*Scot*) *n* a magpie. ◆ *adj* pied. [**pie³**]

■ **pi'oted** *adj*.

pyracanth /pī'rə-kanth/ or **pyracantha** /pī-rə-kan'thə/ *n* a thorny evergreen shrub of the genus *Pyracantha*, related to the hawthorn. [Gr *pyrakantha*, from *pȳr* fire, and *akanthos* thorn]

pyral see under **pyre**.

pyralis /pir'ə-lis/ *n* an insect once supposed to live or breed in fire (*obs*); (with *cap*) a genus of moths, giving name to a heterogeneous family, the **Pyralidae** /pir-al'i-dē/. [Gr *pyralis*, from *pȳr* fire]

■ **pyr'alid** *n* and *adj* (a member) of this family.

pyramid /pir'ə-mid/ *n* (*pl* **pyr'amids**, also (*obs*) **pyramides** /pir-am'i-dēz/ and (*poetic*) **pyram'ids** and **pyram'ides** (3 syllables)) a solid figure on a triangular, square, or polygonal base, with triangular sides meeting in a point; any object or structure of that or a similar form, *esp* a huge ancient Egyptian monument; a crystal form of three or more faces each cutting three axes (*crystallog*); (in *pl*) a game played on a billiard table in which the balls are arranged in pyramid shape. ◆ *vi* (chiefly *US*) to increase one's holdings, profits, etc during a boom period by using paper profits for further purchases. [Gr *pyramis, -idos*]

■ **pyram'idal**, **pyram'id'ic** or **pyramid'ical** *adj* having the form of a pyramid. **pyram'idally** or **pyramid'ically** *adv*. **pyramid'ion** *n* the small pyramidal apex of an obelisk. **pyram'idist** or **pyramidol'ogist** *n* someone who studies the Egyptian pyramids. **pyramidol'ogy** *n*. **pyram'idon** *n* an organ stop with pipes like inverted pyramids. **pyr'amis** *n* (*pl* **pyram'ides** /-i-dēz/ or **pyr'amises**) (*Shakesp*, etc) a pyramid.

❑ **pyramid of numbers** *n* the relative decrease in numbers at each stage of a food chain, characteristic of animal communities. **pyramid selling** *n* a method of distributing goods by selling batches to agents who then sell batches at increased prices to sub-agents, and so on.

pyrargyrite /pī- or pi-rär'ji-rīt/ *n* ruby-silver ore, sulphide of silver and antimony. [Gr *pȳr* fire, and *argyros* silver]

pyre /pīr/ *n* a pile of combustible material for burning a dead body. [L *pyra*, from Gr *pyrā*, from *pȳr* fire]

■ **pyr'al** *adj*.

Pyrenaean see **Pyrenean**.

pyrene¹ /pī'rēn/ (*bot*) *n* a fruit-stone. [Gr *pȳrēn, -ēnos* fruit-stone]

■ **pyrē'nocarp** *n* (Gr *karpos* fruit) a perithecium. **pyrē'noid** *n* a small round albuminous body concerned in starch formation, found in the chloroplasts of some algae, etc. **Pyrēnomycē'tes** *n pl* (Gr *mykēs* fungus) a group of Ascomycetes whose characteristic fructification is the perithecium. **pyrēnomycē'tous** *adj*.

pyrene² /pī'rēn/ *n* a tetracyclic hydrocarbon ($C_{16}H_{10}$) obtained by dry distillation of coal. [Gr *pȳr* fire]

Pyrenean or (*obs*) **Pyrenaean** /pir-ə-nē'ən/ *adj* of the *Pyrenees*, the mountains between France and Spain. ◆ *n* a native of the Pyrenees; (in *pl*) the Pyrenees (*obs*). [L *Pȳrēnaeus*, from Gr *Pȳrēnaios*]

■ **pyrenē'ite** *n* a black garnet.

❑ **Pyrenean mountain dog** *n* a large dog with a dense white coat, bred in the Pyrenees to guard flocks.

pyrenoid, etc see under **pyrene¹**.

Pyrethrum /pī-rē'thrəm, or (*esp US*) pī-reth'rəm or (*rare*) pi-reth'rəm/ *n* a former genus of composite plants, including feverfew, now considered as belonging to the genus *Chrysanthemum*; (without *cap*) a name still applied to various garden flowers, *esp* varieties of *Chrysanthemum coccineum*; (without *cap*) insect-powder made from the flower-heads of various species of pyrethrum; (without *cap*) in pharmacy, the root of pellitory of Spain (see **pellitory²**). [L, from Gr *pyrethron* pellitory of Spain]

■ **pyrēth'rin** (or (*esp US*) /-reth'/) *n* either of two insecticidal oily esters prepared from pyrethrum flowers. **pyrēth'roid** (or (*esp US*) /-reth'/) *n* any of various synthetic compounds related to the pyrethrins, and sharing their insecticidal properties.

pyretic /pī- or pi-ret'ik/ *adj* of, of the nature of, for the cure of, fever. [Gr *pyretikos* feverish, from *pyretos* fever, from *pȳr* fire]

■ **pyretol'ogy** *n* the study of fevers. **pyretother'apy** *n* treatment by inducing a high body temperature.

Pyrex® /pī'reks/ *n* a type of glassware containing oxide of boron and so resistant to heat. [An arbitrary coinage, from **pie¹**; appar nothing whatever to do with Gr *pȳr* fire]

pyrexia /pī-rek'si-ə/ (*med*) *n* fever. [Gr *pyrexis*, from *pyressein* to be feverish, from *pȳr* fire]

■ **pyrex'ial** and **pyrex'ic** *adj*.

pyrheliometer /pir-hē-li-om'i-tər or pīr-hē-li-om'i-tər/ *n* an instrument for measuring the heating effect of the sun's rays. [Gr *pȳr* fire, *hēlios* sun, and *metron* measure]

■ **pyrheliometric** /-ō-met'rik/ *adj*.

pyridine /pir'i-dēn or pir'i-din/ *n* a strong-smelling, colourless, strongly basic liquid heterocyclic hydrocarbon, C_5H_5N, obtained in the distillation of bone-oil, coal tar, etc. [Gr *pȳr* fire]

■ **pyridox'al** *n* a member of the vitamin B complex, a derivative of pyridoxin. **pyridox'in** or **pyridox'ine** *n* a pyridine derivative, a member of the vitamin B complex. **pyrim'idine** *n* a six-membered heterocyclic compound containing two nitrogen atoms in the 1, 3 positions, eg cytosine, thymine and uracil, important bases found in DNA and RNA.

pyriform /pir'i-förm/ *adj* pear-shaped. [L *pyrum*, misspelling of *pirum* a pear, and *förma* form]

pyrimethamine /pi-ri-meth'ə-mēn or pī-ri-meth'ə-mēn/ *n* an antimalarial drug. [Gr *pȳr* fire, **methyl**, and **amine**]

pyrimidine see under **pyridine**.

pyrites /pī- or pi-rī'tēz/ *n* a brassy yellow mineral, iron disulphide, crystallizing in the cubic system, occurring in octahedra, pyritohedra, etc (also called **pyrite** /pī'rīt/, **iron pyrī'tēs**, **fool's gold**); extended to a large class of mineral sulphides and arsenides. [Gr *pyrītēs* striking fire, from *pȳr* fire]

■ **pyritic** /pir-it'ik or pīr-it'ik/ or **pyrit'ical** *adj*. **pyritif'erous** *adj*. **pyr'itize** or **-ise** *vt* to convert into, or replace by, pyrites. **pyritohē'dral** *adj*. **pyritohē'dron** *n* (*pl* **pyritohē'dra**) a pentagonal dodecahedron. **pyr'itous** *adj*.

■ **arsenical pyrites** mispickel. **cockscomb pyrites** or **spear pyrites** a twinned form of marcasite. **copper pyrites** sulphide of copper and iron, chalcopyrite, a mineral very similar to iron pyrites. **magnetic pyrites** pyrrhotite.

pyrithiamine /pi-ri-thī'ə-mēn or -min/ *n* an antivitamin causing thiamine (vitamin B₁) deficiency. [Gr *pȳr* fire, and **thiamine**]

pyro /pī'rō/ *n* a short form of **pyrogallol** or **pyromaniac**.

pyro- /pī-rō-/ *combining form* denoting: fire, heat, fever; obtained by heating or as if by heating, or by removing (theoretically) a molecule of water, as in **pyro-acet'ic**, **pyrophosphor'ic**, **pyrosulphu'ric**, **pyrotartar'ic**, etc **acid**, related in this way to acetic, phosphoric, etc acid, and in the derivative salts **pyrophos'phate**, **pyrotar'trate**, etc (*chem*). [Gr *pỹr* fire]

■ **pyroballogy** /-bal'ə-ji/ *n* (Gr *ballein* to throw, and **-logy**; *Sterne*) the science of artillery. **pyrochem'ical** *adj* relating to, producing, or produced by, chemical changes at high temperatures. **pyroclas'tic** *adj* (Gr *klastos* broken; *geol*) (of rocks) formed of fragments thrown out by volcanic action. **pyroclas'tics** *n pl* ash and other debris ejected by a volcano (also *n sing* **py'roclast**). **pyro-elec'tric** *adj* (*phys*) becoming positively and negatively electrified at opposite poles on heating or cooling; of pyro-electricity. **pyro-electric'ity** *n* the property of being pyro-electric; the study of the phenomena shown by pyro-electric crystals. **pyrogallol** /-gal'ol/ *n* a phenol obtained by heating gallic acid, used in photographic developing (also called **pyrogall'ic acid**). **py'rogen** /-jen/ *n* (see **-gen**; *med*) a substance causing heat or fever. **pyrogenic** /pī-rō-jen'ik/, **pyrogenetic** /-jin-et'ik/ or **pyrogenous** /-roj'ə-nəs/ *adj* produced by, or producing, heat or fever. **pyrognostic** /pī-rog-nos'tik/ *adj* (see **-gnostic** under **gnosis**) relating to the testing of minerals by flame. **pyrognos'tics** *n pl* the properties of a mineral revealed by such testing. **pyrography** /pī-rog'rə-fi/ *n* (see **-graphy**) poker work. **pyrogravure** /-grə-vūr'/ *n* (Fr *gravure* engraving) pyrography. **pyrokinesis** /-kī-nē'sis or -ki-nē'sis/ *n* (Gr *kīnēsis* movement) the ability to start fires by thought alone. **pyrolater** /pī-rol'ə-tər/ *n* a fire-worshipper. **pyrol'atry** *n* (see **-latry**) fire-worship. **pyroligneous** /-lig'ni-əs/ *adj* (L *ligneus*, from *lignum* wood; *chem*) obtained by distillation of wood (**pyroligneous acid** wood vinegar, a mixture of acetic acid, methyl alcohol, etc; **pyroligneous alcohol** wood spirit, methyl alcohol). **pyrolusite** /-lū'sīt or -loo'sīt/ *n* (Gr *lousis* washing, from its use in decolorizing molten glass; *geol*) naturally-occurring manganese dioxide. **py'rolyse** or (*N Am*) **-yze** *vt* to decompose by pyrolysis. **pyrolysis** /pi-rol'i-sis/ *n* (see **lysis**) decomposition of a substance by heat. **pyrolytic** /-lit'ik/ *adj*. **pyromancy** /-man-si/ *n* (see **-mancy**) divination by fire. **pyromā'nia** *n* an obsessive urge to set light to things. **pyromā'niac** *n* and *adj*. **pyromaniacal** /-mə-nī'ə-kl/ *adj*. **pyroman'tic** *adj* relating to pyromancy. **pyromeride** /pī-rom'ər-īd/ *n* (Gr *meros* part, as if meaning only partly fusible; *geol*) a nodular rhyolite. **pyrometallurgy** /-met'əl-ûr-ji or -met-al'ər-ji/ *n* the art and science of treating metals with high temperatures. **pyrometer** /pī-rom'i-tər/ *n* (see **-meter**) an instrument for measuring high temperatures. **pyrometric** /pī-rō-met'rik/ or **pyromet'rical** *adj* (**pyrometric cones** same as **Seger cones**). **pyrom'etry** *n*. **pyromorphite** /-mör'fīt/ *n* (Gr *morphē* form) a minor ore (chloride and phosphate) of lead, so called because the globule formed by heating a small quantity of ore crystallizes on cooling. **pyrophobia** /-fō'bi-ə/ *n* (see **phobia**) an irrational fear of fire. **pyrophō'bic** *n* and *adj*. **py'rophone** /-fōn/ *n* (Gr *phōnē* sound) an organ producing interference-tones by pairs of flames in tubes, invented by Eugène Kastner (1852–82). **pyrophoric** /-rō-for'ik/ and **pyroph'orous** *adj*. **pyrophorus** /pī-rof'ə-rəs/ *n* (Gr *pyrophoros* fire-carrier) a substance that takes fire on exposure to air (*chem*); (with *cap*) a genus of tropical American fireflies, the elaterid beetles. **pyrophosphate** *n* see above. **pyrophosphoric** *adj* see above. **pyropho'tograph** *n* a burnt-in photograph, eg on glass or porcelain. **pyrophotograph'ic** *adj*. **pyrophotog'raphy** *n*. **pyrophyllite** /-fil'īt/ *n* (Gr *phyllon* leaf) a clay mineral that separates into layers on heating with a blowpipe. **py'roscope** /-skōp/ *n* (see **-scope**) an instrument for measuring the intensity of radiant heat. **pyrosis** /pī-rō'sis/ *n* (Gr *pyrōsis*) water brash, heartburn. **Pyrosoma** /-sō'mə/ *n* (Gr *sōma* body) a genus of compound tunicates, with brilliant phosphorescence. **py'rosome** *n*. **py'rostat** /-stat/ *n* a type of thermostat for use at high temperatures. **pyrostat'ic** *adj*. **pyrosulphate** *n* see above. **pyrosulphuric**, **pyrotartaric**, etc *adj* see above. **pyrotech'nic** or **pyrotech'nical** *adj*. **pyrotech'nically** *adv*. **pyrotechnician** /-nish'ən/ *n* a person who makes fireworks or puts on firework displays. **pyrotechnics** /-tek'niks/ *n sing* (Gr *technikos* skilled, from *technē* art) the art of making fireworks; (also *n pl*) a display (or the displaying) of fireworks; (also *n pl*) showy display in talk, music, etc; (also *n pl*) a display of temper. **pyrotech'nist** *n* a pyrotechnician; a person given to pyrotechnics. **py'rotechny** *n* pyrotechnics. **pyroxene** /pī-roks'ēn/ *n* (Gr *xenos* stranger, because the 18c French mineralogist Haüy thought that pyroxene crystals in lava had been caught up accidentally) a general name for an important group of minerals distinguished from amphiboles by a cleavage angle of about 87°, metasilicates of calcium, magnesium, aluminium and other metals, *usu* green or black, very common in igneous rocks such as augite, diopside, enstatite, etc. **pyroxenic** /-sen'ik/ *adj*. **pyrox'enite** /-ən-īt or -ēn'īt/ *n* a rock compound essentially of pyroxene. **pyroxyle** /-rok'sil/ *n* same as **pyroxylin** below. **pyroxylic** /-sil'ik/ *adj* (*obs*) pyroligneous. **pyroxylin** or **pyroxyline** /-rok'si-lin/ *n* (Gr *xylon* wood) any of the nitrocelluloses.

pyroballogy...to...**pyrokinesis** see under **pyro-**.

Pyrola /pir'ə-lə/ *n* the wintergreen genus, giving name to the family **Pyrolā'ceae**, related to the heaths. [Dimin of *pyrus*, a misspelling of L *pirus* a pear-tree]

pyrolater...to...**pyromorphite** see under **pyro-**.

pyrope /pī'rōp/ *n* a fiery-red gemstone (also *poetic* **pyrō'pus**); a red magnesia-alumina garnet, used in jewellery (*mineralogy*). [Gr *pyrōpos* fiery-eyed, from *pỹr* fire, and *ōps, ōpos* eye, face]

pyrophobia...to...**pyroxyline** see under **pyro-**.

Pyrrhic /pir'ik/ *adj* relating to or associated with *Pyrrhus*, king of Epirus (c.319–272BC).
  ❑ **Pyrrhic victory** *n* a victory gained at too great a cost, in allusion to Pyrrhus's exclamation after his defeat of the Romans at Heraclea on the Siris (280), 'Another such victory and we are lost'.

pyrrhic /pir'ik/ *n* an ancient Greek war dance; a foot of two short syllables (*prosody*). ◆ *adj* relating to the dance or to the foot. [Gr *pyrrichē* (*orchēsis*) pyrrhic dance, said to be from *Pyrrichos*, the inventor]
  ■ **pyrrhicist** /pir'i-sist/ *n* (*hist*) a pyrrhic dancer.

Pyrrhonism /pir'ə-ni-zm/ *n* the complete scepticism of *Pyrrho* (Gr *Pyrrōn*) of Elis (3c BC).
  ■ **Pyrrhonian** /pir-ō'ni-ən/ *adj* and *n*. **Pyrrhonic** /-on'ik/ *adj*. **Pyrrh'onist** *n*.

pyrrhotite /pir'ō-tīt or -ə-/ *n* magnetic pyrites, an iron sulphide, often containing nickel (also **pyrrh'otine** /-tēn/). [Gr *pyrrotēs* redness, from *pỹr* fire]

pyrrhous /pir'əs/ *adj* reddish. [Gr *pyrros* flame-coloured, from *pỹr* fire]

pyrrole /pir'ōl/ (*chem*) *n* a colourless toxic liquid found in many naturally-occurring compounds, eg porphyrins and chlorophyll. [Gr *pyrros* flame-coloured, and L *oleum* oil]
  ■ **pyrrolidine** /pi-rol'i-dēn/ *n* a colourless strongly alkaline heterocyclic base, C_4H_9N, both occurring naturally and produced from pyrrole.

Pyrus /pī'rəs/ *n* the pear and apple genus of the rose family. [Misspelling of L *pirus* pear-tree]

pyruvate /pī-roo'vāt/ (*chem*) *n* a salt or ester of pyruvic acid. [Gr *pỹr* fire, and L *ūva* grape]
  ❑ **pyruvic acid** /-roo'vik/ *n* an organic acid, an intermediate in the metabolism of proteins and carbohydrates.

Pythagorean /pī- or pi-thag-ə-rē'ən/ *adj* relating to or associated with the Greek philosopher *Pythagoras* of Samos (6c BC), or to his philosophy; transformed, as if by transmigration of the soul (a doctrine taught by Pythagoras); vegetarian; of a diatonic scale perfected by Pythagoras, with its intervals based on mathematical ratios (*music*). ◆ *n* a follower of Pythagoras.
  ■ **Pythagorē'anism** or **Pythag'orism** *n* the doctrines of Pythagoras.
  ❑ **Pythagoras'** or **Pythagorean theorem** *n* the theorem that the square on the hypotenuse of a right-angled triangle is equal to the sum of the squares on the other two sides. **Pythagorean letter** or **Samian letter** *n* the Greek letter Y which was, for Pythagoras, a symbol of the parting of the ways for vice and virtue.

Pythia /pith'i-ə/ (*hist*) *n* the priestess who delivered the oracles of Pythian Apollo at Delphi. [Gr *Pythō*, the former name of Delphi; see **python**]
  ■ **Pyth'ian** *adj* of Delphi, the oracle there, the priestess, or the games held nearby. ◆ *n* a native or inhabitant of Delphi; the priestess of Apollo there; Apollo. **Pyth'ic** *adj* Pythian; ecstatic.
  ❑ **Pythian games** *n pl* one of the four national festivals of ancient Greece, in honour of Apollo, held every four years at Delphi. **Pythian verse** *n* (*prosody*) the dactylic hexameter.

pythium /pith'i-əm/ *n* a fungus of the genus *Pythium*, a cause of damping-off of seedlings. [Gr *pythein* to cause to rot]

pythogenic /pī-thō-jen'ik/ *adj* produced by filth. [Gr *pythein* to rot, and **-genic**]

Python /pī'thən/ (*comput*) *n* a high-level programming language. [Named in honour of the television series *Monty Python's Flying Circus* (see **Pythonesque**)]

python /pī'thən/ *n* a large snake that crushes its victims, *esp* and properly, one of the Old World genus *Python*, related to the boas; a familiar or possessing spirit; someone possessed by a spirit; someone who utters oracles. [*Python*, the great snake killed, according to Greek mythology, at Pythō (Delphi), the name being associated with Gr *pythein* to rot, because the snake's body rotted]
  ■ **Py'thoness** *n* the priestess of the oracle of Apollo at Delphi; (without *cap*) a witch. **pythonic** /-thon'ik/ *adj*. **python'omorph** /-ō-mörf/ *n* and *adj* (see **-morph**) (a member) of the **Pythonomor'pha**, in some classifications an extinct suborder of *Squamata*, large marine reptiles of the Cretaceous period, with long, scaly bodies and paddle-shaped limbs.

Pythonesque /pī-thə-nesk'/ adj (of humour) bizarre and surreal, as in the British television comedy programme *Monty Python's Flying Circus* (1969–74).

pyuria /pī-ū'ri-ə/ (med) n the presence of pus in the urine. [Gr *pyon* pus, and *ouron* urine]

pyx or **pix** /piks/ n a box; a vessel in which the host is kept after consecration, now *usu* that in which it is carried to the sick (*RC*); a box at the Mint in which sample coins are kept for testing. ◆ vt to test the weight and fineness of eg the coins deposited in the pyx.

[L *pyxis* a box, from Gr *pyxis*, *-idos*, and dimin *pyxidion*, from *pyxos* box-tree]

■ **pyxid'ium** n (pl **pyxid'ia**) (bot) a capsule that opens by a transverse circular split. **pyx'is** n (pl **pyx'ides** /-id-ēz/) a little box or casket for jewels, drugs, toilet materials, etc.

■ **trial of the pyx** trial by weight and assay of gold and silver coins by a jury of goldsmiths; the periodic official testing of sterling coinage.

pzazz same as **pizzazz**.

Q q

a b c d e f g h i j k l m n o p q r s t u v w x y z

Quorum Designed by Ray Baker in 1977. UK.

Q¹ or **q** /*kū*/ *n* the seventeenth letter in the modern English alphabet, sixteenth in the Roman, derived from the archaic Greek letter *koppa* (ϙ) (qv). —In English, Q represents the sound /*k*/ and is normally followed by *u* (*qu* being pronounced /*kw*/, or in words from or modelled on French, Spanish, etc sometimes /*k*/), but sometimes without following *u* in transliteration of the related Semitic letters qoph (Hebrew) and qaf (Arabic) as in *qadi* (more *usu cadi* or *kadi*); Old English used the spelling *cw* instead of *qu*, and medieval Scots had the spelling *quh* for the sound /*hw*/ (English spelling *wh*). [L *cū*]
☐ **Q-Celt** or **Q-Kelt** *n* a speaker of **Q-Celtic** (see under **Celt**).

Q² /*kū*/ (*US*) *n* trichosanthin, a drug used as an experimental treatment for AIDS (also **compound Q**). [Perh because it is an extract from a Chinese *cu*cumber root]

Q or **Q.** *abbrev*: Qatar (IVR); quality; quarto; Quebec (also **Que.**); queen (in cards and chess); Queensland (also **Qld**); query; question; quetzal (Guatemalan currency).
☐ **Q'-boat** or **Q'-ship** *n* (*hist*) a merchant vessel manned by navy personnel and with concealed guns, used to deceive and destroy submarines. **Q'-fever** *n* an acute disease characterized by fever and muscular pains, transmitted by the bacterium *Coxiella burnetii*. **Q'-sort** *n* a psychological test designed to discover subjects' personality types by having them rank traits in the order most appropriate to their own personalities. **Q'-train** *n* a special train carrying railway police and with closed-circuit TV, used to deal with railway vandals and trespassers (named after **Q-boat** above).

Q *symbol*: (as a medieval Roman numeral) 500; a measure of the efficiency of an electrical component as a ratio between stored energy and energy loss (also **Q factor**); a unit of heat energy equal to 10^{18} British thermal units (*US*).
☐ **Q₁₀** *n* (*biol*) temperature coefficient (qv).

Q *symbol*: electric charge (*phys*); quality or quality-value.

Q̄ *symbol*: (medieval Roman numeral) 500000.

q or **q.** *abbrev*: quart; quarter; query; quintal.

QA *abbrev*: quality assurance.

qa- Arabic and Hebrew words spelt this way are in most cases given at **ka-** or **ca-**.

QAA *abbrev*: Quality Assurance Agency for Higher Education.

qabalah see **cabbala**.

Qaddish same as **Kaddish**.

qadi same as **cadi**.

QADS *abbrev*: quality assurance data system.

qaimaqam same as **kaimakam**.

Qajar /*kä-* or *ka-jär'*/ *n* the dynasty that united and ruled Iran from 1779 to 1925. ◆ *adj* of this dynasty, its period, or its art, porcelain, etc.

qalamdan same as **kalamdan**.

QALY /*kwol'i* or *kä'li*/ *abbrev*: quality-adjusted life year, a cost-benefit unit used to assess different surgical operations and medical treatments in terms of the length and quality of life they produce, measured against their cost.

QAM *abbrev*: quadrature amplitude modulation, a method of transmitting digital signals by modulating two out-of-phase carrier waves.

qanat /*kä-nät'*/ *n* an underground tunnel for carrying irrigation water. [Ar *qanāt* pipe]

Q&A *abbrev*: question and answer.

QANTAS /*kwon'təs*/ *abbrev*: Queensland and Northern Territory Aerial Service (the Australian international airline).

QARANC *abbrev*: Queen Alexandra's Royal Army Nursing Corps.

QARNNS *abbrev*: Queen Alexandra's Royal Naval Nursing Service.

qasida /*ka-sē'də*/ *n* a formal Arabic poem of praise or mourning. [Ar]

qat see **khat¹**.

Qatari /*kat'ə-ri* or *kə-tä'ri*/ *adj* of or relating to the State of *Qatar* in the Arabian Gulf, or its people. ◆ *n* a native or citizen of Qatar.

qawwali /*kə-vä'li*/ *n* devotional Sufi music, *usu* sung in Persian or Turkish. [Ar *qawwālī*]
■ **qawwal'** *n* a male singer of this music.

QB *abbrev*: Queen's Bench.

QC *abbrev*: quality circle; quality control; Queen's College; Queen's Counsel.

QCA *abbrev*: Qualifications and Curriculum Authority.

QCD *abbrev*: quantum chromodynamics.

QE *abbrev*: quantitative easing.

qe- Arabic and Hebrew words spelt this way are in most cases given at **ke-** or **ce-**.

QED *abbrev*: quantum electrodynamics; *quod erat demonstrandum* (*L*), which was to be demonstrated (or proved; also **q.e.d.**).

QEF *abbrev*: *quod erat faciendum* (*L*), which was to be done.

QEH *abbrev*: Queen Elizabeth Hall (on London's South Bank).

QEI *abbrev*: *quod erat inveniendum* (*L*), which was to be found.

QE2 *abbrev*: Queen Elizabeth the Second (the liner).

QGM *abbrev*: Queen's Gallantry Medal.

qi see **chi²**.

qi- Arabic and Hebrew words spelt this way are in most cases given at **ki-** or **ci-**.

qibla same as **kiblah**.

QIC *abbrev*: quarter-inch cartridge, a standard for computer tapes.

qid *abbrev*: (in prescriptions) *quater in die* (*L*), four times a day.

qigong or **qi gong** /*kē-gong'*/, or **chi kung** /*chē-goong'*/ *n* a system of meditational exercises for promoting physical and spiritual health by deep breathing. [Chin *qì* breath, energy, and *gōng* skill, exercise]

qin see **guqin**.

qinghaosu /*ching-how-soo'*/ *n* a crystalline compound extracted from the artemisia plant, used *esp* to treat malaria (also called **artemisinin**). [Chin, from *qīng* green, *hāo* plant, and *sù* basic element]

qintar /*kin-tär'*/ or **qindar** /*kin-där'*/ *n* an Albanian monetary unit, $\frac{1}{100}$ of a lek. [Albanian]

qiviut /*kiv'i-ət*/ *n* the wool of the undercoat of the arctic musk ox. [Inuit]

QL (*comput*) *abbrev*: query language.

ql *abbrev*: (in prescriptions) *quantum libet* (*L*), as much as you please; quintal.

Qld *abbrev*: Queensland.

QM *abbrev*: Quartermaster.

QMG *abbrev*: Quartermaster-General.

QMS *abbrev*: Quartermaster-Sergeant.

QMV *abbrev*: qualified majority voting.

qo- Arabic and Hebrew words spelt this way are in most cases given at **ko-** or **co-**.

qoph same as **koph**.

Qoran same as **Koran**.

QPM *abbrev*: Queen's Police Medal.

qq *abbrev*: quartos.

qqv or **qq.v.** *abbrev*: *quae vide* (*L*), which see (used instead of qv when referring to more than one item).

qr *abbrev*: quarter.

QR code® /*kū-är' kōd*/ *n* an arrangement, readable by computer or smart phone, of black squares in a larger square, and encoding a URL, text, or other data. [Quick *R*esponse code]

qs *abbrev*: (in prescriptions) *quantum sufficit* (*L*), a sufficient quantity.

---

fāte; fär; mē; fûr; mīne; mōte; för; mūte; pūt; dhen (then); *el'ə-mənt* (element) • For other sounds see detailed chart of pronunciation

QSM (*NZ*) *abbrev* : Queen's Service Medal.

QSO *abbrev* : quasi-stellar object; Queen's Service Order (*NZ*).

QT see **on the quiet** under **quiet**.

qt *abbrev* : quantity; quart.

q.t. see **on the quiet** under **quiet**.

QT interval or **period** /kū-tē' in'tər-vəl or pē' ri-əd/ (*med*) *n* the period between the start and finish of electrical activity in the ventricles during a single heartbeat. [QRS complex and *T* wave, the two points on an electrocardiogram from which the interval is calculated]

Q-Tip® /kū'tip/ (*US*) *n* a small paper stick with a piece of cotton wool on each end, designed for cleaning small bodily orifices.

qto *abbrev* : quarto.

QTOL *abbrev* : quiet take-off and landing.

QTS *abbrev* : Qualified Teacher Status.

qty *abbrev* : quantity.

Qu. *abbrev* : Queen; question.

qu. or **quar.** *abbrev* : quart; quarter; quarterly.

qu- Arabic and Hebrew words spelt this way are in most cases given at **ku-** or **cu-**.

qua /kwā or kwä/ *adv* in the capacity of. [L *quā*, adverbial ablative fem of *quī* who]

Quaalude® /kwā'lood or -lūd, also kwä'/ (*US*) *n* proprietary name for the drug methaqualone.

quack[1] /kwak/ *n* the cry of a duck. ◆ *vi* to utter a quack. [Imit]
■ **quack'er** *n*. **quack'le** *vi* (*dialect*) to quack.

quack[2] /kwak/ *n* someone who claims, and practises under the pretence of having, knowledge and skill (*esp* in medicine) that he or she does not possess; a doctor (*sl*); a charlatan. ◆ *adj* fraudulent. ◆ *vi* to behave like a quack. ◆ *vt* to advertise, sell or treat in the manner of a quack. [Du *quacksalver* (now *kwakzalver*) perh someone who quacks about their salves (remedies)]
■ **quack'ery** *n* the pretensions or practice of a quack, *esp* in medicine. **quack'ish** *adj*.
□ **quack'salver** *n* (*obs*) a quack. **quack'salving** *adj* (*obs*).

quack grass /kwak gräs/ *n* couch grass. [Altered from *quick*, from **quitch**[1]]

quad[1] /kwod/ *n* short form of **Quaalude**® (*US*; *inf*), **quadrangle**, **quadraphonic** (see under **quadraphonics**), **quadraphonics**, **quadraphony** (see **quadraphonics**), **quadrat**, **quadriceps**, **quadrillion**, **quadruped** (ie horse), **quadruplet** (see under **quadruple**). ◆ *adj* short form of **quadraphonic**, **quadruple**. ◆ *vt* (*printing*) to fill with quadrats.

quad[2] or **Quad** /kwod/ *n* a small, powerful four-wheel-drive vehicle, used eg in military, agricultural and sporting activities (also **quad bike**). [quadruple]

quad[3] same as **quod**[2].

quadr- see **quadri-**.

quadragenarian /kwod-rə-ji-nā'ri-ən/ *n* a person who is forty years old, or between forty and fifty (also *adj*). [L *quadrāgēnārius* relating to forty, from *quadrāgintā* forty]
■ **quadragenary** /-jē'nə-ri/ *adj* (*rare*) of, containing, based on, forty; quadragenarian (also *n*).

Quadragesima /kwo-drə-jes'i-mə/ *n* the first Sunday in Lent; the forty days of Lent (*obs*). [L *quadrāgēsimus* fortieth, from *quadrāgintā* forty]
■ **quadrages'imal** *adj* of Lent; lasting forty days.

quadrangle /kwo-drang'gl or kwod'rang-gl/ *n* a plane figure with four angles (and therefore four sides); an object or space of that form; a court or open space, *usu* rectangular, enclosed by a building (such as a college); a block of buildings containing a quadrangle. [Fr, from L *quadrangulum*, from *quattuor* four, and *angulus* an angle]
■ **quadrang'ular** /-gū-lər/ *adj*. **quadrang'ularly** *adv*.
■ **complete quadrangle** a figure composed of four points and the six straight lines that join these points.

quadrans /kwod'ranz or kwad'ränz/ (*ancient hist*) *n* (*pl* **quadran'tēs**) a Roman copper coin, the fourth part of an as. [L]

quadrant /kwod'rənt/ *n* the fourth part of a circle or its circumference; a sector or an arc of 90° (also *adj*); an area, object or street of that form; an instrument with an arc of 90° for taking altitudes; one of the four segments or areas into which something is divided. [L *quadrans, -antis* a fourth part, from *quattuor* four]
■ **quadrantal** /-rant'l/ *adj*.

quadraphonics or **quadrophonics** /kwo-drə-fon'iks/ *n sing* a system of sound transmission using a minimum of four speakers fed by four, or sometimes three, separate channels (also **quadraph'ony** or **quadroph'ony**). [L *quadri-* four, and Gr *phōnē* sound]
■ **quadraphon'ic** or **quadrophon'ic** *adj*.

quadraplegia, -plegic non-standard forms of **quadriplegia, -plegic**.

quadrat /kwod'rət/ *n* a piece of type metal less high than the letters, used in spacing between words and filling out blank lines (commonly called a **quad**; *printing*); a small area (*usu* one square metre) of ground marked off for the detailed investigation of animal and plant life (*ecology*). [L *quadrātus*, pap of *quadrāre* to square, from *quattuor* four]
■ **quad'rate** /-rāt or -rit/ *adj* square; rectangular; squarish; squared; square, as a power or root (*obs maths*); complete (*obs*); corresponding, consistent (*obs*). ◆ *n* a square or quadrate figure or object; the quadrate bone, suspending the lower jaw in vertebrates other than mammals; quartile (*obs astron*). ◆ *vt* and *vi* to square; to make consistent. **quadratic** /-rat'ik/ *adj* of or like a quadrate; involving the square but no higher power, as a *quadratic equation* (*maths*); tetragonal (*crystallog*). ◆ *n* a quadratic equation; (in *pl*) the branch of algebra dealing with quadratic equations. **quadrat'ical** *adj*. **quadrā'trix** *n* a curve by which a curved figure (such as a circle) may be squared. **quad'rature** /-rə-chər/ *n* squareness (*obs*); the finding of a square with an area equal to a given figure (*maths*); an angular distance of 90°; the position of a heavenly body at such an angular distance from another body, or the time of its being there; a phase angle of 90° within a cycle (*electronics*); a square space (*Milton*). **quadrā'tus** *n* (*anat*) the name of several flat rectangular muscles.
■ **B quadrā'tum** quadrate B (see under **B**). **quadrature of the circle** see under **square**.

quadratura /kwo-drə-too'rə/ (*art*) *n* (*pl* **quadratur'e** /-re/) a work having a trompe l'œil effect, eg a wall or ceiling painted with arches, colonnades, etc in strong perspective. [Ital]

quadrella /kwo-drel'ə/ (*Aust*) *n* a group of four (*esp* the last four) horse races at a meeting, for which the punter selects the four winners. [L *quadr-* four, and *-ella*, dimin sfx]

quadrennium /kwo-dren'i-əm/ *n* (*pl* **quadrenn'ia**) (a period of) four years. [**quadri-** and L *annus* year]
■ **quadrenn'ial** *adj* lasting four years; once in four years. ◆ *n* an event that takes place every four years. **quadrenn'ially** *adv*. —The forms **quadrienn'ium, quadrienn'ial**, etc are etymologically correct but now less usual.

quadri- /kwo-dri-/ or sometimes before a vowel **quadr-** /kwo-dr-/ *combining form* denoting: four; square. [L *quadri-*, from *quattuor* four]
■ **quad'ric** *adj* (*geom*) of the second degree. ◆ *n* (*geom*) a curve, etc of the second degree. **quadricentennial** /kwod-ri-sen-ten'i-əl/ (modelled on **centennial**) *adj* lasting four hundred years; once in four hundred years. ◆ *n* a four-hundredth anniversary. **quadricone** /kwod'ri-kōn/ *n* a quadric cone, or cone having a conic as base. **quadriennial** *adj* see **quadrennium**. **quadrifarious** /kwod-ri-fā'ri-əs/ *adj* (L *quadrifārius*, poss from *fāri* to speak) fourfold; in four rows. **quadrifid** /kwod'ri-fid/ *adj* (L, from the root of *findere* to cleave; *bot*) cleft in four. **quadrifoliate** /kwod-ri-fō'li-āt/ *adj* (L *folium* a leaf) four-leaved. **quadriform** /kwod'ri-förm/ *adj* (L *förma* form) fourfold; having four forms or aspects. **quadriga** /kwod-rī'gə or kwad-rē'ga/ *n* (*pl* **quadri'gae** /-jē or -gī/) (L, a later singular from *quadrīgae* a team of four, for *quadrijugae*, from *jugum* yoke) in Greek and Roman times, a two-wheeled chariot drawn by four horses abreast. **quadrigeminal** /kwod-ri-jem'i-nl/ *adj* (L *geminī* twins) having four similar parts (also **quadrigem'inate** and **quadrigem'inous**). **quadrilateral** *adj* and *n* see separate entry. **quadrilingual** /-ling'gwəl/ *adj* (L *lingua* tongue) using four languages. **quadriliteral** /kwod-ri-lit'ər-əl/ *adj* (L *lītera* a letter) consisting of four letters. ◆ *n* a word or a root of four letters. **quadrillion** *n*, etc see separate entry. **quadrilocular** /kwod-ri-lok'ū-lər/ *adj* (L *loculus*, dimin of *locus* place) having four compartments. **quadringenary** /kwod-rin-jē'nər-i/ *n* (L *quadringēnārius* of four hundred each) a four-hundredth anniversary or its celebration. **quadrinomial** /kwod-ri-nō'mi-əl/ *adj* (modelled on **binomial**; *maths*) consisting of four terms. ◆ *n* an expression of four terms. **quadripartite** *adj* see separate entry. **quadriplegia** *n*, etc see separate entry. **quadrireme** /kwod'ri-rēm/ *n* (L *rēmus* an oar) an ancient ship with four sets of oars. **quad'risect** *vt* to divide into four, *usu* equal, parts. **quadrisection** /kwod-ri-sek'shən/ *n* (L *sectiō, -onis* cutting) division into four equal parts. **quadrisyllab'ic** *adj*. **quadrisyllable** /kwod-ri-sil'ə-bl/ *n* a tetrasyllable. **quadriv'alence** (or /-vā'/) *n*. **quadrivalent** /kwod-riv'ə-lənt or -vā'lənt/ *adj* having a valency of four. ◆ *n* the structure formed by the pairing of four homologous chromosomes during meiosis in tetraploid organisms. **quadriv'ial** *adj*. **quadrivium** /kwod-riv'i-əm/ *n* (L, the place where four roads meet, from *via* a way) in medieval education, the four branches of mathematics (arithmetic, geometry, astronomy, music).

quadriceps /kwod'ri-seps/ (*anat*) *n* the large muscle that runs down the front of the thigh and extends the leg. [Modelled on **biceps** with **quadri-** as pfx]
■ **quadricipital** /-sip'i-tl/ *adj*.

quadrilateral /kwo-dri-lat'ə-rəl/ *adj* four-sided. ◆ *n* a plane figure bounded by four straight lines (*geom*); a group of four fortresses, *esp*

Mantua, Verona, Peschiera and Legnago in N Italy. [**quadri-** and L *latus, lateris* side]

■ **complete quadrilateral** a figure consisting of four straight lines intersecting in six points or vertices.

quadriliteral...to...**quadrivium** see under **quadri-**.

quadrille[1] /k(w)ə-dril'/ *n* a square dance for four couples or more, in five movements; music for such a dance; one of four groups of horsemen (*obs*). ◆ *vi* to dance quadrilles. [Fr, from Sp *cuadrilla* a troop, appar from *cuadra*, from L *quadra* a square]

■ **quadrill'er** *n*.

quadrille[2] /k(w)ə-dril'/ *n* a four-handed game with 40 cards, similar to ombre. ◆ *vi* (*rare*) to play quadrille. [Fr, perh from Sp *cuatrillo* the game of quadrille, or *cuartillo* fourth part]

quadrillion /kwo- or kwə-dril'yən or -i-ən/ *n* a thousand raised to the fifth power (10^{15}); (*esp* formerly, in Britain) a million raised to the fourth power (10^{24}). ◆ *adj* being a quadrillion in number. [Fr, from L *quadr-* four, and **million**]

■ **quadrill'ionth** *adj* and *n*.

quadripartite /kwo-dri-pär'tīt/ *adj* in four parts; having four participants; split in four nearly to the base (*bot*); (of eg a vault) divided into four compartments (*archit*). [**quadri-** and L *partīrī, -ītum* to divide]

■ **quadriparti'tion** *n*.

quadriplegia /kwo-dri-plē'j(i-)ə or -jyə/ (*med*) *n* paralysis of both arms and both legs. [**quadri-** and Gr *plēgē* a blow]

■ **quadripleg'ic** *n* and *adj*.

quadripole /kwo'dri-pōl/ (*electronics*) *n* a network with two input and two output terminals. [Fr *quadripôle*, from **quadri-** and **pole**[1]]

quadroon /kwo-droon'/, also **quarteroon** /kwör-tə-roon'/ (*old*) *n* a person of one-quarter black descent; extended to refer to any person or animal of similarly mixed ancestry. [Sp *cuarterón*, from *cuarto* a fourth]

quadrophonic(s), quadrophony see **quadraphonics**.

quadru- /kwo-drŭ-/ a variant of **quadri-**.

■ **quadru'man** /-mən/ or **quadrumane** /-mān/ *n*. **quadrumanous** /kwod-roo'mən-əs/ *adj* (L *manus* a hand) belonging to the **Quadru'mana**, a former name for the primates other than man, which have all four feet with an opposable digit. **quadrumvir** /kwod-rum'vər/ *n* (L *vir* a man) a member of a **quadrum'virate**, a group of four men acting together in some capacity.

quadruped /kwod'rə-ped/ *n* a four-footed animal, *usu* a mammal, *esp* a horse. ◆ *adj* four-footed. [**quadru-**, and L *pēs, pedis* a foot]

■ **quadrupedal** /-roo'pi-dəl/ *adj*.

quadruple /kwod'rə-pl or (*esp Scot*) -roo'/ *adj* fourfold; having four parts, members or divisions. ◆ *n* four times as much; a coin worth four pistoles (*hist*). ◆ *vt* to increase fourfold, multiply by four; to equal four times. ◆ *vi* to become four times as much. [Fr, from L *quadruplus*, from the root of *plēre* to fill]

■ **quad'ruplet** (or /-roo'/) *n* any combination of four things; one of four (children or animals) born at one birth (*inf* short form **quad**); a group of four notes performed in the time of three (*music*); a cycle for four riders. **quad'ruply** /-pli or -roo'pli/ *adv* in a fourfold manner.

□ **Quadruple Alliance** a league formed in 1718 by Britain, France, Austria and Holland against Spain, or one formed in 1813 by Britain, Prussia, Austria and Russia against Napoleon. **quadruple time** *n* (*music*) a time with four beats to the bar.

quadruplex /kwod'rə-pleks/ *adj* fourfold; (of a Morse telegraphic system) capable of sending four messages at once, two each way, over one wire. ◆ *n* an instrument of this kind; a videotape recording and reproduction system using four rotating heads to produce transverse tracks on magnetic tape. ◆ *vt* to make quadruplex. [L *quadruplex, -icis* fourfold, from *plicāre, -ātum* to fold]

■ **quadru'plicate** *adj* fourfold. ◆ *n* one of four corresponding things; fourfoldness. ◆ *vt* to make fourfold. **quadruplicā'tion** *n*. **quadruplicity** /-plis'i-ti/ *n*. **quad'ruply** /-plī/ *n* (*Scots law*) a reply to a triply.

quadrupole /kwod'rə-pōl/ (*phys*) *n* a collection of four equal monopoles or two unequal dipoles. [**quadru-**]

quaere /kwē'rē or kwī're/ *interj* inquire (suggesting doubt, or desirability of investigation). ◆ *n* a query, question. —See also **query**. [L *quaerere, quaesītum* to inquire]

■ **quaeritur** /kwē-ri'tər or kwī'ri-tūr/ *vi* (*impers*) the question is asked. **quaesitum** /kwē-sī'təm or kwī-sē'tŭm/ *n* something sought for; the true value.

quaestionary /kwēs'chə-nə-ri/ (*Walter Scott*) *n* a pardoner. [Med L *questiōnārius*]

quaestor /kwē'stör, -stər or kwī'stor/ *n* an ancient Roman magistrate, in early times an investigator, prosecutor or judge in murder cases, later a financial officer with various other functions; an officer of the European Parliament charged with supervising the administrative and

financial concerns of MEPs; in the Middle Ages (*usu* **ques'tor**) a church official who granted indulgences, a pardoner; a treasurer. [L *quaestor, -ōris*, from *quaerere, quaesītum* to seek]

■ **quaestorial** /-tō'ri-əl or -tō'/ *adj*. **quaes'torship** *n*. **quaes'tuary** *adj* moneymaking; seeking profit. ◆ *n* (*obs*) someone who seeks profits; a pardoner.

quae vide see **quod**[1].

quaff [1] /kwäf or kwof/ *vt* to drink or drain in large draughts. ◆ *vi* to drink deeply or eagerly. ◆ *n* a draught. [Origin obscure]

■ **quaff'able** *adj* pleasant to drink in large amounts. **quaff'er** *n*.

quaff[2] /kwäf/ an obsolete variant of **quaich**.

quag /kwag or kwog/ *n* a boggy place, *esp* one that moves or quivers underfoot. [Cf **quake**]

■ **quagg'iness** *n*. **quagg'y** *adj*.

quagga /kwag'ə/ *n* an extinct S African wild ass (*Equus quagga*), less fully striped than the zebras, to which it was related. [Perh Khoikhoi *quacha*]

quagmire /kwag'mīr or kwog'/ *n* wet, boggy ground that yields, moves or quivers under the feet; a difficult, problematic situation. ◆ *vt* to entangle, as in a quagmire. [Appar **quag** and **mire**]

■ **quag'miry** *adj*.

quahog /kwŏ'hog or kwə-hog'/, **quahaug** /-hög or -hög'/, or sometimes **cohog** /kō'hog or kə-hog'/ *n* an edible clam (*Venus mercenaria*) of the N American Atlantic coast, also known as **round clam**; another variety of clam, *Cyprina islandica*, also known as **black quahog**. [Native Am (Narraganset) *poquauhock*]

quaich or **quaigh** /kwähh/ (*Scot*) *n* a shallow drinking cup, *orig* of staves and hoops, now *usu* of silver or pewter. [Gaelic *cuach* a cup]

Quai d'Orsay /kā dör-sä'/ *n* the French Foreign Office. [Name of a quay on the Seine where it is situated]

quail[1] /kwāl/ *n* a genus (*Coturnix*) of small birds of the partridge family; in N America extended to various small game birds, such as the California quail (genus *Lophortyx*) and the bobwhite; a whore (*Shakesp*). [OFr *quaille* ; prob Gmc]

□ **quail'-pipe** *n* a whistle for luring quails into a net (also **quail'-call**); the throat (*obs*).

quail[2] /kwāl/ *vi* to flinch; to fail in spirit; to slacken (*Shakesp*); to languish, decline (*archaic*). ◆ *vt* (*obs*) to subdue; to daunt. [ME *quayle* ; origin obscure]

■ **quail'ing** *n* (*Shakesp*).

quaint /kwānt/ *adj* pleasantly odd; whimsical; charmingly old-fashioned; skilful, *esp* in use of language (*Shakesp*); cunning (*obs*); ingenious (*obs*); fine (*Spenser* and *Milton*); affectedly fanciful or elaborate (*obs*); affectedly fastidious or prim (*Spenser*). [OFr *cointe*, from L *cognitus* known; perh confused with *comptus* neat]

■ **quaint'ly** *adv*. **quaint'ness** *n*.

quair obsolete variant of **quire**[1].

quake /kwāk/ *vi* to quiver or vibrate; to tremble, *esp* with cold or fear. ◆ *vt* to cause to tremble (*Shakesp*); to cause to vibrate. ◆ *n* a tremor; an earthquake; a shudder. [OE *cwacian* ; perh related to *quick*]

■ **quā'ker** *n*. **quā'kiness** *n*. **quā'king** *n*. **quā'kingly** *adv*. **quā'ky** *adj* shaky.

□ **quaking ash** *n* the aspen. **quā'king-grass** *n* a moorland grass of the genus *Briza*, with pendulous, panicled, tremulous spikelets.

Quaker /kwā'kər/ *n* one of the Religious Society of Friends, founded by George Fox (1624–91); a dummy cannon (also called **Quaker gun**). ◆ *adj* of Quakers; of Philadelphia ('the Quaker city', because founded by William Penn (1644–1718), Quaker) (*US*). [Nickname (not adopted by themselves, and earlier applied to another sect) given them by Justice Bennet at Derby, because Fox told them to *quake* at the word of the Lord]

■ **Quā'kerdom** *n*. **Quā'keress** *n*. **Quā'kerish** or **Quā'kerly** *adj* like a Quaker. **Quā'kerism** *n*.

□ **Quā'ker-bird** *n* the sooty albatross. **Quā'ker-buttons** *n pl* the round seeds of nux vomica. **Quā'ker-colour** *n* a grey or dull-brown colour.

quale /kwā'li or kwä'li or -lā/ (*logic*) *n* (*pl* **qua'lia** /-li-ə/) a quality or property of something. [L, neuter of adj *qualis* of what kind]

qualify /kwol'i-fī/ *vi* (**qual'ifying; qual'ified**) to take the necessary steps to fit oneself for a certain position, activity or practice; to fulfil a requirement; to have the necessary qualities or qualifications; to be eligible (for a final round, etc) after successfully completing one or more qualifying rounds. ◆ *vt* to ascribe a quality to; to characterize; to add a quality to the connotation of (a word) (*grammar*); to render capable or suitable; to provide with legal power; to limit by modifications; to moderate, mitigate; to appease; to abate, reduce the strength of; to vary; to prove, confirm (*Scots law*). [Fr *qualifier* or LL *quālificāre*, from L *quālis* of what sort, and *facere* to make]

■ **qual'ifiable** /-fī-ə-bl/ *adj*. **qualification** /-fi-kā'shən/ *n* qualifying; distinctive quality; modification; restriction; that which qualifies;

a quality that fits a person for a task, etc; a certificate gained, examination passed, etc indicating a level of competence; a necessary condition; an accomplishment (*obs*); the attaching of quality to, or the distinction of affirmative and negative in, a term (*logic*). **qual'ificātive** *adj* and *n*. **qual'ificātor** *n* (*RC*) a person who examines and prepares ecclesiastical cases for trial. **qual'ificātory** *adj*. **qual'ified** /-*fīd*/ *adj* fitted, competent, having the necessary qualification; modified; limited. **qual'ifiedly** /-*fīd-li*/ *adv*. **qual'ifier** /-*fī-ər*/ *n*. **qual'ifying** *n* and *adj*.
❑ **qualification test** *n* the evaluation of an article to be used in space flight to verify that it functions correctly under the conditions occurring during flight. **qualifying round** *n* a preliminary round in a competition, to limit the number of competitors.
■ **qualified majority voting** a system of majority voting, without veto, used in the EU Council of Ministers, in which each vote is weighted according to the size of the country. **Qualified Teacher Status** accredited status required by any schoolteacher wishing to teach in England and Wales.

qualis ab incepto /*kwä'lis ab in-sep'tō* or *kwä'lis ab in-kep'tō*/ (*L*) as from the beginning.

quality /*kwol'i-ti*/ *n* grade of goodness; excellence; that which makes a thing what it is; nature; character; kind; property; attribute; social status; high social status; persons of the upper class collectively; profession, *esp* (*Shakesp*) the actor's profession; manner (*Shakesp*); skill, accomplishment; timbre, that characteristic of a sound that depends on the overtones present, distinguished from loudness and pitch (*acoustics*); the character of a vowel that depends on the position of the mouth and tongue when it is uttered (*phonetics*); the character of a proposition as affirmative or negative (*logic*); approximate penetrating power (*radiog*); (*usu in pl*) a quality newspaper. ◆ *adj* of a high grade of excellence; (of newspapers, etc) of a high standard of journalism. [OFr *qualité*, from L *quālitās*, *-tātis*, from *quālis* of what kind]
■ **qual'itātive** *adj* relating to, or concerned with, quality, *esp opp* to *quantitative*. **qual'itātively** *adv*. **qual'itied** *adj* endowed with a quality or qualities.
❑ **qualitative analysis** *n* (*chem*) identification of the constituents of a sample without regard to their relative amounts (cf **quantitative analysis** under **quantity**). **quality assurance** *n* the maintenance of set standards in production or services. **quality circle** *n* a meeting of an organization's employees (as distinct from its management) aimed at improving production or efficiency (*abbrev* **QC**). **quality control** *n* the inspection, testing, etc of samples of a product, *esp* at various stages of production, to ensure maintenance of high standards. **quality factor** *n* a measure of the relative biological effectiveness of ionizing radiation. **quality time** *n* time during which one is not distracted but devotes one's attention to one's companion, child, etc.
■ **quality of life** non-material standard of living measured by environmental and cultural amenities, etc. **total quality** a work ethos according to which continuous efforts are made to perform all aspects of one's work better (also *adj*).

qualm /*kwäm* or *kwöm*/ *n* a sudden feeling of faintness or sickness; a sickly feeling; an uneasiness, eg of conscience; a misgiving. [Perh OE *cwealm* death, murder, torment, pain]
■ **qualm'ing** *adj*. **qualm'ish** *adj*. **qualm'ishly** *adv*. **qualm'ishness** *n*. **qualm'less** *adj*. **qualm'y** *adj*.

quamash see **camass**.

quandang see **quandong**.

quandary /*kwon'd(ə-)ri* or (formerly) *kwon-dā'ri*/ *n* a state of perplexity; a dilemma; a hard plight (*obs*). [Origin obscure]

quand même /*kã mem'*/ (*Fr*) nevertheless, whatever the consequences may be.

quandong /*kwan'* or *kwon'dong*/, also **quandang** /-*dang*/ or **quantong** /-*tong*/ *n* a small Australian tree (*Santalum acuminatum*) of the sandalwood family; its edible drupe (*native peach*) or edible kernel (**quan'dong-nut**); an Australian tree (*Elaeocarpus grandis*) (**silver**, **blue** or **brush quandong**); a disreputable person, *esp* a sponger or parasite (*Aust inf*). [From an Aboriginal language]

quango /*kwang'gō*/ *n* (*pl* **quan'gos**) a board funded by, and with members appointed by, central government, to supervise or develop activity in areas of public interest. [*quasi-autonomous non-governmental* (sometimes *national government*) *organization*]

quannet /*kwon'it*/ *n* a flat file used like a plane. [Origin unknown]

quant[1] /*kwant*/ *n* a punting or jumping pole, with a flat end. ◆ *vt* to punt. [Cf **kent**[1]; poss connected with L *contus*, Gr *kontos*]

quant[2] /*kwont*/ (*finance*; *inf*) *n* a person who uses statistical models to predict fluctuations in the stock market. [From *quant*itative analyst]
❑ **quant analysis** same as **quantitative analysis** (see under **quantitative**).

quanta, **quantal** see **quantum**.

quantic /*kwon'tik*/ (*maths*) *n* a rational integral homogeneous function of two or more variables. [L *quantus* how great]
■ **quan'tical** *adj*.

quantify /*kwon'ti-fī*/ *vt* (**quan'tifying**; **quan'tified**) to fix or express the quantity of; to express as a quantity; to qualify (a term in a proposition) by stating the quantity (*logic*). [L *quantus* how great, and *facere* to make]
■ **quan'tifiable** *adj*. **quantification** /-*fi-kā'shən*/ *n*. **quan'tifier** *n*.
■ **quantification of the predicate** (*logic*) the attachment of a sign of quantity to the predicate.

quantity /*kwon'ti-ti*/ *n* the amount of anything; bulk; size; a sum; a determinate amount; an amount, portion; a considerable amount or large portion; a fragment, scrap (*Shakesp*); length or shortness of duration of a sound or syllable (*acoustics*; *phonetics*); extension (*logic*); the character of a proposition as universal or particular; anything which can be increased, divided or measured; proportion (*Shakesp*). [OFr *quantité*, from L *quantitās*, *-tātis*, from *quantus* how much]
■ **quan'titate** *vt* to specify or express the quantity of, quantify. **quan'titātive** or **quan'titive** *adj* relating to, or concerned with, quantity, *esp opp* to *qualitative*. **quan'titātively** or **quan'titively** *adv*.
❑ **quantitative analysis** *n* identification of the relative amounts of substances making up a sample (cf **qualitative analysis**; *chem*); the use of statistics to make stock or market decisions (*finance*). **quantitative easing** *n* (*finance*) the policy of increasing the amount of money in circulation in order to stimulate economic activity. **quantity discount** *n* (*commerce*) a reduction in the unit price of goods when large quantities are purchased. **quantity surveyor** *n* a person who estimates quantities required, obtains materials, evaluates work done, etc for construction work. **quantity theory** *n* the economic theory that prices vary with the amount of money in circulation.
■ **unknown quantity** a quantity whose mathematical value is not known; a factor, person or thing whose importance or influence cannot be foreseen (*fig*).

quantivalence /*kwon-tiv'ə-ləns* or *-ti-vā'ləns*/ (*chem*; now *rare*) *n* valency. [L *quantus* how much, and *valēns*, *-entis*, prp of *valēre* to be worth]
■ **quantiv'alent** (or /-*vā'*/) *adj*.

quantize see under **quantum**.

quantometer or (*US formerly*) **Quantometer**® /*kwon-tom'i-tər*/ *n* an instrument that shows by spectrographical analysis the percentages of the various elements present in a metallic sample. [L *quantus* how much, and **meter**[1]]

quantong see **quandong**.

quantum /*kwon'təm*/ *n* (*pl* **quan'ta**) quantity; amount (*esp law*); a naturally fixed minimum amount of some entity which is such that all other amounts of that entity occurring in physical processes in nature are integral multiples of it (*phys*). ◆ *adj* (loosely) sudden, spectacularly different. [L *quantum*, neuter of *quantus* how much]
■ **quan'tal** *adj* of, or pertaining to, a quantum (*phys*); having one of only two possible states or values. **quantizā'tion** or **-s-** *n*. **quan'tize** or **-ise** *vt* to express in terms of quanta or in accordance with the quantum theory.
❑ **quantum chromodynamics** *n sing* a theory of strong interactions (qv) between elementary particles, including the interaction that binds protons and neutrons to form a nucleus. **quantum computer** *n* a computer that makes of use of quantum mechanics to perform operations on data. **quantum computing** *n*. **quantum dot** *n* a tiny cluster of electrons that act as a switch in a quantum computer. **quantum efficiency** *n* in a photocell or in photosynthesis, the number of electrons released per photon of incident radiation of specified wavelength (also **quantum yield**). **quantum electrodynamics** *n sing* a relativistic quantum theory of electromagnetic interactions. **quantum field theory** *n* the overall theory of fundamental particles and their interactions. **quantum gravity** *n* an area of theoretical physics that seeks to unify gravitational physics with quantum field theory. **quantum jump** or **leap** *n* the sudden transition of an electron, atom, etc from one energy state to another; a sudden spectacular advance, *esp* one which dramatically skips over intermediate stages of understanding or development. **quantum mechanics** *n sing* a branch of mechanics based on the quantum theory, used in predicting the behaviour of elementary particles. **quantum number** *n* any of a set of integers or half-integers which together describe the state of a particle or system of particles; the **principal quantum number**, for instance, specifies the electron shell in an atom that an electron occupies. **quantum physics** *n sing* the branch of physics concerned with quantum theory and its effects. **quantum state** *n* the state of a system expressed in terms of quantum numbers. **quantum theory** *n* a theory, developed by Max Planck, of the emission and absorption of energy not continuously but in finite quanta. **quantum yield** see **quantum efficiency** above.

■ words derived from main entry word; ❑ compound words; ■ idioms and phrasal verbs

quantum meruit /kwon'təm mer'ū-it or kwan'tŭm mer'ŭ-it/ (law) a fair reward for services rendered where there is no agreed rate of payment. [L, as much as he or she has earned]

quantum sufficit /kwon'təm suf'i-sit or kwan'tŭm sŭf'i-kit/ (L) a sufficient quantity.

Quapaw /kwö'pö/ n (a member of) a Native American people, orig from Arkansas, most of whom moved to Oklahoma in the 19c (pl **Qua'paws** or **Qua'paw**); the Siouan language of this people. [Quapaw, literally, people going with the current]

quaquaversal /kwā-kwə-vûr's(ə)l or kwā-kwä-/ adj dipping outward in all directions from a centre (geol); facing or bending all ways. [L quāquā whithersoever, and vertere, versum to turn]
■ **quaquaver'sally** adv.

quar. see qu.

quarantine¹ /kwor'ən-tēn/ n a time (orig for a ship forty days) of compulsory isolation or detention to prevent spread of contagion or infection; isolation or detention for such a purpose; the place where the time is spent; any period of enforced isolation; a period of forty days (obs law). ◆ vt to subject to quarantine. [Ital quarantina, from quaranta forty, from L quadrāgintā]
□ **quarantine flag** n a yellow flag displayed by a ship in quarantine, with a black spot if there is contagious disease on board.

quarantine² see **quarrender**.

quare /kwär/ adj dialect variant of **queer**.

quare impedit /kwā'rē im'pə-dit or kwä'rā im-ped'it/ (law) n a writ issued in cases of disputed presentation to a benefice, requiring the defendant to state his or her reasons for hindering the presentation. [L, why does he (or she) hinder?]

quarenden, quarender see **quarrender**.

quark¹ /kwärk or kwörk/ (phys) n a fundamental subatomic particle (thought to exist in six types: bottom, top, up, down, charmed and strange) which is not directly observable but is suggested as a unit out of which other subatomic particles are formed. [From word coined by James Joyce in Finnegans Wake (1939)]

quark² /kwärk or kwörk/ n a low-fat, soft cheese made from skimmed milk. [Late MHGer twarc, quarc, or zwarc]

quarrel¹ /kwor'əl/ n an unfriendly contention or dispute; a breach of friendship; ground of complaint or action; a cause that is fought for; a complaint, charge (obs); an objection (obs); an action at law (obs); quarrelsomeness (Shakesp); a quarreller (Shakesp). ◆ vi (**quarr'elling**; **quarr'elled**) (often with with) to cavil, find fault; to dispute violently; to fall out; to disagree violently. ◆ vt to call in question (obs); to object to (obs); to chide (now Scot); to bring or render by quarrelling (obs). [OFr querele, from L querēla, from querī, questus to complain]
■ **quarr'eller** n. **quarr'elling** n and adj. **quarr'ellous** adj (Shakesp) quarrelsome. **quarr'elsome** adj disposed to quarrel. **quarr'elsomely** adv. **quarr'elsomeness** n.
■ **quarrel with one's bread and butter** to act in a way prejudicial to one's means of subsistence. **take up a quarrel** (Shakesp) to settle a dispute.

quarrel² /kwor'əl/ n a square-headed arrow as for a crossbow (Spenser **quar'le**); a diamond-shaped pane of glass; a square tile. [OFr quarrel (Fr carreau), from LL quadrellus, from quadrus a square]
□ **quarr'el-pane** n.

quarrender, quarender /kwor'ən-dər/, **quarantine** /-ən-tin/, **quarenden** /-dən/ or **quarrington** /-ing-tən/ (SW Eng) n a kind of early-ripening red apple. [Perh cf Fr quarantain, appar applied to quick-growing peas and maize]

quarry¹ /kwor'i/ n an open excavation for building-stone, slate, etc; any source of building-stone, etc; a great mass of stone or rock (obs); a source from which information can be extracted (fig). ◆ vt (**quarr'ying**; **quarr'ied**) to dig from, or as from, a quarry; to cut into or cut away; to extract (information) from a source. [LL quareia, for quadrāria, from L quadrāre to square]
■ **quarr'iable** adj. **quarr'ier** n a quarryman.
□ **quarr'yman** n a man who works in a quarry. **quarr'ymaster** n the owner of a quarry. **quarr'y-sap** or **quarr'y-water** n the water in the pores of unquarried or newly quarried stone.

quarry² /kwor'i/ n a hunted animal; a bird flown at by a hawk; a person or thing pursued; prey; a victim; a hunter's heap of dead game; a deer's entrails given to the hounds (obs); a hawk's reward for a kill (obs); a heap of corpses (Shakesp); found in some editions of Shakespeare's Macbeth (I.2.15) perhaps meaning slaughter, spoil. [OFr cuiree, curee, said to be from cuir, from L corium a hide]

quarry³ /kwor'i/ n a quarrel of glass; a square paving-tile or slab. [A form of **quarrel²**; or perh from OFr quarré, from L quadrātus squared]
□ **quarry tile** n a square unglazed floor tile.

quart¹ /kwört/ n the fourth part of a gallon, or two pints (in UK, 1.14 litres, in USA, 0.946 litre in liquid measure, 1.1 litres in dry measure);

a quarter, region (Spenser); a fourth (obs music). [Fr quart, -e, from L quārtus fourth, from quattuor four]
■ **quartā'tion** n the mixing of gold with three parts of silver as a stage towards purification.
□ **quart'-pot** n.

quart² or **quarte** /kärt/ n a sequence of four cards in piquet, etc; the fourth of eight parrying or attacking positions in fencing (also **carte**). [Fr quarte, from Ital and L quarta fourth]
■ **quart and tierce** practice between fencers.

quartan /kwör'tən/ adj (of a fever) occurring every third (by inclusive reckoning fourth) day. ◆ n quartan malaria. [L quārtānus of the fourth]

quarte see **quart²**.

quarter /kwör'tər/ n a fourth part; a 25-cent piece, 25 cents, quarter of a dollar (N Am); the fourth part of an hour, of the year, of the moon's period (or the moon's position at the end of it), of the world, etc; one of the four periods of play into which certain games are divided; the fourth part of a cwt = 28 (or in US 25) lb avoirdupois; 8 bushels (perh orig a fourth of a ton of corn); (also **quarter-pound**) a quarter of a pound, 4oz (inf); a cardinal point, or any point, of the compass; the region about any point of the compass; a region generally; a town district inhabited by a particular class; an unspecified person or group regarded as a source of information, support, etc; a part of an army, camp, etc (Shakesp); (usu in pl) lodging, esp for soldiers; an assigned station or position; terms, relations, treatment, esp favourable (Shakesp); mercy granted to an antagonist (perh from sending to quarters); the part of a ship's side to the rear of its widest point; a limb with adjacent parts of the trunk, esp (hist) of the dismembered body of an executed person, or of an animal carcass; a haunch of a live animal; each of the two pieces on a boot or shoe from the centre of the heel to the vamp; each side of a horse's hoof; one of the four parts of a quartered shield (heraldry); an ordinary occupying one-fourth of the field (heraldry); a quartering (heraldry). ◆ vt to divide into four equal or nearly equal parts; to dismember (the body of a traitor, etc) (hist); to divide into parts or compartments; to station, lodge or put in quarters; to bear, place or divide quarterly (heraldry); (esp of dogs) to range for game, to search thoroughly. ◆ vi to be stationed; to lodge; (of a dog) to range for game; to drive a carriage or cart with the wheels between the ruts, or the horse(s) astride a rut; to drive to the side of the road, or from side to side; (of the wind) to blow onto a ship's quarter. ◆ combining form (denoting adjectivally) one-fourth part (of); (denoting adverbially) to the extent of one-fourth. [OFr quarter, from L quārtārius a fourth part, from quārtus fourth]
■ **quar'terage** n a quarterly payment; quarters, lodging. **quar'tered** adj. **quar'tering** adj (of a ship) sailing nearly before the wind; (of a wind) striking on the quarter of a ship. ◆ n assignment of quarters; a series of small upright posts for forming partitions, lathed and plastered only, or boarded also (archit); the division of a coat by horizontal and vertical lines (heraldry); one of the divisions so formed; the marshalling of coats in these divisions, indicating family alliances; any one of the coats so marshalled. **quar'terly** adj relating to a quarter, esp of a year; recurring, or published, once a quarter; divided into or marshalled in quarters (heraldry). ◆ adv once a quarter; in quarters or quarterings (heraldry). ◆ n a quarterly periodical.
□ **quart'erback** n (American football) the player between the linemen and the halfbacks, who directs the attacking play of the team. **quar'ter-binding** n a type of bookbinding in which the spine and a small part of the sides are covered with a different material than the rest of the book. **quar'ter-blood** n a person of one-quarter Native American descent. **quar'ter-bound** adj bound using quarter-binding. **quar'ter-boy** or **quar'ter-jack** n an automaton that strikes the quarter-hours. **quar'ter-bred** adj (of horses, cattle, etc) having only one-fourth pure blood. **quarter day** n the day on each of the year's quarters on which rent or interest is due to be paid. **quar'terdeck** n the part of the deck of a ship abaft the mainmast, used by cabin passengers and by superior officers (and saluted on warships). **quar'terdecker** n (naval sl) a stickler for naval etiquette. **quar'ter-evil** or **quarter-ill** n black-quarter (qv). **quar'ter-fi'nal** n the round before the semi-final in a knockout competition. **quar'ter-gallery** n a projecting balcony on a ship's quarter. **quar'ter-guard** n a guard of a battalion in camp. **quar'ter-gunner** n (US; hist) a naval petty-officer, under the gunner, a gunner's mate. **quar'ter-horse** n (US) a horse that can run a quarter of a mile or so at great speed. **quarter hour** n a period of fifteen minutes; a point marking such a period on a clock, etc. **quarter-hour'ly** adv. **quar'ter-jack** n see **quarter-boy** above; a quartermaster (sl). **quar'terlight** n a small triangular window in a car for ventilation. **quar'termaster** n (also fem **quar'termistress**) an officer who is responsible for the accommodation, weapons and supplies of a group of soldiers; a petty officer who attends to the helm, signals, etc (naut). **quartermaster-gen'eral** n a staff-officer who deals with transport, marches, quarters, fuel, clothing, etc. **quartermaster-ser'geant** n a senior non-commissioned officer with administrative duties. **quarter-mil'er** n an athlete whose speciality is the 400 metres or quarter-mile race. **quarter note** n a crotchet (N Am); a quarter-tone. **quar'ter-plate**

see under **plate**. **quarter-pound'er** *n* a burger weighing a quarter of a pound. **quar'ter-rail** *n* a rail stretching from a ship's gangway to its stern. **quar'ter-repeating** *adj* (of a repeating watch or clock) that strikes the quarter hours. **quar'ter-road** *n* a road divided into four strips by ruts and horse-track. **quar'ter-round** *n* a moulding whose section is about a quadrant, an ovolo. **quar'ter-saw** *vt* (*pat* and *pap* **quar'ter-sawed** or **quar'ter-sawn**) to saw (timber) from quartered logs, so that the face of the planks is at an angle of at least 45° to the growth rings. **quar'ter-seal** *n* the seal kept by the director of the Chancery of Scotland, known also as 'the testimonial of the Great Seal'. **quarter section** *n* (*N Am*) an area of land half a mile square, 160 acres. **quar'ter-sessions** *n pl* a court formerly held quarterly by justices of the peace (superseded in England and Wales in 1972 by crown courts). **quar'terstaff** *n* a long wooden pole with an iron tip, an old weapon of defence; the use of this weapon. **quar'ter-tone** *n* half a semitone. **quar'ter-wind** *n* a wind blowing on a ship's quarter.
■ (**a**) **quarter after** or **past** fifteen minutes after (a specified hour). (**a**) **quarter to** fifteen minutes before the hour. **at close quarters** in very near proximity; hand-to-hand. **keep a quarter** or **a bad quarter** (*obs*) to make a disturbance. **keep good quarter** (*Shakesp*) to keep good watch or good order.

quartern /kwör'tə(r)n/ (*obs*) *n* a quarter, *esp* of various measures, such as a peck, a stone, a pound (weight), a pint or a hundred. [Anglo-Fr *quartrun*, OFr *quarteron*, from *quart*(e) fourth part]
❏ **quartern loaf** *n* a four-pound loaf, made from a quarter of a stone of flour.

quarteroon see **quadroon**.

quartet, **quartette** or **quartett** /kwör-tet'/ *n* a set of four; a composition for four voices or instruments; a set of performers or instruments for such compositions. [Ital *quartetto*, dimin of *quarto*, from L *quārtus* fourth]

quartetto /kwär-tet'tō/ (*Ital*) *n* (*pl* **quartet'ti** /-tē/) a quartet.

quartic /kwör'tik/ (*maths*) *adj* of the fourth degree. ◆ *n* a function, curve or surface of the fourth degree. [L *quārtus* fourth]

quartier /kär-tjā'/ (*Fr*) *n* a specified district in a French town or city.
❏ **quartier latin** /la-tẽ/ *n* the 'Latin quarter' of Paris, on the left bank of the Seine, formerly inhabited by writers, artists and students.

quartile /kwör'tīl/ *n* an aspect of planets when their longitudes differ by 90° (*astrol*); in frequency distribution, a value such that a fourth, a half, or three-quarters of the numbers under consideration fall below it. [L *quārtus* fourth]
❏ **quartile deviation** *n* (*stats*) the distance between the values below which the lowest fourth and above which the highest fourth fall.

quarto /kwör'tō/ *adj* (of paper) having the sheet folded into four leaves or eight pages (often written **4to**); (**demy quarto** $8\frac{3}{4} \times 11\frac{1}{4}$in; **medium quarto** $9 \times 11\frac{1}{2}$in; **royal quarto** $10 \times 12\frac{1}{2}$in). ◆ *n* (*pl* **quar'tos**) a book consisting of sheets so folded, or of such a size. [L (*in*) *quārtō* (in) one-fourth]
■ **small quarto** a square octavo; a book having eight leaves to a sheet but the shape of a quarto.

quartodeciman /kwör-tō-des'i-mən/ *n* an early Christian who celebrated Easter on the 14th of Nisan (the Jewish Passover) without regard to the day of the week (also *adj*). [LL *quartodecimānus*, from L *quārtus decimus* fourteenth]

quartz /kwörts/ *n* the commonest rock-forming mineral, composed of silica, occurring in hexagonal crystals (clear and colourless when pure) or cryptocrystalline. ◆ *adj* made or composed of or with quartz. [Ger *Quarz*, from MHGer *quarz*, from WSlav *kwardy* hard]
■ **quartzif'erous** *adj* quartz-bearing. **quartz'ite** *n* a metamorphosed sandstone with the grains welded together. **quartzitic** /-it'ik/ *adj* of or like quartzite. **quartz'ose** *adj* of, like or rich in quartz. **quartz'y** *adj*.
❏ **quartz clock** or **watch** *n* one in which a quartz crystal, energized by a microcircuit, does the work of the pendulum or hairspring of the traditional clock or watch. **quartz crystal** *n* a disc or rod cut in certain directions from a piece of piezoelectric quartz and ground so that it vibrates naturally at a particular frequency. **quartz glass** *n* fused quartz resistant to high temperatures and transparent to ultraviolet radiation. **quartz lamp**, **quartz-halogen lamp** or **quartz-iodine lamp** *n* a compact source of light used for high-intensity floodlighting of large areas, in car (fog-)lamps, cine projectors, etc. **quartz'-mill** *n* a mill or machine for crushing gold-bearing quartz. **quartz-por'phyry** *n* an igneous rock with crystals of quartz and feldspar in a compact or finely crystalline ground-mass of the same. **quartz'-rock** *n* quartzite. **quartz'-schist** *n* a schistose quartzite with mica.

quasar /kwā'sär, -zär or -sər/ *n* a (starlike) point source of radiation (radio waves, etc) outside our galaxy, *usu* with a very large red shift, forming the most distant and most luminous class of bodies so far discovered. [*quasi-stellar* object]

quash /kwosh/ *vt* to crush; to subdue or extinguish suddenly and completely; to annul, reject as invalid. [OFr *quasser* (Fr *casser*), from L *quassāre*, frequentative of *quatere* to shake]

Quashee or **Quashie** /kwosh'i/ *n* a personal name among W African peoples; (without *cap*) a black person, *esp* in the W Indies; a stupid or unsophisticated black person (*W Indies*). [Twi name given to a person born on Sunday]

quasi /kwā'sī, -zī or kwä'zē/ *adv* as if, as it were. ◆ *combining form* denoting: in a certain manner, sense or degree; in appearance only, as in *quasi-historical* and *quasi-stellar*. [L]
❏ **qua'si-contract** *n* (*law*) a concept which allows a plaintiff to recover money from a defendant if non-payment would confer an unjust benefit on the latter.

Quasimodo /kwa-si-mō'dō, also -zi-/ *n* the first Sunday after Easter, Low Sunday. [From the first words of the introit for the day from Bible, 1 Peter 2.2: L *quasi modo geniti infantes*, as new-born babes]

quassia /kwosh'ə or kwosh'yə/ *n* a S American tree (*Quassia amara*; family Simarubaceae), with bitter wood and bark used in herbal remedies; a West Indian tree of the same family (*Picraena excelsa*). [Named by Linnaeus after a black slave, *Quassi*, who discovered its value against fever]

quatch see **quich**.

quatch-buttock /kwoch'bu-tək/ (*Shakesp*) *n* appar a flat or squat buttock.

quatercentenary /kwot- or kwat-ər-sen-tē'nə-ri, also -sin-, -ten'ə-ri or -sen'tin-/ *n* a 400th anniversary, or its celebration. [L *quater* four times, and **centenary**]

quaternary /kwə- or kwo-tûr'nə-ri/ *adj* consisting of four; by fours; in fours; of the fourth order; based on four; with four variables; (with *cap*) of or belonging to the most recent period of the Cenozoic era, starting 1.8 million years ago (*geol*); connected to four non-hydrogen atoms (*chem*). ◆ *n* the number four; a set of four; (with *cap*) the Quaternary period or system (*geol*). [L *quaternī* four by four]
■ **quater'nate** *adj* in sets of four. **quater'nion** *n* a set or group of four; the operation of changing one vector into another, or the quotient of two vectors, depending on four geometrical elements and expressible by an algebraical quadrinomial (*maths*); (in *pl*) a calculus concerned with this, invented by Sir William Rowan Hamilton (1805–65). **quater'nion'd** *adj* (*Milton*) divided into groups of four. **quater'nionist** *n* a person who studies quaternions. **quatern'ity** *n* fourfoldness; a set of four; a fourfold godhead.

quatorze /kə-törz'/ *n* (in piquet) the four aces, kings, queens, jacks or tens, which count as 14 points. [Fr *quatorze*, *quatorzaine* fourteen]
■ **quatorzain** /kat'ər-zān or kät-ör'zān/ *n* a stanza or poem of fourteen lines.
❏ **Quatorze Juillet** /ka-torz zhoo-yä/ or **the Quatorze** *n* 14 July, Bastille Day, a French national holiday.

quatrain /kwot'rān/ *n* a stanza of four lines, *usu* rhyming alternately. [Fr]

quatrefoil /kat'ər-foil or kat'rə-foil/ or **quatrefeuille** /-fœ-ē or -fīl/ *n* a four-petalled flower or leaf of four leaflets; an openwork design or ornament divided by cusps into four lobes (*archit*). [OFr *quatre* four, and **foil** (Fr *feuille*) leaf]

quattrocento /kwat- or kwä-trō-chen'tō/ *n* the 15c in reference to Italian art and literature. [Ital, four (for fourteen) hundred]
■ **quattrocent'ism** *n*. **quattrocen'tist** *n*.

quaver /kwā'vər/ *vi* to tremble, quiver; to speak or sing with tremulous uncertainty; to trill. ◆ *vt* to say or sing tremulously. ◆ *n* a trembling, *esp* of the voice; half a crotchet (*music*). [Frequentative from obs or dialect *quave*, early ME *cwavien* to shake; related to **quake**, **quiver**[1]]
■ **quā'verer** *n*. **quā'vering** *n* and *adj*. **quā'veringly** *adv*. **quā'very** *adj*.

quay /kē/, earlier **kay** /kā/ and **key** /kē/ *n* a landing-place; a wharf for the loading or unloading of vessels. [OFr *kay*, *cay*, perh Celtic; partly assimilated to Mod Fr spelling *quai*]
■ **quay'age** *n* provision of quays; space for, or system of, quays; payment for use of a quay.
❏ **quay'side** *n* and *adj*.

quayd /kwād/ (*Spenser*) *adj* daunted. [Perh for **quelled**]

qubit /kū'bit/ *n* the basic unit of information in quantum computing, consisting of an individual atom or subatomic particle considered as forming a binary system by representing its spin state as 1 or 0. [*quantum* and *bit*]

Que. *abbrev*: Quebec (also **Q**).

queach /kwēch/ (*obs*) *n* a thicket. [Origin obscure]
■ **queach'y** or **queech'y** *adj* forming a thicket; boggy; sickly.

quean /kwēn/ *n* a saucy girl (*archaic*); a woman of worthless character (*archaic*); a girl (*Scot*). —In NE Scotland **queyn** or **quine** /kwīn/ and the diminutives **queyn'ie** or **quin'ie** are the ordinary words for a girl. [OE *cwene* woman; cf **queen** (OE *cwēn*)]

queasy or **queazy** /kwē'zi/ *adj* nauseated, squeamish, feeling as if about to vomit; causing nausea; uneasy; (of the mind or conscience) fastidious, scrupulous; (of circumstances) unsettled (*obs*); hazardous (*obs*). [Poss OFr *coisier* to hurt, or ON *kveisa* a boil]
■ **quea'sily** *adv.* **quea'siness** *n.*

Quebec or **quebec** /kwə- or kwi-bek'/ *n* (in international radio communication) a code word for the letter *q*.

Quebecker or **Quebecer** /kwə- or kwi-bek'ər/ *n* an inhabitant of *Quebec*, in Canada.
■ **Québecois** /kā-bek-wa/ *n* (*Fr*) an inhabitant of Quebec, *esp* a French-speaking one (also *adj*).

quebracho /kā-brä'chō/ *n* (*pl* **quebra'chos**) the name of several S American trees yielding very hard wood, *incl* **white quebracho** Aspidosperma (family Apocynaceae), and **red quebracho** Schinopsis (family Anacardiaceae); their wood or bark. [Sp, from *quebrar* to break, and *hacha* axe]

Quechua /kech'wə/ or **Quichua** /kē'chwə/ *n* a people of Peru, including the ancient Inca civilization; a member of this people; their language, serving as a lingua franca. ◆ *adj* of the Quechua or their language. [Sp *Quechua, Quichua*]
■ **Quech'uan** or **Quich'uan** *adj* and *n*.

queechy see under **queach**.

queen /kwēn/ *n* a female monarch; the wife or widow of a king; a presiding goddess; a woman or (*fig*) anything that is pre-eminent in excellence, beauty, etc; a sexually functional female social insect; an adult female cat; a male homosexual, *esp* if effeminate (*sl*); a playing card bearing the picture of a queen, in value next below a king; in chess, either of two pieces, one on each side, *usu* with a top in the shape of a crown, that can move any distance in any straight line; a size of roofing-slate, 3 feet by 2. ◆ *vt* to make a queen of; to make (a pawn) into a queen when it reaches the far side of the chessboard; to rule over as queen; to supply with a queen; (with *it*) to behave like a queen, to lord it. [OE *cwēn*; Gothic *qēns*, ON *kvæn, kvān*, Gr *gynē*; cf **quean**]
■ **queen'craft** *n* skill or policy on the part of a queen. **queen'dom** *n* queenhood; the realm of a queen. **queen'hood** *n* the state of being a queen. **queen'ie** *n* a queen scallop, *esp* in SW Scotland and the Isle of Man. **queen'ing** *n* a variety of apple. **queen'ite** *n* a queen's partisan. **queen'less** *adj.* **queen'let** *n* a petty queen. **queen'-like** *adj* like a queen. **queen'liness** *n.* **queen'ly** *adj* becoming or suitable to a queen; like a queen. ◆ *adv* in the manner of a queen. **queen'ship** *n* the state, condition or dignity of a queen. **queen'side** *n* in chess, the side of the board where the queen stands at the beginning of play. **queen'y** *adj* camp, effeminate.
❑ **Queen Anne** *n* the simplified Renaissance architectural style of the early 18c, or an imitation of it; the furniture style of the early 18c, incorporating greater attention to comfort, the use of walnut, and cabriole legs. **Queen Anne's Bounty** *n* a fund for augmenting poor livings of the Church of England, formed (1703) out of first-fruits and tenths. **Queen Anne's lace** *n* cow parsley. **queen bee** *n* a fertile female bee; a woman who dominates, or is the centre of attention among, her associates; a woman in an important business position. **queen bee substance** or **queen substance** *n* a pheromone secreted by a queen bee which attracts drones and keeps workers infertile. **queen'-cake** *n* a small, soft, sweet cake with currants. **queen consort** *n* the wife of a reigning king. **queen dowager** *n* a king's widow. **queen'fish** *n* a Californian blue-and-silver fish, *Seriphus politus* (also known as **drum'fish**); a tropical food and game fish of the Carangidae. **queen mother** *n* a queen dowager who is mother of the reigning king or queen; a queen or queen bee that is a mother. **Queen of Heaven** *n* Ashtoreth; Juno; the Virgin Mary (*RC*). **queen of puddings** *n* a pudding made with egg, breadcrumbs, fruit or jam, etc, topped with meringue. **Queen of the May** *n* a May queen. **queen-of-the-mead'ow** or **-mead'ows** *n* meadowsweet. **queen olive** *n* a large variety of olive grown in Spain. **queen post** *n* one of two upright posts in a trussed roof, resting on the tie-beam and supporting the principal rafter. **queen-re'gent** *n* a queen who reigns as regent. **queen-reg'nant** *n* a queen reigning as monarch. **queen's'-arm** *n* (*hist*) a musket. **Queen's Bench** (or **King's Bench** in a king's reign) *n* a division of the High Court of Justice. **queen's bounty** see under **bounty**. **queen scallop** *n* a medium-sized scallop (*Chlamys opercularis*). **Queen's Counsel** (or **King's Counsel** in a king's reign) *n* an honorary rank of barristers and advocates; a barrister or advocate of this rank. **queen's English** see **king's English** under **king**. **Queen's Guide** (or **King's Guide** in a king's reign) *n* the rank awarded to a (Girl) Guide upon reaching the highest level of proficiency and in recognition of service to the community; a Guide of this rank. **Queen's highway** (or **King's highway** in a king's reign) *n* a public road, considered as being under royal control. **queen'-size** or **queen'-sized** *adj* (of furnishings, etc, *esp* beds and bedding) larger

than standard size, but smaller than the largest size. **Queen's Proctor** see **King's Proctor** under **king**. **queen's pudding** *n* queen of puddings (see above). **Queen's Regulations** (or **King's Regulations** in a king's reign) *n pl* the regulations governing the British Armed Forces. **Queen's Scout** (or **King's Scout** in a king's reign) *n* a Scout who has reached the highest level of proficiency, etc. **Queen's Speech** (or **King's Speech** in a king's reign) *n* the sovereign's address to parliament at its annual opening ceremony, describing proposed government legislation; an address to the nation and Commonwealth by the sovereign on Christmas day, broadcast on television and radio. **queen'-stitch** *n* an embroidery pattern of square within square. **Queen's tobacco pipe** *n* a kiln at London Docks for burning contraband goods (till 1891). **queen substance** see **queen bee substance** above. **Queen's ware** *n* cream-coloured Wedgwood ware. **queen's yellow** *n* basic mercuric sulphate.
■ **Queen Anne's dead** that is old news. **turn Queen's evidence** see under **evident**.

queene-apple /kwēn'ap-l/ (*Spenser*) *n* appar a quince. [See **quince**]

Queensberry Rules /kwēnz'bə-ri roolz/ *n pl* rules applied to boxing, *orig* published in 1867 and named after the 9th Marquess of *Queensberry* (1844–1900), who took a keen interest in sport; (loosely) standards of proper behaviour in any fight, physical or verbal.

Queensland /kwēnz'lənd/ *adj* of or relating to the state of *Queensland* in NE Australia.
■ **Queens'lander** *n* an inhabitant or native of Queensland.
❑ **Queensland blue** *n* a bluish-skinned variety of pumpkin. **Queensland nut** *n* the macadamia nut.

queer /kwēr/ *adj* odd, singular, quaint; open to suspicion; counterfeit; slightly mad, eccentric; vaguely unwell, faint or giddy; homosexual (*sl, usu derog*). ◆ *vt* (*inf*) to spoil; to put (someone) in a difficult position, or in another's bad books; to ridicule; to cheat. ◆ *n* (*derog sl*) a male homosexual. [Perh Ger *quer* across; cf **thwart**]
■ **queer'dom** *n* (*derog sl*) the state of being homosexual; homosexuals collectively. **queer'ish** *adj.* **queer'ity** *n* oddity. **queer'ly** *adv.* **queer'ness** *n.*
❑ **queer'-basher** *n.* **queer'-bashing** *n* (*sl*) the practice of making gratuitous verbal or physical attacks on homosexuals. **Queer Street** *n* debt or other difficulties; the imaginary place where debtors, etc live.
■ **queer someone's pitch** to spoil someone's chances. **queer the pitch** (*showmen's sl*) to make the place of performance unavailable. **shove the queer** (*old criminal sl*) to pass bad money.

queest /kwēst/, also **quest** /kwest/, **quoist** /kwoist/ and **quist** /kwist/ (*Scot*) *n* the ringdove or wood pigeon. [See **cushat**]

queez-maddam /kwēz-mad'əm/ (*Walter Scott*) *n* a French jargonelle pear. [Fr *cuisse-madame*]

queint[1] /kwānt/ (*Spenser*) *adj* same as **quaint**.

queint[2] /kwānt/ (*obs*) *pap* of **quench**.

quelch /kwelsh/ or kweltsh/ *vi* and *vt* to squelch. [Imit]

quelea /kwē'li-ə/ *n* a bird of the *Quelea* genus of African weaver birds, *esp Q. quelea*, which is very destructive to crops. [From African name]

quell /kwel/ *vt* to extinguish; to crush; to subdue; to disconcert, to abash (*Spenser*); to kill (*obs*). ◆ *vi* to die, perish (*Spenser*); to subside, abate (*Spenser*). ◆ *n* slaying (*Shakesp*); power of quelling (*Keats*). [OE *cwellan* to kill, causal of *cwelan* to die; cf **quail**[2]]
■ **quell'er** *n.*

quelque chose /kel-kə shōz'/ (*Fr*) *n* something unspecified; an unimportant thing.

queme /kwēm/ (*Spenser*) *vt* to please, suit, fit. [OE *cwēman*; Ger *bequem* fit]

quena /kā'nə/ *n* a type of bamboo flute from the Andes, held vertically for playing. [Am Sp, from Quechua]

quench /kwensh/ or kwentsh/ *vt* to put out (a fire, etc); to put out the flame, light or sight of, or the desire for; to stop (a discharge of electrically-charged particles); to reduce luminescence in (excited particles) (*phys*); to cool with liquid; to slake; to damp down; to put an end to; to put to silence; to destroy; to extinguish hope, etc in (*obs*). ◆ *vi* to be extinguished; to die down; to lose zeal; to subside in passion, grow cold (*Shakesp*). [OE *cwencan*, found only in the compound *ācwencan* to quench, causative of *cwincan* (*ācwincan*); cf OFris *kwinka* to go out]
■ **quench'able** *adj.* **quench'er** *n* someone who or something that quenches; a draught or drink; something introduced into a luminescent material to reduce the duration of phosphorescence (*nuclear phys*). **quench'ing** *n* and *adj.* **quench'less** *adj* not to be extinguished. **quench'lessly** *adv.*
❑ **quenched spark** *n* an oscillatory spark discharge extinguished after the first few oscillations.

quenelle /kə-nel'/ *n* a poached dumpling of finely chopped chicken, veal or fish; a gesture of defiance in which one hand touches the opposite shoulder while the other hand is pointed towards the ground. [Fr]

quep *interj* non-standard form of **gup**¹.

Quercus /*kwûr'kəs*/ *n* the oak genus of the beech family. [L *quercus* oak]

■ **quercetin** /*kwûr'sə-tin*/ *n* a bioflavonoid with antioxidant and antihistamine properties found in bracken and many foods *incl* tea, red wine and some vegetables, thought to provide some protection against heart disease. **quercetum** /*kwûr-sē'təm*/ *n* a collection of oak trees. **quer'citron** /*-si-trən*/ *n* a N American oak, the dyer's oak or yellow-barked oak; its inner bark, a source of quercetin and flavin.

querimony /*kwer'i-mə-ni*/ (*formal*) *n* complaint. [L *querimōnia*, from *querī* to complain]

■ **querimonious** /*-mō'ni-əs*/ *adj*. **querimō'niously** *adv*.

querist see under **query**.

quern /*kwûrn*/ *n* a stone mill for grinding corn, worked by hand. [OE *cweorn*; ON *kvern*, Gothic (*asilu-*)*qaírnus* (ass-)mill]
□ **quern'stone** *n*.

querpo see **en cuerpo**.

quersprung /*kver'shprŭng*/ (*skiing*) *n* a jump-turn at right angles. [Ger]

querulous /*kwer'ū-ləs, -ŭ-* or *-ə-*/ *adj* complaining; peevish. [LL *querulōsus*, from *querī* to complain]

■ **quer'ulously** *adv*. **quer'ulousness** *n*.

query or formerly often **quaere** /*kwē'ri*/ *n* an inquiry; a doubt; a question mark (?). ◆ *vt* (pat and pap **que'ried**) to inquire into; to question; to doubt; to mark with a query. ◆ *vi* to question. [L *quaere*, imperative of *quaerere*, *quaesītum* to inquire!

■ **que'rist** *n* an inquirer. **que'rying** *n* and *adj*. **que'ryingly** *adv*.
□ **query language** *n* (*comput*) any of various formalized sets of commands used to search and retrieve information in a database.

quesadilla /*ke-sə-dē'yə* or *-sa-*/ (*Mex cookery*) *n* a tortilla filled with cheese, chillis, etc, folded and fried or grilled. [Mex Sp, dimin of *queseda*, from *queso* cheese]

quest¹ /*kwest*/ *n* the act of seeking; search; pursuit; an adventure, expedition or undertaking with the purpose of achieving or finding some definite object; the object sought for; a searching party; a jury of inquest; inquiry, investigation; the collection of alms or donations (*RC*); a searching for game by dogs, or their baying or barking on finding it. ◆ *vi* to go in search; to go begging; (of dogs) to search for game; (of dogs) to bark, yelp. ◆ *vt* to go in quest of or after. [OFr *queste* (Fr *quête*), from L (*rēs*) *quaesīta* (a thing) sought, from *quaerere*, *quaesītum* to seek]

■ **quest'er** *n* a person who goes on a quest (also (*Shakesp*) **quest'ant** and **quest'rist**). **quest'ing** *n* and *adj*. **quest'ingly** *adv*.

quest² see **queest**.

question /*kwes'chən*/ *n* an inquiry; an interrogation; the putting of a problem; a demand for an answer; an interrogative sentence or other form of words in which an inquiry is put; a unit task in an examination; a problem; a subject of doubt or controversy; discussion, conversation (*Shakesp*); a subject of discussion, *esp* the particular point actually before a group of people or deliberative body; subjection to examination; examination by torture (*hist*); objection, demur; doubt; the measure to be voted upon; (vaguely) a relevant matter. ◆ *vt* to put questions to; to call to account; to examine by questions; to inquire; to inquire concerning; to throw doubt upon; regard as doubtful; to challenge, take exception to. ◆ *vi* to ask questions; to inquire; to discuss, converse (*Shakesp*). [OFr, from L *quaestiō*, *-ōnis*, from *quaerere*, *quaesītum* to ask]

■ **questionabil'ity** *n*. **quest'ionable** *adj* that may be questioned; doubtful, uncertain; open to suspicion; possibly dishonest, improper, immoral, etc; such as questions may be put to, not unwilling to be conversed with (*Shakesp*). **quest'ionableness** *n*. **quest'ionably** *adv*. **quest'ionary** *adj* asking questions (*rare*); in the form of questions. ◆ *n* an asker of questions (*obs*); a questionnaire; a quaestionary (*Walter Scott*). **questionee'** someone who is questioned. **quest'ioner** *n*. **quest'ioning** *n* and *adj*. **quest'ioningly** *adv*. **quest'ionist** *n* a questioner, a doubter; an undergraduate in the final term before proceeding to a degree (*Cambridge University* and *Harvard*; *obs*). **quest'ionless** *adj* unquestioning; beyond question or doubt. ◆ *adv* (*archaic*) certainly.
□ **ques'tion-begging** *n* and *adj* begging the question (see **beg the question** under **beg**¹). **question mark** *n* a point or mark of interrogation (?); a query or unresolved doubt. **question master** *n* someone who presides over a quiz, discussion programme or meeting, and puts the questions to the participants. **question tag** *n* a tag question (qv). **question time** *n* (in parliament) a period during each day when members can put questions to ministers.

■ **at question** questionable, open to question. **in question** under consideration; in dispute, open to question. **make question** to demur. **no question** no possibility; undoubtedly. **out of question** without

any doubt. **out of the question** not to be thought of. **question of fact** (*Eng law*) that part of the issue which is decided by the jury. **question of law** that part decided by the judge.

questionnaire /*kwes-chə-nār'* or (Fr) *kes-tē-o-ner'* or *-tyo-*/ *n* a prepared set of written questions, for purposes of statistical compilation or comparison of the information gathered; a series of questions. [Fr, from *questionner* to question, and *-aire* -ary]

questor see **quaestor**.

questrist see under **quest**¹.

quetch see **quich**.

quethe see **quoth**.

quetsch /*kwech* or *kvech*/ *n* a variety of plum, or brandy distilled from it. [Ger dialect *quetsch*(e) wild plum]

quetzal /*ket-säl', ket'* or *kwet'səl*/ *n* a Central American bird with brilliant green plumage and very long tail feathers (the **resplendent trogon**); the standard monetary unit of Guatemala (100 centavos; *pl* **quetzales** /*-sä'les*/). [Nahuatl *quetzalli* tail feather]

queue /*kū*/ *n* a line of people, etc awaiting their turn for service or attention; a set of data-processing tasks waiting in a buffer to be processed in FIFO order (*comput*); a data-storage system of this kind (*comput*); a braid of hair hanging down the back of the head, a pigtail; the tail of an animal (*heraldry*). ◆ *vt* to place or arrange in a queue. ◆ *vi* to form, or take one's place in, a queue (often with *up*). [Fr, from L *cauda* a tail]

■ **queued** /*kūd*/ *adj* tailed; in a queue. **queu'er** *n*. **queu'ing** or **queue'ing** *n*.
□ **queue'-jump** *vi* and *vt*. **queue'-jumping** *n* going ahead of one's turn in a queue, waiting list, etc (*lit* and *fig*).

quey /*kwā*/ (*Scot*) *n* a heifer; a young cow that has not yet had a calf. [ON *kvīga*; Dan *kvie*]

queyn, queynie see **quean**.

quh- /*hw-*/ obsolete Scots spelling for *wh-*. [OE *hw-*]

quia timet /*kwē'ə tim'et*/ (*law*) of or denoting an (action to obtain an) injunction to prevent a possible future harmful act. [L, because he or she fears]

quibble /*kwib'l*/ *n* an evasive turning away from the point in question to something irrelevant, merely verbal, trivial or insignificant; a petty complaint or observation; a pun, play on words. ◆ *vi* to raise petty or irrelevant objections; to argue over unimportant details; to pun or evade the issue by punning. [Perh dimin of obs *quib* quibble, which may be from L *quibus*, dative or ablative pl of *quī* who, a word frequent in legal use; or a variant of **quip**]

■ **quibb'ler** *n*. **quibb'ling** *n* and *adj*. **quibb'lingly** *adv*. **quib'lin** *n* (*obs*) a quibble.

quich /*kwich*/ (*Spenser*) *vi* to stir, to move (also (*obs* or *dialect*) **quatch**, **quetch** or **quitch**). [OE *cweccan* to shake, causative of *cwacian* to quake]

quiche /*kēsh*/ *n* a flan of plain pastry filled with a cooked egg mixture *usu* containing cheese, onion or other vegetables, ham, etc. [Fr, from Ger dialect *küchen*, dimin of *Kuchen* cake]

Quichua see **Quechua**.

quick¹ /*kwik*/ *adj* swift; speedy; brief; nimble; ready; sensitive; readily responsive; prompt to act; ready-witted; prompt to perceive or learn; hasty; living, alive (*archaic, Bible, church*, etc); pregnant (*archaic*); (of a hedge) composed of living plants; (of a fire, etc) burning briskly; (of an oven) hot; (of sand, etc) mobile, shifting; sharp (*fig*). ◆ *adv* (*inf*) without delay; rapidly; soon. ◆ *n* the sensitive parts of the body surface, *esp* under the nails; the tenderest or deepest feelings; the innermost or vital part; the living flesh (*archaic*); the living (*archaic*); a living thing (*Spenser*); a living plant, *esp* hawthorn in a hedge (also collectively); the life (*archaic*). [OE *cwic*; ON *kvikr* living]

■ **quick'en** *vt* to accelerate; to impart energy or liveliness to; to invigorate; to stimulate; to give life to; to revive. ◆ *vi* to move faster; to become alive or lively; to revive; to be stimulated; (of a pregnant woman) to reach the stage in pregnancy when the movement of the baby can be felt. **quick'ener** *n*. **quick'ening** *n* and *adj*. **quick'ie** or **quick'y** *n* (*inf*) something that takes, or is to be done in, a short time (also *adj*); an alcoholic drink to be rapidly consumed; a brief or hurried act of sexual intercourse. **quick'ly** *adv*. **quick'ness** *n*.
□ **quick-an'swered** *adj* (*Shakesp*) quick at answering. **quick assets** *n pl* readily realizable assets. **quick'-born** *adj* (*archaic*) born alive. **quick'-change** *adj* quick in making a change, *esp* (of a performer) in appearance (**quick-change artist** such a performer; a person who changes rapidly or frequently in mood or opinion). **quick'-conceiving** *adj* (*Shakesp*) quick at understanding. **quick'-eyed** *adj* having a keen eye. **quick fire** *n* rapid and continuous gunfire. **quick'-fire** *adj* (of questions, etc) following in rapid succession; (also **quick'-firing**) designed to allow a quick succession of shots. **quick'-firer** *n*. **quick'-fix** *adj* expedient and temporary as a

solution. **quick'-freeze** n very rapid freezing of food so that its natural qualities are unimpaired (also vt and vi). **quick'-frozen** adj. **quick'-hedge** n a hedge of living plants. **quick'lime** n unslaked lime, calcium oxide. **quick'-lunch** adj (of a café, etc) that serves quickly-eaten lunches with prompt service. **quick march** n (milit) a march at a fast pace. ◆ interj the command to start such a march. **quick'-match** n cotton thread impregnated with an inflammable mixture. **quick'sand** n a loose watery sand which swallows up anyone who walks on it, or objects placed on it; anything similarly treacherous. **quick'-sandy** adj. **quick'-scented** or **quick'-scenting** adj having a keen scent. **quick'-selling** adj. **quick'set** adj formed of living plants set into place. ◆ n a living plant, slip or cutting, esp of hawthorn, or a series of them, set to grow for a hedge; a quickset hedge. **quick-sight'ed** adj having quick sight or discernment. **quick-sight'edness** n. **quick'silver** n mercury. ◆ adj of mercury; quick-moving; mercurial. ◆ vt to overlay or to treat with quicksilver or amalgam. **quick'silvered** adj. **quick'silvering** n the mercury on the back of a mirror. **quick'silverish** or **quick'silvery** adj. **quick'step** n a march step or tune in fast time; a fast foxtrot. ◆ vi to dance a quickstep. **quick'-sticks** or **quick'-stick** adv (inf) without delay. **quick-tem'pered** adj irascible. **quick'thorn** n hawthorn. **quick time** n (milit) a rate of about 120 steps per minute in marching. **quick trick** n (bridge) a card that should win a trick in the first or second round of the suit. **quick'-water** n a solution of nitrate of mercury. **quick-witt'ed** adj able to think quickly and effectively. **quick-witt'edness** n.

■ **a quick one** a quick drink; a quickie. **quick and dirty** produced as a swift, but often inelegant, expedient. **quick off the mark** prompt to act. **quick on the draw** swift to draw a gun from its holster; prompt in response or action.

quick² /kwik/ n couch grass or its rootstocks (also **quick'en** or **quick grass**). (Scot and N Eng form of **quitch¹**]

quicken¹ /kwik'ən/ (Scot and N Eng) n the rowan (also **quick'beam** (Eng), **quick'en-tree**, **wick'en** or **wick'y**). [OE cwicbēam, cwictrēow aspen]

quicken² see **quick¹,²**.

quid¹ /kwid/ (inf) n (pl **quid**; or in sense of ready money (obs) **quids**) a pound sterling (£); formerly, a guinea. [Origin obscure]

■ **not the full quid** (Aust) simple-minded, dopey. **quids in** in a very favourable or profitable situation.

quid² /kwid/ n something chewed or kept in the mouth, esp a piece of tobacco. [**cud**]

quid³ /kwid/ n that which a thing is, substance. [L, what]

quidam /kwī'-/ or /kwē'dam/ n (pl **quidams**) somebody; a certain person. [L quīdam]

quiddany /kwid'ə-ni/ n a jelly or thick syrup made from quince-juice and sugar. [L cotōnea quince, from cydōnia; see **quince**]

quidditch /kwid'ich/ n an imaginary game in which players fly on broomsticks. [Created by children's writer JK Rowling (born 1965)]

quiddity /kwid'i-ti/ or (archaic) **quiddit** /kwid'it/ n the inherent nature or essence of anything; any trifling nicety; a quibble. [Med L quidditās, -tātis, from L quid what]

■ **quidd'itative** adj.

quidnunc /kwid'nungk/ n an inquisitive, gossiping person. [L quid nunc? what now?]

quid pro quo /kwid prō kwō/ n something given or taken as equivalent to another, often as retaliation or in return for a previous favour; the action or fact of giving or receiving thus. [L, literally, something for something]

quiesce /kwi- or kwī-es'/ vi to quiet down; (of consonants in Hebrew) to become silent. ◆ vt (comput) to stop the operations of, make inactive. [L quiēscere to rest]

■ **quiesc'ence** or **quiesc'ency** n rest; inactivity; (in Hebrew) a consonant's becoming silent. **quiesc'ent** adj resting; (of a letter) not sounded; inactive, without input to activate it (comput); still. **quiesc'ently** adv.

quiet /kwī'ət/ adj at rest; calm; undisturbed; free from disturbing noise; without loudness, gaudiness, ostentation, formality or obtrusiveness of any kind; still; without bustle or restlessness; without much activity; peaceful; gentle; inoffensive. ◆ n freedom from noise or disturbance; calm; stillness; rest; peace. ◆ vt and vi to quieten. [L quiētus quiet, calm]

■ **quī'eten** vt and vi to make or become quiet. **quī'etening** n and adj. **quī'eter** n. **quī'eting** n and adj. **quī'etism** n mental tranquillity; the doctrine that religious perfection on earth consists in passive and uninterrupted contemplation of the Deity. **quī'etist** n. **quīetist'ic** adj. **quī'etive** n and adj sedative. **quī'etly** adv. **quī'etness** n. **quī'etsome** adj (Spenser) undisturbed. **quī'etude** n quietness.

■ **keep quiet about** to say nothing about. **keep something quiet** to preserve the secrecy of something by saying nothing about it. **on the quiet** (inf; or sl **on the QT** or **q.t.**) clandestinely, secretly; unobtrusively.

quietus /kwī-ē'təs or kwi-ā'tŭs/ n release from life; extinction, death; silencing, quashing or elimination; discharge from office; an acquittance on payment of money due. [L quiētus est he is at rest or quiet]

quiff /kwif/ n a tuft of hair brushed up and back away from the forehead, or (formerly) a lock of hair oiled and brushed down over the forehead; a prostitute (sl); a male (esp effeminate) homosexual (sl). [Poss **coif**]

quight see **quit**, **quite¹**.

qui-hi or **qui-hye** /kwī'hī'/ n a prosperous Anglo-Indian, esp in Bengal, during British colonial rule. [Hindi koī hai, the call for a servant, Is anyone there?, from koī anyone, and hai is]

quill¹ /kwil/ n the hollow basal part of a feather; a large feather; a porcupine's spine; a goose or other feather used as a pen; a pen generally, or by metonymy, the writer's profession; something made from a quill feather, such as a toothpick, an angler's float or a plectrum; a weaver's bobbin (orig made of reed or other material); a hollow non-rotating shaft (also **quill drive**; engineering); a reed, hollow stalk or internode, etc (obs); a small tube (obs); a musical pipe made from a hollow stem; hence throat, or perh voice (Shakesp); a roll of curled bark, eg of cinnamon; a cylindrical fold (obs). ◆ vt to goffer, crimp; to wind on a bobbin. [Origin obscure; cf LGer quiele, Ger Kiel]

■ **quilled** adj provided with, or formed into quills; tubular. **quill'ing** n a strip of cloth gathered into cylindrical folds; decorative work characterized by longitudinal pleats or grooves.

❑ **quill'-driver** n (derog) a clerk (now milit sl); an assiduous writer. **quill'-driving** n. **quill'-feather** n a large stiff wing or tail feather. **quill'man** n (obs) a clerk. **quill'-nib** n a quill-pen shortened for use with a holder. **quill'-pen** n a quill used as a pen. ◆ adj using or suggestive of old-fashioned, slow and protracted methods or style (in office or literary work). **quill'wort** n any plant of the genus Isoetes (from the quill-like leaves).

quill² /kwil/ (Shakesp) n a combination (in the phrase **in the quill** in a body, in concert). [Fr cueille a gathering]

quillai /ki-lī'/ n the soapbark tree. [Am Sp]

■ **Quillaja** or **Quillaia** /ki-lī'ə or -lē'ə/ n a genus of S American rosaceous trees whose bark has soaplike properties; a quillai.

quillet /kwil'it/ n a subtlety in argument; a quibble. [Perh L quidlibet what you will]

quillon /kē-yõ'/ n either arm of the cross guard of a sword-handle. [Fr]

quilt /kwilt/ n a bedcover consisting of padding between two outer layers of cloth stitched through all three layers into compartments or channels; any material or piece of material so treated; a duvet, continental quilt; a patchwork quilt; a thick coverlet; a thick covering placed over beehive frames; the inner part of a cricket or hockey ball. ◆ vt to pad, cover or line with a quilt; to form into a quilt; to stitch in; to seam like a quilt; to cover with interlaced cord; to thrash (Aust inf). [OFr cuilte (Fr couette), from L culcita a cushion]

■ **quilt'ed** adj. **quilt'er** n a person or machine that makes quilting. **quilt'ing** n the act of making a quilt or quilted material; something which is quilted; cloth for making quilts; cloth with a pattern like a quilt; a covering of rope yarn; a thrashing with a rope's end.

❑ **quilting bee** or **party** n a gathering of women to help someone in making a quilt, combined with social amusement. **quilt'ing-cotton** n cotton wadding. **quilt'ing-frame** n an adjustable frame for holding a fabric for quilting.

quim /kwim/ (vulgar sl) n the female genitalia. [Origin uncertain; a relationship with **coomb¹**, **cwm** has been suggested]

quin see **quintuplet** under **quintuple**.

quina, kina or **china** /kē'nə/ n (also **quinaquina, kinakina, chinachina** /kē-nä-kē'nə/ or **quinquina** /kin- or king-kē'nə, also kwing-kwī'nə/) cinchona bark; any tree yielding it; quinine. [Sp quina, quinaquina, from Quechua kina, kina-kina, kinkina bark]

■ **quinic** /kwin'ik/ adj.

❑ **quinic acid** n an acid obtained from cinchona bark.

quinacrine /kwin'ə-krēn/ (pharm) n another name for **mepacrine**. [quinine and acridine]

quinary /kwī'nə-ri/ adj fivefold; by or in fives; of the fifth order; based on five; with five variables. ◆ n a set of five. [L quīnī five by five]

■ **qui'nate** adj (bot) consisting of five leaflets.

quince /kwins/ n a golden, round or pear-shaped, fragrant, acid fruit, used esp for jellies, marmalade, etc; the tree or shrub (Cydonia oblonga), related to pear and apple, that bears it; extended to the closely related Japanese quince (see **japonica** under **Japonic**) and to the unrelated Bengal quince, the bael-fruit. [Orig pl of quine, from OFr *coin* (Fr *coing*), from L *cotōneum*, from Gr *kydōnion*, from *Kydōniā* a town in Crete]

quincentenary /kwin-sen-tēʹnə-ri, -sin-tenʹə-ri or -senʹtin-ə-ri/ n and adj a five-hundredth anniversary or its celebration. [Irregularly formed from L *quinque* five, and **centenary**]
■ **quincentennial** /-tenʹi-əl/ adj and n.

quinche /kwinsh/ (*Spenser*) vi to stir, move. [Ety uncertain]

quincunx /kwinʹkungks/ n an arrangement of five things at the corners and centre of a square (eg as seen on cards and dice), or of a great number of things (*esp* trees) spaced in the same way; an aspect of 150° between two heavenly bodies (*astrol*). [L *quīncunx*, from *quīnque* five, and *uncia* a twelfth part]
■ **quincuncial** /-kunʹshl/ adj of or in a quincunx; (of aestivation) having two leaves overlapping at each edge, two underlapping at each edge, and one overlapping and underlapping (*bot*). **quincunʹcially** adv.

quine see **quean**.

quinella /kwi-nelʹə/ (*orig US*, now *esp Aust*) n a form of bet in which the punter has to select the two horses (or dogs, etc) which will come in first and second but not give their order of placing. [Am Sp *quiniela*]

quingentenary /kwin-jen-tēʹnə-ri, -tenʹə-ri or -jenʹtə-nə-ri/ n a quincentenary (also *adj*). [L *quīngentī* five hundred]

quinic see under **quina**.

quinie see **quean**.

quinine /kwi-nēnʹ, kwinʹēn or (*N Am*) kwīʹnīn/ n a colourless, odourless, very bitter alkaloid ($C_{20}H_{24}O_2N_2.3H_2O$), obtained from cinchona bark, or one of its salts, used as an antipyretic and analgesic, formerly widely used to treat malaria. [See **quina**]
■ **quinʹidine** /-i-dēn/ n a crystalline alkaloid drug, isomeric with quinine, used to treat irregularities in the heart rhythm. □ **quinine water** n a beverage made by flavouring water with quinine, lemon, etc.

quink-goose /kwingkʹgoos/ (*dialect*) n the brent goose. [Prob imit]

quinnat /kwinʹət/ n the king salmon. [From a Native American name]

quinoa /kēʹnō-ə or kēnʹwä/ n a S American goosefoot, with seeds used like rice, and leaves used like spinach. [Sp *quínoa*, from Quechua *kinua*]

quinol /kwinʹol/ n a reducing agent and photographic developer, $C_6H_4(OH)_2$, obtained by reduction of quinone (also called **hydroquinone** and **1,4-dihydroxybenʹzene**). [**quina**]
■ **quinoid** /kwinʹoid/ or **quinonoid** adj. **quinoidʹal** adj a quinonoid substance. **quinʹoline** /-ə-lēn/ n a pungent, colourless, oily liquid (C_9H_7N), extracted from coal tar. **quinʹolone** n any of a group of antibiotics *esp* effective against infections of the urinary and respiratory tracts resistant to conventional antibiotics. **quinone** /kwinʹōn or kwin-ōnʹ/, also **kinone** /kēʹnōn/ n a golden-yellow crystalline compound ($C_6H_4O_2$) *usu* prepared by oxidizing aniline; a reddish or colourless isomer of this; a general name for a benzene derivative in which two oxygen atoms replace two hydrogen. **quinonoid** /kwi-nōʹnoid or kwinʹən-oid/ adj like a quinone.

quinqu- /kwin-kw-/ or **quinque-** /kwin-kwi-/ combining form denoting five. [L *quīnque* five]
■ **quinquecostate** /kwin-kwi-kosʹtāt/ adj (L *costa* rib) five-ribbed. **quinquefarious** /kwin-kwi-fāʹri-əs/ adj (L -*fārius*, *poss* from *fārī* to speak) fivefold; in five rows. **quinquefoliate** /kwin-kwi-fōʹli-āt/ adj (L *folium* leaf) with five leaflets. **quinquennʹiad** n quinquennium. **quinquennʹial** adj occurring once in five years; lasting five years. ◆ n a fifth anniversary or its celebration. **quinquennʹially** adv. **quinquennium** /kwin-kwenʹi-əm/ n (*pl* **quinquennʹia**) (L *annus* year) a period of five years. **quinquereme** /kwinʹkwi-rēm/ n (L *rēmus* an oar) an ancient ship with five banks of oars. **quinquevʹalence** (or /-väʹ/) n. **quinquevalent** or **quinquivalent** /kwin-kwevʹə-lənt or -kwi-väʹ/ adj having a valency of five.

quinquagenarian /kwin-kwə-ji-nāʹri-ən/ n a person who is fifty years old, or between fifty and sixty (also *adj*). [L *quinquāgēnārius* relating to fifty, from *quinquāgintā* fifty]
■ **quinquagenary** /-jēʹnə-ri/ adj (*rare*) of, containing, based on, fifty; quinquagenarian (also *n*).

Quinquagesima /kwin-kwə-jesʹi-mə/ n (also **Quinquagesima Sunday**) the Sunday before Lent begins, *appar* as being fifty days before Easter Sunday (by inclusive reckoning). [L *quinquāgēsimus* fiftieth, from *quinquāgintā* fifty]
■ **quinquagesʹimal** adj of the number fifty; of fifty days.

quinque-, **quinquennium**, etc see **quinqu-**.

quinquina see **quina**.

quinquivalent see under **quinqu-**.

quinsy /kwinʹzi/ n suppurative tonsillitis, acute inflammation of the tonsil with the formation of pus around it. [LL *quinancia*, from Gr *kynanchē*; see **cynanche**]

■ **quinʹsied** adj suffering from quinsy.
□ **quinʹsy-berry** n the blackcurrant. **quinsʹy-wort** n squinancy wort.

quint¹ /kwint/ n an organ stop a fifth above the basic pitch; a fifth (*obs music*); the E string of a violin; a five-stringed tenor viol (also **quinte**); /kint or (*old*) kent/ a sequence of five cards in piquet, *esp* **quint major** ace to ten, and **quint minor** jack to seven. [Fr *quinte*, from L *quīntus* fifth]

quint² see **quintuplet** under **quintuple**.

quint- /kwint-/ combining form denoting fifth. [L *quīntus* fifth]

quinta /kinʹtə/ n a country house in Spain or Portugal. [Sp and Port]

quintain /kwinʹtin or -tən/ (*hist*) n a post for tilting at, often with a turning crosspiece to strike the unskilful tilter; the sport of tilting at such a post. [OFr *quintaine*, thought to be from L *quīntāna via* the road adjoining the fifth maniple in a Roman military camp]

quintal /kwinʹt(ə)l/ n 100 kilograms; formerly, a hundredweight. [Fr and Sp *quintal*, from Ar *qintār*, from L *centum* a hundred]

quintan /kwinʹtən/ adj (of a chill or fever) occurring every fourth (or by inclusive reckoning fifth) day. [L *quīntānus* of the fifth]

quinte¹ /kãt/ (*fencing*) n the fifth of eight parrying or attacking positions. [Fr]

quinte² see **quint¹**.

quintessence /kwin-tesʹəns or kwinʹte-səns/ n the pure concentrated essence of anything; the most essential part, form or embodiment of anything; a dynamical field that is repulsed by gravity and induces a vacuum energy, exerting a negative, outward pressure that is thought to cause the acceleration of the expansion of the universe (*astron*); *orig* a fifth entity, in addition to the four elements. [Fr, from L *quīnta essentia* fifth essence]
■ **quintessential** /-ti-senʹshl/ adj. **quintessenʹtialize** or **-ise** vt. **quintessenʹtially** adv.

quintet, **quintette** or **quintett** /kwin-tetʹ/ n a composition for five voices or instruments; a set of performers or instruments for such compositions; a group of five people or things. [Ital *quintetto*, dimin of *quinto*, from L *quīntus* fifth]

quintetto /kwēn-tetʹtō/ (*Ital*) n (*pl* **quintetʹti** /-tē/) a quintet.

quintic /kwinʹtik/ (*maths*) adj of the fifth degree.

quintile /kwinʹtīl/ n any of four values which divide the items of a frequency distribution into five groups; any of the five groups so formed; an aspect of 72° between two heavenly bodies (*astrol*). [L *quīntus* fifth]

quintillion /kwin-tilʹyən or -i-ən/ n a thousand raised to the sixth power (10^{18}); (*esp* formerly, in Britain) a million raised to the fifth power (10^{30}). ◆ adj being a quintillion in number. [Fr, from L *quīntus* fifth, and **million**]
■ **quintillʹionth** adj and n.

quintroon /kwin-troonʹ/ (*old*) n the offspring of a person of European descent and an octoroon; a person who is fifth (inclusive) in descent from a black person. [Sp *quinterón*, from L *quīntus* fifth]

quintuple /kwinʹtū-pl, kwin-tūʹpl or -tooʹ/ adj fivefold; having five parts, members or divisions. ◆ n five times as much. ◆ vt and vi to multiply by five. [L *quīntus* fifth, on the model of **quadruple**]
■ **quinʹtuplet** (also /-tūʹ/) n a set of five things; a group of five notes played in the time of four; one of five (children or animals) born at one birth (*inf* short form **quin** or (*N Am*) **quint**). **quinʹtuply** /-pli or -tūʹpli/ adv.

quintuplicate /kwin-tūʹpli-kāt/ adj fivefold. ◆ n one of five corresponding things; fivefoldness. ◆ vt to make fivefold. [L *quīntuplex*, -*icis*, from *quīntus* fifth, and *plicāre* to fold]
■ **quintuplicaʹtion** n.

quinze /kwinz/ n a card game, like vingt-et-un, the object being to score as close to fifteen as possible without going above it. [Fr, fifteen]

quip /kwip/ n a short, clever remark; a gibe; a quibble; a fanciful jest or action; a knick-knack (*archaic*). ◆ vi to utter a quip or quips. ◆ vt (*obs*) to assail with quips. [Perh from obs *quippy*, which may be from L *quippe* forsooth]
■ **quipʹish** adj. **quipʹster** n a person given to making clever remarks.

quipu /kēʹpoo/ n a mnemonic device consisting of various colours of knotted cords, used by the ancient Incas (also **quipʹo** (*pl* **quipʹos**)). [Quechua *quipu* knot]

quire¹ /kwīr/ (*printing*) n the twentieth part of a ream, 24 sheets of paper (now often 25) of the same size and quality; formerly, four sheets of paper or parchment folded together to make eight leaves; (also **quair** /kwār/) a (quire-filling) book or poem (*obs*). ◆ vt to fold in quires. [OFr *quaier* (Fr *cahier*), prob from LL *quaternum* a set of four sheets, from L *quattuor* four]

quire² /kwīr/ n an obsolete spelling of **choir**.
■ **quirister** /kwirʹis-tər/ n (*obs*) chorister.

Quirinus /kwi-rī'nəs or kwi-rē'nŭs/ n (Roman myth) an Italic god of war, etc, afterwards identified with the deified Romulus. [L *Quirīnus*]

■ **Quirinal** /kwir'in-əl/ n one of the hills of Rome; the Italian government, as opposed to the Vatican (from the palace on the hill). **Quirinalia** /kwir-i-nā'li-ə/ n pl (*ancient Rome*) a festival held in honour of Quirinus, on 17 February.

quirister see under **quire²**.

Quirites /kwi-rī'tēz or kwi-rē'tās/ n pl the citizens of ancient Rome in their civil capacity. [L *Quirītēs*, orig the Samnite people of *Cures* (united with the Romans)]

quirk /kwûrk/ n a trick or peculiarity of action, style or behaviour; a sudden turn, twist, jerk or flourish; an acute sharp-edged groove alongside a moulding (*archit*); an artful evasion; a quibble; a quip; a trick, knack, way (*Shakesp*). ◆ vi to quip; to move jerkily. ◆ vt to provide with a quirk. [Origin unknown]

■ **quirk'ily** adv. **quirk'iness** n. **quirk'ish** adj. **quirk'y** adj.

quirt /kwûrt/ n a braided hide riding whip. ◆ vt (*US*) to strike with a quirt. [Mex Sp *cuarta*]

quisling /kwiz'ling/ n a person who aids the enemy; a native puppet prime minister set up by an occupying foreign power. [Vidkun *Quisling*, Norwegian prime minister during German occupation (1940–45)]

quist see **queest**.

quit /kwit/ or (*archaic*) **quite** (*Spenser* **quight** or **quyte**) /kwīt/ vt (**quitt'ing** (*archaic* **quit'ing**); **quitt'ed** or **quit** (*archaic* **quit'ed**)) to depart from; to cease to occupy; (*with of*) to rid (oneself); to let go; to leave off, cease (*esp N Am*); to resign from; to behave, acquit (oneself; *archaic*); to absolve, release from obligation; to clear off, discharge (a debt, etc); to repay, requite (*obs*); to free, rid (*obs*); to clear of blame, etc, acquit (*obs*). ◆ vi to leave off, cease (*esp N Am*); to resign; to depart. ◆ adj (**quit**) set free; clear, rid; quits; released from obligation. [OFr *quiter* (Fr *quitter*), from LL *quiētāre* to pay, from L *quiētāre* to make quiet, from *quiētus* quiet]

■ **quits** adj even; neither owing nor owed. **quitt'al** n (*Shakesp*) requital. **quitt'ance** n a release; a discharge from debt; a receipt; requital. ◆ vt (*obs*) to repay. **quitt'er** n a shirker; a person who gives up easily.

□ **quit'claim** n (*law*) a deed of release, as of relinquishment of a claim or portion of mining ground. ◆ vt to relinquish claim or title to; to release, discharge. **quit'-rent** n a (*usu* nominal) rent in money or kind in lieu of services.

■ **call it quits** or **cry quits** (or formerly **quittance**) to declare oneself even with another, and so satisfied. **double or quits** see under **double**. **quit scores** to balance accounts.

qui tam /kwī tam or kwē tam/ n a legal action by an informer partly on his or her own behalf, partly on the state's. [From the first words, L *quī tam* who as much (for the king as for himself)]

quitch¹ /kwich/ or **quitch grass** n couch grass. [OE *cwice*; cf **couch grass**, **quick²**]

quitch² see **quich**.

quite¹ (*Spenser* **quight**) /kwīt/ adv completely, wholly, entirely; really, actually; somewhat, fairly; (often **quite so**) exactly, indeed, yes (*inf*). [**quit**]

■ **quite a** (*inf*) (with *adj* and *n*) a very; (with *n* alone) an outstanding or exceptional. **quite something** (*inf*) something remarkable or excellent.

quite² see **quit**.

quittance see under **quit**.

quitter¹ see under **quit**.

quitter² or **quittor** /kwit'ər/ n pus (*obs* except *W Indies*); (**quittor**) a fistulous sore on a horse's hoof (*vet*). [Poss OFr *quiture* cooking, from L *coctūra*]

quiver¹ /kwiv'ər/ vi to shake with slight and tremulous motion; to tremble; to shiver. ◆ vt (of a bird) to cause (the wings) to move rapidly. [Prob imit, perh connected with **quiver³**]

■ **quiv'er** or **quiv'ering** n. **quiv'eringly** adv. **quiv'erish** adj. **quiv'ery** adj.

quiver² /kwiv'ər/ n a case for arrows. [OFr *cuivre*; prob Gmc in origin; cf OHGer *kohhar* (Ger *Kocher*), OE *cocer*]

■ **quiv'ered** adj provided with a quiver; kept in a quiver. **quiv'erful** n (*fig*) a large family (Psalm 127.5).

quiver³ /kwiv'ər/ (*Shakesp*) adj nimble, active. [ME *cwiver*, from OE *cwifer*, found in the adverbial form *cwiferlīce* zealously]

qui vive /kē vēv/ n a state of alertness, in the phrase *on the qui vive*. [From the French sentry's challenge, literally (long) live who?, ie whom do you support?, from *qui* who, and *vive*, 3rd pers sing pr subjunctive of *vivre* to live, from L *vīvere*]

quixotic /kwik-sot'ik/ adj like Don Quixote, the knight in the romance of Cervantes (1547–1616), extravagantly romantic in ideals or chivalrous in action; (of ideals, actions) absurdly generous and unselfish.

■ **quixot'ically** adv. **quix'otism** n. **quix'otry** n.

quiz /kwiz/ n (pl **quizz'es**) a set of questions (designed for amusement or entertainment), such as a test on general knowledge or on a special subject; a TV or radio programme, or organized event, in which contestants are asked a prepared set of questions; an interrogation; an oral test (*N Am*); the remaining noun senses are *obs*: an odd-looking person or (*Austen*) thing; a monocle, often with a handle; a piece of banter or quiet mockery; a mocking look; a hoax; a person who practises any of these; a bandalore. ◆ vt (**quizz'ing**; **quizzed**) to question, interrogate; to test (a class, etc) orally (*N Am*); to poke fun at (*obs*); to eye, *esp* with an air of mockery (*obs*). ◆ vi (*obs*) to poke fun. [Origin obscure]

■ **quizz'er** n. **quizz'ery** n. **quizz'ical** adj mocking, questioning; mildly perplexed; amusing, comical. **quizzical'ity** n. **quizz'ically** adv. **quizzifica'tion** n quizzing. **quizz'ify** vt (*obs*) to cause to look odd. **quizz'iness** n (*rare*) oddness. **quizz'ing** n.

□ **quiz'master** n a question master. **quiz show** n a TV or radio quiz. **quizzing glass** n (*obs*) a monocle.

quo' /kə, ko, kō or kwō/ vt a Scots form of **quoth**.

■ **quod** n an obsolete form of **quoth**, used *esp* at the end of a poem, followed by the poet's name.

quoad /kwō'ad/ (*L*) so far as.

■ **quoad hoc** /hōk or hok/ as far as this. **quoad omnia** /om'ni-ə or -a/ in respect of all things. **quoad sacra** /sā'krə or sa'kra/ (*Scot*) as far as concerns sacred matters (applied to a parish created and functioning for ecclesiastical purposes only).

quod¹ /kwod/ (*L*) which.

■ **quod erat demonstrandum** /er'at dem-ən-stran'dəm or dām-ōn-stran'dŭm/ which was to be proved or demonstrated (*abbrev* QED). **quod erat faciendum** /fā-shē-en'dəm or fa-ki-en'dŭm/ which was to be done (*abbrev* QEF). **quod erat inveniendum** /in-vā-ni-en'dəm/ which was to be found (*abbrev* QEI). **quod vide** /vī'dē, vi' or wī'de/ (*pl* **quae vide** /kwē, kwī/) which see.

quod² /kwod/ (*sl*) n prison. ◆ vt to imprison. [Origin unknown]

quod³ see under **quo'**.

quodlibet /kwod'li-bet/ n a philosophical argument or disputation, *esp* as an exercise; a humorous medley of tunes. [L, what you please, from *quod* what, and *libet* it pleases]

■ **quodlibetā'rian** n a person who engages in quodlibets. **quodlibet'ic** or **quodlibet'ical** adj.

quodlin /kwod'lin/ an obsolete form of **codlin** (see **codling¹**).

quoif /koif/ same as **coif**.

quoin /koin/ n a salient angle, *esp* of a building; a cornerstone, *esp* a dressed cornerstone; a keystone; a voussoir (qv); a wedge, *esp* for locking type in a chase, or for raising a gun. ◆ vt to wedge; to secure or raise by wedging. [See **coin**]

■ **quoin'ing** n.

quoist see **queest**.

quoit /koit or kwoit/ n a flat ring for throwing so as to encircle a hob or pin; a dolmen cover; a dolmen; same as **coit**; (in *pl*, treated as *sing*) the game played with quoits. ◆ vi to play at quoits. ◆ vt to throw like a quoit. [Origin obscure]

■ **quoit'er** n.

quo jure? /kwō joo'rē or yoo're/ (*L*) by what right?

quokka /kwok'ə/ n a small-tailed wallaby (*Setonix brachyurus*) found in SW Australia. [From an Aboriginal language]

quoll /kwol/ n any of several small Australian marsupials, a native cat. [From an Aboriginal language]

quondam /kwon'dam/ adj former. [L, formerly]

quonk /kwongk/ (*inf*) n any accidental noise made too close to a microphone and thus disrupting a radio or television programme. ◆ vi to make such a noise. [Imit]

Quonset hut® /kwon'set or kwon'sit hut/ n the US equivalent of the Nissen hut.

quooke /kwŭk/ (*Spenser*) pat of **quake**.

quop /kwop/ (*obs* or *dialect*) vi to throb. [ME *quappe*; imit]

Quorn® /kwörn/ n a vegetable protein composed of minute filaments, derived from a type of fungus, used as a low-calorie, cholesterol-free meat substitute that absorbs flavours in cooking.

quorum /kwō' or kwö'rəm/ n a minimum number of persons necessary for transaction of business in any body; *orig* a number of specially named justices of the peace who had to be present before any business could be done (*obs*); (loosely) the whole body of justices (*obs*). [L *quōrum* of whom, from the wording of the commission, of whom we will that you, so-and-so, be one (two, etc)]

■ **quo'rate** adj having or being (at least) a quorum.

quot. *abbrev* : quotation.

quota /kwō'tə/ *n* (pl **quo'tas**) a proportional share, a part assigned; a regulated quantity of goods allowed by a government to be manufactured, exported, imported, etc; a regulated number of immigrants allowed into a country per year, students allowed to enrol for a course, fish allowed to be caught, etc. [L *quota (pars)* the how-manieth (part), from *quotus* of what number, from *quot* how many] ❑ **quo'ta-hopper** *n*. **quo'ta-hopping** *n* the practice of registering a fishing vessel in a port of another country in order to use the fish quota of that country. **quota immigrant** *n* an immigrant (to the USA) admitted as one of the yearly quota allowed to his or her country of origin, as opposed to a **non-quota immigrant** (eg as child or spouse of a resident citizen). **quota quickie** *n* a quickly-produced, low-budget, poor-quality film made in Britain (but *usu* US-financed) in the 1920s and 30s to exploit a government measure requiring UK cinemas to show a set quota of British-made films. **quota sample** *n* a proportional sample of people in a specific category or categories of the population defined in terms of age, sex, social class, etc. **quota sampling** *n* the use of quota samples to obtain data, as for opinion polls and marketing purposes. **quota system** *n* the imposition of specified quotas by a government or other agency.

quote /kwōt or formerly kōt/ (*Shakesp* **coat**, **coate** or **cote**) *vt* to cite as evidence, authority, illustration or example; to give the actual words of; *orig* to divide into chapters, verses, etc, number the chapters of, or mark with references (*obs*); to give the current price of, *esp* to state the market price of (shares, etc) on the Stock Exchange list; to enclose within quotation marks; to examine, scrutinize (*Shakesp*); to record, note, set down, mention, in writing or mentally (*obs*); to set down in the prompter's book as due to be called (*theatre*). ◆ *vi* to give the actual words, used as an interjection to indicate that what follows immediately is a quotation; to give a statement of price and terms (*commerce*). ◆ *n* (*inf*) a quotation; a quotation mark. [LL *quotāre* to divide into chapters and verses, from L *quotus* of what number, from *quot* how many] ■ **quo'table** *adj* lending itself, herself or himself to quotation; fit to quote. **quo'tableness** or **quotabil'ity** *n*. **quo'tably** *adv*. **quota'tion** *n* the act of quoting; something that is quoted; a short passage of music, written or played, extracted from a longer piece; a statement of price and terms submitted to a prospective purchaser (*commerce*); the current price of shares, etc on the Stock Exchange list; registration of a company, etc with the Stock Exchange so that shares may be listed; a quadrat for filling blanks in type (*orig* those between marginal references). **quota'tious** *adj* given to quoting. **quo'tative** *adj* quotatious; indicating or consisting of a quotation. **quo'ter** *n*. **quote'worthy** *adj*.

❑ **quotation mark** *n* either of the marks (*printing* and *inf* **quotes**) used to note the beginning and end of a quotation (see also **inverted commas** under **comma**). **quoted company** *n* one whose shares are quoted on the Stock Exchange.

quoth /kwōth/ (*archaic*) *vt* (*1st and 3rd pers sing, pat,* of the otherwise obsolete verb **quethe**) said (followed by its subject). [OE *cwæth*, preterite of *cwethan* to say; cf **bequeath**] ■ **quō'tha** *interj* forsooth, indeed (literally, quoth he; see **a**[2]).

quotidian /kwō- or kwo-tid'i-ən/ *adj* daily; (of a fever, etc) recurring daily; (of any activity of a living creature or a living part) that follows a regular recurrent pattern; everyday, commonplace. ◆ *n* a fever or chill that recurs daily. [L *quotīdiānus*, from *quotīdiē* daily, from *quot* how many, and *diēs* day]

quotient /kwō'shənt/ (*maths*) *n* the number of times one quantity is contained in another; a ratio, *usu* multiplied by 100, used in giving a numerical value to ability, etc (see **achievement quotient** under **achieve** and **intelligence quotient** under **intelligent**); a measure of the extent or significance of something (*inf*). [L *quotiens*, *quotiēs* how often, from *quot* how many (with -*t* erroneously added as though from the genitive ending of the present participle, -*entis*)]

quotition /kwō-tish'ən/ *n* a division regarded as repeated subtraction or measuring. [From L *quot* how many]

quotum /kwō'təm/ *n* quota. [L, neuter of *quotus*; see **quota**]

quo vadis? /kwō vä'dis/ (*L*) where are you going?, the words used by Peter to Christ (Bible, John 16.5; Vulgate version) and, in tradition, by Christ later appearing to Peter as he fled from Rome.

quo warranto /kwō wo-ran'tō/ (*legal hist*) *n* a writ (abolished 1938) calling upon a person to show by what warrant he or she held (or claimed) a franchise or office. [L *quō warrantō* by what warrant]

Quran, Qur'an /ko- or kŭ-rän'/ see **Koran**.

qursh /koorsh/ *n* (pl **qursh**) a Saudi Arabian monetary unit, $\frac{1}{5}$ of a riyal. [From Ar *qirsh*]

quyte see **quit**.

qv or **q.v.** *abbrev* : *quantum vis* (*L*), as much as you wish; *quod vide* (*L*), which see (pl **qqv** or **qq.v.**).

qwerty or **QWERTY** /kwûr'ti/ *n* the standard arrangement of keys on an English-language typewriter keyboard; a keyboard having its keys laid out as on a standard typewriter (also **qwerty keyboard**). ◆ *adj* of or having such a keyboard. [From the letters at the top left-hand side of the keyboard]

qy *abbrev* : query.

■ words derived from main entry word; ❑ compound words; ■ idioms and phrasal verbs

Rr

a b c d e f g h i j k l m n o p q r s t u v w x y z

Rotis Semi Sans Designed by Otl Aicher in 1989. Germany.

R or **r** /är/ n the eighteenth letter in the modern English alphabet, seventeenth in the Roman (sometimes called the 'dog letter', from the trilling of the tip of the tongue in its pronunciation in rhotic accents); anything shaped like the letter R.

◻ **R months** n pl the time when oysters are in season (from the spelling of the names of the months from September to April). ■ **the three R's** reading, writing and arithmetic.

R or **R.** abbrev : rand (South African currency); Réaumur's thermometric scale (also **Réau**); Rector; regina (L), Queen; Republican (US); rex (L), King; River; Röntgen unit; rook (in chess); ruble(s); run(s) (cricket); rupee(s).

R symbol : (as a medieval Roman numeral) 80.

R symbol : electrical resistance.

R̄ symbol : (medieval Roman numeral) 80000.

® symbol : registered trademark.

r or **r.** abbrev : radius; recipe (L), take; right; rule (law).

RA abbrev : Rear Admiral; Republic of Argentina (IVR); rheumatoid arthritis; Royal Academician; Royal Academy of Arts; Royal Artillery.

Ra /rä/ or **Re** /rā/ n the ancient Egyptian sun-god.

Ra (chem) symbol : radium.

RAAF abbrev : Royal Australian Air Force.

rabanna /rə-ban'ə/ n a Madagascan raffia fabric. [Malagasy]

rabat or **rabatte** /rə-bat'/ (geom) vt to rotate into coincidence with another plane. [Fr rabattre to lower]
■ **rabat'ment** or **rabatte'ment** n. **rabatt'ing** n.

rabato /rə-bä'tō/ same as **rebato**.
■ **rabatine** /rab'ə-tēn/ n (Walter Scott) a low collar.

Rabb. abbrev : Rabbinical.

rabbet /rab'it/ n a groove cut to receive an edge. ◆ vt (**rabb'eting**, **rabb'eted**) to groove; to join by a rabbet. [Fr rabat, from rabattre to beat back]
◻ **rabb'eting-machine** n. **rabb'eting-plane** n. **rabb'eting-saw** n. **rabb'et-joint** n.

rabbi (with cap when prefixed, as in Chief Rabbi) /rab'ī/ n (pl **rabb'is**) a Jewish expounder or doctor of the law (also **rabbin** /rab'in/ (pl **rabb'ins**); archaic); the leader of a Jewish synagogue. [Heb rabbi my great one, from rabh great master]
■ **rabb'inate** n the post or tenure of office of a rabbi; a body or gathering of rabbis. **rabbin'ic** or **rabbin'ical** adj relating to the rabbis or to their opinions, learning and language. **Rabbin'ic** n the late Hebrew language. **rabbin'ically** adv. **rabb'inism** n the doctrine or teaching of the rabbis; a rabbinical peculiarity of expression; the late Jewish belief which regarded the oral and written laws as being of equal value. **rabb'inist** or **rabb'inite** n a person who adheres to the Talmud and traditions of the rabbis. **rabboni** /rab-ō'ni or -nī/ interj (Bible) my great master.

rabbit¹ /rab'it/ n a small burrowing mammal of any of several genera of the family Leporidae, related to the hare; its flesh (as food); its fur; an inferior player at golf, cricket, etc; a timid person; an unimportant, insignificant person; same as **go-devil** (see under **go¹**) (mining); (in pl; also **white rabbits**) spoken before anything else on the first day of the month, to invoke good luck. ◆ vi to hunt rabbits; to talk at length and in a rambling fashion (inf; often with on; orig rhyming slang rabbit and pork, talk). [ME rabet; poss from ONFr]
■ **rabb'iter** n a person who hunts rabbits. **rabb'itry** n a place where rabbits are kept; the practice of playing as a rabbit in games. **rabb'ity** adj.
◻ **rabbit fever** n another term for **tularaemia**. **rabb'itfish** n a cartilaginous fish of the genus Chimaera; any of several other fish thought to resemble a rabbit. **rabbit food** n (derog inf) salad or other vegetables eaten raw. **rabbit hole** n a rabbit's burrow. **rabbit hutch** n a box for housing rabbits. **rabbit punch** n a blow on the back of the neck. **rabb'it-squirrel** n a viscacha of the genus Lagidium, found in the mountainous parts of western S America. **rabb'it-sucker** n (Shakesp) a sucking rabbit. **rabbit warren** see under **warren¹**.
■ **be at it like rabbits** (sl) to have sexual intercourse frequently and eagerly. **Welsh rabbit** see **rarebit** under **rare¹**. **white rabbits** see **rabbit** (n) above.

rabbit² /rab'it/ vt to confound (often in od rabbit, d'rabbit, or drabbit, for God rabbit). [Perh a facetious substitution for **rat¹**]

rabble¹ /rab'l/ n a disorderly gathering or crowd; a mob; (with the) the lowest class of people; a confused stream of words. ◆ adj of or like a rabble. ◆ vt and vi to gabble. ◆ vt to mob. [Cf Du rabbelen to gabble, LGer rabbeln]
■ **rabb'lement** n a rabble; tumult. **rabb'ling** n (esp Scot hist) the mobbing and ousting of the Episcopal 'curates' at the Revolution.
◻ **rabb'le-rouse** vi. **rabb'le-rouser** n a person who stirs up the common people to discontent and violence esp by inflammatory speeches, a demagogue. **rabb'le-rousing** n. **rabble rout** n (obs) the mob, rabble.

rabble² /rab'l/ n a device for stirring molten iron, etc in a furnace. ◆ vt to stir with a rabble. [Fr râble, from L rutābulum a poker]
■ **rabb'ler** n.

rabboni see under **rabbi**.

Rabelaisian /ra-bə-lā'zi-ən/ n a follower, admirer or student of François Rabelais (died 1553 or 1554). ◆ adj of or like Rabelais; extravagantly humorous; robustly outspoken; coarsely indecent.
■ **Rabelais'ianism** n.

rabi /rub'ē/ n the spring grain harvest in India, Pakistan, etc. [Ar rabī' spring]

rabid /rab'id/ adj raging; fanatical (fig); affected with rabies. [L rabidus (adj), rabiēs (noun), from rabere to rave]
■ **rab'ic** adj of rabies. **rabid'ity** or **rab'idness** n. **rab'idly** adv. **rabies** /rā'bēz, -bi-ēz or ra'/ n the disease called hydrophobia (fear of water being a symptom), caused by a virus transmitted by the bite of an infected animal.

RAC abbrev : Royal Armoured Corps; Royal Automobile Club.

raca /rä'kə/ (Bible) adj worthless. [Chaldee rēkā (a term of reproach)]

racahout or **raccahout** /rak'ə-hoot/ n acorn meal. [Fr, from Ar rāqaut]

raccoon or **racoon** /ra- or rə-koon'/ n a smallish American carnivore (Procyon lotor, or other species) with black-striped tail and face, related to the bears; its fur. [Algonquian]
◻ **raccoon'-berry** n a member of the Podophyllum. **raccoon'-dog** n a raccoon-like wild dog (genus Nyctereutes) of E Asia.

race¹ /rās/ n a competitive trial of speed as by running, driving, sailing, etc; (in pl) a meeting for horse- or dog-racing; a competition in getting ahead of others figuratively; a running or racing place (rare); a run or onward rush (archaic and Scot); a fixed course, track or path over which anything runs; a channel bringing water to or from a millwheel; a groove in which anything runs (such as ball-bearings or a rope); a passage through which sheep pass, eg to be dipped (Aust and NZ); a regular traverse of a fixed course, as of the sun; a rapid flow or current of the tides. ◆ vi to run, go, drive, sail, etc swiftly; to contend in speed with others; (of an engine, propeller, etc) to run wildly when resistance is removed; to own racehorses or watch horse-racing as a hobby. ◆ vt to cause (a car, horse, etc) to race; to rush (an action); to contend in speed or in a race with. [ON rās; OE ræs]
■ **ra'cer** n a person or that which races; any of several non-venomous N American snakes of the genus Coluber. **ra'cing** n. **ra'cy** adj.
◻ **race'-ball** n a ball held in connection with a race meeting. **race'card** n a programme for a race meeting. **race'course, race'path** or **race'track** n a course for running races over. **race'-cup** n a piece of plate forming a prize at a race. **race'goer** n an attender at race meetings. **race'going** n. **race'horse** n a horse bred for racing. **race meeting** n an organized occasion for horse-racing. **race'-walker** n.

race'-walking *n* a form of racing in which the competitors walk as fast as possible, but must not run. **race'way** *n* a millrace; a channel or groove for directing or controlling movement; a track for running races over. **racing bit** *n* a light jointed ringbit. **racing car** *n*. **racing certainty** *n* a thing certain to happen.

race² /rās/ *n* the descendants of a common ancestor, *esp* those who inherit a common set of characteristics; such a set of descendants, narrower than a species; a breed; a stud or herd (*obs*); ancestry, lineage, stock; the condition of belonging by descent to a particular group; inherited disposition; a class or group, defined otherwise than by descent; a sex (*obs*); peculiar flavour, as of wine, by which its origin may be recognized; raciness, piquancy. [Fr, from Ital *razza*, of doubtful origin]

■ **racial** /rā'shl, -shyəl* or *-shi-əl/ adj* of or relating to race. **ra'cialism** *n* racism. **ra'cialist** *n* and *adj* racist. **racialis'tic** *adj*. **ra'cially** *adv*. **racia'tion** *n* formation locally of new, distinct biological groups smaller than species. **rac'ism** *n* hatred, rivalry or bad feeling between races; belief in the inherent superiority of some races over others, *usu* with the implication of a right to be dominant; discriminative treatment based on such belief. **rac'ist** *n* and *adj*.

❑ **race'-baiting** *n* persecution on the grounds of race; incitement of racial hatred. **race hatred** *n* animosity accompanying difference of race. **race memory** *n* folk-memory. **race relations** *n pl* social relations between members of different races living in the same country or community. **race riot** *n* a riot caused by perceived discrimination on the grounds of race. **race suicide** *n* voluntary cessation of reproduction, leading to the extinction of the race. **racial unconscious** same as **collective unconscious** (see under **collect**). ■ **play the race card** to introduce the topic of race for one's own advantage, often to impute racism to an opponent or to appeal to a racist audience.

race³ /rās/ (*Shakesp*) *n* a rootstock of ginger. [OFr *rais*, from L *rādīx*, *-īcis* a root]

race⁴ /rās/ *n* a white streak down an animal's face (also **ratch** or **rach**). [Origin unknown]

race⁵ /rās/ *vt* to scratch; to raze (*Spenser*); to erase (*Spenser*); to slash (*Shakesp*). ◆ *n* a cut, slit or scratch. [An otherwise obs form of **raze¹**]

race⁶ /rās/ (*Spenser*) *vt* to tear away or off, to pluck, snatch (also (*Shakesp*) **rase**). [OFr *arrachier*]

raceme /ra-, rə- or rā-sēm', or ras'ēm/ (*bot*) *n* an inflorescence in which stalked flowers are borne in acropetal succession on a main stalk or lateral branches; a similar group of spore-cases. [L *racēmus* a bunch of grapes]

■ **racemate** /ras'i-māt/ *n* a racemic mixture. **racemation** /ras-i-mā'shən/ *n* a gleaning or gathering of grapes; a residue; a cluster or bunch of anything, *esp* grapes. **racemed** (also /ras' or ra-sē'/) *adj* in or having racemes. **racemic** /ra-sē'mik or -sem'ik/ *adj* applied to an acid obtained from a certain kind of grape, an optically inactive form of tartaric acid; hence applied to similar mixtures of dextrorotatory and laevorotatory enantiomorphs. **rac'emism** *n* the quality of being racemic. **racemizā'tion** or **-s-** *n* a change into a racemic form. **rac'emize** or **-ise** *vt* and *vi*. **racemose** /ras'i-mōs/ *adj* of the nature of, or like, a raceme or racemes; of, in or having racemes; like a bunch of grapes.

rache, rach or **ratch** /rach/ (*archaic*) *n* a dog that hunts by scent. [OE *racc* setter; ON *rakki*]

rachis or **rhachis** /rā'kis/ *n* (pl **rachises, rhachises** /rak'i-sēz/, **rachides** or **rhachides** /rāk'i-dēz/) the spine; an axis, eg of a feather, an inflorescence or a pinnate leaf, etc. [Gr *rhachis*, *-ios*, or *-eōs* spine]

■ **ra'chial** *adj*. **rachidial** /rə-kid'/ (*rare*) or **rachid'ian** *adj*. **rachilla** /rə-kil'ə/ *n* the axis of a grass spikelet. **rachischisis** /ra-kis'ki-sis/ *n* (Gr *schisis* cleavage) a severe form of spina bifida.

rachitis or **rhachitis** /ra- or rə-kī'tis/ (*med*) *n* rickets. [Gr *rhachītis* inflammation of the spine, adopted by Dr Gleeson in 1650 in the belief that it was the etymon of **rickets**]

■ **rachitic** /-kit'ik/ *adj*.

Rachmanism /rak'ma-ni-zm* or *-mə-/ *n* the conduct of a landlord who charges extortionate rents for property in which very bad slum conditions prevail. [From the name of one such landlord exposed in 1963]

■ **Rach'manite** *adj*.

racial, etc, **racism**, etc see under **race²**.

raciness see under **racy¹**.

racino /rə-sē'nō/ (*US*) *n* (pl **raci'nos**) a racetrack that offers additional facilities for gambling. [**race¹** and **casino**]

rack¹ /rak/ *n* an instrument for stretching, *esp* an instrument of torture; an extreme pain, anxiety or doubt (*fig*); stress, *esp* of weather; a framework, grating, shelf, etc on or in which articles are laid or set aside; a grating from which farm animals, etc may pull down fodder; a bar or framework as for chaining a prisoner (*Spenser*); a bar with teeth to work into those of a wheel, pinion, cog, etc. ◆ *vt* to stretch or move forcibly or excessively; to strain; to wrest, overstrain, distort; to torture; to practise rapacity upon; to extort (*Spenser*); to put in a rack; to separate (ore) by washing it on an inclined plane (*mining*); to move or adjust by rack and pinion. [Prob MDu *recke* (Du *rek, rak*) or LGer *reck, recke, rack*; cf ON *rakkr* straight, Ger *Rack* rail, *recken* to stretch; Eng **reach¹**]

■ **racked** *adj* (also, *non-standard*, **wracked**) tortured, tormented; (in combination) denoting tortured or distressed by, as in *disease-racked*, etc. **rack'er** *n*. **rack'ing** *n* and *adj*.

❑ **rack and pinion** *n* a means of turning rotatory into linear or linear into rotatory motion by a toothed wheel engaging in a rack. **rack price** *n* (*N Am*) the price at which a product is made available to a retailer or dealer, wholesale price. **rack rail** *n* a cogged rail, as on a rack-and-pinion railway. **rack railway** *n* a mountain railway with a rack in which a cogwheel on the locomotive works. **rack'-rent** *n* a rent stretched to the utmost annual value of the property rented, an exorbitant rent; a rack-renter. ◆ *vt* to subject to such rents. **rack'-renter** *n* a person who charges or pays rack-rent. **rack'work** *n* a mechanism with a rack.

■ **on the rack** extremely anxious or distressed; (of skill, etc) stretched to limits. **rack and manger** wasteful abundance (*esp* in the phrase *live at rack and manger*); waste and destruction (*perh* from confusion with *rack and ruin*). **rack one's brains** to use one's memory or reasoning powers to the utmost. **rack up** to accumulate points (in a score).

rack² /rak/ *n* same as **wrack¹**, destruction; a crash (*Milton*). [**wrack¹**, or ON *rek* wreckage]

■ **rack and ruin** a state of neglect and collapse.

rack³ /rak/ *vt* to draw off from the lees. [Provençal *arracar*, from *raca* husks, dregs]

rack⁴ /rak/ *n* the neck and spine of a forequarter of a carcass, *esp* as a cut of meat (*orig dialect*); a vertebra (*obs*); a horse's bones. [Perh OE *hracca* occiput]

rack⁵ /rak/ (now *esp US*) *n* a horse's gait in which the legs at the same side move nearly together. ◆ *vi* to walk with such a gait. [Origin obscure]

■ **rack'er** *n*.

■ **rack off** (*Aust inf*) to go away (often as *imperative*).

rack⁶ /rak/ *n* flying cloud (*Shakesp*); driving mist; a track; a shallow ford (*Scot*). ◆ *vi* (*Shakesp*) to drift, to drive. [Appar ON *rek* drifting wreckage, or some related form; cf **wrack²**, **wreck¹** and **wreak¹**; OE *wrecan* to drive]

rack⁷ /rak/ *n* aphetic for **arrack**.

❑ **rack'-punch** *n*.

rack⁸ /rak/ *n* a young rabbit's skin. [Origin unknown]

racket¹ /rak'it/ *n* a bat with *usu* roughly elliptical head, of wood or metal strung with catgut or nylon, for playing tennis, badminton, etc; a snowshoe of similar design. ◆ *vt* to strike with a racket. [Fr *raquette*, poss from Ar *rāhat*, colloquial form of *rāha* the palm of the hand]

■ **rack'ets** *n sing* a simplified derivative of the old game of tennis, similar to squash, played by two or four people in a four-walled court.

❑ **rack'et-court** *n*. **rack'et-ground** *n*. **rack'et-press** *n* a press for keeping a racket in shape. **rack'et-tail** *n* a hummingbird with two long racket-shaped feathers. **rack'et-tailed** *adj*.

racket² /rak'it/ *n* din; clamour; hubbub; hurly-burly; fuss; noisy or hustling gaiety; dissipation; a noisy merry-making; a dodge; fraudulent, violent, or otherwise unscrupulous moneymaking activities; strain of excitement; responsibility; liability for expenses; job or occupation (*sl*). ◆ *vi* to make or engage in a racket; to go about making a great, unnecessary noise (often with *about*); to have a full and exciting social life (*archaic*; often with *about*). ◆ *vt* to disturb, stir or affect by racket. [Prob imit]

■ **racketeer'** *n* a person who extorts money or other advantage by threats or illegal interference. ◆ *vi* to act as a racketeer. **racketeer'ing** *n*. **rack'eter** *n* a noisy or dissipated person. **rack'etry** *n*. **rack'ety** *adj* noisy; energetic and excitable.

■ **stand the racket** to endure the strain; to take the consequences or responsibility; to pay expenses.

racket³ or **rackett** /rak'it/ *n* a Renaissance or Baroque wind instrument developed in Germany, sounded through a double reed, the forerunner of the bassoon. [Ger *Rachett*, orig *raggett*, of uncertain origin]

raclette /ra-klet'/ *n* a semi-soft cow's milk cheese, *orig* from the Valais region of Switzerland; a dish comprising melted raclette scraped from a large section of the cheese while it is heated, often served with boiled potatoes. [Fr, a small scraper]

racloir /ra-klwär'/ (*Fr*) *n* a scraper.

racon /rā'kon/ *n* a radar beacon. [*radar* and *beacon*]

raconteur /ra-kon-tûr'/ or /rä-kɔ̃-tœr'/ n a teller of anecdotes (also fem **raconteuse** /-tœz/). [Fr]
■ **raconteur'ing** n.

racoon see **raccoon**.

Racovian /rə-kō'vi-ən/ n a member of a group of 17c Polish Socinians whose seminary was at Raków (also adj).

racquet /rak'it/ n same as **racket**[1].
□ **racq'uetball** or **rack'etball** n (N Am) a game played by two or four players in a walled court with rubber balls and short-handled strung rackets.

racy[1] /rā'si/ adj (**ra'cier**; **ra'ciest**) exciting the mind by strong thought or language; spirited; pungent; zestful; risqué; (of wine) having a distinctive flavour imparted by the soil. [**race**[2]]
■ **ra'cily** adv. **ra'ciness** n the quality of being racy.

racy[2] see under **race**[1].

RAD abbrev : reflex anal dilatation.

rad[1] /rad/ (Spenser) pat and pap of **read**[1], and pat of **ride**.

rad[2] /rad/ (Scot) adj afraid. [ON hræddr]

rad[3] /rad/ n (also with cap) short form of **radical** (in politics). ◆ adj (sl, esp and orig US) excellent, radically and admirably up to date (short for **radical**).

rad[4] /rad/ n (pl **rad** or **rads**) a unit of dosage of any radiation, equal to 100 ergs of energy for one gram of mass of the material irradiated. [**radiation**]

rad symbol : radian (SI unit).

rad. abbrev : radiator; radius; radix (L), root.

RADA /rä'də/ abbrev : Royal Academy of Dramatic Art.

RADAR abbrev : Royal Association for Disability and Rehabilitation.

radar /rā'där/ n the use of high-powered radio pulses, reflected or regenerated, for locating objects or determining one's own position; equipment for sending out and receiving such pulses. [Acronym from radio detection and ranging, appropriately a palindrome word]
□ **radar altimeter** n a high altitude radio altimeter. **radar astronomy** n the use of pulsed radio signals to measure distances and map the surfaces of objects in the solar system. **radar beacon** n a fixed radio transmitter whose signals enable an aircraft, by means of its radar equipment, to determine its position and direction. **radar gun** n a speed gun (qv) that operates by means of radar. **ra'darscope** n a cathode-ray oscilloscope on which radar signals can be seen. **radar trap** n a device using radar which enables the police to identify motorists exceeding the speed limit over a particular section of the road (see also **speed trap** under **speed**).

RADC abbrev : Royal Army Dental Corps.

raddle[1] /rad'l/ n reddle or ruddle (red ochre). ◆ vt to colour or mark with red ochre; to rouge coarsely. [See **ruddle**]
■ **radd'led** adj (of a person) aged and worsened by debauchery; coloured as by raddle.
□ **radd'leman** n.

raddle[2] /rad'l/ n a flexible rod or strip of wood used to make hurdles, fences or (with plaster) walls, by weaving between uprights; a hurdle, door, fence, etc so made; a hedge formed by interweaving the branches of trees; a wooden bar used in weaving. ◆ vt to interweave; to thrash (N Eng). [Anglo-Fr reidele rail]

raddocke /rad'ək/ (Shakesp) same as **ruddock**.

rade /rād/ Scot and N Eng form of **rode**[1]. [See **ride**]

radge /raj/ (Scot) adj angry, obstreperous; sexually excited, lustful. ◆ n a bad temper, a rage; an unpleasant person. [Variant of **rage**, perh influenced by Romany raj]

radial /rā'di-əl/ adj relating to a ray or radius; along, or in the direction of, a radius or radii; having rays, spokes or parts diverging from a centre; arranged like spokes or radii; near the radius of the arm (med). ◆ n a radiating part; a radial artery, nerve, engine, plate, tyre, etc. [LL radiālis, from L radius]
■ **radiale** /-ā'li (L ra-di-ä'le)/ n (pl **radia'lia**) a wrist-bone in line with the radius. **rādiality** /-al'/ n radial symmetry. **radialization** or **-s-** /rād-yəl-ī-zā'shən/ n. **ra'dialize** or **-ise** vt to arrange radially. **rā'dially** adv in the manner of radii or of rays.
□ **radial artery** n the smaller branch of the brachial artery at the elbow. **radial drill** n (engineering) a large drilling machine in which the drilling head is capable of radial movement along a horizontal arm, which is itself adjustable in angle. **radial engine** n one with its cylinders radially arranged (as opposed to in line). **radial keratotomy** n eye surgery involving cuts around the cornea. **radial-ply tyre** n a tyre in which layers or plies of fabric in the carcass are wrapped in a direction radial to the centre of the wheel. **radial symmetry** n symmetry about several planes intersecting in a common axis. **radial tyre** n a radial-ply tyre. **radial velocity** n the speed of motion along the observer's line of sight, esp to or from a star.

radian /rā'di-ən/ n the derived SI unit of plane angle (symbol **rad**), equal to the angle between two lines which, when drawn from the centre of a circle, divide off on its circumference an arc equal to its radius, nearly 57.3°. [L radius]

radiant /rā'di-ənt or rā'dyənt/ adj emitting rays; issuing in rays; transmitted by radiation; glowing; shining; with happy emotion, lit up, beaming. ◆ n that which emits radiations; a point from which rays emanate; the centre from which meteoric showers seem to emanate; a straight line from a point about which it is conceived to revolve (geom). [L radiāns, -antis, prp of radiāre to radiate, from radius]
■ **rā'diance** or **rā'diancy** n the state of being radiant; a measure of the amount of electromagnetic radiation being transmitted from or to a point (on a surface). **rā'diantly** adv.
□ **radiant energy** n energy given out as electromagnetic radiation. **radiant heat** n heat transmitted by electromagnetic radiation.

radiata /rä-di-ä'tə or -ā'tə/ n an orig Californian variety of pine tree, now grown esp in New Zealand and Australia for timber (also **radiata pine**).

radiate /rā'di-āt/ vi to emit rays; to shine; to issue in rays; to diverge from a point or points; to transmit without the use of cables, by radio. ◆ vt to send out in or by means of rays; to communicate by radio, without wires; to broadcast. ◆ adj /-it, -āt or -āt/ having rays; having ray-florets; spreading like a ray or rays; radial; radially arranged; of or belonging to the Radiata. ◆ n an animal of the Radiata. [L radiāre to shine, radiātus rayed, from radius]
■ **Rādia'ta** n pl in Cuvier's obsolete classification, the lowest sub-kingdom of animals, radially symmetrical, including echinoderms, coelenterates, polyzoans, etc. **rā'diated** adj. **rā'diately** adv. **rādiā'tion** n the act of radiating; the emission and diffusion of rays; that which is radiated; energy, esp nuclear rays, transmitted in electromagnetic waves; radial arrangement. **rādiā'tional** adj. **ra'diative** or **rādiā'tory** adj. **rā'diātor** n that which radiates; an apparatus for radiating or diffusing heat, eg for warming a room, or cooling an engine; a radio transmitting aerial.
□ **radiation belts** see **Van Allen (radiation) belts**. **radiation oncologist** see **radiologist** under **radio-**. **radiation pattern** n a graphic representation of the electromagnetic field strength produced by an antenna. **radiation sickness** n an illness due to excessive absorption of radiation in the body, marked by diarrhoea, vomiting, internal bleeding, decrease in blood cells, loss of teeth and hair, reduction of sperm in the male, etc.

radical /rad'i-kl/ adj relating to, constituting, proceeding from or going to the root; fundamental; original; intrinsic; inherent; thorough; primary; primitive; implanted by nature; not derived; proceeding from near the root (bot); of or concerning the root of a word (linguistics); of or concerning the roots of numbers (maths); favouring, involving or necessitating thoroughgoing but constitutional social and political reform (politics; usu with cap); (with cap) of or relating to a political party holding such beliefs; fine, excellent (sl). ◆ n a root, in any sense; (often with cap) an advocate of radical reform or a member of the Radical party; a group of atoms behaving like a single atom and passing unchanged from one compound to another, now usu confined to electrically neutral entities as distinguished from charged ions (also **rad'icle**; chem). [L rādīx, -īcis a root]
■ **Rad'icalism** n the principles or spirit of a Radical. **radicality** /-kal'i-ti/ n. **radicalizā'tion** or **-s-** n. **rad'icalize** or **-ise** vt and vi to make or become radical. **rad'ically** adv. **rad'icalness** n. **rad'icand** n a quantity written under the root sign in a mathematical expression, indicating the root to be calculated. **rad'icant** adj rooting from the stem. **rad'icāte** adj rooted; deeply rooted; firmly established; fixed. ◆ vt to root; to plant or fix deeply and firmly. **rad'icāted** adj rooted, established. **radicā'tion** n rooting; implanting; rootedness; general character of the root-system. **rad'icel** /-sel/ n a rootlet. **rad'icellose** adj. **radicicolous** /-sik'ə-ləs/ adj inhabiting or parasitic on roots. **radiciform** /rə-dis'/ adj like a root. **radiciv'orous** adj root-eating. **rad'icle** n a little root; the part of a seed that becomes the root; a rhizoid; a radical (chem); the rootlike origin of a vein or nerve. **radic'ūlar** adj relating to a radicle, a rootlet, or the root of a tooth, nerve, etc. **rad'icūle** n. **radic'ulose** adj having many rootlets or rhizoids.
□ **radical axis** n the locus of a point of equal potency with respect to two circles. **radical chic** n (chiefly US) the trend amongst socialites of the late 1960s and early 1970s of mixing with and affecting the views, dress, style, etc of radicals. **radical mastectomy** see under **mastectomy**. **radical sign** n the symbol √ indicating a square root. ■ **free radical** see under **free**.

radicchio /ra-dē'ki-ō/ n a purple-leaved variety of chicory from Italy, used raw in salads. [Ital]

radices see **radix**.

radicle see **radical**.

radiesthesia /rā-di-es-thē'zi-ə, -zyə or -zhə/ n sensitivity to forms of radiation from any source, eg detecting water with a dowsing-rod, diagnosing illness with a pendulum, etc, considered an extrasensory power. [L *radius* ray; New L *esthesia* feeling].
■ **radiesthē'sist** n. **radiesthet'ic** adj of or relating to radiesthesia.

radii see **radius**.

radio /rā'di-ō/ n (pl **rā'dios**) a generic term applied to methods of signalling through space, without connecting wires, by means of electromagnetic waves generated by high-frequency alternating currents; a wireless receiving, or receiving and transmitting, set; a wireless message or broadcast; the business of sound broadcasting; a broadcasting channel. ◆ adj of, for, transmitted or transmitting by electromagnetic waves. ◆ vt and vi to communicate by transmitting (a radio message). [L *radius* a rod, spoke, radius, ray]
❑ **radio altimeter** see under **altimeter**. **radio amateur** n a person licensed to send and receive radio messages privately on certain shortwave bands. **radio assay** n analysis of a substance from the radiation it emits. **radio astronomy** n astronomical study by means of radar; study of radio waves generated in space. **radio beacon** n an apparatus that transmits signals for direction-finding. **radio communication** n wireless telegraphy or telephony. **radio compass** n a radio direction-finding instrument. **radio fix** n the identification of a ship's or aircraft's position from radio signals it emits. **radio frequency** n a frequency suitable for radio transmission, about 3kHz to 300GHz (**radio-frequency heating** heating, such as dielectric heating, by means of a radio-frequency electric current). **radio galaxy** n a galaxy emitting a particularly high level of radio-frequency energy. **radio ham** n (inf) a radio amateur. **radio microphone** n a microphone with a miniature radio transmitter, and therefore not requiring any cable. **radio pill** n an ingestible capsule containing a tiny radio transmitter that will send out information about bodily processes. **radio spectrum** n the range of radio frequencies. **radio star** n a discrete source of radio waves in outer space, generally corresponding with no visual object and known only by radio astronomy. **radio station** n a place where radio transmitters and (if radio-communication is involved) receivers are installed; a broadcasting company, association, etc. **radio telescope** n an apparatus for the reception, analysis and transmission in radio astronomy of radio waves from and to outer space. **radio wave** n an electromagnetic wave of radio frequency.

radio- /rā-di-ō-/ combining form (some of the following words may also be hyphenated) denoting: rays; radiation; radium; radius; radio, wireless; (of product or isotope) radioactive, as in **rādio-actin'ium** and **rādio-tho'rium**, both isotopes of thorium, or **rādioel'ement** (chem). [Ety as for **radio**]
■ **rādioact'ive** adj emitting radiation (**radioactive waste** any radioactive waste material, esp spent fuel from a nuclear reactor). **rādioact'ively** adv. **rādioactiv'ity** n spontaneous disintegration, first observed in certain naturally occurring heavy elements (radium, actinium, uranium, thorium) with emission of α-rays, β-rays, and γ-rays; the subatomic particles or radiation emitted by this process; disintegration brought about by high-energy bombardment. **rādioaut'ograph** n another term for **autoradiograph**. **rādiobiol'ogist** n. **rādiobiol'ogy** n the study of the effects of radiation on living tissue. **rādiocar'bon** n a radioactive isotope of carbon, specif carbon-14 (**rādiocarbon dating** a method of establishing the age of any organic material, eg wood or paper, by measuring the content of carbon-14). **rādiochem'ical** adj. **rādiochem'ist** n. **rādiochem'istry** n the chemistry of radioactive elements and compounds. **rādioel'ement** n a radioisotope. **rādiogenic** /-jen'ik/ adj produced by radioactive disintegration; suitable for broadcasting. **rādiogoniom'eter** n a radio direction-finder. **rā'diogram** n an X-ray photograph, a radiograph; a wireless telegram; (for **rādio-gram'ophone**) a combined wireless receiver and gramophone. **rā'diograph** /-gräf/ n a recorded image, usu a photograph, produced by X-rays; formerly, the wireless telegraph. **rādiog'rapher** n a technician involved in radiology, eg in the taking of radiographs or in radiotherapy. **rādiographic** /-graf'ik/ adj. **rādiograph'ically** adv. **rādiography** /-og'rə-fi/ n photography of the interior of a body or specimen by radiations other than light, such as X-rays, etc; formerly, radiotelegraphy; the study of radioactivity. **rā'dioimmunoass'ay** (or /-as-ā'/) n an immunoassay of a substance which has been labelled (qv) with a radioactive substance. **rādioī'sotope** n a radioactive isotope of a stable element. **rādioīsotop'ic** adj. **rādiola'belled** adj labelled (qv) with a radioactive substance. **rādiolocā'tion** n position-finding by radio signals; radar. **rādiolog'ic** or **rādiolog'ical** adj. **rādiolog'ically** adv. **rādiol'ogist** n a doctor specializing in the use of X-rays and in methods of imaging the internal structure of the body for diagnosis and treatment of disease (now often called a **radiation oncologist**). **rādiol'ogy** n the study of radioactivity and radiation or their application to medicine, eg as X-rays, or as treatment for certain diseases. **rādiolu'cent** adj transparent to electromagnetic radiation. **rādioluminesc'ence** n luminous radiation arising from radiation from a radioactive material.

rādiol'ysis n chemical decomposition induced by ionizing radiation. **rādiolyt'ic** adj. **rādiometeor'ograph** n same as **radiosonde** below. **rādiom'eter** n any instrument that measures radiant energy. **rādiomet'ric** adj (**radiometric age** the radiometrically determined age of a fossil, mineral, rock, event, etc, usu given in years (also **absolute age**); **radiometric dating** the method of obtaining a geological age by measuring the relative abundance of radioactive parent and daughter isotopes in geological materials). **rādiomet'rically** adv. **rādiom'etry** n. **rādiomimet'ic** adj (of drugs) imitating the physiological action of X-rays. **rādion'ics** n sing diagnosis and treatment at a distance on radiesthetic principles, using a device that tunes in to radiations from samples of hair, nail clippings, etc. **rādionū'clide** n any radioactive atom of an element identified by the number of neutrons and protons in its nucleus, and its energy state (**radionuclide imaging** (radiol) the use of radionuclides to image the physiology or anatomy of the body). **rā'diopager** n a radio receiver which functions as a pager. **rā'diopaging** n. **rādiopaque** /-pāk'/ adj opaque to radiation (esp X-rays). **rā'diophōne** n an instrument for producing sound by radiant energy; a radiotelephone. **rādiophonic** /-fon'ik/ adj (of music) produced electronically; producing electronic music. **rādiophon'ics** n sing. **rādiophonist** /-of'ə-nist/ n. **rādioph'ony** n. **rādioresist'ant** adj able to withstand considerable radiation doses without injury. **rā'dioscope** n a machine used in **rādios'copy**, examination by X-rays, etc. **rādioscopic** /-skop'ik/ adj. **rādioscop'ically** adv. **rādiosen'sitive** adj quickly injured or changed by radiation. **rādiosen'sitize** or **-ise** vt to make (eg cancer cells) more radiosensitive. **rā'diosonde** n (Fr sonde plummet, probe) an apparatus for ascertaining atmospheric conditions at great heights, consisting of a hydrogen-filled balloon, radio transmitter(s), etc (also **rādiometeor'ograph**). **rādio-stron'tium** n a radioactive isotope of strontium, esp strontium-90. **rādiotel'egram** n. **rādiotel'egraph** n. **rādioteleg'raphy** n. **rādiotelem'eter** n see under **telemeter**. **rādiotel'ephone** n a device which receives and transmits by means of radio waves (rather than wires) and which functions as a telephone (eg in cars and other vehicles). **rādioteleph'ony** n. **rādiotel'etype** n a teleprinter that receives and transmits by radio. **rādiother'apy** or **rādiotherapeut'ics** n treatment of disease, esp cancer, by radiation, eg by X-rays, etc. **rādiother'apist** n. **rādiotox'ic** adj of or relating to the toxic effects of radiation or radioactive material.

Radiolaria /rā-di-ō-lā'ri-ə/ n pl an order of marine Protozoa, or unicellular animals, with fine radial tentacles for feeding and movement. [LL *radiolus*, dimin of L *radius* radius]
■ **radiola'rian** adj and n.
❑ **radiolarian ooze** n a deep-sea deposit in which the siliceous skeletons of Radiolaria predominate.

radiothon /rā'di-ō-thon/ (US) n a very long radio programme used as a fund-raising event. [**radio** mara*thon*; cf **telethon**]

radish /rad'ish/ n a plant (especially *Raphanus sativus*) of the genus *Raphanus* (family Cruciferae); its pungent root, eaten raw as a salad vegetable. [Fr *radis*, from Provençal *raditz* or Ital *radice*, from L *rādīx*, -*īcis* a root]

radium /rā'di-əm/ n a radioactive metallic element (symbol Ra; atomic no 88) discovered by the Curies in 1898, found in pitchblende and other minerals, remarkable for its active spontaneous disintegration. [L *radius* a ray]
❑ **radium A, B**, etc n successive products in the disintegration of radon. **radium bomb** n an apparatus containing radium, emitting gamma rays for medical treatment (more commonly called **teleradium unit**). **radium emanation** n radon.

radius /rā'di-əs/ n (pl **radii** /rā'di-ī/ or **ra'diuses**) a straight line from the centre to the circumference of a circle or surface of a sphere (geom); a radiating line; anything placed like a radius, such as the spoke of a wheel, the movable arm of a sextant, etc; a radial plane of symmetry in a coelenterate; a line from a fixed point (eg the focus of a conic) to a point on a curve; the outer bone (in supine position) of the forearm in humans, or its equivalent in other animals; a barbule of a feather; the third vein of an insect's wing; a ray-flower or the ray-flowers of a head collectively (rare); a distance from a centre, conceived as limiting an area or range. [L *radius* a rod, spoke, ray]
■ **ra'dial** adj see separate entry.
❑ **radius of curvature** n (geom) of any curve, the radius of the circle which can be superimposed on it on the concave side. **radius vector** n (pl **radii vectō'res** /-rēz/) a straight line joining a fixed point and a variable point.

radix /rā'diks or rā'dēks/ n (pl **radices** /rā'di-sez or rā-dē'kās/) a root, root-number, root-word (obs); a source; a basis; the quantity on which a system of numeration, or of logarithms, etc is based. [L *rādīx*, -*īcis* root]

radome /rā'dōm/ n a protective covering for microwave radar antennae. [*radar dome*]

radon /rā′don/ *n* a radioactive gaseous element (symbol **Rn**; atomic no 86), the first disintegration product of radium, radium emanation (formerly called **niton**). [**radium** and **-on**, as in *argon, xenon*, etc]

radula /rad′ū-lə/ *n* (pl **rad′ulae** /-lē/) a mollusc's tongue or rasping ribbon. [L *rādula* a scraper, from *rādere*]
- **rad′ular** *adj.* **rad′ulate** *adj.* **rad′uliform** *adj* rasp-like.

radwaste /rad′wāst/ (*esp US*) *n* radioactive waste. [Contraction]

RAEC *abbrev* : Royal Army Educational Corps (now replaced by **ETS**).

RAeS *abbrev* : Royal Aeronautical Society.

Raetia and **Raetian** see **Rhaetia**.

RAF /är-ā-ef′ or (*inf*) raf/ *abbrev* : Royal Air Force.

rafale /rä-fäl′/ *n* a burst of artillery in quick rounds; a drum roll. [Fr, gust of wind]

raff /raf/ (*archaic*) *n* a heap, a quantity; riff-raff; one of the riff-raff; a rakish, flashy or blackguardly person. ◆ *adj* rakish. [Cf **riff-raff**]

Rafferty's rules /raf′ər-tiz roolz/ *n pl* no rules at all. [Origin uncertain]

raffia /raf′i-ə/ *n* ribbon-like fibres obtained from the leaves of the Raphia palm, used in weaving mats, baskets, etc. [**Raphia**]

raffinose /raf′i-nōs/ *n* a trisaccharide sugar. [Fr *raffiner* to refine]
- **raff′inate** *n* liquid left after a desired solute has been extracted.

raffish /raf′ish/ *adj* rakish, dashing; flashy. [From **raff**]
- **raff′ishly** *adv.* **raff′ishness** *n.*

raffle[1] /raf′l/ *n* an old game of dice, the stakes going to the thrower of a pair-royal; a lottery for an article. ◆ *vt* to dispose of by raffle. ◆ *vi* to engage in a raffle. [Fr *rafle* a pair-royal]
- **raff′ler** *n.*
- **raff′le-ticket** *n* a ticket with a number printed on it, bought by raffle participants and drawn to determine the winner(s).

raffle[2] /raf′l/ *n* a rabble; riff-raff; lumber; rubbish; a jumble; a tangle. [Cf **raff**]

raffle[3] /raf′l/ *vt* to notch; to crumple. [Ety uncertain]

Rafflesia /rə- or ra-flē′zi-ə/ *n* a genus (giving name to the family **Rafflesiā′ceae**, related to the birthwort family) of parasitic plants in Sumatra, Java, etc, one species having the largest known flowers, over 1m across, carrion-scented, the rest of the plant reduced to threads within the tissues of its host-plant. [Sir T Stamford *Raffles* (1781–1826), British governor in Sumatra (1818)]

raft[1] /räft/ *n* a flat, floating mass of logs or other material (ice, vegetation, etc); a flat structure of logs, etc for support or for conveyance on water; a dense mass of floating waterfowl (*US*); a wide layer of concrete to support a building on soft ground. ◆ *vt* to transport on a raft; to form into a raft; to cross, travel down, etc by raft. ◆ *vi* to manage a raft; to travel by raft; to form into a raft; (of ice, etc) to pile up by overriding. [ON *raptr* rafter]
- **raft′er** *n* a raftsman. **raft′ing** *n* the sport of travelling on a raft, *esp* over rapids.
- **raft′-bridge** *n* a raft used as a bridge; a bridge supported on rafts. **raft′man** *n* a raftsman. **raft′-port** *n* (in ships) a large port for timber. **raft′-rope** *n* a rope for towing blubber. **rafts′man** *n* a person who works on a raft.

raft[2] /räft/ (*esp N Am*) *n* a large number, a heap; a crowd; a miscellaneous lot. [**raff**]

raft[3] /räft/ an obsolete *pat* and *pap* of **reave**: in Keats *pap* of **rive**.

rafter[1] /räf′tər/ *n* an inclined beam supporting a roof; a person who fits rafters. ◆ *vt* to equip with rafters; to plough so that a strip is overturned upon unploughed ground. [OE *ræfter* a beam]
- **raft′ered** *adj* having (*esp* visible) rafters. **raft′ering** *n.*
- **raft′er-bird** *n* the spotted flycatcher.

rafter[2] and **raftsman** see under **raft**[1].

rag[1] /rag/ *n* a worn, torn or waste scrap of cloth; a tatter; a shred, scrap or tiny portion; a farthing (*old sl*); a jagged projection; a flag, handkerchief, sail, theatre curtain, garment, newspaper, or paper money (*derog* or *joc*); the pithy part of an orange, lemon, etc; a worthless or beggarly person; a person in a state of exhaustion; (in *pl*) tattered clothing; ragtime; a piece of ragtime music. ◆ *adj* of, for or dealing in rags. ◆ *vt* (**ragg′ing**; **ragged** /ragd/) to tear to rags; to make ragged; to perform in ragtime. ◆ *vi* to become ragged, to fray; to dress (with *out* or *up*; *old US sl*). [OE *ragg*, inferred from the adj *raggig* shaggy; ON *rögg* shagginess, tuft]
- **ragged** /rag′id/ *adj* shaggy; rough-edged; jagged; made or performed unevenly; raguly (*heraldry*); torn or worn into rags; wearing ragged clothes. **ragg′edly** *adv.* **ragg′edness** *n.* **ragg′edy** *adj* ragged-looking. **ragg′ery** *n* rags or ragged people collectively; clothes, *esp* women's (*sl*); raggedness. **ragg′y** *adj* rough; ragged; of the nature of a rag.
- **rag-and-bone′-man** *n* a person who collects or deals in goods of little value, eg old clothes, furniture, etc. **rag baby** *n* (*archaic*) a rag doll. **rag′bag** *n* a bag for rags and thrown-away garments; a random

or confused collection (*fig*); a slattern. **rag′bolt** *n* a bolt with barbs to prevent withdrawal. **rag′-book** *n* a child's book printed on cloth. **rag′-bush** *n* a bush to which shreds of cloth are tied as offerings to the local spirit, often near a well. **rag doll** *n* a doll made of rags; a slattern. **rag′-dust** *n* finely divided rags, used for making flock-paper. **rag′-fair** *n* an old-clothes market; a kit inspection (*milit sl*). **ragged-la′dy** *n* a garden flower (*Nigella damascena*) of the buttercup family having blue or white flowers, love-in-a-mist. **ragged Robin** *n* a campion (*Lychnis floscuculi*) with ragged-edged petals. **ragged school** *n* (*hist*) a voluntary school for destitute children in the 19c. **ragged staff** *n* (*heraldry*) a stick with branch stubs. **rag′head** *n* (*derog sl; offensive*) an Arab. **rag′man** *n* a person who collects or deals in rags; a devil (*obs*). **rag′-money** *n* (*sl*) paper money. **rag′-out** *n* a newspaper article or headline reproduced in a later issue with a ragged edge as if torn out; an unofficial strike (*sl*). **rag paper** *n* paper made from rags. **rag′picker** *n* a person who collects rags from bins, heaps, etc. **rag′-roll** *vt* a technique, used in house decoration, of rolling a folded cloth over a specially painted surface to produce a randomly shaded effect. **rags-to-rich′es** *adj* (of a story, etc) describing a person's progression from poverty to wealth. **rag′tag** *n* the rabble (also **ragg′le-tagg′le**). ◆ *adj* of or like the rabble; ragged, disorderly. **rag′time** *n* a form of jazz music of black American origin, with highly syncopated melody; a tune, song or dance in ragtime. **rag′timer** *n.* **rag′top** *n* (*US inf*) a folding canvas roof on a sports car; a car with this, a convertible. **rag trade** *n* (*inf*) the trade concerned with designing, making and selling clothes. **rag′-trader** *n* (*inf*). **rag′weed** *n* ragwort; any species of the composite genus *Ambrosia* (*US*). **rag′wheel** *n* a toothed wheel; a polishing-wheel made of cloth discs clamped together. **rag′-woman** *n.* **rag′-wool** *n* shoddy. **rag′worm** *n* a pearly white burrowing marine worm (*Nereis diversicolor*) used as bait by fishermen. **rag′wort** *n* a common coarse yellow-headed composite weed (*Senecio jacobaea*) of pastures; any similar species of the genus *Senecio* with long rays (from the cut leaves).
- **glad rags** see under **glad**[1]. **on the rag** (*N Am* and *Aust sl*) menstruating. **rag-tag and bobtail** riff-raff.

rag[2] /rag/ *vt* (**ragg′ing**; **ragged** /ragd/) to banter; to assail or beset with silly questions, ridicule or horseplay; to scold. ◆ *vi* to wrangle, argue; to indulge in a rag. ◆ *n* an outburst of organized horseplay, *usu* in defiance of authority; riotous festivity, *esp* and *orig* of undergraduates (now, in British universities, associated with the raising of money for charity). [Perh shortened from **bullyrag**; perh from **rag**[1] as in *red rag*]
- **ragg′ing** *n.* **ragg′y** *adj* (*sl*) irritated.
- **rag day** or **rag week** *n* in British universities, the particular day or week during which moneymaking activities, such as processions, etc for charity are organized.
- **lose one's rag** (*inf*) to lose one's temper.

rag[3] or **ragg** /rag/ *n* a rough hard stone of various kinds, *esp* one breaking in slabs; a large rough slate (3ft by 2ft). [Poss from **rag**[1]]
- **rag′stone** *n.* **rag′work** *n* undressed masonry in slabs.

raga /rä′gə/ *n* a traditional Hindu musical form or mode, a rhythmic or melodic pattern used as the basis for improvisation; a piece composed in such a mode. [Sans *rāga* colour, tone (in music)]

ragamuffin /rag′ə-muf-in or -muf′/ *n* a ragged, disreputable child; ragga; (with *cap*) the name of a devil (*obs*). [Poss **rag**[1]]

rag'd or **ragde** /ragd/ *adj* Shakespearean forms of **ragged**, in the sense of shaggy, jagged; *perh* unruly; *poss* also /rājd/ for **raged**, irritated (as if *pap* of *vt*).

rage /rāj/ *n* madness; overpowering passion of any kind, such as desire or *esp* anger; inspired frenzy; ardour; a fit of any of these; a mania or craze (for something); a vogue (*inf*); something in vogue; violence, stormy or furious activity; a flood (*Shakesp*); a party (*sl, esp Aust*); (in combination) uncontrolled anger or aggression arising from a particular situation or environment, as in *road rage, air rage*. ◆ *vi* to behave or speak with passion, *esp* with furious anger; to be violent; to storm; to be prevalent and violent; to scold (with *at* or *on*; *Scot*); to be violently bent on (*Milton*); to attend a party, etc, to have a good time (*sl, esp Aust*). ◆ *vt* see **rag'd**. [Fr, from L *rabiēs*, from *rabere* to rave]
- **rage′ful** *adj.* **rā′ger** *n.* **rā′ging** *adj* and *n.* **rā′gingly** *adv.*
- **all the rage** very much in fashion.

ragee see **ragi**.

ragg see **rag**[3].

ragga /rag′ə/ *n* a type of rap music developed from reggae and influenced by dance rhythms (also **rag′amuffin** or **ragg′amuffin**). [Short form of **ragamuffin**, because of the lifestyle associated with the music]

ragged, **raggedy** and **raggery** see under **rag**[1].

raggee see **ragi**.

raggle /rag'l/ (*Scot*) *n* a groove in masonry, *esp* to receive the edge of a roof. ◆ *vt* to make a raggle in. [Origin obscure]

raggle-taggle see **ragtag** under **rag¹**.

raggy see under **rag¹,²** and **ragi**.

ragi, **ragee**, **raggee** or **raggy** /rä'gē or rag'i/ *n* a millet (*Eleusine coracana*) much grown in India, Africa, etc. [Hindi (and Sans) *rāgī*]

ragini /rä'gi-nē/ *n* a modified raga. [Sans *rāginī* coloured]

raglan /rag'lən/ *n* an overcoat with sleeve in one piece with the shoulder; any garment made in this style, *esp* knitted. ◆ *adj* (of a sleeve) in one piece with the shoulder; (of a garment) having sleeves of this kind. [Lord *Raglan* (1788–1855), British commander in the Crimea]

ragman¹ /rag'mən/ or **ragment** /rag'mənt/ *n* a catalogue (*obs*); a document with pendent seals (*obs*); a rigmarole (*obs Scot*). [Origin obscure]

❑ **Ragman Rolls** *n pl* a collection of instruments by which the Scottish nobles, etc subscribed allegiance to Edward I.

ragman² see under **rag¹**.

ragmatical /rag-mat'i-kl/ (*Fielding* and *Smollett*) *adj appar*, riotous, disorderly. [Perh from **rag¹**, after **pragmatical**]

ragment see **ragman¹**.

Ragnarök /rag'nə-rok or rag'na-rək or -ræk/ (*Norse myth*) *n* the coming mutual destruction of the gods and the powers of evil, and the end of this world, to be superseded by a better. [ON *ragna rök* history or judgement of the gods, from *rögn*, *régin* gods, and *rök* reason, judgement, sophisticated into *ragna rökr* twilight of the gods, from *rökr* darkness]

ragout /ra-goo'/ *n* a highly seasoned stew of meat and vegetables; a mixture. ◆ *vt* to make a ragout of. [Fr *ragoût*, from *ragoûter* to restore the appetite]

ragstone and **ragwork** see under **rag³**.

ragtime, **ragweed**, **ragwheel**, **ragworm** and **ragwort** see under **rag¹**.

ragu /ra-goo'/ *n* in Italian cookery, a meat and tomato sauce. [Ital, from Fr *ragoût*]

raguly /rag'ū-li/ (*heraldry*) *adj* with projections like oblique stubs of branches (also **rag'üled**). [Origin obscure]

rah or **'rah** /rä or rö/ *interj*, n and vi short form of **hurrah**.

Rahu /rä'hoo/ (*Hindu myth*) *n* the demon that swallows the sun and moon at eclipses.

rai /rī/ (also with *cap*) *n* a modern, N African form of popular music, blending traditional Arabic and Spanish with Western dance rhythms. [Ar ra'y opinion, view]

RAID (*comput*) *abbrev* : Redundant Array of Inexpensive (or Independent) Disks, a set of disk drives used to store data in such a way that should a disk fail, the data can be recovered from the remainder.

raid¹ /rād/ *n* a sudden swift inroad, *orig* by horsemen, for assault or seizure; an air attack; an invasion unauthorized by government; an incursion of police for the purpose of making arrests, etc; an onset or onslaught for the purpose of obtaining or suppressing something; concerted selling by a group of speculators in order to lower the price of a particular stock (*stock exchange sl*). ◆ *vt* to make a raid on. ◆ *vi* to go on a raid. [Scot form of **road** (revived by Sir Walter Scott), from OE *rād* riding]

■ **raid'er** *n* a person who raids; a raiding aeroplane.

■ **corporate raider** a person who buys up a large proportion of a company's shares so as to be in a position to take it over or influence management policy. **dawn raid** see under **dawn**. **raid the market** to upset prices of stocks artificially for future gain.

raid² see **ride**.

raik /rāk/ (*Scot* and *N Eng*) *n* course, journey; range; pasture. ◆ *vi* to go; to range. [ON *reik* (noun), *reika* (verb) walk; coalescing later with **rake⁴**]

rail¹ /rāl/ *n* a bar extending horizontally or at a slope between supports or on the ground, often to form a support, a fence, a guard, a track for wheels, etc; the railway as a means of travel or transport; a horizontal member in framing or panelling (as in a door); the capping part of bulwarks; (in *pl*) a racecourse barrier; (in *pl*) railway shares. ◆ *vt* to enclose or separate with rails; to provide with rails; to send by railway. ◆ *vi* (*archaic*) to travel by railway. [OFr *reille*, from L *rēgula* a ruler]

■ **rail'age** *n* (chiefly *S Afr*) (the cost of) transportation by railway. **rail'ing** *n* fencing; fencing materials; (often in *pl*) a barrier or ornamental structure, *usu* of upright iron rods secured by horizontal connections. **rail'less** *adj*.

❑ **rail'bed** *n* the roadbed of a railway track. **rail'-borne** *adj* carried by railway. **rail'bus** *n* a lightweight railway coach powered by a bus-type diesel engine, or otherwise resembling a bus. **rail'car** *n* (*US*) a railway carriage; a self-propelled railway carriage. **rail'card** *n* any of various cards entitling its holder (eg a young person, old-age pensioner, etc) to reduced train fares. **rail'-fence** *n* (*US*) a fence of wooden posts and rails. **rail'head** *n* the furthest point reached by a railway under construction; a railway terminal. **rail'man** or **rail'woman** *n* a railway employee. **rail'-motor** *n* a self-propelled railway carriage. **rail'road** *n* (chiefly *N Am*) a railway. ◆ *vt* (*inf*) to force or push forward unduly (a person into a particular course of action, a bill through parliament, etc) (*orig US*); to get rid of, *esp* by sending to prison on a false charge. **railroad car** *n* (*US*) a railway carriage or a railway van or truck. **rail'roader** *n* (*US*) a railway worker or official. **rail'-splitter** *n* (*US*) a person who splits logs for fence-rails. **rail'way** *n* a track laid with rails for wheels to run on, *esp* for locomotives with passengers and goods wagons; a system of such tracks together with their equipment and organization; the company owning such a system. ◆ *adj* of or relating to a railway. **railway carriage** *n* a railway vehicle for passengers. **railway crossing** *n* an intersection of railway lines or of road and railway, *esp* without a bridge. **rail'wayman** *n* a railway employee. **rail'way-stitch** *n* a name for various quickly worked stitches.

■ **off the rails** mad, deranged; morally degenerate; not functioning; disorganized. **thin as a rail** (of a person) extremely thin.

rail² /rāl/ *vi* to scoff; to use vigorously or mockingly reproachful language; to banter; to revile (*usu* with *at* or *against*). ◆ *vt* to bring or render by raillery. ◆ *n* (*Spenser* **rayle**) reviling. [Fr *railler*]

■ **rail'er** *n*. **rail'ing** *adj* and *n*. **rail'ingly** *adv*. **raillery** /rāl'ər-i or (*archaic*) ral'/ *n* railing or mockery; banter; playful satire.

rail³ /rāl/ *n* any bird of the genus *Rallus*, *esp* the water rail, or other member of the family **Rall'idae**, *esp* the corncrake or land-rail. [OFr *rasle* (Fr *râle*)]

rail⁴ (*Spenser* **rayle** or **raile**) /rāl/ (*archaic*) *vi* to flow, gush. [Origin obscure]

rail⁵ /rāl/ (*obs* except in **night-rail**) *n* a garment; a cloak; a neckerchief. [OE *hrægl*]

■ **raill'y** *n* (*Scott*) a jacket.

raiment /rā'mənt/ *n* (*archaic* or *poetic*) clothing. [**arrayment**]

rain¹ /rān/ *n* water that falls from the clouds in drops; a shower; a fall of anything in the manner of rain; (in *pl*) the rainy season in tropical countries. ◆ *vi* to fall as or like rain; to send down rain. ◆ *vt* to shower. [OE *regn*; Du *regen*, Ger *Regen*; ON *regn*]

■ **rain'iness** *n*. **rain'less** *adj*. **rain'y** *adj* (**rain'ier**; **rain'iest**).

❑ **rain'band** *n* a dark band in the solar spectrum, due to water vapour in the earth's atmosphere. **rain'bird** *n* a bird, such as the green woodpecker and various kinds of cuckoo, supposed to foretell rain. **rain'-bound** *adj* detained by rain. **rain'bow** *n* the coloured bow caused by refraction and internal reflexion of light in raindrops; any similar array of colours; (with *cap*; in full **Rainbow Guide**) a member of the most junior section of the Guides; a highly discoloured bruise (*sl*); a rainbow trout; a S American hummingbird, the cock with rainbow-coloured head. ◆ *adj* of, or coloured like, the rainbow; consisting of a wide range or assortment; involving people of different ethnic origins or political views. **rain'bow-chaser** *n* a visionary, someone who tries to reach the end of the rainbow (**chase rainbows** to pursue an impossible aim). **rainbow coalition** *n* a political alliance between minority groups or parties of varying opinions. **rain'bow-coloured** *adj*. **rainbow dressing** *n* a gaudy display of flags on a ship. **rain'bowed** *adj*. **Rainbow Guide** see **rainbow** above. **rainbow therapy** *n* a form of colour therapy based on drinking water that is considered to have taken on the energy specific to the colour of its container. **rain'bow-tint'ed** *adj*. **rainbow trout** *n* a finely marked and coloured trout (*Salmo gairdneri*) *orig* N American. **rain'bowy** *adj*. **rain'-chamber** *n* a compartment for condensing noxious fumes by spray. **rain'check** *n* (*US*) a ticket for future use given to spectators when a game or a sports meeting is cancelled or stopped because of bad weather (**take a raincheck** (on) (*inf*; *orig US*) to promise to accept an invitation (for) at a later date). **rain'-cloud** *n* nimbus, a dense dark sheet of cloud that may shed rain or snow. **rain'coat** *n* a light overcoat capable of protecting the wearer against moderate rain. **rain dance** *n* a religious ceremonial dance performed by Native Americans in the belief that it will bring rain. **rain'date** *n* (*US*) an alternative date set for an event in case of rain or bad weather. **rain'-doctor** *n* a rainmaker. **rain'drop** *n* a drop of rain. **rain'fall** *n* a shower of rain; the amount (by depth of water) of rain that falls. **rain'forest** *n* broad-leaved, evergreen tropical forest with very heavy rainfall. **rain gauge** *n* an instrument for measuring rainfall. **rain'maker** *n* a person in tribal societies who professes to bring rain; a high-powered employee who generates a great deal of income for his or her employers (*sl*). **rain'making** *n* attempting to cause rainfall by techniques such as seeding clouds. **rain'-plover** *n* the golden plover. **rain'-print** *n* a little pit made by a raindrop in clay, etc, sometimes preserved in rocks. **rain'proof** *adj* more or less impervious to rain. ◆ *vt* to make rainproof. ◆ *n* a rainproof overcoat. **rain shadow** *n* an area sheltered by hills from the prevailing winds and having a lighter

■ words derived from main entry word; ❑ compound words; ■ idioms and phrasal verbs

rainfall than the windward side of the hills. **rain'-stone** *n* a stone used in magic rites aimed at bringing rain. **rain'storm** *n*. **rain'tight** *adj* rainproof. **rain tree** *n* a S American tree (*Samanea saman*) of the family Mimosaceae, under which there is a constant rain of juice ejected by cicadas. **rain'wash** *n* the washing away of earth, etc by rain; downward creep of superficial deposits soaked in rain; matter so transported. **rain'water** *n* water that falls or has fallen as rain. **rain'wear** *n* articles of rainproof clothing.

■ **a rainy day** (*fig*) a possible future time of need. **chase rainbows** see **rainbow-chaser** above. **come rain or shine** whatever the weather or circumstances. **rain cats and dogs** see under **cat**[1]. **rained off** (of a sport, outdoor activity, etc) cancelled because of rain. **rain in** (of rain) to penetrate a roof, tent, badly-fitting window, etc. **right as rain** (*inf*) perfectly in order. **take a raincheck (on)** see **raincheck** above.

rain[2], **raine** (*Spenser*) same as **reign**.

raird see **reird**.

raise[1] /rāz/ *vt* to cause to rise; to make higher or greater; to lift; to exalt; to advance; to elevate; to cause to stand up or upright; to rouse; to stir up; to elate; to rear, grow or breed (children, animals, etc); to produce; to give rise to; to build, erect; to bring into being; to bring to life (from the dead); to utter (*esp* a question); to establish; to institute; to bring forward into consideration or notice; to bring into relief; to intensify; to call up; to cause (land) to rise in view by approaching (*naut*); to contact by radio; to make a higher bid than (*cards*); to levy, get together, collect (taxes, an army, etc); to cause (a lump) to swell; to extol; to remove, take off; to produce a nap on. ◆ *n* an act of raising or lifting; a rising road; an increase in wages or salary (*inf*; *esp N Am*). [ME *reisen*, from ON *reisa*, causative of *rīsa* to rise; cf **rise** and **rear**[2]]

■ **rais'able** or **raise'able** *adj*. **rais'er** *n* someone who or something that raises a building, etc; the riser of a step. **rais'ing** *n*.

□ **raised beach** *n* (*geol*) an old sea margin above the present water level. **raised bog** *n* a type of sphagnum bog, convex in shape and caused by the upward growth of vegetation and failure of dead plant material to decompose. **raised pastry** or **pie** *n* a pastry or pie without support of a dish at the sides. **rais'ing-bee** *n* (*US*) a gathering of neighbours to help in raising the frame of a house, etc.

■ **raise a hand to** to hit, or generally treat badly. **raise an eyebrow** or **raise one's eyebrows** to look surprised (at). **raise a siege** to abandon, or put an end to, a siege. **raise Cain** or **raise the roof** (*inf*) to make a lot of noise; to be extremely angry. **raise hell** or **raise the devil** (*inf*) to make a lot of trouble. **raise money on** to get money by pawning or selling, *esp* privately. **raise one's glass** to drink a health (to). **raise one's hat** to take one's hat off in salutation (to). **raise the market (upon)** (*stock exchange*) to bring about a rise in prices (to the disadvantage of). **raise the wind** (*sl*) to get together the necessary money by any means.

raise[2] /rāz/ (*N Eng*) *n* a cairn. [ON *hreysi*]

raisin /rā'zn/ *n* a dried grape. [Fr, grape, from L *racēmus* a bunch of grapes]

■ **rai'siny** *adj*.

raison d'état /rā-zɔ̃ dā-ta'/ (*Fr*) *n* literally, reason of state; the principle that national interests take precedence over strict individual rights, morality, etc.

raison d'être /rā-zɔ̃ de'tr'/ (*Fr*) *n* reason for existence (purpose or cause).

raisonné /rā-zo-nā'/ (*Fr*) *adj* logically set out, systematically arranged, and (*usu*) provided with notes.

raisonneur /rā-zo-nœr'/ *n* (in a play or novel) a character who embodies the author's point of view and expresses his or her opinions. [Fr, an arguer]

rait same as **ret**.

raita /rā-ē'tə or rī'tə/ *n* an Indian dish of chopped vegetables, *esp* cucumber, in yoghurt. [Hindi]

raiyat and **raiyatwari** same as **ryot** and **ryotwari**.

raj /räj/ *n* rule, sovereignty; government, *esp* (with *cap*) the British government of India, 1858–1947. [Hindi *rāj*, *rājā*, from Sans *rājan* a king (cognate with L *rēx*)]

■ **ra'ja** or **ra'jah** *n* an Indian prince or king; a Malay or Javanese chief. **ra'jaship** or **ra'jahship** *n*. **raj'pramukh** /-mŭk'/ *n* the head of a state or states union in the Democratic Republic of India. **Rajput** or **Rajpoot** /räj'poot/ *n* (Hindi *putra* son) a member of a race or class claiming descent from the original Hindu military and ruling caste.

□ **raja yoga** *n* a form of yoga stressing control of the energy of the mind via meditation.

Rajya Sabha /rä'jyə sub'ə/ *n* the upper house of the Indian parliament. [Hindi *rajya* state, and *sabha* assembly]

rake[1] /rāk/ *n* a toothed bar on a handle, for scraping, gathering together, smoothing, etc; a tool for various purposes, toothed, notched or bladed and with a long handle (eg a croupier's implement for drawing in money); a wheeled field implement with long teeth for

gathering hay, scraping up weeds, etc; a connected set (of railway carriages or wagons); an extremely thin person or horse. ◆ *vt* to scrape, smooth, clear, break up, draw, gather, remove, cover, uncover, search, ransack, with a rake or as if with a rake; to cover (a fire) with ashes so as to keep it smouldering; to graze, scrape; to pass over violently and swiftly; to fire (bullets, etc) across the entire line of one's enemy; to provide or take a view all over or completely through. ◆ *vi* to work with or as if with a rake; to search minutely. [OE *raca*; Ger *Rechen* rake; ON *reka* shovel]

■ **rā'ker** *n* a person who rakes; a scavenger; a raking implement; (in games) a long, fast, low-flying shot (*perh* partly from **rake**[4]). **rā'king** *n* and *adj*.

□ **rake'-off** *n* (*sl*) monetary share, *esp* unearned or dishonest. **rake'shame** *n* (*obs*) a base, dissolute wretch.

■ **rake in** (*inf*) to acquire rapidly and in great quantity. **rake up** to revive from oblivion (*usu* something scandalous); to collect together.

rake[2] /rāk/ *n* a debauched or dissolute person, *esp* a man of fashion. ◆ *vi* to lead a rake's life; to make a practice of lechery. [Shortening of **rakehell**]

■ **rā'kery** *n* dissoluteness. **rā'kish** *adj*. **rā'kishly** *adv*. **rā'kishness** *n*.

rake[3] /rāk/ *n* inclination from the vertical or horizontal, eg of a ship's funnel, a theatre stage, etc; an angle, eg between the face of a cutting tool and the surface on which it is working, or the wings and body of an aircraft. ◆ *vi* to incline. ◆ *vt* to slope; to cut aslant. [Ety dubious]

■ **rā'ker** *n* a sloping support or strut. **rā'kish** *adj* with raking masts; swift-looking; pirate-like; dashing; jaunty. **rā'kishly** *adv*.

rake[4] /rāk/ (now *dialect*) *vi* to proceed, *esp* swiftly; to roam, range about; (of a hawk) to fly wide; (of a dog) to follow the scent wanderingly along the ground. [OE *racian* to go forward, hasten]

■ **rā'ker** *n* a very fast pace; a plunge in betting. **rā'king** *adj* advancing swiftly.

rake[5] /rāk/ (*N Eng*) *n* a track, *esp* up a hill or in a gully or a pasture; a pasture; a journey, *esp* in fetching things; the amount carried at one journey, load, gang; an irregular, *usu* vertical, vein of ore; a string, eg of wagons. ◆ *vi* (eg of sheep) to form into single file. [ON *rāk* stripe; partly coalescing with **raik**]

rakee see **raki**.

rakehell /rāk'hel/ *n* an utterly debauched person (see also **rake**[2]). ◆ *adj* debauched. [Prob **rake**[1] and **Hell**, ie such as might be found by raking out hell]

■ **rake'helly** *adj*.

raker see under **rake**[1,3,4].

rakery see under **rake**[2].

rakeshame see under **rake**[1].

raki /rä'kē or rak'i/ *n* an aniseed-flavoured spirit of Turkey and the E Mediterranean (also **rak'ee**). [Turk *rāqī*]

rakia /ra-kē'ə/ *n* the Bulgarian name for **rakija**.

rakija /ra-kē'ə/ *n* any of several alcoholic spirits distilled in the Balkans from fermented fruit juice, including raki and slivovitz. [Serbo-Croat]

rakish, etc see under **rake**[2,3].

rakshas /räk'shəs/ or **rakshasa** /-shə-sə/ (*Hindu myth*) *n* an evil spirit. [Sans *rākṣasa*]

raku /rä'koo/ *n* a type of Japanese coarse-grained, lead-glazed pottery fired at low temperature, used *esp* to produce tea bowls. [Jap, literally pleasure, enjoyment]

râle or **rale** /räl/ (*pathol*) *n* a rattling sound from a diseased lung. [Fr]

rall. /ral/ (*music*) *abbrev* : rallentando.

rallentando /ral-ən-tan'dō/ (*music*) *adj* and *adv* becoming slower (*abbrev* **rall.**). ◆ *n* (*pl* **rallentan'dos** or **rallentan'di** /-dē/) a passage played in this way; a slowing. [Ital, prp of *rallentare* to slacken]

rallier see under **rally**[1,2].

Rallus /ral'əs/ *n* the water-rail genus of birds, giving name to the family **Rall'idae**. [Latinized from Fr *râle*]

■ **rall'ine** /-īn/ *adj*.

rally[1] /ral'i/ *vt* (**rall'ying**; **rall'ied**) to reassemble; to gather to one's support; to bring together for united effort; to muster (eg the faculties) by an effort; to pull together, revive. ◆ *vi* to come together, *esp* from dispersal, or for renewed effort, or in support of a leader, friend or cause; to recover; to recover in some degree lost health, power, vigour, value, etc; (of a share price or currency value) to improve after a period of decline or decrease; to drive in a rally. ◆ *n* an assembly or reassembly for renewed effort; a gathering for a common purpose; a mass meeting; a competition to test skill in driving, and ability to follow an unknown route (*US* also **rall'ye**), or to test quality of motor vehicles (see also under **rely**); a pantomime mêlée; a temporary or partial recovery (from an illness, etc); a quick exchange of blows in boxing; a series of to-and-fro strokes in deciding a point, as in tennis. [OFr *rallier*, from pfx *re-* and *allier*; see **ally**[1]]

■ **rall'ier** *n.* **rall'ying** *n* long-distance motor-racing over public roads. **rall'yist** *n.*

❑ **rall'ycross** *n* motor-racing round a circuit consisting partly of paved road and partly of rough ground. **rall'ying-cry** *n* a slogan to attract support for a cause, etc. **rall'ying-point** *n* a place of assembly, *esp* for a mass meeting.

■ **rally round** to support, help someone in need.

rally² /ral'i/ *vt* and *vi* (**rall'ying; rall'ied**) to banter. [Fr *railler*; cf **rail²**]
■ **rall'ier** *n.* **rall'yingly** *adv.*

rallye see **rally¹**.

raloxifene /rə-lok'si-fēn/ *n* a non-hormonal drug that mimics the action of oestrogen, used to prevent osteoporosis in postmenopausal women by increasing bone density.

RAM *abbrev*: random access memory (/ram/; *comput*); Royal Academy of Music.

❑ **RAM disk** *n* (*comput*) a memory area used to emulate a very fast temporary disk drive.

ram /ram/ *n* a male sheep, a tup; (with *cap* and *the*) Aries; a battering-ram; a ship's beak, a pointed device on a warship's prow for striking holes in an enemy ship's hull; a warship with such a beak; a water ram or hydraulic ram (see **hydraulic**); the falling weight of a pile-driver; the striking head of a steam-hammer; a piston applying pressure, operated by hydraulic or other power; a machine with such a piston; a rammer; an act of ramming. ◆ *vt* (**ramm'ing, rammed**) to thrust roughly, cram (also *fig*); to block up; to beat hard; to drive hard down; to strike, batter or pierce with a ram; to strike or dash into violently. [OE *ram, rom*; Ger *Ramm*]

■ **ramm'er** *n* a person or thing that rams, *esp* a tool for compressing earth before paving, etc. **ramm'ish** *adj* rank in smell or taste (now *dialect*); lecherous, lustful (*obs*).

❑ **ram-air turbine** *n* a small turbine driven by air used as an emergency power source for aircraft, etc, or to provide power in guided weapons. **ram'cat** *n* a male cat. **ram'jet** or **ramjet engine** *n* a simple form of aero-engine, consisting of forward air-intake, combustion chamber and rear expansion nozzle, in which thrust is generated by compression due solely to forward motion. **ram'-raid** *n* the action of smashing into shop windows, etc with a stolen car and subsequent stealing of the goods inside. ◆ *vi* and *vt* to perform such a raid (on). **ram'-raider** *n.* **ram'-raiding** *n.* **ram'rod** *n* a rod for ramming down a charge into, or for cleaning, a gun-barrel; a stern, inflexible person; a strict disciplinarian. ◆ *adj* rigid, inflexible; stern. ◆ *vt* (**ram'rodding; ram'rodded**) to push or drive with great force. **ram's'-horn** *n* the horn of a ram; any article made of or resembling this, eg a trumpet or snuff-box. ◆ *adj* made of ram's-horn. **ramshorn snail** *n* a freshwater snail (*Planorbis*) often kept in aquariums.

r.a.m. *abbrev*: relative atomic mass.

Rāma /rä'mä/ *n* an incarnation of Vishnu.
■ **Rāmāyana** /rä-mä'yä-na/ *n* the Sanskrit epic of *Rāma*.

Ramadan or **Ramadhan** /ra-mə-dän' or ram'ə-dan/ *n* the ninth month of the Muslim calendar, during which fasting is observed between dawn and dusk; the fast observed at this time. [Ar *Ramadān*]

ramakin see **ramekin**.

ramal, ramate, etc see under **ramus**.

Raman effect /rä'mən i-fekt'/ *n* a change in frequency of light passing through a transparent medium, used in the study of molecules. [Sir Chandrasekhara V *Raman* (1888–1970), Indian physicist]

Ramapithecus /rä-ma-pith'i-kəs/ *n* an early Pliocene genus of primates, *poss* an ancestor of modern man, known from fossil remains found in N India. [**Rāma**, with reference to his birth as a prince of Oudh, and Gr *pithēkos* ape]
■ **ramapith'ecine** *n* and *adj.*

Rāmāyana see under **Rāma**.

ramble /ram'bl/ *vi* to go wherever one's fancy leads; to wander; to walk for recreation or pleasure; to wander in mind or discourse; to be desultory, incoherent or delirious; (of a plant, etc) to straggle or trail randomly. ◆ *n* a roving about; an irregular, unorganized excursion; a walk for pleasure; rambling. [ME *romblen*; appar connected with **roam**]
■ **ram'bler** *n* a person who rambles; a trailing climbing plant, *esp* a rose with small clustered flowers. **ram'bling** *n* and *adj.* **ram'blingly** *adv.*

Rambouillet /rom'boo-yā, ram'boo-lā or (Fr) rã-boo-le'/ *n* a hardy breed of sheep bred for its fine merino-like wool. [*Rambouillet*, town in N France]

rambunctious /ram-bungk'shəs/ *adj* difficult to control, boisterous, exuberant. [Perh **rumbustious**]
■ **rambunc'tiously** *adv.* **rambunc'tiousness** *n.*

rambutan /ram-boo'tən/ *n* a sapindaceous tree (*Nephelium lappaceum*) of the same family as the lychee, found throughout SE Asia; its fruit with edible, translucent flesh and thick red shell covered with hooked hairs. [Malay *rambūtan*, from *rambut* hair]

RAMC *abbrev*: Royal Army Medical Corps.

ramcat see under **ram**.

rameal see under **ramus**.

Ramean see under **Ramism**.

ramee see **rami**.

ramekin, ramequin or **ramakin** /ram'ə-kin/ *n* a small, round baking dish or mould for single portions of food; a mixture of cheese, eggs, etc baked in small moulds, or served on toast. [Fr *ramequin*, from obs Flem *rammeken*]

ramen /rä'mən/ *n* a Japanese dish of clear broth containing vegetables, noodles and often pieces of meat. [Jap *rāmen*]

ramentum /rə- or ra-men'təm/ *n* (pl **rament'a**) a chaffy scale, such as on ferns. [L *rāmentum* a scraping, from *rādere* to scrape]

rameous see under **ramus**.

ramequin see **ramekin**.

ramet see under **ramus**.

ramfeezle /ram-fē'zl/ (*Scot*) *vt* to weary out.

ramgunshoch /ram-gun'shohh/ (*Scot*) *adj* rough.

rami, ramie or **ramee** /ram'ē/ *n* a plant (*Boehmeria nivea*) of the nettle family long cultivated in China (also called **rhea** or **China grass**); its fibre, used for weaving, paper-making, etc; a garment made of this. [Malay *rami*]

ramification /ram-i-fi-kā'shən/ *n* branching; arrangement of branches; a single branch or part of a complex arrangement, or of a situation or problem, *esp* a consequence that must be taken into account. [Ety as for **ramus**]
■ **ram'iform** *adj* having a branched shape. **ram'ify** *vt* and *vi* to divide into branches (also *fig*).

Ramilie, Ramillie /ram'i-li/, **Ramilies** or **Ramillies** /ram'i-liz/ (*hist*) *n* a name for several articles and modes of dress in fashion after Marlborough's victory at *Ramillies* (1706), *esp* a form of cocked hat, and a wig with a long plaited tail (also *adj*).

ramin /ram'in/ *n* a Malaysian tree of the genus *Gonystylus*; a hardwood obtained from this, commonly used in making moulding, frames, etc. [Malay]

Ramism /rä'mi-zm/ *n* the system of logic of Peter *Ramus* (1515–72).
■ **Rä'mean** or **Rä'mist** *n* and *adj.*

ramjet see under **ram**.

rammer and **rammish** see under **ram**.

rammy /ram'i/ (*Scot*) *n* a row, free-for-all fight. [Perh from Scot *rammle* an uproar, noisy drinking spree]

ramose and **ramous** see under **ramus**.

ramp¹ /ramp/ *n* an inclined plane, a slope; a low hump made across a road, eg to slow down traffic; a set of movable stairs for entering or leaving an aircraft; an inclined slip road (*N Am*); the slope of a wall-top, or anything similar, between two levels; an upwardly concave bend in a handrail; a swindle; an act of ramping; a stunt worked for private profit; a worked-up excitement or craze, *esp* for some gain; an exploitation of a special situation to increase prices, etc; a romp, tomboy (*archaic*); a disorderly or loose woman (*archaic*). ◆ *vi* to climb; to grow rankly; to rear as if climbing; to slope from one level to another; to rage; to dash about wildly. ◆ *vt* to provide with a ramp; to bend into a ramp; to snatch; to rob; to hustle into paying a fictitious debt; to swindle; to increase (the price of something) dishonestly, and to a large extent (usu with *up*). [Fr *ramper* to creep, to clamber]
■ **rampa'cious** *adj* (*Dickens*) rampageous. **rampall'ian** (*Shakesp*) a term of abuse. **ramp'er** *n* a person who ramps, *esp* someone who makes a disturbance to cover the activities of others; a rampsman. **ramp'ing** *n* (*business*) the practice of causing large, false increases in the price of shares, etc by dishonest means.
❑ **ramp shot** same as **dilscoop**. **ramps'man** *n* (*sl*) a person who ramps bookmakers.

ramp² /ramp/ *n* a kind of wild onion native to N America; a ramson. [OE *hramsa*]

rampage /ram'pāj or -pāj'/ (*Scot* **rampauge** /-pöj'/) *n* turbulently or aggressively excited behaviour or rushing about. ◆ *vi* to storm; to rush about wildly. [Ety as for **ramp¹**]
■ **rampā'geous** *adj.* **rampā'geousness** *n.* **ram'pager** *n.* **rampag'ing** *n.*
■ **on the rampage** storming about, behaving wildly and violently in anger, exuberance, etc.

rampant /ram'pənt/ *adj* rearing; standing in profile, on the left hindleg (*heraldry*); high-spirited; fierce; unrestrained; unchecked in growth or prevalence; (of an arch) having springers on different levels. [Ety as for **ramp¹**]
■ **ramp'ancy** *n.* **ramp'antly** *adv.*

---

rampart /ram'pärt or -pərt/ n a flat-topped defensive mound; that which defends. ◆ vt to fortify or surround with ramparts. [Fr rempart, from OFr rempar, from remparer to defend, from L pfx re-, ante-, and parāre to prepare]

rampauge see **rampage**.

Ramphastos see **Rhamphastos** under **rhamphoid**.

rampick /ram'pik/ or **rampike** /-pīk/ (archaic and US) n a dead tree, or one decayed at the top, broken off or partly burned. [Origin obscure]
■ **ram'pick** or **ram'picked** adj.

rampion /ram'pyən or -pi-ən/ n a bellflower (Campanula rapunculus) whose root is eaten as a salad vegetable; any species of the related genus Phyteuma. [Cf Ital raponzolo, Ger Rapunzel, Fr raiponce]

rampire /ram'pīr/ (archaic) n same as **rampart**.
■ **ram'pired** adj.

ram-raid, etc and **ramrod** see under **ram**.

Ramsar site /ram'sär sīt/ n an area of wetland considered to be of international importance and worthy of conservation according to the criteria established at a convention in the Iranian city of Ramsar in 1971.

ramshackle /ram'sha-kl/ adj tumbledown; badly constructed or organized, etc. [Perh from ramshackled, pap of an obs form of ransackle (see **ranshackle**)]

ramson /ram'zən/ n (usu in double plural form **ramsons**) wild or broad-leaved garlic. [Orig the plural of rams (now a dialect word); from OE hramsa, hramse, hramsan (pl)]

ramstam /ram'stam/ (Scot and N Eng) adj and adv headlong. [Poss **ram**]

ramus /rā'məs/ n (pl rā'mī) a branch of anything, esp a nerve; a process of a bone; the mandible, or its ascending part; a feather barb. [L rāmus a branch]
■ **rā'mal**, **rā'meal**, **rā'meous** or **rā'mous** adj of a branch. **rā'mate**, **rā'mous** or **ramose** /rə-mōs'** or /rā'mōs/ adj branched. **rā'met** n a physically and physiologically independent individual plant, whether grown from a sexually produced seed or derived by vegetative reproduction. **ram'ūlar** adj of a branch. **ram'ūlose** or **ram'ūlous** adj having ramuli. **ram'ūlus** n (pl **ram'ūlī**) a little branch.

RAN abbrev : Royal Australian Navy.

ran /ran/ pat of **run**.

Rana /rā'nə/ n the typical genus of frogs, giving name to the family **Ranidae** /ran'i-dē/. [L rāna, dimin rānula a frog, ranula]
■ **ranarian** /rə-nā'ri-ən/ adj froggy. **ranā'rium** n a place where frogs are reared. **raniform** /ran'/ adj frog-like. **ranine** /rā'nīn/ adj of the underside of the tongue (seat of ranula). **ranivorous** /rə-niv'ər-əs/ adj frog-eating. **ranula** /ran'ū-lə/ n a cyst in the gland under the tongue (poss from an imagined resemblance to a small frog).

rana /rā'nä or -nə/ n a Rajput prince. [Hindi]

ranarium see under **Rana**.

rance /rans/ (chiefly Scot) n a prop, shore; a bar. ◆ vt to prop; to bar. [Fr ranche]

rancel see **ranzel**.

ranch[1] /ränch, ranch, ränsh or ransh/ n a stock farm, as in western N America, often taken to include its buildings and the people employed on it; an establishment for rearing any commercially-important animal, such as a cattle ranch, etc. ◆ vi to own, manage or work on a ranch. ◆ vt to use (land) as a ranch. [Am Sp rancho, from Sp, mess, mess-room]
■ **ranched** adj (of a fur coat) made from skins of animals from a ranch. **ranch'er** or **ranch'man** n a person who ranches. **rancheria** /ran-chä-rē'a or (Sp) rän-che-rē'a/ n a herdsmen's hut or village; a small village or settlement of native peoples in Mexico or SW USA; a rancherie (obs). **rancherie** /ranch'ə-ri/ n a Native Canadian village or settlement, esp on a reserve. **ranchero** /ran-chä'rō or (Sp) rän-che'rō/ n (pl **ranche'ros**) in Mexico and SW USA, a rancher. **ranch'ing** n. **rancho** /ran'chō or (Sp) rän'chō/ n (pl **ranch'os**) a rude hut, or group of huts, esp for travellers; a ranch.

ranch[2] /ränch, ranch, ränsh or ransh/ (Dryden) vt to tear. [Cf **race**[5]]

rancid /ran'sid/ adj rank in smell or taste, as of butter or oil that is going bad. [L rancidus]
■ **rancid'ity** or **ran'cidness** n.

rancour or US **rancor** /rang'kər/ n harboured bitterness of mind, speech, etc; deep-seated enmity; spite; virulence; sourness (Shakesp). [OFr, from L rancor, -ōris an old grudge, from rancēre to be rancid]
■ **ran'corous** adj. **ran'corously** adv.

rand[1] /rand/ n (pl rand or rands) a border, margin; a strip, esp of flesh or of leather; /ront or rand/ a ridge overlooking a valley (S Afr); the

standard monetary unit of South Africa (100 cents). [OE and Du rand border]
■ **the Rand** the Witwatersrand goldfield.

rand[2] /rand/ vi an old form of **rant**.

R&A or **R and A** abbrev : Royal and Ancient Golf Club of St Andrews.

randan[1] /ran-dan' or ran'dan/ n a din, uproar; riotous conduct; a spree. [Origin obscure; cf **random**]

randan[2] /ran-dan' or ran'dan/ n a boat rowed by three, the second with two oars (also **randan gig**). [Origin obscure]

R&B abbrev : rhythm and blues.

R&D abbrev : research and development.

randem /ran'dəm/ n, adj and adv (in) a tandem with three horses.

randie see **randy**.

randle-balk /ran'dl-bök/, **randle-perch** /-pûrch/ or **randle-tree** /-trē/ (Scot and N Eng) n a bar in a chimney for hanging pots (also **rann'el-balk**, **rann'ell-balk**, **rann'le-balk** or **ran'tle-balk**, etc). [Cf Norw randa-tre, from rand space above a fireplace]

random /ran'dəm/, also formerly (Spenser and Shakesp) **randon** /-dən/ adj haphazard, chance; uncontrolled; irregular; fired at an elevation. ◆ n irregular masonry; uncontrolled or unguarded state, freedom (Spenser); chance (archaic); a rush, full speed (obs); elevation of a gun (obs). [OFr randon, from randir to gallop]
■ **randomīzā'tion** or **-s-** n. **ran'domize** or **-ise** vt to arrange or set up so as to occur in a random manner. **ran'domizer** or **-s-** n. **ran'domly** or **ran'domwise** adv. **ran'domness** n.
❑ **random access** n (comput) access to any data in a large store of information without affecting other data. **random access memory** n a computer memory that can be read from and written to by a program, and in which the data are accessed directly (not serially, as in magnetic tape) (abbrev **RAM**). **random variable** n (stats) one which can take any from a range of values which occur randomly. **random walk** n a series of processes, quantities, variables, etc following no discernible pattern.

R and R (inf; orig US) abbrev : rest and relaxation (or recreation).

randy or **randie** /ran'di/ adj (**ran'dier**; **ran'diest**) sexually excited; lustful (inf); boisterous (dialect); aggressively or coarsely loud-spoken (Scot). ◆ n (Scot and N Eng) a violent beggar, esp a woman; a coarse virago; a romping girl. [Poss **rand**[2]]
■ **ran'dily** adv. **ran'diness** n.

ranee see **rani**.

rang /rang/ pat of **ring**[2,3].

rangatira /ran-gə-tē'rə/ n a Maori leader or chief. [Maori]
■ **rangatiratang'a** n leadership, chieftaincy.

range /rānj/ vt to set in a row or rows; to assign a place among others to; to classify; to arrange; to straighten, level, align; to traverse freely or in all directions; to sail along or about (naut); to bring to bear. ◆ vi to lie in a direction; to extend; to take or have a position in a line, or alongside; to take sides; to lie evenly, align; to move, have freedom of movement, occur or vary within limits; to rove freely, in all directions; to beat about, as for game; to be inconstant, fluctuate; to have a range. ◆ n a row or rank; a system of points in a straight line; anything extending in line, such as a chain of mountains or a row of connected buildings; a stretch of open country, esp one used for grazing; a north and south strip of townships six miles wide (US); line of lie; an act of ranging; scope, compass, extent, limits; movement, freedom of movement or variation between limits; space or distance between limits; the area or distance within which anything moves, can move, occurs, is possible, acts efficiently or varies; a place for practice in shooting; effective shooting distance of a gun, etc, ie between gun, etc and target; an enclosed kitchen fireplace fitted with appliances of various kinds. [Fr ranger to range, from rang a rank]
■ **ran'ger** n a forest or park officer; a member of a body of troops, usu mounted and employed in policing an area; a soldier specially trained for raiding combat; (with cap) a member of a senior branch of the Guides (also **Ranger Guide**); a dog that beats the ground. **rang'ership** n. **rang'iness** n. **ran'gy** adj (**rang'ier**; **rang'iest**) disposed or well able to roam; roomy; long-legged and thin; mountainous (Aust).
❑ **range'finder** n an instrument for finding the distance of an object; same as **tacheometer**. **range'finding** n. **range'land** n (often in pl) land suitable for grazing, but too dry for growing crops. **range** (or **ranging**) **pole** or **rod** n a pole or rod used to mark positions in surveying.
■ **free-range** see under **free**. **range oneself** to side (with), to take sides; (Fr se ranger) to settle down to reputable ways, esp on marrying.

rangoli /rung-gō'li/ n a traditional Hindu form of decoration on floors or doorsteps, forming patterns of coloured sand and riceflour. [Hindi]

rani or **ranee** /rä'nē/ fem of **raja**. [Hindi rānī, from Sans rājñī queen, fem of rājan]

Ranidae, raniform, ranine, etc see **Rana**.

rank[1] /rangk/ *n* a row; a row of soldiers standing side by side (cf **file**[1]); any row thought of as so placed (eg of squares along the player's side of a chessboard); (in *pl*) soldiers, *esp* private soldiers, (with *the*, private soldiers collectively); (in *pl*) persons of ordinary grade; a row of taxis awaiting hire; a place where taxis are allowed to stand for hire (also **taxi rank**); a set of organ pipes of the same type; arrangement in line; order, grade or degree; an official post ordered in superiority (*esp milit*); position in society, etc; high standing, *esp* social. ◆ *vt* to place in a line; to assign to a particular class or grade; to place on the list of claims against a bankrupt; to be superior to in position, grade, etc, outrank (*US*). ◆ *vi* to have a place in a rank, grade, scale or class; to move in rank; to be admitted as a claim against the property of a bankrupt (*Scots law*). [OFr *renc* (Fr *rang*), perh from OHGer *hring*, *hrinc* ring]
■ **ranked** *adj* (*Shakesp*) *appar* bordered with rows. **rank'er** *n* a person who serves or has served as a private soldier; an officer who has risen from the ranks. **rank'ing** *adj* having a high military, political, etc position; highest in rank of those present. ◆ *n* a position in a graded scale, a rating.
■ **break rank** or **ranks** (*esp milit*) to fall or move out of line. **close ranks** see under **close**[2]. **pull rank** to use one's rank to exert authority, get one's own way. **rank and file** common soldiers; ordinary people; those in an organization, etc not involved in its management. **take rank of** to take precedence over.

rank[2] /rangk/ *adj* growing high and luxuriantly; coarsely or excessively overgrown; out-and-out, absolute, utter; over-productive; offensively strong-scented or strong-tasting; gross; foul; (of an amount of money) excessive (*law*); abundant (*Spenser*); swollen (*Shakesp*); dense (*Spenser*, now *N Eng*); lustful, in heat (*Shakesp*); grossly obvious (*rare*); deep-cutting; strong, lusty, vigorous (*obs* or *dialect*); violent (*obs*). ◆ *adv* violently (*Spenser*); utterly (now *dialect*). [OE *ranc* proud, strong]
■ **rank'ly** *adv*. **rank'ness** *n*.
□ **rank'-rī'der** *n* a hard rider; a mosstrooper; a highwayman. **rank'-rī'ding** *adj*.

ranke /rangk/ (*Shakesp, As You Like It* III.2.88) *n appar* a jog-trot (*perh* a misprint for **rack**[5]); passage otherwise explained as meaning a repetition of the same rhyme like a file (rank) of so many butterwomen.

Rankine /rang'kin/ *adj* of or designating an absolute scale of temperature on which the units are the same as those on the Fahrenheit scale. [William JM *Rankine* (1820–72), Scottish engineer and scientist]

rankle /rang'kl/ *vi* to go on vexing, irritating or embittering; to fester (*archaic*); to cause festering (*archaic*). ◆ *vt* to cause to fester; to poison; to embitter; to fester (*archaic*); to cause festering (*archaic*). ◆ *n* (*archaic*) a continual irritation. [OFr *rancler*, *raoncler*, from *draoncler*, appar from LL *dra(cu)nculus* an ulcer, dimin of L *dracō*, from Gr *drakōn* dragon]

rannel-balk, rannell-balk, rannle-balk, etc see **randle-balk**.

ransack /ran'sak/ or *-sak'*/ *vt* to search thoroughly; to plunder; to pillage. ◆ *n* (*archaic*) eager search. [ON *rannsaka*, from *rann* house, and *sœkja* to seek]
■ **ran'sacker** *n*.

ransel see **ranzel**.

ranshackle or **ranshakle** /ran-shak'l/ (*Walter Scott*) *vt* to search, ransack. [Dialect Eng *ransackle*, *ram-*, from **ransack**]

ransom /ran'səm/ *n* price of redemption or reclamation; redemption from captivity; atonement, redemption (*relig*); an extortionate price. ◆ *vt* to pay, demand or accept ransom for; to redeem; to redeem, atone (*relig*). [Fr *rançon*, from L *redemptiō*, *-ōnis* redemption]
■ **ran'somable** *adj*. **ran'somer** *n*. **ran'somless** *adj*.
□ **ransomware** *n* (*comput sl*) software designed to inhibit the operation of a system until a ransom is paid.
■ **a king's ransom** a very large sum of money. **hold to ransom** to retain until a ransom is paid; to blackmail into concessions (*fig*). **put to ransom** to offer to release for ransom.

rant /rant/ *vi* to declaim bombastically; to storm or scold with great anger; to sing, play, or make merry, noisily. ◆ *vt* to utter in a high-flown, self-important way. ◆ *n* empty speechifying; bombast; an angry tirade; a noisy frolic (*Scot*); a lively tune. [Obs Du *ranten* to rave; LGer *randen*, Ger *ranzen*]
■ **ran'ter** *n* a person who rants; an extravagant preacher; a member of a Commonwealth antinomian sect; (as a byname) a Primitive Methodist; a roisterer; a noisy musician (*Scot*). **ran'terism** *n*. **rant'ing** *n* and *adj*. **rant'ingly** *adv*.

rantle-balk, etc see **randle-balk**.

ranula see under **Rana**.

ranunculus /rə-nung'kū-ləs/ *n* (*pl* **ranun'culī** or **ranun'culuses**) any plant of the buttercup genus *Ranunculus*. [L *rānunculus*, dimin of *rāna* a frog]
■ **ranunculā'ceous** *adj* of the buttercup family (**Ranunculā'ceae**).

ranz-des-vaches /rä(s)-dā-väsh'/ *n* (*pl* **ranz-des-vaches**) a French Swiss herdsman's song or alpenhorn melody. [Swiss Fr; *ranz*, of uncertain meaning, and Fr *des vaches* of the cows]

ranzel /ran'zl/, **rancel** or **ransel** /ran'sl/ *n* formerly in Orkney and Shetland, a search for stolen goods. [Older Scot *ransell*; ON *rannsaka*; **ranshackle**]
□ **ran'zelman,** etc (*Walter Scott* **Ran'zellaar**) *n* an official who did this.

RAOC *abbrev*: Royal Army Ordnance Corps (now replaced by **RLC**).

raoulia /ra-oo'li-ə/ *n* any plant of the *Raoulia* genus of large, white caespitose cushion plants (family Compositae) of New Zealand. [New L, from Étienne FL *Raoul* (died 1852)]

rap[1] /rap/ *n* a sharp blow; the sound of a knock; a crime or criminal charge (*sl*). ◆ *vt* and *vi* (**rapp'ing; rapped**) to strike or knock sharply; to swear or testify, *esp* falsely (*obs sl*); to communicate or sound out by raps. ◆ *vt* to censure, reprove (*inf*); to utter sharply. ◆ *vi* to rattle, patter. [Imit]
■ **rapp'er** *n* a person who raps; a doorknocker; a great lie or oath (*archaic*); a spirit-rapper. **rapp'ing** *n* the process of loosening a pattern in a foundry mould by inserting in it and tapping a spike or similar object.
□ **rap sheet** *n* (chiefly *US sl*) a criminal record; a charge sheet.
■ **beat the rap** (*N Am sl*) to be acquitted of a crime; to avoid punishment. **take the rap** (*sl*) to take the blame or punishment, *esp* in place of another.

rap[2] /rap/ (*inf*) *n* an informal talk, discussion, chat, etc; a rhythmic monologue delivered over a musical background; a type of music consisting of such monologues (also **rap music**). ◆ *vi* (**rapp'ing; rapped**) to have a talk, discussion, etc; to get along well, sympathize; to deliver a rhythmic monologue to music. [Perh from **rapport**]
■ **rapp'er** *n*. **rapp'ing** *n*.
□ **rap artist** *n* a performer of rap music. **rap group** *n* (*US*) a group which meets for informal discussions. **rap session** *n* an informal discussion.

rap[3] /rap/ *n* an 18c Irish counterfeit halfpenny; as a type of worthlessness, a whit, *esp* in *not worth a rap*. [Origin obscure]

rap[4] /rap/ *vt* (**rapp'ing; rapped** or **rapt**) to snatch; to grab; to carry away in spirit or with joy (*Shakesp*). [Perh partly related to MLGer *rappen*, Swed *rappa* to snatch; mainly a back-formation from **rapt**]

rap[5] or **wrap** /rap/ (*Aust*) *vt* (**rapp'ing; rapped**) (*usu* with *up*) to boost, commend, praise highly. ◆ *n* a boost, acclamation, high praise. [Appar erroneously from the obs sense of **rap**[4], to transport with joy, etc]

rapacious /rə-pā'shəs/ *adj* grasping; greedy for gain; living by taking prey. [L *rapāx*, *-ācis*, from *rapere* to seize and carry off]
■ **rapā'ciously** *adv*. **rapā'ciousness** *n*. **rapacity** /-pas'/ *n*.

rape[1] /rāp/ *n* unlawful sexual intercourse (by force) with another person without that person's consent; violation, despoliation; rapine, plunder, seizure (*obs*). ◆ *vt* to commit rape upon; to violate, despoil; to seize and carry off (*obs*); to ravish or transport, as with delight (*obs*). [Prob L *rapere* to snatch, confused with **rap**[4]]
■ **rā'per** *n*. **rā'ping** *adj* tearing prey (*heraldry*); ravishing, delighting (*obs*). **rā'pist** *n*.
■ **date rape** see under **date**[1]. **statutory rape** see under **statute**.

rape[2] /rāp/ *n* the refuse left after wine-making. [Fr *râpe*]

rape[3] /rāp/ *n* a plant (*Brassica napus*) closely related to the turnip and producing brilliant yellow flowers, cultivated for its herbage and oil-producing seeds; applied to various closely related species or varieties. [L *rāpa*, *rāpum* a turnip]
□ **rape cake** *n* refuse of rapeseed after the oil has been expressed. **rape oil** or **rapeseed oil** *n* oil expressed from rapeseed. **rape'seed** *n*.

rape[4] /rāp/ *n* a division of Sussex. [Origin obscure]

Raphanus /raf'ə-nəs/ *n* the radish genus. [Gr *rhaphanis*]
■ **raphania** /rə-fā'ni-ə/ *n* ergotism (attributed by Linnaeus to wild radish seeds).

raphe or **raphé** /rā'fē/ *n* a seam-like junction; the ridge on the side of an anatropous ovule continuing the funicle to the chalaza (*bot*); a broad connecting ridge, eg that between the halves of the vertebrate brain. [Gr *rhaphē* a seam]

Raphia /rā'fi-ə or raf'i-ə/ *n* a genus of handsome pinnately-leaved palms; (*without cap*) raffia. [Malagasy]

raphis, rhaphis /rā'fis/, **raphide** or **rhaphide** /rā'fīd/ *n* (*pl* **raphides** or **rhaphides** /raf'i-dez or rā'fīdz/) a needle-like crystal, *usu* of calcium oxalate, occurring in plant cells. [Gr *rhaphis*, *-idos* a needle, from *rhaptein* to sew]

■ words derived from main entry word; □ compound words; ■ idioms and phrasal verbs

rapid /rap'id/ adj swift; quickly accomplished; sloping steeply; requiring short exposure (photog). ◆ n a very swift-flowing part of a river with steep descent and often broken water but no actual drop (usu in pl). [L rapidus, from rapere to seize]
■ **rapidity** /rə-pid'i-ti/ n. **rap'idly** adv. **rap'idness** n.
❏ **rapid dominance** n (milit) a strategy of launching an overwhelming attack at the start of a conflict in order to break the enemy's will to resist. **rapid eye movement** n the rapid movement of the eyes in unison behind closed lids that accompanies phases of sleep during which dreams are particularly vivid (abbrev **REM**). **rapid fire** n the firing of guns, asking of questions, etc in quick succession. **rap'id-fire** adj.

rapier /rā'pi-ər/ n a long slender sword, suitable for thrusting. [Fr rapière]

rapine /rap'īn or -in/ n seizure, plundering; prey; ravishment, transport (Milton). [L rapīna, from rapere to seize]

rapist see under **rape**[1].

raploch /rap'lohh/ (Scot) n and adj homespun. [Origin unknown]

rapparee /ra-pə-rē'/ n a wild Irish plunderer, orig of the late 17c. [Ir rapaire half-pike, robber]

rappee /ra-pē'/ n a coarse, strong-flavoured snuff. [Fr râpé rasped, grated, from râper to rasp]

rappel /ra- or rə-pel'/ n abseiling; call to arms by the beating of a drum (milit). ◆ vi (**rappell'ing**; **rappelled'**) same as **abseil**. [Fr]
■ **rappell'ing** n.

rappen /räp'ən/ n (pl **rapp'en**) a monetary unit in Switzerland and Liechtenstein, $\frac{1}{100}$ of a Swiss franc. [Ger Rappe raven]

rapper and **rapping** see under **rap**[1,2].

Rappist /rap'ist/ or **Rappite** /-īt/ n a Harmonist (qv under **harmony**), a follower of George Rapp.

rapport /ra- or rə-pōr'/ n relation; connection; sympathy; emotional bond; spiritualistic touch. [Fr]

rapporteur /ra-pör-tœr'/ n a person whose task it is to carry out an investigation and/or draw up a report (for a committee, etc). [Fr, from rapporter to bring back]
■ **rapportage** /ra-pör-täzh'/ n the description of real events in writing; flat description, lacking in imagination.

rapprochement /ra-prosh-mã'/ n a drawing together; establishment or renewal of cordial relations. [Fr]

rapscallion /rap-skal'yən or -i-ən/ n a rascal; a low, mean wretch (joc). [**rascal**]

rapt /rapt/ adj snatched or carried away (archaic); abducted (archaic); carried out of this world; transported, enraptured, entranced; wholly engrossed; very pleased, thrilled (Aust and NZ inf). [L raptus, pap of rapere to seize and carry off; but partly also pap of **rap**[4]]
■ **rapt'ly** adv.

raptor /rap'tər/ n a rapist (archaic); a plunderer (archaic); a bird of prey (esp diurnal), member of the abandoned order Raptores /-tō'rēz/; a fierce predatory dinosaur (usu short for **velociraptor**). [L raptor, -ōris a plunderer, from rapere to seize]
■ **raptatō'rial** or **raptō'rial** adj predatory; adapted to predatory life.

rapture /rap'chər/ n extreme delight; transport; ecstasy; a paroxysm; (among some fundamentalist Christians) the transporting of the faithful to heaven at the Second Coming; a seizing and carrying away (archaic). ◆ vt to enrapture. [**rapt**]
■ **rap'tured** adj. **rap'tureless** adj. **rap'turist** n. **rap'turize** or **-ise** vi to go into raptures. **rap'turous** adj. **rap'turously** adv. **rap'turousness** n.
■ **rapture of the deep** or **depth** nitrogen narcosis.

rara avis /rä'rə ā'vis or rä'ra ä'wis/ (L) n a rare bird; a rare person or thing. [Juvenal, 6.165]

ra-ra skirt /rä'rä skûrt/ n a very short gathered or pleated skirt, orig as worn by cheerleaders. [Prob from **hurrah**]

rare[1] /rār/ adj seldom encountered; uncommon; excellent; especially good; extraordinary; used as a mere intensive, esp with and (inf); (of the atmosphere) thin; not dense; sparse. [Fr, from L rārus]
■ **rarefac'tion** /rār-i- or rar-i-/ n rarefying. **rarefac'tive** adj. **rar'efiable** adj. **rar'efied** adj (of the atmosphere) thin; refined, exclusive, esoteric. **rar'efy** vt and vi (**rar'efying; rar'efied**) to make or become less dense, to refine. **rāre'ly** adv seldom; choicely; remarkably well. **rāre'ness** n. **rarity** /rār' or rar'i-ti/ n the state of being rare; thinness; something valued for its scarcity; uncommonness.
❏ **rare bird** n an exceptional person or thing. **rare'bit** n (often called **Welsh rarebit**) melted cheese, with or without ale, on hot toast (also **rabbit** or **Welsh rabbit**). **rare earth** n an oxide of a **rare-earth element**, any of a group of metallic elements (some of them rare) closely similar in chemical properties and very difficult to separate; now more usu a rare-earth element itself. **rare gas** n inert gas. **rare**

groove n a genre of music that mixes 1970s soul and funk with sampling and electronically generated sounds.

rare[2] /rār/ adj (of meat) underdone; (of eggs) lightly cooked (obs or dialect). [**rear**[3] influenced by **rare**[1]]

rare[3] /rār/ or **rear** /rēr/ (obs) adj and adv early. [**rathe**]
■ **rear'ly** adv.
❏ **rare'-ripe** adj early ripe.

rarebit see under **rare**[1].

raree-show /rā'rē-shō/ n a show carried about in a box, a peepshow; a spectacle. [Appar representing a foreign pronunciation of rare show]

raring /rā'ring/ adj eager (for), full of enthusiasm and sense of urgency, esp in phrase raring to go. [**rear**[2]]

rarity see under **rare**[1].

RAS abbrev : Royal Astronomical Society.

ras /räs/ n a headland; an Ethiopian prince. [Ar ras, ra's head]

rascaille /rä-skä'ē/ (Walter Scott, etc) n and adj an archaic form of **rascal**, in the sense of rabble.

rascal /räs'kl/ n a rogue, scamp; (playfully) a fellow; a deer out of condition (Shakesp); the rabble (obs); one of the rabble (obs). ◆ adj knavish; wretched; of the rabble; out of condition. [OFr rascaille (Fr racaille) scum of the people]
■ **ras'caldom** n the world or conduct of rascals. **ras'calism** n. **rascality** /-kal'/ n the rabble; character or conduct of rascals. **ras'cal-like** adj. **rascallion** /-kal'yən/ or **rapscall'ion** n a rascal; a low, mean wretch. **ras'cally** adj (superl (Shakesp) **ras'calliest**).

rascasse /ras'kas/ n same as **scorpion fish** (see under **scorpion**).

raschel /räsh'əl/ n a type of light loosely-knitted fabric. [Ger Raschelmaschine, a kind of knitting machine]

rase /rāz/ same as **race**[3] or **raze**[1] (see also **race**[5,6] and **rise**).

rash[1] /rash/ adj over-hasty; lacking in caution; operating suddenly (Shakesp); calling for haste (Shakesp). ◆ adv rashly. [Cf Dan and Swed rask; Du and Ger rasch rapid]
■ **rash'ly** adv. **rash'ness** n.

rash[2] /rash/ n an outbreak of red spots or patches on the skin; a large number of instances of anything happening at the same time or in the same place. [Perh OFr rasche (Fr rache)]

rash[3] /rash/ (obs) vt to tear, drag. [OFr arrachier to uproot; cf **race**[6]]

rash[4] /rash/ (Spenser) vt to slash. [Variant of **raze**[1]]

rash[5] /rash/ vi (obs) to dash, rush. ◆ vt (Shakesp) to stick, thrust forcibly. [Origin obscure]

rash[6] /rash/ n a Scots form of **rush**[2].

rasher /rash'ər/ n a thin slice of bacon. [Poss from **rash**[4]]

Raskolnik /ra-skol'nik/ (hist) n a dissenter from the Russian Orthodox Church. [Russ, from raskól separation]

rasorial /ra-, rə-sō'ri-əl or -sō'/ adj scraping the ground for food. [L rāsor, -ōris scraper]
■ **Rasō'res** /-rēz/ n pl an obsolete order, gallinaceous birds with or without the pigeons.

rasp[1] /räsp/ n a coarse file; anything with a similar surface; a mollusc's tongue; an insect's stridulating apparatus; a risp at a door; a grating sound or feeling. ◆ vt to grate as if with a rasp; to grate upon; to risp; to utter gratingly. ◆ vi to have a grating effect; to scrape, as on a fiddle. [OFr raspe (Fr râpe); perh Gmc]
■ **rasp'atory** n a surgeon's rasp. **rasp'er** n someone or something that rasps; in hunting, a difficult fence (inf). **rasp'ing** n a filing; (in pl) fine breadcrumbs used as a coating for food before frying, etc. ◆ adj grating, harsh. **rasp'ingly** adv. **rasp'y** adj rough.
❏ **rasp'-house** n (Du rasphuis) a former type of prison in Germany and Holland, where dyewood was rasped.

rasp[2] /räsp/ (now inf and Scot) n a raspberry. [Earlier raspis; origin unknown]
■ **raspberry** /räz'bər-i/ n the fruit of Rubus idaeus; the plant producing it; extended to some similar species; a sign of disapproval, esp a noise produced by blowing hard with the tongue between the lips (sl); a refusal or rebuke (sl). ◆ adj of, made with, or like raspberry; of the red colour of a raspberry.
❏ **raspberry bush** n. **raspberry jam tree** n an Australian acacia (from the smell of its wood).

rasse /ras or ras'ə/ n a small civet, Viverricula indica. [Javanese rase]

rast /räst or räst/ a Spenserian pap of **race**[5,6].

Rastafarian or **Ras Tafarian** /ras-tə-fä'ri-ən/ (also without cap) n a member of a West Indian (esp Jamaican) religious movement, which rejects Western culture and ideas and regards Haile Selassie, the former Emperor of Ethiopia, as divine (also **Ras'ta** or **Ras'taman**). ◆ adj of or relating to this movement (also **Ras'ta** or **Rastafari** /-ä'ri/). [From Haile Selassie's title and name, Ras Tafari]
■ **Rastafā'rianism** n.

---

fāte; fär; mē; fûr; mīne; mōte; för; mūte; pŭt; dhen (then); el'ə-mənt (element) ◆ For other sounds see detailed chart of pronunciation

raster /ras'tər/ (*TV*) *n* a complete set of scanning lines appearing on a television or computer screen as a rectangular patch of light on which the image is reproduced. [Perh from L *rāstrum*, as for **rastrum**]
■ **ras'terize** or **-ise** *vt*.

rastrum /ras'trəm/ *n* a music-pen. [L *rāstrum* rake]

rasure or **razure** /rā'zhər/ *n* the act of scraping or shaving; erasure; obliteration. [L *rāsūra*]

rat[1] /rat/ *n* a genus (*Rattus*) of animals closely allied to mice, but larger; extended to various related or superficially similar animals; a renegade or turncoat (from the rat's alleged desertion of a doomed ship; *inf*); a strike-breaker (*inf*); someone who works for less than recognized wages (*inf*); a miserable or ill-looking specimen (*inf*); a despicable person (*inf*). ◆ *vi* (**ratt'ing**; **ratt'ed**) to hunt or catch rats; to desert or change sides for unworthy motives; to act as an informer; (of a worker) to work as a rat. [OE *ræt*; cf Ger *Ratte*]
■ **rats** *interj* (*sl*) expressing irritation, annoyance, etc. **ratt'ed** *adj* (*sl*) drunk. **ratt'er** *n* a killer of rats, *esp* a dog; a person who rats. **ratt'ery** *n* apostasy; a place where rats are kept or are abundant. **ratt'ily** *adv* in a rat-like or ratty manner. **ratt'iness** *n* the quality of being rat-like or ratty. **ratt'ing** *n* apostasy; rat-hunting. **ratt'ish** *adj* rat-like; rat-infested. **ratt'y** (**ratt'ier**; **ratt'iest**) *adj* rat-like; rat-infested; wretched; unkempt, untidy; angry, irritable (*inf*).
◻ **rat'-arsed** *adj* (*vulgar sl*) drunk. **rat'bag** *n* (*sl*) a term of abuse; a despicable person. **rat'bite fever** *n* a disease caused by infection with bacteria conveyed by the bite of a rat. **rat'-catcher** *n* a professional killer of rats; unconventional hunting garb (*sl*). **rat'-catching** *n*. **rat'fish** *n* another name for **rabbitfish** (see under **rabbit**[1]); an edible chimera of the N Pacific (*Hydrolagus colliei*). **rat'-flea** *n* a flea that infests rats. **rat'-guard** *n* a metal disc put on a hawser to prevent rats from boarding a ship in port. **rat'hole** *n*. **rat'-hunting** *n*. **rat'-kangaroo** *n* the potoroo, a marsupial of various species about the size of a rabbit, related to the kangaroo. **rat'pack** *n* (*sl*) a rowdy gang of young people; a group of photographers aggressively pursuing famous people. **rat'-pit** *n* an enclosure where rats are worried by dogs. **rat'-poison** *n* any poison for rats. **rat'proof** *adj*. **rat race** *n* a continual round of hectic and futile activity; the scramble to get on in the world by fair means or foul. **rat run** *n* (*inf*) a minor road heavily used by traffic trying to avoid major road congestion. **rats'bane** *n* poison for rats, *esp* white arsenic; a name for many poisonous plants. **rat snake** *n* any of several rodent-eating colubrid snakes, *esp* of the S Asian genus *Ptyas*, or the N American *Elaphe*. **rat's'-tail** or **rat'-tail** *n* the tail of a rat; anything like a rat's tail; a thin coherent dangling lock of hair; an excrescence on a horse's leg; (**rat'-tail**) the grenadier fish. **rat's'-tail**, **rat'-tail** or **rat'-tailed** *adj* having a tail like a rat; like a rat's tail; (of a spoon) ridged along the back of the bowl. **rat trap** *n* a trap for catching rats; a toothed bicycle pedal; an unpleasantly restricting situation.
■ **rat on** to inform against (also **rat out**); to betray the interests of; to desert. **smell a rat** to have a suspicion that something is afoot.

rat[2] /rat/ *vt* (**ratt'ing**; **ratt'ed**) (in imprecations) used for **rot**. [Cf **drat**]

rata /rä'tə/ *n* a myrtaceous New Zealand tree (*Metrosideros robusta*) with hard red wood and bearing crimson flowers. [Maori]

ratable or **rateable** /rā'tə-bl/ *adj* see under **rate**[1].

ratafia /ra-tə-fē'ə/ *n* a flavouring essence made with the essential oil of almonds; a cordial or liqueur flavoured with fruit-kernels; an almond biscuit or cake. [Fr; ety doubtful; cf **tafia**]

ratan /ra-tan'/ *n* same as **rattan**[1].

rataplan /ra-tə-plan'/ *n* a drumming sound. [Fr]

rat-a-tat /rat-ə-tat'/ same as **rat-tat**.

ratatouille /ra-tə-too'i or ra-ta-twē' or -tooy'/ *n* a stew of tomatoes, aubergines, peppers, onions and other vegetables, with olive oil. [Fr, from *touiller* to stir]

ratbag see under **rat**[1].

ratch[1] /rach/ *n* a ratchet; a ratchet-wheel. [Cf Ger *Ratsche*, Fr *rochet*]
■ **ratch'et** *n* a pawl and/or ratchet-wheel. ◆ *vt* and *vi* to move by, or as if by, a ratchet mechanism, by steady, progressive degrees (with *up* or *down*).
◻ **ratchet screwdriver** *n* (*building*, etc) a screwdriver with a ratchet mechanism to make it operate in one direction only. **ratch'et-wheel** *n* a wheel with inclined teeth with which a pawl engages.

ratch[2] /rach/ *n* same as **rache**. ◆ *vi* to wander or prowl (often with *about*; Scot and N Eng). [Ety as for **rache**]

ratch[3] same as **race**[4].

rate[1] /rāt/ *n* amount corresponding; ratio, *esp* time-ratio, speed; amount determined according to a rule or basis; price or cost; a standard; a class or rank, *esp* of ships or sailors; manner, mode; extent, degree; (often in *pl*) an amount levied by a local authority according to the assessed value of property; a clock's gain or loss in unit time; estimated amount or value (*Shakesp*); estimation (*Shakesp*); a fixed quantity (*obs*). ◆ *vt* to estimate; to value; to settle the relative rank, scale or position of; to esteem, regard as; to deserve, be worthy of; to value for purpose of rate-paying; to think highly of (*inf*); to allot (*Shakesp*); to calculate (*Shakesp*). ◆ *vi* to be placed in a certain class. [OFr, from LL (*pro*) *ratā* (*parte*) according to a calculated part, from *rērī*, *ratus* to think, judge]
■ **ratabil'ity** or **rateabil'ity** *n*. **rat'able** or **rate'able** *adj*. **rat'ably** or **rate'ably** *adv*. **rat'er** *n* a person who makes an estimate; (in combination) a ship, etc of a given rate (such as *second-rater*). **rat'ing** *n* a fixing of rates; classification according to grade; the class of any member of a crew; a sailor of such a class; the tonnage-class of a racing yacht; the proportion of viewers or listeners who are deemed to watch or listen to a particular programme or network.
◻ **ratable** (or **rateable**) **value** *n* a value placed on a property, and used to assess the amount of rates payable to the local authority each year. **rate'-cap** *vt*. **rate'-capping** *n* the setting by central government of an upper limit on the rate that can be levied by a local authority. **rate'-cutting** *n* a lowering of charges to obtain traffic. **rated altitude** *n* the height, measured in the international standard atmosphere, at which an aero-engine delivers its maximum power. **rated capacity** *n* a general term for the output of a piece of equipment under specified conditions. **rate-determining step** *n* (*chem eng*) the step, in a process involving a series of consecutive steps, with the slowest rate, largely determining the overall rate of the process. **rate fixing** *n* the determination of the time allocated for a specific task, *usu* as a basis for remuneration. **rate of exchange** see **exchange rate** under **exchange**. **rate'payer** *n* a person who pays a local rate. **rate support grant** *n* money contributed by central government to make up the difference between the rate levied and the amount required for local authority spending. **rate tart** *n* (*inf*) a person who frequently moves money between different savings accounts in order to take advantage of the most favourable rates of interest.
■ **at any rate** in any case, anyhow.

rate[2] /rāt/ *vt* to scold; to chide; to reprove; to drive by scolding. ◆ *vi* to scold. ◆ *n* a reproof to a dog. [ME *raten*; origin obscure]
■ **rā'ting** *n* a sharp scolding.

rate[3] same as **ret**.

ratel /rā'təl or rä'təl/ *n* an animal of the badger-like genus (*Mellivora*) of Africa and India, related to the wolverine (also **honey badger**). [Afrik; origin uncertain]

ratfink /rat'fingk/ (*derog sl*, *esp* N Am) *n* a mean, deceitful, despicable person (also *adj*). [**rat**[1] and **fink**]

rath[1] /räth/ or **rathe** /rädh/ (*archaic*) *adj* quick; eager; early (*compar* **rather** /rädh'ər/ (*Spenser*) earlier; *superl* **rath'est** (*obs* or *dialect*) earliest). [Compar of archaic *rath* quick, ready, eager; OE *hræd* (rarely *hræth*) quick, *hræthe*, *hrathe* quickly; ON *hrathr*]
■ **rathe** /rädh/ *adv* (*compar* **rather** (see **rather** separate entry); *superl* (*obs*) **rath'est**) (*Milton*) early.

rath[2] /räth/ *n* a prehistoric hill fort. [Ir]

rath[3] /ruth/ or **ratha** /ruth'ə/ *n* a four-wheeled horse-drawn carriage or chariot. [Hindi]

rathe see **rath**[1].

rather /rä'dhər/ *adv* (*irreg superl* **ra'therest** (*Shakesp*)) sooner, more quickly (*Shakesp*); more readily; more willingly; in preference; more than otherwise; more properly; somewhat, in some degree. ◆ *interj* (sometimes affectedly /rä-dhûr'/) I should think so; yes, indeed. [Compar of **rath**[1]; OE *hrathor*]
■ **ra'therish** *adv* (*inf*).
■ **the rather** all the more.

ratheripe /rädh'rīp/ or **rathripe** /räth'rīp/ (*archaic and dialect*) *adj* early ripe. ◆ *n* an early-ripening variety. [**rath**[1] and **ripe**[1]]

ratify /rat'i-fī/ *vt* (**rat'ifying**; **rat'ified**) to approve and sanction, *esp* by signature; to give validity or legality to; to confirm the correctness of (*obs*). [Fr *ratifier*, from L *ratus*, pap of *rērī* (see **rate**[1]), and *facere* to make]
■ **rat'ifīable** *adj*. **ratificā'tion** *n*. **rat'ifier** *n*.

ratine or **ratteen** /ra-tēn'/ *n* a rough, open dress fabric (also **rat'iné** /-i-nā/). [Fr *ratine*]

rating see under **rate**[1,2].

ratio /rā'shi-ō or -shyō/ *n* (*pl* **rā'tios**) the relation of one thing to another of which the quotient is the measure; quotient; proportion; a portion, allowance (*rare*); (also **ratio decidendi**) the reason or principle which underlies a decision and which is the basis for using that decision as a precedent in future cases (*law*). [L *ratiō*, *-ōnis* reason, from *rērī*, *ratus* to think]
■ **compound ratio** see under **compound**[1]. **inverse ratio** see under **inverse**.

ratiocinate /ra-shi-os'i-nāt or -ti-/ *vi* to reason. [L *ratiōcinārī*, *-ātus*]
■ **ratiocinā'tion** *n*. **ratioc'inative** or **ratioc'inatory** *adj*. **ratioc'inātor** *n*.

ration /rash'ən or formerly rä'shən/ n a fixed allowance or portion, esp of food and other provisions in time of shortage; (in pl) food (inf). ◆ vt to put on an allowance; to supply with rations; to restrict the supply of to so much for each. [Fr, from L ratiō, -ōnis]
❑ **ration book** or **ration card** n a book or card of coupons or vouchers for rationed commodities. **ration money** n money in lieu of rations.

rational[1] /rash'ə-nəl/ adj of the reason; endowed with reason; agreeable to reason; sane; intelligent; judicious; commensurable with natural numbers. ◆ n a rational being or quantity; (in pl) rational dress, ie knickerbockers instead of skirts for women (hist). [L ratiōnālis, -e, from ratiō]
■ **rationale** /rash-ə-näl'/ n underlying principle; a rational account; a theoretical explanation or solution. **rat'ionalism** n a system of belief regulated by reason, not authority; a disposition to apply to religious doctrines the same critical methods as to science and history, and to attribute all phenomena to natural rather than miraculous causes. **rat'ionalist** n. **rationalist'ic** adj. **rationalist'ically** adv. **rationality** /rash-ən-al'i-ti/ n the quality of being rational; the possession or due exercise of reason; reasonableness. **rationalization** or **-s-** /rash-nəl-ī-zā'shən/ n. **rat'ionalize** or **-ise** vt to make rational; to free from irrational quantities; to conform to reason; to reorganize scientifically; to interpret rationalistically; to substitute conscious reasoning for unconscious motivation in explaining; to organize (an industry) so as to achieve greater efficiency and economy. ◆ vi to think or argue rationally or rationalistically; to employ reason, rationalism or rationalization. **rat'ionalizer** or **-s-** n. **rat'ionally** adv.
❑ **rational dress** n (hist) knickerbockers for women instead of skirts. **rational horizon** see under **horizon**. **rational number** n a number expressed as the ratio of two integers.

rational[2] /rash'ə-nəl/ (hist) n the Jewish high-priest's breastplate; a bishop's vestment like the pallium. [L ratiōnāle, Vulgate translation of Gr logion oracle]

rationale[1] see under **rational**[1].

rationale[2] obsolete form of **rational**[2].

ratite /rat'īt/ (ornithol) adj having a keel-less breastbone; of the **Ratitae** /rä-tī'tē/, flightless birds, such as the ostrich, rhea, emu, kiwi, etc. [L ratis raft]

ratlin, **ratline**, **ratling**, **rattlin**, **rattline** or **rattling** /rat'lin, rat'ling/ n any of the small lines forming steps of the rigging of ships. [Ety uncertain]

ratoo see **ratu**.

ratoon /ra- or rə-toon'/ n a new shoot from the ground after cropping, esp of sugar-cane or cotton. ◆ vi to send up ratoons. ◆ vt to cut down so as to obtain ratoons. [Sp retoño shoot]
■ **ratoon'er** n a plant that ratoons.

rat-rhyme /rat'rīm/ (Scot) n a bit of doggerel; a screed.

rattan[1] or **ratan** /ra-tan'/ n any of various climbing palms, esp of the genus Calamus, with a very long thin stem; a cane made from the stem; the stems collectively as wickerwork. [Malay rōtan]

rattan[2] /rə-tan'/ n the continuous beat of a drum. [Imit]

rat-tat /rat'tat/ n a knocking sound. [Imit]

ratted see under **rat**[1].

ratteen same as **ratine**.

ratten /rat'n/ vt to practise sabotage against (worker or employer). [Origin uncertain]
■ **ratt'ening** n (found earlier than verb).

ratter, **rattery**, **ratting**, etc see under **rat**[1].

rattle /rat'l/ vi to make a quick succession or alternation of short hard sounds; to move along rapidly making such a sound; to chatter briskly and emptily. ◆ vt to cause to rattle; to fluster, disconcert or irritate (inf); to assail with rattling (Shakesp); to utter glibly, as by rote (often with off); to perform or push through to completion in a rapid, perfunctory or noisy manner; to scold loudly (obs). ◆ n an instrument or toy producing a rattling sound when shaken; an instrument for making a whirring noise, formerly used by watchmen; a similar device used at festive gatherings; a dice-box (old sl); a plant whose seeds rattle in the capsule, applied to two scrophulaceous plants, **yellow rattle** or cock's-comb (Rhinanthus crista-galli) and **red rattle** or marsh lousewort (Pedicularis palustris); the rings of a rattlesnake's tail; a vivacious prattler; a spell of lively chattering; the sound of rattling; the crackling of paper; a sound in the throat of a dying person (also **death rattle**); racket. [ME ratelen; cf Ger rasseln, Du ratelen to rattle; connection with OE plant names hratele, hrætelwyrt is questioned]
■ **ratt'ler** n a rattle; a coach (old sl); a rattlesnake (inf); a telling blow (inf); an excellent specimen of the kind (inf). **ratt'ling** n. ◆ adj making a rattle; smart, lively; strikingly good (inf). ◆ adv strikingly. **ratt'ly** adj (**ratt'lier**; **ratt'liest**) making a rattling noise; inclined to rattle.

❑ **ratt'lebag** n a rattle or rattling apparatus; a person who causes commotion (Scot). **ratt'lebrain**, **ratt'lehead** or **ratt'lepate** n a shallow, voluble, volatile person. **ratt'le-brained**, **ratt'le-headed** or **ratt'le-pated** adj. **ratt'lesnake** n a venomous American pit-viper (genus Crotalus) with rattling horny rings on the end of its tail. **ratt'letrap** n (inf) a contemptuous name for any apparatus, equipment, finery, bric-à-brac; a rickety vehicle; the mouth.
■ **rattle someone's cage** (inf) to stir someone up to anger or excitement.

rattlin, **rattline** and **rattling** same as **ratlin**.

ratton /rat'n/ (now N Eng) n a rat. [Fr raton]

ratty see under **rat**[1].

ratu /rä'too/ n a local chief or ruler in Indonesia and Fiji (also **ra'too**).

raucle /rö'kl/ (Scot) adj rough; vigorous; hale.

raucous /rö'kəs/ adj hoarse, harsh. [L raucus hoarse]
■ **rau'cously** adv. **rau'cousness** n. **raucid** /rö'sid/ adj (Lamb) raucous.

raught /röt/ obsolete or archaic pat and pap of **reach**[1,2] and **reck**.

raun (Walter Scott) same as **rawn**[1].

raunch[1] /rönsh/ (Spenser) vt same as **race**[6].

raunch[2] see under **raunchy**.

raunchy /rön' or rän'chi/ (inf) adj (**raunch'ier**; **raunch'iest**) coarsely or openly sexual; earthy, bawdy, lewd; carelessly untidy, shabby. [Origin unknown]
■ **raunch** n (orig US) coarseness, bawdiness. **raunch'ily** adv. **raunch'iness** n.

raunge /rönj/ obsolete form of **range**.

Rauwolfia /rö-wol'fi-ə/ n a tropical genus of apocynaceous trees and shrubs, of which Rauwolfia serpentina and other species yield valuable drugs. [Leonhard Rauwolf (died 1596), German botanist]

RAuxAF abbrev : Royal Auxiliary Air Force.

rav /rav/ n a rabbi, esp one in authority; a teacher or mentor; (with cap) a title preceding a personal name, used by orthodox rabbis.

ravage /rav'ij/ vt and vi to lay waste; to destroy; to pillage. ◆ n devastation; ruin. [Fr ravager, from ravir to carry off by force, from L rapere]
■ **rav'ager** n.

RAVC abbrev : Royal Army Veterinary Corps.

rave[1] /rāv/ vi to rage; to talk as if mad or delirious; to write or speak with extreme enthusiasm (with about or over; inf); to attend a rave. ◆ vt to utter wildly. ◆ n infatuation (inf); extravagant praise (inf); a rave-up (inf); a mass gathering of young people to dance to loud music under bright flashing lights, often associated with the use of certain drugs, esp Ecstasy. ◆ adj (inf) extravagantly enthusiastic; crazy. [Perh OFr raver, which may be from L rabere to rave]
■ **rā'ver** n a person who raves; a lively, uninhibited person (inf). **rā'ving** n and adj. **rā'vingly** adv.
❑ **rave'-up** n (inf) a lively celebration; a wild, uninhibited, thoroughly enjoyable party. **raving mad** adj frenzied; very angry (inf).

rave[2] /rāv/ n a side piece of a wagon. [Ety obscure]

rave[3] /rāv/ (Scot) pat of **rive**.

ravel /rav'l/ vt (**rav'elling**; **rav'elled**) to entangle; to disentangle, untwist, unweave, unravel (usu with out). ◆ vi to become entangled; to be untwisted or unwoven; to search (with into; obs). ◆ n a tangle; a broken thread. [Appar Du ravelen]
■ **rav'elling** n a ravelled out thread. **rav'elment** n.

ravel bread /rav'l bred/ (obs or dialect) n wholemeal bread, intermediate between white and brown (also **ravelled bread**). [Origin unknown]

ravelin /rav'lin/ (fortif) n a detached work with two embankments raised before the counterscarp. [Fr]

ravelment see under **ravel**.

raven[1] /rā'v(ə)n/ n a large, glossy black species of crow (Corvus corax). ◆ adj shiny black like a raven. [OE hræfn; ON hrafn]
❑ **rā'ven-bone** or **rā'ven's-bone** n the gristle on the spoon of the brisket, formerly thrown to the ravens after a hunt. **rā'ven-duck** or **rā'ven's-duck** n fine hempen sail-cloth.

raven[2] /rav'in/ n same as **ravin** (n). ◆ vt to take away by force (obs); to devour hungrily or greedily (literary). ◆ vi to prey rapaciously (on or upon); to be intensely hungry; to hunger intensely (for); to roam about hungrily after prey. [OFr ravine plunder, from L rapīna plunder]
■ **rav'ener** n. **rav'ening** adj plundering; rapacious; voracious; intensely hungry. **rav'enously** adv. **rav'enousness** n.

ravin, **raven** or **ravine** /rav'in/ n rapine; preying; prey (Spenser and Milton). ◆ adj (Shakesp) ravening. ◆ vt and vi same as **raven**[2] (v). [Ety as **raven**[2]]
■ **rav'in'd** adj (Shakesp) prob sated, gorged.

ravine[1] /rə-vēn'/ n a deep, narrow gorge. [Fr, from L rapīna rapine, violence]
■ **ravined'** adj scored with ravines; trenched.

ravine[2] see **ravin**.

ravioli /ra-vi-ō'li/ n small, square pasta cases with a savoury filling of meat, cheese, etc. [Ital, pl of raviòlo]

ravish /rav'ish/ vt to seize or carry away by violence; to abduct; to snatch away from sight or from the world; to rape; to enrapture. [Fr ravir, ravissant, from L rapere to seize and carry off]
■ **rav'isher** n. **rav'ishing** adj delightful; lovely; transporting. **rav'ishingly** adv. **rav'ishment** n.

raw /rö/ adj not altered from its natural state; not cooked or dressed; unwrought; not prepared or manufactured; not refined; not corrected; not mixed; having the skin abraded or removed (also fig); showing through the skin (Spenser); crude; hard, harsh, cruel; untrained; out of condition (Spenser); red and inflamed; immature; inexperienced; chilly and damp; naked; (of statistics, data for a computer, etc) not yet checked, sorted, corrected, etc. ◆ n (with the) a skinned, sore or sensitive place; the raw state; that which is raw. [OE hrēaw; Du rauw, ON hrār, Ger roh]
■ **raw'ish** adj. **raw'ly** adv. **raw'ness** n.
❑ **raw bar** n (US) a restaurant or counter at which uncooked shellfish is served. **raw'bone** (Spenser) or **raw'boned** adj with little flesh on the bones; gaunt. **raw'head** or **raw'head-and-blood'y-bones** n a bugbear or pair of bugbears to frighten children. **raw'hide** adj of untanned leather. ◆ n a rope or whip of untanned leather. **raw material** n material (often in its natural state) that serves as the starting-point of a manufacturing or technical process; that out of which something is or can be made, or may develop (fig). **raw sienna** see **sienna** under **Sienese**. **raw silk** n natural untreated silk threads; fabric made from these.
■ **a raw deal** harsh, inequitable treatment. **in the raw** in its natural state; naked.

rawing see **rowen**.

Rawlplug® /röl'plug/ n a tubular plug for fixing screws, etc in masonry. [Manufacturers' name]

rawn[1] or **raun** /rön/ (Scot) n fish-roe; a female fish. [Cf Dan ravn roe]

rawn[2] see **rowen**.

RAX abbrev : rural automatic exchange.

rax /raks/ (Scot and N Eng) vt to stretch; to strain; to reach; to reach out, hand. ◆ vi to stretch; to reach out. ◆ n a stretch; a strain. [OE raxan]

ray[1] /rā/ n a line along which light or other energy, or a stream of particles, is propagated; a narrow beam; a gleam of intellectual light; a look or glance; a radiating line or part; the radially extended fringing outer part of an inflorescence; a supporting spine in a fin. ◆ vt to radiate; to provide with rays. ◆ vi to radiate. [OFr rais (accusative rai), from L radius a rod]
■ **rayed** adj. **ray'less** adj. **ray'let** n a small ray.
❑ **ray flower** or **floret** n any of the small flowers radiating out from the margin of the flower-head of certain composite plants. **ray fungus** n a bacterium (genus Actinomyces) that forms radiating threads, some species pathogenic. **ray gun** n (in science fiction) a gun that fires destructive rays. **ray of sunshine** n a happy person, someone who cheers up others.

ray[2] /rā/ n a skate, thornback, torpedo, or any similar flat-bodied elasmobranch fish. [Fr raie, from L raia]

ray[3] same as **re**[2].

ray[4] /rā/ n (obs) array. ◆ vt to array (obs); to dress (obs); to defile, dirty (Shakesp). [**array**]

rayah /rī'a/ (hist) n a non-Muslim subject of the Ottoman Empire. [Ar ra'īyah, from ra'ā to pasture]

Ray-Bans® /rā'banz/ n pl a type of designer sunglasses.

rayle obsolete or Spenserian spelling of **rail**[2,4].

Rayleigh criterion /rā'lē krī-tē'ri-ən/ (phys) n a criterion for the resolution of interference fringes, spectral lines and images. [JW Strutt, Lord Rayleigh (1842–1919), English physicist]

Rayleigh disc /rā'lē disk/ n a small light disc hung by a fine thread at an angle to a progressive sound wave, its deflection being used to measure the intensity of the sound. [Ety as for **Rayleigh criterion**]

Rayleigh scattering /rā'lē skat'ə-ring/ n scattering of light by fine dust or suspensions of particles. [Ety as for **Rayleigh criterion**]

Rayleigh wave /rā'lē wāv/ (acoustics) n a non-dispersive surface wave on a solid body with a free surface. [Ety as for **Rayleigh criterion**]

raylet, etc see under **ray**[1].

Raynaud's disease /rā'nōz di-zēz'/ (med) n constriction of the blood supply to digits due to a paroxysmal disorder of the arteries, the fingers (or toes) turning white and then blue usu in response to cold or stress

(called **Raynaud's phenomenon** in the context of an underlying disease of connective tissues). [Maurice Raynaud (1834–81), French physician]

rayne obsolete or Spenserian spelling of **reign**.

rayon /rā'ən or -on/ n a ray (Spenser); artificial silk fabric made from cellulose (see **silk**). [Fr rayon ray]

raze[1] or **rase** /rāz/ vt to lay (a building) level with the ground; to demolish; to graze; to scrape; to erase; to slash, cut into ornamental devices. [Fr raser, from L rādere, rāsum to scrape]
■ **razed** or **rased** adj.

raze[2] /rāz/ (Shakesp) n same as **race**[3].

razee /rā-zē'/ (hist) n a ship cut down by reducing the number of decks. ◆ vt to remove the upper deck or decks of. [Fr rasé cut down]

razmataz see **razzmatazz**.

razoo /rə-zoo'/ (Aust and NZ inf) n a (non-existent) coin of insignificant value, esp in phrases not have a (brass) razoo, give someone every last razoo, etc. [Origin obscure]

razor /rā'zər/ n a sharp-edged implement for shaving. ◆ vt to cut with a razor. ◆ adj (fig) sharp, keen, precise. [OFr rasour; see **raze**[1]]
■ **rā'zorable** adj (Shakesp) fit to be shaved.
❑ **rā'zorback** n a sharp ridge; a rorqual; a ridge-backed pig. ◆ adj sharply ridged. **rā'zorbill** n a species of auk, with a compressed bill. **razor blade** n a sharp blade used in a razor. **razor cut** n a haircut done with a razor. **rā'zor-cut** vt. **razor edge** n a very fine sharp edge, such as that on which a balance swings; a critically balanced situation. **rā'zorfish** or **rā'zorclam** n a lamellibranch mollusc (genus Solen and Ensis), with a shell like an old-fashioned razor handle. **razor shell** n its shell, or the animal itself. **rā'zor-strop** n. **razor wire** n thick wire with sharp pieces of metal attached, used like barbed wire, for fences, etc.
■ **Occam's razor** see under **Occamism**.

razure same as **rasure**.

razz /raz/ (sl) n a raspberry. ◆ vt and vi (N Am) to jeer (at).

razzamatazz see **razzmatazz**.

razzia /raz'ya or -i-ə/ n a pillaging incursion, esp one carried out by N African Moors. [Fr, from Algerian Ar ghāzīah]

razzle-dazzle /raz'l-daz'l/ (sl) n (also **razz'le**) a rowdy, lively spree; dazzling show, confusion, etc. [Appar from **dazzle**]
■ **on the razzle** having a spree or bout of heavy drinking.

razzmatazz, **razmataz** /raz'mə-taz or -taz'/ or **razzamatazz** /raz'-ə-mə-taz or -taz'/ n to-do, hullabaloo; razzle-dazzle.

RB abbrev : formerly, Rifle Brigade.

Rb (chem) symbol : rubidium.

RBI (baseball) abbrev : run batted in.

RBMK reactor /är-bē-em-kā ri-ak'tər/ n a graphite-moderated, boiling water-cooled, pressure-tube reactor, unique to the former USSR. [Abbrev Russ reaktor bolshoy moshchnosti kanalnӯy, high-power channel reactor]

RC abbrev : Red Cross; Roman Catholic (Church); Taiwan (official name Republic of China; IVR).

RCA abbrev : Central African Republic (ie République Centrafricaine; IVR); Radio Corporation of America; Royal Canadian Academy; Royal College of Art.

RCAF abbrev : Royal Canadian Air Force.

RCB abbrev : Republic of Congo (IVR).

RCC abbrev : Roman Catholic Church.

RCD abbrev : residual current device.

RCGP abbrev : Royal College of General Practitioners.

RCH abbrev : Republic of Chile (IVR).

RCM abbrev : Regimental Court-martial, abolished in 1955; Royal College of Music.

RCMP abbrev : Royal Canadian Mounted Police.

RCN abbrev : Royal College of Nursing.

RCO abbrev : Royal College of Organists.

RCOG abbrev : Royal College of Obstetricians and Gynaecologists.

RCP abbrev : Royal College of Physicians.

RCPS abbrev : Royal College of Physicians and Surgeons.

RCR abbrev : Royal College of Radiologists.

RCS abbrev : Royal College of Science; Royal College of Surgeons; Royal Corps of Signals.

RCSLT abbrev : Royal College of Speech and Language Therapists.

RCT abbrev : Royal Corps of Transport (now replaced by **RLC**).

RCU abbrev : remote control unit.

RCVS abbrev : Royal College of Veterinary Surgeons.

RD *abbrev* : (Naval) Reserve Decoration; refer to drawer (written on a returned bank cheque); Rural Dean.

Rd *abbrev* : Road (in addresses).

rd *abbrev* : rutherford.

RDA *abbrev* : recommended daily (or dietary) allowance.

RDC *abbrev* : Rural Development Council.

RDF *abbrev* : radio direction-finding (or -finder); refuse-derived fuel.

rDNA *abbrev* : recombinant DNA (see **recombine**).

RDS *abbrev* : radio data system, a method of broadcasting in which a digital signal is transmitted along with the radio signal, *esp* to facilitate automatic tuning.

RDX *abbrev* : Research Department Explosive (also called **cyclonite**).

RE *abbrev* : Reformed Episcopal; religious education (in schools); Royal Engineers; Royal Society of Painter-Printmakers (formerly known as the Royal Society of Etchers and Engravers).

Re see **Ra** (*n*).

Re or **re** *abbrev* : rupee.

Re (*chem*) *symbol* : rhenium.

re¹ /rē/ (*commercial jargon*) *prep* concerning, with reference to. [L *in rē* (ablative of *rēs* thing) in the matter]

re² /rā/ (*music*) *n* the second note of the scale in sol-fa notation (also anglicized in spelling as **ray**). [See **Aretinian**]

re- /rē-/ *pfx* denoting: again; again and in a different way. [L]

> Words formed using the prefix **re-** are listed as separate entries in the main word list or, if their meaning is self-evident, at the foot of the page.

're /r/ short form of **are¹**.

reach¹ /rēch/ *vt* (pat and pap **reached** or (*obs*) **raught** /röt/) to stretch forth, hold out; to hand, pass; to succeed in touching or getting; to communicate with; to arrive at; to extend to; to deal, strike (*archaic*); to get at; to take, snatch, seize (*obs*); to stretch, lengthen out (*obs*). ◆ *vi* to stretch out the hand; to extend; to amount; to attain to (*usu* with *for* or *after*); to succeed in going or coming. ◆ *n* act or power of reaching; extent of stretch; range, scope; (*usu pl*) level or rank; the number of people estimated to be exposed at least once to a particular advertisement (*marketing*); a conclusion that is barely justifiable or demands an effort of the imagination (*N Am*); artifice (*obs*); a stretch or portion between defined limits, as of a stream between bends; the distance traversed between tacks (*naut*); a bay (*obs*). [OE *rǣcan* (pat *rǣhte, rāhte* ; pap *gerǣht*); Ger *reichen* to reach]
 ■ **reach'able** *adj.* **reach'er** *n.* **reach'ing** *adj.* **reach'less** *adj* unattainable.
 ❑ **reach'-me-down** *adj* ready-made or second-hand. ◆ *n* (often in *pl*) ready-made or second-hand attire; trousers.

reach² /rēch/ obsolete or dialect form of **retch¹**.

react¹ /ri-akt/ *vi* to return an impulse in the opposite direction; to act in return; to act with mutual effect; to act in resistance; to swing back in the opposite direction; to respond to a stimulus; to undergo chemical change produced by a reagent; to act, behave; (of share prices) to fall sharply after a rise. [LL *reagere, -actum*, from *agere* to do]
 ■ **reac'tance** *n* (*electronics*) the component of impedance due to inductance or capacitance. **reac'tant** *n* (*chem*) a substance taking part in a reaction. **reac'tion** *n* action resisting other action; mutual action; an action or change in an opposite direction; backward tendency from revolution, reform or progress; response to stimulus; the chemical action of a reagent; a physical or mental effect caused by medicines, drugs, etc; a transformation within the nucleus of an atom; acidity or alkalinity; feeling or thought aroused by, or in response to, a statement, situation, person, etc. **reac'tional** *adj.* **reac'tionarism** *n.* **reac'tionarist** *n.* **reac'tionary** *adj* of or favouring reaction, *esp* against revolution, reform, etc. ◆ *n* a person who tends to oppose political change or who attempts to revert to past political conditions. **reac'tionism** *n.* **reac'tionist** *n* and *adj* reactionary. **reac'tive** *adj* of or relating to reaction; readily acted upon or responsive to stimulus; produced by emotional stress; relating to or having a reactance (*electronics*). **reac'tively** *adv.* **reac'tiveness** or **reactiv'ity** *n.* **reac'tor** *n* someone or something that undergoes a reaction; a device which introduces reactance into an electric circuit; a container in which a chemical reaction takes place; a nuclear reactor (qv).
 ❑ **reaction formation** *n* (*psychol*) a mechanism whereby a person adopts a mode of behaviour that is the opposite of his or her true disposition. **reaction time** *n* the interval between stimulus and reaction. **reaction turbine** *n* a turbine in which the fluid expands progressively in passing alternate rows of fixed and moving blades, the kinetic energy continuously developed being absorbed by the latter.

react² /rē-akt/ *vt* to act a second, etc time.

reactivate /rē-ak'ti-vāt/ *vt* to restore to an activated state. [**re-**]
 ■ **reactiva'tion** *n.*

reactive see under **react¹**.

read¹ /rēd/ *vt* (pat and pap **read** /red/) to look at and comprehend the meaning of written or printed words in; to understand as by interpretation of signs; to collect the meaning of; to go over progressively with silent understanding of symbols or with utterance aloud of words or performance of notes; to accept or offer as that which the writer intended; to learn from written or printed matter; to find recorded; to observe the indication of; to solve; to register, indicate; to teach, lecture on; to study; to impute by inference (as to read a meaning into); to retrieve (data) from a storage device (*comput*); to advise (*archaic*; see **rede**); to make out; to interpret; to expound; to make known (*Spenser*); to declare; to name (*Spenser*). ◆ *vi* to perform the act of reading; to practise much reading; to study; to find mention; to give the reader an impression; to endure the test of reading; to deliver lectures; to have a certain wording. ◆ *n* a spell of reading; reading-matter; an opportunity of reading (*Scot*); counsel, a saying, an interpretation (*Spenser*). ◆ *adj* /red/ versed in books; learned. [OE *rǣdan* to discern, read, from *rǣd* counsel]
 ■ **readabil'ity** /rēd-/ *n.* **read'able** *adj* legible; easy to read; interesting without being of highest quality. **read'ableness** *n.* **read'ably** *adv.* **read'er** *n* someone who reads or reads much; a person who reads prayers or passages of scripture, etc at a church service; a lecturer, *esp* a higher grade of university lecturer; a proof-corrector; a person who reads and reports on manuscripts for a publisher; a reading-book; a pocketbook (*criminal sl*); a device that projects a large image of a piece of microfilm onto a screen, for reading; a document reader (*comput*). **read'ership** *n* the post of reader in a university; the total number of readers (of a newspaper, etc). **read'ing** *adj* addicted to reading. ◆ *n* the action of the verb *read*; perusal; study of books; public or formal recital, *esp* of a bill before Parliament (see **first, second** and **third reading** below); the actual word or words that may be read in a passage of a text; the indication that can be read off from an instrument; matter for reading; lettering; an interpretation; a performer's conception of the meaning, rendering; knowledge gained from having read books.
 ❑ **reader advertisement** *n* an advertising feature in a magazine which follows the style of the editorial part of the magazine, often with accompanying photographs or drawings. **readers' inquiry card** or **readers' service card** *n* a business reply card bound into a magazine with numbers corresponding to advertised products. **read'-in** *n* input of data to a computer or storage device. **reading age** *n* reading ability calculated as equivalent to the average ability at a certain age. **read'ing-book** *n* a book of exercises in reading. **read'ing-boy** *n* (*printing*; *obs*) a reader's assistant. **read'ing-desk** *n* a desk for holding a book or paper while it is read; a lectern. **reading group** same as **book group** (see under **book**). **read'ing-lamp** *n* a lamp for reading by. **read'ing-machine** *n* a reader for microfilm; a document reader (*comput*). **reading matter** *n* printed material, eg books, magazines. **read'ing-room** *n* a room for consultation, study or investigation of books in a library; a room with papers, periodicals, etc resorted to for reading; a proofreaders' room. **read'me file** *n* (*comput*) a text file supplied with computer software that contains information about the software, such as advice on installation and bugs. **read'-only** *adj* (*comput*) of a storage device or file, capable of being read but not altered. **read'-out** *n* the output unit of a computer; the retrieval of data from a computer; data from a computer, printed or registered on magnetic tape or punched paper tape, or displayed on a screen; data from a radio transmitter. **read-write head** *n* (*comput*) in a disk drive, a head that can both retrieve and record data. **read-write memory** *n* (*comput*) one that allows retrieval and input of data.
 ■ **first, second** and **third reading** the three successive formal readings of a bill before parliament, when (in Britain) it is introduced, discussed

rēabsorb' *vt.*	**rēaccus'tom** *vt.*	**rēac'tuate** *vt.*
rēabsorp'tion *n.*	**rēacquaint'** *vt.*	**rēadapt'** *vt* and *vi.*
rēacclī'matize or **rēacclī'matise** *vt* and *vi.*	**rēacquaint'ance** *n.*	**rēadapta'tion** *n.*
	rēacquire' *vt.*	**rēaddress'** *vt.*

in general, and reported on by a committee. **read between the lines** to detect a meaning not expressed but implied. **read in** to transfer data from a storage device into the main memory of a computer. **read into** to find in a person's writing, words, behaviour, etc (meanings which are not overtly stated and may not have been intended). **read off** to take as a reading from an instrument. **read (oneself) in** in the Church of England, to enter into possession of a benefice by reading the Thirty-nine Articles. **read out** to read aloud; to retrieve data from a computer, etc; to expel from a political party or a society (chiefly *N Am*). **read someone's mind** to guess accurately what someone is thinking. **read up** to amass knowledge of by reading. **take as read** /red/ to presume; to understand to be, and accept as, true.

read² /rēd/ *n* a ruminant's fourth stomach, the abomasum. [OE *rēad*]

ready /red'i/ *adj* (**read'ier**; **read'iest**) prepared; willing; inclined; about or liable (to); dexterous; prompt; quick; handy; at hand; immediately available; dressed, attired (*obs*); direct; also used as *combining form*, as in *ready-mix*, *ready-to-wear*, etc. ◆*adv* readily (now only in *compar* and *superl*). ◆*n* (*usu* with *the*) the position of a firearm ready to be fired; ready money (*sl*; also in *pl*); time of, or for, making ready (*inf*). ◆*vt* (**read'ying**; **read'ied**) to make (*usu* oneself) ready. [OE (ge)*ræde*; cf Ger *bereit*]

■ **read'ily** *adv* willingly; quickly and without difficulty. **read'iness** *n*. ▫ **read'y-made** *adj* made before sale, not made to order; unoriginal; immediately usable, not requiring construction or preparation. ◆*n* a ready-made article, *esp* a garment. **ready meal** *n* a packaged meal that has been pre-cooked and requires only to be reheated. **read'y-mix** *adj* (of cake, etc ingredients) prepared and blended so that *usu* only liquid need be added before cooking; (also **ready-mixed'**) (of concrete) mixed in the vehicle in which it is being transported to the site where it is to be used. **ready money** *n* money ready at hand; cash. **read'y-money** *adj* paying, or for payment, in money on the spot. **read'y-moneyed** or **read'y-monied** *adj* having, or of the nature of, ready money. **ready reckoner** *n* a book of tables used as a calculation aid, *esp* one giving the value of so many things at so much each, and interest on any sum of money from a day upwards. **read'y-wash** *n* (*sl*) crack (cocaine). **read'y-witted** *adj* quick-witted.

■ **at the ready** (of a firearm) ready to be fired; prepared for instant action. **make** or **get ready** to dress, put on one's clothes (*obs*); to prepare (*esp* a forme for printing). **ready, steady, go** words used by the starter of a race to the competitors.

reaedify same as **re-edify**.

reafforest /rē-ə-for'ist/ *vt* to replant (a previously forested area) with trees. [**re-**]
■ **reafforesta'tion** *n*.

Reaganism /rā'gə-ni-zm/ *n* the political policies and practices characteristic of Ronald *Reagan*, US President 1981–89, *esp* the advocacy of supply-side economics (**Rea'ganomics**).
■ **Rea'ganite** *n* and *adj*.

reagent /rē-ā'jənt/ *n* a substance with characteristic reactions, used as a chemical test. [See **react¹**]
■ **reā'gency** *n*.

reagin /rē-ā'jin/ *n* an antibody that fixes to tissue cells of the same species so that, in the presence of an antigen, histamine and other vasoactive agents are released. [Ger *reagieren* to react, and **-in** (3)]

reak¹ or **reik** /rēk/ (*obs*) *n* a prank, *usu* in *pl* **reaks** or **rex** /reks/, sometimes with an allusion to L *rēx* king. [Origin obscure]

reak² obsolete spelling of **reck**.

real¹ /rē'(ə)l/ or /ri'əl/ *adj* actually existing; not counterfeit or assumed; true; genuine; sincere; authentic; involving or containing only real numbers (*maths*); relating to things fixed, eg lands or houses (*law*). ◆*adv* (*inf*; *N Am* and *Scot*) really, quite, truly. ◆*n* a real thing; that which is real; a realist; a realtone. [LL *reālis*, from L *rēs* a thing]

■ **realia** /rē-ā'li-ə/ *n pl* (LL neuter plural of *reālis* real) realities; objects, etc used as teaching aids to relate classroom work to real life. **rē'alism** *n* the medieval philosophical doctrine that general terms stand for real existences, *opp* to *nominalism*; the philosophical doctrine that in external perception the objects immediately known are real existences; the tendency to regard, accept or represent things as they really are (often in their most ignoble aspect); (often with *cap*) a style in art, literature, etc that seeks to present an unglamorized, unromanticized view of the world; literalness and precision of detail, with the effect of reality; the taking of a practical view in human problems. **rē'alist** *n*. **realist'ic** *adj* relating to the realists or to realism;

lifelike. **realist'ically** *adv*. **reality** /ri-al'i-ti or rē-/ *n* the state or fact of being real; that which is real and not imaginary; truth; verity; the fixed permanent nature of real property (*law*). **rē'ally** *adv* in reality; actually; genuinely, very. ◆*interj* expressing suprise, interest, doubt or disapproval. **rē'alness** *n*. **rē'alo** *n* (*pl* **rē'alos**) a member of the less radical section of the German Green Party, advocating co-operation with other parties, industry, etc (cf **fundie**). **re'altie** *n* (*Milton*) sincerity, honesty. **Realtor**® or **rē'altor** *n* (*N Am*; irregularly formed) an agent for the buying and selling of landed property, *esp* one who is a member of the National Association of Real Estate Boards. **rē'alty** *n* (*law*) land, with houses, trees, minerals, etc on it; the ownership of, or property in, lands (also (*esp N Am*) **real estate**).

▫ **real account** *n* one that records transactions relating to a tangible asset so that the value of the asset can be seen. **real ale** or **beer** *n* beer that continues to ferment and mature in the cask after brewing. **re'al-estate** *adj* (*esp N Am*) concerned with or dealing in property in land. **real food** *n* food that has not undergone commercial processing, does not contain additives, etc. **real image** see under **image**. **real income, wages**, etc *n* income, wages, etc measured in terms of their actual purchasing power. **reality check** *n* (*inf*) a reminder of the true, as opposed to the imagined, state of affairs. **reality principle** *n* (*psychol*) the principle that modifies the pleasure principle (qv), accommodating the demands of the real world. **reality TV** *n* a genre of television programme (**reality show**) that takes members of the general public as subjects, either presenting their daily lives as if they were soap operas or observing them in artificially contrived situations. **real life** *n* everyday life as lived by ordinary people, as opposed to glamorous fictional life. **real number** *n* any rational or irrational number. **real presence** see under **presence**. **real price** *n* the price of a commodity calculated after correcting for changes in the general price level. **real property** *n* same as **realty** above. **real school** *n* (Ger *Realschule* /rā-äl'shoo'la/) a German school teaching modern languages, science, and technical subjects, not classics, the highest grade being the **real gymnasium** (Ger *Realgymnasium* /rā-äl'gim-nä'zi-ŭm/), as opposed to the gymnasium proper, or classical school. **real terms** *n pl* (*econ*) the cash value, adjusted according to eg a price index, of goods or a service. **real'time** *adj* (*comput*) relating to or designating a system in which the processing of data occurs as it is generated (also *n*). **real'tone** *n* a ringtone that closely resembles an original sound recording.

■ **for real** (*inf*) in reality; serious or seriously; intended to be carried out or put into effect. **get real** (*N Am sl*; *usu* in *imperative*) to wake up to the realities of the situation. **in reality** actually. **keep it real** (*inf*) to be true to the original spirit of something; to continue to be genuine and honest in one's character and endeavours. **the real Mackay** or **McCoy** the genuine article, *esp* good whisky (the expression has been variously explained). **the real thing** the genuine thing, not an imitation or a cheap substitute.

real² /rē'əl/ (*obs*) *adj* royal. [OFr, from L *rēgālis* royal]
■ **re'alty** *n* (*obs*) royalty.
▫ **real tennis** *n* royal tennis, the original form of the game, as opposed to lawn tennis (also **court tennis**).

real³ /rā-äl'/ *n* the standard monetary unit of Brazil (100 centavos). [Port, from L *rēgālis* royal]

real⁴ /rā-äl'/ or /rē'əl/ (*hist*) *n* (*pl* **reals** or **reales**) a quarter of a peseta; a former Spanish coin, one-eighth of a dollar. See also **reis²**. [Sp, from L *rēgālis* royal]

realgar /ri-al'gär/ or /-gər/ *n* a bright-red monoclinic mineral, arsenic monosulphide. [Med L, from Ar *rahj-al-ghār* powder of the mine or cave]

realia see under **real¹**.

realign /rē-ə-līn'/ *vt* to align afresh; to group or divide on a new basis. [**re-**]
■ **realign'ment** *n*.

reality see under **real¹**.

realize or **-ise** /rē'ə-līz/ *vt* to feel strongly; to comprehend completely; to bring home to one's own experience; to make real, or as if real; to bring into being or act; to accomplish; to convert into real property or money, *esp* to convert (an asset) into cash by selling; to obtain, as a possession; to provide a detailed artistic version of music where the composer has (as was often the case in the 17c and 18c) left much to be filled in by the performer; to articulate (*linguistics*); to provide the drawings for an animated cartoon. [Fr *réaliser*; see **real¹**]

Some words formed with the prefix **re-**.

rēadjust' *vt* and *vi*.	**rēadmit'** *vt*.	**rēadop'tion** *n*.
rēadjust'ment *n*.	**rēadmitt'ance** *n*.	**rēadvance'** *n*, *vt* and *vi*.
rēadmiss'ion *n*.	**rēadopt'** *vt*.	**rēad'vertise** *vt* and *vi*.

■ **rēalīzabil'ity** or **-s-** *n* the ease with which an asset may be converted into cash. **rēalī'zable** or **-s-** (or /*rē'*/) *adj* able to be realized; *specif* of an asset, able to be converted into cash. **rēalī'zably** or **-s-** (or /*rē'*/) *adv*. **rēalīzā'tion** or **-s-** (or /-*li-*/) *n*. **rē'alizer** or **-s-** *n*. **rē'alizing** or **-s-** *adj*.

really[1] /*rē-ə-lī'*/ (*obs*) *vt* to rally; (*Spenser* **reallie**) to form again. [Obs Fr *realier = rallier*; see **rally**[1]]

really[2] see under **real**[1].

realm /*relm*/, *obs* **reame** /*rēm*/ *n* a kingdom; a domain, province, region; a field of study or sphere of action. [OFr *realme*, from hypothetical LL *rēgālimen*, from L *rēgālis* royal]
■ **realm'less** *adj*.

realo see under **real**[1].

realpolitik /*rā-äl-po-li-tēk'* or *rā-äl'po-li-tēk*/ *n* practical politics based on the realities and necessities of life, rather than moral or ethical ideas. [Ger]
■ **realpolit'iker** *n*.

realtie, etc see under **real**[1].

realty see under **real**[1,2].

ream[1] /*rēm*/ *n* a quantity of 480 or 500 sheets of paper, equal to 20 quires; (in *pl*) a large quantity (*inf*). [Ar *rizmah* a bundle]
■ **printer's ream** 516 sheets of paper.

ream[2] /*rēm*/ (*Scot*) *n* cream; froth. ◆ *vi* to cream; to froth; to overflow. ◆ *vt* to skim. [OE *rēam*]
■ **ream'ing** *adj* (*Scot*) foaming; brimming. **ream'y** *adj* (**ream'ier**; **ream'iest**) (*Scot*) creamy, frothy.

ream[3] /*rēm*/ *vt* to enlarge the bore of. [Appar OE *rӯman* to open up, to make room, from *rūm* room]
■ **ream'er** *n* a rotating instrument for enlarging, shaping or finishing a bore; a spiral-bladed drill for enlarging root canals (*dentistry*); a lemon squeezer (*N Am*).
❑ **ream'ing-bit** *n*.

reame /*rēm*/ (*Spenser*, etc) *n* see **realm**.

rean see **rhine**.

reanimate /*rē-an'i-māt*/ *vt* to restore to life; to infuse new life or spirit into. ◆ *vi* to revive. [**re-**]
■ **reanimā'tion** *n*.

reanswer /*rē-än'sər*/ (*Shakesp*) *vt* to be equivalent to. [**re-**]

reap /*rēp*/ *vt* to cut down, as grain; to clear by cutting a crop; to derive as an advantage or reward. [OE *rīpan* or *ripan*]
■ **reap'er** *n* a person who reaps; a reaping machine; the grim reaper.
❑ **reap'ing-hook** *n* a sickle. **reaping machine** *n* a machine for cutting grain. **reap'-silver** *n* (*hist*) money paid in commutation for service in reaping.
■ **the grim reaper** (*fig*) death.

reappropriate /*rē-ə-prō'pri-āt*/ *vt* (*US*) to carry over funds remaining unused at the end of one fiscal year into the next. [**re-**]
■ **reapprōpriā'tion** *n*.

rear[1] /*rēr*/ *n* the back or hindmost part or position, *esp* of an army or fleet; a position behind; the buttocks (*euphem*); a public or school, etc lavatory (also in *pl*; *sl*). ◆ *adj* placed behind; hinder. ◆ *vt* (*Bunyan*) to attack in the rear. [Aphetic for **arrear**; also partly from OFr *rere* (Fr *arrière*)]
■ **rear'most** *adj* last of all; nearest the back. **rear'ward** or **rere'ward** *adj* in or toward the rear. ◆ *adv* backward; at the back. ◆ *n* (*archaic*) rear; rearguard (partly from Anglo-Fr *rerewarde*).
❑ **rear admiral** *n* an officer next below a vice-admiral, *orig* one in command of the rear. **rear'-arch**, **rear'-dorse**, **rear'-dos**, **rear'-dorter** see under **rere-**. **rear'-end'** *vt* to hit the rear of (another motor vehicle) with the front of one's own vehicle. **rear'guard** *n* (OFr *rereguarde*) the rear of an army; a body of troops protecting it. ◆ *adj* from a defensive or losing position; from the rear, as characteristic of a rearguard. **rear lamp** or **light** *n* a light attached to the back of a vehicle. **rear'-rank** *n*. **rear-view mirror** *n* a mirror that shows what is behind a vehicle. **rear'-wheel drive** *n* a system in which the driving power of a vehicle is transmitted to the rear wheels.
■ **bring up the rear** to come last (in a procession, etc).

rear[2] /*rēr*/ *vt* to raise, cause or help to rise; to set up or upright; to originate, to bring into being (*Spenser*); to erect; to build up; to lift up or off; to hold up; to take up; to take away (*Spenser*); to bring up; to breed and foster; to rouse, stir up (now *dialect*); to drive (a hunted animal) from cover (*obs*). ◆ *vi* to rise up, tower (often with *up*); (of a quadruped) to rise on the hindlegs; to be roused suddenly to anger, etc (*fig*). [OE *ræran* to raise, causative of *rīsan* to rise]
■ **rear'er** *n*.
❑ **rear'horse** *n* a praying mantis (from its stance).
■ **rear its ugly head** (*fig*) (of a question, situation, etc) to arise unwelcomely.

rear[3] /*rēr*/ *adj* (now *obs* or *dialect*; see **rare**[2]) lightly cooked (*orig* applied to eggs). [OE *hrēr*]
❑ **rear'-boiled** *adj*. **rear'-roasted** *adj*.

rear[4], **rearly** see **rare**[3].

rearmouse same as **reremouse**.

reascend /*rē-ə-send'*/ *vt* and *vi* to ascend again; to go back up; to climb again. [**re-**]
■ **reascen'sion** or **reascent'** *n*.

reason /*rē'z(ə)n*/ *n* ground, support or justification of an act or belief; a premise, *esp* when placed after its conclusion; a motive or inducement; an underlying explanatory principle; a cause; the mind's power of drawing conclusions and determining right and truth; the exercise of this power; sanity; conformity to what is fairly to be expected or called for; moderation; fair treatment, eg satisfaction by a duel, or doing one's fair share in drinking (*archaic*); a remark, a sentatious saying (*Shakesp*); proportion (*Spenser*). ◆ *vi* to exercise the faculty of reason; to deduce inferences from premises; to argue; to debate; to converse (*Shakesp*). ◆ *vt* to examine or discuss; to debate; to think out; to set forth logically; to bring by reasoning. [Fr *raison*, from L *ratiō*, *-ōnis*, from *rērī*, *ratus* to think]
■ **rea'sonable** *adj* endowed with reason; rational; acting according to reason; agreeable to reason; just; not excessive; not expensive; moderate. ◆ *adv* (now *non-standard*) reasonably. **rea'sonableness** *n*. **rea'sonably** *adv*. **rea'soned** *adj* argued out. **rea'soner** *n*. **rea'soning** *n*. **rea'sonless** *adj*.
■ **by reason of** on account of; in consequence of. **do someone reason** (*obs*) to give someone the satisfaction of a duel; to drink without shirking. **it stands to reason** it is obvious or logical. **listen to reason** listen to, and take heed of, the reasonable explanation, course of action, etc. **no reason but** (*Shakesp*) no reason for it being otherwise, hence, no possible alternative. **principle of sufficient reason** that nothing happens without a sufficient reason why it should be as it is and not otherwise. **pure reason** reason absolutely independent of experience. **within** or **in reason** within the bounds of what is possible, sensible, etc.

reassure /*rē-ə-shoor'*/ *vt* to relieve apprehension or worry; to give confidence to; to confirm; to assure anew; to reinsure. [**re-**]
■ **reassur'ance** *n*. **reassur'er** *n*. **reassur'ing** *adj*. **reassur'ingly** *adv*.

reast[1], **reest** or **reist** /*rēst*/ *vi* to become rancid (*esp* of bacon). [ME *rest*, *reest*, rancid]
■ **reast'iness**, etc *n*. **reast'y**, etc *adj*.

reast[2] same as **reest**[2].

reata or **riata** /*rē-ä'tä* or *'tə*/ *n* a lariat. [Sp, from *reater* to tie again]

reate /*rēt*/ *n* water-crowfoot. [Origin obscure]

reattribute /*rē-ə-trib'ūt*/ *vt* to judge (a work of art) to be by a different artist than that to whom it was previously attributed. [**re-**]
■ **reattribū'tion** *n*.

Réau *abbrev* : Réaumur's thermometric scale.

Réaumur /*rā'ə-mūr* or (Fr) *rā-ō-mür'*/ *adj* (of a thermometer or thermometer scale) having the freezing point of water marked 0° and boiling point 80°. [RAF de *Réaumur* (1683–1757), French physicist who introduced the scale]

reave, also (*orig Scot*) **reive** /*rēv*/ (*archaic*) *vt* and *vi* (pat and pap **reft** (*obs* **raft**)) to plunder; to rob. [OE *rēafian* to rob; cf Ger *rauben* to rob]
■ **reav'er** or **reiv'er** *n*.

Reb /*reb*/ (*Judaism*) *n* a title corresponding to *Mr*, given to a man who is not a rabbi. [Yiddish]

reback /*rē-bak'*/ *vt* to put a new back on. [**re-**]

rebadge /*rē-baj'*/ *vt* to market (a product) under a new name or brand. [**re-**]

re-bar /*rē'bär*/ *n* a steel bar in reinforced concrete. [reinforcing *bar*]

rebarbative /*ri-bär'bə-tiv*/ *adj* repellent. [Fr *rébarbatif*, from *barbe* beard]

Some words formed with the prefix **re-**.

readver'tisement *n*.	**reaffirmā'tion** *n*.	**reallot'** *vt*.
readvise' *vt* and *vi*.	**reall'ocate** *vt*.	**reallot'ment** *n*.
reaffirm' *vt*.	**reallocā'tion** *n*.	**rē-ally'** *vt* and *vi*.

---

rebate[1] /ri-bāt'/ vt to reduce; to abate; to dull; to blunt; to repay a part of; to diminish by removal of a projection (heraldry). ◆ n (or /rē'/) discount; repayment, refund. [Fr rabattre to beat back, from pfx re- and abattre to abate]
■ **rebat'able** or **rebāte'able** adj. **rebāte'ment** n abatement; reduction; discount; a narrowing (Bible). **re'bater** n.

rebate[2] /rē'bāt or rab'it/ same as **rabbet**.

rebato /rə-bä'tō/ (Shakesp) n (pl **reba'toes**) a stiff collar or support for a ruff (also **reba'ter** or **raba'to** (pl **raba'toes**)). [Fr rabat]

rebbe /reb'ə/ n a rabbi or spiritual leader of a Hasidic Jewish group (also with cap as a title). [Yiddish, from Heb rabbī]

rebbetzin /reb'ət-sən/ n a rabbi's wife; a female religious teacher. [Yiddish]

rebec see **rebeck**.

Rebecca /ri-bek'ə/ (hist) n the leader of those who demolished tollgates in the **Rebecca riots** in Wales from 1843. [Alluding to Bible, Genesis 24.60]
■ **Rebecc'aism** n. **Rebecc'aite** n.

rebeck or **rebec** /rē'bek/ n a medieval instrument of the viol class shaped like a mandolin, usu with three strings. [OFr rebec, from Ar rebāb, rabāb (change of ending unexplained); other forms occur in European languages, including, in ME ribibe and ribible]

rebel /reb'(ə)l/ n a person who rebels; a person who resents and resists authority or oppressive conditions; someone who refuses to conform to the generally accepted modes of behaviour, dress, etc. ◆ adj rebellious. ◆ vi /ri-bel'/ (often with against) (**rebell'ing**; **rebelled'**) to renounce the authority of the laws and government, or to take up arms and openly oppose them; to oppose any authority; to revolt; to offer opposition; to feel repugnance. [Fr rebelle, from L rebellis insurgent, from pfx re- and bellum war]
■ **reb'eldom** n. **rebell'er** n (now rare). **reb'el-like** adv (Shakesp). **rebell'ion** /-yən/ n the act of rebelling; revolt. **rebell'ious** adj engaged in rebellion; characteristic of a rebel or rebellion; inclined to rebel; refractory. **rebell'iously** adv. **rebell'iousness** n.

rebellow /rē-bel'ō/ (Spenser) vi to bellow in return; to echo back a loud noise. [re-]

rebid /rē-bid'/ vt and vi to bid again, esp (bridge) on the same suit as a previous bid. ◆ n /rē'/ a renewed bid, esp on one's former suit. [re-]

rebind /rē-bīnd'/ vt (pat and pap rē'bound') to give a new binding to; to bind again. [re-]

rebirth /rē'bûrth/ n reincarnation; revival of, eg an interest; spiritual renewal. ◆ vt to practise rebirthing. [re-]
■ **rebirth'er** n. **rebirth'ing** n a type of psychotherapy involving the reliving of the experience of being born, in order to release anxieties, etc by screaming, special breathing, etc (see also **primal therapy** under **primal**).

rebite /rē-bīt'/ vt (in engraving) to freshen (a plate) by a new application of acid. [re-]

reblochon /rə-blo-shȝ'/ n a delicately-flavoured soft cheese, made chiefly in the Savoie region of France. [Fr, from Savoyard dialect reblochi processed for a second time]

reboant /reb'ō-ənt/ (poetic) adj rebellowing; loudly resounding. [L reboāns, -antis, prp of reboāre, from re- again, and boāre to cry aloud]
■ **reboā'tion** n.

reboot /rē-boot'/ (comput) vt to restart (a computer) by reloading the disk-operating-system program into working memory. ◆ n /rē'/ the act of rebooting. [re-]

rebore /rē-bōr' or -bör'/ vt to bore again (the cylinder of a car engine) so as to clear it. ◆ n /rē'bōr or -bör/ an instance of this. [re-]

reborn /rē-börn'/ adj born again; revitalized, transformed. [re-]

rebound[1] /ri-bownd'/ vi to bound back from collision; to spring back, often with unexpected results (lit and fig); to re-echo; to recover quickly after a setback. ◆ vt to throw back; to re-echo. ◆ n /rē'/ the act of rebounding. [Fr rebondir; see **bound**[4]]
■ **on the rebound** after colliding; while reacting against a setback, disappointment, etc, esp in love affairs.

rebound[2] see **rebind**.

rebozo /ri-bō'zō/ n (pl **rebo'zos**) a long scarf covering the head and shoulders, worn by women in Latin America. [Sp rebozar to muffle]

rebrand /rē-brand'/ vt to use a new name or image to market a product (also fig). [re-]

rebreather /rē-brē'dhər/ n an aqualung that recycles air exhaled by the diver. [re-]

rebuff /ri-buf'/ n a sudden check, curb or setback; unexpected refusal or rejection; a snub or slight; a blowing back (Milton). ◆ vt to snub; to beat back; to check; to repulse or reject. [OFr rebuffe, from Ital ributfo a reproof, from Ital ri- (= L re-) back, and buffo puff]

rebuke /ri-būk'/ vt to reprove sternly; to check, restrain, beat back (obs); to put to shame (archaic). ◆ n a reproach; stern reproof, reprimand; a check (obs); a putting to shame (obs). [Anglo-Fr rebuker (OFr rebucher), from pfx re- and bucher to strike]
■ **rebūk'able** adj. **rebūke'ful** adj. **rebūke'fully** adv. **rebūk'er** n. **rebūk'ingly** adv.

rebus /rē'bəs/ n (pl **re'buses**) an enigmatical representation of a word or name by pictures representing the component parts of the name, as in a puzzle or a coat of arms; such a puzzle. [L rēbus by things, ablative pl of rēs thing]

rebut /ri-but'/ vt (**rebutt'ing**; **rebutt'ed**) to drive back; to repel; to meet in argument or proof; to disprove; to refute. ◆ vi to recoil (Spenser); to adduce evidence or arguments countering those of the other party (law). [OFr rebo(u)ter, rebuter to repulse; see **butt**[1]]
■ **rebut'ment** n. **rebutt'able** adj. **rebutt'al** n. **rebutt'er** n a person or an argument that rebuts; a defendant's reply to a plaintiff's surrejoinder (law).

REC abbrev : regional electricity company.

rec /rek/ (inf) n recreation; a recreation ground.

rec. abbrev : receipt; recipe; recipe (L), take; record.

recal see **recall**.

recalcitrate /ri-kal'si-trāt/ vt and vi (rare) to kick back. ◆ vi (usu with at or against) to show strong objection or opposition; to be refractory. [L recalcitrāre to kick back, from calx, calcis the heel]
■ **recal'citrance** n strong objection or opposition; refractoriness. **recal'citrant** adj refractory; obstinate in opposition. ◆ n a recalcitrant person. **recalcitrā'tion** n.

recalesce /rē-ka-les'/ vt to display again a state of glowing heat. [L re- again, and calēscere to grow hot]
■ **recales'cence** n (phys) the renewed glowing of iron at a certain stage of cooling from white heat. **recales'cent** adj.

recall (rarely **recal**) /ri-köl'/ vt to call back; to command to return; to bring back as by a summons; to remove from office by vote (US); to revoke; to call back to mind. ◆ n /rē'/ act, power or possibility of recalling or revoking; a signal or order to return; the calling back of a performer to the stage or platform by applause; a right of electors to dismiss an official by a vote (US); remembrance of things learned or experienced, esp in the phrase **total recall** (power of) remembering accurately in full detail. [re-]
■ **recall'able** adj capable of being recalled. **recal'ment** or **recall'ment** n.
■ **beyond recall** unable to be stopped or cancelled.

recant /ri-kant'/ vt to retract. ◆ vi to revoke a former declaration; to unsay what has been said, esp to declare one's renunciation of one's former religious belief. [L recantāre to revoke, from cantāre to sing, to charm]
■ **recantā'tion** /rē-/ n. **recant'er** /ri-/ n.

recap /rē-kap' or rē'kap/ short form of **recapitulate** and **recapitulation**.

recapitalize or **-ise** /rē-kap'i-tə-līz/ vt to supply again with capital. [re-]
■ **recapitalīzā'tion** or **-s-** n.

recapitulate /rē-kə-pit'yə-lāt/ vt to go over again the chief points of; (of an embryo) to repeat (stages in the development of the species) during embryonic development; to repeat (an earlier passage) in a musical work. [L recapitulāre, -ātum, from re- again, and capitulum heading, chapter, from caput head]
■ **recapitulā'tion** n the act of recapitulating; summing up; the reproduction, in the developmental stages of an individual embryo, of the evolutionary stages in the life history of the race or type (biol); the final repetition of the subjects in sonata form after development (music). **recapit'ūlative** or **recapit'ūlatory** adj repeating again; of the nature of a recapitulation.

Some words formed with the prefix **re-**.

rē-al'ter vt.	**rēamend'ment** n.	**rēappar'el** vt.
rē-alterā'tion n.	**rēannex'** vt.	**rēappear'** vi.
rēamend' vt.	**rēannexā'tion** n.	**rēappear'ance** n.

---

recaption /rē-kap'shən/ n reprisal; taking back by peaceable means goods, children, etc from someone who has no right to detain them (*law*). [**re-**]

recapture /rē-kap'chər/ vt to capture back, eg a prize from a captor; to recover by effort. ◆ n the act of retaking; recovery; a thing recaptured. [**re-**]
■ **recap'tor** or **recap'turer** n.

recast /rē-käst'/ vt (pat and pap **recast'**) to cast or mould again or in a new form; to reconstruct, remould; to recalculate (*poetic*); to reassign parts in a theatrical production; to give (an actor) a different part. ◆ n /rē'käst or rē'käst/ shaping again or afresh, reconstruction; that which has been shaped again or afresh. [**re-**]

recce /rek'i/ (*milit sl*) n (pl **recc'es**) reconnaissance (also (*esp RAF sl*) **recc'o** (pl **recc'os**)). ◆ vt and vi (**recc'eing**; **recc'ed** or **recc'eed**) to reconnoitre.

reccy /rek'i/ (*milit sl*) n, vt and vi (**recc'ying**; **recc'ied**) another spelling of **recce**.

recd *abbrev* : received.

recede /ri-sēd'/ vi to go back, go farther off, become more distant (*lit and fig*); to go or draw back (from; *lit and fig*); to differ (from; *archaic*); to grow less, decline; to bend or slope backward; to give up a claim, renounce a promise, etc. [L *recēdere, recēssum*, from *re-* back, and *cēdere* to go, yield]
■ **reced'ing** adj.

re-cede or **recede** /rē-sēd'/ vt to cede again or back. [**re-**]

receipt /ri-sēt'/ n receiving; place of receiving; capacity (*obs*); a written acknowledgement of anything received; that which is received; a recipe, *esp* in cookery (*archaic*); anything prepared after a recipe (*obs*). ◆ vt to mark as paid; to give a receipt for (chiefly *N Am*). [OFr *receite, recete* (Fr *recette*), from L *recepta*, fem pap of *recipere* to receive, with *p* restored after L]

receive /ri-sēv'/ vt to take, get or catch, *usu* more or less passively; to have given or delivered to one; to experience; to take in or on; to admit; to accept; to meet or welcome on entrance; to harbour (ideas, etc); to await in resistance; to bear the weight of; to experience, or learn of, and react towards; to accept as authority or as truth; to take into the body; to buy or deal in (stolen goods); to be acted upon by, and transform, electrical signals. ◆ vi to be a recipient; to participate in communion (*Christianity*); to receive signals; to hold a reception of visitors; to buy or deal in stolen goods. [Anglo-Fr *receivre* (Fr *recevoir*), from L *recipere, receptum*, from *re-* back, and *capere* to take]
■ **receivabil'ity** or **receiv'ableness** n. **receiv'able** adj. **receiv'ables** n pl amounts owed, assets. **receiv'al** n (*rare*). **received'** adj generally accepted. **receiv'er** n a person who receives; an officer who receives taxes; a person appointed by a court to manage property under litigation, receive money, etc; an official receiver (see below); a person who receives stolen goods (*inf*); a vessel for receiving the products of distillation, or for containing gases (*chem*); the glass vessel of an air-pump in which the vacuum is formed; an instrument by which electrical signals are transformed into audible or visual form, eg a telephone receiver; a receiving-set; a player on the offensive team eligible to catch forward passes (*American football*); the catcher (*baseball*); the part of a firearm that guides the round into the chamber. **receiv'ership** n the state of being in the control of a receiver; the office or function of a receiver. **receiv'ing** n and adj.
□ **Received (Standard) English** n the English generally spoken by educated British people and considered the standard of the language. **Received Pronunciation** n the particular pronunciation of British English which is generally regarded as being least regionally limited, most socially acceptable, and is considered the standard (*abbrev* **RP**). **receiver general** n an officer who receives revenues. **receiv'ing-house** n a depot; a house where letters, etc are left for transmission. **receiving line** n a number of people standing in line formally to receive a VIP, guests, etc on arrival. **receiv'ing-office** n a branch post-office for receipt of letters, etc. **receiving order** n formerly, an order putting a receiver in temporary possession of a debtor's estate, pending bankruptcy proceedings. **receiv'ing-room** n a room where patients, inmates, etc are received. **receiv'ing-set** n apparatus for receiving radio communications. **receiv'ing-ship** n a stationary ship for naval recruits.
▨ **official receiver** an official appointed by a govenment agency to manage the estate of a person, company, etc declared bankrupt, until a trustee has been appointed.

recency see under **recent**.

recense /ri-sens'/ vt to revise critically. [L *recēnsiō, -ōnis*, from *re-* again, and *cēnsēre* to value, to assess]
■ **recen'sion** n a critical revision of a text; a text established by critical revision; a review.

recent /rē'sənt/ adj done, made, etc not long ago or not long past; fresh; modern; (with *cap*) of or belonging to the Holocene epoch, Post-Glacial (also n). [L *recēns, recentis*]
■ **rē'cency** n. **rē'cently** adv. **rē'centness** n.

recept /rē'sept/ n an image or idea formed by repeated similar perceptions. [L *receptum*, pap of *recipere* to receive, after *concept*, etc]

receptacle /ri-sep'tə-kl also, eg Shakesp, res'ip-tə-kl/ n that in which anything is or may be received or held; the enlarged end of an axis bearing the parts of a flower or the crowded flowers of an inflorescence; in flowerless plants, a structure bearing reproductive organs, spores or gemmae. [L *receptāculum*, from *recipere, receptum* to receive]
■ **receptacular** /res-ip-tak'ū-lər/ adj. **receptac'ulum** n (pl **receptac'ula**) a receptacle.

receptibility and **receptible** see under **reception**.

reception /ri-sep'shən/ n the act, fact or manner of receiving or of being received; taking in; the act or manner of taking up signals; the quality of received radio or television signals; a formal receiving, as of guests; a social function (eg *wedding reception*) at which guests are *usu* received formally; the part of a hotel, suite of offices, etc where visitors, guests, etc are received; a reception room; treatment on arrival; capacity for receiving (*Milton*). [L *recipere, receptum* to receive]
■ **receptibil'ity** /ri-/ n receivability. **recept'ible** adj capable of receiving (with *of*); able to be received. **recep'tionist** n a person employed to receive callers, hotel-guests, patients, customers, etc and make arrangements. **recep'tive** adj capable of receiving; quick to receive or take in *esp* ideas; relating to reception or receptors. **recep'tively** adv. **recep'tiveness** or **receptivity** /res-ep-tiv'i-ti/ n. **recep'tor** n a receiver; an element of the nervous system adapted for reception of stimuli, eg a sense-organ or sensory nerve-ending; a chemical grouping on the surface of the cell to which a specific antigen may attach itself; a site in or on a cell to which a drug or hormone can become attached, stimulating a reaction inside the cell.
□ **reception centre** n a building, office, etc where people are received for immediate assistance before being directed to specific centres of help, treatment, etc as in the case of drug addicts or victims of fire, natural disasters, etc. **reception class** n a class for the new intake of children at a school. **reception order** n an order for the reception and detention of a person in a mental hospital. **reception room** n a room for formal receptions; any public room in a house. **reception theory** n the idea that the way in which the audience of a film, performance, etc or the reader of a text responds to it is an important component of its meaning.

recess /rē-ses' or rē'ses/ n part of a room formed by a receding of the wall; a niche or alcove; a secluded spot, a nook; a hidden, inner or secret place (often in *pl*); a small indentation or depression; a sinus; temporary cessation of business, *esp* the adjournment of a lawcourt, or of Parliament during a vacation; a break or interval during a school day (*N Am*); a holiday period during the academic year (*N Am*); a going back or withdrawing; retirement (*obs*); seclusion (*obs*). ◆ vt to make a recess in; to put into a recess; to suspend temporarily (*N Am*). ◆ vi to adjourn. [See **recede**]
■ **recessed'** adj. **recession** /ri-sesh'ən/ n the act of receding; withdrawal; the state of being set back; part of a wall, etc that recedes; a slight temporary decline in a country's trade, *specif* one identified by two successive quarters without growth. **recessional** /ri-sesh'ən-əl/ adj. ◆ n a hymn sung during recession or retirement of clergy and choir after a service. **recess'ionary** adj of or relating to an economic recession. **recessionista** /-ēs'tə/ n (*inf*) a woman who strives to remain fashionable despite financial constraints arising from a recession. **recessive** /-ses'/ adj tending to recede; of an ancestral character, apparently suppressed in crossbred offspring in favour of the alternative character in the other parent, though it may be transmitted to later generations (*genetics*; also n); of stress, tending to move toward the beginning of the word (*linguistics*). **recess'ively** adv. **recess'iveness** n.
□ **recessed arch** n one arch within another.

Some words formed with the prefix **re-**.

rēapplicā'tion n.	**rēappoint'ment** n.	**rēapprais'al** n.
rēapply' vi.	**rēappor'tion** vt.	**rēappraise'** vt.
rēappoint' vt.	**rēappor'tionment** n.	**rēappraise'ment** n.

recession[1] /rē-sesh'ən/ n a ceding again or back. [**re-**]

recession[2] see under **recess**.

Rechabite /rek'ə-bīt/ n a descendant of Jonadab, son of Rechab, who did not drink wine or dwell in houses (Bible, Jeremiah 35.6–7); a total abstainer from intoxicating drinks, esp a member of the order so named; a tent-dweller.
- **Rech'abitism** n.

rechate (Shakesp) see **recheat**.

réchauffé /rā-shō'fā/ n a reheated dish; a fresh concoction of old material. ◆ adj reheated; rehashed. [Fr]

recheat /ri-chēt'/ or **rechate** /ri-chāt'/ (Shakesp) n a horn-call to assemble hounds. ◆ vi to sound the recheat. [OFr racheter, rachater to reassemble]

recheck /rē-chek'/ vi and vt to make a further check (on). ◆ n /rē'/ a further check. [**re-**]

recherché /rə-shār'shā or (Fr) rə-sher-shā/ adj carefully chosen; particularly choice; (too) far-fetched or tenuous; rare or exotic. [Fr]

rechie see **reechy** under **reech**.

rechip /rē-chip'/ vt to change the electronic identity of (a stolen mobile phone). [**re-**]
- **rechipp'ing** n.

rechlesse /rech'lis/ (Spenser) adj same as **reckless**.

recidivism /ri-sid'i-vi-zm/ n the habit of relapsing into crime. [Fr récidivisme, from L recidīvus falling back]
- **recid'ivist** n and adj. **recidivist'ic** adj.

recipe /res'i-pi/ n (pl **rec'ipes**) directions for making something, esp a food or drink; a prescription (archaic); a method laid down for achieving a desired end. [L recipe take, imperative of recipere]

recipient /ri-sip'i-ənt/ adj receiving; receptive. ◆ n a person or thing that receives. [L recipiēns, -entis, prp of recipere to receive]
- **recip'ience** or **recip'iency** n a reception; receptivity.

reciprocal /ri-sip'rə-kl/ adj acting in return; mutual; complementary; inverse; alternating; interchangeable; giving and receiving or given and received; expressing mutuality (grammar); reflexive. ◆ n that which is reciprocal; the multiplier that gives unity (maths). [L reciprocus]
- **reciprocality** /-kal'i-ti/ n. **recip'rocally** adv. **recip'rocant** n (maths) a differential invariant. **recip'rocāte** vt to give and receive mutually; to requite; to interchange; to alternate. ◆ vi to move backward and forward; to make a return or interchange (inf). **reciprocā'tion** n. **recip'rocātive** adj characterized by or inclined to reciprocation. **recip'rocātor** n a person or thing that reciprocates; a double-acting steam-engine. **reciprocity** /res-i-pros'i-ti/ n reciprocal action; mutual relation; concession of mutual privileges or advantages, esp mutual tariff concessions.
- **reciprocal cross** n (biol) a cross made both ways with regard to sex, ie A♂×B♀ and B♂×A♀. **reciprocal translocation** n (biol) mutual exchange of non-homologous portions between two chromosomes. **reciprocating engine** n an engine in which the piston moves to and fro in a straight line. **reciprocity failure** n (photog) failure of the reciprocity rule for extremely long or short exposure times, or at very high or low light intensities. **reciprocity principle** n (phys) one stating that the interchange of radiation source and detector will not change the level of radiation at the latter, whatever the shielding arrangement between them. **reciprocity rule** n (photog) the principle that an increase in light intensity should be compensated for by a proportionate decrease in time exposure and vice versa.

recision /ri-sizh'ən/ n cutting back (obs); rescinding. [L recīsiō, -ōnis, from recīdere to cut off]

récit /rā-sē'/ n a narrative, esp the narrative in a book as opposed to the dialogue; a book consisting largely of narrative; a solo part, for voice or instrument (music); a principal part in a concerted piece (music); a swell organ (music). [Fr]

recite /ri-sīt'/ vt to repeat from memory; to declaim; to read aloud (rare); to narrate; to enumerate; to give (the details of); to repeat to a teacher, have heard a lesson in (US); to give a recitation; to repeat, or have heard, a lesson (N Am). [L recitāre, from citāre, -ātum to call]
- **recī'table** adj. **recī'tal** n the act of reciting; setting forth; enumeration; narration; a public performance of music, usu by one performer or composer, or of some particular character; that part of a

deed which recites the circumstances (law). **recī'talist** n. **recitation** /res-i-tā'shən/ n the act of reciting; a piece for declaiming; the repeating or hearing of a prepared lesson (N Am); hence a lesson generally (N Am). **recitā'tionist** n a declaimer. **recitative** /-tə-tēv'/ or **recitativo** /re-sit-ä-tē'vō or (Ital) rā-chē-tä-tē'vō/ n (pl **recitatives'**, **recitati'vos** or (Ital) **recitati'vi** /-vē/) a style of song resembling speech in its succession of tones and freedom from melodic form; a passage to be sung in this manner. ◆ adj in the style of recitative. **reciter** /ri-sīt'ər/ n.
- **recitā'tion-room** n (N Am) a classroom. **recit'ing-note** n the note on which, in a Gregorian chant, the greater part of a verse is sung.

reck /rek/ (usu with a neg) vt (pat and pap **recked**, obs or archaic **raught** /röt/) to care, desire (with infinitive; archaic); to care about, heed; (used impers) to concern. ◆ vi (usu with of) to care, concern oneself; (used impers) to matter. ◆ n care; heed. [OE reccan, rēcan; cf OHGer ruoh care, Ger ruchlos regardless]
- **what reck?** (Scot) what does it matter?

reckan /rek'ən/ (Walter Scott, ostensibly Cumberland dialect) adj perh a form of **racked** or **ricked**.

reckless /rek'ləs/ adj careless; heedless of consequences; rash. [**reck** and **less**]
- **reck'lessly** adv. **reck'lessness** n.

reckling /rek'ling/ n the weakest, smallest or youngest of a litter or family. ◆ adj puny. [Origin obscure; poss from ON reklingr an outcast]

reckon /rek'(ə)n/ vt to estimate, judge to be; to think, believe, suppose or expect; to count; to calculate (often with up); to include (in an account); to place or class; to think much of (sl); to attribute (to; archaic); to enumerate (archaic). ◆ vi to calculate; to judge; to go over or settle accounts (with); to concern oneself (with); to count or rely (on or upon). [OE gerecenian to explain; Ger rechnen]
- **reck'oner** n. **reck'oning** n counting; calculation, esp of a ship's position; a tavern bill; settlement of accounts; judgement.
- **to be reckoned with** of considerable power and influence.

reclaim /ri-klām'/ vt orig to call back (eg a hawk); to win back; to win from evil, wildness, waste or submersion; /rē-klām'/ to claim back. ◆ vi /ri-klām'/ to exclaim in protest (archaic); to appeal (Scots law). ◆ n recall; possibility of reform. [OFr reclamer, from L reclāmāre]
- **reclaim'able** adj. **reclaim'ably** adv. **reclaim'ant** n. **reclaim'er** n.

reclamation /rek-lə-mā'shən/ n the act of reclaiming; the state of being reclaimed. [L reclāmātiō, -ōnis, from reclāmāre, from clāmāre to cry out]

réclame /rā-klām'/ n the art or practice by which publicity or notoriety is secured; publicity. [Fr]

recline /ri-klīn'/ vt to lean or lay on the back; to incline or bend (properly backwards). ◆ vi to lean in a recumbent position, on back or side; (of the plane of a sundial) to make an angle with the vertical; to rely (on or upon; archaic). ◆ adj or adv (Milton) recumbent. [L reclīnāre, -ātum, from clīnāre to bend]
- **reclī'nable** adj. **reclinate** /rek'li-nāt/ adj bent down or back. **reclinā'tion** /rek-li-/ n reclining; bending back; angle of a dial with the vertical. **reclīned'** adj recumbent; reclinate. **reclī'ner** n someone or something that reclines, esp a type of easy chair with a back that can be lowered towards a horizontal position. **reclī'ning** adj.

recluse /ri-kloos'/ n a religious devotee who lives in an enclosed or secluded place; a person who lives retired from the world. ◆ adj enclosed, eg as an anchorite; secluded; retiring; solitary. [L reclūsus, pap of reclūdere to open, in later Latin, shut away, from re- back, away, and claudere]
- **recluse'ly** adv. **recluse'ness** n seclusion from society; retirement. **reclusion** /-kloo'zhən/ n religious seclusion; the life of a recluse; seclusion in prison. **reclu'sive** /-siv/ adj of or living in, etc seclusion. **reclu'sory** n a recluse's cell.

recognize or **-ise** /rek'əg-nīz/ vt to know again; to identify as known or experienced before; to show sign of knowing (a person); to see or acknowledge the fact of; to acknowledge (that); to acknowledge the validity of (a claim); to acknowledge the status or legality of (eg a government); to allow someone to speak in court proceedings, formal debate, etc (US); to reward (meritorious conduct). [L recognōscere and OFr reconoistre, reconoiss-; see **cognosce** and **cognition**]
- **recognition** /rek-əg-nish'ən/ n the act of recognizing; state of being recognized; acknowledgement; acknowledgement of status; a sign,

---
Some words formed with the prefix **re-**.

rēapprais'er n.	**rēarm'ament** n.	**rēarrange'** vt.
rēarise' vi.	**rēarous'al** n.	**rēarrange'ment** n.
rēarm' vt and vi.	**rēarouse'** vt.	**rēarrest'** n and vt.

---

recoil /ri-koil'/ (*Spenser* **recoyle**, **recule** or **recuile**) *vi* to start back; to stagger back; to shrink in horror, etc; to rebound; (of a gun) to kick; to degenerate (*Shakesp*); to retreat, fall back (*archaic*); to revert (*obs*). ◆ *vt* (*obs*) to force back. ◆ *n* (or /rē'/) retreat (*archaic*); a starting or springing back; rebound; the kick of a gun; change in motion of a particle caused by ejection of another particle, or (sometimes) by a collision (*nuclear phys*). [Fr *reculer*, from *cul*, from L *cūlus* the hind parts]
■ **recoil'er** *n*. **recoil'less** *adj*.
❏ **recoil atom** *n* an atom that experiences a sudden change of direction or reversal, after the emission from it of a particle or radiation. **recoil escapement** same as **anchor escapement** (see under **anchor**). **recoil nucleus** same as **recoil atom** above.

recoin /rē-koin'/ *vt* to coin again, *esp* by melting and passing again through a mint. [**re-**]
■ **recoin'age** *n*.

recollect[1] /re-ka-lekt'/ *vt* to recall to memory; to remember, *esp* by an effort; to absorb in mystical contemplation (*archaic*); to recall to the matter in hand, or to composure or resolution (*usu reflexive*). ◆ *n* /rek'/ (also (*Fr*) **récollet** /rā-kol-ā/) a Franciscan friar of a reformed branch, aiming at detachment from creatures and recollection in God. [L *recolligere* to gather again or gather up, from *colligere*; see **collect**]
■ **recollect'ed** *adj*. **recollect'edly** *adv*. **recollect'edness** *n*. **recollec'tion** /rek-/ *n* the act or power of recollecting; a memory, reminiscence; a thing remembered; mystical contemplation (*archaic*). **recollec'tive** *adj*. **recollec'tively** *adv*.
❏ **recollected terms** *n pl* (*Shakesp*) variously explained as: known by heart, picked, studied, lacking spontaneity.

recollect[2] or **re-collect** /rē-kə-lekt'/ or -*ko-*/ *vt* to gather together again; to summon up; to bring back again (*Milton*); to collect (*obs*). [Partly **recollect**[1]; partly **re-** and **collect**]

recombine /rē-kəm-bīn'/ *vt* and *vi* to join together again. [**re-**]
■ **recombinant** /ri-kom'bi-nənt/ *adj* and *n*. **recombina'tion** *n* the act or result of recombining; the reassortment of genes or characters into combinations different from those in the parents, done in linked genes by crossing over (qv under **cross**; *biol*).
❏ **recombinant DNA** *n* genetic material produced by the combining of DNA molecules from different organisms (*abbrev* **rDNA**; see also **genetic manipulation** under **genetic**).

recomfort /ri-kum'fərt/ (*archaic*) *vt* to comfort; to console; to reinvigorate; to refresh. [**re-**]
■ **recom'fortless** *adj* (*Spenser*) comfortless. **recom'forture** *n* (*Shakesp*) consolation.

recommend /re-kə-mend'/ *vt* to commend or introduce as suitable for acceptance, favour, appointment or choice; to make acceptable; to advise; to commend, commit or consign (*archaic*); to inform (*Shakesp*). ◆ *vi* to advise. [**re-**]
■ **recommend'able** *adj*. **recommend'ably** *adv*. **recommenda'tion** *n*. **recommend'atory** *adj*. **recommend'er** *n*.

recompense /rek'əm-pens/ *vt* to return an equivalent to or for; to repay. ◆ *n* (formerly **recompence**) return of an equivalent; that which is so returned; reward; retribution; requital. [OFr *recompenser*, from L *compēnsāre* to compensate]
■ **rec'ompensable** *adj*. **rec'ompenser** *n*.

recon /rē'kon/ (*US milit sl*) *n* reconnaissance.

reconcile /rek'ən-sīl/ *vt* to restore or bring back to friendship or union; to bring to agreement or contentment; to pacify; to make, or to prove consistent; to admit or restore to membership of a church; to adjust or compose; to regain, conciliate (*Spenser*); to reconsecrate (a desecrated holy place). [L *reconciliāre*, -*ātum*, from *conciliāre* to call together]
■ **rec'oncilability** (or /-sīl'/) *n*. **rec'oncilable** (or /-sīl'/) *adj*. **rec'oncilableness** (or /-sīl'/) *n*. **rec'oncilably** (or /-sīl'/) *adv*. **rec'oncilement** (or /-sīl'/) *n*. **rec'onciler** *n*. **reconcilia'tion** /-sil-/ *n*. **reconciliatory** /-sīl'i-ə-tər-i/ *adj*.

recondite /ri-kon'dīt or rek'ən-dīt/ *adj* hidden; obscure; abstruse; profound. [L *recondere*, -*itum* to put away, from *re-* again, and *condere* to establish, store]
■ **recon'ditely** (or /rek'/) *adv*. **recon'diteness** (or /rek'/) *n*.

recondition /rē-kən-dish'ən/ *vt* to repair and refit; to restore to original or sound condition. [**re-**]

reconfigure /rē-kon-fig'(y)ər/ *vt* to shape in a new way; to set up in a different way (*comput*). [**re-**]

reconnaissance /ri-kon'i-səns/ *n* reconnoitring; a preliminary survey. [Fr]
■ **reconnaissance in force** an attack by a large body to discover the enemy's position and strength.

reconnoitre or (*esp N Am*) **reconnoiter** /re-kə-noi'tər/ *vt* to examine with a view to military operations or other purpose; to remember (*obs*). ◆ *vi* to make preliminary examination. ◆ *n* a reconnaissance. [Fr *reconnoître* (now *reconnaître*), from L *recognōscere* to recognize]
■ **reconnoi'trer** or (*esp N Am*) **reconnoi'terer** *n*.

reconsider /rē-kon-sid'ər or -kən-/ *vt* to consider (a decision, etc) again, with a view to altering or reversing it. [**re-**]
■ **reconsiderā'tion** *n*.

reconstitute /rē-kon'sti-tūt/ *vt* to constitute anew; to reorganize; to restore the constitution of (*esp* dried foods by adding water). [**re-**]
■ **reconstit'uent** /-kən-/ *adj* and *n*. **reconstitūt'able** *adj*. **reconstitū'tion** *n* constituting afresh; refounding; restoration to original condition; theoretical reconstruction on the spot of the details of a crime.

reconstruct /rē-kən-strukt'/ *vt* to construct again; to rebuild; to remodel; to restore in imagination or theory. [**re-**]
■ **reconstruc'table** or **reconstruc'tible** *adj*. **reconstruc'tion** *n* the act of reconstructing; a thing reconstructed; reorganization; a model representing a series of sections; a theoretical representation or view of something unknown; the upbuilding of moral and material public wellbeing after a great upheaval; (with *cap*) the process of restoring the Seceding States to the rights and privileges of the Union after the Civil War (*US*). **reconstruc'tional** *adj*. **reconstruc'tionary** *adj*. **reconstruc'tionist** *n*. **reconstruc'tive** *adj*. **reconstruc'tor** *n*.
❏ **reconstructive surgery** *n* plastic surgery either to correct a disfigurement or make cosmetic changes to the body.

reconvalescence /ri-kon-və-les'əns/ (*archaic*) *n* recovery from illness. [**re-**]

reconvert /rē-kən-vûrt'/ *vt* to convert again to a former state, religion, etc. [**re-**]
■ **reconver'sion** *n*.

reconvey /rē-kən-vā'/ *vt* (of an estate, etc) to transfer again to a former owner. [**re-**]
■ **reconvey'ance** *n*.

record /ri-körd'/ *vt* to set down in writing or other permanent form; to register (on an instrument, scale, etc); to trace a curve or other representation of; to perform before a recording instrument; to make a recording of (music, speech, etc); to mark, indicate; to bear witness to; to put on record (an offence, etc) without taking further measures against the offender; to register (as a vote or verdict); to celebrate; to call to mind (*archaic*); to get by heart (*obs*); to go over in one's mind (*Spenser*); to repeat from memory (*Spenser*); to narrate, set forth (*archaic*); to sing in an undertone, practise quietly (*esp* of birds; *obs*). ◆ *vi* to make a record; to sing, warble, *esp* in quiet rehearsal (*obs*). ◆ *n* /rek'örd, formerly ri-körd'/ a register; a formal writing of any fact or proceeding; a book of such writings; past history; a witness, a memorial; memory, remembrance; anything entered in the rolls of a court, *esp* the formal statement or pleadings of parties in a litigation; a group of related fields forming a complete piece of information, such as a name and address, and constituting one of the basic elements of a database (*comput*); a curve or other representation of phenomena made by an instrument upon a surface; a disc (or formerly a cylinder) on which sound is registered for reproduction by an instrument such as a record player; a performance or occurrence not recorded to have been surpassed; a list of a person's criminal convictions. ◆ *adj* /rek'örd/ not surpassed. [OFr *recorder*, from L *recordārī* to call to mind, get by heart, from *cor*, *cordis* the heart]
■ **record'able** /ri-/ *adj* able to be recorded; worthy of record. **recordā'tion** (or (*Shakesp*) /rek'/) *n* remembrance; recording; commemoration. **record'er** /ri-/ *n* a person who records or registers,

Some words formed with the prefix **re-**.

rēassem'blage *n*.	**rēassert'** *vt*.	**rēassess'ment** *n*.
rēassem'ble *vt* and *vi*.	**rēasser'tion** *n*.	**rēassign'** *vt*.
rēassem'bly *n*.	**rēassess'** *vt*.	**rēassign'ment** *n*.

fāte; fär; mē; fûr; mīne; mōte; för; mūte; pŭt; dhen (then); *el'ə-mənt* (element) • For other sounds see detailed chart of pronunciation

esp the rolls, etc of a city; (with *cap*) a judge of a city or borough court of quarter-sessions (*hist*); in England, a barrister or solicitor appointed as a part-time judge; a person who performs before a recording instrument; a recording apparatus; a fipple flute, once called the 'English flute', much used in the 16c–18c and revived in the 20c (from the obsolete meanings of the verb). **record'ership** *n* the office of recorder or the time of holding it. **record'ing** *n* a record of sound or images made for later reproduction, eg on magnetic tape, film or disc; the process of registering these sounds and images. ◆ *adj* relating to the production of records. **record'ist** *n* a person who records (*esp* the sound for a cinema film).

❏ **record-breaking** *adj* outdoing the highest achievement yet recorded. **recorded delivery** *n* a service of the Post Office in which a record is kept of the collection and delivery of a letter, parcel, etc. **recording angel** *n* an angel supposed to keep a book in which every misdeed is recorded against the doer. **Record Office** *n* a place where public records are kept. **record player** *n* a small, portable instrument for playing audio records, run on batteries or mains electricity; a larger, more sophisticated, etc device for the same purpose. **record sleeve** *n* a cardboard case for a record.

■ **beat** or **break a** (or **the**) **record** to outdo the highest achievement yet recorded. **close the record** an act of a Scottish judge after each party has said all he or she wishes to say by way of statement and answer. **court of record** a court (such as the supreme court, county courts and others) whose acts and proceedings are permanently recorded, and which has the authority to fine or imprison persons for contempt. **for the record** (*inf*) in order to get the facts straight. **go on record** to make a public statement. **off the record** not to be made public (**off'-the-record** *adj*). **on record** recorded in a document, etc; publicly known. **public records** contemporary officially authenticated statements of acts and proceedings in public affairs, preserved in the public interest. **set** (or **put**) **the record straight** to put right a mistake or false impression. **trial by record** (*obs*) a common-law mode of trial when a former decision of the court was disputed and the matter settled by producing the record.

recount[1] /ri-kownt'/ *vt* to narrate or relate the particulars of; to detail. [OFr *reconter*, from *conter* to tell]
■ **recount'al** *n*. **recount'ment** *n* (*Shakesp*) relation in detail.

recount[2] or **re-count** /rē-kownt'/ *vt and vi* to count over again. ◆ *n* /rē'kownt/ a second or new counting (as of votes). [**re-**]

recoup /ri-koop'/ *vt* to make good (a loss); to indemnify, compensate; *orig* to deduct or keep back (from what is claimed by a counterclaim) (*law*; *obs*). [Fr *recouper* to cut back, from *couper* to cut]
■ **recoup'able** *adj*. **recoup'ment** *n*.

recoure or **recower** /ri-kowr'/ (*Spenser*) *vt* variant of **recover** see also **recure**.

recourse /ri-kōrs'* or *-körs'/ *n* access; resort; freedom to return; a source of aid or protection; right to payment, *esp* by the drawer or endorser of a bill of exchange not met by the acceptor; flowing back (*archaic*); withdrawal (*archaic*); recurrence (*archaic*); flow (*Shakesp*); return (*archaic*). ◆ *vi* (*Spenser*) to return, go back or revert in the mind. [Fr *recours*, from L *recursus*, from *re-* back, and *currere, cursum* to run]
■ **have recourse to** to go to for help, protection, etc. **without recourse** (*law and commerce*) a qualified endorsement of a bill or promissory note indicating that the endorser takes no responsibility for non-payment.

recover /ri-kuv'ər/ *vt* to get or find again; to regain; to reclaim; to extract (a valuable substance) from an ore, etc, or (usable material) from waste; to bring back; to retrieve; to cure (*archaic*); to revive; to restore; to rescue; to succeed in reaching; to attain; to obtain as compensation; to obtain for injury or debt. ◆ *vi* to regain health or any former state; to get back into position; to obtain a judgement (*law*). ◆ *n* recovery (*obs*); possibility of recovery (*obs*); return to a former position, as in rowing or exercise with a weapon; the position so resumed. [OFr *recover*, from L *recuperāre*; see **recuperate**]
■ **recoverabil'ity** *n*. **recov'erable** *adj*. **recov'erableness** *n*. **recoveree'** *n* a person against whom a judgement is obtained in common recovery. **recov'erer** *n* a person who recovers. **recov'eror** *n* a person who recovers a judgement in common recovery. **recov'ery** *n* the act, fact, process, possibility or power of recovering, or state of having recovered, in any sense; a verdict giving right to the recovery of debts or costs (*law*).

❏ **recovered memory** *n* (*psychol*) memory of repressed childhood experiences, *esp* of being sexually abused, (apparently) recovered by psychoanalysis. **recovery position** *n* in the medical treatment of unconscious or semiconscious casualties, a position of the body on its side with the face tilted slightly upwards. **recovery stock** *n* (*finance*) a share that has fallen in price but is considered likely to rise again. **recovery time** *n* the minimum time interval between two separately-recorded events or states. **recovery vehicle** *n* a vehicle used to carry away another vehicle that has broken down or been involved in an accident; a vehicle used to collect isolated personnel or disabled vehicles from a battlefield (*mil*).

■ **common recovery** a former method of transferring an entailed estate by a legal fiction. **recover the wind of** (*Shakesp*) to get to windward of (so as to drive a hare into a toil, or take the wind out of someone's sails); to gain an advantage over.

re-cover or **recover** /rē-kuv'ər/ *vt* to cover again. [**re-**]

recower see **recoure**.

recoyle see **recoil**.

recpt *abbrev* : receipt.

recreant /rek'ri-ənt/ (*archaic*) *adj* surrendering; cowardly; false; apostate. ◆ *n* a person who yields in combat; a coward; a mean-spirited wretch; an apostate; a renegade. [OFr, prp of *recroire* to yield in combat, from LL *recrēdere* to surrender, from L *crēdere* to entrust]
■ **rec'reance** or **rec'reancy** *n*. **rec'reantly** *adv*.

recreate /rē-krē-āt'/ *vt* to create again; in the following senses /rek'ri-āt/ (*rare*) to reinvigorate; to refresh; to indulge, gratify or amuse by sport or pastime. ◆ *vi* to take recreation. [**re-**]
■ **recreation** /rē-krē-ā'shən/ *n* the act of creating anew; a new creation. **rēcreā'tive** *adj* creating anew.

recreation /rek-ri-ā'shən/ *n* pleasurable occupation of leisure time; an amusement or sport; a source of amusement; refreshment after toil, sorrow, etc. [**re-**]
■ **recrea'tional** *adj*. **recreative** /rek'ri-ā-tiv/ *adj* serving as recreation, amusing.

❏ **recreational drug** *n* one taken for its intoxicating effects, not for medical reasons. **recreational vehicle** *n* one having living, sleeping, etc facilities in the back (*abbrev* **RV**). **recreation ground** *n* an open area for games, sports, etc. **recreation room** *n* a room in a hospital, hotel, etc where people can relax, play games, etc.

recrement /rek'ri-mənt/ *n* waste, dross; a secretion that is reabsorbed. [L *recrēmentum* dross, from *cernere* to sift]
■ **recremental** /-ment'l/ *adj*. **recrementitial** /-mən-tish'l/ *adj*. **recrementi'tious** *adj*.

recriminate /ri-krim'i-nāt/ *vi* to charge an accuser. [L *crīminārī* to accuse]
■ **recrimina'tion** *n* act of accusing in return; countercharge. **recrim'inative** *adj*. **recrim'inator** *n*. **recrim'inatory** *adj*.

recrudesce /rē-kroo-des'/ *vi* to break out afresh. [L *recrūdēscere*, from *crūdus* raw]
■ **recrudesc'ence** *n*. **recrudesc'ency** *n*. **recrudesc'ent** *adj*.

recruit /ri-kroot'/ *n* a newly enlisted member, eg a soldier, police officer, etc; a new supply (of men, money, health, etc; *archaic*); renewal; restoration; a reinforcement (*obs*). ◆ *vi* to enlist new soldiers or other recruits; to obtain fresh supplies; to recover in health or strength; to recoup expenses (*obs*). ◆ *vt* to enlist or raise (recruits); to reinforce; to replenish; to restore; to reinvigorate. [Obs Fr *recrute* reinforcement, prob pap fem of *recroître*, from L *recrēscere* to grow again]
■ **recruit'able** *adj*. **recruit'al** *n* renewed supply; restoration. **recruit'er** *n*. **recruit'ing** *adj*. **recruit'ment** *n* the action or practice of recruiting, *esp* for employment; in deafness of neural cause, the distressing exaggeration of loud sounds, while soft sounds may be audible.
❏ **recruiting ground** *n* a place where recruits may be obtained.

recrystallize or **-ise** /rē-kris'tə-līz/ *vt and vi* to dissolve and reform (a crystalline substance), as when purifying chemical compounds. ◆ *vi* (in metal) to replace deformed crystals by newly generated ones which absorb them. [**re-**]
■ **recrystallīzā'tion** or **-s-** *n*.

Rect *abbrev* : Rector; Rectory.

recta, **rectal**, etc see **rectum**.

Some words formed with the prefix **re-**.

rēassume' *vt*.	**rēattach'ment** *n*.	**rēawake'** *vt and vi*.
rēassump'tion *n*.	**rēattain'** *vt*.	**rēawak'en** *vt and vi*.
rēattach' *vt and vi*.	**rēattempt'** *vt, vi and n*.	**rēawak'ening** *n*.

---

rectangle /rek'tang-gl or -tang'gl/ n a four-sided plane figure with all its angles right angles, *esp* one with unequal adjacent sides. [LL *rēct(i)angulum*, from L *angulus* an angle]
■ **rec'tangled** *adj* having a right angle. **rectang'ūlar** *adj* of the form of a rectangle; at right angles; right-angled. **rectangūlar'ity** *n*. **rectang'ūlarly** *adv*.
▫ **rectangular coordinates** *n pl* a pair of coordinates whose axes are at right angles. **rectangular hyperbola** *n* one whose asymptotes are at right angles. **rectangular solid** *n* one whose axis is perpendicular to its base.

recti see **rectus**.

recti- /rek-ti-/, or before a vowel **rect-** /rekt-/ *combining form* denoting: right; straight. [L *rēctus* straight, right]
■ **rectilineal** /rek-ti-lin'i-əl/ or **rectilinear** /rek-ti-lin'i-ər/ *adj* (L *līnea* a line) in a straight line or lines; straight; bounded by straight lines. **rectilinearity** /-ar'i-ti/ *n*. **rectilin'early** or **rectilin'eally** *adv*. **rectipetality** /rek-ti-pi-tal'i-ti/ or **rectipetaly** /-pet'əl-i/ *n* (L *petere* to seek; *bot*) tendency to grow in a straight line. **rectirostral** /rek-ti-ros'trəl/ *adj* (L *rōstrum* a beak) straight-billed. **rectiserial** /rek-ti-sēr'i-əl/ *adj* (L *seriēs* a row) in straight rows.

rectify /rek'ti-fī/ *vt* (**rec'tifying** (or) **rec'tified**) to set right; to correct; to redress; to adjust; to purify by distillation (*chem*); to determine the length of (an arc); to change (an alternating current) to a direct current. [Fr *rectifier*, from LL *rēctificāre*, from *facere* to make]
■ **rec'tifiable** *adj*. **rectifica'tion** *n*. **rec'tifier** *n* a person who rectifies (*esp* alcohol); apparatus for rectifying (*esp* spirit, an alternating current, or electromagnetic waves).

rectilineal, etc see under **recti-**.

rection /rek'shən/ (*grammar*) *n* syntactical government. [L *rēctiō, -ōnis* government]

rectipetality…to…**rectiserial** see under **recti-**.

rectitis and **rectitic** see under **rectum**.

rectitude /rek'ti-tūd/ *n* rightness; uprightness; integrity; straightness (*obs*). [Fr, from LL *rēctitūdō*, from L *rēctus* straight]
■ **rectitū'dinous** *adj* manifesting moral correctness; over-obviously righteous.

recto /rek'tō/ (*printing*) *n* (pl **rec'tos**) the right-hand page of an open book, the front page of a leaf, *opp* to *verso*. [L *rēctō* (*foliō*) on the right (leaf)]

recto- /rek-tō-/ *combining form* signifying of or relating to the rectum.
■ **rec'tocele** *n* a hernia of the rectum into the vagina.

rector /rek'tər/ *n* in the Church of England, a clergyman of a parish where the tithes were formerly paid to the incumbent; an Episcopal clergyman with charge of a congregation in the USA or (since 1890) Scotland; the headmaster of certain schools in Scotland, *esp* those called academies; the chief elective officer of many Scottish (*Lord Rector*) and foreign universities; the head of certain university colleges; an ecclesiastic in charge of a congregation, an important mission, a college or a religious house, *esp* the head of a Jesuit seminary (*RC*); a ruler, governor or controller (*obs*). [L *rēctor, -ōris*, from *regere, rēctum* to rule]
■ **rec'toral** *adj* of God as a ruler. **rec'torate** *n* a rector's office or term of office. **rec'toress** or **rec'tress** *n* a female rector; a rector's wife (*inf*). **rectorial** /-tō'ri-əl/ *adj* of a rector. ◆ *n* an election of a Lord Rector. **rec'torship** *n*. **rec'tory** *n* the province or residence of a rector.
▫ **Rector Magnificus** *n* the head of a German university.
■ **lay rector** a layman who enjoys the great tithes of a parish.

rectrix /rek'triks/ *n* (pl **rectrices** /rek'tri-sēz or rek-trī'sēz/) a female governor (*rare*); a bird's long tail feather, used in steering. [L *rēctrīx, -īcis*, fem of *rēctor*]
■ **rectricial** /-trish'l/ *adj*.

rectum /rek'təm/ *n* (pl **rec'ta** or **rec'tums**) the terminal part of the large intestine. [L neuter of *rēctus* straight]
■ **rec'tal** *adj*. **rec'tally** *adv*. **rectitic** /-tit'ik/ *adj*. **rectitis** /rek-tī'tis/ *n* inflammation of the rectum.

rectus /rek'təs/ (*anat*) *n* (pl **rec'tī**) a straight muscle. [L]

recuile or **recule** /ri-kūl'/ (*Spenser*) same as **recoil**.

recumbent /ri-kum'bənt/ *adj* reclining; (of an organ, etc) resting against the anatomical structure from which it extends. [L *recumbere*, from *cubāre* to lie down]
■ **recum'bence** or **recum'bency** *n*. **recum'bently** *adv*.

▫ **recumbent fold** *n* (*geol*) an overturned fold with a more or less horizontal axial plane.

recuperate /ri-koo'pə-rāt or -kū'/ *vi* to recover from an illness, etc. ◆ *vt* to recover (a loss). [L *recuperāre* to recover]
■ **recu'perable** *adj* recoverable. **recuperā'tion** *n*. **recu'perative** /-ə-tiv/ *adj*. **recu'perātor** *n* an arrangement by which something lost is regained, such as the heat of waste gases in a furnace. **recu'peratory** *adj*.

recur /ri-kûr'/ *vi* (**recurr'ing** (or /-kur'/); **recurred'** /-kûrd/) to come up or come round again, or at intervals; to come back into one's mind; to revert (*archaic*); to have recourse (*archaic*). [L *recurrere*, from *currere* to run]
■ **recurr'ence** or **recurr'ency** /-kur'/ *n*. **recurr'ent** /-kur'/ *adj* returning at intervals; running back in the opposite direction or toward the place of origin (*anat*). **recurr'ently** *adv*. **recur'sion** /-kûr'/ *n* (*rare*) a going back, return. ◆ *adj* (*maths*; of a formula) enabling a term in a sequence to be computed from one or more of the preceding terms. **recur'sive** *adj* (*maths*; of a definition) consisting of rules which allow values or meaning to be determined with certainty.
▫ **recurring decimal** *n* a decimal fraction in which after a certain point one figure (*repeating decimal*) or a group of figures (*circulating*) is repeated to infinity. **recursive subprogram** or **subroutine** *n* (*comput*) one which includes among its program statements a call to the subprogram itself.

recure /ri-kūr'/ *vt* to cure, remedy, heal, bring back to a better state (*Spenser, Shakesp* and *Milton*); to recover, get back (*Spenser*). ◆ *vi* (*obs*) to recover, get well. ◆ *n* (*obs*) cure; recovery. [Partly L *recūrāre* to cure, partly for **recoure**]
■ **recure'less** *adj* (*obs*) incurable.

recurve /ri-kûrv'/ *vt* and *vi* to bend back. [L *recurvāre*; *rōstrum* beak]
■ **recurv'ature** *n*. **recurved'** *adj*. **recurviros'tral** *adj* with up-bent bill.

recuse /ri-kūz'/ *vt* to reject, object to (eg a judge) (*archaic*); to declare (oneself) unable to judge, participate, etc due to bias or conflict of interest (chiefly *N Am* and *S Afr*). [L *recūsāre*, from *causa* a cause]
■ **recū'sal**, **recusance** /rek' or ri-kū'/ or **recusancy** /-i/ *n*. **recusant** /rek'ū-zənt or ri-kū'zənt/ *n* a person (*esp* a Roman Catholic) who refused to attend the Church of England when it was legally compulsory (*hist*); a dissenter; a person who refuses, *esp* to submit to authority. ◆ *adj* refusing; dissenting. **recusā'tion** *n* (*law*) an objection or appeal.

recycle /rē-sī'kl/ *vt* to pass again through a series of changes or treatment; to remake into something different; to cause (material) to be broken down by bacteria and then reconstitute it; to direct into a different channel. [**re-**]
■ **recy'clable** *adj* and *n*. **recy'clate** *n* material that has been recycled. **recy'clist** *n*.

red[1] /red/ *adj* (**redd'er**; **redd'est**) of a colour like blood; extended traditionally to mean golden, and by custom to other colours more or less near red; having a red face (from shame, heat, embarrassment, etc; see also **red face** below); (of the eyes) bloodshot or with red rims; revolutionary, or supposedly revolutionary; communist (*derog inf*); (of a US state) tending to vote Republican. ◆ *n* the colour of blood; an object of this colour in a set of similar objects; a red pigment; red clothes; red wine; the red traffic-light, meaning 'stop'; a revolutionary or person who favours sweeping changes, variously applied to radical, republican, anarchist, socialist, communist, etc; a former squadron of the British fleet; a red cent. [OE *rēad*; cf Ger *rot*, L *ruber, rūfus*, Gr *erythros*, Gaelic *ruadh*]
■ **redd'en** *vt* to make red. ◆ *vi* to grow red; to blush. **redd'ish** *adj*. **redd'ishness** *n*. **redd'y** *adj*. **red'ly** *adv*. **red'ness** *n*.
▫ **red admiral** *n* a common butterfly (*Vanessa atalanta*) with reddish-banded wings. **red alert** *n* a state of readiness for imminent crisis, eg war or natural disaster. **red algae** *n pl* one of the great divisions of seaweeds, the Rhodophyceae or Florideae, containing a red pigment. **red ant** *n* any of several reddish-coloured ants, *esp* the Pharaoh ant. **red'back** *n* (*Aust*) a poisonous spider (*Latrodectus hasselti*), the female of which has a red strip on its back. **red beds** *n pl* (*geol*) red sedimentary rocks, *usu* sandstones, silicates and shales. **red'belly** *n* the char, or other red-bellied fish; the slider, a terrapin. **red biddy** *n* (*inf*) a drink made of red wine and methylated spirit. **red'-blood'ed** *adj* having red blood; abounding in vitality, and usually in crudity. **red'-blood'edness** *n*. **red book** *n* a book bound in red, *esp* a court guide, peerage, directory of persons in the service of the state, official

---

Some words formed with the prefix **re-**.

rēbap'tism *n*.	**rēbloss'om** *vi*.	**rēbrace'** *vt*.
rēbaptize' or **rēbaptise'** *vt*.	**rēboil'** *vt* and *vi*.	**rēbroad'cast** *vt* and *n*.
rēbloom' *vi*.	**rēborr'ow** *vt*.	**rēbuild'** *vt*.

---

regulations, etc. **red box** *n* a government minister's red-covered box for official papers. **red'breast** *n* the robin. **red brick** *n* a brick, made from clay containing iron compounds that are converted into ferric oxide. **red'brick** *adj* denoting an English university founded in the 19c or first half of the 20c, contrasted with Oxford and Cambridge. **Red Brigade** *n* any of a group of left-wing terrorist groups in Italy. **red'bud** *n* the American Judas tree (*Cercis canadensis*), producing heart-shaped leaves and pink bud-like flowers. **red bush tea** see **rooibos tea**. **red cabbage** *n* a purplish cabbage often used for pickling. **red'cap** *n* a goldfinch; a Scottish castle goblin (also **red'-cowl**); a military policeman (*sl*); a railway porter (*N Am*). **red card** *n* (*football*) a red-coloured card that a referee holds up to show that he or she is sending a player off. **red'-card** *vt*. **red carpet** *n* a strip of carpet put out for the highly favoured to walk on; treatment as a very important person (*fig*). **red'-car'pet** *adj* (*usu fig*). **red cedar** *n* a name for various species of *Cedrela* and of juniper. **red cell** *n* a red corpuscle. **red cent** *n* a cent (formerly made of copper) considered as a very small amount (*inf*; *esp N Am*); a whit. **red clay** *n* a clayey deposit of oceanic abysses, stained reddish or brown by manganese and iron oxides; cave-earth. **red'coat** *n* a British soldier (*hist*); an entertainment organizer at a Butlins holiday camp, wearing a red blazer as uniform; a mountie (*Can inf*). **red cock** *n* (*fig*) an incendiary fire. **red coral** *n* any of various corals of warm seas, *esp Corallium nobile*, the smooth pink skeleton of which is used in making jewellery. **red corpuscle** *n* an erythrocyte, a blood cell which carries oxygen in combination with the pigment haemoglobin, and removes carbon dioxide. **Red Crag** *n* a middle division of the English Pliocene. **Red Crescent** *n* the Red Cross Society in Islamic countries. **Red Cross** *n* a red cross on a white ground, the national flag of England (in Spenser's **Redcross Knight**, representing holiness and the Church of England); the Swiss flag with colours reversed, the copyrighted symbol of an organization (known as **the Red Cross**) for tending sick, wounded in war, etc, enjoying privileges under the Convention of Geneva (1864). **Red Crystal** *n* a diamond-shaped emblem used by the Red Cross Society as a politically and religiously neutral alternative to the Red Cross and Red Crescent. **redcurr'ant** *n* the small red berry of a shrub of the gooseberry genus. **red'currant** *adj*. **red deer** *n* the common stag or hind, reddish-brown in summer. **Red Delicious** *n* a red-skinned variety of eating apple. **Red Devils** *n pl* the display unit of the Parachute Regiment; the regiment itself (*inf*). **red diesel** *n* diesel fuel that is intended for use by agricultural vehicles only, and is therefore subject to a reduced rate of excise duty and is chemically marked and dyed red to identify it. **red dog** *n* a dhole. **red'-dog** *n* the lowest grade of flour in high milling. **red dwarf** *n* a red star of low luminosity. **Red Ensign** *n* (also (*sl*) **Red Duster**) a red flag with the Union Jack in the top left corner, until 1864 the flag of Red Squadron, now flown by British merchant ships. **red'-eye** *n* the rudd; poor-quality whisky (*US*); a drink of beer and tomato juice (*Can sl*); a common fault in amateur flash photography which causes the pupils of the subject's eyes to appear red; an overnight aeroplane journey (*N Am sl*; also *adj*). **red face** *n* a blushing from embarrassment or disconcertion. **red'-faced** *adj*. **red'-figure** or **red'-figured** *adj* designating a style of ancient Greek pottery in which the background is painted with a fine clay solution which turns and remains black after firing in a reducing atmosphere (cf **black-figure** under **black**). **red'fish** *n* a male salmon when, or just after, spawning; any of various red-fleshed fish, of the genus *Sebastes*. **red flag** *n* a flag used as a signal of danger, defiance, no mercy, or an auction sale; the banner of socialism or of revolution; (with *caps*) a socialist's song. **red fox** *n* a common fox, native to Europe, parts of Asia, N Africa and N America, having a reddish-brown coat and white underparts. **red giant** *n* a red star of high luminosity. **red grouse** *n* another name for the common grouse. **Red Guard** *n* a member of a strict Maoist youth movement in China, *esp* active in the cultural revolution of the late 1960s. **red gum** *n* an eruption of the skin in teething infants; a Eucalyptus (of various kinds) with red gum; the hard red timber from this tree. **red'-haired** *adj*. **red hand** *n* the bloody hand (see under **hand**). **redhand'ed** *adj* and *adv* in the very act, or immediately after, as if with bloody hands. **red hat** *n* a cardinal; a cardinal's hat (award of this to cardinals was discontinued in 1969); a staff officer (*milit sl*). **red'head** *n* a person with red hair; any of several birds with reddish head, *esp* the pochard. **red'-headed** *adj* having a red head or red hair; angrily excited (*sl*). **red heat** *n* the temperature at which something is red-hot. **red'-heeled** *adj*. **red herring** *n* a herring cured and dried, of reddish appearance; a subject introduced to divert discussion or attention as a

herring drawn across a track would throw hounds out. **red'-hot** *adj* heated to redness; extremely hot; extreme; marked by extreme emotion of any kind; (of information) very recently received (*inf*); (of a telephone line) very busy with calls (*inf*); (of the favourite in a sporting contest) considered almost certain to win. **red-hot poker** *n* the plant Kniphofia or Tritoma. **Red Indian** *n* (*inf*; *offensive*) a Native American, *esp* of N America (also *adj*). **Red Lane** see under **lane**[1]. **red'-latt'ice** *adj* (*Shakesp*) savouring of the alehouse (whose lattice was conventionally painted red). **red lead** *n* an oxide of lead (Pb_3O_4) of a fine red colour, used in paint-making (also called **minium**). **red'leg** *n* (*W Indies*) a *derog* term for a poor white person, *esp* a descendant of original white settlers. **red'-legged** *adj*. **red'-letter** *adj* marked with red letters, as holidays or saints' days in the old calendars; deserving to be so marked, special. **red light** *n* a rear light; a danger-signal; the red traffic-light, meaning 'stop'; a brothel (*inf*). **red'-light** *adj* (*inf*) of or relating to brothels, as in *red-light district*. **red line** *n* the centre line on an ice-hockey rink; on the agenda of a meeting, a line marked in red ink below a point on which one is not prepared to compromise; (also **red-line issue**) a point on which one is not prepared to compromise. **red'-line** *vt* to mark or cancel (a date, name, etc) by circling or scoring through with a red line; to subject to red-lining. **red'-lining** *n* (*inf*; *orig US*) the practice of refusing credit or insurance to all those living in an area considered to be a poor financial risk. **red'-looked** *adj* (*Shakesp*) having a red look. **red'-mad**[1] *adj* (*Scot*) stark mad. **red man** *n* a Native American (*archaic*); *prob* red mercuric sulphide (*alchemy*). **red meat** *n* dark-coloured meat, eg beef and lamb. **red mist** *n* (*inf*) a source of impaired judgement that is said to descend over a person during moments of extreme rage. **red mud** *n* a type of industrial waste resulting from alumina processing, consisting of silicon oxide, iron oxide, etc. **red mullet** see under **mullet**[1]. **red'neck** *n* (*derog*) a poor white farm labourer in SW USA; a poorly educated person with intolerant and reactionary opinions. ◆ *adj* ignorant, intolerant, narrow-minded; pertaining to, or characteristic of, poor white farm labourers. **red panda** *n* a panda with chestnut fur and white patches on its face, found in mountain forests in Asia. **red pepper** see under **pepper**. **red pine** *n* any of various coniferous trees yielding reddish timber. **red'-plague** or **-murrain** *n* (*Shakesp*) bubonic plague. **red'poll** *n* a name for two birds (*lesser* and *mealy redpoll*) related to the linnet; an animal of a red breed of polled cattle. **red'-polled** *adj* having a red poll; red and polled. **red rag** *n* the tongue (*sl*); a cause of infuriation (as red is said to be to a bull). **red rattle** *n* lousewort. **red ribbon** or **riband** *n* the ribbon of the Order of the Bath. **red river hog** *n* a bush pig (qv under **bush**[1]). **red'root** *n* a genus (*Ceanothus*) of the buckthorn family, New Jersey tea. **red rot** *n* a disease of oaks, etc caused by *Polyporus*, the wood becoming brown and dry. **red route** *n* a system of traffic control in large cities, designated by red lines painted along the edge of the road where it is operational. **red salmon** *n* any of various types of salmon with red flesh, *esp* the sockeye salmon. **red sanders** *n* a papilionaceous tree (*Pterocarpus santalinus*) of tropical Asia, with heavy dark-red heartwood, used as a dye, etc (see also **sandal**[2]). **redsear, redshare, redshire** see **redshort**. **red seaweed** *n* any of the red algae, *esp* one of the genus *Polysiphonia*. **red seed** *n* the food of mackerel, small floating crustaceans, etc. **red setter** *n* an Irish setter. **red'shank** *n* a sandpiper with red legs; a Highlander or an Irishman (*inf*; *derog*); (**red shank**) a polygonaceous annual plant with a red stem. **red shift** *n* a shift of lines in the spectrum towards the red, considered to occur because the source of light is receding (see **Doppler principle**, etc). **red'-shifted** *adj*. **Red Shirt** *n* (*hist*) a follower of Garibaldi (1807–82), from his garb; a revolutionary or anarchist. **red'shirt** *n* (in American collegiate sport) a player who is not selected for a representative team for one year in order to prolong his or her period of eligibility. ◆ *vt* and *vi* to designate or be designated as a redshirt. **red'skin** *n* (*derog sl*; *offensive*) a Native American. **red snapper** *n* a fish of the Lutjanidae with reddish colouring, common off the east coast of America. **red snow** *n* snow coloured by a microscopic red alga. **red spider** or **red spider mite** *n* a spinning mite that infests leaves. **red squirrel** *n* a squirrel of reddish-brown colour (*Sciurus vulgaris*) native to Europe and Asia, in Britain now rarely found outside the Scottish Highlands; a small squirrel (*Sciurus hudsonicus*) of N America. **red'start** *n* (OE *steort* tail) a European bird (*Ruticilla* or *Phoenicurus*) with a conspicuous chestnut-coloured tail; an American warbler, superficially similar. **red'streak** *n* an apple with streaked skin. **red tape** *n* the tape used in government offices to bind official documents, etc; rigid formality of intricate official routine; bureaucracy. **red'-tape** *adj*. **red-tap'ism** *n*. **red-tap'ist** *n*. **red tide** *n* a

---

Some words formed with the prefix **re-**.

rebur'ial *n*.	**recal'culate** *vt*.	**rechall'enge** *vt* and *n*.
rebur'y *vt*.	**recatch'** *vt* and *vi*.	**recharge'** *vt*.
rebutt'on *vt*.	**recen'tre** *vt*.	**recharge'able** *adj*.

■ words derived from main entry word; ◻ compound words; ■ idioms and phrasal verbs

bloom of red dinoflagellates which colours the sea, etc red. **red'top** *n* (*US*) a kind of bent grass (*Agrostis stolonifera*). **red'-top** *n* any tabloid newspaper whose masthead is printed in red, noted *esp* for sensationalism and prurience (also *adj*). **red'water** *n* a cattle disease due to a protozoan parasite in the blood, that is transmitted by ticks and destroys the red blood cells, causing red-coloured urine to be passed (also called **babesiasis** or **babesiosis**). **red wine** *n* wine coloured by (red) grape skins during fermentation (cf **rosé**). **red'wing** *n* a thrush with reddish sides below the wings. **red'wood** *n* a species of *Sequoia* with reddish wood much used commercially; any wood or tree yielding a red dye. **red-wood'** or (*Scot*) **red-wud'** *adj* stark mad. ■ **in the red** overdrawn at the bank, in debt. **red out** to experience a red hazy field of vision, etc as a result of aerobatics. **reds under the bed(s)** the supposed influence of communist infiltrators, *esp* during the Cold War. **Royal Red Cross** a decoration for nurses, instituted 1883. **see red** to grow furious; to thirst for blood. **the Red Planet** Mars.

red² see **redd**[1,2].

redact /ri-dakt'/ *vt* to edit, work into shape; to frame. [L *redigere, redactum* to bring back, from pfx *red-*, and *agere* to drive]
■ **redac'tion** *n*. **redac'tional** *adj*. **redac'tor** *n*. **redactō'rial** /re- or rē-/ *adj*.

redan /ri-dan'/ (*fortif*) *n* a fieldwork of two faces forming a salient. [OFr *redan*, from L *re-*, and *dēns, dentis* a tooth]

redargue /ri-där'gū/ (*obs* or *Scot*) *vt* to refute; to confute. [L *redarguere*, from *re(d)-* again, and *arguere* argue]

redd¹ or **red** /red/ (chiefly *Scot*) *vt* (**redd'ing**; **redd** or **red**) to put in order, make tidy; to clear up; to disentangle; to comb; to separate in fighting. ◆ *vi* to set things in order, tidy up (*usu* with *up*). ◆ *n* an act of redding; refuse, rubbish. ◆ *adj* (*Scots law*) vacated. [Partly OE *hreddan* to free, rescue (cf Ger *retten* to rescue); prob partly from or influenced by OE *rǣdan* (see **rede, read¹**); cf also **rid¹**]
■ **redd'er** *n*. **redd'ing** *n*.
❑ **redd'ing-comb** or **-kame** *n* a hair-comb. **redd'ing-straik** *n* a stroke received in trying to separate fighters. **redd'ing-up'** *n* setting in order, tidying up.

redd² or **red** /red/ *pat* and *pap* of **read¹** (*Spenser*); same as **rede** (*pres* tense; *Scot*).

redd³ /red/ *n* a place on a river bed excavated by a salmon for nesting; fish or frog spawn (*Scot*). [Origin obscure; perh from **redd¹**]

redden, etc see under **red¹**.

reddendum /ri-den'dəm/ (*law*) *n* (pl **redden'da**) a clause in a lease stating the rent and the time when it is payable. [L, to be rendered, gerundive of *reddere*]
■ **redden'do** *n* (pl **redden'dos**) (*Scots law*) service to be rendered or money to be paid by a vassal, or the clause in a charter specifying it.

reddle and **reddleman** see **ruddle**.

rede /rēd/ *vt* an old spelling of **read¹** retained as an archaism in the senses of 'to counsel or advise, expound, relate'. ◆ *n* (*archaic*) advice; resolution; saying, tale; interpretation (*Browning*).
❑ **rede'craft** *n* (*archaic*) logic. **rede'less** *adj* (*archaic*) without counsel or wisdom.

redeem /ri-dēm'/ *vt* to buy back; to act so as to settle or discharge (a burden, obligation, etc); to recover or free by payment; to free oneself from (a promise) by fulfilment; to ransom; to rescue, deliver, free; (of God or Christ) to deliver from sin; to get back; to reclaim; to exchange (tokens, vouchers, etc) for goods, or (bonds, shares, etc) for cash; to pay the penalty of; to atone for; to compensate for; to put (time) to the best advantage. [L *redimere* (perh through Fr *rédimer*), from *red-* back, and *emere* to buy]
■ **redeemabil'ity** *n*. **redeem'able** *adj*. **redeem'ableness** *n*. **redeem'ably** *adv*. **redeem'er** *n*. **redeem'ing** *adj*. **redeem'less** *adj* not to be redeemed.
■ **the Redeemer** the Saviour, Jesus Christ.

redeliver /rē-di-liv'ər/ *vt* to restore; to free again; to report the words of (*Shakesp*). [**re-**]
■ **redeliv'erance** *n*. **redeliv'erer** *n*. **redeliv'ery** *n*.

redemption /ri-dem(p)'shən/ *n* the act of redeeming; anything that redeems; atonement. [L *redimere, redemptum*; cf **redeem**]
■ **redemp'tible** *adj* (*rare*) redeemable. **redemp'tioner** *n* an emigrant to N America bound to service until his or her fare was made up. **Redemp'tionist** *n* a Trinitarian friar. **redemp'tive** *adj*. **redemp'tively**

adv. **Redemp'torist** *n* a missionary priest of a congregation founded by Alfonso Liguori in 1732 for work among the poor. **redemp'tory** *adj*.
❑ **redemption yield** *n* (*finance*) the total return from a stock, including annual interest and any capital gain, calculated as a percentage of the price to be repaid at a fixed future date.

redeploy /rē-di-ploi'/ *vt* to transfer (eg military forces, supplies, industrial workers) from one area to another (also *vi*). [**re-**]
■ **redeploy'ment** *n*.

redia /rē'di-ə/ *n* (pl **rē'diae** /-ē/) a form in the life cycle of the trematodes. [Francesco *Redi* (died prob 1698), Italian naturalist]

redid *pat* of **redo**.

Rediffusion® /rē-di-fū'zhən/ *n* an early broadcasting system by which television or radio programmes were relayed along a wire rather than being transmitted directly.

redingote /red'ing-gōt/ *n* a long double-breasted (*orig* man's, later woman's) overcoat. [Fr, from Eng *riding coat*]

redintegrate /re-din'ti-grāt/ *vt* to restore to wholeness; to re-establish. ◆ *adj* restored; renewed. [L *redintegrāre, -ātum*, from *red-* again, and *integrāre* to make whole, from *integer*]
■ **redintegrā'tion** *n* restoring to wholeness; the recurrence of a complete mental state when any single element of it recurs, eg when a piece of music reminds one of an occasion on which it was played (*psychol*). **redin'tegrative** *adj*.

redisburse /rē-dis-bûrs'/ (*Spenser*) *vt* to refund. [**re-**]

redistrict /rē-dis'trikt/ (chiefly *US*) *vt* and *vi* to divide (a country, state, etc) into new administrative or electoral districts. [**re-**]

redo /rē-doo'/ *vt* (pat **redid'**; *pap* **redone'**) to do again; to redecorate (a room, house, etc). ◆ *n* /rē'/ a further attempt. [**re-**]

redolent /red'ə-lənt/ *adj* fragrant; smelling (of, or with); suggestive (of), imbued (with). [L *redolēns, -entis*, from *red-* again, and *olēre* to emit smell]
■ **red'olence** or **red'olency** *n*. **red'olently** *adv*.

redouble /ri-dub'l/ *vt* and *vi* to double; to repeat; to re-echo; to increase; /rē'dub'l/ to double after previous doubling (*bridge*). ◆ *n* /rē'dub-l/ an act or fact or redoubling, as in bridge. [**re-**]
■ **redoub'lement** /ri-/ *n*.

redoubt¹ /ri-dowt'/ (*fortif*) *n* a fieldwork enclosed on all sides; an inner last retreat. [Fr *redoute*, from Ital *ridotto*, from LL *reductus* refuge, from L, retired, from *redūcere*; the *b* from confusion with **redoubt²**]

redoubt² /ri-dowt'/ *vt* (*archaic*) to fear. [OFr *redouter* to fear greatly, from L *re-* back, and *dubitāre* to doubt]
■ **redoubt'able** *adj* formidable; valiant. **redoubt'ably** *adv*. **redoubt'ed** *adj* (*archaic*) redoubtable.

redound /ri-downd'/ *vi* to overflow (*Spenser*); to be in excess (*Milton*); to surge (*Spenser*); to be filled (*Spenser*); to flow back; to return; to rebound, be reflected or echoed; to turn, recoil, be reflected, as a consequence (to one's credit, discredit, advantage, etc); to conduce; to rise one above another in receding series (*Spenser*). ◆ *vt* (*fig*) to cast, reflect. ◆ *n* the coming back, as an effect or consequence, return. [Fr *rédonder*, from L *redundāre*, from *red-* back, and *undāre* to surge, from *unda* a wave]
■ **redound'ing** *n* and *adj*.

redowa /red'ō-va/ *n* a Bohemian dance; music for it, *usu* in quick triple time. [Ger or Fr, from Czech *rejdovák*]

redox /rē'doks/ *adj* of a type of chemical reaction in which one of the reagents is reduced, while another is oxidized. [*reduction* and *oxidation*]

redraft /rē'dräft/ *n* a revised draft or copy; a new bill of exchange which the holder of a protested bill draws on the drawer or endorsers, for the amount of the bill, with costs and charges. ◆ *vt* /-dräft'/ to make a revised draft of. [**re-**]

redress /ri-dres'/ *vt* to set right; to readjust; to restore (*Spenser*); to remedy; to compensate. ◆ *n* relief; reparation. [Fr *redresser* (see **dress**); partly from **re-** and **dress**]
■ **redress'able** /ri-/ *adj*. **redress'al** *n* an act or an instance of redressing. **redress'er** *n* a person who redresses abuses or injuries. **redress'ive** *adj* (*rare*) affording redress.

re-dress /rē-dres'/ *vt* and *vi* to dress again; to dress in different clothes. [**re-**]

Some words formed with the prefix **re-**.

rēchart' *vt*.	**rēcir'culate** *vt* and *vi*.	**rēclimb'** *vt*.
rēchart'er *vt* and *vi*.	**rēclassificā'tion** *n*.	**rēclose'** *vt*.
rēchrist'en *vt*.	**rēclass'ify** *vt*.	**rēclothe'** *vt*.

redruthite /red'rŭ-thīt/ n copper-glance, a mineral found at Redruth in Cornwall.

redshort /red'shört/ adj brittle at red-heat (also **red'sear**, **red'share** or **red'shire**). [Swed rödskör, from röd red, and skör brittle]

reduce /ri-dūs'/ vt to make smaller or less, to lessen; to diminish in weight or girth; to bring into a lower state; to concentrate or thicken (a sauce) by boiling to evaporate water and reduce the volume; to weaken; to degrade (milit); to impoverish; to subdue; to subject to necessity; to drive into (a condition; with to); to change to another form; to express in other terms; to range in order or classification; to adapt, adjust; to translate; to put into (writing, practice, etc; with to); to break up, separate, disintegrate; to disband (milit; obs); to bring to the metallic state; to put back into a normal condition or place (eg a dislocation or fracture) (surg); to remove oxygen from, or combine with hydrogen, or lessen the positive valency of (an atom or ion) by adding electrons; to annul (Scots law); to bring back (archaic); to restore to an old state (archaic); to bring into a new state (archaic). ◆ vi to become smaller or less; (of a sauce, etc) to thicken or become concentrated; to resolve itself; to slim, or lessen weight or girth. [L redūcere, reductum, from re- back, and dūcere to lead]
■ **reduced'** adj in a state of reduction; weakened; impoverished; diminished; simplified in structure. **reduc'er** n a person who reduces; a means of reducing; a joint-piece for connecting pipes of varying diameter. **reducibil'ity** n. **reduc'ible** adj that may be reduced. **reduc'ibleness** n. **reduc'ing** adj. **reduc'tant** n a reducing agent. **reduc'tase** n an enzyme which brings about the reduction of organic compounds. **reduction** /-duk'shən/ n the act of reducing or state of being reduced; diminution; lowering of price; subjugation; changing of numbers or quantities from one denomination to another (maths); a settlement of S Americans converted by the Jesuits to Christianity, and governed by them (hist). **reduc'tionism** n the belief that complex data and phenomena can be explained in terms of something simpler. **reduc'tionist** n and adj. **reductionist'ic** adj. **reduc'tive** adj bringing back (archaic); reducing, narrowing, limiting. **reduc'tively** adv. **reduc'tiveness** n.
□ **reducing agent** n (chem) a substance with a strong affinity for oxygen, or the like, serving to remove it from others. **reducing flame** n a hot luminous blowpipe flame in which substances can be reduced. **reduction division** n (biol) meiosis. **reduction works** n smelting works.
■ **in reduced circumstances** (euphem) impoverished. **reduce to the ranks** to demote, for misconduct, to the condition of a private soldier.

Reductil® /ri-duk'til/ n a proprietary name for a drug, sibutramine hydrochloride monohydrate, which is used to treat obesity by suppressing the appetite.

reductio ad absurdum /ri-duk'shi-ō ad ab-sûr'dəm or re-dŭk'ti-ō ad ab-soor'dŭm/ reduction to absurdity; the proof of a proposition by proving the falsity of its contradictory; the application of a principle so strictly that it is carried to absurd lengths. [L]

reduit /rā-dwē'/ n an inner fortified retreat for a garrison. [Fr réduit]

redundant /ri-dun'dənt/ adj superfluous; (of a word or phrase) excessive, able to be removed from the sentence, etc without affecting meaning; (of workers) no longer needed and therefore dismissed; surging (Milton); overflowing (obs); copious; over-copious. [L redundāns, -antis, prp of redundāre to overflow]
■ **redun'dance** n. **redun'dancy** n the state of being redundant; a dismissal, or a person dismissed, from a job because of redundancy; the presence of multiple components which improve the reliability of a system (comput). **redun'dantly** adv.
□ **redundancy payment** n a minimum statutory payment to be made to an employee who is made redundant, its amount based on age, pay, and length of service.

reduplicate /ri-dū'pli-kāt/ vt to double; to repeat. ◆ vi to double; to exhibit reduplication (grammar). ◆ adj /-kit/ doubled; showing reduplication (grammar); in aestivation, valvate with edges turned outwards (bot). [L reduplicāre, -ātum, from duplicāre to double]
■ **reduplica'tion** n a folding or doubling; the doubling of the initial part, in inflection and word-formation, as in L fefellī, perf of fallō, Gr tetypha, perf of typtō (grammar); the reduplicated element in a word; the combination of two rhyming, alliterative, etc words (the second sometimes a coinage for the purpose) to form one, as in hurry-skurry, popsy-wopsy or mishmash. **redū'plicātive** adj.

reduviid /rə-dū'vi-id/ adj belonging to the **Redū'viidae** family of predaceous bugs. ◆ n an insect of this family. [New L Reduvius, and -id²]

redux /rē'duks/ adj returned, revived, brought back. [L, from redūcere to bring back]

ree¹ /rē/ see **reeve³**.

ree² /rē/ or **reed** /rēd/ (Scot) n an enclosure, esp a (partially-)roofed walled yard, eg for coal, for wintering cattle, for confining sheep, etc. [Poss cognate with Du rede roadstead]

reebok /rē'bok or rā'/ n a S African antelope. [Du]

reech /rēch/ same as **reek**.
■ **reech'y** (Shakesp **rechie** or **reechie**) adj smoky, grimy.

re-echo /rē-ek'ō/ vt to echo back; to repeat as if an echo. ◆ vi to give back echoes; to resound. ◆ n a re-echoing. [re-]

reed¹ /rēd/ n a tall stiff hard-culmed marsh or water grass of various kinds, esp Phragmites australis; a thing made, or formerly made, of a reed or reeds, eg a pen, an arrow, a measuring rod, a music pipe, the vibrating tongue of an organ-pipe or woodwind instrument (with or without the parts to which it is attached), a weaver's appliance for separating the warp threads and beating up the weft; thatching; a small reedlike moulding; a reed instrument; the metal reed of an organ pipe used as the plate of a capacitor for electronic amplification. ◆ adj reedlike (Shakesp); having a vibrating reed (music); milled, ribbed. ◆ vt to thatch. [OE hrēod; cf Du riet and Ger Riet]
■ **reed'ed** adj covered with reeds or reed moulding; having reed(s). **reed'en** adj of reed. **reed'er** n a thatcher. **reed'ily** adv. **reed'iness** n. **reed'ing** n the milling on the edge of a coin; a reed moulding. **reed'ling** n a Eurasian bird, Panurus biarmicus (also called **bearded tit**). **reed'y** adj (**reed'ier**, **reed'iest**) abounding with reeds; resembling a reed; sounding like a reed instrument, esp in being thin and piping. □ **reed'-band** n a band of reed instruments. **reed'bed** n. **reed'-bird** n the bobolink. **reed'buck** n an African antelope (Redunca) with inward curving horns and a whistling call. **reed bunting** n a European bunting which breeds in marshy places and reedbeds. **reed'-drawing** n the combing out of rough straw by means of a frame. **reed'-grass** n a reedlike grass of various kinds (eg Phalaris or Arundo). **reed instrument** n a woodwind with reed, such as a clarinet, oboe or bassoon. **reed'-knife** n a tool for organ-tuning. **reed'-mace** n a tall erect herb of the genus Typha, growing esp in marshy areas (also called **cat's-tail**). **reed organ** n a keyboard instrument with free reeds, such as the harmonium, or the American organ. **reed'-pheasant** n the bearded titmouse. **reed pipe** n an organ-pipe whose tone is produced by the vibration of a reed, the pipe acting as resonator. **reed'-rand** or **-rond** n (E Anglia) a reed thicket. **reed'-sparrow** n the reed-bunting; the sedge-warbler. **reed stop** n a set of reed-pipes controlled by a single organ stop. **reed warbler** n a warbler that frequents marshy places and builds its nest on reeds (also called **reed'-wren**, the **reed'-thrush** being a larger species (greater reed-warbler)).
■ **broken reed** (fig) a person who is too weak or unreliable to be depended upon. **free reed** a reed vibrating in an opening without touching the sides.

reed², **reede** (Spenser) same as **rede**.

reed³ see **ree²**.

re-edify /rē-ed'i-fī/ vt to rebuild (also (Spenser) **reæd'ifye**). [L aedificāre to build]
■ **re-edifica'tion** n. **re-ed'ifier** n.

re-educate /rē-ed'ū-kāt/ vt to educate again; to change a person's (esp political) beliefs. [re-]
■ **re-educa'tion** n.
□ **re-education camp** n a detention camp in some totalitarian states where dissidents and others are sent to be re-educated.

reedy see under **reed¹**.

reef¹ /rēf/ n a chain of rocks at or near the surface of water; a shoal or bank; a gold-bearing lode or vein (orig Aust); the encasing rock of a diamond-mine, all ground in the mine other than diamondiferous (S Afr). [Du rif, from ON rif]
□ **reef'-builder** n a coral-animal that forms reefs.

reef² /rēf/ n a portion of a sail that may be rolled or folded up. ◆ vt to reduce the exposed surface of (a sail, etc); to gather up in a similar way. [ON rif]
■ **reef'er** n a person who reefs; a midshipman (sl); a reefing-jacket (also **reefer jacket**); a cigarette containing marijuana (sl). **reef'ing** n.

Some words formed with the prefix **re-**.

recode' vt.	**recommence'** vt and vi.	**recommit'** vt.
recoloniza'tion or **recolonisa'tion** n.	**recommence'ment** n.	**recommit'ment** n.
recol'onize or **recol'onise** vt.	**recommiss'ion** n, vt and vi.	**recommitt'al** n.

■ words derived from main entry word; □ compound words; ■ idioms and phrasal verbs

❏ **reef band** *n* a strengthening strip across a sail. **reef'ing-jacket** *n* a short thick double-breasted jacket. **reef knot** *n* a flat knot used in tying reef points consisting of two loops passing symmetrically through each other. **reef point** *n* a short rope on a reef band to secure a reefed sail.

reefer[1] /rē'fər/ (*sl*) *n* a refrigerated railway car; a refrigerated ship. [**refrigerator**]

reefer[2] see under **reef**[2].

reek /rēk/ *n* a smell, *esp* an offensive one; smoke; vapour; fume. ◆ *vi* to emit smoke, fumes, or (*esp* offensive) smell; to exhale. ◆ *vt* to expose to smoke; to exhale. [OE *rēc*; ON *reykr*, Ger *Rauch*, Du *rook* smoke; a Scot and N Eng form; cf **reech**]
■ **reek'ing** *adj*. **reek'y** (or *Scot* **reek'ie**) *adj* smoky; smoked; reeking; foul (*Shakesp*).
■ **Auld Reekie** Edinburgh.

reel /rēl/ *n* a cylinder, drum, spool, bobbin or frame on which thread, fishing-line, wire, cables, photographic film, etc may be wound; a length of material so wound; a loud rattling, a din (*Scot*); a whirl, a stagger; a lively dance, *esp* Highland or Irish; a tune for it, *usu* in 4–4, sometimes in 6–8 time; (in *pl*) revelry (*Shakesp*). ◆ *vt* to wind on a reel; to take off by or from a reel; to draw (in) by means of a reel; to cause to whirl or roll (*Spenser*); to stagger along (*Shakesp*). ◆ *vi* to whirl; to seem to swirl or sway; to totter; to stagger; (of eg line of battle) to waver; to rattle (*Scot*); to dance a reel. [OE *hrēol*, but poss partly of other origin; Gaelic *righil* (the dance) may be from English]
■ **reel'er** *n* a person who reels; the grasshopper-warbler. **reel'ing** *n* and *adj*. **reel'ingly** *adv*.
❏ **reel'man** *n* (*Aust*) the member of a surf life-saving team who operates the reel on which the line is wound. **reel'-to-reel** *adj* (of recording equipment) using magnetic tape which is wound from one reel to another (as opposed to cassette or cartridge); (of a magnetic tape) which passes between two reels, as used with a reel-to-reel tape recorder.
■ **off** or **right off the reel** in uninterrupted course or succession; without stop or hesitation. **reel off** to utter rapidly and fluently. **Virginia reel** an American country dance.

reen see **rhine**.

re-enact /rē-in-akt'/ *vt* to enact over again; to reconstruct in action. [**re-**]
■ **re-enact'ment** *n*. **re-enact'or** *n*.

re-enchant /rē-in-chänt'/ *vt* to add new enchantment to (something that has lost its charm). [**re-**]
■ **re-enchant'ment** *n*.

re-enforce /rē-in-förs'/ or -förs'/ *vt* to enforce again; to reinforce (*rare*); to reassemble, rally (*Shakesp*). [**re-**]
■ **re-enforce'ment** *n* reinforcement.

re-engineering /rē-en-ji-nē'ring/ *n* the reorganization of business operations so as to increase efficiency. [**re-**]

re-enter /rē-en'tər/ *vt* and *vi* to enter again or afresh; (in engraving) to cut deeper. [**re-**]
■ **re-en'tering** *adj* entering again; pointing inwards; reflex (*maths*). **re-en'trance** *n* the act or achievement of entering again; the fact of being re-entrant (in this sense also **re-en'trancy**). **re-en'trant** *adj* re-entering, *opp* to **salient**; reflex (*maths*); returning upon itself at the ends (*electronics*). ◆ *n* a re-entering angle; a valley, depression, etc running into a main feature; the concavity between two salients. **re-en'try** *n* entering again, *esp* the action of a spacecraft entering the earth's atmosphere again; resumption of possession (*law*); the re-opening of an oil well for further drilling; a card allowing a hand to take the lead again.
❏ **re-entry corridor** *n* a narrow corridor available to a spacecraft returning to Earth, bounded by excessive heating below and low atmospheric density above, preventing slowdown.

reest[1] see **reast**[1].

reest[2], **reist** or **reast** /rēst/ (*Scot*) *vt* to dry or cure with smoke. ◆ *vi* to be smoke-dried. [Origin obscure]

reest[3] or **reist** /rēst/ (*Scot*) *vi* (of a horse) suddenly to refuse to move, to baulk. ◆ *n* a sudden fit of stubbornness. [Perh **rest**[1] or **arrest**]
■ **reest'y** *adj*.

reeve[1] /rēv/ (*hist*) *n* a high official, chief magistrate of a district; a bailiff or steward. [OE *gerēfa*; cf **grieve**[2] (*Scot*)]

reeve[2] /rēv/ *vt* (pat and pap **reeved** or **rove**) to pass the end of a rope through; to pass through any hole; to thread one's way through; to fasten by reeving. [Origin obscure]

reeve[3] /rēv/ or **ree** /rē/ *n* the female of the ruff. [Origin obscure]

re-export /rē-eks-pört'/ *vt* to export (goods that have been imported) to another country. ◆ *n* /-eks'/ an act of re-exporting; a re-exported product. [**re-**]
■ **re-exportā'tion** *n*. **re-export'er** *n*.

ref /ref/ (*inf*) *n*, *vt* and *vi* (**reff'ing**; **reffed**) short form of **referee**.

ref. *abbrev* : reference.

Ref. Ch. *abbrev* : Reformed Church.

refection /ri-fek'shən/ *n* refreshment or relief (*lit* and *fig*); a meal; in rabbits, hares and other herbivores, the habit of eating freshly-passed faeces (*zool*). [L *reficere*, *refectum*, from *facere* to make]
■ **refect** /-fekt'/ *vt* (back-formation) to refresh. ◆ *vi* to take a meal. **refec'tioner** or **refectorian** /rē-fek-tō' or -tö'ri-ən/ *n* the officer in charge of the refectory and its arrangements. **refectory** /ri-fek'tər-i (sometimes *ref'ik-*)/ *n* a dining-hall, *esp* in a monastery, convent or university.
❏ **Refection Sunday** *n* Refreshment Sunday. **refectory table** *n* a long narrow dining table supported on two shaped pillars each set in a base.

refel /ri-fel'/ (*obs*) *vt* (**refell'ing**; **refelled'**) to refute; to disprove; to confute; to repulse. [L *refellere*, from *fallere* to deceive]

refer /ri-fûr'/ *vt* (**referr'ing**; **referred'**) to assign (to); to impute (to); to attribute (to); to bring into relation (to); to deliver, commit or submit (to); to hand over for consideration (to); to direct for information, confirmation, testimonials, or whatever is required (to); to direct the attention of (to); to postpone (*obs*); to recount (*archaic*); to direct to sit an examination again; to reproduce, represent (*obs*). ◆ *vi* (with *to* in all cases) to have relation or application, to relate; to direct the attention; to turn for information, confirmation, etc; to turn, apply or have recourse; to make mention or allusion. [L *referre* to carry back, from *ferre* to carry]
■ **referable** /ref'ər-ə-bl/ or **ri-fûr'i-bl/** (sometimes **referrable** /-fûr'/ or **referrible** /-fer'/) *adj* that may be referred or assigned. **referee** /ref-ə-rē'/ *n* (*inf* shortening **ref**) a person to whom anything is referred; an arbitrator, umpire or judge; a person willing to provide a testimonial. ◆ *vt* to act as referee for. ◆ *vi* to act as referee. **ref'erence** *n* the act of referring; a submitting for information or decision; the act of submitting a dispute for investigation or decision (*law*); relation; allusion; a person who is referred to; a testimonial; a person willing to provide this; a direction to a book or passage; a book or passage used for reference. ◆ *vt* to make a reference to; to provide (a book, etc) with references to other sources. ◆ *adj* (of a price, point on a scale, etc) providing a standard to which others may be referred for comparison. **referendary** /-end'ə-ri/ *n* (*obs*) a referee; formerly a court official who was the medium of communication with the Pope, emperor, etc. **referen'dum** *n* (*pl* **referen'da** or **referen'dums**) the principle or practice of submitting a question directly to the vote of the entire electorate. **ref'erent** *n* the object of reference or discussion; the first term in a proposition. **referential** /-en'shl/ *adj* containing a reference; having reference (to); used for reference. **referen'tially** *adv*. **referr'al** *n* act or instance of referring or being referred, *esp* to another person or organization for, eg consideration, treatment, etc. **referr'er** *n*.
❏ **reference book** *n* a book to be consulted on occasion, not for consecutive reading; a pass book (*S Afr*). **reference library** *n* a library whose books may not be taken away on loan. **ref'erence-mark** *n* a character, such as *, †, or a superscript figure, used to refer to notes, etc. **referred pain** *n* pain felt in a part of the body other than its source.
■ **terms of reference** a guiding statement defining the scope of an investigation or similar piece of work; the scope itself.

reffo /ref'ō/ (*Aust sl*; *offensive*) *n* (*pl* **reff'os**) a refugee.

refigure /rē-fig'(y)ər/ *vt* to represent again, reproduce (*Shakesp*); to restore to form; to recalculate. [**re-**]

refill /rē-fil'/ *vt* to fill again. ◆ *n* /rē'fil/ a fresh fill; a duplicate for refilling purposes. [**re-**]
■ **refill'able** *adj*.

refinancing /rē-fi-nan'sing or -fī'/ (*finance*) *n* payment of a debt by borrowing additional money (*inf* short form **rē'fī**).

Some words formed with the prefix **re-**.

recompact' *vt*.	**recompress'** *vt*.	**recondense'** *vt* and *vi*.
recompose' *vt* and *vi*.	**recompress'ion** *n*.	**reconfirm'** *vt*.
recomposi'tion *n*.	**recondensā'tion** *n*.	**reconnect'** *vt*.

---

refine /ri-fīn'/ vt to purify; to clarify; (usu with out) to get rid of (impurities, etc) by a purifying process; to free from coarseness, vulgarity or crudity; to make more cultured. ◆ vi to become more fine, pure, subtle or cultured; to apply or affect subtlety or nicety; to improve by adding refinement or subtlety (with on or upon). [L re- denoting change of state, and **fine**[1]]
■ **refined'** adj. **refin'edly** adv in a refined manner; with affected elegance. **refin'edness** n. **refine'ment** n the act or practice of refining; state of being refined; culture in feelings, taste and manners; an improvement; a subtlety; an excessive nicety. **refin'er** n. **refin'ery** n a place for refining. **refin'ing** n.

refit /rē-fit'/ vt to fit out afresh and repair. ◆ vi to undergo refitting. ◆ n /rē'fit/ the process of refitting or being refitted. [re- and **fit**[1]]
■ **refit'ment** or **refitt'ing** n.

refl. abbrev : reflection; reflective; reflex; reflexive.

reflag /rē-flag'/ vt (**reflagg'ing**; **reflagged'**) to replace the national flag of (a ship) with that of a more powerful nation, so that it sails under its protection; to change the country of registration of (a ship), usu for commercial advantage. [re-]

reflation /rē-flā'shən/ n increase in the amount of currency, economic activity, etc after deflation; a general increase, above what would normally be expected, in the spending of money. [re- and inflation]
■ **rēflate'** vt (back-formation). **reflā'tionary** adj.

reflect /ri-flekt'/ vt to bend or send back or aside; to throw back after striking; to give an image of in the manner of a mirror; to express, reproduce (fig); to cast, shed (eg credit or discredit) (fig); to consider meditatively (that, how, etc). ◆ vi to bend or turn back or aside; to be mirrored; to cast a light (Shakesp); to meditate (on); to cast reproach or censure (on or upon); to bring harmful results. [L reflectere, reflexum, from flectare to bend]
■ **reflect'ance** or **reflecting factor** n ratio of reflected radiation to incident radiation. **reflect'ed** adj cast or thrown back; turned or folded back; mirrored. **reflect'er** n (Swift) a person who casts reflections. **reflect'ing** adj. **reflect'ingly** adv meditatively; with implication of censure. **reflection**, also (now chiefly in scientific use) **reflexion** /ri-flek'shən/ n a turning, bending or folding aside, back or downwards; folding upon itself; rebound; change of direction when an electromagnetic wave or sound wave strikes on a surface and is thrown back; reflected light, colour, heat, etc; an image in a mirror; (production of) a mirror image of a line or figure (by reflecting it in an axis of symmetry); the conformal transformation in which a figure is reflected in a fixed line; the action of the mind by which it is conscious of its own operations; attentive consideration; contemplation; a thought or utterance resulting from contemplation; a consideration leading to discredit, censure or reproach. **reflec'tionless** adj. **reflect'ive** adj reflecting; reflected; contemplative. **reflect'ively** adv. **reflect'iveness** n. **reflectiv'ity** n the ability to reflect rays; reflectance. **reflec'togram** or **reflec'tograph** n an image produced by reflectography. **reflectog'raphy** n a technique used to detect underdrawing, etc in a painting, in which infra-red light is bounced off the lowest, gessoed layer and the resulting image viewed on a TV monitor. **reflectom'eter** n any of various instruments for measuring the properties of reflected light, colour, etc. **reflect'or** n a reflecting surface, instrument or body; a reflecting telescope.
□ **reflecting factor** see reflectance above. **reflecting microscope** n one using a system of mirrors instead of lenses. **reflecting telescope** n one (eg the Gregorian or Newtonian) which has a concave mirror instead of an object glass (lens or lenses). **reflective binary code** see Gray code.
■ **angle of reflection** the angle between a reflected ray and the normal to the surface it falls on.

reflet /rə-flā' or -flā'/ (Fr) n an iridescent or metallic lustre. [Ital reflesso reflection]

reflex /rē'fleks, formerly ri-fleks'/ adj bent or turned back; reflected; reciprocal; (of an angle) more than 180°; turned back upon itself; involuntary, produced by or concerned with response from a nerve-centre to a stimulus from without; illuminated by light from another part of the same picture (art); using the same valve or valves for high- and low-frequency amplification (radio). ◆ n reflection; reflected light; a reflected image; an expression, manifestation, outward representation; a reflex action; (in pl) the ability to perform such actions; a reflex radio receiving set; an element of speech that has developed from a corresponding earlier form (linguistics). ◆ vt /-fleks'/

to bend back; to project, direct (Shakesp). [L reflexus, from reflectere ; cf reflect]
■ **reflexed'** adj (bot) bent abruptly backward or downward. **reflexibil'ity** n. **reflex'ible** adj. **reflex'ion** n see reflection under reflect. **reflex'ive** adj (grammar) indicating that the action turns back upon the subject; relating to a reflex. ◆ n a reflexive pronoun or verb. **reflex'ively** adv. **reflex'iveness** or **reflexiv'ity** n. **reflex'ly** (or /rē'/) adv. **reflexolog'ical** adj. **reflexol'ogist** n. **reflexol'ogy** n the study of the body's reflexes as a guide to behaviour (psychol); a form of therapy for treating particular bodily ailments and general stress, carried out through massage on the soles of the feet, on the principle that specific areas of the feet relate to specific parts and organs of the body.
□ **reflex anal dilatation** n involuntary widening of the anus on examination. **reflex arc** n the simplest functional unit of the nervous system, by which an impulse produces a reflex action. **reflex camera** n one in which the image is reflected onto a glass screen for composing and focusing, either through the camera lens (**sing'le-lens reflex**) or through a separate lens of the same focal length (**twin'-lens reflex**). **reflex light** n a lens with a reflecting back or a prism with internal reflection, returning a beam of light when the headlight, eg of a motor car, shines on it.

reflow /rē-flō'/ vi to ebb; to flow again. ◆ n an ebb; a reflux. [re-]
■ **reflow'ing** n.

refluent /ref'loo-ənt/ (rare) adj flowing back; ebbing; tidal. [L refluēns, -entis, prp of refluere, from fluere, fluxum to flow]
■ **ref'luence** n flowing back; ebb.

reflux /rē'fluks/ n a flowing back, an ebb; the process of boiling a liquid in a flask with a condenser attached so that the vapour condenses and flows back into the flask, avoiding loss by evaporation (chem; also vi and vt); the condensed vapour involved in this process. [Ety as for refluent; L fluxus, -ūs a flow]

reforest /rē-for'ist/ vt same as reafforest. [re-]
■ **reforestā'tion** n same as reafforestation (see under reafforest).

reform /ri-förm'/ vt to transform; to restore, rebuild (Milton); to amend; to make better; to remove defects from; to redress; to bring to a better way of life; to chastise (Spenser); to prune (Milton); to break up in reorganization, hence to disband, dismiss (milit hist). ◆ vi to abandon evil ways. ◆ n amendment or transformation, esp of a system or institution; a stricter offshoot or branch of a religious order; an extension or better distribution of parliamentary representation. [L reförmāre, -ātum, from förmāre to shape, from förma form]
■ **reformabil'ity** n. **reform'able** /-ri-/ adj. **reformation** /ref-ər-mā'shən/ n the act of reforming; amendment; improvement; (with cap) the great religious revolution of the 16c, which gave rise to the various evangelical or Protestant organizations of Christendom. **reformā'tional** adj. **reformā'tionist** n. **reformative** /ri-förm'ə-tiv/ adj tending to produce reform. **reform'atory** adj reforming; tending to produce reform. ◆ n in the UK and USA, formerly, an institution for reclaiming young delinquents. **reformed'** adj changed; amended; improved; (with cap) Protestant, esp Calvinistic, in doctrine or polity. **reform'er** n a person who reforms anything; someone who advocates political reform; (with cap) one of those who took part in the Reformation of the 16c. **reform'ism** n any doctrine or movement advocating gradual social and political change within a democratic framework rather than revolutionary change. **reform'ist** n a reformer; an advocate of reformism.
□ **Reformed Presbyterian** n a Cameronian. **Reform flask** n a salt-glazed stoneware flask made in the likeness of one of the figures connected with the 1832 parliamentary Reform Bill. **Reform Judaism** n a form of Judaism, originating in the 19c, in which the Jewish Law is adapted so as to be relevant to contemporary life. **reform school** n a reformatory.

re-form /rē-förm'/ vt and vi to form again or anew (also **reform**). [re-]
■ **rē-formā'tion** n. **rē-formed'** adj.

reformado /ref-ör-mä'dō or -mä'dō/, also (obs) **reformade** /-mäd'/ (hist) n (pl **reforma'does**, **reforma'dos** or **reformades'**) a disbanded or dismissed soldier; an officer whose company has been disbanded or who is for other reason without a command; a volunteer serving as an officer; a reformed person; a reformer. ◆ adj in the position of a reformado. [Sp reformado reformed]

refract /ri-frakt'/ vt of a medium, to deflect (rays of light, sound, etc passing into it from another medium); to measure the

---

Some words formed with the prefix **re-**.

rēconnec'tion n.	**rēcon'secrate** vt.	**rēconsolidā'tion** n.
rēcon'quer vt.	**rēconsecrā'tion** n.	**rēcontin'ue** vt and vi.
rēcon'quest n.	**rēconsol'idate** vt and vi.	**rēconvene'** vt and vi.

■ words derived from main entry word; □ compound words; ■ idioms and phrasal verbs

refractive capacity of (the eye, a lens, etc); to produce by refraction (*rare*). ◆ *adj* (*rare*) refracted. [L *refringere*, *refrāctum*, from *frangere* to break]
■ **refract'able** *adj* refrangible. **refrac'ted** *adj* deflected on passage into another medium; bent sharply back from the base (*bot*). **refract'ing** *adj*. **refrac'tion** *n*. **refrac'tional** *adj*. **refrac'tive** *adj* refracting; of refraction. **refrac'tively** *adv*. **refractivity** /rē-frak-tiv'i-ti/ *n*. **refractom'eter** *n* an instrument for measuring refractive indices. **refractomet'ric** *adj*. **refractom'etry** *n*. **refrac'tor** /ri-/ *n* anything that refracts; a refracting telescope.
❑ **refracting telescope** *n* one in which the principal means of focusing the light is an object glass. **refraction correction** *n* (*astron*) the correction made in the calculation of the altitude of a star, planet, etc to allow for the refraction of its light by the earth's atmosphere. **refractive index** *n* the ratio of the sine of the angle of incidence to that of the angle of refraction when a ray passes from one medium to another.
■ **angle of refraction** the angle between a refracted ray and the normal to the bounding surface. **double refraction** the separation of an incident ray of light into two refracted rays, polarized in perpendicular planes.

refractory (formerly **refractary**) /ri-frak'tə-ri/ *adj* unruly; unmanageable; obstinate; perverse; resistant to ordinary treatment, stimulus, disease, etc; *esp* difficult to fuse; fire-resistant. ◆ *n* a substance that is able to resist high temperatures, etc, used in lining furnaces, etc. [L *refrāctārius* stubborn]
■ **refrac'torily** *adv*. **refrac'toriness** *n*.
❑ **refractory period** *n* (*biol*) for an organism or an excitable tissue, the period of zero response following a previous response.

refrain[1] /ri-frān'/ *n* a burden, a line or phrase recurring, *esp* at the end of a stanza; the music of such a burden. [OFr *refrain*, from *refraindre*, from L *refringere*, from *frangere* to break]

refrain[2] /ri-frān'/ *vi* to keep oneself from action, forbear; to abstain (from; *obs* with *to*). ◆ *vt* to curb (*archaic*); to restrain (*archaic*); to abstain from (*Shakesp*); to keep away from (*obs*). [OFr *refrener*, from LL *refrēnāre*, from *re-* back, and *frēnum* a bridle]

refrangible /ri-fran'ji-bl/ *adj* that may be refracted. [See **refract**]
■ **refrangibil'ity** or **refran'gibleness** *n*.

refresh /ri-fresh'/ *vt* to make fresh again; to freshen up; to give new vigour, life, liveliness, spirit, brightness, fresh appearance, coolness, moistness, etc to; to replenish a supply; to update the display of data on a screen (*comput*). ◆ *vi* to become fresh again; to take refreshment, *esp* drink (*inf*). [OFr *refrescher*, from *re-*, and *freis* (fem *fresche*) fresh]
■ **refresh'en** *vt* to make fresh again. **refresh'ener** *n*. **refresh'er** *n* someone or something that refreshes; a cool drink (*inf*); a fee paid to counsel for continuing his or her attention to a case, *esp* when adjourned; a douceur to encourage further exertions (*inf*); a subsequent course of training or instruction to maintain or reattain one's former standard, study new developments, etc (also *adj*). **refresh'ful** *adj* (*archaic*) full of power to refresh; refreshing. **refresh'fully** *adv*. **refresh'ing** *adj* pleasantly cooling, inspiriting, reviving or invigorating. **refresh'ingly** *adv*. **refresh'ment** *n* the act of refreshing; the state of being refreshed; renewed strength or spirit; that which refreshes, such as food or rest; (in *pl*) drink or a light meal.
❑ **refresh'ment-room** *n*. **Refreshment** or **Refection Sunday** *n* the fourth Sunday in Lent, when the story of the loaves and fishes is traditionally read.

refrigerant /ri-frij'ə-rənt/ *adj* cooling; giving a feeling of coolness; refreshing. ◆ *n* a freezing or cooling agent; that which gives a cool feeling. [L *refrigerāre*, *-ātum*, from *re-* (denoting change of state) and *frīgerāre*, from *frīgus* cold]
■ **refrig'erāte** *vt* to freeze; to make cold; to make to feel cold; to expose (food, etc) to great cold for preservation. ◆ *vi* to become cold. **refrigerā'tion** *n*. **refrig'erative** /-rə-tiv/ *adj* cooling. **refrig'erator** /-rā-tər/ *n* an apparatus or chamber for producing and maintaining a low temperature (contracted to **fridge**, *esp* when in domestic use). **refrig'eratory** /-rə-tər-i/ *adj* cooling; refrigerative. ◆ *n* (*archaic*) a refrigerator; a chamber in which ice is formed; a water-filled vessel for condensing in distillation.

refringe /ri-frinj'/ *vt* (*obs*) to refract. [L *refringere* ; see **refract**]
■ **refring'ency** *n* refractivity. **refring'ent** *adj*.

reft /reft/ *pat* and *pap* of **reave**.

refuel /rē-fū'əl/ *vt* to supply (a vehicle, aircraft, etc) with more fuel. ◆ *vi* to take on more fuel. [**re-**]
■ **refū'elable** or **refū'ellable** *adj*.

refuge /ref'ūj/ *n* shelter or protection from danger or trouble; an asylum or retreat; *specif* an establishment set up to provide emergency accommodation, protection, support, etc for eg battered wives; a street island for pedestrians; recourse in difficulty. ◆ *vt* and *vi* (*archaic*) to shelter. [Fr, from L *refugium*, from *fugere* to flee]
■ **refugee** /ref-ū-jē'/ *n* a person who flees for refuge to another country, *esp* from religious or political persecution; a fugitive. **refugium** /ri-fū'ji-əm/ *n* (*pl* **refū'gia** /-ji-ə/) a region that has retained earlier geographical, climatic, etc conditions, and thus becomes a haven for older varieties of flora and fauna.
■ **house of refuge** a shelter for the destitute.

refulgent /ri-ful'jənt/ *adj* casting a flood of light; radiant; beaming. [L *refulgēns*, *-entis*, prp of *refulgēre*, from *re-* (intensive) and *fulgēre* to shine]
■ **reful'gence** or **reful'gency** *n*. **reful'gently** *adv*.

refund[1] /ri-* or *rē-fund'/ *vt* to pour back (now *rare*); to repay. ◆ *vi* to restore what was taken. [L *refundere*, from *fundere* to pour]
■ **refund** /rē'fund* or *ri-fund'/ *n*. **refund'able** *adj*. **refund'er** *n*. **refund'ment** /ri-/ *n*.

refund[2] or **re-fund** /rē-fund'/ *vt* to fund anew; to replace (an old issue of bonds) by a new; to borrow so as to pay off (an old loan). [**re-**]

refurb /rē'fûrb/ (*inf*) *vt* to refurbish. ◆ *n* an act of refurbishment.
refurbish /rē-fûr'bish/ *vt* to renovate; to brighten up, redecorate. [**re-**]
■ **refur'bishment** *n*.

refuse[1] /ri-fūz'/ *vt* to decline to take or accept; to renounce; to decline to give or grant; (of a horse) to decline to jump over; to fail to follow suit to (*cards*); to decline to meet in battle; to hold back from the regular alignment in action (*milit*). ◆ *vi* to make refusal. [Fr *refuser*, from L *refūsum*, pap of *refundere*, from *fundere* to pour; cf **refund**[1]]
■ **refus'able** /ri-/ *adj*. **refus'al** *n* the act of refusing; the option of taking or refusing; a thing refused. **refusenik** or **refusnik** /ri-fūz'nik/ *n* (see **-nik**) formerly, a dissident Soviet citizen, *esp* a Soviet Jew wishing to emigrate; generally, a dissident (*inf*). **refus'er** *n*.

refuse[2] /ref'ūs/ *n* that which is rejected or left as worthless; rubbish, waste. ◆ *adj* rejected as worthless; waste. [Fr *refus* ; see **refuse**[1]]

refute /ri-fūt'/ *vt* to disprove; to deny. [L *refūtāre* to drive back]
■ **refutable** /ref'ūt-ə-bl* or *ri-fūt'ə-bl/ *adj*. **ref'utably** (or /ri-fūt'/) *adv*. **refu'tal** or **refutā'tion** /ref-/ *n* the act of refuting; that which disproves. **refu'ter** *n*.

reg /rej/ *n* short form of **registration number** (see under **register**).

regain /ri-* or *rē-gān'/ *vt* to gain or win back; to get back to. ◆ *n* recovery. [Fr *regaigner* (now *regagner*)]
■ **regain'able** *adj*. **regain'er** *n*. **regain'ment** *n*.

regal[1] /rē'gl/ *adj* royal; kingly. [L *rēgālis*, from *rēx* a king, from *regere* to rule]
■ **regalian** /ri-gā'li-ən/ *adj* (*archaic*) regal. **regalism** /rē'gəl-izm/ *n* royal supremacy, *esp* in Church matters. **rē'galist** *n*. **regality** /ri-gal'i-ti/ *n* state of being regal; royalty; sovereignty; a territorial jurisdiction formerly conferred by the king (*Scot hist*). **rē'gally** *adv*.
❑ **regal lily** *n* a variety of lily (*Lilium regale*) producing fragrant, white flowers.

regal[2] /rē'gl/ *n* a small portable organ. [Fr *régale*]

regale[1] /ri-gāl'/ *vt* to treat to (stories, etc; with *with*); to give pleasure to; to feast. ◆ *vi* (*archaic*) to feast. ◆ *n* (*archaic*) a feast; a choice dish. [Fr *régaler*, from Ital *regalare*, perh from *gala* a piece of finery]
■ **regale'ment** *n*.

regale[2] see **regalia**[1].

regalia[1] /ri-gā'li-ə* or *rā-gā'li-ə/ *n pl* royal privileges or powers, as (*hist*) that of enjoying the revenues of vacant sees, etc (*sing* **regale** /ri-gā'lē/); the insignia of royalty, ie crown, sceptre, etc; any insignia or special garb, such as that of the Freemasons. [L *rēgālis* royal, neuter sing *-e*, pl *-ia*]

regalia[2] /ri-gā'li-ə/ *n* a big cigar. [Sp, royal right]

regalism, **regality**, etc see under **regal**[1].

regar see **regur**.

regard /ri-gärd'/ *vt* to look at; to observe; to heed; to look to; to esteem or consider; to esteem highly; to have kindly feelings for;

---

to respect; to take into account; to have respect or relation to. ◆ *vi* to look; to give heed. ◆ *n orig* look; a thing seen (*Shakesp*); intention (*Shakesp*); attention with interest; observation; estimation; esteem; kindly, affectionate or respectful feeling; care; consideration; a thing to be considered; repute; respect; relation; reference; (in *pl*) in messages of greeting, respectful good will. [Fr *regarder*, from *garder* to keep, watch]

■ **regard'able** *adj* worthy of consideration. **regard'ant** *adj* attentive; looking backward (*heraldry*). **regard'er** *n*. **regard'ful** *adj* heedful; respectful. **regard'fully** *adv*. **regard'fulness** *n*. **regard'ing** *prep* concerning. **regard'less** *adj* heedless; inconsiderate; without regard to consequences; careless (of). ◆ *adv* nevertheless, anyway; despite or without concern for the consequences. **regard'lessly** *adv*. **regard'lessness** *n*.

■ **as regards** with regard to, concerning. **in regard of** or **to** (*archaic*) in comparison with; in reference to; out of consideration for (*Shakesp*). **in this regard** in this respect. **with regard to** concerning; so far as relates to.

regatta /ri-gat'ə/ *n* a yacht or boat race-meeting. [Ital (Venetian) *regata*]

regd *abbrev*: registered.

regelation /rē-ji-lā'shən/ *n* freezing together again (as of ice melted by pressure when the pressure is released). [**re-** and L *gelāre* to freeze]
■ **rē'gelāte** *vt* and *vi*.

regency /rē'jən-si/ *n* the office, term of office, jurisdiction or dominion of a regent; a body entrusted with vicarious government; *specif* in French history, the minority of Louis XV, 1715–23, when Philip of Orleans was regent; in British history, the years 1811–20, when the Prince of Wales (George IV) was Prince Regent. ◆ *adj* of, or in the style prevailing during, the French or English regency. [L *regēns*, *-entis*, prp of *regere* to rule]

■ **rē'gence** *n* (*obs*) government. **rē'gent** *adj* ruling; invested with interim or vicarious sovereign authority. ◆ *n* a ruler; a person invested with interim authority on behalf of another; formerly in Scotland and elsewhere, a professor; a master or doctor who takes part in the regular duties of instruction and government in some universities. **rē'gentship** *n*.

❑ **rē'gent-bird** *n* a bowerbird (*Sericulus chrysocephalus*) named in honour of George, the Prince Regent.

regenerate /ri-jen'ə-rāt/ *vt* to produce anew; to renew spiritually (*theol*); to put new life or energy into; to reform completely; to reproduce (a part of the body); to magnify the amplitude of an electrical output by relaying part of the power back into the input circuit (*electronics*); to produce again in the original form (*chem*, *nucleonics*, etc). ◆ *vi* to undergo regeneration; to be regenerated. ◆ *adj* /-it or -āt/ regenerated, renewed; changed from a natural to a spiritual state. [L *regenerāre*, *-ātum* to bring forth again, from *re-* again, and *generāre* to generate]

■ **regen'erable** *adj*. **regen'eracy** /-ə-si/ *n*. **regenerā'tion** *n* renewal of lost parts; spiritual rebirth; reformation; recovery of waste heat or other energy that would have been lost; rebuilding or revitalizing of an area, eg the centre of a city. **regen'erative** *adj*. **regen'eratively** *adv*. **regen'erātor** *n* someone or something that regenerates; a chamber in which waste heat is, by reversal of draught, alternately stored up and given out to the gas and air entering. **regen'eratory** /-ə-tər-i/ *adj*.

regent see under **regency**.

regest /ri-jest'/ (*Milton*) *n* a register. [See **register**]

reggae /reg'ā or rä'gä/ *n* a strongly rhythmic form of music originating in Jamaica in the 1960s. [Origin unknown; perh from Jamaican English *rege-rege* quarrel, row]
■ **reggaeton** /reg-ā-ton'/ *n* a Puerto Rican dance music influenced by reggae and hip-hop.

reggo or **rego** /rej'ō/ (*Aust inf*) *n* short form of (motor vehicle) **registration** (see under **register**).

regicide /rej'i-sīd/ *n* the killing or killer of a king. [L *rēx*, *rēgis* a king, on the analogy of **homicide**, **parricide**, etc]
■ **regicī'dal** *adj*.

régie /rā-zhē'/ (*Fr*) *n* a system of government monopoly, *esp* in tobacco; the department concerned; tobacco sold by it.

regift /rē-gift'/ *vt* to give (an unwanted present) as a gift to another person, in a process which is likely to continue indefinitely. [**re-**]

regime or **régime** /rā-zhēm'/ *n* regimen; system of government; a particular government; administration. [Fr, from L *regimen*]

regimen /rej'i-mən or -men/ *n* government; system of government; course of treatment, such as (*med*) a prescribed combination of diet, exercise, drugs, etc; grammatical government; prevailing system or set of conditions. [L *regimen*, *-inis*, from *regere* to rule]
■ **regim'inal** *adj*.

regiment /rej'(i-)mənt/ *n* (often /rej'mənt/) a large permanent unit within an army, in the British Army *usu* containing *approx* 650 soldiers, commanded by a colonel; a large number (*fig*); government (*archaic*); control (*archaic*); rule (*archaic*); regimen (*archaic*); a region under government (*archaic*). ◆ *vt* /rej'i-ment or -ment/ to form into a regiment or regiments; to systematize, classify; to organize; to subject to excessive control. [LL *regimentum*, from L *regere* to rule]

■ **regimental** /-i-ment'l/ *adj* of a regiment. ◆ *n* (in *pl*) the uniform of a regiment. **regiment'ally** *adv*. **regimentation** /-i-men-tā'shən/ *n*.
❑ **regimental sergeant-major** see under **sergeant**.

regiminal see under **regimen**.

regina /ri-jī'nə/ *n* queen; (with *cap*) title of a reigning queen (*abbrev* **R**). [L *rēgīna*]
■ **reginal** /-jī'nl/ *adj* of a queen; siding with a queen.

region /rē'jən/ *n* a tract of country; any area or district, *esp* one characterized in some way; (from 1975 to 1996) a unit of local government in Scotland; a realm; a portion or division, as of the body; a portion of space; the atmosphere, or a division of it, *esp* the upper air (*Shakesp* and *Milton*); the heavens (*obs*). ◆ *adj* (*Shakesp*) of the air. [Anglo-Fr *regiun*, from L *regiō*, *-ōnis*, from *regere* to rule]

■ **rē'gional** *adj*. **rē'gionalism** *n* regional patriotism or particularism. **rē'gionalist** *n* and *adj*. **regionalīzā'tion** or **-s-** *n* the division of a country into regions for local government administration. **re'gionalize** or **-ise** *vt*. **rē'gionally** *adv*. **rē'gionary** *adj*.
❑ **regional council** *n* a council elected to govern the affairs of a region.
■ **in the region of** near; about, approximately.

régisseur /rā-zhē-sœr'/ (*Fr*) *n* a manager; a stage manager; (in a ballet company) a director.

register /rej'i-stər/ *n* a written record or official list regularly kept; the book containing such a record; an entry in it; a recording or indicating apparatus, such as a cash register; a registrar (now *rare* or *US*); apparatus for regulating a draught; a register-plate; an organ stop or stop-knob; the set of pipes controlled by an organ stop, or a set of strings in a harpsichord; part of the compass of any instrument having a distinct quality of tone (also *fig*); the compass of an instrument or voice; the range of tones of a voice produced in a particular manner; the form of language used in certain circumstances, situations, or when dealing with certain subjects, eg legal, technical or journalistic; exact adjustment of position, as of colours in a picture, or letterpress on opposite sides of a leaf (*printing*); registration; a certificate of registration; a location in the central processor of a computer, used for special purposes only. ◆ *vt* to enter or cause to be entered in a register; to record; to indicate; to put on record; to express; to represent by bodily expression; to adjust in register; to send by registered post. ◆ *vi* to enter one's name (*esp* as a hotel guest); to correspond in register; to make an impression, reach the consciousness (*inf*). [OFr *registre* or LL *registrum*, for L *pl regesta* things recorded, from *re-* back, and *gerere* to carry]

■ **reg'istered** *adj* recorded, entered or enrolled (as a voter, a letter requiring special precautions for security, etc); made with a register-plate. **reg'istrable** *adj*. **reg'istrant** *n* a person who registers, or has registered (a trademark, etc). **reg'istrar** /-trär or -trär'/ *n* a person who keeps a register or official record; someone who makes an official record of births, deaths and marriages registered locally; a hospital doctor in one of the intermediate grades (**medical** or **surgical registrar**). **reg'istrarship** *n* office of a registrar. **reg'istrary** *n* (now only at Cambridge University) a registrar. **registrā'tion** *n* the act or fact of registering; something registered; the act or art of combining stops in organ-playing. **reg'istry** *n* registration; an office or place where a register is kept; a register; an entry in a register.
❑ **Registered General Nurse** *n* a nurse who has passed the examination of the General Nursing Council for Scotland (*abbrev* **RGN**). **registered office** *n* the officially recorded address of a company, to which legal documents, etc are sent. **registered post** *n* a postal service in which a number is given to an item on payment of a

---

Some words formed with the prefix **re-**.

rēdescribe' *vt*.	**rēdeter'mine** *vt*.	**rēdi'al** *vt* and *vi*.
rēdesign' *vt*.	**rēdevel'op** *vt*.	**rēdip'** *vt*.
rēdeterminā'tion *n*.	**rēdevel'opment** *n*.	**rēdirect'** *vt*.

---

registration fee, and compensation paid for loss or damage during delivery; mail sent using this service. **registered trademark** *n* a trademark that has been officially registered to prevent it being used by others (symbol ®). **Register House** *n* the building in Edinburgh where Scottish records are kept. **register office** *n* a record-office; an employment office; the less common but strictly correct term for a registry office (see below). **reg'ister-plate** *n* (in rope-making) a disc with holes to give each yarn its position; a chimney damper. **register ton** see under **ton**¹. **Registrar General** *n* an officer having the superintendence of the registration of all births, deaths and marriages. **registration number** *n* the combination of letters and numbers shown on a motor vehicle's number plates, by which its ownership is registered. **registration plate** *n* (*Aust* and *NZ*) a number plate. **registry office** *n* an office for putting domestic servants in touch with employers; a registrar's office, (strictly, **register office**) where births, etc are recorded and civil marriages are celebrated. ▪ **gross** or **net register** (**tonnage**) gross or net tonnage. **Lord Clerk-Register** an officer of the General Register House with duties concerned with the election of Scottish representative peers, formerly custodian of records and registers. **parish register** a book in which births, deaths and marriages are recorded. **Registrar of Companies** the government official responsible for recording certain information about British companies, such as the memorandum of association, address of registered office, etc. **ship's register** a document showing the ownership of a vessel.

regius /rē'ji-əs or rā'gi-ŭs/ *adj* royal, eg **regius professor** one whose chair was founded by a king or queen. [L *rēgius*, from *rēx* king] ❑ **regium donum** /rē'ji-əm dō'nəm/ *n* a former annual grant of public money to nonconformist ministers in England, Scotland, and *esp* Ireland.

reglet /reg'lit/ *n* a flat, narrow moulding (*archit*); a fillet; a strip for spacing between lines (*printing*). [Fr *réglet*, dimin of *règle*, from L *rēgula* a rule]

regma /reg'mə/ (*bot*) *n* (pl **reg'mata**) a fruit that splits into dehiscent parts. [Gr *rhēgma, -atos* a breaking]

regnal /reg'nl/ *adj* of a reign. [L *rēgnālis*, from *rēgnum* a kingdom, *rēgnāns, -antis*, prp of *rēgnāre* to reign] ▪ **reg'nant** *adj* reigning (often after the noun, eg **queen regnant** a reigning queen, not a *queen consort*); prevalent.

regolith /reg'ə-lith/ *n* mantle-rock. [Gr *rhēgos* a blanket, and *lithos* a stone]

regorge /ri- or rē-görj'/ *vt* to disgorge, regurgitate; to swallow again (*rare*); to gorge to repletion (*Milton*). ◆ *vi* to gush back. [**re-** and **gorge**; or Fr *regorger* to overflow, abound]

Reg. Prof. *abbrev*: Regius Professor.

regrate /ri-grāt'/ (*hist*) *vt* to buy and sell again in or near the same market, thus raising the price (formerly a criminal offence in England). [OFr *regrater*; of doubtful origin] ▪ **regrā'ter** or **regrā'tor** *n* a person who regrates goods (*hist*); a middleman (*SW Eng*). **regrā'ting** *n*.

regrede /ri-grēd'/ *vi* (*rare*) to retrograde. [L *regredī*, from *re-*, and *gradī* to go] ▪ **regrē'dience** *n* (*Herrick*).

regreet /ri-grēt'/ *vt* to greet in return; to greet again (*Shakesp*); to greet (*Shakesp*). ◆ *vi* to exchange greetings. ◆ *n* a greeting, *esp* in return; (in *pl*) greetings, salutation (*Shakesp*). [**re-**]

regress /rē'gres/ *n* passage back; return; reversion; backward movement or extension; right or power of returning; re-entry. ◆ *vi* /ri-gres'/ to go back; to recede; to return to a former place or state; to revert; to move from east to west (*astron*). ◆ *vt* to cause to regress or return to a former state or condition; to calculate the degree of association between one parameter and other parameters (*stats*). [L *regressus*, from *regredī*; see **regrede**] ▪ **regression** /ri-gresh'ən/ *n* the act of regressing; reversion; return towards the mean; return to an earlier stage of development, as in an adult's or adolescent's behaving like a child. **regressive** /ri-gres'iv/ *adj* going back; reverting; returning; (of taxation) in which the rate decreases as the amount to be taxed increases. **regress'ively** *adv* in a regressive manner; by return. **regress'iveness** /ri-/ *n*. **regressiv'ity** /rē-/ *n*.

❑ **regression therapy** *n* (*psychol*) a therapeutic technique which aims to return a patient to the emotional state of a child in order to identify the causes of psychological problems.

regret /ri-gret'/ *vt* (**regret'ing**; **regret'ed**) to remember with a sense of loss or a feeling of having done wrong; to wish otherwise. ◆ *n* sorrowful wish that something had been otherwise; sorrowful feeling of loss; compunction; (*usu* in *pl*) an intimation of regret or refusal. [OFr *regreter, regrater*; poss connected with **greet**²] ▪ **regret'ful** *adj* feeling regret. **regret'fully** *adv*. **regrett'able** *adj* to be regretted. **regrett'ably** *adv* in a regrettable way; I'm sorry to say, unfortunately.

regt *abbrev*: regiment.

reguerdon /ri-gûr'dən/ (*Shakesp*) *n* reward. ◆ *vt* to reward. [OFr *reguerdon*]

regula /reg'ū-lə/ *n* (pl **reg'ulae** /-lē/) the rule of a religious order; a fillet, *esp* under the Doric taenia, below each triglyph (*archit*). [L *rēgula*, from *regere* to rule]

regular /reg'ū-lər/ *adj* governed by or according to rule, law, order, habit, custom, established practice, mode prescribed or the ordinary course of things; placed, arranged, etc at regular intervals in space or time; (of a marriage) celebrated by a church minister after proclamation of banns; normal; medium-sized (*orig US*); ordinary; without pretensions (*US*); habitual; constant; steady; uniform; periodical; duly qualified; inflected in the usual way, *esp* of weak verbs (*grammar*); symmetrical, *esp* (*bot*) radially symmetrical or actinomorphic; having all the sides and angles equal or all faces equal, equilateral and equiangular, the same number meeting at every corner (*geom*); also (of a pyramid) having a regular polygon for base and the other faces similar and equal isosceles triangles; subject to a monastic rule, *opp* to *secular*; permanent, professional, or standing, *opp* to *militia*, *volunteer* and *territorial* (*milit*); (of a satellite) that keeps or scarcely deviates from a circular orbit around its planet (*astron*); thorough, out-and-out, *esp* (*US*) in party politics (*inf*); of the same way of thinking as the speaker, hence ready to help or abet him or her, loyal, swell (*sl*); veritable (*inf*). ◆ *n* a member of a religious order who has taken the three ordinary vows; a soldier of the regular army; a regular customer; a loyal supporter of the party leader (*US politics*). [L *rēgula* a rule, from *regere* to rule] ▪ **reg'ulable** *adj*. **regularity** /-lar'i-ti/ *n* state, character or fact of being regular. **regularīzā'tion** or **-s-** *n*. **reg'ularize** or **-ise** *vt* to make regular. **reg'ularly** *adv*. **reg'ulate** *vt* to control; to adapt or adjust continuously; to adjust by rule. ◆ *vi* to make regulations. **regulā'tion** *n* the act of regulating; state of being regulated; a rule or order prescribed; a form of legislation used to bring the provisions of an Act of Parliament into force; in the EU, a proposal from the commission which is approved by the council and immediately becomes law in all member states. ◆ *adj* prescribed by regulation; normal, usual. **reg'ulative** /-ə-tiv/ *adj* tending to regulate. **reg'ulatively** *adv*. **reg'ulātor** *n* someone or something that regulates; a controlling device, *esp* for the speed of a clock or watch; a change in the taxation rate introduced by the Chancellor of the Exchequer between budgets to regulate the economy. **reg'ulatory** /-lə-tər-i/ *adj*. ❑ **regulating rod** *n* (*nuclear eng*) a fine control rod of a reactor. **regulatory gene** *n* (*biol*) a gene whose product controls the expression of other genes (cf **structural gene**).

reguline see under **regulus**.

Regulo® /reg'ū-lō/ *n* a thermostatic control system for gas ovens; loosely (with a given numeral) one of the graded scale of temperatures on a gas oven (also without *cap*).

regulus /reg'ū-ləs/ *n* (pl **reg'uluses** or **reg'uli** /-lī/) an impure metal, an intermediate product in smelting of ores; antimony; (with *cap*) a first-magnitude star in Leo; (with *cap*) the goldcrest genus of birds. [L *rēgulus*, dimin of *rēx* a king] ▪ **reg'uline** *adj*. **reg'ulize** or **-ise** *vt* to reduce to regulus.

regur or **regar** /rā' or rē'gər/ *n* the rich black cotton soil of the Indian subcontinent, full of organic matter. [Hindi *regar*]

regurgitate /ri- or rē-gûr'ji-tāt/ *vt* to cast out again; to pour back; to bring back into the mouth after swallowing. ◆ *vi* to gush back. [LL *regurgitāre, -ātum*, from *re-* back, and *gurges, gurgitis* a gulf] ▪ **regur'gitant** *adj*. **regurgitā'tion** *n*.

reh /rā/ *n* an efflorescence of sodium salts on the soil in India, etc. [Hindustani]

Some words formed with the prefix **re-**.

rēdirec'tion *n*.	**rēdiscov'er** *vt*.	**rēdissolu'tion** *n*.
rēdiscount' *vt*.	**rēdiscov'erer** *n*.	**rēdissolve'** *vt*.
rēdis'count *n*.	**rēdiscov'ery** *n*.	**rēdistil'** *vt*.

---

rehab /rē'hab/ abbrev : rehabilitate; rehabilitation; rehabilitation centre.

rehabilitate /rē-(h)ə-bil'i-tāt/ vt to reinstate, restore to former privileges, rights, rank, etc; to clear the character of; to bring back into good condition, working order or prosperity; to make fit, after disablement, illness or imprisonment, for earning a living or playing a part in the world; to rebuild or restore (a building or housing area) to good condition. [LL rehabilitāre, -ātum ; see **habilitate**]
■ **rehabilitā'tion** n. **rehabil'itative** adj tending to rehabilitate. **rehabil'itator** n.

rehash /rē'hash or rē-hash'/ n something made up of materials formerly used, without appreciable change or improvement, esp a restatement in different words of ideas already expressed by oneself or someone else (also vt). [**re-** and **hash**[1]]

rehear /rē-hēr'/ vt to hear again; to retry (a lawsuit). [**re-**]
■ **rehear'ing** n.

rehearse /ri-hûrs'/ vt to repeat, say over or read aloud; to enumerate; to recount, narrate in order; to perform privately for practice or trial; to practise beforehand. ◆ vi to take part in rehearsal. [OFr rehercer, reherser, from re- again, and hercer to harrow, from herce (Fr herse), from L hirpex, -icis a rake, a harrow]
■ **rehears'al** n the act of rehearsing; repetition; enumeration; narration; a performance for trial or practice. **rehears'er** n. **rehears'ing** n.

reheat /rē-hēt'/ vt to heat again. ◆ n /rē'hēt/ a device to inject fuel into the hot exhaust gases of a turbojet in order to obtain increased thrust; the use of this. [**re-**]
■ **reheat'er** n a person who reheats; an apparatus for reheating.

rehoboam /rē-(h)ō-bō'əm or -(h)ə-/ n a large liquor measure or vessel (esp for champagne), the size of six normal bottles (approx 156 fluid oz). [Rehoboam, Biblical king of Israel; cf **jeroboam**]

rehouse /rē-howz'/ vt to provide with a new house or houses. [**re-**]
■ **rehous'ing** n.

rehydrate /rē-hī'drāt or rē-hī-drāt'/ vi to absorb water after dehydration. ◆ vt to add water to (a dehydrated substance); to enable a dehydrated person to absorb water. [**re-**]
■ **rēhydrā'tion** n.

Reich /rīhh/ n the German state; Germany as an empire (the **First Reich** Holy Roman Empire, 962–1806, **Second Reich** under Hohenzollern emperors, 1871–1918, and **Third Reich** as a dictatorship under the Nazi regime, 1933–45). [Ger, OE rīce kingdom; cf **bishopric**]
❑ **Reichsbank** /rīhhs'bängk/ n the German state bank. **Reichsland** /-länt/ n German imperial territory, ie Alsace-Lorraine, 1871–1919. **reichsmark** /-märk/ n the German monetary unit 1924–48 (see **mark**[2]). **Reichsrat**, earlier **Reichsrath** /-rät/ n the upper house of the parliament of the former Austrian Empire; a deliberative Council of the Weimar Republic in Germany (1919–33), representing the States. **Reichstag** /-tähh/ n the lower house of the parliament of Germany during the Second Reich and the Weimar Republic; the building in which it met.

Reichian /rī'hhi-ən/ adj of or relating to the theory or practice of Wilhelm Reich, Austrian-born psychiatrist (1897–1957), esp the concept of a universal, sexually-generated life energy called 'orgone'. ❑ **Reichian therapy** n (also without cap) therapy designed to release inhibited or disturbed energies by the use of massage, controlled breathing, etc (also called **bioenerget'ics**).

reif /rēf/ (Scot) n spoliation. [OE rēaf ; cf **reave**]

reify /rē'i-fī/ vt (**re'ifying**; **re'ified**) to think of as a material thing; to convert into a material thing, to materialize. [L rēs a thing]
■ **reification** /-fi-kā'shən/ n materialization, turning into an object; depersonalization (esp in Marxist terminology). **reifica'tory** adj. **re'ifier** n.

R18 symbol : (a certificate) designating a film for restricted distribution only, in venues (or from premises) to which no one under eighteen may be admitted.

reign /rān/ n rule, actual or nominal, of a monarch; time of reigning; predominance; predominating influence; kingdom (obs); realm (obs); domain (obs). ◆ vi to be a monarch; to be predominant; to prevail. [OFr regne, from L rēgnum, from regere to rule]

reik same as **reak**[1].

reiki /rā'kē/ n a form of Japanese natural therapy involving the laying on of hands or gentle massage. [Jap, universal energy]

Reil's island see **insula**.

reimagine /rē-im-aj'in/ vt to present a fundamentally new interpretation of (a subject, esp an artistic work). [**re-**]

reimbattell'd /rē-im-bat'ld/ (Milton) adj drawn up again in battle array. [**re-**]

reimburse /rē-im-bûrs'/ vt to repay; to pay an equivalent to for loss or expense. [LL imbursāre, from in in, and bursa purse]
■ **reimburs'able** adj. **reimburse'ment** n. **reimburs'er** n.

reim-kennar /rīm'ke-nər/ n an enchanter or enchantress. [Appar invented by Sir Walter Scott, from Ger Reim rhyme, and Kenner knower]

reimplant /rē-im-plänt'/ (med) vt to replace severed body tissue, esp an organ or member, in its original site surgically. ◆ n /-im'/ a section of the body which has been reimplanted. [**re-**]
■ **reimplantā'tion** n.

reimport /rē-im-pört'/ vt to import (goods that have been manufactured from exported materials) back into a country. ◆ n /-im'/ an act of reimporting; a reimported product. [**re-**]
■ **reimportā'tion** n. **reimport'er** n.

reimpression /rē-im-presh'ən/ n a second or later impression of an edition of a book, etc; a reprint. [**re-**]

rein[1] /rān/ n the strap or either half of the strap from the bit, by which a horse is controlled; (in pl) a device with a similar strap for guiding a small child (also called **walking reins**); any means of curbing or governing (fig). ◆ vt to fasten or tie by the rein (Shakesp); to provide with reins; to govern with the rein; to restrain or control; to stop or check (with in or up). ◆ vi to answer (Shakesp); to stop or slow up. [OFr rein, resne, rene (Fr rene), perh through (hypothetical) LL retina, from L retinēre to hold back]
■ **rein'less** adj without rein or restraint.
❑ **rein'-arm**, **rein'-hand** n normally the left arm and hand respectively, opp to whip-hand. **reins'man** n a skilful horse-driver or rider.
■ **draw rein** to pull up, stop riding. **give rein** or **a free rein** or **the reins to** to allow free play to, apply no check to. **keep a tight rein** (**on**) to control closely. **rein back** to make a horse step backwards by pressure on the reins; (of a horse) to step backwards (also fig). **rein in** to check, stop. **take** (**up**) **the reins** to take control.

rein[2] see **reindeer** and **reins**.

reincarnate /rē-in-kär'nāt or rē-in-kär-nāt'/ vt to cause to be born again in another body or form; to embody again in flesh. ◆ adj (poetic) reborn. [**re-**]
■ **rēincarnā'tion** n. **rēincarnā'tionism** n belief in reincarnation of the soul. **rēincarnā'tionist** n.

reindeer /rān'dēr/ n (pl **rein'deer** or **rein'deers**) a large heavy deer (Rangifer tarandus), wild and domesticated, of northern regions, antlered in both sexes, the N American variety being called the caribou (also (rare) **rein**). [ON hreinndȳri, or ON hreinn (OE hrān) and **deer**]
❑ **Reindeer Age** n (archaeol) the Magdalenian. **reindeer moss** n a lichen (Cladonia rangiferina), the winter food of the reindeer.

reinette /rā-net'/ same as **rennet**[2].

re infecta /rē or rā in-fek'tə or -tä/ (L) without finishing the business.

reinflation /rē-in-flā'shən/ n (excessive) reflation which, rather than stimulating the economy, causes further inflation. [**re-**]

reinforce /rē-in-förs' or -förs'/ vt to strengthen with new force or support; to strengthen; to increase by addition; to encourage (the response to a stimulus) by giving or not giving a reward (psychol); to enforce again (rare). ◆ vi (Shakesp) to get reinforcements. ◆ n something that reinforces; a reinforced part near the rear of a gun. [Alteration by 17c, of **renforce**]
■ **reinforce'ment** n the act of reinforcing; additional force or assistance, esp of troops (usu in pl).
❑ **reinforced concrete** n concrete strengthened by embedded steel bars or mesh.

reinform /rē-in-förm'/ vt to inform anew; to give form to again; to reanimate. [**re-**]

reinfund /rē-in-fund'/ (Swift) vi to flow in again. [**re-** and L infundere, from fundere to pour]

Some words formed with the prefix **re-**.

rēdistillā'tion n.	**rēdistrib'utive** adj.	**rēdraw'** vt and vi.
rēdistrib'ute vt.	**rēdivide'** vt and vi.	**rēdrive'** vt.
rēdistribu'tion n.	**rēdivis'ion** n.	**rē-ed'it** vt.

■ words derived from main entry word; ❑ compound words; ■ idioms and phrasal verbs

reins /rānz/ *n pl* (*rare* or *obs* in *sing*) the kidneys, *esp* as formerly believed to be the centre of emotion; the loins. [OFr *reins*, from L *rēn*, pl *rēnēs*]

reinstall /rē-in-stöl'/ *vt* to install again. [**re-**]
■ **reinstal'ment** *n*.

reinstate /rē-in-stāt'/ *vt* to instate again; to restore to or re-establish in a former station or condition. [**re-**]
■ **reinstāte'ment** *n*. **reinstā'tion** *n* (*rare*).

reinsure /rē-in-shoor'/ *vt* to insure against the risk undertaken by underwriting an insurance; to insure again. [**re-**]
■ **reinsur'ance** *n*. **reinsur'er** *n*.

reintegrate /rē-in'ti-grāt or -tə-/ *vt* to integrate again; to redintegrate.
■ **reintegrā'tion** *n*.

reintermediation /rē-in-tər-mē-di-ā'shən/ *n* the return into the banking system of borrowing previously financed outside it to evade corset (qv) controls. [**re-**]

reinvent /rē-in-vent'/ *vt* to invent again; to recreate in a different or spurious form. [**re-**]
■ **reinven'tion** *n*.
■ **reinvent the wheel** to return, *usu* by a circuitous and complex process, to a simple device or method.

reinvest /rē-in-vest'/ *vt* to clothe again; to endow again; to invest again (also *vi*). [**re-**]
■ **reinvest'ment** *n*.

reinvigorate /rē-in-vig'ə-rāt/ *vt* to put new vigour into. [**re-**]
■ **reinvigorā'tion** *n*.

reioyndure (*Shakesp*) see **rejoin²**.

reird /rērd/ or **raird** /rārd/ (*Scot*) *n* an uproar, clamour, din. [OE *reord*]

reis¹ /rīs/ same as **rice²**.

reis² /rās/ *n pl* (*sing* **real** /rā-äl'/) an obsolete Portuguese and Brazilian money of account, 1000 reis making a *milreis*. [Port]

reist same as **reast¹**, or as **reest²,³**.

reistafel see **rijstafel**.

REIT *abbrev* : Real Estate Investment Trust.

reiter /rī'tər/ (*hist*) *n* a German cavalry soldier. [Ger]

reiterate /rē-it'ə-rāt/ *vt* to repeat; to repeat again and again. ◆ *adj* /-īt/ repeated (also **reit'erated**). [**re-**]
■ **reit'erance** *n*. **reit'erant** *adj* reiterating. **reit'eratedly** *adv*. **reiterā'tion** *n* act of reiterating; the printing of the second side of a sheet. **reit'erative** *adj* characterized by repetition. ◆*n* a word expressing reiteration of utterance or act; a word formed by reduplication, the second element *usu* differing from the first (eg *helter-skelter*).

reive and **reiver** same as **reave** and **reaver**.

reject /ri-jekt'/ *vt* to throw away; to discard; to refuse to accept, admit or accede to; to refuse; to renounce; (of the body) not to accept tissue, a transplanted organ, etc from another source (*med*). ◆*n* (*usu* /rē'/) someone or something that is rejected; an imperfect article, not accepted for export, normal sale, etc, and often offered for sale at a discount. [L *rejicere*, *rejectum*, from *re-* back, and *jacere* to throw]
■ **rejec'table** or **rejec'tible** *adj*. **rejectamen'ta** *n pl* refuse; excrement. **rejec'tion** *n*. **rejec'tionist** *adj* (of a policy, attitude, etc) rejecting or clearly inclined towards rejection of eg an offer, proposal or (*esp* peace) plan (also *n*). **rejec'tive** *adj* tending to reject. **reject'or** or **reject'er** *n*.

rejig, re-jig /rē-jig'/ or **rejigger** /-jig'ər/ *vt* to re-equip; to change or rearrange in a new or unexpected way that is sometimes regarded as unethical (*commerce*). ◆*n* /rē'/ an act of rejigging. [**re-**]

rejoice /ri-jois'/ *vi* to feel or express great joy, to exult; to make merry. ◆ *vt* to gladden; to make joyful (*archaic*); to be joyful because of (*Shakesp*). [OFr *resjoir*, *resjoiss-* (Fr *réjouir*), from L *re-*, ex and *gaudēre* to rejoice]
■ **rejoice'ful** *adj*. **rejoice'ment** *n* rejoicing. **rejoic'er** *n*. **rejoic'ing** *n* act of being joyful; expression, subject or experience of joy; (in *pl*) festivities, celebrations, merry-makings. **rejoic'ingly** *adv*.
■ **rejoice in** to be happy because of; to have (*facetious*).

rejoin¹ /ri-join'/ (*law*) *vt* to say in reply, retort. ◆ *vi* to reply to a charge or pleading, *esp* to a plaintiff's replication. [OFr *rejoindre*]
■ **rejoin'der** /ri-/ *n* an answer to a reply; an answer, *esp* a sharp or clever one; the defendant's answer to a plaintiff's replication (*law*).

rejoin² /ri- or rē-join'/ *vt* and *vi* to join again. [**re-**]
■ **rejoin'dure** (*Shakesp* **reioyn'dure**) *n* a joining again.

rejón /re-hhōn'/ (*Sp*) *n* (*pl* **rejo'nes** /-nāz/) a lance with a wooden handle, used in bullfighting.
■ **rejoneador** /re-hhōn-ā-ad-ör'/ or *-ör/ n* (*pl* **rejoneador'es** /-āz/) a mounted bullfighter who uses rejones (also *fem* **rejoneador'a**). **rejoneo** /re-hhōn-ā'ō/ *n* the art of bullfighting on horseback using rejones.

rejourn /ri-jûrn'/ (*Shakesp*) *vt* to postpone, defer. [Cf **adjourn**]

rejuvenate /ri-joo'vi-nāt/ *vt* to make young again; to restore to youthful condition or appearance or to activity; to restore (by uplift) to an earlier condition of active erosion (*geol*). ◆ *vi* to rejuvenesce. [**re-** and L *juvenis* young, from *juvenēscere* to become young]
■ **rejuvenā'tion** *n*. **reju'venator** *n*. **rejuvenesce** /-es'/ *vi* to grow young again; to recover youthful character; to undergo change in cell-contents to a different, *usu* more active, state (*biol*); to resume growth. ◆*vt* to rejuvenate. **rejuvenesc'ence** *n*. **rejuvenesc'ent** *adj*. **reju'venize** or **-ise** *vt* to rejuvenate.

reke /rēk/ (*Spenser*) *vi* to reck. [OE *rēcan*]

rel. *abbrev* : related; relating; relation; relative.

relâche /rə-läsh'/ (*Fr*) *n* relaxation; rest; no performance.

relapse /ri-laps'/ *vi* to slide, sink or fall back, *esp* into evil or illness; to return to a former state or practice; to backslide; to fall away. ◆ *n* (also /rē'/) a falling back into a former bad state; the return of a disease after partial recovery (*med*). [L *relābī*, *relāpsus*, from *lābī* to slide]
■ **relapsed'** *adj* having relapsed. **relap'ser** *n*. **relap'sing** *adj*.
□ **relapsing fever** *n* an infectious disease characterized by recurrent attacks of fever with enlargement of the spleen, caused by a spirochaete transmitted by ticks and lice.

relate /ri-lāt'/ *vt* to recount, narrate, tell; to give an account of (*Milton*); to bring back (*Spenser*); to refer, bring into connection or relation. ◆ *vi* to date back in application (*law*); to have reference or relation; to connect; to get on well (with) (often with *to*; *inf*); to discourse (*Shakesp*). ◆*n* (with *cap*) in Britain, a marriage guidance service. [L *relātus*, used as pap of *referre* to bring back, from *re* and *ferre*]
■ **relā'table** *adj*. **relā'ted** *adj* narrated; referred (to) (*rare*); connected; allied by blood or marriage (also *fig*); (of a key) sharing notes with another key or keys (*music*). **relā'tedness** *n*. **relā'ter** *n* a person who relates. **relā'tion** *n* act of relating; state or mode of being related; narrative or recital; statement; an information (*law*); way in which one thing is connected with another; a quality that can be predicated, not of a single thing, but only of two or more together (*philos*); respect, reference; a relative by birth or marriage; (in *pl*) mutual dealings; (in *pl*) sexual intercourse (*euphem*). **relā'tional** *adj* concerning, expressing, or of the nature of relation, *esp* syntactic relation in grammatical structures. **relā'tionally** *adv*. **relā'tionism** *n* (*philos*) the doctrine that relations have an objective existence; the doctrine of relativity of knowledge. **relā'tionist** *n*. **relā'tionless** *adj* kinless; unrelated. **relā'tionship** *n* a state or mode of being related; relations; an emotional or sexual affair. **relā'tival** /rel-ə-tī'vl/ *adj* concerning relation, *esp* grammatical relation. **rel'ative** /-ə-tiv/ *adj* in or having relation; correlative; corresponding; having the same key-signature (*music*); relevant; comparative; not absolute or independent; relating, having reference (to); referring to an antecedent (*grammar*). ◆*n* that which is relative; a relative word, *esp* a relative pronoun; a person who is related by blood or marriage. **rel'atively** *adv*. **rel'ativeness** *n*. **rel'ativism** *n* relationism; a doctrine of relativity; the view that accepted standards of right and good vary with environment and from person to person. **rel'ativist** *n*. **relativis'tic** *adj* relating to relativity, or to relativism. **relativis'tically** *adv*. **relativ'itist** *n* a person who studies or accepts relativity. **relativ'ity** *n* state or fact of being relative; (in *pl*) related aspects of pay, working conditions, etc between different jobs or the same job in different areas; a principle which asserts that only relative, not absolute, motion can be detected in the universe (Einstein's **Special Theory of Relativity**, 1905, starts from two fundamental postulates: (1) that all motion is relative, (2) that the velocity of light is always constant relative to an observer; his **General Theory of Relativity**, 1916, which embraces the Special Theory, deals with varying velocities or accelerations, whereas the Special Theory dealt with constant relative velocity, or zero acceleration, and it is much concerned with gravitation; in each case Einstein derived important equations and made predictions). **relativīzā'tion** or **-s-** *n*. **rel'ativize** or **-ise** *vt* and *vi* to make or become relative. **relator**

Some words formed with the prefix **re-**.

rē-elect' *vt*.	**rē-elevā'tion** *n*.	**rē-embark'** *vt* and *vi*.
rē-elec'tion *n*.	**rē-eligibil'ity** *n*.	**rē-embarkā'tion** *n*.
rē-el'evate *vt*.	**rē-el'igible** *adj*.	**rē-embod'iment** *n*.

/ri-lā'tər/ n a person who relates; a narrator; a person who lays an information before the Attorney-General, enabling him to take action (law).

□ **relational database** n (comput) a database that is constructed so that related items of data can be accessed or retrieved together. **relative abundance** n a rough measure of population density, eg number of birds seen per hour, or the percentage of sample plots occupied by a species of plant (ecology); see **abundance** (phys). **relative address** n a location in the memory of a computer described in terms of its distance from another location. **relative aperture** n (in a camera) the ratio of the diameter of the lens to the focal length usu expressed as the f-number. **relative atomic mass** n the inferred weight of an atom of an element relatively to that of oxygen as 16 or, more recently, carbon-12 taken as 12. **relative density** n the weight of any given substance as compared with the weight of an equal bulk or volume of water or other standard substance at the same, or at standard, temperature and pressure. **relative humidity** n the ratio of the amount of water vapour in the air to the amount that would saturate it at the same temperature. **relative majority** n an excess number of votes won in an election over a runner-up when no candidate has more than fifty per cent. **relative molecular mass** n weight of a molecule relatively to that of an atom of carbon-12 taken as 12. **relativity of knowledge** n the doctrine that the nature and extent of our knowledge is determined not merely by the qualities of the objects known but necessarily by the conditions of our cognitive powers.

relative, etc see under **relate**.

relaunch /rē-lönch' or -lönsh'/ vt to reintroduce (a product or service) to the market, usu with some change to the item or its marketing. ◆ n /rē'lönch or rē'lönsh/ an instance of this. [**re-**]

relax /ri-laks'/ vt and vi to loosen; to slacken; to make or become less close, tense, rigid, strict or severe. ◆ n a relaxing. [L relaxāre, -ātum, from laxus loose]

■ **relax'ant** adj and n (a substance) having the effect of relaxing; laxative (archaic). **relaxā'tion** /re- or rē-/ n the act of relaxing; the state of being relaxed; partial remission (law); the return of a system towards equilibrium (phys); release from outlawry (Scots law; obs); recreation. **relax'ative** adj. **relaxed'** adj. **relax'edly** adv. **relax'in** n a hormone which has a relaxing effect on the pelvic muscles, and is used to facilitate childbirth. **relax'ing** adj enervating.
□ **relaxation therapy** n a form of therapy which focuses on learning to relax certain muscle groups.

relay[1] /ri-lā', also rē'lā or rē-lā'/ n orig a supply of horses, etc to relieve others on a journey; a fresh set of dogs in hunting (archaic); a station for either of these; a relieving shift of men; a supplementary store of anything; a relay race, or one of its stages; an electrically-operated switch employed to effect changes in an independent circuit; any device by which a weak electric current or other small power is used to control a strong one; a relayed programme, or act or fact of relaying it. ◆ vt (pat and pap **relayed**) to place in, relieve, control, supply or transmit by relay; to rebroadcast (a programme received from another station or source). ◆ vi to obtain a relay; to operate a relay. [OFr relais relay of horses or dogs; origin obscure]
□ **relay race** n a race between teams, each person running part of the total distance.

relay[2] /rē-lā'/ vt (pat and pap **relaid'**) to lay again. [**re-**]

rel. d abbrev : relative density.

release[1] /ri-lēs'/ vt to let loose; to set free; to let go; to relieve; to slacken; to undo; to remit; to relinquish; to surrender, convey, give up a right to (law); to make available, authorize sale, publication, exhibition, etc of; to make available for public knowledge. ◆ n a setting free; liberation; discharge or acquittance; remission; mode of releasing; the giving up of a claim, conveyance; a catch for holding and releasing; authorization to make available on a certain date; a thing so made available; a film, video, record or other recording made available for sale by its production company (esp as new release). [OFr relaissier, from L relaxāre to relax]
■ **releas'able** adj. **releasee'** n a person to whom an estate is released. **release'ment** n release. **releas'er** n. **releas'or** n (law).

release[2] /rē-lēs'/ vt to grant a new lease of. [**re-**]

relegate /rel'i-gāt/ vt to consign to an inferior or less important place or position; to move to a lower division of a league (sport); to assign (to a class); to refer (to another or others) for decision or action; to banish; to

refer (a person, for something, to another; archaic). [L relēgāre, -ātum, from re- away, and lēgāre to send]
■ **rel'egable** adj. **relegā'tion** n.

relent /ri-lent'/ vi to soften, become less severe; to give way (Spenser and Milton); to abate, slacken (Spenser); to slacken pace (Spenser); to melt (obs). ◆ vt to soften, cause to relent (Spenser and Burns); to relax, moderate (Spenser); to slow down (Spenser); to regret, repent (Spenser). ◆ n relenting; slowing (Spenser); melting (obs). [L re- back, and lentus sticky, sluggish, pliant]
■ **relent'ing** n and adj. **relent'less** adj unrelenting; inexorable; merciless, stern. **relent'lessly** adv. **relent'lessness** n. **relent'ment** n (rare).

Relenza® /ri-len'zə/ n a drug used in treating influenza, acting by inhibiting the neuraminidase that allows the virus to spread in the subject's system.

relevant /rel'ə-vənt or -i-/ adj bearing upon or applying to the matter in hand, pertinent; related, proportional (to); sufficient legally. [L relevāns, -antis, prp of relevāre to raise up, relieve; from the notion of helping; cf **relieve**]
■ **rel'evance** or **rel'evancy** n. **rel'evantly** adv.

reliable, **reliant**, etc see under **rely**.

relic or (archaic) **relique** /rel'ik/ n that which is left after loss or decay of the rest; a corpse (usu in pl; archaic); any personal memorial of a saint, held in reverence as an incentive to faith and piety (RC); a souvenir; a memorial of antiquity or object of historic interest; anything, such as a custom, that is a survival from the past. [Fr relique, from L reliquiae ; see **reliquiae**]
□ **rel'ic-monger** n a person who deals in or collects relics.

relict /rel'ikt/ n a species occurring in circumstances different from those in which it originated (ecology); a survivor or surviving trace (archaic); a widow (archaic); a relic (obs). ◆ adj /ri-likt'/ left behind; surviving; formed by removal of surrounding materials (geol). [L relictus left, pap of relinquere to leave]
□ **relict organ** n an organ of the body that no longer has any function and is therefore seen as evidence of Darwinian evolution.

relie /ri-lī'/ (obs) vt (pap **relied** or (Spenser) **relide**) to assemble, collect together. [**rely**]

relied and **relier** see **rely**.

relief /ri-lēf'/ n the lightening or removal of any burden, discomfort, evil, pressure or stress; release from a post or duty; a person who releases another by taking his or her place; that which relieves or mitigates; aid in danger, esp deliverance from siege; assistance to the poor; fresh supply of provisions; feeding or seeking food (hunting; obs); a certain fine paid to the overlord by a feudal tenant's heir on coming into possession (hist); release from obligation, or right to reimbursement of expenses (Scots law); anything that gives diversity; projection or standing out from the general surface, ground or level; a sculpture or other work of art executed in relief; appearance of standing out solidly; distinctness by contrast, esp in outline. ◆ adj providing relief in cases of overloading, distress, danger or difficulty. [OFr relef, from relever ; see **relieve**, also **relievo**]
■ **relief'less** adj.
□ **Relief Church** n a body that left the Church of Scotland because of oppressive exercise of patronage, organized in 1761, united with the United Secession Church in 1847 to form the United Presbyterian Church. **relief map** n a map in which the form of the country is shown by elevations and depressions of the material used, or by the illusion of such elevations and depressions, or (loosely) by other means.

relieve /ri-lēv'/ vt to bring, give or afford relief to; to release; to release from duty by taking the place of; to ease (eg a burden); (reflexive) to urinate or to defecate; to mitigate; to raise the siege of; to set off by contrast; to break the sameness of; to lift up (Shakesp); to bring into relief; to feed (obs). [OFr relever, from L relevāre to lift, relieve, from levāre to raise, from levis light]
■ **reliev'able** adj. **relieved'** adj freed from anxiety or concern. **reliev'er** n. **reliev'ing** adj.
□ **relieving arch** n an arch in a wall to relieve the part below it from a superincumbent weight. **relieving officer** n (hist) an official formerly appointed to superintend the relief of the poor.
■ **relieve someone of** to take from someone's possession, with or without that person's approval; to steal from someone; to free someone from (a necessity, restriction, etc).

Some words formed with the prefix **re-**.

rē-embod'y vt.	**rē-em'phasize** or **rē-em'phasise** vt.	**rē-endorse'ment** n.
rē-emerge' vi.	**rē-encour'age** vt.	**rē-endow'** vt.
rē-emer'gence n.	**rē-endorse'** vt.	**rē-endow'ment** n.

---

relievo /ri-lē'vō/, also (from Ital) **rilievo** /rē-lyä'vō/ (art) n (pl **relie'vos** or **rilie'vi** /-vē/) relief; a work in relief; appearance of relief. [Ital *rilievo*]

religieux /rə-lē-zhyø'/ (Fr) n a monk or friar.
■ **religieuse** /-zhyœz/ n a nun; a cake made of two balls of choux pastry set one on top of the other, with icing and a creamy filling in matching flavours.

religio- /re-lij-i-ō-/ combining form denoting: relating to religion or religious matters.

religion /ri-lij'ən/ n belief in, recognition of or an awakened sense of a higher unseen controlling power or powers, with the emotion and morality connected with such; rites or worship; any system of such belief or worship; devoted fidelity; monastic life; a monastic order; Protestantism (obs). [L *religiō, -ōnis*, noun, *religiōsus*, adj, perh connected with *religāre* to bind]
■ **relig'ionary** adj (rare) religious. ◆ n a member of a religious order; a Protestant (obs). **relig'ioner** n a member of an order; a Protestant (obs). **relig'ionism** n religiosity; bigotry. **relig'ionist** n a person attached to a religion; a bigot; someone professionally engaged in religion, eg an evangelist (US). **relig'ionize** or **-ise** vt to imbue with religion. ◆ vi to make profession of being religious. **relig'ionless** adj. **religiose** /-lij'i-ōs or -i-ōs'/ adj morbidly or sentimentally religious. **religiosity** /-os'it-i/ n spurious or sentimental religion; religious feeling. **relig'ious** /-əs/ adj of, concerned with, devoted to or imbued with religion; scrupulous; bound to a monastic life (RC); strict, very exact. ◆ n a person bound by monastic vows. **relig'iously** adv. **relig'iousness** n.

religiose, etc see under **religion**.

religioso /rə-lij-i-ō'sō/ (Ital) adj and adv (music) in a devotional manner.

reline /rē-līn'/ vt to mark with new lines; to renew the lining of. [**re-**]

relinquish /ri-ling'kwish/ vt to give up; to let go. [OFr *relinquir, relinquiss-*, from L *relinquere, relictum*, from pfx *re-*, and *linquere* to leave]
■ **relin'quishment** n.

relique /rel'ik or ri-lēk'/ n an archaic form of **relic**. [Fr]
■ **reliquaire** /rel-i-kwār'/ or **rel'iquary** /-kwər-i/ n a receptacle for relics. **rel'iquary** adj of relics; residual.

reliquiae /ri-lik'wi-ē or re-lik'wi-ī/ n pl remains, esp fossil remains. [L, from *relinquere* to leave]

relish¹ /rel'ish/ n a flavour; characteristic flavour; enough to give a flavour; appetizing flavour; zest-giving quality or power; an appetizer; condiment; zestful enjoyment; gusto; pleasureful inclination. ◆ vt to like the taste of; to be pleased with; to enjoy; to appreciate discriminatingly; to give a relish to; to taste, experience (obs). ◆ vi to savour, smack; to have an agreeable taste; to give pleasure. [OFr *reles, relais* remainder, from *relaisser* to leave behind]
■ **rel'ishable** adj.

relish² or **rellish** /rel'ish/ n a musical ornament. ◆ vt (Shakesp) to warble. [Origin obscure]

relive /rē-liv'/ vt and vi to live again; /rē-līv'/ to revive (Spenser).

reliver /ri-liv'ər/ (Shakesp) vt to deliver back. [OFr *relivrer*; also **re-** and *liver* to deliver, obs and dialect]

rellie /rel'i/ (Aust and NZ inf) n a relative.

rellish see **relish²**.

relocate /rē-lō-kāt'/ vt to locate again; to move (a firm, workers, etc) to a different area or site. ◆ vi to move one's place of business or residence. [**re-**]
■ **reloca'tion** n.

relucent /ri-loo'sənt or -lū'-/ (archaic) adj reflecting; shining. [L *relūcēns, -entis*, prp of *relūcēre* to shine back]

reluct /ri-lukt'/ (archaic) vi to be unwilling (with *at*); to hold back. [L *reluctārī*, from *re-* against, and *luctārī* to struggle]
■ **reluc'tance** n unwillingness; opposition, resistance (Milton); magnetomotive force applied to whole or part of a magnetic circuit divided by the flux in it. **reluc'tancy** n. **reluc'tant** adj unwilling; struggling (Milton); resisting. **reluct'antly** adv. **reluct'āte** vi to be reluctant. **reluctā'tion** /rel-/ n (archaic) repugnance.

relume /ri-lūm' or -loom'/ (archaic) vt to light or light up again; to rekindle. [L *relūmināre*, from *lūmen, -inis* light]
■ **relu'mine** /-in/ vt (archaic) to relume.

rely /ri-lī'/ vi (**rely'ing**; **relied'**) to depend confidently (on or upon); to rally (obs); to rest as on a support (obs). [OFr *relier*, from L *religāre* to bind back]
■ **reliabil'ity** n. **relī'able** adj to be relied on, trustworthy. **relī'ableness** n. **relī'ably** adv. **relī'ance** n trust; that in which or in whom one trusts. **relī'ant** adj. **relī'er** n (Shakesp).
❑ **reliability test** or **trial** n a public test of the qualities of motor vehicles (now known as a **rally**). **reliance loss** n (law) the loss incurred by the plaintiff in a breach of contract action due to relying on the defendant's promise to enter into the contract.

REM /rem or är-ē-em'/ abbrev : rapid eye movement.
❑ **REM sleep** n any of the phases of sleep accompanied by rapid eye movement.

rem /rem/ n a former unit of radiation dosage, the amount which has the same effect as one rad of X-radiation. [*röntgen equivalent man or mammal*]

remain /ri-mān'/ vi to stay or be left behind; to continue in the same place; to dwell, abide (Shakesp); to be left after or out of a greater number; to continue in one's possession or mind; to continue unchanged; to continue to be; to be still to be dealt with (often without subject *it*); to await (Spenser and Milton). ◆ n stay, abode (Shakesp); a surviving part (archaic). [OFr *remaindre*, from L *remanēre*, from *re-* back, and *manēre* to stay]
■ **remain'der** n that which remains or is left behind after the removal of a part or after division; the residue, rest; balance of an account (Shakesp); an interest in an estate to come into effect after a certain other event happens (law); right of next succession to a post or title; residue of an edition when the sale of a book has fallen off. ◆ adj (Shakesp) left over. ◆ vt to sell (a book) as a remainder. **remains'** n pl (occasionally with sing verb) that which is left; relics; a corpse; the literary productions of a dead person.
❑ **remain'der-man** n a person to whom a legal remainder is devised.

remake /rē-māk'/ vt to make anew. ◆ n something made again, esp (a new version of) a film; the act of making anew; a remade. [**re-**]
■ **rēmade'** adj made anew. ◆ n a thing made over again from the original materials.

remand /ri-mänd'/ vt to send back (esp a prisoner into custody or on bail to await further evidence). ◆ n act of remanding; recommittal. [OFr *remander*, or LL *remandāre*, from *mandāre* to order]
❑ **remand centre** n in the UK, a place of detention for those on remand or awaiting trial. **remand home** n formerly a place where young people were detained as punishment.
■ **on remand** having been remanded.

remanent /rem'ə-nənt/ adj remaining. ◆ n a remainder; a remnant. [L *remanēns, -entis*, prp and *remanet*, 3rd pers sing pr indic of *remanēre*]
■ **rem'anence** n something that remains, esp (phys) the magnetization after an exciting magnetic field has been removed from ferromagnetic materials. **rem'anency** n. **rem'anet** n a remainder; a postponed case or parliamentary bill.

remanié /rə-mä-nyā'/ (geol) n a fossil or other relic of an older rock preserved as a fragment in a later deposit. [Fr, pap of *remanier* to rehandle]

remark¹ /ri-märk'/ vt to mark out (Milton); to notice; to comment (that), or say incidentally (that). ◆ vi to comment, make an observation (often with *on* or *upon*). ◆ n noteworthiness; observation; comment; (also as Fr, **remarque'**) a marginal drawing or other distinguishing mark on an engraving or etching indicating an early state of the plate; a plate, print or proof bearing this special remark. [OFr *remarquer*, from *re-* (intensive) and *marquer* to mark]
■ **remark'able** adj noteworthy; unusual, singular, strange. ◆ n a remarkable thing. **remark'ableness** n. **remark'ably** adv. **remarked'** adj conspicuous; (also **remarqued'**) bearing a remark (eg of an etching). **remark'er** n.

remark² or **re-mark** /rē-märk'/ vt to mark again, esp in an examination. ◆ n the act or an instance of marking something again. [**re-**]

remarque see **remark¹**.

remaster /rē-mäs'tər/ vt to make a new master recording of. [**re-**]

rematch /rē'mach/ (sport) n a second match or return match (also vt /rē-mach'/). [**re-**]

Some words formed with the prefix **re-**.

rē-engage' vt and vi.	**rē-enlist'** vt and vi.	**rē-equip'** vt and vi.
rē-engage'ment n.	**rē-enlist'er** n.	**rē-erect'** vt.
rē-engineer' vt.	**rē-enlist'ment** n.	**rē-erec'tion** n.

---

remblai /*rä-ble*'/ *n* earth used to form a rampart, embankment, etc; stowage in a mine. [Fr]

remble /*rem*'*bl* or *rem*'*l*/ (*NE Eng*) *vt* to remove, clear. [Origin obscure]

Rembrandtesque /*rem-bran-tesk*' or -*bran*-/ *adj* like the work of *Rembrandt* (1606–69), *esp* in his contrast of high lights and deep shadows.
■ **Rem'brandtish** *adj*. **Rem'brandtism** *n*.

REME /*rē*'*mi*/ *abbrev* : Royal Electrical and Mechanical Engineers.

remead see **remedy**.

remeasure /*rē-mezh*'*ər*/ *vt* to measure anew; to retrace (*Spenser*). [**re**-]
■ **remeas'urement** *n*.

remedy /*rem*'*i-di*/, *obs* and *Scot* **remede**, **remeid** or **remead** /*ri-mēd*'/ *n* any means of curing a disease, redressing, counteracting or repairing any evil or loss; reparation; redress; range of tolerated variation in the weight of a coin. ◆ *vt* (**rem'edying**; **rem'edied**) to put right, repair, counteract; to cure (a person or diseased part) (*archaic*). [Anglo-Fr *remedie*, OFr *remede*, from L *remedium*]
■ **remē'diable** *adj*. **remē'diably** *adv*. **remē'dial** *adj* tending or intended to remedy; of or concerning the teaching of children with learning difficulties (*obs*). **remē'dially** *adv*. **remē'diat** or **remē'diate** *adj* (*Shakesp*) remedial. **remediā'tion** *n*. **rem'ediless** (formerly /-*med*'/) *adj* without remedy; incurable. **rem'edilessly** (or /-*med*'/) *adv*. **rem'edilessness** (or /-*med*'/) *n*.
■ **no remedy** (*Shakesp*) of necessity. **what remedy?** (*obs*) how can it be helped or avoided?

remember /*ri-mem*'*bər*/ *vt* to keep in or recall to memory or mind; to bear in mind as someone or something deserving of honour or gratitude, or as someone to be rewarded, tipped or prayed for; to bear in mind as something to be mentioned (*Shakesp*); to mention, record (*obs*); to commemorate (*obs*); to remind (*archaic* or *dialect*); to recollect (*reflexive*; *Shakesp*); to occur to (*impers*; *archaic*); to regain one's good manners after a temporary lapse (*reflexive*); to recall to the memory of another (often as a greeting). ◆ *vi* to have the power or perform the act of memory; to have memory (with *of* ; *Shakesp* and *Milton*; now *Scot* and *US*). [OFr *remembrer*, from L *re-* again, and *memor* mindful]
■ **remem'berable** *adj*. **remem'berably** *adv*. **remem'berer** *n*. **remem'brance** *n* memory; that which serves to bring to or keep in mind; a reminder; a souvenir; a memorandum; a memorial; the reach of memory; (in *pl*) a message of friendly greeting. **remem'brancer** *n* someone or something that reminds; a recorder; an officer of exchequer responsible for collecting debts due to the Crown (**King's** or **Queen's Remembrancer**); an official representative of the City of London to Parliamentary committees, etc.
❑ **Remembrance Sunday** *n* the Sunday nearest to 11 November commemorating the fallen of the two World Wars (see **Armistice Day** under **armistice**).

remen /*rē*'*mən*/ *n* a unit of measurement used by the ancient Egyptians (equivalent to 52.4cm or 20.62in), also known as a **royal cubit**. [Ancient Egyp]

remercy /*ri-mûr*'*si*/ (*obs*) *vt* (pat (*Spenser*) **remer'cied**) to thank. [(O)Fr *remercier*]

remerge /*rē-mûrj*'/ *vt* to merge again. [**re**-]

remex /*rē*'*meks*/ *n* (pl **remiges** /*rem*'*i-jēz*/) any of the large feathers of a bird's wing, either primary or secondary. [L *rēmex*, -*igis* a rower]
■ **remigate** /*rem*'*i-gāt*/ *vi* (*rare*) to row. **remigā'tion** *n*. **remigial** /*ri-mij*'*i-əl*/ *adj*.

remigrate /*rem*'*i-grāt*, also *rē-mī-grāt*' or -*mī*'/ *vi* to change back; (also /*rē-mī-grāt*'/) to migrate again or back. [**re**-]
■ **remigrā'tion** /*rem-i*- or *rē-mī*-/ *n*.

remind /*ri-mīnd*'/ *vt* to put in mind (of), to cause to remember. [**re**- and **mind** vt]
■ **remind'er** *n* that which reminds. **remind'ful** *adj* mindful; reminiscent, prompting memories.

remineralize or **-ise** /*rē-min*'*ə-rə-līz*/ (*med*) *vi* (of bone) to regain depleted minerals, eg calcium. ◆ *vt* to replace the depleted mineral content of (bones, teeth, etc). [**re**-]
■ **remineralizā'tion** or **-s-** *n*.

reminiscence /*rem-i-nis*'*əns*/ *n* recollection; an account of something remembered; the recurrence to the mind of the past. [L *reminīscēns*, -*entis*, prp of *reminīscī* to remember]
■ **reminisce** /-*nis*'/ *vi* (back-formation) to recount reminiscences. **reminisc'ent** *adj* suggestive, remindful; addicted to reminiscences (also *n*); relating to reminiscence. **reminiscen'tial** /-*sen*'*shl*/ *adj* of, or of the nature of, reminiscence. **reminisc'ently** *adv*.

remise /*ri-mīz*'/ *n* surrender of a claim (*law; hist*); /*rə-mēz*'/ an effective second thrust after the first has missed (*fencing*); a coach house (*obs*); a livery-carriage (*obs*). ◆ *vt* /*ri-mīz*'/ to surrender. ◆ *vi* (*fencing*) to make a remise. [Fr *remis, remise*, from *remettre*, from L *remittere* to send back, remit, relax]

remiss /*ri-mis*'/ *adj* negligent; slack; lax; lacking vigour. [L *remittere*, *remissum*; see **remit**]
■ **remissibil'ity** *n*. **remiss'ible** *adj* that may be remitted. **remission** /*ri-mish*'*ən*/ *n* the act of remitting; slackening; abatement; relinquishment of a claim; the lessening of a term of imprisonment; pardon; forgiveness. **remiss'ive** *adj* remitting; forgiving. **remiss'ively** *adv*. **remiss'ly** *adv*. **remiss'ness** *n*. **remiss'ory** *adj* of remission.

remit /*ri-mit*'/ *vt* (**remitt'ing**; **remitt'ed**) to refrain from exacting or inflicting; to give up; to desist from; to transfer; to transmit (money, etc); to put again in custody; to refer to another court or authority, etc; to refer for information; to send or put back; to relax; to pardon (*archaic*). ◆ *vi* (*esp* of pain, an illness, etc) to abate; to relax; to desist. ◆ *n* /*rē*'*mit* or *ri-mit*'/ reference of a case or matter to another (*law*); scope, terms of reference; a matter submitted (to a conference or other body) for consideration (*politics*, *esp NZ*). [L *remittere*, *remissum*, from *re-* back, and *mittere* to send]
■ **remit'ment** *n* remission; remitting; remittance. **remitt'able** *adj*. **remitt'al** *n* remission; reference to another court, etc. **remitt'ance** *n* the sending of money, etc to a distance; the sum or thing sent. **remittee** /-*ē*'/ *n* the person to whom a remittance is sent. **remitt'ent** *adj* remitting at intervals. **remitt'ently** *adv*. **remitt'er** or **remitt'or** *n* a person who makes a remittance.
❑ **remittance man** *n* a man living abroad dependent upon remittances from home. **remittent fever** *n* a severe type of malaria in which the temperature falls slightly from time to time.

remix /*rē-miks*'/ *vt* to mix (a sound recording) again in a different way. ◆ *n* /*rē*'/ a remixed recording. [**re**-]

remnant /*rem*'*nənt*/ *n* a fragment or a small number surviving or remaining after destruction, defection, removal, sale, etc of the greater part; *esp* a remaining piece of cloth; a tag or quotation; a surviving trace; trace of a fact (*Walter Scott*). ◆ *adj* remanent, remaining. [**remanent**]

remonetize or **-ise** /*rē-mun*'*ə-tīz* or -*mon*'/ *vt* to re-establish as legal tender. [**re**-]
■ **remonetizā'tion** or **-s-** *n*.

remonstrance /*ri-mon*'*strəns*/ *n* a strong or formal protest, expostulation. [L *re-* again, and *mōnstrāre* to point out]
■ **remon'strant** *adj* remonstrating; (with *cap*) Dutch Arminian. ◆ *n* a person who remonstrates; (with *cap*) a Protester (*Scot hist*); (with *cap*) a member of the Dutch Arminian party whose divergence from Calvinism was expressed in five articles in the Remonstrance of 1610. **remon'strantly** *adv*. **rem'onstrāte** (earlier /-*mon*'/) *vi* to make a remonstrance. ◆ *vt* to say or (*obs*) state in remonstrance; to demonstrate (*obs*). **rem'onstratingly** *adv*. **remonstrā'tion** /*rem-ən*-/ *n*. **remon'strative** or **remon'stratory** /-*strə-tər-i*/ *adj* expostulatory. **rem'onstrator** (or /-*mon*'/) *n*.
■ **Grand Remonstrance** a statement of abuses presented to Charles I by the House of Commons in 1641.

remontant /*ri-mon*'*tənt*/ *adj* (of a plant) flowering or fruiting more than once in the same season. ◆ *n* a remontant plant, *esp* a rose. [Fr]

remora /*rem*'*ə-rə*/ *n* the sucking-fish, formerly believed to stop ships by attaching its sucker; an obstacle (*fig*). [L *remora* delay, hindrance, from *mora* delay]

remoralize or **-ise** /*rē-mor*'*ə-līz*/ *vt* to restore morality to. [**re**-]
■ **remoralizā'tion** or **-s-** *n*.

remorse /*ri-mörs*'/ *n* feeling of regret and guilt for past wrongdoing; compunction; pity, compassionate feeling (*Spenser, Shakesp* and *Milton*); mitigation (*Shakesp*); *prob* matter of conscience (*Shakesp*); bite (*Spenser*). [OFr *remors* (Fr *remords*), from LL *remorsus*, from

---

Some words formed with the prefix **re-**.

rē-estab'lish *vt*.	rē-examinā'tion *n*.	rē-exist'ence *n*.
rē-estab'lishment *n*.	rē-exam'ine *vt*.	rē-expand' *vt* and *vi*.
rē-eval'uate *vt*.	rē-exist' *vi*.	rē-expan'sion *n*.

■ words derived from main entry word; ❑ compound words; ■ idioms and phrasal verbs

L *remordēre*, *remorsum* to bite again, from *re-* again, and *mordēre* to bite]
■ **remorse'ful** *adj* penitent; compassionate (*obs*). **remorse'fully** *adv*. **remorse'fulness** *n*. **remorse'less** *adj* without remorse; cruel; without respite. **remorse'lessly** *adv*. **remorse'lessness** *n*.

remote /ri-mōt'/ *adj* far removed in place, time, chain of causation or relation, resemblance or relevance; aloof; widely separated; very indirect; located separately from the main processor but having a communication link with it (*comput*). ◆ *n* an outside broadcast (*TV* and *radio*, *esp US*); a remote control device. [L *remōtus*, pap of *removēre*; see **remove**]
■ **remote'ly** *adv*. **remote'ness** *n*. **remō'tion** *n* removal (*Shakesp*); remoteness (*rare*).
❑ **remote access** *n* (*comput*) access from a terminal at another site. **remote control** *n* control of a device from a distance by the making or breaking of an electric circuit or by means of radio waves; a hand-held unit for controlling a television, video, etc from a distance. **remote-controlled**' *adj*. **remote handling equipment** *n* (*nuclear eng*) equipment enabling an operator to manipulate highly radioactive materials from behind a shield or from a safe distance. **remote job entry** *n* (*comput*) input of data or programs to a computer from a distant input device (eg a card reader). **remote sensing** *n* a method in which remote sensors are used to collect data for transmission to a central computer; observation and collection of scientific data without direct contact, *esp* observation of the earth's surface from the air or from space using electromagnetic radiation.

remoud /ri-mood'/ *pat* (*Spenser*) for **removed**.

remoulade or **rémoulade** /rā-mü-läd'/ *n* a sauce made with eggs, herbs, capers, etc, or sometimes with mayonnaise, and served with fish, salad, etc. [Fr dialect *ramolas* horseradish, from L *armoracea*]

remould /rē'mōld/ *n* a used tyre which has had a new tread vulcanized to the casing and the walls coated with rubber. ◆ *vt* /rē-mōld'/ to treat a tyre in this way. —*Cf* **retread**. [re-]

remount /rē-mownt'/ *vt* and *vi* to mount again. ◆ *n* /rē'/ a fresh horse or supply of horses. [re-]

remove /ri-moov'/ *vt* to put or take away; to transfer; to withdraw; to displace; to make away with; (in *passive*; *Thackeray*) of a dish on the table, to be succeeded (by). ◆ *vi* to go away; to move house, change location. ◆ *n* removal; the raising of a siege (*Shakesp*); absence (*Shakesp*); step or degree of remoteness or indirectness; in some schools, an intermediate class; promotion; a dish removed to make way for another, or taking the place of one so removed. [OFr *remouvoir*, from L *removēre*, *remōtum*, from *re-* away, and *movēre* to move]
■ **removabil'ity** *n*. **remov'able** *adj*. **remov'ably** *adv*. **remov'al** *n* the act of taking away; displacing; change of place; transference; going away; change of home or location; murder (*euphem*). **remov'alist** *n* see **remover** below. **removed**' *adj* remote; distant by degrees, as in descent or relationship. **remov'edness** *n*. **remov'er** *n* someone or something that removes; a person employed to convey furniture and other house contents from house to house (also (*Aust* and *NZ*) **removalist**).
❑ **removal terms** *n pl* (*Scot*) 28 May and 28 November, called Whitsunday and Martinmas.

remuage /rə-mü-äzh' or -moo-/ *n* the process of turning or shaking wine bottles so that the sediment collects at the cork end for removal. [Fr, from *remuer* to move or turn]
■ **remueur** /rə-mü-œr' or -moo-ûr'/ *n* in wine-making, the person who turns the bottles.

remuda /ri-mū'də or rā-moo'dha/ (*N Am*) *n* a supply of remounts on a ranch, etc. [Sp, exchange]

remunerate /ri-mū'nə-rāt/ *vt* to recompense; to pay for service rendered. [L *remunerārī* (late *-āre*), *-ātus*, from *mūnus*, *-eris* a gift]
■ **remū'nerable** *adj*. **remūnerā'tion** *n* recompense; reward; pay. **remū'nerative** *adj* profitable. **remū'nerativeness** *n*. **remū'nerātor** *n*. **remū'neratory** /-ə-tər-i/ *adj* giving a recompense.

remurmur /ri-mûr'mər/ *vt* and *vi* to echo, repeat, or resound in murmurs. [re-]

ren see **run**.

renague see **renege** under **renegade**.

renaissance /ri-nā'səns, ren'i-säns or -säns'/ *n* a new birth; (with *cap*) the revival of arts and letters, the transition from the Middle Ages to the modern world. ◆ *adj* of the Renaissance. [Fr; cf **renascence**]
❑ **Renaissance man** or **woman** *n* a person who typifies the renaissance ideal of wide-ranging culture and learning.

renal /rē'nl/ *adj* of the kidneys. [L *rēnālis*, from *rēnēs* (sing *rēn* is rare), the kidneys]

renascent /ri-nas'ənt, also -nā'sənt/ *adj* coming into renewed life or vitality. [L *renāscēns*, *-entis*, prp of *renāscī*, from *nāscī* to be born]
■ **renasc'ence** *n* being born anew; (with *cap*) Renaissance.

renay, **reney** /ri-nā'/ or **reny** /ri-nī'/ (*obs*) *vt* (**renay'ing** or **reny'ing**; **renayed**' or **renied**') to renounce, abjure, forswear; to deny. [OFr *renaier*, *renier*, from L *renegāre*]

rencounter /ren-kown'tər/ or (*Fr*) **rencontre** /rā-kɔ̃'tr'/ *n* a chance meeting; an encounter; a casual combat; a collision; an informal meeting of scientists. ◆ *vt* to meet; to encounter. [Fr *rencontre*]

rend /rend/ *vt* (pat and pap **rent**) to tear apart with force; to split; to tear away. ◆ *vi* to become torn. [OE *rendan* to tear]

render /ren'dər/ *vt* to give up; to give back, return, give in return; to make up; to deliver; to hand over; to give; to surrender; to yield; to tender or submit; to show forth; to represent or reproduce, *esp* artistically; to perform; to translate; to perform or pay as a duty or service; to present or betake (with *at*; *reflexive*); to cause to be or become; to melt; to extract, treat or clarify by melting; to plaster with a first coat; (in computer graphics) to convert a description of (an image) into pixels; to transfer (an accused person) to another country without formal extradition proceedings. ◆ *n* an act of rendering; that which is rendered. [OFr *rendre*, from LL *rendere*, appar formed by influence of *prendere* to take, from L *reddere*, from *re-* back, and *dare* to give]
■ **ren'derable** *adj*. **ren'derer** *n*. **ren'dering** *n* the action of the verb; a first coat of plaster, etc. **rendi'tion** *n* surrender; rendering; a performance; a translation (**extraordinary rendition** see under **extraordinary**).
❑ **render farm** *n* (*film* and *TV*) a group of linked computers used to render images so that they can be manipulated to create special effects.

rendezvous /rä'dā-voo or ron'di-/ *n* (*pl* **rendezvous** /-vooz/ or (*obs*) **rendezvous'es**) appointed meeting-place; a meeting by appointment; a general resort; an arranged meeting, and *usu* docking, of two spacecraft (*space technol*). ◆ *vi* (pat and pap **rendezvoused** /rä'dā-vood, or ron'di-/) to assemble at any appointed place. [Fr *rendez-vous* present yourselves, from *rendre* to render]

rendition see under **render**.

rendzina /rend-zē'nə/ *n* a fertile soil-type derived from a calcium-rich bedrock and typical of grass or open woodland in humid to semi-arid climates. [Russ, from Pol *redzina*]

renegade /ren'ə-gād/ or **renegate** /-gāt/ *n* a person who betrays or deserts a principle, party or religion; an apostate; a turncoat; *specif* a Christian convert to Islam. ◆ *adj* apostate. ◆ *vi* (**renegade**) to turn renegade. [LL *renegātus*, from L *re-* (intensive) and *negāre*, *-ātum* to deny; partly through Sp *renegado*]
■ **renegā'do** (or /-ä'dō/) *n* (*pl* **renega'dos**) (*archaic*) a renegade. **renegā'tion** *n*. **renege** or **renegue** /ri-nēg' or -nāg'/, also (*Irish*) **renig** /-nig'/ or **renague** /-nāg'/ ◆ *vt* to renounce; to apostatize from. ◆ *vi* to deny (often with *on*); to refuse (often with *on*); to revoke at cards. **reneg'er** or **reneg'uer** *n*.

renew /ri-nū'/ *vt* to renovate; to transform to new life, revive; to begin again; to repeat; to make again; to invigorate; to substitute new for; to restore; to regenerate; to extend (eg the period of a loan, validity of a lease, etc). ◆ *vi* to be made new; to begin again. [re- and new (adj)]
■ **renewabil'ity** *n*. **renew'able** *adj*. ◆ *n* (often in *pl*) any form of renewable energy (see below). **renew'al** *n* renewing; short form of **urban renewal** (see under **urban**). **renew'edness** *n*. **renew'er** *n*. **renew'ing** *n*.
❑ **renewable energy** *n* an alternative source of energy, such as waves, wind or sun, that can be considered inexhaustible (also called **alternative energy**). **renewable resource** *n* a supply of living organisms that, after harvesting, can be replaced by regrowth or reproduction.

reney see **renay**.

renfierst /ren-fērst'/ (*Spenser*) *adj* made fierce. [Appar modelled on **renforce**]

Some words formed with the prefix **re-**.

rē-exportā'tion *n*.	**rēfash'ionment** *n*.	**rēflow'ering** *n*.
rēface' *vt*.	**rēfloat'** *vt*.	**rēfo'cus** *vt*.
rēfash'ion *vt*.	**rēflow'er** *vi*.	**rēfoot'** *vt*.

---

renforce /ren-fōrs' or -förs'/ (*obs*) *vt* (pat (*Spenser*) **re'nforst'**; *pap* (*Spenser*) **renforst'**) to reinforce; to force again. ◆ *vi* to renew efforts. [(O)Fr *renforcer*]

renga /ren'gə/ same as **linked verse** (see under **link¹**).

reni- /rē-ni-/ *combining form* denoting relating to the kidneys. [*renal*]

renied see **renay**.

reniform /ren'i-förm/ *adj* kidney-shaped. [L *rēnēs* (sing *rēn*) the kidneys, and *förma* form; see **renal**]

renig see **renege** under **renegade**.

renin /rē'nin/ *n* a protein enzyme secreted by the kidneys into the bloodstream, where it helps to maintain the blood pressure. [L *rēnēs* (sing *rēn*) the kidneys]

renitent /ri-nī'tənt or ren'i-tənt/ (*rare*) *adj* resistant; reluctant; recalcitrant. [L *renītēns, -entis*, prp of *renītī* to resist]
■ **renī'tency** (or /ren'i/) *n*.

renminbi /ren'min-bē/ (also with *cap*) *n* the currency of the People's Republic of China since 1948; the standard monetary unit of China (100 fen), also called **yuan**. [Chin *rénmín* the people, and *bì* money]

renne /ren/ (*Spenser*) *vi* to run (also *pap*). [See **run**]
■ **renn'ing** *n*.

rennet¹ /ren'it/ *n* any means of curdling milk, *esp* a preparation of calf's stomach. [OE *rinnan* to run; cf **earn²**]
❑ **renn'et-bag** *n* the fourth stomach of a ruminant.

rennet² /ren'it/ *n* an apple of certain old varieties. [Fr *reinette, rainette*; origin uncertain]

rennin /ren'in/ *n* an enzyme found in gastric juice, which causes coagulation of milk. [*rennet*]

renormalization or **-s-** /rē-nör-mə-lī-zā'shən/ (*phys*) *n* a method of obtaining finite answers to calculations (rather than infinities) by redefining the parameters, *esp* of mass and charge. [**re-**]
■ **renorm'alize** or **-ise** *vt* to subject to or calculate using renormalization.

renounce /ri-nowns'/ *vt* to disclaim; to disown; to reject publicly and finally; to recant; to abjure. ◆ *vi* to fail to follow suit at cards. ◆ *n* a failure to follow suit. [OFr *renuncer*, from L *renuntiāre*, from *re-* away, and *nuntiāre, -ātum* to announce]
■ **renounce'able** *adj*. **renounce'ment** *n*. **renoun'cer** *n*.

renovate /ren'ō-vāt or -ə-/ *vt* to renew or make new again; to make as if new; to regenerate. [L *re-* again, and *novāre, -ātum* to make new, from *novus* new]
■ **renovā'tion** *n*. **ren'ovātor** *n*.

renown /ri-nown'/ *n* fame. ◆ *vt* (*literary*) to make famous; to celebrate. [OFr *renoun* (Fr *renom*), from L *re-* again, and *nōmen* a name]
■ **renowned'** *adj* famous. **renown'er** *n* (*Milton*) a person who gives another renown.

rensselaerite /ren'sə-lə-rīt or ren-sə-lā'rīt/ *n* a kind of firm-textured talc, used for carved or lathe-turned ornaments. [Stephen Van *Rensselaer* (1764–1839), N American statesman]

rent¹ /rent/ *n* periodical payment for use of another's property, *esp* houses and lands; revenue. ◆ *vt* to hold or occupy by paying rent; to let or hire out for a rent; to charge with rent. ◆ *vi* to be let at a rent. [Fr *rente*, from L *reddita* (*pecūnia*) money paid, from *reddere* to pay; cf **render**]
■ **rentabil'ity** *n*. **rent'able** *adj*. **rent'al** *n* the act of renting; a rent roll; rent; annual value; something rented or hired (*US*); a lease held by a kindly tenant (*qv*; *Scot*). **rent'aller** *n* (*Scot*) a kindly tenant. **rent'er** *n* a tenant who pays rent; a person who lets out property; a farmer of tolls or taxes (*hist*); a theatre shareholder (*archaic*); a distributor of commercial films to cinemas.
❑ **rent-a-** or before a vowel **rent-an-** *combining form* (*facetious*) denoting: (as if) rented or hired, organized for a specific occasion or purpose, instantly or artificially created, etc, as in *rent-a-crowd, rent-a-mob* or *rent-an-army*. **rental library** *n* (*US*) a lending-library which takes fees for books borrowed. **rent boy** *n* a young male prostitute. **rent'-charge** *n* a periodical payment charged upon rent. **rent'-collector** *n*. **rent'-day** *n*. **rent'-free** *adj* and *adv* without payment of rent. **rent restriction** *n* restriction of a landlord's right to raise rent. **rent roll** *n* a list of property and rents; total income from property.
■ **for rent** (*orig US*) to let.

rent² /rent/ pat and pap of **rend**. *n* an opening made by rending; a fissure. ◆ *vt* and *vi* (*obs* or *dialect*) to rend. [**rend**]

rente /rãt/ *n* annual income; (in *pl*; /rãt/) French or other government securities or income from them. [Fr]
■ **rentier** /rã-tyā/ *n* a fundholder; a person who has, or who lives on, an income from rents or investments.

renunciation /ri-nun-si-ā'shən/ *n* the act of renouncing; self-resignation; the act of surrendering to another the right to buy new shares in a rights issue (*stock exchange*). [L *renūntiāre* proclaim; see **nuncio**]
■ **renun'ciative** /-shə-tiv, -syə-tiv or -si-ā-tiv/ or **renun'ciatory** /-shə-tər-i or -si-ə-tər-i/ *adj*.

renverse /ren-vûrs'/ (*archaic*) *vt* (pat and pap **renversed'** or **renverst'** (*Spenser*)) to reverse; to upset. [Fr *renverser*, from pfx *re-* and *enverser* to overturn]
■ **renversement** /-vûrs'mənt/ *n* (*aeronautics*) *specif*, a half-roll and a half-loop in a combined manoeuvre; any aerial manoeuvre involving a reverse in direction of travel.

renvoi or (*esp* formerly) **renvoy** /ren-voi'*, Fr rã-vwä'/ *n* sending back by a government of an alien to his or her own country; a referring or relegation of a legal dispute to another jurisdiction. [Fr]

reny see **renay**.

reopen /rē-ō'pən/ *vt* and *vi* to open again; to begin again. [**re-**]
❑ **reopening clause** *n* in collective bargaining, a clause enabling any issue in a contract to be reconsidered before the contract expires (also **reopener** or **reopener clause**).

reorient /rē-ö'ri-ənt or -ō'/ *adj* rising again. ◆ *vt* /-ent/ to orient again. [**re-**]
■ **reō'rientate** *vt* to reorient. **reōrientā'tion** *n*.

Rep. *abbrev*: Representative (*US*); Republic; Republican (*US*).

rep¹ /rep/ (*inf*) *n* short form of: repeat; repertory (*theatre*); repetition (*school*, etc); representative (*esp commerce*); reprobate; reputation (early 18c and *US*).

rep² /rep/ *vi* (**repp'ing**; **repped**) (*commercial jargon*) to work or act as a commercial representative. [**rep¹**, from **represent**]
■ **repp'ing** *n*.

rep³ or **repp** /rep/ *n* a corded cloth (also **reps** /reps/). [Fr *reps*, perh from Eng **ribs**]
■ **repped** /rept/ *adj* transversely corded.

rep⁴ /rep/ *n* a unit of radiation dosage, now superseded by **rad**. [**r**öntgen **e**quivalent **p**hysical]

repaid pat and pap of **repay**.

repaint /rē-pānt'/ *vt* to paint over or again. ◆ *n* /rē'pānt/ an act of repainting; a repainted thing. [**re-**]
■ **repaint'ing** *n*.

repair¹ /ri-pār'/ *vt* to mend, fix, put right (something broken, out of order or condition, etc); to make amends for; to make good; to restore, refresh, revivify (*Shakesp*). ◆ *n* restoration after injury, loss or deterioration; sound condition; condition in terms of soundness; a part that has been mended or made sound. [OFr *reparer*, from L *reparāre*, from *parāre* to prepare]
■ **repair'able** *adj* capable of being mended (*esp* of material things); liable to be repaired (with *by*; *law*). **repair'er** *n*. **reparability** /rep-ər-ə-bil'i-ti/ *n*. **reparable** /rep'ər-ə-bl/ *adj* capable of being made good or (*rare*) being mended; falling to be repaired. **rep'arably** *adv*. **reparā'tion** *n* repair; supply of what is wasted; amends; compensation, often (in *pl*) to a country after it has suffered by war. **reparative** /ri-par'ə-tiv/ or **repar'atory** *adj*.
❑ **repair'man** *n* a person who does repairs, *esp* on something mechanical. **repair'-shop** *n*.

repair² /ri-pār'/ *vi* to take oneself; to go; to resort; to return (*Shakesp*). ◆ *vt* (*Spenser*) to restore to its position; to withdraw. ◆ *n* resort; place of resort; concourse. [OFr *repairer* to return to a haunt, from LL *repatriāre* to return to one's country, from L *re-* back, and *patria* native country]

repand /ri-pand'/ (*bot* and *zool*) *adj* slightly wavy. [L *repandus*, from *re-* back, and *pandus* bent]

reparable, etc see under **repair¹**.

repartee /re-pär-tē'/ *n* a ready and witty retort; skill in making such retorts. ◆ *vt* and *vi* to retort with ready wit. [OFr *repartie*, from *repartir*, from *partir* to set out, from L *partīrī* to divide]

Some words formed with the prefix **re-**.

refor'mat *vt*.	**refort'ify** *vt*.	**refound'er** *n*.
reform'ulate *vt*.	**refund'** *vt*.	**refrac'ture** *n* and *vt*.
refortificā'tion *n*.	**refoundā'tion** *n*.	**reframe'** *vt*.

■ words derived from main entry word; ❑ compound words; ■ idioms and phrasal verbs

repartition /rē-pär- or rep-ər-tish'ən/ n distribution; /rē-pär-/ a second partition; a division into smaller parts. ◆ vt /rē-pär-/ to partition again or differently. [**re-**]

repass /rē-päs'/ vt and vi to pass again; to pass in the opposite direction. [**re-**]
■ **repassage** /rē-pas'ij/ n.

repast /ri-päst'/ (formal) n a meal; refreshment of sleep (Spenser). ◆ vt and vi (Shakesp) to feed. [OFr repast (Fr repas), from LL repastus, from L pascere, pastum to feed]
■ **repas'ture** n (Shakesp) food.

repatriate /rē-, ri-pā'tri-āt or -pat'/ vt to restore or send (someone) back to his or her own country. ◆ n a repatriated person. [LL repatriāre, -ātum to return to one's country, from L patria]
■ **repatria'tion** n the act or fact of being repatriated; the return of capital, invested abroad, to investment in its country of origin (finance). **repat'riator** n.

repay /rē-pā' or ri-pā'/ vt (**repay'ing**; **repaid'**) to pay back; to make return for; to recompense; to pay or give in return. ◆ vi to make repayment. [**re-**]
■ **repay'able** adj that is to be repaid; due. **repay'ment** n.

repeal /ri-pēl' or -pē'əl/ vt to revoke; to annul; to quash, repress, set aside (Spenser and Milton); to recall from banishment (obs); to try to have restored to favour (Shakesp). ◆ n abrogation; (with cap) dissolution of the Union between Great Britain and Ireland called for by O'Connell (hist). [OFr rapeler, from pfx re-, and apeler to appeal]
■ **repeal'able** adj. **repeal'er** n a person who repeals; (with cap) an advocate of Repeal (hist).

repeat /ri-pēt'/ vt to say, do, perform or go over again; to iterate; to quote from memory; to say off; to recount; to celebrate (Milton); to say or do after another; to tell to others, divulge; to cause to recur; to reproduce; to repeat the words or actions of (reflexive); to seek again (obs); to ask back (obs). ◆ vi to recur; to make repetition; to strike the last hour, quarter, etc when required; to fire several shots without reloading; to rise so as to be tasted after swallowing; to vote (illegally) more than once (US). ◆ n a repetition; a retracing of one's course; a passage repeated or marked for repetition (music); dots or other mark directing repetition; a unit of a repeated pattern; an order for more goods of the same kind; a radio or television programme broadcast for the second, third, etc time. ◆ adj done or occurring as a repetition. [Fr répéter, from L repetere, repitītum, from re- again, and petere to seek]
■ **repeatabil'ity** n. **repeat'able** adj able to be done again; fit to be told to others. **repeat'ed** adj done again; reiterated. **repeat'edly** adv many times repeated; again and again. **repeat'er** n someone or something that repeats, or does a thing that he, she or it has done before; a decimal fraction in which the same figure (or sometimes figures) is repeated to infinity; a watch, clock or firearm that repeats; a ship that repeats an admiral's signals; an instrument for automatically retransmitting a message (telegraphy); a thermionic amplifier inserted in a telephone circuit (also **repeating coil**) or in a cable. **repeat'ing** n and adj.
❑ **repeat purchasing** n (marketing) the buying of products that are used frequently, such as newspapers or bread.
■ **repeat oneself** to say again what one has said already.

repechage /rep'ə-shäzh or (Fr) rə-pe-shäzh'/ (sport, esp rowing and fencing) n a supplementary heat or competition giving competitors eliminated in the first heat or earlier competitions a second chance to go on to the final (also adj). [Fr repêchage a fishing out again]

repel /ri- or rə-pel'/ vt (**repell'ing**; **repelled'**) to drive off or back; to repulse; to reject; to hold off; to provoke aversion in; to repudiate. [L repellere, from pellere to drive]
■ **repell'ence** or **repell'ency**, also **repell'ance** or **repell'ancy** n. **repell'ent**, also **repell'ant** adj driving back; able or tending to repel; distasteful. ◆ n anything that repels. **repell'ently**, also **repell'antly** adv. **repell'er** n. **repell'ing** adj. **repell'ingly** adv.

repent[1] /ri-pent'/ vi to regret, be sorry for, or wish to have been otherwise, what one has done or left undone (with of); to change from past evil or misconduct; to feel contrition; to sorrow (Spenser). ◆ vt (reflexive or impers) to affect with contrition or with regret (archaic); to regret or feel contrition for (an action). ◆ n (Spenser) repentance. [OFr repentir, from L paenitēre to cause to repent]
■ **repent'ance** n the act of repenting; the state of being penitent. **repent'ant** adj experiencing or expressing repentance. ◆ n (rare) a penitent. **repent'antly** adv. **repent'er** n. **repent'ingly** adv.

repent[2] /rē'pənt/ (bot) adj lying on the ground and rooting (also **rep'tant**). [L repēns, -entis, prp of repere to creep]

repercuss /rē-pər-kus'/ vt (obs, or now inf) to drive back, reflect, reverberate or have consequences. [L repercutere, -cussum, from re-, per and quatere to strike]
■ **repercussion** /-kush'ən/ n driving back; reverberation; echo; reflection; a return stroke, reaction or consequence. **repercussive** /-kus'iv/ adj driving back; reverberating; echoing; repeated.

repertory /rep'ər-tə-ri/ n a stock of pieces that a person or company is prepared to perform; repertory theatres collectively; a storehouse, repository. [LL repertōrium, from L reperīre to find again, from parere to bring forth]
■ **repertoire** /rep'ər-twär/ n (Fr répertoire) a performer's or company's repertory; a full set of the codes and instructions which a computer can accept and execute (comput).
❑ **repertory theatre** n a theatre with a repertoire of plays and a stock or permanent company of actors, called a **repertory company**.

repetend /rep'i-tend or rep-i-tend'/ n the figure(s) that recur(s) in a recurring decimal number (maths); a recurring note, word, refrain, etc; anything that recurs or is repeated. ◆ adj to be repeated. [L repetendum that which is to be repeated, from L repetere to repeat]

répétiteur /ri-pe-ti-tûr' or (Fr) rā-pā-tē-tœr'/ n a coach, tutor; a person who rehearses opera singers, etc. [Fr; cf **repeat**]

repetition /rep-i-tish'ən or -ə-/ n the act of repeating; recital from memory; a thing repeated; power of repeating a note promptly. [L repetere; see **repeat**]
■ **repeti'tional**, **repeti'tionary** or **repetitious** /-tish'əs/ adj of the nature of, or characterized by, repetition. **repeti'tiously** or **repet'itively** adv. **repeti'tiousness** or **repet'itiveness** n. **repetitive** /ri-pet'i-tiv/ adj iterative; overinclined to repetition.
❑ **repetitive strain** (or **stress**) **injury** n inflammation of the tendons and joints of the hands and lower arms, caused by repeated performance of identical manual operations (abbrev **RSI**).

rephrase /rē-frāz'/ vt to put in different words, usu so as to make more understandable, acceptable, etc. [**re-**]

repine /ri-pīn'/ vi to fret (with at or against); to feel discontent; to murmur. ◆ vt (obs) to lament; to grudge. ◆ n (Shakesp) a repining. [Appar from **pine**[2]]
■ **repine'ment**. **repīn'er** n. **repīn'ing** n and adj. **repīn'ingly** adv.

repique /ri-pēk'/ n at piquet, the winning of thirty points or more from combinations in one's own hand, before play begins. ◆ vt to score a repique against. ◆ vi to score a repique. [Fr repic]

repla see **replum**.

replace /ri- or rē-plās'/ vt to put back; to provide a substitute for; to take the place of, supplant. [**re-**]
■ **replace'able** adj. **replace'ment** n the act of replacing; a person or thing that takes the place of another; the occurrence of a face or faces in the position where the principal figure would have a corner or edge (crystallog); the process by which one mineral gradually forms from another in crystalline form by solution and redeposition (geol). **replac'er** n a substitute.
❑ **replaceable hydrogen** n hydrogen atoms that can be replaced in an acid by metals to form salts.

replant /rē-plänt'/ vt and vi to plant again. ◆ vt to replace surgically (a severed limb, digit, etc). [**re-**]
■ **replanta'tion** n.

replay /rē-plā'/ vt to play again (a game, match, record, recording, etc). ◆ n /rē'plā/ a game or match played again; a recording played again, esp (also **action replay**) of a part of a broadcast game or match, often in slow motion. [**re-**]

replenish /ri-plen'ish/ vt to fill again; to fill completely; to stock abundantly; to people. [OFr replenir, -iss-, from replein full, from L re- again, and plēnus full]
■ **replen'ished** adj (Shakesp) complete, consummate. **replen'isher** n a person who replenishes; an apparatus for maintaining an electric charge. **replen'ishment** n.

replete /ri-plēt'/ adj full; completely filled; filled to satiety; abounding (with with). ◆ vt to fill to repletion. [L replētus, pap of replēre, from plēre to fill]
■ **replete'ness** or **replē'tion** n superabundant fullness; surfeit; fullness of blood (med); plethora.

Some words formed with the prefix **re-**.

refreeze' vt.	**refu'sion** n.	**regrade'** vt.
re'fried adj.	**regath'er** vt and vi.	**regrant'** n and vt.
refur'nish vt and vi.	**regive'** vt.	**regrind'** vt.

---

replevy /ri-plev'i/ (law) vt (**replev'ying**; **replev'ied**) to bail (archaic); to recover, or restore to the owner (goods distrained) upon pledge to try the right in legal proceedings. ◆ n replevin. [OFr replevir, from plevir to pledge]

■ **replev'iable** or **replev'isable** /-i-səb-l/ adj. **replev'in** n replevying; a writ or action in such a case. ◆ vt to recover by replevin (Swift, etc).

replica /rep'li-kə/ n a duplicate, esp one by the original artist; a facsimile; a repeat (music). [Ital, from L replicāre to repeat]

replicate /rep'li-kāt/ vt orig to fold back; to repeat; to make a replica of; to reply. ◆ vi (of molecules of living material) to reproduce molecules identical with themselves. ◆ n /-kit or -kət/ (music) a tone one or more octaves from a given tone; a repetition. ◆ adj /-kit or -kət/ folded back; being a replicate or repetition. [L replicāre, -ātum to fold back, from plicāre to fold]

■ **rep'licant** n (in science fiction) an artificially created or cloned biological creature, esp in human form. **replicā'tion** n a reply; the plaintiff's answer to the defendant's plea; doubling back; copy, reproduction; reverberation, echo (Shakesp). **rep'licative** adj. **rep'licator** n. **rep'licon** n (biol) a part of a DNA molecule replicated from a single origin.

❑ **replication fork** n (biol) the site of simultaneous unwinding of duplex DNA and synthesis of new DNA.

replum /rep'ləm or rē'pləm/ n (pl **rep'la**) a partition in a fruit formed by ingrowth of the placentas, as in Cruciferae. [L replum the upright in the frame of a folding door]

reply /ri-plī'/ vt (**reply'ing**; **replied'**) to say in answer. ◆ vi to answer; to respond in action, as by returning gunfire; to echo; to answer a defendant's plea. ◆ n an answer, response; a replication (Scots law); the answer in a fugue (music). [OFr replier, from L replicāre; see replicate]

■ **repli'er** n.

repo /rē'pō/ (inf) n (pl **rē'pōs**) short form of **repossession**; a repurchase agreement (see under **repurchase**; finance).

■ **rē'pōman** n a person employed to repossess unpaid-for goods.

repoint /rē-point'/ vt to repair (stone or brickwork) by renewing the mortar, etc. [**re-**]

répondez s'il vous plaît /rā-p̄ɔ̄-dā sēl voo ple'/ (Fr) please answer (this invitation) (abbrev **RSVP**).

repone /ri-pōn'/ (Scots law) vt to restore to office or status; to allow a person to defend an action after a decree in absence has been passed against him or her. [L repōnere to put back, from pōnere to put]

report /ri-pōrt' or -pört'/ vt to convey (Spenser); to bring back, as an answer, news or account of anything; to give an account of, esp a formal, official, or requested account; to state in such an account; to relate; to circulate publicly; to transmit as having been said, done or observed; to write down or take notes of, esp for a newspaper or radio or television programme; to lay a charge against; to echo back; (reflexive) to make personal announcement of the presence and readiness of. ◆ vi to make a statement; to write an account of occurrences; to make a formal report; to report oneself; to act as a reporter; (with to) to be responsible to someone or be under their authority. ◆ n a statement of facts; a formal or official statement, such as of results of an investigation or matter referred; a statement on a school pupil's work and behaviour or the like; an account of a matter of news, esp the words of a speech; reporting, testimony (Shakesp); general talk; rumour; hearsay; repute (Bible); explosive noise. [OFr reporter, from L reportāre, from re- back, and portāre to carry]

■ **report'able** adj. **report'age** n journalistic reporting, style or manner; gossip; a documentary presented through pictures (in film or photographs) without comment or written or spoken narrative. **report'edly** adv according to report. **report'er** n a person who reports, esp for a newspaper or legal proceedings. **report'ing** n and adj. **report'ingly** adv (Shakesp) by common report. **reportō'rial** /rep-ər- or -ör-/ adj. **reportō'rially** adv.

❑ **reported speech** n indirect speech. **reported verses** n pl (Fr vers rapportés) verses that combine a number of parallel sentences by collocation of corresponding parts, such as Sidney's 'Virtue, beauty, and speech did strike, wound, charm, My heart, eyes, ears, with wonder, love, delight'. **report program** n (comput) a program designed to search a file and print out an analysis of its data. **report**

stage n the stage at which a parliamentary bill as amended in committee is reported to the House, before the third reading.

repose /ri-pōz'/ vt to lay at rest; to rest (oneself) in confidence (on; archaic); to give rest to, refresh by rest; to place (eg confidence) in a person or thing; to place in trust. ◆ vi to rest; to be still; to rely, place one's trust, be based (with on or upon; archaic). ◆ n rest; quiet; stillness; calm; ease of manner; serenity; restful feeling or effect; a place of rest (Milton). [Fr reposer, from LL repausāre; confused with **reposit**]

■ **repōs'al** (Shakesp **repos'all**, another reading **repōs'ure**) n reposing. **repōsed'** adj calm; settled. **repō'sedly** adv. **repōs'edness** n. **repōse'ful** adj. **repōse'fully** adv.

reposit /ri-poz'it/ vt to lay away, deposit. [L repōnere, repositum to put back, lay aside, from pōnere to put; confused with **repose**]

■ **reposition** /rep-ə-zish'ən/ n replacing; reinstatement (Scot); laying up. **repos'itor** n an instrument for replacing a displaced organ. **repos'itory** n a place or receptacle in which anything is deposited or contained; a collection or museum (now rare); a mart, esp for horses; an abode of souls (archaic); a tomb, sepulchre (archaic); a storehouse, magazine, as of information; a place of accumulation; a confidant.

re-position or **reposition** /rē-pə-zish'ən/ vt to put in a different position. [**re-**]

repossess /rē-pə-zes'/ vt to regain possession of; to take back (goods or property acquired on credit or by hire-purchase) because payment has not been made; to put again in possession. [**re-**]

■ **repossession** /-esh'ən/ n the act of repossessing anything; a property, etc that has been repossessed. **rēpossess'or** n.

repost same as **riposte**.

reposure see under **repose**.

repoussé /rə-poo-sā' or -poo'/ adj (of metal) raised in relief by hammering from behind or within; embossed. ◆ n repoussé work; an article made from this. [Fr, from repousser to push back]

■ **repoussage** /-säzh'/ n. **repoussoir** /rə-poo-swär/ n a figure or object in the foreground of a painted, etc composition intended to draw the viewer's eye into the picture.

repp same as **rep³**.

repr. abbrev: reprint(ed).

repreeve (Shakesp) see **reprieve**.

reprehend /re-pri-hend'/ vt to find fault with; to reprove. [L repraehendere, -hēnsum, from re-, intens, and praehendere to lay hold of]

■ **reprehend'er** n. **reprehensibil'ity** n. **reprehen'sible** adj blameworthy. **reprehen'sibly** adv. **reprehen'sion** n reproof; censure. **reprehen'sive** adj containing reproof; given in reproof. **reprehen'sively** adv. **reprehen'sory** adj.

represent /rep-ri-zent'/ vt to exhibit the image of; to use, or serve, as a symbol for; to stand for; to exhibit, depict, personate, show an image of, by imitative act; to act; to be a substitute, agent, deputy, member of parliament, etc, for; to correspond or be in some way equivalent or analogous to; to serve as a sample of, typify; to present earnestly to mind; to give out, make to appear, allege (that). [L repraesentāre, -ātum, from praesentāre to place before]

■ **representabil'ity** n. **represent'able** /rep-ri-/ adj. **representā'men** n (psychol) the product of representation. **represent'ant** n a representative. **representation** /-zən-tā'shən/ n act, state or fact of representing or being represented; anything which represents; an image; picture; dramatic performance; a mental image; a presentation of a view of facts or arguments; a petition, remonstrance, expostulation; a statement; assumption of succession by an heir (law); a statement by a party entering into a contract that influences the other party's view of the contract, but falls short of being a condition (law); a body of representatives. **representā'tional** /rep-ri-zən-/ adj (esp of art) depicting objects in a realistic rather than an abstract form. **representā'tionalism** n representational art; the doctrine that in the perception of the external world the immediate object represents another object beyond the sphere of consciousness (also **representā'tionism**). **representā'tionist** n and adj. **representative** /rep-ri-zent'ə-tiv/ adj representing; exhibiting a likeness; typical; relating to representation. ◆ n a sample; a typical example or embodiment; a person who represents another or others, as a deputy,

---

Some words formed with the prefix **re-**.

rēgroup' vt and vi.	**rēheel'** vt.	**rēilluminā'tion** n.
rēgrowth' n.	**rēhire'** vt.	**rēillum'ine** vt.
rēhand'le vt.	**rēhome'** vt.	**rēimpose'** vt.
rēhand'ling n.	**rē-ignite'** vt.	**rēimposi'tion** n.
rēhang' vt.	**rēillume'** vt.	**rēincrease'** vt.

■ words derived from main entry word; ❑ compound words; ▪ idioms and phrasal verbs

delegate, ambassador, member of parliament, agent, successor or heir; the head of a family (*Austen*); a representative legislative body (*obs*). **represent'atively** *adv*. **represent'ativeness** *n*. **representee'** *n* (*law*) a person to whom a representation has been made. **represent'er** *n*. **represent'ment** *n*. **represent'or** *n* (*law*) a person who makes a representation in the course of contractual negotiations. ❑ **representative peers** *n pl* Scottish and Irish peers chosen by their fellows to sit in the House of Lords.

■ **House of Representatives** the lower branch of the United States Congress, consisting of members chosen biennially by the people; also of various State and other legislatures.

re-present /rē-pri-zent'/ *vt* to present again. [**re-**]
■ **re'presentā'tion** or **rē'present'ment** *n*.

repress /ri-pres'/ *vt* to restrain; to keep under control; to put down; to exclude from the conscious mind. [L *reprimere, repressum*, from *premere* to press]
■ **repressed'** *adj* having a tendency to repress unacceptable thoughts, feelings, etc. **repress'er** *n*. **repress'ible** *adj*. **repress'ibly** *adv*. **repression** /-presh'ən/ *n*. **repress'ive** *adj*. **repress'ively** *adv*. **repress'iveness** *n*. **repress'or** *n* someone or something that represses; a protein which binds to an operator site and prevents transcription of the associated gene (*biol*).

re-press /rē-pres'/ *vt* to press again. [**re-**]

repriefe /ri-prēf'/ (*Spenser*) *n* reproach, insult, shame, reproof. [Same root as **reproof**; for vowel see **prove**]
■ **reprieve** /-prēv'/ *vt* to reprove.

reprieve /ri-prēv'/ (*Shakesp*) **repreeve** /-prēv'/; *Spenser* **reprive** or **repryve** /-prīv'/) *vt* to delay the execution of; to give a respite to; to rescue, redeem. ◆ *n* a suspension of a criminal sentence, *esp* a death sentence; interval of ease or relief. [Supposed to be from Anglo-Fr *repris*, pap of *reprendre* to take back (see **reprise**); the *v* appar by confusion, perh with **reprieve** reprove]
■ **repriev'al** *n*.

reprimand /rep'ri-mänd or -mand/ *n* a severe reproof. ◆ *vt* (also /-mänd' or -mand'/) to reprove severely, *esp* publicly or officially. [Fr *réprimande*, from L *reprimere, repressum* to press back, from *premere* to press]

reprime /ri-prīm'/ (*rare*) *vt* to repress. [See **repress**]

reprint /rē-print'/ *vt* to print again; to print a new impression of, *esp* with little or no change. ◆ *vi* to be reprinted. ◆ *n* /rē'/ the act of reprinting; a later impression (of eg a book); printed matter used as copy. [**re-**]
■ **reprint'er** *n*.

reprise (*Spenser* **reprize**) /ri-prīz', now *usu* -prēz'/ *vt* to renew, repeat, reissue; to gain anew (*obs*); to recapture (*obs*). ◆ *n* a renewed or alternating spell of action; resumption of an earlier subject (*music*; also *vt*); a yearly charge or deduction; reprisal (*Dryden*). [Fr *reprise*, from *reprendre*, from L *repraehendere*]
■ **reprīs'al** *n* an act of retaliation; recapture; compensation; seizure in retaliation; a prize (*Shakesp*).

reprivatize or **-ise** /rē-prī'və-tīz/ *vt* to return (a company, etc) to private ownership. [**re-**]
■ **rēprivatizā'tion** or **-s-** *n*.

reprive (*Spenser*) see **reprieve**.

repro /rē'prō or rep'rō/ *n* and *adj* short form of **reproduction**, *esp* designating modern copies of period styles of furniture. ◆ *n* /rē'prō/ (*pl* **re'pros**) short for **reproduction proof**.

reproach /ri-prōch'/ *vt* to upbraid, rebuke; to blame (oneself, etc; with *for* or *with*); to reprove gently; to bring into discredit; to cast (something) in someone's teeth (with *to, against*, also *on*; *Dryden*, etc). ◆ *n* upbraiding; reproof; censure; disgrace; a source or matter of disgrace or shame. [Fr *reprocher*, perh from L *prope* near; cf **approach**; or from *reprobāre*; see **reprobate**]
■ **reproach'able** *adj*. **reproach'er** *n*. **reproach'ful** *adj* reproving; deserving of reproach, disgraceful (*obs*). **reproach'fully** *adv*. **reproach'fulness** *n*. **reproach'less** *adj* irreproachable.
■ **above** or **beyond reproach** excellent, too good to be criticized. **the Reproaches** antiphons chanted in Roman Catholic churches on Good Friday, in which Christ reproaches the Jewish people.

reprobate /rep'rə- or rep'rō-bāt/ *n* a dissolute or profligate person; someone lost to shame; a villain or rogue; (often *joc*) a scamp; a person rejected by God. ◆ *adj* given over to sin; depraved; unprincipled; base; rejected by God; condemnatory; failing to pass a test (*esp* of silver) (*archaic*). ◆ *vt* to reject; to disapprove of; to censure; to disown (*obs*). [L *reprobāre, -ātum* to reprove, contrary of *approbāre*, from *probāre* to prove]
■ **rep'robacy** /-bə-si/ *n* state of being a reprobate. **rep'robance** *n* (*Shakesp*) reprobation. **rep'robāter** *n*. **reprobā'tion** *n* the act of reprobating; rejection; predestination to eternal damnation; utter abandonment; severe censure or condemnation. **rep'robātive** or **rep'robatory** *adj* condemnatory. **rep'robātor** *n* (*Scots law*) an action to prove a witness perjured or biased.

reprocess /rē-prō'ses/ *vt* to process again, *esp* to remake used material, eg spent nuclear fuel, into a new material or article (see **fuel reprocessing** under **fuel**). [**re-**]

reproduce /rē-prə-dūs'/ *vt* to produce a copy of; to form again or afresh; to propagate; to reconstruct in imagination. ◆ *vi* to produce offspring; to prove suitable for copying in some way; to turn out (well, badly, etc) when copied. [**re-**]
■ **reprodū'cer** *n*. **reprodū'cible** *adj*. **reproduction** /-duk'shən/ *n* the act of reproducing; the act of producing new organisms, ie the whole process whereby life is continued from generation to generation; regeneration; a copy, facsimile; a representation. ◆ *adj* (of furniture, etc) copied from an original piece. **reproduc'tive** *adj*. **reproduc'tively** *adv*. **reproduc'tiveness** or **reproductiv'ity** *n*.
❑ **reproduction proof** *n* (*printing*) a high-quality proof made from strips of typeset copy and photographed to produce a plate for printing from (often shortened to **repro proof** or **repro**).

reprography /ri-prog'rə-fi/ *n* the reproduction of graphic or typeset material, eg by photocopying. [Fr *reprographie*]
■ **reprog'rapher** *n*. **reprograph'ic** *adj*. **reprograph'ically** *adv*.

reproof /ri-proof'/ *n* a reproving; rebuke; censure; reprehension; shame, disgrace (*Shakesp*); disproof (*obs*); /rē-/ a second or new proof. ◆ *vt* /rē-/ to make waterproof again. [OFr *reprover* (Fr *réprouver*), from L *reprobāre* ; see **reprobate**]
■ **reprovable** /ri-proo'və-bl/ *adj*. **repro'val** *n* reproof. **repro've** *vt* to rebuke; to censure, condemn; to disprove or refute (*obs*); to accuse or convict (of; *Bible*, Authorized Version). **repro'ver** *n*. **repro'ving** *adj*. **repro'vingly** *adv*.

repryve see **reprieve**.

reps /reps/ see **rep³**.

rept *abbrev* : receipt; report.

reptant see **repent²** and **reptation**.

reptation /rep-tā'shən/ *n* the act of squirming along or up a smooth-walled narrow passage. [L *reptāre* to creep]
■ **rep'tant** *adj* (*old biol*) creeping.

reptile /rep'tīl/ *n* any animal of the **Reptilia** /-til'i-ə/, a class of cold-blooded scaly vertebrates that breathe through lungs and typically lay eggs on land; a creeping thing; a base, malignant, abject or treacherous person. ◆ *adj* creeping; like a reptile in nature. [LL *reptilis, -e*, from *repere* to creep]
■ **reptilian** /-til'i-ən/ or **rep'tiloid** *adj* and *n*. **reptil'ianly** *adv*. **reptilif'erous** *adj* (of rock) bearing fossil reptiles. **reptil'ious** *adj* like a reptile.

republic /ri-pub'lik/ *n* a form of government without a monarch, in which the supreme power is vested in the people and their elected representatives; a state or country so governed; the state (*archaic*). [L *rēspublica* commonwealth, from *rēs* affair, and *publica* (fem) public]
■ **repub'lican** *adj* of or favouring a republic; (with *cap*) of the Republican party. ◆ *n* a person who advocates a republican form of government; (with *cap*) in USA, *orig* an Anti-Federal, now a member of the political party opposed to the Democrats, and favouring an extension of the powers of the national government; (with *cap*) in Northern Ireland, a person who advocates the union of Northern Ireland and the Republic of Ireland. **repub'licanism** *n*. **repub'licanize** or **-ise** *vt*.

Some words formed with the prefix **re-**.

rēindustrializā'tion or **rēindustrialīsā'tion** *n*.	**rēinhab'it** *vt*.	**rēinspec'tion** *n*.
rēindus'trialize or **rēindus'trialise** *vt* and *vi*.	**rēin'jure** *vt*.	**rēinspire'** *vt*.
	rēinsert' *vt*.	**rēinspir'it** *vt*.
rēinfuse' *vt*.	**rēinser'tion** *n*.	**rēinter'** *vt*.
	rēinspect' *vt*.	**rēinter'ment** *n*.

❑ **Republican era** n the era adopted by the French after the downfall of the monarchy, beginning with 22 September 1792. **republic of letters** n the world of books and authors.

repudiate /ri-pū'di-āt/ vt to cast off, disown; to refuse or cease to acknowledge (debt, authority, claim, etc); to deny as unfounded (a charge, etc); (of a husband) to divorce (archaic). [L repudiāre, -ātum, from repudium divorce, from re- away, and the root of pudēre to be ashamed]

■ **repū'diable** adj. **repūdiā'tion** n. **repūdiā'tionist** n a person who favours repudiation of public debt. **repū'diative** adj. **repū'diātor** n.

repugn /ri-pūn'/ vt to fight against, to oppose (Shakesp); to be repugnant to (archaic). ◆ vi (archaic) to be repugnant. [L repugnāre, from re- against, and pugnāre to fight]

■ **repugnance** /ri-pug'nəns/ n aversion; inconsistency. **repug'nancy** n repugnance (now chiefly law); opposition (Shakesp). **repug'nant** adj distasteful; disgusting; inconsistent with (with to); (of things) incompatible; resisting, unwilling (archaic). **repug'nantly** adv.

repulse /ri-puls'/ vt to drive back; to beat off; to rebuff, reject; to cause aversion. ◆ n a driving back; a beating off; a check; a refusal; a rebuff. [L repulsus, pap of repellere, from re- back, and pellere to drive]

■ **repulsion** /-pul'shən/ n driving off; a repelling force, action or influence; driving force, effect or influence; action or effect; raison d'être. **repul'sive** adj that repulses or drives off; repelling; cold, reserved, forbidding; causing aversion and disgust. **repul'sively** adv. **repul'siveness** n.

repunit /rep'ū-nit/ (maths) n a number consisting of two or more identical integers, eg 22, 333. [repeating unit]

repurchase /rē-pûr'chəs/ vt to purchase again, buy back (also n). [re-] ❑ **repurchase agreement** n (finance) one in which a seller of bonds, etc undertakes to buy them back after an agreed period.

repurify /rē-pū'ri-fī/ or **repure** /ri-pūr'/ vt to purify again; to refine thoroughly. [re-]

repurpose /rē-pûr'pəs/ vt to find a new application for. [re-]

repute /ri-pūt'/ vt (also (archaic) vi with of) to account, deem. ◆ n general opinion or impression; attributed character; widespread or high estimation; fame. [L reputāre, -ātum, from putāre to reckon]

■ **reputable** /rep'ūt-ə-bl/ adj in good repute; respectable; honourable; consistent with reputation. **rep'ūtably** adv. **repūtā'tion** /rep-/ n repute; estimation; character generally ascribed; good report; fame; good name. **rep'ūtative** adj reputed; putative. **rep'ūtatively** adv by repute. **reputed** /ri-pūt'id/ adj supposed, reckoned to be such; of repute. **repūt'edly** adv in common repute or estimation. **repute'less** adj (Shakesp) without good repute. **reput'ing** n (Shakesp) pluming oneself.

❑ **reputed owner** n a person who has to all appearance the title to the property. **reputed pint** or **quart** n that which is commonly called a pint or quart though not necessarily of legal standard (sometimes as little as half the legal amount).

requere /ri-kwēr'/ (Spenser) vt to require.

request /ri-kwest'/ n the asking of a favour; a petition; a favour asked for; the state of being sought after. ◆ vt to ask as a favour; to ask politely; to ask for. [OFr requeste (Fr requête), from L requīsītum, pap of requīrere, from re- away, and quaerere to seek]

■ **request'er** n.

❑ **request note** n an application for a permit to remove excisable goods. **request stop** n a bus stop at which a bus will stop only if signalled to do so.

■ **Court of Requests** a former English court of equity, abolished 1641; a local small debt court, superseded by the County Court (also called **Court of Conscience**). **on request** if, or when, requested.

requicken /rē-kwik'(ə)n/ (Shakesp) vt to give new life to. [re-]

requiem /rek'wi-əm or rē'kwi-əm/ n a mass for the rest of the soul of the dead; music for it; any music of similar character; rest (obs). [L, accusative of requiēs, from re-, intens, and quiēs rest; first word of the introit]

❑ **requiem shark** n any of the large voracious, chiefly tropical, sharks of the family Carcharhinidae.

requiescat /re-kwi-es'kat/ n a prayer for the rest of the soul of the dead. [L, third pers sing subjunctive of requiescere]

■ **requiescat in pace** /in pä'sē, pä'chä or pä'ke/ may he or she rest in peace (abbrev **RIP**).

requight a Spenserian spelling of **requite**.

require /ri-kwīr'/ vt to demand, exact; to direct (a person to do something); to call for, necessitate; to request (archaic); to ask for (obs); to ask (someone) a question (obs). ◆ vi to ask. [L requīrere; partly through OFr requerre, later assimilated to L]

■ **requir'able** adj. **required'** adj compulsory as part of a curriculum. **require'ment** n a need; a thing needed; a necessary condition; a demand. **requir'er** n. **requir'ing** n.

requisite /rek'wi-zit/ adj required; needed; indispensable. ◆ n that which is required, necessary or indispensable. [L requīsītus, pap of requīrere; see **require**]

■ **req'uisitely** adv. **req'uisiteness** n. **requisi'tion** n the act of requiring; a formal demand or request; a formal call for the doing of something that is due; a demand for the supply of anything for military purposes; a written order for the supply of materials; the state of being in use or service. ◆ vt to demand a requisition from; to demand or take by requisition; to seize; to call in; to press into service. **requisi'tionary** adj. **requisi'tionist** or **requis'itor** n a person who makes a requisition. **requis'itory** adj.

requite /ri-kwīt'/ vt (pat **requit'ed** (Spenser **requit'**); pap **requit'ed** (Shakesp **requit'** or **requitt'ed**)) to repay (an action); to avenge; to repay (a person, for); to retaliate on; to counterbalance, compensate for (obs). ◆ n (rare) requital. [re- and **quit**]

■ **requit** /-kwit'/ vt (pap (Shakesp) **requitt'ed**) (obs) to requite. ◆ n (Burns) requital. **requi'table** adj. **requi'tal** n the act of requiting; payment in return; recompense; reward. **requite'ful** adj. **requite'less** adj without requital, free. **requite'ment** n. **requi'ter** n.

requoyle a Shakespearean spelling of **recoil**.

reradiate /rē-rā'di-āt/ vt to radiate again, esp as a result of having absorbed an amount of radiation previously. [re-]

■ **reradiā'tion** n.

rerail /rē-rāl'/ vt to replace on the rails. [re-]

rere- /rēr-/ combining form same as **rear**[1].

■ **rere'-arch** or **rear'-arch** n an arch supporting the inner part of a wall's thickness, as in a splayed window. **rere'brace** /-brās/ n (Fr bras arm) armour for the arm from shoulder to elbow. **rere'dorse**, **rere'dosse** or **rere'dos** n (L dorsum, Fr dos back) a screen or panelling behind an altar or seat; a choirscreen; the back of a fireplace (archaic). **rere'dorter** n (hist) a lavatory built behind a monastic dormitory. **rere'-supper** n a late meal, after supper. **rere'ward** adj rearward.

reread /rē-rēd'/ vt (pat and pap **re'read'** /-red'/) to read again. [re-]

rerun /rē-run'/ vt to run (a race, etc) again; to broadcast (a radio or television series) again (also fig). ◆ n /rē'run/ an instance of rerunning. [re-]

RES abbrev : Royal Economic Society.

res or **rez** /rez/ (US inf) short form of (Native American) **reservation** (see under **reserve**).

res. abbrev : research; reserve; residence; resolution.

resale /rē'sāl or rē-sāl'/ n the selling again of an article. [re-]

■ **resale price maintenance** the setting of a fixed minimum price on an article by the manufacturer (abbrev **RPM**).

resalgar /re-sal'gər/ obsolete variant of **realgar**.

resat see **resit**.

re-scale or **rescale** /rē-skāl'/ vt to plan or form on a new (usu reduced) scale. [re-]

reschedule /rē-shed'ūl or -sked'/ vt to schedule again; to arrange a new time or timetable for; to rearrange (a debt-repayment programme) usu to alleviate liquidity problems (econ). [re-]

■ **resched'uling** n.

rescind /ri-sind'/ vt to cut away; to annul, abrogate. [L rescindere, rescissum, from rē back, and scindere to cut]

■ **rescind'able** adj. **rescission** /-sizh'ən/ or **rescind'ment** n abrogation; cutting off (obs). **rescissory** /-sis'ər-i/ adj annulling.

rescore /rē-skōr' or -skör'/ vt to rewrite a musical score for different instruments, voices, etc. [re-]

rescript /rē'skript/ n the official answer of a pope or an emperor to any legal question; an edict or decree; a rewriting. ◆ vt to rewrite. [L rescrīptum, from re-, and scrībere, scrīptum to write]

rescue /res'kū/ (**res'cuing**; **res'cued**) to free from danger, captivity or evil plight; to deliver forcibly from legal custody; to recover by force. ◆ n the act of rescuing; deliverance from danger or evil; forcible

---

Some words formed with the prefix **re-**.

reinter'pret vt.	**reinterr'ogate** vt.	**reintroduc'tion** n.
reinterpretā'tion n.	**reinterrogā'tion** n.	**reinvolve'** vt.
reinter'pretative adj.	**reintroduce'** vt.	**reiss'uable** adj.

■ words derived from main entry word; ❑ compound words; ■ idioms and phrasal verbs

recovery; forcible release from arrest or imprisonment; relief of a besieged place; a beach-rescue; a rescuer or rescuing party (*archaic*); a person or thing rescued; a bid (**rescue bid**) to bring one's partner out of a dangerous situation (*bridge*). [OFr *rescourre*, from L *re-* and *excutere*, from *ex* out, and *quatere* to shake]

■ **res'cuable** *adj.* **res'cuer** *n.*
❑ **rescue cat** (or **dog**) a domestic cat (or dog) that has been officially taken away from an abusive or neglectful owner. **Rescue Remedy**® *n* a combination of five Bach remedies, used for its calming effect.

rescue-grass /res'kū-gräs/ *n* a S American brome-grass, *Bromus catharticus*. [Origin unknown]

research /ri-sûrch' or rē'sûrch/ *n* a careful search; investigation; systematic investigation towards increasing the sum of knowledge. ◆ *vi* and *vt* to make researches (into or concerning). [Obs Fr *recerche* (Mod Fr *recherche*); see **search**[1]]
■ **research'able** *adj.* **research'er** *n.* **research'ful** *adj.*
■ **research and development** the process of investigating the need for new or better products and the means of producing them.

re-search /rē-sûrch'/ *vt* to search again. [**re-**]

reseat /rē-sēt'/ *vt* to seat in a different place; to return to a former position or office; to renew the seat of (a chair, etc); to provide (a theatre, etc) with new seats. [**re-**]

réseau /rā-zō'/ *n* (*pl* **réseaux** /rā-zō'/ or **réseaus** /rā-zōz'/) a fine-meshed ground for lacework; a network of lines for reference in star-photographs. [Fr, network]

resect /ri-sekt'/ *vt* to cut away part of, *esp* the end of a bone. [L *resecāre*, *-sectum* to cut off, from *secāre* to cut]
■ **resection** /-sek'shən/ *n* cutting away, *esp* bone (*surg*); a positional fix of a point by sighting it from three or more known stations (*surveying*). **resec'tional** *adj.*

Reseda /res'i-də or ri-sē'də/ *n* the mignonette genus, giving name to the family **Resedā'ceae**; /re'/ (without *cap*) a pale green colour (often as Fr **réséda** /rā-zā-dā/; also *adj*). [L *resēda*, said to be from *resēdā morbīs* assuage diseases, first words of a charm used in applying it as a poultice]

reseize /rē-sēz'/ (*Spenser*) *vt* to reinstate. [**re-** and **seise**]

resemble /ri-zem'bl/ *vt* to be like; to compare (*archaic*); to depict (*obs*). ◆ *vi* to be like each other; to be like (with *to*; *archaic*). [OFr *resembler* (Fr *ressembler*), from *re-* again, and *sembler* to seem, from L *simulāre* to make like, from *similis* like]
■ **resem'blance** *n* likeness; appearance; an image. **resem'blant** *adj.* **resem'bler** *n.* **resem'bling** *adj.*

resent /ri-zent'/ *vt* to take in, consider as an injury or affront; to feel anger, bitterness or ill-will towards (a person or thing); to feel joy or sorrow because of (*obs*); to receive (a person), well or badly (*obs*). ◆ *vt* (*obs*) to savour (of). [OFr *ressentir*, from L *re-* in return, and *sentīre* to feel]
■ **resent'er** *n.* **resent'ful** *adj.* **resent'fully** *adv.* **resent'ingly** *adv.* **resent'ive** *adj.* **resent'ment** *n.*

reserpine /ri-sûr', ri-zûr'pin or -pēn/ *n* a drug obtained from *Rauwolfia serpentina*, formerly used against high blood pressure and as a tranquillizer.

reserve /ri-zûrv'/ *vt* to hold back; to save up, *esp* for a future occasion or special purpose; to keep, retain; to preserve; to spare; to set apart; to book, engage. ◆ *n* the keeping of something reserved; state of being reserved; that which is reserved; a reservation; a reserved store or stock; a reserve price; a tract of land reserved for a special purpose; a public park (*Aust and NZ*); in Canada, a Native American reservation; a substitute kept in readiness (*sport*); (*esp* in *pl*) a military force kept out of action until occasion serves; (*esp* in *pl*) a force not *usu* serving but liable to be called up when required; (*often pl*) resources of physical or spiritual nature available in abnormal circumstances; part of assets kept readily available for ordinary demands; (*usu* in *pl*) an unexploited quantity of a mineral (*esp* oil, gas or coal) calculated to exist in a given area; (in *pl*) amounts of gold and foreign currencies held by a country; (in *pl*) elements of equity other than the face value of share capital (*account*); artistic restraint; restrained manner; reticence; aloofness; a secret information withheld (*archaic*); limitation, restriction; a mental reservation. ◆ *adj* kept in reserve; of a reserve or reserves. [OFr *reserver*, from L *reservāre*, from *re-* back, and *servāre* to save]

■ **reserv'able** *adj.* **reservā'tion** /rez-/ *n* the act of reserving or keeping back, or keeping for oneself; an expressed or tacit proviso, limiting condition, or exception; something withheld; a tract of public land reserved for some special purpose, eg for preserving game, forest, etc; in the USA, an area of land set aside by treaty for the use of a particular Native American tribe or group; the Pope's retention to himself of the right to nominate to a benefice; a limitation; the booking of a seat, room, passage, etc; a booked seat, room, etc; the strip of grass, etc between the two roads of a dual carriageway; a clause of a deed by which a person reserves for himself or herself a right, interest, etc in a property he or she is granting, as that of ordinary rent (*law*); the act of reserving such a right or interest (*law*). **reservatory** /ri-zûrv'ə-tər-i/ *n* (*obs*) a receptacle; a reservoir. **reserved'** *adj* reticent; uncommunicative; aloof in manner; booked; having the original colour of the surface or background (*ceramics*). **reserv'edly** *adv.* **reservedness** /ri-zûrvd'nis/ *n.* **reserv'er** *n.* **reserv'ist** *n* a member of a reserve force.
❑ **reserve bank** *n* any of the US Federal Reserve banks; a central bank holding reserves for other banks (*esp Aust* and *NZ*). **reserve currency** *n* any stable and easily convertible foreign currency that a government holds in its foreign exchange reserves and uses to finance a large part of its international trade. **reserved list** *n* a list of retired officers in the armed services who may be recalled for active service in the event of war. **reserved occupation** *n* employment of national importance that exempts from service in the armed forces. **reserved word** *n* (*comput*) a word with a specific use in a programming language that cannot therefore be used as an identifier, etc. **reserve grade** *n* (*Aust*) a sporting competition of the second division or rank. **reserve price** *n* the minimum price acceptable to the vendor of an article for sale or auction. **reserve ratio** *n* (*econ*) the government-imposed minimum ratio that must be maintained by a bank between its total deposit liabilities and the cash reserves it retains with the central bank.
■ **judgement reserved** see under **judge**. **mental reservation** a reservation made mentally but not openly expressed. **reservation of the sacrament** the practice of reserving part of the consecrated bread of the Eucharist for the communion of the sick. **without reserve** frankly, not holding back any information; fully, without reservation; without restrictions or stipulations regarding sale; without a reserve price.

re-serve /rē-sûrv'/ *vt* to serve again. [**re-**]

reservoir /rez'ər-vwär or -vwör/ *n* a receptacle; a store; a receptacle for fluids, *esp* a large basin, artificial lake or tank for storing water. ◆ *vt* to store. [Fr]
❑ **reservoir rock** *n* porous rock containing producible oil and/or gas.

reset[1] /rē-set'/ *vt* to set again. [**re-**]
■ **resett'er** *n.*

reset[2] /ri-set'/ (*Scot*) *vt* and *vi* to receive (stolen goods) knowingly; to harbour (*archaic*). ◆ *n* /rē'/ receiving of stolen goods; harbouring of a proscribed person (*archaic*). [OFr *recet(t)er*, from L *receptāre*, from *recipere* to receive]
■ **resett'er** *n.*

res extincta /rāz eks-tingk'tə/ (*law*) the thing does not exist, ie the subject matter of a contract no longer exists or had never existed when it was drawn up, and therefore no contract will ensue. [L]

res gestae /rēz jes'tē or räs ges'tī/ (*L*) *n pl* exploits; facts relevant to the case and admissible in evidence (*law*).

resh /räsh/ *n* the twentieth letter of the Hebrew alphabet. [Heb]

reshoot /rē-shoot'/ *vt* to photograph (a film scene, etc) for a second time. ◆ *n* /rē'/ a film scene, etc that has been reshot; the act of reshooting. [**re-**]

reshuffle /rē-shuf'l/ *vt* to shuffle again; to rearrange, *esp* cabinet or government posts. ◆ *n* /rē'shuf-l/ an instance of reshuffling. [**re-**]

resiant /rez'i-ənt or -ant/ (*obs* or *archaic*) *adj* and *n* resident. [OFr *reseant*, prp of *reseoir*, from L *residēre*]
■ **res'iance** *n* (*obs* or *archaic*).

reside /ri-zīd'/ *vi* to make one's home permanently; to be in residence; to abide; to be vested; to inhere. [L *residēre*, from *re-* back, and *sedēre* to sit]
■ **residence** /rez'i-dəns/ *n* the act or duration of dwelling in a place; the act of living in the place required by regulations or performance of functions; a stay in a place; a dwelling-place; a dwelling-house, *esp* one of some pretensions; that in which anything permanently inheres

Some words formed with the prefix re-.

rēiss'ue *vt* and *n.*	**rēkin'dle** *vt* and *vi.*	**rēlight'** *vt* and *vi.*
rējudge' *vt.*	**rēlearn'** *vt.*	**rēload'** *vt* and *vi.*
rēkey' *vt.*	**rēlet'** *vt.*	**rēman'** *vt.*

or has its seat. **res'idency** *n* a residence; the official abode of a resident or governor of a protected state; an administrative district under a resident; a resident's post at a hospital, or the period during which it is held; a band's or singer's regular or permanent engagement at a venue. **res'ident** *adj* dwelling in a place for some time; residing on one's own estate, or the place of one's duties, or the place required by certain conditions; (of computer files, programs, etc) stored in the permanent memory; not migratory; not moving (*obs*); inherent. ◆ *n* a person who resides; an animal that does not migrate; a doctor who works in, and *usu* resides at, a hospital to gain experience in a particular field; a registered guest at a hotel; a representative at a foreign court of lower rank than an ambassador (*hist*); a representative of a governor in a protected state; the governor of a residency or administrative district (*esp* in the former Dutch East Indies). **res'identer** (or (*Scot*) **/-dent'/**) *n* an inhabitant. **residential** /-den'shl/ *adj* of, for, or connected with residence; suitable for or occupied by houses, *esp* of a better kind. **residen'tially** *adv*. **residentiary** /-den'shə-ri/ *adj* resident; officially bound to reside; relating to or involving official residence. ◆ *n* an inhabitant; a person bound to reside, such as a canon. **residen'tiaryship** *n*. **res'identship** *n*. **resi'der** *n*.
❑ **resident commissioner** *n* a representative from a dependency who is allowed to speak but not vote in the US House of Representatives. **residential school** *n* (*Can*) a boarding school.

residue /rez'i-dū or US also -doo/ *n* that which is left, remainder; what is left of an estate after payment of debts, charges and legacies (*law*). [L *residuum*, from *residēre* to remain behind]
■ **resid'ual** *adj* remaining as residue or difference; formed by accumulations of rock waste where the rock has disintegrated (*geol*). ◆ *n* that which remains as a residue or as a difference; a payment to an artist, etc for later use of a film, etc in which he or she appears. **resid'ually** *adv*. **resid'uary** *adj* of, or of the nature of, a residue, *esp* of an estate. **resid'uous** *adj* (*rare*) residual. **residuum** /rə-zij'ū-əm, -wəm or rez-id'ū-əm/ *n* (*pl* **resid'ua**) a residue.
❑ **residual activity** *n* in a nuclear reactor, the activity remaining after the reaction is shut down following a period of operation. **residual current device** *n* a circuit breaker used to protect electrical equipment or its operator. **residual value** *n* (*finance*) the expected selling price of an asset at the end of its useful life.

resign /ri-zīn'/ *vt* to give up (one's position, employment, etc); to yield up; to submit calmly; to relinquish (often with *from*); to entrust. ◆ *vi* to give up office, employment, etc; to submit (*rare*). [OFr *resigner*, from L *resignāre, -ātum* to unseal, annul, from *signāre* to seal, from *signum* a mark]
■ **resignation** /rez-ig-nā'shən/ *n* the act of resigning; a document stating one's intention to resign; the state of being resigned or quietly submissive; the form by which a vassal returns the feu into the hands of a superior (*Scots law*). **resigned** /ri-zīnd'/ *adj* calmly submissive. **resignedly** /ri-zīn'id-li/ *adv*. **resign'edness** *n*. **resign'er** *n*. **resign'ment** *n*.

re-sign /rē-sīn'/ *vt* to sign again; to engage for a further period. ◆ *vi* to commit to engagement for a further period. [**re-**]

resile /ri-zīl'/ *vi* to recoil; to rebound; to recover form and position elastically; to draw back from a statement, agreement or course of action; to back out (*esp Scot*). [L *resilīre* to leap back, from *salīre* to leap]

resilient /ri-zil'i-ənt/ *adj* recoiling, rebounding; able to recover form and position elastically; able to withstand shock, suffering, disappointment, etc. [L *resiliēns, -entis*, prp of *resilīre*; see **resile**]
■ **resilience** /ri-zil'i-əns/ or **resil'iency** *n* recoil; the quality of being resilient. **resil'iently** *adv*.

resin /rez'in/ *n* any of a number of substances or products obtained from the sap of certain plants and trees (**natural resins**), used in plastics, etc; any of a large number of substances made by polymerization or condensation (**synthetic resins**) which, though not related chemically to natural resins, have some of their physical properties, very important in the plastics industry, etc. ◆ *vt* to treat with resin; to remove resin from; to rosin. [Fr *résine*, from L *rēsīna*]
■ **res'inate** *n* a salt of any of the acids occurring in natural resins. ◆ *vt* to impregnate with resin. **res'iner** *n* a resin gatherer. **resinif'erous** *adj* yielding resin. **resinifica'tion** *n*. **res'inify** *vt* and *vi* to make or become a resin or resinous. **res'inize** or **-ise** *vt* to treat with resin. **res'inoid** *n* and *adj* (a substance) of, like or containing resin. **resinō'sis** *n* abnormal flow of resin. **res'inous** *adj* of, like, containing or of the

nature of resin; of the lustre of resin; negative (as produced by rubbing a resin) (*electronics*; *obs*). **res'inously** *adv*.

resinata /re-zi-nä'tə/ *n* Greek white wine with resinous flavour. [L *rēsīnāta* (fem) resined]

resipiscence /re-si-pis'əns/ *n* recognition of error, change to a better frame of mind (also **resipisc'ency**). [L *resipīscentia*, from *resipīscere*, from *re-* again, and *sapere* to be wise]
■ **resipisc'ent** *adj*.

res ipsa loquitur /rēz ip'sə lok'wi-tər or (L) rās ip'sə lok'wi-tŭr/ (*law*) the thing speaks for itself, applied in cases in which the mere fact that an accident has happened is deemed to be evidence of negligence unless the defendant proves otherwise.

resist /ri-zist'/ *vt* to strive against, oppose; to withstand; to refuse; to hinder the action of; to be little affected by; to be distasteful to (*Shakesp*). ◆ *vi* to make opposition. ◆ *n* a protective coating, *esp* one on parts of a textile to protect the blank areas of the design that is being printed, an acid-proof coating on parts of a metal plate, or a light-sensitive coating on a silicon wafer (also *adj*). [L *resistere*, from *re-* against, and *sistere* to make to stand]
■ **resis'tance** *n* the act or power of resisting; opposition; the body's ability to resist disease; (with *cap*) an organization of (armed) opposition to an occupying enemy force, *esp* that of the French in World War II (also **resistance movement**); the opposition of a body to the motion of another; that property of a substance in virtue of which the passage of an electric current through it is accompanied with a dissipation of energy; an electrical resistor. **resis'tant** *n* someone or something that resists. ◆ *adj* (less *usu* **resis'tent**) making resistance; (eg of parasites, germs, antibiotics, corrosion) withstanding adverse conditions. **resis'ter** *n* a person who resists. **resistibil'ity** *n*. **resis'tible** *adj*. **resis'tibly** *adv*. **resis'tingly** *adv*. **resis'tive** *adj*. **resis'tively** *adv*. **resistiv'ity** /rez-/ *n* capacity for resisting; (also **specific resistance**) a property of a conducting material expressed as resistance multiplied by cross-sectional area over length. **resist'less** *adj* (*archaic*) irresistible; unable to resist. **resist'lessly** *adv*. **resist'lessness** *n*. **resist'or** *n* anything that resists; a piece of apparatus used to offer electric resistance.
❑ **resistance box** *n* a box containing resistors. **resistance coil** *n* a coil of wire used to offer resistance to the passage of electricity. **resistance movement** see above. **resistance pyrometer** or **thermometer** *n* a device for measuring high temperatures by means of the variation in the electrical resistance of a wire as the temperature changes. **resistance thermometry** *n* temperature measurement of this kind. **resistance welding** see under **weld¹**.
■ **consumer** or **market resistance** unwillingness of consumers to buy marketed products (also **sales resistance**). **line of least resistance** the easiest course of action.

resit /rē-sit'/ *vi* and *vt* (pat and pap **resat**) to sit (an examination) again after failing. ◆ *n* /rē'/ an opportunity or act of resitting. [**re-**]

resize /rē-sīz'/ *vt* to enlarge or decrease in size.

res judicata /rēz joo-di-kä'tə or rās yoo-di-kä'ta/ (L) *n* a case or suit already decided.

reskew or **reskue** (*Spenser*) same as **rescue**.

reskill /rē-skil'/ *vt* to retrain (employees) to do new work. [**re-**]

resnatron /rez'nə-tron/ *n* a high-power, high-frequency tetrode. [*reso*nator and **-tron**]

resoluble /ri-zol'ū-bl or rez'ə-lū-bl/ *adj* that may be resolved or analysed. [L *resolvere, resolūtum*, from *re-*, intens, and *solvere* to loose]
■ **resolubil'ity** *n*. **resol'ubleness** *n*. **resolute** /rez'əl-oot or -ūt/ *adj* having a fixed purpose; constant in pursuing a purpose; determined. ◆ *n* (*Shakesp*) a determined person. **res'olutely** *adv*. **res'oluteness** *n*. **resolution** /rez-əl-oo'shən or -ū-shən/ *n* act of resolving; analysis; separation of components; melting; solution; the separation of an optically inactive mixture or compound into its optically active components (*chem*); the definition of a graphic or text image on a computer monitor, fax printer, TV screen, etc often measured in dots per unit area; the smallest measurable difference, or separation, or time interval (*phys, electronics* and *nucleonics*); resolving power (qv below); state of being resolved; fixed determination; that which is resolved; removal of or freedom from doubt; progression from discord to concord (*music*); a formal proposal put before a meeting, or its formal determination thereon; substitution of two short syllables for a

---

Some words formed with the prefix **re-**.

rēmap' *vt*.	**rēmint'** *vt*.	**rēmort'gage** *vt* and *n*.
rēmarr'iage *n*.	**rēmod'el** *vt*.	**rēname'** *vt*.
rēmarr'y *vt* and *vi*.	**rēmod'ify** *vt*.	**rēnegō'tiable** *adj*.

■ words derived from main entry word; ❑ compound words; ■ idioms and phrasal verbs

long; the making visible of detail; the disappearance or dispersion of a tumour or inflammation; /rē-sol-/ renewed or repeated solution. **resolu'tioner** /rez-əl-/ n one who joins in or accepts a resolution; (with cap) a person who approved of the resolutions of 1650 admitting to civil and military office all persons except those excommunicate and hostile to the Covenant, opp to Protester (Scot hist). **resolu'tionist** n. **res'olutive** adj. **resolvability** /ri-zolv-ə-bil'i-ti/ n. **resolv'able** adj. **resolve'** vt to separate into components; to make visible the details of; to analyse; to break up; to melt; to transform; to relax; to solve; to dissipate; to free from doubt or difficulty; to convince (of; obs); to assure (obs); to inform (obs); to answer (a question; obs); to dispel (fears; Shakesp); to pass as a resolution; to determine; to disperse (eg a tumour); to make (a discord) pass into a concord (music). —The obsolete senses are also used reflexively. ◆ vi to undergo resolution; to come to a determination (often with on to indicate the course chosen); to decide to go to a place (with on; Shakesp); to take counsel (Spenser); to lapse (law). ◆ n (a) resolution; fixed purpose; firmness of purpose; solution (obs). **resolved'** adj fixed in purpose. **resolvedly** /ri-zol'vid-li/ adv resolutely. **resol'vedness** n. **resol'vent** adj having power to resolve. ◆ n that which causes or helps solution or resolution. **resol'ver** n.
❑ **resolving power** n the ability of a telescope, microscope, etc to distinguish very close, or very small, objects; the ability of a photographic emulsion to produce finely detailed images.

re-soluble /rē-sol'ū-bl/ adj able to be dissolved again. [re-]
■ **re-solubil'ity** n. **re-sol'ubleness** n.

resolute, etc, **resolve**, etc see under **resoluble**.

resonance /rez'ə-nəns/ n resounding; sonority; the sound heard in auscultation; sympathetic vibration; the ringing quality of the human voice when produced in such a way that sympathetic vibration is caused in the air-spaces in the head, chest and throat; the state of a system in which a large vibration (is) produced by a small stimulus of approx the same frequency as that of the system (phys and electronics); such a large vibration (phys and electronics); increased probability of a nuclear reaction when the energy of an incident particle or photon is around a certain value appropriate to the energy level of the compound nucleus; a property of certain compounds, in which the most stable state of the molecule is a combination of theoretically possible bond arrangements or distributions of electrons (chem); the complex of bodily responses to an emotional state, or of emotional responses to a situation. [L resonāre, -ātum, from re- back, and sonāre to sound]
■ **res'onant** adj resounding, ringing; of giving its characteristic vibration in sympathy with another body's vibration. **res'onantly** adv. **res'onate** vi to resound; to vibrate sympathetically. **res'onātor** n a resonating body or device, such as for increasing sonority or for analysing sound.
❑ **res'onance-box** n a chamber in a musical instrument for increasing its sonority by vibration in sympathy with the strings.

resorb /ri-sörb' or -zörb'/ vt to absorb back. [L resorbēre to suck back]
■ **resorb'ence** n. **resorb'ent** adj.

resorcin /ri-zör'sin/ n a colourless phenol, $C_6H_4(OH)_2$, used in dyeing, photography and medicine (also **resor'cinol**). [resin and orcin (see orcinol)]

resorption /ri-sörp'shən or -zörp'/ n resorbing, esp of a mineral by rock magma; the breaking down and assimilation of a substance (med). [See resorb]
■ **resorp'tive** adj.

resort¹ /ri-zört'/ vi to have recourse; to apply; to go or be habitually; to go (to); to take oneself; to revert (obs). ◆ n act of resorting; a place much frequented, esp by holidaymakers; a haunt; that which one has or may have recourse to; concourse; thronging; repair. [OFr resortir (Fr ressortir) to rebound, retire, from sortir to go out; origin obscure]
■ **resort'er** n a frequenter.
■ **in the last resort** orig (a Gallicism, en dernier ressort), without appeal; hence as a last expedient.

resort² /rē-sört'/ vt to sort again or differently. [re-]

resound /ri-zownd'/ vt to echo; to sound with reverberation; to sound (the praises of a person or thing). ◆ vi to echo; to re-echo, reverberate; to sound sonorously; to be widely known or celebrated. **resound'ing** adj echoing; thorough, decisive, as in resounding victory. **resound'ingly** adv.

re-sound /rē-sownd'/ vi to sound again. [re-]

resource /ri-sōrs', -sörs', -zörs', -zörs' or rē'sörs/ n source or possibility of help; an expedient; (in pl) money or means of raising money; means of support; means of occupying or amusing oneself; resourcefulness. ◆ vt to provide the (esp financial) resources for. [OFr ressource, from resourdre, from L resurgere to rise again]
■ **resource'ful** adj fertile in expedients; clever, ingenious; rich in resources. **resource'fully** adv. **resource'fulness** n. **resource'less** adj. **resource'lessness** n.

respeak /rē-spēk'/ (Shakesp) vt to echo. [re-]

respect /ri-spekt'/ vt to treat with consideration, refrain from violating; to feel or show esteem, deference, or honour to; to look to, regard, consider, take into account; to heed; to refer to, relate to, have reference to (archaic); to value (a thing; Shakesp); to face, look at (obs and heraldry). ◆ vi (rare) to face (towards). ◆ n heed (Spenser); an aspect (obs); a particular; a relation; reference; regard; consideration; partiality or favour towards (with of); deferential esteem; (often in pl) a greeting or message of esteem, as in pay one's respects. ◆ interj (sl) expressing admiration. [L respicere, respectum, from re- back, and specere to look]
■ **respectabil'ity** n. **respec'tabilize** or **-ise** vt to make respectable. **respec'table** adj worthy of respect; considerable; passable; mediocre; of good social standing (obs); fairly well-to-do; decent and well-behaved; reputable; seemly; presentable; timidly or priggishly conventional. **respec'tableness** n. **respec'tably** adv. **respec'tant** adj facing each other (heraldry); looking back. **respec'ter** n a person who respects, esp in respecter of persons, someone or something that singles out an individual or individuals for unduly favourable treatment (usu in neg). **respect'ful** adj showing or feeling respect. **respect'fully** adv. **respect'fulness** n. **respect'ing** prep concerning; considering. **respec'tive** adj having respect; regardful, considerate (Shakesp); heedful; discriminating; respectful (obs); worthy of respect (Shakesp); relative; particular or several, relating to each distributively. **respec'tively** adv. **respec'tiveness** n. **respect'less** adj regardless.
■ **in respect of** in the matter of; because of (obs); in comparison with (obs). **respect of persons** undue favour, eg for wealth, etc. **with respect to** with regard to.

respire /ri-spīr'/ vi to breathe; to take breath. ◆ vt to breathe; to exhale; to carry out respiration. [L respīrāre, -ātum, from spīrāre to breathe]
■ **respirable** /res'pər-ə-bl or ri-spīr'ə-bl/ adj fit for breathing. **respiration** /res-pər-ā'shən/ n breathing; the taking in of oxygen and giving out of carbon dioxide, with associated physiological processes; a breath; a breathing space. **res'pirator** n an appliance which provides artificial respiration (med); an appliance worn on the mouth or nose to filter or warm the air breathed; a gas mask. **respiratory** /res'pər-ə-tər-i, ri-spī'rə-tər-i or -spī'/ adj of, relating to, or serving for, respiration. **respirom'eter** n an apparatus for measuring breathing.
❑ **respiratory quotient** n the ratio of molecules of carbon dioxide exhaled to molecules of oxygen absorbed in the process of respiration.

respite /res'pīt or -pit/ n temporary cessation of something that is tiring or painful; postponement requested or granted; temporary suspension of the execution of a criminal (law); delay in action (obs); leisure (obs). ◆ vt to grant a respite to; to relieve by a pause (obs); to delay, put off; to grant postponement to; to prolong (Shakesp); to give up, cease from (obs). ◆ vi (obs) to rest (from). [ME respit, from OFr (Fr répit), from L respectus, respicere; see respect]
❑ **respite care** n temporary residential care for an elderly, disabled or ill person to provide relief for the person's usual carer.

resplend /ri-splend'/ vi to shine brilliantly. [L resplendēre, from re-, intens, and splendēre to shine]
■ **resplend'ence** or **resplend'ency** n. **resplend'ent** adj shining, brilliant and splendid. **resplend'ently** adv.

respond /ri-spond'/ vi to answer; to utter liturgical responses; to act in answer; to react. ◆ n a response to a versicle in liturgy; a half-pillar or half-pier attached to a wall to support an arch (corresponding to one at the other end of an arcade, etc). [L respondēre, respōnsum, from re- back, and spondēre to promise]
■ **respond'ence** n response (Spenser); correspondence, agreement. **respond'ency** n correspondence. **respond'ent** adj answering; corresponding; responsive. ◆ n a person who answers; a response to a specific stimulus; a person who refutes objections; a defendant, esp in a divorce suit. **respondentia** /res-pon-den'sha/ n a loan on a ship's cargo, payable only on safe arrival. **respond'er**, **respons'er** or **respons'or** /ris-/ n a person or thing that responds; the part of a transponder which replies automatically to the correct interrogation

Some words formed with the prefix **re-**.

rēnegō'tiate vt.	**rēoccupā'tion** n.	**rēoffend'** vi.
rēnegōtiā'tion n.	**rēocc'upy** vt.	**rēordain'** vt.
rēnum'ber vt.	**rēoccur'** vi.	**rēor'der** vt.

signal. **Respon'sa** *n pl* a branch of rabbinical literature consisting of written decisions from authorities in reply to questions, problems, etc submitted to them (**respon'sum** one of these decisions). **response'** *n* an answer; an oracular answer; an answer made by the congregation to the minister or priest during divine service; a responsory; a reaction, *esp* sympathetic; the ratio of the output to the input level of a transmission system at any particular frequency (*electronics*). **response'less** *adj*. **responsibil'ity** *n* state of being responsible; a trust or charge for which one is responsible. **respon'sible** *adj* liable to be called to account as being in charge or control; answerable (*to* a person, etc *for* something); deserving the blame or credit of (with *for*); governed by a sense of responsibility; being a free moral agent; morally accountable for one's actions; trustworthy; able to meet one's financial obligations; respectable-looking; involving responsibility; correspondent (*obs*). **respon'sibleness** *n*. **respon'sibly** *adv*. **respon'sions** /-shənz/ *n pl* formerly, the first of three examinations for the BA degree at Oxford, 'smalls'. **respon'sive** *adj* ready to respond; answering; correspondent; with responses. **respon'sively** *adv*. **respon'siveness** *n*. **responsorial** /ri- or rē-spon-sō'ri-əl or -sō'ri-əl/ *adj* responsive. ◆ *n* an office-book containing the responsories. **respon'sory** *adj* making answer. ◆ *n* an anthem sung after a lesson; a liturgical response.
❑ **response time** *n* (*comput*) the time taken by a computer to reply to a command given to it by a user, eg to display a website after the address has been entered.

respray /rē-sprā'/ *vt* to spray (a vehicle) again with a new coat of paint. ◆ *n* /rē'/ the act of respraying; a resprayed vehicle. [**re-**]

ressaldar same as **risaldar**.

rest[1] /rest/ *n* repose, refreshing inactivity; intermission of or freedom from motion or disturbance; tranquillity; repose of death; invigoration by resting (*Shakesp*); a place for resting; a prop or support (eg for a book, a snooker cue, a violinist's chin); motionlessness; a pause in speaking or reading; an interval of silence in music, or a mark indicating it. ◆ *vi* to repose; to be at ease; to be still; to be supported (*on*); to lean (*on*); to put trust in (with *on*); to have foundation in (with *on*); to settle, alight; to remain; (*esp* of an actor or actress) to be temporarily unemployed (*inf*; *facetious*); to finish the introduction of evidence in a case (*law*). ◆ *vt* to give rest to; to place or hold in support (*on*); to lean (*on*); to base (*on*); (*reflexive*) to give (oneself) rest or (*obs*) to rely (upon). [OE *rest*, *ræst*; Ger *Rast*, Du *rust*; converging and merging in meaning with **rest**[2,3]]
■ **rest'er** *n*. **rest'ful** *adj* at rest; rest-giving; tranquil. **rest'fully** *adv*. **rest'fulness** *n*. **rest'ing** *n* and *adj*. **rest'less** *adj* unresting, not resting, sleeping or relaxing; never still; uneasily active; impatient (of) (*Pope*); impatient of inactivity or of remaining still; never-ceasing; unrestful, giving or allowing no rest. **rest'lessly** *adv*. **rest'lessness** *n*.
❑ **rest centre** *n* a place of shelter for numbers of people driven from their homes by an emergency. **rest cure** *n* treatment consisting of inactivity and quiet. **rest day** *n* a day of rest; the first day of a three days' visit. **rest home** *n* an establishment for those who need special care and attention, eg invalids, elderly people, etc. **rest house** *n* a house of rest for travellers. **resting place** *n* a place of rest; a stair-landing (**one's last resting place** one's grave). **resting potential** *n* the potential difference (qv) across the membrane of a nerve cell that is not conducting an impulse. **resting spore** *n* a spore that can germinate after a period of dormancy. **resting stage** *n* a state of suspended activity. **rest mass** *n* (*phys*) the mass of an object when it is at rest. **rest room** *n* a room in a building other than a private house with adjoining lavatories, etc. **rest stop** *n* (*N Am*) a lay-by.
■ **at rest** stationary; in repose, *esp* asleep or dead; free from disquiet. **lay to rest** to bury or inter.

rest[2] /rest/ *n* remainder; all others; reserve fund; a rapid continuous series of returns (*tennis*, etc); (in primero) a stake whose loss ends the game. ◆ *vi* to remain (see also **rest**[1]). [Fr *reste*, from L *restāre* to remain, from *re-* back, and *stāre* to stand]
■ **for the rest** as regards other matters. **set up one's rest** (*archaic*) to make one's final stake; to take a resolution; to take up abode.

rest[3] /rest/ (*hist*) *n* a device on a breastplate to prevent the spear from being driven back. ◆ *vt* (*Shakesp*) to arrest. [Aphetic for **arrest**]

restart /rē-stärt'/ *vi* and *vt* to start again. ◆ *n* a fresh or subsequent start; (with *cap*) in the UK, a government scheme of courses, etc intended to help the unemployed find retraining or new employment. [**re-**]
■ **restart'er** *n*.

restaurant /res't(ə-)rönt or -rənt or -rä/ *n* a place where food or meals are prepared and served, or are available, to customers. [Fr, from *restaurer* to restore]
■ **restaurateur** /res-tər-ə-tûr' or -tær'/ *n* the keeper of a restaurant. **restaura'tion** *n* the business, skill or art of a restaurateur.
❑ **restaurant car** *n* a dining-car.

restem /rē-stem'/ (*Shakesp*) *vt* to force (a way) back against the current. [**re-**]

restenosis /re- or rē-stə-nō'sis/ *n* (*pl* **resteno'sēs**) the recurrence of stenosis, *esp* in a coronary artery or valve after heart surgery. [**re-**]

restharrow /rest'ha-rō/ *n* a papilionaceous plant (genus *Ononis*) with long, tough, woody roots. [**rest**[3] and **harrow**[1]]

restiff /res'tif/ an obsolete form of **restive**.

restiform /res'ti-förm/ *adj* cordlike. [L *restis* a cord, and *fōrma* form]

restitute /res'ti-tūt/ (*archaic*) *vt* to restore. ◆ *vi* (*archaic*) to make restitution. [L *restituere*, *-ūtum*, from *re-* and *statuere* to make to stand]
■ **restitu'tion** *n* an act or instance of restoring; compensation; (also **restitū'tionism**) restorationism (*esp US*). **restitū'tionist** *n*. **restitutive** /res'ti-tūt-/ or /res'tit-/ *adj*. **res'titūtor** *n*. **restit'ūtory** *adj*.

restitutio in integrum /res-ti-tū'ti-ō in in-teg'rəm/ (*law*) the restoration of the parties to a contract to the relative positions occupied by them before the contract was made. [L]

restive /res'tiv/ *adj* uneasy, as if ready to break from control; unwilling to go forward; obstinate, refractory; inert (*obs*). [OFr *restif*, from L *restāre* to rest]
■ **res'tively** *adv*. **res'tiveness** *n*.

restore /ri-stōr' or -stör'/ *vt* to repair; to bring, put or give back; to make good; to reinstate; to bring back to a (supposed) former state, or to a normal state; to reconstruct mentally, by inference or conjecture. ◆ *n* (*Spenser*) restitution. [OFr *restorer*, from L *restaurāre*, *-ātum*]
■ **restor'able** *adj*. **restor'ableness** *n*. **restoration** /res-tō-rā'shən or -tö-, -tə-, -to-/ *n* the act or process of restoring; (*usu* with *cap*) a reinstatement of a monarch or monarchy (eg the Restoration of the Stuarts or the Bourbons); renovations and reconstruction (sometimes little differing from destruction) of a building, painting, etc; a reconstructed thing or representation. ◆ *adj* (with *cap*) occurring during, or relating to, the period of the Restoration of Charles II. **restorā'tionism** *n* (*theol*) the receiving of a sinner to divine favour; the belief that after a purgation all sinners and angels will be restored to the favour of God. **restorā'tionist** *n* an adherent of restorationism, a universalist. **restorative** /ris-tor'ə-tiv or -tör'/ *adj* tending to restore, *esp* to strength and vigour. ◆ *n* a medicine that restores. **restor'atively** *adv*. **restor'er** *n*.

restrain /ri-strān'/ *vt* to hold back; to control; to subject to forcible repression; to tighten (*Shakesp*); to forbid (*Milton*). ◆ *vi* (*rare*) to refrain. [OFr *restraindre*, *restrai(g)n-*, from L *restringere*, *restrictum* from *re-* back, and *stringere* to draw tightly]
■ **restrain'able** *adj*. **restrained'** *adj* controlled; self-controlled; displaying restraint; forbidden (*Shakesp*). **restrain'edly** *adv*. **restrain'edness** *n*. **restrain'er** *n* a person or thing that restrains; an ingredient of a photographic developer which checks the development and reduces the tendency to fog. **restrain'ing** *n* and *adj*. **restraint'** *n* the act of restraining; state of being restrained; a restraining influence; restriction; forcible control; artistic control or reticence; lack of liberty; reserve.
■ **restraint of princes** embargo. **restraint of trade** interference with free play of economic forces, eg by monopolies.

restrict /ri-strikt'/ *vt* to limit; to confine within limits; to limit circulation or disclosure of for security reasons. [L *restringere*, *restrictum*]
■ **restrict'ed** *adj*. **restrict'edly** *adv*. **restrict'edness** *n*. **restric'tion** *n*. **restric'tionist** *n* a person who favours restriction (also *adj*). **restric'tive** *adj* restricting; tending to restrict; expressing restriction, as in relative clauses, phrases, etc that limit the application of the verb to the subject, eg *people who like historic buildings should visit Edinburgh*. **restric'tively** *adv*. **restric'tiveness** *n*. **restringe** /ri-strinj'/ *vt* to restrict. **restrin'gent** *n* and *adj* astringent.
❑ **restricted area** *n* one from which the general public is excluded; one within which there is a speed limit. **restriction endonuclease** or **enzyme** *n* a class of endonucleases with different specificities, often recognizing four or six base pairs and able to cleave DNA at a such a sequence, widely used in genetic manipulation. **restriction fragment**

Some words formed with the prefix **re-**.

rēordinā'tion *n*.	**rēpack'** *vt* and *vi*.	**rēpaginā'tion** *n*.
rēorganizā'tion or **rēorganisā'tion** *n*.	**rēpack'age** *vt*.	**rēpā'per** *vt*.
rēor'ganize or **rēor'ganise** *vt*.	**rēpag'inate** *vt*.	**rēpeo'ple** *vt*.

---

n one of the segments into which a gene has been divided by a restriction enzyme. **restrictive covenant** *n* a deed that restricts the use of land or property to preserve the value and/or enjoyment of adjoining land or property. **restrictive practice** *n* a trade practice that is against the public interest, such as an agreement to sell only to certain buyers, or to keep up resale prices; used also of certain trade union practices, such as the closed shop, demarcation, working to rule, etc. **restrictive temperature** *n* (*biol*) the temperature at which a temperature sensitive mutant organism will not grow (cf **permissive temperature**).

restringe see under **restrict**.

restructure /rē-struk'chər/ *vt* to reorganize (a business or company) and redeploy its personnel so as to improve efficiency. [**re-**]
■ **restruc'turing** *n*.

resty /rest'i/ *adj* restive; sluggish (*Shakesp*); inoperative, ineffectual (*Spenser*). [**restive**, or partly **rest¹**]

result /ri-zult'/ *vi* to issue (with *in*); to follow as a consequence; to rebound (*obs*); to be the outcome; to revert (*law*). ◆ *n* consequence; outcome; outcome aimed at; quantity obtained by calculation; decision, resolution, eg of a council (*obs* and *US*); in games, the (*usu* final) score; in games, etc, a successful final score, a win, as in *get a result* (*inf*). [L *resultāre* to leap back, from *saltāre* to leap]
■ **result'ant** *adj* resulting; resulting from combination (as of tones sounded together). ◆ *n* a force compounded of two or more forces; a sum of vector quantities; a resultant tone; a result of combination. **result'ative** *adj* expressing result. **result'ful** *adj*. **result'ing** *adj*. **result'less** *adj*. **result'lessness** *n*.

resume /ri-zūm'/ or -*zoom'*/ *vt* to take back; to summarize, make a résumé of (*archaic*); to assume again; to take up again; to begin again. ◆ *vi* to take possession again; to begin again in continuation. [L *resūmere*, -*sūmptum*, from *re*- and *sūmere* to take]
■ **resum'able** *adj*. **résumé** /rā-zū-mā or rez'ū-mā/ *n* (Fr *pap*) a summary; /rez'-/ a curriculum vitae (*N Am*). **resumption** /ri-zump'shən or -*zum'*/ *n* the act of resuming. **resumptive** /-zump'* or -*zum'*/ *adj*. **resump'tively** *adv*.

resupinate /ri-soo'pi-nāt or -*sū'*/ *adj* (*bot*) upside down by twisting. [L *resupīnāre*, -*ātum* and *resupīnus*, from *re*- back, and *supīnus* bent backward]
■ **resupinā'tion** *n*. **resupine** /rē-sū-pīn' or -*soo-*/ *adj* lying on the back.

resurface /rē-sûr'fis/ *vt* to put a new surface on (a road, etc). ◆ *vi* to rise again to the surface; to appear or become known again. [**re-**]

resurge /ri-sûrj'/ (*rare*) *vi* to rise again. [L *resurgere*, *resurrēctum*, from *re*- and *surgere* to rise]
■ **resur'gence** *n*. **resur'gent** *adj*. **resurrect** /rez-ər-ekt'/ *vt* (back-formation) to restore to life; to revive; to disinter. ◆ *vi* to come to life again. **resurrection** /-ek'shən/ *n* a rising from the dead, *esp* (with *cap*) that of Christ; resuscitation; revival; a thing resurrected; body-snatching (*hist*). **resurrec'tional** *adj*. **resurrec'tionary** *adj*. **resurrec'tionism** *n*. **resurrec'tionist** *n* (*hist*; also **resurrection man**) a person who stole bodies from the grave for dissection. **resurrec'tionize** or -**ise** *vt*. **resurrect'ive** *adj*. **resurrect'or** *n*.
□ **resurrection pie** *n* a dish comprising remnants of former meals. **resurrection plant** *n* a plant that curls into a ball during a drought and spreads again when moist, such as the rose of Jericho, or some selaginellas.

resurvey /rē-sər-vā'/ *vt* to make a further survey of. ◆ *n* /-sûr'/ a further survey. [**re-**]

resuscitate /ri-sus'i-tāt/ *vt* and *vi* to bring back or be brought back to life or consciousness; to revive. [L *resuscitāre*, -*ātum*, from *re*-, *sus*-, *sub*- from beneath, and *citāre* to put into quick motion, from *ciēre* to make to go]
■ **resusc'itable** *adj*. **resusc'itant** *adj* and *n* (a person or thing) having a resuscitating effect. **resuscitā'tion** *n*. **resusc'itātive** *adj* tending to resuscitate; reviving; revivifying; reanimating. **resusc'itātor** *n* a person or thing that resuscitates; an oxygen-administering apparatus used to induce breathing after asphyxiation.

resveratrol /rez-vē'rə-trol/ *n* a fungicidal phenol with antioxidant properties found in grape skins, thought to protect against heart disease.

ret /ret/, **rate** or **rait** /rāt/ *vt* (**rett'ing**, **rāt'ing** or **rait'ing**; **rett'ed**, **rāt'ed** or **rait'ed**) to expose to moisture. ◆ *vt* and *vi* to soak; to soften, spoil or rot by soaking or exposure to moisture; to rot. [Appar related to **rot**]
■ **rett'ery** *n* a place where flax is retted.

ret. *abbrev* : retain; retired; return.

retable /ri-tā'bl/ *n* a shelf or ornamental setting for panels, etc behind an altar. [Fr *rétable*, from LL *retrōtabulum*]

retail /rē'tāl, formerly (now *rare*) ri- or rē-tāl'/ *n* the sale of goods directly to the consumer, or in small quantities (cf **wholesale**). ◆ *adj* in, of, engaged in or concerned with such sale. ◆ *adv* by retail; at retail price. ◆ *vt* to sell by retail; to repeat in detail; to put about, hand on by report. ◆ *vi* to sell. [OFr *retail* piece cut off, from *tailler* to cut]
■ **re'tailer** *n*. **retail'ment** *n*.
□ **retail bank** same as **commercial bank** (see under **commerce**). **retail price index** *n* a monthly index of the retail prices of specific household goods and services, used as a measure of the rate of inflation (*abbrev* **RPI**). **retail price maintenance** *n* same as **resale price maintenance** (see under **resale**). **retail therapy** *n* (*facetious*) shopping, regarded as a means of improving one's mental state.

retain /ri-tān'/ *vt* to keep; to hold back; to continue to hold; to keep up; to employ or keep engaged, eg by a fee paid; to keep in mind. [Fr *retenir*, from L *retinēre*, from *re*- back, and *tenēre* to hold]
■ **retain'able** *adj*. **retain'er** *n* a person or thing that retains; a dependant of a person of rank, owing some service to him or her (*hist*); a family servant of long standing; an authorization; a retaining fee (in legal usage, **general** to secure a priority of claim on a counsel's services, **special** for a particular case); an appliance worn in the mouth to keep straightened teeth in position. **retain'ership** *n*. **retain'ment** *n*.
□ **retaining fee** *n* the advance fee paid to a lawyer to defend a cause. **retaining wall** *n* a wall to hold back solid material, such as earth or (loosely) water (also called **revetment**).

retake /rē-tāk'/ *vt* (*pat* **retook'**; *pap* **retā'ken**) to take again; to take back, recapture. ◆ *n* /rē'/ an act of retaking something; an examination that is taken for a second time; a second or repeated photographing or photograph, *esp* for a film. [**re-**]
■ **retāk'er** *n*. **retāk'ing** *n*.

retaliate /ri-tal'i-āt/ *vt* to repay in kind (now *usu* an injury; sometimes *upon* a person). ◆ *vi* to return like for like (*esp* in hostility). [L *retāliāre*, -*ātum*, from *re*-, and *tāliō*, -*ōnis* like for like, from *tālis* such]
■ **retaliā'tion** *n* return of like for like; imposition of a tariff against countries that impose a tariff. **retalia'tionist** *n*. **retal'iātive** *adj*. **retal'iātor** *n*. **retal'iatory** /-āt-ər-i or -ət-ər-i/ *adj*.

retama /re-tä'mə/ *n* a name for various desert switch-plants, either papilionaceous or caesalpiniaceous, including Spanish broom. [Sp, from Ar *retām* (pl)]

retard /ri-tärd'/ *vt* to slow; to keep back development or progress of; to delay; to postpone (*rare*); to delay the timing of (an ignition spark). ◆ *vi* to slow down; to delay. ◆ *n* delay; lag; /rē'/ (chiefly *US*; *offensive sl*) a person of low intelligence. [L *retardāre*, -*ātum*, from *re*- and *tardāre* to slow]
■ **retar'dant** *n* and *adj* (a substance) serving to delay or slow down a chemical reaction, such as rusting. **retar'date** *n* (*psychol*) a person who is mentally retarded or backward. **retardā'tion** /rē-/ or **retard'ment** *n* slowing; delay; lag. **retardative** /ri-tard'ə-tiv/ *adj*. **retar'datory** *adj*. **retar'ded** *adj* delayed or slowed down; slow in development, *esp* mental, or having made less than normal progress in learning (*old*). **retar'der** *n* a retardant; a substance that delays or prevents setting of cement. **retard'ment** *n* see **retardation** above.

retch¹ /rech, also rēch/ *vi* to strain as if to vomit. ◆ *n* an act of retching. [OE *hræcan*, from *hrāca* a hawking]

retch² /rech/, **retchless**, etc obsolete forms of **reck**, **reckless**, etc.

retd *abbrev* : retired; returned.

rete /rē'tē/ (*anat*) *n* (pl **retia** /rē'shi-ə or rē'ti-ə/) a network, eg of blood vessels or nerves. [L *rēte* net]
■ **retial** /rē'shi-əl/ *adj*.

retene /rē'tēn or ret'ēn/ *n* a hydrocarbon ($C_{18}H_{18}$) obtained from tar. [Gr *rhētinē* pine resin]
■ **retinalite** /ret' or ri-tin'/ *n* a resinous-lustred form of serpentine. **retinis'pora** or **retinos'pora** *n* a cypress or related conifer in a perpetuated juvenile form, once placed in a separate genus. **ret'inite** *n*

Some words formed with the prefix **re-**.

rēperus'al *n*.	**rēpop'ulate** *vt*.	**rēpro'grammable** *adj*.
rēperuse' *vt*.	**rēpot'** *vt*.	**rēpro'gramme** or **rēpro'gram** *vt*.
rēplan' *vt* and *vi*.	**rēpott'ing** *n*.	**rēpublicā'tion** *n*.

---

pitchstone (*obs*); a fossil resin. **ret'inoid** *adj* resembling resin. ◆ *n* (*biochem*) a chemical variant of vitamin A, with powerful effect when used as a drug. **ret'inol** *n* an oil distilled from resin; vitamin A.
□ **retinō'ic acid** *n* a derivative of vitamin A that is important in morphogenesis and embryo development; a lotion containing this used in treating acne and other skin conditions.

retention /ri-ten'shən/ *n* the act or power of retaining; memory; custody; inability to void or get rid of fluid, etc (*med*). [L *retentiō*, *-ōnis*; OFr *retentif*; see **retain**]
■ **reten'tionist** *n* a person who advocates the retaining of a policy, etc, *esp* that of capital punishment. **reten'tive** *adj* retaining; tenacious; retaining moisture. **reten'tively** *adv*. **reten'tiveness** or **retentiv'ity** /rē-/ *n*.

retexture[1] /rē-teks'chər/ *vt* to treat (a material) so as to restore firmness lost through the action of spirit in the process of dry-cleaning. [**re-** and **texture** to give a texture to]

retexture[2] /rē-teks'chər/ *n* weaving anew. [L *retexere* to weave anew, earlier to unweave]

rethink /rē-thingk'/ *vt* to consider again and come to a different decision about. ◆ *n* /rē'thingk/ an act of rethinking. [**re-**]

retia and **retial** see **rete**.

retiarius /rē-shi-ā'ri-əs or rā-ti-ā'ri-ŭs/ (*hist*) *n* (pl **retia'rii** /-ri-ī or -ri-ē/) a gladiator armed with a net. [L *retiārius*, from *rēte* net]
■ **retiary** /rē'shi-ər-i/ *adj* of nets; using a net as a weapon, as a gladiator or a spider.

reticella /re-ti-chel'ə/ *n* an early form of needlepoint lace produced in Italy in the 16c and 17c, made by working cutwork designs on a linen background. [Ital, dimin of *rete* net]

reticent /ret'i-sənt/ *adj* reserved or communicating sparingly or unwillingly. [L *reticēns, -ēntis*, prp of *reticēre*, from *re-*, and *tacēre* to be silent]
■ **ret'icence** or **ret'icency** *n*. **ret'icently** *adv*.

reticle /ret'i-kl/ *n* an attachment to an optical instrument consisting of a network of lines of reference. [L *rēticulum*, dimin of *rēte* net]
■ **reticular** /ri-tik'ū-lər/ *adj* netted; netlike; reticulated; of the reticulum. **retic'ularly** *adv*. **retic'ulary** *adj*. **retic'ulate** /-lāt/ *vt* to form into or mark with a network; to distribute (eg water or electricity) by a network. ◆ *vi* to form a network. ◆ *adj* /-lət or -lit/ netted; marked with network; net-veined. **retic'ulāted** *adj* reticulate; (of masonry) consisting of lozenge-shaped stones, or of squares placed diamond-wise; (of rusticated work) having ridges of uniform width between irregular sinkings. **retic'ulately** *adv*. **reticula'tion** *n* network; netlike structure. **reticule** /ret'i-kūl/ *n* a reticle; a small, woman's handbag, *esp* and *orig* of network. **retic'ulocyte** *n* an immature red blood cell that exhibits a reticulated appearance when stained. **retic'ulum** *n* (pl **retic'ula**) a network; the second stomach of a ruminant; (with *cap*) a southern constellation, also called the **Net**, between Hydrus and Dorado.
□ **reticulo-endothelial system** *n* (*immunol*) the network of phagocytic cells extending throughout lymphoid and other organs which is involved in the uptake and clearance of foreign particles from the blood.

retiform /rē'ti-förm/ *adj* having the form of a net. [L *rēte* net, and *fōrma* form]

retina /ret'i-nə/ *n* (pl **ret'inas** or **ret'inae** /-nē/) the light-sensitive tissue that lines much of the back layer of the eyeball. [LL *rētina*, appar from L *rēte* net]
■ **ret'inal** *adj*. **retini'tis** *n* inflammation of the retina. **retinoblastō'ma** *n* a cancerous tumour of the eye. **ret'inoscope** *n* an optical instrument used in **retinos'copy**, examination of the eye by observing a shadow on the retina. **retinoscop'ically** *adv*. **retinos'copist** *n*. **retinula** /ri-tin'ū-lə/ *n* (pl **retin'ulae** /-lē/) a cell playing the part of a retina to an ommatidium. **retin'ular** *adj*.
□ **retina camera** *n* an instrument that photographs the minute blood vessels at the back of the eye in full colour. **retinitis pigmentosa** /pig-mən-tō'sə/ *n* a familial and hereditary disease in which chronic and progressive degeneration of the choroid in both eyes causes progressive loss of vision.

retinaculum /ret-i-nak'ū-ləm/ *n* (pl **retinac'ula**) a connecting band; a means of retention; the apparatus that holds an insect's forewing and hindwing together; the sticky attachment of a pollen-mass, as in

orchids. [L *retināculum* a holdfast, from *retinēre*; see **retain** and **retention**]
■ **retinac'ūlar** *adj*.

retinal see under **retina**.

retinalite, retinispora, retinite see under **retene**.

retinitis, retinoblastoma see under **retina**.

retinoic acid, retinoid, retinol see under **retene**.

retinoscope, etc see under **retina**.

retinue /ret'i-nū, formerly ri-tin'ū/ *n* a body of people accompanying and often attending an important person; a suite or train. [Fr *retenue*, fem pap of *retenir*; see **retain**]

retinula, etc see under **retina**.

retire /ri-tīr'/ *vi* to withdraw; to retreat; to recede; to withdraw from society, office, public or active life, business, profession, etc; to go into seclusion or to bed; to return (*obs*). ◆ *vt* to withdraw; to draw back; to withdraw from currency; to cause to retire. ◆ *n* (now *rare*) retirement; retreat (*obs*); a place of retirement (*obs*); return (*obs*); a signal to retreat. [Fr *retirer*, from *re-* back, and *tirer* to draw]
■ **reti'racy** *n* (*US*) seclusion; enough to retire on. **reti'ral** *n* giving up of office, business, etc; withdrawal. **retired'** *adj* withdrawn; reserved in manner; secluded, sequestered; withdrawn from business or profession; recondite (*obs*). **retired'ly** (or /ri-tī'rid-li/) *adv*. **retired'ness** (or /ri-tī'rid-nis/) *n*. **reti'ree** *n* a person who retires or has retired from work. **retire'ment** *n* the act of retiring; the state of being or having retired; solitude; privacy; a time or place of seclusion. **reti'rer** *n*. **reti'ring** *adj* reserved; unobtrusive; retreating; modest; given to someone who retires from a public office or service. **reti'ringly** *adv*. **reti'ringness** *n*.
□ **retired list** *n* a list of officers who are relieved from active service but receive a certain amount of pay (**retired pay**). **retirement pension** *n* (*Brit*) a state pension paid to men of 65 and over, and women of 60 and over (formerly **old age pension**). **retirement pregnancy** *n* an artificially induced pregnancy in an elderly or postmenopausal woman.

retook see **retake**.

retool /rē-tool'/ *vt* to re-equip with new tools (in a factory, etc; also *vi*); to remake, refashion (chiefly *US*). [**re-**]

retorsion see under **retort**.

retort /ri-tört'/ *vt* to throw back; to return upon an assailant or opponent; to answer in retaliation; to answer sharply or wittily; to reject (*Shakesp*); to purify or treat in a retort (*chem*); to sterilize (food in a sealed container) by heating it with steam, etc (*US*). ◆ *vi* to make a sharp reply. ◆ *n* retaliation; a ready and sharp or witty answer; the art or act of retorting; a vessel in which substances are placed for carrying out a chemical process, typically a flask with a long bent-back neck used for distillation. [L *retorquēre, retortum*, from *re-* back, and *torquēre* to twist]
■ **retor'ted** *adj* bent back; thrown back; turned back. **retor'ter** *n*. **retortion** /-tör'shən/ (also **retor'sion**) *n* retorting; bending, turning or casting back; retaliation. **retor'tive** *adj*.

retouch /rē-tuch'/ *vt* to touch again; to touch up with the intention of improving. ◆ *n* /rē'/ an act of touching up, *esp* of a photograph by pencil-work on the negative; an article or detail altered in this way. [**re-**]
■ **retouch'er** *n*.

retour /ri-toor'/ *n* a return; an extract from chancery of the service of an heir to his or her ancestor (*Scots law*; *obs*). ◆ *vt* to return as heir; to return to chancery. [OFr *retour* return]

retrace /ri- or rē-trās'/ *vt* to trace back; to go back upon; to run over with the eye or in the memory; /rē-/ to trace again; /rē-/ to renew the outline of. [Fr *retracer*]
■ **retrace'able** /ri-/ *adj*.

retract /ri-trakt'/ *vt* to draw back; to withdraw; to revoke; to unsay; in chess, to undo (the previous move); to pronounce with tongue drawn back. ◆ *vi* to take back, or draw back from, what has been said or granted. [Mainly from L *retrahere, retractum*; partly from *retractāre, retractātum*, from *re-* back, and *trahere* to draw]
■ **retrac'table** or **retrac'tible** *adj* able to be retracted; that can be drawn up into the body or wings (*aeronautics*); that can be drawn up towards the body of a vehicle. **retractā'tion** /rē-/ *n* revoking; recantation. **retrac'ted** *adj* drawn in; turned back; cancelled; revoked;

Some words formed with the prefix **re-**.

rēpub'lish *vt*.	**rēquote'** *vt* and *vi*.	**rēreg'ulate** *vt*.
rēpub'lisher *n*.	**rērecord'** *vt*.	**rēregulā'tion** *n*.
rēpulp' *vt*.	**rēreg'ister** *vt* and *vi*.	**rērelease'** *vt* and *n*.

■ words derived from main entry word; □ compound words; ■ idioms and phrasal verbs

pronounced with tongue drawn in. **retrac'tile** /-tīl/ *adj* that may be drawn back, as a cat's claws. **retractility** /rē-trak-til'i-ti/ *n.* **retraction** /ri-trak'shən/ *n* drawing back; retractation. **retrac'tive** *adj* tending to retract; in chess, involving the reversal of the previous move. **retrac'tively** *adv.* **retrac'tor** *n* a device or instrument for holding parts back, *esp* a surgical instrument for this purpose; a muscle that pulls in a part; in chess, a problem involving the reversal of the previous move.

retraict, **retrait** and **retraite** /ri-trāt'/ obsolete forms of **retreat**.

retraitt see **retrate**[2].

retral /rē'trəl or ret'rəl/ (*biol*) *adj* at or towards the rear. [L *retro* backwards]
■ **re'trally** *adv.*

retranslate /rē-trans-lāt' or -träns- or -tranz- or -tränz-/ *vt* to translate anew; to translate back into the original language; to transfer back. [**re-**]
■ **retranslā'tion** *n.*

retransmit /rē-träns-mit', -tränz-, -trans- or -tranz-/ *vt* to transmit again; to transmit back; to transmit a stage further. [**re-**]
■ **retransmiss'ion** *n.*

retrate[1] /ri-trāt'/ (*Spenser*) *n* and *vi* same as **retreat**.

retrate[2] or **retraitt** /ri-trāt'/ (*Spenser*) *n* a portrait, portraiture. [Ital *ritratto*]

retread /rē-tred'/ *vt* to tread again (*pat* **retrod'**; *pap* **retrodd'en**); to remould (a tyre) (*pat* and *pap* **retread'ed**). ◆ *n* /rē'tred/ a used tyre which has been given a new tread; someone or something returned to use, made useful again, eg a retired person who takes up new work, an MP who is returned to the Commons having previously lost his or her seat (*sl*); a soldier who fought in both the First and Second World Wars (*Aust* and *US*). [**re-**]

retreat /ri-trēt'/ *n* a withdrawal; an orderly withdrawal before an enemy, or from a position of danger or difficulty; a signal (by bugle or drum) for withdrawal or for retirement to quarters (*milit*); recall of pursuers (*Shakesp*); retirement; seclusion; retirement for a time for religious meditation; a time of such retirement; a place of privacy, seclusion, refuge or quiet; an institution for the care and treatment of the elderly, the mentally ill, alcoholics, etc. ◆ *vi* to draw back; to relinquish a position; to retire; to recede. ◆ *vt* (*rare*) to withdraw. [OFr *retret*, *-e*, *pap* of *retraire*, from L *retrahere* to draw back]
■ **retreat'ant** *n* a person taking part in a religious, etc retreat.

re-treat or **retreat** /rē-trēt'/ *vt* to treat again. [**re-**]
■ **retreat'ment** *n.*

retrench /ri-trench' or -trensh'/ *vt* to cut off, out or down; to protect by a retrenchment; to make (an employee) redundant (*Aust*). ◆ *vi* to cut down expenses. [OFr *retrencher* (Fr *retrancher*), from *re-* off, and *trencher*; see **trench**]
■ **retrench'ment** *n* an act or instance of retrenching; economy; a work within another for prolonging defence (*fortif*).

retrial see under **retry**.

retribute /ri-trib'ūt or ret'ri-būt/ *vt* to give in return; to give in return for. ◆ *vi* to make requital. [L *retribuere*, *-ūtum* to give back, from *re-* back, and *tribuere* to give]
■ **retribution** /ret-ri-bū'shən/ *n* requital (now *esp* of evil). **retrib'ūtive** /ri-/ *adj* repaying; rewarding or punishing suitably. **retrib'ūtively** *adv.* **retrib'ūtor** *n.* **retrib'ūtory** *adj.*

retrieve /ri-trēv'/ *vt* to search for and fetch, as a dog does game; to recover, repossess; to rescue (from or out of); to save (time); to restore (honour or fortune); to make good (a loss or error); to return successfully (*tennis*); to get possession of (a shot, pass, etc that is difficult to reach) (*football*). ◆ *vi* to find and fetch (as a dog does). ◆ *n* retrieving. [OFr *retroev-*, *retreuv-*, stressed stem of *retrover* (Fr *retrouver*), from *re-* again, and *trouver* to find]
■ **retriev'able** *adj.* **retriev'ableness** *n.* **retriev'ably** *adv.* **retriev'al** *n* retrieving; the extraction of data from a file (*comput*). **retrieve'ment** *n* (*rare*). **retriev'er** *n* a dog (of a breed that can be) trained to find and fetch game that has been shot; a person who retrieves. **retriev'ing** *n* and *adj.*

retro or **Retro** /ret'rō/ *adj* reminiscent of, reverting to, or recreating the past, *esp* for effect. ◆ *n* (*pl* **ret'ros**) design, style, etc which deliberately reverts to or recreates the past; short form of **retro-rocket**. [Ety as for **retro-**]

retro- /ret-rō-/ *combining form* denoting: backwards; behind. [L *retrō*]

retroact /re-trō-akt'/ *vi* to act retrospectively, or apply to the past (*law*); to react. [L *retroagere*, *-actum* from *agere* to do]
■ **retroac'tion** *n.* **retroac'tive** *adj* applying to or affecting things past; operating backward. **retroac'tively** *adv.* **retroactiv'ity** *n.*
❏ **retroactive inhibition** or **interference** *n* (*psychol*) the tendency for retention of learned material to be impaired by subsequent learning.

retrobulbar /re-trō-bul'bər/ *adj* behind the eyeball. [**retro-** and L *bulbus* onion]

retrocede /ret-rō-sēd'/ *vi* to move back or (*med*) inwards; to reinsure (a reinsurance contract). ◆ *vt* to cede back, grant back; to reinsure (a reinsurance contract). [L *retrōcēdere*, *-cēssum*, from *cēdere* to go, yield; partly from **retro-** and **cede**, or Fr *céder*]
■ **retrocé'dent** *adj.* **retrocession** /-sesh'ən/ *n.* **retrocessionaire'** *n* a reinsurer who contractually accepts from another reinsurer a portion of the ceding company's underlying reinsurance risk. **retrocess'ive** *adj.*

retrochoir /ret'rō-kwīr/ (*archit*) *n* an extension of a church behind the position of the high altar. [**retro-**]

retrocognition /ret-rō-kog-ni'shən/ *n* extrasensory knowledge of past events. [**retro-**]

retrod and **retrodden** see **retread**.

retrofit /ret'rō-fit/ *vt* (**ret'rofitting**; **ret'rofitted**) to modify (a house, aircraft, nuclear reactor, etc) some time after construction by incorporating or substituting more up-to-date parts, etc. ◆ *n* (the addition of) a more up-to-date component or accessory. [**retro-**]
■ **ret'rofitting** *n.*

retroflex /ret'rō-fleks/ *adj* bent back (also **retroflect'ed** or **ret'roflexed**); cacuminal (also **ret'roflexed**; *phonetics*). ◆ *vt* and *vi* to turn or bend back. [LL *retroflexus*, from L *retro-* back, from L *flectere*, *flexum* to bend]
■ **retroflexion** or **retroflection** /-flek'shən/ *n.*

retrograde /ret'rō-grād/ *adj* moving or directed backward or (*astron*) from east to west, relatively to the fixed stars; inverse; habitually walking or swimming backwards; degenerating; reverting; contrary (*Shakesp*). ◆ *n* a person who goes back or degenerates; backward movement. ◆ *vi* to go back or backwards, recede; to deteriorate; to have a retrograde movement (*astron*). ◆ *vt* to cause to go back. [L *retrōgradus* going backward, from *retrō-* backward, and *gradī*, *gressus* to go]
■ **retrogradation** /-grə-dā'shən/ *n* (*esp astron*) retrogression. **ret'rogradely** *adv.*

retrogress /ret'rō-gres/ *n* backward movement; degeneration. ◆ *vi* /-gres'/ to retrograde, go backwards; to revert to an earlier, *esp* worse, state or condition. ◆ *vt* to cause to retrogress. [L *retrōgressus* retrogression, from *retrō-* backward, and *gradī*, *gressus* to go]
■ **retrogression** /-gresh'ən/ *n* a going backward or reversion; a decline in quality or merit; retrograde movement (*astron*). **retrogress'ional** or **retrogress'ive** *adj.* **retrogress'ively** *adv.*

retroject /ret'rō-jekt/ *vt* to throw backwards, opp to *project*. [**retro-** and **project**]
■ **retrojec'tion** *n.*

retrolental /ret-rō-len'təl/ *adj* behind the or a lens, *esp* that of the eye. [**retro-** and L *lēns*, *lentis* (see **lens**)]

retromingent /ret-rō-min'jənt/ *adj* urinating backward. ◆ *n* a retromingent animal. [**retro-** and L *mingere* to urinate]
■ **retromin'gency** *n.*

retronym /ret'rə-nim/ *n* a new word or term coined to refer to a concept for which a word already exists, and used to distinguish it from a newer concept, eg *snail mail* (coined after the development of *electronic mail*). [**retro-** and Gr *onyma*, *onoma* name]

retro-operative /ret-rō-op'ə-rə-tiv/ *adj* retrospective in effect. [**retro-**]

retrophilia /ret-rō-fil'i-ə/ *n* love of anything, *esp* material objects, from, connected with or evoking the past. [**retro-**]
■ **retrophil'iac** *n* and *adj.*

retropulsion /ret-rō-pul'shən/ *n* pushing backwards; a tendency to fall backwards experienced by some people with Parkinson's disease. [**retro-** and *pulsion* (*rare*), from L *pulsiō*, *-ōnis*]
■ **retropul'sive** *adj.*

retroreflector /ret-rō-rə-flek'tər or -ri-/ *n* a device, placed on a satellite or a celestial object, that reflects light or radiation back to its source. [**retro-**]
■ **retroreflect'ive** *adj.*

Some words formed with the prefix **re-**.

rē'vise *vt* and *n.*	**rēsalute'** *vt.*	**rēseal'able** *adj.*
rē-roof' *vt.*	**rēsay'** *vt.*	**rēselect'** *vt.*
rē'route *vt.*	**rēseal'** *vt.*	**rēselect'ion** *n.*

---

retro-rocket /ret'rō-rok-it/ *n* a rocket whose function is to slow down, fired in a direction opposite to that in which a body, eg a spacecraft or an artificial satellite, is travelling. [**retro-**]

retrorse /ri-trörs'/ (*biol*) *adj* turned back or downward. [L *retrōrsus*, from *retrōversus*]
■ **retrorse'ly** *adv*.

retrospect /ret'rə-spekt/ *n* reference, regard; a backward view; a view or a looking back; a contemplation of the past. ◆ *vi* to look back. ◆ *vt* to look back on. [L *retrōspicere*, from L *specere*, *spectum* to look]
■ **retrospec'tion** *n*. **retrospec'tive** *adj* looking back; relating to or of the nature of a retrospective; retroactive. ◆ *n* an exhibition, etc presenting the life's work of an artist, musician, etc, or a representative selection of this; an exhibition, etc which looks back over the history or development (of something). **retrospec'tively** *adv*.

retrotransposon /ret-rō-trans-pō'zon/ *n* a type of transposon that replicates by producing an RNA transcript of itself and translating this back into a DNA copy, which can then be inserted at a different site in a chromosome or in a different chromosome in the same cell. [**retro-**]

retroussé /rə-troos'ā or rə-trūs'ā/ *adj esp* of the nose, turned up. [Fr *retrousser* (pap *retroussé*) to turn up]
■ **retroussage** /-äzh'/ *n* wiping aside of ink on an engraved plate to soften tones.

retrovert /ret-rō-vûrt' or ret'rō-vûrt/ *vt* to turn back. [L *retrōvertere*, *-versum*, from *vertere* to turn]
■ **retrover'sion** *n* a turning or falling back; backward displacement. **ret'roverted** *adj*.

Retrovir® /ret'rō-vēr/ *n* the brand name for the drug AZT. [From **retrovirus**]

retrovirus /ret'rō-vī-rəs/ *n* any of a group of eukaryotic viruses whose genetic material is encoded in the form of RNA rather than DNA and which are known to cause a number of diseases. [*reverse transcriptase* (the active enzyme in these viruses) and **virus**]
■ **ret'roviral** *adj*.

retry /rē-trī'/ *vt* (**retry'ing**; **retried'**) to try again (judicially). [**re-**]
■ **rētrī'al** *n*.

retsina /ret-sē'nə/ *n* a Greek resin-flavoured wine. [Gr]

retted, **rettery** and **retting** see **ret**.

Rett's syndrome /rets sin'drōm/ *n* a genetic neurological disorder that mainly affects baby girls, causing dyspraxia and impaired communication. [Andreas *Rett* (1924–97), Austrian paediatrician]

retund /ri-tund'/ *vt* to blunt. [L *retundere* to blunt]

retune /rē-tūn'/ *vt* to alter the tone of (a musical instrument); to readjust (a radio, TV, etc) to produce the optimum response to an incoming signal. ◆ *n* /rē'/ an act or instance of retuning. [**re-**]

return /ri-tûrn'/ *vi* to come or go back; to revert; to recur; to turn away (*Bible*); to continue with change of direction (*archit*). ◆ *vt* to give, put, cast, bring or send back; to answer; to retort; to report officially; to report as appointed or elected; to elect to parliament; to give in return; to lead back or hit back (*sport*); to requite; to repay; to respond to in a similar manner; to render; to yield; to make a turn at an angle (*archit*); to turn round (*Shakesp*); to turn back (*Spenser*); to come back over (*Shakesp*). ◆ *n* the act of returning; a recurrence; reversion, continuation, or a continuing stretch, at an angle, *esp* a right angle (*archit*, etc); that which comes in exchange; proceeds, profit, yield; recompense; requital; an answer; an answering performance; a thing returned, *esp* an unsold newspaper; (in *pl*) a light-coloured mild tobacco (*orig* refuse); the rendering back of a writ by the sheriff, with a report (*law*); an official report or statement, eg of one's taxable income (*tax return*) or (*esp* in *pl*) of the votes cast in an election; election to parliament; a return ticket; the enter key (qv) on a computer keyboard. ◆ *adj* returning; for return; in return; at right angles. [Fr *retourner*, from *re-* back, and *tourner* to turn]
■ **return'able** *adj*. **returnee'** *n* someone who returns or is returned, *esp* home from abroad or war service. **return'er** *n* a person who returns to paid employment after a period of absence, *esp* a woman doing so after having had children. **return'ik** (see **-nik**) a person, *esp* an E European, allowed or deciding to return to his or her country of origin after changes to its political system. **return'less** *adj*.
❑ **return crease** see under **crease**[1]. **returning officer** *n* the officer who presides at an election. **return key** *n* same as **enter key** (see under **enter**). **return match** *n* a second match played at a different

venue by the same teams of players. **return order** *n* (*law*) an order granted by a court at the request of a creditor to the effect that a consumer returns the goods to the creditor. **return shock** *n* an electric shock due to induction sometimes felt after a lightning-flash. **return ticket** *n* a ticket entitling a passenger to travel to a place and back to his or her starting-point.
■ **by return** or **return of post** by the next post leaving in the opposite direction. **in return** in exchange; in reply. **many happy returns** (**of the day**) a conventional expression of good wishes said to a person on his or her birthday.

re-turn /rē-tûrn'/ *vt* and *vi* to turn again or back. [**re-**]

retuse /ri-tūs'/ (*bot*) *adj* with the tip blunt and broadly notched. [L *retūsus*, from *retundere* to blunt]

Reuben sandwich /roo'bən sand'wich or -wij/ *n* a hot sandwich containing corned beef, melted cheese and sauerkraut. [Prob named after its inventor]

reunify /rē-ū'ni-fī/ *vt* to unify (*esp* a country or title that has been divided) again or anew. [**re-**]
■ **rēūnifica'tion** *n*.

reunion /rē-ū'nyən or -ni-ən/ *n* a union, or a meeting, after separation; a social gathering of friends or persons with something in common. [Fr *réunion*, from *re-* again, and *union* union]
■ **reun'ionism** *n*. **reun'ionist** *n* and *adj* (a person) in favour of the reuniting of the Anglican and Roman Catholic Churches. **reunionis'tic** *adj*.

reunite /rē-ū-nīt'/ *vt* and *vi* to join after separation. [**re-**]

re-up /rē-up'/ (chiefly *US*) *vi* to re-enlist for military service. ◆ *vt* to renew. [**re-**]

Rev. *abbrev*: (the Book of) the Revelation of St John, Revelations (*Bible*); Reverend (also **Revd**); revise, revised or revision (also **rev.**).

rev /rev/ *n* a revolution in an internal-combustion engine; an act of revving an engine. ◆ *vt* (**revv'ing**; **revved**) to increase the speed of revolution in (often with *up*). ◆ *vi* to revolve; to increase in speed of revolution. [**revolution**]
❑ **revved-up** *adj* (*fig*) excited, eagerly anticipating something.

revalenta /re-və-len'tə/ *n* lentil-meal (earlier **ervalen'ta**). [*Ervum lens*, Linnaean name of the lentil, from L *ervum* bitter vetch, and *lēns*, *lentis* lentil]

revalorize or **-ise** /rē-val'ə-rīz/ *vt* to give a new value to, *esp* to restore the value of (currency). [**re-**]
■ **rēvalorīza'tion** *n* or **-s-** *n*.

revalue /rē-val'ū/ or **revaluate** /-āt/ *vt* to make a new valuation of; to give a new value to. [**re-**]
■ **rēvaluā'tion** *n*.

revamp /rē-vamp'/ *vt* to renovate, revise, give a new appearance to (also *n*). [**re-**]

revanche /ri-vänch' or (*Fr*) rə-väsh'/ *n* revenge; a policy directed towards recovery of territory lost to an enemy. [Fr; connected with **revenge**]
■ **revanch'ism** *n*. **revanch'ist** *n* and *adj*.

Revd see **Rev.**

reveal[1] /ri-vēl'/ *vt* to make known, as by divine means or inspiration; to disclose; to divulge; to make visible; to allow to be seen. ◆ *n* an act or instance of revealing. [OFr *reveler* (Fr *révéler*), from L *revēlāre*, from *re-* back, and *vēlāre* to veil, from *vēlum* a veil]
■ **reveal'able** *adj*. **reveal'er** *n*. **reveal'ing** *n* and *adj*. **reveal'ingly** *adv*. **reveal'ment** *n* revelation.
❑ **revealed religion** *n* religion based on divine revelation.

reveal[2] /ri-vēl'/ *n* the side surface of a recess, or of the opening for a doorway or window between the frame and the outer surface of the wall. [OFr *revaler* to lower]

revegetate /rē-vej'i-tāt/ *vi* (of plants) to produce new growth. [**re-**]
■ **revegetā'tion** *n*.

reveille /ri-val'i, ri-vel'i, ri-vāl'yi or (*US*) rev'ə-lē/ *n* the sound of the drum or bugle at daybreak to awaken soldiers; a summons to awake, get up or begin. [Fr *réveillez* awake, imperative of *réveiller*, from L *re-* and *vigilāre* to watch]

revel /rev'l/ *vi* (**rev'elling**; **rev'elled**) to feast or make merry in a riotous or noisy manner; to take intense delight, to luxuriate (with *in*). ◆ *vt* to

---

Some words formed with the prefix **re-**.

rēsell' *vt*.	**rēshape'** *vt*.	**rēsole'** *vt*.
rēsent'ence *vt*.	**rēship'** *vt* and *vi*.	**rēspell'** *vt*.
rēsett'le *vt* and *vi*.	**rēship'ment** *n*.	**rēstaff'** *vt*.
rēsett'lement *n*.	**rē-site'** *vt*.	**rēstage'** *vt*.

■ words derived from main entry word; ❑ compound words; ■ idioms and phrasal verbs

spend in revelry. ◆ *n* a riotous feast; merrymaking; a festival or (often in *pl*) occasion of merrymaking, dancing, masquerading, etc. [OFr *reveler*, from L *rebellāre* to rebel]

■ **rev'eller** *n*. **rev'elling** *n*. **rev'elry** *n* revelling.

❑ **rev'el-rout** *n* boisterous revelry; a crowd of revellers.

■ **Master of the Revels** an official organizer of entertainments, *esp* at court or in the Inns of Court.

revelation /re-və-lā'shən or -vi-/ *n* the act or experience of revealing; that which is revealed; a disclosure; an enlightening experience; divine or supernatural communication; **Revelation (of St John)** or, popularly, **Revelations** (*n sing*) the Apocalypse or last book of the New Testament. [L *revēlāre*, *-ātum*; see **reveal**[1]]

■ **revelā'tional** *adj*. **revelā'tionist** *n* a believer in divine revelation; a person who makes a revelation; the author of the Apocalypse or an apocalyptic book. **rev'elātive** *adj*. **rev'elātor** *n*. **rev'elatory** *adj*.

revenant /rəv-nä' or rev'ə-nənt/ *n* a person who returns after a long absence, *esp* from the dead; a ghost. ◆ *adj* returned, *esp* from the dead. [Fr, prp of *revenir* to come back]

revendicate /rē-ven'di-kāt/ *vt* to make formal claim to, or recover by such claim (eg lost territory); to endeavour to have unpaid-for and undamaged goods restored when the buyer is bankrupt. [Variant, through Fr, of **vindicate**]

■ **revendicā'tion** *n*.

revenge /ri-venj'/ *vt* to inflict injury in retribution for; (*esp reflexive*) to avenge. ◆ *vi* to take vengeance. ◆ *n* (the act of inflicting) malicious injury in return for injury received; the desire for retaliation of evil (also in *pl*; *Shakesp*); avenging (*Shakesp*); in games, opportunity of retaliation in a return game; punishment (*obs*). [OFr *revenger*, *revencher* (Fr *revancher*) from L *re-*, and *vindicāre* to lay claim to]

■ **revenge'ful** *adj* ready to seek revenge. **revenge'fully** *adv*. **revenge'fulness** *n*. **revenge'less** *adj*. **revenge'ment** *n* (now *rare*). **reveng'er** *n*. **reveng'ing** *n* and *adj*. **reveng'ingly** *adv*. **reveng'ive** *adj* (*Shakesp*).

revenue /rev'i-nū or -ə- (formerly also ri-ven'ū)/ *n* receipts or return from any source; income; the income of a state; a government department concerned with it. [Fr *revenue*, pap (fem) of *revenir* to return, from L *revenīre*, from *re-* back, and *venīre* to come]

■ **rev'enued** *adj*.

❑ **revenue cutter** *n* (*hist*) an armed vessel employed in preventing smuggling. **revenue tariff** *n* a tariff imposed to generate public revenue.

■ **Inland Revenue** revenue from excise, income tax, etc; the department of the civil service which collects this.

reverb /ri-vûrb'/ or **reverb unit** /ū'nit/ (*music*) *n* a device which creates an effect of reverberation, used in recording or with electrically amplified instruments. [Short form of **reverberate** and **reverberation**]

reverberate /ri-vûr'bə-rāt/ *vt* to beat or send back; to reflect; to echo; to heat in a reverberatory furnace. ◆ *vi* to recoil, rebound; to be reflected; to re-echo; to resound. ◆ *adj* reverberated (*poetic*); reverberating (*Shakesp*). [L *reverberāre*, *-ātum*, from *re-* back, and *verberāre* to beat, from *verber* a lash]

■ **reverb'** (after *Shakesp*). **rever'berant** *adj* reverberating. **rever'berantly** *adv*. **reverberā'tion** *n*. **rever'berātive** (or /-ət-/) *adj*. **rever'berātor** *n*. **rever'beratory** /-ət-ər-i or -āt-/ *adj*.

❑ **reverberation time** *n* (*acoustics*) the time required for the decay of the average sound intensity in a closed room over an amplitude range of 60db. **reverberatory furnace** *n* a furnace in which the flame is turned back over the substance to be heated.

revere /ri-vēr'/ *vt* to regard with high respect; to venerate. [OFr *reverer* (Fr *révérer*), from L *reverērī*, from *re-*, intens, and *verērī* to feel awe]

■ **revēr'able** *adj*. **reverence** /rev'ər-əns/ *n* high respect; respectful awe; veneration; the state of being held in high respect; a gesture or observance of respect. ◆ *vt* to venerate. **rev'erencer** *n*. **rev'erend** *adj* worthy of reverence; clerical; (with *cap*; *usu* written **Rev**) a title prefixed to the name of a member of the clergy. ◆ *n* (*inf*) a member of the clergy. **rev'erent** *adj* feeling or showing reverence. **reverential** /-en'shl/ *adj* proceeding from reverence; respectful; submissive. **reveren'tially** *adv*. **rev'erently** *adv*. **reverer** /ri-vēr'ər/ *n*.

■ **His** (or **Your**) **Reverence** (now *Irish* or *playful*) a mode of referring to or addressing a member of the clergy. **Most Reverend** is used of an archbishop, **Right Reverend**, a bishop, or Moderator of the Church of Scotland, **Very Reverend**, a dean, a former Moderator, or (if a

member of the clergy) a Scottish University principal. **Reverend Mother** a Mother Superior of a convent. **save** or **saving** (**your**) **reverence** (*obs* contracted to **sir-reverence**) with all due respect to you (used when apologizing for introducing an unseemly word or subject).

reverie or **revery** /rev'ə-ri/ *n* an undirected train of thoughts or fancies in meditation; a fanciful notion (*archaic*); mental abstraction; a piece of music expressing such a state of mind. [Fr *rêverie*, from *rêver* to dream]

■ **rev'erist** *n*.

revers /ri-vēr', also (*US*) -vûr' or rə-ver'/ *n* (*pl* **revers** /pronounced as *sing*, or ri-vērz'/) any part of a garment that is turned back, such as a lapel. [Fr, from L *reversus*]

reverse /ri-vûrs'/ *vt* to turn the other way about, as upside down, inside out, in the opposite direction, etc; to invert; to set moving backwards; to overturn (a decision) on appeal to a higher court (*law*); to annul; to bring back (*Spenser*); to turn aside (*Spenser*). ◆ *vi* to move backwards or in the opposite direction; to set an engine, etc moving backwards; to return (*Spenser*). ◆ *n* the contrary, opposite; the back, *esp* of a coin or medal, *opp* to *obverse* ; a setback, misfortune, defeat; a backhanded sword-stroke; the act of reversing; a backwards direction; a direction or order opposite to normal; reverse gear. ◆ *adj* contrary, opposite; turned about; acting in the contrary direction; reversing; backhanded (*obs*); of the rear (*milit*). [L *reversāre* to turn round; partly through Fr]

■ **rever'sal** *n* the act of reversing. **reversed'** *adj*. **rever'sedly** *adv*. **reverse'less** *adj* unalterable. **reverse'ly** *adv*. **rever'ser** *n* someone or something that reverses; a reversing device; a borrower on wadset (*Scots law* ; *obs*). **rever'si** /-sē/ *n* a game in which a captured piece is not removed from the board but turned upside down to show the captor's colour; reversis. **reversibil'ity** *n*. **rever'sible** *adj* able to be reversed (in any sense); of tissues, etc, able to be restored to a normal state (*med*). ◆ *n* a fabric having both sides well finished. **rever'sibly** *adv*. **rever'sing** *n* and *adj*. **rever'sion** /-shən/ *n* the act or fact of reverting or of returning; anything which reverts or returns; the return, or the future possession, of any property after some particular event; the property to which one has such a right; the right to succeed to possession or office; a sum payable upon death; that which is left over, remains; the process by which a mutant phenotype is restored to normal by another mutation of the same gene (also called **back-mutation**; *biol*). **rever'sional** *adj*. **rever'sionally** *adv*. **rever'sionary** *adj* of, relating to, or of the nature of reversion. ◆ *n* a person who has a reversion. **rever'sioner** *n* a reversionary. **rever'sis** *n* an old card game in which the taker of fewest tricks wins. **rever'so** *n* (*pl* **rever'sos**) a verso; a backhanded sword-stroke.

❑ **reversal colour film** *n* film in which the negative image in the respective colour layers is reversed in processing to give a positive transparency. **reverse** (or **reversed**) **discrimination** *n* discrimination in favour of any group previously discriminated against. **reverse engineering** *n* the taking apart of a competitor's product to see how it works, eg with a view to copying it or improving on it. **reverse gear** *n* a gear combination which causes an engine, etc to go in reverse. **reverse genetics** *n sing* the process of removing a gene from an organism, treating it in a known way, reinserting it, and testing the organism for any altered function. **reverse osmosis** *n* (*chem*) purification of water by forcing it under pressure through a membrane impermeable to the impurities to be removed. **reverse pass** *n* (*football*) a pass made when a player runs in one direction and passes in the opposite direction. **reverse printer** *n* (*comput*) a bidirectional printer. **reverse proxy** *n* (*comput*) a proxy server (qv) which controls access from external users to a group of servers on a network. **reverse swing** *n* (*cricket*) a phenomenon that causes a cricket ball that has become roughened on one side to swing in the opposite direction to a new ball. **reverse takeover** *n* (*business*) one in which the company that has been taken over controls the new organization; one in which a smaller company takes over a large company. **reverse transcriptase** *n* the enzyme in a retrovirus which makes a DNA copy of an RNA genome. **reverse yield gap** *n* (*commerce*) the amount by which the average yield on the shares making up the Financial Times ordinary index, or the return on any particular stocks, falls short of the return on $2\frac{1}{2}$% consolidated annuities. **reversible reaction** *n* a chemical reaction that can occur in both directions and, as a mixture of reactants and reaction products is obtained, is incomplete; a

---

Some words formed with the prefix **re-**.

rēstate' *vt*.	**rēstruc'ture** *vt*.	**rēsynchronizā'tion** or
rēstate'ment *n*.	**rēstyle'** *vt*.	**rēsynchronisā'tion** *n*.
rēstock' *vt*.	**rēsubmiss'ion** *n*.	**rēsyn'chronize** or **rēsyn'chronise** *vt*.
rēstring' *vt*.	**rēsubmit'** *vt*.	**rētell'** *vt*.

---

chemical reaction that can be made to proceed in one direction or the other by altering the conditions. **reversing layer** *n* a layer of the sun's chromosphere that reverses bright lines of the spectrum to dark absorption lines. **reversing light** *n* a light on the back of a motor vehicle which comes on when the vehicle is put into reverse gear, providing illumination for the driver, a warning to other road-users, etc. **reversionary bonus** *n* a bonus added to the sum payable on death or at the maturation of an insurance policy.

■ **go into reverse** to engage reverse gear; to move backwards. **reverse the charges** to charge a telephone call to the person who receives it instead of to the caller.

revert /ri-vûrt'/ *vt* to turn back; to reverse. ◆ *vi* to return; to fall back to a former state; to recur to a former subject; to return to the original owner or his or her heirs. [L *re-* back, and *vertere* to turn]

■ **rever'ted** *adj* reversed; turned backwards. **revert'ible** *adj*. **revert'ive** *adj* (*rare*).

revery same as **reverie**.

revest /ri-vest'/ *vt* to clothe again (*Spenser*); to vest again. ◆ *vi* to vest again. [OFr *revestir*, or *re-* and *vestir*, from L *revestīre*, *vestīre* to clothe again, to clothe]

■ **revest'iary** or **revest'ry** *n* a vestry.

revet /ri-vet'/ *vt* (**revett'ing**; **revett'ed**) to face with masonry, etc. [Fr *revêtir* to reclothe]

■ **revet'ment** *n* a retaining wall, facing.

rêveur /re-vœr'/ or (*fem*) **rêveuse** /re-vœz'/ (*Fr*) *n* a daydreamer.

revie /rē-vī'/ *vt* (**rēvy'ing; rēvied'**) to stake more than an opponent has proposed on (eg the taking of a trick); to bandy (words) in emulation (*obs*). ◆ *vi* (*obs*) to stake higher. ◆ *n* (*obs*) an instance of revying. [Fr *renvier*, from L *re-* and *invītāre* to invite]

review /ri-vū'/ *n* a viewing again (also **re-view** /rē'vū'/); a looking back, retrospect; a reconsideration; a survey; a revision; a critical examination; a critique; a periodical with critiques of books, etc; a display and inspection of troops or ships; the judicial revision of a higher court (*law*). ◆ *vt* to see, view or examine again (also **rē-view'**); to look back on or over; to survey; to examine critically; to write a critique on; to inspect, eg troops; to revise. ◆ *vi* to write reviews. [Partly **re-** and **view**; partly Fr *revue*, pap (fem) of *revoir*, from L *revidēre*, from *vidēre* to see]

■ **review'able** *adj* capable of being reviewed. **review'al** *n* a review of a book; reviewing. **review'er** *n* a writer of critiques; a writer in a review.

❑ **review body** *n* a committee set up to review (salaries, etc). **review copy** *n* a copy of a book sent by the publisher to a periodical for review.

revile /ri-vīl'/ *vt* to assail with bitter abuse. ◆ *vi* to rail, use abusive language. ◆ *n* (*obs*) revilement. [OFr *reviler*, from L *re-* and *vīlis* worthless]

■ **revile'ment** *n* the act of reviling; a reviling speech. **revil'er** *n*. **revil'ing** *n* and *adj*. **revil'ingly** *adv*.

revindicate /ri-vin'di-kāt/ *vt* to claim and get back; to vindicate again. [**re-**]

■ **revindicā'tion** *n*.

revise /ri-vīz'/ *vt* to examine and correct; to make a new, improved version of; to study anew; to look at again (*obs*). ◆ *vi* to study in preparation for an examination. ◆ *n* the act of revising or being revised; review; a proof in which previous corrections have been incorporated (*printing*). [Fr *reviser* and L *revīsere*, from *re-* back, and *vīsere*, intensive of *vidēre* to see]

■ **revīs'able** *adj* liable to revision. **revī'sal** *n* a revision. **revī'ser** *n* (also **revī'sor**). **revision** /-vizh'ən/ *n* the act or product of revising. **revi'sional** or **revi'sionary** *adj* relating to revision. **revi'sionism** *n*. **revi'sionist** *n* an advocate of revision (eg of a treaty, of established doctrines, etc); a Communist favouring modification of stricter orthodox Communism and evolution, rather than revolution, as a means of achieving world domination; (a derogatory name for) a Communist who does not hold to what some other Communist considers to be orthodox Communism (also loosely and *fig*); a reviser of the Bible. **revī'sory** *adj*.

❑ **Revised Version** *n* an English translation of the Bible issued 1881– 5 (Apocrypha 1895), further revised 1946–52 (**Revised Standard Version**). **revising barrister** *n* till 1918, a barrister appointed to revise the parliamentary voters' roll.

revisit /rē-viz'it/ *vt* to visit again; to experience or consider (something) again. ◆ *n* the act of revisiting a place or experience. [**re-**]

revitalize or **-ise** /rē-vī'tə-līz/ *vt* to imbue with new life or energy. [**re-**]

■ **rēvītalizā'tion** or **-s-** *n*.

revive /ri-vīv'/ *vt* and *vi* to bring back or come back to life, vigour, being, activity, consciousness, memory, good spirits, freshness, vogue, notice, currency, use, the stage, or natural metallic form. [L *revīvere* to live again, from *vīvere* to live]

■ **revīvabil'ity** *n*. **revī'vable** *adj*. **revī'vably** *adv*. **revī'val** *n* the act or fact of reviving; the state of being revived; recovery from languor, neglect, depression, etc; renewed performance, a restaged production, of a play, etc; renewed interest or attention; a time of extraordinary religious awakening or sometimes worked-up excitement; a series of meetings to encourage this; quickening; renewal; awakening. **revī'valism** *n*. **revī'valist** *n* a person who promotes religious, architectural or other revival; an itinerant preacher. **revivalist'ic** *adj*. **revive'ment** *n* (*rare*). **revī'ver** *n* someone or something that revives; a renovating preparation; a stimulant (*sl*). **revī'ving** *n* and *adj*. **revī'vingly** *adv*. **revī'vor** *n* (*law*; *obs*) the revival of a suit which was abated by the death of a party or other cause.

■ **Gothic Revival** the reintroduction of Gothic style architecture in (and before) the 19c. **Revival of Learning** the Renaissance. **Romantic Revival** see under **romantic**.

revivescent see **reviviscent**.

revivify /ri-viv'i-fī/ *vt* (**reviv'ifying; reviv'ified**) to restore to life; to put new life into; to reactivate. ◆ *vt* and *vi* (*chem*) to revive, restore (eg metal) to its uncombined state. [LL *revīvificāre*, from *re-*, *vīvus* alive, and *facere* to make]

■ **revivificā'tion** *n*.

reviviscent /re-vi-vis'ənt/ or /rē-vī-/ or **revivescent** /-ves'ənt/ *adj* reviving. [L *revīvīscere*, *-ēscere*]

■ **revivisc'ence** or **revivisc'ency** *n* (also **revivesc'ence** or **revivesc'ency**).

revoke /ri-vōk'/ *vt* to recall, call back (now *rare*); to annul; to retract; to withdraw (*Spenser*); to check (*Spenser*). ◆ *vi* to make revocations; to neglect to follow suit at cards. ◆ *n* revocation, recall; the act of revoking at cards. [L *revocāre*, from *vocāre* to call]

■ **revocable** /rev'ō-kə-bl/ *adj*. **rev'ocableness** or **revocabil'ity** *n*. **rev'ocably** *adv*. —Also **revokable**, etc. **revocā'tion** *n* recall; the act of revoking. **rev'ocatory** *adj*. **revoke'ment** *n* (*Shakesp*) revocation. **revōk'er** *n* someone who revokes at cards.

revolt /ri-vōlt'/ or /-volt'/ *vi* to renounce allegiance; to rise in opposition; to turn or rise in disgust, loathing or repugnance. ◆ *vt* to inspire revulsion or repugnance in; to turn back (*Spenser*); to cause to rise in revolt (*obs*). ◆ *n* a rebellion; insurrection; secession; revulsion (*Shakesp*); a rebel (*Shakesp*). [Fr *révolter*, from L *re-* and *volūtāre*, frequentative of *volvere*, *volūtum* to turn]

■ **revolt'ed** *adj* shocked, outraged; insurgent. **revol'ter** *n*. **revol'ting** *adj*. **revol'tingly** *adv*.

revolute see under **revolve**.

revolution /re-və-loo'shən/ or /-lū'/ *n* the act or condition of revolving; movement in an orbit, as distinguished from rotation; (less commonly) rotation; a complete turn by an object or figure, through four right angles, about an axis; a cycle of phenomena or of time; recurrence in cycles; turning over in the mind (*archaic*); mutation (*Shakesp*); a great upheaval; a complete change, eg in outlook, social habits or circumstances; a radical change in government; a time of intensified change in the earth's features (*geol*). [LL *revolūtiō*, *-ōnis*]

■ **revolu'tional** *adj* of revolution in movement. **revolu'tionary** *adj* of, favouring, or of the nature of revolution, *esp* in government or conditions. ◆ *n* a person who takes part in, supports or advocates a revolution. **revolu'tioner** *n* (*hist*) a supporter of a revolution, *esp* that of 1688. **revolu'tionism** *n*. **revolu'tionist** *adj* and *n* (a person) supporting or advocating revolution. **revolu'tionize** or **-ise** *vt* to cause radical change, or a revolution, in; to make revolutionary.

❑ **Revolutionary Calendar** *n* the calendar used in France from 1793 to 1805 (see **Vendémiaire**, **Brumaire**, **Frimaire**, **Nivôse** under **nival**, **Pluviôse** under **pluvial**, **Ventôse** under **ventose**, **Germinal**, **Floréal** under **flora**, **Prairial**, **Messidor**, **Thermidor** and **Fructidor**).

■ **the American Revolution** the change from the condition of British colonies to national independence effected by the thirteen states of the American Union in 1776. **the French Revolution** the overthrow of

---

Some words formed with the prefix **re-**.

rētell'er *n*.	**rēti'tle** *vt*.	**rēturf'** *vt*.
rētie' *vt*.	**rētrain'** *vt* and *vi*.	**rētweet'** *vt*.
rētile' *vt*.	**rētrans'fer** *vt* and *n*.	**rē-type'** *vt*.
rētime' *vt*.	**rētrim'** *vt*.	**rēuphol'ster** *vt*.

■ words derived from main entry word; ❑ compound words; ■ idioms and phrasal verbs

the old French monarchy and absolutism (1789). **the glorious Revolution** the expulsion of James II from the British throne (1688–9) that established the power of Parliament over the monarch.

revolve /ri-volv'/ *vt* and *vi* to turn round on a centre or axis; to rotate; to ponder; to roll back, return (*obs*). ◆ *n* turning, revolution; a part of the stage which can be revolved by hand or electrical means, providing one method of scene-changing (*theatre*). [L *revolvere, revolūtum,* from *volvere* to roll]

■ **revolute** /rev'əl-ūt or -oot/ *adj* (*bot*) rolled backward and *usu* downward. **revol'vable** *adj*. **revol'vency** *n* revolution; a tendency to revolve. **revol'ver** *n* a revolving device of various kinds; a pistol with a rotating magazine. **revol'ving** *n* and *adj*.

❑ **revolving credit** *n* credit which is automatically renewed as the sum previously borrowed is paid back, so allowing the borrower to make repeated use of the credit so long as the agreed maximum sum is not exceeded. **revolving door** *n* a door consisting of *usu* four leaves fixed around a central axis and standing within a cylindrical structure open at opposite sides to allow entrance and egress; (used *attrib*) designating the process whereby retiring government employees are offered senior consultative positions in companies with whom they had had contact through their previous job (*fig*); a company or organization that people join and leave very quickly (*fig*). **revolving fund** *n* a fund that is being replenished as withdrawals are made, *usu* by income from invested finances.

revue /ri-vū'/ *n* a loosely constructed theatrical show, more or less topical and musical. [Fr, review]

revulsion /ri-vul'shən/ *n* withdrawal; disgust; a sudden change or reversal, *esp* of feeling; diversion to another part, *esp* by counter-irritation (*med*). [L *revellere, revulsum* to pluck back, from *vellere* to pluck]

■ **revul'sionary** *adj*. **revul'sive** /-siv/ *adj*.

revved, etc see **rev**.

Rev. Ver. *abbrev* : Revised Version.

revying see **revie**.

rew /roo/ (*Spenser*) same as **rue**[1,2] and **row**[1].

reward /ri-wörd'/ *n* that which is given in return for good (sometimes evil), or in recognition of merit, or for performance of a service. ◆ *vt* to give or be a reward to or for; to give as a reward (*Bible*). [OFr *rewarder, regarder,* from *re-* again, and *warder, garder* to guard; see **regard, guard** and **ward**]

■ **reward'able** *adj* capable or worthy of being rewarded. **reward'ableness** *n*. **reward'er** *n*. **reward'ful** *adj* yielding reward. **reward'ing** *adj* profitable; yielding pleasure or satisfaction; yielding a result well worthwhile. **reward'less** *adj* unrewarded.

rewarewa /rē'wə-rē'wə or rä'wə-rä'wə/ *n* a New Zealand tree (*Knightia excelsa*) whose wood is used in furniture-making (in NZ also called **honeysuckle**). [Maori]

rewild /rē-wīld'/ *vt* to release (an animal) from captivity into the wild; to return (land) to a natural, undeveloped state. [**re-**]

rewind /rē-wīnd'/ *vt* (pat and pap **rēwound'**) to wind again; to wind back (a film, tape recording, etc) to the beginning or a specific place. ◆ *n* /rē'wīnd/ the action of rewinding; a thing rewound; a mechanism for rewinding. [**re-**]

■ **rewind'er** *n*.

rewire /rē-wīr'/ *vt* to fit (a house) with new electrical wiring. [**re-**]

■ **rewir'able** or **rewire'able** *adj*.

reword /rē-wûrd'/ *vt* to repeat, re-echo (*Shakesp*); to put into different words. [**re-**]

■ **reword'ing** *n*.

rework /rē-wûrk'/ *vt* to alter, revise or refashion, *esp* in order to use again. [**re-**]

■ **rework'ing** *n*.

rewound pat and pap of **rewind**.

rewrite /rē-rīt'/ *vt* (pat **rewrote'**; pap **rewritt'en**) to write again or anew; to retain (data) in an area of a store by recording it in the area from which it has been read (*comput*). ◆ *n* /rē'rīt/ an act of rewriting; something that has been rewritten. [**re-**]

■ **rewrīt'able** *adj* (*comput*) (of data) capable of being recorded in the area from which it has been read.

rewth /rooth/ (*Spenser*) same as **ruth**.

Rex /reks/ *n* king; the title used by a reigning king (*abbrev* **R**); a type of cat of either of two varieties, Devon Rex or Cornish Rex, with a curly but thin coat (also **Rex cat**); a type of domestic rabbit in which the hair that would normally form the outer coat is shorter than that of the under coat (also **Rex rabbit**), one variety, **Astrex** /as'treks/ (*Ast*rakhan) having curly or wavy fur.

rex see **reak**[1].

Rexine® /rek'sēn/ *n* a type of artificial leather.

Reye's syndrome /rīz sin'drōm/ (*med*) *n* a rare, acute and often fatal disease of children, affecting the brain and the liver. [RDK *Reye* (1912–78), Australian paediatrician]

Reynard or **reynard** /rā'närd, ren'ärd or -ərd/ *n* a fox, from the fox in the famous animal fable of Late German origin, *Reynard the Fox* (also (*Spenser*) **Reyn'old**). [MDu *Reynaerd,* from OHGer *Reginhart,* literally, strong in counsel]

Reynolds number /ren'əldz num'bər/ (*mech*) *n* a number designating type of flow of a fluid in a system, obtained from the product of the fluid's density, velocity and dimension at a particular point, divided by its viscosity. [Osborne *Reynolds* (1842–1912), British physicist]

rez see **res**.

rezone /rē-zōn'/ *vt* to alter (the boundaries of) a zone. [**re-**]

RF *abbrev* : radio frequency; *République française* (*Fr*), French Republic.

Rf (*chem*) *symbol* : rutherfordium.

rf (*music*) *abbrev* : rinforzando.

RFA *abbrev* : Royal Fleet Auxiliary.

RFC *abbrev* : (until 1918) Royal Flying Corps; Rugby Football Club.

RFID *abbrev* : Radio Frequency Identification, a method of storing and retrieving information by means of tiny tags that can transmit and receive radio signals.

RFS *abbrev* : Register of Friendly Societies (now replaced by **FSA**).

RFU *abbrev* : Rugby Football Union.

RG *abbrev* : Republic of Guinea (IVR).

Rg (*chem*) *symbol* : roentgenium.

RGB *abbrev* : Republic of Guinea-Bissau (IVR).

RGN *abbrev* : Registered General Nurse.

RGS *abbrev* : Royal Geographical Society (now often **RGS-IBG** since amalgamation with the Institute of British Geographers).

Rgt *abbrev* : regiment.

RGV *abbrev* : Remote Guidance Vehicle.

RH *abbrev* : Republic of Haiti (IVR); Royal Highness.

Rh *abbrev* : rhesus; Rhesus factor.

Rh *symbol* : rhodium (*chem*).

rh *abbrev* : right hand or right-hand.

RHA *abbrev* : Regional Health Authority (replaced by **DHSC**); Royal Hibernian Academy; Royal Horse Artillery.

rhabdus /rab'dəs/ *n* a rodlike sponge spicule. [Latinized from Gr *rhabdos* rod]

■ **rhab'doid** *adj* rodlike. ◆ *n* a rodlike body. **rhab'dolith** *n* (Gr *lithos* stone) a calcareous rod in some Protozoa. **rhab'dom** *n* (Gr *rhabdōma* bundle of rods) a fourfold rod in the compound eye of an arthropod. **rhab'domancer** *n*. **rhab'domancy** *n* (Gr *manteiā* divination) divination by rod, *esp* divining for water or ore. **rhab'domantist** *n*. **rhabdomyol'ysis** *n* (Gr *lysis* dissolution) the breaking down of muscle tissue, *esp* following skeletal trauma. **rhabdomyō'ma** *n* (*pl* **rhabdomyō'mas** or **rhabdomyō'mata**) a tumour of striped muscle. **Rhabdoph'ora** *n pl* the graptolites. **rhab'dosphere** *n* an aggregation of rhabdoliths in oceanic ooze.

rhachis same as **rachis**.

rhachitis same as **rachitis**.

Some words formed with the prefix **re-**.

rēurge' *vt*.	**rēval'idate** *vt*.	**rēwash'** *vt*.
rēūs'able *adj*.	**rēvalidā'tion** *n*.	**rēwat'er** *vt*.
rēuse' *vt* and *n*.	**rēvar'nish** *vt*.	**rēwax'** *vt*.
rēutt'er *vt*.	**rēvict'ual** *vt* and *vi*.	**rēweigh'** *vt*.
rēvac'cinate *vt*.	**rēvis'itant** *n*.	**rēweight'** *vt*.
rēvaccinā'tion *n*.	**rēvisitā'tion** *n*.	**rēwrap'** *vt*.

Rhadamanthine /ra-də-man'thīn/ adj rigorously just and severe, like *Rhadamanthus* (Gr -os), a judge of the lower world.

Rhaetia or **Raetia** /rē'shə or rē'shyə/ n (hist) a province of the Roman Empire, roughly Grisons and Tyrol, to which Vindelicia was added.
■ **Rhae'tian** adj (also **Rae'tian**) from Rhaetia; (also **Rhaetic** /rē'tik/) of the Upper Triassic (also **Keuper**) or (according to others) Lower Jurassic (geol). ◆ n (also **Rae'tian**) a person from Rhaetia; (also **Rhae'tic**) the Rhaetian epoch.
◻ **Rhaeto-Roman'ic**, **Rhae'tic** or **Rhaeto-Romance'** n and adj (of) a group of Romance dialects spoken from SE Switzerland to Friuli (Romansch, Ladin and Friulian).

rhagades /rag'a-dēz/ (med) n pl cracks or fissures in the skin. [Gr *rhagas*, pl *rhagades* a tear, rent]
■ **rhagad'iform** adj.

Rhamnus /ram'nəs/ n the buckthorn genus, giving name to the family **Rhamnā'ceae**. [Latinized from Gr *rhamnos*]
■ **rhamnā'ceous** adj.

rhamphoid /ram'foid/ adj hook-beak-shaped. [Gr *rhamphos* a hooked beak]
■ **Rhamphast'os**, now usu **Ramphast'os** n the typical genus of toucans. **Rhamphorhynchus** /ram-fō-ring'kəs/ n (Gr *rhynchos* snout) a genus of pterodactyls. **rhamphothē'ca** n (Gr *thēkē* case) the horny sheath of a bird's bill.

rhaphe same as **raphe**.

rhaphide, **rhaphis** see **raphis**.

rhapontic /ra-pon'tik/ n the common rhubarb, *Rheum rhaponticum*. [LL *rhā ponticum* Pontic rhubarb; see **rhubarb**]

rhapsody /rap'sə-di/ n an ecstatic utterance of feeling; an irregular, emotional piece of music; an epic or instalment of an epic recited at one sitting (Gr hist); a patching or stringing together of poems (obs); an orderless, unconnected composition, or collection of things said, beliefs, etc (obs). [Gr *rhapsōidia* an epic, a rigmarole, from *rhaptein* to sew, and *ōidē* a song]
■ **rhapsode** /raps'ōd/ n a reciter of Homeric or other epics. **rhapsodic** /-od'ik/ adj of rhapsodes or rhapsodies; of the nature of rhapsody. **rhapsod'ical** adj rhapsodic; unrestrainedly enthusiastic, rapt. **rhapsod'ically** adv. **rhaps'odist** n a rhapsode; a person who rhapsodizes. **rhaps'odize** or **-ise** /-ə-dīz/ vt to recite in rhapsodies; to piece together (obs). ◆ vi to write or utter rhapsodies.

rhatany /rat'ə-ni/ n either of two S American caesalpiniaceous plants (species of *Krameria*); the astringent root of either plant. [Sp *ratania*, from Quechua *rataña*]

rhea[1] /rē'ə/ n a small flightless S American bird of the genus *Rhea*, resembling the ostrich; (with cap) the fifth satellite of Saturn. [*Rhea*, daughter of Uranus and Ge in Gr myth]

rhea[2] /rē'ə/ n rami. [Assamese *rihā*]

rhebok same as **reebok**.

Rheinberry see under **Rhine**.

rhematic /rē-mat'ik/ adj of words or verbs; forming a word or words. [Gr *rhēma*, *-atos* word, verb]

Rhemish /rē'mish/ adj of Rheims (Reims) in NE France.
■ **Rhē'mist** n a translator of the Rhemish version.
◻ **Rhemish version** n the English translation of the New Testament by Roman Catholics of the English college at Rheims (1582).

Rhenish /ren'ish or rē'nish/ adj of the river *Rhine*. ◆ n (also **Rhenish wine**) Rhine wine, esp hock. [L *Rhēnus* the Rhine]
■ **rhenium** /rē'ni-əm/ n a chemical element (symbol **Re**; atomic no 75) discovered by X-ray spectroscopy in Germany in 1925.

rheo- /rē-ō-/ combining form denoting current or flow. [Gr *rheos* flow]
■ **rhē'ochord** or **rhē'ocord** n a wire rheostat. **rheolog'ic** or **rheolog'ical** adj. **rheol'ogist** n. **rheol'ogy** n the science of the deformation and flow of matter. **rheom'eter** n an instrument for measuring a current of fluid; a galvanometer (obs). **rheomet'rical** adj. **rhē'ostat** n an instrument for varying an electric resistance. **rheostat'ic** adj. **rheotax'is** n rheotropism. **rhē'otome** n (electronics) an interrupter. **rhē'otrope** n a commutator for reversing an electric current. **rheotrop'ic** adj. **rheot'ropism** n (biol) response to the stimulus of flowing water.

rhesus /rē'səs/ or **rhesus monkey** /mung'kē/ n a macaque, the bandar (*Macacus rhesus* or *Macaca mulatta*), a monkey of the Indian Subcontinent, used extensively in medical research. [Gr *Rhēsos*, a king of Thrace, arbitrarily applied]
◻ **Rhesus baby** n a baby born with a blood disorder because its rhesus-positive blood is incompatible with the mother's rhesus-negative blood. **Rhesus factor**, **Rh-factor** or **Rh** n any of a group of weakly antigenic agglutinogens usu found in human red blood cells and in those of rhesus monkeys, inherited according to Mendelian

laws, **Rh-positive** people being those who have the factor, and **Rh-negative** those (a very much smaller number) who do not (a difference important in blood transfusion and as explaining haemolytic disease of the newborn).

rhet. abbrev : rhetoric.

rhetor /rē'tōr/ n (Gr hist) a teacher of rhetoric; a professional orator. [Gr *rhētōr*]
■ **rhetoric** /ret'ər-ik/ n the theory and practice of eloquence, whether spoken or written, the whole art of using language so as to persuade others; the art of literary expression, esp in prose; false, showy, artificial, or declamatory expression. **rhetoric** /ri-tor'ik/ (rare) or **rhetor'ical** adj relating to rhetoric; oratorical; inflated, over-elaborate or insincere in style. **rhetor'ically** adv. **rhetorician** /ret-ər-ish'ən/ n a person who teaches the art of rhetoric; an orator; a user of rhetorical language. **rhetorize** or **-ise** /re'/ vi (obs) to use rhetorical language. ◆ vt (Milton) to address rhetorically.
◻ **rhetorical question** n a question in form only, made for effect and not calling for an answer.

Rheum /rē'əm/ n the rhubarb genus. [Latinized from Gr *rhēon*]

rheum /room/ n a mucous discharge, esp from the nose; tears (poetic); a cold in the head (obs); (in pl) rheumatic pains (rare); ill humour (obs). [Gr *rheuma*, *-atos* flow, from *rheein* to flow]
■ **rheumatic** /roo-mat'ik or (Shakesp) roo'/ adj of the nature of, relating to, apt to cause or affected with rheumatism or (obs) rheum. ◆ n a person who suffers from rheumatism; (in pl) rheumatic pains (inf). **rheumat'ical** adj. **rheumat'ically** adv. **rheumat'icky** adj. **rheumatism** /roo'mə-tizm/ n a condition characterized by pain and stiffness in muscles and joints (dialect **rheu'matiz**, **rheu'matize**, **rheu'matise** or **rheu'mateese**). **rheumatis'mal** adj. **rheum'atoid** adj resembling rheumatism; relating to rheumatoid arthritis. **rheumatolog'ical** adj. **rheumatol'ogist** n. **rheumatol'ogy** n the study of rheumatism and related disorders of the joints and muscles. **rheumed** adj. **rheum'y** adj of or like rheum; (esp of air) cold and damp.
◻ **rheumatic fever** n an acute disease characterized by fever, multiple arthritis, and liability of the heart to be inflamed, caused by a streptococcal infection. **rheumatoid arthritis** n a disease or diseases characterized by inflammation and swelling of joints, often leading to their complete stiffening.

rhexis /rek'sis/ n rupture, esp of a blood vessel. [Gr *rhēxis* breach]

RHF abbrev : Royal Highland Fusiliers.

Rh-factor see under **rhesus**.

RHG abbrev : Royal Horse Guards.

rhime an obsolete spelling of **rhyme**.

rhin- see **rhino-**.

rhinal see under **rhino-**.

Rhincodon /rin'kō-don/ n a genus of sharks occurring in tropical and temperate seas. [Gr *rhynchos* a snout, and *odous*, *odontos* a tooth]

Rhine /rīn/ n a river of W and Central Europe. [Ger *Rhein*; Du *Rijn*]
◻ **Rhine'berry** or **Rhein'berry** n the buckthorn berry; the buckthorn. **Rhine'grave** n (Du *Rijngrave*, now *-graaf*; hist) a count with possessions on the Rhine. **Rhine'gravine** /-ēn/ n (Du *Rijngravin*) a female Rhinegrave; the wife or widow of a Rhinegrave. **Rhine'stone** n (also without cap) an imitation diamond made of paste. **Rhine wine** n wine made from grapes grown in the Rhine valley, esp hock.

rhine /rēn/ (Somerset, etc) n a ditch or watercourse (also spelt **reen**, **rean** or **rhyne**).

rhinencephalic and **rhinencephalon** see under **rhino-**.

Rhineodon /rī-nē'ō-don/, also **Rhinodon** /rī'nō-don/ n former names of the whale-shark genus *Rhincodon*. [Gr *rhīnē* a file, and *odous*, *odontos* a tooth]

rhinitis see under **rhino-**.

rhino[1] /rī'nō/ n (pl **rhī'nos**) short for **rhinoceros**.
◻ **rhino bars** n pl (E Afr) bullbars (qv under **bull**[1]).

rhino[2] /rī'nō/ (archaic sl) n money. [Connection with **rhino**[1] and **rhinoceros** obscure]
■ **rhinocerical** /-ser'i-kl/ adj (archaic sl) rich.

rhino- /rī-nō-/ or before a vowel **rhin-** /rīn-/ combining form denoting nose. [Gr *rhīs*, *rhīnos* nose]
■ **rhī'nal** adj of the nose. **rhinencephalic** /-al'ik/ adj. **rhinencephalon** /rīn-en-sef'ə-lon/ n (Gr *enkephalon* brain) the olfactory lobe of the brain. **rhinī'tis** n inflammation of the mucous membrane of the nose. **rhinolalia** /-lā'li-ə/ n (Gr *laliā* talk) nasal speech. **rhī'nolith** n (Gr *lithos* stone) a concretion in the nose. **rhinolog'ical** adj. **rhinol'ogist** n a nose specialist. **rhinol'ogy** n the study of the nose; nasal pathology. **rhinopharyngitis** /rī-nō-far-in-jī'tis/ n inflammation of the nose and pharynx. **rhinophyma** /-fī'/ n (Gr *phȳma* growth, tumour) overgrowth of skin and subcutaneous tissue of the nose. **rhinoplas'tic** adj. **rhī'noplasty** n plastic surgery of

---

■ words derived from main entry word; ◻ compound words; ■ idioms and phrasal verbs

the nose. **rhinorrhagia** /rī-nō-rā'jyə/ n (Gr *rhēgnynai* to break) excessive nose-bleeding. **rhīnorrhoea** /-rē'ə/ n (Gr *rhoiā* flow) excessive mucous discharge from the nose. **rhīnorrhoe'al** adj. **rhīnoscleroma** /-sklē-rō'mə/ n a disease with hard swelling in the nose, etc. **rhī'noscope** n an instrument for examining the nose. **rhīnoscop'ic** adj. **rhīnos'copy** n. **rhīnothē'ca** n (Gr *thēkē* case) the sheath of a bird's upper mandible. **rhī'novirus** n a virus belonging to a subgroup of picornaviruses thought responsible for the common cold and other respiratory diseases.

rhinoceros /rī-nos'ə-rəs/ or ri-/, (obs) **rhinocerot** /-rot/ or **rhinocerote** /-rōt/ n (pl **rhinoc'eroses**, obs rhinocerotes /-ō'tēz/) a large ungulate of several species in Africa and S Asia, constituting a family (**Rhīnocerot'idae**) characterized by one or two horns on the nose. [Gr *rhīnokerōs*, from *rhīs*, *rhīnos* nose, and *keras* horn]
- **rhinocerot'ic** adj.
- **rhinoceros beetle** n a very large beetle (of various genera) with a large upcurved horn on the head. **rhinoceros bird** n an oxpecker that alights on the rhinoceros; a hornbill.

Rhinodon see **Rhineodon**.

rhinolalia...to...**rhinovirus** see under **rhino-**.

rhipidate /rip'i-dāt/ adj fan-shaped. [Gr *rhīpis*, *rhīpidos* a fan]
- **rhipid'ion** n in the Greek Orthodox Church, the Eucharistic fan or flabellum. **rhipid'ium** n (bot) a fan-shaped cymose inflorescence. **Rhipip'tera** or **Rhipidop'tera** n pl the Strepsiptera.

RHistS abbrev : Royal Historical Society.

rhizo- /rī-zō-/ or before a vowel **rhiz-** /rīz-/ combining form denoting root. [Gr *rhiza* root]
- **rhīzan'thous** adj (bot) seeming to flower from the root. **rhī'zic** adj of the root of an equation. **rhī'zine** /-zin/ n a lichen rhizoid. **rhizō'bium** n (pl **rhizō'bia**) a bacterium of the *Rhizobium* genus of bacteria, important in nitrogen fixation by leguminous plants. **rhī'zocarp** n (Gr *karpos* fruit) a water fern or heterosporous fern; a plant with sporangia on rootlike processes; a perennial herb; a plant fruiting underground. **rhīzocar'pic** or **rhīzocar'pous** adj. **rhī'zocaul** n (Gr *kaulos* stalk) the rootlike stalk of a hydrozoan colony. **Rhīzoceph'ala** n pl (Gr *kephalē* head) an order of Cirripedes parasitic on crabs. **rhīzogen'ic** or **rhīzogenet'ic** or **rhīzog'enous** adj producing roots. **rhī'zoid** n a short hairlike organ in the lower plants, serving as a root. **rhīzoi'dal** adj. **rhīzō'matous** adj. **rhī'zome** n (Gr *rhizōma* a root-mass) a rootstock, an underground stem producing roots and leafy shoots. **rhī'zomorph** n (Gr *morphē* form) a rootlike mass of fungal hyphae. **rhīzomorph'ous** adj having the form of a root. **rhīzoph'agous** adj root-eating. **rhīzoph'ilous** adj growing on roots. **Rhīzoph'ora** n the mangrove genus, with great development of aerial roots, giving name to the family **Rhīzophorā'ceae**. **rhī'zophore** n a root-bearing structure, esp in *Selaginella*. **rhī'zoplane** n the surface of a root together with the soil adhering to it. **rhī'zopod** n any member of the **Rhīzop'oda**, protozoa with rootlike pseudopodia. **rhī'zopus** n a mould of the *Rhizopus* genus. **rhī'zosphere** n the region in the soil surrounding a plant's root system, affected by its excretions and characterized by considerable microbiological activity.

Rh-negative see **Rhesus factor** under **rhesus**.

rho /rō/ n (pl **rhos**) the seventeenth letter (P or ρ) of the Greek alphabet, corresponding to R; as a numeral ρ' = 100, ‚ρ = 100000. [Gr *rhō*]

rhod- /rōd-/ or **rhodo-** /rō-dō-/ combining form signifying: rose; rose-coloured. [Gr *rhodon* rose]
- **rhō'damine** /-mēn/ n (see *amine*) a synthetic dyestuff, usu red, related to fluorescein. **rhō'danate** n (in dyeing) a thiocyanate. **rhōdan'ic** adj thiocyanic. **rhō'danize** or **-ise** vt to electroplate with rhodium. **rhō'dic** adj of rhodium in higher valency. **Rhodites** /rō-dī'tēz/ n a gallfly that forms bedeguars on the wild rose. **rhō'dium** n a metallic element (symbol **Rh**; atomic no 45) of the platinum group, forming rose-coloured salts (**rhodium-wood** the scented wood of Canary Island convolvulus, yielding **oil of rhodium**). **rhodochrosite** /rō-dō-krō'sīt/ n (Gr *rhodochrōs* rose-coloured) manganese spar, a pink rhombohedral mineral, manganese carbonate. **rhōdodaph'ne** (or /rod-/) n (Gr *daphnē* laurel; *Spenser*) oleander. **rhō'dolite** n a pink or purple garnet (gemstone). **rhō'donite** n a rose-red anorthic pyroxene, manganese silicate. **rhō'dophane** n (Gr *phainein* to show) a red pigment in the retinal cones of birds, etc. **Rhodophyceae** /-fish'i-ē/ n pl (Gr *phȳkos* seaweed) the red seaweeds (including some forms that are neither red nor found in the sea), one of the main divisions of the algae, in which the chlorophyll is usually masked by a red pigment. **rhōdop'sin** n (Gr *opsis* sight) visual purple. **rhō'dous** adj of rhodium in lower valency. **Rhodymenia** /rō-di-mē'ni-ə/ n (Gr *hymēn* a membrane) the dulse genus of red seaweeds.

Rhode Island red /rōd ī'lənd red/ n an American breed of domestic fowl with dark reddish-brown feathers. [*Rhode Island*, the US state]

Rhodesian /rō-dē'z(h)yən or -z(h)i-ən, also -s(h)yən or -s(h)i-ən/ adj of or relating to *Rhodesia*, a former region of southern Africa consisting of

Zambia (formerly *Northern Rhodesia*) and Zimbabwe (formerly *Southern Rhodesia*, later simply *Rhodesia*). ◆ n a native or inhabitant of Rhodesia.
- **Rhodesian man** n an extinct type of man represented by a skull found in Northern Rhodesia in 1921. **Rhodesian ridgeback** /rij'bak/ n a hunting dog with a ridge of hair along the back.

Rhodian /rō'di-ən/ adj of or relating to *Rhodes*, an island and ancient city state of the Aegean (also n).
- **Rhodian laws** n pl the earliest system of marine law. **Rhodian school** n a school of Hellenistic sculpture.

rhodic see under **rhod-**.

rhodie or **rhody** /rō'di/ (inf) n rhododendron.

Rhodites...to...**rhododaphne** see under **rhod-**.

rhododendron /rō-də-den'drən or ro-də-den'drən/ n (pl **rhododen'drons** or **rhododen'dra** /-drə/) any member of the *Rhododendron* genus of trees and shrubs of the heath family, with leathery leaves and large showy slightly zygomorphic flowers, some species being called *Alpine rose*. [Gr *rhodon* rose, and *dendron* tree]

rhodolite see under **rhod-**.

rhodomontade same as **rodomontade**.

rhodonite...to...**rhodopsin** see under **rhod-**.

rhodora /rō-dō'rə or -dō'/ n a N American species of *Rhododendron*, or separate related genus. [L *rhodōra* meadow-sweet, said to be a Gallic plant-name]

rhodous and **Rhodymenia** see under **rhod-**.

rhody see **rhodie**.

Rhoeadales /rē-ə-dā'lēz/ n pl an order of dicotyledons including poppies, Cruciferae, etc. [Gr *rhoias*, *-ados* corn poppy]
- **rhoe'adine** /-dēn/ n an alkaloid found in poppies.

rhoicissus /rō-i-sis'əs/ n any climbing plant of the genus *Rhoicissus* of the family Vitaceae, esp the **grape ivy** (*Rhoicissus rhomboidea*) with rhomboid, toothed leaves, often grown as a foliage pot plant. [New L, from Gr *rhoia* pomegranate]

rhomb /rom(b)/ n an equilateral parallelogram (usu excluding the square); a lozenge-shaped object; anything that whirls, such as (*Milton*) the wheel of day and night (obs); a magic wheel; a rhombohedron (crystallog). [Gr *rhombos* bull-roarer, magic wheel, rhombus]
- **rhombencephalon** /rom-ben-sef'ə-lon/ n (Gr *enkephalon* brain) the hind-brain. **rhombenporphyr** /rom-ben-pör'fēr/ (from Ger), **rhombenpor'phyry** or **rhomb'por'phyry** n an intermediate, moderately fine-grained igneous rock with feldspar phenocrysts rhombic in section. **rhombic** /rom'bik/ adj shaped like a rhombus; orthorhombic (crystallog). **rhombohē'dral** adj of a rhombohedron; trigonal (crystallog). **rhombohē'dron** (pl **rhombohē'dra** or **rhombohē'drons**) (Gr *hedrā* seat) a crystal form of six rhombi, in the trigonal or hexagonal system, a hemihedral form of the hexagonal pyramid. **rhom'boid** adj like a rhombus; nearly square, with the petiole at one of the acute angles (bot). ◆ n a figure approaching a rhombus, a parallelogram, usu one that is not a rhombus nor a rectangle. **rhomboid'al** adj more or less like a rhomboid. **rhomboi'dēs** n (rare or obs) a rhomboid. **rhomboi'deus** n (pl **rhomboi'dei** /-di-ī/) either of two muscles connecting the spinal vertebrae to the scapulae. **rhom'bos** n (pl **rhom'boi**) a bull-roarer. **rhom'bus** n (pl **rhom'bī** or **rhom'buses**) a rhomb (geom); an object shaped like a rhomb.

rhonchus /rong'kəs/ n (pl **rhonch'ī**) a bronchial sound, heard in auscultation. [Latinized from Gr *rhonchos* wheezing]
- **rhonch'al** or **rhonch'ial** adj of rhonchus; of snoring.

rhone same as **rone**.

rhopalic /rō-pal'ik/ adj (of a verse) having each word a syllable longer than the one before. [Gr *rhopalikos* club-like, *rhopalon* a club]
- **rho'palism** n.

Rhopalocera /rō-pə-los'ə-rə/ n pl a sub-order of insects with clubbed antennae, ie butterflies as distinguished from moths. [Gr *rhopalon* a club, and *keras* a horn]
- **rhopaloc'eral** or **rhopaloc'erous** adj.

rhotacize or **-ise** /rō'tə-sīz/ vt and vi to change to an *r*- sound (esp from *z*). [Gr *rhōtakizein*, from *rhō* the Greek R]
- **rho'tacism** n excessive, exceptional or exceptionable sounding of *r*; burring; a change or tendency to change to *r*. **rhōtacizā'tion** or **-s-** n.

rhotic /rō'tik/ (phonetics) adj r-pronouncing, ie denoting a dialect or accent, or speaking a dialect or with an accent, in which *r* is pronounced when it occurs before a consonant or before a pause. [Gr *rhō* the Greek R]
- **rhoticity** /-tis'i-ti/ n.

Rh-positive see **Rhesus factor** under **rhesus**.

RHS *abbrev*: Royal Highland Show; Royal Historical Society; Royal Horticultural Society; Royal Humane Society.

rhubarb /*roo'bärb* or -*bərb*/ *n* any species of the genus *Rheum*, of the dock family; the rootstock (chiefly of *Rheum officinale*) used for its purgative properties; the leaf-stalks (chiefly of *Rheum rhaponticum*) cooked and used as if fruit; a squabble, row, rumpus (*sl*); a word muttered repeatedly to give the impression of indistinct background conversation (*theatre*); nonsense. [OFr *reubarbe*, from LL *rheubarbarum*, for *rhābarbarum*, from Gr *rhā* rhubarb, from *Rhā* the Volga, and L *barbarum* (neuter), from Gr *barbaron* foreign; infl by *rhēum*, Gr *rhēon*]

■ **rhu'barbing** *n* (*theatre*) the use or practice of muttering rhubarb or a similar sound. **rhu'barby** *adj*.

❑ **monk's rhubarb** patience dock.

rhumb /*rum*/ (*naut*) *n* a loxodromic curve; a course following such a fixed line; any point of the compass. [Fr *rumb*, or Sp or Port *rumbo*, from L *rhombus*; see **rhomb**]

❑ **rhumb course** *n*. **rhumb line** *n*. **rhumb'-sailing** *n*.

rhumba same as **rumba**.

rhus /*rus*/ *n* a plant of the sumach genus (*Rhus*) of the cashew-nut family. [L, from Gr *rhous*]

rhy (*Spenser*) same as **rye**[1].

rhyme or (*archaic*) **rime** /*rīm*/ *n* in two or more words, identity of sound from the last stressed vowel to the end, the consonant or consonant group preceding not being the same in both or all cases; extended to other correspondences in sound, such as **head-rhyme** or alliteration, to inexact correspondences, such as **eye-rhyme**, and to variations such as French, **rich rhyme**, or **rime riche** (where the consonants immediately preceding the stressed vowel are alike), and **identical rhyme** (where like-sounding words of different meaning are used); a word or group of words agreeing in this way with another; versification, verses, a poem or a short piece of verse, in which this correspondence occurs at the ends of lines (or within the lines, in **internal rhyme**); a jingle. ◆ *vi* to be in rhyme; to correspond in sound; to make or find a rhyme or rhymes; to harmonize; to chime; to make rhymes or verses. ◆ *vt* to put into rhyme; to compose in rhyme; to use or treat as a rhyme. [OFr *rime*, from L *rhythmus*, from Gr *rhythmos*; see **rhythm**[1]; associated and confused with OE *rīm* number]

■ **rhymed** or (*archaic*) **rimed** /*rīmd*/ *adj* in rhyme. **rhyme'less** *adj*. **rhy'mer** or (*archaic*) **ri'mer** *n* a user of rhyme; a poet; an inferior poet; a minstrel. **rhyme'ster** *n* a poetaster; a would-be poet. **rhym'ist** *n* a versifier.

❑ **rhyme letter** *n* the alliterating letter. **rhyme royal** *n* (*appar* a commendatory name) a seven-line stanza borrowed by Chaucer from the French, its lines rhyming in the pattern *ababbcc*. **rhyme scheme** *n* the pattern of rhymes in a stanza, etc. **rhyme word** *n* a word used as a rhyme. **rhyming slang** *n* a form of slang in which a word is replaced by another word, or part or all of a phrase, which rhymes with it.

■ **identical rhyme** and **rich rhyme** see *n* above. **rhyme or reason** reasonable or sensible purpose or explanation.

rhyncho- /*ring-kō-*/ or before a vowel **rhynch-** /*ringk-*/ *combining form* denoting snout. [Gr *rhynchos* a snout]

■ **Rhynchobdell'ida** *n pl* (Gr *bdella* leech) an order of leeches with proboscis but no jaw. **Rhynchocephalia** /-*si-fə'li-ə*/ *n pl* (Gr *kephalē* head) a primitive order of reptiles extinct except for the New Zealand tuatara. **rhynch'ocoel** /-*sēl*/ *n* (Gr *koilos* hollow) the cavity in which the proboscis of a nemertine lies. **rhynch'odont** *adj* (Gr *odous, odontos* tooth) with toothed beak. **Rhynchonell'a** *n pl* a genus of hinged brachiopods with prominent beak. **Rhynchoph'ora** *n pl* (Gr *pherein* to bear) a group of beetles with snouts, the weevils. **rhynchoph'orous** *adj* of or belonging to the Rhynchophora; snouted. **Rhynchō'ta** *n pl* the Hemiptera.

rhyne see **rhine**.

Rhyniaceae /*rī-ni-ā'si-ē*/ *n pl* a family of very simple land plants (order Psilophytales) found as Old Red Sandstone fossils at *Rhynie* in Grampian Region, Scotland.

rhyolite /*rī'ə-* or *rī'ō-līt*/ *n* an acid igneous rock with a glassy or cryptocrystalline groundmass and generally phenocrysts of quartz and alkali-feldspar (also called **liparite**). [Irregularly, from Gr *rhyax, -akos* a (lava) stream, and *lithos* a stone]

■ **rhyolitic** /-*lit'ik*/ *adj*.

rhyparography /*ri-pə-rog'rə-fi*/ *n* genre or still-life pictures of sordid subjects. [Gr *rhyparos* dirty, and *graphein* to write]

■ **rhyparog'rapher** *n*. **rhyparographic** /-*graf'ik*/ *adj*.

rhythm[1] /*ridhm* or *rithm*/ *n* regular recurrence, *esp* of stress or of long and short sounds; a pattern of recurrence; an ability to sing, move, etc rhythmically; a regular and harmonious pattern of shapes, colours, etc (*art*). [L *rhythmus*, from Gr *rhythmos*, from *rheein* to flow; cf **rhyme**]

■ **rhyth'mal** *adj*. **rhythmed** /*ridhmd* or *rithmd*/ *adj*. **rhyth'mic** or **rhyth'mical** *adj*. **rhyth'mic** *n* (also **rhyth'mics** *sing*) the science or theory of rhythm. **rhyth'mically** *adv*. **rhythmic'ity** *n*. **rhyth'mist** *n* a person skilled in rhythm. **rhyth'mize** or **-ise** *vt* to subject to rhythm. ◆ *vi* to act in or observe rhythm. **rhythm'less** *adj*. **rhythmom'eter** *n* a kind of metronome. **rhythmopoeia** /-*ō-pē'yə*/ *n* (Gr *poieein* to make) the art of composing rhythmically. **rhyth'mus** *n* rhythm.

❑ **rhythm and blues** *n sing* a type of music combining the styles of rock'n'roll and the blues. **rhythmic gymnastics** *n sing* a form of gymnastics in which routines are based around apparatus such as balls, hoops, and ropes. **rhythm method** *n* a method of birth control requiring the avoidance of sexual intercourse during the period in which conception is most likely to occur. **rhythm section** *n* in a band, those instruments whose main function is to supply the rhythm (*usu* percussion, guitar, double bass and piano); the players of such instruments.

rhythm[2] /*rīm*/ an obsolete spelling of **rhyme**.

rhytidectomy /*rī-ti-dek'tə-mi*/ *n* an operation for smoothing the skin of the face by removing wrinkles, a facelift. [Gr *rhytis* a wrinkle, and *ektomē* cutting out]

rhytina /*ri-tī'nə*/ *n* an aquatic mammal of the now extinct *Rhytina* genus of Sirenia (also called **Steller's sea-cow**). [Gr *rhytis* a wrinkle]

Rhytisma /*ri-tiz'mə*/ *n* a genus of fungi that cause black spots on maple leaves. [Gr *rhytisma* a patch or darn]

rhyton /*rī'ton*/ *n* (*pl* **rhy'ta**) a drinking cup or pottery horn (Greek, etc) with a hole in the point to drink by. [Gr *rhyton*, neuter of *rhytos* flowing]

RI *abbrev*: *Regina et Imperatrix* (*L*), Queen and Empress; *Rex et Imperator* (*L*), King and Emperor; religious instruction; Republic of Indonesia (IVR); Rhode Island (US state); (Member of the) Royal Institute of Painters in Water Colours.

Ri *abbrev*: Royal Institution of Great Britain, a society for the promotion of science.

RIA *abbrev*: radioimmunoassay; Royal Irish Academy.

ria /*rē'ə*/ (*geol*) *n* a normal drowned valley. [Sp *ría* river mouth]

riad /*rē'ad*/ *n* a traditional Moroccan house or palace, built round an interior garden. [Ar, garden]

rial[1] /*rī'əl*/ same as **ryal**.

rial[2] /*rē'əl, rī'əl* or *rē-äl'*/ *n* the standard monetary unit of Iran, Oman and (also **riyal**) Saudi Arabia and the Yemen Arab Republic. [Pers *rial*, Ar *riyal*; see **riyal**]

Rialto /*rē-al'tō*/ *n* a district and island of Venice, with a famous bridge over the Grand Canal. [Ital, contracted from *rivo alto* deep channel, or possibly *rialzato* raised]

RIAM *abbrev*: Royal Irish Academy of Music.

riant /*rī'ənt*/ *adj* laughing; merry. [Fr, prp of *rire*, from L *rīdēre* to laugh]

■ **rī'ancy** *n*.

RIAS *abbrev*: Royal Incorporation of Architects in Scotland.

riata see **reata**.

rib[1] /*rib*/ *n* any of the bones that curve round and forward from the backbone; a piece of meat containing one or more ribs; a curved member of the side of a ship running from keel to deck; a strengthening bar; a rodlike structure supporting or strengthening a membrane, such as one of the greater veins of a leaf, a nervure in an insect's wing, a member supporting the fabric of an aeroplane wing or of an umbrella; a bar of a grate (*Scot*); the shaft of a feather; any of the parallel supports of a bridge; the side of a guitar, violin, etc; a framing timber; a purlin; a vein of ore in a rock; a raised band; a prominence running in a line; a ridge; one of the raised lines on the spine of a book where the stitching runs across (*bookbinding*); a ridge raised in knitting, by alternating plain and purl stitches, or a similar ridge raised in weaving; the pattern of ribs so formed (also called **ribbing**); a moulding or projecting band on a ceiling; a wife (from Bible, Genesis 2.21–23; *facetious*). ◆ *vt* (**rib'bing**; **ribbed**) to provide, form, cover or enclose with ribs; to plough with spaces between the furrows (**rib'-plough**). [OE *ribb* rib, *ribbe* ribwort; Ger *Rippe* rib]

■ **ribbed** *adj* having ribs; ridged. **ribb'ing** *n* an arrangement of ribs. **ribb'y** *adj* having many or prominent ribs; nasty, seedy, squalid (*sl*). **rib'less** *adj*. **rib'let** *n* a small, narrow or shallow rib. **rib'like** *adj*.

❑ **rib bone** *n* a rib. **rib'cage** *n* the enclosing wall of the chest formed by the ribs, etc. **rib eye** or **rib'eye** *n* a choice cut of beefsteak, cut from the ribs. **rib'-grass** *n* the ribwort plantain. **rib'-roast** *vt* (*obs*) to beat soundly. **rib'-roaster** *n* (*archaic*) a severe blow on the ribs. **rib'-roast'ing** *n* (*archaic*). **rib'-tickler** *n* a very funny joke or story. **rib'-tickling** *adj* very funny, inclining one to laugh uproariously. **rib'-vaulting** *n*. **rib'work** *n*. **rib'wort** (or **ribwort plantain**) *n* a common weed (*Plantago lanceolata*) with narrow, strongly ribbed leaves and short brown heads.

■ **false rib** one joined indirectly to the breastbone or (**floating rib**) not at all. **true rib** one joined directly by its cartilage.

■ words derived from main entry word; ❑ compound words; ■ idioms and phrasal verbs

rib² /rib/ (sl) vt to tease, ridicule, make fun of. [Perh **rib¹** from the tickling of one's ribs causing laughter]
■ **ribb'ing** n.

RIBA abbrev : Royal Institute of British Architects.

ribald, also (Spenser) **ribaud** or **rybauld** /rib'əld/ adj low, base, mean; licentious; foul-mouthed or coarse; sometimes loosely, jeering, floutingly derisive. ◆ n an obscene speaker or writer; a menial of the lowest grade (obs); a loose, low character (obs). [OFr ribald, ribaut (Fr ribaud); origin uncertain]
■ **rib'aldry**, also (obs) **rib'audry** or (Spenser) **rybaudrye** /-öd-ri/ n obscenity; coarse jesting. **rib'audred** adj (Shakesp) an obscure word, perh for ribaud-rid, ridden by a ribald, or for ribaldried, composed of ribaldry.

riband or **ribband** /rib'ən or rib'ənd/ n a spelling of **ribbon**, used (now esp in heraldry or sport) in derivatives and compounds, eg blue riband.

ribattuta /rē-bät-too'tä/ (music) n the slow beginning of a trill. [Ital]

ribaud and **ribaudred** see **ribald**.

ribband see **riband**.

ribble-rabble /rib'l-rab'l/ n a mob; gabble. [**rabble¹**]

ribbon /rib'ən/ n fine material, usu of silk or synthetic fibre, tightly woven in narrow bands or strips and used for decoration, trimming, etc; a strip of this or other material; anything resembling such a strip, such as a road or a stripe of colour; a torn strip, a tatter or shred; a watchspring; an endless saw; a mollusc's radula; a strip of inking cloth, eg for a typewriter; a diminutive of the bend, one-eighth of its width (heraldry); (in pl) driving reins. ◆ adj made of ribbon; of the shape of a ribbon, forming a narrow band or strip; having bands of different colours. ◆ vt to decorate with, mark into, or make into ribbon; to stripe; to streak. ◆ vi to form into strips; to streak. [OFr riban; origin obscure]
■ **Ribb'onism** n an Irish secret society movement, at its height about 1835–55, opposed to the Orangemen, named from its badge, a green ribbon. **ribb'onry** n ribbons collectively. **ribb'ony** adj.
❑ **ribbon building** or **ribbon development** n unplanned building, growth of towns, in long strips along the main roads. **ribb'onfish** n a long, slender, laterally compressed fish of the family Trachypteridae, esp the oarfish. **ribb'on-grass** n gardener's garters, a striped canary-grass. **Ribb'on-man** n a member of the Ribbonism movement. **ribbon microphone** n a microphone in which the sound is picked up by a thin metallic strip. **ribbon parachute** n a parachute in which the canopy is made from light webbing, giving greater strength for deployment at high speed. **ribb'on-seal** n a banded N Pacific seal. **ribb'on-weed** n sugar-wrack. **ribbon worm** n a nemertine.

Ribes /rī'bēz/ n the black and red currant genus of the saxifrage family (generally including gooseberry), in some classifications giving name to a separate family **Ribēsiā'ceae**. [LL ribes, from Ar rībās sorrel]

ribibe /rib'ib or ri-bīb'/ (obs) n a rebeck; an old crone. [See **rebeck**]
■ **ribible** /ri-bib'l or ri-bī'bl/ n a rebeck.

ribose /rī'bōs/ (chem) n a pentose, $C_5H_{10}O_5$. [From **arabinose**, by transposition of letters]
■ **riboflavin** /rī-bō-flā'vin/ or **riboflā'vine** /-vēn/ n (L flāvus yellow) a member of vitamin B complex, in yellowish-brown crystals, promoting growth in children. **ribonuclease** /ri-bō-nū'kli-ās or -āz/ n an enzyme in the pancreas, etc, the first enzyme to be synthesized (1969). **ribonu'cleotide** n a nucleotide containing ribose. **riboso'mal** adj. **ribosome** /rī'bō-sōm/ n a small particle, found in large numbers in most cells and composed of RNA and protein, on which protein synthesis takes place. **rī'bōzyme** n an RNA-derived molecule displaying enzyme-like activity.
❑ **ribonucleic acids** /rī'bō-nū-klē'ik/ n pl nucleic acids containing ribose, present in living cells, where they play an important part in the synthesis of proteins (abbrev **RNA**). **ribosomal RNA** n the major component of ribosomes.

ribston or **ribstone** /rib'stən/ n (in full **Ribston pippin**) a variety of winter apple brought from Normandy to Ribston Hall in Yorkshire.

RIC (hist) abbrev : Royal Irish Constabulary.

Ricardian /ri-kär'di-ən/ adj relating to the economist David Ricardo (1772–1823), or his theories. ◆ n a follower of Ricardo.

Riccia /rik'si-ə/ n a genus of liverworts. [P Francisco Ricci, Italian botanist]

rice¹ /rīs/ n a grass (Oryza sativa) grown in warm climates, usu in flooded paddy-fields; its grain, an important cereal food. ◆ vt (esp N Am) to form soft food, esp cooked potatoes, into strands by passing through a ricer, sieve, etc. [OFr ris, from L oryza, from Gr oryza a word of Eastern origin]
■ **rīc'er** n (esp N Am) a kitchen utensil used for ricing food. **rice'y** or **ri'cy** adj.
❑ **rice beer** n a fermented drink made from rice. **rice'bird** n the bobolink (as a feeder on true rice or so-called wild rice); the paddy

bird or Java sparrow. **rice biscuit** n a sweet biscuit made of flour mixed with rice. **rice bowl** n a small dish for eating rice; a fertile area that produces large quantities of rice. **rice cake** n a light, usu round cake made from puffed rice grains, eaten alone or spread with other foods. **rice crispies** or **Rice Krispies**® n pl puffed grains of rice, eaten esp as breakfast cereal. **rice field** n. **rice flour** n. **rice glue** n a cement made by boiling rice flour in soft water. **rice grain** n a marking like a grain of rice on the sun's photosphere; a decoration in pottery made by pressing rice or other seeds into the clay before firing. **rice grass** n cord grass. **rice milk** n milk boiled and thickened with rice. **rice paper** n sliced and flattened edible pith of an Asiatic tree of the Araliaceae; a similar material made from other plants, or from linen trimmings. **rice polishings** n pl the parts rubbed off in milling rice. **rice pudding** n. **rice soup** n. **rice water** n an invalid's drink of water in which rice has been boiled; a cholera patient's evacuation, of similar appearance.
■ **Canada**, **Indian**, **water** or **wild rice** see zizania.

rice² or **reis** /rīs/ (obs except dialect) n twigs or small branches collectively, brushwood; a twig or small branch. [OE hrīs; Ger Reis]

ricercar /rē-chər-kär'/, **ricercare** /-kä'rā/ or **ricercata** /-kä'tä/ (music) n orig a contrapuntal forerunner of the fugue; later, a very elaborate form of fugue. [Ital, from ricercare to seek again with effort]

rich /rich/ adj having many possessions; wealthy; fortunate in having any good thing; abundantly supplied or stocked; having any ingredient or quality in great abundance; productive; fertile; deep in colour; full-toned; full-flavoured; containing a high proportion of fat, sugar, fruit or seasonings; (of the mixture in an internal-combustion engine) having a high proportion of fuel to air; full; splendid and costly; sumptuous; elaborately decorated; ample; providing good opportunities for laughter, full of comic potential; (of a remark, etc) outrageous, ridiculous (inf). ◆ vt (Shakesp) to enrich. ◆ vi (obs) to grow rich. ◆ combining form well-provided with a specified thing, as in oil-rich. [OE rīce great, powerful; Ger reich, Du rijk, Gothic reiks; perh reinforced by Fr riche rich]
■ **rich'en** vt and vi to make or become richer. **rich'ly** adv. **rich'ness** n.
❑ **rich'-left** adj (Shakesp) left heir to much wealth. **rich rhyme** see **rhyme**.

Richardia /ri-chär'di-ə/ n an older name for Zantedeschia. [LCM Richard (1754–1821), French botanist, and his son]

Richard Roe see **John Doe** under **John**.

riches /rich'iz/ n (now usu treated as pl) wealth (also (Spenser) **rich'esse**). [OFr richesse, from riche rich]

richt /rihht/ Scots form of **right**.

Richter scale /rik'- or rihh'tər skäl/ n a seismological scale of measurement. [Dr Charles F Richter (1900–85), its inventor]

ricin /rī'sin or ris'in/ n a highly toxic albumin found in the beans of the castor-oil plant. [See **Ricinus**]

Ricinulei /ris-i-nū'li-ī/ n pl the Podogona, a rare order of blind arachnids with male organs on the third leg. [L ricinus a tick]

Ricinus /ris'i-nəs/ n a genus of one species (Ricinus communis, castor-oil plant) of the spurge family. [L ricinus the castor-oil plant]
■ **ricinolē'ic** (or /-ō'lē-ik/) adj relating to castor oil, as in **ricinoleic acid** ($C_{18}H_{34}O_3$), an oily acid obtained from castor oil.

rick¹ /rik/ n a stack; a heap; a set of shelves for storing barrels (N Am). ◆ vt to stack. [OE hrēac; ON hraukr]
■ **rick'er** n an implement for shocking hay.
❑ **rick'-barton** n a stack-yard. **rick'-burner** n an incendiary who fired stacks. **rick'-lifter** n. **rick'stand** n a flooring for a stack. **rick'stick** n a toothed stick for combing thatch on a stack. **rick'yard** n.

rick² /rik/ vt and n see **wrick**.

rick³ /rik/ same as **ricket**.

ricker /rik'ər/ n a spar or young tree trunk. [Perh Ger Rick pole]

ricket /rik'it/ (sl) n a mistake or blunder. [Origin unknown]

rickets /rik'its/ n sing a disease of children, characterized by softness of the bones caused by deficiency of vitamin D. [First recorded in SW England in the 17c, perh ME wrikken to twist; or Gr rhachitis (see **rachitis**)]
■ **rick'etily** adv shakily. **rick'etiness** n unsteadiness. **rick'ety** adj (formerly, now rare **rick'etty**) affected with or relating to rickets; feeble, unstable; tottery; threatening to collapse.

rickettsia /ri-ket'si-ə/ n (pl **rickett'siae** /-ē/ or **rickett'sias**) a member of the Rickettsia genus of micro-organisms found in lice and ticks and, when transferred to humans by a bite, causing typhus and other serious diseases, or of the family **Rickettsia'ceae** /-ā'si-ē/, order **Rickettsia'les** /-ā'lēz/, to which it belongs (also **Rickettsia body**). [Howard Taylor Ricketts (1871–1910), US pathologist]
■ **rickett'sial** adj.

rickety see under **rickets**.

rickey /rik'ē/ (N Am) n a cocktail of gin or vodka, lime juice and soda water with ice. [Origin uncertain]

rickle /rik'l/ (Scot) n a loose heap; a rickety or ramshackle structure or collection. [Poss Scand; connection with **rick**[1] very doubtful]
■ **rick'ly** adj.

rick-rack or **ric-rac** /rik'rak/ n a decorative braid in even zigzag form, or openwork made with it. [**rack**[1]]

rickshaw or **ricksha** /rik'shö/ or -shä/ n (also **jinrick'sha**, **jinrick'shaw** or **jinrik'isha**) a small two-wheeled, hooded carriage drawn by a man or men, or powered by a man on a bicycle (also **bicycle rickshaw** or **ricksha**) or motorcycle (also **auto rickshaw** or **ricksha**). [Jap jin man, riki power, and sha carriage]

RICO /rē'kō/ (US) abbrev : Racketeer Influenced and Corrupt Organizations.

ricochet /rik'ə-shā or ri-kə-shā', also -shet/ n a glancing rebound or skip, such as that of a projectile flying low. ◆ vi (**ricocheting** /-shā'ing/ or rik'/ or **ricochetting** /-shet'ing/ or rik'/; **ricocheted** /-shād'/ or rik'/ or **ricochetted** /-shet'id/ or rik'/) to glance; to skip along the ground. [Fr]

ricotta /ri-kot'ə/ n a type of soft Italian curd cheese of sheep's or cow's milk, often used in ravioli, lasagne, etc. [Ital, from L recocta, fem pap of recoquere to cook again]

ric-rac see rick-rack.

RICS abbrev : Royal Institution of Chartered Surveyors.

rictus /rik'təs/ (zool) n (pl **ric'tus** or **ric'tuses**) the gape, esp of a bird; the chink or aperture of a lipped corolla; unnatural gaping of the mouth, eg in horror. [L rictus, -ūs]
■ **ric'tal** adj of the gape; at the corners of the mouth.

rid[1] /rid/ vt (**ridd'ing**; **rid** or **ridd'ed**) to free; to deliver; to clear; to disencumber; to expel; to remove, eg by banishment or murder, make away with (obs). [ON rythja to clear; with senses converging upon **redd**[1]]
■ **ridd'ance** n clearance; removal; disencumberment; deliverance; a thing that one is well rid of. **ridd'er** n.
■ **good riddance** a welcome relief. **get rid of** to disencumber oneself of. **rid way** (Shakesp) to cover ground, make progress.

rid[2] and **ridden** see ride.

riddle[1] /rid'l/ n a piece of verse, etc giving cryptic clues as to the identity of something which the hearer or reader is asked to name; a puzzling question; anything puzzling. ◆ vt to solve; to puzzle. ◆ vi to make riddles; to speak obscurely. [OE rǣdelse, from rǣdan to guess, to read, from rǣd counsel; cognate with Du raad, Ger Rat]
■ **ridd'le-like** adj and adv (Shakesp). **ridd'ler** n. **ridd'ling** n propounding of riddles; speaking in riddles. ◆ adj enigmatic, obscure, puzzling; speaking in riddles; explaining riddles. **ridd'lingly** adv.
❏ **ridd'le-me-ree'** n (a fanciful modification of riddle me a riddle, or riddle my riddle) a rigmarole.

riddle[2] /rid'l/ n a large coarse sieve. ◆ vt to pass through or sift with a riddle; to make full of holes like a riddle, as with shot; to fill, spread throughout. ◆ vi to use a riddle; to sift. [OE hriddel, earlier hridder]
■ **ridd'ler** n. **ridd'ling** n. **ridd'lings** n pl the less desirable part of anything, whether finer or coarser, separated by riddling and usu rejected; refuse.

ride /rīd/ vt (pat **röde**, archaic **rid**, Scot **raid** or **rade**; pap **ridd'en**, archaic **rid** or **rode**) to travel or be borne on the back of an animal, on a bicycle, or in a vehicle, boat, on a broomstick, the waves, a whirlwind, etc (usu with in, on or upon); to float or seem to float buoyantly; to go on horseback on a raid (archaic), in procession, across a ford, etc; to serve as a cavalryman; to lie at anchor (naut); to remain undisturbed or unchanged; to sit or move as if on horseback; to turn, rest or grate upon something; to work up out of position; (of an animal, etc) to allow itself to be ridden; to weigh when mounted; to have sexual intercourse (vulgar sl). ◆ vt to traverse, trace, ford or perform on horseback, on a bicycle, etc; to sit on; to sit astride; to sit on and control; to travel on; to control at will, or oppressively; to oppress, domineer over, badger, annoy; to improvise on (a theme) (jazz); to rest upon; to overlap; to mount upon; to sustain, come through, esp while riding at anchor (naut; also fig); to give a ride to, or cause to ride; to convey by vehicle (US); to have sexual intercourse with (vulgar sl). ◆ n a journey on horseback, on a bicycle, or in a vehicle; the animal, vehicle, etc providing this; a spell of riding; an act of riding with particular regard to the rider's, driver's, etc degree of comfort or discomfort, etc; a lift in a vehicle (N Am); the person providing such a lift; an experience or course of events of a specified nature, eg a rough ride; a fairground entertainment on or in which people ride; a road for horse-riding, esp one through a wood; an excise officer's district; an act of sexual intercourse (vulgar sl); a sexual partner (esp female) (vulgar sl). [OE rīdan; Du rijden, Ger reiten]
■ **ridabil'ity** n fitness for riding or driving, or for riding or driving along or across. **rī'dable** or **ride'able** adj. **-ridden** combining form

oppressed by the dominance or prevalence of a specified thing (eg hag-ridden or cliché-ridden). **rī'der** n a person who rides or can ride; a commercial traveller (obs); a mosstrooper; an object that rests on or astride of another, such as a piece of wire on a balance for fine weighing; a clause or corollary added to an already complete contract or other legal document; a list of specific personal requirements, such as food and drink, included in the contract of a performing artist; a proposition that a pupil or candidate is asked to deduce from another; a gold coin bearing a mounted figure (Du and Flem rijder). **rī'dered** adj. **rī'derless** adj. **rī'ding** n the action of the verb to ride; the art or practice of horse-riding; a track, esp through woodland, for riding on; an excise-officer's district; anchorage.
❏ **riding boot** n a high boot worn in riding. **riding breeches** n pl breeches for riding, with loose-fitting thighs and tight-fitting legs. **riding cloak** n. **riding clothes** n pl. **riding coat** n a coat of a style worn by horse-riders. **riding committee** n a committee of ministers sent by the General Assembly to carry out an ordination or induction, where the local presbytery refused to act, under the 18c Moderate domination in Scotland. **riding crop** n. **riding glove** n. **riding habit** n a woman's dress for riding, esp one with a long skirt for riding side-saddle. **riding hood** n a hood formerly worn by women when riding. **riding horse** n. **rī'ding-in'terest** n (Scots law) an interest depending on other interests. **riding light** n (naut) a light hung out in the rigging at night when a vessel is riding at anchor. **riding master** n a teacher of horse-riding. **rī'ding-rhyme** n the heroic couplet, perh from Chaucer's use of it in the Canterbury Tales. **riding robe** n a riding habit. **riding rod** n a light cane for equestrians. **riding school** n. **riding skirt** n. **riding suit** n. **riding whip** n.
■ **let (something) ride** to let (something) alone, not try to stop it. **ride a hobby** see under **hobby**[1]. **ride and tie** to ride and go on foot alternately, each tying up the horse, or leaving the bicycle by the roadside, and walking on (also **ride'-and-tie'** n, adv and vi). **ride down** to overtake by riding; to charge and overthrow or trample. **ride for a fall** to court disaster. **ride herd on** (orig US) to guard (a herd of cattle, etc) by riding on its perimeter; to control, keep watch on (fig). **ride on** to depend, rest or turn on. **ride out** to keep afloat throughout (a storm); to cut out from a herd by riding; to survive, get safely through or past (a period of difficulty, etc). **ride (someone) off** (polo) to bump against (another player's horse) moving in the same direction. **ride to hounds** to take part in foxhunting. **ride up** (of a garment) to move gradually up the body out of position. **riding high** currently very successful, popular, etc. **riding the fair** the ceremony of opening a fair by a procession. **take for a ride** to play a trick on, dupe; to give (someone) a lift in a car with the object of murdering him or her in some remote place.

rident /rī'dənt/ (literary) adj laughing or smiling radiantly, beaming. [L rīdēns, -entis, prp of rīdēre to laugh]

ridge /rij/ n a narrow elevation or raised strip along any surface; a strip of arable land, usu between furrows; the earth thrown up by the plough between the furrows; a rib on a knitted garment, etc; a long narrow top or crest; the horizontal line of a rooftop; a hill-range; a long narrow area of high pressure, often associated with fine weather and strong breezes (meteorol); the back (obs). ◆ vt and vi to form into ridges; to wrinkle. [OE hrycg; ON hryggr, Ger Rücken, back]
■ **ridged** adj having ridges. **ridg'er** n a type of plough which forms furrows on either side of the blade. **ridg'ing** n the forming of ridges; covering with ridge tiles. **ridg'y** adj having ridges.
❏ **ridge'back** n a Rhodesian ridgeback (qv). **ridge bone** n the spine. **ridgepiece** or **ridgepole** n the timber forming the ridge of a roof; the pole forming the roof of a tent. **ridge rope** n the central rope of an awning. **ridge tile** n a tile shaped to cover the ridge of a roof. **ridge'way** n a track along a hill-crest.

ridgel or **ridgil** /rij'əl/ (now dialect) n a male animal with only one testicle in position or remaining (also **ridgling** /rij'ling/, **rig** /rig/ or (in Scotland and N England) **rigg'ald**, **rig'ling** or **rig'lin** /rig'/). [Appar from **ridge**, from the undescended testicle near the back]

ridic /ri-dik'/ (sl) adj ridiculous.

ridicule[1] /rid'i-kūl/ n derision; mockery; absurdity (rare). ◆ vt to laugh at; to make fun of; to deride; to mock. [L rīdiculus, from rīdēre to laugh]
■ **rid'iculer** n. **ridic'ūlous** adj deserving or causing ridicule; absurd. **ridic'ūlously** adv. **ridic'ūlousness** n.

ridicule[2] /rid'i-kūl/ (now dialect) n same as **reticule** (see under **reticle**).

Riding /rī'ding/ n one of the three former divisions of Yorkshire; a political constituency (Can). [For thriding, from ON thrithi third]

riding see under ride.

ridotto /ri-dot'ō/ n (pl **ridott'os**) a public dancing party in the 18c and 19c. [Ital]

riebeckite /rē'bek-īt/ (*mineralogy*) *n* a monoclinic amphibole, silicate of sodium and iron. [Emil *Riebeck* (1853–85), German traveller]

riel /rē'əl or rē-el'/ *n* the standard monetary unit of Cambodia (100 sen).

riem /rēm/ *n* a rawhide thong. [Afrik]
■ **riempie** /rēm'pē/ *n* (dimin of *riem*) a long riem about the width of a shoelace, used as string, for the weaving of chair-backs and seats, etc.

Riemannian /rē-man'i-ən/ *adj* relating to the German mathematician Georg Friedrich Bernhard *Riemann* (1826–66), or to his work or concepts, *esp* to **Riemannian geometry**, the geometry of **Riemannian space**.

riempie see under **riem**.

rien ne va plus /ri-ɛ̃ or ryɛ̃ nə va plü'/ (*Fr*) a term used by croupiers to indicate that no more bets may be placed. [Literally, nothing goes any more]

Riesling /rīs', rīz' or rēz'ling/ *n* a type of grape grown *esp* in Germany; a dry white table wine produced from it. [Ger]

rieve and **riever** same as **reave** and **reaver**.

rifacimento /rē-fä-chi-men'tō/ *n* (pl **rifacimen'ti** /-tē/) a recasting of a literary or musical work. [Ital]

rifampicin /ri-fam'pə-sin/ *n* an antibiotic drug used in treating tuberculosis, leprosy and meningitis. [Altered from *rifamycin*, an earlier antibiotic, and *piperidine*]

rife /rīf/ *adj* prevalent; abounding; current. [OE *rȳfe*, *rīfe* ; Du *rijf*, ON *rīfr*]
■ **rife'ly** *adv*. **rife'ness** *n*.

riff /rif/ *n* a musical phrase or figure played repeatedly. ◆ *vi* to play riffs; to improvise on a theme. [Perh *refrain*]
■ **riff'age** *n* (in rock or jazz music) use of riffs.

riffle[1] /rif'l/ *vt* and *vi* to turn or stir lightly and rapidly (eg the pages of a book), often in cursory search for something; to scan a book in this way (with *through*); to shuffle by allowing the corner of a card from one part of the pack to fall alternately with that of a card in the other; to make or form ripples on the surface of. ◆ *n* a shallow section in a river where the water flows swiftly (*N Am*); a ripple on the surface of water (*N Am*); an act of riffling. [Cf **ripple**[1]]

riffle[2] /rif'l/ *n* (eg in gold-washing) a groove or slat in a sluice to catch free particles of ore. [Cf **rifle**[1]]

riffler /rif'lər/ *n* a small file with curved ends used by sculptors, wood- or metalworkers, etc for intricate work. [Fr *rifloir*, from *rifler* to scrape or file]

riff-raff /rif'raf/ *n* undesirable, common people, scum; rubbish. ◆ *adj* rubbishy. [ME *rif and raf*, from OFr *rif et raf*]

rifle[1] /rī'fl/ *vt* to groove spirally; (also *vi*) to shoot with a rifle; to hit (a ball) very hard at a target. ◆ *n* a firearm with a spirally grooved barrel; a groove on the inside bore of a gun; (in *pl*) riflemen. [OFr *rifler* to scratch; cf Ger *riefeln* and **rifle**[2]]
■ **ri'fling** *n* the spiral grooving of a gun-bore; the act of making such grooving.
▫ **rifle bird** or **rifleman bird** *n* any of several Australian birds of paradise with a call like a whistling bullet; a New Zealand bushwren. **rifle corps** *n* a body of soldiers armed with rifles. **rifle green** *n* a dark green, the colour of a rifleman's uniform (also *adj*). **rifle grenade** *n* a grenade or bomb fired from a rifle. **ri'fleman** *n* a soldier armed with a rifle; a rifle bird. **rifle pit** *n* a pit to shelter riflemen. **rifle range** *n* the range of a rifle; a place for rifle practice. **rifle shot** *n*.

rifle[2] /rī'fl/ *vt* to plunder; to ransack; to disarray; (of a hawk) to seize only the feathers of; to injure. [OFr *rifler*]
■ **ri'fler** *n*. **ri'fling** *n*.

rift[1] /rift/ *n* a cleft; a fissure; a chink; a riven fragment (*Spenser*). ◆ *vt* and *vi* to cleave, split. [Cf Dan and Norw *rift* a cleft]
■ **rift'less** *adj*. **rift'y** *adj*.
▫ **rift valley** *n* a valley formed by subsidence of a portion of the earth's crust between two faults. **Rift Valley fever** *n* an infectious disease of cattle and sheep in Africa, to which humans are also susceptible, characterized by high fever and hepatitis, and caused by a virus *prob* transmitted by mosquitoes.

rift[2] /rift/ (*Scot*) *vi* to belch. ◆ *n* a belch. [ON *ryfta*]

rifte /rift/ (*Spenser*) *pap* of **rive**.

rig[1] /rig/ *vt* (**rigg'ing**; **rigged**) to fit with sails and tackling (*naut*); to fit up or fit out; to equip; to set up, set in working order (also *vi*); to dress, clothe (now *inf*). ◆ *n* the form and arrangement of masts, sails and tackling; an outfit; garb; general appearance; equipment; a team of horses and carriage (*N Am*); an articulated lorry (*inf*, *esp N Am*); a well-boring plant, an oil rig. [Origin obscure; perh connected with Norw *rigga* to bind]
■ **-rigged** *combining form* with masts and sails arranged in the manner indicated. **rigg'er** *n* a person who rigs ships; a person who puts together and attends to the rigging of aircraft; someone who puts up and looks after the scaffolding and lifting apparatus, etc that is used for building operations and theatrical and musical productions, etc; an outrigger; (in machinery) a narrow drum. ◆ *combining form* denoting a ship rigged in the manner indicated. **rigg'ing** *n* tackle; the system of cordage which supports a ship's masts and extends the sails; the system of wires and cords in an aircraft.
▫ **rigging loft** *n* a long workshop where rigging is fitted; the place in a theatre from which the scenery is manipulated. **rig'-out** *n* an outfit.
■ **rig out** to provide with complete dress, full equipment, etc. **rig up** to dress or equip; to put up quickly from available, *esp* inadequate, materials.

rig[2] /rig/ (*inf*) *vt* (**rigg'ing**; **rigged**) to manipulate unscrupulously or dishonestly; to set up fraudulently. ◆ *n* a frolic, prank; a trick, swindle. [Origin obscure]
■ **rigg'ing** *n* manipulating unscrupulously or dishonestly, as in *price-rigging*, *vote-rigging*, etc.
■ **run a rig** (now *dialect*) to play a trick (on).

rig[3] /rig/ (*Scot* and *N Eng*) *n* same as **ridge**.
■ **rigg'ing** *n* the roof.
▫ **rigg'ing-tree** *n* a roof-tree.

rig[4] /rig/ *n* (now *dialect*) a wanton person. ◆ *vi* (**rigg'ing**; **rigged**) to behave in a wanton manner; to romp about. [Origin obscure]
■ **rigg'ish** *adj* (*Shakesp*) wanton.

rig[5] see **ridgel**.

rigadoon /ri-gə-doon'/ *n* a lively jig-like dance for one couple; the music for this. [Fr *rigaudon*]

rigatoni /ri-gə-tō'ni/ *n* pasta in the form of large, fluted tubes. [Ital, augmentative pl of *rigato*, pap of *rigare* to draw lines, from *riga* line]

Rigel /rī'gəl or -jəl/ *n* a first-magnitude star appearing in the foot of the constellation Orion. [Ar *rijl* foot]

rigg /rig/ (*dialect*) *n* the dogfish. [Ety unknown]

riggald see **ridgel**.

right[1] /rīt/ *adj* straight; direct; perpendicular; forming one-fourth of a revolution; with axis perpendicular to base; true; genuine; veritable; characteristic; truly judged or judging; appropriate; in accordance, or identical, with what is true and fitting; not mistaken; accurate; fit; sound; intended to be exposed (such as a side, eg of cloth); morally justifiable or incumbent; just; in accordance with what should be; equitable; justly to be preferred or commended; on, for, or belonging to that side or part of the body, etc which in man has normally the stronger and more skilful hand, *opp* to *left*; on that side from the point of view of a person looking downstream, a soldier looking at the enemy, a president looking at an assembly, an actor looking at the audience; on the east side from the point of view of a person looking north; sitting at the president's right hand (in Continental assemblies); hence, conservative or inclined towards conservatism, right-wing. ◆ *adv* straight; straightway; quite; completely, absolutely; just, exactly; in a right manner; justly; correctly; very (*archaic* and *dialect* or in special phrases); on or towards the right side. ◆ *n* that which is right or correct; rightness; fair treatment; equity; truth; justice; just or legal claim; what one has a just claim to; due; (in *pl*) a stag's brow, bez and trez antlers (*archaic*); territory (*Spenser*); the right hand; the right side; a glove, shoe, etc for the right hand, foot, etc; a punch with the right hand; the region on the right side; a right turn; the right wing; the conservatives. ◆ *vt* to set right; to set in order; to rectify; to redress; to vindicate; to do justice to; to avenge; to set right side up or erect. ◆ *vi* to recover an erect position. ◆ *interj* expressing agreement, acquiescence or readiness. [OE *riht* (noun and adj), *rihte* (adv), *rihten* (verb); cf Ger *recht* and L *rēctus* straight, right]
■ **right'able** *adj* capable of being righted. **right'en** *vt* (*archaic*) to set right. **right'er** *n* a person who sets right or redresses wrong. **right'ful** *adj* having a just claim; according to justice; belonging to right. **right'fully** *adv*. **right'fulness** *n* righteousness; justice. **right'ing** *n*. **right'ish** *adj*. **right'ism** *n*. **right'ist** *adj* and *n* (an adherent) of the political right. **right'less** *adj* (*Scot*) without rights. **right'ly** *adv*. **right'ness** *n*. **righto'** or **right-oh'** *interj* (*inf*) expressing acquiescence. **right'ward** *adj* and *adv* towards the right; on the right side; more right-wing. ◆ *n* (*rare*) the region on the right side. **right'wardly** or **right'wards** *adv*.
▫ **right about** *n* the directly opposite quarter (in drill or dismissal; also **right about face**). ◆ *adv* in the opposite direction. ◆ *vi* to turn to face the opposite direction. **right'-and-left'** *adj* having a right and a left side, part, etc; bilaterally symmetrical; on both sides; from both barrels. ◆ *n* a shot or a blow from each barrel or hand. ◆ *adv* on both sides; on all hands; towards one side, then the other; in all directions. **right-ang'led** *adj* having a **right angle**, one equal to a fourth of a revolution. **right ascension** see under **ascend**. **right'-bank** *adj* on the right bank. **right'-click** *vi* to press and release the right-hand button on a computer mouse. ◆ *n* an act of doing this. **right-down'** *adj* and *adv* out-and-out. **right'-drawn** *adj* (*Shakesp*) drawn in a just cause. **right'-field** *n* in baseball, the area in the outfield to the right

facing from the plate. **right'-foot'ed** adj performed with the right foot; having more skill or strength in the right foot. **right'-hand** adj on the right side; towards the right; performed with the right hand; with thread or strands turning to the right; chiefly relied on (as one's right-hand man). **right-hand drive** n a driving mechanism on the right side of a vehicle which is intended to be driven on the left-hand side of the road; a vehicle with a driving mechanism of this type. **right-hand'ed** adj using the right hand more easily than the left; with or for the right hand; with rotation towards the right, or clockwise. ◆ adv in the manner of a right-handed person. **right-hand'edly** adv. **right-hand'edness** n. **right-hand'er** n a blow with the right hand; a right-handed person. **right-hand man** see **right-hand** above. **Right Honourable** n and adj a title of distinction given to peers below the rank of marquis, to privy councillors, to present and past cabinet ministers, to certain Lord Mayors and Lord Provosts, etc. **right'-lined** adj rectilinear. **right-mind'ed** adj having a mind disposed towards what is right, just or according to good sense; sane. **right-mind'edness** n. **right'-of-cen'tre** adj inclining slightly towards the more conservative policies of a group, party or political system. **right of search** see under **search**[1]. **right-of-way'** n (pl **right'-of-ways'** or **rights'-of-way'**) a track over which there is a **right of way** (see below); the strip of land occupied by a railway track, a road, etc (US). **right-on'** adj absolutely correct; trendy, belonging to or in keeping with the latest social, moral, political, etc ideas or fashions. **Right Reverend** n and adj see under **revere**. **rights issue** n (commerce) an issue of new shares which shareholders of a company may buy, usu below the market price, in proportion to their current holdings. **right'size** vt (euphem) to adapt (an organization, etc) to an appropriate size, esp by means of redundancies. **right'-thinking** adj of approved opinions; right-minded. **right-to-life'** adj (esp N Am) same as **pro-life** (see under **pro-**[1]). **right-to-lif'er** n (esp N Am) same as **pro-lifer** (see under **pro-**[1]). **right triangle** n (N Am) a right-angled triangle. **right whale** n a whale of the genus Balaena or Eubalaena, esp the Greenland whale. **right wing** n the political right; the wing on the right side of an army, football pitch, etc. **right'-wing** adj of or on the right wing; relating to the political right; (having opinions which are) conservative, opposed to socialism, etc. **right'-wing'er** n a player on the right wing; a person with right-wing views or who supports the right wing of a party, etc.

■ **all right** see under **all**. **a right one** (inf) a foolish or eccentric person. **at right angles** forming or in such a way as to form a right angle. **bill of rights** (often with caps) an accepted statement of the rights and privileges of the people or of individuals, which the government or state must not infringe (eg that embodied in the Bill of Rights, 1689, or in the US Constitution). **by rights** or (formerly **right**) rightfully; if all were right. **civil rights** see under **civil**. **do someone right** or **do right by someone** to do someone justice; to keep pace with someone in drinking; to drink someone's health. **have a right** (or **no right**) to be entitled (or not entitled); to be under a moral obligation (or no obligation) (non-standard or dialect). **have right** (archaic) to be right. **in one's own right** by absolute and personal right, not through another; by one's own abilities, etc, not through connection with another. **in one's right mind** quite sane. **in right of** by virtue of; by title vested in. **in the right** right; maintaining a justifiable position. **put** or **set to rights** to set in order; to correct. **right as a trivet** see under **trivet**. **right as rain** see under **rain**[1]. **right away** straightaway, immediately; without delay. **right down** or **right enough** plainly. **right, left and centre** same as **left, right and centre** (see under **left**[1]). **right of common** (law) a right to take something from, or pasture animals on, the land of another. **right of entry** a legal right to enter a place. **right off** without delay. **right of way** the right of the public to pass over a piece of ground (see also **right-of-way** above). **right on** (US) an exclamation expressing enthusiastic agreement or approval (see also **right-on** above). **right out** (Shakesp) outright. **right the helm** to put it amidships, in a line with the keel. **send**, etc **to the right about** (inf) to dismiss summarily, or force to retreat. **she'll be right** (Aust) an expression of assurance or confidence.

right[2] (Shakesp and Milton) for **rite**.

righteous /rī'chəs/ adj just, upright; provoked or supported by a moral standpoint or premise; excellent, honest (US sl). [OE rihtwīs, from riht right, and wīs wise, prudent, or wīse wise, manner]
■ **right'eously** adv. **right'eousness** n rectitude; a righteous act.

rigid /rij'id/ adj stiff; unbending; unyielding; rigorous; strict; (of an airship) having a rigid structure to maintain shape; (of a truck or lorry) not articulated. ◆ n a strict or unyielding person (rare); a rigid airship. [L rigidus, from rigēre to be stiff]
■ **rigid'ify** vt and vi to make or become rigid. **rigid'ity** n. **rig'idize** or **-ise** vt to rigidify. **rig'idly** adv. **rig'idness** n.

Rigil /rī'gəl, -jəl or rij'il/ n a first-magnitude double star in the foot of the Centaur, usu known as Alpha Centauri. [Cf **Rigel**]

riglin or **rigling** see **ridgel**.

rigmarole /rig'mə-rōl/ n a long rambling discourse; a long, complicated series of actions, instructions, etc, often rather pointless, boring or irritating. ◆ adj prolix and incoherent. [**Ragman Rolls** (see under **ragman**[1])]

rigol or **rigoll** /rig'əl/ n a gutter or water channel; a groove, esp an encircling groove; a circlet (Shakesp). [Fr rigole gutter, groove]

rigor /rī'gör or rig'ər/ n a sense of chilliness with contraction of the skin, a preliminary symptom of many diseases (med); failure to react to stimulus, under unfavourable conditions (bot); a rigid irresponsive state caused by a sudden shock, as when an animal is said to sham dead (zool); /rig'ər/ another, chiefly American, spelling of **rigour**. [L rigor, from rigēre to be stiff]
■ **rigorism** /rig'ər-izm/ n extreme strictness; the doctrine that in doubtful cases the strict course should be followed. **rig'orist** n. **rig'orous** adj rigidly strict or scrupulous; exact; unsparing; severe; harsh, violent (Spenser). **rig'orously** adv. **rig'orousness** n. **rigour** /rig'ər/ n stiffness; hardness; rigor; severity; unswerving enforcement of law, rule or principle; strict exactitude; austerity; extreme strictness; severity of weather or climate.
❑ **rigor mortis** /mör'tis or mor'tis/ n (L) stiffening of the body after death.

RIGS abbrev: regionally important geological site.

Rigsdag /rigz'dag or rēgz'däg/ n the former parliament of Denmark, replaced in 1953 by the Folketing. [Dan, from rige a kingdom, and dag a day, diet]

Rigveda /rig-vā'də or -vē'/ (Hinduism) n the first of the four Vedas. [Sans ṛic a hymn, and veda knowledge]

rigwiddie or **rigwoodie** /rig-wid'i, -wûd'i, -wud'i or rig'/ (Scot) n a cart-horse's back-band. ◆ adj lean and tough; stubborn; a vague word of reproach, with a suggestion of the widdy, or halter. [**rig**[3] and **widdy**[1]]

RIIA abbrev: Royal Institute of International Affairs.

rijstafel, **rijsttafel** or **reistafel** /rīs'tä-fəl/ n an Indonesian meal consisting of several rice dishes served with a variety of foods. [Du rijst rice, and tafel table]

rikishi /ri-kish'i/ n (pl **rikish'i**) a sumo wrestler. [Jap]

Riksdag /riks'dag/ n the parliament of Sweden. [Swed, from rike a kingdom, and dag a day, diet]

Riksmål /riks'mol/ n former name for **Bokmål**. [Norw, from riks, genitive of rik kingdom, and möl language]

rile /rīl/ vt to annoy or irritate; to make angrily excited (also with up); to agitate (water, etc) (N Am). [Variant of **roil**]
■ **riley** /rī'li/ adj (US) turbid, roily; irritable.

Riley see **the life of Riley** under **life**.

rilievo see **relievo**.

rill /ril/ n a very small brook; a runnel; a small trench; a narrow furrow on the moon or Mars (also **rille** from Ger Rille); a fricative produced by forcing air out of a small gap formed between the tongue and the roof of the mouth (phonetics). ◆ vi to flow in a rill or rills. [Cf Du ril, Ger (orig LGer) Rille channel, furrow]
■ **rilled** adj. **rill'et** n a little rill.
❑ **rill'mark** n (geol) a marking produced by water trickling down a beach or bank.

rillettes /ri-yet'/ n pl a French type of potted meat made by simmering shreds of lean and fat pork, etc until crisp, and pounding them to form a paste. [Fr]

RIM abbrev: Mauritania (ie République Islamique de Mauritanie; IVR).

rim[1] /rim/ n the outermost circular part of a wheel, not including the tyre; an edge, border, brim, or margin, esp when raised or more or less circular; an encircling band, mark or line. ◆ vt (**rimm'ing; rimmed**) to provide with a rim; to edge. [OE rima (found in compounds)]
■ **rim'less** adj. **rimmed** adj.
❑ **rim brake** n a brake acting on the rim of a wheel. **rim'-fire** adj (of a cartridge) having the primer in the rim of the base; (of a firearm) for use with such cartridges. **rim lock** n a lock mechanism in a metal case that is screwed to the inner face of a door (cf **mortise lock**). **rim'rock** n rock forming the boundaries of a gravel deposit, esp the cliff at the edge of a plateau. **rim'-shot** n (esp in jazz) a drum-stroke which hits the rim and skin of the drum simultaneously.

rim[2] /rim/ n a membrane (obs); the peritoneum (now dialect). [OE rēoma; cf **riem**]

rim[3] /rim/ (vulgar sl) vi and vt (**rimm'ing; rimmed**) to stimulate the anus (of), esp orally; to practise anilingus (on). [Perh variant of **ream**[3]]
■ **rimm'ing** n.

rima /rī' or rē'mə/ n (pl **rimae** /rī'mē or rē'mī/) a chink; specif the gap between vocal cords and arytaenoid cartilages. [L rīma]
■ **rime** /rīm/ n (obs) a chink, fissure. **rī'mose** (or /-mōs'/) or **rī'mous** adj full of chinks; covered with cracks.

rime¹ /rīm/ n hoarfrost or frozen dew; ice deposited by freezing of supercooled fog (*meteorol*). ◆ *vt* to cover with rime. [OE *hrīm*; Du *rijm*, Ger *Reif*]

■ **rī'my** *adj*.

rime² and **rimer**, etc same as **ream³** and **reamer**, **rhyme** and **rhymer**, etc.

rime³ see under **rima**.

rime⁴ /rēm/ (*Fr*) *n* rhyme.

❑ **rime riche** /rēsh/ *n* literally, rich rhyme (see **rhyme**). **rime suffisante** /sü-fē-zät/ *n* literally, sufficient rhyme, corresponding to ordinary rhyme in English.

rimu /rē'moo/ *n* a coniferous tree of New Zealand, *Dacrydium cupressinum*. [Maori]

rin /rin/ a Scots form of **run**.

rind¹ /rīnd/ *n* bark; peel; crust; outside. ◆ *vt* to bark. [OE *rinde*; Du *rinde*, Ger *Rinde*]

■ **rīnd'ed** *adj*. **rīnd'less** *adj*. **rīnd'y** *adj*.

rind² or **rynd** /rīnd/ *n* a fitting that supports an upper millstone, cross-shaped with expanded ends. [Cf MDu *rijn*, MLGer *rîn*]

rinderpest /rin'dər-pest/ *n* a malignant and contagious disease of cattle causing fever, severe diarrhoea, and discharges from the mucous membranes, etc. [Ger, cattle-plague]

rine /rīn/ (*Spenser*, etc) *n* same as **rind¹**.

rinforzando /rin-för-tsan'dō/ (*music*) *adj* and *adv* with sudden accent. [Ital, reinforcing]

ring¹ /ring/ *n* a small, circular band, *esp* one of metal, worn on the finger, in the ear, nose, or elsewhere; any object, mark, arrangement, group or course of a similar form; an encircling band; a rim; a short cylinder for holding a table-napkin; (*usu* in *pl*) either of two cylindrical handles suspended from a rope, used for gymnastic exercises; a link of chain mail; an encircling cut in bark; a zone of wood added in a season's growth, as seen in sections; a mark of fungus growth in turf (**fairy ring**); a flat crowd of very small satellites encircling Saturn; an annulus; a segment of a worm, caterpillar, etc; a closed chain of atoms; a system of elements in which addition is associative and commutative and multiplication is associative and distributive with respect to addition (*maths*); a circular ripple; a circular earthwork or rampart; an arena; a space set apart for boxing, wrestling, circus performance, riding display of animals, etc; an enclosure for bookmakers at a race-course; pugilism; prize-fighters or bookmakers with their associates collectively; a combination or clique, *esp* one organized to control the market or for other self-seeking purpose; a system operated by some antique dealers who refrain from bidding against each other at an auction, so that one of their number may buy cheaply, and then share the profit made by subsequent resale; a computer system suitable for local network use, with several microcomputers or peripheral devices connected by cable in a ring; the anus (*vulgar sl*). ◆ *vt* (pat and pap **ringed**; formerly sometimes, and still in sheep-shearing competitions, **rung**) to encircle; to put a ring on or in; to put on in the manner of a ring; to cut a ring in the bark of; to cut into rings; to go in rings round; to excel, be the quickest sheepshearer among (*Aust*). ◆ *vi* to move in rings; to gather or be in a ring. [OE *hring*; ON *hringr*; Ger *Ring*, Dan and Swed *ring*]

■ **ringed** *adj* surrounded by, or marked with, a ring or rings; ring-shaped; composed of rings. **ringer** /ring'ər/ *n* a person who rings; a throw of a quoit that encircles the pin; a quoit so thrown; a person or thing of the highest excellence; a station hand or stockman (*Aust*); the quickest, most expert of a group of shearers (*Aust*). **ringette'** *n* a team sport, similar to ice hockey, in which skaters attempt to send a rubber ring into the opponents' goal. **ring'ing** *n* and *adj*. **ring'less** *adj*. **ring'let** *n* a little ring; a fairy ring; a fairy dance in a ring; a long curl of hair; a type of butterfly (*Aphantopus hyperantus*) with small ring marks on its wings. **ring'leted** *adj*. **ring'ster** *n* a member of a ring, *esp* in a political or price-fixing sense. **ring'wise** *adv*.

❑ **ring'-ar'mature** *n* one with a ring-shaped core. **ring'-bark** *vt* to strip a ring of bark from. **ring binder** *n* a loose-leaf binder with metal rings along the inside spine which open to hold perforated sheets of paper. **ring'bit** *n* a horse's bit with rings at the ends. **ring'bolt** *n* a bolt with a ring through a hole at one end. **ring'bone** *n* a bony callus on a horse's pastern-bone; the condition caused by this. **ring'-canal** *n* a circular canal within the rim of a jellyfish; a circular vessel of the water-vascular system of echinoderms. **ring'-carrier** *n* (*Shakesp*) a go-between. **ring circuit** *n* (*electronics*) an electrical supply system in which a number of power-points are connected to the main supply by a series of wires, forming a closed circuit. **ring'-compound** *n* a chemical compound with a closed chain. **ring'-cross** *n* a circle with crossed diameters. **ring dance** *n* a round dance. **ring dial** *n* a portable sundial. **ring dotterel** *n* the ringed plover. **ring'dove** *n* the wood pigeon, from the broken white ring or line on its neck. **ring'-dropping** *n* a sharper's trick of pretending to find a dropped ring and selling it. **ring dyke** *n* (*geol*) a dyke with more or less circular outcrop. **ringed**

plover *n* a ring-necked plover of various kinds. **ring'-fence** *n* a fence continuously encircling an estate; a complete barrier; the compulsory reservation of funds for use within a specific, limited sector or department (of government, of a company, etc). ◆ *vt* to enclose within a ring-fence; to apply a ring-fence to. **ring'-fencing** *n*. **ring finger** *n* the third finger, *esp* of the left hand, on which the wedding ring is worn. **ring flash** *n* (*photog*) a circular flash tube fitting round the lens to produce a light without shadows. **ring fort** *n* (*archaeol*) a type of defended dwelling-site of the Iron Age and later, enclosed within a strong circular wall. **ring gauge** *n* a gauge in the form of a ring; either a collection of graded rings or a graduated stick for measuring ring- or finger-size. **ring'leader** *n* a person who takes the lead in mischief or trouble. **ring main** *n* (*electronics*) an electrical supply system in which the power-points and the mains are connected in a ring circuit. **ring'man** *n* the ring-finger (*obs* or *dialect*); a bookmaker. **ring mark** *n* a ring-shaped mark. **ring'master** *n* a person in charge of performances in a circus-ring. **ring money** *n* money in the form of rings. **ring'-necked** /-nekt/ *adj* having the neck marked with a ring. **ring network** *n* (*comput*) one forming a closed loop of connected terminals. **ring ouzel** or **ousel** see under **ouzel**. **ring'-porous** *adj* having annual rings marked by large pores. **ring pull** *n* the tongue of metal and the ring attached to it, which one pulls from or on the top of a can of beer, lemonade, etc to open it. **ring road** *n* a road or boulevard encircling a town or its inner part. **ring roller** *n* a type of roller consisting of a number of closely-packed wheels on an axle, the rims of the wheels narrowing to form a wedge shape (also **Cambridge roller**). **ring rot** *n* a disease of potatoes caused by the bacterium *Clavibacter michiganensis*, characterized by the browning and decay of the ring of vascular bundles in the tubers. **ring'-rusty** *adj* (of a boxer, etc) impaired by lack of recent competition. **ring'-shake** *n* a defect in timber, separation along the annual rings. **ring'side** *n* the seating area immediately next to a circus-ring, etc. **ring'sider** *n* a spectator at prize-fights. **ringside seat** or **view** *n* (*fig*) (a position which allows one to have) a very clear view. **ring'-small** *adj* small enough to pass through a ring of standard size. ◆ *n* stones of such a size. **ring snake** *n* a common English snake, the grass-snake (also **ringed snake**); a harmless American snake with yellow collar. **ring spanner** *n* a spanner in the form of a notched ring in which diametrically opposite notches fit over the nut. **ring'stand** *n* a stand for chemical vessels, with rings clamped to a vertical rod; a stand for finger-rings. **ring stopper** *n* a rope for securing an anchor-ring to the cathead. **ring'-straked** (*Bible*) or **ring'-streaked** *adj* streaked in rings. **ring'tail** *n* a studding-sail set upon the gaff of a fore-and-aft sail (*naut*); a light sail set abaft and beyond the spanker (*naut*); the female or young male of the hen harrier, from a rust-coloured ring on the tail feathers; a ring-tailed cat (see **cacomistle**). **ring'-tail** or **-tailed** /-tāld/ *adj* having the tail marked with bars or rings of colour, as a lemur; having a prehensile tail curled at the end, as do certain species of opossum. **ring taw** *n* a game of marbles, with rings marked on the ground. **ring'-time** *n* (*Shakesp*) time for giving rings. **ring walk** *n* an encircling walk. **ring wall** *n* an enclosing wall. **ring'way** *n* a ring road. **ring'-winding** *n* winding that threads a ring. **ring'work** *n* work executed in rings, such as circular fortifications. **ring'worm** *n* a skin disease characterized by ring-shaped patches, caused by fungi.

■ **hold** or **keep the ring** to watch a fight and keep others from interfering. **make** or **run rings round** to be markedly superior to. **ride** or **tilt at the ring** to practise the sport of riding rapidly and catching a hanging ring on a spear. **ring the shed** (*Aust*) to win a sheep-shearing competition. **throw one's hat into the ring** (*inf*) to offer oneself as a candidate or challenger; to issue a challenge, institute an attack.

ring² /ring/ *vi* (pat **rang**, (now rare) **rung**, (*obs*) **rong**; *pap* **rung**) to give a metallic or bell-like sound; to sound aloud and clearly; to give a characteristic or particular sound; to resound, re-echo; to be filled with sound, or a sensation like sound; to be filled with talk or news of (with *with*); to cause a bell or bells to sound, *esp* as a summons or signal. ◆ *vt* to cause to give a metallic or bell-like sound; to sound in the manner of a bell; to summon, usher or announce by a bell or bells; to call on the telephone; to re-echo, resound, proclaim; to disguise (a stolen vehicle) by exchanging its frame, engine number, etc with those of a legitimate vehicle (*sl*). ◆ *n* a sounding of a bell; the characteristic sound or tone, as of a bell or a metal, or of a voice; a ringing sound; a set of bells; a telephone call; a suggestion or impression. [OE *hringan*; ON *hringja*; Ger *ringen*; Dan *ringe*]

■ **ringed** *adj* (*sl*) (of a car) put together from parts of other cars. **ring'er** *n* someone or something that rings; a horse raced under the name of another horse, or an athlete or other contestant competing under a false name or otherwise disguised (*esp US*); a car put together from parts of other cars; an outsider, an impostor (*US sl*); (also **dead ringer**) a person or thing (almost) identical to some other person or thing (with *for*; *inf*). **ring'ing** *n* and *adj*. **ring'ingly** *adv*.

❑ **ringing tone** *n* a telephone tone indicating to the caller that a telephone is ringing (ie not engaged or disconnected) at the number called. **ring'tone** *n* a characteristic sound or tune made by a mobile phone when ringing.

■ **ring a bell** see under **bell**[1]. **ring back** to telephone (a previous caller) in response to his or her call; to follow up a telephone call with a second one. **ring down** to give the signal for lowering the curtain (*theatre*); (with *on*) to bring (something) to a close (*fig*). **ring in** to ring more rapidly before stopping, as a final intimation to lingering churchgoers; to report by telephone. **ring in** or **out** to usher in or out (*esp* the year) with, or as if with, bellringing. **ring off** to put an end to a telephone conversation by replacing the receiver. **ring out** to sound loudly, clearly and suddenly. **ring the bell** and **ring the bells backward** see under **bell**[1]. **ring true** to sound genuine (like a tested coin). **ring up** to summon by a bell; to call (someone) on the telephone; to enter (an amount, a total) in eg a shop till. **ring up the curtain** to give the signal for raising the curtain (*theatre*); (with *on*) to open, set (something) in motion (*fig*).

ring[3] /*ring*/ *n* and *vi* (pat **rang**) an obsolete Scots form of **reign**.

Ringelmann chart /*ring'g(ə)l-man chärt* or *-mən*/ *n* a chart giving a scale of shades of grey against which density of smoke may be gauged. [After the deviser]

ringent /*rin'jənt*/ *adj* gaping. [L *ringēns, -entis*, prp of *ringī*]

Ringer's solution /*ring'(g)əz sə-loo'shən* or *-lū'shən*/ *n* a salt solution that is isotonic with mammalian cells. [S *Ringer* (1835–1910), British physiologist]

ringgit /*ring'git*/ *n* the standard monetary unit of Malaysia (100 sen). [Malay]

ringhals /*ring'hals*/ or **rinkhals** /*ring'kals* or *ringk'hals*/ *n* a S African snake (*Haemachatus haemachatus*) which spits or sprays its venom at its victims. [Afrik *ring* a ring, and *hals* a neck]

rink /*ringk*/ *n* a course for tilting or racing; a portion of a bowling green, curling pond, etc allotted to one set of players; a division of a side playing on such a portion; a piece of ice prepared for skating, ice-hockey or curling; a building or enclosure containing this; a building or floor for roller-skating. ◆ *vi* to skate on a rink. [Orig Scot; origin obscure]

rinkhals see **ringhals**.

rinky-dink /*ring'ki-dingk*/ (chiefly *N Am sl*) *n* something old-fashioned; something old and run down or worn-out; something cheap, trite or trivial; a cheap place of entertainment. ◆ *adj* old-fashioned; trite; cheap.

rinse /*rins*/ *vt* to wash lightly by pouring water in or over, or by dipping in water (also with *out*); to wash in clean water to remove soap traces; to apply a hair rinse to. ◆ *n* an act of rinsing; liquid used for rinsing; a solution used in hairdressing, *esp* one to tint the hair slightly and impermanently. [OFr *rinser* (Fr *rincer*)]

■ **rins'able**, **rinse'able** or **rins'ible** *adj*. **rins'er** *n* a device for rinsing, or for holding rinsed articles. **rins'ing** *n* and *adj*. **rins'ings** *n pl* liquid in which something has been rinsed.

Rioja /*rē-ok'ə* or (*Sp*) *rē-ō'hhä*/ *n* a red or white Spanish table wine. [La *Rioja*, in N Spain]

riot /*rī'ət*/ *n* wild revelry; debauchery; loose living; unrestrained squandering or indulgence; tumult; a great, *usu* boisterous, success; a striking display of colour, etc; a wildly enjoyable or amusing event or occasion (*sl*); a hilarious person (*sl*). ◆ *vi* to take part or indulge in riot; to revel. [OFr *riot, riotte*]

■ **rī'oter** *n*. **rī'oting** *n*. **rī'otise** /*-is, -ēz* or *-īz*/ or *-ize* /*-īz*/ *n* (*obs*) riot, extravagance. **rī'otous** *adj*. **rī'otously** *adv*. **rī'otousness** *n*. **rī'otry** *n*.

❑ **Riot Act** *n* a statute designed to prevent riotous assemblies; a form of words read as a warning to rioters to disperse. **riot agent** *n* a chemical substance such as tear gas used to control or disperse rioters. **riot girl** or **riot grrr(r)l** *n* a young woman who plays or enjoys an aggressively feminist style of punk rock music. **riot police** *n* police specially equipped with **riot gear** (shields, tear gas grenades, etc) for dealing with rioting crowds.

■ **read the riot act** (*fig*) to give vehement warning that something must stop. **run riot** to act or grow without restraint.

RIP *abbrev* : *requiescat in pace*, (*L*) may he (or she) rest in peace.

rip[1] /*rip*/ *vt* (**ripp'ing**; **ripped** or (*archaic*) **ript**) to slash or tear open, apart, off or out; to make by such an action; to reopen (a wound; with *up*); to shred, tear into pieces (with *up*); to split or saw (timber) with the grain; to strip (a building or its roof); to utter explosively (with *out*); to criticize severely (*sl, esp N Am*); to copy (digital data) from a CD or DVD onto a hard disk (*comput, inf*). ◆ *vi* to come apart in shreds; to break out violently; to rush, go forward unrestrainedly. ◆ *n* a rent, tear; an unchecked rush; a ripsaw; a rip-off (*N Am*). [Origin uncertain; cf Fris *rippe*, Flem *rippen*, Norw *rippa*]

■ **ripped** *adj* torn, rent; extremely drunk or high on drugs (*sl*). **ripp'er** *n* a person who rips; a tool for ripping; a person or thing especially

admirable (*sl, esp Aust*). **ripp'ing** *n* the action of the verb. ◆ *adj* and *adv* (*old sl*) excellent. **ripp'ingly** *adv*.

❑ **rip'cord** *n* a cord for opening a balloon's gasbag or enabling a parachute to open. **rip'-off** *n* (*sl*) (financial) exploitation; a theft, stealing, cheating, etc; a swindle, confidence trick; a film, etc that exploits the success of another by imitating it. **ripp'ing-saw** or **rip'saw** *n* a saw for cutting along the grain. **rip'-roaring** *adj* wild and noisy. **rip'-roaringly** *adv*. **rip'snorter** *n* (*sl*) a fast and furious affair or person; a gale. **rip'snorting** *adj*. **rip'snortingly** *adv*. **rip'stop** *adj* of a synthetic fabric (*esp* nylon), woven with a series of raised areas throughout to prevent or reduce ripping.

■ **let it rip** to allow an action or process to go on in an unrestrained or reckless way. **let rip** to express oneself, or to act, violently or without restraint; to make a sudden increase in speed, volume, etc. **rip into** (*sl*) to criticize severely. **rip off** (*sl*) to steal; to steal from; to exploit, cheat, overcharge, etc.

rip[2] /*rip*/ *n* stretch of broken water (chiefly *US*); disturbed state of the sea. [Perh **rip**[1]]

❑ **rip current** or **rip'tide** *n* tidal rip.

rip[3] /*rip*/ *n* an inferior horse; a disreputable person. [Poss **reprobate**]

rip[4] /*rip*/ (*dialect*) *n* a wicker basket; a coop. [ON *hrip* basket]

■ **ripp'er** or **ripp'ier** *n* (*obs*) a person who carries fish inland to sell.

rip[5] or **ripp** /*rip*/ (*Scot*) *n* a handful, *esp* a plucked handful, of grass or corn. [Poss **rip**[1]; connection with **reap** involves difficulty]

RIPA *abbrev* : Royal Institute of Public Administration (now defunct).

riparian /*rī-pā'ri-ən*/ *adj* of or inhabiting a riverbank. ◆ *n* an owner of land bordering a river. [L *rīpārius*, from *rīpa* a riverbank]

■ **ripā'rial** *adj*.

ripe[1] /*rīp*/ *adj* ready for harvest; arrived at perfection; fit for use; fully developed; finished; ready for a particular purpose or action; resembling ripe fruit; mature; (of cheese) mature, strong-smelling; (of language, etc) somewhat indecent or over-colourfully expressive; rich and strong in quality; complete, thorough (*sl*); excellent (*sl*); excessive (*sl*). ◆ *vt* and *vi* to ripen. [OE *rīpe* ripe, *rīpian* to ripen; connected with *rīp* harvest, and perh **reap**; cf Du *rijp*, Ger *reif*]

■ **ripe'ly** *adv*. **rī'pen** *vt* and *vi* to make or grow ripe or riper. **ripe'ness** *n*.

ripe[2] /*rīp*/ (*Scot*) *vt* and *vi* to grope, search, ransack. [OE *rȳpan* to rob]

■ **rī'per** *n*.

ripeck see **ryepeck**.

RIPH *abbrev* : Royal Institute of Public Health.

ripidolite /*rī-, ri-pid'ō-līt* or *-ə-*/ *n* clinochlore. [Gr *rhīpis, -idos* fan]

ripieno /*ri-pyä'nō*/ (*music*) *adj* supplementary, reinforcing; for all, or nearly all, the orchestra or choir. ◆ *n* (*pl* **ripie'nos** or **ripie'ni** /*-nē*/) a supplementary instrument or performer; same as **tutti** (*n*). [Ital, full]

■ **ripie'nist** *n* a supplementary instrumentalist.

riposte /*ri-post'* or *-pōst'*/ *n* a quick return thrust after a parry (*fencing*); a repartee. ◆ *vt* and *vi* to answer with a riposte. [Fr, from Ital *risposta* reply]

ripp same as **rip**[5].

ripper see under **rip**[1,4].

rippier see under **rip**[4].

ripping see under **rip**[1].

ripple[1] /*rip'l*/ *n* light fretting of the surface of a liquid; a little wave; a similar appearance on any surface; a type of ice cream with coloured syrup lightly mixed throughout to give a marbled appearance; small periodic variations in a steady current or voltage (*electronics*); a sound as of rippling water; (in *pl*) repercussions, reverberations; a method of firing missiles, etc in succession. ◆ *vt* to ruffle the surface of; to mark with ripples. ◆ *vi* to move or run in ripples; to sound like ripples. [Origin obscure]

■ **ripp'let** *n* a small ripple. **ripp'ling** *n* and *adj*. **ripp'lingly** *adv*. **ripp'ly** *adj*.

❑ **ripple effect** *n* a process in which a trend or situation spreads outward from its initial location to affect areas distant from it. **ripple mark** *n* an undulatory ridging produced in sediments by waves, currents and wind, often preserved in sedimentary rocks. **ripp'le-marked** *adj*. **ripple tank** *n* a shallow tank of water used to demonstrate the behaviour of waves.

ripple[2] /*rip'l*/ *n* a toothed implement for removing seeds, etc from flax or hemp. ◆ *vt* to clear of seeds by drawing through a ripple; to remove by a ripple. [Cf LGer and Du *repel* a ripple, hoe, Ger *Riffel*]

■ **ripp'ler** *n*.

Rippon /*rip'ən*/ (*obs*; in full **Rippon spur**) *n* a spur made at *Ripon*, once famous for the manufacture of such.

rip-rap or **riprap** /*rip'rap*/ *n* loose broken stones, used to form a foundation on soft ground or under water, or in the construction of revetments and embankments; a foundation formed of these. [From an obs word imit of the sound of repeated blows]

Ripstone pippin (*Dickens*) for **Ribston pippin** (see **ribston**).

ript see **rip**[1].

Ripuarian /ri-pū-ā'ri-ən/ *adj* applied to the Franks on the lower Rhine and their laws. ◆ *n* a Ripuarian Frank. [Generally said to be from L *rīpa* a riverbank]

Rip Van Winkle /rip van wing'kl/ *n* a person very much behind the times, after a character of that name in a story by Washington Irving, who returned home after having slept in the mountains for twenty years.

risaldar /ri-säl-där'/ *n* the commander of a troop of Indian cavalry. [Hindi *risāldār*]

RISC *abbrev* : reduced instruction set computer (ie one having a central processor with a very small instruction set, allowing faster processing, etc).

rise /rīz/ *vi* (pat **rose** /rōz/, *Scot* **raise** or **rase** /rāz/, *US dialect* **riz**; *pap* **risen** /riz'n/, *US dialect* **riz**) to get up; to become erect, stand up; to come back to life; to become hostile; to revolt (often with *up*); to close a session; to break up camp; to raise a siege; to move upward; to come up to the surface; to fly up from the ground; to come above the horizon; to grow upward; to advance in rank, fortune, etc; to swell (*med*); (of dough) to swell under the action of yeast; to increase; to increase in price; to become more acute in pitch; to be excited; to be cheered; to come into view, notice or consciousness; to spring up; to take origin; to have source; to come into being; to extend upward; to tower; to slope up; to come to hand, chance to come; to respond (eg to provocation, or to a challenging situation); to excavate upward; to feel nausea (also *fig*). ◆ *vt* to cause to rise; to surmount (*US*); to raise, view better by nearing (*naut*). ◆ *n* rising; ascent; a coming up to the surface, as that of a fish; the sport of making a butt of someone by deception; increase in height; vertical difference or amount of elevation or rising; increase of salary or price, etc; an upward slope; a sharpening of pitch; source, origin; occasion (*obs*); a response, *esp* an angry or excited one; the riser of a step; a shaft excavated from below. [OE *rīsan*; ON *rīsa*, Gothic *reisan*, Ger *reisen*]
■ **rīs'er** *n* a person who rises, *esp* from bed; that which rises; the upright portion of a step; a vertical pipe, eg in a building or an oil rig. **rīs'ing** *n* the action or process of the verb in any sense; a revolt; a prominence; a swelling; a hill. ◆ *adj* ascending; increasing; coming above the horizon; advancing; growing up; approaching the age of; quite as much as (*US*).
❑ **rising damp** *n* wetness rising through bricks and mortar in a wall. **rising tide** *n* (*fig*) an increase in the frequency or occurrence of a specified thing, a growing trend or tendency.
■ **give rise to** to cause, bring about. **on the rise** in process of rising, *esp* in price. **rise above** to remain unaffected, unlimited or unconstrained by. **rise and shine** a facetiously cheerful invitation or instruction to get out of bed briskly, *esp* in the morning. **rise from the ranks** to work one's way up from private soldier to commissioned officer; to become a self-made man or woman. **rise to it** or **rise to the bait** (*fig*, from fishing) to take the lure. **rise to the occasion** to prove equal to an emergency. **take a rise out of** to lure into reacting to provocation, or loosely, to make sport of. **take rise** to originate. **the rise of** (*US*) more than.

rishi /rish'i/ *n* a sage or poet. [Sans]

risible /riz'i-bl/ *adj* able or inclined to laugh; of laughter; ludicrous. [L *rīsibilis*, from *rīdēre*, *rīsum* to laugh]
■ **risibil'ity** *n* laughter; inclination to laugh; faculty of laughter. **ris'ibly** *adv*.

risk, also (*obs*) **risque** /risk/ *n* hazard, danger, chance of loss or injury; the degree of probability of loss; a person, thing or factor likely to cause loss or danger. ◆ *vt* to expose to risk, endanger; to incur the chance of (an unfortunate consequence) by some action. [Fr *risque*, from Ital *risco*; origin uncertain]
■ **risk'er** *n*. **risk'ful** *adj*. **risk'ily** *adv*. **risk'iness** *n*. **risk'y** *adj* (**risk'ier**; **risk'iest**) dangerous, liable to accident or mishap; risqué (now *rare*).
❑ **risk analysis** *n* a methodical investigation process undertaken to assess the financial and physical risks affecting a business venture. **risk assessment** *n* a complete description of the safety of something, eg a nuclear plant, to evaluate the likelihood and consequence of any possible accident. **risk-averse** *adj* disinclined to take risks. **risk capital** see **venture capital** under **venture**. **risk factor** *n* a factor, such as smoking, that increases the likelihood of a person developing a particular medical condition. **risk money** *n* allowance to a cashier to compensate for ordinary errors.
■ **at risk** in a situation or circumstances where loss, injury, physical abuse, etc are possible; susceptible (**at'-risk** *adj*). **at the risk of** with the possibility of. **run** (or **take**) **a risk** to be in, or get into, a risky situation. **run a** (or **the**) **risk of** to risk (failing, etc).

risoluto /rē-zō-loo'tō/ (*music*) *adj* and *adv* with emphasis, boldly. [Ital]

risorgimento /ri-sör-ji-men'tō/ *n* (pl **risorgimen'tos**) a revival, rebirth; (with *cap*) the Renaissance; (with *cap*) the liberation and unification of Italy in the 19c (*hist*). [Ital, from L *resurgere* to rise again]

risorius /ri-zō'ri-əs/ or **-sö'**/ *n* a facial muscle situated at the corner of the mouth (also **risorius muscle**). [L *risor* laughter]

risotto /ri-zot'ō/ *n* (pl **risott'os**) a dish of rice cooked in stock with meat or seafood, onions and other vegetables, and cheese, etc. [Ital, from *riso* rice]

risp /risp/ (*Scot*) *vt* to rasp; to grate. ◆ *vi* to make a grating sound; to tirl. ◆ *n* a rasp or coarse file; a baker's grater; a roughened bar, on which a ring is grated, used instead of a knocker or doorbell; a grating sound. [ON *rispa* to scratch]
■ **risp'ings** *n pl* portions risped off.

risperidone /ris-per'i-dōn/ *n* an antipsychotic drug used to treat schizophrenia and other conditions.

rispetto /rē-spet'ō/ *n* (pl **rispet'ti** /-tē/) a type of Italian folk song with eight-line stanzas, or a piece of music written in the same style. [Ital]

risque see **risk**.

risqué /rē'skä/ or *ri*-skä'/ *adj* audaciously bordering on the unseemly. [Fr, pap of *risquer* to risk]

Riss /ris/ (*geol*) *n* the third stage of glaciation in the Alps (also *adj*). [From a tributary of the Danube in Württemberg]
■ **Riss'ian** *adj*.

rissole /ris'ōl or rē-sōl'/ *n* a fried ball or cake of minced seasoned meat or fish coated in breadcrumbs. [Fr]

Risso's dolphin /ris'ōz dol'fin/ *n* another name for the **grampus**. [Giovanni *Risso* (1777–1845), Italian naturalist]

risus /rī'səs or rē'sŭs/ *n* a laugh; a grin. [L *rīsus*, *-ūs* laugh]
❑ **risus sardonicus** /sär-don'ik-əs or *-ŭs'* / *n* (*pathol*) a sardonic grin, or drawing back of the corners of the mouth by spasm of the muscles, as in tetanus.

rit or **ritt** /rit/ (*Scot*) *vt* to score; to scratch; to slit. ◆ *n* a scratch; a slit. [ME *ritten*; cf Ger *ritzen*]

rit. (*music*) *abbrev* : ritardando; ritenuto.

Ritalin® /rit'ə-lin/ *n* a proprietary name for methylphenidate.

ritardando /rē-tär-dan'dō/ (*music*) *adj* and *adv* with diminishing speed. ◆ *n* (pl **ritardan'dos**) a ritardando passage; a slowing down. [Ital]

rite /rīt/ *n* a ceremonial form or observance, *esp* religious; a liturgy. [L *rītus*]
■ **rite'less** *adj*.
❑ **rite of passage** or (*Fr*) **rite de passage** /rēt də pas-äzh/ *n* (pl **rites of passage** or **rites de passage**) a term, first used by the French anthropologist Arnold van Gennep, for any of the ceremonies (such as those associated with birth, puberty, marriage or death) which mark or ensure a person's transition from one status to another within society.

ritenuto /ri-tə-nū'tō/ (*music*) *adj* restrained, indicating a sudden slowing-down of tempo. ◆ *n* (pl **ritenu'tos**) a ritenuto passage. [Ital, pap of *ritenere* to restrain, hold back]

ritonavir /ri-ton'ə-vīr/ *n* a protease inhibitor used as a drug in the treatment of HIV.

ritornello /ri-tör-nel'ō/ (*music*) *n* (pl **ritornel'li** /-lē/ or **ritornel'os**) a short instrumental passage in a vocal work, eg a prelude or refrain; a passage for the whole orchestra in a concerto. —Also **ritornel'**, **ritornell'**, **ritornelle'** or **ritournelle'**. [Ital]

ritt see **rit**.

ritter /rit'ər/ (*archaic*) *n* a knight. [Ger *Ritter*, *Rittmeister*]
❑ **ritt'-master** *n* a captain of cavalry.

ritual /rit'ū-əl/ *adj* relating to, or of the nature of, rites. ◆ *n* the manner of performing divine service, or a book containing it; a body or code of ceremonies; an often repeated series of actions; the performance of rites; a ceremonial. [L *rituālis*, from *rītus*; see **rite**]
■ **rit'ualism** *n* attachment of importance to ritual, *esp* with the implication of undue importance. **rit'ualist** *n* a person skilled in or devoted to a ritual, often to an excessive degree; a member of the High Church party in the Church of England. **ritualist'ic** *adj*. **ritualist'ically** *adv*. **ritualizā'tion** or **-s-** *n*. **rit'ualize** or **-ise** *vi* to practise or turn to ritualism. ◆ *vt* to make ritualistic. **rit'ually** *adv*.
❑ **ritual abuse** *n* child abuse involving elements of satanic ritual. **ritual choir** *n* part of a church used as a choir. **ritual murder** *n* the killing of a human being as part of a tribal religious ceremony.

rituximab /ri-tuk'si-mab/ *n* a therapeutic antibody used to treat arthritis and non-Hodgkin's lymphoma. [*ri* (arbitrary syllable), *tumour*, *xi* (denoting a chimaeric antibody), and *mono*clonal anti*b*ody]

Ritz /rits/ *n* an expensive, stylish and luxurious establishment (often with *neg*); ostentatious luxury (chiefly *N Am*). [The *Ritz* hotels]
■ **ritz'ily** *adv*. **ritz'iness** *n*. **ritzy** /rit'zi/ *adj* (**ritz'ier**; **ritz'iest**) (*sl*) stylish, elegant, ostentatiously rich.

■ **put on the Ritz** or **ritz** to get dressed up to impress; to dress or act ostentatiously.

riva /riv'ə/ or /rē'va/ (*Shetland*) *n* a cleft in rock. [ON *rīfa*]

rivage /riv'ij/ or /rī'vij/ (*poetic*) *n* a bank, shore. [Fr, from L *rīpa* a bank]

rival /rī'vl/ *n* a person pursuing an object in competition with another; a person who strives to equal or excel another; a person for whom, or thing for which, a claim to equality might be made; a partner, fellow (*Shakesp*). ◆ *adj* standing in competition; having similar pretensions or comparable claims. ◆ *vt* (**rī'valling**; **rī'valled**) to stand in competition with; to try to gain the same object against; to try to equal or excel; to be worthy of comparison with. [L *rīvālis*, said to be from *rīvus* river, as a person who draws water from the same river]
■ **rī'valess** *n* (*archaic*) a female rival. **rī'vality** /-val'i-ti/ *n* rivalry; equality (*Shakesp*). **rī'valize** or **-ise** *vi* to enter into rivalry. **rī'valess** *adj.* **rī'valrous** *adj.* **rī'valry** *n* the state of being a rival; competition; emulation; the feeling of a rival. **rī'valship** *n* emulation.
❑ **rī'val-hating** *adj* (*Shakesp*).

rivastigmine /riv-ə-stig'mēn or rī'və-/ *n* a drug used to treat Alzheimer's disease.

rive /rīv/ (*poetic* or *archaic*) *vt* (pat **rīved** or (*Scot*) **rave** /rāv/; pap **riven** /riv'n/ or **rived** /rīvd/, also *Spenser* **rive** /riv/ and *Keats* **raft**) to tear apart; to tear; to rend; to split; to discharge as if with rending (*Shakesp*); to pierce (*obs*); to plough up (*Scot*). ◆ *vi* to tug, tear; to split. [ON *rīfa*]

rivel /riv'l/ (now *dialect*) *vt* and *vi* to wrinkle. [OE *rifelede* rivelled]
■ **riv'elled** *adj.*

river /riv'ər/ *n* a large stream of water flowing over the land; sometimes extended to a strait or inlet; a place for hawking (*archaic*); a stream in general; (also **river card**) the fifth community card dealt in some forms of poker. ◆ *adj* of a river or rivers; dwelling or found in or near a river or rivers. [OFr *rivere* (Fr *rivière*), from L *ripārius* (adj), from *rīpa* bank; cf Ital *riviera*]
■ **riv'erain** /-ān/ *adj* of a river or its neighbourhood. ◆ *n* a riverside dweller. **riv'ered** *adj* watered by rivers. **riv'eret** *n* (*archaic*) a small river. **riv'erine** /-īn or -ēn/ *adj* of, on, or dwelling in or near a river. **riv'erless** *adj.* **riv'erlike** *adj.* **riv'erworthiness** *n.* **riv'erworthy** *adj* fit to sail, etc on a river. **riv'ery** *adj* of or like a river; having many rivers. ❑ **riv'erbank** *n.* **river basin** *n* the whole region drained by a river with its affluents. **river bed** *n* the channel in which a river flows. **river blindness** *n* a W African disease, onchocerciasis (qv). **riv'erboat** *n* a boat with a flat bottom or shallow draft, for use on rivers. **river bottom** *n* (*US*) alluvial land along the margin of a river. **riv'ercraft** *n* small vessels that ply on rivers. **river dolphin** *n* any of various species of a small, toothed whale found in rivers and brackish water in S Asia and S America. **riv'er-dragon** *n* Pharaoh (*Milton*, an allusion to Bible, Ezekiel 29.3); a crocodile. **river drift** *n* old alluvia of rivers. **riv'er-driver** *n* (*US*) a person who conducts logs downstream. **river flat** *n* a piece of alluvial land by a river. **riv'erfront** *n* land, quays, buildings, etc facing a river. **river god** *n* the tutelary deity of a river. **river head** *n* the source of a river. **riv'er-hog** *n* the capybara; an African wild pig. **river horse** *n* the hippopotamus; the kelpie; a pole which a person sits astride to cross a river (*S Afr*). **riv'er-jack** (or **river-jack viper**) *n* a W African viper. **riv'erman** *n* a person who lives and works on or along a river. **river mouth** *n.* **river mussel** *n* a freshwater mussel. **river novel** same as **roman fleuve** (see under **roman**). **riv'er-rat** *n* a thief who prowls about a river. **river sand** *n* sand from a river bed. **riv'erscape** *n* a picture of river scenery. **riv'erside** *n* the bank or neighbourhood of a river. ◆ *adj* beside a river. **riv'er-terrace** *n* a terrace formed when a river eats away its old alluvium deposited when its flood-level was higher. **riv'er-tide** *n* the current of a river; the tide from the sea rising or ebbing in a river. **riv'erwalk** *n* a footpath along the side of a river. **river wall** *n* a wall confining a river within bounds. **river water** *n.* **riv'erway** *n* a river as a waterway. **riv'erweed** *n* any plant of the genus *Podostemon*.

rivet[1] /riv'it/ *n* a bolt with a head at one end, used to join two or more pieces of metal, etc by hammering down the projecting, headless end. ◆ *vt* (**riv'eting**; **riv'eted** (formerly often **riv'etting** and **riv'etted**)) to fasten with rivets; to fix immovably; to attract or fix (one's attention, etc) on something; to enthral or fascinate; to clinch or hammer out the end of. [OFr *rivet*, from *river* to clinch; origin obscure]
■ **riv'eter** *n* a person who rivets; a machine for riveting. **riv'eting** *n.* ◆ *adj* gripping, enthralling, arresting. **riv'etingly** *adv.*
❑ **rivet head** *n.* **rivet hearth** *n* a forge for heating rivets. **rivet hole** *n* a hole to receive a rivet.

rivet[2] /riv'it/ *n* bearded wheat. [Origin obscure]

riviera /ri-vi-ā'rə/ *n* a warm coastal district reminiscent of the Riviera in France and Italy on the Mediterranean Sea. [Ital, coast]

rivière /rē-vyer' or ri-vi-er'/ *n* a necklace of diamonds or other precious stones, *usu* in several strings; a row of openwork (*needlework*). [Fr, river]

rivlin /riv'lin/ (*Scot*) *n* a shoe moulded from untanned hide, worn with the hair to the outside; (in *pl*) tatters, rags. [OE *rifling*, ON *hriflinger* hide shoe]

rivo /rē' or rī'vō/ (*Shakesp*) *interj* a drinking-cry.

rivulet /riv'ū-lit/ *n* a small river. [L *rīvulus*, dimin of *rīvus* a stream, perh through Ital *rivoletto*, from *rivolo*, from *rivo*]

rix-dollar /riks'do-lər/ (*hist*) *n* a silver coin, current in various European countries and colonies in the 16c–19c. [Obs Du *rijcksdaler* (Du *rijksdaalder*), from Du *rijk* kingdom (OE *rīce*), and *daler* dollar]

riyal /ri-yäl'/ *n* the standard monetary unit of Qatar (100 dirhams); (also spelt **rial**) the standard monetary unit of Saudi Arabia (100 halala) and the Yemen Arab Republic (100 fils). [Ar *riyāl*, from Sp *real*; see **real**[4]]

riz /riz/ (*US dialect*) pat and pap of **rise**.

riza /rī'zə/ *n* an ornamental (*usu* silver) plate covering a Russian icon, with shaped holes through which to see the face and other features. [Russ, from OSlav, garment]

rizard see **rizzer**[2].

Rizla® /riz'lə/ *n* a brand of cigarette paper.

rizzer[1], **rizzar** or **rizzor** /riz'ər/ (*Scot*) *vt* to dry, *esp* in the sun. ◆ *n* a rizzered haddock. [Cf obs Fr *ressorer* to dry]

rizzer[2], **rizzar** /riz'ər/, **rizard** /riz'ərd/ or **rizzart** /riz'ərt/ (*Scot*) *n* a red currant. [Earlier *razour*; origin unknown]

RJE (*comput*) *abbrev*: remote job entry.

RJET (*comput*) *abbrev*: remote job entry terminal.

RL *abbrev*: reference library; Republic of Lebanon (IVR); Rugby League.

RLC *abbrev*: Royal Logistic Corps.

RLO *abbrev*: returned letter office.

rly *abbrev*: railway.

RM *abbrev*: Republic of Madagascar (IVR); Resident Magistrate; Royal Mail; Royal Marines.

rm *abbrev*: ream (*printing*); room.

RMAS *abbrev*: Royal Military Academy, Sandhurst.

RMetS same as **RMS**.

RMI *abbrev*: Retail Motor Industry Federation.

RMM *abbrev*: Republic of Mali (IVR).

RMN *abbrev*: Registered Mental Nurse.

RMO *abbrev*: Resident Medical Officer.

RMP *abbrev*: Royal Military Police.

RMS *abbrev*: Royal Meteorological Society.

rms (*maths*) *abbrev*: root mean square.

RMT *abbrev*: National Union of Rail, Maritime and Transport Workers.

RN *abbrev*: Registered Nurse (*N Am*); Republic of Niger (also IVR); Royal Navy.

Rn (*chem*) *symbol*: radon.

RNA (*biochem*) *abbrev*: ribonucleic acid.
■ **RNase'** *n* an enzyme that promotes the hydrolysis of RNA into smaller molecules.

RNAS *abbrev*: Royal Naval Air Service (until 1918); Royal Naval Air Station.

RNCM *abbrev*: Royal Northern College of Music.

RNIB *abbrev*: Royal National Institute of the Blind.

RNID *abbrev*: Royal National Institute for Deaf People.

RNLI *abbrev*: Royal National Lifeboat Institution.

RNR *abbrev*: Royal Naval Reserve.

RNT *abbrev*: Royal National Theatre.

RNVR *abbrev*: Royal Naval Volunteer Reserve.

RNZAF *abbrev*: Royal New Zealand Air Force.

RNZN *abbrev*: Royal New Zealand Navy.

RO *abbrev*: Romania (IVR).

ro *abbrev*: recto (*printing*); run out (*cricket*).

roach[1] /rōch/ *n* a silvery freshwater fish of the carp family, with pale red ventral and tail fins; applied to various N American fishes resembling this. [OFr *roche*]
■ **as sound as a roach** perfectly sound.

roach[2] /rōch/ *n* a cockroach (*US*); (the butt of) a marijuana cigarette (*sl*; *esp US*).
❑ **roach clip** *n* a clip used to hold (the butt of) a marijuana cigarette when it has become too short to hold without burning the fingers.

roach[3] /rōch/ n (naut) a concave curve in the foot of a square sail. ◆ vt to arch; to cut short, trim (a horse's mane); to cut, or cut the hair or mane of, in an upright ridge. [Origin uncertain]
■ **roached** adj arched convexly; cut in an upright ridge.

road (Shakesp, Spenser, etc, **rode**) /rōd/ n a track suitable for wheeled traffic, esp for through communication (often in street-names); a highway; a roadway; a way of approach; course; an anchorage in an area of sea protected by guns, etc; a mine-passage; (often in pl) a roadstead; a railway (US); journeying; travelling, tour; a ride, horseback journey (Shakesp); a raid, incursion (Shakesp and Spenser); dismissal (inf); a prostitute (Shakesp). [OE rād a riding, raid; cf **raid**[1] and **ride**]
■ **road'ie** n (inf) a member of the crew who transport, set up and dismantle equipment for musicians, esp a rock group, on tour. **road'less** adj. **road'ster** n a horse, cycle or car suitable for ordinary use on the road; a coach driver or other traveller by road (obs); an open car (orig US) with a rumble seat or large boot instead of a rear seat, and a single seat for two or three in front. **road'worthiness** n. **road'worthy** adj fit for the road.
□ **road agent** n (US; hist) a highwayman. **road'bed** n the foundation of a railway track; the material laid down to form a road. **road'block** n an obstruction set up across a road, eg to prevent the escape of a fugitive. **road book** n a guide-book to the roads of a district. **road'-borne** adj carried by road. **road bridge** n a bridge carrying a road. **road'craft** n knowledge and skill useful to drivers and other road-users. **road end** n the place where a road branches off from another. **road fund licence** n a former name for vehicle excise duty. **road game** n (US) a game played by a sports team while on tour; loosely, an away game. **road'header** n a tunnelling machine used in mining that excavates with a combination of cutting heads and pressurized water jets. **road hog** n a swinishly selfish or boorishly reckless motorist or other user of the road. **road'-hoggish** adj. **road'holding** n the extent to which a motor vehicle grips the road when in motion. **road'house** n a roadside public house, refreshment-room or inn catering for motorists, cyclists, etc. **road hump** n any of a series of low ridges built into a road surface to slow traffic down, a sleeping policeman. **road kill** n (esp N Am) the killing of an animal by a vehicle on a road, esp intentionally as a form of sport; the animal killed. **road maker** n. **road'-making** n. **road'man** n a person who keeps a road in repair; a person who uses the roads, an itinerant; a competitor in road races. **road manager** n the tour manager for a rock band or other group, entertainer, etc, responsible for organizing venues, equipment, crew, etc. **road map** n a map representing the road network in a particular area; a plan for achieving a goal via a series of intermediate stages (fig). **road mender** n. **road'-mending** n. **road metal** n broken stones for roads. **road'-metalling** n. **road movie** n a film with a narrative based on a journey, the latter often undertaken as an escape and having no definite destination. **road pricing** n the system of charging the driver of a vehicle for the use of a road (eg to reduce traffic in a city centre). **road rage** n uncontrolled anger or aggression between road users, often involving violence and injury. **road roller** n a heavy roller used in making roads. **road'runner** n a type of cuckoo of the Californian and Mexican chaparral that is capable of running at great speed. **road scraper** n an implement for clearing roads of loose material. **road sense** n aptitude for doing the right thing in driving or road-using in general. **road'show** n a touring group of theatrical or musical performers; (a live broadcast from one of a series of venues, presented by) a touring disc jockey and his or her retinue; a promotional tour undertaken by any body or organization seeking publicity for its policies or products; their performances. **road'side** n the border of a road; wayside. ◆ adj by the side of a road. **road sign** n a sign along a road, motorway, etc giving information on routes, speed limits, etc to travellers. **roads'man** n a roadman. **road'stead** n a place near a shore where ships may ride at anchor. **road surveyor** n a person who supervises roads. **road tax** n vehicle excise duty. **road test** n a test of a vehicle on the road for performance and roadworthiness (also fig). **road'-test** vt. **road train** n (Aust) a number of linked trailers towed by a truck, for transporting cattle, etc. **road warrior** n (inf, chiefly US) a person who travels extensively, esp for work. **road'way** n the way or part of a road or street used by traffic; the road surface. **road'work** n running on roads as a method of training for marathon runners, boxers, etc. **road'works** n pl the building or repairing of a road, or work involving the digging up, etc of part of a road.
■ **down the road** (chiefly N Am) in the future. **hit the road** see under **hit**. **in** or **out of the** (or **one's**) **road** in or out of the way. **one for the road** a last alcoholic drink before setting off. **on the road** travelling, esp as a commercial traveller or a tramp; on the way to some place. **road up** road surface being repaired. **rule of the road** see under **rule**. **take the road** to set off, depart. **take to the road** to become a highwayman (archaic), or a tramp; to set off for, or travel to, somewhere.

roading see under **rode**[3].

roadster and **roadstead** see under **road**.

roam /rōm/ vi to rove about; to ramble; to use a mobile phone in a place outside the standard area of coverage. ◆ vt to wander over; to range. ◆ n a wandering; a ramble. [ME romen; origin obscure]
■ **roam'er** n. **roam'ing** n and adj.

roan[1] /rōn/ adj bay or dark, with spots of grey and white; of a mixed colour with a decided shade of red. ◆ n a roan colour; a roan animal, esp a horse. [OFr roan (Fr rouan)]

roan[2] /rōn/ n grained sheepskin leather. ◆ adj of roan. [Poss Roan, early form of Rouen]

roan[3] same as **rone**.

roar /rōr or rör/ vi to make a full, loud, hoarse, low-pitched sound, as a lion, fire, wind, the sea, cannon, etc; to bellow; to bawl; to guffaw; (of a diseased horse) to take in breath with a loud noise; to behave in a riotous, bullying, noisy manner (obs); to rush forward with loud noise from the engine. ◆ vt to utter vociferously; to shout (encouragement, abuse, etc); to encourage by shouting (with on). ◆ n a sound of roaring. [OE rārian; but partly from MDu roer stir, disturbance]
■ **roar'er** n a person who roars; a horse that roars as a result of disease; a roaring boy (obs). **roar'ing** n the action of the verb in any sense; a disease of horses marked by roaring. ◆ adj uttering or emitting roars; riotous; proceeding with very great activity or success. **roar'ingly** adv. **roar'y** or **roar'ie** adj (Scot) noisy; garish, too bright.
□ **roaring boy** n (obs) a boisterous bullying reveller, swaggerer or brawler. **roaring drunk** adj very drunk (and typically rowdy). **roaring forties** see under **forty**.
■ **do a roaring trade** to do very brisk and profitable business. **the roaring game** curling.

roast /rōst/ vt to cook before a fire; to bake; to parch by heat; to heat strongly; to dissipate the volatile parts of (esp sulphur) by heat; to criticize excessively, even sarcastically; to banter (sl). ◆ vi to undergo roasting; (of a person) to be very hot (inf). ◆ adj roasted. ◆ n a joint, esp of beef, roasted or to be roasted; an open-air party at which roasted meat is cooked and eaten (N Am); an operation of roasting; banter (sl). [OFr rostir (Fr rôtir); of Gmc origin]
■ **roas'ter** n an apparatus for roasting; a pig, etc suitable for roasting; a very hot day (inf). **roast'ie** n (inf) a roast potato. **roast'ing** n the action of the verb; a severe reprimand (sl); a form of group sexual activity in which a person is penetrated in more than one orifice at the same time (sl). ◆ adj (inf) very hot.
□ **roast beef** n. **roast-beef plant** n the fetid iris (from its smell). **roasting jack** n an apparatus for turning a joint in roasting.
■ **rule the roast** (mistakenly **roost**) to lord it, predominate.

roate an old spelling (Shakesp) of **rote**[1].

rob[1] /rob/ vt (**robb'ing**; **robbed**) to deprive wrongfully and forcibly; to steal from; to plunder; to deprive; to take as plunder; to carry off. ◆ vi to commit robbery. [OFr rober, of Gmc origin; cf **reave**, OHGer roubōn, Ger rauben]
■ **robb'er** n a person who robs. **robb'ery** n theft from the person, aggravated by violence or intimidation; plundering. **robb'ing** n.
□ **Robber Council** or **Synod** n a council held at Ephesus in 449, afterwards repudiated, which reinstated Eutyches (from the violence of its proceedings). **robber crab** n a large coconut-eating land crab of the Indian Ocean; a hermit crab. **robber fly** n any fly of the Asilidae, large, bristly, insect-eating flies.
■ **daylight robbery** glaring extortion. **rob Peter to pay Paul** to deprive one person in order to satisfy another; to raise a loan to pay off a debt.

rob[2] /rob/ n a fruit syrup. [Ar robb]

robalo /rob'ə-lō/ n (pl **rob'alos**) an American pike-like fish (genus Centropomus), of a family related to the sea-perches. [Sp róbalo bass]

robe[1] /rōb/ n a gown or loose outer garment; a gown or dress of office, rank or state; a rich dress; a woman's dress; a dressing-gown; (in pl) clothes, garb; a dressed bison hide, or the like. ◆ vt to dress; to invest in robes. ◆ vi to assume official garments. [Fr robe, orig booty; cf **rob**[1], **reave**, OHGer raup (Ger Raub) booty]
■ **rob'ing** n the putting on of robes or clothes; apparel; a trimming on a robe.
□ **robe-de-chambre** /rob-də-shã-br'/ n (pl **robes-de-chambre** /rob-də-shã-br'/) (Fr) a dressing-gown. **robe maker** n a maker of official robes. **robing room** n a room in which official robes may be put on.
■ **Mistress of the robes** the head of a department in a queen's household. **the robe** or **the long robe** the legal profession.

robe[2] or **'robe** /rōb/ n short for **wardrobe**.

robertsman /rob'ərdz-man/ n (obs) a stout robber (also **rob'ertsman**). [Appar from Robert; allusion unknown]

robin[1] /rob'in/ n the redbreast or **robin redbreast** (Erithacus rubecula), a widely-spread singing bird with reddish-orange breast; extended to other birds, eg a red-breasted thrush of N America (**American robin**). [A form of Robert; cf Jackdaw, and Magpie]

❑ **Robin Goodfellow** n (folklore) a mischievous English spirit or creature (also called **Puck**). **Robin Hood** n a legendary medieval English outlaw who robbed the rich to give to the poor. **Robin-run'-in-the-hedge** or **Robin-run'-the-hedge** n cleavers or goosegrass; ground-ivy; also various other hedgeside plants. **robin's-egg blue** n (chiefly N Am) a light greenish-blue colour.

robin² /rō'bin/ (obs) n trimming on a gown. [**robing**]

robinia /ro-bin'i-ə/ n any plant of the locust or false acacia genus (Robinia) of Papilionaceae. [Jean Robin (1550–1629), Parisian gardener who introduced it to cultivation]

roble /rō'blä/ n a name for various species of oak (genus Nothofagus), and other trees. [Sp, from L rōbur oak]

robo- /rō-bō-/ combining form denoting a robot or something that is controlled by computer technology. [**robot**]

roborant /rob'ə-rənt/ n a strengthening drug or tonic. ◆ adj (also **rob'orating**) strengthening. [L rōborāns, -antis, prp of rōborāre to strengthen, invigorate]

robot /rō'bot/ n a mechanical man; a machine, now esp computer-controlled, able to perform complex physical tasks, eg welding; esp in S Africa, an automatic traffic signal. [Czech robota statute labour; from Karel Čapek's play RUR (1920)]
■ **robot'ic** adj. **robot'icist** n an expert in the field of robotics. **robot'ics** n sing the branch of technology dealing with the design, construction and use of robots; a form of street dance in which a mechanical effect is achieved by making sharp movements keeping the body stiff (also called **robotic dancing**). **rō'botize** or **-ise** vt to cause (a job, etc) to be done by, or (a house, etc) to be looked after by, a robot or robots. **rō'bot-like** adj.

roburite /rō'bə-rīt/ n a flameless explosive substance, chlorinated dinitrobenzene with ammonium nitrate. [L rōbur strength]

robust /rō-bust'/ adj stout, strong and sturdy; constitutionally healthy; vigorous; thickset; over-hearty. [L rōbustus, from rōbur strength, oak]
■ **robust'ious** /-yəs/ adj robust; violent (Shakesp); strong or rough (Milton). **robust'iously** adv. **robust'iousness** n. **robust'ly** adv. **robust'ness** n.

robusta /rō-bus'tə/ n coffee produced from the shrub Coffea robusta, grown esp in E Africa.

ROC abbrev : Royal Observer Corps (now defunct).

roc /rok/ n an enormous bird described in Arabian legend, strong enough to carry off an elephant (also **rok**, **ruc** or **rukh** /rook/). [Pers rukh]

rocaille /rō-kä'ē/ n artificial rockwork or similar ornament; scroll ornament; rococo. [Fr]

rocambole /rok'əm-bōl/ n a plant closely related to garlic. [Fr]

Roccella /rok-sel'ə/ n a genus of lichens, yielding archil and litmus. [Ital orcella, remodelled on rocca rock; see **archil**]

roch see **rotch**.

Roche limit /rōsh or rosh lim'it/ (astron) n the lowest orbit which a satellite can maintain around its parent planet without being pulled apart by the tidal forces it creates. [Edouard Roche (1820–83), French astronomer]

Rochelle /rō-shel'/ adj relating to the town of La Rochelle in France.
❑ **Rochelle'-powder** n seidlitz powder. **Rochelle'-salt** n sodium potassium tartrate, discovered in 1672 by a Rochelle apothecary.

roche moutonnée /rosh moo-to-nā'/ (geog) n (pl **roches moutonnées** /-nā'/ or -nāz'/) a smooth, rounded, hummocky rock-surface due to glaciation. [Fr roche a rock, and moutonnée a kind of wig; applied by De Saussure]
■ **roche moutonnéed'** adj.

rochet /roch'it/ n a mantle (obs); a close-fitting surplice-like vestment worn by bishops and abbots. [OFr, of Gmc origin; cf Ger Rock, OE rocc]

rock¹ /rok/ n a large outstanding natural mass of stone; a natural mass of one or more minerals consolidated or loose (geol); any variety or species of such an aggregate; a diamond or other precious stone (sl); crack, the drug, or a piece of this (sl); a stone, pebble or lump of rock (N Am and Aust); (in pl) testicles (vulgar sl); a type of hard confectionery made in sticks; a sure foundation or support, anything immovable; a danger or obstacle (fig); for rockfish, rock pigeon or Plymouth Rock fowl; a coin (old US sl). ◆ adj of rock; found on, in or among rocks. ◆ vt to stone (US sl); to clear of calcareous deposit. [OFr roke, from LL rocca]
■ **rock'er** or **rock'ier** n the rock dove. **rock'ery** n a heap of soil and rock fragments in a garden, for growing rock plants. **rock'iness** n. **rock'like** adj. **rock'ling** n a small fish of the cod family with barbels on both jaws. **rock'y** adj full of rocks; made of rocks; like rocks; rough, difficult (inf).
❑ **rock'-alum** n alum prepared from alunite. **rock'-badger** n the Cape hyrax; a dassie. **rock'-basin** n a lacustrine hollow in rock, excavated

by glacier-ice. **rock bass** n a freshwater game fish (Ambloplites rupestris) of eastern N America. **rock'-bird** n a puffin or other bird that nests or lives on rocks. **rock boots** or **shoes** n pl tight-fitting boots or shoes with rubber soles, designed for climbing. **rock borer** n any mollusc or other animal that bores into rocks. **rock bottom** n bedrock; the very bottom, esp of poverty or despair. **rock'-bott'om** adj the lowest possible; to, or at, the lowest possible level. **rock'-bound** adj hemmed in by rock; rocky. **rock brake** n parsley fern. **rock breaker** n a machine for breaking stones. **rock butter** n a butter-like exudation from rocks, containing alum. **rock cake** n a small hard bun with irregular top. **rock candy** n (N Am) rock (the confectionery). **rock climber** n. **rock climbing** n mountaineering on rocky faces. **rock cod** n a cod found on rocky sea-bottoms; a name for various Australian and other fishes, mostly of the sea-bass family. **rock cook** n the small-mouthed wrasse. **rock cork** n mountain cork. **rock cress** n a cruciferous plant of the genus Arabis. **rock crystal** n colourless quartz, esp when well crystallized. **rock dove** n a pigeon that nests on rocks, source of the domestic varieties. **rock drill** n a tool for boring rock. **rock elm** n an elm of N America with a corky bark. **Rock English** n the Gibraltar dialect. **rock'fall** n a fall of rock; a mass of fallen rock. **Rock fever** n undulant fever (from Gibraltar). **rock'fish** n any of various types of fish that live among rocks or rocky bottoms; applied as a name to several such fishes, such as wrasse, striped bass, black goby; rock salmon. **rock flour** n finely divided rock material, such as is found under glaciers. **rock'-forming** adj occurring as a dominant constituent of rocks. **rock garden** n a rockery; a garden containing rockeries. **rock guano** n a rock phosphatized by percolations from guano. **rock'-hewn** adj hewn out of rock. **rock'hopper** n a small crested penguin. **rock house** n (sl) a crack- or cocaine-dealer's den. **rock lark** n the rock pipit. **rock leather** n mountain leather. **rock lizard** see **rock scorpion** below. **rock lobster** see under **lobster**. **rock melon** n (Aust) the cantaloupe. **rock oil** n petroleum. **rock perch** n a scorpion-fish. **rock pigeon** n the rock dove. **rock pipit** n a pipit inhabiting rocky coasts. **rock plant** n a plant adapted to growing on or among rocks. **rock rabbit** n a hyrax; a pika. **rock'-ribbed** adj (N Am) unyielding. **rock rose** n a plant of either of the genera Cistus and Helianthemum of the family Cistaceae. **rock salmon**, **rock turbot** n dogfish or wolffish when being sold as food-fish. **rock salt** n salt as a mineral, halite; salt in crystalline form. **rock shoes** see **rock boots** above. **rock scorpion** n a person born in Gibraltar (also **rock lizard**). **rock snake** n a python; a krait. **rock socks** n pl an orig Japanese form of rubber socks, with a separate big-toe section, worn for walking over rocks, coral, etc. **rock'-sol'id** adj steady; dependable; firm; unwavering; unbeatable. **rock sparrow** n a genus (Petronia) related to the true sparrow. **rock-stead'y** adj absolutely steady. **rock tar** n petroleum. **rock temple** n a temple hewn out of the solid rock. **rock tripe** n an edible arctic lichen of various kinds. **rock violet** n a violet-scented alga growing on mountain rocks. **rock'water** n water issuing from a rock. **rock'weed** n bladderwrack or related seaweed growing on rocks. **rock wood** n a wood-like asbestos. **rock wool** n mineral wool, used as an insulating material. **rock'work** n masonry in imitation of rock (archit); rocks in a rockery; rock climbing.
■ **between a rock and a hard place** in a situation where one has to choose between two equally undesirable alternatives. **get one's rocks off** to have an orgasm (vulgar sl); to derive excitement (sl). **have rocks in one's head** (US sl) to lack brains. **on the rocks** penniless; (of whisky, etc) on ice; (of a marriage) broken down, failed. **Rocky Mountain goat** a white N American animal intermediate between goat and antelope. **the Rock** Gibraltar. **the Rockies** the Rocky Mountains.

rock² /rok/ vt and vi to sway to and fro, tilt from side to side; to startle, stagger (inf). ◆ vt to do, play, wear, etc very successfully (sl). ◆ vi to dance to rock'n'roll music; to play rock music in a powerful and compelling way; to be highly enjoyable, exciting or admirable (sl). ◆ n a rocking movement; (also **rock music**) a form of music with a strong beat, which developed from rock'n'roll but which is more varied and often more complex in style, and less influenced by blues and country-and-western music; rock'n'roll. ◆ adj relating to rock music or rock'n'roll. [OE roccian]
■ **rock'er** n someone or something that rocks; a curved support on which anything rocks; a rocking horse; a rocking chair; (with cap) a member of a teenage faction of the 1960s who wore leather jackets, rode motorcycles, and were rivals of the Mods; a rock'n'roll song (inf); a mining cradle; a skate with curved blade; a 180°-turn in skating, so that the skater continues backwards in the same direction; a mezzotint engraver's tool for preparing a surface. **rock'ily** adv. **rock'iness** n. **rock'ing** n and adj. **rock'y** adj tending to rock; shaky; tipsy; unpleasant, unsatisfactory (sl).
❑ **rock'abilly** n a form of rock'n'roll with elements of hillbilly music; a devotee of this music. **rock and roll** see **rock'n'roll** below. **rocker arm** n a rocking lever, esp in an internal-combustion engine, that transmits the motion of a cam or pushrod to the valve. **rocker panel** n

the part of a vehicle's bodywork below the door-sills of the passenger compartment. **rocker switch** *n* an electric light, etc switch on a central pivot, the bottom being pushed back to switch on, the top to switch off. **rocking chair** *n* a chair mounted on rockers. **rocking horse** *n* the figure of a horse mounted on rockers or on some other supports which allow the horse to rock when ridden by a child. **rocking stone** *n* a logan, or finely poised boulder that can be made to rock. **rocking tool** *n* an engraver's tool for roughing a plate. **rock''n'roll'** or **rock and roll** *n* a simple form of music deriving from jazz, country-and-western and blues music, with a strongly accented, two-beat rhythm; dancing to the music. ◆ *vi* to play or dance to this music. **rock''n'roll'er** or **rock and roller** *n*. **rock'shaft** *n* in engines, a shaft that oscillates instead of revolving. **rock'steady** *n* a 1960s style of dance music, *orig* from Jamaica, slow in tempo with a heavily stressed offbeat.

■ **off one's rocker** out of one's right mind. **rock the boat** to make things difficult for one's colleagues, create trouble. **rock up** (*inf*) to arrive without giving prior notification.

rock³ /rok/ (*archaic*) *n* a distaff. [ME *roc*; cf MDu *rocke*; ON *rokkr*; Ger *Rocken*]

■ **rock'ing** *n* (*Scot*) an evening party, *orig* for spinning.

rockaway /rok'ə-wā/ *n* an American four-wheeled horse-drawn carriage, formerly made at *Rockaway*, New Jersey.

rockery see under **rock¹**.

rocket¹ /rok'it/ *n* a cylinder full of inflammable material, projected through the air for signalling, carrying a line to a ship in distress, or for firework display; a missile projected by a rocket system; a system or vehicle obtaining its thrust from a backward jet of hot gases, all the material for producing which is carried within the rocket; a severe reprimand (*inf*). ◆ *vi* to move like a rocket; (of a game bird) to fly straight up rapidly when flushed; (of eg prices) to rise very rapidly (*fig*); to come to an important position with remarkable speed (*fig*). ◆ *vt* to attack with rockets; to propel by means of a rocket; to reprimand severely (*inf*). [Ital *rocchetta*, of Gmc origin]

■ **rocketeer'** *n* a rocket technician or pilot; a specialist in rocketry, *esp* a designer of rockets. **rock'eter** *n* a game bird which rockets. **rock'etry** *n* the scientific study of rockets.

❑ **rocket engine** or **motor** *n* a jet engine or motor which uses an internally stored oxidizer instead of atmospheric oxygen, for combustion. **rocket launcher** *n*. **rocket plane** *n* an aeroplane driven by rocket motor. **rocket range** *n* a place for experimentation with rocket projectiles. **rocket science** *n* rocketry; (*usu* with *neg*) any complex and intellectually demanding activity (*inf*). **rocket scientist** *n* a person engaged in rocketry; a person who devises schemes to take advantage of price differentials on money markets (*stock exchange sl*); an extremely clever person (*inf*).

rocket² /rok'it/ *n* a cruciferous salad plant (*Eruca sativa*) of Mediterranean countries; extended to dame's violet (genus *Hesperis*) and other plants of the same family (**sea rocket** *Cakile*; **wall rocket** *Diplotaxis*; **yellow rocket** winter cress, *Barbarea*) or of other families (**blue rocket** monkshood; larkspur; **dyer's rocket** weld). [OFr *roquette*, from L *ērūca*]

rocklay see **rokelay**.

rockumentary /rok'ū-men-t(ə-)ri/ (*inf*) *n* a documentary film about a rock band or artist. [From *rock* docu*mentary*]

rococo /rə-, rō-kō'kō or rō-kō-kō'/ *n* (pl **rococos**) a style of architecture, decoration and furniture-making prevailing in Louis XV's time, marked by endless multiplication of ornamental details unrelated to structure, with rockwork, shells, scrolls and unsymmetrical broken curves, a lighter, freer development of the baroque; the equivalent of this style in other arts, *esp* music. ◆ *adj* in the style of rococo; florid, extravagant in style; grotesque; old-fashioned and odd (*obs*). [Fr, prob from *rocaille* rockwork]

rocquet /rok'it/ *n* a rochet. [OFr, a Northern form of *rochet*]

rod /rod/ *n* a long straight shoot; a slender stick; a slender bar of metal or other matter; such a metal bar forming part of the framework under a railway carriage (see also **ride the rods** below); a sceptre or similar emblem of authority; a stick or bunch of twigs as emblem or instrument of punishment; a stick or wand for magic or divination; a riding crop; a slender pole or structure carrying a fishing-line; an angler using this; a measuring stick; a pole or perch ($5\frac{1}{2}$ yards, or $16\frac{1}{2}$ feet); a square pole ($272\frac{1}{4}$ sq ft); (of brickwork) 272 sq ft of standard thickness of $1\frac{1}{2}$ bricks or 306 cu ft; race or tribe (*Bible*); a rod-shaped body of the retina sensitive to light; a rod-shaped bacterium; a revolver, a pistol (*US sl*); the penis (*sl*). ◆ *vt* (**rodd'ing**; **rodd'ed**) to push a rod through (a drain, etc) so as to clear it. [OE *rodd*; cf ON *rudda* club]

■ **rodd'ing** *n*. **rod'less** *adj*. **rod'like** *adj*. **rod'ster** *n* (*archaic*) an angler.

❑ **rod'fisher** *n*. **rod'fishing** *n*. **rod'man** or **rods'man** *n* a person who holds, carries or uses a rod, *esp* an angler. **rod puppet** *n* a glove

puppet held on one hand, its arms being manipulated by rods held in the other hand.

■ **a rod in pickle** punishment in reserve. **kiss the rod** to accept punishment with submission. **make a rod for one's own back** to do something that will cause problems for oneself at a later date. **Napier's rods** see under **Napierian**. **ride the rods** (*old US*) to travel illegally on the railway, supporting oneself on the rods of railway carriages.

rode¹ /rōd/ *pat of* **ride**.

rode² /rōd/ (*Spenser* and *Shakesp*) *n* an old spelling of **road**.

■ **rode'way** *n* (*Shakesp*).

rode³ /rōd/ *vi* (*esp* of woodcock) to perform a regular evening flight. [Origin obscure]

■ **rōd'ing** or **road'ing** *n* a woodcock's evening flight.

rode⁴ /rōd/ (*N Am*) *n* an anchor rope or chain. [Origin unknown]

rodent /rō'dənt/ *n* a mammal of the order **Rodentia** /rō-den'shə or -shyə/, which have prominent incisor teeth and no canines, eg the squirrel, beaver or rat. ◆ *adj* gnawing; belonging to the Rodentia. [L *rōdēns, -entis*, prp of *rōdere* to gnaw]

■ **rodenticīd'al** *adj*. **roden'ticide** *n* a substance that kills rodents. **ro'dent-like** *adj*.

❑ **rodent officer** *n* an official rat-catcher. **rodent ulcer** *n* a slow-growing malignant tumour on the face.

rodeo /rō'di-ō or rō-dā'ō/ *n* (pl **ro'deos**) a place where cattle are assembled; a round-up of cattle; an exhibition of cowboy skill; a contest suggestive of a cowboy rodeo involving eg motorcycles. [Sp, from *rodear* to go round, from L *rotāre* to wheel]

rodgersia /ro-jûr'zi-ə/ *n* any of a group of flowering perennial herbs (family Saxifragaceae) native to E Asia, with large divided leaves and small, white panicled flowers. [John *Rodgers* (1812–82), US admiral]

rodomontade /rod-ō-mon-tād'/ *n* extravagant boasting. ◆ *vi* to bluster. [After the boasting of *Rodomonte* in Ariosto's *Orlando Furioso*]

■ **rodomontā'der** *n*.

roe¹ /rō/ *n* a mass of fish eggs (also **hard roe**); the testis of a male fish containing mature sperm (also **soft roe**). [ME *rowe*; cf ON *hrogn*, MHGer *roge*, Ger *Rogen*]

■ **roed** *adj* containing roe.

❑ **roe'stone** *n* oolite.

roe² /rō/ *n* a small species of deer (also **roe deer**), sometimes applied to the female red deer. [OE *rā, rāha*; Ger *Reh*, Du *ree*]

❑ **roe'buck** *n* the male roe. **roe'buck-berry** or **roe'-blackberry** *n* the stone-bramble.

roemer /roo'mər/ *n* a rummer. [Du]

roentgen, roentgenium see **röntgen**.

roesti or **rösti** /ræs'ti/ *n* a dish of grated potatoes shaped into a pancake and fried. [Swiss Ger]

rogan josh /rō'gən josh/ *n* an Indian dish of curried meat in a tomato-based sauce. [Urdu]

rogation /rō-gā'shən/ (*relig*) *n* an asking; supplication. [L *rogātiō, -ōnis*, from *rogāre* to ask]

■ **rogatory** /rog'ə-tə-ri/ *adj* (**letters rogatory** see under **letter¹**).

❑ **Rogation Days** *n pl* the three days before Ascension Day, when supplications were recited in procession. **Rogation flower** *n* the milkwort, which was carried in Rogation Day processions. **Rogation Sunday** *n* that before Ascension Day. **Rogation Week** *n* the week in which the Rogation Days occur.

roger /roj'ər/ *n* (with *cap*) a male personal name; a goose (*sl*); the penis (*vulgar sl*); a word used in signalling and radio-communication for R, in the sense of *received* (and understood). ◆ *vt and vi* (*vulgar sl*) of a man, to copulate (with). [Fr, of Gmc origin, equivalent to OE *Hrōthgār*]

■ **rog'ering** *n*.

■ **Jolly Roger** the pirates' skull-and-crossbones flag. **Roger** (or **Sir Roger**) **de Coverley** /də-kuv'ər-li/ an English country dance (whence the name of the *Spectator* character).

Rogerian /ro-jē'ri-ən/ *adj* denoting a type of psychological therapy developed by Carl *Rogers* in the 1940s, in which the therapist tries to discover his patients' needs by involving himself in a positive and understanding relationship with them, by means of one-to-one counselling or group discussion.

rogue /rōg/ *n* an unprincipled person, a rascal; a prankster; a mischievous person (often *playfully* or *affectionately*); a vagrant (*archaic*); a plant that falls short of a standard, or is of a different type from the rest of the crop; a variation from type; a horse, person or object that is troublesome, unruly or unco-operative; a savage elephant or other wild animal which lives apart from or has been driven from its herd. ◆ *adj* mischievous; disruptive; diverging from type; operating in disregard of the accepted regulations or system, as in a *rogue state*. ◆ *vi* to act or behave as a rogue. ◆ *vt* to cheat; to eliminate rogues or inferior plants from (a crop, etc). [Cant; origin unknown]

■ **roguer** /*rōg'ər*/ *n*. **rōg'uery** *n* rascally tricks; mischievousness; joking; fraud. **rogue'ship** *n* (*archaic*). **roguing** /*rōg'ing*/ *adj* roaming (*archaic*); behaving like a rogue. **roguish** /*rōg'ish*/ *adj* rascally; mischievous; waggish; villainous; confounded. **rog'uishly** *adv*. **rog'uishness** *n*. **rog'uy** *adj* (*obs*).

❑ **rogue money** *n* a former assessment in Scotland for the expense of catching, prosecuting and maintaining rogues. **rogues' gallery** *n* a police collection of photographs of criminals; any group of disreputable people. **rogues' Latin** *n* cant. **rogues' march** *n* derisive music played at a drumming-out. **rogue value** *n* (*comput*) a number or set of characters, outside the generally expected range, which is used to terminate a list of data items.

ROH *abbrev* : Royal Opera House.

Rohypnol® /*rō-hip'nol*/ *n* a powerful sedative drug.

ROI *abbrev* : Republic of India; Republic of Ireland; return on investment.

roi fainéant /*rwä fä-nā-ā̃'*/ (*Fr*) *n* a king without royal power (see **fainéant**).

roil /*roil*/ (now *dialect* and *US*) *vt* to make turbid or turbulent; same as **rile**. ◆ *vi* to move turbulently, billow. [Origin doubtful]

■ **roil'y** *adj* turbid.

roin same as **royne**.

roinish same as **roynish**.

roister or **royster** /*roi'stər*/ *n* a blusterer; a noisy reveller. ◆ *vi* to bluster, swagger; to revel noisily. [OFr *rustre* a rough, rude fellow, from OFr *ruste*, from L *rusticus* rustic]

■ **roist** or **royst** *vi* (back-formation from the noun) to roister. **rois'terer** or **roys'terer** *n*. **rois'tering** *n*. **rois'terous** or **roys'terous** *adj*. **rois'terously** *adv*. **rois'ting** or **roys'ting** *adj* blustering, boisterous; rousingly defiant (*Shakesp*).

roji /*rō'ji*/ *n* a form of Japanese garden design incorporating a path of stepping stones which are sprinkled with water to concentrate the viewer's eye and mind on objects in the immediate field of vision. [Jap]

ROK *abbrev* : Republic of Korea (South Korea; IVR).

rok same as **roc**.

roke /*rōk*/ (*dialect*) *n* a vapour; steam; mist; light rain; smoke. ◆ *vt* and *vi* to steam; to smoke. [Perh Scand]

■ **rōk'y** *adj*.

rokelay or **rocklay** /*rok'(ə-)lā*/ (*Scot*) *n* a woman's short cloak, worn in the 18c. [Fr *roquelaire* ; see **roquelaure**]

roker /*rō'kər*/ *n* any ray other than skate, *esp* the thornback. [Perh Dan *rokke*, Swed *rocka* ray]

rokkaku /*rō-kak'oo*/ *n* (pl **rokkak'u**) a Japanese fighting kite used in competition. [Jap]

roky see under **roke**.

rolag /*rō'lag*/ *n* a roll of combed sheep's wool ready for spinning. [Gaelic *ròlag*, dimin of *rola* a roll]

Roland /*rō'lənd*/ *n* a hero of the Charlemagne legend; hence, a hero; a worthy match (with allusion to a drawn contest between Roland and his comrade-in-arms, Oliver).

■ **a Roland for an Oliver** tit for tat; as good as one got.

role or **rôle** /*rōl*/ *n* a part played by an actor; a function, part played in life or in any event. [Fr *rôle*, orig a roll of paper containing an actor's lines]

❑ **role model** *n* a person whose character and behaviour, etc is imitated by others who would like to be in the same or a similar position or situation, etc. **role'-play** or **role'-playing** *n* the performing of imaginary roles, *esp*, as a method of instruction, training or therapy, the acting-out of real-life situations in which the subject might find himself or herself. **role'-play** *vt* and *vi*. **role reversal** *n* (*psychol*) the reversing of roles formerly taken by two people in relation to each other.

Rolfing /*rol'fing*/ *n* a therapeutic technique for correcting postural faults and improving physical wellbeing through manipulation of the muscles and connective tissue, so that the body is realigned symmetrically and the best use of gravity made in maintaining balance (also without *cap*). [Dr Ida *Rolf* (1897–1979), originator of the technique]

■ **Rolf'er** or **rolf'er** *n* a practitioner of this technique.

roll /*rōl*/ *n* a scroll; a sheet of paper, parchment, cloth or other material bent spirally upon itself into a nearly cylindrical form; a document in such form; a register; a list, *esp* of names; a supply of money, *esp* a wad of notes rolled together (*N Am* and *Aust*); a spirally wound cake, or one of dough turned over to enclose other material; a small, individually-baked portion of bread formed into any of various shapes,

that can be cut open and filled with other foods, preserves, etc; a revolving cylinder; a roller; a more or less cylindrical package, mass or pad; a cylindrical moulding; a volute; a bookbinder's tool with a small wheel for impressing designs; a part turned over in a curve; an act of rolling; a swaying about an axis in the direction of motion; a full rotation about an axis in the direction of motion, as an aeronautical manoeuvre; a continuous reverberatory or trilling sound; a pattern of drumming; an undulation; a wavelike flow. ◆ *vi* to move like a ball, a wheel, a wheeled vehicle or a passenger in one; to perform revolutions; to sway on an axis in the direction of motion; to turn over or from side to side; to swagger; to wallow; to go with a roll; to move in, on, or like waves; to flow; to undulate; to wander; to sound with a roll; to use a roller; to curl; to start; to get under way; to start operating; to make progress. ◆ *vt* to cause to roll; to turn on an axis; (of the eyes) to move with a circular sweep; to wrap round on itself; to enwrap; to curl or to wind; to drive forward; to move upon wheels; to press, flatten, spread out, thin or smooth with a roller or between rollers; to round by attrition; to beat (a drum) rapidly; to rumble; to peal; to trill; to pour in waves; to wind (a clock; *Scot*); to attack and rob (*sl*); to rob (someone who is helpless, *esp* drunk or asleep; *N Am* and *NZ sl*); to have sexual intercourse with (*sl*, *esp N Am*). [OFr *rolle* (noun), *roller* (verb), from L *rotula*, dimin of *rota* a wheel]

■ **roll'able** *adj*. **rolled** *adj*. **roll'er** *n* a person or thing that rolls; a revolving or rolling cylinder; a contrivance including a heavy cylinder or cylinders for flattening roads or turf; a long, coiled-up bandage (**roller bandage**) a strap buckled round a horse to keep its blanket in place; a long heavy sea wave; a small solid wheel; a cylinder on which hair is wound to curl it; a kind of tumbler pigeon; a bird (genus *Coracias*) of a family related to the kingfishers, with a habit of flight like a tumbler pigeon (Ger *Roller*); a kind of canary with a soft trilling song; a Rolls-Royce car (*inf*). ◆ *adj* relating to, performed or carried out on roller skates. **roll'ing** *n*. ◆ *adj* (of landscape) characterized by a gentle undulation; extremely rich (*sl*); staggering with drunkenness (*sl*); (of a contract, etc) subject to periodic review; occurring in different places in succession; (of planned events, etc) organized to take place successively, on a relay or rota system, with a steadily maintained or escalating effect.

❑ **roll'-about** *adj* podgy. **roll'away** *n* a bed mounted on rollers so as to be easily moved, stored away, etc. **roll'back** *n* a decrease, *esp* in wages, prices, etc. **roll'bar** *n* a metal bar that strengthens the frame of a vehicle, lessening the danger to the occupants if the vehicle overturns. **roll'-call** *n* the calling of a list of names, to ascertain attendance. **roll'collar** *n* a collar of a garment turned back in a curve. **rolled gold** *n* metal coated with gold rolled very thin. **rolled oats** *n pl* oats which have been husked, steamed and flattened with rollers, used *esp* to make porridge. **roll'erball** *n* a pen having a moving ball as a writing point. **roller bearing** *n* a bearing consisting of two races between which a number of parallel or tapered rollers are located, *usu* in a cage, suitable for heavier loads than ball-bearings. **Roll'erblade**® or **roll'erblade** *n* a type of roller skate with wheels set in a line resembling the blade of an ice skate (also *vi*). **roll'erblader** *n*. **roll'erblading** *n*. **roll'erblind** *n* a window screen on a roller. **roll'ercoaster** *n* a type of switchback railway popular at carnivals, etc, along which people ride in open cars at great speed; an action or process moving at great speed and seemingly unstoppable; a series of unexpected changes of fortune or emotional swings. ◆ *vt* to direct or cause to move with great speed, *esp* in a set direction. **roller derby** *n* a speed skating race on roller skates. **roller hockey** *n* a form of hockey played by teams on roller skates. **roller skate** *n* a skate with four wheels instead of a blade, set at the corners of the shoe. **roll'er-skate** *vi* to move, dance, etc on roller skates. **roll'er-skater** *n*. **roll'er-skating** *n*. **roller towel** *n* a continuous towel on a roller. **rolling hitch** *n* a hitch knot used for fastening one rope to another or to a spar. **rolling launch** *n* (*marketing*) the gradual introduction of a new product or service onto the market. **rolling mill** *n* a factory or machine for rolling metal into various shapes between rolls. **rolling news** *n* the continuous broadcasting of news information, *usu* on a twenty-four-hour basis. **rolling pin** *n* a cylinder pushed between the hands for rolling out dough, etc. **rolling stock** *n* the stock or store of engines and vehicles that run upon a railway; the stock of vehicles of a trucking company (*US*). **rolling stone** *n* see phrases below. **rolling strike** *n* a strike by several groups of workers in succession, so that not all of them are on strike at any one time. **roll'-neck** *adj* (of a jersey, etc) having a high neck which is made to be folded over loosely on itself. **roll'-off** *adj* denoting a frequency at which the response of an amplifier or filter is three decibels below maximum. **roll'-on** *adj* (of a deodorant, etc) contained in a bottle which has a rotating ball in its neck, by means of which the liquid is applied to the skin; (of a boat, etc) roll-on roll-off. ◆ *n* a roll-on deodorant, etc; a corset that fits on by stretching. **roll-on roll-off** *n* and *adj* (a ferry-boat, cargo boat, or ferry or cargo service) designed to allow goods vehicles to embark and disembark without unloading and passenger traffic to drive straight on and off. **roll'out** *n* the first public display of a prototype of an aircraft; the public launch or announcement of a new product or service (*fig*);

that part of an aeroplane's landing during which it slows down after touch-down. **roll'over** *n* the deferring of a payment to later time; (also **mouse'over**) an explanatory message or image that is displayed when the cursor rests over a certain point on a computer screen. **roll'-top** *adj* (of a desk) having a flexible cover of slats that rolls up. **roll'-up** *adj* suitable for rolling up. ◆ *n* an accumulator bet; a hand-rolled cigarette (*inf*); attendance, turn-out (*Aust*). **roll-up fund** *n* an offshore fund which returns interest earned from bank deposits back into the fund rather than paying it out to investors, so avoiding incurring income tax. ■ **a rolling stone gathers no moss** a wandering person does not grow rich, but is free from responsibilities and ties. **be rolling in** to have large amounts of (eg money). **heads will roll** severe punishments will be meted out, *esp* loss of status or office. **Master of the Rolls** head of the Civil Division of the Court of Appeal (for England and Wales), formerly head of the Public Record Office, *orig* custodian of the court records (rolls). **on a roll** (*inf*) having continuing luck or success, on a winning streak. **roll along** to arrive by chance, or with a casual air. **roll back** to change back to a former state; to postpone to a later time. **rolled into one** combined in one person or thing. **roll in** to arrive in quantity. **roll in the hay** (*sl*) sexual intercourse or activity. **roll on** may (a specified event) come quickly. **roll out** to launch (a new product or service). **roll over** to defer demand for the repayment of (a loan, etc); to defer indeterminately or indiscriminately; (of a lottery prize) to be added to the next round because it has not been won (see also **rollover** above). **roll up** (*inf*) to assemble, arrive. **roll with the punches** (of a boxer) to move the body away to cushion the impact of the opponent's blows (also *fig*). **strike off the roll** to remove the right to practise from (a doctor, solicitor, etc) after professional misconduct.

Roller see **Rolls-Royce**®.

rollick¹ /rol'ik/ *vi* to behave in a carefree, playful or boisterous manner. ◆ *n* a boisterous romp. [Origin unknown]
■ **roll'icking** *adj* playful, boisterous; joyous, carefree.

rollick² /rol'ik/ (*sl*) *vt* to rebuke severely. ◆ *n* a severe scolding. [Perh alteration of **bollock**]
■ **roll'icking** *n* (also **roll'ocking**).

rollmop /rol'mop/ *n* a fillet of herring rolled up, *usu* enclosing a slice of onion, and pickled in spiced vinegar. [Ger *Rollmops*, from *rollen* to roll, and *Mops* a pug-dog]

rollock see **rowlock**.

rollocking see **rollicking** under **rollick**².

Rolls-Royce® /rōlz-rois'/ *n* a superior make of car, produced by *Rolls-Royce* Ltd (also *inf* **Rolls** or **Roll'er**); anything thought of as being of superior quality (*fig*; also *adj*).

Rolodex® /rō'lə-deks/ *n* a proprietary brand of rotary index (qv under **rota**).

roly-poly /rō'li-pō'li/ *n* a pudding made of a sheet of dough, covered with jam or fruit, rolled up, and baked or steamed (also **roly-poly pudding**); a round, podgy person; the children's game of rolling over and over down a grassy slope; an old game in which balls are bowled into holes or thrown into hats placed on the ground; any of several bushy plants, especially *Salsola kali*, that break off and roll in the wind (*Aust*). ◆ *adj* round, podgy. [Prob **roll**]

ROM /rom/ (*comput*) *abbrev* : read-only memory, a storage device whose contents cannot be altered by a programmer.

Rom. (*Bible*) *abbrev* : (the Letter to the) Romans.

rom /rom/ *n* (pl **rō'ma**) a gypsy man. [Romany, man, husband]
■ **Rō'ma** *n pl* the travelling people, gypsies; (as *sing*) a member of this community.

rom. *abbrev* : roman (type).

Roma see under **rom**.

romage /rum'ij/ (*Shakesp*) *n* tumult. [**rummage**]

Romaic /rō-mā'ik/ *n* and adj modern Greek. [Mod Gr *Rhōmaikos* Roman (ie of the Eastern Roman Empire), from *Rhōmē* Rome]
■ **romā'ika** *n* a modern Greek dance.

romaine /rō-mān'/ (*N Am*) *n* a cos lettuce. [Fr]

romaji /rō'mä-ji/ *n* a system for writing Japanese using the Roman alphabet. [Jap, Roman letters]

romal /rō-mäl'/ or **rumal** /roo-mäl'/ *n* a handkerchief; a headcloth. [Pers *rūmāl*]

Roman /rō'mən/ *adj* relating to Rome, *esp* ancient Rome, its people, or the empire founded by them; relating to the Roman Catholic religion, papal; (without *cap*) (of type) of the ordinary upright kind, *opp* to *italic*; (of numerals) written in letters, eg IV, iv, etc (cf **Arabic**); (of handwriting) round and bold; (of a nose) high-bridged. ◆ *n* a native or citizen of Rome; a Roman Catholic; (without *cap*) roman letter or type. [L *Rōmānus*, from *Rōma* Rome]
■ **Romanic** /rō-man'ik/ *adj* of Roman or Latin origin; Romance. ◆ *n* the Romance language or languages collectively. **Ro'manish** *adj* (*usu derog*) Roman Catholic; reminiscent of, or having elements of, Roman

Catholicism. **Ro'manism** *n* Roman Catholicism or a slavish adherence to its doctrine. **Ro'manist** *n* a Roman Catholic; a specialist in Romance philology or Roman law or antiquities. ◆ *adj* Roman Catholic. **Romanist'ic** *adj*. **Romanization** or **-s-** /rō-mə-nī-zā'shən/ *n*. **Ro'manize** or **-ise** *vt* to make Roman or Roman Catholic; to bring under Roman or Roman Catholic influence; to represent by the Roman alphabet. ◆ *vi* to accept Roman or Roman Catholic ways, laws, doctrines, etc; to become Roman Catholic. **Ro'manizer** or **-s-** *n*. **Romano-** /rō-mä-nō-/ *combining form* signifying: Roman; Romanized; Roman and (as in *Romano-British*).
□ **Roman alphabet** *n* the alphabet developed by the ancient Romans for writing Latin, used for most writing in W European languages. **Roman candle** *n* a firework discharging a succession of white or coloured stars; a bad landing by aeroplane (*sl*); a landing by parachute when the parachute fails to open (*sl*). ◆ *vi* to make such a landing. **Roman Catholic** *adj* recognizing the spiritual supremacy of the Pope or Bishop of Rome. ◆ *n* a member of the Roman Catholic Church. **Roman Catholicism** *n* the doctrines and polity of the Roman Catholic Church collectively. **Roman cement** *n* a hydraulic cement made from calcareous nodules from the London Clay. **Roman Empire** *n* the ancient empire of Rome, divided in the 4c into the Eastern and Western Empires (see also **Holy Roman Empire** under **holy**). **Roman holiday** *n* entertainment or profit derived from the suffering of others (from Byron *Childe Harold's Pilgrimage* 4.141). **Roman law** *n* the system of law developed by the ancient Romans, civil law. **Roman nettle** *n* a nettle, rare in Britain, with female flowers in heads, traditionally introduced by the Romans. **Roman numerals** see **Roman** (*adj*) above. **Roman snail** *n* the edible snail (*Helix pomatia*) much valued by the Romans.

roman /ro-mä'/ *n* a medieval romance, tale of chivalry; a novel. [Fr]
□ **roman à clef** or **clefs**, **clé** or **clés** /ro-mä-nä klā/ *n* (literally, novel with a key) a novel with characters based on real people under disguised names. **roman à thèse** /ro-mä-nä tez/ *n* a novel that sets out to demonstrate a thesis or proposition. **roman à tiroirs** /ro-mä-nä tēr'wär/ *n* (literally, novel with drawers) a novel with an episodic structure, a picaresque. **roman fleuve** /flœv/ *n* (literally, river novel) a novel written as a series of self-contained narratives telling the story of a family or other social group over successive generations (also called **saga novel**).

romance /rō-mans', rō'mans or rō'məns/ *n* (with *cap*) a general name for the vernacular languages that developed out of popular Latin, ie French, Provençal, Italian, Spanish, Portuguese, Romanian and Romansch, with their various dialects; a tale of chivalry, *orig* one in verse, written in one of these vernaculars; any fictitious and wonderful tale; a fictitious narrative in prose or verse which passes beyond the limits of ordinary life; a Spanish historical ballad; a piece of romantic fiction; romantic fiction as a literary genre; a romantic occurrence or series of occurrences; a love affair; romantic atmosphere or feeling; a leaning towards the romantic; an imaginative lie; romanticism; a composition of romantic character (*music*). ◆ *vi* to write or tell romances; to talk extravagantly or with an infusion of fiction; to lie; to build castles in the air. ◆ *vt* to woo. ◆ *adj* (with *cap*) of or relating to Romance; of or relating to romantic fiction. [OFr *romanz*, from (hypothetical) LL *rōmānicē* (adv), in (popular) Roman language]
■ **roman'cer** *n*. **roman'cical** *adj* (*Lamb*) dealing with romance. **roman'cing** *n* and *adj*.

Romanes see **Romany**.

romanesco /rō-mə-nes'kō/ *n* (pl **rōmanes'cos**) a vegetable of the Brassica family with spiral rosettes that exhibit fractal geometry (also **romanesco broccoli**, **romanesco cauliflower**). [Ital *broccolo romanesco* Romanesque broccoli]

Romanesque /rō-mə-nesk'/ *adj* of the transition from Roman to Gothic architecture, characterized by round arches and vaults. ◆ *n* the Romanesque style, art or architecture. [Fr]

Romani see **Romany**.

Romanian /rō-mā'ni-ən/, **Rumanian** or **Roumanian** /roo-/, also (*archaic*) **Ruman** or **Rouman** /roo'mən/ *adj* of or relating to the republic of *Romania* in SE Europe, its inhabitants or their language. ◆ *n* a native or citizen of Romania, or member of the same people; the Romance language of Romania. [Romanian *România*, from L *Rōmānus* Roman]

Romanism, **Romanize**, etc see under **Roman**.

Romano /rō-mä'nō/ *n* a sharp-tasting hard cheese. [Ital]

Romansch, **Romansh**, **Roumansch**, **Rumansch** /rō-, roo-mansh' or -mänsh/, or **Rumonsch** /-monsh/ *n* and adj Rhaeto-Romanic; sometimes confined to the Upper Rhine dialects. [Romansch]

romantic /rō-man'tik/ *adj* relating to, or of the nature of, romance, inclining towards, or savouring of, romance, *esp* feelings of love or the idea of sentimentalized love; fictitious; extravagant; wild; fantastic; (of literature, art, music, etc) of or in the style of romanticism. ◆ *n* a romanticist. [Fr *romantique*, from OFr *romant* romance]

■ **roman'tical** *adj.* **romantical'ity** *n.* **roman'tically** *adv.* **roman'ticism** /-*sizm*/ *n* romantic quality, feeling, tendency, principles or spirit; (often with *cap*) literature and art typical of the Romantic Revival. **roman'ticist** *n.* **romanticīzā'tion** or **-s-** *n.* **roman'ticize** or **-ise** /-*ti-sīz*/ *vt* to make seem romantic. ◆ *vi* to have or express romantic ideas.
❑ **Romantic Revival** *n* the late 18c and early 19c revolt against classicism or neoclassicism to a more picturesque, original, free and imaginative style in literature and art.

Romany, Romani /rō'mə-ni/ or /rom'ə-ni/, also **Rommany** /rom'ə-ni/ *n* a gypsy; (also **Romanes** /rom'ə-nes/) the Indic language of the gypsies (in pure form not now common in Britain). ◆ *adj* of Romanies or their language; gypsy. [Romany, from *rom* man]
❑ **Romany rye** /rī/ *n* a man who associates with gypsies, though not one himself.

romaunt /rō-mönt'/ (*archaic*) *n* a romance. [OFr *romant*; see **romance**]

romcom or **rom-com** /rom'kom/ (*film*) *n* a romantic comedy.

Rome /rōm, formerly *room*/ *n* the capital of the Roman Empire, now of Italy; often used for the Roman Catholic Church or Roman Catholicism. [L *Rōma*]
■ **Rome'ward** *adj* and *adv.* **Rome'wards** *adv.* **Rōm'ic** *n* a phonetic notation devised by Henry Sweet, based upon the original Roman values of the letters. **Rōm'ish** *adj* Roman Catholic (*derog*); Roman (*obs*).
❑ **Rome'-penny** or **-scot** *n* (*obs*) Peter's penny. **Rome'-runner** *n* (*obs*) a self-seeking cleric who had much resort to Rome.

Romeo¹ /rō'mi-ō/ *n* (pl **Rō'meos**) a young man very much in love; a Don Juan in the making. [Shakespearean character]

Romeo² or **romeo** /rō'mi-ō/ *n* (in international radio communication) a code word for the letter *r*.

Rommany see **Romany**.

romneya /rom'ni-ə/ *n* a plant of the *Romneya* genus of papaveraceous shrubs, with large white poppy-like flowers with yellow centres. [Thomas *Romney* Robinson (1792–1882), British astronomer and physicist]

Romo /rō'mō/ *n* a revival of the New Romantic (qv) movement in pop music. [*romantic* and *modern*]

romp /romp/ *vi* to frolic actively; to move along easily and quickly, *esp* in winning a race. ◆ *n* a person, *esp* a girl, who romps; a tomboy; a vigorous frolic, *esp* a sexual one; a light-hearted outing; a swift easy run. [**ramp¹**]
■ **romp'er** *n* a person who romps; (*usu* in *pl*) a young child's one-piece suit for play (also **romper suit**). **romp'ingly** *adv.* **romp'ish** *adj.* **romp'ishly** *adv.* **romp'ishness** *n.*
■ **romp home** to win easily. **romp through** to do (something) quickly and easily.

roncador /rong-kə-dör'/ or /-dör'/ *n* a name for various fishes of the N American Pacific coast, *esp* of the maigre family, from the sounds they emit. [Sp, snorer]

rondache /ron-dash'/ or /-däsh'/ *n* a buckler. [Fr]

rondavel /ron-dav'əl/ or /ron'/ *n* in S Africa, a round hut, *usu* with a grass roof; a more sophisticated building of similar shape, used eg as a guest house. [Afrik *rondawel*]

ronde /rond/ *n* a script printing-type. [Fr, round (*fem*)]

rondeau /ron'dō/ or /rə-dō'/ *n* (pl **ron'deaux** /-dōz/) a form of poem characterized by closely-knit rhymes and a refrain, and, as defined in the 17c, consisting of thirteen lines, divided into three unequal strophes, not including the burden (repeating the first few words) after the eighth and thirteenth lines, brought into vogue by Swinburne; a rondo (*music*). [Fr *rondeau*, earlier *rondel*, from *rond* round]
■ **ron'del** *n* a verse form of thirteen or fourteen lines on two rhymes, the seventh and thirteenth being identical with the first, and the eighth and (if present) the fourteenth with the second; a circular part or ornament in jewellery; a circular badge. **rondino** /-dē'nō/ *n* (pl **rondi'nos**) (from *Ital dimin*) a short rondo. **ron'do** *n* (pl **ron'dos**) (*orig Ital*, from Fr) a musical composition whose principal subject recurs in the same key in alternation with other subjects, often the last movement of a sonata. **rondolet'to** *n* (pl **rondolet'tos**) a short rondo.

rondure /rond'yər/ *n* a Shakespearean form of **roundure**.

rone, roan or **rhone** /rōn/ (*Scot*) *n* a roof-gutter (also **rone'pipe** or **roan'pipe**). [Origin unknown]

Roneo® /rō'ni-ō/ *n* an early duplicating machine. ◆ *vt* (without *cap*) to produce copies of (a document) using such a machine.

rong /rong/ (*obs*) *pat of* **ring².**

ronggeng /rong'geng/ *n* a Malaysian dancing-girl; a kind of dancing, often with singing, in Malaysia. [Malay *rónggeng*]

ronin /rō'nin/ (*hist*) *n* a lordless samurai. [Jap]

ronne and **ronning** (*Spenser*) same as **run** (*infinitive* and *pap*) and **running.**

ront or **ronte** (*Spenser*) same as **runt.**

röntgen or **roentgen** /rænt'yən, also *rent'*, *ront'* or *runt'yən*, also -*gən*/ (sometimes with *cap*) *adj* of the German physicist Wilhelm Conrad *Röntgen* (1845–1923), discoverer of the **röntgen rays** or X-rays (see **X**). ◆ *n* the international unit of dose of X-rays or gamma rays, defined in terms of the ionization it produces in air under stated conditions.
■ **roent'genium** *n* an artificially produced radioactive transuranic element (symbol **Rg**; atomic no 111), formerly called **unununium.** **rönt'genize** or **-ise** *vt* to treat by röntgen rays. **rönt'genogram** *n* a photograph made with these rays. **röntgenog'raphy** *n* photography by these rays. **röntgenol'ogy** *n* the study of the rays. **röntgenos'copy** *n* observation by means of these rays. **röntgenother'apy** *n* treatment of disease by means of them.

ronyon or **runnion** /run'yən/ (*Shakesp*) *n* a term of reproach to a woman. [Some connect with Fr *rogne* mange]

roo /roo/ (*Aust inf*) *n* short form of **kangaroo.**
❑ **roo bar** *n* a strong metal bar or grid fitted to the front of a road vehicle as protection in case of collision with a kangaroo or other animal on an outback road, etc.

rood /rood/ *n* Christ's cross; a cross or crucifix, *esp* at the entrance to a church chancel; a rod, pole or perch, linear or square, varying locally in value; a quarter of an acre, or 0.10117 hectares. [OE *rōd* gallows, cross]
❑ **rood beam** *n* a beam for supporting the rood. **Rood Day (Holyrood Day** or **Rood'mas Day**) *n* the feast of the Exaltation (14 September) or of the Invention (3 May) of the Cross. **rood loft** *n* a gallery over the rood screen. **rood screen** *n* an ornamental partition separating choir from nave. **rood'-steeple, rood'-tower** *n* the steeple and tower over the crossing of a church. **rood'-tree** *n* (*obs*) Christ's cross.

roof /roof/ *n* (pl **roofs**) the top covering of a building or vehicle; a ceiling; the overhead surface, structure or stratum of a vault, arch, cave, excavation, etc; the upper covering of the mouth (the palate) or of any cavity; a dwelling; a culmination; a high or highest plateau (eg *the roof of the world*, the Pamir); an upper limit; an aeroplane's ceiling or limiting height. ◆ *vt* to cover with a roof; to shelter. [OE *hrōf*; Du *roef*]
■ **roofed** *adj.* **roof'er** *n* a person who makes or mends roofs; a roof board; a letter of thanks for hospitality (*inf*). **roof'ing** *n* covering with a roof; materials for a roof; the roof itself; shelter. ◆ *adj* for roofing. **roof'less** *adj* (of a building) having no roof; (of a person) having neither permanent nor temporary accommodation, living on the streets. **roof'lessness** *n.* **roof'like** *adj.* **roof'y** *adj* having a roof or roofs.
❑ **roof board** *n* a board lying under slates or tiles. **roof garden** *n* a garden on a flat roof. **roof guard** *n* a device to prevent snow from sliding off a roof. **roof plate** *n* a wall plate that receives the lower ends of the rafters of a roof. **roof rack** *n* a rack which may be fitted to the roof of a car, etc to carry luggage, etc. **roof'scape** *n* a view of a skyline formed by the tops of buildings against the sky. **roof'top** *n* the outside of a roof. **roof'tree** *n* the ridgepole of a roof; the roof.
■ **have a roof over one's head** to have somewhere to live. **hit** (or **go through**) **the roof** to become very angry. **raise the roof** to make a great noise or commotion; to hit the roof.

Roofie /roo'fi/ (*sl*) *n* a tablet of the sedative Rohypnol.

rooibos tea /roi'bos tē/ *n* (also **red bush tea**) tea prepared from the leaves of any of several species of *Borbonia* or *Aspalanthus*. [Afrik *rooi* red, and *bos* bush]

rooikat /roi'kat/ *n* a S African lynx, *Felis caracal*. [Afrik *rooi* red, and *kat* cat]

rooinek /roi'nek/ *n* an Afrikaans nickname for a British or English-speaking person. [Afrik, red neck, from Du *rood nek*, from the complexion]

rook¹ /rook/ *n* a gregarious species of crow; a card-sharp (*sl*); a simpleton (*obs*). ◆ *vt* to fleece. [OE *hrōc*]
■ **rook'ery** *n* a breeding-place of rooks in a group of trees; a breeding-place of penguins, seals, etc; a crowded cluster of slum tenements (*archaic*); a place unpleasantly overcrowded with a particular group or type (*fig*); a disturbance (*sl* or *dialect*). **rook'ish** *adj.* **rook'y** *adj* (*Shakesp*) full of rooks, or *poss* black, murky (see **roky** under **roke**).

rook² /rook/ *n* in chess, any of four pieces, two on each side, *usu* shaped like a tower with battlements, that can move in a vertical or horizontal line over any number of empty squares (also called **castle**). [OFr *roc*, from Pers *rukh*]

rook³ /rook/ (*Shakesp*) same as **ruck⁴.**

■ words derived from main entry word; ❑ compound words; ■ idioms and phrasal verbs

rookie or **rooky** /rŏŏk'i/ (*inf*) *n* a raw beginner; a callow recruit; someone new to or inexperienced in eg a sport, sporting event, profession, etc. ◆ *adj* of or relating to a rookie. [Appar from **recruit**]

room /room/ or /rŭm/ *n* space; necessary or available space; space unoccupied; opportunity, scope or occasion; stead; a particular place; an assigned place, as in a theatre (*obs*); a seat (*Bible*); appointment, office; a holding of land (*obs*); a compartment; a chamber; a cottage sitting room; company in a room. ◆ *vt* and *vi* (chiefly *N Am*) to lodge; to share a room or rooms (with *with*). [OE *rūm* ; Ger *Raum*, Du *ruim*]
■ **roomed** *adj* having rooms. **room'er** *n* (*N Am*) a lodger, *usu* taking meals elsewhere. **roomette'** *n* (*N Am*) a sleeping compartment in a train; a small bedroom to let. **room'ful** *n* (*pl* **room'fuls**) as much or as many as a room will hold. **room'ie** *n* (*US inf*) a roommate. **room'ily** *adv*. **room'iness** *n*. **rooms** *n pl* a set of rooms in a house, etc rented as a separate unit. **room'some** *adj* (*obs*) roomy. **room'y** (**room'ier**; **room'iest**) *adj* having ample room; wide; spacious.
❑ **room'-divider** *n* a low wall or piece of furniture serving as one, dividing a room into two separate sections. **room'-fellow** *n* (*archaic*) a person who shares a room. **rooming house** *n* (*N Am*) a house with furnished rooms to let. **rooming-in'** *n* (*N Am*) shared accommodation, *esp* for a mother and her newborn baby. **room'mate** *n* a fellow lodger (*N Am*); a person who shares a room. **room'-ridden** *adj* confined to one's room. **room service** *n* the serving of food, etc to people in their room(s) in a hotel, etc. **room temperature** *n* the average temperature of a living room, taken to be about 20°C.
■ **leave the room** (*euphem*) *esp* of children in school, to go to the toilet.

roon /rŭn/ or **rund** /run(d), rŭn(d) or rŏn(d)/ (*Scot*) *n* a list or selvage; a strip or thread of cloth (also **royne** /roin/). [Origin obscure]

roop[1] /roop/ *vi* (*Scot*) to make a hoarse sound. ◆ *n* a hoarse sound; hoarseness. [Variant of **roup**[2]]
■ **roop'it** or **roop'y** *adj* (*Scot*) hoarse.

roop[2] see **stoop and roop** under **stoop**[4].

roosa see **rusa**[2].

roose /rooz/ or (*Scot*) *rüz/* (*dialect*) *vt* to praise. [ME *rosen*, from ON *hrōsa* to praise]

roost[1] /roost/ *n* a perch or place for a sleeping bird; a hen house; a sleeping-place; a bed; a set of fowls resting together; a loft or garret or its roof (*Scot*). ◆ *vi* to settle or sleep on a roost or perch; to perch; to go to rest for the night. [OE *hrōst* ; Du *roest*]
■ **roost'er** *n* a domestic cock.
■ **come home to roost** to recoil upon oneself (**the chickens have come home to roost**) one's actions have had unpleasant consequences for oneself); to return to a place (*usu* after travel) in order to settle down. **rule the roost** see under **roast**.

roost[2] /roost/ (*Orkney and Shetland*) *n* a tidal race. [ON *röst*]

root[1] /root/ *n* (ordinarily and popularly) the underground part of a plant, *esp* when edible; that part of a higher plant which never bears leaves or reproductive organs, ordinarily underground and descending, and serving to absorb salts in solution, but often above-ground, often arising from other parts, often serving other functions, though morphologically comparable (*bot*); the source, cause, basis, foundation or occasion of anything, eg an ancestor, or an element from which words are derived; an embedded or basal part, as of a tooth, a hair, a dam; a growing plant with its root; the factor of a quantity which, taken so many times, produces that quantity (*maths*); any value of the unknown quantity for which an equation is true (*maths*); the fundamental note on which a chord is built (*music*); (in *pl*) one's ancestry, family origins; (in *pl*) one's ethnic or cultural origins; (in *pl*) a feeling of belonging in a town, community, etc; a sexual partner (*Aust and NZ sl*). ◆ *vi* to fix the root; to be firmly established; to develop a root; to have sexual intercourse (*Aust and NZ sl*). ◆ *vt* to plant in the earth; to implant deeply; to fix by the root (also *fig*); to have sexual intercourse with (*Aust and NZ sl*); to uproot (*usu* with *up*); to remove entirely by uprooting, clear away, eradicate, extirpate (*usu* with *out*). [Late OE *rōt*, from ON *rōt* ; Dan *rod* ; Gothic *waurts*, OE *wyrt*]
■ **root'age** *n* the act of striking root; the state of being rooted; roothold; a root system. **root'ed** *adj* having roots; fixed by roots or as by roots; firmly established. **root'edly** *adv*. **root'edness** *n*. **root'er** *n*. **root'less** *adj* having no roots; belonging nowhere, having no home and so constantly shifting about. **root'lessness** *n*. **root'let** *n*. **root'like** *adj*. **roots** *adj* expressing or concerned with one's ethnic or cultural identity; of or relating to roots music (see below). **root'siness** *n*. **root'sy** *adj* (*esp* of music) reminiscent of or incorporating traditional or folk styles. **root'y** *adj* (**root'ier**; **root'iest**) abounding in, consisting of, or like roots; rank.
❑ **root-and-branch'** *adj* and *adv* without leaving any part; thorough(ly), complete(ly). **root ball** *n* the spherical mass formed by the roots of a plant, with the surrounding soil. **root beer** *n* a drink made from roots of dandelion, sassafras, etc. **root'bound** *adj* rooted to the ground (*Milton*); pot-bound. **root canal** *n* the narrow passage through which nerves and blood vessels enter the pulp cavity of a tooth. **root cap** *n* a sheath of cells at the tip of a root. **root cause** *n* fundamental cause. **root climber** *n* a plant that climbs by means of roots, such as ivy. **root crop** *n* a crop of esculent roots. **root directory** *n* (*comput*) the highest level of directory in a directory structure. **root eater** *n*. **root'-fallen** *adj* fallen, by roots giving way. **root'-fast** *adj* firmly rooted. **root hair** *n* a fine tubular outgrowth from a cell by which a young root absorbs water. **root'hold** *n* maintenance of position by roots; a footing. **root house** *n* a summerhouse built of tree roots; a storehouse for potatoes, etc. **rooting compound** *n* (*bot*) a preparation, containing plant growth substances, in which a cutting is dipped to promote root growth. **root'kit** *n* (*comput*) software embedded within an operating system that performs operations without informing the user. **root'-knot** *n* an enlargement of a root caused by a nematode. **root mean square** *n* the square root of the sum of the squares of a set of quantities divided by the total number of quantities. **root nodule** *n* (*bot*) the swelling on the root of a leguminous plant containing nitrogen-fixing bacteria. **root parasite** *n* a plant parasitic on a root. **root planing** *n* (*dentistry*) a treatment for gum disease in which the parts of teeth below the gum are cleaned and smoothed. **root pressure** *n* an upward forcing of sap, shown by the bleeding of plants. **root'-prune** *vt* to prune the roots of. **root'-pruning** *n*. **root rubber** *n* rubber obtained from the roots of certain African apocynaceous plants. **root sheath** *n* the sheath of the root of an orchid, hair, feather, etc. **roots music** *n* popular music based on traditional forms, often reflecting an ethnic identity. **root'stock** *n* a rhizome, *esp* if short, thick, and more or less erect (*bot*); a source, ancestral form. **root system** *n*. **root tubercle** *n* a root nodule. **root vegetable** *n* a vegetable which has an esculent root; the root itself.
■ **put down roots** to settle in a place. **strike** or **take root** to root, to become established.

root[2], earlier **wroot** /root/ *vt* to turn up with the snout. ◆ *vi* (of pigs) to burrow into the ground with the snout; to grub; to rummage; to poke about. ◆ *n* an act of rooting. [OE *wrōtan*, from *wrōt* a snout; see also **rout**[2]]
■ **root'er** *n*. **root'ing** *n* and *adj*. **root'le** *vt* and *vi* to grub.

root[3] /root/ (*orig US*) *vi* to shout, applaud, support or encourage (a contestant, etc) (with *for* or *on*). [Prob from **rout**[4]]
■ **root'er** *n*.

rootsiness and **rootsy** see under **root**[1].

rooty[1] /roo'ti/ (*milit sl*) *n* bread. [Ety as for **roti**]

rooty[2] see under **root**[1].

rope /rōp/ *n* a stout twist of fibre, wire, etc, technically over 1 inch round; a string of pearls, onions, etc; a glutinous stringy formation; a local lineal measure, 20 feet; a climbing party roped together. ◆ *vt* to fasten, bind, enclose, mark off, or (*US and Aust*) catch with a rope; to hold back to avoid winning (*horse-racing*). ◆ *vi* to form into a rope. [OE *rāp* ; ON *reip*, Ger *Reif*]
■ **rop'able** or **rope'able** *adj* (*Aust and NZ sl*; of cattle or horses) wild, unmanageable; very angry. **roped** /rōpt/ *adj*. **rō'per** *n* a rope-maker; a person who ropes a horse; a decoy (also **rō'per-in'**). **rōp'ery** *n* ropework; trickery, knavery (*archaic*). **rōp'ily** *adv*. **rōp'iness** *n*. **rōp'ing** *n* and *adj*. **rō'py** or **rō'pey** (**rō'pier**; **rō'piest**) *adj* stringy; glutinous; wrinkled like loops of rope; bad of its kind (*sl*); slightly unwell (*sl*).
❑ **rope dance** *n* a tightrope performance. **rope dancer** *n*. **rope'-drilling** *n* boring by a drill alternately raised by a rope and then dropped. **rope house** *n* a storehouse for ropes; a house where salt is crystallized from brine trickling along ropes. **rope ladder** *n* a ladder of ropes. **rope machine** *n*. **rope'-maker** *n*. **rope'-making** *n*. **rope'-ripe** *adj* deserving to be hanged. **rope's end** *n* (*hist*) the end of a rope used for flogging; a hangman's noose. **rope's'-end** *vt* (*hist*) to beat with a rope's end. **rope'-soled** *adj* having a sole of rope. **rope stitch** *n* satin stitch worked in stitches laid diagonally side by side. **rope trick** *n* a disappearing trick with a rope; *poss* a rhetorical figure, or, according to some, a trick deserving the gallows (*Shakesp*). **rope'-walk** *n* a long narrow shed or alley for twisting strands into rope. **rope'-walker** *n* a tight-rope performer. **rope'-walking** *n*. **rope'way** *n* a means of transmission by ropes. **rope'work** *n* a rope-walk or rope factory (**rope'works** *n sing*); a system of ropes. **rope yarn** *n* yarn for making ropes, or obtained by untwisting ropes. **roping-down'** *n* (*inf*) abseiling.
■ **give someone (enough) rope (to hang himself** or **herself)** to allow a person full scope to defeat his or her own ends. **know the ropes** see under **know**. **on the high ropes** elated; arrogant. **on the ropes** driven back against the ropes of a boxing ring; nearing defeat, desperate. **rope in** to bring in, enlist (*esp* someone who is reluctant). **ropes of sand** a bond with no cohesion. **the rope** capital punishment by hanging.

roque see under **roquet**.

Roquefort /rok'för/ n a creamy, blue-veined, strong-flavoured cheese made from ewe's milk and matured in natural caves at *Roquefort* commune in S France.

roquelaure /rok'ə-lör or -lör/ n a knee-length cloak worn in the 18c and early 19c. [Fr, after the Duc de *Roquelaure* (1656–1738)]

roquet /rō'kā/ n (in croquet) a stroke by which the striker's ball is played against another ball. ◆ vt to strike by a roquet. ◆ vi to play a roquet. [Prob formed from **croquet**]

■ **roque** /rōk/ n (back-formation) a version of croquet played in N America on a walled, hard-surfaced court.

roquette /rō-ket'/ n same as **rocket²**.

roral see **roric**.

rore /rör or rör/ an obsolete spelling (*Shakesp*) of **roar** (tumult).

roric /rō' or rō'rik/, **rorid** /rö' or rö'rid/ or **roral** /rö' or rö'rəl/ adj dewy. [L *rōs, rōris* dew]

ro-ro /rō'rō/ adj and n (pl **ro'-ros**) short form of **roll-on roll-off** (see under **roll**).

rorqual /rör'kwəl/ n any whale of the genus *Balaenoptera* (finback). [Fr, from Norw *røyrkval*, from ON, literally red whale]

Rorschach test /rör'shak test/ n a test designed to show intelligence, personality and mental state, in which the subject interprets ink-blots of standard type. [Hermann *Rorschach* (1884–1922), Swiss psychiatrist]

rorty /rör'ti/ (*Aust inf*) adj lively and enjoyable; rowdy. [Ety doubtful]

■ **rort** n a racket; a lively or riotous party. ◆ vi to shout, protest loudly; (at a race meeting) to call the odds; to falsify accounts, etc, commit fraud. **ror'ter** n a spiv, a con man. **ror'ting** n.

rory or **rorie** same as **roary** (see under **roar**).

Rosa /rō'zə or roz'ə/ n the rose genus, giving name to the family **Rosā'ceae**. [L *rosa* rose; *rosāceus, roseus* rosy]

■ **rosace** /rō-zās' or -zäs'/ n (from Fr; *archit*) a rosette; a rose window. **rosacea** /rō-zā'shi-ə/ n (*med*) same as **acne rosacea** (see under **acne**). **rosaceous** /rō-zā'shəs/ adj of the rose family; roselike. **rosā'rian** n a rose-fancier. **rosā'rium** n (pl **rosā'riums** or **rosā'ria**) (L) a rose garden.

rosaker /ro-sā'kər/ n obsolete variant of **realgar**.

rosalia /rō-zā'lyä/ (*music*) n a series of repetitions of the same passage, each a tone higher. [Said to be from an Italian folk song, *Rosalia cara mia*]

rosaniline /rō-zan'i-lin, -lēn or -līn/ n a base derived from aniline, with red salts used in dyeing. [**rose¹** and **aniline**]

rosarian and **rosarium** see under **Rosa**.

rosary /rō'zə-ri/ n a rose garden or rose-bed (also **rō'sery**); a chaplet (*obs*); a series of prayers; a string of beads used by Roman Catholics and some other religions as a guide to devotions. [L *rosārium* rose garden]

rosa-solis /rō-zä-sō'lis/ (*obs*) n the sundew; a cordial, *orig* flavoured with sundew juice, afterwards with various spices. [Orig L *rōs sōlis* dew of the sun, altered to *rosa* rose]

rosbif /rōz-bēf'/ (Fr) n a contemptuous term applied by the French to any person who has the misfortune to be British. [Literally, roast beef]

Roscius /rosh'i-əs or rō'ski-ūs/ n a famous Roman actor (died 62BC); hence, a great actor. [L *Rōscius*]

■ **Rosc'ian** adj.

rose¹ /rōz/ n the flower of any species of the genus *Rosa*, national emblem of England; a shrub bearing it, mostly prickly, with white, yellow, pink, orange, or red flowers, numerous stamens and carpels, and achenes enclosed in the receptacle; extended to various flowers or plants in some way resembling the true rose (see eg **guelder rose**, **rock rose** under **rock¹**); a paragon; a rosette, *esp* on a shoe; a rose-cut stone; a rose window; a perforated nozzle; a circular moulding from which eg a door-handle projects; a circular fitting in a ceiling from which an electric light flex hangs; the typical colour of the rose, pink or light crimson; (in *pl*) (in white-skinned peoples) the pink glow of the cheeks in health; erysipelas. ◆ adj of, for or like the rose or roses; rose-coloured. ◆ vt to make like a rose, in colour or scent. [OE *rōse*, from L *rosa*, prob from Gr *rhodeā* a rosebush, *rhodon* rose]

■ **roseal** /rō'zi-əl/ adj roselike. **rō'seate** /-zi-it or -zi-āt/ adj rosy; rose-scented; of roses; unduly favourable or sanguine. **rosed** adj flushed (*Shakesp*); having a rose or roses. **rose'less** adj. **rose'like** adj. **rō'sery** n a rose garden (see **rosary**). **rosier** /rō'zhər/ (Fr *rosier*) or (*Spenser*) **rosiere** /rō-zi-ār', -ēr'/ n a rose tree or bush. **rō'sily** adv. **rō'siness** n. **rō'sy** adj (**rō'sier**; **rō'siest**) of or covered in roses; roselike; rose-red; blooming; blushing; bright; hopeful; promising. ◆ n (*old sl*) wine. ◆ vt and vi to redden.

❑ **rose apple** n an East Indian tree of the clove genus; its edible fruit. **rose'bay** n the oleander (also called **rosebay laurel** or **rose-laurel**); any rhododendron (*N Am*). **rosebay willowherb** n a willowherb common where woods have been felled or land cleared by fire (also

called **fireweed**). **rose beetle** n the rose chafer; the rose bug. **rose'bowl** n an ornamental bowl for cut flowers. **rose'bud** n. **rose bug** n an American beetle that eats roses. **rose'bush** n. **rose campion** n a garden species of campion (*Lychnis coronaria*). **rose chafer** n a beetle (*Cetonia aurata*) that eats roses. **rose'-cheeked** adj. **rose colour** n pink. **rose'-coloured** adj pink; seeing or representing things in too favourable a light. **rose comb** n a fowl's low red crest; a fowl with such a crest. **rose'-combed** adj. **rose cross** n a cross within a circle; a Rosicrucian. **rose'-cut** adj (of a gem) cut in nearly hemispherical form, with flat base and many small facets rising to a low point above. **rose diamond** n a rose-cut diamond. **rose drop** n a rose-flavoured sweet; a red eruption on the nose. **rose elder** n the guelder-rose. **rose engine** n a lathe attachment for carving swirling patterns. **rose'finch** n any of various finches of the genus *Carpodacus* found in Europe and Asia, the males more or less covered with red or pink plumage, especially *Carpodus erythrinus*, the common rosefinch. **rose'fish** n the bergylt. **rose garden** n. **rose geranium** n a pelargonium (*Pelargonium graveolens*) with small pink flowers and fragrant leaves. **rose'hip** n the fruit of the rose. **rose'-hued** adj (*archaic*) rose-coloured. **rose knot** n a rosette of ribbon, etc. **rose laurel** n oleander. **rose leaf** n the leaf of a rose; *usu* a rose-petal. **rose'-lipped** adj having red lips. **rose madder** n a pale pink colour, made from madder pigment. **rose'maling** n painting or carving furniture in floral motifs. **rose mallow** n hollyhock; hibiscus. **rose noble** n an old English gold coin with the figure of a rose. **rose of Jericho** n a cruciferous plant (*Anastatica hierochuntica*) of N Africa and Syria, that curls in a ball in drought. **rose of Sharon** n (in the Bible, *Song of Solomon*) *prob* a narcissus; now applied to a species of hibiscus, and to a species of *Hypericum*. **rose oil** n a fragrant oil expressed from rose petals. **rose'-pink** adj rose-coloured; sentimental. ◆ n a pink colour; a pink pigment. **rose quartz** n a rose-coloured quartz. **rose rash** n roseola. **rose'-red** adj red as a rose. **rose'root** n a stonecrop (*Sedum rosea*) with rose-scented root. **rose'-tinted** adj rose-coloured (*lit* and *fig*). **rose topaz** n a topaz coloured pink by heat. **rose tree** n a standard rose. **rose'water** n water distilled from rose petals. ◆ adj sentimental; superfine; comfortable. **rose window** n a round window with tracery of radiating compartments. **rose'wood** n a valuable heavy dark-coloured wood of many trees, *esp* Brazilian and Indian species of *Dalbergia* (family Papilionaceae), said to smell of roses when fresh-cut. **rosewood oil** n oil of rhodium. **ro'sy-bos'omed** adj. **ro'sy-cheeked** adj. **ro'sy-col'oured** adj. **rosy cross** n the emblem of the Rosicrucians. **rosy drop** n rose drop. **rosy finch** n any of a genus (*Leucosticte*) of finches of western N America and E Asia with bright pink tinted plumage. **ro'sy-fing'ered** adj Homer's favourite epithet (*rhododaktylos*) of the dawn. **ro'sy-foot'ed** adj.

■ **all roses** see **roses all the way** below. **bed of roses** see under **bed¹**. **come out** (or **up**) **smelling of roses** to emerge from a series of events, etc seemingly innocent, with image untainted or undamaged. **look** or **see through rose-coloured** (or **rose-tinted** or **rosy**) **spectacles** or **glasses** to view matters over-optimistically. **roses all the way** or **all roses** pleasant, happy; without difficulties, problems, etc. **under the rose** in confidence; privately. **Wars of the Roses** a disastrous dynastic struggle in England (1455–85) between the Houses of Lancaster and York, from their respective emblems, the red and the white rose.

rose² pat of **rise**.

rosé /rō'zā/ n a pinkish table wine produced either by removing red grape skins, or by mixing red and white wines, early in fermentation (cf **red wine** under **red¹**). [Fr, literally pink]

roseal, roseate, etc see under **rose¹**.

Roseland /rōz'land/ (*sl*) n the areas of SE England outside London. [*Rest of South East* and **land¹**, with deliberate suggestion of **rose²**]

rosella /rō-zel'ə/ n any of several varieties of Australian parakeet with brightly-coloured plumage, first observed at Rose Hill near Sydney. [For *rosehiller*]

roselle or **rozelle** /rō-zel'/ n an East Indian hibiscus.

rosemary /rōz'mə-ri/ n a small fragrant pungent Mediterranean labiate shrub (genus *Rosmarinus*), whose leaves are widely used as a flavouring in food, and in perfumes. [L *rōs marīnus* sea dew]

roseola /rō-zē'ə-lə/ n rose-coloured rash; German measles (also called **rubella**). [Dimin from L *roseus* rosy]

■ **rosē'olar** adj.

rosery see **rosary**.

roset, rosit, rozet or **rozit** /roz'it/ (*Scot*) n a rosin. ◆ vt to rosin. [**rosin**]

■ **ros'ety** (sometimes **ros'etty**), etc adj.

Rosetta stone /rō-zet'ə stōn/ n a tablet, found near Rosetta in Egypt in 1799, which carried the same inscription in hieroglyphics and demotic script and also in Greek and thus enabled a beginning to be made in deciphering hieroglyphics; any comparable first clue.

■ words derived from main entry word; ❑ compound words; ■ idioms and phrasal verbs

rosette /rō-zet'/ *n* a knot of radiating loops of ribbon or the like in concentric arrangement, *esp* worn as a badge showing affiliation, or awarded as a prize; a close radiating group of leaves, *usu* pressed to the ground; a rose-shaped ornament (*archit*); any structure, arrangement or figure of similar shape; a curve whose polar equation is $r = a \sin m^\theta$; a disc, *esp* of copper, formed by throwing water on molten metal; any of several diseases of plants (also **rosette disease**). ◆ *vt* to award a rosette to. ◆ *vi* (*med*; of a cell or group of cells) to form into a rosette. [Fr, dimin of *rose*]
 ■ **rosett'ed** *adj*. **rosett'ing** *n* the development of abnormal leaves as a symptom of disease.

Rosh Hashanah or **Rosh Hashana** /rosh hə-shä'nə/ *n* the Jewish festival of New Year. [Heb, literally head of the year]

Rosicrucian /roz-i- or rō-zi-kroo'sh(y)ən/ *n* a member of an alleged secret society whose members made great pretensions to knowledge of the secrets of Nature, transmutation of metals, elemental spirits, magical signatures, etc, affirmed to have been founded (1459) by Christian *Rosenkreutz*; a member of any of various modern esoteric quasi-religious fraternities. ◆ *adj* of or relating to the Rosicrucians. [Prob a Latinization of *Rosenkreuz* rose cross, L *rosa* rose, and *crux* cross]
 ■ **Rosicru'cianism** *n*.

Rosie Lee or **Rosy Lee** /rō'zi lē/ (*rhyming sl*) *n* tea.

rosier, rosily and **rosiness** see under **rose**[1].

rosin /roz'in/ *n* a resin obtained when turpentine is prepared from dead pine wood, used to make waxes, varnishes, etc and for preparing the bows used to play stringed musical instruments (also called **colophony**). ◆ *vt* to rub with rosin; to add rosin to. [**resin**]
 ■ **ros'inate** *n* a resinate. **ros'ined** *adj*. **ros'iny** *adj*.
 ❑ **rosin oil** *n* an oil distilled from rosin. **rosin plant** or **ros'inweed** *n* *Silphium* or compass plant.

Rosinante or **Rozinante** /ro-zi-nan'ti/ *n* Don Quixote's horse; a pitiful, worn-out nag. [Sp *Roucinante*, explained as *rocin antes*, formerly a rouncy]

rosinate and **rosiny** see under **rosin**.

rosit see **roset**.

rosmarine[1] /roz'mə-rīn/ (*Spenser*) *n* a walrus, or a sea-monster supposed to lick dew off the rocks. [Dan *rosmar* walrus; influenced by **rosmarine**[2]]

rosmarine[2] /roz'mə-rīn or -rēn/ *n* rosemary (*Spenser*); sea dew (*Jonson*). [See **rosemary**]

Rosminian /roz- or ros-min'i-ən/ *adj* of Antonio *Rosmini*-Serbati (1797–1855), his philosophy, or the Institute of Charity founded by him. ◆ *n* a follower of Rosmini.
 ■ **Rosmin'ianism** *n*.

rosolio or **rosoglio** /rō-zō'lyō/ *n* a sweet cordial made with raisins (formerly, it is said, with sundew). [Ital *rosolio*, from L *rōs sōlis* dew of the sun]

RoSPA /ros'pə/ *abbrev*: Royal Society for the Prevention of Accidents.

rosser variant spelling of **rozzer**.

rost an old spelling of **roast**.

rostellum /ro-stel'əm/ *n* a little beak; a beak-like outgrowth from an orchid column; the forepart of a tapeworm's head. [L *rōstellum*, dimin of *rōstrum* beak]
 ■ **rostell'ar** or **rostell'ate** *adj*.

roster /ros'tər or rō'stər/ *n* a list of employees, army personnel, etc with assigned (turns of) duties; any roll of names (*inf*). ◆ *vt* to put in a roster. [Du *rooster*, orig gridiron (from the ruled lines), from *roosten* to roast]
 ■ **ros'tering** *n*.

rösti see **roesti**.

rostrum /ros'trəm or rō'strəm/ *n* a platform for public speaking, etc (from the *Rostra* in the Roman forum, adorned with the beaks of captured ships); a beak; a part resembling a beak (*biol*); a raised platform on a stage (*theatre*); a platform carrying a camera (*film* and *TV*). [L *rōstrum* beak, from *rōdere, rōsum* to gnaw]
 ■ **ros'tral** *adj* of or like a rostrum; of or near the front part of the body, *esp* the nose or mouth (*anat*). **ros'träte** or **ros'trated** *adj* beaked. **rostrocarinate** /ros-trō-kar'in-āt/ *adj* (L *carīna* keel) beaked and keeled. ◆ *n* a supposed flint implement with beak and keel.

rosula /roz'ū-lə/ *n* a leaf-rosette. [LL dimin of L *rosa* rose]
 ■ **ros'ulate** *adj* in a rosette.

rosy see under **rose**[1].

Rosy Lee see **Rosie Lee**.

ROT *abbrev*: registered occupational therapist.

rot /rot/ *vi* (**rott'ing**; **rott'ed**) to putrefy; to decay; to become corrupt; to become weak; to suffer from wasting disease, *esp* in prison, or sheep-rot; to talk nonsense, to joke (*sl*). ◆ *vt* to cause to rot, to ret; to tease, banter with (*sl*). ◆ *n* decay; putrefaction; corruption; collapse,

disintegration (often *fig*); applied to various diseases of sheep, timber, etc; worthless or rotten stuff (*inf*); nonsense (*inf*). ◆ *interj* expressing contemptuous disagreement. [OE *rotian*, pap *rotod*; cf **rotten**[1]]
 ■ **rott'er** *n* a thoroughly depraved or worthless person.
 ❑ **rot'grass** *n* soft grass, butterwort, pennywort or other plant reputed to cause sheep-rot. **rot'gut** *n* (*inf*) cheap poor-quality alcoholic drink. **rot'-stone** *n* rottenstone.

rota /rō'tə/ *n* a roster; a course, round, routine or cycle of duty, etc; (with *cap*) the Roman Catholic supreme ecclesiastical tribunal; a round, a canon, a rondo or other composition with much repetition. [L *rota* a wheel, *rotāre, -ātum* to run]
 ■ **rō'tal** *adj*. **Rō'tameter**® *n* a device for measuring the rate of flow of a fluid, in which a tapered float moves vertically in a transparent tube in accordance with the speed of flow. **rō'taplane** *n* rotor plane. **Rōtarian** /-tā'ri-ən/ *n* a member of a Rotary club (also *adj*). **Rōtā'rianism** *n*. **rotary** /rō'tər-i/ *adj* turning like a wheel; of the nature of rotation; working by rotation of a part; (with *cap*) of an international system of clubs, formed to encourage service to and within the community, with a wheel as a badge, each member being of a different occupation. ◆ *n* a rotary apparatus; (with *cap*) a Rotary club; (with *cap*) Rotarianism; a traffic roundabout (*N Am*). **rotāt'able** *adj*. **rōtāte'** *vt* and *vi* to turn like a wheel; to put, take, go or succeed in rotation. **rō'tate** *adj* (*bot*) wheel-shaped; with united petals in a plane with almost no tube. **rotā'tion** *n* a turning round like a wheel; succession in definite order, as of crops; recurrent order; the conformal transformation in which a particular arrangement is rotated about a fixed point (*maths*, etc). **rotā'tional** *adj*. **rotative** /rō'tə-tiv/ *adj*. **rotā'tor** *n* a person or thing that rotates; a muscle that rotates a part of the body on its axis (*anat*). **rotatory** /rō'tə-tər-i or rō-tāt'ər-i/ *adj* rotary. **rō'tavate** or **rō'tovate** *vt* (back-formation) to till by means of a rotavator. **Rō'tavator**® or **Rō'tovator**® *n* (*rotary cultivator*; also without *cap*) a motor-powered, hand-operated soil-tilling machine. **rō'tavirus** *n* a wheel-shaped virus causing gastroenteritis.
 ❑ **rotary engine** *n* an engine with cylinders set in a circle, rotating around a fixed crankshaft. **rotary index** *n* a filing box with a central, rotating spine to which index cards are attached at one edge and rolled vertically. **rotary press** *n* a machine for printing from a revolving cylindrical forme.

ROTC /rot'si/ (*US*) *abbrev*: Reserve Officers' Training Corps.

rotch, rotche or **roch** /roch/ *n* the little auk (also **rotch'ie**). [Cf Du *rotje* petrel; Fris *rotgies*, pl of *rotgoes* brent goose]

rote[1] /rōt/ *n* mechanical memory, repetition or performance without regard to the meaning. ◆ *vt* (*Shakesp* **roate**) to fix by rote (according to others, to root); to discourse by rote. [Origin obscure; L *rota* a wheel, and OFr *rote* road, have been conjectured]
 ■ **by rote** by repetition.

rote[2] /rōt/ *n* a medieval stringed instrument. [OFr *rote* a fiddle, prob through Gmc from Celtic; Welsh *crwth*, Gaelic *cruit*]

rote[3] /rōt/ (now *US*) *n* the roar of surf. [Ety obscure]

rotenone /rō'ti-nōn/ *n* an insecticide and fish-poison prepared from derris and other plants. [Jap *roten* derris, and **-one**]

rother /rodh'ər/ (*obs*) *n* an ox, cow. [OE *hrȳther* an ox, a cow; cf Ger pl *Rinder* horned cattle]
 ❑ **roth'er-beast** *n*.

roti /rō'tē/ *n* (pl **rō'tis**) (in Indian and Caribbean cooking) a cake of unleavened bread; a kind of sandwich made of this wrapped around curried vegetables, seafood or chicken. [Hindi, bread]

rotifer /rō'ti-fər/ *n* a wheel-animalcule, or member of the **Rotif'era**, minute aquatic animals whose rings of waving cilia suggest a rotating wheel. [L *rota* a wheel, and *ferre* to carry]
 ■ **rotif'eral** or **rotif'erous** *adj*.

rotisserie or **rôtisserie** /rō-tis'ə-ri or rō-tēs-rē'/ *n* a cooking apparatus incorporating a spit; a shop or restaurant in which meats are cooked by direct heat. [Fr, cookshop, from *rôtir* to roast]

rotl /rot'l/ *n* (pl **rot'ls** or **ar'tal**) a unit of weight of variable amount, used in the E Mediterranean. [Ar *ratl*]

rotograph /rō'tə-gräf/ *n* a photograph (eg of a manuscript) made directly by throwing a reversed image on a roll of sensitive paper. ◆ *vt* to photograph by this method. [L *rota* a wheel, and Gr *graphein* to write]

rotogravure /rō-tō-grə-vūr'/ *n* a photogravure process using a rotary press; a print so produced. [L *rota* a wheel, and Fr *gravure* engraving]

rotolo /rot'ə-lō or rō'tō-lō/ (pl **ro'tolos**) an Italian form of **rotl**.

rotor /rō'tər/ *n* a rotating part, *esp* of a dynamo, motor or turbine; a revolving cylinder for propulsion of a ship; a revolving aerofoil; a large, closed eddy sometimes formed under lee waves and associated with severe turbulence (*meteorol*). [For **rotator**]
 ❑ **ro'torcraft** or **rotor plane** *n* a helicopter or autogyro. **rotor ship** *n*. **ro'tor-station** *n* an aerodrome designed specially for helicopters.

rototiller /rō'tō-til-ər/ (N Am) n a Rotavator.

Rotovator® see under **rota**.

rottan /rot'n/ same as **ratton**.

rotten[1] /rot'n/ adj putrefied; decaying; affected by rot; corrupt; unsound; disintegrating; deplorably bad (inf); miserably out of sorts (inf). ◆ adv (sl) very much. [ON rotinn; cf **rot**]

■ **rott'enly** adv. **rott'enness** n.

□ **rotten apple** n a corrupt person. **rotten borough** n a borough that still (till 1832) sent members to parliament though it had few or no inhabitants. **rott'enstone** n a decomposed silicious limestone that has lost most of its calcareous matter, used for polishing metals. ◆ vt to polish with rottenstone.

rotten[2] /rot'n/ same as **ratton**.

rotter, rotting, etc see **rot**.

Rottweiler /rot'vī-lər or -wī-/ n a large, powerfully built black German dog with a smooth coat and tan markings on the chest and legs (also without cap); a rudely aggressive or brutish person (fig). ◆ adj vicious and unscrupulous, brutal, as Rottweiler politics, etc. [Rottweil, in SW Germany]

rotula /rot'ū-lə/ n (pl **rot'ūlae** /-lē/ or **rot'ūlas**) the knee-cap (anat); a radial piece of Aristotle's lantern in sea-urchins (zool). [L rotula, dimin of rota a wheel]

rotund /rō-tund'/ adj round; rounded; nearly spherical; convexly protuberant; (of speech, etc) impressive or grandiloquent; plump. ◆ vt to round. [L rotundus, from rota a wheel]

■ **rotund'a** n a round (esp domed) building or hall. **rotund'ate** adj rounded off; orbicular. **rotund'ity** n roundness; a round mass. **rotund'ly** adv.

roturier /ro-tü-ryä'/ n a plebeian. [Fr, prob from LL ruptūra ground broken by the plough, from L rumpere, ruptum to break]

ROU abbrev : Republic of Uruguay (also IVR).

rouble or **ruble** /roo'bl/ n the standard monetary unit of Russia and Belarus, and formerly of the Soviet Union (100 kopecks). [Russ rubl', perh from rubit' to cut; or Pers rūpīya a rupee]

roucou /roo-koo'/ n annatto. [Fr, from Tupí urucú]

roué /roo'ā/ (old) n a profligate, rake, debauched man, esp an old man. [A name given by Philippe, Duke of Orléans, Regent of France 1715–23, to his dissolute companions, from Fr roué broken on the wheel, from pap of rouer, from roue, from L rota a wheel]

Rouen cross /roo-ã kros/ n a cross in fretwork as a brooch or pendant. [Rouen in France]

rouge[1] /roozh/ n cosmetic powder used to redden the face, orig a mixture of safflower and talc; a polishing powder of hydrated ferric oxide (also **jeweller's rouge**); French red wine (for vin rouge). ◆ vt to colour with rouge. ◆ vi to use rouge; to blush. [Fr rouge, from L rubeus red]

□ **Rouge Croix** /krwä/, **Rouge Dragon** n two of the pursuivants of the Heralds' College. **rouge-et-noir** /roozh-ā-nwär/ n a gambling card game played on a table with two red and two black diamond marks on which stakes are laid (also called **trente-et-quarante**).

rouge[2] /rooj/ (Eton) n a scrimmage (obs); a touchdown in football. [Origin unknown]

rough /ruf/ adj uneven; rugged; unshorn; unshaven; unpolished; harsh; crude; unelaborated; without attention to minute correctness; (of a horse, etc) unbroken; coarse; rude; unrefined; ungentle; turbulent; aspirate; astringent; unpleasant, nasty (inf); difficult, harrowing (inf); feeling unwell, tired or hung over (inf). ◆ adv roughly; with roughness or risk of discomfort. ◆ n rough state; that which is rough; rough ground, esp uncut grass, etc beside a golf fairway or green; a piece inserted in a horse's shoe to keep it from slipping; a hooligan, a rowdy; a crude preliminary sketch, etc. ◆ vt to make rough; to ruffle; to roughen the shoes of; to shape roughly; to treat roughly (usu with up). [OE rūh rough; Ger rauch, rauh, Du ruig]

■ **rough'age** n refuse of grain or crops; bran, fibre, etc in food; coarse food that promotes intestinal movement. **rough'en** vt to make rough. ◆ vi to become rough. **rough'er** n a person who performs preliminary operations. **rough'ie** n a dry bough, esp one used as a torch (Walter Scott); a rough or rowdy person (sl); an outsider in horse-racing or dog-racing (Aust sl); an unfair trick, twist or incident, etc (Aust sl). **rough'ish** adj. **rough'ly** adv. **rough'ness** n the quality of being rough; a rough place; roughage (US dialect). **rough'y** n same as **roughie** above.

□ **rough'-and-read'y** adj ready to hand or easily improvised, and serving the purpose well enough; (of a person) lacking refinement or social graces but pleasant enough. **rough'-and-tumb'le** adj haphazard and scrambling (also adv). ◆ n a scuffle; haphazard struggling. **rough breathing** n in ancient Greek, the sound h. **rough'cast** vt to shape roughly; to cover with roughcast. ◆ n plaster mixed with small stones or shells, used to coat the outside walls of buildings; a rough or preliminary model, etc. ◆ adj coated with roughcast. **rough'-coated** adj given an initial coat of plaster. **rough collie** n a shaggy-coated breed of collie. **rough cut** n a roughly edited, preliminary version or sequence of a film. **rough diamond** see under **diamond**. **rough'-draft** or **-draw** vt to draft roughly. **rough'-dry** vt to dry without smoothing. ◆ adj (of linen, clothes, etc) ready for pressing. **rough'-footed** adj with feathered feet. **rough'-grained** adj coarse-grained. **rough grazing** n uncultivated ground, used for pasture. **rough-grind'** vt to grind roughly. **rough-hand'le** vt to treat roughly. **rough-hew'** vt (Shakesp) to hew or shape into a rough form. **rough-hew'er** n. **rough-hewn'** adj shaped roughly; uncouth, unrefined. **rough hound** n a small species of dogfish. **rough'-house** n (orig US; also **rough house**) a disturbance; a brawl. ◆ vi to brawl; to make a disturbance. ◆ vt to handle roughly, maltreat. **rough justice** n approximate justice, hastily assessed and carried out; a verdict or sentence that is appropriate, though formed without careful attention to the forms and processes of a legal code. **rough'-legged** adj with feathered or hairy legs. **rough'neck** n (inf; orig N Am) an unmannerly lout; a hooligan or tough; a member of an oil rig crew employed to deal with equipment on the rig floor. ◆ vi to work as a roughneck on an oil rig. **rough'-out** n a leather or a leather article, having the reverse side from the grain outermost. **rough passage** n a stormy sea voyage; a difficult, trying time. **rough'-per'fect** adj nearly perfect in the memorizing of a part. **rough puff-pastry** n quick puff-pastry made without allowing the pastry to rest between the repeated rolling out and folding. **rough'rider** n a rider of untrained horses; a horse-breaker; an army riding master's assistant; an irregular cavalryman. **rough'shod** adj provided with horse-shoes with projecting nails to afford extra grip. **rough shooting** n shooting over moorland (mainly grouse). **rough'-spoken** adj rough in speech. **rough string** n an intermediate support for the steps of a wooden stairway. **rough stuff** n coarse paint laid on after the priming, and before the finish; violent behaviour. **rough trade** n (sl) violent or sadistic male prostitute(s) or casual sexual partner(s), esp homosexual. **rough'-wrought** adj shaped out or done roughly, or in a preliminary way.

■ **a bit of rough** (inf) a person, esp a man, whose unrefined manner is seen as sexually attractive. **cut up rough** see under **cut**. **ride roughshod over** to treat arrogantly, domineer over without consideration. **rough in** to sketch in roughly. **rough it** to live in rough or basic conditions (to which one is unaccustomed); to take whatever hardships come. **rough on** hard luck for; pressing hard upon. **rough out** to shape out roughly. **sleep rough** to sleep out-of-doors, esp because of being homeless.

rought /rōt/ an obsolete pat of **reck**.

rouille /roo-ē'y'/ n a Provençal sauce made from pounded red chillis, garlic and breadcrumbs blended with olive oil or stock, served esp with bouillabaisse. [Fr, rust]

roul and **roule** obsolete forms of **roll**.

roulade /roo-läd'/ n melodic embellishment (music); a run, turn, etc sung to one syllable (music); meat, cake or soufflé mixture served rolled up, usu with a filling (cookery). [Fr]

rouleau /roo-lō'/ n (pl **rouleaus** or **rouleaux** /-lōz'/) a roll or coil, often of ribbon; a cylindrical pile or column of coins, blood corpuscles, or other discs. [Fr]

roulette /roo-let'/ n literally, a little roller or wheel; a game of chance in which a ball rolls from a rotating disc into one or other of a set of compartments answering to those on which the players place their stakes; a tool with a toothed disc for engraving rows of dots, for perforating paper, etc; a cylinder for curling hair or wigs; the locus of a point carried by a curve rolling upon a fixed curve (geom). [Fr]

roum /room/ an old spelling of **room**.

■ **roum'ing** n (see **souming and rouming** under **soum**).

Rouman and **Roumanian** see **Romanian**.

Roumansch see **Romansch**.

rounce /rowns/ n in a hand printing-press, the apparatus, or its handle, for moving the carriage. [Du ronse]

rounceval /rown'si-vl/ n a giant (obs); a large, boisterous woman (obs); a marrowfat pea. ◆ adj (obs) gigantic. [Poss Roncesvalles, in the Pyrenees]

rouncy /rown'si/ (archaic) n a riding horse; a nag. [OFr ronci]

round[1] /rownd/ adj having a curved outline or surface; approaching a circular, globular or cylindrical form; in a course returning upon itself; enveloping; with horizontal swing; plump; pronounced with lips contracted to a circle (phonetics); smooth and full-sounding; sonorous; well finished off; (of a sentence) periodic; approximate, without regarding minor denominations; (of a number) without fractions; full; not inconsiderable in amount; plain-spoken; candid; honest; unsparing; without mincing; (of pace) vigorous; (of a strong statement, etc) unqualified. ◆ adv about; on all sides; every way; in a ring; in a curve; along the circumference; in rotation; from one to another successively; indirectly; circuitously; towards the opposite quarter; roundly (*Shakesp*); in the neighbourhood. ♦ *prep* about; around; on every side of; all over; to every side of in succession; past, beyond. ♦ *n* a round thing or part; a ring, circumference, circle or globe, *esp* the earth or the sky; a ladder rung or similar rounded connecting part; a whole slice of bread or toast; a sandwich made with two complete slices of bread; a cut of beef across the thigh bone; a brewer's vessel for beer during fermentation; a projecting corner turret (not necessarily round in shape); a carving in the round; a coil; a bend; a circuit; a course returning upon itself; a dance in a ring, or its tune; a canon sung in unison; a sequence in which each bell in a set or peal is rung once; a cycle or recurring series of events or doings; a complete revolution or rotation; an accustomed walk; a prescribed circuit; a patrol; a series of calls made by a doctor, postman, etc; a complete series of holes in golf; scope; routine; a volley, eg of firearms or applause; ammunition of one shot; a fixed number of arrows shot from a prescribed distance (*archery*); a successive or simultaneous action of each member of a company or player in a game; a portion dealt around to each; a set of drinks bought at one time for all the members of a group; a subdivision of a bout, as in boxing; a defined stage in a competition; roundness; the condition of being visible from all sides, not merely in relief (*sculpt*). ♦ *vt* to make round; to surround; to go round; to turn round; to finish off; to give finish to; to pronounce (a sound) with rounded lips. ♦ *vi* to become round; to go round; to go the rounds. [OFr *rund* (Fr *rond*), from L *rotundus*, from *rota* a wheel.] ■ **round'ed** *adj* made round or curved; (of a sound) round; finished, complete, developed to perfection. **round'edness** *n*. **round'er** *n* a person or thing that rounds; a thing that is round (see also **roundure**); a person who goes the round of anything; a complete circuit in rounders. **round'ers** *n sing* a bat-and-ball game in which players run from station to station. **round'ing** *n* (*comput*) the process of raising (*up*) or lowering (*down*) a number to an approximation which has fewer decimal places. **round'ish** *adj*. **round'ly** *adv* in a round way; so as to be round; frankly, bluntly. **round'ness** *n*. □ **round'about** *adj* circuitous; indirect; cut evenly, without tails or train; plump. ♦ *n* a circular revolving platform with handles, seats, etc at playgrounds, etc; a merry-go-round; a place where traffic circulates in one direction; a devious way; a round earthwork; a round dance; a short jacket (*US*). ♦ *vi* to go round and round. **roundabouta'tion** or **roundaboutil'ity** *n* (*facetious*). **roundabout'edly** or **round'aboutly** *adv*. **round'aboutness** *n*. **round angle** same as **perigon**. **round'arch** or **round'arched** *adj* having semicircular arches. **round'-arm** *adj* and *adv* with nearly horizontal swing of the arm. ♦ *n* a throw made in this way. **round'-backed** *adj*. **round dance** *n* a dance in a ring; a dance in which couples revolve about each other. **round'-down** *n* an instance of rounding down (see **rounding** above). **round'-eared** *adj*. **round'-eyed** *adj*. **round'-faced** *adj*. **round fish** *n* any fish other than a flat fish; the carp; an American whitefish. **round game** *n* a game, *esp* a card game, in which each plays for his or her own hand. **round'hand** *n* a style of penmanship in which the letters are well-rounded and free. **Round'head** *n* a supporter of Parliament during the English Civil War, a Puritan (from the close-cut hair). **round'-headed** *adj* puritanical; having a round head, top or end; brachycephalic. **round'house** *n* a lock-up (*obs*); a cabin on the after part of the quarterdeck (*hist*); an engine-house with a turntable (*N Am*); (a boxing style using) a wild swinging punch (*orig US*); a circular domestic building dating from the Bronze or Iron Age (*archaeol*). **roundhouse kick** *n* (in martial arts) a kick delivered with a semicircular turn of the body. **rounding error** *n* (*comput*) an error in a computation caused by repeated rounding. **round'-leaved** *adj*. **round mouth** *n* a cyclostome. **round'-mouthed** *adj*. **round'-nosed** *adj* having a rounded nose or tip. **round robin** or **Robin** *n* a paper with signatures in a circle, so that no one may seem to be a ringleader; any letter, petition, etc signed by many people; a circular letter sent to friends and family, *esp* with a Christmas card; (in sports) a tournament in which each player plays every other player (also called **American tournament**). **round'-shouldered** *adj* with shoulders bending forward from the back. **rounds'man** *n* a person who goes round *esp* one sent by a shopkeeper to take orders and deliver goods; a policeman who acts as a supervisor (*US*); a reporter covering a specified area (*Aust* and *NZ*). **round table** *n* a meeting or conference at which the participants meet on equal terms; (with *caps*) an organization for men aged from 18 to 45, with social and charitable aims. **round'-table** *adj* meeting on equal terms, like the inner circle of King Arthur's knights, who sat at a round table. **round-the-clock'** *adj* lasting through the day and night, twenty-four-hour (also *adv*, without *hyphens*). **round top** *n* a mast-head platform. **round tower** *n* a tall tapering tower of circular section, of early Christian origin, common in Ireland. **round trip** *n* a trip to a place and back again; an instance of roundtripping (*inf*). **round-trip** *adj* (*esp N Am*) return. **roundtripp'ing** *n* (*inf*) the financial practice of a company re-lending money at a rate higher than that at which they themselves have

borrowed it. **round'-up** *n* a driving together or assembling, as of all the cattle on a ranch, a set of people wanted by the police, a collection of facts or information, etc; an instance of rounding up (see **rounding** above). **round window** *n* (in vertebrates) the lower of the two membrane-covered openings between the middle ear and the inner ear. **round'-winged** *adj*. **round'wood** *n* small pieces of timber taken from near the tops of trees and used for furniture. **round'worm** *n* a threadworm or nematode, a member of the *Nematoda*, unsegmented animals with long rounded bodies, mostly parasitic.

■ **bring round** see under **bring**. **come round** see under **come**. **get round to** to have the time or inclination to do (something) after delay. **go** or **make the rounds** to go or be passed from place to place or person to person; to circulate; to patrol. **in round numbers** or **figures** to the nearest convenient large number, ie ten, a hundred, a thousand, etc; roughly, approximately. **in the round** capable of being viewed from all sides, not merely in relief; taking everything into consideration; with all features, etc fully displayed. **round about** an emphatic form of round; the other way about; approximately. **round down** to lower (a number) to the nearest convenient figure, *usu* ten, a hundred, etc. **round off** to finish off neatly. **round on** to turn on, attack verbally. **round out** to fill out to roundness. **round the bend** see under **bend¹**. **round the clock** see **round-the-clock** above. **round the twist** see under **twist**. **round to** to turn the head of a ship to the wind. **round up** to ride round and collect; to gather in (wanted persons, facts, etc); to raise (a number) to the nearest convenient figure, *usu* ten, a hundred, etc.

round² /rownd/ (*archaic*) *vt* to whisper (*to*). ♦ *vi* to whisper. [OE *rūnian* to whisper; cf **rune**]

roundel /rown'dl/ *n* anything circular; a circle; a disc; a ladder rung; a ring-dance, a rondel; a round turret; a circular device (*heraldry*). [OFr *rondel*, *-le*, *rondelet*, dimins of *rond* round]
■ **roun'delay** *n* a song with a refrain; a dance in a ring. **roun'dle** *n* a roundel. **round'let** /-lit/ *n* a little circle or disc. **rown'dell** *n* (*Spenser*) a bubble.

roundure /rown'dyər/ *n* (also (*Shakesp*) **round'er** or **rond'ure**) roundness; a round form or space; a circle, circuit; a globe. [Fr *rondeur*, from *rond* round]

roup¹ /rowp/ (*Scot*) *n* a sale by public auction. ♦ *vt* to sell by public auction; to sell up (with *out*). [Scand]
□ **rouping'-wife** *n* (*obs*) a woman auctioneer or buyer at auctions.

roup² /roop/ *n* an infectious disease of the respiratory passages of poultry; hoarseness (*Scot*). [Perh imit]
■ **roup'it** *adj* (*Scot*). **roup'y** *adj*.

roup³ see **stoop and roup** under **stoop⁴**.

rousant see under **rouse¹**.

rouse¹ /rowz/ *vt* to stir up; to awaken; to start, as from cover or lair; to excite; to put in action; to haul in (eg a cable); to disturb (*rare*); to shake the feathers of (*orig reflexive*; *obs*); to ruffle, set up (*obs*). ♦ *vi* to awake; to be excited to action; to shake oneself (*obs*); to rise from cover (*rare*); to stand erect (of hair; *Shakesp*). ♦ *n* a shake of the feathers, body, etc (*obs*); reveille. [Origin obscure]
■ **rous'ant** *adj* (*heraldry*) rising as a bird. **rouse'about** *n* (*Aust* and *NZ*) an odd-job man on a sheep station. **rouse'ment** *n* (*US*) religious excitement. **rous'er** *n* a person or thing that rouses; anything astonishing. **rous'ing** *adj* awakening; stirring; vigorously active; great; violent. **rous'ingly** *adv*. **roust** *vt* to stir up; to rout out. ♦ *vi* to move energetically. **roust'about** *n* a wharf labourer (*N Am*); a person who does odd jobs (*N Am*); a rouseabout (*N Am* and *Aust*); a general labourer employed on an oil rig or in a circus. **roust'er** *n* a roustabout.
■ **rouse on** (*Aust*) to reprove.

rouse² /rowz/ (*archaic*) *n* a carousal; a bumper. [Prob from **carouse**; poss Scand *rus* drunkenness]

roussette /roo-set'/ *n* a fruit bat; a dogfish. [Fr]

roust, roustabout and **rouster** see under **rouse¹**.

rout¹ /rowt/ *n* a defeated body; an utter defeat; disorderly retreat; a tumultuous crowd; a rabble; a pack, herd, or flock; a large party or reception (*archaic*); a fashionable evening gathering (*archaic*); a gathering of three or more people for the purpose of committing an unlawful act (*law*); disturbance; brawl; riot; clamour; a fuss. ♦ *vi* to behave riotously. ♦ *vt* to defeat utterly; to cause to retreat in disorderly confusion. [OFr *route*, from the pap of L *rumpere*, *ruptum* to break]
■ **rout'ing** *n* (*archaic*) going to receptions. **rout'ous** *adj* (*archaic*). **rout'ously** *adv* (*archaic*).
□ **rout'-cake** *n* (*archaic*) a rich sweet cake formerly served at receptions. **rout'-seat** *n* (*archaic*) a bench hired out for large social gatherings.

rout² /rowt/ *vt* (of a pig) to grub up; to hollow or scoop out (often with *out*); to turn up; to turn out, fetch out; to rummage out; to bring to light. ♦ *vi* to grub; to poke about. [An irreg variant of **root³**]

■ **rout'er** *n* a person or thing that routs; a tool of various styles for hollowing out, grooving, etc.

rout³ /rowt/ *vi* (now *Scot* and *dialect*) to snore. [OE *hrūtan*]

rout⁴ /rowt/ (*Scot* and *N Eng*) *vi* and *vt* to roar, bellow. [ON *rauta*]

route /root/ or (*US* and *milit*) /rowt/ *n* a way or course that is or may be travelled; marching orders; any regular journey; a regular series of calls, a round (*N Am*). ◆ *vt* (**route'ing** or (*esp N Am*) **rout'ing**; **rout'ed**) to fix the route of; to send by a particular route. [Fr, from L *rupta* (*via*) broken (way); see **rout**¹]

■ **rout'er** *n* (*comput*) a device on a network used for communication between two networks which can operate on different protocols. ❑ **route'man** *n* (*N Am*) a shopkeeper's roundsman. **route march** *n* a long march of troops in training. **route one** *n* (*football*) the strategy of playing long high passes towards a tall central striker. **route-proving flight** *n* a flight of aeroplanes sent out to test the possibilities and advantages of variants of a new service. **route'-step** *n* an order of march in which soldiers are not required to keep step.

routh or **rowth** /rowth/ (*Scot*) *n* abundance. ◆ *adj* plentiful. [Origin obscure]

■ **routh'ie** *adj*.

routine /roo-tēn'/ *n* regular, unvarying or mechanical course of action or round; the set series of movements gone through in a dancing, skating or other performance; a comedian's or singer's, etc act (*inf*); a part of a program performing a specific and separate function (*comput*). ◆ *adj* unvarying; standard, ordinary; keeping an unvarying round; forming part of a routine. [Fr, dimin of *route*]

■ **routineer'** *n* a person who follows a routine. **routine'ly** *adv*. **routi'nism** *n*. **routi'nist** *n* and *adj* (a person) advocating or fond of routine. **routinizā'tion** or **-s-** *n*. **routinize'** or **-ise'** *vt* to render mechanical or uniform; to remove interest from.

routous see under **rout**¹.

roux /roo/ (*cookery*) *n* (pl **roux** /roo or rooz/) a thickening made of equal quantities of butter and flour cooked together. [Fr (*beurre*) *roux* brown (butter)]

ROV *abbrev* : remotely-operated vehicle.

rove¹ /rōv/ *vt* to wander over or through; to discharge (an arrow, etc) at random (*obs*). ◆ *vi* to wander about; to ramble; to change about inconstantly; to troll with live bait; to practise piracy (*obs*); to aim or shoot arrows, etc at random (with *at* ; *obs*). ◆ *n* wandering; a mode of incomplete ploughing (*dialect*). [Partly at least from Du *rooven* to rob, *roofer* robber, from *roof* plunder; perh partly from a Midland form of obs *N Eng* *rave* to wander]

■ **rō'ver** *n* a pirate (*archaic*); a robber (*obs*); a random or distant mark (*archery*); an arrow for shooting at rovers (*obs*); a wanderer; an inconstant person; a croquet ball or player ready to peg out; a player with no fixed position who forms part of the rucks (*Aust rules*); formerly a member of a senior branch of the (Boy) Scout organization (also **rover scout**); a remotely-controlled vehicle for exploring the surface of the moon, etc. **rō'ving** *adj* wandering; not confined to a particular place, eg *roving ambassador*, *roving commission*, etc. **rō'vingly** *adv*. ❑ **rove'-over** *adj* (of a kind of verse in sprung rhythm) having an extra syllable at the end of one line, which forms a foot with the beginning of the next line. **rover ticket** *n* a ticket permitting unlimited travel during a specified period.

■ **at rovers** (*archaic*) at a distant mark; at random; conjecturally. **have a roving eye** to tend to show a fleeting sexual interest in successive members of the opposite sex.

rove² /rōv/ *vt* to twist (cotton, wool, etc) slightly in preparation for spinning. ◆ *n* a roved sliver. [Origin obscure]

■ **rō'ver** *n* a machine for roving; a person who operates it. **rō'ving** *n* the process of giving the first twist to yarn; rove.

rove³ /rōv/ *n* a metal plate or ring through which a rivet is put and clenched over. [ON *ró*]

rove⁴ /rōv/ *pat* and *pap* of **reeve**².

rove beetle /rōv bē'tl/ *n* the devil's coach-horse, or other beetle of the family Staphylinidae. [Cf Du *roof-kever*, literally, reif chafer, from *roof* robbery]

row¹ /rō/ *n* a line or rank of people or things, eg seats, houses, turnips, etc; a series in line, or in ordered succession; a complete line of stitches (*knitting*); often in street-names, of a single or double line of houses. ◆ *vt* (*rare*) to set in or with a row or rows. [OE *rāw* ; Ger *Reihe*, Du *rij*]

❑ **row house** *n* (*N Am*) a terraced house.

■ **a hard row to hoe** a destiny fraught with hardship. **death row** see under **death**. **in a row** in unbroken sequence. **twelve-tone row** or **twelve-note row** see under **twelve**.

row² /rō/ *vt* to propel through water by making strokes with an oar or oars; to transport by rowing; to direct in a particular course of action, etc (*fig*); to achieve, render, perform or effect by use of oars; to take

part in or race against in competitive rowing; to use (an oar) or make (a stroke) in rowing. ◆ *vi* to work with the oar; to be moved by oars; to race in rowing boats for sport. ◆ *n* an act or spell of rowing; a journey in a rowing boat; a distance rowed. [OE *rōwan*]

■ **row'able** *adj* capable of being rowed or rowed on. **row'er** *n*. **row'ing** *n*.

❑ **row barge** *n* (*hist*) a barge worked by oars. **row'boat** *n* (*N Am*). **rowing boat** *n*. **rowing machine** *n* an exercise machine with movable seat and arms to simulate the action of rowing. **row port** *n* (*naut*) a small square hole for an oar in a vessel's side.

■ **row over** to win a (heat in a) rowing race by rowing the course unopposed.

row³ /row/ *n* a noisy squabble; a brawl; a din, hubbug; a scolding or rebuking. ◆ *vi* to make a disturbance; to quarrel. ◆ *vt* to rag, assail (*archaic*); to scold. [A late 18c word, poss a back-formation from **rouse**²]

row⁴ /row/ *n* and *v* a Scots form of **roll**.

row⁵ /row/ an obsolete or dialect form of **rough**.

rowan¹ /row'ən, also rō'ən/ *n* the mountain-ash (*Sorbus*, or *Pyrus*, *aucuparia*), a tree of the rose family with pinnate leaves; its small, red berry-like fruit. [Cf Norw *raun*, Swed *rönn*]

❑ **row'an-berry** *n*. **rowan tree** *n*.

rowan² see **rowen**.

row-dow /row'dow'/ or **row-dow-dow** /row'dow'dow'/ *n* the sound of a drum. [Echoic]

■ **rowdedow'** or **rowdydow'** *n* hubbub. **row'dy-dow'dy** *adj* uproarious.

rowdy¹ /row'di/ *n* orig a lawless American backwoodsman; a noisy, turbulent person. ◆ *adj* orig of the nature of or belonging to a rowdy, lawless; noisy and disorderly, or having a tendency to behave so. [Origin unknown]

■ **row'dily** *adv*. **row'diness** *n*. **row'dyish** *adj*. **row'dyism** *n*.

rowdy² /row'di/ (*obs sl*) *n* money.

rowdydow and **rowdy-dowdy** see under **row-dow**.

rowel /row'əl/ *n* a small, spiked wheel on a spur; the rowel-head; a knob, ring or disc on a horse's bit; a disc used as a seton for animals. ◆ *vt* (**row'elling**; **row'elled**) to prick (a horse) with the rowel; to treat (an animal) with a rowel. [Fr *rouelle*, from LL *rotella*, dimin of L *rota* a wheel]

❑ **row'el-head** *n* the axis of a rowel. **row'el-spur** *n* a spur with a rowel.

rowen /row'ən/ *n* a second mowing of grass in the same season, an aftermath (also **row'an**, **row'ing**, **raw'ing** or **rawn** /rön/). [From a Northern form of OFr *regain*]

rowlock /rol'ək, rul'ək or rō'lək/ *n* a contrivance serving as fulcrum for an oar (also **roll'ock** or **rull'ock**). [Prob for **oarlock**, from OE *ārloc*]

rowme /rowm/ (*Spenser*) *n* a room; place, station. [**room**]

rownd an obsolete spelling of **round**¹,².

rowndell see under **roundel**.

rowt same as **rout**².

rowth see **routh**.

Roxburghe /roks'bə-rə/ *n* a style of binding for books, with cloth or paper sides, plain leather back, gilt top, other edges untrimmed. [Duke of *Roxburghe* (1740–1804), book-collector]

Roy /roi/ (*obs Aust sl*; *derog*) *n* a fashion-conscious, young, Australian male. [From male given name *Roy*]

royal /roi'əl/ *adj* of, relating to or befitting a king or queen; kingly or queenly; being a king or queen; of a reigning family; founded, chartered or patronized by a king or queen; magnificent; of exceptional size or quality; of writing paper, 19 × 24in, of printing-paper, 20 × 25in (**royal octavo** a book size 6¼ × 10in). ◆ *n* a royal person (often in *pl* with *the* ; *inf*); a gold coin of various kinds; a sail immediately above the top gallant sail; the third (*orig* the second) tine of a stag; a stag with twelve or more points. [Fr, from L *rēgālis* regal]

■ **roy'alet** *n* (*derog*, now *rare*) a petty king or other ruler. **roy'alism** *n* support of the institution of monarchy. **roy'alist** *n* (also with *cap*) an adherent of royalism, a monarchist; a cavalier during the English civil war; (in American history) a supporter of the British government during the American Revolution; (in French history) a supporter of the Bourbons. ◆ *adj* of or relating to the royalists. **roy'alize** or **-ise** *vt* (*Shakesp*) to make royal or (*Milton*) royalist; to give royal character, sanction or status to. ◆ *vi* to play the king. **roy'ally** *adv*. **roy'alty** *n* sovereignty; the state or office of a king or queen; royal or majestic character or quality; the person of the sovereign, majesty (*Shakesp*); the members of a royal family collectively or (*inf*) any such member; a queen bee, queen termite, etc; sovereign rule, monarchy; royal authority; a right or prerogative granted by a king or queen, *esp* a right over minerals; a payment made by oil companies, etc to the owners of the mineral rights in the area in which they operate; payment to an author, composer, etc for every copy sold or every public performance of a particular work; the area of a royal domain, a realm; a royal burgh (*Scot*).

❏ **Royal Academy** *n* an academy of fine arts in London, founded in 1768, to which members and associates are elected (in very limited number); a teaching, degree-giving academy of music in London. **royal assent** see under **assent. royal blue** *n* a bright, deep-coloured blue. **Royal British Legion** see under **legion. royal burgh** see under **burgh. royal commission** *n* (also with *caps*) a body of people nominated by the Crown to inquire into and report on a particular matter. **royal duke** *n* a duke who is also a royal prince. **royal fern** *n* (*Osmunda regalis*) the most striking of British ferns, with large fronds. **royal fish** *n* a 'fish' that is the monarch's perquisite when cast ashore or caught near the land (whale, sturgeon, porpoise). **royal flush** see under **flush**[3]. **royal icing** *n* a kind of hard icing made with egg white, used *esp* on rich fruitcakes. **royal jelly** *n* a secretion produced by worker bees, the food of young larvae and of a developing queen bee. **royal marriage** *n* (*bezique*) king and queen of trumps. **royal mast** *n* (*naut*) the fourth and highest part of the mast, *usu* made in one piece with the top-gallant mast. **royal palm** *n* a palm (*Oreodoxa regalis*) of the cabbage palm genus. **Royal Peculiar** *n* an ecclesiastical peculiar whose superior is the sovereign. **royal prerogative** see under **prerogative. royal purple** *n* a deep rich purple colour. **royal road** *n* a short and easy way of circumventing difficulties. **royal standard** *n* a banner bearing the British royal arms, flown wherever the monarch is present. **royal tennis** *n* the earlier form of the game of tennis, distinguished from lawn tennis, and played in a walled court (also called **real** or **court tennis**). **royal warrant** *n* an official authorization to supply goods to a royal household. **Royal We** *n* (also without *caps*) a monarch's use of the first person plural when speaking of himself or herself.

■ **the Royals** formerly the first regiment of foot in the British Army (the Royal Scots); (without *cap*) see *n* above.

royne[1] /*roin*/ (*Spenser*) *vi* to mutter, growl, roar. [Prob connected with **groin**[3]]

royne[2] see **roon**.

roynish /*roi'nish*/ (*Shakesp*) *adj* scurvy, mangy; mean. [OFr *roigne* mange]

royster, etc same as **roister**, etc.

rozelle same as **roselle**.

rozet and **rozit** see **roset**.

Rozinante see **Rosinante**.

rozzer /*roz'ər*/ (*sl*) *n* a policeman. [Origin obscure]

RP *abbrev*: Received Pronunciation; Reformed Presbyterian; Regius Professor; Republic of the Philippines (IVR); retinitis pigmentosa; Royal Society of Portrait Painters.

RPB *abbrev*: recognized professional body.

RPC *abbrev*: Rail Passengers Council.

RPG *abbrev*: report program generator, a computer programming language used in business; rocket-propelled grenade; role-playing game.

RPI *abbrev*: retail price index.

RPM *abbrev*: retail or resale price maintenance.

rpm *abbrev*: revolutions per minute.

RPN *abbrev*: reverse Polish notation.

RPO *abbrev*: Royal Philharmonic Orchestra.

RPR *abbrev*: *Rassemblement pour la République* (*Fr*), a neo-Gaullist, right-wing political party in France.

RPS *abbrev*: Royal Photographic Society.

rps *abbrev*: revolutions per second.

RPSGB *abbrev*: Royal Pharmaceutical Society of Great Britain.

RPT *abbrev*: registered physiotherapist; registered professional turner.

rpt *abbrev*: repeat; report.

RPV (*milit*) *abbrev*: remotely-piloted vehicle, a miniature aircraft designed to identify the exact position of enemy targets.

RR *abbrev*: Right Reverend.

RRP *abbrev*: recommended retail price.

RS *abbrev*: Royal Society, a UK body of eminent scientists.

Rs *abbrev*: rupees.

RSA *abbrev*: Republic of South Africa; Returned Services Association (*NZ*); Royal Scottish Academy or Academician; Royal Society of Arts (officially the Royal Society for encouragement of Arts, Manufactures and Commerce).

RSA encryption /*är es ā in-krip'shən*/ (*comput*) *n* an encryption algorithm based on a public-key system used to secure authentication

requests between networks. [Initial letters of *Rivest, Shamir* and *Adleman* who devised it in 1977]

RSAMD *abbrev*: Royal Scottish Academy of Music and Drama.

RSC *abbrev*: Royal Shakespeare Company; Royal Society of Chemistry.

RSE *abbrev*: Royal Society of Edinburgh, a body of eminent scientists in Scotland.

RSFSR *abbrev*: Russian Federated Soviet Socialist Republic.

RSI *abbrev*: Relative Strength Index, a measure of share market activity; repetitive strain or stress injury.

RSJ *abbrev*: rolled steel joist.

RSL *abbrev*: Returned Services League (*Aust*); Royal Society of Literature.

RSM *abbrev*: Regimental Sergeant-Major; Republic of San Marino (IVR); Royal School of Music; Royal Society of Medicine.

RSNC *abbrev*: Royal Society for Nature Conservation.

RSNO *abbrev*: Royal Scottish National Orchestra.

RSNZ *abbrev*: Royal Society of New Zealand.

RSPB *abbrev*: Royal Society for the Protection of Birds.

RSPCA *abbrev*: Royal Society for the Prevention of Cruelty to Animals.

RSS (*comput*) *abbrev*: rich site summary (or, popularly, really simple syndication), a system that allows computer users to view the content of many web pages in a single screen.

RSSA *abbrev*: Royal Scottish Society of Arts.

RSSPCC *abbrev*: Royal Scottish Society for the Prevention of Cruelty to Children (now known as Children 1st).

RSTM&H *abbrev*: Royal Society of Tropical Medicine and Hygiene.

RSV *abbrev*: Revised Standard Version (of the Bible).

RSVP *abbrev*: *répondez s'il vous plaît* (*Fr*), please reply.

RT *abbrev*: radio telegraphy or telephony.

rt *abbrev*: right.

RTA *abbrev*: road traffic accident.

rtd *abbrev*: retired.

RTE *abbrev*: *Radio Telefís Éireann* (*Irish Gaelic*), Irish Radio and Television.

RTF (*comput*) *abbrev*: Rich Text Format, a standard format for text files.

Rt Hon. *abbrev*: Right Honourable.

RTPI *abbrev*: Royal Town Planning Institute.

Rt Rev. *abbrev*: Right Reverend.

RU *abbrev*: Republic of Burundi (IVR); Rugby Union.

Ru (*chem*) *symbol*: ruthenium.

ruana /*roo-ä'nə*/ *n* a woollen outer garment resembling a poncho, worn in parts of S America. [Am Sp]

rub[1] /*rub*/ *vt* (**rubb'ing; rubbed**) to apply friction to; to move something with pressure along the surface of; to move with pressure along the surface of something; to clean, polish or smooth by friction; to remove, erase or obliterate by friction (*usu* with *away, off* or *out*); to grind, sharpen, chafe or treat by friction; to cause to pass by friction (with *in, through*, etc); to impede (*Shakesp*); to irritate, fret; to take a rubbing of. ◆ *vi* to apply, or move with, friction; to meet an impediment (*esp* in *bowls*); to chafe; to grate; to fret; to make shift, to get along somehow; to be able to be rubbed. ◆ *n* process or act of rubbing; an impediment, or a meeting with an impediment (*bowls*); an inequality or uneven place; a difficulty; a hitch; an irritating experience. [Cf LGer *rubben*]

■ **rubb'ing** *n* application of friction; experience of rubs (*Shakesp*); an impression of an inscribed surface produced by rubbing heelball or plumbago upon paper laid over it.

❏ **rubbing alcohol** *n* denatured ethyl alcohol used as an antiseptic or in massage. **rubbing post** *n* one for cattle to rub against. **rubbing stone** *n* a stone for smoothing. **rub'down** *n* an act or experience of rubbing down. **rub'out** *n* an act of rubbing out; a murder (*sl*). **rub'stone** *n* a whetstone.

■ **rub along** (*inf*) to get along, to manage somehow; to be on more or less friendly terms (with). **rub down** to rub from head to foot; to remove (a surface) by rubbing in order to repaint, etc; to search by passing the hands over the body. **rub in** to force into the pores by friction; to mix (fat) into flour by rubbing together with the fingertips (*cookery*); to be unpleasantly insistent in emphasizing. **rub off on** (**to**) (*fig*) to pass to (another person or thing) by close contact, association, etc. **rub of** (or **on**) **the green** chance events over which one has no control (*orig* an outside interference with the ball in golf). **rub one's hands** to rub one's palms together, *esp* as a sign of satisfaction. **rub out** to erase; to murder (*sl*). **rub shoulders** or (*US*) **elbows** to come into social contact (with). **rub someone's nose in it** (*inf*) to remind someone insistently of a mistake, fault, misdeed, etc. **rub** (or **rub up**) **the wrong way** to irritate by tactless handling. **rub up** to polish; to freshen one's memory of.

rub² see **rubber²**.

rub³ /rub/ (pat **rubb'it** or **rubb'et**) a Scots form of **rob¹**.

rub-a-dub-dub /rub'ə-dub-dub'/ n the sound of a drum. [Echoic]

rubai /roo-bä'ē/ n (pl **rubaiyat** /roo'bä-yat/) a Persian verse form consisting of four-line stanzas; *specif* (in *pl*; with *cap*) those written in Persia by Omar Khayyam in the late 11c or early 12c, and translated by Edward Fitzgerald in 1859. [Arabic *rubā'īyāt*, pl of *rubā'īyah* quatrain]

rubato /roo-bä'tō/ (*music*) *adj*, *adv* and *n* (pl **ruba'ti** /-tē/ or **ruba'tos**) (in) modified or distorted rhythm. [Ital, pap of *rubare* to steal]

rubber¹ /rub'ər/ n a person or thing that rubs or massages; an eraser; a thing for rubbing with, such as a hard brush, a file, a whetstone, emery cloth, a coarse towel, etc; a rubbing part of a machine; a cabinetmaker's pad for polishing; a soft brick that can be cut and smoothed; an uneven place; a rub or impediment in bowls; a rebuff or irritating experience; caoutchouc, india-rubber, or a substitute; a piece of india-rubber, *esp* for erasing, or as part of a brake; (in *pl*) plimsolls or india-rubber overshoes (*orig US*); a rubberneck (*US*); a condom (chiefly *N Am*); (in *pl*) a sheep disease with heat accompanied by itchiness. ◆ *adj* of, yielding or concerned with india-rubber. ◆ *vt* to coat, cover or provide with rubber. ◆ *vi* (*US*) to rubberneck. [Ety as for **rub¹**]
■ **rubb'eriness** n. **rubb'erize** or **-ise** vt to treat or coat with rubber. **rubb'ery** *adj* resembling rubber in appearance or texture.
□ **rubber band** n a thin loop of rubber used to hold things together. **rubber bullet** n a hard rubber cylinder fired from a special type of gun, used in riot control. **rubber cement** n an adhesive made of rubber dissolved in a solvent. **rubber cheque** or (*N Am*) **check** n (*facetious*) a cheque that bounces. **rubb'er-cored** *adj* (of a golf ball) having a tightly wound band of rubber enclosed in a guttapercha cover. **rubber goods** n pl (*euphem*) condoms. **rubb'erneck** n (*orig US sl*) an over-inquisitive or gaping person; a tourist, *esp* one who sightsees from a tour coach. ◆ *vi* to behave as a rubberneck. ◆ *vt* to stare at. **rubber plant** n any of various plants from whose sap rubber is made, especially *Ficus elastica*, often grown as an ornamental pot-plant; a rubber tree. **rubber room** n (*US sl*) a room padded with foam rubber in a psychiatric hospital, etc; a tedious job with poor working conditions (**rubb'er-room** *adj*; *fig*). **rubber solution** n a solution of rubber in naphtha or carbon disulphide, for repairing pneumatic tyres. **rubber stamp** n a stamp of rubber for making inked impressions; a person unquestioningly devoted to routine or officialdom; an automatic or unthinking agreement or authorization; a person or people making such an agreement, etc. **rubb'er-stamp** vt to imprint with a rubber stamp; to approve without exercise of judgement. **rubber tree** n a tropical American tree (*Hevea brasiliensis*) grown for its latex, a source of rubber. **rubb'erwear** n rubber clothing.

rubber² /rub'ər/, also **rub** /rub/ n formerly in bowls (also **rubbers**, *sing* or *pl*), now chiefly in bridge and whist, the winning of, or play for, the best of three games (sometimes five); any spell of card-playing; used generally of a series of games in various sports, such as cricket, tennis, etc; a rub (*bowls*; see **rub¹**). [Origin obscure]

rubberize, **rubbery**, etc see under **rubber¹**.

rubbet see **rub³**.

rubbish /rub'ish/ n waste matter; litter; trash; rubble; trumpery; nonsense; a worthless or despicable person or people. ◆ *adj* of or relating to rubbish; of poor quality (*inf*). ◆ *vt* to criticize, think of or talk about as rubbish. [Origin obscure; appar connected with **rubble**]
■ **rubb'ishing** *adj*. **rubb'ishly** *adj* (*rare*). **rubb'ishy** *adj* worthless; paltry; trashy.
□ **rubbish heap** n.

rubbit see **rub³**.

rubble /rub'l/ n loose fragments of rock or ruined buildings; undressed irregular stones used in rough masonry and in filling in; masonry of such a kind. ◆ *adj* of rubble. [Origin obscure; cf **rubbish**]
■ **rubb'ly** *adj*.
□ **rubble stone** n. **rubb'lework** n coarse masonry.

rube /roob/ (*N Am sl*) n a country bumpkin; an uncouth, unsophisticated person. [*Reuben*]

rubefy /roo'bi-fī/ vt (**ru'bifying**; **ru'bified**) to redden. [L *rubefacere*, from *rubeus* red, and *facere* to make]
■ **rubefacient** /-fā'shənt/ *adj* reddening. ◆ n any external application that reddens the skin, *esp* a counter-irritant. **rubefaction** /-fak'shən/ n reddening or redness of the skin.

Rube Goldberg /roob gōld'bûrg/ or **Goldbergian** /gōld-bûr'gi-ən/ (*N Am*) *adj* same as **Heath-Robinson**. [Reuben ('Rube') L Goldberg (1883–1970), US cartoonist]

rubella /roo-bel'ə/ n German measles, an infectious disease producing a pink rash, like measles but milder except for its possible effect on the fetus of an expectant mother infected early in pregnancy. [Dimin from L *rubeus* red]
■ **rubell'an** (or /roo'/) n an altered biotite. **rubell'ite** (or /roo'/) n a red kind of mineral with varying composition, a red tourmaline.

rubeola /roo-bē'ə-lə/ n measles. [Dimin from L *rubeus* red]

rubescent /roo-bes'ənt/ (*literary*) *adj* growing red; blushing. [L *rubescere* to grow red]

Rubia /roo'bi-ə/ n the madder genus, giving its name to the **Rubiá'ceae**, a family of sympetalous dicotyledons related to the Caprifoliaceae. [L *rubia* madder, from *rubeus* reddish]
■ **rubiá'ceous** *adj*.

rubicelle /roo'bi-sel/ n an orange-coloured spinel. [Fr, prob from *rubis* ruby]

Rubicon /roo'bi-kon/ or **-kən/** n a stream of Central Italy (*perh* the Fiumicino), separating Caesar's province of Gallia Cisalpina from Italia proper, its crossing by Caesar (49BC) being thus a virtual declaration of war against the republic; hence, a point of no return; (without *cap*) in piquet, the winning of a game before one's opponent scores 100. ◆ *vt* (without *cap*) to defeat in this way. [L *Rubicō, -ōnis*]
■ **cross the Rubicon** (*fig*) to take a decisive, irrevocable step.

rubicund /roo'bi-kund* or *-kənd/ *adj* ruddy. [L *rubicundus*, from *rubēre* to be red]
■ **rubicund'ity** n.

rubidium /roo-bid'i-əm/ n a soft silvery-white metallic element (symbol **Rb**; atomic no 37). [L *rubidus* red (so called from two red lines in its spectrum)]
□ **rubid'ium-stron'tium dating** n a method of determining the age of rocks that are more than 10 million years old by measuring the relative amounts of rubidium-87 and its beta decay product strontium-87.

rubify (now *rare*) same as **rubefy**.

rubiginous /roo-bij'i-nəs/ or **rubiginose** /-nōs/ *adj* rust-coloured; rusty. [L *rūbīgō* or *rōbīgō, -inis* rust]

Rubik's Cube® /roo'biks kūb/ n a cube-shaped puzzle composed of 26 small pieces (cubes or partial cubes) with faces coloured in any of six colours, fixed to a central spindle that allows them to be rotated on three axes, the solved puzzle presenting a uniform colour on each face. [Developed by Ernö Rubik, Hungarian designer, in 1974]

rubin, **rubious**, etc see under **ruby**.

ruble see **rouble**.

rubric /roo'brik/ n a heading, guiding rule, entry or liturgical direction, *orig* one in red ink; a flourish after a signature; a thing definitely settled; red ochre (*obs*). ◆ *adj* in red; ruddy; inscribed with book titles (*obs*). [L *rubrīca* red ochre, from *ruber* red]
■ **ru'brical** *adj*. **ru'brically** *adv*. **ru'bricate** vt to mark with red; to write or print in red; to make a red-letter saint; to provide with rubrics; to regulate by rubric. **rubricā'tion** n. **ru'bricātor** n. **rubrician** /roo-brish'ən/ n a person who follows, or is versed in, liturgical rubrics.

Rubus /roo'bəs/ n the raspberry and bramble genus of the rose family. [L *rubus* a bramble-bush]

ruby /roo'bi/ n a precious stone, a pure transparent red corundum; extended to other stones, such as varieties of spinel and garnet; the colour of a ruby, a deep crimson; (in *pl*) the lips (*poetic*); blood (*boxing sl*); a deep-red wine or port; ruby glass (see below); a type smaller than nonpareil and larger than pearl (5½ points; *printing*). ◆ *adj* red as a ruby. ◆ *vt* (**ru'bying**; **ru'bied**) to redden. [OFr *rubi* and *rubin*, from L *rubeus*, from *ruber* red]
■ **ru'bied** *adj* red as a ruby. **ru'bin** or **ru'bine** /-bin/ n (*Spenser*) a ruby. **rubin'eous** *adj*. **ru'bious** *adj* ruby, red, ruddy.
□ **ru'by-coloured** *adj*. **ruby glass** n glass coloured a deep red by the addition of mineral oxides. **ruby-red'** *adj* deep crimson. **ruby silver** n proustite; pyrargyrite. **ruby spinel** n a ruby-red spinel (also **spinel-ruby**). **ru'by-tail** n a gold-wasp, or cuckoo-fly. **ru'bythroat** n a hummingbird with a ruby gorget. **ru'bythroated** *adj*. **ruby wedding** n a fortieth wedding anniversary.

RUC *abbrev* : Royal Ulster Constabulary (now replaced by **PSNI**).

ruc same as **roc**.

RUCC *abbrev* : Rail Users' Consultative Committee (now known as **RPC**).

ruche /roosh/ n a frill of lace or other material, *esp* pleated. ◆ *vt* to trim with a ruche. [Fr; prob of Celtic origin]
■ **ruched** *adj*. **ruch'ing** n.

ruck¹ /ruk/ n a heap, stack or mass of anything, such as fuel, hay, etc; a multitude; the mass of ordinary people or things; in Rugby Union, a gathering of players around the ball when it is on the ground; the three players who do not have fixed positions but follow the ball about the field (*Aust rules*). ◆ *vt* to heap. ◆ *vi* (in Rugby Union) to form a ruck; to play as a member of the ruck (*Aust rules*). [Prob Scand]

ruck² /ruk/ *n* a wrinkle, fold or crease. ◆ *vt* and *vi* to wrinkle or crease (often with *up*). [ON *hrukka* a wrinkle]
■ **ruck'le** *n* a pucker, crease. ◆ *vt* and *vi* to pucker, crease.

ruck³ /ruk/ (*prison sl*) *n* a fight. [**ruckus**]

ruck⁴ /ruk/ *vi* to squat; to crouch down; to cower; to huddle. ◆ *vt* (*Shakesp* **rook** /rŭk/; *reflexive*) to set squatting. [Prob Scand; cf Norw dialect *ruka* to crouch]

ruckle¹ /ruk'l/ (*Scot*) *n* a rattle in the throat; a gurgle. ◆ *vi* to rattle; to gurgle. [Cf Norw dialect *rukl*]

ruckle² see under **ruck²**.

rucksack /ruk', rŭk'sak or -zak/ *n* a bag carried on the back by hikers, campers, etc. [Ger dialect *ruck* (Ger *Rücken*) back, and Ger *Sack* bag]
■ **ruck'seat** *n* a folding seat with aluminium frame, attached to a rucksack for camping.

ruckus /ruk'əs/ (*orig US*) *n* a disturbance. [Perh a combination of **ruction** and **rumpus**]

rucola /roo-kō'lə/ *n* same as **rocket²**. [Ital]

ructation /ruk-tā'shən/ (*obs*) *n* eructation. [L *ructāre* to belch]

ruction /ruk'shən/ (*inf; esp in pl*) *n* a noisy disturbance; a rumpus, row. [Poss for **insurrection**]

rud /rud/ (*archaic or dialect*) *n* redness; flush; complexion; ruddle. ◆ *vt* (pap **rudd'ed**) (*Spenser*) to redden. [OE *rudu* redness, *rēodan* to redden]

rudaceous /roo-dā'shəs/ *adj* (of conglomerate, breccia, etc) composed of coarse-grained material. [L *rudis* coarse, rough, and **-aceous**]

rudas /roo'dəs/ (*Scot*) *n* a foul-mouthed old woman; a randy, a hag. ◆ *adj* coarse. [Origin obscure]

rudbeckia /rud- or rŭd-bek'i-ə/ *n* any of the N American composite plants of the genus *Rudbeckia*, of the sunflower subfamily. [Olaf Rudbeck (1660–1740), Swedish botanist]

rudd /rud/ *n* the red-eye, a fish closely related to the roach. [Prob OE *rudu* redness]

rudder /rud'ər/ *n* a steering apparatus; a flat structure hinged to the stern of a ship or boat for steering; a vertical control surface for steering an aeroplane to right or left; anything used for steering, such as an aquatic animal's tail; something, eg a principle, that guides a person in life (*fig*). [OE *rōthor* oar; Ger *Ruder* oar]
■ **rudd'erless** *adj*.
◻ **rudd'erfish** *n* the pilot fish, or other fish that accompanies ships.

ruddle /rud'l/, also **raddle** /rad'l/ or **reddle** /red'l/ *n* red ochre. ◆ *vt* to mark with ruddle; to rouge coarsely. [Cf **rud**]
◻ **rudd'leman, radd'leman** or **redd'leman** *n* a person who digs or deals in ruddle.

ruddock /rud'ək/ *n* the redbreast (now *dialect*); a gold coin (*obs sl*); a kind of apple (*obs*). [OE *rudduc*; cf **rud**]

ruddy /rud'i/ *adj* (**rudd'ier**, **rudd'iest**) red; reddish; of the colour of healthy skin in white-skinned people; rosy, glowing, bright; bloody (*euphem*; also *adv*). ◆ *vt* (**rudd'ying**; **rudd'ied**) to make red. [OE *rudig*; cf **rud** and **red¹**]
■ **rudd'ily** *adv*. **rudd'iness** *n*.
◻ **ruddy duck** *n* a small N American duck (*Oxyura jamaicensis*), the male of which has a brownish-red neck and upper body.

rude /rood/ *adj* uncultured; unskilled; discourteously unmannerly; vulgar; harsh; crude; undeveloped; unwrought; coarse; rugged; rough; roughly or unskilfully fashioned; violent; (of health) robust. ◆ *adv* (*rare*) rudely. ◆ *n* (*sl*) a rude boy (see below). [L *rudis* rough]
■ **rude'ly** *adv*. **rude'ness** *n*. **rud'ery** (*inf*). **rudesby** /roodz'bi/ *n* (*Shakesp*) an uncivil person. **rud'ie** *n* (*sl*) a rude boy (see below). **rud'ish** *adj*.
◻ **rude boy** *n* (*orig in Jamaica*) a member of a youth movement wearing smart clothes.

ruderal /roo'də-rəl/ (*bot*) *n* and *adj* (a plant) growing in wasteland or among rubbish. [L *rūdus, -eris* rubbish]

Rüdesheimer or **Rudesheimer** /rü' or roo'dəs-hī-mər/ *n* a white Rhine wine. [*Rüdesheim*, opposite Bingen]

rudie see under **rude**.

rudiment /roo'di-mənt/ *n* (*usu in pl*) a first principle or element; anything in a rude or first state; an organ in the first discernible stage; often applied to an organ that never develops beyond an early stage (*biol*). [L *rudīmentum*, from *rudis* rough, raw]
■ **rudimental** /-ment'l/ *adj* rudimentary. **rudimen'tarily** *adv*. **rudimen'tariness** *n*. **rudimen'tary** *adj* of rudiments; elementary; crude, primitive or makeshift; in an early or arrested stage of development (*biol*).

rue¹ /roo/ *vt* (**rue'ing** or **ru'ing**; **rued**) to be sorry for; to repent of; to wish not to have been or happened; to feel compassion for; to cause to feel regret, grieve (*archaic*). ◆ *vi* to feel remorse or regret; to take pity; to change one's mind, contemplate backing out. ◆ *n* (*archaic*) repentance; regret; sorrow; pity. [OE *hrēow* (noun), *hrēowan* (verb); cf Ger *Reue*, OHGer *hriuwa* mourning]
■ **rue'ful** *adj* sorrowful; piteous; deplorable; mournful; melancholy. **rue'fully** *adv*. **rue'fulness** *n*. **rue'ing** or **ru'ing** *n* repentance.
◻ **rue'-bargain** *n* (*dialect*) a forfeit for withdrawing from a bargain.
■ **take the rue** (*Scot*) to change one's mind, *esp* about an intended marriage.

rue² /roo/ *n* a strong-smelling shrubby Mediterranean plant (*Ruta graveolens*), with pinnately divided leaves and greenish-yellow flowers, punningly (see **rue¹**) symbolic of repentance, compunction or compassion; any other member of its genus; extended with qualification to other plants (see **goat's-rue** under **goat**, **meadow-rue** under **meadow** and **wall rue** under **wall**). [Fr *rue*, from L *rūta*, from Peloponnesian Gr *rhytē*]
◻ **rue'-leaved** *adj*.

rueda /roo-ā'dä/ *n* a Cuban street dance, performed in a circle, featuring many turns and changes of partner. [Sp, wheel]

ruelle /rü-el'/ *n* the space between a bed and the wall; a bedchamber where aristocratic French women held receptions in the morning in the 17c and 18c; a morning reception; in France, a narrow lane. [Fr, dimin of *rue* street]

ruellia /roo-el'i-ə/ *n* any plant of the *Ruellia* genus of the acanthus family. [Jean *Ruel* (1479–1537), French botanist]

rufescent /roo-fes'ənt/ (*bot* and *zool*) *adj* inclining to redness. [L *rūfescens, -entis*, prp of *rūfescere* to turn reddish, from *rūfus* reddish]

ruff¹ /ruf/ *n* a frill, *usu* starched and pleated, worn round the neck, *esp* in the Elizabethan and Jacobean periods; an animal's or bird's collar of long hair or feathers; a ruffed breed of domestic pigeon. ◆ *vt* to provide with a ruff; to ruffle (*Spenser*); to strike without securing (*falconry*; *obs*). [Cf **ruffle¹**]
■ **ruffed** /ruft/ *adj* having a ruff.
◻ **ruffed grouse** *n* a N American game bird (*Bonasa umbellus*) with neck feathers that can be extended into a ruff.

ruff² /ruf/ *n* an old card game similar to whist or trumps (also called **ruff and honours**); an act of trumping. ◆ *vt* and *vi* to trump. [Perh connected with OFr *roffle*, Ital *ronfa* a card game]

ruff³ /ruf/ *n* a kind of sandpiper (*Philomachus pugnax*), the male of which has an erectile ruff during the breeding season (see also **reeve³**). [Poss **ruff¹**]

ruff⁴ or **ruffe** /ruf/ *n* the pope, a small freshwater fish of the perch family, with one dorsal fin. [Perh **rough**]
■ **ruff'in** *n* (*Spenser*) the ruff.

ruff⁵ /ruf/ *n* a low vibrating beat of a drum; applause, *esp* with the feet (*Scot*). ◆ *vt* and *vi* to beat or be beaten with a ruff; to applaud (*Scot*). [Prob imit]
■ **ruff'-a-duff'** *n* drumming. **ruff'le** *n* a ruff of drums. ◆ *vi* to ruff.

ruff⁶ /ruf/ a variant of **rough**.

ruff⁷ or **ruffe** /ruf/ (*obs*) *n* pitch or height of exaltation; elation; excitement. [Cf Swed *ruff* spirit]

ruffian /ruf'i-ən or ruf'yən/ *n* a brutal, violent person; a bully. ◆ *adj* brutal; ruffianly; violent. ◆ *vi* to behave like a ruffian. [OFr *ruffian* (Fr *rufien*); source obscure]
■ **ruff'ianish** *adj*. **ruff'ianism** *n*. **ruff'ianlike** *adj*. **ruff'ianly** *adj*.

ruffin see under **ruff⁴**.

ruffle¹ /ruf'l/ *vt* to make uneven, disturb the smoothness of; to cause (feathers) to stand up or erect; to wrinkle; to gather into a ruff or ruffle; to disorder; to agitate; to turn the leaves of hastily; to disturb the equanimity of, irritate, discompose. ◆ *vi* to wrinkle; to grow rough; to flutter; to become irritated or discomposed. ◆ *n* a frill on a garment, *esp* at the wrist or neck; a bird's ruff; a ripple or disturbance on an otherwise even surface; annoyance; a quarrel; agitation. [Cf LGer *ruffelen*]
■ **ruff'led** *adj* having a ruffle. **ruff'ler** *n* a plate attached to a sewing machine, for making ruffles. **ruff'ling** *n* and *adj*.

ruffle² /ruf'l/ (*archaic*) *vi* to struggle; to bluster; to swagger. ◆ *vt* to handle roughly or offensively; to snatch (*Shakesp*). ◆ *n* an encounter, a tumult; bustle (*Shakesp*). [Origin obscure]
■ **ruff'ler** *n* a beggar posing as a maimed soldier or sailor (*obs*); a swaggerer.

ruffle³ see under **ruff⁵**.

ruffler see under **ruffle¹,²**.

rufiyaa /roo'fi-yä/ *n* (pl **rufiyaa**) the standard monetary unit of the Maldives (100 lari).

rufous /roo'fəs/ adj and n (of) a reddish or brownish-red colour. [L *rūfus*, related to *ruber* red]

rug[1] /rug/ n a thick, heavy floor-mat; a thick covering or wrap, eg for travelling; a coarse, rough, woollen fabric (obs); a toupee (sl; orig and esp N Am). ◆ adj made of rug. [Cf Norw *rugga*, *rogga* coarse coverlet, Swed *rugg* coarse hair]
■ **rugg'ing** n.
▫ **rug gown** n a gown of rug; a watchman (obs). **rug'-head'ed** adj (Shakesp) shock-headed. **rug rat** n (N Am sl) a child, esp one not yet walking.
■ **pull the rug (out) from under** (fig) to leave (a person) without support, defence, etc by a sudden action or discovery.

rug[2] /rug/ (Scot) vt (**rugg'ing; rugged**) to pull roughly. ◆ n a tug; a haul, share. [Prob Scand]
■ **rugg'ing** n.

rug[3] /rug/ (old sl) adj secure; snug.

rugate see **rugose**.

rugby /rug'bi/ n a form of football using an oval ball which (unlike association football) permits carrying the ball (also (inf) **rugg'er**). [*Rugby* school, Warwickshire]
▫ **Rugby fives** n sing the most usual version of fives, played with a back, as well as front and side walls to the court. **Rugby League** n (also without caps) a modified form of the game of rugby, with 13 players on each side. **rugby shirt** or **jersey** n a thick cotton shirt of a style worn for rugby, usu in a strong, single colour or stripes, with white collar and placket. **Rugby Union** n (also without caps) the original form of the game of rugby, with 15 players on each side. **rugger bugger** n (sl) a young man equally devoted to sport, esp rugby, and boorish behaviour.

rugelach or **ruggelach** /roo'gə-lahh/ (Jewish cookery) n pl small, crescent-shaped pastries filled with fruit, nuts, cheese, etc. [Yiddish *rugelekh*, pl of *rugele*]

rugged /rug'id/ adj rough; uneven; uncouth; involving physical hardship; (of facial features) giving an appearance of strength or suggesting experience of (esp physical) hardships; sturdy and rough; massively irregular; robust, vigorous; stormy (now US). [Prob related to **rug**[1]]
■ **ruggedīzā'tion** or **-s-** n. **rugg'edize** or **-ise** vt to make rugged; to make so as to withstand rough handling. **rugg'edly** adv. **rugg'edness** n. **rugg'y** adj (dialect) rough; uneven.

ruggelach see **rugelach**.

rugger see **rugby**.

rugose /roo'gōs or roo-gōs'/ adj (also **ru'gate** /-gāt or -gət/ or **ru'gous**) wrinkled; covered with sunken lines. [L *rūgōsus*, from *rūga* a wrinkle]
■ **ru'gosely** (or /-gōs'/) adv. **rugosity** /-gos'i-ti/ n. **ru'gūlose** adj finely rugose.

ruin /rū'in or roo'in/ n downfall; collapse; overthrow; complete destruction; wreck; loss of fortune or means; bankruptcy; undoing; seduction or loss of chastity; a downfallen, collapsed, wrecked or irretrievably damaged state (often in pl); the cause of a person's ruin; broken-down remains, esp of a building (often in pl); devastation; inferior gin (esp as *blue ruin* and *mother's ruin*; sl). ◆ vt to reduce or bring to ruin; to spoil. ◆ vi (archaic) to fall headlong; to go to ruin. [L *ruīna*, from *ruere* to tumble down]
■ **ru'inable** adj. **ru'inate** vt to ruin, to destroy (Shakesp); to demolish (archaic); to reduce to poverty (archaic); to fling headlong (Spenser; reflexive). ◆ adj (archaic) in ruins; ruined. **ruinā'tion** n the act of ruining; the state of being ruined. **ru'ined** adj. **ru'iner** n. **ru'ining** n and adj. **ru'inous** adj fallen to ruins; decayed; bringing ruin; (of noise) of or resembling crashing (Milton). **ru'inously** adv. **ru'inousness** n.
▫ **ruin agate** or **marble** n agate or marble with irregular markings like ruins.

ruing see under **rue**[1].

rukh same as **roc**.

rule /rool/ n a straight-edged strip used as a guide in drawing straight lines or as a measuring-rod, or means of mechanical calculation; a type-high strip of metal for printing straight lines; a straight line printed or drawn on paper, etc; a dash; a straight-edge used for securing a flat surface in plaster or cement; a straight shaft of light (Milton); government; control; prevalence; that which is normal or usual; conformity to good or established usage; well-regulated condition; conduct (obs); misrule (obs); a principle; a standard; a code of regulations, such as of a religious order; a regulation, whether imposed by authority or voluntarily adopted; an order of a court; a guiding principle; a method or process of achieving a result; a regulation that must not be transgressed; a maxim or formula that it is generally best, but not compulsory, to follow; (in pl) an area around a prison in which privileged prisoners were allowed to live (hist); the privilege of living there (hist); (in pl) Australian rules football (see under **Australian**). ◆ vt to draw with a ruler; to mark with (esp parallel)

straight lines; to govern; to control; to manage; to prevail upon; to determine or declare authoritatively to be; to determine, decree. ◆ vi to exercise power (with over); to decide; to be prevalent; to stand or range in price. [OFr *reule* (Fr *règle*), from L *rēgula*, from *regere* to rule]
■ **ru'lable** adj governable; allowable (US). **rule'less** (Spenser **ru'lesse**) adj unruly, lawless; without rules. **ru'ler** n a strip or roller for ruling lines; a person who rules. ◆ vt to strike with a ruler. **ru'lership** n. **ru'ling** adj predominant; prevailing; reigning; exercising authority. ◆ n a determination by a judge, esp an oral decision; the act of making ruled lines. **ru'ly** adj orderly in behaviour.
▫ **Rule 43** n a UK prison rule allowing a prisoner who is thought to need protection from other prisoners to be held in solitary confinement; a prisoner held under this rule. **rule-of-thumb'** adj according to rule of thumb (see below).
■ **as a rule** usually. **be ruled** take advice. **rule of faith** in polemical theology, the authoritative sources of the doctrines of the faith. **rule of the road** the regulations to be observed in traffic by land, water or air (eg in Britain drivers, riders and cyclists take the left side in meeting, and the right in overtaking). **rule of three** the method of finding the fourth term of a proportion when three are given. **rule of thumb** any rough-and-ready practical method. **rule (or rules) OK** (sl; orig a gang slogan, chiefly found in graffiti) to be dominant, have the ascendancy. **rule out** to exclude as a choice or possibility. **rule the roost** see under **roast**.

rullion /rul'yən/ (Scot) n a rawhide shoe. [OE *rifeling*]

rullock see **rowlock**.

ruly see under **rule**.

rum[1] /rum/ n a spirit distilled from fermented sugar-cane juice or from molasses; intoxicating drink generally (N Am). [Perh from **rumbullion** or related form]
■ **rum'bo** n (pl **rum'bos**) rum punch. **rumm'y** adj.
▫ **rum baba** n baba au rhum (see under **baba**). **rum blossom** or **rum bud** n a pimple on the nose. **rum butter** n a mixture of butter and sugar with rum, etc. **rum punch** n punch made with rum. **rum'-runner** n (hist) a person involved in smuggling alcohol into the USA during Prohibition, esp by boat. **rum'-running** n. **rum shop** n. **rum shrub** n a liqueur of rum, sugar, lime or lemon juice, etc.

rum[2] /rum/ adj (**rumm'er; rumm'est**) good (obs sl); queer, droll, odd, strange (sl). ◆ n (archaic) a strange person. [Cant]
■ **rum'ly** adv. **rumm'ily** adv. **rumm'iness** n. **rumm'ish** adj. **rumm'y** adj. **rum'ness** n.

rumal see **romal**.

Ruman and **Rumanian** see **Romanian**.

Rumansch and **Rumonsch** see **Romansch**.

rumba or **rhumba** /rum'bə or rum'bə/ n a lively Afro-Cuban dance following a square pattern; a ballroom dance based on a modification of this; a piece of music for the dance. ◆ vi to dance the rumba. [Sp]

rumbelow /rum'bi-lō/ n a meaningless word, occurring as a refrain in old sea-songs.

rumble[1] /rum'bl/ vi to make a low heavy grumbling or rolling noise; to move with such a noise; to be involved in a gang fight (sl, esp N Am). ◆ vt to give forth, or to agitate or move, with such a sound; to inform against, betray to the police (sl). ◆ n a sound of rumbling; low-frequency noise produced in vinyl disc recording when the turntable is not dynamically balanced (acoustics); a seat for servants behind a carriage, or for extra passengers in a two-seater car (also **rumble seat**); a quarrel, disturbance, gang fight (N Am sl). [Cf Du *rommelen*, Ger *rummeln*]
■ **rum'bler** n someone or something that rumbles; a machine for peeling potatoes. **rum'bling** n and adj. **rum'blingly** adv. **rum'bly** adj.
▫ **rum'bledethump** or **rum'bledethumps** n (Scot) a dish of mashed potatoes with butter and seasoning, or mixed with cabbage or turnip. **rumble strip** or **rumble area** n one of a set of rough-textured strips or areas set into a road surface to warn drivers (by tyre noise) of a hazard ahead. **rum'ble-tum'ble** n a rumble seat; a lumbering vehicle; a tumbling motion; scrambled eggs (Anglo-Ind).

rumble[2] /rum'bl/ (sl) vt to grasp; to see through, discover the truth about. [Origin obscure]

rumblegumption see **rumgumption**.

rumbo see under **rum**[1].

rumbullion /rum-bul'yən/ (obs) n an older name for **rum**[1]. [Origin obscure]

rumbustious /rum-bust'yəs/ (inf) adj boisterous (also (archaic) **rumbus'tical**). [Prob **robust**]
■ **rumbust'iously** adv. **rumbust'iousness** n.

rume a Shakespearean spelling of **rheum**.

rumelgumption see **rumgumption**.

rumen /roo'men/ n (pl **ru'mina** or **ru'mens**) the paunch or first stomach of a ruminant. [L *rūmen, -inis* gullet]

Rumex /roo'meks/ n the dock and sorrel genus of Polygonaceae. [L *rumex*, *-icis* a kind of dart, also sorrel (from its hastate leaves)]

rumfustian /rum-fus'chən/ (*archaic*) n a hot drink, a kind of negus. [**rum**[1] and **fustian**]

rumgumption /rum-gum(p)'shən/ (*Scot*) n common sense (also **rumelgump'tion**, **rummelgump'tion**, **rumlegump'tion**, **rummlegump'tion** or **rumblegump'tion** /rum'l-/).

rumina see **rumen**.

ruminant /roo'mi-nənt/ n an animal that chews the cud. ◆ adj cud-chewing; meditative. [L *rūmināre, -ātum*, from *rūmen, -inis* the gullet] ■ **Ruminantia** /-an'shyə or -shə/ n pl the cud-chewing division of the even-toed ungulates. **ru'minantly** adv. **ru'mināte** vi to chew the cud; to regurgitate for chewing; to meditate (on or upon). ◆ vt to chew over again; to muse on. ◆ adj (*bot*) mottled as if chewed. **ru'minātingly** adv. **ruminā'tion** n. **ru'minative** adj contemplative. **ru'minatively** adv. **ru'minātor** n someone who ruminates.

rumkin[1] /rum'kin/ (*obs*) n a kind of drinking vessel.

rumkin[2] /rum'kin/ n a tailless fowl. [Appar from **rump** and **-kin**]

rumlegumption see **rumgumption**.

rummage /rum'ij/ n an unsystematic or untidy search; things at or for a rummage sale (*N Am*); a thorough search of a ship by customs officers; *orig* stowage of casks, etc in a ship's hold; (*Shakesp* **romage**) commotion, upheaval. ◆ vt to arrange, *orig* in a ship's hold (*archaic*); to ransack; to overhaul; to search; to stir. ◆ vi to make a search. [Fr *arrumage* (now *arrimage*) stowage]
■ **rumm'ager** n.
❑ **rummage sale** n (*N Am*) a sale at which buyers are allowed to rummage among the goods; any sale of odds and ends or unwanted goods.

rummelgumption or **rummlegumption** see **rumgumption**.

rummer /rum'ər/ n a large drinking-glass; the quantity contained in this. [Du *roemer*; Ger *Römer*]

rummy[1] /rum'i/ n a card game in which players try to collect sequences or sets of three or four cards of the same kind. [Origin uncertain]

rummy[2] see under **rum**[1,2].

Rumonsch see **Romansch**.

rumour or (*N Am*) **rumor** /roo'mər/ n general talk, hearsay; gossip; a current story, *esp* unverified or based on partial evidence; repute, renown (*Shakesp* and *Milton*); clamour, outcry (*archaic*). ◆ vt to circulate or make known by rumour. [OFr, from L *rūmor, -ōris* a noise]
■ **ru'morous** adj resounding (*archaic*); full of rumours; of the nature of rumours; vaguely heard. **ru'mourer** n.
❑ **rumour mill** n a place or institution that continually creates or spreads rumours.

rump /rump/ n the hind part of an animal's body, the root of the tail with parts adjoining; a cut of beef between the loin and the round; (in birds) the uropygium; the buttocks; a remnant (*usu contemptuous*). ◆ vt to turn one's back upon; to clean out of money (*Scot*). [Scand; cf Dan *rumpe*, Swed and Norw *rumpa*, ON *rumpr*, Ger *Rumpf*, Du *romp*]
■ **Rump'er** n (*Eng hist*) a member or supporter of the Rump Parliament (see below). **rum'ple** n (*Scot*) a rump. **rump'less** adj. **rump'y** n a Manx cat; a tailless chicken.
❑ **rump bone** n the coccyx. **rump'-end** n. **rump'-fed** adj (*Shakesp*) *prob* with well-nourished rump. **rump'le-bane** n (*Scot*) rump bone. **rump'-post** n the share bone or pygostyle of a bird. **rump steak** n beef steak cut from the thigh near the rump.
■ **the Rump** or **Rump Parliament** (*Eng hist*) the remnant of the Long Parliament, after Pride's expulsion (1648) of about a hundred Presbyterian royalist members.

rumple[1] /rum'pl/ n (now *rare*) a fold, crease or wrinkle. ◆ vt to crush out of shape, crease, wrinkle; to make uneven or disordered. [Du *rompel*; cf OE *hrimpan* to wrinkle]
■ **rum'pled** adj creased; dishevelled. **rum'ply** adj.

rumple[2] see under **rump**.

rumpus /rum'pəs/ n an uproar; a disturbance. [Origin unknown]
❑ **rumpus room** n (*orig N Am*) a room in which children can play freely.

rumpy see under **rump**.

rumpy-pumpy /rum-pi-pum'pi/ (*sl*) n sexual intercourse, *esp* when casual or playful (also **rump'y**).

rumti-iddity /rum-ti-id'i-ti/, **rumpti-iddity** /rump-ti-id'i-ti/ or **rum-ti-tum** /rum'ti-tum'/ interj a meaningless refrain.

run /run/, also (formerly) **ren** /ren/, (*Scot*) **rin** /rin/ vi (**runn'ing**; **ran**; **run**) to proceed by lifting one foot before replacing the other; to go swiftly, at more than a walking pace; to hasten; to proceed quickly; to take oneself somewhere; to flee (*esp* with *away* or *off*); to progress,

esp smoothly and quickly; to go about freely; to ride at a running pace; to roll; to revolve; (of a film, video or audio tape, etc) to be rolling between spools, be playing or recording; to go with a gliding motion; to slip; to go on wheels; to travel, cover a distance; to make a short journey; to swim in shoals; to ascend a river for spawning; to ply; (of notes, words, etc) to have a definite sequence; (*esp* of a machine) to proceed through a sequence of operations, to work or go; to follow a course; (of a play or film) to be staged or screened regularly over a period of time; to flow; to spread, diffuse (*esp* of a colour), to spread through a fabric when wetted; (of a pipe, tap, etc) to emit or transmit a flow; to overflow, leak; (of the nose, a sore, etc) to discharge a fluid; (of a bath) to be being filled with water from the taps; to melt; to fuse; to curdle (now *dialect*); to have a course, stretch or extent; (of a bill, etc) to amount to, total (with *to*); to range; to average; to elapse; to tend; to come to be, become, pass (*archaic*); to be current; to be valid; to recur repeatedly or remain persistently (in the mind, in the family, etc); to come undone, eg by the dropping or breaking of a stitch or thread; to compete in a race; to be a candidate (*N Am*). ◆ vt to cause to run; to chase, hunt; to drive forward; to thrust; to pierce; to drive; to pass quickly; to drive through (a red traffic light or stop signal; chiefly *N Am*); to range, run about or throughout; to hurry through; to enter, promote, put forward (eg a horse, candidate or protégé); to render, by running or otherwise; to conduct, manage; to follow; to traverse; to cause to extend, form in a line; to sew lightly and quickly; to shoot along or down; to perform, achieve or score by running, or as if by running; to flee or desert from; to incur; to risk and pass the hazard of; to smuggle; to have or keep current or running; to publish (a regular paper, magazine, etc); to publish (an article or advertisement) in a newspaper or magazine, *esp* in successive issues; to show (a film, video or TV programme); to provide pasture for (*Aust* and *NZ*); to compete with in a race; to press or put to it, in competition or difficulty; to coagulate; to fuse; to emit, discharge, flow with; to be filling (a bath) with water from the taps; to execute (a program; *comput*); to control the activities of (*esp* a spy); to take an uninterrupted succession of tricks in (a suit) (*bridge*). ◆ n an act, spell or manner of running; a journey, trip; distance, time or quantity run; a circuit of duty, such as a delivery round, etc; a continuous stretch, spell, series, or period; a shoal, migration or migrating body; a roulade (*music*); a chance, go, opportunity; a spell of being in general demand (*usu* with *on*); a rush for payment, as upon a bank; a unit of scoring in cricket; a batsman's passage from one popping crease to the other; a circuit in baseball; flow or discharge; a mark made by the spreading of dye, paint, etc; course; prevalence; the ordinary or average kind, the generality; a track; a path made by animals; a small stream (*US*); a range of feeding-ground; a tract of land used for raising stock (*Aust* and *NZ*); an enclosure for chickens, etc; freedom of access to all parts; the playing of a salmon; general direction; a ladder in knitting or knitted fabrics, *esp* stockings; the part of a ship's hull near the stern where it curves upwards and inwards; the complete execution of a program, suite of programs or routine (*comput*); (in *pl*, with *the*) diarrhoea (*inf*). ◆ adj having been poured, smuggled or coagulated; having run. [OE *rinnan*, *irnan*, *iernan* to run; causative *rennan* to curdle; see also **earn**[2]]
■ **run'let** n a runnel. **runn'able** adj (of a stag) fit for hunting; (of a machine, etc) in a fit state to drive, be operated, etc. **runn'er** n a person or thing that runs or can run; a fugitive; a racer; a messenger; an agent; a tout; a person employed to collect information; a rooting stem that runs along the ground; a rope to increase the power of a tackle; a smuggler; a Bow Street officer (*hist*); a ring, loop, etc through which anything slides or runs; the part on which a sledge, a skate or a drawer slides; the passage by which metal is poured into a mould; a strip of cloth, *usu* embroidered, as a table ornament; a revolving millstone, *esp* the upper of a pair; a slice across a carcase of beef below the breast (*Scot*); a climbing plant *Phaseolus multiflorus* of the kidney bean genus, (also called **runner bean** or **scarlet runner**); a breed of domestic duck (also called **runner duck**); any of various fish of the jack family found in tropical waters, such as *Caranx crysos*; a vessel for conveying fish, oysters, etc; a long narrow strip of carpet used for passages and staircases; a player who runs between the wickets in place of an injured teammate who is able to bat but not run (*cricket*); (*usu* in *pl*) a running shoe. **runn'ing** adj racing; habitually going at a run; current; successive; continuous; flowing; discharging; easy; cursive; itinerant; done at or with a run; hasty. ◆ n the action of the verb; the pace; the lead; the competitive state. **runn'ingly** adv. **runn'y** (**runn'ier**; **runn'iest**) adj inclined to run or liquefy; watery.
❑ **run'about** n a gadabout; a vagabond; a small light car, boat or aeroplane. **run'around** n a runabout (car); see also **give (someone) the runaround** below. **run'away** n a fugitive; a horse that bolts; a flight. ◆ adj fleeing; done by or during flight; uncontrolled; overwhelming. **run'back** n the area behind the baseline at either end of a tennis court. **run chart** n (*comput*) a diagram prepared from a systems flowchart which represents the sequence of computer operations. **run-down**[1] adj in weakened health; (of a building, etc) dilapidated. ◆ n (*usu* **run'down**) a reduction in numbers; a statement

bringing together all the main items, a summary (see also **run down** below). **run'flat** *n* and *adj* (a tyre) able to be safely driven on for a considerable distance when punctured, without sustaining further damage. **run'-in** *n* an approach; a quarrel, argument (*inf*; see also **run in** below). **run length** *n* (*comput*) the number of consecutive identical digits in binary data. **run'-length limited** *adj* (*comput*) denoting a coding strategy used in magnetic and optical recording to eliminate the error caused by long runs of consecutive identical digits, which cannot be counted accurately, by ensuring that the number of consecutive identical digits is never less than three or more than eleven. **runner-up'** *n* (*pl* **runners-up'**) a competitor (*orig* a dog) that holds out to the last heat; the competitor next after the winner; any of a number of contestants coming close behind the winner. **running back** *n* (*American football*) a back who is expected to advance the ball from the scrimmage by running with it. **running balance** *n* one computed and shown every time a transaction or an alteration to an account occurs, such as in a bank statement (also called **continuous balance**). **running banquet** or **running buffet** *n* a slight or hasty collation. **running battle** *n* a battle between pursuers and pursued; a continuing skirmish (also *fig*). **running belay** *n* (*mountaineering*) a device attached to the rockface through which a rope runs freely. **running board** *n* a footboard along the side of a motor car or (*US*) locomotive. **running commentary** *n* a commentary accompanying a text; a broadcast description of a game or other event in progress. **running costs** *n pl* the costs of materials and labour, etc required for the normal operation of a machine, office or business company. **running dog** *n* (*derog*) in political jargon, a slavish follower. **running fight** *n* a fight between pursuer and pursued. **running fire** *n* (*milit*) a rapid succession of firing. **running footman** *n* a servant who ran before or alongside a horse-rider or carriage. **running gag** *n* (*inf*) a joke that continually reappears throughout a play, programme, etc. **running gear** *n* the wheels and axles of a vehicle. **running hand** *n* a cursive handwriting script produced without lifting the pen, etc between letters of the same word. **running head** or **headline** same as **running title** below. **running knot** *n* a knot that will form a noose on pulling. **running lights** *n pl* the lights shown by vessels between sunset and sunrise; small lights at the front and rear of a car which remain on while the engine is running. **running mate** *n* a runner who makes the pace for another; a horse teamed with another, or making the pace for another; the candidate for the less important of two associated offices, *esp* the candidate for the vice-presidency considered in relation to the presidential candidate (*US politics*). **running ornament** *n* an ornament in which the design is continuous. **running repairs** *n pl* minor temporary repairs. **running rigging** *n* (*naut*) all the rigging except the shrouds, stays and lower masthead pendants. **running shoe** *n* (*usu* in *pl*) a lightweight shoe designed for running or for casual wear. **running sore** *n* one which discharges pus; a continual irritation, a long-standing problem. **running stitch** *n* a straight stitch worked in a line with stitches and spaces between of equal length, often used to gather fabric. **running time** *n* the duration, *usu* given in minutes, of a cinema film. **running title** *n* the title of a book, chapter, etc printed repeatedly in the upper margin of each or every alternate page. **running water** *n* an uninterrupted flow of water from a main or tap; water in or taken from a flowing stream. **run'-off** *n* a race held to resolve a dead heat or other uncertain result (also *fig*); rainwater which drains into rivers, rather than being absorbed into the soil; urination (*sl*). **run-of-the-mill'** *adj* constituting an ordinary fair sample, not selected; mediocre. **run-on'** *adj* in verse, carrying the sense on beyond the end of the line (see also **run on** below). **run'-out** *n* (*cricket*) a dismissal of a batsman by running him or her out. **run'-resist** *adj* (of stockings or tights) knitted with a stitch that does not ladder readily. **run'-through** *n* an instance of running through (see **run through** below). **run time** *n* the time needed for the execution of a computer program. **run-time error** *n* (*comput*) same as **execution error** (see under **execute**). **run-time system** *n* (*comput*) a complete set of software which supports a high-level language and enables programs to be executed. **run'-up** *n* an approach (*lit* and *fig*; see also **run up** below). **run'way** *n* a trail, track or passageway; a firm strip of ground for aircraft to take off from and land on; a catwalk; an enclosure for domestic animals.

■ **do a runner** (*inf*) to run away, *esp* to leave a shop, restaurant, etc quickly, without paying. **give** (**someone**) **the runaround** (*inf*) to behave repeatedly in a vague, indecisive or deceptive way towards; to reply to a question or meet a request with evasion. **in the long run** in the end or final result. **in** or **out of the running** competing with or without a fair chance of success. **make** or **take up the running** to take the lead; to set the pace. **on the run** (*inf*) pursued, *esp* by the police. **run across** to come upon by accident. **run after** to pursue. **run along** (*inf*) to leave (often as *imperative*). **run a temperature** to be feverish. **run away with** to take away; to win (a prize, etc) easily; to be over-enthusiastic about (an idea, etc). **run by** (or **past**) to mention (a plan, idea, etc) to (someone) in order to ascertain his or her opinion of it. **run down** to pursue to exhaustion or capture; to collide with and knock over or sink; to treat or speak to disparagingly; to become

unwound or exhausted. **run dry** to cease to flow; to come to an end. **run for it** (*inf*) to attempt to escape, run away from. **run hard** or **close** to press hard behind. **run high** (of rivers or feelings) to be close to overflowing. **run in** to go in; to arrest and take to a lock-up; to insert a word, etc without making a break or new paragraph (*printing*); to bring (new machinery, a car, etc) into full working condition by a period of careful operation. **run in the blood** or **family** to be a hereditary characteristic or quality. **run into** to meet, come across; to collide with; to extend into. **run into debt** to get into debt. **run it fine** to allow very little margin of time, etc. **run itself** (of a business enterprise, etc) to need little supervision or active direction. **run low** to run short. **run off** to cause to flow out; to take impressions of, to print; to repeat, recount. **run off one's feet** exhausted by overwork. **run off with** (*inf*) to take away, steal; to elope with; to win comfortably. **run on** to talk on and on; to continue in the same line, and not in a new paragraph (*printing*); to print extra copies of something, eg an advertisement for trade distribution. **run one's eyes over** to look at cursorily. **run out** to run short; to terminate, expire; to leak, let out liquid; to dismiss (a batsman running between the wickets and not yet in his ground) by breaking the wicket with the ball; dismissed thus; to force to leave (chiefly *N Am sl*). **run out of** to have no more of. **run out on** (*inf*) to abandon, desert. **run over** to overflow; to go beyond (a limit, etc); to overthrow; to go over cursorily; (of a road vehicle) to knock down (a person or animal). **run scared** (*sl*) to be frightened. **run short** to come to be short, lacking or exhausted. **run through** to pierce through with a sword, etc; to spend wastefully; to read or perform quickly or cursorily but completely. **run to** to be sufficient for. **run to earth** see under **earth**. **run together** to mingle or blend. **run to ground** see under **ground'**. **run to seed** see under **seed'**. **run up** to make or mend hastily; to build hurriedly; to string up, hang; to send the ball rolling or flying low towards the hole (*golf*); to incur increasingly. **run up against** to be faced with (a challenge, difficulty, etc). **run with** to associate habitually with; to agree to, proceed with. **take a running jump** (*sl*) an expression of impatience, contempt, etc. **take up the running** (in a race) to take over as pacesetter.

runagate /run'ə-gāt/ *n* and *adj* (a) vagabond; (a) renegade; (an) apostate; (a) fugitive. [**renegade** influenced by **run** and **agate²**]

runch /runsh/ (*Scot* and *Eng*) *n* charlock; wild radish. [Origin obscure]

runcible /run'si-bl/ *adj appar* a nonsense-word of Edward Lear's, whose phrase *runcible spoon* has been applied to a pickle-fork with broad prongs and one sharp, curved prong.

runcinate /run'si-nāt/ (*bot*) *adj* with backward-pointing lobes. [L *runcina* a plane, formerly misunderstood as a saw]

rund same as **roon**.

rundale /run'dāl/ *n* a system of holding land in single holdings made up of detached pieces; land or a share of it so held. [**run** and **dale**, N Eng form of **dole¹**]

rundle /run'dl/ *n* a round, a ladder rung; a ring, circle, disc or ball. [**roundel**]
■ **run'dled** *adj*.

rundlet /rund'lit/ or **runlet** /run'lit/ (*archaic*) *n* a liquid measure equal to *approx* 15 gallons (USA 18 gallons); a small barrel. [Fr *rondelet*]

rune /roon/ *n* any of the letters of the futhork or ancient Germanic alphabet; any of a set of tiles inscribed with such letters used for fortune-telling; a secret, a mystic symbol, sentence, spell or song; a song, stanza or canto of a Finnish poem, *esp* of the *Kalevala* (Finn *runo*, related to ON *rūn*). [OE and ON *rūn* mystery, rune; Gothic and OHGer *rūna*]
■ **runed** *adj*. **ru'nic** *adj* of, relating to, written in or inscribed with runes; ancient Scandinavian or Scot and N Eng; in the style of ancient Northumbrian and Celtic interlacing ornament.
❑ **rune'craft** *n* knowledge of runes. **rune'-singer** *n*. **rune'-stave** *n* (OE *rūnstæf*) a runic letter.

rung¹ /rung/ *n* a spoke; a crossbar or rail; a ladder round or step; a ship's floor timber; a cudgel (*Scot*). [OE *hrung*; Ger *Runge*]
■ **rung'less** *adj*.

rung² /rung/ see **ring¹,²**.

rung³ /rung/ *adj* having a ring through the nose. [**ring¹**]

runic see under **rune**.

runkle /rung'kl/ *n* a wrinkle, crease. ♦ *vt* and *vi* to wrinkle; to crease. [Prob Scand; cf **ruck²** and **ruckle²**]

runlet¹ see under **run**.

runlet² see **rundlet**.

runnable see under **run**.

runnel /run'l/ *n* a little brook; a gutter. [OE *rynel*, dimin of *ryne* a stream, from *rinnan* to run]

runner and **running** see under **run**.

runnet dialect variant of **rennet**¹.

runnion see **ronyon**.

runny see under **run**.

runrig /run'rig/ (*Scot*) *n* a form of land-tenure, the same as **rundale**. [**run** and **rig**³]

runt /runt/ *n* a small, stunted or old ox or cow; a small pig, *esp* the smallest of a litter; anything undersized; a large breed of domestic pigeon; a dead tree stump or trunk; a cabbage stem, *esp* withered; an apple core (*Scot*); a vague term of reproach, *esp* to the old or boorish. [Origin uncertain]
  ■ **runt'ed** *adj*. **runt'ish** *adj*. **runt'y** *adj*.

Runyonesque /run-yə-nesk'/ *adj* in the style of the American writer A Damon *Runyon* (1884–1946), portrayer of gangsters in their milder moments.

rupee /roo-pē'/ *n* a nickel (*orig* silver) coin and the standard monetary unit of India, Pakistan and Bhutan (100 paisas), Nepal (100 pice), and Sri Lanka, Mauritius and the Seychelles (100 cents). [Urdu *rūpiyah*, from Sans *rūpya* wrought silver]

rupestrian /roo-pes'tri-ən/ *adj* composed of rock; inscribed on rock. [L *rūpēs* rock]

rupia /roo'pi-ə/ *n* a skin ulcer covered by crusts of dried secretion and dead tissue. [Gr *rhypos* filth]

rupiah /roo'pi-ə/ *n* (*pl* **ru'piah** or **ru'piahs**) the standard monetary unit of Indonesia (100 sen). [Hindi, rupee]

rupicoline /roo-pik'ō-līn/ or **rupicolous** /roo-pik'ō-ləs/ *adj* rock-dwelling. [L *rūpēs* a rock, and *colere* to inhabit]

rupture /rup'chər/ *n* a breach, breaking or bursting; the state of being broken; breach of harmony, relations, or negotiations; a hernia, *esp* abdominal. ◆ *vt* and *vi* to break or burst. [LL *ruptūra*, from L *rumpere*, *ruptum* to break]
  □ **rup'turewort** *n* a caryophyllaceous plant (genus *Herniaria*), once thought to cure hernia.

rural /roo'r(ə)l/ *adj* of, relating to or suggesting the country or countryside. ◆ *n* (*obs*) a country-dweller. [L *rūrālis*, from *rūs*, *rūris* the country]
  ■ **ru'ralism** *n*. **ru'ralist** *n*. **rurality** /-al'i-ti/ *n*. **ruralizā'tion** or **-s-** *n*. **ru'ralize** or **-ise** *vt* to render rural. ◆ *vi* to become rural; to adopt rural habits, way of life, etc, to rusticate. **ru'rally** *adv*. **ru'ralness** *n*. **ruridecanal** /roo-ri-di-kā'nl/ (sometimes *-dek'ən-l*) *adj* of a rural dean or deanery.
  □ **rural dean** see under **dean**¹.

Ruritania /roo-ri-tā'nyə/ or *-ni-ə*/ *n* a fictitious land of historical romance (in SE Europe) created by Anthony Hope; any idealistically exciting or romantic place, situation, etc.
  ■ **Ruritān'ian** *n* and *adj*.

rurp /rûrp/ (*orig US*) *n* a very small hook-like piton used in mountaineering. [realized *u*ltimate *r*eality *p*iton]

ruru /roo'roo/ (*NZ*) *n* same as **mopoke**. [Maori]

RUS *abbrev* : Russia (IVR).

rusa¹ /roo'sə/ *n* any large Asian deer formerly of the genus *Rusa*, *esp* the sambar. [Malay *rūsa*]
  ■ **ru'sine** /-sīn/ *adj*.

rusa² or **roosa** /roo'sə/ *n* an Indian grass (**rusa grass**) from which an aromatic oil (**rusa oil**) is distilled. [Hindi *rūsā*]

rusalka /roo-sal'kə/ *n* a Russian water nymph. [Russ]

ruscus /rus'kəs/ *n* any plant of the *Ruscus* genus of European evergreen shrubs (family Liliaceae). [L *rūscum* butcher's-broom]

ruse /rooz/ *n* a trick, stratagem, artifice. [OFr *ruse*, from *ruser*, *reüser* to get out of the way, double on one's tracks; see **rush**¹]
  ■ **rusé** /rü-zā/ *adj* (*Fr*) artful, deceitful, cunning.
  □ **ruse contre ruse** /rüz kõtr' rüz/ *n* (*Fr*) cunning against cunning. **ruse de guerre** /də ger/ *n* (*Fr*) a stratagem of war.

rush¹ /rush/ *vi* to move forward with haste, impetuosity or rashness; to flow, spread, etc quickly, suddenly or forcefully; to run with the ball, or gain ground by so doing · (*American football*). ◆ *vt* to force out of place; to hasten or hustle forward, or into any action; to move, transport, drive or push in great haste; to capture, secure, surmount or pass by a rush; to provide a series of social entertainments for (a freshman) as an inducement to join a fraternity or sorority (*US*); to defraud (*inf*); to overcharge (*inf*). ◆ *n* a swift impetuous forward movement; a sudden simultaneous or general movement (eg a *gold rush*); an onset; a stampede; a move to push through a line of defenders while in possession of the ball (*rugby* and *American football*); a migratory movement or body; a run upon, or

sudden great demand for, anything; (in *pl*) an unedited print of a motion picture scene or series of scenes for immediate viewing by the film makers; the viewing of such a print; rapidly increased activity; bustling activity; a series of social entertainments provided for prospective members of a fraternity or sorority (*N Am*); a feeling of euphoria experienced after the taking of a drug, eg heroin or amphetamine (*sl*); a sound of rushing; a collective name for a group of pochards. ◆ *adj* (*inf*) done or needing to be done quickly, such as *rush job*, *rush order*, etc. [Anglo-Fr *russcher*, OFr *reusser*, *reüser*, *ruser* (Fr *ruser*); see **ruse**]
  ■ **rushee'** *n* (*US*) a prospective member of a fraternity or sorority taking part in a rush. **rush'er** *n* a person or thing that rushes; a player who specializes in rushing (*American football*).
  □ **rush hour** *n* one of the times during the day of maximum movement of people or traffic. **rush'-hour** *adj*.
  ■ **rushed off one's feet** frantically busy. **rush one's fences** to act precipitately.

rush² /rush/ *n* any plant of the grasslike marsh-growing genus *Juncus*; a stalk or round stalklike leaf of such a plant; extended to various more or less similar plants (eg *bulrush*, *clubrush*, *Dutch rush*); a rushlight, a rush wick; a type of something of no value or importance; a rush ring (*Shakesp*). ◆ *adj* of rush or rushes. ◆ *vt* to make or strew with rushes. ◆ *vi* to gather rushes. [OE *risce* ; Ger *Risch*]
  ■ **rush'en** *adj* (*archaic*) made of rushes. **rush'iness** *n*. **rush'like** *adj*. **rush'y** *adj* rushlike; full of or made of rushes.
  □ **rush bearing** *n* a traditional annual festival in rural N England marked by carrying rushes to strew the local church; the day of this festival. **rush'-bottomed** *adj* (of a chair, etc) having a seat made with rushes. **rush candle** or **rush'light** *n* a candle or night-light having a wick of rush-pith; a small, feeble light. **rush'-grown** *adj* overgrown with rushes. **rush holder** *n* a stand for a rushlight. **rush ring** *n* a ring of plaited rush, formerly sometimes used as an improvised wedding ring. **rush'y-fringed** *adj*.

rusine see under **rusa**¹.

rus in urbe /roos in ûr'bā/ (*L*) the country in the city, ie a rural atmosphere within a town or city. [Martial XII.57.21]

rusk /rusk/ *n* a small, hard, crisp cake, made by rebaking slices of enriched bread, *esp* given to young children. [Sp *rosca* a roll, twist; origin unknown]

rusma /ruz'mə/ *n* a depilatory of lime and orpiment. [Appar Turk *khirisma*, from Gr *chrīsma* ointment]

russel /rus'l/ *n* a ribbed cotton and woollen material. [Poss Flem *Rijssel* Lille]
  □ **russ'el-cord** *n* a kind of rep made of cotton and wool.

Russell Group /rus'əl groop/ *n* an association of those British universities considered to embody the highest academic standards. [Hotel *Russell*, London, original meeting place]

Russellite /rus'ə-līt/ (*offensive*) *n* and *adj* (a member) of the Jehovah's Witnesses, founded as the International Bible Students' Association by the American Pastor CT *Russell* (1852–1916).

russet /rus'it/ *n* a reddish-brown colour; a reddish-brown variety of apple (also **russet apple**); a coarse homespun cloth or dress. ◆ *adj* reddish-brown; made of russet; homespun, homely, rustic (*archaic*); of brown leather. ◆ *vt* and *vi* to make or become russet in colour. [OFr *rousset*, from L *russus* red]
  ■ **russ'eting** *n* a russet apple. **russ'ety** *adj*.

Russian /rush'ən or rush'yən/ *adj* of or relating to *Russia*, its people or their language; (loosely) of the former Soviet Union or its people. ◆ *n* a native or citizen of Russia, or (formerly) the Soviet Union; the Slavonic language of most Russians, formerly the official language of the Soviet Union.
  ■ **Russ** /rus/ *n* and *adj* (a) Russian. **Russia** /rush'ə or -yə/ *adj* Russian. ◆ *n* (without *cap*) russia leather. **Russ'ianism** *n*. **Russ'ianist** *n*. **Russianīzā'tion** or **-s-** *n*. **Russ'ianize** or **-ise** *vt* to give Russian characteristics to; to make Russian. **Russ'ianness** *n*. **Russification** /rus-i-fi-kā'shən/ *n*. **Russ'ify** *vt* to Russianize. **Russ'ky** or **Russ'ki** *n* and *adj* (*derog sl*, *esp N Am*) (a) Russian. **Russocen'tric** *adj* centred or focused on Russia, *esp* without due consideration of states allied to it, or (formerly) of other Soviet republics. **Russocen'trism** *n*. **Russocen'trist** *n* and *adj*. **Russ'ophil** or **Russ'ophile** *n* a person who shows admiration for or is enthusiastic about the culture, language, political system, etc of Russia or (formerly) the Soviet Union (also *adj*). **Russoph'ilism** *n*. **Russoph'ilist** *n*. **Russ'ophobe** *n* a person who dreads or hates the Russians, or (formerly) the Soviet Union, its citizens, political system, etc (also *adj*). **Russophō'bia** *n*. **Russophō'bic** *adj*. **Russoph'obist** *n*.
  □ **russia** (or **Russia**) **leather** *n* a fine brownish-red leather impregnated with birch tar oil, used *esp* in bookbinding. **Russian boots** *n pl* wide-topped, calf-length leather boots. **Russian doll** *n* one of a set of hollow wooden brightly painted dolls of gradually

decreasing size, designed to fit inside each other. **Russian dressing** *n* mayonnaise sharpened with chilli sauce, chopped pickles, etc. **Russian roulette** *n* an act of bravado, *specif* that of loading a revolver with one bullet, spinning the cylinder, and firing at one's own head. **Russian salad** *n* a salad of mixed vegetables, diced and served with a Russian dressing. **Russian tea** *n* tea with lemon and no milk, *usu* served in a glass. **Russian thistle** or **tumbleweed** *n* a tumbleweed (*Salsola kali teniufolia*) with narrow, prickly leaves, native to Russia. **Russian vine** *n* a Central Asian climbing plant (*Polygonum baldschuanicum*) of the knotgrass family, producing white or pink flowers. **Russo-Byzan'tine** *adj* in or relating to the Byzantine style as developed in Russia.

Russniak /*rus'ni-ak*/ *n* and *adj* (a) Ruthenian; (a) Ukrainian or Little Russian. [Ruthenian *Rusnjak*]

russula /*rus'ū-lə*/ *n* (pl **russ'ulas** or **russ'ulae** /-*lē*/) any fungus of the genus *Russula*, having a characteristic toadstool shape and often brightly coloured.

rust /*rust*/ *n* the reddish-brown coating on iron exposed to moisture; any similar coating or appearance; a plant disease characterized by a rusty appearance, caused by various fungi of the Uredineae; a fungus causing such disease, notably *Puccinia graminis*, which attacks wheat; corrosion; injurious influence or consequence, *esp* of mental inactivity or idleness; the colour of rust. ◆ *vi* to become rusty; to affect with rust; to become dull or inefficient by inaction. ◆ *vt* to make rusty; to impair by time and inactivity. [OE *rūst*; Ger *Rost*]
■ **rust'ed** *adj*. **rust'ily** *adv*. **rust'iness** *n*. **rust'ing** *n* and *adj*. **rust'less** *adj* free from rust; proof against rust. **rust'y** *adj* (**rust'ier**; **rust'iest**) covered with rust; impaired by inactivity, out of practice; dull; affected with rust-disease; rust-coloured; of a rusty black; time-worn; rough; raucous; obstinate; discoloured.
❑ **rust belt** *n* those areas of the Midwestern and NE USA in which declining heavy industries, *esp* steel production, are concentrated (also with *caps*); extended to any similar area in other industrialized countries. **rust'-belt** *adj* of or relating to such an area. **rust bucket** *n* (*inf*) a badly rusted car. **rust'-coloured** *adj*. **rust fungus** *n* see *n* above. **rust'proof** *adj*. **rust'proofing** *n*. **rust'-resistant** *adj*. **rust'y-back** *n* the scale-fern. **rust'y-coloured** *adj*. **rusty nail** *n* (*inf*) an alcoholic cocktail containing whisky and Drambuie.

rustic /*rus'tik*/ *adj* of or characteristic of the country or country people; living in or belonging to the country; like, or like that of, country people; simple and plain; awkward; uncouth; unrefined; roughly made; made of rough branches; (of masonry) with sunken or chamfered joints, sometimes with roughened face. ◆ *n* a peasant; a clown; a rough-surfaced brick or stone; rustic masonry; (in showjumping) a fence made of rough branches, etc. [L *rūsticus*, from *rūs* (dialect) the country]
■ **rus'tical** *adj* and (*rare*) *n*. **rus'tically** *adv*. **rust'icate** *vt* to send into the country; to banish for a time from town or college because of wrongdoing; to make rustic in style; to build in rustic masonry. ◆ *vi* to live or go to live in the country; to become rustic. **rust'icated** *adj*. **rustica'tion** *n*. **rust'icator** *n*. **rusticial** /-*tish'l*/ *adj* (*Walter Scott*, as a false archaism). **rust'icism** /-*sizm*/ *n* a rustic saying or custom. **rusticity** /-*tis'i-ti*/ *n* rustic manner; simplicity; rudeness. **rus'ticize** or **-ise** /-*ti-sīz*/ *vt* and *vi*.
❑ **rustic capitals** *n pl* a type of Roman script using simplified, squared capital letters. **rus'ticware** *n* a terracotta of a light brown paste, having a brown glaze. **rus'ticwork** *n* rusticated masonry; summerhouses, etc of rough branches.

rustle /*rus'l*/ *vi* to make a soft, whispering sound, like that of dry leaves; to go about with such a sound; to stir about, hustle (*N Am inf*); to steal cattle (*US*). ◆ *vt* to cause to rustle; to get by rustling (*US*). ◆ *n* a quick succession of small sounds, as that of dry leaves; a rustling; bustle (*US*). [Imit; cf Flem *ruysselen*]
■ **rus'tler** *n* a person who steals cattle or horses. **rus'tling** *n* and *adj*. **rus'tlingly** *adv*.
■ **rustle up** to arrange, gather together, *esp* at short notice.

rustre /*rus'tər*/ (*heraldry*) *n* a lozenge pierced with a circular opening. [Fr]
■ **rus'tred** *adj*.

rusty[1] see under **rust**.

rusty[2] /*rus'ti*/ (now *dialect*) *adj* variant of **reasty**, etc (see under **reast**[1]).

rut[1] /*rut*/ *n* a furrow made by wheels; a fixed, often tedious, course difficult to get out of or away from. ◆ *vt* (**rutt'ing**; **rutt'ed**) to furrow with ruts. [Origin obscure; prob not Fr *route*]
■ **rutt'y** *adj*.
■ **in a rut** following a tedious routine from which it is difficult to escape.

rut[2] /*rut*/ *n* the annual period of sexual excitement in male deer; also in other male ruminants, such as sheep, goats, etc. ◆ *vi* (**rutt'ing**; **rutt'ed**) to be in such a period of sexual excitement. ◆ *vt* (*Dryden*) to copulate with. [OFr *ruit*, *rut*, from L *rugītus*, from *rugīre* to roar]
■ **rutt'ing** *n* and *adj*. **rutt'ish** *adj* (*Shakesp*) lustful.
❑ **rut'-time** *n*.

Ruta /*roo'tə*/ *n* the rue genus of dicotyledons, giving its name to the family **Rutā'ceae** which is *usu* made to include the orange, etc. [L *rūta*; see **rue**[2]]
■ **rutā'ceous** *adj*.

rutabaga /*roo-tə-bā'gə*/ (*N Am*) *n* a swede. [Swed dialect *rotabagge*]

rutaceous see under **Ruta**.

ruth /*rooth*/ (*archaic*) *n* pity; remorse; sorrow; matter for pity; misfortune, calamity (*obs*). [ME *ruthe*, *reuth*; see **rue**[1]; ending influenced by Scand, as ON *hryggth*]
■ **ruth'ful** *adj* pitiful, sorrowful; piteous, causing pity. **ruth'fully** *adv*.

Ruthenian /*roo-thē'ni-ən*/ or (now *rare*) **Ruthene** /*roo-thēn'*/ *n* a member of a branch of the Ukrainian people inhabiting both sides of the Carpathians; the language of the Ruthenians, a dialect of Ukrainian. ◆ *adj* of or relating to the Ruthenians or their language.

ruthenium /*roo-thē'ni-əm*/ *n* a metallic element (symbol **Ru**; atomic no 44) of the platinum group, found in the Ural Mountains. [LL *Ruthenia* Russia]
■ **ruthē'nic** *adj* of or concerning ruthenium, *esp* with a high valency. **ruthē'nious** *adj* of or concerning ruthenium, *esp* with a low valency.

rutherford /*rudh'ər-fərd*/ *n* a unit of radioactive disintegration, equal to a million disintegrations a second (*abbrev* **rd**). [Baron *Rutherford* (1871–1937), New Zealand-born British physicist]
■ **rutherford'ium** *n* an artificially produced radioactive transuranic element (symbol **Rf**; atomic no 104), formerly called **unnilquadium**, **dubnium**, and by the Russians **kurchatovium**; a former name for **seaborgium**.

ruthful, etc see under **ruth**.

ruthless /*rooth'ləs*/ *adj* pitiless, brutal; severe, unsparing. [**ruth** and **-less**]
■ **ruth'lessly** *adv*. **ruth'lessness** *n*.

rutilant /*roo'ti-lənt*/ (*rare*) *adj* shining; glowing ruddily. [L *rutilāns*, *-antis*, prp of *rutilāre* to be reddish]

rutile /*roo'tīl*/ *n* a reddish-brown mineral of the tetragonal system, titanium oxide. [L *rutilus* reddish]
■ **rutilated** /*roo'til-āt-id*/ *adj* enclosing needles of rutile.

rutin /*roo'tin*/ *n* a drug used against the fragility of small blood vessels. [Formed from **Ruta**]

rutter /*rut'ər*/ (*obs*) *n* a mercenary cavalryman. [MDu *rutter*, from OFr *routier*]

rutty, etc see under **rut**[1].

RV *abbrev*: recreational vehicle; Revised Version (of the Bible).

RW *abbrev*: Right Worshipful; Right Worthy.

RWA *abbrev*: Rwanda (IVR).

Rwandan /*roo-(w)an'dən*/, also **Rwandese** /*roo-(w)an-dēz'*/ *adj* of or relating to the Republic of *Rwanda* in central Africa, or its inhabitants. ◆ *n* a native or citizen of Rwanda.

RWS *abbrev*: Royal Watercolour Society (formerly known as the Royal Society of Painters in Water Colours).

Rwy or **Ry** *abbrev*: Railway.

ry- in many words an old spelling of *ri-*.

RYA *abbrev*: Royal Yachting Association.

rya /*rē'ə*/ *n* a type of Scandinavian knotted-pile rug with a distinctive colourful pattern (also **rya rug**); the weave, pattern or style typical of a rya. [Swed, connected with Finn *ryjiy*]

ryal or **rial** /*rī'əl*/ *adj* (*obs*) royal. ◆ *n* a royal person; any of various coins, such as an old English gold coin worth about ten shillings, a Spanish real, and others (*hist*). [OFr *rial* royal]

rybat /*rib'ət*/ (*Scot*) *n* a dressed stone at the side of a door, window, etc. [Prob connected with **rebate**[2] and **rabbet**]

rybaudrye and **rybauld** see **ribald**.

rye[1] /*rī*/ *n* a grass (*Secale*, especially *Secale cereale*) related to wheat and barley; its grain, used for making bread; rye grass; rye whisky; rye bread (chiefly *N Am*). ◆ *adj* of rye. [OE *ryge*; ON *rugr*, Ger *Roggen* (also *Rocken*)]
❑ **rye'bread** *n*. **rye coffee** *n* a coffee substitute made from roasted grains of rye. **rye corn** *n* (*Aust*) rye. **rye'flour** *n*. **rye grass** *n* a pasture and fodder grass (species of *Lolium*), with flat spikelets appressed edgewise in a two-rowed spike. **rye'-roll** *n* a dark treacly cookie,

understood not to be of rye. **rye'-straw** *n* and *adj*. **rye whisky** *n* whisky distilled chiefly from rye. **rye wolf** *n* (Ger *Roggenwolf*) an evil creature of German folklore lurking in the rye-fields.

rye² /rī/ *n* a gypsy word for gentleman. [Romany *rei*, *rai* lord]

ryepeck, **rypeck** or **ripeck** /rī'pek/ (*dialect*) *n* a pole used for mooring a punt. [Origin obscure]

ryfe /rīf/ (*Spenser*) *adj* same as **rife**.

ryke /rīk/ a Scots form of **reach¹**.

rymme an old spelling of **rim¹,²**.

rynd same as **rind²**.

ryokan /rē-ō'kən/ *n* a traditional Japanese inn. [Jap]

ryot or **raiyat** /rī'ət/ *n* in the Indian subcontinent, a peasant or tenant farmer. [Hindi *raiyat*, *raiyatwārī*, from Ar *ra'īyah* a subject]
■ **ry'otwari** or **raiy'atwari** /-wä-rē/ *n* a system of land-tenure by which each peasant holds directly of the state.

rype /rü'pə/ *n* (*pl* **ry'per**) a ptarmigan. [Dan]

RYS *abbrev*: Royal Yacht Squadron.

S or **s** /es/ n the nineteenth letter in the modern English alphabet, eighteenth in the Roman, its usual sound a voiceless sibilant (ie pronounced /s/), but often voiced (ie pronounced /z/), and sometimes a voiceless postalveolar fricative (represented *usu* by *sh*), or voiced (as in *pleasure*); anything shaped like the letter S.
  ■ **collar of SS** same as **collar of esses** (see under **ess**).

S or **S.** abbrev: Sabbath; Saint; schilling; Society; soprano (*music*); South; Southern; spades (*cards*); special; square; stokes; strangeness (*phys*); sun; Sweden (IVR).

S symbol: entropy (*phys*); (as a medieval Roman numeral) 7 or 70; siemens (SI unit); sulphur (*chem*); (in the form $) dollar.

Š symbol: (medieval Roman numeral) 70000.

s or **s.** abbrev: second(s); section; shilling; singular; son(s); succeeded.

s symbol: second (SI unit).

's /z or s/ a sentence element used to form the possessive of singular nouns (eg *John's*, *the dog's*), some pronouns (eg *one's*), and plural nouns not ending in *-s* or a similar sound (eg *the children's*); often also to form the plural lower-case letters (eg *m's*), of numbers (eg *3's*) or symbols; a shortened form of **has** and **is** (eg *she's taken it*, *he's not here*); a shortened form of **us** (pronounced *s*; eg *let's go*).

SA abbrev: Salvation Army; sex appeal; *Société anonyme* (*Fr*), limited liability company; Society of Antiquaries (**SAL** of London; **SAS** of Scotland); Society of Arts; South Africa; South America; South Australia; *Sturmabteilung* (*Ger*), the Nazi terrorist militia (literally, storm section).

sa abbrev: *secundum artem* (*L*), according to art; *sine anno* (*L*), without date (literally, without year).

sa' /sä/ vt an obsolete contraction of **save**.

saag or **sag** /säg/ (*Ind cookery*) n spinach. [Hindi]

Saam, Saame, Sabme, Sabmi or **Sami** /sä'mē/ n (pl **Saame** or **Samit**) a Lapp. ◆ adj Lappish. [Lappish]

Saanen /sä'nən/ n a Swiss breed of white, short-haired goat. [*Saanen*, a town in Switzerland]

sab¹ /sab/ (*Scot*) n a form of **sob**.

sab² /sab/ (*inf*) n a saboteur. ◆ vi to act as a saboteur.
  ■ **sabb'ing** n the performance of organized acts of sabotage.

Saba /sä'bä/ n the Sheba, an ancient people of Yemen. [Gr *Saba*, from Ar *Saba'*; Heb *Shebā*]
  ■ **Sabaean** or **Sabean** /-bē'ən/ n a member of the Sheba; an adherent of Sabaism or Sabianism (*non-standard*). ◆ adj of or relating to the Sheba; of or relating to Sabaism or Sabianism (*non-standard*).

sabadilla /sab-ə-dil'ə/ n (the seeds of) a plant, *Schoenocaulon officinale*, yielding the alkaloid veratrine (also **cebadill'a** or **cevadill'a**). [Sp *cebadilla*, dimin of *cebada* barley]

Sabaean see under **Saba**.

Sabahan /sə-bä'hən/ n a citizen or inhabitant of *Sabah*, a Malaysian state (formerly North Borneo). ◆ adj of, from or relating to Sabah.

Sabaism /sä'bā-izm/ n a mystical religion involving communication with angels. [Heb *tsābā* the angelic host]

Sabal /sä'bal/ n an American genus of palms, the palmettos. [Origin unknown]

Sabaoth /sa-bā'oth/ (*Bible*) n pl armies, used only in the phrase *Lord of Sabaoth*; /sab'əth/ used erroneously for Sabbath (*Spenser*). [Heb *tsebāōth* (transliterated *sabaōth* in Gr), pl of *tsabā* an army]

sabaton /sab'ə-ton/ (*hist*) n a foot-covering, *esp* square- or round-toed, worn as part of a suit of armour; a shoe or half-boot made of cloth, etc. [Provençal *sabató*; cf **sabot**, Sp *zapata*]

sabayon see **zabaglione**.

Sabbath /sab'əth/ n (among Jews) Saturday, set apart for rest from work; (among most Christians) Sunday; sometimes also used for the Muslim day of rest, Friday; a sabbatical year of the Jews; (without *cap*)

a time of rest; (also **sabb'at**) a witches' midnight meeting. ◆ adj of or appropriate to the Sabbath. [Heb *Shabbāth*]
  ■ **Sabbata'rian** n a person who observes Saturday as Sabbath; a person who believes in or practises observance, or strict observance, of the Sabbath (Saturday or Sunday). ◆ adj (sometimes without *cap*) of or relating to Sabbatarians. **Sabbata'rianism** n. **Sabb'athless** adj. **sabbatical** /sə-bat'i-kəl/ adj relating to, or resembling, the Sabbath (also **sabbat'ic**); enjoying or bringing rest; on or relating to leave from one's work (as in *sabbatical leave*, *sabbatical visit*, etc). ◆ n a period of leave from one's work, *esp* for teachers and lecturers, also *esp* to undertake a separate or related project. **sabb'atine** adj relating to Saturday. **sabb'atism** n sabbatical rest; observance of the Sabbath. **sabb'atize** or **-ise** vt to observe as a Sabbath. ◆ vi to keep a Sabbath. □ **Sabb'ath-breaker** n. **Sabb'ath-breaking** n (also adj). **Sabb'ath-day** n (also adj). **Sabbath-day's journey** n (*hist*) 2000 cubits, or about one kilometre, which a Jew was permitted to walk on the Sabbath. **Sabbath school** n (chiefly *US*) a Sunday school. **sabbatical year** n every seventh year, in which the Israelites allowed their fields and vineyards to lie fallow; a year off, for study, travel, etc.

SABC abbrev: South African Broadcasting Corporation.

Sabean see under **Saba**.

sabella /sə-bel'ə/ n a worm of the *Sabella* genus of tube-building seaworms. [L *sabulum* sand]

Sabellian¹ /sə-bel'i-ən/ n and adj originally, Sabine; now generally used in a wide sense to include related ancient peoples and languages. [L *Sabellus*, poetic dimin of *Sabīnus*]

Sabellian² /sə-bel'i-ən/ n a follower of *Sabellius*, a Libyan priest of the 3c (also adj).
  ■ **Sabell'ianism** n the teaching of Sabellius, that Father, Son, and Holy Ghost are one and the same God in different aspects.

saber N American spelling of **sabre**.

sabermetrics /sä'bər-met-riks/ (*inf*) n sing the application of statistical methods to the analysis of baseball. [Acronym of *Society of American Baseball Research* and **metrics** (see under **metric¹**)]

sabha /sab'hä/ or **subha** /sŭb'hä/ n a set of beads used by Muslims during prayer. [Ar]

Sabian /sā'bi-ən/, **Tsabian** /tsä'-/ or **Zabian** /zä'-/ n and adj (an adherent) of a religion or a group of religions (*esp* a semi-Christian sect of Babylonia) mentioned in the Koran as entitled to toleration, *prob* related to the Mandaeans; (a) Mandaean; sometimes applied erroneously to a Sabaean, sometimes to an adherent of Sabaism. [Ar *Sābi'*]
  ■ **Sa'bianism** n.

sabin /sab'in or sä'bin/ (*phys*; now *obs*) n a unit of acoustic absorption, equal to the absorption, considered complete, of 1 square foot of a perfectly absorbing surface. [WC *Sabine* (1868–1919), US physicist]

Sabine /sab'īn/ (*hist*) n a member of an ancient people of central Italy, united with the Romans about 300BC (also adj). [L *Sabīnus*]

Sabine's gull /sa-bēnz' gul/ n a small gull, *Larus sabini*, with a forked tail, grey and white plumage with black outer feathers on the wing tips, and a black, yellow-tipped bill. [Sir Edward *Sabine* (1788–1883), Irish general and explorer]

Sabin vaccine /sā'bin vak'sēn or -sin/ n a live-virus poliomyelitis vaccine taken orally. [AB *Sabin* (1906–93), US microbiologist]

sabkha, sabkhah /sab'kə or sab'hə/ or **sabkhat** /-kət or -hhət/ (*geol*) n a broad, salt-encrusted coastal plain, above the level of normal tides and subjected to only occasional flooding, common in Arabia. [Ar]

sable¹ /sä'bl/ n an arctic and subarctic marten, *esp Martes zibellina* of N Asia; its lustrous dark-brown fur; an artist's paintbrush made of its hair. ◆ adj made of sable fur. [OFr; prob from Slav]

■ words derived from main entry word; □ compound words; ■ idioms and phrasal verbs

sable² /sā'bl/ *n* and *adj* black (*orig heraldry*, now chiefly *poetic*); dark. ◆ *n* a sable antelope; (in *pl*) mourning garments (*obs*). ◆ *vt* (*poetic*) to darken. [Fr *sable*; poss the same as **sable¹**]
▫ **sable antelope** *n* a large predominantly black antelope of S and E Africa (*Hippotragus niger*), with long, ringed backward-curving horns. **sa'ble-coloured** *adj*. **sa'blefish** *n* a Pacific food-fish (*Anoplopoma fimbria*).

Sabme, **Sabmi** see **Saam**.

sabot /sab'ō/ *n* a wooden shoe or clog, as formerly worn by French peasants; an attachment to guide a projectile through the bore of a firearm. [Fr]
■ **sabotier** /sa-bo-tyā/ *n* someone who wears wooden shoes; a Waldensian (*rare*).

sabotage /sa-bo-täzh', now *usu* sab'ə-täzh, also -tij/ *n* malicious or deliberate destruction or damage of machinery, etc, by discontented workers, rebels, etc; action taken to prevent the fulfilment of any plan, aim, etc. ◆ *vt* and vi to perform an act of sabotage (on). [Fr *sabot*]
■ **saboteur** /-tœr'/ *n* a person who sabotages (*inf* **sab**).

sabra /sä'brə/ *n* a native-born Israeli, not an immigrant. [Mod Heb *sābrāh*, a type of desert pear, prickly on the outside and soft inside, common in coastal areas of Israel]

sabre or (*N Am*) **saber** /sā'bər/ *n* a curved single-edged cavalry sword; a light sword used in fencing; a cavalry soldier armed with a sabre. ◆ *vt* to wound or kill with a sabre. [Fr *sabre*, from Ger dialect *Sabel* (now *Säbel*); perh from Pol *szabla* or Hung *szablya*]
■ **sabreur** /-rœr'/ *n* a person, *esp* a cavalry soldier, who fights with a sabre.
▫ **sa'bre-cut** *n*. **sa'bre-rattle** *vi*. **sa'bre-rattling** *n* an aggressive display of military power, military bluster intended to intimidate (also *adj*). **sa'bretooth** *n* any extinct feline carnivore of the Tertiary period, eg the **sabre-toothed tiger** (genus *Smilodon*), with extremely long upper canine teeth. **sa'brewing** *n* a hummingbird of a group with bent outer primaries in the male.

sabretache /sab'ər-tash/ *n* a flat bag slung from a cavalry officer's sword-belt. [Fr *sabretache*, from Ger *Säbeltasche*, from *Säbel* sabre, and *Tasche* pocket]

sabulous /sab'ū-ləs/ or **sabulose** /sab'ū-lōs/ *adj* sandy; gritty; (of plants) growing in sandy places (also **sab'uline**). [L *sabulum* sand]

saburra /sə-bur'ə/ *n* a granular deposit, as in the stomach. [L *saburra* sand]
■ **saburr'al** *adj*. **saburrā'tion** *n* (*med*) the application of hot sand as a treatment.

SAC *abbrev*: Scottish Arts Council; Special Area of Conservation; Strategic Air Command (in the USA).

sac¹ /sak/ *n* (*biol*) a pouch or bag-like structure. [Fr, from L *saccus* a bag; see **sack¹**]
■ **sacc'ate** *adj* pouched; pouchlike; gibbous; enclosed in a sac. **sacciform** /sak'si-förm/ or **sacc'ular** *adj* saclike. **sacc'ulate** or **sacc'ulated** *adj* formed in a series of saclike enclosures; enclosed in a sac. **saccula'tion** *n*. **sacc'ule** or **sacc'ulus** *n* (*pl* **sacc'ules** or **sacc'ulī**) a small sac, eg the smaller of two sacs in the vestibule of the ear. **saccū'liform** *adj* in the shape of a small sac. **sac'like** *adj*.

sac² /sak/ (*old Eng law*) *n* the conveyance to a lord of manor of certain rights of jurisdiction, eg holding courts (see also **soc**). [OE *sacu* strife, litigation]
■ **sac'less** *adj* (*Walter Scott*) unchallengeable, not to be molested; see also separate entry **sackless**.

sacaton /sak'ə-tōn/ *n* a type of coarse perennial grass growing in alkaline regions of the southern USA, used for making hay. [Am Sp *zacatón*]

saccade /sa-käd', sə- or -kād'/ *n* the sharp lateral movement of the eye as it switches swiftly from one fixation point to another, eg in reading; a short rapid tug on a horse's reins; any short jerky movement. [Fr *saccade* a jerk, from OFr *saquer* to pull]
■ **saccad'ic** *adj* jerky; consisting of or relating to saccades. **saccad'ically** *adv*.

sacchar- /sak-ər-/, **sacchari-** /sak-ə-ri-/ or **saccharo-** /sak-ə-rō-, -rə-/ *combining form* denoting sugar. [L *saccharum*, through Gr *sakcharon* sugar, ult from Sans *śarkarā* gravel, grit]
■ **sacch'arase** *n* same as **invertase** (see under **invert**). **sacch'arate** *n* a salt of saccharic acid. **sacch'arated** *adj* sugared, sweetened. **sacchar'ic** *adj* of or obtained from saccharin, a saccharine substance or **saccharic acid**, an acid (COOH(CHOH)₄COOH) obtained by oxidation of sugar (**saccharic ester** an ester obtained from saccharic acid). **sacch'aride** *n* a carbohydrate; a compound with sugar. **saccharif'erous** *adj* sugar-yielding. **sacchar'ification** *n*. **sacchar'ify** (or /sak'-/) *vt* to convert or break down into sugar or sugars. **saccharim'eter** *n* an instrument for testing the concentration of sugar solutions. **saccharim'etry** *n*. **sacch'arin** or **sacch'arine** /-in or -ēn/ *n* an intensely sweet, white crystalline semi-soluble compound (C₆H₄COSO₂NH) used as an artificial sweetener; sickly sweetness (*fig*). **sacch'arine** /-īn, -ēn/ *adj* of sickly sweetness; sugary; of, containing, or of the nature of sugar or saccharine. **saccharinity** /-in'i-ti/ *n*. **sacchariza'tion** or **-s-** *n*. **sacch'arize** or **-ise** *vt* to saccharify. **sacch'aroid** or **saccharoid'al** *adj* (*geol*) like loaf sugar in texture, *usu* applied to marbles and quartzites of fine to medium grain with closely interlocking crystals. **saccharom'eter** *n* a hydrometer or other instrument for measuring concentration of sugar solutions. **Saccharomyces** /-ō-mī'sēz/ *n* (Gr *mykēs* fungus) the yeast genus of ascomycete fungi. **sacch'arose** /-ōs/ *n* any carbohydrate, *esp* cane sugar. **Sacch'arum** *n* the sugar-cane genus of grasses; (without *cap*) cane sugar or its invert form.

sacciform see under **sac¹**.

saccos same as **sakkos**.

saccular, **sacculate**, etc see under **sac¹**.

sacellum /sə-sel'əm/ *n* (*pl* **sacell'a**) a tomb or monument in the form of a chapel within a church (*archit*); a little chapel; a roofless temple consecrated to an ancient Roman deity. [L dimin of *sacrum* a holy place, from *sacer* consecrated]

sacerdotal /sas-ər-dō'tl, sak-/ *adj* priestly. [L *sacerdōs, -ōtis* a priest, from *sacer* sacred, and *dare* to give]
■ **sacerdō'talism** *n* the spirit, principles, etc of the priesthood; devotion to priestly interests; priestcraft; the belief that the presbyter is a priest in the sense of offering a sacrifice in the Eucharist; the attribution to a priesthood of special or supernatural powers; excessive influence of priests over people's thoughts and actions (*derog*). **sacerdō'talist** *n*. **sacerdō'talize** or **-ise** *vt* to render sacerdotal. **sacerdō'tally** *adv*.

sachem /sā'chəm/ (*US*) *n* a Native American chief, a sagamore; a political leader, *esp* one of the officials of Tammany Hall (qv). [Narraganset *sachim*]
■ **sā'chemdom** or **sā'chemship** *n*. **sachemic** /sā-chem'ik/ *adj*.

Sachertorte /sähh'ər-tör-tə, zä-, -k-/ *n* a rich chocolate cake with apricot jam filling and chocolate icing, *orig* made and served at *Sacher*'s hotel in Vienna (also **Sacher torte**). [See **torte**]

sachet /sa'shā/ *n* a small *usu* plastic envelope, containing a liquid, cream, etc, such as shampoo; a small bag containing potpourri or other scented material; a bag for holding handkerchiefs, etc. [Fr]

sack¹ /sak/ *n* a large bag made of coarse fabric, thick paper, etc; a sackful; a varying, *usu* large measure of capacity; (with *the*) dismissal from employment (*inf*); (with *the*) a form of the death penalty by which the criminal was condemned to be sewn up in a sack and drowned (*hist*); bed (*sl*); an instance of sacking a quarterback (*American football*). ◆ *vt* to put into a sack; to dismiss from employment (*inf*); to tackle (a quarterback) behind the line of scrimmage and before he or she can pass the ball (*American football*). [OE *sacc*, from L *saccus*, from Gr *sakkos*; prob Phoenician]
■ **sack'able** *adj*. **sack'ful** *n* (*pl* **sack'fuls**) as much as a sack will hold; a large quantity (*inf*). **sack'ing** *n* coarse cloth used in making sacks, sackcloth. **sack'like** *adj*.
▫ **sack'cloth** *n* coarse cloth used for making sacks; coarse material, formerly worn in mourning or penance. **sack-doudling** /-düd'lin/ *adj* (*Walter Scott*) bagpiping (cf **doodle²** and Ger *Dudelsack*). **sack race** *n* one in which each runner's legs are enclosed in a sack. **sack tree** *n* the upas (from the use of its inner bark to make sacks). ■ **hit the sack** (*sl*) to go to bed. **in sackcloth and ashes** showing extreme regret, penitence, etc (often *facetious*); in deep mourning. **sad sack** (*esp US sl*) a person who seems to attract mishap and disaster, a misfit.

sack² /sak/ *n* plundering or devastation (of a town or city); pillage. ◆ *vt* to plunder; to pillage. [Fr *sac*; according to some the same as **sack¹** (putting (one's) loot) in a bag)]
■ **sack'age** (*rare*) or **sack'ing** *n*. **sack'er** *n*.

sack³ /sak/ *n* the old name of various dry white wines from Spain and the Canaries. [Fr *sec*, from L *siccus* dry]
▫ **sack'-poss'et** *n* posset made with sack. ■ **burnt sack** mulled sack.

sack⁴ or **sacque** /sak/ (*hist*) *n* a woman's loose-fitting gown (also **sack dress**); a train of silk hanging from the shoulders of such a gown; a woman's hip-length coat with a loose-fitting back. [See ety for **sack¹**; infl by Fr *sac*]

sackbut /sak'but/ *n* an early wind instrument with a slide like the trombone; a mistranslation of Aramaic *sabbekā*, the sambuca (*Bible*). [Fr *saquebute*, perh OFr *saquier* to draw out, and *bouter* to push]

sackless /sak'lis/ (*archaic* and *Scot*) *adj* innocent; guileless; feeble; dispirited (see also under **sac²**). [OE *sacleās*, from *sacu*; **sac²**, **sake²**]

SACN *abbrev*: Scientific Advisory Committee on Nutrition.

sacque see **sack⁴**.

sacra see **sacrum**.

sacral[1] /sā'krəl/ adj of or relating to sacred rites (see also **sacrum**). [L *sacrum* a sacred object]

■ **sacral'ity** n. **sacraliza'tion** or **-s-** n endowing something with sacred status or properties; treating something as if it were sacred. **sac'ralize** or **-ise** vt.

sacral[2] see under **sacrum**.

sacrament /sak'rə-mənt/ n a religious rite variously regarded as a channel to and from God or as a sign of grace, amongst Protestants generally *Baptism* and the *Lord's Supper*, amongst Roman Catholics and members of the Eastern Orthodox Church also *Confirmation, Penance, Holy Orders, Matrimony* and *Extreme Unction*; the Lord's Supper specially; the bread or wine taken in celebration of the Lord's Supper; a symbol of something spiritual or secret; a sign, token, or pledge of a covenant; a religious mystery; a Roman soldier's oath on enlistment; a pledge deposited by each party to a suit (*Roman law*); a solemn oath; an oath of purgation; materials used in a sacrament. ◆ vt to bind by an oath. [L *sacrāmentum* an oath, pledge, from *sacrāre* to consecrate, from *sacer* sacred]

■ **sacramental** /-ment'l/ adj of or relating to a sacrament or sacraments. ◆ n (RC) an act or object which may transmit or receive grace. **sacramen'talism** n. **sacramen'talist** n a person who attaches importance to the spiritual nature of the sacraments. **sacramental'ity** n. **sacramen'talize** or **-ise** vt. **sacramen'tally** adv. **sacramentā'rian** n and adj (a person) holding a high or extreme view of the efficacy of the sacraments; (someone) not accepting the real presence in the sacrament of the Lord's Supper (*obs*). **sacramentā'rianism** n. **sacramen'tary** adj relating to the sacrament or sacraments; sacramentarian. ◆ n a book containing all the prayers and ceremonies used at the celebration of the Roman Catholic sacraments; a person who denies the doctrine of the real presence.

❑ **sacrament house** n an ambry where the sacrament is kept.

■ **take the sacrament upon** or **to** to take communion in confirmation of (an oath).

sacrarium /sa-, sā-krā'ri-əm or sa-krā'ri-ŭm/ n (pl **sacra'ria**) a place where sacred objects were kept, either in a temple or house (*ancient Rome*); the sanctuary of a church; the piscina (RC church). [L *sacrārium*, from *sacer* holy]

sacred /sā'krid/ adj consecrated; devoted; set apart or dedicated to religious use, *esp* to God; holy; emanating from God; religious; entitled to veneration or worship; not to be violated, breached, etc; accursed (*rare*). [Pap of obs *sacre*, from OFr *sacrer*, from L *sacrāre*, from *sacer* sacred]

■ **sa'credly** adv. **sa'credness** n.

❑ **sacred ape** n the hanuman of India. **sacred beetle** n an Egyptian scarab. **sacred cat** n the house cat of Egypt, sacred to Pasht or Bast. **Sacred College** n the body of cardinals of the Roman Catholic Church. **sacred cow** n (*inf*) an institution, custom, etc, so venerated that it is above criticism (in allusion to the animal being sacrosanct in Hinduism). **sacred fish** n oxyrhynchus. **Sacred Heart** n (RC) the physical heart of Christ, adored with special devotion since the 18c. **sacred mushroom** n any of various hallucinogenic mushrooms, eg of the genus *Psilocybe* of N and S America, and *Amanita* of Europe and Asia, used in religious rituals and ceremonies; a mescal button used in a similar way.

sacrifice /sak'ri-fīs, sometimes (*esp poetic*) -fīz/ n the slaughter of an animal, person, etc on an altar as an offering to a god; any offering, tangible or symbolic, to a god; Christ's offering of himself as mankind's saviour (*theol*); destruction, surrender, or foregoing of anything valued for the sake of anything else, *esp* a higher consideration; loss sustained by selling something at less than its value; a victim offered in sacrifice; a play where a batter deliberately makes an out in order to enable a baserunner to score or gain a base (*baseball*). ◆ vt to offer up in sacrifice; to make a sacrifice of; to give up, surrender, for a higher good or for mere advantage; to make a victim of; to sell at a loss; to allow to come to destruction or evil. ◆ vi to offer sacrifice(s). [L *sacrificium*, from *sacer* sacred, and *facere* to make]

■ **sac'rificer** n. **sacrificial** /-fish'l/ adj of or relating to sacrifice; (of an object or substance) protecting another from corrosion by its own exposure to and damage by the corrosive, as in *sacrificial anode, sacrificial plate, sacrificial metal* (*technol*). **sacrifi'cially** adv. **sac'rify** vt and vi (pap (*Spenser*) **sac'rifide**) (*obs*) to sacrifice.

sacrilege /sak'ri-lij/ n profanation or disregard of anything holy; the outrage of breaking into a place of worship and stealing from it; extreme disrespect for anything generally regarded as worthy of extreme respect. [Fr *sacrilège*, from L *sacrilegium*, from *sacer* sacred, and *legere* to gather]

■ **sacrilegious** /-lij'əs/ adj. **sacrile'giously** adv. **sacrile'giousness** n. **sacrile'gist** n.

sacring /sā'kring/ (*archaic*) n the act or ritual of consecration. [**sacred**]

❑ **sacring bell** n (RC church) a small bell rung to call attention to the more solemn parts of the service of the Mass.

sacrist /sak'rist, sā'krist/ n a sacristan; in a cathedral, someone who copied music for the choir and looked after the books (*hist*). [LL *sacrista, sacristānus* a sacristan, *sacristia* a vestry, from L *sacer* sacred]

■ **sacristan** /sak'ri-stən/ n an officer in a church who has care of the sacred vessels and other movables; a sexton. **sacristy** /sak'-/ n a room in a church where the sacred utensils, vestments, etc, are kept; a vestry.

sacro- /sak-rō-/ or (sometimes before a vowel) **sacr-** /sakr-/ combining form denoting sacrum. [**sacrum**]

■ **sacrococcygeal** /-kok-sij'i-əl/ adj relating to the sacrum and the coccyx. **sacrocos'tal** adj connected with the sacrum and having the character of a rib (also n). **sacroïl'iac** adj relating to the articulation of the sacrum and ilium. ◆ n this joint. **sacroiliitis** /-il-i-ī'tis/ n inflammation of the sacroiliac joint.

sacrosanct /sak'rō-sangkt/ adj inviolable, protected by sacred or quasi-sacred rules. [L *sacrōsanctus*, from *sacer* sacred, and *sanctus*, pap of *sancīre* to hallow]

■ **sacrosanc'tity** or **sac'rosanctness** n.

sacrum /sā'krəm or sak'rəm/ (*anat*) n (pl **sa'cra**) a triangular bone composed of five fused vertebrae (**sacral vertebrae**) wedged between the two innominate bones, so as to form the keystone of the pelvic arch in humans. [L (*os*) *sacrum* holy (bone), so called for unknown reason]

■ **sa'cral** adj. **sacralgia** /-ral'ji-ə/ n pain in the sacrum or region of the sacrum. **sacraliza'tion** or **-s-** n abnormal fusion of the sacrum with the fifth lumbar vertebra.

SAD abbrev : seasonal affective disorder.

sad /sad/ adj (**sadd'er**; **sadd'est**) sorrowful; inspiring sorrow or pity; deplorable (often *joc*); (of a person) inspiring ridicule, *esp* because lacking in taste (*sl*); (of baking) heavy, stiff, doughy; sober, dark-coloured; serious, earnest, grave (*archaic*); staid, sedate (*archaic*); steadfast, constant (*obs*); heavy (*obs*); sated (*obs*). [OE *sæd* sated, weary; cf Du *zat*, Ger *satt*; L *sat*, *satis*]

■ **sadd'en** vt to make sad. ◆ vi to grow sad. **sadd'ish** adj. **sadd'o** or **sadd'ie** n (*sl*) a dull or unsociable person. **sad'ly** adv in a sad manner; unfortunately, sad to relate. **sad'ness** n.

❑ **sad'iron** n a flatiron pointed at both ends. **sad sack** see under **sack**[1].

■ **in sober sadness** in serious earnest.

saddhu see **sadhu**.

saddle /sad'l/ n a seat for a rider on a horse, bicycle, etc; a pad for the back of a draught animal; anything of similar shape, eg a mountain col between two peaks; that part of the back of an animal on which the saddle is placed; a mark on that part; a butcher's cut including a part of the backbone with the ribs; the rear part of a male fowl's back; a worm's clitellum; the part of a lathe that slides on the bed, between the headstock and tailstock; a block surmounting one of the towers of a suspension bridge, supporting or fixing the suspension cables. ◆ vt to put a saddle on; to encumber; to impose upon (someone) as a burden or encumbrance; (of a trainer) to be responsible for preparing and entering (a racehorse) for a race; to ride or mount (a horse, bicycle, etc) (*rare*). ◆ vi to get into the saddle of a horse, bicycle, etc. [OE *sadol, sadel*; cf Du *zadel*, Ger *Sattel*]

■ **sadd'leless** adj. **sadd'ler** n a maker or seller of saddles and related goods; a soldier in charge of cavalry saddles (also **sadd'ler-cor'poral** and **sadd'ler-ser'geant**; *hist*); a saddle horse (US *inf*). **sadd'lery** n the occupation of a saddler; a saddler's shop or stock-in-trade; a saddle-room at a stables, etc.

❑ **sadd'leback** n a saddle-shaped hill, coping, animal or object; the great black-backed gull; the hooded crow; the male harp seal; a breed of goose; a breed of pig; a rare New Zealand wattlebird, *Philesturnus carunculatus*; a saddle roof. ◆ adj (also **sadd'lebacked**) saddle-shaped; having a depression in the middle (of the back); having a saddle-shaped mark on the back; (of a coping) sloping from the middle to each side. **sadd'lebag** n a bag carried at, or attached to, the saddle; (in pl) excessive fat in the abdominal region (*inf*). ◆ adj (of furniture) upholstered in cloth in imitation of camels' saddlebags. **saddle bar** n a bar for supporting stained glass in a window. **saddlebill** or **saddle-bill stork** n a large black-and-white stork, *Ephippiorhynchus senegalensis*, of sub-Saharan Africa, with a red and black bill that has a yellow saddle-like structure at the base. **saddle blanket** n a folded blanket used as a saddlecloth. **sadd'lebow** /-bō/ n the arched front of a saddle. **sadd'lecloth** n a cloth placed under a saddle to prevent rubbing. **sadd'le-fast** adj firmly seated in the saddle. **saddle feather** or **hackle** n one of the long, slender feathers drooping from a male fowl's saddle. **sadd'le-girth** n a band that holds the saddle in place. **saddle horse** n a riding horse. **sadd'le-lap** n the skirt of a saddle. **sadd'le-nose** n flattening of the bridge of the nose, eg as a result of congenital syphilis. **sadd'le-nosed** adj. **saddle pillar** or **pin** n the support of a cycle saddle, which fits a socket in the frame. **saddle reef** n (*geol*) an ore deposit occurring in concavo-convex formations of igneous rocks, *esp* in Australia. **saddle roof** *n* a roof with a ridge and two gables. **sadd'leroom** *n* a room where saddles and harness are kept. **sadd'le-shaped** *adj* arched; concave and convex in sections at right angles to each other. **saddle soap** *n* a kind of oily soap used for cleaning and treating leather. **saddle sore** *n* a sore resulting from chafing of the saddle. **sadd'le-sore** *adj* (of a rider) with buttocks and inner thighs sore or chafed from riding. **saddle spring** *n* a spring supporting a cycle saddle. **saddle stitch** *n* needlework consisting of long stitches on the top surface and short stitches on the underside of the material; one such stitch; a method of stitching or stapling (a booklet, magazine, etc) together through the back centre fold. **sadd'le-stitch** *vt* and *vi* to sew using saddle stitch. **sadd'letree** *n* the frame of a saddle.

■ **in the saddle** on horseback; in control. **put the saddle on the right horse** to impute blame where it is deserved. **saddle up** to saddle a horse; to mount (*S Afr*).

Sadducee /sad'ū-sē/ *n* a member of a Jewish priestly and aristocratic party of traditionalists, whose reactionary conservatism resisted the progressive views of the Pharisees, and who rejected, among various other beliefs, resurrection of the body. [Gr *Saddoukaios*, from Heb *Tsadûqîm*, from *Zadok* the High Priest, the founder]

■ **Sadducaean** or **Sadducean** /-sē'ən/ *adj*. **Sadd'uceeism** or **Sadd'ucism** *n* the principles of the Sadducees; scepticism.

sade see **sadhe**.

sadhana /sä'dha-nä/ (*Hinduism*) *n* an exercise carried out repeatedly in order to achieve spiritual perfection. [Sans]

sadhe or **sade** /sä'dē/ *n* the eighteenth letter of the Hebrew alphabet. [Heb]

sadhu or **saddhu** /sä'doo/ *n* a Hindu holy man, ascetic and mendicant. [Sans *sādhu*, from adj, straight, pious]

sadism /sä'di-zm/ *n* pleasure, *esp* sexual satisfaction, obtained by inflicting pain or suffering on another person; love of cruelty. [Comte (called Marquis) de *Sade* (1740–1814), who died insane, notoriously depicted this form of pleasure in his novels]

■ **sa'dist** *n*. **sadistic** /sə-dis'/ *adj*. **sadis'tically** *adv*. **sadomasochism** /sā-dō-mas'ə-kizm/ *n* the combination of sadism and masochism in one person; pleasure, *esp* sexual gratification, obtained by inflicting pain on another person and having pain inflicted on one by another person. **sadomas'ochist** *n*. **sadomasochist'ic** *adj*.

sadza /sad'zə/ *n* a type of porridge made from maize flour, a staple food in southern Africa. [Shona]

SAE *abbrev* : Society of Automotive Engineers (in the USA).

sae /sā/ *adv* Scottish form of **so**[1].

sae or **s.a.e.** *abbrev* : stamped addressed envelope.

saeculum or **seculum** /sek'ū-ləm/ *n* an astronomical or geological age. [L, a generation]

SAEF *abbrev* : Seaq Automatic Execution Facility (see also **SEAQ**).

saeter /set'ər or sä'tər/ *n* (in Norway) an upland meadow which provides summer pasture for cattle, and where butter and cheese are made; a hut on a saeter providing shelter for those looking after the animals. [Norw]

saeva indignatio /sē'və in-dig-nä'shi-ō or sī'wa, also sī'va, in-dig-nä'ti-ō/ (*L*) fierce indignation.

safari /sə-fä'ri/ *n* an expedition, *esp* for hunting or animal-watching in Africa; the people, vehicles, equipment, etc that go on safari; a long expedition involving difficulty and requiring planning, *usu* in tropical climes. ♦ *vi* to go on safari. [Swahili, from Ar *safarīya* a journey]

■ **safar'ist** *n* a person who goes on safari.

□ **safari park** *n* an enclosed park where wild animals (mostly non-native) are kept uncaged on view to the public. **safari suit** *n* a suit, typically of cotton and consisting of a square-cut **safari jacket** with four pockets and a belt, and long or short trousers or a skirt.

safe /sāf/ *adj* unharmed; free from danger; secure; sound, free from risk; certain, sure; reliable, trustworthy; cautious; good, fine (*sl*); having reached base before being thrown out by the fielding side (*baseball*). ♦ *n* a metal box, often set in a wall, secure against fire, thieves, etc; a ventilated box or cupboard for meat, etc; a condom (*N Am sl*). ♦ *adv* in a safe manner or condition. ♦ *vt* to make safe (*obs*); to bring safely (*Shakesp*). ♦ *prep* (*Spenser*) save. [OFr *sauf*, from L *salvus*]

■ **safe'ly** *adv*. **safe'ness** *n*. **safe'ty** *n* (in Spenser often /sā'fi-ti/) the state or fact of being safe; a safety shot in snooker or billiards; a device designed to prevent injury, *esp* a safety catch; (also **safe'tyman**) one of two defensive players positioned furthest back in the field (*American football*); a play in which the defensive team scores two points when an offensive player is tackled or downs the ball on or behind his own goal-line (*American football*).

□ **safe'-blower** *n*. **safe'-blowing** *n* the forcing of safes, using explosives. **safe'-breaker** or **safe'-cracker** *n*. **safe'-breaking** or **safe'-cracking** *n* illegal opening of safes. **safe'-con'duct** *n* a permit to pass or travel through an area with guarantee of freedom from interference or arrest. ♦ *vt* /-kon', -dukt'/ to conduct (a person) safely; to give a safe-conduct to. **safe'-deposit** or **safe'ty-deposit** *n* a vault, etc providing safe storage for valuables. **safe'guard** *n* a device, condition, or arrangement ensuring safety; a precaution; a safe-conduct. ♦ *vt* to protect (*esp* interests or rights); to protect (eg domestic manufacturers and industry) against foreign competition. **safe haven** *n* an area, *esp* in a war zone or a country with internal conflict, set aside for the protection of ethnic or religious minorities. **safe house** *n* (*inf*) a place (*esp* one kept by the intelligence services or care agencies) unknown to one's pursuers, where one can safely hide. **safe'keeping** *n* keeping in safety; safe custody. **safe light** *n* a light used in a photographic darkroom, etc, which emits light of an intensity and colour which will not damage the materials being processed. **safe period** *n* that part of the menstrual cycle during which conception is most unlikely. **safe seat** *n* a parliamentary seat that the incumbent political party will almost certainly win again in an election. **safe sex** *n* sexual intercourse minimizing the risk of transmission of disease, eg by the use of condoms. **safety arch** *n* an arch built into the body of a wall to relieve the pressure of weight from above. **safety belt** *n* a belt for fastening a person to a fixed object while carrying out a dangerous operation; a belt for restraining the occupant of a seat in a car, aircraft, etc, a precaution against injury in a crash. **safety bicycle** *n* (*old*) a low-wheeled bicycle for general use. **safety bolt** *n* the safety lock of a firearm. **safety cage** *n* a cage with a safety catch to prevent it falling if the hoisting rope breaks (*mining*); (in a motor-vehicle chassis) a specially strengthened framework around the seating part to give maximum protection to driver and passengers in a crash (also **safety cell**). **safety catch** *n* any catch to provide protection against something, such as the accidental firing of a gun. **safety curtain** *n* a fireproof curtain between stage and audience in a theatre. **safety factor** *n* the ratio between the breaking stress in a member, structure, or material, and the safe permissible stress in it. **safety film** *n* photographic or cinematographic film with a non-flammable or slow-burning base of cellulose acetate or polyester. **safety fuse** *n* a slow-burning fuse that can be lit at a safe distance; a fuse inserted for safety in an electric circuit. **safety glass** *n* a laminate of plastic between sheets of glass, used eg in vehicle windscreens; glass reinforced with wire, or otherwise toughened to avoid shattering (also **laminated glass**). **safety lamp** *n* a miners' lamp that will not ignite inflammable gases. **safety light** *n* a warning light; a light that will not readily cause a fire. **safety lock** *n* a lock that cannot be picked by ordinary means; (in firearms) a device for preventing accidental discharge, a safety catch. **safety match** *n* a match that can be ignited only on a specially prepared surface. **safety net** *n* a net stretched beneath an acrobat, etc, during a rehearsal or performance, in case he or she should fall; any precautionary measure or means of protection from injury, hardship, etc. **safety officer** *n* an official whose responsibility is to ensure that safety regulations are adhered to. **safety paper** *n* paper difficult to imitate or tamper with without detection, such as that used for banknotes. **safety pin** *n* a pin in the form of a clasp with a guard covering its point; a pin for locking a piece of machinery or a device, eg that used to prevent detonation of a grenade, a mine, etc. **safety plug** *n* an electrical plug with a fuse that melts when the temperature rises too high. **safety razor** *n* a razor incorporating a guard for the blade which prevents deep cutting of the skin. **safety rein** *n* a rein for preventing a horse from running away. **safety shot** *n* (in snooker and billiards) a shot intended to prevent one's opponent from scoring with his or her next shot. **safety valve** *n* a valve that opens when the pressure becomes too great; any harmless outlet for pent-up emotion, energy, etc. **safe word** *n* a word prearranged to be uttered by a person indulging in masochistic sexual activity when they genuinely wish to stop.

■ **be** or **err on the safe side** to choose the safer alternative. **place of safety order** (until 1991) a legal order, effective for not more than 28 days, allowing a child to be taken into care to avoid further or possible physical harm by parents, etc. **play safe** to act in a manner that minimizes the risk of defeat, injury or loss; to act in a cautious way. **safe and sound** secure and uninjured. **safe as houses** (*inf*) very safe.

saffian /saf'i-ən/ *n* leather tanned with sumac and dyed in bright colours. [Russ *saf'yan*]

safflower /saf'lowr/ *n* a thistle-like composite plant (*Carthamus tinctorius*) cultivated in India; its dried petals, used in cosmetics and for making a red dye. [Cf Du *saffloer*, OFr *saffleur*]

□ **safflower oil** *n* an oil produced from this plant and used in cooking, etc.

saffron /saf'rən/ *n* a species of crocus, *Crocus sativus*, with purple flowers; its orange-coloured stigmas, dried and used as a dye and flavouring; an orange-yellow colour. [OFr *safran*, from Ar *za'farān*]

■ **saff'roned** *adj* coloured or flavoured with saffron. **saff'rony** *adj* coloured somewhat like saffron or having a flavour like saffron. **saf'ranin** or **saf'ranine** *n* any of various coal tar dyes, giving various colours. **safronal** /saf'rə-nəl/ n a spicy-tasting chemical constituent of saffron.

□ **saffron cake** n a cake flavoured with saffron. **saffron milk cap** n an edible orange toadstool (*Lactarius deliciosus*).

■ **false, mock** or **bastard saffron** safflower. **meadow saffron** see under **meadow**.

S Afr *abbrev* : South Africa; South African.

safranin(e) see under **saffron**.

safrole /saf'rōl/ n a *usu* colourless oily liquid obtained from sassafras, formerly used in perfumes, soaps and insecticides. [*sassafras* and **-ol**²]

sag¹ /sag/ vi (**sagg'ing; sagged**) to bend, sink, or hang down, *esp* in the middle; to yield or give way, from or as if from weight or pressure; to flag; (of industrial activity, prices, etc) to decline; to droop; to move along in a slow, laboured manner; to move or drift to leeward. ◆ n an act or instance of sagging; a part or area that sags, eg a depression in an area of glacial deposition. ◆ *adj* sagging. [Cf Swed *sacka* to sink down; LGer *sacken* to sink]

■ **sagg'ing** n and *adj*. **sagg'y** *adj* inclined to sag.

□ **sag bag** n a large bag filled with a substance, *usu* polystyrene granules, which allows it to be pushed into any shape and used as a chair, cushion, bed, etc.

sag² see **saag**.

saga¹ /sä'gə/ n a prose narrative of the deeds of Icelandic or Norwegian heroes in the old literature of Iceland; a body of legend about some subject; a series of novels dealing with the history of a family (also **saga novel**); a long, detailed story (*inf*). [ON *saga*; cf **saw**³]

□ **sa'gaman** n a narrator of Icelandic or Norwegian sagas.

saga² see **sagum**.

sagacious /sə-gā'shəs/ adj keen in perception or thought; discerning and judicious; wise. [L *sagāx, -ācis*]

■ **sagā'ciously** *adv*. **sagā'ciousness** or **sagacity** /-gas'i-ti/ n.

sagaman see under **saga**¹.

sagamore /sag'ə-mör/ n a Native American chief. [Penobscot *sagamo*; cf **sachem**]

sagapenum /sag-ə-pē'nəm/ n a gum resin, the juice of *Ferula persica*, formerly used to stimulate menstruation and as an antispasmodic. [Gr *sagapēnon*]

sagathy /sag'ə-thi/ (*obs*) n a lightweight fabric, a mixture of wool and silk or silk and cotton. [Origin unknown; cf Fr *sagatis*, Sp *sagatí*]

sage¹ /sāj/ n a garden labiate plant (*Salvia officinalis*) whose grey-green leaves are used as a flavouring; any plant of the *Salvia* genus, such as clary; extended to wood germander (*wood sage*). [OFr *sauge* (Ital *salvia*), from L *salvia*, from *salvus* safe]

■ **sā'gy** *adj*.

□ **sage apple** n an edible gall formed on Mediterranean sage. **sage'brush** n a subshrub of the genus *Artemisia*, that grows in arid regions of N America. **sage cheese** n a cheese flavoured and mottled with sage leaves. **sage Derby** n a kind of sage cheese. **sage green** n the greyish-green colour of sage leaves. **sage-green'** *adj*. **sage grouse** or **cock** n a large N American grouse, *Centrocercus urophasianus*, that feeds on and lives in sagebrush. **sage rabbit** n a small hare found amongst sagebrush. **sage tea** n an infusion of sage leaves, used domestically as a tonic. **sage'-thrash'er** n the mountain mockingbird.

sage² /sāj/ *adj* wise. ◆ n a (*usu* old) man of great wisdom. [Fr *sage*, ult from L *sapere* to be wise]

■ **sage'ly** *adv*. **sage'ness** n.

■ **Seven Sages** see under **seven**.

sagene /sə-jēn'/ n (*rare*) a fishing-net; a network. [Gr *sagēnē* dragnet]

■ **sagenite** /saj'ə-nīt or sə-jē'nīt/ n (*mineralogy*) rutile in the form of a network of needle-like crystals. **sagenitic** /saj-ə-nit'ik/ *adj*.

saggar or **sagger** /sag'ər/ or **saggard** /sag'ərd/ or **seggar** /seg'ər/ n a clay box in which pottery is packed for baking. [Perh **safeguard**]

sagged, sagging see **sag**¹.

sagger see **saggar**.

saginate /saj'i-nāt/ (*rare*) vt to fatten (animals). [L *sagināre* to fatten]

■ **sagina'tion** n.

sagitta /sə-jit'ə/ n (with *cap*) the Arrow, a northern constellation; a keystone; a versed sine of an arc (*geom*); the middle stroke of the letter epsilon. [L *sagitta* an arrow]

■ **sagittal** /saj'it-l/ *adj* shaped like an arrow; like a sagitta; relating or parallel to the sagittal suture. **sag'ittally** *adv*. **Sagitta'ria** n the arrowhead genus. **Sagittar'ian** n and *adj* (relating to or characteristic of) a person born under the sign of Sagittarius. **Sagitta'rius** n the Archer, a constellation giving its name to, and formerly coinciding with, a sign of the zodiac (*astron*); the ninth sign of the zodiac, between Scorpio and Capricorn (*astrol*); a person born between 23 November and 22 December, under the sign of Sagittarius (*astrol*; *pl*

Sagitta'rius or Sagitta'riuses). **sag'ittary** n a centaur; an archer. **sag'ittate** or **sagitt'iform** *adj* (of leaves) shaped like an arrowhead with the barbs pointing backwards.

□ **sagittal suture** n the serrated join between the two parietal bones forming the top and sides of the skull.

sago /sā'gō/ n a nutritive cereal substance produced from the pith of the sago palm. [Malay *sāgū*]

□ **sago grass** n a tall grass, *Paspalidum globoideum*, used as fodder for cattle in Australia. **sago palm** n any of various palms (including *Metroxylon, Arenga, Caryota, Oreodoxa*) and certain cycads, yielding sago.

sagoin or **sagouin** see **saguin**.

saguaro /sä-gwä'rō/ n (pl **sagua'ros**) a giant cactus, *Carnegiea gigantea*, of SW USA and Mexico, with a tree-like trunk, white flowers and edible red fruits. [Mex Sp]

saguin, sagoin or **sagouin** /sag'win or sa-goin'/ n a small S American monkey. [Fr *sago(u)in*, from Port *saguim*, from Tupí *saguin*]

sagum /sā'gəm, sag'ŭm/ n (pl **sa'ga**) a Roman military cloak. [L *sagum*; prob Gaulish]

Saharan /sə-hä'rən/ adj of, resembling, or characteristic of, the *Sahara* desert in N Africa.

Sahelian /sə-hē'li-ən or -hel'i-ən/ adj of or concerning the countries south of the Sahara desert, *incl* Chad, Niger, Mali and Mauritania, generally between the desert and savanna regions. [Ar *sāhel* coastal strip]

sahib /sä'ib/ n a form of address used in India to people of rank and, during the period of British rule, to Europeans; Sir or Mr; a European; a refined, cultured man (*inf*). [Ar *sāhib*, orig, friend]

■ **sah'iba** or **sah'ibah** n (*rare*) a female equivalent of this (see also **memsahib**).

Sahrawi /sa-hrä'wē/ n a member of an indigenous people of the W Sahara; another name for **Hassaniya**. ◆ *adj* of the Sahrawis or their language. [Ar *Sahrāwī* Saharan]

sai /sä'i/ n the capuchin monkey. [Tupí, monkey]

saibling /zīp'ling/ n a freshwater fish, the char. [Ger dialect]

saic, saick or **saique** /sä-ēk' or sä'ik/ n a vessel like a ketch, used in the E Mediterranean. [Fr *saïque*, from Turk *shāïqā*]

saice same as **syce**.

said¹ /sed/ *pat* and *pap* of **say**¹. *adj* previously- or already-mentioned.

said² see **sayyid**.

saiga /sī'gə/ n a Eurasian antelope, *Saiga tatarica*, with a swollen nose ending in a pig-like snout. [Russ]

saikless /sāk'lis/ adj a Scots form of **sackless**.

sail¹ /sāl/ n a sheet of canvas, framework of slats, or other structure, spread to catch the wind, so as to propel a ship, drive a windmill, etc; a specified type of sail on a boat or ship (often shortened to **s'l**), as in *foresail* or *fores'l*; sails collectively; a ship or ships; a trip in a vessel (which may or may not have sails); an act or distance of sailing; any sail-like organ or object; a wing, *esp* a hawk's; a submarine's conning-tower. ◆ vi to progress, travel or make trips in sailing-craft or any other type of ship; to set out on a voyage; to glide or float smoothly along (*fig*). ◆ vt to direct the course or movements of (a ship), navigate; to cause (a toy boat, etc) to sail; to pass over or along in a ship; to go through or get through effortlessly (*fig*). [OE *segel*; cf Du *zeil*, Ger *Segel*]

■ **sail'able** *adj* navigable. **sailed** *adj* having sails. **sail'er** n a boat or ship that can sail in a stated manner. **sail'ing** n travelling, or a journey, by sails or on water; (the time of) a ship's departure from port; the art or activity of directing a ship's course. ◆ *adj* of or relating to this activity. **sail'less** *adj*. **sail'or** n a person who is employed in the operation of a ship, *esp* one who is not an officer; a mariner, seaman; a navigator; a person regarded in terms of ability to tolerate the heaving motion of a ship (as in *good* or *bad sailor*); a sailor hat (*inf*). **sail'oring** n occupation as a sailor. **sail'orless** *adj*. **sail'orlike** or **sail'orly** *adj*.

□ **sail arm** n one of the arms of a windmill. **sail'board** n a simple apparatus for sailing, *usu* consisting of a surfboard fitted with a single flexible mast, the sail being controlled by a hand-held boom. **sail'boarder** n someone who goes in for sailboarding. **sail'boarding** n the sport of sailing a sailboard, windsurfing. **sail'boat** n (*esp* N Am) a (*usu* small) sailing boat. **sail'cloth** n a strong cloth used for sails; heavy cotton cloth used for garments. **sail'fish** n a large game fish of the genus *Istiophorus*, related to the swordfish, with a large sail-like dorsal fin; another name for the basking shark. **sail'-flying** n flying in a sailplane. **sailing boat** n a boat moved by sails, though often having auxiliary motor power. **sailing master** n an officer in charge of navigation, *esp* of a yacht; formerly a warrant officer in the US Navy. **sailing orders** n pl instructions to the captain of a ship at setting forth on a voyage. **sailing ship** n a ship driven by sails. **sail loft** n a large room or loft with sufficient floor area to allow sails to be spread out while they are being made or repaired. **sail'maker** *n.* **sail'making** *n.* **sailor hat** *n* a round hat with a wide, upcurved brim. **sail'or-man** *n* a seaman. **sailor suit** *n* a child's outfit resembling that of a sailor. **sail'plane** *n* a glider that can rise with an upward current. ◆ *vi* to fly in a sailplane. **sail'room** *n* a room aboard a vessel for storing sails in. **sail'-yard** *n* the yard on which sails are extended.

■ **full sail** with all sails raised and filled with the wind. **good** (or **bad**) **sailor** a person who is unaffected (or made ill) by the motion of a ship. **make sail** to spread more canvas, raise more sails; to set off on a voyage. **put on sail** to set more sails in order to travel more quickly (also *fig*). **sail close to** (or **near**) **the wind** see under **wind**[1]. **sail under false colours** to pretend to be what one is not. **set sail** to spread the sails; to set forth on a voyage (with *for*). **shorten sail** to reduce its extent. **strike sail** to lower a sail or sails; to retreat from one's stated position, eat humble pie. **trim one's sails** to adjust or modify one's plans, policy or opinion to take account of changed circumstances. **under sail** having the sails spread; propelled by means of sails.

sail[2] /sāl/ *vi* to project. ◆ *n* projection. [OFr *saillir* to jut, from L *salīre* to leap]

saim (*Scot*) see **seam**[2].

saimiri /sī-mē'rē/ *n* a squirrel monkey. [Tupí *sai* monkey, and *miri* little]

sain /sān/ (*archaic*) *vt* to make the sign of the cross over; (by association with L *sānāre*) to heal. [OE *segnian*, from L *signāre*, from *signum* mark]

saine /sān/ a Spenserian form of the infinitive and the present indicative pl of **say**[1]; an editor's reading for **faine** (see **fain**[2]) (*Love's Labours Lost* III.1.77) taken as a *pap* of **say**[1] (*Shakesp*).

sainfoin /sān'foin/ *n* a leguminous plant, *Onobrychis viciaefolia*, used as fodder (also **saint'foin**). [Fr *sainfoin*, prob from *sain* wholesome, and *foin* hay, from L *sānum fēnum*]

saint /sānt/, when prefixed to a name *sint, snt*/ *adj* (or *n* in apposition) holy. ◆ *n* a canonized person, a person formally recognized by the Christian (*esp* RC) Church as having lived a life of holiness and exceptional virtue, and to whom the right to be venerated is therefore accorded; a person of outstanding virtue or kindness; an Israelite, a Christian, or one of the blessed dead (*Bible*); an angel (*Bible*, *Milton*); a member of various religious bodies, *esp* Puritans, as used of themselves or as a nickname; a sanctimonious person. ◆ *vt* to make a saint of; to hail as a saint. [Fr, from L *sanctus* holy].

■ **saint'dom** *n.* **saint'ed** *adj* made a saint, canonized; like a saint; sacred; gone to heaven. **saint'ess** *n* (*obs*). **saint'hood** *n.* **saint'ish** *adj.* **saint'ism** *n* the character or quality of a saint; sanctimoniousness. **saint'like** *adj.* **saint'liness** *n.* **saint'ling** *n.* **saint'ly** *adj* of, like, characteristic of, or befitting a saint. **saint'ship** *n.*

❑ **saint's day** *n* a day set apart for the commemoration of a particular saint. **St Agnes's Eve** *n* 20 January, when, according to tradition, having performed certain rites, one may dream of the person that will be one's husband or wife. **St Agnes's flower** *n* the snowflake (qv under **snow**[1]). **St Andrew's cross** *n* a cross in the form of the letter X; a white cross of this type on a blue background, as borne on the banner of Scotland. **St Andrew's Day** *n* 30 November. **St Anthony's cross** *n* the tau cross, a cross shaped like the Greek letter T. **St Anthony's fire** *n prob* an old name for ergotism; see under **Anthony**. **St Barbara's cress** *n* yellow rocket. **St Barnaby's thistle** *n* a knapweed flowering about the saint's day (11 June). **St Bernard's dog** or **St Bernard** *n* a breed of very large dog, named after the hospice of the Great St Bernard on the Swiss–Italian border, used, *esp* formerly, to rescue travellers lost in the snow. **St Crispin's Day** *n* a shoemakers' festival, 25 October. **St Cuthbert's beads**, **St Cuthbert's duck** see under **Cuthbert**. **St Dabeoc's heath** *n* a rare Irish shrub (genus *Daboecia*). **St David's Day** *n* 1 March. **St Elmo's fire** *n* an electrical charge forming a glow around a church spire, ship's mast, etc, a corposant. **St George's cross** *n* a red upright cross on a white background. **St George's Day** *n* 23 April. **St Hubert's disease** *n* another name for hydrophobia. **St Ignatius's bean** *n* the poisonous seed of a plant (*Strychnos ignatii*) related to nux vomica. **St James's** *n* the British royal court. **St John's bread** *n* another name for the carob bean. **St John's Day** *n* 27 December. **St Johnston's ribbon** or **tippet** *n* the hangman's rope (*St Johnston* or *St John's toun* being Perth, associated in the 18c with hangings). **St John's wort** *n* any of the plants of the *Hypericum* genus. **St Julien** *n* an esteemed red Bordeaux wine from the Médoc region. **St Leger** *n* a horse race run annually at Doncaster, so called since 1778 from Colonel *St Leger*. **St Luke's summer** *n* a spell of pleasant weather about the middle of October. **St Martin's evil** *n* drunkenness. **St Martin's summer** *n* a spell of mild, damp weather in late autumn. **St Nicholas's clerks** *n pl* thieves. **St Patrick's Day** *n* 17 March. **St Peter's fish** *n* a name applied to several fish, eg the dory and the tilapia. **St Peter's wort** *n* square-stalked St John's wort; extended to several other plants. **St Stephen's** *n* the Houses of Parliament. **St Stephen's Day** *n* 26 December. **St Swithin's Day** *n* 15 July. **St**

Tibb's (or **St Tib's**) **Eve** or **Tib(b)'s Eve** *n* never. **St Trinian** *adj* of, relating to or typical of St Trinian's; applied to or denoting unruly or riotous behaviour, exploits, or spectacularly untidy dress, *usu* of schoolgirls (*inf*). ◆ *n* a pupil of St Trinian's. **St Trinian's** *n* a fictitious girls' school created by the English cartoonist Ronald Searle (1920–2011) and popularized in humorous films. **St Valentine's Day** *n* 14 February (see also under **valentine**). **St Vitus's dance** *n* a non-technical name for **Sydenham's chorea**.

saintfoin see **sainfoin**.

saintpaulia /sānt-pö'li-ə/ *n* a tropical African flowering plant of the genus *Saintpaulia*, commonly grown as a pot plant, the African violet. [New L, from Baron Walter von *Saint Paul* (1860–1910), who discovered it]

Saint-Simonism /sānt- or sint-sī'mə-ni-zm/ *n* the socialist system of the French philosopher Comte de *Saint-Simon* (1760–1825).

■ **Saint-Simō'nian** *n* (also *adj*). **Saint-Simō'nianism** *n.* **Saint-Si'monist** *n.*

saique see **saic**.

sair /sār/ Scots form of **sore**[1], **savour**, **serve**.

saist (*Spenser* and *Milton*) same as **sayest** (see **say**[1]).

saith[1] /seth/ (*archaic*) 3rd *pers sing present indicative* of **say**[1].

saith[2] or **saithe** /sāth/ *n* another name for the coalfish. [ON *seithr*]

Saiva /shī'və, sī'/ or **Shaiva** /shī'/ *n* a member of a sect devoted to the Hindu god Siva.

■ **Sai'vism** or **Shai'vism** *n.* **Sai'vite** or **Shai'vite** *n.*

sajou /sä-zhoo' or -joo'/ or **sapajou** /sap'ə-joo/ *n* a capuchin or spider monkey. [Fr, from Tupí *sai* monkey, and augmentative -*uassu*]

Sakai /sä'kī/ *n* (*pl* **Sakai**) a group of forest tribes of Malaysia; an individual of this group; their language, of the Mon-Khmer group. ◆ *adj* of or relating to the Sakai or their language.

sake[1] /sāk/ *n* a cause; account, behalf; advantage, benefit; purpose, aim, object. [OE *sacu* strife, a lawsuit; Du *zaak*, Ger *Sache* ; OE *sacan* to strive, Gothic *sakan* ; cf **sac**[2], **sackless**, **seek**]

■ **for goodness** (or **heaven's, pete's**, etc) **sake** an expression of frustration, irritation, urgency, etc. **for old sake's sake** (*obs*) or **old time's sake** for the sake of old times or friendship, for auld lang syne. **for the sake of** for the purpose of; on account of.

sake[2] /sä'ki or sä'kē/ *n* a Japanese alcoholic drink made from fermented rice (also **saké** or **saki**). [Jap]

saker /sā'kər/ *n* a species of falcon (*Falco cherrug*) used in falconry; an obsolete small cannon. [Fr *sacre*, prob from Ar *saqr*]

■ **sa'keret** *n* the male saker.

saki[1] /sä'ki or -kē/ *n* a S American monkey of the genus *Pithecia* or *Chiropotes*, with a long bushy non-prehensile tail. [Fr, for Tupí *sai* or *saguin* ; cf **sai, saguin**]

saki[2] see **sake**[2].

sakieh, sakiyeh or **sakia** /sä'ki-yə, -ki-ə/ *n* a water wheel used in Middle Eastern countries. [Ar *sāqiyah*]

sakkos /sak'os/ *n* in the Eastern Church, a bishop's vestment like an alb or a dalmatic (also **sacc'os**). [Gr *sakkos* a bag]

saksaul same as **saxaul**.

Sakti /shäk'ti, shuk', säk'/ or **Shakti** /shäk', shuk'/ (*Hinduism*) *n* the feminine aspect of divine energy, *esp* as personified in the wife of Siva or other god. [Sans *śakti* divine energy]

■ **Sak'ta** or **Shak'ta** *n* a worshipper of the Sakti. **Sak'tism** or **Shak'tism** *n.*

sal[1] /sal/ (*chem* and *pharm*) *n* a salt. [L *sāl* salt]

❑ **sal alembroth** *n* (an alchemists' word of unknown origin) mercury ammonium chloride, also called **salt of wisdom**. **sal ammoniac** *n* ammonium chloride. **sal prunella** or **sal prunelle** *n* saltpetre cast in cakes. **sal volatile** /vol-at'i-li/ *n* ammonium carbonate, or a solution of it in alcohol and/or ammonia in water; smelling salts.

sal[2] /säl/ *n* a large N Indian tree, *Shorea robusta*, yielding valuable timber similar to teak. [Hindi *sāl*]

sal[3] /säl/ a Scot and N Eng form of **shall**.

sal[4] see **sial**.

salaam /sä-läm'/ *n* a word and gesture of salutation in the Middle East, chiefly among Muslims; obeisance; (in *pl*) greeting, compliments. ◆ *vi* to perform the salaam, a low bow with the palm of the right hand on the forehead. [Ar *salām* peace; cf Heb *shālōm*]

■ **salaam aleikum** peace be with you.

salable, salableness, salably see under **sale**[1].

salacious /sə-lā'shəs/ *adj* lustful; lecherous; arousing lustful or lecherous feelings. [L *salāx, -ācis*, from *salīre* to leap]

■ **salā'ciously** *adv.* **salā'ciousness** or **salacity** /-las'i-ti/ *n.*

salad /sal'əd/, also (*archaic*) **sallad** and **sallet** /sal'it/ *n* a cold dish of vegetables or herbs (either raw or pre-cooked), generally mixed with or without oil and vinegar or other dressing, sometimes including egg, meat, fish etc; a plant grown for or used in salads; a savoury seasoning (*obs*); a diverse or confused mixture. [Fr *salade*, from L *sāl* salt]

■ **sal'ading** *n* herbs and vegetables for salads.

❑ **salad bowl** *n*. **salad burnet** *n* the common burnet. **salad cream** *n* a type of bottled mayonnaise for dressing salad. **salad days** *n pl* one's youth, *esp* if carefree and showing inexperience. **salad dodger** *n* (*facetious*) a person with an unhealthy diet. **salad dressing** or **oil** *n* sauce, olive oil, etc used in dressing salads. **salad herb** *n*. **salad plant** *n*. **salad plate** *n*.

■ **fruit salad** see under **fruit**. **word salad** see under **word**.

salade same as **sallet**[1].

salade niçoise /*sa-lad nē-swäz'*/ *n* a cold dish consisting of salad vegetables, French beans, hard-boiled eggs, anchovies, olives and herbs. [Fr, salad of Nice]

Salafism /*sə-laf'izm*/ *n* a movement within Islam whose aim is to restore the purity of the faith in its early generations. [Ar *as-salaf as-saalih* pious predecessors]

■ **Salaf'i** or **Salaf'ist** *n* and *adj*.

salal or **sallal** /*sal'al*/ *n* a NW American ericaceous shrub (*Gaultheria shallon*). [Chinook Jargon]

❑ **salal berry** or **sallal berry** *n* its edible fruit.

salamander /*sal'ə-man-dər* or *-man'*/ *n* a tailed amphibian, closely related to the newts (genus *Salamandra* or related genera); (in ancient myth) a lizard-like monster supposed to inhabit fire and able to extinguish it by the chill of its body; (in medieval philosophy) an elemental spirit believed to live in fire; a person who survives exposure to fire unscathed (*fig*); a poker used red-hot for kindling fires; a hot metal plate for browning meat, etc; a portable stove, used during the construction of a building, in a greenhouse, etc; a residual deposit of metal or slag on a furnace wall. [Fr *salamandre*, from L *salamandra*, from Gr *salamandrā*; prob of Eastern origin]

■ **salaman'der-like** *adj* (also *adv*). **salaman'drian** or **salaman'drine** *adj*. **salaman'droid** *adj* (also *n*).

salami /*sə-lä'mi*/ *n* (*pl* **salamis**) a highly seasoned sausage, *usu* sliced very thinly. [Ital, *pl* of *salame*, from an assumed Vulgar L *sālāre* to salt]

❑ **salami strategy** or **tactics** *n* a policy of cutting away, one by one, undesirable elements, eg particular people from an organization. **salami technique** *n* (*esp comput*) a fraud involving the deduction of almost indiscernible sums of money from numerous and scattered transactions.

salamon see **salmon**[2].

salangane /*sal'ang-gän*/ *n* a swiftlet (genus *Collocalia*) that builds edible nests. [Tagálog *salangan*]

salary /*sal'ə-ri*/ *n* a periodical payment (*usu* made monthly) for one's (*usu* non-manual) labour. ◆ *vt* to pay a salary to. [OFr *salarie* (Fr *salaire*), from L *salārium* salt-money, from *sāl* salt]

■ **salariat** /*sə-lä'ri-ət*/ *n* the salary-earning class or body collectively. **sal'aried** *adj*.

❑ **sal'aryman** *n* (in Japan) an office worker.

salat /*sä-lät'*/ *n* a set of prayers performed by Muslims five times a day while facing towards Mecca. [Ar, *pl* of *ṣalāh* prayer]

sal Atticum /*sal at'i-kəm* or *säl at'i-kŭm*/ (*L*) *n* Attic salt (see under **Attic**).

salband /*säl'band* or *zäl'bänt*/ (*geol*) *n* a crust or coating of mineral. [Ger *Salband* selvage, from *Selb* self, and *Ende* end]

salbutamol /*sal-bū'tə-mol*/ *n* a bronchodilator drug, used in the treatment of bronchial asthma, emphysema, etc.

salchow /*sal'kō* or *-kov*/ (*ice skating*) *n* a jump in which the skater takes off from the inside back edge of one skate, spins in the air and lands on the outside back edge of the other skate. [Ulrich *Salchow* (1877–1949), Swedish skater]

sale[1] /*sāl*/ *n* an act or instance of selling; the exchange of anything for money; the power or opportunity of selling; demand, volume of selling; the offer of goods at reduced prices for a limited period; the offer of goods at public auction; the state of being on offer to buyers. ◆ *adj* intended for selling, in general, by auction, or *esp* at reduced prices. [Late OE *sala*, perh from ON *sala*]

■ **saleabil'ity** or **salabil'ity** *n*. **sale'able** or **sal'able** *adj* suitable for selling; in good demand. **sale'ableness** or **sal'ableness** *n*. **sale'ably** or **sal'ably** *adv*.

❑ **sale'-cat'alogue** *n*. **sale of work** *n* a sale of things made by members of a church congregation, club or association to raise money. **sale price** *n* the price asked at a sale. **sale'ring** *n* an enclosed area, often circular, at a market, where livestock for sale are paraded. **sale'room** or (*N Am*) **sales'room** *n* a room where goods for sale, *esp* at auction, are displayed. **sales'clerk** *n* (*N Am*) a sales assistant in a store or shop. **sales drive** *n* a special effort to increase sales, using a variety of techniques. **sales engineer** *n* a salesperson with technical knowledge of the company's product(s) or goods. **sales'man**,

sales'woman or **sales'person** *n* a person who sells goods, *esp* in a shop; a commercial traveller. **sales'manship** *n* the art of selling; skill in presenting wares in the most attractive light or in persuading purchasers to buy. **sales pitch** *n* sales talk, *esp* the individual technique used by a salesperson. **sales resistance** *n* unwillingness of potential customers to buy, or resistance to aggressive selling techniques. **sales talk** *n* persuasive talk designed to effect a sale. **sales tax** *n* (*esp N Am*) a tax levied on retail goods and services. **sale'yard** *n* (*Aust* and *NZ*) an enclosure in which livestock for auction are kept.

■ **forced sale** a sale compelled by a creditor. **sale or return** or **sale and return** an arrangement by which a retailer may return to the wholesaler any goods not sold.

sale[2] see **seal**[5].

salep /*sal'əp*/ *n* dried orchid tubers; a food or drug prepared from them. [Turk *sālep*, from Ar]

saleratus /*sal-ə-rā'təs*/ (*N Am*) *n* potassium or sodium bicarbonate, used in raising agents such as baking powder. [L *sāl aerātus* aerated salt]

Salesian /*sə-lē'zhən*/ *adj* of St Francis of *Sales* or his order of nuns, the Visitants. ◆ *n* a follower of St Francis; a member of his order of nuns.

salet see **sallet**[1].

salewd (*Spenser*) *pat* of **salue**.

salfern /*sal'fərn*/ *n* gromwell (*Lithospermum arvense*).

Salian[1] /*sā'li-ən*/ *adj* relating to a tribe of Franks who established themselves along the Yssel river in the 4c. ◆ *n* a member of this tribe. [L *Saliī* Salians]

■ **Salic** /*sal'ik* or *sā'lik*/ or **Salique** /*sal'ik* or *sa-lēk'*/ *adj*.

❑ **Salic law** *n* a law among the Salian Franks limiting the succession of certain lands to males; a law so named by extension, excluding women from the succession to the French crown, first invoked in 1316.

Salian[2] /*sā'li-ən*/ *adj* relating to the *Saliī*, or priests of Mars in ancient Rome.

saliaunce see under **salient**.

Salic see under **Salian**[1].

salic /*sal'ik* or *sā'lik*/ *adj* (of minerals) rich in silicon and aluminium. [*sil*icon and *al*uminium]

salicaceous /*sal-i-kā'shəs*/ *adj* of or belonging to the **Salicā'ceae**, a family of trees and shrubs *incl* the willows and poplars. [L *salix*, *salicis* a willow]

■ **sal'icet** /*-set*/ or **salicional** /*sə-lish'ə-nəl*/ *n* an organ stop with tones like those of willow pipes. **salicetum** /*-sē'təm*/ *n* (*pl* **salicē'tums** or **salicē'ta**) a thicket or plantation of willows. **sal'icin** or **sal'icine** /*-sin*/ *n* a bitter crystalline glucoside ($C_{13}H_{18}O_7$) obtained from willow-bark, etc and used medicinally as an analgesic, etc. **salicyl'amide** *n* an amide of salicylic acid, formerly used as an analgesic. **salicylate** /*sə-lis'i-lāt*/ *n* a salt of salicylic acid. ◆ *vt* to treat with salicylic acid. **salicylic** /*sal-i-sil'ik*/ *adj* (Gr *hȳlē* matter, material). **sal'icylism** *n* poisoning due to overdose of salicylate-containing drugs such as aspirin.

❑ **salicylic acid** *n* an acid ($C_7H_6O_3$) *orig* prepared from salicin, and used in the manufacture of aspirin, fungicides, etc.

saiices see **salix**.

salicornia /*sal-i-kör'ni-ə*/ *n* any plant, such as glasswort, of the *Salicornia* genus of goosefoots, found on salt marshes and pebbly seashores, having jointed cactus-like stems. [Perh L *sāl* salt, and *cornū* a horn]

salient /*sā'li-ənt* or *-lyənt*/ *adj* outstanding, prominent, striking; projecting outwards (*archit*); leaping or springing (now *usu* biol or heraldry). ◆ *n* an outward-pointing angle, *esp* of a fortification or line of defences. [L *saliēns*, *-entis*, *prp* of *salīre* to leap]

■ **sā'lience** (*Spenser* **saliaunce** onslaught) or **sā'liency** *n*. **salientian** /*-en'shyən*, *-shən*/ *n* and *adj* (an animal) of the order **Salien'tia**, amphibians *incl* frogs and toads. **sā'liently** *adv*.

saliferous /*sə-lif'ə-rəs*/ *adj* salt-bearing. [L *sāl*, *salis* salt, and *ferre* to bear]

salify /*sal'i-fī*/ *vt* (**sal'ifying**; **sal'ified**) to combine or impregnate with, or form into, a salt. [Fr *salifier*, from L *sāl*, *salis* salt, and *facere* to make]

■ **sal'ifiable** *adj*. **salificā'tion** *n*.

saligot /*sal'i-got*/ *n* another name for the water chestnut. [Fr]

salimeter same as **salinometer** (see under **saline**).

salina /*sə-lē'nə* or *-lī'*/ *n* a salt lagoon, lake, marsh, or spring. [Sp, from L *salīna* (in *pl* only), from *sāl* salt]

saline /*sā'līn* or *sal'īn*, also *sə-līn'*/ *adj* salt; salty; containing salt; of the nature of a salt; abounding in salt; of the salts of alkali metals and magnesium; adapted to an environment with salt. ◆ *n* /*sə-līn'*/, also *sā'līn*/ a salina; a salt; an effervescent laxative powder; a salt solution, *esp* (*med*) an isotonic solution containing sodium chloride used as a plasma substitute, etc. [L *salīnus*, cf **salina**]

■ **salinity** /sə-lin'i-ti/ *n*. **saliniza'tion** or **-s-** or **salinā'tion** *n* the accumulation of (too much) salt in soil, fresh water, etc, *esp* through flooding by seawater. **salinometer** /sal-i-nom'i-tər/ or **salim'eter** *n* a hydrometer for measuring the amount of salt in a solution.

Salique see under **Salian**[1].

Salish /sā'lish/ *n* a group of Native American language dialects of the Mosan phylum spoken in the NW USA and W Canada; (with *the*) the peoples speaking these dialects. ◆ *adj* (also **Sa'lishan**) of or relating to the Salish or their dialects.

saliva /sə-lī'və/ *n* a liquid secreted in the mouth to soften food and begin the process of digestion. [L *salīva*]

■ **salī'val** *adj* (*rare*). **salivary** /sə-lī'vər-i or *sal'i-*/ *adj* relating to, secreting, or conveying, saliva. **sal'ivate** *vi* to produce or discharge saliva, *esp* in excess, *usu* in eager anticipation of food (also *fig*). ◆ *vt* to cause to secrete excess of saliva. **saliva'tion** *n* flow of saliva, *esp* in excess, and in anticipation of (food, etc).
□ **salivary gland** *n* a saliva-secreting gland. **salivary gland chromosome** *n* a giant conspicuously banded chromosome found in the salivary glands of larvae of dipteran insects.

salix /sal'iks or sā'liks/ *n* (pl **salices** /sal'i-sēz or sā'/) any tree or plant of the willow genus *Salix*. [L *salix, -icis*]

Salk vaccine /sök, solk or sölk vak'sēn or *-sin*/ *n* the first vaccine developed against poliomyelitis, administered by injection. [Developed by Dr JE *Salk* (1914–95), US microbiologist, and others]

sallad see **salad**.

sallal see **salal**.

salle /sal/ (*Fr*) *n* a hall.

sallee or **sally** /sal'ē/ (*Aust*) *n* any of various species of acacia; a species of eucalyptus with pale-coloured bark, the snow gum. [From a native word, or **sally**[3]]

sallee-man or **sally-man** /sal'ē-man/ *n* a Moorish pirate ship (also **sall'ee-rover**; *obs*); a hydrozoan with a sail-like crest. [*Sallee*, on the coast of Morocco]

sallenders /sal'ən-dərz/ *n* a skin disease affecting the hocks of horses. [Cf Fr *solandre*]

sallet[1] or **salet** /sal'it/ *n* (in medieval armour) a light helmet extending over the back of the neck (also **salade** /sä-läd'/). [Fr *salade*; cf Ital *celata*; perh from L *galea caelāta* engraved helmet]

sallet[2] an archaic or dialect form of **salad**.

sallow[1] /sal'ō/ *adj* (*esp* of a person's skin) of a pale-yellowish colour. ◆ *vt* to make sallow. [OE *salo, salu*; cf OHGer *salo*]
■ **sall'owish** *adj*. **sall'owness** *n*. **sall'owy** *adj*.

sallow[2] /sal'ō/ *n* a willow, *esp* the broader-leaved kinds with comparatively brittle twigs, such as *Salix cinerea*, the common sallow (also (*Scot*) **sauch, saugh** /söhh/). [OE (Anglian) *salh*, late stem *salg-* (WSax *sealh, sēales*); cf Ger *Sal(weide)*, L *salix*]
■ **sall'owy** *adj*.
□ **sallow kitten** *n* a small puss moth whose larvae feed on sallow. **sall'ow-thorn** *n* sea-buckthorn.

sally[1] /sal'i/ *n* a sudden rushing forth of troops to attack besiegers; an outrush, a sortie; a going forth, excursion, outing, jaunt; a witty remark or retort; a projection; an angle cut into the end of a timber to allow it to rest on a cross-timber (*building*); a ship's leaping, bounding or swaying motion (*naut*). ◆ *vi* (**sall'ying; sall'ied**) (*archaic* or *facetious*; *usu* with *forth*) to rush out suddenly; to go or come forth, set off on an excursion, outing, etc; (of a ship) to sway, rock or bound (*naut*). ◆ *vt* (*naut*) to rock (a ship) by running from side to side to urge it on. [Fr *saillie*, from *saillir* (Ital *salire*), from L *salīre* to leap]
□ **sall'yport** *n* a gateway or opening for making a sally from a fortified place; a large port for the escape of the crew from a fireship.

sally[2] /sal'i/ (*bellringing*) *n* the raising of a bell by a pull of the rope; the woolly grip of a bell-rope. ◆ *vt* to bring into position of sally. [Perh from **sally**[1]]

sally[3] /sal'i/ a variant of **sallee** and of **sallow**[2].

Sally Army /sal'i är'mi/ (*inf*) *n* the Salvation Army.

Sally Lunn /sal'i lun/ *n* a sweet teacake, *usu* served hot with butter. [From a girl who sold them in the streets of Bath, c.1797]

sally-man see **sallee-man**.

sallyport see under **sally**[1].

salmagundi or **salmagundy** /sal-mə-gun'di/ *n* a dish of minced meat with eggs, anchovies, vinegar, pepper, etc; a medley, miscellany. [Fr *salmigondis*; origin obscure]

salmanazar or **salmanaser** /sal-ma-nā'zər/ (also with *cap*) *n* a large wine bottle, *usu* holding the equivalent of 12 standard bottles. [Allusion to Shalmaneser, king of Assyria, in Bible, 2 Kings 17.3]

salmi or **salmis** /sal'mē/ *n* (pl **salmis** /sal'mē/) a ragout, *esp* of previously cooked game. [Fr; perh from **salmagundi**, or from Ital *salame* sausage]

Salmo /sal'mō/ *n* the salmon and trout genus of fishes, giving name to the family **Salmonidae** /sal-mon'i-dē/. [L *salmō, -ōnis* salmon]
■ **sal'monid** *n*. **sal'monoid** *n* and *adj*.

salmon[1] /sam'ən/ *n* (pl **salmon** or (in referring to different kinds of salmon) **salmons**) a large, soft-finned fish (*Salmo salar*), with silvery sides, that ascends rivers to spawn and is highly prized as a food and game fish; extended to many closely related fishes, and to some that resemble it superficially in some respects; the flesh of any of these as food; the colour of salmon flesh, a pinkish orange. ◆ *adj* salmon-coloured. [OFr *saumon*, from L *salmō, -ōnis*, from *salīre* to leap]
■ **salm'onet** *n* a samlet. **sal'monid** *n* and *adj* (a fish) of the family Salmonidae, soft-finned fishes including the salmon, trout, etc. **sal'monoid** *adj* and *n* (of) any member of the suborder Salmonoidea. **salm'ony** *adj*.
□ **salm'onberry** *n* a salmon-coloured N American raspberry, *Rubus spectabilis*. **salmon coble** *n* a boat used on rivers and estuaries by salmon fishermen. **salm'on-colour** *n* an orange-pink. **salm'on-coloured** *adj*. **salmon disease** *n* a bacterial disease of salmon formerly attributed to a fungus (genus *Saprolegnia*). **salm'on-fisher** *n*. **salmon fishery** *n*. **salm'on-fishing** *n*. **salmon fly** *n* any artificial fly used in salmon-fishing. **salmon fry** *n* young salmon in their second year. **salmon ladder** *n* a series of steps built eg into the side of a river bed so as to permit salmon to pass upstream avoiding obstructions such as a dam, hydroelectric installation, etc. **salmon leap** *n* a waterfall which salmon ascend by leaping. **salmon leister** or **spear** *n* an instrument for spearing salmon. **salmon pink** *n*. **salmon-pink'** *adj*. **salmon trout** *n* a name applied to various forms of fish of the species *Salmo trutta*, resembling the salmon, *esp* the sea trout; applied to various kinds of trout and char (*US*).
■ **Burnett salmon** the Australian lungfish (from the Burnett River).

salmon[2] /sam'ən/ or **salamon** /sal'ə-mən/ (*obs*) *n* a word used in old oaths such as *by* (*the*) *salmon*, supposed to refer to the Mass. [Origin obscure]

salmonella /sal-mə-nel'ə/ *n* (pl **salmonell'as** or **salmonell'ae** /-ē/) a member of a large genus of rod-like bacteria (*Salmonella*), many of which are associated with poisoning by contaminated food; food poisoning caused by such bacteria (also called **salmonellō'sis**). [New L, from DE *Salmon* (1850–1914), US veterinarian]

salmonet, salmonid, salmonoid see under **salmon**[1].

Salomonic same as **Solomonic** (see under **Solomon**).

salon /sal'on or sal-ɔ̃/ *n* a drawing room; a reception room; a social gathering of distinguished people at the house of a lady of fashion, literary hostess, etc; a somewhat elegant shop or business establishment whose purpose is to provide cosmetic, hairdressing, etc services (eg *beauty salon*); a room or hall for the exhibiting of paintings, sculptures, etc; (with *cap*) a great annual exhibition of works by living artists in Paris. [Fr]

saloon /sə-loon'/ *n* a large public room (for billiards, for hairdressing, for dancing, for exhibitions, etc); a large public cabin or dining room for passengers on a ship, luxury train, etc; a saloon carriage; a saloon bar; an establishment where alcoholic drink is served (*N Am*); a motor car with two or four doors and enclosed compartment for driver and passengers, not an estate, coupé or sports model (also **saloon car**). [Fr *salon*]
□ **saloon bar** *n* an area in a public house, quieter and more comfortably furnished than the public bar, *usu* (*esp* formerly) separated from it. **saloon carriage** *n* a railway carriage with its interior open from end to end, not divided into compartments, etc. **saloon deck** *n* an upper deck on a ship reserved for saloon or first-class passengers. **saloon'-keeper** *n* (*N Am*) a publican. **saloon pistol** or **saloon rifle** *n* one for use in a shooting gallery.

saloop /sə-loop'/ *n* a hot drink made from an infusion of salep, later from sassafras, formerly used as a tonic. [**salep**]

salop a variant of **saloop**.
■ **salop'ian** *adj* (*Lamb*).

salopettes /sal-ə-pets'/ *n pl* a type of ski suit consisting of *usu* quilted trousers extending to the chest and held up with shoulder-straps. [Fr]

Salopian /sə-lō'pi-ən/ *adj* of or from Shropshire (formerly called *Salop*); of or from Shrewsbury School. ◆ *n* a native or inhabitant of Shropshire; a person educated at Shrewsbury School. [*Salop*, from Anglo-Fr *Sloppesberie*, from OE *Scrobbesbyrig*]

salpa /sal'pə/ *n* (pl **sal'pae** /-pē/ or **sal'pas**) any free-swimming planktonic tunicate or urochordate of the genus *Salpa*, having a transparent barrel-shaped body and lacking a larval stage (also **salp** /salp/). [L from Gr *salpē*, a kind of fish]
■ **sal'pian** *n* and *adj*. **sal'piform** *adj*.

salpicon /sal'pi-kon/ n a mixture of chopped meat, fish or vegetables, esp mushrooms or truffles, in a sauce, used in pâtés, or as fillings for pastries, etc. [Fr, from Sp salpicar to sprinkle with salt]

salpiglossis /sal-pi-glos'is/ n any plant of the genus Salpiglossis, some of which bear bright, trumpet-shaped flowers. [Gr salpinx a trumpet, and glōssa tongue]

salpinx /sal'pingks/ n the Eustachian tube, leading from the middle ear to the pharynx (anat); either of the Fallopian tubes, leading from the ovary to the uterus (anat); a trumpet or tuba of ancient Greece (hist). [Gr salpinx, -ingos a trumpet]
■ **salpingectomy** /-pin-jek'tə-mi/ n surgical removal of a Fallopian tube. **salpingian** /-pin'ji-ən/ adj. **salpingit'ic** adj of, or of the nature of, salpingitis. **salpingitis** /-jī'tis/ n inflammation of a tube, esp one or both Fallopian tubes.

salsa /sal'sə/ n the name given to a type of rhythmic Latin-American big-band music, with elements of jazz and rock; a dance performed to this music; a spicy sauce made with tomatoes, onions and chillis (Mex cookery). ◆ vi to dance the salsa. [Sp and Ital salsa sauce]
❑ **salsa verde** n Italian green sauce, made with anchovies, garlic, capers, oil and herbs.

salse /sals/ (geol) n a mud volcano. [Fr, from Ital salsa, prob from Sassuolo, name of one near Modena]

salsify /sal'si-fi, also sōl', -fī/ n the oyster plant or vegetable oyster, a purple-flowered European composite plant, Tragopogon porrifolius, cultivated for its edible root tasting like oysters, and its tender spring shoots boiled like asparagus. [Fr salsifis, prob from Ital sassefrica]
■ **black salsify** scorzonera, a plant like a dandelion, with an edible root.

salsolaceous /sal-sə-lā'shəs/ (bot) adj of, characteristic of, or relating to the saltwort genus Salsola of the goosefoot family. [Obs Ital salsola, dimin of salso, from L salsus salt (adj)]

salsuginous /sal-soo'ji-nəs/ adj salty, brackish; growing in salty soil. [L salsūgō, -inis saltness]

SALT /sölt or solt/ abbrev : Strategic Arms Limitation Talks or Treaty.

salt¹ /sölt or solt/ n chloride of sodium, occurring naturally as a mineral (rock salt) and in solution in seawater, saltwater springs, etc, used as a condiment and preservative; a saltcellar; a compound in which metal atoms or electropositive radicals replace one or more of the replaceable hydrogen atoms of an acid (chem); piquancy, liveliness; dry or pungent wit; a salt marsh or salting; an influx of salt water; a sailor, esp an experienced sailor; (in pl) smelling salts; (in pl) Epsom salts or other salt or mixture of salts used medicinally, esp as a purgative; money collected at montem (qv). ◆ adj containing salt; tasting of salt; seasoned or cured with salt; covered over with, or immersed in, salt water; growing in salt soil; inhabiting salt water; pungent; expensive, dear (archaic sl). ◆ vt to sprinkle, season, preserve or impregnate with salt; to season, or add piquancy to; to acclimatize; to assign an excessive value to or in (sl); to add gold, ore, etc to (a mine, etc) in order to give a false appearance of riches (mining sl); to immunize (an animal) by inoculation, etc (old). [OE (Anglian) salt (WSax sealt); cf Ger Salz, also L sāl, Gr hals]
■ **salt'ed** adj. **salt'er** n a person who makes or deals in salt or salted foods; a dealer in gums, dyes, etc, a drysalter. **salt'ily** adv. **saltine** /sōl-tēn'/ n (N Am) a crisp salted biscuit. **salt'iness** n. **salt'ing** n the act of preserving, seasoning, etc with salt; a meadow flooded by the tides (cf **ing**); the montem (qv) ceremony. **salt'ish** adj. **salt'ishly** adv. **salt'ishness** n. **salt'less** adj. **salt'ly** adv. **salt'ness** n. **salt'y** adj tasting of, containing, etc salt; piquant, racy, witty.
❑ **salt bath** n (metallurgy) a bath of molten salts in which steel is heated, hardened or tempered. **salt'box** n a box for holding salt, esp an old-fashioned one with a sloping clapper lid, once used as a percussion instrument in burlesque music; a house with one fewer storey at the back than at the front and a gable roof that slopes steeply at the rear (US). **salt'bush** n any shrubby plant (genus Atriplex) of the goosefoot family, of arid regions. **salt'-butter** adj (Shakesp) fed on nothing better than salt butter, gross. **salt cake** n impure sodium sulphate. **salt'cat** n a salt mixture given as a digestive to pigeons. **salt'cellar** n (OFr saliere, from L salārium, from sāl salt) a container for holding salt when used as a condiment; a depression behind the collarbone. **salt'chuck** n (Can) a body of salt water. **salt'-cote** n (obs) a building where salt is prepared for use as a condiment. **salt dome** or **plug** n (geol) a diapir formed by a column of rock salt forced up by pressure through rock stata. **salt eel** see under eel. **salt'-fat** or (non-standard) **salt'-foot** n formerly, a large saltcellar marking the class boundary at table; a pickling-tub. **salt'fish** n (W Indies) salted cod. **salt flat** n a stretch of flat, salt-covered land left by the evaporation of an area of salt water. **salt glaze** n a glaze produced on pottery by volatilization of common salt in the kiln; pottery produced with this glaze. **salt'-glazed** adj. **salt glazing** n. **salt horse** (also (naut) **salt'-junk**) n (sl) salt beef. **salt lake** n an inland lake of saline water. **salt lick** n a place to which animals go to obtain salt; a block of

salt, often also containing other essential minerals, given to domestic animals as a dietary supplement. **salt marsh** n land liable to be flooded with salt water. **salt'-mine** n a mine of rock salt. **salt'-money** n an allowance for salt; money collected at montem (qv). **salt of sorrel** n acid potassium oxalate, formerly used for removing ink-stains. **salt of tartar** n a commercial name for purified potassium carbonate. **salt of vitriol** n sulphate of zinc. **salt of wisdom** n sal alembroth. **salt of wormwood** n potassium carbonate. **salt pan** n a large basin for obtaining salt by evaporation; a natural depression in which salt accumulates or has accumulated by evaporation. **salt pit** n a pit for obtaining salt by evaporation. **salt plug** see **salt dome** above. **salt rheum** n a discharge of mucus from the nose (Shakesp); eczema or other skin eruption (N Am; old). **salt spoon** n. **salt spring** n a brine spring. **salt'water** adj of, containing or inhabiting salt water. **salt'wort** n a place where salt is refined. **salt'wort** n a fleshy, prickly plant of the genus Salsola, of the goosefoot family, eg S. kali found on sandy seashores; sometimes applied to the glasswort (genus Salicornia).
■ **above** (or **below**) **the salt** among those of high (or low) social class, the saltcellar formerly marking the boundary at table when all dined together. **lay, put** or **cast salt on someone's tail** to find or catch someone, from the jocularly recommended method of catching a bird. **like a dose of salts** (inf) very quickly. **rub salt in a wound** to aggravate someone's sorrow, shame, regret, etc. **salt away** to store away; to hoard, esp in a miserly way. **salt down** to preserve with salt; to lay by, store up. **salt of the earth** the choice few of the highest excellence (from Bible, Matthew 5.13). **salt out** to obtain as a precipitate by adding a salt. **take with a pinch** (or **grain**) **of salt** to believe (something or someone) only with great reservations. **worth one's salt** valuable, useful, orig worth the value of the salt one consumes.

salt² /sölt or solt/ (obs) n sexual desire, esp in bitches. ◆ adj in heat; salacious. [L saltus, -ūs leap]

salt³ /sölt or solt/ n see **sault**.

saltando /säl-tän'dō/ or **saltato** /-tä'tō/ adv and n arco saltando (qv). [Gerund and pap respectively of Ital saltare to jump, skip]

saltant /sal'tənt or söl'tənt/ adj (of an organism) resulting from or exhibiting saltation (biol); dancing, jumping (obs); salient (heraldry). ◆ n (biol) a changed or mutated form of an organism that has developed suddenly. [L saltāre, -ātum, intens of salīre to leap]
■ **sal'tate** vi to undergo saltation. **salta'tion** n an abrupt variation or mutation (biol); a leaping or jumping; the movement of a particle being transported by wind or water, resembling a series of leaps (geol). **salta'tionism** n the process or concept of saltation, specif the evolutionary theory that new species come about by saltation. **salta'tionist** n someone who supports saltationism as a theory. **saltato'rial, saltato'rious** or **sal'tatory** adj of or for leaping or jumping (biol); of or displaying saltation.

saltarello /sal-tə-rel'ō/ n (pl **saltarell'os** or **saltarell'i**) a lively Italian dance with a hop executed at the beginning of each measure; its music, in triple time. [Ital saltarello, Sp saltarelo, from L saltāre to dance]

saltate, etc see under **saltant**.

saltato see **saltando**.

saltern /sölt' or solt'ərn/ n a saltworks; a place where pools of sea water evaporate to produce a natural reserve of salt. [OE s(e)altern, from s(e)alt salt, and ærn house]

saltier¹ see **saltire**.

saltier² /söl'ti-ər/ n a word used in Shakespeare's Winter's Tale (IV.4.320) perhaps meant to mark a rustic confusion of satyr and saultier (jumper).

saltimbanco /sal-tim-bang'kō/ (obs) n (pl **saltimbanc'os**) a mountebank, a quack. [Ital, from saltare in banco to leap onto a bench, so as to harangue a crowd; see also **mountebank**]

saltimbocca /sal-tim-bok'ə/ n and adj (of) an Italian dish of rolled slices of veal and ham, with cheese or herbs. [Ital, literally, it leaps into the mouth]

saltire or **saltier** /söl' or sal'tīr/ n an armorial emblem in the form of a St Andrew's cross (heraldry); loosely, the national flag of Scotland, a white St Andrew's cross on a blue background. [OFr saultoir, sautoir, from LL saltātōrium a stirrup, from L saltāre to leap]
■ **sal'tirewise** adj.

salto /sal'tō or säl'tō/ n (pl **sal'tos**) a daring leap (also fig); a somersault (gym). ◆ vi (pat and pap **sal'toed**) to perform a salto. [Ital, a jump, leap; also salto mortale, literally, a mortal leap, a somersault]

saltpetre or (N Am) **saltpeter** /solt- or sölt-pē'tər/ n potassium nitrate. [OFr salpetre, from LL salpetra, prob for L sāl petrae salt of stone]
❑ **saltpe'treman** (hist) someone authorized to search for saltpetre; someone who prepares saltpetre. **saltpe'tre-paper** n touch paper.

■ words derived from main entry word; ❑ compound words; ■ idioms and phrasal verbs

■ **Chile saltpetre** or **cubic saltpetre** sodium nitrate. **Norway saltpetre** calcium nitrate.

saltus /sal'təs/ (*logic*) *n* (*pl* **saltuses**) a breach of continuity; a jump to a conclusion. [L, a leap, *pl* saltūs]

salubrious /sə-loo'bri-əs/ or -lū'/ *adj* health-giving, promoting wellbeing; loosely, pleasant, decent, respectable. [L salūbris, from salūs, salūtis health]
■ **salu'briously** *adv*. **salu'briousness** or **salu'brity** *n*.

salue /sa-loo' or -ū', also sal'/ (*obs*) *vt* (*pat* (*Spenser*) **salewd'**, also **sal'ued**) to salute. [Fr saluer, from L salutāre]

saluki /sə-loo'kē or -ge/ *n* a tall, slender, silky-haired breed of dog, *orig* from Arabia and Persia. [Ar seluqi]

salutary /sal'ū-t(ə-)ri/ *adj* promoting health or safety; wholesome; containing, bringing, etc a timely warning. [L salūtāris, from salūs health]
■ **sal'ūtarily** *adv*. **sal'ūtariness** *n*.

salute /sə-loot' or -lūt'/ *vt* to greet with words or (now *esp*) with a gesture or with a kiss; to honour formally by a discharge of cannon, striking of colours, or *esp* with any of various recognized gestures with the arm (*milit*); to pay tribute to; to affect, act upon (*Shakesp*). ◆ *vi* to perform the act of saluting, *esp* in the military manner. ◆ *n* the act or position of saluting; a greeting, *esp* in the form of a gesture or a kiss; a complimentary discharge of cannon, dipping of colours, presenting of arms, etc, eg to honour a person or occasion. [L salūtāre, -ātum (verb), and salūs, salūtis (noun), and partly through Fr salut]
■ **salutation** /sal-ū-tā'shən/ *n* the act of, or words used in, greeting; a formal visit (*esp Roman hist*); a quickening (of the blood), excitement (*Shakesp*); the Angelic Salutation (see **ave**). **salūtā'tional** *adj*. **salutatorian** /sə-loo-tə-tō'ri-ən or -tö'/ *n* in American colleges, the graduand who pronounces the address of welcome. **salu'tatorily** *adv*. **salu'tatory** *adj* of salutations. ◆ *n* an address of welcome, *esp* in American colleges; an audience chamber (*hist*). **salu'ter** *n* someone who salutes; in Spain, someone who professed to work miracles in the name of St Catherine (Sp saludador; *hist*).

salutiferous /sal-ū-tif'ə-rəs/ (*formal*) *adj* conducive to health or wellbeing. [L salūtifer, from salūs, salūtis health, and ferre to bring]

salvable, etc see under **salve²**.

Salvadorian /sal-və-dö'ri-ən/ or **Salvadoran** /-dö'rən/ *adj* of or relating to the Republic of *El Salvador* in Central America, or its inhabitants. ◆ *n* a native or citizen of El Salvador.

salvage¹ /sal'vij/ *n* the raising of sunken or wrecked ships; a reward paid by a ship's owner to those involved in its rescue, or the rescue of its cargo, from danger or loss; the rescue of property from fire or other peril; the saving of waste material for utilization; anything saved in any of these ways. ◆ *vt* to save from danger of loss or destruction; to manage to retain (one's pride, etc); to recover or save as salvage. [LL salvāgium, from salvāre to save]
■ **sal'vageable** *adj*. **sal'vager** *n*.
□ **salvage corps** *n* a body of people employed in salvage work.

salvage² /sal'vij/ (*Spenser, Shakesp*, etc) *n* and *adj* same as **savage**.

salvarsan /sal'vər-san/ or sal-vär'san/ *n* a compound of arsenic, first used by Paul Ehrlich (1854–1915) as a remedy for syphilis (since superseded by antibiotics). [L salvus safe, whole, and Ger Arsen arsenic]

salvation, etc see under **salve²**.

salve¹ /salv, säv/ *n* a soothing ointment; a remedy; anything to soothe the feelings or conscience. ◆ *vt* to anoint; to smear; to heal; to soothe. [OE s(e)alf ointment; Ger Salbe, Du zalf]
■ **salv'ing** *n* and *adj*.

salve² /salv/ *vt* to salvage; to save (an opinion) from objection (*obs*); to vindicate (*obs*); to preserve unhurt or undamaged (*obs*); to explain by hypothesis (*obs*); to explain, clear up, harmonize (*obs*). ◆ *n* a way out of a difficulty. [LL salvāre to save; partly back-formation from **salvage¹**]
■ **salvabil'ity** *n*. **salv'able** *adj*. **salvā'tion** *n* the act of saving; the means of preservation from any serious evil; the saving of humankind from the power and penalty of sin, the conferring of eternal happiness (*theol*). **Salvā'tionism** *n*. **Salvā'tionist** *n* a member of the Salvation Army. ◆ *adj* of or relating to the Salvation Army. **sal'vatory** *n* a repository for safe storage. ◆ *adj* (*rare*) saving. **salvif'ic** or **salvif'ical** *adj* having the purpose or intention of saving. **salvif'ically** *adv* (*obs*).
□ **Salvation Army** *n* an organization for the spread of religion among the poor, founded by William Booth in 1865.

salve³ /sal'vi, sal'wā/ *interj* hail (addressed to one person). ◆ *n* a greeting; a piece of church music beginning *Salve Regina* (*RC*). [L salvē, imperative of salvēre to be well]
■ **salvete** /sal-vē'tē, sal-wā'tā/ *interj* and *n* (addressed to more than one person).

salver¹ /sal'vər/ *n* a tray or (silver) plate on which anything is presented. [Sp salva, the precautionary tasting of food, as by a prince's taster, hence the tray on which it was presented to the prince, from salvar to save, from LL salvāre]
□ **sal'ver-shaped** or **sal'verform** *adj* (*bot*) (of a corolla) having a long tube with terminal petals spread out flat.

salver² see **salvor**.

salvia /sal'vi-ə/ *n* any labiate of the genus *Salvia*, *incl* sage. [L salvia sage]

salvific, etc see under **salve²**.

Salvinia /sal-vin'i-ə/ *n* a genus of water ferns, giving name to a family **Salvinia'ceae**. [Named after Antonio Maria *Salvini* (1653–1729), Italian Greek scholar]
■ **salvinia'ceous** *adj*.

Salvo /sal'vō/ (*Aust inf*) *n* (*pl* **Sal'vos**) a member of the Salvation Army.

salvo¹ /sal'vō/ *n* (*pl* **sal'vos** or **sal'voes**) a simultaneous discharge of artillery in salute or otherwise; a simultaneous discharge of bombs, etc; a sudden round of applause; a burst (of repeated criticisms, insults, attacks, etc). [Ital salva salute, from L salvē hail]

salvo² /sal'vō/ *n* (*pl* **sal'vos**) a saving clause, reservation (*esp law*); an excuse, pretext (*obs*); an expedient for saving appearances, avoiding offence, etc. [L salvō, ablative of salvus safe, (one's right, honour, etc) being saved]

salvo jure /sal'vō joo'rē, also sal'wō yoo're/ (*L*) without prejudice, keeping one's rights (literally, the right being saved).

sal volatile see under **sal¹**.

salvor or **salver** /sal'vər/ *n* a person who salvages.

salwar see **shalwar**.

SAM /sam/ *abbrev* : self-assembled monolayer, a monolayer that forms spontaneously when a solution is applied to a surface (*chem*); surface-to-air missile.

Sam. (*Bible*) *abbrev* : (the Books of) Samuel.

sam /sam/ (*Spenser*) *adv* together. [OE samen]

sama /sam'ə/ (*Jap*) *n* a title given to an exalted or distinguished person. Cf **san³**.

samadhi /sə-mä'di/ *n* a state of super-awareness brought about by profound yogic meditation, in which the yogi becomes one with the object of the meditation. [Hindi]

saman /sa-män'/ *n* the rain tree (qv) (also **samaan'**). [Am Sp samán, from Carib zamang]

samara /sam'ə-rə or sə-mä'rə/ *n* a dry one-seeded fruit, with a winglike appendage that facilitates distribution on air currents. [L samara, samera elm seed]
■ **sama'riform** *adj*.

Samaritan /sə-mar'i-tən/ *adj* of *Samaria*, in Palestine. ◆ *n* a native of Samaria; an adherent of the religion of Samaria, differing from Judaism in that only the Pentateuch is accepted as holy scripture, with Moses the sole prophet of God; the Aramaic dialect of Samaria; a good Samaritan; a member of a voluntary organization formed to help people who are distressed or despairing, *esp* by talking to them on the telephone. [L Samarītānus]
■ **Samar'itanism** *n*.
□ **Samaritan Pentateuch** *n* a recension of the Hebrew Pentateuch accepted by the Samaritans as alone canonical.
■ **good Samaritan** a person who charitably gives help to those in need (from Bible, Luke 10.30–37).

samarskite /sə-mär'skīt/ *n* a black mineral containing uranium. [Named in honour of Colonel *Samarski*, 19c Russian engineer]
■ **samarium** /sə-mä'ri-əm/ *n* a metallic element (symbol **Sm**; atomic no 62) observed spectroscopically in samarskite.

Sama-Veda or **Samaveda** /sä-mä-vā'dä/ (*Hinduism*) *n* the name of one of the four books of the Veda, containing ritual chants for sacrifices. [Sans Sāmaveda]

samba /sam'bə/ *n* a Brazilian dance in duple time with syncopation; a ballroom dance developed from it; music for either of these dances. ◆ *vi* to dance the samba. [Port]

sambal /säm'bäl/ *n* any of various foods served with curries in Malaysia and Indonesia, eg peppers, pickles, salt fish, coconut, etc. [Malay]

sambar or **sambur** /sam'bər/ *n* a large deer, *Cervus unicolor*, of S Asia, Indonesia and China. [Hindi sābar]

sambo¹ /sam'bō/ (*offensive*) *n* (*pl* **sam'bos**) the offspring of a black person and a Native American or mulatto; a black person, *esp* a man, sometimes used as a form of address (*sl*). [Sp zambo, said to be from L scambus, from Gr skambos, bow-legged; perh partly Fulah sambo uncle]

sambo² /sam'bō/ n a form of wrestling using judo techniques. [Russ *samozashchita bez oruzhiya* self-defence without weapons]

Sam Browne /sam brown/ n a military or police officer's belt with a shoulder strap. [General Sir Samuel James *Browne* (1824–1901), who invented it]

sambuca /sam-bū'kə, -bū' or -boo'/ n an ancient musical instrument like a harp; an Italian liquorice-flavoured liqueur made from aniseed. [L *sambūca*, from Gr *sambȳkē*, prob an Asiatic word; cf Aramaic *sabbekā*]

sambur same as **sambar**.

same /sām/ adj identical (commonly with *as*, or a relative clause introduced by *that*; also with *with*); not different; unchanged; unvaried; (*esp* with *the*) mentioned before. ◆ *pronoun* (*inf*) the aforesaid, it, them, they, etc. ◆ n (*rare*) an identical thing. [OE *same* (only in phrase *swā same* likewise); Gothic *sama*; L *similis* like, Gr *homos*]
■ **same'ly** adj unvaried. **same'ness** n being the same; tedious monotony. **sā'mey** adj (*inf*) (boringly) alike; monotonous. **sā'meyness** n.
❑ **same'-sex** adj denoting relations between people of the same sex; homosexual.
■ **all** (or **just**) **the same** for all that, nevertheless. **at the same time** simultaneously; notwithstanding. **same here** (*inf*) me too. **the same** the same thing or person; the aforesaid or aforementioned; in the same way.

samekh /sä'mək or sam'ehh/ n the fifteenth letter of the Hebrew alphabet. [Heb]

samel /sam'l/ adj (of a brick, tile, etc) underburnt. [Appar OE pfx *sam-* half, and *æled* burned]

samen /sā'mən/ an obsolete Scots form of **same**.

samey see under **same**.

samfoo or **samfu** /sam'foo/ n an outfit worn by Chinese women, consisting of a jacket and trousers. [Cantonese]

Sami see **Saam**.

Samian /sā'mi-ən/ adj of the Greek island of *Samos*. ◆ n a native of Samos (also **Sa'miot** or **Sa'miote**).
❑ **Samian earth** n an argillaceous astringent soil. **Samian letter** n the Pythagorean letter. **Samian stone** n a goldsmiths' polishing stone. **Samian ware** n brick-red or black earthenware pottery with a highly-polished surface, produced in Italy in 1c BC; a later imitation made in Roman Gaul and elsewhere in the Roman Empire.

samiel /sā'mi-əl/ n a hot desert wind, the simoom. [Ar *samm* poison, and Turk *yel* wind]

Samiot, Samiote see **Samian**.

samisen /sam'i-sen/ or **shamisen** /sham'/ n a Japanese guitar-like instrument with three strings. [Jap]

samite /sam'īt/ n a kind of heavy silk fabric, often interwoven with gold or silver threads, used for clothing in medieval times. [OFr *samit*, from LL *examitum*, from Gr *hexamiton*, from *hex* six, and *mitos* thread]

samiti /sam'i-ti/ n (in India) an organization or committee of workers, *usu* involved in political activity. [Hindi]

samizdat /sam'iz-dat/ n in the former Soviet Union, the clandestine or illegal printing and distribution of underground literature, *usu* expressing views contrary to those endorsed by the state (also *adj*). [Russ *sam* self, and *izdatelstvo* publishing]

samlet /sam'lit/ n a young salmon. [**salmon¹**, and **-let**]

samlor /sam'lör/ or -*lōr*/ n a three-wheeled vehicle common in Thailand, *usu* motorized and used as a taxi. [Thai]

Sammy /sam'i/ n a noodle (*sl*); an American expeditionary soldier (*milit sl*; from *Uncle Sam*). [*Samuel*]

Samnite /sam'nīt/ n a member of an ancient people of central Italy, thought to be a branch of the Sabines, frequently in conflict with the Romans; their language; a Roman gladiator armed in the style of the Samnites. ◆ adj of or relating to the Samnites or their language. [L *Samnīs, -ītis*]

samnitis /sam-nī'tis/ (*Spenser*) n an unknown poisonous plant.

Samoan /sə-mō'ən or sä-/ adj of or relating to the state of *Samoa* in the SW Pacific, its people or its language. ◆ n a native or citizen of Samoa; the language of Samoa.

Samoed see **Samoyed**.

samosa /sa-mō'sə/ n (pl **samo'sas** or **samo'sa**) a small, fried, triangular, pastry turnover stuffed with spiced vegetables or meat, an Indian savoury. [Hindi]

samovar /sam'ə-vär or -vär'/ n a Russian metal urn for boiling water for making tea, etc, often elaborately decorated, traditionally heated by a central charcoal-filled pipe. [Russ *samovar*, literally, self-boiler]

Samoyed /sam-ō-yed' or sam'/ n a member of a Ugrian people of NW Siberia; their Ural-Altaic language; /sa-moi'ed/ a breed of Siberian dog with a thick white coat and curled tail. ◆ adj of or relating to the Samoyeds or their language (also (*Milton*) **Sam'oed**). [Russ *Samoyed*]
■ **Samoyed'ic** adj.

samp /samp/ (*N Am* and *S Afr*) n a coarsely ground maize; porridge made from it. [From Narraganset *nasaump*]

sampan /sam'pan/ n in E Asia, a boat propelled by a sail or oar(s) (also **san'pan**). [Chin *sān* three, and *băn* board]

samphire /sam'fīr/ or **sampire** /-pīr/ n an umbelliferous plant (*Crithmum maritimum*) which grows on sea-cliffs; extended to other plants, eg *Inula crithmoides*, a plant related to elecampane (*golden samphire*), to glasswort (*marsh samphire*), and to saltwort (*prickly samphire*). [Fr (*herbe de*) *Saint Pierre* Saint Peter('s herb)]

sampi /sam'pī, sam'pi or -pē/ n the supposed name of a Greek numerical character, τ, , or , representing 900 and *perh orig* the same as the letter san. [Gr *sampī*]

sampire see **samphire**.

sample /säm'pl/ n a specimen, a small portion to show the quality or nature of the whole; a digitally recorded sound that has been programmed into a synthesizer; an example for imitation (*Spenser, Shakesp*) or (*obs*) warning. ◆ adj serving as a sample. ◆ vt to take, try or offer, a sample or samples of; to match (*obs*); (in popular music) to mix (a short extract) from one recording into a different backing track; to record (a sound) and program it into a synthesizer which can then reproduce it at the desired pitch. [ME *essample*; see **example**]
■ **sam'pler** n a collection of samples; a person or device that takes and tests samples; the equipment that samples sound. **sam'pling** n the taking, testing, etc of a sample; the examination and analysis of data obtained from a random group in order to deduce information about the population as a whole; the mixing of short extracts from previous sound recordings into a different backing track.
❑ **sample space** n (*stats*) the set of all possible outcomes of an experiment. **sampling error** n (*stats*) variation due to a sample group necessarily giving only incomplete information about the whole population. **sampling frame** n (*stats*) a list of the items or people from which a sample is taken.

sampler /säm'plər/ n an exemplar, type, pattern (*obs*); a test-piece of embroidery, commonly including an alphabet, with figures, names, etc. [OFr *essemplaire*, from L *exemplar*; see **exemplar**]
■ **sam'plery** n.
❑ **sam'pler-work** n.

samsara /səm-sä'rə/ n the never-ending cycle of birth and death and rebirth (*Hinduism*); the passage of a person's soul into another body or state (*Buddhism*). [Sans *saṁsāra* passing through]
■ **samsa'ric** adj.

samshoo or **samshu** /sam'shoo/ n a Chinese alcoholic drink made from fermented rice. [Pidgin; origin doubtful]

Samson /sam's(ə)n/ n an exceptionally strong man (from the biblical character of Judges 13–16).
❑ **Samson's post** n a strong post on a ship; a kind of mousetrap.

Samsonite® /sam'sə-nīt/ n a kind of strong composite material, used to make luggage, etc.

samurai /sam'ŭ-rī or -ū-rī/ (*Jap hist*) n (pl **sam'urai**) a military retainer of a feudal Japanese nobleman; a member of the military caste in feudal Japan. [Jap, from *samurau* to attend (one's lord)]

San /san/ n (pl **San**) (also **Bushman**) a member of an almost-extinct nomadic race of huntsmen in S Africa; the group of Khoisan languages spoken by this people. [Nama (a Khoisan language) *san* aboriginals]

san¹ /san/ (*old inf*) n a sanatorium.

san² /san/ n a discarded letter of the Greek alphabet (Ϲ) *perh orig* the same as sampi. [Doric Gr *san* sigma]

san³ /san, sän or sun/ n a Japanese title or form of address equivalent to Mr or Mrs, placed after the name.

sanative /san'ə-tiv/ adj healing. [L *sānāre, -ātum* to heal]
■ **sanatō'rium** or (imitation Latin; *esp N Am*) **sanitā'rium** n (pl **sanatō'riums** or **sanatō'ria**) a hospital for convalescents and the chronically ill, *orig esp* for people suffering from tuberculosis; a health farm, health resort or health station; a ward or building for the isolation and treatment of sick pupils at a boarding school, etc. **san'atory** adj healing; of healing.

sanbenito /san-be-nē'tō/ n (pl **sanbeni'tos**) a garment, either yellow with a red cross worn by penitents in the Inquisition, or black with painted flames, devils, etc worn by impenitents at an auto-da-fé. [Sp *San Benito* St Benedict, from its resemblance to St Benedict's scapular]

sancai /san'sī/ n in Chinese ceramics, a three-colour glaze. [Chin *sān* three, and *căi* colour]

Sancerre /sä-ser'/ n a white wine produced around *Sancerre* in the Loire valley.

sancho or **sanko** /sang'kō/ n (pl **san'chos** or **san'kos**) a W African guitar. [Ashanti *osanku*]

sanctify /sangk'ti-fī/ vt (**sanc'tifying**; **sanc'tified**) to make, declare, consider or show to be, sacred or holy; to set apart for sacred use; to free from sin or evil; to consecrate, bless; to invest with sacredness, blessedness or holiness; to sanction (*obs*). [Fr *sanctifier*, from L *sanctificāre*, from *sanctus* holy, and *facere* to make]
■ **sanctifi'able** *adj*. **sanctificā'tion** n. **sanc'tified** *adj* made holy. **sanc'tifiedly** /-fī-id-li/ *adv*. **sanc'tifier** /-fī-ər/ n a person or thing that sanctifies; (*usu* with *cap*) the Holy Spirit. **sanc'tifying** n and *adj*. **sanc'tifyingly** *adv*.

sanctimony /sangk'ti-mə-ni/ n outward, affected, or simulated holiness; holiness (*obs*). [L *sanctimōnia*, from *sanctus*]
■ **sanctimonious** /-mō'ni-əs/ *adj* giving the appearance of holiness, *esp* hypocritically; holy (*obs*). **sanctimō'niously** *adv*. **sanctimō'niousness** n.

sanction /sangk'shən/ n the act of ratifying, or giving permission or authority; support; official permission, authority; motive, rationale for obedience to any moral or religious law (*ethics*); a penalty or reward expressly attached to non-observance or observance of a law or treaty (*law*); a military or economic measure taken by one country against another as a means of coercion (*politics*). ◆ vt to give validity to; to authorize; to countenance, permit; to penalize, *esp* for failing to observe a law or treaty. [L *sanctiō*, *-ōnis*, from *sancīre*, *sanctum* to ratify]
■ **sanc'tionable** *adj*. **sanctioneer'** n a person who advocates (*esp* political) sanctions.
❑ **sanc'tions-busting** n the breaching (*usu* by commercial concerns) of economic sanctions imposed on a country.

sanctitude /sangk'ti-tūd/ n saintliness. [L *sanctitūdō*, *-inis*]

sanctity /sangk'ti-ti/ n the quality of being sacred or holy; purity; godliness; inviolability; saintship; (in *pl*) holy feelings, obligations, or objects. [L *sanctitās*, *-ātis* sanctity]

sanctuary /sangk'tū-ə-ri or sangk'chū-ri, *-chə-ri/ n a holy place; a place of worship; the most holy part of a temple, church, etc; the chancel; a place affording immunity from arrest, persecution, etc; the privilege of refuge in such a place; a place of refuge or private retreat; a nature, animal, or plant reserve. [L *sanctuārium*]
■ **sanc'tuarize** or **-ise** vt to afford sanctuary to.

sanctum /sangk'təm/ n (*esp* in the phrase *inner sanctum*) a sacred place; a (very) private room. [L, from *sanctus* holy]
❑ **sanctum sanctorum** n the holy of holies, the inner chamber of the Jewish tabernacle; any specially reserved retreat or room (*inf*).

Sanctus /sangk'təs/ n the hymn *Holy, holy, holy* (from the Bible, Isaiah 6); music for it. [L]
❑ **sanctus bell** n a bell rung at the singing of the Sanctus; a small bell rung to call attention to more solemn parts of the Mass (*RC church*).

sand /sand/ n a mass of rounded grains of rock, *esp* quartz; (in *pl*) a tract covered with this, as on a seashore or desert; (in *pl*) sandstones; (in *pl*) moments of time, from the use of the grains in an hourglass; firmness of character, grit (*N Am inf*); a light yellowish-brown colour. ◆ *adj* made of sand; of the colour of sand. ◆ vt to sprinkle, cover or mix with sand; to smooth or polish with abrasive material, *esp* sandpaper. [OE *sand*; Du *zand*, Ger *Sand*, ON *sandr*]
■ **sand'ed** *adj* sprinkled, covered, or mixed with sand; smoothed or polished with sandpaper, etc; yellow (*Shakesp*). **sand'er** n a tool (*esp* power-driven) with an abrasive surface, or with a pad to which sandpaper, etc can be fitted, used to sand wood, etc. **sand'iness** n sandy quality, *esp* in colour. **sand'ing** n. **sand'-like** *adj*. **sand'ling** n the launce or sand eel. **sand'y** *adj* consisting of, covered with, containing, or like sand; measured by sand (*Shakesp*); coloured like sand, yellowish-beige. **sand'yish** *adj*.
❑ **sand'bag** n a bag of sand or earth, used *esp* to protect against bomb blasts, floods, etc; a small bag of sand, etc, used as a cosh; an engraver's leather cushion. ◆ vt (*pat* **sand'bagged**) to provide with sandbags; to attack with a sandbag; to attack unexpectedly and with force; to obstruct or outmanoeuvre. **sand'bagger** n. **sand'bank** n a bank of sand in a river, river mouth, etc, often above water at low tide. **sand bar** n a long sandbank in a river or the sea. **sand bath** n a bath in sand; a vessel for heating without direct exposure to the source of heat. **sand bed** n a layer of sand, *esp* one used in founding or moulding; a toper (*Scot*). **sand'-binder** n a plant whose roots or rootstocks fix shifting sands. **sand'blast** n a sand-laden wind; sand blown by a blast of air or steam under pressure for glass-engraving, finishing metal surfaces, cleaning stone and metal surfaces, etc (also vt). **sand'blaster** n. **sand'blasting** n. **sand'-blind** *adj* see separate entry. **sand blow** n (*geol*) the removal of large amounts of sand from a place by the wind. **sand'box** n a box for sand, eg for sprinkling on railway lines or roads; a sandpit; the explosive capsule of a tropical American tree (**sandbox tree**, *Hura crepitans*) of the spurge family, formerly used to sprinkle sand on wet ink. **sand'boy** n a boy selling

sand, proverbially happy. **sand break** n a barrier to prevent sand being blown into crops, etc. **sand bunker** n. **sand'-cast** vt to cast in a mould of sand. **sand'-casting** n. **sand'castle** n a model of a castle made *esp* by children at play on a beach or in a sandpit. **sand crack** n a crack in a horse's hoof, often causing lameness. **sand dab** n any of various kinds of small Pacific flatfishes often eaten as food. **sand dance** n a dance performed on a sanded surface. **sand'-dart** n a British noctuid moth. **sand'-devil** n a small whirlwind. **sand dollar** n a flat sea urchin of shallow coastal waters. **sand'-dune** n a ridge of loose sand drifted by the wind. **sand eel** or **sand lance** n the launce. **sand'-flag** n a fissile sandstone. **sand flea** n the chigoe or jigger; a sandhopper. **sand'fly** n a small biting midge (genus *Simulium*); a small moth-like midge (*Phlebotomus papatasii*) that transmits **sandfly fever**, an influenza-like viral infection. **sand'glass** n a glass instrument, eg an hourglass, for measuring time by the running out of sand. **sand grain** n. **sand grass** n any grass that grows on sand. **sand'groper** n (*Aust*) a pioneer at the time of the gold rush; a W Australian (*joc*). **sand grouse** n any bird of the genera *Pterocles* and *Syrrhaptes*, with long pointed wings, once classified as grouse because of their feathered legs but now considered as a suborder (Pterocletes) related to pigeons. **sand'heap** n. **sand'hill** n. **sand'hog** n (*N Am sl*) a person who works on underground or underwater construction projects in an enclosed work area supplied with compressed air. **sand'hopper** n an amphipod crustacean (*Talitrus, Orchestia*, etc) of the seashore and tidal estuaries that jumps by suddenly straightening its bent body. **sand iron** n another name for a sand wedge. **sand lance** n the sand eel or launce. **sand'-lark** n a name applied to various small shore birds; a sandpiper. **sand leek** n the rocambole. **sand lizard** n an oviparous lizard (*Lacerta agilis*) of Europe and S England. **sand'man** n (with *the*) a fairy who supposedly puts children to sleep at bedtime by sprinkling sand on their eyes. **sand martin** n a small European bird, *Riparia riparia*, of the martin family that nests in tunnels hollowed out of sandy banks. **sand mason** n a tube worm that makes its tube out of sand. **sand mole** n an African mole-rat, *Bathyergus*. **sand painting** n the making of designs with coloured sand, as in various Native American ceremonies. **sand'paper** n the popular term for glasspaper, a stiff paper coated with powdered glass, used as an abrasive; an early form of glasspaper, coated with sand. ◆ vt to smooth or polish with sandpaper. **sand'papery** *adj*. **sand'-peep** n (*US*) any small sandpiper. **sand pipe** n a tubular hollow in chalk, *usu* filled with clay, sand, etc from above. **sand'piper** n the name for a large number of birds of the Scolopacidae family of ground-dwelling, wading birds intermediate between plovers and snipe, frequenting sandy shores and riverbanks and uttering a clear piping note. **sand'pit** n a place from which sand is dug; an enclosure filled with sand for children to play in. **sand plough** n a vehicle like a snow plough, for clearing roads, railway lines, etc of sand. **sand pride** n a small river lamprey. **sand'pump** n a pump for raising wet sand or mud. **sand saucer** n the egg mass of certain sea snails. **sand'-screw** n a burrowing amphipod (from its wriggling movements). **sand'shoe** n a shoe for walking or playing on the sands in, *usu* with a canvas upper and rubber sole, a plimsoll. **sand'-skipper** n a sandhopper. **sand'-snake** n a short-tailed, boa-like genus (*Eryx*) of Old World snakes. **sand sole** see **lemon**². **sand'spout** n a moving pillar of sand drawn up by a whirlwind. **sand'-star** n an ophiurid, *esp* of the short-armed kind, such as Ophiura. **sand'stone** n a rock formed of compacted and hardened sand. **sand'storm** n a storm of wind carrying along clouds of sand. **sand'sucker** n a ship or other device that clears blockages of sand; a European flounder. **sand table** n a tray for moulding sand on or for demonstration of military tactics; an inclined trough for separating heavier particles from a flow of liquid, as in ore-dressing, paper-making (also **sand trap**). **sand'-thrower** n a tool for throwing sand on newly sized or painted surfaces. **sand trap** n a bunker on a golf course; a sand table. **sand wasp** n a solitary burrowing insect of several families related to the true wasps. **sand wedge** n a golf club specially designed to hit the ball out of bunkers. **sand'worm** n the lugworm or other worm that lives on the sand. **sand'wort** n any species of *Arenaria*, plants related to the chickweed. **sand yacht**, **sand'-yachting** see under **yacht**. **sandy blight** n (*Aust*) any of various eye infections. **sand'y-lav'erock** n (*Scot*) a sand-lark.

sandal¹ /san'dl/ n a type of footwear with an openwork upper, or consisting of a sole bound to the foot by straps; an ornate shoe or slipper; a strap for tying round a shoe; a lightweight rubber overshoe. [L *sandalium*, from Gr *sandalion*, dimin of *sandalon* sandal]
■ **san'dalled** *adj* wearing or fastened with sandals.
❑ **sandal shoon** n pl (*archaic*) sandals.

sandal² /san'dl/ or **sandalwood** /-wŭd/ n a compact and fine-grained very fragrant Indian wood; the parasitic tree yielding it, *Santalum album* (**white sandalwood**), or other species; extended to other woods, such as red sanders and Barbados pride (genus *Adenanthera*), both called **red sandalwood**. [LL *santalum*, from Gr *sandanon*, from Sans *candana*, of Dravidian origin]

sandal³ /san'dal/ n a long narrow N African boat. [Turk, Pers, and Ar]

sandarach or **sandarac** /san'də-rak/ n arsenic monosulphide, realgar; the resin (in full **gum sandarach** or **sandarac resin**) of the Moroccan **sandarach tree** (*Collitris quadrivalvis*) powdered to form pounce and used in making varnish. [L *sandaraca*, from Gr *sandarakē*, -*chē*]

sand-blind /sand'blīnd/ adj half-blind. [Prob OE pfx *sam-* half, and **blind**, affected by **sand**]

Sandemanian /san-di-mā'ni-ən/ n a follower of Robert *Sandeman* (1718–71), leader of a religious sect developed from the Glassites (also *adj*).

sander¹ see **zander**.

sander² see under **sand**.

sanderling /san'dər-ling/ n a species of sandpiper (*Crocethia alba*), without a hind toe. [Appar from **sand**]

sanders /san'- or sän'dərz/ or **sanderswood** /-wŭd/ n sandalwood, *esp* red sandalwood (**red sanders**; see under **red**¹). [OFr *sandre*, variant of *sandal*, *santal* sandalwood]

sandhi /sän'dē/ n (*linguistics*) modification of the sound of a word or affix caused by the context in which it is uttered. [Sans *saṃdhi* placing together]

Sandinista /san-di-nē'stə/ n a member of the left-wing revolutionary movement in Nicaragua which overthrew President Somoza in 1979. [Augusto César *Sandino* (murdered in 1933), Nicaraguan rebel general]
■ **Sandinismo** /-nēz'mō/ n the beliefs and practices of the Sandinistas.

sandiver /san'di-vər/ n glass-gall, a scum formed on molten glass. [OFr *suin de verre*, literally, exudation of glass]

S & L *abbrev*: savings and loan (association).

sandling see under **sand**.

S & M (*inf*) *abbrev*: sadomasochistic (practices).

S and T *abbrev*: Signalling and Telecommunications.

sandwich /sand'wich, -wij/ n any sort of food between two slices of bread, said to be named after the fourth Earl of *Sandwich* (1718–92), who ate a snack of this kind in order not to have to leave the gaming-table; anything in a similar arrangement. ◆ vt to lay or place between two layers; to fit tightly or squeeze between two others or two of another kind; to intercalate. ◆ adj of the nature of, relating to or resembling, a sandwich or sandwich course.
□ **sandwich boards** n pl a pair of advertising placards worn over the chest and back on shoulder straps by a person employed to walk the streets. **sandwich construction** n (*aeronautics*) structural material, consisting of two thin skins either side of a thick core, having an exceptionally high stiffness/weight ratio. **sandwich course** n an educational course consisting of alternating periods of study and paid employment. **sandwich man** n a man who carries a pair of sandwich boards (qv above). **sandwich technique** n (*immunol*) a technique for the detection of antibody in histological preparations, involving the sandwiching of an antigen layer between the preparation and a layer of labelled antibody. **sandwich tern** n a European tern, *Sterna sandvicensis*.

Sandy /san'di/ (*obs*) n a Scot. [From *Alexander*]

sane /sān/ adj sound in mind; rational; sound in health (*rare*); sensible, reasonable. [L *sānus*]
■ **sane'ly** adv. **sane'ness** n.

Sanforized® /san'fə-rīzd/ adj (of cotton or linen fabrics) treated by a mechanical process that compresses the fibres to ensure against further shrinking. [*Sanford* L Cluett (1874–1968), US inventor of the process]

sang¹ /sang/ pat of **sing**¹. n a Scots form of **song**¹.

sang² /säng/ n a Chinese organ played by mouth. [Chin *shēng*]

sang³ /sang or (*heraldry*) sä/ n blood (*Scot*; *heraldry*); anthrax (*vet*). [Fr, blood]

sangar or **sungar** /sung'gər/ n a stone breastwork; a lookout post. [Pashto *sangar*]

sangaree /sang-gə-rē'/ n a West Indian drink of diluted and sweetened wine, similar to sangria. [Sp *sangría*]

sang-de-boeuf /sä-də-bœf'/ n a deep red colour, as found on old Chinese porcelain. [Fr, literally, ox-blood]

sangeet /san-gēt'/ n (in Indian theatre) a light-hearted musical drama; a celebration held shortly before a Hindu wedding. [Hindi, music]

sangfroid /sä-frwä'/ n coolness, composure, self-possession. [Fr, literally, cold blood]

sangha /sung'gə/ n the Buddhist community; the Buddhist monastic order. [Sans *saṃgha* community]

sangiovese /san-jə-vā'zē/ n a type of black grape grown *esp* in central Italy; a red wine produced from this grape. [Ital, from L *sanguis Jovis* blood of Jupiter]

sanglier /sang'gli-ər/ (*obs* and *heraldry*) n a wild boar. [Fr, from L *singulāris* solitary]

sangoma /sang-gom'ə/ (*S Afr*) n a witch doctor. [Zulu *isangoma*]

Sangraal, Sangrail or **Sangreal** /sang-grāl', sang'grāl or san-/ n the holy grail (see **grail**¹). [**saint** and **grail**¹]

Sangrado /sang-grä'dō or san-/ n (pl **Sangra'does**) a bloodletter. [After Dr *Sangrado* in Alain Le Sage's novel *Gil Blas* (1715–35); from Sp *sangrador* one who lets blood]

sangria /sang-grē'a or sang'gri-ə/ n a Spanish wine punch with fruit and soda water or lemonade. [Sp *sangría*]

sangui- /sang-gwi-/ *combining form* denoting blood. [L *sanguis*, -*inis* blood; adjs *sanguineus*, *sanguinārius*, *sanguinolentus*; partly through Fr *sanguin*]
■ **sanguiferous** /-gwif'ər-əs/ adj (L *ferre* to bear) blood-carrying. **sanguifica'tion** n blood-making. **sang'uify** /-fī/ vi to make blood. ◆ vt to turn into blood. **sanguinaria** /-gwi-nā'ri-ə/ n the dried rhizome of the bloodroot *Sanguinaria* used as an emetic. **sang'uinarily** /-gwin-ə-ri-li/ adv. **sang'uinariness** n. **sang'uinary** adj bloody; bloodthirsty. **sanguine** /sang'gwin/ adj (in old physiology) of the complexion or temperament in which blood was supposed to predominate over the other humours; confident and inclined to hopefulness; abounding in blood; blood-red; bloody; ruddy; florid; of blood (*rare*). ◆ n a blood-red colour; a red chalk; a drawing in red chalks. ◆ vt (*obs*) to colour blood-red; to stain with blood. **sang'uinely** adv. **sang'uineness** n. **sanguin'eous** adj referring or relating to blood; of or having blood; blood-red; bloody; sanguine; full-blooded. **sanguin'ity** n sanguineness. **sanguin'olent** adj bloody. **Sanguisorba** /-sör'bə/ n (L *sorbēre* to absorb) a genus of rosaceous plants, supposed to have styptic qualities. **sanguiv'orous** or **sanguiniv'orous** adj (L *vorāre* to devour) feeding on blood.

Sanhedrin /san'i-drin/, also -*hed'* or -*hēd'* or **Sanhedrim** /-drim/ (*hist*) n a Jewish council or court, *esp* the supreme council and court at Jerusalem. [Heb *sanhedrīn*, from Gr *synedrion*, from *syn* together, and *hedrā* a seat]
■ **San'hedrist** n a member of the Sanhedrin.

sanicle /san'i-kl/ n a woodland umbelliferous plant (in full **wood sanicle**; *Sanicula europaea*) with glossy leaves, headlike umbels, and hooked fruits; any plant of the genus *Sanicula*; extended to various other plants. [OFr, perh from L *sānāre* to heal, from its once-supposed power]

sanidine /san'i-dēn/ n a clear glassy variety of potash feldspar, *usu* tabular. [Gr *sanis*, *sanidos* a board]

sanies /sā'ni-ēz/ n a watery, *usu* foul-smelling discharge from wounds or sores, made up of serum, blood and pus. [L *saniēs*]
■ **sa'nious** adj.

sanify /san'i-fī/ vt (**san'ifying**; **san'ified**) to make healthy. [L *sānus* sound, and *facere* to make]

sanitary /san'i-t(ə-)ri/ adj relating to, or concerned with, the promotion of health, *esp* connected with drainage and sewage disposal; conducive to health. [Fr *sanitaire*, from L *sānitās* health]
■ **sanitā'rian** n and adj (a person) favouring or studying sanitary measures. **sanitā'rianism** n. **san'itarily** adv. **san'itariness** n. **san'itarist** n. **sanitā'rium** n (pl **sanita'ria** or **sanita'riums**) (sham Latin; *esp* N Am) a sanatorium. **san'itate** vt (back-formation) to make sanitary; to furnish with sanitary appliances or ware. **sanitā'tion** n measures for the promotion of health and prevention of disease, *esp* drainage and sewage disposal. **sanitā'tionist** n. **sanitizā'tion** or **-s-** n. **san'itize** or **-ise** vt to make sanitary; to make clinically or starkly, unwelcomingly clean; to clean up, make more acceptable by removing offensive elements, words, connotations, etc. **san'itizer** or **-s-** n.
□ **sanitary engineer** n. **sanitary engineering** n the branch of civil engineering dealing with provision of pure water supply, disposal of waste, etc. **sanitary inspector** n formerly, an official with responsibility for ensuring that standards of hygiene, etc were adhered to, both in commercial and domestic establishments (cf **environmental health officer** under **environment**). **sanitary napkin** n (*US*) a sanitary towel. **sanitary towel** n a pad of absorbent material for wearing during menstruation, etc. **sanitary ware** n coarse-glazed earthenware for sewer pipes; plumbing fixtures such as sinks, baths, lavatories, etc.

sanity /san'i-ti/ n soundness of mind; rationality; health (*archaic*). [L *sānitās*, from *sānus* healthy]

sanjak /san'jak/ n formerly, a subdivision of a Turkish vilayet or eyalet. [Turk *sancak* flag, sanjak]

San Jose scale /san hō-zā' skāl'/ *n* an E Asian scale insect, *Quadraspidiotus perniciosus*, introduced into the USA, where it causes great damage to fruit trees.

sank /sangk/ *pat* of **sink**.

Sankhya /säng'kyə/ *n* one of the six great systems of orthodox Hindu philosophy, teaching that salvation is gained through the eternal interaction between spirit and matter. [Sans *sāṁkhya*, literally, based on calculation]

sanko see **sancho**.

sannie /san'i/ (*Scot inf*) *n* a sandshoe.

sannup /san'əp/ *n* a married male Native American. [Abenaki *senanbe*]

sannyasi /sun-yä'si/ *n* a Hindu ascetic or hermit who lives by begging (also **sannya'sin**). [Hindi, from Sans *saṃnyāsin* one who has cast away (all worldly desires)]

sanpan see **sampan**.

Sans. *abbrev* : Sanskrit.

sans /sä or sanz/ *prep* without. [Fr]
□ **sans-appel** /säz-a-pel/ *n* a person against whose decision there is no appeal.
■ **sans cérémonie** /sä-rä-mon-ē/ without ceremony, informally. **sans gêne** /zhen/ at ease, unconstrained, unceremonious. **sans nombre** /nōbr'/ (*heraldry*) repeated often, and covering the field. **sans phrase** /fräz/ without phrases (of courtesy), without circumlocution. **sans souci** /soo-sē/ without care or worry.

sansa /san'sə/ same as **zanze**.

sansculotte /sä-kü-lot'/ *n* in the French Revolution, the court party's nickname for an extreme republican (*appar* as wearing pantaloons instead of knee-breeches); hence generally, a strong republican, democrat, or violent revolutionary. [**sans**, and Fr *culotte* knee-breeches]
■ **sansculotterie** /-rē or -ə-rē/ *n*. **sansculott'ic** *adj*. **sansculottides** /-ēd'/ *n pl* a proposed name (in honour of the most ardent revolutionaries) for the supplementary days in the French revolutionary calendar. **sansculott'ism** *n*. **sansculott'ist** *n*.

sansei /san'sā' or san-sā'/ *n* a resident of the Americas born of the offspring of Japanese immigrant parents (cf **issei, nisei**). [Jap, third generation]

sanserif or **sans serif** /san-ser'if/ (*printing*) *n* a type without serifs (also *adj*). [**sans** and **serif**]

sansevieria /san-se-vi-ē'ri-ə or san-si-vē'ri-ə/ *n* any plant of the genus *Sansevieria*, *esp* a houseplant with sword-like leaves, known as mother-in-law's tongue, and *incl* plants yielding bowstring-hemp. [Named after the Neapolitan inventor Raimondo di Sangro, Prince of *San Severo* (1710–71)]

Sansk. *abbrev* : Sanskrit.

Sanskrit or (*old*) **Sanscrit** /san'skrit/ *n* the ancient Indo-European literary language of India. ◆ *adj* of or relating to Sanskrit. [Sans *saṃskṛta* put together, perfected, from *sam* together, and *karoti* he makes, cognate with L *creāre* to create]
■ **Sanskrit'ic** *adj*. **Sans'kritist** *n* a person skilled in Sanskrit.

sans serif see **sanserif**.

sant /sant/ *n* (also with *cap* when used as title) a devout person, saint (*esp* in Sikhism). [Hindi]

Santa Claus /san'tə klöz'/ *n* a fat white-bearded old man dressed in a red coat or robe who by tradition brings children Christmas presents (also known as **Father Christmas**); an improbable source of improbable benefits. [Orig US modification of Du dialect *Sante Klaas* St Nicholas]

santal /san'təl/ *n* sandalwood. [Gr *santalon*]
■ **santalā'ceous** *adj* of or characteristic of the sandalwood genus *Santalum*, or sandalwood family Santalaceae. **san'talin** *n* the colouring matter of red sandalwood.

Santeria /san-tə-rē'ə/ *n* a Caribbean religion which includes elements of traditional African religion and Roman Catholicism. [Sp *santería* holiness]

santim /san'tēm/ *n* (pl **san'tim**) a Latvian monetary unit, $\frac{1}{100}$ of a lat. [Latvian, from **centime**]

santir /san-tēr'/, **santur**, **santoor** or **santour** /-toor'/ *n* an Asian dulcimer. [Ar *santīr*, Pers and Turk *sāntūr*]

santolina /san-tō-lē'nə/ *n* a plant of the *Santolina* genus of fragrant Mediterranean shrubs related to the camomile, with dissected leaves and clustered flower-heads. [Ital *santolina*, from L *sanctus* holy, and *līnum* flax]

santon /san'ton/ *n* a Muslim holy man, a dervish. [Sp *santón*, from *santo* holy, from L *sanctus* holy]

santonica /san-ton'i-kə/ *n* the dried unexpanded flower-heads of a species of wormwood. [Gr *santonikon*, as found in the country of the *Santones* in Gaul]
■ **san'tonin** /-tən-/ *n* an anthelminthic extracted from santonica.

santoor, santour, santur see **santir**.

saola /sow-la'/ *n* a small ox-like mammal found in Vietnam and Laos (also called **vu quang ox** or **vu quang bovid**). [Viet *sao la* spindle horn]

Saorstát Eireann /se'ər-stät e'ə-rən/ (*Irish*) *n* Irish Free State.

saouari same as **souari**.

sap¹ /sap/ *n* vital juice that circulates in plants; juice generally; energy or vitality; sapwood; a saphead (*inf*); a plodding student (*inf*); any object used as a bludgeon. ◆ *vi* (*archaic inf*) to play the part of a ninny; to be studious. ◆ *vt* to drain or withdraw the sap from; to drain the energy from, exhaust; to strike with, or as if with, a sap. [OE *sæp*; LGer *sapow* juice, Ger *Saft*]
■ **sap'ful** *adj* full of sap. **sap'less** *adj*. **sap'lessness** *n*. **sap'ling** *n* a young tree (also *adj*); a young, immature person; a young greyhound. **sapp'ily** *adv*. **sapp'iness** *n*. **sapp'y** *adj*.
□ **sap'-green** *n* a green paint made from the juice of buckthorn berries; its colour (also *adj*). **sap'head** *n* (*inf*) a fool, a weak or foolish person. **sap'headed** *adj*. **sap'sucker** *n* any of several N American woodpeckers (genus *Sphyrapicus*) that feed on the sap of trees. **sap'wood** *n* alburnum.

sap² /sap/ *n* sapping; a trench (*usu* covered or zigzag) by which approach is made towards a hostile position. ◆ *vt* (**sapp'ing; sapped**) to undermine or weaken. ◆ *vi* to make a sap; to proceed insidiously. [Ital *zappa* and Fr *sappe* (now *sape*); cf LL *sappa* a pick]
■ **sapp'er** *n* someone who saps; a private in the Royal Engineers (formerly Royal Sappers and Miners).
□ **sap'head** *n* the furthest point reached by a sap.

sapajou see **sajou**.

sapan same as **sappan**.

sapego see **serpigo**.

sapele /sa-pē'lē/ *n* a wood resembling mahogany, used for furniture; a W African tree of the genus *Entandrophragma* yielding this wood, *esp E. cylindricum*. [W African name]

saphead see under **sap¹,²**.

saphena /sə-fē'nə/ (*anat*) *n* either of two large superficial veins of the leg draining blood from the foot. [New L, from Ar *ṣāfin*]
■ **saphe'nous** *adj*.

saphir d'eau /sa-fēr dō'/ (*mineralogy*) *n* an intensely blue variety of cordierite found in Sri Lanka. [Fr, water sapphire]

sapid /sap'id/ *adj* having a perceptible or decided taste; savoury; agreeable; relishing, exhilarating. [L *sapidus*, from *sapere* to taste]
■ **sapid'ity** or **sap'idness** *n*. **sap'idless** *adj* (*Lamb*) insipid.

sapient /sā'pi-ənt/ *adj* (*often ironic*) showing wisdom, sagacious. [L *sapientia*, from *sapere* to be wise]
■ **sa'pience** *n* (*often ironic*) discernment, judgement; wisdom. **sāpiential** /-en'shl/ *adj*. **sapien'tially** *adv*. **sā'piently** *adv*.

sapindaceous /sap-in-dā'shəs/ *adj* of, belonging to, or characteristic of the *Sapindus* genus of plants, *incl* soapwort. [New L genus name *Sapindus*, from L *sāpō Indicus* Indian soap]

sapi-outan see **sapi-utan**.

Sapium /sā'pi-əm/ *n* a genus of tallow trees.

sapi-utan or **sapi-outan** /sä-pi-oo'tän/ *n* a wild ox found in Indonesia. [Malay *sāpi* cow, and *hūtan* wild, wood]

sapling see under **sap¹**.

sapodilla /sap-ə-dil'ə/ *n* (also called **naseberry, sapota**) a large evergreen sapotaceous tree of the West Indies, etc (*Achras zapota*); its edible fruit (also **sapodilla plum**); its durable timber. [Sp *zapotilla*, dimin of *zapote*, from Nahuatl *tzapotl*]

saponaceous /sap-ə-nā'shəs/ *adj* soapy; soaplike. [L *sāpō, -ōnis* soap, prob from Gmc]
■ **sapogenin** /-jen'in/ *n* a compound derived from saponin, often used in synthesizing steroid hormones. **sapona'ria** *n* any plant of the soapwort genus *Saponaria*. **saponifiable** /sap-on'i-fī'ə-bl/ *adj*. **saponifica'tion** *n* the process of turning into or forming soap; hydrolysis of esters into acid and alkali. **sapon'ify** *vt* to convert (*esp* a fat) into soap. ◆ *vi* to become soap; (of esters) to undergo hydrolysis into acid and alkali. **saponin** /sap'ə-nin/ *n* a glucoside derived from various plants such as soapwort, that gives a soapy froth. **sap'onite** *n* a soapy amorphous silicate of magnesium and aluminium found in cavities in serpentine.

sapor /sā'pör/ (*formal*) *n* a property of a substance that is perceived by the sense of taste; flavour. [L *sapor, -ōris*]
■ **sapori'fic** *adj*. **sā'porous** /-pər-əs/ *adj*.

sapota /sə-pō'tə/ n another name for sapodilla. [Sp zapote, from Nahuatl tzapotl]
■ **sapotà'ceous** adj of, belonging to, or characteristic of a family of tropical plants and trees (**Sapotà'ceae**), incl sapodilla, gutta-percha, etc.

sappan or **sapan** /sap'an or -ən/ n brazil-wood (Caesalpinia sappan), usu **sapp'anwood** or **sap'anwood**. [Malay sapang]

sapped, **sapper**, **sapping** see sap[2].

sapperment /sap-ər-ment'/ interj a German oath. [Ger Sakrament sacrament]

Sapphic /saf'ik/ adj relating to or associated with the Greek lyric poetess Sappho (c.600BC) of Lesbos or her poetry; (also without cap) lesbian. ◆ n (usu in pl; also without cap) verses in a form said to have been invented by Sappho in stanzas of four lines each, three Lesser Sapphics (–∪–∪––∪∪–∪–∪) followed by an Adonic (–∪∪–∪).
■ **Sapph'ism** n (also without cap) lesbianism, with which she was charged by ancient writers. **sapph'ist** n a lesbian.

sapphire /saf'īr/ n a brilliant precious variety of corundum, generally of a beautiful blue; the blue colour of a sapphire. ◆ adj made of sapphire; deep pure blue. [OFr safir, from L sapphīrus, from Gr sappheiros lapis lazuli]
■ **sapph'ired** adj coloured with sapphire blue. **sapph'irine** /-ir-īn/ adj made of, or like, sapphire. ◆ n a blue mineral, aluminium-magnesium silicate.
❑ **sapph'ire-quartz** n a blue quartz. **sapph'ire-wing** n a blue-winged hummingbird.

sapple /sap'l/ (Scot) vt to wash (clothes) by hand in soapy water.
■ **sapp'les** n pl soapsuds.

sappy see under sap[1].

sapro- or before a vowel **sapr-** /sap-r(ō)-, -r(ə)- or -r(o)-/ combining form denoting: rotten or decaying matter; putrefaction. [Gr sapros rotten]
■ **sapraemia** /sap-rē'mi-ə/ n (Gr haima blood) blood poisoning resulting from the presence of toxins of saprophytic bacteria in the blood. **saprae'mic** adj. **saprobe** /sap'rōb/ n (Gr bios life) an organism living in foul water. **saprobiot'ic** adj feeding on dead or decaying plants or animals. **saprogenic** /-jen'ik/ or **saprogenous** /sə-proj'i-nəs/ adj (Gr root of gignesthai to produce) growing on decaying matter; causing or caused by putrefaction. **saprolegnia** /-leg'ni-ə/ n (Gr legnon border) any fungus of the genus Saprolegnia, one species of which grows on diseased salmon and was formerly thought to be the cause of the disease. **sap'rolite** n (Gr lithos stone) a soft, partially decomposed rock that has remained in its original site. **sap'ropel** /-pel/ n (Gr pēlos clay, mud) slimy sediment laid down in water, largely organic in origin. **sapropel'ic** adj relating to, living in, or derived from, sapropel. **sapropel'ite** n coal formed from sapropel. **saproph'agous** adj (see -phagous under phag-) feeding on decaying organic matter. **sap'rophyte** /-fīt/ n (see -phyte under phyt-) a fungus or bacterium that feeds upon dead and decaying organic matter. **saprophytic** /-fit'ik/ adj. **saprophyt'ically** adv. **sap'rophytism** n. **sap'rotroph** n (Gr trophē food) an organism living on dead or decaying organic matter. **saprotroph'ic** adj. **saprozō'ic** adj (Gr zōion an animal) feeding on dead or decaying organic material.

sapsago /sap-sā'gō or sap'sə-gō/ n (pl **sapsagos**) a hard Swiss green cheese made from skimmed milk and melilot. [Altered from Ger Schabziger, from schaben to scrape, and dialect Ger ziger, a kind of cheese]

sapucaia /sap-ū-kä'yə/ n a Brazilian tree (genus Lecythis) whose urn-shaped fruit (monkey pot) contains a number of finely-flavoured oval seeds or nuts. [Tupí]
❑ **sapuca'ia-nut** n.

saquinavir /sə-kwin'ə-vir/ n a protease inhibitor used as a drug in the treatment of HIV.

SAR abbrev : search and rescue; Special Administrative Region (of the People's Republic of China); synthetic aperture radar.

sar[1] /sär/ see sargus.

sar[2], **sa'r** /sär/ (Scot) n and vt (**sa'ring**; **sared**) a form of savour.

saraband or **sarabande** /sar'ə-band/ n a slow Spanish dance or dance tune; a suite-movement in its rhythm, in 3–4 time strongly accented on the second beat (a dotted crotchet or minim). [Sp zarabanda]

Saracen /sar'ə-sən/ n a Syrian or Arab nomad (hist); any Arab; a Muslim, esp an opponent of the Crusaders; a Moor or Berber; a non-Christian (obs). ◆ adj of or relating to the Saracens. [OE Saracene (pl), from L Saracēnus, from late Gr Sarakēnos, perh from Ar sharq sunrise]
■ **Saracenic** /-sen'ik/ or **Saracen'ical** adj. **Sar'acenism** n.
❑ **Saracenic architecture** n a general name for Muslim architecture. **Saracen's-stone** same as sarsen.

sarafan /sar-ə-fan' or sar'/ n a Russian peasant woman's cloak. [Russ]

Saran® /sə-ran'/ n a thermoplastic resin based on a co-polymer of vinylidene chloride and vinyl chloride, used in making fibre, moulded articles, etc.
❑ **Saran Wrap** n a US proprietary brand of clingfilm.

sarangi /sä'rung-gē/ n an Indian stringed instrument, played like a fiddle. [Hindi]

sarape same as serape.

Sarapis see Serapis.

Saratoga /sar-ə-tō'gə/ (US) n (in full **Saratoga trunk**) a large travelling trunk. [Saratoga Springs, resort in New York State]

sarbacane /sär'bə-kān/ (hist) n a blowpipe for shooting animals, etc with. [Fr]

sarcasm /sär'ka-zm/ n language expressing scorn or contempt, often but not necessarily ironical; a gibe; the use or quality of such language. [L sarcasmus, from Gr sarkasmos, from sarkazein to tear flesh like dogs, to speak bitterly, from sarx, sarkos flesh]
■ **sarcas'tic** adj containing or inclined to sarcasm. **sarcas'tically** adv.

sarcenchyme /sär-seng'kīm/ n a soft tissue of sponges with close-packed cells and reduced gelatinous matrix. [Gr sarx, sarkos flesh, and enchyma an infusion]
■ **sarcenchymatous** /-kim'ə-təs/ adj.

sarcenet see sarsenet.

sarco- /sär-kō-, -kə- or -ko-/ or before a vowel **sarc-** /särk-/ combining form denoting flesh or fleshy tissue. [Gr sarx, sarkos flesh]
■ **sar'cocarp** n (Gr karpos fruit; bot) the fleshy pericarp of a stone fruit. **sarcocystis** /-sis'tis/ n (Gr kystis a bladder) a sporozoan of the genus Sarcocystis, parasitic in muscles of mammals. **sarcolemma** /-lem'ə/ n (Gr lemma husk) the cell membrane enclosing a muscle fibre. **sarcolemm'al** adj. **sarcol'ogy** n (see -logy) the anatomy of the fleshy parts of the body. **sar'comere** /-mēr/ n (Gr meros part) a unit of myofibril in muscle. **sarcopē'nia** n (Gr penia poverty) loss of muscle strength associated with aging. **sar'coplasm** n the protoplasmic substance separating the fibrils in muscle fibres. **sarcoplas'mic** adj. **Sarcoptes** /-kop'tēz/ n (irreg, from Gr koptein to cut) a genus of small mites including Sarcoptes scabiei, the human itch mite. **sarcop'tic** adj. **sarcosaprophagous** /-sap-rof'ə-gəs/ adj (Gr sapros rotten, and see -phagous under phag-) feeding on decaying flesh. **sarcous** /sär'kəs/ adj of flesh or muscle.

sarcocolla /sär-kō-kol'ə/ n a Persian gum from Astragalus or other plants, reputed to heal wounds. [Gr sarkokolla, from sarx, sarkos flesh, and kolla glue]

sarcocystis see under sarco-.

sarcode /sär'kōd/ n protoplasm, esp of protozoans. [Gr sarkōdēs, sarkoeidēs, from sarx, sarkos flesh, and eidos form]
■ **Sarcodes** /sär-kōd'ēz/ n the Californian snow-plant genus. **sarcodic** /-kod'ik/ adj protoplasmic; flesh-like. **Sarcodina** /-kō-dī'nə/ n pl a class of Protozoa with pseudopodia. **sar'coid** adj flesh-like. ◆ n a fleshy tumour; short for sarcoidosis. **sarcoidō'sis** n a chronic disease of unknown cause characterized by the formation of nodules in the lymph nodes, lungs, skin, etc.

sarcolemma, **sarcology** see under sarco-.

sarcoma /sär-kō'mə/ n (pl **sarco'mas** or **sarcō'mata**) a tumour of connective tissue; any fleshy excrescence; a fleshy disc (bot). [Gr sarkōma, from sarx, sarkos flesh]
■ **sarcomatō'sis** n a condition characterized by the formation of sarcomas in many areas of the body. **sarcō'matous** adj.

sarcomere see under sarco-.

sarconet see sarsenet.

sarcopenia see under sarco-.

Sarcophaga /sär-kof'ə-gə/ n a genus of flies whose larvae feed on flesh. [Gr sarkophagos flesh-eating, from sarx, sarkos flesh, and phagein (aorist) to eat]
■ **sarcoph'agal** adj flesh-eating; of or relating to sarcophagi. **sarcoph'agous** adj feeding on flesh. **sarcoph'agus** n (pl **sarcoph'agi** /-jī or -gī/ or **sarcoph'aguses**) a limestone used by the Greeks for coffins, thought to consume the flesh of corpses; a stone coffin, esp one with carvings; a tomb or cenotaph of similar form.

sarcoplasm...to...**sarcous** see under sarco-.

Sard /särd/ n and adj Sardinian. [L Sardus]

sard /särd/ or **sardius** /sär'di-əs/ n a deep-red or brownish variety of chalcedonic silica. [L sarda, sardius, and Gr sardion, also sardios (lithos) the Sardian (stone), from Sardeis Sardis, in Lydia]

sardana /sär-dä'nə/ n a Catalan dance in a ring formation; the music for this, played esp on the flute and drum. [Catalan sardana]

sardar see sirdar.

sardel /sär-del'/ or **sardelle** /-del'/ or **-del'ə/ n a small fish related to the sardine.

sardine[1] /sär-dēn' or sär'dēn/ n a young pilchard, commonly tinned in oil; applied at various times and places to other fishes. [Fr sardine, from Ital sardina, from L sardina; Gr sardīnos, sardīnē]
  ■ **packed like sardines** crowded closely together.

sardine[2] /sär'dīn or -dĭn/ n a precious stone mentioned in the Bible (Revelation 4.3). [Gr sardinos (lithos) sard (stone), from sardios; see **sard**]

Sardinian /sär-dĭn'i-ən or -yən/ adj of the island or former kingdom of Sardinia, or of its inhabitants or their language. ◆ n a native, citizen, or member of the people of Sardinia; their language or dialect of Italian.

sardius see **sard**.

sardonic /sär-don'ik/ adj mockingly scornful, heartless or bitter; sneering. [Fr sardonique, from L sardonius, from late Gr sardonios, doubtfully referred to sardonion, a plant of Sardinia (Gr Sardō) which was said to screw up the face of the eater]
  ■ **sardō'nian** adj (obs). **sardon'ical** adj. **sardon'ically** adv. **sardon'icism** /-i-sizm/ n.

sardonyx /sär'də-niks/ n an onyx with bands of cornelian or sard. [Gr sardonyx, from Sardios Sardian, and onyx a nail]

saree see **sari**.

sargasso /sär-gas'ō/ n (pl **sargass'os**) gulfweed; a floating mass or expanse of it, as in the **Sargasso Sea** in the N Atlantic. [Port sargaço]

sargassum /sär-gas'əm/ n any brown seaweed of the genus Sargassum, of warm seas, with air-sacs enabling it to float on the surface of the water. [New L; see **sargasso**]

sarge /särj/ (inf) n sergeant.

sargus or **sargos** /sär'gəs/ n a marine fish of the genus Sargus (also **sar** and **sar'go** (pl **sar'gos**)). [Gr sargos]

sari or **saree** /sä'ri or sä'rē/ n a garment consisting of a long cloth wrapped round the waist and passed over the shoulder and head, worn esp by Hindu women. [Hindi sārī]

sarin /sä'rin/ n a compound of phosphorus ($C_4H_{10}FPO_2$) used as a lethal nerve gas. [Ger]

sark /särk/ or **serk** /serk/ n (Scot) a shirt or chemise; a surplice. [OE serc; ON serkr]
  ■ **sark'ing** n (Scot and NZ) a lining for a roof, usu of wood or felt.

sarky /sär'ki/ (inf) adj sarcastic.
  ■ **sar'kily** adv. **sar'kiness** n.

Sarmatia /sär-mā'shyə or -shi-ə/ n the ancient name for a region reaching from the Vistula and Danube to the Volga and Caucasus; Poland (poetic).
  ■ **Sarmā'tian** n and adj. **Sarmatic** /-mat'ik/ adj.

sarment /sär'mənt/ n a sarmentum; a long weak twig; a cut twig or cutting (obs). [L sarmentum a twig, from sarpere to prune]
  ■ **sar'mentose** /-tōz/, **sarmen'tous** or **sarmentaceous** /-tā'shəs/ adj (of plants) having sarmenta or runners; creeping. **sarmen'tum** n (pl **sarment'a**) a stem in the form of a runner, as in the strawberry.

sarnie or **sarney** /sär'ni/ (inf) n a sandwich.

sarod /sar'od/ n an Indian instrument like a cello, with strings that are plucked. [Hindi]

sarong /sə-rong' or sä'rong/ n a Malay skirtlike garment for a man or woman; a cloth for making it; a Western adaptation of this garment, often used by women as beachwear. [Malay sārung]

saros /sä'ros or sä'ros/ n an astronomical cycle of 6585 days and 8 hours, after which relative positions of the sun and moon recur; a Babylonian cycle of 3600 years. [Gr saros, from Babylonian shāru 3600]
  ■ **saronic** /sə-ron'ik/ adj.

sarpanch /sär'punch/ n an elected head of a village council in India. [Hindi sar head, and panca five]

sarracenia /sar- or sär-ə-sē'ni-ə/ n an American insectivorous flowering plant of the genus Sarracenia (family **Sarracenia'ceae**), with leaves modified to form pitchers for trapping insects. [Dr Sarrazin, 17c botanist, who sent them to Europe from Quebec]
  ■ **sarracenia'ceous** adj of or belonging to the Sarraceniaceae.

sarrasin or **sarrazin** /sar' or sär'ə-zin/ n buckwheat. [Fr (blé) sarrasin Saracen (corn)]

sarrusophone /sə-rus'ə-fōn/ n a double-reed brass instrument, devised by a 19c French bandmaster, Pierre-Auguste Sarrus. [Gr phōnē voice]

SARS /särz/ abbrev: severe acute respiratory syndrome, a contagious lung infection, the main symptoms of which are high fever, a dry cough and difficulty in breathing.

sarsaparilla /sär-sə-pə-ril'ə or sär-spə-ril'ə/ n any tropical American plant of the genus Smilax; its dried root; a soft drink flavoured with this; a medicinal preparation from it; extended to various plants or roots of similar use. [Sp zarzaparilla, from zarza bramble (from Basque), and a dimin of parra vine]

SARSAT /sär'sat/ abbrev: Search and Rescue Satellite Aided Tracking, a system that picks up emergency transmissions from international shipping, etc (now known as **COSPAS-SARSAT**).

sarsen /sär'sn/ n a grey-wether (also **sars'den**, **sar'sen-stone** or **Sar'acen's-stone**). [Appar forms of **Saracen**]

sarsenet, **sarcenet**, **sarconet** or **sarsnet** /särs'nit, -net/ n a thin tissue of fine silk. ◆ adj made of sarsenet. [Anglo-Fr sarzinett, prob from Sarzin Saracen]

sartor /sär'tör/ (facetious) n a tailor. [L sartor a patcher]
  ■ **sartorial** /-tō'ri-əl or -tō'/ adj of or relating to a tailor, tailoring, dress, or to the sartorius. **sarto'rially** adv. **sarto'rian** adj (rare). **sarto'rius** n (anat) a narrow ribbon-like muscle at the front of the thigh, the longest muscle in the body, helping to flex the knee.

Sartrian /sär'tri-ən/ adj relating to or associated with the French philosopher, dramatist and novelist Jean-Paul Sartre (1905–80). ◆ n a follower or admirer of Sartre.

Sarum use /sā'rum ūs/ n the system of religious rites peculiar to Salisbury cathedral in medieval times. [Sarum, ancient name of Salisbury]

sarus /sä'rəs, sä'rəs/ n an Indian crane (also **sarus crane**). [Hindi sāras]

Sarvodaya /sär-vō'da-ya/ n in India, the promotion of the welfare of the community as a whole. [Sans sārva all, and udayā prosperity]

SAS abbrev: Special Air Service.

sa sa /sä sä'/ interj of incitement; a fencer's exclamation on thrusting. [Fr ça ça, there there]

sasarara same as **siserary**.

sash[1] /sash/ n a band or scarf worn round the waist or over the shoulder. ◆ vt to dress or adorn with a sash. [Ar shāsh a turban cloth]

sash[2] /sash/ n a frame, esp a sliding frame, for windowpanes. ◆ vt to provide with sashes. [Fr châssis]
  ❑ **sash cord** n a cord attaching a weight to the sash in order to hold it open at any height. **sash weight** n either of two counterweights in a sash window. **sash window** n a window with a sash or sashes, as opposed to a casement window.

sashay /sa-shā'/ (inf) vi to walk or move in a gliding or ostentatious way. ◆ n an excursion. [Alteration of **chassé**]

sashimi /sash'i-mi, sa-shē'mi/ n a Japanese dish of thinly-sliced raw fish served with soy sauce, grated radish, etc. [Jap, literally, pierce flesh]

sasin /sas'in/ n the blackbuck or common Indian antelope. [Nepalese]

sasine /sā'sin/ (Scots law) n the act of giving legal possession of feudal property, infeftment. [Legal L sasina, a variant of **seisin**]

saskatoon /sas-kə-toon'/ n a small tree or shrub, Amelanchier alnifolia, of NW USA and Canada; its edible purple fruit. [Cree misaskwatomin]

sasquatch /sas'kwach or -kwoch/ n another name, esp in W Canada, for **Bigfoot** (see under **big**[1]). [Salish name]

sass /sas/ (N Am inf) n impertinent talk or behaviour. ◆ vi to speak or behave impertinently. ◆ vt to be impertinent to. [**sauce**]
  ■ **sass'ily** adv. **sass'iness** n. **sass'y** adj impertinent.

sassaby /sə-sä'bi/ n the bastard hartebeest, a large S African antelope. [Tswana tsessébe]

sassafras /sas'ə-fras/ n a tree (Sassafras officinale) of the laurel family, common in N America; the bark, esp of its root, a powerful stimulant; an infusion of it; extended to various plants with similar properties. [Sp sasafrás]
  ❑ **sassafras nut** n the pichurim bean (qv), whose oil smells like sassafras oil. **sassafras oil** n a volatile aromatic oil distilled from sassafras.

Sassanid /sas'ə-nid/ n one of the **Sassan'idae**, the dynasty that ruled Persia from 226 to 641AD.
  ■ **Sassā'nian** adj.

sassarara same as **siserary**.

sasse /sas/ (obs) n a sluice or lock. [Du sas]

Sassenach /sas'ə-nahh/ (esp Scot; usu derog) n an English person; a Lowlander. ◆ adj English; of the Lowlands. [Gaelic Sasunnach Saxon, English]

sassolite /sas'ə-līt/ n native boric acid, first found near Sasso in Italy (also **sass'olin**).

sassy see under **sass**.

sastra see **shaster**.

---

sastruga /sa-stroo'gə/ n (pl **sastru'gi** /-gē/) one of the long parallel ridges of snow and ice that form on open windswept plains in snowy regions. [Russ zastruga]

SAT abbrev : scholastic aptitude test; standard assessment task (educ).

Sat. abbrev : Saturday.

sat /sat/ pat and pap of **sit**.

sat /sat/ abbrev : satellite.

Satan /sā'tən/ or (old) sat'ən/ n the chief evil spirit, adversary of God and tempter of humankind, the Devil; the chief fallen angel, Lucifer; a devil. —Also (obs) **Satanas** /sat'ən-as/, **Sathan** /sā'thən/, **Sathanas** /sath'/. [Gr and L Satān, Satanās, from Heb sātān enemy, from sātan to be adverse]
■ **satanic** /sə-tan'ik/ or **satan'ical** adj. **satan'ically** adv. **satan'icalness** n (rare). **sā'tanism** n Satan-worship; devilish disposition. **sā'tanist** n and adj. **satanity** /sə-tan'/ n devilishness. **sātanol'ogy** n. **sātanoph'any** n (Gr phainein to show) an appearance of Satan. **sātanophō'bia** n (see **phobia**) fear of the Devil.
❏ **satanic abuse** n mental and physical (esp sexual) abuse as part of the rituals associated with certain forms of satanism. **Satanic school** n Southey's name for Byron, Shelley, Keats and others whom he considered immoral because of their interest in the exotic and their rejection of orthodox Christianity. **Satan monkey** n the black saki.

satang /sa-tang'/ n (pl **satang'**) a monetary unit of Thailand, $\frac{1}{100}$ of a baht. [Thai satān]

satara /sə- or sā-tä'rə or sat'ə-rə/ n a ribbed, hot-pressed and lustred woollen cloth. [Sátara in India]

satay /sat'ā/ n a Malaysian dish of marinated meat barbecued on skewers, usu served with a spicy peanut sauce (also **sate**). [Malay]

SATB abbrev : soprano, alto, tenor, bass (when combined in choral music).

satchel /sach'l/ n a small bag, usu with shoulder strap(s), esp as traditionally carried by schoolchildren. [OFr sachel, from L saccellus, dimin of saccus; see **sack¹, sac¹**]
■ **satch'elled** adj.

sate¹ /sāt/ vt to satisfy fully; to glut. [Blend of ME sade (cf **sad**) and L sat enough, or **satiate** shortened]
■ **sāt'ed** adj. **sāt'edness** n. **sāte'less** adj insatiable.

sate² /sat/, also (in rhyme) sāt/ an archaic form of **sat**.

sate³ see **satay**.

sateen /sa-tēn'/ n a glossy cotton or woollen fabric resembling satin.

satellite /sat'ə-līt/ n a body revolving around a planet, esp now a man-made device used for communication, etc (see **artificial satellite** below); a small piece of chromosomal material attached to a chromosome by a narrow filament (biol); a smaller companion to anything; a subordinate or dependent state, community, etc; an obsequious follower; an attendant. ◆ adj of, relating to or transmitted by a satellite. ◆ vt to transmit by satellite. [L satelles, satellitis an attendant]
■ **satelles** /sa-tel'ēz/ n (pl **satell'ites** /-i-tēz/) (obs) a satellite. **satellitic** /-lit'ik/ adj. **satellitium** /-lit'i-əm/ n (astrol) a group of several planets in one sign of the zodiac. **sat'ellitize** or **-ise** vt to bring satellite(s) into use in (meteorology, broadcasting, etc).
❏ **satellite broadcasting** or **television** n broadcasting of television programmes via artificial satellite. **satellite dish** n a saucer-shaped receiver for satellite television. **satellite state** or **country** n one which relies on and obeys the dictates of a larger, more powerful state. **satellite town** n a town, often a garden city, limited in size, built near a larger town to house excess population.
■ **artificial** or **earth satellite** any man-made body, incl spacecraft, launched by rocket into space and put into orbit round the earth.

satem languages /sä'təm lang'gwi-jiz or -jəz/ n pl the group of Indo-European languages in which an original palatal consonant developed as a sibilant (cf **centum languages**). [From Avestic satem hundred (exemplifying the consonant so developed)]

Sat Guru /sät goo'roo/ n a Sikh term for God, literally, the true guru. [Hindi]

Sathan and **Sathanas** see **Satan**.

sati same as **suttee**.

satiate /sā'shi-āt/ vt to gratify fully; to satisfy to excess. ◆ adj glutted. [L satiāre, -ātum, from satis enough]
■ **sātiabil'ity** n. **sā'tiable** adj. **sātiā'tion** or **satiety** /sə-tī'ə-ti/ n the state of being satiated; surfeit.

satin /sat'in/ n a closely-woven silk with a lustrous and unbroken surface showing much of the warp. ◆ adj of or like satin; clad in satin. ◆ vt to make satiny. [Fr satin, appar from LL sēta silk (L saeta bristle), or from Ar zaytūn from Zaitūn (Tsinkiang), a town in China where it was produced]

■ **satinet'** or **satinette'** (Walter Scott **satinett'a**) n a thin satin; a modification of satin with a slightly different weave; a cloth with a cotton warp and a woollen weft. **sat'iny** adj.
❏ **satin bird** n an Australian bowerbird with satiny blue and black plumage. **satin finish** n a satiny polish. **satin flower** n a species of stitchwort. **satin paper** n a fine, glossy writing paper. **satin sheeting** n a twilled cotton and silk fabric with a satin surface. **satin spar** n a satiny fibrous calcite, aragonite, or gypsum. **satin stitch** n an embroidery stitch worked in adjacent parallel lines, giving a satiny appearance. **satin stone** n a fibrous gypsum. **sat'inwood** n a smooth, satiny ornamental wood from India; the rutaceous tree (Chloroxylon swietenia) yielding it; extended to several more or less similar woods and trees.

satire /sat'īr/ n a literary composition, orig in verse, essentially a criticism of folly or vice, which it holds up to ridicule or scorn, its chief instruments being irony, sarcasm, invective, wit and humour; such writing as a genre; its spirit; the use of, or inclination to use, its methods; satirical denunciation or ridicule in which such methods are employed; (through confusion with **satyr**) a satirist (obs). [L satira, satura (lanx) full (dish), a medley]
■ **satiric** /sə-tir'ik/ or **satir'ical** adj relating to, or conveying, satire; sarcastic; abusive. **satir'ically** adv. **satir'icalness** n. **sat'irist** n a writer or performer of satire; a person who frequently uses satire. **satiriza'tion** or **-s-** n. **satirize** or **-ise** /sat'ər-īz/ vt to make the object of satire; to ridicule. ◆ vi to write satire.

satisfice /sat'is-fīs/ vi to aim for or achieve that which will satisfy or suffice, rather than a potential maximum. [Alteration of **satisfy**]
■ **sat'isficing** n.

satisfy /sat'is-fī/ vt (**sat'isfying; sat'isfied**) to give enough to; to be enough for; to supply fully; to fulfil the conditions of; to meet the requirements of; to make content; to pay (a debt, etc) in full; to compensate or atone for; to free from doubt; to convince. ◆ vi to remove the need or desire for more; to give contentment; to make payment or atonement. [OFr satisfier, from L satisfacere, from satis enough, and facere to make]
■ **satisfaction** /-fak'shən/ n the act of satisfying; the state of being satisfied; contentment; payment; quittance; gratification; comfort; something which satisfies; atonement; reparation; the satisfying of honour, as by fighting a duel; conviction. **satisfac'torily** adv. **satisfac'toriness** n. **satisfac'tory** adj satisfying; providing contentment; such as might be wished; making amends or payment; atoning; convincing. **sat'isfiable** adj. **sat'isfied** adj. **sat'isfier** n. **sat'isfying** adj. **sat'isfyingly** adv.
❏ **satisfaction theory** n the Christian orthodoxy that Christ made satisfaction to Divine justice for the guilt of human sin by suffering as the human representative, and that thus Divine forgiveness was made possible.

satis verborum /sā'tis vur-bō'rəm or -bō' or sat'is ver- or wer-bō'rŭm/ (L) enough of words; enough said.

sative /sā'tiv/ (obs) adj cultivated. [L sativus]

Sativex® /sat'i-veks/ n a selective cannabinoid developed to relieve spasticity in patients with multiple sclerosis.

satnav /sat'nav/ (inf) abbrev : satellite navigation (system).

satori /sa-tō'rē or -tö'/ n a state of sudden enlightenment, sought in Zen Buddhism. [Jap, from toshi be quick]

satrap /sat'rap, -rəp or sā'trap/ n a viceroy or governor of an ancient Persian province; a provincial governor, esp if powerful or ostentatiously rich; a tyrannical person. [Gr satrapēs, from Old Pers khshathrapāvan country-protector]
■ **sat'rapal** adj. **sat'rapy** n a satrap's province, office, or period of office.

sat sapienti /sat sap-i-en'tī or -tē/ (L) enough for the wise, a nod to the wise.

satsuma /sat-soo'mə/ n a thin-skinned seedless type of mandarin orange; the tree bearing this. [Satsuma, a province of SW Japan]
❏ **Satsuma ware** /sat'/ n a yellowish pottery with gilding and enamel made in Satsuma from the end of the 16c.

saturate /sat'ū-rāt or sach'ə-rāt/ vt to soak; to imbue; to fill to the fullest extent possible; to satisfy all the valencies of (chem); to cover (a target area) completely with bombs dropped simultaneously. ◆ adj /-rət, -rāt/ saturated; pure in colour, free from dilution with white, grey or black. ◆ n /-rət/ (chem) a saturated compound. [L saturāre, -ātum, from satur full, related to satis enough]
■ **saturabil'ity** n. **sat'urable** adj. **sat'urant** adj tending to saturate. ◆ n a saturating substance. **sat'urated** adj (of a solution) containing as much of a solute as can be dissolved at a particular temperature and pressure; (esp of a fat) containing no carbon-carbon double bonds in the molecule and consequently not susceptible to addition reactions (chem); thoroughly wet; soaked. **saturā'tion** n the state of being saturated; the state of the atmosphere when fully saturated with water vapour at a given temperature; the state of a ferromagnetic material

which has been magnetized to the fullest possible extent (*phys*); the conversion of an unsaturated compound to a saturated compound (*chem*); the condition where a field applied across an ionization chamber is sufficient to collect all ions produced by incident radiation (*nuclear eng*); the degree to which a colour departs from white and approaches a pure spectral wavelength, *desaturation* being the inverse of this (*phys*). ◆ *adj* of very great, or greatest possible, intensity (eg *saturation bombing*). **sat'urātor** *n*.

□ **saturated fat** *n* an animal fat (*usu* solid, eg lard, butter) containing a high proportion of saturated fatty acids. **saturation coefficient** *n* (*building*) the ratio between a building material's natural capacity to absorb moisture and its porosity. **saturation diving** *n* diving to great depths using a chamber at the same pressure as the water, to which the diver can return frequently for rest spells, etc, thus reducing the frequency of (and hence time spent in) decompression. **saturation point** *n* the point at which saturation is reached; dewpoint; the limit in numbers that can be taken in, provided with a living, used, sold, etc; the limit of emotional response, endurance, etc.

Saturday /sat'ər-dā or -di/ *n* the seventh day of the week, the Jewish Sabbath. [OE *Sæter-*, *Sætern(es)dæg*, transl of L *diēs Saturni* the day of Saturn]

■ **Sat'urdays** *adv* on Saturdays.

Saturn /sat'ərn/ *n* the ancient Roman god of agriculture; commonly used for the Greek Kronos, with whom he came to be identified; the second in size and sixth in distance from the sun of the major planets, believed by the astrologers to induce a cold, melancholy, gloomy temperament; the metal lead (*alchemy*). [L *Sāturnus*, from *serere*, *satum* to sow]

■ **Saturnā'lia** *n pl* (*Roman hist*) the festival of Saturn in mid-December, a time of great gift-giving and revelry when slaves had temporary freedom; hence (often as *sing* without *cap*) a wild party or orgy. **saturnā'lian** *adj* of the Saturnalia; riotously merry. **Satur'nia** /sat- or sət-/ *n* a genus of very large moths. **Satur'nian** *adj* relating to Saturn, whose legendary reign was called the golden age; hence happy, pure, simple; in the metre in which early Latin poems were written; of the planet Saturn; saturnine. ◆ *n* a person born under Saturn, or of saturnine temperament; the son of Saturn (Jupiter or Zeus); a fancied inhabitant of Saturn. **satur'nic** *adj* (*med*) suffering from lead-poisoning. **saturniid** /-ni-id/ *n* any large moth of the family Saturniidae, *incl* the emperor moth (also *adj*). **sat'urnine** *adj* grave; gloomy; phlegmatic; caused or poisoned by lead. **sat'urninely** *adv*. **sat'urnism** *n* lead-poisoning. **sat'urnist** *n* (*obs*) a gloomy person.

□ **Saturn's tree** *n* an arborescent deposit of lead from a solution of a lead salt.

satyagraha /sut'ya-gru-ha/ or -grä/ *n* orig Mahatma Gandhi's policy of passive resistance to British rule in India, now any non-violent campaign for reform. [Sans, reliance on truth]

■ **satyagra'hi** /-hē/ *n* an exponent of passive resistance.

satyr /sat'ər/ *n* a Greek god of the woodlands, with a tail and long ears, represented by the Romans as part goat; a very lecherous man; an orang-utan; a desert demon (*Bible*, Isaiah); any butterfly of the Satyridae family; (formerly, by confusion) a satire or satirist. [L *satyrus*, from Gr *satyros*]

■ **sat'yra** or **sat'yress** *n* a female satyr. **sat'yral** *n* (*heraldry*) a monster compounded of man, lion, and antelope. **satyresque'** *adj*. **satyrī'asis** *n* (*med*) overpowering sexual desire in men, corresponding to nymphomania in women. **satyric** /sə-tir'ik/ or **satyr'ical** *adj* of satyrs; having a chorus of satyrs. **sat'yrid** *n* any butterfly of the family Satyridae, a subfamily of Nymphalidae, *incl* meadow-browns, heaths, marbled whites, etc. **sat'yrisk** *n* a little satyr.

□ **satyr play** *n* in ancient Greek drama, a play performed as comic relief after a series of three tragedies, in which the hero is presented with a chorus of satyrs.

sauba /sä-oo'bə or sö'bə/ *n* (also **sauba ant**) a S American leaf-carrying ant. [Tupí]

sauce /sös/ *n* any dressing poured over food; any (semi-) liquid mixture in which food is cooked and/or served; anything that gives relish, interest or excitement; vegetables eaten with meat (*US*); stewed fruit (*N Am*); a solution of salt, etc, used in individual processes; a pert or impudent person (*obs*); pert or impertinent language or behaviour (*inf*); (with *the*) alcoholic drink (*US inf*). ◆ *vt* to add or give sauce to; to make piquant or pleasant; to be impertinent to (*inf*); to rebuke (*Shakesp*); to make to pay dear (*Shakesp*); to belabour (*obs*). [Fr *sauce*, from L *salsa*, from *sallere*, *salsum* to salt, from *sāl* salt]

■ **sauce'less** *adj*. **sauc'ily** *adv*. **sauc'iness** *n*. **sauc'y** *adj* (**sauc'ier**; **sauc'iest**) like or tasting of sauce; pert, forward; piquantly audacious, *esp* arousing sexual desire; (eg of a ship) smart and trim; disdainful; lascivious (*Shakesp*).

□ **sauce-alone'** *n* the plant garlic mustard. **sauce boat** *n* a container from which sauce is poured over food. **sauce'box** *n* (*inf*) an impudent person. **sauce-crayon** /sös-krā-yõ'/ *n* (Fr) a soft black pastel used for backgrounds. **sauce'pan** /-pən/ *n* a handled and *usu* lidded

metal pan for boiling, stewing, etc, *orig* for sauces. **sauce'pan-fish** *n* the king crab.

saucer /sö'sər/ *n* orig a dish for salt or sauce; a shallow dish, *esp* one placed under a tea or coffee cup; anything of similar shape. [OFr *saussiere*, from LL *salsārium*, from L *salsa* sauce]

■ **sau'cerful** *n* (*pl* **sau'cerfuls**). **sau'cerless** *adj*.

□ **saucer eye** *n* a large round eye. **sau'cer-eyed** *adj*.

■ **flying saucer** see under **fly**.

sauch or **saugh** /söhh/ a Scots form of **sallow**[2].

saucisse /sō-sēs'/ or **saucisson** /-sē-sõ'/ (*milit*) *n* a long canvas tube filled with powder for use as a fuse, eg when firing a mine. [Fr, sausage]

Saudi /sow'di/ or **Saudi Arabian** /ə-rā'bi-ən/ *adj* of or relating to the Kingdom of *Saudi Arabia* in SW Asia, or its people. ◆ *n* a native or citizen of Saudi Arabia.

sauerbraten /sow' or zow'ər-brä-tən/ *n* a German dish of beef marinaded in vinegar and braised. [Ger, sour roast]

sauerkraut /sow' or zow'ər-krowt/ *n* a German dish of cabbage allowed to ferment with salt, etc (also **sour'-crout**). [Ger, sour cabbage]

saufgard /söf-gärd'/ (*Spenser*) *n* same as **safeguard** (see under **safe**).

sauger /sö'gər/ *n* a small N American pike-perch, *Stizostedion canadense*.

saugh see **sauch**.

saul a Scots form of **soul**.

saulge /söj/ (*Spenser*) *n* same as **sage**[1].

saulie /sö'li/ (*archaic Scot*) *n* a hired mourner. [Origin obscure]

sault /sölt/ *n* (also **salt**) a leap (*obs*); /soo/ a waterfall or rapid (*Can*). [Fr *saut*, 17c *sault*, from L *saltus*, *-ūs* leap]

sauna /sö'na or sow'na/ *n* (a building or room equipped for) a Finnish form of steam bath. [Finn]

saunt /sönt/ a Scots form of **saint**.

saunter /sön'tər/ *vi* to walk in a casual or leisurely manner; to wander about without purpose; to stroll; to dawdle (*obs*). ◆ *n* a sauntering gait; a leisurely stroll. [Origin obscure]

■ **saun'terer** *n*. **saun'tering** *n* and *adj*. **saun'teringly** *adv*.

saurel /sö-rel' or sö'rəl/ (*US*) *n* the horse-mackerel, scad. [Fr]

saurian /sö'ri-ən/ *adj* of or resembling a lizard; of, characteristic of, or belonging to the Sauria, an order of reptiles in some classifications, *incl* the lizards. ◆ *n* an old name for a lizard. [Gr *saurā*, *sauros* a lizard]

■ **saurischian** /-is'ki-ən/ *adj* (Gr *ischion* hip joint) of or belonging to the Saurischia, an order of Triassic dinosaurs *incl* the sauropods and theropods. ◆ *n* any dinosaur of the Saurischia. **saurog'nathous** *adj* (see **-gnathous** under **gnathic**; *zool*) having a lizard-like arrangement of the palate-bones (as eg woodpeckers). **saur'oid** *adj* lizard-like. **saur'opod** *n* any gigantic quadrupedal herbivorous dinosaur of the suborder Sauropoda, one of the two main groups of lizard-hipped dinosaurs, including *Apatosaurus* (*Brontosaurus*), *Diplodocus* and *Brachiosaurus*. **saurop'odous** *adj*. **saurop'sidan** *n* and *adj* (Gr *opsis* appearance) (a member) of the Sauropsida, one of the main divisions of Vertebrata *incl* birds and reptiles. **Sauropterygia** /sö-rop-tər-ij'i-ə/ *n pl* (Gr *pterygion* a fin) an order of fossil reptiles, aquatic or amphibious, *incl* Plesiosaurus. **sauropteryg'ian** *adj*. **Saururae** /-roo'rē/ *n pl* (Gr *ourā* tail) an extinct (Jurassic) subclass of birds, with teeth and jointed tail (eg Archaeopteryx, etc).

saury /sö'ri/ *n* a long sharp-beaked, marine fish (*Scombresox saurus*) related to the garfish. [Perh Gr *sauros* lizard]

sausage /sos'ij/ *n* chopped or minced meat with fat, cereal, etc seasoned and stuffed into a length of intestine or now *usu* a synthetic tube-shaped casing, or formed into the shape of a tube; anything of similar shape. [Fr *saucisse*, from LL *salsīcia*, from L *salsus* salted]

□ **sausage bassoon** *n* the rackett. **sausage dog** *n* (*inf*) a dachshund. **sausage machine** *n* a machine that makes sausages by forcing meat into a continuous tube which is then divided into links; something (or someone) that produces identical items in a steady, monotonous manner. **sausage meat** *n* meat prepared for making sausages. **sausage poisoning** *n* (*old*) botulism (qv). **sausage roll** *n* minced meat cooked in a roll of pastry.

■ **not a sausage** (*inf*) nothing at all.

saussurite /sö-sū'rīt or sö'sū-rīt/ *n* a dull opaque mass of zoisite, albite, etc, formed by the alteration of feldspar. [HB de *Saussure* (1740–99), Swiss geologist]

■ **saussuritic** /-it'ik/ *adj*.

saut /söt/ a Scots form of **salt**[1].

sauté /sö'tā/ (*cookery*) *adj* fried lightly and quickly. ◆ *vt* (**sau'téing** or **sau'téeing**; **sau'téed**) to fry lightly and quickly. ◆ *n* (*pl* **sautés**) a dish of food that has been sautéed. [Fr *sauter* to jump]

Sauterne or **Sauternes** /sō-tûrn' or -tern'/ n sweet white wine produced at *Sauternes* in the Gironde, France.

sautoir /sō'twär/ n a long necklace, or a pendant on a long chain or ribbon. [Fr, from LL *saltātōrium* a stirrup; cf **saltire**]

sauve qui peut /sōv kē pœ'/ (Fr) n a state of panic; a stampede. [Literally, save (himself) who can]

Sauvignon /sō'vē-nyō/ n a variety of grape *orig* grown in Bordeaux and the Loire valley; wine made from this grape variety.

savable, etc see under **save**.

savage /sav'ij/, also (obs) **salvage** /sal'vij/ adj in a state of nature; untamed; wild; uncivilized; ferocious; furious. ◆ n a human being in a wild, primitive or uncivilized state; a brutal, fierce, or cruel person; an enraged horse or other animal; a wild beast (obs; rare). ◆ vt to attack savagely, esp with the teeth; to make savage. ◆ vi (obs; rare) to play the savage. [OFr *salvage*, from L *silvāticus* relating to the woods, from *silva* a wood]
■ **sav'agedom** n a savage state; savages collectively. **sav'agely** adv. **sav'ageness** n the state of being savage. **sav'agery** /-ri or -ər-i/ n fierceness; ferocity; uncivilized condition; wildness; savage behaviour; savages collectively; wild ruggedness of landscape; wild, overgrowing vegetation (obs). **sav'agism** n.

savanna or **savannah** /sə-van'ə/ n a tract of level land, covered with low vegetation, treeless, or dotted with trees or patches of wood, as in tropical or subtropical Africa. [Sp *zavana* (now *sabana*), said to be from Carib: not from *sábana* sheet]
□ **savanna flower** n a West Indian apocynaceous plant (genus *Echites*). **savann'a-forest** n parklands. **savann'a-sparr'ow** n a N American sparrow (genus *Passerculus*). **savann'a-watt'le** n fiddlewood.

savant /sa'vä or sä-vä'/ or fem **savante** /-vãt'/ n a learned person, a scholar. ◆ adj learned, accomplished. [Fr obs prp of *savoir* to know]
□ **savant syndrome** n the syndrome observed in an **idiot savant**.

savarin /sav'ə-rin/ n a ring-shaped cake made with yeast, containing nuts, fruit, etc, and often flavoured with rum. [Antheline Brillat-*Savarin* (died 1826), French politician and gourmet]

savate /sä-vät'/ n a method of boxing in which the feet (as well as the fists) are used. [Fr]

save /sāv/ vt to rescue; to bring or keep out of danger; to bring safely out of evil; to protect; to preserve; to prevent or avoid the loss, expenditure, or performance of, or the gain of by an opponent; to reserve; to spare; to deliver from the power of sin and from its consequences; to be economical in the use of; to hoard; to (enter an instruction to) store (data) on a tape or disk (comput); to prevent (a goal) from being scored; to obviate, to prevent; to be in time for (eg the post; archaic). ◆ vi to be economical; to reserve esp money for future use; to act as a saviour. ◆ prep except. ◆ conj were it not that; unless. ◆ n an act of saving, esp in games; an instance by a relief pitcher of successfully preserving a narrow lead at the end of a game (baseball); a computer instruction to save material onto a tape or disk. [Fr *sauver*, from L *salvāre*, from *salvus* safe]
■ **sav'able** adj. **sav'ableness** n. **saved** adj. **sa'ver** n. **sa'ving** adj protecting; preserving; redeeming; securing salvation (theol); frugal; making a reservation (esp law); directed towards the avoidance of loss rather than the making of profit. ◆ prep excepting. ◆ n the action of the verb; something which is saved; (in pl) money laid aside for future use; a reservation (law). **sa'vingly** adv. **sa'vingness** n.
□ **save'-all** n a contrivance intended to save anything from being wasted or damaged; a pinafore or overall (dialect); a miser. ◆ adj stingy. **save as you earn** n a government-operated savings scheme in which regular deductions are made from one's earnings (abbrev **SAYE**). **save'gard** vt (Spenser) to guard, protect. **saving clause** n a legal clause, or a statement, in which a reservation or condition is made. **saving game** n a policy or procedure aimed rather at avoiding loss than at making a profit. **saving grace** see under **grace**. **savings and loan association** n (US) a building society. **savings bank** n a bank established to encourage thrift by taking small deposits, investing under regulations for safety, and giving compound interest. **savings certificate** n a certificate of having invested a sum of money in government funds, the investment being free of income tax and capital gains tax. **savings ratio** n the percentage of disposable income that is saved in an economy.
■ **save appearances** to keep up an appearance of wealth, comfort, consistency, harmony, propriety, etc; to make hypothesis agree with observation (astron, Milton). **save (some)one's bacon, save one's face, save one's neck, save one's skin, save the mark** see under **bacon, face, neck, skin** and **mark¹**. **save up** to accumulate or hold for some purpose by refraining from spending or using. **save you** (archaic) a greeting, God keep you.

saveloy /sav'ə-loi/ n a highly seasoned sausage, orig made of brains. [Fr *cervelat*, *cervelas* a saveloy, from Ital *cervellata*, from *cervello* brain, from L *cerebellum*, dimin of *cerebrum* the brain]

savey see **savvy**.

savin or **savine** /sav'in/ n a species of juniper (*Juniperus sabina*) with very small imbricated leaves; an irritant volatile oil extracted from the tops of this plant, an anthelminthic and abortifacient; extended to Virginian juniper ('red cedar') and other plants. [OFr *sabine*, from L *sabīna* (*herba*) Sabine (herb)]

saviour or (US) **savior** /sā'vyər/ n someone who saves from evil, danger or destruction; (with cap) a title applied by Christians to Jesus Christ. [ME *sauveur*, from OFr *sauveour*, from L *salvātor*, from *salūs*, *salūtis* health, wellbeing, safety]
□ **saviour sibling** n a child conceived primarily as an organ donor for an older sibling who suffers from a life-threatening illness.

savoir-faire /sa-vwär-fer'/ n the faculty of knowing just what to do and how to do it; tact. [Fr]

savoir-vivre /sa-vwär-vē'vr'/ n good breeding; knowledge of polite usages. [Fr]

savory /sā'və-ri/ n a labiate flavouring herb (genus *Satureia*), esp S. *hortensis* (summer savory) or S. *montana* (winter savory). [Appar from L *satureia*]

savour or (N Am) **savor** /sā'vər/ n taste; odour; the distinctive quality of something; flavour; relish; a hint or trace; repute (Bible). ◆ vi to taste or smell (with of); to have a flavour; to have a suggestion (with of). ◆ vt to flavour, season; to taste, smell; to be conscious of; to relish; to taste with conscious direction of the attention. [OFr *sav(o)ur* (Fr *saveur*), from L *sapor*, from *sapere* to taste]
■ **sā'vorous** adj (rare) pleasant to the taste. **sā'voured** adj having a savour. **sā'vourily** adv. **sā'vouriness** n. **sā'vourless** adj. **sā'vourly** adv (obs) relishingly; feelingly; understandingly. **sā'voury** adj of good savour or relish; fragrant; having savour or relish; appetizing; salty, piquant or spiced, opp to *sweet* (also fig); morally pleasing, respectable; savouring of edification or holiness (archaic). ◆ n a savoury course or dish or small item of food.

Savoy /sə-voi'/ n a district of the former kingdom of Sardinia, now (and usu referred to by the French name **Savoie** /sav-wa/) a region of SE France, giving name to a former palace and sanctuary and to a theatre in London; (without cap) a winter cabbage with a large compact head and wrinkled leaves, orig from *Savoy*. [Fr *Savoie*, *Savoyard*]
■ **Savoyard** /sav'oi-ärd/ n a native or inhabitant of Savoy, or of the Savoy precinct in London; (also without cap) a performer in, or devotee of, the Gilbert and Sullivan operas produced at the *Savoy* Theatre. ◆ adj of or relating to Savoy; of or relating to the operas of Gilbert and Sullivan.

savvy, savvey or **savey** /sav'i/ (inf) vt and vi to know; to understand. ◆ n general ability; common sense; know-how, skill. ◆ adj knowledgeable, shrewd. [Sp *sabe*, from *saber* to know, from L *sapere* to be wise]

SAW abbrev : surface acoustic wave.

saw¹ /sö/ pat of **see¹**.

saw² /sö/ n any of numerous cutting tools with a toothed blade, hand-operated or power-driven, used esp for cutting wood. ◆ vt (pat **sawed**; pap **sawed** or (usu) **sawn**) to cut with, or as with, or as, a saw; to play harshly or crudely (as a violinist). ◆ vi to use a saw; to make to and fro movements, as if with a saw. [OE *saga*; Ger *Säge*]
■ **sawed** adj. **saw'er** n (rare). **saw'ing** n and adj. **saw'like** adj. **sawn** adj. **saw'yer** n a person who makes a living by sawing timber; a stranded tree that bobs in a river (N Am).
□ **saw'bill** n a merganser; a motmot; any of various hummingbirds with serrated bills. **saw'blade** n. **saw'bones** n sing (sl) a surgeon or doctor. **saw'buck** n (N Am) a sawhorse; a ten-dollar bill (sl). **saw doctor** n a person who sharpens sawblades. **saw'dust** n dust or small particles of wood, etc detached in sawing. ◆ vt to sprinkle with sawdust. **saw'dusty** adj. **saw'-edge** n. **saw'-edged** adj serrated. **saw'fish** n a sharklike ray (genus *Pristis*) with a long, flattened, serrated jaw. **saw'fly** n a hymenopterous insect of various kinds with a sawlike ovipositor. **saw frame** n the frame in which a saw is set. **saw gate** or **saw kerf** n the gap made by a saw. **saw'grass** n a sedge (*Cladium jamaicense*) with serrated leaves, growing in coastal areas of SE USA. **saw'horse** n a trestle for supporting wood that is being sawn; a straight-line diagram showing the three-dimensional structure of a molecule. **saw'mill** n a factory in which timber is cut into planks, etc. **sawn'-off** adj (also **sawed'-off**) shortened by cutting with a saw; short in stature (inf). ◆ n a sawn-off shotgun. **saw palmetto** n a small prickly N American palm tree whose berries are used as an aphrodisiac and to treat disorders of the prostate. **saw'pit** n a pit in which one sawyer stands while another stands above. **saw set** n an instrument for turning sawteeth to right and left. **saw'shark** n a shark (genus *Pristiophorus*) with a long flattened serrated jaw. **saw'-tones** n pl harsh notes. **saw'tooth** n and adj. **saw'-toothed** adj serrated, like the edge of a sawblade. **saw'-wort** n a name for various composite plants with serrate leaves, eg *Serratula tinctoria*.

saw[3] /sö/ n a saying; a proverb; a decree (Spenser). [OE sagu, from the root of secgan to say, tell]

saw[4] /sö/ a Scots form of **sow**[1] and of **salve**[1].

sawah /saw'a/ n an irrigated paddy-field. [Malay]

sawder /sö'dər/ vt to flatter, blarney. ◆ n flattery, esp in the phrase soft sawder. [Prob **solder**]

sawn /sön/ pap of **saw**[2]; also (Scot and N Eng) of **sow**[1]; (Shakesp) perh of **sow**[1], perh of **see**[1].

Sawney or **Sawny** /sö'ni/ n an old nickname for a Scotsman. [For Sandy, from Alexander]

sawney /sö'ni/ (sl) n a fool. [Origin obscure; perh developed from **zany**]

sawyer see under **saw**[2].

sax[1] /saks/ (inf) n short for **saxophone**.

sax[2] /saks/ n a chopper for trimming slates. [OE sæx (WSax seax) a knife]

sax[3] /saks/ a Scots form of **six**.

saxatile /sak'sə-tīl or -til/ adj rock-dwelling. [L saxātilis, from saxum a rock]

saxaul or **saksaul** /sak'söl/ n a low, thick, grotesquely contorted tree (genus Haloxylon) of the goosefoot family, found on the salt steppes of Asia.

Saxe /saks/ adj (of china, etc) made in, or characteristic of, Saxony; (also without cap) of a deep shade of light blue (also **Saxe** or **saxe blue**). ◆ n Saxon blue, a dye colour; an albuminized paper (photog). [Fr Saxe Saxony]

saxhorn /saks'hörn/ n a valved brass instrument having a long winding tube with a bell opening, invented by Antoine (also known as Adolphe) Sax (1814–94).

saxicavous /sak-sik'ə-vəs/ adj rock-boring. [L saxum a rock, and cavāre to hollow]

saxicolous /sak-sik'ə-ləs/ or **saxicoline** /sak-sik'ə-lēn/ adj living or growing among rocks. [L saxum a rock, and colere to inhabit]

saxifrage /sak'si-frij or -frāj/ n any plant of the London pride genus Saxifraga, alpine or rock plants with tufted foliage and small white, yellow or red flowers, giving name to the family **Saxifragā'ceae**; extended to certain other plants (see **burnet saxifrage** under **burnet**, **golden saxifrage** under **golden**). [L saxifraga, from saxum a stone, and frangere to break (from growing in clefts of rock, or, according to Pliny, from its supposed efficacy in breaking up a calculus in the bladder)]

■ **saxifragā'ceous** adj.

saxitoxin /sak-si-tok'sin/ n a nerve poison found in molluscs feeding on dinoflagellates of the genus Gonyaulax. [Saxidomus giganteus, the Alaskan butter clam, from which the toxin has been isolated]

Saxon /sak'sən/ n a member of a N German people that conquered most of Britain in the 5c and 6c (including or excluding the Angles and Jutes); the language of that people on the Continent (Old Saxon) or in Britain (Anglo-Saxon, Old English); an English or lowland Scots person; someone whose native language is English; the English language; a native, inhabitant, or citizen of Saxony in the later German sense (now in S Germany). ◆ adj relating to the Saxons in any sense, their language, culture, or architecture. [L Saxonēs (pl); of Ger origin; cf OE Seaxe; Ger Sachsen; perh connected with OE sæx (WSax seax), OHGer sahs knife, short sword]

■ **Sax'ondom** n the Anglo-Saxon or English-speaking world. **Saxonian** /saks-ō'ni-ən/ n (geol) a division of the Permian system in W Europe. **Saxonic** /-on'ik/ adj. **Sax'onism** n a Saxon or English idiom; a preference for native English words, institutions, etc. **Sax'onist** n a scholar in Old English. **Sax'onize** or **-ise** vt and vi to make or become Saxon. **sax'ony** n a soft woollen yarn or cloth.

❑ **Saxon architecture** n a style of building in England before the Norman Conquest, marked by the peculiar 'long and short' work of the quoins, projecting fillets running up the face of the walls and interlacing like woodwork, and baluster-like shafts between the openings of the upper windows resembling the turned woodwork of the period. **Saxon** or **Saxony blue** n a dye produced by dissolving indigo in sulphuric acid. **Saxon Shore** n (L Litus Saxonicum) in Roman times, the coast districts from Brighton to the Wash, peculiarly exposed to the attacks of the Saxons, or perhaps already partly settled by them, and so placed under the authority of a special officer, the 'Count of the Saxon Shore'.

saxonite /sak'sə-nīt/ n an ultrabasic igneous rock consisting of olivine and enstatite. [**Saxon** and **-ite**]

saxophone /sak'sə-fōn/ n a wind instrument with a reed, an S-shaped (properly metal) tube, and about twenty finger-keys, used esp in jazz and dance bands. [Sax, the inventor (see **saxhorn**), and Gr phōnē the voice]

■ **saxophonic** /-fon'ik/ adj. **saxophonist** /-sof'ən-ist/ n.

say[1] /sā/ vt (2nd pers sing present indicative (archaic) **say'est** /sā'ist/ or **sayst** /sāst/; 3rd pers sing **says** /sez or saz/ or (archaic) **saith** /seth/; prp **say'ing**; pat and pap **said** /sed/; 2nd pers sing (archaic) **said'est** /sed'ast/ or **saidst** /sedst/) to utter or set forth, as words or in words; to speak; to assert, affirm, state, declare; to express; to tell; to suppose as a hypothesis; to go through in recitation or repetition. ◆ vi to make a statement; to speak; to declare, set forth in answer to a question. ◆ n opportunity of speech; a voice, part, or influence in a decision; something said; a remark; a speech; what one wants to say; a saw (obs). ◆ adv approximately; for example. ◆ interj (N Am) expressing surprise, protest, sudden joy, etc; used to attract attention; used to introduce a rhetorical question (esp 18c poetic). [OE secgan (sægde, gesægd); ON segia, Ger sagen]

■ **say'able** adj. **say'er** n. **say'ing** n an expression; a maxim; something said.

❑ **say'-so** n authority; an authoritative saying; a rumour; hearsay.

■ **don't say** (inf) surely it's not, let's hope it's not, the case that (eg don't say I've no money with me!). **I'll say!** (inf) a response expressing wholehearted agreement. **I say!** an exclamation calling attention or expressing surprise, protest, sudden joy, etc. **it goes without saying** it is obvious. **it is said** or **they say** it is commonly reputed. **it says (that)** (inf) the text runs thus. **nothing to say for oneself** no defence of oneself to offer; no small talk. **nothing to say to** no dealings or conversation with. **not to say** indeed one might go further and say. **says I**, **says you**, **he**, etc (in non-standard or joc use) ungrammatical substitutes for said I, you, he, etc. **says you** an interjection expressing incredulity. **that is to say** in other words. **there's no saying** it is impossible to guess or judge. **to say nothing of** not to mention. **to say the least** at least; without exaggeration. **what do you say to?** how about?; are you inclined towards? **you can say that again** (inf) you are absolutely right, I agree entirely. **you don't say!** (inf) an astonished rejoinder, or ironic response to the obvious or unamusing.

say[2] /sā/ (obs; Spenser, Shakesp) n, vt and vi an aphetic form of **assay**.
■ **say'er** n.
❑ **say'-master** n. **say'-piece** n.

say[3] /sā/ (archaic) n a woollen fabric like serge. ◆ adj made of say. [OFr saie, from L saga, pl of sagum military cloak]
■ **say'on** n a medieval peasant's sleeveless jacket.

SAYE abbrev : save as you earn.

sayid see **sayyid**.

sayne /sān/ (Spenser) infinitive and pl of prt of **say**[1].

sayonara /sä-yo-nä'ra/ (Jap) n or interj goodbye.

sayyid, sayid or **said** /sī' or sā'yid, sā'id, also säd/ n a descendant of Mohammed's daughter Fatima; an honorary title given to some Muslims. [Ar]

saz /saz/ n a stringed instrument of Turkey, N Africa and the Middle East. [Pers sāz a musical instrument]

Sazerac® /saz'ə-rak/ n (US) a cocktail based on Pernod and whisky.

sazhen /sä-zhen'/ n a Russian measure, about 2 metres. [Russ]

Sb (chem) symbol : antimony. [L stibium]

sb. abbrev : substantive.

sbirro /zbir'rō/ n (pl **sbirr'i** /-rē/) an Italian police officer. [Ital]

'sblood /zblud/ (archaic) interj an exclamatory oath. [God's blood]

SBN abbrev : Standard Book Number.

'sbodikins /zbod'i-kinz/ or **'sbuddikins** /zbud'/, also **'zbud** /zbud/ (obs) interj an exclamatory oath. [God's body]

SBS abbrev : sick building syndrome; Special Boat Service.

SC abbrev : School Certificate (Aust and NZ); Signal Corps; South Carolina (US state); special constable.

Sc (chem) symbol : scandium.

sc (printing) abbrev : small capitals.

sc. abbrev : scilicet (L), namely; sculpsit (L), he/she sculpted (this work).

s/c abbrev : self-catering; self-contained.

SCAA abbrev : School Curriculum and Assessment Authority (now replaced by **QCA**).

scab /skab/ n a crust formed over a wound or sore, or in various diseases; vaguely, a skin disease, esp with scales or pustules, and esp one caused by mites (as in sheep scab); a fungal disease of various kinds in potatoes, apples, etc; a scoundrel (derog); a blackleg (inf). ◆ vi to develop a scab; to act as a blackleg. [Appar from an ON equivalent of OE scæb, sceabb (see **shabby**) infl by association with L scabiēs]

■ **scabbed** /skabd or skab'id/ adj affected or covered with scabs; diseased with scab; vile, worthless (archaic). **scabb'edness** n. **scabb'iness** n. **scabb'y** adj. **scab'like** adj.

scabbard /skab'ərd/ n a sheath, esp for a sword. ◆ vt to sheathe. [ME scauberc, appar from Anglo-Fr escaubers (pl), prob Gmc]
■ **scabb'ardless** adj.
▫ **scabbard fish** n a long narrow fish (genus Lepidopus) having a whiplike tail.

scabble /skab'l/ same as **scapple**.

scaberulous /skə-ber'ū-ləs/ (archaic) adj somewhat scabrous. [From dimin of L scaber rough, scurfy]

scabies /skā'bēz or -bi-ēz/ n a contagious skin infection caused by the itch mite, Sarcoptes scabiei, characterized by intense itching and the formation of vesicles and pustules. [L scabiēs, from scabere to scratch]

scabious /skā'bi-əs/ adj having scabs. ◆ n any plant of the genus Scabiosa of the teasel family, long thought efficacious in treating skin diseases. [L scabiōsus, from scabiēs the itch]
■ **devil's-bit scabious** a small plant (Scabiosa succisa) with purplish flowers. **sheep's-bit** (or **sheep's**) **scabious** a plant (genus Jasione) of the bellflower family, of similar appearance.

scablands /skab'ləndz/ (geol) n pl an area of bare, usu volcanic rock, in the NW USA, that has been deeply channelled by glacial meltwaters. [**scab**]

scabrid /skab'rid/ (archaic) adj scabrous. [L scabridus, from scaber rough]
■ **scabrid'ity** n.

scabrous /skā'brəs/ adj rough; rough with projecting points; scurfy; harsh; beset with difficulties; bordering on the indecent. [L scabrōsus, scabridus, from scaber rough]
■ **scab'rously** adv. **scā'brousness** n.

scad¹ /skad/ n a carangoid fish (genus Trachurus) with an armoured and keeled lateral line, superficially like a coarse mackerel, also called **horse mackerel**. [Appar Cornish dialect; perh **shad**]

scad² /skad/ (esp US; inf) n (usu in pl) a large amount, a lot (esp of money). [Of uncertain origin; poss from dialect scald multitude]

scaff /skaf/ n food (Scot); riff-raff (also **scaff'-raff**). [Perh Du or Ger schaffen to procure food; cf **scoff²**]

scaffie /skaf'i/ (Scot inf) n short for **scavenger** (a street-cleaner).

scaffold /skaf'əld/ n a temporary framework of platforms erected around a building, from which repairs, construction work, etc can be carried out; a raised platform, eg for performers, spectators, or executions; a raised framework, eg for hunters, or among some primitive peoples for disposal of the dead; a framework; (with the) capital punishment, hanging (fig). ◆ vt to supply with a scaffold; to put on a scaffold; to sustain. [OFr escadafault (Fr échafaud), of obscure origin; cf Ital catafalco]
■ **scaff'oldage** (Shakesp **scaff'olage**) n a scaffolding; the gallery of a theatre. **scaff'older** n. **scaff'olding** n a framework of platforms for painters, builders, etc at work; materials for scaffolds; a frame, framework (fig); the erection of scaffolds.

scag or **skag** /skag/ (N Am sl) n heroin. [Origin obscure]

scaglia /skal'yə/ n an Italian limestone, usu reddish. [Ital scaglia scale]

scagliola /skal-i-ō'lə/ n a polished imitation marble consisting of ground gypsum bound with glue. [Ital, dimin of scaglia a chip of marble]

scail same as **skail**.

scaith see **scathe**.

scala /skā'lə or skä'lə/ n (pl **scā'lae** /-lē or -lī/) a ladder-like structure, such as any of the spiral canals of the cochlea. [L scāla a ladder]
■ **scalar** /skā'lər/ adj ladder-like; numerical; represented by a point in a scale; having magnitude only, not direction (phys and maths). ◆ n a scalar quantity. **scalariform** /skə-lar'i-förm/ adj ladder-like.
▫ **scalar product** n (maths) a number equal to the product of the magnitudes of two vectors and the cosine of the angle between them.

scalade /skə-lād'/, also **scalado** /-lä'dō, -lä'dö/ n (pl **scalades'** or **scala'dos**) an escalade. [Ital scalada, from scāla a ladder]

Scalaria /skə-lā'ri-ə/ n the wentletrap genus. [Mod L, from scāla a ladder]

scalawag same as **scallywag**.

scald¹ /sköld/ vt to injure with hot liquid or steam; to cook or heat short of boiling; to treat with very hot water; to burn, scorch (now dialect). ◆ vi to be scalded; to be hot enough to scald. ◆ n a burn caused by hot liquid. [OFr escalder (Fr échauder), from LL excaldāre to bathe in warm water, from ex from, and calidus warm, hot]
■ **scald'er** n. **scald'ing** n and adj. **scald'ings** interj (old) a cry of warning to get out of the way, as if of hot water.

scald² same as **skald**.

scald³ /sköld/ (obs) adj scabby; scurfy; paltry. ◆ n scurf on the head; a scurvy fellow. [For **scalled**]
▫ **scald'berry** n the blackberry (from a belief that it causes scaldhead). **scald'-crow** n (Irish) the hooded crow. **scald'fish** n the smooth sole,

Argoglossus laterna. **scald'head** n a diseased scalp; scalp disease of various kinds.

scaldino /skal- or skäl-dē'nō/ n (pl **scaldi'ni** /-nē/) an Italian earthenware brazier. [Ital scaldare to warm]

scale¹ /skāl/ n a graduated series or order; a graduated measure; a system of definite tones used in music; a succession of these performed in ascending or descending order of pitch through one octave or more; the compass or range of a voice or instrument; a numeral system; a system or scheme of relative values or correspondences; the ratio of representation to object; relative extent; a ladder (obs); a scaling ladder (Milton); a flight of steps (obs). ◆ vt to mount (as by a ladder); to climb; to change according to scale (often with up or down); to estimate how much timber will be obtained from (a log or tree) (N Am). ◆ vi to mount. [L scāla a ladder, from scandere to mount]
■ **scalabil'ity** or **scaleabil'ity** n. **scal'able** or **scale'able** adj able to be scaled; esp of computer systems, easily variable in size. **scal'ableness** or **scale'ableness** n. **scal'ably** or **scale'ably** adv. **scal'er** n an instrument incorporating more than one **scaling circuit**, a device that counts very rapid pulses, by recording at the end of each group of specified numbers instead of after individual pulses; a scaling circuit itself. **scal'ing** n climbing; adjustment to or in a scale.
▫ **scale model** n a model of something made in reduced size but accurate proportion. **scale stair** or **staircase** n (Scot) stairs in straight flights. **scaling ladder** n a ladder for climbing the walls of a fortress, etc; a firefighter's ladder.
■ **full-scale** see under **full¹**. **on a large**, **small**, etc **scale** in a great, small, etc way. **on the scale of** in the ratio of. **scale and platt** (Scot) stairs with straight flights and landings. **to scale** in proportion corresponding to actual dimensions.

scale² /skāl/ n a thin plate on a fish, reptile, etc; a readily detached flake; a lamina; an overlapping plate in armour; a small, flat, detachable piece of cuticle; a reduced leaf or leaf-base, often membranous, or hard and woody; any of the small flat structures covering a butterfly's or moth's wing; the waxy shield secreted by a scale insect; an encrustation, esp that left inside a kettle, etc by hard water; a deposit of tartar on the teeth; a film, as on iron being heated for forging; a side piece of a razor or clasp-knife handle. ◆ vt to clear of scale or scales; to peel off in thin layers. ◆ vi to come off in thin layers or flakes; to form scales; to become encrusted with scale. [ME scāle, from OFr escale husk, chip of stone, of Gmc origin; cf **scale³**, **shale²**, **shell**]
■ **scaled** adj having scales; cleared of scales. **scale'less** adj. **scale'like** adj. **scal'er** n a person who scales fish, boilers, etc; an instrument for scaling, as for removing tartar from the teeth. **scal'iness** n. **scal'ing** n formation, peeling off, shedding, removal, or arrangement, of scales or scale; a scaled-off piece. **scal'y** adj covered with scales; like scales; shabby; formed of scales; inclined to scale.
▫ **scale armour** n armour of overlapping scales. **scale board** n a very thin slip of wood. **scale fern** n a fern (Ceterach officinarum) whose back is densely covered with rusty-coloured scales. **scale fish** n a dry-cured fish, such as haddock, hake, pollack; a fish with scales. **scale insect** n any insect of the homopterous family Coccidae, in which the sedentary female fixes on a plant and secretes a waxy shield. **scale leaf** n a scale that is homologically a leaf. **scale moss** n a liverwort with small leaflike structures, as Jungermannia. **scale'work** n imbricated ornament. **scaly anteater** n the pangolin. **scal'y-bark** n hickory; hickory-nut. **scal'y-leg** n a disease of the legs and feet in poultry, caused by a mite.

scale³ /skāl/ n (usu in pl; treated by Shakespeare as sing) a device for weighing; a balance pan; (in pl; usu with cap) Libra, a constellation and a sign of the zodiac. ◆ vt to weigh; to weigh up. ◆ vi to weigh or be weighed, as a jockey (often scale in). [A Scot and N Eng form from ON skāl bowl, pan of balance; cf OE scealu shell, cup, Du schaal, Ger Schale, and **scale²**]
▫ **scale beam** n the beam of a balance.
■ **tip the scale(s)** see under **tip²**.

scale⁴ /skāl/ same as **skail**.

scale⁵ /skāl/ (Shakesp, Coriolanus I.1.90) vt variously explained as to spread, disseminate (see **skail**), to lay bare, make clear (see **scale²**) or as a misprint for 'stale'.

scalene /skā'lēn or ska-lēn'/ adj (of a triangle) with three unequal sides; (of a cone or cylinder) with the axis oblique to the base (maths); denoting a scalenus muscle (anat). [Gr skalēnos uneven]
▫ **scalenohē'dron** n (Gr hedrā seat; crystallog) a hemihedral form bounded in the hexagonal system by twelve, in the tetragonal by eight, faces, each a scalene triangle.

scalenus /ska-lē'nəs or skā-/ (anat) n (pl **scaleni** /-nī/) one of the paired muscles in the neck extending to the first and second ribs, being obliquely situated and unequal-sided. [New L, from LL scalēnus, from Gr skalēnos; see **scalene**]

scall /sköl/ (*obs*) *n* scabbiness, *esp* of the scalp. ◆ *adj* scurvy; mean. [ON *skalli* bald head]
■ **scalled** *adj* (see **scald**³).

scallawag same as **scallywag**.

scallion /skalˈyən/ *n* the shallot (*dialect*); the leek; an onion with a slim bulb; a spring onion. [ONFr *escalogne*, from L *Ascalōnia* (*cēpa*) Ascalon (onion)]

scallop /skolˈəp or skalˈəp/, also **scollop** /skolˈ/ *n* a bivalve mollusc (*esp* genus *Pecten*) having a sub-circular shell with sinuous radiating ridges and an eared hinge-line; a valve of its shell; a dish or other object of similar form; a shallow dish in which oysters, etc are cooked, baked, and browned; hence, the cooked oysters, etc themselves; a potato slice cooked in batter; one of a series of curves in the edge of anything; an escalope. ◆ *vt* to cut into scallops or curves; to cook in a scallop with sauce and *usu* breadcrumbs. ◆ *vi* to gather or search for scallops. [OFr *escalope*; of Gmc origin; cf Du *schelp* shell; Ger *Schelfe* husk]
■ **scall'oped** *adj* having the edge or border cut into scallops or curves. **scall'oper** *n*.
□ **scallop shell** *n* the shell of a scallop, *esp* that of a Mediterranean species used (*esp hist*) as the badge of a pilgrim to the shrine of St James of Compostela in NW Spain.

scally /skalˈi/ (*sl*) *n* a rogue or scoundrel. [Short for **scallywag**]

scallywag /skalˈi-wag/, **scallawag** or **scalawag** /-ə-wag/ *n orig* an undersized animal of little value; a good-for-nothing; a rascal, scamp; a Southerner who co-operated with the Republicans in the Reconstruction period (*US hist*). [Origin obscure; association with *Scalloway* in Shetland, in allusion to its small cattle or ponies, is regarded as a joke]

scaloppine /skal-ə-pēˈni/ *n pl* escalopes of meat, *usu* veal, fried and served in a sauce. [Ital *scaloppina* (sing), dimin of *scaloppa* a fillet]

scalp¹ /skalp/ (*Scot* **scaup** /sköp/) *n* the outer covering of the skull; the skull (*obs*); the top or hairy part of the head; the skin on which the hair of the head grows; a piece of that skin torn off as a token of victory by some tribes of Native Americans (*hist*); a bare rock or mountain-top (*esp Scot*); a bed of oysters or mussels (*dialect*). ◆ *vt* to cut the scalp from; to buy cheap in order to resell quickly at a profit; to buy up and sell (theatre, travel, or other tickets) at inflated prices (*N Am*); to destroy the political influence of (*N Am*). [ME *scalp*; perh Scand; cf ON *skälpr* sheath; cf **scallop**]
■ **scalp'er** *n*. **scalp'ing** *n*. **scalp'less** *adj*.
□ **scalp'ing-knife** *n* a knife for scalping enemies. **scalp'ing-tuft** *n* a scalp lock. **scalp lock** *n* a long tuft of hair left unshaven as a challenge by Native Americans.

scalp² /skalp/ (*rare*) *vt* and *vi* to scrape; to cut; to engrave. [L *scalpere* to scrape, cut]
■ **scalp'el** *n* a small knife for dissecting or operating. **scalpell'iform** *adj* shaped like a scalpel. **scalp'er** *n* a scalprum; an engraver's scauper. **scalp'riform** *adj* chisel-shaped. **scalp'rum** *n* a surgeon's rasping instrument.

scalpins /skalˈpinz/ *n pl* small stones used for drainage in excavations, and as hardcore. [Origin unknown]

scaly see under **scale**².

scam /skam/ (*sl*) *n* a swindle. ◆ *vt* to swindle. [Origin unknown]
■ **scamm'er** *n*.

scamble /skamˈbl/ *vi* to scramble (for eg something scattered); to get along somehow (*obs*); to shamble (*dialect*); to sprawl (*dialect*). ◆ *vt* to get together with effort (now *dialect*); to remove piecemeal; to scatter as for a scramble (*dialect*); to squander (*dialect*). [Origin obscure; appar related to **shamble**¹ and **scramble**]
■ **scam'bler** *n* (*Scot*) a mealtime sponger. **scam'bling** *n* (*obs*) scrambling; a haphazard meal. **scam'blingly** *adv* strugglingly.
□ **scam'bling-days** *n pl* (*obs*) days of makeshift meals in Lent.

scamel /skamˈl/ (*Shakesp*) *n* alleged to be a Norfolk name for the bar-tailed godwit; or a misprint for **staniel** or **stannel**.

scammony /skamˈə-ni/ *n Convolvulus scammonia*, a twining Mediterranean plant with arrow-shaped leaves; its dried root; a cathartic gum resin obtained from its root or that of a substitute. [Gr *skammōniā*]

scamp¹ /skamp/ *n* a rascal; a lively, mischievous person, *esp* a child; a highwayman (*obs*). ◆ *vi* to go about idly (*dialect*); to take to the highway (as a robber; *obs*). [OFr *escamper* or Ital *scampare* to decamp, relating to the obs verb sense above]
■ **scamp'ish** *adj*. **scamp'ishly** *adv*. **scamp'ishness** *n*.

scamp² /skamp/ *vt* to do or execute perfunctorily or without thoroughness. [Poss ON *skemma* to shorten; cf **skimp**, **scant**]
■ **scamp'er** *n*. **scamp'ing** *n*.
□ **scamp'-work** *n*.

scamper /skamˈpər/ *vi* to run or skip about briskly; to decamp (*obs*). ◆ *n* an act of scampering. [Related to **scamp**¹]

scampi /skamˈpi/ *n pl* crustaceans of the species *Nephrops norvegicus* (called the Norway lobster or Dublin (Bay) prawn), *esp* (treated as *sing*) when cooked (often in breadcrumbs) and served as a dish. [Pl of Ital *scampo* a shrimp]

scan /skan/ *vt* (**scann'ing**; **scanned** (*archaic* **scand**)) to examine critically or closely; to scrutinize; to analyse metrically (*prosody*); to recite so as to bring out the metrical structure (*prosody*); to judge (*obs*); to interpret, read (*Shakesp*); to make out; to examine all parts of in systematic order; (in television) to pass a beam over every part of in turn; to make pictorial records of (the body or part of it) by various techniques, eg ultrasonics (*med*); to examine data on (a magnetic disk, etc); to search out by swinging the beam (*radar*); to glance over quickly; loosely, to cast an eye negligently over; to climb, scale (*archaic*). ◆ *vi* (*prosody*) to conform with the rules of metre; to analyse or recite verse metrically. ◆ *n* a scanning; the image, etc produced by scanning or by a scanner. [L *scandere*, *scānsum* to climb]
■ **scann'able** *adj*. **scann'er** *n* a person who scans or can scan; a perforated disc (also **scann'ing-disc**) used in early television; the rotating aerial by which the beam is made to scan (*radar*); an instrument which scans, *esp* (*med*) one that makes an image of an internal organ. **scann'ing** *n* and *adj*. **scan'sion** *n* the act, art, or mode of analysing the metrical patterns of verse; scanning in television.
□ **scanning electron microscope** *n* an electron microscope that produces a three-dimensional image, allowing the surface structure of a specimen to be examined (*abbrev* **SEM**). **scanning speech** *n* (*med*) a speech disorder caused by cerebellar disease in which syllables are improperly separated and given equal stress.

Scand. or **Scan.** *abbrev*: Scandinavian.

scand see **scan**.

scandal /skanˈdl/ *n* anything that causes moral discredit or injury to reputation; something said which is injurious to reputation; a false imputation; malicious gossip; slander; opprobrious censure; a disgraceful fact, thing, or person; a shocked feeling; a stumbling-block to religious faith (*obs*); anything that brings discredit upon religion (*obs*). ◆ *vt* (*obs*) to defame; to disgrace; to shock. [L *scandalum*, from Gr *skandalon* a stumbling-block]
■ **scandalīzā'tion** or **-s-** *n*. **scan'dalize** or **-ise** *vt* to give scandal or offence to; to shock; to disgrace (*obs*); to slander (*obs*). ◆ *vi* (*rare*) to talk scandal. **scandal'izer** or **-s-** *n*. **scan'dalled** *adj* (*obs*) disgraceful; slandered. **scan'dalous** *adj* giving scandal or offence; openly vile; defamatory. **scan'dalously** *adv*. **scan'dalousness** *n*.
□ **scan'dal-bearer** *n* a propagator of malicious gossip. **scan'dalmonger** *n* a person who spreads or relishes scandal. **scan'dalmongering** *n*. **scandal sheet** *n* a newspaper with a reputation for publishing scandal or gossip. **scan'dalum magnā'tum** *n* defamation of well-known or important people (*abbrev* **scan. mag.**).

scandent /skanˈdənt/ *adj* (*esp* of plants) climbing. [L *scandēns*, *-entis*]

Scan'dinavian /skan-di-nāˈvi-ən/ *adj* of, or characteristic of, *Scandinavia*, the peninsula divided into Norway and Sweden, but, in a historical sense, applying also to Denmark and Iceland; N Germanic (*philology*). ◆ *n* a native of Scandinavia; a member of the dominant Nordic race of Scandinavia; any of the group of N Germanic languages spoken in Scandinavia. [L *Scandināvia* (from Gmc word which did not have *n* before *d*), applied to the southern part of the peninsula]
■ **Scan'di** (*inf*) *n* and *adj* Scandinavian. **Scan'dian** *n* and *adj* (a) Scandinavian. **Scan'dic** *adj*.

scandium /skanˈdi-əm/ *n* a rare metallic element (symbol **Sc**; atomic no 21) found in various rare minerals *incl* the Scandinavian mineral *euxenite* in which it was discovered in 1879, used in superconductors and lasers. [Scandinavian]

scan. mag. see **scandalum magnatum** under **scandal**.

scanner, **scansion** see under **scan**.

scansorial /skan-söˈri-əl or -sôˈri-əl/ (*zool*) *adj* climbing, *esp* denoting birds of the old order Scansores; adapted for climbing, *esp* denoting a bird's foot having two forward-facing and two rear-facing toes. [L *scandere*, *scānsum* to climb]

scant /skant/ *adj* not full or plentiful; scarcely sufficient; deficient; short, poorly supplied; sparing. ◆ *n* scarcity. ◆ *adv* barely; scantily. ◆ *vt* to stint; to restrict; to reduce; to dispense sparingly; to treat inadequately; to slight. [ON *skamt*, neuter of *skammr* short]
■ **scant'ies** *n pl* (*inf*) underwear, *esp* women's brief panties. **scant'ily** *adv*. **scant'iness** *n*. **scant'ity** *n* (*rare*). **scant'ly** *adv*. **scant'ness** *n*. **scant'y** *adj* meagre; deficient; skimpy; lacking fullness; parsimonious.
□ **scant'-o'-grace** *n* (*Scot*) a good-for-nothing.

scantle[1] /skan'tl/ (obs) vt to stint; to make scant; to shorten (sail). ◆ vi to become scant. ◆ n (Shakesp; variant reading for **cantle**) a portion. [Prob **scant**, with senses merging in **scantling**[1]]
■ **scant'ling** n a small portion. ◆ adj petty.

scantle[2] see under **scantling**[1].

scantling[1] /skant'ling/ n the dimensions of a cross-section, eg of timber used in building, shipbuilding, etc; a sample or pattern; a narrow piece of timber; a small quantity or amount (archaic); a gauge (obs). [OFr escantillon, eschantillon, of uncertain ety, senses merging in **scantle**]
■ **scan'tle** n a gauge for slates. ◆ vt to adjust to measure.

scantling[2] see under **scantle**[1].

scanty see under **scant**.

scapa see **scarper**.

scape[1] /skāp/, also **scapus** /skā'pəs/ n (pl **scapes** or **sca'pi** /-pī/) a flower-stalk rising from the ground, without foliage leaves (bot); the basal part of an antenna (zool); the shaft or stem of a feather; the shaft of a column (archit). [L scāpus a shaft]
■ **scape'less** adj. **scapigerous** /skə-pij'ər-əs/ adj having a scape.

scape[2] /skāp/ n an escape; an escapade; a transgression; a slip. ◆ vt and vi (also **'scape**) to escape. [escape]
■ **scape'less** adj not to be escaped. **scape'ment** n an escapement. ❏ **scape'gallows** n sing a person who deserves hanging. **scape'grace** n an incorrigible rascal. **scape'-wheel** n an escape wheel.

scape[3] /skāp/ n the cry of the snipe when flushed; the snipe itself. [Prob imit]

-scape /-skāp/ sfx indicating a type of scene or view, as in seascape, streetscape. [landscape]

scapegoat /skāp'gōt/ n a goat on which, once a year, the Jewish high-priest symbolically laid the sins of the people, and which was then allowed to escape into the wilderness (Bible, Leviticus 16); someone who is made to bear or take the blame for the failings, misfortunes or misdeeds of another. ◆ vt to make into or treat as a scapegoat. [escape and goat]
■ **scape'goating** n the practice of making (someone) into or using someone as a scapegoat, esp involving harsh or violent treatment; a psychological syndrome of this nature.

scapegrace see under **scape**[2].

scaphocephalus /skaf-ō-sef'ə-ləs, -kef'/ n an abnormally long and narrow boat-shaped skull. [Gr skaphē a boat, and kephalē a head]
■ **scaphocephal'ic** or **scaphoceph'alous** adj. **scaphoceph'aly** n.

scaphoid /skaf'oid/ n (also **scaphoid bone**) a boat-shaped bone of the wrist or ankle joint, the navicular bone. ◆ adj boat-shaped; referring or relating to the scaphoid bone. [Gr skaphē a boat, and eidos form]

scaphopod /skaf'ə-pod/ n a member of the class of marine molluscs Scaphopoda (tooth or tusk shells), in which the foot is trilobed or has a terminal disc and the mantle forms a tube enclosed by the tubular univalve shell (also adj). [Gr skaphos a spade, and pous, podos a foot]

scapi see **scape**[1].

scapigerous see under **scape**[1].

scapolite /skap'ə-līt/ n any of a group of rare minerals, silicates of aluminium, calcium, and sodium with some chlorine, crystallizing in the tetragonal system. [Gr skāpos a rod, and lithos a stone]

scapple /skap'l/ or **scabble** /skab'l/ vt to work or shape (eg stone) roughly, without smoothing to a finish. [OFr escapeler to dress timber]

scapula /skap'ū-lə/ n (pl **scap'ulas** or **scap'ulae** /-lē/) the shoulder blade. [L scapula the shoulder blade]
■ **scap'ular** adj of the shoulder blade or shoulder. ◆ n orig ordinary working clothes, now the mark of the monastic orders, a long strip of cloth with an opening for the head, worn hanging in front and behind over the habit; two pieces of cloth tied together over the shoulders, worn by members of certain lay confraternities (RC church); a supporting bandage worn over the shoulder; any of the small feathers lying along the shoulder in birds. **scap'ulary** adj and n scapular. **scap'ulated** adj (zool) with noticeable scapular feathers. **scap'ulimancy** or **scap'ulomancy** n (see **-mancy**) divination by means of the cracks appearing in a burning shoulder blade. **scapūliman'tic** or **scapūloman'tic** adj.

scapus see **scape**[1].

scar[1] /skär/ n the mark left by a wound or sore; any mark or blemish; any mark, trace, or result of injury, eg of a material, moral or psychological, etc nature; a mark at a place of former attachment, eg of a leaf. ◆ vt (scarr'ing; scarred) to mark with a scar. ◆ vi to become scarred. [OFr escare, from L eschara, from Gr eschara a hearth, brazier, burn, scar]

■ **scar'less** adj without scars; unwounded. **scarred** adj. **scarr'ing** n and adj. **scarr'y** adj.

scar[2] /skär/ or **scaur** /skör/ n a precipitous bare place on a hill-face; a cliff; a reef in the sea. [Appar ON sker, skera to cut]
■ **scarr'y** adj.

scar[3] /skär/ n (also **scar'fish**) a parrot-wrasse. [L scarus, from Gr skaros]
■ **Scarus** /skā'rəs/ n the parrot-wrasse genus, giving name to the family **Scaridae** /skar'i-dē/.

scar[4] or **scarre** /skär/ (pat and pap **scarred** or **scarr'd**) an archaic or Scots form of **scare**.

scarab /skar'əb/ n any scarabaeid beetle, esp the dung-beetle, Scarabaeus sacer, the sacred beetle of the ancient Egyptians, or related species; a gem carved in the form of a beetle, used by the ancient Egyptians as an amulet, seal, etc; a term of abuse (obs). [L scarabaeus; cf Gr kārabos]
■ **scarabaeid** /skar-ə-bē'id/ or **scarabaean** /-bē'ən/ n and adj (any lamellicorn beetle) of the family Scarabaeidae, incl the dung-beetles, chafers, stag beetles, etc. **scarabae'ist** n a person who studies scarabaeid beetles. **scarabae'oid** adj resembling a scarabaeid. ◆ n a scarabaeid or a gem carved in the shape of one. **scarabae'us** n (pl **scarabae'uses** or **scarabaei** /-bē'ī/) a beetle of the Scarabaeus genus of lamellicorn beetles, the typical genus of the Scarabaeidae. **scar'abee** n (archaic) a scarabaeid beetle. **scar'aboid** n a carved gem only vaguely resembling a beetle in shape; a scarabaeid (also adj).

Scaramouch or **Scaramouche** /skar'ə-moosh or (rare) -mowch/ n a stock character in an old Italian comedy, dressed in the black costume of a Spanish don, and characterized as a boastful coward; (without cap) a bragging, cowardly buffoon. [Fr Scaramouche, from Ital Scaramuccia]

scarce /skärs/ adj by no means plentiful; not often found; hard to get; in short supply; sparing (obs). ◆ adv scarcely; with difficulty (Milton); hardly ever. [ONFr escars (Fr échars) niggardly, from a LL substitute for L excerptus, pap of excerpere, from ex out, and carpere to pick]
■ **scarce'ly** adv only just; not quite; hardly ever; not at all; scantily (obs). **scarce'ness** n. **scarc'ity** n the state or fact of being scarce; shortness of supply, esp of necessaries; dearth; deficiency; niggardliness (obs).
■ **make oneself scarce** (inf) to leave quickly, unobtrusively, for reasons of prudence, tact, etc.

scarcement /skärs'mənt/ (Scot) n a ledge formed by the setting back of a wall, buttress, or bank. [Poss from **scarce**]

scare /skär/ vt to startle, frighten; to drive or keep off by frightening. ◆ vi to become frightened. ◆ n a fright; a panic; a short-lived and often unwarranted public alarm. [ME skerre, from ON skirra to avoid, from skiarr shy; vowel history obscure]
■ **scared** adj frightened. **scar'er** n. **scarify** /skär'i-fī/ vt (non-standard) to frighten. **scar'ily** adv. **scar'iness** n. **scar'y** or **scare'y** adj frightening; timorous.
❏ **scare'crow** n anything set up to scare birds; a vain cause of terror, a bogy; a shabbily-dressed person; a person so thin that his or her clothes appear ill-fitting. **scared'y-cat** n a term of abuse used, esp by children, in addressing someone who is afraid to undertake some dangerous or illicit act; a coward. **scare'-head**, **scare'-heading** or **scare'-line** n a newspaper heading designed to raise a scare. **scare'monger** n an alarmist, someone who causes panic by initiating or encouraging rumours of trouble. **scare'mongering** n and adj. **scare quotes** n pl quotation marks used to indicate that the enclosed expression is in some way questionable. **scare tactics** n pl actions or words solely intended to intimidate. **scare'ware** n (comput sl) malicious software designed to deceive users into buying useless or dangerous products.
■ **run scared** to panic. **scare the (living) daylights out of** or **scare the pants off** (both inf) to frighten considerably. **scare up** to beat up (game) (US and dialect); to hunt out; to produce (eg a meal) quickly, to rustle up (inf).

scarf[1] /skärf/ n (pl **scarfs** or **scarves**) a light, usu decorative piece of material thrown loosely on the shoulders about the neck, or tied around the head, etc; a strip of woollen or other warm fabric to tie or tuck round the neck; a muffler; a military or official sash; a band worn around the neck with ends hanging in front, formerly the mark of a clergyman of some degree of dignity, esp a nobleman's chaplain; hence, a chaplaincy; a veil; a necktie; a cravat; a sling for an injured limb (obs). ◆ vt (rare) to cover, as if with a scarf; to wrap as a scarf does. [Perh ONFr escarpe (Fr écharpe) sash, sling]
■ **scarfed** adj wearing a scarf, decorated with scarves. **scarf'wise** adv in the manner of a scarf or sash, over the shoulder, diagonally across the chest and back, and secured under the arm.
❏ **scarf'-pin** n an ornamental pin worn in a scarf; a tie-pin. **scarf'-ring** n an ornamental ring through which the ends of a scarf are drawn.

scarf² /skärf/ n a joint between pieces placed end to end, cut so as to fit with overlapping like a continuous piece; an end so prepared; a longitudinal cut in a whale's carcase. ◆ vt (also **scarph**) to join with a scarf-joint; to make a scarf in. [Perh Scand]
- **scarf'ing** n.
- ❑ **scarf'-joint** n.

scarf³ /skärf/ (N Am sl) vt to devour greedily (often with up, down or out). [Origin uncertain; perh variant of **scoff²**]

scarfskin /skärf'skin/ n the surface skin. [Origin doubtful; perh **scarf¹**; perh related to **scurf**]

Scaridae see **Scarus** under **scar³**.

scarify¹ /skar'i-fī/ vt (**scar'ifying**; **scar'ified**) to make a number of scratches or slight cuts in; to break up the surface of (esp soil); to lacerate (the skin) with a series of small punctures, as in inoculation; to criticize harshly and severely. [LL scarīficāre, -ātum, for L scarīfāre, from Gr skarīphasthai, from skarīphos an etching tool]
- **scarification** /-fi-kā'shən/ n. **scar'ificātor** n a surgical instrument for scarifying; a scarifier. **scar'ifier** n someone who scarifies; an implement for breaking the surface of the soil or of a road.

scarify² see under **scare**.

scarious /skā'ri-as/ adj thin, dry, stiff, and membranous (bot); scaly, scurfy (zool). [Origin unknown]

scarlatina /skär-lə-tē'nə/ (med) n scarlet fever. [Ital scarlattina]

scarlet /skär'lit/ n orig a fine cloth, not always red; a brilliant red; a brilliant red cloth, garment, or garb, or its wearer. ◆ adj of the colour scarlet; dressed in scarlet. ◆ vt to redden. [OFr escarlate (Fr écarlate), thought to be from Pers saqalāt scarlet cloth]
- ❑ **scarlet bean** n another name for scarlet runner. **scarlet fever** n an infectious streptococcal fever, usu marked by a sore throat, sickness and a scarlet rash, scarlatina. **scarlet geranium** n a scarlet-flowered pelargonium. **scarlet hat** n a cardinal's red hat. **scarlet letter** n (hist) a scarlet-coloured letter A worn by women convicted of adultery in the Puritan communities of New England. **scarlet pimpernel** n a flowering plant, Anagallis arvensis, of the primrose family, with small red, white or purple flowers that close when the weather is cloudy. **scarlet runner** n a scarlet-flowered climber (Phaseolus multiflorus) of the kidney bean genus, with edible beans. **scarlet woman** n the woman referred to in the Bible (Revelation 17), variously interpreted as pagan Rome, Papal Rome, or the world in its anti-Christian sense; a whore.

scarmoge /skär'mɔj/ n an archaic form of **skirmish**.

scarp¹ /skärp/ n an escarp; an escarpment. ◆ vt to cut into a scarp. [Ital scarpa]
- **scarped** adj. **scarp'ing** n.

scarp² /skärp/ (heraldry) n a diminutive of the bend-sinister, half its width. [OFr escarpe; cf **scarf¹**]

scarper /skär'pər/ (inf) vi to run away, escape, leave without notice (also **scar'pa** and **sca'pa**). [Ital scappare to escape; poss strengthened by Cockney scapa, from World War I rhyming slang Scapa Flow go]

scarph see **scarf²**.

scarpines /skär'pinz/ n pl an instrument of torture for the feet. [Ital scarpino, scarpetto, dimins of scarpa shoe]
- **scarpet'to** n (pl **scarpet'ti** /-tē/) a hemp-soled shoe or climbing boot.

scarre¹ /skär/ (Shakesp) n word of unknown meaning in All's Well That Ends Well IV.2.38, probably a misprint, but never satisfactorily explained.

scarre² see **scar⁴**.

scarred, scarring, scarry see under **scar¹,²,⁴**.

SCART or **Scart** /skärt/ n a plug with 21 pins used to connect parts of a video or audio system. [Acronym from Syndicat des Constructeurs des Appareils Radiorécepteurs et Téléviseurs, the name of the European syndicate that developed it]

scart¹ /skärt/ (Scot) vt to scratch; to scrape. ◆ n a scratch or scrape; a dash or stroke of a pen. [See **scrat**]
- ❑ **scart'-free** adj (Scot).

scart², **scarth** see **skart**.

Scarus see under **scar³**.

scarves see **scarf¹**.

scary see under **scare**.

scat¹ /skat/ (inf) interj (used orig and esp to animals) go away! ◆ vt (**scatt'ing**; **scatt'ed**) to scare away. ◆ vi to go away quickly.

scat² /skat/ (jazz) n the use of nonsense syllables and other wordless effects in singing (also adj). ◆ vi (**scatt'ing**; **scatt'ed**) to sing in this way. [Perh imit]

scat³ or **skat** /skat/ n an animal-dropping. [Gr skōr, skatos dung]

- **scatolog'ical** adj. **scatol'ogy** n the scientific study of excrement, as in (pathol) diagnosis by study of the faeces, or (palaeontol) classification or identification of fossils by study of their fossilized excrement; obscene literature; interest in or preoccupation with the obscene. **scatoph'agous** adj (see **-phagous** under **phag-**) dung-eating. **scatoph'agy** /-ji/ n the practice of feeding on dung.

scat⁴ /skat/ n a small brightly-coloured marine fish of the family Scatophagidae, often living around sewage. [Gr skatophagos dung-eating]

scat⁵, **scatt** or **skat** /skat/ (hist) n tribute; a tax; esp a udaller's land tax, in Orkney and Shetland, paid to the Crown. [ON skattr; cf OE sceatt money, Du schat, Ger Schatz]

scat⁶ or **skatt** /skat/ (Devon and Cornish dialect) n a blow; a throw or break; a spell; a sudden rain shower. ◆ adv in collapse; to bankruptcy.
- **scatt'ing** n pebble-dashing.

scatch /skach/ n a stilt. [ONFr escache (Fr échasse); cf **skate¹**]

scathe /skādh/ (Scot **scaith**, **skaith** /skāth/; Spenser **scath** /skath/) vt (often in neg) to injure; to blast; to scorch with invective. ◆ n (archaic or dialect) injury, harm. [ON skathe; cf OE sceatha an injurer; Ger Schade injury]
- **scathe'ful** adj hurtful. **scathe'fulness** n. **scathe'less** (Scot **scaith'less**, **skaith'less**) adj without injury. **scath'ing** adj scornfully critical; detrimental. **scath'ingly** adv.

scatole same as **skatole**.

scatological, scatophagous, etc see under **scat³**.

scatt see **scat⁵**.

scatted see **scat¹,²**.

scatter /skat'ər/ vt to disperse; to throw loosely about; to strew; to sprinkle; to dispel; to reflect or disperse irregularly (waves or particles). ◆ vi to disperse; to fire shot loosely. ◆ n a scattering; a sprinkling; dispersion; the extent of scattering. [Origin obscure; scatered occurs in the Anglo-Saxon Chronicle (1137); cf **shatter**]
- **scatt'erable** adj. **scatt'ered** adj dispersed irregularly, widely, in all directions, or here and there; thrown about; casually dropped (archaic); (of one's thoughts, etc) distracted. **scatt'eredly** /-ərd-li/ adv. **scatt'erer** n. **scatt'ering** n dispersion; that which is scattered; a small proportion occurring sporadically; the deflection of the path of subatomic particles as a result of collisions with other particles or atoms (phys); the deflection of light by the fine particles of solid, liquid or gaseous matter, from the main direction of the beam (phys); the deflection of radiation resulting from interactions between the photons radiated and the nuclei or electrons in the material through which the radiation is passing, or with another radiation field (phys). **scatt'eringly** adv. **scatt'erling** n (archaic) a vagrant. **scatterom'eter** n an instrument carried in a meteorological satellite for measuring the backscatter of light from the surface of the sea, used to gather information on wind speed. **scatt'ery** adj dispersed; sparse; giving an effect of scattering.
- ❑ **scatt'erbrain** n someone incapable of sustained attention or thought. **scatt'erbrained** adj. **scatter diagram** n a graph plotting two variables, with axes at right angles to one another. **scatt'ergood** n a spendthrift. **scatt'er-gun** n a shotgun. **scattering matrix** n (phys) a matrix in which particles that result from high-energy collisions are made to scatter in various directions (also **S'-matrix**). **scatter rugs**, **scatter cushions** n pl small rugs and cushions which can be placed anywhere in a room. **scatt'ershot** adj random, indiscriminate and wide-ranging, like shot fired from a gun.
- **elastic scattering** see **elastic collision** under **collide**. **inelastic scattering** see **inelastic collision** under **collide**.

scattermouch /skat'ər-mowch/ (old naut sl) n any Mediterranean person. [**Scaramouch** infl by **scatter**]

scatting see **scat¹,²,⁶**.

scatty /skat'i/ (inf) adj mentally disorganized; slightly crazy and unpredictable in conduct. [Poss scatterbrain]
- **scatt'ily** adv. **scatt'iness** n.

scaturient /ska-tū'ri-ənt/ (formal) adj flowing out; gushing. [L scatūriēns, -entis, from scatūrīre to gush out]

scaud /sköd/ a Scots form of **scald¹**.

scaup /sköp/ n a mussel bed; any of various diving ducks of the genus Aythya that feeds on molluscs and crustaceans, esp Aythya marila, the male of which has a black, pale grey and white plumage (also **scaup duck**). [**scalp¹**]

scauper /skö'pər/ or **scorper** /skör'/ n a gouging chisel with a semicircular face, used by engravers and woodcarvers. [**scalper**]

scaur¹ /skör/ a Scots form of **scare**.

scaur² same as **scar²**.

scaury /skö'ri or skö'/ (Orkney and Shetland) n a young gull (also **scou'rie** or **scow'rie**). [ON skāri]

scavage /skav'ij/ n a toll formerly levied in boroughs on goods offered for sale by outsiders; street refuse (obs). [Anglo-Fr scawage inspection; prob of Gmc origin; cf OE scēawian to inspect; see **show**]

■ **scav'ager** n the officer who collected the toll, later charged with keeping the streets clean. **scav'enge** /-inj or -inzh/ vt (back-formation from **scavenger** below) to search (for useful items) among refuse; to cleanse; to remove impurities from (a substance) (chem). ◆ vi to act as a scavenger. ◆ n the sweeping out of waste gases from an internal-combustion engine. **scav'enger** /-jər/ n a person who searches for and gathers discarded items from garbage bins, etc; a person who cleans the streets; a person or apparatus that removes waste; an animal that feeds on garbage or carrion; someone who deals or delights in filth. ◆ vi to act as a scavenger. **scav'engering** n. **scav'engery** n. **scav'enging** n.

❑ **scavenge pump** n in certain internal-combustion engines, an oil pump that returns used oil from the crank case to the oil tank. **scavenger hunt** n a game, usu played outdoors, in which players are given a list of items they must acquire without resorting to buying them.

scavenger[1] /skav'in-jər/ n a perversion of the name of Skevington, Lieutenant of the Tower under Henry VIII, inventor of an instrument of torture known as the **scavenger's**, or **Skevington's**, or **Skeffington's daughter**.

scavenger[2] see under **scavage**.

scaw same as **skaw**.

scawtite /skö'tīt/ n a carbonate or silicate of calcium, occurring naturally as small colourless crystals. [Scawt Hill, Co. Antrim, where it is found]

scazon /skā'zon/ (prosody) n (pl **sca'zons** or **scazontes** /skə-zon'tēz/) (also **scazon iambus**) a choliamb (qv). [Gr skazōn limping]
■ **scazontic** /skə-zon'tik/ n and adj.

ScB abbrev: Scientiae Baccalaureus (L), Bachelor of Science.

SCBU /ski-boo'/ abbrev: special care baby unit.

SCCL abbrev: Scottish Council for Civil Liberties (now known as **SHRC**).

ScD abbrev: Scientiae Doctor (L), Doctor of Science.

SCE abbrev: Scottish Certificate of Education (now replaced by **SQC**).

sceat or **sceatt** /shat/ (hist) n (pl **sceatt'as**) a small silver (or gold) coin of Anglo-Saxon times. [OE]

scedule see **schedule**.

scelerate /sel'ə-rāt or -rit/ (obs) adj wicked. ◆ n (also **scelerat** after Fr scélérat) a villain. [L scelerātus, from scelus crime]

scena /shā'na/ n (pl **scene** /shā'nā/) an operatic scene; an elaborate dramatic recitative followed by an aria. [Ital, from L scēna, scaena, from Gr skēnē tent, stage]

scenario /si-nä'ri-ō/ n (pl **scena'rios**) an outline of a dramatic work, film, etc, scene by scene; an outline of future development, or of a plan to be followed, which shows the operation of causes and where points of decision or difficulty occur; loosely, any imagined, suggested or projected sequence of events, plan of action, situation, etc. [Ital, from L scēnārius, from scēna; see **scena**]
■ **scena'rist** n. **scenariza'tion** or **-s-** n. **scenarize** or **-ise** /-nä'rīz or -nä'/ vt to make a scenario of. **scenary** /sē'nə-ri/ n (obs) disposition of scenes; scenery.

scend see **send**.

scene[1] /sēn/ n a landscape, picture of a place or action; a view or spectacle; the activity, publicity, etc surrounding a particular business or profession, eg the pop music scene (inf); one's area of interest or activity (inf); a situation, state of affairs (inf); orig the stage; a stage performance (obs); the place of action in a play (hence in a story, an actual occurrence, etc); its representation on the stage; a painted slide, hanging, or other object, used for this purpose; a curtain, veil, or screen (archaic); a division of a play marked off by the fall of the curtain, by a change of place, or (in Latin, French, and some English plays) by the entry or exit of any important character; an episode; a dramatic or histrionic incident, esp an uncomfortable, untimely, or unseemly display of feelings. ◆ vt to set in a scene. [L scēna, scaena, from Gr skēnē a tent, stage building]
■ **scēn'ery** n theatrical slides, hangings, etc collectively; views of beautiful, picturesque, or impressive country; dramatic action (obs). **scēne'ster** n (inf) a person who identifies with a particular cultural scene. **scenic** /sē'nik or sen'ik/ adj relating to scenery; having beautiful or remarkable scenery; belonging or relating to the stage or stage scenery; dramatic, theatrical; (of painting, sculpture, etc) representing a scene or incident, eg of historical action. **scen'ical** adj (rare). **scen'ically** adv. **scēnograph'ic** or **scēnograph'ical** adj. **scēnograph'ically** adv. **scēnog'raphy** n perspective drawing; scene-painting.

❑ **scene dock** or **bay** n the space where scenery is stored. **scene'man** n a scene-shifter. **scene-of-crime officer** n a police officer responsible for gathering evidence at the scene of a crime. **scene'-painter** n a person who paints scenery for theatres. **scene'-shifter** n a person who sets and removes the scenery in a theatre. **scene'-shifting** n. **scenic railway** n a miniature railway running through artificial representations of picturesque scenery; a roller-coaster, eg in an amusement park. **scenic reserve** n (NZ) an area of picturesque scenery protected against development and accessible to the public for recreational purposes.

■ **behind the scenes** at the back of the visible stage; away from the public view (lit and fig); in a position to know what goes on; in private. **come on the scene** to arrive. **set the scene** to describe the background to an event, etc.

scene[2] see **scena**.

scène à faire /sen a fār' or fer'/ n the climactic scene in a play or opera. [Fr, scene of action]

scent, earlier **sent** /sent/ vt to track, find, or discern by smell, or as if by smell; to perfume. ◆ vi to give out a smell; to sniff; to smell. ◆ n odour; sense of smell; a substance used for the sake of its smell, perfume; the smell left by an animal, etc, by which it may be hunted; a series of clues or findings; paper strewn by the pursued in the game of hare and hounds. [Fr sentir, from L sentīre to perceive]
■ **scent'ed** adj having a smell, fragrant; impregnated or sprinkled with perfume; endowed with a sense of smell. **scent'ful** adj (archaic) odoriferous; with an acute sense of smell. **scent'ing** n and adj. **scent'less** adj.

❑ **scent bag** n a scent gland; a sachet; a bag containing a strong-smelling substance dragged over the ground for a drag hunt. **scent bottle** n a small bottle for holding perfume. **scent box** n. **scent gland** n a gland that secretes a substance of distinctive smell, for recognition, attraction, or defence. **scent organ** n a scent gland; a smelling organ. **scent scale** n on male butterflies' wings, a scale that gives off a scent.
■ **put** (or **throw**) **someone off the scent** to mislead someone.

scepsis or (esp US) **skepsis** /skep'sis/ n philosophic doubt. [Gr skepsis query, doubt, hesitation, from skeptesthai; see **sceptic**]

sceptic or (esp US) **skeptic** /skep'tik/ adj (with cap) relating to the philosophical school of Pyrrho and his successors, who asserted nothing positively and doubted the possibility of knowledge; sceptical (rare). ◆ n a person who doubts prevailing doctrines, esp in religion; a person who tends to disbelieve; (with cap) a Sceptic philosopher or adherent of the Sceptic school. [L scepticus, from Gr skeptikos thoughtful, from skeptesthai to consider]
■ **scep'tical** or (esp US) **skep'tical** adj of or inclined to scepticism; doubtful or inclined towards incredulity. **scep'tically** or (esp US) **skep'tically** adv. **scep'ticism** or (esp US) **skep'ticism** n doubt; the doctrine that no facts can be certainly known; agnosticism; sceptical attitude towards Christianity; general disposition to doubt.

sceptre or (US) **scepter** /sep'tər/ n a staff or baton carried as an emblem of monarchic authority; hence, monarchic authority itself. [L scēptrum, from Gr skēptron a staff, from skēptein to prop, stay]
■ **scep'tral** adj regal. **scep'tred** or (US) **scep'tered** adj bearing a sceptre; regal. **scep'treless** or (US) **scep'terless** adj. **scep'try** adj (Keats) sceptred.

scerne /sûrn/ (archaic) vt to discern. [**discern**, or Ital scernere]

sceuophylax /skū-of'i-laks or sū-of'/ (Gr church) n a sacristan. [Gr skeuos a vessel, and phylax a watcher]
■ **sceuophylacium** /-lā'si-əm/ n a sacristy.

SCF abbrev: Save the Children Fund.

SCG abbrev: Serbia and Montenegro (ie Srbija i Crna Gora; IVR).

Sch. abbrev: schilling; (also **sch.**) school.

schadenfreude /shä'dən-froi-də/ n malicious pleasure in the misfortunes of others. [Ger, from Schade hurt, and Freude joy]

Schafer's method /shā'fərz meth'əd/ n a method of artificial respiration in which pressure is exerted on the prone patient's lower back at intervals of several seconds (cf **kiss of life**). [Sir Edward Sharpey-Schafer (1850–1935), English physiologist]

schalstein /shäl'shtīn/ n a slaty diabase tuff. [Ger, from Schale shell, scale, and Stein stone]

schanse /shan'sə/, **schanze** or **schantze** /shant'sə/ (S Afr) n a heap of stones used as a protection against rifle fire. [Du schans, schantze; see **sconce**[2]]

schappe /shap'ə/ n a fabric of waste silk, with gum, etc partly removed by fermentation. ◆ vt to subject to this process. [Swiss Ger]

schapska see **chapka**.

schechita(h), **shechita(h)**, **shehita(h)** /she-hhē'ta/ (Judaism) n the slaughtering of animals in accordance with rabbinical law. [Heb shehītāh slaughter]

schecklaton see **checklaton**.

■ words derived from main entry word; ❑ compound words; ■ idioms and phrasal verbs

schedule /shed'ūl/ or (*esp* N Am) /sked'ūl/ *n* (formerly **scedule** /sed'ūl/) *orig* a slip or scroll with writing; a list, inventory, or table; a supplementary, explanatory, or appended document; an appendix to a bill or act of parliament; a form for filling in particulars, or such a form filled in; a timetable, plan, programme, or scheme. ◆ *vt* to make a schedule or enter in a schedule; to plan or arrange to take place at a certain time. [OFr *cedule* (Fr *cédule*), from LL *sc(h)edula*, dimin of *scheda* a strip of papyrus, from Gr *schedē*]

■ **sched'ular** *adj*. **sched'uled** *adj* entered in a schedule; planned, appointed, arranged (to happen at a specified time); (of a building) entered in a list of buildings to be preserved for historic or architectural reasons (see also **listed building** under **list¹**). **sched'uler** *n*.

❑ **scheduled castes** *n pl* (in India) the former untouchables. **scheduled territories** *n pl* (*hist*) the sterling area. **scheduled tribes** *n pl* (in India) indigenous tribes officially given some protection and privileges.

■ **behind schedule** not keeping up to an arranged programme; late. **on schedule** on time.

Scheele's green /shā'ləz or shēlz grēn/ *n* a poisonous yellowish-green pigment, copper hydrogen arsenite, formerly used in wallpapers. [KW *Scheele* (1742–86), who first prepared it; see ety for **scheelite**]

scheelite /shē'līt/ *n* a greenish or brownish mineral, calcium tungstate, crystallizing in the tetragonal system, an important source of tungsten. [KW *Scheele* (1742–86), Swedish chemist, who investigated it]

schefflera /shef'lə-rə/ *n* any of various evergreen tropical or subtropical shrubs of the family Araliaceae, having large compound leaves and clusters of small flowers followed by berries. [Mod L, named after JC *Scheffler*, Polish physician]

schellum same as **skellum**.

schelly or **skelly** /skel'i/ *n* a freshwater white fish, *Coregonus lavaretus*, of the Lake District, a local variation of the powan with spotted flanks.

schelm older form of **skelm**.

schema /skē'mə/ *n* (*pl* **sche'mata** or **sche'mas**) a scheme, plan; a diagrammatic outline or synopsis; a mental picture of a thing in the imagination, which the mind uses to help perceive or understand it more clearly (*psychol*); a kind of standard or principle which the mind forms from past experiences, and by which new experiences can be evaluated to a certain extent. [Gr *schēma, -atos* form, from the reduced grade of the root of *echein* to have (as in the future *schēsein*)]

■ **schematic** /ski-mat'ik/ *n* a schematic diagram, *esp* of an electrical circuit. ◆ *adj* (also **schemat'ical**) following, or involving, a particular plan or arrangement; representing something by a diagram, plan, etc. **schemat'ically** *adv*. **sche'matism** *n* form or outline of a thing; arrangement, disposition in a scheme. **sche'matist** *n*. **schematizā'tion** or **-s-** *n*. **sche'matize** or **-ise** *vt* to reduce to or represent by a scheme.

scheme /skēm/ *n* a systematic plan of action for achieving an end; a plan for building operations of various kinds, or the buildings, etc, constructed, or the area covered (eg *housing scheme, irrigation scheme*); a plan pursued secretly, insidiously, by intrigue, or for private ends; a project; a programme of action; a diagram of positions, *esp* (*astrol*) of planets; a table; a system; an arrangement; a rhetorical figure (*obs*); an escapade (*obs*). ◆ *vt* to plan; to reduce to a system; to lay schemes for. ◆ *vi* to form a plan; to lay schemes, to plot or intrigue; to indulge in an escapade (*obs*). [**schema**]

■ **sche'mer** *n*. **sche'mie** *n* (*Scot*; *sl*) a working-class youth from a council estate. **sche'ming** *n* and *adj*.

schemozzle see **shemozzle**.

Schengen agreement /sheng'gen ə-grē'mənt/ *n* an agreement (initially between France, Germany, Belgium, Luxembourg and the Netherlands, but since joined by ten additional countries) to remove all border controls between themselves and to exchange information on criminal activities, etc. [From the Luxembourg village of *Schengen*, where the agreement was first discussed]

scherzo /sker'tsō or skûr'/ (*music*) *n* (*pl* **scher'zos** or **scher'zi** /-tsē/) a lively busy movement in triple time, *usu* with a trio, now generally taking the place of the minuet in a sonata or a symphony. [Ital, from Gmc; cf Ger *Scherz* jest]

■ **scherzan'do** *adj* and *adv* in a playful manner. ◆ *n* (*pl* **scherzan'dos** or **scherzan'di** /-dē/) a scherzando passage or movement.

Scheuermann's disease /shoi'ər-mənz di-zēz'/ *n* a form of osteochondrosis of the vertebrae, affecting children and adolescents. [HW *Scheuermann* (1877–1960), Danish surgeon]

schiavone /skyä-vō'nā/ *n* a 17c basket-hilted broadsword used by the Doge's bodyguard of Slavs. [Ital *Schiavoni* Slavs]

Schick('s) test /shik(s) test/ *n* a test for susceptibility to diphtheria, made by injecting the skin with a measured amount of diphtheria toxin. [Bela *Schick* (1877–1967), US paediatrician]

schiedam /skē'dam/ or **-dam**/ *n* Holland gin, chiefly made at Schiedam /s'hhē-däm'/, near Rotterdam.

Schiff('s) base /shif(s) bās/ *n* a benzylidene aniline. [Hugo *Schiff* (1834–1915), German chemist]

Schiff's reagent /shifs rē-ā'jənt/ *n* a reagent for testing for the presence of aldehydes. [Ety as for **Schiff base**]

schiller /shil'ər/ (*geol*) *n* a peculiar bronze-like lustre in certain minerals, such as hypersthene, due to diffraction caused by minute plates of haematite, etc, developed in separation planes. [Ger]

■ **schillerizā'tion** or **-s-** *n* the development of such plates. **schill'erize** or **-ise** *vt* to impart a schiller to.
❑ **schiller spar** *n* schillerized enstatite (bronzite).

schilling /shil'ing/ *n* a former unit of currency in Austria, replaced by the euro. [Ger; cf **shilling**]

Schilling test /shil'ing test/ (*med*) *n* a test to assess capacity to absorb vitamin B_{12} from the bowel, used in the diagnosis of pernicious anaemia. [RF *Schilling* (born 1919), US physician]

schimmel /shim'l/ *n* a roan horse. [Ger, a white horse; also Du]

schindylesis /skin-di-lē'sis/ (*anat*) *n* an articulation formed by the fitting of the crest of a bone into a groove in another. [Gr *schindylēsis* cleaving]

■ **schindyletic** /-let'ik/ *adj*.

schipperke /skip'ər-kə/ or **-ki**, also **ship'** or **shhip'**/ *n* a small tailless breed of dogs, *orig* used as watchdogs on Dutch barges. [Du, little boatman]

schism /si- or ski-zm/ *n* a breach, *esp* in the unity of a church; promotion of such a breach; a body so formed. [Gr *schisma* a split, rent, cleft, partly through OFr *(s)cisme*]

■ **schisma** /skiz'mə/ *n* (*music*) half the difference between twelve perfect fifths and seven octaves. **schismatic** /siz-mat'ik or skiz-/ *n* someone who favours a schism or belongs to a schismatic body; a Catholic who avoided penalties by occasional conformity (*RC*). ◆ *adj* (also **schismat'ical**) tending to, favouring, or of the nature of, a schism. **schismat'ically** *adv*. **schismat'icalness** *n*. **schis'matize** or **-ise** *vi* to practise schism; to make a schism.
❑ **schism house** or **shop** *n* (*old, esp* 19c) contemptuous Anglican terms for a nonconformist church.

■ **great Eastern** (or **Greek**) **schism** the separation of the Greek church from the Latin, finally completed in 1054. (**great**) **Western schism** the division in the Western Church from 1378 to 1417, when there were antipopes under French influence at Avignon.

schist /shist/ *n* any crystalline foliated metamorphic rock not coarse and feldspathic enough to be called gneiss, such as mica-schist, hornblende-schist; sometimes extended to shaly rocks. [Fr *schiste*, from Gr *schistos* split; pronunciation due to Ger influence]

■ **schist'ose** *adj*. **schistosity** /-os'i-ti/ *n*. **schist'ous** *adj*.

Schistosoma /shis-tə-sō'mə or skis-/ *n* a genus of blood flukes (also called **Bilharzia**), some species of which are parasites of humans. [Gr *schistos* split]

■ **schis'tosome** *n* a member of the genus. **schistosomī'asis** *n* a disease caused by infestation by schistosomes (also called **bilharzia**).

schizo /skit'sō/ (*derog inf*) *adj* and *n* (*pl* **schiz'os**) (a) schizophrenic.

schizo- or (before a vowel) **schiz-** /skit-s(ō)-, -s(ə)- or -s(o)-, also *skid-z(ō)-*, etc and *skī-z(ō)-*, etc/ *combining form* denoting a split, cleft or division. [Gr *schizein* to cleave]

■ **Schizaea** /-zē'ə/ *n* a tropical genus of ferns giving name to the family **Schizaeā'ceae**, with sporangia splitting longitudinally by an apical annulus. **schizaeā'ceous** *adj*. **schizanthus** /-an'thəs/ *n* (Gr *anthos* flower) a Chilean flowering plant of the genus *Schizanthus*, frequently cultivated for its showy orchid-like blooms. **schizo-affect'ive** *adj* marked by symptoms of schizophrenia and manic-depressiveness. **schi'zocarp** /-kärp/ *n* (Gr *karpos* fruit; *bot*) a dry fruit that splits into several indehiscent one-seeded portions. **schizocar'pous** or **schizocar'pic** *adj* (*bot*). **schizogenesis** /-jen'i-sis/ *n* (see **genesis**) asexual reproduction by fission. **schizogen'ic** or **schizogenetic** /-ji-net'ik/ *adj* reproducing, reproduced, or formed by fission or splitting. **schizognathous** /-og'nə-thəs/ *adj* (see **-gnathous** under **gnathic**) (of some birds) having the bones of the palate separate. **schizog'onous** *adj*. **schizog'ony** *n* (Gr *gonē* generation) reproduction in protozoans by multiple fission. **schizoid** /skit'soid or skid'zoid/ *adj* (see **-oid**) showing qualities of a schizophrenic personality, such as asocial behaviour, introversion, tendency to fantasy, but without definite mental disorder. ◆ *n* a schizoid person. **schizoid'al** *adj*. **schizomycete** /-sēt'/ *n* any microscopic organism of the class **Schizomycetes**. **schizomycet'ic** or **schizomycē'tous** *adj*. **schiz'ont** *n* in protozoans, a mature trophozoite about to reproduce by schizogony. **schiz'ophrene** /-frēn/ *n* (Gr *phrēn* mind) a person who suffers from schizophrenia. **schizophrenet'ically** *adv*. **schizophrenia** /-frē'ni-ə/ *n* a psychosis marked by introversion, dissociation, inability to distinguish reality from unreality, delusions, etc. **schizophrenic** /-fren'ik/ n a schizophrene. ♦ adj (also **schizophrenet'ic** or **schizophrenet'ical**) suffering from schizophrenia. **schizophrenogenic** /-jen'ik/ adj (see **-genic**) causing or tending to cause schizophrenia. **schizophyceous** /-fī'shəs or -fī'/ adj of or belonging to the **Schizophyceae** /-fī'si-ē/ (Gr phykos seaweed), a group of algae, bluish-green in colour, that grow in fresh or salt water, and can be responsible for the pollution of drinking water. **schiz'ophyte** /-fīt/ n (see **-phyte** under **phyt-**) a plant of the **Schizoph'yta**, an obsolete grouping of organisms that multiply only by fission, incl bacteria and blue-green algae. **schizophytic** /-fit'ik/ adj. **schi'zopod** /-pod/ n (see **-pod**) a shrimp-like crustacean of the former order **Schizop'oda**, having each leg divided into exopodite and endopodite (also adj). **schizop'odal** or **schizop'odous** adj. **schizothymia** /-thī'mi-ə/ n (Gr thymos mind, temper; psychiatry) manifestation of schizoid traits within normal limits. **schizothy'mic** adj.

schläger /shlä'gər/ n the sword used by students in some German universities where the duelling tradition has been preserved. [Ger, from schlagen to beat]

schlemiel, schlemihl or **shlemiel** /shlə-mēl'/ (sl) n a clumsy person, a pitiful bungler, fool. [Yiddish, prob from Shelumiel, a biblical general notorious for losing battles, with spelling influenced by A von Chamisso's character Peter Schlemihl (1814)]

Schlemm's canal /shlemz kə-nal'/ (anat) n a channel at the junction of the cornea and the sclera in the eye, through which aqueous humour drains. [F Schlemm (1795–1858), German anatomist]

schlep, schlepp or **shlep** /shlep/ (sl) vt (**schlepp'ing; schlepped**) to carry or pull with effort; to drag. ♦ n a clumsy, stupid, incompetent person; a person of no importance; a journey or procedure requiring great effort or involving great difficulty. [Yiddish]
■ **schlepp'er** or **shlepp'er** n an incompetent or nonentity. **schlepp'y** adj.

schlich /shlihh/ (mining) n the finer portions of crushed ore, separated by water. [Ger]

schlieren /shlē'rən/ n pl streaks of mineral of different colour, structure, or composition in igneous rocks; visible streaks in a transparent fluid, caused by the differing refractive indices of fluid of varying density (phys). [Ger, pl of Schliere streak]
❑ **schlieren photography** n the technique of photographing a flow of air or other gas, the variations in refractive index according to density being made apparent under a special type of illumination, often used in the testing of models in wind tunnels.

schlimazel or **shlimazel** /shli-mä'zl/ (US sl) n a persistently unlucky person. [Yiddish; see **shemozzle**]

schlock or **shlock** /shlok/ (esp US sl) adj of inferior quality. ♦ n something of inferior quality, esp shoddy merchandise (also **schlock'er**). [Yiddish]
■ **schlock'y** adj.

schlong /shlong/ (US vulgar sl) n the penis. [Yiddish]

schloss /shlos/ n a castle, palace, manor house. [Ger]

schlub or **shlub** /shlub/ (sl) n a pathetic or foolish person. [Yiddish]

schlumbergera see **Christmas cactus** under **Christmas**.

schmaltz or **shmaltz** /shmolts, shmölts or shmälts/ n mush; a production in music or other art that is very sentimental, or showy; sickly sentimentality. [Yiddish, from Ger Schmalz cooking fat, grease]
■ **schmaltz'y** or **shmaltz'y** adj old-fashioned, old-style, outmoded; sentimental.

schmeck or **shmek** /shmek/ (US sl) n a taste or sniff; heroin (see also **smack⁴**). [Yiddish]

schmelz /shmelts/ n glass used in decorative work. [Ger Schmelz enamel]

Schmidt telescope /shmit tel'i-skōp/ n a type of optical telescope with a wide field, used to survey extensive areas of sky. [BV Schmidt (1879–1935), its Estonian inventor]

Schmitt trigger /shmit trig'ər/ n a bistable circuit that gives accurately-shaped constant amplitude rectangular pulse output for any input pulse above the triggering level. [OH Schmitt (1913–98), US scientist]

schmo, schmoe, or **shmo** /shmō/ (US sl) n (pl **schmoes** or **shmoes**) a stupid or a boring person, a fool. [Yiddish]

schmock see **schmuck**.

schmoe see **schmo**.

schmooze or **shmooze** /shmooz/ or **shmoose** /shmoos/ (orig US sl) vi to gossip, to chat in a friendly or intimate manner. ♦ n (also **schmooz**) such a chat, esp at a social gathering. [Yiddish]
■ **schmooz'er** or **shmooz'er** n. **schmooz'y** or **shmooz'y** adj.

schmuck or **shmuck** /shmuk/ or **schmock** or **shmock** /shmok/ (orig US sl) n orig, a euphemism for the penis; a pitiful, stupid or obnoxious person. [Yiddish, from Ger Schmuck ornament]

schmutter /shmut'ər/ (sl) n clothing; rag. [Yiddish schmatte rag]

schnapper /shnap'ər/ n see **snapper** under **snap**. [Germanized]

schnapps or **schnaps** /shnaps/ n any of various strong alcoholic drinks, esp Holland gin. [Ger Schnapps a dram]

schnauzer /shnow'tsər/ n a German breed of wire-haired terrier. [Ger Schnauze snout]

schnecken /shnek'ən/ (esp N Am) n pl (sing **schneck'e**) sweet bread rolls containing nuts and flavoured with cinnamon. [Ger Schnecke snail (the bread being baked in a spiral shape reminiscent of a snail's shell)]

Schneiderian /shnī-dē'ri-ən/ adj relating to the German anatomist Konrad Victor Schneider (1614–80).
❑ **Schneiderian membrane** n the olfactory mucous membrane, studied by him.

schnell /shnel/ (Ger) adj quick. ♦ adv quickly.

schnitzel /shnit'sl/ n a veal cutlet (see also **Wiener schnitzel** under **wiener**). [Ger]

schnook /shnŭk/ (orig US sl) n a pathetic, timid or unfortunate person. [Yiddish, prob from Ger Schnuck small sheep]

schnorkel see **snorkel**.

schnorrer /shnō'rər, shnö'** or **shno'/ (US sl) n a sponger; a beggar. [Yiddish]
■ **schnorr** /shnör or shnör/ vi to beg, esp in such a way as to make the giver feel in some way beholden.

schnozzle /shnoz'əl/ (sl) n nose. [Yiddish shnoitsl, dimin of Ger Schnauze snout]

schola cantorum /skō'lə kan-tō'rəm/ n a choir or choir school attached to a church, cathedral, etc; the part of a church, etc in which the choir is placed for services. [L, school of singers]

scholar /skol'ər/ n someone whose learning (formerly esp in Latin and Greek) is extensive and exact, or whose approach to learning is scrupulous and critical; a pupil; a disciple; a student; (in times of less widespread education) someone who could read and write, or an educated person; generally, a holder of a scholarship. [OE scōlere, and (in part) OFr escoler, both from LL scholāris, from schola; see **school¹**]
■ **schol'ar-like** adj like or befitting a scholar. **schol'arliness** n. **schol'arly** adj of or natural to a scholar; having the learning of a scholar; intended for serious students who already have some knowledge of the subject. ♦ adv (Shakesp) as becomes a scholar. **schol'arship** n scholarly learning; a foundation or grant for the maintenance of a pupil or student; the status and emoluments of such a pupil or student.
❑ **scholar's mate** n in chess, a simple mate accomplished in four moves.

scholarch /skō'lärk/ n the head of a school, esp of philosophy. [Gr scholarchēs]

scholastic /skə-las'tik or sko-/ adj relating to schools, universities, etc, or to teachers, teaching or students; referring or relating to medieval scholasticism; subtle; pedantic. ♦ n a teacher or scholar, one who adheres to the method or subtleties of the medieval schools, a schoolman; a Jesuit who has taken first vows only; a university teacher (esp with implication of pedantry). [Gr scholastikos, from scholē; see **school¹**]
■ **scholas'tical** adj (archaic). **scholas'tically** adv. **scholas'ticism** /-sizm'/ n the aims, methods, and products of thought which constituted the main endeavour of the intellectual life of the Middle Ages; the method or subtleties of the schools of philosophy; the collected body of doctrines of the schoolmen.

scholion /skō'li-on, -ən/ or **scholium** /-əm/ n (pl **scho'lia**) an annotation in the nature of an explanation or supplementary comment, such as those written in the margins of manuscripts of the classical authors; an observation or note added to a mathematical proposition. [Gr scholion (Mod L scholium), from scholē; see **school¹**]
■ **scho'liast** n (Gr scholiastēs) a writer of scholia; an annotator; a commentator. **scholias'tic** adj.

school¹ /skool/ n a place for instruction; an institution for education, esp primary or secondary, or for the teaching of a specific subject or subjects (eg a ballet school); a division of such an institution; a building or room used for that purpose; the work of such an institution; the time during which pupils, etc attend it; the body of pupils in it; the disciples of a particular teacher; a group of artists whose work shares a common style, from the circumstance of their having received instruction at the same place or under the same master, sometimes used by way of rough attribution where a work is by an unknown hand; those who hold a common doctrine or follow a common tradition; a particular environment or set of experiences seen as a training ground; a group of people meeting in order to play card games, *usu* for money (*inf*); a method of instruction; an instruction book (now *usu* in music); the body of instructors and students in a university, college, faculty, or department; a group of studies in which honours may be taken; (in *pl*) academic institutions; (in *pl*) an academic disputation; (in *pl*) the BA examinations at Oxford; (in *pl*) a university building comprising rooms for lectures, disputations or (in modern Oxford use) examinations. ◆ *adj* of school, schools, or the schools. ◆ *vt* to educate in a school; to train, to drill; to instruct; to coach in a part to be played; to teach overbearingly; to discipline; to admonish (*obs*). [OE *scōl*, from L *schola*, from Gr *scholē* leisure, a lecture, a school]

■ **schooled** *adj* trained; experienced. **school'ery** *n* (*archaic*) something taught, precepts. **school'ie** *n* (*Aust inf*) a school teacher; a school pupil; a school-leaver. **school'ing** *n* instruction or maintenance at school; tuition; training; discipline; school fees; reproof; reprimand. **school'ward** *adj* and *adv*. **school'wards** *adv*. □ **school age** *n* the age at which children attend school. **school'-age** *adj*. **school'bag** *n* a bag for carrying school books. **school bell** *n* a bell to announce time to begin or end lessons at school. **school board** *n* formerly, an elected board of school managers for a parish, town, or district; now, a board made up of elected parents, teachers and community representatives with responsibility for the management of an individual school. **school book** *n* a book used in school. **school'boy** *n* a boy attending school. ◆ *adj* of or appropriate for schoolboys. **school'boyish** *adj*. **school'-bred** *adj*. **School Certificate** *n* (formerly in England, Wales and New Zealand) a secondary-school qualification gained by succeeding in public examinations. **school'child** *n*. **school'craft** *n* (*archaic*) learning. **school dame** *n* the mistress of a dame-school (qv under **dame**¹). **school'day** *n* a day on which schools are open; (in *pl*) time of being a school pupil. **school'-divine** *n*. **school'-divin'ity** *n* scholastic or seminary theology. **school doctor** *n* a physician appointed to examine or attend the pupils of a school or schools; a schoolman; a schoolteacher (*obs*). **school experience** same as **teaching practice** (see under **teach**). **school'fellow** *n* someone taught at the same school at the same time as oneself. **school'-friend** *n* someone who is or has been one's friend at school. **school'-friend'ship** *n*. **school'girl** *n* a girl attending school. ◆ *adj* of or appropriate for schoolgirls. **school'girlish** *adj*. **school'going** *n* and *adj*. **school'house** *n* a building used as a school; a house provided for a schoolteacher (**school house** a headmaster's or headmistress's boarding house; its boarders). **school inspector** *n* an official appointed to examine schools. **school'-leaver** *n* someone who is leaving, or has just left, school because he or she has reached the statutory age, or the stage, for doing so. **school'-leaving** *n* and *adj*. **school'ma'am** *n* a schoolmarm. **school'maid** *n* (*old*) a schoolgirl. **school'man** *n* a philosopher or theologian of medieval scholasticism; a teacher or educator (*US*; *rare*). **school'marm** *n* (*inf*; a form of **schoolma'am**) a schoolmistress (*N Am*); a prim pedantic woman (*inf*). **school'marmish** *adj*. **school'master** *n* a male schoolteacher or head of a school; a tutor (*Shakesp*); a person or thing that instructs. ◆ *vt* and *vi* to act as a schoolmaster (to). **school'mastering** *n* and *adj*. **school'masterish** *adj*. **school'masterly** *adj*. **school'mastership** *n*. **school'mate** *n* a school-friend; a schoolfellow. **school'mistress** *n* a female schoolteacher or head of a school. **school'mistressy** *adj*. **school night** *n* a night before a school day. **school nurse** *n* a registered nurse employed to visit schools and promote children's health through screening procedures, immunization, etc. **school phobia** *n* an irrational fear of attending school. **school point** *n* a point for scholastic disputation. **school'room** *n* a school classroom; in a house, a room for receiving or preparing lessons in. **school run** *n* a regular car journey made to escort children to and from school. **school ship** *n* a training ship. **school'-taught** *adj* taught at school or in the schools. **school'teacher** *n* a person who teaches in a school. **school'teaching** *n*. **school term** *n* a division of the school year; a word or term in use in the schools or among schoolmen. **school'tide** *n* (*Walter Scott*) schooldays. **school'time** *n* the time at which a school opens, or during which it remains open; schooldays. **school'-trained** *adj* trained at school. **school'work** *n*. **school year** *n* the period of (more or less) continual teaching during the year comprising an academic unit during which a child or student remains in the same basic class, ie, in Britain, from autumn to early summer.

■ **old school** see under **old**. **the schoolmaster is abroad** a phrase (coined by Henry Brougham in the 19c) implying that education and intelligence are now widely spread.

school² /skool/ *n* a shoal of fish, whales, or other swimming animals; a flock, troop, assemblage (*esp* of birds). ◆ *vi* to gather or go in schools. ◆ *adj* going in schools. [Du *school*; cf **shoal**¹]
■ **school'ing** *n* and *adj*.
□ **school'master** *n* the leader of a school of whales, etc.

schoole (*Shakesp*, *Macbeth* I.7.6) same as **shoal²** (*n*).

schooner /skoo'nər/ *n* a swift sailing-ship, generally two-masted, fore-and-aft rigged, or with top and topgallant sails on the foremast; a covered wagon used in the 19c to travel across the N American prairies (also **prairie schooner**); a large beer glass (*esp* N Am and Aust); a large sherry glass. [Origin uncertain; said to be from a dialect Eng word *scoon* to skim]
□ **schoon'er-rigged** *adj*.

schorl /shörl/ (*mineralogy*) *n* black tourmaline. [Ger *Schörl*]
■ **schorlā'ceous** *adj*. **schorlomite** /shör'lə-mīt/ *n* a black variety of garnet rich in titanium dioxide.
□ **schorl'-rock** *n* (*geol*) a rock composed of aggregates of schorl and quartz.

schottische /sho-tēsh'** or *shot'ish*/ *n* a dance, or dance tune, similar to the polka. [Ger (*der*) *schottische* (*Tanz*), (the) Scottish (dance); pronunciation sham French]

Schottky defect /shot'ki dē'fekt/ (*phys*) *n* deviation from the ideal crystal lattice by removal of some molecules to the surface, leaving vacancies in the lattice. [Walter *Schottky* (1886–1976), German physicist]

Schottky effect /shot'ki i-fekt'/ (*electronics*) *n* the removal of electrons from the surface of a semiconductor when a localized field is present. [Ety as for **Schottky defect**]

Schottky noise see **shot noise** under **shot**¹.

schout /skowt/ *n* a municipal officer. [Du]

schrecklich /shrek'lihh/ (*Ger*) *adj* frightful.
■ **Schreck'lichkeit** /-kīt/ *n* frightfulness.

schreech-owl see under **shriek**.

Schrödinger equation /shrə'ding-ər i-kwā'zhən/ *n* a fundamental equation of wave mechanics which describes the behaviour of a particle in a field of force. [Erwin *Schrödinger* (1887–1961), Austrian physicist]

schtick, schtik see **shtick**.

schtook, schtuck see **shtook**.

schtoom see **shtoom**.

schtum same as **shtoom**.

schuit or **schuyt** /skoit/ *n* a Dutch flat-bottomed boat, used on canals and along the coast. [Du]

schul see **shul**.

schuss /shŭs/ (*skiing*) *n* a straight slope on which it is possible to make a fast run; such a run. ◆ *vi* to make such a run. [Ger]

Schutzstaffel /shŭts'shtaf-əl/ (*Ger*) *n* Hitler's bodyguard of élite police, later forming military units in Nazi Germany (*abbrev* **SS**).

schuyt see **schuit**.

schwa or **shwa** /shwä/ or *shvä*/ (*phonetics*) *n* an indistinct vowel sound; a neutral vowel (ə). Cf **sheva**. [Ger, from Heb *schewa* a diacritic indicating lack of vowel sound]

schwag /shwag/ (*sl*) *n* cheap merchandise given away to the public at promotional events; poor-quality marijuana. [Humorous version of **swag**]

Schwann cell /shvan sel/ (*zool*) *n* a large nucleated cell that lays down myelin in peripheral nerve fibres. [Theodor *Schwann* (1810–82), German physiologist]

schwarzlot /shvarts'lōt/ *n* a type of black enamel decoration on glass, pottery and porcelain. [Ger, black lead]

Schwarzschild radius /shvarts'shilt rä'di-əs/ (*astron*) *n* the critical radius at which an object becomes a black hole if collapsed or compressed indefinitely. [K *Schwarzschild* (1873–1916), German astronomer]

Schwenkfelder /shvengk'fel-dər/ *n* a member of a religious sect founded by the German theologian Kaspar *Schwenkfeld* (1490–1561). Also **Schwenkfeld'ian**.

sci. *abbrev*: science; scientific.

scia- /sī'ə-* or *sī-a-*/ *combining form* denoting shadow. See also words listed under **skia-**.

sciaenid /sī-ē'nid/ or **sciaenoid** /sī-ē'noid/ *n* and *adj* (of or relating to) any member of the genus *Sciaena* or the family **Sciae'nidae**, marine percoid tropical and subtropical fishes, *incl* the croakers and drums. [Gr *skiaina* a kind of fish]

sciamachy /sī-am'ə-ki/ *n* same as **skiamachy** (see under **skia-**).

sciarid /sī-ar'id/ *n* a minute, dark-coloured, two-winged fly of the family Sciaridae (also *adj*). [Gr *skiaros* shady, dark-coloured, from *skia* shadow]

sciatic /sī-at'ik/, also **sciatical** /-i-kəl/ *adj* of, or in the region of, the hip; referring or relating to the sciatic nerve; affected by sciatica. [LL *sciaticus*, fem *-a*, from Gr *ischion* hip joint]

■ **sciat'ica** *n* neuritis of the sciatic nerve. **sciat'ically** *adv*.
□ **sciatic nerve** *n* the major nerve of the leg, passing down the back of the thigh from the base of the spine.

SCID (*med*) *abbrev*: severe combined immunodeficiency.

science /sī'əns/ *n* knowledge ascertained by observation and experiment, critically tested, systematized and brought under general principles, *esp* in relation to the physical world; a department or branch of such knowledge or study; knowledge (*archaic*); a skilled craft (*obs*); trained skill, *esp* in boxing (now *usu joc*). [L *scientia*, from *sciēns*, *-entis* prp of *scīre* to know]
■ **sci'enced** *adj* (*archaic*) versed, learned. **sci'ent** *adj* (*archaic*) having knowledge or skill. **sciential** /-en'shl/ *adj* (*rare*) of, having, or producing, science; scientific. **scientif'ic** *adj* (L *facere* to make) relating to or based on the principles of science or of a branch of science; devoted to or versed in science; used in science; *orig* (of a syllogism) demonstrative, producing knowledge. **scientif'ical** *adj* (*rare*). **scientif'ically** *adv*. **scientificity** /sī-ən-tif-is'i-ti/ *n*. **sci'entism** *n* the methods or mental attitudes of scientists; a belief that the methods used in studying natural sciences should be employed also in investigating all aspects of human behaviour and condition, eg in philosophy and social sciences; scientific or pseudo-scientific language. **sci'entist** *n* a person who studies or practises any science, *esp* natural science. **scientis'tic** *adj*. **sci'entize** or **-ise** *vt* to treat in a scientific way. **Scientol'ogist** *n*. **Scientol'ogy**® *n* a religious movement founded in the USA in the 1950s by L Ron Hubbard, which claims that an individual's full spiritual potential may be realized through study and psychotherapy.
□ **science fiction** *n* a literary genre dealing with speculative scientific and technological developments, *esp* the imaginative presentation, often set in the future, of people and environments on the earth, on other planets or in space (*inf* short form **sci-fi** /sī'fī'/). **science park** *n* a centre for industrial research, etc attached to a university, set up for the purpose of co-operation between the academic and the commercial world. **scientific whaling** *n* whaling carried out actually or ostensibly for the purposes of research.
■ **the (noble) science** the art of boxing.

scienter /sī-en'tər/ (*law*) *adv* having knowledge, being aware; knowingly, wilfully. [L]

sci. fa. *abbrev*: *scire facias* (qv).

sci-fi /sī'fī'/ (*inf*) *n* and *adj* science fiction.

scilicet /sī'li-set or skē'li-ket/ *adv* to wit, namely (*abbrev* **scil.** or **sciz.**). [L *scīlicet*, from *scīre licet* it is permitted to know]

scilla /sil'ə/ *n* any plant of the squill genus *Scilla* of the lily family, *incl* some bright-blue bell-shaped flowers. [L, from Gr *skilla* the officinal squill]

Scillonian /si-lō'ni-ən/ *adj* of, belonging to or concerning the *Scilly* Isles, off the SW coast of Britain. ◆ *n* an inhabitant of these islands.

scimitar /sim'i-tər/ *n* a short, single-edged, curved sword, broadest at the point end, used by the Turks and Persians. [Poss through Fr *cimeterre* or Ital *scimitarra*, from Pers *shamshīr*; but doubtful]

scincoid /sing'koid/ or **scincoidian** /-koi'di-ən/ *adj* resembling a skink. ◆ *n* an animal resembling a skink. [Gr *skinkos* a skink, and see **-oid**]

scintigraphy /sin-tig'rə-fi/ *n* a diagnostic technique in which the pattern of gamma rays emitted by a radioactive isotope injected into the body is represented in diagrammatic form, and a record or map of the radioactivity in various parts of the body may be built up by scanning the body, section by section. [*scint*illation, and **-graphy**]
■ **scint'igram** *n* a diagram so produced. **scintigraph'ic** *adj*. **scin'tiscan** *n* a scan made by scintigraphy. **scin'tiscanner** *n* a device for producing scintiscans.

scintilla /sin-til'ə/ *n* a spark; a hint, trace. [L, a spark]
■ **scin'tillant** *adj* sparkling. **scin'tillate** *vi* to sparkle; (of an atom) to emit a unit of light after having been struck by a photon or a particle of ionizing radiation; to be dazzlingly impressive or animated; to talk wittily. ◆ *vt* to emit in sparks; to sparkle with. **scin'tillating** *adj*. **scin'tillatingly** *adv*. **scintilla'tion** *n* a flash of light produced in a phosphor by an ionizing particle, eg an alpha particle, or a photon; the twinkling of stars due to rapid changes in their brightness caused by variations in the density of the atmosphere through which their light rays pass. **scin'tillator** *n* an instrument for detecting radioactivity; a phosphor that produces scintillations. **scintill'iscan** *n* same as **scintiscan** (see under **scintigraphy**). **scintillom'eter** *n* an instrument for detecting and measuring radioactivity. **scintill'oscope** or **scintill'ascope** *n* an instrument which shows scintillations on a screen, used to produce a scintigram.
□ **scintillation counter** *n* a scintillometer.

scio- /sī-ō-, sī-ə- or sī-o-/ *combining form* denoting shadow. See also words listed under **skia-**.

sciolism /sī'ə-li-zm/ *n* superficial pretensions to knowledge. [L *sciolus*, dimin of *scius* knowing, from *scīre* to know]
■ **sci'olist** *n* someone who pretends to have knowledge. **sciolis'tic** *adj*. **sci'olous** *adj*.

sciolto /shol'tō/ (*music*) *adj* and *adv* in a free manner. [Ital]

scion /sī'ən/ *n* a detached piece of a plant capable of propagating, *esp* by grafting; a young member of a family; a descendant, offshoot. [OFr *sion*, *cion*; origin obscure]

sciosophy /sī-os'ō-fi or -ə-fi/ *n* a system of what claims to be knowledge but is without basis in ascertained scientific fact, such as astrology. [Gr *skiā* a shadow, and *sophiā* wisdom]

scire facias /sī'ri fā'shi-as or skē're fak'i-äs/ (*law*) *n* a writ requiring a person to appear and show cause why a record should not be enforced, annulled or vacated (*abbrev* **sci. fa.**). [L *scīre faciās* make him to know]

sciroc and **scirocco** see **sirocco**.

Scirpus /sûr'pəs/ *n* the clubrush genus of the sedge family. [L, a rush]

scirrhus /skir'əs or sir'əs/ (*med*) *n* a hard swelling; a hard fibrous carcinoma. [Latinized from Gr *skirros*, *skīros* a tumour]
■ **scirr'hoid** or **scirr'hous** *adj*.

scissel, also **scissil** /sis'(ə)l/ *n* metal clippings; scrap metal left when blanks have been cut out. [OFr *cisaille*, from *ciseler*, from *cisel* a chisel; for the spelling cf **scissors**]

scissile /sis'īl/ *adj* capable of being cut; readily splitting. [L *scissilis*, from *scindere*, *scissum* to cut, to split, cleave]
■ **scission** /sish'ən or sizh'ən/ *n* cutting; division; splitting; schism. **scissiparity** /sis-i-par'i-ti/ *n* (L *parere* to bring forth) reproduction by fission. **scissure** /sish'ər/ *n* a cleft; a splitting, fissure; a rupture; a division; cutting.

scissors /siz'ərz/ *n pl* or (*rare*) *n sing* a cutting instrument with two blades pivoted to close together and overlap, *usu* smaller than shears; a position or movement like that of scissors; movement of the legs suggesting opening and closing of scissors (*gym*, etc); (also **scissors** or **scissor hold**) locking the legs round the body or head of an opponent (*wrestling*); a style of high jump in which the leg nearest the bar leads throughout; a pass executed on the run to another player who is crossing one's path (*rugby*). [OFr *cisoires*, from LL *cīsōrium* a cutting instrument, from *caedere*, *caesum* to cut; the spelling *sc-* is due to erroneous association with *scindere*, *scissum*; cf **scissile**]
■ **sciss'or** *vt* and *vi* to cut with scissors. ◆ *vi* (*rugby*) to execute a scissors pass. **sciss'orer** *n* a scissors-and-paste compiler. **sciss'orwise** *adv*.
□ **sciss'orbill** *n* a skimmer. **scissor blade** *n*. **scissor case** *n*. **scissor cut** *n*. **sciss'or-leg** *n* a disability in which one leg is permanently crossed over the other, occurring in stroke victims and in certain brain-damaged children. **scissors-and-paste'** *n* literary or journalistic matter collected from various sources with little or no original writing (also *adj*). **scissors** or **scissor kick** *n* a kick used in some swimming strokes in which the legs are moved in a scissorlike action; (in football) a type of kick in which the player jumps in the air with one leg outstretched then brings forward the other leg to kick the ball. **sciss'ortail** *n* an American flycatcher. **sciss'or-tooth** *n* a *usu* long, large tooth in a carnivore, used for tearing flesh.

scissure see under **scissile**.

Scitamineae /sit-ə-min'i-ē/ *n pl* an order of monocotyledons *incl* the banana, ginger, Indian shot, and arrowroot families (also called **Musales**). [Appar from L *scītāmenta* delicacies]
■ **scitamin'eous** *adj*.

sciurine /sī-ū'rīn or sī'/ *n* a member of the genus *Sciurus* or family **Sciur'idae** of rodents, *incl* the squirrels, marmots and chipmunks. ◆ *adj* of, belonging to or characteristic of *Sciurus* or the Sciuridae. [L *sciūrus*, from Gr *skiouros*, from *skiā* shadow, and *ourā* tail]
■ **sciuroid** /-ū'/ *adj*. **Sciurop'terus** *n* (Gr *pteron* wing) a former genus of flying squirrels.

sciz. see **scilicet**.

SCL *abbrev*: Student of Civil Law.

sclaff /sklaf or skläf/ *n* a light slap or its sound (*Scot*); a stroke in which the sole of the club scrapes the ground before striking the ball (*golf*); any horribly mishit shot (*sport*). ◆ *vt* and *vi* to strike or play with a sclaff. [Imit]

sclate /sklāt or slāt/ *n* a Scots form of **slate**[1].
□ **sclate'-stane** *n* a piece of slate (such as money obtained from the Devil turned into).

sclaunder /sklön'dər/ an obsolete form of **slander**.

Sclav an obsolete form of **Slav**.

sclave an obsolete form of **slave**.

Sclavonian an obsolete form of **Slavonian**.

sclera /sklē'rə/ n the outermost membrane of the eyeball, the sclerotic. [Gr *sklēros* hard]
■ **sclē'ral** adj. **sclerot'ic** adj.

sclero- /sklē-rō-, -rə-, sklə-ro-/ or (before a vowel) **scler-** /sklēr- or sklər-/ combining form denoting hard; denoting the sclera. [Gr *sklēros* hard]
■ **sclere** /sklēr/ n (zool) a supporting element; a sponge spicule. **sclereid** or **sclereide** /sklēr'i-id/ n (bot) a thick-walled cell. **sclerema** /sklər-ē'mə/ n hardening of (esp subcutaneous) tissues. **sclerenchyma** /sklə-reng'ki-mə/ n (Gr *enchyma* in-filling) plant tissue consisting of cells with thick lignified walls; hard skeletal tissue, as in corals. **sclerenchymatous** /sklēr-eng-kim'ə-təs/ adj. **sclerī'asis** n hardening of tissue, scleroderma; a hard tumour; an induration. **sclē'rite** n a hard skeletal plate or spicule. **scleritis** /sklər-ī'tis/ n sclerotitis. **sclerocaulous** /sklēr-ō-kö'ləs/ adj. **sclē'rocauly** n (Gr *kaulos* stem) possession of a hard, dry stem. **scleroderm** /sklēr'/ n a hard integument. **scleroder'ma** or **scleroder'mia** n hardness and contraction of the body's connective tissue in which the skin becomes thickened by substitution of fibrous tissue for subcutaneous fat. **scleroder'matous**, **scleroder'mic** or **scleroder'mous** adj hard-skinned; relating to a scleroderm or to sclerodermia. **scleroder'mite** n the integument of a segment in arthropods. **sclē'roid** adj (bot and zool) hard; hardened. **sclerō'ma** n (pl **sclerōmata** /-rō'mə-tə/ or **sclerō'mas**) hardening; morbid hardening; a hardened area of mucous membrane or skin, eg forming nodules in the nose. **scleromalacia** /-mə-lā'shi-ə/ n thinning of the sclerotic coat resulting from inflammation. **sclerom'eter** n an instrument for measuring the hardness of minerals. **scleromet'ric** adj. **sclerophyll** /sklēr'ə-fil/ n a hard, leathery leaf; a woody plant, esp of hot, arid regions, with such leaves. **sclerophyll'ous** adj. **scleroph'ylly** n possession of sclerophylls. **scleroprō'tein** n insoluble protein forming the skeletal parts of tissues. **sclero'sal** adj affected with sclerosis. **sclerose** /sklə-rōs' or sklēr'/ vt to harden; to affect with sclerosis. ◆ vi to become sclerotic. **sclerosed'** (or /sklēr'/) adj. **sclerosis** /sklə-rō'sis/ n (pl **sclerō'ses** /-sēz/) hardening; morbid hardening, eg of arteries by deposition of fatty plaques (med); hardening of tissue by thickening or lignification (bot) (**disseminated sclerosis** an older name for **multiple sclerosis** (see under **multiple**)). **sclerō'tal** adj sclerotic. ◆ n a bony plate in the sclerotic of some animals. **sclerot'ic** adj hard, firm; of sclerosis; sclerosed, affected with sclerosis; see also under **sclera**. ◆ n the sclera, the fibrous outer membrane of the eyeball (also **sclerotic coat**). **sclerotin** /sklē'rə-tin/ n (in insects) a protein in the cuticle that becomes hard and dark. **sclerō'tioid** or **sclerō'tial** adj of, relating to, or resembling a sclerotium. **sclerotī'tis** n inflammation of the sclerotic. **sclerotium** /sklə-rō'shi-əm/ n (pl **sclerō'tia**) a hard, tuberlike body consisting of a compact mass of hyphae, the resting stage of many fungi. **sclerotizā'tion** or **-s-** n. **scle'rotize** or **-ise** vt (zool) to harden or darken. **sclerot'omy** n (med) incision into the sclera. **sclē'rous** adj hard or indurated; ossified or bony.

scliff or **skliff** /sklif/ (Scot) n a small segment or piece. [Imit]

sclim or **sklim** /sklim/ Scots forms of **climb**.

SCM abbrev : State Certified Midwife; Student Christian Movement.

SCN abbrev : St Kitts and Nevis (IVR).

SCODA /skō'də/ abbrev : Standing Conference on Drug Abuse (now known as DrugScope).

scoff¹ /skof/ n mockery; a gibe, jeer; an object of derision. ◆ vi to jeer (with at). ◆ vt (Shakesp) to jeer at. [Cf obs Dan *skof* jest, mockery, OFris *schof*]
■ **scoff'er** n. **scoff'ing** n and adj. **scoff'ingly** adv.

scoff² or **skoff** /skof/ (dialect and inf) vt to devour; to plunder. ◆ vi to feed quickly or greedily. ◆ n food; a meal. [Appar **scaff**, reinforced by Afrik, from Du *schoft* a meal]

scofflaw /skof'lö/ (US inf) n a person who is contemptuous of, or flouts, the law. [**scoff¹** and **law¹**]

scog see **skug¹**.

Scoggin or **Scogan** /skog'ən/ n a popular 16c jestbook said to be the work of John *Scogan*, reputed to be court fool to Edward IV; hence a buffoon.

scoinson /skoin'sən/ same as **scuncheon**.

scold /skōld/ n a person, usu a woman, who constantly finds fault in a strident or clamorous manner; a scolding. ◆ vi to brawl; to use abrasive language; to find fault vehemently or at some length. ◆ vt to chide; to rebuke. [Appar ON *skāld* poet (through an intermediate sense, lampooner)]
■ **scold'er** n. **scold'ing** n and adj. **scold'ingly** adv.
❑ **scold's bridle** see **branks**.

scolecite /skol'ə-sīt or skōl'/ n a white mineral of the zeolite group, a hydrated silicate of calcium and aluminium. [**scolex** and **-ite**]

scolex /skō'leks/ n (pl **scoleces** /skō-lē'sēz/ or (non-standard) **scō'lices**) the head of a tapeworm having hooks and suckers by which it attaches itself to its host. [Gr *skolēx, -ēkos* a worm]
■ **scole'cid** n a worm of the Scolecida, the tapeworm class (also adj). **scōleciform** /-lēs'i-förm/ adj. **Scōleciform'ia** n pl the lugworm order. **scōlecoid** /-lē'koid/ adj like a scolex.

scolion see **skolion**.

scoliosis /skol-i-ō'sis/ n abnormal curvature of the spine (also **scoliō'ma**). [Gr *skoliōsis*, from *skolios* crooked]
■ **scoliotic** /-ot'ik/ adj.

scollop¹ same as **scallop**.

scollop² /skol'əp/ n a flexible wooden rod, pointed at both ends, used in Ireland to pin down thatch. [Ir *scolb*]

scolopaceous /skol-ə-pā'shəs/ adj of, belonging to, or characteristic of, the genus *Scolopax* or family Scolopacidae of birds incl the woodcock and snipe. [Gr *scolopax, -akos* a woodcock]

scolopendra /skol-ə-pen'drə/ n a centipede of the genus *Scolopendra* of myriapods, incl large tropical centipedes up to a foot in length, giving name to the family Scolopendridae; a fabulous fish that vomited up the hook with its viscera, which it then re-swallowed. [Gr *skolopendra*]
■ **scolopen'drid** n any centipede of the family Scolopendridae. **scolopen'driform** or **scolopen'drine** adj. **scolopen'drium** n a fern with undivided leaves of the genus *Scolopendrium*, incl hart's tongue, so called from the resemblance of the sori to a centipede.

Scolytus /skol'i-təs/ n the typical genus of Scolytidae /-it'i-dē/, a family of bark-beetles. [Gr *skolyptein* to strip]
■ **scol'ytid** n a member of the Scolytidae (also adj). **scol'ytoid** adj and n.

Scomber /skom'bər/ n the mackerel genus, giving name to the family **Scom'bridae** /-bri-dē/. [L *scomber*, from Gr *skombros* a mackerel]
■ **Scom'bresox** n (L *esox* pike) the skipper genus, giving name to the **Scombresoc'idae**. **scom'brid** n a fish of the Scombridae (also adj). **scom'broid** n a member of the Scombroidea, a suborder of marine spiny-finned fish incl the mackerel, tunny and swordfish (also adj).

scomfish /skum'fish/ (Scot) vt to stifle; to disgust. [From *discomfish*, a by-form of **discomfit**, from the stem appearing in the Fr prp]

sconce¹ /skons/ n a candlestick or lantern with a handle; a bracket candlestick; a street wall-lamp. [OFr *esconse*, from LL *absconsa* a dark lantern, from *abscondere* to hide]

sconce² /skons/ n a small protective fortification or earthwork; a shelter. ◆ vt to entrench; to screen. [Du *schans*]
■ **build a sconce** to run up a debt (eg in a tavern) and have to keep away.

sconce³ /skons/ n (at Oxford University) a fine imposed for some breach of university rules or etiquette (paid in ale or in attempting to drink a large amount of ale without taking a breath, or otherwise); a two-handled mug used for the purpose (holding about a quart); a forfeit. ◆ vt to fine. [Origin obscure]

sconce⁴ /skons/ (archaic and dialect) n the head; the crown of the head; brains, wits. [Origin obscure]

sconcheon same as **scuncheon**.

scone /skon, sometimes anglicized as skōn/ (Scot) n a flattish, usu round or quadrant-shaped plain cake of dough without much fat, with or without currants, baked on a girdle or in an oven. [Perh from Du *schoon* (*brot*) fine (bread)]

scontion same as **scuncheon**.

SCONUL /skō'nəl or -nül/ abbrev : Society of College, National and University Libraries (formerly known as Standing Conference of National and University Libraries).

scoog see **skug¹**.

scoop /skoop/ n a container for bailing water; a concave shovel or lipped container for skimming or shovelling up loose material; a kitchen utensil, a deeply concave spoon, often fitted with a mechanical device for unloading it, used for dispensing a serving of pulpy food, eg ice cream or mashed potato; an instrument for gouging out apple-cores, samples of cheese, etc; anything of similar shape; an act of scooping; a quantity scooped; a sweeping stroke; a scooped-out place; anything got by or as by scooping, a haul; the forestalling of other newspapers in obtaining a piece of news; an item of news so secured (also adj). ◆ vt to bail out; to lift, obtain, remove, hollow, or make with, or as if with, a scoop; to secure in advance of or to the exclusion of others. ◆ vi (music) to slide up to a pitch. [Prob partly MLGer or MDu *schōpe* bailing-vessel, partly MDu *schoppe* shovel]
■ **scooped** adj. **scoop'er** n someone or something that scoops; an engraver's tool; another name for the avocet. **scoop'ful** n (pl **scoop'fuls**). **scoop'ing** n and adj.

❏ **scooped'-out** *adj.* **scoop neck** *n* a low rounded neckline. **scoop net** *n* a long-handled dipping net; a net for scooping along the bottom.

■ **scoop the pool** see under **pool**[2].

scoosh or **skoosh** /skoosh/ *vt* and *vi* to squirt. ◆ *n* a squirt; a fizzy drink; something that is easily done (*inf*). [Imit]

scoot[1] /skoot/ *vt* and *vi* (*Scot*) to squirt. ◆ *vi* to slip suddenly (*Scot*); to make off quickly (*inf*); to travel on a scooter (*inf*). ◆ *n* a squirt (*Scot*); an act of scooting. [Prob from ON, related to **shoot**[1]]

■ **scoot'er** *n* someone or something that scoots; a child's toy, a wheeled footboard with steering handle, pushed along with the foot; a small-wheeled motorcycle with a protective front fairing; a boat for sailing on ice and water (*US*); a swift motor-boat; a simple form of plough (*US*). **scoot'erist** *n* a person who rides on or is enthusiastic about scooters.

scoot[2] /skŭt/ (*Scot*) *n* an insignificant person.

scop /skop/ *n* (pl **scopas**) an Anglo-Saxon poet or minstrel. [OE, jester, someone who scoffs; see also **scoff**[1]]

scopa /skō'pə/ *n* (pl **sco'pae** /-pē/) a brushlike tuft of hairs on the hind legs of bees, used for collecting pollen. [L *scōpae* twigs, a broom]

■ **sco'pate** *adj* tufted. **scopula** /skop'ū-lə/ *n* a little tuft of hairs. **scop'ulate** *adj.*

scope[1] /skōp/ *n* range; field or opportunity of activity; capacity or room for action; potential or natural ability; spaciousness; a point aimed at (*obs*); purpose or aim (*archaic*); a length of cable on an anchor that provides slack to allow a vessel to move with the tides, etc; (with *cap*) a UK charity that helps people with cerebral palsy. [Ital *scopo*, from Gr *skopos* watcher, point watched, (*fig*) aim, from *skopeein* to view]

scope[2] /skōp/ *n* short for **microscope**, **telescope**, **horoscope**, etc; a visual display unit, *esp* a radar screen; a cinema (short for **bioscope**; *S Afr inf*). ◆ *vt* to examine (the internal organs) with a viewing instrument; to catch sight of (*inf*); to investigate (with *out*; *inf*); to discover as the result of an investigation (with *out*; *inf*).

❏ **scoping review** *n* a preliminary survey of the literature about a subject, often performed to establish which aspects of the subject require further research.

-scope /-skōp/ *combining form* an instrument for viewing, examining, or detecting, as in *telescope*, *oscilloscope*, *stethoscope*. [Gr *skopeein* to view]

Scopelus /skop'ə-ləs/ *n* a genus of deep-water fishes with luminous spots, giving name to the family Scopelidae. [Gr *skopelos* a rock, thought by Georges Cuvier to mean a kind of fish]

■ **scop'elid** or **scop'eloid** *n* a member of the Scopelidae (also *adj*).

scopolamine /skə- or sko-pol'ə-mēn/ *n* an alkaloid obtained from plants of the genus *Scopolia* and other plants of the Solanaceae (see **hyoscine** under **Hyoscyamus**) with sedative properties, used eg to prevent muscle spasm and travel sickness and as a premedication before anaesthesia. [Named after *Scopoli* (1723–88), Italian naturalist, and **amine**]

scopophilia /skop-ə-fil'i-ə/ *n* the practice of obtaining sexual pleasure from things seen, as eg naked bodies. [Gr *skopeein* to view, and **-philia**]

■ **scopophil'iac** *n.* **scopophil'ic** *adj.*

scopophobia /skop-ə-fō'bi-ə/ *n* fear of being looked at. [Gr *skopeein* to view, and **phobia**]

Scops owl /skops owl/ *n* any of various owls of the genus *Otus*. [Gr *skōps*]

scoptophilia same as **scopophilia**.

scoptophobia same as **scopophobia**.

scopula, scopulate see under **scopa**.

-scopy /-skə-pi/ *combining form* indicating viewing, examining, or observing, as in *autoscopy*, *poroscopy*, *ornithoscopy*. [Gr *skopeein* to view]

scorbutic /skör-bū'tik/ *adj* of, like, of the nature of, or affected with, scurvy. [LL *scorbūticus*, poss from MLGer *schorbuk*]

■ **scorbū'tically** *adv.*

scorch[1] /skörch/ *vt* to burn slightly or superficially; to parch; to dry up, wither, or affect painfully or injuriously by heat or as if by heat; to wither with scorn, censure, etc. ◆ *vi* to be burned on the surface; to be dried up; to cycle or drive very quickly (*inf*). ◆ *n* an act of scorching; damage or an injury by scorching. [Perh ME *skorken*; cf ON *skorpna* to shrivel; poss affected by OFr *escorcher* to flay]

■ **scorched** *adj.* **scorch'er** *n* a person who or thing which scorches; a day of scorching heat (*inf*); something remarkable (*inf*); anything stinging or caustic. **scorch'ing** *n* and *adj.* **scorch'ingly** *adv.* **scorch'ingness** *n.*

❏ **scorched earth policy** *n* in warfare, the policy of destroying everything in an area that may be of use to an advancing army; any

policy or manoeuvre in which action is taken to reduce useful assets in order to minimize their value to future occupants, owners, etc.

scorch[2] /skörch/ (*Shakesp*; *Walter Scott*) *vt* to slash (in *Macbeth* III.2.13, *scotch'd* conjecturally read for *scorch'd* by L Theobald, 18c editor). [Perh **score**, infl by **scratch**]

scordato /skör-dä'tō/ (*music*) *adj* put out of tune. [Ital]

■ **scordatura** /-too'rə/ *n* a temporary departure from the normal tuning of a stringed instrument.

score /skör or skōr/ *n* a notch, gash, or scratch; an incised line; a boldly drawn line, *esp* one marking a deletion; a line marking a boundary, starting-place, or defined position; an arrangement of music on a number of staves (*perh orig* with the bar divisions running continuously through all); a composition so distributed; music for a film, television or radio play or the music and songs for a stage or film musical; a notch in a tally; an account of charges incurred (as in a tavern) by tallies or (later) chalk marks or the like; a debt incurred; a reckoning, account; a grievance, grudge; the full total; the total or record of points made in a game; an addition made thereto; the result of a test or examination (*N Am*); a successful attempt to obtain drugs for illegal use (*sl*); a set of twenty (sometimes verging upon numeral *adj*); (in *pl*) applied also to an indefinitely large number; twenty or twenty-one pounds in weight; a distance of twenty paces (*obs*); a fixed number (20 to 26) of tubs of coal. ◆ *vt* to mark with or by scores; to record in or with a score; to make a score through as a mark of deletion (with *out* or *through*); to write as a score (*music*); to break down (a musical composition) into parts for individual (groups of) instruments, and write the appropriate music; to make as a score; to add to a score; to achieve; to enumerate; to record; to mark (a test or examination) (*N Am*); to rebuke or criticize harshly (*N Am*). ◆ *vi* to keep or run up a score; to make a point; to achieve a success; to be worth a certain number of points; to keep a record of points gained during a game; (of a man) to succeed in having sexual intercourse (*sl*); to obtain illegal drugs (*sl*). [Late OE *scoru*, from ON *skor*, *skora*; cf OE *sceran* (pap *scoren*) to shear]

■ **score'less** *adj.* **scor'er** *n* a person who or thing that scores. **scor'ing** *n* the act of scoring; orchestration.

❏ **score'board** or **scoring board** *n* a board on which the score is exhibited, as at cricket. **score'card**, **scoring card** or **score'sheet** *n* a card or sheet, for recording the score in a game. **score draw** *n* (*esp football*) a drawn match in which both teams have scored at least once. **score'line** *n* a score in a match, etc.

■ **go off at score** (*old*) to make a spirited start. **know the score** to know the hard facts of the situation; to know what is required, without having to be told. **on that score** as regards that matter. **over the score** (*inf*) beyond reasonable limits; unfair. **pay off** (or **settle**) **old scores** to deal decisively with old grudges. **run up a score** to run up a debt. **score an own goal** (*inf*) to do something unintentionally to one's own disadvantage. **score off** or **score points off** (*inf*) to achieve a success against, get the better of.

scoria /skō'ri-ə or skô'/ *n* (pl **sco'riae** /-ri-ē/) dross or slag from metal-smelting; a mass of lava with steam-holes. [L, from Gr *skōriā*, from *skōr* dung]

■ **sco'riac** or **scoriaceous** /-ri-ā'shəs/ *adj.* **scorificā'tion** *n* reduction to scoria; assaying by fusing with lead and borax. **sco'rifīer** *n* a dish used in assaying. **sco'rify** *vt* to reduce to scoria; to rid metals of (impurities) by forming scoria. **sco'rious** *adj.*

scorn /skörn/ *n* extreme contempt; an expression, or the object, of contempt (*archaic*). ◆ *vt* to feel or express scorn for; to refuse with scorn; to make a mock of (*obs*). ◆ *vi* (*obs*) to scoff. [OFr *escarn* mockery; of Gmc origin; cf OHGer *skern* mockery]

■ **scorn'er** *n.* **scorn'ful** *adj.* **scorn'fully** *adv.* **scorn'fulness** *n.* **scorn'ing** *n.*

■ **think scorn of** (*archaic*) to disdain or think beneath one.

scorodite /skor'ə-dīt/ (*mineralogy*) *n* an orthorhombic hydrated arsenate of iron and aluminium. [Gr *skorodon* garlic, from its smell when heated]

scorpaenid /skör-pē'nid/ *n* a member of the genus *Scorpaena* or family Scorpaenidae, spiny-finned marine fish with large armoured heads, *incl* the scorpion fish and rock fish (also *adj*). [Gr *skorpaina* a kind of fish]

■ **scorpae'noid** *adj* and *n.*

scorper see **scauper**.

Scorpio /skör'pi-ō/ *n* the Scorpion, a constellation giving its name to, and formerly coinciding with, a sign of the zodiac (also **Scor'pius**; *astron*); the eighth sign of the zodiac, between Libra and Sagittarius (*astrol*); a person born between 23 October and 22 November, under the sign of Scorpio (*astrol*; *pl* **Scor'pios**). [L, scorpion; see **scorpion**]

■ **Scor'pian** *n* and *adj* (relating to or characteristic of) a person born under the sign of Scorpio. **Scor'pionic** *adj* relating to or characteristic of a person born under the sign of Scorpio.

scorpioid /skör'pi-oid/ *adj* (*zool*) like a scorpion, or a scorpion's curled tail. ◆ *n* (*bot*) a cincinnus or cicinnus, an inflorescence in which the plane of each daughter axis is at right angles, to right and left alternately, with its parent axis, that of the whole coiled in bud. [Gr *skorpios* scorpion, and **-oid**]

scorpion /skör'pi-ən/ *n* any arachnid of the genus *Scorpio* or order Scorpionida with head and thorax united, pincers, four pairs of legs, and a segmented abdomen including a tail with a venomous sting; (with *cap* and *the*) Scorpio; a form of barbed scourge (*Bible*); an old contraption for hurling stones, a ballista; any person of virulent hatred or animosity. [L *scorpiō*, *-ōnis*, from Gr *skorpios* scorpion]
■ **scorpion'ic** *adj*.
❑ **scorpion fish** *n* any of the family Scorpaenidae, having venomous spines on the fins. **scorpion fly** *n* an insect of the order Mecoptera (from the male's scorpion-like tail). **scorpion grass** *n* another name for forget-me-not. **scorpion spider** *n* a whip scorpion.

Scorpius see **Scorpio**.

scorrendo /sko-ren'dō/ (*music*) *adj* gliding. [Ital]

scorse¹ /skörs or skörs/ (*obs*) *vt* to chase. [Ital *scorsa* a run, from *scorrere*, from L *excurrere*]

scorse² /skörs or skörs/ (*obs*) *n* exchange. ◆ *vt* and *vi* to exchange (also **scourse**). [Poss from *horse-scorser* for **horse-courser**]
■ **scors'er** *n* someone who barters.

scorzonera /skör-zə-nē'rə/ *n* a plant of the genus *Scorzonera*, *esp S. hispanica* (black salsify). [Ital]

Scot /skot/ *n* a native or inhabitant of Scotland; a member of a Gaelic-speaking people of Ireland, afterwards also in Argyllshire (*hist*). [OE *Scottas* (pl), from LL *Scottus* and *Scōtus*; see also **Scotch**, **Scots**, **Scottish**]
■ **Scotland** /skot'lənd/ *n* the country forming the northern member of the United Kingdom; Ireland (*hist*). **Scot'landite** *n* naturally-occurring lead sulphite, first identified in Lanarkshire, Scotland. **Scott'y** or **Scott'ie** *n* a nickname for a Scotsman; a Scotch terrier.
❑ **Scotland Yard** *n* the earliest or (**New Scotland Yard**) two more recent headquarters (1890 and 1967) of the Metropolitan Police; hence, the London Criminal Investigation Department.
■ **Irish Scot** (*obs*) a Highlander.

Scot. *abbrev* : Scotland; Scottish.

scot /skot/ *n* (*hist*) a payment, *esp* a customary tax; a share of a reckoning (also **shot**). [OE *scot*, *sceot*; but prob partly from ON *skot*, and OFr *esco*; see **shot¹**, **escot**]
❑ **scot and lot** *n* an old local tax entitling all who paid to vote in parliamentary elections; an old legal term embracing all forms of tax; hence, all forms of responsibility, duty, etc. **scot-free'** *adj* and *adv* free from scot, untaxed (*hist*); entirely free from expense, injury, penalty, punishment, etc.

Scotch /skoch/ *adj* of or belonging to Scotland or the Scots, a form regarded as incorrect by many Scots, who prefer **Scottish** or **Scots**; applied to products or supposed products of Scotland, *esp* whisky; having the character popularly attributed to a Scotsman, an excessive leaning towards defence of oneself and one's property (*derog inf*). ◆ *n* Scotch whisky, or a glass of it; the Scots language; (as *pl*) the Scots. [From **Scottish**]
■ **Scotch'ness** *n*. **Scot'chy** *n* a nickname for a Scot. ◆ *adj* having Scottish characteristics.
❑ **Scotch and English** *n* prisoners' base (qv under **prison**). **Scotch attorney** *n* (*W Indies*) a climber (genus *Clusia*) that strangles trees. **Scotch barley** *n* hulled barley. **Scotch bluebell** *n* the harebell. **Scotch bonnet** *n* a round flat blue woollen cap with a tuft on the top; the fairy-ring mushroom; the hottest variety of capsicum pepper, used in Mexican, N American and Caribbean cooking (also called **habañera**). **Scotch broth** *n* broth made with pearl barley, mutton or beef stock and plenty of various vegetables chopped small. **Scotch cart** *n* (*S Afr*; *archaic*) a strong, springless, two-wheeled uncovered farm cart with one shaft. **Scotch catch** or **snap** *n* (*music*) a short accented note followed by a longer, not peculiar to Scottish music. **Scotch collops** *n pl* minced beef (sometimes called **scotched collops**). **Scotch cuddy** *n* (Scot *cuddy* a donkey; *archaic*) a Scotch draper. **Scotch curlies** *n pl* a variety of kale. **Scotch draper** *n* (*archaic*) an itinerant dealer differing from a pedlar in not carrying his goods about with him; an itinerant draper (also **Scotch cuddy**). **Scotch egg** *n* a hard-boiled egg (often cut in two) enclosed in sausage-meat and covered with breadcrumbs. **Scotch elm** *n* the wych-elm (*Ulmus montana*); sometimes the common English elm (*Ulmus campestris*). **Scotch fiddle** *n* (*archaic*) scabies (from the movements of the fingers when scratching). **Scotch fir** *n* Scots pine (see under **Scots**). **Scotch hand** *n* a wooden bat for manipulating butter. **Scotch-Ir'ish** *adj* and *n pl* (*US*) Irish of Scottish descent. **Scotch kale** *n* a variety of kale. **Scotch'man** *n* a Scotsman; an old South African name for a florin (from a tradition that a Scotsman passed such coins off to the native people as half-crowns).

Scotch mist *n* a fine rain; something insubstantial, a phantom (*usu ironic*). **Scotch pancake** *n* a drop scone. **Scotch pebble** *n* an agate or similar stone. **Scotch pine** *n* Scots pine (see under **Scots**). **Scotch rose** *n* the burnet rose (*Rosa spinosissima*). **Scotch snap** *n* a Scotch catch (see above). **Scotch terrier** *n* a rough-haired, strongly-built little dog with erect ears (also **Scottish terrier**, **Scottie**, **Scotty**). **Scotch thistle** *n* the cotton thistle, national emblem of Scotland (not native). **Scotch verdict** *n* not proven. **Scotch'woman** *n* a Scotswoman. **Scotch woodcock** *n* scrambled eggs and anchovies on toast.

scotch¹ /skoch/ *vt* to frustrate, put an end to; to quash; to maim, to render harmless by crippling (without killing); to gash (*obs*); to score; (from Theobald's conjecture in *Macbeth*; see **scorch²**). ◆ *n* a gash (*obs*); a line marked on the ground (as for hopscotch). [Origin unknown]

scotch² /skoch/ *n* a strut, wedge, block, etc, to prevent turning or slipping, as of a wheel, gate, ladder. ◆ *vt* to stop or block; to frustrate (plans, etc). [Perh a form of **scratch**]

Scotch tape® /skoch tāp/ (*esp N Am*) *n* a transparent tape, adhering to paper, etc when pressure is applied.

scoter /skō'tər/ *n* (also **scoter duck**) any of several northern sea ducks of the genus *Melanitta*, with black or mainly black plumage in the male. [Origin obscure]

Scotia /skō'shyə, -shə/ *n* (*poetic*) Scotland. [LL *Scōtia*, *Scōticus*]
■ **Scot'ian** *adj* (*rare*).

scotia /skō'ti-ə or -shi-ə/ (*archit*) *n* a concave moulding, *esp* at the base of an Ionic column. [Gr *skotiā*, from *skotos* darkness]

Scotic /skot'ik/ *adj* denoting the branch of English spoken in Scotland; relating to the ancient Scots, incomers from Ireland. [LL *Scōticus* from *Scōtus*]
■ **Scot'ican** *adj* (formed in imitation of *Anglican*; *relig*) of Scotland.

Scoticism, Scotify, etc see **Scotticism, Scottify**, etc.

Scotism /skō'ti-zm/ *n* the metaphysical system of Johannes Duns Scotus (c.1265–1308), a native of Maxton in Roxburghshire (not Duns in Berwickshire, Dunstane in Northumberland, or Down in Northern Ireland), who sought the foundation of Christian theology in practice, not in speculation, his theological descendants being the Franciscans, in opposition to the Dominicans, who followed Aquinas.
■ **Scō'tist** *n* a follower of Duns Scotus. **Scotist'ic** *adj*.

Scoto- /skot-ō-, -ə-, -o-/ *combining form* denoting Scotland and the Scots as in *Scotophobia*, or a Scottish element combined with another, as in *Scoto-Irish*, etc. [LL *Scōtus* a Scot]
■ **Scot'ophile** *n* someone fond of Scotland and its people. **Scotophil'ia** *n*. **Scotophil'ic** *adj*. **Scot'ophobe** *n* a hater of Scotland and its people. **Scotophō'bia** *n*. **Scotopho'bic** *adj*.

scoto- /skot-ō-, -ə-, -o-/ or (before a vowel) **scot-** /skot-/ *combining form* denoting dark, darkness. [Gr *skotos* darkness]
■ **scotodinia** /-din'i-ə/ *n* (Gr *dīnos* whirling) dizziness with headache and impairment of vision. **scotoma** /-ōm'ə/ *n* (*pl* scotō'mata or scotō'mas) (Gr *skotōma* dizziness; *med*) an area of abnormal or absent vision within the visual field, a blind spot due to disease of the retina or optic nerve. **scotō'matous** *adj*. **scoto'meter** *n* an instrument for identifying defects in the visual field. **scotō'mia** and **scot'omy** *n* (*obs*) scotoma, in its obsolete sense of dizziness accompanied by dimness of vision. **scotop'ia** *n* vision in dim light. **scotopic** /-op'/ *adj*.

Scots /skots/ *adj* Scottish (almost always used of money, measures, law, and language). ◆ *n* any of the varieties of the northern branch of English spoken in Scotland, *esp* that of Lowland Scotland preserved in the poetry of Burns and others (see also **Lallans** under **lallan**). [Scot *Scottis* Scottish]
❑ **Scots fir** *n* Scots pine (see below). **Scots Greys** *n pl* a famous regiment of dragoons, established in 1683, amalgamated with the 3rd Carabiniers in 1971. **Scots Guards** *n pl* a Scottish force which served the kings of France from 1418 to 1759, nominally to 1830; a well-known regiment of Guards in the British Army, formerly Scots Fusilier Guards. **Scots'man** or **Scots'woman** *n* a native of Scotland. **Scots mile** see under **mile**. **Scots pine** *n* (often called **Scots fir**) the only native British pine, *Pinus sylvestris*. **Scots pint, pound scots** see **pint, pound¹**.

Scottice or **Scotice** /skot'i-sē, skot'i-kā/ *adv* in Scots. [L]

Scotticism or **Scoticism** /skot'i-si-zm/ *n* a Scottish idiom; Scottish feeling. [LL *Scotticus, Scōticus*]
■ **Scott'icize** or **-ise** *vt* to render Scottish; to put into Scots.

Scottify or **Scotify** /skot'i-fī/ *vt* (**Scot(t)'ifying**; **Scot(t)'ified**) to make Scottish. [**Scottish**]
■ **Scottificā'tion** or **Scotificā'tion** *n*.

Scottish /skot'ish/ *adj* of *Scotland* and the Scots. ◆ *n* the variety of English spoken in Scotland (*usu* **Scots**); (as *pl*) the Scots collectively. ◆ *vt* (*rare*) to put into the Scottish tongue. [OE *Scottisc*, from *Scottas*; see **Scot**]

- **Scott'ishness** n.
□ **Scottish Qualifications Certificate** n (in secondary education in Scotland) a qualification awarded at Intermediate, Higher and Advanced Higher grades for proficiency in one or more subjects. **Scottish terrier** see **Scotch terrier** under **Scotch**.

SCOTVEC /skot'vek/ abbrev: Scottish Vocational Education Council (now replaced by **SQA**).

scoug same as **skug**[1].

scoundrel /skown'drəl/ n an unprincipled or villainous person. [Origin unknown]
- **scoun'drelism** n. **scoun'drelly** adj.

scoup or **scowp** /skowp/ (Scot) vi to bound; to caper; to scamper. [Origin unknown]

scour[1] /skowr/ vt to clean, polish, remove, or form by hard rubbing; to scrub; to cleanse; to free from grease, dirt, or gum; to flush or cleanse by a current; to purge, esp drastically; to clear out; to punish (fig). ◆ vi to scrub and polish; to serve or act as a purgative; (of livestock) to have diarrhoea. ◆ n the action, place, or means of scouring; (often in pl) diarrhoea in cattle, etc; a swig of liquor (Scot). [Prob MDu or MLG schûren, from OFr escurer, from L ex cūrāre to take care of]
- **scour'er** n a person who scours; an instrument or container for scouring; a cathartic. **scour'ing** n scrubbing; vigorous cleansing; clearing; erosion; purging; (often in pl) matter removed or accumulated by scouring.
□ **scouring rush** n any of several horsetails or other plants whose rough stems were formerly used for scouring. **scouring stick** n a rod for scouring a gun.

scour[2] /skowr/ vt to range over or traverse swiftly, vigorously, riotously, or in pursuit; to search thoroughly. ◆ vi to rush or scurry along; to range about, esp in quest or pursuit. [Poss ON skūr storm, shower; cf **shower**]
- **scour'er** or (obs) **scowr'er** n (hist) a member of a roistering band that scoured the streets, maltreating watchmen and others.

scourer[1] /skow'rər/ n a scout. [Aphetic from **discoverer**]

scourer[2] see under **scour**[1,2].

scourge /skûrj/ n a whip; an instrument of divine punishment; a cause of widespread affliction. ◆ vt to whip severely; to afflict. [Anglo-Fr escorge, from L excoriāre to flay, from corium leather (perh as made of a strip of leather, perh as a flaying instrument)]
- **scourg'er** n.

scourie see **scaury**.

scourse see **scorse**[2].

Scouse /skows/ (inf) n a native or inhabitant of Liverpool (also **Scous'er**); the northern English dialect spoken in and around Liverpool; (without cap) a stew or hash, often made with meat scraps. ◆ adj referring or relating to Liverpool, its people or their dialect. [Short for lobscouse a vegetable stew, a sea dish]

scout[1] /skowt/ n someone, or (obs or N Am) a party, sent out to reconnoitre or bring in information; a (military) spy; a member of the Scout Association (formerly **Boy Scout**); (in the USA) a member of the Girl Scouts (an organization similar to the Guides); a patrolman on the roads; a person who watches or attends at a little distance; a person who seeks out new recruits, players, sales opportunities, etc; a ship for reconnoitring; a small light aeroplane orig intended for reconnaissance; a light armoured car for reconnaissance (now usu **scout car**); a college servant (esp at Oxford); a search (inf); watch, spying (archaic). ◆ vt to watch closely. ◆ vi to act as a scout; to reconnoitre (often with about or around). [OFr escoute, from escouter, from L auscultāre to listen]
- **scout'er** n an adult working with instructors, etc, in the Scout Association. **scout'ing** n.
□ **Scout Association** n (formerly, the **Boy Scouts**) a worldwide movement for young people, intended to develop character and a sense of responsibility, founded (for boys) by Lord Baden-Powell in 1908. **scout car** see **scout** (n) above. **scout'craft** n the knowledge and skill appropriate to a scout. **scout law** n the code of rules of the Scout Association. **scout'master** n the leader of a band of scouts, a scouter; formerly, an adult in charge of a troop of Boy Scouts. **scout's pace** n alternately walking and running for a set number of paces.

scout[2] /skowt/ (archaic) vt to mock, flout; to dismiss or reject with disdain. [Cf ON skúta a taunt]

scout[3] same as **scoot**[2].

scouth or **scowth** /skooth or skowth/ (Scot) n free range; scope; plenty.

scouther, **scowther** /skow'dhər/ or **scowder** /skow'dər/ (Scot) vt to scorch, singe; to overheat; to toast slightly; to blight. ◆ vi to drizzle; to threaten to rain or snow. ◆ n a scorch or burn; a slight or brief shower. [Connected with **scald**[1]]

- **scou'thering**, **scow'dering** adj scorching, blighting. ◆ n a scorching, blighting; a sprinkle of snow. **scou'thery** adj.

scow /skow/ n a flat-bottomed boat, esp a barge, or (US) a sailing yacht. [Du schouw]

scowder see **scouther**.

scowl /skowl/ vi to contract the brows in a malevolent and menacing look; to look gloomy and threatening. ◆ n a scowling look. [Cf Dan skule to cast down the eyes, look sidelong]
- **scow'ler** n. **scow'ling** adj. **scow'lingly** adv.

scowp see **scoup**.

scowrer see under **scour**[2].

scowrie see **scaury**.

scowth see **scouth**.

scowther see **scouther**.

SCP abbrev: single-cell protein; Society of Chiropodists and Podiatrists.

SCR abbrev: senior common (or combination) room (see under **senior**).

scr. abbrev: scruple (weight).

scrab /skrab/ (archaic and dialect) vt (**scrabb'ing**; **scrabbed**) to scratch. [Du schrabben to scratch, frequentative schrabbelen; cf **scrape**]
- **scrabb'le** vt and vi to scratch; to scrape; to scrawl. ◆ vi to scramble. ◆ n an act of scrabbling; a scrawl. **scrabb'ler** n.

Scrabble® /skrab'l/ n a word-building game. [**scrabble**]

scrae /skrā/ (Scot) n same as **scree**.

scrag[1] /skrag/ n a sheep's or (inf) human neck; the bony part of the neck; an unhealthily thin person or animal. ◆ vt (**scragg'ing**; **scragged**) to hang; to throttle; to wring the neck of; to grab by the neck; to attack or beat up (inf). [Prob **crag**[2]]
- **scragg'ed** or /skragd/) adj scraggy. **scragg'edness** n. **scragg'ily** adv. **scragg'iness** n. **scragg'y** adj skinny and gaunt.
□ **scrag'-end** n the scrag of a neck.

scrag[2] /skrag/ n a stump; a rough projection. [Cf **scrog**]
- **scragg'ily** adv. **scragg'iness** n. **scragg'ling**, **scragg'ly** or **scragg'y** adj irregular, unkempt, straggling.
□ **scrag'-whale** n a whale with a knobbed back.

scraich or **scraigh** /skrāhh/ (Scot) vi to screech; to make a scratchy sound. ◆ n a screech; a scratchy sound. [Cf **scraugh**, **skreigh**]

scram[1] /skram/ (inf) vi (**scramm'ing**; **scrammed**) (esp in the imperative) to go away. [Perh **scramble**]

scram[2] /skram/ adj (SW Eng) puny; withered. ◆ vt (**scramm'ing**; **scrammed**) to benumb (SW Eng); to paralyse (SW Eng); to shut down (a nuclear reactor), esp in an emergency. ◆ n an emergency shut-down of a nuclear reactor. [Cf **scrimp**]

scram[3] or **scramb** /skram/ (dialect) vt to scratch with claws or nails. [From Du schrammen]

scramble /skram'bl/ vi to make one's way with disorderly struggling haste; to get along somehow; to clamber; to climb or grow upwards over a vertical surface; to dash or struggle for what one can get before others; (of a military aircraft or its crew) to take off immediately, as in an emergency. ◆ vt to put, make, get or push together in a rough hasty manner; to change the frequency of (a transmission) so that it can be made intelligible only by means of an electronic decoding device; to beat (eggs) up and heat to thickness with milk, butter, etc; to make (a radiotelephone conversation) unintelligible by a device that alters frequencies; to order (a military aircraft or its crew) to take off immediately. ◆ n an act or the action of scrambling; a disorderly performance; a dash or struggle for what can be had; an emergency take-off by a military aircraft; a form of motor or motorcycle trial on rough or hilly terrain. [Cf the dialect verb scramb to rake together with the hands]
- **scram'bler** n a person who, or that which, scrambles, esp a telephone device. **scram'bling** adj. ◆ n the action of the verb scramble; participation in motorcycle, etc scrambles. **scram'blingly** adv.
□ **scrambled eggs** n pl eggs cooked as described above; the gold braid on a military officer's cap (sl).

scramjet /skram'jet/ n a jet engine in which compressed air drawn into the engine via turbo fans mixes with fuel to improve combustion at a supersonic speed. [supersonic combustion ramjet]

scran /skran/ (inf) n food, provisions. [Ety doubtful]
- **bad scran to you** (Irish) bad luck to you.

scranch /skranch or skransh/ vt to crunch. [Prob imit; cf Du schransen to eat heartily]

scrannel /skran'l/ (archaic) adj thin; meagre; squeaking; grating; scratchy (Milton).
- **scrann'y** adj thin, scrawny.

scrap[1] /skrap/ n a small fragment; a piece of left-over food; a remnant; a cut-out picture, newspaper cutting, or the like, intended or suited for preservation in a scrapbook; residue after extraction of oil from blubber, fish, etc; metal clippings or other waste, often for recycling or re-using; anything discarded as worn-out, out of date, or useless. ◆ adj consisting of, or of the value of, scrap. ◆ vt (**scrapp'ing**; **scrapped**) to consign to the scrapheap; to discard, cease to use, do away with, abandon. [ON skrap scraps; cf **scrape**]
■ **scrapp'age** n the scrapping of an old or useless item, esp a motor vehicle. **scrapp'ily** adv. **scrapp'iness** n. **scrapp'y** adj fragmentary; disconnected, disorganized; made up of scraps.
❑ **scrap'book** n a blank book for pasting in scraps, cuttings, etc. ◆ vi and vt to keep a scrapbook (of). **scrap'booking** n. **scrap'heap** n a place where old iron or useless material is collected; a rubbish heap (also fig). **scrap iron** or **scrap metal** n scraps of iron or other metal, of use only for remelting. **scrap'-man**, **scrap merchant** or **scrap'-metal merchant** n a person who deals in scrap metal. **scrap'yard** n a premises for the storing and processing of scrap metal.
■ **not a scrap** not even a tiny amount. **throw on the scrapheap** to reject as no longer useful (lit and fig).

scrap[2] /skrap/ (inf) n a fight, usu physical; a battle (euphem). ◆ vi (**scrapp'ing**; **scrapped**) to fight.
■ **scrapp'er** n. **scrapp'y** adj belligerent; quarrelsome.

scrape /skrāp/ vt to pass a sharp edge over; to move with a grating sound over; to smooth, clean, clear, reduce in thickness, abrade, graze, remove, form, collect, bring, render, by such an action; to get together, collect by laborious effort (often with together or up); to achieve with difficulty; to erase; contemptuously, to play (the fiddle). ◆ vi to graze (with against or on); to scratch the ground; to grate; to make a grating sound; to draw back the foot in making a bow; to play the fiddle; to save as much as possible, enduring hardship thereby; to get by with difficulty (with through, along, home, etc). ◆ n an act, process, or period of scraping; a stroke of a violin, etc bow; a grating sound; a stroke (of a pen); a scraped place in the ground; a graze or abrasion, eg on the skin; a shave (facetious); a mass of earth scraped up, eg by a rabbit; a backward movement of one foot accompanying a bow; a scraping or thin layer; thin-spread butter or margarine; a fight or other conflict (inf); a difficult or embarrassing predicament (inf). [OE scrapian or ON skrapa]
■ **scrāp'er** n a person who scrapes; a scraping tool, instrument or machine; a fiddler (derog); a barber (derog); any of several gallinaceous birds that scrape or scratch the ground. **scrāp'ie** n a degenerative disease caused by prions and affecting the central nervous system of sheep, characterized by acute itching, the animals rubbing against trees, etc to relieve it. **scrāp'ing** n the action of the verb; its sound; a thin piece scraped off. **scrapp'age** n a scheme by which an owner of a car or other piece of equipment can claim towards the cost of replacing it.
❑ **scrape'good** n (archaic) a miser. **scrape'gut** n (archaic) a fiddler. **scrape'penny** n (archaic) a miser. **scrap'erboard** n a clay-surface board on which drawings can be made by scraping tints off as well as applying them; such a drawing; this method of making drawings. **scraper ring** n (motoring) a ring fitted on the skirt of an engine piston to prevent excessive oil consumption (also **oil-control ring**).
■ **bow and scrape** to be over-obsequious. **scrape acquaintance with** to contrive somehow to get to know. **scrape the (bottom of the) barrel** see under **barrel**.

scrapie see under **scrape**.

scrapple /skrap'(ə)l/ (US) n a type of meat loaf made with scraps of meat or minced meat, usu pork, cornmeal, seasonings, etc, served sliced and fried. [**scrap**[1]]

scrat /skrat/ (obs or dialect) vt and vi to scratch. [ME scratte; origin doubtful]

Scratch /skrach/ n the Devil (also **Old Scratch**). [Cf ON skratte goblin, monster]

scratch /skrach/ vt to draw a sharp point over the surface of; to hurt, mark, render, seek to relieve an itch in, by so doing; to dig or scrape with the claws; to write hurriedly; to erase or delete (usu with out); to strike along a rough surface; to withdraw from a competition or (esp musical) engagement. ◆ vi to use the nails or claws to inflict injury, relieve an itch, etc; to scrape; to make a grating or screechy noise; to retire from a contest or engagement; to get (along or through) somehow (inf). ◆ n an act, mark, or sound of scratching; a slight wound or graze; a scrawl; formerly, the line in the ring up to which boxers were led to begin fighting; hence a test, trial, as in come up to scratch; the starting-point for a player or competitor without a handicap; a player or competitor who starts from scratch; a fluke, esp in billiards; a scratch-wig; cash, ready money (sl); (in pl) a disease in horses with the appearance of scratches on the pastern or ankle. ◆ adj improvised; casual; hastily or casually got together; (of a player or competitor) having a handicap of zero. [Poss ME cracchen to scratch, modified by **scrat**]

■ **scratch'er** n. **scratch'ily** adv. **scratch'iness** n. **scratch'ing** n the action of the verb; the act of manipulating a gramophone record so that it plays a repeated beat or section of music. **scratch'ingly** adv. **scratch'less** adj. **scratch'y** adj like scratches; uneven; ready or likely to scratch; irritable, bad-tempered, tetchy (esp US); grating or screechy; itchy.
❑ **scratch'back** n a backscratcher. **scratch'board** n a scraperboard. **scratch brush** n a wire brush, used eg in gilding and polishing metal. **scratch'build** vt to build (usu models) from raw materials, as opposed to constructing from kits or buying ready made. **scratch'builder** n. **scratch'building** n. **scratch'built** adj. **scratch'card** n a type of lottery card covered with an opaque film which is scratched off to reveal numbers or symbols which may entitle the holder to a prize. **scratch coat** n a first coat of plaster, scratched to provide a key for the second coat. **scratch pad** n a note-pad, jotter; a facility on a mobile phone that enables the user to record information in the phone's memory during a call. **scratch test** n (med) a test for allergy to a certain substance, made by introducing it to an area of skin that has been scratched. **scratch'-wig** n a wig that covers only part of the head. **scratch'-work** n sgraffito in plaster.
■ **come up to scratch** (fig) to reach an expected standard; to fulfil an obligation. **scratch the surface** see under **surface**. **start from scratch** (fig) to start at the beginning; to embark on (a task, career, etc) without any advantages, experience or without any preparatory work having been done. **you scratch my back and I'll scratch yours** (inf) do me a favour and I'll do you one in return.

scrattle /skrat'l/ (West Country dialect) vi to keep scratching; to scuttle. [Frequentative of **scrat**]

scraugh or **scrauch** /skröhh/ (Scot) n a raucous squawk. ◆ vi to make a scraugh. [Imit]

scraw /skrö/ (archaic) n a thin sod or turf. [Ir sgrath]

scrawl /sköl/ vt and vi to draw or write illegibly, untidily or hastily; to scribble. ◆ n untidy, illegible, or bad writing; a letter, etc, written thus; a small crab (Lincs dialect; Tennyson). [Perh connected with **crawl**[1] or **sprawl**]
■ **scrawl'er** n. **scrawl'ing** n and adj. **scrawl'ingly** adv. **scrawl'y** adj.

scrawm /sköm/ (dialect) vt to scratch. [Prob Du schrammen to graze]

scrawny /skrö'ni/ (orig US) adj unhealthily thin, scraggy; sparse, meagre. [From **scranny**]
■ **scraw'nily** adv. **scraw'niness** n.

scray or **scraye** /skrā/ n the tern. [Cf Welsh ysgräell]

screak /skrēk/ (dialect) vt to screech; to creak. ◆ n a screech; a creak. [Cf ON skrækja]
■ **screak'y** adj.

scream /skrēm/ vt and vi to cry out in a loud shrill voice, as in fear or pain; to laugh shrilly and uncontrollably; to shriek. ◆ vi (of colours) to clash acutely (inf); to be all too loudly evident (inf); to move with a screaming noise. ◆ n a shrill, sudden cry, as in fear or pain; a shriek; a loud whistling sound; anything or anyone supposed to make one scream with laughter (inf). [Late OE scræmen]
■ **scream'er** n a person or thing that screams; a large spur-winged S American bird (**crested** and **black-necked screamer**) with a loud harsh cry; a different S American bird, the seriema (sometimes known as **crested screamer**); anything likely or intended to thrill with emotion, eg a sensational headline (sl); an exclamation mark (printing sl). **scream'ing** n and adj. **scream'ingly** adv.
❑ **screaming farce** n a highly ludicrous situation. **screaming habdabs** or **abdabs** see under **habdabs**. **screaming meemies** see **meemie**.

scree /skrē/ n a sloping mass of loose weathered rock at the base of a cliff or on the face of a mountain. [ON skritha a landslip, from skrītha to slide]

screech /skrēch/ vi to utter a harsh, shrill, and sudden cry or noise, or to speak in that way. ◆ vt to utter in such tones. ◆ n a harsh, shrill, and sudden cry, noise, or tone of voice. [ME scrichen; cf **scritch**]
■ **screech'er** n someone or something that screeches; the swift, barn owl or other screeching bird. **screech'y** adj shrill and harsh, like a screech.
❑ **screech'-hawk** n the nightjar. **screech'-martin** n the swift. **screech owl** n any of various small N American owls characterized by a long quavering cry; the barn owl; a bringer of bad news. **screech'-thrush** n the mistle-thrush; the fieldfare.

screed /skrēd/ n a shred; a strip; a border; a long passage, spoken or written; a drinking bout (obs); a band of plaster laid on the surface of a wall as a guide to the thickness of a coat of plaster to be applied subsequently (building); a layer of mortar finishing off the surface of a floor (also **screed'ing**); a strip of wood or metal for levelling off mortar, sand, etc; a rent, a tear (Scot). ◆ vt to repeat glibly. ◆ vi to tear; to make a shrill or tearing noise. [OE scrēade shred]
■ **screed'er** n a person whose job is to lay screeds on floors or walls.

screen /skrēn/ n a shield against danger, observation, wind, heat, light, or other outside influence; a piece of room furniture in the form of a folding framework or of a panel on a stand; a clothes-horse (Scot); a large scarf or stole (Allan Ramsay); a windscreen; a sheltering row of trees, shrubs, etc; a body of troops or formation of ships intended as a cover for the bulk of the army or fleet; a wall masking a building (also **screen wall**); a partition separating off part of a room, a church choir, or side chapel; a coarse sifting apparatus; in some cameras, a glass plate with a pattern of various kinds on it to aid in focusing; a glass plate with rules or dots of a given coarseness or frequency for printing half-tone photographs; a mosaic of primary colours for colour photography; the surface on which a cinema film, television or computer image or slide projection is seen; (with the) the medium of cinema or television; a white board on the perimeter of a cricket ground, against which the batsman can pick out the ball moving towards him; a screen grid. ◆ vt to shelter or conceal; to sift coarsely; to sort out by, or subject to, tests of ability, trustworthiness, desirability, etc; to test for illness, etc; to protect from stray electrical interference; to prevent from causing outside electrical interference; to project or exhibit on a cinema, television or slide screen or on cinema or TV screens generally; to make a motion picture of. ◆ vi to show up on, or be suitable for, the screen. [Appar related in some way to OFr escran (Fr écran) which may be from OHGer skirm, skerm (Ger Schirm)]
■ **screen'able** adj. **screen'er** n. **screen'ful** n as much information as can be displayed on a computer or TV screen at one time. **screen'ing** n. **screen'ings** n pl material eliminated by sifting.
❑ **screen'ager** n a young person skilled in the use of computers and the Internet. **screen'craft** n the technique of making films. **screen door** n (in N America) a frame of wood or metal with netting panels, to exclude insects when the door proper is open. **screen dump** or **screen grab** n (comput) a record of the display on a computer screen that can be printed or saved as an image file; a single frame from a television or video film saved as a still image. **screen grid** n an electrode placed between the control grid and anode in a valve, having an invariable potential to eliminate positive feedback and instability. **screening test** n a test carried out on a large number of people to identify those who have, or are likely to develop, a specified disease. **screen'play** n the written text for a film, with dialogue, stage directions, and descriptions of characters and setting. **screen printing** and **screen process** same as silkscreen printing and silkscreen process (see **silkscreen** under **silk**). **screen saver** n (comput) a program which, after a period of user inactivity, replaces the screen image with a usu moving pattern. **screen'shot** n an image representing the display of a computer screen at a particular time. **screen test** n a trial filming to determine whether an actor or actress is suitable for cinema work. **screen'-test** vt and vi. **screen'wash** n a liquid that is sprayed onto the windscreen of a motor vehicle so that the windscreen-wipers can clean it. **screen'-wiper** n a windscreen-wiper. **screen'writer** n a writer of screenplays. **screen'writing** n.
■ **screen off** to hide behind, or separate by, a screen; to separate by sifting.

screeve /skrēv/ (sl) vt and vi to write, esp begging letters; to draw on the pavement. ◆ n a piece of writing; a begging letter. [Prob Ital scrivere, from L scrībere to write]
■ **screev'er** n. **screev'ing** n.

screich, screigh see skreigh.

screw /skrōō/ n a cylinder with a helical groove or ridge on its outside (the thread), used as a fastening driven into wood, etc by rotation (a male thread; for female thread, see **female**), mechanically or otherwise; anything of similar form; a screw propeller or ship driven by one; a thumbscrew, an instrument of torture; a corkscrew; a twisted cone of paper, or the portion of a commodity contained in it; the turn of a screw; pressure (fig); a twist; (esp in billiards and snooker) a spin imparted to a ball; a stingy person, an extortionist, a skinflint (old sl); a prison officer (sl); a broken-winded horse; an act of sexual intercourse (vulgar sl); a sexual partner (vulgar sl); salary, wages (sl). ◆ vt to fasten, tighten, compress, force, adjust or extort by a screw or screws, a screwing motion, or as if by a screw; to apply a screw to; to twist; to turn in the manner of a screw; to pucker (often with up); to put sidespin or backspin on (the cue ball) in snooker or billiards; to have sexual intercourse with (vulgar sl); to practise extortion upon; to cheat, defraud or take advantage of (sl); to enter by means of a skeleton key (sl); to burgle, rob (sl). ◆ vi to be capable of being screwed; to wind (with in, up, etc); to have sexual intercourse (vulgar sl). [Earlier scrue; appar OFr escroue, of obscure origin; prob connected with LG schrûve, Ger Schraube]
■ **screw'able** adj. **screwed** adj messed up, spoiled; ruined, defeated; tipsy (sl). **screw'er** n. **screw'iness** n (inf) eccentricity. **screw'ing** n and adj. **screw'y** adj (inf) tipsy; eccentric, slightly mad (inf).
❑ **screw'ball** n (N Am) a ball delivered with spin (baseball); a crazy person, an eccentric (sl; orig US). ◆ adj eccentric or zany. **screw'baller** n (N Am) a screwball comedy (inf); a pitcher who throws screwballs (baseball). **screw bolt** n a bolt with a screw thread.

screw cap n a lid that screws onto a container. **screw'-capped** adj. **screw'-down** adj closed by screwing. **screw'driver** n an instrument for turning and driving screws; a cocktail, the principal ingredients of which are vodka and orange juice. ◆ adj (of factories, assembly plants, etc) assembling components produced elsewhere, usu in a foreign country. **screw eye** n a screw formed into a loop for attaching rope, wire, etc. **screwing die** n (engineering) an internally threaded hardened steel block for cutting externally threaded screws or screwed pieces. **screwing machine** n (engineering) a form of lathe adapted for the continuous production of screws or screwed pieces by screwing dies. **screw jack** n a jack for lifting heavy weights, operated by a screw. **screw nail** n a nail with a screw thread. **screw'-pile** n a pile for sinking into the ground, ending in a screw. **screw pine** n a plant of the genus Pandanus or its family (from the screwlike arrangement of the leaves). **screw plate** n (engineering) a hardened steel plate in which a number of screwing dies of different sizes are formed. **screw press** n (engineering) a press worked by a screw, for punching holes, etc. **screw propeller** n a propeller with helical blades. **screw steamer** n a steamer driven by a screw propeller. **screw tap** n a tool for cutting female screw threads. **screw thread** n the helical ridge of a screw. **screw'top** n a bottle with a stopper that screws in or on, esp a beer bottle of the kind with its contents (also adj); the stopper itself. **screw'-topped** adj. **screw'-worm** n the larva of a dipterous fly (**screw-worm fly**) which develops under the skin of various animals, often causing death. **screw'-wrench** n a tool for gripping screw heads.
■ **have a screw loose** to be defective (esp mentally). **put on** or **tighten** or **turn the screw** to apply (physical, moral, etc) pressure progressively; to exact payment. **put the screws on** to coerce. **screw around** to have many sexual partners (vulgar sl); to act the fool (sl). **screw it, them, you**, etc (vulgar sl) an interjection expressing disgust, scorn, frustration, etc. **screw over** (sl) to cheat or take advantage of (someone). **screw up** to twist or distort; to summon up (courage, etc); to disrupt, spoil or ruin (inf); (usu passive) to cause to become nervous, emotionally disturbed, etc (inf) (**screw'-up** n (inf) a disaster, failure, mess or fiasco; a person who is a failure, whose life is a mess, etc).

scribable, scribacious, etc see under **scribe**.

scribble[1] /skrib'l/ vt and vi to scrawl; to write or draw in a careless or illegible hand; to write paltry, ill-expressed material, esp copiously. ◆ n careless writing or drawing; a scrawl. [A frequentative of **scribe**, or LL scrībillāre, from L scrībere to write]
■ **scribb'lement** n. **scribb'ler** n (derog) a worthless author. **scribb'ling** n. **scribb'lingly** adv. **scribb'ly** adj.
❑ **scribb'ling-book, -pad, -paper** n.

scribble[2] /skrib'l/ vt to comb (wool) roughly. [Prob from LGer]
■ **scribb'ler** n a wool-combing machine; a person who tends it. **scribb'ling** n.

scribe /skrīb/ n a writer; a public or official writer; a medieval clerk, amanuensis or secretary; a copyist; a calligrapher; an expounder and teacher of the traditional law and that of Moses (Bible); a pointed instrument to mark lines on wood, metal, etc. ◆ vt to mark or score with a scribe, etc; to fit by so marking; to incise; to write. ◆ vi to act as a scribe. [L scrība a scribe, and scrībere to write]
■ **scrī'bable** adj capable of being written upon. **scribā'ciousness** n (archaic). **scrī'bal** adj. **scrī'ber** n a scribing tool, a scribe. **scrī'bing** n. **scrī'bism** n.

scriech see skreigh.

scriene (obs) same as **screen**.

scrieve[1] /skrēv/ (Scot) vi to glide swiftly along. [Prob ON skrefa from skref stride]

scrieve[2], **scrieveboard** see scrive.

scriggle /skrig'l/ vi to writhe; to wriggle. ◆ n a wriggling. [Cf **struggle**]
■ **scrigg'ly** adj.

scrike /skrīk/ (archaic and dialect) vi to shriek. ◆ n a shriek. [Prob Scand]

scrim /skrim/ n open fabric used in upholstery, bookbinding, for curtains, etc. [Ety obscure]

scrimmage /skrim'ij/ or **scrummage** /skrum'ij/ n an untidy mêlée, a struggle; (in rugby) a scrum (old); (in American football) play between two teams beginning with the snap (qv) and ending when the ball is dead; a practice session of this; a line of scrimmage. ◆ vi to take part in a scrimmage. [A variant of **skirmish**]
■ **scrimm'ager** or **scrumm'ager** n.
■ **line of scrimmage** or **scrimmage line** (American football) an imaginary line, parallel to the goal lines, behind which the linemen of a team position themselves for start of play, and on which the end of the ball nearest that team's goal line rests.

scrimp /skrimp/ vt to stint; to keep limited, often by necessity. ◆ vi to be sparing or niggardly, often by necessity, usu in the phrase scrimp and save. ◆ adj (rare) scanty; stinted. ◆ adv (obs) barely. [Cf Swed and Dan skrumpen shrivelled, OE scrimman to shrink]

■ **scrimped** *adj.* **scrimp'ily** *adv.* **scrimp'iness** *n.* **scrimp'ly** *adv* sparingly; scarcely. **scrimp'ness** *n.* **scrimp'y** *adj* scanty.

scrimshander, **scrimshandy** see **scrimshaw**.

scrimshank see **skrimshank**.

scrimshaw /skrim'shö/ *n* (also **scrim'shander** or **scrim'shandy**) a sailor's spare-time handicraft, such as engraving or carving fanciful designs on shells, whales' teeth, etc; anything crafted in this way. ◆ *vt* and *vi* to work or decorate in this way. [Origin obscure]
■ **scrim'shoner** *n* someone who does scrimshaw.

scrimure /skrim'yər/ (*obs*) *n* a fencer. [Fr *escrimeur*]

scrine or **scryne** /skrīn/ (*obs*) *n* a box or chest in which written records are kept; a shrine. [OFr *escrin*, from L *scrīnium* a chest; cf **shrine**]

scrip¹ /skrip/ *n* a writing; a scrap of paper or of writing; (for *subscription*) a preliminary certificate, as for shares allotted; share certificates, or shares or stock collectively; a dollar bill, money (*old US sl*); a paper token issued instead of currency in special eg emergency circumstances (*US*). [**script** and **subscription**; partly perh **scrap¹**]
■ **scrip'ophile** or **scripoph'ilist** *n.* **scripoph'ily** *n* the collecting of bond and share certificates as a hobby, *esp* those of historical, etc interest; the items thus collected.
❑ **scrip issue** *n* a bonus issue (qv).

scrip² see **script**.

scrip³ /skrip/ (*obs*) *n* a small bag; a satchel; a pilgrim's pouch. [Cf ON *skreppa* a bag, and OFr *escrep(p)e*]
■ **scripp'age** *n* the contents of a scrip.

Script. *abbrev* : Scripture.

script /skript/ *n* a piece of writing; the actors', director's, etc written copy of the text of a play, film, etc; a text for broadcasting; handwriting, or system or style of handwriting; a set of characters used in writing a language (such as *Cyrillic script*); type in imitation of handwriting; handwriting in imitation of type; an original document (*law*); a candidate's examination answer paper; a list of commands that can be executed by a computer; a list of actors and their parts (*obs*); short for **manuscript** or **typescript**; short for **prescription** (also **scrip**; *inf*). ◆ *vt* to write a script for, or make a script from (eg a novel), *esp* for broadcasting or the theatre or cinema. [L *scrīptum*, from *scrībere* to write]
■ **script'ed** *adj.*
❑ **script doctor** *n* (*inf*) a writer who revises a film script in order to make it suitable for production. **scripting language** *n* (*comput*) a high-level programming language that uses an interpreter (qv) to execute programs. **script kiddie** *n* (*derog inf*) a computer hacker with limited knowledge and skill. **script'writer** *n.* **script'writing** *n.*

scriptorium /skrip-tö'ri-əm/ or /-tö'-/ *n* (pl **scripto'ria**) a writing-room, *esp* in a monastery. [L *scrīptōrium*, from *scrībere* to write]
■ **scripto'rial** *adj.* **scrip'tory** /-tər-i/ *adj* by, in, or relating to writing.

scripture /skrip'chər/ *n* handwriting; something written; (in *sing* or *pl*) the sacred writings of a religion, *esp* (with *cap*) the Bible; a biblical text (*rare*). [L *scrīptūra*, from *scrībere* to write]
■ **scrip'tural** *adj* of, in or according to Scripture; of writing. **scrip'turalism** *n* literal adherence to the Scriptures. **scrip'turalist** *n* a person who adheres to the letter of Scripture; a person who studies Scripture (*obs*). **scrip'turally** *adv.* **scrip'turism** *n.* **scrip'turist** *n* a person versed in Scripture; a person who bases his or her belief on the Bible and the Bible alone.
❑ **scrip'ture-reader** *n* (*hist*) a person who read the Bible in cottages, barracks, etc to those who could not read for themselves.

scritch /skrich/ *n* a screech. ◆ *vt* and *vi* to screech. [ME *scrichen*, as **screech**]
❑ **scritch'-owl** *n.*

scrive /skrīv/ or **scrieve** /skrēv/ (*Scot*) *vt* and *vi* to write, *esp* with copious fluency; to describe; to inscribe.
❑ **scrive'board** or **scrieve'board** *n* a shipbuilder's drawing board.

scrivener /skriv'(ə-)nər/ (*hist*) *n* a scribe; a copyist; a person who draws up contracts, etc; a person who lends money at interest to others. [OFr *escrivain* (Fr *écrivain*), from LL *scrībānus*, from L *scrība* a scribe]
■ **scriv'enership** *n.* **scriv'ening** *n* writing.
❑ **scrivener's palsy** *n* writer's cramp.

scrobe /skrōb/ (*zool*) *n* a groove. [L *scrobis* ditch]

scrobicule /skrō'bi-kūl/ (*biol*) *n* a small pit or depression, as around the tubercles of a sea urchin. [Dimin of L *scrobis* a ditch]
■ **scrobicular** /-bik'ū-lər/ *adj* relating to or surrounded by scrobicules. **scrobic'ulate** /-lət/ or **scrobic'ulated** *adj* pitted all over.

scrod /skrod/ (*N Am*) *n* a young cod or haddock. [Perh obs Du *schrood*, MDu *schrode*]

scroddled /skrod'ld/ *adj* (of pottery) made of clay scraps of different colours. [Cf LGer *schrodel* scrap]

scrofula /skrof'ū-lə/ *n* a former name for tuberculosis of the lymph nodes in the neck (also formerly called **king's evil**). [L *scrōfulae*, from *scrōfa* a sow (supposed to be prone to it)]
■ **scrof'ulous** *adj.*

scrog /skrog/ (*Scot* and *N Eng dialect*) *n* a stunted bush or small tree; a crab-apple (the fruit or tree); a bushy place; scrubby wood; a broken branch; a branch of a tree (*heraldry*). [Origin obscure]
■ **scrogg'ie** or **scrogg'y** *adj* covered with scrogs; stunted.
❑ **scrog'-apple** and **scrog'-bush** (or **-buss**) *n* respectively the crab-apple and crab-apple tree.

scroggin /skrog'in/ (*Aust* and *NZ*) *n* a hiker's snack of mixed fruit, nuts, etc. [Origin uncertain; perh from **scran**]

scroll /skrōl/ *n* a roll of paper, parchment, etc; a ribbonlike decorative strip in painting, architecture, etc, partly coiled or curved, sometimes bearing a motto; a writing in the form of a roll; a draft or copy of a letter, etc (*Scot*); a list, roll or inventory; a spiral ornament or part, such as a flourish to a signature. ◆ *vt* to set in a scroll; to draft (*Scot*); to roll into a scroll or scrolls; to cut into scrolls from a length of material; to move (a text, graphics, etc) up or down or from side to side in order to view data that cannot all be seen on a computer screen at the same time (*comput*). ◆ *vi* to curl; (of a text or graphics) to move up or down or from side to side (*comput*). [Earlier **scrowl**, **scrowle**, formed (perh as dimin) from **scrow**]
■ **scroll'able** *adj* (*comput*) (of data on a computer screen) able to be scrolled up or down. **scrolled** *adj* formed into a scroll; ornamented with scrolls; moved across a screen as described above. **scroll'er** *n* someone or something that scrolls; a two-dimensional computer game in which the background moves behind the image controlled by the player. **scroll'ing** *adj* and *n* (*comput*). **scroll'wise** *adv.*
❑ **scroll bar** *n* (*comput*) a shaded strip at the side of a computer screen, to which the mouse is pointed to scroll down or up. **scroll chuck** *n* (*engineering*) a self-centring chuck, *esp* a *three-jaw chuck* for holding round work. **scroll saw** *n* a saw for cutting scrolls. **scroll'work** *n* ornament in scrolls.

Scrooge /skrooj/ *n* a miser. [From Ebenezer *Scrooge* in Dickens's *A Christmas Carol*]

scrooge see **scrouge**.

scroop /skroop/ (*dialect*) *n* a scraping noise. ◆ *vi* to make a scroop. [Imit]

scrophularia /skrof-ū-lā'ri-ə/ *n* a plant of the figwort genus *Scrophularia*. [L, scrofula plant, from its being reputedly a cure for scrofula]
■ **scrophulariaceous** /-ā'shəs/ *adj* of, belonging to, or characteristic of the Scrophulariaceae, a family of sympetalous dicotyledons with zygomorphic flowers, *incl* foxglove, mullein, speedwell and eyebright.

scrote /skrōt/ (*sl*) *n* the scrotum; a despised person. [**scrotum**]

scrotum /skrō'təm/ *n* (pl **scrō'ta**) the bag of skin that contains the testicles in mammals. [L *scrōtum*]
■ **scrō'tal** *adj.* **scrote** *n* (*sl*) the scrotum; a despised person.

scrouge, **scrowdge** /skrowj/ or **scrooge** /skrooj/ (*dialect*) *vt* and *vi* to squeeze; to crowd. [Cf **scruze**]
■ **scroug'er** *n* (*old US*) a whopper; something large.

scrounge /skrownj/ (*orig milit sl*) *vt* to cadge or beg, or obtain by cadging or begging; to purloin. ◆ *vi* to sponge; to hunt around (with *for*). [Origin doubtful]
■ **scroung'er** *n.* **scroung'ing** *n.*

scrow /skrō/ *n* a scroll; (in *pl*) writings; a clipping or strip of hide used in glue-making. [Anglo-Fr *escrowe*; see **escroll**, **escrow**, **scroll**]

scrowdge see **scrouge**.

scrowl and **scrowle** /skrōl/ old spellings of **scroll**.

scroyle /skroil/ (*obs*) *n* a wretch. [Origin doubtful]

scrub¹ /skrub/ *vt* (**scrubb'ing**; **scrubbed**) to rub hard; to wash or clean by hard rubbing, eg with a stiff brush; to purify (*gas-making*); to cancel, abandon (plans, etc) (*inf*). ◆ *vi* to use a scrubbing-brush; to make a rapid to-and-fro movement as if scrubbing; (of jockeys) to make a similar movement with the arms over a horse's neck to urge it forward (*horse-racing sl*). ◆ *n* an act of scrubbing; a slightly abrasive skin cleansing lotion; a worn or short-bristled brush or broom; a drudge; (in *pl*) the clothes worn by a surgeon, etc while performing or assisting at an operation. [Perh obs Du *schrubben*, or a corresponding lost OE word]
■ **scrubb'er** *n* someone or something that scrubs; an apparatus for freeing gas from tar, ammonia, and hydrogen-sulphur combinations; any device that filters out impurities; an unattractive woman, or one with loose morals (*sl*). **scrubb'ing** *n.*
❑ **scrubb'ing-board** *n* a washboard. **scrubb'ing-brush** *n* a brush with short stiff bristles for scrubbing floors, etc.
■ **scrub round** (*inf*) to cancel; to ignore intentionally. **scrub up** (of a surgeon, etc) to wash the hands and arms thoroughly before performing or assisting at an operation. **scrub up well** to be capable of

rendering one's usual appearance more respectable or attractive when necessary.

scrub² /skrub/ n a stunted tree; stunted trees and shrubs collectively; brushwood; country covered with bushes or low trees, *esp* the Australian evergreen xerophytic dwarf forest or bush of eucalyptus, acacia, etc; hence, a remote place, far from civilization (*Aust inf*); an undersized or inferior animal, *esp* one of indefinite breed; a player in a second or inferior team (*N Am*); a team of inferior players, or one with too few players (*N Am*); an insignificant or undersized person; anything small or insignificant. ◆ *adj* insignificant; undersized; (of a team) improvised, hastily got together for the occasion (*N Am*); (of a player) in a second or inferior team (*N Am*). [A variant of **shrub¹**]
■ **scrubb'ed** *adj* (*Shakesp*) stunted. **scrubb'er** n (*Aust*) an animal that has run wild. **scrubb'y** *adj* covered with scrub; stunted; insignificant.
❑ **scrub bird** n an elusive wren-like Australian bird (genus *Atrichornis*). **scrub'land** n an area covered with scrub. **scrub rider** n (*esp Aust*) a person who looks for cattle that stray into the scrub. **scrub turkey** or **scrub fowl** n a type of ground-living bird of the Australian scrub, a mound-builder. **scrub typhus** n a typhus-like disease caused by a parasitic microorganism and transmitted by a mite to humans (also called **tsutsugamushi disease**).
■ **the Scrubs** an informal name for **Wormwood Scrubs**, an English prison.

scruff¹ /skruf/ n the nape (of the neck). [See **scuft**]

scruff² /skruf/ n scurf; an untidy, dirty person (*inf*). [Metathetic variant of **scurf**]
■ **scruff'ily** *adv*. **scruff'iness** n. **scruff'y** *adj* scurvy (*archaic*); untidy, dirty (*inf*).

scrum /skrum/ n a disorderly struggle, a mêlée; a closing-in of rival forwards round the ball on the ground, or in readiness for its being inserted (by the scrum half) between the two packs (*rugby*); a large number of people crushed into a relatively small space and jostling for position (*inf*). ◆ *vi* (**scrumm'ing**; **scrummed**) to form a scrum. [Short form of **scrummage**; see **scrimmage**, **skirmish**]
❑ **scrum'down** n an act of forming a rugby scrum. **scrum half** n (*rugby*) a halfback whose duty it is to put the ball into the scrum and secure it as soon as it emerges. **scrum'pox** n (*rugby sl*) impetigo spread by rugby players' faces rubbing together in the scrum.

scrummage see **scrimmage**.

scrummy /skrum'i/ (*inf*) *adj* scrumptious.

scrump, skrump /skrump/ or **skrimp** /skrimp/ (*dialect*) *vt and vi* to gather windfalls, hence to steal (apples) from orchards. ◆ *n* anything shrivelled, small or undersized, *esp* an apple; an undersized person. [See **scrimp**]
■ **scrump'y** n very strong cider made from small, sweet apples, *esp* as brewed in the West Country.

scrumple /skrum'pl/ *vt* to crush or crumple. ◆ *vi* to become crushed or crumpled. [Variant of **crumple**]

scrumptious /skrump'shəs/ (*inf*) *adj* delightful; delicious. [Origin uncertain]
■ **scrump'tiously** *adv*. **scrump'tiousness** n.

scrumpy see under **scrump**.

scrunch /skrunch/ or **skrunsh/** *vt* to crunch or crush, *esp* with relation to the noise produced. ◆ *vi* (*esp of paper, snow, hair, etc*) to be crunched or crushed. ◆ *n* the act or sound of scrunching. [Variant of **crunch**]
■ **scrunch'y** *adj* making a scrunching sound. ◆ *n* (also **scrunch'ie**) a tight ring of elastic covered in coloured fabric for holding the hair in a ponytail.
❑ **scrunch'-dry** *vt* to scrunch (hair) into handfuls during blow-drying to give it more body.

scrunt /skrunt/ (*Scot*) n anything stunted (eg an apple, a tree); a niggard.
■ **scrunt'y** *adj*.

scruple /skroo'pl/ n a difficulty or consideration, *usu* moral, obstructing action, *esp* one turning on a fine point or one that is baseless; (in *pl*) moral standards, personal standards of decency which one adheres to; a doubt, disbelief or difficulty; protest, demur; scrupulousness; a small weight (in apothecaries' weight, 20 grains) (*abbrev* **scr.**); a sexagesimal division, as a minute of time or arc (*obs*); a very small quantity (*archaic*). ◆ *vi* to hesitate because of scruples. ◆ *vt* to cause to feel scruples (*obs*); to question, doubt (*archaic*); to have scruples about (*archaic*); to hesitate. [L *scrūpulus*, dimin of *scrūpus* a sharp stone, anxiety]
■ **scru'pler** n. **scrupulosity** /-pū-los'i-ti/ n. **scru'pulous** *adj* directed by scruples; having scruples, doubts, or objections; extremely conscientious or exact; captious (*old*). **scru'pulously** *adv*. **scru'pulousness** n.
■ **make no scruple** (or **no scruples**) **about** or **make scruples about** to offer (no) moral objections to.

scrutin de liste /skrü-tẽ də lēst'/ (*Fr*) n a method of voting used in France, in which several representatives are to be appointed and people may vote for a combination of candidates. [List ballot, from L *scrūtinium*; see **scrutiny**]

scrutiny /skroo'ti-ni/ n close, careful, or minute investigation or examination; a searching look; official examination of votes; examination of the catechumens (*hist*). [L *scrūtinium*, and *scrūtārī* to search even to the rags, from *scrūta* rags, trash]
■ **scru'table** *adj* accessible to scrutiny, open to examination, observable. **scrutā'tor** n a close examiner; a scrutineer. **scrutineer'** n someone who makes a scrutiny, *esp* of votes. **scrutinizā'tion** or **-s-** n. **scru'tinize** or **-ise** *vt and vi* to examine closely. **scru'tinizer** or **-s-** n. **scru'tinizing** or **-s-** *adj*. **scru'tinizingly** or **-s-** *adv*. **scru'tinous** *adj*. **scru'tinously** *adv*.

scrutoire /skrū-twär', -tōr' or -tör'/ n same as **escritoire**.

scruze /skrooz/ (*obs*; now *dialect*) *vt* to squeeze. [Perh **screw** combined with **squeeze**]

scry /skrī/ *vt* (**scry'ing**; **scried**, (*Spenser*) **scryde**) (*archaic and dialect*) to descry. ◆ *vi* to practise crystal-gazing. [Aphetic for **descry**]
■ **scry'er** n. **scry'ing** n.

scryne (*Spenser*) same as **scrine**.

SCSI /skuz'i/ (*comput*) *abbrev*: Small Computer Systems Interface, a control system that allows communication between a computer and several devices (eg hard disks).

scuba /skoo'bə or skū'/ n an apparatus used by skin-divers, consisting of a breathing tube attached to a cylinder or cylinders of compressed air (also *adj*). [self-contained *u*nderwater *b*reathing *a*pparatus]
❑ **scuba diver** n. **scuba diving** n.

scuchin, scuchion Spenserian forms of **scutcheon**.

Scud /skud/ n a surface-to-surface missile of a kind made in the former Soviet Union. ◆ *vt* to attack with Scud missiles (*inf*; also *fig*).

scud¹ /skud/ *vi* (**scudd'ing; scudd'ed**) (*esp of clouds*) to sweep along easily and swiftly; (*esp of sailing vessels*) to drive before the wind. ◆ *vt* to cross swiftly. ◆ *n* an act or the action of scudding; driving cloud, shower or spray; a gust; a swift runner (*school sl*). [Perh alteration of *scut* rabbit's tail, hence meaning 'to run like a rabbit']
■ **scudd'er** n. **scudd'le** *vi* to scuttle.

scud² /skud/ (*Scot*) *vt* (**scudd'ing; scudd'ed**) to slap, to hit with a sharp, glancing blow. ◆ *n* a slap; (in *pl*) a spanking.

scud³ /skud/ (*Scot*) n a state of nudity. [Origin obscure]
■ **in the scud** naked, without clothes.

scuddaler, scudler same as **skudler**.

scuddle see under **scud¹**.

scudo /skoo'dō/ n (*pl* **scu'di** /-dē/) an old Italian silver coin. [Ital, from L *scūtum* a shield]

scuff¹ /skuf/ *vt and vi* to shuffle, drag or scrape (the feet) on the ground; to brush, graze, scrape (*esp shoes or heels while walking*) or become grazed or scraped; to make or become shabby by wear; to scrape the sole of the club against the ground before striking the ball (*golf*). ◆ *vt* (*N Am*) to prod at with the foot. ◆ *n* the act or sound of scuffing; a scrape or scratch caused by scuffing. [Imit]

scuff² /skuf/ n a form of **scuff¹** or **scuft**.

scuffle /skuf'l/ *vi* to struggle confusedly, *esp* while fighting; to shuffle. ◆ *vt* to hoe, scarify; to shuffle; to poke at or scuff with the foot (*N Am*); to gather, scrape together (*esp money*) (with *up*; also *vi* with *up on*; *US*). ◆ *n* an act or sound of scuffling; a confused struggle; a thrust hoe (*US*); an agricultural scuffler. [Cf Swed *skuffa* to shove; Du *schoffelen*; see **shove, shovel, shuffle**]
■ **scuff'ler** n a person who scuffles; an implement for scarifying the soil.

scuft /skuft/ (*dialect*) n the nape of the neck (also **scuff** or **scruff**). [Poss ON *skopt*, *skoft* the hair]

scug see **skug¹**.

scul, scull, sculle /skul/ obsolete spellings of **school²**.

sculduddry /skul-dud'ri/, **sculduddery** or **skulduddery** /-dud'ə-ri/ (*Scot, facetious*) n breach of chastity; bawdy talk or writing. ◆ *adj* bawdy. [Origin obscure]

sculduggery same as **skulduggery**.

sculk obsolete spelling of **skulk**.

scull¹ /skul/ n a short, light spoon-bladed oar for one hand, used in pairs; an oar used over the stern of a boat; a small, light rowing boat propelled by sculls; an act or spell of sculling; (in *pl*) a race between small, light rowing boats rowed by one person. ◆ *vt* to propel with sculls, or with one oar worked like a screw over the stern. ◆ *vi* to row using sculls. [Origin obscure]
■ **scull'er** n a person who sculls; a small boat pulled by one person with a pair of sculls. **scull'ing** n.

scull² or **skull** /skul/ n a shallow basket for fish, etc. [Poss ON *skjōla* pail]

scull³ obsolete spelling of **skull¹**.

scull⁴, **sculle** see **scul**.

scullery /skul'ə-ri/ n a room for rough kitchen work, such as the cleaning of utensils; a kitchen (*obs dialect*). [OFr *escuelerie*, from L *scutella* a tray]
- ❑ **scull'ery-maid** n.

scullion /skul'yən/ n a servant employed for rough work (*archaic*); a mean, contemptible person. [Poss OFr *escouillon* a dishcloth, from L *scōpa* a broom; or from Fr *souillon* scullion, infl by **scullery**]

sculp /skulp/ (*rare*) vt and vi to carve; to engrave; to sculpture. [L *sculpere*; not a back-formation from **sculptor**, **sculpture**]

sculp. or **sculpt.** abbrev: *sculpsit* (qv); sculptor; sculpture.

sculpin /skul'pin/ (*N Am*) n the dragonet, a large-headed spiny fish of no commercial value; a good-for-nothing person or animal (*sl*). [Poss *Scorpaena*, a genus of spiny fishes]

sculpsit /skulp'sit or skŭlp'sit/ (L) (he or she) sculptured (this work), sometimes appended to the signature of the sculptor (*abbrev* **sc.**, **sculp.** or **sculpt.**).

sculpt /skulpt/ vt and vi to carve or otherwise shape stone, or out of stone, to sculpture; to carve. [Fr *sculpter*, from L *sculpere* to carve; not a back-formation from **sculptor**, **sculpture**]

sculptor /skulp'tər/ n an artist who creates images by carving, *esp* in stone (*also fem* **sculp'tress**). [L *sculptor*, *-ōris*, *sculptūra*, from *sculpere*, *sculptum* to carve]
- ■ **sculp'tural** /-chər-əl/ adj. **sculp'turally** adv. **sculp'ture** n the art of carving, *esp* in stone; extended to clay-modelling or moulding for casting; work, or a piece of work, in this art; engraving (*obs*); shaping in relief; spines, ridges, etc, standing out from the surface (*biol*). ◆ vt to carve, shape in relief; to represent in sculpture; to mould, or form, so as to have the appearance, or (*fig*) other quality, of sculpture; to modify the form of (the earth's surface). **sculp'tured** adj carved; engraved; (of features) fine and regular like a classical sculpture; having ridges, etc on the surface (*bot* and *zool*). **sculpturesque'** adj. **sculp'turing** n.

scum /skum/ n matter coming to or floating on the surface of liquid, *esp* in the form of foam or froth; a worthless, despicable person or group of people. ◆ vt (**scumm'ing**; **scummed**) to remove the scum from. ◆ vi to form or throw up a scum. [Cf Dan *skum*, Ger *Schaum* foam]
- ■ **scumm'er** n an instrument for removing scum. **scumm'ings** n pl scum removed from a liquid. **scumm'y** adj.
- ❑ **scum'bag** n (*vulgar sl*) a condom (*esp US*); a general term of abuse.

scumber /skum'bər, skum'ər/ or **skummer** /skum'ər/ (*archaic*) vt and vi to defecate (used *esp* of a dog or fox). ◆ n dung. [Prob OFr *descumbrer* to disencumber]

scumble /skum'bl/ vt (in painting and drawing) to soften the effect of (an outline or colour) by a very thin coat of opaque or semi-opaque colour, or by light rubbing or by applying paint with a dry brush. ◆ n colour laid down in this way; the effect produced. [Frequentative of **scum**]
- ■ **scum'bling** n.

scumfish same as **scomfish**.

scuncheon /skun'shən/, **sconcheon** or **scontion** /skon'shən, skun'-/ n the inner part of a door jamb or window frame. [OFr *escoinson*]

scunge /skunj/ (*dialect*) vi to slink about; to borrow or scrounge (*also* vt). ◆ n a scrounger; a dirty, sneaky person; accumulated sticky dirt (*Aust* and *NZ*). [Cf **scrounge**]
- ■ **scun'gy** adj (*Aust* and *NZ*) dirty; unkempt; sordid.

scunner /skun'ər/ (*Scot*) vi to feel loathing. ◆ vt to produce a feeling of loathing in; to disgust, nauseate. ◆ n an object, or a manifestation, of loathing; an irritation or nuisance. [Perh ME *scurn* to shrink; origin unknown]
- ■ **take a scunner to** to take a strong dislike to.

scup /skup/ or **scuppaug** /skup'ög or -ög'/ n the northern porgy, a common marine fish of Atlantic coastal waters of N America. [Narraganset *mishcuppauog*]

scupper¹ /skup'ər/ n (*usu* in *pl*) a hole allowing water to drain from a ship's deck. [Origin disputed]

scupper² /skup'ər/ (*inf*) vt to do for; to ruin; to sink (a ship). [Perh connected with **scupper¹**]

scuppernong /skup'ər-nong/ n a native American grape, *Vitis rotundifolia*, from the region of the *Scuppernong* river, North Carolina; a sweet wine made from it.

scur /skûr/ same as **skirr**.

---

scurf /skûrf/ n small flakes or scales of dead skin, *esp* on the scalp, dandruff; an incrustation of flakes or scales. [OE *scurf*, *sceorf*]
- ■ **scurf'iness** n. **scurf'y** adj.

scurrier see **scurriour**.

scurril or **scurrile** /skur'il/ adj (*archaic*) like or worthy of a vulgar buffoon; indecently opprobrious or jocular. [L *scurrīlis*; see **scurrilous**]

scurrilous /skur'i-ləs/ adj indecently abusive and unjustifiably defamatory; characterized by vulgar or obscene humour. [L *scurrīlis*, from *scurra* a buffoon]
- ■ **scurrility** /skə-ril'i-ti/ n. **scurr'ilously** adv. **scurr'ilousness** n.

scurriour or **scurrier** /skur'i-ər/ (*obs*) n a scout. [See **discoverer**, **scourer¹**]

scurry /skur'i/ vi to hurry briskly or in a panicky way; to scuttle. ◆ n an act or sound of scurrying; flurried haste; a flurry, as of snow; a short sprint race (*horse-racing*). [From **hurry-skurry**, reduplication of **hurry**; or back-formation of **scurrier**; or from **scour²**]

scurvy /skûr'vi/ adj scurfy; shabby; vile, contemptible. ◆ n a disease caused by a deficiency of vitamin C when the diet is devoid of fresh fruit and vegetables, characterized by spongy and bleeding gums followed by subcutaneous bleeding. [**scurf**; the application to the disease helped by similarity of sound to **scorbutic**]
- ■ **scur'vily** adv in a scurvy manner; meanly, basely. **scur'viness** n.
- ❑ **scurvy grass** n a cruciferous plant (*Cochlearia officinalis*) used by sailors to treat scurvy.

scuse or **'scuse** /skūs, skūz/ n and vt aphetic for **excuse**.

scut /skut/ n a short erect tail, as in a hare, rabbit or deer; a hare; a contemptuous term for a (small) person (*dialect*). [Origin obscure]

scuta plural of **scutum** (see under **scute**).

scutage /skū'tij/ (*hist*) n a tax on a knight's fee, *esp* one in lieu of personal or military service. [LL *scūtāgium*, from L *scūtum* a shield]

scutal, **scutate** see under **scute**.

scutch¹ /skuch/ vt to dress (eg flax) by beating; to switch. ◆ n a tool for dressing flax, a swingle; a bricklayer's cutting tool. [Prob OFr *escousser* to shake off]
- ■ **scutch'er** n a person, tool, or part of a machine that scutches; the striking part of a threshing mill. **scutch'ing** n.

scutch² /skuch/ or **scutch grass** forms of **quitch¹** and **quitch grass** (see also **couch²** and **couch grass**).

scutcheon /skuch'ən/ n an aphetic form of **escutcheon**.

scute /skūt/ n a scutum; an écu, a French coin (*hist*); any coin of small value (*obs*); a hard exoskeletal plate (*zool*). [L *scūtum* a shield]
- ■ **scūt'al** adj. **scūt'ate** adj protected by scutes or scuta; shield-shaped. **scūt'iform** adj. **scūt'iger** n a squire (*facetious*); a centipede of the genus *Scutigera*, giving name to the family **Scutiger'idae** /-i-dē/. **scūt'um** n (*pl* **scūt'a**) the oblong shield of Roman heavy-armed infantry (*hist*); a scute; the second tergal plate of the notum of an insect's thorax (*zool*); (with *cap*) a small southern constellation in the Milky Way.

scutellum /skū-tel'əm/ n (*pl* **scūtell'a**) a scale of a bird's foot; the third tergal plate of the notum of an insect's thorax; a structure in a grass grain, supposed to be the cotyledon, which at germination secretes hydrolytic enzymes into, and absorbs sugars etc from, the adjacent endosperm. [L *scutella* a tray, dimin of *scutra* a platter, confused in scientific use with *scūtulum*, dimin of *scūtum* a shield]
- ■ **scūtell'ar** adj. **scūt'ellate** adj. **scūtellā'tion** n (*zool*) the arrangement of scales or plates on an animal's body.

scutiform see under **scute**.

scutter /skut'ər/ vi to run hastily, scurry. ◆ n a hasty run; a sound of scuttering. [A variant of **scuttle³**]

scuttle¹ /skut'l/ n a shallow basket; a fireside container for coal; the part of a motor car between the bonnet and the windscreen. [OE *scutel*, from L *scutella* a tray]
- ■ **scutt'leful** n.

scuttle² /skut'l/ n an opening in a ship's deck or side; its lid; a shuttered hole in a wall, roof, etc; its shutter or trapdoor. ◆ vt to make a hole in, or open the lids of the scuttles of, *esp* in order to sink; to destroy, ruin (eg plans). [OFr *escoutille* hatchway]
- ❑ **scutt'lebutt** n a cask with a hole cut in it for drinking water on board ship (*also* **scuttle cask**; *hist*); a drinking fountain; rumour, gossip (*esp US sl*).

scuttle³ /skut'l/ vi to move or run with short rapid steps, dash hurriedly, scurry. ◆ n an act or sound of scuttling. [**scud¹**]
- ■ **scutt'ler** n.

scutum see under **scute**.

---

scuzz /skuz/ (N Am sl) n dirt; seediness; something distasteful; an unpleasant, disreputable or worthless person (also **scuzz'ball** or **scuzz'bag**). [Origin uncertain]
■ **scuzz'y** adj.

scybalum /sib'ə-ləm/ n (pl **scyb'ala**) a lump or mass of hard faeces in the intestine. [Latinized from Gr skybalon dung]
■ **scyb'alous** adj.

scye /sī/ (Scot and N Ireland) n an opening in a garment for the insertion of a sleeve. [Origin obscure]

Scylla /sil'ə/ (Gr myth) n a six-headed monster who sat over a dangerous rock on the Italian side of the Straits of Messina, opposite Charybdis (qv), and seized or drowned sailors from passing ships. [Gr Skylla]
■ **between Scylla and Charybdis** (usu fig) forced to steer a perilous or hopeless course between two deadly dangers, avoidance of one meaning almost certain destruction by the other.

scyphus /sī'fəs/ n (pl **scyph'ī**) a large ancient Greek drinking cup; a cup-shaped structure (bot). [Gr skyphos cup]
■ **scyph'iform** adj. **scyphis'toma** n (pl **scyphis'tomas** or **scyphis'tomae**) (Gr stoma mouth) the segmenting polyp stage of a jellyfish. **scyphozo'an** n and adj (relating to) any of a class (Scyphozoa or Scyphomedusae) of medusoid coelenterates, a jellyfish.

scytale /sit'ə-lē/ n a Spartan secret writing on a strip wound around a stick, unreadable without a stick of the same thickness. [Gr. skytalē a staff]

scythe /sīdh/ n an instrument with a large curved blade and wooden handle, for mowing or cropping by hand; a blade attached to the wheel of a war chariot. ◆ vt and vi to mow (down) with a scythe. [OE sīthe; cf ON sigthr, Ger Sense]
■ **scythed** adj armed or cut down with scythes. **scyth'er** n a person who uses a scythe.
❑ **scythe'man** n a scyther. **scythe'-stone** n a whet for scythes.

Scythian /sith'i-ən/ adj of Scythia, an ancient region north and east of the Black Sea, of its nomadic people, or of their language. ◆ n a member of the people; the language of Scythia.
❑ **Scythian lamb** n the barometz plant.

SD abbrev : South Dakota (US state); Swaziland (IVR).

sd abbrev : sine die (L), without a day, without (fixed) date.

sdaine see **sdeigne**.

S.Dak. abbrev : South Dakota (US state).

sdayn see **sdeigne**.

'sdeath /zdeth/ (obs) interj an obsolete oath. [God's death]

sdeigne or **sdeign** /zdān/ (obs) vt and vi to disdain (also **sdein**, **sdaine** or **sdayn**). [Ital sdegnare, aphetic for disdegnare ; or Eng **disdain**]
■ **sdeign'full** adj. **sdeign'fully** adv.

SDI abbrev : Strategic Defense Initiative.

SDLP abbrev : Social Democratic and Labour Party (in Northern Ireland).

SDP abbrev : (formerly in the UK) Social Democratic Party; social, domestic and pleasure (of motor insurance).

SDR or **SDRs** abbrev : Special Drawing Rights.

sdrucciola /zdroot'chō-la/ adj (of rhyme) triple. [Ital, slippery]

SDSL (comput) abbrev : Symmetric Digital Subscriber Line.

SE abbrev : Society of Engineers; south-east; south-eastern.

Se (chem) symbol : selenium.

SEA abbrev : Single European Act.

sea /sē/ n the great mass of salt water covering the greater part of the earth's surface, the ocean; any great expanse of water; a great (esp salt) lake, mainly in proper names; (a given height of) swell or roughness; a great wave; the tide; (with the) a maritime career; a seemingly limitless mass or expanse. ◆ adj marine. [OE sǣ; Du zee, Ger See, ON sǣr, Dan sö]
■ **sea'-like** adj like the sea. ◆ adv in the manner of the sea. **sea'ward** adj and adv towards the (open) sea. ◆ n seaward side, direction or position. **sea'wardly** adj and adv. **sea'wards** adv. **sea'worthiness** n. **sea'worthy** adj (of a vessel) fit for sailing on the sea; able to endure stormy weather.
❑ **sea acorn** n an acorn-shell. **sea adder** n a pipefish; a marine stickleback. **sea air** n the air at sea or at the seaside. **sea anchor** n a floating anchor used at sea to slow a boat down, or maintain its direction. **sea anemone** n a solitary soft-bodied polyp, esp of the order Actiniaria, typically having many tentacles around the mouth cavity. **sea ape** n the sea otter; the thresher shark; a manatee. **sea aster** n a flowering plant, Aster tripolium, of salt marshes. **sea'bank** n the seashore; an embankment to keep out the sea. **sea bass** /bas/ n a perchoid marine fish of various kinds, esp of the Serranidae and the Sciaenidae families. **sea bat** n a name for various fishes with long or outspread fins. **sea'-bather** n. **sea'-bathing** n. **sea beach** n. **sea bean** n the cacoon (genus Entada) or other seed cast up by the sea; a mollusc's operculum, worn as an amulet. **sea bear** n the polar bear; the fur seal. **sea beast** n. **sea'-beat** or **-beaten** adj lashed by the waves. **sea'bed** n the bottom or floor of the sea. **sea beet** n wild beet. **sea belt** n another name for sugar kelp. **sea'bird** n any marine bird. **sea biscuit** n ship biscuit, hardtack. **sea'blite** n a salt-marsh plant (Suaeda maritima) of the goosefoot family. **sea blubber** n a jellyfish. **sea-blue** adj. **sea'board** n the country or land bordering the sea (also adj). **sea boat** n a craft with reference to its seaworthiness in bad weather. **sea boots** n pl long waterproof boots worn by sailors. **sea'-born** adj produced by the sea. **sea'borne** adj carried on or by the sea. **sea'bottle** n a translucent inflated seaweed (genus Valonia); bladderwrack. **sea bottom** n the floor of the sea. **sea boy** n (Shakesp) a sailor boy. **sea breach** n an inroad of the sea. **sea bream** n any fish of the Sparidae family, esp Pagellus centrodontus of European seas; also applied to any fish of the Bramidae, a family related to the mackerels. **sea breeze** n a breeze from the sea, esp owing to convection in the daytime; (with caps) a cocktail containing vodka, cranberry juice and grapefruit juice. **sea brief** see **sea letter** below. **sea buckthorn** n a willow-like seaside shrub (Hippophae rhamnoides) of the family Eleagnaceae. **sea bun** n a common name for the heart urchin. **sea burdock** n another name for cocklebur (genus Xanthium). **sea butterfly** n a pteropod, Clione limacina. **sea cabbage** n sea kale. **sea calf** n the common seal. **sea canary** n the white whale. **sea cap** n (Shakesp) a cap worn on board a ship. **sea captain** n the captain of a merchant ship. **sea card** n a compass card; a sea chart. **sea cat** n a catfish; the great weever, a spiny fish, Trachinus draco ; the wolffish or sea wolf, Anarrhichas lupus ; a shark, Scyllium catulus. **sea change** n (Shakesp) a change effected by the sea; a complete transformation. **sea chart** n. **sea chest** n a seaman's trunk. **sea cliff** n a cliff fronting or formed by the sea. **sea coal** n (archaic) coal in the ordinary sense, mineral coal not charcoal (possibly as first worked where exposed by the sea). **sea'coast** n the land adjacent to the sea. **sea cob** n another name for a seagull. **sea'cock** n a gurnard, a type of fish; a valve communicating with the sea through a vessel's hull; a bold sea rover. **sea colewort** n sea kale; wild cabbage. **sea cook** n a ship's cook (son of a sea cook being an abusive designation). **sea cow** n the walrus (archaic); any sirenian, such as the dugong or manatee; formerly, the hippopotamus (S Afr ; Du zeekoe). **sea'craft** n skill in navigation; seamanship; any seagoing craft. **sea crow** n a name of many birds, such as the skua, chough, cormorant. **sea cucumber** n any burrowing echinoderm of the class Holothuroidea, with an elongated cucumber-like body. **sea dace** n the bass. **sea devil** n the devilfish (qv). **sea dog** n an old or experienced sailor; a pirate; a dogfish; the common or harbour seal (old); a beast like a talbot with a dorsal fin and beaver's tail (heraldry) ; a luminous appearance over the horizon, presaging bad weather (cf **fog-bow**, **fog-dog**). **sea dotterel** n another name for the turnstone. **sea dove** n another name for the little auk. **sea dragon** n any of various fishes, eg the dragonet and types of seahorse. **sea'drome** n a floating aerodrome. **sea duck** n any duck of the pochard group. **sea dust** n dust deposited on the sea from a distant land. **sea eagle** n any of several fish-eating eagles that live near the sea, such as Haliaetus albicilla the white-tailed eagle. **sea ear** n an ormer (genus Haliotis). **sea eel** n a conger. **sea egg** n a sea urchin. **sea elephant** n the elephant seal. **sea fan** n an alcyonarian coral with a fan-like skeleton. **sea'farer** n a traveller by sea, usu a sailor. **sea'faring** n and adj. **sea feather** n a feathery alcyonarian, the sea pen. **sea'-fight** n a battle between ships at sea. **sea fir** n a hydroid whose delicate branched structure resembles a fir. **sea'-fire** n phosphorescence at sea. **sea fish** n any salt-water or marine fish. **sea'-fish'er** n. **sea'-fish'ing** n. **sea floor** n the bottom of the sea. **sea-floor spreading** n (geol) the process by which new oceanic crust is generated at oceanic ridges by the convective upswelling of magma. **sea foam** n the froth on the sea formed by the action of the waves. **sea fog** n a fog on, or coming from, the sea. **sea'folk** n pl seafaring people. **sea'food** n food got from the sea, esp shellfish. **sea'fowl** n a seabird. **sea fox** n another name for the thresher, or foxshark. **sea fret** n a fog coming inland off the sea. **sea'front** n the side of the land, of a town, or of a building that looks towards the sea; a promenade with its buildings fronting the sea. **sea froth** n the foam of the sea; formerly, meerschaum. **sea furbelow** n a brown seaweed (genus Saccorhiza) with a bulb of tentacular outgrowths above the primary holdfast. **sea gate** n a seaward gate of a tidal basin, etc; an outlet to the sea. **sea gherkin** n the sea cucumber, Cucumaria saxicola. **sea gillyflower** n thrift. **sea ginger** n millepore coral. **sea girdle** n a coarse seaweed, esp Laminaria digitata. **sea'-girt** adj (literary and poetic) surrounded by sea. **sea god** or **sea goddess** n a god or goddess ruling over or dwelling in the sea. **sea'-going** adj sailing on the seas; designed or suitable for deep-sea voyages. **sea gooseberry** n a common ctenophore, Pleurobranchia pileus, like a gooseberry in shape. **sea gown** n (Shakesp) a short-sleeved garment worn at sea. **sea grape** n any plant of the genus Ephedra, or its fruit; seaside grape; another

name for glasswort; gulfweed; (in *pl*) cuttlefish eggs in masses. **sea grass** *n* a grass or grasslike plant growing by or in the sea, eg *Enteromorpha*, thrift, grasswrack, etc. **sea green** *n* the bluish-green colour of some seas. **sea-green'** *adj*. **sea-green incorruptible** *n* a person sincerely and unshakably devoted to an ideal or purpose, *esp* in public life (*orig* used by Carlyle of Robespierre). **sea'gull** *n* a gull; a casual dock-labourer not yet admitted to a union (*Aust* and *NZ*); a rugby player who hovers around the periphery of play waiting for the ball (*NZ*). **sea haar** *n* a haar (qv). **sea hare** *n* a tectibranch gastropod, *Aplysia punctata*, with ear-like tentacles. **sea'hawk** *n* a skua. **sea heath** *n* a wiry heath-like pink-flowered plant (*Frankenia laevis*) of salt marshes and chalk cliffs. **sea hedgehog** *n* a sea urchin; a globe fish. **sea'hog** *n* a porpoise. **sea holly** *n* a European plant, *Eryngium maritimum*, with spiny stems, that grows on seashores. **sea'horse** *n* any marine fish of the genus *Hippocampus* with a prehensile tail and a horselike head, that swims in an upright position; the fabulous hippocampus, a sea monster with the head and body of a horse and the tail of a fish; the walrus (*archaic*); the hippopotamus (*obs*). **sea'hound** *n* a dogfish. **sea ice** *n*. **sea'-island** *adj* (of cotton) of the kind grown on the islands off the coast of South Carolina. **sea ivory** *n* a lichen, *Ramalina siliquosa*, found on sea cliffs. **sea jelly** *n* a jellyfish. **sea'kale** *n* a fleshy, sea-green cruciferous seaside plant (*Crambe maritima*) cultivated for its blanched sprouts, eaten as food. **seakale beet** *n* another name for chard. **sea'keeping** *n* maintenance of navigational control and stability, *esp* in rough seas. **sea king** *n* a Viking chief who led raids on the coastal areas of Europe; a king of the merfolk; Poseidon or Neptune. **sea lace** *n* a brown seaweed, *Chorda filum*. **sea lane** *n* a navigable passage, delineated on charts, etc, between islands, ships, ice-floes, etc; an established route taken by ships at sea. **sea lark** *n* any of various shore birds, eg the sandpiper; the rock pipit. **sea lavender** *n* a salt-marsh plant of the plumbaginaceous genus *Limonium*. **sea law** *n* maritime law, *esp* medieval customary law. **sea lawyer** *n* (*naut sl*) a (low-ranking) sailor versed in the intricacies of maritime law, disputatiously standing on his rights, or finding fault with his superiors' decisions; a shark. **sea legs** *n pl* ability to walk on a ship's deck when it is pitching; resistance to seasickness. **sea lemon** *n* a type of sea slug, *Archidoris pseudoargus*, with a warty yellowish body. **sea lentil** *n* gulfweed. **sea leopard** *n* a spotted seal of the southern seas, *esp* of the genus *Ogmorhinus*. **sea letter** or **sea brief** *n* formerly, a document listing a ship's place of origin and her cargo; a document issued to a neutral merchant vessel in wartime, allowing it to pass freely (also **sea pass** or **passport**). **sea lettuce** *n* a seaweed, *Ulva lactuca*, with flat translucent green fronds, green laver (see under **laver**[1]). **sea level** *n* the mean level of the surface of the sea. **sea lily** see **crinoid**. **sea'line** *n* a coastline; the sea horizon. **sea lion** *n* a seal with external ears and with hind flippers turned forward; a lion with the tail of a fish (*heraldry*). **sea loach** *n* a rockling. **sea loch** *n* (*Scot*) a lakelike arm of the sea. **sea longworm** *n* a nemertean worm (genus *Lineus*). **sea lord** *n* (often with *caps*) a naval member of the Board of Admiralty, a division of the Ministry of Defence. **sea lung** *n* a ctenophoran. **sea'maid** *n* (*Shakesp*) a mermaid. **sea'man** *n* a sailor; a man, other than an officer or apprentice, employed aboard ship; a merman. **sea'manlike** *adj* showing good seamanship. **sea'manly** *adj* characteristic of a seaman. **sea'manship** *n* the art of handling ships at sea. **sea marge** or **margin** *n* the shoreline. **sea'mark** *n* a mark of tidal limit; any object serving as a guide to those at sea. **sea mat** *n* hornwrack (genus *Flustra*), a common polyzoan like a flat horny seaweed. **sea maw** *n* (now *Scot*) a sea mew. **sea mell** *n* an alleged variant of **sea mew**. **sea mew** *n* any gull. **sea mile** *n* a geographical or nautical mile. **sea milkwort** *n* a primulaceous plant, *Glaux maritima*, of northern seashores, having small pink flowers. **sea monster** *n* any huge maritime animal, *esp* fabulous. **sea moss** *n* carrageen; seaweed. **sea'mount** *n* a mountain under the sea of at least 3000ft. **sea mouse** *n* an elliptical polychaete, *Aphrodite aculeata*, with coarse iridescent hairs and bristles along its sides. **sea nettle** *n* a jellyfish. **sea nymph** *n* a minor sea goddess. **sea onion** *n* the sea squill. **sea orange** *n* a large globose orange-coloured sponge (also called **sulphur sponge**). **sea otter** *n* a N Pacific animal (*Enhydris lutris*) related to the true otters; its silvery-brown fur, largely unobtainable since the widespread ban on otter-hunting. **sea owl** *n* the lumpsucker. **sea parrot** *n* another name for the puffin. **sea pass** see **sea letter** above. **sea passage** *n* (the cost of) a journey by sea. **sea pen** *n* a featherlike anthozoan coelenterate (*esp Pennatula*); a name for the squid's internal shell. **sea perch** *n* a bass or other fish of the Serranidae. **sea pie** *n* a baked dish of salt meat and vegetables eaten at sea; the oyster-catcher. **sea piece** *n* a picture, poem or piece of music representing (a scene at) sea. **sea'-pig** *n* a porpoise; a dolphin; a dugong. **sea pike** *n* a pike-like marine fish of various kinds, eg robalo or hake. **sea pink** *n* any of several perennial plants generally known as thrift. **sea'plane** *n* an aeroplane with floats instead of wheels, for landing on water. **sea poacher** *n* the pogge. **sea porcupine** *n* another name for the globe fish (genus *Diodon*). **sea'port** *n* a port or harbour on the sea; a place with such a harbour. **sea potato** *n* another name for the heart urchin, *Echinocardium*

cordatum. **sea power** *n* naval strength; a nation with great naval strength. **sea purse** *n* the tough horny egg case of certain sharks, skates or rays, a mermaid's purse; a small whirlpool formed by the meeting of two waves at an angle, dangerous to bathers (*US*). **sea purslane** see under **purslane**. **sea'quake** *n* a seismic disturbance at sea. **seaqua'rium** see **oceanarium** under **ocean**. **sea ranger** *n* in the Guide organization, a ranger who trains specially in seamanship and related matters. **sea'rat** *n* a pirate. **sea raven** *n* a large fish, *Hemitripterus americanus*, related to the bullhead. **sea reed** *n* marram grass. **sea road** *n* a designated route followed by ships, a sea lane. **sea robber** *n* a pirate. **sea robin** *n* an American fish (*esp* of the genus *Prionotus*) of the gurnard family, with red or brown colouring. **sea rocket** *n* a fleshy cruciferous seaside plant (genus *Cakile*). **sea room** *n* space to manoeuvre a ship safely. **sea rosemary** *n* sea lavender. **sea rover** *n* a pirate or pirate ship. **sea'-roving** *n* piracy. **sea salmon** *n* inaptly, coalfish or pollack. **sea salt** *n* salt derived from seawater. ◆ *adj* as salty as the sea. **sea sand** *n*. **sea satyre** *n* a Spenserian sea monster. **sea'scape** *n* a painting, photograph, etc of the sea. **sea scorpion** *n* a scorpion-fish, having a spiny head and fins; another name for the father-lasher (*Cottus scorpius*). **Sea Scout** *n* a member of a marine branch of the Scout movement. **sea serpent** *n* (*myth*) an enormous marine animal of serpent-like form frequently seen and described by credulous sailors, imaginative landsmen and common liars; a sea snake. **sea shanty** same as **shanty**[2]. **sea'shell** *n* the shell of a crustacean or mollusc. **sea'shore** *n* the land immediately adjacent to the sea; the foreshore (*law*). **sea shrub** *n* a sea fan. **sea'sick** *adj* nauseous owing to the rolling movement of a vessel at sea; travel-worn (*Shakesp*). **sea'sickness** *n*. **sea'side** *n* any area that borders the sea, *esp* one popular as a holiday resort (also *adj*). **seaside grape** *n* the grape tree (genus *Coccoloba*) or its fruit. **sea slater** *n* a small crustacean, *Ligia oceanica*, resembling a woodlouse. **sea sleeve** *n* a cuttlefish. **sea slug** *n* a type of shell-less marine mollusc, a nudibranch; a sea cucumber. **sea snail** *n* any snail-like marine gastropod; an unctuous fish (genus *Liparis*) related to the lumpsucker. **sea snake** *n* a snake that lives in the sea, *esp* of the very venomous family Hydrophidae of the Indian and Pacific oceans; a sea serpent. **sea snipe** *n* the sandpiper. **sea'speak** *n* (also with *cap*) a variety of English of restricted unambiguous vocabulary, used by mariners, navigators, etc for communication. **sea spider** *n* a pycnogonid. **sea squill** *n* a Mediterranean plant, *Urginea maritima*, of the lily family with an onion-like bulb, sea onion. **sea squirt** *n* a marine animal shaped like a double-mouthed flask, an ascidian. **sea star** *n* a starfish. **sea stick** *n* a herring cured at sea. **sea storm** *n*. **sea strand** *n*. **sea surgeon** *n* a tropical genus (*Acanthurus*) of spiny-finned fishes with a lancetlike spine ensheathed on each side of the tail. **sea swallow** *n* a tern; the storm petrel; a flying fish. **sea swine** *n* a porpoise; the ballanwrasse. **sea tangle** *n* any of various kinds of brown seaweed, *esp* of the genus *Laminaria*. **sea term** *n* a nautical word. **sea trout** *n* the salmon trout (*Salmo trutta*); extended to various other fishes of the genus *Cynoscion*, of US coastal waters. **sea turn** *n* a gale from the sea. **sea turtle** *n* a marine turtle; the black guillemot. **sea unicorn** *n* a former name for the narwhal. **sea urchin** *n* one of the Echinoidea, a class of echinoderms with a globular, ovoid, or heart-shaped, sometimes flattened body and shell of calcareous plates, without arms. **sea vampire** *n* a giant ray, or devilfish. **sea view** *n* a view of the sea; a seascape. **sea wall** *n* a wall to keep out the sea. **sea'-walled** *adj* walled against or by the sea. **sea'ware** *n* seaweed. **sea wasp** *n* a jellyfish of the class Cubozoa with a highly venomous sting. **sea'water** *n* water of or from the sea. **sea wave** *n*. **sea'way** *n* progress through the waves; a heavy sea; a regular route taken by ocean traffic; an inland waterway on which ocean-going vessels can sail. **sea'weed** *n* marine algae collectively; any marine alga. **sea whistle** *n* a seaweed (*Ascophyllum nodosum*) whose bladders can be made into whistles. **sea'wife** *n* a kind of wrasse. **sea wind** *n*. **sea wing** *n* a sail. **sea wolf** *n* the wolffish (also **loup de mer** /*loo-də-mer*/); the bass; the sea elephant (*obs*); a Viking; a pirate. **sea'woman** *n* a mermaid. **sea'worm** *n* any marine worm. **sea'-worn** *adj* worn by the sea or by seafaring. **sea wrack** *n* coarse seaweeds of any kind; grasswrack.

■ **all at sea** totally disorganized; completely at a loss. **at full sea** at full tide. **at sea** away from land; on the ocean; disorganized, bewildered. **follow the sea** or **go to sea** to become a sailor. **heavy sea** a sea in which the waves run high. **molten sea** (*Bible*) the brazen laver in 1 Kings 7.23–26. **short sea** a sea in which the waves are choppy, irregular, and interrupted. **the four seas** those bounding Great Britain. **the Seven Seas** see under **seven**.

Seabee /*sē'bē*/ (the letters *cb* phonetically represented) *n* a member of a US Navy construction *batt*alion.

seaborgium /*sē-bör'gi-əm*/ *n* an artificially produced radioactive transuranic element (symbol **Sg**; atomic no 106), formerly called **unnilhexium** and **rutherfordium**. [Glenn T *Seaborg* (1912–99), US physicist]

SEAC /sē'ak/ abbrev : formerly, School Examination and Assessment Council; South-East Asia Command (in World War II); Spongiform Encephalopathy Advisory Committee.

seacunny /sē'ku-ni/ n a lascar steersman or quartermaster. [Appar Pers sukkānī, from Ar sukkān rudder, confused with **sea** and **con**³]

seal¹ /sēl/ n a piece of wax, lead or other material, stamped with a device and attached as a means of authentication or attestation; a substitute for this, such as a wafer or circular mark; a piece of wax, etc, stamped or not, used as a means of keeping something closed; the design stamped; an engraved stone or other stamp for impressing a device, or a trinket of similar form; an adhesive label, esp decorative, for a Christmas parcel, etc, sold for charity; a token or symbol to confirm a bargain, etc; any device which keeps something closed; an obligation to secrecy; an impression; a device to prevent the passage of a gas, air, water, etc; water in a gas trap; a road surface sealed with bitumen, etc (Aust and NZ); an animal's, esp an otter's, footprint. ◆ vt to put a seal on; to stamp; to fasten with a seal; to give confirmation of; to ratify; to close up, esp permanently or for a long time; to enclose; to decide, settle irrevocably; to set apart; to seal (a road surface) with bitumen, etc, to tarmac (Aust and NZ); to paint with a protective substance. ◆ vi to set one's seal to something. [OFr seel, from L sigillum, dimin of signum a mark]
■ **seal'able** adj. **seal'ant** n any device or (esp cement-like) substance used to seal a gap to prevent the passage of water, etc. **sealed** adj. **seal'er** n a person or thing that seals; a substance used to coat a surface for protection, impermeability, etc. **seal'ing** n.
□ **sealed'-beam** adj (of car headlights) consisting of a complete unit sealed within a vacuum. **sealed book** n something beyond one's knowledge or understanding (also **closed book**). **seal'-engraving** n the art of engraving seals. **sealing wax** (also obs **seal'wax**) n formerly beeswax, now usu a composition of shellac, turpentine, vermilion or other colouring matter, etc, for making decorative seals. **seal'-pipe** n a dip-pipe. **seal ring** n a signet ring.
■ **Great Seal** (also without caps) the state seal of the United Kingdom. **Lord Privy Seal** formerly the keeper of the Privy Seal, now the senior cabinet minister without official duties. **Privy Seal** (also without caps) formerly, the seal appended to documents that were to receive, or did not require, authorization by the Great Seal, in Scotland used esp to authenticate royal grants of personal rights. **seal off** to make it impossible for any thing or person to leave or enter (eg an area). **set one's seal to** or **on** to give one's authority or assent to. **the seals** symbolically the office of Lord Chancellor or of Secretary of State. **under seal** authenticated. **under sealed orders** under orders only to be opened at a stated time.

seal² /sēl/ n a member of the Pinnipedia, carnivorous marine mammals, incl the eared seals of the family Otariidae (sea lions and fur seals), and the true or earless seals of the family Phocidae (eg the grey seal, common seal, monk seal and elephant seal); sealskin. ◆ adj made of seal or sealskin. ◆ vi to hunt seals. [OE seolh (genitive sēoles); ON selr]
■ **seal'er** n a seal-fisher. **seal'ery** n seal-fishery. **seal'ing** n.
□ **seal'-fish'er** n a hunter of seals; a sealing ship. **seal'-fish'ing** n. **seal'point** n a variety of Siamese cat, with a dark-brown face, paws and tail. **seal rookery** n a seals' breeding-place. **seal'skin** n the prepared fur of the fur seal, or an imitation (eg of rabbit-skin, or of mohair); a garment made of this.

seal³ same as **seel**¹.

seal⁴ /sēl/ vt to tie up. ◆ n a rope or chain for tying up an animal. [OE sǣlan, from sāl rope]

seal⁵ /sēl/ or **sale** /sāl/ n willow; wicker (Spenser). [Form of **sallow**²]

seal⁶ see **seel**².

sealgh or **sealch** /selhh/ (Scot) n a seal (the animal). [**seal**²]

Sealyham /sē'li-əm/ n (also without cap; in full **Sealyham terrier**) a long-bodied, short-legged, wiry-coated terrier, first bred at Sealyham in Pembrokeshire.

seam¹ /sēm/ n a sewn join between edges of cloth; the turned-up edges of such a join on the wrong side of the work; the ornamentation of such a join; a piece of sewing work (old); a weld or other join between edges; a re-stitched surgical incision; a wrinkle; a stratum (of a mineral), esp if thin or valuable; seam bowling (cricket). ◆ vt to join, provide, or mark with seams; to pick out the seams of. ◆ vi (of a cricket ball) to deviate after pitching on the seam. [OE sēam, from sīwian to sew; Du zoom, Ger Saum]
■ **seam'er** n a person or thing that seams; a seam bowler (cricket); a ball delivered by seam bowling (cricket). **seam'free** adj. **seam'less** adj without a seam or seams; unbroken, flowing (fig). **seam'lessly** adv.
□ **seam allowance** n (in dressmaking) the margin allowed for the seams along the edge of the pieces of a garment. **seam bowler** n. **seam bowling** n (cricket) fast or medium-paced bowling in which the seam of the ball is positioned so as to make it deviate after pitching.

seaming lace n a lace, braid, etc, to insert in or cover seams. **seam'set** n a tool for flattening seams in metal, etc. **seam welding** n resistance welding of overlapping sheets of metal using wheels or rollers as electrodes; welding two pieces of sheet plastic along a line by dielectric heating.

seam² or **seame** /sēm/ n grease (Shakesp); lard made from pork fat (Scot **saim** /sām/). ◆ vt to grease. [OFr saim, OE seime; cf L sagīna stuffing, feasting]

seam³ /sēm/ (obs except dialect) n a packhorse load (eg 8 bushels of grain, 9 pecks of apples, 120lb of glass); a cartload. [OE sēam a burden, from LL sauma, from Gr sagma a packsaddle]

seamster /sēm'stər or sem'/ n a person who sews. [Orig a fem form; from OE sēamestre; see **seam**¹]
■ **seam'stress** n a woman who sews. **seam'stressy** n (Sterne) sewing, needlework.

seamy /sē'mi/ adj having or showing seams; sordid; disreputable. [**seam**¹]
■ **seam'iness** n.
□ **seamy side** n the wrong side of a garment (Shakesp); the disreputable, sordid or unpleasant side or aspect (of something, esp life).

sean /sēn/ same as **seine**.

Seanad /shan'ədh/ or **Seanad Eireann** /ā'rən/ n the upper house of the legislature of the Republic of Ireland. [Ir, senate]

séance /sā'ons, sā'äns, or sā'ās/ n a session or meeting of psychical researchers or spiritualists for the purpose of trying to contact the spirits of the dead or promote supernatural manifestations of various kinds. [Fr, from L sedēre to sit]

seannachie /shen'ə-hhē/ n a Highland or Irish genealogist and transmitter of family lore (also **seann'achy** or **senn'achie**). [Gaelic seanachaidh]

SEAQ or **Seaq** /sē'ak/ abbrev : Stock Exchange Automated Quotations.

seaquarium see **oceanarium** under **ocean**.

sear¹ /sēr/ adj (poetic) dry and withered (also **sere**); (Spenser **seare**) burning. ◆ vt to dry up; to scorch; to brand; to cauterize; to render callous or unfeeling. ◆ vi (rarely **sere**) to become sear. ◆ n a mark of searing. [OE sēar dry, sēarian to dry up; LGer soor, Du zoor]
■ **seared** adj. **seared'ness** n. **sear'ing** n and adj. **sear'ness** n.
□ **sear'ing-iron** n.
■ **the sere**, **the yellow leaf** (Shakesp) the autumn of life.

sear² /sēr/ n the catch that holds a gun at cock or half-cock. [Cf OFr serre, from L sera a bar]
■ **tickle** or **tickled a th' sere** (Shakesp) ready to go off.

searce /sûrs/ or **search** /sûrch/ (obs) vt to sift. ◆ n (obs) a sieve. [OFr saas; unexplained]

search¹ /sûrch/ vt to explore all over in trying to find something; to examine closely; to examine for hidden articles; to ransack; to scrutinize (eg one's conscience); to probe; to penetrate all parts of (archaic); to put to the test; to seek (with out). ◆ vi to make an examination, etc; to look or hunt (with for). ◆ n the act or power of searching; a thorough examination; a quest; a search party (obs). [OFr cerchier (Fr chercher), from L circāre to go about, from circus a circle]
■ **search'able** adj. **search'er** n a person who searches; a person appointed to search, eg a custom-house officer; an inspector of various kinds; a probe. **search'ing** adj penetrating; thorough. **search'ingly** adv. **search'ingness** n. **search'less** adj (poetic) unsearchable.
□ **search and replace** see **global exchange** under **globe**. **search engine** n (comput) a software program for retrieving information, esp from the Internet. **search image** n (animal behaviour) a predator's preconception of what its prey looks like and where it is to be found. **search'light** n a lamp and reflector throwing a strong beam of light for illuminating a target or quarry by night; the beam of light so projected. **search party** n a group of people sent out in search of somebody or something. **search warrant** n a legal warrant authorizing the searching of a house, etc, usu by the police.
■ **right of search** the right of a warring country to search neutral ships for contraband of war. **search me** (inf) I don't know.

search² see **searce**.

seare see **sear**¹.

sease see **seize**.

season /sē'z(ə)n/ n one of the four natural divisions of the year, spring, summer, autumn and winter; the usual, natural, legal, or appropriate time, or time of year (for anything); any particular time; a limited period; a season ticket (inf); seasoning (obs). ◆ vt to add herbs, spices, etc to, to make savoury, to flavour; to add interest or liveliness to; to mature; to temper, reduce somewhat; to bring into suitable condition (eg wood by drying it out); to inure; to preserve from decay (Shakesp); to mature, confirm, imbue with the flavour of (Shakesp). ◆ vi to become seasoned, mature or experienced. [OFr *seson* (Fr *saison*), from L *satiō, -ōnis* a sowing]

■ **sea'sonabil'ity** *n.* **sea'sonable** *adj* appropriate to the particular season; timely. **sea'sonableness** *n.* **sea'sonably** *adv.* **sea'sonal** *adj* according to the seasons; available only in certain seasons. **seasonal'ity** *n* the quality of being seasonal. **sea'sonally** *adv.* **sea'soned** *adj.* **sea'soner** *n.* **sea'soning** *n* the process or act by which anything is seasoned; herbs, spices, salt and pepper, added to food to improve its flavour; the process of acclimatization; (in diamond-cutting) the charging of the laps or wheels with diamond-dust and oil; the process of coating dyed leather with liquid albumen. **sea'sonless** *adj* without difference of seasons.

❑ **seasonal affective disorder** *n* a depressive illness experienced by people in winter, thought to be due to the reduction in hours of daylight (*abbrev* **SAD**). **season creep** *n* changes in the timing of the seasons, *esp* the earlier onset of spring, as a result of global warming. **sea'soning-tub** *n* a trough in which dough is set to rise. **season ticket** *n* a ticket valid any number of times within a specified period. ■ **close** or **closed season** see under **close**[1]. **in season** ripe, fit and ready for use; available; (eg in the holiday trade) at the busiest time of the year; allowed to be killed; (of a bitch) ready to mate, on heat; fit to be eaten. **in season and out of season** at all times. **out of season** unripe, not normally grown; (eg in the holiday trade) at any other time than the busiest time of the year, or at the least busy time; at a time of year when hunting is illegal; inopportune.

seasure an obsolete spelling of **seizure**.

seat /sēt/ *n* anything used or intended for sitting on; a chair, bench, saddle, etc; the part of a chair on which one sits; a mode of sitting, *esp* on horseback; a place where one may sit in a theatre, church, etc, or a ticket for this; a right to sit; a parliamentary or local-government constituency; membership, eg of a committee; that part of the body or of a garment on which one sits; that on or in which something rests; site, situation; a place where anything is located, settled, or established; a post of authority; a throne; a capital city; station; a (*usu* country) abode, a mansion. ◆ *vt* to place on a seat; to cause to sit down; to place in any situation, site, location, etc; to establish, fix; to assign a seat to; to provide with a seat or seats; to fit accurately; to make (a skirt, trousers, etc) baggy by sitting. ◆ *vi* to sit or lie down (*obs*); to become baggy by sitting. [ON *sǣti* seat; cf OE *sǣt* ambush]

■ **seat'ed** *adj.* **seat'er** *n* someone or something that seats. ◆ *combining form* denoting a vehicle, sofa, etc, with seats for a specified number, as in *two-seater*. **seat'ing** *n* the taking, provision, allocation or arrangement of seats; a supporting surface; fabric for covering seats. **seat'less** *adj*.

❑ **seat belt** *n* (also **safety belt**) an adjustable belt for holding the occupant firmly in his or her aircraft seat, car seat, etc. **seat earth** *n* a bed of clay underlying a coal seam. **seat rent** *n* (*hist*) payment for a church sitting. **seat'-stick** *n* a walking-stick that can be made to serve as a seat, a shooting-stick.

■ **by the seat of one's pants** instinctively, by intuition (**seat-of-the-pants**' *adj* instinctive). **lord of seat** a Lord of Session. **lose one's seat** to fail to be re-elected to Parliament or local council. **take a back seat** to adopt a passive or subordinate role. **take a seat** to sit down. **take one's seat** to take up one's allocated place, *esp* in Parliament.

SEATO /sē'tō/ *abbrev*: South-East Asia Treaty Organization (now defunct).

seaward, **seawardly**, **seawards** see under **sea**.

seaze see **seize**.

sebaceous see under **sebum**.

Sebat see **Shebat**.

sebesten /si-bes'tən/ *n* a boraginaceous Asian tree (genus *Cordia*); its edible plumlike fruit; a preparation made from the fruit and used as medicine. [Ar *sabastān*]

sebum /sē'bəm/ *n* the fatty secretion that lubricates the hair and skin. [L *sēbum* suet]

■ **sebaceous** /si-bā'shəs/ *adj* like tallow; of, like, of the nature of, or secreting sebum. **sebacic** /-*bas*'/ *adj.* **sebate** /sē'bāt/ *n* a salt of sebacic acid. **sebif'erous** /si-/ *adj* bearing fatty matter. **sebif'ic** *adj* producing fatty matter. **seborrhoea** /seb-ə-rē'ə/ *n* excessive discharge of sebum from the sebaceous glands. **seborrhoe'ic** *adj*.

❑ **sebaceous cyst** *n* a non-specific term for a cyst arising in a sebaceous gland (see also **steatoma** under **stear-**, **wen**[1]). **sebaceous gland** *n* a gland in the skin that secretes sebum. **sebacic acid** *n* a dibasic acid, the esters of which are used in the production of resins and plasticizers.

sebundy /si-bun'di/ *n* (in India) an irregular soldier or soldiers. [Urdu *sibandī*]

SEC *abbrev*: Securities and Exchange Commission.

Sec. *abbrev*: Secretary.

sec[1] /sek/ *n* a second (of time) (*inf*).

sec[2] /sek/ *adj* (of wines) dry. [Fr]

sec[3] /sek/ *abbrev*: secant.

SECAM /sē'kam/ *abbrev*: *séquentiel couleur à mémoire* (*Fr*), a broadcasting system for colour television.

secant /sē'kənt or sek'ənt/ *adj* cutting. ◆ *n* a cutting line; a straight line which cuts a curve in two or more places (*geom*); *orig* a straight line from the centre of a circle through one end of an arc to the tangent from the other end (*maths*); one of the six trigonometrical functions of an angle, the ratio of the hypotenuse to the side of a right-angled triangle formed by dropping a perpendicular from a point on one side of the angle to the other (negative if the base is the side produced) (*abbrev* **sec**). [L *secāns, -antis*, prp of *secāre* to cut]

■ **sec'antly** *adv*.

secateurs /sek'ə-tûrz or -tûrz'/ *n pl* pruning shears. [Pl of Fr *sécateur*, from L *secāre* to cut]

secco /sek'ō/ *adj* plain; (of wine, etc) dry; (of recitative) unaccompanied or with minimal accompaniment, *usu* only continuo. ◆ *n* (pl **sec'cos**) painting on dry plaster. [Ital, dry, from L *siccus*]

secede /si-sēd'/ *vi* to withdraw, *esp* from a party, religious body, federation, or the like. [L *sēcēdere, sēcēssum*, from *sē-* apart, and *cēdere* to go]

■ **sece'der** *n* a country, etc which secedes; any of a body of Presbyterians (**Secession Church**) who seceded from the Church of Scotland about 1733. **secession** /-*sesh*'ən/ *n* the act of seceding; a body of seceders. **secess'ional** *adj.* **secess'ionism** *n.* **secess'ionist** *n* a person who favours or joins in secession (also *adj*).

■ **War of Secession** the American Civil War.

secern /si-sûrn'/ *vt* to discriminate or distinguish; to secrete. [L *sēcernere, sēcrētum* to separate]

■ **secern'ent** *n* and *adj.* **secern'ment** *n*.

secesher /si-sesh'ər/ or **secesh** /si-sesh'/ (*old US sl*) *n* a secessionist.

sech /sesh/ *abbrev*: hyperbolic *sec*ant (see **hyperbolic functions** under **hyper-**).

seckel or **seckle** /sek'l/ *n* a variety of pear. [From the American grower who originated it]

seclude /si-klood'/ *vt* to shut off, *esp* from contact, association or influence. [L *sēclūdere, -clūsum*, from *sē-* apart, and *claudere* to shut]

■ **seclud'ed** *adj* kept apart from the rest of society; in a place not visible to, nor visited by, others, private (and *usu* quiet). **seclud'edly** *adv.* **seclusion** /si-kloo'zhən/ *n* the act of secluding; the state of being secluded; retirement; privacy; solitude; a private place. **seclu'sionist** *n.* **seclu'sive** /-*siv*/ *adj* tending to or favouring seclusion.

seco /sek'ō/ (*Sp*) *adj* (of wine) dry.

secodont /sek'ə-dont/ (*zool*) *adj* with cutting back teeth (also *n*). [L *secāre* to cut, and Gr *odous, odontos* tooth]

Seconal® /sek'ə-nəl/ *n* a hypnotic and soporific barbiturate.

second[1] /sek'ənd/ *adj* next after or below the first; other, alternate; additional; supplementary; another, as it were; inferior; subordinate; referring to the person or persons addressed (*grammar*); singing or playing a part in harmony slightly below others of the same voice or instrument, as in *second soprano, second violin*; helpful, favouring (*obs*). ◆ *adv* next after the first; in the second place, as the second matter, etc. ◆ *n* a person or thing that is second or of the second class; a place in the second class or rank; a person who is second in rank, eg a Boy Scout or Cub Scout who is second-in-command in his patrol; second gear; a person who acts as an assistant to a boxer or duellist; a supporter; a base SI unit, the unit of time (symbol **s**), defined in terms of the resonance vibration of the caesium-133 atom as the interval occupied by a specific number of cycles; the 60th part of a minute of time, or of a minute of angular measurement (short form **sec**); a time interval variously measured (see **atomic second** under **atom**; **ephemeris second** under **ephemera**; **universal second** under **universe**); a very small amount of time (*esp* in short form **sec**; *inf*); a second-class university degree (*inf*); the second person (*grammar*); the interval between successive tones of the diatonic scale (*music*); (in *pl*) goods of a second quality; (in *pl*) a second course or second helping of food (*inf*). ◆ *vt* to follow; to act as second to (a boxer or a duellist); to back, give support to; to further; to assist; to encourage; to support (the mover of) a nomination or resolution; to sing or play second to (*music*); to follow up with another. [Fr, from L *secundus*, from *sequī, secūtus* to follow]

■ **sec'ondarily** *adv.* **sec'ondariness** *n.* **sec'ondary** *adj* subordinate; subsidiary; of lesser importance; of a second stage, *esp* of an electric circuit; not original, derivative; (of a disease or disorder) that results from or follows another; (of a voltage, magnetic field, etc) induced; (of education) between primary and higher or tertiary; (of a feather) growing in the second joint of the wing; (of an industry) involving the production of goods from raw materials; (with *cap*; *geol*) of or belonging to the Mesozoic era. ◆ *n* a subordinate; a delegate or deputy; a feather growing in the second wing joint; a secondary colour; a secondary school; a malignant tumour that has spread from a primary cancer to another part of the body, a metastasis; (the coils and windings of) the second stage of a transformer, etc; the area of the field behind the linebackers (*American football*); the players defending this area. **sec'onder** *n* a person who seconds a motion, resolution, etc; a supporter; a member of a second group. **sec'ondly** *adv* in the second place, as regards the second matter.

❏ **Second Advent** or **Second Coming** *n* a second coming of Christ to earth. **second-ad'ventist** *n* someone who expects a second coming of Christ. **secondary action** *n* secondary picketing. **secondary alcohol** *n* an alcohol, RR′CHOH, in which R and R′ are two similar or dissimilar molecular groups. **secondary battery** or **secondary cell** *n* one on which the chemical action is reversible, and which can therefore be recharged. **secondary coil** *n* one carrying an induced current. **secondary colour** *n* one produced by mixing two primary colours. **secondary electron** *n* an electron in a beam of secondary emission. **secondary emission** *n* emission of electrons from a surface caused by bombardment with higher energy electrons from another source. **secondary mineral** *n* (*geol, mining*) a mineral formed after the formation of the rock enclosing it; a mineral of minor interest in an ore-body undergoing exploitation. **secondary modern** *n* formerly, a type of secondary school offering a less academic, more technical education than a grammar school. **secondary picket** *n*. **secondary picketing** *n* the picketing by workers of a firm with which they are not directly in dispute but which has a trading connection with their own firm, in order to maximize the effects of a strike. **secondary production** *n* (*ecology*) see **production** under **produce**. **secondary (surveillance) radar** *n* radar in which a responder is triggered by received pulses so that it retransmits a signal. **secondary school** *n* any of various types of school for secondary education. **secondary sexual characteristics** *n pl* (*zool*) features other than the reproductive organs which distinguish between the sexes. **secondary shut-down system** *n* a system for shutting down a nuclear reactor should the control rods fail to do so. **secondary smoking** *n* inhalation of tobacco smoke by non-smokers from smokers' cigarettes, etc, passive smoking. **second ballot** *n* a system of election whereby a second vote is taken, the candidate or candidates who received fewest votes in the first ballot being eliminated. **second banana** *n* (*sl*) a subordinate (*orig* a vaudeville performer who played a secondary role). **second best** *n* the next to the best (**come off second best** to be in a position of disadvantage after a contest, to be the loser in a fight, etc). **second-best'** *adj* next after the best; somewhat inferior. **second chamber** *n* in a legislature of two houses, the house with fewer powers, *usu* acting as a check on the other. **second childhood** *n* mental weakness in extreme old age. **second class** *n* the class next to, and in an inferior position relative to, the first. **second-class'** *adj* and *adv*. **second-class citizen** *n* a member of a group in the community which is not given the full rights and privileges enjoyed by the community as a whole. **second-class mail** or **post** *n* mail sent at a cheaper rate, therefore taking longer for delivery. **second cousin** *n* one who has the same pair of great-grandparents as oneself, but different grandparents; loosely, a first cousin's child, or a parent's first cousin (properly, first cousin once removed). **second degree** see under **degree**. **second fix** *n* (*building*) that part of the joinery, plumbing or electrical work that can only be completed after most of the building, including plaster work, is finished (cf **first fix**). **second floor** *n* the floor above the first floor (qv under **floor**). **sec'ond-floor** *adj*. **second growth** *n* a new growth of a forest after cutting, fire, etc; a second crop of grapes in a season. **sec'ond-guess'** *vt* and *vi* (*inf*; *orig US*) to judge, criticize, find fault with, using hindsight; to predict or anticipate (an action), or the future actions or behaviour of; to gain the advantage of, by forethought, anticipation, etc. **second** (or **seconds**) **hand** *n* a hand on a clock or watch that indicates seconds. **second-hand'** *adj* derived from another; not original; already used by a previous owner; dealing in second-hand goods. ◆*adv* indirectly, at one remove; after use by a previous owner. **second home** *n* a holiday home; a house owned in addition to one's main residence; a place where one feels as at home as in one's own house. **second-in-command'** *n* the next under the commanding officer or other person in charge. **second lieutenant** *n* an army officer of lowest commissioned rank (formerly called an ensign or cornet). **second man** *n* a man assisting the driver of a train (formerly, in steam trains, called the fireman). **second mark** *n* the character (v), used for seconds of arc or time or for inches. **second mate** or **second officer** *n* an officer next in command to the first mate/officer on a merchant ship. **second mortgage** *n* a subsequent mortgage on an already-mortgaged property. **second name** *n* a surname. **second nature** *n* a deeply ingrained habit or tendency. **second-rate'** *adj* inferior; mediocre. **second-rat'er** *n*. **second row** *n* (*rugby*) (either of) the two forwards in the middle of a scrum. **sec'ond-row** *adj*. **second self** *n* a person with whom one has the closest possible ties, almost intuitively sharing beliefs, attitudes, feelings and ways of behaving. **second sight** *n* a gift of prophetic vision attributed to certain people, eg Scottish

Highlanders. **second-sight'ed** *adj*. **seconds pendulum** *n* a pendulum that makes one swing per second. **second storey** *n* (*Brit*) the first floor. **second strike** *n* a counter-attack (in nuclear warfare) following an initial attack by an enemy. **second-strike'** *adj* (of a nuclear weapon) specially designed so as to be ready to be used to strike back after a first attack by an enemy and to withstand such an attack. **second string** *n* an alternative choice, course of action, etc. **second thoughts** *n pl* doubts; reconsideration. **second-to-none'** *adj* supreme, best; unsurpassed. **second wind** *n* recovery of breath after a time, during prolonged exertion; a burst of renewed energy or enthusiasm. **Second World** *n* the (former) Communist countries of the world regarded as a political and economic bloc.

■ **at second hand** through an intermediate source, indirectly; by hearsay. **every second** (**day**, **week**, etc) (on) alternate (days, weeks, etc), every other (day, week, etc).

second² /si-kond′/ *vt* to transfer (an officer) to another post or unit (*milit*); to transfer (an employee) temporarily to another branch, company or organization, *usu* to undertake some special task. [From the Fr phrase *en second* in the second rank (said of officers)]

■ **secondee** /sek-on-dē′/ *n* a person who is on secondment. **second'ment** *n* temporary transfer to another position.

seconde /si-kond′ or sə-gȯd′/ (*fencing*) *n* a position in parrying. [Fr]

secondo /si-kon′dō/ (*music*) *n* (pl **secon'di** /-dē/) the lower part in a duet. [Ital]

sec. reg. *abbrev*: *secundum regulam* (L) according to the rule.

secret /sē′krət/ *adj* kept back from the knowledge of others; guarded against discovery or observation; unrevealed, unidentified; hidden; secluded; recondite, occult; preserving privacy. ◆*adv* (*poetic*) secretly. ◆*n* a fact, purpose, method, etc, that is kept undivulged; participation in the knowledge of such a fact; a nostrum (*obs*); anything unrevealed or unknown; the fact of being secret, secret quality, secrecy; a secret or private place (*obs*); a piece of armour hidden by clothes; the key or principle that explains or enables; an inaudible prayer, *esp* in the Mass; (in *pl*) external sex organs (*obs*). [L *sēcernere*, *sēcrētum*, from *sē-* apart, and *cernere* to separate]

■ **secrecy** /sē′krə-si/ *n* the state or fact of being secret; concealment; seclusion; confidentiality; power or habit of keeping secrets; the keeping of secrets. **secretagogue** /si-krēt′ə-gog/ *n* (Gr *agōgos* leading) a substance which stimulates secretion. **sē'cretage** *n* treatment of furs with mercury before felting. **secrete** /si-krēt′/ *vt* to hide; to take away (*usu* an object) secretly; to form and emit by means of bodily functions (*biol* or *zool*). **secrē'tion** *n* the act of secreting; that which is secreted, eg the substance produced by a gland; a mass of mineral matter formed by inward growth in a cavity. **secrē'tional** *adj*. **sē'cretive** (also /si-krē′tiv/) *adj* inclined to, fond of, secrecy; very reticent; indicative of secrecy. **se'cretively** *adv*. **se'cretiveness** *n*. **sē'cretly** *adv* in secret; in concealment; (of prayers) inaudibly. **sē'cretness** *n*. **secrē'tor** *n*. **secrē'tory** *adj* (of a gland, etc) secreting.

❏ **secret agent** *n* someone employed in (the) secret service. **secret police** *n* a police force which operates in secret, *usu* dealing with matters of politics, national security, etc. **Secret Service** *n* a department of the US government service whose operations are covert, not disclosed; its activities; (without *caps*) espionage.

■ **in on** (or **in**) **the secret** admitted to, participating in, or having knowledge of the secret. **in secret** with precautions against being known, found out, etc; in confidence, as a secret; secretly. **keep a secret** not to divulge a secret. **of secret** (*Shakesp*) of a secret character. **open secret** see under **open**. **secret of** (or **secret de** /sə-krā də/) **Polichinelle** (Fr equivalent of the character Punchinello) something that is common knowledge.

secreta /si-krē′tə/ *n pl* products of secretion. [L, things secreted, neuter pl of *sēcrētus*, pap of *sēcernere*; see **secret**]

secretaire /sek′ri-tār or sek-rə-ter′/ *n* a cabinet folding out to form a writing desk, an escritoire. [Fr; cf **secretary**]

❏ **secretaire à abattant** /a a-ba-tä′/ *n* a writing-cabinet with a desk flap that closes vertically.

secretary /sek′ri-t(ə-)ri/ *n* a person who types and deals with correspondence, and does general clerical and administrative work for a company or individual; a person who writes or transacts business for a society, company, etc; the minister at the head of certain departments of state; an ambassador's or government minister's assistant; a writing desk, a secretaire; secretary hand; secretary type. [ME *secretarie*, from LL *sēcrētārius*, from L *sēcrētum*; see **secret**]

■ **secretarial** /-tār′i-əl/ *adj*. **secreta'riat** or **secretā'riate** /-ət/ *n* secretaryship; a secretary's office; the administrative department of a council, organization, legislative or executive body; the staff or premises of such a department; a body of secretaries. **sec'retaryship** *n* the office, duties, or skills of a secretary.

❏ **secretary bird** *n* a long-legged snake-eating African bird of prey (genus *Serpentarius*), said to be named from the tufts of feathers at the back of its head like pens stuck behind the ear. **secretary-gen'eral** *n* the chief administrator of an organization, eg the United Nations. **secretary hand** *n* an old legal style of handwriting. **Secretary of State** *n* a cabinet minister holding one of the more important portfolios; in the USA, the foreign secretary. **secretary type** *n* a type in imitation of secretary hand.

secrete, etc see under **secret**.

secretin /si-krē'tin/ (*physiol*) *n* a hormone secreted by the duodenum, that stimulates the liver and pancreas. [L *sēcrētus*, pap of *sēcernere* (see **secret**), and **-in**]

sect[1] /sekt/ *n* a body of followers, *esp* of an extreme political movement; a school of opinion, *esp* in religion or philosophy; a subdivision of one of the main religious divisions of mankind; an organized denomination, used *esp* by members of the established churches to express their disapproval of the less established or smaller; a dissenting body; a party; a class of people; a sex (*old*). [L *secta* a school or following, from *sequī*, *secūtus* to follow, infl by *secāre* to cut]
   ■ **sectā'rial** *adj* distinguishing a sect (*esp* in India). **sectā'rian** *adj* of or relating to a sect, or between sects; (of a crime, *esp* a murder) motivated solely by a hatred derived from religious bigotry; narrow, exclusive, rigidly adhering to the beliefs of a given sect; denominational. ◆ *n* a member of a sect; a person strongly imbued with the characteristics of a sect, *esp* if bigoted. **sectā'rianism** *n*. **sectā'rianize** or **-ise** *vt*. **sectary** /sek'tə-ri/ *n* a follower, a votary; a member of a sect; a dissenter from the established faith. **sectā'tor** *n* (*rare*) an adherent of a school or party.

sect[2] /sekt/ *n* (*Shakesp*) a cutting. [L *secāre*, *sectum* to cut]
   ■ **sectile** /sek'tīl/ *adj* capable of being cut with a knife without breaking. **sectil'ity** *n*.

sect. *abbrev*: section.

section /sek'shən/ *n* the act of cutting; a division; a portion; one of the parts into which anything may be considered as divided or of which it may be composed; the line of intersection of two surfaces; the surface formed when a solid is cut by a plane; an exposure of rock in which the strata are cut across (*geol*); a numbered subdivision in a body of law; a plan of anything represented as if cut by a plane or other surface; a thin slice for microscopic examination of a specimen; the act or process of cutting or the cut or division made (*surg*); a one-mile square of American public lands; a subdivision of a company, platoon, battery, etc; a number of men detailed for a special service; a district or region (*US*); a subdivision of an orchestra or chorus, containing (players of) similar instruments or singers of similar voice; a frame for a honeycomb; a section mark (*printing*); a building plot (*NZ*). ◆ *vt* to divide into sections; to draw a sectional plan of; to cut a section through (*surg*); to have (a person suffering from mental illness) confined in a mental hospital under the relevant section of mental health legislation. [L *sectiō*, *-ōnis*, from *secāre*, *sectum* to cut]
   ■ **sec'tional** *adj* of a section; in section; of sectionalism; built up of sections. **sec'tionalism** *n* a narrow-minded concern for the interests of a group, area, etc, at the expense of the general or long-term. **sec'tionalist** *adj* and *n*. **sectionalizā'tion** or **-s-** *n*. **sec'tionalize** or **-ise** *vt* to make sectional; to divide into sections. **sec'tionally** *adv*. **sectionizā'tion** or **-s-** *n*. **sec'tionize** or **-ise** *vt* to section; to cut sections or slices from (*bot*, etc).
   ◻ **sec'tion-cutter** *n* an instrument for making sections for microscopic work, commonly microtome. **section mark** *n* the sign y, used to mark the beginning of a section of a book or as a reference mark.

sector /sek'tər/ *n* a plane figure bounded by two radii and an arc; an object of similar shape, *esp* one for measuring angular distance (*astron*); a length or section of a fortified line, army front, guarded area, etc; a mathematical instrument consisting of two graduated rules hinged together, *orig* with a graduated arc; a telescope turning about the centre of a graduated arc; a division, section, eg of a nation's economic operations (as in *private* and *public sector*) or of military operations; the smallest addressable portion of storage (512 bytes) on a disk, etc (*comput*). ◆ *vt* to divide into sectors. [L *sector*, from *secāre*, *sectum* to cut]
   ■ **sec'toral** *adj*. **sectorial** /-tō'ri-əl/ or /-tō'/ *adj* sectoral; adapted for cutting (*zool*). ◆ *n* a tooth designed for flesh-eating; a vein in the wings of insects. **sectorizā'tion** or **-s-** *n*. **sec'torize** or **-ise** *vt* to divide into sectors.
   ◻ **sector scan** *n* (*radar*) a scan in which the antenna moves through only a limited sector.

secular /sek'ū-lər/ *adj* relating to, or coming or observed once in, a lifetime, generation, century or age (in ancient Rome about 100 to 120 years); relating to the present world, or to things not spiritual; civil, not ecclesiastical; lay, not concerned with religion; (of clergy) not bound by monastic rules, *opp* to *regular*; of the secular clergy; lasting for a long time; agelong; age-old; appreciable only in the course of ages or over an extended period; occurring in cycles. ◆ *n* a lay person; a member of the clergy, such as a parish priest, not bound by monastic rules. [L *saeculāris*, from *saeculum* a lifetime, generation]

■ **sec'ularism** *n* the belief that the state, morals, education, etc, should be independent of religion; GJ Holyoake's (1817–1907) system of social ethics. **sec'ularist** *n* and *adj*. **secularist'ic** *adj*. **secularity** /-lar'/ *n*. **seculārizā'tion** or **-s-** *n*. **sec'ularize** or **-ise** *vt* to make secular. **sec'ularly** *adv*.
   ◻ **secular arm** *n* the civil power, authority or courts. **secular games** *n pl* (*Roman hist*) games held at long intervals. **secular hymn** *n* a hymn for the secular games.

seculum see saeculum.

secund /si-kund', also sek'und or sē'kund/ *adj* (*bot*) (of eg leaves) all turned to or positioned on the same side. [L *secundus* following, second]
   ■ **sec'undine** /-in or -īn/ *n* the inner (rarely outer and second-formed) coat of an ovule; (in *pl*) the afterbirth. **secund'ly** *adv*.
   ◻ **secundogeniture** /-jen'/ *n* inheritance by a second child or son.

secundum /si-kun'dum or se-kŭn'dŭm/ (*L*) following, according to.
   ■ **secundum artem** /är'tem/ scientifically; professionally. **secundum naturam** /na-tū'ram/ according to nature. **secundum ordinem** /ör'di-nem/ in order. **secundum quid** /kwid/ in some respects only. **secundum regulam** according to rule (*abbrev* **sec. reg.**).

secure /si-kūr'/ *adj* without care or anxiety; free from danger; safe; confident; over-confident, careless (*archaic*); assured; providing safety; stable; firmly fixed or held; in (police, etc) custody. ◆ *adv* (*poetic*) in security. ◆ *vt* to make safe or certain; to assure the possession of; to establish in security; to prevent (*obs*); to seize and guard; to get hold of; to contrive to get; to plight or pledge (*obs*); to guarantee; to fasten. ◆ *vi* to make sure; to be, or make oneself, safe. [L *secūrus*, from *sē-* without, and *cūra* care]
   ■ **secūr'able** *adj*. **secūr'ance** *n* (*rare*). **secure'ly** *adv*. **secure'ment** *n*. **secure'ness** *n*. **secūr'er** *n*. **secūr'itan** *n* (*obs*) someone who dwells in fancied security. **securitizā'tion** or **-s-** *n* the procedure, practice or policy of making loans, mortgages, etc into negotiable securities. **secur'itize** or **-ise** *vt* to make (debts) into securities. **secūr'ity** *n* the state, feeling, or means of being secure; over-confidence, carelessness (*archaic*); protection from the possibility of future financial difficulty; protection from espionage, theft, attack, etc; staff providing such protection, etc; certainty; a pledge; a guarantee, a surety; a right conferred on a creditor to make him or her sure of recovering a debt; (*usu* in *pl*) a bond or certificate in evidence of debt or property. ◆ *adj* providing security.
   ◻ **secure unit** *n* a government-run institution for the confinement of difficult or mentally disordered persons, juvenile offenders, etc. **security blanket** *n* a blanket, piece of material, etc, that a child comes to depend upon for a sense of comfort and security; something that (irrationally) makes one feel secure or happy (*fig*); an official set of measures, a policy, etc, applied to conceal a matter of (often national) security. **Security Council** *n* a body of the United Nations consisting of five permanent members (China, France, Russia, UK, USA, each with the right of veto) and ten elected two-yearly members, charged with the maintenance of international peace and security. **security guard** *n* a person whose job is to protect a building, person, etc, or to deliver or collect large amounts of money. **security risk** *n* a person considered from his or her political affiliations or leanings to be likely to divulge (*esp* state) secrets.

securiform /si-kū'ri-förm/ *adj* axe-shaped. [L *secūris* axe, from *secāre* to cut, and **-form**]

Securitate /si-kū-ri-tä'tä/ *n pl* a secret police force in Romania before the 1989 revolution. [Romanian, security]

Secy *abbrev*: Secretary.

SED *abbrev*: Scottish Education Department (now called **SEED**).

sed, se'd Miltonic spellings of **said**[1] (*pat* and *pap*).

sedan /si-dan'/ *n* a covered chair for one person, carried on two poles (also **sedan chair**; *hist*); a litter; a palanquin; a large closed motor car, a saloon-car (*N Am* and *NZ*). [Appar not connected with *Sedan* in France; poss Ital *sedere* to sit]

sedate /si-dāt'/ *adj* composed; dignified or staid; slow in a boring or dignified way. ◆ *vt* to calm or quieten by means of sedatives. [L *sēdātus*, pap of *sedāre* to still]
   ■ **sedate'ly** *adv*. **sedate'ness** *n*. **sedā'tion** *n* the act of calming, or state of being calmed, *esp* by means of sedatives. **sedative** /sed'ə-tiv/ *adj* calming; composing; allaying excitement or pain. ◆ *n* a sedative drug or agent.

se defendendo /sē di-fen-den'dō or sā de-fen-den'dō/ (*L*) *adv* in self-defence.

sedent /sē'dənt/ *adj* seated. [L *sedēns*, *-entis* (prp), and *sedentārius*, from *sedēre* to sit]
   ■ **sedentarily** /sed'ən-tər-i-li/ *adv*. **sed'entariness** *n*. **sed'entary** *adj* spending much time sitting and taking little exercise; requiring a person to sit for a long time; inactive; stationary; not migratory; (eg of a

spider) lying in wait, for prey, etc; (eg of a mollusc) attached to a rock or other surface, and so moving very little (*zool*).
□ **sedentary soil** *n* soil remaining where it was formed.

Seder /sā'dər/ (*Judaism*) *n* the ceremonial meal and its rituals on the first night or first two nights of the Passover. [Heb, order]

sederunt /si-dē'runt, si-dā'rənt or sā-dā'rŭnt/ *n* (in Scotland) a sitting, as of a court; a list of persons present. [L *sēdērunt* there sat (the following persons), from *sedēre* to sit]
■ **Acts of Sederunt** ordinances of the Court of Session.

sedes /sē'dēz or sed'ās/ (*L*) *n* a seat.
□ **sedes impedita** /im-pə-dī'tə or im-ped'i-ta/ *n* a papal or episcopal see where there is a partial cessation by the incumbent of his episcopal duties. **sedes vacans** /vā'kanz, va' or wa'kanz/ (also **sede vacante** /sē'dē və-kan'ti, sed'e va- or wa-kan'te/) *n* a term of canon law to designate a papal or episcopal see when vacant.

sedge¹ /sej/ *n* any species of *Carex* or other plant of the Cyperaceae, a family distinguished from grasses by its solid triangular stems and leaf-sheaths without a slit; extended to iris and other plants; (also **sedge fly**) any of several mayflies or caddis flies common along rivers; an artificial fishing fly resembling a sedge fly. [OE *secg*; cf LGer *segge*]
■ **sedged** *adj* of sedge; bordered with sedge. **sedg'y** *adj* of, like, or abounding with sedge.
□ **sedge'land** *n*. **sedge warbler** *n* (also **sedge bird** or **sedge wren**) a common migratory warbler of marshy areas.

sedge² /sej/ *n* see **siege**.

sedigitated /sē-dij'i-tā-tid/ *adj* six-fingered. [L *sēdigitus*, from *sex* six, and *digitus* finger]

sedilia /si-dil'i-ə/ *n pl* (sing **sedile** /si-dī'li, se-dī'le/) seats (*usu* three, often in niches) for the officiating clergy, on the south side of the chancel. [L *sedīle* (pl *sedīlia*) seat]

sediment /sed'i-mənt/ *n* solid matter that settles at the bottom of a liquid; dregs; a deposit; material deposited by water, wind or ice and formed into rock (*geol*). ◆ *vt* to deposit as sediment; to cause or allow to deposit sediment. [L *sedimentum*, from *sedēre* to sit]
■ **sedimentary** /-men'tər-i/ *adj*. **sedimentā'tion** *n* deposition of sediment; the formation of sedimentary rocks. **sedimentolog'ical** *adj*. **sedimentol'ogist** *n*. **sedimentol'ogy** *n* (*geol*) the study of sedimentary rock.
□ **sedimentary rocks** *n pl* those formed by accumulation and deposition of fragmentary materials or organic remains.

sedition /si-dish'ən/ *n* public speech or actions intended to promote disorder; vaguely, any offence against the state short of treason; insurrection (*archaic*). [OFr, from L *sēditiō, -ōnis*, from *sēd-* away, and *īre, ītum* to go]
■ **sedi'tionary** *n* an inciter to sedition; inducement to attempt, otherwise than by lawful means, alteration in church or state. **sedi'tious** *adj*. **sedi'tiously** *adv*. **sedi'tiousness** *n*.

Sedol number /sē'dol num'bər/ *n* a number assigned by the London Stock Exchange to identify a security. [Acronym for *Stock Exchange Daily Official List*]

seduce /si-dūs'/ *vt* to lead astray; to entice; to corrupt; to draw aside from party, belief, allegiance, service, duty, etc; to induce to have sexual intercourse. [L *sēdūcere, sēductum*, from *sē-* aside, and *dūcere* to lead]
■ **sedúce'ment** *n* the act of seducing or drawing aside; allurement. **sedū'cer** *n* someone who seduces, *esp* in the sexual sense. **sedúc'ible** *adj*. **sedū'cing** *n* and *adj*. **sedū'cingly** *adv*. **seduction** /si-duk'shən/ *n* the act or practice of seducing; allurement. **seduc'tive** *adj* tending or intended to seduce; alluring. **seduc'tively** *adv*. **seduc'tiveness** *n*. **seduc'tor** *n* (*obs*) someone who seduces or misleads. **seduc'tress** *n* a female seducer.

sedulous /sed'ū-ləs/ *adj* assiduous or diligent; painstaking. [L *sēdulus*, from *sē dolō* without deception, hence in earnest]
■ **sedulity** /si-dū'li-ti/ or **sed'ulousness** *n*. **sed'ulously** *adv*.

sedum /sē'dəm/ *n* any rock plant of the genus *Sedum*, with white, yellow or pink flowers. [L *sedum* house leek]

see¹ /sē/ *vt* (pat **saw** (also *non-standard* or *dialect* **see**, **seed** and **seen**); *pap* **seen**) to perceive by means of the eye; to perceive mentally; to apprehend; to recognize; to realize; to understand; to learn; to be aware by reading; to look at; to judge, to deem; (with *in*) to find attractive about; to refer to; to ascertain; to regard as likely, or possible; to make sure of having; to wait upon, escort; to spend time with, or meet with regularly, *esp* romantically; to call on; to receive as a visitor; to meet; to consult; to experience; to witness; to meet and accept (another's bet) by staking a similar sum; to spend on seeing (*obs*; with *away*); (as *imperative*, in prefatory reference to a person or thing to be commented on) consider as an example, take, as in *See my brother, he's a great worker* (*inf*, *esp Scot*). ◆ *vi* to have power of vision; to see things well enough; to look or inquire; to be attentive; to understand or realize; to await further developments, to postpone any

decision until more thought has been given to the matter; to consider. ◆ *interj* (or *imperative*) look, behold. ◆ *n* an act of seeing, a look. [OE *sēon*; Ger *sehen*, Du *zien*]
■ **see'able** *adj*. **see'ing** *n* sight; vision; clear-sightedness; atmospheric conditions for good observation (*astron*). ◆ *adj* having sight, or insight; observant; discerning. ◆ *conj* (also **seeing that**) since; in view of the fact that. **seer** /sē'ər/ *n* a person who sees; /sēr/ a person who sees into the future. **seer'ess** *n* a female seer.
□ **seeing stone** *n* a scrying crystal. **see'-through** *adj* (*esp* of fabrics) transparent.
■ **as far as ! can see** to the best of my understanding. **have seen better days** or **one's best days** to be now on the decline. **let me see** a phrase employed to express reflection. **see about** to consider; to do whatever is to be done about; to attend to. **see fit** to think it appropriate (to). **see in** to witness, greet, or celebrate the arrival of. **see off** to accompany (someone) at their departure; to reprimand (*sl*); to get rid of (*inf*). **see one's way clear to** (*inf*) to feel that one will be able to. **see out** to conduct to the door; to see to the end; to outlast. **see over** or **round** to look or be conducted all through (eg premises, property). **see red** see under **red¹**. **see someone right** (*inf*) to take care of someone, *usu* in the sense of giving them a tip or reward. **see the back of** to be rid of or finished with (someone or something unpleasant, difficult, etc). **see the light** to experience a religious conversion; to come round to another's way of thinking, to come to understand and agree with someone (*usu facetious*). **see things** see under **thing**. **see through** to participate in to the end; to back up until difficulties end; to understand the true nature of, *esp* when faults or bad intentions are concealed by a good appearance. **see to** to look after; to make sure about. **see what one can do** to do what one can. **see you (later)** or **be seeing you** (*inf*) goodbye for now. **well** (or **ill**) **seen** well (or ill) versed.

see² /sē/ *n* the office of bishop of a particular diocese; (wrongly according to some) a cathedral city, also a diocese; a throne, *esp* a bishop's (*archaic*); a seat, *esp* of dignity or authority (*obs*). [OFr *se, sied*, from L *sēdēs, -is*, from *sedēre* to sit]
■ **Holy See** the papal court.

see³ /sē/ *n* the third letter of the alphabet (C, c).

seecatch /sē'kach/ *n* (pl **see'catchie**) an adult male Aleutian fur seal. [Russ *sekach*, prob from Aleutian Indian]

SEED *abbrev* : Scottish Executive Education Department.

seed¹ /sēd/ *n* a multicellular structure by which flowering plants reproduce, consisting of embryo, stored food, and seed coat, derived from the fertilized ovule (*bot*); a small hard fruit or part in a fruit, a pip; a seedlike object or aggregate; semen (*literary* or *poetic*); spawn; the condition of having or proceeding to form seed; sown land; grass and clover grown from seed; a first principle; origin, beginning or germ; a crystal introduced to start crystallization; offspring, descendants, race; a small bubble in glass; a tournament player who has been seeded. ◆ *vi* to produce seed; to run to seed. ◆ *vt* to sow; to sprinkle, powder, dust; to remove seeds from; (in sports tournaments) to arrange (the draw) so that the best players do not meet in the early rounds; to deal with (the best players) in this way; to introduce particles of material (into something, eg a chemical solution) to induce crystallization or precipitation; *specif*, to induce rainfall, disperse a storm or freezing fog, etc, by scattering cloud with particles of an appropriate substance (also **cloud-seeding**). [OE *sǣd*; cf *sāwan* to sow; ON *sāth*; Ger *Saat*]
■ **seed'ed** *adj* with the seeds removed; having seeds; bearing seed; full-grown; sown; showing seeds or carpels (*heraldry*); (of a tournament player) who has been seeded. **seed'er** *n* a plant that produces seeds; a seed drill; an apparatus for removing seeds from fruit; a seed-fish. **seed'ily** *adv*. **seed'iness** *n*. **seed'ing** *n* and *adj*. **seed'less** *adj*. **seed'like** *adj*. **seed'ling** *n* a plant reared from the seed; a young plant ready for planting out from a seedbed; a seed oyster. **seed'ness** *n* (*obs*) sowing. **seed'y** *adj* abounding with seed; having the flavour of seeds; not cleared of seeds; run to seed; worn-out; out of sorts; shabby.
□ **seed bank** *n* (*bot*) the total viable seed content of the soil; a collection of seeds in long-term storage, which can be germinated as required for breeding and study. **seed'bed** *n* a piece of ground for receiving seed; an environment, etc, that fosters a particular thing (*esp* something considered undesirable). **seed'box** or **seed'case** *n* a part of a plant in which the seeds are encased. **seed'cake** *n* a cake flavoured with caraway seeds. **seed capital** *n* (*finance*) capital provided to allow a new company to finance the costs of producing the business plan necessary to raise further capital for development. **seed coat** *n* the hard protective covering of the seeds of flowering plants, the testa. **seed coral** *n* coral in small irregular pieces. **seed corn** *n* grain for sowing; assets likely to bring future profit. **seed drill** *n* a machine for sowing seeds in rows. **seed fern** *n* another name for pteridosperm. **seed'-field** *n* a field in which seed is sown. **seed'-fish** *n* a fish about to spawn. **seed'-lac** *n* granular residues of lac after

trituration. **seed leaf** *n* a cotyledon, a leaf contained in a seed. **seed'lip** *n* (OE *sǣdlēap* from *lēap*, basket) a sower's basket. **seed'-lobe** *n* a cotyledon. **seed money** *n* money with which a project or enterprise is set up, seed capital. **seed'-oil** *n* oil expressed from seeds. **seed oyster** *n* a very young oyster. **seed pearl** *n* a very small pearl. **seed'-plant** *n* a spermatophyte or flowering plant; a plant grown from or for seed. **seed plot** *n* a piece of nursery ground, a hotbed. **seed potato** *n* a potato tuber for planting. **seeds'man** *n* a dealer in seeds; a sower. **seed'-stalk** *n* the funicle. **seed time** *n* the season for sowing seeds. **seed vessel** *n* a dry fruit; the ovary of a flower. **seed'y-toe** *n* a disease of a horse's foot.

■ **go** or **run to seed** to grow rapidly and untidily in preparation for seeding, instead of producing the vegetative growth desired by the grower; to disappoint expectation of development; to become exhausted; to go to waste; (*usu* **go**) to become unkempt, shabby. **sow the seed(s) of** to initiate or engender.

seed² see **see¹**.

seek /sēk/ *vt* (pat and pap **sought** /söt/) to look for; to try to find, get, or achieve; to ask for; to aim at; to resort to, take oneself off to; to advance against; to try; to search, examine (*archaic*). ◆ *vi* to make a search; to try or endeavour; to resort (*obs*). [OE *sēcan* (pat *sōhte*, pap *gesōht*); cf Ger *suchen*]

■ **seek'er** *n* a person who seeks; an inquirer; a dissector's probing instrument; a telescopic finder; (with *cap*) a member of a 17c sect who sought for the true church.

■ **seek after** to go in quest of. **seek for** to look for. **seek out** to look for and find; to find after much searching; to bring out from a hidden place. **sought after** in demand. **to seek** not to be found; lacking; at a loss to know (*archaic*; eg *What real good is, I am to seek*); defective (in; *archaic*).

seel¹ /sēl/ *vt* to sew up the eyelids of (eg a hawk); to blindfold; to blind, hoodwink. [OFr *siller*, *ciller*, from *cil*, from L *cilium* eyelid, eyelash]

seel², **sele** or **seal** (*Scot* **seil**) /sēl/ (*dialect*) *n* happiness; good fortune; opportune time; season; time of day. [OE *sǣl* time, due time, happiness; see **silly**]

■ **seel'y** *adj* fortunate, happy, good (*obs*); simple, innocent (*Spenser*); pitiful, wretched, trifling; to be pitied, poor (*obs*); foolish (see **silly**).

■ **pass the seel of the day** to greet in passing.

seel³ /sēl/ (*naut* and *obs*) *vi* to heel over suddenly. ◆ *n* a sudden heeling. [Origin obscure]

seeld /sēld/ a Spenserian form of **seld**.

seeling a Spenserian form of **ceiling**.

seely see under **seel²**.

seem /sēm/ *vi* to appear; to appear to one; to appear to be; to be fitting (*obs*). ◆ *vt* (*archaic*) to beseem, befit. [ON *sǣma* to beseem]

■ **seeme'lesse**, **seem'less** *adj* (*Spenser*) unseemly; indecorous. **seem'er** *n*. **seem'ing** *adj* apparent; ostensible. ◆ *adv* apparently; in appearance only (*esp* in combination, eg *seeming-simple*, *seeming-virtuous*). ◆ *n* appearance; semblance; a false appearance. **seem'ingly** *adv* apparently; as it would appear. **seem'ingness** *n*. **seem'lihed** or **seem'lihead** (*Spenser* **seem'lyhed**) *n* seemliness. **seem'liness** *n*. **seem'ly** *adj* (**seem'lier**; **seem'liest**) becoming; suitable; decent; handsome. ◆ *adv* (*archaic*) in a seemly manner.

■ **it seems** it appears; it would seem. **it would seem** it turns out; I have been told.

seen see **see¹**.

seep /sēp/ *vi* to ooze, percolate. ◆ *n* a place or area where water or other liquid has oozed through the ground, seepage. [Cf **sipe¹**]

■ **seep'age** *n* the action of seeping; liquid that has seeped. **seep'y** *adj*.

seer¹ /sēr/ *n* an Indian weight of widely ranging amount, officially about 2lb. [Pers *sīr*]

seer², **seeress** see under **see¹**.

seer³ see **seir**.

seersucker /sēr'suk-ər/ *n* a thin crinkly Indian linen (or cotton) striped or checked fabric. [Pers *shīr o shakkar*, literally, milk and sugar]

seesaw /sē'sö/ *n* a playground device, a plank balanced at its centre so that children sitting on either end can rise and sink alternately; the activity of rising and sinking on it; alternate up-and-down or back-and-forth motion; repeated alternation. ◆ *adj* (moving up and down) like a seesaw. ◆ *adv* in the manner of a seesaw. ◆ *vi* to play at seesaw; to move or go like a seesaw. ◆ *vt* to make (something) go up and down like a seesaw. [Prob a reduplication of **saw²**, from a sawyer's jingle, from *See saw sack a down*]

seethe /sēdh/ *vi* (pat **seethed** or (*archaic*) **sod**; pap **seethed** or (*archaic*) **sodd'en**) to boil; to surge (*lit* or *fig*); to be agitated (by anger, excitement, etc). ◆ *vt* to boil; to soak to a condition similar to that produced by boiling. [OE *sēothan* (pat *sēath*, pl *sudon*; pap *soden*); ON *sjōtha*, Ger *sieden*]

■ **seeth'er** *n*. **seeth'ing** *n* and *adj*. **seeth'ingly** *adv*.

seewing a Spenserian spelling of **suing** (see **sue**).

Sefer /sā'fər/ (*Judaism*) *n* (pl **Sifrei** /sē'frä/) a scroll on which the Torah or Law is written (also called **Sefer Torah**); any book containing Hebrew religious literature. [Heb *sēpher*, literally, a book]

seg¹ /seg/ (*obs* or *dialect*) *n* same as **sedge¹**.

seg² /seg/ *n* a stud or small metal plate in the sole of a shoe to protect it from wearing down, *esp* at the toe or heel; a callus, *esp* at the base of the finger (*NW Eng dialect*). [ON *sigg* hard skin, a callus]

segar /si-gär'/ *n* a variant of **cigar**.

Seger cones /sā'gər or zā'gər könz/ *n pl* (*engineering*) small clay and oxide cones, used in furnaces to indicate the temperature reached, by softening and bending over within a particular temperature range. [Hermann *Seger* (1839–94), German chemist]

seggar see **saggar**.

seghol or **segol** /se-gōl'/ *n* a vowel point in Hebrew (ֶ) with the sound of *e* in *pen*, placed under a consonant. [Heb, literally, bunch of grapes (from its shape)]

■ **segh'ölate** or **seg'ölate** *n* a disyllabic noun form with a tone-long vowel in the first and a short seghol in the second syllable.

segment /seg'mənt/ *n* a part cut off; a portion; part of a circle, ellipse, etc, cut off by a straight line, or of a sphere, ellipsoid, etc, by a plane; a section; one of a linear series of similar portions, eg of a vibrating string between nodes, a somite or metamere of a jointed animal, or a joint of an appendage; a lobe of a leaf-blade not separate enough to be a leaflet; the smallest sound unit of speech (*phonetics*). ◆ *vt* and *vi* (also /-ment'/) to divide or cut into segments. [L *segmentum*, from *secāre* to cut]

■ **segmental** /-ment'l/ *adj* of a segment; by segments; forming or formed of a segment, segments, arc, or arcs. **segmen'tally** *adv*. **seg'mentary** or **seg'mentate** *adj*. **segmentā'tion** *n* the act or process of dividing into segments; an instance of this; the process of repeated cell division in a fertilized ovum, initially forming a solid mass of cells, followed by the diversification of cells into specific tissue types (*embryol*). **segment'ed** (or /seg'/) *adj*.

□ **segmental arch** *n* an arch forming an arc of a circle whose centre is below the springing. **segmentation cavity** *n* a blastocele.

segno /sā'nyō/ (*music*) *n* (pl **se'gnos**) a sign to mark the beginning or end of repetitions (:$:). [Ital, from L *signum* a mark]

sego /sē'gō/ *n* (pl **sē'gos**) a showy plant (genus *Calochortus*) of the western USA. [Ute Native American name]

segol see **seghol**.

segreant /seg'ri-ənt/ (*heraldry*) *adj* generally understood to mean with raised wings. [Earlier *sergreant*; origin unknown]

segregate /seg'ri-gāt/ *vt* to set apart; to seclude; to isolate; to group apart. ◆ *vi* to separate out in a group or groups or mass; to separate into dominants and recessives (*genetics*). ◆ *adj* /-gət/ set apart. ◆ *n* /-gət/ that which is segregated. [L *sēgregāre*, *-ātum*, from *sē-* apart, and *grex*, *gregis* a flock]

■ **seg'regable** *adj*. **segregā'tion** *n* the act of segregating; the state of being segregated; dispersal (*obs*); the separation of the two alleles in a heterozygote when gametes are formed with the appearance of several genotypes in the progeny (*genetics*); the separation into patches or undistributed areas of impurities, inclusions, and alloying constituents in metals; a segregated mass or group; separation of one particular class of people from another, eg on grounds of race. **segregā'tional** *adj*. **segregā'tionist** *n* a believer in racial or other segregation. **seg'regative** /-gā-tiv/ *adj*.

segue /seg'wā/ (*music*) *vi* (**se'gueing**; **se'gued**) to proceed without pause, to follow on, *usu* as a musical direction (literally, it follows on, apprehended as an imperative) to proceed immediately with the next song, movement, etc (also *fig*). ◆ *n* the term or direction to segue; the act or result of segueing; segued music (live or recorded); a compilation, *esp* in popular recorded music, in which tracks follow on continuously. [Ital]

seguidilla /seg-i-dē(l)'yä/ *n* a Spanish verse form of seven lines; a Spanish dance; a tune for it, in triple time. [Sp, dimin of *seguido* series]

sehri /ser'i/ (*Islam*) *n* a meal eaten before sunrise by those fasting during Ramadan (also **sohur'** or **suhur'**). [Ar, morning meal]

sei /sā/ *n* (also **sei whale**) a kind of rorqual (*Balaenoptera borealis*). [Norw *sejhval* sei whale]

seicento /sā-chen'tō/ *n* (in Italian art, literature, etc) the seventeenth century. [Ital, abbrev of *mille seicento* one thousand six hundred]

■ **seicen'tist** *n*.

seiche /sāsh or sesh/ *n* a periodic fluctuation from side to side of the surface of an enclosed or partly-enclosed body of water, such as a lake, harbour, etc, caused eg by changes in barometric pressure. [Swiss Fr]

Seidlitz powder /sed'lits pow'dər/ *n* a mixture of sodium bicarbonate, sodium potassium tartrate and tartaric acid, used as a laxative when dissolved in water. [*Seidlitz*, Bohemian village producing a mineral water with a laxative effect]

seif /sāf or sīf/ n a long sand-dune lying parallel to the direction of the wind that forms it. [Ar *saif* sword]

seignior /sā' or sē'nyər/ or **seigneur** /sen-yær'/ n a feudal lord, lord of a manor, *esp* in France or French Canada. [Fr *seigneur*, from L *senior*, *-ōris*, compar of *senex* old. In LL *senior* is sometimes equivalent to *dominus* lord]
■ **seign'iorage** or **seign'orage** n lordship; a right, privilege, etc, claimed by an overlord; an overlord's royalty on minerals; a percentage on minted bullion. **seign'ioralty** n seignory. **seignio'rial**, **seigneu'rial**, **seignoral** /sān' or sen'/ or **signo'rial** /sin-/ adj. **seign'iorship** n. **seign'ory** or **seign'iory** n feudal lordship; the council of an Italian city state (*hist*); (also **seigneurie** or **seigneury** /sen'yə-rē/) a domain.
■ **grand** /grä/ **seigneur** a great lord; a man of aristocratic dignity and authority. **Grand Seignior** or **Signior** (*hist*) the Sultan of Turkey.

seik /sēk/ adj a Scots form of **sick**.

seil[1] same as **sile**.

seil[2] (*Scot*) see **seel**[2].

seine, also **sean** /sān or sēn/ n a large vertical fishing-net whose ends are brought together and hauled (also **seine net**). ♦ vt and vi to catch or fish with a seine. [OE *segne*, from L *sagēna*, from Gr *sagēnē* a fishing-net]
■ **sein'er** n. **sein'ing** n.
❑ **seine boat** n. **seine fishing** n. **seine'-shooting** n the casting of seine nets.

seir or **seer** /sēr/ n a scombroid fish, *Cybidium guttatum*, of the eastern coastal waters of India. [Port *serra*, the name of the fish]

seise /sēz/ vt an old spelling of **seize**, still used legally in the sense of to put in possession of (property, etc).
■ **seis'ed** adj (*Spenser*) reached, attained. **seis'in** or (*US*) **seizin** n orig feudal possession, now possession in freehold; an object handed over as a token of possession; sasine (*Scots law*).

seism /sī'zm/ (*rare*) n an earthquake. [Gr *seismos*; see **seismo-**]

seismo- /sīz-mō-, -mə- or -mo-/ combining form denoting an earthquake. [Gr *seismos* a shaking, from *seiein* to shake]
■ **seis'mal**, **seis'mic** or **seis'mical** adj (**seismic array** a system of seismographs, linked together and placed so as to increase sensitivity to the occurrence of earthquakes; **seismic prospecting** investigating the depth and character of subsurface rock formations by noting the travel times of reflected and refracted artificial shock waves; **seismic shock** or **wave** a vibration or shock wave resulting from earth movements). **seis'mically** adv. **seismicity** /-mis'i-ti/ n liability to or frequency of earthquakes. **seis'mism** n earthquake phenomena. **seis'mogram** n a seismograph record. **seis'mograph** n an instrument for registering earthquakes. **seismog'rapher** n. **seismograph'ic** or **seismograph'ical** adj. **seismog'raphy** n. **seismolog'ic** or **seismolog'ical** adj. **seismolog'ically** adv. **seismol'ogist** n. **seismol'ogy** n the science and study of earthquakes. **seismom'eter** n an instrument for measuring the intensity and duration of earthquakes. **seismomet'ric** or **seismomet'rical** adj. **seismom'etry** n. **seismonas'tic** adj. **seis'monasty** n (Gr *nastos* pressed together, compressed; *bot*) response to mechanical shock. **seis'moscope** n an instrument for detecting earthquakes. **seismoscop'ic** adj.

seiten /sī'tən/ n wheat gluten, widely used in vegetarian and Far Eastern cookery.

seity /sē'i-ti/ n a self; selfhood, personal identity. [L *sē* oneself]

seize or (*old or law*) **seise**, also (*Spenser, Shakesp, Milton*) **sease**, **seaze**, **ceaze**, etc /sēz/ vt to grasp suddenly, eagerly, or forcibly; to take by force; to take prisoner; to apprehend; to take possession of; to take legal possession of; to lash or make fast (*naut*); to reach, attain (*naut* and *Spenser*). ♦ vi to take hold, grasp (with *on* or *upon*); to penetrate (*Spenser*); (of mechanical parts) to jam or become partially welded due to lack of lubrication. [OFr *seisir, saisir*, from LL *sacīre*, prob Gmc; cf OHGer *sazzan* to set, Ger *setzen*, Eng *set*]
■ **seiz'able** adj. **seiz'er** n. **seiz'in** n seisin (see **seise**). **seiz'ing** n the action of the verb; a cord to seize ropes with (*naut*). **seizure** /sē'zhər/ n the act of seizing; a thing seized; capture; a sudden fit or attack of illness, *esp* a convulsion.
■ **be seized with** or **by** to have a sudden severe attack of (eg remorse, pneumonia). **seize** or **seise of** to put in possession of. **seized** or **seised of** in (legal) possession of; aware of; in the process of considering. **seize up** to jam, seize, become immovable or stuck.

sejant or **sejeant** /sē'jənt/ (*heraldry*) adj (*esp* of a quadruped) sitting (upright). [OFr *seiant*, Fr *séant*, prp of *seoir*, from L *sedēre* to sit]

Sejm /sām/ n the lower house of parliament of the Republic of Poland. [Pol, assembly]

sekos /sē'kos/ n a sacred enclosure. [Gr *sēkos*]

Sekt or **sekt** /sekt or zekt/ n a German sparkling wine. [Ger]

sel /sel/ (*Scot*) n self.

selachian /si-lā'ki-ən/ n any fish of the subclass Selachii, *incl* sharks, rays, dogfish and skates (also adj). [Gr *selachos*]

seladang /se-lä'dang/ or **sladang** /slä'dang/ n the gaur; the Malayan tapir. [Malay *seladang, saladang*]

selaginella /si-laj-i-nel'ə/ n a plant of the genus *Selaginella*, heterosporous club mosses constituting the family Selaginellaceae. [Dimin of L *selāgō, -inis* a plant mentioned by Pliny]

selah /sē'lə, -lä/ n in the Old Testament psalms, a Hebrew word probably meaning pause.

Selbornian /sel-bör'ni-ən/ adj of *Selborne* in Hampshire, or of Gilbert White (1720–93), author of *The Natural History and Antiquities of Selborne*; of Gault and Upper Greensand (*geol*). ♦ n a devotee of Gilbert White; the Gault and Upper Greensand.

selcouth /sel'kooth/ (*obs*) adj strange, unfamiliar, marvellous. [OE *sel(d)cūth*, from *seldan* seldom, and *cūth* known, from *cunnan* to know]

seld /seld/ (*obs*) adj rare, uncommon. ♦ adv seldom, rarely. [See **seldom**]
■ **seld'seen** adj (*obs*) rarely seen. **seld'shown** adj (*Shakesp*) rarely shown.

seldom /sel'dəm/ adv rarely. ♦ adj infrequent. [OE *seldum*, altered (on the analogy of *hwīlum* whilom) from *seldan*; Ger *selten*]
■ **sel'domness** n. **sel'dom-times** adv.
■ **seldom when** see under **when**.

sele same as **seel**[2].

select /si-lekt'/ vt to pick out from a number by preference; (also **block**) to choose (eg text) for manipulation (*comput*); to free-select (*Aust*). ♦ adj picked out; choice; exclusive. [L *sēligere, sēlectum*, from *sē-* aside, and *legere* to choose]
■ **selec'table** adj. **selec'ted** adj. **select'ee** n a person who is selected, *esp* (*US*) a person selected for military service. **selec'tion** n the act of selecting; a thing or collection of things selected; a potpourri (*music*); the process by which some individuals contribute more offspring than others to the next generation, in *natural selection* through intrinsic differences in fertility and survival, and in *artificial selection* through the breeder's choice of parents (*biol*); a horse selected as likely to win a race; a number or group of things from which to select; free-selection (*Aust*). ♦ adj relating to or consisting of selection. **selec'tionist** n a person who believes that natural selection is responsible for evolution and diversity in natural systems (also adj). **selec'tive** adj having or exercising power of selection; able to discriminate, eg between different frequencies; choosing, involving, etc, only certain things or people. **selec'tively** adv. **selec'tiveness** n. **selectiv'ity** /sel-/ n ability to discriminate. **select'ness** n. **select'or** n. **selecto'rial** adj.
❑ **select committee** n a number of members of parliament chosen to report and advise on some matter. **selective attention** see under **attention**. **selective mating** n the selection of mates, based on some outward characteristic (eg tail length in birds) and/or on competition between members of the same sex. **selective service** n formerly, in the USA, compulsory military service under which men were conscripted selectively. **selective weedkiller** n a weedkiller that does not destroy certain plants. **select'man** n in New England towns, one of a board of officers chosen to manage local business.
■ **select out** (*US; euphem*) to give (someone) the sack.

selegiline /sə-leg'i-lēn/ n a drug used in the treatment of Parkinson's disease.

selenic /si-lē'nik or -len'ik/ adj of or relating to the moon (also **selenian** /sə-lē'ni-ən/); of selenium in higher valency (**selenic acid** H_2SeO_4). [Gr *selēnē* moon]
■ **selenate** /sel'i-nāt/ n a salt of selenic acid. **selenide** /sel'i-nīd/ n a compound of selenium with an element or radical. **selē'nious** or **selē'nous** adj of selenium in lower valency (**selenious acid** H_2SeO_3). **selenite** /sel'i-nīt/ n gypsum, *esp* in transparent crystals (anciently supposed to wax and wane with the moon); a salt of selenious acid. **selenitic** /sel-i-nit'ik/ adj. **selenium** /si-lē'/ n a metalloid element (symbol **Se**; atomic no 34) discovered by Berzelius in 1817 and named from its resemblance to tellurium. **selē'nograph** n a delineation of the moon. **selenog'rapher** /sel-i-nog'rə-fər/ n. **selenographic** /si-lē-nə-graf'ik/ or **selenograph'ical** adj. **selenography** /sel-i-nog'rə-fi/ n mapping of the moon; the study of the moon's physical features. **selēnolog'ical** adj. **selenol'ogist** n a selenographer. **selenol'ogy** n the scientific study of the moon. **selenomorphol'ogy** n the study of the surface of the moon.
❑ **selenium cell** n a photoelectric cell dependent on the circumstance that light increases the electric conductivity of selenium.

selenodont /si-lē'nə-dont/ adj (of the molar teeth of certain animals) having crescent-shaped ridges on the crowns. ♦ n an animal, such as a deer, having such ridges on the teeth. [Gr *selēne* moon, and *odous*, *odontos* tooth]

Seleucid /se-lū′sid/ *n* a member of the dynasty (**Seleu′cidae**) that ruled Syria from 312 to 65BC, beginning with Alexander's general, *Seleucus* I (Nicator). ◆ *adj* of or relating to the Seleucid dynasty. ▪ **Seleu′cidan** *adj*.

self /self/ *pronoun* loosely, oneself, myself, himself, etc. ◆ *n* (pl **selves** /selvz/ or, of things in one colour or one piece, **selfs**) personality, ego; a side of one's personality; identity; what one is; self-interest; a self-coloured plant or animal; a thing (*esp* a bow) made in one piece. ◆ *adj* very, same, identical (*archaic*); own (*archaic*); uniform in colour; made in one piece; made of the same material. ◆ *vt* to fertilize by the same individual (self-fertilize) or by the same strain (inbreed). [OE *self*; Du *zelf*; Ger *selbe*, Gothic *silba*]
▪ **self′hood** *n* personal identity; existence as a person; personality; selfishness (*rare*). **self′ie** *n* (*inf*) a photograph of oneself taken by oneself. **self′ing** *n* (*biol*) self-fertilization or self-pollination. **self′ish** *adj* chiefly or wholly concerned with one's own welfare and interests, *usu* when accompanied by a disregard for others; tending to perpetuate or duplicate itself in the genome without affecting the host or phenotype (*genetics*). **self′ishly** *adv*. **self′ishness** *n*. **self′ism** *n* concentration upon self; the selfish theory of morals, that people act from the consideration of what will give them the most pleasure. **self′ist** *n*. **self′less** *adj* having no regard to self, altruistic. **self′lessly** *adv*. **self′lessness** *n*. **self′ness** *n* egotism; personality.
▪ **one self** (*Shakesp*) one and the same, one only. **one's self** see **oneself** under **one**. **second self** see under **second**[1].

self- /self-/ *combining form* indicating: action upon the agent; action by, of, in, in relation to, etc, oneself or itself; automatic action. [OE *self*; Du *zelf*, Ger *selbe*, Gothic *silba*]
▪ **self-aban′donment** *n* disregard of self. **self-abase′ment** *n* self-humiliation. **self-abnegā′tion** *n* renunciation of one's own interest; self-denial. **self-absorbed′** *adj* wrapped up in one's own thoughts or affairs. **self-absorp′tion** *n* the state of being self-absorbed; self-shielding (*phys*). **self-abuse′** *n* revilement of oneself; masturbation; self-deception (*Shakesp*). **self-abus′er** *n*. **self-accusā′tion** *n*. **self-accus′atory** *adj*. **self-acknow′ledged** *adj*. **self′-act′ing** *adj* automatic. **self-ac′tion** *n* spontaneous or independent action. **self-activ′ity** *n* an inherent power of acting. **self-actualizā′tion** or **-s-** *n* (*psychol*) the realization of one's whole personality and one's understanding and development of all its aspects. **self-addressed′** *adj* addressed to oneself. **self-adhē′sive** *adj* able to stick to a surface without the use of (additional) glue, etc. **self-adjust′ing** *adj* requiring no external adjustment. **self-admin′istered** *adj*. **self-admirā′tion** *n*. **self-advance′ment** *n*. **self-advert′isement** *n*. **self-ad′vertiser** *n*. **self-ad′vocacy** *n* the act or practice of representing oneself, *esp*, in the USA, the practice of people with learning disabilities taking control of their own affairs rather than automatically being represented by others. **self′-affairs** *n pl* (*Shakesp*) one's own affairs. **self-affec′ted** *adj* (*Shakesp*) self-loving. **self-affirmā′tion** *n* assertion of the existence of the self. **self-affrigh′ted** *adj* (*Shakesp*) frightened at oneself. **self-aggrand′izement** or **-s-** *n*. **self-aggrand′izing** or **-s-** *adj*. **self′-anal′ysis** *n*. **self-anneal′ing** *adj* (of metals such as lead, tin, and zinc) recrystallizing at air temperature and so able to be cold-worked with little or no strain-hardening. **self-annihilā′tion** *n* the losing of one's sense of individual existence when contemplating the divine; a sense of union with God. **self-anoin′ted** *adj*. **self-applause′** *n*. **self-appoint′ed** *adj*. **self-appreciā′tion** *n*. **self-approbā′tion** *n*. **self-appro′val** *n*. **self-approv′ing** *adj*. **self-approv′ingly** *adv*. **self-assem′bly** *adj* (of furniture, etc) in parts or sections for assembly by the purchaser. **self-assert′ing** or **self-assert′ive** *adj* given to asserting one's opinion or to putting oneself forward. **self-asser′tion** *n*. **self-assert′iveness** *n*. **self-assess′ment** *n* a system by which taxpayers themselves calculate the amount of tax they are liable to pay; the act of assessing one's own performance or progress. **self-assumed′** *adj* consciously adopted by oneself. **self-assump′tion** *n* conceit. **self-assū′rance** *n* assured self-confidence. **self-assured′** *adj*. **self-assur′edly** *adv*. **self-aware′** *adj*. **self-aware′ness** *n*. **self-bal′ancing** *adj* balancing without outward help; stable. **self-bast′ing** *adj* (*cookery*) not requiring to be basted by hand. **self-begot′** or **self′-begott′en** *adj* (*archaic*) being its own parent, as is the phoenix. **self-betray′al** *n*. **self-bind′er** *n* a reaping machine with automatic binding apparatus; a portfolio that grips loose sheets. **self′-blind′ed** *adj*. **self′-born′** *adj* born of itself, as is the phoenix. **self-boun′ty** *n* native goodness. **self-breath′** *n* (*Shakesp*) one's own utterances. **self-built′** or **self-build′** *adj* built, or to be built, by the purchaser or owner. **self-capac′itance** *n* capacitance. **self-cat′ering** *adj* (of a holiday, accommodation, etc) in which one cooks, etc for oneself. **self-cen′tred** *adj* preoccupied with oneself; selfish; fixed independently. **self-cen′tredly** *adv*. **self-cen′tredness** *n*. **self-certif′icate** *n*. **self-certificā′tion** *n* a system by which an employee declares, on a pre-printed form and without needing the authorization of a doctor, that an absence from work was due to illness; any similar system for

declaring personal information without recourse to authority. **self-char′ity** *n* (*Shakesp*) self-love. **self-clean′ing** *adj*. **self-clōs′ing** *adj* shutting automatically. **self-cock′er** *n* a firearm in which the hammer is raised by pulling the trigger. **self-cock′ing** *adj*. **self-collec′ted** *adj* self-possessed. **self-col′our** *n* uniform colour; natural colour. **self-col′oured** *adj*. **self-command′** *n* self-control. **self-commit′ment** *n*. **self-commun′ion** *n* communing with oneself, introspective meditation. **self-compar′ison** *n* (*Shakesp*) the setting of oneself against another. **self-compat′ible** *adj* (*bot*) (of a plant) capable of self-fertilization (also *n*). **self-complā′cence** *n* satisfaction with oneself, or with one's own performances. **self-complā′cent** *adj*. **self-conceit′** *n* an over-high opinion of oneself, one's own abilities, etc; vanity. **self-conceit′ed** *adj*. **self-conceit′edness** *n*. **self-concentrā′tion** *n* concentration of one's thoughts upon oneself. **self-con′cept** *n* one's concept of oneself. **self-concern′** *n*. **self-condemnā′tion** *n*. **self-condemned′** *adj* condemned by one's own actions or words. **self-condem′ning** *adj*. **self-confessed′** *adj* openly acknowledging oneself as such. **self-con′fidence** *n* confidence in, or reliance on, one's own abilities; self-reliance. **self-con′fident** *adj*. **self-con′fidently** *adv*. **self-confi′ding** *adj* self-reliant. **self-congratulā′tion** *n*. **self-congrat′ulatory** *adj* congratulating oneself. **self-con′jugate** *adj* (*maths*) conjugate to itself. **self-con′scious** *adj* irrationally believing oneself to be the subject of close observation by others, and embarrassed as a result; conscious of one's own mind and its acts and states. **self-con′sciously** *adv*. **self-con′sciousness** *n*. **self-con′sequence** *n* self-importance. **self-con′sequent** *adj*. **self-consid′ering** *adj* deliberating with oneself. **self-consist′ency** *n* consistency of each part with the rest; consistency with one's principles. **self-consis′tent** *adj*. **self-con′stituted** *adj* constituted by oneself. **self-consūmed′** *adj*. **self-consūm′ing** *adj* consuming oneself, or itself. **self-contained′** *adj* calmly independent, not needing the company or reassurance of others; wrapped up in oneself, reserved; (of a house, flat, room, etc) complete in itself. **self-contempt′** *n*. **self-contempt′ūous** *adj*. **self-content′** *n* self-satisfaction, complacency. **self-contradic′tion** *n* the act or fact of contradicting oneself; a statement whose terms are mutually contradictory. **self-contradic′tory** *adj*. **self-control′** *n* power of controlling oneself. **self-controlled′** *adj*. **self-convict′ed** *adj* convicted by one's own acts or words. **self-convic′tion** *n*. **self′-correct′ing** *adj*. **self-cov′ered** *adj* (*Shakesp*) either dissembling, or revealed in one's true colours. **self-creāt′ed** *adj*. **self-creā′tion** *n*. **self-crit′ical** *adj*. **self-crit′icism** *n* critical examination and judgement of one's own works and thoughts. **self-cult′ure** *n* development and education of one's personality by one's own efforts. **self-damn′ing** *adj*. **self-dan′ger** *n* (*Shakesp*) personal risk. **self-deceit′** or **self-decep′tion** *n* deceiving of oneself, *esp* with regard to one's true feelings or motives. **self-deceit′ful** *adj*. **self-deceived′** *adj*. **self-deceiv′er** *n*. **self-defeat′ing** *adj* that defeats its own purpose. **self-defence′** *n* defending one's own person, rights, etc (**art of self-defence** *orig* boxing, now used more loosely to refer to any of various martial arts). **self-defens′ive** *adj*. **self-degradā′tion** *n*. **self-delight′** *n* delight in one's own being or thoughts. **self-delu′sion** *n* the delusion of oneself by oneself. **self-denī′al** *n* forbearing to gratify one's own appetites or desires. **self-deny′ing** *adj*. **self-deny′ingly** *adv*. **self-depen′dence** *n*. **self-depen′dent** *adj*. **self-dep′recating** *adj*. **self-deprēc′iating** *adj* lowering its (or one's) own value; undervaluing oneself or itself. **self′-despair′** *n* a despairing view of one's own nature, prospects, etc. **self-destroy′ing** *adj*. **self-destruct′** *vi* (of a spacecraft, etc) to disintegrate or explode automatically through the operation of a timing-device, etc. **self-destruc′tion** *n* the destruction of anything by itself; suicide. **self-destruc′tive** *adj*. **self-determinā′tion** *n* determination without extraneous impulse; direction of the attention or will to an object; the power of a population to decide its own government and political relations or of an individual to live his or her own life. **self′-deter′mined** and **self′-deter′mining** *adj*. **self-devel′oping** *adj*. **self-devel′opment** *n*. **self-devō′ted** *adj*. **self-devō′tion** *n* self-sacrifice. **self-direc′ted** *adj*. **self-direc′tion** *n*. **self-direc′tor** *n*. **self-dis′charge** *n* (*elec eng*) loss of capacity of a primary cell or accumulator as a result of internal leakage; loss of charge in a capacitor due to finite insulation resistance between plates. **self-dis′cipline** *n*. **self-dis′ciplined** *adj*. **self-disliked′** *adj*. **self-dispar′agement** *n*. **self-displeased′** *adj*. **self-dispraise′** *n*. **self-dissociā′tion** *n* (*chem*) the splitting into ions of the molecules of certain highly polar liquids. **self-distrust′** *n*. **self-doc′umenting** *adj* (of a computer program) that informs the user how to use the program as it runs. **self-doubt′** *n*. **self-dramatizā′tion** or **-s-** *n* presentation of oneself as if a character in a play; seeing in oneself an exaggerated dignity and intensity. **self-drive′** *adj* (of a hired motor vehicle) to be driven by the hirer; (of a holiday) involving driving in one's own or a hired vehicle. **self-driv′en** *adj* driven by its own power. **selfe′-despight′** *n* (*Spenser*) injury to oneself. **self-ed′ucated** *adj* educated by one's own efforts. **self-educā′tion** *n*. **self-efface′ment** *n* keeping oneself in the background out of sight; withdrawing from notice or rights. **self-effac′ing** *adj*. **self-effac′ingly** *adv.* **self-elect'ed** *adj* elected by oneself or itself. **self-elect'ing** or **self-elect'ive** *adj* having the right to elect oneself or itself, as by co-option of new members. **self-elec'tion** *n.* **self-employed'** *adj* working independently in one's own business, or on a freelance basis. **self-employ'ment** *n.* **self'-end** *n* (*obs, esp* 17c) a selfish motive or object. **self-endeared'** *adj* self-loving. **self-enjoy'ment** *n* internal satisfaction. **self-enrich'ment** *n.* **self-esteem'** *n* good opinion of oneself; self-respect. **self-ev'idence** *n.* **self-ev'ident** *adj* obvious, evident without proof. **self-ev'idently** *adv.* **self-evolved'** *adj.* **self-examinā'tion** *n* a scrutiny into one's own state, conduct, etc; examination of one's own body in order to detect changes or abnormalities, *esp* by women of their breasts. **self'-example** *n* one's own example. **self-excīt'ing** or **self-excit'ed** *adj* (*elec*) (of an electrical machine) itself supplying the exciting current. **self-ex'ecuting** *adj* (*law*) automatically coming into effect, not needing legislation to enforce. **self-exer'tion** *n.* **self-ex'iled** *adj.* **self-exist'ence** *n.* **self-exist'ent** *adj* existing of or by oneself or itself, independent of any other cause. **self-explan'atory** or **self-explain'ing** *adj* obvious, understandable without explanation, self-evident. **self-explicā'tion** *n.* **self-express'** *vi.* **self-express'ion** *n* the giving of expression to one's personality, as in art. **self-express'ive** *adj.* **self-faced'** *adj* undressed or unhewn, *esp* of a stone showing a natural cleavage. **self-fed'** *adj* fed by itself or automatically; fed upon itself. **self-feed'er** *n* a device for supplying anything automatically, *esp* a measured amount of foodstuff for cattle, etc. **self-feed'ing** *adj.* **self-feel'ing** *n* one's personal experience. **self-fer'tile** or **self-fer'tilizing** *adj* made fertile or fertilizing by its own pollen or sperm. **self'-fertilizā'tion** or **-s-** *n.* **self-fertil'ity** *n.* **self-fig'ured** *adj* of one's own devising. **self-fill'er** *n* a fountain pen that can be filled without feeding ink through an external tube. **self-finan'cing** *adj* (of a business, enterprise, etc) requiring no finance from outside sources, eg loans, etc. **self-flatt'ering** *adj.* **self-flatt'ery** *n.* **self-fo'cusing** *adj.* **self-forget'ful** *adj* unselfishly forgetful of oneself or one's own interests. **self-forget'fully** *adv.* **self-forget'fulness** *n.* **self'-fulfill'ing** *adj.* **self-fulfil'ment** *n.* **self-gen'erating** *adj.* **self-giv'ing** *adj.* **self-glazed'** *adj* (of pottery, etc) glazed in one tint or colour. **self-glorificā'tion** *n.* **self-glō'rious** *adj* boastful. **self-gov'erning** *adj.* **self-gov'ernment** *n* self-control; autonomy; government without outside interference; democracy. **self-grā'cious** *adj* gracious towards oneself or spontaneously gracious. **self-harm'** *n* and *vi.* **self-har'ming** *adj.* **self-hate'** or **self-hāt'red** *n.* selfheal see separate entry. **self-heal'ing** *n* spontaneous healing; healing oneself (also *adj*). **self-help'** *n* doing things for oneself without assistance from others (also *adj*). **self-het'erodyne** *adj* (*electronics*) autodyne. **selfhood** *n* see under self. **self-humiliā'tion** *n.* **self-hypnō'sis** or **self'-hyp'notism** *n.* **self-iden'tity** *n* identity of a thing with itself; the conscious realization of the individual identity. **self-im'age** *n* an individual's view of his or her own personality and abilities. **self-immolā'tion** *n* offering oneself up in sacrifice; suttee. **self-import'ance** *n* an absurdly high sense of one's own importance; pomposity. **self-import'ant** *adj.* **self-import'antly** *adv.* **self-imposed'** *adj* taken voluntarily on oneself. **self-impregnā'tion** *n* impregnation of a hermaphrodite by its own sperm. **self-improve'ment** *n* improvement, by oneself, of one's status, education, job, etc. **self-incompat'ible** *adj* having reproductive organs that cannot function together. **self-incompatibil'ity** *n.* **self'-induced'** *adj* induced by oneself; produced by self-induction (*electronics*). **self-induc'tance** *n* the property of an electric circuit whereby self-induction occurs. **self-induc'tion** *n* the property of an electric circuit by which it resists any change in the current flowing in it. **self-induc'tive** *adj.* **self-indul'gence** *n* undue or unhealthy gratification of one's appetites or desires. **self'-indul'gent** *adj.* **self'-indul'gently** *adv.* **self-infec'tion** *n* infection of the entire organism from a local lesion. **self'-inflict'ed** *adj* inflicted by oneself on oneself. **self-inject'** *vi.* **self-injec'tion** *n.* **self-insū'rance** *n* the practice of laying aside funds from income, etc to cover losses, rather than taking out an insurance policy. **self-in'terest** *n* private interest; regard to oneself or one's own advantage. **self-in'terested** *adj.* **self-invī'ted** *adj* invited by nobody but oneself. **self-involved'** *adj* wrapped up in oneself or one's own thoughts; inwoven into itself. **self-judge'ment** *n.* **self-justificā'tion** *n.* **self-justificā'tory** *adj.* **self-jus'tifying** *adj* justifying oneself; automatically arranging the length of the lines of type (*printing*). **self-killed'** *adj.* **self-kill'er** *n.* **self-know'ing** *adj.* **self-knowl'edge** *n* knowledge of one's own nature or personality. **self-left'** *adj* left to oneself. **self-lev'elling** *adj* automatically adjusting so as to be level. **self'-life** *n* self-existence; life only for oneself. **self-light'ing** *adj* igniting automatically. **self'-like** *adj* exactly similar. **self-lim'ited** *adj* (*pathol*) running a definite course. **self-lim'iting** *adj.* **self-liq'uidating** *adj* (of a loan, business enterprise, etc) yielding sufficient increase to pay for its own redemption, initial outlay, etc. **self-load'er** *n.* **self-load'ing** *adj* (of a gun) automatically reloading itself. **self-lock'ing** *adj* locking automatically. **self-lost'** *adj* lost or damned through one's own fault. **self-love'** *n* the love of oneself; tendency to seek one's own welfare or advantage; desire of happiness. **self-lov'ing** *adj.* **self-lum'inous** *adj* emitting a light of its

own. **self-made'** *adj* made by oneself; risen from poverty or obscurity to a high position by one's own exertions. **self-man'agement** *n* self-control; the management of a factory, etc, by its own workers. **self-mas'tery** *n* self-command; self-control. **self-mett'le** *n* (*Shakesp*) natural spirit. **self-misused'** *adj* denigrated by oneself. **self-mock'ery** *n.* **self-mo'tion** *n* spontaneous motion. **self-mo'tivated** or **self-mo'tivating** *adj* naturally enterprising; motivated by inherent energy, enthusiasm, ambition, etc, without external impetus. **self-motivā'tion** *n.* **self-mo'ving** *adj* moving spontaneously from within. **self-mur'der** *n* suicide. **self-mur'derer** *n.* **self-mur'dering** *adj.* **self-mutilā'tion** *n.* **self-neglect'** *n.* **self-observā'tion** *n* (*psychol*) the observation of one's own behaviour, personality, mental processes, etc. **self-occ'upied** *adj.* **self-offence'** *n* (*rare*) an attack on, or injury to, oneself; one's own offence (*Shakesp*). **self-o'pening** *adj* opening of its own accord; opening automatically. **self'-op'erating** *adj.* **self-opin'ion** *n* high, or unduly high, opinion of oneself or of one's own opinion. **self-opin'ionated, self-opin'ionative** or **self-opin'ioned** *adj* obstinately adhering to one's own opinion. **self-ordained'** *adj.* **self-par'ody** *n* parody of oneself or one's own work. **self-perpet'uating** *adj.* **self-perpetuā'tion** *n.* **self-pī'ous** *adj* hypocritical. **self-pit'y** *n* pity for oneself. **self-pit'ying** *adj.* **self-pit'yingly** *adv.* **self-plant'ed** *adj* planted without human agency. **self-plea'sing** *adj.* **self-poised'** *adj* balanced without outside help. **self-poll'inated** *adj.* **self-pollinā'tion** *n* the transfer of pollen to the stigma of the same flower (or sometimes the same plant or clone). **self-pollu'tion** *n* (*archaic*) masturbation. **self-por'trait** *n* a portrait of oneself executed by oneself. **self-por'traiture** *n.* **self-possessed'** *adj* having self-possession. **self-possess'ion** *n* collectedness of mind; calmness. **self-pow'ered** *adj.* **self-praise'** *n* the praise of oneself by oneself. **self-preparā'tion** *n.* **self-prepared'** *adj.* **self-preservā'tion** *n* care, action, or instinct for the preservation of one's own life. **self-preser'vative** or **self-preser'ving** *adj.* **self-pride'** *n* self-esteem. **self-proclaimed'** *adj.* **self-produced'** *adj.* **self-professed'** *adj.* **self-prof'it** *n* private interest. **self-prop'agating** *adj* propagating itself when left to itself. **self-propagā'tion** *n.* **self-propelled'** *adj.* **self-propell'ing** *adj* carrying its own means of propulsion. **self-propul'sion** *n.* **self-protec'tion** *n* self-defence. **self-protect'ing** *adj.* **self-protec'tive** *adj.* **self-pru'ning** *adj* naturally shedding twigs. **self-pub'licist** *n* someone who actively creates or seeks publicity for himself or herself. **self-public'ity** *n.* **self-pun'ishment** *n.* **self-ques'tioning** *adj.* **self-raised'** *adj* raised by oneself; grown without cultivation. **self-rais'ing** *adj* (of flour) already mixed with a raising agent (also (*esp N Am*) **self-ris'ing**). **self-realizā'tion** or **-s-** *n* attainment of such development as one's mental and moral nature is capable of. **self-record'ing** *adj* recording its own readings. **self-rec'tifying** *adj* (*radiol*) (of an X-ray tube) in which an alternating voltage is applied directly between target and cathode. **self-referen'tial** *adj* relating or belonging to the self; (of an artistic work) making references to the artist's own life or work. **self-referential'ity** *n.* **self-referen'tially** *adv.* **self-referr'ing** *adj* self-referential. **self-regard'** *n* self-interest; self-respect, *esp* exaggerated. **self-regard'ing** *adj.* **self-reg'istering** *adj* self-recording. **self-reg'ulating** *adj* regulating itself. **self-regulā'tion** *n.* **self-regulāt'ory** (or /-*reg'*/) *adj.* **self-relī'ance** *n* reliance on one's own abilities, resources, etc. **self-relī'ant** *adj.* **self-relī'antly** *adv.* **self-rely'ing** *adj.* **self-renunciā'tion** *n* self-abnegation. **self-repeat'ing** *adj.* **self-repose'** *n.* **self-repress'ion** *n* repression of one's own desires or of expression of one's personality. **self-reproach'** *n* blaming oneself or finding fault with one's own actions. **self-reproach'ful** *adj.* **self-reproof'** or **self-reprov'ing** *n* reproof of conscience. **self-repug'nance** *n.* **self-repug'nant** *adj* self-contradictory; inconsistent. **self'-resem'blance** *n* (*Spenser*) appearance of being what one really is. **self-respect'** *n* proper respect for oneself or one's own character. **self-respect'ful** *adj.* **self-respect'ing** *adj.* **self-restrained'** *adj* restrained by one's own will. **self-restraint'** *n* a refraining from excess; self-control. **self-reveal'ing** *adj.* **self-revelā'tion** *n.* **self-rev'elatory** *adj.* **self-rev'erence** *n* great self-respect. **self-rev'erent** *adj.* **self-right'eous** *adj* having a high opinion of one's own virtue; pharisaical. **self-right'eously** *adv.* **self-right'eousness** *n.* **self-right'ing** *adj* (*esp* of a boat, etc) righting itself when capsized. **self-rig'orous** *adj* rigorous towards oneself. **self-ris'ing** *adj* see **self-raising** above. **self-rolled'** (*Milton* **self-rowld'**) *adj* coiled on itself. **self-rule'** *n.* **self-rul'ing** *adj.* **self-sac'rifice** *n* foregoing one's own needs, etc for the sake of others. **self-sac'rificing** *adj.* **self'same** *n* and *adj* the very same. **self-same'ness** *n.* **self-satisfac'tion** *n.* **self-sat'isfied** *adj* satisfied with oneself, one's efforts, etc; inordinately proud of oneself, smug; unwisely resting on one's laurels. **self-sat'isfying** *adj* giving satisfaction to oneself. **self-schooled'** *adj.* **self-seal'ing** *adj* (of envelopes, etc) that can be sealed by pressing two adhesive surfaces together; (of tyres) that seal automatically when punctured. **self-seed'er** *n* a plant that propagates itself from its own seeds shed around it. **self-seek'er** *n* someone who looks mainly to his or her own interests or advantage; a device which automatically tunes a radio to required wavelengths by means of a push-button control. **self-**

■ words derived from main entry word; ❑ compound words; ■ idioms and phrasal verbs

seek'ing *n* and *adj*. **self-ser'vice** *n* helping oneself, as in a restaurant, petrol station, etc (also *adj*). **self-ser'ving** *adj* taking care of one's own interests before and *usu* to the prejudice of those of other people (also *n*). **self-severe'** *adj* (*Milton*). **self-shield'ing** *n* (*phys*) a radiation emitting material or structure which absorbs part of its own emission. **self-slain'** *adj*. **self-slaugh'ter** *n*. **self-slaugh'tered** *adj*. **self-slay'er** *n*. **self-sov'ereignty** *n* sovereignty over, or inherent in, oneself. **self-sow'** *vi* (of *esp* cultivated plants) to disperse and sow seeds naturally without human agency. **self-sown'** *adj*. **self-stan'ding** *adj* independent, standing or functioning alone, without support. **self-star'ter** *n* an automatic device for starting a motor; a car or other vehicle fitted with one; a person with initiative and drive. **self-ster'ile** *adj* unable to fertilize itself. **self-steril'ity** *n*. **self-stud'y** *n* study on one's own, without a teacher. **self-styled'** *adj* called by oneself; pretended. **self-subdued'** *adj* (*Shakesp*) subdued by one's own power. **self-substan'tial** *adj* (*Shakesp*) composed of one's own substance. **self-suffi'ciency** *n*. **self-suffi'cient** *adj* requiring nothing to be brought from outside; requiring no emotional, etc support from others. **self-suffi'ciently** *adv*. **self-suffic'ing** *adj*. **self-sugges'tion** *n* auto-suggestion. **self-support'** *n*. **self-support'ed** *adj*. **self-support'ing** *adj* able to support or maintain oneself without outside help; of independent means, paying one's way; (of plants, structures, etc) able to stand up without support(s). **self'-surren'der** *n* a yielding up of oneself or one's will. **self-survi'ving** *adj* surviving as a mere ruin of itself. **self-sustained'** *adj* sustained by one's own power. **self-sustain'ing** *adj*. **self-sustain'ment** *n*. **self-sus'tenance** and **self-sustenta'tion** *n*. **self-synch'ronizing** or **-s-** *adj* (*elec eng*) (of a synchronizing machine) that may be switched to alternating current without being in exact synchronism with it. **self-tan'** *vi* to apply a lotion to one's skin to artificially produce the appearance of a suntan. **self-tann'ing** *n* and *adj*. **self-tapp'ing** *adj* (of a screw) made of hard metal with a thread that either deforms a softer metal as it is driven in or grips thin sheets of metal within the thread. **self-taught'** *adj*. **self-temp'ted** *adj*. **self-think'ing** *adj* thinking for oneself. **self-tor'ment** *n*. **self-torment'ing** *adj*. **self-torment'or** *n*. **self'-tor'ture** *n*. **self-trained'** *adj*. **self-transforma'tion** *n*. **self-treat'ment** *n*. **self-trust'** *n* self-reliance; confidence in one's own faithfulness to oneself (*Shakesp*). **self-una'ble** *adj* (*Shakesp*) insufficient in oneself. **self-understand'ing** *n*. **self-vindica'tion** *n*. **self-vī'olence** *n* suicide. **self-will'** *n* obstinacy. **self-willed'** *adj*. **self-wind'ing** *adj* (of a watch) wound by the wearer's spontaneous movements, or by opening and shutting the case; automatically wound by electricity. **self-wor'ship** *n*. **self'-worth** *n* (one's idea of) one's own worth, usefulness, etc; self-esteem. **self-wrong'** *n* (*Shakesp*) injury done to one by oneself.

-self /-*self*/ *combining form* (*pl* **-selves** /-*selvz*/) used to form reflexive and emphatic pronouns.
■ **be oneself**, **himself**, **herself**, etc to be in full possession of one's powers; to be (once more) at one's best or as normal; to be alone (*Scot*). **by oneself**, etc alone.

selfheal /*self'hēl*/ *n* a spreading labiate European plant, *Prunella vulgaris*, with bright purple, pink or white flowers, once widely believed to be a healer of wounds and infections. [**self** and **heal**[1]]

selictar /*se-lik'tär*/ *n* a sword-bearer. [Turk *silihdār*, from Pers *silahdār*, from Ar *silh* weapon]

Seljuk /*sel-jook'*/ *n* a member of any of the Turkish dynasties (11c–13c) descended from *Seljūq* (grandfather of Togrul Beg); a Turk subject to the Seljuks.
■ **Seljuk'** or **Seljuk'ian** *adj*.

selkie see **silkie**.

sell[1] /*sel*/ *vt* (*pat* and *pap* **sold**) to give or give up for money or other equivalent; to betray; to impose upon, trick; to promote the sale of; to make acceptable; to cause someone to accept (eg an idea, plan); to convince (someone) of the value of something; to praise, to cry up (*obs*). ◆ *vi* to make sales; to be sold, to be in demand for sale. ◆ *n* (*inf*) a deception; a disappointment; an act of selling; a particular quality emphasized in order to sell; stocks to be sold; an order to sell stocks. [OE *sellan* to give, hand over; ON *selja*, Gothic *saljan*]
■ **sell'able** *adj* that can be sold. **sell'er** *n* a person who sells; that which finds a sale; a selling race or plate (*inf*).
❑ **sell-by date** *n* a date, indicated on a manufacturer's or distributor's label, after which goods, *esp* foods, are considered no longer fit to be sold (also *fig*). **sellers'** or **seller's market** *n* one in which sellers control the price, demand exceeding supply. **sell'ing-pla'ter** *n* a horse fit only to race in a selling race (also *fig*). **sell'ing-price** *n* the price at which a thing is sold. **selling race** or **plate** *n* a race the winning horse of which must be put up for auction at a price previously fixed (*cf* **claiming race**). **sell'-out** *n* a betrayal; a show, performance, etc for which all seats are sold.
■ **sell down the river** to play false, betray. **sell in** to sell (a product) to a retailer; (of a product) to be sold to a retailer (**sell'-in** *n*). **sell off** to sell cheaply in order to dispose of (**sell'-off** *n*). **sell on** to sell (what

one has bought) to someone else. **sell one's life dearly** to do great injury to the enemy before one is killed. **sell out** to dispose entirely of; to sell one's commission; to betray (one's principles). **sell short** to belittle, disparage; to sell (stocks, etc) before one actually owns them, when intending to buy at a lower price. **sell someone a bargain** see under **bargain**. **sell the pass** to betray a trust. **sell through** to sell (a product) to the end-user, as opposed to a retailer; (of a product) to be sold to the end-user (**sell'-through** *n*). **sell up** to sell the goods of, for debt; to sell all. **to sell** for sale.

sell[2] or **selle** /*sel*/ *n* a seat (*archaic*); a saddle (*obs*). [OFr *selle*, from L *sella*, from *sedēre* to sit]

sell[3] /*sel*/ *n* (*pl* **sells**) a Scots form of **self**.

sella /*sel'ə*/ (*anat*) *n* (also **sella turcica** /*tûr'ki-kə*/) a saddle-shaped area in the sphenoid bone enclosing the pituitary gland. [L, a seat, saddle]

selle see **sell**[2].

Sellotape® /*sel'ə-tāp*/ (also without *cap*) *n* (a brand of) *usu* transparent adhesive tape. ◆ *vt* to stick with Sellotape.

seltzer /*selt'sər*/ *n* a mineral water from Nieder-*Selters* near Wiesbaden in Germany, or an imitation of it.
■ **selt'zogene** /-*sə-jēn*/ *n* a gazogene.

selva /*sel'və*/ *n* (*usu* in *pl* **sel'vas**) a rainforest in the Amazon basin. [Sp, Port, from L *silva* wood]

selvage or **selvedge** /*sel'vij*/ *n* a differently finished edging of cloth, *esp* one woven so as not to fray. ◆ *vt* to border. [**self** and **edge**]
■ **sel'vaged** *adj*. **sel'vagee** (or /-*jē'* /) *n* a marked hank of rope, used as a strap or sling.

selves /*selvz*/ plural of **self**.

SEM *abbrev*: scanning electron microscope.

Sem. *abbrev*: Seminary; Semitic.

sem. *abbrev*: semester; semicolon.

semantic /*si-man'tik*/ *adj* relating to meaning, *esp* of words; relating to semantics. [Gr *sēmantikos* significant]
■ **seman'teme** *n* a unit of meaning, a word or the base of a word, that conveys a definite idea. **seman'tically** *adv*. **seman'ticist** *n*. **seman'tics** *n sing* the area of linguistics dealing with the meaning of words; the meaning attached to words or symbols (*comput*). ◆ *n pl* (loosely) differences in, and shades of, meaning of words. **sememe** /*se'mēm* or *sē'mēm*/ *n* a unit of meaning, *usu specif* the smallest linguistically analysable unit.
❑ **semantic error** *n* (*comput*) an error which results in an ambiguous or erroneous meaning in a program. **semantic memory** *n* a computer memory that recalls vast blocks of information corresponding to whole areas of human knowledge, eg language or mathematics, rather than specific items of data. **semantic web** *n* a development of the World Wide Web by means of which computer programs are enabled to understand human semantic input without further instructions.

semantide /*si-man'tīd*/ (*biol*) *n* a molecule carrying information, eg in a gene or messenger RNA.

semantron /*si-man'tron*/ *n* (*pl* **seman'tra**) a wooden or metal bar that is struck with a mallet, used instead of a bell in Orthodox churches and in mosques. [Gr *sēmantron* sign, signal]

semaphore /*sem'ə-för* or *-för*/ *n* an upright signalling apparatus with arms that can be turned up or down, often replaced by the signaller's own body and arms with flags; this system of signalling. ◆ *vt* and *vi* to signal in this way. [Fr *sémaphore*, from Gr *sēma* sign, signal, and *-phoros* bearing, bearer]
■ **semaphor'ic** *adj*. **semaphor'ically** *adv*.

semasiology /*si-mā-zi-ol'ə-ji* or *-si-*/ *n* the science of semantics. [Gr *sēmasia* meaning]
■ **semasiolog'ical** *adj*. **semasiolog'ically** *adv*. **semasio'logist** *n*.

sematic /*si-mat'ik*/ (*biol*) *adj* (of an animal's colouring) serving for recognition, attraction, or warning. [Gr *sēma* sign]

semble[1] /*sem'bl*/ *vi* (*obs*) to seem; to be like (with *to*). ◆ *vt* (*obs*) to pretend; to make a picture or image of. [Fr *sembler* to seem, to resemble, from L *simulāre*, from *similis* like]
■ **sem'blable** *adj* (*obs*) resembling, similar, like. ◆ *n* (*obs*) one's like, fellow, equal; something similar. **sem'blably** *adv* in like manner. **sem'blance** *n* a likeness or copy; outward appearance; an apparition; an image. **sem'blant** *adj* (*archaic*) resembling; seeming. ◆ *n* (*obs*) a semblance; cheer, countenance, entertainment; demeanour. **sem'blative** *adj* (*obs*) resembling or seeming; simulative.

semble[2] /*sem'bl*/ *vt* to bring together, collect, *esp* as some female moths do males by scent. [Aphetic from **assemble**]
❑ **sembling box** *n* (*zool*) a collector's box enclosing a captive female.

semé or **semée** /*sem'ā, sem'i*/ (*heraldry*) *adj* strewn or scattered over with small bearings, powdered (also **sem'éed**). [Fr, *pap* of *semer*, from L *sēmināre* to sow]

semeio- see **semio-**.

semeion /se-mī'on/ n (pl **semei'a**) (in ancient prosody) the unit of time; one of the two divisions of a foot; a mark of metrical or other division. [Gr *sēmeion* sign]

semeiotic and **semeiotics** see **semiotics**.

semelparous /sem-əl-par'əs/ (*zool*) adj (of an animal) capable of producing offspring only once in the course of a lifetime. [L *semel* once, and *parēre* to bring forth]
- **semelpar'ity** n.

sememe see under **semantic**.

semen /sē'mən or -men/ n the liquid that carries spermatozoa (see also **seminal**). [L *sēmen*, *-inis* seed]

semester /si-mes'tər/ n an academic half-year course or term. [L *sēmēstris*, from *sex* six, and *mēnsis* a month]
- **semesterizā'tion** or **-s-** n the organization of the academic year into two terms, rather than three. **semes'tral** or **semes'trial** adj half-yearly.

semi /sem'i or (N Am) -ī/ (*inf*) n a semi-detached house; a semifinal; a semi-trailer or semi-truck (N Am); a semi-bajan (also **sem'ie**); a semi-finished (qv) article of steel, copper, etc. [semi-]

semi- /sem-i- or (N Am) -ī-/ pfx denoting: half; (loosely) nearly, partly, incompletely; occurring twice in a stated period, as in *semi-annual*. [L *sēmi-* half-; cf Gr *hēmi-*, OE *sam-*]
- **sem'iangle** n a half-angle. **semi-ann'ual** adj (chiefly N Am) half-yearly. **semi-ann'ually** adv. **semi-ann'ular** adj half-ring shaped. **semi-aqua'tic** adj (*esp* of plants) living near or in water. **semi-Ā'rian** n and adj homoiousian. **semi-Ā'rianism** n. **semi-a'rid** adj. **semi-attached'** adj partially bound. **semi-automat'ic** adj partly automatic; (of a firearm) continuously reloading itself, but only firing one bullet at a time. ◆ n a semi-automatic firearm. **semi-automat'ically** adv. **sem'i-axis** n a half-axis. **semi-bā'jan** n (*old*) a second-year student at a Scottish university. **semi-barbā'rian** n and adj. **semi-bar'barism** n. **semibold'** n (*printing*) a typeface between medium and bold; matter printed in this. ◆ adj (of type) printed in semibold. **sem'ibrēve** n (*music*) half a breve (2 minims or 4 crotchets). **sem'ibull** n a pope's bull issued between election and coronation. **semicar'bazide** n a base (H₂NCONHNH₂) reacting with aldehydes and ketones to form **semicar'bazones**. **semi-centenn'ial** adj occurring at the completion of fifty years. ◆ n (US) a jubilee. **semichōr'us** n half, or part of, a chorus; a passage sung by it. **sem'icircle** n half a circle, bounded by the diameter and half the circumference. **sem'icircled** adj. **semicir'cular** adj (**semicircular canals** three curved tubes of the inner ear concerned with balance or equilibrium, with each canal registering movement on a different plane). **semicir'cularly** adv. **sem'icirque** n (*poetic*) a semicircular hollow; a semicircle. **sem'icolon** (or /-kō'lon/) n the punctuation mark (;) marking a division greater than the comma. **semicō'ma** n an unconscious state approaching coma. **semico'matose** adj. **semiconduct'ing** adj. **semiconductiv'ity** n. **sem'iconductor** n an element or compound having a resistivity between that of a conductor and an insulator, being either *intrinsic*, where thermal energy causes charges to cross the forbidden energy gap, or *extrinsic*, where small amounts of donor and acceptor impurities have been added to facilitate the transition. **semicon'scious** adj. **semicrys'talline** or **semicrystall'ic** adj having, or being, a partly crystalline structure. **sem'icyl'inder** n a longitudinal half-cylinder. **semicylin'drical** adj. **sem'idem'isem'iquaver** n (*music*) half a demisemiquaver. **semidepō'nent** adj (*grammar*) passive in form in the perfect tenses only. ◆ n a semideponent verb. **semi-detached'** adj partly separated; joined by a party wall to one other house only; associated with, but not wholeheartedly committed to, a particular group, political doctrine, etc. ◆ n a semi-detached house. **semi-diam'eter** n half the diameter, *esp* the angular diameter. **sem'i-dī'tone** n (*music*) a minor third. **semi-diur'nal** adj accomplished in twelve hours; relating to half the time or half the arc traversed between rising and setting. **semi-divine'** adj half-divine; of, or of the nature of, a demigod. **semidocument'ary** n a cinema film based on real events but with an invented plot and dialogue (also adj). **semi-dome'** n half a dome, *esp* as formed by a vertical section. **semidomes'ticated** adj partially domesticated; half-tame. **semi-doub'le** adj (of flowers) having only the outermost stamens converted into petals. ◆ n such a flower; a religious festival less solemn than a double (qv; *relig*). **semi-dry'ing** adj (of oils) thickening without completely drying on exposure. **semi-ellipse'** n half of an ellipse, bounded by a diameter, *esp* the major axis. **semi-ellip'tical** adj. **semi-ev'ergreen** n a plant which is evergreen in its original habitat but not completely so in other places it now grows, dropping leaves in severe weather conditions (also adj). **semifī'nal** adj (in competitions, sports contests, etc) denoting the contest immediately before the final. ◆ n a last round but one. **semifī'nalist** n a competitor in a semifinal. **semi-fin'ished** adj partially finished, *specif* of metal shaped into rods, sheets, etc, in preparation for further processing into finished goods. **semiflu'id** adj nearly solid but able to flow to some extent (also n /sem'/). **semifredd'o** n (pl **semifredd'os** or **semifredd'i**) (Ital *freddo* cold) a partially frozen Italian dessert. **semiglob'ular** adj. **semi-grand'** n a square piano with a curtailed keyboard (also adj). **semi-im'becile** n and adj. **semi-independ'ent** adj not fully independent. **semi-ju'bilee** n the twenty-fifth anniversary. **sem'i-latus rectum** n (*geom*) half the latus rectum, terminated at the focus. **semi-liq'uid** adj half-liquid. **semilit'eracy** n. **semilit'erate** n and adj (a person) barely able to read and write. **sem'i-log** or **semi-logarith'mic** adj (of graph paper, graphs, etc) having an arithmetical scale on the x-axis and a logarithmic scale on the y-axis (also called **single-log** or **-logarithmic**; cf **log-log** under **log²**). **semilu'cent** adj half-transparent. **semilu'nar** or **semilu'nate** adj half-moon-shaped (as the **semilunar valves** of the aorta and pulmonary artery which prevent regurgitation of blood into the heart). **sem'ilune** /-loon/ n a half-moon-shaped object, body, or structure. **semimanufac'ture** n a manufactured product, material, etc, used to make an end-product. **semimen'strual** adj half-monthly. **semi-met'al** n (*obs*) a metal that is not malleable. **semi-month'ly** adj (chiefly N Am) half-monthly. ◆ n a half-monthly periodical. **semi-mute'** n and adj (a person) having impaired speech due to loss of hearing (considered *offensive* by some people). **semi-nūde'** adj half-naked. **semi-occā'sional** adj (N Am) occurring now and then. **semi-occā'sionally** adv. **semi-offic'ial** adj partly official. **semi-offic'ially** adv. **semi-ō'pal** n a dull variety of opal. **semi-opaque'** adj partly opaque. **semiovip'arous** adj (*zool*) giving birth to partially developed young. **semipal'mate** /-mət, -māt/ or **semipalmā'ted** adj half-webbed; partly webfooted. **semipalmā'tion** n. **semipar'asite** n a partial parasite, feeding partly independently. **semiparasit'ic** adj. **sem'iped** n (*prosody*) a half-foot. **Semi-Pelā'gian** n and adj. **Semi-Pelā'gianism** n the middle course between Augustinian predestination and Pelagian free will. **semipellu'cid** adj imperfectly transparent. **semiperim'eter** n half the perimeter. **semi-perm'anent** adj. **semipermeabil'ity** n. **semiper'meable** adj permeable by a solvent but not by the dissolved substance. **sem'iplume** n a feather with an ordinary shaft but a downy web. **semipor'celain** n a coarse ware resembling porcelain. **semipost'al** adj (chiefly US; *philately*) denoting an issue of postage stamps the profits of which are donated to charity. **semi-prec'ious** adj (*mineralogy*) valuable, but not valuable enough to be considered a gemstone. **semi-pro'** adj and n (pl **semi-pros'**) semi-professional. **semi-profess'ional** adj (of a person) engaging only part-time in a professional activity, *esp* a sport; (of an activity) engaged in by semi-professionals. ◆ n a semi-professional person. **sem'iquāver** n half a quaver. **semi-rig'id** adj (of an airship) having a flexible gasbag and a stiffened keel. **sem'i-ring** n a half-ring. **semi-sag'ittate** adj shaped like half an arrowhead. **Semi-Sax'on** n and adj (*obs*) Early Middle English (c.1150–1250). **semi-skilled'** adj. **sem'i-skimmed** adj (of milk) having some of the cream skimmed. ◆ n semi-skimmed milk. **semi-soft'** adj (of cheese) fairly soft. **semisol'id** adj and n (a substance) of a consistency between liquid and solid. **semisubmers'ible** adj and n (denoting) a floating oilrig (used mainly for exploratory drilling) which has the greater part of its structure below the water. **semiterete'** adj half-cylindrical. **sem'itone** n half a tone, one of the lesser intervals of the musical scale, as from B to C. **semiton'ic** adj. **semi-trail'er** or **semi-truck'** n (N Am) an articulated trailer or lorry. **semitranspa'rency** n. **semitranspa'rent** adj imperfectly transparent. **semi-trop'ical** adj subtropical. **semi-trop'ics** n pl. **semi-tū'bular** adj like half of a tube divided longitudinally. **semi-un'cial** adj (of writing) intermediate between uncial and minuscule. ◆ n a semi-uncial letter. **sem'ivowel** n a sound having the nature of both a vowel and a consonant; a letter representing it, in English, chiefly w and y, and sometimes used of the liquid consonants l and r. **semiwater gas** n see under **water**. **semi-week'ly** adj issued or happening twice a week (also n and adv).

Sémillon /sā-mē-yõ'/ n a grape variety grown worldwide, used to produce various wines, *incl* Sauternes. [Fr, from L *sēmen*, *-inis* seed]

seminal /sem'i-n(ə)l/ adj relating to, or of the nature of, seed or semen; of or relating to the beginnings, first development, of an idea, study, etc, rudimentary; generative; notably creative or influential in future development. [L *sēmen*, *-inis* seed]
- **seminal'ity** n germinating principle; germ. **sem'inally** adv. **sem'ināte** vt to sow; to propagate. **seminā'tion** n sowing; seed-dispersal; seeding. **seminif'erous** adj seed-bearing; producing or conveying semen.
- **seminal fluid** n semen.

seminar /sem'i-när/ n a group of advanced students working in a specific subject of study under a teacher; a class at which a group of students and a tutor discuss a particular topic; a discussion group on any particular subject. [L *sēminārium* a seed plot, from *sēmen* seed]
- **seminarial** /-ā'ri-əl/ adj of a seminary. **seminā'rian** or **sem'inarist** /-ə-rist/ n a student in a seminary or in a seminar; a Roman Catholic priest educated in a foreign seminary; a teacher in a seminary. **sem'inary** /-ə-ri/ n a breeding-place; a place of origin and fostering, a nursery; formerly, a pretentious name for a school (*esp* for young ladies); now, *usu* a theological college providing training and

instruction to ministers, priests, rabbis, etc; a seminary-educated priest (*obs*). ◆ *adj* seminal; of, relating to or educated in a seminary.

Seminole /sem'i-nōl/ *n* a Native American of a group that is a branch of the Creek people, *orig* in Florida, now mostly in Oklahoma; the language of this people. [Creek *Simánole*, literally, runaway]

semio- or **semeio-**, /sē-mi-ə-, sem-i-ə-, -o-/ *combining form* denoting sign. [Gr *sēmeion* sign]
■ **semiochem'ical** *n* a chemical produced by an animal, eg in a scent gland, and used as a means of signalling its presence, readiness to mate, etc. **semiolog'ical** *adj*. **semiol'ogist** *n*. **semiol'ogy** *n* the science or study of signs or signals, *esp* of spoken or written words as signs and their relationships with the objects, concepts, etc they refer to (*linguistics*); the scientific study of signs and symptoms (*pathol*). See also **semiotics**.

semiotics or **semeiotics** /sē-mi-ot'iks or sem-i-/ *n sing* the study of signs and symptoms, symptomatology or semiology (*pathol*); the study of signs, signals and symbols, *esp* in language and communication, semiology. [Gr *sēmeiōtikos*, from *sēmeion* a sign]
■ **semiot'ic** or **semeiot'ic** *adj*. **semiot'ically** or **semeiot'ically** *adv*. **semioti'cian** or **semeioti'cian** *n*.

semis /sē'mis or sā'mis/ *n* a bronze coin of the ancient Roman republic, half an as. [L *sēmis, sēmissis*]

semitar, semitaur obsolete spellings of **scimitar**.

Semite /sem'īt or sē'mīt/ *n* a member of any of the peoples said (in the Bible, Genesis 10) to be descended from Shem, or speaking a Semitic language. [Gr *Sēm* Shem]
■ **Semitic** /si-mit'ik/ *adj* of or relating to Semites or any of their languages. ◆ *n* any Semitic language. **Semit'ics** *n sing* the study of Semitic languages, etc. **Sem'itism** *n* a Semitic idiom or characteristic; Semitic ways of thought; the cause of the Semites, *esp* the Jews. **Sem'itist** *n* a Semitic scholar. **Semitizā'tion** or **-s-** *n*. **Sem'itize** or **-ise** *vt* to render Semitic in language, religion, or otherwise.
□ **Semitic languages** *n pl* Assyrian, Aramaic, Hebrew, Phoenician, Arabic, Ethiopic, and other ancient languages of this Afro-Asiatic subfamily.

semmit /sem'it/ (*Scot*) *n* a vest or undershirt.

Semnopithecus /sem-nō-pith'-ə-kəs/ *n* the genus of monkeys to which the entellus monkey belongs. [Gr *semnos* honoured, and *pithēkos* an ape]

semolina /sem-ə-lē'nə or -lī'nə/ *n* the particles of fine, hard wheat that do not pass into flour in milling, used to make puddings, thicken soups, etc. [Ital *semolino*, dimin of *semola* bran, from L *simila* fine flour]

semper /sem'pər or -per/ (*L*) *adv* always.
■ **semper fidēl'is** always faithful. **semper idem** /i'dem, id'em or ē'dem/ or (*fem*) **semper eadem** /ē'ə- or e'a-/ always the same. **semper paratus** /pə-rä'təs or pa-rä'tŭs/ always ready.

sempervivum /sem-pər-vī'vəm/ *n* any succulent plant of the family Crassulaceae, *incl* the house leek and various ornamental plants. [New L, from L *sempervīvus* ever-living]

sempiternal /sem-pi-tûr'n(ə)l/ (chiefly *poetic*) *adj* everlasting. [L *sempiternus*, from *semper* always, ever]
■ **sempiter'nally** *adv*. **sempiter'nity** *n*. **sempiter'num** *n* (*obs*) a durable woollen cloth.

semple /sem'pl/ *adj* a Scottish form of **simple**, *esp* meaning not of gentle birth.

semplice /sem'plē-che/ (*music*) *adj* and *adv* simple or simply, without embellishments. [Ital]

sempre /sem'pre/ (*music*) *adv* always, in the same manner throughout. [Ital, from L *semper* always]

sempster /sem'stər/ *n* a variant of **seamster**.
■ **semp'stering, semp'stressing** and **semp'stress-ship** *n* sewing. **semp'stress** *n* a seamstress.

semsem /sem'sem/ *n* sesame. [Ar *simsim*]

Semtex® /sem'teks/ *n* a very powerful kind of plastic explosive.

semuncia /si-mun'sh(y)ə/ *n* a Roman half-ounce; a bronze coin, an as in its ultimate value. [L *sēmuncia*, from *sēmi-* half, and *uncia* a twelfth]
■ **semun'cial** *adj*.

SEN *abbrev*: Special Educational Needs; State Enrolled Nurse.

Sen. *abbrev*: senate; senator; senior.

sen¹ /sen/ *n* (*pl* **sen**) a monetary unit of Japan, $\frac{1}{100}$ of a yen; a coin of this value. [Chin *qián* money]

sen² /sen/ *n* a SE Asian monetary unit, $\frac{1}{100}$ of a rupiah, a ringgit, or a riel; a coin of this value. [**cent**]

sen. (*music*) *abbrev*: *senza* (*Ital*), without.

sena /sā'nä/ *n* in India, an army, *esp* used of paramilitary political organizations representing various castes. [Hindi]

senary /sē'nər-i or sen'ər-i/ *adj* of, involving or based on, six. ◆ *n* a set of six; a senarius. [L *sēnārius*, from *sēnī* six each, from *sex* six]
■ **senarius** /si-nā'ri-əs/ *n* (*pl* **sena'rii** /-ri-ī/) a verse of six iambs or equivalents.

senate /sen'it/ *n* the governing body of ancient Rome; a legislative or deliberative body, *esp* the upper house of a national or state legislature; a body of venerable or distinguished people; the governing body of certain British universities (in older Scottish universities, **Senā'tus Academ'icus**). [L *senātus* council of elders, from *senex, senis* an old man]
■ **senator** /sen'ə-tər/ *n* a member of a senate. **senatorial** /sen-ə-tō'ri-əl or -tō'ri-əl/ *adj*. **senato'rially** *adv* with senatorial dignity. **sen'atorship** *n*.
□ **sen'ate-house** *n* the meeting-place of a senate. **Senator of the College of Justice** *n* a Lord of Session (see under **lord**). **senā'tus con'sult** or **senā'tus consultum** /kən-sul'təm/ *n* a decree of the senate, *esp* in ancient Rome.

senatus populusque Romanus /sə-nā'təs pop'ū-ləs-kwē rō-mā'nəs or se-nä'tŭs pop-ŭ-lŭs'kwe rō-mä'nŭs/ (*L*) the Roman senate and people (*abbrev* **SPQR**).

send /send/ *vt* (*pat* and *pap* **sent**; *naut* **send'ed**) to cause, direct, or tell to go; to propel; to cause to be conveyed; to dispatch; to forward; to grant; to cause to pass into a specified state; (*orig* of jazz) to rouse (someone) to ecstasy. ◆ *vi* to dispatch a message or messenger (often with *for*); to pitch into the trough of the sea (sometimes **scend** or **'scend**, as if aphetic from *ascend* or *descend*; *naut*). ◆ *n* a messenger (*Scot*); one or more escorts sent ahead of a bridegroom to fetch the bride (*Scot*); an impetus or impulse; the sound or a movement of breaking waves, a swash. [OE *sendan*; ON *senda*, Gothic *sandjan*, Ger *senden*]
■ **send'able** *adj*. **send'er** *n* a person who sends; a transmitting instrument. **send'ing** *n* dispatching; pitching; transmission; that which is sent.
□ **send'-off** *n* a gathering to express good wishes at departing or starting a journey. **send'-up** *n* a process of making fun of someone or something; a play, film, novel, etc, doing this.
■ **send away** (or **off**) **for** to order (something) by post. **send down** to send to prison (*inf*); to expel from university. **send for** to require, direct or request by message (someone or something) to come or be brought. **send in** to submit (an entry) for a competition, etc. **send off** (in football, etc) to order (a player) to leave the field and take no further part in the game, *usu* after an infringement of the rules; to dispatch (something). **send on** to send in advance; to readdress and repost (a letter or package). **send out** to distribute or dispatch (something). **send round** to circulate. **send up** to make fun of; to sentence to imprisonment (*inf*). **send word** to send an intimation.

sendal /sen'dəl/ *n* a thin silk or linen; a garment made of this. [OFr *cendal*, prob from Gr *sindōn*; see **sindon**]

sene /sen'e or sā'nä/ *n* (*pl* **sen'e** or **sen'es**) a Samoan monetary unit, $\frac{1}{100}$ of a tala. [Samoan]

Seneca /sen'i-kə/ *n* an Iroquois Native American of a tribe in New York state; their language. [From Du *Sennecaas* (pl), collective name for this and related tribes]
■ **Sen'ecan** *adj*.
□ **Seneca oil** *n* crude petroleum, used by this people for medicinal purposes.

Senecan /sen'i-kən/ *adj* of or in the manner of Lucius Annaeus *Seneca*, Stoic philosopher and writer of declamatory tragedies (c.4BC–65AD).

senecio /se-nē'shi-ō or -si-ō/ *n* (*pl* **senē'cios**) any composite plant of the genus *Senecio*, distributed throughout most parts of the world, *incl* groundsel and ragwort and many cultivated varieties (cf **cineraria¹**). [L *senex* an old man, from the hoary pappus]

Senedd /sen'edh/ (*Welsh*) *n* the National Assembly for Wales. [Literally, senate]

senega /sen'i-gə/ *n* an American milkwort, *Polygala senega*; its dried root used as an expectorant and reputed by the *Seneca* Native Americans to be an antidote for snake-bites (also **senega snakeroot**).

Senegalese /se-ni-gə-lēz'/ *adj* of or relating to the Republic of *Senegal* in W Africa, or its people. ◆ *n* a native or citizen of Senegal.

senescent /si-nes'ənt/ *adj* verging on or characteristic of old age; ageing. [L *senēscēns, -entis, prp* of *senēscere* to grow old, from *senex* old]
■ **senesc'ence** *n* the process of growing old, *esp* (*biol*) the physical changes such as slowing down of metabolism and breakdown of tissues that are characteristic of this process.

seneschal /sen'i-shl/ (*hist*) *n* a steward; an administrative and judicial title still retained for certain cathedral officials and a judicial position on Sark (Channel Islands). [OFr (Fr *sénéchal*), of Gmc origin, literally old servant; cf Gothic *sineigs* old, *skalks*, OE *scealc* servant]
■ **sen'eschalship** *n*.

sengreen /sen'grēn/ n the house leek. [OE singrēne evergreen, house leek, periwinkle, from pfx sin- one, always (cf L semel once), grēne green; cf Ger Sin(n)grüne periwinkle]

Senhor /se-nyōr'/ or -nyör'/, fem **Senhora** /se-nyō'rə or -nyö'rə/ and **Senhorita** /-nyə-rē'tə/ n (also without caps) the Portuguese forms corresponding to the Spanish **Señor**, **Señora** and **Señorita** (see under **Señor**).

senile /sē'nīl/ or (esp N Am) sen'īl/ adj characteristic of or accompanying old age; showing the decay of mind or body brought on by old age. [L senīlis, from senex, senis old]
■ **sēn'ilely** adv. **senility** /si-nil'i-ti/ n old age; the mental infirmity of old age; a state of deterioration or decay.
❑ **senile dementia** see **dementia** under **dement**.

senior /sē'nyər or sē'ni-ər/ adj elder; older or higher in standing; more advanced; first. ◆ n a person who is senior; a pupil in the senior part of a school; a fourth-year student at college (US). [L senior, -ōris, compar of senex old]
■ **seniority** /sē-ni-or'i-ti/ n the state or fact of being senior; priority by age, time of service, or standing; a body of seniors or senior fellows.
❑ **senior citizen** n an old-age pensioner. **senior common room** or (Cambridge University) **senior combination room** n in some universities, a common room for the use of staff (cf **junior common room**, **middle common room**; abbrev **SCR**). **senior moment** n (inf) a momentary lapse in memory, esp experienced by an older person. **senior optime** see **optime**. **senior service** n the Royal Navy.

seniti /sen'i-tē/ n (pl **sen'iti**) a monetary unit in Tonga, $\frac{1}{100}$ of a pa'anga. [Tongan, from **cent**]

senna /sen'ə/ n any tropical shrub of the genus Cassia; a laxative drug obtained from its dried leaflets and fruits (**senna pods**). [Ar sanā]
❑ **senna tea** n an infusion of senna.
■ **bladder senna** a papilionaceous shrub (genus Colutea) with similar properties.

sennachie same as **seannachie**.

sennet /sen'it/ (Shakesp) n a trumpet or woodwind announcement of a ceremonial entrance or exit; a fanfare. [Appar a form of **signet**]

sennight or **se'nnight** /sen'īt/ (archaic) n a week. [**seven** and **night**]

sennit /sen'it/ or **sinnet** /sin'it/ n a flat braid or cordage made from several strands of rope, straw or grass. [Origin uncertain]

Senonian /si-nō'ni-ən/ (geol) n a name applied to the European Upper Cretaceous stratigraphic subdivision (also adj). [L Senonēs a tribe of central Gaul]

Señor /se-nyōr'/ or -nyör'/ n a gentleman; (in address) sir; (prefixed to a name) Mr. [Sp, from L senior older]
■ **Señora** /se-nyō'rə or -nyö'/ n a lady; madam; (as a title) Mrs. **Señorita** /sen-yə-rē'tə or -yö-/ n a young lady; Miss. —All words also without cap.

Senoussi see **Senussi**.

sens /sens/ adv (obs) since.

sensate /sen'sāt/ adj endowed with physical sensation; perceived by the senses. [LL sensātus, from L sensus sense]

sensation /sen-sā'shən/ n consciousness of a physical experience, resulting from a certain bodily condition or resulting from stimulation of a sense organ (cf **perception**); function or operation of any of the senses; an effect on the senses; power of sensing; an emotion or feeling, esp of a specified kind; a thrill; a state, or matter, of general excited interest in the public, audience, etc; melodramatic quality, style or method; enough to taste, as of an alcoholic drink (sl). [From Med L sensātiō, -ōnis, from L sensus sense]
■ **sensā'tional** adj causing or designed to cause a strong emotional reaction, esp excitement or horror; excellent (inf); related to sensation or the senses. **sensā'tionalism** n the use of melodramatic style or lurid details in order to achieve a sensational effect; the doctrine that our ideas originate solely in sensation (philos). **sensā'tionalist** n and adj. **sensātionalist'ic** adj. **sensā'tionalize** or -**ise** vt to make (an event, situation, etc) appear more exciting or shocking than it really is. **sensā'tionally** adv. **sensā'tionism** n. **sensā'tionist** n (also **sensā'tion-monger**) a dealer in the sensational.

sense /sens/ n faculty of receiving sensation, general or particular; subjective consciousness; inward feeling; impression; opinion; mental attitude; discernment; understanding; appreciation; feeling for what is appropriate; discerning feeling for things of some particular kind; (usu in pl) one's wits or reason; soundness of judgement; reasonableness; sensible or reasonable discourse; that which is reasonable; plain matter of fact; the realm of sensation and sensual appetite; a sense-organ (Shakesp); a meaning, esp any of a range of meanings that a word or phrase may convey; interpretation; purport; gist; direction (esp in geom, after Fr sens). ◆ adj relating to a sense or senses. ◆ vt to have a sensation, feeling, or appreciation of; to appreciate, grasp, comprehend; to become aware (that); (of computers) to detect (eg a

hole, constituting a symbol, in punched card or tape). [L sensus, from sentīre to feel]
■ **sensed** adj having meaning of a specified kind, etc. **sense'ful** adj significant; full of good sense. **sense'less** adj unconscious; without good sense; meaningless. **sense'lessly** adv. **sense'lessness** n. **sen'sing** n and adj. **sen'sism** n (philos) sensationalism. **sen'sist** n. ❑ **sense datum** n what is received immediately through the stimulation of a sense organ (also called **sensum** /sen'səm/; pl **sen'sa**). **sense organ** n a structure specially adapted for the reception of stimuli, such as eye, ear and nose. **sense perception** n perception by the senses.
■ **bring someone to his** or **her senses** to make someone recognize the facts; to let someone understand that his or her behaviour must be mended. **come to one's senses** to regain consciousness; to start behaving sensibly (again). **common sense** see under **common**. **five senses** the senses of sight, hearing, smell, taste, and touch. **in a sense** in a sense other than the obvious one; in a way; after a fashion. **in** or **out of one's (right) senses** in or out of one's normal rational condition. **make sense** to be understandable, sensible or rational. **make sense of** to understand; to see the purpose in, or explanation of. **sixth sense** an ability to perceive what lies beyond the powers of the five senses. **take leave of one's senses** to go mad, start behaving unreasonably or irrationally.

sensei /sen'sā/ n (pl **sen'sei**) a martial arts instructor. [Jap, from sen previous, and sei birth]

Sensex /sen'seks/ n the indicator of the relative prices of stocks and shares on the Mumbai (Bombay) Stock Exchange. [Shortened from 30-share sensitive index]

sensible /sen'si-bl/ adj having or marked by good sense, reasonable, judicious; perceptible by sense; perceptible, appreciable; easily perceived, evident; having the power of sensation; physically conscious; sensitive, easily or readily affected or altered; cognizant, aware (of); having sensibility (obs). ◆ n something that is or can be sensed; that which is perceptible. [ME, from OFr, from L sensibilis]
■ **sensibil'ity** n sensitiveness, sensitivity; capacity of feeling or emotion; readiness and delicacy of emotional response; sentimentality; (usu in pl) feelings that can be hurt. **sen'sibleness** n. **sen'sibly** adv in a sensible manner; to a sensible or perceptible degree; so far as the senses show.
❑ **sensible horizon** n the visible horizon. **sensible note** n (music) a leading note.

sensile /sen'sīl/ adj sentient; capable of affecting the senses. [L sensilis, from sentīre to feel]

sensillum /sen-sil'əm/ n (pl **sensill'a**) in insects, a small sense organ on the integument. [New L, dimin of L sensus sense]

sensitive /sen'si-tiv/ adj having power of sensation; feeling readily, acutely, or painfully; easily upset or offended; capable of receiving stimuli; reacting to outside influence; ready and delicate in reaction; sensitized; susceptible to the action of light (photog); relating to, or depending on, sensation; stimulating much strong feeling or difference of opinion; (of documents, etc) with secret or controversial contents. ◆ n someone who or that which is sensitive, or abnormally or excessively sensitive. [ME, from OFr, from Med L sensitīvus]
■ **sen'sitively** adv. **sen'sitiveness** or **sensitiv'ity** n response to stimulation of the senses; heightened awareness of oneself and others within the context of personal and social relationships; abnormal responsiveness eg to an allergen; degree of responsiveness to electric current, or radio waves, or to light; (of an instrument) readiness and delicacy in recording changes.
❑ **sensitive flame** n a flame that rises or falls in response to sound. **sensitive plant** n a plant, esp Mimosa pudica, that shows more than usual irritability when touched or shaken, by movements of leaves, etc; a person who is easily upset.

sensitize or -**ise** /sen'si-tīz/ vt to render sensitive, or more sensitive, or sensitive in a high degree. [sensitive and -**ize**]
■ **sensitiza'tion** or -**s**- n. **sen'sitized** or -**s**- adj. **sen'sitizer** or -**s**- n.

sensitometer /sen-si-tom'i-tər/ n an instrument for measuring sensitivity, eg of photographic films. [sensitive and -**meter**]

sensor /sen'sər/ n a device that detects a change in a physical stimulus and turns it into a signal which can be measured or recorded, or which operates a control. [sense and -**or**]

sensori- /sen-sə-ri-/ or **senso-** /sen-sō- or -sə-/ combining form indicating the senses, as in sensorineural and sensoparalysis.
■ **sensorimō'tor** adj relating to the senses and movement (**sensorimotor development** (behaviourism) the development of co-ordination between perception and action, eg hand-eye co-ordination).

sensorial see under **sensorium** and **sensory**.

sensorium /sen-sö'ri-əm or -sö'/ (biol) n (pl **senso'riums** or **senso'ria**) the area of the brain that is the seat of sensation; the brain; the mind; the nervous system. [LL, from L sēnsus felt]
■ **senso'rial** adj relating to the sensorium. **senso'rially** adv.

sensory /sen'sə-ri/ *adj* of the senses or sensation. [L *sensōrius*, from L *sentīre* to feel]

■ **senso'rial** *adj* sensory. **sen'sorily** *adv*.

❏ **sensory deprivation** *n* the reduction to a minimum of all external stimulation reaching the body, a situation used in psychological experiments and sometimes as a method of interrogation.

sensual /sen'sū-əl *or* -shū-əl/ *adj* of the senses, as distinct from the mind; not intellectual or spiritual; connected with gratification, *esp* undue gratification of bodily sense; tending to arouse sexual appetite; carnal; lewd; voluptuous. [LL *sensūalis*, from L *sensus* sense]

■ **sen'sualism** *n* sensual indulgence; the doctrine that all our knowledge is derived originally from sensation, sensationalism (*philos*); the regarding of the gratification of the senses as the highest end. **sen'sualist** *n* a person given to sensualism or sensual indulgence; a debauchee; a believer in the doctrine of sensualism. **sensualist'ic** *adj*. **sensual'ity** *n* the quality of being sensual; indulgence in sensual pleasures. **sensualīzā'tion** *or* **-s-** *n*. **sen'sualize** *or* **-ise** *vt* to make sensual; to debase by carnal gratification. **sen'sually** *adv*. **sen'sualness** *n*.

sensum see **sense datum** under **sense**.

sensuous /sen'sū-əs/ *adj* of or relating to the senses without implication of lasciviousness or grossness (appar coined by Milton to distinguish this sense from those of **sensual**); pleasing to the senses; alive to the pleasures of sensation; connected with sensible objects; (of pleasure) experienced through the senses. [L *sensus*]

■ **sen'suously** *adv*. **sen'suousness** *n*.

Sensurround® /sen'sə-rownd/ *n* a system of sound reproduction used *esp* in films, in which low-frequency output produces physical sensations in the audience and creates the impression of involvement in the action portrayed on screen.

sent[1] /sent/ *pat* and *pap* of **send**.

sent[2] an obsolete spelling of **scent**.

sent[3] /sent/ *n* (*pl* **sen'ti**) an Estonian monetary unit, $\frac{1}{100}$ of a kroon. [Estonian, from **cent**]

sente /sen'tē/ *n* (*pl* **lisen'tē**) a monetary unit in Lesotho, $\frac{1}{100}$ of a loti. [Sotho, from **cent**]

sentence /sen'təns/ *n* a number of words making a complete grammatical structure, in writing generally begun with a capital letter and ended with a full stop or its equivalent; determination of punishment pronounced by a court or a judge; a judgement, opinion or decision; an assertion in logic or mathematics; a maxim, aphorism (*archaic*); a group of two or more phrases forming a musical unit; sense, meaning, matter (*obs*). ◆ *vt* to pronounce sentence or judgement on; to condemn. [Fr, from L *sententia*, from *sentīre* to feel]

■ **sen'tencer** *n*. **sentential** /-ten'shl/ *adj*. **senten'tially** *adv*. **senten'tious** *adj* full of meaning; aphoristic, abounding in maxims; tending to moralize. **senten'tiously** *adv*. **senten'tiousness** *n*.

■ **Master of the Sentences** Peter Lombard (12th century), from his collection of opinions from Augustine, etc. **open sentence** (*maths*) a sentence which, having an undefined variable is, as it stands, neither true nor false.

sentient /sen'ti-ənt, -tyənt *or* -sh(y)ənt/ *adj* conscious; capable of sensation; aware; responsive to stimulus. ◆ *n* that which is sentient; a sentient being or mind. [L *sentiēns*, *-entis*, prp of *sentīre* to feel]

■ **sen'tience** *or* **sen'tiency** *n*. **sen'tiently** *adv*.

sentiment /sen'ti-mənt/ *n* a thought or body of thought tinged with or influenced by emotion; an opinion, attitude or judgement; a thought or feeling expressed in words; a maxim; emotion; feeling bound up with some object or ideal; regard to ideal considerations; sensibility, refined feelings, *esp* as expressed in art or literature; consciously worked-up or partly insincere feeling; sentimentality, mawkishness; a toast, *esp* epigrammatically expressed, proposed for drinking (*old*). [LL *sentimentum*, from L *sentīre* to feel]

■ **sentimental** /-men'tl/ *adj* relating to or expressive of sentiment; easily feeling and expressing tender emotions, *esp* love, friendship and pity; providing or designed to provoke such emotions, *esp* in large measure and without subtlety; closely associated with, or moved (to tears) by, fond memories of the past. **sentimen'talist** *n*. **sentimentality** /-men-tal'i-ti/ *or* **sentimen'talism** *n* the state or quality of being sentimental; the tendency to indulge in sentiment or the affectation of fine feelings; an act or statement that is sentimental; sloppiness. **sentimentalīzā'tion** *or* **-s-** *n*. **sentimen'talize** *or* **-ise** *vi* to behave sentimentally; to indulge in sentimentality. ◆ *vt* to make sentimental; to treat sentimentally. **sentimen'tally** *adv*.

❏ **sentimental value** *n* the value that a person ascribes to an object because of its personal associations, regardless of its monetary worth.

sentinel /sen'ti-nl/ *n* a person posted on guard, a sentry; a character indicating the occurrence of a specified condition, eg the end of a magnetic tape (*comput*). ◆ *adj* acting as a sentinel. ◆ *vt* (**sen'tinelling;**

sen'tinelled) to watch over; to post as a sentinel; to supply with a sentinel or sentinels. ◆ *vi* to keep guard. [Fr *sentinelle*, from Ital *sentinella* watch, sentinel]

❏ **sentinel crab** *n* a crab of the Indian Ocean with long eyestalks.

sentry /sen'tri/ *n* a sentinel; a member of the armed forces set to guard eg a gate or entrance; the watch or guard kept by such a soldier, etc. [Ety obscure, perh shortening of obs *centrinell*, *centronel*, variation of **sentinel**]

❏ **sentry box** *n* a box-like shelter with an open front, in which a sentry can stand for protection from rain, etc. **sen'try-go** *n* a sentry's patrol or duty; a watchtower (*obs*).

Senussi, also **Senoussi** *or* **Senusi** /se-noo'sē/ *n* (*pl* **Senus(s)'i**, etc *or* **Senus(s)'is**, etc) a member of a Muslim sect or confraternity, chiefly in NE Africa, founded by Sidi Mohammed ben Ali es-Senussi (died 1860; named from the *Senus* Mountains).

senvy /sen'vi/ (*obs*) *n* mustard (the plant or seed). [OFr *senevé*, from L *sināpi*, from Gr *sināpi* mustard]

senza /sen'tsä/ (*music*) *prep* without (*abbrev* **sen.**). [Ital]

SEO *abbrev*: search engine optimization; Senior Executive Officer.

Sep. *abbrev*: September.

SEPA *abbrev*: Scottish Environment Protection Agency.

sepad /sə-päd'/ *vt* to suppose; to warrant. [A ghost word; from JM Barrie's mishearing of *I'se* (= I sal) *uphaud*, I shall uphold]

sepak takraw /sē'päk täk-rö'/ *n* a SE Asian game in which two teams of three players kick a ball over a net. [Malay *sepak* kick, and Thai *takraw* ball]

sepal /sep'l, also sē'pl/ *n* any of the separate parts of a flower calyx. [Fr *sépale*, invented by NJ de Necker (1790) from Gr *skepē* cover]

■ **sep'aline** /-īn/ *or* **sep'aloid** *adj* of the form of sepals. **sep'alody** *n* (Gr *eidos* form) transformation of other flower parts into sepals. **sep'alous** *adj* having sepals.

separate /sep'ə-rāt/ *vt* to divide; to part; to sunder; to sever; to disconnect; to disunite; to remove; to isolate; to keep apart; to seclude; to set apart for a purpose; to exclude from cohabitation, *esp* by judicial decree; to remove cream from, using a separator. ◆ *vi* to part; to cease to live together as a (*esp* married) couple; to withdraw; to secede; to come out of combination or contact; to become disunited. ◆ *adj* /sep'ə-rit *or* sep'rit/ separated; divided; apart from another; distinct. ◆ *n* an offprint; (in *pl*) items of dress, eg blouse, skirt, etc, forming separate parts of an outfit. [L *sēparāre*, *-ātum*, from *sē-* aside, and *parāre* to put]

■ **separability** /-ə-bil'i-ti/ *n*. **sep'arable** *adj* that may be separated or disjoined. **sep'arableness** *n*. **sep'arably** *adv*. **sep'arately** *adv*. **sep'arateness** *n*. **separā'tion** *n* the act of separating or disjoining; the state of being separate; disunion; a place or line where there is a division; a gap or interval that separates; chemical analysis; cessation of cohabitation by agreement or judicial decree, without a formal dissolution of the marriage tie. **sep'aratism** /-ə-tizm/ *or* **separā'tionism** *n*. **sep'aratist** *n* a person who withdraws or advocates separation from an established church, federation, organization, etc (also **separā'tionist**); a dissenter; an Independent (*hist*); (by Unionists) a person who advocates Home Rule; a believer in separate authorship of parts, *esp* of the Homeric poems. ◆ *adj* of or relating to separatism or separatists. **sep'arative** /-ə-tiv/ *adj* tending to separate. **sep'arātor** *n* a person who or thing which separates; a machine for separating cream from milk by whirling. **separatory** /sep'ər-ə-tər-i/ *n* an instrument for separating. ◆ *adj* having the function of separating. **sep'arātrix** *n* (*pl* **separātri'cēs**) a separating line, solidus. **separā'tum** *n* a separate offprint.

❏ **separate development** *n* segregation of different racial groups, each supposed to progress in its own way. **separate maintenance** *n* a provision made by a husband for his separated wife. **separate school** *n* (in Canada) a school for pupils belonging to a religious minority. **separation allowance** *n* a government allowance to a serviceman's wife and dependants.

Sephardim /si-fär'dēm *or* -dim/ (*Judaism*) *n pl* the Jews of Spanish, Portuguese or N African descent; loosely, Oriental Jews. [Heb *sephāradhī*, from *sephāradh* a region (thought to be Spain) mentioned in the Bible, Obadiah 20, to which Jews were exiled]

■ **Sephar'di** *n* a member of the Sephardim; the pronunciation of Hebrew used by them. ◆ *adj* of the Sephardim. **Sephar'dic** *adj*.

sephen /sef'en/ *n* a stingray. [Ar *safan* shagreen]

sepia /sē'pi-ə/ *n* cuttlefish ink; a cuttlefish, *esp* of *Sepia* or a related genus; a pigment made from it, or an artificial imitation; its colour, a fine brown; brownish tone produced in certain, *esp* early, photographic processes; a sepia drawing or photograph. ◆ *adj* of the colour of sepia; done in sepia. [L, from Gr *sēpiā* cuttlefish]

■ **sē'piolite** *n* (Gr *lithos* stone) meerschaum. **se'piost** *or* **sepiostaire'** /-stār/ (Fr *sépiostaire*, from Gr *osteon* bone) *or* **se'pium** *n* cuttle-bone.

sepiment /sep'i-mənt/ *n* a hedge, a fence. [L *saepīmentum* a hedge]

sepiolite, sepiost, sepiostaire, sepium see under **sepia**.

sepmag /sep'mag/ adj (of a film, television programme, etc) having sound recorded on separate magnetic tape which is then synchronized with the film, etc as it is run. [*separate* and *mag*netic]

sepoy /sē'poi/ (*hist*) n an indigenous soldier or policeman in India during British rule. [Urdu and Pers *sipāhī* horseman]

seppuku /se-poo'koo/ n hara-kiri. [Jap]

seps /seps/ n a skink of the genus *Seps* with a serpentlike body, the serpent-lizard; a very venomous snake mentioned by classical writers. [Gr *sēps*]

sepsis /sep'sis/ (*med*) n (pl **sep'sēs**) putrefaction; invasion by pathogenic bacteria. [Gr *sēpsis* putrefaction]

Sept. abbrev : September.

sept /sept/ n (*orig* in Ireland) a division of a tribe; a clan. [Prob for **sect¹**, infl by L *saeptum*]
■ **sept'al** adj.

sept- /sept-/, **septi-** /sep-ti-/ or **septem-** /sep-tem- or sep-təm-/ combining form denoting the quantity or amount seven. [L *septem*]
■ **septemfid** /sep'təm-fid/ adj (root of L *findere* to cleave) seven-cleft. **septemvir** /sep-tem'vir/ n (pl **septem'virī** or **septem'virs**) (L *vir* man) one of a board of seven. **septem'virate** n the office of a septemvir; a board of septemviri; a group of seven men. **septilateral** /sep-ti-lat'ə-rəl/ adj (L *latus, lateris* a side) seven-sided.

septa see **septum**.

septal see under **sept** and **septum**.

septarium /sep-tā'ri-əm/ n (pl **septā'ria**) a nodule of mineral substance with a network of cracks filled with another mineral. [Mod L, from L *septum*]
■ **septā'rian** adj.

septate /sep'tāt/ adj partitioned; divided by septa. [**septum**]
■ **septā'tion** n division by partitions or septa.

September /səp- or sep-tem'bər/ n the ninth month of the year. [L *September, -bris*, from *septem* seven; in the original Roman calendar, September was the seventh month of a ten-month year]
■ **Septem'berish** adj. **Septem'brist** n a participant in the September massacres of royalist prisoners in Paris, 2–7 September 1792 (*Fr hist*); a supporter of the successful rising of 1836 in Portugal. **Sep'tembrizer** or **-s-** n a Septembrist (*Fr* and *Port hist*); a partridge-shooter, esp one active in September.
□ **September people** n pl (*inf*; *euphem*) people of late middle age or older.

septemfid…to…septemvirate see under **sept-**.

septenarius /sep-ti-nā'ri-əs/ n a seven-foot verse, esp a trochaic tetrameter catalectic. [L *septēnārius* of seven]
■ **septenary** /sep-tē'nə-ri or sep'tə-nə-ri/ adj numbering or based on seven. ◆ n a seven, set of seven (*esp* years); a septenarius.

septennium /sep-ten'i-əm/ n (pl **septenn'ia**) a period of seven years. [L *septennis*, from *annus* a year]
■ **septenn'ate** n a period of seven years. **septenn'ial** adj happening every seventh year; lasting seven years. **septenn'ially** adv.
□ **Septennial Act** n a statute of 1716, in force until 1911, limiting the length of a parliament to seven years.

septentrion /sep-ten'tri-ən/ (*archaic*) n the north. [L *septentriōnēs*, ie *septem triōnēs* the seven plough-oxen]
■ **septen'trion** (*archaic*), **septen'trial** (*obs*) or **septen'trional** adj northern. **septen'trionally** adv. **septen'trions** or **septentriō'nēs** n pl the seven stars of the Plough; the Great Bear.

septet or **septette** /sep-tet'/ n a musical composition for seven performers; a set of seven (*esp* musicians). [Ger *Septett*, from L *septem*]

sept-foil /set'foil/ n the tormentil plant; a figure divided by seven cusps (*archit*). [Fr *sept* seven, and OFr *foil*, from L *folium* a leaf]

septic /sep'tik/ adj affected by bacteria from a diseased wound, putrefying; caused by such bacteria. [Gr *sēptikos*, from *sēpein* to putrefy]
■ **septicaemia** /sep-ti-sē'mi-ə/ n (Gr *haima* blood) the presence of pathogenic bacteria in the blood. **septicae'mic** adj. **sep'tically** adv. **septicity** /-tis'i-ti/ n.
□ **septic shock** n a severe drop in blood pressure caused by infection. **septic tank** n a tank, usu below ground, in which sewage is decomposed by anaerobic bacteria.

septicidal /sep-ti-sī'dəl/ (*bot*) adj with splitting of septa, as when a fruit dehisces by separation of the carpels. [**septum** and L *caedere* to cut]

septiferous, septiform see under **septum**.

septifragal /sep-tif'rə-gl/ (*bot*) adj with separation of the outer walls of the carpels from the septa. [**septum** and root of L *frangere* to break]

septilateral see under **sept-**.

septillion /sep-til'yən/ n a thousand raised to the eighth power (10^{24}); (*esp* formerly, in Britain) a million raised to the seventh power (10^{42}). ◆ adj being a septillion in number. [Fr, from L *septem* seven, and **million**]
■ **septill'ionth** adj and n.

septimal /sep'ti-ml/ adj relating to or based on the number seven. [L *septimus* seventh, from *septem* seven]
■ **septime** /sep'tēm/ n (*fencing*) the seventh parrying position. **sep'timole** /-mōl/ n (*music*) a group of seven notes to be played in the time of four or six.

septleva /set'lə-vä/ (*cards*) n (in the game of basset) seven times as much added to the first stake. [Fr *sept-et-le-va* seven and the first stake]

septuagenarian /sep-tū-ə-ji-nā'ri-ən/ n a person who is seventy years old, or between seventy and eighty (also adj). [L *septuāgēnārius* relating to seventy, from *septuāgintā* seventy]
■ **septuagenary** /-jē'nə-ri/ adj (*rare*) of, containing, based on, seventy; septuagenarian (also n).

Septuagesima /sep-tū-ə-jes'i-mə/ n the third Sunday before Lent (also **Septuagesima Sunday**), appar in continuation of the sequence Quadragesima, Quinquagesima, etc. [L *septuāgēsimus* seventieth]

Septuagint /sep'tū-ə-jint/ n the Greek Old Testament, traditionally attributed to 72 translators at Alexandria in 3c BC, often written **LXX**. [L *septuāgintā* seventy, from *septem* seven]
■ **Septuagin'tal** adj.

septum /sep'təm/ (*biol* and *anat*) n (pl **sept'a**) a partition or dividing structure in a cavity, tissue, etc. [L *saeptum* (used in pl) a fence, enclosure, from *saepīre* to fence, enclose]
■ **sept'al** adj. **septif'erous** adj having partitions. **sep'tiform** adj in the form of a partition.

septuor /sep'tū-ör/ n a septet. [Fr, from L *septem*, after *quattuor*]

septuple /sep'tū-pl/, also -*tū*', -*tū*- or -*too*'/ adj sevenfold. ◆ vt and vi to multiply sevenfold. [LL *septuplus*, from L *septem* seven; cf **quadruple**]
■ **sep'tūplet** n one of seven children (or animals) born at a single birth; a group of seven notes played in the time of four or six, a septimole (*music*).

sepulchre or (*US*) **sepulcher** /sep'əl-kər/ n a tomb; a recess in a church, usu in the north chancel wall, or a structure placed in it, to receive the reserved sacrament and the crucifix from Maundy Thursday or Good Friday until Easter (**Easter sepulchre**); burial. ◆ vt (formerly sometimes /si-pul'kər/) to entomb; to enclose as a tomb. [L *sepulcrum, sepultūra*, from *sepelīre, sepultum* to bury]
■ **sepulchral** /si-pul'krəl/ adj of, or of the nature of, a sepulchre; as if of or from a sepulchre; funereal, gloomy, dismal; hollow-toned. **sepul'chrally** adv. **sepul'chrous** adj (*rare*). **sepul'tural** adj. **sep'ulture** n the act of burial in a sepulchre; a tomb or burial-place. ◆ vt to entomb.
■ **whited sepulchre** see under **white**.

seq. abbrev : *sequens* (L), following (pl **seqq.**).

sequacious /si-kwā'shəs/ adj ready to follow a leader or authority; compliant; pliant; observing logical sequence or consistency. [L *sequāx, sequācis*, from *sequī* to follow]
■ **sequā'ciously** adv. **sequā'ciousness** or **sequacity** /si-kwas'i-ti/ n.

sequel /sē'kwəl/ n that which follows; consequences; upshot; a resumption of a story already complete in itself, in book, play, film, etc form; sequence (*Shakesp*); an allowance to mill servants in thirlage (*Scots law*; *obs*); followers (*obs*); successors (*obs*). [L *sequēla*, from *sequī* to follow]
■ **sequela** /si-kwē'lə/ n (pl **sequē'lae** /-lē/) (often pl) any abnormal condition following or relating to a previous disease; the psychological, etc aftereffect of any trauma.

sequence /sē'kwəns/ n a state or fact of being sequent or consequent; succession; order of succession; a series of things following in order; a succession of quantities each derivable from its predecessor according to a law (*maths*); a set of three or more cards consecutive in value; that which follows; consequence; successive repetition in higher or lower parts of the scale or in higher or lower keys (*music*); (in cinematography) a division of a film more or less equivalent to a scene in a stage play; (in liturgics) a hymn in rhythmical prose, sung after the gradual and before the gospel. ◆ vt to place in sequence; to discover or determine the sequence or order of. [L *sequēns, -entis*, prp of *sequī* to follow]
■ **se'quencer** n any device which arranges or determines the order of a number of events, operations, items or data, etc, in a sequence; a device connected to a synthesizer that can memorize sequences of notes. **se'quencing** n (*biochem*) the process of determining the order of amino acids in a protein or of nucleotides in DNA or RNA. **se'quent** adj following; consequent; successive; consecutive. ◆ n a follower (*Shakesp*); that which follows. **sequential** /si-kwen'shl/ adj in, or having, a regular sequence; sequent; (of data) stored one after

another (*comput*). **sequentiality** /-shi-al'i-ti/ *n*. **sequen'tially** *adv*. **se'quently** *adv*.

❑ **sequence of tenses** *n* (*grammar*) the relation of the tense used in a subordinate clause to that used in the principal clause. **sequential access** *n* (*comput*) a method of finding data in a file by reading through the file from the beginning (cf **direct access**).

sequester /si-kwes'tər/ *vt* to set aside; to seclude; to set apart; to confiscate; to remove (property, etc) from someone's possession until a dispute can be settled, creditors satisfied, etc; to hold the income of (a vacant benefice) for the benefit of the next incumbent; to sequester the estate or benefice of; to remove or render ineffective (a metal ion) by adding a reagent that forms a complex with it (eg as a means of preventing or getting rid of precipitation in water). ◆ *vi* (*obs*) to seclude oneself. ◆ *n* /sek'wis-tər/ (*Shakesp*) seclusion. [LL *sequestrāre, -ātum*, from L *sequester* a depositary, from *secus* apart]

■ **seques'tered** *adj* retired, secluded. **seques'trable** *adj*. **seques'tral** *adj*. **seques'trant** *n* (*chem*) a substance which removes an ion or renders it ineffective, by forming a complex with the ion. **sequestrate** /sek', sēk' or si-kwes'/ *vt* to sequester; to vest (the property, assets, etc of a bankrupt individual) in a trustee for distribution amongst creditors (*Scots law*); to render (a person) bankrupt (*Scots law*). **sequestrā'tion** /sek-, sēk-/ *n* the act of sequestering; the process of vesting a bankrupt's property, assets, etc, with a trustee for distribution amongst creditors, bankruptcy (*Scots law*); the action of a sequestrant (*chem*); a portion of diseased or dead tissue detached from, or joined abnormally to, surrounding healthy tissue (*med*). **seq'uestrātor** *n*. **seques'trum** *n* (*pl* **seques'tra**) (*pathol*) a fragment of dead or diseased bone that has become detached from healthy bone, as in osteomyelitis.

sequin /sē'kwin/ *n* a spangle used to decorate a garment; an old Italian gold coin. [Fr, from Ital *zecchino*, from *zecca* the mint; of Ar origin]
■ **se'quined** or **se'quinned** *adj*.

sequoia /si-kwoi'ə/ *n* either of two gigantic Californian conifers, the redwood, *Sequoia sempervirens*, and the big tree or giant sequoia, *Sequoiadendron giganteum* (formerly *Sequoia gigantea*, also Wellingtonia), that can grow to heights of 100 metres and may take 2000 years to reach their mature height. [*Sequoiah*, Cherokee scholar]

ser. *abbrev*: serial; series; serine; sermon.

sera see **serum**.

sérac or **serac** /sā-rak' or sā'rak/ *n* one of the cuboidal or pillarlike masses into which a glacier breaks on a steep incline. [Swiss Fr, *orig* a kind of white cheese]

serafile see under **serried**.

serafin same as **xerafin**.

seraglio /sə-rä'li-ō, se- or -lyō/ *n* (*pl* **sera'glios**) women's quarters in a Muslim house or palace; a harem; a collection of wives or concubines; an enclosure; a Turkish palace, *esp* that of the sultans at Constantinople. [Ital *serraglio*, from L *sera* a door-bar, confused with Turk *saray, serāī* a palace]

serai /se-rä'i/ *n* a khan or caravanserai; a harem, a seraglio (*nonstandard*). [Turk (*orig* Pers) *saray, serāī*]

serail /se-rāl'/ *n* a seraglio. [Fr *sérail*]

seral see under **sere²**.

serang /se-rang'/ *n* a boatswain on an Oriental, *esp* Indian, ship. [Pers *sarhang* a commander]

serape or **sarape** /sə-rä'pā/ *n* a *usu* brightly-coloured woollen ridingblanket, often worn around the shoulders by Mexican men. [Mex Sp *sarape*]

seraph /ser'əf/ *n* (*pl* **ser'aphs** or **ser'aphim** /-im/, formerly also **ser'aphin, ser'aphins** or **ser'aphims**, the plurals in *-im* and *-in* also occurring as *obs sing*) a six-winged celestial being (from the Bible, Isaiah 6); an angel of the highest of the nine orders; a person of angelic character or mien. [Heb *Serāphīm* (pl)]
■ **seraphic** /-af'/ or **seraph'ical** *adj* of or like a seraph; serene; blissful. **seraph'ically** *adv*. **ser'aphine** /-ēn/ *n* a keyboard reed instrument, precursor of the harmonium.
❑ **Seraphic Doctor** *n* St Bonaventura; St Teresa. **Seraphic Father** *n* St Francis. **Seraphic Order** *n* the Franciscans.

seraphin¹ same as **xerafin**.

seraphin² see **seraph**.

Serapis or **Sarapis** /sə- or se-rā'pis/ *n* a god of the Greeks of Egypt, identified with Apis and Osiris. [Gr *Sarāpis*, later (also L) *Serāpis*]
■ **Serapeum** /ser-ə-pē'əm/ *n* a temple of Serapis. **Serapic** or **Sarapic** /-ap'ik/ *adj*.

seraskier /ser-a-skēr'/ (*hist*) *n* a Turkish commander-in-chief or war minister. [Turk pronunciation of Pers *ser'asker*, from *ser* head, and Ar 'asker army]
■ **seraskier'ate** *n* the office of seraskier.

Serb /sûrb/ or **Serbian** /sûr'bi-ən/ *n* a native or citizen of Serbia (formerly a kingdom, then a constituent republic of Yugoslavia, now an independent republic); a member of the people principally inhabiting Serbia; the South Slav language of Serbia. ◆ *adj* of Serbia, its people, or their language. [Serb *Srb*]
❑ **Serbo-Cro'at** or **Serbo-Croatian** /-krō-ā'shən/ *n* a member of the South Slavonic branch of the Indo-European family of languages, spoken in Serbia, Croatia, etc (also *adj*).

Serbonian /sər-bō'ni-ən/ *adj* like *Sirbōnis, Serbōnis*, a now dry lake in the NE corner of Egypt, 'Where armies whole have sunk' (Milton, *Paradise Lost* II.594).

Sercial /sûr'si-al/ *n* a Riesling-like grape variety used to make the driest Madeira wine. [Fr]

serdab /sər-däb'/ *n* an underground chamber; a secret chamber in an ancient Egyptian tomb. [Pers *sard* cold, and *āb* water]

sere¹ see **sear¹,²**.

sere² /sēr/ *n* a series of ecological communities succeeding each other and representing stages in the biological development of an area. [L *seriēs* series]
■ **sēr'al** *adj*.
❑ **seral community** *n* an ecological community which is not stabilized but represents a stage in a succession.

sere³ /sēr/ (*obs*) *n* a claw. [OFr *serre*, from *serrer* to hold]

serein /sə-rē'/ *n* in the tropics, fine rain falling from an apparently cloudless sky after sunset. [Fr, from L *sērum* evening, from *sērus* late]

serenade /ser-i-nād'/ *n* a song or tune suitable for or suggestive of the evening, *esp* one with a romantic theme sung or played under a lady's window by a suitor; the performing of such a song or tune in this way; a composition like a symphony, *usu* lighter in tone and in more movements. ◆ *vt* to entertain with a serenade. ◆ *vi* to perform a serenade. [Fr *sérénade*, and Ital *serenata*, prob from Ital *sereno* open air, from L *serēnus* clear, cloudless; meaning infl by L *sērus* late]
■ **serenā'der** *n*. **serenata** /-i-nä'tä/ *n* a (symphonic) serenade; a pastoral cantata. **ser'enate** *n* (*Milton*) a serenade.

serendipity /ser-ən-dip'i-ti/ *n* the faculty of making fortunate or beneficial discoveries by accident. [*Serendip*, a former name for Sri Lanka. Horace Walpole coined the word (1754) from the title of the fairy tale 'The Three Princes of Serendip', whose heroes 'were always making discoveries, by accidents and sagacity, of things they were not in quest of']
■ **serendip'itist** *n* a person who believes in serendipity; a person who has this faculty. **serendip'itous** *adj* discovered by luck or chance; relating to or having serendipity. **serendip'itously** *adv*.

serene¹ /sə-rēn'/ *adj* calm; unclouded; unruffled; (with *cap*) an adjunct to the titles of members of some European royal families (translating Ger *Durchlaucht* Serenity). ◆ *n* (*poetic*) calm brightness; serenity; serene sky or sea; pure air. ◆ *vt* (*archaic*) to tranquillize; to clear. [L *serēnus* clear]
■ **serēne'ly** *adv*. **serēne'ness** *n*. **serenity** /-ren'i-ti/ *n*.
■ **all serene** (*inf*) everything as it should be; all right. **drop serene** (*Milton*) gutta serena or amaurosis, a kind of blindness.

serene² /ser'ēn or sə-rēn'/ (*obs*) *n* a supposedly unwholesome night dew; serein. [**serein**]

Serevent® /ser'ə-vent/ *n* a tradename for the broncho-dilator drug salmerol, a beta-2 agonist used to control asthma.

serf /sûrf/ *n* (*pl* **serfs**) a person in modified slavery, *esp* one bound to work on the land; a villein. [Fr, from L *servus* a slave]
■ **serf'age, serf'dom, serf'hood** and **serf'ship** *n*. **serf'ish** *adj*. **serf'like** *adj*.

Serg. *abbrev*: Sergeant.

serge¹ /sûrj/ *n* a strong twilled fabric, now *usu* of worsted. ◆ *adj* of serge. [Fr, from L *sērica* silk; see **seric**]

serge² see **cerge**.

sergeant or **serjeant** /sär'jənt/ *n* (*usu* with *g*) a non-commissioned officer of one of the higher ranks, ranking above a corporal; (with *g*) an officer of police; (*usu* with *g*) alone or as a prefix, designating certain officials; (with *j*) formerly, a barrister of highest rank (in full **sergeant-at-law**'); *orig* a servant; an officer who made arrests (*obs*). [Fr *sergent*, from L *serviēns, -entis*, prp of *servīre* to serve]
■ **ser'geancy** or **ser'jeancy** *n* the office or rank of sergeant or serjeant. **ser'geantship** or **ser'jeantship** *n*. **ser'jeantry** *n* serjeanty. **ser'jeanty** *n* (*hist*) a condition of feudal tenure by which the tenant either assisted the monarch in person (**grand serjeanty**) or made a small contribution to the defence of the realm (**petty serjeanty**).
❑ **sergeant-** (or **serjeant-)at-arms'** *n* an officer of a legislative body or the Court of Chancery, for making arrests, etc. **Sergeant Baker** *n* a brightly-coloured Australian marine fish (*Aulopus purpurissatus*). **sergeant-drumm'er** *n* a drum-major. **sergeant first class** *n* in the US Army, a sergeant below a master sergeant. **sergeant fish** *n* a fish with stripes, *esp* the cobia (genus *Rhachicentron*) of the SE USA,

related to the mackerel. **sergeant-ma'jor** n formerly, an officer of rank varying from major to major-general; now, the highest non-commissioned officer (**company sergeant-major** the senior warrant officer in a company; **regimental sergeant-major** the senior warrant officer in a regiment); a boldly-striped fish of warm seas.

■ **Common Serjeant** in London, an assistant to the Recorder, a judge of the quarter-session court.

Sergt abbrev : Sergeant.

serial, **seriate** see under **series**.

seriatim /sē-ri-ā'tim/ (L) adv in succession, one after another, one by one. [Med L, from L serēs; see **series**]

seric /ser'ik/ (rare) adj silken; (with cap) Chinese. [Gr sērikos, from Sēres the Chinese people who produced silk in ancient times]

■ **sericeous** /sə-rish'əs/ adj silky; covered with soft silky hairs that are closely pressed together (bot); with a silky sheen. **sericin** /ser'i-sin/ n the gelatinous protein found in raw silk and removed in processing. **ser'icite** n a silky soapy potash mica. **sericitic** /-sit'ik/ adj. **sericitīzā'tion** or **-s-** n conversion (esp of orthoclase) into sericite. **sericterium** /-tē'ri-əm/ n (pl **sericte'ria**) (zool) a silk or spinning gland, as in the silkworm. **sericul'tural** adj. **ser'iculture** n the breeding of silkworms for production of raw silk (also **sericiculture** /ser'i-si-kul-chər/). **sericul'turist** or **sericicul'turist** n. **ser'igraph** n a print made by silkscreen process. **serig'rapher** n. **serigraph'ic** adj. **serig'raphy** n.

sericulture see under **seric**.

seriema /ser-i-ē'mə or -ā'mə/ n either of two S American birds of the family Cariamidae, related to the cranes and the rails, similar to a small crested crane in form (also, now obsolescent, **caria'ma**). [Tupí çariama]

series /sē'rēz or -riz, rarely sē'ri-ēz/ n (pl **se'ries**) a set of things in line or in succession, or thought of in this way; a set of things having something in common, eg of books in similar form issued by the same publishing house; a TV or radio programme in which the same characters appear, or a similar subject is addressed, in regularly broadcast shows; a set of things differing progressively; the sum where each term of a sequence is added to the previous one (maths); a taxonomic group (of various rank); a geological formation; succession; sequence; linear or end-to-end arrangement; a set of notes in a particular order, taken, instead of a traditional scale, as the basis of a composition, eg the twelve-note row of twelve-tone music; an electric circuit whose components are arranged so that the same current passes through each of them in turn. [L seriēs, from serere, sertum to join]

■ **se'rial** adj forming a series; in series; in a row; in instalments; of publication in instalments; using series as the basis of composition (music); (of supernumerary buds) one above another; transferring one bit at a time (comput). ◆ n a publication, esp a story, in instalments; a motion picture, television or radio play appearing in instalments. **se'rialism** n (music) serial technique, or use of it. **se'rialist** n a writer of serials, or of serial music. **seriality** /-al'i-ti/ n. **serializā'tion** or **-s-** n publication in instalments; the use of notes and/or other elements of music in regular patterns. **se'rialize** or **-ise** vt to arrange in series; to publish serially. **se'rially** adv. **se'riate** /-ət/ adj in rows; forming one or more series. ◆ vt /-āt/ to arrange in a series, or in order. **se'riately** adv. **seriā'tion** n.

❑ **serial access memory** n (comput) memory where storage locations can be accessed only in predetermined sequences, eg in magnetic tape. **serial killer** n a person who murders several people over a period, often killing the victims in the same way or choosing victims of the same type, sex, age, etc. **serial monogamy** n the practice of having a sequence of monogamous affairs with different partners. **serial number** n the individual identification number marked on each one of a series of identical products. **serial port** n (comput) a connection on a computer through which data can only be sent one bit at a time. **serial technique** n the technique of music based on series. **serial time** n time regarded as an infinite regression of successive times, each needed for the description of its predecessor (JW Dunne, 1875–1949). **series winding** n (in an electric motor) a winding of the armative coil and field-magnet coil so that they are in series with the external circuit. **series-wound'** adj.

■ **arithmetical series** (maths) a series progressing by constant difference. **geometrical series** (maths) a series progressing by constant ratio. **in series** (phys) of electric components, connected in such a way that a current flows through them (cf **in parallel**).

serif, also (rare) **seriph** or **ceriph** /ser'if/ n a short decorative foot at the end of a stroke on a printed character; any of the styles of type or print which feature such feet. [Origin obscure; poss Du schreef stroke] ■ **ser'iffed** adj.

serigraph, **serigrapher**, etc see under **seric**.

serin /ser'in/ n any of various small finches of the genus Serinus, incl the canary. [Fr, canary]

■ **serinette'** n a small barrel organ for training songbirds.

serine /ser'ēn, sē'rēn or -rin/ n a polar amino acid (HOCH$_2$CH(NH$_2$)COOH), found in protein and synthesized in the body. [From sericin and **-ine**[1]]

seringa /sə-ring'gə/ n a Brazilian tree (genus Hevea) yielding rubber; mock orange (genus Philadelphus). [Port; see **syringa**]

serious /sē'ri-əs/ adj grave; staid; earnest; disinclined to lightness of mood; in earnest; not to be taken lightly; showing firmness of intention or commitment; approaching the critical or dangerous; concerned with weighty matters; professedly religious; significant, notable, or in significant quantities, as in serious money (inf). [LL sēriōsus, from L sērius grave, weighty]

■ **se'riocom'ic** or **seriocom'ical** adj partly serious and partly comic. **seriocom'ically** adv. **se'riously** adv in a serious manner; extremely, as in seriously rich (inf). **se'riousness** n.

seriph see **serif**.

serj. or **serjt.** abbrev : serjeant.

serjeant see **sergeant**.

serk see **sark**.

serkali /ser-kä'lē/ n (in Africa) the Government; (in Africa) white rulers. [Swahili]

sermon /sûr'mən/ n a discourse, esp one delivered, or intended to be delivered, from the pulpit, on a Biblical text; a written version of this; a harangue, reproof or moralizing lecture. ◆ vt and vi (rare) to preach; to discourse. [L sermō, sermōnis speech, prob ult from serere to join]

■ **sermoneer'** or **ser'moner** n (both rare) a preacher; a sermonizer. **sermonet'** or **sermonette'** n a brief sermon. **sermonic** /-mon'ik/ or **sermon'ical** adj. **ser'moning** n. **ser'monize** or **-ise** vi to compose sermons; to preach. ◆ vt to preach to. **ser'monizer** or **-s-** n.

sero- /sē-rō-, -rə-, -ro-/ combining form denoting serum.

■ **serologic** /-loj'ik/ or **serolog'ical** (**serological typing** a technique based on antibody–antigen reactions, for the identification of pathogenic organisms when morphological differentiation is difficult or impossible, serotyping). **serolog'ically** adv. **serol'ogist** n. **serol'ogy** n the study of serums, their constituents and properties. **seroneg'ative** adj (of an individual whose blood has been tested for a specific disease) showing no serological reaction. **seronegativ'ity** n. **seropos'itive** adj showing a serological reaction indicating the presence of a virus or disease, such as AIDS. **seropositiv'ity** n. **seropu'rulent** adj (pathol) containing a mixture of serum and pus, as in infected blisters. **seropus** /sē'rō-pus/ n a mixture of serum and pus. **serotaxon'omy** n serological analysis as a source of information for taxonomic classification. **serother'apy** n treatment or prevention of disease by injecting blood serum containing known antibodies.

seroconvert /sē-rō-kən-vûrt'/ vi to produce specific antibodies in response to the presence of an antigen, such as a virus or vaccine. [**sero-** and **convert**]

■ **seroconver'sion** n. **seroconvert'ed** adj.

serogroup /sē'rō-groop/ n any group of bacteria or other microorganisms (which may comprise several serotypes) that have a certain antigen in common. [**sero-** and **group**]

seron or **seroon** /si-rōn', -ron' or -roon'/ n (archaic) a crate or hamper; a bale wrapped in hide. [Sp serón]

seronegative see under **sero-**.

seroon see **seron**.

seropositive...to...seropus see under **sero-**.

serosa /si-rō'zə or -sə/ (zool) n (pl **serō'sas** or **serō'sae** /-zē or -sē/) an epithelial layer formed in the development of an insect's egg; a serous membrane, such as the peritoneum (see **serous**). [Mod L; fem of serōsus, from serum (see **serum**)]

■ **serō'sal** adj.

serosity see under **serous**.

serotaxonomy, **serotherapy** see under **sero-**.

serotine /ser'ə-tīn or -tin/ adj (biol) late in occurrence, development, flowering, etc (also **serotinal** /-si-rot'i-nəl/). ◆ n an insectivorous bat, Eptesicus serotinus, of Europe, N Africa and SE Asia (also **serotine bat**). [L sērōtinus, from sērus late]

■ **serotinous** /si-rot'i-nəs/ adj.

serotonin /ser-ə- or sē-rə-tō'nin/ (biochem) n a compound that occurs throughout body tissue, esp in the brain, intestinal tissue and blood platelets, acting as a neurotransmitter and powerful vasoconstrictor (also called **5-hydroxytryptamine**). [**sero-**, tonic and **-in**]

serotype /sē'rō-tīp/ n a group or category of bacteria or other microorganisms that have a certain set of antigens in common or against which common antibodies are produced; the combination of antigens by which such a group is categorized. ◆ vt to classify according to the composition of antigens. [**sero-** and **-type**]

■ **serotypic** /-tip'ik/ adj. **ser'otyping** n serological typing.

serous /sē'rəs/ adj of, relating to, like or consisting of serum; watery. [L serōsus, from serum; see **serum**]

■ **seros'ity** n.

❏ **serous membrane** n a serosa, a thin membrane, moist with serum, lining a cavity and enveloping the viscera within, such as the peritoneum or pericardium.

serow /ser'ō/ n either of two SE Asian goat-antelopes, the mainland serow (Capricornis sumatrensis), and the smaller Japanese or Taiwanese serow (Capricornis crispus). [Lepcha (Tibeto-Burman language) sa-ro]

Seroxat® /sə-rok'sat/ n a proprietary name for paroxetine, an antidepressant drug.

serpent /sûr'pənt/ n formerly, any reptile or creeping thing, esp if venomous; (with the) Satan as the tempter (Bible); a snake (literary and dialect); a treacherous or malicious person; a wooden leather-covered wind instrument shaped like a writhing snake; a firework that writhes like a serpent when ignited; (with cap) a northern constellation. ◆ adj serpentlike. [L serpēns, -entis, prp of serpere to creep; cf Gr herpein]

■ **serpentiform** /-pent'-/ adj snake-shaped. **ser'pentine** /-tīn/ adj snakelike; winding; tortuous. ◆ n a winding track; an old kind of cannon; a soft, usu green mineral, a hydrated magnesium silicate, occurring in winding veins and in masses, formed by alteration of olivine, etc; a rock, commonly an altered peridotite, composed mainly of the mineral serpentine. ◆ vt and vi to wind; to insinuate. **ser'pentinely** adv. **serpentinic** /-tīn'ik/ adj. **ser'pentining** n and adj. **serpenti'ningly** adv. **serpentinite** /-pen'-/ n a rock composed mainly of serpentine. **serpentiniza'tion** or **-s-** n. **ser'pentinize** or **-ise** vt to convert into serpentine. **serpenti'nous** adj of serpentine; winding. **ser'pentize** or **-ise** vi to wind. ◆ vt to cause to wind. **ser'pentlike** adj and adv. **ser'pentry** n (rare) serpents collectively.

❏ **ser'pent-eater** n the secretary bird; the markhor. **serpent god** or **goddess** n a deity in the form of a snake; a deified snake. **serpentine verse** n a line that begins and ends with the same word (from the figure of a snake with its tail in its mouth, common as a symbol of eternity). **ser'pent-liz'ard** n the lizard Seps. **ser'pent-star** n a brittlestar. **ser'pent-stone** n an ammonite; a snake-stone. **ser'pent-worship** n.

■ **the old serpent** Satan.

serpigo /sər-pī'gō/ (pathol) n (pl **serpigines** /-pij'in-ēz/ or **serpi'goes**) (Shakesp **sapego** or **suppeago**) any spreading or creeping skin disease, specif ringworm. [LL serpīgō, from L serpere to creep]

■ **serpiginous** /-pij'-/ adj (of certain skin lesions) having an indented or wavy margin.

SERPS or **Serps** /sûrps/ abbrev : (until 2002) state earnings-related pension scheme.

serpulid /sûr'pū-lid/ n a marine polychaete worm of the family **Serpū'lidae**, that constructs and lives within a twisted calcareous tube. [L serpula a snake, from serpere to creep]

■ **ser'pulite** n a fossil resembling a worm tube.

serr, **serre** see under **serried**.

serra /ser'ə/ n (pl **serr'ae** /-ē/ or **serr'as**) a sawlike organ (zool); anything sawlike; a mountain-range (pl **serr'as**). [L and Port (from L) serra a saw]

■ **serradill'a** or **serradell'a** n (Port) a species of clover grown as fodder. **serr'an** n a fish of the genus Serranus, or its family. **serranid** /ser'ən-id/ or **serr'anoid** n a member of the Serranidae (also adj). **Serranus** /sə-rā'nəs/ n the typical genus of Serranidae /-ran'i-dē/, a family of percoid fishes, incl the sea perches, sea basses and groupers. **serrasal'mo** n (pl **serrasal'mos**) (L salmō salmon) a fish of the piranha genus Serrasalmo. **serrate'** vt to notch. **serrā'ted** or **serr'āte** adj notched like a saw; (with sharp forward-pointing teeth (bot and zool). **serrā'tion** n saw-edged condition; (usu in pl) a sawlike tooth. **serratiros'tral** adj (L rōstrum beak) saw-billed. **serratulate** /sə-rat'ū-lāt/ adj minutely serrate. **serrature** /ser'ə-chər/ n serration. **serrā'tus** n (anat) one of several muscles of the thorax. **serricorn** /ser'-/ adj (L cornū horn) having serrate antennae. **serr'ulate** or **serr'ulated** adj finely serrated. **serrulā'tion** n.

serrate, **serrated**, etc see under **serra**.

serried /ser'id/ adj close-set; packed or grouped together without gaps. [Fr serrer or its pap serré, from L sera bar, lock]

■ **serr** or **serre** /sûr/ vt to press close; to close the ranks of. **serrefile** or **serafile** /ser'ə-fīl/ n (see **file**[1]) a file of officers or men detailed to ride in rear of the rear rank of a squadron when in line; a soldier so detailed. **serr'y** vt and vi to close together.

serrulate, etc see under **serra**.

serry see under **serried**.

Sertoli cells /sûr-tō'li selz/ n pl specialized nutritive cells which initiate the formation of seminiferous tubules in the testes and which nourish the developing sperm. [E Sertoli (1842–1910), Italian histologist]

sertularian /sûr-tū-lā'ri-ən/ n any hydroid coelenterate of the common genus Sertularia, having a double row of sessile hydrothecae (also adj). [Mod L, from dimin of serta garland]

seruewe (ie **servewe**) a Spenserian spelling of **surview**.

serum /sē'rəm/ n (pl **sē'rums** or **sē'ra**) a watery liquid, esp that which separates from coagulating blood; blood serum containing antibodies, taken from an animal that has been inoculated with bacteria or their toxins, used to immunize people or animals; the watery part of a plant fluid. [L serum whey]

❏ **serum albumin** n an albumin (or combination of albumins) that makes up more than half the protein in blood plasma and maintains the osmotic pressure of the blood. **serum globulin** n a globulin (or combination of globulins) containing most of the antibodies in blood plasma. **serum hepatitis** n a virus infection of the liver, usu transmitted by transfusion of infected blood or use of contaminated instruments, esp needles, consequently often occurring in drug addicts. **serum sickness** n a hypersensitivity reaction that sometimes occurs after injection of foreign serum, with fever, rashes, and enlargement of the lymph nodes. **serum therapy** n serotherapy (see under **sero-**).

serval /sûr'vl/ n a slender long-legged African cat (Felis serval), with a spotted coat. [Port (lobo) cerval, literally, deer-like wolf]

servant /sûr'vənt/ n someone who is hired to perform service, esp personal or domestic service of a menial kind, or farm labour, for another or others; a person who is in the service of the state, the public, a company, or other body; someone who serves in any capacity; a ministrant; formerly, a man conventionally accepted by a lady (called his mistress) as binding himself to devoted attendance, a lover; in formal letter-writing, formerly in greeting and leave-taking, now usu jocularly, applied in seeming humility to oneself; a designation formerly used in the USA for a slave; (in pl) formerly a designation conceded by a great personage to a company of actors, to evade legal difficulties. ◆ vt (rare) to subject. [Fr, prp of servir, from L servīre to serve]

■ **ser'vantless** adj. **ser'vantry** n (rare) servants collectively. **ser'vantship** n the position or relation of a servant.

❏ **ser'vant-girl**, **ser'vant-lass** or **ser'vant-maid** n a female domestic servant. **ser'vant-man** n a male domestic. **servants' hall** n a servants' dining room and sitting room.

■ **civil servant** a member of the civil service (see **civil**).

serve /sûrv/ vt to be a servant to; to be in the service of; to worship (obs); to work for; to render service to; to perform service for or under; to perform the duties or do the work connected with; (of a male animal) to copulate with (the female); to attend as assistant; to be of use to or for; to avail; to suffice for; to satisfy; to further; to minister to; to attend to the requirements of; to supply; to provide with materials; to provide with quarry (falconry); to help to food, etc; to present (food) in a specified manner; to send or bring to table; to deal; to put into action, bring to bear (archaic); to put into play by striking (tennis, etc); to treat, behave towards; to be opportune to; to conform one's conduct to; to undergo, work out, go through; to bind (rope, etc) with cord, etc in order to strengthen (esp naut); to deliver or present formally, or give effect to (law); to operate or maintain in operation (a gun, etc) (milit); to declare (heir) (Scots law : obs). ◆ vi to be a servant; to be in service or servitude; to render service; to be a member, or take part in the activities, of an armed force; to perform functions; to wait at table; to attend to customers; to act as server, eg at Roman Catholic Mass; to answer a purpose, be of use, do; to be opportune or favourable; to suffice. ◆ n service of a ball in tennis, etc; verbal abuse or mockery (Aust inf); a portion of food (Aust). [Fr servir, from L servīre to serve]

■ **ser'ver** n a person who serves, esp at meals or tennis; a person who acts as assistant to a priest during Mass; a salver; a fork, spoon, or other instrument for distributing or helping at table; (in computer networks) a dedicated computer that stores communal files, processes electronic mail, provides printing facilities, etc. **serv'ery** n a room or rooms adjoining a dining room, from which meals and drinks are served and in which utensils are kept. **serv'ing** n and adj. **serv'let** n (comput) a program, written in the Java language, that is installed on an Internet server and receives and responds to messages from a number of clients.

❏ **server farm** n a series of powerful computers linked together to provide increased processing power and reliability. **serving mallet** n (naut) a mallet with a grooved head used in serving ropes. **serv'ing-man** n (archaic) a manservant.

■ **serve as** to act as; to take the place of. **serve one's time** to pass through an apprenticeship or a term of office (see also **time-served**, etc under **time**). **serve out** to deal or distribute; to punish; to get even with, take revenge on. **serve someone a trick** to play a trick on someone. **serve someone right** (of something unpleasant) to be no more than deserved. **serve the** (or **one's**) **turn** to suffice for one's immediate purpose or need. **serve time** to undergo a term of imprisonment, etc. **serve up** to present for consumption.

servewe a Spenserian spelling of **surview**.

Servian[1] /sûr'vi-ən/ adj of Servius Tullius, legendary king of Rome.

Servian[2] /sûr'vi-ən/ (obs) n and adj (a) Serbian.

service[1] /sûr'vis/ n the condition or occupation of a servant or of any person who serves; work; the act or mode of serving; employ; employment in the armed forces, or in any public organization or department; the personnel so employed; the force, organization, or body employing it (in pl usu the fighting forces); that which is required of its members; that which is required of a feudal tenant; performance of a duty or function; actual participation in warfare; a warlike operation; a performance of religious worship; a liturgical form or office or a musical setting of it; a good turn, good offices, benefit to another or others; duty or homage ceremonially offered, as in health-drinking, correspondence, or greeting; use; hard usage; availability; disposal; supply, eg of water, public transport, etc; expediting; assistance given to customers in a shop, etc; waiting at table; that which is served, a course; the order of dishes; a complete set, eg of dishes for a particular meal; supplementary activities for the advantage of customers; the checking, and (if necessary) repairing and/or replacing of parts, of machinery, etc to ensure efficient operation; (in tennis, squash, badminton, etc) the right of a player to serve the ball, the act of so doing, or the manner, style or game in which an individual player serves; a service charge; the cost of interest and sinking-fund charges; cord or other material for serving a rope; (in pl) a service area. ◆ adj of the army, navy, or air force; (sometimes in pl) of the army, navy and air force collectively; for the use of servants; providing services rather than manufactured products (see eg **service industry** below). ◆ vt to provide or perform service for (eg motor cars); (of a male animal) to mate with (a female). [Fr, from L servitium]
■ **serviceabil'ity** or **ser'viceableness** n. **ser'viceable** adj able or willing to serve; advantageous; useful; capable of rendering long service, durable. **ser'viceably** adv. **ser'viceless** adj.
❑ **service agreement** n a contract stipulating the responsibilities that the provider of a service has to a client. **service area** n a place by a motorway or major road where facilities such as filling stations, garages, restaurants and toilets are available; the range covered by a radio or television transmitter. **service book** n a book of forms of religious service; a prayer book. **service car** n (NZ) a bus used on long-distance journeys. **service ceiling** n the altitude above sea level, in standard atmospheric conditions, at which the rate of ascent of an aircraft falls to a specified rate (cf **absolute ceiling** under **absolute**). **service charge** n a charge made for service in a restaurant or hotel, usu a percentage of the bill. **service contract** n a service agreement. **service court** n in tennis, the area outside of which a served ball must not fall. **service flat** n a flat in which domestic service is provided, its cost being included in the rent. **service hatch** n one connecting dining room to kitchen, etc, through which dishes, etc, may be passed. **service industry** n an industry which provides a service rather than a product, eg catering, entertainment, transport. **service line** n the boundary of the service court, in tennis 21 feet from the net. **ser'viceman** n a male member of the armed forces; a man who maintains esp household machinery. **service mark** n a mark, emblem, device, etc used to identify a certain service, such as catering, insurance, etc and reserved for the exclusive use of providers of that service. **service module** n a self-contained unit housing a spacecraft's fuel and supplies. **service pipe** or **service wire** n a branch from a gas, electric, etc main to a building. **service provider** (comput) see **ISP**. **service reservoir** n a reservoir for supplying water to a particular area. **service road** n a minor road parallel to a main road, providing access to local facilities, eg shops, without obstructing the main road. **service room** n a room in a club or hotel where visitors' requirements are attended to. **service station** n an establishment providing general services, esp the supply of fuel for motorists. **ser'vicewoman** n a female member of the armed forces.
■ **active service** service of a soldier, etc, in the field (widely interpreted by the authorities). **at your service** at your disposal; also a mere phrase of civility. **civil service** see under **civil**. **have seen service** to have fought in war; to have been put to long or hard use. **in service** in use or operation; working as a domestic servant. **out of service** broken, not in operation.

service[2] /sûr'vis/ n (also **service tree**) a Eurasian tree (Sorbus domestica) similar to the rowan, with apple- or pear-shaped fruits used since Roman times to make an alcoholic drink (also called **sorb**); a related European tree (**wild service**), Sorbus torminalis, somewhat like a maple, with clusters of round fruits. [OE syrfe, perh from L cerevisia the cider-like drink made from its fruit, perh from L sorbus]
❑ **ser'viceberry** n the fruit of a service; see also separate entry.

serviceberry /sûr'vis-be-ri/ n any of several N American trees or shrubs of the genus Amelanchier, having clusters of white flowers and edible red or purple berries (also called **shadberry**, **shadbush**, **shadblow**, **Juneberry**); the sweet fruit of several species (also called **shadberry**, **Juneberry**). See also under **service**[2].

servient /sûr'vi-ənt/ (law) adj subordinate; subject to a servitude or easement (qv). [L serviēns, -entis, prp of servīre to serve]

serviette /sûr-vi-et'/ (orig Scot) n a table-napkin, esp a paper one. [Fr]

servile /sûr'vīl/ adj relating to slaves or servants; slavish; fawning or submissive; cringing; controlled, subject; slavishly or unintelligently imitative; expressing mere grammatical relations. ◆ n (rare) a servile person. [L servīlis, from servus a slave]
■ **ser'vilely** adv. **ser'vilism** /-vil-izm/ n systematic or habitual servility; servile spirit; a system based on slavery or advocacy of it. **servility** /-vil'i-ti/ n servitude; slavishness of manner or spirit; slave-like deference.

Servite /sûr'vīt/ n a member of the mendicant order of Servants of the Virgin, founded at Florence in 1233. ◆ adj of or relating to this order.

servitor /sûr'vi-tər/ n (also fem **ser'vitress**) a person who serves; a servant (chiefly poetic); a person who serves in war (obs); an assistant, apprentice, lawyer's clerk, assistant schoolmaster, or the like (Scot, obs); a follower or adherent; formerly, at Oxford University, an undergraduate partly supported by the college, whose duty was to wait on the fellows and gentlemen commoners at table; at Edinburgh University, a classroom janitor. [LL servītor, -ōris, from L servīre to serve]
■ **servito'rial** adj. **ser'vitorship** n.

servitude /sûr'vi-tūd/ n a state of being a slave or (now rare) servant; slavery; subjection; compulsory labour; subjection to irksome conditions; a burden on property restraining its owner from certain uses or allowing certain rights to the owner of an adjacent property (law). [L servitūdō]

servlet see under **serve**.

servo /sûr'vō/ adj and combining form denoting a system in which the main mechanism is set in operation by a subsidiary mechanism and is able to develop a force greater than the force communicated to it. ◆ n (pl **ser'vos**) short for **servomechanism** or **servomotor**. [L servus a servant, slave]
■ **ser'vocontrol** n (in aircraft) a reinforcing mechanism for the pilot's effort, usu a small auxiliary aerofoil. **servomechan'ical** adj. **ser'vomechanism** n a closed-cycle control system in which a small input power controls a larger output power in a strictly proportionate manner. **ser'vomotor** n a motor using a servomechanism.

servus servorum Dei /sûr'vəs sûr-vō'rəm, -vö'rəm, dē'ī, ser'vŭs, -wŭs, ser-vō'rŭm, -wō', de'ē/ (L) n a servant of the servants of God (a title adopted by the popes).

sesame /ses'ə-mi/ n a plant, Sesamum indicum, probably native to SE Asia, cultivated for its seeds which yield a light edible oil (**sesame oil**; also called **benne** or **gingili oil**). [Gr sēsamē a dish of sesame (Gr sēsamon)]
■ **ses'amoid** adj shaped like a sesame seed. ◆ n (anat) (in full **ses'amoid bone**) a small rounded bone formed in the substance of a tendon, eg in the flexor tendon of the big toe.
❑ **sesame grass** n gama grass. **sesame seed** n.
■ **open sesame** see under **open**.

sese a variant reading for **sessa**.

seseli /ses'ə-li/ n a plant of the genus Seseli of the Umbelliferae family. [Gr seseli, a name for several umbellifers of this and other genera]

sesey see **sessa**.

sesh /sesh/ (inf) n a session.

Sesotho /se-soo'too, -tō or -sō'/ n the language of the Besotho, a Bantu people of Lesotho. Also **Sotho**.

sesqui- /ses-kwi-/ combining form denoting the ratio of one-and-a-half to one, or (chem) one-and-a-fraction to one. [L sēsqui, from sēmisque, from sēmis (for sēmi-as) half a unit, and que and]
■ **sesquialter** /-al'tər/ adj (L alter second) as three to two. **sesquial'tera** n (music) a perfect fifth; three notes against two; an organ stop giving the root, the twelfth and the tierce. **sesquicar'bonate** n a salt composed of a carbonate and a hydrogen carbonate. **sesquicente'nary** or **sesquicentenn'ial** n a hundred and fiftieth anniversary (also adj). **sesquiox'ide** n an oxide with three atoms of oxygen to two of the other constituent. **sesquipedā'lianism** or **sesquipedality** /-pi-dal'i-ti/ n. **sesquip'licate** adj (L sēsquiplex, -plicis; maths) of, or as, the square roots of the cubes. **sesquisul'phide** n a compound with three atoms of sulphur to two of the other element or radical. **sesquiter'pene** n any of a group of terpene derivatives of the empirical formula $C_{15}H_{24}$. **sesquiter'tia** n (music) a perfect fourth; a rhythm of three notes against four.

Sess. abbrev: Session.

sess /ses/ *n* same as **cess**.

sessa /ses'ə/ or **sesey** /ses'ē/ (*Shakesp*) *interj* perh meaning 'enough said'. [Poss reduplication of *sa*; poss Sp *cesa*, or Fr *cessez*, cease]

sessile /ses'īl/ or (*esp N Am*) *ses'il/ adj* stalkless; sedentary; fixed or stationary. [L *sessilis* low, squat, from *sedēre*, *sessum* to sit]
□ **sess'ile-eyed** *adj*. **sessile oak** *n* a native British oak, *Quercus petraea*, distinguished from the English oak by its stalkless acorns (also called **durmast oak**).

session /sesh'ən/ *n* a sitting, series of sittings, or time of sitting, eg of a court or public body; the time between the meeting and prorogation of Parliament; a school year (sometimes a school day); (in Scotland) a division of the academic year; the kirk session; formerly, the Court of Session; (in *pl*) quarter-sessions; a period of time spent engaged in any one activity, eg teaching, drinking or making music; the enthronement of Christ at God's right hand; an act of sitting (*obs*); a seated position (*obs*). [Fr, from L *sessiō*, *sessiōnis*, from *sedēre*, *sessum* to sit]
■ **sess'ional** *adj*. **sess'ionally** *adv*.
□ **sess'ion-clerk** *n* the official who records the transactions of a kirk session. **sess'ion-house** *n* a building where sessions are held; the room where a kirk session meets. **session singer** or **musician** *n* a person who provides vocal or instrumental backing at recording sessions.
■ **Court of Session** the supreme civil court of Scotland. **in session** (of a court, committee, etc) conducting or engaged in a meeting; (of a musician) engaged in a live recording.

sesspool same as **cesspool** (see **cesspit**).

sesterce /ses'tûrs/ *n* a Roman coin, the *sestertius*, worth $2\frac{1}{2}$ asses, later 4 asses. [L *sestertius* two and a half, from *sēmis* half, and *tertius* third]
■ **sester'tium** /-shi-əm/ *n* (*pl* **sester'tia**) a Roman money of account equal to 1000 sesterces (*prob orig* genitive plural for *mille sestertium* a thousand sesterces).

sestet, **sestett** or **sestette** /ses-tet'/ *n* a group of six; the last six lines of a sonnet; (also **sestett'o**; *pl* **sestett'os**) a composition for six performers (*music*). [Ital *sestetto*, from *sesto* from L *sextus* sixth]

sestina /ses-tē'na/, also **sestine** /-tēn'/ (*poetry*) *n* an old verse form of six six-lined stanzas having the same end-words in different orders, and a triplet introducing all of them. [Ital, from L *sextus* sixth]

seston /ses'ton/ *n* a very small plankton organism. [Gr *sēston*, from *sēthein* to strain, filter]

SET *abbrev*: Secure Electronic Transaction, a credit-card payment security system on the Internet.

set /set/ *vt* (**sett'ing**; **set**) to put, place, or fix in position or required condition; to dispose, array, arrange; to restore (a broken bone) to its normal alignment; to apply; to cause to be; to plant; to stake; to embed; to frame; to mount; to beset or bestow about; to stud, dot, sprinkle, variegate; to put in type (*printing*); to compose (type); to form or represent, eg in jewels; to adjust to show the correct (or a specified) time, etc; to spread, lay, cover (a table) with the food, dishes, etc for a meal, or (*Scot* and *dialect*) to cover the table with the food, dishes, etc for (a meal); to regulate; to appoint; to ordain; to assign; to prescribe; to propound; to put on a course, start off; to incite, direct; to put in opposition; to posit; to cause to become solid, coagulated, rigid, fixed, or motionless; to begin to form (eg a fruit or seed); to rate, value; to pitch (eg a tune); to compose or fit music to; to position (sails) to catch the wind; to arrange (hair) in a particular style when wet, so that it will remain in it when dry; to seat (*obs* and *dialect*); to put (a hen) on eggs; to put (eggs) under a hen; (of a gundog) to indicate by crouching; to sharpen (eg a razor); to defeat (one's opponent's contract) *usu* by a stated number of tricks (*bridge*); to escort (*Scot and N Eng dialect*); to lease or let to a tenant (*esp Scot*); to become, befit (chiefly *Scot*); conversely, to appear to advantage in (*Scot*). ◆ *vi* to go down towards or below the horizon, to decline; to offer a stake; to become rigid, fixed, hard, solid, or permanent; to coagulate; (of a broken bone) to knit; to settle down; (of eg bone) to begin to develop; to have, take or start along a course or direction; to dance in a facing position; to acquire a set or bend; (of dogs) to point out game; to apply or betake oneself; to hang in position; to be in session; to sit (now *obs* or *dialect*). ◆ *adj* in any of the senses of the participle; prescribed; deliberate, intentional; prearranged; formal; settled; fixed; rigid; determined; regular; established; ready. ◆ *n* a group of persons or things, *esp* of a type that associate, occur, or are used together or have something in common; a clique, coterie, exclusive group; a complete series, collection, or complement; a company performing a dance; a series of dance movements or figures; a complete apparatus, *esp* for receiving radio or television signals; an act, process, mode, or time of setting; a setting; an inclination; a direction; the scenery, properties, etc set up for a scene (*theatre*, etc); the place where filming takes place (*cinematog*); any collection of objects, called 'elements', defined by specifying the elements (*maths*); the basic haploid complement of chromosomes (*biol*); habitual or temporary form, posture, carriage, position, or tendency; the items performed by a singer or band at a

concert; a series of games, the winner being the first side to win at least six games and at least two games more than the opponent, *usu* with a tie-break played to decide the winner if the score reaches six games all (*tennis*); a shot sending the cue ball against an object ball, with the aim of causing a third ball that is touching the object ball to be propelled towards a pocket (*snooker*); a set hairstyle; the hang of a garment; a young cutting, bulb or tuber, for planting; a gun dog's indication of game; bodily build (now *dialect*); permanent effect of strain; the constitution of a burgh; (for the following senses, **set** or **sett**): the number of a weaver's reed, determining the number of threads to the inch; the texture resulting; a square or a pattern of tartan; a paving-block of stone or wood; a tool for setting in various senses; a badger's burrow; a lease or letting (*Scot*); a mining lease or area worked (*Cornwall*, etc); a place with fixed fishing-nets. [OE *settan*; cognate with Ger *setzen*, ON *setja*, Gothic *satjan*; *settan* is the weak causative of *sittan* to sit; the noun is from the verb, but may be partly from OE *set* seat, partly from OFr *sette*, from L *secta* sect]
■ **set'ness** *n*. **sett'er** *n* someone who or something that sets; a dog that sets; a dog of a breed derived from the spaniel and (probably) pointer; a person who finds victims for thieves, etc; a spy. **sett'ing** *n* the act of someone who sets; the direction of current; fixation; surroundings; environment; the scenery and props used in a single scene of a play, film, etc; a level of power, volume, etc, to which a machine or other device can be set; mounting of jewellery; the period of time in which a play, novel, etc, is set; a set of cutlery, crockery and glassware laid out for use by one person; adaptation to music; music composed for a song, poem, etc; a system of dividing pupils in mixed-ability classes into ability groups for certain subjects only; the period of play after a game has been set (to two, three or five) (*badminton*).
□ **set'-aside** *n* (also **land set-aside**) the practice or policy of taking agricultural land out of production (**set-aside scheme** *specif* that introduced to reduce EU grain surpluses, with compensatory payments to farmers). **set'back** *n* a check, reverse, or relapse; a disappointment or misfortune; a receding section in the upper part of a tall building. **set dancing** *n* a traditional form of Irish dancing, *usu* involving a group of four couples in a square formation. **set'-down** *n* a rebuff or snub; a scolding. **set'line** *n* any of various kinds of fishing-line suspended between buoys, etc, and having shorter baited lines attached to it. **set menu** *n* a complete meal with limited options offered by a restaurant at a fixed price. **set'-off** *n* a claim set against another; a crossclaim which partly offsets the original claim; a counterbalance; an ornament; a contrast, foil; a setting forth; an offset (*archit* and *printing*). **set'-out** *n* an outfit; preparations; a display of dishes, dress, etc; company or clique. **set piece** *n* a piece of theatrical scenery with a supporting framework, distinguished from a side-scene or drop-scene; an elaborately arranged display in fireworks; a painstakingly prepared performance; (a carefully planned and executed piece of team-work at) a corner or free kick (*football*, etc). **set'-piece** *adj*. **set point** *n* (*tennis*, etc) a point which wins a set. **set pot** *n* a fixed boiler or copper. **set'screw** *n* a screw used to prevent relative motion by exerting pressure with its point. **set speech** *n* a studied oration. **set square** *n* a right-angled triangular drawing instrument. **set'-stitch'd** *adj* (*Sterne*) perh embroidered. **setter-forth'** *n*. **set terms** *n pl* deliberately chosen, *usu* outspoken language. **setter-off'** *n*. **setter-on'** *n*. **setter-out'** *n*. **setter-up'** *n*. **set theory** *n* (*maths*) the investigation of the properties of sets. **setting lotion** *n* a lotion containing gum or resin used to fix or set a hairstyle. **set-to'** *n* (*pl* **set-tos'** or **set-to's'**) a bout; a fight or argument; a fierce contest. **set'-top' box** *n* a device that allows a conventional television set to receive a digital signal. **set'-up** *n* the arrangement, organization, configuration or structure of anything; the place where an instrument for measuring, surveying, recording, etc is set up; a situation, the outcome of which has been prearranged, eg one in which someone is made a victim (*inf*); a shot, forming part of a scene, consisting of part of the action, close-up or location, etc (*film*); bodily carriage and physique. See also **set up** below.
■ **dead set** determined (on); indisputable (*Aust sl*). **set about** to begin, take in hand; to attack; to spread (rumours). **set against** to assail; to compare or balance. **set (a game) to two, three** or **five** (*badminton*) to set, in the final stages of a game, a new deciding score of two, three, or five points. **set alight, set light to, set fire to** or **set on fire** to cause to break into flame and burn. **set apart** to put aside, or out of consideration; to separate, distinguish. **set aside** to put away or to one side; to reject, annul; to reserve, lay by; to take (agricultural land) out of production, to leave fallow. **set at naught** see under **naught**. **set back** to check, delay, hinder, reverse; to cost (in money; *inf*); to place at some distance behind; to surprise, take aback. **set by** to lay up; to put aside; to value or esteem, to care (*archaic*). **set down** to lay on the ground; to put in writing, record; to appoint a time for (*Shakesp*); to judge, esteem, regard; to snub; to pitch, encamp (*Shakesp*); to attribute, ascribe; to lay down authoritatively; to stop and allow (passengers) to alight from a taxi, bus, car, etc. **set eyes on** to see, catch sight of. **set fair** (of weather) steadily fair; (of future prospects,

outlook, etc) settled and secure; likely, to all appearances (to do the desired thing). **set fire to** see **set alight** above. **set forth** to exhibit, display; to state, expound, declare; to praise, recommend; to publish; to start on a journey. **set free** to release, liberate. **set going** to put in motion. **set hand to** to set to work on. **set in** to begin; to become prevalent or established; (of wind, etc) to run landwards (naut). **set in hand** to undertake; to set someone about doing. **set little, much**, etc, **by** to regard or value little, much, etc. **set off** to start off; to send off; to show in relief or to advantage; to counterbalance; to make an offset, mark an opposite page; to mark off, lay off. **set on** to attack or incite to attack; to instigate; bent or determined upon. **set oneself** to bend one's energies. **set oneself against** to oppose. **set one's face against** see under **face**. **set one's hand to** to start work on, set about; to sign. **set one's heart on** see under **heart**. **set one's teeth** to clench the teeth, as in strong resolution. **set on fire** see **set alight** above. **set on foot** to set going, to start. **set out** to start, go forth; to display; to begin with an intention; to expound; to mark off; to adorn; to equip and send forth. **set sail** see under **sail**[1]. **set to** to affix; to apply oneself; to set (eg a bone) (Shakesp). **set up** to erect; to put up; to exalt, raise up (**set you, him**, etc **up** (Scot; ironic) what a cheek you've, he's, etc got!); to arrange; to begin; to enable to begin; to place in view; to put in type; to begin a career, esp in one's own business; to make pretensions; to arrange matters so as to implicate, incriminate, embarrass or make a fool of (another person) (inf) (**set'-up** n). **set upon** to set on; determined on.

seta /sē'tə/ n (pl **se'tae** /-tē/) a bristle; a bristle-like structure; the stalk of a moss capsule. [L saeta (sēta) bristle]
■ **setaceous** /si-tā'shəs/ or **setose** /sē'tōs or -tōs'/ adj. **sē'tal** adj. **setif'erous** or **setig'erous** adj bearing bristles. **set'iform** adj.

se-tenant /sə-tə-nā'/ (philately) adj denoting two or more stamps joined together in an unsevered row or block, (at least) one of which differs (eg in design or value) from the other(s). [Fr, holding together]

SETI abbrev: search for extraterrestrial intelligence.

seton /sē'tən/ n a thread or similar filament passed through the skin as a counter-irritant and means of promoting drainage; a flow obtained in this way. [LL sētō, -ōnis, appar from L sēta, saeta bristle]

SETS abbrev: Stock Exchange Electronic Trading Service.

sett see **set**.

settee[1] /se-tē'/ n a long seat with a back. [Prob **settle**]

settee[2] /se-tē'/ n a single-decked Mediterranean vessel with a long prow and lateen sails. [Prob Ital saettia]

setter[1], **setting** see under **set**.

setter[2] /set'ər/ (chiefly Scot and N Eng dialect) vt to treat with a seton of setterwort root. ◆ n a flow so produced in cattle. [Perh from MLGer]
❑ **sett'erwort** n stinking hellebore.

settle /set'l/ n a long high-backed bench; a ledge (Bible). ◆ vt to place in a stable, secure, restful or comfortable situation; to adjust; to lower; to compact, cause to subside; to regulate; to fix, arrange; to establish, set up, or install (eg in residence, business, marriage, a parish); to colonize; to make clear; to determine; to decide; to put beyond doubt or dispute; to restore to good order; to quiet; to compose; to secure by gift or legal act; to create successive interests in, use or income going to one person while the corpus of the property remains another's; to make final payment of; to dispose of, put out of action, stun, kill. ◆ vi to alight; to come to rest; to subside; to sink to the bottom (or form a scum); to dispose oneself; to take up permanent abode; to become stable; to fix one's habits (often with down); to grow calm or clear; to come to a decision or agreement; to adjust differences; to settle accounts (often with up). [OE setl seat, setlan to place; the verb may be partly from, or influenced by, late OE sehtlian to reconcile]
■ **sett'leable** adj. **sett'led** adj. **sett'ledness** n. **sett'lement** n an act of settling; the state of being settled; payment; arrangement; the placing of a religious minister in a parish; a subsidence or sinking; a settled colony; a local community; an establishment of social workers aiming at benefit to the surrounding population; a settling of property, an instrument by which it is settled, or the property settled, esp a marriage-settlement; residence in a parish or other claim for poor relief in case of becoming destitute. **sett'ler** n someone who settles; a colonist; a decisive blow, argument, etc. **sett'ling** n. **sett'lor** n (law) a person who settles property on another.
❑ **sett'le-bed** n a settle that may be converted to a bed. **settler's clock** n (Aust) a name formerly used for the kookaburra. **settling day** n a date fixed by the Stock Exchange for completion of transactions. **settling pond** n an artificial pond into which water containing effluent from a mine, etc is discharged and in which harmful sediment is deposited.
■ **settle for** to agree to accept (usu as a compromise). **settle in** to adapt to a new environment; to prepare to remain indoors for the night. **settle with** to come to an agreement with; to deal with.

setule /set'ūl/ n a small seta or bristle. [Mod L setula, dimin of seta]
■ **set'ulose** or **set'ulous** adj.

setwall /set'wol/ n orig the plant zedoary; now, valerian. —Also **setuale** /-ū-āl/ (Spenser), **cet'ywall**, etc. [OFr citoual, from LL zedoāria, from Ar zedwār]

seven /sev'n/ n the cardinal number next above six; a symbol representing that number (7, vii, etc); a set of seven things or people; a score of seven points, strokes, tricks, etc; an article of a size denoted by 7; a playing card with seven pips; the seventh hour after midnight or midday; the age of seven years. ◆ adj of the number seven; seven years old. [OE seofon; Du zeven, Ger sieben, Gothic sibun, Gr hepta, L septem]
■ **sev'enth** adj last of seven; next after the sixth; equal to one of seven equal parts. ◆ n a seventh part; a person or thing in seventh position; a tone or semitone less than an octave; a note at that interval. **sev'enthly** adv in the seventh place.
❑ **Seven against Thebes** n pl (Gr myth) the war of seven heroes to reinstate Polynices in Thebes against Eteocles. **seven-a-side'** n (also called **sev'ens**) a form of Rugby Union played by seven players on each side instead of fifteen (also adj). **Seven Champions of Christendom** n pl St George for England, St Andrew for Scotland, St Patrick for Ireland, St David for Wales, St Denis for France, St James for Spain, St Anthony for Italy. **sev'en-day** adj for seven days. **seven deadly sins** n pl pride, covetousness, lust, anger, gluttony, envy, and sloth. **sev'enfold** adj and adv in seven divisions; seven times as much. **seven hills of Rome** n pl the hills on which ancient Rome was built, the Aventine, Caelian, Capitoline, Esquiline, Palatine, Quirinal and Viminal. **sev'en-league** adj taking seven leagues at a stride (like the ogre's boots acquired by Hop-o'-my-Thumb in the fairy story). **sev'enpence** n the value of seven pennies. **sev'enpenny** adj costing or worth sevenpence. ◆ n a sevenpenny book, bus-ticket, etc. **Seven Sages** n pl Solon of Athens, Thales of Miletus, Pittacus of Mitylene, Bias of Priene in Caria, Chilon of Sparta, Cleobulus tyrant of Lindus in Rhodes, and Periander tyrant of Corinth; an Eastern cycle of tales in which seven wise men compete in story-telling against a woman to save the life of a falsely accused prince. **sev'en-score** n and adj. **Seven Seas** n pl the Arctic, Antarctic, N and S Atlantic, N and S Pacific, and Indian Oceans; all the seas of the world generally. **Seven Sleepers** n pl seven Christian youths at Ephesus said to have slept walled up in a cave c.250–447AD. **Seven Stars** n pl the planets known to the ancients; the Plough; the Pleiades. **seventh day** n Saturday. **sev'enth-day** adj observing Saturday as Sabbath (**Seventh-day Adventists** a sect that expects the Second Coming of Christ and observes Saturday as the Sabbath). **seventh heaven** see under **heaven**. **Seven Wonders of the World** n pl the seven monuments regarded as the most remarkable of the ancient world, the Pyramids, the Hanging Gardens of Babylon, the Temple of Artemis at Ephesus, Phidias's statue of Zeus at Olympia, the Mausoleum at Halicarnassus, the Colossus of Rhodes, and the Pharos of Alexandria. **seven-year itch** n a tendency towards sexual infidelity, held in jocular tradition to be common after about seven years of marriage. **Seven Years' War** n the struggle for Silesia between Frederick the Great and the Empress Maria Theresa (1756–63).

seventeen /sev-n-tēn' or sev'/ n and adj seven and ten. [OE seofontīene; see **seven** and **ten**]
■ **sev'enteenth** (or /-tēnth'/) adj and n. **seventeenth'ly** adv.
❑ **sev'enteen-hund'er** adj (Burns) woven with a reed of 1700 divisions, ie fine linen. **sev'enteen-year locust** see **periodical cicada** under **period**.

seventy /sev'n-ti/ n and adj seven times ten. [OE (hund)seofontig]
■ **sev'enties** n pl the numbers seventy to seventy-nine; the years so numbered in a life or any century; a range of temperature from seventy to just less than eighty degrees. **sev'entieth** adj last of seventy; next after the sixty-ninth; equal to one of seventy equal parts. ◆ n a seventieth part; a person or thing in seventieth position.
❑ **seventy-eight'** n an old type of gramophone record designed to be played at 78 revolutions per minute, standard before the introduction of long-playing microgroove records (usu written **78**).
■ **the Seventy** the Jewish Sanhedrim; the disciples sent out in the Bible, Luke 10; the Septuagint translators (often written **LXX**).

sever /sev'ər/ vt and vi to separate; to divide, part; to cleave, split; to detach; to break off or end. [ME severen, from MFr severer, from L sēparāre to separate]
■ **sev'erable** adj. **sev'erance** n.
❑ **severance pay** n an allowance granted to an employee on the termination of his or her employment.

several /sev'(ə-)rəl/ adj various; sundry; more than one (usu more than three), but not very many; separate; particular; distinct; different; belonging or relating distributively, not jointly (law); privately owned. ◆ n privately owned land, esp enclosed pasture (hist); private property (archaic or law); a detail, particular (Shakesp); an individual person (Shakesp). ◆ pronoun a few. [OFr, from L sēparāre to separate]

■ words derived from main entry word; ❑ compound words; ■ idioms and phrasal verbs

■ **sev'eralfold** *adj* and *adv*. **sev'erally** *adv* separately; respectively. **sev'eralty** *n* separateness; individual ownership of property, *esp* land (*law*).

■ **in several** separately, individually.

severe /si-vēr'/ *adj* rigorous, harsh; very strict; conforming to a rigorous standard; unsparing; hard to endure; dangerous; grave, acute or very bad; critical; stern; austerely restrained or simple in appearance. [L *sevērus*].

■ **severe'ly** *adv*. **severe'ness** *n*. **severity** /si-ver'i-ti/ *n*.

❑ **severe combined immunodeficiency syndrome** *n* a severe form of congenital immunological deficiency in which both T and B lymphocytes are absent (*abbrev* **SCID**).

severy /sev'ə-ri/ (*archit*) *n* a compartment of vaulting. [OFr *civoire*, from L *cibōrium*; see **ciborium**]

Sèvres /sev'r'/ *adj* (of porcelain) made at *Sèvres*, near Paris. ◆ *n* Sèvres porcelain.

sevruga /si-vroo'gə/ *n* a species of sturgeon, *Acipenser stellatus*, of the Black and Caspian seas; a delicately-flavoured caviar obtained from it.

sew[1] /sō/ *vt* (pat **sewed** /sōd/; pap **sewn** /sōn/ or **sewed**) to join, attach, enclose, or work on with a needle and thread, with wire, or with a sewing machine. ◆ *vi* to work with a needle and thread, sewing machine, or in any similar way. [OE *sīwian*, *sēowian*; from OHGer *siuwen*, Gothic *siujan*]

■ **sew'er** *n*. **sew'ing** *n* the act of sewing; something that is being sewn.

❑ **sewing machine** *n* a machine for sewing fabric, leather, etc.

■ **sew up** to enclose or close up by sewing; to complete satisfactorily, or secure a satisfactory result (*inf*); to tire out, bring to a standstill, nonplus, or make drunk (*sl*).

sew[2] /sū/ *vt* (*dialect*) to drain. ◆ *vi* to ooze (*dialect*); to be aground (*naut*). [OFr *essever* to drain off, from L *ex* out, and *aqua* water]

■ **sew'age** *n* refuse or waste carried off by sewers. **sewer** /soo'ər or sū'ər, or (old) shōr or shör/ *n* a channel (*esp* underground) for receiving the discharge from house-drains and streets. ◆ *vt* to provide with sewers. **sew'erage** *n* a system, or the provision, of sewers; sewage. **sew'ering** *n*.

❑ **sewage farm** *n* a place where sewage is treated to render it suitable for use as manure; also, a farm on which sewage is used as fertilizer. **sewage works** *n* a place where sewage is treated and purified before being discharged into a river or the sea. **sewer gas** *n* the contaminated air of sewers produced by the decomposition of sewage. **sewer rat** *n* the brown rat.

sew[3] (*Spenser*) same as **sue**.

sewel see **shewel**.

sewellel /si-wel'əl/ *n* the mountain beaver, *Aplodontia rufa*, a squirrel-like burrowing rodent of NW coastal regions of N America. [Chinook *shewallal* a robe of its skin]

Sewel motion /soo'əl mō'shən/ *n* a motion passed by the Scottish parliament endorsing legislation passed in the British parliament. [Lord *Sewel* (born 1946), British politician]

sewen see **sewin**.

sewer[1] see under **sew**[1].

sewer[2], **sewerage** see under **sew**[2].

sewer[3] /sū'ər/ (*hist*) *n* a high-ranking servant who superintended the service at table in medieval England; later, an officer of the royal household. [OFr *asseour*, from *asseoir* to set down, from L *ad* to, and *sedēre* to sit]

sewin or **sewen** /sū'in/ *n* the Welsh and Irish name for a sea-trout grilse. [Origin unknown]

sewn see **sew**[1].

sex /seks/ *n* the sum of the characteristics which distinguish an animal or plant as male or female; the quality of being male or female; either of the divisions according to this, or its members collectively; the whole area connected with this distinction; sexual intercourse, or behaviour, feelings, desires, etc associated with it. ◆ *adj* of or relating to sex. ◆ *vt* to ascertain the sex of. [L *sexus*, *-ūs*]

■ **sexed** /sekst/ *adj* having sexual characteristics; being male or female; having sexual desires or urges to a specified degree, as in *under-sexed*, *highly-sexed*. **sex'er** *n* a person who ascertains the sex of domestic fowl, etc. **sex'ily** *adv*. **sex'iness** *n*. **sex'ism** *n* discrimination against, stereotyping of, patronizing or otherwise offensive behaviour towards anyone (*orig* women) on the grounds of sex. **sex'ist** *n* and *adj*. **sex'less** *adj* of neither sex; without sex; without sexual feelings; devoid of sexual attractiveness. **sex'lessly** *adv*. **sex'lessness** *n*. **sexolog'ical** *adj*. **sexol'ogist** *n*. **sexol'ogy** *n* the study of (human) sexual behaviour and relationships. **sex'ual** *adj* of, by, having or characteristic of, sex, one sex or other, or organs of sex. **sex'ualism** *n* emphasis on sex. **sex'ualist** *n*. **sexual'ity** *n*. **sexualīzā'tion** or **-s-** *n*. **sex'ualize** or **-ise** *vt* to make sexual; to

attribute sexual significance to. **sex'ūally** *adv*. **sex'y** *adj* (of a person) sexually attractive, stirring sexual interest in others; stimulating sexual instincts; involved in, or concerned with, sexual activity, *esp* sexual intercourse; (of an object, idea, etc) exciting, attractive, fascinating, tempting (*inf*).

❑ **sex aid** *n* any of various articles and devices used to prompt or increase sexual arousal artificially, as sold in sex shops. **sex'-and-shopp'ing** *adj* denoting a style of fiction in which women are portrayed enjoying a glamorous and promiscuous lifestyle (also (*taboo sl*) **shopp'ing-and-fuck'ing**). **sex appeal** *n* the power of attracting, *esp* of exciting sexual desire in others. **sex bomb** *n* (*inf*) a person, *esp* female, with a lot of sex appeal. **sex cell** *n* an egg cell or sperm. **sex change** *n* (*esp* of humans) a changing of sex, *usu* achieved by the surgical transformation and/or recreation of sexual organs. **sex'-change** *adj*. **sex chromosome** *n* the chromosome that determines sex. **sex'-determination** *n* the biological process by which the sex of a new organism is determined. **sex drive** *n* the natural impulse and appetite for sexual relations. **sexed-up'** *adj* made sexy or extra sexy; sexually excited. **sex hormones** *n pl* hormones produced by the gonads that control the development of sexual characteristics. **sex intergrade** *n* an intersex. **sex kitten** *n* a young woman (mischievously) playing up her sex appeal. **sex'-limited** *adj* developed only in one sex. **sex linkage** *n*. **sex'-linked** *adj* (of a trait, disorder, etc) inherited along with sex, that is, by a factor located in the sex chromosome. **sex object** *n* an individual regarded purely in terms of their ability to satisfy sexual desire. **sex offender** *n* a person who has committed a crime of a sexual nature. **sex-pos'itive** *adj* showing a positive attitude towards sexual instincts and desires. **sex'pot** *n* (*sl*) a person of very great or obvious physical attraction. **sex'-reversal** *n* change from male to female or female to male in the life of the individual. **sex shop** *n* a shop selling articles connected with sexual arousal, behaviour, etc. **sex'-starved** *adj* deprived of the pleasures and satisfactions of sexual activity. **sex symbol** *n* a celebrity who is widely acknowledged as being sexually attractive. **sex (or sexual) therapist** *n* a person who deals with problems relating to sexual intercourse. **sex (or sexual) therapy** *n*. **sex tourism** *n* travelling to a foreign country in order to take advantage of permissive attitudes or poor enforcement of laws regarding sexual activity, *esp* concerning prostitution and sex with children. **sex tourist** *n*. **sex typing** *n* the designation of certain behaviours as being either feminine or masculine. **sexual abuse** *n* the subjection of a person to sexual activity likely to cause physical or psychological harm. **sexual athlete** *n* someone who performs sexual intercourse skilfully and/or frequently. **sexual harassment** *n* harassment consisting of misplaced and unwelcome sexual advances, remarks, etc, *esp* in the workplace. **sexual intercourse** *n* the uniting of sexual organs, *esp* involving the insertion of the male penis into the female vagina and the release of sperm. **sexually transmitted disease** or **infection** *n* a venereal disease. **sexual preference** *n* a preference for either homosexual or heterosexual relations. **sexual reproduction** *n* the union of gametes or gametic nuclei preceding the formation of a new individual. **sexual selection** *n* the province of natural selection in which preference for mates having certain characters comes into play. **sexual system** *n* the Linnaean system of plant classification according to sexual organization. **sex worker** *n* a prostitute.

■ **sex on legs** (*sl*) a person who is regarded as extremely attractive or desirable. **sex up** (*sl*) to make more interesting or attractive. **the sex** (*archaic*) the female sex, women.

sex- /seks-/ or **sexi-** /sek-si-/ *combining form* denoting six. [L *sex* six]

■ **sex'fid** *adj* split or divided into six parts. **sex'foil** *n* a window, design, etc, with six lobes or leaves. **sexivā'lent** (or /sek-siv'ə-lənt/) or **sexvā'lent** *adj* (*chem*) of a valency of six. **sexloc'ular** *adj* with six compartments. **sexpart'ite** *adj* parted in six; involving six participants, groups, etc.

sexagenarian /sek-sə-ji-nā'ri-ən/ *n* a person who is sixty years old, or between sixty and seventy (also *adj*). [L *sexāgēnārius* relating to sixty, from *sexāgintā* sixty]

■ **sexagenary** /-jē'nə-ri/ *adj* (*rare*) of, containing, based on, sixty; sexagenarian. ◆ *n* a sexagesimal fraction; a sexagenarian.

Sexagesima /sek-sə-jes'i-mə/ *n* the second Sunday before Lent (also **Sexagesima Sunday**), *appar* so named on the false analogy of Quadragesima, etc. [L *sexāgēsimus* sixtieth]

■ **sexages'imal** *adj* relating to, or based on, sixty. ◆ *n* a sexagesimal fraction. **sexages'imally** *adv* by sixtieths.

sexcentenary /sek-sen- or sek-sin-tē'nə-ri or -ten'ə-ri/ *n* a 600th anniversary or a celebration of this (also *adj*).

sexennial /sek-sen'yəl or -sen'i-əl/ *adj* lasting six years; recurring every six years. [L *sex* six, and *annus* year]

■ **sexenn'ially** *adv*.

sexer see under **sex**.

sexfid, sexfoil see under **sex-**.

sexily...to...**sexist** see under **sex**.

sexivalent see under **sex-**.

sexless, etc see under **sex**.

sexlocular see under **sex-**.

sexology, etc see under **sex**.

sexpartite see under **sex-**.

sexpert /seks'pûrt/ (inf; esp US) n an expert in sexual behaviour. [**sex** and **expert**]

sexploitation /seks-ploi-tā'shən/ n the exploitation of sex for commercial gain in films and other media. [**sex** and **exploitation**]

sext[1] /sekst/ n one of the hours of the Divine Office, orig held at the sixth hour of the day (midday) (RC); a sixth (music). [L sextus sixth, from sex six]

sext[2] /sekst/ vi to send sexually explicit material in a text message. ◆ n a text message that contains sexually explicit material. [**sex** and **text**]
■ **sex'ting** n.

sextan /seks'tən/ (med) adj (of the paroxysms of a fever) recurring every fifth day (sixth by old reckoning). [From Med L sextana (febris) (fever) of the sixth (day)]

sextant /seks'tənt/ n the sixth part of a circle or its circumference, a sector or an arc of 60°; an instrument with an arc of a sixth of a circle, for measuring angular distances, esp a navigating instrument incorporating a small telescope; (with cap; also **Sex'tans**) a constellation, lying over the equator; (also **sex'tans** /-tənz/) a Roman bronze coin worth a sixth of an as (hist). [L sextāns, -antis a sixth]
■ **sextantal** /-tant'l/ adj.

sextet, **sextett**, **sextette** /seks-tet'/ n altered forms (partly through German) of **sestet**.

sextile /seks'tīl or -til/ (astrol) n a position 60° apart on the zodiacal chart (also **sextile aspect**). [L sextīlis sixth]

sextillion /seks-til'yən/ n a thousand raised to the seventh power (10^{21}); (esp formerly, in Britain) a million raised to the sixth power (10^{36}). ◆ adj being a sextillion in number. [Fr, from L sextus sixth, and **million**]
■ **sextill'ionth** adj and n.

sextodecimo /sek-stō-des'i-mō/ adj having sixteen leaves to the sheet. ◆ n (pl **sextodec'imos**) a book with sheets so folded, usu written **16mo**. [L (in) sextō decimō (in) one-sixteenth]

sextolet /seks'tə-let/ (music) n a group of six notes performed in the time of four. [Ger Sextole, from L sex six]

sexton /seks'tən/ n an officer who rings a church bell, attends the clergyman, digs graves, etc; a burying beetle (also **sexton beetle**). [sacristan]
■ **sex'toness** n a female sexton. **sex'tonship** n.

sextuor /seks'tū-ör/ n a sextet. [Fr, from L sex, after quattuor four]

sextuple /seks'tū-pl/ adj sixfold. ◆ n six times as much. ◆ vt and vi to increase or multiply sixfold. [LL sextuplus]
■ **sex'tuplet** n one of six children born at a single birth; a sextolet (music).

sexual, **sexy**, etc see under **sex**.

sey /sī/ (Scot) n part of a carcase of beef incl the sirloin. [Origin obscure]

Seychellois /sā-shel-wä'/ adj of or relating to the Republic of Seychelles in the Indian Ocean, or its inhabitants. ◆ n a native or citizen of the Seychelles.

seyen a Shakespearean spelling of **scion**.

Seyfert galaxy /sī'fûrt or sē'fərt gal'ək-si/ (astron) n one of a small class of galaxies with intensely bright nuclei and inconspicuous spiral arms. [Carl Seyfert (1911–60), US astrophysicist]

seysure a Shakespearean spelling of **seizure**.

sez slang spelling of **says** (see **say**[1]).

Sézary syndrome /sez'ə-ri sin'drōm/ (med) n a rare condition in which abnormal growth of lymphocytes occurs in the skin, liver and lymph nodes. [A Sézary (1880–1956), French physician]

SF abbrev : science fiction; signal frequency; Sinn Fein.

sf (music) abbrev : sforzando.

SFA abbrev : Scottish Football Association; Securities and Futures Authority (now replaced by **FSA**); Sweet Fanny Adams (= nothing at all; sl).

SFAS (US) abbrev : Statement of Financial Accounting Standards.

sferics see **spherics**[1].

SFO abbrev : Serious Fraud Office.

'sfoot /sfūt/ (Shakesp) interj for **God's foot**, an exclamatory oath.

sforzando /sför-tsän'dō/ or **sforzato** /sför-tsä'tō/ (music) adj and adv forced, with sudden emphasis (symbol > or ⌃). ◆ n (pl **sforzan'dos** or

sforzan'di /-dē/, **sforza'tos** or **sforza'ti** /-tē/) a sforzando note. [Ital, prp and pap of sforzare to force, from L ex out, and LL fortia force]

S4C abbrev : Sianel Pedwar Cymru, the Welsh language television channel.

sfumato /sfoo-mä'tō/ (art) n (pl **sfuma'tos**) a misty, indistinct effect achieved by gradually blending together areas of different colour or tone. [Ital, pap of sfumare to shade off, from L ex out, and fūmāre to smoke]

SFX abbrev : special effects.

sfx abbrev : suffix.

sfz (music) abbrev : sforzando.

SG abbrev : Solicitor General.

Sg (chem) symbol : seaborgium.

sg abbrev : specific gravity.

sgd abbrev : signed.

SGHWR abbrev : steam-generating heavy water reactor.

sgian-dubh /skē'ən-doo'/ n same as **skene-dhu** (see under **skene**).

SGML (comput) abbrev : Standard Generalized Mark-up Language, a form of coding of electronic data for printed applications.

SGP abbrev : Singapore (IVR).

sgraffito /sgra- or zgra-fē'tō/ n (pl **sgraffi'ti** /-tē/) a decorative technique in which different colours are revealed by removal of parts of outer layers of material (plaster, slip, etc) laid on; pottery with such decoration. [Ital, from L ex-, and **graffito**]

Sgt abbrev : Sergeant.

sh or **shh** /sh/ interj hush.

s/h abbrev : shorthand.

SHA abbrev : Strategic Health Authority.

Shabbat /sha-bat' or -bät'/ (Judaism) n (pl **Shabbatot** /-bä-tot'/) the Sabbath. [Heb Shabbāth, literally, day of rest]

shabby /shab'i/ adj dingy or dirty; (of eg clothes) threadbare or worn; having a look of poverty; (of behaviour) unworthy, discreditable or contemptible; low; paltry. [Obs or dialect shab scab, from OE sceabb]
■ **shabb'ily** adv. **shabb'iness** n.
❑ **Shabby Chic**® n a style of interior decoration using worn or vintage furniture and pale colours. **shabb'y-genteel** adj keeping up or affecting an appearance of gentility, though really very shabby. **shabby-gentil'ity** n.

shabrack /shab'rak/ (hist) n a trooper's housing or saddlecloth (also **shab'racque**). [Ger Schabracke, prob from Turk çāprāq]

Shabuoth, **Shavuoth** /sha-vū'oth or -ot/, **Shavuot** /-ot/ or **Shevuoth** /shev'ū-oth/ n the Jewish Feast of Weeks, celebrated on the 50th day after Passover, orig marking the end of harvest, now generally taken as a commemoration of the giving of the Law to Moses (also called **Pentecost**). [Heb shabuot(h) weeks]

shack /shak/ n a roughly-built hut. [US; origin obscure]
■ **shack up** (with with; sl; usu of unmarried sexual partners) to live together, or set up house together.

shackle /shak'l/ n a prisoner's or slave's ankle-ring or wrist-ring, or the chain connecting a pair; (in pl) fetters, manacles; a hindrance, constraint; a hobble; a staple-like link, closed with a pin; the curved movable part of a padlock; a coupling of various kinds. ◆ vt to fetter; to couple; to hamper. [OE sceacul]
❑ **shack'le-bolt** n the pin of a shackle. **shack'le-bone** n (Scot) the wrist.

shacko see **shako**.

shad /shad/ n an anadromous fish related to the herring; extended to various other similar but unrelated fishes. [OE sceadd]
❑ **shad'-bellied** adj flat-bellied, opp to pot-bellied; (of a coat) sloping away gradually in front. **shad'berry** n the serviceberry shrub (also **shad'bush** or **shad'blow**); the fruit of the serviceberry, which flowers at shad spawning-time.

shadchan /shad'hhən/ n (pl **shad'chans** or **shad'chanim** /-hhə-nim/) an arranger of marriages for Jewish couples. [Heb shadhkhān, from shiddēkh (see **shidduch**)]

shaddock /shad'ək/ n an E Asian citrus fruit like a very large orange, the pomelo; the tree that bears it. [Introduced to the W Indies c.1700 by a Captain Shaddock]

shade[1] /shād/ n partial or relative darkness; interception of light; obscurity; a shadow; a momentary facial expression; a place or area from which sunlight is excluded; shelter from light or heat; that which casts a shadow; a screen; a window blind (US); a cover to modify or direct the light from a lamp; an inverted glass vessel formerly put over a clock or ornament; a projecting cover to protect the eyes from glare; (in pl) sunglasses (inf); an awning for a shop-window; a lace head-covering (obs); a variety or degree of colour; a hue mixed with black;

the dark part of a picture; a slight difference or amount; (in *pl*; often with *cap*) the darkness of the underworld, the abode of the dead, Hades; the disembodied soul; a ghost (*literary*). ◆ *vt* to screen; to overshadow; to mark with gradations of colour or shadow; to soften down; to darken; to shadow, represent (*obs*); to lower (eg a price) very slightly (*orig US*); to win narrowly (*inf*). ◆ *vi* to pass imperceptibly (*away*, *into*, etc). [OE *sceadu*; see **shadow**]

■ **shā'ded** *adj*. **shade'less** *adj*. **shā'der** *n*. **shā'dily** *adv*. **shā'diness** *n*. **shā'ding** *n* the marking of shadows or shadowlike appearance; the effect of light and shade; fine gradations; nuances; toning down; modification of sound by anything put on top of an organ-pipe; the generation of a non-uniform background level in an image by a television camera tube; slight lowering of prices. **shā'dy** *adj* having, or in, shade; sheltered from light or heat; underhand, disreputable (*inf*); shadowy, mysterious, sinister.

❑ **shade card** *n* a card illustrating the various shades available in a certain type of paint. **shade plant** *n* a plant adapted to light of low intensity. **shade tree** *n* a tree planted to give shade.

■ **in the shade** sheltered from strong light; overlooked, forgotten, in relative obscurity. **on the shady side of** (*inf*) over (a specified age). **put in the shade** to outdo completely. **shades of** used to say that something reminds one in some way of (a specified person or thing).

shade² /*shād*/ (*Scot*) *vt* to part (the hair). [Scot and N Eng form of **shed²**]

shadoof or **shaduf** /*shä-doof'*/ *n* a device for raising water by a bucket on a counterpoised pivoted rod. [Egyp Ar *shādūf*]

shadow /*shad'ō*/ *n* shade cast by the interception of light by an object; the dark figure so projected on a surface, mimicking the object; the dark part of a picture; a reflected image; a mere appearance; an unreal thing; a representation; a person or thing wasted away almost to nothing; an inseparable or constant companion; a spy or detective who follows one; shade; protective shade, shelter; darkness; gloom; trouble; a ghost, spirit. ◆ *adj* unreal; feigned; existing only in skeleton; inactive, or only partly active, but ready for the time when opportunity or need arises; denoting, in the main opposition party, a political counterpart to a member or section of the party in power. ◆ *vt* to shade; to cloud or darken; to indicate obscurely, vaguely, or in dim outline (*usu* with *forth*); to typify; to hide; to attend like a shadow, follow and watch; to maintain a position close to, follow every movement of; to shadowcast. ◆ *vi* to cast a shadow; to darken. [OE *sceadwe*, genitive, dative and accusative of *sceadu* (**shade¹** representing the nominative); cf OHGer *scato*, Gr *skotos* darkness]

■ **shad'ower** *n*. **shad'owiness** *n*. **shad'owing** *n*. **shad'owless** *adj*. **shad'owy** *adj* shady; like a shadow; symbolic; secluded, dim; unsubstantial.

❑ **shadow box** *n* a frame or box-like structure (often with shelves and a clear protective front) used to display articles. **shad'ow-box** *vi*. **shad'ow-boxing** *n* sparring practice with an imaginary opponent; making a show of opposition or other action, as a cover for taking no effective steps. **shadow cabinet** *n* a body of senior politicians from an opposition party, each acting as a spokeperson on a different area of policy. **shad'owcast** *vt* (in microscopy) to cast shadows of projecting parts of (a specimen) by exposing to a stream of vapour of a heavy metal. **shad'owcasting** *n*. **shadow economy** *n* another name for the **black economy** (see under **black**). **shadow effect** *n* a loss of signal strength in broadcast transmissions due to the topography of a region. **shadow fight** *n* a fight between or with shadows or imaginary enemies. **shadow figure** *n* a silhouette. **shad'owgraph** *n* an image produced by throwing a shadow on a screen; a radiograph. **shadow mark** *n* the trace of an archaeological site revealed by observation from the air. **shadow mask** *n* a perforated metal sheet situated behind the phosphor screen in some colour television tubes. **shadow play** *n* one in which the spectators see only shadows on a screen (also **shadow pantomime**); action which is merely symbolic or which mimics real or effective action. **shadow price** *n* an estimated price for a product for which there is no market price.

■ **afraid of one's own shadow** extremely timid. **may your shadow never grow less** may you continue to prosper. **shadow of death** the darkness of death; the threatening approach of darkness or death.

SHAEF /*shāf*/ *abbrev*: (during World War II) Supreme Headquarters Allied Expeditionary Force.

Shafiite /*shaf'i-īt*/ *n* a member of one of the four principal sects of the Sunnites, or orthodox Muslims. [Ar *Shāfiʿī* the name of the founder]

shaft /*shäft*/ *n* anything long and straight; a stem; an arrow; a missile (*esp fig*); the main, upright, straight, or cylindrical part of anything; the part of a cross below the arms; the part of a column between the base and the capital; the rachis of a feather; the bill of a carriage on either side of the horse; a straight handle; a pole; a ray or beam of light; a rotating rod that transmits motion; a well-like excavation or passage; the penis (*vulgar sl*); a woman's body (purely as a sexual object) (*US vulgar sl*). ◆ *vt* to have sexual intercourse with (a woman) (*vulgar sl*); to

dupe, swindle, treat unfairly (*sl*). [OE *sceaft*; perh partly Ger *Schacht* pit-shaft]

■ **shaft'ed** *adj*. **shaft'er** *n* (also **shaft'-horse**) a horse harnessed between shafts. **shaft'ing** *n* the action of the verb in either sense; a system of shafts. **shaft'less** *adj*.

■ **make a shaft or a bolt of it** to venture and take what comes of it, the shaft and the bolt being the arrows of the longbow and the crossbow respectively.

shag /*shag*/ *n* a ragged mass of hair, or anything similar; a long coarse nap; a kind of tobacco cut into shreds; the green cormorant (*appar* from its crest), or other species; an act of sexual intercourse (*vulgar sl*); a partner, *usu* female, in sexual intercourse (*vulgar sl*); a whore (*vulgar sl*); a US dance related to the jitterbug but with shuffling footwork, first popular in the 1950s and 60s; a lively dance of the 1930s. ◆ *adj* shaggy; shaggy-haired. ◆ *vt* (**shagg'ing**; **shagged** /*shagd*/) to make shaggy; to have sexual intercourse with (*vulgar sl*); to chase after (balls hit in the air) as part of fielding practice (*baseball*). ◆ *vi* to have sexual intercourse (*vulgar sl*); to dance the shag; to hang in shaggy clusters (*archaic*). [OE *sceacga*; cf ON *skegg* a beard]

■ **shagg'able** *adj* (*vulgar sl*) sexually attractive. **shagged** /*shagd*/ *adj* shaggy, rough (also /*shag'id*/); tired out, exhausted, as if from strenuous lovemaking (often with *out*) (*sl*). **shagg'edness** *n*. **shagg'er** *n* (*vulgar sl*) a person who engages in sexual intercourse. **shagg'ily** *adv*. **shagg'iness** *n*. **shagg'y** *adj* long, rough, and coarse; having long, rough, coarse hair, wool, vegetation, etc; unkempt; rugged.

❑ **shag'bark** *n* a kind of hickory tree. **shag'-** (or **shagge'-**)**eared** *adj* (*Shakesp*) hairy-eared. **shaggy cap**, **shaggy ink-cap** or **shaggy mane** *n* an edible fungus (*Coprinus comatus*) with a white, cylindrical, shaggy-scaled cap. **shaggy-dog story** *n* (from the shaggy dog featured in many) a whimsically long-drawn-out story humorous because of its length and the inconsequence of its ending. **shag'-haired** *adj*. **shag'pile** *adj* (*esp* of carpets) having a pile of long, thick fibres.

shagreen /*shə-grēn'*/ *n* a granular leather made from horses' or donkeys' skin; the skin of shark, ray, etc, covered with small nodules (formerly **chagrin'**). [Fr *chagrin*, from Turk *sagri* horse's rump, shagreen]

■ **shagreen'** or **shagreened'** *adj* of, or covered with, shagreen.

shagroon /*shə-groon'*/ *n* an early settler in New Zealand of other than British origin. [Perh Ir *seachrán* wandering]

shah /*shä*/ *n* the king of Persia (now Iran) (*hist*); also formerly of certain other Eastern countries. [Pers *shāh*]

■ **shah'dom** *n*.

shahada /*shə-hä'də*/ *n* the Islamic declaration of faith. [Ar *shahāda* witnessing]

shaheed or **shahid** /*shə-hēd'*/ *n* a martyr for the Islamic faith. [Ar]

shahtoosh or **shatoosh** /*sha-toosh'*/ *n* a fine wool made from the throat hairs of the chiru antelope; a shawl made from this wool. [Pers, literally, king of wools]

shaikh same as **sheikh**.

shairn same as **sharn**.

Shaitan /*shī-tän'*/ *n* Satan; (without *cap*) an evil spirit; a devilish person or animal; a dust storm. [Ar *shaitān*, from Heb (see **Satan**)]

Shaiva see **Saiva**.

shake /*shāk*/ *vt* (*pat* **shook** or *obs* **shāked** and **shākt**; *pap* **shāk'en** or *obs* **shāked**, **shākt** and **shook**) to move with quick, short, often violent to-and-fro or up-and-down movements; to brandish; to cause to tremble or to totter; to disturb the stability of; to cause to waver; to disturb; to dismay; to unnerve, shock; to alert, rouse, summon (*sl*); to put, send, render or cause to be, by shaking; to scatter or send down by shaking; to split; to get rid of (*US*; *old*). ◆ *vi* to be agitated; to tremble; to shiver; to shake hands; to trill (*music*); to happen (*sl*). ◆ *n* a shaking; tremulous motion; (in *pl* with *the*) a fit of uncontrollable trembling (*inf*); a damaging or weakening blow; a shaken-up drink (*esp* a milk shake); a trillo (*music*); a fissure or crack (*esp* in rock or in growing timber); a moment (*inf*). [OE *sc(e)acan*]

■ **shake'able** or **shāk'able** *adj*. **shāk'en** *adj*. **shāk'er** *n* a person who shakes; a person who makes things happen, as in the phrase *mover and shaker*; a device for shaking (eg drinks); a perforated container from which something, eg flour, is shaken; (with *cap*; in *pl*) a name popularly applied to an American religious sect, the United Society of Believers in Christ's Second Appearing, as a result of their ecstatic dancing, also formerly to Quakers and sects whose religious fervour manifested itself in violent trembling. **Shāk'erism** *n*. **shāk'ily** *adv*. **shāk'iness** *n*. **shāk'ing** *n* and *adj*. **shāk'y** *adj* shaking or inclined to shake; loose; tremulous; precarious; uncertain; wavering; unsteady; frail from old age or illness; full of cracks or clefts.

❑ **shake'-bag** *n* a fighting cock turned out of a bag; a large fighting cock. **shake'down** *n* a temporary bed (*orig* made by shaking down straw); a trial run, operation, etc to familiarize personnel with procedures and machinery (chiefly *US*; *inf*); an act of extortion or blackmail (*sl*); a thorough search of a person or place *esp* by the police (*sl*). **shaken baby syndrome** *n* a collection of symptoms, including brain damage and paralysis, that can occur when an infant is shaken violently by an adult. **shake'-out** *n* a drastic reorganization or upheaval; a recession in a particular commercial or industrial activity, *esp* when accompanied by cutbacks in the workforce or closure of individual businesses. **shake'-rag** *n* (*obs*) a disreputable ragged man. **shake'-up** *n* (*inf*) a disturbance or reorganization. **shaking palsy** *n* a name for Parkinson's disease.

■ **great shakes** or **no great shakes** (*inf*) of great account or of no account. **shake a leg** (often *imperative*; *inf*) to hurry up, get moving. **shake down** (*sl*) to extort money from by threats or blackmail; to search thoroughly; to frisk (a person for weapons, drugs, etc); to go to bed (*esp* in a temporary bed); to settle by shaking; to cheat of money at one stroke. **shake hands with** to greet (someone) by clasping his or her hand *usu* with an up-and-down movement; to seal a bargain, acknowledge an agreement, settle differences, etc, with (someone) in this way. **shake** or **shiver in one's shoes** to be so afraid that one's body, *esp* one's legs, quiver with fear. **shake off** to get rid of, often by shaking (also *fig*); to get away, escape, from (someone or something that is following, pursuing, etc). **shake off** (or **shake**) **the dust from one's feet** (see Bible, Matthew 10.14) to leave hurriedly or gladly (*lit* and *fig*). **shake on** to conclude (a bargain, agreement, etc) by shaking hands. **shake one's head** to turn one's head from side to side as an indication of reluctance, rejection, denial, disapproval, etc. **shake one's sides** to laugh uproariously. **shake out** to empty or cause to spread or unfold by shaking. **shake up** to rouse, mix, disturb, loosen by shaking; to unnerve or upset; to reorganize (*inf*); to upbraid (*Shakesp*). **two shakes** (**of a lamb's tail**, etc) (*inf*) a very short time.

Shakespearean or **Shakespearian** /shāk-spē'ri-ən/ *adj* of or relating to William *Shakespeare* (1564–1616), or his literary works, etc. ◆ *n* a person who studies Shakespeare.
■ **Shakespeariana** /-i-ä'nə/ *n pl* items, writings or lore relating to Shakespeare.
❑ **Shakespearean sonnet** see under **sonnet**.

shako or **shacko** /shak'ō/ *n* (*pl* **shak'os** or **shak'oes**) a tall, nearly cylindrical military cap with a plume. [Hung *csákó*]

Shakta, **Shakti**, **Shaktism** see **Sakti**.

shakudo /shak'ŭ-dō or -dō'/ *n* an alloy of copper and a small percentage of gold, used in Japanese decorative art, *esp* in sword fittings, to give a blue-black patina. ◆ *adj* made of or with shakudo. [Jap]

shakuhachi /shak-ŭ-hach'ē or shäk-ŭ-häch'ē/ *n* a Japanese end-blown bamboo flute. [Jap]

shale¹ /shāl/ *n* clay rock splitting readily into thin layers along the bedding planes. [Ger *Schale* lamina; or from **shale²**]
■ **shā'ly** *adj*.
❑ **shale gas** *n* natural gas extracted from shale. **shale mine** *n*. **shale'-miner** *n*. **shale oil** *n* oil distilled from oil-bearing shales.

shale² /shāl/ (*Shakesp*) *n* a shell or husk. ◆ *vt* to shell. [OE *sc(e)alu*; cf **scale²**]

shall /shal or shəl/ *vt* (no participles; 2nd pers sing (*archaic*) **shalt**; 3rd pers sing **shall**; *pat* **should** /shŭd or shəd/; 2nd pers sing (*archaic*) **shouldest** or **shouldst**) *orig* expressing debt or moral obligation, now used with the infinitive of a verb (without *to*) to form (in sense) a future tense, expressing in the first person mere futurity (as **will¹** does in the second and third), in the second and third implying also promise, command, decree, or control on the part of the speaker (rules for the use of *shall* and *will* are often ignored); must, will have to, is to, etc (in 2nd and 3rd persons, and interrogatively 1st); may be expected to, may chance to, may well (in all persons); may in future contingency, may come to (in all persons). [OE *sculan*, prt *sceal*, *scealt*, *sceal*; *pat* *sceolde*; cf Ger *soll*, Gothic *skal*, ON *skal*]

shalli see **challis**.

shallon /shal'ən/ *n* salal.

shalloon /shə-lōōn'/ *n* a light woollen fabric used for coat linings, etc. [OFr *chalon*; perh made at *Châlons-sur-Marne*]

shallop /shal'əp/ *n* formerly, a heavy fore-and-aft-rigged boat; a dinghy; a small or light boat. [Fr *chaloupe*; cf **sloop**]

shallot or **shalot** /shə-lot'/ *n* a species of onion (*Allium ascalonicum*) with clusters of oval bulbs (also **eschalot** /e-shə-lot', esh'/). [OFr *eschalote*, variant of *escalogne*; see **scallion**]

shallow /shal'ō/ *adj* of no great depth, concavity, profundity or penetration; superficial. ◆ *adv* at or to no great depth. ◆ *n* a shallow place; (in *pl* with *the*) the shallow part (of the sea, etc). ◆ *vt* to make shallow. ◆ *vi* to grow shallow. [ME *schalowe*, perh related to **shoal²**]
■ **shall'owing** *n* and *adj*. **shall'owly** *adv* simply, foolishly; in a shallow or superficial manner. **shall'owness** *n*.

shalm same as **shawm**.

shalom /sha-lōm' or sha-lom'/ (*Heb*) *interj* (in full **shalom aleichem** /ə-lāhh'əm/) peace (be with you), a greeting or valediction used *esp* by Jewish people.

shalot see **shallot**.

shalt /shalt/ 2nd pers sing of **shall**.

shalwar /shul'vär or shal'war/ or **salwar** /sal'war/ *n* loose-fitting trousers worn (by both sexes) in many parts of S Asia. [Urdu *shalwār*, Hindi *salvar*, from Pers *shalwar*]
❑ **shalwar-kameez'** *n* (Urdu *kamis*, from Ar *qamīs* shirt) a S Asian outfit (for men and women) of loose-fitting trousers and a long tunic.

shaly see under **shale¹**.

sham /sham/ *n* a counterfeit or pretence; a hoax, imposture (*obs*); an imposter. ◆ *adj* pretended; false. ◆ *vt* (**shamm'ing**; **shammed**) to pretend; to feign; to impose upon (*obs*). ◆ *vi* to make false pretences; to pretend to be (as *to sham dead* or *sick*). [First found as slang, late 17c; prob derived from **shame**]
■ **shamm'er** *n*.
❑ **sham Abraham** see under **Abraham-man**.

shama /shä'mə/ *n* an Indian songbird of the thrush family. [Hindi *sāmā*]

shamal see **shimaal**.

shaman /shā' or shä'man or -mən/ *n* (*pl* **sha'mans**) a doctor-priest or medicine man working by magic, *esp* a priest of Asian Shamanism. [Russ, from Tungus *saman*, ult from Sans *śrama* religious practice]
■ **shaman'ic** *adj*. **Sha'manism** *n* (also without *cap*) the religion of certain peoples of N Asia, based essentially on magic and sorcery as practised by shamans. **sha'manist** *n* and *adj*. **shamanist'ic** *adj*.

shamateur /sham'ə-tər, -tūr or -tær/ (*inf*) *n* (*esp* formerly) a sportsperson retaining amateur status while receiving payment for playing or competing. [**sham**, and **amateur**]
■ **sham'ateurism** *n*.

shamba /sham'bə/ *n* (in E Africa) any farm, plot or smallholding used for growing crops. [Swahili]

shamble¹ /sham'bl/ *vi* to walk with an awkward, unsteady gait; to shuffle. ◆ *n* a shambling gait. [Poss from **shamble²**, in allusion to its trestle-like legs]
■ **sham'bling** *n* and *adj*. **sham'bly** *adj*.

shamble² /sham'bl/ *n* a butcher's market stall; (in *pl*; *usu* treated as *sing*) a meat-market, hence, a slaughterhouse. [OE *scamel* (Ger *Schemel*) stool, from LL *scamellum*, dimin of *scamnum* a bench]
■ **sham'bles** *n sing* a mess or muddle; a place of carnage (*fig*). **shambol'ic** *adj* chaotic.

shame /shām/ *n* the humiliating feeling of having appeared unfavourably in one's own eyes, or those of others, by having failed, offended, or been made to appear foolish, or a similar feeling on behalf of anything one associates with oneself; susceptibility to such feeling; fear or scorn of incurring disgrace or dishonour; modesty; bashfulness; disgrace, ignominy; disgraceful wrong; a cause or source of disgrace; a thing to be ashamed of; an instance or a case of hard or bad luck (*inf*); those parts of the body that it is felt to be immodest to expose (*archaic*). ◆ *interj* how shameful, what a disgrace!; an expression of affection, warmth or sympathy (*S Afr*). ◆ *vt* to make ashamed; to disgrace; to cause to seem humiliatingly poor or paltry by greater excellence (often *into*) to drive or compel by shame. ◆ *vi* to be ashamed. [OE *sc(e)amu*; Ger *Scham*]
■ **shame'able** or **sham'able** *adj*. **shamed** *adj* ashamed. **shame'ful** *adj* disgraceful. **shame'fully** *adv*. **shame'fulness** *n*. **shame'less** *adj* immodest, brazen; done without shame. **shame'lessly** *adv*. **shame'lessness** *n*. **shā'mer** *n* someone who or that which causes shame. **shame'worthy** *adj*.
❑ **shame'faced** (formerly **shame'fast**) *adj* (OE *scamfæst*) very modest or bashful; showing shame; abashed. **shame'facedly** /-fāst-li or fā'sid-li/ *adv*. **shame'facedness** (formerly **shame'fastness**) *n* modesty. **shame'-proof** *adj* insensible to shame.
■ **for shame** an interjectional phrase, you should be ashamed. **put to shame** to disgrace, *esp* by excelling. **shame on** (**you**, **them**, etc) (you, they, etc) should be ashamed. **tell the truth and shame the Devil** put the Devil to disgraceful defeat by boldly telling the truth. **think shame** to be ashamed.

shamianah or **shamiana** /shä-mē-ä'nə/ *n* (in India) a large tent, awning or canopy (also **shamiya'nah**). [Hindi *shāmiyāna*; from Pers]

shamisen see **samisen**.

shammes /shä'məs/ or **shammash** /sha-mash'/ (*Judaism*) *n* (*pl* **shammos'im** or **shammash'im**) a caretaker of a synagogue with a similar role to a sexton's; a candle used to light the candles of the menorah. [Yiddish, from Heb *shāmmāsh*, from Aramaic *shemāsh* to serve]

shammy /sham'i/ *n* (in full **shammy leather**) a soft leather, *orig* made from chamois skin, now *usu* from sheepskin, by working in oil; a piece of it, used for polishing, etc. [**chamois**]

■ **sham'oy** (or /-moi'/) *vt* to prepare (skins) by working oil into them.

shampoo /sham-poo'/ *vt* (pat and pap **shampooed'** or **shampoo'd'**) to wash and rub (the scalp and hair) with special lathering preparation; to clean (a carpet, etc) by rubbing with detergent; to massage. ◆ *n* (pl **shampoos'**) an act or process of shampooing; a preparation for the purpose. [Hindi *cāpnā* to squeeze]

■ **shampoo'er** *n*.

shamrock /sham'rok/ *n* the national emblem of Ireland, a trifoliate leaf or plant; (in living popular tradition) the lesser yellow trefoil; (in English poetry) often wood sorrel; according to some, white clover, hop-trefoil, black medick, or some other (or any) leaf or plant with three leaflets. [Ir *seamróg*, Gaelic *seamrag*, dimin of *seamar* trefoil]

shamus /shā'məs or shä'/ (old US sl) *n* (pl **sha'muses**) a detective. [Perh from Yiddish *shammes* a sexton, caretaker, with influence from the Irish name *Seamas*, a form of James]

Shan /shän/ *n* (pl **Shan**) a member of a Mongoloid people of China, Thailand, Myanmar (Burma), and Assam, related to the Thais; their Sino-Tibetan language. ◆ *adj* of or relating to the Shan or their language.

shan see **shand**.

shanachie /shan'ə-hhē/ same as **seannachie**.

shand /shand/ or **shan** /shan/ (obs criminal sl) *n* a base or counterfeit coin. [From dialect *shan* paltry]

Shandean /shan'di-ən or shan-dē'ən/ *adj* characteristic of Tristram Shandy or the Shandy family, or their creator Laurence Sterne. ◆ *n* a person of Shandean character.

shandry /shan'dri/ (N Eng) *n* a light cart on springs. [Origin unknown]
■ **shan'drydan** /-dri-dan/ *n* a shandry; a type of chaise; a rickety vehicle.

shandy /shan'di/ *n* a mixture of beer and ginger beer or lemonade (also (esp US) **shan'dygaff**). [Origin unknown]

Shang /shang/ *n* a Chinese dynasty (17c–11c BC). ◆ *adj* of the dynasty, its time or *esp* its pottery, bronzes, etc.

shanghai¹ /shang-hī'/ *vt* (**shanghai'ing**; **shanghaied'** or **shanghai'd'**) to drug or make drunk and send to sea as a sailor; to trick into performing an unpleasant task. ◆ *n* (darts) the feat of scoring a single, double and treble of the same number with a set of three darts. [*Shanghai* in China]
■ **shanghai'er** *n*.

shanghai² /shang'ī/ (Aust and NZ) *n* a catapult. ◆ *vt* to shoot with a shanghai. [Scot dialect *shangy* cleft stick, from Gaelic *seangan*]

Shangri-la /shang-gri-lä'/ *n* an imaginary pass in the Himalayas, an earthly paradise, described in James Hilton's *Lost Horizon* (1933); hence, any remote or imaginary paradise.

shank /shangk/ *n* the leg from knee to foot; the corresponding part in other vertebrates; the lower part of the foreleg, *esp* as a cut of meat; a shaft, stem, straight or long part; the part of a shoe connecting sole with heel; the leg of a stocking; a long-handled ladle for molten metal; an act of shanking a golf ball; the end, latter part (dialect). ◆ *vi* to be affected with disease of the footstalk (bot); to take to one's legs (also *vt* with *it*). ◆ *vt* to dispatch unceremoniously (Scot); to strike (the ball) by mistake close to the heel of the club so that it makes contact with the hosel, causing the ball to fly to the right (for a right-handed player) (golf). [OE *sc(e)anca* leg; Du *schonk*, LGer *schanke*]
■ **shanked** *adj* having a shank; affected with disease of the shank or footstalk (bot).
▫ **shank'bone** *n*.
■ **on Shanks's pony, mare, nag**, etc on foot.

shanny /shan'i/ *n* the smooth blenny, *Lipophrys pholis*, a small marine fish found in inshore waters and rock pools. [Origin obscure]

shan't or **sha'n't** /shänt/ (inf) a contraction of **shall not**.

shantung /shan-tung' or -toong'/ *n* a plain rough cloth of wild silk; a similar cotton or rayon fabric. [*Shāndōng* province in China]

shanty¹ /shan'ti/ *n* a roughly built hut; a ramshackle dwelling; a rough public house or (hist) a place selling alcohol illicitly (Aust). [Perh Fr *chantier* a timber-yard (in Canada, a woodcutter's headquarters); perh Ir *sean tig* old house]
▫ **shan'tyman** *n* a man, *esp* a logger, who lives in a shanty. **shan'tytown** *n* a town, or an area of one, where housing is makeshift and ramshackle.

shanty² or **shantey** /shan'ti/ *n* a rhythmical song with chorus and solo verses (often extempore) sung by sailors while heaving at the capstan, etc (also **chanty**, **chantie** or **chantey**). [Said to be from Fr *chantez* (imperative) sing]
■ **shan'tyman** *n* the solo-singer in shanties.

SHAPE /shāp/ *abbrev* : Supreme Headquarters Allied Powers Europe.

shape /shāp/ *vt* (pat **shāped** (obs **shope** /shōp/); pap **shāped** (archaic **shāp'en**)) to form; to fashion; to mould into a particular shape or form; to give form to; to embody; to plan, devise; to direct; to determine; to purpose (obs). ◆ *vi* to take shape; to develop; to give promising signs; to conduce (Shakesp); to become fit. ◆ *n* form; figure; disposition in space; guise; form or condition; that which has form or figure; an apparition; a pattern; a mould (cookery); a jelly, pudding, etc, turned out of a mould. [OE *scieppan*, pat *scōp*, pap *scapen*, to create, form, with new present developed from the pap infl by the noun *gesceap* creation, form; cf ON *skapa*, Ger *schaffen, schöpfen*]
■ **shāp'able** or **shape'able** *adj*. **shaped** *adj* having a shape, or a definite, determinate, or adapted shape, often in combination, as in *L-shaped*. **shape'less** *adj* of ill-defined or unsatisfactory shape; without shape; unattractively shaped; purposeless (Shakesp). **shape'lessly** *adv*. **shape'lessness** *n*. **shape'liness** *n*. **shape'ly** *adj* having an attractive, well-proportioned shape or figure. **shap'en** *adj* fashioned; definitely shaped. **shap'er** *n* someone or something that shapes; (in management) a decisive, somewhat bullying leader who carries others along with his or her dynamism (inf). **shap'ing** *n* and *adj*.
▫ **shape'shifter** *n* in folklore, a creature that is able to transform its appearance by supernatural means. **shape'shifting** *n* and *adj*. **shape'-up** *n* (N Am) formerly, a method of hiring workers, *esp* dockers, for a single day's work by selecting the number of men needed from an assembly gathered for this purpose.
■ **in any shape or form** at all. **in good shape** or **in shape** in good condition. **in the shape of** in the guise of; of the nature of. **out of shape** deformed, disfigured; in poor physical condition, unfit. **shape one's course** to direct one's way. **shape up** to assume a shape; to develop, to be promising. **take shape** to assume a definite form or plan; to be embodied or worked out in practice.

shaps /shaps/ *n pl* short form of **chaparajos**.

shard¹ /shärd/ or **sherd** /shûrd/ *n* a gap (now dialect); a scrap, broken piece, *esp* of pottery; a boundary water (archaic). [OE *sceard* cleft, potsherd; cf *sceran* to cut; Ger *Scharte* notch]

shard² /shärd/ (Shakesp) *n* a piece of cow-dung. [Cf **sharn**]
■ **shard'ed** *adj* (archaic) sheltered under dung.
▫ **shard beetle** *n* a dor-beetle, laying its eggs in cow-dung. **shard'-borne** *adj* see separate entry.

shard³ /shärd/ same as **chard**.

shard⁴ /shärd/ (zool) *n* a tough or hard sheath or shell, such as a beetle's wingcase. [From a misunderstanding of Shakespeare's **shard-borne**]

shard⁵ or **shar'd** /shärd/ (Spenser) pat and pap of **share**^{1,2}.

shard-borne /shärd'börn or -börn/ *adj* born in dung (Shakesp); later used as meaning borne on elytra. [**shard²**; cf **shard⁴**]

share¹ /shär/ *n* a part allotted, contributed, owned or taken; a part cut off (archaic); a division, section, portion; a fixed and indivisible section of the capital of a company. ◆ *vt* to divide into shares; to apportion; to give or take a share of; to participate in; to have in common. ◆ *vi* to have, receive, or give a share. [OE *scearu*; cf **shear**]
■ **shar'able** or **share'able** *adj*. **shar'er** *n*. **shar'ing** *n*.
▫ **share bone** *n* the pubis. **share capital** *n* money derived from the sale of shares in a business, and used for carrying it on. **share certificate** *n* a certificate issued to a shareholder by a company indicating ownership of its shares. **share'crop** *vi*. **share'cropper** *n* (esp US) a tenant farmer who supplies, in lieu of rent, a share of the crop. **shared logic** *n* (comput) a shared facility in which the central processing unit is shared by several terminals. **shared ownership** *n* a type of house ownership shared between the householder and a housing association. **share'farmer** *n* (esp Aust) a tenant farmer who pays a share of the proceeds as rent. **share'farming** *n*. **share'holder** *n* a person who owns a share or shares, *esp* in a company. **share'holding** *n*. **share index** *n* an index showing the movement of shares in companies trading on a stock exchange. **share'man** or **shares'man** *n* a fisherman who shares profits with the owners. **share'milker** *n* (NZ) a sharefarmer on a dairy farm. **share option** *n* a scheme enabling employees to buy shares in their company at less than the market rate. **share'-out** *n* a distribution in or by shares. **share'-pusher** *n* a person who seeks to sell shares otherwise than through recognized channels, eg by dubious advertisement, etc. **share shop** *n* a shop or special area in a bank, etc where shares are traded quickly and informally without investment advice. **share size** or **sharing size** *n* a larger than standard packet of a snack food, marketed with the implicit suggestion to the purchaser not to consume the whole packet unaided. **share'ware** *n* (comput sl) software available on free trial, often with restricted features or for a limited time, after which a fee must be paid if regular use is to continue.
■ **go shares** (inf) to share something with others. **lion's share** see under **lion**. **share and share alike** give everyone his or her due share; in equal shares.

share² /*shār*/ *n* a ploughshare, or the corresponding part of another implement. ◆ *vt* (pat and pap **shared**, (*Spenser*) **shard** /*shärd*/) to cut, cleave. [OE *scear*; cf **share¹**, and **shear**]

Sharia /*sha-rēˈə*/ or **Shariat** /*sha-rēˈət*/ (also without *cap*) *n* the body of Islamic religious law (also **Sheria** or **Sheriat**). [Ar *shariˈa* law]

sharif see **sherif**.

shark /*shärk*/ *n* a general name for elasmobranchs other than skates, rays, and chimeras, voracious fishes with a fusiform body, lateral gill slits, and a mouth on the under side; sometimes confined to the larger kinds, excluding the dogfishes; an extortionist; a financial swindler; an underhand or predatory dealer; a sharper. ◆ *vi* and *vt* (*archaic*) to obtain by swindling. [Origin doubtful; Ger *Schurke* scoundrel, Austrian Ger *Schirk* sturgeon, Fr dialect *cherquier* to seek, L *carcharus* dogfish, from Gr *karcharos* jagged, have been suggested]
■ **shark'er** *n*. **shark'ing** *n*.
◻ **shark oil** *n* oil from shark's liver, used like cod-liver oil. **shark patrol** *n* (*esp Aust* and *US*) a regular patrol of the waters close to bathing beaches by boats, aircraft, etc, to look for sharks. **shark repellent** *n* (*finance*) any strategy adopted by a business organization to avoid an unwanted takeover. **shark'skin** *n* a woollen or worsted suiting in twill weave; a heavy rayon material with dull finish; shagreen. **shark'sucker** *n* a remora.

sharn /*shärn*/ (*Scot* and *dialect*) *n* cow-dung or dung generally. [OE *scearn*; cf ON *skarn*]
■ **sharn'y** *adj*.
◻ **sharny peat** *n* a cake of cow-dung mixed with coal.

sharon fruit /*sharˈən froot*/ *n* a persimmon. [From the *Sharon* valley in Israel where it is grown]

sharp /*shärp*/ *adj* cutting; piercing; penetrating; acute; having a thin edge or fine point; affecting the senses as if pointed or cutting; severe; harsh; keen; eager; hungry (*Shakesp*); alive to one's own interests; barely honest; of keen or quick perception; alert; fit, able; pungent, sarcastic; brisk; abrupt; having abrupt or acute corners, etc; sudden in onset; clear-cut; unblurred; well-defined; stylish (*inf*); exceptionally smart or fashionable in dress (*inf*); high in pitch, or too high (*music*); raised a semitone (*music*); voiceless (*obs phonetics*). ◆ *adv* high or too high in pitch; punctually, precisely; sharply. ◆ *n* a note raised a semitone; the symbol for it (x); the key producing it; sharpness (*Milton*); a long slender needle; a small sword or duelling-sword; (in *pl*) sharp instruments, esp used blades or needles disposed of as medical waste; (in *pl*) hard parts of wheat, middlings; (in *pl*) sword-fighting in earnest; a sharper. ◆ *vt* and *vi* (*obs* or *dialect*) to sharpen. [OE *scearp*; ON *skarpr*, Ger *scharf*]
■ **sharp'en** *vt* and *vi* to make or become sharp in any sense. **sharp'ener** *n*. **sharp'er** *n* a cheat or hoaxer, *esp* someone who cheats at cards. **sharp'ie** *n* a flat-bottomed, two-masted vessel with triangular sails, formerly of the US Atlantic coast; a cheat (*inf*); one of a set of stylishly dressed teenagers (*Aust* and *NZ*). **sharp'ing** *n* and *adj* cheating. **sharp'ish** *adj* and *adv*. **sharp'ly** *adv*. **sharp'ness** *n*.
◻ **sharp'-cut** *adj* well-defined; clear-cut. **sharp'-edged** *adj*. **sharp'-eyed** *adj*. **sharp'-ground** *adj* ground to a sharp edge. **sharp'-looking** *adj* (*Shakesp*) hungry-looking. **sharp'-nosed** *adj* having a pointed nose; with a keen sense of smell. **sharp'-pointed** *adj*. **sharp practice** *n* unscrupulous dealing, verging on dishonesty. **sharp'-set** *adj* hungry; keen in appetite for anything, *esp* food or sexual indulgence; (of a tool, etc) set with a sharp edge. **sharp'-shod** *adj* (of a horse) having spikes in the shoes to prevent slipping. **sharp'shooter** *n* an expert marksman; a soldier, police officer, etc employed as a marksman; (loosely) someone with a talent for scoring in any sport. **sharp'shooting** *n* and *adj*. **sharp-sight'ed** *adj* having acute sight; shrewd. **sharp-tailed grouse** *n* a grouse of W Canada and USA whose middle tail feathers are longer than the rest. **sharp-tongued'** *adj* critical, sarcastic, harsh in speech. **sharp-toothed'** *adj*. **sharp-witt'ed** *adj* having an alert intelligence, wit or perception. **sharp-witt'edly** *adv*. **sharp-witt'edness** *n*.
▪ **at the sharp end** in the position of greatest difficulty, danger, stress, etc, in any activity. **look sharp** be quick; hurry up. **sharp's the word** be brisk.

Shar-Pei /*shär-pāˈ*/ *n* a large muscular dog of a Chinese breed, with a distinctive wrinkled nose. [Chin *shā* sand, and *pí* skin]

shash¹ /*shash*/ the earlier spelling of **sash¹**.

shash² /*shash*/ (*telecom*) *n* noisy interference (to a sound or picture signal). [Imit]

shashlik or **shashlick** /*shash-lik*/ or *shashˈ*/ *n* a type of lamb kebab. [Russ *shashlyk*]

Shasta daisy /*shasˈtə dāˈzi*/ *n* a composite flowering plant, *Chrysanthemum maximum*, with large, yellow-centred, white daisy-like flowers. [From Mount *Shasta*, California]

shaster /*shasˈtər*/, **shastra** or **sastra** /*shäsˈträ*/ (*Hinduism*) *n* a holy writing. [Sans *śāstra*, from *śās* to teach]

shat see **shit**.

shatoosh see **shahtoosh**.

shatter /*shatˈər*/ *vt* to dash to pieces; to wreck; to scatter (*archaic*). ◆ *vi* to break into fragments. ◆ *n* a fragment; an impaired state. [Perh LGer; cf **scatter**]
■ **shatt'ered** *adj* (*inf*) exhausted; extremely upset. **shatt'erer** *n*. **shatt'ering** *adj*. **shatt'eringly** *adv*. **shatt'ery** *adj* brittle.
◻ **shatt'er-brain** or **shatt'er-pate** *n* a scatterbrain. **shatt'er-brained** *adj*. **shatt'erproof** *adj*.

shauchle /*shöˈhhl*/ (*Scot*) *vi* to shuffle. ◆ *vt* to put out of shape or make down-at-heel. ◆ *n* a shuffling gait; a down-at-heel shoe. [Origin obscure]
■ **shauch'ly** *adj*.

shave /*shāv*/ *vt* (pap **shaved** or *archaic* **shā'ven**) to scrape or pare off a superficial slice, hair (*esp* of the face), or other surface material from; to tonsure; to remove by scraping or paring; to pare closely; to graze the surface of; to plunder, fleece. ◆ *vi* to remove hair with a razor; to pass or escape with little margin. ◆ *n* the act or process of shaving; a paring; a narrow miss or escape (*esp* in *close shave*); a paring or slicing tool. [OE *sc(e)afan*; Du *schaven*, Ger *schaben*]
■ **shave'ling** *n* a tonsured cleric. **shā'ven** *adj* shaved; tonsured; close-cut; smoothed. **shā'ver** *n* a person who shaves; an electric razor; a barber; a sharp or extortionate dealer; a chap, a youngster (*inf*). **shā'vie** *n* (*Scot*) a trick. **shā'ving** *n* the act of scraping or using a razor; a thin slice, *esp* a curled piece of wood planed off.
◻ **shave'-grass** *n* Dutch rush. **shā'ving-brush** *n* a brush for lathering the face before shaving. **shā'ving-soap** *n* soap for lathering in preparation for shaving. **shā'ving-stick** *n* a cylindrical piece of shaving-soap.

Shavian /*shāˈvi-ən*/ *adj* relating to or associated with the dramatist George Bernard Shaw (1856–1950). ◆ *n* a follower or admirer of Shaw.

Shavuot, Shavuoth see **Shabuoth**.

shaw¹ /*shö*/ *n* a small wood. [OE *sc(e)aga*; ON *skōgr*, Dan *skov*]

shaw² /*shö*/ (*Scot*) *n* the above-ground parts of a potato plant, turnip, etc; show, appearance, display. [Scot form of **show**]

shawl /*shöl*/ *n* a loose-knitted or other covering for the shoulders, wrapping a baby in, etc. ◆ *vt* to wrap in a shawl. [Pers *shāl*]
■ **shawl'ie** or **shawl'ey** *n* (*Irish*) a working woman, *esp* a fisherwoman, who habitually wears a shawl. **shawl'ing** *n*. **shawl'less** *adj*.
◻ **shawl collar** *n* a large rolled collar tapering from the neck to (near) the waistline. **shawl pattern** *n* the pine-cone pattern used on Kashmir shawls and imitated on Paisley shawls in the 19c. **shawl waistcoat** *n* a waistcoat with a large prominent pattern like that of an oriental or Paisley shawl.
▪ **Paisley shawl** see under **paisley**.

shawm /*shöm*/ or **shalm** /*shäm*/ *n* a musical instrument, a predecessor of the oboe, having a double reed and a flat circular piece against which the lips are rested. [OFr *chalemie, -mel*, from L *calamus* reed]

Shawnee /*shö-nēˈ*/ *n* a Native American of an Algonquin people now mostly in Oklahoma; the language of this people. ◆ *adj* of or relating to this people or their language. [Shawnee *Shawunogi*]
◻ **shawnee'-wood** *n* a species of *Catalpa*.

shay /*shā*/ *n* an informal form of **chaise**.

shaya see **chay²**.

shchi or **shtchi** /*shchē*/ *n* cabbage soup. [Russ]

she /*shē*, or when unemphatic *shi*/ *pronoun* (*pl* **they**) the nominative (also, irregularly, ungrammatically or dialectally, accusative or dative) feminine form of the 3rd person pronoun: the female (or thing spoken of as female) named before, indicated, or understood. ◆ *n* (*pl* **shes**) (*nominative, accusative* and *dative*) a female. ◆ *adj* female (*esp* in combination, as in *she-ass, she-bear, she-devil*). [Prob OE *sēo*, fem of the definite article, which in the 12c came to be used instead of the pronoun *hēo*]

s/he a form representing *she* or *he*.

shea /*shē, shēˈə*/ *n* an African tree (**shea tree**, *Butyrospermum parkii*) whose seeds (**shea nuts**) yield **shea butter**, used as a food and in soap manufacture. [Mungo Park's spelling of Mandingo (W Afr language) *si*]

sheading /*shēˈding*/ *n* one of the six divisions or districts of the Isle of Man. [**shedding**]

sheaf /*shēf*/ *n* (*pl* **sheaves** /*shēvz*/) a bundle of things bound side by side, *esp* stalks of corn; a bundle of papers; a bundle of (*usu* 24) arrows. [OE *scēaf*; cf Ger *Schaub*, Du *schoof*]
■ **sheaf** or **sheave** *vt* to bind in sheaves. ◆ *vi* to make sheaves. **sheaf'y** *adj*. **sheaved** *adj* in sheaves; flared; perh, made of straw (*Shakesp*).

sheal¹, **sheel**, **shiel** /shēl/ or **shill** /shil/ (*Shakesp*) *vt* to shell or husk. [Related to **shell**, **shale²**, **scale²**]
□ **sheal'ing-** (or **sheel'ing-**, etc) **hill** *n* a hill where grain is winnowed by the wind.

sheal², **shealing** same as **shiel²**, **shieling**.

shear /shēr/ *vt* (*pat* **sheared** or (*archaic* and *poetic*) **shore**; *pap* **shorn**, also, less commonly in ordinary senses, but always of deformation and *usu* of metal-cutting, **sheared**) to cut, or clip, *esp* with shears; to strip, fleece (also *fig*); to cut superfluous nap from; to achieve or make by cutting; to tonsure; to reap with a sickle (*Scot*); to subject to a shear (*engineering* and *phys*). ◆ *vi* to separate; to cut; to penetrate; to reap with a sickle (*Scot*). ◆ *n* a shearing or clipping; a strain, stress, or deformation in which parallel planes remain parallel, but move parallel to themselves (*engineering* and *phys*). [OE *sceran*; ON *skera* to clip, Ger *scheren* to shave]
■ **shear'er** *n* a person who shears sheep; a reaper (*Scot*). **shear'ing** *n*. **shear'ling** *n* a sheep that has been shorn for the first time; the fleece of such a sheep, *usu* of inferior quality. **shears** *n pl orig* scissors (also *Scot*); now a larger pair of clippers, or any scissorlike cutting instrument, with a pivot or spring; a hoisting apparatus (see **sheers** under **sheer²**).
□ **shear force** *n* a force that tends to cause sliding of adjacent layers relative to each other, in a material. **shear'-hog** *n* a shearling. **shear'-hulk**, **shear'leg** see under **sheer²**. **shearing shed** *n* (*Aust* and *NZ*) a building in which sheep are shorn, *esp* one specially equipped with several power-driven shears, shearing platforms and wool-baling machines. **shear'man** *n* a textile worker who shears superfluous nap from cloth. **shear pin** *n* a pin, which, as a safety mechanism, will shear and halt a machine or power-transmission when the correct load or stress is exceeded. **shear'-steel** *n* steel suitable for making shears, etc. **shear'water** *n* a seabird of the family Procellariidae, related to the petrels, that skims the water when flying low. **shear zones** *n pl* (*geol*) bands in metamorphic rocks consisting of crushed and brecciated material and many parallel fractures.

shears /shērz/ (*engineering*) *n pl* same as **ways** (see under **way¹**).

'sheart /särt/ (*obs*) *interj* for **God's heart**, an exclamatory oath.

sheatfish /shēt'fish/ or **sheathfish** /shēth'-/ *n* a large fish (*Silurus glanis*, the American catfish) introduced into European rivers; any related fish. [Ger *Scheidfisch*; see **sheath**]

sheath /shēth/ *n* (*pl* **sheaths** /shēdhz/) a case for a sword or blade; a close-fitting (*esp* tubular or long) covering; a woman's close-fitting tubular dress (also **sheath dress**); a clasping leaf-base, or any similar protective structure; an insect's wingcase; a contraceptive device for men, a condom. [OE *scēath*, *scǣth*; Ger *Scheide*, ON *skeithir*]
■ **sheathe** /shēdh/ *vt* to put into or cover with a sheath or casing. **sheathed** /shēdhd/ *adj* having, or enclosed in, a sheath. **sheath'ing** /-dh-/ *n* that which sheathes; casing; the covering of a ship's bottom. **sheath'less** *adj*. **sheath'y** /-th-* or *-dh-/ *adj* sheathlike.
□ **sheath'bill** *n* either of two Antarctic seabirds (genus *Chionis*) having a white plumage and a horny sheath at the base of the bill. **sheath dress** see *n* above. **sheathfish** see **sheatfish**. **sheath knife** *n* a knife encased in a sheath. **sheath'-winged** *adj* (*zool*) coleopterous.
■ **sheathe the sword** (*literary*) to end war.

sheave¹ /shēv/ *n* a shive, slice, slab; a grooved wheel, pulley-wheel; a fragment; a speck, particle of impurity, as in paper. [Related to **shive**]

sheave², **sheaves**, etc see **sheaf**.

Sheba /shē'bə/ same as **Saba**.

shebang /shi-bang'/ (*sl, orig US*) *n* a room, house, shop, hut, etc; a vehicle; affair, matter, etc, *esp* in the phrase *the whole shebang*. [Of uncertain origin; perh connected with **shebeen** or Fr *cabane*]

Shebat /shē'bät/ or 'bat/ *n* the fifth (ecclesiastically eleventh) Jewish month, parts of January and February (also **Se'bat** or **She'vat**). [Heb *Sh'bāt*]

shebeen /shi-bēn'/ *n* an illicit liquor shop; (in Ireland) illicit, *usu* home-made, alcohol. ◆ *vi* to keep a shebeen. [Anglo-Irish]
■ **shebeen'er** *n*. **shebeen'ing** *n*.

Shechinah /shi-kī'nə/ *n* same as **Shekinah**.

shechita(h) see **schechita(h)**.

shecklaton see **checklaton**.

shed¹ /shed/ *n* a structure, often open-fronted, for storing or shelter; an outhouse. ◆ *vt* (**shedd'ing**; **shedd'ed**) to store in a shed. [Appar a variant of **shade¹**]
■ **shedd'er** *n* (*NZ*) a person who milks cows in a milking shed. **shed'hand** *n* (*Aust* and *NZ*) a person who works in a shearing shed.
□ **shed'load** *n* (*inf*) a large amount.

shed² /shed/ *vt* (**shedd'ing**; **shed**) to part, separate; to cast off; to give, give away; to drop; to emit; to pour forth; to cast, throw (eg light); to impart; to cause effusion of; to spill (*dialect*); to besprinkle (*archaic*). ◆ *vi* to fall off; to disperse (*archaic*). ◆ *n* (*obs* or *dialect*) a parting. ◆ *adj*

cast; spilt, emitted. [OE *scādan*, *scēadan* (strong verb), to separate; Ger *scheiden*]
■ **shedd'er** *n* a person who or thing that sheds; an animal that moults or casts hair; a female salmon or the like after spawning. **shedd'ing** *n*.

she'd /shēd/ (*inf*) a contraction of **she had** or **she would**.

sheel see **sheal¹**.

sheen /shēn/ *n* shine; lustre; radiance; a very thin slick of oil (on water); glistening attire (*poetic*). ◆ *adj* (*rare* or *poetic*) beautiful; bright; shining. ◆ *vi* (*obs* except *Scot*) to shine; to gleam; to have a lustre. [OE *scēne* (WSax *scīene*, *scȳne*) beautiful; Du *schoon*, Ger *schön*; infl by **shine**]
■ **sheen'y** *adj* lustrous; glistening.

sheeny /shē'ni/ (*obs sl; offensive*) *n* (also with *cap*) a Jew; a pawnbroker. ◆ *adj* Jewish; fraudulent; (of money) counterfeit. [Origin unknown]

sheep /shēp/ *n* (*pl* **sheep**) a beardless, woolly, wild or domestic ruminant animal (genus *Ovis*) of the goat family; the skin of such an animal, with or without the woolly coat; someone who is like a sheep, in being eg a member of a flock (or congregation), a creature that follows meekly, is at the mercy of the wolf or the shearer, displays tameness of spirit, etc. [OE *scēap*; Ger *Schaf*]
■ **sheep'ish** *adj* like a sheep; embarrassed through having done something foolish or wrong. **sheep'ishly** *adv*. **sheep'ishness** *n*. **sheep'like** *adj*. **sheep'o** *n* (*pl* **sheep'os**) (*Aust* and *NZ*) a farm worker who drives sheep into pens for shearing. **sheep'y** *adj* (*rare*) sheeplike.
□ **sheep'-biter** *n* (*obs*) a dog that bites or worries sheep; *prob* an oppressive supervisor (*Shakesp*). **sheep'-biting** *adj* (*obs*) given to biting sheep; sneaking, thieving. **sheep'cote** *n* an enclosure for sheep. **sheep'-dip** *n* a disinfectant insecticidal preparation used in washing sheep; a place for dipping sheep, *specif* the trough of disinfectant through which they are driven; inferior liquor (*sl*). **sheep'dog** *n* a dog trained to watch or drive sheep, or of a breed used for that purpose; a chaperon (*sl*). **sheep'-faced** *adj* sheepish, bashful. **sheep'-farmer** *n*. **sheep'fold** *n*. **sheep'-hook** *n* a shepherd's crook. **sheep ked** *n* a wingless fly (*Melophagus ovinus*) that sucks sheeps' blood. **sheep'-louse** *n* (*pl* **sheep'-lice**) a louse (genus *Trichodectes*) that infests sheep; loosely, a sheep ked. **sheep'-master** *n* an owner of sheep. **sheep meat** *n* mutton or lamb. **sheep'-pen** *n*. **sheep'-plant** *n* vegetable sheep (qv). **sheep'-pox** *n* a contagious eruptive disease of sheep, resembling smallpox. **sheep'-rot** *n* liver rot. **sheep run** *n* a tract of grazing country for sheep. **sheep's'-bit scabious** see under **scabious**. **sheep scab** *n* a mange in sheep transmitted by mites. **sheep'-scor'ing** *n* the counting of sheep (**sheep-scoring numerals** numerals of Welsh origin, used by shepherds, knitters, and in counting-out rhymes by children). **sheep's eyes** *n pl* a wistful amorous look. **sheep's fescue** *n* a temperate tufted pasture grass (*Festuca ovina*). **sheep's'-foot** *n* a printer's claw hammer. **sheep'shank** *n* a nautical knot for shortening a rope; a sheep's leg; something of slender importance (*Scot*). **sheep's'-head** *n* the head of a sheep, *esp* as food (also *adj*); a dolt; an American fish related to the porgie. **sheep'shearer** *n*. **sheep'shearing** *n*. **sheep'-silver** *n* money paid in commutation of some right connected with sheep. **sheep'skin** *n* the skin of a sheep, with or without the fleece attached; an item made from it, eg a rug, horse's noseband, coat, etc; leather or parchment prepared from it. **sheep station** *n* (*Aust*) a large sheep farm. **sheep'-stealer** *n*. **sheep'-stealing** *n*. **sheep tick** *n* strictly, a tick (*Ixodes ricinus*), a parasite of sheep (and other animals, *incl* humans); commonly, a sheep ked. **sheep'track** *n* a terracette. **sheep'walk** *n* a range of pasture for sheep. **sheep'-wash** *n* a sheep-dip. **sheep'-whistling** *adj* (*Shakesp*) tending sheep.
■ **black sheep** the disreputable member of a family or group. **separate the sheep from the goats** to identify (*esp* by some test) the superior members of any group.

sheer¹ /shēr/ *adj* unmingled; mere, downright; plumb; unbroken; vertical or very nearly vertical; thin; pure; bright, clear (*archaic*). ◆ *adv* clear; quite; plumb; vertically. ◆ *n* a very thin fabric. [ME *schēre*, perh from a lost OE equivalent of ON *skærr* bright]
■ **sheer'ly** *adv* completely, thoroughly, wholly, etc. **sheer'ness** *n*.

sheer² /shēr/ *vi* (with *off* or *away*) to deviate; to take oneself off, *esp* to evade something disagreeable; to swerve. ◆ *vt* to cause to deviate. ◆ *n* a deviation; an oblique position; the fore-and-aft upward curve of a ship's deck or sides. [Partly at least another spelling of **shear**; perh partly from the LGer or Du equivalent, *scheren* to cut, withdraw]
■ **sheers** or **shears** *n pl* an apparatus for hoisting heavy weights, having legs or spars spread apart at their lower ends, and hoisting tackle at their joined tops.
□ **sheer'-hulk** or **shear'-hulk** *n* an old dismantled ship with a pair of sheers mounted on it; popularly, a mere hulk, as if from **sheer¹**. **sheer'leg** or **shear'leg** *n* one of the spars of sheers; (in *pl*) sheers.

sheesha see **shisha**.

sheet[1] /shēt/ n a large wide expanse or thin piece of something; a large broad piece of cloth, esp for a bed, a penitent, or a corpse; a piece of paper, esp large and broad; a section of a book printed on one piece of paper, a signature; as much copy as will fill a sheet; a pamphlet, broadsheet, or newspaper; a sail (poetic); a sill (**intrusive sheet**; geol); sheet rubber; one of the separate pieces or planes that make up a surface; aircraft structural material under 6.35mm (0.25in) thick, thinner than 'plate'. ◆ adj in the form of a sheet; printed on a sheet. ◆ vt to wrap or cover with, or as if with, a sheet; to provide with sheets; to form into sheets. ◆ vi to form or run in a sheet; (of rain) to fall fast and heavily. [OE scēte (WSax scīete), scēat; cf **sheet**[2]]

■ **sheet'ed** adj wrapped or covered with a sheet (esp of a corpse); (eg of a cow) marked with a white band or belt; spread out like a sheet. **sheet'ing** n cloth for sheets; protective boarding or metal covering; formation into sheets. **sheet'y** adj.

❑ **sheet copper, iron, lead, metal, rubber, tin**, etc n copper, iron, etc, in thin sheets. **sheet'-feed** vt and n. **sheet'-feeder** n (comput and word processing) a storage cassette that feeds single sheets of paper into a printer as required. **sheet'-glass** n a kind of crown glass made in a cylinder and flattened out. **sheet lightning** n the diffused appearance of distant lightning. **sheet music** n music written or printed on (unbound) sheets.

■ **post-forming sheet** (plastics) a laminated sheet suitable for drawing and forming to shape when heated.

sheet[2] /shēt/ (naut) n a rope attached to the lower corner of a sail; (in pl) the part of a boat between the thwarts and the stern or bow. [OE scēata corner; related to **sheet**[1]]

❑ **sheet bend** n a type of knot used esp for joining ropes of different sizes.

■ **a sheet** (or **three sheets**) **in** or **to the wind** (inf) half-drunk (or drunk).

sheet anchor /shēt ang'kər/ n an extra anchor for an emergency (naut); a chief support; a last refuge. [Formerly shut-, shot- or shoot-anchor; origin doubtful]

SHEFC abbrev : Scottish Higher Education Funding Council.

Sheffield plate /shef'ēld plāt/ n a type of metalware developed in Sheffield and produced between the mid-18c and mid-19c, of copper coated with silver. [Sheffield, city in S Yorkshire, and **plate**]

shehita(h) see **schechita(h)**.

sheikh or **sheik** /shāk or shēk/ n an Arab chief; a Muslim leader; a girl's young man or ideal film hero (old sl); a Hindu convert to Islam. [Ar shaikh, from shākha to be old]

■ **sheikh'a** n the chief wife or consort of a sheikh; a high-class Arab lady. **sheikh'dom** or **sheik'dom** n a sheikh's territory.

sheila /shē'lə/ n a young girl or a woman (Aust inf). [From proper name]

sheiling same as **shieling** (see under **shiel**[2]).

shekel /shek'l/ n an ancient Jewish weight (about 14 grams) and a coin of this weight; the standard monetary unit of present-day Israel (100 agorot); (in pl) money (sl). [Heb sheqel, from shāqal to weigh]

Shekinah or **Shechinah** /shi-kī'nə/ (Judaism) n the divine presence. [Heb shekīnāh, from shākan to dwell]

shelduck /shel'duk/ n (fem or generic) any of various large ducks (genus Tadorna) with bold black, brown and white plumage (in the breeding season) and red feet and bill (also **sheld'duck, shell'duck, shiel'duck**, and (esp masc) **shel'drake, shell'drake, shiel'drake**). [Prob dialect sheld (cf Du schillede) variegation, and **duck**[1], **drake**[1]]

shelf /shelf/ n (pl **shelves** /shelvz/) a board fixed horizontally on a wall, in a bookcase, cupboard, etc, for laying things on; a shelf-ful; a terrace; a ledge; a shoal; a sandbank; an informer (Aust inf). ◆ vt to shelve; to inform upon (Aust inf). [OE scylf shelf, ledge, pinnacle, or LGer schelf; perh partly from some other source]

■ **shelf'-ful** n (pl **shelf'-fuls**) enough to fill a shelf. **shelf'like** adj. **shelf'y** adj.

❑ **shelf'-catalogue** n a library catalogue arranged by shelves. **shelf ice** n ice extending from the land out to sea. **shelf life** n the length of time a product can be stored without deterioration occurring. **shelf mark** n an indication on a book of its place in a library. **shelf'room** n space or accommodation on shelves. **shelf'talker** n a marketing device, eg a notice or mini-poster, attached to a shelf in a shop, to promote a specific product.

■ **off the shelf** immediately available, in stock; (of a company) registered only in order to be sold. **on the shelf** no longer useful; no longer likely to have the opportunity to marry; removed from further prospect of employment.

shell /shel/ n a hard outer covering, esp of a shellfish, a tortoise, an egg, or a nut; a husk, pod, or rind; a shelled mollusc; an outer framework; the outer, often waterproof or showerproof, layer of a lined garment such as a jacket, coat, trousers, etc; a crust; a hollow sphere or the like; a mere outside, empty case, or lifeless relic; any frail structure; a

type of light racing boat; a light coffin; a conch trumpet; a lyre of tortoise-shell; an explosive projectile shot from a cannon, large gun, etc; a cartridge containing explosive for small arms, fireworks, etc; a piece of quicklime; a shell program; in some schools, an intermediate class (from one that met in an apse at Westminster). ◆ adj of, with, or like shell or shells. ◆ vt to separate from the shell; to case; to throw, fire, etc shells at. ◆ vt to peel, scale; to separate from the shell. [OE scell (WSax sciell); Du schil, ON skel]

■ **shelled** adj having a shell; separated from the shell, pod, etc. **shell'er** n. **shell'ful** n. **shell'iness** n. **shell'ing** n. **shell'-less** adj. **shell'-like** adj resembling a mollusc's shell; used as an epithet for the ear (poetic or joc). ◆ n (inf) an ear. **shell'y** adj of or like shell or shells; abounding in shells; having a shell; testaceous.

❑ **shell'back** n an old sailor; a sailor who has crossed the equator. **shell'bark** n a hickory with peeling bark. **shell bean** n (US) a bean removed from, and eaten without, its pod; any of various bean plants suitable for this. **shell'bound** adj (of a baby bird, etc) unable to escape from the shell. **shell company** n a little-known or failing company through which a major company conducts business clandestinely. **shell'-crater** n a hole in the ground made by a bursting shell. **shell'fire** n bombardment with shells. **shell'fish** n a shelled aquatic invertebrate, esp a mollusc or crustacean, or such animals collectively. **shell game** n (N Am) thimblerig. **shell heap** n (archaeol) a heap of domestic refuse consisting mainly of shells, associated with peoples who lived on shellfish. **shell'-hole** n a shell-crater. **shell'-ice** n ice no longer supported by water. **shell jacket** n a tight, short military jacket. **shell lime** n lime made from seashells. **shell'-lime'stone** n a limestone mainly consisting of shells. **shell'-marl** n a white, earthy lacustrine deposit. **shell money** n wampum. **shell mound** n a shell heap. **shell ornament** n a decoration based on the form of a shell. **shell parrakeet** or **parrot** n the budgerigar. **shell pink** n a pale yellow-tinged shade of pink. **shell-pink'** adj. **shell program** n (comput) a program, often concerned with look and feel, that can be developed for particular applications by the user. **shell'proof** adj able to resist shells or bombs. **shell'-sand** n sand consisting in great part of calcareous remains of dead organisms. **shell'shock** n mental disturbance due to war experiences, once thought to be caused by the bursting of shells; mental disturbance due to similar violent, etc experiences. **shell'shocked** adj. **shell star** n (astron) a star surrounded by a gaseous shell. **shell suit** n a type of lightweight tracksuit with a crinkly nylon outer layer and a cotton lining. **shell'work** n work composed of or adorned with shells. **shell'ycoat** n (Scot) a water goblin dressed in shells; a sheriff's messenger.

■ **come out of one's shell** to cease to be shy and reticent. **electron shell** see under **electron**. **shell out** (inf) to pay up; to pay out, spend.

she'll /shēl/ (inf) a contraction of **she shall** or **she will**.

shellac /shə-lak' or shel'ak/ n (also **shell'-lac**) lac (qv) in thin plates, obtained by melting seed-lac, straining and dropping, formerly used for making gramophone records; an old gramophone record whether or not made of shellac; loosely, lac, the resin, used eg as a spirit varnish. ◆ vt (**shellacking**; **shellacked**) to coat with shellac; /shə-lak'/ to trounce, defeat decisively (N Am inf). [**shell** and **lac**[2], transl of Fr laque en écailles lac in scales]

■ **shellack'ing** n.

Shelta /shel'tə/ n a language used by the Travelling People in Britain and Ireland. [Shelrū, poss a perversion of OIr béulra language]

shelter /shel'tər/ n a shielding or screening structure, esp against weather; (a place of) refuge, retreat, or temporary lodging in distress; asylum; screening; protection; (with cap) a UK charity that helps homeless people. ◆ vt to screen; to shield; to afford asylum, protection or lodging to; to harbour. ◆ vi to take shelter. [Origin obscure]

■ **shel'tered** adj affording shelter. **shel'terer** n. **shel'tering** n and adj. **shel'terless** adj. **shel'tery** adj affording shelter.

❑ **shelter belt** n a row of trees providing shelter from the wind. **sheltered housing** n housing for the elderly or disabled consisting of separate units with a resident housekeeper and/or warden to look after the tenants' wellbeing. **shelter tent** n (in the US Army) a tent for two men.

sheltie or **shelty** /shel'ti/ n a Shetland pony or sheepdog. [Perh ON Hjalti Shetlander]

shelve /shelv/ vt to furnish with shelves; to place on a shelf; to put aside, postpone. ◆ vi to slope, incline. ◆ n a ledge; a shelf. [See ety for **shelf**]

■ **shel'ver** n. **shelves** n pl (pl of **shelf** and of **shelve**). **shelv'ing** n provision of, or material for, shelves; shelves collectively; the act of putting on a shelf or setting aside; a slope. ◆ adj shallowing; sloping. **shel'vy** adj having sandbanks; overhanging.

Shema /shə-mä'/ n a Jewish prayer representing a declaration of faith, recited morning and evening. [Heb, hear]

shemale /shē'māl/ (inf) n a person, born a male, who has acquired female physical characteristics as a result of hormone treatment, but has not had surgery to remove the male genitalia. [**she** and **male**[1]]

■ words derived from main entry word; ❑ compound words; ■ idioms and phrasal verbs

Shemite earlier form of **Semite**.

shemozzle /shi-moz'l/ (inf) n (also **shimozz'le**, **shlemozz'le**, **schemozz'le**) a mess; a scrape; a rumpus. ◆ vi to make off. [Yiddish, from Ger schlimm bad, Heb mazzāl luck; cf **schlimazel**]

SHEN® /shen/ n a hands-on therapy effecting release in emotional and psychosomatic disorders. [Specific Human Emotional Nexus]

shenanigan /shi-nan'i-gən/ (inf; usu in pl) n trickery, underhand dealings; mischief, antics. [Origin unknown]

shend /shend/ (archaic or poetic) vt (pat and pap **shent**) to put to shame; to disgrace; to reproach, chide; to punish; to discomfit; to injure. [OE scendan to disgrace]

sheng cycle /sheng sī'kl/ n in traditional Chinese medicine, the cycle in which balance is achieved by each of the five elements being generated by its predecessor and generating its successor (see also **ko cycle**, **wu cycle**).

she-oak /shē'ōk/ (Aust) n an evergreen tree of the genus Casuarina, adapted for dry conditions. [**she**, denoting inferior, and **oak**, from its grain]

She'ol or **Sheol** /shē'ōl/ (Bible) n the place of departed spirits, the abode of the dead; (also without cap) hell. [Heb she'ōl]

shepherd /shep'ərd/ n a person who tends sheep (fem **shep'herdess**); a swain; a pastor. ◆ vt to tend or guide as or like a shepherd; to watch over, protect the interests of, or one's own interests in. ◆ vi to tend sheep. [OE scēaphirde; see **sheep** and **herd**²]
  ■ **shep'herdless** adj. **shep'herdling** n a little shepherd.
  ❑ **shepherd** (or **shepherd's**) **check**, **plaid** or **tartan** n (cloth with) a small black-and-white check. **Shepherd kings** n pl the Hyksos. **shepherd moon** or **satellite** n a moon whose gravitational field confines a planetary ring. **shepherd's club** n another name for mullein. **shepherd's cress** n a small cruciferous plant, Teesdalia. **shepherd's glass** or **weather glass** n the scarlet pimpernel. **shepherd's myrtle** n butcher's-broom. **shepherd's needle** n Venus's comb. **shepherd's pie** n a dish of meat (esp lamb) cooked with mashed potatoes on the top. **shepherd's-purse'** n a cosmopolitan cruciferous weed with flat obcordate pods (Capsella bursa-pastoris). **shepherd's rod** n the small teasel.
  ■ **the Good Shepherd** Jesus Christ (from Bible, John 10.11).

sherardize or **-ise** /sher'ər-dīz/ vt to coat with zinc by heating with zinc-dust in a vacuum. [Sherard Cowper-Coles (1867–1936), English chemist]

Sheraton /sher'ə-tən/ adj of a style of furniture designed by Thomas Sheraton (1751–1806).

sherbet /shûr'bət/ n a fruit-flavoured powder eaten as confectionery, or made into an effervescent drink; a kind of water-ice; a fruit-juice drink; beer (Aust inf). [Turk and Pers sherbet, from Ar; cf **shrub**², **syrup**]

sherd /shûrd/ n see **shard**¹.

shere a Spenserian spelling of **sheer**¹.

Sheria /shə-rē'ə/ or **Sheriat** /shə-rē'ət/ (also without cap) n same as **Sharia**.

sherif or **shereef**, also **sharif** /shə-rēf'/ n a descendant of Mohammed through his daughter Fatima; a prince, esp the Sultan of Morocco; the chief magistrate of Mecca; a Muslim ruler. [Ar sharīf noble, lofty, illustrious]
  ■ **sherif'ian** or **shereef'ian** adj.

sheriff /sher'if/ n the king's representative in a shire, with wide judicial and executive powers (hist); (in England and Wales) the chief officer of the Crown in the county, with duties chiefly honorary rather than judicial; (in Scotland) the chief judge of the sheriff court of a town or region; (in the USA) an elected officer of a county, mainly responsible for maintaining peace and order, attending courts, guarding prisoners, serving processes and executing judgements. [OE scīrgerēfa, from scīr shire, and gerēfa reeve; cf **reeve**¹, **grieve**², Ger Graf count]
  ■ **sher'iffalty** n shrievalty. **sher'iffdom** n the office, term of office, or territory under the jurisdiction of a sheriff; (in Scotland) one of the six divisions of the judicature, made up of sheriff court districts. **sher'iffhood** n. **sher'iffship** n the office of sheriff.
  ❑ **sheriff clerk** n (pl **sheriff clerks**) (in Scotland) the registrar of the sheriff's court, who has charge of the records of the court, organizes its work, etc. **sheriff court** n (in Scotland) a court having jurisdiction over civil and most criminal cases. **sheriff depute** n (pl **sheriff deputes**) (in Scotland) until the abolition of the heritable jurisdictions in 1748, a lawyer who acted as deputy for the sheriff; thereafter sometimes applied to the sheriff or sheriff principal. **sheriff officer** n (in Scotland) an officer connected with the sheriff court, who is responsible for raising actions, enforcing decrees, ensuring attendance of witnesses, etc. **sheriff principal** n (in Scotland) the chief judge of a sheriffdom. **sheriff's post** n (hist) a painted post at a sheriff's door for affixing proclamations. **sheriff substitute** n (pl **sheriffs substitute**) a Scottish acting sheriff, appointed by the Crown, in most cases resident in his judicial district.

■ **high sheriff** an English sheriff proper; the chief executive officer of a district (US). **honorary sheriff substitute** one who may act in the absence of the sheriff substitute. **un'der-sheriff** an English sheriff's deputy who performs the execution of writs.

sherlock /shûr'lok/ n a detective; (also with cap) someone who shows highly developed powers of observation and deduction, as did the detective, Sherlock Holmes, in the stories of Conan Doyle (1859–1930), often used ironically.

Sherpa /shûr'pə/ n (pl **Sher'pa** or **Sher'pas**) a member of a people living mainly in E Nepal, renowned for their skills as mountaineers and guides; their Tibetan language; (also without cap) an aide to, or personal representative of, a head of government participating in a summit conference, and concerned with negotiations behind the scenes and with drafting agreements, communiqués, etc. [Tibetan shar east, and pa inhabitant]

sherris /sher'is/ (archaic) n sherry.
  ❑ **sherr'is-sack** n sack imported from Xeres (now Jerez).

sherry /sher'i/ n a fortified wine from the neighbourhood of Jerez de la Frontera in Spain; a wine of this type from various regions of the world, incl Australia, S Africa, Cyprus, etc. [Xeres, earlier form of Jerez]
  ❑ **sherry-cobb'ler** n a drink made up of sherry, lemon, sugar, ice, etc.

sherwani /shûr-wä'ni/ n (pl **sherwa'nis**) in S Asia, a man's knee-length coat buttoning up to the chin. [Hindi]

she's /shēz/ an informal contraction of **she is** or **she has**.

shet /shet/ obsolete or dialect form of **shut**.

Shetland /shet'lənd/ (also without cap) adj relating to the Shetland Islands off the N coast of Scotland.
  ■ **Shet'lander** n. **Shetlan'dic** adj. ◆ n Shetland dialect.
  ❑ **Shetland pony** n a small, hardy pony with a thick coat, originating in the Shetland Islands (also **shel'tie**). **Shetland sheep** n a breed of sheep of Shetland and formerly Aberdeenshire. **Shetland sheepdog** n a breed of dog developed in the Shetland Islands resembling the collie, though smaller in size and with a thicker coat (also **shel'tie**). **Shetland wool** n a fine loosely twisted wool obtained from Shetland sheep.

sheuch or **sheugh** /shoohh/ (Scot) n a ditch or drain. ◆ vt to plant temporarily. [**sough**²]

sheva /shə-vä'/ n (in Hebrew grammar) a point or sign (:), under a consonant, indicating absence of vowel; a neutral vowel sound, a schwa (phonetics). [Heb shewā]

Shevat see **Shebat**.

Shevuoth see **Shabuoth**.

shew /shō or shoo/ (pap **shewn** /shōn/) an archaic spelling of **show**.

shewbread or **showbread** /shō'bred/ n the twelve loaves placed each Sabbath on the table beside the altar of incense in the sanctuary of the tabernacle by the Jewish priests in ancient Israel. [After Ger Schaubrot, transl Heb lechem pānīm bread of the presence]

shewel /shoo'əl/ (obs or dialect) n (also **sew'el**) a scarecrow; a device to scare deer. [Connected with **shy**¹]

SHF or **shf** abbrev : superhigh frequency.

shh see **sh**.

Shia or **Shiah** /shē'ə/ n the branch of Islam, or a collective name for its adherent sects, that recognizes Ali (Mohammed's cousin and son-in-law) and his successors as the true imams (cf **Sunni**); a member of this branch of Islam, a Shiite. [Ar shī'a sect]
  ■ **Shiism** /shē'izm/ n. **Shiite** /shē'īt/ n and adj (a member) of this (now chiefly Iranian) sect. **Shiitic** /-it'ik/ adj.

shiatsu or **shiatzu** /shi-at'soo or -sŭ/ n acupressure, a Japanese healing and health-promoting therapy using massage with fingers, palms, etc. [Jap, literally, finger pressure]

shibah see **shiva**.

shibboleth /shib'ə-leth/ n the criterion, catchword or catchphrase of a group, party or sect by which members may be identified; a slogan; a peculiarity of speech; the Gileadite test-word to distinguish an Ephraimite, who could not pronounce sh (from Bible, Judges 12.5–6); any such test. [Heb shibbōleth an ear of corn, or a stream]

shibuichi /shi-bū-ich'ē/ n an alloy of three parts copper to one part silver, widely used in Japanese decorative art to give a silver-grey patina. ◆ adj made of or with shibuichi. [Jap shi four, bu part, and ichi one]

shicker /shik'ər/ (esp Aust and NZ sl) n strong drink, liquor; a drunk. [Yiddish shikker, from Heb]
  ■ **shick'ered** adj drunk.

shicksa same as **shiksa**.

shidder /shid'ər/ (Spenser) n a female animal. [**she** and **deer**; cf **hidder**]

shidduch /shid'ahh/ (Judaism) n (pl **shidduchim** /-doo'hhim/) an arranged marriage. [Heb shiddēkh to arrange a marriage]

shied see **shy**[1,2].

shiel[1] same as **sheal**[1].

shiel[2] or **sheal** /shēl/ (chiefly *Scot*) *n* a hut, shieling. [Prob from a lost OE equivalent of ON *skāli* hut]
■ **shiel'ing** or **sheal'ing** *n* a rough hut near summer pasture used as shelter by shepherds or people tending cattle; a summer pasture.

shield /shēld/ *n* a piece of armour, a broad plate carried to deflect weapons, *esp* one with a straight top and tapering curved sides; a protective plate, screen, pad, or other guard; the outer protective covering of certain animals, such as the carapace of a tortoise; someone or something that protects from damage or danger; a tubular framework that supports the ground and protects workers during tunnelling; a shield-shaped design or object, eg an escutcheon used for displaying arms, or a piece of plate awarded as a prize; the large stable area of Precambrian rocks that forms the central part of a continent; a policeman's badge (*US*). ◆ *vt* to protect by sheltering; to hide from view; to ward off; to forfend (*Shakesp*). [OE *sceld* (WSax *scield*); Ger *Schild*, ON *skjöldr*, protection]
■ **shiel'der** *n*. **shiel'ding** *n* (*nuclear eng*; *radiol*) protective use of materials of low atomic number to reduce the energy of strong neutron beams, or of concrete, lead or other heavy materials to shield against radiation. **shield'less** *adj*. **shield'like** *adj*. **shield'ling** *n* a protected person.
❑ **shield'-arm** *n* the left arm. **shield'-bearer** *n* an attendant who carries a warrior's shield. **shield bug** *n* any heteropterous insect of the superfamily Pentatomoidea, typically having flat, broad bodies shaped like heraldic shields. **shielded line** *n* (*elec eng*) a line or circuit shielded from external interference by highly conducting or magnetic material. **shielded pair** *n* (*telecom*) a balanced pair of insulated wires encased in a cable which prevents external interference. **shield fern** *n* any evergreen or semi-evergreen fern of the genus *Polystichum* with scales covering the spore-producing pinnae. **shield'-hand** *n* the left hand. **shield ivy** *n* a variety of common ivy, *Hedera helix*, with heart-shaped leaves (also called **sweetheart ivy**). **shield law** *n* (*N Am*) a law that protects journalists from being forced to reveal confidential information relating to sources, etc. **shield'-maid, -maiden** or **-may** *n* an Amazon; a Valkyrie. **shield of brawn** *n* the thick skin of a pig's side, *esp* when stuffed with meat. **shield pond** or **shielding pond** *n* (*nuclear eng*) a deep tank of water used to shield operators from highly radioactive materials stored and manipulated at the bottom of it. **shield'-shaped** *adj*. **shield volcano** *n* (*geog*) a volcano with a broad, gently sloping dome formed by successive eruptions of lava. **shield'wall** *n* a defence of interlocked shields.

shieldrake, **shieldduck** see **shelduck**.

shieling see under **shiel**[2].

shier, **shies**, **shiest** see under **shy**[1,2].

shift /shift/ *vt* to change; to change the clothes of (*archaic* or *dialect*); to change the position or direction of; to remove; to dislodge; to transfer; to evade (*obs*); to rid; to quit; to swallow, consume (*sl*); to sell, get rid of by selling (*sl*); to put off. ◆ *vi* to manage, get on, do as one can; to change; to change position or direction; to fluctuate; to change one's clothes (*archaic* or *dialect*); to take appropriate or urgent action; to move; to go away; to move quickly (*inf*); to undergo phonetic change. ◆ *n* a group of people who work for a specific period within a working day, alternating with other groups; the time worked by such a group; a change; a change of position or direction; a change in the direction of the wind (*naut*); a general or bodily displacement of a series (as of lines in the spectrum, consonant or vowel sounds, faulted strata); displacement of an ordered set of data to the left or right (*comput*); the movement of two or more offensive players at the same time before the snap (*American football*); (in violin-playing) any change of position of the hand on the fingerboard; a removal; the gear change in a motor vehicle (chiefly *N Am*); an expedient; an artifice or contrivance; a woman's undergarment, a smock, chemise or slip (*old*); a loose dress, roughly triangular or oblong; provision of clothes or (*archaic*) other things for use in rotation or substitution. [OE *sciftan* to divide, allot; ON *skipta*]
■ **shift'able** *adj*. **shift'ed** *adj*. **shift'er** *n* someone who or something that shifts, *esp* a scene-shifter; someone who resorts to shifts, tricks, evasions, or sophistry. **shif'tily** *adv*. **shift'iness** *n*. **shift'ing** *n*. ◆ *adj* moving about; unstable; shifty. **shift'less** *adj* without resource or expedient; inefficient; feckless; aimless; without a smock (*archaic*). **shift'lessly** *adv*. **shift'lessness** *n*. **shift'y** *adj* evasive, tricky, suggesting trickery; dubious, shady, furtive; ready with shifts or expedients.
❑ **shif'ting-boards** *n pl* partitioning to prevent shifting of cargo. **shifting cultivation** *n* a system of cultivating land, in which an area is cleared and farmed until the fertility of the soil is exhausted, then abandoned for a new area. **shifting register** same as **shift register** below. **shifting spanner** *n* an adjustable spanner. **shift key** *n* a key on a typewriter or computer keyboard used to bring a different set of letters (eg capitals) into use. **shift register** *n* (*comput*) a register (qv)

which carries out shifts on data (bits or digits). **shift work** *n* (a system of) working in shifts. **shift worker** *n*. **shift working** *n*.
■ **shift about** to move from side to side; to turn right round to the opposite point. **shift down** or **up** (chiefly *N Am*) to change down or up a gear (also *fig*). **shift for oneself** to depend on one's own resources. **shift one's ground** (*usu fig*) to change the position one has taken, eg in a discussion.

shigella /shi-gel'ə/ *n* a rod-shaped bacterium of the genus *Shigella*, in particular *Shigella dysenteriae*, which causes bacillary dysentery. [K Shiga (1870–1957), the Japanese bacteriologist who discovered it]
■ **shigellosis** /shi-gə-lō'sis/ *n* infestation of the intestinal tract by shigella, causing bacillary dysentery.

shih tzu /shē dzoo/ or **shitzu** /shē' tsoo/ *n* a small long-haired dog bred from the Pekingese and the Lhasa Apso. [Chin *shīzigǒu* lion dog]

Shiism, **Shiite**, **Shiitic** see under **Shia**.

shiitake /shi-i-tä'kä/ *n* (pl **shiita'ke**) the large dark-brown mushroom (*Lentinus edodes*) widely used in Oriental cookery, cultivated on tree logs. [Jap *shii* a type of tree, and *take* mushroom]

shikar /shi-kär'/ (*Anglo-Ind*) *n* hunting, *esp* of big game; game, booty; sport. [Urdu, from Pers *shikār*]
■ **shikar'ee** or **shikar'i** *n* a hunter, *esp* of big game; a professional, *esp* indigenous, hunting guide; a sportsman.

shiksa or **shikse** /shik'sə/ *n* a non-Jewish girl or woman. [Yiddish]

shill[1] see **sheal**[1].

shill[2] /shil/ (*sl*; *esp N Am*) *n* an accomplice to a tradesman, etc, who poses as a genuine customer to encourage trade or interest; a gambler's or con man's sidekick; a decoy. ◆ *vi* to act as a shill. [Prob short form of **shillaber**]

shillaber /shil'ə-bər/ (*old US sl*) *n* an enthusiastic or satisfied customer; a shill. [Origin uncertain]

shillelagh /shi-lā'li or -lā'lə/ *n* in Ireland, an oak or blackthorn cudgel, or any similar stout club, etc (also **shilla'lah**). [*Shillelagh*, an oak wood in County Wicklow, Ireland, or *sail* willow, and *eílle* (genitive) thong]

shilling /shil'ing/ *n* a coin or its value, 12 old pence, equivalent to 5 (new) pence (*hist*); the standard monetary unit of Kenya, Somalia, Tanzania and Uganda (100 cents). ◆ *adj* costing or offered for a shilling; also in combination, as in *two-shilling*, *three-shilling*, etc. [OE *scilling*, Ger *Schilling*]
■ **shill'ingless** *adj*. **shill'ingsworth** *n* as much as can be purchased for a shilling.
❑ **shilling mark** *n* a solidus sign. **shilling shocker** or **shilling dreadful** *n* a short sensational story or novel, *orig* one published at a shilling.
■ **not the full shilling** (*inf*) not having all mental faculties intact. **take the** (**king's** or **queen's**) **shilling** (*hist*) to enlist as a soldier by accepting a recruiting officer's shilling, a practice discontinued in 1879.

shilly-shally /shil'i-shal'i/ *vi* to be indecisive; to hesitate; to vacillate. ◆ *adv* indecisively. ◆ *n* vacillation; someone who vacillates. [A reduplication of *shall I?*]
■ **shill'y-shall'ier** *n*. **shill'y-shallying** *n*.

shilpit /shil'pit/ (*Scot*) *adj* sickly-looking; puny; insipid; watery; inferior. [Ety uncertain]

shily see under **shy**[1].

shim /shim/ *n* a thin slip of metal, wood, etc, used to fill in space or to adjust parts. ◆ *vt* to fill in or adjust using a shim or shims. [Ety uncertain]
❑ **shim rod** *n* a coarse control rod in a nuclear reactor.

shimaal or **shamal** /shə-mäl'/ *n* in the Middle East, a hot dry north wind that carries sand in desert regions. [Ar *shamal* north]

shimmer /shim'ər/ *vi* to gleam tremulously, to glisten. [OE *scimerian*, from *scimian* to shine; Ger *schimmern*]
■ **shimm'er** or **shimm'ering** *n* a tremulous gleam. **shimm'eringly** *adv*. **shimm'ery** *adj*.

shimmy[1] or **shimmey** /shim'i/ (*inf*) *n* a chemise.

shimmy[2] /shim'i/ *n* a body-shaking dance, popular during the 1920s (also **shimm'y-shake**); a shaking of the hips; vibration in a motor vehicle or an aeroplane. ◆ *vi* (**shimm'ying**; **shimm'ied**) to dance the shimmy, or make similar movements; to vibrate. [Origin uncertain]

shimozzle see **shemozzle**.

shin[1] /shin/ *n* the forepart of the leg below the knee; the lower part of a leg of beef. ◆ *vi* to swarm, climb by gripping with the hands and legs (*usu* with *up*); to use one's legs, hasten along. ◆ *vt* to climb by gripping with the hands and legs; to kick on the shins. [OE *scinu* the shin; Du *scheen*; Ger *Schiene* a thin plate]
❑ **shin'-barker** *n* a dog that barks at one's shins. **shin'bone** *n* the tibia. **shin pad** *n* a protective covering for the shin (also **shin guard**). **shin'plaster** *n* (*US*; now *obs*) *orig*, a brown-paper patch for a sore on

the shin; paper money of low value. **shin splints** *n pl* or *n sing* inflammation of the muscles around the shinbone caused by strenuous exercise, *esp* running on hard surfaces.

shin² /shēn/ or **sin** /sēn/ *n* the twenty-first letter of the Hebrew alphabet. [Heb]

shindig /shin'dig/ (*inf*) *n* a lively celebration or party; a row. [Cf **shindy**]

shindy /shin'di/ (*inf*) *n* a row, rumpus. [Perh **shinty**]
■ **kick up a shindy** to make a disturbance.

shine /shīn/ *vi* (pat and pap **shone** /shon/ or (*archaic*, or in the sense 'polished') **shined**) to give off or reflect light; to beam with steady radiance; to glow; to be bright; to be clear or conspicuous; to excel. ◆ *vt* to cause to shine; to direct the light of (a torch, etc). ◆ *adj* (*archaic*) sheen. ◆ *n* brightness; lustre; a dash, brilliant appearance; an act or process of polishing; fine weather, *esp* in the phrase *rain or shine*; a party (*old sl*); a shindy (*old sl*). [OE *scīnan*; Ger *scheinen*; in some senses perh a different word; cf **shindy**]
■ **shine'less** *adj*. **shīn'er** *n* a person who or thing that shines; a coin, *esp* a sovereign (*old sl*); a small fish of various kinds with glittering scales; a black eye (*inf*). **shīn'ily** *adv*. **shīn'iness** *n*. **shīn'ing** *adj* bright or gleaming; excellent or distinguished. **shīn'ingly** *adv*. **shīn'ingness** *n*. **shīn'y** *adj* having a bright or polished surface or appearance; lustrous, glossy. ◆ *n* a shiny or bright object; (with *the*) money (*old sl*). ◆ *adv* (*Spenser*) in a shiny manner.
■ **shine at** to be very good at. **take a shine to** (*inf*) to fancy, take a liking to. **take the shine off** or **out of** (*inf*) to outshine, eclipse; to take the brilliance or pleasure-giving quality out of.

shiness see under **shy¹**.

shingle¹ /shing'gl/ *n* a thin tile, *usu* of wood, laid on a roof or the sides of a building, in overlapping rows; these tiles collectively; a board; a small signboard or plate (*US*); a style of haircut in which the hair is cut short in overlapping layers, emphasizing the shape of the head at the back. ◆ *vt* to cover with shingles; to cut in the manner of a shingle. [LL *scindula* a wooden tile, from L *scindere* to split]
■ **shing'led** *adj*. **shing'ler** *n*. **shing'ling** *n* shingles collectively; the act or process of laying shingles; the act or process of cutting hair in a shingle; the state or condition of overlapping in the manner of shingles.
□ **shing'le-roofed** *adj*.

shingle² /shing'gl/ *n* coarse gravel; small rounded pebbles found *esp* on beaches; a bank or bed of gravel or stones. [Origin obscure]
■ **shing'ly** *adj*.

shingles /shing'glz/ *n sing* the disease *Herpes zoster*, in which acute inflammation of nerve ganglia produces pain and a series of blisters along the path of the nerve, *esp* in the area of the waist and ribs, but sometimes round the head and face. [L *cingulum* a belt, from *cingere* to gird]

shinne /shin/ *n* an archaic form of **chin**.

shinny¹ see **shinty**.

shinny² /shin'i/ (*N Am*) *vi* to shin (*usu* with *up*, *down*, etc). [**shin¹**]

Shinto /shin'tō/ *n* the Japanese nature and hero cult, the indigenous religion of the country. [Jap, from Chin *shén dào*, from *shén* god, and *dào* way, path]
■ **Shin'tōism** *n*. **Shin'tōist** *n* and *adj*.

shinty /shin'ti/ or **shinny** /shin'i/ *n* a game similar to hockey, of Scottish origin, played by teams of 12; the slim curved club (the caman, also **shin'ty-stick**) or leather-covered cork ball (or substitute) used in this game. [Perh from Gaelic *sinteag* a bound, pace]

shiny see under **shine**.

ship /ship/ *n* a large seagoing vessel using engines or sails, formerly *esp* a square-rigged sailing vessel with bowsprit and three masts; a racing-boat with eight oars; any floating craft (also *fig*); an aircraft or airship; a spaceship; a ship's crew. ◆ *vt* (**shipp'ing**; **shipped**) to put, receive, or take on board; to send or convey by ship; to send by land or air; to dispatch, send (off); to engage for service on board; to fix or place in position. ◆ *vi* to embark; to travel by ship; to engage for service on board ship. [OE *scip*; Gothic *skip*, ON *skip*, Ger *Schiff*]
■ **ship'ful** *n*. **ship'less** *adj*. **ship'ment** *n* the act of shipping cargo; a consignment, *orig* by ship, now extended to other forms of transport. **shipp'able** *adj*. **shipped** *adj* provided with a ship or ships (*archaic*); embarked. **shipp'er** *n* a person or company that sends goods by ship or aircraft. **shipp'ing** *n* ships collectively; accommodation on board ship; (the act of) putting aboard ship; transport by ship, the business of a shipper; a voyage (*archaic*).
□ **ship biscuit** *n* a hard biscuit formerly used as a staple food for sailors aboard ship, hardtack. **ship'board** *n* a ship's side, hence a ship. ◆ *adj* occurring on board ship. **ship** (or **ship's**) **boy** *n* a boy that serves on a ship. **ship'-breaker** *n* a person or company that breaks up old ships. **ship'broker** *n* a broker for the sale, insurance, etc, of ships. **ship'builder** *n* a person or company that constructs

ships. **ship'building** *n*. **ship canal** *n* a canal large enough for ships. **ship** (or **ship's**) **carpenter** *n* a carpenter employed on board ship or in a shipyard. **ship** (or **ship's**) **chandler** *n* a dealer in supplies for ships. **ship chandlery** *n*. **ship fever** *n* a form of typhus fever. **ship'-holder** *n* a remora (qv). **ship'lap** *n* an arrangement of boards or plates, used *esp* on a ship's hull, in which the lower edge of one overlaps the upper edge of the adjacent one (also *vt* and *vi*). **ship letter** *n* a letter sent by a private vessel, not by the mail boat. **ship'load** *n* the actual or possible load of a ship. **ship'man** *n* (*pl* **ship'men**) (*archaic*) a sailor; a skipper; a pilot. **ship'master** *n* the captain of a ship. **ship'mate** *n* a fellow sailor. **ship money** *n* (*hist*) a tax imposed by the sovereign to raise money to build a fleet of ships, *esp* that raised without authorization of parliament by Charles I from 1635 onwards. **ship of the desert** *n* the camel. **ship of the line** *n* before steam navigation, a man-of-war large enough to take a place in a line of battle. **ship'owner** *n* the owner of, or owner of a share in, a ship or ships. **shipping agent** *n* a person or company that manages the administrative business of a ship on behalf of the owner. **shipping articles** *n pl* articles of agreement between the captain and his crew. **shipping clerk** *n* a person employed by a shipper to deal with the receiving and dispatching of goods. **ship'pound** *n* in the Baltic ports, twenty lispounds. **ship railway** *n* a railway for carrying ships overland. **ship'-rigged** *adj* having three masts with square sails and spreading yards. **ship's biscuit** same as **ship biscuit** above. **ship'shape** *adj* in a seamanlike condition; trim, neat, proper. **ship's husband** see under **husband**. **ship's papers** *n pl* documents that a ship is required to carry. **ship'-tire** *n* (*Shakesp*) a shiplike headdress. **ship'way** *n* a sliding way for launching ships; a support for ships under examination or repair; a ship canal. **ship'worm** *n* a wormlike lamellibranch mollusc (*esp* of the family Teredinidae) that makes shell-lined tunnels in submerged wood. **ship'wreck** *n* a wrecked ship; the wreck or destruction (*esp* by accident) of a ship; destruction, ruin, disaster; wreckage (*rare*). ◆ *vt* to wreck; to cause to undergo shipwreck; to cause ruin or destruction to. ◆ *vi* to suffer or undergo shipwreck or destruction. **ship'wright** *n* a wright or carpenter employed in shipbuilding. **ship'yard** *n* a yard where ships are built or repaired.
■ **on shipboard** upon or within a ship. **ship a sea** or **ship water** to have a wave come over the side of a ship or boat. **ship it green** to ship waves, not mere spray. **ship the oars** to put the oars in the rowlocks; to bring the oars into the boat. **ship water** see **ship a sea** above. **take ship** or **shipping** to embark, set off on a voyage. **when one's ship comes home** or **in** when one becomes rich.

-ship /-ship/ *sfx* denoting: a condition or state, eg *friendship, fellowship*; position, rank, status, eg *lordship, kingship*; a specified type of skill, eg *craftsmanship, scholarship*; a group of people having something in common, eg *membership*. [OE *-scipe*, connected with **shape**]

shipment, etc see under **ship**.

shippen or **shippon** /ship'n/ (*dialect*) *n* a cowhouse, cattle shed. [OE *scypen*; cf **shop**]

shir see **shirr**.

shiralee or **shirralee** /shir'ə-lē/ (*Aust*; now *obs*) *n* a swagman's bundle. [Origin uncertain, perh from an Aboriginal word]

Shiraz /shē'rāz, shir'äz or -az/ *n* (also called in France **Syrah**) a red wine grape; the dark, tannic red wine made from this. [From *Shiraz* a city in Iran]

shire /shīr/ (in combination *-shir* or *-shər*) *n* an administrative district of England formed for mainly taxation purposes by the Anglo-Saxons; a county; formerly, applied also to certain smaller districts, as with *Richmondshire* and *Hallamshire*; a rural district having its own elected council (*Aust*). [OE *scīr* office, authority]
□ **shire horse** *n* a large, strong draught horse with fringes of hair on the lower legs, once bred chiefly in the Midland shires. **shire'man** *n* a sheriff. **shire'-moot** *n* (OE *scīrgemōt*; *hist*) the court of the shire in medieval England. **shire'-reeve** *n* a sheriff (see ety at **sheriff**).
■ **the Shires** those English counties whose names end in *-shire*, particularly Leicestershire, Northamptonshire, Rutlandshire (later Rutland), and part of Lincolnshire, having strong associations with hunting.

shirk /shûrk/ *vt* to evade (work, a duty, responsibility, etc). ◆ *vi* to go or act evasively; to avoid work or duty. ◆ *n* a person who shirks. [Cf **shark**]
■ **shirk'er** *n*.

Shirley poppy /shûr'li pop'i/ *n* a garden variety of the common poppy first produced at *Shirley* vicarage, Croydon.

Shirley Temple /shûr'li tem'pl/ *n* a soft drink made with ginger ale and grenadine. [Named in honour of *Shirley Temple* (1928–2014), US actress]

Shirodkar's operation /shir'od-kärz op-ə-rā'shən/ (*obstetrics*) *n* an operation in which the neck of the womb is closed with a suture to prevent miscarriage. [NV *Shirodkar* (1900–71), Indian obstetrician]

shirr, **shir** /shûr/ n a puckering or gathering. ◆ vt to pucker, make gathers in; to draw (fabric) into a series of parallel gathered rows using elastic thread; to bake (eggs broken into a dish). [Origin unknown]
■ **shirred** adj. **shirr'ing** n.

shirra /shir'ə/ n an obsolete Scots form of **sheriff**.

shirt /shûrt/ n a loose sleeved garment, esp for men, covering the upper part of the body, typically with a fitted collar and cuffs; a woman's blouse of similar form; an undershirt; a nightshirt; a close covering. ◆ vt (now rare) to put a shirt on. [OE scyrte ; cf **short**]
■ **shirt'ing** n cloth for shirts. **shirt'less** adj.
❑ **shirt'band** n the neckband of a shirt. **shirt button** n. **shirt dress** n a straight dress with a collar like a shirt's, resembling an elongated shirt; a shirtwaister (US). **shirt frill** n a frill on the breast of a shirt. **shirt front** n the breast of a shirt, esp a starched false one, a dickey. **shirt'lifter** n (derog sl) a male homosexual. **shirt pin** n an ornamental pin fastening a shirt at the neck. **shirt'sleeve** n. **shirt'sleeved** adj. **shirt stud** n a decorative stud used to fasten a formal shirt. **shirt tail** n the longer flap at the back of a shirt. **shirt'waist** n (US) a woman's blouse. **shirt'waister** n a tailored dress with a shirtwaist top.
■ **Black Shirt** or **Black'shirt** a fascist. **boiled shirt** a white shirt (with starched front). **Brown Shirt** or **Brown'shirt** a Nazi. **get** or **have one's** (or **someone's**) **shirt out** (old sl) to become (or make someone else) angry (from the dishevelment of uncontrolled rage). **in one's shirt** wearing nothing but a shirt, or nothing over the shirt. **in one's shirtsleeves** with one's jacket or jersey off. **keep one's shirt on** to keep calm. **lose one's shirt** to lose all one has. **put one's shirt on** to bet all one has on. **Red Shirt** a follower of Garibaldi.

shirty /shûr'ti/ (inf) adj ill-tempered, annoyed. [From get or have someone's shirt out ; see under **shirt**]
■ **shirt'ily** adv. **shirt'iness** n.

shisha or **sheesha** /shē'shə/ n tobacco that is flavoured with fruit and molasses; (also **shisha pipe** or **sheesha pipe**) a hookah used for smoking this mixture. [Ar]

shish kebab see **kebab**.

shit /shit/ or (dialect, euphem or joc) **shite** /shīt/ (vulgar sl) n faeces, excrement; the act of defecating; a contemptuous term for a person; rubbish, nonsense; unspecified items, stuff; marijuana or heroin (drug sl). ◆ vi **shitt'ing** or **shī'ting**; **shit**, **shitt'ed**, **shī'ted** or **shat** to evacuate the bowels, defecate. ◆ vt to produce by defecating (also fig); (reflexive) to defecate over one's person, soil (oneself). ◆ interj expressing anger, disgust, disappointment, etc. [OE scitan to defecate]
■ **shit'less** adj and adv in a state where one is unable to function properly, chiefly in the phrase scared shitless. **shitt'iness** n. **shitt'y** adj soiled with or like shit; very bad or unpleasant.
❑ **shit'face** n a contemptible person (often as a term of abuse). **shit'faced** adj (esp N Am) drunk. **shit'head** n a contemptible or unpleasant person; a drug user, esp a user of marijuana. **shit'hole** n a filthy or dilapidated place or establishment. **shit-hot'** adj (usu of a person) very good, excellent, first-rate, admirable. **shit'house** n a lavatory. **shit list** n a notional list of people who are in disgrace. **shit'load** n a very large amount. **shit'-scared** adj very frightened. **shit'-stirrer** n someone who causes unnecessary trouble.
■ **get one's shit together** to compose oneself and one's affairs into a satisfactory state. **in (the) shit** in trouble. **no shit** no fooling; you amaze me (often ironic). **shit a brick** or **bricks** to be very anxious or frightened. **shit oneself** to be very scared. **the shits** diarrhoea. **up shit creek (without a paddle)** see under **creek**. **when the shit hits the fan** when real trouble or conflict begins.

shittim /shit'im/ n (Bible; in full **shitt'im wood**) the wood of the **shitt'ah (tree)**, believed to be a species of acacia; applied also to various other trees. [Heb shittāh, pl shittīm]

shitzu see **shih tzu**.

shiur /shē'ûr/ (Judaism) n (pl **shiurim** /shē-ū-rim'/) a period spent studying the Talmud. [Heb]

shiv see **chiv**.

Shiva see **Siva**.

shiva, **shivah** or **shibah** /shiv'ə/ (Judaism) n a period of mourning observed for seven days after a funeral. [Heb, seven days]

shivaree /shiv-ə-rē'/ (N Am) n a variant of **charivari**.

shive /shīv/ n a slice, eg of bread (Scot); a thin flat cork or bung; (in pl) pale yellow or brown splinters of undigested wood particles in wood pulp or paper; (in pl) small particles of vegetable or woody matter found in flax fibres or newly-shorn wool (textiles). [ME schive ; cf ON skīfa ; Du schijf, Ger Scheibe]

shiver¹ /shiv'ər/ vi to quiver; to tremble; to make an involuntary muscular movement as with cold; (of sails) to tremble or shake when a sailing vessel is brought close to the wind (naut). ◆ vt to cause to quiver or tremble. ◆ n a shivering movement or feeling. [ME chivere]
■ **shiv'erer** n. **shiv'ering** n and adj. **shiv'eringly** adv. **shiv'ery** adj inclined to shiver or to cause shivers.

■ **shiver in one's shoes** see **shake**. **the shivers** (inf) a shivering fit; the ague; a thrill of horror or fear.

shiver² /shiv'ər/ n a splinter or small fragment (now rare); a flake or splinter of stone. ◆ vt and vi to shatter. [Early ME scifre ; cf **shive**, **sheave**; Ger Schiefer]
■ **shiv'ery** adj brittle.
■ **shiver my timbers** a stock nautical exclamation uttered by stage sailors, etc.

shiver³ /shiv'ər/ (dialect; esp Scot) n a cold sore. [Perh **shiver¹**]

shivoo /shi-voo'/ (Aust inf) n a (noisy) party or social occasion. [From N Eng dialect sheevo a shindy; perh connected with Fr chez vous at your house]

Shiv Sena /shēv or shiv sā'nä/ n a nationalist Hindu political organization in India. [Sans, Siva's army]

shlemiel see **schlemiel**.

shlemozzle see **shemozzle**.

shlep see **schlep**.

shlimazel see **schlimazel**.

shlock see **schlock**.

SHM or **shm** (phys) abbrev : simple harmonic motion.

shmaltz see **schmaltz**.

shmo see **schmo**.

shmock see **schmuck**.

shmoose, **shmooze** see **schmooze**.

shmuck see **schmuck**.

Shoah /shō'ə/ n the Jewish Holocaust of World War II. [Heb, literally, destruction]

shoal¹ /shōl/ n a multitude of fishes, etc, swimming together; a flock, swarm, great assemblage. ◆ vi to gather or go in shoals, swarm. [OE scolu troop, prob from MDu schōle troop, group; cf **school²**]
■ **shoal'wise** adv in shoals.

shoal² /shōl/ adj shallow. ◆ n an area of shallow water; a sandbank, esp one exposed at low tide. ◆ vi to become shallow; to sail into shallow water (naut). ◆ vt to sail into (water of decreasing depth); to make shallow. [OE sceald shallow]
■ **shoal'ing** n. **shoal'ness** n. **shoal'y** adj (of a stretch of water) full of shallows; (of a vessel's draught) shallow, and therefore capable of sailing in shoal water (naut).
❑ **shoal mark** n an indication of shoal water. **shoal water** n.

shoat or **shote** /shōt/ n a young pig, esp one that has just been weaned. [From ME; connected with Flem schote]

shochet /shohh'ət/ n (pl **shoch'etim** /-tim/) a slaughterer qualified to kill cattle or poultry according to prescribed Jewish ritual. [Heb shōḥēt, prp of shāḥat to slaughter]

shock¹ /shok/ n a violent impact, orig of charging warriors; a dashing together; a shaking or unsettling blow; a sudden shaking or jarring as if by a blow; a blow to the emotions or its cause, an unpleasant surprise; outrage at something regarded as improper; a convulsive excitation of nerves, eg by electricity; (also **surgical shock**) a state of extreme physical collapse, a suspension of the body's voluntary and involuntary functions caused by trauma, a surgical operation, or excessive sudden emotional disturbance; a stroke of paralysis, eg resulting from cerebral haemorrhage (inf). ◆ vt to meet or assail with a shock; to shake or impair by a shock; to give a shock to; to cause to feel outrage, indignation, disgust, horror, etc. ◆ vi to outrage feelings; to collide with violence. ◆ adj (press) sensational, surprising, unexpected, as in a shock result. [Appar Fr choc (noun), choquer (verb) to strike, or perh directly from a Gmc source; cf Du schok]
■ **shockabil'ity** n. **shock'able** adj. **shocked** adj. **shock'er** n (inf) a sensational story, film or play; any remarkably unpleasant or offensive person or thing; a shock absorber. **shock'ing** adj giving a shock; revolting to the feelings, esp to oversensitive modesty; execrable; deplorably bad. ◆ adv (inf) deplorably. **shock'ingly** adv. **shock'ingness** n.
❑ **shock absorber** n a device for absorbing shock, such as the telescopic oleo leg in aircraft landing gear or the dampers between the chassis and axles in a motor vehicle. **shock'-horror** adj used eg of banner headlines and other sensationalistic devices of the tabloid press (see also **shock horror** below). **shocking pink** n an extremely vivid, glaring shade of pink. **shock jock** n (inf) a radio disc jockey who is intentionally outspoken or offensive. **shock'proof** adj protected in some way from giving, or suffering the effects of, shock or impact; unlikely to be upset, or to feel moral outrage. **shock'stall** n (aeronautics) loss of lift at high speed caused by the formation of shock waves on an aircraft's wings. **shock tactics** n pl orig tactics of cavalry attacking in masses and depending for their effect on the force of impact; any course of action aimed at achieving an object by means of suddenness and overwhelming force (fig). **shock therapy** or

treatment *n* the use of electric shocks in the treatment of mental disorders; the use of violent measures to change someone's way of thinking (*fig*). **shock troops** *n pl* troops trained or selected for attacks demanding exceptional physique and bravery. **shock wave** *n* a wave of the same nature as a sound wave but of very great intensity, caused eg by an atomic explosion, earthquake or by a body moving with supersonic velocity; the reaction to a sensation or a scandal, thought of as spreading in ever-widening circles.

■ **shock and awe** a less formal name for rapid dominance (qv under **rapid**). **shock horror** (*inf*) an ironic expression used in response to something purporting to shock.

shock² /shok/ *n* a mass of thick, shaggy hair; (also **shock dog**) a dog with long shaggy fur (*obs*). [Poss from **shock³**; cf **shough**]
□ **shock'-head** *n*. **shock-head'ed** *adj*.

shock³ /shok/ *n* a stook, or propped-up group of sheaves; three score, sixty. ◆ *vt* to set up in shocks. [ME *schokke*; the corresponding word in some Gmc languages has come to mean sixty]
■ **shock'er** *n*.

shockumentary /shok-ū-men'tə-ri/ *n* a documentary film dealing with shocking subjects in a graphic way. [From *shock* and *documentary*]

shod see **shoe**.

shoddy /shod'i/ *adj* inferior and pretentious; cheap and nasty; sham; made of shoddy; badly made or executed. ◆ *n* woollen fibre obtained by shredding refuse woollen rags; cloth made of it, alone or mixed; anything inferior seeking to pass for better than it is. [Origin unknown]
■ **shodd'ily** *adv*. **shodd'iness** *n*.

shoder /shō'dər/ *n* a set of skins in which gold leaf is beaten the second time (see **cutch²**). [From obs Fr *chaucher* to press; ult from L *calx* heel]

shoe /shoo/ *n* (pl **shoes** /shooz/; also (*archaic* and *dialect*) **shoon** /shoon/, also (*Scot*) **shün** or **shin**/) a stiff outer covering for the foot, not coming above the ankle (or in the USA not much above); a rim of iron nailed to a hoof; anything in form, position, or use like a shoe, as in a metal tip or ferrule, a piece attached where there is friction, a drag for a wheel, the part of a brake that comes in contact with the wheel, etc, the block by which an electric tractor collects current; the short bent part at the bottom of a downpipe that directs water away from the wall (*building*); a box-like device for dispensing playing-cards singly (*gambling*). ◆ *vt* (**shoe'ing**; **shod** /shod/ or **shoed** /shood/) to put shoes or a shoe on. [OE *scōh* (pl *scōs*); Gothic *shōhs*, Ger *Schuh*]
■ **shod** *adj*. **shoe'ing** *n*. **shoe'less** *adj*. **shoer** /shoo'ər/ *n* a person who shoes horses.

□ **shoe'bill** *n* a large African wading bird (*Balaeniceps rex*) with a heavy bill (also called **shoebill stork**, **whale-head**, **whale-headed stork**). **shoe'black** *n* someone who polishes shoes, a bootblack. **shoe brush** *n*. **shoe buckle** *n*. **shoe'horn** *n* a curved implement with a handle used for easing the heel into the back of a shoe; anything serving to facilitate something else (*old*). ◆ *vt* (*fig*) to fit, squeeze or compress into a tight or insufficient space. **shoe'lace** *n* a cord passed through eyelet-holes to fasten a shoe. **shoe latchet** *n* a thong for fastening a shoe, sandal, etc. **shoe leather** *n* leather for shoes; shoes generally. **shoe'maker** *n* a person who makes (now more often only sells or mends) shoes and boots. **shoe'making** *n*. **shoe nail** *n* a nail for fastening a horseshoe; a nail for a shoe sole. **shoe peg** *n* a peg for fastening parts of a shoe together. **shoe'shine** *n* (the act of) polishing shoes; the shiny appearance of polished shoes. **shoe'shiner** *n*. **shoe shop** *n*. **shoe'string** *n* a shoelace (*US*); a minimum of money or capital (*inf*). ◆ *adj* operated, produced, etc on a minimum of money or capital; petty, paltry (*US*). **shoestring fungus** *n* the honey fungus (qv). **shoe tie** *n* a (fancy) shoelace. **shoe'tree** *n* a support, *usu* of wood or metal, inserted in a shoe when it is not being worn, in order to preserve its shape.

■ **another pair of shoes** (*inf*) quite a different matter. **be in, fill** or **step into someone's** (or **a dead man's**) **shoes** to be in, or succeed to, someone's place. **die in one's shoes** to die by violence, *esp* by hanging. **on a shoestring** with an extremely small amount of capital.

shofar /shō'fär/ (*Judaism*) *n* (pl **shō'fars** or **shōfroth** /-frōt'/) a wind instrument made from a ram's horn, blown in Jewish religious ceremonies and in ancient times as a call to battle, etc (also **shophar**). [Heb *shōphār* ram's horn]

shog /shog/ (chiefly *dialect*) *vi* (**shogg'ing**; **shogged**) to shake; to sway, swing; to jog; to move on, go away. ◆ *vt* to shake; to push aside. ◆ *n* a jog, shock. [ME *shogge*, perh related to **shock¹** and OHGer *scoc* a swing]

shoggle /shog'l/ (*dialect*) *vt* to shake, rock. ◆ *vi* to wobble, shake. [Cf **shoogle**, **shog**]
■ **shogg'ly** *adj*.

shogi /shō'gē/ *n* the Japanese form of chess. [Jap *shōgi*]

shogun /shō'gŭn/ or *-goon/* (*Jap hist*) *n* any of the hereditary military governors who were the effective rulers of Japan from the 12c until the 1860s. [Jap, from *sho* to lead, and *gun* army]

■ **shō'gunal** *adj*. **shō'gunate** *n* the office or state of a shogun.

shoji /shō'jē/ *n* (pl **sho'ji** or **sho'jis**) a screen of paper covering a wooden framework, forming a wall or sliding partition in Japanese homes. [Jap, from *sho* to separate, and *ji* a piece]

shola¹ /shō'lə/ *n* a thicket or jungle in S India. [Tamil *çolai*]

shola² same as **sola²**.

sholom same as **shalom**.

Shona /shō'nə/ *n* (also **Mashona**) a group of African peoples living south of the Zambesi; any member of the group; any language spoken by the group; a literary language (**Union Shona**) designed for use by the whole group. ◆ *adj* of or relating to these people or their languages.

shone /shon/ *pat* and *pap* of **shine**.

shoneen /shō'nēn/ (*Irish derog*) *n* an Irishman who imitates the ways and manners of the English. [From Ir *Seoinín*, dimin of *Seon* John (a generic name for an Englishman)]

shonky /shong'ki/ (*Aust inf*) *adj* underhand, illicit; unreliable. [Perh from offensive *shonk* Jew, a mean, money-grubbing person]

shoo /shoo/ *interj* an exclamation used to scare away birds, animals, etc. ◆ *vi* to cry 'Shoo!'. ◆ *vt* to drive away by shouting 'Shoo!'; to cause or allow (a horse) to win a race (*US sl*); to fix (a race) so that a particular horse wins (*US sl*). [Instinctive; cf Ger *schu*, Gr *sou*]
□ **shoo'-in** *n* (*US sl*) a horse that is allowed to win; any certain winner of a race, competition, etc; a sure thing. **shoo'fly** *n* (*US*) a child's toy, a rocker consisting of a seat with end boards shaped and painted like animals. **shoofly pie** *n* (*US*) a sweet open pie filled with molasses and baked.

shoogie /shŭg'ē/ or /shoo'gē/ (*Scot dialect*) *vi* to swing, sway back and forth. ◆ *n* a swinging or swaying movement. [Cf **shoogle**, **shog**]

shoogle /shŭg'l/ (*Scot*) *vi* to shake, joggle; to sway, rock back and forth. ◆ *vt* to shake, joggle. ◆ *n* a swaying, rocking motion. [Cf **shog**, **shoggle**]
■ **shoog'ly** *adj*.

shoo-in see under **shoo**.

shook¹ /shŏok/ *pat* and obsolete *pap* of **shake**.
■ **shook on** (*Aust* and *NZ inf*) keen on.

shook² /shŏok/ *n* a bundle of sheaves, a shock, stook; a set of cask staves and heads, or of parts for making a box, etc. [Origin unknown]

shool¹ or **shoole**, also **shule** /shool/ (*dialect* and *old sl*) *vi* to saunter about, skulk; to go about begging; to sponge. [Perh Ir]

shool² /shool or shōl/, also (*Scot*) **shül** or **shil**/ *n* and *v* a dialect form of **shovel**.

shoon see **shoe**.

shoot¹ /shoot/ *vt* (pat and pap **shot**; see also **shotten**) to let fly with force; to discharge (a bullet, missile, etc); to hit, wound, or kill in this way; to precipitate, launch forth; to tip out, dump; to cast; to kick or hit at goal (*games*); to score, for a hole or the round (*golf*); to thrust forward; to pull (one's shirt cuffs) forward so that they project from the sleeves of one's jacket; to slide along; to slide (a bolt) across or back; to plane (a board) to give it a straight edge; to produce (new growth); to crystallize; to pass rapidly through, under, or over; to pass through (traffic lights at red) without stopping; to photograph, *esp* for motion pictures; to variegate (*usu in pap*); to inject (*esp* oneself) with (a drug) (*sl*); to play (a round of golf, game of pool, etc); to detonate. ◆ *vi* to dart out, back, forward, etc; (of a bowled ball) to keep abnormally low after pitching (*cricket*); to send darting pains; to sprout; (of vegetables) to bolt; to elongate rapidly; to jut out far or suddenly; to begin, *esp* to speak one's mind or to tell what one knows (*inf*; *usu in imperative*); to tower; to send forth a missile, etc; to discharge a shot or weapon; to use a bow or gun in practice, competition, hunting, etc; to crystallize. ◆ *n* a shooting; a shooting match, party, expedition; an area of land within which animals are hunted with firearms for sport; a shot (*archaic*); a shooting pain; a movement of the shuttle; a weft thread; a rapid; the shooting of a film; a photographic modelling session; new growth; a sprout; the stem and leaf parts of a plant; a dump; a chute (see **chute¹**). ◆ *interj* (*US inf*) expressing anger, disgust, disappointment, etc. [OE *scēotan*; Du *schieten*, Ger *schiessen*; in some senses merging with Fr *chute* fall]

■ **shoot'able** *adj* capable of being shot, or shot over. **shoot'er** *n* a cricket ball that shoots (see above); a gun, etc (*inf*); someone who shoots, a hired killer, etc (*inf*); a small drink of alcoholic spirit (*inf*). **shoot'ing** *n* the action of the verb in any sense; a twinge of quick pain; the killing of game with firearms over a certain area; the right to do so; the district so limited; the planing of edges that are to be joined. **shoot'ist** *n* (*sl*; now *esp US*) someone who shoots; a skilled marksman.
□ **shoot'-'em-up** *n* (*inf*; *orig US*) a film, television programme or computer game featuring or involving scenes of violent action, gunfights, etc. **shooting board** *n* a board for steadying a piece of wood for shooting. **shooting box** or **lodge** *n* a small house in the

country for use in the shooting season. **shooting brake** n (old) an estate car. **shooting gallery** n a long room used for practice or amusement with firearms; a place where addicts gather to inject drugs (sl). **shooting iron** n (sl) a firearm, esp a revolver. **shooting jacket** n a short coat for shooting in. **shooting range** n a place for shooting at targets. **shooting script** n (film) a final version of a script with instructions for the cameraman indicating the order in which scenes will be shot. **shooting star** n a meteor (inf); a N American plant of the primrose family. **shooting stick** n a printer's tool used for locking and unlocking formes by tapping the quoins; a walking-stick with a two-part handle that opens out to form a seat. **shooting war** n actual war as distinct from cold war. **shoot'-out** n a gunfight, esp to the death or other decisive conclusion (also fig).

■ **get shot of** (sl) to get rid of. **have shot one's bolt** see under **bolt¹**. **shoot a line** (inf) to brag, exaggerate (**line'-shooter** n). **shoot down** to kill, or to bring down (an aeroplane) by shooting; to rout, defeat. **shoot down in flames** (inf) to reprimand severely; to destroy, humiliate, esp by the strength of one's argument. **shoot from the hip** (inf) to speak bluntly or hastily, without preparation or without concern for the consequences. **shoot home** to hit the target (also fig). **shoot it out** to settle (a dispute, competition, etc) conclusively by shooting (also fig). **shoot off** to discharge a gun; to begin; to rush away. **shoot oneself in the foot** (inf) to harm one's own interests by ineptitude. **shoot one's mouth off** see under **mouth**. **shoot the breeze** (inf) to chat inconsequentially. **shoot the crow** (sl) to leave. **shoot the sun** (naut) to take the sun's altitude. **shoot the works** (sl) to risk one's all on one play (gambling); hence, to make one's maximum effort. **shoot through** (inf; esp Aust) to go, depart in haste. **shoot up** to kill or injure by shooting; to grow very quickly; to inject (a drug, esp heroin) (sl). **the whole (bang) shoot** or **shooting match** (inf) the whole lot.

shoot² same as **shoat**.

shoot³ same as **chute¹**.

shop /shop/ n a building or room in which goods are sold or services provided; a spell of shopping, esp for food and/or household items; a place where mechanics work, or where any kind of industry is pursued, a workshop; a place of employment or activity, esp a theatre; prison (old sl); shop talk. ◆ vi (**shopp'ing; shopped**) to visit shops, esp for the purpose of buying. ◆ vt to imprison, or cause to be imprisoned (sl); to betray or inform against (someone) to the police, etc (sl); to give employment to (obs). [OE sceoppa a treasury]

■ **shopahol'ic** n a compulsive shopper (see **-aholic**). **shop'ful** n. **shopp'er** n a person who shops; a shopping bag or basket. **shopp'ing** n the activity of visiting shops to buy or see goods; goods thus bought. ◆ adj for shopping. **shopp'y** adj commercial; having many shops; given to talking shop; concerning one's own pursuit.

□ **shop assistant** n a person who serves customers in a shop. **shop bell** n a bell, fitted to the door of a shop, that rings when the door is opened. **shop'board** n a counter; a bench on which tailors work. **shop'bot** n (comput) a website used to compare prices for shopping (see **bot²**). **shop boy** or **shop girl** n esp formerly, a boy or girl employed in a shop. **shop'breaker** n a person who breaks into a shop. **shop'breaking** n. **shop'fitter** n a person who installs counters, shelves, etc in a shop. **shop'fitting** n. **shop floor** n that part of a factory, etc, housing the production machinery and in which that part of the workforce directly involved with production is employed; the people who work on the shop floor, esp those workers organized in a union. **shop'-floor** adj. **shop'front** n the part of a shop, with display windows, etc, that faces onto the street. **shop-in-shop'** adj (of a supplier of particular goods or services) having a retail outlet within a larger shop or store. **shop'keeper** n a person who keeps a shop of his or her own. **shop'keeping** n. **shop'lift** vt and vi. **shop'lifter** n. **shop'lifting** n stealing from a shop. **shop'man** or **shop'woman** n a person who serves in a shop; a shopkeeper (rare); a person who is employed in a workshop (US). **shopping bag** or **basket** n a receptacle for goods bought. **shopping-bag lady** same as **bag lady** (see under **bag**). **shopping centre** n a place where there is a concentration of shops of different kinds. **shopping list** n a list of items to be bought; a list of items to be obtained, done, acted upon, considered, etc (fig). **shopping mall** see under **mall**. **shopping precinct** see under **precinct**. **shop sign** n a sign over a shop indicating the occupier's name and trade. **shop'soiled** adj somewhat faded or worn by display in a shop (also fig). **shop steward** n a representative of the employees of a factory or workshop, elected from their own number. **shop talk** n talk about one's own business, esp when carried on outside business hours. **shop walker** n a shop employee who walks about in a shop to see that customers are attended to. **shop window** n a window of a shop in which wares are displayed; any means of displaying what is on offer to advantage. **shopwoman** see **shopman** above. **shop'worn** adj shopsoiled (also fig).

■ **all over the shop** (inf) dispersed all around. **on the shop floor** among the workers in a factory or workshop. **set up shop** to open a

trading establishment; to begin operations generally. **shop around** to compare prices and quality of goods at various shops before making a purchase (also fig). **shut up shop** to close a shop, etc, at the end of a working day, week, etc; to close a business permanently. **talk shop** to talk about one's own work or business. **the Shop** the former Royal Military Academy at Woolwich. **the wrong shop** (inf) the wrong place to look for eg sympathy or help.

shope /shōp/ obsolete pat (Spenser) of **shape**.

shophar see **shofar**.

shoran /shö'ran/ n a system of navigation in an aircraft or other vehicle using the measurement of the time taken for dispatched radar signals to return from two known fixed points. [Short range navigation]

shore¹ /shōr or shör/ n the land bordering on the sea or a large expanse of water; the foreshore; land as opposed to the sea; (in pl) lands, countries. ◆ vt to set on shore. [ME schore; cf Du schoor, schor]

■ **shore'less** adj having no shore, unlimited, boundless. **shore'ward** adj and adv. **shore'wards** adv.

□ **shore'bird** n any of various birds that live on the shore or close to water, a wader. **shore boat** n a boat plying near or to the shore. **shore crab** n a crab (Carcinus maenas) very common between tidemarks. **shore due** n (Scot) a harbour due. **shore effect** n (telecom) horizontal refraction of a radio wave as it crosses a shoreline, causing direction-finding errors (also **coastline effect**). **shore'-going** adj going, or for going, ashore; land-dwelling. **shore leave** n leave of absence granted to members of a ship's crew to go ashore. **shore'line** n the line of meeting of land and water; a rope connecting a net with the land. **shore'man** n a dweller on the shore; a landsman; (US also **shores'man**) a person who has an onshore job connected with fishery. **shore'side** n the area near the shore (also adj). **shore'weed** n a plant (Litorella lacustris) of the plantain family found on lake margins.

■ **on shore** on the land; ashore.

shore² /shōr or shör/ n a temporary prop used to support a wall, excavation, etc, to prevent slipping, sagging, etc. ◆ vt to prop (often with up; also fig). [MDu schōre prop; related to ON skortha]

■ **shor'er** n. **shor'ing** n supporting by shores; a set of props.

shore³ /shōr or shör/ (Aust and NZ or archaic) pat of **shear**.

shore⁴ /shōr or shör/ (Scot) vt to warn, threaten; to offer. ◆ n threatening, menace. [Origin obscure]

shore⁵ /shōr or shör/ (archaic and dialect) n a sewer, drain, usu (as Shakesp) **common-shore**. [Perh **sewer**; perh **shore¹**]

shorn /shörn/ pap of **shear**.

short /shört/ adj of little length, tallness, extent, or duration; in the early future (as short day, date); concise; curt or abrupt; snappish; (of pastry, etc) crisp yet readily crumbling; on the near side; (of memory) not retentive; failing to go far enough or reach the standard or level required; deficient; lacking (in); scanty, in inadequate supply; in default; unable to meet engagements; relating to the sale of what one cannot supply; not being in possession of shares, etc at the time of sale in anticipation of a fall in prices before their delivery date (finance); (of a vowel sound) being the briefer of two possible lengths of vowel (phonetics); in accentual verse, loosely, unaccented (prosody); (of an alcoholic drink) undiluted with water, neat (inf); having short wool; (of glass) fast-setting; (of metal) brittle (mining); (of certain fielding positions) relatively near the batsman (cricket); (of a bowled ball) bouncing at some distance from the batsman (cricket). ◆ adv briefly; abruptly; curtly; without leaving a stump; on this or the near side; at a disadvantage (eg taken short); see **sell short** under **sell¹**. ◆ n that which is short; shortness, abbreviation, summary; a short circuit; (in pl) short trousers (ie thigh- or knee-length, as opposed to ankle-length); (in pl) undershorts (US); (in pl) the bran and coarse part of meal, in mixture; (in pl) short-dated securities; someone who sells short (stock exchange); a short film subordinate to a main film in a programme; a drink of spirits (inf); (in pl) a deficiency (N Am). ◆ vt to short-change. ◆ vt and vi to shorten (obs); to short-circuit; to fall short of, or perhaps cause to fail (archaic). [ME, from OE sc(e)ort; related to OHGer scurz, ON skera to cut]

■ **short'age** n a lack, deficiency. **short'en** vt to make shorter; to make to seem short or to fall short; to draw in or back; to check; to make friable (by adding butter, lard, etc); to put (a baby) in short clothes (old). ◆ vi to become shorter. **short'ener** n. **short'ening** n making or becoming shorter; fat for making pastry short. **short'ie** or **short'y** n (inf) a very short person, garment, etc (also adj). **short'ish** adj. **short'ly** adv soon; briefly; curtly; for a short time (rare); a little; with shortness in that which is indicated. **short'ness** n.

□ **short'-acting** adj (of a drug) having effects that wear off quickly. **short'arm** adj (boxing, etc) (of a blow) using a bent (rather than extended) arm. **short'arse** n (derog sl) a small person. **short'bread** n a brittle crumbling biscuit of flour, butter and sugar. **short'cake** n shortbread or other friable cake; a light cake, prepared in layers with fruit between, served with cream (orig N Am). **short-change'** vt to give less than the correct change to; to deal dishonestly with (a person). ◆ adj relating to cheating. **short-chan'ger** n. **short circuit** n a new and unwanted path of comparatively low resistance accidentally created between two points of a circuit, often causing damage to components (elec); an artificial connection between two normally separate tubular organs or parts (surg). **short-cir'cuit** vt to establish a short circuit in; to interconnect where there was obstruction between (surg); to provide with a short cut (fig). ◆ vi to cut off current by a short circuit; to save a roundabout passage. **short clothes** or **short coats** n pl formerly, the shortened skirts of a child when the first long clothes are left off. **short'-coat** vt (old) to put into short coats. **short'coming** n the circumstance of coming or falling short; a neglect of, or failure in, duty; a defect, failing. **short commons** n pl minimum rations. **short'-cord** adj (elec eng) (of an armature winding) employing coils whose span is less than the pole pitch. **short corner** n (hockey) same as **penalty corner** (see under **penalty**). **short covering** n (stock exchange) the buying of securities, etc, to cover a short sale; the securities, etc, bought for this purpose. **short'crust** adj (of pastry) short. **short cut** n a shorter route than the usual (also fig). **short'-cut** vi to use a shorter route (also fig). ◆ adj and n (denoting) tobacco cut in short shreds. **short'-dated** adj (of a bill) having little time to run from its date; (of securities) redeemable in under five years. **short-day plant** n (bot) one that will flower only if the daily period of light is shorter than some critical length (cf **day-neutral plant**, **long-day plant**). **short division** n division without writing down the working out. **short'fall** n the fact or amount of falling short. **short fuse** n (inf) a quick temper. **short game** n (golf) play on and around the green(s). **short'gown** n (old Scot) a woman's short jacket. **short'hand** n a system of writing in which whole words and phrases are represented by (combinations of) simple strokes, used for recording speech at speaking pace; writing of such a kind. ◆ adj relating to or written in shorthand. **short-hand'ed** adj short of an adequate number of workers; with a small or reduced number on the team, in the crew, etc. **short'-haul** adj involving transportation, etc, over (relatively) short distances. **short'-head** vt (inf) to beat by a short head (see also below). **short'hold** adj (law) in England and Wales, of or being a tenancy of only a few (orig between one and five) years. **short'horn** n any of the various types of beef and dairy cattle developed from a short-horned breed originating in NE England, usu having a red and white, roan or white coat (also called **Durham**). **short hundredweight** see **hundredweight** under **hundred**. **short iron** n (golf) an iron club used to play shots from close to the green. **short leg** n (cricket) a fielder, or a fielding position, very near (and in line with) the batsman on the legside. **short'-life** adj having a short duration, existence, etc. **short'list** n (see also **leet³**) a list of the most suitable candidates for an office, post, etc, from which the successful candidate will be selected. ◆ vt to include (someone) in a shortlist. **short'-lived** (or /-lĭvd/) adj living or lasting only for a short time. **short measure** n less than the amount promised or paid for. **short metre** n (poetry) a form of four-line stanza of which the first, second and last lines have six syllables and the third line eight. **short odds** n pl (in betting) a nearly even chance, favourable odds in terms of risk, unfavourable in terms of potential gain. **short-oil** see **oil length** under **oil**. **short order** n (N Am) (an order for) food that can be prepared quickly. **short'-order** adj. **short'-priced** adj having short odds. **short'-range** adj of or relating to a short distance or period of time. **short rib** n a floating rib. **short sale** n a sale of something which the seller does not yet own. **short score** n a musical score with some of the parts omitted. **short sea** n (naut) one in which the distance between the wave crests is comparatively short. **short selling** see **sell short** under **sell¹**. **short sharp shock** n a brief severe regime imposed by a prison or detention centre, esp on young offenders. **short sheep** n short-woolled sheep. **short shrift** see under **shrift**. **short-sight'ed** adj able to see clearly only those objects that are relatively near; myopic; lacking foresight. **short-sight'edly** adv. **short-sight'edness** n. **short-spo'ken** adj curt in speech. **short-staffed'** adj having a reduced or inadequate number of staff. **short-stā'ple** adj (of wool, cotton, etc fibre) short. **short'stop** n (baseball) the fielding position (or the defending player positioned) between the second and third base. **short story** n a work of prose narrative shorter than a novel and usu concentrating on a single episode or experience and its effect. **short subject** n (chiefly US) a short film shown before the main film in a cinema. **short'sword** n a sword with a short blade. **short-tem'pered** adj easily moved to anger, quick-tempered. **short tennis** n a form of tennis for children, using a smaller court and modified equipment and rules. **short'-term** adj extending over a short time; concerned with the immediate present and future as distinct from time further ahead. **short-term'ism** n (a tendency towards) the adopting of only short-term views, solutions to problems, etc. **short-term'ist** n and adj. **short-term memory** n (psychol) a section of the memory with limited capacity, capable of storing information for a short time only. **short time** n (the condition of) working fewer than the normal number of hours per week. **short'-time** adj. **short ton** see **ton¹**. **short'-track** (skating or) **speedskating** n speedskating in

which contestants race in packs around a 111.12-metre track, over any of several distances between 500m and 5000m. **short wave** n a radio wave with a frequency of between 10m and 100m. **short'-wave** adj. **short-wind'ed** adj quickly becoming breathless.

■ **by a short head** by a distance less than the length of a horse's head; narrowly, barely (fig). **caught short** (inf) having a sudden, uncontrollable need to urinate or defecate. **cut short** see under **cut**. **draw the short straw** to be given an unpleasant task, duty, etc, or the most unpleasant of several. **fall short** see under **fall¹**. **for short** as an abbreviation. **go short** (inf) to have an insufficient amount (esp of money or food). **have someone by the short and curlies** (vulgar sl) to have someone over a barrel, at one's mercy, in a position difficult to wriggle out of. **in short** in a few words, briefly. **in short supply** not available in desired quantity, scarce. **in the short run** over a brief period of time. **make short work of** to settle or dispose of promptly. **run short** see under **run**. **short and sweet** surprisingly or gratifyingly brief, used eg of a speech expected to be of greater length (and tedium); (ironically) curt or abrupt. **short for** a shortened form of. **short of** less than; without going so far as; having insufficient supplies of. **short on** (inf) deficient in. **stop short** to come to a sudden standstill. **taken short** same as **caught short** above. **take** (or **take up**) **short** to take by surprise or at a disadvantage; to interrupt curtly. **the short and the long (of it)** (Shakesp) same as **the long and the short** (see under **long¹**).

Shoshone or **Shoshoni** /shō-shō'nē/ n (a member of) a Native American people of the West Central area of the USA; their Aztec-Tanoan language.
■ **Shosho'nean** n and adj.

shot¹ /shot/ n an act of shooting; a blast; an explosive charge; a single photographic exposure, or a length of cinematic film taken without a break with a single camera; a camera's range or extent of view, as in out of shot; a stroke, throw or hit in sports and games; an attempt (inf); a spell (inf); a turn (inf); a guess (inf); the casting of a net; a set of nets or length of net cast; an aggressive remark; an injection (inf); a dram (inf); a person that shoots, a marksman; a projectile, esp one that is solid and spherical, without bursting charge; a cannonball; a weight for putting (athletics); a bullet; a small pellet of which several are shot together; such pellets collectively; the launch of a rocket to a specified destination; flight of a missile, or its distance; range, reach; a plot of land; (also scot) a payment, esp of a bill or one's share of a bill; a contribution. ◆ vt (shott'ing; shott'ed) to load with shot. [OE sc(e)ot, gesc(e)ot; cf **shoot**]
■ **shott'ed** adj.
□ **shot'-blast** vt. **shot'-blasting** n the cleaning of metal, etc, by means of a stream of shot. **shot'firer** n (mining) in blasting, the worker who fires the charge. **shot'-free** adj scot-free; safe from shot. **shot'gun** n see separate entry. **shot'hole** n a hole made by a shot, or in timber by a boring insect, or in a leaf by a fungus; a hole in a wall for shooting from; a hole bored in rock for a blasting charge. **shot'maker** n (sport, esp tennis and golf) a person who produces winning, attacking or skilful shots or strokes. **shot'making** n. **shot noise** n (electronics) inherent noise resulting from variations in the current output of an electronic device caused by the random pulses of electron emission from the electrode (also called **flicker noise**, **Schottky noise**). **shot'proof** adj able to withstand shot. **shot put** n the athletics event of putting the shot. **shot'-putter** n. **shot tower** n formerly, a tower where small shot is made by dropping molten lead into water from a given height. **shot window** n (obs) appar a hinged or casement window.
■ **a shot across the bows** one thus directed so as to warn a ship off rather than damage it (often fig). **a shot in the arm** an injection in the arm (med); a revivifying injection, eg of money, new effort, renewed confidence, fresh talent (fig). **a shot in the dark** a random guess or wild speculation. **big shot** (inf) a person of importance. **call the shots** see under **call¹**. **have a shot** (with at) (inf) to have a try or go (at something); to jeer or carp (at someone) (Aust). **hotshot** see under **hot¹**. **like a shot** instantly, quickly; eagerly, willingly. **shot to nothing** (snooker) an attempt to pot a ball played in such way that, if the shot is missed, one's opponent will not be left with an easy opportunity. **stand shot** (obs and dialect) to pay the bill. **still have shot in the** (or **one's**) **locker** to be still potent; to have something yet in reserve.

shot² /shot/ pat and pap of **shoot**. adj hit or killed by shooting; exhausted (inf); ruined (inf); elongated by rapid growth; advanced (in years; archaic); with warp and weft of different colours, as in shot silk; showing a play of colours; rid (with of; inf). ◆ n (agric) a reject animal from a herd or flock.

shote, **shot** or **shotte** n variant spellings of **shoat**.

shotgun /shot'gun/ n a smooth-bore gun for firing shot or slugs at relatively short range, used esp for shooting birds and other small game, clay pigeons, etc; an offensive formation in which the quarterback stands well behind the line of scrimmage (American football). ◆ adj relating to a shotgun; involving coercion or duress (eg *shotgun merger, shotgun wedding*); covering a wide field in random, haphazard fashion with resultant hit-and-miss effect. ■ **ride shotgun** to protect a vehicle and its occupants from attack by riding on it (or following close behind it) carrying a firearm or firearms (also *fig*); to be positioned alongside the driver of a vehicle.

Shotokan /shō-tō-kan'/ *n* the most widely practised style of karate, characterized by aggressive, staccato movements. [*Shoto*, pen name of Gichin Funakoshi (1870–1957), Japanese poet and calligrapher]

shott /shot/ (*geog*) *n* in N Africa and the Middle East, a shallow watercourse or lake that tends to dry up in certain seasons.

shotten /shot'n/ old or dialect *pap* of **shoot**. *adj* (of a herring, etc) having ejected the spawn and of little food value; effete, exhausted, worthless; bursting or shooting out, as something violently dispersed.

shottle see **shuttle²**.

shough or (*Shakesp*) **showghe** /shog, shok or shuf/ *n* a shaggy kind of lapdog. [Perh **shock²**]

should /shood/ *pat* of **shall**. [OE *sceolde*]

shoulder /shōl'dər/ *n* the part of a human or other vertebrate animal's body around the junction with the arm or forelimb; the upper joint of an animal's foreleg as a cut of meat; part of a garment covering the shoulder; a coathanger (*old*); a bulge, protrusion, offshoot, etc resembling the human shoulder, eg near the summit of a mountain; a curve like that between the shoulder and the neck or side, as on a stringed instrument; either edge of a road, *usu* applied to the strip on which vehicles do not normally travel; the flat surface on a piece of type from the foot of the bevel to the body (*printing*); the part of a ring where the setting joins the band (*jewellery*); the part of a characteristic curve where levelling off is perceptible (*electronics*). *vt* to thrust with the shoulder; to take upon the shoulder or in a position of rest against the shoulder; to undertake; to take responsibility for; to set shoulder to shoulder; to fashion with a shoulder or abutment; to embezzle from or defraud (one's employer) (also *vi; old sl*). *vi* to jostle. [OE *sculdor*; Ger *Schulter*, Du *schouder*]
■ **shoul'dered** *adj* having a shoulder or shoulders. **shoul'dering** *n* and *adj*.
▫ **shoulder bag** *n* a bag suspended from a strap worn over the shoulder. **shoulder belt** *n* a belt that passes across the shoulder. **shoulder blade** *n* the broad, flat, blade-like bone forming the back of the shoulder, the scapula. **shoulder bone** *n* the shoulder blade. **should'er-clapper** *n* (*Shakesp*) a bailiff. **shouldered arch** *n* (*archit*) a lintel supported over an opening, eg for a door, by corbels. **shoulder girdle** *n* the pectoral girdle. **shoulder-height** *adv* as high as the shoulder. **shoulder-high'** *adj* and *adv* as high as the shoulder. **shoulder joint** *n*. **shoulder knot** *n* a knot worn as an ornament on the shoulder; a bailiff (*old sl*). **shoulder mark** *n* (*US*) a badge of naval rank worn on the shoulder. **shoulder note** *n* (*printing*) a note at the upper outside margin of a page level with the first line of type. **shoulder-of-mutton sail** *n* a triangular sail. **shoulder pad** *n* a pad inserted into the shoulder of a garment to raise and square it. **shoulder plane** *n* a rebate plane with reversed cutting bevel, used in woodworking for fine trimming. **shoul'der-shotten** *adj* (*Shakesp*) with a dislocated or sprained shoulder. **shoulder slip** *n* a sprain of the shoulder. **shoul'der-slipped** *adj*. **shoulder strap** *n* a strap worn on or over the shoulder, *esp* one that holds up a garment, etc; a narrow strap of cloth edged with gold lace worn on the shoulder with a uniform to indicate rank (*US*). **shoulder surfing** *n* (*inf*) the practice of looking over the shoulder of a person who is entering a personal security code. ■ **a shoulder to cry on** a person to tell one's troubles to. **cold shoulder** see under **cold**. **put one's shoulder to the wheel** to set to work in earnest. **rub shoulders** see under **rub¹**. **shoulder arms** (*milit*) (of soldiers on parade, etc) to bring a firearm, etc to an upright position close to the right side of the body. **shoulder to shoulder** side by side; close together, united, in unity. (**straight**) **from the shoulder** frank(ly) and forceful(ly).

shouldest, **shouldst** see **shall**.

shouldn't /shood'ənt/ (*inf*) a contraction of **should not**.

shout /showt/ *n* a loud cry; a call; a call for a round of drinks (*inf*); a turn to buy a round of drinks (*inf*); a term used by the emergency services (firefighters, police and ambulance) for a call-out (*inf*). *vi* to utter a shout; to speak in a raised, *esp* angry, voice (with *at*); to stand drinks all round (*inf*); to write in upper-case letters for emphasis, *esp* in email. *vt* to utter with or as a shout; to buy (something, *esp* a drink) for someone (*Aust* and *NZ inf*). [Ety doubtful, poss as **scout²**, connected with ON *skuta* a taunt]
■ **shout'er** *n*. **shout'ing** *n* and *adj*. **shout'ingly** *adv*. **shout'y** *adj* (*inf*) communicating in a loud and aggressive manner.
▫ **shouting match** *n* (*inf*) a quarrel or argument in which both sides loudly insult each other. **shout'line** *n* (*inf*) a short line of text, *usu* printed in bold type, drawing attention to a major selling point in an advertisement or promotional material. **shout'-out** *n* (*inf*) a greeting or mention of one's name, as by a DJ.

■ **all over bar the shouting** (of a happening, contest, etc) as good as over, virtually finished or decided. **go on the shout** (*orig Aust*; *sl*) to go on a drinking bout, drink to excess. **in with a shout** (*inf*) having a reasonable chance. **shout down** to make (another speaker) inaudible by shouting or talking loudly. **within shouting distance** nearby; within reach.

shouther /shoo'dhər/ Scots form of **shoulder**.

shove /shuv/ *vt* and *vi* to thrust; to push; to jostle; to place roughly or hastily. *n* a push, thrust. [OE *scūfan*; Du *schuiven*, Ger *schieben*]
■ **shov'er** *n* someone or something that shoves; a punning form of **chauffeur**.
▫ **shove'-groat** *n* (*obs*) shovelboard (**shove-groat shilling** a smooth-worn shilling suitable for playing shovelboard). **shove-half'penny** *n* a gambling game similar to shovelboard.
■ **shove it!** (*sl*) an expression of contemptuous refusal or dismissal. **shove off** to push (a boat) from the shore; to go away (*inf*).

shovel /shuv'l/ *n* a broad spadelike tool for scooping, the blade *usu* curved up at the sides; (a part of) a machine having a similar shape or function; a scoop; a shovelful; a shovel hat. *vt* (**shov'elling**; **shov'elled**) to move with, or as if with, a shovel; to gather in large quantities. *vi* to use a shovel. [OE *scofl*, from *scūfan* to shove]
■ **shov'elful** *n* (*pl* **shov'elfuls**) as much as a shovel will hold. **shov'eller** or (*US*) **shov'eler** *n* someone who shovels; a dabbling duck (*Spatula clypeata*) of marshes and muddy shallows, with a long, rounded, spadelike bill (*usu* **shov'eler**).
▫ **shovel hat** *n* a hat with a broad brim, turned up at the sides, and projecting in front, as formerly worn by Anglican clergy. **shov'elhead** *n* a shark (*Sphyrna tiburo*) of the hammerhead family, having a flattish shovel-like head; a shovelnose. **shov'elnose** *n* a freshwater sturgeon (*Scaphorhynchus platorhynchus*) of N American rivers, having a broad shovel-like snout. **shov'elware** *n* (*comput sl*) data, *esp* originating from traditional media, published in electronic form without appropriate adaptation to the new format.

shovelboard /shuv'l-bōrd/ or **shuffleboard** /shuf'l-bōrd/ *n* an old game in which a coin or other disc was driven along a table by the hand; a modern development played in America; a deck game played with wooden discs and cues; a table for the game; a shove-groat shilling (*Shakesp*). [Appar **shove** and **board**, confused with **shovel** and **shuffle**]

show or (now rarely) **shew** /shō/ *vt* (pat **showed** or (rarely) **shewed** /shōd/; *pap* **shown** or (rarely) **shewn** /shōn/, or **showed** or (rarely) **shewed**) to present to view; to exhibit, display or set forth; to cause or allow to be seen or known; to instruct by demonstrating; to prove; to manifest; to indicate; to usher or conduct (with *in, out, over, round, up*, etc). *vi* to appear; to come into sight; to be visible; to arrive, turn up (*inf*). *n* an act of showing; display; exhibition; a sight or spectacle; an entertainment; parade; a demonstration; appearance; plausibility; pretence; a sign, indication; an indication of the presence of oil or gas in an exploratory well; performance; any thing, affair or enterprise (*inf*); in childbirth, a small discharge of blood and mucus at the start of labour; a chance, opportunity (*N Am, Aust* and *NZ*). *adj* of the nature of, suitable for, or connected with, a show; for show. [OE *scēawian* to look; from Du *schouwen*, Ger *schauen* to behold]
■ **shower** /shō'ər/ *n*. **show'ily** *adv*. **show'iness** *n*. **show'ing** *n* the act of displaying, pointing out, etc; appearance; performance; a film screening; a setting forth, representation. **show'y** *adj* cutting a dash; making a show; ostentatious; gaudy; flashy.
▫ **show-and-tell'** *n* an activity of young schoolchildren in which an object is brought to the class by each child to be displayed and described, demonstrated and talked about. **show bill** *n* a bill or poster announcing a play or show. **show'boat** *n* a riverboat, *usu* a paddle steamer, serving as a travelling theatre. *vi* to behave in an ostentatious manner; to show off. **show'boater** *n*. **show'box** *n* a showman's box out of which he takes his materials. **show'bread** see **shewbread**. **show business** *n* the entertainment business, *incl* theatre, film and television (also (*inf*) **show'biz** or **show biz**). **show'biz** or **show'bizzy** *adj* (*inf*) of, relating to or typical of the entertainment business. **show card** *n* a shopkeeper's advertising card; a card of patterns; a show bill. **show'case** *n* a glass display case for a museum, shop, etc; any setting in which something or someone can be displayed to advantage (also *adj*). *vt* to display, exhibit. **show'down** *n* in poker, the exposure of players' cards face up on the table at the end of a game; the name of a card game similar to poker; an open disclosure of plans, means, etc; a confrontation or clash by which a contested issue, argument, etc may be finally settled. **show'girl** *n* a girl who takes part in variety entertainments *usu* as a dancer or singer. **show'ground** *n* a plot of land on which an outdoor show is held. **show home** or **house** *n* a decorated and furnished house shown to prospective buyers as an example of the type of house available on a new or incomplete housing estate. **show'jump** *vi*. **show'jumper** *n* a horse or rider in a showjumping competition.

show'jumping *n* a competition in which a succession of riders on horseback have to jump a series of obstacles of different kinds (also *adj*). **show'man** *n* a person who exhibits, or owns, a show; a person who is skilled at public display and self-advertisement. **show'manly** *adj*. **show'manship** *n* skilful display, or a talent for it. **show'-off** *n* a person who behaves in an ostentatious manner in an effort to win admiration or public attention. **show of hands** *n* a vote indicated by raising hands. **show'piece** *n* something considered an especially fine specimen of its type, etc; an exhibit, something on display, etc. **show'place** *n* a place visited or shown as a sight; a place where shows are exhibited. **show pony** *n* a pony trained to take part in competitions; an ostentatious but ineffective performer (*sl*). **show'room** *n* a room where goods or samples are displayed. **show-stopper**, **show-stopping** see **stop the show** below. **show'time** *n* the time when a performance is due to begin; the time for decisive action (*fig*). **show trial** *n* a trial at which the opportunity to expose the accused to public opprobrium is given priority over the impartial prosecution of justice. **show'yard** *n* a yard for cattle shows.

■ **for show** for the sake of outward appearances; to attract notice. **give the show away** to let out a secret. **good** (or **bad**) **show** well (or not well) done; fortunate (or unfortunate) occurrence or circumstances. **run the show** (*inf*) to take or be in charge; to take over, dominate. **show a leg** (*inf*) to get out of bed. **show fight** to show a readiness to resist. **show forth** to manifest, proclaim. **show off** to display or behave ostentatiously; to display to good effect. **show up** to expose; to appear to advantage or disadvantage; to show (*esp* faults) clearly by contrast; to embarrass, put to shame (*inf*); to be present; to appear, arrive (*inf*); to lodge, hand in, as a school exercise. **steal the show** to win the most applause; to attract the most publicity or admiration. **stop the show** to be applauded with so much enthusiasm as to interrupt the show, play, etc (hence **show'-stopper** *n* the act, line, etc, so applauded; **show'-stopping** *adj* generating so much applause as to interrupt the show, etc); to have a sensational effect.

showbiz see under **show**.

shower /show'ər or showr/ *n* a short fall of rain, etc; a fall of drops of liquid; a fall, flight, or accession of many things together, such as meteors, sparks, arrows, blows, volcanic dust or (*esp N Am*) wedding gifts, gifts for an expected baby, etc; a party at which gifts are presented (*N Am*); a device with a nozzle for spraying water to wash the body; a wash thus taken; a booth or compartment containing such a device; an attack, a pang (*obs*); a large number of fast particles arising from a high-energy particle; a disparaging term applied to any particular group of people one disapproves of (*sl*). ◆ *vt* and *vi* to drop in a shower or showers; to sprinkle; to water. ◆ *vi* to wash under a shower. [OE *scūr*; ON *skūr*, Ger *Schauer*]
■ **show'erful** *adj*. **show'eriness** *n*. **show'ering** *n* and *adj*. **show'erless** *adj*. **show'ery** *adj* marked by showers; raining by fits and starts.
❑ **shower bath** *n* (*old*) a bathroom shower, or a wash taken under one. **shower curtain** *n* a plastic curtain drawn around a person taking a shower to prevent water from escaping. **show'erproof** *adj* impervious to light rain. ◆ *vt* to render showerproof. **shower tray** *n* a moulded plastic or tiled tray with a drain hole used for standing in while taking a shower.

showghe see **shough**.

shoyu /shō'ū/ *n* a rich soy sauce made from soya beans naturally fermented with wheat or barley, used as flavouring in oriental, *esp* Japanese, cookery. [Jap *shōyu*]

shpt. *abbrev* : shipment.

shr. (*stock exchange*) *abbrev* : share(s).

shraddha see **sraddha**.

shrank /shrangk/ *pat* of **shrink**.

shrapnel /shrap'nl/ *n* a shell filled with musketballs with an explosive charge, invented by General Henry *Shrapnel* (1761–1842), or any later improved version of this; such shells collectively; pieces scattered by the bursting of a shrapnel or other shell; loose coins (*inf*).

SHRC *abbrev* : Scottish Human Rights Centre.

shred /shred/ *n* a scrap, fragment; a paring, *esp* a curled paring; a ragged strip. ◆ *vt* (**shredd'ing**; **shredd'ed** or **shred**) to cut or cut off; to cut, tear or scrape into shreds; to prune (*obs*). ◆ *vi* to be reduced to shreds. [OE *scrēade*, ult from Gmc base *skraud-*, *skreud-*, *skrud-* cut; cf **screed**, **scroll**, **shroud**[1]; Ger *Schrot*]
■ **shredd'ed** *adj*. **shredd'er** *n* a device or machine for shredding eg vegetables, documents. **shredd'ing** *n* the action of the verb to shred; snowboarding, *esp* downhill at high speed while moving one's weight from one edge of the board to the other (*inf*). **shredd'y** *adj*. **shred'less** *adj*.
❑ **shred'-pie** *n* (*archaic*) mince pie.

shreek and **shreik** obsolete spellings of **shriek**.

shrew /shroo/ *n* a small mouselike insectivorous mammal of the family Soricidae, with a long snout, formerly thought to be venomous to cattle; an evil being (*obs*); a brawling, troublesome person, in later use only a woman, a scold. ◆ *vt* (*Shakesp*) to curse, beshrew. [OE *scrēawa* a shrewmouse]
■ **shrew'ish** *adj* of the nature of a shrew or scold; ill-natured. **shrew'ishly** *adv*. **shrew'ishness** *n*.
❑ **shrew mole** *n* any of various moles of Asia and N America having a long snout and tail. **shrew'mouse** *n* (*pl* **shrew'mice**) a shrew.

shrewd /shrood/ *adj* showing keen practical judgement, astute; wily, crafty; evil, hurtful, spiteful, ill-natured, ill-conditioned, mischievous (*obs* or *dialect*); severe, hard (*obs*); formidable (*obs*); uncomfortably near the mark; biting, keen, piercing (*archaic*); shrewish, vixenish (*obs*). ◆ *adv* (*Shakesp*) keenly. [**shrew**]
■ **shrewd'ie** *n* (*inf*) a shrewd person. **shrewd'ly** *adv*. **shrewd'ness** *n*.

Shri see **Sri**.

shriche-owl see under **shriek**.

shriech see **shriek** and **shritch**.

shriek /shrēk/ *n* a shrill cry; a wild piercing scream; an exclamation mark (*sl*). ◆ *vi* to utter a shriek. ◆ *vt* to utter shriekingly. —Also **shreek** (*Shakesp*, *Spenser*), **shreik** (*Milton*), **shriech** (*Spenser*). [Cf **screak**, **screech**]
■ **shriek'er** *n*. **shriek'ing** *n* and *adj*. **shriek'ingly** *adv*.
❑ **shriek'-owl**, also (*Spenser*) **shriech-**, **shriche-**, etc, (*Shakesp*) **screech-** *n* a screech owl.

shrieval /shrē'vl/ *adj* relating to a sheriff. [**shrieve**, obs form of **sheriff**]
■ **shriev'alty** *n* the office, term of office, or area of jurisdiction, of a sheriff.

shrieve /shrēv/ same as **shrive**.

shrift /shrift/ *n* (*archaic*) *orig* a prescribed penance; absolution; confession; a confessional (*Shakesp*). [OE *scrift*, from *scrīfan* to shrive]
❑ **short shrift** *n* a short time for confession before execution; summary treatment of a person or a matter.

shright /shrīt/ (*Spenser*) *n* a shriek (see also **shritch**). [Perh a misreading of Chaucer, *Troilus* IV.1147]

shrike[1] /shrīk/ *n* a butcherbird, any passerine bird of the family Laniidae, some species of which prey on smaller birds and small mammals, impaling them on thorns or barbed wire for later consumption. [Perh from OE *scrīc* thrush, MLGer *schrīk* corncrake; cf **shriek**]

shrike[2] /shrīk/ *vi* to shriek (*archaic*); (of birds) to sing (*obs* or *dialect*). ◆ *n* (*archaic*) a shriek. [Cf **scrike**, **shriek**]

shrill /shril/ *adj* high-pitched and piercing; keen; excessively strident. ◆ *adv* shrilly; often in combination, as in Shakespeare's *shrill-shriking*. ◆ *n* a piercing sound. ◆ *vt* and *vi* to sound or cry shrilly. [Cf LGer *schrell*, whence prob Ger *schrill*]
■ **shrill'ing** *n* and *adj*. **shrill'ness** *n*. **shrill'y** *adj*. **shril'ly** *adv*.
❑ **shrill-gorged'** *adj* (*Shakesp*) shrill-voiced. **shrill-tongued'** *adj*. **shrill-voiced'** *adj*.

shrimp /shrimp/ *n* a small edible crustacean, *esp* a decapod of *Crangon* or related genera; the colour of a shrimp, a bright pink; a very small or puny person (*inf*). ◆ *vi* to fish for shrimps. [Cf **scrimp**, and OE *scrimman* to shrink]
■ **shrimp'er** *n*. **shrimp'ing** *n* and *adj*. **shrimp'y** *adj*.
❑ **shrimp net** *n*. **shrimp plant** *n* a small Mexican plant (*Justicia brandegeana*) of the acanthus family with shrimp-like, pendent bracts enclosing small white flowers.

shrine /shrīn/ *n* *orig* a chest or cabinet; a container for relics or the place in which such a container is kept; the tomb of a saint or other holy person; a place hallowed by its association with a sacred object or person; a niche, alcove or shelf for a religious image; an image (*Shakesp*). ◆ *vt* to enshrine. [OE *scrīn*, from L *scrīnium* a case for papers, from *scrībere* to write]
■ **shri'nal** *adj*. **shrine'like** *adj*. **Shri'ner** *n* (*N Am*) a member of the Ancient Arabic Order of Nobles of the Mystic Shrine, a male fraternity with social and charitable aims.

shrink /shringk/ *vi* (*pat* **shrank** or (*old*) **shrunk**; *pap* **shrunk** or **shrunk'en**) to contract; to become smaller in size or extent; to shrivel; to wither; to dwindle; to give way; to draw back, retreat; to withdraw; to show or feel repugnance or reluctance; to recoil; to shrink-wrap (*inf*). ◆ *vt* to cause to contract, shrink or dwindle; to withdraw; to fix by allowing to contract. ◆ *n* an act of shrinking; contraction; withdrawal or recoil; a psychiatrist, contracted from **headshrinker** (*sl*, *orig US*). [OE *scrincan*, *scranc*, *gescruncen*]
■ **shrink'able** *adj*. **shrink'age** *n* an act of shrinking; extent of such diminution; in meat marketing, the loss of carcase weight during shipping, preparation for sale, etc; in manufacturing, etc, the loss of goods resulting from pilfering, breakages, etc. **shrink'er** *n*. **shrink'ing**

adj. **shrink'ingly** *adv*. **shrunk** or **shrunk'en** *adj* contracted, reduced, shrivelled.
❑ **shrinking violet** see under **violet**. **shrink'pack** *n* a shrink-wrapped package. **shrink'-proof** or **shrink-resis'tant** *adj* that will not shrink on washing. **shrink'-resistance** *n*. **shrink'-wrap** *vt* to package (goods) in a clear plastic film that is subsequently shrunk (eg by heating) so that it fits tightly (also *n*).

shritch /shrich/ (*obs* or *dialect*) *vi* (pat (*Spenser*) **shright** /shrīt/) to shriek, screech. ◆ *n* (*Spenser* **shriech**) a shriek. [Cf **scritch**]
❑ **shritch'-owl** *n* screech owl.

shrive /shrīv/, also (after *Spenser*) **shrieve** /shrēv/ (*RC church*) *vt* (pat **shrōve**, **shrīved** or **shrieved** /shrēvd/; pap **shriven** /shriv'ən/, **shrīved** or **shrieved**) to hear a confession from, impose a penance on and give absolution to; to confess; to disburden by confession or otherwise. ◆ *vi* to receive or make confession. [OE *scrīfan* to write, to prescribe penance, from L *scrībere*]
■ **shrī'ver** *n* a confessor. **shrī'ving** *n* (*Spenser*) shrift.
❑ **shrī'ving-time** *n* (*Shakesp*) time for confession.

shrivel /shriv'l/ *vi* and vt (**shriv'elling** or (*US*) **shriv'eling**; **shriv'elled** or (*US*) **shriv'eled**) to contract into wrinkles; to lose or cause to lose potency, vitality, etc. [Cf Swed dialect *skryvla* to wrinkle]

shroff /shrof/ (*Anglo-Ind*) *n* a moneylender, moneychanger, or banker; in the Far East, an expert who identifies and separates counterfeit money from that which is genuine. ◆ *vt* to examine or test (money) in order to detect counterfeit coins. ◆ *vi* to practise money-changing. [Ar *sarrāf*]
■ **shroff'age** *n* commission for such examination.

shroom /shroom/ (*sl*) *n* (*usu* in *pl*) a mushroom, *esp* referring to magic mushrooms. [Contraction of *mushroom*]

shroud[1] /shrowd/ *n* a garment or piece of cloth used to wrap a corpse, a winding sheet; a garment, clothes (*obs*); an enveloping or protective covering, screen, shelter, or shade; (in *pl*) a set of ropes from the masthead to a ship's sides to give lateral support to the mast; an extension from the rear of a fixed aerofoil surface covering the leading edge of eg a flap hinged to it (*aeronautics*); a streamlined covering used to protect the payload during launch (*space*); an extension of the metal parts in electrical devices (subject to high voltages) to protect the insulating dielectric (*telecom*). ◆ *vt* to enclose in a shroud; to cover, envelop; to hide; to shelter. ◆ *vi* to take shelter. [OE *scrūd*; ON *skrūth* clothing, gear, from Gmc base *skraud-, skreud-, skrud-* cut; see also **shred**]
■ **shroud'ed** *adj*. **shroud'ing** *n* and *adj*. **shroud'less** *adj* without a shroud. **shroud'y** *adj* giving shelter.
❑ **shroud-laid**' *adj* (of a rope) having four strands twisted round a central strand or heart. **shroud line** *n* any one of the cords of a parachute by which the load is suspended from the canopy.

shroud[2] /shrowd/ (*dialect*) *n* (*usu* in *pl*) a branch; loppings. ◆ *vt* to lop. [Prob same as **shroud**[1] from the root meaning of cut]

Shrove /shrōv/ *n* (*obs*) Shrovetide. [Related to OE *scrīfan* to shrive]
■ **shrove** *vi* (*obs*) to celebrate Shrovetide (*go a-shroving*, to go round singing for money at Shrovetide).
❑ **Shrove'tide** *n* the three days preceding Ash Wednesday. **Shrove Tuesday** *n* the day before Ash Wednesday.

shrove /shrōv/ *pat* of **shrive**.

shrow /shrō/, **shrowd** /shrōd/ Shakespearean forms of **shrew**, **shrewd**.

shrub[1] /shrub/ *n* a low woody plant smaller than a tree, a bush, *esp* one with little or no trunk; a scrub (*obs*). ◆ *vt* to lop; to cudgel (*obs*). [OE *scrybb* scrub]
■ **shrubb'eried** *adj*. **shrubb'ery** *n* a plantation or growth of shrubs. **shrubb'iness** *n*. **shrubb'y** *adj* of, like or having the character of, a shrub; covered with shrubs. **shrub'less** *adj*. **shrub'like** *adj*.

shrub[2] /shrub/ *n* a mixed drink of lemon or other citrus fruit juice, sugar, spices and a spirit, *esp* rum; a cordial of fruit juice (eg raspberry) and vinegar (*US*). [Ar *sharāb*, for *shurb* drink; cf **sherbet**, **syrup**]

shrug /shrug/ *vi* (**shrugg'ing**; **shrugged**) to raise (and lower) the shoulders in an abrupt movement, a gesture expressive of doubt, indifference, etc; to shudder, shiver (*rare* or *obs*). ◆ *vt* to raise (the shoulders) in a shrug; to shrink (*obs*). ◆ *n* an expressive raising of the shoulders; a jerk; a *usu* woollen garment covering the arms, shoulders and top of the back. [Origin obscure]
■ **shrug off** to shake off, get rid of; to show indifference to or dismiss as unimportant (eg responsibility, a difficulty).

shrunk, shrunken see under **shrink**.

sht. *abbrev* : sheet(s).

shtchi see **shchi**.

shtetl or **shtetel** /shtet'əl/ *n* (pl **shtet'lach** /-läk/ or **shtetls**) formerly, a Jewish community in an E European town or village. [Yiddish, small town, from MHGer *stetel*, dimin of *stat* town]

shtg. *abbrev* : shortage.

shtick, schtick or **schtik** /shtik/ (*sl*) *n* a familiar routine, line of chat, etc, adopted by, and associated with, a particular comedian, etc; an attention-catching device. [Yiddish *shtik* piece, part, slice, from MHGer *stücke*]

shtook, schtook, shtuck or **schtuck** /shtŭk/ (*sl*) *n* trouble, bother. [Origin unknown]
■ **in shtook**, etc (*sl*) in trouble.

shtoom, schtoom, shtum, shtumm or **stumm** /shtŭm/ (*sl*) *adj* silent, dumb, quiet. [Yiddish, from Ger *stumm* silent]
■ **keep** or **stay shtoom**, etc remain silent, be quiet.

shtup /shtŭp/ (*vulgar sl*) *vt* and *vi* (**shtupp'ing**; **shtupped**) to have sexual intercourse (with), to copulate. ◆ *n* an act of sexual intercourse. [Yiddish, from Ger *stupsen* to push]

shubunkin /shŭ-bung'kin or -bŭng'/ *n* a type of variegated large-finned goldfish. [Jap]

shuck /shuk/ (*N Am*) *n* a husk, shell, or pod. ◆ *vt* to remove the shuck from; to strip or peel off or away, to discard (with *off*). [Origin unknown]
■ **shuck'er** *n*. **shuck'ing** *n*. **shucks** *interj* (*inf*) a mild exclamation expressive of disappointment, irritation or embarrassment.
■ **not worth shucks** (*inf*) worthless.

shudder /shud'ər/ *vi* to shiver, eg from cold or horror; to vibrate. ◆ *n* a tremor caused by cold or horror; an act or instance of vibrating or trembling. [From ME *shod(d)er*, from MLGer *schōderen*; cf OHGer *skutten* to shake]
■ **shudd'ering** *n* and *adj*. **shudd'eringly** *adv*. **shudd'ersome** *adj*. **shudd'ery** *adj*.

shuffle /shuf'l/ *vt* to mix at random (*esp* playing-cards); to jumble; to put (*out, in, off*, etc) surreptitiously, evasively, scramblingly, or in confusion; to manipulate unfairly; to patch up; to drag (the feet) along without lifting them clear; to perform with such motions. ◆ *vi* to mix cards in a pack; to scramble; to behave shiftily; to shift ground; to evade fair questions; to move by dragging the feet along; to shamble; to dance the shuffle. ◆ *n* act of shuffling; a shuffling gait, dance or dance step; an evasion or artifice. [Early modern; cf **scuffle**, **shove**, **shovel**; LGer *schüffeln*]
■ **shuff'ler** *n*. **shuff'ling** *n* and *adj*. **shuff'lingly** *adv*.
❑ **shuff'le-cap** *n* an old game in which the stake is money shaken in a cap.
■ **shuffle off** to thrust aside, put off, wriggle out of.

shuffleboard see **shovelboard**.

shufti or **shufty** /shuf'ti/ (*inf*) *n* a look, glance. [Colloquial Ar *shufti* have you seen?, from *shaffa* to see]

shul or **schul** /shool/ *n* (pl **s(c)huln** or **s(c)huls**) a synagogue. [Yiddish, from MHGer *schuol* school]

shule see **shool**[1].

shun /shun/ *vt* (**shunn'ing**; **shunned**) to avoid deliberately. [OE *scunian*]
■ **shun'less** *adj* (*Shakesp*) not to be shunned. **shunn'able** *adj*. **shunn'er** *n*.
■ **upon the shun** (*old*) bent on evading notice.

'shun /shun/ (*milit inf*) *interj* attention!

shunamitism /shoo'nə-mi-ti-zm/ *n* rejuvenation of an old man by means of a young woman. [Abishag the *Shunammite* (Bible, 1 Kings 1.3)]

shunt /shunt/ *vt* and vi to turn or move aside; to move (railway rolling stock) to another track, *esp* a side track; to divert or be diverted by means of a shunt (*electronics* or *med*). ◆ *vt* to bypass; to sidetrack; to shelve; to get rid of; to crash (a car) (*sl*). ◆ *vi* (*inf*) to be off. ◆ *n* an act of shunting; a conductor connected in parallel with eg a measuring instrument, diverting part of an electric current; a switch; a passage (resulting from congenital abnormality or created surgically) in which two anatomical channels are connected and blood (or, in the brain, cerebrospinal fluid) is diverted from one to the other (*med*); a road accident, crash, mishap (*orig motor-racing sl*). [Perh connected with **shun**]
■ **shunt'er** *n*. **shunt'ing** *n* and *adj*.
❑ **shunt'-winding** *n*. **shunt'-wound** *adj* (of an electric motor, etc) having the field and armature circuits connected in parallel.

shura /shoo'rə/ *n* in Afghanistan, a traditional regional or village council. [Ar, consultation]

shuriken /shoo'ri-ken/ *n* a hand-held throwing weapon, either long and thin or flat and star-shaped, used by ninja warriors. [Jap *shu* hand, *ri* release, and *ken* blade]

shush /shush/ *vt* and *vi* to (cause to) be quiet. ◆ *interj* hush! be quiet!

shut /shut/ *vt* (**shutt'ing**; **shut**) to place so as to stop an opening; to stop or cover the opening of; to lock; to fasten; to bar; to forbid entrance into; to bring together the parts or outer parts of; to confine;

to catch or pinch in a fastening; to end the operations of (a business, etc); to shoot (eg a bolt; *obs*). ◆ *vi* to become closed; to be capable of being closed; to close in; (of a business, etc) to cease to operate. ◆ *adj* made fast; closed; rid (with *of* ; *inf*). ◆ *n* an act or time of shutting. [OE *scyttan* to bar; cf *scēotan*, to shoot]

❑ **shut'down** *n* a temporary closing, eg of a factory; the reduction of power in a nuclear reactor to the minimum, *usu* carried out as a safety or emergency measure. **shut'-eye** *n* (*inf*) sleep. **shut'-in** *n* (*N Am*) a disabled person confined indoors. **shut'-off** *n* a device that stops the flow or operation of something; a stoppage. **shut'out** *n* (in sports, etc) a game in which one team is prevented from scoring. **shut'-out bid** *n* (*bridge*) one to deter opponents from bidding.

■ **shut away** to keep hidden or repressed; to isolate; to confine. **shut down** to close down, or stop the operation of, often temporarily. **shut in** to enclose, to confine; to settle down, or fall (said, eg, of evening). **shut off** to exclude; to switch off; to stop the flow of. **shut one's eyes to** to ignore; to refuse to acknowledge (*esp* something disagreeable). **shut out** to prevent from entering; to hide or screen from view; to prevent (the opposing team) from scoring. **shut up** to close finally or completely; to confine; to cease speaking (*inf*); to reduce to silence (*inf*).

shute see **chute**[1].

shutter /shut'ər/ *n* something or someone that shuts; an external or internal cover for a window, *esp* one of a (*usu* wooden or metal) hinged pair; a device for regulating the opening of an aperture, as in photography and cinematography; a removable cover, gate, or piece of shuttering. ◆ *vt* to close or fit with a shutter or shutters. [**shut**]

■ **shutt'ered** *adj*. **shutt'ering** *n* closing and fitting with a shutter; material used as shutters; temporary support for concrete work. **shutt'erless** *adj*.

❑ **shutter'bug** *n* (*inf*) a camera or photographic enthusiast. **shutter priority** *n* a facility enabling a camera to select the aperture automatically once the shutter speed has been selected by the photographer.

■ **put up the shutters** (*inf*) to stop trading, either for the day or permanently (also *fig*).

shuttle[1] /shut'l/ *n* an instrument used for shooting the thread of the woof between the threads of the warp in weaving or through the loop of thread in a sewing machine; anything that makes similar movements; rapid movement to and fro between two points; a shuttle service or the vehicle, craft, etc, used for this; a shuttlecock. ◆ *vt* and *vi* to move to and fro like a shuttle; to move or travel regularly between two points. [OE *scytel* dart; *scēotan* to shoot; Dan and Swed *skyttel*]

■ **shutt'lewise** *adv* to and fro like a shuttle.

❑ **shutt'lecock** *n* a lightweight cone consisting of a rounded cork stuck with feathered flights (or a moulded plastic version of this) to be hit to and fro with badminton rackets; an old game played with battledores; something tossed to and fro repeatedly. ◆ *vt* and *vi* to shuttle. **shuttle diplomacy** *n* the exercise, undertaken by an intermediary, of travelling to and fro between two heads of state, in order to bring about agreement between them. **shuttle service** *n* a train or other transport service moving constantly between two points.

shuttle[2] /shut'l/ or **shottle** /shot'l/ (*esp Scot*) *n* a small drawer, *esp* in a cabinet or chest. [Perh **shut**; perh OE *scyttel* bolt, bar]

shwa see **schwa**.

shy[1] /shī/ *adj* (**shy'er** or **shi'er**; **shy'est** or **shi'est**) shrinking from notice or approach; bashful; chary; disposed to avoidance (with *of* ; also used in combination, as in *workshy*); secluded; warily reluctant; unproductive; scanty; short, lacking (with *of*) (*N Am inf*); of doubtful repute; (*esp* in poker) short in payment. ◆ *vi* (**shy'ing**; **shied**) to recoil, to shrink (with *away*, *off*); to start aside, like a horse from fear. ◆ *vt* to shun. ◆ *n* (*pl* **shies**) a sudden swerving aside. [OE *scēoh* timid; cf **skeigh**, MHGer *schiech*]

■ **shi'er** or **shy'er** *n*. **shy'ish** *adj*. **shy'ly** or **shi'ly** *adv*. **shy'ness** or (*obs*) **shi'ness** *n*.

■ **fight shy of** to shrink from.

shy[2] /shī/ *vt* and *vi* (**shy'ing**; **shied**) to fling, toss. ◆ *n* (*pl* **shies**) a throw; a fling; a gibe; an attempt, shot; a thing to shy at. [Origin obscure]

■ **shi'er** or **shy'er** *n*.

Shylock /shī'lok/ *n* a ruthless creditor; an avaricious, grasping person. [From Shylock in Shakespeare's *Merchant of Venice*]

shyster /shī'stər/ (*inf*) *n* an unscrupulous or disreputable lawyer; an unscrupulous practitioner in any profession or business. [Appar from **shy**[1] in sense of 'of doubtful repute']

SI *abbrev* : South Island (of New Zealand); Système International (d'Unités), the modern scientific system of units (**SI units**), used in the measurement of all physical quantities, the principal units being the metre, kilogram, second, ampere, kelvin, candela, and mole.

Si (*chem*) *symbol* : silicon.

si /sē/ (*music*) *n* the seventh note of the scale, a later addition to the six Aretinian syllables, but superseded by *ti*. [Perh from the initial letters of

Sancte Ioannes, the last line of the hymn from which the Aretinian syllables were taken]

sial /sī'al/ or *-əl*/ *n* the lighter upper part of the earth's continental crust composed of rocks rich in *si*lica and *al*umina (also **sal** /sal/).

■ **sial'ic** *adj*.

siala- /sī-ə-lə-/ or /sī-al-ə-/ or **sialo-** /sī-ə-lō-, -lə-, -lo-, sī-al-ō-, -lə-/ or **sial-** /sī-əl-, sī-al-/ *combining form* denoting saliva. [Gr *sialon* saliva]

■ **sialagogue** or **sialogogue** /sī-al'ə-gog/ *n* (Gr *agōgos* leading) anything that stimulates a flow of saliva (also *adj*). **sialagog'ic** or **sialogog'ic** *adj* of or relating to saliva (**sialic acid** (*biochem*) any of a group of amino sugars that form covalently linked sugar residues in glycoproteins). **sial'ogram** *n* an X-ray of the salivary tract. **sialog'raphy** *n*. **sī'aloid** *adj* resembling saliva. **sial'olith** *n* (Gr *lithos* a stone) a calculus in a salivary gland. **sialorrhoe'a** *n* (Gr *rhoiā* flow) excessive secretion of saliva, ptyalism.

sialic see under **sial** and **siala-**.

sialon /sī'ə-lon/ *n* any of various ceramic materials consisting of silicon, aluminium, oxygen, and nitrogen. [From the chemical symbols of the constituent elements, *Si, Al, O, N*]

siamang /sē'ə-mang/ or /syä'mang/ *n* a large black gibbon, *Symphalangus* (or *Hylobates*) *syndactylus*, found in the Indonesian island of Sumatra and the Malay Peninsula. [Malay]

Siamese /sī-ə-mēz'/ *adj* of Siam, the former name of Thailand. ◆ *n* (*pl* **Siamese**) a native, or citizen, or the language of Siam; a Siamese cat.

■ **siamese'** or **-eze'** *vt* (*old*) to join (eg pipes) in a way suggestive of the union of Siamese twins.

❑ **Siamese cat** *n* a domestic fawn-coloured cat, with blue eyes and a small head, probably descended from the jungle cat of India, Africa, etc. **Siamese fighting fish** *n* a brilliantly coloured freshwater fish of SE Asia, the males having elongated sail-like fins and being extremely pugnacious. **Siamese twins** *n pl orig* a set of Chinese twins (1811–74), born in Siam, joined from birth by a fleshy ligature; (also **conjoined twins**) any set of twins who are physically joined; an inseparable pair (*fig*).

SIB *abbrev* : Securities and Investments Board (now known as **FSA**); Special Investigations Branch.

sib (*Spenser* **sybbe**, *Walter Scott* **sibb**) /sib/ *n* kinship (*rare*); kindred (*rare*); a kinsman or kinswoman; a blood relation; a brother or sister; a group descended from one ancestor (*anthrop* or *genetics*). ◆ *adj* akin, related by blood; (of canaries) inbred. [OE *sibb* relationship, *gesibb* related; Ger *Sippe*]

■ **sib'ling** *n* a person who has both parents in common with oneself, a brother or sister; a person who has a parent or an ancestor in common with oneself. ◆ *adj* of or relating to siblings. **sib'ship** *n* a group of sibs; blood relationship; clan relationship.

Siberian /sī-bē'ri-ən/ *adj* relating to the region of *Siberia* in NE Asia.

❑ **Siberian ginseng** same as **eleutherococcus** (see under **eleutherian**).

sibilate /sib'i-lāt/ *vt* and *vi* to pronounce (words) with, or produce, a hissing sound. [L *sībilāre*, *-ātum* to hiss]

■ **sib'ilance** or **sib'ilancy** *n*. **sib'ilant** *adj* hissing; pronounced with a hissing sound. ◆ *n* a hissing consonant sound, as of *s* and *z*. **sib'ilantly** *adv*. **sibilā'tion** *n*. **sib'ilator** *n*. **sib'ilatory** /-ə-tə-ri/ or **sib'ilous** *adj*.

sibling see under **sib**.

sibyl /sib'il/ *n* (also with *cap*) any of several female oracles or prophets of ancient Rome, Greece, Babylonia, Egypt, etc, each believed to be inspired by an individual deity; loosely, a prophetess, witch or female fortune-teller; an old crone. [Gr *Sibylla*]

■ **sibyll'ic** or **sibyl'ic** *adj*. **sib'ylline** /-īn/ *adj*. **Sib'yllist** *n* a believer in the Sibylline prophecies.

❑ **Sibylline Books** *n pl* prophetic books said to have been offered to the Roman king Tarquinius Superbus by the Sibyl of Cumae, of which he ultimately bought three for the price he had refused to give for nine, these three being held in the Capitol and referred to by the Roman senate in times of emergency and disaster (a later set was made after the first collection was destroyed by fire in 83BC).

sic[1] /sik/ or /sēk/ (L) so, thus (often printed within brackets in quoted matter to show that the original is being faithfully reproduced even though incorrect or apparently so).

■ **sic passim** /pas'im/ so throughout, used to indicate that a word, spelling, etc has been printed in the same form throughout in a book, article, etc.

sic[2] /sik/ *adj* a Scots form of **such**.

■ **sicc'an** *adj* (for *sic kin* such kind) such; (in exclamations) what, what a. **sic'like** *adj* suchlike. ◆ *adv* in like manner.

sic[3] same as **sick**[2].

Sican /sik'ən/ *n* a native of Sicily. [L *Sīcānus, Sicānus*, from Gr *Sikanos*]

■ **Sicanian** /-ā'ni-ən/ *n* and *adj*.

siccan see under **sic²**.

siccar same as **sicker**.

siccative /sik'ə-tiv/ adj drying. ◆ n a drying agent. [L siccus dry]
■ **siccity** /sik'si-ti/ n dryness.

sice¹ /sīs/ or **size** /sīz/ n the number six in a game of dice. [OFr sis]

sice² same as **syce**.

Sicel /sis'əl/ or **sik'əl**/ or **Siceliot** /si-sel'i-ot or -kel'/ see **Sikel**.

sich /sich/ adj an archaic form of **such**.

Sicilian /si-sil'yən or -sil'i-ən/ adj of or relating to the island of Sicily; denoting a cloth of cotton and mohair.
■ **siciliano** /si-sil-yä'nō/ n (pl **sicilia'nos**) a Sicilian pastoral dance, dance tune, or movement, in 6–8 or 12–8 time.
❑ **Sicilian Vespers** n sing the massacre of the French in Sicily in 1282, beginning, according to a late tradition, at the first stroke of the vesper-bell.

siciliana /sē-chē-lyä'nä/ (Ital) n (pl **sicilia'ne** /-nā/) a siciliano. [Ital, Sicilian]

sicilienne /si-si-lyen'/ n a ribbed silk fabric; a siciliano. [Fr, Sicilian]

sick¹ /sik/ adj unwell, ill; diseased; astonishing, extraordinary (sl); vomiting or inclined to vomit; pining; mortified; disgusted; thoroughly wearied; out of condition; sickly; of or for people who are ill; (of humour, comedy, a joke, etc) gruesome, macabre, tending to exploit topics not normally joked about, such as illness, death, etc; disappointed (inf); (sl) excellent. ◆ vi (Shakesp) to grow sick. ◆ vt (inf) to vomit (with up). ◆ n (inf) vomited matter. [OE sēoc; Ger siech, Du ziek]
■ **sick'en** vt to make sick; to disgust; to make weary of anything. ◆ vi to become sick; to be disgusted (with at); to become disgusting or tedious; to become weakened. **sick'ener** n something that provokes nausea, disgust, etc; a poisonous toadstool (Russula emetica). **sick'ening** n and adj. **sick'eningly** adv. **sick'ie** n (inf) a day's sick leave (orig Aust and NZ); a sick person, whether mentally or physically (N Am). **sick'ish** adj. **sick'ishly** adv. **sick'ishness** n. **sick'lied** adj. **sick'lily** adv. **sick'liness** n. **sick'ly** adj inclined to be ailing; feeble; languid; pallid; suggestive of sickness; slightly or insipidly sickening; mawkish; of sickness or the sick. ◆ adv in a sick manner; feebly. ◆ vt (obs) to make sickly-looking, impart an unhealthy hue to; to make sentimental or mawkish. **sick'ness** n. **sick'o** n (pl **sick'os**) (chiefly N Am) a mentally ill person; a crazy or deranged person; a pervert. ◆ adj perverted; macabre.
❑ **sick bag** n a small paper bag, provided for each passenger on an aircraft, which may be used by those suffering from travel sickness to vomit into. **sick bay** n a compartment for sick and wounded on a ship (also **sick berth**); an infirmary or sanatorium at a boarding school, etc. **sick'bed** n a bed on which someone lies sick. **sick benefit** or **sickness benefit** n a benefit paid to someone who is out of work through illness. **sick building syndrome** n a set of symptoms, such as headaches, dizziness and general fatigue, experienced by occupants of buildings which have inadequate ventilation or air-conditioning. **sick'-fallen** adj (archaic) struck with sickness. **sick-feath'ered** adj (of birds) with immature feathers at moulting. **sick flag** n a quarantine flag. **sick headache** n a headache with nausea. **sick leave** n leave of absence owing to sickness. **sick list** n a list of the sick. **sick'-listed** adj entered on the sick list. **sick'-making** adj (inf) sickening. **sick note** n (inf) in Britain, a note (signed either by the employee or the employee's doctor) given to an employer to certify that absence from work was due to illness. **sick'nurse** n (old) a nurse who attends the sick. **sick'nurs'ing** n. **sick'-out** n (N Am and W Indies) a form of industrial action in which all workers at a particular factory, workplace, etc, absent themselves simultaneously on the pretext of sickness. **sick'room** or (old) **sick chamber** n a room to which one is confined by sickness. **sick-thought'ed** adj (Shakesp) lovesick. **sick-tired'** adj.
■ **be sick** to vomit; to be ill. **look sick** (inf) to appear inadequate in comparison. **sick (and tired** or **to death) of** tired of; wearied to the point of disgust by. **sick as a dog** (inf) vomiting profusely and unrestrainedly. **sick as a parrot** (inf) extremely disappointed. **sicken for** to show early symptoms of. **sick to one's stomach** about to vomit; disgusted.

sick² /sik/ vt to set upon, chase; to incite (eg a dog) to make an attack (on). [A dialect variant of **seek**]

sicker or **siccar** /sik'ər/ adj (archaic and Scot) sure, certain, firm. ◆ adv (archaic) surely, certainly. [OE sicor, from L sēcūrus; Ger sicher]
■ **sick'erly** adv (Scot). **sick'erness** n (Scot).

sickle¹ /sik'l/ n an implement with a curved blade and a short handle, for cutting crops, etc, a reaping-hook; a sickle feather. [OE sicol, sicel, perh from L secula, from secāre to cut]
■ **sick'led** adj bearing a sickle.
❑ **sick'lebill** n a bird of paradise, hummingbird, etc, with a sickle-shaped bill. **sickle-cell** (or **-celled**) **anaemia** n (also called **sickle'mia**)

a severe hereditary anaemia, mainly affecting black people, in which the red blood cells become distorted into a sickle shape and are subsequently destroyed by the body's defence system. **sickle-cell trait** n a mild, usu symptomless, condition with some of the characteristics of sickle-cell anaemia. **sickle feather** n a cock's elongated tail feather. **sick'leman** n a reaper. **sick'le-shaped** adj.

sickle² /sik'l/ (Shakesp) n a shekel. [OFr sicle, from Heb sheqel]

Siculian /si-kū'li-ən/ adj and n (a member) of the Siculi, or Sikels, an ancient people that colonized Sicily from Italy.

sida /sī'də/ n any plant of the Queensland hemp genus Sida, of the mallow family, tropical herbs yielding a fibre. [Gr sidē a plant name]

sidalcea /si-dal'si-ə/ n a plant of the genus Sidalcea of the mallow family, a herbaceous perennial with tall spikes of white, pink, or purple flowers. [Mod L from Gr sidē a kind of plant, and alkea mallow]

siddhi /sid'i/ (also with cap) n (in Hinduism, Buddhism and Jainism) the supernatural powers that come with the spiritual perfection attained by meditation, etc (sing and pl). [Sans, fulfilment]
■ **sidd'ha** n someone who has attained perfection (also **sid'ha**).
❑ **siddha yoga** see **maha yoga**.

siddur /sid'oor/ (Judaism) n (pl **siddur'im** or **-im'**) a Jewish prayer book used in daily liturgy. [Heb siddūr order, arrangement]

side¹ /sīd/ n a line or surface forming part of a boundary; the part near such a boundary; a surface or part turned in some direction, esp one more or less upright, or one regarded as right or left, not front or back, top or bottom; the part of the body between armpit and hip; half of a carcase divided along the medial plane; either of the extended surfaces of anything in the form of a sheet; a page; a portion of space lying in this or that direction from a boundary or a point; the father's or mother's part of a genealogy; a department or division, eg of a school or prison; an aspect; a direction; a particular district; a border or bank; the slope of a hill; the wall of a vessel or cavity; any party, team, interest, or opinion opposed to another; part (as in on my side, for my part); the womb (Milton); a spin given to a ball causing it to swerve and regulating its angle of rebound (snooker, etc); a pretentious air, arrogance (inf); a speech in a play; a television channel (inf). ◆ adj at or toward the side; sideways; subsidiary. ◆ vi to ally oneself with a particular side in an argument, etc, to take sides (with with). ◆ vt to cut into sides; to thrust or set aside; to adjudge or assign to one side or other (Shakesp); to assign in this way to (Shakesp); to be on the side next to (archaic). [OE sīde; cf Ger Seite, Du zijde]
■ **sid'ed** adj having sides; flattened on one or more sides. ◆ combining form having a (specified) number or kind of sides, as in three-sided, many-sided, unequal-sided. **side'ling** adj and adv sideways; with a slope. **side'long** adj oblique; sloping; tilted; sideways. ◆ adv in the direction of the side; obliquely; on the side. **sid'er** n someone who takes a side. **side'ward** adj and adv. **side'wards** adv. **side'ways** or **side'wise** adj and adv toward or on one side. **sid'ing** n a short railway track for shunting or lying by; material used to weatherproof the outside of a building (N Am). ◆ n and adj taking sides.
❑ **side'arm** n (usu in pl) a weapon worn at the side or in a belt. **side'band** n (radio) a frequency band above or below the carrier frequency, containing additional frequencies constituting the information to be conveyed, introduced by modulation. **side'bar** n a short newspaper article alongside, and dealing in detail with some aspect of, a longer article (N Am); a toolbar or taskbar that appears at the side of a screen or window (comput); a private conference between lawyers and the judge in court during a criminal trial (N Am). **side'-bar** n (in S Africa) solicitors, as opposed to barristers (who belong to the bar). **side'board** n a piece of dining-room furniture for holding plates, etc, often with drawers and cupboards; a board at the side, eg of a cart; a side table (archaic); (in pl) side whiskers. **side'bones** n pl ossifications of the lateral cartilages of a horse's hoof. **side box** n a box at the side of a theatre. **side'burns** n pl two strips of hair grown along the side of the face, a modification of the rather more extensive growth pioneered by the US General Burnside (1824–81). **side'car** n a small car attached to the side of a motorcycle usu for the carriage of a passenger; a jaunting car; a kind of cocktail consisting of brandy, orange liqueur and lemon juice. **side chain** n (chem) a chain of atoms forming a branch attached to a ring. **side comb** n a small comb in the hair at the side. **side cutting** n an excavation along the side of a railway or canal to get material for an embankment. **side dish** n a supplementary dish. **side door** n a door at the side of a building or of a main door. **side'-dress** vt to place fertilizers on or in the soil near the roots of (a crop, etc). **side drum** n a small double-headed drum with snares, slung from the drummer's side or sitting on a stand. **side effect** n a subsidiary effect; an effect, often undesirable, additional to the effect sought. **side'-foot** vt (inf) to kick (a ball) with the side of the foot. **side glance** n a sidelong glance; a passing allusion. **side issue** n something subordinate, incidental, not important in comparison with the main issue. **side'kick** n (inf) a partner, deputy; a special friend. **side'light** n a light on the side of a

vessel or vehicle; a window above or at the side of a door; a window, as opposed to a skylight; light coming from the side; any incidental illustration. **side'line** *n* a line attached to the side of anything; a branch route or track; a subsidiary trade or activity; (in *pl*) (the area just outside) the lines marking the edge of a football pitch, etc, hence, a peripheral area to which spectators or non-participants are confined. ◆ *vt* to remove (a player) from a team and confine to the sidelines; to suspend from normal operation or activity; to confine to a peripheral area; to relegate (someone) to a minor, peripheral position, prevent his or her participation in the main or most important area of activity, *esp* in business. **side'lined** *adj.* **side'lock** *n* a lock of hair at the side of the head. **side'man** *n* (*pl* **side'men**) (*jazz*) one of the members of a band or orchestra, other than the leader or featured artist, who performs occasional solo passages demonstrating virtuosity on a particular instrument. **side meat** *n* (*US*) meat cut from the side of a pig, salt pork or bacon. **side'note** *n* a comment written in a margin. **side-on** *adj* and *adv* with a side facing forwards or leading. **side'path** *n* a byway, footpath or sidewalk. **side plate** *n* a small plate used for food, such as bread or salad, which accompanies the main meal. **side post** *n* a doorpost; a post supporting a roof at the side. **side'road** *n* a minor road. **side'saddle** *n* a saddle designed for women wearing long riding habits, on which the rider sits with both legs on the same side (also *adv*). **sidesaddle flower** *n* a N American pitcher plant, *Sarracenia.* **side'shoot** *n* (*bot*). **side'show** *n* an exhibition subordinate to a larger one; any subordinate or incidental activity. **side'slip** *n* an oblique offshoot; a bastard (*obs*); a sideways skid; a lateral movement of an aircraft; a side-on downward slide (*skiing*). ◆ *vi* to slip sideways. **sides'man** or **sides'woman** *n* a deputy churchwarden; a partisan (*archaic*). **side'-splitting** *adj* extremely funny, making one laugh until one's sides ache. **side'step** *n* a step taken to one side; a step attached to the side. ◆ *vi* to step aside. ◆ *vt* to avoid, as by a step aside. **side'stepper** *n.* **side'stream** *adj* denoting smoke exhaled by smokers of cigarettes, etc that is inhaled involuntarily by non-smokers. **side street** *n* a minor street, *esp* if opening off a main street. **side'stroke** *n* a stroke performed by a swimmer lying on his or her side; a stroke performed sideways. **side'swipe** *n* a blow dealt from the side, not struck head-on; a criticism made in passing, incidentally to the main topic. ◆ *vt* to deal (someone) a sideswipe. **side'swiper** *n.* **sideswoman** see **sidesman** above. **side table** *n* a table used as a sideboard, or placed against the wall, or to the side of the main table. **side tone** *n* (*telecom*) a signal reaching the receiver of a radiotelephone station from its own transmitter. **side'track** *n* a railway siding. ◆ *vt* to divert or turn aside; to shelve. **side valve** *n* (in an engine) a valve situated at the side of the cylinder block. **side view** *n* a view on or from one side. **side'walk** *n* (*N Am*) a pavement or footpath. **side'wall** *n* the side portion of a tyre, between tread and wheel rim. **side'-wheel** *adj* with paddle wheels at the side. **side'-wheeler** *n* a side-wheel paddle steamer. **side whiskers** *n pl* hair grown by a man down either side of the face, in front of the ears. **side wind** *n* a lateral wind; indirect means. **side'winder** *n* a rattlesnake (*Crotalus cerastes*) of the southern USA that progresses by lateral looping motions; the name of an air-to-air missile directed at its target by means of a homing device; a hard blow struck from the side (*US*). ■ **bit on the side** see under **bit**[1]. **choose sides** to pick teams. **get on the right** (or **wrong**) **side of** to gain (or lose) the regard, approval, favour, etc of. **let the side down** to fail one's colleagues, associates, etc, by falling below their standard. **on the short, long, tight,** etc, **side** rather too short, long, etc. **on the side** in addition to or apart from ordinary occupation, income, etc, *esp* applied to dishonest or underhand dealings. **put on** (or **to**) **one side** to shelve; to set apart. **put on side** (*inf*) to assume pretentious airs. **right** (or **wrong**) **side** the side intended to be turned outward (or inward). **side by side** close together; abreast. **split one's sides** see under **split**. **take sides** to range oneself with one party or other. **the other side** the spiritual world, to which one passes after death. **this side of** between here and (somewhere specified); short of.

side[2] /*sīd*/ (now *dialect*; *Shakesp*) *adj* long. [OE *sīd* ample]
■ **side'long** *adj* and *adv* (*Spenser*).

sidereal /*sī-dē'ri-əl*/ *adj* of, like, or relating to the stars. [L *sīdus, sīderis* a star, constellation]
■ **sideral** /*sid'ər-əl*/ *adj* sent from the stars, said *esp* of a malign influence. **sid'erate** *vt* to blast or strike. **siderā'tion** *n* (now *rare*) a blast, blight, or stroke; sudden paralysis of (any part of) the body; erysipelas. **sid'erostat** *n* a mirror, or telescope with a mirror, for reflecting the rays of a star in a constant direction, on the principle of the coelostat.
❑ **sidereal day** *n* the time the earth takes to make a revolution on its axis, relative to the time between two successive transits of a particular star. **sidereal month** see under **month**. **sidereal period** *n* the time a celestial body takes to return to the same position in relation to the stars. **sidereal time** *n* time based on the sidereal day. **sidereal year** see under **year**.

sidero- /*sid-ə-rō-* or *-rə-*/ or **sider-** /*sid-ər-*/ *combining form* denoting iron. [Gr *sidēros* iron]
■ **siderite** /*sid'ə-rīt*/ *n* chalybite, or ferrous carbonate, one of the ores of iron; a meteorite mainly of metallic iron. **sideritic** /*-it'ik*/ *adj*. **sid'erolite** *n* (Gr *lithos* stone) a meteorite made up partly of stone and partly of iron. **sideropēn'ia** *n* (*med*) deficiency of iron. **sid'erophile** *n* (*geol*) an element with an affinity for iron, whose geochemical distribution is influenced by this property (also *adj*). **siderophil'ic** *adj*. **siderō'sis** *n* lung disease caused by breathing in iron or other metal particles.

siderostat see under **sidereal**.

sidesman, siding, etc see under **side**[1].

sidha see under **siddhi**.

sidie /*sī'dl*/ *vi* to go or edge along (sideways), *esp* in a furtive or ingratiating manner. ◆ *n* a sidling movement. [Prob back-formation from *sideling* sideways]

SIDS or **Sids** *abbrev* : sudden infant death syndrome.

siege /*sēj*/ *n* the act or process of surrounding a town or fortress, cutting off its supply lines and subjecting it to persistent attack with the intention of forcing surrender by its defenders and capturing it; any persistent attack, offensive, attempt to gain control, etc; a long period of persistent illness or troubles; a seat or throne (*archaic*); rank, distinction or class (*obs*); a privy (*obs*); dung (*Shakesp*); a mason's or bricklayer's workbench (*building*); the floor of a pot furnace or tank furnace (*glass-making*); a company of herons or bitterns (also **sedge**). ◆ *vt* to besiege. [OFr *sege* (Fr *siège*) seat, from L *sēdēs* seat]
■ **sieg'er** *n* a besieger.
❑ **siege'-artillery** or **siege'-gun** *n* heavy artillery or a gun designed for use in sieges rather than in the field. **siege basket** *n* a gabion. **siege'craft** *n* the art of the besieger. **siege economy** *n* an economy in which imports are restricted in order to protect national industries and production. **siege mentality** *n* a mental state in which one imagines one is constantly under attack. **siege piece** *n* a coin, generally of imperfect workmanship, issued in a besieged place; a siege-gun. **siege train** *n* a train of artillery for besieging a place. **siege'works** *n* a besieger's engineering works.
■ **lay siege to** to besiege. **state of siege** a condition of suspension of civil law or its subordination to military law.

Sieg Heil /*sēg* or *zēk hīl'*/ (*Ger*) victory hail, used as a Nazi salute.

sield /*sēld*/ a Spenserian spelling of **ceiled**.

siemens /*sē'mənz* or *-menz*/ *n* a derived SI unit, the unit of electrical conductance (symbol **S**), defined as the reciprocal of ohm. [Sir William *Siemens* (1823–83), German-born British inventor and industrialist]

sien /*sī'ən*/ (*Shakesp*) *n* same as **scion**.

Sienese or **Siennese** /*sē-ə-nēz'*/ *adj* of *Siena* (also *Sienna*) or its school of painting. ◆ *n* a native of Siena.
■ **sienna** /*sē-en'ə*/ *n* a fine pigment made from ferruginous ochreous earth, originally browny-yellow (**raw sienna**) but warm reddish-brown when roasted (**burnt sienna**); its colour.

sient /*sī'ənt*/ (*archaic*) *n* same as **scion**.

Sierra or **sierra** /*si-er'ə*/ *n* (in international radio communication) a code word for the letter *s*.

sierra /*si-er'ə*/ *n* a mountain range, *esp* in Spanish-speaking countries and the USA. [Sp, from L *serra* saw]
■ **sierr'an** *adj*.
❑ **Sierra Leonean** /*lē-ō'ni-ən*/ *adj* of or relating to the Republic of Sierra Leone in W Africa, or its people. ◆ *n* a native or citizen of Sierra Leone.

siesta /*si-es'tə*/ *n* a midday or afternoon nap. [Sp, from L *sexta* (*hōra*) sixth (hour)]

sieth a Shakespearean spelling of **scythe**.

sieve /*siv*/ *n* a utensil with a meshed or perforated bottom for sifting or straining, generally finer than a riddle; a refuse-basket (*Shakesp*). ◆ *vt* and *vi* to sift. [OE *sife*; Ger *Sieb*]
■ **sieve'-like** *adj* perforated like a sieve; (of a memory) extremely unreliable.
❑ **sieve plate** *n* (*bot*) a perforated area by which a sieve tube connects with another. **sieve tube** *n* (*bot*) a conducting element in phloem, consisting of thin-walled cells connected end to end with sieve plates between adjacent members.
■ **have a head** (or **memory**) **like a sieve** to be very forgetful.

sievert /*sē'vərt*/ *n* a derived SI unit, the unit of radiation dose equivalent (symbol **Sv**), equal to one joule per kilogram, subject to a quality and a weighting factor depending on the radiation and tissue involved. [RM *Sievert* (1896–1966), Swedish physicist]

sifaka /*si-fä'kə*/ *n* a lemur, typically long-tailed and black-and-white (genus *Propithecus*), native to Madagascar. [Malagasy]

siffle /*sif'l*/ *vi* to whistle, hiss. [Fr *siffler*, from L *sībilāre*]

■ **siffleur** /-*flær*/ and **siffleuse** /-*flæz*/ *n* respectively, a male or female professional whistler.

Sifrei see **Sefer**.

sift /*sift*/ *vt* to separate eg by passing through a sieve; to remove lumps from in this way; to sprinkle eg from a sieve; to examine closely and discriminatingly. ◆ *vi* to use a sieve; to pass through, or as if through, a sieve, to filter; (with *through*) to go through or investigate item by item. ◆ *n* a sifting. [OE *siftan*, from *sife* a sieve]
■ **sift'er** *n*. **sift'ing** *n* putting through a sieve; separating or sprinkling by a sieve; (in *pl*) material separated by a sieve and rejected. **sift'ing** *adj*. **sift'ingly** *adv*.

SIG *abbrev* : special interest group.

Sig. *abbrev* : signor; signore.

sig. *abbrev* : signature.

sigh /*sī*/ *vi* to produce a long, deep, audible respiration expressive of yearning, dejection, relief, etc; (of the wind, etc) to make a sound similar to this. ◆ *vt* to utter, express, etc with sighs. ◆ *n* an act of, or the sound made by, sighing. [Prob a back-formation from the weak pat of ME *siche*, from OE (strong) *sīcan*; Swed *sucka*]
■ **sigh'er** *n*. **sigh'ful** *adj*. **sigh'ing** *adj*. **sigh'ingly** *adv*.
■ **sigh for** to yearn for.

sight[1] /*sīt*/ *n* the faculty of seeing, vision; an opportunity or act of seeing; a view, glimpse; estimation, judgement; a beginning or coming to see; an instrumental observation, eg an astronomical altitude observation using sextant and chronometer to determine a ship's position when out of sight of land; visual range; anything that is seen; a spectacle; an object of especial interest; perusal; anything unsightly, odd or ridiculous in appearance; a visor (*Shakesp*); a guide to the eye on a gun or optical or other instrument; a sight-hole; skill, insight (*obs*); a great many or a great deal (*inf*). ◆ *vt* to catch sight of; to view; to take a sight of; to adjust the sights of (a gun, etc). ◆ *vi* to take a sight. [OE *sihth, gesiht*; Ger *Sicht*]
■ **sight'able** *adj*. **sight'ed** *adj* having sight, not blind; (of a gun, etc) equipped with a sight. ◆ *combining form* denoting sight of a particular kind, as in *long-sighted*. **sight'er** *n* a practice shot in archery, etc. **sight'ing** *n* an instance or the act of taking or catching sight. **sight'less** *adj* blind; invisible (*Shakesp*); unsightly (*Shakesp*). **sight'lessly** *adv*. **sight'lessness** *n*. **sight'liness** *n*. **sight'ly** *adj* pleasing to look at; comely. **sight'worthy** *adj* worth looking at.
□ **sight'-hole** *n* an aperture for looking through. **sight'line** *n* the line from the eye to the perceived object; (in *pl*) the view afforded, eg of the stage in a theatre or the screen in a cinema. **sight'-player, -reader, -singer** *n* someone who can read or perform music at first sight of the notes. **sight'-playing, -reading, -singing** *n*. **sight'-read** *vi* and *vt*. **sight'-sing** *vi* and *vt*. **sight screen** *n* (*cricket*) a large (*usu* white) screen placed on the boundary behind the bowler, providing a backdrop against which the batsman can more easily see the approaching ball. **sight'see** *vi* to go about visiting sights, buildings, etc of interest. **sight'seeing** *n*. **sight'seer** /-*sē-ər*/ *n*. **sights'man** *n* a local guide, cicerone.
■ **at first sight** when seen initially and without the benefit of a detailed study or investigation. **at** or **on sight** without previous view or study; as soon as seen; on presentation; (of a bill, draft, etc, payable) as soon as presented. **at so many days' sight** (of a bill, draft, etc, payable) so many days after it is presented. **catch sight of** to get a glimpse of, begin to see. **in sight** within view, visible; (also **within sight**; with *of*) in a position to see, or be seen from or by; close at hand, expected soon. **keep sight of** or **keep in sight** to keep within seeing distance of; to remain in touch with. **know by sight** to recognize or be familiar with by appearance. **lose sight of** to cease to see; to get out of touch with. **out of sight** (with *of*) not in a position to be seen (from or by) or to see; out of range of vision; not visible, hidden; beyond comparison, marvellous (*inf*). **put out of sight** to remove from view; to eat or drink up (*sl*). **raise** (or **lower**) **one's sights** to set oneself a more (or less) ambitious target. **set one's sights on** to aim for (eg a specified goal). **sight for sore eyes** a most welcome sight. **sight unseen** without having seen the object in question.

sight[2] /*sīt*/ an old *pat* of **sigh**.

sigil /*sij'il*/ *n* a seal, signet; a magical mark or sign. [L *sigillum*, dimin of *signum* sign]
■ **sigillā'rian** *n* and *adj*. **sigillā'rid** *n* (*geol*) any fossil lycopod tree of the genus *Sigillaria*, having parallel rows of seal-like leaf-scars and found chiefly in coal deposits. **sig'illary** /-*ə-ri*/ *adj* relating to a seal. **sig'illate** *adj* sealed; with seal-like impressions. **sigillā'tion** *n*.

sigisbeo /*sē-jēs-bā'ō* or *si-jis-*/ *n* (*pl* **sigisbe'i** /-*ē*/) same as **cicisbeo**. [Ital]

sigla /*sig'lə*/ *n pl* abbreviations, symbols and signs, as used in manuscripts, seals, etc. [L, *pl* of *siglum*, dimin of *signum* sign]

sigma /*sig'mə*/ *n* the eighteenth letter (Σ, early form C; σ, or when final, ç) of the Greek alphabet, corresponding to S; as a numeral

σ' = 200, ‚σ = 200000; the symbol Σ, used in mathematical notation to indicate summation of the numbers or quantities given. [Gr *sīgma*]
■ **sig'mate** /-*māt*/ *adj* shaped like Σ, C, or S. ◆ *vt* to add σ or ç to. **sigmatic** /-*mat'ik*/ *adj* characterized by σ. **sigmā'tion** /-*shən*/ *n* the adding of σ or ç at the end of a syllable. **sig'matism** *n* repetition of the *s*-sound. **sig'matron** *n* a machine consisting of two accelerators (cyclotron and betatron; see under **accelerate**), for the generation of very high-energy X-rays. **sig'moid** or **sigmoid'al** *adj* C-shaped; S-shaped. **sigmoid'ally** *adv*. **sigmoidec'tomy** *n* (*surg*) removal of the sigmoid colon. **sigmoid'oscope** *n* an instrument inserted through the anus and used for examining the interior of the rectum and sigmoid colon. **sigmoidoscopic** /-*skop'ik*/ *adj*. **sigmoidos'copy** *n*.
□ **sigma particles** *n pl* (*phys*) three hyperons of medium mass, having respectively positive, neutral and negative charge. **sigmoid flexure** *n* (*zool*, etc) a C-shaped or S-shaped bend; (also **sigmoid colon**) the S-shaped terminal part of the descending colon that leads to the rectum.

sign /*sīn*/ *n* a gesture expressing a meaning; a signal; a mark with a meaning; a symbol; an emblem; a token; a portent; a miraculous token; an ensign, banner (in *pl* insignia; *archaic*); an indication of positive or negative value, or that indicated; a device marking an inn, etc (formerly also a house) instead of a street number; a board or panel giving a shopkeeper's name or trade, displaying information for public view, etc; an effigy (*obs*); a mere semblance (*obs*); an indication; an outward or objective indication of a disorder or disease, perceptible to an examining doctor (cf **symptom**); a trail or track of a wild animal, perceptible to a tracker; a trace; a twelfth part (30°) of the zodiac, bearing the name of, but not now coincident with, a constellation. ◆ *vt* to indicate, convey, communicate, direct or mark by a sign or signs; to mark; to attach a signature to; to write as a signature; to designate by signature; to engage by signature; to betoken (*archaic*); to cross, make the sign of the cross over; to make the sign of. ◆ *vi* to make a sign; to sign one's name; to enter into employment by the signing of a contract; to use sign language; to bode, promise (*obs*). [Fr *signe*, from L *signum*]
■ **sign'age** *n* another term for **signing** below; the arrangement or design of a sign or signs; signs collectively. **signary** /*sig'nə-ri*/ *n* a system of symbols, as an alphabet or syllabary. **sign'er** *n*. **sign'ing** *n* the use of sign language (*esp* by the deaf) as a means of communication; an act or instance of this. **sign'less** *adj*.
□ **sign'board** *n* a board bearing a notice or serving as a shop or inn sign. **sign language** *n* a means of communication using finger and hand movements, used eg by deaf people. **sign-man'ual** *n* a signature, *esp* a king's. **sign of the cross** *n* a gesture of tracing the form of a cross as an invocation of God's grace. **sign'-painter** *n* a person who paints signs for shops, etc. **sign'post** *n* a post for an inn sign; a fingerpost or post supporting road signs; an indication, clue. ◆ *vt* to provide with a signpost or signposts; to point out as a signpost does, clearly and conspicuously. **sign'-writer** *n* an expert in lettering for shop signs, etc. **sign'-writing** *n*.
■ **sign away** or **over** to transfer or relinquish by signing. **sign in** or **out** to sign one's name on coming in or going out. **sign off** to record departure from work; to stop work, etc; to discharge from employment; (of a doctor) to state that someone is entitled to be absent from work due to illness; to announce the end of broadcasting or a broadcast; to make a bid that is intended to be the final bid in the auction (*bridge*); to remove oneself from the register of unemployed people; (often with *on*) to give final assent to (a document or a course of action). **sign on** to engage (*vt* or *vi*) for a job, etc, by signature (also **sign up**); to record arrival at work; to register for Jobseeker's Allowance. **sign on the dotted line** to give one's consent, thereby binding oneself, to a proposed scheme, contract, etc; to do this docilely or without proper investigation. **sign out** see **sign in** above. **sign up** to enlist in the armed forces; see also **sign on** above.

signal /*sig'nl*/ *n* a token; an intimation, eg of warning, conveyed over a distance; a transmitted effect conveying information; the apparatus used for the purpose; a piece of play intended to give information to one's partner (*cards*); an intimation of, or event taken as marking, the moment for action; an initial impulse. ◆ *vt* (**sig'nalling** or (*US*) **sig'naling** or **sig'nalled** or (*US*) **sig'naled**) to intimate, convey, or direct by signals; to signalize. ◆ *vi* to make signals. ◆ *adj* remarkable; notable. [Fr *signal*, from L *signum*]
■ **sig'nalize** or **-ise** *vt* to mark or distinguish signally. **sig'naller** or (*US*) **sig'naler** *n*. **sig'nalling** or (*US*) **sig'naling** *n*. **sig'nally** *adv* notably.
□ **signal box** *n* a railway signalman's cabin or an automatic or semi-automatic control point for the signals for all railway lines in a section. **signal letters** *n pl* (*naut*) four letters by which an individual ship may be identified. **sig'nalman** *n* a person who transmits signals; a person who operates railway signals. **signal peptide** *n* a short N-terminal peptide sequence involved in the passage of a protein across a membrane (also **signal sequence**). **signal-to-noise ratio** *n*

(*acoustics*) the relationship, *usu* expressed in decibels, between the wanted signal and the unwanted background noise.

signary see under **sign**.

signatory see under **signature**.

signature /sig'nə-chər or -ni-/ n a signing; a signed name; a distinctive mark or stamp; an indication of key, also of time, at the beginning of a line of music, or where a change occurs; the part of a medical prescription indicating how often the medication should be taken and in what quantities (*US*); a letter or numeral at the foot of a page to indicate sequence of sheets; a sheet so marked; the pages formed by such a sheet when folded and cut; in a plant, a distinctive feature of shape or marking once believed (according to the **doctrine of signatures**) to be a symbolic indication of its (*esp* medicinal) properties, a kidney-shaped leaf, for instance, indicating the plant's capacity to cure kidney disease; a signature tune; the indication of the presence of eg an aeroplane on a radar screen or a submarine on a sonar screen. ◆ *adj* distinctive or characteristic of a particular individual or organization. [LL *signātūra*, from L *signāre*, *-ātum* to sign] ■ **sig'natory** n a person who has signed a document, agreement, treaty, etc (also *adj*). ▫ **signature tune** n a tune used to introduce, and hence associated with, a particular radio or television programme, group of performers, etc.

signet /sig'nit/ n a small seal; the impression of such a seal; a signet ring; one of the royal seals for authenticating grants (for **Writer to the Signet** see under **write**). ◆ *vt* to stamp or authenticate with a signet. [From Med L *signētum* a small seal, from *signum*] ■ **sig'neted** *adj*. ▫ **signet ring** n a ring with a signet.

signeur a Shakespearean spelling of **senior**. ■ **sign'eurie** n (*Shakesp*) seniority. **sign'ieur** n (*Shakesp*) seigneur.

signify /sig'ni-fī/ *vt* (**sig'nifying**; **sig'nified**) to be a sign for; to mean; to denote, betoken; to indicate or declare. ◆ *vi* to be of consequence. [L *significāre*, *-ātum*, from *signum* a sign, and *facere* to make] ■ **sig'nifiable** *adj*. **signif'icance** /-i-kəns/ n meaning; import; the quality of being significant (also **signif'icancy**); a value of probability at which a particular hypothesis is held to be contradicted by the results of a statistical test (*stats*). **signif'icant** *adj* having a meaning; full of meaning; important, worthy of consideration; indicative; having statistical significance. ◆ n that which carries a meaning; a sign. **signif'icantly** *adv*. **signif'icate** n a thing signified. **significa'tion** n meaning; that which is signified; importance. **signif'icative** /-kə-tiv/ *adj* indicative; significant. **signif'icatively** *adv*. **signif'icator** n (*astrol*) a planet ruling a house. **signif'icatory** /-kə-tər-i/ *adj*. **signif'ics** n *sing* the science of meaning. **sig'nifīer** n. ▫ **significance test** n (*stats*) a test which is used to demonstrate the probability that observed patterns cannot be explained by chance. **significant figures** or (*esp N Am*) **significant digits** n pl (*maths*) the figures 1 to 9, or zeroes occurring medially, used to express a magnitude (eg the numbers 3.15, 0.0127 and 1.01 are each expressed to three significant figures). **significant other** n a person's sexual partner. ■ **most** (or **least**) **significant bit** (*comput*) the bit with the greatest (or lowest) place value in a computer data word.

Signor, Signior /sē'nyör/ or **Signore** /sē-nyō'rā or -nyö'/ n an Italian title or form of address equivalent to *Mr* or *Sir*; (without *cap*; *pl* **sig'nors** or **signo'ri**) a gentleman. [Ital *signor*, *signore*] ■ **Signora** /sē-nyō'rə or -nyö'/ n feminine of *Signor*, Mrs, madam; (without *cap*; *pl* **signo're**) a lady. **signoria** /-rē'ä/ n (*hist*) a seignory, the governing body of an Italian city state. **Signorina** /sē-nyə-rē'nə or -nyö'/ n Miss; (without *cap*; *pl* **signori'ne** /-nā/) an unmarried lady, a young lady. **Signorino** /sē-nyə-rē'no/ n Master; (without *cap*; *pl* **signori'ni**) a young man, a young gentleman. **si'gnory** n seignory; a signoria. ■ **Grand Signior** see under **seignior**.

signorial see under **seignior**.

sijo /sē'jō/ n a Korean verse form of three lines each of four groups of syllables, *orig* sung with musical accompaniment. [Korean, literally, melody of the times]

sika /sē'kə/ n a deer, *Cervus nippon* (of the subfamily Cervidae), of Japan and E Asia, similar to the fallow deer in size and with a spotted coat in summer. [Jap *shika*]

sike¹ or **syke** /sīk/ (*Scot*) n a rill or small ditch. [Scot and N Eng, from OE *sīc*]

sike² Spenserian spelling of **sic²**.

Sikel /sik'əl/ n and adj Sicilian (also **Sic'el**). [Gr *Sikelos*, *Sikeliōtēs*] ■ **Sikelian** or **Sicelian** /-el'/ *adj*. **Sikel'iot** or **Sicel'iot** n an ancient Greek colonist in Sicily.

Sikh /sēk/ n an adherent of a monotheistic religion established in the 15c by former Hindus who rejected the authority of the Vedas. ◆ *adj* of or relating to the Sikhs. [Hindi, disciple] ■ **Sikh'ism** n.

sikorsky /si-kör'ski/ (also with *cap*) n any of various helicopters that are versions of the first successful helicopter that flew in 1939, designed by Igor *Sikorsky* (1889–1972), Russian-born US aeronautical engineer.

silage /sī'lij/ n any green crop (such as grass or clover) harvested, compressed, fermented and stored for use as animal fodder, ensilage. ◆ *vt* (*prp* **si'laging** or **si'lageing**) to harvest and store (a green crop) in this way. [**ensilage**, after **silo**]

silane /sil'ān/ n a gas, silicon hydride, SiH₄, used in the production of semiconductors; also applied to a group of silicon hydrides *incl* disilane and trisilane. [From **silica** and chem *sfx* -*ane*]

Silastic® /si-las'tik/ (also without *cap*) n a flexible silicone rubber, used in the manufacture of artificial limbs, etc.

sild /sild/ n a young herring. [Norw]

sildenafil /sil-den'ə-fil/ n any of several compounds, *esp* **sildenafil citrate**, that increase blood flow to the penis, used in treating male impotence.

sile or **seil** /sīl/ (*dialect*) *vt* to strain. ◆ *vi* to rain heavily. ◆ n a strainer (also **sī'ler**). [Scand; cf Swed and Norw *sila* to pass through a strainer]

silen see **silenus**.

silence /sī'ləns/ n absence of sound, stillness; omission of, or abstention from, sounding, speech, mention, or communication; a time of such absence or abstention; a state of not, or no longer, being spoken about; taciturnity; the state of being forgotten, oblivion; secrecy; (of distilled spirits) flavourlessness, odourlessness. ◆ *vt* to cause to be silent. ◆ *interj* be silent. [L *silēre* to be silent] ■ **si'lenced** *adj* brought to silence; (of a priest) forbidden to preach. **si'lencer** n a person who or a thing that silences; a device for reducing the sound of escaping gases by gradual expansion, used, eg for small arms and internal combustion engines. **si'lent** *adj* noiseless; without sound; unaccompanied by sound; refraining from speech, mention, or divulging; taciturn; not pronounced; (of distilled spirit) without flavour or odour; inoperative; (of the new moon) not yet visible (*Milton*). ◆ n a time of silence (*archaic*); a silent film. **si'lently** *adv*. **si'lentness** n. ▫ **silent call** n an instance of answering a ringing telephone only to find that no-one is there, often because the number has been dialled automatically in a telemarketing exercise. **silent film** n a cinema film which has no accompanying synchronized soundtrack. **silent majority** n those, in any country the bulk of the population, who are assumed to have sensible, moderate opinions though they do not trouble to express them publicly. **silent partner** n a sleeping partner (*qv*).

silene /sī-lē'ni/ n a flowering plant of the genus *Silene* (family Caryophyllaceae), *incl* the campions, catchfly and many cultivated species. [Mod L, prob from L *Sīlēnus*; see **silenus**]

silent, etc see under **silence**.

silentiary /sī-len'shi-ə-ri/ n an official who calls for silence, *esp* (*hist*) an official of the Byzantine court; someone who observes or recommends silence. [From L *silentiarius* a confidential servant, privy councillor]

silentium altum same as **altum silentium**.

silenus /sī-lē'nəs/ n (also **si'len** /-lin/) a woodland god or elderly satyr (*pl* **sile'ni** /-nī/); (with *cap*) the chief of the satyrs, foster-father of Bacchus, represented as a pot-bellied, bald, snub-nosed old man; (with *cap*) the lion-tailed macaque genus. [L *Sīlēnus*, from Gr *Seilēnos*]

silesia /sī-lē'zi-ə, -zhə, or -shə/ n a thin, twilled cotton or linen used for lining clothes, etc, *orig* made in *Silesia* (now part of Poland).

silex /sī'leks/ n silica or quartz; a heat-resistant and shock-resistant glass formed of fused quartz. [L *silex*, *silicis* flint]

silhouette /si-lū-et' or -lū-/ n a pictorial representation of an object or *esp* a person, in profile, consisting of an outline filled in with black; an image of anything against a lighter background in which only the outline is seen in detail; an outline. ◆ *vt* to represent or show in silhouette. [Étienne de *Silhouette* (1709–67), French minister of finance in 1759; reason disputed]

silica /sil'i-kə/ n silicon dioxide or silicic anhydride, occurring in nature as quartz, chalcedony, etc, and (amorphous and hydrated) as opal. ◆ *adj* composed of silica. [L *silex*, *silicis* flint] ■ **sil'icate** n one of the largest group of minerals, all of which are composed of silicon, oxygen and one or more metals, with or without hydrogen; any salt of silicic acid or derived from silicon. ◆ *vt* to combine, coat, or impregnate with silica or silicates. **siliceous** or **silicious** /-ish'əs/ *adj* of or containing silica. **silicic** /-is'ik/ *adj* relating to, or obtained from, silica (**silicic acid** a general name for a group of acids, eg **orthosilic'ic**, H₄SiO₄; **metasilic'ic**, H₂SiO₃). **silicicolous** /-sik'/ adj (L colere to cultivate, inhabit) growing on siliceous soil. **sil'icide** /-sīd/ n a compound of silicon and another element. **silicif'erous** adj containing silica. **silicification** /si-lis-i-fi-kā'shən/ n. **silicified** /-lis'-/ adj. **silic'ify** vt to render siliceous; to impregnate or cement with or replace by silica. ◆ vi to become siliceous. **sil'icon** /-kon or -kən/ n a non-metallic element (symbol **Si**; atomic no 14), forming grey crystals or brown amorphous powder and having semiconducting properties (formerly called **silicium** /-lis'- or -lish'/). **sil'icone** n any of a number of extremely stable organic derivatives of silicon, used in rubbers, lubricants, polishes, etc. **silicosis** /-kō'sis/ n a lung disease caused by the prolonged inhalation of silica dust. **silicot'ic** n and adj.

❑ **silica gel** n an absorbent form of silica used as a drying agent, and as a catalyst in many chemical processes. **silicon carbide** n a hard, crystalline compound, widely used as an abrasive and in cutting, grinding and polishing instruments. **silicon chip** see under **chip**. **silicon valley** n a district or area in which there is a concentration of information technology industries (from the orig Silicon Valley in California).

silicle, **silicula**, etc see under **siliqua**.

siliqua /sil'i-kwə/ or **silique** /si-lēk'/ (bot) n a type of dry fruit consisting of a long, somewhat cylindrical pod of two carpels divided by a partition, which splits to allow the seeds to escape, characteristic of cruciferous plants. [L siliqua pod, dimin silicula]

■ **silicula** /-ik'ū-lə/ n a dry fruit consisting of a short, broad pod of similar structure to a siliqua (also **sil'icle** or **sil'icule**). **silic'ulose** adj. **sil'iquose** adj.

silk /silk/ n a fibre produced by the larva of a silkworm moth, mainly of fibroin coated with sericin, formed by the hardening of a liquid emitted from spinning-glands; a similar fibre from another insect or a spider; an imitation (**artificial silk**) made by forcing a viscous solution of modified cellulose through small holes; a thread, cloth, garment, or clothing made from such fibres; the silk gown, or the rank, of a Queen's (or King's) Counsel; hence, a QC or KC (inf); the styles of maize; silky lustre in the ruby, etc. ◆ adj of or relating to silk; silky (Shakesp). ◆ vt to cover or clothe with silk. [OE seolc, from L sēricum; see **seric**]

■ **silk'en** adj of, like or clad in silk; glossy; soft and smooth; ingratiating; luxurious. ◆ vt to make silken. **silk'ily** adv. **silk'iness** n. **silk'-like** adj. **silk'y** adj.

❑ **silk cotton** n the silky seed-covering of Eriodendron anfractuosum and other trees of the family Bombacaceae. **silk gland** n a gland (at a silkworm's mouth, on a spider's abdomen) from which silk is spun. **silk'-grass** n a name for various plants with fibrous leaves, eg Karatus (Bromeliaceae), Yucca, Agave. **silk'grower** n a breeder of silkworms for silk. **silk hat** n a top hat. **silk'-man** n (Shakesp) a dealer in silks. **silk'screen** n a print produced by the **silkscreen process** (or **silkscreen printing**), a printmaking process in which silk (or now more usually a synthetic fibre) is stretched and attached to a frame with stencils attached to the underside of the fabric mesh, colour then being forced through the upper side of the mesh, using a rubber squeegee, onto those areas of the print not blocked out by the stencil. **silk'tail** n the waxwing. **silk'-thrower** or **-throwster** n a person who makes raw silk into thread. **silk'weed** n same as **milkweed** (see under **milk**). **silk'worm** n any of various moths (esp Bombyx mori) whose larvae produce silk; opprobriously, a wearer of silk (obs); someone who haunts drapers' shops without buying (obs). **silk'worm-gut** n the drawn-out glands of the silkworm. **silky oak** n any of several Australian trees of the genus Grevillea, yielding smooth timber.

■ **take silk** to become a Queen's (or King's) Counsel.

silkie or **silky** /sil'ki/, also **selkie** /sel'/ (Scot) n in folklore, a creature that appears as a seal in the water, but assumes human form on land; a seal. [Old Scottish selich, OE seolh seal]

sill /sil/ n (also **cill**) a horizontal length of timber, stone, etc at the foot of an opening, eg for a door, window, embrasure, port, dock-entrance, etc; the bottom of a title-page, a plough, a ledge; a bed of rock (mining); a sheet of intrusive rock more or less parallel to the bedding (geol). [OE syll; ON syll; Ger Schwelle]

sillabub same as **syllabub**.

silladar /sil'ə-där/ n an irregular cavalryman. [Urdu and Pers silāhdār]

siller /sil'ər/ n a Scots form of silver, usu used in the sense of money (also adj).

Sillery /sil'ə-ri/ n champagne from Sillery, near Rheims.

sillimanite /sil'i-mə-nīt/ n a mineral, Al₂SiO₅, aluminium silicate in the form of orthorhombic crystals, occurring in argillaceous metamorphic rocks (see also **fibrolite** under **fibre**). [Benjamin Silliman (1779–1864), US scientist]

sillock /sil'ək/ (N Scot) n a young coalfish. [Cf ON silungr a small salmon]

silly /sil'i/ adj foolish, stupid; lacking in good sense; feeble-minded; not well-thought-out; frivolous; nonsensical, absurd; dazed, stunned (eg from a blow); harmless (said of eg sheep); defenceless (archaic); simple, humble (obs); pitiable, feeble (obs); (of a fielding position) very near the batsman (cricket). ◆ n a silly person. [OE sælig; see **seely**]

■ **sill'ily** adv. **sill'iness** n.

❑ **silly-bill'y** n (inf) a foolish person. **sill'y-how** n (OE hūfe headdress; archaic and Scot) a (child's) caul. **silly money** n (inf) absurdly or unthinkably large quantities of cash. **silly season** n a time of year, usu late summer, when newspapers print trivial matter for lack of more newsworthy material. **Silly String**® n a substance that sets quickly into long, coloured threads when expelled from a pressurized container, used as a children's toy or a party entertainment.

silo /sī'lō/ n (pl **si'los**) a pit or airtight chamber for storing grain, or for ensilage, or for storing other loose materials; a storage tower above ground, typically tall and cylindrical; an underground chamber housing a guided missile ready to be fired. ◆ vt (pap **si'lo'd** or **si'loed**) to put or keep in a silo. [Sp from L sīrus, from Gr siros, sīros, seiros a pit]

siloxane /si-lok'sān/ n any of various polymers containing silicon and oxygen, with a wide range of industrial applications. [sil icon, oxygen and methane]

silphium /sil'fi-əm/ n (pl **sil'phia** or **sil'phiums**) a plant (perh the umbelliferous Ferula tingitana) imported from Cyrenaica by the Greeks for use as a food and in medicine (hist); (cap) a genus of American composites, compass plants. [L, from Gr silphion]

silt /silt/ n fine sediment deposited by a body of water. ◆ vt to choke, block, cover, etc with silt (with up). ◆ vi to become silted up. [ME sylt; cf Dan and Norw sylt salt marsh]

■ **silta'tion** n. **silt'y** adj.

❑ **silt'stone** n rock formed of hardened silt.

Silurian /sī- or si-loo'ri-ən or -lū'/ adj of the Silures, an ancient British tribe, or the district around the Welsh/English border which they inhabited; of or belonging to a period of the Palaeozoic era, between 440 and 415 million years ago (geol). ◆ n a member of the Silures; the Silurian period.

■ **sil'urist** n (also with cap) a Silurian, a name adopted by the poet Henry Vaughan (1621 or 1622–95).

silurid /si-loo'rid or -lū'/ n any freshwater fish of the family **Silū'ridae**, including the European catfish, wels or sheatfish, Siluris glanis, having an elongated, slimy, scaleless body and a long anal fin (also adj). [L silūrus, from Gr silouros]

■ **silu'roid** adj and n.

silva or **sylva** /sil'və/ n (pl **sil'vas**, **syl'vas**, **sil'vae** or **syl'vae** /-vē/) the assemblage of trees in a region. [L silva (sometimes sylva) a wood]

■ **silvan** adj and n see **sylvan**.

silver /sil'vər/ n a whitish-grey element (symbol **Ag**; atomic no 47), one of the precious metals; a whitish-grey colour; silver money; silverware; cutlery, sometimes even when not of silver; a silver medal. ◆ adj of or like silver; silver-coloured; belonging or relating to elderly people (inf); clear and ringing in tone. ◆ vt to cover with silver; to make silvery. ◆ vi to become silvery. [OE silfer, seolfor; ON silfr, Ger Silber]

■ **sil'veriness** n. **sil'vering** n coating with, or of, silver or quicksilver. **sil'verize** or **-ise** vt to coat or treat with silver. **sil'verling** n (Bible) a small silver coin. **sil'verly** adv with the appearance or sound of silver. **sil'vern** adj (poetic) made of silver; silvery. **sil'very** adj like silver; silver-coloured; light in tone; having a clear ringing sound.

❑ **Silver Age** n the reign of Zeus, second of the ages of the world, following and less innocent than the Golden Age of Kronos (classical myth); in Latin literature, the time of Martial, Tacitus and Juvenal. **sil'verback** n an older male gorilla with grey hair on its back and flanks. **sil'ver-bath** n (photog) a solution of a silver salt, or a vessel for it, for sensitizing plates. **sil'ver-beater** n a person who beats silver into foil. **silver bell** n any of various deciduous trees or shrubs of the genus Halesia, native to N America and China, having bell-shaped silvery-white flowers (also called **snowdrop tree**). **sil'verbill** n the name of three species of the genus Lonchura of weaver-finches, with a silvery sheen to their bills. **silver birch** n a species of birch, Betula pendula, with silvery-white peeling bark. **silver bullet** n a bullet made of silver, supposedly the only variety fatal to a werewolf; any wonderful solution to a difficult problem. **sil'vereye** n an Australasian songbird with a white ring around the eyes. **silver fern** n another name for the ponga. **silver fir** n a European fir, Abies alba, with shiny needles, green on top and silvery beneath, an important timber tree; a small Japanese fir, Abies veitchii, with notched needles banded with silver underneath. **sil'verfish** n any wingless primitive insect of the genus Lepisma (order Thysanura), eg L. saccharina, which feeds on starch in wallpaper, bookbindings, etc; a silvery-white goldfish, or other silvery fish. **silver foil** n silver leaf. **silver fox** n an American red fox in a colour phase in which the fur is black with white tips; this fur. **silver gate** see **ivory gate** under **gate**¹. **silver-gilt'** n gilded silver (also adj). **sil'ver-glance** n native sulphide of silver. **sil'ver-grain** n medullary rays in longitudinal section. **silver iodide** n a yellow powder that darkens when exposed to light, is used in photography, is scattered on clouds to cause rainfall, and has various medical uses. **silver jubilee** n a twenty-fifth anniversary. **Silver Latin** n that written by authors of the Silver Age. **silver leaf** n silver beaten into thin leaves; a disease of plum trees. **silver lining** n a redeeming aspect of an otherwise unpleasant or unfortunate situation. **silver medal** n (in athletics competitions, etc) the medal awarded as second prize. **sil'ver-mount'ed** adj. **silver nitrate** n a poisonous colourless crystalline salt that turns grey or black in the presence of light or organic matter, and has uses in photography, as an antiseptic, etc. **silver paper** n silver foil; (usu) tinfoil (sometimes with a backing of greaseproof paper); fine white tissue paper. **silver pheasant** n a white-tailed E Asian pheasant, introduced to Europe, etc. **silver plate** n utensils, esp tableware, made of silver; electroplate. **silver-plā'ted** adj. **sil'verpoint** n the process or product of drawing with a silver-tipped pencil. **silver salmon** n the coho. **silver screen** n the cinema screen; (with the) the film industry (inf). **silver service** n a method of serving food in restaurants, etc, in which the waiter or waitress uses a spoon and fork held in one hand to transfer food from the serving dish to the diners' plates. **sil'verside** n a cut of beef taken from the rump, below the aitchbone. **sil'versides** n sing any small fish of the family Atherinidae, eg Atherina presbyter, the sand smelt. **sil'verskin** n the fine skin of a coffee bean. **sil'versmith** n a worker in silver. **sil'versmithing** n. **silver steel** n a type of carbon steel containing silicon, manganese and chromium, and low in phosphorus and sulphur. **sil'ver-stick** n a palace officer, from his silvered wand. **silver surfer** n (inf) an older person who enjoys using the Internet. **silver'tail** n (obs Aust inf) a wealthy socialite; a social climber. **silver thaw** n (Can) ice formed by rain freezing rapidly as it hits the ground or other surface. **sil'ver-tongued** adj plausible, eloquent. **silver tree** n a silvery-leaved S African proteaceous tree (Leucadendron argenteum). **sil'ver-voiced** adj. **sil'verware** n items, esp tableware or sporting trophies, made from or coated with silver. **silver wedding** n the twenty-fifth wedding anniversary. **sil'verweed** n a creeping plant (Potentilla anserina) with silvery leaves and yellow flowers whose starchy roots were used as food from prehistoric times. **silver white** see **China white** under **white. sil'ver-white** adj of a lustrous greyish-white colour. **silver Y** n a noctuid moth (Autographa gamma) with Y-shaped markings on the forewings.

■ **born with a silver spoon in one's mouth** born to affluence. **tree of silver** see under **tree**.

silvestrian, **silviculture**, etc see under **sylvan**.

sim¹ /sim/ n a contraction of **simulation**.
□ **sim game** n a computer game that attempts to replicate the sort of events encountered in the real world.

sim² see **Simeonite**.

sima /sī'mə/ n the part of the earth's crust underlying the sial. [From silicon and magnesium]

simar, **simarre** /si-mär'/ same as **cymar**.

simaruba or **simarouba** /sim-ə-roo'bə/ n any tropical American tree of the Simaruba genus, esp Simaruba amara of Brazil, Guyana, etc; the bark of Simaruba amara that has therapeutic qualities. [Carib name]
■ **simaruba'ceous** or **simarouba'ceous** adj of, belonging or relating to the Simarubaceae, a family of tropical trees related to the Rutaceae.

simazine /sim'ə-zēn/ (also with cap) n an organic herbicide used as a general weedkiller.

SIM card /sim kärd/ n a removable electronic card inside a mobile phone that stores information about the subscriber. [Subscriber Identification Module]

Simeonite /sim'i-ə-nīt/ n (often shortened to **sim**) a follower of Charles Simeon (1759–1836); a Low-Churchman or evangelical.

simi /sim'i/ n (in E Africa) a short two-edged sword or large knife. [Swahili sime]

simian /sim'i-ən/ adj of the apes; ape-like. ◆ n an ape. [L sīmia ape]
■ **sim'ial** or **sim'ious** adj (rare).

similar /sim'i-lər/ adj (with to) like; resembling; exactly corresponding in shape, without regard to size (geom). [Fr similaire, from L similis like]
■ **similarity** /-lar'i-ti/ n. **sim'ilarly** adv.

simile /sim'i-li/ (rhetoric) n (pl **sim'iles**) a figure of speech in which a person or thing is described by being explicitly likened to another, usu preceded by as or like; the use of such figures of speech. [L neuter of similis like]
■ **sim'ilative** adj expressing similarity. **simil'itude** n likeness; semblance; comparison; parable. **sim'ilize** or **-ise** vt to liken. ◆ vi to use simile.

simillimum /si-mil'i-mum/ n (in homeopathy) a remedy chosen because it would produce in a healthy person the same symptoms as those exhibited by the patient. [L, neuter superl of similis like]

similor /sim'i-lör/ n a yellow alloy used for cheap jewellery. [Fr, from L similis like, and aurum gold]

simious see under **simian**.

simitar same as **scimitar**.

simkin or **simpkin** /sim'kin/ (Anglo-Ind) n an Urdu corruption of **champagne**.

SIMM (comput) abbrev : single in-line memory module.

Simmental /zim'ən-täl/ n a breed of cattle, orig native to Switzerland, used in many parts of Europe for meat and milk (also **Simm'enthal** or **Simm'enthaler** /-tä-lər/). [From the Simmental or Simme valley]

simmer /sim'ər/ vi and vt to boil gently. ◆ vi to be close to an outburst of emotion, esp anger. ◆ n a simmering state. [Earlier simper ; origin unknown]
■ **simmer down** to calm down.

'simmon /sim'ən/ n short for **persimmon**.

simnel /sim'nl/ n a sweet fruitcake, usu covered with marzipan and traditionally eaten at Easter, or sometimes Christmas or Mothering Sunday (also **simnel bread** or **cake**). [OFr simenel, from L siminellus fine bread, from simila fine flour]

Simon Pure /sī'mən pūr'/ n the real person (or thing). [From a character in Susannah Centlivre's comedy, A Bold Stroke for a Wife (1717)]
■ **sī'mon-pure** adj real, genuine.

simony /sī'mə-ni or sim'ə-ni/ n the buying or selling of an ecclesiastical benefice. [Simon Magus (from the Bible: Acts 8)]
■ **simō'niac** n and adj (a person) guilty of simony. **simonī'acal** adj. **simonī'acally** adv. **simō'nious** adj (obs). **si'monist** n a person who practises or defends simony.

simoom /si-moom'/ or **simoon** /-moon'/ n a hot suffocating desert wind in Arabia and N Africa. [Ar samūm, from samm to poison]

simorg same as **simurg**.

simp see **simpleton** under **simple**.

simpai /sim'pī/ n the black-crested langur of Sumatra. [Malay]

simpatico /sim-pat'i-kō/ (inf) adj sympathetic in the sense of congenial. [Ital and Sp]

simper /sim'pər/ vi to smile in a silly, weak or affected manner. ◆ vt to express by simpering. ◆ n a silly or affected smile, or one displaying or suggestive of weakness. [Cf Norw semper smart]
■ **simp'erer** n. **sim'pering** adj. **sim'peringly** adv.

simpkin see **simkin**.

simple /sim'pl/ adj consisting of one thing or element; not complex or compound; in or relating to simple time (music); not divided into leaflets (bot); easy; plain; unornate; unpretentious; mean, sorry; mere, sheer; ordinary; unlearned or unskilled; of humble rank or origin; unaffected; artless; guileless; unsuspecting; credulous; weak in intellect; silly. ◆ n (archaic) a simple or humble person (also used collectively) or thing; a simpleton; an irreducible component of a compound; a medicine having only one constituent; hence a medicinal plant. ◆ vi (archaic) to gather medicinal plants. [Fr simple, and L simplus, simplex]
■ **sim'pleness** n. **sim'pler** n (archaic) a gatherer of medicinal plants. **sim'plesse** n (Spenser) simplicity. **sim'pleton** n a weak or foolish person, one easily imposed on (inf short form **simp**, esp N Am). **simplicity** /-plis'-/ n. **simplifica'tion** n the process, or an instance, of making simple or simpler. **sim'plificātor** adj. **sim'plificātor** and **sim'plifier** n. **sim'plify** vt to make simple, simpler, or less difficult. **sim'pling** n (archaic) the act or process of gathering medicinal herbs. **sim'plism** n affected simplicity; oversimplification of a problem or situation. **sim'plist** n (archaic) a person having an expert knowledge of simples or medicinal herbs. **simplis'tic** adj tending to oversimplify, making no allowances for the problems and complexities that exist or inevitably arise; naïve. **simplis'tically** adv. **sim'ply** adv in a simple manner; considered by itself; alone; merely; without qualification; truly; absolutely; really (inf).
□ **simple fraction** n a fraction that has whole numbers as numerator and denominator. **simple fracture** see **fracture**. **simple harmonic motion** n (phys) the motion of a particle or system subjected to a force which is proportional to the displacement of the particle or system from a fixed point and is directed towards that point (abbrev **SHM**). **simple-heart'ed** adj (archaic) guileless; frank, sincere. **simple interest** n interest calculated on the principal only. **simple-mind'ed** adj lacking intelligence; foolish. **simple-mind'edly** adv. **simple-mind'edness** n. **simple sentence** n a sentence with one predicate. **simple time** n (music) any measure or time in which there are two, three or four beats to the bar, each divisible by two (see also **compound time** under **compound¹**).

simplex /*sim'pleks*/ *n* (pl **sim'plices** /*-pli-sēz*/) a figure with the minimum number of vertices for space of a particular number of dimensions (eg a triangle in 2-dimensional space) (*geom*); a simple word, as opposed to a compound word (*linguistics*). ◆ *adj* simple, single; allowing transmission and reception in one direction only (*comput* and *telecom*). [L]

simpliciter /*sim-plis'i-tər, -plik'i-ter*/ (*L*) *adv* simply, not relatively; naturally, unconditionally.

simplicity, **simplify**, etc see under **simple**.

simpliste /*sĕ-plēst'*, *sim-plēst'* or *sim'plist*/ *adj* simplistic, naïve. [Fr]

simul /*sim'əl*/ (*chess*) *n* and *adj* a short form of **simultaneous**.

simulacrum /*sim-ū-lā'krəm*/ *n* (pl **simula'cra** or **simula'crums**) an image (also **simulacre** /*-lā'kər*/); a semblance, superficial likeness. [L *simulācrum*]

simulate /*sim'ū-lāt*/ *vt* to feign; to have or assume a false appearance of; to mimic; to recreate the conditions of, for the purposes of training or experimentation. ◆ *adj* feigned. [L *simulāre, -ātum*; cf **similar**, **simultaneous**] ■ **sim'ulant** *adj* simulating; mimicking (*biol*). ◆ *n* a simulator. **sim'ular** *adj* counterfeit; feigned. ◆ *n* (*archaic*) a person or thing that simulates. **sim'ulated** *adj* (of a material, eg fur, leather, wood) not of such a material but made (*usu* in an inferior material) to look like it; not genuine, feigned. **simula'tion** *n* feigning; mimicry; the re-creation of a situation, environment, etc with working replicas or by computers for the purpose of demonstration or for analysis of problems. **sim'ulative** *adj*. **sim'ulātor** *n* someone who or something that simulates; a device used for simulating required conditions, etc, eg for training purposes. **sim'ulatory** *adj*. ❑ **simulated pearl** *n* a bead resembling a pearl.

simulcast /*sim'əl-käst*/ *n* a programme broadcast simultaneously on radio and television, or on two or more radio wavebands or television channels; the transmission of such a programme. ◆ *vt* to transmit (a programme) simultaneously. [*simul*taneous and broad*cast*]

simulium /*si-mū'li-əm*/ *n* a small black bloodsucking fly of the genus *Simulium*, of temperate and tropical regions, that breeds in fast-flowing streams. [L *simulāre* to imitate] ■ **Simuli'idae** /*-dē*/ *n pl* the family of flies of which the *Simulium* is the type genus, some species of which are the carriers of diseases such as onchocerciasis.

simultaneous /*sim-əl-tā'nyəs, -ni-əs* or (*N Am*) *sī'mul-*/ *adj* being or happening at the same time; (of equations) satisfied by the same roots (*maths*). ◆ *n* in chess, an exhibition in which one player plays several opponents at once (*usu* shortened to **simul**). [L *simul* at the same time] ■ **simultaneity** /*-tə-nē'i-ti* or *-nā'-*/ *n* the quality of being simultaneous, coincidence; a basic consequence of relativity, that two events that are simultaneous for one observer may occur at different times for another observer in another reference frame moving relative to the first (*phys*). **simultā'neously** *adv*. **simulta'neousness** *n*. ❑ **simultaneous translation** *n* a simultaneously running translation of a speaker's or actor's words into the language, or respective languages, of audience members, *esp* relayed through earphones.

simurg, **simurgh** /*si-moorg'* or *-mûrg'*/ or **simorg** /*-mörg'*/ *n* a monstrous bird of Persian fable. [Pers *sīmurgh*]

simvastatin /*sim-və-stat'in*/ *n* a statin drug used to lower the amount of fatty substances, eg cholesterol, in the blood.

sin[1] /*sin*/ *n* moral offence or shortcoming, *esp* from the point of view of religion; the condition of offending in this way; an offence generally; a shame or pity (*old inf*). ◆ *vi* (**sinn'ing**; **sinned**) to commit sin (often with *against*). ◆ *vt* to commit; to burden with sin (as in *sin one's soul*); to bring, drive, or render by sin (hence *sin one's mercies* to be ungrateful). [OE *synn*; ON *synth*; Ger *Sünde*; perh L *sōns, sontis* guilty] ■ **sin'ful** *adj* tainted with sin; wicked; involving sin; morally wrong. **sin'fully** *adv*. **sin'fulness** *n*. **sin'less** *adj*. **sin'lessly** *adv*. **sin'lessness** *n*. **sinn'er** *n*. ❑ **sin bin** *n* (in ice hockey, etc) an enclosure to which a player is sent for a statutory length of time when suspended from a game for unruly behaviour; a room or other place to which disruptive school pupils are sent. **sin'-bin** *vt* to send (a person) to the sin bin. **sin'-eater** *n* (*hist*) a person who by eating bread and salt at a funeral was supposed to take upon himself the sins of the dead person, so that the soul might be delivered from purgatory. **sin'-eating** *adj*. **sin'-offering** *n* a sacrifice in expiation of sin. **sin tax** *n* (*inf*) a tax levied on items such as cigarettes and alcohol. ■ **live in sin** (*old*) to cohabit without being married. **original sin** see under **origin**. **sinner it** (*Pope*) to act as a sinner.

sin[2] or **sin'** /*sin*/ *prep*, *conj* and *adv* (*archaic* or *Scot*) since. [Shortened from **sithen**] ■ **long sin** (*Spenser*) for a long time in the past.

sin[3] see **sine**[1].

sin[4] see **shin**[2].

Sinaean /*si-* or *sī-nē'ən*/ (*rare*) *adj* Chinese. [LL *Sīnae*, Gr *Sīnai* Chinese (pl)]

Sinaitic /*sī-nā-it'ik*/ *adj* of Mount *Sinai* or the Sinai peninsula.

Sinanthropus /*sin-* or *sīn-an'thrə-pəs* or *-thrō'*/ *n* Peking (fossil) man. [Gr *Sīnai* (the) Chinese, and *anthrōpos* man]

sinapism /*sin'ə-pi-zm*/ *n* a mustard plaster. [Gr *sināpi*]

sinarchism /*sin'är-ki-zm*/ or **sinarquism** /*sin'är-ki-zm* or *-kwi-zm*/ (also with *cap*) *n* the fascist movement in Mexico, prominent around the time of the Second World War. [Sp *sinarquismo*, from *sin* without, and *anarquismo* anarchism] ■ **sin'archist** or **sin'arquist** *n* and *adj*.

since /*sins*/ *adv* from that time on; after that time; past; ago. ◆ *prep* after; from the time of. ◆ *conj* from the time that; seeing that; because. [ME *sins, sithens*; see under **sith**[1]]

sincere /*sin-sēr'*/ *adj* unfeigned; genuine; free from pretence; the same in reality as in appearance; *orig* pure, unmixed; unadulterated. [Fr *sincère*, from L *sincērus* clean] ■ **sincēre'ly** *adv*. **sincēre'ness** or **sincerity** /*-ser'*/ *n*. ■ **yours sincerely** used in moderately formal conclusion to a letter.

sinciput /*sin'si-put*/ (*anat*) *n* (pl **sin'ciputs** or **sincip'ita**) the forepart of the head or skull. [L, from *sēmi-* half, and *caput* head] ■ **sincip'ital** *adj*.

sind see **synd**.

Sindhi or **Sindi** /*sin'dē*/ *n* a native or inhabitant of *Sind*, in SE Pakistan; the Indic language spoken mainly in Sind. ◆ *adj* of Sind, its people or its language.

sindon /*sin'dən*/ (*archaic*) *n* fine (*esp* linen) cloth, or a garment, etc, made from it; a shroud, *esp* that preserved as Jesus's at Turin, Italy. [Gr *sindōn* fine cloth, winding sheet] ■ **sindonol'ogist** *n*. **sindonol'ogy** *n* the study of the Turin Shroud and its history. **sindonoph'any** *n* (Gr *phainein* to show) the periodic exhibiting of the Turin Shroud to the public.

sine[1] /*sīn*/ (*maths*) *n* one of the six trigonometrical functions of an angle, the ratio in a right-angled triangle of the side opposite the angle to the hypotenuse (*abbrev* **sin**); *orig* the perpendicular from one end of an arc to the diameter through the other. [L *sinus* a bay] ■ **sinical** /*sin'i-kl*/ *adj*. ❑ **sine curve** *n* a curve showing the relationship between the size of an angle and its sine, a sinusoid. **sine wave** *n* any oscillation whose graphical representation is a sine curve.

sine[2] /*sī'nē* or *si'ne*/ (*L*) *prep* without. ❑ **sine qua non** *n* /*kwä non* or *kwä nōn*/ an indispensable condition. ■ **sine die** /*dī'ē* or *di'ā*/ without a day (appointed); (of a meeting or other business) indefinitely adjourned. **sine dubio** /*dū'bi-ō* or *doob'i-ō*/ without doubt. **sine prole** /*prō'lē* or *prō'le*/ without issue, without children.

sine[3] same as **syne**[1], **synd**.

sinecure /*sin'i-kūr* or *sī'ni-*/ *n* a church benefice without spiritual charge; an office without work, a cushy job. ◆ *adj* relating to or having a sinecure. [L *sine* without, and *cūra* care] ■ **sin'ecurism** *n*. **sin'ecurist** *n*.

sinew /*sin'ū*/ *n* a piece of strong fibrous tissue that joins a muscle to a bone, a tendon; physical strength, muscle; (often *pl*) (a source of) strength or power of any kind. ◆ *vt* (*poetic*) to bind as if by sinews; to strengthen. [OE *sinu*, genitive *sinwe*] ■ **sin'ewed** *adj*. **sin'ewless** *adj*. **sin'ewy** *adj*. ■ **sinews of war** money.

sinfonia /*sin-fō'ni-ə, sin-fō-nē'ə*/ *n* a symphony; a symphony orchestra. [Ital] ■ **sinfonietta** /*-nyet'ə*/ *n* a simple, or light, short symphony; a small symphony orchestra. ❑ **sinfonia concertante** /*kon-chər-tan'ti*/ *n* an orchestral work with parts for more than one solo instrument.

sing[1] /*sing*/ *vi* (pat **sang** or (now rarely) **sung**; pap **sung**) to utter melodious sounds in musical succession while articulating words; to perform songs, *esp* as a profession; to emit more or less songlike sounds; to give a cantabile or lyrical effect; (of the ears) to ring; to be capable of being sung; to write poetry (*literary*); to confess, to turn informer, to squeal (*sl*, *esp N Am*). ◆ *vt* to utter or perform by voice, musically; to chant; to celebrate; to proclaim, relate, in song or verse or in comparable manner; to bring, drive, render, pass, etc by singing. ◆ *n* (*inf*) an act or period of singing. [OE *singan*; Ger *singen*, Gothic *siggwan*] ■ **sing'able** *adj*. **sing'ableness** *n*. **sing'er** *n* a person, bird, etc, that sings; a person who sings as a profession; an informer (*sl*, *esp N Am*); a poet (*obs*). **sing'ing** *n*. **sing'ingly** *adv*. ❑ **singer-song'writer** *n* a person who performs songs that he or she has also written. **sing'ing-bird** *n* a songbird. **singing flame** *n* a flame that gives a musical note in a tube. **sing'ing-gallery** n a gallery occupied by singers. **singing hinny** n (Scot and N Eng) a currant cake that hisses on the griddle. **sing'ing-man** n (Shakesp) a man employed to sing, eg in a church choir. **singing master** n a teacher of singing. **singing sand** n musical sand (qv). **singing telegram** n a method of delivering a greeting by employing a person specializing in this service to sing the greeting to the recipient. **sing'-sing'** n (in New Guinea) a tribal get-together for singing, dancing and feasting. **sing'song** n a ballad; jingly verse; (monotonous) up-and-down intonation; an informal gathering of friends at which there is singing; a meeting for community singing. ♦ adj of the nature of singsong. ♦ vt and vi to sing, speak or utter, in a singsong way.

■ **all-sing'ing-all-dan'cing** (inf) incorporating the full range of features and elaborations. **sing along** (orig US) of an audience, to join in the familiar songs with the performer (with with; **sing'along** n). **sing another** (or **a different**) **song** or **tune** to change to a humbler tone; to express an opinion different from that of someone else, or esp from one's own earlier one, to change one's mind. **sing out** to call out distinctly, to shout; to inform, peach (inf). **sing small** to assume a humble tone.

sing² or **sing.** abbrev : singular.

Singaporean /sing-gə-pö'ri-ən/ adj of or relating to the republic of Singapore in SE Asia, or its inhabitants. ♦ n a native or citizen of Singapore.
□ **Singapore Sling** n a cocktail containing brandy, gin, orange juice, lime juice, Cointreau, Benedictine and grenadine.

singe /sinj/ vt (**singe'ing**; **singed**) to burn on the surface; to scorch; to remove by scorching. ♦ vi to become scorched. ♦ n a burning on the surface; a slight burn. [OE sen(c)gan]
□ **singed cat** n a person who is better (in any respect) than outward appearance suggests.

Singhalese see **Sinhalese**.

single /sing'gl/ adj consisting of one only or one part; unique, individual; one-fold; uncombined; unmarried; for the use of or sufficient for one; (of combat) person-to-person; slight, poor (Shakesp); (of ale) weak, small; undivided; unbroken; determined; (of a flower) without development of stamens into petals, or having ligulate instead of tubular florets; sincere, honest (rare); (of a travel ticket) valid for the outward journey only, not return. ♦ adv singly. ♦ n anything single; (usu in pl) an unmarried, unattached person; (in pl; in tennis, etc) a game played by one against one; a hit for one run (cricket); a talon of a hawk; a gramophone record with usu only one tune, or other short recording, on each side; a one-pound note or coin or a one-dollar note. ♦ vt to separate; to pick (out); to pick out challengingly (Milton); to take aside; to thin. ♦ vi (Spenser) to come forth alone. [OFr, from L singulī one by one]
■ **sing'ledom** or **sing'lehood** n the state of being unmarried. **sing'leness** /-gl-nis/ n. **sing'let** /-glit/ n a thing that is single; an undershirt or sleeveless vest; a state in which there are no unpaired electrons (chem); a single sharp line in atomic spectroscopy (phys); an elementary particle with an isotopic spin number of 0 (phys). **sing'leton** /-gl-tən/ n a single card of its suit in a hand; anything single. **sing'ling** /-gling/ n. **sing'ly** /-gli/ adv one by one; alone; by oneself.
□ **sing'le-acting** adj (of a reciprocating engine, etc) acting effectively in one direction only. **sing'le-action** adj and n (a firearm) having a hammer which requires to be cocked manually before firing. **sing'le-blind'** adj denoting a comparative experiment or trial in which the identities of the control group are known to the experimenters but not the subjects. **single bond** n (chem) a covalent bond involving the sharing of one pair of electrons. **sing'le-breasted** adj with one thickness over the breast and one row of buttons. **sing'le-cell protein** n protein-rich material from cultured algae, fungi or bacteria, used esp as a food supplement (abbrev **SCP**). **sing'le-chamber** adj having one legislative house. **single combat** n fighting between two individuals, usu with weapons. **single cream** n cream with a low fat content that will not thicken when beaten. **sing'le-cross** n (genetics) a first-generation hybrid of two inbred lines. **single currency** n a centralized currency used by members of an economic group in preference to individual national currencies. **sing'le-cut** adj (of a file) having teeth in one direction only. **single-deck'er** n a vessel or vehicle, esp a bus, with only one deck. **sing'le-digit** adj of a number or percentage smaller than ten. **sing'le-end** n (Scot) a one-room dwelling, esp in a tenement. **sing'le-ended** adj (electronics) of a unit or system, having one input and one output terminal permanently earthed. **sing'le-entry** n a system of bookkeeping in which each entry appears only once on one side or other of an account. **sing'le-eyed** adj one-eyed; devoted, unselfish. **sing'le-figure** adj. **single figures** n pl a score, total, etc, of any number from 1 to 9. **single file** see under **file¹**. **sing'le-foot** n (dressage) a brisk walking pace with each foot striking the ground separately, a rack or amble. ♦ vi (of a horse) to walk in this way. **single-hand'ed** adj and adv by oneself; unassisted; with or for one

hand. **single-hand'edly** adv. **single-heart'ed** adj sincere; without duplicity; dedicated, devoted in one's attitude. **single-heart'edly** adv. **single house** n a house one room deep or wide. **single in-line memory module** n (comput) a small printed circuit board carrying a number of memory chips which are inserted into the motherboard (abbrev **SIMM**). **single-lens reflex** see **reflex camera** under **reflex**. **single market** or **single European market** n a market allowing freedom of trade and movement of goods between members of the European Union. **single-mind'ed** adj bent upon one sole purpose; ingenuous. **single-mind'edly** adv. **single-mind'edness** n. **single parent** n a mother or father bringing up children alone (hence **single-parent family**). **sing'le-phase** adj (of an alternating electric current) requiring one outward and one return conductor for transmission. **sing'le-priced** adj (stock exchange) of a share, etc in which buyers and sellers deal at the same price. **single pricing** n. **singles bar** or **club** n one esp for unmarried or unattached people, where friendships (and implicitly sexual relationships) can be formed. **single-seat'er** n a car, aeroplane, etc fitted with one seat only. **sing'le-sex** adj (of schools, etc) for pupils, members, etc of one sex only. **single soldier** n (Walter Scott) a private. **sing'le-soled** adj (of shoes) having one layer in the sole. **single-step'** vt (comput) to carry out a single instruction on (a program). **sing'lestick** /-gl-stik/ n a fighting stick for one hand; a fight or game with singlesticks. **single tax** n a tax on ground-rent or land-values to supersede all other taxes. **single ten** n (Shakesp) the ten of a card suit. **single transferable vote** see under **transfer**. **sing'le-wicket** adj denoting a form of cricket in which individual players take it in turns to bat for a limited number of overs.

singletree /sing'gl-trē/ n same as **swingletree** (see under **swingle**).

sing-sing, **singsong** see under **sing¹**.

singspiel /sing'spēl/ or (Ger) zing'shpēl/ n a semi-dramatic representation in dialogue and song. [Ger, from singen to sing, and Spiel play]

singular /sing'gū-lər/ adj single; unique; proper; private; denoting or referring to one; pre-eminent; pre-eminently good or efficacious; extraordinary; peculiar; strange; odd. ♦ adv singularly. ♦ n an individual person or thing; the singular number or a word in the singular number (grammar). [L singulāris]
■ **sing'ularism** n a philosophy that recognizes one principle only, opp to pluralism. **sing'ularist** n someone who affects singularity; an upholder of singularism. **singularity** /-lar'i-ti/ n the fact or state of being singular; peculiarity; individuality; oddity; oneness; anything curious or remarkable; a point in space-time at which matter is compressed to an infinitely great density (astron). **singularīzā'tion** or **-s-** n. **sing'ularize** or **-ise** vt to make singular; to signalize. **sing'ularly** adv in a singular manner; peculiarly; strangely; singly; pre-eminently (archaic).

sinh /shīn/ or /sīn-āch'/ abbrev : hyperbolic sine (see **hyperbolic functions** under **hyper-**).

Sinhalese /sin'hə-lēz or -lēz'/ or **Singhalese**, **Cingalese** /sing'gə-lēz or -lēz'/, also **Sinhala** /sin'hə-la/ adj of the majority population of Sri Lanka; of or in their language, similar to Pali. ♦ n a member of the Sinhalese people; their language. [Sans Siṁhala Sri Lanka]

Sinic /sin'ik/ adj Chinese. [From Med L Sinicus Chinese; see also **Sinaean**]
■ **Sin'icism** /-sizm/ n a Chinese custom, idiom, etc. **sin'icize** or **-ise** vt and vi to make or become Chinese or of Chinese character.

sinical see under **sine¹**.

sinister /sin'i-stər, formerly also sin-is'tər/ adj suggestive of threatened evil, ominous; malign; underhand; left or on the left side; on the left side from the point of view of the bearer of the shield, not the beholder (heraldry), and similarly sometimes in description of an illustration, etc; inauspicious; unlucky; misleading (obs). [L, left, on the left side]
■ **sinisterity** /-ter'i-/ n (rare) left-handedness; sinister quality. **sin'isterly** adv. **sin'isterness** n. **sin'isterwise** adv. **sin'istral** adj positioned on or relating to the left side; turning to the left; left-handed; (of flatfish) lying left side up; (of a shell) coiled contrary to the normal way. ♦ n a left-handed person. **sinistral'ity** n. **sin'istrally** adv. **sinistrous** /si-nis' or sin'is-/ adj inauspicious; sinister (obs). **sin'istrously** adv.

sinistrodextral /si-ni-strō-dek'strəl/ adj moving, going or extending from left to right. [**sinister** and **dexter¹**]

sinistrorse /sin-i-strörs' or sin'/, also **sinistrorsal** /-strör'səl/ (biol) adj (of a climbing plant) rising helically and turning to the right, ie crossing an outside observer's field of view from right to left upwards (like an ordinary spiral stair). [L sinistrōrsus, sinistrōversus towards the left side, from sinister left, and vertere, versum to turn]
■ **sinistrors'ally** adv. **sinistrorse'ly** adv.

Sinitic /si-nit'ik/ adj denoting a group of languages belonging to the Sino-Tibetan family, used mainly in China. ♦ n the languages forming this group. [See **Sino-**]

sink /singk/ vi (pat **sank** or (now rarely) **sunk**; pap **sunk** or **sunk'en**) to become submerged, wholly or partly; to subside; to fall slowly; to

go down passively; to pass to a lower level or state; to penetrate or be absorbed; to slope away, dip; to diminish; to collapse; to be or become withdrawn inwards. ◆ *vt* to cause or allow to sink; to complete successfully (a putt or shot) by causing the ball to run into the hole (*golf*); to cause (a ball) to fall into a pocket (*snooker*, etc); to suppress; to degrade; to conceal; to appropriate surreptitiously; to excavate; to let in, insert; to abandon; to abolish; to merge; to pay (a debt); to lose under the horizon; to invest, *esp* unprofitably or beyond easy recovery; to damn or ruin (*esp* in imprecation); to drink quickly (*inf*). ◆ *n* a kitchen or scullery basin with a drain, for washing dishes, etc; a receptacle or drain for filth or dirty water; a place where things are engulfed or where foul things gather; a cesspool; a depression in a surface; an area without surface drainage; a swallow hole (*geol*); a shaft; a natural or artificial means of absorbing or discharging heat, fluid, etc (*phys*, etc). ◆ *adj* populated by individuals who are not wanted elsewhere, as in *a sink school*. [OE *sincan* (vi); Ger *sinken*, Du *zinken*]
■ **sink'able** *adj*. **sink'age** *n* the process of sinking; amount of sinking; a sunken area or depression; shrinkage. **sink'er** *n* a person who sinks; a weight for sinking anything, such as a fishing-line; a doughnut (*US inf*); a mistletoe root. **sink'ing** *n* and *adj*. **sink'y** *adj* yielding underfoot.
❑ **sink'hole** *n* a hole for filth; a swallow hole (*N Am*). **sinking fund** *n* a fund formed by setting aside income to accumulate at interest to pay off debt. **sink unit** *n* a fitting consisting of sink and draining board, with cupboards, etc underneath.
■ **sink in** to be absorbed; to be understood.

sink-a-pace or **sinke-a-pace** same as **cinque-pace** (see under **cinque**).

sinner, etc see under **sin**[1].

sinnet /*sin'it*/ same as **sennit**.

Sinn Fein /*shin fān*/ *n* a political movement and party in Ireland championing a republic, opposing partition and later campaigning for reunification. [Ir, we ourselves]
■ **Sinn Fein'er** *n*. **Sinn Fein'ism** *n*.

sinningia /*si-nin'ji-ə*/ *n* any Central and S American plant of the genus *Sinningia* of the Gesneriaceae family, *esp Sinningia speciosa*, popularly known as gloxinia and grown in greenhouses for its bell-shaped, velvety flowers. [W *Sinning*, German gardener]

Sino- /*sī-nō-, -nə-, sin-*/ *pfx* denoting Chinese, as in *Sino-American*. [Gr *Sīnai* Chinese (pl)]
■ **Sinolog'ical** /*-loj'*/ *adj*. **Sinologist** /*-ol'ə-jist*/ *n*. **Si'nologue** *n* a person with knowledge of Chinese language, culture, etc, a Sinologist. **Sinol'ogy** *n* the study of Chinese language, culture, etc. **Si'nophil** or **Si'nophile** *n* and *adj* (someone who is) friendly to the Chinese or attracted by Chinese culture. **Sinoph'ily** or **Sinoph'ilism** *n*. **Si'no-Tibet'an** *adj* denoting the family of languages spoken in China and Myanmar (Burma). ◆ *n* the languages forming this group.

sino- /*sin-ō-* or *sī-nō-*/ *pfx* denoting sinus, as in *sino-nasal*.

sinopia /*si-nō'pi-ə*/, also **sinopis** /*-pis*/ *n* a reddish-brown pigment used for one of the preparatory drawings of a fresco, obtained from **sin'opite**, an iron ore; a drawing so made. [L *sinopis* sinopite]

sinsemilla /*sin-sə-mil'ə*/ *n* marijuana containing high levels of the narcotic tetrahydrocannabinol; the plant, a seedless female strain of *Cannabis sativa*, from which it is obtained. [Am Sp *sin* without, and *semilla* seed]

sinsyne /*sin-sīn'*/ (*Scot*) *adv* since that time. [**sin**[2] and **syne**[1]]

sinter /*sin'tər*/ *n* a deposit from hot springs. ◆ *vt* to heat (a mixture of powdered metals) sometimes under pressure, to the melting-point of the metal in the mixture which has the lowest melting-point, the melted metal binding together the harder particles. ◆ *vi* to coalesce under heat without liquefaction. [Ger *Sinter*; cf **cinder**]
■ **sin'tery** *adj*.

sinuate /*sin'ū-āt*/ or **sinuated** /*sin'ū-ā-tid*/ *adj* having a wavy edge or margin; winding; sinuous. [L *sinuātus* curved, bent, from *sinus* bend]
■ **sin'uately** *adv*. **sinuā'tion** *n*.

sinuous /*sin'ū-əs*/ *adj* wavy; bending in a supple manner. [L *sinuōsus*, from *sinus*, bend]
■ **sinuose** /*sin'ū-ōs*/ *adj* sinuous. **sinuosity** /*-os'*/ *n*. **sin'uously** *adv*. **sin'uousness** *n*.

sinus /*sī'nəs*/ *n* (pl **si'nuses**) an air-filled cavity in the bones of the skull, connecting with the nose; a narrow cavity through which pus is discharged; a cavity; an indentation; a notch between two lobes in a leaf (*bot*). [L *sinus, -ūs* a bend, fold, bay]
■ **sinupall'ial** /*sī-nū-*/ or **sinupall'iate** *adj* (of certain bivalve molluscs) having an indented pallial line for the retraction and expansion of the pallial siphons. **sinusi'tis** or **sinui'tis** /*sī-nū-*/ *n* inflammation of a sinus, *esp* one in the skull communicating with the nose. **sinusoid** /*sī'nə-soid*/ *n* the curve of sines (*y* = *a*sinx); a small blood vessel in certain organs, such as the liver, heart, etc. ◆ *adj* similar to or referring to a sinus. **sinusoid'al** *adj*. **sinusoid'ally** *adv*.

Sioux /*soo*/ *n* (pl **Sioux** /*soo* or *sooz*/) a Native American of a tribe now living in the Dakotas, Minnesota, and Montana; any of the group of languages spoken by them. ◆ *adj* of or relating to the Sioux or their languages. [Fr, from a native word]
■ **Siou'an** *adj* relating to the Sioux, or to a larger group to which the Sioux belong; relating to the languages of this group. ◆ *n* the group of languages spoken by the Siouan peoples.

sip /*sip*/ *vt* and *vi* (**sipp'ing**; **sipped**) to drink, or drink from, in small quantities by action of the lips. ◆ *n* the act of sipping; the quantity sipped at once. [Cf **sup**; OE *sypian*; LGer *sippen*]
■ **sipp'er** *n* someone who or something that sips; a drinking straw (*N Am*).

sipe[1] or **sype** /*sīp*/ (*dialect*) *vi* to soak through; to seep or ooze. [OE *sipian* to soak]

sipe[2] /*sīp*/ *n* a tiny groove or slit in the tread of a tyre, aiding water dispersal and improving the tyre's grip. [From **sipe**[1]]

siphon or **syphon** /*sī'fən*/ *n* a bent tube or channel by which a liquid may be drawn off over a higher point to a lower level; a tubular organ for intake and output of water, as in lamellibranchs; an aerated-water bottle that discharges by a siphon. ◆ *vt* (often with *off*) to convey, remove by means of (or as if by means of) a siphon; to divert (funds, money, etc). [Gr *sīphōn, siphōn* siphon]
■ **sī'phonage** *n*. **sī'phonal** or **sīphon'ic** *adj*. **Sīphonap'tera** *n pl* the flea order of insects. **sīphonap'teran** *n* and *adj*. **sī'phonate** *adj* having a siphon. **sī'phonet** *n* an aphid's honeydew tube. **sīphon'ogam** *n* a seed plant. **sīphonog'amy** *n* (*bot*) fertilization by pollen tube. **sī'phonophore** (or /*sī-fon'*/) *n* a colonial hydrozoan of the order Siphonophora. **sīphonostele** /*-stē'lē* or *-stēl'*/ *n* (*bot*) a hollow cylinder of vascular tissue. **sī'phuncle** *n* a tube connecting the chambers of a nautilus; a siphonet.

Siporex® /*sip'ə-reks*/ *n* a material used by builders, and also by artists, a form of aerated concrete, which can be sawn, etc.

SIPP /*sip*/ *abbrev* : self-invested personal pension.

sippet /*sip'it*/ *n* a morsel, *esp* of bread to be eaten with soup. [Cf **sip** and **sup**]
■ **sipp'le** *vt* and *vi* to sip at leisure.

sipunculid /*sī-pung'kū-lid*/ *n* any marine worm of the group Sipunculacea, having a retractile proboscis (also *adj*). [Mod L, from L *siphunculus* a little pipe]
■ **sipunc'uloid** *n* and *adj*.

si quis /*sī* or *sē kwis*/ *n* a public notice, *esp* one announcing the impending ordination of a parish priest, allowing for objections to be raised. [L *sī quis* if anybody (wants, knows, has found, etc)]

Sir. (*Bible*) *abbrev* : (the Apocryphal Book of) Wisdom of Jesus the son of Sirach (also called **Ecclesiasticus**).

sir /*sûr*/ *n* a word of respect (or disapprobation) used in addressing a man; a gentleman; (with *cap*) prefixed to the Christian name of a knight or baronet; (with *cap*) a word of address to a man in a formal letter; formerly used as a translation of L *dominus*, bachelor of arts (as distinguished from *magister*, master of arts). ◆ *vt* (**sirr'ing**; **sirred**) to address as 'sir'. [OFr *sire*, from L *senior* an elder]

Sirah see **Petite Sirah** under **petit**.

sircar or **sirkar**, also **circar** /*sər-kär'* or *sûr'*/ (*Anglo-Ind*) *n* the state or government; the authorities; a province or district; an Indian clerk or factotum. [Urdu *sarkār* a superintendent, from Pers *sar* head, and *kār* agent]

sirdar or **sardar** /*sər-där'* or *sûr'*/ *n* a military leader in India and other Eastern countries; a commander-in-chief, *specif* (formerly) the British commander-in-chief of the Egyptian army. [Urdu *sardār*, from Pers *sar* head, and *dār* holding]

sire /*sīr*/ *n* a father, *esp* of a horse or other animal; an ancestor; a master, lord, man of high rank (*obs*); a term of address to a king (*hist*); a senior or elder (*obs*). ◆ *vt* (of animals) to father. [See **sir**]
■ **sir'ing** *n*.

siren /*sī'rən*/ *n* a signalling or warning instrument that produces a loud wailing sound, *usu* by the escape of air or steam through a rotating perforated plate; a fascinating woman, insidious and deceptive; a bewitching singer; (with *cap*) one of certain sea nymphs, part woman, part bird, whose seductive songs lured sailors to their deaths on rocks (*Gr myth*); a mermaid; any eel-like amphibian of the family Sirenidae, having no hind legs and with external gills. ◆ *adj* deceptively alluring. [Gr *Seirēn*]
■ **sirē'nian** *adj* of, relating or belonging to the Sirenia, an order of aquatic mammals now represented by the dugong and the manatee. ◆ *n* a member of this order, having paddlelike forelimbs and no hind limbs. **sirenic** /*-ren'*/ *adj*. **sire'nize** or **-ise** *vt* to bewitch, allure or enchant.
❑ **siren suit** *n* a close-fitting trousered overall *orig* designed for use in air-raids.

sirgang /sûr'gang/ n a green Asiatic jay-like bird. [Prob from native name]

sirih or **siri** /sē'ri/ n betel. [Malay *sīrih*]

Sirius /sir'i-əs/ n the Dogstar. [L *Sīrius*, from Gr *Seirios*]
■ **Sir'ian** *adj*. **sirī'asis** *n* sunstroke.

sirkar see **sircar**.

sirloin or rarely **surloin** /sûr'loin/ n the upper part of a loin of beef. [From a by-form of OFr *surlonge*, from *sur* over, and *longe* (cf **loin**)]

sirname an obsolete form of **surname**.

sirocco /si-rok'ō/ or **scirocco** /shi-rok'ō/ n (pl **sirocc'os** or **scirocc'os**) a hot, dry, dusty and gusty wind blowing from N Africa to the north Mediterranean coast, becoming moist further north (also **siroc'** or **sciroc'**); any oppressive south or south-east wind; a wind from the desert; a drying machine. [Ital *s(c)irocco*, from Ar *sharq* east wind]

sirrah /sir'ə/ n (*archaic*) sir (used in anger or contempt). [An extension of **sir**]
❑ **sirree'** /sə-rē'/ n (*US*) a form of sir or sirrah used for emphasis, *esp* with *yes* or *no*.

sir-reverence /sə-rev'ə-rəns/ (*obs*) a corruption of the phrase *save reverence*, used apologetically when anything vulgar or disgusting has to be mentioned. *n* (a piece of) excrement.

sirtuin /sûr-too'-in/ n any of a group of enzymes which regulate cell metabolism and aging. [*s*ilent mating type *i*nformation *r*egulation *t*wo, and **-in** (2)]

sirup see **syrup**.

sirvente /sēr-vãt'/ n a medieval verse form of satirical or heroic character as composed and performed by troubadours. [Fr]

SIS *abbrev* : Satellite Information Services; Secret Intelligence Service; Security Intelligence Service (in New Zealand).

sis¹ or **siss** /sis/ (*esp* N Am) n a contracted form of **sister** (used as a form of address).
■ **siss'ified** *adj* cissy. **siss'iness** *n*. **siss'y** *n* and *adj* (*orig* chiefly N Am) cissy. **siss'yish** *adj*.

sis² /sis/ (S Afr *inf*) *interj* expressing disgust, contempt, etc. [Afrik]

-sis /-sis/ n sfx signifying: action, process; condition caused by. [Gr]

sisal /sī'səl/ or *sī'zəl*/ n a Mexican agave whose leaves yield a fibre; agave fibre, used for making rope, etc (also **sisal hemp** or **grass**). [First exported from *Sisal*, in Yucatán]

siserary or **sisserary** /sis-ə-rā'ri/, also **sasarara** or **sassarara** /sas-ə-rā'rə/ (*dialect*) n a scolding; a blow. [Corruption of **certiorari**]
■ **with a siserary** suddenly; on the spot.

siskin /sis'kin/ n a yellowish-green Eurasian finch, *Carduelis spinus*. [Ger dialect *sisschen*; appar Slav]

siss see **sis¹**.

sisserary see **siserary**.

sissoo /sis'oo/ n a papilionaceous Indian timber tree (genus *Dalbergia*) or its wood. [Hindi *sīsū*]

sissy see under **sis¹**.

sist /sist/ (Scots *law*) *vt* to stop, stay; to make (a person) a party to a case. *n* a stay. [L *sistere* to make to stand]

sista /sis'tə/ (US *sl*) n an African-American woman. [Altered form of **sister**]

sister /sis'tər/ n a daughter of the same parents; a half-sister; formerly, a sister-in-law; a female fellow; a member of a sisterhood; a nun; a senior nurse, *esp* one in charge of a ward. *adj* of the same origin; fellow; built on the same model. *vt* to be a sister to; to call sister. [Appar ON *systir*; OE *sweostor*; Du *zuster*, Ger *Schwester*]
■ **sis'terhood** *n* the act or state of being a sister; the relationship of sister; a society, *esp* an active religious community, of women; a set or class of women. **sis'tering** *adj* (*Shakesp*) neighbouring. **sis'terless** *adj*. **sis'terlike** *adj*. **sis'terliness** *n*. **sis'terly** *adj* like or befitting a sister; kind; affectionate.
❑ **sister-chromatid exchange** *n* reciprocal exchange of DNA between the chromatids of a single chromosome. **sister hook** *n* one of a pair of hooks that close each other. **sis'ter-in-law** *n* (pl **sis'ters-in-law**) a husband's or wife's sister, or a brother's wife; a husband or wife's brother's wife.

Sistine /sis'tīn or -tēn or -tin/ *adj* of Pope *Sixtus*, *esp* Sixtus IV (1471–84) or V (1585–90).
❑ **Sistine Chapel** *n* the Pope's chapel in the Vatican, built by Sixtus IV.

sistrum /sis'trəm/ n (pl **sis'tra**) an ancient Egyptian wire rattle used in Isis-worship. [L *sīstrum*, from Gr *seistron*]

Sisyphean /sis-i-fē'ən/ *adj* relating to *Sisyphus*, king of Corinth, condemned in Tartarus to roll ceaselessly up a hill a huge stone which would roll back to the foot of the hill again each time he neared the top; hence, endless, laborious and futile.

sit /sit/ *vi* (**sitt'ing**; **sat**, (*archaic*) **sate** /sat or sāt/) to rest on the buttocks and thighs with the upper body more or less vertical; (of birds) to perch; to brood; to have a seat, eg in parliament; to be in session; to reside; to be a tenant; to be located, have a specific position or (of the wind) direction; to pose, be a model; to undergo an examination, be a candidate; to weigh, bear, press; to be disposed in adjustment, hang, fit; to befit. *vt* to seat; to have a seat on, ride; to undergo or be examined in; (often in combination) to stay in or with in order to look after, as in *baby-sit*. *n* a mode or spell of sitting. [OE *sittan*; Ger *sitzen*, L *sedēre*]
■ **sitt'er** *n* someone who sits; someone who sits as a model for an artist or with a medium; a baby-sitter; someone who looks after a house, pet, etc in the absence of its owner; a sitting bird; an easy shot; an easy dupe (*inf*); anything difficult to fail in; a sitting room (*sl*). **sitt'ing** *n* the state of being seated or act of taking a seat; a period of being seated, *esp* when engaged in some activity; brooding on eggs; a clutch; one or two or more groups into which a large number of diners are divided, or the period set aside for each group to occupy the dining room, etc; a continuous meeting of a body; a spell of posing for an artist, etc; a seat; a church seat. *adj* seated; brooding; currently holding office; in the course of a parliamentary session.
❑ **sit'-down** *n* a spell of sitting. *adj* (of a meal) that one sits down to; (of a strike) in which workers down tools but remain in occupation of the plant, workshop, etc. **sit'fast** *n* a lump in a horse's skin under the saddle. **sit'-in** *n* the occupation of a building, etc, as an organized protest against some (alleged) injustice, etc (also *adj*). **sitt'er-in** *n* a baby-sitter. **sitting room** *n* a room in which members of a family commonly sit; a space for sitting. **sitting target** or **sitting duck** *n* an easy target or victim. **sitting tenant** *n* the tenant currently occupying a property. **sit'-up** *n* an exercise in which the head and torso are raised from a lying position while the legs remain still. **sit'-upon** *n* (*inf*) the buttocks.
■ **sit back** to take no active part, or no further active part. **sit by** to look on without taking any action. **sit down** to take a seat; to pause, rest; to take up positions prior to beginning a siege; to accept meekly (with *under*). **sit in** to act as a baby-sitter; to be present as a visitor, and (*usu*) take part, eg at a conference or discussion; to have or take part in a sit-in; to act as a substitute. **sit on** or **upon** to hold an official inquiry regarding; to be a member of; to repress, suppress, check or delay dealing with (*inf*). **sit out** to sit apart without participating; to sit to the end of; to outstay. **sit tight** to maintain one's seat; to keep one's position quietly and unobtrusively. **sitting pretty** see under **pretty**. **sit under** to be in the habit of hearing the preaching of (a particular priest, minister, etc). **sit up** to rise from a recumbent to a sitting position, or from a relaxed to an erect seat; to become alert or startled; to remain up instead of going to bed; to keep watch during the night.

sitar /sit'är or si-tär'/ n an Indian instrument with a long neck and a rounded body, played by plucking the strings (also **sittar'**). [Hindi *sitār*]

sitatunga /si-tə-toong'gə or -tung'gə/, also **situtunga** /si-tə- or si-tū-/ n a species of African antelope, *Tragelaphus spekei*, notable for its elongated hooves which allow it to walk on marshy ground. [Swahili]

sitcom /sit'kom/ (*inf*) n a *sit*uation *com*edy.

site /sīt/ n the situation, *esp* of a building, town, etc; the area or ground occupied or set apart for a building, etc; an area set aside for some specific purpose, activity, etc; a website; posture (*obs*). *vt* to locate, position. [L *situs* situation, from *sineri*, *situs* to be placed, from *sinere* to allow]
❑ **site-specific mutagenesis** *n* the possibility of altering a DNA sequence at a defined position, eg by synthesizing an alternative sequence and reinserting it into the host chromosome.

sitella or **sittella** /si-tel'ə/ n an Australasian bird of the genus *Daphoenositta*. [*Sittella*, former genus name, from Gr *sittē* nuthatch]

sith¹ /sith/ (*Shakesp*) *adv*, *prep* and *conj* since (also **sith'en**, (*Spenser*, *Shakesp*) **sith'ence** and **sith'ens**). [OE *siththan*, for *sīth than* (instrumental), after that; cf **since**, **syne¹**]

sith², **sithe** or **sythe** /sīdh/ n (pl **sith**, **sithes** or **sythes**) time. [OE *sīth* time]

sithe¹ /sīdh/ (*archaic*) *n* and *vt* same as **scythe**.

sithe² /sīdh/ *n* and *vi* an obsolete or dialect form of **sigh**.

sithe³ see **sith²**.

sithen, **sithence**, **sithens** see **sith¹**.

sitiology, **sitiophobia** see **sitology**.

Sitka spruce /sit'kə sproos/ n a spruce tree, *Picea sitchensis*, with sharp blue-green needles, grown for its timber in both N America and Europe. [*Sitka* in Alaska]

sitology /sī-tol'ə-ji/ or **sitiology** /sit-i-ol'ə-ji/ n dietetics. [Gr *sītos*, dimin *sītion* grain, food]

■ **sitophō'bia** or **sitiophō'bia** *n* morbid aversion to food.

sitrep /*sit'*rep/ (*inf*) *n* a report on the current military position (also *fig*). [*sit*uation *rep*ort]

Sitta /*sit'ə*/ *n* the nuthatch genus. [Gr *sittē* nuthatch]
■ **sitt'ine** *adj*.

sittar see **sitar**.

sittella see **sitella**.

sitter, sitting, etc see under **sit**.

sittine see under **Sitta**.

Sittlichkeit /*zit'*lihh-kīt/ (*Ger*) *n* morals, morality; that which is becoming or suitable.

situate /*sit'*ū-āt/ *vt* to set, place, locate; to circumstance. ◆ *adj* /-*ū-it*/ (now *esp law*) situated. [LL *situātus*, from L *situere* to place]
■ **sit'uated** *adj* set, located; circumstanced. **sit'uatedness** *n* (*philos* and *psychol*) the idea that an agent interacts with its environment, receiving sensory information from it and acting in ways that affect it. **situā'tion** *n* location; place; position; momentary state; condition; a set of circumstances, a juncture; a critical point in the action of a play or the development of the plot of a novel; office, employment. **situā'tional** *adj*. **situā'tionally** *adv*. **situā'tionism** *n* the theory that behaviour is determined by surrounding situations rather than by personal qualities. **situā'tionist** *n* and *adj*.
□ **situation comedy** *n* a comedy, now *esp* in a television or radio series in which the same characters appear in each episode, which depends for its humour on the behaviour of the characters in particular, sometimes contrived, situations (*inf* short form **sitcom**). **situation ethics** see under **ethic**.

situla /*sit'*ū-lə/ (*ancient hist*) *n* (*pl* **sit'ūlae** /-*lē*/) a bucket. [L]

situs /*sī'*təs/ *n* (*pl* **sī'tus** /-*z*/) position; the normal position of an organ in the body. [L, site, position]

situtunga see **sitatunga**.

sit. vac. /*sit* vak/ *abbrev*: situation vacant (*pl* **sits vac**).

sitz-bath /*sits'*bäth/ *n* a therapeutic hip bath in hot water. [Ger *Sitzbad*]

sitzkrieg /*sits'*krēg or *zits'*krēk/ *n* the period (September 1939 to May 1940) of comparative military quiet at the opening of World War II, or any similar period in any war. [Ger *sitzen* to sit, and *Krieg* war; cf **blitzkrieg** (see **blitz**)]

Sium /*sī'*əm/ *n* the water-parsnip genus. [Gr *sion*]

SIV (*finance*) *abbrev*: structured (or special) investment vehicle.

Siva or **Shiva** /*sē'*və or *siv'*ə, *shē'*və or *shiv'*ə/ *n* the third god of the Hindu triad, destroyer and reproducer. [Sans *śiva* friendly, gracious]
■ **Si'vaism** or **Shi'vaism** *n*. **Sivaist'ic** or **Shivaist'ic** *adj*. **Si'vaite** or **Shi'vaite** *n*. **Sivapithē'cus** (or /-*pith'*/) *n* an Indian Miocene fossil anthropoid. **Sivathē'rium** *n* a gigantic giraffe-like Indian Pliocene fossil animal.

Sivan /*sē-văn'*/ *n* the ninth month of the Jewish civil year, third of the ecclesiastical year, part of May and June. [Heb *sīwān*]

siver see **syver**.

siwash /*sī'*wosh/ (*NW US derog inf*; also with *cap*) *n* a north-western Native American (also *adj*). ◆ *vi* to camp out without a tent. [Chinook, from Fr *sauvage* wild]

six /*siks*/ *n* the cardinal number next above five; a symbol representing that number (6, vi, etc); a set of six things or people (syllables, leaves, rowers, etc); a score of six points, strokes, tricks, etc; an article of a size denoted by 6; a playing card with six pips; a six-cylinder engine or car; a division of a Brownie Guide or Cub Scout pack; the sixth hour after midnight or midday; the age of six years. ◆ *adj* of the number six; six years old. [OE *siex*; Ger *sechs*; Gaelic *sè*; L *sex*, Gr *hex*, Sans *şaş*]
■ **six'er** *n* anything counting for six or indicated by six; the leader of a Brownie Guide or Cub Scout six. **six'fold** *adj* and *adv* in six divisions; six times as much. **sixth** *adj* last of six; next after the fifth; equal to one of six equal parts. ◆ *n* a sixth part; a person or thing in sixth position; an interval of five (conventionally called six) diatonic degrees (*music*); a combination of two tones separated by such an interval (*music*). **sixth'ly** *adv* in the sixth place.
□ **six'-day** *adj* of or for six days (ie *usu* excluding Sunday). **six'-foot** *adj* measuring six feet. **six'-foot'er** *n* a person six feet tall. **six'-gun** *n* a six-shooter. **Six Nations** *n pl* a more recent grouping of N American peoples, comprising the Five Nations (qv) and the Tuscaroras. **six'-pack** *n* a pack which comprises six items sold as one unit, *esp* a pack of six cans of beer; a set of well-defined abdominal muscles (*inf*). **six'pence** *n* a coin worth six old pence; its value. **six'penny** *adj* costing or worth sixpence; cheap; worthless. ◆ *n* formerly, a sixpenny book. **six'score** *n* and *adj*. **six'-shooter** *n* a six-chambered revolver. **sixth form** *n* (the classes studying in) the (*usu*) two years of preparation for A-level examinations in England or, in Scotland, the one year of preparation for higher level examinations and sixth-year studies. **sixth'-form college** *n* a school which provides the sixth-form education for the pupils of an area. **sixth'-former** *n*. **sixth sense** see **sense**.
■ **at sixes and sevens** in disorder. **hit** or **knock for six** to overcome completely; to take by surprise. **long** or **short sixes** candles weighing six to the pound, about 8 or 4 inches long respectively. **six (of one) and half a dozen (of the other)** equal, attributable to both parties equally; having alternatives which are considered equivalent, equally acceptable, etc. **six of the best** (*inf*) six strokes of the cane as a punishment, or a beating generally; also in extended reference to a choice of six things. **the Six Counties** Northern Ireland.

sixain or **sixaine** /*sik-sān'*/ (*prosody*) *n* a stanza of six lines. [Fr]

sixte /*sikst*/ (*fencing*) *n* a parry with hand on guard opposite the right breast, sword point a little raised to the right. [Fr]

sixteen /*siks-tēn'* or *siks'tēn*/ *n* and *adj* six and ten. [OE *siextēne* (-*tīene*); see **six** and **ten**]
■ **sixteen'er** *n* a verse of sixteen syllables. **sixteen'mo** *n* (*pl* **sixteen'mos**) and *adj* sextodecimo, written 16mo. **sixteenth'** (or /*siks'*/) *adj* last of sixteen; next after the fifteenth; equal to one of sixteen equal parts. ◆ *n* a sixteenth part; a person or thing in sixteenth position. **sixteenth'ly** *adv*.
□ **sixteenth note** *n* (*N Am*) a semiquaver.

sixty /*siks'*ti/ *n* and *adj* six times ten. [OE *siextig*]
■ **six'ties** *n pl* the numbers sixty to sixty-nine; the years so numbered in a life or century; a range of temperature from sixty to just less than seventy degrees. **six'tieth** *adj* last of sixty; next after the fifty-ninth; equal to one of sixty equal parts. ◆ *n* a sixtieth part; a person or thing in sixtieth position.
□ **sixty-fourth note** *n* (*N Am*) a hemidemisemiquaver. **sixty-four-(thousand-)dollar question** *n* (from a US quiz game), the final and most difficult question one has to answer, from the sixty-four-(thousand-)dollar top prize money awarded; hence, a hard question to answer, the supreme or crucial question. **sixty-nine'** same as **soixante-neuf**.

size¹ /*sīz*/ *n* bigness; magnitude; any of a series of graded measurements into which eg clothes, shoes, are divided; an allowance (*obs*); a portion of food and drink (*obs*); an assize (*obs*). ◆ *vt* to arrange according to size; to measure; formerly at various universities, to get (food or drink) on credit. ◆ *vi* (*rare*) to draw a size; to assume size. [**assize**]
■ **sī'zable** or **size'able** *adj* of a considerable size. **sī'zably** or **size'ably** *adv*. **sī'zar** (also **sī'zer**) *n* at Cambridge University and Trinity College, Dublin, a student receiving a college allowance towards expenses. **sī'zarship** *n*. **sized** *adj* having a particular size (often in combination, as in *medium-sized*). **sī'zer** *n* a measurer; a gauge; a thing of considerable or great size (*sl*). **sī'zing** *n* sorting by size. **sī'zism** or **sī'zeism** *n* discrimination against overweight people. **sī'zist** or **sī'zeist** *n* and *adj*.
□ **size-exclusion chromatography** *n* chromatographic separation of particles according to size, a solid phase of material of restricted pore size functioning as a molecular sieve. **size zero** *n* (*US*) (in women's clothing) a very small size, equivalent to the UK size 4.
■ **of a size** of the same size. **size up** to take mental measure of (also *fig*). **the size of it** (*inf*) an assessment of the present situation.

size² /*sīz*/ *n* a weak glue or gluey material used for stiffening paper or rendering it sufficiently water-resistant to accept printing ink without over-absorption, for stiffening fabric and for preparing walls before plastering or wallpapering. ◆ *vt* to cover or treat with size. [Origin obscure]
■ **sized** *adj*. **sī'zer** *n*. **sī'ziness** *n*. **sī'zing** *n* application of size, or material for the purpose. **sī'zy** *adj*.

size³ /*sīz*/ same as **sice¹**.

sizel /*siz'*l/ same as **scissel**.

sizzle /*siz'*l/ *vi* (of food) to make a hissing sound while frying; to be extremely hot (*inf*); to be in a state of intense emotion, *esp* anger or excitement (*inf*). ◆ *vt* and *vi* to fry, scorch, sear. ◆ *n* a hissing sound, as of frying food; extreme heat. [Imit]
■ **sizz'ler** *n* a sizzling heat or day; a thing strikingly fierce or effective. **sizz'ling** *n* a hissing. ◆ *adj* very hot; very striking. **sizz'lingly** *adv*.

SJ *abbrev*: Society of Jesus (see **Jesuit**).

sjambok /*sham'*bok/ (*S Afr*) *n* a whip of dried hide. ◆ *vt* to flog. [Afrik, from Malay *samboq*, from Urdu *chābuk*]

SJC (*US*) *abbrev*: Supreme Judicial Court.

Sjögren's syndrome /*shœ'*grenz sin'drōm/ *n* a condition, often associated with rheumatoid arthritis and lupus erythematosus, in which secretion from the mucous membrane becomes deficient, with resulting dryness of eg the mouth and eyes. [HSC *Sjögren* (1899–1986), Swedish ophthalmologist]

SK *abbrev*: Saskatchewan (Canadian province); Slovakia (IVR).

Sk *abbrev*: Slovak koruna.

---

ska /skä/ *n* a form of Jamaican music similar to reggae. [Origin obscure]

skag see **scag**.

skail, **scail** or **scale** /skāl/ (*Scot*) *vt* and *vi* to disperse; to scatter; to spill. [Ety doubtful; prob not connected with Gaelic *sgaoil*]

skaines mate /skānz māt/ (*Shakesp*) *n* perh a companion, a scapegrace.

skaith see **scathe**.

skald or **scald** /sköld/ *n* a poet; a Scandinavian bard. [ON *skāld*]
■ **skald'ic** or **scald'ic** *adj*. **skald'ship** or **scald'ship** *n*.

skank /skangk/ *vi* to dance to reggae music, lifting the knees up in rapid, jerky movements. ◆ *n* such a dance, or a spell of this kind of dancing. [Origin uncertain]
■ **skank'ing** *n*.

skanky /skang'ki/ (*sl*) *adj* dirty and unattractive. [African-American slang *skank* dirt]
■ **skank** *n* a promiscuous girl or woman.

skart, **scart** /skärt/, **scarth** or **skarth** /skärth/ (*Scot*) *n* a cormorant. [ON *skarfr*]

skat[1] /skät/ *n* a three-handed card game using 32 cards. [OFr *escart* laying aside]

skat[2] same as **scat**[5].

skat[3] see **scat**[3].

skate[1] /skāt/ *n* a boot mounted on a blade (for moving on ice); the blade itself; a roller skate; a spell of skating. ◆ *vi* to go on skates. [Du *schaats*, from ONFr *escache* stilt, from LGer *schake* shank]
■ **skā'ter** *n*. **skā'ting** *n*.
□ **skate'board** *n* a narrow board made of wood, fibreglass, etc, mounted on small wheels, on which the user balances and rides, *usu* in a standing position. ◆ *vi* to ride on a skateboard. **skate'boarder** *n*. **skate'boarding** *n*. **skate'park** *n* an area set aside for skateboarding, *usu* including specially designed ramps, etc. **skating rink** *n*.
■ **get one's skates on** (*inf*) to hurry. **skate around** or **round** (*fig*) to avoid discussing or answering directly. **skate on thin ice** see under **ice**. **skate over** (*fig*) to hurry over lightly.

skate[2] /skāt/ *n* a large edible kind of ray of tropical and temperate waters (*Raja batis*, or related species). [ON *skata*]

skatole /skat'ōl or skä'tōl/ *n* a crystalline compound (C_9H_9N) found in faeces and coal tar. [Gr *skōr, skatos* dung]

skatt same as **scat**[6].

skaw or **scaw** /skö/ *n* a low cape or headland (in place names). [ON *skagi*]

skean see **skene**.

skear and **skeary** dialect forms of **scare** and **scary**.

skedaddle /ski-dad'l/ (*inf*) *vi* to run off hurriedly. ◆ *n* a hasty flight. [Ety uncertain]
■ **skedadd'ler** *n*.

skeechan /skē'hhən/ (*Scot*) *n* a kind of beer made by mixing malt liquor, a by-product of the brewing process, with treacle. [Gaelic *caochan* fermented liquor]

skeely /skē'li/ (*Scot*) *adj* skilful. [**skill**]

skeer and **skeery** dialect forms of **scare** and **scary**.

skeesicks /skē'ziks/ (*US*) *n* a rascal.

skeet /skēt/ *n* a form of clay-pigeon shooting in which targets are released in opposite directions and at different elevations. [ON *skōta* to shoot]

skeeter /skē'tər/ (*US*) *n* an informal short form of **mosquito**.

Skeffington's daughter see **scavenger**[1].

skeg or **skegg** /skeg/ (*naut*) *n* (in early sailing vessels) a short length of keel projecting aft beyond the sternpost to protect the rudder; (in steamships) an extension or projection from the keel to protect the propellers; (in modern yachts) a short keel used in conjunction with a fin keel; a stabilizing fin projecting from the underside at the rear of a surfboard or sailboard. [Du *scheg* cutwater, from Scand]

skegger /skeg'ər/ *n* a young salmon, a salmon fry. [Scand; perhaps related to **skeg**]

skeigh /skēhh/ (*Scot*) *adj* shy; coy; aloof; skittish. [Cf OE *scēoh* shy]

skein /skān/ *n* a loosely tied coil or standard length of thread or yarn; a tangle (also *fig*); a web; a loose or confused bundle of things; a flock of wild geese in flight; the chromosomal network in a cell when at the mitosis stage (*cytology*; *obs*). [OFr *escaigne*]

skelder /skel'dər/ *vi* and *vt* to beg or obtain (money) by begging; to swindle, cheat. [Cant; perh perverted from Du *bedelen* to beg]

skeleton /skel'i-t(ə)n/ *n* the internal or external framework of bones of a person or an animal; the veins of a leaf; a framework or outline of anything; a scheme reduced to its essential or indispensable elements;

a workforce, etc reduced to its lowest strength; an emaciated person or animal (*inf*). ◆ *adj* of or like a skeleton; (of a workforce, etc) reduced to its lowest strength. [Gr *skeleton* (*sōma*), dried (body), from *skellein* to dry]
■ **skel'etal** *adj*. **skel'etally** *adv*. **skeletogenous** /-toj'| *adj* skeleton-forming. **skel'etonize** or **-ise** *vt* to reduce to a skeleton or minimum framework; to create the basic framework for.
□ **skeleton bob** or **bobsleigh** *n* a small flat sledge with no steering mechanism on which one person races head-first down an ice-covered course. **skeleton key** *n* a key with its serrated edge or the shaped part of its bit filed down, so that it can open many locks. **skeleton shrimp** *n* a ghostly-looking amphipod (genus *Caprella*). **skeleton suit** *n* (*hist*) an early-19c boy's suit with the trousers buttoning over the coat.
■ **a skeleton in the cupboard** or (*US*) **closet** a hidden domestic sorrow or shame.

skelf /skelf/ (*Scot* and *N Eng*) *n* a splinter of wood, *esp* one that becomes embedded in the skin; a very thin person. [Prob from obs Du *schelf*]

skell /skel/ (*sl*) *n* a homeless person who lives on the streets, often obtaining money, etc by begging. [Prob from **skelder** or **skellum**]

skellie see **skelly**[1].

skelloch /skel'əhh/ (*Scot*) *vi* to yell. ◆ *n* a yell.

skellum, **schellum** or **skelum** /skel'əm/ (*dialect* and *Scot*) *n* a ne'er-do-well; a scamp, rascal. [Du *schelm* a rogue; cf **skelm**]

skelly[1] or **skellie** /skel'i/ (*Scot*) *vi* to squint. ◆ *n* a sideways glance. ◆ *adj* (also **skelly-eyed'**) cross-eyed. [Prob ON; cf OE *sceolh* squint]

skelly[2] same as **schelly**.

skelm or **schelm** /skelm/ (*S Afr*) *n* a rascal. [Du *schelm*, Ger *Schelm*]

skelp /skelp/ (*Scot* and *N Eng*) *vt* to slap. ◆ *vi* to move briskly along; to bound along. ◆ *n* a slap. [Gaelic *sgealp* a slap with the palm of the hand]
■ **skelp'ing** *adj* very big or full; smacking; lusty. ◆ *n* a smacking.

skelter /skel'tər/ *vi* to scurry. ◆ *n* a scurry.

skene /skēn/ or **skean** /skē'ən/ *n* an Irish or Highland dagger, knife, or short sword. [Ir and Gaelic *sgian* knife]
□ **skene-dhu** or **skean-dhu** /-doo'| *n* (Irish and Gaelic *dhu* black) a dirk, a dagger stuck in the stocking in full Highland dress. **skene-occle** /-ok'l/ *n* (Irish and Gaelic *achlais* armpit) a dirk, dagger or knife carried in the sleeve.

skeo same as **skio**.

skep /skep/ *n* a large round basket of wickerwork or straw; a beehive, *esp* one made of straw. ◆ *vt* (**skepp'ing**; **skepped**) to collect into a hive. [ON *skeppa* bushel]
■ **skep'ful** *n*.

skeptic, skepsis same as **sceptic, scepsis**.

sker same as **skirr**.

skerrick /sker'ik/ (*dialect*; *esp N Am, Aust* and *NZ*) *n* a minute quantity, a scrap, chiefly in the phrase *not a skerrick*. [Ety uncertain]

skerry /sker'i/ *n* a reef of rock or a small rocky island. [ON *sker*]

sketch /skech/ *n* a drawing, slight, rough, or without detail, *esp* as a study towards a more finished work; an outline or short account; a short and slightly constructed play, dramatic scene, musical entertainment, etc; a short descriptive essay. ◆ *vt* to make or give a sketch of; to outline, or give the principal points of. ◆ *vi* to practise sketching. [Du *schets*, prob from Ital *schizzo*, from L *schedium* an extempore, from Gr *schedios* offhand]
■ **sketchabil'ity** *n*. **sketch'able** *adj* worth sketching. **sketch'er** *n*. **sketch'ily** *adv*. **sketch'iness** *n*. **sketch'y** *adj* like a sketch; incomplete, slight, vague; imperfect, inadequate.
□ **sketch'book** or **sketch book** *n* a book of or for sketches (in drawing, literature or music).

skeuomorph /skū'ə-mörf/ *n* a decoration or decorative feature in architecture, etc, derived from the nature of the material (originally) used, or the way of working it; a retained but no longer either functional or incidental characteristic of an artefact, eg the 'casting seams' knapped onto a flint knife, imitated from those on a cast bronze knife (*archaeol*); also applied to modern decorative features such as the imitation stitching on plastic upholstery. [Gr *skeuos* vessel, tool, and *morphe* shape]
■ **skeuomorph'ic** *adj*. **skeuomorph'ism** *n*.

Skevington's daughter see **scavenger**[1].

skew[1] /skū/ *adj* oblique; biased; asymmetrical; (of lines) not lying in the same plane (*maths*); (of statistics or a curve representing them) not symmetrical about the mean. ◆ *adv* awry. ◆ *n* obliquity. ◆ *vt* and *vi* to set, go, or look obliquely. [Appar ONFr *eskiu(w)er*, from OFr *eschuer*; see **eschew**; or MDu *schuwe* to shun; cf **shy**[1]]
■ **skewed** *adj* distorted; skew. **skew'ness** *n*.

❑ **skew arch** *n* an arch set obliquely on its abutments. **skew'back** *n* (*archit*) the part or inclined surface on which a segmented arch abuts. **skew bridge** *n* a bridge having a skew arch. **skew-whiff'** *adj* and *adv* (*inf*) crooked, awry.

skew² /skū/ *n* the coping or a coping-stone of a gable. [OFr *escu*, from L *scūtum* a shield]

❑ **skew'-corbel**, **skew'-put** or **skew'-table** *n* the cornerstone supporting the coping of a gable.

skewbald /skū'böld/ *adj* (of an animal, *esp* a horse) marked in white and another colour (not black). ◆ *n* a skewbald horse. [From **skew¹** and pie*bald*]

skewer /skū'ər/ *n* a long pin of wood or metal, *esp* for holding pieces of meat together for cooking. ◆ *vt* to fasten or pierce with a skewer; to transfix. [**skiver**]

ski /skē, formerly also *shē*/ *n* (*pl* **skis** or **ski**) a long narrow runner *orig* of wood, now also of metal or synthetic materials, fastened to the foot to enable the wearer to slide across snow, etc; a water-ski. ◆ *vi* (**ski'ing**; **skied** or **ski'd**) to travel on skis. [Norw, from ON *skíth* snow-shoe, piece of split wood; OE *scíd*]

■ **ski'able** *adj* (of a surface) in a condition suitable for skiing on. **ski'er** *n*. **ski'ing** *n*.

❑ **ski'bob** *n* a vehicle resembling a bicycle used for gliding down snow-slopes, consisting of a short front-pivoting ski, turned by handlebars, and a longer fixed rear ski with a seat attached (also *vi*). **ski'bobber** *n*. **ski'bobbing** *n*. **ski bum** *n* (*inf*) a devotee of skiing who travels the world seasonally in search of snowy conditions. **ski'-flying** *n* ski jumping from a high take-off point, so that a longer time is spent in the air. **skijor'er** *n*. **skijoring** /-jör' or -jör'/ or (*Norw*) **skikjöring** /shihh-yûr'ing/ *n* the sport of being towed on skis by a horse or motor vehicle. **ski jump** *n* a steeply sloping, snow-covered track ending in an elevated platform from which a skier jumps; a jump by a skier from such a platform. **ski jumper** *n*. **ski jumping** *n*. **ski'-kiting** *n* water-skiing holding on to a bar on a kitelike device. **ski lift**, **ski tow** *n* devices for taking skiers uphill. **ski mask** *n* a knitted covering for the whole head except the eyes, worn for protection by skiers and bank robbers. **ski pants** *n pl* tightly-fitting trousers made of stretch fabric and having a strap which is worn under the foot, *orig* designed for skiing but now more often worn by women as everyday wear. **ski'plane** *n* an aeroplane with skis attached to its undercarriage to enable it to take off from and land on snow and ice. **ski run** *n* a slope for skiing on. **ski school** *n*. **ski slope** *n*. **ski stick** or **ski pole** *n* one of a pair of sticks, *usu* pointed with a disc near the tip, used by skiers for balance or propulsion. **ski touring** *n* the sport of journeying on skis across country, as distinct from downhill skiing on a particular slope.

skia- /skī'ə- or skī-a-/ or **scia-** /sī-ə- or sī-a-/ *combining form* denoting shadow. [Gr *skiā* a shadow]

■ **ski'agram** or **ski'agraph** *n* a shadow picture or photograph, eg an X-ray photograph. **skiamachy** /-am'ə-ki/ *n* (Gr *machē* a fight) a sham fight; a fight with shadows. **skias'copy** *n* retinoscopy. **ski'atron** *n* a cathode-ray tube in which an electron beam varies the transparency of a phosphor, which is illuminated from behind so that its image is projected onto a screen.

skid /skid/ *vi* (**skidd'ing**; **skidded**) to slide along without rotating, as does a wheel to which a brake has been applied; to slip, *esp* sideways; (of an aeroplane) to slide sideways when banking; to slip or slide losing grip or traction. ◆ *vt* to check with a skid; to cause to skid. ◆ *n* a side-slip; a skidding; a support on which something rests, is brought to the desired level, or slides; an aeroplane runner; a ship's wooden fender; a shoe or other device to check a wheel on a down-slope. [Prob related to **ski**]

■ **skidd'er** *n* a person or thing that skids; a tractor with thick tyres used for hauling logs (*forestry*). **skidd'y** *adj*.

❑ **skid lid** (*sl*) a crash-helmet. **skid mark** *n* the black trace left on a road surface by the tyre of a skidding vehicle; (*vulgar sl*) a faecal stain on one's underwear. **skid pan** or **pad** *n* a piece of slippery ground on which motorists can learn to control a skidding car. **skid'pan** *n* (*sl*) a drag for a wheel (also *fig*). **skid'proof** *adj* (of a road surface, tyre, etc) designed to prevent skids. **skid road** *n* (*N Am*) a road covered with greased logs over which timber can be hauled; same as **skid row** below. **skid row** *n* (*esp N Am*) a squalid quarter where vagrants, drunks, etc live.

■ **put the skids on** or **under** (*sl*) to cause to hurry; to put a stop to, thwart. **the skids** (*fig*; *inf*) a downward path.

Ski-doo® or **skidoo** /ski-doo'/ *n* a motorized sledge, fitted with tracks at the rear and steerable skis at the front.

skier¹ see under **ski**.

skier² and **skiey** see under **sky**.

skiff¹ /skif/ *n* a small light boat. [Related to **ship**]

skiff² /skif/ (*Scot*) *vi* and *vt* to skim. ◆ *n* a skimming or grazing movement or blow; a slight touch; a sketch; a puff. [Prob imit]

skiffle¹ /skif'l/ *n* a strongly accented form of music played on guitars, drums, and often unconventional instruments, etc, popular in the late 1950s. [Origin obscure]

skiffle² /skif'l/ (*dialect*) *n* light rain, drizzle. [Prob from **skiff²**]

skijoring, **skikjöring** see under **ski**.

skill /skil/ *n* expertness; a craft or accomplishment; (in *pl*) aptitudes and competencies appropriate for a particular job; expert knowledge (*archaic*); reason (*Shakesp*); discrimination (*obs*). ◆ *vt* and *vi* (*archaic*) to matter; to make (a difference); to signify. [ON *skil* distinction, *skilja* to separate]

■ **skil'ful** or (*N Am*) **skill'ful** *adj*. **skil'fully** or (*N Am*) **skill'fully** *adv*. **skil'fulness** or (*N Am*) **skill'fulness** *n*. **skilled** *adj* expert; skilful; (of a job) requiring special training. **skill'-less** or **skil'less** *adj*. **skill'y** or **skeel'y** *adj* (*Scot*) skilful.

❑ **skill'centre** *n* formerly in Britain, a Government-funded training establishment to assist those who wish to develop new occupational skills. **skill set** *n* (*commercial jargon*) a range of job-related aptitudes. **skills gap** *n* a situation in which there are insufficient numbers of workers with the appropriate level of training in the skills required by industry; a shortage of skilled workers.

skillet /skil'it/ *n* a small, long-handled pan; a frying-pan (*esp N Am*). [Origin doubtful]

skilligalee, **skilligolee** see under **skilly¹**.

skilling¹ /skil'ing/ *n* an obsolete coin of Scandinavian countries, of small value. [Dan]

skilling² see **skillion**.

skillion /skil'yən/ (*Aust*) *n* an outhouse or lean-to, *esp* one with a sloping roof (also **skill'ing**). [Eng dialect *skilling* an outhouse, lean-to]

❑ **skillion roof** *n* a roof slanting out from the wall of a building.

skilly¹ /skil'i/ *n* thin gruel (also **skilligalee'** or **skilligolee'**). [Ety uncertain]

skilly² see under **skill**.

skim /skim/ *vt* (**skimm'ing**; **skimmed**) to remove floating matter from the surface of; to remove (floating matter) from the surface of a liquid (often with *off*; also *fig*); to glide lightly over; to throw (something) over a surface so as to make it bounce; to read superficially, skipping parts (often with *over* or *through*). ◆ *vi* to pass over lightly; to glide along near the surface; to become coated over; (of an organized criminal group) to fail to declare certain income in order to avoid tax payment (*sl*); to copy information stored on a credit card in order to create a counterfeit card with the same account data (*sl*). ◆ *n* the act of skimming; skimmed milk; a thin layer covering a surface. [Appar related to **scum**]

■ **skimm'er** *n* someone who or something that skims; a utensil for skimming milk; an apparatus for clearing water of floating debris or pollutants, eg in a swimming-pool; a seabird of the genus *Rhyncops*, related to the tern, that skims the water; another name for the shearwater. **skimm'ing** *n*. **skimm'ingly** *adv*.

❑ **skimmed milk** or **skim milk** *n* milk from which the cream has been skimmed.

skimble-skamble /skim'bl-skam'bl/ (*archaic*) *adj* wild, rambling, incoherent. [A reduplication of **scamble**]

skimmia /skim'i-ə/ *n* any Asiatic shrub of the genus *Skimmia*, cultivated for its holly-like leaves and fragrant panicles of flowers. [Jap *shikimi*]

skimmington /skim'ing-tən/ *n* (in rural Britain) the old custom of forming a burlesque procession to ridicule an unfaithful husband or nagging wife. [Origin unknown]

skimp /skimp/ *vt* and *vi* to scrimp; to stint. ◆ *vt* to carry out hurriedly or recklessly. ◆ *adj* scanty, spare. [Poss **scamp²** combined with **scrimp**]

■ **skimp'ily** *adv*. **skimp'iness** *n*. **skimp'ingly** *adv*. **skimp'y** *adj* (of clothes) scanty; stingy, mean.

skin /skin/ *n* the natural outer covering of tissue of a person or an animal; a hide; a thin outer layer or covering; the outer surface other than fabric of an aircraft (*aeronautics*); the programs that determine the visual appearance of a document on the World Wide Web but can be substituted without altering its content or functionality (*comput*); an integument; a membrane; a wine-vessel made of an animal's skin; a drum (*inf*); a cigarette paper for making a joint of marijuana (*sl*); short for **skinhead** below (*sl*). ◆ *adj* of skin. ◆ *vt* (**skinn'ing**; **skinned**) to cover with a skin; to strip the skin from; to injure by scraping the skin; to swindle or fleece (*sl*). ◆ *vi* to become covered with skin, or with any membranous layer; to slip through or away. [ON *skinn*; late OE *scinn*]

■ **skin'ful** *n* (*inf*) as much alcoholic drink as one can hold. **skin'less** *adj*. **skin'-like** *adj*. **skinned** *adj* stripped of skin; having skin, *esp* (in combination) of a specified type or quality, as in *fair-skinned*, *thick-skinned*. **skinn'er** *n* a person who prepares hides. **skinn'iness** *n*. **skinn'y** *adj* of or like skin; thin, *esp* unattractively thin, too thin; (of a pullover, etc) tight-fitting (*inf*). ◆ *n* (*sl*; *usu* with *the*) information.

■ words derived from main entry word; ❑ compound words; ■ idioms and phrasal verbs

❑ **skin'care** *n* care of the skin, using cosmetics, etc. **skin'-deep** *adj* superficial; shallow, not deeply fixed. ◆ *adv* superficially. **skin'-diver** *n* orig, a naked pearl diver; a person involved in skin diving. **skin diving** *n* diving and swimming underwater, with breathing equipment carried on the back, not wearing the traditional diver's helmet and suit. **skin effect** *n* the tendency, increasing with frequency, for an alternating current to be greater in the surface layer of a conductor. **skin'flick** *n* (*sl*) a cinema film in which there is much nudity and sexual activity, *esp* a (cheaply made) pornographic film. **skin'flint** *n* a very niggardly person. **skin'food** *n* a cosmetic intended to nourish the skin. **skin game** *n* a swindling trick. **skin graft** *n* the transplantation of a piece of skin from one part of the body to another where there has been an injury, *esp* a burn. **skin'head** *n* a young person with closely cropped hair, *esp* applied to a member of a gang wearing simple, severe clothes and displaying aggressive anti-establishment behaviour. **skin magazine** *n* (*sl*) a magazine featuring photographs of naked women (or men). **skinn'y-dip** *vi* (*inf*) to bathe naked. **skinn'y-dipper** *n*. **skinn'y-dipping** *n*. **skinny latte** see under **latte**. **skinn'y-rib** *n* (*inf*) a tight-fitting sweater of ribbed wool or similar fibre (also *adj*). **skin'-pop** *vi* (*sl*) to inject drugs. ◆ *n* the injection of a drug. **skin'-popper** *n*. **skin'-popping** *n*. **skin'suit** *n* a one-piece skintight garment worn by cyclists, athletes, etc. **skin test** *n* a test made by applying a substance to, or introducing a substance beneath, a person's skin, to test for an allergy, immunity from a disease, etc. **skin'tight** *adj* fitting close to the body, like a skin. **skin'tights** *n pl* close-fitting garments. **skin wool** *n* wool from a dead sheep.

■ **by** or **with the skin of one's teeth** very narrowly. **get under someone's skin** to annoy someone; to interest someone seriously, to become an obsession with someone. **have a thin** (or **thick**) **skin** to possess (or lack) a sensitive nature. **no skin off one's nose** (*inf*) a matter about which one feels unconcerned or indifferent because it does not harm or inconvenience one, or because it may be to one's benefit. **save one's skin** to save one's life. **skin up** (*sl*) to make a marijuana joint (see the corresponding sense of the *n* above).

skink¹ /*skingk*/ *n* any lizard of the family Scincidae, of Africa, Asia, and Australia, with an elongated body and short limbs. [L *scincus*, from Gr *skinkos*]

skink² /*skingk*/ *n* (*Scot*) soup, *orig* made with stock from a shin of beef, now *usu* made with fish; a shin of beef. [MDu *schenke*, LGer *schinke*]

skink³ /*skingk*/ *vi* and *vt* to pour out. ◆ *n* (*Scot*) alcoholic drink. [Perh LGer *schenken*; cf OE *scencan*; Ger *schenken*]
■ **skink'er** *n*. **skink'ing** *adj* (*Scot*) thin, watery.

skinny see under **skin**.

skint /*skint*/ (*sl*) *adj* without money, hard up. [**skinned**]

skio or **skeo** /*skyō*/ (*Orkney* and *Shetland*) *n* (*pl* **skios** or **skeos**) a hut; a shed. [Norw *skjaa*]

skip¹ /*skip*/ *vi* (**skipp'ing**; **skipped**) to progress by hopping on each foot alternately; to spring or hop lightly; to make jumps over a twirling rope; to pass lightly, inattentively, etc (with *through*, *over*, etc); to pass discontinuously. ◆ *vt* to overleap; to omit; to cut, not go to (eg a class); to make (a stone) skim over a surface. ◆ *n* a skipping movement; an act of skipping; a belt of inaudibility in wireless transmission; a college servant in some older universities. [Cf ON *skopa* to run]

■ **skipp'er** *n* a person who skips; a dancer; a young and thoughtless person (*Shakesp*); a stout hairy-bodied butterfly of the family Hesperiidae, with wings of the same length as its body, so called because of its short jerky flight; the saury. **skipp'ing** *adj* flighty, giddy. ◆ *n* the art or activity of jumping over a twirling rope. **skipp'ingly** *adv*. **skipp'y** *adj* (*inf*) frolicsome; exuberant.

❑ **skip'jack** *n* any of a number of species of fish that jump out of, or swim at the surface of, the water, such as the bonitos, the bluefish, the saurel, and either of two species of tuna (the **skipjack tuna**, *Katsuwonus pelamis*, and the **black skipjack**, *Euthynnus yaito*); a type of sailing boat sometimes used for oystering (*US*); another name for the click beetle; a pert fop (*archaic*); a jumping toy made of a fowl's wishbone (*hist*). **skip'-kennel** *n* (*obs*) a lackey. **skipp'ing-rope** *n* a rope for skipping with. **skip-tooth saw** *n* a saw from which alternate teeth are cut away. **skip zone** *n* an area round a broadcasting station where transmissions cannot be received.
■ **skip it!** (*inf*) never mind, forget it!

skip² /*skip*/ *n* a box or truck for raising minerals and workers from a mine; a large container for transporting building materials, etc, theatrical costumes or refuse. [**skep**]

skip³ /*skip*/ *n* the captain of a rink in bowls or curling. ◆ *vt* and *vi* (**skipp'ing**; **skipped**) to act as a skip. [**skipper**]

skipjack see under **skip¹**.

skipper¹ /*skip'ər*/ *n* a ship's captain; the captain of an aeroplane; the captain of a team. ◆ *vt* to act as skipper. [Du *schipper*]
❑ **skipper's daughters** *n pl* white-topped waves.

skipper² see under **skip¹**.

skipper³ /*skip'ər*/ (*old sl*) *n* a barn, outhouse, etc, *esp* as a sleeping-place for vagrants. ◆ *vi* to sleep rough in barns, etc. [Perh Cornish *sciber* or Welsh *ysgubor* barn]
■ **skipp'ering** *n* (*sl*) sleeping rough.

skippet /*skip'it*/ *n* a flat box for protecting a seal (eg of a document). [Origin unknown]

skirl /*skirl* or *skûrl*/ (*Scot*) *vt* and *vi* to shriek or sing shrilly. ◆ *vi* to make the sound of the bagpipes. ◆ *n* a shrill cry; the sound of the bagpipes. [Scand]
■ **skirl'ing** *n* a shrill sound.
❑ **skirl-in-the-pan'** *n* the noise of frying; a fried dish.

skirmish /*skûr'mish*/ *n* a minor irregular fight between small or marginal parties. ◆ *vi* to engage in a skirmish. [OFr *escarmouche*]
■ **skir'misher** *n*. **skir'mishing** *n*.

skirr, **sker**, **scur** or **squirr** /*skûr*/ *vt* to scour, search, range over (*Scot*); to send skimming. ◆ *vi* (*Shakesp*) to scurry. [Origin doubtful]

skirret /*skir'it*/ *n* a water parsnip (*Sium sisarum*) with edible roots. [ME *skirwhit*, as if *skire white*, pure white, but perh altered from OFr *eschervis*]

skirt /*skûrt*/ *n* a garment, or part of a garment, generally a woman's, that hangs from the waist; the lower part of a gown, coat, or other garment or anything suggesting this; a flap hanging from a saddle; a midriff (of meat); a rim, border, margin; a part of, or attachment to, an object that suggests a skirt, eg the flap of material hanging down around the base of a hovercraft to contain the air-cushion, or a similar flap around a racing-car; the lower edges of a sheep's fleece (*Aust* and *NZ*); a woman (also **bit of skirt**) or women collectively (*offensive sl*). ◆ *vt* to border; to pass along the edge of; to scour the outskirts of; to avoid confronting. ◆ *vi* to be on or pass along the border (*usu* with *along*, *around*, etc); (of dogs) to leave the pack (*hunting*). [ON *skyrta* a shirt, kirtle; cf **shirt**]

■ **skir'ted** *adj* wearing or having a skirt. **skir'ter** *n* someone who removes skirts from fleeces (*Aust* and *NZ*); a huntsman who dodges jumps by going round about. **skir'ting** *n* material for skirts; skirting-board; (in *pl*) dirty wool from the skirts of a fleece. **skirt'less** *adj*.
❑ **skirt chaser** *n* (*inf*) a womanizer. **skirt'-dancing** *n* dancing characterized by the waving of flowing skirts. **skir'ting-board** *n* the narrow board next to the floor round the walls of a room.
■ **divided skirt** trousers made to look like a skirt.

skit /*skit*/ *n* a satirical sketch in dramatic or literary form; a humorous hit; a hoax; a sudden slight shower of rain or snow, etc (*dialect*). [Perh related to ON *skjóta* to shoot]
■ **skite** or **skyte** /*skīt*/ *vi* (*Scot*) to dart or glide obliquely. ◆ *n* a glancing blow; a spree; a trick; a queer person.

skite /*skīt*/ (*Aust & NZ inf*) *vi* to boast. ◆ *n* a boastful person; boastful chatter. [**blatherskite**]

skitter /*skit'ər*/ *vi* to skim over the surface of water; to fish by drawing the bait over the surface; to scamper lightly. [Perh from **skite** (see **skit**)]

skittish /*skit'ish*/ *adj* unsteady; light-headed; frivolous; frisky; playful; lively; volatile; changeable; nervous; wanton; coy (*rare*). [Perh connected with **skit**]
■ **skitt'ishly** *adv*. **skitt'ishness** *n*.

skittle /*skit'l*/ *n* a pin for the game of **skittles**, a form of ninepins in which a ball or cheese (see **cheese¹**) is used. ◆ *vt* to knock down. [Prob alteration of **kail¹** (see ety for **squail**), through intermediate *kittle*; see **kittle-pins**]
❑ **skitt'le-alley** *n*. **skitt'le-ball** *n*. **skitt'le-ground** *n*.
■ **beer and skittles** see under **beer¹**. **skittle out** (*cricket*; *inf*) to dismiss (a batsman or team) for a low score, *usu* quickly.

skive¹ /*skīv*/ (*inf*) *vt* and *vi* (often with *off*) to evade (a duty, work, etc). ◆ *n* an instance of skiving. [Origin uncertain]
■ **ski'ver** *n*. **skī'vy** *adj*.

skive² /*skīv*/ *vt* to pare or split leather. [ON *skīfa*; cf **shive**]
■ **ski'ver** *n* split sheepskin leather; a person or machine that skives. **skī'ving** *n*.

skiver /*skiv'ər*/ (*dialect*) *n* and *vt* same as **skewer**. [Origin unknown]

skivie /*skī'vi*/ (*obs Scot*) *adj* deranged; askew. [Cf ON *skeifr*]

skivvy¹ /*skiv'i*/ (*inf*) *n* a disrespectful word for a (*esp female*) domestic servant; a drudge. ◆ *vi* to work as a skivvy, to drudge. [Origin uncertain]

skivvy² /*skiv'i*/ *n* a man's undervest (*esp N Am sl*); (in *pl*) men's underwear (*esp N Am sl*); a knitted cotton polo-necked sweater (*Aust* and *NZ*). [Ety uncertain]

sklate /*sklāt*/ Scottish form of **slate¹**.

sklent /*sklent*/ Scottish form of **slant¹**.

skliff same as **scliff**.

sklim same as **sclim**.

skoal /skōl/ or **skol** /skol/ *interj* hail!; a friendly exclamation in salutation before drinking, etc. [ON *skål*; Norw *skaal* a bowl, Swed *skå*; cf **scale**[2,3]]

skoff see **scoff**[2].

skokiaan /skō'ki-än/ (*S Afr*) *n* a strong home-brewed drink made from yeast. [Afrik]

skol see **skoal**.

skolion or **scolion** /skō'li-on or skol'ī-/ *n* (pl **skō'lia** or **scō'lia** (or /skol'/)) a short drinking-song of ancient Greece, taken up by the guests in irregular succession. [Gr *skolion*]

skolly or **skollie** /skol'i/ (*S Afr derog*) *n* a young hooligan or gang member of Coloured race. [Afrik, prob from Du *schoelje* rascal]

skoosh see **scoosh**.

skran same as **scran**.

skreen same as **screen** (*esp* in the sense of a partition of wood or stone).

skreigh, skriech, skriegh, screich, screigh or **scriech** /skrēhh/ (*Scot*) *n* and *v* (to) screech, shriek. [Imit improvement upon **screak**]
▫ **skreigh of day** *n* cock-crow, daybreak.

skrik /skrik/ (*S Afr*) *n* a fright. [Afrik, from Du *schrik* fright]

skrimmage same as **scrimmage**.

skrimp see **scrump**.

skrimshank or **scrimshank** /skrim'shangk/ (*milit sl*) *vi* to evade work or duty. ◆ *n* evasion of work. [Origin obscure]
■ **skrim'shanker** *n*.

skronk /skronk/ *n* a loud, energetic style of music that contains elements of jazz and funk. [Imit]

skrump see **scrump**.

skry, skryer same as **scry, scryer**.

Skt or **Skr** *abbrev* : Sanskrit.

skua /skū'ə/ *n* any of several large predatory gull-like birds of the genus *Stercorarius*. [ON *skūfr*]

skudler, scuddaler or **scudler** /skud'lər/ (*Shetland*) *n* the leader of a band of guisers; the conductor of a festival. [Origin obscure]

skug[1] or **scug** /skug/ (*Scot* **scoug, scoog** /skŭg/ or **scog** /skog/) *n* *orig* shadow; shelter. ◆ *vt* and *vi* to shelter. [ON *skuggi* shadow]

skulduddery see **sculduddry**.

skulduggery or (*N Am*) **skullduggery** /skul'dug'ə-ri/ *n* underhand malpractices; trickery. [Perh **sculduddery**]

skulk /skulk/ *vi* to sneak out of the way; to lurk; to malinger. [Scand, as in Dan *skulke*]
■ **skulk** or **skulk'er** *n* a person who skulks. **skulk'ing** *n* and *adj*. **skulk'ingly** *adv*.
▫ **skulk'ing-place** *n*.

skull[1] /skul/ *n* the bony case that encloses the brain; the head, the brain (*inf*); a skullcap, *esp* of metal; a crust of solidified metal on a ladle, etc. [ME *scolle*; perh Scand]
▫ **skull and crossbones** see **crossbones** under **cross**. **skull'cap** *n* a close-fitting brimless cap; a protective cap of metal for the top of the head; the top of the skull; any labiate plant of the genus *Scutellaria*, with helmet-like calyx.
■ **out of one's skull** (*inf*) mad, crazy; extremely drunk.

skull[2] see **scull**[2].

skulpin same as **sculpin**.

skummer see **scumber**.

skunk /skungk/ *n* a small American musteline animal, typically with a black-and-white coat and a squirrel-like tail, that emits an offensive fluid from a gland near its anus to deter predators; its fur; a despised person (*abusive sl*); a type of cannabis smoked for its particularly strong narcotic effects (*sl*). ◆ *vt* (*US*) to defeat without allowing to score. [Algonquian *segonku*]
▫ **skunk'bird** or **skunk-black'bird** *n* the bobolink (from its colouring). **skunk cabbage** *n* a foul-smelling plant (*Symplocarpus foetidus*) of the arum family.

Skupstina or **Skupshtina** /skŭp'shti-nə/ *n* a national assembly in Serbia or Montenegro; the national assembly of Yugoslavia (*hist*). [Serb]

skurry same as **scurry**.

skutterudite /skŭt'ə-rŭ-dīt/ *n* a cubic mineral, cobalt arsenide. [*Skutterud* in Norway, a source]

skuttle same as **scuttle**[3].

sky /skī/ *n* (pl **skies**) the apparent canopy over our heads; the heavens; the weather; the upper rows of pictures in a gallery; sky blue. ◆ *vt* (**sky'ing; skied**) to raise aloft; to hit high into the air; to hang above the line of sight. [ON *skȳ* cloud]

sky'er or **skī'er** *n* (*cricket*) a ball hit high into the air. **sky'ey** or **skī'ey** *adj* of the weather; or of like the sky. **sky'ish** *adj* (*Shakesp*) like or approaching the sky, lofty. **sky'less** *adj*. **sky'ward** *adj* and *adv*. **sky'wards** *adv*.
▫ **sky'-aspiring** *adj* (*Shakesp*). **sky blue** *n* light blue like the sky. **sky-blue'** *adj*. **sky-blue pink** *n* an imaginary colour. **sky'born** *adj* of heavenly birth. **sky'-bred** *adj*. **skybridge** see **skywalk** below. **sky'clad** *adj* naked. **sky'-coloured** *adj*. **sky'dive** *vi*. **sky'diver** *n*. **sky'diving** or **sky'jumping** *n* jumping by parachute as a sport, using a special steerable parachute, and delaying opening it for a specified time. **sky-high'** *adj* (*esp* of prices) very high (also *adv*). **sky'hook** *n* a hook at the end of a length of cable and hung beneath eg a helicopter, used to attach a load; a type of grappling-iron used by climbers to secure a rope above, on a sheer face. **sky'jack** *vt* (*inf*) to hijack (an aeroplane). **sky'jacker** *n*. **sky'jacking** *n*. **sky'lab** *n* an orbiting experimental space-station, *specif* (with *cap*) that launched and manned by the USA, 1973–4. **sky'lark** *n* the common lark. ◆ *vi* to frolic boisterously. ◆ *vt* to trick. **sky'larker** *n*. **sky'larking** *n* running about the rigging of a ship in sport; frolicking. **sky'light** *n* a window in a roof or ceiling; light from or in the sky; light through the bottom of an empty glass. **skylight filter** *n* (*photog*) a slightly pink filter that absorbs ultraviolet light. **sky'line** *n* the horizon; a silhouette or outline against the sky. **sky'man** *n* a paratrooper. **sky marshal** *n* an armed plain-clothes officer on an air-flight, having the job of protecting passengers and dealing with hijack attempts. **sky parlour** *n* (*old inf*) an attic. **sky pilot** *n* (*sl*) a clergyman, a military chaplain. **sky'rocket** *n* a firework that bursts high in the sky. ◆ *vi* to shoot up high; to rise high and fast. **skysail** /skī'sl/ *n* a square sail above the royal on a square-rigged ship. **sky'scape** *n* a view or a picture of the sky. **sky'scraper** *n* a very tall building; a triangular skysail; anything very high. **skyscraper ad** *n* an advertisement positioned down the side of a page on the Internet. **sky sign** *n* an elevated advertising sign, eg a neon sign on a high building. **sky surfing** *n* the sport of free-falling from an aeroplane with a modified surfboard attached to the feet, which is used to ride the air currents. **sky'-tinc'tured** *adj* of the colour of the sky. **sky troops** *n pl* paratroopers; airborne troops. **sky'walk** or **sky'bridge** *n* a passageway between two elevated points, often with views over a valley or street below. **sky wave** *n* a radio wave reflected from the ionosphere. **sky'way** *n* a route for aircraft. **sky'writing** *n* tracing of words by smoke from an aircraft.
■ **the sky's the limit** (*inf*) there are no restrictions on amount or extent (of something). **to the skies** (*inf*) in a lavish or vociferously enthusiastic manner as in *applaud to the skies*.

Skye /skī/ *n* (in full, **Skye terrier**) a small long-haired Scotch terrier. [From the island of *Skye*]

Skype® /skīp/ *n* a network that allows telephone calls to be made using VOIP (*qv*) technology. ◆ *vi* and *vt* to communicate (with someone) by means of Skype.

skyr /shür or skēr/ *n* curds; a yoghurt-like curd cheese. [Scand, from ON]

skyre /skīr/ (*Scot*) *vi* to shine, be gaudy, flaunt. [Origin obscure]

skyrmion /skûr'mi-on/ (*phys*) *n* (in a non-linear field theory) a soliton (*qv*) with spin and statistics different from those of the underlying fields. [Tony *Skyrme* (1922–87), English physicist]

skyte see under **skit**.

SL *abbrev* : Serjeant-at-Law; Solicitor at Law.

slab[1] /slab/ *n* a thin flat piece of stone, etc; a large thick slice of cake, etc; an outer plank sawn from a log; a plane-sided plate. ◆ *vt* to cut slabs from; to form into slabs; to cover with slabs. [Origin obscure]
■ **slabbed** *adj*. **slabb'y** *adj*.
▫ **slab'-sided** *adj* (*N Am*) flat-sided; tall and lank. **slab'stone** *n* flagstone.

slab[2] /slab/ *adj* semi-liquid, viscous. ◆ *n* mud. [Scand; cf Norw, Swed *slabb* wet filth]
■ **slabb'iness** *n*. **slabb'y** *adj* muddy.

slabber /slab'ər/ *vi* to slaver, to drivel. ◆ *vt* to cover with spittle; to gobble sloppily and grossly. [Cf LGer and Du *slabberen* and **slobber**]
■ **slabb'erer** *n*. **slabb'ery** *adj*.

slack[1] /slak/ *adj* lax or loose; not firmly extended or drawn out; not holding fast; remiss; promiscuous (*sl*); not strict; not eager or diligent, inattentive; not busy; not violent or rapid, slow; pronounced with wide, not tense, tongue (*phonetics*). ◆ *adv* in a slack manner; partially; insufficiently. ◆ *n* the slack part of a rope, belt, etc; a time, occasion, or place of relaxed movement or activity; a slack-water haul of a net; (in *pl*) long, loose trousers for casual wear. ◆ *vi* and *vt* to slacken. [OE *slæc* (*sleac*); cf Swed *slak*, ON *slakr*]
■ **slack'en** *vi* to become loose or less tight; to be remiss; to abate; to become slower; to fail or flag; to be inactive or lax. ◆ *vt* to make slack or less tight; to loosen; to slow, retard; to be remiss or dilatory in; to relax; to slake (lime). **slack'ening** *n* and *adj*. **slack'er** *n* an idler; a person who is reprehensibly inactive; a shirker; (*US*) a young person

taking an apathetic or cynical attitude to mainstream culture. **slack'erdom** *n.* **slack'ly** *adv.* **slack'ness** *n.*

❑ **slack'-bake** *vt* to half-bake. **slack-hand'ed** *adj* remiss. **slack jaw** *n* (*sl*) impudent talk. **slack line** *n* a slack rope. **slack'lining** *n* walking along a slack rope (qv below). **slack rope** *n* a loosely stretched rope for a funambulist. **slack water** *n* turn of the tide; a stretch of still or slow-moving water. **slack'-water** *adj* relating to slack water.

■ **cut someone some slack** (*esp N Am inf*) to allow someone to act without undue criticism or pressure. **slack away** to ease off freely. **slack in stays** (of a ship, etc) slow in going about. **slack off** or **slacken off** to ease off. **slack up** or **slacken up** to ease off; to slow.

slack² /slak/ *n* coal dross. [Cf Ger *Schlacke*]

slack³ /slak/ (*Scot*) *n* a cleft between hills; a boggy place. [ON *slakki* dell]

sladang same as **seladang**.

slade¹ /slād/ *n* a small valley or dell; a piece of low, moist ground. [OE *slæd* dell]

slade² /slād/ Scots *pat* of **slide**.

slae /slā/ a Scots form of **sloe**.

slag¹ /slag/ *n* solid scum on molten metal; vitrified cinders; scoriaceous lava; coalmining waste; a piece of slag. ◆ *vt* and *vi* to form into slag. [MLGer *slagge*; cf Ger *Schlacke* dross]

■ **slagg'y** *adj.*

❑ **slag heap** *n* a small hill of coalmining waste. **slag wool** *n* fibre made from molten slag, mineral wool.

slag² /slag/ (*sl*) *n* a slovenly or dissolute woman (or, more recently, man). [**slag¹**]

slag³ /slag/ (*sl*) *vt* (**slagg'ing**; **slagged**) to criticize, mock, deride (*esp* with *off*). [**slag¹**]

slag⁴ /slag/ (*Aust sl*) *n* spit. ◆ *vi* (**slagg'ing**; **slagged**) to spit. [Prob **slag¹**]

slaid /slād/ same as **slade²**.

slain /slān/ *pap* of **slay**.

slàinte /slän'chə/ (*Gaelic*) *interj* good health!

slairg /slärg/ (*Scot*) *vt* to spread or smear sloppily. ◆ *vi* to eat messily. ◆ *n* a dollop; a smear. [Cf Ger dialect *schlarggen* to smear]

slaister /slā'stər/ (*Scot* and *N Eng*) *n* a sloppy mess; wet slovenly work. ◆ *vt* to bedaub. ◆ *vi* to do anything in a wet, dirty, slovenly way. [Origin obscure]

■ **slais'tery** *adj.* ◆ *n* slops; drudgery.

slake¹ /slāk/ *vt* to quench; to extinguish; to deaden; to moisten; to refresh with moisture; to hydrate (eg lime); to abate, mitigate, allay, reduce, moderate (*poetic*); to slacken. ◆ *vi* to become slaked; to subside; to abate; to die down. [OE *slacian, sleacian* to grow slack, from *slæc, sleac* slack]

■ **slake'less** *adj* that cannot be slaked.

slake² /slāk/ (*Scot*) *vt* and *vi* to lick, smear, daub. ◆ *n* a slabbery daub; a smear. [ON *sleikja* to lick; Ger *schlecken* to lick]

slake³ /slāk/ (*Scot* and *N Eng*) *n* mud; slime; a mudflat.

slalom /slä'ləm/ *n* a race in which tactical skill is required, *esp* a downhill or zigzag ski-run among posts or trees, or between hanging poles in canoes. ◆ *vi* and *vt* (*fig*) to move in a zigzag course. [Norw]

■ **sla'lomer** *n.*

slam¹ /slam/ *vt* or *vi* (**slamm'ing**; **slammed**) to shut or strike with violence and noise; to bang; to censure, harshly criticize (*inf*); (of a telecommunications provider) to transfer a customer's account to another supplier without permission (*inf*). ◆ *n* the act or sound of slamming; a harsh criticism (*inf*); (also **poetry slam**) a competitive event at which poets take turns to perform their work and are judged on content and delivery. ◆ *adv* with a slam (also *fig*). [Cf Norw *slemma*]

■ **slamm'er** *n* (*sl*) prison; a fizzy cocktail, *usu* made with tequila, imbibed in a single swift motion shortly after the glass has been slammed against a table or similar surface; a slam dancer. **slamm'ing** or **slamm'in'** *adj* (*sl*) excellent, admirable; lively, energetic.

❑ **slam'-bang** *adv* (chiefly *N Am*) a variant of **slap-bang**; carelessly. **slam'-dance** *vi.* **slam dancer** *n.* **slam dancing** *n* (at, *esp* heavy metal, rock concerts) the practice of leaping in the air and crashing into others in the crowd (also **slamm'ing**). **slam dunk** *n* an act of jumping above the basket and forcing the ball downwards to score (*basketball*); a dramatic and unqualified success (*fig*). **slam'-dunk** *vt* and *vi* (*basketball*) to jump up and force the ball down through the basket. **slamming stile** *n* (*building*) the upright member of a doorcase against which the door shuts and into which the bolt of a rim lock engages.

slam² /slam/ *n* an old card game, also called **ruff** or **trump**; (in whist) the winning of every trick; (in bridge) the winning of every trick (**grand**

slam) or of all but one (**small** or **little slam**). ◆ *vt* to inflict a slam upon. [Origin unknown]

slander /slän' or slan'dər/ *n* a false or malicious report; injurious defamation by spoken words or by looks, signs, or gestures (distinct from *libel*; *law*); defamation whether spoken or written (*Scots law*); calumny. ◆ *vt* to defame; to calumniate. [OFr *esclandre*, from L *scandalum*, from Gr *skandalon* snare, scandal]

■ **slan'derer** *n.* **slan'derous** *adj.* **slan'derously** *adv.* **slan'derousness** *n.*

slane /slān/ *n* a turf-cutting spade. [Ir *sleaghan*]

slang¹ /slang/ *n* words and usages not forming part of standard language, only used very informally, *esp* in speech; *orig* a jargon of thieves and disreputable people; the jargon of any class, profession, or set. ◆ *adj* of or relating to this sort of language. ◆ *vt* (*inf*) to scold, vituperate. [Of cant origin; connection with **sling¹** very doubtful]

■ **slang'ily** *adv.* **slang'iness** *n.* **slang'ing** *n* and *adj* (a) scolding. **slang'ingly** *adv.* **slang'ish** *adj.* **slang'ular** *adj* (*Dickens*). **slang'y** *adj.* ❑ **slanging match** *n* a bitter verbal quarrel, *usu* involving an exchange of insults. **slang'-whang** *vt* and *vi* to rail, to rant. **slang'-whanger** *n.*

■ **back-slang** see under **back¹**.

slang² /slang/ (*old sl*) *n* a short weight or measure; a travelling show, or performance (*obs*); a hawker's licence. [Cant; origin obscure]

■ **slang'er** *n* a hawker; a dealer in illegal drugs (*US sl*).

slang³ /slang/ *n* a watch chain; any chain; (in *pl*) leg-irons, fetters. [Perh Du *slang* snake]

slangish, slangular, slangy see under **slang¹**.

slanguage /slang'gwij/ (*inf*, chiefly *N Am*) *n* a type of language containing many slang elements. [Blend of **slang¹** and **language**]

slant¹ /slänt or slant/ *vt* and *vi* to slope; to turn, strike, fall, obliquely; to be biased. ◆ *vt* to bias in a certain direction in presentation. ◆ *n* a slope; obliquity; a sloping surface, line, ray, or movement; a divergence from a direct line; a glance (*N Am inf*); a gybe; a point of view, way of looking at a thing; bias; a chance (*sl*). ◆ *adj* sloping; oblique; inclined from a direct line. [ME *slent*; cf Norw *slenta*, Swed *slinta* to slope, slip]

■ **slant'ed** *adj* biased, prejudiced. **slantendic'ular** or **slantindic'ular** *adj* (*joc inf*) oblique; neither horizontal nor perpendicular. **slant'ing** *adj.* **slant'ingly**, **slant'ingways** or **slant'ly** *adv.* **slant'ways** or **slant'wise** *adj* and *adv.*

❑ **slant'-eyed** *adj* (*offensive*) having slanting eyes, *esp* applied to people from E Asia. **slant rig** *n* (*mining*) a rig with facilities for digging at an angle from the vertical.

slant² /slänt or slant/ *n* a transitory breeze. [Earlier *slent*; Scand; cf Norw *slett*]

slap¹ /slap/ *n* a blow with the hand or anything flat; the sound made by this; a snub, rebuke; stage make-up (*theatre sl*); hence, make-up generally. ◆ *vt* (**slapp'ing**; **slapped**) to give a slap to; to bring or send with a slap; to rebuke (also with *down*); to apply without much care or attention (*usu* with *on*). ◆ *adv* with a slap; suddenly, violently; directly, straight. [Related to LGer *slapp*, Ger *Schlappe*; imit]

■ **slapp'er** *n* someone who or something that slaps; a whopper, a thing very big of its kind (*sl*); a promiscuous woman (*sl*). **slapp'ing** *adj* (*sl*) whopping.

❑ **slap and tickle** *n* (*inf*) amorous frolicking, with kissing, petting, etc. **slap'-bang** *adv* violently, all at once; directly, straight. ◆ *adj* dashing, violent. ◆ *n* a cheap eating-house; a simple firework that makes a noise when thrown down. **slap bass** *n* (in popular music) a style of playing the bass guitar or double bass in which strings are plucked and released sharply against the fingerboard. **slap'dash** *adv* in a hasty, careless way. ◆ *adj* hastily and carelessly done. ◆ *n* roughcast; careless work. ◆ *vt* to do in a hasty, imperfect manner; to roughcast. **slap-happ'y** *adj* (*inf*) recklessly or boisterously happy; slapdash, happy-go-lucky; punch-drunk. **slap'head** *n* (*sl*) a person with a bald or shaved head. **slap'jack** *n* (*US*) a flapjack, griddle-cake; a card game in which players try to win the pack by being the first to slap a hand over the jack, as it is turned over on top of the pile. **slap'shot** *n* (in ice hockey) a fast powerful shot. **slap'stick** *n* a harlequin's double lath that makes a noise like a slap; (also **slapstick comedy**) knockabout low comedy or farce. **slap'-up** *adj* (*inf*) first-class, lavish, sumptuous.

■ **slap in the face** (*inf*) an insult or rebuff. **slap on the back** (*inf*) a mark of congratulations. **slap on the wrist** (*inf*) a mild reprimand.

slap² /slap/ (*Scot*) *n* a gap in a fence, wall, hedge, etc; a hill pass; a passage in a salmon cruive; hence the weekly period when the passage is open and fishing is prohibited. ◆ *vt* to breach; to pierce. [Du or LGer *slop*]

slash¹ /slash/ *vt* to cut by striking with violence and often at random; to make long cuts in; to slit so as to show lining or material underneath; to lash; to criticize very harshly; to crack (eg a whip); to cut down, reduce drastically or suddenly (*inf*); to clear by felling trees. ◆ *vi* to strike violently and at random with a cutting or sharp instrument; to strike right and left. ◆ *n* a long cut; a slant or solidus (/); a cut at random; a cut in cloth to show colours or material underneath; a stripe on a non-commissioned officer's sleeve; débris of trees (*N Am*); a forest clearing, *esp* littered with débris (*N Am*). [Perh OFr *esclachier* to break; or connected with **lash**[1]]

■ **slashed** *adj* cut with slashes; gashed. **slash'er** *n* a person who or thing that slashes; a slasher film (*sl*); a machine for sizing warp threads (*weaving*); a circular saw for slicing logs into regular lengths. **slash'ing** *n* a slash or slashes; the felling of trees as a military obstacle; felled trees; a clearing. ◆ *adj* cutting mercilessly, unsparing; dashing; very big, slapping.

❑ **slash-and-burn'** *adj* denoting a method of agriculture in which trees and natural undergrowth are cut down and burned, leaving the soil bare before cultivation begins. **slasher film** or **movie** *n* (*sl*) a horror film in which people are slashed with knives, razors, etc. **slash fiction** *n* a form of explicit fiction in which the central character has a homosexual relationship.

slash[2] /*slash*/ (*US*) *n* a low-lying, swampy area. [Poss alteration of **plash**[3]]

slash[3] /*slash*/ (*vulgar sl*) *vi* to urinate. ◆ *n* an act of urinating. [Cf Scot *slash* a large splash, poss from OFr *esclache*]

slat[1] /*slat*/ *n* a thin strip of wood, etc; a slate or roofing slab (*dialect*). [OFr *esclat*]

■ **slatt'ed** *adj* having, or composed of, slats.

slat[2] /*slat*/ *vt* and *vi* to strike, beat; to flap. ◆ *n* a sudden sharp blow. [Poss ON *sletta* to slap, splash]

slatch /*slach*/ (*naut*) *n* the slack parts of a cable or rope lying outside a ship.

slate[1] /*slāt*/ *n* a fine-grained argillaceous rock which by regional metamorphism has developed a cleavage along close-spaced planes independent of the bedding, *usu* a dull blue, grey, purple, or green; a slab of this material (or a substitute) for roofing, or for writing on with chalk; a preliminary list (eg of political candidates; *esp N Am*); slate-colour. ◆ *adj* of slate; slate-coloured, dull bluish-grey. ◆ *vt* to cover with slate or slates; to enter on a slate; to clear (hide) of fine hair with a slater; to enter on a list; to note down for nomination or appointment (*US*); to propose; to schedule (*US*). [OFr *esclate*; cf **slat**[1]]

■ **slat'ed** *adj* covered with slates. **slat'er** *n* a person who covers roofs with slates; a tool with a slate blade for removing fine hair from hides; a woodlouse (*Scot and N Eng dialect, Aust* and *NZ*). **slat'iness** *n*. **slat'ing** *n* covering with slates; a covering of slates; materials for slating. **slat'y** *adj* of or like slate.

❑ **slate axe** *n* a slater's sax. **slate club** *n* an informally organized communal fund to which members contribute regularly, as insurance against hard times or savings towards eg Christmas expenses. **slate'-coloured** *adj* dull bluish-grey. **slate-grey'** or **-gray'** *adj* of a light slate colour. **slate pencil** *n* a cut or turned stick of soft slate, compressed slate powder, or pyrophyllite, for writing on. **slate'-writer** *n*. **slate'-writing** *n* in spiritualism, the mysterious process of producing writing on a covered slate. **slaty cleavage** *n* (*geol*) fissility like that of slate along planes independent of bedding.

■ **a clean slate** see under **clean**. **a slate loose** (*inf*) a slight mental derangement. **on the slate** (*inf*) on credit. **wipe the slate clean** to allow a person to make a fresh start in a job, relationship, etc by ignoring past mistakes, crimes, etc.

slate[2] /*slāt*/ *vt* to abuse; to review or comment on very unfavourably; to reprimand; to bait with dogs (*dialect*); to set on (*dialect*). [From the ON word answering to OE *slǣtan* to bait]

■ **slā'ting** *n*.

slather /*sladh'ər*/ (*esp N Am and dialect*) *n* a large quantity. ◆ *vt* to slop or smear; to squander. [Origin uncertain]

■ **open slather** (*Aust and NZ*) carte blanche, a free rein; a free-for-all.

slattern /*slat'ərn*/ *n* a dirty, untidy or slovenly woman. [Appar **slat**[2]]

■ **slatt'er** *vi* (*dialect*) to be untidy or slovenly. ◆ *vt* (*dialect*) to spill, splash, slop about. **slatt'ernliness** *n*. **slatt'ernly** *adj* and *adv* slovenly. **slatt'ery** *adj* (*dialect*) sloppy; slovenly.

slaughter /*slö'tər*/ *n* the killing of animals, *esp* for food; the killing of great numbers, *usu* of people; wanton or inexcusable killing, *esp* of the helpless; carnage; butchery; bodies of the slain. ◆ *vt* to kill in any of these ways; to criticize severely, or demolish in argument (*inf*); to defeat resoundingly (*inf*). [ON *slātr* butchers' meat, whence *slātra* to slaughter (cattle)]

■ **slaugh'terable** *adj* fit or due for slaughter. **slaugh'tered** *adj* (*sl*) very drunk. **slaugh'terer** *n*. **slaugh'terous** *adj* inclined to slaughter, murderous; destructive. **slaugh'terously** *adv*. **slaugh'tery** *n* (*rare*) slaughter; a slaughterhouse.

❑ **slaugh'terhouse** *n* a place where animals are killed prior to being butchered. **slaugh'terman** *n* a man employed in killing or butchering animals.

Slav /*släv*/ *n* a person whose language is Slavonic, ie belongs to that division of the Indo-European tongues that includes Russian, Polish, Wendish, Czech, Slovak, Serbian, Slovenian, and Bulgarian. [Med L *Sclavus*, from Late Gr *Sklabos*, from the stem of Slav *slovo* word, *sloviti* to speak; cf **Slovene**]

■ **Slav** or **Slav'ic** *adj*. **Slav'dom** *n* the Slavs collectively, the Slavonic world. **Slav'ify** *vt* to assimilate to the Slavs. **Sla'vism** *n* a Slavonic idiom used in another language; enthusiasm for Slavic ways or culture; anything characteristic of the Slavs. **Slavonia** /*slə-* or *slä-vō'ni-ə*/ *n* a region bounded by the Danube, Sava, and Drava. **Slavo'nian** *adj* and *n* (a person) from Slavonia; (a) Slav. **Slavonic** /-*von'ik*/ *adj* of the group of languages indicated above, or the peoples speaking them. ◆ *n* the forerunner of the group of languages indicated above, or the umbrella term for the group. **Slavon'icize** or **-ise** or **Slav'onize** or **-ise** *vt* to make Slavonic. **Slav'ophil** or **Slav'ophile** *adj* and *n* (someone who is) favourable or friendly to Slavs. **Slav'ophobe** *adj* and *n* (someone who is) hostile to Slavs.

slave /*slāv*/ *n* a person kept as property, *usu* made to work as a servant; a person who is submissive under domination; a person who is submissively devoted to another; a person whose will has lost power of resistance, *esp* to an influence, drug, etc; a person who works extremely hard, as if in bondage, a drudge; a mechanism controlled by another mechanism, eg in computing, by the central processor, or by remote control; a master-slave manipulator (qv under **master**). ◆ *vi* to work like or as a slave; to drudge. ◆ *vt* to enslave; to treat as a slave; *perh* make subservient to one's own views (*Shakesp, King Lear* IV.1.69). [OFr (Fr) *esclave*, orig a Slav]

■ **slav'er** *n* a slave-trader; a ship employed in the slave trade. **slav'ery** *n* the state of being a slave or enslaved; the institution of ownership of slaves; drudgery. **slav'ey** *n* (*inf*) a domestic drudge, a maid of all work. **slav'ish** *adj* of or belonging to slaves; befitting a slave; servile; abject; servilely following or conforming (eg to fashion); unoriginal; laborious. **slav'ishly** *adv*. **slav'ishness** *n*. **slāvoc'racy** *n* (*esp US hist*) slave-owners collectively; their power, interests, etc. **slāv'ocrat** *n*.

❑ **slave ant** *n* an ant captured and kept as a worker in a community of another species. **slave'-driver** *n* a person who superintends slaves at their work; a hard taskmaster (*fig*). **slave'-fork** *n* a long and heavy forked branch fixed on the neck of a slave to prevent escape. **slave'holder** *n* an owner of slaves. **slave'holding** *n*. **slave'-hunt** *n* a hunt after runaway slaves or after people to enslave. **slave labour** *n* (the work of) people employed as slaves (*lit* and *fig*). **slave ship** *n* a ship used for transporting slaves. **slave states** *n pl* those states of the American Union which maintained domestic slavery before the Civil War, namely Delaware, Maryland, Virginia, North and South Carolina, Georgia, Florida, Alabama, Mississippi, Louisiana, Texas, Arkansas, Missouri, Kentucky and Tennessee. **slave trade** or **slave traffic** *n* the buying and selling of slaves. **slave'-trader** or **slave-traff'icker** *n*.

slaver[1] /*slav'ər*/ or (*esp Scot*) /*slāv'ər*/ *n* spittle running from the mouth, *esp* in anticipation of food. ◆ *vi* to let spittle run out of the mouth; to drivel; to fawn over (a person), *esp* with lust. ◆ *vt* to cover with slaver. [Related to **slabber**]

■ **slav'erer** *n*. **slav'ering** *adj* and *n*. **slav'eringly** *adv*. **slav'ery** *adj* slabbery.

slaver[2] see under **slave**.

Slavic see under **Slav**.

slavocracy, slavocrat see under **slave**.

Slavonian, Slavonic, etc see under **Slav**.

slaw /*slö*/ *n* cabbage salad. [Du *sla*, from *salade*]

slay /*slā*/ (*literary and archaic*) *vt* (pat **slayed**, sometimes **slew**; pap **slayed**) and *vi* (pat **slew** /*sloo*/; pap **slain** /*slān*/) to kill. ◆ *vt* (*inf*) to amuse very much; to impress greatly. [OE *slēan* to strike, to kill; ON *slā*, Gothic *slahan*, Ger *schlagen* to strike]

■ **slay'er** *n*.

SLBM *abbrev* : submarine-launched ballistic missile.

SLD *abbrev* : Social and Liberal Democrats (now called Liberal Democrats).

sld *abbrev* : sailed.

sleave /*slēv*/ *n* (*Shakesp*) a fine filament that can be separated from a silk fibre. ◆ *vt* (*dialect*) to separate (eg threads). [OE *slǣfan* to divide]

■ **sleaved** *adj* used in the term **sleaved silk**, floss silk.

sleazy /*slē'zi*/ *adj* corrupt, squalid, *esp* in sexual ways (*inf*); slatternly (*inf*). [Origin doubtful]

■ **sleaze** *n* (back-formation) sleaziness, *esp* corruption or immoral behaviour in public life (*inf*); a sleazy person, *esp* a man (*sl*). **sleaz'ily** *adv*. **slea'ziness** *n*.

❑ **sleaze'ball** *n* (also **sleaze'bag**) (*sl*) a sleazy person, *esp* an unprincipled man who tries to take advantage of women.

sleb /*sleb*/ (*sl*) *n* a celebrity. [Short form]

sled /sled/ n a sledge, esp a small one; a drag or wheelless structure for conveying goods, esp on snow, formerly for taking the condemned to execution. ◆ vt (**sledd'ing**; **sledd'ed**) to convey by sled. ◆ vi to go on a sled. [MDu or MLGer sledde; Ger Schlitte, ON slethi; cf **sledge**[1], **sleigh**, **slide**]
■ **sledd'ed** adj (Shakesp) having sleds. **sledd'ing** n.

sleded see **sleided**.

sledge[1] /slej/ n a conveyance with runners for sliding on snow; a framework without wheels for dragging goods along; an iron- or flint-studded board for threshing corn (hist). ◆ vt and vi to convey, or travel, by sledge. [MDu sleedse; cf **sled**]
■ **sledg'er** n. **sledg'ing** n.
❑ **sledge'-chair** n a chair mounted on runners for ice.

sledge[2] /slej/ n a sledgehammer. ◆ vi and vt (cricket sl, orig Aust) to seek to upset the batsman's concentration by making offensive remarks. [OE slecg, from slēan to strike, slay]
■ **sledg'ing** n.
❑ **sledge'hammer** n a large, heavy, long-handled hammer wielded in both hands. ◆ vt to hit with, or as if with, a sledgehammer.

slee /slē/ Scots form of **sly**.

sleech /slēch/ n slimy mud; a mudflat. [Origin uncertain]
■ **sleech'y** adj.

sleek /slēk/ adj pleasingly smooth; glossy; having an oily, plastered-down look; insinuating, slick in manner; suggestive of material wealth; prosperous in appearance. ◆ vt to make smooth or glossy; to calm or soothe. ◆ vi to glide. ◆ adv smoothly, oilily. [A later form of **slick**]
■ **sleek'en** vt to make sleek. **sleek'er** n a moulding tool for smoothing over small irregularities in the mould (also **smooth'er**). **sleek'ing** n. **sleek'it** adj (Scot) smooth, sleek; sly, cunning, sneaking. **sleek'ly** adv. **sleek'ness** n. **sleek'y** adj smooth; sly, untrustworthy.
❑ **sleek'-headed** adj. **sleek'stone** n a polishing stone.

sleep /slēp/ vi (pat and pap **slept** /slept/) to take rest by surrendering consciousness; to slumber; to be motionless, inactive, or dormant; to appear still or restful; to take or have the nocturnal position, to display nyctitropism (bot); to be dead (euphem); to rest in the grave (euphem); (of a limb) to go or be numb from pressure, etc; (of a top) to spin steadily without movement of the axis. ◆ vt to spend (time) in sleep; to enjoy a period of (sleep, as cognate object); to outsleep; to provide, contain sleeping accommodation for. ◆ n the state of being asleep; a period of sleeping; dormancy; death (euphem); vertical disposition of leaves at night, nyctitropism (bot); mucous matter which collects at the corners of the eyes (inf). [OE slǣpan (verb), slǣp (noun); Ger Schlaf, Gothic slēps]
■ **sleep'er** n a person who sleeps; a horizontal beam supporting and spreading a weight, esp a support for railway rails; a sleeping car; a compartment or berth in a sleeping car; a sleeping tablet (inf); (chiefly Brit) a small gold hoop worn in a pierced ear to prevent the hole from closing up; a fish of the genus Dormitator, resembling the gobies; an agent who spends a long time (often years) establishing himself or herself as an inoffensive citizen preparing for the moment when he or she will be required to pass on information, spy for a foreign power, etc; someone or something not recognized for what it is; a record, film, etc which becomes popular after an initial period of not being so, or an item whose true value is not recognized and which is sold too cheaply as a result (inf). **sleep'ery** or **sleep'ry** adj (Scot) sleepy. **sleep'ily** adv. **sleep'iness** n. **sleep'ing** n sleep; abeyance. ◆ adj in a state of, occupied with, or for, sleeping; dormant. **sleep'less** adj without sleep; unable to sleep. **sleep'lessly** adv. **sleep'lessness** n. **sleep'y** adj inclined to sleep, drowsy; inducing or suggesting sleep; characterized by quietness and lack of activity; partially decayed internally, esp of a pear, soft and lacking juice.
❑ **sleep apnoea** see **apnoea**. **sleeping bag** n a quilted bag for sleeping in, used by travellers, campers, etc. **sleeping berth** n. **sleeping car**, **carr'iage** or **coach** n a railway carriage with berths for sleeping in. **sleeping draught** n a drink containing a drug to induce sleep. **sleeping partner** n a person who has money invested in a business but takes no part in its management. **sleeping pill** n one containing a sleep-inducing drug. **sleeping policeman** n a low transverse hump built into the surface of a road, intended to slow down traffic. **sleeping sickness** n a deadly disease of tropical Africa, characterized by headache, great drowsiness, and exhaustion, caused by a trypanosome introduced by the bite of a tsetse-fly; sometimes erroneously applied to sleepy sickness. **slee'ping-suit** or **sleep'suit** n a baby's all-in-one garment for sleeping in. **sleep learning** same as **hypnopaedia** (see under **hypno-**). **sleep mode** n (comput) the facility of temporarily restricting electrical power in a computer to those parts that are needed to restore it to full operation, so that it can be left switched on when not in use. **sleep'out** n a partitioned-off section of a veranda for use as a sleeping area (Aust and NZ; see also **sleep out** below). **sleep'walk** vi. **sleep'walker** n a person who walks in his or her sleep, a somnambulist. **sleep'walking**

n. **sleep'yhead** n a lazy or sleepy-looking person. **sleepy hollow** n a very quiet place (from A Legend of Sleepy Hollow (1820) by Washington Irving). **sleepy sickness** n encephalitis lethargica, a feature of which is great drowsiness; formerly applied to sleeping sickness.
■ **get to sleep** to manage to fall asleep. **go to sleep** to fall asleep; (of a limb) to become numb through pressure or positioning that cuts off the blood supply. **in one's sleep** while asleep. **on sleep** (Bible) asleep. **put to sleep** to anaesthetize; to kill (an animal) painlessly (euphem). **sleep around** (inf) to be sexually promiscuous. **sleep in** to oversleep, wake or get up later than intended; to sleep later than usual; to sleep at one's place of work. **sleep off** to recover from (eg a hangover) by sleeping. **sleep on** to consider overnight, postpone a decision on. **sleep out** to sleep outdoors overnight (**sleep'out** n); to sleep away from one's place of work. **sleep over** to sleep at another person's house overnight, esp after a party (**sleep'over** n). **sleep together** (euphem) to have sexual relations with each other. **sleep with** (euphem) to have sexual relations with.

sleet /slēt/ n rain mingled with snow or hail; a coating of ice formed when rain or sleet freezes on a cold surface (US). ◆ vi to hail or snow simultaneously with rain. [Prob an unrecorded OE (Anglian) slēt; Ger Schlosse a hailstone]
■ **sleet'iness** n. **sleet'y** adj.

sleeve /slēv/ n the part of a garment covering, or partially covering, the arm; a tube into which a rod or other tube is inserted; a tube, esp of a different metal, fitted inside a metal cylinder or tube, as protection or to decrease the diameter (engineering); a thin cardboard container for a gramophone record; a wind sleeve; a drogue. ◆ vt to provide with sleeves. [OE (Anglian) slēfe (WSax sliefe)]
■ **sleeved** adj having sleeves; (in combination) having sleeves of a stated type, as in long-sleeved. **sleeve'less** adj without sleeves; futile, vain (see **errand**). **sleev'er** n an old, esp Welsh, measure for beer, containing about three quarters of a pint; a straight-sided beer glass. **sleev'ing** n tubular flexible insulation for threading over bare conductor wires.
❑ **sleeve board** n a small board for ironing sleeves. **sleeve dog** n (old) a little dog that could be carried in the sleeve. **sleeve fish** n the squid. **sleeve'hand** n (Shakesp) a wristband. **sleeve notes** n pl the text on a record sleeve. **sleeve nut** n a double nut for attaching the joint-ends of rods or tubes. **sleeve'-valve engine** n a type of engine in which two cylindrical metal sleeves, one inside the other, slide up and down on a film of oil, providing intake and exhaust passages as the port openings pass each other. **sleeve** or **sleeved waistcoat** n a long-sleeved waistcoat, as worn by hotel porters, etc.
■ **keep something up one's sleeve** to keep something, eg information, in secret reserve. **laugh in** or **up one's sleeve** to laugh privately or unperceived. **roll up one's sleeves** to get down wholeheartedly to a job, esp an unpleasant manual one. **wear one's heart on one's sleeve** see under **heart**.

sleeveen /slē'vēn/ (Irish) n a crafty, smooth-talking person. [Ir slíbhín]

sleezy same as **sleazy**.

sleided and **sleded** /slē'did/ (Shakesp) adj appar irregular forms of **sleaved**.

sleigh /slā/ n (esp N Am) a sledge. ◆ vi to travel by sleigh. [Du slee]
■ **sleigh'er** n. **sleigh'ing** n.
❑ **sleigh bell** n a small bell attached to a sleigh or its harness.

sleight (obs **slight**) /slīt/ n cunning; dexterity; an artful trick; a juggling trick; trickery; a design, device, pattern (Spenser). [ON slœgth cunning, slœgr sly]
❑ **sleight of hand** n deceptive movement of the hands, esp in order to conceal or remove something, as in conjuring, legerdemain. **sleight'-of-hand** adj.

slender /slen'dər/ adj thin or narrow; slim; slight; meagre. [Origin obscure]
■ **slen'derize** or **-ise** vt and vi to make or become slender. **slen'derly** adv. **slen'derness** n.

slept /slept/ pat and pap of **sleep**.

sleuth /slooth/ n a relentless tracker, a detective (esp joc); a bloodhound, a sleuth-hound (obs); a track or trail (obs). ◆ vt and vi to track. ◆ vi to work as a detective. [ON slōth track]
❑ **sleuth'-hound** n a bloodhound or other dog trained to track people; a detective.

slew[1] /sloo/ pat of **slay**.

slew[2] or **slue** /sloo/ vt and vi to turn about the axis; to swing round, esp suddenly and uncontrollably. ◆ n a turn, twist or swing round; a position so taken. [First recorded as a sailor's word: origin unknown]
■ **slewed** or **slued** adj (sl) drunk.
❑ **slew rate** n (electronics) the rate at which an amplifier can respond to a change in input level.

slew³ or **slue** /sloo/ (*N Am inf*) *n* a large number or amount. [Ir *slua* a multitude]

sley /slā/ *n* a weaver's reed. [OE *slege*, from *sléan* to strike]

slice /slīs/ *n* a thin broad piece or segment; a flat or broad-bladed instrument of various kinds, *esp* a broad knife for serving fish; a slash, swipe; an inadvertent stroke causing the ball to move in the air from left to right (for a right-handed player) or from right to left (for a left-handed player) (*golf*); a share (of something) (*inf*); a representative section. ◆ *vt* to cut into slices; to cut a slice from; to cut as a slice; to hit (the ball) so that it inadvertently moves in the air from left to right (for a right-handed player), or from right to left (for a left-handed player) (*golf*). ◆ *vi* to slash; to cut in the manner of slicing; (of a boat) to move through the water in a smooth, cutting manner; (of a ball) to move in the air from left to right (for a right-handed player), or from right to left (for a left-handed player) (*golf*). [OFr *esclice*, from OHGer *slīzan* to split]

■ **slice'able** *adj*. **slī'cer** *n*. **slī'cing** *n* and *adj*.

slick /slik/ *adj* sleek; smooth; smooth-tongued, glib; adroit; trim, smart. ◆ *adv* smoothly; glibly; deftly; quickly; altogether. ◆ *n* a smooth place or surface; a slicker; a film or expanse of spilt oil; a smooth racing-car tyre; a glossy magazine. ◆ *vt* to polish, make glossy; to tidy up; to smooth (hair; with *back* or *down*). [ME *sliken*, from OE *slician*, (in composition) to smooth]

■ **slick'en** *vt* to smooth, polish. **slick'er** *n* a smoothing tool; a waterproof, *esp* oilskin (*US*); a swindler, shifty person; a sophisticated city-dweller. **slick'ered** *adj*. **slick'ing** *n*. **slick'ly** *adv*. **slick'ness** *n*. □ **slick'enside** *n* (*geol*) a smooth, polished or striated rock surface produced by friction. **slick'ensided** *adj*. **slick'stone** *n* a sleekstone.

slid see **slide**.

'slid /slid/ (*archaic*) *interj* for **god's lid** (**eyelid**), an exclamatory oath.

slidder /slid'ər/ *vi* to slip, slide. ◆ *n* a steep path or trench down a hillside. [OE *slidor* slippery, *sliderian* to slip]

■ **slidd'ery** *adj* slippery.

slide /slīd/ *vi* (pat **slid** /slid/, (*obs*) **sli'ded**, (*Scot*) **slade**, **slaid**; *pap* **slid**, (*obs*) **sli'ded**, (*rare*) **slidd'en**) to slip or glide; to pass along, over, down, etc smoothly; to glide or slip in a standing position (without skates or snowshoes) over ice or other slippery surface; to lapse, fall out of use; to pass quietly, smoothly, or gradually; to take its own course; to decamp (*inf*). ◆ *vt* to cause to slip or glide along. ◆ *n* a slip; a polished slippery track (on ice); a chute or shoot; a slippery sloping surface, eg in a park, for children to slide down; a bed, groove, rail, etc, on or in which a thing slides; a sliding part, eg of a trombone; a sliding clasp, *esp* for women's hair; a flat piece of glass for mounting objects for the microscope; a case (*dark slide*) for photographic plates or its sliding cover; a translucent photograph for projection on a screen, a transparency; a sliding lid; a sledge; a runner; a sliding seat, *esp* in a rowing boat; a landslip; a gliding from one note to another (*music*); a falling (in value, popularity, etc); (with *the*) a rhythmic dance. [OE *slīdan* to slide]

■ **slīd'able** *adj*. **slīd'er** *n* a person who or thing that slides; a sliding part; ice-cream between wafers (*Scot*); a red-bellied terrapin; a pitch that breaks in a horizontal plane (*baseball*). **slīd'ing** *n* and *adj*. **slīd'ingly** *adv*.

□ **slide fastener** *n* (*N Am*) a zip fastener. **slide guitar** *n* a method of playing the guitar using a metal tube which is drawn across the frets. **slide projector** *n* a device which projects an enlarged image of a photographic slide onto a wall or screen. **slide rest** *n* (*engineering*) an apparatus for carrying the cutting tool of a lathe, etc. **slide rule** *n* a calculating device consisting of two logarithmic graduated scales sliding one against the other (also **slid'ing-rule**). **slide trombone** *n* a trombone. **slide valve** *n* a valve in which openings are covered and uncovered by a sliding part. **sliding keel** *n* a centreboard. **sliding scale** *n* a scale, eg of taxes, varying according to variation in something else, eg prices; a slide rule. **sliding seat** *n* a racing-boat seat, moving with the swing of the rower's body.

■ **let slide** to take no action over; to allow to deteriorate through negligence.

'slife /slīf/ or **'slight** /slīt/ (*archaic*) *interj* for **God's life** or **light**, exclamatory oaths.

slight¹ /slīt/ *adj* lacking solidity, massiveness, weight, significance; slim; slender; trifling; flimsy; small; smooth (*obs*); slighting (*obs*). ◆ *adv* slightly; slightingly, meanly. ◆ *vt* to ignore or overlook disrespectfully; to insult; to toss contemptuously (*Shakesp*); to smooth (*obs*); to raze, level to the ground (*archaic*). ◆ *n* contemptuous indifference; discourteous disregard; an affront by showing neglect or lack of respect. [Cf OE *eorthslihtes* close to the ground; ON *slёttr*, OLGer *slicht* plain, Du *slecht* bad, Ger *schlecht* bad]

■ **slight'ing** *adj*. **slight'ingly** *adv*. **slight'ish** *adj*. **slight'ly** *adv*. **slight'ness** *n*.

■ (**not**) **in the slightest** (not) at all. **slight off** (*Shakesp*) to put off, set aside, with contempt. **slight over** to ignore.

slight² old spelling of **sleight**.

slily /slī'li/ *adv* see under **sly**.

slim /slim/ *adj* (**slimm'er**; **slimm'est**) (of people) attractively thin; slender; only slight; crafty (reintroduced from Afrik, now again *rare*). ◆ *n* (also with *cap*) the name used in Africa for AIDS (from the severe weight loss associated with the disease). ◆ *vt* (**slimm'ing**; **slimmed**) to make thin; to decrease (*fig*). ◆ *vi* to make oneself more slender, by dieting, taking exercise, etc; (of a company, etc) to become more efficient or economical, *esp* by reducing the workforce. [Du, LGer, Fris *slim* crafty; Dan *slem* worthless, Ger *schlimm* bad]

■ **slim'ly** *adv*. **slimm'er** *n*. **slimm'ing** *n* and *adj*. **slimm'ish** *adj*. **slim'ness** *n*. **slim'sy** *adj* (*US*) frail, flimsy.

□ **slim'line** *adj* slim, or conducive to slimness (also *fig*). **slimmers' disease** *n* anorexia nervosa.

■ **slim down** to make or become slimmer or more economical (**slimmed-down'** *adj*).

slime /slīm/ *n* any very fine, thin, slippery, or gluey mud-like substance, *esp* when considered unpleasant; bitumen (*obs*); any thick organic semi-liquid secretion, such as mucus; matter, *esp* as forming the human body; moral filth; obsequiousness, oily servility; (in *pl*) finely crushed ore in mud form. ◆ *vt* to smear or cover with slime; to grind to slime; to clear of slime. ◆ *vi* to go or move slimily. [OE *slīm*; Ger *Schleim*]

■ **slim'ily** *adv*. **slim'iness** *n*. **slim'y** *adj* thick and slow-flowing, only semi-liquid; covered with slime; disgusting; obsequiously servile (*inf*). □ **slime'ball** *n* (*sl*) a disgusting person (also *adj*). **slime fungus** or **slime mould** *n* a myxomycete. **slime pit** *n* a hole where bitumen is obtained; a pit for receiving metallic slimes.

sling¹ /sling/ *n* a strap or pocket with a string attached to each end, for hurling a stone; a catapult; a ballista; a loop for hoisting, lowering, or carrying a weight; a hanging support for an injured arm or foot; a strap attached to something for carrying it; an act of throwing; a sweep or swing; a bribe (*Aust inf*). ◆ *vt* (pat and pap **slung**) to throw with a sling; to hang loosely; to put up (a hammock, etc); to move or swing by means of a rope; to hurl, toss or fling (*inf*); to pass, give, etc (*sl*). ◆ *vi* to discharge, eg stones, from a sling; to bound along with swinging steps. [Prob from several sources; cf ON *slyngva* to fling, OE *slingan* to wind, twist, LGer *sling* noose]

■ **sling'er** *n*.

□ **sling'back** or **slingback shoe** *n* one without a covering for the heel, supported by a strap fastening round the heel. **sling fruit** *n* a fruit that ejects its seeds by elastic tissue. **sling'shot** *n* (*esp N Am*) a catapult. **sling'stone** *n* a stone for throwing from a sling.

■ **sling ink** (*sl*) to write for the press. **sling off at** (*Aust* and *NZ inf*) to jeer at. **sling one's hook** (*sl*) to go away, remove oneself.

sling² /sling/ *n* an *orig* American drink, spirits and water sweetened and flavoured. [Perh **sling¹** in the sense of toss; poss Ger *schlingen* to swallow]

slink /slingk/ *vi* (pat and pap **slunk**) to go sneakingly or ashamedly; to move in a lithe and seductive manner; (of an animal, *esp* a cow) to miscarry. ◆ *vt* to slip; to droop; (of an animal, *esp* a cow) to give birth to prematurely. ◆ *n* a prematurely born calf or other animal; its flesh or hide; an illegitimate child; a slinking gait. ◆ *adj* prematurely born; lean, starved; mean. [OE *slincan*; LGer *slinken*]

■ **slink'er** *n*. **slink'ily** *adv*. **slink'iness** *n*. **slink'y** *adj* slinking; lean; sinuous; close-fitting.

□ **slink butcher** *n* a dealer in slink and diseased meat. **slink'skin** *n* the skin of a slink, or leather made from it. **slink'weed** *n* rosebay willowherb or other plant believed to cause cows to slink.

slinter /slin'tər/ (*Aust* and *NZ inf*) *n* a dodge or trick (also (*obs*) **slen'ter**). [Du *slenter*]

slip¹ /slip/ *vi* (**slipp'ing**; **slipped** or (formerly) **slipt**) to move quietly, easily, unobtrusively or stealthily; to glide; to escape; to get out of position accidentally; (of animals, *esp* horses) to give birth prematurely; to slide, fall, etc, *esp* accidentally; to lose one's former skill, grip, or control of the situation (*inf*); to lose one's footing; to make a slight mistake inadvertently rather than from ignorance; to lapse morally; (of a motor clutch) to fail to engage correctly. ◆ *vt* to cause or allow to slide or fall; to put with a sliding motion; to convey quietly or secretly; to let pass; to let slip; to cast; to disengage, let loose; to escape from or elude; (of animals, *esp* horses) to give birth to prematurely; to dislocate (a spinal disc). ◆ *n* an act of slipping; an inadvertent mistake; a slight error or transgression; a lapse, *esp* in morals or principles; an escape; an incline, sloping down to the water; a slight dislocation; a landslide; a pillow case; a garment easily slipped into, *esp* one worn under a dress, a full-length version of a petticoat; a leash; the difference between the pitch of a propeller and the distance actually travelled; any of several fielders (eg *first slip*, *second slip*, etc) positioned in a row next to the wicketkeeper on the offside (*cricket*); (often in *pl*) their position; the runner of a sledge; (in *pl*) the place at the side of the stage for slipping scenery from; the side of a theatre gallery. [Perh LGer or Du *slippen*; but OE has *slipor* slippery, and *slȳpescōh* slipper]

■ **slip'age** *n* (the extent of) failure to reach a set target; the act, an instance or the amount of slipping. **slipp'er** *adj* (*archaic*) slippery. **slipp'erily** *adv*. **slipp'eriness** or **slipp'iness** *n*. **slipp'ery** or **slipp'y** *adj* so smooth, wet or slimy as to allow or cause slipping; elusive; evasive; untrustworthy; apt to slip; unstable; uncertain, unpredictable. □ **slip angle** *n* in vehicles, the attitude angle. **slip'-board** *n* a board sliding in grooves. **slip'-carriage** or **slip-coach** *n* a railway carriage that can be left behind without stopping the train. **slip'case** *n* a box-like case for a book or set of books, open at one end to leave the spine(s) visible. **slip cover** *n* a loose cover for an item of furniture; a book jacket. **slip'-dock** *n* a dock with a slipway. **slip'form** *n* (*building*) a form that can be moved slowly as work progresses (also *adj*). **slipform paver** *n* a machine for laying continuously a concrete road surface. **slip gauge** *n* (*engineering*) an accurately ground rectangular block used to measure with great accuracy the distance between components or faces. **slip'knot** *n* a knot that adjusts tightness by slipping along a rope; a knot easily untied by pulling an end. **slip'-on** or **slip'-over** *adj* slipped on or over; (of a garment) slipped easily over the head without unbuttoning. ◆ *n* a garment easily slipped on; a garment slipped over the head. **slipped disc** see **disc**. **slippery elm** *n* a N American elm; its mucilaginous bark used as a demulcent. **slip'rail** *n* (*Aust*) a movable rail serving as a gate; a gap closed by such a rail. **slip ring** *n* a device in an electric motor or alternator which conveys power to or from the rotor without changing polarity. **slip road** *n* a local bypass; a road by which vehicles move off or onto a motorway. **slip sheet** *n* (*printing*) a sheet of paper placed between sheets as they are printed to avoid offset. **slip'shod** *adj* careless, carelessly executed; shod with slippers, or with shoes down at the heel; slovenly. **slip'-shoe** *n* (*obs*) a slipper. **slip stitch** *n* a concealed sewing stitch used on hems, facings, etc in which only a few threads of the material forming the main body of the garment are caught up by the needle for each stitch. **slip'-stitch** *vt* to join using slip stitches. **slip'stream** *n* the stream of air driven back by an aircraft propeller or the stream of air behind any (*usu* quickly) moving vehicle or other object. ◆ *vt* and *vi* to follow (another car, bicycle, etc) closely and thus benefit from the decreased wind resistance created by its slipstream. **slip'-string** *n* (*obs* or *dialect*) a rogue, someone who richly deserves hanging (also *adj*). **slip'-up** *n* (*inf*) an error or failure. **slip'way** *n* a pier in a dock or shipyard that slopes down into the water.

■ **give someone the slip** to escape from someone, *usu* by cunning. **let slip** to reveal accidentally; to miss (an opportunity). **look slippy** (*inf*; *esp* in *imperative*) to be quick, to hurry. **slip a cable** or **mooring** to let a cable or mooring go overboard instead of waiting to weigh anchor. **slip off** to fall off; to take off quickly; to go away quietly. **slip of the tongue** or **pen** a word, etc said, or written, in error when something else was intended. **slip on** to put on loosely or in haste. **slip one's ways** (*Scot*) to make one's way quietly. **slip the cable** to die. **slip up** to make a mistake, to fail (*inf*); to deceive or disappoint (*Aust*).

slip² /*slip*/ *n* a strip; anything slender or narrow; a small piece of paper, etc; a cutting; a descendant; a young or slender person; a young pig (*dialect* and *Aust*); a small sole (fish); a galley proof; a memorandum giving details of the kind of cover required, to be signed by the underwriters (*insurance*). ◆ *vt* to take cuttings from; to tear obliquely (*heraldry*). [Perh MDu or MLGer *slippe* strip]

slip³ /*slip*/ *n* a creamy paste of clay and water for coating, decorating and casting pottery. [OE *slipa* or *slypa* slime, paste] □ **slip'ware** *n* pottery decorated with slip.

slip⁴ /*slip*/ *n* (*obs*) a counterfeit coin. [Perh **slip¹**]

slipe /*slīp*/ *n* a skip or sledge (*mining*); a runner. [Appar LGer *slîpe*]

slippage see under **slip¹**.

slipper /*slip'ər*/ *n* a shoe easily slipped onto the foot, *esp* a loose indoor shoe; a lightweight dancing shoe; a person who slips; (*esp* formerly) a device attached to a wheel eg of a coach to slow its speed when going downhill; the runner of a sledge. ◆ *vt* to provide with slippers; to beat with a slipper. [Ety as for **slip¹**]

■ **slipp'ered** *adj*.

□ **slipper animalcule** see **Paramecium**. **slipper bath** *n* a partially covered bath, shaped like a slipper; (*esp* formerly) one of a number of single baths for hire at public baths. **slipper limpet** *n* an American mollusc (genus *Crepidula*) with a somewhat slipperlike shell. **slipper orchid** *n* any terrestrial orchid of the genus *Cypripedium*, with flowers made up of fused lateral sepals, a large dorsal sepal and a conspicuous slipperlike lip (see also **lady's-slipper** under **lady**). **slipper satin** *n* fine satin with a dull finish. **slipper socks** *n pl* thick *esp* patterned socks with a reinforced sole, for use as slippers. **slipp'erwort** *n* a S American genus of flowering plants, calceolaria.

slippery, **slipshod**, **slipstream**, etc see under **slip¹**.

slipt see **slip¹**.

slipware see under **slip³**.

slish /*slish*/ (*Shakesp*) *n* a cut. [**slash¹**]

slit /*slit*/ *vt* (**slitt'ing**; **slit**) to make a long cut in, *esp* lengthwise; to split; to cut into strips. ◆ *n* a long cut; a narrow opening. ◆ *adj* cut with a long opening, *esp* lengthwise; cut open; having a slit. [ME *slitten*, appar related to OE *slītan*; Ger *schlitzen*]

■ **slitt'er** *n*.

□ **slit pocket** *n* an overcoat pocket reached through an opening in the form of a slit. **slit trench** *n* (*milit*) a narrow trench for one person or a few people.

slither /*slidh'ər*/ *vi* to slide, *esp* on the belly. ◆ *adj* slippery. ◆ *n* a slithering movement; a scree. [**slidder**]

■ **slith'ery** *adj* slippery.

slive /*slīv*/ (*dialect*) *vt* and *vi* (*pat* **slove** or **slived**; *pap* **slived** or **sliven** /*sliv'ən*/) to slip. [Cf OE *slēfan* to slip (on)]

sliver /*sliv'ər* or *slī'vər*/ *vt* to split, tear off lengthwise or slice thinly. ◆ *vi* to break into slivers. ◆ *n* a thin or small piece cut or torn off, a slice or splinter; a continuous strand of loose untwisted wool or other fibre. [OE (*tō-*)*slīfan* to cleave]

slivovitz /*sliv'ə-vits*/ *n* a dry plum brandy (also **sliv'ovic** /-*vits*/, **sliv'ovica** /-*sə*/ or **sliv'owitz**). [Serbo-Croat *šljivovica*, from *šljiva* plum]

SLO *abbrev*: Slovenia (IVR).

sloan /*slōn*/ (*Scot*) *n* a snub; a reproof. [Ety uncertain]

Sloane Ranger /*slōn rān'jər*/ *n* a young person, typically upper- or upper-middle-class and female, favouring expensively casual clothing suggestive of rural pursuits, speaking in distinctively clipped tones, evincing certain predictable enthusiasms and prejudices, and resident (during the week) in the *Sloane* Square area of London or a comparable part (also **Sloane**). [Coined in mid-1970s by Peter York, punning on *The Lone Ranger* a television cowboy hero]

■ **Sloan'ey** *adj*.

slob /*slob*/ *n* sludge, mud, ooze; a mudflat; a slovenly, lazy person (*inf*); a person with wealth but no refinement, a boor (*sl*). ◆ *vi* to move or behave in a lazy, untidy or slovenly way (*usu* with *about* or *around*). [Ir *slab*]

■ **slobb'ish** *adj*. **slobb'ishness** *n*. **slobb'y** *adj*.

□ **slob ice** *n* (*Can*) sludgy floating ice. **slob'land** *n* a mudflat; reclaimed alluvial land.

slobber /*slob'ər*/ *vt* and *vi* to slaver. [Cf Du *slobberen* to eat or work in a slovenly way; **slabber**, **slubber**]

■ **slobb'ery** *adj*.

slockdolager, **-iger**, **-oger** see **sockdolager**.

slocken or **sloken** /*slok'n*/ or *slō'kn*/ (*Scot*) *vt* to quench; to slake; to moisten; to extinguish. [ON *slokna* to go out]

sloe /*slō*/ *n* the blackthorn fruit or bush. ◆ *adj* of blackthorn wood; made with sloes; black. [OE *slā*, *slāg* or *slāh*; Du *slee*]

□ **sloe'bush** *n*. **sloe'-eyed** *adj* dark-eyed, slant-eyed, or both. **sloe gin** *n* gin flavoured by having sloes steeped in it. **sloe'thorn** *n*. **sloe'tree** *n*.

slog /*slog*/ *vt* (**slogg'ing**; **slogged**) and *vi* to hit hard. ◆ *vi* to work or walk doggedly, with great effort. ◆ *n* a hard blow (generally with little regard to direction); a strenuous spell of work; something which requires strenuous, *esp* protracted, effort. [Origin uncertain]

■ **slogg'er** *n*.

slogan /*slō'gən*/ *n* an advertising catchphrase; a party political catchword; *orig*, a clan war cry. [Earlier *slogorne*, *sloggorne*, *sloghorne*; said to be from Gaelic *sluagh* army, and *gairm* cry; see **slughorn**]

■ **sloganeer'** *n* an enthusiastic inventor and user of slogans. ◆ *vi* to invent or make heavy use of slogans. **sloganeer'ing** *n*. **slo'ganize** or **-ise** *vi* to utter or repeat slogans, *esp* as a substitute for reasoned discussion. **slo'ganizing** or **-s-** *n*.

sloid see **sloyd**.

sloken see **slocken**.

slo-mo /*slō'mō'*/ (*inf*) *n* and *adj* slow-motion.

sloom /*sloom*/ (*N Eng dialect*) *n* slumber. ◆ *vi* to slumber. [OE *slūma*]

■ **sloom'y** *adj*.

sloop /*sloop*/ *n* a light boat; a one-masted cutter-rigged vessel, differing from a cutter in having proportionally smaller sails and sometimes no bowsprit; (also **sloop'-of-war**) formerly a vessel (of whatever rig) between a corvette and a gun vessel, under a commander, carrying from ten to eighteen guns. [Du *sloep*; cf **shallop**]

sloosh /*sloosh*/ (*inf* or *dialect*) *vt* to wash or rinse with (*usu* large quantities of) water or other liquid (often with *out*); to pour (*usu* large quantities of) water or some other liquid (over). ◆ *vi* (of a quantity of liquid) to make or move with a rushing, splashing, pouring sound. ◆ *n* a washing or rinsing with water, etc; an act or instance of pouring, or the sound of this. [Prob imit]

sloot see **sluit**.

slop[1] /*slop*/ *n* slush; spilled liquid; a puddle; (in *pl*) urine and faeces collected in a bucket; (in *pl*) waste food; (in *pl*) weak or insipid liquor or semi-liquid food, *esp* as fed to pigs; (in *pl*) wishy-washy sentiment. ◆ *vt* and *vi* to spill; to splash with slops; to slobber. ◆ *vt* (**slopp'ing**; **slopped**) to wash away; to feed slops to. ◆ *vi* to walk carelessly in slush or water; to express oneself effusively (*esp N Am*). [OE (*cū-*)*sloppe* (cow-)droppings, from *slūpan* to slip]
■ **slopp'ily** *adv*. **slopp'iness** *n*. **slopp'y** *adj* wet or muddy; wishy-washy, watery; (of work or language) slipshod; over-sentimental; maudlin; (of clothes) baggy.
❏ **slop basin** or **slop bowl** *n* a basin for waste liquids at table. **slop bucket** or **slop pail** *n* a pail for removing bedroom slops or used by prisoners to slop out.
■ **slop out** (of a prisoner) to take away and empty out a bucket containing urine and faeces; to take slops from (a cell).

slop[2] /*slop*/ *n* a loose garment, such as a gown, cassock or smock-frock; (in *pl*) wide baggy trousers or breeches; the wide part of these; (in *pl*) poor quality ready-made clothing; (in *pl*) clothes and bedding issued to seamen. [Cf OE *oferslop* loose outer garment; MDu *slop*; ON *sloppr*]
❏ **slop'-built** *adj* jerry-built. **slop'-chest** *n* a supply of clothing taken on board a ship to sell to seamen; a seaman's chest for keeping clothes and bedding in. **slop'-clothing** *n*. **slop'-pouch** *n*. **sloppy joe** *n* (*inf*) a large, loose sweater; a runny mixture of minced beef and sauce served on a half roll (*N Am*). **slop'-seller** *n*. **slop'-shop** *n* a shop for ready-made clothes. **slop'work** *n* the making of slop-clothing; cheap inferior work.

slop[3] /*slop*/ (*obs*) *n* a policeman. [Back-slang]

slope /*slōp*/ *n* an incline; an inclined surface; an inclined position; an inclination, upward or downward slant. ◆ *adj* slanting (*poetic*); moving on a slope (*Milton*). ◆ *adv* aslant. ◆ *vt* to form with a slope, or obliquely; to put in a sloping position or positions; to turn downwards, to bow. ◆ *vi* to have or take a sloping position or direction; to move down a slope; to decamp or disappear (*inf*). [Aphetic from **aslope**, from OE *āslopen* pap of *āslūpan* to slip away]
■ **slope'wise** *adv* obliquely. **slop'ing** *adj*. **slop'ingly** *adv*. **slop'y** *adj* sloping.
■ **at the slope** (of a rifle) on the shoulder with the barrel sloping back and up. **slope arms** to place or hold a rifle at the slope. **slope off** (*inf*) to go away, *esp* suddenly or furtively, to decamp.

sloppy see under **slop**[1,2].

slops see under **slop**[1,2].

slosh /*slosh*/ *n* slush; a watery mess; the sound of splashing or spilling; a heavy blow (*sl*). ◆ *vi* to flounder or splash in slush; to loaf around (*N Am*); to hit (*sl*). ◆ *vt* to splash; to hit hard, beat (*sl*). [**slush**]
■ **sloshed** *adj* (*inf*) drunk, intoxicated. **slosh'ing** *n* (*space technol*) the bulk motion of liquid propellants in their tanks, particularly at launch. **slosh'y** *adj*.

slot[1] /*slot*/ *n* a long narrow depression or opening, such as one to receive a coin, an armature winding or part of a mechanism, or opening in an aerofoil or into the conduit of an electric or cable tramway or railway; the hollow down the middle of the breast (now *Scot*); a slit; a (*usu* regular) place or position in eg a radio or television programme or schedule of programmes; a niche in an organization; a point in an airport's timetable at which a given aircraft may take off. ◆ *vt* (**slott'ing**; **slott'ed**) to make a slot in, provide with a slot; to pass through a slot; to put into a slot; to fit into a small space (*lit* or *fig*; with *in* or *into*). ◆ *vi* to fit into a slot in something (with *in* or *into*); to fit into a story, puzzle, etc (*fig*). [OFr *esclot*]
■ **slott'er** *n* a person or machine that cuts slots.
❏ **slot-car racing** *n* racing on a track by tiny model cars powered and controlled electrically. **slot machine** *n* one operated by inserting a coin in a slot, such as a vending machine or a fruit machine. **slotted aerofoil** *n* any aerofoil having an air-passage (or slot) directing the air from the lower to the upper surface in a rearward direction. **slott'ing-machine** *n* a machine for cutting slots.

slot[2] /*slot*/ *n* a bar or bolt; a crosspiece that holds other parts together. [LGer or Du *slot* lock]

slot[3] /*slot*/ *n* tracks, *esp* a deer's footprints. ◆ *vt* to track. [OFr *esclot*, from ON *slōth*; cf **sleuth**]

sloth /*slōth* or *sloth*/ *n* laziness, sluggishness; a slow-moving, tree-dwelling, tropical American edentate mammal. ◆ *vt* and *vi* to spend (time) in sloth. [ME *slawthe*, altered from OE *slǣwth*, from *slāw* slow]
■ **sloth'ful** *adj* inclined to sloth, inactive, lazy. **sloth'fully** *adv*. **sloth'fulness** *n*.
❏ **sloth bear** *n* a black Indian bear (*Melursus ursinus*), with a long snout.

slouch /*slowch*/ *n* a loose, ungainly stooping gait; a stoop; a droop; an inefficient person (*US inf*); a slouch hat; an ungainly person. ◆ *adj* drooping. ◆ *vi* to go or carry oneself slouchingly; to droop. ◆ *vt* to turn down the brim of (a hat). [Cf ON *slōkr* a slouching fellow]
■ **slouch'er** *n*. **slouch'ing** *adj*. **slouch'y** *adj*.
❏ **slouch hat** *n* a soft, broad-brimmed hat. **slouch'-hatted** *adj*.
■ **be no slouch** (*inf*) (of a person) to be very good, efficient, etc (*usu* with *at*).

slough[1] /*slow*/ *n* a hollow filled with mud; a marsh; /*sloo*/ a backwater, a marshland creek (*US*). [OE *sloh*]
■ **sloughed** /*slowd*/ *adj* bogged down or swallowed up in a slough. **slough'y** *adj*.
■ **the Slough of Despond** (the state of) extreme despondency, great depression.

slough[2] /*sluf*/ *n* a cast skin; a coating; dead tissue in a sore. ◆ *vi* to come away as a slough (with *off*); to cast the skin; to develop a slough. ◆ *vt* to cast off, eg a snake's skin. [ME *sloh*; origin uncertain]
■ **slough'y** *adj*.

sloughi /*sloo'gi*/ *n* (pl **slough'is**) a breed of dog, *orig* from NW Africa, with a smooth coat, lean body, and excellent vision. [Ar *seluqi*; cf **saluki**]

Slovak /*slō'vak* or *slō-vak'*/ *adj* of or relating to the Republic of *Slovakia* in E Europe, its people or their language. ◆ *n* a native or citizen of Slovakia; a member of a Slavonic people living east of the Czechs; their language. [Slovak *Slovák*]
■ **Slovakian** /*-vak'*/ or /*-vāk'*/ *n* and *adj*.

slove see **slive**.

sloven /*sluv'n*/ *n* a person who is habitually carelessly or dirtily dressed or slipshod in work (also *adj*). [Cf ODu *slof*, *sloef*, LGer *sluf* slow, indolent]
■ **slov'enlike** *adj*. **slov'enliness** *n*. **slov'enly** *adj* and *adv*. **slov'enry** *n* (*Shakesp*) slovenliness.

Slovene /*slō-vēn'* or *slō'vēn*/ *adj* of or relating to the *Slovenian* Republic in Central Europe, its people or its language. ◆ *n* a native or citizen of the Slovenian Republic; the language of Slovenia; a member of a branch of the Southern Slavs found chiefly in Slovenia and adjoining areas; their language. [OSlav *Slovēne*]
■ **Slovē'nian** *n* and *adj*.

slow /*slō*/ *adj* not fast, not quick; late; behind in time; not hasty; not ready; not progressive; boring; (of wit and intellect) dull; (of a road lane) for slow-moving traffic; (of business) slack; (of a cooker, etc) heating gently, cooking slowly; lessening the speed of the ball, players, etc (*sport*); acting, etc slowly; (of photographic film) comparatively less sensitive to light. ◆ *n* anything that is slow. ◆ *adv* (or in compounds) slowly. ◆ *vt* to delay, retard, or reduce the speed of. ◆ *vi* to reduce speed. [OE *slāw*; Du *slee*, ON *sljōr*]
■ **slow'ing** *n* a lessening of speed. **slow'ish** *adj*. **slow'ly** *adv*. **slow'ness** *n*.
❏ **slow'back** *n* (*obs*) a lazy person. **slow burn** *n* a slow or delayed but finally strong response, reaction, etc. **slow'-burn** *adj*. **slow'coach** *n* a person who works, moves, etc slowly and who lags behind; a slow or sluggish person. **slow cooker** *n* an electric casserole dish that cooks at very low power over a long period. **slow'down** see **slow down** below. **slow food** *n* (a movement promoting the use of) locally produced, carefully prepared food. **slow'-footed** *adj* moving with a slow pace. **slow'-gaited** *adj* (*Shakesp*) accustomed to walk slowly. **slow handclap** see under **hand**. **slow march** *n* a march at a slow pace. **slow'-march** *vi*. **slow match** *n* a slowly burning rope for firing explosives. **slow motion** *n* a technique in cinema, television, etc for showing motion more slowly than it actually occurs. **slow-mo'tion** *adj* happening or appearing to happen in slow motion. **slow-mov'ing** *adj*. **slow neutron** same as **thermal neutron** (see under **thermal**). **slow'-paced** *adj*. **slow'poke** *n* (*esp N Am*) an irritatingly slow person, a slowcoach. **slow-release'** *adj* (of a medicinal capsule, fertilizer, etc) releasing its active ingredient little by little over a period of time. **slow-sight'ed** *adj*. **slow track** *n* a course of action involving slow progress. **slow virus** *n* a transmissible agent which may take years to induce symptoms.
■ **go slow** and **go-slow** see under **go**[1]. **slow down** or **up** to go more slowly (**slow'down** and **slow'-up** *n*).

slow-hound /*slō'hownd*/ *n* appar a form of **sleuth-hound**, assimilated to **slow**.

slow-worm /*slō'wûrm*/ *n* the blindworm, a harmless snakelike legless lizard. [OE *slāwyrm*, prob from root of *slēan* to strike, and *wyrm* worm, assimilated to **slow**]

sloyd or **sloid** /*sloid*/ *n* a Swedish system of using woodwork to teach basic manual skills, co-ordination, etc. [Swed; from ON *slœgth* dexterity; cf **sleight**]

SLR *abbrev* : single-lens reflex; self-loading rifle.

SLT *abbrev* : Speech and Language Therapist.

slub[1] or **slubb** /*slub*/ vt to twist (fibre) after carding to prepare it for spinning. ◆ n a piece of fibre twisted in this way.
■ **slubb'er** n. **slubb'ing** n.

slub[2] /*slub*/ n a lump in yarn. ◆ adj lumpy, knobbly in texture. [Origin obscure]
■ **slubbed** or **slubb'y** adj.

slubb see **slub**[1].

slubbed see under **slub**[2].

slubber[1] /*slub'ər*/ vt to smear, soil or daub; to perform hurriedly and carelessly, to slur over; to gobble. ◆ vi to wallow. [Du *slobberen* to lap, LGer *slubbern*]
■ **slubberdegull'ion** n a dirty, slovenly person. **slubb'ering** n and adj. **slubb'eringly** adv.

slubber[2] see under **slub**[1].

slubby see under **slub**[2].

sludge /*sluj*/ n soft mud or mire; half-melted snow; a slimy precipitate, such as from sewage; a dark yellowish or brownish green. [Cf **slush**]
■ **sludg'y** adj miry; muddy.

slue same as **slew**[2,3].

slug[1] /*slug*/ n a land mollusc with a rudimentary shell or none at all; the similar larvae of some insects, esp sawflies; a sea slug; a heavy, lazy person; anything slow-moving. ◆ vi to be inert; to go sluggishly; to hunt for slugs. ◆ vt to make sluggish. [Cf Norw dialect *slugg* a heavy body, *sluggje* a slow heavy person, Swed dialect *slogga* to be sluggish]
■ **slugg'ard** n a person who is habitually inactive (also adj). **slugg'ardize** or **-ise** vt (*Shakesp*) to make lazy. **slugg'ardliness** n. **slugg'ardly** adj. **slugg'ish** adj habitually lazy; slothful; slow-moving, slow-acting, etc; inactive. **slugg'ishly** adv. **slugg'ishness** n.
❑ **slug'-a-bed** or **slugg'abed** n (*Shakesp*) a person who lies in bed a long time.

slug[2] /*slug*/ n a lump of crude ore (*mining*); a lump of metal, esp one for firing from a gun; a bullet (*inf*); a unit of fuel in a nuclear reactor (*nuclear eng*); a metal token used in a slot machine; a solid line or section of type cast by a composing machine (*printing*); a strip of metal thicker than a lead, for separating type (*printing*); the gravitational unit of mass, *approx* 32.174 pounds (= 14.5939kg) in the **slug-foot-second** system (47.88kg in slug-metre-second reckoning). [Perh connected with **slug**[1] or **slug**[3]]

slug[3] /*slug*/ vt and vi to strike heavily. ◆ n a heavy blow. [Cf **slog**]
■ **slugg'er** n a person who slugs; a batter who specializes in hitting home runs (*baseball*).
❑ **slug'fest** n (Ger *Fest* festival, celebration; *inf*) a match or struggle, characterized by heavy blows.

slug[4] /*slug*/ (now esp US) n a gulp, a swallow; an alcoholic drink. ◆ vt to take a slug or slugs of or from. [Poss Gaelic *slug* a gulp]

sluggard, **sluggish**, etc see under **slug**[1].

slughorn or **slughorne** /*slug'hörn*/ n an old form of **slogan**; imagined by Thomas Chatterton (followed by Browning) to be a musical instrument not unlike a hautboy, or a kind of clarion.

sluice /*sloos*/ n a structure with a gate for stopping or regulating flow of water; a floodgate or watergate; a regulated outlet or inlet; a drain or channel for water; a trough for washing gold from sand, etc; an act of sluicing. ◆ vt to let out or drain by a sluice; to wet or drench copiously; to wash in or by a sluice; to flush or swill by flinging water on; to dash with water. [OFr *escluse* (Fr *écluse*), from LL *exclūsa* (*aqua*) a sluice, ie (water) shut out, pap of L *exclūdere* to shut out]
■ **sluic'y** adj streaming as from a sluice; sluicelike; soaking.
❑ **sluice'gate** n.

sluit /*slū'it* or *sloot*/ (S Afr) n a narrow water channel (also **sloot**). [Du *sloot* ditch]

slum[1] /*slum*/ n an overcrowded, squalid neighbourhood. ◆ vi to visit slums, esp for pleasure; (also vt with *it*) to adopt a lower standard of social behaviour, a less sophisticated level of cultural or intellectual activity, etc than is or would be normal for oneself. [Cant]
■ **slumm'er** n. **slumm'iness** n. **slumm'ing** n. **slumm'y** adj.
❑ **slum'-dweller** n. **slum'lord** n (esp N Am) a landlord of slum dwellings.

slum[2] /*slum*/ n the non-lubricating part of crude oil. [Perh from **slime**]

slumber /*slum'bər*/ vi to sleep, esp lightly; to be inattentive or inactive (*fig*). ◆ vt to spend in slumber. ◆ n (often in pl) light sleep; repose. [ME *slūmeren*, from OE *slūma* slumber]
■ **slum'berer** n. **slum'berful** adj. **slum'bering** n and adj. **slum'beringly** adv. **slum'berless** adj. **slum'berous** or **slum'brous** adj inviting or causing slumber; sleepy. **slum'berously** or **slum'brously** adv. **slum'bersome** adj. **slum'bery** or **slum'bry** adj sleepy, drowsy.
❑ **slum'berland** n the state of slumber. **slumber party** n (N Am) a gathering of girls at one house where they spend the night, *usu* including eating, playing music and talking, in their nightwear.

slumgullion /*slum-gul'yən*/ (N Am) n a watery stew, made with cheap or left-over meat. [Origin uncertain]

slummock /*slum'ək*/ vi to move slowly and awkwardly. ◆ n (dialect or inf) a slovenly person, esp a woman, a slut.

slummy see under **slum**[1].

slump[1] /*slump*/ vi to flop, to relax carelessly and completely; to fall or sink suddenly into water or mud; to fail or fall through helplessly; (of prices, trade, etc) to fall suddenly or heavily; to plump (*obs*). ◆ n a boggy place; a sinking into mud, etc; the sound so made; a (time of) sudden or serious fall of prices, business, etc, *opp* to **boom**. [Cf Norw *slumpe* to slump or plump, LGer *schlump* marshy place]
■ **slump'y** adj marshy.
❑ **slumpflā'tion** n an economic situation in which there is a marked decline in investment in industry, at the same time as a marked rise in inflation. **slumpflā'tionary** adj. **slump test** n (*civil eng*) a test for determining the consistency of concrete by measuring subsidence in a cone of known dimensions.

slump[2] /*slump*/ (Scot) vt to throw into a lump or mass, to lump. ◆ vi to flow lumpily. ◆ n a gross amount, a lump. [Cf LGer *slump*, Du *slomp* mass]
❑ **slump sum** n a lump sum.

slung /*slung*/ pat and pap of **sling**[1].
❑ **slung shot** n a weight attached to a cord, used as a weapon.

slunk /*slungk*/ pat and pap of **slink**.

slur /*slûr*/ n an aspersion, stain, imputation of blame or wrongdoing; disparagement; discredit to one's reputation; a slight; a blur; a running together resulting in indistinctness in writing or speech; a smooth or legato effect (*music*); a curved line indicating that notes are to be sung to one syllable, played with one bow, or with a smooth gliding effect; a gliding movement in dancing (*obs*); a gliding throw in cheating with dice (*obs*); thin mud (*dialect*). ◆ vt (**slurr'ing**; **slurred**) to disparage, cast aspersions on; to smear or besmirch (*dialect*); to glide over slyly so as to mask or to avoid attracting attention; to blur; to sound (*esp* speech) indistinctly; to sing or play legato; to go through perfunctorily; to slip glidingly out of the dice-box (*obs*); to cheat (*obs*). [Origin obscure, perh different words that have run together]
■ **slurred** adj. **slurr'y** /*slur'i*/ n a thin paste or semi-fluid mixture, eg a thin liquid cement, liquid waste from farm animals, liquid waste or residue from mining, coal-washing, etc.

slurb /*slûrb*/ (*inf*) n an area combining the appearance and qualities of a *slum* and a su*burb*.

slurp /*slûrp*/ vt to drink (liquid) or eat (semi-liquid food) noisily. ◆ vi to flow with, or produce the sound of, a slurp or slurps. ◆ n the noise produced by, or similar to that produced by, slurping food or drink. [Du *slurpen* or *slorpen* to sip audibly, gulp]
■ **slurp'er** n. **slurp'y** adj.

slurry see under **slur**.

sluse a Miltonic spelling of **sluice**.

slush /*slush*/ n melting snow; liquid mud; a protective coating for metal; worthless sentimental drivel or gush. ◆ vt to splash or cover with slush; to sluice, wash by throwing water; to fill the joints of (brick, etc) with mortar (with *up*). ◆ vi to splash in slush; to make a slushing sound. [Cf **slosh**]
■ **slush'iness** n. **slush'y** adj.
❑ **slush fund** or **money** n (*orig* US) a fund of money used, *usu* corruptly, in political campaigning and propaganda, bribery, undeclared commissions, etc. **slush pile** n (*sl*) a collection of unsolicited manuscripts received by a publishing company.

slut /*slut*/ n a dirty, untidy woman; a promiscuous or otherwise disreputable woman; a bitch, female dog (*archaic*); a greased rag used as a candle (*obs*). [Cf Ger dialect *schlutt(e)*]
■ **slutt'ish** or **slutt'y** adj. **slutt'ishly** or **slutt'ily** adv. **slutt'ishness**, **slutt'iness** or **slutt'ery** n.

sly /*slī*/ adj (**sly'er** or **sli'er**; **sly'est** or **sli'est**) skilful in doing anything (esp anything wrong) without being observed; cunning; wily; secretive; surreptitious; done with artful dexterity; with hidden meaning; illicit (*Aust*); expert (*obs* or dialect); cunningly made (*obs*). [ON *slægr*; cf **sleight**; cf Ger *schlau*]
■ **sly'ish** adj. **sly'ly** adv (also **slī'ly**). **sly'ness** n.
❑ **sly'boots** n sing a sly or cunning person or animal.
■ **on the sly** surreptitiously.

slype /*slīp*/ n a passage between walls, esp a covered passage from a cloister between transept and chapterhouse. [Perh **slip**[2]]

SM abbrev : sadomasochism (also **s-m** or **s/m**); Sergeant-Major; short metre.

Sm (*chem*) symbol : samarium.

sma /*smö*/ (*Scot*) adj small.

smack[1] /*smak*/ vt to strike smartly, slap loudly; to kiss roughly and noisily; to make a sharp noise with (eg the lips by first compressing and then parting them); to taste with relish or with a smacking sound. ◆ *vi* to make such a sound. ◆ *n* a sharp sound; a crack; a slap; a hearty kiss. ◆ *adv* sharply, straight, absolutely. [Prob imit; Du or LGer *smakken* to smite, Ger *schmatzen* to smack]

■ **smack'er** *n* (*inf*) a pound sterling; a dollar; an enthusiastic or exaggerated kiss. **smack'ing** *n* and *adj*.

❑ **smack'down** *n* (*N Am sl*) a chastisement or defeat; a confrontation.

■ **talk smack** (*N Am sl*) to make abusive or disparaging remarks, *esp* without justification.

smack² /smak/ *n* a taste; a distinctive or distinguishable flavour; a trace or tinge; a mere tasting, enough to taste. ◆ *vi* to taste or have the flavour (of); to have a suggestion or trace (of) (*fig*). [OE *smæc*]

smack³ /smak/ *n* a small decked or half-decked coaster or fishing-vessel, *usu* rigged as a cutter, sloop, or yawl; a fishing-vessel containing a well in which fish can be kept alive (*esp US*). [Du *smak*; Ger *Schmacke*]

smack⁴ /smak/ (*sl*) *n* heroin. [Perh Yiddish *schmeck*, with same meaning]

❑ **smack'head** *n* (*sl*) a heroin addict.

smacker, smacking see under **smack¹**.

smaik /smāk/ (*Scot*) *n* a contemptible fellow, rascal.

small /smöl/ *adj* little in size, extent, quantity, value, power, importance, or degree; young; slender; narrow; fine in grain, texture, gauge, etc; unimposing, humble; (of thought or action) ungenerous, petty, ignoble; short of the full standard; dilute; operating on no great scale; soft or gentle in sound; minor. ◆ *n* a small thing, portion or piece; the narrow part (*esp* of the back); small-coal; (in *pl*) small-clothes; (in *pl*; *euphem* and *joc*) underclothes; (in *pl*) formerly at Oxford, the examination called responsions (corresponding to little go at Cambridge); a size of roofing slate, 12 × 8in (305 × 203mm). ◆ *adv* in a low tone; gently; into small pieces; on a small scale; only slightly (*Shakesp*). ◆ *vt* and *vi* (*rare*) to make or become small. [OE *smæl*; Ger *schmal*]

■ **small'ish** *adj*. **small'ness** *n*.

❑ **small ads** *n pl* classified advertisements. **small ale** *n* ale made with little malt and no hops. **small'-and-earl'y** *n* (*inf*; *Dickens*, etc) an informal evening party. **small arm** *n* (*usu* in *pl*) a weapon that can be carried by a person, *esp* a handgun or short weapon. **small beer** see under **beer¹**. **small'-bore** *adj* (of a firearm) having a barrel with a small bore, of a calibre not more than .22in. **small calorie** see **calorie**. **small capitals** (*inf* **small caps**) *n pl* capital letters of the height of lower case. **small change** *n* coins of low value; hence, someone or something of little importance. **small chop** *n* (*W Afr*) snacks served with drinks. **small circle** see under **circle**. **small claims** *n pl* claims for small amounts of money (in England and Wales up to d5000, in Northern Ireland up to d2000, in Scotland up to d750) that can be dealt with through a simpler legal procedure than larger claims. **small'-clothes** *n pl* knee-breeches, *esp* those of the close-fitting 18c form. **small'-coal** *n* coal in small pieces. **small craft** *n* small vessels generally. **smallest room** *n* (*euphem*) a lavatory, *esp* in a house. **small fry** *n* a small person; an unimportant or insignificant person (or people). **small goods** *n pl* (*Aust* and *NZ*) cooked meat products, such as sausages. **small'-hand** *n* writing such as is ordinarily used in correspondence. **small'holder** *n*. **small'holding** *n* a holding of land smaller than an ordinary farm, *esp* one provided by the local authority; the working of such land. **small hours** *n pl* the hours immediately after midnight. **small intestine** see **intestine**. **small lady** *n* a size of roofing slate, 14 × 12in (356 × 305mm). **small letter** *n* (*usu* in *pl*) a lower-case letter. **small-mind'ed** *adj* petty. **small-mind'edly** *adv*. **small-mind'edness** *n*. **small'mouth** *n* a N American freshwater fish (*Micropterus dolomieu*). **small pica** see under **pica¹**. **small'-pipes** *n pl* the form of bagpipes played *esp* in S Scotland and N England, smaller than the Highland bagpipes and with the bag inflated by bellows under the arm rather than by air from the lungs. **small potatoes** *n pl* (*orig N Am*) someone or something (*esp* a sum of money) of little importance, value, significance, etc. **small'pox** *n* (*orig pl*) a contagious, febrile disease, characterized by fever and pockmarks on the skin. **small print** *n* details of a contract, insurance policy, etc, the small type having a tendency to obscure limitations or legal rights. **small'sat** *n* (*inf*) a relatively small, inexpensive communications satellite. **small'-scale** *adj* (of maps, models, etc) representing a large area without giving fine detail; (of a business enterprise) having a limited size and scope. **small screen** *n* television. **small'-screen** *adj*. **small sword** *n* a light thrusting sword for fencing or duelling. **small talk** *n* light or trifling conversation. **small'-time** *adj* (*inf*) unimportant; insignificant. **small-tim'er** *n*. **small-tooth comb** *n* a comb with a row of fine teeth on each side; an arrangement for minute investigation (*fig*). **small'-town** *adj* provincial, petty; naïve, unsophisticated. **small wares** *n pl* small articles such as tape, braid, buttons and hooks; trifles.

■ **by small and small** (*Shakesp*) little by little. **feel small** to feel insignificant, cheap, ashamed, etc. **in a small way** with little capital or stock; unostentatiously, on a small scale. **in small** on a small scale. **in the smallest** (*Shakesp*) in the least. **look small** to look silly or insignificant; to be snubbed.

smallage /smö'lij/ *n* wild celery. [**small** and Fr *ache*, from L *apium* parsley]

smalm see **smarm**.

smalt /smölt/ *n* glass coloured with cobalt oxide; its powder, used as a pigment; its deep blue colour; smalto. ◆ *adj* deep blue. [Ital *smalto*, from OHGer *smalzjan* (Ger *schmelzen*) to melt]

■ **smalt'ite** *n* a cubic mineral, (Co,Ni)As₂, cobalt arsenide. **smalto** /smöl'tō or zmäl'tō/ *n* (*pl* **smal'tos** or **smal'ti** /-tē/) coloured glass or enamel for mosaic work; a cube of it.

smaragd /smar'agd/ (*archaic*) *n* an emerald. [L *smaragdus*, from Gr *smaragdos*]

■ **smarag'dine** /-dīn, -dēn or -dīn/ *adj* emerald green. **smarag'dite** *n* a mineral, a green amphibole.

smarm /smärm/ or (*obs*) **smalm** /smäm/ *vt* and *vi* to smear, daub or plaster (*dialect*); to sleek. ◆ *vi* to fawn ingratiatingly and fulsomely; to be unctuous. ◆ *n* smarminess. [Origin obscure]

■ **smarm'ily** or (*obs*) **smalm'ily** *adv*. **smarm'iness** or (*obs*) **smalm'iness** *n*. **smarm'y** or (*obs*) **smalm'y** *adj*.

smart /smärt/ *vi* to feel or be the location of a prolonged stinging pain (also *fig*); to be punished (for). ◆ *vt* to cause to smart. ◆ *n* a smarting pain; smart money; a dandy (*old sl*). ◆ *adj* sharp and stinging; brisk; acute, witty; clever, brainy; pert, vivacious; trim, spruce, fine; fashionable; keen, quick, and efficient in business; considerable (*esp US*); technologically advanced and able to respond to changing conditions (*comput*); computer-guided or electronically controlled, as in *smart house, smart bomb, smart weapon*, etc (*inf*). ◆ *adv* smartly. [OE *smeortan*; Du *smarten*]

■ **smart'en** *vt* and *vi* to make or become smart, to brighten (with *up*). **smartie** see **smarty** below. **smart'ingly** *adv*. **smart'ish** *adj* somewhat smart. ◆ *adv* (*inf*) quickly. **smart'ly** *adv*. **smart'ness** *n*. **smart'y** or **smart'ie** *n* (*usu* ironic or contemptuous) a would-be smart person.

❑ **smart Al'ick, Al'eck, Al'ec** or **alec** *n* a would-be clever person or one too clever for their own good (also *adj*, with *hyphen*). **smart'-alecky** *adj*. **smart'ass** or **smart'arse** (*derog sl*) a smarty (also *adj*). **SMART®** **board** a brand of interactive whiteboard (qv under **white**). **smart bomb** or **missile** *n* a bomb or missile that is able to alter its direction and/or find its target using computer-aided or electronically-controlled guidance and detection systems. **smart card** *n* a plastic card like a banker's card fitted with a microprocessor (including a memory) rather than a magnetic strip, used in commercial transactions, telecommunications, etc, its design intended to combat fraud. **smart drug** *n* a non-technical name for a drug that can radically enhance mental powers, a cognitive enhancer. **smart missile** see **smart bomb** above. **smart money** *n* money staked or invested by experienced or clever gamblers or investors; the people staking or investing this money; money paid by a recruit for his release before being sworn in (*obs*); money paid for escape from any unpleasant situation or engagement; excessive damages; money allowed to soldiers and sailors for wounds, or to employees for injuries received (*obs*). **smart'phone** or **smart phone** *n* a portable device combining a mobile phone and a computer; a telephone with electronically-controlled automatic dialling. **smart'-tick'et** *n* (*obs*) a certificate granted to someone entitled to smart money. **smart'watch** *n* a wristwatch that can perform some of the functions of a computer. **smart'weed** *n* water pepper, from its acridity. **smart'ypants** or **smart'y-boots** *n sing* (*inf*; *pl* the same) a smarty.

■ **look smart** (*inf*) to be quick, hurry. **smart sanctions** sanctions that are intended to coerce the government of a country without causing hardship to the civilian population.

smash /smash/ *vt* to dash or shatter violently; to ruin, cause to fail; to strike overhand with great force (*tennis*, etc). ◆ *vi* to fly into pieces; to be ruined, fail; to be dashed or shattered violently; to smash a tennis ball, etc. ◆ *n* an act or occasion of smashing, destruction, ruin, bankruptcy; an accident, *esp* in road traffic; a smash hit; cash (*sl*). ◆ *adv* with a smash. [Imit; cf Swed dialect *smaske* to smack]

■ **smashed** *adj* (*sl*) drunk or under the influence of drugs. **smash'er** *n* a person or thing that smashes; a person who passes bad money (*old sl*); anything great or extraordinary (*inf*); a person of dazzling charm (*inf*). **smasheroo'** *n* (*sl*) a person or thing of superlative quality, importance, etc, eg a smash-hit (also *adj*). **smash'ing** *n* the action of the verb. ◆ *adj* crushing, shattering; dashing; strikingly good, wonderful (*inf*). **smash'ingly** *adv*.

❑ **smash-and-grab'** *adj* and *n* (a robbery) effected by smashing a shop-window and grabbing goods. **smash hit** *n* (*inf*) an overwhelming success, *esp* in entertainment of any kind. **smash'-up** *n* a serious accident.

smatch /smach/ (*obs*) *n* smack, taste; tincture (*Shakesp*); a touch; a smattering. ◆ *vi* to smack, have a flavour. ◆ *vt* to smack of. [**smack²**]

smatter /smat'ər/ n a smattering. ◆ vi to talk superficially; to have a superficial knowledge; to dabble. ◆ vt to talk or utter smatteringly; to dabble in. [ME *smateren* to rattle, to chatter; connections doubtful]
- **smatt'erer** n. **smatt'ering** n a scrappy, superficial knowledge; a small amount scattered around. **smatt'eringly** adv.

smaze /smāz/ n smoky haze.

SMD (*electronics*) abbrev : surface-mounted device.

SME abbrev : small or medium-sized enterprise; Suriname (IVR).

smear /smēr/ n a rub with, or a mark or patch of, anything sticky or oily; the matter so applied, *esp* to a slide for microscopic study; a fine glaze for pottery; a slur, defamatory accusation; grease (*obs*). ◆ vt to spread something sticky or oily over; to apply in a smear or smears; to rub smearily; to anoint; to defame. [OE *smeru* fat, grease; Ger *Schmer* grease; ON *smjör* butter]
- **smear'er** n. **smear'ily** adv. **smear'iness** n. **smear'y** adj sticky; greasy; ready to smear; showing smears.
- □ **smear campaign** n a series of verbal or written attacks intended to defame or discredit. **smear'-dab** see **lemon²**. **smear tactics** n pl tactics employed in a smear campaign. **smear test** n a test involving the microscopic study of a smear, as for example a cervical smear (qv under **cervix**).

smeath see **smee**.

smectic /smek'tik/ (*chem*) adj used of a substance whose state is intermediate between solid and liquid and whose atoms or molecules are oriented in parallel planes. [L *smecticus* cleansing, from Gr *smektikos* detergent (from the soapy consistency of a smectic substance)]

smectite /smek'tīt/ n the family of minerals that are constituents of clays, *incl* bentonite, fuller's earth and saponite. [See **smectic**]

smeddum /smed'əm/ n fine powder; spirit, mettle (*Scot*). [OE *smed(e)ma, smeodoma* fine flour]

smee /smē/, **smeath** or **smeeth** /smēth/ (*dialect*) n names for various ducks, such as the smew, pochard, wigeon and pintail.

smeech /smēch/ (*SW Eng dialect*) and **smeek** /smēk/ (*Scot*) forms of **smoke**.

smeeth see **smee**.

smegma /smeg'mə/ n a sebaceous secretion, *esp* that under the foreskin. [Gr *smēgma, -atos* soap]

smeik and **smeke** /smēk/ Scots forms of **smoke**.

smell /smel/ n the sense by which the odours of gases, vapours and very finely divided substances are perceived, located in the higher animals in the mucous membrane of the nose; the specific sensation excited by such a substance; the property of exciting it; an act or instance of exercising the sense; a pleasant scent or (often) an unpleasant one; a smack, savour, sense, property of suggesting, intimation (*fig*). ◆ vi (pat and pap **smelled** or **smelt**) to affect the sense of smell; to have an odour (*esp* unpleasant), or an odour (of); to have or use the sense of smell; to have a savour, give a suggestion (of something) (*fig*). ◆ vt to perceive, detect, find, by smell (often with *out*); to be aware of by intuition; to take a smell at; to impart a smell to; to emit a smell of. [Very early ME *smel*, prob OE but not recorded]
- **smell'able** adj. **smell'er** n. **smell'iness** n. **smell'ing** n and adj. **smell'-less** adj. **smell'y** adj having an unpleasant smell.
- □ **smell'-feast** n (*obs*) a sponger. **smelling bottle** n a bottle of smelling salts or the like. **smelling salts** n pl a preparation of ammonium carbonate with lavender, etc, used as a stimulant in cases of fainting, etc. **smell'-trap** n a drain-trap.
- ▪ **smell a rat** see under **rat¹**. **smell at** to sniff at, take a smell at. **smelling of roses** see under **rose¹**. **smell of** to have the smell of; to savour of. **smell out** to find out (eg a scandal) by prying; to detect by witchcraft (*S Afr*).

smelt¹ /smelt/ vt to melt in order to separate metal from ore. [Prob MLGer or MDu *smelten*; cf Norw *smelta*, Swed *smälta*]
- ▪ **smel'ter** n. **smel'tery** n a place for smelting. **smel'ting** n.
- □ **smel'ting-furnace, -house, -works** n.

smelt² /smelt/ n any fish of the family Osmeridae, related to the salmon family, with a cucumber-like smell; any of various similar fish, such as those of the family Retropinnidae of Australia and Tasmania. [OE *smelt*]

smelt³ /smelt/ a pat and pap of **smell**.

smelt⁴ /smelt/ (*obs sl*; *Walter Scott*) n a half-guinea. [Origin obscure]

smeuse /smūs/ or /smūz/ n a dialect form of **meuse¹**.

smew /smū/ n a sea duck, a small species of merganser. [Origin uncertain]

smicker /smik'ər/ (*obs*) adj beautiful; smirking, wanton. ◆ vi to look amorously. [OE *smicer* beautiful]
- ▪ **smick'ering** n an amorous inclination. **smick'ly** adv amorously.

smicket /smik'it/ n a smock. [Prob dimin]

smiddy /smid'i/ a Scots form of **smithy**.

smidgen, **smidgeon** or **smidgin** /smij'ən/ or -*in*/ (*inf*) n a very small amount. [Ety uncertain]

smifligate /smif'li-gāt/ same as **spiflicate**.

smight a Spenserian spelling of **smite**.

smilax /smī'laks/ n any plant of the genus *Smilax*, of the lily family, mostly climbers with net-veined leaves, some yielding sarsaparilla; a southern African twining plant of the asparagus family, with bright-green foliage, much used by florists as decoration. [Gr *smīlax*]

smile /smīl/ vi to express amusement, slight contempt, favour, pleasure, etc by a slight drawing up of the corners of the lips; to look joyful; to be favourable (*fig*); to drink, *esp* whisky (*old sl*). ◆ vt to express, drive (away), etc, by smiling; to smile at (*Shakesp*); to give (a smile). ◆ n an act of smiling; the expression of the features in smiling; favour (*fig*); a drink, treat (*old sl*). [ME *smīlen*; poss from LGer]
- ▪ **smile'ful** adj. **smile'less** adj. **smil'er** n (*Shakesp*) a little smile. **smil'ey** adj smiling; cheerful. ◆ n a set of characters representing a smiling face when read sideways (*comput*; see also **emoticon**); an icon of a smiling face as a symbol of peace and happiness (now *usu* associated with drug-taking). **smil'ing** n and adj. **smil'ingly** adv. **smil'ingness** n the state of being smiling.
- ▪ **smile at** to show amusement at, disregard of. **smile on** (*fig*) to show favour to, be propitious to.

smilodon /smī'lə-don/ n a member of an extinct genus (*Smilodon*) of large, short-limbed, sabre-toothed tigers which inhabited the Americas during the Pleistocene epoch. [LL, from Gr *smilē* a knife, and *odous, odontos* a tooth]

smir see **smur**.

smirch /smûrch/ vt to besmear or dirty; to sully. ◆ n a stain. [Earlier *smorch*, supposed to be from OFr *esmorcher* to hurt, infl by **smear**]

smirk /smûrk/ vi to smile affectedly, smugly or foolishly; to look affectedly soft. ◆ n an affected, smug or foolish smile. ◆ adj trim, spruce. [OE *smercian*]
- ▪ **smirk'er** n. **smirk'ily** adv. **smirk'ing** adj. **smirk'ingly** adv. **smirk'y** adj simpering.

smirr see **smur**.

smit¹ /smit/ (*obs* or *poetic*) pat and pap of **smite**.

smit² /smit/ (*Scot and N Eng dialect*) vt to stain; to mark with ruddle; to infect. ◆ n a stain (*obs*); ruddle; a ruddle mark on a sheep; an infection. [OE *smittian* to befoul or infect, intens of *smītan* to smear; *smitte* spot]
- ▪ **smitt'le** adj infectious.

smite /smīt/ (*literary* or *archaic*) vt (pat **smōte** or (*archaic* or *poetic*) **smit**; pap **smitt'en** or (*archaic* or *poetic*) **smit**) to strike; to beat; to kill; to overthrow in battle; to affect with feeling; to afflict. ◆ vi to strike; to meet forcibly. [OE *smītan* to smear]
- ▪ **smi'ter** n.
- ▪ **smite off** to cut off.

smith /smith/ n a person who forges metals with a hammer; a worker in metals; (often in combination) a person who makes anything or who makes skilful use of anything, as in *wordsmith*. ◆ vt to forge; to fashion. ◆ vi to work as a smith. [OE *smith*; Ger *Schmied*]
- ▪ **smith'ery** n a smithy; smith's work, smithing. **smithy** /smidh'i or smith'i/ n a smith's workshop. ◆ vt and vi to smith.
- □ **smith'craft** n.

smithereens /smidh-ə-rēnz'/ n pl shivers, tiny fragments (also **smith'ers**). [Ir *smidirín*, dimin of *smiodar* a fragment]
- ▪ **smithereen'** vt (*rare*) to break into tiny pieces; to shatter.

Smithsonian parity /smith-sō'ni-ən par'i-ti/ n parity agreed for major currencies at an international conference at the *Smithsonian* Institution, Washington, in 1971.

smithsonite /smith'sə-nīt/ n a white mineral, carbonate of zinc, occurring in calcareous rocks (also called **calamine**). [James *Smithson* (1765–1829), British chemist and mineralogist]

smithy see under **smith**.

smitten /smit'n/ pap of **smite** (*literary* or *archaic*); obsessed (with), in love (with) (*inf*).

smittle see under **smit²**.

SMM abbrev : *Sancta Mater Maria* (*L*), Holy Mother Mary.

SMMT abbrev : Society of Motor Manufacturers and Traders.

SMO abbrev : Senior Medical Officer.

smock /smok/ n a loose, protective garment, *usu* of coarse cloth, worn by artists, etc; an outer garment of coarse white linen formerly worn by farm workers in the south of England; a woman's long loose-fitting blouse; a loose dress worn by pregnant women; a woman's shift, a chemise (*archaic*); a woman or wench (*obs*). ◆ vt to clothe in a smock; to decorate with smocking. [OE *smoc*]
- ▪ **smock'ing** n honeycomb stitching, as on the yoke and cuffs of a smock.

❑ **smock'-faced** *adj* pale-faced. **smock'-frock** *n* a farm worker's smock. **smock mill** *n* a windmill with a fixed tower and revolvable cap above it bearing the sails (also called **tower mill**). **smock'-race** *n* formerly, a race run by women or girls for the prize of a smock.

smog /*smog*/ *n* smoky fog.
■ **smogg'y** *adj*.

smoile or **smoyle** /*smoil*/ old forms of **smile**.

smoke /*smōk*/ *n* the gases, vapours, and fine particles that are emitted by burning material; solid particles suspended in a gas; fumes; vapour; fog; a cloud or column of fumes; something which may be smoked, eg tobacco, a cigarette, or a cigar (*inf*); an instance or spell of smoking; South African brandy (**Cape smoke**); tear gas (*inf*). ◆ *vi* to exhale or emit smoke, vapour, dust, etc; to reek; to send smoke (*esp* in a wrong direction); to move like smoke; to dash along in a cloud of smoke, vapour, spray, or dust; to suffer (*orig* at the stake), to smart; to take into the mouth and puff out the smoke of tobacco or something similar; to permit, or lend itself to, smoking. ◆ *vt* to dry, scent, preserve, fumigate, suffocate, blacken, taint, drive or render by smoke; to inhale and emit the smoke from; to scent out, suspect, have an inkling of (*archaic*); to observe (*archaic*); to quiz, ridicule (*archaic*); to thrash (*archaic*). [OE *smoca* (noun), *smocian* (verb); Ger *Schmauch*]
■ **smok'able** or **smoke'able** *adj* fit to be smoked. **smoked** *adj*. **smoke'less** *adj* (eg of a fuel) emitting no smoke; containing little or no smoke. **smoke'lessly** *adv*. **smoke'lessness** *n*. **smok'er** *n* a person who smokes tobacco; a smoking carriage or compartment; an apparatus for emitting smoke; a vent in the sea bed which issues hot water and minerals; a person who smoke-dries meat, or an apparatus for doing this; a smoking concert. **smokie** see **smoky** below. **smok'ily** *adv*. **smok'iness** *n*. **smok'ing** *n* and *adj*. **smok'o** *n* (*pl* **smok'os**) (*inf*) a smoke-ho. **smok'y** *adj* giving out smoke; like smoke; coloured like or by smoke; filled, or liable to be filled, with smoke; tarnished or made unattractive or offensive by smoke; suspicious (*archaic*). ◆ *n* (*Scot*) a smoked haddock (also **smok'ie**).
❑ **smoke abatement** *n* (measures directed to) reducing the amount of smoke in the atmosphere of towns. **smoke alarm** *n* a device that detects smoke from a fire in a room, building, etc and sounds a warning bell or buzzer. **smoke ball** *n* a shell emitting smoke as a screen or to drive out an enemy. **smoke'-black** *n* lampblack. **smoke'board** *n* a board suspended before the upper part of a fireplace to prevent the smoke coming out into the room. **smoke bomb** *n* a bomb that emits smoke on bursting. **smoke'box** *n* part of a steam boiler where the smoke is collected before passing out at the chimney. **smoke bush** or **smoke tree** *n* a sumach with light feathery or cloudlike panicles. **smoke'-consumer** *n* an apparatus for removing all the smoke from a fire. **smoke control area** *n* one in which the emission of smoke from chimneys is prohibited. **smoke detector** *n* a device that activates an alarm when it detects smoke in the air, a smoke alarm. **smoke'-dried** *adj*. **smoke'-dry** *vt* to cure or dry by means of smoke. **smoke'-filled room** *n* (*inf*) a place away from the public view where political decisions are taken by a small but influential group of people (characterized as typically being smokers). **smoke helmet** *n* a head-covering for firefighters or others who work in dense smoke. **smoke-ho'** *n* (*pl* **smoke-hos'**) (*Aust inf*) *orig* a break for a smoke during the working day, now a rest, a tea-break. **smoke hole** *n* a fumarole; a hole allowing smoke to escape. **smoke'hood** *n* a protective hood that prevents the wearer from inhaling smoke and poisonous fumes, eg from a fire on an aircraft. **smoke'house** *n* a building where meat or fish is cured by smoking, or where smoked meats are stored. **smoke'-jack** *n* a contrivance for turning a spit by means of an ascending current of air (*hist*); a muddled brain (*obs*). **smokeless fuel** *n* a fuel that produces little or no smoke and is thus permitted in a smoke control area. **smokeless zone** *n* a smoke control area. **smoke'proof** *adj* impervious to smoke. **smoke room** *n* a smoking room (see below). **smoke'-room story** *n* one unsuitable for telling elsewhere. **smoke'-sail** *n* a small sail hoisted to drive off the smoke from the galley. **smoke'screen** *n* a cloud of smoke raised to conceal movements (also *fig*). **smoke signal** *n* (often in *pl*) a signal or message conveyed by means of patterns of smoke (also *fig*). **smoke'stack** *n* the funnel of a ship or railway engine; a (*usu* tall industrial) chimney. **smokestack industry** *n* a traditional heavy industry, *esp* one employing methods of production and technology that adversely affect the environment. **smoke test** *n* a method of testing for leaks in drain pipes or chimneys by introducing dense smoke, often by using a smoke bomb. **smoke'tight** *adj* impervious to smoke. **smoke tree** see **smoke bush** above. **smoke tunnel** *n* a wind tunnel into which smoke is put at certain points in order to make wind effects visible. **smoking cap**, **smoking jacket** *n* a light ornamental cap and jacket formerly worn by smokers. **smoking carriage**, **compartment** or **room** *n* a railway carriage, compartment or room, set apart for smokers. **smoking concert** *n* a concert at which smoking (euphemistically) is allowed. **smoking gun** *n* (*inf*) a piece of evidence that leaves no doubt as to someone's involvement in a crime. **smoky quartz** *n* Cairngorm stone.

■ **end** or **go up in smoke** (of eg hopes) to vanish; (of eg plans) to come to nothing. **like smoke** very quickly. **sell smoke** (L *fūmum vendere* to make empty promises) to swindle. **smoke and mirrors** the use of deception, *esp* to achieve one's aims in spite of being in a weak position. **smoke out** to discover; to drive out of a hiding place by smoke or fire. **the (Big) Smoke** (*inf*; also without *caps*) a metropolitan area characterized by atmospheric pollution, *esp* London; the (nearest) city or major town (*orig* a phrase used by the Australian aborigines), now *esp* Melbourne or Sydney.

smoko see under **smoke**.

smolder American spelling of **smoulder**.

smolt /*smōlt*/ *n* a young river salmon when it is bluish along the upper half of the body and silvery along the sides. [*Orig* Scot; see **smout**[2]]

smooch /*smooch*/ (*inf*) *vi* to kiss or pet; to dance slowly while in an embrace. ◆ *n* an act or period of smooching. [Origin uncertain; poss related to **smouch**[1]]
■ **smooch'er** *n*. **smooch'y** *adj* (of music) suitable for slow dancing; (of dancing) performed by couples in a close embrace.

smoor see **smore**.

smoot /*smoot*/ (*sl*) *n* a compositor who does odd jobs in various printing houses. ◆ *vi* to work in this way. [Origin obscure]

smooth /*smoodh*/ *adj* having an even surface; without roughness of texture or taste; evenly spread; glossy; hairless; of even consistency; slippery; gently flowing; easy; bland; fair-spoken; charming, perhaps self-consciously so; classy or elegant (*inf*). ◆ *adv* smoothly. ◆ *vt* to make smooth, not rough, lumpy, etc; to free from obstruction, difficulty or harshness; to reduce from a diphthong to a simple vowel; to remove by smoothing (often with *away*; often *fig*); to calm or soothe; to blandish; to make (difficulties or problems) seem less serious or less important (often with *over*). ◆ *vi* to become smooth; to flatter, blandish or behave ingratiatingly (also *vt* with *it*; Shakesp). ◆ *n* a smooth place, part or side; an act of smoothing. [OE *smōth* (usu *smēthe*)]
■ **smooth'able** *adj*. **smooth'en** *vt* to make smooth. **smooth'er** *n* a person or thing that smooths; a smoothing tool, a sleeker; a flatterer (*obs*). **smooth'ie** *n* a plausible or smooth-spoken person (*inf*); a person elegant or suave in manner or appearance, *esp* insincerely or excessively so (*inf*); a thick drink of smooth consistency made with puréed fruit, milk, yoghurt or ice cream. **smooth'ing** *n* and *adj*. **smooth'ish** *adj*. **smooth'ly** *adv*. **smooth'ness** *n*.
❑ **smooth'-bore** *adj* (of a firearm) not rifled (also **smooth'-bored**). ◆ *n* a gun with a smooth-bored barrel. **smooth'-browed** *adj* with unwrinkled brow. **smooth'-chinned** *adj* beardless. **smooth'-coated** *adj* not shaggy-haired. **smooth dab** see **lemon**[2]. **smooth-ditt'ied** *adj* (*Milton*) set to words that smoothly fit the tune or, possibly, having a smooth ditty, or set of words. **smooth'-faced** *adj* having a smooth face or surface; pleasant-looking; beardless; unwrinkled; plausible. **smooth hound** *n* a small shark of the genus *Mustelus*. **smoothing iron** *n* a flatiron. **smoothing plane** *n* a small fine plane used for finishing. **smooth'-leaved** *adj*. **smooth muscle** *n* unstriated muscular tissue (eg in the walls of the intestines) whose action is slow rhythmic contraction and relaxation, independent of the will. **smooth'-paced** *adj* having a regular easy pace. **smooth'pate** *n* (*archaic*) a bald person. **smooth'-shod** *adj* having shoes without spikes. **smooth snake** *n* a harmless European snake (*Coronella austriaca*), with smooth scales and a dark horizontal line on the side of its head. **smooth'-spoken**, **smooth'-talking** or **smooth'-tongued** *adj* conciliatory, plausible, flattering, persuasive, or soft in speech. **smooth'-talk** *vt*. **smooth'-talker** *n*.

smørbrød /*smör'broo* or *smær'brö*/ (*Norw*), or **smørrebrød** /*smæ'rə-brædh* or *smö'rə-bröd*/ (*Dan*) *n* literally, bread and butter; hors d'œuvres served on slices of buttered bread.

smore /*smōr* or *smör*/ or **smoor** /*smoor*/ (*Scot*) *vt* and *vi* to smother or suffocate; to put out (a fire or light). ◆ *n* (**smoor**) smoke. [OE *smorian*]

smörgåsbord /*smör'gas-börd* or *smær'gŏs-boord*/ *n* a Swedish-style table assortment of hors d'œuvres and many other dishes to which one helps oneself. [Swed]

smørrebrød see **smørbrød**.

smorzando /*smört-san'dō* or *zmort-sän'dō*/ or **smorzato** /*-sä'tō*/ (*music*) *adj* and *adv* with a gradual fading away; growing slower and softer. [Ital; gerund and pap of *smorzare* to tone down, extinguish]

smote /*smōt*/ *pat* of **smite**.

smother /*smudh'ər*/ *vt* to suffocate by excluding the air, *esp* by a thick covering; to stifle (*lit* and *fig*); to envelop closely; to cover up thickly; to suppress; to conceal. ◆ *vi* to be suffocated or suppressed; to smoulder. ◆ *n* smoke; thick floating dust; a smouldering fire or condition; a welter; suffocation. [ME *smorther*, from OE *smorian* to smother; cf **smore**]

■ **smoth'ered** *adj.* **smoth'erer** *n.* **smoth'eriness** *n.* **smoth'ering** *n* and *adj.* **smoth'eringly** *adv.* **smoth'ery** *adj* tending to smother; stifling.
□ **smothered mate** or **smother mate** *n* in chess, checkmate by a knight, the king having been prevented from moving by the positions of his own forces. **smother'-fly** *n* an aphis.

smouch¹ /smowch/ (*dialect*) *n* a smack, a hearty kiss. ◆ *vt* to kiss. [Cf Ger *Schmutz*]

smouch² /smowch/ or **smouse** /smowz/ *n* a Jew (*obs sl*); a pedlar (*S Afr*). ◆ *vi* (*S Afr*) to trade as a pedlar. [Afrik *smous*, perh from Heb *sh'mū'ōth* news]
■ **smous'er** *n* (*S Afr*) a pedlar.

smouch³ /smowch/ *vt* to filch. ◆ *vi* to cheat.

smouch⁴ /smowch/ *n* a form of **smutch** and **smudge¹**.

smoulder /smōl'dər/ *vt* to smother. ◆ *vi* to burn slowly or without flame; to linger on in a suppressed or hidden state; to harbour suppressed and often hidden emotions. ◆ *n* smother; smouldering fire. [ME *smolder*; origin obscure]
■ **smoul'dering** *n* and *adj.* **smoul'deringly** *adv.* **smoul'dry** *adj* (*Spenser*).

smouse, smouser see **smouch²**.

smout¹ /smowt/ same as **smoot**.

smout² or **smowt** /smowt/ *n* Scots form of **smolt**; a small person or child.

smoyle see **smoile**.

SMR *abbrev*: standardized mortality rate.

SMS *abbrev*: short message service, a service for sending text messages.

SMTP (*comput*) *abbrev*: Simple Mail Transfer Protocol, a protocol used for the transmission of email between servers.

smudge¹ /smuj/ *n* a smear; a blur; a rubbed blot. ◆ *vt* to smear; to blur; to soil; to daub. ◆ *vi* to become or cause a smudge. [Cf **smutch**]
■ **smudge'less** *adj.* **smudg'er** *n.* **smudg'ily** *adv.* **smudg'iness** *n.* **smudg'y** *adj.*

smudge² /smuj/ *n* a choking smoke; fuel for obtaining smoke. ◆ *vt* to fumigate with smoke. [Origin obscure]
■ **smud'gy** *adj* smoky.
□ **smudge box, pot**, etc *n* a container for or of materials which produce smoke to protect people, plants, etc against insects, etc.

smug¹ /smug/ *adj* (**smugg'er**; **smugg'est**) offensively self-complacent; neat, prim, spruce; smooth; sleek; affectedly smart. ◆ *n* a smug person; an industrious student who does not take part in social activities (*obs university sl*). ◆ *vt* to make trim. [Connection with LGer *smuk* trim is unlikely, as the *g* presents difficulty]
■ **smug'ly** *adv.* **smug'ness** *n.*
□ **smug'-faced** *adj.*

smug² /smug/ (*sl*) *vt* to seize without ceremony; to steal; to hush up. [Origin obscure]

smuggle¹ /smug'l/ *vt* to import or export illegally or without paying duty; to convey secretly. [LGer *smuggeln*; Ger *schmuggeln*]
■ **smugg'led** *adj.* **smugg'ler** *n* a person who smuggles; a vessel used in smuggling. **smugg'ling** *n* and *adj.*

smuggle² /smug'l/ *vt* to fondle or cuddle. [Origin obscure]

smur /smûr/, **smirr** or **smir** /smir/ (*Scot*) *n* fine misty rain. ◆ *vi* to drizzle, rain very finely.
■ **smurr'y** or **smirr'y** *adj.*

smut /smut/ *n* soot; worthless or bad coal; a flake or spot of dirt, soot, etc; a black spot; a disease of plants, *esp* cereals, giving an appearance of soot; the fungus causing it; mildly obscene conversation, remarks, material, etc. ◆ *vt* to soil, spot or affect with smut. ◆ *vi* to become smutty. [Cf LGer *schmutt*; Ger *Schmutz* dirt]
■ **smutt'ed** *adj.* **smutt'ily** *adv.* **smutt'iness** *n.* **smutt'y** *adj* stained with smut; affected with smut disease; mildly obscene.
□ **smut fungus** *n* any member of the Ustilaginales, an order of Basidiomycetes, parasitic on plants, causing smut and bunt.

smutch /smuch/ *vt* to smut; to sully. ◆ *n* a dirty mark; soot; grime; a stain. [Cf **smudge¹**]

smytrie /smī'tri/ (*Scot*) *n* a collection of small things. [Cf Flem *smite*]

SN *abbrev*: Senegal (IVR).

Sn (*chem*) *symbol*: tin. [L *stannum*]

sn *abbrev*: *secundum naturam* (L), according to nature.

snab see **snob**.

snabble see **snaffle**.

snack /snak/ *n* a light meal; a share; a small quantity; a taste; a snap, bite (*dialect*). ◆ *vi* to eat a snack; to snap (*Scot*); to share (*obs*). [Cf MDu *snacken* to snap; **snatch**]
□ **snack bar** or **snack counter** *n* a place where light meals can be bought.

■ **snack on** to make a light meal from.

snaffle /snaf'l/ *n* a jointed bit for horses (less severe than the curb). ◆ *vt* to put a snaffle on; to control by a snaffle; (the following meanings *sl*; also **snabb'le**) to arrest; to capture; to purloin; to get possession of. [Ety doubtful; cf Du *snavel*, Ger *Schnabel* beak, mouth]
□ **snaff'le-bit** *n.* **snaff'le-bridle** *n.* **snaff'le-rein** *n.* **snaff'ling-lay** *n* the trade of highwayman.

snafu /sna-foo'/ or /sna'foo/ (*N Am sl, orig milit*) *n* chaos. ◆ *adj* chaotic. ◆ *vt* to throw into chaos. [situation normal all fouled (or fucked) up]

snag /snag/ *n* a catch, a (hidden) obstacle or drawback; a caught thread in a stocking; a stump, eg of a branch or tooth; a jag; a short tine; an embedded tree, dangerous for boats; (*usu pl*) sausage (*Aust sl*). ◆ *vt* (**snag'ing**; **snagged**) to catch on a snag; to tear on a snag; to hack so as to form snags; to clear of snags; to obtain, secure (*N Am inf*). [Cf ON *snagi* peg]
■ **snagged** *adj.* **snagg'y** *adj.*

snaggletooth /snag'l-tooth/ *n* (pl **snagg'leteeth**) a broken, irregular or projecting tooth. [Appar from **snag** and **tooth**]
■ **snagg'le-toothed** *adj.*

snail /snāl/ *n* any terrestrial or air-breathing gastropod mollusc with a well-developed coiled shell; extended to other shelled gastropods and (*dialect*) to slugs; a sluggish person or animal; a snail wheel; any of several medicks with coiled pods. ◆ *vi* to crawl, go very slowly (also *vt* with *it*). [OE *snegl*, *snægl*, *snēl*]
■ **snail'ery** *n* a place where edible snails are bred. **snail'-like** *adj* and *adv.* **snail'y** *adj.*
□ **snail darter** *n* a small American freshwater fish (*Percina tanasi*). **snail'fish** *n* the fish also called the **sea snail**. **snail flower** *n* any flower pollinated by snails. **snail mail** *n* (*facetious*) normal, in contrast to electronic, mail. **snail'-paced** *adj.* **snail'-shell** *n.* **snail'-slow** *adj.* **snail's pace** *n* a very slow speed. **snail wheel** *n* a cam that controls the striking of a clock.
■ **giant African snail** a 10-inch snail, a serious plant pest except in its place of origin, E Africa.

'snails /snālz/ (*obs*) *interj* for **God's nails**, an exclamatory oath.

snake /snāk/ *n* a serpent, or member of the Ophidia, a suborder of elongated limbless (or all but limbless) scaly carnivorous reptiles, often venomous, with forked tongue, no eyelids or external ears, and teeth fused to the bones that bear them; an ungrateful or treacherous person (in allusion to one of Aesop's fables); a wretch or drudge; anything snakelike in form or movement; (also **plumber's snake**) an apparatus for clearing blocked pipes; an apparatus for blasting a passage through a minefield; formerly, the band (narrower than the tunnel allowed by the IMF on the world market) within which the relative values of certain EC currencies were allowed to float. ◆ *vi* to move sinuously or follow a winding course; to creep. ◆ *vt* to drag. [OE *snaca*]
■ **snake'like** *adj.* **snake'wise** *adv* in the manner of a snake. **snāk'ily** *adv.* **snāk'iness** *n.* **snāk'ish** *adj.* **snāk'ishness** *n.* **snāk'y** *adj* snakelike; treacherous.
□ **snake'bird** *n* the darter; the wryneck. **snake'bite** *n* the bite of a venomous snake; the condition or symptoms of a victim of a snakebite; a drink made of lager and cider in equal measures. **snake'-charmer** *n* a person who handles snakes and gets them to perform rhythmical movements. **snake cult** *n* serpent-worship. **snake dance** *n* a religious dance of the Hopi people in which snakes are handled. **snake eel** *n* an eel without a tail fin. **snake eyes** *n sing* a score of two ones made when two dice are thrown. **snake fence** *n* (*US*) a worm fence (qv). **snake fly** *n* a neuropterous insect (genus *Raphidia*) with a necklike prothorax. **snake'head** *n* a freshwater fish of tropical Asia and Africa with a snakelike body; a member of a Chinese criminal gang specializing in transporting illegal migrants to other countries. **snake'-hipped** *adj* slim-hipped. **snake'-house** *n* a place where snakes are kept. **snake lizard** *n* a legless lizard of Australia and New Guinea. **snake'-oil** *n* any substance or mixture without medicinal value but sold as medicine. **snake'-pit** *n* (*fig*) a mental hospital; a place, or circumstances, characterized by disordered emotions and relationships. **snake'root** *n* bistort, milkwort, *Aristolochia*, or any other plant whose root has been thought good for snakebites. **snake's'-head** *n* fritillary. **snake'skin** *n* the skin of a snake, *esp* when made into leather (also *adj*). **snake'stone** *n* a fossil ammonite; a stone thought to cure snakebite. **snake'weed** *n* bistort. **snake'wood** *n* letterwood.
■ **snake in the grass** (*fig*) someone who injures treacherously or furtively; a lurking danger. **snakes and ladders** a board game played with counters and dice in which 'ladders' afford short cuts to the finish, but 'snakes' oblige players to descend to nearer the starting-point.

snap /snap/ *vi* (**snapp'ing**; **snapped**) to make a bite (often with *at*); to speak tartly in sudden irritation; to grasp (with *at*); to shut suddenly, eg by a spring; to make a sharp noise; to go with a sharp noise; to break suddenly; to lose one's temper or self-control (*inf*). ◆ *vt* to bite suddenly; to seize, secure promptly (*usu* with *up*); to answer or interrupt sharply (often with *up*); to shut with a sharp sound; to cause to make a sharp sound; to send or put with a sharp sound; to say snappishly (sometimes with *out*); to break suddenly; to pass (the ball) from the line of scrimmage back to the quarterback (*American football*); to take a quick photograph of, *esp* with a hand-held camera. ◆ *n* an act, instance, or noise of snapping; a small catch or lock; an earring (*rare*); (in *pl*) a kind of handcuffs; a share; a scrap; a whit; a snack; a crack; a crisp, ginger biscuit (also **gingersnap**); a quick, crisp, incisive, epigrammatic quality in style; lively energy; a brief theatrical engagement (*sl*); an easy and profitable place or task; a sharper, a cheat (*old sl*); a riveter's or glass-moulder's tool; a snapshot; a sudden cold spell (also **cold snap**); a type of card game in which the first player to shout 'snap' on spotting a matching pair of cards wins all the cards on the table; the play that involves snapping the ball (*American football*). ◆ *adj* sudden, unexpected; offhand; (of a decision or judgement) made on the spur of the moment without deep consideration of all possibilities; snapping shut. ◆ *adv* with a snap. ◆ *interj* used in claiming cards in the game of snap; also, on meeting or discovering two matching items, circumstances, etc. [Prob Du *snappen* to snap; Ger *schnappen*]

■ **snapp'er** *n* an animal that snaps; someone who snaps or snaps up; an attachment at the end of a whiplash to make it crack; a snapping-turtle; any fish of the family Lutjanidae, related to the basses; (also **schnapper**) any of several highly esteemed food-fish of the family Sparidae, found in Australian and New Zealand waters; a photographer (*sl*); a Christmas or party cracker (*N Am*). **snapp'ily** *adv*. **snapp'ing** *n* and *adj*. **snapp'ingly** *adv*. **snapp'ish** *adj* inclined to snap; quick and tart. **snapp'ishly** *adv*. **snapp'ishness** *n*. **snapp'y** *adj* snappish; snapping; having the quality of snap; instantaneous; lively; smart, fashionable, polished (as in *snappy dresser*).

◻ **snap bean** *n* (*N Am*) a variety of bean with edible pods. **snap'-brim** *adj* (of a hat) having a brim that turns down springily. **snap'dragon** *n* a plant (genus *Antirrhinum*) of the figwort family whose flower when pinched and released snaps like a dragon; another name for **flap-dragon** (see under **flap**). **snap'-fastener** *n* a press-fastener, a press-stud. **snap'-link** *n* a link with a side opening closed by a spring. **snapp'ing-turtle** *n* a large aggressive American freshwater turtle. **snap roll** *n* an aerobatic manoeuvre in which an aircraft turns in a longitudinal circle while maintaining its flight direction. **snap'shooter** *n*. **snap'shooting** *n*. **snap'shot** *n* a hasty shot; a photograph taken quickly and informally, with simple equipment; an instant record of an event, situation, etc at a particular time, *esp* a stage in a process or sequence (*fig*; also *adj*); a record of the placement of stored data at a specific stage in a program run (*comput*).

■ **look snappy, make it snappy** (*inf*) to hurry. **Scotch snap** see under **Scotch**. **snap into it** to get going quickly. **snap one's fingers** to flick a finger and thumb together with a sharp noise, *usu* to attract attention or peremptorily demand service. **snap out of it** (*inf*) to give (eg a mood or habit) up at once. **snap someone's head** or **nose off** to answer irritably and rudely. **snap up** to take or purchase eagerly and quickly.

snaphaunce /*snap'häns* or *-höns*/, **snaphance** /*-häns* or *-hans*/ or **snaphaunch** /*-hönsh*/ (*obs*) *n* a freebooter; a flintlock or a weapon with one; a spring catch or trap. [Cf Du *snapshaan*, from *snappen* to snap, and *haan* a cock]

snapper[1] /*snap'ər*/ (*Scot*) *n* a stumble; a slip in conduct; a scrape. ◆ *vi* to stumble. [Cf Ger dialect *schnappen* to stumble]

snapper[2] see under **snap**.

snar /*snär*/ (*Spenser*) *vi* to snarl. [Cf Du and LGer *snarren*]

snare /*snār*/ *n* a running noose for trapping; a trap; an allurement, temptation, entanglement or moral danger; a loop for removing tumours, etc; a string stretched across the lower head of a side drum. ◆ *vt* to catch, entangle or trap in a snare; to remove with a snare. [OE *sneare* or ON *snara* ; prob partly from Du *snaar* or LGer *snare*]
■ **snar'er** *n*. **snar'ing** *n*. **snar'y** *adj*.
◻ **snare drum** *n* a side drum.

snarf /*snärf*/ (*inf*) *vt* to devour greedily. [Origin uncertain]

snark /*snärk*/ *n* an imaginary animal created by Lewis Carroll (1876).

snarky /*snär'ki*/ (*sl*) *adj* irritable; snide and sarcastic. [Du and LGer *snorken* to snort]
■ **snark** *n* a snide or sarcastic comment. ◆ *vi* to make such a comment; to act irritably.

snarl[1] /*snärl*/ *vi* to make a noise with a show of teeth; to speak in a surly manner. ◆ *vt* to utter snarlingly. ◆ *n* an ill-natured growling sound or facial expression; an act of snarling. [*snar*]
■ **snarl'er** *n*. **snarl'ing** *n* and *adj*. **snarl'ingly** *adv*. **snarl'y** *adj*.

snarl[2] /*snärl*/ *n* a knot; a tangle; a knot in wood. ◆ *vt* to ensnare (*dialect*); to tangle; to raise with a snarling-iron. ◆ *vi* to tangle. [*snare*]
■ **snarled** *adj*. **snarl'er** *n*. **snarl'ing** *n*.
◻ **snarl'ing-iron** or **-tool** *n* a curved tool for raised work in metal.

■ **snarl up** (used *esp* in *pap* and *participial adj* forms) to make muddled or tangled and thus stop operating, moving, etc smoothly (**snarl'-up** *n* a tangle; a traffic jam).

snash /*snash*/ (*Scot*) *n* insolence, abusive language. ◆ *vi* to talk impudently. [Prob imit]

snaste /*snāst*/ (now *dialect*) *n* the burnt wick of a candle. [Origin obscure]

snatch /*snach*/ *vt* to seize suddenly; to pluck away quickly; to grab; to take as opportunity occurs. ◆ *vi* to make a snap or seizure. ◆ *n* a snap (*Shakesp*); an act of snatching or snatching at; a grab; a short spell; a fragment, eg of song or verse; a snack; a robbery or kidnapping (*inf*); a catch (of the voice) (*Shakesp*); a quibble (*Shakesp*); (in weightlifting) a type of lift in which the weight is raised from the floor to an overhead position in one movement; the female genitals (*vulgar sl*). [ME *snacchen* ; poss related to **snack**]
■ **snatch'er** *n*. **snatch'ily** or **snatch'ingly** *adv*. **snatch'y** *adj* irregular.
◻ **snatch block** *n* a block with a side opening for the bight of a rope. **snatch'-purse** or **-thief** *n* a thief who snatches. **snatch squad** *n* a group of policemen, etc who force a sudden quick passage into eg a disorderly or rioting crowd in order to arrest troublemakers or ringleaders; a swift, organized sally by a group of people in order to seize something.
■ **snatch at** to try to snatch or seize.

snath /*snath*/, **snathe** /*snādh*/, **snead** /*snēd*/, **sneath** /*snēth*/ or **sned** /*sned*/ *n* the curved handle or shaft of a scythe. [OE *snæd* a scythe handle, a slice]

snazzy /*snaz'i*/ (*inf*) *adj* very attractive or fashionable; flashy. [Origin obscure]

SNCF *abbrev* : Société Nationale des Chemins de fer Français (*Fr*), French national railways.

snead see **snath**.

sneak /*snēk*/ *vi* (pat and pap **sneaked** or (*N Am* or *inf*) **snuck**) to go furtively or meanly; to slink or skulk; to creep meanly; to tell tales. ◆ *vt* to pass furtively; to steal (*sl*). ◆ *n* a sneaking person; a person who sneaks or sneaks away; a sneaking thief; a telltale. [Connection with OE *snīcan* to crawl is obscure]
■ **sneak'er** *n* a person who or thing that sneaks; a soft-soled, *usu* canvas, shoe; a sandshoe. **sneak'ily** *adv*. **sneak'iness** *n*. **sneak'ing** *adj* mean, crouching; secret, underhand, not openly avowed; slight but persistent; lurking under other feelings. **sneak'ingly** *adv*. **sneak'ish** *adj* befitting a sneak. **sneak'ishly** *adv*. **sneak'ishness** *n*. **sneaks'by** *n* (*archaic*) a sneak. **sneak'y** *adj* sneaking; cunning.
◻ **sneak'-cup** *n* in some editions of Shakespeare (*1 Henry IV* III.3.84), probably a misreading of a blurred **sneakeup** (same as **sneak-up** below) in the first quartos, but by some taken to be a correction and explained as one who balks his cup, or a stealer of cups. **sneak preview** *n* a special private screening or viewing of a film, exhibition, etc before it is officially released, made available, etc to the public. **sneak'-raid** *n* a bombing or other raid made under conditions of concealment. **sneak thief** *n* a thief who steals through open doors or windows without breaking in. **sneak'-thievery** *n*. **sneak'-up** *n* a sneak, shirker or skulker.

sneap /*snēp*/ *vt* to nip, pinch; to put down, repress, snub. ◆ *n* a snub, check. [Earlier *snape*, from ON *sneypa*]
■ **sneap'ing** *adj* (*Shakesp*).

sneath see **snath**.

sneb and **snebbe** old forms of **snib**[2], **snub**.

sneck[1] /*snek*/ (*Scot and N Eng*) *n* a latch; a door catch. ◆ *vt* to fasten with a sneck. [Cf **snack**, **snatch**]
◻ **sneck drawer**, also **sneck draw** *n* someone who lifts the latch; an insinuating or crafty person. **sneck'-drawing** *n* and *adj*.

sneck[2] see **snick**[1].

sneck up see **snick up**.

sned[1] /*sned*/ *vt* to cut; to lop; to prune. [OE *snǣdan*]

sned[2] see **snath**.

snee /*snē*/ (*obs*) *vi* to cut. [Du *snijden* to cut]
■ **snick and snee, snick or snee, stick or snee** see **snickersnee**.

sneer /*snēr*/ *vi* to show cynical contempt by the expression of the face, as by drawing up the lip (sometimes with *at*); to express such contempt in other ways; to grin (*obs*). ◆ *vt* to utter sneeringly; to sneer at (*obs*); to render or drive by sneering. ◆ *n* a sneering expression; an act of sneering. [Perh related to Fris *sneere* to scorn]
■ **sneer'er** *n*. **sneer'ing** *n* and *adj*. **sneer'ingly** *adv*. **sneer'y** *adj*.

sneesh /*snēsh*/ (*Scot*) *n* a pinch of snuff; snuff. [Poss **sneeze**, **sneezing**; or imit; cf **snush**]
■ **sneesh'in, sneesh'ing** or **sneesh'an** *n* snuff; a pinch of snuff.
◻ **snee'shin-mull** *n* a snuff box.

sneeze /*snēz*/ *vi* to make a sudden, involuntary and audible expiration through the nose and mouth, due to irritation of the inner nasal

---

membrane. ◆ *n* an act of sneezing. [ME *snesen*, *fnesen*, from OE *fnēsan* to sneeze; Du *niezen*]

■ **sneez'er** *n*. **sneez'ing** *n*. **sneez'y** *adj*.

❑ **sneeze box** *n* (*sl*) a snuffbox. **sneeze'weed** *n* an American composite plant (genus *Helenium*). **sneeze'wood** *n* a S African meliaceous timber tree (genus *Ptaeroxylon*), or its wood, whose sawdust causes sneezing. **sneeze'wort** *n* a species of yarrow (*Achillea ptarmica*) once used as a substitute for snuff; white hellebore.

■ **not to be sneezed at** not to be despised.

snell[1] /*snel*/ (*Scot*) *adj* (of eg wind or weather) keen, sharp or severe. [OE *snell* active; Ger *schnell* swift]

■ **snel'ly** *adv*.

snell[2] /*snel*/ (*angling*) *n* a short piece of hair, gut, etc attaching a hook to a line. ◆ *vt* to attach (a hook) to a line. [Origin obscure]

Snell's law see under **law**[1].

SNG *abbrev*: synthetic natural gas.

snib[1] /*snib*/ (chiefly *Scot*) *n* a small bolt; a catch for a window sash. ◆ *vt* to fasten with a snib. [Cf LGer *snibbe* beak]

snib[2] same as **snub**.

snick[1] /*snik*/ (*Walter Scott* **sneck** /*snek*/) *vt* to cut out, snip, nick; to deflect slightly by a touch of the bat (*cricket*). ◆ *n* a small cut; a slight deflection off the edge of the bat (*cricket*). [Origin doubtful]

■ **snick and snee** or **snick or snee** see **snickersnee**.

snick[2] /*snik*/ *n*, *vt* and *vi* click. [Imit]

snicker /*snik'ər*/ *vi* to snigger; to nicker or neigh. ◆ *vt* to say gigglingly. ◆ *n* a giggle; a neigh. [Imit; cf **nicker**[2], **snigger**[1]]

snickersnee /*snik'ər-snē*/ *n* a large knife for fighting; fighting with knives (*obs*). ◆ *vi* (*obs*) to fight with knives (also earlier **snick'-a-snee**, **snick and snee**, **snick or snee**, **stick or snee**). [Appar Du *steken* to thrust, and *snijden* to cut]

snicket /*snik'it*/ (*dialect*) *n* a narrow passage or backstreet; a ginnel. [Origin obscure]

snick up /*snik up*/ (*Shakesp*) *vi* (*usu imperative*) go hang (also **sneck up**).

snide /*snīd*/ *adj* sham; counterfeit; base; mean; dishonest; derogatory in an insinuating way (also **snī'dey**); showing malice (also **snī'dey**). ◆ *n* a snide person; snide behaviour. [Ety doubtful]

■ **snide'ly** *adv*. **snide'ness** *n*.

sniff /*snif*/ *vt* to draw in with the breath through the nose; to smell; to suspect or detect by smell or as if by smell. ◆ *vi* to draw in air sharply and audibly through the nose; to draw up mucus or tears escaping into the nose; to smell tentatively; to express disapprobation with reticence by a slight sound in the nose; to snuffle; to inhale a dangerous or addictive substance (eg glue or cocaine). ◆ *n* an act or a sound of sniffing; a smell; a small quantity inhaled by the nose; a slight intimation or suspicion (*fig*). [Imit; cf **snuff**[1]]

■ **sniff'er** *n* a person or thing that sniffs; a program or tool used to monitor traffic and capture data on a network (*comput*). ◆ *adj* (of a dog, apparatus, etc) trained, designed, etc to seek out or locate (*esp* illicit or dangerous substances) by smell. **sniff'ily** *adv*. **sniff'iness** *n*. **sniff'ing** *n* and *adj*. **sniff'ingly** *adv*. **sniff'le** *vi* to snuffle slightly, to sniff. ◆ *n* an act of sniffling; the sound made by sniffling; (often in *pl* with *the*) a slight cold; (often in *pl* with *the*) liquid mucus running out of or blocking the nose. **sniff'ler** *n* someone who sniffles; a slight breeze. **sniff'ly** *adj* having a slight cold. **sniff'y** *adj* inclined to be disdainful.

■ **not to be sniffed at** not to be despised.

snift /*snift*/ *vi* to sniff or snivel; to blow out steam, etc. [Ety as for **sniff**]

■ **snift'er** *vt* and *vi* to sniff. ◆ *n* a sniff; (in *pl*) blockage of the nasal passages in catarrh, the sniffles; a dram (*sl*); a strong breeze; a brandy glass (*US*). **snift'y** *adj* (*sl*) having a tempting smell; inclined to sniff in disdain.

❑ **snift'er-** or **snift'ing-valve** *n* an air valve of a cylinder, etc.

snig /*snig*/ (*dialect*) *n* a river eel, *esp* an immature (olive and yellow) eel. ◆ *vt* to drag a load with chains or ropes. [Origin obscure]

■ **snigg'er** *vt* to catch (salmon) with a weighted hook. **snigg'le** *vi* to fish for eels by thrusting the bait into their hiding places; to fish for salmon, etc, by hooking them with a quick turn of the wrist. ◆ *vt* to catch in this way. ◆ *n* a baited hook. **snigg'ler** *n*. **snigg'ling** *n*.

snigger[1] /*snig'ər*/ *vi* to laugh in a half-suppressed way, often derisively or mockingly. ◆ *vt* to say with a snigger. ◆ *n* a half-suppressed laugh. [Imit]

■ **snigg'erer** *n*. **snigg'ering** *n* and *adj*. **snigg'eringly** *adv*.

snigger[2] see under **snig**.

snip /*snip*/ *vt* (**snipp'ing**; **snipped**) to cut eg with scissors; to snatch or snap (*obs*). ◆ *n* a small cut, eg with scissors; a small shred; a small, slender or despicable person; a small piece; a notch, slit or slash; the sound of a stroke of scissors; a white or light patch or stripe on a horse,

esp on the nose; a share; a tailor (*sl*); a certainty; a bargain. [LGer or Du *snippen*; Ger dialect *schnippen*]

■ **snipp'er** *n*. **snipp'ing** *n* a clipping. **snipp'y** *adj* fragmentary; stingy; snappish. **snips** *n pl* hand-shears for sheet metal.

❑ **snipp'er-snapper** *n* a whippersnapper. **snip-snap'** *n* the action or sound of scissors (also *interj*); quick snappy dialogue. ◆ *adj* and *adv* with a snapping sound. ◆ *vi* to make a snapping sound. **snipt taffeta fellow** *n* (*Shakesp*) one who goes about in slashed silk.

snipe /*snīp*/ *n* (pl usu **snipe** of the bird, **snipes** of species of the bird, and in other senses) any of several wading birds of the genus *Gallinago*, breeding in marshes and having a long straight bill; any of several similar or related species; a fool or contemptible person (*Shakesp*); the butt of a cigar or cigarette (*US sl*); a sniping shot; a verbal attack, criticism. ◆ *vi* to shoot snipe for sport, go snipe-shooting; to shoot at individuals from a position of (*usu* distant) cover; to attack or criticize, *esp* from a position of security (*fig*; often with *at*). ◆ *vt* to pick off by rifle-fire from (*usu* distant) cover. [Prob Scand; the OE word is *snīte*]

■ **snip'er** *n*. **snip'ing** *n*. **snip'y** *adj* snipe-like; snipe-beaked; frequented by snipe.

❑ **snipe'fish** *n* the trumpetfish. **snipe fly** *n* a long-legged fly that preys on other insects.

snipper see under **snip**.

snippet /*snip'it*/ *n* a little piece snipped off; a scrap, of literature, news, etc. [**snip**]

■ **snipp'etiness** *n*. **snipp'ety** *adj* trivial, fragmentary.

snippy see under **snip**.

snip-snap-snorum /*snip-snap-snö'rəm*/ *n* a children's game of turning up cards, to the calls of 'snip', 'snap' and 'snorum'. [LGer *snipp-snapp-snorum*]

snirt /*snirt*/ or *snûrt*/ (*Scot*) *n* a smothered laugh. [Imit]

■ **snirt'le** *vi* to snicker.

snit /*snit*/ (*N Am*) *n* a fit of bad temper or sulking. [Origin unknown]

snitch /*snich*/ (*sl*) *n* the nose; a fillip on the nose (*obs*); an informer. ◆ *vi* to inform or sneak. ◆ *vt* to pilfer.

■ **snitch'er** *n* an informer; (*usu* in *pl*) a handcuff (*obs sl*).

snivel /*sniv'l*/ *n* mucus of the nose; a sniff; a hypocritical snuffle; cant. ◆ *vi* (**sniv'elling**; **sniv'elled**) to run at the nose; to sniff; to snuffle; to whimper or cry; to complain self-pityingly. ◆ *vt* to utter with snivelling. [OE *snofl* mucus]

■ **sniv'eller** *n*. **sniv'elling** *adj*. **sniv'elly** *adj*.

SNO *abbrev*: Senior Nursing Officer.

snob /*snob*/ *n* a person who sets too much value on social standing, wishing to be associated with the upper class and their mores, and treating those viewed as inferior with condescension and contempt; someone having similar pretensions as regards specified tastes, such as *wine snob*, *intellectual snob*; a shoemaker, shoemaker's apprentice, cobbler (*old inf* and *dialect*; Scot **snab**); a townsman (*Cambridge University sl*); a person of ordinary or low rank (*obs*); an ostentatious vulgarian (*obs*); a blackleg, scab (*obs*). [Orig slang]

■ **snobb'ery** *n* snobbishness; snobbish behaviour. **snobb'ish** *adj*. **snobb'ishly** *adv*. **snobb'ishness** *n*. **snobb'ism** *n*. **snobb'y** *adj*. **snob'ling** *n* a little snob. **snoboc'racy** or **snobboc'racy** *n* snobs as a powerful class. **snobog'rapher** *n*. **snobog'raphy** *n* the description of snobs and snobbery.

❑ **snob value** *n* perceived superior worth deriving from high price or exclusivity.

SNOBOL /*snō'böl*/ *n* String Oriented Symbolic Language, a high-level computer language for handling strings of symbols.

Sno-cat /*snō'kat*/ *n* a type of motorized, tracked vehicle for use on snow. [From **snow**[1] and **caterpillar**]

snod /*snod*/ (*Scot*) *adj* smooth, neat, trim, snug. ◆ *vt* (pat and pap **snodd'ed** or **snodd'it**) to trim, set in order (with *up*). [Poss connected with ON *snothinn* bald]

snoek see **snook**[1].

snog /*snog*/ (*sl*) *vi* to embrace, cuddle, kiss, indulge in lovemaking (also *n*). [Origin obscure]

snoke see **snook**[3].

snood /*snood*/ *n* a band for the hair, once worn by unmarried women in Scotland as the badge of virginity; an ornamental hairnet supporting the back of a woman's hair; a tube of knitted or other material worn as a hood; the length of fine line, gut, etc, by which a fish-hook is fixed to the line. ◆ *vt* to bind, dress or fasten with or in a snood. [OE *snōd*]

■ **snood'ed** *adj*.

snook[1] /*snook*/ *n* any of several marine fishes, including the cobia, robalo, garfish, or (in S Africa and now elsewhere also **snoek** /*snook*/) the barracouta (*Thyrsites atun*). [Du *snoek* pike]

snook[2] /snŭk or snook/ n the gesture of putting the thumb to the nose with the fingers held upright and spread out, to express derision, defiance, etc (also **snooks**). [Origin obscure]
■ **cock a snook** to make that gesture (also *fig*).

snook[3] /snook/, **snoke** /snōk/ or (*Scot*) **snowk** /snowk/ vi to snuff or smell about; to lurk, prowl or sneak about. [ME *snoken* to lurk, from MLGer *snoken*, orig from Scand]

snooker /snoo'kər/ n a variety of the game of pool, played with 15 red balls, 1 white cue ball and 6 balls of other colours, the object being to pocket the non-white balls in a certain order and gain more points in so doing than one's opponent; a situation in snooker where the path between the cue ball and the ball to be played is blocked, forcing an indirect shot to be played. ◆ *vt* to render a direct stroke impossible for; to thwart (a person or plan) by placing an obstacle in the way (*fig*). [Popularly believed to be a coinage, at the game's inception in India in 1875, from old military slang *snooker* a raw cadet, perh from **snook**[3]]

snool /snool/ (*Scot*) n someone who submits tamely to wrong or oppression. ◆ *vt* to keep in subjection; to snub. ◆ *vi* to be tamely submissive. [Ety doubtful]

snoop /snoop/ vi to go about sneakingly, to pry. ◆ *n* a person who snoops. [Du *snoepen* to eat, steal]
■ **snoop'er** n. **snoop'y** adj.
❑ **snoop'erscope** n a device which converts infrared radiation reflected from an object into an image on a fluorescent screen, used for locating or identifying objects in darkness.

snoot /snoot/ n the nose (*sl*); an expression of contempt; a snobbish person (*sl*). ◆ *vt* to regard contemptuously (also *vi*). [Cf Du *snuit* snout, face]
■ **snoot'ful** n (*inf*) enough alcohol to make one drunk. **snoot'ily** adv. **snoot'iness** n. **snoot'y** adj (*inf*) haughtily supercilious, snobbish.

snooze /snooz/ vi to doze, take a nap. ◆ *n* a nap; something boring and soporific (*sl*). [Origin obscure; perh orig slang]
■ **snooz'er** n. **snooz'y** adj.
❑ **snooze button** n a device on an alarm clock which stops the alarm and allows a few minutes respite before it sounds again.

snore /snōr or snör/ vi to breathe roughly and hoarsely during sleep with vibration of the uvula and soft palate, or of the vocal cords; to snort. ◆ *vt* to pass in snoring; to render by snoring. ◆ *n* a noisy breathing of this kind; a boring person, thing or event (*sl*). [Imit; cf **snort**]
■ **snör'er** n. **snör'ing** n.

snorkel /snör'kl/, also **schnorkel** /shnör'/ n a retractable tube or set of tubes by means of which a submarine takes in air and releases exhaust gases; a short stiff tube with a mouthpiece, by means of which a submerged swimmer can breathe. [Ger *Schnorchel*]
■ **snor'keller** n. **snor'kelling** n swimming with a snorkel.

snort /snört/ vi to force air with violence and noise through the nostrils, as horses do; to snore (*Shakesp*); to inhale a powdered drug, eg cocaine, through the nose (*sl*). ◆ *vt* to express by or utter with a snort; to force out, as by a snort; to inhale (a powdered drug, *esp* cocaine) through the nose (*sl*). ◆ *n* an act or sound of snorting; a quick drink (*inf*); the snorkel on a submarine. [Imit]
■ **snort'er** n someone who or something that snorts; anything characterized by extreme force, *esp* a gale (*inf*); anything exceptional, eg in size, strength (*inf*). **snort'ing** n and adj. **snort'ingly** adv. **snort'y** adj snorting; inclined to snort (*inf*); contemptuous and ready to take offence.

snot /snot/ n nasal mucus; a contemptible person. ◆ *vt* and vi (chiefly *dialect*) to blow the nose. [OE *gesnot*; *snytan* to blow the nose; cf Du *snot*; allied to **snout**]
■ **snott'er** vi to breathe through an obstruction in the nostrils; to sob, snuffle, blubber. ◆ *n* the wattles of a turkey cock; snot (*Scot*). **snott'ery** n snot, filthiness. ◆ *adj* (*Scot*) snotty, foul with snot. **snott'ily** adv. **snott'iness** n. **snott'y** adj like, or foul with, snot; superciliously standoffish, with the nose in the air; mean, of no importance. ◆ *n* (*naval sl*) a midshipman (also **snott'ie**).
❑ **snot'-nosed** or **snott'y-nosed** adj. **snot'rag** n (*sl*) a handkerchief.

snotter /snot'ər/ (*naut*) n the fitting that supports the inboard end or heel of a sprit (qv). [Origin obscure]

snout /snowt/ n the projecting muzzle of an animal, *esp* a pig; the nose (*sl*); any similar projection; the lower end of a valley glacier (*geog*); a cigarette, tobacco (*prison sl*); a police informer (*sl*). ◆ *vt* to provide with a snout. [ME *snūte*, prob from unrecorded OE; cf Swed *snut*; Ger *Schnauze*, Du *snuit*; also **snot**]
■ **snout'ed** adj. **snout'y** adj like a snout; snouted; haughtily supercilious (see **snooty** under **snoot**).
❑ **snout beetle** n another name for **weevil**.

snow[1] /snō/ n atmospheric vapour frozen in crystalline form, whether in single crystals or aggregated in flakes; a snowfall; a mass or expanse

of snow; a winter; any substance resembling snow, such as carbonic acid snow (frozen carbon dioxide); snowlike specks on the screen caused by electrical interference (*TV* and *radar*); anything white, such as hair (*fig*); a white-fleshed variety of apple; linen, *esp* drying or bleaching (*old sl*); cocaine, morphine, heroin (*sl*). ◆ *adj* of snow. ◆ *vi* to shower snow; to fall as snow or like snow. ◆ *vt* to shower like snow; to strew as with snow; to whiten, whiten the hair of (*fig*); (with *up* or *under*) to bury, block, shut in or overwhelm, with or as if with snow; to mislead, persuade, overwhelm or convince with insincere and complex information (*N Am sl*). [OE *snāw*; Ger *Schnee*, L *nix, nivis*]
■ **snow'ily** adv. **snow'iness** n. **snow'ish** adj resembling snow. **snow'less** adj. **snow'like** adj. **snow'y** adj abounding or covered with snow; white, like snow; pure.
❑ **snow'ball** n a ball made of snow pressed hard together, used as a missile, *esp* by children; a snowball tree; a dance begun by one couple who then separate and choose new partners, and so on until everyone present is dancing; a drink of advocaat and lemonade; a round white pudding, cake, or sweetmeat; (*ironically*) a black person, chimney-sweep, etc; something that grows like a snowball rolled in snow, *esp* a distribution of begging letters, each recipient being asked to send out so many copies; a mixture of cocaine and heroin (*sl*). ◆ *vt* to throw snowballs at. ◆ *vi* to throw snowballs; to grow greater ever more quickly. **snowball tree** n a deciduous flowering shrub of the genus *Viburnum*, eg *V. plicatum*, having dense rounded heads of sterile white flowers; the guelder rose. **snow'berry** n the white berry of a N American shrub (*Symphoricarpos albus*) of the honeysuckle family; the shrub itself. **snow'bird** n any finch of the N American genus *Junco*, white underneath, which migrates to the USA from Canada in winter; applied to various other birds that appear in winter; a person who regularly moves to, or holidays in, a warmer climate in winter (chiefly *US sl*); a cocaine addict or user (*sl*). **snow'blading** n a form of skiing without poles, using short skis. **snow'-blind** adj. **snow blindness** n amblyopia caused by excessive exposure to ultraviolet light reflected from snow. **snow'blink** n a reflection from fields of snow, like iceblink. **snow'blower** n a snow-clearing machine which takes in the snow in front of it and blows it to the side of the road. **snow board** n (*building*) a horizontal board fixed above a roof gutter to prevent snow falling off in a mass (also **gutter board** or **snow guard**). **snowboard cross** n a cross-country snowboarding race. **snow'boarder** n a person who goes snowboarding. **snow'boarding** n skiing on a **snow'board**, a board, similar to a skateboard but without wheels, on which the user balances, guiding the board with movements of the feet and body. **snow'boot** n a boot or overshoe for walking in snow. **snow'bound** adj shut in or prevented from travelling by snow. **snow box** n a theatrical apparatus for representing a snowfall. **snow brake** n a fern (*Pteris ensiformis*) with dark green fronds marked with greyish-white along the mid-rib. **snow'-broth** n melted or melting snow. **snow bunting** n an Arctic bunting (*Plectrophenax nivalis*), a winter visitor to Britain. **snow bush** n a small evergreen shrub (*Breynia nivosa* or *Phyllanthus nivosus*), having rounded green leaves with white marbling; (also **snow'bush**) any of several white-flowered ornamental N American shrubs. **snow cannon** see **snow gun** below. **snow'cap** n a cap of snow as on the polar regions or a mountain-top. **snow'-capped** or **snow'-capt** adj. **snow chains** n pl tyre chains. **snow cone** n (*N Am*) a confection consisting of a paper cone filled with crushed ice flavoured with a syrup. **snow'dome** n an indoor arena in which winter sports can be carried out all year round; see also **snowstorm**. **snow'drift** n a bank of snow drifted together by the wind. **snow'drop** n a drooping white flower of early spring, or a plant (of the genus *Galanthus*, *esp G. nivalis*) of the amaryllis family that bears it. **snow'-dropper** or **snow'-gatherer** n (*old sl*) a linen thief. **snowdrop tree** n the fringe tree; any of several American styraceous trees or shrubs of the genus *Halesia* with white, pendent bell-shaped flowers (also called **silver bell**). **snow'-eyes** n sing an Inuit device to prevent snow blindness, a piece of wood with slits. **snow'fall** n a fall of snow; the amount falling in a given time. **snow'-fed** adj (of a stream, etc) begun or increased by melted snow. **snow fence** n a paling fence erected to prevent snow drifting onto a road, railway, etc. **snow'field** n a wide expanse of snow, *esp* where permanent. **snow finch** n a bird of mountainous areas of S Europe, similar to the snow bunting. **snow'flake** n a feathery clump of snow crystals; any of several flowering plants of the genus *Leucojum*, cultivated for their white or pink flowers that resemble the snowdrop; (also **snow'fleck** or **snow'flick**) the snow bunting. **snow flea** n a springtail living in or on snow. **snow-gatherer** see **snow-dropper** above. **snowglobe** see **snowstorm** below. **snow'-goggles** n pl goggles for protection against snow blindness; snow-eyes. **snow goose** n a white Arctic American goose (*Anser* or *Chen caerulescens*), with black-tipped wings. **snow guard** n a snow board. **snow gun** or **cannon** n a device for spreading artificial snow on ski slopes. **snow'-hole** n a hole dug in snow as a temporary shelter. **snow'-ice** n ice formed from freezing slush or compacted snow. **snow-in-summ'er** n a white-flowered, mat-forming garden mouse-ear chickweed, *Cerastium tomentosum* or *biebersteinii*. **snow**

job n (N Am sl) an attempt to mislead, persuade or convince by means of insincere or flattering words, exaggeration, inaccurate or complex information, etc. **snow leopard** n the ounce (Panthera uncia), an animal related to the leopard, found in the mountainous regions of Central Asia. **snow'line** n the level or line above or beyond which an area, esp an upland area, is under permanent snow. **snow'man** n a figure resembling a person fashioned from packed snow; the abominable snowman (see under **abominate**). **snow'mobile** /-ma-bēl/ n a motorized sleigh or a tractorlike vehicle capable of travelling over snow. ◆ vi to ride on a snowmobile. **snow-on-the-mount'ain** n a N American annual plant, Euphorbia marginata, cultivated for its ornamental leaves which become edged and veined with white as the plant matures. **snow'pack** n an accumulation of packed snow that lingers throughout the winter. **snow pea** n another name for the mangetout or sugar pea. **snow plant** n a red Californian saprophyte (Sarcodes sanguinea) of the wintergreen family that grows through snow in mountainous regions; the organism of **red snow** (see under **red**[1]). **snow'plough** n an implement for clearing snow from roads and railways; a skiing position in which the skis form a V, with the tips touching, used to slow down or stop. ◆ vi (in skiing) to assume the snowplough position. **snow'scape** n a snowy landscape. **snow'shoe** n a wooden or metal frame, broad at the front and tapering at the back, with a network of thongs, strapped to the foot for walking on snow; a ski (obs). ◆ vi to walk or travel on snowshoes. **snowshoe rabbit** or **snowshoe hare** n a N American hare, white in winter, brownish with white feet in summer. **snow'slip** n a small avalanche of snow. **snow'storm** n a storm in which snow falls heavily; (also **snowdome, snowglobe**) an ornament depicting a winter scene which can be shaken so that small white particles suspended inside move about like falling snow. **snow'surfing** n the sport of skiing downhill on a large single ski controlled like a surfboard. **snow tyre** n a soft rubber tyre with deep treads, designed to maintain grip in ice and snow. **snow'-water** n water from melted snow. **snow-white'** adj as white as snow; spotless, pure. **snow'-wreath** n a snowdrift. **snowy egret** n a small white American egret, Egretta thula. **snowy owl** n a great white owl of northern regions.

■ **not a snowball's chance** (**in hell** or **in an oven**) (inf) no chance at all. **snowed in** or **up** blocked or isolated by snow. **snowed under with** overwhelmed with a heap or rapid accumulation of.

snow[2] /snō/ n a vessel like a brig, with a trysail-mast. [Du snaauw]

snowk see snook[3].

SNP abbrev: Scottish National Party; /snip/ single nucleotide polymorphism, any of the variations in single nucleotides in a DNA sequence that contribute to human individuality.

Snr or **snr** abbrev: senior.

snub /snub/ vt (**snubb'ing; snubbed**) to take up, cut short, rebuff, in a humiliating or mortifying manner; to rebuke; to check or stop; to bring to a sudden stop, eg to bring (a boat, unbroken horse, etc) to a stop by means of a rope secured to a post or stake; to cut or break short. ◆ n an act of snubbing; a check; a snub nose; (archaic **snubbe**) a stub, snag, knob. ◆ adj flat, broad, blunt and turned up; (of a polyhedron) having undergone secondary truncation (geom). [ON snubba to chide, snub]

■ **snubb'er** n someone who snubs; a device for stopping a rope; a shock absorber (N Am). **snubb'ing** n and adj. **snubb'ingly** adv. **snubb'ish** or **snubb'y** adj inclined to snub or check; somewhat snub. ❑ **snubbing post** n a post for passing a rope round, so as to stop a boat or horse. **snub cube** n (geom) a polyhedron obtained by repeated truncation of a cube, having 38 faces, six of which are squares, the rest being equilateral triangles. **snub nose** n a short, blunt turned-up nose. **snub'-nosed** adj having a snub nose; having a blunt end or front.

snuck /snuk/ a pat and pap of sneak (dialect or N Am inf).

snudge[2] /snuj/ vi to save in a miserly way. ◆ n a mean stingy person. [Origin unknown]

snuff[1] /snuf/ vi to draw in air violently and noisily through the nose; to sniff; to smell at anything doubtfully; to take snuff. ◆ vt to draw into the nose; to smell, to examine, suspect, or detect by smelling. ◆ n a powdered preparation of tobacco or other substance for inhaling through the nose; a pinch of snuff or act of snuffing; a sniff; resentment, huff. [MDu snuffen; Ger schnaufen to snuff]

■ **snuff'er** n. **snuff'iness** n. **snuff'ing** n and adj. **snuff'y** adj like, smelling of, soiled with or showing traces of, snuff; touchy, huffy. ❑ **snuff'box** n a small lidded (usu metal) box for snuff. **snuffbox bean** n the cacoon. **snuff'-colour** or **snuff'-brown** n a yellowish or greyish brown, slightly paler than bistre. **snuff'-coloured** adj. **snuff'-dipper** n. **snuff'-dipping** n orig in the USA, the practice of rubbing the teeth and gums with a wet stick dipped in snuff; now, the practice of sucking a pinch or sachet of snuff held between the gum and the inside of the cheek. **snuff mill** n a factory or a hand-mill for grinding tobacco into snuff; a snuff-mull. **snuff'-mull** n a snuffbox (see **mill**[1]). **snuff'-paper** n (Walter Scott; contemptuous) banknotes. **snuff**

spoon n a spoon for taking snuff from a snuffbox. **snuff'-taker** n. **snuff'-taking** n.

■ **take it in snuff** (Shakesp) to take offence, be angered by. **up to snuff** alert, knowing, not likely to be taken in or imposed upon; up to scratch, in good order; of a high or suitable standard.

snuff[2] /snuf/ n the sooty burnt part of a wick; a worthless or offensive residue; a heeltap. ◆ vt to put out as with snuffers (with out; also fig); to remove the snuff from; to make brighter. [ME snoffe; connection with snuff[1] and with LGer snuppen, Ger schnappen, is obscure]

■ **snuff'er** n (in later use **snuffers**, or **pair of snuffers**) an instrument like a pair of scissors for removing snuffs from the wicks of candles or oil-lamps; an instrument with a cap-shaped part for extinguishing candles; an attendant, esp in a theatre, who snuffed candles. ❑ **snuff'-dish** n a dish or tray for candle snuffs. **snuff film, movie** or **video** n an illegal, usu pornographic, film or video recording depicting scenes of violence and torture climaxing in the actual killing of an unsuspecting member of the cast.

■ **snuff it** (sl) to die. **snuff out** (sl) to kill or be killed.

snuffle /snuf'l/ vi to breathe hard or in an obstructed manner through the nose; to sniff; to speak through the nose. ◆ vt to sniff; to say or utter nasally. ◆ n an act or sound of snuffling; a snuffling tone; cant; (in pl) an obstructed condition of the nose, esp in infants. [Frequentative of snuff[1]; cf snivel and Du snuffelen, Ger schnüffeln]

■ **snuff'ler** /snuf'lər or snuf'l-ər/ n. **snuffling** /snuf'ling or snuf'l-ing/ n and adj. **snuff'ly** adj.

snug /snug/ adj (**snugg'er; snugg'est**) lying close and warm; comfortable; sheltered; not exposed to view or notice; in good order; compact; fitting close. ◆ n a snuggery. ◆ vi (**snugg'ing; snugged**) to lie close. ◆ vt to make snug; to stow away snugly. [Origin obscure]

■ **snugg'ery** n a snug room or place, esp a bar-parlour or (dialect) a separate small compartment in a bar. **snugg'le** vi to nestle. ◆ vt to hug close; to wrap close. **snug'ly** adv. **snug'ness** n.

snush /snush/ (obs) n snuff. ◆ vt and vi to snuff. [Poss imit; cf **sneesh**, Dan and Swed snus]

snuzzle /snuz'l/ (dialect) vi to grub or root; to rub or poke and sniff; to nuzzle. [Cf **nuzzle**[1] and **snoozle**]

snye or **sny** /snī/ (Can) n a side channel of a river. [From Can Fr chenail, from Fr chenal channel]

SO abbrev: Signal Officer; Somalia (IVR); special order; Staff Officer; standing order.

So abbrev: south.

so[1] /sō/ adv merging into conj or interj in this, that, or such manner, degree, or condition; to such an extent; likewise; accordingly; well; therefore; in due course, thereupon, thereafter; as; soever; thus; for the same or the said reason; in a high degree; as has been stated; provided; in case; in order that (inf); be it; that will do; very good; a meaningless interjection used to start a sentence (inf); so what? (see under **what**). [OE swā; ON svā, Gothic swa, Ger so]

❑ **so'-and-so** n this or that person or thing; such-and-such a person or thing; used to replace a descriptive oath (inf; also adj). **so'-called** adj styled thus, usu implying doubt or denial of the meaning or implications of the following term, or a wish to disassociate oneself from the implications of the term.

■ **and so on** or **and so forth** (or as one phrase **and so on and so forth**) and more of the same or the like; and the rest of it. **just so** exactly right, impeccable; quite so. **or so** or thereabouts; approximately. **quite so** just as you have said, exactly. **so as** in such a manner as or that; in order (with to; inf); if only, on condition that. **so be it** used to express acceptance or resignation. **so far** to that, or to such an extent, degree, or point. **so far so good** everything is all right up to this point. **so long!** and **so long as** see under **long**[1]. **so many** such-and-such a number of. **so much** such-and-such an amount; in such a degree; to such an extent; such an amount (of); that amount of; an equal amount. **so much as** as much as; even. **so much for** that disposes of; that is the end of; no more of. **so much so** to such an extent (that). **so so** see separate entry **so-so**. **so that** with the purpose that; with the result that; if only. **so then** thus then it is, therefore. **so to say** (or **speak**) if one may use that expression. **so what?** see under **what**.

so[2] /sō/ see **sol**[1].

s.o. (stock exchange, finance) abbrev: seller's opinion; shipping order.

soak /sōk/ vt (pap **soaked** or (rarely) **soak'en**) to steep in a liquid; to drench; to saturate; to absorb (liquid) (with up; also fig); to draw through the pores; to bathe thoroughly (N Am); to beat, pummel (sl); to overcharge, tax heavily, etc (inf). ◆ vi to be steeped in a liquid; to pass through pores; to drink (usu alcohol) to excess, to guzzle; to soften by heating. ◆ n the process or act of soaking; a drenching; a marshy place; a heavy or habitual drinker. [ME soke, from OE socian, a weak verb related to sūcan to suck]

■ **soak'age** n the process or period of soaking; liquid that has percolated. **soak'er** n someone who or something that soaks; a small

piece of sheet lead used to form a watertight joint with slates or tiles at a chimney or wall where it projects above the surface of a roof. **soak'ing** *n* and *adj*. **soak'ingly** *adv*.
❑ **soak'away** *n* a depression or excavated pit into which water percolates.

soap /sōp/ *n* an alkaline salt of a higher fatty acid; *esp* such a compound of sodium (**hard soap**) or potassium (**soft soap**) which reacts with water to produce a lather that acts as a cleaning agent in washing; smooth words, flattery (*obs sl*; cf **soft soap**); money, *esp* used for bribery and other secret political purposes (*US sl*); girls or women collectively, *esp* as sex objects (*sl*); a soap opera. ♦ *vt* to rub with soap; to flatter. [OE *sāpe* ; Du *zeep*, Ger *Seife*]
■ **soap'ie** *n* (*N Am*) a soap opera. **soap'ie** *n* (*Aust*) a soap opera. **soap'ily** *adv*. **soap'iness** *n*. **soap'land** *n* (*sl*) a red-light district (also *adj*). **soap'less** *adj*. **soap'y** *adj*.
❑ **soap'-ball** *n* soap made into a ball, often with starch, as an emollient. **soap'bark** *n* a S American rosaceous tree (*Quillaja saponaria*), or its bark, used as a substitute for soap. **soap'berry** *n* the fruit of *Sapindus saponaria*, a S American tree, or related species, used as a substitute for soap. **soap boiler** *n* a manufacturer of soap. **soap boiling** *n*. **soap'box** *n* a box for packing soap; such a box used as an improvised platform by a speaker or campaigning politician in the street, etc. **soap bubble** *n* a globe of air enclosed in a film of soapsuds. **soap dish** *n*. **soap flakes** *n pl*. **soap opera** *n* a sentimental, melodramatic radio or television serial concerned with the day-to-day lives of the members of a family or other small group (also *fig*; *orig* American and often sponsored by soap manufacturers); broadcast drama of this sort. **soap powder** *n*. **soap'root** *n* any of certain species of *Gypsophila*, *Saponaria*, and other plants whose roots can be used as a substitute for soap. **soap'stone** *n* a popular name for steatite, or French chalk, a compact kind of talc with a greasy or soapy feel. **soap'suds** *n pl* soapy water, *esp* when frothy. **soap test** *n* a test for determining hardness of water by amount of standard soap solution required to make a lather. **soap tree** *n* the soapbark tree, the soapberry tree, or other yielding saponin. **soap'-works** *n* a factory manufacturing soap. **soap'wort** *n* a tall herb (*Saponaria officinalis*, or other species) of the pink family, whose roots and leaves contain saponin.

soar[1] /sōr or sör/ *vi* to rise or fly high in the air; to rise to a great height (*lit* or *fig*); to glide high in the air, *esp* on a rising current; to increase rapidly in number or amount. ♦ *vt* to reach, traverse, or accomplish in upward flight. [Fr *essorer* to expose to air, raise into air, from L *ex* out, and *aura* air]
■ **soar'er** *n*. **soar'ing** *n* and *adj*. **soar'ingly** *adv*.
❑ **soar'away** *adj* making spectacular progress.

soar[2] and **soare** see **sore**[2].

Soave /swä'vā/ *n* a dry, pale white wine from a small region east of Verona in NE Italy. [From the town of *Soave*]

Soay /sō'ā/, or in full **Soay sheep** /shēp/ *n* a breed of small, wild, dark-coloured sheep found *esp* on the island of *Soay* in the Outer Hebrides.

SOB or **S.O.B.** see **s.o.b.**

sob /sob/ *vi* (**sobb'ing**; **sobbed**) to catch the breath convulsively in distress or other emotion; to make a similar sound; to weep noisily. ♦ *vt* to utter with sobs; to bring (oneself) to a certain state by sobbing. ♦ *n* a convulsive catch of the breath; any similar sound. [Imit]
■ **sobb'ing** *n* and *adj*. **sobb'ingly** *adv*.
❑ **sob sister** *n* (*inf*) an actor, writer, etc who seeks to arouse sentimental feelings in his or her audience, readers, etc; a journalist who answers questions in a woman's magazine. **sob story** *n* a pitiful tale told to arouse sympathy. **sob stuff** *n* cheap and extravagant pathos, to stir tears; maudlin or highly sentimental stories, films or scenes.

s.o.b. *abbrev* : son of a bitch (also **S.O.B.** or **SOB**).

soba /sō'bə/ *n* in Japanese cookery, a thin noodle made from buckwheat flour. [Jap]

sobeit /sō-bē'it/ (*archaic*) *conj* provided. [**so be it**]

sober /sō'bər/ *adj* not drunk; not intoxicated by drugs (*US*); temperate, *esp* in use of intoxicants; moderate; restrained; without excess or extravagance; serious; sedate; quiet in colour; sombre; sane, rational (*obs*); poor, feeble (*Scot*). ♦ *vt* to make sober (often with *up*). ♦ *vi* to become sober (often with *up*). [Fr *sobre*, from L *sōbrius*, from *sē-* apart, not, and *ēbrius* drunk]
■ **so'bering** *adj* making sober; causing to become serious, grave or thoughtful. **so'beringly** *adv*. **so'berize** or **-ise** *vt* to make sober. **so'berly** *adv*. **so'berness** or **sobriety** /sō- or sə-brī'i-ti/ *n* the state or habit of being sober; calmness; gravity.
❑ **so'ber-minded** *adj*. **so'ber-mind'edness** *n* the state of being sober-minded; freedom from inordinate passion; calmness. **so'bersides** *n* (*pl* **so'bersides**) a sedate, serious-minded and solemn person. **so'ber-suited** *adj* dressed in sombre-coloured clothes.

sobole /sō'bōl/ or **soboles** /sob'ō-lēz/ (*bot*) *n* (pl **sob'ōlēs**) a creeping underground stem producing roots and buds. [L *sobolēs*, *subolēs* a shoot, from *sub* under, and the root of *alere* to nourish, sustain]
■ **sobolif'erous** *adj* having soboles.

Sobranje /sō-brän'ye/ *n* the national assembly of Bulgaria (also **Sobran'ye**). [Bulgarian]

sobriquet /sō'bri-kā/ or **soubriquet** /soo'/ *n* a nickname; an assumed name. [Fr *sobriquet*, earlier *soubriquet* a chuck under the chin]

Soc. *abbrev* : Socialist; Society.

soc /sok/ (*law; hist*) *n* the right of holding a local court. [OE *sōcn* inquiry, jurisdiction, franchise]
■ **soc'age** or **socc'age** *n* feudal tenure of lands by service fixed and determinate in quality (other than military service); a payment made by a socager. **soc'ager** or **soc'man** *n* a tenant by socage (also **sōke'man**). **soke** /sōk/ *n* soc; a district under a particular jurisdiction. **soke'manry** *n* tenure by socage. **sōk'en** *n* a district under a particular jurisdiction.

SOCA /sok'ə or sō'kə/ *abbrev* : Serious and Organized Crime Agency.

soca /sō'kə/ *n* a variety of Caribbean calypso music incorporating elements of American soul music and having a strong pounding rhythm (also **sokah**). [*soul* and *calypso*]

so-called see under **so**[1].

soccer /sok'ər/ (*inf*) *n* association football.
■ **Socceroos'** *n pl* (*soccer* and kanga*roos*) the Australian national association football team.
❑ **soccer mom** *n* (*chiefly US*) a mother who dedicates many hours to driving her children to, and supporting them at, organized recreational activities.

socdolager, -iger, -oger see **sockdolager**.

sociable /sō'shə-b(ə)l/ *adj* tending to live in groups or communities, rather than in isolation; companionable; favourable to social intercourse; friendly, fond of others' company. ♦ *n* a four-wheeled open horse-drawn carriage with side seats facing each other; a seat, tricycle, aeroplane, etc, for two people side by side; a social (*US*). [Fr, from L *sociābilis*, from *sociāre* to write, from *socius* companion]
■ **sociabil'ity** or **so'ciableness** *n*. **so'ciably** *adv*.

social /sō'sh(ə)l/ *adj* relating to life in an organized community; relating to welfare in such a community; growing or living in communities; relating to, or characterized by, friendly association; convivial; gregarious, sociable; relating to fashionable circles; sympathetic (*obs*). ♦ *n* an informal party or gathering of a club, church, etc; (with *the*) social security (*inf*). [L *socius* a companion]
■ **so'cialism** *n* the theory, principle, or scheme of social organization which places the means of production of wealth and the distribution of that wealth in the hands of the community. **so'cialist** *n* an adherent of socialism. ♦ *adj* relating to socialism or socialists. **socialist'ic** *adj*. **socialist'ically** *adv*. **so'cialite** *n* (*inf*) a person having a place in fashionable society. **sociality** /sō-shi-al'i-ti/ *n* the quality or fact of being social; social relations, association, or intercourse; sociability; a social function or formality. **socializā'tion** or **-s-** *n* the act or process of socializing; the process by which infants and young children become aware of society and their relationships with others. **so'cialize** or **-ise** *vt* to render social; to put on a socialistic footing. ♦ *vi* (*inf*) to behave in a sociable manner, eg at parties, etc; to spend time in the company of others. **so'cially** *adv*. **so'cialness** *n*. **so'ciate** /-shi-āt/ *n* (*archaic*) an associate (also *adj*). **socia'tion** *n* a plant community; the smallest area in which a full range of plants making up such a plant community may be found. **so'ciātive** *adj* expressing association.
❑ **social anthropologist** *n*. **social anthropology** *n* the branch of anthropology which deals with the culture, customs and social structure of (*esp* primitive) societies. **social assistance** *n* (*Can*) social security. **social capital** *n* the benefits accruing to society from cooperative behaviour; the perceived value to an individual, company, etc of personal social relationships. **Social Chapter** *n* a social charter forming a section of the Treaty of Maastricht agreed by members of the European Community in 1991 and ratified in 1993 as a basis for the European Union. **social charter** *n* a charter laying down conditions of employment, *incl* minimum pay, maximum working hours, etc, *esp* that forming the basis of the Social Chapter of the European Union. **social cleansing** *n* (*euphem*) the forced removal of social minorities from an area. **social climber** *n* (often *derog*) a person who tries to become accepted into a higher social stratum by a deliberate policy of getting to know and associating with people belonging to it. **social climbing** *n*. **social contract** or **compact** *n* the voluntary agreement between individuals upon which an organized society, its rights, functions, and the relationships within it are founded. **social credit** *n* (*econ*) a system stressing

the element of unearned increment in the returns of industry and advocating the achievement of social wellbeing by the stable adjustment of production and consumption through monetary reform; (with *cap*) a theory that the government should distribute national dividends in order to spread purchasing power and thus increase consumption (regarded as a benefit). **social democracy** *n* the practices and policies of socialists who believe that socialism can and should be achieved by a gradual and democratic process. **social democrat** *n* a supporter of social democracy; (with *caps*) a member or supporter of a Social Democratic party. **social democratic** *adj*. **social disease** *n* (*euphem*) a venereal disease. **social dumping** *n* the practice of reducing wage rates and conditions of employment in order to attract or keep investment. **social engineer** *n*. **social engineering** *n* the furtherance of social change and the development of social institutions in accordance with an overall plan. **social enterprise** *n* a self-sustaining business organization whose primary aim is to have a beneficial effect on society rather than to maximize its profits. **social evil** *n specif* prostitution (*archaic*); any factor which has a damaging, unhealthy or negative effect on or with society as a whole. **social exclusion** *n* the effective loss of the benefits of living in a society experienced by people who are subject to multiple deprivations, such as poverty, unemployment, lack of education, poor health, etc. **social fund** *n* in Britain, a social security fund from which discretionary loans or grants may be made (*esp* for basic household items) to those in extreme need. **social gaming** *n* playing games online as a form of social interaction. **social housing** *n* houses provided by the government for rent. **social insurance** *n* state insurance by compulsory contributions against sickness, unemployment, and retirement. **socialist realism** *n* the official form of art and literature in the former Soviet Union and other Communist states, intended to present an optimistic image of the lives of working people. **social media** *n* websites used for social interaction. **social mobility** *n* the upward or downward movement of an individual or group within a social hierarchy. **social networking** *n* interaction between individuals for their mutual benefit, *esp* online. **social ownership** *n* (*euphem*) nationalization. **social realism** *n* a form of art intended to present an unromanticized view of the world. **social science** *n* the scientific study of human society and behaviour, including such disciplines (the *social sciences*) as anthropology, sociology, economics, political science and history. **social secretary** *n* one who is responsible for organizing the social activities of a person, club, association, etc. **social security** *n* security against sickness, unemployment, retirement, provided by a social insurance scheme; income support. **social service** *n* welfare work (also in *pl*); (in *pl*) the public bodies carrying out such work. **social software** *n* (*comput*) software that allows users of the Internet to interact. **social studies** *n sing* a branch of knowledge concerned with various aspects of human society. **Social War** *n* the war (90–88BC) of Rome's Italian allies (*Socii*) against Rome for admission to Roman citizenship. **social whale** *n* the ca'ing whale (see under **ca'**). **social work** *n* any of various forms of welfare work intended to promote the wellbeing of those regarded as socially disadvantaged. **social worker** *n*.
■ **socialism of the chair** professorial socialism, the doctrines of a school of political economists (c.1872) in Germany whose aim was mainly to better the condition of the working classes by factory acts, savings banks, insurance against sickness and old age, etc.

société anonyme /so-syä-tä a-no-nēm'/ (*Fr*) *n* literally, anonymous society; a joint-stock company.

society /sə-sī'ə-ti or -i-ti/ *n* fellowship, companionship; company; association; a community; the conventions and opinions of a community; the fashionable world; a corporate body; any organized association. ◆ *adj* of fashionable society. [OFr *societé*, from L *societās*, from *socius* a companion]
■ **soci'etal** *adj* relating to society, social. **soci'etally** *adv*.
□ **Society of Friends** see under **friend**. **Society of Jesus** see **Jesuit**.

Socinian /sō-sin'i-ən/ *adj* relating to or following the Unitarian teachings of the Italian theologians Laelius (1525–62) and Faustus (1539–1604) *Socinus* (also *n*).
■ **Socin'ianism** *n*. **Socin'ianize** or **-ise** *vt* (*rare*).

socio- /sō-si-ō- or sō-shi-ō-/ *combining form* denoting social, or relating to society, as in *sociocultural, socioeconomic, sociopolitical*. [L *socius* a companion]
■ **sociobiolog'ical** *adj*. **sociobiol'ogist** *n*. **sociobiol'ogy** *n* a scientific discipline combining biology and the social sciences which attempts to establish that social behaviour and organization in humans and animals has a genetic basis and is to be explained in terms of evolution and genetics. **socioeconom'ic** *adj* involving sociological and economic factors. **so'ciogram** /-gram/ *n* a chart representing personal interrelationships within a social group. **so'ciolect** *n* (*linguistics*) a variety of language used by members of a particular social class or group. **sociolingu'uist** *n*. **sociolinguis'tic** *adj* of or relating to sociolinguistics; relating to language as it functions as a social tool. **sociolinguis'tics** *n sing* the study of language as it functions in society

and is affected by social and cultural factors. **sociologese** /-ol-ə-jēz'/ *n* the jargon of sociology. **sociolog'ical** or **sociolog'ic** *adj* relating to sociology; dealing or concerned with social questions and problems of human society; social. **sociol'ogism** *n* a concept or explanation taking into consideration social factors only, and disregarding others. **sociol'ogist** *n*. **sociologis'tic** *adj*. **sociol'ogy** *n* the study of the origin, development, structure and functioning of human society. **sociomet'ric** *adj*. **sociom'etrist** *n*. **sociom'etry** *n* the measurement of social phenomena; the study of personal interrelationships within a social group. **so'ciopath** *n* a person suffering from a personality disorder characterized by asocial or antisocial behaviour, such as a psychopath. **sociopath'ic** *adj*. **sociop'athy** *n*.

sock[1] /sok/ *n* a covering for the foot and part or all of the lower leg; an insole placed in a shoe for warmth, to improve the fit, etc; a light shoe, worn by Greek Roman actors of comedy (*obs* except *hist* and allusively; cf **buskin**); a windsock; anything resembling a sock in shape or function. [OE *socc*, from L *soccus*]
■ **sockette** /sok-et'/ *n* a covering for the foot only.
□ **sock puppet** *n* a rudimentary puppet made by placing a sock over the hand; (on an Internet forum) a fictional persona created to post approving remarks (*inf*).
■ **knock the socks off** (*inf*) to surpass, defeat, overtake, etc in competitions. **pull up one's socks** to brace oneself for doing better. **put a sock in it** (*sl; usu imperative*) to become silent, stop talking. **sock away** (*inf*) to save or put aside for the future.

sock[2] /sok/ (*dialect and sl*) *vt* to thrust hard; to strike hard; to drub, thrash. ◆ *n* a violent blow, *esp* with the fist. [Ety dubious]
■ **sock'ō** *adj* (*US and theatre sl*) excellent, successful, knockout; having an impact, full of energy. **socks** *n pl* a beating, *esp* in the phrase *give someone socks*.
■ **sock it to** (*sl*) to speak, behave, etc in a manner that creates an impact on.

sock[3] /sok/ *n* a ploughshare. [OFr *soc*, from Celtic, Breton *souc'h*, Gaelic *soc*]

sockdolager, sockdoliger or **sockdologer**, also **sockdolager**, etc, **sogdolager**, etc, **slockdolager**, etc /s(l)ok-dol'ə-jər/ (*old US sl*) *n* a conclusive argument; a hard or decisive blow; anything unusually big, a whopper. [Cf **sock**[2]; infl by **doxology** as the closing act of a service]

socket /sok'it/ *n* a hollow into which something is inserted or into which something fits, such as the receptacle of the eye, of a bone, of a tooth, of the shaft of an iron golf club, the hollow of a candlestick, etc; a device in which an electric plug or light bulb may be inserted to make a connection; a stroke with the socket of a golf club. ◆ *vt* (**sock'eting; sock'eted**) to provide with or place in a socket; to strike with the socket (*golf*). [OFr *soket*, dimin of *soc*; see **sock**[3]]
■ **sock'eted** *adj*.
□ **socket chisel** *n* a robust chisel with a socketed metal shaft into which the wooden handle is fitted. **socket head screw** *n* a screw with a hexagonal recess in its head, turned by means of a hexagonal bar formed into a key (also **cap screw**). **socket set** *n* a range of socketed heads for use with a socket wrench. **socket spanner** *n* a spanner with a socketed head made to fit over a nut or a bolt. **socket wrench** *n* a wrench with a handle to which a variety of socketed heads can be fitted.

sockette see under **sock**[1].

sockeye /sok'ī/ or **sockeye salmon** *n* a Pacific salmon, *Oncorhynchus nerka*, of coastal areas from Japan to California (also called **red** or **blueback salmon**). [By folk ety from Salish (Native American) *sukai* the fish of fishes, the native name of the Fraser River, Canada]

socking /sok'ing/ (*inf*) *adj* huge, whacking (*usu* followed by *great*). [Prob **sock**[2]]

socle /sō'kl or sok'l/ (*archit*) *n* a plain face or plinth at the foot of a wall, column, etc. [Fr, from Ital *zoccolo*, from L *socculus*, dimin of *soccus* a shoe]

Socratic /sō-krat'ik or so-/ *adj* relating to or associated with the Greek philosopher Socrates (c.469–399BC), to his philosophy, or to his method of teaching by a series of simple questions revealing to his interlocutors their own ignorance. ◆ *n* a follower of Socrates.
■ **Socrat'ically** *adv*. **Socratize** or **-ise** /sok'rə-tīz or sok'/ *vi* to practise the Socratic method.
□ **Socratic irony** *n* (*philos*) a means by which a questioner pretends to know less than a respondent, while actually knowing more. **Socratic method** *n* (*philos*) a method of questioning unaffected by preformed conclusions, used by Socrates to expose feeble arguments or develop latent ideas in his pupils.

Socred /sō'kred/ (*Can*) *n* a person or political party espousing a *social cred*it policy.

sod[1] /sod/ *n* a turf, *usu* one cut in rectangular shape; sward; the ground (*poetic*). ◆ *adj* of sod. ◆ *vt* to cover with sod. [MLGer *sode*; Ger *Sode*]
■ **sodd'y** *adj* covered with sod; turfy.

sod² /*sod*/ (chiefly *Brit* and *Aust vulgar sl*) *n* an obnoxious person, *usu* applied to a man or boy; a non-pejorative term for a chap or fellow, now also sometimes applied to a woman or girl, as in the phrase *you lucky sod!* ♦ *interj* (*vulgar sl*) a term expressing annoyance, exasperation, etc (sometimes behaving as a verb with *it*, *him*, etc as object). [Short form of **sodomite** (see under **Sodom**)]
■ **sodd'ing** *adj*.
❑ **Sod's law** *n* (*facetious*) the precept that states that the most inconvenient thing is the most likely to happen, or if there is a possibility that something will go wrong, it will.
■ **sod all** nothing at all. **sod off** (*vulgar sl*; *usu imperative*) to go away.

sod³ /*sod*/ see **seethe**.

soda /*sō'də*/ *n* any of a number of common sodium compounds, *incl* sodium oxide (Na₂O), sodium hydroxide (**caustic soda**), sodium carbonate (**washing-soda**), and sodium bicarbonate (**baking soda**); soda water (*inf*); a fizzy drink made of soda water with flavouring, ice-cream, etc (*N Am*); any fizzy soft drink (*N Am*). ♦ *adj* of or containing soda or sodium. [Ital and LL *soda*; origin doubtful]
■ **sodaic** /*sō-dā'ik*/ *adj* containing or relating to soda. **so'dalite** *n* a cubic mineral, a complex feldspathoid consisting of sodium aluminium silicate and sodium chloride in crystalline form, occurring in igneous rocks. **so'damide** /*-mīd*/ *n* a compound (NaNH₂) formed when ammonia gas is passed over hot sodium (also called **sodium amide**). **so'dic** *adj*.
❑ **soda ash** *n* anhydrous sodium carbonate in powdered form for commercial use. **soda bread** *n* bread leavened with baking soda. **soda cracker** *n* (*N Am*) a crisp biscuit leavened with baking soda. **soda fountain** *n* (*N Am*) an apparatus for supplying soda water; a shop or counter where sodas, ice-cream, etc are served. **soda jerk** or **soda jerker** *n* (*N Am sl*) a person who serves at a soda fountain. **so'da-lake** *n* a lake containing and depositing a large amount of sodium salts. **soda lime** *n* a mixture of caustic soda and quicklime. **soda nitre** *n* sodium nitrate (also called **Chile saltpetre**, **nitratine**). **soda pop** *n* (*US*) a carbonated soft drink of any flavour. **soda scone** *n* a scone made with baking soda. **so'da-siphon** *n* a siphon which dispenses soda water. **soda water** *n* water charged with carbon dioxide.

sodain, **sodaine** obsolete spellings of **sudden**.

sodality /*sō-dal'i-ti*/ *n* a fellowship or fraternity. [L *sodālitās*, from *sodālis* a comrade]

sodden /*sod'n*/ *pap* of **seethe**. *adj* soaked thoroughly; boggy; doughy, not well baked; bloated or saturated with drink; boiled (*rare*). ♦ *vt* and *vi* to make or become sodden; to soak.
■ **sodd'enness** *n*.
❑ **sodden-witt'ed** *adj* (*Shakesp*) heavy, stupid.

soddy see under **sod¹**.

sodger /*soj'ər*/ *n* a dialect word for **soldier**.

sodium /*sō'di-əm*/ *n* a bluish-white alkaline metallic element (symbol **Na**; atomic no 11), occurring in nature in combination, eg as a nitrate, chloride, etc. [**soda**]
❑ **Sodium Amytal**®️ /*am'i-tal*/ *n* a salt of the barbiturate drug amobarbital. **sodium ascorbate** *n* a compound used as a meat preservative and also in the treatment of vitamin C deficiency. **sodium benzoate** *n* a compound used as an antiseptic and as a food preservative. **sodium bicarbonate** see under **bicarbonate**. **sodium carbonate** *n* a soluble compound widely used in the making of glass, ceramics, etc and as a cleaning agent. **sodium chlorate** *n* a colourless crystalline compound used in explosives, as an antiseptic, and as weedkiller. **sodium chloride** *n* common table salt, occurring naturally as halite and in seawater. **sodium cromoglycate** *n* a drug which blocks the release of histamine, used to treat asthma and various allergies. **sodium hydroxide** *n* caustic soda, manufactured by treating quicklime with a solution of hot sodium carbonate, and used as a reagent, in the manufacture of soap, rayon and sodium compounds. **sodium lamp** *n* a street lamp using sodium vapour and giving orange or yellow light. **sodium nitrate** *n* a white crystalline solid compound used in explosives, as a fertilizer and food preservative (also called **soda nitre**). **sodium pump** *n* (*biochem*) a mechanism by which sodium is removed through cell membranes, eg in the axon of a neurone and certain kidney cells, the energy for the process being derived from the breakdown of ATP. **sodium thiosulphate** *n* a white soluble substance used as a fixer in photography. **sodium vapour lamp** *n* a sodium lamp.

Sodom /*sod'əm*/ *n* one of the 'cities of the plain' (in the Bible, Genesis 18–19); any place of utter depravity (*fig*).
■ **Sod'omite** /*-īt*/ *n* an inhabitant of Sodom; (without *cap*) someone who practises sodomy. **sodomitic** /*-it'ik*/ or **sodomit'ical** *adj*. **sodomit'ically** *adv*. **sod'omize** or **-ise** *vt* to practise sodomy upon. **sod'omy** *n* anal intercourse (with a man or woman) or copulation with an animal, imputed to the inhabitants of Sodom.
■ **apple of Sodom** see under **apple**.

SOE *abbrev* : Special Operations Executive.

soever /*sō-ev'ər*/ *adv* to an indefinite degree, in any way (*esp* as combining form, as in *whatsoever*, *howsoever*, etc).

sofa /*sō'fə*/ *n* a long upholstered seat with back and arms. [Ar *suffah* a raised platform used as a bench]
❑ **sofa bed** *n* a sofa whose parts can be unfolded to form a bed. **sofa table** *n* a narrow table with a flap at each end, used as a writing table from c.1790.

sofar /*sō'fär*/ *n* a method of calculating the location of an underwater explosion from measurements of the time taken for the sound vibrations to reach three widely separated shore stations (used in searching for survivors, who drop into the sea). [*sound fixing and ranging*]

soffioni /*sof-yō'nē*/ *n pl* volcanic steam-holes. [Ital]

soffit /*sof'it*/ *n* a ceiling, now generally restricted to the ornamented underside of a stair, entablature, archway, etc. [Ital *soffitto*, from L *suffixus*, pap of *suffigere* to fasten beneath, from *sub* under, and *figere* to fix]

Sofi, **Sofism** see **Sufi**.

S. of S. (*Bible*) *abbrev* : Song of Songs or Song of Solomon.

soft /*soft*/ *adj* easily yielding to pressure; easily cut; easily scratched (*mineralogy*); malleable; yielding; not rigorous enough; (of sounds) not loud, low; not glaring; diffused; slightly blurred; weak in muscle or mind; out of training; smooth; pleasing or soothing to the senses; tender; mild; politically moderate, not radical or extreme, as in *soft left*; sympathetic; (with *on*) infatuated with; gentle; effeminate; unable to endure rough treatment or hardship; (relatively) unprotected; (of a vehicle) unarmoured (*milit*); gently moving; easy; (of water) free from calcium and magnesium salts; (of coal) bituminous; (of money) paper rather than metallic; (of paper) unsized; rainy (*dialect*); pronounced with a somewhat sibilant sound, not guttural or explosive; voiced or sonant; (of silk) freed from natural gum; (of diet) consisting of semi-liquid and easily digestible foods; apt to fall in price; (of drugs) not habit-forming in an obvious degree; (of pornography) not explicit; (of radiation) having short wavelengths and therefore not highly penetrating; (in typesetting and word processing) denoting a space, hyphen or carriage return that can be removed automatically when its environment changes to make it redundant. ♦ *n* a softy, a fool; (in *pl*) soft commodities. ♦ *adv* softly; gently; quietly. ♦ *vt* (*Spenser*) to soften. ♦ *interj* (*archaic*; also **soft you**) hold; not so fast. [OE *sōfte*, *sēfte*; Du *zacht*, Ger *sanft*]
■ **soften** /*sof'n*/ *vt* to make soft or softer; to mitigate; to tone down, make smoother or less glaring. ♦ *vi* to grow soft or softer. **softener** /*sof'nər*/ *n*. **softening** /*sof'ning*/ *n*. **soft'ie** *n* a softy. **soft'ish** *adj* rather soft. **soft'ling** *n* (*archaic*) a weakling; an effeminate man or boy; a soft object. **soft'ly** *adv* in a soft manner. ♦ *adj* (*Spenser*) soft; slack in enterprise. **soft'ness** *n*. **soft'y** *n* (*inf*) a silly person, a weak fool; someone who is soft-hearted or sentimental.
❑ **soft'back** or **soft'cover** *n* a paperback (also *adj*). **soft'ball** *n* an American game similar to baseball, played on a smaller diamond with a soft ball; the ball itself. **soft benefits** *n pl* non-financial benefits offered to employees, such as health insurance or childcare. **soft-billed'** *adj*. **soft-bod'ied** *adj*. **soft'-boil** *vt*. **soft-boiled'** *adj* boiled not long enough to be quite solid; soft-hearted (*inf*). **soft-cen'tred** *adj*. **soft commodities** *n pl* foodstuffs, coffee, cotton, etc, as opposed to metals. **soft-con'scienc'd** *adj* (*Shakesp*) having a not very rigorous conscience. **soft copy** *n* (*comput*) material that is coded or stored on disk as distinct from data that is printed out. **soft'-core** *adj* (of obscene or pornographic material) not explicit, blatant or graphic. **softcover** see **softback** above. **soft currency** *n* one unstable in value in the international money market through fluctuation in its gold backing. **soft drink** *n* a non-alcoholic drink. **soft-finned'** *adj* without fin-spines. **soft focus** *n* (*photog*, *cinematog*) deliberate slight blurring of a picture or scene. **soft-fo'cus** *adj*. **soft-foot'ed** *adj* softly treading. **soft fruit** *n* small, stoneless, edible fruit, such as berries and currants. **soft furnishings** *n pl* curtains, coverings, rugs, etc. **soft goods** *n pl* cloth and cloth articles, as opposed to hardware, etc. **soft'-grass** *n* a worthless grass (*Holcus mollis* or other species) similar to oats. **soft'head** *n* a simpleton. **soft-head'ed** *adj*. **soft-heart'ed** *adj* kind, generous; tender-hearted. **soft hyphen** *n* (in word processing) one inserted in a word only if necessary for word division at the end of a line. **soft iron** *n* iron that is low in carbon content and does not retain magnetism. **soft landing** *n* a landing by a spacecraft, etc without uncomfortable or damaging impact (also *fig*). **soft launch** *n* (*commerce*) the introduction of a new product to a restricted group of customers before it has been fully developed. **soft lens** *n* a flexible contact lens of a hydrophylic material which allows some oxygen to reach the cornea. **soft line** *n* a flexible or lenient attitude, policy, etc. **soft loan** *n* one without conditions attached; a cheap or interest-free loan, *usu* to a developing country. **softly-soft'ly** *adj* cautious, careful, delicate. **softly-spright'ed** *adj* (*Shakesp*) tame-spirited. **soft mark** see under **mark¹**. **soft meat** *n* regurgitated food given by pigeons to their young. **soft'-nosed** *adj* (of a bullet) with a tip that expands on striking.

soft option *n* an alternative that is easy to carry out, undergo, etc. **soft palate** *n* the fleshy back part of the palate. **soft'-paste** *adj* (of porcelain) made of a paste of various kinds requiring less heat in firing than china clay. **soft pedal** *n* a pedal for reducing tone in the piano, *esp* by causing the hammer to strike only one string. **soft-ped'al** *vt* and *vi* to play with the soft pedal down; to subdue, tone down, avoid emphasizing or alluding to (*sl*). **soft power** *n* (*esp US*) the power of a nation to influence others by displaying the advantages of its own cultural, social, financial, etc systems without the use of military power. **soft radiation** *n* (*radiol*) radiation which has very limited penetrating power. **soft return** *n* (*comput*) a line feed which is inserted by a word processor or text editor to justify the text and which can be moved or deleted. **soft rock** *n* a form of rock music, *usu* more melodious and slower in tempo than hard rock (qv under **hard**¹). **soft-rock geology** *n* (*inf*) the geology of sedimentary rocks. **soft rot** *n* a bacterial disease of plant tissues which reduces them to soft, mushy, foul-smelling rot. **soft sawder** or **sowder** *n* flattery. **soft-saw'der** or **soft-sow'der** *vt* to flatter. **soft science** *n* any of the scientific disciplines in which rules or principles of evaluation are difficult to obtain, such as social sciences (cf **hard science** under **hard**¹). **soft-sect'ored** *adj* (*comput*) (of a floppy disk) formatted by means of software (cf **hard-sectored**). **soft'-sect'oring** *n*. **soft sell** *n* selling or sale by preliminary softening up or other indirect method; mild persuasion, or mildly persuasive tactics. **soft-sell'** *adj*. **soft'-shell** or **-shelled'** *adj* having a soft shell; moderate in policy or principles. **soft'-shell** *n* a soft-shell crab, clam, or river-turtle; a moderate. **soft'-shoe** *adj* characteristic of or relating to a form of tap-dancing done in soft-soled shoes. **soft skills** *n pl* personal qualities or aptitudes that may be seen as indirectly qualifying someone for a particular job. **soft'-slow** *adj* (*Shakesp*) soft and slow. **soft soap** *n* a kind of soap containing potash; flattery; blarney. **soft'-soap** *vt* to rub or cover with soft soap; to flatter for some end. **soft sore** *n* chancroid, a sexually-transmitted disease resulting in enlargement and ulceration of the lymph nodes in the groin. **soft sowder** see **soft sawder** above. **soft-spo'ken** *adj* having a mild or gentle voice; affable; suave; plausible in speech. **soft spot** see under **spot**. **soft thing** *n* an easy task; a snug job. **soft top** *n* a convertible car with a fabric roof. **soft'-top** *adj*. **soft touch** see under **touch**. **soft underbelly** *n* the vulnerable part. **soft'ware** *n* computer programs that control the operation of computer hardware (qv); computer program (or analogous) accessories (other than the actual parts of a computer, etc); video cassettes and discs; material recorded in microform. **software engineering** *n* the production of software and its modification for particular applications. **software house** *n* a commercial organization that specializes in the design of software. **soft wheat** *n* a variety of wheat with soft kernels and a high starch content. **soft'wood** *n* (timber of) a conifer (also *adj*).

■ **be** or **go soft on** to be lenient with. **softening of the brain** a softening of brain tissues; marked deterioration of mental faculties (*inf*). **soften up** to lessen resistance in (*inf*); to wear down by continuous shelling and bombing.

softa /*sof'tə*/ *n* (*hist*) a student of Islamic theology in the Ottoman Empire. [Turk *sŏfta*]

sog /*sog*/ *n* (*dialect*) a soft wet place. ◆ *vt* and *vi* to soak. [Ety dubious] ■ **sogged** *adj*. **sogg'ing** *n* and *adj*.

sogdolager, -iger, -oger see **sockdolager**.

soger /*sō'jər*/ *n* a dialect word for **soldier**.

sogged see under **sog**.

soggy /*sog'i*/ *adj* soaked; soft or heavy with moisture; boggy; soppy; sultry; spiritless. [**sog**] ■ **sogg'ily** *adv*. **sogg'iness** *n*.

soh see **sol**¹.

SOHO /*sō'hō*/ *abbrev* : Small Office/Home Office, a large market for computer hardware and software.

so-ho or **soho** /*sō-hō'*/ (*Shakesp*) *interj* a form of call from a distance, a huntsman's halloo. [Anglo-Fr]

sohur /*sə-hûr'*/ *n* another name for **sehri**.

soi-disant /*swä-dē-zä'*/ *adj* self-styled, pretended, would-be. [Fr]

soigné, *fem* **soignée**/*swa-nyä'*/ *adj* well-groomed; elegantly simple; carefully done. [Fr]

soil¹ /*soil*/ *n* the ground; the mould in which plants grow; the mixture of disintegrated rock and organic material which nourishes plants; land. ◆ *adj* having soil. [OFr *soel, suel, sueil*, from L *solum* ground] ■ **soil'less** *adj*.

❑ **soil'-bound** *adj* attached to the soil. **soil creep** *n* (*geol*) the very slow but continuous movement of soil and rock fragments down a slope. **soil mechanics** *n sing* a branch of civil engineering concerned with the ability of different soils to withstand the use to which they are put. **soil science** *n* the study of the composition and uses of soil.

soil² /*soil*/ *n* dirt; dung; filth; sewage; a spot or stain; a wallowing-place (*obs*); a watery place where a hunted animal takes refuge. ◆ *vt* to make dirty; to stain; to manure. ◆ *vi* to become dirty or stained; to tarnish. [OFr *soil, souil* (Fr *souille*) wallowing-place]

■ **soiled** *adj*. **soil'iness** *n* (*rare*) stain; foulness. **soil'ing** *n* and *adj*. **soil'less** *adj*. **soil'ure** *n* (*archaic*) stain; pollution. **soil'y** *adj*.

❑ **soil pipe** *n* an upright pipe which carries away waste water and sewage from a building into a sewer or drain.

soil³ /*soil*/ *vt* to feed (livestock) on fresh-cut green food; to purge by so doing; to fatten. [OFr *saouler*, from *saol, saoul*, from L *satullus*, from *satur* full; or from **soil**²]

■ **soil'age** *n* green fodder for livestock.

soirée /*swä'rä*/ *n* an evening party; an evening social meeting with tea, etc. [Fr, from *soir* evening, from L *sērus* late]

soixante-neuf /*swa-sät-nœf'*/ (*Fr*) *n* a sexual position in which both partners simultaneously orally stimulate each other's genitalia. [Literally, sixty-nine, from the position adopted]

soja see **soy**.

sojourn /*soj'*/ or *suj'ərn, -ûrn*/ *vi* to stay for a day; to dwell for a time. ◆ *n* a temporary residence. [OFr *sojourner*, from L *sub* under, and *diurnus* of a day, from *diēs* a day]

■ **so'journer** *n*. **so'journing** or **so'journment** *n*.

Soka Gakkai /*sō'kə gak'ī*/ *n* an international Buddhist society founded in Japan in 1930. [Jap, value creating society]

sokah see **soca**.

sokaiya /*so-kī'yə*/ *n* (pl **sokai'ya**) in Japan, a corporate racketeer, who extorts money from companies by threatening to disrupt shareholders' meetings, expose scandals, etc. [Jap *sokai* meeting, and *ya* dealer]

soke, sokeman, soken see under **soc**.

Sol /*sol*/ *n* the sun personified, Helios or Phoebus; gold (*alchemy*); the tincture or (*heraldry*). [L *sōl* sun]

Sol. or **Solr** *abbrev* : Solicitor.

sol¹ /*sol*/ (*music*) *n* the fifth note of the scale in sol-fa notation (also **so** or **soh** /*sō*/). [See **Aretinian**]

sol² /*sol*/ *n* a colloidal suspension in a liquid (cf **gel**¹). [Short for **solution**]

■ **solā'tion** *n* liquefaction of a gel.

sol³ /*sōl*/ *n* (pl **soles** /*sō'lās*/) the standard monetary unit of Peru (100 céntimos) (also **nuevo sol**); an old coin bearing a sun with rays. [Am Sp, from L *sōl* sun]

sol⁴ /*sol*/ *n* an old French coin, one-twentieth of a livre. [OFr *sol* (now *sou*), from L *solidus* solid]

sol. *abbrev* : solution.

sola¹ /*sō-lä'*/ *interj* a cry to a person at a distance.

sola² or **solah** /*sō'lə*/ *n* spongewood, an Indian papilionaceous plant (*Aeschynomene aspera* or *indica*; also known as the **hat-plant**); its pithlike stems used in making lightweight hats. ◆ *adj* made of sola. [Hindi *śolā*]

❑ **sola hat**, **helmet**, **topee** or **topi** *n* a sun helmet made of sola pith (also, incorrectly, **solar**).

sola³ see **solus**.

solace /*sol'is*/ or *sol'əs*/ *n* consolation, comfort in distress; pleasure, amusement; a source of comfort or pleasure. ◆ *vt* to comfort in distress; to console; to allay. ◆ *vi* to take comfort. [OFr *solas*, from L *sōlātium*, from *sōlārī, -ātus* to comfort in distress]

■ **sol'acement** *n*. **solacious** /*-ā'shəs*/ *adj* (*archaic*) giving solace.

solah see **sola**².

solan /*sō'lən*/ or **solan goose** /*goos*/ *n* an old name for the gannet. [Scand *soland*; ON *sūla*]

solanaceous see under **solanum**.

solander /*sə-* or *sō-lan'dər*/ *n* a box in the form of a book, invented by the Swedish botanist Daniel *Solander* (1736–82).

solanine see under **solanum**.

solano /*sō-lä'nō*/ *n* (pl **sola'nos**) a hot, dust-laden south-easterly wind in Spain. [Sp, from L *sōlānus* (*ventus*), the east wind, from *sōl* the sun]

solanum /*sə-* or *sō-lā'nəm*/ *n* any herbaceous plant of the genus *Solanum*, incl the potato, bittersweet and certain nightshades. [L *sōlānum* nightshade]

■ **solanā'ceous** *adj* of, related or belonging to the **Solanaceae** /*sōl-ə-nā'si-ē*/, a family of dicotyledonous flowering plants with fused petals, many of which contain poison and/or tropane alkaloids used in medicine, and incl potato, tomato, peppers, tobacco, henbane and certain nightshades. **solanine** /*sol'* or *sōl'ə-nēn*/ *n* a glucoside obtained from potato sprouts and other solanaceous plants.

solar[1] /sō'lər/ adj of, from, like, or relating to the sun; measured by the sun; influenced by the sun; powered by energy from the sun's rays; with branches radiating like the sun's rays. ◆ n (also **sō'ler**, **sollar** or **soller** /sol'ər/; OE solor, or OFr soler; archaic) an upper room; a garret; a landing between ladders in a mine. [L sōlāris solar, sōlārium a sundial, from sōl the sun]

■ **solarimeter** /-im'it-ər/ n a device for measuring solar radiation. **sō'larism** n excessive use of solar myths in the explanation of mythology. **sō'larist** n. **solā'rium** n a sundial; a place for sunbathing or equipped with sunbeds; a conservatory or other room allowing exposure to sunlight. **sōlarīzā'tion** or **-s-** n the act, process, or effect of solarizing; the reversal of an image by over-exposure (photog); the interruption of photosynthesis by long exposure to bright light (bot). **sō'larize** or **-ise** vt to expose to sunlight or affect by such exposure, esp excessive or injurious exposure. ◆ vi to be so affected.

❑ **solar battery** n a battery of solar cells. **solar cell** n a photoelectric cell converting sunlight into electric power. **solar constant** n (astron) the rate at which the sun's energy reaches the earth's surface, equal to approx 1370 watts per square metre. **solar day** see under **day**. **solar eclipse** n an eclipse of the sun by the interposition of the moon. **solar energy** n energy obtained from the sun's rays, esp when used for home-heating, etc. **solar flare** n a short-lived bright outburst in the sun's chromosphere, generally associated with sun spots and often the cause of radio and magnetic disturbances on earth. **solar furnace** n a furnace using sunlight (guided and focused by a system of mirrors) as a heat source. **solar heating** n a method of providing hot water, esp for domestic heating systems, by collecting heat radiated by the sun in water passed through solar panels. **solar microscope** n an obsolete apparatus for projecting an enlarged image. **solar month** see under **month**. **solar myth** n a sun-myth, or a myth allegorizing the course of the sun. **solar noise** n a hissing background noise heard in radio communication, due to radiation from the sun and its atmosphere. **solar panel** n a panel of solar cells, esp when used to provide domestic heating or power for spacecraft, etc. **solar plexus** n (anat) a network of sympathetic nerves high in the back of the abdomen (so called from its radiating nerves; also called **coeliac plexus**). **solar power** n solar energy. **sō'lar-powered** adj. **solar prominences** n pl large prominent or protruding parts of the great volumes of heated gas surrounding the sun. **solar salt** n salt got by evaporation of seawater by the sun. **solar system** n the sun with its attendant bodies, ie major and minor planets, meteors, comets, satellites. **solar time** see under **time**. **solar wind** n charged particles emitted by the sun, travelling at about one and a half million kilometres an hour. **solar year** see under **year**.

solar[2] /sō'lər/ see **sola**[2].

solation see under **sol**[2].

solatium /sō-lā'shi-əm or sō-lä'ti-ŭm/ n (pl **sola'tia**) (esp law) compensation for disappointment, inconvenience, wounded feelings. [L sōlātium]

sold[1] /sōld/ pat and pap of **sell**[2].
■ **sold on** extremely enthusiastic or convinced about.

sold[2] /sold/ (Spenser) n pay, remuneration (also (rare) **solde**). [Fr solde, from L solidus a piece of money]

soldado /sōl-dä'dō/ n (pl **solda'dos**) a soldier. [Sp]

soldan /sol'dən/ (archaic) n a sultan, esp of Egypt. [Fr; see **sultan**]

soldatesque /sol-də-tesk'/ adj soldierlike. [Fr, from soldat a soldier]

solde see **sold**[2].

solder /sōl'dər or sol-, also (N Am) sod'ər or sō'dər/ n a fusible alloy for uniting metals. ◆ vt to attach with solder; to join; to mend, patch up. ◆ vi to adhere. [OFr soudre, souldure, from souder, soulder to consolidate, from L solidāre to make solid]
■ **sol'derer** n. **sol'dering** n.
❑ **soldering iron** n a tool with a pointed or wedge-shaped copper bit for use in soldering.

soldi see **soldo**.

soldier /sōl'jər/ n a person engaged in military service; a private; a person of military skill; a low-ranking member of a criminal organization, such as the Mafia, esp one who carries out shootings and other violent acts (sl); a shirker (naut); an ant, or white ant, of a specialized fighting caste; a scarlet, pugnacious, or armoured animal of various kinds (beetle, fish, etc); a red herring (sl); the ribwort plantain (used by children for a game of soldiers); a diligent worker for a cause; a brick set upright in a wall; a narrow strip of bread-and-butter or toast, esp for a child to eat (inf). ◆ vi to serve as a soldier; to shirk. [OFr soldier, from L solidus a piece of money, the pay of a soldier]
■ **sol'diering** n. **sol'dierlike** adj having the appearance of a soldier; soldierly. ◆ adv in the manner of a soldier. **sol'dierliness** n. **sol'dierly** adj befitting a soldier; having the qualities of or befitting a soldier. **sol'diership** n the state or quality of being a soldier; military qualities;

martial skill. **sol'diery** n soldiers collectively; a military body or class; military qualities.
❑ **soldier beetle** n a beetle of the family Cantharidae. **soldier crab** n a hermit crab. **soldier of fortune** n a mercenary; someone ready to serve anywhere for pay or his or her own advancement.
■ **old soldier** see under **old**. **soldier on** to continue doggedly in face of difficulty or discouragement.

soldo /sol'dō/ n (pl **sol'di** /-dē/) a former Italian coin, one-twentieth of a lira. [Ital, from L solidus]

sole[1] /sōl/ n the underside of the foot; the bottom of a boot or shoe; the undersurface of a clubhead (golf); the floor of an oven or furnace; a sill (now dialect); the bottom, understructure, floor, or undersurface of various things; a thrustplane (geol). ◆ vt to put a sole on. [OE and OFr sole, from L solea sole, sandal, from solum bottom]
❑ **sole'plate** n a bedplate or similar object.

sole[2] /sōl/ n an elliptical flatfish of the genus Solea, esp S. solea, the European or Dover sole, having a twisted mouth with teeth on the underside only and dorsal and anal fins that extend to the tail. [Fr sole, from L solea]
■ **solenette** /sōl-net' or sōl-ə-net'/ n a small European species of sole, Buglossidium luteum, with distinctive dark-coloured rays on the dorsal and anal fins.
■ **lemon sole** see under **lemon**[2].

sole[3] /sōl/ adj alone; only; without husband or wife (law); without another; solitary; consisting of one person; exclusive; uniform. [Fr, from L sōlus alone]
■ **sole** adv. **sole'ly** adv alone; only; singly. **sole'ness** n.

sole[4] /sōl/ (Shakesp) vt to pull (by the ears) (also (dialect) **sowl**, **sowle** or **soole** /sowl, sēl or sool/). [Origin obscure]

solecism /sol'i-si-zm/ n a breach of syntax or a nonstandard grammatical usage; any absurdity, impropriety, or incongruity; a breach of good manners or etiquette. [Gr soloikismos, said to come from the corruption of the Attic dialect among the Athenian colonists (oikizein to colonize) of Soloi in Cilicia]
■ **sol'ecist** n. **solecist'ic** or **solecist'ical** adj. **solecist'ically** adv. **sol'ecize** or **-ise** vi to commit a solecism or solecisms.

solein an old form (Spenser) of **sullen**.

solemn /sol'əm/ adj attended with or marked by special (esp religious) ceremonies, pomp, or gravity; attended with an appeal to God, as an oath; grave; in serious earnestness; with formal dignity; awed; awe-inspiring; stately; pompous; glum; sombre. [OFr solempne, solemne (Fr solennel), from L sollemnis customary, appointed]
■ **solemnify** /sə-lem'ni-fī/ vt to make solemn. **solemnity** /-lem'ni-ti/ n a solemn ceremony; high seriousness; affected gravity. **solemnization** or **-s-** /sol-əm-nī-zā'shən/ n. **sol'emnize** or **-ise** /-nīz/ vt to perform religiously or solemnly; to celebrate with rites; to make solemn. **sol'emnizer** or **-s-** n. **sol'emnly** adv. **sol'emnness** n (also **sol'emness**).
❑ **solemn mass** n High Mass.

solenette see under **sole**[2].

solenodon /sō-len'ə-don/ n either of two shrewlike West Indian insectivorous mammals with elongated snouts and hairless tails, growing to about two feet in length. [New L, from L sōlēn, from Gr sōlēn a pipe]

solenoid /sol'ə- or sol'lə-noid/ n a cylindrical coil of wire, acting as a magnet when an electric current passes through it, converting electrical energy to mechanical energy. [From Gr sōlēn a pipe, and -oid]
■ **solenoid'al** adj. **solenoid'ally** adv.

soler see **solar**[1].

solera /sō-lā'rä or -rə/ n a system of sherry production involving blending wines of various ages from a series of graded casks to achieve uniformity; collectively, the casks used in this process. ◆ adj relating to or used in this process. [Sp, from L solus ground, base]

soles see **sol**[3].

soleus /sō'li-əs/ (anat) n a broad flat muscle, in the calf of the leg beneath the gastrocnemius, that flexes the foot. [New L, from L soles sole]

sol-fa /sol'fä'/ (music) n a system of syllables (do or ut, re, mi, fa, sol or so, la, si or ti) representing and sung to the notes of the scale. ◆ adj belonging to the system. ◆ vt and vi (**sol-faing** /-fä'ing/; **sol-faed** or -**fa'd** /-fäd'/) to sing to sol-fa syllables. [**sol**[1] and **fa**]
■ **sol-fa'ism** n singing by syllables; solmization. **sol-fa'ist** n a teacher, practiser, or advocate of solmization. **solfège** /-fej'/ n (Fr) solfeggio. **solfeggio** /-fed'jō/ n (pl **solfeggi** /-fed'jē/ or **solfeggios**) (Ital) an exercise in sol-fa syllables.
■ **tonic sol-fa** see under **tonic**.

solfatara /sol-fä-tä'rə/ n (pl **solfata'ras**) a volcanic vent emitting only gases, esp one emitting acid gases (hydrochloric acid and sulphur

dioxide). [From the *Solfatara* volcano (literally, sulphur-mine, sulphur-hole) near Naples, from Ital *solfo* sulphur]
■ **solfata'ric** *adj.*

solfeggio see under **sol-fa**.

solferino /sol-fə-rē'nō/ *n* (pl **solferi'nos**) the colour of rosaniline, a purplish-red, discovered soon after the battle of *Solferino* in Italy (1859).

sol-gel or **solgel** /sol'jel/ *adj* of or relating to alteration between **sol²** and **gel¹** states.

Sol.-Gen. *abbrev* : Solicitor-General.

soli see **solo**.

solicit /sə-lis'it/ *vt* to petition; to importune; to seek after; to call for, require; to invite or urge to immorality; to incite; to conduct, manage; to extract gently (*obs*). ♦ *vi* to petition; to act as solicitor; (of prostitutes) to make advances so as to win custom; (of beggars) to importune for alms. ♦ *n* (*Shakesp*; another reading **solic'ity**) a solicitation. [L *sōlicitāre, sollicitāre,* from *sō-, sollicitus,* from *sollus* whole, and *citus* aroused, from *ciēre* to cite]
■ **solic'itant** *n* a person who solicits (also *adj*). **solicitā'tion** *n* a soliciting; an earnest request; an invitation. **solic'iting** *n* any action of the verb, *esp* (of prostitutes) the making of advances. **solic'itor** *n* a person who is legally qualified to act for another in a court of law (*esp* formerly a court of equity); a lawyer who advises, prepares deeds, manages cases, instructs counsel in the higher courts, and acts as an advocate in the lower courts; a person who asks earnestly; a canvasser (*N Am*); a law officer responsible for the legal affairs of a town or city (*N Am*). **solic'itorship** *n*. **solic'itous** *adj* soliciting or earnestly asking or desiring; anxious; concerned; considerate; careful. **solic'itously** *adv*. **solic'itousness** or **solic'itude** *n* the state of being solicitous; anxiety or uneasiness of mind; trouble.
□ **solic'itor-ad'vocate** *n* in Scotland, a solicitor empowered to represent clients in the High Court or Court of Session. **Solic'itor-Gen'eral** *n* in England, the law officer of the crown next in rank to the Attorney-General, and in Scotland, the law officer of the crown next in rank to the Lord-Advocate; (in the US) the representative of the federal government at the Supreme Court.

solid /sol'id/ *adj* resisting change of shape, having the particles firmly cohering, *opp* to *fluid* (distinguished from *liquid* and *gaseous*); hard; compact; full of matter; not hollow; strong; having or relating to three dimensions; substantial; worthy of credit; weighty; of uniform undivided substance; financially sound, wealthy; reliable; sensible; unanimous; unbroken; unvaried. ♦ *n* a substance, body, or figure that is solid; a solid mass or part; (in *pl*) non-liquid food. [L *solidus* solid]
■ **solidare** /sol'i-dār/ *n* (*Shakesp*) a small coin. **sol'idarism** /-də-rizm/ *n*. **sol'idarist** *n* an advocate of solidarity. **solidarity** /-dar'i-ti/ *n* unity of interests, aims, opinions, etc. **sol'idary** /-dər-i/ *adj* marked by solidarity; jointly responsible; joint and several. **sol'idate** *vt* (*rare*) to consolidate. **solidifiable** /sə-lid'i-fī-ə-bl/ *adj*. **solidifica'tion** *n*. **solid'ify** *vt* to make solid or compact. ♦ *vi* to grow solid. **sol'idish** *adj*. **sol'idism** *n* the doctrine that refers all diseases to alterations of the solid parts of the body. **sol'idist** *n* a believer in solidism. **solid'ity** *n* the state of being solid; fullness, substance, actuality; strength or firmness, moral or physical; soundness, sturdiness; volume; a solid thing (*Shakesp*). **sol'idly** *adv*. **sol'idness** *n*.
□ **solid angle** *n* one of the eight cone-shaped three-dimensional angles defined by the intersection of three plane surfaces. **solid colour** *n* a colour covering the whole of an object; a uniform colour. **sol'id-hoofed** *adj* (of animals) with uncloven hoofs. **solid matter** *n* (*printing*) matter set without leads between the lines. **solid of revolution** *n* a solid figure regarded as formed by a plane figure turning round on an axis. **solid propellant** *n* (*space*) rocket propellant in solid state, *usu* in caked, plastic-like form. **solid solution** *n* an arrangement of atoms or molecules of different species within the same crystal lattice. **sol'id-state** *adj* of, consisting of, or relating to solid substances; of, consisting of or relating to semiconductor materials (and their electrical properties). **solid-state light** *n* light produced by means of a semiconductor device. **solid-state physics** *n sing* a branch of physics which covers all properties of solid materials, now *esp* electrical conduction in crystals of semiconductors, and superconductivity and photoconductivity.
■ **solid with** packed tight with; on a firm footing of understanding with; supporting fully.

solidago /sol-i-dā'gō or -dā'/ *n* (pl **solida'gos**) goldenrod, any herbaceous composite plant of the genus *Solidago*, typically having plumelike clusters of golden-yellow flowers. [New L, from Med L *soldago,* from *soldāre* to strengthen (from its supposed healing qualities)]

solidi see **solidus**.

solidum /sol'i-dum/ *n* the die of a pedestal (*archit*); a complete sum (*Scots law*). [See ety for **solid**]

solidungulate /sol-i-dung'gū-lāt/ (*zool*) *adj* having uncloven hoofs (also **solidung'ulous**). [L *solidus* solid, and *ungula* a hoof]

solidus /sol'i-dəs/ *n* (pl **solidi** /-dī/) the stroke, oblique or slash (/), a sign used for various purposes, as in writing fractions and to separate alternatives, ratios, etc (eg 3/4, and/or); a line in a constitutional diagram, eg of alloys, indicating the temperatures at which solidification is completed or melting begins (*chem*; cf **liquidus**); a Roman gold coin introduced by Constantine, later called the *bezant*; a medieval silver coin of 12 denarii. [ME, from LL *solidus* (*nummus*) a solid (coin); used to denote the former English shilling, representing the old lengthened *s* (d. s. d. = *librae, solidi, denarii* pounds, shillings, pence)]

solifidian /sō-li-fid'i-ən/ (*Christianity*) *n* and *adj* (a person) maintaining that only faith can bring redemption. [L *sōlus* only, and *fidēs* faith]
■ **solifid'ianism** *n*.

solifluxion or **solifluction** /sol-i-fluk'shən/ (*geol*) *n* the slow movement of soil or scree down a slope resulting from alternate freezing and thawing. [L *solum* soil, and *fluxiō, -ōnis* flow]

Solifugae /sol-i-fū'jē/ *n pl* an order of spider-like arachnids, with head and three-jointed thorax distinct. [See **Solpuga**; modified by popular association with L *sōl* the sun, and *fugere* to flee]

soliloquy /so-, sō- or sə-lil'ə-kwi/ *n* an act of talking to oneself; a speech of this nature made by a character in a play, etc. [L *sōliloquium,* from *sōlus* alone, and *loquī* to speak]
■ **solil'oquize** or **-ise** *vi* to speak to oneself; to utter a soliloquy in a play, etc. **solil'oquizer** or **-s-**, or **solil'oquist** *n*.

solion /sol'ī-ən or so-lī'on/ *n* a low-frequency amplifier that controls the flow of ions in solution. [*solution* and **ion**]

soliped /sol'i-ped/ *n* an animal with uncloven hoofs. ♦ *adj* of or relating to a soliped. [L *sōlus* alone, and *pēs, pedis* a foot]
■ **solip'edous** *adj*.

solipsism /sol'ip-si-zm/ (*philos*) *n* the theory that holds that self-existence is the only certainty, otherwise described as absolute egoism, the extreme form of subjective idealism. [L *sōlus* alone, and *ipse* self]
■ **sol'ipsist** *n* and *adj*. **solipsis'tic** *adj*. **solipsis'tically** *adv*.

solitaire /sol-i-tār'/ *n* a game played by one person with a board and balls, pegs, etc; patience (the card game) (*esp N Am*); a gemstone, *esp* a diamond, set by itself; a recluse; a large loose silk necktie as worn in the 18c; a gigantic flightless pigeon (*Pezophaps solitarius*) of Rodriguez, extinct since the 18c; an American or West Indian fly-catching thrush. [Fr, see **solitary**]
□ **solitaire board** *n* a board with cups, holes, etc for playing solitaire.

solitary /sol'i-t(ə-)ri/ *adj* alone; single, separate; living alone, not social or gregarious; without company; remote from society; retired, secluded; lonely; growing singly (*bot*). ♦ *n* someone who lives alone; a hermit; solitary confinement (*inf*). [L *sōlitārius,* from *sōlus* alone]
■ **solitarian** /-tā'ri-ən/ *n* a hermit. **sol'itarily** *adv*. **sol'itariness** *n*.
□ **solitary confinement** *n* imprisonment in a cell by oneself.

solito /sol'i-tō/ (*music*) *adv* in the usual manner. [Ital]

soliton /sol'i-tən/ (*phys*) *n* a solitary wave; a quantum which corresponds to a solitary wave in its transmission. [**solitary**]

solitude /sol'i-tūd/ *n* solitariness; absence of company; a lonely place or desert. [L *sōlitūdō,* from *sōlus*]
■ **solitūdinā'rian** *n*. **solitūd'inous** *adj*.

solive /so-lēv'/ *n* a joist or beam of secondary importance. [Fr, from L *sublevāre* to support]

sollar, soller see **solar¹**.

solleret /sol'ə-ret/ *n* a jointed steel shoe worn as part of protective armour. [OFr, dimin of *soler* slipper]

solmization or **-s-** /sol-mi-zā'shən/ (*music*) *n* sol-faing; a recital of the notes of the gamut. [**sol¹** and **mi**]

solo /sō'lō/ *n* (pl **sō'los** or (*music*) **soli** /sō'lē/) a piece or passage for one voice or instrument, accompanied or unaccompanied; any performance in which no other person or instrument participates; a single-seater motorcycle or bicycle as opposed to motorcycle with sidecar, tandem, etc; a card game (**solo whist**) based on whist, in which various declarations are made and the declarer may or may not have a partner. ♦ *adj* performed, or for performances, as a solo; performing a solo; for one; single. ♦ *adv* alone. ♦ *vi* to fly solo; to play (a) solo. [Ital, from L *sōlus* alone]
■ **sō'loist** *n*.
□ **solo parent** *n* (*Aust* and *NZ*) a single parent. **solo stop** *n* an organ stop for imitating a solo performance on another instrument.

Solomon /sol'ə-mən/ *n* a person of unusual wisdom, from *Solomon,* king of Israel (Bible, 1 Kings 3.5–15).
■ **Solomonian** /-mō'ni-ən/ or **Solomonic** /-mon'ik/ *adj*.
□ **Solomon's seal** *n* any species of *Polygonatum,* a genus of the lily family, with small dangling greenish flowers (*perh* from the scars on

the rootstock); a symbol formed of two triangles interlaced or superposed, forming a six-pointed star.

Solon /sō'lon or -lən/ n a famous lawgiver of Athens (594BC), one of the Seven Sages; a sage; a wiseacre; a Congressman or member of any other legislative assembly (US).
■ **Solō'nian** adj.

solonchak /sol-on'chak/ n a pale or grey soil type found in arid to subhumid, poorly drained conditions. [Russ, salt marsh, from sol salt]

solonetz or **solonets** /sol-o-nets'/ n an alkaline soil type having a hard, dark subsoil under a thin friable topsoil, formed by the leaching of salts from a solonchak. [Russ, salt not produced by boiling]
■ **solonet'zic** adj. **soloniza'tion** or **-s-** n the process by which a solonetz is formed.

so-long or **so long** /sō-long'/ (inf or sl) interj goodbye. [Prob **so**[1] and **long**[1]; poss **salaam**]

Solpuga /sol-pū'gə/ n a genus of very venomous members of the Solifugae. [L solpūga, salpūga, solipūga, solipugna, a venomous animal supposedly the same, a word originating in Spain]
■ **solpu'gid** n and adj (a member) of the genus.

Solr abbrev : Solicitor.

solstice /sol'stis/ n the time when the sun reaches its maximum distance from the equator, touching the tropic of Cancer or Capricorn (**summer solstice** about 21 June in the northern hemisphere, 21 December in the southern hemisphere; **winter solstice** about 21 December in the northern hemisphere, 21 June in the southern hemisphere); the turning point then reached. [Fr, from L sōlstitium, from sōl the sun, sistere, statum to make to stand, from stāre]
■ **solstitial** /-stish'l/ adj relating to, or happening at, a solstice, esp at the summer solstice. **solstit'ially** adv.

soluble /sol'ū-bl/ adj capable of being solved, dissolved, or resolved. [L solvere, solūtum to loosen]
■ **solūbil'ity** n (a measure of) the ability of a substance to dissolve. **solubiliza'tion** or **-s-** n. **sol'ubilize** or **-ise** vt to render soluble; to make more soluble.
□ **soluble glass** n waterglass (qv).

solum /sō'ləm/ n ground, soil; a piece of ground. [L solum the ground]

solus /sō'ləs/ or (fem) **sola** /sō'lə/ adj alone, orig in dramatic directions; (of a poster, newspaper advertisement, etc) having no other advertisement next to it. ◆ n a poster or advertisement appearing in isolation from any others. [L sōlus alone]

solution /sə-loo'shən or -lū'shən/ n the act of solving or dissolving; the condition of being dissolved; the preparation resulting therefrom; the separating of parts; abnormal separation; an explanation; the removal of a doubt; the solving of, answer to, a problem; the crisis of a disease; a breach (as of continuity); the payment of a debt, or similar discharge of an obligation; a solution of rubber. ◆ vt to mend or cement with rubber solution; to apply or treat with a solution, solve (a problem) (esp N Am). [**soluble**]
■ **sol'ūtal** adj of or relating to a solute. **sol'ūte** n a dissolved substance. ◆ adj /sol' or -ūt'/ loose; free; not adhering; dissolved. **solutional** /-oo' or -ū'/ adj. **solu'tionist** n a solver (as of puzzles). **sol'ūtive** adj tending to dissolve; laxative.
□ **solution of triangles** n (maths) finding the values of the remaining sides and angles, some being given. **solution set** n (maths) the set of all the values that solve an equation.

Solutrean or **Solutrian** /so-loot'ri-ən or -lūt' or -trē'/ adj belonging to an upper Palaeolithic European culture which succeeded the Aurignacian and preceded the Magdalenian. [Solutré, in Saône-et-Loire, where objects of this culture have been found]

Solvay process /sol'vā prō'ses/ n a process for manufacturing sodium carbonate in which carbon dioxide is passed through a concentrated solution of sodium chloride saturated with ammonia with the resulting precipitate of sodium bicarbonate being heated to produce the carbonate. [Ernest Solvay (1838–1922), Belgian chemist]

solve /solv/ vt to settle; to clear up or explain; to find an answer to or a way out of; to unbind; to dissolve. [L solvere to loosen, prob from sē-, se- aside, and luere to loosen]
■ **solvabil'ity** n. **sol'vable** adj capable of being solved; capable of being paid, dissolved, or resolved (rare or obs); solvent (obs). **sol'vate** n a definite combination of solute and solvent. ◆ vt and vi to (cause to) undergo solvation. **solvā'tion** n the association of the molecules of a solvent with solute ions or molecules. **sol'vency** n. **sol'vent** adj able to solve or dissolve; able to pay all debts. ◆ n a substance that dissolves another; that component of a solution which is present in excess, or whose physical state is the same as that of the solution; something which provides a solution. **sol'ver** n.
□ **solvent abuse** n self-intoxication by inhaling the fumes given off by various solvents in adhesives, petrol, etc.

solvitur ambulando /sol'vi-toor am-bū-lan'dō/ (L) literally, it is solved by walking (ie the problem of reality of motion); hence, the problem is solved by practical experiment, by actual performance.

Som. abbrev : Somerset.

som /sōm/ n (pl **sōm**) the standard monetary unit of Kyrgyzstan (100 tiyin).

soma[1] /sō'mə/ n (pl **sō'mas** or **sō'mata**) the body; the body of an animal or plant excluding the germ cells (biol). [Gr sōma body]
■ **somascope** /sō'mə-skōp/ n (Gr skopeein to view) an instrument using ultrasonic waves converted into a television image to show the character of diseased internal tissues of the body. **somatic** /-mat'ik/ adj. **somat'ically** adv. **so'matism** /-mə-tizm/ n materialism. **so'matist** n (also adj). **somatogenic** /sō-mə-tō-jen'ik/ adj originating in body cells. **somatolog'ic** or **somatolog'ical** adj. **somatol'ogy** n the science of the properties of matter; the science of the human body. **somatomedin** /sō-mə-tō-mē'din/ n a hormone, produced in the liver, that stimulates growth of bone and muscle. **so'matoplasm** n protoplasm of the somatic cells. **so'matopleure** /-ploor/ n (Gr pleurā side) the outer body-wall or the layer that gives rise to it. **somatosens'ory** adj relating to sensory stimuli perceived in the skin. **somatostatin** /sō-mə-tō-stat'in/ n a peptide of the hypothalamus which controls the secretion of somatotropin by the pituitary. **somatotens'ic** adj that which restores the equilibrium of an organism (applied esp to certain plants when eaten as food). **somatotōn'ia** n a pattern of temperament and body type in which alertness and aggression are combined with mesomorphic build. **somatotonic** /-ton'/ adj. **somatotrop'ic** or **somatotroph'ic** adj promoting bodily growth. **somatotrop'in** or **somatotroph'in** n a polypeptide growth hormone. **somat'otype** n a type consisting of a physical build paired with a particular temperament. ◆ vt to place with regard to somatotype. **somital** /sō'mi-tl/ or **somit'ic** adj. **so'mite** n (zool) a body segment of a vertebrate embryo or of a segmented invertebrate.
□ **somatic cell** n one of the non-reproductive cells of the body, as distinct from the reproductive or germ cells. **somatic cell hybrid** n a cell formed by fusion of two somatic cells from the same or different species. **somatic mutation** n a mutation occurring in somatic cells, and therefore not inheritable.

soma[2] /sō'mə/ (also with cap) n a plant (perh an asclepiad), or its intoxicating juice, used in ancient Indian religious ceremonies, and personified as a god. [Sans soma (Avestan haoma juice)]

soma[3] /sō'mə/ n an imaginary perfect drug described by Aldous Huxley in Brave New World; (**Soma**®) a drug which relieves pain and is a muscle-relaxant. [**soma**[2]]

Somali /sə- or so-mä'li/ adj of or relating to the republic of Somalia in NE Africa, its people or its language. ◆ n a native or citizen of Somalia; the language of Somalia.

soman /sō'mən/ n an organophosphate nerve agent developed for use in chemical warfare, causing sweating, vomiting, convulsions and death, if inhaled. [Origin unknown]

somascope...to...**somatotype** see under **soma**[1].

sombre or (N Am) **somber** /som'bər/ adj dark and gloomy; serious; melancholy, dismal. ◆ vt and vi to make or become sombre. [Fr sombre (cf Sp sombra shade), perh from L sub under, and umbra a shade]
■ **som'brely** adv. **som'breness** n. **som'brous** adj sombre.

sombrerite /som-brā'rīt/ n rock guano. [Sombrero in the West Indies]

sombrero /som-brā'rō/ n (pl **sombre'ros**) a broad-brimmed hat, esp as worn in Mexico. [Sp, hat, from sombra shade]

some /sum/ indefinite pronoun an indefinite part of the whole number or quantity; (a) certain (undetermined) one(s); a great deal (N Am); a good deal more, esp as and then some (esp N Am); one, one or other (obs). ◆ adj one or other; in an indefinite number or quantity; a little; not a little; considerable; a certain; certain unspecified; several; a few; in approximate number, length, etc, more or less; remarkable, outstanding, of note (inf, esp US; also ironic). ◆ adv somewhat, in some degree, rather, a little (dialect); very much (N Am); sometimes (Shakesp). [OE sum; Gothic sums, ON sumr]
■ **some'body** n (or pronoun) (pl **some'bodies**) some person; a person of importance. **some'day** adv at an unspecified time in the future. **some'deal** or **some'dele** adv (archaic) in some degree, somewhat. **some'gate** adv (Scot) somewhere, somehow. **some'how** adv in some way or other. **some'one** n (or pronoun) somebody. **some'place** adv (N Am) somewhere. **some'thing** n or pronoun an undefined thing; a thing of some account; a portion. ◆ adv in some degree; to an extreme degree. ◆ adj that is some account. ◆ combining form indicating an unspecified or unknown number greater than or in addition to, as in thirty-something. —Also used as substitute for any word or component of any word forgotten, indefinite or avoided. **some'time** adv at a time not fixed; at one time or other; formerly. ◆ adj former; late; occasional. **some'times** adv at times; now and

then; sometime (*obs*). ◆*adj* (*Shakesp*) sometime. **some'way**, **some'ways** or **some'wise** *adv* in some way; somehow. **some'what** *adv* in some degree. ◆*n* an unfixed quantity or degree; something. **some'when** *adv* (*rare*) some time or other. **some'whence** *adv* (*rare*). **some'where** *adv* in or to some place. **some'while** or **some'whiles** *adv* (*rare*) sometimes. **some'whither** *adv* (*rare*). **some'why** *adv* (*rare*). **somewise** see **someway** above.

❑ **someone else** *n* some other person. **something else** *n* some other thing; an exceptional person or thing (*inf*).

-some[1] /-*sum* or -*səm*/ *sfx* (1) forming adjectives with the meaning full of, eg *troublesome*, *wholesome*; (2) forming nouns denoting a group with a certain number of members, eg *twosome*, *threesome*. [OE *-sum*; Ger *-sam*; cf **same**]

-some[2] /-*sōm*/ *sfx* forming nouns denoting a body, eg *chromosome*. [Gr *soma* body]

somersault or **summersault** /*sum'ər-sölt* or -*solt*/, also sometimes **somerset** or **summerset** /*sum'ər-set*/ *n* a leap or other movement in which a person (or animal) turns heels over head. ◆*vi* to turn a somersault. [OFr *sombre saut* (Fr *soubresaut*), from L *suprā* over, and *saltus*, -*ūs* a leap, from *salīre* to leap]

somital, **somite**, **somitic** see under **soma**[1].

sommelier /*som'ə-lyā*/ *n* a butler; a wine waiter or steward in a restaurant. [Fr]

somnambulance /*som-nam'bū-ləns*/ *n* sleepwalking. [L *somnus* sleep, and *ambulare* to walk]

■ **somnam'būlant** *adj* and *n*. **somnam'būlar** or **somnam'būlary** *adj*. **somnam'būlate** *vi* to walk in one's sleep. **somnambūlā'tion** *n*. **somnam'būlātor** or **somnam'būle** *n* a sleepwalker. **somnam'būlic** *adj*. **somnam'būlism** *n* walking in sleep; a hypnotic trance in which acts are performed that are not remembered afterwards. **somnam'būlist** *n*. **somnambūlis'tic** *adj*.

somnial /*som'nyəl* or -*ni-əl*/ *adj* (*rare*) relating to dreams. [L *somnus* sleep]

■ **som'niate** *vt* to dream. ◆*vi* to make drowsy, stupefy. **som'niative** or **som'niatory** *adj*.

somnifacient /*som-ni-fā'shənt* or -*shi-ant*/ *adj* sleep-inducing or promoting (also **somnif'erous** or **somnif'ic**). ◆*n* a somnifacient drug. [L *somnus* sleep, and *faciens*, *facientis* prp of *facēre* to do]

somniloquence /*som-nil'ə-kwəns*/, **somniloquism** /-*nil'ə-kwi-zm*/ or **somniloquy** /-*nil'ə-kwi*/ *n* (the act of) talking in one's sleep. [L *somnus* sleep, and *loquī* to talk]

■ **somnil'oquist** *n*. **somnil'oquize** or **-ise** *vi*.

somnolence /*som'nə-ləns*/ *n* sleepiness, drowsiness (also **som'nolency**). [ME *sompnolence*, from OFr, from L *somnolentia*, from *somnus* sleep]

■ **som'nolent** *adj*. **som'nolently** *adv*. **somnolesc'ent** *adj* half-asleep.

somoni /*sō-mō'nē*/ *n* (pl **somo'ni**) the standard monetary unit of Tajikistan (100 dirams).

son /*sun*/ *n* a male child or offspring; formerly extended to a son-in-law; a descendant, or one so regarded or treated; a disciple; a native or inhabitant; the product of anything; a familiar (sometimes patronizing) mode of address to a boy or to a male younger than oneself. [OE *sunu*; Du *zoon*, Ger *Sohn*]

■ **son'less** *adj*. **sonn'y** *n* a little son; a familiar mode of address to a boy. **son'ship** *n* the state or character of a son.

❑ **son'-in-law** *n* (pl **sons'-in-law**) a daughter's husband; formerly, a stepson. **son of a bitch** see **sonofabitch**. **son of a gun** see under **gun**. **son of man** *n* a man; (with *caps*) a title applied to Jesus Christ or the Messiah. **son of the manse** *n* a minister's son.

■ **son of...** (often *facetious*) a person (or thing) that is a derivative, copy or product of an original. **the Son** the second person in the Trinity, Jesus Christ.

sonant /*sō'nənt*/ (*phonetics*) *adj* voiced; syllabic. ◆*n* a voiced sound; a syllabic consonant. [L *sonāns*, -*antis*, prp of *sonāre* to sound]

■ **so'nance** *n* a sounding. **so'nancy** *n* sonant character.

sonar /*sō'när*/ *n* a system for detecting and locating a submarine or other underwater object by means of ultrasonic waves echoed back from the object; natural equipment that provides echo location in bats and some marine animals; echo-sounding equipment in general. [*sound navigation and ranging*]

❑ **sonar buoy** same as **sonobuoy** (see under **sono-**).

sonata /*sə-* or *so-nä'tə*/ (*music*) *n* orig, an instrumental composition; a composition *usu* of three or more movements designed chiefly for a solo instrument. [Ital, fem pap of *sonare*, from L *sonāre* to sound]

■ **sonatina** /*son-ə-tē'nə*/ *n* a short sonata.

❑ **sonata form** *n* the form usual in the first movement of a sonata or symphony, divided into three sections: exposition, development and recapitulation.

sonce see **sonse**.

sondage /*sɔ̃-däzh'*/ *n* a trial bore or excavation (*mining* and *archaeol*); a sounding (*naut*); sounding out of opinion, an opinion poll. [Fr]

sonde /*sond*/ *n* any device for obtaining information about atmospheric and weather conditions at high altitudes. [Fr]

sondeli /*son'de-li*/ *n* the Indian musk shrew. [Kanarese *sundili*]

sone /*sōn*/ *n* a unit of sound on a scale such that the numerical value is proportional to the perceived loudness. [L *sonus* sound]

soneri /*son'ə-* or *sō'nə-rē*/ *n* cloth of gold. [Hindi *sonā* gold]

son et lumière /*son ā lüm'yər* or -*yär*/ *n* a dramatic spectacle presented after dark, involving lighting effects on natural features of the country or on a chosen building and an appropriate theme illustrated by spoken words and by music. [Fr]

Song see **Sung**.

song[1] /*song*/ *n* that which is sung; a short poem or ballad suitable for singing or set to music; the melody to which it is sung; an instrumental composition of similar form and character; singing; the melodious outburst of a bird; any characteristic sound; a poem, or poetry in general; a theme of song; a habitual utterance, manner, or attitude towards anything; a fuss; a mere trifle (as in **going for a song** being sold for a trifling sum). [OE *sang*, from *singan* to sing; Gothic *saggws*, ON *söngr*]

■ **song'ful** *adj* abounding in song; melodious; songlike; like singing; ready to break into song. **song'fully** *adv*. **song'fulness** *n*. **song'less** *adj*. **song'like** *adj*. **song'ster**, *fem* **song'stress** *n* a singer.

❑ **song'bird** *n* a bird that sings; any bird of the suborder Oscines. **song'book** *n* a book of songs; a service-book (*obs*). **song'craft** *n* (*rare*) the art of writing or singing songs. **song cycle** *n* a sequence of songs connected in subject. **song'fest** see **fest**. **song form** *n* the form of composition usual in songs. **song'man** *n* (*Shakesp*) a singer; a choir singer. **Song of Songs** or **of Solomon** *n* Canticles, a book of the Old Testament long attributed to Solomon. **song school** *n*. **song'smith** *n* a composer of songs. **song sparrow** *n* an American songbird (*Melospiza melodia*). **song thrush** *n* a common European thrush, with a song consisting of a series of short repeated calls (see also **thrush**[1]). **song'writer** *n* one who composes music and/or words for (*esp* popular) songs.

■ **make a song** (**and dance**) **about** to make overmuch of; to make an unnecessary fuss about. **on song** (*inf*) performing well, on form.

song[2] /*song*/ (*Spenser*) pat of **sing**[1].

SONIA /*son'yə*/ (*finance*) *abbrev*: sterling overnight interbank average rate.

sonic /*son'ik*/ *adj* relating to or using sound waves; travelling at about the speed of sound. [L *sonus* sound]

■ **son'ics** *n sing* the study of the technological application of sounds, *esp* supersonic waves.

❑ **sonic bang** or **boom** *n* (*aeronautics*) a loud double report caused by shock waves projected outward and backward from the leading and trailing edges of an aircraft as it reaches supersonic speed. **sonic barrier** *n* the sound barrier. **sonic mine** *n* an acoustic mine.

sonne an obsolete spelling of **son** or **sun**.

sonnet /*son'it*/ *n* formerly, a short (*esp* lyrical) poem; a short poem of fourteen lines of ten or eleven syllables, rhymed according to one or other of certain definite schemes, forming an octave and a sestet, properly expressing two successive phases of one thought. ◆*vi* to write sonnets. ◆*vt* to celebrate in sonnets. [Ital *sonetto*, dimin of *suono*, from L *sonus* a sound]

■ **sonn'etary** *adj*. **sonneteer'** *n* a writer of sonnets; a poetaster (*obs*). **sonn'etize** or **-ise** *vi* to compose sonnets.

❑ **sonnet sequence** *n* a connected series of sonnets by one poet.

■ **Miltonic sonnet** a sonnet with the rhyme scheme *abbaabba cdecde*. **Petrarchan** (or **Petrarchian**) **sonnet** a sonnet with the rhyme scheme *abbaabba cdcdcd*. **Shakespearean sonnet** a sonnet with the rhyme scheme *ababcdcd efefgg*.

Sonnite see **Sunna**.

sonny see under **son**.

sono- /*son-ō-*/ *combining form* meaning sonic. [L *sonus* sound]

■ **sonobuoy** /*son'ō-boi* or (*N Am*) -*boo-ē*/ *n* sonar equipment dropped to float on the sea and pick up underwater noise, eg from a submarine, and to transmit bearings of the source to aircraft. **son'ogram** *n* a visual representation of a sound produced by a sonograph (*acoustics*); a sonogram produced by ultrasonography (*med*). **son'ograph** *n* an instrument for scanning and recording sound and its component frequencies. **sonog'rapher** *n*. **sonog'raphy** *n*. **sonoluminesc'ence** *n* luminescence produced by sound waves.

sonofabitch /*sun'ə-və-bich'*/ (*sl*; *esp N Am*) *n* (pl **sons of bitches**) son of a bitch, an abusive term of address or of description, or vulgar exclamation.

sonorous /*sə-nö'rəs* or *son'ə-rəs*/ *adj* sounding, *esp* loudly, deeply, impressively, etc; full-sounding; full of impressive language; sounding or ringing when struck. [L *sonōrus*, from *sonor, -ōris* a sound, from *sonāre* to sound]

■ **son'orant** *n* (*phonetics*) a frictionless continuant or nasal (*l, r, m, n, ng*) capable of fulfilling a vocalic or consonantal function; the consonants represented by *w* and *y*, having consonantal or vocalic articulations. **sonority** /*sŏ-* or *sə-nor'i-ti*/ *n* sonorousness; type, quality, etc, of sound. **sono'rously** (or /*son'*/) *adv*. **sono'rousness** (or /*son'*/) *n* sonorous quality or character.

□ **sonorous figures** *n pl* (*acoustics*) the visual patterns produced by a fine powder on a vibrating plate (also called **Chladni figures**).

sonse or **sonce** /*sons*/ (*Scot*) *n* good luck; abundance. [Gaelic *sonas* good fortune]

■ **sons'y** or **sons'ie** *adj* bringing luck; comely; comfortable-looking; good-natured; plump, buxom; robust.

sontag /*son'tag* or *zon'täk*/ *n* a woman's knitted cape, tied down round the waist. [From the famous German singer Henriette *Sontag* (1806–54)]

sonties /*son'tiz*/ *n pl* a word used in an oath in Shakespeare's *Merchant of Venice* (II.2.43) *perh* meaning sanctities.

sook[1] /*sook*/ *n* a soft, timid or cowardly person (*inf, esp Aust*); someone who sucks up, a toady (*dialect*). [Perh from earlier *suck* (*-calf*), a hand-reared calf, infl by Scot pronunciation of **suck**]

sook[2] same as **souk**.

soole see **sole**[4].

soom /*soom*/ a Scots form of **swim**.

soon /*soon*/ *adv* (**soon'er**; **soon'est**) in a short time; without delay; early; readily; willingly. [OE *sōna*]

■ **soon'est** *adv* (*inf* and *milit jargon*) as soon as possible, immediate. ■ **no sooner…than** immediately. **soon at** (*Shakesp*) about. **sooner or later** eventually.

soop /*soop*/ (*Scot*) *vt* to sweep. [ON *sōpa*; cf **sweep, swoop**]

■ **soop'ing** *n* (*Scot*). **soop'stake** *adv* (*Shakesp*) with a sweep of the stakes (another reading **swoop'-stake-like**).

soot[1] /*sŭt*/ *n* a black deposit from imperfect combustion of carbonaceous matter (wood, coal, etc); a smut. ◆ *vt* to cover, smear, dirty, clog, or treat with soot. [OE *sōt* ; Dan *sod*]

■ **soot'erkin** *n* (now *rare*) an imaginary afterbirth of which Dutch women were reported to be delivered, thought to be the offspring of the stoves over which they huddled; a Dutchman; a black person; a chimney-sweep; anything supplementary, fruitless, or imperfect. **soot'ily** *adv*. **soot'iness** *n*. **soot'less** *adj*. **soot'y** *adj*.

□ **soot'flake** *n* a smut of soot. **sooty mould** *n* a disease of plants in which a dark-coloured fungus grows on the sticky secretions of certain insects.

soot[2] or **soote** /*soot*/ *adj* and *n* (*obs*) sweet. ◆ *adv* (*Spenser*) sweetly. [ODu *soet* sweet]

sooterkin see under **soot**[1].

sooth /*sooth*/ *n* truth, verity, reality (*archaic*); blandishment (*Shakesp*); an augury, foretokening (*obs; Spenser* **soothe**). ◆ *adj* true; truthful; smooth, soft (*Keats*). ◆ *adv* in truth; indeed. [OE *sōth* truth, true; ON *sannr*]

■ **sooth'fast** *adj* truthful, honest, faithful. **sooth'fastly** *adv*. **sooth'fastness** *n*. **sooth'ful** *adj* truthful; faithful. **sooth'ly** or **sooth'lich** *adv* (*Spenser*) truly, indeed.

□ **sooth'say** *vi* to foretell, to divine. ◆ *n* a prediction; (also *Spenser*) /*-sā'*/) an omen. **sooth'sayer** *n* (also *Spenser*) /*-sā'*/) someone who foretells, a diviner or prognosticator; a truth-teller (*obs*). **sooth'saying** *n*.

soothe[1] /*soodh*/ *vt* to calm, comfort, compose, tranquillize; to appease; to allay, soften; to blandish, cajole, flatter; to gloss over (*obs*); to prove or declare true (*obs*); to confirm, support, back up (*obs*). ◆ *vi* to have a tranquillizing effect. [OE (ge)*sōthian* to confirm as true, from *sōth* true]

■ **sooth'er** *n* someone who, or something that, soothes; a dummy teat for a baby, a comforter or pacifier. ◆ *vt* (*Irish*) to flatter, blandish. **sooth'ing** *n* and *adj*. **sooth'ingly** *adv*.

soothe[2] see **sooth**.

sootily, sootiness, sootless, sooty see under **soot**[1].

SOP *abbrev*: significant other person (eg a cohabiting partner); standard operating procedure.

sop /*sop*/ *n* bread or other food dipped or soaked in liquid; a puddle; a soaking; a propitiatory gift or concession (from the drugged sop the Sibyl gave to Cerberus to enable Aeneas to enter the Underworld in Virgil, *Aeneid* 6.420). ◆ *vt* (**sopp'ing; sopped**) to steep in alcohol; to take up by absorption (with *up*); to soak. ◆ *vi* to soak in, percolate; to be soaked. [OE *sopp* (noun), *soppian* (verb); prob connected with *sūpan* to sup]

■ **sopp'ily** *adv*. **sopp'iness** *n*. **sopp'ing** *n, adj* and *adv*. **sopp'y** *adj* drenched; thoroughly wet; sloppily sentimental.

sop. *abbrev*: soprano.

soph /*sof*/ *n* a short form of **sophister** and of **sophomore**.

sopherim /*sŏ'fə-rim*/ *n pl* the scribes, the expounders of the Jewish oral law. [Heb *sōferīm*]

■ **sopheric** /*-fer'ik*/ *adj*.

Sophi same as **Sophy**.

sophism /*sof'i-zm*/ *n* a plausibly deceptive fallacy. [Gr *sophiā* wisdom, *sophisma* skill]

■ **soph'ist** *n* a captious or intentionally fallacious reasoner; *orig* one of a class of public teachers of rhetoric, philosophy, etc, in ancient Greece. **soph'ister** *n* a sophist (*Shakesp*); *esp* formerly, a second- or third-year student at certain British universities, or a third- or fourth-year student at Trinity College, Dublin. **sophis'tic** or **sophis'tical** *adj* relating to, or of the nature of, a sophist or sophistry; fallaciously subtle. **sophis'tically** *adv*. **soph'istry** *n* (an instance of) plausibly deceptive or fallacious reasoning; the art of reasoning speciously.

sophisticate /*sə-fis'ti-kāt*/ *vt* to give a fashionable air of worldly wisdom to; to make (eg a machine) highly complex and efficient; to make sophistic; to adulterate, falsify. ◆ *vi* to practise sophistry. ◆ *n* a sophisticated person. ◆ *adj* (*old*) sophisticated. [Med L *sophisticāre* to adulterate, from *sophisticus* sophistic; see **sophism**]

■ **sophis'ticāted** *adj* very refined and subtle; devoid or deprived of natural simplicity, complex; with qualities produced by special knowledge and skill; (of a person) accustomed to an elegant, cultured way of life; with the most up-to-date devices; worldly-wise; adulterated, falsified. **sophisticā'tion** *n*. **sophis'ticātor** *n*.

sophistry see under **sophism**.

Sophoclean /*sof-ō-klē'ən*/ *adj* relating to or associated with the Athenian tragic poet *Sophocles* (c.496–c.406BC).

sophomore /*sof'ə-mör*/ (*esp US*) *n* a second-year student (also *adj*). [Prob from *sophom* (obs form of *sophism*) and *-or*, as if from *sophos* wise, and *mōros* foolish]

■ **sophomoric** /*-mor'*/ or **sophomor'ical** *adj* of a sophomore; bombastic.

Sophy /*sŏ'fi*/ (*obs*) *n* the shah of Persia. [From the Ṣafī or Safawi dynasty (1502–1736) descended from Ṣafi-ud-dīn]

sopite /*sō-pīt'*/ (now *rare*) *vt* to dull, lull, put to sleep; to put an end to. [L *sōpītus*, pap of *sōpīre* to put to sleep, calm, settle]

sopor /*sŏ'pör*/ (*pathol*) *n* unnaturally deep sleep. [L *sopor, -ōris* deep sleep, and *ferre* to bring, *facere* to make]

■ **soporiferous** /*sop-* or *sōp-ər-if'ər-əs*/ *adj* inducing sleep. **soporif'erously** *adv*. **soporif'erousness** *n*. **soporif'ic** *adj* inducing sleep (also *fig*). ◆ *n* a sleep-inducing agent. **sop'orōse** or **sop'orous** *adj* sleepy.

sopped, sopping, soppy see **sop**.

sopra /*sŏ'pra*/ (*music*) *adv* above. [Ital, from L *suprā* above]

soprano /*sə-prä'nō*/ *n* (*pl* **sopra'nos** or **sopra'ni** /*-nē*/) the highest variety of voice, treble; a singer with such a voice; a part for such a voice. ◆ *adj* of, or possessing, a treble voice or a part for it; in a group of instruments of the same type but of different sizes, that with the range close to the range of a soprano voice. [Ital, from *sopra*, from L *suprā* or *super* above]

■ **sopranino** /*sō-prə-nē'nō*/ *adj* (of an instrument) higher than the corresponding soprano. ◆ *n* (*pl* **soprani'nos** or **soprani'ni**) such an instrument. **sopra'nist** *n* a soprano singer.

SOR *abbrev*: sale or return.

sora /*sŏ'rə*/ or *sö'*/ *n* a N American short-billed rail, *Porzana carolina* (also **so'ree**). [Native American name]

sorage see under **sore**[2].

soral see under **sorus**.

Sorb /*sörb*/ *n* a Wend. [Ger *Sorbe*; cf **Serb**]

■ **Sor'bian** or **Sor'bish** *n* and *adj* Wendish.

sorb[1] /*sörb*/ *n* the service tree, the wild service tree, or (sometimes) the rowan tree; its fruit (also **sorb'-apple**). [L *sorbus* (the tree), *sorbum* (the fruit)]

■ **sor'bate** *n* a salt of sorbic acid.

□ **sorbic acid** *n* an acid obtained from the rowanberry, used in food preservation.

sorb[2] /*sörb*/ *vt* to absorb or adsorb. [L *sorbēre* to suck in]

■ **sorbefacient** /*-i-fā'shənt*/ *adj* promoting absorption (also *n*). **sor'bent** *n* and *adj*.

sorbaria /*sör-bā'ri-ə*/ *n* any shrub of a small Asiatic genus (*Sorbaria*) of deciduous shrubs of the family Rosaceae, with long pinnate leaves and large clusters of white flowers. [L *sorbus*; see **sorb**[1]]

sorbate see under **sorb**[1].

sorbefacient, sorbent see under **sorb**[2].

■ words derived from main entry word; □ compound words; ■ idioms and phrasal verbs

sorbet /sör'bət or sör'bā/ n sherbet; water ice. [Fr, from Ital *sorbetto*; cf **sherbet**]

Sorbian see under **Sorb**.

sorbic acid see under **sorb**[1].

Sorbish see under **Sorb**.

sorbite /sör'bīt/ (*metallurgy*) n a fine-grained constituent of steel formed of ferrite and cementite, produced by tempering martensite at over 450°C.
■ **sorbit'ic** adj. **sorbitiza'tion** or **-s-** n. **sorb'itize** or **-ise** vt to turn (a metal) into a form containing sorbite.

sorbitol /sör'bi-tol/ n a white crystalline substance ($C_6H_8(OH)_6$) derived from (and used as a substitute for) sugar. [**sorb**[1]]

Sorbonne /sör-bon'/ n a theological college of the medieval university of Paris, founded in 1253 by Robert of *Sorbon*, long dominant in matters of doctrine, suppressed 1792, revived 1808, seat of the faculties of science and letters (arts).
■ **Sorbon'ical** or **Sorbonn'ical** adj. **Sor'bonist** or **Sor'bonnist** n a doctor or student of the Sorbonne.

sorbo rubber /sör'bō rub'ər/ n a spongy type of rubber. [From **absorb**]

sorbus /sör'bəs/ n (pl **sorb'uses**) any plant of a large genus of deciduous shrubs and trees (*Sorbus*) of the family Rosaceae, incl the service tree and the rowan. [L; see **sorb**[1]]

sorcery /sör'sə-ri/ n divination by the assistance of evil spirits; enchantment; magic; witchcraft. [OFr *sorcerie*, from L *sors, sortis* lot]
■ **sor'cerer**, fem **sor'ceress** n. **sor'cerous** adj.

sord[1] /sörd or sörd/ (*Milton*) n a form of **sward**.

sord[2] /sörd or sörd/ n a flock of mallards. [OFr *sordre*, from L *surgere* to rise]

sordamente see under **sordo**.

sordid /sör'did/ adj dirty, squalid; mean; contemptibly avaricious; mercenary; of low or unworthy ideals. [L *sordidus* dirty]
■ **sor'didly** adv. **sor'didness** n.

sordo /sör'dō/ or (*fem*) **sorda** /sör'da/ (*music*) adj muted, damped. [Ital, from L *surdus* deaf, noiseless]
■ **sordamente** /-dä-men'tā/ adv gently, softly. **sordino** /-dē'nō/ n (pl **sordini** /-nē/) a mute or damper to soften or deaden the sound of an instrument.
■ **con sordino** with mute. **senza sordino** without mute.

sore[1] /sör or sör/ n a painful or tender injured or diseased spot; an ulcer or boil; grief; an affliction. ◆ adj wounded; tender; readily sensitive to pain; irritable; touchy; painful; afflicted; vexed; irritated; causing pain; painful to contemplate; grievous (*archaic* or *Bible*); aching (*Scot*); bringing sorrow or regret; aggrieved (*inf*). ◆ adv painfully; grievously; severely; distressingly; in distress; hard; eagerly; very much. ◆ vt to make sore; to wound. [OE *sār*; Ger *sehr* very, ON *sārr* sore]
■ **sore'ly** adv. **sore'ness** n.
❑ **sore'head** n (*orig* and *esp N Am*) someone discontented, eg with a reward; an irritable or grumpy person. **sore'head'ed** adj. **sore point** n a subject about which someone feels touchy, angry or aggrieved.
■ **a sore thumb** something obtrusive, too painful or too awkward to be ignored. **stick out like a sore thumb** (*inf*) to be painfully obvious, noticeable, etc.

sore[2], **soar** or **soare** /sör or sör/ (*obs*) adj sorrel, reddish-brown; (of hawks, etc) in the reddish-brown first-year plumage. ◆ n a hawk in its first year (*obs*); a buck in its fourth year (*Shakesp*). [Anglo-Fr and OFr *sor* (Fr *saur, saure*) sorrel, reddish; cf **sorrel**[2]]
■ **sor'age** n the first year of a hawk.

soredium /sō-rē'di-əm or sö-/ n (pl **sorē'dia**) a small vegetative reproductive body in lichens, consisting of a few algal cells enclosed in fungal hyphae. [Gr *sōros* a heap]
■ **sorē'dial** or **sorē'diate** adj.

soree see **sora**.

sorehon /sör'hon or sör'/ n an ancient Irish exaction of free accommodation by a lord from a freeholder or tenant. [See **sorn**]

sorel, sorell see **sorrel**[2].

sorex /sō'reks or sö'/ n any member of the common shrew genus *Sorex*, of the family Soricidae. [L *sōrex, -icis* shrew; cf Gr *hyrax*]
■ **soric'ident** adj (L *dēns, dentis* tooth) having teeth like the shrew. **soricine** /sor'i-sīn or -sin/ adj of the shrew; shrewlike. **sor'icoid** /-koid/ adj shrewlike.

sorghum /sör'gəm/ n any grass of the tropical Old World genus (*Sorghum*) of grasses closely related to sugarcane, including durra and kaffir corn; molasses made from its juice (*US*). [Ital *sorgo*, prob from an Indonesian word, or poss from (unattested) vulgar L *Syricum* (*grānum*) Syrian (grain)]

■ **sor'go** or **sor'gho** n (pl **sor'gos** or **sor'ghos**) a variety of durra from which sugar is prepared (**sweet sorghum**, or Chinese sugarcane).

sori see **sorus**.

soricident, **soricine**, **soricoid** see under **sorex**.

sorites /sö-rī'tēz or sö-/ (*logic*) n a string of propositions in which the predicate of one is the subject of the next (or the same in reverse order); a sophistical puzzle on the model of 'How many grains make a heap?' [Gr *sōreitēs*, from *sōros* a heap]
■ **sorit'ic** or **sorit'ical** adj.

SORN abbrev: Statutory Off-Road Notification.

sorn /sörn/ (*Scot*) vi to obtrude oneself as an uninvited guest. [Obs Ir *sorthan* free quarters]
■ **sor'ner** n. **sorn'ing** n.

soroban /sö'rə-bän/ n a Japanese abacus. [From Jap, from Chin words meaning 'calculating board']

soroche /so-rō'chā/ n mountain sickness. [Sp, from Quechua *surúcht* antimony (present in the Andes and formerly believed to cause the sickness)]

Soroptimist /sə- or so-rop'ti-mist/ adj of an international organization of clubs for professional women. ◆ n a member of one of these clubs. [L *soror* sister, and **optimist**]

sororal /sor-ō'rəl, -ö'/ or **sororial** /-ri-əl/ adj sisterly; of, or of the nature of, a sister. [L *soror* sister]
■ **soro'rate** (or /sor'ər-āt/) n a custom that allows or requires marriage with a wife's sister. **soro'rially** adv. **sororicide** /-or'i-sīd/ n (L *caedere* to kill) the killing or killer of a sister. **sorority** /sor-or'i-ti/ n a sisterhood; a women's academic society (*N Am*). **sororize** or **-ise** /sor'ər-īz/ vi to associate in a sisterly way. **sorō'sis** n (*US*) a women's club.

sorosis[1] /so-, sö- or sə-rō'sis/ n a fleshy fruit formed from a crowd of flowers, as the pineapple. [Gr *sōros* a heap]

sorosis[2] see under **sororal**.

SORP (*account*) abbrev: Statement of Recommended Practice.

sorption /sörp'shən/ n absorption and/or adsorption.

sorra see **sorrow**.

sorrel[1] /sor'l/ n any of the acid-tasting species of herbs of the dock genus, *Rumex* (**common sorrel** *R. acetosa*; **sheep's sorrel** *R. acetosella*; **French** or **Roman sorrel** *R. scutatus*) or the related *Oxyria digyna* (**mountain sorrel**); applied also to other plants such as roselle and wood sorrel. [OFr *sorele, surele* (Fr *surelle*), from *sur* sour, from OHGer *sûr* (Ger *sauer*) sour]
❑ **sorrel tree** n the sourwood (qv).
■ **salts of sorrel** a very poisonous combination of potassium acid oxalate and oxalic acid.

sorrel[2] /sor'l/ adj reddish-brown or light chestnut. ◆ n a reddish-brown colour; a sorrel horse; (also **sorel** or **sorell** /sör'el or sör'/; *Shakesp*) a buck in its third year. [OFr *sorel*, from *sor* (Fr *saur, saure*) sorrel; poss LGer; cf **sore**[2]]

sorrow /sor'ō/ n grief, sadness; affliction; pain of mind; lamentation; a person or thing causing any such state of mind; the Devil (in imprecations, as an emphatic negative, and applied as a term of abuse; *Irish* **sorra**). ◆ vt and vi to grieve. [OE *sorg, sorh*; Ger *Sorge*, ON *sorg*]
■ **sorr'owed** adj (*Shakesp*) accompanied with sorrow. **sorr'ower** n. **sorr'owful** adj full of sorrow; causing, showing, or expressing sorrow; sad; dejected. **sorr'owfully** adv. **sorr'owfulness** n. **sorr'owing** n and adj. **sorr'owless** adj free from sorrow.
■ **drown one's sorrows** to become drunk in order to forget one's troubles.

sorry /sor'i/ adj (**sorr'ier**; **sorr'iest**) regretful; expressing pity, sympathy, etc; (often merely formally) apologetic; distressing; poor, miserable, wretchedly bad, contemptible, worthless. ◆ interj expressing (often slight) apology; (as a question) I beg your pardon?, what did you say? (*inf*). [OE *sārig* wounded, from *sār* pain; Du *zeerig*; infl in meaning by **sorrow**, but not connected in origin]
■ **sorr'ily** adv. **sorr'iness** n. **sorr'yish** adj.

sort /sört/ n a class, kind, or species; quality or rank; one, a specimen or instance, of a kind (often ungrammatically in the singular with *these* or *those*, to denote examples of this or that kind); something of the nature but not quite worthy of the name; the arranging of data or the product of this (*comput*); a letter, stop, or other character in a fount of type (*printing*); manner; a person (*inf*); a woman, *esp* an attractive one (*sl, orig Aust*); a company, group, collection, parcel (*obs*); a lot (in sortilege) (*Shakesp*). ◆ vt to separate into lots or classes; to group, classify, arrange; to pick out, select; to put in good order; to adjust, put to rights, attend to (*Scot*); to geld; to beat, punish (*inf*); to deal effectively with (*esp* in a vague threat) (*inf*); to provide (*Scot*); to procure (*Scot*); to allot, assign (*Shakesp*); to dispose (*Shakesp*); to befit (*rare*). ◆ *vi* to come about, turn out (*obs*); to fit, accord (*rare*); to agree (*Scot*); to consort (*dialect*). [L *sors, sortis* a lot, *sortīrī* to draw lots; partly through OFr]

■ **sort'able** *adj* capable of being sorted; assorted; suitable, befitting (*rare*). **sort'ance** *n* (*Shakesp*) suitableness, agreement. **sortā'tion** *n* a sorting out. **sort'ed** *adj* put into order; classified; well-organized or -equipped, *esp* with drugs (*sl*); well-balanced, *esp* emotionally (*inf*). **sort'er** *n* someone who (or something which) separates and arranges (eg letters). **sort'es** /-*ēz* or -*ās*/ *n pl* divination by chance opening of the Bible, Homer, Virgil, etc. **sort'ing** *n* and *adj*. **sorti'tion** *n* the casting of lots. **sort'ment** *n* a sorting out; an assortment.

❑ **sort code** *n* a sequence of numbers used to identify a bank and an account held at that bank. **sorting office** *n* a place where mail that has been posted is sorted by destination.

■ **after a sort** to some extent. **a good sort** a decent fellow. **in a sort** in a manner. **in some sort** in a way; as it were. **in sort** in a body (*Shakesp*); inasmuch (*Spenser*). **of a sort** or **of sorts** vague, rough, inexact; inferior. **out of sorts** out of order, slightly unwell; with some sorts of type in the fount exhausted (*printing*). **sort of** (*inf*; used adverbially and parenthetically) as it were; to an extent; rather. **sort out** to classify, separate, arrange, etc; to deal with, punish, etc. **that's your sort** that's right; well done; go on.

sortie /*sör*'ti/ *n* a sally from a besieged party to attack their besiegers; a raiding excursion; a flight by a military aircraft; a short return trip (*inf*). ◆ *vi* to sally. [Fr, from *sortir* to go out, to issue]

sortilege /*sör*'ti-lij/ *n* divination by drawing lots. [L *sortilegus* a diviner] ■ **sortil'eger** *n*. **sortil'egy** *n*.

sorus /*sō*'rəs or *sö*'/ (*bot*) *n* (*pl* **so'rī**) a cluster of sporangia or soredia. [Gr *sōros* a heap] ■ **so'ral** *adj*.

SOS /*es-ō-es*'/ *n* an appeal for help or rescue, *esp* at sea by Morse code (...−−−...). ◆ *vi* to make such an appeal. [Chosen for ease of transmission in Morse]

sosatie /*sə-sä*'ti/ *n* a S African dish of spiced or curried meat grilled on a skewer. [Afrik]

so-so, also **so so** /*sō*'sō/ *adj* neither very good nor very bad; tolerable; indifferent. ◆ *adv* tolerably well. [**so**[1]]

soss /*sos*/ (*dialect, esp Scot*) *n* a mess; a dish of sloppy food; a puddle; a heavy fall; a plump. ◆ *vt* to dirty; to slobber up; to throw carelessly about. ◆ *vi* to plump down; to splash about. ◆ *adv* plump. [Imit] ■ **soss'ing** *n*.

sostenuto /*sos-te-noo*'tō or -*nū*'/ (*music*) *adj* sustained. ◆ *adv* with full time allowed for each note. ◆ *n* (*pl* **sostenu'tos**) a piece played in this manner. [Ital]

SOT *abbrev* : stay-on tab (see under **stay**[1]).

sot[1] /*sot*/ *n* someone stupefied by alcohol; a habitual drunkard; a fool (*obs*). ◆ *vi* to be a sot. [OFr *sot*] ■ **sott'ed** *adj* besotted. **sott'ing** *n*. **sott'ish** *adj* like a sot; foolish; stupid with drink. **sott'ishly** *adv*. **sott'ishness** *n*.

sot[2] /*sot* or *sut*/ (*Scot*) *adv* the emphatic correlative of *not*, meaning on the contrary, etc, used to contradict a negative assertion. [Variant of **so**[1] infl by **not**]

Sotadic /*sō-tad*'ik/ or **Sotadean** /*sō-* or *so-tə-dē*'ən/ *adj* relating to *Sōtadēs*, a lascivious and scurrilous Greek poet (*fl* 276BC), or his writings, or his metre; coarse and scurrilous; palindromic. ◆ *n* a satire in his manner; a catalectic tetrameter of ionics *a majore* (see **Ionic**).

soterial /*sō-tē*'ri-əl/ (*theol*) *adj* relating to salvation. [Gr *sōtēriā* salvation, from *sōtēr* a saviour] ■ **sōtēriolog'ical** *adj*. **sōtēriol'ogy** *n* the doctrine of salvation.

Sothic /*soth*'ik or *sō*'thik/ *adj* of or relating to Sirius. [Egyptian name of Sirius, given in Gr as *Sōthis*] ❑ **Sothic period** or **cycle** *n* a period of 1460 years, after which the beginning of the Egyptian year of 365 days again coincides with the beginning of the **Sothic year**, which was reckoned from the heliacal rising of Sirius.

Sotho /*soo*'tŭ or *sō*'tō/ *n* see **Basotho**.

sotted, etc see under **sot**[1].

sottisier /*so-tē-zyä*'/ *n* a collection of jokes, ridiculous remarks, quotes, etc. [Fr, from *sottise* folly]

sotto voce /*sot*'tō vō'che/ *adv* in an undertone or aside. [Ital, below the voice]

sou /*soo*/ *n* a French five-centime piece (*hist*); a tiny amount of money. [Fr, from L *solidus*; cf **sold**[2], **soldier**, **soldo**]

souari or **saouari** /*sow-ä*'ri/ *n* a tropical American tree (genus *Caryocar*) yielding a durable timber and edible butternuts. [Fr *saouari*, from Galibi] ❑ **soua'ri-nut** or **saoua'ri-nut** see **butternut** under **butter**[1].

soubise /*soo-bēz*'/ *n* an 18c cravat; a sauce made from, or a side dish of, puréed onions. [Fr, after the French Marshal Prince de *Soubise* (1715–87)]

soubrette /*soo-bret*'/ *n* a pert, coquettish, intriguing maidservant in comedy (*theatre*); a singer of light songs of similar character; a maidservant, lady's maid. [Fr, from Provençal *soubreto* (fem), coy]

soubriquet see **sobriquet**.

souce, **souct** old spellings (*Spenser* and *Shakesp*) of **souse**[2], **soused**.

souchong /*soo-shong*' or *soo-chong*'/ *n* a fine sort of black China tea. [Chin *xiǎo* small, and *zhǒng* sort]

Soudanese same as **Sudanese**.

souffle /*soo*'fl/ (*med*) *n* a murmuring sound heard in auscultation. [Fr]

soufflé /*soo*'flā/ *n* a light dish, properly one made with eggwhites whisked into a froth. ◆ *adj* prepared in this style. [Fr, pap of *souffler*, from L *sufflāre* to blow]

sough[1] /*sow* or *suf*, or (*Scot*) *sŭhh*/ *vi* to sigh, as the wind does. ◆ *vt* to whine out; to sigh out; to hum. ◆ *n* a sighing of the wind; a deep sigh; a vague rumour; a whining tone of voice. [OE *swōgan* to rustle] ■ **keep a calm sough** to keep quiet.

sough[2] /*suf*/ *n* a drain, sewer, adit. [Cf Flem dialect *zoeg* a small ditch] ❑ **sough'ing-tile** *n* a drain-tile.

sought /*söt*/ *pat* and *pap* of **seek**.

souk /*sook*/ *n* in Muslim countries, a marketplace (also **suk**, **sukh** or **suq**). [Ar *sūq*]

soukous /*soo*'koos/ *n* a form of Central African dance music, originating in the Democratic Republic of Congo, heavily influenced by Latin American rhythms. [From Fr *secouer* to shake]

soul /*sōl*/ *n* that element of a being which thinks, feels, desires, etc, regarded by some as distinct from the physical, material form, and as immortal; a spirit, embodied or disembodied; the ego; innermost being or nature; moral and emotional nature, power, or sensibility; nobleness of spirit or its sincere expression; a complete embodiment or exemplification; the essential part; essence; an element; an indwelling or animating principle; the moving spirit, inspirer, leader; a person (*inf*); the lungs of a goose, etc; a violin sound-post; (also **soul music**) the popular music *orig* and *esp* of black Americans, typically emotional and earthy, a blend of blues, jazz, gospel and pop elements; life (*obs*). ◆ *adj* of or relating to soul music; of or characteristic of black Americans or their food, music, culture, etc. ◆ *interj* by or upon my soul. [OE *sāwol*; Ger *Seele*] ■ **souled** *adj* having a soul, *esp*, in compounds, of this or that kind. **soul'ful** *adj* having or expressive of deep or elevated feeling or emotion. **soul'fully** *adv*. **soul'fulness** *n*. **soul'less** *adj* without a soul; (of a person) lacking animation, spirit, or nobleness of mind; (of a place, etc) empty, lifeless, bleak; (of a job) mechanical, dehumanized. **soul'lessly** *adv* in a soulless manner. **soul'lessness** *n*. ❑ **soul brother** or **sister** *n* a fellow black person. **soul'-confirming** *adj* (*Shakesp*) ratifying the devoting of the soul. **soul'-cūrer** *n* (*Shakesp*) a parson. **soul'-destroying** *adj* (of a task, situation, etc) extremely monotonous, unrewarding, etc. **soul'-fearing** *adj* (*Shakesp*) terrifying the soul. **soul food** *n* (*US inf*) food such as chitterlings, cornbread, etc, traditionally eaten by African Americans of the Southern states. **soul'-force** *n* (a term for) satyagraha. **soul'-killing** *adj* (*Shakesp*). **soul mate** *n* a person to whom one is deeply emotionally or spiritually attached. **soul music** see **soul** (*n*) above. **soul patch** *n* (*inf*) a tuft of beard beneath the lower lip. **soul'-search'ing** *n* a critical examination of one's actions, motives, etc (also *adj*). **soul'-shot, -scot** or **-scat** *n* a payment to the church on behalf of a dead person, a funeral payment. **soul'-sick** *adj* morally diseased. **soul sister** see **soul brother** above. **soul'-sleeper** *n* a psychopannychist. **soul'-stirring** *adj*. ■ **upon my soul!** an exclamation of surprise, etc.

souldan an old form of **soldan**.

souldier an old spelling of **soldier**.

soum or **sowm** /*sŭm*/ (*Scot*) *n* the proportion of sheep or cattle suitable for any pasture; pasture for one cow or its equivalent in sheep, etc. ◆ *vt* and *vi* to determine in terms of soums. [Form of **sum**[1]] ■ **soum'ing** *n*.

■ **souming and rouming** the determination of the number of soums appropriate to a common pasture, and their apportionment (according to ability to supply fodder through winter) to the various roums or holdings.

sound[1] /*sownd*/ *n* the sensation of hearing; a transmitted disturbance perceived or perceptible by the ear, *esp* a tone produced by regular vibrations, *opp* to *noise*; mere noise, without meaning or sense or distinguished from sense; a mental impression; quality or level of noise; a particular type or quality of music; (in *pl*) music, *esp* popular (*inf*); spoken commentary, music, etc accompanying visual material such as filmed news footage (*broadcasting* and *cinematog*); radio, as opposed to television (*broadcasting*); earshot. ◆ *vi* to give out a sound; to resound; to be audible; to be sounded; to be famed; to give an impression on hearing; to call, as by trumpet; to tend (*obs*). ◆ *vt* to cause to make a sound; to produce, utter or make the sound of; to utter audibly; to pronounce; to announce, publish, proclaim, celebrate, signal or direct by sound; to mean (*obs*); to examine by percussion and listening (see also **sound³**); to tease, goad, provoke (*US sl*). [ME *soun*, from Anglo-Fr, from L *sonus*; for *d* cf **pound³**]

■ **sound'er** *n* that which sounds; a telegraph-receiving instrument in which Morse signals are translated into sound signals. **sound'ing** *n* emission of sound; a signal by trumpet, bell, alarm, etc; examination by percussion. ◆ *adj* making a sound; sonorous; resounding; having a magnificent sound. **sound'ingly** *adv*. **sound'less** *adj*. **sound'lessly** *adv*.

❏ **sound'-alike** *n* a person whose voice closely resembles that of another person. **sound barrier** *n* (*aeronautics*) a resistance met at or about the speed of sound when power required to increase speed rises steeply. **sound'bite** or **sound bite** *n* a brief memorable phrase used by someone, *esp* a politician, when being interviewed on television or radio. **sound'board** *n* a thin resonating plate of wood or metal in a musical instrument; (in an organ) the apparatus that conveys the air from the wind chest to the appropriate pipes; a sounding board. **sound boarding** *n* boards between joists carrying pugging to make a floor soundproof. **sound body** *n* a resonance box. **sound bow** *n* the thick edge of a bell, against which the hammer strikes. **sound'box** *n* a resonance box; part of a gramophone supporting the diaphragm. **sound broadcasting** or **radio** *n* broadcasting by radio as opposed to television. **sound card** *n* a printed circuit board that enables a computer to produce enhanced sound effects. **sound'-carrier** *n* a medium, such as a record, tape or compact disc, on which sound is recorded. **sound'check** *n* a check or test made on sound equipment prior to its use at a concert or for recording. **sound effects** *n pl* sounds other than dialogue or music used in films, radio and television. **sound engineer** *n* (*broadcasting*, etc) one responsible for sound. **sound film** *n* a cinema film with a synchronized soundtrack. **sound hole** *n* an *f*-shaped hole in the belly of a stringed musical instrument. **sounding board** *n* a structure for carrying a speaker's voice towards the audience; a soundboard; any person, object or institution used to test the acceptability or effectiveness of an idea, plan, etc. **sound'man** *n* a member of a television or film crew whose job it is to record sound. **sound mixer** *n* the person who controls the tone and volume of sound(s) to be recorded for a motion picture, musical recording, etc; the machine used in performing this task. **sound poem** *n* a poem consisting of a series of euphonic syllables. **sound poet** *n*. **sound post** *n* a short post connecting the belly and back of a violin, etc under the bridge. **sound'proof** *adj* impenetrable by sound. ◆ *vt* to render soundproof. **sound'proofing** *n*. **sound radio** see **sound broadcasting** above. **sound ranging** *n* (*acoustics*) the calculation of position by timing the arrival of sound waves from (three or more) known positions. **sound'scape** *n* *esp* in pop music, a mixture of sounds producing an overall effect. **sound'seeing** *n* listening to a recording of sounds from a distant place, eg on a podcast, to gain an impression of it. **sound shadow** *n* a region of silence behind a barrier to sound. **sound shift** *n* a series of regular changes in stop-consonants differentiating Germanic from other Indo-European languages, or (*second shift*) High German from other Germanic. **sound spectrogram** *n* a record produced by a **sound spectrograph**, an electronic instrument which makes a graphic representation of the qualities of a sound, eg frequency, intensity, etc. **sound spectrography** *n*. **sound stage** *n* the soundproof area of a motion-picture studio on which the actors perform and sets are built. **sound system** *n* an electronic system, *incl* amplifier, speakers and one or more devices for playing recorded sound; a highly sophisticated or accessorized music system, eg a mobile disco. **sound therapy** *n* a therapeutic technique based on sound, using both its rhythmic patterns and its frequencies. **sound'track** *n* (on a cinema film) the magnetic tape on which sounds are recorded; a recording of the sound (*esp* musical) accompaniment to a film. **sound wave** *n* a longitudinal disturbance propagated through air or other medium.

■ **sound off** (**about** or **on**) to speak loudly and freely (about or on), *esp* in complaint; to boast (about).

sound² /*sownd*/ *adj* safe; whole; uninjured, unimpaired; in good condition; healthy; wholesome; (of sleep) deep; whole or solid; (of eg a beating) thorough; well-founded; well-grounded; trustworthy; of the right way of thinking, orthodox; excellent (*inf*). ◆ *adv* soundly, completely fast (as in sleep). [OE *gesund*; Ger *gesund*]

■ **sound'ly** *adv*. **sound'ness** *n*.

■ **sound as a bell** see under **bell¹**.

sound³ /*sownd*/ *vt* to measure the depth of; to probe; to examine with a sound (*med*); to try to discover the inclinations, thoughts, etc of (*esp* with *out*). ◆ *vi* to take soundings; to dive deep (of eg a whale). ◆ *n* (*med*) a probe for examining the bladder, etc. [OE *sund-* (in

compounds), cf **sound⁴**; or perh OFr *sonder* to sound, which may be from Gmc]

■ **sound'er** *n* a person who sounds; apparatus for taking soundings. **sound'ing** *n* the action of something which or someone who sounds; an ascertained depth; (in *pl*) waters in which an ordinary sounding line will reach the bottom; a test or measurement of depth, *esp* of water by means of an echo-sounder or sounding line; penetrating a particular environment to obtain sample readings, eg of temperature; (*usu* in *pl*; also with *out*) sample testing of opinion, inclination, etc, *usu* of an unofficial kind.

❏ **sounding lead** *n* the weight at the end of a sounding line. **sounding line** *n* a line with a plummet at the end for soundings. **sounding rocket** *n* a rocket devised to gather high-altitude meteorological data and to radio it back to earth. **sounding rod** *n* a rod for measuring water in a ship's hold.

sound⁴ /*sownd*/ *n* a strait; an inlet of the sea; a fish's swimming bladder. [OE *sund* swimming]

sound⁵ /*sownd*/ (*obs*) *n* and *vi* same as **swoon**.

sounder /*sown'dər*/ *n* a herd of pigs; a young boar. [OFr *sundre*; of Gmc origin; cf OE *sunor*]

soup /*soop*/ *n* any liquid food made by stewing pieces of meat, vegetables or grains; loosely, anything resembling soup in consistency, etc; a photographic developer (*inf*); stolen plate melted down (*sl*); nitroglycerine (*US inf*). [OFr *soupe*; cf **sop**]

■ **soup'er** *n* in Ireland, someone who dispenses soup as a means of proselytizing; a person really or supposedly converted in this way. **soup'y** *adj*.

❏ **souped'-up** *adj* (*sl*) (of eg an engine) having had the power increased; enlivened. **soup kitchen** *n* a place for supplying soup to the poor; a mobile kitchen (*milit*). **soup maigre** (or **meagre**) *n* a thin fish or vegetable soup, originally for fast-days. **soup plate** *n* a large deep plate for serving soup. **soup run** *n* a regular journey by charity workers to a place where they can supply hot food and drinks to the needy. **soup'spoon** *n* a spoon with a large, rounded bowl for taking soup. **soup'-ticket** *n* a ticket entitling someone to eat at a soup kitchen. **soup tureen** *n*.

■ **in the soup** (*inf*) in difficulties or trouble. **soup up** (*sl*) to increase the power of; to enliven. **the ticket for soup** (*sl*) exactly the right thing.

soupçon /*soop-son'* or *-sɔ̃'*/ *n* a hardly perceptible quantity, a dash. [Fr, suspicion]

souple¹ /*soo'pl*/ *adj* a dialect form of **supple¹**; (of silk) lightly scoured; clever (*Scot*). ◆ *vt* to make supple or souple.

souple² /*soo'pl*/ *n* a Scots form of **swipple**; a cudgel (*Walter Scott*).

sour /*sowr*/ *adj* having an acid taste or smell; turned, rancid or fermented; rank; (of animals) heavy, strong; cold and wet; embittered, crabbed, or peevish; disagreeable; inharmonious (*lit* and *fig*); bad, unsuccessful; containing sulphur compounds; (of soil) lacking in lime and thus unfruitful for crops. ◆ *vt* to make sour; to treat with dilute acid. ◆ *vi* to become sour. ◆ *n* an acid drink, such as a gin or whisky cocktail that contains lemon or lime juice; an acid solution used in bleaching, curing skins, etc. [OE *sūr*; Ger *sauer*, ON *sūrr*]

■ **sour'ing** *n* the process of turning or becoming sour; vinegar; the crab-apple; treatment with dilute acid in bleaching. **sour'ish** *adj*. **sour'ishly** *adv*. **sour'ly** *adv*. **sour'ness** *n*.

❏ **sour'-cold** *adj* (*Shakesp*). **sour cream** *n* cream soured by a ferment. **sour'-crout** see **sauerkraut**. **sour'dough** *n* leaven; a piece of dough reserved to leaven a new batch; bread made in this way; in Canada and Alaska, an old-timer. **sour'-eyed** *adj* morose-looking. **sour gas** *n* (*mining*) natural gas containing impurities, mainly hydrogen sulphide. **sour'-gourd** *n* the cream of tartar tree; a tropical grass related to millet; sorrel. **sour grapes** see under **grape¹**. **sour mash** *n* (*US*) new mash mixed with old to increase acidity and promote fermentation; whiskey made in this way. **sour'puss** *n* (*inf*) a sour-tempered person. **sour'wood** *n* a deciduous tree of eastern N America (*Oxydendrum arboreum*) with acid-tasting leaves, the sorrel tree.

source /*sōrs* or *sörs*/ *n* a spring; the head of a stream; an origin; a rise; (*Spenser* **sourse**) *perh* a surging; an originating cause; something from which anything rises or originates; a book or document serving as authority for history, or furnishing matter or inspiration for an author; any person, publication, etc providing information. ◆ *vt* (in *passive*) to come from, originate; to obtain (from a particular source). [OFr *sorse* (Fr *source*), from *sourdre*, from L *surgere* to rise]

■ **sourc'ing** *n*.

❏ **source'book** *n* a book of original documents for (*esp* historic) study. **source code** *n* a computer code that requires translation by a compiler before it can be executed by the computer (cf **object code**).

sourdeline /*soor'də-lēn*/ *n* a small bagpipe. [Fr]

sourdine /*soor-dēn'*/ (*music*) *n* a mute or sordino. [Fr; cf **sordino** under **sordo**]

sourock /*soo'rək*/ (*Scot*) *n* sorrel (the plant). [**sour**]

sourse see **source**.

soursop /sow'ər-sop/ n a West Indian tree (*Annona muricata*); its large, sour, pulpy fruit. [**sour** and **sop**]

sousaphone /soo'zə-fōn/ n a large type of tuba, named after the American bandmaster and composer JP *Sousa* (1854–1932).

sous-chef /soo'shef/ n a chef next in rank to the head chef in a hotel, restaurant, etc. [Fr *sous* under, and **chef**]

souse[1] or **sous** /sows/ (*obs*) n (pl **souse** or **sous'es**) same as **sou**.

souse[2] /sows/ vt to pickle; to marinade and cook in spiced wine or vinegar; to plunge, immerse or duck; to drench or soak; to make drunk; to dash; to fling down; to smite; to swoop down upon. ◆ vi to be drenched or soaked; to wash oneself thoroughly; to get drunk; to strike; to impinge; to fall heavily; to swoop like a hawk. ◆ n pickled meat, esp pig's feet or ears; an ear (*dialect* or *facetious*); pickling liquid; a plunge in pickling or other liquid; a ducking or drenching; a wash; a sluicing with water; an act of getting drunk (*inf*); a drunkard (*US*); a heavy blow or fall; a thump; an impact; a rising from the ground, taking wing (in the falconer's phrase *at souse*, *at the souse*, when the hawk gets a chance of striking); hence, the downward swoop of a bird of prey. ◆ adv with a plunge; with a heavy impact; plump; suddenly. —Also **souce**, **sowce**, **sowse**, **sowsse** in old writers. [Partly OFr *sous*, *souce*, from OHGer *sulza*, from the root of **salt**[1]; partly imit (cf German *Saus*); partly **source** in its old sense of rising] ■ **soused** adj pickled; very wet; drunk (*inf*). **sous'ing** n and adj.

souslik same as **suslik**.

sou-sou see **susu**.

sous-vide /soo-vēd'/ adj of or relating to a cookery method in which food is vacuum-packed in a plastic bag before being cooked in a water bath. [Fr *sous* under, and *vide* vacuum]

sout (*Spenser*) same as **soot**[1].

soutache /soo-tāsh'/ n a narrow braid used for trimming. [Fr]

soutane /soo-tän'/ n a cassock. [Fr, from Ital *sottana*, from L *subtus* beneath]

soutar see **souter**.

souteneur /soot'nær/ n a prostitute's bully or exploiter. [Fr, supporter, protector; cf **sustain**]

souter /soo'tər/ (*Scot*) n a shoemaker, a cobbler (also **sow'ter** or **sou'tar**). [OFr *sūtere* (ON *sūtari*), from L *sūtor*, from *suere* to sew] ■ **sou'terly** adj. □ **souter's clod** n (*Walter Scott*) a brown wheaten roll.

souterrain /soo-te-rē'* or *soo'tə-rān/ n an underground chamber; an earth-house. [Fr]

south /sowth/ n the point of the horizon or that pole of the earth or sky which at equinox is towards the sun at noon in Europe or elsewhere on the same side of the equator, or opposite the sun in the other hemisphere; one of the four cardinal points of the compass; (often with *cap* and *the*) the south part of the earth or of a region, country or town; (with *cap* and *the*) the part of the USA lying south of Pennsylvania and the Ohio River, esp those states south of the Mason-Dixon line during the civil war; (*usu* with *cap*) in bridge, the player or position occupying the place designated 'south' on the table; the south wind (*poetic*). ◆ adj situated towards the south; forming the part that is towards the south; (of wind) blowing from the south; (of a pole of a magnet) *usu* turning to the south. ◆ adv towards the south. ◆ vi /sowdh/ (*archaic*) to turn or move south; to cross the meridian. [OE *sūth*; ON *suthr*] ■ **souther** /sowdh'ər/ n a south wind or gale. ◆ vi /sudh'ər/ to move or veer towards the south. **southering** /sudh'/ adj. **southerliness** /sudh'/ n. **southerly** /sudh'/ adj situated in the south; towards the south; (esp of the wind) coming from the south. ◆ adv on the south; towards the south; from the south. ◆ n a south wind. **southern** /sudh'/ adj situated in the south or further to the south; coming from the south; towards the south; connected with the south; living in the south; (with *cap*) of, from or relating to the South. ◆ n a southerner. **southerner** /sudh'/ n (sometimes with *cap*) a native or inhabitant of the south, esp of the southern USA or the southern counties of England. **southernism** /sudh'/ n a form of expression or characteristic peculiar to the south, esp the Southern states of the USA. **southernize** or **-ise** /sudh'/ vt to give a southern character to. **southernly** /sudh'/ adj southerly. ◆ adv towards the south. **southernmost** /sudh'/ or **southmost** /sowth'/, also (*obs*) **south'ermost** adj situated furthest south. **southing** /sowdh'/ n distance, deviation, tendency or motion to the south; meridian passage. **southron**, **Southron** or **Southroun** /sudh'rən/ adj (*Scot*) southern, esp English as distinguished from Scots. ◆ n a southerner; an Englishman; the English of England. **southward** /sowth'wərd/ or (*naut*) *sudh'ərd*/ adv towards the south (also adj and n). **south'wardly** adv and adj. **south'wards** adv southward. □ **south'about** adv towards the south. **South African** adj of or relating to the Republic of South Africa, or its people. ◆ n a native or citizen of South Africa. **south'bound** adj travelling in a southward

direction. **south'-by-east'** n the direction midway between south and south-south-east. **south'-by-west'** n the direction midway between south and south-south-west. **south-east'** (or /sowth'/) n the direction midway between south and east; the region lying in that direction; the wind blowing from that direction. ◆ adj and adv in or towards the south-east; (of a wind) from the south-east. **south-east'-by-east'** n the direction midway between south-east and east-south-east. **south-east'-by-south'** n the direction midway between south-east and south-south-east. **south-east'er** n a strong wind from the south-east. **south-east'erly** adj situated in the south-east; towards the south-east; (esp of the wind) coming from the south-east. ◆ adv on the south-east; towards the south-east; from the south-east. ◆ n a south-east wind. **south-east'ern** adj situated in the south-east or further to the south-east; coming from the south-east; towards the south-east; connected with the south-east; living in the south-east. **south-east'ward** adv towards the south-east (also adj and n). **south-east'wardly** adv and adj. **south-east'wards** adv south-eastward. **Southern Comfort**® n a whisky liqueur originally produced in the southern USA. **Southern Cross** n a conspicuous southern constellation with four bright stars placed crosswise. **southern hemisphere** n (also with *caps*) the hemisphere of the world which is south of the equator. **southern lights** n pl the aurora australis. **southernwood** /sudh'/ n an aromatic S European shrub (*Artemisia abrotanum*), of the wormwood genus. **south'land** n the south (also adj). **south'lander** n. **south'paw** adj (*inf*) left-handed; (in boxing) leading with the right hand. ◆ n (*inf*) a left-handed person, esp in sport; a boxer who leads with his right hand. **south polar** adj. **south pole** n the end of the earth's axis in Antarctica; its projection on the celestial sphere (*astron*); (*usu*) that pole of a magnet which when free points to the earth's south magnetic pole (logically the other end). **South Sea** or **Seas** n the Pacific Ocean. **south'-seeking** adj turning towards the earth's magnetic south pole. **south'-south-east'** n the direction midway between south and south-east (also adj and adv). **south'-south-west'** n the direction midway between south and south-west (also adj and adv). **south-west'** or (*archaic* or *poetic*) **sou'-west** /sowth'* or *sow'/, also *-west'/ n the direction midway between south and west; the region lying in that direction; the wind blowing from that direction. ◆ adj and adv in or towards the south-west; (of a wind) from the south-west. **south-west'-by-south'** n the direction midway between south-west and south-south-west. **south-west'-by-west'** n the direction midway between south-west and west-south-west. **south-west'er** n a strong wind from the south-west (see also separate entry **sou'wester**). **south-west'erly** adj situated in the south-west; towards the south-west; (esp of the wind) coming from the south-west. ◆ adv on the south-west; towards the south-west; from the south-west. ◆ n a south-west wind. **south-west'ern** adj situated in the south-west or further to the south-west; coming from the south-west; towards the south-west; connected with the south-west; living in the south-west. **south-west'ward** adv towards the south-west (also adj and n). **south-west'wardly** adv and adj. **south-west'wards** adv south-westward.

Southcottian /sowth-kot'i-ən/ n a follower of Joanna *Southcott* (1750–1814) who was expected to give birth to a Shiloh or Prince of Peace (also adj).

Southdown /sowth'down/ adj relating to the *South Downs* in Hampshire and Sussex, the famous breed of sheep so named, or their mutton. ◆ n a sheep of this breed, or its mutton.

southerly, **southern**, etc see under **south**.

Southern blot /sudh'ərn blot/ (*biol*) n a technique for the separation and identification of DNA fragments. [From its pioneer, EM *Southern* (born 1938), British molecular biologist]

southsay, etc same as **soothsay**, etc (see under **sooth**).

souvenir /soo'və-nēr* or *-nēr'/ n a memento; an item kept as a reminder of a place, occasion, etc. ◆ vt (*orig Aust* and *NZ*; *inf*) to collect as a 'souvenir', to steal, purloin. [Fr *souvenir*, from L *subvenīre* to come up, to come to mind, from *sub* under, and *venīre* to come]

souvlaki /soov-lä'kē/ or **souvlakia** /-ki-a/ n (pl **souvla'ki** or **souvla'kia**) a Greek dish of lamb, similar to a shish kebab. [Gr *soublāki*, pl *soublākia*, dimin of *soúbla* a skewer]

sou'wester /sow-wes'tər/ n a gale from the south-west (*inf*; esp *naut*); a waterproof hat with a large flap at the back of the neck, as worn by seamen. [Orig *southwester*]

sov see **sovereign**.

sovenance /soo'və-näns/ (*archaic*) n remembrance, memory. [OFr *sovenance* (Fr *souvenance*), from *so(u)venir*, see **souvenir**]

sovereign /sov'rin* or *sov'rən/ n a supreme ruler or head; a monarch; an Irish mayor (*obs*); a gold coin (from the time of Henry VII to Charles I worth 22s. 6d. to 10s., from 1817 to 1914 a pound sterling; *inf* short form **sov** /sov/). ◆ adj supreme; excelling all others; having supreme power residing in itself, himself or herself; of sovereignty; highly efficacious. [OFr *sovrain* and Ital *sovrano*, from L *super* above]

■ **sov'ereignly** adv supremely; as a sovereign. **sov'ereigntist** adj (in Canadian politics) favouring devolution of sovereignty to a province or provinces. **sov'ereignty** n pre-eminence; supreme and independent power; self-government; the territory of a sovereign or of a sovereign state.
□ **sovereign debt** n money owed by the government of a country.

soviet /sō'vi-ət or sov'yet/ n a council, esp one of those forming the machinery of local and national government in the former Union of Soviet Socialist Republics, the local councils elected by workers, peasants, and soldiers, the higher councils consisting of deputies from the lower; (with cap) a citizen of the former USSR. ◆ adj (with cap) of or relating to the USSR. [Russ sovét council]
■ **soviet'ic** adj. **so'vietism** n the principles and practices of a soviet government, specif communism; a characteristic mannerism indicative of soviet ideology. **so'vietize** or **-ise** vt to transform to the soviet model. **Sovietolog'ical** adj (also without cap). **Sovietol'ogist** n (also without cap) a person making a special study of the theory and practice of government in the USSR and of Soviet affairs.
■ **Supreme Soviet** see under **supreme**.

sovran /sov'ran/ n an archaic and poetic form of **sovereign**.
■ **sov'ranly** adv. **sov'ranty** n.

sow[1] /sō/ vt (pat sowed /sōd/; pap sown /sōn/ or sowed) to scatter on, or put in, the ground; to plant by scattering; to scatter seed over; to spread, strew, disseminate. ◆ vi to scatter seed for growth. [OE sāwan; Ger säen, ON sā, Gothic saian]
■ **sow'er** n. **sow'ing** n.
■ **sow the seeds of** to initiate or implant.

sow[2] /sow/ n a female pig; the female of various other animals, eg the badger; an abusive term for a fat, lazy, greedy, or sluttish person, esp a woman; a main channel for molten iron, leading to metal pigs (qv); the metal solidified there; a movable shed for protecting besiegers (milit hist). [OE sū, sugu; Ger Sau, ON syr; L sūs, Gr hȳs]
□ **sow'back** n (geol) same as **hogback** (see under **hog**[1]). **sow'bread** n a cyclamen, esp Cyclamen europaeum, so called because its tubers are eaten by pigs. **sow bug** n (N Am) a woodlouse. **sow'-drunk** adj (obs inf) extremely and inhumanly drunk. **sow'-skin** n and adj. **sow thistle** n a thistle-like genus of plants (Sonchus) with milky juice, yellow flowers and prickly leaves.

sowans see **sowens**.

sowar /sō-wär'/ (Anglo-Ind) n an Indian trooper, mounted policeman, or attendant. [Urdu sawār horseman]
■ **sowarr'y** or **sowarr'ee** n a mounted retinue, cavalcade.

sowce see **souse**[2].

sowens or **sowans** /sō'ənz/ (Scot) n pl a dish made from the fine meal remaining among the husks of oats, flummery. [Supposed to be from Gaelic sùghan the liquid of sowens, from sùgh juice]

sowf, sowff see **sowth**.

sowl, sowle see **sole**[4].

sowm see **soum**.

sownd[1] /sownd/ (Spenser) vt appar, to wield.

sownd[2] /sownd/ (Spenser) n same as **swoon**.

sowne /sown/ (Spenser) n same as **sound**[1].

sowp /sowp/ (Scot) n a spoonful, sip, small drink. [ON saup; cf **sop**, **sup**]

sowse or **sowsse** /sows/ (Spenser; Shakesp) v and n same as **souse**[2].

sowter see **souter**.

sowth /sowth/ (Scot) vi and vt to whistle or hum over softly (also **sowf** or **sowff** /sowf/). [Scot forms of obs solf, from Fr solfier to sol-fa]

sox /soks/ n pl an informal spelling of **socks**.

soy /soi/ or **soya** /sō'yə or soi'ə/, also **soja** /sō'yə or sō'jə/ n a dark, salty sauce made from fermented soy beans and wheat flour (also **soy** (or **soya**) **sauce**); the soy bean, rich in oil and protein; the E Asiatic papilionaceous plant (Glycine soja, Glycine hispida or max) producing it. ◆ adj made from soy beans or soy flour. [Jap shō-yu, colloquial form soy, Du soya, soja, from Chin jiàng yóu soy sauce]
□ **soya milk** n a liquid made from soy flour and water, used as a substitute for cow's milk. **soy** (or **soya**) **bean** n. **soy** (or **soya**) **flour** n.

soyle /soil/ (Spenser) n apparently body or prey. [Unexplained]

Soyuz /sō'yooz/ n a vehicle used by the former USSR for ferrying crews to and from its orbiting space stations. [Russ soyuz union]

soz /soz/ interj (sl) sorry.

sozzle /soz'l/ vt (N Am and dialect) to splash; to make sloppy; to intoxicate; to perform sluttishly. ◆ n (N Am and dialect) slops; sluttishness; a slattern. [Cf **soss**]
■ **sozz'led** adj (inf) drunk. **sozz'ly** adj (N Am and dialect) sloppy.

SP abbrev: starting price.

sp abbrev: sine prole (L), without issue.

sp. abbrev: special; species (pl **spp.**); spelling.

SPA abbrev: Special Protection Area.

spa /spä, formerly spö/ n a mineral spring; a resort where such a spring is located; an establishment offering steam baths and other health treatments; a heated bath or pool of aerated water (also **spa bath** or **pool**); a device which circulates water or some other solution in which parts of the body may be immersed or bathed, such as a foot spa. ◆ vi to stay at a spa. [Spa in Belgium]
■ **spa'ing** n.
□ **spa town** n.

SPAB abbrev: Society for the Protection of Ancient Buildings.

space /spās/ n that in which material bodies have extension; a portion of such; room; intervening distance; an interval; an open or empty place; regions remote from the earth; an interval between lines or words; a type used for making such an interval (printing); an interval between the lines of the stave (music); a portion, extent, or interval of time; a short time; an individual's immediate environment for personal activity (see also **personal space** under **personal**); opportunity or leisure to do what one wants (inf); see also **mark/space ratio** under **mark**[1]. ◆ vt to make, arrange, or increase intervals between. ◆ vi (Spenser) to walk about. [Fr espace, from L spatium; Gr spaein to draw]
■ **spaced** adj. **space'less** adj. **spac'er** n someone who, or something which, spaces; an instrument for reversing a telegraphic current; a space bar; a space traveller or spacecraft (sci-fi); a space plate (see below). **spacey** see **spacy** below. **spacial** /spā'shl/ adj spatial. **spacing** /spās'ing/ n a space or spatial arrangement; the existence or arrangement of spaces, or of objects in spaces. **spacious** /spā'shəs/ adj of a great extent or area; ample; roomy; wide; broad in scope. **spa'ciously** adv. **spa'ciousness** n. **spac'y** or **spac'ey** adj (sl; chiefly N Am) dreamy; behaving as if spaced out; eccentric, unconventional.
□ **space age** n the present time when exploration of, and ability to travel in, space up to the limit of and beyond the earth's atmosphere are increasing. **space'-age** adj characteristic of the space age; very modern, up-to-date, using sophisticated modern technology. **space band** n a wedge for justifying the line in mechanical typesetting. **space bar** n a bar on a typewriter or computer keyboard which is pressed to insert a space. **space blanket** n a light plastic aluminium-coated cover used to wrap climbers, runners, etc in order to prevent loss of body heat. **space'borne** adj carried through space; effected or operated in space. **space cadet** n a trainee spaceman or spacewoman; a space-travel enthusiast; a person (acting as if) habitually high on drugs (inf). **space capsule** n a spacecraft, or a part of one, that houses the crew and instruments in a self-contained unit. **space charge** n a net electric charge distributed through a finite volume. **space'craft** n a vehicle, manned or unmanned, designed for putting into space, orbiting the earth, or reaching other planets. **space'faring** adj concerned with or engaged in space travel (also n). **space heater** n a device which warms the air in a room or similar enclosed area. **space-heat'ing** n. **Space Invaders**® n an early computer game, involving 'shooting' at graphic representations of supposed invaders from outer space. **space lattice** n an arrangement of points in three-dimensional space at the intersections of equally spaced parallel lines, such as the arrangement of atoms in a crystal disclosed by X-ray spectroscopy. **space'man** or **space'woman** n a traveller in space. **space medicine** n the branch of medicine concerned with effects of conditions in space on the human body. **space opera** n a science fiction film, novel, etc. **space'plane** n a craft (eg HOTOL and the space shuttle) designed to take off like a plane, enter into space orbit (eg to deliver payloads) and return to earth landing horizontally like a glider. **space platform** or **space station** n a platform in space planned as an observatory and/or a landing stage in space travel. **space'port** n a place from which spacecraft are launched. **space probe** n a spacecraft designed to obtain, and usu transmit, information about the environment into which it is sent. **spacer plate** n (archaeol) a flat bead, eg of jet or amber, with several parallel holes, for separating the threads of a multi-string necklace. **space'ship** n a spacecraft. **space shuttle** n a spacecraft designed to transport men and materials to and from space stations, in-orbit experiments, satellite repair, etc. **space station** see **space platform** above. **space'suit** n a suit specially designed for use in space travel. **space-time**[1] n normal three-dimensional space plus dimension of time, modified by gravity in relativity theory. **space-time continuum** n physical space or reality, regarded as having four dimensions (length, breadth, height and time) in which an event can be represented as a point fixed by four co-ordinates. **space travel** n. **space traveller** n. **space travelling** n. **space vehicle** see under **vehicle**. **space walk** n an excursion by an astronaut outside his or her craft while in space. **space'-walk** vi. **spacewoman** see **spaceman** above. **space writer** n a writer paid according to the space filled. **spacious times** n pl days of expansion (in knowledge, trade, etc) and scope (for discovery, adventure, and the like), as in the reign of Queen Elizabeth I.

■ **spaced out** (*sl*) in a dazed or stupefied state (as if) caused by the taking of drugs. **space out** to set wide apart or wider apart; to lapse into a drugged, dazed, delirious or light-headed state.

spackle /spak'l/ (*US*) *n* a type of plaster used for filling cracks and holes. [Orig a trademark]

SPAD /spad/ *abbrev* : signal passed at danger, an instance of a train passing a signal ordering it to stop.

spadassin /spad'ə-sin/ *n* a swordsman, a bravo. [Fr, from Ital *spadaccino*, from *spada* a sword]

spade¹ /spād/ *n* a broad-bladed digging tool; a whaler's knife; a spade's depth or spit. ◆ *vt* to dig or remove with a spade. [OE *spadu*, *spædu*; related to Gr *spathē* (see **spade²**)]
■ **spade'ful** *n* (*pl* **spade'fuls**) as much as a spade will hold. **spade'like** *adj*. **spa'der** *n*.
❏ **spade bone** *n* another name for the scapula. **spade'fish** *n* a marine fish (*Chaetodipterus*, *esp C. faber*) of N American coastal waters, having a deep, flattened body. **spade foot** *n* a rectangular, spade-shaped furniture foot. **spade guinea** *n* a guinea with spade-shaped shield, coined 1787–99. **spade'man** or **spades'man** *n* a worker with the spade. **spade'work** *n* preparatory drudgery.
■ **call a spade a spade** to speak plainly without euphemism.

spade² /spād/ *n* a playing card with black leaf-shaped (on Spanish cards sword-shaped) pips; a black or other non-white person (*offensive*). [Sp *espada* sword, from L *spatha*, from Gr *spathē* a broad blade]
■ **in spades** (*orig US sl*) extremely, emphatically; to a great(er) extent.

spade³ see **spado**.

spade⁴ see **spayad**.

spadger /spaj'ər/ (*sl*) *n* a sparrow. [Form of *sparrow*]

spadiceous, **spadices**, etc see **spadix**.

spadille /spə-dil'/ *n* the ace of spades in the games of ombre and quadrille (also (*obs*) **spadill'o** or **spadill'io**). [Fr, from Sp *espadilla*, dimin of *espada*; see **spade²**]

spadix /spā'diks/ (*bot*) *n* (*pl* **spādices** /-dī'sēz/) a fleshy spike of flowers. [Gr *spādix*, *-īkos* a torn-off (palm) branch, in L date-coloured, bay]
■ **spadiceous** /spā-dish'əs/ *adj* having, like, of the nature of, a spadix; coloured like a date; shaped like a palm branch. **spadicifloral** /spā-dī-si-flō'rəl* or *-flō'* / *adj* having flowers in a spathe, as do arum, palms, and some other monocotyledons.

spado /spā'dō or spā'* / *n* (*pl* **spadones** /spā-dō'nēz or -nās/, **spā'dos** or **spā'does**) a castrated or impotent person or animal (also (*rare*) **spade**). [L *spadō*, *-ōnis*, from Gr *spadōn*, *-ōnos*, from *spaein* to pull, tear]

spadroon /spə-droon'/ (*hist*) *n* a cut-and-thrust sword; swordplay with it. [Fr (Genevan dialect) *espadron*]

spae /spā/ (*Scot*) *vt* and *vi* to foretell, divine. [ON *spā*]
■ **spä'er** *n*.
❏ **spae'man** *n*. **spae'wife** *n* a, *usu* old, woman supposed to be able to tell the future.

spag /späg/ (*Aust offensive sl*) *n* an Italian person. ◆ *adj* relating to anything Italian. [From *spaghetti*]

spag bol /spag bol/ (*inf*) *n* spaghetti bolognese.

spageric see **spagyric**.

spaghetti /spə-get'i/ *n* pasta in the form of long cordlike strings. ◆ *adj* denoting similarity to spaghetti, *esp* in terms of numerous intertwining strands, etc. [Ital, pl of *spaghetto*, dimin of *spago* a cord]
■ **spaghettini** /spä-ge-tē'ni/ *n* particularly thin spaghetti.
❏ **spaghetti bolognese** /bol-on-yāz' or bol-ən-āz'/ *n* in full **spaghetti alla bolognese** /al-a/, spaghetti served with a meat and tomato sauce. **spaghetti strap** *n* a thin cordlike strap on a woman's dress, etc. **spaghetti western** *n* a film about the American West, *usu* made in Europe by an Italian director, characterized by a violent and melodramatic content and a baroque style.

spagyric /spə-jir'ik/ *adj* (also **spagyr'ical**, **spagir'ic**, **spager'ic**, etc) alchemical. ◆ *n* (also **spagyrist** /spaj'ər-ist/) an alchemist. [Prob coined by Paracelsus]

spahi or **spahee** /spä'hē/ *n* formerly, a Turkish or French Algerian cavalryman. [Turk (from Pers) *sipāhi*; cf **sepoy**]

spain see **spane**.

spairge see **sparge**.

spake /spāk/ see **speak**.

spald see **spauld**.

spale /spāl/ (*Scot*) *n* a splinter; a chip. [See **spall¹**]

spall¹ /spöl/ *vt* and *vi* to split or splinter, to chip. ◆ *n* a chip or splinter, *esp* of stone. [Cf ME *spalden* to split; Ger *spalten*]

■ **spallā'tion** *n* (*phys*) any nuclear reaction in which several particles result from a collision, eg cosmic rays with atoms of the atmosphere, or a chain reaction in a nuclear reactor or weapon; spalling. **spall'ing** *n* the breaking off of fragments of stone or concrete from a surface, *usu* caused by water ingress through fine cracks (*building, civil eng*); the process of breaking off splinters from a block of stone being dressed. **spalt** *vt* and *vi* to split, splinter. ◆ *adj* brittle. **spalt'ed** *adj* split, splintered; (of wood) having been attacked by fungus, often resulting in an attractive decorative pattern.

spall², **spalle** see **spauld**.

spalpeen /spal-pēn'/ *n* a rascal, a mischievous fellow; a boy. [Ir *spailpín* a (migratory) labourer]

spalt, **spalted** see under **spall¹**.

Spam® /spam/ *n* a type of luncheon meat made from pork, spices, etc. [*Spiced ham*]
■ **spamm'y** *adj* tasting of, containing or like spam or luncheon meat; loosely, bland, unexciting, corny (*inf*).

spam /spam/ *n* electronic junk mail. ◆ *vi* (**spamm'ing**; **spammed**) to send out spam. [Associated in various ways with **Spam**®]
■ **spamm'er** *n*. **spamm'ing** *n*.

span¹ /span/ *n* the total spread or stretch; the distance between abutments, piers, supports, etc, or the portion of a structure (eg a bridge); the distance between the wing tips of an aeroplane; a stretch of time, *esp* of life; the space from the end of the thumb to the end of the little finger when the fingers are extended; nine inches. ◆ *vt* (**spann'ing**; **spanned**) to stretch over; to arch over; to bridge; to encompass; to measure by spans; to measure. [OE *spann*; cf Ger *Spanne*]
■ **span'less** *adj* that cannot be spanned or measured.
❏ **span'-counter** or **span'-farthing** *n* a game in which one tries to throw a counter or coin within a span of one's opponent's. **span loading** *n* (*aerodynamics*) the gross weight of an aircraft divided by the square of the span. **span'-long** *adj* of the length of a span. **span roof** *n* a roof with equal slopes.

span² /span/ *n* a pair of horses; a team of oxen; a securing rope or chain (*naut*). ◆ *vt* to yoke; to wind up (*obs*). [Du and LGer *span*]

span³ /span/ *adj* fresh, short for **span new** quite new, new as a fresh-cut chip. [ON *spān-nyr*, from *spān* chip (cf **spoon¹**), *nyr* new]
■ **spick and span** see under **spick¹**.

span⁴ /span/ see **spin**.

spanaemia /spa-nē'mi-ə/ *n* deficiency of red corpuscles in the blood. [Gr *spanos* lacking, and *haima* blood]
■ **spanae'mic** *adj*.

spanakopita /span-ə-kop'i-tə/ *n* a Greek dish of spinach and feta cheese in filo pastry. [Mod Gr, spinach pie]

spancel /span'sl/ *n* a hobble, *esp* for a cow. ◆ *vt* to hobble. [Du or LGer *spansel*, from *spannen* to stretch]
■ **span'celled** *adj*.

spandex /span'deks/ *n* a synthetic elastic fibre made chiefly from polyurethane; (**Spandex**®) a fabric made from this fibre. [Metathesis of **expand**]

spandrel or **spandril** /span'drəl/ *n* the space between the curve of an arch and the enclosing mouldings, string-course, or the like (*archit*); a self-contained area of surface space (*esp* triangular) available for decorative use, eg in graphic design or forming part of a structure. [Poss connected with **expand**]

spane, **spain** or **spean** /spān/ (*Scot*) *vt* to wean. [MDu or MLGer *spanen*, or OFr *espanir*; cf Ger *spänen*]

spang¹ /spang/ *n* a glittering ornament (*obs*); a clasp (*archaic*). ◆ *vt* (*obs*) to sprinkle with spangs. [OE *spang* clasp; cf Du *spang*, Ger *Spange*, *Spängel*]
■ **spangle** /spang'gl/ *n* a small, thin, glittering plate of metal; a sequin; a sparkling speck, flake, or spot. ◆ *vt* to decorate with spangles. ◆ *vi* to glitter. **spang'led** *adj*. **spang'ler** *n*. **spang'let** *n* (*Shelley*). **spang'ling** *n* and *adj*. **spang'ly** *adj*.

spangle, etc see under **spang¹**.

Spanglish /spang'glish/ *n* a mixture of *Span*ish and En*glish* spoken *esp* in Hispanic communities in the USA.

Spaniard /span'yərd/ *n* a native or citizen of *Spain*; a Spanish ship (*archaic*). [ME *Spaignarde*, from OFr *Espaignart*]

spaniel /span'yəl/ *n* a kind of dog, *usu* liver-and-white, or black-and-white, with large pendent ears; a fawning person. ◆ *adj* like a spaniel; fawning, mean. ◆ *vt* (*Shakesp*) to follow or fawn on like a spaniel. ◆ *vi* (or *vt* with *it*) to play the spaniel. [OFr *espaigneul* (Fr *épagneul*), from Sp *español* Spanish]
■ **span'iel-like** *adj* and *adv*.
■ **Blenheim spaniel** a red-and-white spaniel named from the Duke of Marlborough's seat. **Cavalier King Charles spaniel** a larger variety of King Charles spaniel. **clumber spaniel** a lemon-and-white spaniel

formerly bred at *Clumber*, Notts. **field-** or **land-spaniel** hunting breeds (eg *cockers, springers*). (**Irish**) **water spaniel** a (liver-coloured) spaniel for retrieving water fowl. **King Charles spaniel** a breed of small spaniel, made fashionable by *Charles II*. **Sussex spaniel** a golden-liver or -brown spaniel. **toy spaniel** any of the smaller breeds (eg *Blenheim, King Charles*).

spaniolate /span'yō-lāt/ or **spaniolize** or **-ise** /-līz/ *vt* to hispanicize. [OFr *Espaignol* a Spaniard]

Spanish /span'ish/ *adj* of or relating to *Spain*. ◆ *n* the language of Spain, also used as the official language in much of Central and S America.
▫ **Spanish bayonet** *n* a yucca with straight sword-shaped leaves. **Spanish broom** *n* a Mediterranean shrub (*Spartium junceum*) resembling broom, with showy yellow fragrant flowers. **Spanish chalk** *n* soapstone, French chalk. **Spanish chestnut** *n* the true chestnut. **Spanish cress** *n* a species of pepperwort. **Spanish customs** see **Spanish practices** below. **Spanish dagger** *n* a yucca plant (*Yucca gloriosa*) with tough, sword-shaped leaves and white flowers. **Spanish fly** *n* the blister beetle, *Lytta vesicatoria*; a preparation made from the dried bodies of these beetles yielding cantharides (qv) formerly used medicinally to produce blisters or as an aphrodisiac. **Spanish fowl** *n* a breed of domestic hen, also called **white-faced black Spanish**. **Spanish grass** *n* esparto. **Spanish guitar** *n* a six-stringed acoustic guitar. **Spanish influenza** *n* a severe form of influenza, which, first noted in Spain, spread all over the world in 1918. **Spanish Inquisition** see under **inquisition**. **Spanish juice** *n* extract of liquorice root. **Spanish mackerel** *n* a large Atlantic fish of the mackerel family. **Spanish Main** *n* (ie mainland) the mainland coast of the Caribbean Sea; often (*popularly*) the Caribbean Sea itself. **Spanish moss** *n* any of various plants which grow in tropical and sub-tropical areas in long, trailing strands from tree branches, *esp Usnea longissima* or *Tillandsia usneoides*. **Spanish needles** *n pl* an American weed of the bur-marigold genus with hooked fruits. **Spanish omelette** *n* an omelette made with various vegetables. **Spanish onion** *n* a large mild type of onion. **Spanish practices** or **customs** *n pl* irregular or restrictive practices by a group of workers, such as overmanning and excessive overtime, which are costly, inefficient, etc (*orig* called **old Spanish practices** or **customs**). **Spanish rice** *n* a dish of rice with peppers, tomatoes and onions. **Spanish sheep** *n* a merino. **Spanish soap** *n* Castile soap. **Spanish topaz** *n* an orange-brown variety of quartz (not a true topaz) used as a gemstone. **Spanish walk** *n* the piaffer gait in horsemanship. **Spanish windlass** *n* (*esp naut*) a stick or short bar used in ropemaking to twist and tighten the strands.
▪ **ride the Spanish mare** (*obs naut*) to be made to sit astride the ship's boom as a punishment. **walk Spanish** to compel or be compelled to walk on tiptoe, lifted by the collar and the seat of the trousers; hence, to proceed or act under duress or compulsion.

spank[1] /spangk/ *vt* to strike, *esp* with the flat of the hand, to smack; to defeat heavily (*inf*). ◆ *n* a loud slap, *esp* on the buttocks. [Prob imit]
▪ **spank'ing** *n*.

spank[2] /spangk/ *vt* and *vi* to move or drive briskly. [Poss back-formation from **spanking**]
▪ **spank'er** *n* a person or thing that spanks; any person or thing particularly striking or dashing; a fore-and-aft sail on the aftermost mast of a sailing ship (*naut*); a gold coin (*obs sl*). **spank'ing** *adj* spirited, going freely; (of a wind) fresh and brisk; striking, beyond expectation; very large. *adv* very. **spank'ingly** *adv*.

spanner /span'ər/ *n* a wrench for nuts, screws, etc; an instrument for winding up a spring (*obs*). [Ger *Spanner*, from *spannen* to stretch; cf **span**[1]]
▪ **throw a spanner in the works** to cause confusion or difficulty, upset plans.

spansule /span'sūl/ *n* a type of pill, generally a capsule containing grains coated with varying amounts of a soluble substance, so that the medicine is released into the body slowly over a period of time. [**span**[1] and cap*sule*]

spar[1] /spär/ *n* a rafter; a pole; a bar or rail (chiefly *Scot*; also *archaic* **sparre**); an undressed tree stem of medium girth; a general term for masts, yards, booms, gaffs, etc (*naut*). ◆ *vt* to fasten with a spar (also *archaic* **sperre**); to fasten; to shut; to fit with spars. [OE *gesparrian* to bar; Du *spar* (noun), *sperren* (verb); ON *sparri* (verb); Ger *sperren* (verb)]
▫ **spar deck** *n* (*naut*) a temporary deck laid in any part of a ship; a light upper deck of a flush-decked ship.

spar[2] /spär/ *vi* (**sparr'ing**; **sparred**) to box, or make the actions of boxing; to dispute, argue; (of gamecocks) to fight with spurs. ◆ *n* a boxing match or demonstration; a cock fight; a dispute. [Perh OFr *esparer* (Fr *éparer*) to kick out; prob Gmc]
▪ **sparr'er** *n*. **sparr'ing** *n*.
▫ **sparring partner** *n* a person, *usu* another boxer, with whom a boxer practises; a friend with whom one enjoys lively arguments.

spar[3] /spär/ *n* any transparent to translucent, lustrous, non-metallic mineral, with clean cleavage planes (*esp* in compounds, eg *calcspar, fluorspar, feldspar*); a crystal or fragment of this; an ornament made of it. [MLGer *spar*, related to OE *spærstān* gypsum]
▪ **sparry** /spär'i/ *adj* of or like spar.

sparable /spar'ə-bl/ *n* a small headless nail used by shoemakers. [Altered from **sparrow-bill** from its shape]

Sparagmite /spä-rag'mīt/ (*geol*) *n* a general name for the late Precambrian rocks of Scandinavia, containing conglomerates, quartzites, breccias and arkoses. [**spar**[3] and stal*agmite*]
▪ **sparag'matic** *adj*.

sparaxis /spa-rak'sis/ *n* any plant of the S African *Sparaxis* genus of cormous iridaceous plants, having colourful star-shaped flowers with lacerated spathes. [LL, from Gr *sparassein* to tear, lacerate]

spard /spärd/ archaic form of **spared**.

spare[1] /spär/ *vt* to do without, part with voluntarily; to afford; to allow oneself, concede to oneself (*archaic*); to abstain from using; to refrain from hurting, injuring, punishing, killing or ending; to treat mercifully; to relieve or save from; to avoid; to avoid incurring; to use frugally (*archaic*); to save, hoard (*obs*). ◆ *vi* (*archaic* or *rare*) to be frugal; to refrain; to be merciful. ◆ *adj* not in actual use; not required; kept or available for others or for such purposes as may occur; lean; frugal, scanty, meagre; sparing. ◆ *adv* sparely. ◆ *n* a spare part, thing or person; a duplicate kept or carried for emergencies, etc; (in skittles or tenpin bowling) overturning all the pins with the first two balls, ie with a ball to spare (a **double spare** with first ball only); the score for so doing. [OE *sparian* to spare, *spær* sparing; Ger *sparen*]
▪ **spare'less** *adj* unmerciful. **spare'ly** *adv*. **spare'ness** *n*. **spär'er** *n*. **spär'ing** *adj* tending or wanting to make savings, frugal, economical. **spär'ingly** *adv*. **spär'ingness** *n*.
▫ **spare part** *n* a part for a machine ready to replace an identical part if it becomes faulty (**spare-part surgery** surgery involving the replacement of organs, by transplants or artificial devices). **spare rib** *n* a piece of pork consisting of ribs with a little meat adhering to them. **spare room** *n* a bedroom that is not normally used, available for visitors. **spare time** *n* leisure time. **spare'-time** *adj*. **spare tyre** *n* an extra tyre for a motor vehicle, carried in case of a puncture; a roll of fat around the midriff (*inf*).
▪ **go spare** (*sl*) to become furious or frenzied. **to spare** over and above what is required.

spare[2] /spär/ (now *Scot*) *n* the opening or slit at the top of a skirt, pair of trousers, etc. [Origin obscure]

sparganium /spär-gā'ni-əm/ *n* a plant of the bur-reed genus *Sparganium* that grows in marshes and shallow water, typically having straplike leaves and globelike flower-heads made up of either male or female flowers. [Gr *sparganion*]

sparge /spärj/ or (*Scot*) **spairge** /spārj/ *vt* to sprinkle (with moisture). [L *spargere* to sprinkle]
▪ **spar'ger** *n* a sprinkler.

spar-hawk /spär'hök/ *n* same as **sparrowhawk**.

sparid or **sparoid** /spar'id or -oid/ *n* any marine fish of the family Sparidae, *incl* the sea breams, porgies, dentex, etc, with slim streamlined bodies and well-developed teeth adapted to their individual feeding habits. [Gr *sparos* the fish sargus]

spark /spärk/ *n* a glowing or glittering particle; anything of this appearance or character, eg easily extinguished, ready to cause explosion or burning hot; a flash; an electric discharge across a gap; anything active or vivid; a bright sprightly person; a small diamond (*inf*); an electrician (*inf*; see also **sparks** below); a lover, a beau (*archaic*). ◆ *vi* to emit sparks; to produce a spark; to sparkle; to play the gallant or lover (*archaic*). ◆ *vt* to cause to begin, kindle or animate (often with *off*). [OE *spærca, spearca*; Du *spark*]
▪ **spark'ish** *adj* jaunty, showy. **spark'ishly** *adv*. **spark'less** *adj*. **spark'lessly** *adv*. **spark'let** *n* a small spark. **sparks** *n sing* a ship's wireless operator (*naut inf*); (also **spark** or *esp Aust* **spark'ie**) an electrician (*inf*). **spark'y** *adj* producing sparks; jaunty; sprightly.
▫ **spark chamber** *n* a radiation detector, consisting of a chamber containing inert gas and electrically charged metal plates, in which tracks of particles can be detected and studied by photographing the spark caused by their ionization of the gas. **spark coil** *n* an induction coil; a connection of high resistance used to prevent sparking in electrical apparatus. **spark gap** *n* the space between electrodes across which electric sparks pass; apparatus with such a space. **spark plug** or **spark'ing-plug** *n* in an internal-combustion engine, a plug carrying wires between which an electric spark passes to fire the explosive mixture of gases.
▪ **bright spark** (often *ironic*) a person who has many good ideas. **make sparks fly** to cause or arouse sudden anger. **spark off** see **spark** (*vt*) above. **spark out** (*sl*) to fall asleep; to pass out; to die (**spark-** or **sparked-out** *adj*).

---

fāte; fär; mē; fûr; mīne; mōte; för; mūte; pŭt; dhen (then); *el'ə-mənt* (element³) ◆ For other sounds see detailed chart of pronunciation

sparke /spärk/ (*Spenser*) *n* a weapon of some kind, *perh* an error for **sparthe**.

sparkle /spär'kl/ *n* a little spark; glitter; scintillation; emission of sparks; the appearance of effervescence (as of carbon dioxide in wine); vivacity; spirited animation; scintillating wit. ◆ *vi* to emit sparks; to glitter; to effervesce with small shining bubbles; to be bright, animated, vivacious or witty. ◆ *vt* to cause to sparkle; to throw out as, in, or like sparks. [Dimin and frequentative of **spark**]
■ **spark'ler** *n* that which sparkles; a diamond or other gem (*inf*); a small firework that gives off a shower of tiny sparks and which can be held in the hand. **spark'ling** *n* and *adj*. **spark'lingly** *adv*. **spark'ly** *adj* having sparkles; sparkling. ◆ *n* (*pl* **spark'lies**) (*inf*) something that sparkles.
□ **sparkling wine** *n* wine that effervesces, either as a result of secondary fermentation or by the introduction of carbon dioxide.

sparling /spär'ling/, **sperling** or **spirling** /spûr' or spir'ling/ *n* a dialect (*esp Scot*) name for the smelt. [Partly OFr *esperlinge* (of Gmc origin), partly MLGer *spirling* or MDu *spierling*]

sparoid see **sparid**.

sparre see **spar**[1].

sparrer, **sparring**, etc see under **spar**[2].

sparrow /spar'ō/ *n* any member of a family of small finch-like birds of the genus *Passer* and related genera (eg *P. domesticus*, the house sparrow, and *P. montanus*, the tree sparrow); extended to many other, *usu* brown, birds, such as the hedge sparrow. [OE *spearwa*; Gothic *sporwa*, ON *spörr*, Ger *Sperling*]
□ **sparr'ow-bill** see **sparable**. **sparr'owhawk** *n* any of several long-legged, round-winged birds of prey of the genus *Accipiter*, *esp A. nisus*, a European hawk that preys on smaller birds.

sparrow-grass or **sparrow grass** /spar'ō-gräs/ (*dialect* and *inf*) *n* a corruption of **asparagus** (also **spara'grass**).

sparry see under **spar**[3].

sparse /spärs/ *adj* thinly scattered; scanty. [L *sparsus*, pap of *spargere* to scatter; Gr *speirein* to sow]
■ **spars'edly** *adv* (now *rare*). **sparse'ly** *adv*. **sparse'ness** *n*. **spars'ity** *n*.

spart /spärt/ *n* esparto; Spanish broom (*obs*). [L *spartum* Spanish broom, esparto, and Sp *esparto*]
■ **sparterie** /-ə-rē/ *n* (*Fr*) articles made of esparto.

Spartacist /spär'tə-sist/ *n* a follower of *Spartacus*, leader of the slaves that revolted against Rome in the Third Slave War (73–71BC); a member of an extreme German communist group that staged an uprising in 1918.

spartan /spär'tən/ *adj* simple, hardy, rigorous, frugal, laconic, militaristic, despising culture (thought to be characteristic of the ancient Greek city of *Sparta*, capital of Laconia); bleak, rigorous, austere. ◆ *n* someone or something displaying spartan qualities; (with *cap*) a citizen or native of Sparta or Laconia. [Gr *Spartē* (Doric *Spartā*)]

sparteine /spär'tē-ēn or -in/ *n* an oily three-ringed alkaloid (C$_{15}$H$_{26}$N$_2$), obtained from the branches of the common broom plant and the seeds of the lupin, sometimes used to treat heart irregularities. [New L *Spartium*, from Gr *spartos* broom]

sparterie see under **spart**.

sparth or **sparthe** /spärth/ (*archaic*) *n* a long battle-axe. [ON *spartha*]

sparticle /spär'ti-kl/ (*phys*) *n* any of several types of hypothetical heavy particle that are predicted by string theory. [From supersymmetric *particle*]

spasm /spaz'm/ *n* a sustained involuntary muscular contraction; a sudden convulsive action, movement, or emotion; a brief period, a spell (*inf*); a section of a performance, eg a verse of a song, stanza of a poem, etc (*joc sl*). ◆ *vi* to go into spasm; to experience a spasm or spasms. [Gr *spasma*, *-atos*, and *spasmos*, *-ou* convulsion, from *spaein* to draw, convulse]
■ **spasmat'ic** or **spasmat'ical** *adj* (*rare*). **spasm'ic** *adj*. **spasmod'ic** or **spasmod'ical** *adj* relating to, or occurring in, spasms; convulsive; intermittent. **spasmod'ically** *adv*. **spas'modist** *n* (*rare*) a person whose work is spasmodic. **spasmolyt'ic** *n* and *adj* (an) antispasmodic.
□ **Spasmodic School** *n* a group of 19c British poets, PJ Bailey, Sydney Dobell, Alexander Smith, etc, whose works were marked by over-strained and unnatural sentiment and expression.

spastic /spas'tik/ *adj* of the nature of spasm; characterized or affected by spasms, as in *spastic colon*; spasmodic; awkward, clumsy, useless (*offensive sl*). ◆ *n* a person affected with cerebral palsy (*old*); a useless or stupid person (*offensive sl*). [Gr *spastikos*, from *spaein* to draw, convulse; see eg at **spasm**]
■ **spas'tically** *adv*. **spasticity** /-tis'i-ti/ *n* a tendency to spasm.
□ **spastic paralysis** *n* a former name for **cerebral palsy** (see under **cerebrum**).

spat[1] /spat/ pat and pap of **spit**[1].

spat[2] /spat/ *n* a slap (*rare*); a large drop, as of rain; a splash, spattering; a petty quarrel. ◆ *vt* (*rare*) to slap, strike lightly. ◆ *vi* to engage in a petty quarrel. [Prob imit; cf Du *spat* spot, stain, spatter]

spat[3] /spat/ *n* a short gaiter; a fairing covering an aircraft wheel. [**spatterdash**]

spat[4] /spat/ *n* the spawn of shellfish; a shellfish larva. ◆ *vi* and *vt* to spawn. [ME; origin uncertain]
■ **spat'fall** *n* a mass of planktonic shellfish larvae which has settled on the seabed prior to developing into adults; the location or occurrence of this settlement.

spatangoid /spa- or spə-tang'goid/ *n* a heart urchin, a member of the Spatangoidea, an order of more or less heart-shaped sea urchins with eccentric anus. [Gr *spatangēs* a kind of sea urchin]

spatchcock /spach'kok/ *n* a fowl slit lengthways, opened out, and cooked (*usu* grilled) flat; *orig* a fowl dressed and cooked immediately after being killed. ◆ *vt* to treat in this way; to interpolate, insert (words, a sentence, etc) hastily into a narrative, etc. [Prob **dispatch** and **cock**[1]; cf **spitchcock**]

spate /spāt/ (*orig Scot* and *N Eng dialect*) *n* (also (*rare*) **speat**) a flood; a sudden rush or increased quantity. [Origin doubtful]
■ **in spate** (of a river) in a swollen, fast-flowing condition.

spathe /spādh/ (*bot*) *n* a sheathing bract, *usu* a conspicuous one enclosing a spadix. [Gr *spathē* a broad blade]
■ **spathaceous** /spə-thā'shəs/ or **spathed** /spādhd/ *adj* having a spathe.

spathic /spath'ik/ (*mineralogy*) *adj* of the nature of, or like, spar; lamellar. [Ger *Spat(h)* spar]
■ **spath'ose** (or /-ōs'/) *adj* spathic.
□ **spathic iron** *n* another name for **siderite** (see under **sidero-**).

spathiphyllum /spa-thi'fi-lum/ *n* any araceous tropical plant of the genus *Spathiphyllum* (eg *S. wallisii*, the peace lily) with lance-shaped leaves and fleshy white spadices of flowers in white spathes. [New L, from Gr *spathē* a broad blade, and *phyllon* leaf]

spathulate /spath'ū-lāt/ same as **spatulate** (see under **spatula**).

spatial or **spacial** /spā'sh(ə)l/ *adj* relating to space. [L *spatium* space]
■ **spatiality** /spā-shi-al'i-ti/ *n*. **spā'tially** *adv*. **spatiotemp'oral** *adj* of space-time or space and time together.

Spätlese /shpāt'lā-zə/ (*Ger*) *n* literally, a late harvest; a sweet white wine made from grapes harvested after the main vintage (also without *cap*).

spattee /spa-tē'/ *n* a protective outer stocking or long gaiter. [**spat**[3] and **puttee**]

spatter /spat'ər/ *vt* to throw out or scatter upon or about; to sprinkle, *esp* with mud or liquid. ◆ *vi* to fly or fall in drops; to fall, rain down or fly about. ◆ *n* a spattering; something spattered. [Cf Du and LGer *spatten*]
□ **spatt'erdash** *n* roughcast (*US*); an old type of long gaiter or legging to protect the trouser leg from being spattered with mud, etc. **spatt'erdock** *n* (*US*) the yellow water lily of the genus *Nuphar*. **spatt'erwork** *n* reproduction of designs by covering the surface with the pattern and spattering colour on the parts exposed.

spatula /spat'ū-lə/ *n* a broad, blunt, flexible blade or flattened spoon. [L *spatula*, *spathula*, dimin of *spatha*, from Gr *spathē* a broad blade]
■ **spat'ular** *adj*. **spat'ulate** *adj* shaped like a spatula; broad and rounded at the tip and tapering at the base. **spat'ule** *n* a spatula.

spauld /spöld/ (now chiefly *Scot*) *n* (also **spald**, **spall**, **spaul** or (*Spenser*) **spalle**) the shoulder; the shoulder of an animal used as food; a limb. [OFr *espalde* (Fr *épaule*), from L *spatula* (see **spatula**)]
□ **spauld'-bone** *n* shoulder-blade. **spauld'-ill** *n* the cattle disease black-quarter.

spavin /spav'in/ (*vet*) *n* a disease of the hock joint of horses, resulting from inflammation, in which a bony growth (**bone** or **bony spavin**), or distension of the tissues and veins associated with the joint (**bog spavin**) occurs; the growth or enlargement so formed. [OFr *espa(r)vain* (Fr *éparvin*)]
■ **spavie** /spā'vē/ *n* (*Scot*) spavin. **spav'ined** *adj* affected with spavin; lame; broken down, decrepit.

spaw /spö/ an obsolete form of **spa**.

spawl /spöl/ (*archaic*) *n* spittle, slaver, saliva. ◆ *vi* to spit (also *fig*). [Origin unknown]

spawn /spön/ *n* a mass of eggs laid in water; fry; brood; (contemptuously) offspring; mushroom mycelium. ◆ *vt* to produce as spawn; to give rise to; (contemptuously) to generate, *esp* in mass. ◆ *vi* to produce or deposit spawn; to teem; to come forth as or like spawn. [OFr *espandre* to shed, from L *expandere* to spread out]
■ **spawn'er** *n*. **spawn'ing** *n* and *adj*. **spawn'y** *adj* of or like spawn; lucky (*sl*).

■ words derived from main entry word; □ compound words; ■ idioms and phrasal verbs

❑ **spawn brick** or **cake** *n* a consolidated cake of horse dung with mushroom spawn. **spawn'ing-bed** or **-ground** *n* a bed or place in the bottom of a stream on which fish deposit their spawn; a place where new ideas, etc are generated.

spay[1] see **spayed**.

spay[2] /spā/ *vt* to remove or destroy the ovaries of (a female animal). [Anglo-Fr *espeier*, from *espee* (Fr *épée*) sword]

spayad /spā'ad/, **spayd**, **spade** /spād/ or **spay** /spā/ (*obs*) *n* a male deer in his third year. [Origin obscure]

spaz or **spazz** /spaz/ (*sl*) *vi* (*usu* with *out*) to lapse into a delirious state; to lose control. [Altered from **spastic** used as a derogatory slang word]

SPCK *abbrev* : Society for Promoting Christian Knowledge.

SPD *abbrev* : *Sozialdemokratische Partei Deutschlands*, the German Social Democratic Party.

speak /spēk/ *vi* (*pat* **spoke** or (*archaic* or *dialect*) **spake**; *pap* **spō'ken** or (*archaic*) **spoke**) to utter words; to talk or converse; to make a speech; to sound; to give voice; to give expression, information, or intimation by any means. ◆ *vt* to pronounce; to utter; to express; to declare; to mention; to describe (*archaic*); to hail or communicate with; to use or talk in (a language); to bring or render by speaking. ◆ *combining form* (*inf*) a particular jargon or style of language, such as *technospeak*, *doublespeak*, *airspeak*, *seaspeak*, etc. [Late OE *specan* (for *sprecan*); Ger *sprechen*]
■ **speak'able** *adj* able or fit to be spoken or expressed in speech; able to speak (*rare*). **speak'er** *n* a person who speaks; the president (*orig* the mouthpiece) of a legislative body, such as the House of Commons; a loudspeaker. **speak'ership** *n* the office of speaker. **speak'ing** *n* the act of expressing ideas in words; conversation, discussion. ◆ *adj* uttering or transmitting speech; seeming to speak, lifelike. ◆ *adj combining form* able to speak a particular language, as in *English-speaking*. **speak'ingly** *adv*.
❑ **speak'easy** *n* (*US*) during Prohibition, an illicit bar selling alcohol, a shebeen. **speak'erphone** *n* a type of telephone incorporating a loudspeaker and microphone. **speaking clock** *n* a British telephone service which states the exact time when dialled. **speaking tube** *n* a tube for speaking through to another room. **speak'ing-voice** *n* the kind of voice normally used in speaking.
■ **on speaking terms** see under **term**. **so to speak** as one might put it, as it were. **speak a ship** to hail and speak to someone on board her. **speak fair** (*archaic*) to address in conciliatory terms. **speak for** to speak on behalf of or in favour of; to be a proof of or witness to; to bespeak or engage. **speak in tongues** see under **tongue**. **speak one's mind** see under **mind**. **speak out** to speak boldly, freely, unreservedly, or so as to be easily heard (**speak'out** *n*). **speak the same language** see under **language**. **speak to** to converse with, address; to rebuke, scold; to attest, testify to; to comment on, discuss. **speak up** to speak so as to be easily heard; to state one's opinions boldly. **to speak of** worth mentioning.

speal /spēl/ *n* see **spule**.

spean see **spane**.

spear /spēr/ *n* a long weapon made of a pole with a pointed head; a barbed fork for catching fish; anything sharp or piercing; a spearman; a spire; a spiky shoot or blade; a reed. ◆ *vt* to pierce with a spear. [OE *spere* ; Ger *Speer* ; with some senses from **spire**[1]]
■ **speared** *adj* armed with the spear. **spear'y** *adj*.
❑ **spear carrier** *n* (*inf*) an actor in a minor non-speaking role; a minor participant. **spear'fish** *n* marlin or any similar large game fish. **spear grass** *n* a name for many spearlike grasses. **spear gun** *n* an underwater hunting gun which fires spears. **spear'head** *n* the head of a spear; the front of an attack (also *fig*). ◆ *vt* to lead an attack (also *fig*). **spear'man** *n* a man armed with a spear. **spear'mint** *n* a common garden mint used in cooking and flavouring. **spear'-point** *n*. **spear'-running** in a tourney. **spear'-shaft** *n*. **spear side** *n* the male side or line of descent, *opp* to **spindle side**, or **distaff side**. **spear tackle** *n* (rugby, etc) a dangerous tackle in which a player is lifted up and thrown down head first. **spear thistle** *n* a common thistle (*Cnicus lanceolatus* or *Cirsium lanceolatum*). **spear'-thrower** *n* a throwing stick. **spear'wort** *n* any of various Eurasian plants of the genus *Ranunculus* with lance-shaped leaves, eg *R. lingua*, **greater spearwort**, and *R. flammula*, **lesser spearwort**.

speat see **spate**.

spec[1] /spek/ *n* an informal shortening of **speculation** (see under **speculate**).
❑ **spec'-built** *adj* (of houses, etc) built as a speculative investment by the builder.
■ **on spec** as a gamble, on the chance of achieving something.

spec[2] /spek/ *n* an informal shortening of **specification** (see under **specify**).

speccy or **specky** /spek'i/ (*inf*) *n* and *adj* (someone) habitually wearing spectacles. [Cf **specs**, **spectacle**]

special /spesh'(ə)l/ *adj* particular; peculiar; distinctive; exceptional; additional to ordinary; detailed; intimate; designed for a particular purpose; confined or mainly applied to a particular subject. ◆ *n* any special or particular person or thing; any person or thing set apart for a particular duty, such as a constable, a railway train, etc; a dish offered exceptionally as an addition to a restaurant menu, often at a lower price; a newspaper extra, a dispatch from a special correspondent. [L *speciālis*, from *speciēs* species]
■ **spec'ialism** *n* (devotion to) some particular study or pursuit. **spec'ialist** *n* a person whose work, interest or expertise is concentrated on a particular subject; an organism with a narrow range of food and habitat preferences (*ecology*); a secondary school teacher (*educ*). **specialist'ic** *adj*. **speciality** /spesh-i-al'i-ti/ or (*N Am* or *med*) **specialty** /spesh'əl-ti/ *n* the particular characteristic skill, use, etc of a person or thing; a special occupation or object of attention. **specializa'tion** or **-s-** *n*. **spec'ialize** or **-ise** *vt* to make special or specific; to differentiate; to adapt to conditions; to specify; to narrow and intensify; to become or be a specialist in (with *in*). ◆ *vi* to become or be a specialist; to become differentiated; to be adapted to special conditions. **spec'ialized** or **-s-** *adj*. **spec'ializer** or **-s-** *n*. **specially** /spesh'ə-li/ *adv*. **spec'ialness** *n*. **spec'ialogue** *n* a mail order catalogue aimed at a specific target group of customers. **spec'ialty** *n* something special or distinctive; any special product, article of sale or of manufacture; any special pursuit, department of study, etc; speciality (chiefly *N Am* or *med*); a special contract for the payment of money; a deed under seal (*law*).
❑ **Special Air Service** *n* a regiment of the British Army specializing in operations behind enemy lines, etc (*abbrev* **SAS**). **special area** an earlier name for **development area** (see under **develop**). **Special Boat Service** *n* a Royal Marines force specializing in reconnaissance, sabotage and spearheading amphibious assaults. **Special Branch** *n* a British police department which deals with political security. **special constable** see under **constable**. **special correspondent** *n* a person employed to send reports to a newspaper, agency, etc on a particular area of news. **special delivery** *n* the delivery of mail by special messenger outside normal delivery times. **Special Drawing Rights** *n pl* (also without *caps*) a reserve of International Monetary Fund assets which members of the fund may draw on in proportion to their IMF contributions (*abbrev* **SDR** or **SDRs**). **special education** *n* education for children with special educational needs. **special educational needs** *n pl* requirements for educational provision in excess of that usually provided, *esp* due to physical or learning disability. **special effects** *n pl* techniques such as computer-generated imagery, lighting, manipulation of film, etc used to contribute to the illusion in film, television and theatre. **special hospital** *n* a secure hospital for mentally ill patients who are also dangerous. **special intention** *n* (*RC church*) the purpose for which prayers are being said or mass celebrated. **Special K** *n* a slang name for **ketamine**, used as a recreational drug. **special licence** see under **licence**. **special needs** same as **special educational needs** above. **special offer**, **pleading**, **verdict** see under **offer**, etc. **special school** *n* a school designed for the teaching of children with special educational needs. **Special Theory of Relativity** see under **relate**.
■ **in special** (*archaic*) in particular; especially.

spécialité de la maison /spā-sya-lē-tā də la me-zõ'/ *n* the dish regarded by a restaurant as its best and most distinctive. [Fr, speciality of the house]

speciate, **speciation** see under **species**.

specie /spē'shē or -shi-ē/ *n* coined money. [L, ablative of *speciēs* kind; formerly used of payment or requital in the same kind (*in speciē*)]
■ **in specie** in coin; in kind.

species /spē'sēz, -siz, -shēz, -shiz/ *n* (*pl* **spē'cies**) a group of individuals having common characteristics, specialized from others of the same genus (*logic*); a group of individuals which can interbreed with themselves but not with other such groups, and which show morphological variation which is distinct from other such groups, taxonomically placed under a genus and with their names in italics without a capital (*biol*); a type of atom, molecule or ion (*chem*); a kind, sort, type; outward appearance, visible form (*obs* except *theol*); a Eucharistic element; a visual image (*obs*). [L *speciēs*, pl -*ēs* appearance, kind, species, from *specere* to look at]
■ **spē'ciate** *vt*. **specia'tion** *n* formation of new biological species. **speciesism** /spē'shēz-izm/ *n* the assumption that man is superior to all other species of animals and that he is therefore justified in exploiting them to his own advantage. **spe'ciesist** *n*. **speciocide** /spē'shē-ə-sīd/ *n* the destruction of a whole animal species.

specif. *abbrev* : specific; specifically.

specify /spes'i-fī/ *vt* (**spec'ifying**; **spec'ified**) to mention particularly; to make specific; to set down as required. [OFr *specifier*, from LL *specificāre*, from L *speciēs* kind, and *facere* to make]

■ **spec'ifiable** (or /-fī'/) *adj.* **specific** /spi-sif'ik/ *adj* of special application or origin; specifying; precise; constituting or determining a species; relating to or peculiar to a species; (of a parasite) restricted to one particular host; (of a stain) colouring certain structures or tissues only; (of a physical constant) being the ratio per unit volume, area, (or *esp*) mass, etc. ◆ *n* a remedy or medicine for a particular disease or part of the body; anything that is specific, *esp* a specific detail or factor. **specif'ical** *adj.* **specif'ically** *adv.* **specif'icate** *vt* to specify. **specifica'tion** /spes-/ *n* making, becoming, or being specific; the act of specifying; any point or particular specified; a detailed description of requirements, etc; the description of his or her invention presented by an inventor applying for a patent. **specificity** /spes-i-fis'i-ti/ *n.* **spec'ified** *adj.*
□ **specific charge** *n* (*phys*) the ratio of electric charge to mass in an elementary particle. **specific gravity** *n* relative density. **specific heat** or **specific heat capacity** *n* (*phys*) the number of heat units necessary to raise the unit of mass of a given substance one degree in temperature. **specific impulse** *n* a measure of the efficiency of a rocket engine, the ratio of the thrust obtained to the fuel consumed, *usu* per second. **specific name** *n* in biological nomenclature, the name of the species, ie the second name, the first being the generic name. **specific performance** *n* (*law*) the compulsory performance of an obligation ordered by a court. **specific resistance** *n* resistivity.

specimen /spes'ə-mən, also -i-, -min/ *n* an object or portion serving as a sample, *esp* for purposes of study, collection or consideration; a remarkable type; a urine, blood or tissue sample (*med*); derogatorily, a person (*inf*). ◆ *adj* for use as, or of the nature of, a specimen; representative. [L *specimen*, from *specere* to see]

specious /spē'shəs/ *adj* plausible, but wrong or inaccurate in reality; showy; looking good at first sight; beautiful (*obs*). [L *speciōsus* showy, from *speciēs* form, from *specere* to look at]
■ **speciosity** /-shi-os'i-ti/ or **spe'ciousness** *n.* **spe'ciously** *adv.*

speck[1] /spek/ *n* a small spot; a particle. ◆ *vt* to mark with specks. [OE *specca*]
■ **speck'less** *adj.* **speck'y** *adj.*

speck[2] or **spek** /spek/ *n* a kind of spiced smoked ham; fatty bacon or pork; whale blubber. [Ger *Speck*, Du *spek* fat; cf OE *spic* fat bacon]
■ **specktioneer** or **specksioneer** /spek-shən-ēr'/ *n* the chief harpooner in whale-fishing.

speckle /spek'l/ *n* a little spot, *esp* of colour; a grainy pattern on or forming a photographic image, caused by atmospheric interference (*astron* and *phys*). ◆ *vt* to mark with speckles. [Dimin of **speck**[1]]
■ **speck'led** *adj.* **speck'ledness** *n.*
□ **speckled trout** *n* a freshwater trout native to N America, introduced to Europe where it is often known as the brook trout. **speckle interferogram** *n* a visual record produced by speckle interferometry. **speckle interferometry** *n* (*astron* and *phys*) a method of obtaining information, *esp* a visual image, of a distant stellar object by the processing and analysis of a number of short-exposure speckle photographs.

specktioneer see under **speck**[2].

specky see **speccy**.

specs /speks/ (*inf*) *n pl* a pair of spectacles (also **specks**).

spectacle /spek'tə-kl/ or -ti-kl/ *n* a sight; a show, pageant or exhibition; (in *pl*) a pair of lenses (for correcting the eyesight) mounted in frames with side-pieces that sit over the ears; (in *pl*) a marking (on an animal) resembling spectacles. [L *spectāculum*, from *spectāre*, *-ātum*, intensive of *specere* to look at]
■ **spec'tacled** *adj* wearing spectacles; having rings around the eyes (*fig*). **spectacular** /-tak'ū-lər/ *adj* of the nature of, or marked by, display; sensational, extremely impressive. ◆ *n* a theatrical show, *esp* on television, or any display, that is large-scale and elaborate. **spectacularity** /-lar'i-ti/ *n.* **spectac'ularly** *adv.*
■ **make a spectacle of oneself** to behave in a way that attracts attention, ridicule, etc. **pair of spectacles** (*cricket sl*) a duck in both innings.

spectator /spek-tā'tər/ *n* a person who looks on. [L *spectātor*, from *spectāre* to look]
■ **spectate'** *vi* (back-formation) to look on. **spectatorial** /-tə-tō'ri-əl or -tō'/ *adj.* **specta'torship** *n* the action, office, or quality of a spectator. **specta'tress** or **specta'trix** *n* (*rare*) a female spectator.
□ **spectator sport** *n* a sport that has great appeal for spectators.

spectinomycin /spek-ti-nə-mī'sin/ *n* a substance obtained from the bacterium *Streptomyces spectabilis*, formerly prescribed as an antibiotic.

spectra see **spectrum**.

spectral, **spectrality** see under **spectre** and **spectrum**.

spectre or (*N Am*) **specter** /spek'tər/ *n* an apparition; a ghost, phantom; a haunting fear or premonition. [Fr *spectre*, from L *spectrum*, from *specere* to look at]

■ **spec'tral** *adj* relating to, or like, a spectre. **spectral'ity** *n* the state of being spectral; a spectral object. **spec'trally** *adv.* **spectrolog'ical** *adj.* **spectrolog'ically** *adv.* **spectrol'ogy** *n* the study of ghosts.
□ **spectre bat** *n* a leaf-nosed bat. **spectre crab** *n* a glass crab. **spectre insect** *n* a phasmid. **spectre lemur** *n* the tarsier. **spectre shrimp** *n* a skeleton shrimp.

spectro- /spek-trō- or -tro-/ *combining form* signifying: spectre; spectrum.

spectrum /spek'trəm/ *n* (pl **spec'tra**) the range of colour produced by a prism or diffraction grating; any analogous range of radiations in order of wavelength; the range of frequencies of sound or a sound; the range of effectiveness of a drug, *esp* an antibiotic (*pharmacol*); a range of opinions, activities, etc (*fig*); an after-image. [L *spectrum* an appearance, from *specere* to look at]
■ **spec'tral** *adj* relating to, or like, a spectrum. **spectral'ity** *n.* **spec'trochemistry** *n* chemical spectroscopy. **spec'trogram** *n* a photograph of a spectrum; a sound spectrogram (see under **sound**[1]). **spec'trograph** *n* a spectroscope designed for use over a wide range of frequencies (well beyond visible spectrum) and recording the spectrum photographically (see also **mass spectrograph** under **mass**[1]). **spectrograph'ic** or **spectrograph'ical** *adj.* **spectrog'raphy** *n.* **spectrohē'liogram** *n* a photograph of the sun by monochromatic light. **spectrohē'liograph** *n* an instrument for taking it. **spectrohē'lioscope** *n* a similar instrument with which one can observe an image of the whole solar disc in the light of a single particular wavelength. **spectrolog'ical** *adj.* **spectrolog'ically** *adv.* **spectrol'ogy** *n* the science of the spectrum or spectrum analysis. **spectrom'eter** *n* an instrument for measuring refractive indices; one used for measurement of wavelength or energy distribution in a heterogeneous beam of radiation (see also **mass spectrometer** under **mass**[1]). **spectromet'ric** *adj.* **spectrom'etry** *n.* **spectrophotom'eter** *n* an instrument for measuring intensity of each colour or wavelength present in an optical spectrum. **spectrophotom'etry** *n.* **spec'troscope** *n* a general term for an instrument (*spectrograph*, *spectrometer*, etc) used in spectroscopy, the basic features of which are a slit and collimator for producing a parallel beam of radiation, a prism or grating for 'dispersing' different wavelengths through differing angles of deviation, and a telescope, camera or counter tube for observing the dispersed radiation. **spectroscop'ic** or **spectroscop'ical** *adj.* **spectroscop'ically** *adv.* **spectroscopist** /spek-tros'kə-pist or spek'trə-skop-ist/ *n.* **spectros'copy** (or /spek'/) *n* the study of spectra.
□ **spectral type** *n* (*astron*) one of the different groups into which stars can be classified according to characteristics of their spectra. **spectroscopic binary** *n* (*astron*) a binary star whose components are too close to be resolved visually, but can be resolved spectroscopically. **spectrum analysis** *n* determination of chemical composition by observing the spectrum of light or X-rays coming from or through the substance.

specula see **speculum**.

specular /spek'ū-lər/ *adj* mirrorlike; having a speculum; by reflection; visual; giving a wide view. [L *speculāris*, from *speculum* a mirror, and *specula* a watchtower]
□ **specular iron** *n* a brilliant steely crystallized haematite. **specular stone** *n* any transparent or semitransparent mineral, such as mica, selenite, talc.

speculate /spek'ū-lāt/ *vi* to reflect; to theorize; to make conjectures or guesses; to take risk in hope of gain, *esp* in buying and selling. ◆ *vt* to look at or into, view, examine (*lit* or *fig*; *archaic*); to observe (*archaic*); to view in a mirror (*obs*); to make conjectures about (*obs*). [L *speculātus*, pap of *speculārī*, from *specula* a lookout, from *specere* to look at]
■ **specula'tion** *n* an act of speculating or its result; theorizing; conjecture; mere guesswork; a more or less risky investment of money for the sake of unusually large profits; a card game in which trumps are bought and sold; vision (*obs*); viewing (*obs*); an observer (*Shakesp*). **spec'ulatist** *n* a speculative philosopher; a speculator. **spec'ulative** (or /-ət-/) *adj* of the nature of, based on, given to, speculation or theory. **spec'ulatively** *adv.* **spec'ulativeness** *n.* **spec'ulator** *n* someone who speculates in any sense; a watchman, lookout (*archaic*). **spec'ulatory** *adj* exercising speculation; adapted for spying or viewing (*archaic*). **spec'ulatrix** *n* (*rare*) a female speculator.

speculum /spek'ū-ləm/ *n* (pl **spec'ula**) a mirror; a reflector, *usu* of polished metal; an instrument for inserting into and holding open a cavity of the body so that the interior may be inspected (*med*); a bright patch on a wing, *esp* a duck's. [L *speculum* a mirror, from *specere* to look at]
□ **speculum metal** *n* an alloy of copper and tin, with or without other ingredients, which can be highly polished and used for mirrors, lamp reflectors, etc.

sped /sped/ *pat* and *pap* of **speed**.

---

speech /spēch/ n that which is spoken; language; the power of speaking; a manner of speaking; a continuous spoken utterance; a discourse, oration; a talk; a colloquy; a mention; the sounding of a musical instrument; parole (qv) (*linguistics*); a rumour (*obs*); a saying (*obs*). ◆ vt and vi (*rare* or *dialect*) to harangue. [Late OE *spēc, spǣc*, OE *sprēc, sprǣc*; Ger *Sprache*]

■ **speech'ful** adj loquacious; expressive. **speech'fulness** n. **speechifica'tion** n (*inf*). **speech'ifier** n. **speech'ify** vi to make speeches, harangue (implying contempt). **speech'less** adj destitute or deprived of the power of speech. **speech'lessly** adv. **speech'lessness** n.

❑ **speech act** n (*philos* and *linguistics*) an utterance, such as a directive, defined in terms of the content, the intention of the speaker and the effect on the listener. **speech community** n a community based on a common language or dialect. **speech'craft** n philology; rhetoric. **speech'-crī'er** n (*hist*) a hawker of broadsides giving hanged criminals' dying speeches. **speech day** n in some schools, the public day at the close of a school year, or on which prizes won during the previous year are presented. **speech'maker** n someone who speaks, or is accustomed to speaking, in public. **speech'making** n. **speech pathologist** n. **speech pathology** n the study and treatment of speech and language defects. **speech reading** n lip-reading. **speech recognition** n the understanding of an individual's speech patterns, or of continuous speech, by a computer. **speech'-song** n (*music*) sprechgesang. **speech synthesis** n the generation of spoken sounds by a computer from input text. **speech therapist** n someone who is professionally qualified to provide speech therapy. **speech therapy** n the treatment of speech and language defects. **speech'-train'ing** n training in clear speech. **speech'writer** n someone whose job is to write speeches for a public figure.

speed /spēd/ n quickness, swiftness, dispatch; the rate at which a distance is covered; the time taken for a photographic film to accept an image; amphetamine (*sl*); success, good fortune (*archaic*); a help to success (*archaic*). ◆ vi (pat and pap **sped** (also **speed'ed**)) to move quickly; to hurry; to drive at high, or at dangerously, unduly, or illegally high, speed; to succeed, fare (*archaic*); to be under the influence of an amphetamine (*sl*). ◆ vt to send swiftly; to push forward; to hasten; to betake with speed; to urge to high speed; to set or regulate the speed of; to give or bring success to, to further (*archaic*); to send forth with good wishes (*archaic*); to bring to an end or finished state (*archaic*); to bring to a sorry plight, to do for (in *passive*; *archaic*). [OE *spēd*; Du *spoed*]

■ **speed'er** n someone who or something that speeds or promotes speed. **speed'ful** adj. **speed'fully** adv. **speed'ily** adv. **speed'iness** n quickness. **speed'ing** n progressive increase of speed (often with *up*); motoring at excessive speed; success; promotion, furtherance. ◆ adj travelling at (excessive) speed. **speed'less** adj. **speedom'eter** n a device indicating the speed at which a vehicle is travelling (*inf* shortening **speed'o** (*pl* **speed'os**)). **speed'ster** n a speedboat; a fast (sports) car; someone who speeds, *esp* in driving. **speed'y** adj swift; prompt; soon achieved.

❑ **speed'ball** n a team sport with eleven players a side, combining many elements of soccer, basketball and rugby; a mixture of cocaine and opiates, *esp* heroin or morphine (*sl*). **speed'balling** n (*sl*) injecting or sniffing speedballs. **speed'boat** n a very swift motorboat. **speed'boating** n. **speed bump** or **speed hump** n a low hump across a road intended to slow down traffic. **speed camera** n an automatic camera installed at the side of a road to measure and record the speed of vehicles (often shortened to **speed cam**). **speed cop** n (*sl*) a policeman who watches out for motorists who are exceeding a speed limit. **speed dating** n the practice of attending an organized social event during which people have a series of short meetings (**speed dates**) with potential romantic partners. **speed dial** or **speed dialling** n a facility of some telephones that enables numbers to be stored in the telephone's memory and dialled automatically by pressing a single button or a short combination of buttons. **speed'freak** n (*sl*) a habitual user of amphetamine as a recreational drug; an enthusiast of fast driving. **speed gun** n a hand-held radar or laser device used by police at the side of a road to measure and record the speed of passing vehicles. **speed hump** see **speed bump** above. **speed limit** n the maximum speed at which motor vehicles may be driven legally on certain roads. **speed merchant** n (*inf*) someone who drives, runs, bowls, etc with exceptional speed. **speed reading** n a technique of very rapid reading, by which words are taken in in phrases or other groups instead of singly. **speed'skating** n a sport in which two or more ice- or roller-skaters race on an oval track. **speed trap** n a section of road over which the police (often using radar) check the speed of passing vehicles and identify drivers exceeding the limit (see also **radar trap** under **radar**). **speed'-up** n an acceleration, *esp* in work. **speed'way** n the sport of motorcycle racing on a short oval cinder track; such a track; a road for fast traffic. **speed'well** n any species of the scrophulariaceous genus *Veronica*, typically blue-flowered, with posterior petals united and lacking a posterior sepal.

Speed'writing® n a type of shorthand, in which letters of the alphabet stand for words or sounds, as *u* for *you*. **speedy cut** or **cutting** n injury to a horse's foreleg by the opposite shoe.

■ **speed up** to quicken the rate of working. **up to speed** at full or high speed; fully informed.

speel¹ /spēl/ (*Scot*) vt and vi to climb. ◆ n a climb. [Poss LGer *speler* a performer]

■ **speel'er** n an acrobat (*obs*); a climber; a climbing iron.

speel² /spēl/ (*Scot and N Eng dialect*) n a splinter of wood, etc. [Scand, cf Norw *spela, spila*, Swed *spjela, spjele*]

speir or **speer** /spēr/ (*Scot*) vt and vi to ask, inquire. [OE *spyrian* to inquire after, *spor* a trace]

■ **speir'ings** or **speer'ings** n news.

speisade see **lance prisado**.

speiss /spīs/ n a mass of arsenides and commonly antimony compounds, a first product in smelting certain ores. [Ger *Speise*]

❑ **speiss cobalt** n smaltite.

spek see **speck²**.

spekboom /spek'bōm/ n a S African succulent shrub of the purslane family. [Du, bacon tree]

spelaean, etc see **spelean**, etc.

speld /speld/ or **spelder** /spel'dər/ (*Scot*) vt to spread open or sprawlingly; to slit and lay open. [Cf ME *spalden* to split; Ger *spalten*]

■ **spel'ding**, **speld'ring**, **spel'din** or **speld'rin** n a haddock (or other fish) split open and dried.

spelean or **spelaean** /spi-lē'ən/ adj cave-dwelling. [Gr *spēlaion* cave]

■ **speleological** or **spelaeological** /spē-li-ə-loj'i-kl or spel-/ adj. **speleol'ogist** or **spelaeol'ogist** n. **speleol'ogy** or **spelaeol'ogy** n the scientific study of caves; the exploration of caves. **speleo'them** or **spelaeo'them** n a term for depositional features, such as stalactites and stalagmites, found in caves.

spelk /spelk/ (*Scot and N Eng dialect*) n a splinter, of wood, etc. [OE *spelc*]

spell¹ /spel/ vt (pat and pap **spelled** or **spelt**) to read laboriously, letter by letter; to name or set down in order the letters of; to constitute or represent orthographically; to make out, come to understand; to scan; to signify, indicate, amount to (*fig*). ◆ vi to spell words, *esp* correctly; to contemplate (*poetic*); to express or hint a desire. ◆ n a mode of spelling. [OFr *espeller* (Fr *épeler*), of Gmc origin; cf **spell²**]

■ **spell'able** adj. **spell'er** n. **spell'ing** n. **spell'ingly** adv letter by letter.

❑ **spell'check** or **spell'checker** n a program in a word processor that checks the accuracy of the operator's spelling (also *adj*). **spell'-check** vt and vi. **spell'down** n (*US*) a spelling competition. **spelling bee** n a spelling competition. **spelling book** n a book for teaching how to spell. **spelling pronunciation** n (*linguistics*) a pronunciation of a word that, as a side-effect of literacy, closely represents its spelling, superseding the traditional pronunciation, eg *forehead* as /för'hed/ (*orig* /for'id/).

■ **spell backward** to spell in reverse order; perversely to mispresent or misconstrue the qualities of. **spell baker** to do something difficult, probably because *baker* was one of the first disyllables in old spelling books. **spell it out** or **spell out** to be extremely specific in explaining something.

spell² /spel/ n a magic formula; a magic influence; enchantment; entrancement. ◆ vt to say a spell over; to bind with a spell; to enchant. ◆ vi (*obs*) to discourse. [OE *spell* narrative, discourse, *spellian* to speak, announce; cf Gothic *spill*, ON *spjall* tale]

■ **spell'ful** adj magical.

❑ **spell'bind** vt (back-formation). **spell'binder** n an orator, *usu* political or evangelical, who holds his or her audience spellbound; any person or thing that entrances. **spell'binding** adj. **spell'bound** adj bound by a spell; entranced. **spell'stopt** adj (*archaic*) brought to a standstill by a spell.

spell³ /spel/ n a shift; a turn at work; a bout, turn; a short time; a stretch of time; a number of overs bowled consecutively by a bowler (*cricket*); a rest; a fit (of irritation, illness, etc). ◆ vt (**spell'ing**; **spelled**) to take the place of at work; to relieve, give a rest to; to take a turn at. ◆ vi to take turns; to rest. [OE *spelian* to act for another; cf Du *spelen*, Ger *spielen* to play]

spell⁴ /spel/ (*dialect*) n a splinter; a rung; a trap for throwing up the knur in knur and spell. [Perh *speld*; but cf Ger *spellen* to split]

spellican see under **spill²**.

spelt¹ see **spell¹**.

spelt² /spelt/ n an inferior species of wheat (*Triticum spelta*), grown in the mountainous parts of Europe. [OE *spelt*]

spelter /spel'tər/ n zinc, *esp* impure zinc. [Cf LGer *spialter*]

spelunker /spi-lung'kər/ n a person who explores caves as a hobby. [From L *spēlunc, -a*, from Gr *spēlynx* a cave]

■ **spelunk'ing** n.

spence /spens/ n a larder (dialect); a pantry (dialect); an inner room, parlour (Scot). [OFr despense a buttery, from despendre, from L dispendere]

spencer[1] /spen'sər/ n a kind of wig; a short double-breasted overcoat; a woman's short undergarment, formerly over-jacket. [After various persons of the name]

spencer[2] /spen'sər/ n (in ships and barques) a fore-and-aft trysail abaft the fore- and mainmasts. [Perh the name Spencer]

Spencerian /spen-sē'ri-ən/ adj relating to the synthetic philosophy or evolutionary cosmology of Herbert Spencer (1820–1903). ♦ n a follower of Spencer.
■ **Spencē'rianism** n.

spend /spend/ vt (pat and pap **spent**) to expend; to pay out; to give, bestow, employ, for any purpose; to shed; to consume; to use up; to exhaust; to waste; to pass (time, etc). ♦ vi to make expense. ♦ n an act of, or the sum of money available (usu on a regular basis) for, spending. [OE spendan, from L expendere or dispendere to weigh out]
■ **spen'dable** adj. **spen'der** n. **spen'ding** n. **spent** adj used up; exhausted; (of fish) exhausted by spawning; (of a mast or yard) broken during bad weather (naut). **spen'dy** adj (**spen'dier**; **spen'diest**) (sl) expensive; profligate.
□ **spend'all** n a spendthrift. **spending money** n pocket money. **spend'thrift** n someone who spends the savings of thrift; a prodigal. ♦ adj excessively lavish. **spent force** n a person or thing whose former strength, usefulness, etc is exhausted.
■ **spend a penny** (euphem) to urinate.

Spenglerian /speng-glē'ri-ən/ adj relating to or associated with the German historian Oswald Spengler (1880–1936) and his work, esp the theory that all world civilizations are subject to the same inevitable cycle of growth and decline. ♦ n a follower of Spengler.

Spenserian /spen-sē'ri-ən/ adj relating to or associated with Edmund Spenser (1552–99) or esp his stanza in The Faerie Queene, of eight decasyllabic lines and an Alexandrine, rhymed ababbcbcc.

spent /spent/ see under **spend**.

speos /spē'os/ n (pl **spe'oses**) a temple or tomb in the form of a grotto. [Gr, cave]

Spergula /spûr'gū-lə/ n the spurrey genus of plants, related to chickweed. [LL]
■ **Spergulā'ria** n the related sandwort-spurrey genus.

sperling /spûr'ling/ same as **sparling**.

sperm /spûrm/ n semen; spermatozoa; any generative substance; eggs, spawn, brood, offspring (obs); the chalaza of a hen's egg (formerly believed to be contributed by the cock) (obs); a sperm whale; sperm oil; a sperm candle; spermaceti. ♦ combining form denoting seed. [Gr sperma, -atos seed, semen, from speirein to sow]
■ **sper'maduct** or **sper'miduct** n a duct conveying spermatozoa. **-spermal** and **-spermous** adj combining forms. **spermā'rium** or **sper'mary** n (pl **spermā'ria** or **sper'maries**) the male germ gland. **spermat'ic** adj (also **spermat'ical**) of, relating to, associated with or conveying sperm; generative. ♦ n a spermatic vessel. **sper'matid** n a cell that develops directly into a spermatozoon. **sper'matist** n a person who believes in the doctrine that the sperm contains all the material from which future generations are created. **spermatium** /-mā'shəm/ n (pl **spermā'tia**) a non-motile male gamete in red seaweeds; a sporelike structure, part of the reproductive system in some fungi and lichens. **sper'mic** adj spermatic. **spermici'dal** adj. **sper'micide** n any substance which kills spermatozoa. **spermiduct** n see spermaduct above. **spermiogen'esis** n same as spermatogenesis (see under spermato-). **sper'mogone** or **spermogō'nium** n (pl **sper'mogones** or **spermogō'nia**) a flask-shaped structure in some fungi and lichens in which spermatia are produced. **sper'mous** adj spermatic; of, derived from, or relating to the sperm whale.
□ **spermatic artery** n (anat) either of two arteries that supply blood to the testes. **spermatic cord** n (anat) the cord, consisting of the vas deferens, blood vessels and nerves, that runs from the abdominal cavity to the testicle. **sperm bank** n a refrigerated store of semen for use in artificial insemination. **sperm candle** n a candle made from spermaceti. **sperm cell** n a male gamete. **sperm count** n a measure of male fertility found by estimating the concentration of spermatozoa in semen. **sperm oil** n oil from the sperm whale. **sperm whale** n the cachalot, Physeter catodon, a whale from which spermaceti is obtained.

spermaceti /spûr-mə-set'i/ n a waxy substance obtained from oil from the head of whales, esp the sperm whale. [L sperma cētī (genitive of cētus a whale, from Gr kētos) whale's sperm, from a wrong notion of its origin]

spermaduct...to...**spermatium** see under **sperm**.

spermato- /spûr-mə-tō- or spûr-mə-to-/ or **spermat-** /spûr-mət-/ combining form denoting: (1) sperm; (2) organs or ducts conveying, or associated with, sperm. [Gr sperma, -atos seed, semen]
■ **sper'matoblast** n (Gr blastos a shoot) a spermatid. **spermatoblas'tic** adj. **sper'matocele** n (Gr kēlē tumour) a cystic swelling of the testicle arising from the epididymis and containing sperm. **sper'matocyte** n (Gr kytos vessel) a male sex cell that gives rise to spermatids or develops into an antherozoid. **spermatogenesis** /-jen'/ or **spermatogeny** /-ə-toj'i-ni/ n the process of sperm production in the testes. **spermatogenet'ic**, **spermatogen'ic** or **spermatog'enous** adj. **spermatogonium** /-gō'ni-əm/ n one of the cells that by repeated division form the spermatocytes. **sper'matophore** n a case enclosing the spermatozoa of certain crustaceans, molluscs and amphibians. **spermat'ophyte**, **sperm'aphyte** or **sperm'ophyte** n any member of the **Spermatophyta**, one of the four phyla of the plant kingdom, incl all seed-bearing plants. **spermatophytic** /-fit'ik/ (also **sperma'phytic** or **spermo'phytic**) adj. **spermatorrhoe'a** or **spermatorrhe'a** n (Gr rhoiā flow) involuntary discharge of semen. **spermatothē'ca** or **spermathē'ca** n (Gr thēkē receptacle) in female insects, etc, a receptacle in which sperms received are stored. **spermatothē'cal** or **spermathē'cal** adj. **spermatozō'al**, **spermatozō'an** or **spermatozō'ic** adj. **spermatozō'id** or **spermatozō'on** n (pl **spermatozō'ids** or **spermatozō'a**) (Gr zōion animal) a male sex cell, any of the millions contained in semen.

spermic...to...**spermogone** see under **sperm**.

spermophile /spûr'mō-fīl or -fīl/ n a ground squirrel (Spermophilus, Citellus, etc), a N American rodent related to the true squirrels and regarded as a pest in many areas. [Gr sperma seed, and phileein to love]

spermophyte see spermatophyte under spermato-.

spermous see under **sperm**.

sperre /spûr/ (Spenser) vt to bolt, bar; in Shakespeare, Troilus and Cressida, Prologue line 19, **stirre** is probably a misprint for **sperre**. [spar[1]]

sperrylite /sper'i-līt/ n a white lustrous metallic mineral, platinum diarsenide in cubic crystalline form. [FL Sperry, with Gr lithos stone]

sperse /spûrs/ (archaic) vt and vi (pat and pap (Spenser) **sperst**; also **spersed**) an aphetic form of **disperse**.

sperthe same as **sparth**.

spessartite /spes'ər-tīt/ or **spessartine** /-tīn/ n a dark, orange-red garnet, a silicate of manganese and aluminium, used as a gemstone. [From Spessart in Bavaria]

SPET or **Spet** /spet/ abbrev : single photon emission tomography.
□ **SPET scanner** n a scanner used to pinpoint areas of the cerebral cortex that are not functioning, by measuring the blood flow.

spet /spet/ (archaic and dialect) vt and vi a form of **spit**[1].

spetch /spech/ n a piece of hide, undressed leather used in making glue. [Scot and N Eng dialect speck a patch of leather or cloth]

Spetsnaz or **Spetznaz** /spets'naz/ n (also without cap) a select intelligence unit in the former Soviet Union, specializing in undercover activities, counter-insurgency tactics, raids, etc. ♦ adj (usu without cap) of or relating to the Spetsnaz. [Russ]

spew or (archaic) **spue** /spū/ vt to vomit. ♦ vi to vomit; to ooze, run. ♦ n vomited matter; a marshy spot (dialect). [OE spīwan, spīowan to spit; Du spuwen, Ger speien; also L spuere, Gr ptyein]
■ **spew'er** n. **spew'iness** n. **spew'y** adj boggy (dialect); awful, despicable (Aust sl); very angry (Aust).

SPF abbrev : sun protection factor (of a sunscreen, lotion, etc).

SPFL abbrev : Scottish Professional Football League.

SPG abbrev : formerly, Special Patrol Group.

sp.gr. abbrev : specific gravity (now relative density).

sphacelus /sfas'ə-ləs/ (pathol) n (an instance of) necrosis, mortification. [Gr sphakelos convulsive movement, painful spasm, gangrene]
■ **sphac'elate** vt to cause, or affect with, gangrene or mortification (also vi). ♦ adj (also **sphac'elated**) necrosed; dark and shrunken, as rye affected with ergot (bot). **sphacelā'tion** n.

sphaere, **sphaer** obsolete forms of **sphere**.

sphaeridium /sfē-rid'i-əm/ n (pl **sphaerid'ia**) a minute spheroidal body on the surface of a sea urchin, perhaps a sense organ. [Gr sphaira a ball]
■ **sphae'rite** n a hydrous aluminium phosphate. **sphaerocō'baltite** n cobalt carbonate, occurring in rounded masses. **sphaerocrys'tal** n a rounded crystalline mass. **sphaerosid'erite** n concretionary clay-ironstone.

sphagnum /sfag'nəm/ n any moss of the genus Sphagnum of boggy areas in temperate regions, forming peat as it decays and used in

---

■ words derived from main entry word; □ compound words; ■ idioms and phrasal verbs

horticulture, etc for its water-retentive properties (also called **peat moss** or **bog moss**). [Gr *sphagnos* a name for various plants]
■ **sphagnic'olous** *adj* (L *colere* to inhabit) living in peat moss. **sphagnol'ogist** *n*. **sphagnol'ogy** *n* the study of the sphagnum mosses. **sphag'nous** *adj*.

sphalerite /sfal'ǝ-rīt/ (*mineralogy*) *n* zinc blende, a lustrous black or brown crystalline zinc sulphide, the commonest source of zinc. [Gr *sphaleros* deceptive, from its resemblance to galena]

spheare or **sphear** archaic forms of **sphere**.

sphendone /sfen'do-nē/ *n* a headband or fillet worn by women in ancient Greece; an elliptical or semi-elliptical auditorium. [Gr *sphendonē* a sling]

sphene /sfēn/ *n* the mineral titanite, occurring as wedge-shaped crystals in igneous and metamorphic rocks. [Gr *sphēn, sphēnos* a wedge]
■ **sphē'nic** *adj* wedge-like. **Spheniscifor'mes** /sfē-nis-i-för'mēz/ *n pl* the penguin order of birds. **Sphenis'cus** /-kǝs/ *n* the jackass-penguin genus. **Sphē'nodon** *n* (Gr *odous, odontos* a tooth) the reptilian genus, also known as *Hatteria*, to which the tuatara (qv) belongs; (without *cap*) an animal of this genus. **sphē'nogram** *n* a cuneiform character. **sphē'noid** *adj* wedge-shaped, applied to a set of bones at the base of the skull. ◆ *n* a sphenoid bone; a wedge-shaped crystal form of four triangular faces. **sphenoid'al** *adj*.

sphere /sfēr/ *n* a solid figure bounded by a surface of which all points are equidistant from a centre, any cross-section of which is a circle; its bounding surface or the space enclosed by it; the apparent sphere of the heavens, upon which the stars are seen in projection; any one of the concentric spherical shells which were once supposed to carry the planets in their revolutions; a circle of society or class, *orig* of the higher ranks (as if a planetary sphere); domain, scope, range; a field of activity; condition of life; a world, mode of being; a ball, globe; a spherical object, *esp* a planet; an orbit (*archaic*). ◆ *combining form* denoting: the shape of a sphere; an area around a planet, as in *ionosphere*. ◆ *vt* to round; to place in a sphere; to encompass; to send about. [Gr *sphaira*]
■ **sphēr'al** *adj*. **sphered** *adj*. **sphere'less** *adj*. **sphere'like** *adj*. **spheric** /sfer'ik/ or **spher'ical** *adj* of a sphere or spheres; having the form of a sphere. **spherical'ity** *n*. **spher'ically** *adv*. **spher'icalness** or **sphericity** /-is'i-ti/ *n* the state or quality of being spherical. **spheristē'rion** *n* (Gr *sphairistērion*) a room or court for ball games. **spher'ocyte** *n* an abnormal red blood cell that is spherical rather than disc-shaped. **spherocyto'sis** *n* the presence of spherocytes in the blood, as in certain haemolytic anaemias. **sphē'roid** *n* a form of ellipsoid that is a body or figure which is nearly, but not quite, spherical (**oblate spheroid** a slightly flattened sphere; **prolate spheroid** a slightly lengthened sphere). **sphēroi'dal** *adj*. **sphēroidi'city** *n*. **sphēroidizā'tion** or **-s-** *n*. **sphēr'oidize** or **-ise** *vt* to develop spherulitic or granular structure in. **sphērom'eter** *n* an instrument for measuring curvature of surfaces. **spherular** /sfer'/ *adj*. **spher'ule** *n* a small sphere or spherical object. **spher'ūlite** *n* a radiating spherical group of minute crystalline fibres occurring in certain rocks. **spherūlitic** /-lit'ik/ *adj*. **sphē'ry** *adj* spherical, round; belonging to the celestial spheres.
□ **sphere'-born** *adj* (Milton) of celestial origin. **spherical aberration** *n* (*phys, optics*) loss of image definition which occurs when light strikes a lens or mirror with a spherical surface. **spherical angle** *n* an angle formed by arcs of great circles on the surface of a sphere. **spherical coordinates** *n pl* a set of coordinates locating a point in three-dimensional space. **spherical geometry** *n* the branch of geometry dealing with the properties of figures on the surface of spheres. **spherical polygon** *n* a closed figure bounded by three or more arcs of great circles on the surface of a sphere. **spherical triangle** *n* a three-sided figure on the surface of a sphere, bounded by arcs of great circles. **spherical trigonometry** *n* the branch of trigonometry concerned with the measurement of these.
■ **music** (or **harmony**) **of the spheres** the music, inaudible to mortal ears, produced according to Pythagoras by the motions of the celestial spheres in accordance with the laws of harmony. **sphere of influence** any region over which one nation has a dominant influence.

spherics[1] or (*N Am*) **sferics** /sfer'iks or sfē'riks/ *n pl* a shortened form of **atmospherics**.

spherics[2] *n sing* the geometry and trigonometry of the sphere.

sphincter /sfingk'tǝr/ (*anat*) *n* a ringlike muscle whose contraction narrows or shuts an orifice, eg the anus. [Gr *sphinktēr*, from *sphingein* to bind tight]
■ **sphinc'teral, sphincterial** /-tē'ri-ǝl/ or **sphincteric** /-ter'ik/ *adj*.

sphingomyelin /sfin-go-mī'ǝ-lin/ (*biol*) *n* a phospholipid derived from sphingosine, occurring in cell membranes. [From Gr *sphingein* to bind, and **myelin**]

sphingosine /sfin'gǝ-sīn/ (*biol*) *n* a hydrophobic amino alcohol, a component of sphingomyelins and cerebrosides. [From Gr *sphingein* to bind, and **-ine**[1]]

Sphinx or **sphinx** /sfingks/ *n* (pl **sphinx'es** or **sphinges** /sfin'jēz/) a monster of Greek mythology, with the head of a woman and the body of a lioness, that lay outside Thebes and proposed riddles to travellers, strangling those who could not solve them; any similar monster or representation of one, *esp* any of numerous massive stone statues built by the ancient Egyptians; an enigmatic or inscrutable person (from the facial expression of the huge stone sphinx at El Gîza). [Gr, from *sphingein* to draw tight]
■ **sphingid** /sfin'jid/ *n* and *adj* (a member) of the Sphingidae, the hawk moth family, so called because the posture of its larvae resembles that of the sphinx. **sphinx'like** *adj*.
□ **sphinx moth** *n* (*N Am*) the hawk moth.

sphragistic /sfrǝ-jis'tik/ *adj* relating to seals and signets. [Gr *sphrāgistikos*, from *sphrāgis* a seal]
■ **sphragist'ics** *n sing* the study of seals and signets.

sphygmus /sfig'mǝs/ *n* the pulse. [Latinized from Gr *sphygmos* pulse]
■ **sphyg'mic** *adj*. **sphyg'mogram** *n* a sphygmograph record. **sphyg'mograph** *n* an instrument for recording the pulse, showing the rate and strength of the beats. **sphygmograph'ic** *adj*. **sphygmog'raphy** *n*. **sphyg'moid** *adj* resembling a pulse. **sphygmol'ogy** *n* the science or study of the pulse. **sphygmōmanom'eter** or **sphygmom'eter** *n* an instrument for measuring arterial blood pressure, consisting of an inflatable cuff for the arm connected to a column of mercury which indicates systolic and diastolic pressure in millimetres. **sphyg'mophone** *n* an instrument that records and transmits pulse beats as sounds. **sphyg'moscope** *n* an instrument for making arterial pulsations visible.

spial /spī'ǝl/ (*obs*) *n* observation, watch; a spy, scout. [Aphetic from **espial**]

spic[1], **spick** or **spik** /spik/ (*esp US derog sl*) *n* a person from a Spanish-speaking American country, or of Mexican, S American, etc origin; a member of one of the Mediterranean races. [Origin uncertain]

spic[2] see **spick and span** under **spick**[1].

spica /spī'kǝ/ *n* (pl **spi'cae** or **spi'cas**) a bandage wound around an injured limb in repeated figures-of-eight forming a series of overlapping V-shapes suggesting an ear of barley; in birds, a spur. [L *spīca* an ear of corn]
■ **spī'cate** or **spī'cated** *adj* (*esp bot*) in, having, or forming a spike; spikelike. **spicilege** /spī'si-lij/ *n* (L *spīcilegium*, from *legere* to gather) a gleaning; an anthology. **spicula** /spik'ū-lǝ/ *n* a spicule, prickle, or splinter. **spic'ūlar** *adj* of the nature of or like a spicule. **spic'ūlate** *adj* having spicules. **spic'ūle** *n* a minute needlelike body, crystal, splinter, or process; a small splinter of bone (*med*); one of the spikelike forms seen forming and reforming on the edge of the sun, caused by ejections of hot gas several thousand miles above its surface. **spic'ūlum** *n* (pl **spic'ūla**) a little spine; a spicula; a snail's dart.

spiccato /spik-kä'tō/ (*music*) *adj* and *adv* with staccato bowing. ◆ *n* (pl **spicca'tos**) spiccato playing, or a spiccato passage. [Ital]

spice /spīs/ *n* any aromatic and pungent vegetable substance used as a condiment and for seasoning food, eg pepper, cayenne pepper, pimento, nutmeg, mace, vanilla, ginger, cinnamon, cassia, etc; such substances collectively or generally; a characteristic smack, flavour; anything that adds piquancy or interest; an aromatic odour; sweetmeats (*dialect*); a touch, tincture (*fig*). ◆ *vt* to season with spice; to tincture, vary, or diversify; (with *up*) to add an interesting quality to. [OFr *espice* (Fr *épice*), from LL *speciēs* kinds of goods, spices, from L *speciēs* a kind]
■ **spiced** *adj* impregnated with a spicy odour; seasoned with spice; over-scrupulous (*obs*). **spīc'er** *n* (*obs*) a dealer in spices or drugs. **spīc'ery** *n* spices in general; a repository of spices; spiciness. **spīc'ily** *adv*. **spīc'iness** *n*. **spīc'y** *adj* producing or abounding with spices; fragrant; pungent; piquant, pointed; racy; risqué; showy.
□ **spice'berry** *n* any of several plants having spicy edible berries, eg a small American tree, *Eugenia rhombea*, with black or orange fruits; the fruit of this tree. **spice box** *n* a box, often ornamental, for keeping spices. **spice'bush** *n* an aromatic American shrub (*Lindera benzoin*) of the laurel family. **spice cake** *n* any spiced cake.

spicilege see under **spica**.

spick[1] /spik/ *n* a nail, a (wooden) spike. ◆ *adj* tidy, fresh. [**spike**[1]]
■ **spick** (or **spic**) **and span** trim and speckless (like a newly cut spike or a newly split chip). **spick and span new** brand-new.

spick[2] see **spic**[1].

spicknel see **spignel**.

spicule, etc see under **spica**.

spicy see under **spice**.

spide an obsolete spelling of **spied** (see **spy**).

spider /spī'dər/ n an arachnid of the order Araneae, the body divided into two distinct parts, an unsegmented cephalothorax with four pairs of legs, and a soft unsegmented abdomen with spinnerets; formerly, a light high-wheeled horse-drawn carriage (in full **spider phaeton**); a frying-pan, properly one with feet; any of various spiderlike radiating structures, instruments, tools, etc; a rest for a cue in snooker or billiards, specif one with legs arched wide and offering several cueing positions; an arrangement of elastic straps with hooks attached, used to fasten luggage, etc onto the roof rack of a car or onto a motorcycle, etc; a computer program that performs automatic searches on the Internet. [OE spīthra, from spinnan to spin; cf Dan spinder, Ger Spinne]
■ **spi'derlike** adj. **spi'dery** adj spiderlike; thin and straggling; abounding in spiders. □ **spider beetle** n a long-legged wingless beetle of the Ptinidae family. **spider crab** n a crab with long thin legs. **spider flower** n an annual plant of the genus Cleome, bearing clusters of white or pink flowers with long stamens reminiscent of spider's legs. **spider hole** n (milit) a hole in the ground to conceal a sniper. **spi'der-hunting wasp** n a large solitary digger wasp that preys on spiders. **spider leg** n a long thin leg. **spi'der-legged** adj. **spider line** n a thread of silk spun by a spider; any fine thread in an optical instrument, for measurement, position-marking, etc. **spi'derman** n a building worker who erects the steel structure of a tall building. **spider mite** n any web-spinning mite of the family Tetranychidae, feeding on, and often a serious pest of, plants, eg the **red spider mite** (Panonychus ulmi). **spider monkey** n an American monkey of the genus Ateles, with long slender legs and tail. **spider plant** n any of various plants of the genus Chlorophytum, with spiky, variegated leaves, esp Chlorophytum comosum which grows new plantlets on trailing stems; spiderwort. **spider spanner** see **spider wrench** below. **spider stitch** n a stitch in lace or netting in which threads are carried diagonally and parallel to each other. **spider web** n the snare spun by a spider. **spider wheel** n (in embroidery) a circular pattern with radiating lines. **spi'derwork** n lace worked by spider stitch. **spi'derwort** n any plant of the American commelinaceous genus Tradescantia, esp T. virginiana, with deep-blue or reddish-violet flowers. **spider wrench** or **spanner** n a box-spanner having heads of different sizes at the ends of radial arms.

spie (Spenser, Milton, etc) an archaic spelling of **spy**.

spied see **spy**.

spiegeleisen /spē'gl-ī-zn/ n a white cast iron containing manganese, largely used in the manufacture of steel by the Bessemer process. [Ger, from Spiegel, from L speculum a mirror, and Ger Eisen iron]

spiel /spēl or shpēl/ n a (esp plausible) story or line of talk. ◆ vi to talk glibly, tell the tale (also vt). [Ger spielen to play]
■ **spiel'er** n a person with a glib, persuasive line of talk; a swindler or a card-sharper; a gambling den (criminal sl).

spies see **spy**.

spiff /spif/ (dialect) adj smart, spruce (also **spiff'y**). ◆ vt (with up) to smarten up, make more attractive. [Origin obscure]
■ **spiff'ing** adj (old inf) excellent.

spifflicate or **spifflicate** /spif'li-kāt/ (esp school sl) vt to destroy; to quell; to confound; to handle roughly.
■ **spifflicā'tion** or **spifflicā'tion** n.

Spigelia /spī-jē'li-ə/ n the pink-root genus of Loganiaceae. [Adrian van den Spiegel (1578–1625), Belgian physician and anatomist]
■ **Spigē'lian** adj of van den Spiegel or of Spigelia; applied to the lobulus Spigelii, one of the lobes of the liver.

spight /spīt/ v and n (Spenser and Shakesp) same as **spite**.

spignel /spig'nl/ n baldmoney or meu, a European plant, Meum athamanticum, of mountainous regions (also (obs) **spick'nel**). [Origin obscure]

spigot /spig'ət/ n a peg for a vent-hole, or peg used to close the opening of a tube or pipe; an end of a pipe that fits into another; a tap or faucet (N Am); an interface (comput). [Provençal espigot, from L spīculum]

spik see **spic¹**.

spike¹ /spīk/ n a hard thin pointed object; a large nail; a sharp metal projection, eg one of those forming a row along the top of a railing, etc; a sharp-pointed metal rod set upright on a base, on which to impale documents requiring attention, etc; (in pl) spiked shoes, worn, esp by athletes, to prevent slipping; a bayonet (milit sl); a hypodermic needle (sl); a workhouse or its casual ward (old sl); a dosshouse (Brit sl); a short period of increased activity, eg a sudden surge of power on an electronic circuit. ◆ vt to fasten, set, pierce or damage with a spike or spikes; to make (eg a gun) useless, orig by driving a spike into the vent; to frustrate, put a stop to; to make (a drink) stronger by adding spirits or other alcohol (inf); to contaminate (eg food) by the addition

of a harmful substance (inf); to reject (a news article, etc) (press); to hit (a volleyball) so that it flies forcefully downwards into the opposing team's court; to inject with a drug (inf). ◆ vi to form a spike or peak; to inject oneself with a drug (inf). [OE spīcing a spike-nail; poss from L spīca an ear of corn]
■ **spiked** adj. **spīk'ily** adv. **spīk'iness** n. **spīk'y** adj having or provided with spikes; having a sharp point; irritable, acerbic; characterized by irritable, difficult or jarring disagreements or incidents.
□ **spike'fish** n (US) a kind of sailfish. **spike heel** n a very narrow metal heel on a woman's shoe. **spike'-nail** n a large small-headed nail.

spike² /spīk/ n an ear of corn; an inflorescence in which sessile flowers or spikelets are arranged on a long axis (bot); a kind of lavender (**spike lavender**). ◆ vi to develop a spike. [L spīca an ear of corn]
■ **spike'let** n (in grasses, etc) a small crowded spike, itself forming part of a greater inflorescence.
□ **spike grass** n Uniola or other American grass with conspicuous spikelets. **spike oil** n the oil of spike lavender. **spike'-rush** n any of several sedges of the genus Eleocharis, closely related to the true sedges, with stiff tufted stems and solitary spikelets.

spike³ /spīk/ n a very High-Church Anglican, an Anglo-Catholic. [From **spiky** (see under **spike¹**)]
■ **spīk'ery** n. **spīk'y** adj very High-Church.

spikenard /spīk'närd/ n an aromatic oil or balsam yielded by an Indian valerianaceous herb (Nardostachys jatamansi; also called **nard**) or a synthetic substitute for this; the plant itself. [L spīca nardi]
■ **ploughman's spikenard** a European and N African spikenard with yellow flowers and aromatic roots (Inula conyzae).

spile /spīl/ n a plug; a spigot; a pile for a foundation; a stake, or post for fencing. ◆ vt to pierce and provide with a spile; to shape (the timbers of a wooden vessel or the ribs of a steel vessel) to form a gradual slope towards the bow and/or stern (naut). [Cf LGer spile, Du spijl, Ger Speil]
■ **spī'ling** n.
■ **soft spile** in beer-making, a wooden peg driven into a cask to allow carbon dioxide to escape during secondary fermentation.

spilikin see under **spill²**.

spilite /spī'līt/ (geol) n a fine-grained igneous rock of basaltic composition, often developed as submarine lava-flows. [Gr spilos a spot]
■ **spilitic** /-it'ik/ adj. **spī'losite** n a spotted slate, formed by contact metamorphism.

spill¹ /spil/ vt (pat and pap **spilled** or **spilt**) to allow to run out of a container; to shed; to waste; to throw from a vehicle or the saddle (inf); to empty from the belly of a sail or empty of wind for reefing; to overlay as if by spilling (Spenser); to kill (obs); to destroy (obs). ◆ vi to overflow; to be shed; to be allowed to fall, be lost, or wasted; to come to grief or ruin (obs). ◆ n a fall, a throw; a spilling. [OE spillan; Du spillen, ON spilla to destroy]
■ **spill'age** n the act of spilling; that which is spilt. **spill'er** n. **spill'ing** n. **spilth** n spilling; anything spilt or poured out lavishly; excess.
□ **spilling line** n a rope for spilling the wind out of a square sail. **spill'over** n an overflow (also fig). **spill'-stream** n an overflow channel; a bayou. **spill'way** n (inf) a passage for overflow water.
■ **spill one's guts** (inf) to confess all that one knows. **spill over** to overflow (also fig). **spill the beans** see under **bean**.

spill² /spil/ n a spile; a thin strip of wood or paper for lighting a candle, a pipe, etc. [Connection with **spile** or with **spell⁴** doubtful]
■ **spill'ikin**, **spill'ikin** or **spell'ican** n a small slip of wood, ivory, etc, to be picked out from a heap without disturbing the others in the game of **spillikins**.

spillage, etc see under **spill¹**.

spilosite see under **spilite**.

spilt /spilt/ pat and pap of **spill¹**.

spilth see under **spill¹**.

spin /spin/ vt (**spinn'ing**; **spun**, archaic **span**; **spun**) to draw out and twist into threads; to draw out a thread as spiders do; to form by spinning; to draw out; to make to last (usu with out); to send hurtling; to twirl, set revolving rapidly; to spin-dry; to play (a record, CD, etc); to put a favourable slant on (an item of news, policy, etc); to fish with a swivel or spoonbait; to reject at an examination (sl). ◆ vi to practise the art or trade or perform the act of spinning; to rotate rapidly; to whirl; to hurtle; to go swiftly, esp on wheels; to spurt; to stream vigorously; to lengthen out, last (usu with out); to present information in a misleadingly favourable form; to fish with rotating bait. ◆ n the act or result of spinning; a rotatory motion; a playing of a record, etc; a cycle ride; a short trip in a motor car; a spurt at high speed; a spiral descent (lit and fig); a favourable slant on an item of news, policy, etc; the practice of applying this; a period of time, an experience (Aust and NZ

inf); the intrinsic angular momentum of an electron, nucleus or elementary particle, quantized in integral multiples of half of **Dirac's constant** (Planck's constant divided by 4π) (*phys*); confused excitement; the sum of five dollars (*Aust*). [OE *spinnan* ; Ger *spinnen*] ■ **spin'ar** *n* (*astron*) a rapidly spinning galactic body. **spinn'er** *n* someone who or something that spins; a spider (*Shakesp*); a spinneret; a spinning-machine; a ball with imparted spin, causing it to deviate after pitching (*cricket*); a spin bowler; an artificial fly that revolves in the water (*angling*); a rotating display stand (eg for books) in a shop, etc; a spin doctor. **spinn'eret** *n* a spinning organ in spiders, etc; a plate with holes from which filaments of plastic material are expressed (also **spinnerette**). **spinn'erule** /-ə-*rool* or -*rūl*/ *n* one of the tubules of a spinneret. **spinn'ery** *n* a spinning-mill. **Spinn'ing**® *n* an aerobic exercise performed on stationary indoor bicycles, and involving frequent changes of pace. **spinn'ing** *n* and *adj*. **spintron'ic** *adj*. **spintron'ics** *n sing* (*phys*) the study of the spin of electrons with a view to creating systems that allow very fast storage and retrieval of information.
□ **spin bowler** *n*. **spin bowling** *n* (*cricket*) a style of slower bowling in which the ball is given a twisting motion by the bowler's wrist or fingers, in order to make it deviate after striking the ground. **spin doctor** or **spin'-doctor** *n* (*orig US*) someone (often a public relations expert) employed by a politician, etc to influence public opinion, *esp* by presenting information to the public in the most favourable light. **spin drier** or **spin dryer** *n* a device that dries washed clothes without wringing, to a point ready for ironing, by forcing the water out of them under pressure of centrifugal force in a rapidly revolving drum. **spin-dry'** *vt* (*pat* and *pap* **spin-dried'** or **spun-dry'**). **spinn'ing-house** *n* (*hist*) a place of correction where lewd and incorrigible women were made to spin. **spinning jenny** *n* a machine by which a number of threads can be spun at once; a cranefly (*dialect*). **spinn'ing-mill** *n* a factory where thread is spun. **spinning mule** *n* an early form of spinning machine. **spinning top** see **top²**. **spinn'ing-wheel** *n* a machine for spinning yarn, consisting of a wheel driven by the hand or by a treadle, which drives one or two spindles. **spin'-off** *n* a process of transference of business on the US stock-market; a by-product that proves profitable on its own account; an incidental benefit. ◆ *adj* (of a product or benefit) arising incidentally from another process. **spin'out** *n* a spinning skid that throws a motor vehicle off the road, track, etc. **spin'-out** *adj* having its origins in another process or organization. **spin stabilization** *n* the stabilizing of the flight of a projected bullet, space rocket, etc by giving it a spinning motion. **spin'-the-bott'le** *n* a party game in which an empty bottle is spun on its side in the centre of a circle of people, the person to whom the neck of the bottle points when it comes to rest being chosen to perform some task such as kissing another person.
■ **flat spin** a state of panic. **on the spin** (*inf*) in succession, without a break. **spin a yarn** to tell a story. **spin off** (*business*) to make (a subsidiary company) independent of the parent company. **spin out** to prolong, protract; (of a vehicle) to execute a spinning skid and leave the road, etc; (of an educational establishment) to create (a company) to exploit commercial opportunities identified by its research.

spina bifida /*spī'*nə *bif'*i-də/ *n* a congenital defect in which one or more vertebrae fail to unite during the embryo stage, resulting in exposure of part of the spinal cord and often permanent paralysis. [See **spine** and **bifid**]

spinach /*spin'*ij or -*ich*/ or **spinage** /-*ij*/ *n* a plant (*Spinacia oleracea*) of the goosefoot family; its young leaves used as a vegetable; extended to various other plants. [OFr *espinage, espinache* ; of doubtful origin, poss from L *spīna*, poss Ar *isfīnāj*]
■ **spinaceous** /*spin-ā'*shəs/ *adj*.
□ **spinach beet** *n* a kind of beet used like spinach.

spinal see under **spine**.

spinar see under **spin**.

spinate see under **spine**.

spindle /*spin'*dl/ *n* the pin by which thread is twisted; a pin on which anything turns; the fusee of a watch; anything very slender; a spindle-shaped structure containing microtubules, formed within the nucleus or cytoplasm at the end of prophase during mitosis and meiosis (*biol*). ◆ *vi* to grow long and slender. [OE *spinel*, from *spinnan* to spin; Ger *Spindel*]
■ **spin'dling** *n* a person or thing too long and slender; a slender shoot. ◆ *adj* long and slender. **spin'dly** *adj* disproportionally long and slender.
□ **spin'dle-legged** or **spin'dle-shanked** *adj* having long thin legs, like spindles. **spin'dle-legs** or **spin'dle-shanks** *n pl* long slim legs; hence (as *sing*) a person with long thin legs. **spindle moulder** *n* (*building*) a woodworking machine with a revolving spindle to which cutters of various shapes can be fixed. **spindle oil** *n* very light and fluid lubricating oil. **spin'dle-shaped** *adj* shaped like a spindle, thickest in the middle and tapering to both ends. **spindle shell** *n* a gastropod (genus *Fusus*) with a spindle-shaped shell. **spindle side** *n*

the female side or line of descent, distaff side, *opp* to *spear side*. **spindle tree** *n* a shrub (*Euonymus europaeus*) of the Celastraceae, whose hard-grained wood was used for making spindles. **spindle whorl** *n* a heavy ring giving momentum to the spindle.

spindrift /*spin'*drift/ *n* the spray blown from the crests of waves; fine snow or sand driven by wind. [See **spoon²** and **drift**]

spine /*spīn*/ *n* a thorn, *esp* one formed by a modified branch or leaf; a long sharp process of a leaf; a thin, pointed spike, *esp* in fishes; the spinal column; firmness of character; any ridge extending lengthways; heartwood; the back of a book; a pay scale organized on linear but flexible principles. [L *spīna* a thorn]
■ **spī'na** *n* the spinal column; a quill of a spinet; a lengthwise barrier in a Roman circus (*ancient hist*). **spī'nal** *adj* of the backbone. **spī'nate** or **spined** *adj* having a spine or spines. **spine'less** *adj* having no spine; weak; vacillating; lacking courage, *esp* moral courage. **spine'lessly** *adv*. **spine'lessness** *n*. **spinesc'ence** *n*. **spīnesc'ent** *adj* tapering or developing into a spine; tending to become spinous; somewhat spiny. **spīnif'erous** *adj* thornbearing. **spī'niform** *adj* like a thorn. **spīnig'erous** *adj* bearing spines. **spī'nigrade** *adj* moving by means of spines, as an echinoderm does. **spī'niness** *n*. **spī'nose** (or /-*nōs'*/) *adj* full of spines; thorny. **spīnos'ity** *n* thorniness. **spī'nous** *adj* spinose; like a thorn or spine in appearance (*anat*, etc). **spin'ūlate** *adj*. **spinule** /*spin'* or *spīn'*/ *n* (*biol*) a small or minute spine. **spinūlesc'ent** *adj*. **spinūlif'erous** *adj*. **spin'ūlōse** or **spin'ūlous** *adj*. **spī'ny** *adj* full of spines; thorny; troublesome; perplexed.
□ **spina bifida** *n* see separate entry. **spinal anaesthesia** *n* injection of an anaesthetic into the spinal canal, producing suppression of sensation in part of the body but not unconsciousness; loss of sensation in part of the body due to injury to, or disease of, the spinal cord. **spinal canal** *n* a passage running through the spinal column, containing the spinal cord. **spinal column** *n* in vertebrates, the articulated series of vertebrae extending from the skull to the tip of the tail, forming the axis of the skeleton and enclosing the spinal cord. **spinal cord** or **chord** *n* the main neural axis in vertebrates. **spinal tap** *n* (*N Am*) a lumbar puncture. **spine'-bashing** *n* (*Aust sl*) loafing, lying down, sleeping. **spine'-basher** *n*. **spine'-chiller** *n* a frightening story, thought or happening. **spine'-chilling** *adj*. **spine'-tingling** *adj* causing a frisson of fear, pleasure or excitement. **spiny anteater** *n* an echidna. **spiny lobster** *n* a marine crustacean similar to the lobster but smaller and without claws, the langouste.

spinel /*spi-nel'* or *spin'*əl/ *n* any mineral of a group of aluminates, ferrates, and chromates of magnesium, iron, zinc, etc crystallizing in octahedra. [Ital *spinella*]
□ **spinel ruby** *n* ruby spinel, a variety of magnesian spinel with the colour of a true ruby.

spinescence, etc see under **spine**.

spinet or **spinette** /*spin'*it or *spi-net'*/ *n* a musical instrument like a small harpsichord (also **spinnet**). [Ital *spinetta*, poss from maker G *Spinetti* (*fl* 1500)]

Spinhaler® /*spin-hā'*lər/ *n* a device for inhaling anti-asthmatic drugs.

spiniferous see under **spine**.

spinifex /*spin'*i-, *spī'*ni-*feks*/ *n* a sharp-pointed Australian grass (genus *Spinifex*), of arid regions, whose spiny heads blow about and disseminate seed; popularly applied in Australia to porcupine grass. [L *spīna* spine, and the root of *facere* to make]

spiniform, **spinigerous**, etc see under **spine**.

spink¹ /*spingk*/ (now *dialect*) *n* a finch, *esp* the chaffinch. [Perh imit]

spink² /*spingk*/ *n* the lady's smock or cuckoo flower. [Ety dubious]

spinnaker /*spin'*ə-kər/ (*naut*) *n* a three-cornered lightweight sail, normally set forward of a yacht's mast to increase sail area when running before the wind or on a broad reach, and which on racing yachts has a great deal of flow in the belly of the canvas and is often brightly coloured. [Perh from **spin** and **moniker**, or from *spinxer* a word coined when it was first introduced on the yacht *Sphinx* in the 1870s]

spinner, **spinneret**, etc see under **spin**.

spinnet see **spinet**.

spinney or **spinny** /*spin'*i/ *n* (*pl* **spinn'eys** or **spinn'ies**) a copse or small clump of trees. [OFr *espinei*, from L *spīnētum* a thorn hedge, thicket, from *spīna* thorn]

spino- /*spī-nō-*/ *combining form* signifying spine.

spinode /*spī'*nōd/ *n* a cusp or stationary point of a curve. [L *spīna* thorn, and *nōdus* knot]

spinose, **spinous**, etc see under **spine**.

Spinozism /*spi-nō'*zi-zm/ (*philos*) *n* the doctrines of the Dutch philosopher Benedict (or Baruch) *Spinoza* (1632–77), *esp* the definitions, axioms and theorems of his metaphysical treatise *Ethics* ; the pantheistic monism of Spinoza.

■ **Spinō′zist** n a follower of Spinoza or adherent of Spinozism. **Spinōzis′tic** adj.

spinster /spin′stər/ n an unmarried woman; an old maid; a woman fit for the spinning-house (obs); a spinner (obs and Shakesp). [**spin**, and **-ster**]

■ **spin′sterdom** n the world of old maids collectively. **spin′sterhood** n. **spinsterial** /-stē′ri-əl/ adj. **spinstē′rian** adj. **spin′sterish** adj. **spin′sterly** adj. **spin′stership** n. **spin′stress** n a woman who spins; a spinster.

spintext or **spin-text** /spin′tekst/ n a clergyman, a long-winded preacher. [**spin** and **text**]

spinthariscope /spin-thā′ri-skōp/ n an instrument for counting alpha particles by observing the sparks produced by their impact on a fluorescent screen. [Gr spintharis a spark, and skopeein to observe]

spinto /spin′tō/ (music) adj denoting a voice (or the music written for it) having dramatic lyrical qualities. [Ital, pap of spingere to push]

spinule, spiny, etc see under **spine**.

spiracle /spī′rə-kl/ n a breathing hole (zool); a vent, orifice, passage (geol). [L spīrāculum, from spīrāre to breathe]

■ **spīracular** /-ak′ū-lər/ adj. **spīrac′ulate** adj. **spīrac′ulum** n (pl **spīrac′ula**).

spiraea or (esp N Am) **spirea** /spī-rē′ə/ n a plant or shrub of the rosaceous genus Spiraea, having flattened or plume-shaped heads of small pink or white flowers. [Gr speiraiā privet, from speira a coil (from its coiled fruits)]

spiral, etc see under **spire**[1,2].

spirant /spī′rənt/ (phonetics) adj fricative, open, produced by narrowing without stopping the air-passage. ◆ n a spirant consonant (including or excluding nasals, liquids, and semi-vowels). [L spīrāre to breathe]

■ **spīrā′tion** n breathing; the procession of the Holy Ghost (theol).

spiraster, spirated see under **spire**[2].

spire[1] /spīr/ n a tapering or conical body, esp a tree-top; a flower spike; a tall slender architectural structure tapering to a point; a shoot, sprout; a stalk, esp a long slender one; a reed or reedlike plant (also collectively); a deer's tine; a spike; a cone; a summit, peak. ◆ vi to sprout; to shoot up. ◆ vt to furnish with, or form into, a spire; to put forth as a shoot or fruit (Spenser). [OE spīr shoot, stem; cf **spike**[2], **spine**]

■ **spīr′al** adj (rare) towering and tapering. **spir′alism** n advancement through, or the concept of, a spirally structured career (or social, etc) system. **spir′alist** n someone engaged in spiralism; loosely, an ambitious person. **spir′ally** adv. **spired** adj having a spire; tapering, conical; peaked; spiked; sprouted. **spire′less** adj. **spire′wise** adv. **spīr′y** adj shooting into spires; spire-like; tapering; abounding in spires.

❑ **spire′-steeple** n a steeple with a spire.

spire[2] /spīr/ n a coil; a spiral; the helical part of a shell, excluding the body-whorl. ◆ vi to wind, mount, or proceed in spirals. [Gr speira a coil, a tore]

■ **spīr′al** adj (in general but non-technical usage) winding like the thread of a screw; with parts arranged in spirals (bot). ◆ n a spiral line, course, or object; a two-dimensional curve, the locus of a point whose distance from a fixed point varies according to some rule as the radius vector revolves (maths); (in general but non-technical usage) a helix; a gradual but continuous rise or fall, as of prices. ◆ vi to go in a spiral; (of stocks and shares) to decrease in value uncontrollably (inf). ◆ vt to make spiral. **spīral′iform** adj in or based on the shape of a spiral. **spīrality** /-al′i-ti/ n. **spīr′ally** adv. **spīras′ter** n (Gr astēr star) a coiled sponge spicule with radiating spines. **spīr′āted** adj spirally twisted. **spīr′ēme** n in mitosis, the coiled thread formed by nuclear chromatin. **spīr′ic** adj like a tore or anchor-ring. ◆ n a curve, the plane section of a tore. **spīrill′ar** adj. **spīrillō′sis** n infection with a spirillum. **spīrill′um** n (pl **spīrill′a**) any rigid, spiral-shaped bacterium of the genus Spirillum, eg S. minus that causes ratbite fever. **spī′roid** adj with the form of, or like, a spiral. **spīr′y** adj spirally coiled.

❑ **spiral arm** n an arm of a spiral galaxy. **spiral binding** n a method of binding a book or notebook by threading a wire or plastic spiral through punched holes at the spine of each page. **spiral bound** adj. **spiral fracture** n (med) a fracture of a bone caused by a sudden violent twisting movement. **spiral galaxy** n (astron) one of a large class of galaxies, with two spiral arms emerging from a bright central ellipsoidal nucleus about which they rotate. **spiral ratchet screwdriver** n a ratchet screwdriver which can be made to turn in either direction by downward pressure on a sleeve which applies torque to helical grooves in the shaft. **spiral staircase** n a staircase in the form of a spiral, with a central column around which the steps are built.

spirea see **spiraea**.

spirit /spir′it/ n the vital principle; the principle of thought; the soul; a disembodied soul; a ghost; an incorporeal being; enthusiasm; actuating emotion, disposition, frame of mind; a leading, independent, or lively person; animation; verve; courage; mettle; real meaning; essence, chief quality; a breath of wind (archaic or poetic); a breath (obs); a breathing (Gr grammar); a kidnapper (obs); (usu in pl) a formerly supposed subtle substance in the body; (in pl) cheerful or exuberant vivacity; (in pl) state of mind, mood; (in pl) mental powers (obs); (in pl) spirituous liquor; (the following also in pl, sometimes with verb in sing) a distilled liquid; an aqueous solution of ethyl alcohol; a solution in alcohol. ◆ vt to give spirit to; to inspirit, encourage, cheer; to convey away secretly, to kidnap (often with away, off). [L spīritus a breath, from spīrāre to breathe]

■ **spir′ited** adj full of spirit, life, or fire; animated; possessed by a spirit. **spir′itedly** adv. **spir′itedness** n. **spir′itful** adj. **spir′iting** n the action of someone who spirits in any sense; the behaviour of a spirit or sprite. **spir′itism** n spiritualism; animism. **spir′itist** n. **spiritist′ic** adj. **spir′itless** adj without spirit, cheerfulness, or courage; dejected; dead. **spir′itlessly** adv. **spir′itlessness** n. **spir′itous** adj of the nature of spirit, pure; ardent, spirituous. **spir′itousness** n. **spir′itūal** adj of, of the nature of, relating to, spirit, a spirit, spirits, the mind, the higher faculties, the soul; highly refined in thought and feeling, habitually or naturally looking to things of the spirit; incorporeal; ecclesiastical, religious; witty, clever, as a Gallicism; spirituous (obs or rare). ◆ n that which is spiritual; a black American religious song. **spir′itualism** n the condition of being spiritual; the philosophical doctrine that nothing is real but soul or spirit; the doctrine that spirit has a real existence apart from matter; the interpretation of a varied series of abnormal phenomena as for the most part caused by spiritual beings acting upon specially sensitive persons or mediums (also **spir′itism**). **spir′itualist** n someone who has a regard only to spiritual things; (sometimes with cap) someone who holds the doctrine of spiritualism or spiritism. **spiritualist′ic** adj. **spirituality** /-al′i-ti/ n the state of being spiritual; that which is spiritual; property held or revenue received in return for spiritual service (hist); the clergy (hist). **spiritualīzā′tion** or **-s-** n. **spir′itualize** or **-ise** vt to make spiritual; to imbue with spirituality; to refine; to free from sensuality; to give a spiritual meaning to. **spir′itualizer** or **-s-** n. **spir′itually** adv. **spir′itualness** n the state or quality of being spiritual. **spir′itualty** n (obs or hist) spirituality; the clergy. **spirituel**, also fem (indiscriminately used) **spirituelle** /spē-rē-tü-el′ or (inf) spir-it-ū-el′/ adj showing refined and witty grace and delicacy. **spirituos′ity** n spirituous character; immateriality. **spir′ituous** adj sprightly (obs); spiritual (obs); of the nature of, or containing, a volatile substance (archaic); alcoholic. **spir′ituousness** n. **spiritus** /spīr′ or spir′i-tas or spē′ri-tūs/ n spirit; a breathing (Gr grammar; **spiritus asper** rough breathing, **spiritus lenis** smooth breathing). **spir′ity** adj (dialect or inf) spirited; spirituous.

❑ **spir′it-blue** n aniline blue. **spirit duck** n another name for the bufflehead, from its rapid diving. **spirit duplicator** n one that uses a solution of alcohol in the copying process. **spirit gum** n a preparation used by actors for attaching false beards, etc. **spirit lamp** n a lamp burning methylated or other spirit to give heat. **spirit level** n a glass tube nearly filled with usu alcohol, showing perfect levelness when the bubble is central. **spirit master** n the master sheet used in a spirit duplicator. **spirit photography** n the taking of photographs of people in which other shadowy figures appear. **spirit rally** n (US) a mass meeting held to arouse enthusiasm, celebrate achievements, honour deserving individuals, etc. **spirit rapper** n someone who claims to receive messages from disembodied spirits by raps or knocks. **spir′it-rapping** n. **spir′it-stirring** adj rousing the spirit. **spiritual healing** n the transfer of healing energy by the laying on of hands or (in absent or distant healing) by visualizing its transfer. **spirit varnish** n shellac or other resin in a volatile solvent, usu alcohol. **spirit world** n the world of disembodied spirits.

■ **animal spirits** a form of energy formerly believed to be sent along the nerves from the brain in order to cause sensation and motion; hence, constitutional liveliness. **Holy Spirit** or **the Spirit** see **Holy Ghost** under **holy. in spirits** cheerfully vivacious. **out of spirits** depressed. **spirit** (or **spirits**) **of ammonia** sal volatile. **spirit** (or **spirits**) **of salt** hydrochloric acid in water. **spirit** (or **spirits**) **of wine** alcohol.

spiritoso /spir-i-tō′sō or -zō/ (music) adj and adv with spirit. [Ital]

spirling see **sparling**.

spiro-[1] /spī-rō-/ or **spir-** /spir-/ combining form denoting spiral, as in spirochaete. [Gr speira a coil]

spiro-[2] /spī-rō-/ combining form denoting breathing, respiration. [L spīrāre to breathe]

■ **spī′rogram** n a record obtained from a spirograph. **spī′rograph** n an instrument for recording breathing movements. **spīrog′raphy** n. **spīrom′eter** n an instrument for measuring lung capacity. **spīromet′ric** adj. **spīrom′etry** n. **spī′rophore** n (Gr phoros bringing) an apparatus for inducing artificial respiration by means of an airtight case for the body and an air-pump.

spirochaete /spī'rō-kēt/ n a spirally coiled bacterium (*Spirochaeta* and related genera) lacking a rigid cell wall, the cause of syphilis and other diseases. [Gr *speira* a coil, and *chaitē* hair, mane]
■ **spirochaetae'mia** n the presence of spirochaetes in the blood, as in the later stages of syphilis. **spirochaetō'sis** n infection with a spirochaete, as in syphilis, relapsing fever, etc.

spirogyra /spī-rō-jī'rə or -gī'/ n any freshwater alga of the genus *Spirogyra* with chlorophyll in spiral bands. [Gr *speira* a coil, and *gȳros* a ring]

spiroid see under **spire**².

spironolactone /spī-rō-nō-lak'tōn/ n a synthetic corticosteroid drug used in the treatment of hypertension and as a diuretic. [**spiro-**² and **lactone**]

spirt¹ /spûrt/ vi to shoot out forcibly, or in a fine strong jet. ◆ vt to squirt in a fine strong jet. ◆ n a sudden fine jet. [Origin uncertain; cf Ger dialect *spirzen* to spit; **spurt**]

spirt² /spûrt/ (*Shakesp*) vi to sprout, shoot up. [OE *spryttan*; cf **sprout**]

spirtle same as **spurtle**.

spirulina /spē-rə-lī'nə/ n (pl **spirulī'nas** or **spirulī'nae** /-nē/) any of several bacteria of the genus *Arthrospira* (formerly classified as *Spirulina*) used in dietary supplements. [L, small spiral]

spiry see under **spire**¹,².

spit¹ /spit/ vt (prp **spitt'ing**; pat and pap **spat**, *archaic* **spit**, *obs* pap **spitt'en** or (*Bible*) **spitt'ed**) to throw out from the mouth; to eject with violence; to utter with hate, scorn or violence; to spawn. ◆ vi to throw out saliva from the mouth; to rain in scattered drops; to make a spitting sound; to sputter; to feel or be furious (*inf*). ◆ n saliva, spume; a light fall of rain or snow; an exact replica (*sl*; *usu dead* or *very spit*, from the phrase *as like him as if he had spit him out of his mouth*). [Northern OE *spittan*, ON *spȳta*, Ger dialect *spitzen*, *spützen*]
■ **spitt'er** n. **spitt'ing** n the act of ejecting saliva; the ejection of oxygen, with drops of molten metal, when silver or platinum heated in air cools slowly; the resulting surface appearance. **spitt'le** n spit, saliva. **spittoon'** n any (*usu* bucket-like) container for spitting in, formerly a common feature of public houses, etc.
□ **spit box** n a spittoon. **spit curl** n (*inf*) a curl pressed flat on the temple. **spit'fire** n that which emits fire, eg a volcano, cannon; (with *cap*) a type of fighting aeroplane used in World War II; a hot-tempered person, *esp* a woman. **spitting image** n (from *spitten image*, a dialect form of *spit and image*) the exact likeness of (see n above). **spitt'lebug** or **spittle insect** n a frog-hopper or froth-fly.
■ **spit and polish** cleaning up of uniform and equipment, *esp* to excess; ceremony and formality. **spit and sawdust** of or referring to a floor left rough and covered with sawdust, wood chippings, etc, or *esp* a bar having this type of floor; also, the character, quality, etc of such a bar, spartan earthiness. **spit blood** or **feathers** to rage, be furious. **spit (it) out** to speak out, tell (it). **spit up** to regurgitate.

spit² /spit/ n a long thin rod, *usu* of metal, on which a joint of meat, etc is skewered for roasting; a sword (*joc*); a long narrow tongue of land or sand running into the sea; a wire or spindle holding a spool in a shuttle. ◆ vt (**spitt'ing**; **spitt'ed**) to transfix; to string on a rod or wire. [OE *spitu*; Du *spit*, Ger *Spiess*]
■ **spitt'ed** adj. **spitt'er** n a young deer with unbranched antlers. **spitt'ing** n (an act of or) the action of piercing.

spit³ /spit/ vt and vi to dig; to plant with a spade. ◆ n a spade's depth; this amount of earth, a spadeful. [OE *spittan*, or (M)Du and (M)LGer *spit*]

spital see **spittle**².

spitchcock /spich'kok/ n an eel split and broiled. ◆ vt to split and broil (an eel). [Origin unknown; cf **spatchcock**]

spitcher /spich'ər/ (*naval sl*) adj done for. [Maltese *spiċċa*, pronounced *spitch'a* finished, ended]

spite /spīt/ n a grudge; lasting ill-will; hatred; a cause of vexation (*archaic*). ◆ vt to vex; to thwart; to hate. [**despite**]
■ **spite'ful** adj full of spite; wanting or intended to vex or injure another; malignant. **spite'fully** adv. **spite'fulness** n.
■ **in spite of** in opposition to all efforts of, in defiance of, in contempt of; notwithstanding. **spite (of)** despite.

spitten obsolete pap of **spit**¹.

spitter see under **spit**¹,².

spittle¹, **spittoon** see under **spit**¹.

spittle², also **spital** /spit'l/ (*archaic*) n a hospital, *esp* one for infectious diseases, a lazar-house. [**hospital**]
□ **spitt'le-house** n.

spitz /spits/ n a Pomeranian dog; a group of breeds of dog generally having long hair, pointed ears and a tightly curled tail, *incl* husky, Samoyed, Pomeranian, etc. [Ger]

spiv /spiv/ (*inf*) n a flashily dressed man, *esp* one regularly involved in commercial dealings of doubtful legality or morality; an idler. [Back-formation of dialect *spiving* smart; perh connected with **spiff**]
■ **spivv'ery** n the world or the practices of spivs. **spivv'y** adj.

SPL abbrev: Scottish Premier League (now replaced by SPFL).

splanchnic /splangk'nik/ (*zool*) adj visceral, intestinal. [Gr *splanchnon*, pl *splanchna* entrails]
■ **splanch'nocele** /-sēl/ n (Gr *koilos* hollow) a visceral cavity; the posterior part of the coelom. **splanchnol'ogy** n the study of the viscera.

splash /splash/ vt to spatter, as with water or mud; to throw (liquid) about unevenly or scatteringly; to dash liquid on or over; to effect by or with splashing; to variegate as if by splashing; to display, print very prominently. ◆ vi to dabble; to dash liquid about; to move or go with a throwing about of liquid; to fly about dispersedly; (of bullets) to throw about fragments or molten metal on striking. ◆ n the dispersion of liquid suddenly disturbed, as by throwing something into it or by throwing it about; liquid thrown on anything; a spot formed by or as if by throwing liquid; a little soda water, tonic, etc (with a spirit); lead thrown about by a bullet on striking; ostentation, publicity, display; an instance of this; a sensation, excitement, dash; a prominently printed slogan or (a story, article, introduced by such a) headline. [**plash**³]
■ **splash'er** n someone who, or something that, splashes; a guard against splashing; a board attached to the foot for walking on mud. **splash'ily** adv. **splash'ing** n and adj. **splash'y** adj splashing; with splashing; wet and muddy; full of puddles; ostentatious, showy.
□ **splash'back** n a piece of glass, plastic, etc, or area of tiles covering the part of a wall behind a washbasin, sink or cooker to protect against splashing. **splash'board** n a mudguard; a dashboard. **splash'down** n (the moment of) the landing of a spacecraft on the sea. **splash page** n (*comput*; *inf*) a page incorporating highly decorative or arresting graphics, displayed as the introduction to a website. **splash'proof** adj.
■ **make a splash** to gain recognition. **splash down** (of spacecraft) to land on the sea at the end of a mission. **splash out (on)** (*inf*) to spend a lot of money (on).

splat¹ /splat/ n the sound made by a soft, wet object striking a surface. ◆ vi to strike a surface with a splat; to cause (droplets of molten metal) to strike and spread over a metal surface, driven by shock waves (*metallurgy*). ◆ adv with this sound. [Onomatopoeic]
■ **splatt'ing** n.
□ **splat cooling** or **splat quenching** n the technical process of cooling metal rapidly by splatting.

splat² /splat/ n a thin strip forming the upright middle part of a chairback. [**plat**³]

splatch /splach/ (*Scot* and *US*) n a splash or clot of dirt or colour; a splotch. ◆ vt to splotch. [Cf **splotch**]

splatter /splat'ər/ vt and vi to spatter; to splash; to display prominently; to sputter. ◆ n a splash; a spattering. [Cf **spatter**]
□ **splatter film** or **movie** n (*sl*) a film in which graphic scenes of gory mutilation, amputation, etc are depicted, employing various special effects. **splatt'erpunk** n a genre of fiction containing much graphically described violence.

splay¹ /splā/ vt and vi to spread out; to display (*obs*); to slope, slant, or bevel (*archit*). ◆ n a slant or bevel, as of the side of a doorway, window, etc. ◆ adj having a splay; turned outwards. ◆ adv with a splay. [**display**]
□ **splay foot** n a flat foot turned outward. **splay'-foot** or **-footed** adj. **splay'-mouthed** adj wide-mouthed.

splay² /splā/ (*N Am sl*) n marijuana. [Origin obscure]

spleen /splēn/ n a soft, pulpy, ovoid organ close to the stomach, that produces lymphocytes in the newborn and contains phagocytes which remove worn-out blood cells and other waste matter from the bloodstream, and once thought the seat of anger and melancholy; hence various meanings (mostly *Shakesp* and *obs*) such as spite, boredom, ill-humour, melancholy, mirth, caprice, impulse, high spirit. [L *splēn*, from Gr *splēn*]
■ **spleen'ful** adj. **spleen'ish** adj. **spleen'less** adj. **spleen'y** adj (*Shakesp*). **splē'native** adj (*obs*) hot-tempered. **splenec'tomy** /splin-/ n (Gr *ek* out, and *tomē* a cutting) surgical excision of the spleen. **splenetic** /splin-et'ik/ (formerly *splēn'i-tik*/) adj of the spleen; affected with spleen; bad-tempered, irritable or irritated, peevish; melancholy. ◆ n a splenetic person. **splenet'ical** adj. **splenet'ically** adv. **splenic** /splē'nik or splen'/ adj of the spleen. **splenī'tis** /splin-/ n inflammation of the spleen. **splēnīzā'tion** or **-s-** n conversion (eg of the lung) into a spongy, spleenlike substance. **splēnomeg'aly** n (Gr *megas, megalē, mega* big) enlargement of the spleen.
□ **spleen'stone** n (*obs*) jade. **spleen'wort** n any fern of the genus *Asplenium*. **splenic fever** n anthrax.

splendent /splen'dənt/ (*archaic*) adj brightly shining; brilliant, magnificent, gorgeous; renowned (*fig*). [L *splendens, -ent-* pap of *splendēre* to shine]

splendid /splen'did/ adj brilliant, resplendent; magnificent; excellent (inf). [L splendēre to shine, splendidus, splendor]

■ **splendid'ious** adj (obs). **splen'didly** adv. **splen'didness** n. **splen'didous** adj (obs). **splendif'erous** adj (now only inf). **splen'dorous** or **splen'drous** adj. **splen'dour** or (N Am) **splen'dor** /-dər/ n brilliance; magnificence; something splendid.

splendide mendax /splen'di-dā men'daks/ (L) splendidly false, nobly lying, untruthful for a good reason. [Horace Odes III.11.35]

splenectomy, splenetic, etc see under **spleen**.

splenial /splē'ni-əl/ adj splint-like; of the splenium or the splenius. [Gr splēnion pad, compress]

■ **splē'nium** n (anat) the round padlike posterior border of the corpus callosum, the bundle of fibres uniting the two cerebral hemispheres. **splē'nius** n (anat) a large thick muscle on the back of the neck.

splenic, splenomegaly, etc see under **spleen**.

splent see **splint**.

spleuchan /sploohh'ən/ (Scot and Irish) n a tobacco pouch; a purse. [Gaelic spliùc(h)an]

splice /splīs/ vt to unite by interweaving the strands; to join together by overlapping; to unite, esp (inf; also vi) in matrimony. ◆ n the act of splicing; a joint made by splicing; the part of the handle of a cricket bat, etc that fits into the blade. [Du (now dialect) splissen]

■ **splic'er** n.
■ **get spliced** (inf) to be married. **sit on the splice** (cricket sl) to bat defensively, with no attempt to gain runs. **splice the mainbrace** (naut sl) to serve out an allowance of alcoholic spirits; to partake of alcoholic spirits.

spliff /splif/ (sl, orig W Indies) n a marijuana cigarette, a joint; the act of smoking such a cigarette. [Origin uncertain]

spline /splīn/ n a key to make a wheel and shaft revolve together; a thin strip or slat; a flexible instrument used in drawing curves. ◆ vt to put splines on. [Orig East Anglian]

splint /splint/ n (also **splent**) a contrivance for holding a broken bone, etc in position; a bony enlargement on a horse's leg along the line of the splint bone between knee and fetlock; the growth of such an enlargement; a strip, slip of wood, lath; a splinter; an overlapping strip in armour; splint coal. ◆ vt to put in splints. [MDu splinte (Du splint) or (M)LGer splinte, splente; Du and LGer splinter, Ger Splenter]

■ **splint'er** n a piece of wood, metal, etc split off; a needlelike piece; a slender strip of wood, esp one used as a torch; a splint (obs). ◆ vt and vi to split into splinters. ◆ vt (Shakesp) to put in splints, hence join, piece. **splint'ery** adj made of, or like, splinters; apt to splinter. ▫ **splint armour** n armour of narrow overlapping plates. **splint bone** n a small bone alongside the cannon bone in the horse, etc, the second or the fourth metacarpal or metatarsal (also **splent bone**); the fibula. **splint coal** n a hard coal of uneven fracture that does not cake. **splinter bar** n the crossbar of a coach, supporting the springs. **splinter bone** n the fibula. **splinter group** or **party** n a group or party formed by a breakaway from a larger body. **splint'er-proof** adj proof against the splinters of bursting shells or bombs, or against splintering. **splintery fracture** n (mineralogy) the property of breaking with a surface like broken wood. **splint'wood** n sapwood.

splish /splish/ vt, vi and n a usu humorous variant of **splash**.

split /split/ vt (**splitt'ing**; **split**, Shakesp, etc **splitt'ed**) to break in pieces, wreck; to rend; to divide or separate lengthwise; to divide, share; to disunite; to divulge (inf). ◆ vi to be dashed to pieces (often with up); to suffer shipwreck; to divide or come apart (often with up); to divulge secrets (inf); to divide one's votes instead of plumping; to burst with laughter; to go at full speed; to leave, to make oneself scarce (sl); to break off relations (with) (inf; often with up). ◆ n a crack or rent lengthwise; a schism; a half-bottle of aerated water, etc, a half-glass of spirits; (in pl with the) the acrobatic feat of going down to the floor with the legs spread out laterally or one forward and one back; a division, share-out (usu of money, stolen goods, etc) (inf); a kind of rough suede made from an inner separated layer of hide, so having the same finish on both sides (also **split leather**); a sweet dish, usu of sliced-open fruit and cream, ice-cream, etc; a piece of wood split for kindling or basket-weaving (Can); a split-level house or apartment (US); a split time. ◆ adj having been split; having a split or break. [Du splitten, related to splijten, Ger spleissen]

■ **splitt'er** n someone who, or that which, splits; someone who splits hairs in argument, classification, etc; a splitting headache (inf); a fastball thrown with the middle and index fingers spread apart, causing it to break sharply downwards (baseball). **splitt'ing** adj rending; cleaving; ear-splitting; (of a headache) very severe; very rapid. **splitt'ism** n. **splitt'ist** n and adj (a person) advocating the withdrawal of a group from a large centralized body.
▫ **split'-brain** adj (med) of or involving separation of the cerebral hemispheres by dividing the corpus callosum. **split cane** n bamboo split to form triangular strips then glued to form a hexagonal rod, used to make strong but flexible fishing rods. **split capital trust** n an

investment trust having several kinds of security with differing rights, and with a limited life (also **split cap**, **split investment trust**, **split-level trust** and **split trust**). **split decision** n a decision that is not unanimous but is arrived at by a majority, esp in awarding victory in a boxing match. **split end** n the end of a hair that has split; an offensive end player who lines up some distance from the formation (American football). **split image** n a bisected image, produced in a focusing system in which the two halves are displaced if the camera is out of focus (photog); a spitting image (also **splitt'ing image**). **split-image rangefinder** n an optical device, used to assist camera focusing, in which the image is split when out of focus and whole when focused. **split infinitive** n an infinitive with an adverb between 'to' and the verb, as in to boldly go. **split investment trust** see **split capital trust** above. **split leather** see **split** (n) above. **split-lev'el** adj on more than one level (see also below). **split-level house** n a one-storey house with rooms on more than one level. **split-level trust** see **split capital trust** above. **split mind** n a mental disorder in which the thoughts may become separated from the emotions; loosely, a divided or dual opinion or feeling (about something). **split'-new** adj (Scot) brand-new. **split'-off** n (US finance) an exchange of the stock in a subsidiary company with part of the stock in the parent company. **split pea** see under **pea**[1]. **split personality** n dual personality. **split pin** n a pin made of a doubled piece of metal formed into a ring at the head and usu inserted in a hole in a bolt to hold a nut, etc firmly. **split ring** n a ring made up of two or more loops of metal that may be stretched apart, as for keeping keys together. **split screen** n a cinematic technique of showing different scenes simultaneously on separate parts of the screen, also used in television; a facility whereby separate areas of the screen may be used to display and carry out separate functions simultaneously (comput). **split'-screen** adj. **split second** n a fraction of a second. **split'-second** adj timed to a fraction of a second. **split-seconds hand** n a double seconds hand in a chronograph, of which first one and then the other member can be stopped by pressing a button. **split shift** n a working shift divided into two separate periods during the day. **split time** n the time indicated by the split-seconds hand of a chronograph. **split trust** see **split capital trust** above. **split'-up** n a separation, esp of a married couple.
■ **full split** at full speed. **split hairs** see under **hair**. **split on** (inf) to betray, give (a person) away. **split on a rock** to meet some unforeseen and disastrous difficulty, to go to ruin. **split one's sides** to laugh immoderately. **split the difference** to divide equally the sum of matter in dispute, to take the mean.

splodge, splodgily, etc see **splotch**.

splog /splog/ (comput sl) n an automatically generated and maintained weblog, usu offering products for sale. [Short for spam blog]

splore /splōr or splör/ (Scot) n a frolic; a spree; an escapade; a row; a scrape. [Origin obscure]

splosh /splosh/ n, vi and vt a usu humorous variant of **splash**.

splotch /sploch/ or **splodge** /sploj/ n a big or heavy splash, spot, or stain. ◆ vt to mark with splotches or splodges. ◆ vi to trudge flounderingly or splashily. [Perh connected with OE splott spot]

■ **splotch'ily** or **splodg'ily** adv. **splotch'iness** or **splodg'iness** n. **splotch'y** or **splodg'y** adj.

splurge /splûrj/ n any boisterous or extravagant display; a bout of extravagance. ◆ vi to make such a display; to spend a lot of money (on). [Imit]

■ **splur'gy** adj.

splutter /splut'ər/ vi to eject drops; to scatter ink upon a paper, as a bad pen does; to scatter liquid with spitting noises; to make a series of disconnected choking noises, as a failing engine does; to articulate confusedly as in rage. ◆ vt to utter splutteringly. ◆ n an act or noise of spluttering. [Prob imit; cf **sputter**]

■ **splutt'erer** n. **splutt'ering** n and adj. **splutt'eringly** adv. **splutt'ery** adj.

spod /spod/ (derog inf) n a socially inept person, esp a student seen as being excessively studious. [Origin unknown]

Spode /spōd/ (also without cap) n a porcelain made with addition of bone ash by Josiah Spode (1754–1827) at Stoke-on-Trent (also adj).

spodium /spō'di-əm/ (now rare) n powder obtained from various substances by calcination; bone-black. [Gr spodos, dimin spodion ashes]

spodo- /spō-dō-/ or **spod-** /spōd-/ combining form signifying ashes, dross. [Gr spodos ashes]

■ **spō'dogram** n (bot) a preparation of the ash from (the section of) a plant, used in investigating structure in microscopy. **spodomancy** /spod'ə-man-si/ n divination by means of ashes. **spodoman'tic** adj.

spodumene /spod'ū-mēn/ (mineralogy) n a monoclinic pyroxene, a silicate of aluminium and lithium occurring in granite pegmatites. [From Gr spodoumenos (contracted participle) burnt to ashes, from its appearance under the blowpipe]

spoil /spoil/ vt (pat and pap **spoiled** or (only in sense of damage) **spoilt**) to mar; to impair; to make useless; to treat over-indulgently; to harm the character of by so doing; to take by force (*archaic*); to plunder; to despoil; to strip; to deprive; to corrupt; to destroy, end (*Shakesp*). ◆ vi to go bad; to deteriorate; to practise spoliation. ◆ n (*usu* in *pl*) plunder, booty; acquisitions, prizes; spoliation; pillage; a cast or stripped-off skin; remains of an animal body; material cast out in excavation; damage, impairment (*rare*); a thing spoiled in making (*rare*). [OFr *espoille*, from L *spolium* spoil]

■ **spoil'age** n the act of spoiling; waste by spoiling; material so wasted. **spoiled** adj. **spoil'er** n any thing or person that spoils; an aerodynamic device fitted to the wings of an aircraft to reduce lift and assist descent; a similar device fitted to motor vehicles, *esp* racing and sports cars, to lessen drag and reduce the tendency to become unstable through a lifting effect at high speeds; an electronic device incorporated in a piece of recording equipment which prevents unauthorized recording, *usu* by using a **spoiler signal** which renders useless any recording made; a newspaper article, speech, etc intended to lessen the impact of another published or made on the same subject elsewhere; a piece of information about the plot of a film, television show, etc, made public with the intention of lessening interest in the work; a third candidate in a two-way political election, whose only effect is to reduce the number of votes for one of the main candidates (*US*). **spoil'ful** (*Spenser* **spoylefull**) adj plundering.

❑ **spoil bank** or **heap** n a deposit of spoil. **spoil'five** n a card game drawn or *spoiled* if no player wins three out of five tricks. **spoil'ing tactics** n *pl* activities that have no purpose other than to hinder someone or something else. **spoils'man** n (*US*) someone who looks for profit out of politics or who advocates the spoils system. **spoil'sport** n someone who stops or interferes with sport or other people's pleasure; a meddler. **spoils system** n (*chiefly US*) the practice of appointing supporters of the political party gaining or in power, to nonelective public offices, on the principle that 'to the victor belong the spoils'. **spoilt paper** n in a ballot, a voting paper marked, *esp* deliberately, in such a way as to render it invalid.

■ **spoiling for** more than ripe or ready for (a fight, etc); intent on. **spoilt for choice** presented with so many attractive options that picking one is difficult.

spoke[1] /spōk/ pat of **speak**.

spoke[2] /spōk/ n one of the radiating bars of a wheel; one of the rungs of a ladder. [OE *spāca*; Du *speek*, Ger *Speiche*]

■ **spoked** adj. **spoke'wise** adv.

❑ **spoke'shave** n a two-handled planing tool for curved work.

■ **put a spoke in someone's wheel** to thwart or hinder someone.

spoken /spō'kn/ pap of **speak**. *combining form* denoting speech or speaking, as in *plain-spoken*, *soft-spoken*.

■ **spoken for** chosen, reserved; romantically attached, not free or single (*inf*).

spokesman /spōks'mən/ or **spokesperson** /-pûr-sən/, *fem* **spokeswoman** /-wŭ-mən/ n (pl **spokes'men**, **spokes'persons** or **spokes'people**, *fem* **spokes'women**) a person who speaks for another, or for others. [**speak** and **man**[1], **person**, **woman**]

spolia opima /spō'li-ə ō'pi-mə or spol'i-a o-pē'ma/ (*L*) the richest spoils, *orig* applied to the arms taken in single combat by a leader from a leader; hence, supreme achievement.

spoliate /spō'li-āt/ vt and vi to despoil, plunder. [L *spoliāre*, *-ātum*, from *spolium* spoil]

■ **spōliā'tion** n. **spō'liātive** adj serving to take away or diminish. **spō'liātor** n. **spō'liatory** /-ə-tər-i/ adj.

spondee /spon'dē/ (*prosody*) n a foot of two long syllables. [L *spondēus* (*pēs*), from Gr *spondeios* (*pous*) (a foot) used in the slow solemn hymns sung at a *spondē* or drink-offering, from *spendein* to pour out, make a libation]

■ **spondaic** /-dā'ik/ adj. **spondā'ical** adj.

spondulicks, **spondoolicks** or **spondulix** /spon-doo'liks or -dū'/ (*orig US*; *inf*) n *pl* money. [From Gr *spondylikos*, from *spondylos* a seashell used as currency]

spondyl /spon'dil/ (*zool*) n a vertebra; a thorny oyster (genus *Spondylus*). [Gr *sp(h)ondylos* a vertebra]

■ **spondylit'ic** adj affected by spondylitis. ◆ n a person suffering from spondylitis. **spondylī'tis** n (*med*) inflammation of the synovial joints of the backbone. **spondylolisthe'sis** n a partial dislocation of the (*usu* lower) vertebrae in which a vertebra slips forward over the one below. **spondylol'ysis** n disintegration of one or more vertebrae. **spondylō'sis** n vertebral ankylosis. **spondylōsyndesis** /-sin'də-sis/ n surgical fusion of the joints between the vertebrae. **spon'dylous** adj.

sponge /spunj/ n any member of the phylum Porifera, sessile aquatic animals with a single cavity in the body, with numerous pores; the fibrous skeleton of such an animal, remarkable for its power of holding water; a piece of such a skeleton, or a synthetic substitute, used for washing, absorbing, etc; a swab for a cannon; any spongelike substance, such as leavened dough, a cake or pudding, or swampy ground; a bedeguar; a hanger-on or parasite (*inf*); a drunkard (*inf*); an application of a sponge; the life or behaviour of a sponger upon others (*inf*). ◆ vt to wipe, wipe out, soak up or remove with a sponge; to drain, as if by squeezing a sponge; to gain by the art of the parasite. ◆ vi to suck in, as a sponge does; to fish for sponges; to live on others parasitically (often with *on* or *off*). [OE *sponge*, *spunge*, and OFr *esponge*, from L *spongia*, from Gr *spongiā*]

■ **spon'geable** adj. **spongeous** /spun'jəs/ adj spongy. **spong'er** n a person who uses a sponge; a sponge fisher; a sponge fishing boat; an apparatus for sponging cloth; a sponge or parasite. **spongicolous** /spun- or spon-jik'ə-ləs/ adj (L *colere* to inhabit) living in association with, *usu* within, a sponge. **spon'giform** adj like or related to a sponge. **spon'gily** adv in a spongy way or manner. **spongin** /spun'jin/ n a horny substance in the skeletons of various sponges. **spon'giness** n. **spongiose** /spun'- or -ōs'/ adj. **spongious** /spun'jəs/ adj. **spongoid** /spong'goid/ adj. **spongologist** /spong-gol'ə-jist/ n. **spongol'ogy** n the science of sponges. **spongy** /spun'ji/ adj absorptive; porous; wet and soft; drunken; (of vehicle suspension, brakes, etc) lacking firmness or responsiveness.

❑ **sponge'bag** n a waterproof bag for carrying a sponge and toiletries; (in *pl*) checked or striped trousers. ◆ adj checked. **sponge bath** n a washing of the body by or from a sponge, as for a sick or bedridden person. **sponge cake** n a very light sweet cake of flour, eggs, and sugar. **sponge cloth** n a cotton cloth of open texture similar to a sponge. **sponge'-down** see **sponge down** below. **sponge finger** n a finger-shaped sponge cake. **sponge fisher** n. **sponge fishing** n. **sponge rubber** n rubber processed into spongelike form. **sponge'ware** n (*ceramics*) pottery, etc on which patterns, colours, etc are applied using a sponge. **sponge'wood** n sola, an Indian plant also known as the **hat plant**. **spon'ging-house** or **spun'ging-house** n (*obs*) a bailiff's lodging-house for debtors in his custody before their committal to prison. **spongy parenchyma** n (*bot*) a loose tissue in leaves with much intercellular space. **spongy platinum** or **platinum sponge** n platinum in a finely divided state.

■ **set a sponge** to leaven a small mass of dough for use in leavening a large quantity. **sponge down** to clean or wipe with a sponge (**sponge'-down** n). **throw up** (or **in**) **the sponge** to acknowledge defeat by throwing into the air the sponge with which a boxer is rubbed down between rounds (cf **throw in the towel**); to give up any struggle.

sponsal /spon'sl/ adj spousal.

■ **sponsā'lia** n *pl* espousals.

sponsible /spon'si-bl/ (now *dialect*) adj aphetic for **responsible** in the sense of respectable (see under **respond**).

sponsing see **sponson**.

sponsion /spon'shən/ n the act of becoming surety for another; an agreement or promise made on behalf of another, *esp* by an individual on behalf of his or her government. [L *spondēre*, *spōnsum* promise]

■ **spon'sional** adj.

sponson /spon'sn/ n (also **spon'sing**) a platform extending out from a ship's deck, for mounting a gun, a paddle, wheel, etc; a wing section giving extra lift; an air-filled tank on the side of a canoe to give buoyancy; a structure to give a seaplane stability on the water. [Ety dubious]

sponsor /spon'sər/ n a person who promises solemnly for another; a surety; a godfather or godmother; a promoter; a person or organization financing an event, a broadcast, etc in return for self-advertisement at the event, etc; a person or organization who promises to pay a specified sum to a person for taking part in a fund-raising event or activity on behalf of a charity, etc. ◆ vt to act as a sponsor. [L *spondēre*, *spōnsum* promise]

■ **spon'sored** adj. **sponso'rial** adj. **spon'sorship** n.

spontaneous /spon-tā'nyəs or -ni-əs/ adj of one's free will; acting by its own impulse or natural law; produced of itself; impulsive; unpremeditated. [L *spontāneus*, from *sponte* of one's own accord]

■ **spontaneity** /-tə-nē'i-ti or -nā'i-ti/ n. **spontā'neously** adv. **spontā'neousness** n.

❑ **spontaneous abortion** n miscarriage. **spontaneous behaviour** n (*behaviourism*) behaviour occurring in the apparent absence of any stimuli. **spontaneous combustion** n catching fire by causes at work within, *esp* slow oxidation of a mass of matter. **spontaneous generation** n the supposed production of living organisms from non-living matter. **spontaneous remission** n recovery without treatment.

sponte sua /spon'te soo'ä/ (*L*) of one's own accord, unsolicited.

spontoon /spon-toon'/ n a small-headed halberd formerly carried by some infantry officers. [Fr *sponton*, from Ital *spontone*, from *punto*, from L *punctum* a point]

spoof /spoof/ (*sl*) n a parody, take-off, satire; *orig*, a hoaxing game invented and named by Arthur Roberts (1852–1933), comedian; a

card game; ejaculated semen (*Aust*). ◆ *adj* bogus. ◆ *vt* and *vi* to hoax; to parody; to send electronic-mail messages under a fraudulent identity.
■ **spoof'er** *n*. **spoof'ery** *n*. **spoof'ing** *n*.

spook /spook/ *n* a ghost; a spy, an undercover agent (*sl*, *orig US*). ◆ *vi* to play the spook; to take fright; (of a horse) to shy away. ◆ *vt* to frighten, startle. ◆ *adj* ghostly. [Appar LGer; cf Ger *Spuk*, Du *spook*]
■ **spook'ery** *n* things that are spooky; matters relating to spooks. **spook'ily** *adv*. **spook'iness** *n*. **spook'ish** or **spook'y** *adj*.

spool /spool/ *n* a cylinder, bobbin or reel on which yarn, etc is wound. ◆ *vt* to wind on spools (also *vi*); to transfer to a memory store for later printing or processing (*comput*). [LGer *spóle*; Du *spoel*, or ONFr *espole*; Ger *Spule*]
■ **spool'er** *n*.

spoom, spooming see **spoon²**.

spoon¹ /spoon/ *n* an (eating, or serving, etc) instrument with a shallow bowl and a handle; anything of similar shape, such as an oar; an old-fashioned woodenheaded golf club with the face slightly hollowed, commonly used to refer to a three-wood; a spoonbait (*inf*); a stroke with such a club; the wooden spoon (*Cambridge University*; see **wooden**); a simpleton; courtship, *esp* when mawkish or sentimental; a person who engages in such courtship; (in the management of chronic pain) one of a finite number of units of energy regarded as being available to a person each day (*inf*). ◆ *vt* to transfer with, or as if with, a spoon; to shove, scoop, or hit softly up into the air, instead of striking cleanly and definitely; to court, *esp* in a sentimental way; to fish with a spoonbait; to pack together like spoons. ◆ *vi* to indulge in (*esp* sentimental) courtship; to fish with a spoonbait; to lie close in bed together, front to back, like spoons. [OE *spōn* sliver, chip, shaving, Ger *Span* chip, ON *spānn*, *spōnn* chip, spoon]
■ **spooney** see **spoony** below. **spoon'ful** *n* (*pl* **spoon'fuls**) as much as fills a spoon; a small quantity. **spoon'ily** *adv*. **spoon'ways** or **spoon'wise** *adv* like spoons packed closely together. **spoon'y** or **spoon'ey** *adj* silly; foolishly and demonstratively fond. ◆ *n* someone who is spoony.
□ **spoon'bait** or **spoon'hook** *n* a lure on a swivel, used in trolling for fish. **spoon'bill** *n* any bird of the genus *Platalea*, similar to the ibises, with a long, flat, broad bill, spoon-shaped at the tip; a shoveler (the duck). **spoon'-fed** or **spoon'fed** *adj* fed with a spoon; artificially fostered (*fig*); taught by doled-out doses of cut-and-dried information. **spoon'-feed** *vt*. **spoonhook** see **spoonbait** above. **spoon'worm** *n* a marine invertebrate of the phylum Echiuroidea with a spoon-like mouthpiece.
■ **born with a silver spoon in one's mouth** see under **silver**.

spoon² /spoon/ *vi* (also **spoom**) to scud before the wind; to run before a gale with reduced canvas (*old naut*). [Origin unknown]
■ **spoom'ing** *adj* (*Keats*) foaming. **spoon'drift** or (*orig Scot and N Eng*) **spin'drift** *n* light spray borne on a gale.

spoonerism /spoo'nə-ri-zm/ *n* a transposition of initial sounds of spoken words, eg 'shoving leopard' for 'loving shepherd'. [Rev WA *Spooner* (1844–1930), noted for transpositions of this kind]

spoor /spoor/ *n* a track or trail, *esp* that of a hunted animal. ◆ *vt* and *vi* to track. [Du *spoor* a track; cf OE and ON *spor*, Ger *Spur*; also **speir**]
■ **spoor'er** *n*.

spoot /spoot/ (*Orkney*) *n* the razor shell mollusc.

sporadic /spə-, spo-rad'ik/ or (*rare*) **sporadical** /-kəl/ *adj* scattered; occurring here and there or now and then; occurring casually. [Gr *sporadikos*, from *sporas*, *sporados* scattered, from *speirein* to sow]
■ **sporad'ically** *adv*.

spore /spōr or spör/ (*biol*) *n* a unicellular asexual reproductive body; sometimes extended to other reproductive bodies. [Gr *sporā* a seed, from *speirein* to sow]
■ **sporangial** /spor-an'ji-əl/ *adj*. **sporan'giole** or **sporan'giolum** (or /-jī'/) *n* (*pl* **sporan'gioles** or **sporan'giola**) a sporangium containing one or few spores. **sporan'giophore** *n* the part that bears sporangia. **sporan'giospore** *n* a spore developed in a sporangium. **sporan'gium** *n* (*pl* **sporan'gia**) a hollow, walled structure or sac in which spores are produced (also **spore case**). **spor'idesm** *n* (Gr *desmos* a bond) a multicellular body or group of spores, of which every cell is capable of germinating. **sporid'ial** *adj*. **sporid'ium** *n* (*pl* **sporid'ia**) a spore borne on a promycelium. **spor'ocarp** *n* (Gr *karpos* fruit) a structure containing the sori and sporangia in aquatic ferns; a multicellular structure in which spores are formed in certain fungi, algae, etc. **spor'ocyst** *n* a rounded, thick-walled structure produced, as by protozoans, in the process of sporulation; the cyst-like larva of a trematode. **sporocyst'ic** *adj*. **sporogen'esis** *n* production of or by spores (also **sporogeny** /-oj'/). **sporog'enous** *adj* producing spores. **sporogonium** /-gō'/ *n* (*pl* **sporogo'nia**) the capsule or asexual generation in mosses and liverworts. **sporog'ony** *n* (Gr *gonē* generation) the formation of spores in sporozoans. **spor'ophore** *n* a spore-bearing stalk or structure, as in fungi. **sporophor'ic** or

sporoph'orous *adj*. **spor'ophyll** or **spor'ophyl** *n* (Gr *phyllon* leaf) a leaf (often modified) that bears sporangia. **spor'ophyte** *n* (Gr *phyton* plant) the spore-bearing or asexual generation in the lifecycle of a plant. **sporophytic** /-fit'ik/ *adj*. **sporotrichosis** /spŏr-ō-trik-ō'sis/ *n* an infection of the skin (and rarely of muscles and bones) caused by the fungi of the genus *Sporotrichum*, resulting in granulomatous lesions. **sporozō'an** *n* any parasitic protozoan of the class **Sporozō'a**, reproducing by spores, including the causal organism of malaria (also *adj*). **sporozō'ite** *n* (Gr *zōion* an animal) a minute, mobile, pre-adult, *usu* infective spore developed by sporozoans. **spor'ūlar** *adj*. **spor'ūlate** *vi* to produce spores. **sporūlā'tion** *n* formation or production of spores; breaking up into spores. **spor'ule** *n* a small spore.

spork /spŏrk or spörk/ *n* a piece of cutlery with both the shallow bowl of a *spoon* and the prongs of a *fork*.

sporocarp...to...**sporozoite** see under **spore**.

sporran /spor'ən/ *n* an ornamental pouch of leather and/or fur worn in front of the kilt as part of Scottish Highland dress. [Gaelic *sporan*]

sport /spōrt or spört/ *n* recreation; a pastime; play; a game or activity, *esp* one involving physical exercise; a specific, *esp* outdoor, amusement, activity or recreation; success in or pleasure from shooting, fishing, or the like; amusement, fun, good-humoured mirth; mockery, contemptuous mirth; an object of mockery, a laughing stock; a plaything (*esp fig*); dalliance, amorous behaviour; a person of sportsmanlike character, a good fellow; a form of address, used *esp* between males (*Aust* and *NZ*); an animal or plant that varies singularly and spontaneously from the normal type. ◆ *vi* to enjoy oneself, have a good time; to frolic (also *vt* with *it*); to play (*archaic*); to take part in a specific amusement, activity or recreation, *esp* outdoor; to make fun (of) (often with *with*); to trifle (with); to deviate from the normal (*biol*). ◆ *vt* to wear, use, exhibit, set up, publicly or ostentatiously; to wager; to squander (often with *away*; *rare*); to amuse (*obs*); to force open (*obs*). ◆ *adj* see **sports** below. [Aphetic for **disport**]
■ **sportabil'ity** *n* (*rare*) sportiveness. **sport'able** *adj* (*rare*). **sport'ance** *n* (*rare*) play. **sport'er** *n* someone who sports; a sportsman. **sport'ful** *adj* full of sport; merry; full of jesting. **sport'fully** *adv*. **sport'fulness** *n*. **sport'ily** *adv*. **sport'iness** *n*. **sport'ing** *adj* relating to, engaging in, or fond of sports or gambling; willing to take a chance; sportsmanlike; fair and generous; (in the UK) relating to one of the two major classes of dogs recognized by the Kennel Club (the other being *non-sporting*), comprising hounds, gundogs, and terriers; (in the USA) relating to one of the six recognized groups of breeds, essentially comprising the gundogs (as opposed to hounds, terriers, etc). **sport'ingly** *adv*. **sport'ive** *adj* inclined to sport; playful; merry; amorous, wanton. **sport'ively** *adv*. **sport'iveness** *n*. **sport'less** *adj* (*rare*) without sport or mirth; sad. **sports** *n pl* a meeting for races and other competitive events. ◆ *adj* (also *esp N Am*) **sport**) of, or suitable for, sport, as in *sports shoes*. **sport'y** *adj* sportsmanlike (*inf*); (of a person) who enjoys, takes part in or is proficient at sport; (of a car) looking or handling like a sports car; stylish, lively.
□ **sporting chance** *n* as good a chance of winning or being successful as of losing or failing. **sporting house** *n* a public house, hotel, etc, patronized by sportsmen or gamblers (*archaic*); a brothel (*euphem*; *esp US*). **sports car** *n* a low car, *usu* for two, capable of attaining high speed. **sports'cast** *n* (*orig US*) a broadcast about sport. **sports'caster** or **sport'caster** *n* (*orig US*) a presenter on a sports programme. **sports coat** *n* (*N Am*, *Aust* and *NZ*) a sports jacket. **sports ground** *n* an area with equipment and facilities designed for, *esp* competitive, outdoor sports. **sports injury** *n* any injury that is sustained or arises during participation in sports. **sports jacket** *n* a man's jacket, *usu* tweed, for casual wear. **sports'man**, **sports'person** or (*fem*) **sports'woman** *n* someone who practises, or is skilled in, sport; someone who shows fairness and good humour in sport. **sports'manlike** *adj*. **sports'manship** *n*. **sports medicine** *n* the branch of medicine concerned with the treatment of medical disorders, injuries, etc related to sport, and with assessment and improvement of fitness. **sportsperson** see **sportsman** above. **sports shirt** *n* a man's casual shirt. **sports'wear** *n* clothing designed to be worn for sport; designer clothes, *esp* matching separates, for casual wear. **sportswoman** see **sportsman** above. **sports'writer** *n* a journalist who writes on sporting matters. **sports'writing** *n*. **sport utility bicycle** *n* a bicycle with long frame, intended to carry extra passengers or loads. **sport utility vehicle** *n* a four-wheel-drive vehicle.
■ **sport one's oak** see under **oak**.

sporular, sporulate, etc see under **spore**.

sposh /sposh/ (*US*) *n* slush. [Imit]
■ **sposh'y** *adj*.

SPOT /spot/ *abbrev* : Satellite Probatoire pour l'Observation de la Terre (a French satellite that gathers information about the Earth by remote sensing).

spot /spot/ n a mark made by a drop of something wet; a blot; a small discoloured or differently coloured place; a locality, place or limited geographical area; a precise place, location; an eruption on the skin, a pimple; a moral flaw; one of the marked points on a snooker or billiard table, from which balls are played; a relatively dark area on the surface of the sun; a small quantity of anything (inf); a spotlight (inf); a white pigeon with a spot on the forehead; a name for various American fishes; a job, piece of work (obs); a place of entertainment; a place on eg a television or radio programme; a turn, performance, esp a short one; an awkward position or situation; a spot deal or commodity (finance). ◆ vt (**spott'ing**; **spott'ed**) to mark with spots; to tarnish, eg a reputation; to reprehend (Spenser); to pick out, detect, locate, identify, discern (inf); to watch for and record the sighting of; to free from spots (often with out); to place on a spot, as in snooker; to allow or yield an advantage, concession, etc to, esp in order to give (an opponent) an even chance of winning (inf); to lend or give (N Am inf). ◆ vi to become spotted; (of fabric) to be susceptible to spotting; to rain slightly, with few and intermittent drops (usu as spot with rain) (inf). ◆ adj on the spot, random (see **spot check** below); of monetary or commodity transactions, etc, to be paid (usu in cash) or delivered immediately (as in spot market, spot price, etc); involving payment in cash only. [Cf obs Du, LGer spot, ON spotti]

■ **spot'less** adj without a spot or blemish; very clean; untainted; pure. **spot'lessly** adv. **spot'lessness** n. **spott'ed** adj. **spott'edness** n. **spott'er** n someone who or something (such as a plane) that spots, observes or detects. **spott'ily** adv. **spott'iness** n. **spott'ing** n. **spott'y** adj marked with spots; inconsistent, uneven.

◻ **spot advertising** n advertising by means of brief items, usu in dramatized form, on television or radio. **spot'-barred** adj (billiards) under the condition that the spot stroke may not be played more than twice consecutively. **spot cash** n money down. **spot check** n a check made without prior warning; a check of random samples to serve in place of a general check. **spot'-check** vt. **spot dance** n a dance after which a prize is given to the couple spotlighted when the music stopped. **spot dealer** n (commerce) one dealing in the spot market. **spot'-fixing** n the illegal manipulation of an incident in a sporting contest by a participant. **spot height** n on a map, a number giving the height above mean sea level at that point. **spot kick** n (football) a kick made from the penalty spot. **spot'light** n a, usu powerful, light that projects a circle of light on an actor, a small part of a stage, or that illuminates a small area; any adjustable, focused-beam lamp, such as a car lamp additional to fixed lights; a focusing of attention (fig). ◆ vt to turn the spotlight on; to draw attention to (fig). **spot market** n (commerce) a market in which commodities are bought and sold for cash or immediate delivery. **spot-on'** adj (inf) on the target; exactly right, accurate; precisely what is required, excellent. **spot stroke** n (billiards) a stroke by which the player pockets the red ball from the spot, leaving his own ball in position to repeat the stroke. **spotted dick** n a pudding or loaf with currants. **spotted dog** n a Dalmatian dog; a spotted dick. **spotted fever** n any of several febrile diseases, such as cerebrospinal fever and Rocky Mountain spotted fever, characterized by small spots on the skin. **spotted flycatcher** n a European songbird (Muscicapa striata). **spotted owl** n a N American owl (Strix occidentalis). **spot'-weld** vt to join metal with single circular welds. ◆ n a weld of this kind. **spot'-welder** n.

■ **high spot** the most memorable or exciting moment. **in a spot** in a difficult situation. **knock (the) spots off** to surpass or outdo easily. **on the spot** at the very place; there and then; alert, equal to the occasion; in difficulty or danger (eg put on the spot, orig to doom to be murdered) (**on-the-spot'** adj). **soft spot** (inf) affectionate feeling or weakness (for); a fontanelle (inf). **tight spot** (inf) a dangerous or difficult situation. **weak spot** (inf) a weakness; an area in which one is not knowledgeable.

-spot /-spot/ combining form forming verbs signifying to note or identify, as in talent-spot. [Ety as for **spot**]

■ **-spotter** n combining form. **-spotting** n combining form.

spouse /spows or spowz/ n a husband or wife. ◆ vt (obs) to betroth; to marry. [OFr spus(e), espous(e) (Fr époux, fem épouse), from L spōnsus, pap of spondēre to promise]

■ **spous'age** n marriage. **spous'al** adj nuptial; matrimonial. ◆ n (usu in pl) nuptials; marriage. **spouse'less** adj.

spout /spowt/ vt to throw out in a jet; to declaim; to pawn (obs sl). ◆ vi to issue in a jet; to blow as a whale; to declaim (derog). ◆ n a projecting lip or tube for discharging liquid from a container, a roof, etc; a gush, discharge, or jet; an undivided waterfall; a waterspout; the blowing or the blowhole of a whale; a chute; a lift in a pawnshop (obs); hence, a pawnshop (obs). [ME spouten; cf Du spuiten to spout, ON spȳta to spit]

■ **spout'er** n someone who, or that which, spouts; a declaimer; a spouting oil well; a spouting whale; a whaling-ship. **spout'ing** n the action of the verb; a rainwater downpipe or the system of downpipes on the outside of a building (NZ). **spout'less** adj. **spout'y** adj.

◻ **spout'-hole** n a blowhole.

■ **up the spout** (sl) pawned; failed, gone wrong, ruined; pregnant.

spoylefull (Spenser) see **spoil**.

spp. see **sp.**

SPQR abbrev: Senatus Populusque Romanus (L), the Senate and the People of Rome.

SPR abbrev: Society for Psychical Research.

Spr abbrev: Sapper.

sprachgefühl /sprahh'gə-fül or (Ger) shprahh'/ n an instinctive feeling and aptitude for a language, its essential character, word patterns, usage, etc. [Ger Sprache language, and Gefühl feeling]

sprack /sprak/ (W Midland and SW Eng dialect) adj vigorous, sprightly, alert (also (after the pronunciation of Sir Hugh Evans in Shakespeare, Merry Wives of Windsor IV.1.75) **sprag**). [Origin obscure]

sprackle /sprä'kl/ or **spraickle** /sprā'kl/ (Scot) vi to clamber. [Origin obscure]

sprad /sprad/ (obs) pap of **spread**.

sprag¹ /sprag/ n a mine prop; a bar inserted to stop a wheel; a device to prevent a vehicle from running backwards. ◆ vt (**spragg'ing**; **spragged**) to prop, or to stop, by a sprag. [Origin obscure]

sprag² see **sprack**.

spraickle see **sprackle**.

spraid see **spray³**.

sprain /sprān/ vt to overstrain the muscles of. ◆ n a wrenching of a joint with tearing or stretching of ligaments. [Connection with OFr espreindre to squeeze out, is disputed]

spraint /sprānt/ n (usu in pl) otter's dung. [OFr espraintes, literally, pressed out]

sprang /sprang/ pat of **spring¹**.

sprangle /sprang'gəl/ (now US and dialect) vi to sprawl; to straggle; to ramify; to struggle. ◆ n a straggle. [ME spranglen]

sprat /sprat/ n a fish like the herring, but much smaller; a term of contempt (Shakesp). [OE sprot; Du sprot, Ger Sprotte]

◻ **sprat'-weather** n the dark days of November and December.

■ **a sprat to catch a mackerel**, **herring** or **whale** a small risk taken in order to make a great gain.

sprattle /sprat'l/ (Scot) vi to scramble. [Cf Swed sprattla]

sprauchle /sprö'hhl/ (Scot) a later form of **sprackle**.

sprauncy /sprön'si/ adj smart, dapper. [Origin obscure, poss connected with dialect sprouncey cheerful, jolly]

sprawl /spröl/ vi to lie, fall or crawl with limbs spread out; to straggle; to toss or kick the limbs about (archaic). ◆ vt to spread stragglingly. ◆ n a sprawling posture, movement, or mass. [OE sprēawlian to move convulsively]

■ **sprawl'er** n. **sprawl'ing** adj. **sprawl'y** adj.

spray¹ /sprā/ n a cloud of small flying drops; an application or dispersion of such a cloud; an apparatus or a preparation for so dispersing; harsh criticism (Aust). ◆ vt to sprinkle in or with fine mistlike jets; to spray-paint; to make the target of a stream of bullets. [MDu sprayen]

■ **spray'er** n. **spray'ey** adj.

◻ **spray'-dried** adj. **spray drift** n spray, esp a chemical pesticide or herbicide, which remains suspended in the air and is blown away from the original site of spraying by the wind. **spray drying** n the rapid drying of a liquid by spraying it into a flow of hot gas. **spray gun** n a device for applying paint, etc, by spraying. **spray'-on** adj applied in a spray, usu by an aerosol. **spray paint** n paint that is applied in the form of a spray, usu an aerosol. **spray'-paint** vt to use spray paint (on something); to apply with spray paint. **spray'-painting** n. **spray steel** n steel made by pouring molten iron through a ring of oxygen jets, a method of rapidly oxidizing impurities.

spray² /sprā/ n a shoot or twig, esp one spreading out in branches or flowers; an ornament, casting, etc, of similar form. ◆ vi to spread or branch in a spray. [Poss connected with **sprig** or with OE spræc twig]

■ **spray'ey** adj branching.

spray³ /sprā/, **spreathe**, **spreethe** /sprēdh/, **spreaze** or **spreeze** /sprēz/ (SW Eng dialect) vt and vi to chap, roughen, usu in pap **sprayed**, **spraid**, etc. [Origin obscure]

sprayey see **spray¹·²**.

spread /spred/ vt (pat and pap **spread**) to cause to extend more widely or more thinly; to scatter or disseminate abroad or in all directions; to stretch; to extend, esp over a surface; to apply (a soft substance) by smoothing it over a surface; to open out so as to cover a wider surface; to force apart; to overlay; to set with provisions, as a table. ◆ vi to extend or expand; to be extended or stretched; to become bigger or fatter; to open out; to go or be forced further apart; to unfold; to be capable of being spread; to be propagated, circulated or disseminated.

◆ *n* extent; compass; reach; expanse; an expanded surface; the act or degree of spreading; an expansion; the process of becoming bigger or fatter; an array of food, a feast; anything for spreading on bread; a cover, *esp* a bedcover; a ranch (*N Am*); a double page, ie two facing pages (*printing*); a large property with grounds (*inf*); the gap between the bid and offer price of shares (*stock exchange*); the anticipated winning margin in a sporting event (*gambling*). ◆ *adj* extended; (of sounds) made with the lips stretched sideways (*phonetics*); (of a gemstone) flat and shallow. [OE *sprǣdan*; Du *spreiden*, Ger *spreiten*] ■ **spread'able** *adj*. **spread'er** *n* a machine for spreading bulk materials, eg *manure spreader*; a spatula or similar implement for spreading, eg butter, paint, etc; a device for spreading and keeping apart parallel objects, eg rails, electric wires; someone who, or something that, spreads. **spread'ing** *n* and *adj*. **spread'ingly** *adv*. ❑ **spread betting** *n* a form of gambling in which people stake money on whether the numerical outcome of an event will be higher or lower than a stated amount. **spread eagle** *n* a heraldic eagle with the wings and legs stretched out, the emblem of the USA; (anything adopting or placed in) a position in which the limbs are stretched out; a skating figure. **spread'-eagle** *adj* in, or adopting, the position of a spread eagle; bombastic, boastful, and frothy, *esp* in American patriotism. ◆ *vt* to tie up with outstretched limbs; to spread out; to outrun. ◆ *vi* to cut, do or make, spread eagles; to lie, fall, etc with outstretched limbs; to talk in spread-eagle strain. **spread-ea'gleism** *n*. **spread-ea'glewise** *adv*. **spread'-over** *n* an act of spreading out; an elastic distribution of working hours. **spread'sheet** or **spreadsheet program** *n* (*comput*) a program with which data, formatted in rows and columns of cells, can be viewed on a screen and manipulated to make projections, calculations, etc. ■ **spread a plate** (*horse-racing*) (of a horse) to lose a shoe or racing plate, *esp* before or during a race. **spread oneself too thin** to attempt so many tasks at once that none is done satisfactorily. **spread one's wings** to try one's powers or capabilities; to increase the area of one's activities.

spreagh /sprähh or sprehh/ *n* a prey; a foray, cattle raid. [Gaelic *sprèidh* cattle]
■ **spreaghery** or **spreachery** /sprehh'/ *n* cattle-stealing; petty possessions, *esp* plunder.

spreathe, spreaze see **spray³**.

sprechery see under **spreagh**.

sprechgesang /shprehh'gə-zang/ (*music*) *n* a style of vocalization between singing and speaking, first used in Humperdinck's *Königskinder* (1897). [Ger, speaking-song, speaking voice] ■ **sprech'stimme** /-shtim-ə/ *n* music using this form of vocalization.

spreckled /sprek'ld/ (now *dialect*) *adj* speckled. [Cf obs Ger *gespreckelt*]

spred, spredd, spredde obsolete spellings of **spread** (*prt*, *pat* or *pap*).

spree /sprē/ *n* a merry frolic; a drunken bout; a bout of self-indulgence or other enjoyable activity; a gathering or party at which a prospective bride displays her wedding gifts (*old Scot*). ◆ *vi* to carouse. [Orig slang]

spreethe, spreeze see **spray³**.

sprent /sprent/ (*archaic*) *adj* sprinkled. [Pap of obs *sprenge*, from OE *sprengen*, *sprengan*, causative of *springan* to spring]

sprew see **sprue³**.

sprig /sprig/ *n* a small shoot or twig; a scion, a young person (*usu disparagingly*); an ornament like a spray; a headless or almost headless nail, a brad; a spriglike object, ornament, or design, *esp* embroidered or applied. ◆ *vt* (**sprigg'ing**; **sprigged**) to decorate or embroider with representations of twigs; to nail with sprigs. [Origin obscure]
■ **sprigged** *adj*. **sprigg'y** *adj* full of or like sprigs.

spright /sprīt/ *n* a variant of **sprite**, *obs* except perhaps in the sense of a supernatural being, impish person. ◆ *vt* (*Shakesp*) to haunt.
■ **spright'ful** *adj* (*obs*) spirited. **spright'fully** *adv* (*Shakesp*). **spright'fulness** *n* (*obs*). **spright'less** *adj* (*obs*) spiritless. **spright'liness** *n*. **spright'ly** *adj* vivacious; animated; lively; brisk; ghostly (*Shakesp*).

spring¹ /spring/ *vi* (pat **sprang**; pap **sprung**) to move suddenly, as by elastic force; to bound; to start up suddenly; to break forth; to appear; to issue; to come into being; to take origin; to sprout; to dawn (*Bible*); to branch off; to begin to arch; to give way, split, burst, explode, warp, or start; (with *for*) to pay (*N Am*). ◆ *vt* to cause to spring up; to start; to release the elastic force of; to let off, allow to spring; to cause to explode; to make known suddenly (with *on* or *upon*); (of a leak) to open; (of a mast) to crack; to bend by force, strain; to start from an abutment, etc (*archit*); to leap over; to set together with bevel-joints; to attach or fit with springs; to procure the escape of (a prisoner) from jail (*sl*). ◆ *n* a leap; a sudden movement; a recoil or rebound; elasticity; an elastic contrivance *usu* for setting in motion or for reducing shocks; a

source of action or life; a rise; a beginning; a cause or origin; a source; an outflow of water from the earth; the time of beginning (*Shakesp*); the dawn (*Bible*); (often with *cap*) the season of the year when plants spring up and grow, lasting approximately from March to May in the northern hemisphere and from September to November in the southern hemisphere; in the astronomical year, the period of time between the vernal equinox and the summer solstice; a shoot (*obs*); a youth (*Spenser*); a copse (*obs*); undergrowth (*Spenser*); high water; spring tide; a lively dance tune (*Scot*); a Norwegian dance or dance tune; a flock of teal; the springing of an arch; a split, bend, warp, etc, *esp* a crack in a mast. ◆ *adj* of the season of spring; sown, appearing, or used in spring; having or worked by a spring. [OE *springan*; Ger *springen*]

■ **spring'al** or **spring'ald** *n* (*archaic*) an active young man, a youth. **spring'er** *n* someone who or something that springs; a kind of spaniel, useful in copses; the bottom stone of an arch (*archit*); a spring chicken (chiefly *N Am*); a springing cow (qv below); a spring salmon. **spring'ily** *adv*. **spring'iness** *n*. **spring'ing** *n* the act of leaping, sprouting, starting, rising, or issuing; the beginning of curvature of an arch; a place of branching; providing with springs. ◆ *adj* leaping; arising; dawning; sprouting; with the freshness of youth; resilient; starting; beginning to curve. **spring'less** *adj*. **spring'let** *n* a little spring. **spring'like** *adj*. **spring'y** *adj* elastic; resilient; abounding with springs. See also **sprung**.
❑ **spring balance** or (*esp N Am*) **spring scaie** *n* an instrument for weighing by the elasticity of a spiral spring. **spring beauty** *n* an American flowering plant *Claytonia virginica* of the purslane family. **spring beetle** *n* a click beetle. **spring'-bladed** *adj* (of a knife) having a blade that springs out on pressure of a button. **spring'board** *n* a springy board for jumping or diving from; anything which serves as a starting point, or from which one can launch ideas, projects, etc. **spring'bok** *n* a S African antelope, *Antidorcas marsupialis*, that moves in leaps when alarmed (also **spring'buck**); (with *cap*) a South African international sportsman (from emblems of sporting teams, originally the 1906 rugby team; shortened to **Bok**); hence also any South African, *esp* when overseas. **spring box** *n* a box or barrel in which a spring is coiled; the frame of a sofa, etc in which the springs are set. **spring'-carriage**, **spring'-cart** *n* one mounted on springs. **spring chicken** *n* a young chicken, *usu* between two and ten months old, particularly tender when cooked (chiefly *N Am*; also **spring'er**); a young, lively, sometimes naïve, person. **spring-clean'** *vt* and *n*. **spring'-clean'er** *n*. **spring'-clean'ing** *n* a thorough cleaning (*esp* of a house), *usu* in spring. **spring clip** *n* a spring-loaded clip. **spring fever** *n* spring lassitude (*facetious*); restlessness. **spring'form** *adj* denoting a type of baking tin with detachable sides and base, held together by a spring. **spring'haas** /-häs/ *n* (*pl* **spring'haas** or **spring'hase**) (Du *haas* hare) a S African nocturnal rodent, *Pedetes capensis* (also called **spring hare**). **spring'halt** *n* (*vet*) a jerking lameness in which a horse suddenly twitches up its leg or legs (also called **string'halt**). **spring hare** see **springhaas** above. **spring'head** *n* a fountainhead, source; a head- or end-piece for a carriage spring. **spring'-heeled** *adj* having springs on one's heels, as in **spring-heeled Jack**, supposed to do great leaps and play pranks or commit robberies. **spring'house** *n* (*esp US*) a larder, dairy, etc built over a spring or brook in order to keep the contents cool. **springing cow** *n* a cow about to calf. **spring'keeper** *n* a salamander. **spring ligament** *n* a ligament of the sole of the foot. **spring line** *n* a mooring line (*naut*); one of the strips of rubber, steel or wood inserted in and running down the handle of a cricket bat, hockey stick, etc. **spring-load'ed** *adj* having or operated by a spring. **spring lock** *n* a lock in which the bolt is spring-loaded; one that opens when a spring is touched. **spring mattress** *n* a mattress of spiral springs in a frame. **spring onion** *n* a type of onion, its small bulb and long leaves being eaten raw in salads. **spring peeper** *n* a N American tree frog that makes a high-pitched call in spring. **spring roll** *n* a deep-fried Chinese savoury pancake enclosing a mixture of vegetables, pork, prawns, etc. **spring scale** see **spring balance** above. **spring'tail** *n* any member of the Collembola order of primitive, wingless insects. **spring'tide** *n* springtime. **spring tide** *n* a tide of maximum amplitude after new and full moon, when the forces of the sun and moon act in the same direction; any great rush or flood (*fig*). **spring'time** *n* the season of spring. **spring'water** *n* water of or from a spring. **spring wheat** *n* wheat sown in the spring, rather than autumn or winter. **spring'wood** *n* secondary wood with larger and thinner-walled elements formed in spring and early summer. **spring'wort** *n* a root thought to be magical, *perh* mandrake.
■ **spring a leak** to begin to leak. **spring a mine** to cause it to explode.

spring² see **springe¹**.

springal, springald see under **spring¹**.

springe¹ /sprinj/, also **spring** /spring/ *n* a snare with noose and spring; a gin. ◆ *vt* (**spring'ing**; **springed** /sprinjd/) to snare in a springe. [Earlier *sprenge*, from a probable OE *sprencg*; cf **sprent**, **spring¹**]
■ **springle** /spring'gl/ *n* a snare.

springe² /sprinj/ (*George Eliot*) *adj* active, nimble. [Ety unknown]

sprinkle /spring'kl/ *vt* to scatter in small drops or particles; to scatter on; to baptize with a few drops of water; to strew, dot, diversify. ◆ *vi* to scatter in drops. ◆ *n* a sprinkling; an aspersorium or utensil for sprinkling. [Frequentative from OE *sprengan*, the causative of *springan* to spring; cf Ger *sprenkeln*]
  ■ **sprin'kler** *n* any thing or person that sprinkles; any of various devices for scattering water in drops, eg over growing plants, as fire extinguishers, etc (**sprinkler system** a system of such fire extinguishers which operate automatically on a sudden rise in temperature). **sprin'kling** *n* the act of someone who sprinkles; a small quantity sprinkled (also *fig*); (in bookbinding) the mottling of the edges of pages by scattering a few drops of colour.

sprint /sprint/ *n* a short run, row, cycle or race at full speed. ◆ *vi* to run, etc at full speed. ◆ *vt* to perform a sprint over a (given distance). [Cf ON *spretta*, Swed *spritta*]
  ■ **sprin'ter** *n*. **sprin'ting** *n*.

sprit /sprit/ (*naut*) *n* a spar set diagonally to extend a fore-and-aft sail. [OE *sprēot* pole; Du *spriet* and Ger *Spriet* sprit]
  ❑ **spritsail** /sprit'sl/ *n* a sail extended by a sprit.

sprite /sprīt/ *n* a goblin, elf, imp, impish or implike person; (in computer graphics) an icon formed of pixels, which can be moved around a screen by means of a software program. [OFr *esprit*; cf **spirit, spright**]
  ■ **sprite'ful** *adj*. **sprite'ly** *adj* same as **sprightly** (see under **spright**).

spritsail see under **sprit**.

spritz /sprits/ *vt* to spray (liquid). ◆ *n* a spray of liquid. [Ger, as for **spritzer**]

spritzer /sprit'sər/ *n* a drink of white wine and soda water. [Ger *spritzen* to spray, squirt]

spritzig /shprit'sig/ (*Ger*) *adj* sparkling (*esp* of wine). ◆ *n* a slightly sparkling (*usu* German) white wine; the tangy quality of such a wine.

sprocket /sprok'it/ *n* a tooth on the rim of a wheel or capstan for engaging the chain; a toothed cylinder for driving a film, tape, etc; a sprocket wheel; a piece of wood used to build a roof out over eaves. [Origin unknown]
  ❑ **sprocket wheel** *n* a wheel with sprockets.

sprod /sprod/ (*Scot and N Eng dialect*) *n* a young salmon in its second year. [Origin obscure]

sprog /sprog/ *n* a recruit (*milit sl*); a child, infant (*inf*). [Poss from frogspawn or a recruit's confusion of **sprocket** and **cog¹**]

sprong /sprong/ (*archaic*) *pat* and *pap* of **spring¹**.

sprout /sprowt/ *n* a new growth; a young shoot; a side bud, as in Brussels sprout; a scion, descendant; sprouting condition. ◆ *vi* to shoot; to push out new shoots. ◆ *vt* to put forth as a sprout or bud; to cause to sprout; to remove sprouts from (*dialect*). [OE *sprūtan* (found in compounds), Du *spruiten*, Ger *spriessen*]
  ■ **sprout'ed** *adj*. **sprout'ing** *n* and *adj*.

spruce¹ /sproos/ *n* any conifer of the genus *Picea*, with long shoots only, four-angled needles, and pendulous cones; its wood; spruce beer. ◆ *adj* of spruce or its wood. [OE *Spruce* Prussia, altered from *Pruce*, via OFr from L *Prussia*]
  ❑ **spruce beer** *n* a drink made from a fermentation of sugar or treacle and the green tops of spruce. **spruce budworm** *n* the larva of a N American moth that feeds on conifer buds. **spruce fir** *n* the spruce tree; extended to some other trees. **spruce pine** *n* a name given to various American pine trees; extended to some varieties of spruce.

spruce² /sproos/ *adj* smart; neat, dapper; over-fastidious, finical. ◆ *adv* sprucely. ◆ *vt* to smarten. ◆ *vi* to become spruce or smart (often with *up*). [Prob from **spruce¹**, from 'spruce leather' a fine soft leather used for making jackets (obtained from *Pruce* or *Prussia*) in the 16c]
  ■ **spruce'ly** *adv*. **spruce'ness** *n*.

sprue¹ /sproo/ *n* a passage by which molten material runs into a mould; the material that solidifies in it, also called **dead-head**. [Origin obscure]

sprue² /sproo/ *n* infantile thrush (*obs*); either of two disorders, *tropical sprue* and *coeliac disease*, in which the intestines fail to absorb nutrients adequately. [Du *spruw*]
  ■ **tropical sprue** a disease characterized by loss of appetite and weight, diarrhoea, inflammation of the mouth and tongue, and atrophy of the lining of the small intestine.

sprue³ or **sprew** /sproo/ (*esp SE Eng dialect*) *n* very thin, inferior asparagus.

sprug /sprug/ (*Scot*) *n* a sparrow.

spruik /sprook/ (*Aust and NZ*) *vi* (of a showman, etc) to harangue people in public. [Origin uncertain]
  ■ **spruik'er** *n*.

spruit /sprāt, sprü'it or sprīt/ (*S Afr*) *n* a small, deepish watercourse, dry except during and after rains. [Du, sprout]

sprung /sprung/ *pat* and *pap* of **spring¹**. *adj* strained; split; loosed; furnished with springs; tipsy (*inf*).
  ❑ **sprung rhythm** *n* a poetic rhythm close to the natural rhythm of speech, with mixed feet, and frequent single stressed syllables.

sprush /sproosh or sprush/ *adj*, *adv* and *vt* a Scots form of **spruce²**.

spry /sprī/ *adj* (**spry'er**; **spry'est**) nimble; agile. [Origin doubtful]
  ■ **spry'ly** *adv*. **spry'ness** *n*.

SPUC *abbrev*: Society for the Protection of Unborn Children.

spud /spud/ *n* a potato (*inf*); a small narrow digging tool with a spadelike blade; a stumpy person or thing; a blunt needle used to remove foreign bodies embedded in the eye (*med*); a support for earthmoving or drilling machinery. ◆ *vt* and *vi* to dig with a spud; (to position (machinery) in order) to start excavating or drilling (eg an oil-well). [Origin obscure]
  ■ **spudd'ing** *n* (also **spudd'ing-in**) the process of starting to excavate or drill (eg an oil-well by boring a hole in the seabed). **spudd'y** *adj* podgy.
  ❑ **spud'-bashing** *n* (*sl*) peeling potatoes. **spudding bit** *n* (*mining*) a large drill bit for making an initial bore hole, eg into which the casing of an oil-well is cemented.

spue an old-fashioned spelling of **spew**.

spuilzie see **spulzie**.

spule /spûl or spül/ (*Scot*) *n* the shoulder (also **speal** /spēl/). [Relation to **spauld** obscure]
  ❑ **spule'bane**, **spule'bone** or **spule'blade** *n*.

spulzie, spuilzie, spulye or **spulyie** /spül'yi/ (*Scot*) *n* spoliation. ◆ *vt* and *vi* to plunder. [See **spoil**]

spumante /spoo-man'ti/ *n* a sparkling Italian white wine. [Ital, sparkling, from *spumare* to froth]

spume /spūm/ *n* foam; scum. ◆ *vi* to foam. ◆ *vt* to throw up or off as foam or scum. [L *spūma*, from *spuere* to spew]
  ■ **spumesc'ence** *n*. **spumesc'ent** *adj* foamy, frothing. **spū'mous** *adj*. **spū'my** *adj*.

spumone or **spumoni** /spoo-mō'ni/ *n* ice cream served in layers of different colours or flavours. [Ital, from *spuma* foam]

spun /spun/ *pat* and *pap* of **spin**.
  ❑ **spun'-out** *adj* unduly lengthened. **spun silk** *n* a fabric made from waste silk fibres, sometimes mixed with cotton. **spun sugar** *n* sugar spun into fine fluffy threads, as in candyfloss. **spun'yarn** *n* a line or rope made from one or more yarns twisted (not laid) into a cord.

spunge /spunj/ obsolete spelling of **sponge**.
  ❑ **spun'ging-house** see under **sponge**.

spunk /spungk/ *n* spirit, mettle, courage, pluck; a small but spirited person (*dialect*); a spark (*dialect, esp Scot*); a match (*dialect*); a fungus from which tinder is made (*dialect*); touchwood, tinder (*obs*); semen (*vulgar sl*). ◆ *vi* to take light, flame up (*archaic*); to fire up; to show spirit (*usu* with *up*; *US*); to come to light (*Scot*; with *out*). [Cf Ir *sponc* tinder, sponge, from L *spongia* a sponge, from Gr *spongiā*]
  ■ **spunk'ie** *n* (*Scot*) a will-o'-the-wisp; a fiery or mettlesome person; whisky (*Burns*). **spunk'iness** *n*. **spunk'y** *adj* spirited; fiery-tempered.

spur /spûr/ *n* a goading instrument on a horse rider's heel; incitement, stimulus; a hard sharp projection; a clawlike projection at the back of a cock's or other bird's leg; an artificial substitute for this on a gamecock; a short, *usu* flowering or fruit-bearing, branch; a great lateral root; ergot; a tubular pouch at the base of a petal; an expansion of a leaf base; anything that projects in the shape of a spur, eg an extension from an electrical circuit; a lateral branch, as of a hill range; a siding or branch line of a railway; a strut; a structure to deflect the current from a bank. ◆ *vt* (**spurr'ing**; **spurred**) to apply the spur to; to urge on; to provide with a spur or spurs; to prune into spurs. ◆ *vi* to press forward with the spur; to hasten; to kick out. [OE *spura, spora*; ON *spori*, Ger *Sporn*]
  ■ **spur'less** *adj*. **spurred** *adj* having or wearing spurs or a spur; in the form of a spur; urged; (eg of rye) affected with ergot. **spurr'er** *n*. **spurr'ier** *n* a maker of spurs. **spurr'ing** *n* and *adj*. **spurr'y** *adj* like, of the nature of, or having a spur.
  ❑ **spur'-gall** *vt* (*Shakesp*) to gall or wound with a spur. **spur gear** or **wheel** *n* a gear wheel with straight teeth parallel to its axis, as used in **spur gearing**, a system of such gears connecting two parallel shafts. **spur'-heeled** *adj* having a long straight hind claw. **spur leather** *n* a strap for fastening a spur. **spur rowel** *n* the rowel of a spur. **spur'-roy'al, -ry'al** or **-rī'al** *n* a former English fifteen-shilling piece of gold, bearing a star like a spur rowel. **spur'way** *n* (*dialect*) a bridle road. **spur'-whang** *n* (*Scot*) a spur leather. **spur wheel** see **spur gear** above. **spur'-winged** *adj* with a horny spur on the pinion of the wing.
  ■ **gilt spurs** a mark of knighthood. **on the spur of the moment** without premeditation. **set spurs to** to apply the spur to (a horse) and

ride off quickly; to urge on; to hasten the progress of. **win one's spurs** to gain distinction by achievement; *orig* to earn a knighthood.

spurge /spûrj/ *n* any species of *Euphorbia*, a genus of very varied habit, with milky, generally poisonous, juice, and an inflorescence (cyathium) of flowers so reduced as to simulate a single flower. [OFr *espurge* (Fr *épurge*), from L *expurgāre* to purge, from *ex* off, and *purgāre* to clear]
□ **spurge laurel** *n* a European evergreen shrub (*Daphne laureola*) with yellowish-green flowers, thick leaves, and poisonous berries.

spurious /spū'ri-əs/ *adj* not genuine; false; sham; forged; simulating but essentially different; bastard, illegitimate. [L *spurius* false]
■ **spūr'iae** /-i-ē/ *n pl* in birds, feathers of the bastard wing. **spurios'ity** *n*. **spūr'iously** *adv*. **spūr'iousness** *n*.

spurling /spûr'ling/ same as **sparling**.

spurn /spûrn/ *vt* to reject with contempt; to tread, *esp* in contempt; to kick (*archaic*). ◆ *vi* to trip (*obs*); to kick (often with *at* or *against*; *archaic*). ◆ *n* a kick or kicking (*archaic*); disdainful rejection. [OE *spornan*, *spurnan*, related to **spur**]
■ **spurn'er** *n*. **spurn'ing** *n* and *adj*.

spurne /spûrn/ (*Spenser*) *vt* to spur.

spurrey, sometimes **spurry** /spu'ri/ *n* any plant of the genus *Spergula*; applied to related plants, *Spergularia rubra* (**sand spurrey**) and *Sagina nodosa* (**knotted spurrey**). [Du *spurrie*]

spurrier see under **spur**.

spurry see **spur** and **spurrey**.

spurt /spûrt/ *vt* to spout, or send out in a sudden stream or jet. ◆ *vi* to gush out suddenly in a small stream; to flow out forcibly or at intervals; to make a sudden short intense effort. ◆ *n* a sudden or violent gush; a jet; a short spell, *esp* of intensified effort, speed, etc. [Variant of **spirt**[1]]

spurtle /spûr'tl/ (*Scot*) *n* a stick for stirring porridge; a sword (also **spur'tle-blade**). [Origin doubtful]

sputa see **sputum**.

sputnik /spŏŏt' or spŏŏt'nik/ *n* any of a series of artificial Earth satellites launched by the former Soviet Union. [After the Russian *Sputnik* ('travelling companion') 1, the first such satellite, put in orbit in 1957]

sputter /spŏŏt'ər/ *vi* to spit or throw out moisture in scattered drops, to splutter; to speak rapidly and indistinctly, to jabber, to stutter; to make a sputtering noise. ◆ *vt* to spit out or throw out in or with small drops; to utter hastily and indistinctly; to remove atoms from a cathode by positive ion bombardment, the unchanged atoms being deposited on a surface, and the process being used for coating glass, plastic, another metal, etc with a thin film of metal. ◆ *n* an instance of, or the process or sound of sputtering; matter sputtered out. [Imit; cf Du *sputteren*, and **spit**[1]]
■ **sputt'erer** *n*. **sputt'ering** *n* and *adj*. **sputt'eringly** *adv*. **sputt'ery** *adj*.

sputum /spū'təm/ *n* (pl **spū'ta**) matter coughed up and spat out. [L *spūtum*, from *spuere* to spit]

sp. vol. *abbrev*: specific volume.

spy /spī/ *n* (pl **spies**) a secret agent employed to watch others or to collect information, *esp* of a military nature; a spying; a look; an eye (*fig*). ◆ *vt* (**spy'ing**; **spied**) to watch, observe, investigate, or ascertain secretly (often with *out*); to catch sight of, make out; to discover. ◆ *vi* to act as a spy. [OFr *espie* (noun), *espier* (verb); cf **espy**]
■ **spy'al** (*Spenser*) a spy (see **spial**). **spy'ing** *n* and *adj*.
□ **spy'cam** *n* a camera set up for hidden surveillance purposes, *esp* a webcam relaying pictures to a computer. **spy'glass** *n* a small hand-held telescope. **spy'hole** *n* a peephole, eg in a door. **spy'master** *n* a person who controls and co-ordinates the activities of undercover agents. **spy'-money** *n* money paid for secret intelligence. **spy'plane** *n* an aeroplane specially equipped to collect information on enemy positions, military manoeuvres, etc. **spy'ware** *n* computer software that gathers information about the user and transmits it to another computer user.
■ **spy in the cab** (*inf*) a tachograph fitted in a lorry or truck.

spyre obsolete spelling (*Spenser*) of **spire**[1].

sq. *abbrev*: *sequens* (L), following (*pl* **sqq** *sequentes* or *sequentia*); (also **Sq.**) square or Square (in addresses).

SQA *abbrev*: Scottish Qualifications Authority.

SQC *abbrev*: Scottish Qualifications Certificate.

SQL (*comput*) *abbrev*: standard (or structured) query language, a programming language used to retrieve information from a database.

sqn *abbrev*: squadron.

Sqn Ldr *abbrev*: squadron leader.

squab /skwob/ *adj* fat, clumsy; unfledged, newly hatched; shy, coy; curt, abrupt (*obs*); having a squab. ◆ *n* a young pigeon or rook; a fledgling; a young chicken (*US*); a short stumpy person (*inf*); a soft thick cushion; a padded sofa or ottoman; a carriage cushion; the back part of a motor car seat. ◆ *vt* to upholster or stuff thickly and sew through in places. ◆ *vi* to fall heavily. ◆ *adv* plump and squashily. [Poss Scand; cf Swed dialect *sqvabb* loose flesh, *sqvabbig* flabby]
■ **squabb'ish** *adj* thick, heavy. **squabb'y** *adj* squat.
□ **squab pie** *n* a pie made of mutton or pork, onions, and apples.

squabash /skwə-bash'/ (*inf*) *vt* to crush, smash, defeat. ◆ *n* a crushing blow. [Prob **squash**[1] and **bash**[1]]
■ **squabash'er** *n*.

squabbish see under **squab**.

squabby see under **squab**.

squacco /skwak'ō/ *n* (pl **squacc'os**) a small crested European heron, *Ardeola ralloides*. [Ital dialect *sguacco*]

squad /skwod/ *n* a small group of soldiers drilled or working together; any working party; a set or group; a number of players trained in readiness for the selection of a team (*sport*). [Fr *escouade*; cf Sp *escuadra*, Ital *squadra*]
■ **squadd'ie** or **squadd'y** *n* (*milit inf*) a private, an ordinary soldier.
□ **squad car** *n* a police car.
■ **awkward squad** a group, *esp* within a political party, that is inclined to be rebellious; *orig* a body of recruits not yet competent in drill, etc.

squadron /skwod'rən/ *n* a group of aeroplanes forming a unit under one command; a detachment, body, group; a division of a regiment, *esp* a cavalry regiment, under a major or captain; a section of a fleet under a flag-officer; a body of soldiers drawn up in a square (*obs*). ◆ *vt* to form into squadrons. [Ital *squadrone*, from *squadra* square]
■ **squad'ronal** *adj*. **squad'roned** *adj*.
□ **squadrone** (**volante**) /skwa-drō'nā (vō-län'tā)/ *n* (Ital, flying squadron) an early 18c Scottish political party opposed to the Argathelians. **squadron leader** *n* a Royal Air Force officer corresponding in rank to a lieutenant-commander or major.

squail /skwāl/ *n* a counter for playing squails; (in *pl*) a parlour-game similar to tiddlywinks, in which small discs are snapped from the edge of the table to a centre mark; (in *pl*) ninepins; a stick for throwing. ◆ *vi* to throw sticks (as at birds or fruit). ◆ *vt* to pelt with sticks; to hit by throwing a stick. [Cf **kail**[1] (obs *skail*, *skayle*), a ninepin]
■ **squail'er** *n* a throwing stick. **squail'ing** *n*.

squalene /skwā'lēn/ (*biochem*) *n* a symmetrical triterpine, an intermediate in the synthesis of cholesterol, present in mammalian and plant tissue (formerly called **spinacene**). [From New L *squalus*, genus name of the shark in which it was originally found]

squalid /skwol'id/ *adj* filthy, foul; neglected, uncared-for, unkempt; sordid and dingy; morally repulsive; poverty-stricken. [L *squālidus* stiff, rough, dirty, from *squālor*, *-ōris*]
■ **squalid'ity** *n*. **squal'idly** *adv*. **squal'idness** *n*. **squal'or** *n* the state of being squalid; dirtiness; filthiness.

squall /skwöl/ *n* a brief violent storm or sudden strong wind; a loud cry or yell. ◆ *vi* (of wind) to blow in a squall; to cry out violently; to yell; to sing loudly and unmusically. ◆ *vt* to sing or utter loudly and unmusically. [Prob imit]
■ **squall'er** *n*. **squall'ing** *n* and *adj*. **squall'y** *adj* of, abounding in, or disturbed with, squalls or gusts of wind; gusty, blustering; threatening a squall.
□ **squall line** *n* (*meteorol*) a band of storms occurring along a cold front.
■ **white squall** see under **white**.

squaloid /skwā'loid/ *adj* of or relating to sharks of the suborder **Squaloid'ea**; like a shark. [L *squālus* a sea fish of the shark or dogfish group]

squalor see under **squalid**.

squama /skwā'mə or skwä'mə/ *n* (pl **squa'mae** /-mē or -mī/) a scale; a scalelike structure; a thin plate of bone; the exopodite of an antenna in Crustacea. [L *squāma* a scale]
■ **Squamā'ta** /skwə-/ *n pl* (*zool*) an order of reptiles comprising snakes and lizards. **squa'mate** *adj* scaly. **squamā'tion** /skwə-/ *n* scaliness; the mode of arrangement of scales. **squame** /skwām/ *n* a scale or squama. **squamell'a** /skwə-/ *n* a little scale. **squa'miform** *adj* like a scale. **squamosal** /skwə-mō'sl/ *n* a paired membrane bone of the vertebral skull, the squamous portion of the temporal bone (also *adj*). **squā'mose** or **squā'mous** *adj* scaly; (of epithelium) consisting of a layer of flattened scalelike cells. **squāmos'ity** *n*. **squamula** /skwam'ū-lə or skwäm'-/ *n*. **squam'ule** *n* a little scale. **squam'ūlose** *adj*.
□ **squamous cell carcinoma** *n* a tumour of the flattened, scalelike cells in the skin.

squander /skwon'dər/ *vt* to spend lavishly or wastefully; to scatter, disperse (*obs*). ◆ *vi* to wander, roam, straggle; to scatter. ◆ *n* (*rare*) a squandering. [Origin obscure]
■ **squan'dered** *adj*. **squan'derer** *n*. **squan'dering** *n* and *adj*. **squan'deringly** *adv*. **squandermā'nia** *n* (*sl*) a spirit of reckless expenditure (eg in a government).

square /skwār/ n a geometric figure having four equal sides and four right angles; an object, piece, space, figure, of approximately that shape, eg a windowpane, paving-stone, space on a chessboard, a silk headscarf; an open space, commonly but not necessarily of that shape, in a town, along with its surrounding buildings; a rectangular area in the centre of a cricket ground, on which the wickets are prepared; a rectangular block of buildings (US); a body of troops drawn up in that form; the product of a quantity multiplied by itself (maths); the yoke of a garment (Shakesp); a unit of flooring, 100 square feet; an instrument for drawing or testing right angles; a carpenter's measure; a piece of timber cut square, of side up to six inches; a canon, standard, criterion, rule (obs); squareness; quartile aspect (old astron); due proportion; order; honesty, equity, fairness; a quarrel, dissension (obs); poss a part, compartment (Shakesp, King Lear I.1.73); an unopened cotton flower (US); a person of boringly traditional outlook and opinions, esp in musical taste or dress (inf); a square meal (inf). ◆ adj having or approaching the form of a square; relatively broad, thick-set; right-angled; (in football, etc) in a line, position, etc across the pitch; equal to a quantity multiplied by itself; measuring an area in two dimensions, ie length multiplied by width or breadth; exact, suitable, fitting; true, equitable, fair, honest; even, leaving no balance, equal in score; directly opposed; complete, unequivocal; solid, full, satisfying; (of taste in music, dress, etc) boringly traditional and orthodox (inf); bourgeois in attitude (inf). ◆ vt to make square or rectangular, esp in cross-section; to make nearly cubical; to form into squares; to mark with squares; to construct or determine a square equal to; to multiply by itself; to reduce to any given measure or standard, to adjust, regulate; to bring into accord, reconcile; to place at right angles with the mast or keel (naut); to make equal; to pay; to bribe; (with with) to get (someone's) agreement, approval or permission for something. ◆ vi to suit, fit; to accord or agree; to adopt a position of offence and defence, as a boxer does (often with up to; see also below); to swagger (obs); to make the score or account even. ◆ adv at right angles; solidly; directly; evenly; fairly, honestly. [OFr esquarre (Fr équerre), from L ex and quadra a square] ■ **squared** adj. **square'ly** adv. **square'ness** n. **squar'er** n someone who or something that squares; a fighting, quarrelsome person, or perh a swaggerer (Shakesp). **square'wise** adv. **squar'ing** n and adj. **squar'ish** adj.
□ **square B** see **B quadratum** under **B** (n). **square'-bashing** n (milit sl) parade ground drill. **square bracket** n a bracket. **square'-built** adj of a form suggesting squareness; broad in proportion to height. **square centimetre, metre**, etc n an area equal to that of a square whose side measures a centimetre, metre, etc. **square'-cut** adj cut in a square shape; (of a person's chin) having a strong, squared outline. **square dance** n (esp N Am) a folk dance done by a group of four couples in a square formation. **square'-dance** vi. **square'-dancing** n. **squared circle** n a wrestling ring. **square deal** n (inf) a fair and honest arrangement, transaction, etc. **square'-eyed** adj. **square eyes** n pl an imaginary condition affecting those who watch too much television. **square'-face** n (S Afr) gin (from the shape of the bottle). **square foot, inch, mile**, etc n an area equal to that of a square whose side measures a foot, inch, mile, etc. **square'head** n (old derog sl) a Scandinavian or German. **square knot** n a reef knot. **square leg** n (cricket) a fielder, or a fielding position, on the legside in a line with the popping crease. **square matrix** n (maths) a matrix with an equal number of rows and columns. **square meal** n a full, satisfying meal. **square measure** n a system of measures for surfaces, its unit the square of the lineal unit. **square mile** see **square foot** above; (usu with caps) the City of London, specif the area around and incl the Bank of England; financial life, activities, etc in the City of London (fig). **square number** n a number the square root of which is an integer. **square peg** see under **peg**. **square'-pierced** adj (heraldry) having a square opening so as to show the field. **square-rigged'** adj (naut) having square sails extended by yards suspended by the middle at right angles to the masts, opp to fore-and-aft. **square-rigg'er** n (naut) a square-rigged ship. **square root** n a number or quantity which being multiplied by itself produces the quantity in question, eg 3 is the square root of 9. **square'-sail** /-sl/ n (naut) a four-sided sail extended by yards suspended by the middle generally at right angles to the mast. **square sausage** same as **Lorne sausage**. **square shooter** n (chiefly US inf) a frank and honest person. **square shooting** n. **square-shoul'dered** adj with broad, straight shoulders. **square-toed'** adj (of shoes, etc) ending square at the toes. **square'-toes** n (pl) square-toed shoes; (sing) an old-fashioned, punctilious person (archaic).
■ **back to square one** back to the original position with the problem, etc, unchanged. **how squares go** (obs) what is doing; how things are going. **on the square** at right angles; openly, honestly; an expression identifying someone as a member of the Freemasons (sl). **square away** to set (sails) at right angles to the keel (naut); to make neat and tidy (N Am). **square off** (inf) to adopt an offensive or defensive stance, as in boxing before any blows are struck. **square up** (inf) to settle (a bill, account, etc). **square up to** to face up to and tackle. **squaring the circle** finding a square of the same area as a circle, which for

hundreds of years was attempted by Euclidean means (ie with straight-edge and compass) until in 1882 it was proved impossible (also **squaring the quadrature of the circle**); any impossible task.

squarial /skwā'ri-əl/ n a flat diamond-shaped (as opposed to round) aerial formerly used for receiving satellite television broadcasts. [square and aerial]

squarrose /skwar'ōs, skwor'ōs or -ōs'/ (biol) adj rough with projecting or downward-bent scales, bracts, etc; standing out straight or bent down. [L squarrōsus scurfy]

squarson /skwär's(ə)n/ n a clergyman who is also a squire or landowner in his parish. [squire and parson] ■ **squar'sonage** n his residence.

squash[1] /skwosh/ vt to press into pulp; to crush flat; to squeeze; to put down, suppress; to snub or crush. ◆ vi to form a soft mass as from a fall; to crowd; to squelch; to become crushed or pulpy. ◆ n a drink made from fruit juice or a concentrated syrup; anything soft and unripe or easily crushed; a crushed mass; a crushed condition; a close crowd; a squeezing; a game for two or four players played with a small rubber ball, which is struck with a racket against the walls of an enclosed court (also **squash rackets** or **racquets**); a soft rubber ball for playing squash; an unripe peapod (Shakesp). ◆ adv with a squash. [OFr esquacer (Fr écacher) to crush, from L ex (intensifying), and quassāre to shatter; see **quash**] ■ **squash'able** adj. **squash'er** n. **squash'ily** adv. **squash'iness** n. **squash'y** adj pulpy; squelching; sopping.
□ **squash tennis** n a game for two players similar to squash rackets (see above) but played with an inflated ball and larger rackets.

squash[2] /skwosh/ (chiefly N Am) n the fruit of various marrow-like plants of the genus Cucurbita, with edible flesh; any of the plants bearing such fruit. [Narragansett askutasquash]
□ **squash bug** n an insect that is a pest of squashes.

squat /skwot/ vi (squatt'ing; squatt'ed) to crouch down on the hams or heels; to hunch or crouch small and low like an animal; to settle on land or in unoccupied buildings without legal right, or (Aust hist) to settle on land with a view to acquiring legal title. ◆ vt to cause to squat. ◆ adj crouching; short and thick, dumpy. ◆ n the act of squatting; a building in which people are squatting (inf); a squat thrust; a weightlifting exercise in which a weight is lifted by a person rising from a squatting position. [OFr esquatir to crush, from L ex (intensifying), and coactus, pap of cōgere to force together]
■ **squat'ness** n. **squatt'er** n someone who squats; a large landowner (Aust). **squatt'iness** n. **squatt'le** vt and vi to squat down. **squattoc'racy** n (Aust) the powerful land-owning class. **squatt'y** adj short and thick.
□ **squat lobster** n a variety of lobster (family Galatheidae) with the tail tucked under the body. **squat shop** n a business, usu selling cheap goods, that occupies an empty or disused shop illegally, pays no rent or rates and trades for the time taken by the owner to obtain an eviction order from a court. **squat thrust** n a gymnastic exercise performed by thrusting the legs backwards to their full extent from a squatting position while supporting the weight on the hands.

squatter[1] /skwot'ər/ vi to splash along. ◆ n a fluttering; a splashing, spattering. [Prob imit]

squatter[2], **squattle**, **squatty** see under **squat**.

squaw /skwö/ (offensive) n a Native American woman, esp a wife. [Massachuset squa]
□ **squaw'man** n a white man with a Native American wife.

squawk /skwök/ n a croaky call or cry; a loud complaint or protest (inf); a signal on a radar screen identifying an aircraft and its flight level (sl). ◆ vi to utter a squawk; to complain loudly (inf). ◆ vt to utter with a squawk. [Imit]
■ **squawk'er** n. **squawk'ing** n and adj. **squawk'y** adj.
□ **squawk box** n (inf) an intercom or telephone with loudspeaker.

squeak /skwēk/ vi to give forth a high-pitched nasal-sounding note or cry, or produce a similar noise; to inform or confess (inf). ◆ vt to utter, sing or render squeakily. ◆ n a squeaky sound; a narrow escape; a bare chance; the slimmest of margins; a tiny amount; a feeble newspaper (old sl). [Imit; cf Swed sqväka to croak, Ger quieken to squeak]
■ **squeak'er** n someone who or something that squeaks; a young bird; an informer; a squeaking toy; a narrow victory (inf). **squeak'ery** n. **squeak'ily** adv. **squeak'iness** n. **squeak'ing** n and adj. **squeak'ingly** adv. **squeak'y** adj.
□ **squeaky clean** adj orig, of wet hair, so clean that it squeaks when pulled; spotlessly clean; (of a person) impeccable, wholesome, virtuous, above criticism or reproach (often slightly derog).
■ **squeak through** to succeed, pass, win, etc only by a narrow margin.

squeal /skwēl/ vi to make a high-pitched cry or noise; to cry out in pain; to complain; to turn informer (inf). ◆ vt to utter, sing, render or express with squealing. ◆ *n* a high-pitched cry or noise. [Imit; cf Swed dialect *sqväla* to cry out]

■ **squeal'er** *n* someone who or something that squeals, *esp* a piglet or a bird of various kinds, eg a young pigeon; an informer (*inf*). **squeal'ing** *n* and *adj*.

squeamish /*skwē′mish*/ *adj* feeling nauseous, sick; easily nauseated; easily shocked, disgusted, or offended; fastidious; coy; reluctant from scruples or compunction. [ME *scoymous*, from Anglo-Fr *escoymous*; ety dubious]

■ **squeam'ishly** *adv*. **squeam'ishness** *n*.

squeegee /*skwē′jē* or *-jē′*/ or **squilgee** /*skwil′jē*/ *n* an implement with a blade or pad of rubber, leather, etc, for clearing water or mud from decks, floors, windows, etc or used to apply ink in screen printing; a photographer's roller or brush for squeezing out moisture from wet prints or negatives. ◆ *vt* to clear, press, or smooth with a squeegee. [Appar **squeeze**]

□ **squeegee merchant** *n* a person who approaches vehicles when they are stopped in traffic and cleans their windscreens, *usu* unsolicited and with aggressive demands for payment.

squeeze /*skwēz*/ *vt* to crush, press hard, compress; to grasp tightly; to embrace; to force by pressing; to effect, render, or put by pressing; to crush the juice or liquid from; (with *off*) to fire (a bullet); to force to discard winning cards; to fleece, extort from; to take a rubbing of. ◆ *vi* to press; to crowd; to crush; to force a way; to yield to pressure. ◆ *n* the act of squeezing; pressure; a restriction or time of restriction (*usu* financial or commercial); a crowded assembly; an embrace; a close grasp; a portion withheld and appropriated as by an official; a rubbing; a few drops obtained by squeezing; play that forces an opponent to discard a potentially winning card (also **squeeze play**; *bridge*); a girlfriend or boyfriend (*inf*). [Origin obscure]

■ **squeezabil'ity** *n*. **squeez'able** *adj*. **squeez'er** *n* someone who squeezes; an instrument, machine or part for squeezing; a playing card marked in the corner with suit and value. **squeez'ing** *n* and *adj*. **squeez'y** *adj* squeezable; confined, cramped, contracted.

□ **squeeze'-box** *n* (*inf*) a concertina, accordion. **squeezy bottle** or (*esp US*) **squeeze bottle** *n* a flexible plastic bottle, eg for washing-up liquid, that is squeezed to force out the contents.

■ **put the squeeze on** (*inf*) to extort money from. **squeeze home** to win, succeed, etc with difficulty or narrowly.

squegging /*skweg′ing*/ (*electronics* and *telecom*) *n* and *adj* (of) a type of oscillation in which the oscillations build up to a certain value and then stop for a time before resuming. [Origin uncertain, poss from *self-quenching*]

■ **squeg** *vi* (back-formation) to oscillate intermittently or irregularly. **squegg'er** *n* a squegging oscillator.

squelch /*skwelch* or *skwelsh*/ *n* a gurgling and sucking sound as of walking in wet mud; a heavy blow on, or fall of, a soft body; its sound; a pulpy mass; a disconcerting or quashing retort or rebuff; a circuit which automatically controls the audio-frequency amplifier of a radio receiver in accordance with certain input characteristics, eg to suppress background noise at very low signal levels; the operation of this circuit. ◆ *vi* to make, or walk with, the sound of a squelch. ◆ *vt* to crush under heel; to put down, suppress, snub, crush. [Imit; cf **quelch**]

■ **squelch'er** *n* someone who or something that squelches; an overwhelming blow, retort, etc. **squelch'ing** *n* and *adj*. **squelch'y** *adj*.

squeteague /*skwi-tēg′*/ *n* an Atlantic American spiny-finned food-fish of the genus *Cynoscion*, misnamed salmon or trout. [Narragansett *pesukwiteaug*, literally, they make glue]

squib /*skwib*/ *n* a firework, consisting of a paper tube filled with explosive powder, which burns noisily and explodes; a short piece of satire, a lampoon; a short, *esp* humorous, piece of journalism; a paltry fellow (*archaic*). ◆ *vt* to aim squibs at; to lampoon. ◆ *vi* to write lampoons; to use squibs; to sound or skip about like a squib. [Perh imit]

■ **squibb'ing** *n* and *adj*.

■ **damp squib** see under **damp**.

SQUID /*skwid*/ (*phys*) *abbrev* : superconducting *q*uantum *i*nterference *d*evice (any of several devices used to measure extremely small currents, voltages and magnetic fields).

squid /*skwid*/ *n* (*pl* **squid** or **squids**) any large-headed cephalopod mollusc, *esp* of the genera *Loligo* and *Ommastrephes*, with a long tapering body, ten tentacles and triangular tail fins; a bait or lure of, or in imitation of, a squid; an antisubmarine mortar; a pound sterling, a quid (*sl*); a lead puck used in the game of octopush. ◆ *vi* to fish with a squid. [Origin obscure]

squidge /*skwij*/ *vt* to squeeze or squash (something soft, moist, pulpy, etc). ◆ *n* something soft, wet and gooey. [Imit]

■ **squid'gy** *adj* squashy; soft, wet and springy; gooey.

squier see **squire²**.

squiffer /*skwif′ər*/ (*sl*) *n* a concertina.

squiffy /*skwif′i*/ (*inf*) *adj* tipsy (also **squiff**). [Origin unknown]

squiggle /*skwig′l*/ *vi* to squirm, wriggle; to make wriggly lines. ◆ *n* a twist, wriggle, or wriggly line. [Imit, or poss from *squirm* and *wriggle*]

■ **squigg'ly** *adj*.

squilgee see **squeegee**.

squill /*skwil*/ *n* any plant of the genus *Scilla*, eg spring squill, *S. verna*, with strap-like leaves and blue star-shaped flowers; the sea onion (*Urginea maritima*), formerly included in that genus; (*usu* in *pl*) its dried bulbs used as a diuretic and expectorant; a mantis shrimp of the genus *Squilla* (also **squill'a**). [L *squilla*, *scilla* sea onion, shrimp, from Gr *skilla* sea onion]

squillion /*skwil′yən*/ (*inf*) *n* an indefinite but definitely large number. [Coinage based on **million**]

squinancy /*skwin′ən-si*/ (*obs*) *n* quinsy, suppurative tonsillitis. [LL *squinanchia*, a combination of Gr *synanchē* sore throat, and *kynanchē* (see **cynanche**)]

□ **squinancy wort** *n* a species of woodruff, *Asperula cynanchica*, once thought good for quinsy.

squinch¹ /*skwinch* or *skwinsh*/ (*archit*) *n* an arch or other support across a re-entrant or interior angle. [**scuncheon**]

squinch² /*skwinch*/ (*N Am*) *vt* to screw up (one's face or eyes); (also *vi*) to contract (the body) in order to take up less space. [Perh **squeeze** and **pinch**]

squinny /*skwin′i*/ or **squiny** /*skwī′ni*/ (*Shakesp* and *dialect*) *vi* to squint, peer, look askance. [Prob related to **squint**]

squint /*skwint*/ *adv* obliquely, to one side. ◆ *adj* looking obliquely; looking askance; squinting; strabismic; oblique; indirect. ◆ *vi* to look obliquely; to have the eyes focusing in different directions, either by purposely crossing them, or by strabismus; to have a side reference or allusion; to glance aside or casually; to glance (*inf*); to give an impression of disapproval in one's glance. ◆ *vt* to cause to squint; to direct or divert obliquely. ◆ *n* the act or habit of squinting; strabismus; an oblique look; a glance; a peep; an oblique reference, hint, tendency, or aim; an oblique opening in a wall, eg a hagioscope. [Aphetic for **asquint**; perh related to Du *schuinte* slope, slant, from *schuin* sideways, sloping]

■ **squint'er** *n*. **squint'ing** *n* and *adj*. **squint'ingly** *adv*. **squint'y** *adj*.

□ **squint'-eye** or **squint'-eyes** *n* (*offensive*) someone who squints. **squint'-eyed** *adj*.

squiny see **squinny**.

squire¹ /*skwīr*/ *n* an esquire, an aspirant to knighthood attending a knight (*hist*); a man who escorts or attends a lady; an English or Irish landed gentleman, *esp* of old family; a title applied to a justice of the peace, local judge, etc (*US*); in some parts of Britain, a form of sometimes ironically respectful address. ◆ *vt* to escort or attend. [**esquire**]

■ **squire'age** or **squir'age** *n* landed gentry collectively (also **squiral'ity** or **squir'alty**). **squire'arch** or **squir'arch** *n* a member of the squirearchy. **squirearch'al**, **squirarch'al**, **squirearch'ical** or **squirarch'ical** *adj*. **squire'archy** or **squir'archy** *n* the rule of or government by squires; squires collectively and their social or political power. **squire'dom** *n*. **squireen'** *n* (Ir dimin sfx -*ín*; Anglo-Irish) a petty squire, a squireling. **squire'hood** *n*. **squire'like** or **squire'ly** *adj* and *adv*. **squire'ling** *n* a squire of small possessions. **squire'ship** *n*. **squir'ess** *n* a squire's wife.

□ **squire of dames** *n* a man who devotes himself to the ladies, from a character in Spenser (*Faerie Queene* III.7.53).

squire² or **squier** /*skwīr*/ (*Spenser* and *Shakesp*) *n* a carpenter's square or rule; a canon, rule. [See **square**]

■ **by the squire** precisely.

squirm /*skwûrm*/ *vi* to writhe or move with wriggling motion; to display or feel deep discomfort or distress, as from guilt, pain, embarrassment, etc. ◆ *n* a wriggle. [Prob imit]

■ **squirm'y** *adj*.

squirr same as **skirr**.

squirrel /*skwir′əl*/ *n* a nimble, bushy-tailed arboreal rodent (*Sciurus* or kindred genus); the pelt of such an animal; a person who hoards things (*fig*). ◆ *adj* made of squirrel pelts. ◆ *vt* to hoard (*usu* with *away*). [OFr *escurel*, from LL *scurellus*, dimin of L *sciūrus*, from Gr *skiouros*, from *skiā* shade, and *ourā* tail]

■ **squirr'elly** or **squirr'ely** *adj* like a squirrel; nervous, jumpy.

□ **squirrel cage** *n* a cage with a treadwheel for a squirrel (or other small animal); in an induction motor, a rotor whose winding suggests this; any seemingly endless and purposeless situation, task, etc. **squirrel fish** *n* any of various brightly-coloured marine fishes of the family Holocentridae of shallow tropical waters, so called because their large eyes resemble those of the squirrel. **squirrel monkey** *n* a small golden-haired S American monkey, *Saimiri sciureus*. **squirrel shrew** *n* a tree shrew. **squirr'el-tail** *n* a grass (*Hordeum marinum*) of European marshland with long hairlike awns (in full **squirrel-tail**

■ words derived from main entry word; □ compound words; ■ idioms and phrasal verbs

grass); a broad-tailed lobworm (*Walton*); a cap of squirrel skins, with a tail hanging down behind.

squirt /*skwûrt*/ *vt* to throw out in a jet; to splash or spray with (water, etc) from a jet. ◆ *vi* to spurt. ◆ *n* an instrument for squirting; a jet; an unimportant and irritatingly pretentious person (*inf*). [Cf LGer *swirtjen*, *swürtjen*]
　■ **squirt'er** *n*. **squirt'ing** *n* and *adj*.
　❑ **squirt gun** *n* (*N Am*) a water pistol or spray gun. **squirting cucumber** *n* a Mediterranean cucurbitaceous plant (*Ecballium elaterium*) that squirts out its ripe seeds.

squish /*skwish*/ *vi* to make a squelching or squirting sound. ◆ *vt* to crush (something soft). ◆ *n* the sound of squishing; bosh (*old sl*); marmalade (*public school sl*). [Imit]
　■ **squish'y** *adj*.

squit /*skwit*/ (*inf*) *n* a contemptible person; nonsense; (in *pl* with *the*) same as **squitters**. [Cf **squirt**]

squitch /*skwich*/ *n* quitch grass.

squitters /*skwit'ərz*/ (*sl*) *n pl* (with *the*) diarrhoea. [Cognate with **squirt**]

squiz /*skwiz*/ (*Aust* and *NZ inf*) *n* a quick, close look. [Perh **squint** and **quiz**]

SR *abbrev* : Southern Region.

Sr *abbrev* : senior; Señor; Sir; Sister.

Sr (*chem*) *symbol* : strontium.

sr *symbol* : steradian (SI unit).

SRA *abbrev* : Strategic Rail Authority.

sraddha or **shraddha** /*srä'dä* or *shrä'dä*/ (*Hinduism* and *Buddhism*) *n* an offering to the spirit of an ancestor. [Sans *śrāddha*]

SRAM (*comput*) *abbrev* : static random access memory.

SRC *abbrev* : Student Representative Council.

SRCh *abbrev* : State Registered Chiropodist.

Sri or **Shri** /*shrē*/ in India, a title of great respect given to a man, now generally used as the equivalent of *Mr*. [Sans *śrī* majesty, holiness]
　■ **Srimati** or **Shrimati** /*shrē-mä'ti*/ *n* a title of great respect given to an Indian woman, now generally used as the equivalent of *Mrs*.

Sri Lankan /*sri-* or *shri-lang'kən*/ *adj* of or relating to the republic of *Sri Lanka* in the Indian Ocean, or its people. ◆ *n* a native or citizen of Sri Lanka.

SRN *abbrev* : State Registered Nurse.

SRO *abbrev* : self-regulatory organization; standing room only.

SRU *abbrev* : Scottish Rugby Union.

SS *abbrev* : Saints; *Schutzstaffel* (*Ger*), literally, protection department, an élite Nazi corps.

ss *abbrev* : screw steamer; steamship.

SSA *abbrev* : standard spending assessment (a government assessment of the funds that a local authority will require for its services in a given year).

SSAFA *abbrev* : Soldiers, Sailors, Airmen and Families Association (now known as SSAFA Forces Help).

SSAP *abbrev* : Statement of Standard Accounting Practice.

SSAS *abbrev* : small self-administered (pension) scheme.

SSB *abbrev* : single sideband transmission.

SSC *abbrev* : *Societas Sanctae Crucis* (*L*), Society of the Holy Cross; Solicitor before the Supreme Courts (of Scotland).

SSD *abbrev* : *Sanctissimus Dominus* (*L*), Most Holy Lord (the Pope); Social Services Department.

SSE *abbrev* : south-south-east.

SSL (*comput*) *abbrev* : Secure Sockets Layer, a proprietary standard for secure communication between computers in a network, widely used on the Internet.

SSM *abbrev* : surface to surface missile.

SSN *abbrev* : Standard Serial Number.

SSP *abbrev* : Scottish Socialist Party; statutory sick pay.

ssp. *abbrev* : subspecies (*pl* **sspp.**).

SSR *abbrev* : Soviet Socialist Republic.

SSRB *abbrev* : Review Body on Senior Salaries.

SSRC *abbrev* : Social Science Research Council.

SSRI *abbrev* : selective serotonin reuptake inhibitor, any of various drugs used in treating depression.

SSSI *abbrev* : site of special scientific interest.

SST *abbrev* : supersonic transport.

SSVC *abbrev* : Services Sound and Vision Corporation.

SSW *abbrev* : south-south-west.

ST *abbrev* : São Tomé and Príncipe (IVR).

St or **St.** *abbrev* : Saint; Strait; Street.

st or **'st** /*st*/ *interj* hush; a sound made to attract someone's attention.

st *abbrev* : stone (the weight); stumped (*cricket*).

'st /*st*/ a shortened form of **hast**.

Sta *abbrev* : (railway) station.

stab /*stab*/ *vt* (**stabb'ing**; **stabbed**) to wound or pierce by driving in a pointed weapon; to give a sharp pain (also *fig*); to roughen (brickwork) with a pick so as to provide a key for plaster (*building*); to pierce near the back edges, for the passage of thread or wire (*bookbinding*). ◆ *vi* to thrust or pierce with a pointed weapon. ◆ *n* an act of stabbing; a wound with a pointed weapon. [Origin uncertain; cf **stob**]
　■ **stabb'er** *n*. **stabb'ing** *n* and *adj*. **stabb'ingly** *adv*.
　■ **a stab in the dark** a random guess. **have a stab at** (*inf*) to have a go at, attempt. **stab in the back** (*lit* and *fig*) to injure in a treacherous manner.

Stabat Mater /*stä'bat mä'tər* or *stä'bat mä'ter*/ *n* a Latin hymn commemorating the sorrows of the Virgin Mary; a musical setting of it. [From its opening words, the mother stood]

stabile, **stability**, **stabilize**, etc see under **stable**[1].

stable[1] /*stā'b(ə)l*/ *adj* standing firm; firmly established; durable; firm in purpose or character; constant; not ready to change; not radioactive. [Fr, from L *stabilis*, from *stāre* to stand]
　■ **stā'bilate** *n* (*biol*) a population, *usu* of a micro-organism, preserved in a viable condition on a unique occasion, eg by freezing. **stā'bile** /*-bīl* or *-bil*/ *adj* stable (*rare*); not moving; not fluctuating; not decomposing readily, eg under moderate heat. ◆ *n* an abstract art construction of metal, wire, wood, differing from a mobile in having no movement. **stability** /*stə-bil'i-ti*/ *n* the state of being stable; steadiness; fixity; the power of recovering equilibrium; the fixing by vow of a monk or nun to one convent for life. **stabilization** or **-s-** /*stab-*, *stāb-i-lī-zā'shən*, or *-li-*/ *n*. **sta'bilizātor** or **-s-** *n*. **stabilize** or **-ise** /*stab'* or *stāb'*/ *vt* to render stable or steady; to fix; to fix the value of; to establish, maintain, or regulate the equilibrium of. **stab'ilizer** or **-s-** *n* anything that stabilizes; an additional plane or other device for giving stability to an aircraft; a gyroscope or other means of steadying a ship; any measure, such as progressive taxation, reduction of subsidy, etc, taken to control production, restrict fluctuations in prices, etc (*econ*); a substance that retards chemical action, eg an additive to food; (in *pl*) an extra pair of small wheels attached to (*usu* the back wheels of) a child's bicycle. **stā'bleness** *n*. **stā'bly** *adv*.
　❑ **stable equilibrium** *n* the condition in which a body will return to its old position after a slight displacement.

stable[2] /*stā'b(ə)l*/ *n* a building for horses, or sometimes other animals; a set of horses kept together; a horse-keeping establishment, organization or staff (as a horse-keeping establishment often *pl* in form but treated as *sing*); a number of skilled trained (*esp* young) people who work together under one head or one manager; a group of commercial (*esp* publishing) enterprises under the same ownership or management; an establishment in which a group of Japanese sumo wrestlers live and receive training; (in *pl*) a cavalry soldier's duty in the stable, or the call summoning to it. ◆ *vt* to put or keep in a stable. ◆ *vi* to live in a stable, or as if in a stable. [OFr *estable* (Fr *étable*), from L *stabulum*, from *stāre* to stand]
　■ **sta'bler** *n* (*Scot* or *archaic*) a stable-keeper, an inn-keeper. **sta'bling** *n* the act of putting into a stable; accommodation for horses, cattle, cycles, etc.
　❑ **sta'bleboy** or **sta'bleman** *n* someone who works at a stable. **stable companion** *n* (*inf*) someone who lodges in the same place or is a member of the same club, etc. **stable door** *n* a door with upper and lower halves able to be closed independently. **stable fly** *n* a two-winged, bloodsucking fly, *Stomoxys calcitrans*, a common pest of humans and domestic animals. **stable lad** or **lass** *n* someone whose job is to look after the horses at a racing-stable. **stableman** see **stableboy** above. **sta'blemate** *n* a horse from the same stable as another; anything manufactured, originated, produced, etc in the same place as another (eg different models of the same car), or a person from the same club, etc as another (*fig*).
　■ **out of the same stable** having the same background, training, etc.

Stableford /*stā'bl-fərd*/ *n* a golf competition in which points are awarded for scores achieved on each hole, the player's handicap and the stroke index being used to help calculate the points. [Frank Stableford (1870–1959), English doctor who devised it]

stablish /*stab'lish*/ *vt* an archaic form of **establish**.

staccato /*stə-kä'tō* or *stäk-kä'tō*/ (*music*) *adj* and *adv* with each note detached or disconnected, *opp* to *legato*. ◆ *n* (*pl* **stacca'tos**) a staccato performance, manner, or passage. [Ital, *pap* of *staccare*, for *distaccare* to separate]
　■ **staccatis'simo** *adj* and *adv* (*superl*).

---

fāte; fär; mē; fûr; mīne; mōte; för; mūte; pŭt; dhen (then); *el'ə-mənt* (element) ◆ For other sounds see detailed chart of pronunciation

stachys /stā'kis/ n any labiate plant of the genus *Stachys*, esp *S. byzantina* or *lanata* (lamb's-ears), or *S. officinalis* (betony). [New L, from Gr *stachys* ear of corn]

stack¹ /stak/ n a large built-up pile (eg, of hay, corn, wood, etc or of goods or equipment); a group or cluster of chimneys or flues, or a single tall chimney; the chimney or funnel of a steamer, steam-engine, etc; a vertical exhaust pipe on a lorry, etc; an isolated pillar of rock, often rising from the sea; a set of compactly arranged bookcases for storing books not on the open shelves of a library; a temporary storage area for data in a computer memory; a pyramid of three rifles, etc; an ordered, built-up pile; a standard quantity of gambler's chips bought at one time; aircraft waiting to land and circling at definite heights according to instructions; a large amount (*inf*). ♦ vt to pile into a stack; to fill; to shuffle or arrange the order of (cards) for cheating; to arrange (aircraft waiting to land) in a stack (see above). [ON *stakkr* a stack of hay]

■ **stack'able** *adj*. **stacked** *adj* piled in a stack; filled; (of shoe-heels) made of horizontal layers of leather; (of a woman) having a large bust (also **well-stacked**'; *sl*). **stack'er** n a person who stacks; a machine for stacking (eg products in a factory). **stack'ing** n.

□ **stack'room** n in a library, a room where books are stored in stacks. **stack** or **stacking system** n a modular hi-fi system which stacks one component on top of the other. **stack'yard** n a yard for stacks.

■ **stack against** (or **in favour of**) to arrange (circumstances) to the disadvantage (or advantage) of (**have the cards stacked against** (or **in favour of**) to be faced with circumstances arranged in this way). **stack up** to pile or load high; to compare; to add up (*inf*).

stack² see **stick²**.

stacket /stak'it/ (*obs Scot*) n a palisade. [Du *staket*]

stacte /stak'tē/ (*Bible*) n a sweet-smelling spice, liquid myrrh, used in incense by the ancient Hebrews. [Gr *staktos* dropping]

■ **stactom'eter** or **staktom'eter** n a pipette with a hollow bulb in the middle for counting drops.

stadda /stad'ə/ n a combmaker's double-bladed handsaw. [Origin unknown]

staddle /stad'l/ n a support, esp for a stack of hay, etc; the bottom of a stack; a small tree left unfelled; a stump left for coppice. [OE *stathol* foundation; Ger *Stadel*]

□ **staddle stone** n a low mushroom-shaped arrangement of a conical and flat, circular stone, used as a support for a haystack.

stade see under **stadium**.

stadholder see **stadtholder**.

stadia¹ /stā'di-ə/ (*surveying*) n a graduated rod used in measuring distances at one observation, by the angle subtended by the distance between two hairs (**stadia hairs** or **lines**) in the telescope (also **stadia rod**); the telescope so used (*US*). [Ety dubious]

stadia², **stadial** see **stadium**.

stadium /stā'di-əm/ n (pl **stā'dia** or **stadiums**) a race course, sports ground; an ancient Greek measure of length equivalent to 184 metres or 606¾ feet; a stage in development (eg of a glacier, culture, geological or evolutionary period); a stage in the course of a disease (*med*). [Latinized from Gr *stadion*]

■ **stade** /stād/ n a stadium. **stād'ial** n a substage within a period of glaciation or the life of a glacier during which the temperature drops or the ice advances. ♦ *adj* of or relating to a stage, stadium or stadial.

□ **stadium rock** n rock music that is unsubtle and overblown, designed to impose itself on the audience at a large venue such as a sports stadium.

stadtholder /stat'hōl-dər or stät'/ or **stadholder** /stad' or städ'/ n a Dutch viceroy or provincial governor; the head of the Dutch republic (*hist*). [Du *stadhouder*, literally, stead-holder (Ger *Statthalter*, Fr *lieutenant*), from *stad* place (now only town), and *houder* holder; spelling influenced by Ger *Stadt* town]

staff¹ /stäf/ n a stick carried in the hand; a prop or support; a long piece of wood; a pole; a flagstaff; a long handle; a stick or ensign of authority; a token authorizing an engine-driver to proceed along a section of single-track railway; a set of lines and spaces on which music is written or printed; a stanza; (in a watch or clock) the spindle of a balance wheel (these meanings have *pl* **staffs** or **staves** /stāvz/; see also **stave**); a body of officers who help a commanding officer, or perform special duties; a body of people employed in an establishment, *usu* on management, administration, clerical, etc work as distinct from manual; the body of teachers or lecturers in a school, college, university, etc (these three meanings have *pl* **staffs** /stäfs/). ♦ *adj* (or in combination) belonging or attached to the staff; applied also to officers on the staff of a commanding officer, at central headquarters, etc. ♦ vt to provide with a staff. [OE *stæf*, ON *stafr*, Ger *Stab*]

■ **staff'er** n a member of the permanent staff of a business, etc, *usu* as opposed to temporary or casual employees; a member of the editorial staff of a newspaper (*press*).

□ **staff college** n (*milit*) a college that trains officers for staff appointments. **staff corps** n (*milit*) a body of officers and men assisting a commanding officer and his or her staff; formerly, a body that supplied officers to the Indian Army. **staff duty** n (*milit*) the occupation of an officer who serves on a staff, having been detached from his or her regiment. **staff notation** n musical notation in which a staff is used, as opposed to the tonic sol-fa system. **staff nurse** n a nurse immediately below a sister in rank. **staff officer** n (*milit*) an executive officer serving on a staff. **staff of life** n staple food, *esp* bread. **staff'room** n a room for the use of the staff, as of a school. **staff sergeant** n (*milit*) a non-commissioned officer ranking above a sergeant and below a warrant officer. **staff surgeon** n a navy surgeon of senior grade; an army surgeon on the staff of a hospital, not with his or her regiment. **staff'-sys'tem** n a block-system that uses a staff. **staff'-tree** n any of various American shrubs and climbing plants of the family Celastraceae (**staff'-tree family**) *incl* bittersweet and burning bush.

staff² /stäf/ n a building material consisting of plaster and hair used for temporary or decorative work. [Origin unknown]

staffage /sta-fäzh'/ n decorative accessories in a picture, or subordinate additions in any work of art. [Sham Fr, from Ger *staffieren* to garnish]

Staffordshire bull terrier /staf'ərd-shər bŭl ter'i-ər/ n a breed of bull terrier with a short broad head.

Staffs. /stafs/ *abbrev*: Staffordshire.

stag /stag/ n a male deer, *esp* a red deer over four years old; a male of various kinds (cock, turkey cock, etc); a man who goes to dances, etc unaccompanied by a woman; a stag party (*US*); (*Scot* **staig** /stāg/) a colt or stallion; (*Scot* **staig**) an animal castrated in maturity; a person who applies for shares in order to sell them at once at a profit (*stock exchange sl*); an informer (*obs sl*). ♦ *adj* male; of or for males. ♦ vt to follow, dog, shadow. ♦ vi to deal as a stag (also vt with *it* or *the market*; *stock exchange sl*); (of a man) to go as a stag. [OE *stagga* stag; cf ON *steggr* cockbird, gander]

■ **stagg'ard** n a deer, *esp* a red deer, in its fourth year.

□ **stag beetle** n any beetle of the family Lucanidae, from the large antler-like mandibles of the males. **stag'-dance** n one of men only. **stag-head'ed** *adj* (of a tree) dying back giving an antler-like appearance. **stag'horn** n a stag's antler; the material of which antlers are composed. **staghorn coral** n a stony coral with antler-like branches. **staghorn fern** n a fern (genus *Platycerium*) with antler-like leaves. **staghorn moss** n common club moss. **stag'hound** n the buck hound; the Scottish deerhound. **stag hunt** n. **stag party** or **night** n a party for men only, *esp* one held for a man about to be married. **stag's horn** same as **staghorn** above.

stage /stāj/ n an elevated platform, *esp* for acting on; the theatre; theatrical representation; the theatrical calling; any scene or field of action; a place of rest on a journey or road; the portion of a journey between two such places; a fare stage (qv); a point reached in, or a section of, life, development, or any process; a subdivision of a geological series or formation; one of the sections in a rocket jettisoned during flight; one of the elements in a complex piece of electronic equipment; (in a microscope, etc) the support for an object to be examined; a tier, shelf, floor, storey; a tiered structure for plants; a scaffold; a stagecoach. ♦ *adj* relating to the stage, acting or the theatre; as conventionally represented on the stage (eg a *stage rustic*). ♦ vt to represent or put on the stage; to contrive dramatically, organize and bring off. ♦ vi (or vt with *it*) (*obs*) to travel by stages or by stagecoach. [OFr *estage* (Fr *étage*) a storey of a house, from inferred LL *staticus*, from L *stāre* to stand]

■ **staged** *adj* in storeys or tiers; put on the stage. **sta'ger** n someone who has had much experience in anything, an old hand (**old stager**); a stage horse; an actor (*archaic*). **sta'gery** n theatrical contrivances. **sta'gily** *adv*. **stag'iness** n. **sta'ging** n scaffolding; stagecoaching; putting on the stage; the jettisoning of any of the stages of a rocket. **sta'gy** or **sta'gey** *adj* savouring of the stage, acted, assumed, affected; of a style or level of competence in acting such that the artificiality is apparent.

□ **stage'coach** n formerly, a coach that ran regularly with passengers from stage to stage. **stage'coaching** n. **stage'coachman** n. **stage'craft** n skill in the technicalities of the theatre. **stage direction** n in a copy of a play, an instruction to the actor to do this or that. **stage'-dive** vi to jump from the stage onto the crowd at a rock concert or similar venue. **stage'-diver** n. **stage door** n the actors' entrance to a theatre. **stage effect** n theatrical effect. **stage fever** n a passion to go on the stage. **stage flower** n a flower exhibited on a tiered stand. **stage fright** n nervousness before an audience, *esp* for the first time (also *fig*). **stage hand** n a workman employed about the stage. **stage horse** n a stagecoach horse. **stage-man'age** vt (back-formation; used

lit; also *fig*) to arrange (an event) effectively as if it were a stage scene. **stage manager** *n* a person who superintends the performance of plays, with general charge behind the curtain. **stage name** *n* a name assumed professionally by an actor or actress. **stage play** *n* a play played or intended to be played on a stage, as opposed to on radio or television. **stage'-player** *n*. **stage rights** *n pl* legal rights to perform a play. **stage'-struck** *adj* passionate about all things theatrical, *esp* with a strong desire to act. **stage whisper** *n* an audible utterance conventionally understood by the audience to represent a whisper; a loud whisper meant to be heard by people other than the person addressed. **staging area** or **base** *n* a point for the assembly of troops en route for an operation. **staging post** *n* a regular point of call on an air route.
■ **stage left** (or **right**) at the left (or right) of the stage, facing the audience.

stagflation /stag-flā'shən/ *n* an economic situation in which there is stagnation in industrial output and consumer demand at the same time as a marked rise in inflation. [*stagnant* and in*flation*]
■ **stagflā'tionary** *adj*.

staggard see under **stag**.

stagger /stag'ər/ *vi* to reel; to go reeling or tottering; to waver. ◆ *vt* to cause to reel; to give a shock to; to cause to waver; to nonplus, confound; to dispose alternately or variously, or to arrange so that one thing or part is ahead of another. ◆ *n* a staggering; a wavering; a staggered arrangement (eg in aircraft, *positive* where the upper plane of a biplane is advanced, *negative* where the lower); (in *pl*, often treated as *sing*) giddiness, also any of various kinds of disease causing horses, sheep, etc to stagger (**grass** or **stomach staggers** an acute indigestion; **mad** or **sleepy staggers** an inflammation of the brain). [Earlier *stacker*, from ON *stakra*, frequentative of *staka* to push]
■ **stagg'ered** *adj*. **stagg'erer** *n*. **stagg'ering** *n* and *adj*. **stagg'eringly** *adv*.

Stagirite or (*non-standard*) **Stagyrite** /staj'i-rīt/ *n* a native or inhabitant of *Stagira* in Macedonia, *esp* in reference to Aristotle (384–322BC).

stagnant /stag'nənt/ *adj* (of water) still, standing, without current; (of water) foul, unwholesome, or dull from stillness (also *fig*); inert. [L *stagnāre*, *-ātum*, from *stagnum* pond]
■ **stag'nancy** *n*. **stag'nantly** *adv*. **stagnate'** (or /stag'/) *vi* to be or become stagnant. **stagnā'tion** *n*.
❑ **stagnation point** *n* the point at or near the nose of a body in motion in a fluid, where the flow divides.

stagy see under **stage**.

Stagyrite see **Stagirite**.

Stahlhelm /shtäl'helm/ *n* a German old soldiers' conservative nationalist and militaristic organization after World War I. [Ger, steel helmet]
■ **Stahl'helmer** or **Stahl'helmist** *n*.

Stahlian /stäl'i-ən/ *adj* relating to or associated with Georg Ernst *Stahl* (1660–1734), German physician, or his theory of animism.
■ **Stahl'ianism** or **Stahl'ism** *n*.

staid /stād/ *adj* steady; sober, grave or sedate, often implying a dull or boring quality; permanent (*rare*). [**stayed**, from pat and pap of **stay**]
■ **staid'ly** *adv*. **staid'ness** *n*.

staig see **stag**.

stain /stān/ *vt* to impart a new colour to; to tinge; to dye; to impregnate with a substance that colours some parts so as to show composition and structure; to tarnish; to sully; to bring reproach on; to deprive of colour (*obs*); to pale by comparison (*obs*). ◆ *vi* to take or impart a stain. ◆ *n* a dye or colouring matter; discoloration; a spot; the taint of guilt; pollution; a cause of reproach; shame. [**distain**]
■ **stained** *adj*. **stain'er** *n*. **stain'ing** *n* and *adj*. **stain'less** *adj* free from stain; not liable to stain, rust, or tarnish. **stain'lessly** *adv*. **stain'lessness** *n*.
❑ **stained glass** *n* glass painted with certain pigments fused into its surface. **stainless steel** *n* a steel that will not rust, containing 10.5 to 25 per cent of chromium.

stair /stār/ *n* a series of steps, *usu* in *pl*, a flight from landing to landing, but in Scotland, in *sing*, the whole series from floor to floor; one such step. [OE *stæger*, from *stīgan* to ascend; Ger *steigen* to climb, Norw *steg* step]
■ **staired** *adj* having, or arranged like, stairs. **stair'wise** *adv* by steps; in the manner of a stair.
❑ **stair carpet** *n* a long carpet for stairs. **stair'case** *n* the structure enclosing a stair; stairs with banisters, etc. ◆ *vi* (*sl*) (of an individual who has a house in a shared-ownership scheme) to buy that part of the property which he or she did not previously own, thus achieving full ownership, and then sell the house on the open market. **stair'casing** *n*. **stair'foot** *n* the level place at the foot of stairs.

stair'head *n* the level place at the top of stairs. **stair'lift** *n* a lift, mounted on the staircase in a house, on which a disabled or elderly person sits to be carried upstairs (and downstairs). **stair rod** *n* a rod for holding a stair carpet in place. **stair'way** *n* a staircase; a passage by stairs. **stair'well** *n* the well of a staircase. **stair'work** *n* backstairs intriguing.
■ **below stairs** in the basement; among the servants.

staithe or **staith** /stāth/ (*dialect, esp N Eng*) *n* a wharf; a structure for shipping coal; an embankment. [OE *stæth* bank, and ON *stöth* landing stage]

stake[1] /stāk/ *n* a stick or pole pointed at one end; a post; a post to which someone condemned to be burned was tied (*hist*); hence, death or martyrdom by burning; a tinsmith's anvil; an administrative division of the Mormon Church. ◆ *vt* to fasten to or with, to protect, shut, support, furnish, pierce, with a stake or stakes; to mark the bounds of with stakes (often with *off* or *out*). [OE *staca* stake]
❑ **stake boat** *n* a boat anchored as a marker for a boat race, or to which other boats may be moored. **stake net** *n* a net hung on stakes.
■ **stake a claim** (*for* or *to*) to assert one's right to or desire to possess. **stake out** (*inf*) to place (a person, etc) under surveillance (**stake'-out** *n*).

stake[2] /stāk/ *vt* to deposit as a wager; to risk, hazard; to furnish, supply, fit out, whether free or in expectation of return (with *with* or *to*; *orig* US). ◆ *n* anything pledged as a wager; a prize; anything to gain or lose; an interest, concern; the condition of being at hazard; a grubstake; (in *pl*) a race for money staked or contributed (also *fig*). [Perh MDu *staken* to place]
❑ **stake'holder** *n* someone who holds the stake in a bet; someone with an interest or concern in a business or enterprise. **stakeholder economy** or **society** *n* an economy or society in which all individuals are regarded as having an interest and as wishing to contribute to its success. **stakeholder pension** *n* a type of pension arranged as part of a private scheme complying to certain requirements established by the government.
■ **at stake** hazarded; in danger; at issue.

stakhanovite /stə-kan'ō-vīt/ *n* (in the former Soviet Union) a worker who received recognition for his or her part in increasing the rate of production in a factory, etc (also *adj*). [AG *Stakhanov* (1906–77), Russian miner]
■ **stakhan'ovism** *n*.

staktometer same as **stactometer** (see under **stacte**).

stalactite /stal'ək-tīt or sta-lak'tīt/ *n* an icicle-like object hanging from a cave roof, formed by the evaporation of water percolating through limestone; the material it is composed of; anything of similar form. [Gr *stalaktos*, *stalagma*, *stalagmos* a dropping, from *stalassein* to drip]
■ **stalac'tic**, **stalac'tical**, **stalac'tiform**, **stalacti'tal**, **stal'actited** (also /-ak'/), **stalactitic** /-tit'ik/ (the usual *adj*), **stalactit'ical**, **stalactitiform** /-tīt'/ or **stalactitious** /-tish'əs/ *adj*. **stalactit'ically** *adv*. **stalag'ma** *n* a stalagmite. **stal'agmite** (also /-ag'/) *n* an upward-growing conical formation on the floor, formed by the drip from the roof or from a stalactite. **stalagmitic** /-mit'ik/ or **stalagmit'ical** *adj*. **stalagmit'ically** *adv*. **stalagmom'eter** *n* an instrument for determining surface tension by drops. **stalagmom'etry** *n*.

stalag /stal'ag, shtä'lak or shtä'lähh/ *n* a German camp for prisoners of war (non-commissioned officers and men). [Ger *Stamm* base, and *Lager* camp]

stalagma, **stalagmite**, etc see under **stalactite**.

stal'd /stöld/ (*archaic*) pap of **stall**[1].

stale[1] /stāl/ *adj* no longer fresh; past the best; out of condition by over-training or overstudy; impaired by lapse of time; tainted; vapid or tasteless from age; (of liquor) old, clear, and strong (*obs*). ◆ *vt* and *vi* to make or become stale, over-familiar, or insipid. [Perh from the root *sta-*, as in **stand**]
■ **stale'ly** *adv*. **stale'ness** *n*.

stale[2] /stāl/ *n* urine, now *esp* of horses. ◆ *vi* to urinate. [Cf Du *stalle*, Ger *Stall*, OFr verb *estaler*]

stale[3] /stāl/ *n* a decoy bird (*dialect*); a thief's accomplice, acting as a decoy (*obs*); a lure; a prostitute employed as a decoy by thieves, or generally (*Shakesp*); a stalking-horse, cover to a real purpose (*Shakesp*); a pretext; a lover made a butt of by or for one preferred. [Cf Anglo-Fr *estal*, *-e* pigeon used to entice a hawk, OE *stælhrān* decoy-reindeer, Ger *Stellvogel* decoy bird; prob from root of OE *stellan* to place]

stale[4] /stāl/ (*dialect*) *n* a handle, shaft; a stalk. [OE *stalu*, appar part of a harp]

stale[5] /stāl/ *n* and vt (now *rare* or *obs*) stalemate. [Cf Anglo-Fr *estale*, perh from **stall**[2]]
❑ **stale'mate** *n* in chess, a situation where a player not actually in check has no possible legal move, resulting in a draw; an inglorious deadlock. ◆ *vt* to subject to a stalemate.

stale[6] see **steal**[1].

Stalinism /stal'i-ni-zm or stä'li-ni-zm/ n the rigorous rule of the Soviet Communist dictator Joseph *Stalin* (1879–1953), *esp* in its concentration of all power and authority in the Communist world in the former Soviet Union.
■ **Sta'linist** n and adj.

stalk[1] /stök/ n the stem of a plant; a slender connecting part; a shaft; a tall chimney. ◆ vt to remove the stalk from. [Dimin from the root of OE *stela, stalu* stalk]
■ **stalked** adj having a stalk. **stalk'less** adj. **stalk'y** adj running to stalk; like a stalk.
❑ **stalk'-eyed** adj having the eyes on stalks.

stalk[2] /stök/ vi to stride stiffly or haughtily; to go after game, keeping under cover; to follow a person, *esp* an enemy, in a similar manner. ◆ vt to approach under cover; to stalk over or through (a tract of country, etc). ◆ n an act of stalking; a stalking gait. [OE *(bi)stealcian*, frequentative of **steal**[1]]
■ **stalk'er** n a person who stalks game; someone who obsessively follows another person, often with a sinister purpose. **stalkerazzi** /stök-ə-rat'sē/ n pl (sl) members of the paparazzi who pursue celebrities to an extreme degree in order to obtain photographs and information. **stalk'ing** n and adj.
❑ **stalk'ing-horse** n a horse or substitute behind which a hunter hides while stalking game; a candidate in an election standing only to facilitate the success of another; anything put forward to mask plans or efforts.

stalko /stö'kō/ (Anglo-Irish) n (pl **stalk'oes**) a gentleman without fortune or occupation. [Perh Ir *stócach* idler]

stall[1] /stöl/ n a standing-place; a stable, cowshed, or the like; a compartment for one animal; a bench, table, booth or stand for the display or sale of goods, or used as a working place; a church seat with arms, *usu* one of those lining the choir or chancel on both sides, reserved for cathedral clergy, for choir, for monks, or for knights of an order; an office entitling one to such a seat; a doorless pew; an individual seat with arms in a theatre, etc, *esp* (in pl) on the ground floor; a working place in a mine; a covering for a finger (as in *fingerstall*); a starting stall (qv under **start**); an instance of stalling in aircraft or engine; a standstill; (Scot **staw**) a surfeit. ◆ vt to put or keep in a stall; to induct, install; to bring to a standstill; to cause (an aeroplane) to fly in such a way that the angle between the aerofoils and the direction of motion is greater than that at which there is maximum lift, and so lose control; to stop (an engine) by sudden braking, overloading, etc; to cause (a vehicle) to become stuck in mud or snow; (*esp* in Scots form **staw**) to surfeit; (pap **stal'd** /stöld/) to release on payment by instalments (Spenser). ◆ vi to come to a standstill; to stick in mud or snow; (of an aircraft or engine) to be stalled; to inhabit a stall; to dwell (obs); to share a dwelling (obs). [OE *stall, steall*, ON *stallr*, Ger *Stall*]
■ **stallage** /stöl'ij/ n rent paid for erecting a stall in a fair or market. **stalled** adj kept or fed in a stall; fatted; having a stall or stalls; stuck; sated (Scot **stawed**). **stall'ing** n stabling. **stall'inger** or **stall'enger** /-in-jər/ n (hist) a keeper of a stall; a person who paid for the privilege of trading in a burgh of which he was not a freeman.
❑ **stall'-fed** adj (of domestic animals) fed and fattened in a stall. **stall'-feed** vt to confine (an animal) to its stall and fatten it. **stall'holder** n a keeper of a market stall. **stall'ing-ken'** n (obs sl) a house for receiving stolen goods. **stall'man** n a keeper of a stall, *esp* a bookstall. **stall'master** n (Ger *Stallmeister*) a master of horse. **stall plate** n a plate with a knight's arms affixed to his stall.

stall[2] /stöl/ vt to delay or obstruct; to stave off (with off). ◆ vi to hang back, play for time; to be obstructive, evasive or deceptive. ◆ n a ruse, trick; an evasive manoeuvre; a decoy, *esp* someone who diverts attention from a criminal action. [**stale**[3]]

stallage, stallenger, stallinger see under **stall**[1].

stallion[1] /stal'yən/ n an uncastrated male horse, *esp* one kept for breeding. [OFr *estalon* (Fr *étalon*), from OHGer *stal* stall]

stallion[2] /stal'yən/ (obs) n a courtesan. [Fr *estalon*; cf **stale**[3]]

stallion[3] (Shakesp) same as **staniel**.

stalwart /stöl'wərt/ adj stout, strong, sturdy; determined or committed in support or partisanship. ◆ n (also (archaic) **stal'worth** /-wərth/) a resolute person; a loyal supporter. [Orig Scot form (popularized by Walter Scott) of *stalworth*, from OE *staélwierthe* serviceable, from *staél* place (from *stathol* foundation), and *wierthe* worth]
■ **stal'wartly** adv. **stal'wartness** n.

stamen /stä'mən/ n (pl **stä'mens** or **stamina** /stam'i-nə/) the pollen-producing part of a flower, consisting of anther and filament. [L *stāmen, stāminis* a warp thread (upright in an old loom), from *stāre* to stand]
■ **stä'mened** adj having stamens. **stam'inal** adj of stamens or stamina. **stam'inate** adj having stamens but no carpels, male. **stamineal** /stə- or stä-min'i-əl/ or **stamin'eous** adj (both rare).

staminif'erous /stam- or stäm-/ adj having stamens. **stam'inode** or **staminō'dium** n a sterile stamen. **stam'inody** n metamorphosis of other parts into stamens. **stam'inoid** adj like, or metamorphosed into, a stamen.

stamina[1] /stam'i-nə/ n sustained energy, staying power, whether physical, mental or emotional. [Pl of *stamen* warp, understood as the threads of life spun out by the Fates]

stamina[2] see **stamen**.

stammel /stam'l/ (hist) n a kind of woollen cloth, *usu* dyed red, and used to make underclothes; the bright-red colour of this cloth. ◆ adj of stammel; bright-red. [Fr *estamel*, or independently formed ME *stamin*, from OFr *estamin*, both from L *stāmina* warp threads]

stammer /stam'ər/ vi to falter in speaking; to speak with involuntary hesitations, to stutter. ◆ vt to utter falteringly or with a stutter. ◆ n involuntary hesitation in speech, a stutter; a faltering mode of utterance. [OE *stamerian*; Du *stemeren*]
■ **stamm'erer** n. **stamm'ering** n and adj. **stamm'eringly** adv.

stamnos /stam'nos/ n (pl **stam'noi**) an ancient Greek short-necked jar. [Gr]

stamp /stamp/ vt to bring the foot forcibly down upon; to trample; to bring the sole of (the foot) down flat, heavily or with force; to impress, imprint, or cut with a downward blow, as with a die or cutter; to mint, make or shape by such a blow; to fix or mark deeply; to crush, grind or pound (ore, etc); to impress with a mark attesting official approval, ratification, payment, etc; to affix an adhesive stamp to; to attest, declare, prove to be; to characterize. ◆ vi to bring the foot down forcibly and noisily; to walk with a heavy tread. ◆ n the act of stamping; an impression; a stamped device, mark, imprint; an adhesive paper used as a substitute for stamping, *esp* one affixed to show that postage has been paid; attestation; authorization; a coin (Shakesp); pounded maize (S Afr); cast, form, character; a distinguishing mark, imprint, sign, evidence; an instrument or machine for stamping; national insurance contributions, *orig* recorded by sticking a stamp onto an official card (inf). [ME *stampen*, from an inferred OE *stampian* from the same root as *stempan*; Ger *stampfen*]
■ **stamp'er** n. **stamp'ing** n and adj.
❑ **Stamp Act** n an act of parliament imposing or regulating stamp duties, *esp* that of 1765 imposing them on the American colonies. **stamp album** n a book for keeping a collection of postage stamps in. **stamp collecting** n philately. **stamp collector** n a person who makes a hobby of collecting postage stamps; formerly, a receiver of stamp duties. **stamp duty** n a tax on legal documents, its payment being confirmed by the affixation of a stamp. **stamp hinge** see under **hinge**. **stamp'ing-ground** n an animal's usual resort; a place where a person often spends time. **stamping machine** n a machine used for stamping coins, in the stamping of brasswork, or in crushing metallic ores. **stamp mill** or **stamping mill** n a machine for crushing ores. **stamp note** n a certificate from a customs officer for goods to be loaded as freight of a ship. **stamp office** n an office where stamp duties are received and stamps issued. **stamp paper** n paper bearing a government revenue stamp.
■ **stamp out** to put out, extinguish by tramping; to get rid of entirely; to make by stamping from a sheet with a cutter.

stampede /stam-pēd'/ n a sudden mass rush of a panic-stricken herd; a headlong scramble by a crowd of people; any mass rush to do something. ◆ vi to rush in a stampede. ◆ vt to send rushing in a stampede. [Sp *estampida* crash, from *estampar* to stamp]
■ **stampē'do** n and vt (obs) stampede.

stance /stans/ n a posture adopted in standing; the standing position of someone about to play the ball in golf, etc; a point of view taken, an attitude; a place occupied by market stalls, a taxi rank, etc (Scot); a place where a mountain climber may belay; a stanza (obs). [Fr *stance* (now meaning 'stanza'), from Ital *stanza* a stopping-place, station, from L *stāre* to stand]

stanch[1] /stänch or stänsh/ or **staunch** /stönch or stönsh/ vt to stop the flowing of (*esp* blood); to quench, allay. ◆ vi (Bible) to cease to flow. ◆ n a styptic; a floodgate. [OFr *estancher* (Fr *étancher*), from LL *stancāre* to stanch, from L *stagnāre* to be or make stagnant, from *stagnum* a pond]
■ **stanch'able** or **staunch'able** adj. **stanch'er** or **staunch'er** n. **stanch'ing** or **staunch'ing** n. **stanch'less** or **staunch'less** adj that cannot be quenched or stopped.

stanch[2] see **staunch**[1].

stanchel, stancher see **stanchion**.

stanchion /stän'shən or stan'shən/ n (also (Scot) **stanchel** /stän'/ or *stän'/ or **stan'cher**) an upright beam, bar, rod, shaft, etc acting as a support, a strut. ◆ vt to support by means of, or fasten to, a stanchion. [OFr *estançon*, from *estance* prop, from L *stāre* to stand]
■ **stan'chioned** adj.

stanck /stangk/ (Spenser) adj faint. [Ital *stanco*]

---

stand /stand/ vi (pat and pap **stood**; Scot **stood'en**, **studd'en**; infinitive, Spenser, **stand'en**) to be, become, or remain upright, erect, rigid, or still; to be on, or rise to, one's feet; to be a particular height, as in He stands six feet tall; to be steadfast; to have or take a position; to assume the attitude and duties of (guard, sentinel); to be or remain; to be set or situated; to be likely, be in a position (to lose or gain something); to come to a stop, be stationary or remain still; used with and to introduce a second verb, eg stand and stare; to be set down; to hold a course or direction (with for; naut); to hold good; to endure, continue to exist; to be, at the moment in question, as in the score stands at 3 to 1, as things stand; to be a representative, representation or symbol (with for); to be a candidate (with for); (of a vehicle) to park, wait (N Am). ◆ vt to withstand; to tolerate; to endure; to sustain; to suffer, undergo; to abide by; to be at the expense of, offer and pay for; to station, cause to stand; to set erect, in place, or in position. ◆ n an act, manner, or place of standing; a taking up of a position for resistance; resistance; an attitude or position adopted; the partnership of any two batsmen at the wicket, the period of time of the partnership, or the runs made during it (cricket); a standing position; a standstill; a stoppage; a post, station; a stall or position occupied by a trader or an organization at an exhibition, for the display of goods, etc; a place, sometimes under cover, for awaiting game; a place for vehicles awaiting hire; a structure, with or without a roof, with sitting or standing accommodation for spectators, eg at a football or rugby game; a stop on tour to give one or more performances, or the place where it is made (theatre); a platform; a witness box (N Am); a base or structure for setting things on; a piece of furniture for hanging things from; a company of plovers; a complete set, esp (Scot) a suit of clothes or armour; a shearer's position in a shed (Aust and NZ); a standing growth or crop; a young tree left standing; a tub or vat. [OE standan; Gothic standan; cf Ger stehen, Gr histanai to place, L stāre to stand]

■ **standee'** n a person standing as opposed to sitting (esp US); a cardboard figure that is able to stand upright. **stand'er** n. **stand'ing** adj established; settled; permanent; fixed; stagnant; erect; having a base; done as one stands; from a standing position, without preliminary movement (eg standing jump, standing start). ◆ n the action of someone who or something that stands; duration or continuance; a place to stand in or on; position, status or reputation in one's profession or in society; a current ranking within a graded scale, esp in sport; a right or capacity to sue or maintain an action.
□ **stand'-alone** adj (of a system, device, etc) able to operate unconnected to and unaided by any other. ◆ n a stand-alone system or device. **stand'-by** n that which, or someone whom, one relies on or readily resorts to; something or someone available for use in an emergency (see also **on stand-by** below). ◆ adj (of an airline passenger, ticket, fare, etc) occupying, or for, an aircraft seat not booked in advance but taken as available, usu with some price reduction, at the time of departure. **stand'-down** n (milit) a return to normal duties after an alert; an off-duty period. **stand'er-by** n (pl **stand'ers-by**) (Shakesp) a bystander. **stand first** n (press) an introductory paragraph in bigger and/or bolder type summarizing the contents of a newspaper or magazine article. **stand'-in** n a substitute. **standing bed** n a high bedstead, not a truckle bed. **standing committee** n one permanently established to deal with a particular matter. **standing crop** n a growing crop; the total biomass in a particular environment at a particular time. **standing joke** n a subject that raises a laugh whenever it is mentioned. **standing-off dose** n (radiol) the absorbed dose after which occupationally exposed radiation workers must be transferred to duties not involving further exposure. **standing order** n an instruction from a customer to his or her bank to make regular payments from his or her account (also called **banker's order**); an order placed with a shopkeeper, etc for the regular supply of a newspaper or other goods; a military order with long-term application; (in pl) regulations for procedure adopted by a legislative assembly (also **standing rules**). **standing ovation** n applause from an audience that rises to its feet in its enthusiasm. **standing rigging** n the fixed ropes in a ship. **stand'ing-room** n room for standing, without a seat. **standing stone** n (archaeol) a great stone set erect in the ground, thought to be of religious significance to prehistoric peoples. **standing wave** n the pattern of maxima and minima when two sets of oppositely travelling waves of the same frequency interfere with each other (phys); (in pl) a long-lasting layered cloud-formation seen in hilly regions (meteorol). **stand'-off** n a rugby halfback who stands away from the scrum as a link between scrum-half and the three-quarters (also **stand-off half**); a tie, draw or deadlock (chiefly N Am); any object that stands, projects or holds another a short distance away, eg on a ladder, an attachment that holds it away from the surface supporting it. **stand'off** adj standoffish (N Am); (of a missile) capable of being released at a long distance from its target. **standoff'ish** adj inclined to hold aloof, keep others at arm's length. **standoff'ishness** n. **stand oil** n a drying oil used in paints, varnishes, etc. **stand'out** n someone or something exceptional or of high quality. **standpatt'er** n (US) someone who refuses to

accept or consider change; a political diehard. **standpatt'ism** n. **stand'pipe** n an open vertical pipe connected to a pipeline, to ensure that the pressure head at that point cannot exceed the length of the pipe; a pipe fitted with a tap, used to obtain water, eg from an attached hose. **stand'point** n a viewpoint. **stand'still** n a complete stop. ◆ adj stationary; unmoving; forbidding or refraining from movement. **standstill agreement** n an agreement between parties to respect the status quo, esp granting more time for repayment of a debt. **stand'-to** n a precautionary parade or taking of posts. **stand'-up** adj erect; done or taken in a standing position; (of a fight) in earnest; delivering, or consisting of, a comic monologue without feed or other support. ◆ n stand-up comedy; one who performs this; something that stands upright, either independently or with a support to hold it in position; a broken date (between two people) (inf).
■ **all standing** everything remaining as it stands; without unrigging; fully clad. **it stands to reason** it is only logical to assume. **make a stand** to halt and offer resistance. **one-night stand** see under **one**. **on stand-by** in readiness to provide assistance, or work, in an emergency. **stand against** to resist. **stand by** to support; to adhere to, abide by; to be at hand; to hold oneself in readiness; to prepare to work at; to look on without taking action. **stand down** to leave the witness box; (esp of a member or members of the armed forces) to go off duty; to withdraw from a contest or from a controlling position. **stand fast** to be unmoved. **stand fire** to remain steady under the fire of an enemy (also fig). **stand for** to be a candidate for; to direct the course towards (naut); to be a sponsor for; to represent, symbolize; to champion; to put up with, endure (inf). **stand from** (naut) to direct the course from. **stand in** to cost; to become a party; to have an understanding, be in league; to deputize, act as a substitute (with for). **stand in with** to support, act together with. **stand low** (printing) to fall short of the standard height. **stand off** to keep at a distance; to direct the course from (naut); to forbear compliance or intimacy (Shakesp); to suspend temporarily from employment. **stand off and on** (naut) to sail away from shore and then towards it. **stand on** to continue on the same tack or course (naut); to insist on; to set store by (see also under **ceremony**); to behove; to found upon. **stand one's ground** to maintain one's position. **stand one's hand**, **stand sam** (inf), **stand shot** and **stand treat** to treat the company, esp to drinks. **stand on one's own (two) feet** to manage one's own affairs without help. **stand out** to project, be prominent; not to comply, to refuse to yield, take an independent stand (with against or for). **stand over** to keep (someone who is working, etc) under close supervision; to postpone or be postponed. **stand pat** (US) to play one's hand in poker as it was dealt, without drawing any cards; to adhere to an established, esp political, principle, resisting all compromise (fig). **stand to** to fall to, set to work; to back up; to uphold; to take up a position in readiness for orders. **stand to gain**, **win**, etc to be in a position to gain, win, etc. **stand up** to get to one's feet; to take position for a dance; to prove, or remain, valid; to be clad (with in); to fail to keep an appointment with (inf). **stand up for** to support or attempt to defend. **stand upon** to stand on; to attack (Bible). **stand up to** to meet (an opponent, etc) face to face, to show resistance to; to fulfil (an obligation, etc) fairly; to withstand (hard wear, etc). **stand well** to be in favour. **stand with** to be consistent.

standard /stan'dərd/ n an established or accepted model; (often in pl) a principle of behaviour or morality; a criterion; a definite level of excellence or adequacy required, aimed at, or possible; an overall level achieved; an authorized model for a unit of measurement; the legally required weight and purity of the metal used in coins; the commodity, eg gold or silver, that is taken as the basis of value in a currency; a measure of wood in board form, equivalent to 4.7 cubic metres, 165 cubic feet or 1980 board-feet (board-foot = a piece of wood one foot square and one inch thick); a flag or military symbolic figure on a pole, marking a rallying point; a rallying point (also fig); a long tapering flag notched and rounded at the end, bearing heraldic symbols and fixed in the ground (heraldry); a flag generally; a regimental flag; a standard-bearer; a standing shrub or tree not trained on an espalier or a wall; a fruit tree or other tree grafted and trained so as to have an upright stem without branches; an upright post, pillar, stick; a tree left growing amidst coppice; a song or piece of music that has remained popular over the years; a class or grade in an elementary school; the uppermost petal of a papilionaceous flower; a streaming wing feather; a structure erected at a conduit (obs); an accepted authoritative statement of a church's creed; that which stands or is fixed. ◆ adj serving as or conforming to a standard; of the normal, regular quality, size, etc, without additions or variations; of accepted and enduring value; growing as a standard; standing upright. [OFr estandart; prob connected either with **extend** or **stand**, and in any case influenced by or partly from **stander**]
■ **standardizā'tion** or **-s-** n. **stand'ardize** or **-ise** vt to make, or keep, of uniform size, shape, etc. **stand'ardizer** or **-s-** n.
□ **standard assessment task** n (educ) in England and Wales, a component of the standardized testing procedures employed, as part

of the national curriculum, to determine a pupil's level of attainment in a particular subject (*abbrev* **SAT**). **standard atmosphere** *n* 101325 newtons per square metre, or 1 013 250 dynes per square centimetre; a standard of measurement of atmospheric conditions used in comparing the performance of aircraft (*aeronautics*, etc). **stand'ard-bearer** *n* a person who carries a standard or banner; an outstanding leader. **standard bread** *n* bread made with flour containing 80 per cent of the wholewheat including germ and semolina. **Stand'ardbred** *n* a breed of horse *orig* developed in the USA as harness racehorses for trotting or pacing to a standard minimum speed. ♦ *adj* relating to this breed of horses. **standard candle** see **candle**. **standard cost** *n* an estimated cost of a manufacturing process, etc against which the actual cost is assessed. **standard deviation** *n* in a frequency distribution, the root of the average of the squares of the differences from their mean of a number of observations, used as a measure of dispersion. **standard English** *n* the form of English taught in schools, etc, and used, *esp* in formal situations, by the majority of educated English-speakers. **standard error** *n* standard deviation; standard deviation divided by the root of the number of observations in a sample. **standard gauge** see under **gauge**. **Standard grade** *n* a former educational qualification awarded in Scotland; a subject offered, or satisfactory assessment obtained, at Standard grade. **standardized mortality rate** *n* (*med*) the ratio of observed to expected deaths in a subpopulation (*abbrev* **SMR**). **standard lamp** *n* a lamp on a tall support. **standard of living** *n* a measure indicating the relative wealth and comfort in which people live. **standard solution** *n* a solution of known concentration, used for purposes of comparison, commonly containing the equivalent, in grammes, of the solute to a litre of solution (*normal solution*) or some simple fraction (as *decinormal*, one-tenth normal). **standard temperature and pressure** *n* a temperature of 0°C and a pressure of 101325N/m^2 (*abbrev* **stp**). **standard wing** *n* a bird of paradise of the Moluccas with a pair of erectile white feathers at the bend of the wing.

standgale /stand'gāl/ *n* a corrupt form of **staniel**.

standish /stan'dish/ (*archaic*) *n* an inkstand. [Poss for *stand-dish*]

stane /stān/ Scots form of **stone**.

stang^1 /stang/ *n* a stake, pole. [ON *stöng*; cf OE *stæng*, Du *stang*] ■ **riding the stang** (*hist*) punishment by being carried around sitting astride a stang.

stang^2 /stang or stöng/ (*Scot*) *vi* to sting. ♦ *n* a sting. [ON *stanga* to prick]

stanhope /stan'əp or -hōp/ *n* a light open one-seated carriage first made for Fitzroy *Stanhope* (1787–1864). ▫ **Stanhope press** *n* a printing press invented by the third Earl *Stanhope* (1753–1816).

staniel, **stanyel** /stan'yəl/ or **stannel** /stan'l/ (*Shakesp* **stallion** /stal'yən/) *n* the kestrel. [OE *stāngella*, literally, stone yeller]

Stanislavski method or **system** /stan-i-slav'ski or -släf'/ *n* method acting (qv). [K *Stanislavski* (1863–1938), Russian actor and director]

stank^1 /stangk/ *pat* of **stink**.

stank^2 /stangk/ (*chiefly Scot*) *n* a ditch, pool; a dam; a drain in the street. [OFr *estanc* a pond, from L *stagnum* a pond]

Stanley knife® /stan'li nīf/ *n* a type of trimming knife with a hollow metal handle into which a renewable, extremely sharp blade is fitted, used for trimming various materials, such as carpet, hardboard, etc. [FT *Stanley*, US businessman who founded the Stanley Rule and Level Company in 1843]

stann- /stan-/ *combining form* signifying tin. [L *stannum* tin] ■ **stann'ary** /-ə-ri/ *n* a tin-mining district, *esp* the **Stannaries** in Cornwall and Devon. ♦ *adj* of a stannary or (with *cap*) relating to the Stannaries (**Stannary Courts** courts (abolished 1896) for the tinners of the Stannaries; **Stannary Parliament** the ancient parliament of tinners, comprising 24 representatives (stannators) for all Cornwall, reconvened in 1974 after a lapse of more than 200 years). **stann'ate** *n* a salt of stannic acid. **stannā'tor** *n* one of the members of the Stannary Parliament. **stann'ic** /stan'ik/ *adj* (*chem*) relating to tin in its quadrivalent state (**stannic acid** H$_2$SnO$_3$). **stannif'erous** *adj* tin-bearing. **stann'ite** /stan'īt/ *n* a mineral composed of tin, copper, iron, and sulphur, occurring in tin-bearing veins (*mineralogy*); a salt of stannous hydroxide, Sn(OH)$_2$, acting as a weak acid (*chem*). **stann'otype** *n* a photomechanical process in which an exposed and developed bichromated film is coated with tinfoil and used directly for pressure printing. **stann'ous** *adj* of bivalent tin.

stannel see **staniel**.

stanozolol /sta-nō'zə-lol/ *n* an anabolic steroid that is illegally used as a performance-enhancing drug by some athletes.

stanyel see **staniel**.

stanza /stan'zə/ *n* (also (*Shakesp*) **stanze** or **stan'zo** (*pl* **stan'zoes** or **stan'zos**)) a group of lines of verse forming a definite pattern, *usu* constituting one of a series of units in a poem; a pattern so composed. [Ital *stanza*, from L *stāre* to stand] ■ **stanzā'ic** *adj*.

stap /stap/ *vt* an obsolete affectation for **stop**, *esp* in the sense of choke or obstruct; also /stap or stäp/ a Scots form, in the senses of stuff, thrust, cram.

stapedectomy, **stapedial**, **stapedius** see under **stapes**.

stapelia /stə-pē'li-ə/ *n* any succulent plant of the carrion-flower genus *Stapelia*, native to S Africa, having toothed, four-angled stems and large, star-shaped, blotched flowers that smell of carrion. [JB van *Stapel* (died 1636), Dutch botanist]

stapes /stā'pēz/ *n* (*pl* **stā'pēs** or **stapē'dēs**) the stirrup-shaped bone, the innermost ossicle of the middle ear that articulates with the incus. [LL *stapēs*, *-edis* a stirrup] ■ **stapedectomy** /stap-i-dek'tə-mi/ *n* the surgical removal of the stapes. **stapedial** /stə-pē'di-əl/ *adj*. **stape'dius** *n* the muscle of the stapes.

staph see **staphylococcus** under **staphylo-**.

staphylo- /staf-i-lō-/ or **staphy-** /staf-i-/ *combining form* denoting: (1) uvula; (2) resembling a bunch of grapes. [Gr *staphylē* a bunch of grapes, a swollen uvula] ■ **staph'yline** *adj* like a bunch of grapes. **staphylī'tis** *n* inflammation of the uvula. **staphylococc'al** *adj*. **staphylococc'us** *n* (*pl* **staphylococc'i**) (Gr *kokkos* a grain) a Gram-positive spherical bacterium of the genus *Staphylococcus*, found in clustered masses and producing exotoxins which can cause serious infections such as osteomyelitis, pneumonia, boils, abscesses, etc (*inf* shortening **staph**). **staphylō'ma** *n* abnormal protrusion of the sclera or of the cornea. **staph'yloplasty** *n* (*surg*) plastic surgery involving the soft palate and the uvula. **staphylorrh'aphy** *n* (Gr *rhaphē* stitching) the operation of uniting a cleft palate.

staple^1 /stā'pl/ *n* a U-shaped rod or wire for driving into a wall, post, etc as a fastening; a similarly shaped piece of wire that is driven through sheets of paper and compressed, to fasten them together; the curved bar, etc that passes through the slot of a hasp, receives a bolt, etc; the metallic tube to which the reed is fastened in the oboe, etc. ♦ *vt* to fasten with a staple. [OE *stapol* post, support; cf **staple^2**] ■ **stā'pler** *n* an instrument for (dispensing and) inserting staples into papers, etc. ▫ **staple gun** *n* a hand-held tool that propels staples into a wall, post etc. **stapling machine** *n* a machine that stitches paper with wire.

staple^2 /stā'pl/ *n* a leading commodity or raw material; a main element (as of diet, reading, conversation); unmanufactured wool or other raw material; textile fibre, or its length and quality; a settled mart or market (*medieval hist*). ♦ *adj* constituting a staple; leading, main. ♦ *vt* to grade (wool, cotton, etc) according to staple. [OFr *estaple*, from LGer *stapel* heap, mart] ■ **stā'pler** *n* a merchant of a staple; a person who grades and deals in wool. ■ **merchant of the staple** a member of a medieval association of merchants privileged to trade in a staple commodity, *esp* wool, at the **staple town** (or **staple towns**) appointed by the king.

staple^3 or **stapple** /stap'l/ (*Scot*) see **stopple^2**.

star^1 /stär/ *n* any of those heavenly bodies visible by night that are really gaseous masses generating heat and light, whose places are relatively fixed (**fixed stars**); more loosely, these and the planets, comets, meteors and even, less commonly, the sun, moon and earth; a planet as a supposed influence, hence (*usu in pl*) one's luck, or an astrologer's summary of planetary influences; an object or figure with pointed rays, most commonly five; an asterisk; a starfish; a radial meeting of ways; a star-shaped badge or emblem, denoting rank, honour or merit, used eg in grading or classification, as in *three-star general, four-star petrol, five-star* (ie luxurious) *hotel*; a white mark on an animal's forehead, *esp* a horse's; a pre-eminent or exceptionally brilliant person; a leading performer, or one supposed to draw the public; a networking conformation in which the central control point is linked individually to all workstations (*comput*). ♦ *adj* of stars; marked by a star; leading, pre-eminent, brilliant. ♦ *vt* (**starr'ing**; **starred**) to make a star of; to have (a specified person) as a star performer; to mark with a star; to shatter or crack in a radiating form; to set with stars; to bespangle. ♦ *vi* to shine, as a star; to attract attention; to appear as a principal or star performer. [OE *steorra*; cf **stern^3**, Ger *Stern*, L *stēlla* (for *sterula*), Gr *astēr*] ■ **star'dom** *n* the state of being or status of a star performer, *esp* of stage or screen. **star'less** *adj*. **star'let** *n* a kind of starfish (genus *Asterina*); a little star; a young film actress, *esp* one hailed as a future star. **star'like** *adj* and *adv*. **starred** *adj* adorned or studded with stars; influenced by or having a star; decorated or marked with a star; turned into a star; star-shaped; radially cracked, fissured. **starr'ily** *adv*. **starr'iness** *n*. **starr'ing** *n* and *adj*. **starr'y** *adj* abounding or adorned with stars; consisting of, or proceeding from, the stars; like, or shining like, the stars.

❑ **star anise** n a Chinese evergreen tree (genus *Illicium*) of the magnolia family, with aromatic oil; the star-shaped dried seed pods of this tree, imparting an aniseed flavour when used in cookery. **star'-apple** n the edible fruit of the West Indian sapotaceous tree *Chrysophyllum cainito*. **star billing** n prominent display of the name of a performer, etc on posters, etc. **star'-blasting** n the noxious influence of the stars. **star'-bright'** adj bright as a star or with stars. **star'burst** n a pattern of lines radiating from a central point. **star catalogue** n a list of stars, with their places, magnitudes, etc. **star connection** n a Y-shaped three-phase electrical connection. **star'-crossed** or (*archaic*) **star'-crost** adj thwarted by the stars; ill-fated. **star'drift** n a common proper motion of a number of fixed stars in the same region. **star'dust** n an imaginary dust that blinds the eyes to reality and fills them with romantic illusions; cosmic dust, meteoric matter in fine particles; distant stars seen like dust grains. ◆ adj glittering, romantic, magical. **star'fish** n any member of the Asteroidea, a class of echinoderms with five arms merging in a disc, and tube-feet on the undersurface; sometimes extended to the ophiuroids. **star'flower** n any plant with star-shaped flowers, *esp* the star of Bethlehem. **star fruit** n the fruit of the carambola tree, star-shaped in cross-section. **star'-gaze** vi. **star'gazer** n an astrologer; an astronomer; someone who gazes at the sky, or in abstraction; a dreamer or wool-gatherer; a small supplementary sail set above the moonsail and skysail on a square-rigged ship; any fish of the family Uranoscopidae with upward-looking eyes set on top of its head, enabling it to see when it conceals itself in the sand on the sea bottom. **star'gazey pie** n a savoury Cornish fish pie in which whole fish are baked in pastry with their heads protruding through the crust. **star'gazing** n. **star grass** n a name for many grasslike plants with star-shaped flowers or leaf arrangement (see also **star²**). **star jump** n a gymnastic exercise performed by jumping into the air and simultaneously thrusting out the legs and arms. **star'-led** adj guided by a star. **star'light** n light from the stars; an unknown plant, otherwise called astrophel or penthia (*Spenser*). ◆ adj of or with starlight; lighted by the stars; bright as a star. **star'lit** adj lighted by the stars. **star map** n a map showing the positions of stars. **star'monger** n an astrologer. **star-nosed mole** n a N American aquatic mole (*Condylura cristata*) with a starlike fringe of sensory tentacles around its nose. **star of Bethlehem** n a plant (genus *Ornithogalum*) of the lily family with yellow starlike flowers. **Star of David** n the Jewish religious symbol of a six-pointed star, Solomon's seal. **star-of-the-earth'** n buck's-horn plantain, *Plantago coronopus*, so called because its serrated leaves radiate outwards along the ground. **star'-pav'd** adj (*Milton*) paved with stars. **star'-read** n (*Spenser*) astronomy. **star ruby** or **star sapphire** n a ruby or sapphire manifesting asterism. **starr'y-eyed** adj out of touch with reality; innocently idealistic; radiantly happy. **Stars and Bars** n sing the flag of the Confederate States of America. **Stars and Stripes** n sing the flag of the United States of America, with thirteen stripes alternately red and white, and a blue field containing as many stars as there are states. **star sapphire** see **star ruby** above. **star'-shaped** adj shaped like a conventional star, with pointed rays. **star shell** n a shell that explodes high in the air, lighting up the scene. **star'shine** n starlight. **star'ship** n (in science fiction) a craft capable of transporting travellers across solar systems. **star sign** n a sign of the zodiac. **star'-spang'led** adj spangled or studded with stars (**Star-spangled Banner** the Stars and Stripes; the American national anthem). **star'spot** n an area of relative darkness on the surface of a star. **star'stone** n a sapphire, ruby, or other stone showing asterism. **star'-struck** adj in awe of the famous. **star'-studded** adj covered with stars; (of the cast of a film, play, etc) having a high proportion of famous performers. **star thistle** n a species of *Centaurea* with radiating spiny bracts. **star trap** n a stage trap of several wedge-shaped pieces meeting in a centre. **star turn** n the chief item in an entertainment; a pre-eminent performer. **Star Wars** n sing (also without *caps*) an informal term for the Strategic Defence Initiative (qv under **strategy**). ◆ adj denoting the technology proposed for this initiative. **star wheel** n a spur wheel with V-shaped teeth. **star'wort** n any plant of the genus *Aster* (not the China aster); stitchwort; a water plant (**water starwort** *Callitriche*). **star-ypointing** /stär'i-point'ing/ adj (*Milton*; incorrectly formed; see **y-** pfx) pointing to the stars.

■ **see stars** (*inf*) to see spots of light, as a result eg of a blow on the head; to be in a dazed condition. **thank one's lucky stars** to consider oneself extremely fortunate.

star² or **starr** /stär/ (*Scot*) n *Ammophila* or any other coarse seaside grass, sedge, or rush (also **star grass** or **starr grass** (see also under **star¹**)). [ON *störr*]

staragen /star'ə-gən/ (*obs*) n the tarragon plant. [Cf Sp *estragón*, Fr *estragon* tarragon]

starboard /stär'bərd or -börd/ n the right-hand side of a ship. ◆ adj and adv of, to, towards, or on, the right. ◆ vt to turn to the right (see note at **port²**), *opp* to *port*. [OE *stēorbord*, from *stēor* steering, and *bord*

board, side of a ship (ancient Gmc ships being steered by a paddle at the right side)]

starch /stärch/ n the principal reserve food material stored in plants, chemically a carbohydrate, $(C_6H_{10}O_5)_x$ (also called **amylum**), used in laundry as a stiffener; stiffness, formality. ◆ adj made of starch; stiff, rigid, formal. ◆ vt to stiffen or stick with starch. [OE *stercan* to stiffen, inferred from *stercedferhth* stiff-spirited; cf Ger *Stärke* strength, vigour, starch, and **stark**]

■ **starched** adj. **starchedly** /stärcht'li/ or /stär'chid-li/ adv. **starchedness** /stärcht'nis/ or /stär'chid-nis/ n. **starch'er** n. **starch'ily** adv. **starch'iness** n. **starch'y** adj of or like starch; stiff, formal, strait-laced, prim; precise.

❑ **starch blocker** n a slimming aid which is thought to prevent the body from digesting starch. **starch'-grain** n a rounded or irregular mass of starch in the plastids of plants. **starch gum** n dextrin. **starch hyacinth** n the grape hyacinth, from its smell. **starch paper** n a test paper for iodine, coated with starch and potassium iodide. **starch'-reduced** adj (of bread, etc for the use of slimmers) containing less than the usual amount of starch.

Star Chamber /stär chăm'bər/ n a court (abolished 1641) with a civil and criminal jurisdiction, which met in the old council chamber at Westminster and was empowered to act without a jury and to use torture; (also without *caps*) generally, an over-zealous or secret inquiry or investigation; a closed meeting in which important decisions, resolutions, etc are made, *esp* on matters of public concern; a group of senior ministers of the British Cabinet, who meet occasionally to decide how government spending is to be allocated amongst various ministries. [Prob named from the gilt *stars* on the ceiling, not from the Jewish bonds (*starrs*) kept in it]

stare¹ /stār/ vi to look with a fixed gaze; to glare; to be insistently or obtrusively conspicuous, to be all too obvious. ◆ vt to put into a particular state by staring. ◆ n a fixed look. [OE *starian*, from root seen in Ger *starr* rigid; also in Eng **stern¹**]

■ **star'er** n someone who stares; (in *pl*; *old inf*) a lorgnette. **star'ing** n, adj and adv. **star'ingly** adv.

■ **stare down** or **out** to force (someone) to drop his or her gaze through the steadiness and power of one's own. **stare (someone) in the face** to be perfectly evident; to be imminent or apparently inevitable.

stare² /stār/ n a starling. [OE *stær*]

staretz or **starets** /stär'(y)ets/ n (in Russia) a holy man, a religious teacher or spiritual adviser. [Russ *starets*]

stark /stärk/ adj stern; harsh; plain, bare, unadorned; sheer; out-and-out; harshly apparent; all too clear; stark-naked (qv). ◆ adv utterly. ◆ vt and vi (*archaic*) to stiffen. [OE *stearc* hard, strong; ON *sterkr*, Ger *stark*]

■ **stark'en** vt and vi (*obs* or *dialect*) to make or become stark. **starkers** adj see **stark-naked**. **stark'ly** adv. **stark'ness** n.

stark-naked /stärk'nā'kid/, earlier (now *dialect*) **start-naked** /stärt'-/ adj utterly naked; quite bare (shortened to **stark** or (*inf*) **stark'ers**). [ME *stert-naked*, from OE *steort* tail, and *nacod* naked; infl by **stark**]

starlet see under **star¹**.

starling¹ /stär'ling/ n a bird (*Sturnus vulgaris*) with black, brown-spotted, iridescent plumage, a good mimic; any other member of its genus (*Sturnus*) or family (Sturnidae). [OE *stærling*, dimin of *stær*, see **stare²**]

starling² /stär'ling/ n piling protecting a bridge pier. [Prob for *staddling* from **staddle**]

starn same as **stern³**; also (*naut* or *dialect*) for **stern²**.

starnie see under **stern³**.

starosta /stä'rə-stə/ (*hist*) n a Russian village headman; a Polish noble holding a **star'osty** or domain bestowed by the crown. [Russ and Pol, elder]

starr¹ see **star²**.

starr² /stär/ n a Jewish deed or bond, eg of acquittance of debt. [Heb *sh'tār* a writing]

starrily, starry, etc see under **star¹**.

START /stärt/ abbrev : Strategic Arms Reduction Talks (or Treaty).

start /stärt/ vi to begin, commence; to shoot, dart, move suddenly forth, or out; to spring up or forward; to strain forward; to break away; to make a sudden involuntary movement as of surprise or becoming aware; to spring open, out of place, or loose; to begin to move; (of a car, engine, etc) to begin to work, to fire, combust; to set forth on a journey, race, career; to take to grumbling, to begin an argument, quarrel, etc (*inf*). ◆ vt to begin; to set going; to set on foot; to set up; to cause to begin (doing something); to conceive (a baby) (*inf*); to drive (an animal or bird) from a lair or hiding-place; to cause or undergo displacement or loosening of; to startle (*obs*); to break in (a young horse); to pour out or shoot. ◆ n a beginning; a beginning of movement, *esp* of a journey, race or career; a setting in motion; the time or place at which something starts, eg a race; a help in or opportunity of beginning; an advantage in being early or ahead; the extent of such an advantage in time or distance; a sudden movement; a sudden involuntary motion of the body; a startled feeling; a queer occurrence (*inf*); a spurt, spasm, burst; a beginning of building work on a new house site (*esp* as *house* or *housing starts*). [ME *sterten*; closely related to Du *storten* to plunge, Ger *stürzen*]

■ **start'er** *n* one of the competitors or horses assembled for the start of a race; a person who gives the signal for starting; a dog that drives out game; an apparatus or device for starting a machine, such as that (also called **self-starter**) for starting an internal-combustion engine; anything used to begin a process, such as a bacterial culture in making butter or cheese; (also in *pl*) the first course of a meal (see also **for starters** below); a potentially successful or profitable idea, project, etc (*commercial jargon*). **start'ful** *adj* apt to start. **start'ing** *n* and *adj*. **start'ingly** *adv* (*Shakesp*) by starts. **start'ish** *adj* apt to start, skittish. ❑ **starter home** *n* a small house or flat built, or considered by the seller, to suit and be affordable by a first-time buyer, *esp* a young couple. **starting block** *n* (*usu* in *pl*) a device for helping a sprinter make a quick start to a race, consisting of a framework with blocks of wood or metal attached, on which the sprinter braces his feet. **starting gate** *n* a movable barrier behind which the runners in a horse race are contained until the start; starting stalls (*US*). **starting gun** see **starting pistol** below. **starting handle** see under **crank**[1]. **starting hole** *n* a hiding place; an evasive trick. **starting pistol** or **gun** *n* a small pistol used to give the signal for starting a race. **starting point** *n* the point from which anything starts, or from which motion begins. **starting post** *n* the post or barrier from which the competitors start in a race. **starting price** *n* odds on a horse when the race begins (*inf abbrev* **SP**). **starting stalls** *n pl* a line of compartments in which runners wait before the start of a horse race, fitted with gates that are sprung open at the start. **start'-up** *n* an upstart (*Shakesp*); a rustic half-boot or short legging (*obs*); the process of setting up a company or business; such a company or business. ◆ *adj* of or denoting (the process of setting up) a new company or business.

■ **for a start** in the first place, as a preliminary consideration. **for starters** (*inf*) as the first course of a meal; in the first place, for a start. **give (someone) a start** to give (someone) an advantage at the start of, or in beginning, an enterprise, race, etc; to startle (someone); to give (someone) a job, *esp* a manual job (*inf*). **start a hare** see under **hare**. **start in** to begin. **start (in) on** (*inf*) to turn on, scold, berate. **start out** to begin; to begin a journey. **start over** (*N Am*) to begin again from the beginning, start all over again. **start up** to rise suddenly; to come suddenly into notice or being; to set in motion; to set up, initiate, establish (**start'-up** *n* see above). **to start with** at the beginning; in the first place, as a primary consideration. **under starter's orders** (of racehorses) about to be released by the starter at the beginning of a race; ready to start (*fig*).

startle /stär'tl/ *vt* to surprise or frighten suddenly; to cause to start with alarm; to take aback; to cause to awake with a start. ◆ *vi* to start with alarm; to awake with a start; (of a horse) to shy. ◆ *n* sudden alarm or surprise. [ME *stertle*, from OE *steartlian* to stumble, struggle, kick, or formed afresh from **start**]

■ **start'led** *adj*. **start'ler** *n*. **start'ling** *n* and *adj*. **start'lingly** *adv*. **start'lish** or **start'ly** *adj* apt to start. ❑ **startle colours** *n pl* (*zool*) bright colours on the bodies of animals or wings of birds which often resemble vertebrate eyes and act as an anti-predator device.

start-naked see **stark-naked**.

starve /stärv/ *vi* to suffer extreme hunger (or cold); to be in want (with *for*); to die, now only of hunger or (chiefly *Scot* and *N Eng* dialect) cold; to deteriorate (*obs*). ◆ *vt* to cause to die of hunger; to afflict with hunger (or cold); to deprive of food; to force, subdue or cure by depriving of food; to deprive (with *of*). [OE *steorfan* to die; Du *sterven*, Ger *sterben* to die]

■ **starvā'tion** *n*. **starved** *adj*. **starve'ling** *n* a lean, hungry, weak, or pining person, animal, or plant (also *adj*). **starv'ing** *n* and *adj*.

stash /stash/ *vt* to stow in hiding (often with *away*); to stop, desist, quit (*old sl*). ◆ *n* a secret store, or its hiding-place; a hidden store of a drug, or the drug itself (*sl*; *esp US*). [Origin obscure]

stashie see **stooshie**.

Stasi /stä'zi/ *n* the secret police force of the former state of East Germany. [Ger *Staatssicherheitsdienst* state security service]

stasidion, stasimon, etc see under **stasis**.

stasis /stä'sis/ or /stas'is/ *n* cessation, arrest, *esp* of growth, of blood circulation or bleeding, or of the contents of the bowels; (maintenance of) a state of equilibrium, or a constant state; in punctuated equilibrium, the period of equilibrium which is interrupted by a period of rapid change (*palaeontol, biol*). [Gr, stoppage, stationariness]

■ **stasid'ion** *n* (*Mod Gr dimin*) a stall in a Greek church. **stas'imon** *n* (*pl* **stas'ima**) (Gr, stationary) in Greek tragedy, an ode sung after the

chorus had taken their places, or without interruption by dialogue. **stas'imorphy** *n* structural modification by arrested development.

-stasis /-sta-sis/ (chiefly *med*) *combining form* denoting cessation or slowing. [Gr *stasis* stoppage, stationariness]

stat /stat/ (*inf*) a statistic; short for **Photostat**® (see under **photo-**[1]), **thermostat** (see under **thermo-**), etc.

stat. *abbrev*: *statim* (*L*), immediately.

-stat /-stat/ *combining form* designating a regulating device that causes something to remain constant or stationary, as in *barostat*, *hygrostat*, *thermostat*. [Gr *-statēs* causing to stand, from *histanai* to cause to stand]

statant /stā'tənt/ (*heraldry*) *adj* standing on four feet. [L *stāre* to stand]

state /stāt/ *n* a condition; a perturbed condition of mind (*inf*); an untidy condition (*inf*); a mode of existence; a set of circumstances that exist at any time; a phase or stage; an impression taken at a stage of progress in engraving or etching or in printing a book; status; station in life; high station; grave import (*Shakesp*); pomp, display, ceremonial dignity; a seat of dignity (*Shakesp*); a canopy (*Milton*); an estate, order, or class in society or the body politic; hence (in *pl*) the legislature (*hist*); an exalted personage (*Milton*); public welfare; the constitution; a republic (*obs*); the civil power; a political community under one government; one of a number of political communities forming a federation under a central government; the territory of such a community; high politics; an interest in property (*Spenser*); property, estate (*Shakesp*); a body of people united by profession; a statement, report (now chiefly *milit*). ◆ *adj* of, belonging to, or relating to, the state or a federal state; run or financed by the state; public; ceremonial; pompous; affectedly solemn and mysterious; magnificent. ◆ *adv* or *adj* (*Spenser*) explained in old gloss as stoutly (*perh* pompous). ◆ *vt* to set forth; to express the details of; to set down fully and formally; to assert, affirm; to install, establish, endow, place in a condition (*esp* favourable; *archaic*); to set in state; to specify; *perh* to determine the value of (*Milton*); to settle. [L *status, -ūs*, from *stāre, statum* to stand; partly through OFr (see **estate**)]

■ **stat'able** *adj* capable of being stated. **stāt'al** *adj* of a federal state. **stāt'ed** *adj* settled; established; declared; regular; circumstanced (*obs*). **stāt'edly** *adv*. **state'hood** *n* the status of a state. **state'less** *adj* without nationality; unworthy to be accounted a state; without pomp. **state'lessness** *n*. **state'let** *n* a minor state. **state'lily** *adv*. **state'liness** *n*. **state'ly** *adj* showing state or dignity; majestic, greatly impressive. ◆ *adv* majestically; loftily. **state'ment** *n* the act of stating; that which is stated; a formal account, declaration of facts, etc; an instruction in a source language or any directive input to a program that converts a source language into machine code (*comput*); a financial record, eg one issued regularly by a bank to a customer, stating his or her personal balance and detailing debits and credits; (in the UK) a written undertaking, legally binding, by an education authority to provide certain stated resources in the education of a particular child with learning difficulties. ◆ *vt* to issue a statement about the special educational needs of (a child). **state'mented** *adj*. **state'menting** *n*. **stāt'er** *n*. **state'wide** *adj* (*US*) applied throughout the state. **stāt'ism** *n* (the belief in) state control of economic and social affairs. **stāt'ist** *n* and *adj* (see also separate entry).

❑ **state-aid'ed** *adj* receiving contributions from the state. **state bank** *n* (in the USA) a bank that is awarded its charter by a state government. **state cabin** *n* a stateroom on a ship. **state capitalism** *n* control by the state of the means of production and use of capital. **state'craft** *n* the art of managing state affairs. **State Department** *n* the US government department dealing with foreign affairs. **State Enrolled Nurse** *n* a nurse who has passed a particular examination of the General Nursing Council of England and Wales or the General Nursing Council of Scotland (*abbrev* **SEN**; see also **State Registered Nurse** below). **state house** *n* (*usu* with *caps*) the building in which a state legislature sits; (sometimes with *cap*) a building where state ceremonies are held; a house built by the government for renting (*NZ*). **stately home** *n* a large, fine old house, *esp* one open to the public. **statement of claim** *n* the pleading in which the plaintiff in an action at law sets forth his or her case against the defendant. **state'-monger** *n* (*derog*) one who would like to be thought a statesman. **state of affairs** or **events** *n* a situation, set of circumstances. **state of emergency** see **emergency** under **emerge**. **state of play** *n* the situation as it currently stands. **state of repair** *n* physical condition, soundness. **state of the art** *n* the level or position at a given time, *esp* the present, of generally accepted and available knowledge, technical achievement, etc in a particular field, etc; the level of technological development as yet unsurpassed in a particular field. **state-of-the-art'** *adj*. **state paper** *n* an official paper or document relating to affairs of state. **state prison** *n*. **state prisoner** *n* a prisoner confined for offence against the state. **State Registered Nurse** *n* in England and Wales, a nurse who has passed a more advanced examination of the General Nursing Council of England and Wales than a State Enrolled Nurse (*abbrev* **SRN**; see also **Registered General Nurse** under **register**). **state religion** *n* a

---

religion recognized by the state as the national religion. **state'room** *n* a private cabin or railway compartment; a large room for formal or ceremonial occasions, *esp* in a palace. **state school** *n* one controlled by a public authority, and financed by taxation. **States General** *n* the representative body of the three orders (nobility, clergy, burghers) of the French kingdom (*hist*); the Dutch parliament. **State'side** *adj* and *adv* (*inf*; also without *cap*) of, in, towards or to the USA. **states'man**, *fem* **states'woman** *n* a person skilled in government; a person who takes an important part in governing the state, *esp* with wisdom and broad-mindedness; a person who farms his or her own estate, a small landholder (*N Eng*). **states'manlike** or **states'manly** *adj* befitting a statesman or stateswoman. **states'manship** *n* a political system in which the state controls industry and the banking system. **states'person** *n*. **state trial** *n* a trial for an offence against the state. **state trooper** *n* (in the US) a member of a state police force. ■ **Council** (or **House**) **of States** see under **council**. **lie in state** (of a corpse) to be laid out in a place of honour before being buried. **state of the Union message** (in the US) an annual report by the President, required by statute, on the state of the nation and on legislative plans. **States of the Church** (*hist*) an area of central Italy ruled by the popes as a temporal domain (also **Papal States**). **the States** the United States. **turn State's evidence** see under **evident**.

stater /stā'tər/ *n* an ancient Greek standard coin of various kinds, the gold daric, silver tetradrachm, etc. [Gr *statēr*, orig a pound weight, from *histanai* to set, establish, weigh]

static /stat'ik/ *adj* (also **stat'ical**) relating to statics; relating to bodies, forces, charges, etc in equilibrium; stationary; stable; resting; acting by mere weight; relating to sense of bodily equilibrium. ◆ *n* statics (*obs*); atmospheric disturbances in radio reception; white specks or flashes on a television picture; crackling on a vinyl record; static electricity. [Gr *statikos* bringing to a standstill, from *histanai* to cause to stand, to place in the balance, weigh] ■ **stat'ically** *adv*. **stat'ics** *n sing* the science of forces in equilibrium. ❑ **static electricity** *n* electrical charges that are stationary, not moving along in a current. **static line** *n* a cord joining a parachute pack to the aircraft so that when the wearer of the pack jumps, the parachute is automatically opened. **static memory** *n* (*comput*) random access memory in which information does not need refreshing and is retained as long as power is maintained. **static pressure** *n* the pressure normal to the surface of a body moving through a fluid.

statice /stat'i-sē/ *n* any plumbaginaceous plant of the sea lavender genus (*Limonium*), many of which are cultivated for their everlasting flowers. [L, thrift, from Gr *statikē*, fem of *statikos* (see **static**), in medical usage meaning astringent]

statim /stat'im/ (*L*) *adv* immediately, at once.

statin /stat'in/ *n* any of a class of drugs that inhibit an enzyme used in cholesterol production, used to treat heart disease. [**-stat** and **-in**]

station /stā'shən/ *n* a standing-place; a fixed stopping-place, *esp* one on a railway with associated buildings and structures; a place set apart and equipped for some particular purpose; a place where a person stands; a local office, headquarters, or depot; a television or radio channel; a building from which broadcasts are made; a branch post office (*US*); a mode of standing; a position; a chosen fixed point; a standing still (now *rare*); a habitat; an actual spot where a species has been found; an assigned place or post; an assigned region for naval duty; a place in India where officials and officers reside; a stock farm (*Aust* and *NZ*); a position in life (*esp* a high position) or in the scale of nature; a holy place visited as one of a series, *esp* one of (*usu* fourteen) representations of stages in Christ's way to Calvary, disposed around a church interior or elsewhere (*RC*). ◆ *adj* of a station. ◆ *vt* to assign a station to; to set; to appoint to a post, place, or office. [L *statiō, -ōnis*, from *stāre* to stand] ■ **sta'tional** *adj*. ❑ **station hand** *n* (*Aust*) a man employed on a station. **station house** *n* a lock-up at a police station; a police station or fire station (*US*); a small railway station. **sta'tionmaster** or **sta'tion-manager** *n* the person in charge of a railway station. **station wagon** *n* (*N Am, Aust* and *NZ*) an estate car.

stationary /stā'shə-nə-ri* or *stā'shən-ri, -shnə-ri/ *adj* still; not moving; fixed; static, not changing; settled; permanently located; continuously resident. [L *statiōnārius* belonging to a military station, as for **station**] ■ **sta'tionariness** *n*. ❑ **stationary bicycle** *n* an exercise bicycle. **stationary wave** same as **standing wave** (see under **stand**).

stationer /stā'shə-nər/ *n* a shop that sells paper and writing materials; a bookseller or publisher (*obs*). [L *statiōnārius* a shopkeeper, in the Middle Ages a university bookseller, distinguished from an itinerant] ■ **sta'tionery** *n* the goods sold by a stationer. ◆ *adj* belonging to a stationer. ❑ **Stationers' Hall** *n* the hall in London of the Company of Stationers, who until the passing of the Copyright Act in 1842 enjoyed absolute control over printing and publishing. **Stationery Office** *n* an office for

providing books, stationery, etc to government offices and for arranging the printing of public papers.

statism see under **state**.

statist /stā'tist/ *n* a statesman; a politician; an advocate of statism (qv under **state**); a statistician.

statistic /stə-tis'tik/ *n* (in *pl*) tabulated numerical facts, *orig* those relating to a state, or (with *sing* verb) the classification, tabulation, and study of such facts; one such fact; a statistician. ◆ *adj* statistical; political (*obs*); relating to status. [Ital *statista* and Ger *Statistik*, from L *status* state] ■ **statist'ical** *adj* of, concerned with, or of the nature of statistics. **statist'ically** *adv*. **statistician** /stat-is-tish'ən/ *n* a person skilled in statistics; a compiler or student of statistics. ❑ **statistical mechanics** *n sing* (*phys*) theoretical predictions of the behaviour of a macroscopic system by applying statistical laws to the behaviour of component particles.

stative /stā'tiv/ *adj* permanent, fixed (now only of a Roman camp); indicating a physical state or reflex action (of certain Hebrew verbs); indicating a state, as opposed to an action, etc (*linguistics*). ◆ *n* a stative verb. [L *statīvus*, from *stāre* to stand]

stato- /stat-ō-/ *combining form* signifying standing. [Gr *statos* set, placed] ■ **statoblast** /stat'ō-blast/ *n* (Gr *blastos* bud) a reproductive body in bryozoans. **statocyst** /stat'ō-sist/ *n* (Gr *kystis* bladder) an organ of equilibrial sense in crustaceans and other invertebrates, containing statoliths; a cell with starch grains by which a plant is supposed to be sensitive to gravity. **stat'olith** *n* (Gr *lithos* stone) a starch grain or other free solid body in a statocyst. **stat'oscope** *n* a sensitive barometer for detecting minute differences.

stator /stā'tər/ *n* (*mech, elec eng*) a stationary part within which a part rotates. [L *stator* stander]

statue /stach'ū or stat'ū/ *n* a representation (*usu* near or above life-size) of a human or animal form in the round (also (*obs*) **stat'ua**). [L *statua*, from *statuere* to cause to stand, from *stāre*] ■ **stat'uary** *adj* of, relating to, or suitable for sculpture; sculptured; statuesque. ◆ *n* sculpture; statues. **stat'ued** *adj* furnished with statues; sculptured. **statuesque** /-esk'/ *adj* like a statue; (of a person, *esp* a woman) tall and well-proportioned in figure, or dignified and imposing in appearance. **statuesque'ly** *adv*. **statuesque'ness** *n*. **statuette'** *n* a small statue, figurine.

stature /stach'ər or stat'yər/ *n* body height; eminence. [L *statūra*] ■ **stat'ured** *adj* having a stature.

status /stā'təs/ *n* (*pl* (*rare*) **status** /-tūs/ or **statuses**) a state of affairs; condition; standing; position, rank, importance, in society or in any group; high rank or standing; a person's legal position or classification with regard to marriage, citizenship, etc. [L *status*] ❑ **status bar** *n* (*comput*) a line on a screen which gives information, eg the number of the page being worked on. **status symbol** *n* a possession or a privilege considered to mark a person out as having a high position in his or her social group.

status quo /stā'təs or stat'ŭs kwō/ (*L*) *n* the existing condition, unchanged situation; (also **status quo ante** /an'ti/) the condition or situation existing before a particular change. [Literally, the state in which]

statute /stat'ūt or stach'ūt/ *n* a law expressly enacted by the legislature (as distinguished from a customary or common law); a written law; the act of a corporation or its founder, intended as a permanent rule or law; a bond or other proceeding based on a statute; a hiring-fair (*obs*). [L *statūtum* that which is set up, from *statuere*] ■ **stat'utable** *adj* prescribed, permitted, recognized by, or according to statute. **stat'utably** *adv*. **stat'utorily** *adv*. **stat'utory** *adj* of or relating to statute; prescribed; enacted or recognized by statute; depending on statute for its authority; so common or frequent as to seem the rule (as though prescribed by statute) (*inf*). ❑ **sta'tute-barred** *adj* disallowed by the statute of limitations. **statute book** *n* a record of statutes or enacted laws. **statute cap** *n* (*Shakesp*) a kind of cap enjoined by statute (1571) to be worn on Sundays by all below a certain rank. **statute labour** *n* (*old*) compulsory labour on roads, etc. **statute law** *n* law in the form of statutes (also **statutory law**). **statute mile** see under **mile**. **statute of limitations** *n* a statute prescribing the period of time within which proceedings must be taken to enforce a right or bring a legal action. **Statute of Westminster** *n* an act (1931) of the United Kingdom parliament conferring independent sovereign status on the self-governing dominions. **statutory declaration** *n* a declaration made on oath to a statutory authority, eg to change one's name. **statutory rape** *n* (*US*) the criminal offence of having sexual intercourse with a child who is below the age of consent.

staun /stön/ *v* (*pat* and *pap* **stude** /stood/) a Scots form of **stand**.

staunch[1] /stönch or stönsh/ or **stanch** /stänch or stänsh/ adj firm in principle, pursuit, or support; trusty, hearty, constant, loyal, zealous; stout and firm; watertight; seaworthy. [OFr *estanche* ; see **stanch**[1]]
■ **sta(u)nch'ly** adv. **sta(u)nch'ness** n.

staunch[2] (vt) see **stanch**[1].

staurolite /stö'rə-līt/ n (*mineralogy*) a silicate of aluminium with ferrous oxide, magnesia, and water, sometimes occurring as twinned cruciform crystals. [Gr *stauros* cross, and *lithos* stone]
■ **staurolitic** /-lit'ik/ adj.

stauroscope /stö'rə-skōp/ n an optical instrument for studying the structure of mineral crystals under polarized light. [Gr *stauros* cross, and *skopeein* to look at]
■ **stauroscop'ic** adj.

stave /stāv/ n one of the strips of wood of which a barrel or tub is made; a staff, rod, bar, shaft, *esp* wooden, as the rung of a ladder; a staff (*music*); a stanza, verse of a song. ◆ vt (pat and pap **staved** or **stove**) to break a stave or the staves of (a boat or barrel; with *in*); to break; to burst inward (with *in*); to drive off, as with a staff; to delay, ward off or keep back (with *off*); to put together, repair or fit with staves; to sprain, jar violently (fingers, toes, etc) (*Scot*). ◆ vi to thrust onward (*Scot*); to break up. [By-form of **staff**[1]]

stave-church /stāv'chûrch/ n an ancient Norwegian wooden church supported on masts, with gabled roofs rising one above another. [Norw *stav-kirke*, from *stav* staff, stave, and *kirke* church]

staves /stāvz/ plural of **staff**[1] and of **stave**.

stavesacre /stāvz'ā-kər/ n a tall larkspur whose seeds were formerly used against lice. [OFr *stavesaigre*, from LL *staphisagria*, from Gr *staphis* raisins, and *agrios* wild]

staw /stö/ a Scots form of **stall**[1] (n and vt) and **stole**[2].

stay[1] /stā/ vi (pat and pap **stayed**) to remain, continue to be, in a place, position or condition; to reside temporarily, as in *stay at a hotel* ; to live, dwell (*Scot and S Afr*); to wait in order to participate in or be present at; to pause, wait, tarry; to be kept waiting; to wait, attend as a servant (*Shakesp*); to stop, cease, desist (*archaic*); to stand firm (*archaic*); to hold out, last, endure; (in a race, etc) to maintain one's pace over a long distance; to keep pace or keep up (with *with*); (in poker) to match a bet in order to stay in the game. ◆ vt to reside, remain for a specific period, as in *stay for a week* ; to hold, restrain, check the action of; to delay or hinder; to stop, suspend, discontinue or postpone (judgement, proceedings, etc); to hold in abeyance; to endure or remain to the end; to satisfy, appease or allay; to quell, suppress (*archaic*); to stop for, be stopped by (*archaic*); to detain (*archaic*); to await (*archaic*). ◆ n (a period of) staying, temporary residence; a visit; a sojourn; a suspension or postponement of legal proceedings; a check or restraint; the act of stopping or being stopped; staying power, endurance; an obstacle (*obs*); a permanent state (*obs*). [From Anglo-Fr *estaier* to stay, from OFr *ester*, from L *stāre* to stand]
■ **stay'er** n a person or animal (*esp* a horse or greyhound) of good lasting or staying qualities for a race.
❑ **stay'-at-home** adj keeping much at home; tending or preferring to stay at home, in one's own area or country; untravelled, unadventurous. ◆ n a stay-at-home person. **stay'away** n (*S Afr*) a strike; a person participating in a strike. **staying power** n the ability to continue or sustain effort, *esp* over a long period, without flagging. **stay-on tab** n a ring pull that does not pull entirely off, but bends into the can. **stay stitching** n (*dressmaking*) a line of stitching in the seam allowance to prevent stretching and fraying of the fabric.
■ **be here** (or **have come**) **to stay** to have become permanent or established. **stay in** to remain at home. **stay on** to remain, tarry after the normal or expected time for departing. **stay out** to remain away from home; to remain throughout or beyond the end of. **stay over** (*inf*) to remain overnight, stay the night. **stay put** not to move from the place or position in which one has been put. **stay someone's hand** (*literary*) to stop someone on the point of doing something. **stay the course** to endure to the end of the race or other trial of one's stamina and staying power. **stay up** to remain out of bed and awake after the normal time of going to sleep.

stay[2] /stā/ n a prop or support; one of a number of strips of bone or metal sewn into a corset to stiffen it; (in *pl*) a corset thus stiffened (often **pair of stays**). ◆ vt to prop or support (with *up*); to sustain, comfort, strengthen (with *up*; *archaic* or *literary*); to cause to rely or depend (with *upon*; *archaic*). [OFr *estaye*]
■ **stayed** adj wearing stays. **stay'less** adj without stays; unsupported.
❑ **stay bolt** n a bolt or rod binding together opposite plates. **stay lace** n a lace for fastening a corset. **stay'maker** n a maker of corsets. **stay tape** n a stay lace.

stay[3] /stā/ n (*naut*) a rope bracing a mast, etc, a guy; a brace generally. ◆ vt to brace or support (a mast, etc) using stays. ◆ vi to bring the head of a sailing vessel up to the wind in order to tack or go about; (of a mast) to incline (forward). [OE *staeg*; cf ON *stag*, MLGer *stach*, Norw *stagle* wooden post]

❑ **staysail** /stā'sl/ n a triangular, auxiliary fore-and-aft sail spread or set on a stay. **stay'-tackle** n hoisting tackle hung from a ship's mainmast.
■ **at short** (or **long**) **stay** (of an anchor cable) taut and leading to the anchor at a steep (or acute) angle near (or at some distance away from) the bow. **in stays** (of a sailing vessel during tacking) hanging with head to windward without moving to the opposite tack. **miss** (or **refuse**) **stays** (of a sailing vessel) to fail in going about from one tack to another.

staycation /stā-kā'shən/ n (*inf*) a period of holiday spent at one's own home. [**stay**[1] and **vacation** (see under **vacate**)]

stayne an old spelling (*Spenser*, etc) of **stain**.

stayre an old spelling (*Spenser*, etc) of **stair**.

stays see **stay**[2].

STD abbrev : sexually transmitted disease; subscriber trunk dialling.

std abbrev : standard.

Ste abbrev : Sainte (*Fr*), fem of *saint*.

stead /sted/ n the place, function, role or position of another, as in *act in someone's stead*; service, avail, advantage, as in **stand someone in good stead** to be advantageous to someone; a space of time (*Spenser*); circumstances, case, condition (*Spenser*). ◆ vt (pat and pap **stead'ed** or **stead** /sted/) to avail, help, serve (*archaic*); to fulfil in substitution (*Shakesp* **steed up**). [OE *stede* place]

steadfast /sted'fäst/ adj firm; constant; resolute. [OE *stede faest*]
■ **stead'fastly** adv. **stead'fastness** n.

Steadicam® /sted'i-kam/ (*cinematog*) n a device for steadying a hand-held camera, consisting of a shoulder and waist harness with a shock-absorbing arm attached, to which the camera is fitted.

steading /sted'ing/ n the range of buildings surrounding a farmhouse, a farmstead. [OE *stede* place]

steady /sted'i/ adj (**stead'ier**; **stead'iest**) standing firmly; fixed; stable; constant; resolute; consistent; regular; uniform; sober, industrious; (with *to*) (of a hound) seldom diverted from the trail of (a deer, hare, etc); (with *from*) (of a horse or hound) seldom distracted, upset or diverted by (another animal, a noise, etc). ◆ vt (**stead'ying**; **stead'ied**) to make steady; to support; to make or keep firm. ◆ n a rest or support, as for the hand, a tool, or a piece of work; a regular boyfriend or girlfriend (*inf*). ◆ interj be careful!; keep calm!; hold the present course (*naut*); see **ready, steady, go** under **ready**. [OE *stede*]
■ **stead'ily** adv. **stead'iness** n.
❑ **stead'y-going** adj having or showing steady habits or action. **steady state** n a state or condition of dynamic equilibrium with entropy at its maximum (*phys*); any oscillation system that continues unchanged indefinitely (*telecom*). **steady-state theory** n (*astron*) in cosmology, a theory that asserts the universe is in a steady state, being infinitely old and containing the same density of matter at all points and all times, with new matter being created to compensate for the space left by the observed expansion of the universe (cf **Big Bang theory** under **bang**[1]; also called **continuous creation**).
■ **go steady** (*inf*) (*esp* of a boy and girl not yet engaged to be married) to have a steady relationship, to go about regularly together. **steady on!** keep calm!; don't be so foolish, hasty, etc.

steak /stāk/ n any of several cuts of beef graded for frying, braising, stewing, etc; a slice of meat (*esp* hindquarters of beef) or fish. [ON *steik* ; *steikja* to roast on a spit]
❑ **steak diane** /dī-an'/ n steak served in a rich seasoned sauce. **steak'house** n a restaurant specializing in fried or grilled beefsteaks. **steak knife** n a knife with a serrated blade for eating steak. **steak tartare** n minced beef steak served raw mixed with onions, raw egg and seasonings (also **tartar steak**).

steal[1] /stēl/ vt (pat **stole** (*obs* **stale**; *Scot* **staw, stealed** or **stealt**); pap **sto'len** (*obs* **stole**; *Milton* **stoln**; *Scot* **stown, stealed** or **stealt**)) to take without right or permission, *esp* secretly; to take, gain or win, by beguiling talk, by contrivance, unexpectedly, insidiously, gradually, or furtively; to snatch; to hole (a long putt) by a delicate stroke (*golf*); to gain (a base) without the help of a hit or error, by running to it without being tagged out (*baseball*); to put surreptitiously, smuggle. ◆ vi to be a thief; to pass quietly, unobtrusively, gradually, or surreptitiously. ◆ n (*inf*) an act of stealing, a theft; something acquired without right or permission; a bargain; the stealing of a base (*baseball*). [OE *stelan* ; related to Ger *stehlen*, Du *stelen*, Swed *stjäla*, Dan *stjæle*]
■ **steal'er** n. **steal'ing** n and adj. **steal'ingly** adv.
■ **steal a march on** see under **march**[1]. **steal a marriage** to marry secretly. **steal someone's thunder** to make use of another's invention against him or her (as when John Dennis's stage thunder was used in a rival's play); to rob someone of the opportunity of achieving a sensational effect by forestalling him or her. **steal the show** see under **show**.

steal[2], **steale, steel, stele** or **steil** /stēl/ (*dialect* and *Spenser*) n a handle, shaft. [OE *stela* stalk, cf Ger *Stiel*; connected with **stale**[4]]

stealed, **stealt** see **steal**[1].

stealth /stelth/ n a secret procedure or manner; furtiveness; a theft (Spenser, Shakesp); a thing stolen (Milton); secret or unobtrusive going or passage (Shakesp). ◆ adj (milit jargon) of, using, or associated with technological means of avoiding detection, such as (in aircraft) reducing noise, infrared emissions, radar reflections and (in personnel) wearing clothing that reduces the risk of observation by infrared night-sights. ◆ vt and vi to approach (an enemy, etc) without being detected, as certain martial arts experts are trained to do. [From **steal**[1]]
■ **stealth'ily** adv. **stealth'iness** n. **stealth'ing** n the act or process of approaching, eg an enemy, without being detected. **stealth'y** adj acted or acting with stealth; furtive.
❑ **stealth bomber** or **fighter** n a military aircraft of a design that enables it to escape radar detection. **stealth tax** n (inf) a tax that is applied in such a way that taxpayers are unaware of its imposition.

steam /stēm/ n water in the form of a gas or vapour, or of a mist or film of liquid drops; a steamed dish; steam power; a spell of travel by steam power; energy, force, spirit (inf). ◆ adj of, for, using or worked by steam; outdated, old-fashioned, not using the latest technology (facetious). ◆ vi to rise or pass off in steam or vapour; to emit or generate steam, vapour, or smell; to move by means of steam power; to move fast (inf). ◆ vt to expose to steam, apply steam to; to cook by means of steam; to exhale (smoke from a pipe) (old sl). [OE stēam; Du stoom]
■ **steamed** adj. **steam'er** n a steamship; a cooking apparatus for steaming food; one of a gang of muggers that attack by the method of steaming (sl); a wetsuit (sl); stewed kangaroo flavoured with pork (Aust sl). **steam'ie** n (Scot) a public laundry. **steam'ily** adv. **steam'iness** n. **steam'ing** n the action or process of emitting, moving by, applying, or cooking by, steam; a form of mugging used by gangs, eg on the London Underground, who rush en masse through crowds, snatching whatever they can (sl). ◆ adj (inf) in an advanced state of drunkenness; very angry. **steam'y** adj of, like, full of, covered with or emitting, steam or vapour; erotic, sexy, lubricious (inf).
❑ **steam bath** n a steam-filled compartment, eg one at a Turkish bath, etc in which to refresh oneself by sweating, etc, or one in a laboratory for sterilizing equipment. **steam'boat**, **steam'ship** or **steam vessel** n a vessel driven by steam. **steam boiler** n a boiler for generating steam. **steam car** n a car propelled by steam. **steam chest** n (engineering) a chamber above a steam boiler serving as a reservoir for steam and in which the slide valve works. **steam coal** n coal suitable for raising steam. **steam'-driv'en** adj. **steam engine** n any engine worked by steam. **steamer clam** n a soft-shell clam. **steamer duck** n a large duck of S America whose swimming action is suggestive of the motion of a steamer with a paddle wheel on each side. **steam gauge** n a pressure gauge for steam. **steam governor** n the governor (qv) of a steam engine. **steam hammer** n a vertical hammer worked by steam. **steam'-haul** vt and vi to draw (a conveyance for goods, passengers, etc) along rails by means of chains, etc attached to a stationary steam engine. **steaming lights** n pl (naut) compulsory white navigation lights carried on the masts of all vessels at sea, indicating their presence (and course) at night. **steam iron** n an electric iron having a compartment in which water is heated to provide steam to dampen fabrics for easier ironing. **steam jacket** n a hollow casing formed around a steam engine cylinder and supplied with steam to prevent condensation of the steam in the main cylinder. **steam launch** n a large steam-driven boat. **steam locomotive** n a self-propelled steam engine and boiler mounted on a wheeled frame, such as a railway engine. **steam navvy** or **shovel** n an excavator driven by steam. **steam organ** n a calliope. **steam packet** n a steam vessel plying between certain ports. **steam port** n an opening from the valve-face to the cylinder of a steam engine for the passage of steam. **steam power** n the force or agency of steam when applied to machinery. **steam'punk** n a genre of science fiction set in an era of steam power, esp Victorian Britain, and usu featuring innovative inventions or alternative histories. **steam radio** n (facetious) sound radio, considered old-fashioned in comparison with television. **steam'-roller** n a steam engine with heavy rollers for wheels, used in road-mending, etc; any weighty crushing force (fig). ◆ vt (inf) to crush (objections, etc); to force (eg legislation through parliament, etc). **steam room** n a room filled with steam, for use as a steam bath. **steamship** see **steamboat** above. **steam shovel** see **steam navvy** above. **steam'tight** adj impervious to steam. **steam trap** n a contrivance for allowing the passage of water but not of steam. **steam turbine** n an engine in which expanding steam acts on blades attached to a drum. **steam vessel** see **steamboat** above. **steam whistle** n a whistle sounded by the passage of steam.
■ **full steam ahead** forward at the greatest speed possible; with maximum effort. **get up steam** to build up steam pressure; to collect one's forces; to become excited. **let off steam** to release steam into the atmosphere; to work off energy; to give vent to anger or annoyance. **run out of steam** (inf) to be forced to stop through loss of impetus, strength or energy. **steamed up** (inf) indignant (see also

steam up below). **steam open** to soften the gum of, and peel open (sealed envelopes) under exposure to steam. **steam up** (of windows, etc) to become or cause to become dimmed with condensed vapour. **under one's own steam** by one's own unaided efforts.

stean[1], **steane** or **steen** /stēn/ (dialect or archaic) n a stone or earthenware container with two handles. [OE stǣne]

stean[2] see **steen**[1].

steane see **stean**[1].

steapsin /stē-ap'sin/ same as **lipase** (see under **lip-**).

stear, **steard**, **stearage**, **stearsman** obsolete spellings of **steer**[1], **steered**, etc.

stear- /stē-ər- or -ar-/, also **steato-** /-ə-tō- or -at-/ or **steat-** /-ət- or -at-/ combining form denoting suet, fat, fatty tissue. [Gr steār, steātos suet, tallow]
■ **stearate** /stē'ər-āt/ n a salt of stearic acid. **stearic** /stē-ar'ik/ adj of stearin (**stearic acid** a solid fatty acid, $C_{18}H_{36}O_3$, derived from animal and vegetable fats). **ste'arin** /stē'ə-rin/ n glyceryl ester of stearic acid; a mixture of stearic and palmitic acids (also **ste'arine**); the solid part of a fat. **ste'arine** /-rīn/ adj (of candles, etc) made of stearin. **steatite** /stē'ə-tīt/ n soapstone. **steatitic** /-tit'ik/ adj. **steat'ocele** n (Gr kēlē tumour) a fatty tumour in the scrotum. **steatō'ma** n a tumour of a sebaceous gland or sebaceous cyst. **steatom'atous** adj. **steatopygia** /stē-ə-tō-pī'ji-ə or -pij'i-ə/ n (Gr pȳgē buttock) the accumulation of fat in the buttocks. **steatorrhoea** or **steatorrhea** /stē-ə-tə-rē'ə/ n (Gr rhoia a flow) accumulation of abnormal levels of fat in the faeces. **steatō'sis** n fatty degeneration; the accumulation of fat in hepatocytes, occurring eg in pregnancy, alcoholism and as an effect of some drugs.

steare /stēr/ (archaic) same as **steer**[2].

stearsmate another spelling of **steersmate**.

steat-, **steato-** see **stear-**.

sted, **stedd**, **stedde**, **stede** (Spenser) or **steed** (Shakesp) obsolete forms of **stead** (n and vt).

steddy, **steedy** old spellings of **steady**.

stedfast an obsolete spelling (Shakesp, Milton, etc) of **steadfast**.

steed[1] /stēd/ n a horse, esp a spirited horse. [OE stēda stud horse, stallion; cf OE stōd stud; Ger Stute stud mare, Gestüt stud]

steed[2] see **sted**.

steek /stēk/ (Scot) n a stitch. ◆ vt and vi (pat and pap **steek'it**) to stitch. ◆ vt to pierce; to fasten; to shut. [Partly at least OE stice stitch, puncture; perh partly confused with **stick**[2]]

steel[1] /stēl/ n iron containing a little carbon, with or without additional ingredients; a weapon of steel, a sword (literary); a rough-surfaced steel implement for sharpening knives; a piece of steel, eg for stiffening a corset; a steel engraving; extreme hardness, staying power, trustworthiness (fig); formerly, any medicine containing an iron compound; (in pl) bonds and shares of steel companies (stock exchange). ◆ adj of or like steel. ◆ vt to cover, point or edge with steel; to harden; to nerve; to make obdurate. [OE stȳle; Ger Stahl]
■ **steeled** adj made of, covered, protected, provided or edged with, steel; hardened; nerved. **steel'iness** n. **steel'ing** n. **steel'y** adj of or like steel.
❑ **steel band** n a West Indian band, using steel drums, etc. **steel'-blue** n and adj grey-blue like a reflection from steel. **steel'-clad** adj clad in armour. **steel collar** (or **steel-collar worker**) n a term applied to a robot, used in manfacturing industry, esp in the automation of assembly lines, to carry out tasks formerly done by a worker or workers. **steel drum** n a percussion instrument usu made from the top of an oil drum, hammered out into a bowl-like shape and faceted so as to produce different notes (also called **steel pan**). **steel engraving** n the act or process of engraving on steel plates; an impression or print resulting from this. **steel erector** n a spiderman. **steel'-grey** or **steel-gray** n and adj bluish-grey like steel. **steel'head** n a silvery N Pacific rainbow trout. **steel-head'ed** adj. **steel'man** n (more often in pl **steel'men**) a worker in the steel industry. **steel pan** see **steel drum** above. **steel plate** n a plate of steel; one on which a design is engraved; a print from it. **steel-plat'ed** adj plated with steel. **steel trap** n one with steel jaws and spring. **steel'ware** n articles of steel collectively. **steel wool** n steel shavings used for cleaning and polishing. **steel'work** n work executed in steel; a framework for (part of) a building, made of steel; (in pl) a factory where steel is made. **steel'worker** n. **steel'working** n.

steel[2] see **steal**[2].

steelbow /stēl'bō/ (Scots law; hist) n stock and goods received from a landlord with obligation to return a like amount and value when the lease expires; a contract or tenure on these terms. ◆ adj relating to such an agreement. [**steel**[1], in the sense of rigidly fixed, and obs bow, from ON bú stock of cattle]

steeld see **stell**.

steeled see under **steel**[1], and **stellar**.

steelyard /stēl'yärd/ n a weighing-machine consisting of a lever with a short arm for the thing weighed and a long graduated arm on which a single weight moves. [Prob **steel**[1] and **yard**[1], but suggested or fixed in use by the *Steelyard* or *Stålhof* (LGer; properly, sample yard, mistranslated steel yard), the Hanse headquarters in London]

steem /stēm/ (*archaic*) vt same as **esteem**; also same as **steam**.

steen[1], **stean** or **stein** /stēn/ vt to line (a well or other excavation) with stone. ◆ n such a lining. [OE *stǣnan*]
■ **steen'ing**, **stean'ing** or **stein'ing** n such a lining or the process of making it.

steen[2] see **stean**[1].

steenbok /stān' or stēn'bok/ n a small S African antelope, *Raphicerus campestris* (also **steinbock**). [Du from *steen* stone, and *bok* buck]

steenbras /stēn'bras/ (*S Afr*) n any of several edible estuarine S African fish. [Afrik, from Du *steen* stone, and *brasem* bream]

steenkirk /stēn'kûrk/ (*hist*) n a neckcloth or cravat with long lace ends (also **steinkirk**). [From the battle of *Steenkerke*, 3 August 1692, in which the French won a victory over the English]

steep[1] /stēp/ adj rising or descending with great inclination; precipitous; headlong; lofty (*obs*); difficult; excessive, exorbitant (*inf*); a lot to ask anyone to believe, exaggerated, incredible (*inf*). ◆ n a precipitous place. ◆ vt (*SW Eng*) to cause to stoop, slope. ◆ vi to rise or fall precipitously. [OE *stēap*; cf **stoop**[1]]
■ **steep'en** vt and vi to make or become steeper. **steep'iness** n (*obs*). **steep'ish** adj. **steep'ly** adv. **steep'ness** n. **steep'y** adj (*poetic*) steep. ❑ **steep(e)'downe** adj (*Shakesp*) precipitous. **steep(e)'up** adj (*Shakesp*) precipitous. **steep'-to** adj (*naut*) going down precipitously into the water.

steep[2] /stēp/ vt to soak; to wet thoroughly; to saturate; to imbue. ◆ vi to undergo soaking or thorough wetting. ◆ n a soaking process; a liquid for steeping anything in; rennet. [ME *stepen*; perh connected with **stoup**[1]]
■ **steep'er** n someone who steeps; a vessel for steeping in.
■ **steeped in** imbued with; deeply familiar or involved with.

steeple /stē'pl/ n a church or other tower with or without, or including or excluding, a spire; a structure surmounted by a spire; the spire alone. [OE *stēpel*, *stȳpel*, *stīpel*, from root of **steep**[1]]
■ **steep'led** adj having a steeple or steeples or the appearance of steeples. **steep'ling** adj rising on a high trajectory.
❑ **steep'lebush** n the spiraea plant, *esp* the American spiraea or hardhack. **steep'lechase** n orig an impromptu horse race with some visible church steeple as goal; a horse race across country; a horse race over a course with obstacles to be jumped; a race of this kind run on foot. ◆ vi to ride or run in a steeplechase. **steep'lechaser** n. **steep'lechasing** n. **steep'le-crown** n a high conical hat (also *adj*). **steep'le-crowned** adj. **steeple fair** n (*obs*) a market held in the grounds of a vicarage, manse, etc. **steeple hat** n a steeple-crowned hat. **steeple house** n (*obs*) a church building. **steep'lejack** n a person who repairs steeples and high chimneys.

steer[1] /stēr/ vt to move (a vehicle or ship) in the direction desired by means of a steering wheel, helm or similar device; to guide; to govern, control the course of. ◆ vi to direct a ship, vehicle, etc in its course; to move, follow a course, in response to the wheel, helm, etc. ◆ n an act of steering, as in a **bum steer** (*US*) a piece of misinformation. [OE *stēoran*, *stȳran* to steer]
■ **steer'able** adj. **steer'age** n the act or practice of steering; the effect of a rudder on the ship; a course; government; the apparatus for steering; the part (in front of the great cabin) from which a ship used to be steered; the part of a passenger ship with lowest fares (also *adj*). **steer'er** n. **steer'ing** n an act of or the process of steering; the mechanism or interconnected parts that make up a steering system. ❑ **steerage way** n (*naut*) sufficient movement of a vessel to allow the rudder to grip the water, thus enabling it to be controlled by the helm. **steering column** n in a motor vehicle, the shaft on which the steering wheel or handlebars are mounted. **steering committee** n a group who decide what measures shall be brought forward and when. **steering gear** n the mechanism that transmits motion from the steering wheel, etc so that a vehicle, aircraft, etc may be steered. **steering wheel** n the wheel by which a ship's rudder is turned, or a motor car, etc is guided. **steers'man** or (*obs*) **steers'mate** n the person who steers a vessel, a helmsman.
■ **steer clear of** to avoid.

steer[2] /stēr/ n a young ox, *esp* a castrated one from two to four years old. [OE *stēor*; Ger *Stier*]
■ **steer'ling** n a little or young steer.

steer[3] /stēr/ n, vt and vi a Scots form of **stir**[1].
■ **steer'y** n (*Walter Scott*) commotion.

steeve[1] /stēv/ n the angle of elevation, *esp* of a bowsprit, in relation to the horizontal. ◆ vt and vi to incline to the horizon. [Origin unknown]

steeve[2] or **stieve** /stēv/ (*Scot*) adj stiff, firm; sturdy. ◆ adv stiffly, firmly; sturdily. [ME *stef*; ety doubtful]
■ **steeve'ly** or **stieve'ly** adv.

steeve[3] /stēv/ (*naut*) vt to stuff, pack tightly (cargo, eg cotton) into a ship's hold. ◆ n a derrick or spar with a block on the end for packing cargo into a ship's hold. [Perh Fr *estiver*, from L *stīpāre* to stuff]
■ **steev'ing** n.

stegano- /steg-ə-nə- or -o-/ or **stego-** /steg-ə- or -o-/ combining form signifying covered, roofed, hidden, watertight. [Gr *steganos* covered, watertight, *stegein* to cover, hold water, protect, hide, *stegnoein* to make constipated, *stegos* roof]
■ **steganogram** /steg'ən-ə-gram/ or **steg'anograph** n a cryptogram. **steganographer** /-og'/ n a person who works with ciphers. **steganograph'ic** adj. **steganog'raphist** n. **steganog'raphy** n the practice of concealing digital data within some of the pixels of an image (*comput*). **steg'anopod** n (Gr *pous*, *podos* foot) any bird of the Steganopodes, the pelican order of birds, with all four toes webbed together. **steganop'odous** adj. **stegno'sis** n constriction of the pores and vessels; constipation. **stegnot'ic** adj. **stegocarp'ous** adj (Gr *karpos* fruit) with a lidded capsule. **Stegocephalia** /-se-fă'li-ə/ n pl (Gr *kephalē* head) an extinct order of amphibians (Labyrinthodon, etc) having the skull protected by bony plates. **stegocephā'lian** adj and n. **stegocephalous** /-sef'ə-las/ adj. **stegodon** or **stegodont** /steg'ə-don or -dont/ n (Gr *odons*, *odontos* tooth) an extinct mammal with ridged teeth, related to the mastodon and the elephant. **stegoph'ilist** n a person who climbs buildings for sport. **stegoph'ily** n. **steg'osaur** n (Gr *sauros* lizard) any of several ornithischian, quadrupedal, herbivorous dinosaurs of the Jurassic period, having armour of various kinds made up of bony plates. **stegosaur'ian** adj. **Stegosaur'us** n (also without *cap*) a member of the class of stegosaurs, having two lines of kite-shaped plates along the backbone.

steil see **steal**[2].

stein[1] /stēn, stīn or shtīn/ n a large beer mug, often earthenware and frequently with a hinged lid; the amount held by such a mug. [Ger]

stein[2] see **steen**[1].

Steinberger /stīn'bûr-gər or shtīn'ber-gər/ n an esteemed white Rhine wine, from *Steinberg*, near Wiesbaden.

steinbock /stīn'bok/ n the Alpine ibex; another name for **steenbok**. [Ger *Stein* stone, and *Bock* buck]

steining see **steen**[1].

steinkirk same as **steenkirk**.

stele[1] /stē'lē/ n (pl **stē'lae** /-lē/) an upright stone slab or tablet (also **stē'la**); /stē'lē or stēl/ the central cylinder (vascular bundles with pith and pericycle) in stems and roots of the higher plants (*bot*). [Gr *stēlē*, from root of *histanai* to set, stand]
■ **stē'lar** or **stē'lene** adj.

stele[2] see **steal**[2].

stelene see under **stele**[1].

stell /stel/ vt (pap **steeld** /steld/) to establish (a law) (*obs*); to fix, post (*Scot*); to delineate (*obs* or *archaic*; *Shakesp*). ◆ n (*Scot*) an enclosure (*usu* a ringwall) for sheltering sheep, etc. [OE *stellan* to fix, put]
■ **stelled** adj fixed (see also under **stellar**).

stellar /stel'ər/ adj of the stars; of the nature of, relating to, belonging to or characteristic of a star; starry; relating to a star performer or performance; excellent (*sl*). [L *stēlla* a star]
■ **stell'arator** n (*stellar* and *generator*) a twisted torus in which plasma can be confined by a magnetic field, used for producing thermonuclear (ie stellar) power by nuclear fusion. **stell'ate** adj star-shaped; with branches radiating from a point; with sides that intersect one another, giving a starlike effect, as in the pentagram. **stella'ted** adj stellate; starred. **stell'ately** adv. **stell'erid** or **stell'eridan** n (*zool*) an old name for starfish (also *adj*). **stellif'erous** adj having or bearing stars or starlike marks or forms. **stell'ified** adj. **stell'iform** adj star-shaped. **stell'ify** vt to turn into a star; to set among the stars; to set with stars (*obs*). **stell'ifying** n. **stell'ūlar** or **stell'ūlate** adj like a little star or little stars; set with little stars. ❑ **stellar evolution** n the sequence of events and changes covering the entire life cycle of a star. **stellar wind** n material radiating from the atmosphere of a very hot star.

Stellenbosch /stel'ən-bosh/ (*milit sl*) vt to relegate to a post where incompetence matters less; to supersede. [From *Stellenbosch*, Cape of Good Hope, such a dumping-ground]

stelliferous, etc see under **stellar**.

stellion /stel'yən/ or **stellio lizard** /stel'i-ō liz'ərd/ n an E Mediterranean lizard (*Agama stellio*) with starry spots. [L *stēlliō*, *-ōnis* from *stēlla* star]

---

stellionate /stel'yə-nāt/ (Scots law) n a fraud for which there is no specific name. [L stelliōnatus fradulent person, from stelliō, -ōn, from stella star]

stellular, **stellulate** see under **stellar**.

stem[1] /stem/ n the leaf-bearing axis of a plant; a stalk; anything stalklike, such as the slender vertical part of a written musical note, or of a wineglass, or the winding shaft of a watch; an upright stroke of a letter; the main line (or sometimes a branch) of a family; a race or family; the base of a word, to which inflectional suffixes are added (philology). ◆ vt to provide with a stem; to deprive of stalk or stem. ◆ vi to grow a stem; to spring, take rise. [OE stemn, stefn; Ger Stamm; perh connected with **stand**]
■ **stem'less** adj. **stem'let** n. **stemmed** adj.
❑ **stem-and-leaf' diagram** n (stats) a type of diagram representing grouped data, in which class intervals are shown on a vertical line (the **stem**) with observations given beside each class interval on a horizontal line (a **leaf**). **stem cell** n (biol) a generalized parent cell that gives rise to cells that specialize. **stem cup** n a Chinese porcelain goblet first produced in the Ming Dynasty, having a roomy bowl mounted on a stem that broadens to form the base. **stem form** n ancestral form. **stem ginger** n the underground stem of the ginger plant. **stem stitch** n an overlapping stitch used in embroidery. **stem'ware** n glasses and other stemmed vessels. **stem'winder** n (US) a keyless watch.

stem[2] /stem/ n a curved timber at the prow of a ship; the forepart of a ship. ◆ vt to make slight headway or hold position against (a contrary tide or current); hence, to make way against, breast; to ram. [ON stemn, stefn; cf LGer, Du steven, ON stamn, stafn]
■ **stem'son** n a curved timber behind the apron of a wooden-hulled ship.
■ **from stem to stern** from one end of a vessel to the other; throughout.

stem[3] /stem/ vt (**stemm'ing**; **stemmed**) to stop, check; to dam; to plug or tamp (mining); to staunch; to slow down by pushing the heels apart (skiing). ◆ n (in skiing) the process of stemming, used in turning. [ON stemma, OHGer stemmen]
■ **stemm'er** n (mining) a metal bar used to tamp down a charge in a blasting hole. **stemm'ing** n.
❑ **stem turn** n (skiing) a turn performed by stemming one ski and bringing the other ski down parallel with it.

stembuck /stem'buk/ or **stembok** /-bok/ same as **steenbok**.

steme /stēm/ (archaic) vt for **steam**, ie evaporate.

stemma /stem'ə/ n (pl **stemm'ata**) a garland; a scroll; a pedigree, family tree; a diagrammatic tree drawn up (using the internal evidence of manuscripts, etc) to show the descent and relationships of the texts of a literary work; an ocellus. [Gr stemma, usu in pl stemmata]
■ **stemm'atous** adj. **stemme** /stem/ vt (Spenser) to encircle.

stempel or **stemple** /stem'pl/ n a cross-timber in a shaft, as support or step. [Cf Ger Stempel]

stemson see under **stem**[2].

sten (also **Sten**) **gun** /sten gun/ n a small lightweight submachine-gun. [Shepherd and Turpin, the designers, and Enfield, as in **Bren gun**]

sten see **stend** and **sten gun**.

stench /stench/ or /stensh/ n a stink. ◆ vt (rare) to cause to stink. [OE stenc smell (good or bad); cf **stink**; Ger Stank]
■ **stench'y** adj.
❑ **stench trap** n a device to prevent the rise of gases in drains.

stencil /sten'sl/ or /sten'sil/ n a plate perforated with a design, lettering, etc from which copies are made by applying paint, etc through it onto paper or other material; the design or lettering so produced; a piece of waxed paper, etc on which letters are cut by typewriter or stylus so that ink will pass through. ◆ vt (**sten'cilling** or US **sten'ciling**; **sten'cilled** or US **sten'ciled**) to produce (lettering or a design) from a stencil; to mark or decorate (a material) using a stencil. [OFr estinceller to spangle, from estincelle, from L scintilla a spark]
■ **sten'cilled** adj. **sten'ciller** n. **sten'cilling** n.
❑ **stencil plate** n.

stend /stend/, also **sten** /sten/ (Scot) vi to bound, stride vigorously. ◆ n a bound or great stride; a dart of pain. [Poss L extendere]

stengah /steng'ga/ n a drink of whisky and soda, a stinger. [Malay se tengah one half]

stenlock /sten'lək/ (Scot) n a coalfish; an overgrown coalfish. [Origin doubtful]

steno /sten'ō/ (N Am inf) n (pl **sten'os**) a stenographer; stenography.

steno- /sten-ō- or -ə-/ combining form denoting narrow, constricted, contracted. [Gr stenos narrow]
■ **stenocar'dia** n (Gr kardia heart) another name for the heart disease angina pectoris. **sten'ochrome** /-krōm/ n (Gr chrōma colour) a print by stenochromy. **sten'ochromy** (or /-ok'rə-mi/) n printing in several

colours at one printing. **sten'ograph** n a shorthand character or report; (**Stenograph**®) a machine for reproducing letters or characters in a shorthand system. ◆ vt to write in shorthand. **stenog'rapher** n (N Am) a shorthand typist. **stenograph'ic** /sten-ə-graf'ik/ adj. **stenograph'ically** adv. **stenog'raphist** n. **stenog'raphy** n the art, or any method, of writing very quickly; shorthand. **stenohaline** /-hā'līn or -lēn/ adj (Gr hals salt) able to tolerate only a narrow range of salinity. **stenopaeic** /-pē'ik/ adj (Gr opaios holed, opē an opening) with a narrow opening (also **stenopa'ic**). **steno'phyllous** adj (bot) having narrow leaves. **stenosed** /sti-nōst'/ adj (med) contracted as a result of disease. **steno'sis** n (pl **steno'sēs**) (med) constriction, narrowing of a tube or passage; constipation. **sten'othermal** adj able to tolerate only a narrow range of temperature. **stenotic** /sti-not'ik/ adj. **sten'otopic** adj (ecology) able to tolerate only a small degree of environmental change (also **sten'otropic**). **Sten'otype**® /sten'ə-tīp/ n a form of typewriter used for recording speech in phonetic shorthand. **sten'otyper** n. **sten'otypist** n. **sten'otypy** n.

stent[1] /stent/ n, vt and vi same as **stint**[1], with meanings shading off into those of **stent**[2].

stent[2] /stent/ (Scot) n an assessment; a valuation; a tax. ◆ vt to assess; to tax; to levy. [**extent**, or OFr estente; see also **stent**[1] and **stint**[1]]
■ **stent'or** or **stent'our** n stentmaster.
❑ **stent'master** n a person who determines the amount of tax to be paid.

stent[3] /stent/ (med) n a device used as a temporary splint inside a bodily vessel to keep it open; such a device used to support or immobilize a body part onto which skin has been grafted. ◆ vt to insert a stent into. [CT Stent (1807–85), English dentist]

stentor /sten'tər or -tör/ n a person with a loud powerful voice; a trumpet-shaped protozoan. [Stentōr, the loud-voiced Greek herald in Homer's Iliad]
■ **stentorian** /-tö'ri-ən/ adj (of a voice) loud, powerful, carrying.

stentour see under **stent**[2].

step /step/ n a pace; a movement of the leg in walking, running, or dancing; the distance so covered; a footstep, footfall; a footprint; gait; a small space; a short walk or journey; a degree of a scale; a stage upward or downward; one tread of a stair; a rung of a ladder; a doorstep; something to put the foot on in mounting or dismounting; a stairlike rise or drop in level; a stage on the way up or down; a move towards an end or in a course of proceeding; coincidence in speed and phase; a support for the end of a mast, pivot, etc; step aerobics; (in pl) walk, direction taken in walking; (in pl) a stepladder (often a **pair of steps**); (in pl) a flight of stairs. ◆ vi (**stepp'ing**; **stepped** or (archaic) **stept**) to advance, retire, mount, or descend by taking a step or steps; to pace; to walk; to walk slowly or gravely; to walk a short distance. ◆ vt to perform by stepping; to measure by pacing; to arrange or organize in a steplike formation or arrangement, stagger; to set (foot) (old US); to fix (a mast, etc). [OE (Mercian) steppe (WSax stæpe); Du step, Ger Stapfe]
■ **stepp'er** n. **step'wise** adv in the manner of steps.
❑ **step aerobics** n sing an aerobics exercise based on stepping on and off a block of adjustable height, usu in time to music. **step change** n a fundamental change. **step'-cut** adj (of diamonds and other stones) cut in steplike facets. **step dance** n a dance involving an effective display of steps by an individual dancer. **step'dancer** n. **step'dancing** n. **step'-down** n a decrease in rate, quantity, output, etc. ◆ adj reducing voltage; decreasing by stages. **step fault** n (geol) one of a series of parallel faults throwing in the same direction. **step function** n (maths) a function which makes an instant change in value from one constant value to another with an infinite number of harmonics present. **step'-in** n a garment that is put on by being stepped into, esp one that needs no fastening (also adj). **step'ladder** n a ladder with flat treads and a hinged prop. **stepped-index fibre** n (telecom) an optical fibre in which there is an abrupt transition from the higher refractive index of the information-bearing core to the lower refractive index of the cladding (cf **graded-index fibre**). **stepp'ing-stone** n a large stone in a shallow stream, etc stepped on to cross the stream, etc; a means to gradual progress (fig). **step rocket** n one made in sections operating successively and then discarded. **step stone** n a door step. **step'-up** n an increase in rate, quantity, output, etc. ◆ adj increasing or changing by steps; raising voltage.
■ **break step** to change the sequence of right and left foot, so as to get out of step. **in step** with simultaneous putting forward of the right (or left) feet in marching, etc (with others); in conformity or agreement (with others). **keep step** to continue in step. **out of step** not in step; not in conformity, at odds (with others). **step by step** gradually, little by little. **step down** to withdraw, retire, resign, from a position of authority, etc; to decrease the voltage of; to reduce the rate of. **step in** or **step into** to enter easily or unexpectedly; to intervene (in). **step on** to put or press the foot down on; to crush or subdue. **step on it** (sl; see also under **gas** and **juice**) to hurry. **step out** to go out a little way; to increase the length of the step and so the speed; to have a busy social

life. **step out of line** to depart from the usual, or accepted, course of action. **step short** to shorten the length of one's step. **step up** to come forward; to build up into steps; to raise by a step or steps; to increase the voltage of; to increase the rate or level of. **take steps** to take action. **watch one's step** to go carefully, *esp* with a view to not giving offence or cause for complaint.

step- /*step-*/ *pfx* indicating relationship by a second or subsequent marriage or mating. [OE *stēop-* (as in *stēopmōdor*), orig meaning orphan; Ger *stief-*]
■ **step'bairn** *n* (*Scot*) stepchild. **step'brother** or **-sister** *n* the son or daughter of a stepfather or stepmother. **step'child, -daughter** or **-son** *n* a wife's or husband's but not one's own child, daughter or son. **step'dame** *n* (*archaic*) a stepmother. **step'father** *n* a mother's husband not one's own father. **step'mother** *n* a father's wife not one's own mother; a bird that hatches another's eggs. **step'motherly** *adj*. **step'-parent** *n*. **step'-parenting** *n*.

stephane /*stef'ə-nē*/ *n* an ancient Greek headdress like a diadem. [Gr *stephanē*, from *stephein* to encircle]

stephanite /*stef'ə-nīt*/ *n* a brittle silver ore, composed of silver, sulphur, and antimony. [Archduke *Stephan* (1817–67), Austrian mining director]

stephanotis /*stef-ə-nō'tis*/ *n* any asclepiad plant of the genus *Stephanotis*, of Madagascar, etc, cultivated for their waxy, scented flowers. [Gr *stephanōtis* fit for a wreath, from *stephanos* a crown, wreath]

stepney /*step'ni*/ (*old sl*) *n* a spare wheel (often *fig*); a mistress, *esp* that of a white slaver. [Said to be from the name of a street where the wheels were made]

steppe /*step*/ *n* a dry, grassy, generally treeless, uncultivated and sometimes salt plain, as in central Europe and in Asia. [Russ *step'*]

stept see **step**.

ster. *abbrev* : sterling.

-ster /*-stər*/ *sfx* used to denote a person with a particular characteristic, as in *youngster*, or activity, as in *mobster*, *prankster*, etc. [OE sfx *-estre*]

steradian /*stə-* or *sti-rā'di-ən*/ *n* the derived SI unit of solid angle (symbol **sr**), defined as the angle subtended at the centre of a sphere by an area on its surface numerically equal to the square of the radius. [Gr *stereos* solid, and **radian**]

stercoraceous /*stûr-kə-rā'shəs*/ (*esp med*) *adj* of, relating to, like or of the nature of faeces. [L *stercus, -oris* dung]
■ **sterc'oral** *adj* stercoraceous. **sterc'oranism** *n* formerly, a name for the belief that the sacramental bread is digested and evacuated from the body like other food. **sterc'oranist** *n*. **stercorā'rious** or **sterc'orary** *adj*. **sterc'orate** *vt* to evacuate the bowels.

sterculia /*star-kū'li-ə*/ *n* any tree or shrub of the genus *Sterculia* (family Sterculiaceae) related to the mallows, including kola and cacao. [L *Sterculius* god of manuring, from *stercus* dung, from the stinking flowers]
■ **sterculiā'ceous** *adj*.

stere /*stēr*/ *n* a timber measure, a cubic metre (about 35.315 cubic feet), used as *combining form* as in *decastere*, 10 steres, *decistere*, a tenth of a stere. [Fr *stère*, from Gr *stereos* solid]

stereo /*ster'i-ō* or *stē'ri-ō*/ *n* (pl **ster'eos**) stereophonic reproduction of sound; stereoscopic vision; a piece of stereophonic equipment, such as a record player, tape recorder, etc; a unit comprising such pieces; (in printing) a stereotype. ◆ *adj* stereophonic; stereoscopic.

stereo- /*ster-i-ō-* or *stē-ri-ō-*/ *combining form* meaning solid, hard, three-dimensional. [Gr *stereos* solid]
■ **stereoacū'ity** *n* the degree to which a person is aware of the separation of objects along the line of sight. **ster'eobate** *n* (root of Gr *bainein* to go, walk) a substructure, foundation. **stereobatic** /*-bat'ik*/ *adj*. **ster'eoblind** *adj* having two-dimensional rather than normal three-dimensional vision. **ster'eocard** *n* a card on which a pair of stereoscopic pictures are mounted. **stereochem'istry** *n* the study of the spatial arrangement of atoms in molecules. **ster'eochrome** *n* (Gr *chrōma* colour). **ster'eochromy** *n* mural painting fixed with waterglass. **stereoflu'oroscope** *n* a fluoroscope giving a three-dimensional view. **ster'eogram** *n* a picture or diagram suggestive of solidity; a stereographic double picture; *esp* formerly, a radiogram for reproducing stereophonic records. **ster'eograph** *n* a stereogram (in first two senses). **stereograph'ic** *adj*. **stereog'raphy** *n*. **stereoī'somer** *n* an isomer having the same chemical composition, molecular weight and structure, but differing spatial arrangement of atoms. **stereoīsomer'ic** *adj*. **stereoīsom'erism** *n* the property of substances which are stereoisomers. **ster'eome** *n* mechanical tissue in plants. **stereom'eter** *n* an instrument for measuring specific gravity or for measuring solids. **stereomet'ric** or **stereomet'rical** *adj*. **stereomet'rically** *adv*. **stereom'etry** *n*. **stereophon'ic** *adj* giving the effect of sound from different directions in three-dimensional space.

stereophon'ically *adv*. **stereoph'ony** *n* stereophonic reproduction of sound. **stereops'is** *n* (Gr *opsis* vision) binocular stereoscopic vision. **stereopt'icon** *n* a double projecting lantern, by means of which the one picture dissolves into another. **stereop'tics** *n sing* the optics of stereoscopy. **ster'eoscope** *n* an instrument by which the images of two pictures differing slightly in point of view are seen one by each eye and so give an effect of solidity and depth. **stereoscop'ic** *adj*. **stereoscop'ical** *adj*. **stereoscop'ically** *adv*. **stereos'copist** *n*. **stereos'copy** *n*. **stereoson'ic** *adj* stereophonic. **stereospecif'ic** *adj* relating to, or (of atoms) having, a fixed spatial arrangement. **stereotac'tic** or **stereotac'tical** *adj* (Gr *tassein* to arrange) of stereotaxis (*biol*); (also **stereotax'ic**) relating to the precise location of particular brain structures by three-dimensional survey (*med*). **stereotax'ia** *n* (*med*) the electrical destruction of a small area of brain tissue, using stereotactic methods, to relieve disorders such as epilepsy and Parkinsonism. **stereotax'is** *n* the reaction of an organism to the stimulus of contact with a solid body (*biol*); stereotaxia. **stereot'omy** *n* (Gr *tomē* a cut) section-cutting of solids; stone-cutting. **stereotrop'ic** *adj*. **stereot'ropism** *n* (Gr *tropos* a turn) the tendency to bend or turn in response to contact with a solid object. **ster'eotype** *n* a fixed conventionalized or stock image, or a person or thing that conforms to it; a solid metallic plate for printing, cast from a mould (made of papier-mâché or other material) of composed type; the art, method, or process of making such plates. ◆ *adj* relating to, or done with, stereotypes. ◆ *vt* to make a stereotype of; to print with stereotypes; to characterize or categorize (*esp* a person) too readily or simplistically. **ster'eotyped** *adj* fixed, unchangeable, as opinions; conventionalized, conforming to a stock image or cliché; transferred as letterpress from set-up movable type to a mould, and thence to a metal plate. **ster'eotyper** *n*. **stereotyp'ic** or **stereotyp'ical** *adj*. **ster'eotyping** *n*. **ster'eotypy** *n* the producing of stereotype plates; the repetition of senseless movements, actions or words that is characteristic of certain forms of mental illness (*med*).

steric /*ster'ik*/ *adj* relating to the spatial arrangement of atoms in a molecule. [Gr *stereos* solid, and **-ic**]

sterigma /*ste-rig'mə*/ (*bot*) *n* (pl **sterig'mata**) a stalk that bears a sporangium, basidiospore or conidium. [Gr *stērigma* support]

sterile /*ster'īl* or (US) *-il*/ *adj* unfruitful; barren; not producing, or unable to produce, offspring, fruit, seeds, or spores; (of a flower) without pistils; (of a glume) not subtending a flower; sterilized; destitute of ideas or results; lacking in creativity or inspiration. [L *sterilis* barren]
■ **ster'ilant** *n* a sterilizing agent. **steril'ity** *n* the quality of being sterile; unfruitfulness, barrenness, in regard to reproduction. **sterilization** or **-s-** /*ster-i-lī-zā'shən*/ *n*. **ster'ilize** or **-ise** *vt* to cause to be fruitless; to deprive of power of reproduction; to destroy micro-organisms in. **ster'ilizer** or **-s-** *n* one who, or that which, sterilizes; any apparatus for destroying germs.

sterlet /*stûr'lit*/ *n* a small sturgeon. [Russ *sterlyad*]

Sterling /*stûr'ling*/ *n* a submachine-gun that fires bursts or single shots, and does not jam. [From the makers' name]

sterling[1] /*stûr'ling*/ *n* British money of standard value; an old English silver penny (*obs*). ◆ *adj* of standard British money; genuine, authentic; of authority; of thoroughly good character, solidly worthy and reliable; (of silver) of standard quality, ie containing at least 92.5 per cent silver (*usu* alloyed with copper). [Prob a coin with a star, from OE *steorra* star, from some early Norman pennies being so marked]
❑ **sterling area** *n* (*hist*) a group of countries with currencies tied to sterling and freely settling transactions among themselves through London. **sterling effective rate** see under **effect**.

sterling[2] /*stûr'ling*/ same as **starling**[2].

stern[1] /*stûrn*/ *adj* severe; austere; rigorous; hard, unyielding, inflexible; unrelenting. ◆ *adv* (*archaic*) in a stern manner. [OE *styrne*]
■ **stern'ly** *adv*. **stern'ness** *n*.

stern[2] /*stûrn*/ *n* the hind part of a vessel; the rump or tail; steering-gear, helm, the steersman's place (*obs*; Shakesp). ◆ *vt* to back, to row backward. [ON *stjörn* a steering, or lost OE equivalent]
■ **stern'age** *n* (*Shakesp*) sterns collectively. **-sterned** *adj combining form* having a stern of a specified type. **stern'most** *adj* farthest astern. **stern'ward** *adj* and *adv*. **stern'wards** *adv*.
❑ **stern'board** *n* the backward motion of a ship; loss of way in tacking. **stern'-chase** *n* a chase in which one ship follows directly in the wake of another. **stern'-chaser** *n* a cannon in the stern of a ship. **stern'fast** *n* a rope or chain for making fast a ship's stern to a wharf, etc. **stern-fore'most** *adv*. **stern frame** *n* the framework of a ship's stern. **stern'port** *n* a port or opening in the stern of a ship. **stern'post** *n* the aftermost timber of a ship, supporting the rudder. **stern'sheet** *n* (*usu* in *pl*) the part of a boat between the stern and the rowers. **stern'son** *n* the hinder extremity of a ship's keelson, to which the sternpost is bolted. **stern'way** *n* the backward motion of a vessel.

---

stern-wheel'er n (US) a small vessel with one large paddlewheel at the stern. **stern'works** n pl hinder parts.

stern³ /stûrn or stern/ or **starn** /stärn/ (obs and Scot) n a star. [ON stjarna]
- **starn'ie** n (dimin).

sternite, etc see under **sternum**.

Sterno® /stûr'nō/ n a form of flammable hydrocarbon jelly used as cooking fuel. [Sternau, original US manufacturer]

sternson see under **stern²**.

sternum /stûr'nəm/ n (pl **ster'na** or **ster'nums**) the breastbone in humans, and the corresponding bone in other vertebrates; the under part of a somite in arthropods. [Latinized from Gr sternon chest]
- **ster'nal** adj. **sternal'gia** n (Gr algos pain; med) pain around the sternum, angina pectoris. **sternal'gic** adj. **ster'nebra** n (modelled on vertebra) a segment of the breastbone. **ster'nite** n the ventral plate of a segment in arthropods. **sternit'ic** adj. **ster'notribe** adj (Gr tribē a rub) pollinated by touching an insect's undersurface.

sternutation /stûr-nū-tā'shən/ n sneezing. [L sternūtāre, intensive of sternuere to sneeze]
- **sternū'tative** or **sternū'tatory** adj that causes sneezing. ◆ n (also **ster'nūtātor**) a substance that causes sneezing.

steroid /ster'oid or stē'roid/ n any of a class of compounds including the sterols, bile acids, adrenal hormones, sex hormones, vitamin D, etc; a drug containing such a compound. [**sterol** and **-oid**]
- **steroid'al** adj.
- **steroid receptors** n pl discrete regions in the cell responsible for DNA binding, steroid binding, and gene activation and repression. **steroid regulated genes** n pl sets of genes whose expression is modulated by steroid hormones, resulting in the altered physiology of the target tissue.

sterol /stē'rol or ster'ol/ n a solid higher alcohol, such as cholesterol or ergosterol. [See **cholesterol**]

stertorous /stûr'tə-rəs/ adj with a snoring sound. [L stertere to snore]
- **ster'torously** adv. **ster'torousness** n.

sterve /stûrv/ vt and vi an old form (Spenser) of **starve** (to starve, to die).

stet /stet/ vt (**stett'ing**; **stett'ed**) to restore after marking for deletion. ◆ n a written direction to do this. [L, let it stand, 3rd pers sing present subjunctive of stāre to stand; written on a proof sheet with dots under the words to be retained]

stethoscope /steth'ə-skōp/ (med) n an instrument with which to listen to the sounds produced by the heart, lungs, etc, with a hollow circular part that is applied to the body-wall, from which sound is transmitted by tubes into earpieces. [Gr stēthos chest, and skopeein to look at, examine]
- **stethoscopic** /steth-ə-skop'ik/ adj. **stethoscop'ically** adv. **stethoscopist** /-os'kə-pist/ n (rare). **stethos'copy** n.

Stetson® /stet'sn/ n a man's felt hat with a broad brim and a soft, high crown. [JB Stetson (1830–1906), US hat maker]

stevedore /stē'və-dōr or -dör/ n a person who loads and unloads shipping vessels. ◆ vt and vi to load and unload (cargo or a ship). [Sp estibador packer, from estibar to stow, from L stīpāre to press]

steven /stev'n/ n a voice (now dialect); an outcry (Spenser). [OE stefn voice]

stevengraph /stē'vn-gräf/ n a silk picture woven in colours. [T Stevens (1828–88), English weaver]

stevia /stē'vi-ə/ n a S American plant (Stevia rebaudiana) cultivated for its sweet-tasting leaves; an extract of this plant used to sweeten foods. [Pedro Jaime Esteve (1500–56), Spanish botanist]

stew¹ /stū/ n a dish of food, esp meat with vegetables, cooked in water or a stock; a troublesome situation (inf); a state of mental agitation (inf); an overheated or sweaty state (inf); a hot bath (old); a room for hot-air baths (old); a boiling pot (Spenser and Shakesp); (usu in pl) a brothel, or prostitutes' quarter; a prostitute (obs); someone who studies hard, esp unintelligently (old sl). ◆ vt to simmer or boil slowly with some moisture; to over-infuse (eg tea); to keep in a swelter or narrow confinement; to bathe in sweat; to bathe in hot air or water. ◆ vi to swelter, esp in a confined space; to be cooked by stewing; to be in a state of worry or agitation (inf); to study hard (old sl). [OFr estuve (Fr étuve) stove; prob connected with **stove¹**]
- **stewed** adj cooked by stewing; (of tea) over-infused; drunk (inf). **stew'er** n. **stew'ing** n and adj. **stew'y** adj like a stew; sweltering.
- **stew'-can** n (naval sl) a destroyer. **stew'pan** or **stew'pot** n a pan or pot used for stewing.
- **in a stew** in a state of worry, agitation. **stew in one's own juice** to be left to reap the consequences of one's own actions.

stew² /stū/ n a fish pond; a fish tank; an artificial oyster bed. [OFr estui (Fr étui)]
- **stew'pond** n.

steward /stū'ərd/ n a person who manages the domestic concerns of a family or institution; one who superintends another's affairs, esp an estate or farm; the person who oversees catering arrangements and general passenger comfort on a ship, aircraft, etc; a male member of the team responsible for these; a college caterer; someone who helps in arrangements, marshalling, etc at races, a dance, a wedding, an entertainment; an overseer; a foreman; the treasurer of a congregation, guild, society, etc; a shop steward. ◆ vt to serve as a steward of. [OE stig-weard, from stig hall ('sty'), and weard ward, keeper]
- **stew'ardess** n a female steward (esp on a ship, aircraft, etc). **stew'ardship** or **stew'ardry** n the office of a steward; management; the individual's function in the practical work of the Christian church involving obligation to give a share of his or her time and goods to others. **stew'artry** n (Scot) a stewardship, or the extent of a stewardship, applied nominally to the county of Kirkcudbright (now part of Dumfries and Galloway).
- **stewards' enquiry** n (horse-racing) an examination of the evidence relating to an allegation of contravention of the rules of racing, carried out by the stewards after a race, the result of which is signalled by the hoisting of flags on the racecourse.
- **Lord High Steward** one of the great officers of state, and anciently the first officer of the crown in England.

stey /stī/ (Scot) adj steep. [Cf **stile¹**, **stirrup**]

STFC abbrev : Science and Technology Facilities Council.

stg abbrev : sterling.

Sth abbrev : South.

sthenic /sthen'ik/ adj strong, robust; morbidly active (med). [Gr sthenos strength]

STI abbrev : sexually transmitted infection.

stiacciato /sti-ə-chi-ä'to/ (sculpt) n very low relief, as on coins. [Ital]

stibble /stib'l/ n a Scots form of **stubble**.
- **stibb'ler** n a horse turned out to feed on stubble; a person who cuts the handfuls left by the reaper; a probationer (Walter Scott).

stibium /stib'i-əm/ n antimony. [L, from Gr stibi, stimmi, from Egyp stm (Coptic stēm)]
- **stib'ial** adj. **stib'ialism** n antimony poisoning. **stib'ine** /-ēn or -īn/ n antimony hydride, a poisonous gas. **stib'nite** n native antimony trisulphide.

sticcado /sti-kä'dō/ or **sticcato** /-tō/ n (pl **sticca'dos, sticca'does, sticca'tos** or **sticca'toes**) a kind of xylophone. [Perh Ital steccato palisade]

stich /stik/ n a line of verse, or section of prose of comparable length. [Gr stichos a row, from steichein to march]
- **stichar'ion** n a Greek vestment like the Western alb. **stichē'ron** n a short hymn. **stich'ic** adj of or relating to stichs. **stichid'ium** (pl **stichid'ia**) n (bot) a branch producing tetraspores, in red seaweeds. **stichol'ogy** n metrical theory. **stichomet'ric** or **stichomet'rical** adj. **stichomet'rically** adv. **stichom'etry** n (prosody) measurement by lines; division into lines (often of a prose text into lines that mimic verse, units of meaning with a regular rhythm); a statement of such measurements. **stichomythia** /-mith'i-ə/ n (Gr stichomythiā) dialogue in alternate lines. **stichomyth'ic** adj. **stich'os** n (pl **stich'oi**) a stichometric line of a manuscript, etc; a verse or versicle (Gr church). **-stichous** combining form signifying having a certain number of lines or rows, eg distichous.

stick¹ /stik/ n a rod of wood, esp for walking with or for beating; a twig; anything shaped like a rod of wood; a timber tree or trunk; a piece of firewood; a tally; an instrument for beating a percussion instrument; an instrument for playing hockey or another game; a bow for a fiddle, or the wooden part of it; a person of stiff manner; a person who lacks enterprise; a person of a specified character; a rod; any oblong or cylindrical piece; a control rod of an aeroplane; a group of bombs, or of paratroops, released at one time from an aeroplane; a piece of furniture, esp one of few (usu in pl); a ray of a fan; a support for a candle; (in pl) hurdles in steeplechasing; a printer's composing stick; a stickful; blame, criticism, punishment (inf). ◆ adj in the form of a stick; made of sticks. ◆ vt (pat and pap **sticked**) to support (a plant) with sticks; to arrange in a composing stick (printing). [OE sticca; ON stika]
- **stick'ful** n (printing) as much as a composing stick holds.
- **stick force** n (aeronautics) the force exerted on the control column by the pilot when applying aileron or elevator control. **stick'handle** vi to control the puck or ball in a game played with a stick. **stick'handling** n. **stick insect** n a twiglike phasmid insect. **stick'leader** n the leader of a stick of paratroops. **stick shift** n (N Am) a hand-operated gear mechanism in a motor vehicle. **stick'work** n skill in using one's stick in any game played with one.
- **beat to sticks** to defeat and surpass utterly. **carrot and stick** see under **carrot**. **give someone stick** (inf) to subject someone to censure or abuse. **in a cleft stick** in a dilemma. **the big stick** force, coercion.

the right (or **wrong**) **end of the stick** a true (or mistaken) understanding of the situation. **the sticks** (*inf*) rural areas, the backwoods. **up sticks** (*inf*) to move, go and live somewhere else, make off. **up the stick** (*sl*) pregnant.

stick² /stik/ *vt* (pat **stuck**, *Scot* **stack**; *pap* **stuck**, *Scot* **stick'it**) to pierce, transfix; to stab; to spear; to thrust; to fasten by piercing; to insert; to set in position; to set or cover with things fastened on; to cause to adhere, fix with an adhesive; to endure (*esp* with *it*) (*inf*); to function successfully (*inf*); to bring to a standstill or nonplus; to leave someone (with) (something unpleasant) (*inf*); (*usu passive*) to confine; (*esp* in *imperative*) used to dismiss something with disgust, scorn, etc (*vulgar sl*). ◆ *vi* to be fixed by insertion; to jut, protrude; to adhere; (of a charge or accusation) to be accepted as valid; to become or remain fixed; to remain; to be detained by an impediment; to jam; to fail to proceed or advance; to scruple; to hold fast, keep resolutely (with *to*). ◆ *n* adhesiveness; a hitch; a stoppage (*obs*); a difficulty (*archaic*). [OE *stician* ; cf **stick¹**, **stitch**]

■ **stickabil'ity** *n* (*inf*; *facetious*) the ability to stick at something, persistence, perseverance. **stick'er** *n* a gummed label or poster; a person who kills pigs, etc; a person who or thing that sticks; a piercing weapon (*inf*); a person or thing difficult to get rid of; someone who is constant or persistent; a poser; a piano jack; an upright rod that transmits motion from an organ key. ◆ *vt* to apply stickers (gummed labels) to. **stick'ily** *adv*. **stick'iness** *n*. **stick'ing** *n* and *adj*. **stick'y** *adj* adhesive; tenacious; gluey; muggy; difficult (*inf*); unpleasant (*inf*); (of a website) tending to attract visitors and retain their attention (*inf*). ◆ *vt* to make sticky. ◆ *n* (*pl* **stick'ies**) an adhesive label or note.
□ **stick'ing-plaster** *n* an adhesive plaster for covering wounds. **stick'ing-point** or **-place** *n* the point beyond which a thing cannot proceed. **stick'-in-the-mud** *n* an old fogey (also *adj*). **stickit minister** *n* (*Scot*) a licentiate who never gets a pastoral charge. **stick'jaw** *n* a stodgy pudding or sweetmeat. **stick pin** *n* (*US*) a tie-pin. **stick'seed** *n* a plant of the borage family with barbed seeds. **stick'-up** *n* a hold-up; a stand-up collar. **stick'weed** *n* any plant with clinging seeds, *esp* ragweed. **stick'ybeak** *n* (*Aust* and *NZ inf*) a Nosey Parker. ◆ *vi* to pry. **sticky end** *n* an unpleasant end, disaster. **sticky ends** *n pl* single-stranded ends of DNA that has been cut with a restriction endonuclease, able to pair with complementary ends on, and thus joining, other fragments. **stick'y-fing'ered** *adj* (*inf*) prone to pilfering. **sticky wicket** *n* a difficult situation to cope with. **sticky willie** *n* (*Scot*) cleavers (qv under **cleave²**). **stuck-up'** *adj* self-importantly aloof.

■ **get stuck in** (or **into**) (*inf*) to deal with, consume, attack in a vigorous, aggressive, eager, etc manner. **stick around** (*inf*) to remain or linger. **stick at** to hesitate or scruple at (often with *nothing*); to persist at. **stick by** to be firm in supporting, adhere closely to. **stick 'em up!** hold up your hands (or be shot)! **stick in** (*Scot*) to persevere assiduously; also (of a dressing, etc) to adhere to a wound. **stick in one's throat** or **craw** to be difficult, or against one's conscience, for one to countenance. **stick it to** to overcharge systematically; to gain a victory over (someone). **stick one's neck out** see under **neck**. **stick or snee** see **snickersnee**. **stick out** to project; to be obvious; to continue to resist. **stick out for** to insist upon. **stick to** to persevere in holding to. **stick together** to be allies; to support each other. **stick to one's guns** see under **gun**. **stick up** to stand up; to rob at gunpoint, waylay and plunder (*esp US*; **stick'-up** *n*). **stick up for** to speak or act in defence of. **stick with** to remain with; to force (a person) to cope with (something unpleasant), often in the phrase *be stuck with*. **stuck for** unable to proceed because of the lack of. **stuck on** (*inf*) enamoured of.

stickit (*Scot*) see **stick²**.

stickle¹ /stik'l/ *vi* to be scrupulous or obstinately punctilious; to regulate a contest (*obs*); to mediate (*obs*); to interpose (*obs*); to contend, stand up (with *for*). ◆ *vt* to scruple; to compose (*obs*); to stop contention between (*obs*); to contend (*obs*). [Prob ME *stightle*, from OE *stihtan* to set in order]

■ **stick'ler** *n* a punctilious and pertinacious insister or contender, *esp* for something trifling; a regulator or umpire, a mediator (*obs* except *dialect*); a second (*obs*); a backer (*obs*). **stick'ler-like** *adj* or *adv* (*Shakesp*).

stickle² /stik'l/ (*SW Eng dialect*) *adj* steep; rapid. ◆ *n* a rapid. [OE *sticol* steep]

stickleback /stik'l-bak/ *n* a small spiny-backed river-fish. [OE *sticel* sting, prick, and **back¹**]

sticky see under **stick²**.

stiction /stik'shən/ *n* the frictional force occurring when one surface is set against another. [**stick²** and **friction**]

stiddie /stid'i/ same as **stithy**.

stie an old spelling of **sty¹,³**.

stieve same as **steeve²**.

stiff /stif/ *adj* not easily bent; rigid; lacking suppleness; moved or moving with difficulty or friction; dead; approaching solidity; thick,

viscous, not fluid; dense, difficult to mould or cut; resistant; difficult; tough, tiring, arduous; pertinacious; stubborn; formidable; (of an alcoholic drink) strong; (of a breeze) blowing strongly; firm, high, or inclining to rise (in price, etc); excessive; not natural and easy; constrained; formal; keeping upright (*naut*); certain (not to run, to win, to lose; *sl*); unlucky (*esp Aust*); (used predicatively) to an extreme degree, as in *bore* or *scare someone stiff*. ◆ *adv* stiffly; stark; very, extremely (*inf*). ◆ *n* (*sl*) someone who or something that is stiff; a corpse; a good-for-nothing; a racehorse that is a notably poor bet; a customer who fails to tip; a negotiable paper; a forged paper; an illegal letter sent or received by a prisoner. ◆ *vt* (*sl*) to cheat; to rob; to fail to tip; to murder; to cause to fail, get nowhere (also *vi*). [OE *stíf* stiff; Du *stijf*, Ger *steif*]

■ **stiff'en** *vt* and *vi* to make or become stiff or stiffer. **stiff'ener** *n* a person who or thing that stiffens; a strong alcoholic drink (*inf*); a cigarette card or the like, used to stiffen a package. **stiff'ening** *n* and *adj*. **stiff'ish** *adj*. **stiff'ly** *adv*. **stiff'ness** *n* the state or quality of being stiff; in a mechanical vibrating system, the restoring force per unit of displacement (the reciprocal of **compliance**). **stiff'y** or **stiff'ie** *n* an erect penis (*vulgar sl*); someone who is physically not very fit or agile (*Scot*).
□ **stiff'-arm** *n* (*sport*) an act of fending off an opponent while keeping the arm straight and the palm unclenched. ◆ *vt* to fend off (an opponent) in this way. **stiff bit** *n* a horse's jointless bit. **stiff'-hearted** *adj* (*Bible*) obstinate, stubborn. **stiff neck** *n* a condition affecting the neck muscles, making it painful to turn the head; torticollis. **stiff'-necked** *adj* obstinate; haughty; formal and unnatural. **stiff'-necked'ness** *n*.
■ **a stiff upper lip** see under **lip**. **stiff with** (*inf*) full of, crowded with.

stifle¹ /stī'fl/ *vt* to stop the breath of by foul air or other means; to make breathing difficult for; to suffocate, smother; to choke down; to suppress; to repress; to make stifling. ◆ *vi* to suffocate. ◆ *n* a stifling atmosphere, smell, or condition. [Origin obscure]

■ **sti'fled** *adj*. **sti'fler** *n* someone who stifles; the gallows. **sti'fling** /-fling/ *n* and *adj*. **sti'flingly** *adv*.

stifle² /stī'fl/ *n* the joint of a horse, dog, etc corresponding to the human knee. [Connection with **stiff** doubtful]
□ **stifle bone** *n* the knee-cap. **sti'fle-joint** *n*.

stigma /stig'mə/ *n* (*pl* **stig'mata** (or, *esp* in religion /-mä'tə/); also (*esp bot* or in sense of *disgrace* or *reproach*) **stig'mas**) a disgrace or reproach attached to a person; a mark of infamy; any special mark; a spot; a scar; a mark on the skin indicative of a particular disease; a spot sensitive to light; the part of a carpel that receives pollen (*bot*); a spiracle; a pore; (in *pl*) the marks of Christ's wounds or marks resembling them, claimed to have been impressed on the bodies of certain holy people, notably Francis of Assisi in 1224. [Gr *stigma, -atos* tattoo-mark, brand, *stigmē* a point]

■ **Stigmā'ria** *n* the pitted underground part of a fossil tree, *esp* of the genus *Sigillaria*. **stigmā'rian** *adj* (also *n*). **stigmatic** /-mat'ik/ *adj* of, relating to, of the nature of, a stigma; marked or branded with a stigma; giving infamy or reproach; anastigmatic, or not astigmatic. ◆ *n* a person who bears the stigmata; someone who is branded; /stig'/ a deformed person (*Shakesp*). **stigmat'ical** *adj*. **stigmat'ically** *adv*. **stigmatif'erous** *adj* (*bot*) stigma-bearing. **stig'matism** *n* an impression of the stigmata; anastigmatism. **stig'matist** *n* someone impressed with the stigmata. **stigmatīzā'tion** or **-s-** *n* the act of stigmatizing; the production of stigmata or of bleeding spots on the body, as by hypnotism. **stig'matize** or **-ise** *vt* to mark with a stigma or the stigmata; to brand, denounce, describe condemnatorily (with *as*). **stigmatophil'ia** *n* excessive enthusiasm for stigmata, ie tattooing or body piercing. **stigmatoph'ilist** *n*. **stig'matose** *adj*. **stig'mē** *n* (in Greek manuscripts) a dot used as a punctuation mark.

stilb /stilb/ *n* the CGS unit of intrinsic brightness, one candela/cm². [Gr *stilbein* to shine]

■ **stilbene** /stil'bēn/ *n* a crystalline hydrocarbon, used in dye manufacture.

stilbestrol see **stilboestrol**.

stilbite /stil'bīt/ *n* a pearly zeolite. [Gr *stilbein* to shine]

stilboestrol or (*US*) **stilbestrol** /stil-bē'strəl/ *n* a synthetic oestrogen. [Gr *stilbos* glistening and **oestrus**]

stile¹ /stīl/ *n* a step, or set of steps, built into a wall or fence. [OE *stigel*; cf OE *stīgan*, Ger *steigen* to mount]

stile² /stīl/ *n* an upright member in framing or panelling. [Perh Du *stijl* pillar, doorpost]

stile³ an older spelling of **style**.

stilet see **stylet** under **style**.

stiletto /sti-let'ō/ *n* (*pl* **stilett'os**) (a shoe with) a stiletto heel; a dagger with a narrow blade; a pointed instrument for making eyelets. ◆ *vt* (**stilett'oing**; **stilett'oed**) to stab with a stiletto. [Ital, dimin of *stilo* a dagger, from L *stilus* a style]

❑ **stiletto heel** *n* a high, thin heel on a woman's shoe. **stilett'o-heeled** *adj*.

still[1] /stil/ *adj* motionless; inactive; silent; calm; quiet; not sparkling or effervescing; continual, constant (*Shakesp*). ◆ *vt* to quiet; to silence; to appease; to restrain. ◆ *vi* to become still. ◆ *adv* without motion; up to the present time or time in question; as before; yet, even (*usu* with a *compar*); even so, even then; nevertheless, for all that; inactively; quietly; always, constantly (*archaic*). ◆ *n* calm; quiet; an ordinary photograph, or one taken from a cinematographic film and used for publicity, etc purposes. [OE *stille* quiet, calm, stable; Du *stil*, Ger *still*] ■ **still'er** *n* someone who, or something which, stills or quiets, or prevents splashing over. **still'ing** *n* and *adj*. **still'ness** *n*. **still'y** *adj* (*poetic*) still; quiet; calm. ◆ *adv* /stil'li/ (*archaic*) silently; gently. ❑ **still air range** *n* the theoretical ultimate range of an aircraft without wind and with allowances only for take-off, climb to cruising altitude, descent and alighting. **still'birth** *n* the birth of an already dead child (or animal); anything born without life. **still'born** *adj* dead, or in suspended animation, when born (also *fig*). **still hunt** or **hunting** *n* (*US*) stalking. **still'-hunt** *vt* and *vi* (*US*). **still'-hunter** *n* (*US*). **still life** *n* (*pl* **still lifes**) the class of pictures representing inanimate objects; a picture of this class. **still'-life** *adj* relating to the representation of inanimate objects. **still-peer'ing** *adj* (*Shakesp*) *perh* a misprint for **still-piecing** (ie repairing) or **still-piercing**. **still'-stand** *n* a standstill (*Shakesp*); an armistice (*obs*). **still video** *adj* (*photog*) of or relating to (an image photographed by) a camera which records images on a floppy disk and enables them to be transferred direct to a computer. ■ **still and all** (*inf*) nevertheless (also (*Scot*) **still and on**. **still and anon** or **still and end** (*Shakesp*) from time to time.

still[2] /stil/ *n* an apparatus for distillation. ◆ *vt* to exude or cause to fall by drops; to distil. ◆ *vi* to fall in drops. [Aphetic for **distil**] ■ **still'er** *n* a distiller. ❑ **still'-head** *n* the head of a still. **still'house** *n* (*US*) a distillery. **still'room** *n* a room, in a large house, where liquors, preserves, etc are kept, and where tea, etc is prepared for the table; a housekeeper's pantry. **still'room-maid** *n*.

stillage /stil'ij/ *n* a frame, stand, or stool for keeping things off the floor; a box-like container for transporting goods; a cask stand. [Prob Du *stellage*, *stelling*, from *stellen* to place] ■ **still'ing** or **still'ion** *n* a cask stand.

stillatory /stil'ə-tə-ri/ *n* a still; a distillery. [LL *stillātōrium*, from L *stillāre* to drip, *stilla* a drop]

stillicide /stil'i-sīd/ *n* a drip; eavesdrop; an urban servitude for allowing one's eavesdrop to fall on a neighbour's ground (otherwise forbidden; *Roman law*). [L *stillicidium*, from *stilla* drop, and *cadere* to fall]

stilling, **stillion** see under **stillage**.

Still's disease /stilz di-zēz'/ *n* a disease of children causing arthritis leading to ankylosis, possibly a type of rheumatoid arthritis. [Sir GF *Still* (1868–1941), English physician who first described it]

Stillson wrench® /stil'sən rench or rensh/ *n* an adjustable wrench whose grip is tightened by pressure on the handle. [DC *Stillson* (1830–99), US inventor]

stilly see under **still**[1].

stilpnosiderite /stilp-nō-sid'ə-rīt/ *n* limonite. [Gr *stilpnos* shining, and *sidēros* iron]

stilt /stilt/ *n* a thin wooden prop with a footrest enabling one to walk supported high above the ground; any tall support, eg for keeping a house above water level; a plough handle (now *dialect*); a very long-legged wading bird (*Himantopus candidus* or other species) related to the avocets (also **stilt'bird** or **stilt'-plover**). ◆ *vt* to raise on stilts or as if on stilts. [ME *stilte*; cf Du *stelt*, Ger *Stelze*, Swed *stylta*] ■ **stilt'ed** *adj* stiff and pompous; laboured and unnatural; elevated on stilts; (of an arch) springing from above the capital (*archit*). **stilt'edly** *adv*. **stilt'edness** *n*. **stilt'er** *n*. **stilt'iness** *n*. **stilt'ing** *n*. **stilt'ish** or **stilt'y** *adj*. ❑ **stilted arch** *n* an arch that springs from above the capital. **stilt'-walker** *n*.

Stilton® /stil'tən/ *n* a rich white, often blue-veined, cheese first sold chiefly at *Stilton* in Cambridgeshire.

stime and **stimie** or **stimy** see **styme** and **stymie**.

stimpmeter /stimp'mē-tər/ (*golf*) *n* a device that measures the speed of a putting green by propelling a golf ball down a ramp at a standard initial velocity and measuring how far it travels. [Edward *Stimpson* (died 1985), its US inventor]

stimulus /stim'ū-ləs/ *n* (*pl* **stim'ulī**) an action, influence, or agency that produces a response in a living organism; anything that rouses to action or increased action; a sting or stinging hair (*archaic*). [L *stimulus* a goad] ■ **stim'ulable** *adj* responsive to stimulus. **stim'ulancy** *n*. **stim'ulant** *adj* stimulating; increasing or exciting vital action. ◆ *n* anything that stimulates or excites; a stimulating drug; an alcoholic liquor.

stim'ulate *vt* to incite; to instigate; to excite; to inspire enthusiasm in; to produce increased action in (*physiol*). ◆ *vi* to act as a stimulant. **stim'ulating** *adj*. **stimulā'tion** *n*. **stim'ulātive** *adj* tending to stimulate. ◆ *n* that which stimulates or excites. **stim'ulātor** *n* a person who stimulates; an instrument for applying a stimulus. **stim'ulātory** *adj*.

stimy see **styme**.

sting[1] /sting/ *n* in some plants and animals a weapon (hair, modified ovipositor, tooth, etc) that pierces and injects poison; the act of inserting a sting; the pain or the wound caused; any sharp, tingling, or irritating pain or its cause (also *fig*); the point of an epigram; the pain inflicted by wounding words, etc; stinging power; pungency; a goad; an incitement; (a substantial sum of money gained through) a deception, theft, etc (*sl*); a trap for criminals set up by the police (*sl*). ◆ *vt* (pat and pap **stung**) to pierce, wound, pain, or incite with or as if with a sting; to goad or incite (with *into*); to rob, cheat, or involve in expense (*sl*). ◆ *vi* to have or use a power of stinging; to have a stinging feeling. [OE *sting* puncture, *stingan* to pierce] ■ **stinged** *adj* having a sting. **sting'er** *n* someone who or something that stings; anything stinging or pungent; a device of raised spikes thrown across the road by police to bring a speeding driver, *esp* of a stolen vehicle, to a halt; see also separate entry. **sting'ing** *n* and *adj*. **sting'ingly** *adv*. **sting'less** *adj*. **sting'y** *adj* (*inf*). ❑ **sting'bull** or **sting'fish** *n* the weever. **stinging nettle** *n* a common plant of the genus *Urtica*, with stinging hairs. **sting'ray** or (*US* and *Aust*) **stingaree** /sting'gə-rē, -ə-rē or -rē'/ *n* a ray (*Trygon* or related genus) with a formidable barbed dorsal spine on its tail. ■ **sting in the tail** an unlooked-for final unpleasantness or irony. **take the sting out of** (*inf*) to soften the pain of (*lit* and *fig*).

sting[2] /sting/ (*Scot*) *n* a pole. [OE *steng*] ■ **sting and ling** with a rope slung from a pole; by force (*fig*).

stingaree see under **sting**[1].

stinger[1] /sting'ər/ *n* same as **stengah**; (*esp US*) a cocktail containing brandy and white crème de menthe. [**stengah**, infl by **sting**[1]]

stinger[2] see under **sting**[1].

stingo /sting'gō/ *n* (*pl* **stin'gos**) strong malt liquor (*obs sl*); vigour, energy, punch (*inf*; also *adj*). [**sting**[1]]

stingy[1] see under **sting**[1].

stingy[2] /stin'ji/ *adj* niggardly; bad-tempered (*dialect*). [Prob **sting**[1]] ■ **stin'gily** *adv*. **stin'giness** *n*.

stink /stingk/ *vi* (pat **stank** or **stunk**; pap **stunk**) to give out a strong, offensive smell; to be offensive, have a bad reputation, suggest or imply evil or dishonesty (*fig*). ◆ *vt* to impart a bad smell to (a room, etc; with *out*); to drive by a bad smell (with *out*, etc). ◆ *n* an offensive smell; an outraged reaction, a furore; (in *pl*) chemistry or science, a science master (*school sl*). [OE *stincan* to smell (well or bad)] ■ **stink'ard** *n* someone who stinks, an offensive person (*rare* or *obs*); a name given to various foul-smelling animals, eg the **stinking badger** of Java. **stink'er** *n* a person or thing that stinks; a disagreeable person or thing (*inf*); a very difficult question, task, etc; a stinkard; a fulmar or petrel that ejects a foul-smelling oil from its stomach (*naut sl*). **stink'ing** *adj* offensive or evil in smell, reputation, etc. ◆ *adv* (*inf*) very, extremely, *esp* as in *stinking rich*, *stinking drunk*. **stink'ingly** *adv*. **stink'y** *adj* having an offensive smell; highly unpleasant. ❑ **stink ball** or **stink pot** *n* (*hist*) a ball or jar filled with a stinking, combustible mixture, used to create a suffocating smoke when boarding an enemy's vessel. **stink'bird** see **hoatzin**. **stink bomb** *n* a *usu* small bomblike container which releases foul-smelling gases when exploded. **stink bug** *n* a shield bug that releases foul-smelling secretions. **stink'horn** *n* a stinking gasteromycete fungus, *Phallus impudicus*. **stinking camomile** *n* mayweed. **stink'pot** *n* a foul-smelling person or thing; an unpleasant person (*derog*); a N American turtle that releases foul-smelling secretions. **stink pot** see **stink ball** above. **stink'stone** *n* a limestone that gives a fetid urinous smell when rubbed. **stink'weed** *n* any foul-smelling plant. **stink'wood** *n* the foul-smelling wood of various trees, *esp* the lauraceous *Ocotea bullata* of S Africa. ■ **like stink** (*inf*) very much, to a great extent; intensely. **raise a stink** to complain; to cause trouble, *esp* disagreeable publicity. **stink out** (*inf*) to drive out by a bad smell; to fill (a room, etc) with a bad smell.

stinko /sting'kō/ (*sl*) *adj* drunk.

stint[1] /stint/ *vt* to keep short; to be niggardly with or towards; to allot stingily; to spare; to serve successfully, get with foal, lamb, etc; to limit; to check (*archaic*); to restrain (*archaic* or *dialect*); to stop (*obs*); to allot, apportion (*archaic*); to set as a task or as a day's work (*archaic*); to restrict (*obs*). ◆ *vi* to be sparing or mean (with *on*); to go short (*dialect*); to cease, stop (*obs*). ◆ *n* cessation of action, motion, etc (*obs*); a limit (*obs*); restraint, restriction; a proportion allotted, fixed amount; an allowance; a set task; a (conventional) day's work. [OE *styntan* to dull, from *stunt* stupid; cf **stent**[1], **stunt**[1]]

■ **stint'ed** adj. **stint'edly** adv. **stint'edness** n. **stint'er** n. **stint'ing** n and adj. **stint'ingly** adv. **stint'less** adj. **stint'y** adj.

stint² /stint/ n any small wading bird of the genus *Calidris* (eg the little stint, *C. minuta*, and Temminck's stint, *C. temminckii*) that *usu* winters in Africa and is a passage migrant in Britain. [Origin obscure]

stinty see under **stint¹**.

stipa /stī'pə/ n any grass of the feather-grass genus *Stipa*. [L *stipa* tow]

stipe /stīp/ n a stalk, *esp* of the fruiting body of a fungus, a fern-leaf, a pappus, or an ovary (also **stipes** /stī'pēz or stē'pes/ (pl **stipites** /stip'i-tēz or stē'pi-tās/)). [L *stīpes*, *-itis* post, stock]

■ **stipitate** /stip'/ adj.

stipel /stī'pl/ (bot) n a stipule-like appendage at the base of a leaflet. [Dimin from **stipule**]

■ **stipellate** /stī'pəl-āt or stip-el'āt/ adj having stipels.

stipend /stī'pend or -pənd/ n a soldier's pay; (also (Scot) /stēp'ənd/) a salary, *esp* a Scottish parish minister's; a periodical allowance. [L *stīpendium*, from *stips* payment, dole, *pendere* to weigh]

■ **stipendiary** /sti-pen'di-ə-ri or stī-/ adj receiving a stipend. ◆ n a person who performs services for a salary, *esp* a paid magistrate. **stipen'diate** vt to provide with a salary.

stipes, stipitate, stipites see **stipe**.

stipple /stip'l/ vt to engrave, paint, draw, etc in dots or separate touches. ◆ n painting, engraving, etc in this way; the effect so produced; a brush for stippling. [Du *stippelen*, dimin of *stippen* to dot]

■ **stipp'led** adj. **stipp'ler** n. **stipp'ling** n.

stipulaceous, stipular, etc see under **stipule**.

stipulate /stip'ū-lāt/ vt to set or require as a condition of an agreement; to specify, insist on, as an essential part of an agreement (with *for*); to guarantee (*rare*). ◆ vi to make stipulations; to become surety (*obs*). [L *stipulārī*, *-ātus*, prob from Old L *stipulus* firm, connected with *stīpāre* to press firm, but thought by some to be from *stipula* straw, from the ancient custom of breaking a straw to seal a bargain]

■ **stipulā'tion** n the act of stipulating; a contract; a condition of agreement; a requiring of such a condition. **stip'ulator** n. **stip'ulatory** /-lə-tər-i/ adj.

stipule /stip'ūl/ n a paired, *usu* leafy, appendage at a leaf base. [L *stipula* straw, stalk, dimin of *stīpes*; new meaning assigned by Linnaeus]

■ **stipulā'ceous** adj. **stip'ular** or **stip'ulary** adj. **stip'ulāte** or **stip'uled** adj.

stir¹ /stûr/ (Scot **steer** /stēr/, Spenser **stire** or **styre** /stīr/) vt (**stirr'ing; stirred**) to set in motion; to move around; to move (something, *esp* in liquid or powder form) around by continuous or repeated, *usu* circular, movements of a spoon or other implement through it, eg in order to mix its constituents; to disturb; to rouse; to move to activity; to excite; to move, raise, moot (eg a question) (now *rare*). ◆ vi to make a movement; to begin to move; to be able to be stirred; to go about; to be active or excited; (*esp* in *prp*) to be out of bed; to go forth; to cause trouble or dissension (*inf*). ◆ n movement; slight movement; activity; commotion; sensation; an act of stirring. [OE *styrian*; Du *storen*, Ger *stören* to disturb]

■ **stir'less** adj without stir. **stirred** adj. **stirr'er** n a person who or thing that stirs; a person that stirs up trouble, a troublemaker (*inf*). **stirr'ing** n and adj. **stirr'ingly** adv.

❑ **stir'about** n (Anglo-Irish) porridge; a bustle or commotion; a bustling person. ◆ adj busy, active. **stir'-fry** vt and vi to fry (food) rapidly while stirring it in the pan. ◆ n a dish so prepared.

■ **stir abroad, forth** or **out** (old or dialect) to go out of doors. **stir up** to excite; to incite; to arouse; to mix by stirring.

stir² /stûr/, **stirrah** or **stirra** /stir'ə/ (Scot) n apparently corruptions of **sir** and **sirrah**, applied to both sexes.

stir³ /stûr/ (sl) n prison. [Perh OE *stēor*, *stȳr* punishment, or various Romany words, eg *staraben*, *steripen*]

❑ **stir-crā'zy** adj (N Am) unbalanced from confinement, *esp* in prison.

stire /stīr/ an archaic form of **steer¹** and **stir¹**.

stirk /stûrk/ n a yearling or young ox or cow. [OE *stirc* calf]

Stirling engine /stûr'ling en'jin/ n a closed-cycle external-combustion engine using heated air (devised by Scottish minister Dr Robert Stirling, 1790–1878), or a more sophisticated 20c version using, eg, helium under pressure.

stirps /stûrps/, also **stirp** /stûrp/ n (pl **stirpes** /stûr'pēz or stir'pās/ or **stirps**) (a person and his or her descendants forming) a branch of a family (*esp law*); pedigree; a category in biological classification, eg (*zool*) a superfamily, family or subfamily, or (*bot*) a rootstock that retains characteristics in cultivation. [L *stirps, stirpis*]

■ **stirp'iculture** n selective breeding.

stirrah, stirra see **stir²**.

stirre see **sperre**.

stirrup /stir'əp/ n a support for a rider's foot, *usu* consisting of a metal hoop suspended on a strap from the saddle; a footrest, clamp or support of more or less similar shape or function; the stirrup bone; a short rope hanging from a yard on a square-rigged sailing vessel, having a thimble in its lower end for supporting a foot-rope (*naut*). [OE *stigrāp*, from *stīgan* to mount, and *rāp* rope]

❑ **stirrup bone** n the stapes. **stirrup cup** n a drink taken on horseback on departing, or arriving (also **stirrup dram**); a container in the form of a fox's head from which a stirrup cup was drunk (*rare*). **stirrup iron** n the metal part of a stirrup, *usu* regarded as the stirrup itself. **stirrup leather** or **strap** n the strap of a stirrup. **stirrup pants** n pl ski pants. **stirrup pump** n a portable water pump held in position by the foot in stirrup-like bracket, for fighting small fires.

stishie see **stooshie**.

stishovite /stish'ə-vīt/ n a high-density form of silica formed at high pressure, *esp* found in meteor craters. [SM *Stishov* (born 1937), Russian mineralogist]

stitch /stich/ n a complete movement of the needle in sewing, knitting, surgery, etc; a loop or portion of thread, etc so used; a surgical suture; a mode of stitching or knitting; a fastening with thread or wire through all sections (*bookbinding*); the least scrap of clothing, sails, etc; a sharp pricking pain in the side brought on by running, etc; a ridge of land (*dialect*); a shock of corn (*dialect*). ◆ vt to join, adorn, or enclose with stitches. ◆ vi to sew. [OE *stice* prick; cf **stick²**]

■ **stitched** adj. **stitch'er** n. **stitch'ery** n. **stitch'ing** n.

❑ **stitch'craft** n the art of needlework. **stitch-up** see **stitch up** below. **stitch'work** n. **stitch'wort** n any plant of the chickweed genus *Stellaria*, *esp* the greater stitchwort (*S. holostea*), once thought good for easing stitches in the side.

■ **a stitch in time** (**saves nine**) a timely repair or corrective measure (avoids the need for more extensive repairs or measures). **drop a stitch** (in knitting) to let a stitch fall off the knitting needle. **in stitches** in pained helplessness with laughter. **stitch up** (sl) to incriminate by informing on; to swindle (**stitch'-up** n).

stithy /stidh'i/ or **stiddie** /stid'i/ (archaic or dialect) n an anvil; a smithy. ◆ vt to forge on an anvil. [ON *stethi*; Swed *städ* an anvil]

stive /stīv/ (dialect) vt and vi to enclose or be enclosed in a close hot place; to stifle, suffocate. [Cf **stew¹**]

■ **stived** (also **stived'-up**) without fresh air. **stiv'y** adj stuffy.

stiver /stī'vər/ n formerly, a Dutch coin *approx* equivalent in value to a penny; a very small coin or sum; the smallest possible amount. [Du *stuiver*]

stivy see under **stive**.

stoa /stō'ə/ n (pl **sto'as, sto'ae** or **sto'ai** /-ī/) in ancient Greece, a portico or covered colonnade; *esp* the public area, *Stoa Poikilē* (the Painted Porch), in Athens where Zeno gave his lectures. [Gr *stoā*]

stoat /stōt/ n a small carnivorous mammal, *Mustela erminea*, of the weasel family, distinguishable by its black-tipped tail, and called ermine when its coat turns white in winter in colder northern regions. [ME *stote*]

stob /stob/ (Scot) n a stake, stump, or stub; an awl. [Variant of **stub**]

stobie pole /stō'bi pōl/ (Aust) n a steel and concrete pole for supporting electricity wires. [JC *Stobie* (1895–1953), Australian design engineer]

stoccado /sto-kä'dō/ or **stoccata** /-tə/ n (pl **stocca'dos** or **stocca'tas**) a straight thrust in fencing. [Ital *stoccata* thrust, stab, from *stocco* rapier, from Ger *Stock* stick]

stochastic /stə-kas'tik/ adj conjectural (*obs*); random. [Gr *stochastikos* skilful in aiming]

stocious or **stotious** /stō'shəs/ (Irish and Scot) adj drunk. [Origin uncertain; poss from **stot¹**]

stock¹ /stok/ n a fund; capital of a company, divisible into shares, or a unit of ownership of a company, consisting of a group of shares; an individual share in a company (*US*); supply, store, equipment; raw material, equipment, etc for use or in hand, as in *rolling stock, film stock* (unused film, etc); a supply of goods, material or equipment for sale; the animals kept on a farm; shares of a public debt; (in *pl*) public funds; a tally for money paid to the exchequer (*obs*); a repertoire of plays done by a stock company (see below); repute, estimation (*fig*); the undealt part of a pack of cards or set of dominoes; liquor from simmered meat, bones, etc used as a basis for soups, stews, etc; a trunk or main stem; the perennial part of a herbaceous plant; the rooted trunk that receives a graft, rootstock; a log; a post; a block; a stump; an upright beam; the wooden part of a gun; a handle; a part to which others are attached; any cruciferous garden plant of the genus *Matthiola* having heavily scented spikes of flowers (see also **Virginia stock** under **Virginia**); anything fixed and solid; an intrusive boss (*geol*); a stocking (*archaic* or *dialect*); a stiff band worn as a cravat, often fastened with a buckle at the back; (in *pl*) a device for holding a delinquent by the ankles, and often wrists; (in *pl*) a framework on which a ship is built, keel blocks; the horizontal crosspiece of certain old types of anchor set at right angles to the arms; a box or trough; a fireside ledge (*dialect*); the original progenitor; source; race; kindred; family. ◆ *vt* to store or supply with (goods, etc); to keep (goods) in stock for sale; to put in the stocks; to fit (a gun) with a stock; to supply or furnish with stock (eg a river with fish); to keep (a cow) unmilked before selling; to root up (trees, etc); to stunt the growth of (a plant or animal) (*dialect*). ◆ *vi* (of a plant) to send out new shoots; to take in or lay up a stock or supply (*usu* with *up*); (of a plant or animal) to be stunted in growth (*dialect*). ◆ *adj* concerned with stock or stocks; kept in stock; conventionally used, standard; banal, trite; used for breeding purposes; used or intended for livestock. [OE *stocc* a stick; Ger *Stock*] ■ **stock'er** *n* an animal kept while being fattened or matured for slaughter (*N Am*); a person who stocks or makes stocks. **stock'ist** *n* a person who keeps a commodity in stock. **stock'less** *adj*.

❑ **stock agent** *n* (*Aust* and *NZ*) a dealer in livestock. **stock appreciation** *n* (*econ*) business profit from increase in the value of goods held in stock. **stock'breeder** *n* a person who raises livestock. **stock'breeding** *n*. **stock'broker** *n* a stock exchange member who buys and sells stocks or shares for clients, having been officially superseded in the British Stock Exchange, on 27 October 1986, by the broker/dealer, combining the jobs of stockbroker and stockjobber (**stockbroker belt** the area outside a city, *esp* that to the south of London, in which wealthy businessmen live). **stock'broking** *n*. **stock car** *n* a specially adapted and strengthened ordinary saloon car used for a type of racing (**stock car racing**) in which cars are often damaged or destroyed in collisions; a cattle-truck (*N Am*). **stock company** *n* (*N Am*) a joint-stock company; a permanent repertory company attached to a theatre. **stock cube** *n* a cube of compressed meat, fish or vegetable extract used for making stock. **stock dove** *n* a dove (*Columba oenas*), like a small wood pigeon (so called from its habit of nesting in tree stumps or rabbit burrows, or from the erroneous supposition that it represents the ancestor of the domestic breeds). **stock exchange** *n* a place for the buying and selling of stocks and shares; an association of people transacting such business; (with *caps*) the institution in London where such business is done. **stock farm** *n* a farm specializing in the rearing of livestock. **stock'-farmer** *n* a farmer who rears livestock. **stock'-feeder** *n* a person who fattens livestock. **stock-gill'yflower** *n* an old name for the garden flower, stock. **stock'holder** *n* someone who holds stocks in the public funds, or in a company; a person who owns livestock (*Aust*). **stock'horse** *n* (*Aust*) a horse trained for working with sheep and cattle. **stock'-in-trade** *n* all the goods which a shopkeeper has for sale; standard equipment or devices necessary for a particular trade or profession; a person's basic intellectual and emotional resources (often implying inadequacy or triteness). **stock'jobber** *n* a stock exchange member who deals only with other members (in some special group of securities), this job having been abolished in the British Stock Exchange on 27 October 1986, with the introduction of the job of broker/dealer, combining the jobs of stockbroker and stockjobber; a stockbroker (*US*); an unscrupulous speculator. **stock'jobbery** *n*. **stock'jobbing** *n*. **stock'list** *n* a list of stocks and current prices regularly issued. **stock'lock** *n* a lock with wooden case. **stock'man** *n* a man in charge of livestock (*esp Aust*); a storeman (*US*). **stock market** *n* a stock exchange; stock exchange business. **stock'pile** *n* an accumulated reserve supply (also *vt*). **stock'piling** *n* accumulating reserves, eg of raw materials. **stock'pot** *n* a pot in which stock for soup is made and kept. **stock'punisht** *adj* (*Shakesp*) put in the stocks. **stock'-raising** *n* breeding of stock. **stock rider** *n* (*Aust*) a herdsman on horseback. **stock'room** *n* a storeroom; a room in a hotel for the display of commercial travellers' wares. **stock route** *n* (*Aust* and *NZ*) a right of way for travelling stock. **stock saddle** *n* a type of saddle with a high pommel and low curved seat, as *orig* used by American cowboys. **stock-still'** *adj* and *adv* utterly still (as a post or log). **stock'take** *n* an act of stocktaking (also *vi*). **stock'taking** *n* inventorying and valuation of stock (also *fig*). **stock whip** *n* a herdsman's whip with short handle and long lash. **stock'yard** *n* a large yard with pens, stables, etc, where cattle are kept for slaughter, market, etc.

■ **in** (or **out of**) **stock** available (or not available) for sale. **on the stocks** in preparation but unfinished. **put** or **take stock in** to trust to, attach importance to. **stockbrokers' Tudor** (*archit*) imitation Tudor. **stocks and stones** inanimate idols. **take stock (of)** to make an inventory of goods on hand; to make an estimate of.

stock² /stok/ (*Shakesp*) *n* a stoccado. [Ital *stocco* rapier]

stockade /sto-kād'/ *n* a barrier of stakes. ◆ *vt* to surround with a stockade for defence. [Fr *estacade*, from Sp *estacada*; cf **stake¹**]

stock and horn /stok ənd hörn/ *n* a primitive Scottish musical instrument made of a cow's horn, a sheep's thigh bone or elder pipe, with stops and a single reed (also called **stock in horn** or **stockhorn**). [OE (Northumbrian) *stocc* trumpet]

stockfish /stok'fish/ *n* unsalted dried hake, cod, etc, commonly beaten with a stick before cooking. [Prob Du *stokvisch*]

Stockholm syndrome /stok'hō(l)m sin'drōm/ (*psychol*) *n* a mental condition sometimes experienced by hostages and kidnap victims in which positive feelings develop towards their captors which are difficult to reconcile with normal moral standards, *esp* after their release. [Named after the siege of a bank in Stockholm in 1973 in which bank robbers took hostages]

stockinet or **stockinette** /stok-i-net'/ *n* an elastic knitted fabric for undergarments, etc. [Poss orig *stocking-net*]
❑ **stockinette stitch** *n* (*US*) stocking stitch.

stocking /stok'ing/ *n* a close-fitting covering for the whole leg, *usu* made of fine knitted fabric, worn by women; a close-fitting covering for the foot and lower leg, made from knitted wool or similar fibre, as worn by men in Highland dress; distinctive colouring or feathering of an animal's leg. [**stock¹** in archaic sense of *stocking*, perh from comparison of the *stocks* to a pair of leggings]
■ **stock'inged** *adj* wearing stockings (but *usu* not shoes). **stock'inger** /-ing-ər/ *n* a maker of stockings. **stock'ingless** *adj*.
❑ **stocking cap** *n* a conical knitted hat with a hanging tapering tail. **stocking filler** *n* a small present for a Christmas stocking. **stock'ing-foot'** *n* the foot of a stocking. **stocking frame** *n* a knitting machine. **stocking mask** *n* a nylon stocking pulled over the head to distort and so disguise the features. **stocking-sole'** *n*. **stocking stitch** *n* a style of knitting in which a row of plain stitch alternates with a row of purl. **stocking stuffer** *n* (*N Am*) a stocking filler.
■ **in one's stocking-feet** or **-soles** with stockings or socks but no shoes.

stockwork /stok'wərk/ (*mining*) *n* a mass of veins, impregnations, etc of ore that can be worked as one deposit. [Anglicized from Ger *Stockwerk*]

stocky /stok'i/ *adj* sturdy, thickset. [**stock¹**, in the sense of a stout piece of wood, and sfx *-y*]
■ **stock'ily** *adv*. **stock'iness** *n*.

stodge /stoj/ *n* dense, sticky stuff; heavy, often uninteresting, food. ◆ *vt* to stuff, cram or gorge with food; to sate (*archaic*); to bog (*archaic*). ◆ *vi* (*archaic*) to trudge or plod through mud, etc; to work doggedly (with *at*). [Perh imit]
■ **stodg'er** *n* a heavy, dull, spiritless, or unenterprising person. **stodg'ily** *adv*. **stodg'iness** *n*. **stodg'y** *adj* heavy and sticky; solemnly dull.

stoechiology, stoechiometry, etc see **stoichiology**.

stoep /stoop/ (*S Afr*) *n* (also (*US*) **stoop**) a platform along the front, and sometimes the sides, of a house, an open porch; a verandah. [Du; cf **step**]

stogy, stogey or **stogie** /stō'gi/ (*US*) *n* a long, inexpensive cigar. [From Conestoga, Pennsylvania]

stoic /stō'ik/ *n* a stoical person; (with *cap*) a disciple of the philosopher Zeno (died c.261BC), who taught in the *Stoa Poikilē* (Painted Porch) at Athens. ◆ *adj* stoical; (with *cap*) relating to the Stoics, or to their philosophy. [Gr *stoa* a porch]
■ **stō'ical** *adj* indifferent to pleasure or pain; uncomplaining in suffering. **stō'ically** *adv*. **stō'icalness** *n*. **stō'icism** /-sizm/ *n* the philosophy of the Stoics; indifference to pleasure or pain; limitation of wants; austere impassivity; uncomplaining fortitude in suffering.

stoichiology, stoicheiology or **stoechiology** /stoi-ki-ī-ol'ə-ji/ *n* the branch of biology that deals with the elements comprising animal tissues. [Gr *stoicheion* an element]
■ **stoichiolog'ical, stoicheiolog'ical** or **stoechiolog'ical** *adj*. **stoichiomet'ric, stoicheiomet'ric** or **stoechiomet'ric** *adj*. **stoichiometry, stoicheiometry** or **stoechiometry** /stoi-ki-om'i-tri/ *n* the branch of chemistry that deals with the numerical proportions in which substances react.

stoit /stoit/ (*Scot*) *vi* (also **styte**) to bounce; to stumble, stagger, lurch. [Perh Du *stuiten* to bounce]
■ **stoit'er** *vi* (*Scot*) to stagger; to falter in speech.

stoke /stōk/ *vt* to feed with fuel. ◆ *vi* to act as stoker. [Du *stoker* stoker, from *stoken* to stoke]
■ **stoked** *adj* (*inf*) delighted; exhilarated. **stok'er** *n* a person who or thing which feeds a furnace with fuel.
❑ **stoke'hold** *n* a ship's furnace chamber; a stokehole. **stoke'hole** *n* the area around the mouth of a furnace; the space allotted to the stokers; a hole in a reverberatory furnace for introducing a stirring tool.
■ **stoke up** to fuel a fire or furnace (also *fig*); to have a good large meal (*inf*).

stokes /stōks/, also (*esp US*) **stoke** /stōk/ *n* (pl **stokes**) the CGS unit of kinematic viscosity, equal to 10^{-4} square metres per second. [Sir G Stokes (1819–1903), British physicist]
❑ **Stokes' law** *n* either of two laws in physics: (1) the frequency of luminescence excited by radiation is usually less than the frequency of the radiation which excites it; (2) the force needed to move a sphere

through a viscous fluid is directly proportional to the velocity of the sphere, its radius, and the viscosity of the fluid.

STOL /stol/ n a system by which aircraft land and take off over a short distance; an aircraft operating by this system. See also **VTOL**. [short *t*ake-off and *l*anding]
  ▫ **STOL'port** n an airport for such aircraft.

stole[1] /stōl/ n a narrow ecclesiastical vestment worn on the shoulders, hanging down in front; a woman's outer garment of similar form; loosely, a gown, a surplice. [OE *stole*, from L *stola* a Roman matron's long robe, from Gr *stolē* equipment, garment, from *stellein* to array]
  ■ **stoled** /stōld/ adj wearing a stole.

stole[2] /stōl/ pat and obsolete pap of **steal**[1].

stolen /stō'lən/ pap of **steal**[1].
  ■ **stol'enwise** adv (archaic) by stealth.

stolid /stol'id/ adj impassive; showing little or no interest; unemotional. [L *stolidus*]
  ■ **stolid'ity** or **stol'idness** n. **stol'idly** adv.

stollen /shtol'ən/ n rich, sweet German bread made with raisins, etc and coated with icing sugar. [Ger, a prop, strut, from the shape of the loaf]

stolon /stō'lən/ n a runner, a shoot from the base of a plant, rooting and budding at the nodes (bot); a stemlike structure or budding outgrowth from a colony (zool). [L *stolō*, *-ōnis* twig, sucker]
  ■ **stōlonif'erous** adj producing stolons.

STOLport see under **STOL**.

stoma /stō'mə/ n (pl **stō'mata**) a mouthlike opening in some animals (zool); a pore by which gases pass through the epidermis of the green parts of a plant (bot); the artificial opening of a tube that has been brought to the surface of the body, as in colostomy or after a laryngectomy (surg). [Gr *stoma*, *-atos* mouth]
  ■ **stō'mal** adj. **stomatal** /stōm'* or *stom'ə-tl*/ or **stomat'ic** adj. **stomati'tis** n inflammation of the mucous membrane of the mouth. **stomatodaeum** /-dē'əm/ n (Gr *hodaios* on the way) in embryology, the invagination that forms the anterior part of the digestive tract (also **stomod(a)e'um**). **stomatogas'tric** adj of or relating to the mouth and stomach, or the upper alimentary tract. **stomatol'ogy** n the study of the mouth. **stom'atoplasty** n plastic surgery of the mouth. **stom'atopod** n a crustacean of the order Stomatopoda, the mantis shrimps, with legs mostly near the mouth. **-stomous** combining form denoting a particular kind of mouth.
  ▫ **stoma therapist** or **stoma-care nurse** n (med) a nurse specially trained in the care of surgical stomata.

stomach /stum'ək/ n the strong muscular bag into which food passes from the gullet, and where some initial digestion takes place; the cavity in any animal for the digestion of its food; (loosely) the belly (also euphem); appetite, relish for food, inclination generally; disposition, spirit, courage, pride, spleen. ◆ vt to bear or put up with; to digest; to turn the stomach of (archaic); to resent (archaic); to find offensive (archaic). ◆ adj of the stomach. [OFr *estomac*, L *stomachus*, Gr *stomachos* throat, later stomach, from *stoma* a mouth]
  ■ **stom'achal** adj. **stom'ached** adj. **stom'acher** /-chər or -kər/ n a covering or ornament for the chest, esp one worn under the lacing of a bodice. **stom'achful** n (pl **stom'achfuls**) as much as the stomach will hold. ◆ adj (archaic) spirited; haughty; obstinate; resentful; angry. **stom'achfulness** n. **stomachic** /stəm-ak'ik/ adj of the stomach; promoting digestion. ◆ n a stomachic medicine. **stomach'ical** adj. **stom'achless** adj. **stom'achous** adj (archaic) resentful; haughty; spirited; courageous. **stom'achy** adj (archaic or dialect) haughty; easily offended; spirited; paunchy.
  ▫ **stom'achache** n. **stomach pump** n a syringe with a flexible tube for withdrawing fluids from the stomach, or injecting them into it. **stomach stapling** n the surgical practice of reducing the capacity of the stomach for food using a gastric band and staples.

stomatal, stomatodaeum, etc see under **stoma**.

stomp /stomp/ vi to stamp the feet; to dance the stomp (inf). ◆ n an early jazz composition with heavily accented rhythm; a lively dance with foot stamping (inf); an act of stamping the feet. [Variant of **stamp**]
  ■ **stom'per** n.
  ▫ **stomping ground** n a favourite meeting place, a stamping ground.

-stomy /-stəm-i/ combining form denoting a surgical operation to form a new opening into an organ, as in *jejunostomy, ileostomy*. [Gr *stoma* a mouth]

stond /stond/ n a Spenserian form of **stand**.

stone /stōn/ n a detached piece of rock, usu small; the matter of which rocks consist; a gem; a shaped piece of stone designed for a particular purpose; a mirror (Shakesp); a concretion, esp in a bodily organ or vessel such as the kidney; a diseased state characterized by formation of a concretion in the body; a testicle (sl, now rare); a hard fruit-kernel; the hard seed of any of several fruits; the colour of stone, usu a dull,

light brownish-grey; (with pl usu **stone**) a standard weight of 14lb avoirdupois (other stones have been in use, as that of 24lb for wool, 22lb for hay, 16lb for cheese, etc); a tombstone; a hailstone; a curling-stone (qv under **curl**); a printer's table for imposing (obs). ◆ adj of stone; of the colour of stone; of stoneware; of the Stone Age; (of an animal) not castrated (rare). ◆ vt to pelt with stones; to remove stones from (fruit); to lay or wall with stones; to rub or sharpen with a stone; to turn to stone (Shakesp). ◆ vi to form a stone. [OE *stān*; Ger *Stein*, Du *steen*]
  ■ **stoned** adj having or containing a stone or stones; with the stone or stones removed; very drunk, or very high on drugs (sl). **stone'less** adj. **ston'en** or **ston'ern** adj (obs or dialect) of stone. **ston'er** n a person who stones; a person who habitually takes drugs, esp cannabis (inf); used in combination to denote a person who weighs, or a horse that carries, so many stone. **ston'ily** adv. **ston'iness** n. **ston'ing** n. **ston'y** adj of or like stone; abounding with stones; hard; pitiless; obdurate; rigid; petrifying; stony-broke.
  ▫ **Stone Age** n a stage of culture before the general use of metal, divided into the Old (Palaeolithic), Middle (Mesolithic) and the New Stone Age (Neolithic). **Stone'-Age** or **stone'-age** adj (often fig). **stone axe** n an axe made of stone; a two-edged axe for cutting stone. **stone bass** /bas/ n a large marine perch (Polyprion americanus) of the Atlantic, Mediterranean and Tasman Sea, reputed to frequent wrecked ships (also called **wreck fish**). **stone'-blind** adj completely blind. **stone'boat** n (N Am) a low sled for carrying rocks or other heavy objects. **stone boiling** n a primitive method of boiling water by putting hot stones in it. **stone'borer** or **stone'-eater** n any boring mollusc. **stone bramble** n a bramble (Rubus saxatilis) of rocky places. **stone'brash** n a soil of finely broken rock. **stone'break** n another name for saxifrage. **stone'-breaker** n a person who or thing that breaks stones; a stone-crushing machine. **stone-broke** see stony-broke below. **stone canal** n a calcified vertical tube in the water-vascular system of echinoderms. **stone'cast** or **stone's'-cast** n a stone('s) throw. **stone cell** n (bot) a cell not much longer than it is broad, with thick lignified walls. **stone'chat** n a small European songbird (Saxicola torquata) of gorse heathland, with a call resembling the sound of two stones being banged together. **stone circle** n a circle of prehistoric standing stones. **stone coal** n mineral coal, as opposed to charcoal; any hard coal; anthracite. **stone-cold** adj cold as a stone (**stone-cold sober** completely free of (esp alcohol-induced) excitement or passion, utterly sober). **stone'-colour** n and adj light brownish-grey. **stone'-coloured** adj. **stone crab** see **king crab** under **king**. **stone'-crazy** or **stone'-mad** adj completely crazy or mad. **stone'crop** n any plant of the crassulaceous genus Sedum; any similar plant that grows on rocks and walls. **stone curlew** n a large ploverlike wading bird (Burhinus oedicnemus), that habitually nests on stony ground (also called **thick knee**). **stone'cutter** n a person who hews stone; a machine for dressing stone. **stone'cutting** n. **stone'-dead** adj dead as a stone, completely lifeless; (of a golf ball) so close to the hole as to make a putt a mere formality. **stone'-deaf** adj completely deaf. **stone dresser** n a person who prepares stones for building, a stonemason. **stone-eater** see stoneborer above. **stone-faced'** or **stony-faced'** adj revealing no emotion. **stone falcon** or **stone hawk** n the merlin, from its habit of using a stony outcrop as a 'plucking-post'. **stone'fish** n any poisonous tropical scorpaenid fish of the family Synanceiidae, which resembles a stone on the seabed. **stone'fly** n a plecopterous insect (Perla) whose larvae live under stones in streams. **stone fruit** n any fruit with a stone, a drupe. **stone'ground** adj (of flour) ground between millstones. **stone hammer** n a hammer for breaking stones; a hammer with a stone head. **stone'hand** n (printing) a person who sets the type in the chase. **stone'-hard** adj (Shakesp) as hard as a stone. **stone hawk** see stone falcon above. **stone'horse** n (rare) a stallion. **stone-lil'y** n a fossil crinoid. **stone loach** n a scaleless, bottom-living fish, Noemacheilus barbatulus, of European rivers, and sometimes lakes. **stone-mad** see stone-crazy above. **stone marten** n a white-breasted marten (Martes foina) of European woodland (also called **beech marten**); its highly valued fur. **stone'mason** n a mason who works with stone. **stone'masonry** n. **stone parsley** n an umbelliferous plant (Sison amomum) similar to parsley, with aromatic seeds. **stone pine** n a Mediterranean pine (Pinus pinea) with umbrella-shaped branches and edible seeds or nuts. **stone pit** n a quarry. **stone plover** n another name for the stone curlew. **stone'rag** or **stone'raw** n (OE ragu lichen) a lichen (Parmelia saxatilis) yielding a dye. **stone saw** n a toothless saw for cutting stone. **stone's-cast** see stonecast above. **stone'shot** n a stone's-throw; stones or a stone used as shot. **stone snipe** n a N American plover, Totanus melanoleucus. **stone's'-throw** n the distance a stone may be thrown, hence, a fairly short distance. **stone'-still** adv and adj (Shakesp) as still as a stone. **stonewall'** vi to hold up progress, (in parliament) by obstructing discussion, (in cricket) by batting extremely defensively. ◆ vt to delay (a bill in parliament) by stonewalling. **stonewall'er** n. **stonewall'ing** n. **stone'ware** n a coarse kind of pottery baked hard and glazed; a high-fired, vitrified, non-porous ceramic material or objects made of it. **stone'washed** adj

---

■ words derived from main entry word; ▫ compound words; ■ idioms and phrasal verbs

(of new clothes) given an old faded appearance using small pieces of pumice. **stone'work** n work in (usu dressed) stone. **stone'wort** n any plant of the Characeae (from the limy crust); stone parsley. **stony-broke'** adj (sl) penniless, or nearly so (also **ston'y**, **stone-broke'**). **stony coral** n any variety of coral that forms reefs. **stony-faced** see **stone-faced** above. **stony-heart'ed** adj hard-hearted. **ston'y-iron meteorite** n one containing both metal and stony material.

■ **leave no stone unturned** to do everything that can be done in order to secure the effect desired. **mark with a white stone** to mark as particularly fortunate. **set in stone** (as if) engraved on stone and hence fixed and unalterable. **stone me!** and **stone the crows!** (sl) expressions of astonishment.

stonen, **stonern** see under **stone**.

stong old form of **stung**.

stonied (Spenser) see **stony**[2].

stonker[1] /stong'kər/ (sl) vt to kill, destroy, overthrow, thwart. [Ety dubious]
■ **stonk** /stongk/ n (back-formation; milit sl) intense bombardment. **stonk'ered** adj drunk.

stonker[2] /stong'kər/ (sl) n an extremely big, impressive, etc one of its kind, a whopper. [Presumably **stonker**[1]]
■ **stonk'ing** adj.

stonn and **stonne** old forms of **stun**.

stony[1] see under **stone**.

stony[2] /ston'i/ (obs) vt aphetic for **astony** (see **astonish**; pap, Spenser, **ston'ied**).

stood /stŏŏd/ pat and pap of **stand**.

stooden /stŏŏd'ən/ (Scot) pap of **stand**.

stooge /stōōj/ n an actor who feeds lines to a comedian, etc and is used as the butt of the jokes; a performer speaking from the auditorium; a subordinate or drudge; a scapegoat. ◆ vi to act as a stooge. [Origin unknown]
■ **stooge around** (old) to wander about leisurely, purposelessly, or idly.

stook /stŏŏk/ n a group of sheaves, set up in the field. ◆ vt to set up in stooks. [Cf LGer stuke bundle]
■ **stook'er** n.

stookie /stŏŏk'i/ (Scot) n plaster of Paris; a plaster cast on a broken limb; a statue. [**stucco**]

stool[1] /stŏŏl/ n a seat without a back; a low support for the feet or knees; formerly, a seat used in evacuating the bowels; hence, defecation; (usu in pl) faeces; a chair, seat of authority or dignity, throne (obs); a stand; a tree or shrub cut back to ground level and allowed to produce new shoots (hortic); a stump from which sprouts shoot up; a growth of shoots; the wicket in stoolball; a piece of wood to which a bird is fastened as a decoy in hunting. ◆ vi to put forth shoots; to lure wildfowl with a stool; to evacuate the bowels (archaic). [OE stōl; Ger Stuhl; cf Ger stellen to place]
■ **stoolie** n see **stool pigeon** below.
□ **stool'ball** n an old game resembling cricket. **stool pigeon** n a decoy pigeon; a decoy; a police informer (shortened form **stool'ie**; sl).
■ **fall between two stools** to lose both possibilities by hesitating between them, or trying for both. **stool of repentance** a place, esp in Scottish churches, where delinquents, esp fornicators, were exposed.

stoop[1] /stŏŏp/ vi to bend the body forward; to lean forward; to submit; to descend from rank or dignity; to condescend; to lower oneself by unworthy behaviour; (of a bird of prey) to swoop down. ◆ vt to bend, incline, lower, or direct downward. ◆ n a bending of the body; inclination forward; descent; condescension; a swoop. [OE stūpian; ON stūpa; the vowel preserved by the following p]
■ **stooped** adj having a stoop, bent. **stoop'er** n. **stoop'ing** adj. **stoop'ingly** adv.
□ **stoop'-gallant** n (obs; also (Spenser) **stoope-gallaunt**) that which humbles gallants, orig the sweating-sickness (also adj).

stoop[2] /stŏŏp/ (US) n a raised platform, verandah, porch, or set of outside steps leading to the front door of a house. [See **stoep**]

stoop[3] see **stoup**[1].

stoop[4] or **stoup** /stŏŏp/ n a post (dialect); a prop, supporter, patron (Scot); a massive supporting pillar of coal in a mine (dialect). [ON stolpi post]
■ **stoop and roop** or **stoup and roup** (Scot) stump and rump, completely.

stoope see **stoup**[1].

stoope-gallaunt see **stoop-gallant** under **stoop**[1].

stoor[1] or **stour** /stŏŏr/, **sture** /stŭr/ or **stowre** /stowr/ (obs) adj great, formidable; stiff, harsh, austere; stubborn, obstinate, surly. [Partly ME stūr harsh (cf MLGer stūr), partly OE stōr, great]

stoor[2] /stŏŏr/ see **stour**[2].

stooshie /stōō'shi/ (Scot) n (also **stash'ie**, **stish'ie** or **stush'ie**) fuss, ado, disturbance; a frolic. [Poss from aphetic form of **ecstasy**]

stooze /stōōz/ (sl) vi to borrow money offered at zero or very low interest and invest it to make a profit. ◆ n an instance of stoozing. [From Stooz, name adopted by a contributor to a financial website who advocated this activity]
■ **stooz'er** n.

stop /stop/ vt (**stopp'ing**; **stopped**) to cause to cease; to bring to a standstill; to hinder or prevent the passage of; to prevent; to cease from, leave off, discontinue; to obstruct; to snuff, block, plug, choke, close up (often with up); to thrust, cram (obs except as Scots **stap**); to bring down, hit with a shot; to withhold; to instruct one's bank to withhold payment of (a cheque); to restrain; to limit the vibrating length of, esp by pressure of a finger (music); to punctuate; to pinch off (the tip of a growing stem) (hortic); to be struck by (a bullet, blow, etc) (inf); to adjust the aperture of, with a diaphragm (photog); to place a pause in, esp at the end of a line or couplet (prosody); to make fast by lashing (naut). ◆ vi to come to a standstill, halt; to cease; to desist; to come to an end; to stay, tarry, sojourn (inf). ◆ n an act of stopping; the state of being stopped; cessation; a halt; a pause or interruption; a halting-place; a hindrance; an obstacle; a contrivance that limits motion; a card that interrupts the run of play; a diaphragm (photog and optics); an aperture setting (photog); the stopping of an instrument or string; a fret on a guitar, etc; a fingerhole, a key for covering it, or other means of altering pitch or tone; a set of organ pipes of uniform tone quality; a knob operating a lever for bringing them into use; a mechanism on a harpsichord for bringing particular strings into play; (also **stop'-consonant**) a sound requiring complete closure of the breath passage, a mute (phonetics); a punctuation mark; a stud on a football boot (Aust); the angle between the forehead and muzzle in a dog or cat, taken as an indication of proper structure in breeding and showing. [OE stoppian found in the compound forstoppian to stop up, from L stuppa tow, from Gr styppē]
■ **stop'less** adj. **stopp'age** n an act of stopping; the state of being stopped; a stopping of work, as for a strike; obstruction; an amount stopped off pay. **stopped** adj. **stopp'er** n a person who stops; that which stops; a plug; a plug (usu glass) for a bottle; a short rope for making something fast (naut). ◆ vt to close or secure with a stopper. **stopp'ing** n the action of one who or that which stops in any sense (**double-stopping** simultaneous stopping of and playing on two strings); stuffing or filling material, esp for teeth.
□ **stop-and-search** n a police policy of random searching of people in the streets, to look for concealed weapons, etc usu during or just after a period of civil disobedience (also adj). **stop'bank** n (NZ) an embankment to prevent flooding. **stop bath** n a substance in which a photographic negative or print is immersed in order to halt the action of the developing solution. **stop'cock** n a short pipe opened and stopped by turning a key or handle; loosely, the key or handle. **stop codon** n (biol) one of three specific codons which do not code for an amino acid but cause protein synthesis to stop. **stop-frame camera** n a film camera that can be adjusted to take a reduced number of frames, used in creating the effect of pixilation (qv). **stop'gap** n a temporary expedient or substitute (also adj). **stop-go'** adj (of policy) alternately discouraging and encouraging forward movement. ◆ n a stop-go economic policy, etc. **stop hit** n (fencing) a thrust made at the moment the opponent draws breath for his or her thrust. **stop'light** n a brake light on a vehicle (N Am); a traffic light. **stop'-loss** adj (stock exchange) of or relating to an order to a stockbroker to sell shares when their value drops below a certain level, to minimize losses. **stop'-motion** adj of or relating to **stop-motion animation**, a technique in which filming is repeatedly stopped to allow very slight changes of position in the subjects being filmed, creating the illusion of movement when the film is run. **stop'-off** or **stop'off** n a stopover. **stop'-out** n (inf) a person who goes out for the evening and remains away from home until late or for the whole night. **stop'over** n a break in a journey, esp a short stay overnight in the course of a journey. **stoppage time** n (sport) additional time allowed for play to compensate for time lost in dealing with injuries and other interruptions. **stopp'ing-out** n selective use (of a protective covering against acids in etching, against light in photography) to create special effects. **stopp'ing-place** n. **stopping power** n (phys) the energy loss resulting from a particle traversing a material. **stop'-press** or **stop press** n late news inserted in a newspaper after printing has begun; a space for it. **stop'watch** n an accurate watch readily started and stopped, used in timing a race, etc.
■ **pull out all the stops** to do one's utmost, using all one's energy and efforts. **pull out a…stop** to emphasize a (specified) emotional element in a situation. **stop at nothing** see under **nothing**. **stop down** (of a camera lens) to reduce the size of the aperture. **stop off**, **stop over**, **stop in** or (N Am) **stop by** to break one's journey, pay a visit to (usu with at). **stop out** to remain away from home all night. **stop the show** see under **show**. **stop thief!** a cry for help to catch a thief.

stope[1] /stōp/ n a steplike excavation in mining. ◆ vt to excavate, or extract in this way. [Perh connected with **step**]
■ **stop'ing** n.

stope[2] see **stoup**[1].

stopple[1] /stop'l/ (rare) n a stopper; a plug. ◆ vt to stopper, plug. [**stop**]

stopple[2] /stop'l/ n a tobacco pipe stem (also (Scot) **stapp'le** or **stap'le**). [MDu stapel stem]

storable, **storage** see under **store**.

storax /stö'raks/ n the resin of any of the tropical trees or shrubs of the genus Styrax, once used in medicine; now that of Liquidambar orientalis (**liquid storax**); any of the trees or shrubs producing this resin. [L storax, from Gr styrax]

store /stōr or stör/ n a hoard; a stock laid up for future use; sufficiency or abundance (of eg necessities); keeping; a storehouse, warehouse; a shop; a co-operative shop or one with many departments or branches; an animal being fattened for the market; livestock; value, esteem; a computer memory unit, in which programs and data are stored; (in pl) supplies of provisions, ammunition, etc, for an army, ship, etc. ◆ adj and adv (archaic and dialect) in abundance. ◆ adj of a store; (of animals) bought or kept for fattening, as in store cattle, store lambs, etc; sold or purchased in a shop. ◆ vt to furnish or supply; to lay up, keep in reserve; to deposit in a repository; to give storage to; to put (data) into a computer memory. [OFr estor, estoire, from L instaurāre to provide]
■ **stor'able** adj. **stor'age** n placing, accommodation, reservation, or safekeeping, in store; reservation in the form of potential energy; the keeping of information in a computer memory unit; a charge for keeping goods in store. **stor'er** n.
❑ **storage battery** n an accumulator. **storage capacity** n the maximum amount of information that can be held in a computer store. **storage device** n any of several pieces of computer equipment, such as magnetic disks, on which data may be stored. **storage heater** n an electric heater with a large thermal capacity that accumulates and stores heat during the off-peak periods and releases it over a longer period. **store card** n a credit card issued by a shop to its customers. **store cattle** n pl cattle kept for fattening. **stored program** n (comput) a program wholly contained, and capable of being altered, in store. **store farm** n (Scot) a stock farm, a cattle farm. **store farmer** n. **store'front** n (N Am) the façade of a shop or store. **store'house** n a house for storing goods of any kind; a repository; a treasury. **store'keeper** n a man in charge of stores, eg in a warehouse; a shopkeeper (chiefly N Am). **store'keeping** n. **store'man** n a storekeeper (N Am); a person who looks after stores or a storeroom. **store'room** n a room in which stores are kept; space for storing. **store ship** n a vessel used for carrying naval stores. **store teeth** n (US) false teeth.
■ **in store** in hoard for future use, ready for supply; in reserve, awaiting, imminent (**in-store** adj within a shop or store). **set** or **lay** (**great**) **store by** to value greatly.

storey or (esp N Am) **story** /stō'ri or stö'/ n (pl **stor'eys** or **stor'ies**) all that part of a building on the same floor; a tier. [Prob same word orig as **story**[1]]
■ **stor'eyed** or **sto'ried** adj having storeys.
❑ **first**, **second**, etc **storey** n the ground, first, etc floor.

storge /stör'gē or -jē/ n natural, esp parental, affection. [Gr]

storiated see under **story**[1].

storied see under **story**[1] and **storey**.

storiette, **storiology**, etc see under **story**[1].

stork /störk/ n any large wading bird of the family Ciconiidae, with a sturdy bill and legs, eg the white stork (Ciconia ciconia), widely distributed in Europe, Asia and Africa; the bringer of babies (facetious). [OE storc; Ger Storch]
❑ **storks'bill** or **stork's bill** n any plant of the genus Erodium closely related to the geraniums, having elongated beaked fruits and small, usu saucer-shaped, pink, yellow or purplish-red flowers.

storm /störm/ n a violent disturbance of the weather with high winds and usu rain, snow, hail and/or thunder and lightning; a tempest; a wind of force 10 on the Beaufort scale, reaching speeds of 55 to 63mph (meteorol); any intense meteorological phenomenon; a heavy fall of snow, rain, hail, etc; a violent commotion or outbreak of any kind; a paroxysm; a violent, direct assault (milit). ◆ vi to be stormy; to rage; to rush violently or in attack; to upbraid angrily (often with at). ◆ vt to take or try to take by assault; to disturb by a storm. [OE storm; ON stormr; from root of **stir**[1]]
■ **storm'er** n (inf) something particularly good. **storm'ful** adj stormy. **storm'fully** adv. **storm'fulness** n. **storm'ily** adv. **storm'iness** n. **storm'ing** n and adj. **storm'less** adj. **storm'y** adj having many storms; agitated with violent winds; boisterous; violent; passionate.
❑ **storm beach** n shingle or sand thrown up by heavy seas beyond the level of normal tides. **storm'-beat'en** adj beaten by repeated

storms. **storm belt** n an area extending around the earth in which storms are frequent. **storm'bird** n a petrel. **storm'bound** adj delayed, cut off, confined to port by storms. **storm cellar** n an underground shelter affording protection against hurricanes, etc. **storm centre** n the position of lowest pressure in a cyclonic storm; any focus of controversy or strife. **storm cloud** n. **storm'cock** n the mistle-thrush. **storm collar** n a high collar on a coat, jacket, etc that may be fastened tightly around the neck. **storm cone** n a black canvas cone or cones hoisted, eg at coastguard stations, as a storm signal, the position of the cone or cones signifying the direction of the wind. **storm cuff** n an extra elasticated cuff let into the cuff opening of a jacket, etc, to give extra warmth and protection. **storm door** n an additional outer door used as protection in stormy weather. **storm drain** n a large drain for carrying away large volumes of rainwater. **storm glass** n a tube containing a solution supposed to change appearance with the weather. **storm jib** n (naut) a small, strong sail carried at the front of the mast in very bad weather. **storm lantern** n a lantern with flame protected from wind and weather. **storm petrel** or (popularly) **stormy petrel** see under **petrel**. **storm'proof** adj proof against storms or storming. **storm sail** n a storm trysail. **storm shutter** n an outside window shutter. **storm signal** n a signal hoisted in warning of the approach of a storm. **storm'-stay** n a stay on which a storm sail is set. **storm'-stayed** adj hindered from proceeding by storms. **storm surge** n an unusual, rapid rise in tide level caused by a combination of low pressure over the sea and strong onshore winds. **storm'-tossed** adj tossed about by storms; much agitated by conflicting passions. **storm trooper** n. **storm troops** n pl shock troops; a body formed in Germany by Adolf Hitler, disbanded 1934. **storm trysail** n a small strong sail replacing the mainsail in very bad weather. **storm warning** n. **storm window** n a window raised above the roof, slated above and at the sides; an additional outer casement.
■ **a storm in a teacup** a great commotion in a narrow sphere, or about a trifle. **go down a storm** (inf) to be received with great enthusiasm. **take by storm** to take by assault; to captivate totally and instantly (fig).

stornello /stör-nel'ō/ n (pl **stornell'i** /-ē/) an Italian folk verse form, usu of three lines and often beginning with an invocation of a flower. [Ital, literally, turning aside]

Storting or **Storthing** /stör'ting or stör'/ n the legislative assembly of Norway, comprising the Lagting and Odelsting. [Norw stor great, and ting (ON thing) assembly]

story[1] /stō'ri or stö'/ n a narrative of incidents in their sequence; a fictitious narrative; a tale; an anecdote; the plot of a novel or drama; a theme; an account, report, statement, allegation; a news article; a lie, fib (inf); a legend; history (obs). ◆ vt to tell or describe historically, to relate (rare); to adorn (a pot, etc) with scenes from history. ◆ vi (rare) to relate. [Anglo-Fr estorie, from L historia]
■ **sto'riated** adj decorated with elaborate ornamental designs (also **historiated**). **sto'ried** adj told or celebrated in a story; having a history; adorned with scenes from history. **storiette'** or **storyette'** n a short tale. **storiol'ogist** n. **storiol'ogy** n the scientific study of folk tales. **sto'rying** n and adj.
❑ **sto'ryboard** n (a board on which is mounted) a series of rough sketches showing the sequence of film images to be used in an advertisement, cinema film, television programme, etc. **sto'rybook** n a book of tales true or fictitious, esp one for children. ◆ adj unreal, fantastic; rather luckier or happier than in real life. **sto'ryline** n the main plot of a novel, film, television series, etc, or line along which the plot is to develop. **sto'ryteller** n a person who relates tales; a liar (inf). **sto'rytelling** n.
■ **cut a long story short** to come quickly to the point without lingering over details. **end of story** (inf) the matter or discussion is closed. **the same old story** an often-repeated event or situation. **the story goes** it is generally said.

story[2] see **storey**.

stoss /stos/ n the side of a hill, crag, or other feature facing upstream or towards the flow of a glacier. [Ger, from stossen to push, thrust]
❑ **stoss and lee** n a type of glaciated landscape in which only those parts facing the flow of the glacier show erosion.

stot[1] /stot/ (Scot) vi to bound, bounce; to stagger, walk unsteadily; to walk with a springy step. ◆ vt to cause to bounce. ◆ n a bounce, spring; a sharp blow; rhythm, beat. [Origin obscure]
■ **stott'er** n a stagger, stumble; a person or thing that is admired, a smasher.

stot[2] /stot/ (dialect) n a bullock, steer; a stupid, clumsy person. [OE stot horse]

stotin /sto-tēn' or -tin'/ n a former monetary unit of Slovenia, $\frac{1}{100}$ of a tolar. [Slovene]

stotinka /sto-ting'kə/ n (pl **stotin'ki**) a Bulgarian monetary unit, $\frac{1}{100}$ of a lev. [Bulgarian]

stotious see **stocious**.

---

stotter see under **stot**[1].

stottie or **stotty** /stot'i/ n a round bread loaf traditionally baked in NE England (also **stotty cake**). [Origin unknown]

stoun /stoon/ (Spenser) vt (pat and pap **stound**) same as **stun**.

stound[1] or **stownd** /stownd or stoond/ (archaic and Scot) n a period of time, moment; a time of trouble; a pang, an ache; an assault, stroke; a shock; a din. ◆ vi to shoot like a pang; to ache, throb. [OE stund]

stound[2] /stownd or stoond/ (Spenser) vt to stun, astound. ◆ n a stunned or astounded condition. [**stoun** or **astound**]

stoup[1] or **stoop** /stoop/ (Shakesp **stoope** or **stope** /stōp/) n a vessel for holy water; a drinking vessel (archaic); a bucket (obs). [Cf ON staup and Du stoop; OE stēap]

stoup[2] see **stoop**[4].

stour[1] see **stoor**[1].

stour[2], **stowre** or **stoor** /stowr or stoor/ n a battle, assault; tumult; turmoil; dust (Scot). [OFr estour tumult]
■ **stour'y** adj (Scot) dusty.

stoush /stowsh/ (Aust and NZ) n a fight, brawl; a war. ◆ vt and vi to fight. [Variant of Scot **stooshie**]

stout /stowt/ adj resolute; dauntless; vigorous; enduring; robust; strong; thick; fat; fierce (obs); proud, arrogant (obs); unyielding (obs or dialect); stubborn (obs). ◆ adv stoutly. ◆ n strong dark beer flavoured with malt or barley. [OFr estout bold, from Du stout; Ger stolz proud]
■ **stout'en** vt and vi to make, or grow, stout or stouter. **stout'ish** adj. **stout'ly** adv. **stout'ness** n.
◻ **stout-heart'ed** adj. **stout-heart'edly** adv. **stout-heart'edness** n.

stouth /stooth/ (obs Scot) n theft. [ON stuldr theft]
■ **stouth'rie** or **stouth'erie** n theft; stolen goods; equipment, furniture. **stouth'rief** n (old Scots law) theft with violence (later only in a dwelling-house).
■ **stouth and routh** plenty, abundance (cf **stoop and roop** under **stoop**[4]).

stovaine /stō-vā'in or stō' or -vän'/ n a local anaesthetic, a substitute for cocaine, used for spinal analgesia. [**stove**[1], Eng transl of Fr fourneau, after the name of E Fourneau (1872–1949), French pharmacologist, who first prepared it]

stove[1] /stōv/ n a closed heating or cooking apparatus; a fire-grate; a kiln or oven for various manufacturing operations; a hot-air bath (archaic); a heated room or chamber (archaic); a hothouse. ◆ vt to put, keep, heat, or dry in a stove; to stew (Scot). [OE stofa; Ger Stube]
■ **stov'ies** n pl (Scot) stewed potatoes; a thick stew of potatoes, lard, onions and sausage meat or corned beef; Irish stew. **stov'ing** n drying a specially prepared paint quickly by application of heat.
◻ **stove enamel** n a type of heatproof enamel produced by heating an enamelled article in a stove. **stove'pipe** n a metal pipe for carrying smoke and gases from a stove; a tall silk hat (in full **stovepipe hat**; inf). **stove plant** n a hothouse plant.

stove[2] /stōv/ pat and pap of **stave**, also used as the present tense.

stover /stō'vər/ (archaic) n fodder. [Aphetic for **estover**]

stovies see under **stove**[1].

stow[1] /stō/ vt to place, put, lodge; to put away; to store; to put under hatches; to put down one's throat (joc); to desist from, esp in the phrase stow it (sl); to pack; to have room for; to arrange. ◆ vi (with away) to hide as a stowaway; to be able to be stowed away when not in use. [OE stōw place]
■ **stow'age** n an act or manner of stowing; the state of being laid up; room for stowing; a place for stowing things; money paid for stowing goods; things stowed. **stow'er** n. **stow'ing** n.
◻ **stow'away** n a person who hides in a ship, etc to get a passage. ◆ adj travelling as a stowaway; that can be packed up and stored, carried, etc. **stow'down** n the process of stowing down in a ship's hold.

stow[2] /stoo/ (Scot) vt to crop. [ON stūfr stump]

stown /stown/ a Scots form of **stolen**.
■ **stown'lins** or **stow'lins** adv (Scot) by stealth.

stownd see **stound**[1].

stowre see **stoor**[1] and **stour**[2].

STP abbrev : Sanctae Theologiae Professor (L), Professor of Theology.

stp abbrev : standard temperature and pressure.

STR (genetics) abbrev : short tandem repeat, an analytical technique that enables accurate identification of genes.

str abbrev : steamer.

str. abbrev : straight; strong.

strabism /strā'bi-zm/ or **strabismus** /strə-biz'məs/ or -bis'/ n a muscular defect of the eye, preventing parallel vision; a squint. [Gr strabos and strabismos squinting; cf strephein to twist]

■ **strabis'mal**, **strabis'mic** or **strabis'mical** adj. **strabismom'eter** /strab-iz-/ or **strabom'eter** n an instrument for measuring strabismus. **strabot'omy** n (Gr tomē a cut) the surgical operation for the cure of squinting.

stracchino /strä-kē'nō/ n (pl **stracchi'ni** /-nē/) a N Italian soft cheese. [Ital, from stracco weak]

strack see **strike**.

strad see **Stradivarius**.

straddle /strad'l/ vi to part the legs wide; to sit, stand, or walk with legs far apart; to seem favourable to both sides, to be noncommittal (inf). ◆ vt to bestride; to set (the legs) far apart; to overshoot and then shoot short of, in order to get the range; to cover the area of with bombs; to adopt a noncommittal attitude or position towards. ◆ n an act of straddling; a noncommittal position; a stock transaction in which the buyer obtains the privilege of either a put or a call; a vertical timber in a mine supporting a set; the combination of a shot beyond the mark and one short of it; a style of high jump in which the legs straddle the bar while the body is parallel to it. ◆ adv astride. [Frequentative of **stride**]
■ **stradd'leback** adv with a leg on each side.
◻ **straddle carrier** n a high self-propelled vehicle which can straddle a container and lift, carry, and deposit where required. **stradd'le-legged** adj having the legs wide apart.

stradiot /strad'i-ot/ (hist) n a Venetian light horseman from Albania or Greece. [Ital stradiotto, from Gr stratiōtēs soldier]

Stradivarius /strad-i-vä'ri-əs or -vä'/ or **Stradivari** /-vä'rē/ n (also **Stradūa'rius**) a stringed instrument, usu a violin, made by Antonio Stradivari (c.1644–1737) of Cremona (inf short form **strad**).

strae /strā/ n a Scots form of **straw**[1].
◻ **strae death** n natural death in bed.

strafe or **straff** /sträf or strāf/ (orig World War I sl) vt to rake with machine-gun fire from low-flying aeroplanes; to punish; to bombard; to assail. ◆ n an attack. [Ger strafen to punish, used in the phrase Gott strafe England God punish England, a German slogan of World War I]

straggle /strag'l/ vi to wander from the main group or course; to linger behind; to be absent without leave but not long enough to be counted a deserter; to stretch dispersedly or sprawlingly; to grow irregularly and untidily. ◆ n a straggling line or group; a person who straggles, a straggler; a stray; a vagrant. [Origin obscure]
■ **strag** n (dialect) a straggler. **stragg'ler** n. **stragg'ling** n (phys) variation of energy or range of particles in a beam passed through absorbing material, resulting from random interactions (also adj). **stragg'lingly** adv. **stragg'ly** adj straggling; irregularly spread out.

straicht see **straucht**.

straight[1] /strāt/ adj uncurved; in a line without bends or curves; direct; upright; flat, horizontal; in good order; accurate; frank and honourable; respectably conducted; balanced, even, square; settled; downright; normal; with all debts and favours repaid, even; conventional in tastes, opinions, etc (inf); heterosexual (inf); in sequence (poker); (of games, sets won) in succession (tennis); (of a theatrical part) not comic; (of a drink, esp alcohol) undiluted, neat; uninterrupted; consistent; not under the influence of, or not in the habit of taking, drugs or alcohol (sl). ◆ n a straight condition; good behaviour; a straight line, part, course, flight, esp the last part of a racecourse; a sequence of five cards, irrespective of suit, or the hand containing it (poker); a conventional person (inf); a person who does not take drugs (sl); a heterosexual person (inf). ◆ adv in a straight line; directly; all the way; immediately; upright; outspokenly; honestly. [OE streht, pap of streccan; see **stretch**]
■ **straight'en** vt and vi to make or become straight (see also **straighten out** below). **straight'ener** n something that straightens; a bribe (criminal sl). **straight'forth** adv directly forward; straight away, immediately. **straight'ish** adj. **straight'ly** adv in a straight line or manner; directly. **straight'ness** n. **straight'way** or **straight'ways** adv (archaic) directly; immediately; without loss of time.
◻ **straight angle** n a right angle (obs); an angle of 180°. **straight'-arm** adj (of a rugby tackle) with the arm extended straight. **straight arrow** n (N Am) a person who is moral, honest, dependable, etc. **straight'away** adj straight forward. **straight chain** n (chem) a chain of atoms with no branches. **straight'-cut** adj (of tobacco) cut lengthwise of the leaf; cut in a straight line. **straight'edge** n a strip or stick for testing straightness or drawing straight lines. **straight'-faced** adj without smiling. **straight fight** n (esp in politics) a contest in which only two individuals or sides take part. **straightfor'ward** adj going forward in a straight course; without digression; without evasion; easy to understand, not complex; honest; frank. ◆ adv straightforwardly. **straightfor'wardly** adv. **straightfor'wardness** n. **straight'jacket** same as **straitjacket** (see under **strait**). **straight'-jet** adj (of aircraft or engine) driven or driving by jet directly, without a propeller. **straight man** n an actor who acts as stooge to a comedian. **straight'-out** adj (N Am, esp in party politics) out-and-out; see also **straight out** below.

straight'-pight adj (Shakesp) straight, erect. **straight play** n a play without music; a serious drama as opposed to a comedy. **straight razor** n (N Am) an open razor. **straight shooter** n (N Am) a person who is moral, honest and truthful. **straight talk** n a candid outspoken talk. **straight talking** n. **straight'-talking** adj. **straight ticket** see under **ticket**. **straight tip** n a racing tip that comes straight from the owner or trainer; inside information that can be relied on.

■ **go straight** to give up criminal activities. **keep a straight bat** (fig) to behave honourably. **keep a straight face** to refrain from smiling. **straight away** immediately. **straighten out** to disentangle, resolve; to abandon an unconventional or immoral way of life (inf). **straight from the shoulder** frankly, without equivocation (also **straight-from-the-shoulder** adj). **straight off** (inf) straight away, without hesitation. **straight out** frankly, directly. **straight up** honestly, really (inf; often interrog). **the straight and narrow** the virtuous or law-abiding way of life.

straight² see **straucht**.

straight³ see **strait**.

straik¹ /strāk/ n and v a Scots form of **stroke¹,²**. ♦ n (Walter Scott) the proportion of malt in brewing.

straik² see **strake¹**.

strain¹ /strān/ vt to stretch; to draw tight; to draw with force; to exert to the utmost; to injure by overworking; to force unnaturally, unduly, or wrongly; to exalt emotionally; to change in form or bulk by subjecting to a stress; to constrain (obs); to urge, insist upon, press for (Shakesp); to press to oneself, embrace; to squeeze, press; to grip, grasp tightly; to compress; to restrain; to squeeze out, express; to sing or play; to filter or sieve (esp coarsely). ♦ vi to make violent efforts; to tug; to retch; to have difficulty in swallowing or accepting (with at); to make efforts at evacuation of the bowels; to be percolated or filtered. ♦ n the act of straining; a violent effort; an injury by straining, esp a wrenching of the muscles; any change of form or bulk under stress; in a material subjected to a force, the ratio of the change in a dimension to the original value of the dimension (engineering); a section of a melody; a melody; an outpouring or flow of language; emotional tone, key, manner. [OFr estraindre, from L stringere to stretch tight]

■ **strained** adj having been strained; tense, forced or unnatural. **strain'edly** (or /strānd'li/) adv. **strain'er** n someone who or something that strains; a sieve, colander, etc. **strain'ing** n and adj. ◻ **strain gauge** n a device for measuring strain (deformation) in a machine or structure. **strain hardening** n a process by which metal is deformed in order to increase its hardness. **straining sill** n (building) a piece of timber lying on the tie-beam of a timber roof and butting against the bottoms of the queen posts. **strain viewer** n (phys) an eyepiece or projector of a polariscope.

■ **strain a point** to waive a doubt or principle. **strain courtesy** (Shakesp, Romeo and Juliet) to treat with scant courtesy, or (Venus and Adonis) to be over-punctilious in courtesy.

strain² /strān/ n a breed, race, stock, line of descent; offspring (archaic); a natural, esp inherited, tendency or element in one's character; a variety of bacterium or other organism; a kind, type (archaic). [Appar OE (ge)strēon gain, getting, begetting (see **strene**), with altered vowel by confusion with **strain¹**]

straint /strānt/ (Spenser) n pressure. [**strain¹**, on the model of **constraint**, etc]

strait, also (old or non-standard) **straight** or (Spenser and Milton) **streight** /strāt/ n a narrow part, place, or passage, esp (often in pl) by water; (usu in pl) difficulty, distress, hardship. ◆ adj (obs or rare) close; narrow; strict; rigorous; hard-pressed, needy; sparing in giving; tight (Shakesp). ◆ adv (obs or rare) tightly; closely; narrowly; strictly; rigorously; with hardship. ♦ vt (obs or rare) to tighten; to narrow; to put in a difficulty; to reduce to hardship. [OFr estreit (Fr étroit), from L strictus, pap of stringere to draw tight]

■ **strait'en** vt to distress; to put into difficulties; to run short; to narrow (archaic); to confine (archaic); to tighten (obs). ♦ vi (archaic) to narrow. **strait'ened** adj. **strait'ly** adv (obs or archaic) tightly; narrowly; closely; strictly. **strait'ness** n (rare). ◻ **strait'jacket** n a garment for restraining a person with violent tendencies, consisting of a padded jacket with arms crossing in front and tying behind (also **strait'waistcoat**); anything which inhibits freedom of movement or initiative (fig). ◆ vt to put into a straitjacket; to inhibit severely. **strait-laced'** adj narrow in principles of behaviour; prudish.

strak see **strike**.

strake¹ or **straik** /strāk/ n a line of planking or plating in a ship, running the length of the hull; a section of a cartwheel rim; a stripe (archaic); a strip; a trough for washing ore. [Related to **stretch**, coalescing with **streak**]

strake² /strāk/ an obsolete pat of **strike**.

stramaçon see **stramazon**.

stramash /strə-mash'/ (Scot) n a tumult, disturbance; a broil; a wreck. ◆ vt to wreck, smash. [Perh an elaboration of **smash**]

stramineous /strə-min'i-əs/ adj strawy; light, worthless; straw-coloured. [L strāmineus, from strāmen straw]

strammel /stram'l/ see **strummel**.

stramonium /strə-mō'ni-əm/ n the thorn apple; a substance similar to belladonna obtained from its seeds and leaves and formerly used to treat asthma and nervous disorders. [New L, poss from a Tatar word]

stramp /stramp/ (Scot) vt and vi to tread, stamp, or trample. ◆ n a stamp of the foot.

strand¹ /strand/ n a shore or beach (poetic); a landing-place (archaic). ◆ vt to run aground (also vi); to leave in a helpless position. [OE strand; Ger Strand, ON strönd border]

■ **strand'ed** adj driven on shore; left helpless without further resource. ◻ **strand'flat** n in Norway, a gently sloping coastal platform extending seaward. **strand'wolf** n the brown hyena (Hyaena brunnea), that scavenges along the shores in S Africa.

strand² /strand/ n a yarn, thread, fibre, or wire twisted or plaited with others to form a rope, cord, or the like; a thread, filament; a tress; an element, component part. ◆ vt to break a strand of (archaic); to insert a strand in (archaic); to form of strands. [Origin obscure]

■ **strand'ed** adj (of a fur garment) made by resewing skins after they have been cut diagonally into strips; (of a rope) having one of its strands broken.

strand³ /strand/ (Scot) n a rivulet; a gutter. [Origin obscure] ◻ **strand'-scouring** n searching of gutters.

strange /strānj/ adj alien; from elsewhere; not of one's own place, family, or circle; not one's own; not formerly known or experienced; unfamiliar (often with to); foreign (Shakesp); interestingly unusual; odd; surprising; not easy to explain; (of an elementary particle) exhibiting strangeness; estranged; like a stranger; distant or reserved; shy; unacquainted, unversed (often with to); crazy, silly, stupid (Aust inf); exceedingly great, exceptional (obs). [OFr estrange (Fr étrange), from L extrāneus, from extrā beyond]

■ **strange'ly** adv. **strange'ness** n the quality of being strange; a property of certain elementary particles, conserved in strong but not in weak interactions and represented by a quantum number (**strangeness number**) equal to the particle's hypercharge number minus its baryon number (phys). **strān'ger** n a foreigner; a person whose home is elsewhere; a person unknown or little known; a person who is outside one's familiar circle or kindred; a visitor; a newborn child (humorous); a non-member; an outsider; a person not concerned; a person without knowledge, experience, or familiarity (with to). ◆ vt (Shakesp) to make a stranger. ◻ **strange attractor** n (maths) an orderly but non-repeating pattern within a chaotic system. **strange matter** n (phys) a hypothetical form of matter composed of up, down and strange quarks. **strangeness number** see **strangeness** above. **strange particles** n pl kaons and hyperons, which have a non-zero strangeness number (qv above). **strange quark** n (phys) one of six categories of quark, having a charge of $-\frac{1}{3}$, spin of $\frac{1}{2}$ and mass of 195. **strangers' gallery** n a public gallery, esp in the House of Commons.

■ **make it strange** (Shakesp) to make difficulties, show reluctance.

strangle /strang'gl/ vt to kill by compressing the throat, to throttle; to choke; to kill (obs); to constrict; to choke back, suppress, stifle; to impede or prevent the development of. [OFr estrangler (Fr étrangler), from L strangulāre; see **strangulate**]

■ **strang'lement** n (rare). **strang'ler** n. **strang'les** n pl a contagious bacterial disease of horses caused by infection with streptococci (also called **equine distemper**). ◻ **strang'lehold** n a choking hold in wrestling; complete power over a person or situation that prevents any freedom of action. **strang'le-weed** n a name applied to various parasitic plants, eg dodder, broomrape, that have a strangling effect on crop plants.

strangulate /strang'gū-lāt/ vt to strangle; to compress (eg a vein) so as to suppress or suspend circulation or other function. [L strangulāre, -ātum, from Gr strangalaein to strangle, strangos twisted] ■ **strang'ulated** adj strangled; constricted, much narrowed. **strangulā'tion** n.

strangury /strang'gū-ri/ (med) n severe pain in the urethra with intense desire to pass urine or painful passage of a few drops of urine. [L strangūria, from Gr strangouriā, from stranx a drop, trickle, and ouron urine]

strap /strap/ n a narrow strip, usu of leather or similar material; a thong; a strop (obs or dialect); a metal band or plate for holding things in position; a narrow flat projection, as on a strap-hinge; a looped band; a string or long cluster; anything strap-shaped; an application of the strap or tawse in punishment; a barber (sl, after Hugh Strap in Smollett's Roderick Random); a term of abuse to a woman (Anglo-Irish); credit, esp for liquor (old sl). ◆ vt (strapp'ing; strapped) to beat or bind with a strap; to strop; to hang (Scot); to make suffer from scarcity, *esp* of money; to allow credit for (goods) (*old sl* or *dialect*). ◆ *vi* to work vigorously; to suffer strapping, or be capable of being strapped. [Scot and N Eng form of **strop**[1]]

■ **strap'less** *adj* without a strap or straps, *esp* (of woman's dress) without shoulder-straps. **strapp'er** *n* a person who works with straps, *esp* a groom; an energetic worker; a tall robust person (*inf*); a whopping lie. **strapp'ing** *n* fastening with a strap; materials for straps; strengthening bands; a thrashing. ◆ *adj* tall and robust. **strapp'y** *adj* having (many) straps (used *esp* of clothing and footwear).

❑ **strap'-game** *n* the game of fast-and-loose. **strap'-hang** *vi*. **strap'-hanger** *n* a standing passenger in a train, bus, etc who holds on to a strap for safety; any person who commutes using public transport. **strap hinge** *n* a hinge fastened by a long leaf or flap. **strap'line** *n* (*publishing*) a subsidiary headline in a newspaper or magazine, *esp* one beneath the title. **strap'-oil** *n* (*old sl*) a thrashing. **strap'-on** *adj* able to be held in place by a strap or straps. **strap'-shaped** *adj*. **strap work** *n* (*archit*) ornamentation of crossed and interlaced fillets. **strap'wort** *n* a seaside caryophyllaceous plant (*Corrigiola littoralis*) of SW England, etc, with strap-shaped leaves.

■ **strapped for** short of (*esp* cash).

strapontin /stra-pɔ̃-tɛ̃'/ (*Fr*) *n* a folding seat, as in a taxi, theatre, etc.

strappado /stra-pā'dō or -pä'dō/ *n* (*pl* **strappa'dos**) a form of torture in which the victim was hoisted on a rope tied around the wrists and then allowed to drop with a sudden jerk to the length of the rope. ◆ *vt* to torture or punish by the strappado. [Sham Spanish, from Ital *strappata*, from *strappare* to pull]

strapper, etc see under **strap**.

strass /stras/ *n* paste for making false gems. [Josef *Strasser*, 18c German jeweller, its inventor]

strata /strä'tə or strä'/ plural of **stratum**.

stratagem /strat'ə-jəm/ *n* a plan for deceiving an enemy or gaining an advantage; any artifice generally. [Fr *stratagème*, from L, from Gr *stratēgēma* a piece of generalship, trick; see **strategy**]

strategy /strat'i-ji/ *n* generalship, or the art of conducting a campaign and manoeuvring an army; any long-term plan; artifice or finesse generally. [Gr *stratēgia*, from *stratēgos* a general, from *stratos* an army, and *agein* to lead]

■ **strateget'ic** or **strateget'ical** *adj* (*rare*) strategic(al). **strategic** /strə-tēj'ik/ or **strate'gical** *adj* relating to, dictated by, of value for, strategy; (of weapons, bombings, etc) for use against an enemy's homeland rather than on the battlefield. **strateg'ically** *adv*. **strate'gics** *n sing* (*esp military*) strategy. **strat'egist** *n* a person skilled in strategy.

❑ **Strategic Defence Initiative** *n* a strategic defence system proposed by the USA involving laser-equipped satellites deployed in space for destroying enemy missiles (*abbrev* **SDI**; also called **Star Wars**). **strategic materials**, **strategic metals** *n pl* materials or metals used for military purposes or necessary for carrying on a war. **strategic position** *n* a position that gives its holder a decisive advantage.

strath /strath/ *n* in the Highlands of Scotland, a broad valley. [Gaelic *srath* a valley, from L *strāta* a street]

strathspey /strath-spā'/ *n* a Scottish dance, similar to and danced alternately with the reel; a tune for it, differing from the reel in being slower, and abounding in the jerky motion of dotted notes and semiquavers. [*Strathspey*, the valley of the *Spey*]

stratify, etc see under **stratum**.

Stratiotes /strat-i-ō'tēz/ *n* the water-soldier genus. [Gr *stratiōtēs* a soldier]

stratocracy /stra- or strə-tok'rə-si/ *n* military rule or despotism. [Gr *stratos* an army]

■ **stratocrat** /strat'ō-krat/ *n*. **stratocrat'ic** *adj*. **stratonic** /-on'ik/ *adj* of an army.

stratum /strä'təm or strä'/ *n* (*pl* **stra'ta**) a layer; a bed of sedimentary rock; a layer of cells in living tissue; a region determined by height or depth; a level of society. [L *strātum*, -*ī*, *strātus*, -*ūs* something spread or laid down, from *strātum* neuter pap of *sternere* to spread out, lay down]

■ **stra'tal** *adj*. **strati'culate** *adj* (of rocks) composed of thin parallel strata. **stratifica'tion** /strat-/ *n*. **stratifica'tional** *adj*. **strat'ified** *adj*. **strat'iform** *adj* layered; forming a layer. **strat'ify** *vt* to deposit, form or arrange in layers; to classify according to a graded scale (*science* and *social science*). ◆ *vi* to form, settle, compose into layers or layers. **stratig'rapher** or **stratig'raphist** *n*. **stratigraph'ic** or **stratigraph'ical** *adj*. **stratigraph'ically** *adv*. **stratig'raphy** *n* the geological study of strata and their succession; stratigraphical features. **stra'tose** *adj* in layers. **stratosphere** /strat' or strät'ō-sfēr/ *n* a region of the atmosphere beginning about 4½ to 10 miles up, in which temperature does not fall as altitude increases. **stratospheric** /-sfer'ik/ *adj* of or in the stratosphere; (of prices, etc) extremely high (*inf*). **stra'tous** *adj* of stratus. **stra'tus** *n* a wide-extended horizontal sheet of low cloud.

❑ **stratificational grammar** *n* (*linguistics*) a model that views language as a system of related layers of structure. **stratocruiser** /strat' or strät'/ *n* an aeroplane for the stratosphere. **stratocū'mulus** *n* a cloud in large globular or rolled masses, not rain-bringing. **stra'topause** *n* the transitional layer between the stratosphere and the mesosphere. **strat'otanker** *n* a type of aeroplane which refuels other planes at high altitudes. **stratovolca'no** *n* a volcano consisting of alternating layers of ash and lava.

straucht or **straught** /ströht/ (*Scot*) *vt* a form of **stretch**, *esp* in the sense to lay out (a corpse). ◆ *adj* and *adv* (also **straicht** or **straight** /strehht/) a form of **straight**[1].

straunge /strönj/ (*archaic*) *adj* same as **strange**, in the sense foreign, borrowed.

stravaig /stra-vāg'/ (*Scot*) *vi* to wander about idly. [Cf **stray** and **extravagant**]

■ **stravaig'er** *n*.

straw[1] /strö/ *n* the stalk of corn; dried stalks, etc of corn, or of peas or buckwheat, etc used as fodder, bedding, packing, for making hats, etc; a narrow tube for sucking up a beverage; a straw hat (*old*); a trifle, a whit. ◆ *adj* of straw; of the colour of straw. [OE *strēaw*; Ger *Stroh*; cf **strae**, **strew**]

■ **straw'en** *adj* (*archaic*) of straw. **straw'less** *adj*. **straw'like** *adj*. **straw'y** *adj* of or like straw.

❑ **straw'board** *n* a thick cardboard, made of straw. **straw boss** *n* (*US*) an assistant, temporary, or unofficial foreman. **straw'-breadth** *n* the breadth of a straw. **straw'-colour** *n* and *adj* delicate brownish-yellow. **straw'-coloured** *adj*. **straw'-cutter** *n* an instrument for cutting straw. **straw'flower** or **straw flower** *n* any Australian composite flowering plant of the genus *Helichrysum*, *esp H. bracteatum* (or *macranthum*) with everlasting flowers in a wide variety of colours. **straw'-hat** *adj* (*US*) of or relating to summer theatre. **straw man** *n* a man of straw (see under **man**[1]). **straw'-plait** *n* plaited straw for hats. **straw poll** or **vote** *n* an unofficial vote taken to get some idea of the general trend of opinion. **straw'-stem** *n* the fine stem of a wineglass pulled out from the material of the bowl, instead of being attached separately; a wineglass having such a stem. **straw'weight** same as **mini flyweight** (see **flyweight** under **fly**). **straw wine** *n* a sweet wine obtained from grapes dried on straw. **straw'-work** *n* work done in plaited straw. **straw'worm** *n* another name for a caddis fly larva.

■ **catch**, **clutch** or **grasp at straws** or **at a straw** to resort to an inadequate remedy in desperation. **draw the short straw** to be entrusted with an unpleasant task (as a result of, or as if by, drawing straws). **last straw** see under **last**[1]. **man of straw** see under **man**[1]. **straw in the wind** a sign of possible future developments.

straw[2] /strö/ *vt* (*pat* **strawed**; *pap* **strawed** or **strawn**) an archaic form of **strew**.

strawberry /strö'b(ə-)ri/ *n* the fruit (botanically the enlarged receptacle) of any species of the rosaceous genus *Fragaria*, related to *Potentilla*; the plant bearing it. ◆ *adj* of the colour (pinkish-red) or flavour of strawberries. [OE *strēawberige*, poss from the chaffy appearance of the achenes]

❑ **strawberry blonde** *n* and *adj* (a woman with hair that is) reddish-yellow. **strawberry cactus** *n* a clump-forming cactus, *Mammillaria prolifera*, with pale yellow flowers and red strawberry-flavoured berries. **strawberry leaf** *n* the leaf of the strawberry plant; symbolically (*esp in pl*) the rank of duke or duchess, from the ornaments like strawberry leaves on a duke's (also a marquess's or earl's) coronet. **strawberry mark** *n* a reddish birthmark. **strawberry roan** *n* a horse with a reddish-brown coat flecked with white. **strawberry shrub** *n* calycanthus. **strawberry tomato** *n* the Cape gooseberry. **strawberry tree** *n Arbutus unedo*, a small tree of the heath family with red berries.

■ **barren strawberry** a plant of the genus *Potentilla*, distinguished from the wild strawberry by its dry fruit.

strawen, **strawy** see under **straw**[1].

stray /strā/ *vi* to wander; to wander away, *esp* from control, or from the right way; to digress; to get lost. ◆ *vt* (*Shakesp*) to set astray. ◆ *n* a domestic animal that has strayed or is lost; a straggler; a waif; anything occurring casually, isolatedly, or out of place; a body of strays (*archaic*); a common; (*in pl*) atmospherics; a straying (*Shakesp*). ◆ *adj* gone astray; casual; isolated. [OFr *estraier* to wander, from L *extrā* beyond, and *vagārī* to wander]

■ **strayed** *adj* wandering, gone astray. **stray'er** *n*. **stray'ing** *n* and *adj*. **stray'ling** *n* a stray.

❑ **stray field** *n* (*elec eng*) a magnetic field set up around electric machines or current-carrying conductors that has no use and may interfere with the operation of measuring instruments, etc. **stray radiation** *n* (*phys*) direct and secondary radiation from irradiated objects that has no use.

streak /strēk/ *n* an irregular stripe; the colour of a mineral in powder, seen in a scratch; a scratch; a strain, vein, interfused or pervading character; a line of bacteria, etc (placed) on a culture medium; the line or course as of a flash of lightning; a rush, swift dash; a dash made by a naked person through a public place (*inf*); a course or succession, as of luck. ◆ *vt* to mark with streaks. ◆ *vi* to become streaked; to rush past; to run naked, or in a state of indecent undress, in public (*inf*). [OE *strica* a stroke, line, mark; Ger *Strich*; cf **strike**]

■ **streaked** *adj* streaky, striped. **streak'er** *n* a person or thing that streaks; a person who runs naked through a public place (*inf*). **streak'ily** *adv*. **streak'iness** *n*. **streak'ing** *n*. **streak'y** *adj* marked with streaks, striped; fat and lean in alternate layers; uneven in quality.
■ **like a streak** like (a flash of) lightning.

stream /strēm/ *n* a small body of running water; a river or brook, *esp* a rivulet; a flow or moving succession of anything; a large number or quantity coming continuously; a division of pupils in a school consisting of those of roughly equal ability or those following a particular course of study; any similar division of people; a current; a drift; a tendency. ◆ *vi* to flow, issue, or stretch, in a stream; to pour out abundantly; to float out, trail; to wash earth, etc in search of ore. ◆ *vt* to discharge in a stream; to wave, fly; to wash (earth, etc) for ore; to divide (pupils, etc) into streams; to play (sound or video) on a computer in real time as it is downloaded from the Internet. [OE *strēam*; Ger *Strom*, ON *straumr*]

■ **stream'er** *n* a flag, ribbon, plume, or the like streaming or flowing in the wind; a luminous beam or band of light, as of the aurora; one who washes detritus for gold or tin; a large bold headline (*press*); a narrow roll of coloured paper that streams out when thrown; a tape cartridge for backing up large quantities of data (*comput*). **stream'ered** *adj*. **stream'iness** *n*. **stream'ing** *n* and *adj*. **stream'ingly** *adv*. **stream'less** *adj* not watered by streams; waterless; without a current. **stream'let** or **stream'ling** *n* a little stream. **stream'y** *adj* abounding in streams; flowing in a stream.
◻ **stream anchor** *n* a small anchor used in warping or for stemming an easy current. **stream'-gold** *n* placer-gold. **stream'-ice** *n* pieces of drift ice swept down in a current. **stream'line** *n* a line followed by a streaming fluid; the natural course of air streams. ◆ *vt* to make streamlined. **stream'lined** *adj* having boundaries following streamlines so as to offer minimum resistance; a term of commendation with a variety of meanings, such as efficient, without waste of effort, up-to-the-minute, of superior type, graceful (*inf*). **stream'-tin** *n* tin-ore found in alluvial ground.
■ **on stream** see **on-stream** under **on**. **stream of consciousness** the continuous succession of thoughts, emotions, and feelings, both vague and well-defined, that forms an individual's conscious experience, often used to describe a narrative style which imitates this, as in James Joyce's *Ulysses*.

streek /strēk/ *vt* and *vi* (*orig Scot and N Eng*) a form of **stretch**, used *esp* (*Scot*) in the sense of to lay out for burial.

streel /strēl/ (*Irish*) *vi* to trail; to stream; to wander. [Cf Ir *straoillim* to trail]

street /strēt/ *n* a paved road; a road lined with houses, broader than a lane, including or excluding the houses and the footways; those who live in a street or are on the street; (with *cap*) used in street names; a passage or gap through or among anything. ◆ *adj* of or characteristic of the streets, *esp* in densely populated cities, or of the people who frequent them, *esp* the poor, the homeless, prostitutes, petty criminals, etc (also in compounds). [OE *strǣt* (Du *straat*, Ger *Strasse*, Ital *strada*), from L *strāta* (*via*) a paved (way), fem form of *strātus*, pap of *sternere* to spread out]

■ **street'age** *n* (*US*) a toll for street facilities. **street'ed** *adj* having streets. **street'ful** *n* (*pl* **street'fuls**). **street'ward** /-wərd/ *adv* and *adj* towards or facing the street. **street'wards** *adv*. **street'y** *adj* savouring or characteristic of the streets.
◻ **street arab** see **Arab**. **street'boy** *n* a boy who lives mainly on the street. **street'car** *n* (*N Am*) a tramcar. **street credibility** *n* (often shortened to **street cred**) trust, believability, popularity, support or trust from the man in the street; convincing knowledge of popular fashions, modes of speech, etc. **street-cred'ible** *adj* (*inf* short form **street-cred'**). **street cries** *n pl* the slogans of hawkers. **street door** *n* the door of a house that opens on to the street. **street food** *n* food cooked and sold by street vendors to be eaten straight away. **street furniture** *n* the various accessorial public items sited in the street, eg litter bins, parking meters, road signs. **street hockey** *n* (*orig US*) a type of hockey played on roller skates, *orig* in the street. **street'keeper** *n* an official formerly employed to keep order in a street or streets. **street'lamp** or **street'light** *n* one set high on a lamppost to light a street. **street'-level** *adj* and *n* (at) ground level; (in or relating to) the urban street environment, *esp* street-trading; (relating to) the general population. **street name** *n* a common or slang name for an illegal drug. **street'-raking** *adj* (*Walter Scott*) ranging the streets. **street'room** *n* space enough in the street. **street'scape** *n* a scene or view of a street; the specific characteristics of, or improvements made to, a street. **street'smart** *adj* (*N Am*) streetwise. **street smarts** *n pl* (*N Am sl*) the quality of being streetsmart. **street style** *n* an informal but

strongly assertive style, *esp* in fashion and music, influenced by urban culture and the need for alternatives to normal conventions. **street sweeper** *n* a person who or machine that sweeps the streets clean. **street theatre** *n* dramatic entertainments performed in the street. **street value** *n* the cash value of an item when sold directly to the customer in the street, *esp* illegally or on the black market. **street'walker** *n* any one who walks in the streets, *esp* a prostitute who solicits in the street. **street'walking** *n* and *adj*. **street'wise** *adj* familiar with the ways, needs, etc of the people who live and work on the city streets, eg the poor, the homeless, the petty criminals, etc; experienced in, and able to cope with, the harsher realities of city life; cynical; wily.
■ **not in the same street as** much inferior to. **on the street** (*sl*) homeless, destitute. **on the streets** (*sl*) practising prostitution. **streets ahead of** far superior to. **streets apart** very different. **up one's street** (*fig*) in the region in which one's tastes, knowledge or abilities lie.

Strega® /strā'gə/ *n* a sweet, bright-yellow Italian liqueur flavoured with herbs.

streight /strīt/ an archaic form of **strait** and **straight**[1].

streigne an old spelling of **strain**[1].

strelitz /strel'its/ *n* (*pl* **strel'itzes** or **strel'itzi**) a soldier of the Muscovite guards, abolished by Peter the Great. [Russ *strelets* bowman]

strelitzia /strə-lit'si-ə/ *n* a plant of the S African genus *Strelitzia*, of the banana family, with large showy flowers. [From Queen Charlotte (1744–1818), wife of George III, of the house of Mecklenburg-*Strelitz*]

strene /strēn/ (*Spenser*) *n* a form of **strain**[2], in the sense race.

strength /strength/ *n* the quality, condition, or degree of being physically or mentally strong; the power of action or resistance; the ability to withstand great pressure or force; force; degree or intensity; vigour; potency; a beneficial characteristic; complement (as of a workforce, team, etc); a military force; the number on the muster roll, or the normal number; the point, the truth (*Aust and NZ*). [OE *strengthu*, from *strang* strong]

■ **strength'en** *vt* to make strong or stronger; to confirm. ◆ *vi* to become stronger. **strength'ener** *n*. **strength'ening** *n* and *adj*. **strength'ful** *adj*. **strength'less** *adj* without strength.
■ **get the strength of** (*esp Aust and NZ*) to comprehend. **go from strength to strength** to move successfully forward, through frequent triumphs or achievements. **in strength** in great numbers. **on the strength** on the muster roll. **on the strength of** in reliance upon; founding upon.

strenuous /stren'ū-əs/ *adj* active; vigorous; urgent; zealous; requiring exertion. [L *strēnuus*]

■ **strenuity** /stri-nū'i-ti/ *n* (*rare*). **strenuosity** /stren-ū-os'i-ti/ or **stren'uousness** *n*. **stren'uously** *adv*.

strep see **strepto-**.

Strephon /stref'on or -ən/ *n* a love-sick rustic. [After the love-sick shepherd in Sir Philip Sidney's *Arcadia*]

strephosymbolia /stref-ō-sim-bō'li-ə/ *n* a visual disorder in which items are seen in mirror image; a reading problem in which letters, symbols, words, etc are reversed, transposed or confused. [LL, from Gr *strephein* to twist, turn, and *symbolon* a symbol]

strepitant, strepitation see under **strepent**.

strepitoso /strep-i-tō'sō/ (*music*) *adj* noisy, boisterous (also *adv*). [Ital; see **strepent**]

strepitous see under **strepent**.

strepsipterous /strep-sip'tə-rəs/ *adj* of, relating or belonging to an order of insects (Strepsiptera) parasitic on other insects, the females wormlike, the males with twisted forewings. [Gr *strepsis* a twist, and *pteron* a wing]

strepto- /strep-tō-/ *combining form* denoting bent, flexible, twisted quality. [Gr *streptos* twisted, flexible]

■ **streptocar'pus** *n* any flowering plant of the Cape primrose genus *Streptocarpus*, with foxglove-shaped flowers. **streptococcal** /-kok'l/ or **streptococcic** /-kok'sik/ *adj*. **Streptococcus** /-kok'əs/ *n* (Gr *kokkos* a grain) a genus of bacteria forming bent chains, certain species of which can cause scarlet fever, pneumonia, etc; (without *cap*; *pl* **streptococ'ci** /-kok'sī or -kok'ī/) any bacterium of this genus (*inf* short form **strep**; **strep throat** an informal name for an acute streptococcal infection of the throat). **streptokin'ase** *n* an enzyme which catalyzes the dissolution of thrombi; a generic thrombolytic drug, used to treat heart attack victims. **streptomycin** /-mī'sin/ *n* (Gr *mykēs* fungus) an antibiotic drug obtained from the bacterium *Streptomyces griseus*, used as the first effective drug treatment for tuberculosis, and in the treatment of certain rare infections such as tularaemia, brucellosis and glanders. **Streptoneura** /-nū'rə/ *n pl* (Gr *neuron* nerve) a subclass of gastropods with twisted visceral nerve-loop, including limpets, whelks, etc. **streptosol'en** *n* an evergreen solanaceous flowering shrub of the genus *Streptosolen*, with panicles of tubular orange flowers.

■ words derived from main entry word; ◻ compound words; ■ idioms and phrasal verbs

Strepyan /strep'i-ən/ adj of the oldest known Palaeolithic culture. [Strépy, a village near the Belgian town of Charleroi, where stone implements of this stage occur]

stress /stres/ n strain; a constraining influence; physical, emotional or mental pressure; a disturbed physiological state resulting from being continually under emotional or mental pressure; force; the system of forces applied to a body; the insistent assigning of weight or importance; emphasis; relative emphasis placed on a syllable or word; distraint (law); hardship, straits (obs). ◆ vt to apply stress to; to subject to stress or strain; to lay stress on; to emphasize. ◆ vi (inf) to experience stress or anxiety. [Aphetic for **distress**; prob partly also from OFr estrece, from L strictus, from stringere to draw tight]
■ **stressed** adj. **stress'ful** adj. **stress'less** adj. **stress'or** n an agent or factor that causes stress. **stress'y** adj (inf) causing or affected by stress.
❑ **stressed'-out'** adj (inf) exhausted from stress or nervous tension. **stressed-skin construction** n that of aircraft structures in which the skin carries a large proportion of the loads. **stress fracture** n (med) a fracture of a bone resulting from repetitive jarring, most commonly occurring in runners and other athletes. **stress mark** n a mark used to indicate that a written syllable is stressed when spoken. **stress test** n a test to determine whether a system is able to cope with adverse conditions. **stress-test** vt.
■ **stress out** (inf) to make (a person) exhausted from stress or nervous tension.

stretch /strech/ vt to extend (in space or time); to draw out; to expand, make longer or wider by tension; to spread out; to reach out; to exaggerate, strain, or carry further than is right; to lay at full length; to lay out; to place so as to reach from point to point or across a space; to hang by the neck (sl). ◆ vi to be drawn out; to reach; to extend (with over, across, etc); to be sufficient; to be extensible without breaking; to straighten and extend fully one's body and limbs; to exaggerate; to go swiftly. ◆ n the act of stretching; the state of being stretched; reach; extension; utmost extent; strain; undue straining; exaggeration; a demanding task; extensibility; a single spell; a continuous journey; an area, expanse; a straight part of a course; a term of imprisonment (sl); a stretch limo (sl); a pitching stance that is more upright than the wind-up (qv under **wind²**), used in order to prevent a runner from stealing a base (baseball). ◆ adj capable of being stretched. [OE streccan]
■ **stretched** adj. **stretch'er** n a person who stretches; anything used for stretching eg gloves, hats, etc; a frame for stretching a painter's canvas; a frame for carrying the sick or wounded; a rower's footboard; a crossbar or horizontal member; a brick, stone, sod, sandbag, etc laid horizontally with others in the forming of a wall; an exaggeration or lie (inf). ◆ vt to transport (a sick or injured person) by stretcher; (with off) to carry (esp an injured player) from the field of play on a stretcher. **stretch'less** adj no longer liable to stretch. **stretch'y** adj able, apt, or inclined to stretch.
❑ **stretch'er-bearer** n a person who carries injured from the field. **stretch'er-bond** or **stretch'ing-bond** n a method of building with stretchers only, the joints of one course falling between those above and below. **stretching course** n a brick course entirely of stretchers. **stretching frame** n a machine for stretching cotton rovings; a frame on which starched fabrics are dried. **stretching iron** n a currier's tool for dressing leather. **stretch limo** n (inf; in full **stretch limousine**) a luxurious, custom-made limousine that has been lengthened to provide extra seating, etc. **stretch marks** n pl marks left on the skin where it has been stretched, esp after pregnancy.
■ **at a stretch** continuously, without interruption; with difficulty. **stretch a point** to go further, esp in concession, than the strict rule allows. **stretch one's legs** to take a walk, esp for exercise.

stretto /stret'ō/ (music) n (pl **strett'i** /-ē/) part of a fugue in which subject and answer are brought closely together; (also **strett'a**, pl **strett'e** /-tā/) a passage, esp a coda, in quicker time. [Ital, contracted]

streusel /stroi'zl or stroo'/ n a crumbly topping for cakes, pastries, etc. [Ger, from streuen to sprinkle]

strew /stroo/ vt (pat **strewed**; pap **strewed** or **strewn**) to scatter loosely; to cover dispersedly; to spread (rare); to level (poetic). ◆ n an assemblage of things strewn. [OE strewian, streowian]
■ **strew'age** n. **strew'er** n. **strew'ing** n. **strew'ment** n (Shakesp) strewings.

strewth /strooth/ interj an oath (from God's truth).

stria /strī'ə or strē'a/ n (pl **stri'ae** /strī'ē or strē'ī/) a fine streak, furrow, or threadlike line, usu parallel to others; one of the fillets between the flutes of columns, etc (archit). [L stria a furrow, flute of a column]
■ **strī'ate** vt to mark with striae. ◆ adj marked with striae. **strī'ated** adj. **striā'tion** n. **striā'tum** n the corpus striatum, the great ganglion of the forebrain. **strī'ature** n mode of striation.
❑ **striated muscle** n a voluntary muscle, or muscular tissue, whose fibres are transversely striated.

strich /strich/ (archaic) n the screech owl. [L strix, prob modified by scritch]

stricken /strik'n/ (literary and poetic, or in certain compounds such as grief-stricken) adj struck, affected; afflicted. [Archaic pap of **strike**]

strickle /strik'l/ n an instrument for levelling the top of a measure of grain or shaping the surface of a mould; a template; a tool for sharpening scythes. ◆ vt to level (a measure of grain) or shape the surface of (a mould) with a strickle. [OE stricel]

strict /strikt/ adj exact; rigorous; allowing no laxity; austere; observing exact rules, regular; severe; exactly observed; thoroughgoing; tight (Shakesp); narrow (archaic); stiff and straight (bot); close, intimate (obs); restricted. [L strictus, pap of stringere to draw tight]
■ **strict'ish** adj. **strict'ly** adv. **strict'ness** n. **strict'ure** n an adverse remark or criticism; a restriction; strictness (Shakesp); abnormal narrowing of a passage (med); a binding; a closure; tightness. **strict'ured** adj abnormally narrowed.

stridden see **stride**.

stride /strīd/ vi (pat **strōde**; pap **stridd'en** /strid'n/) to walk with long steps; to take a long step; to straddle. ◆ vt to stride over; to cover (a distance) by striding. ◆ n a long step; a striding gait; the length of a long step; stride piano (jazz); (in pl) trousers (sl, esp Aust). [OE strīdan to stride]
■ **striddle** /strid'l/ vi (back-formation from stridling) to straddle. **stri'der** n. **stride'ways** or **stridling** /strid'/ adv (dialect) astride.
❑ **stride'legs** or **stride'legged** adv (Scot) astride. **stride piano** n (jazz) a rhythmic style of piano-playing derived from ragtime, popularized in Harlem during the 1920s.
■ **be into**, **get into** or **hit one's stride** to achieve one's normal or expected level of progress, efficiency, degree of success, etc. **make great strides** to make rapid progress. **take in one's stride** to accomplish without undue effort or difficulty.

strident /strī'dənt/ adj (of a voice) loud and grating; urgent, commanding attention. [L strīdēre and strīdere to creak]
■ **strī'dence** or **strī'dency** n. **strī'dently** adv. **strī'dor** n a harsh shrill sound; a harsh whistling sound of obstructed breathing (med). **stridūlant** /strid'/ adj stridulating; relating to stridor. **strid'ulantly** adv. **strid'ūlate** vi to make a chirping or scraping sound, like a grasshopper. **stridūlā'tion** n the act of stridulating. **strid'ūlātor** n an insect that makes a sound by scraping; the organ it uses. **strid'ūlatory** adj. **strid'ūlous** adj.

stridling see under **stride**.

stridor...to...**stridulous** see under **strident**.

strife /strīf/ n contention or conflict; variance; striving; any sort of trouble, hassle. [OFr estrif; see **strive**]
■ **strife'ful** adj. **strife'less** adj. **strift** /strift/ n (archaic) a struggle.
❑ **strife'-torn** adj severely disrupted, damaged, etc by conflict.

strig /strig/ (S Eng dialect) n a stalk. ◆ vt (prp **strigg'ing**) to remove the stalk from. [Origin obscure]

striga /strī'gə/ n (pl **strigae** /strī'jē/) a stria; a bristle, usu one closely pressed to, but not united with, others (bot and zool). [L strīga a swath, a furrow, a flute of a column]
■ **strī'gate** or **strī'gose** (or /-gōs'/) adj (bot and zool) marked with streaks; having bristles.

Striges /strī'jēz, strig'ās/ or **Strigiformes** /strij-i-för'mēz/ n pl in some classifications, the order comprising the owls. [L strix, strigis an owl]
■ **strig'iform** adj. **strī'gine** adj owl-like; of the owls.

strigil /strij'il/ n (in ancient Greece and Rome) a scraper used to clean the skin after bathing; (in bees) a mechanism for cleaning the antennae. [L strigilis]

strigine see under **Striges**.

Strigops /strī'gops/ or **Stringops** /string'gops/ n the kakapo or owl-parrot genus. [Gr strinx or strix, stringos owl, and ōps face]

strigose see under **striga**.

strike /strīk/ vt (pat and pap **struck**) to give a blow to or with; to hit, smite; to come into forcible contact with; to deal, deliver, or inflict; to bring forcibly into contact; to impel; to put, send, move, render, or produce by a blow or stroke; to render as if by a blow; to impress; to impress favourably; to afflict; to assail, affect; to affect strongly or suddenly; to mark off; (of a line, path, etc) to draw, describe, give direction to; to arrive at, estimate, compute, fix, settle (as a balance, an average, prices); to make (a compact or agreement), to ratify; to occur to; to assume (a pose or an attitude); to lower (eg a sail, flag, tent); to take down the tents of (strike camp); to dismantle; to sound by percussion or otherwise; to announce by a bell; to come upon, reach; to stamp; to coin; to print; to delete, cancel; to constitute (orig by cutting down a list); to broach (Shakesp); to fight (a battle) (Shakesp); to blast, bewitch; to hook (a fish) by a quick turn of the wrist; to smooth (dialect); to strickle (dialect); to stroke (obs and Bible). ◆ vi to make one's way; to set out; to take a direction or course; to dart, shoot, pass quickly; to penetrate; to jerk the line suddenly in order to impale the hook in the mouth of a fish; to put forth roots; to chance, alight, come by chance; to interpose; to deal or aim a blow, perform a stroke; to sound or be sounded or announced by a bell; to hit out; to seize the bait; to strike something, as a rock, sail, flag; to attempt to hook the ball (*rugby*); to touch; to run aground; to surrender; to go on strike; to blast, blight (*Shakesp*). —There are numerous archaic and obsolete forms of the past tense (**strake**, **stroke**, **strook**, **strooke** and (*Scot*) **strack**, **strak**) and of the past participle (**strick'en**, **strik'en**, **strook**, **strooke**, **strook'en** and **struck'en**). ♦ *n* a stroke, striking; an attack, *esp* by aircraft; a raid; the direction of a horizontal line at right angles to the dip of a bed (*geol*); a find (as of oil), a stroke of luck; a cessation of work, or other obstructive refusal to act normally, as a means of putting pressure on employers, etc; the part that receives the bolt of a lock; (in tenpin bowling) the knocking down of all the pins with the first ball bowled, or the score resulting from this; a ball thrown by the pitcher into the strike zone (*baseball*); a ball at which the batter swings and misses (*baseball*); the position of facing the bowling, licence to receive the next delivery (*cricket*); blackmail, *esp* by introducing a bill in the hope of being bought off (*old US sl*); the quantity of coins, etc made at one time; a strickle (*dialect*); a proportion of malt (cf **straik**[1]). [OE *strīcan* to stroke, go, move]

■ **strik'er** *n* someone who or something that strikes; a footpad (*Shakesp*); an attacker, *esp* one whose task is to attempt to score goals (*football*); the batsman facing the bowling (*cricket*). **strik'ing** *n* the action of the verb. ♦ *adj* that strikes or can strike; impressive, arresting, noticeable. **strik'ingly** *adv*. **strik'ingness** *n*.

□ **strike'bound** *adj* closed or similarly affected because of a strike. **strike'breaker** *n* a person who works during a strike or who does the work of a striker, *esp* if brought in with a view to defeating the strike. **strike'breaking** *n*. **strike fault** *n* (*geol*) a fault parallel to the strike. **strike force** *n* a force designed and equipped to carry out a strike (*milit*); a special police unit trained to strike suddenly and forcefully to suppress crime. **strikeout** see **strike out** below. **strike pay** *n* an allowance paid by a trade union to members on strike. **strike'-slip fault** *n* (*geol*) a fault in which movement is parallel to the strike. **strike zone** *n* (*baseball*) the area above home plate extending from the batter's knees to the middle of the torso. **striking circle** *n* (*hockey*) the area in front of goal from within which the ball must be hit in order to score. **striking price** *n* (*stock exchange*) a stipulated price at which a holder may exercise his or her put or call option (also **exercise** or **strike price**).

■ **be struck off** (of doctors, lawyers, etc) to have one's name removed from the professional register because of misconduct. **on strike** taking part in a strike; (of a batsman) facing the bowling (*cricket*). **strike a match** to light it by friction or a grazing stroke. **strike at** to attempt to strike, aim a blow at. **strike back** to return a blow; to backfire, burn within the burner. **strike down** to fell; to make ill or cause to die. **strike hands** to join or slap together hands in confirmation of agreement. **strike home** to strike right to the point aimed at (also *fig*). **strike in** to enter suddenly; to interpose; to agree, fit (*obs*). **strike into** to enter upon suddenly, break into. **strike it lucky** (*inf*) to experience good luck. **strike it rich** (*inf*) to make a sudden large financial gain, eg through discovering a mineral deposit, etc. **strike off** to erase from an account, deduct; to remove (from a roll, register, etc); to print; to separate by a blow. **strike oil** see under **oil**. **strike out** to efface; to bring into light; to direct one's energy and efforts boldly outwards; to swim away; to dismiss or be dismissed by means of three strikes (*baseball*); to fail completely (*inf, esp N Am*; **strike'out** *n*); to remove (testimony, an action, etc) from the record (*law*); to strike from the shoulder; to form by sudden effort. **strike root** see under **root**[1]. **strike through** to delete with a stroke of the pen. **strike up** to begin to beat, sing, or play; to begin (eg an acquaintance). **struck on** enamoured of. **take strike** (*cricket*) (of a batsman) to prepare to face the bowling.

Strimmer® /strim'ər/ *n* a machine for cutting grass, *esp* in areas inaccessible to a lawn mower, using a filament or length of strong cord (instead of a blade) that rotates rapidly within a protective guard.

■ **strim** *vt* and *vi* (back-formation).

Strine /strīn/ (*inf*) *n* a jocular name given to Australian English in terms of its vernacular pronunciation (with frequent assimilation, elision, etc). ♦ *adj* Australian. [Alleged pronunciation of *Australian*, coined by Alastair Morrison (pseudonym Afferbeck Lauder), esp in his book *Let Stalk Strine* (1965)]

string /string/ *n* a small cord or a piece of it; cord of any size; a hangman's rope; a piece of anything for tying; anything of similar character, such as a tendon, nerve or fibre; a leash; a shoelace (*N Am*); a stretched piece of catgut, silk, wire, or other material in a musical instrument; (in *pl*) the stringed instruments played by a bow in an orchestra or other combination; (in *pl*) their players; the cord of an archery bow; in theoretical physics, a minute, one-dimensional entity in space (see **string theory** below); the thread of a necklace or the like; anything on which things are threaded; a

filing cord; a set of things threaded together or arranged as if threaded; a train, succession, file, or series; a sequence of alphanumeric characters (*comput*); (of horses, camels, etc) a drove or number; a long bunch; the buttons strung on a wire by which the score is kept (*billiards*); hence, the score itself; a sloping joist supporting the steps in wooden stairs; a string course; a hoax (*sl*); (in *pl*) awkward or undesirable conditions or limitations. ♦ *adj* of, like or for string or strings. ♦ *vt* (*pat* and *pap* **strung**) to fit or furnish with a string or strings; to put in tune (*poetic*); to make tense or firm; to tie up; to hang; to extend like a string; to put on or in a string; to take the strings or stringy parts off; to hoax, humbug (*sl*). ♦ *vi* to stretch out into a long line; to form into strings; (of glues, etc) to become stringy; to be hanged (*Scot*); (in billiards) to drive the ball against the end of the table and back, to decide who is to begin. [OE *streng*; cf Du *streng*, Ger *Strang*, ON *strengr*]

■ **stringed** /stringd/ *adj* having strings; of stringed instruments. **stringer** /string'ər/ *n* someone who or that which strings; a horizontal member in a framework (*archit*); an interior horizontal plank, supporting the beam-ends of a ship (*naut*); a narrow mineral vein; a journalist employed part-time by a newspaper or news agency to cover a particular (*esp* remote) town or area. **string'ily** *adv*. **string'iness** *n*. **string'ing** *n*. **string'less** *adj*. **string'y** *adj* consisting of, or abounding in, strings or small threads; fibrous; capable of being drawn into strings; like string or a stringed instrument.

□ **string-bag** *n* a bag made of string, or (**string'-bag**) for holding string. **string band** *n* a band of stringed instruments. **string bass** *n* a double bass. **string bean** *n* the French bean. **string'board** *n* a board facing the well hole of a staircase, and receiving or covering the ends of the steps. **string course** *n* a projecting horizontal course of bricks or line of mouldings running quite along the face of a building. **string figure** *n* a structure of string looped around the fingers in a symmetrical pattern that can be altered by manipulation, as in cat's-cradle. **string orchestra** *n* a small orchestra of stringed instruments. **string pea** *n* a pea with edible pods. **string piece** *n* a long, heavy, *usu* horizontal timber used to support a framework; the string of a staircase. **string quartet** *n* a musical ensemble of two violins, a viola and a cello; music for such an ensemble. **string theory** *n* (*phys*) the theory that all fundamental particles in the cosmos arise from strings (invisibly small, one-dimensional, elastic entities) and that the characteristic properties of each particle are determined by the vibration and rotation of the string, much in the same way as the tension, etc of a violin string determines the sound produced; further developed as **superstring theory** a supersymmetrical version of the original theory. **string tie** *n* a narrow necktie of uniform width. **string vest** *n* a vest made of a netlike fabric. **string'y-bark** *n* one of a class of Australian eucalypts with very fibrous bark.

■ **highly-strung** see under **high**[1]. **more than one string to one's bow** (capable of or expert in) more than one area of knowledge, function, etc. **no strings** or **no strings attached** with no conditions or limitations (**no'-strings** *adj*). **on a string** under complete (*esp* emotional) control; kept in suspense. **pull (the) strings** to use influence behind the scenes, as if working puppets (**string'-pulling** *n*). **string along** to string, fool; to give someone false expectations; to go along together, co-operate. **string out** (*inf*) to be under the influence of or addicted to a drug. **string up** (*inf*) to hang by the neck. **strung out** (*orig US*) suffering from drug withdrawal symptoms; weak, ill or distressed as a result of drug addiction; addicted to a drug. **strung up** nervously tensed.

stringendo /strin-jen'dō/ (*music*) *adj* and *adv* (played) with increasing speed. [Ital]

stringent /strin'jənt/ *adj* tight; binding; rigorous; demanding close attention to detail, set procedure, etc; characterized by difficulty in finding money. [L *stringēns, -entis*, prp of *stringere* to draw together]

■ **strin'gency** *n*. **strin'gently** *adv*. **strin'gentness** *n*.

stringer see under **string**.

stringhalt /string'hölt/ *n* a catching up of a horse's legs, *usu* of one or both hindlegs, caused by a muscle spasm in the hock (also **spring'halt**). [Appar **string** (sinew) and **halt**[2]]

Stringops see **Strigops**.

stringy see under **string**.

strinkle /string'kl/ (*Scot*) *vt* to sprinkle. [Cf **sprinkle**]

■ **strink'ling** *n*.

strip /strip/ *vt* (**stripp'ing**; **stripped**) to pull, peel, or tear off; to doff; to divest; to undress; to reduce to the ranks; to deprive of a covering; to skin, peel, husk; to lay bare, expose; to deprive; to clear, empty; to dismantle; to clear of fruit, leaves, stems, midribs, or any other part; to press out the last milk from (a cow, etc) or obtain (milk) in this way; to press out the roe or milt from; to handle as if milking a cow; to cut in strips; to put strips on; to outstrip, press (*obs*); to remove a constituent from a substance by boiling, distillation, etc (*chem*); to break the thread of (a screw, etc) or a tooth of (a gear); to unload (*esp* a container or lorry). ♦ *vi* to undress; to perform a striptease; (of a screw) to be stripped of the thread; to come off; to go swiftly (*obs*). ◆ *n* a long narrow piece; a long thin piece of rolled metal, such as *steel strip*; a narrow space in a newspaper in which a story is told in pictures (also **strip cartoon**); a lightweight uniform, *esp* one displaying the club colours, for running, football, etc; a striptease; an airstrip; a row of three or more connected stamps; a road lined with shops and other business premises (*N Am*). [OE *strȳpan*; Ger *streifen*; perh partly from other sources]

■ **strip'ogram** or **stripp'ergram** *n* a message delivered by a messenger who performs a striptease act for the recipient. **stripp'er** *n* someone who or something that strips; a striptease artist. **stripp'ings** *n pl* the last milk drawn at a milking.

◻ **strip cartoon** see *n* above. **strip cell** *n* a secure room without furnishings or fittings, in eg a psychiatric hospital, in which seriously disturbed patients are confined. **strip club** *n* one which regularly features striptease artists. **strip cropping** *n* the cultivation of different crops in bands to prevent erosion. **strip joint** *n* (*inf*) a strip club. **strip'-leaf** *n* tobacco stripped of stalks. **strip light** *n* a light containing a long fluorescent tube. **strip lighting** *n*. **strip mall** *n* (*US*) a shopping mall in which the shops are arranged in a row along a roadside. **strip map** *n* a map showing a long narrow strip of country, used *esp* by airmen. **strip mill** *n* a mill where steel is rolled into strips. **strip mine** *n* an opencast mine in which the overburden is removed (stripped) before the valuable ore is excavated. **stripped atom** *n* an ionized atom from which one or more electrons have been removed. **stripped-down'** *adj* reduced to the bare essentials. **strip-po'ker** *n* poker in which losses are paid by removing articles of clothing. **strip search** *n* a search of a person's body (for hidden items, eg drugs, contraband) for which their clothes are removed. **strip'-search** *vt*. **striptease'** *n* an act of undressing slowly and seductively, *esp* as entertainment.

■ **strip down** to dismantle, remove parts from. **strip off** (*inf*) to take one's clothes off. **strip out** (*commerce*) to remove (one or more items) from a balance sheet, *usu* to give a truer picture of a firm's trading and financial position.

stripe /strīp/ *n* a band of colour; a chevron on a sleeve, indicating non-commissioned rank or good behaviour; a striped cloth or pattern; a strip; a strain; a kind, particular sort (*US*); a blow, *esp* with a lash; magnetic sound track(s) on cinema film for sound-film reproduction. ◆ *vt* to make stripes on; to mark with stripes; to lash. [Perh different words; cf Du *streep* (earlier *strijpe*); Ger *Streif* stripe, ON *strīp* striped fabric, Du *strippen* to whip]

■ **striped** *adj* having stripes of different colours; marked with stripes. **stripe'less** *adj*. **stripes** *n* (*old inf*) a tiger. **stripey** see **stripy** below. **strip'iness** *n*. **strip'ing** *n*. **strip'y** or **strip'ey** *adj* stripelike; having stripes.

◻ **striped bass** /bas/ *n* a large dark-striped bass of coastal N American seas that breeds in rivers.

stripling /strip'ling/ (*literary* and *facetious*) *n* a youth. [Dimin of **strip**]

stripper see under **strip**.

stripy see under **stripe**.

strive /strīv/ *vi* (pat **strove** /strōv/, *Shakesp* **strived**; *pap* **striven** /striv'n/, *Shakesp* **strove**, *Bible* **strived**) to contend; to be in conflict (with *against*); to struggle (with *for*); to endeavour earnestly (with *to*); to make one's way with effort. [OFr *estriver*; poss Gmc, from the root of **stride**, or of Ger *streben* to strive]

■ **striv'er** *n*. **striv'ing** *n* and *adj*. **striv'ingly** *adv*.

stroam /strōm/ (*dialect*) *vi* to wander idly about; to stride. [Perh **stroll** and **roam**]

strobe /strōb/ *n* the process of viewing vibrations with a stroboscope; a stroboscope or stroboscopic light. ◆ *vi* (of a stroboscopic light) to flash on and off. [**strobic**]

■ **strob'ing** *n* an unwanted jerky effect in a television or cinematic image.

strobic /strob'ik/ *adj* like a spinning-top; spinning or seeming to spin. [Gr *strobos* a whirling, from *strephein* to twist]

strobila /stro-bī'lə/ (*biol*) *n* (pl **strobi'lae** /-lē/) (in the lifecycle of jellyfishes) a chain of segments, cone within cone, that separate to become medusoids; a chain of segments forming the body of a tapeworm. [Gr *strobīlē* a conical plug of lint, *strobīlos* a spinning-top, whirl, pine cone, from *strobos* (see foregoing)]

■ **strobilaceous** /strob-i-lā'shəs/ *adj* of or like a strobile; bearing strobiles. **strob'ilate** *vi* to undergo strobilation. ◆ *adj* of the nature of a strobilus. **strobila'tion**, **strobilīzā'tion** or **-s-** *n* production or reproduction by strobilae. **strobile** /strob' or strōb'īl/ or **-il** /-il/ or a strobila; a strobilus. **strobiliform** /-il'-/, **strob'iline** or **strob'iloid** *adj*. **strobi'lus** *n* (pl **strobi'li** /-lī/) a close group of sporophylls with their sporangia, a cone; a scaly spike of female flowers, as in the hop.

stroboscope /strō'bə-skōp or strob'ə-/ *n* an instrument for studying rotating machinery or other periodic phenomena by means of a flashing lamp which can be synchronized with the frequency of the

periodic phenomena so that they appear to be stationary; an optical toy giving an illusion of motion from a series of pictures seen momentarily in succession. [**strobic**]

■ **stroboscopic** /strob- or strōb-ə-skop'ik/ *adj*.

◻ **stroboscopic** (more commonly **strobe**) **lighting** *n* periodically flashing light, or the equipment used to produce it.

stroddle /strod'l/ (*obs* or *dialect*) same as **straddle**.

strode /strōd/ pat of **stride**.

strodle /strod'l/ (*obs* or *dialect*) same as **straddle**.

stroganoff /strog'ə-nof/ *adj* (of meat) cut thinly and cooked with onions, mushrooms and seasoning in a sour cream sauce, as in *beef stroganoff*; also applied to vegetables cooked in this way, as in *mushroom stroganoff*. ◆ *n* a dish cooked in this way. [Count Paul Stroganoff (1772–1817), Russian diplomat]

stroke[1] /strōk/ *n* an act or mode of striking; a hit or attempt at hitting; a blow; a striking by lightning; a reverse; damage to part of the brain caused by diminished blood flow or leakage of blood through the walls of blood vessels, leading to (often permanent) impairment of sensation, function or movement in those parts controlled by the damaged area; the striking of a clock or its sound; a dash or line; a touch of pen, pencil, brush, etc; an oblique line, solidus; a trait (*obs*); a beat, pulse; a sudden movement or occurrence; a particular way of hitting the ball in cricket, tennis, etc; a particular named style or manner of swimming; a single complete movement in a repeated series, as in swimming, rowing or pumping; a stroke oar; a single action towards an end; an effective action, feat, achievement. ◆ *vt* to put a stroke through or on; to cross (commonly with *out*); to row as stroke in or for; to row at the rate of; to encourage, flatter (*inf*). ◆ *vi* to row as the stroke-oar; to make a stroke, as in swimming. [OE (inferred) *strāc*; cf Ger *Streich*]

◻ **stroke index** *n* a measure of the relative difficulty of the holes on a golf course. **stroke oar** *n* the oar nearest the stern in a boat; its rower, whose stroke leads the rest. **stroke play** or **stroke'play** *n* (in cricket, tennis, etc) the ability to execute a range of strokes successfully; scoring in golf by counting the total number of strokes played (rather than the number of holes won).

■ **at a stroke** in one action. **off one's stroke** operating less effectively or successfully than usual. **on the stroke (of)** punctually (at). **stroke of luck** a fortunate occurrence.

stroke[2] /strōk/ *vt* to rub gently in one direction; to rub gently in kindness or affection; to put or direct by such a movement; to reassure or flatter with attention (*N Am*); to milk, strip; to tool in small flutings; to whet; to set in close gathers; to strike, move (a ball, etc) smoothly. ◆ *n* an act of stroking. [OE *strācian*, from *strāc* stroke (noun); cf Ger *streichen* to rub]

■ **stroke'able** or **strok'able** *adj* able to be stroked; (appearing to be) pleasant to stroke. **strok'er** *n*. **strok'ing** *n*.

stroke[3] /strōk/ or **stroken** /strō'kn/ obsolete forms (*Spenser* and *Shakesp*) of **struck** (see **strike**).

stroll /strōl/ *vi* to walk at a leisurely pace; to saunter; to wander from place to place. ◆ *n* a leisurely walk; a stroller (*N Am*). [Perh Ger *strolchen* (obs *strollen*), from *Strolch* vagrant]

■ **stroll'er** *n* a person who strolls; a wanderer; a saunterer; a vagrant; an itinerant; a pushchair (*N Am*). **stroll'ing** *n* and *adj*.

◻ **strolling player** *n* (*hist*) an itinerant actor.

■ **stroll on!** an exclamation of surprise, disbelief (often used ironically).

stroma /strō'mə/ *n* (pl **strōm'ata**) a supporting framework of connective tissue (*zool*); a dense mass of hyphae in which a fungus fructification may develop (*bot*); the matrix of the chloroplast, in which the dark reactions of photosynthesis take place. [Gr *strōma* a bed, mattress]

■ **strō'mal**, **strōmatic** /-mat'ik/ or **strō'matous** *adj*. **stromat'olite** *n* (*bot*) a rounded, multi-layered structure up to *approx* 1 metre across, found in rocks dating back at least 2800 million years, having present-day equivalents that result from the growth, under special conditions, of blue-green algae.

stromb /strom or stromb/ *n* a very large gastropod related to the whelk; its shell with short spire and expanded lip. [Gr *strombos* a spinning-top, snail, whirlwind]

■ **strombūlif'erous** *adj* bearing spirally coiled organs or parts. **strombū'liform** *adj* shaped like a spinning top; spirally twisted. **strom'bus** *n* the stromb, any gastropod mollusc of the genus *Strombus*; a spirally coiled pod.

strond /strond/ (*Spenser* and *Shakesp*) *n* same as **strand**[1].

strong /strong/ *adj* (**stronger** /strong'gər/; **strongest** /strong'gist/) powerful; forcible; forceful; (of wind) fast-moving; vigorous; hale; robust; of great staying power; firm; resistant; difficult to overcome; steadfast; excelling; efficient; of great tenacity of will and effective in execution; able, competent; well-skilled or versed; rich in resources or means to power; well-provided; numerous; numbering so many; of vigorous growth; stiff, coarse, and abundant, indicating strength; (of language) without ambiguity, obscurity, or understatement; (of language) intemperate, offensive and unseemly; gross; violent; grievous; having great effect; intense; ardent and convinced; performed with strength; powerfully, or unpleasantly powerfully, affecting the senses; rank; vivid; marked; (of a syllable) stressed, emphasized; bold in definition; in high concentration; showing the characteristic properties in high degree; (of prices, markets, currency) steady or tending to rise; (of Germanic and similar verbs) showing vowel variation in conjugation (*grammar*); (of Germanic nouns and adjectives) having a stem originally ending in a vowel or a consonant other than *n*; of the strongest type of interaction between nuclear particles, occurring at a range of less than (approximately) 10^{-15}cm and accounting for the stability of the atomic nucleus (*phys*). ◆ *adv* strongly (*rare*); very (*obs*). [OE *strang* strong; ON *strangr*, Ger *streng* tight]

■ **strongish** /strong'gish/ *adj*. **strong'ly** *adv*.
▫ **strong'arm** *n* a person who uses violence. ◆ *adj* by, having, or using, physical force. ◆ *vt* to treat violently, show violence towards. **strong'box** *n* a safe or strongly made coffer for valuables. **strong breeze** *n* (*meteorol*) a wind of force 6 on the Beaufort scale, reaching speeds of 25 to 31mph. **strong drink** *n* alcoholic liquors. **strong flour** or **wheat** *n* one rich in gluten, giving bread that rises well. **strong force** *n* (*phys*) the force that binds quarks together and holds neutrons and protons together to form atomic nuclei. **strong gale** *n* (*meteorol*) a wind of force 9 on the Beaufort scale, reaching speeds of 47 to 54mph. **strong head** *n* power to withstand alcohol or any dizzying influence. **strong'hold** *n* a fastness or fortified refuge; a fortress; a place where anything is in great strength. **strong interaction** *n* an interaction between particles completed in a time of the order of 10^{-23}s, such an interaction binding protons and neutrons together in the nuclei of atoms. **strong'-knit** *adj* firmly jointed or compacted. **strong'man** *n* a person who performs feats of strength, in a circus, etc; a person, group, etc that wields political, economic, etc power. **strong meat** *n* solid food, not milk (*Bible*, Hebrews 5.12–14); anything tending to arouse fear, repulsion, etc. **strong-mind'ed** *adj* resolute, determined, having a vigorous mind. **strong-mind'edness** *n*. **strong'point** *n* (*milit*) a favourably situated and well-fortified defensive position. **strong point** *n* that in which one excels, one's forte. **strong'room** *n* a room constructed for the safekeeping of valuables or prisoners. **strong wheat** see **strong flour** above.
■ **a strong stomach** resistance to nausea. **come on strong** see under **come. going strong** see under **going**[2].

strongyle or **strongyl** /stron'jil/ *n* a blunt rhabdus; a parasitic threadworm (*Strongylus* or related genera). [Gr *strongylos* round]
■ **stron'gyloid** *adj* and *n*. **strongyloidiasis** /-dī'ə-sis/ *n* an intestinal disease caused by infestation with a type of tropical or subtropical threadworm of the genus *Strongyloides*, *esp S. stercoralis*. **strongylō'sis** *n* infestation with strongyles.

strontium /stron'shi-əm, -shəm or stron'ti-əm/ *n* a yellow metallic element (symbol **Sr**; atomic no 38) found in celestite.
■ **stron'tia** *n* its oxide. **stron'tian** /-shi-ən/ *n* (loosely) strontium, strontia or strontianite. **stron'tianite** *n* its carbonate, an orthorhombic mineral (first found in 1790 near *Strontian* in NW Scotland).
▫ **stron'tium-90** *n* a radioactive isotope of strontium, an important element in nuclear fallout. **strontium unit** *n* a measure of the concentration of strontium-90 in organic material (*abbrev* **SU**).

strook or **strooke** /strŭk/ obsolete *pat* and *pap* (also **strooken** /strŭk'ən/) of **strike**.
■ **strooke** /strōk/ *n* (*obs*) a stroke.

strop[1] /strop/ *n* a strip of leather, etc for sharpening razors; a rope or band round a deadeye (*naut*). ◆ *vt* (**stropp'ing; stropped**) to sharpen on a strop. [Older form of **strap**, from OE *strop*, prob from L *struppus* a thong]

strop[2] /strop/ (*inf*) *n* (a fit of) bad temper; censure, criticism, *esp* in the phrase *give someone strop*. [Perh back-formation from **stroppy**]

strophanthus /stro- or strō-fan'thəs/ *n* a plant of the African and Asiatic genus *Strophanthus*, of the periwinkle family; its dried seeds used in medicine or yielding poison used to make poison arrows. [Gr *strophos* twisted band, and *anthos* flower, from the ribbonlike prolongation of the petals, twisted in bud]
■ **strophan'thin** *n* a very poisonous glucoside in its seeds.

strophe /strof'i or strō'fi/ (*prosody*) *n* (in a Greek play) the song sung by the chorus as it moved towards one side, answered by an exact counterpart, the **an'tistrophe**, as it returned; part of any ode answered in this way; (loosely) a stanza. [Gr *strophē* a turn]
■ **stroph'ic** *adj*.

strophiole /strof'i-ōl/ (*bot*) *n* a caruncle. [Gr *strophiolon* a fringe, from *strophos* a twisted band]
■ **stroph'iolate** or **stroph'iolated** *adj*.

stroppy /strop'i/ (*inf*) *adj* quarrelsome, bad-tempered; rowdy, obstreperous and awkward to deal with. [Perh **obstropalous**]

strossers /stros'ərz/ (*Shakesp*) *n pl* trousers. [Cf **trousers**]

stroud /strowd/ (*obs* or *rare*) *n* a blanket *orig* made for trading with Native Americans. [Prob made at *Stroud*, Gloucestershire]
■ **stroud'ing** *n* its material, coarse wool.

stroup /stroop/ (*Scot*) *n* a spout, nozzle, eg of a kettle, jug, pump, etc; a water tap. [Cf Swed *strupe* throat]
■ **stroup'ach** or **stroup'an** *n* a drink of tea.

strout /strowt/ (*dialect*) *vi* to bulge, swell; to stand out, protrude; to flaunt; to strut. ◆ *vt* to cause to protrude. [OE *strūtian* to protrude]

strove /strōv/ *pat* of **strive**.

strow (*pat* **strowed**; *pap* **strown**), **strower, strowing** same as **strew, strewer, strewing**.

stroy /stroi/ (*obs* or *dialect*) *vt* to destroy. ◆ *n* (*Bunyan*) destruction. [**destroy**]

struck see **strike**.

structure /struk'chər/ *n* the manner or (*obs*) act of putting together; construction; the arrangement of parts; the manner of organization; a thing constructed; an organic form. ◆ *vt* to organize, build up; to construct a framework for; to allot to (a linguistic element) its function or syntactical relationship. [L *structūra*, from *struere, structum* to build]
■ **struc'tural** *adj*. **struc'turalism** *n* the belief in and study of unconscious, underlying patterns in thought, behaviour, social organization, etc, *esp* as a technique in literary criticism. **struc'turalist** *n* and *adj*. **struc'turally** *adv*. **structurā'tion** *n* (*rare*) forming (something) into or applying an organized structure to (something), creating a formal structure. **struc'tured** *adj* having a certain structure; having a definite structure or organization. **struc'tureless** *adj*.
▫ **structural formula** *n* a chemical formula showing the arrangement of atoms in the molecule and the bonds between them. **structural gene** *n* a gene specifying the amino acid sequence of a protein needed for cell structure or metabolism (cf **regulatory gene**). **structural isomerism** *n* (*chem*) the property of substances which are isomers (qv) and differ in molecular structure, often having distinct physical and chemical properties (cf **stereoisomerism**). **structural linguistics** *n sing* the study of language in terms of the interrelations of its basic phonological, morphological and semantic units. **structural psychology** *n* a type of psychology dealing with the nature and arrangement of mental states and processes. **structural steel** *n* a strong mild steel suitable for construction work. **structural unemployment** *n* unemployment due to changes in the structure of society or of a particular industry.

strudel /stroo'dl or shtrü'dl/ *n* very thin pastry enclosing fruit, or cheese, etc. [Ger, eddy, whirlpool, from the way the pastry is rolled]

struggle /strug'l/ *vi* to strive vigorously in resistance, contention, or coping with difficulties; to make great efforts or exertions; to contend strenuously; to make one's way with difficulty; to move convulsively. ◆ *n* a bout or course of struggling; strife; a hard contest with difficulties; a convulsive movement. [ME *strogelen*; origin unknown]
■ **strugg'ler** *n*. **strugg'ling** *n* and *adj*. **strugg'lingly** *adv*.

Struldbrug /struld'brug/ *n* one of a class among the Luggnaggians in Swift's *Gulliver's Travels*, endowed with immortality, but doomed to decrepitude after 80, and most wretched. [A capricious coinage]

strum /strum/ *vt* and *vi* (**strumm'ing; strummed**) to sound the strings of a guitar, etc with a sweep of the hand; to play in this way (rather than plucking individual strings). ◆ *n* a strumming. [Cf **thrum**[1]]
■ **strumm'er** *n*.

struma /stroo'mə/ *n* (*pl* **stru'mae** /-mē or -mī/) scrofula or a scrofulous tumour (*pathol*); goitre (*pathol*); a cushion-like swelling (*bot*). [L *strūma* a scrofulous tumour]
■ **strumatic** /strü-mat'ik/, **strumose** /stroo'mōs/ or **stru'mous** *adj*. **strumī'tis** *n* inflammation of the thyroid gland.

strummel /strum'l/ or **strammel** /stram'l/ (*obs sl*) *n* straw; hence, hair. [Cf L *strāmen* straw]

strumose, strumous see under **struma**.

strumpet /strum'pit/ (*archaic*) *n* a whore. ◆ *adj* like a strumpet; inconstant; false. ◆ *vt* to make a strumpet of; to call a strumpet. [Origin obscure]

strung /strung/ *pat* and *pap* of **string**.

strunt[1] /strunt/ (*Scot*) *vi* to strut. [Cf Norw *strunta*]

strunt[2] /strunt/ (*Scot*) *n* alcoholic liquor. [Ety dubious]

strunt[3] /strunt/ (*Scot*; often in *pl*) *n* the huff, the sulks. [Origin unknown]

strut[1] /strut/ *vi* (**strutt'ing; strutt'ed**) to walk stiffly in vanity or self-importance; to walk in an ostentatious, swaggering manner; to stand stiffly upright (*obs*); to flaunt, glory (*obs*); to bulge, protrude (*obs*). ◆ *n* a strutting gait. [OE *strūtian* or some similar form; see **strout**]
■ **strutt'er** *n*. **strutt'ing** *n* and *adj*. **strutt'ingly** *adv*.

■ **strut one's stuff** (*sl*; *orig US*) to dance; to show off one's talent (at a public activity, etc); to show off generally.

strut² /*strut*/ *n* a rod or member that resists pressure; a prop. ◆ *vt* to support as, or with, a strut or struts. [Cf LGer *strutt* rigid, and **strut¹**]

struthious /*stroo'thi-əs*/ *adj* (of birds) resembling or related to the ostrich or belonging to the order of flightless birds (**Struthiones**) to which the ostrich belongs. [L, from Gr *strouthiōn* an ostrich]

■ **stru'thioid** *adj* and *n*.

strychnine /*strik'nēn* or *-nin*/ *n* a very poisonous alkaloid ($C_{21}H_{22}O_2N_2$) obtained from the seeds of the nux vomica plant. ◆ *vt* to poison with strychnine. [Gr *strychnos* nightshade (of various kinds)]

■ **strych'nia** *n* (now *rare*) strychnine. **strych'nic** *adj*. **strych'ninism** or **strych'nism** *n* strychnine poisoning.

Stuart /*stū'ərt*/ *adj* of or relating to the royal house that reigned in Britain from 1603 to 1714.

stub /*stub*/ *n* a short piece (eg of a cigarette or a pencil) left after the larger part has been used; something blunt and stunted; a counterfoil; a stump; (also **stub'-nail**) a short thick nail or worn horseshoe nail, *esp* in *pl*, old nails used as scrap. ◆ *vt* (**stubb'ing**; **stubbed**) to strike as against a stub; to extinguish by pressing the end on something (often with *out*); to remove stubs from; to grub (up); to wear or cut to a stub; to wound with a stub. [OE *stubb, stybb*]

■ **stubbed** *adj* cut or worn to a stub; cleared of stubs; stumpy; blunt; (*esp* of a digit) injured by striking against something. **stubb'iness** *n*. **stubb'y** *adj* abounding with stubs; short, thick, and strong. ◆ *n* (*Aust*) a small, squat beer bottle or the beer it contains.

stubble /*stub'l*/ *n* a stump of reaped corn; such stumps collectively; straw; a reaped field; unshaven growth of beard. [OFr *estuble*, from LL *stupula*, from L *stipula*; see **stipule**]

■ **stubb'led** *adj* stubbly. **stubb'ly** *adj* like or covered with stubble. ❑ **stubb'le-fed** *adj* fed on the natural grass growing among stubble. **stubble field** *n*. **stubble goose** *n* a goose fed on stubble. **stubble rake** *n* a rake with long teeth for raking stubble.

stubborn /*stub'ərn*/ *adj* obstinate, *esp* unreasonably or troublesomely so; pertinacious; refractory; hard to work or treat; inflexible (*lit* and *fig*); rigid. ◆ *vt* (*obs*) to make stubborn. [Connection with **stub** is obscure]

■ **stubb'ornly** *adv*. **stubb'ornness** *n*.

stubby see under **stub**.

STUC *abbrev* : Scottish Trades Union Congress.

stucco /*stuk'ō*/ *n* any kind of plaster or cement used to coat exterior walls or make architectural mouldings; a decorative work on a building done in stucco (*pl* **stucc'ōs**). ◆ *vt* (pat and pap **stucc'oed** or **stucc'o'd**) to face or overlay with stucco; to form in stucco. [Ital *stucco* ; from OHGer *stucchi* crust, coating]

■ **stucc'oer** *n* a worker or dealer in stucco.

stuck¹ see **stick²**.

stuck² /*stuk*/ (*Shakesp*) *n* a thrust. [**stock²**]

stuck-up /*stuk-up*/ (*inf*) *adj* snobbish, arrogant.

stud¹ /*stud*/ *n* a projecting boss, knob, or pin; a large-headed nail; a stud bolt; a type of fastener consisting of two interlocking discs; a small rounded earring; one of several rounded projections on the soles of certain types of (*esp* sports) footwear, improving the grip; a spur, stump, or short branch; an upright in a timber framework or partition; a crosspiece strengthening a link in a chain; a wooden post (*obs*); a tree trunk (*Spenser*); the height of a room (*US*). ◆ *vt* (**studd'ing**; **studd'ed**) to adorn, set, or secure with studs; to set at intervals. [OE *studu* post]

■ **studd'ed** *adj*. **studd'ing** *n*. ❑ **stud bolt** *n* a bolt with a thread on each end, screwed into a fixed part at one end, receiving a nut on the other. **stud'work** *n* brickwork walls between studs; studded leather.

stud² /*stud*/ *n* a horse-breeding establishment; the animals kept there; a collection of horses or other animals, or of cars, belonging to the same owner; a stud horse; a sexually potent or active man, or one who thinks he is (*inf*); stud poker. ◆ *adj* kept for breeding; of a stud. [OE *stōd*; cf **steed¹**; Ger *Stute* mare, *Gestüt* stud]

■ **stud'ly** *adj* (*sl*) strong and powerful; (of a man) sexually attractive. ❑ **stud'book** *n* a record of horses' (or other animals') pedigrees. **stud'farm** *n* a horse-breeding farm. **stud groom** *n* a groom at a stud, *esp* the head groom. **stud horse** *n* a stallion kept for breeding. **stud muffin** *n* (*N Am inf*) a sexually attractive young man. **stud poker** *n* a variety of the game of poker in which bets are placed on hands containing some cards dealt face up.

■ **at stud** or **out to stud** being used for breeding purposes.

studden see **stand**.

studdingsail or **studding-sail** /*stun'sl*/ *n* a narrow additional sail set at the outer edges of a square sail when wind is light and abaft the beam (also **stun'sail** or **stun's'l**). [Origin unknown]

studdle /*stud'l*/ *n* a post; a prop. [OE *stodla*]

stude see **staun**.

student /*stū'dənt*/ *n* a person who studies; a person devoted to books or to any study; a person who is enrolled for a course of instruction, *esp* at a higher or further education establishment; an undergraduate; a member of the foundation of Christ Church, Oxford, equivalent to a fellow elsewhere; the holder of a studentship; a school pupil; a person learning a specified profession, etc (as *student teacher, student nurse*). [L *studēre* (prp *studēns, -entis*) to be zealous, from *studium* (OFr *estudie* ; Ital *studio*) zeal, study]

■ **stu'dentry** *n* students collectively. **stu'dentship** *n* an endowment for a student in a college; in Christ Church, Oxford, the equivalent of a fellowship; the condition or time of being a student. **stū'denty** *adj* relating to the lifestyle or fashions typically associated with students. **studied** /*stud'id*/ *adj* well considered; deliberately contrived, designed; over-elaborated with loss of spontaneity; well prepared by study; well-read; versed. **stud'iedly** *adv*. **stud'iedness** *n*. **stud'ier** *n*. **studio** /*stū'di-ō*/ *n* (*pl* **stu'dios**) an artist's workroom; a workshop for photography, cinematography, radio or television broadcasting, the making of sound recordings, etc; a company that makes films. **studious** /*stū'di-əs*/ *adj* devoted to or assiduous in study; studied; painstaking or painstakingly carried out; deliberate. **stu'diously** *adv*. **stu'diousness** *n*. **study** /*stud'i*/ *vt* (**stud'ying**; **stud'ied**) to apply the mind to in order to acquire knowledge or skill; to examine; to consider; to scrutinize; to look contemplatively at; to take into consideration; to consider the wishes, advantage, feelings of; to devise; to think out; to instruct (*Shakesp*). ◆ *vi* to apply the mind closely to books, nature, acquisition of learning or of skill; to take an educational course; to rack one's mind; to muse, meditate, reflect. ◆ *n* an object of endeavour, solicitude, or mental application; (in *pl*) related objects of mental application or departments of knowledge; a state of consideration; attentive and detailed examination; a scrutiny; a reverie; application of the mind to the acquisition of knowledge or skill; a department of knowledge; a preliminary essay towards a work of art; an exercise in art; a musical composition serving as an exercise in technique; a presentation in literature or art of the results of study; a room devoted to study, actually or ostensibly; the committing to memory, hence a memorizer (*theatre*); inclination; interest; zeal. ❑ **studio couch** *n* a couch, sometimes without a back, that can be converted into a bed. **studio flat** *n* a small flat consisting of one main room, or an open-plan living area. **studio pottery** *n* pottery individually produced by the potter in a studio, rather than factory-made. **study group** *n* a group of people studying a specific subject, who meet informally at regular intervals to discuss their work or some other topic.

studio see under **student**.

studly see under **stud²**.

study, etc see under **student**.

stuff /*stuf*/ *n* matter; substance; essence; material; a preparation used or commodity dealt in in some particular industry or trade; garden produce; cloth, *esp* woollen; a medicinal mixture; goods; luggage; provision; furniture; money; literary or journalistic copy; liquor (**good stuff** often whisky); a broad category or collection of indeterminate or unspecified things (*inf*); rubbish; nonsense; stuffing, filling (*obs*); indecent matter (*obs*). ◆ *adj* (*archaic*) woollen. ◆ *vt* to garrison (*obs*); to store, furnish (*Shakesp*); to provision (*obs*); to line; to be a filling for; to fill very full; to thrust in; to crowd; to cram; to obstruct, clog; to cause to bulge out by filling; to fill (eg a fowl) with seasoning; to fill the skin of (an animal) so as to reproduce the living form; to hoax (*sl*); (of a man) to have sexual intercourse with (*vulgar*); to fill (envelopes) with copies of printed material, *esp* promotional leaflets; to load (a freight container); (in electronics manufacturing, etc) to assemble the internal components of a machine in its external casing; to defeat very convincingly (*sl*). ◆ *vi* to feed gluttonously; to practise taxidermy. [OFr *estoffe* stuff, from *estoffer* to furnish, equip, from Gmc *stopfōn*, earlier *stoppōn*, from LL *stuppāre* to plug, stop up, from L *stuppa*, from Gr *styppē* coarse fibres, tow]

■ **stuffed** *adj* provisioned; well-stored; filled; filled out with stuffing; clogged in nose or throat, etc (often with *up*); utterly defeated (*sl*). **stuff'er** *n* a person or thing that stuffs; a person who conceals illegal substances, *esp* drugs, in a body passage such as the rectum or vagina (*sl*). **stuff'ily** *adv*. **stuff'iness** *n*. **stuff'ing** *n* that which is used to stuff or fill anything, straw, sawdust, feathers, hair, etc; savoury ingredients put into meat, poultry, etc in cooking. **stuff'y** *adj* badly ventilated; musty; stifling; stout, sturdy (*Scot*); stodgy (*sl*); strait-laced; sulky (*US*); (of a nose) blocked up with mucus, etc. ❑ **stuffed shirt** *n* a pompous, unbendingly correct person, *esp* if of little real importance. **stuff gown** *n* a gown of stuff, not silk, *esp* that of a junior barrister. **stuffing box** *n* a device for preventing leakage of gases or liquids along a reciprocating rod or rotating shaft, consisting of a ring-shaped chamber packed to provide a pressure-tight seal. ■ **and stuff** (*inf*) and that sort of thing or rubbish. **bit of stuff** (*offensive sl*) a girl or woman considered sexually. **do one's stuff** to do what is expected of one. **get stuffed!** (*vulgar sl*) an interjection expressing anger, derision, contemptuous dismissal, etc. **hot stuff** (*inf*) denoting a very attractive, effective, etc person or thing. **knock the stuffing out of** to reduce (an opponent) to helplessness. **know one's stuff** to have a thorough knowledge of the field in which one is concerned. **stuff it** (or **them, you,** etc) (*sl*) an interjection expressing disgust, scorn, frustration, etc. **stuff up** (*inf*) to make a mess of things. **that's the stuff!** excellent! **the hard stuff** strongly alcoholic drink, *esp* whisky.

stull /stul/ (*mining*) *n* a horizontal prop in a stope. [Cf Ger *Stollen*]
■ **stulm** /stulm/ *n* an adit; a small draining-shaft.

stultify /stul'ti-fī/ *vt* (**stul'tifying; stul'tified**) to dull the mind of; to cause to appear foolish or ridiculous; to destroy the force of, as by self-contradiction; to allege or prove to be of unsound mind (*law*). [L *stultus* foolish]
■ **stultificā'tion** *n*. **stul'tifīer** *n*.

stum /stum/ *n* must, grape-juice unfermented; new wine used to revive dead or vapid wine; a mixture used to impart artificial strength, etc to weak beer or wine; wine revived by the addition of stum or by a second fermentation. ◆ *vt* (**stum'ming; stummed**) to renew or doctor with stum; to fume (eg a cask of liquor) with burning sulphur. [Du *stom* must, from *stom* mute; Ger *stumm* dumb]

stumble /stum'bl/ *vi* to take a false step or come near to falling in walking; to move or speak unsteadily or with hesitations; to err; to lapse into wrongdoing; to flounder; to come upon by chance or error (with *across* or *on*). ◆ *vt* to disconcert. ◆ *n* a trip; a false step; a lapse; a blunder. [ME *stomble, stumble*; cf Norw *stumla*, and **stammer**]
■ **stum'bler** *n*. **stum'blingly** *adv*. **stum'bly** *adj* apt to stumble or to cause stumbling.
□ **stum'blebum** *n* (*sl; orig* and *esp US*) an awkward, inept, ineffectual person. **stum'bling-block** *n* an obstacle; a cause of perplexity or error.

stumer /stū'mər/ (*sl*) *n* a counterfeit coin or note; a forged or worthless cheque; a sham; a dud; a failure, bankruptcy; a horse sure to lose; a stupid mistake, clanger; a stupid person (*Scot*). [Origin obscure]

stumm /shtum/ same as **shtoom**.

stummel /stum'l/ *n* the bowl and adjacent part of a pipe. [Ger]

stump /stump/ *n* the part of a felled or fallen tree left in the ground; a short thick remaining basal part, *esp* of anything that projects; a short thick branch; a leg (*facetious*); a wooden leg; anything stumpy; a stumping walk or its sound; a pencil of soft material for softening hard lines, blending, etc (also **tortillon**); one of the three sticks forming (with the bails) a wicket (*cricket*); a challenge to perform a feat (*US*); a tree stump or similar, used as a platform, eg by a public speaker. ◆ *adj* reduced to a stump; stumpy. ◆ *vt* to reduce to a stump; to remove stumps from; (of the wicketkeeper; sometimes with *out*) to dismiss by breaking the wicket when the striker is out of his or her ground (*cricket*); to clear out of money (*sl*); to nonplus, foil, defeat; to soften or tone with a stump; to walk over or strike heavily and stiffly; to traverse (an area) making political speeches; to dare, challenge (*US*). ◆ *vi* to walk stiffly and heavily, as if on wooden legs; to make political speeches from improvised platforms. [Cf Du *stomp*, MLGer *stump*, ON *stumpr*, Ger *Stumpf*]
■ **stump'age** *n* (*US*) standing timber, its monetary value, or money paid for it. **stump'er** *n*. **stump'ily** *adv*. **stump'iness** *n*. **stump'ing** *n*. **stumps** *n sing* (*cricket*) the end of play. **stump'y** *adj* short and thick; full of stumps (*US*). ◆ *n* (*sl*) cash.
□ **stump orator** *n* one who speaks from an improvised platform, *usu* with an implication of rant; (in the USA) a political public speaker in general. **stump oratory** *n*. **stump speech** *n*. **stump work** *n* elaborate raised embroidery of the 15c–17c using various materials and raised by stumps of wood or pads of wool.
■ **draw stumps** (*cricket*) to end play (also *fig*). **on the stump** engaged in a (political) speech-making tour, campaign. **stir one's stumps** to move, be active. **stump up** to pay up, fork out.

stun /stun/ *vt* (**stunn'ing; stunned**) to render unconscious by a blow or similar; to stupefy or daze, eg with din or sudden emotion; to astound; to abrade, bruise. ◆ *n* a shock, stupefying blow; stunned condition. ◆ *adj* (of a weapon) designed to stun rather than kill. [OFr *estoner* (Fr *étonner*) to astonish; cf OE *stunian* to make a din, from *stun* a din]
■ **stunn'er** *n* someone who or something that stuns; a person or thing supremely excellent (*inf*); a very attractive person (*inf*). **stunn'ing** *n* stupefaction. ◆ *adj* stupefying, dazing; supremely excellent (*inf*); very attractive (*inf*). **stunn'ingly** *adv*.
□ **stun grenade, gun,** etc *n* one designed to stun its target temporarily without causing serious injury.

Stundist /s(h)tŭn'dist/ *n* a member of a Russian Protestant evangelical sect. [Ger *Stunde* hour, lesson, from their Bible-reading meetings]
■ **Stun'dism** *n*.

stung /stung/ *pat* and *pap* of **sting**[1].

stunk /stungk/ *pat* and *pap* of **stink**.

stunkard /stung'kərd/ (*Scot*) *adj* sulky; sullen. [Origin obscure]

stunsail, stuns'l /stun'sl/ see **studdingsail**.

stunt[1] /stunt/ *vt* to hinder from growth, to dwarf, check. ◆ *n* a check in growth; a stunted animal. [OE *stunt* dull stupid; ON *stuttr* short]
■ **stunt'ed** *adj* dwarfed. **stunt'edness** *n*.

stunt[2] /stunt/ *n* a difficult, often showy, performance, enterprise, or turn; anything done to attract attention. ◆ *adj* of, used in or relating to a stunt. ◆ *vi* to perform stunts. [Perh a variant of **stint**[1], **stent**[1]; cf **stunt**[1]; or perh Ger *Stunde* hour, lesson]
□ **stunt'man** or **stunt'woman** *n* one paid to perform dangerous and showy feats (*esp* a stand-in for a film actor).

stupa /stoo'pə/ *n* a dome-shaped Buddhist memorial shrine, a tope. [Sans *stūpa*]

stupe[1] /stūp/ (*archaic*) *n* a medicated piece of tow or cloth used in fomentation. ◆ *vt* to treat with a stupe. [L *stūpa* for *stuppa*, from Gr *styppē* tow]

stupe[2] see **stupid**.

stupefy /stū'pi-fī/ *vt* (**stū'pefying; stū'pefied**) to make stupid or senseless (as with alcohol, drugs, etc); to stun with amazement, fear, etc. ◆ *vi* to become stupid or dull. [L *stupēre* to be struck senseless, and *facere* to make]
■ **stupefacient** /-fā'shənt/ *adj* stupefying. ◆ *n* a stupefying drug. **stupefaction** /-fak'shən/ *n* the act of stupefying; the state of being stupefied; extreme astonishment. **stupefac'tive** *adj* stupefying. **stu'pefied** *adj*. **stu'pefier** *n*. **stu'pefying** *adj*.

stupendous /stū-pen'dəs/ (formerly, as *Milton*, **stupendious** /-i-əs/) *adj* astounding; astoundingly huge; often used as an informal term of approbation or admiration. [L *stupendus*, gerundive, and *stupēns, -entis*, prp of *stupēre* to be stunned]
■ **stupen'dously** *adv*. **stupen'dousness** *n*. **stu'pent** *adj* (*rare*) astounded; dumbfounded.

stupid /stū'pid/ *adj* stupefied or stunned; senseless; insensible; deficient or dull in understanding; showing lack of reason or judgement; foolish; dull; boring. ◆ *n* (*inf*) a stupid person (also *inf* **stupe**). [L *stupidus*]
■ **stupid'ity** or **stu'pidness** *n*. **stu'pidly** *adv*.

stupor /stū'pər/ *n* torpor; lethargy; a state of near-unconsciousness (as caused by alcohol, drugs, etc); a daze. [L *stupor, -ōris*, from *stupēre*]
■ **stu'porous** *adj*.

stuprate /stū'prāt/ (*archaic*) *vt* to ravish, violate. [L *stuprāre, -ātum*]
■ **stuprā'tion** *n*.

sturdy /stûr'di/ *adj* robust; stout; firmly built or constructed; *orig*, giddy; impetuous, violent, rough (*obs*); refractory; obstinate; resolute. ◆ *n* gid, a disease of sheep characterized by staggering, due to a bladderworm in the brain; a sturdy person. [OFr *estourdi* (Fr *étourdi*) stunned, giddy]
■ **stur'died** *adj* affected with sturdy. **stur'dily** *adv*. **stur'diness** *n*.

sture see **stoor**[1].

sturgeon /stûr'jən/ *n* any member of a genus (*Acipenser*) of large fishes of northern temperate waters, with a cartilaginous skull, long snout, heterocercal tail, and rows of bony shields on the skin, yielding caviar and isinglass. [Anglo-Fr from OFr *estourgeon*, of Gmc origin (OHGer *sturjo*)]

Sturge-Weber syndrome /stûrj-web'er sin'drōm/ *n* a rare congenital condition in which abnormal distension and knotting of the blood vessels in part of the brain (causing weakness on the opposite side of the body, seizures, etc) is associated with a large purple birthmark spreading over one side of the face, including the eye. [WA *Sturge* (1850–1919) and FP *Weber* (1863–1962), British physicians]

Sturmabteilung /shtŭrm'ap-tī-lŭng/ *n pl* storm troops (qv), Brownshirts. [Ger *Sturm* storm, and *Abteilung* division]

Sturmer /stûr'mər/ or **Sturmer Pippin** /pip'in/ (also without *caps*) *n* a variety of dessert apple named after *Sturmer*, a village in Essex where it was developed; an apple of this variety.

Sturm und Drang /shtŭrm ŭnt drang/ *n* a German literary movement of the latter half of the 18c, characterized by realism, extravagant passion and rousing action; storm and stress, turmoil. [Ger, literally, storm and stress, title of a play by German dramatist FM von Klinger (1752–1831)]

sturnus /stûr'nəs/ *n* any bird of the starling genus (*Sturnus*) giving name to the family **Stur'nidae** /-ni-dē/. [L *sturnus* starling]
■ **stur'nine** or **stur'noid** *adj*.

sturt /stûrt/ (chiefly *Scot*) *n* contention, strife, annoyance; a disturbance. ◆ *vt* to trouble, annoy, disturb. ◆ *vi* to start with fear. [**strut**[1]]

stushie see **stooshie**.

stutter /stut'ər/ *vi* and *vt* to speak, say, or pronounce with spasmodic repetition of (*esp* initial) sounds, *usu* consonants; to stammer. ◆ *n* a speech impediment characterized by such repetition. [A frequentative of obs dialect *stut* to stutter, ME *stutten*; cf ON *stauta*; Ger *stossen*]
■ **stutt'erer** *n*. **stutt'ering** *n* and *adj*. **stutt'eringly** *adv*.

STV *abbrev* : Scottish Television; Single Transferable Vote.

sty[1] or rarely **stye** /stī/ *n* (*pl* **sties** or **styes**) a pen for pigs; any extremely filthy place; any place of gross debauchery. ◆ *vt* and *vi* (**sty'ing**; **stied** or **styed**) to put or keep in a sty. [OE *stig* pen, hall; Ger *Steige*]

sty[2] or **stye** /stī/ *n* a small inflamed swelling at the edge of the eyelid, caused by bacterial infection (also called (*med*) **hordeolum**). [Obs or dialect *stian, styan*, from OE *stīgend*, from *stīgan* to rise]

sty[3] /stī/ (*obs*) *vi* to mount, rise, climb (also **stye** or **stie**). ◆ *n* a path; a ladder. [OE *stīgan* to mount, rise, ascend, *stīg* path, and ON *stige* path, OE *stīge* ascent or descent]

stye see **sty**[1,2,3].

Stygian /stij'i-ən or -yən/ *adj* of the *Styx*, one of the rivers of Hades, across which Charon ferries the spirits of the dead (*Gr myth*); hellish, infernal, gloomy; black as the Styx. [Gr *Styx*; cf *stygein* to hate]
❑ **Stygian oath** *n* an inviolable oath, like that of the gods, by the Styx.

stylar, **stylate** see under **style**.

style /stīl/ *n* the manner of writing, mode of expressing thought in language or of expression, execution, action or bearing generally; a literary composition (*obs*); the distinctive manner peculiar to an author or other; the particular custom or form observed, as by a printing house in optional matters (**house style**), or by lawyers in drawing up deeds; designation; manner, form, fashion, *esp* when considered superior or desirable; an air of fashion or consequence; a kind or type; a slender structure of various kinds (*biol*); the slender part of the pistil of a flower connecting the stigma and the ovary (*bot*); a hand, pointer, index; the gnomon of a dial; a pointed instrument for writing on wax tablets; a similar instrument or tool of various kinds, such as a graver, a blunt probe, a tracing or cutting point; a mode of reckoning dates, ie *Old Style*, according to the Julian calendar, as in Britain until 1752, Russia until 1917, and *New Style*, according to the Gregorian calendar, adopted in Britain by omitting eleven days, 3 to 13 September 1752. ◆ *vt* to arrange or dictate the fashion or style of; to designate. ◆ *adj* and *adv combining form* in the style of, resembling. [L *stilus* a writing instrument, literary composition or style, confused with Gr *stȳlos* a column; in some senses perh from the Gr word]
■ **sty'lar** *adj*. **sty'late** *adj* having a style or a persistent style. **style'less** *adj*. **sty'ler** *n* a device for styling the hair. **sty'let** or **stī'let** *n* a probe; a wire in a catheter; a small bristle-like projection (*biol*); an engraving tool; a writing instrument; a piercing part of an insect's jaws; a stiletto. **stylif'erous** *adj* (*bot* and *zool*) bearing a slender structure of various kinds. **sty'liform** *adj* (*bot* and *zool*) shaped like a style or a bristle. **sty'lish** *adj* displaying style; fashionable; showy; imposingly smart. **sty'lishly** *adv*. **sty'lishness** *n*. **sty'list** *n* a person with a distinctive and fine (*esp* literary, etc) style; a person who creates or arranges a style, *esp* in hairdressing. **stylist'ic** *adj* and *n*. **stylist'ically** *adv*. **stylis'tics** *n sing* the science of the variations in language, including the effective values of different words, forms, and sounds, that constitute style in the literary and also the wider sense. **styliza'tion** or **-s-** *n*. **sty'lize** or **-ise** *vt* to give an elaborate, *esp* non-naturalistic, style to; to conventionalize. **sty'loid** *adj* (*bot* and *zool*) like a style or bristle; forming a slender process. ◆ *n* a spiny process, *esp* that of the temporal bone in the skull.
❑ **style'book** *n* a book of forms for deeds, etc, or rules for printers and editors. **style'sheet** *n* (*comput*) a set of type specifications, layout instructions, etc used as a template for documents in desktop publishing or in assembling web pages.
■ **in style** in a grand manner.

styli see **stylus**.

stylite /stī'līt/ *n* one of a class of ascetics that lived on the tops of pillars in ancient times. [Gr *stylītēs*, from *stȳlos* a pillar]

stylize, -ise see under **style**.

stylo see **stylograph** under **stylography**.

stylobate /stī'lō-bāt/ (*archit*) *n* a continuous pedestal supporting a row of columns. [Gr *stȳlobatēs*, from *stȳlos* a column, and *batēs* someone who treads, from the root of *bainein* to walk]

stylography /stī-log'rə-fi/ *n* a mode of writing or engraving with a style. [Gr *stȳlos* a style, and *graphein* to write]
■ **styl'ograph** /stī'lə-gräf/ *n* a pencil-like pen from which ink is liberated by pressure on a needle-point (*inf* short form **sty'lo**, *pl* **sty'lōs**). **stylographic** /-graf'ik/ *adj*. **stylograph'ically** *adv*.

styloid see under **style**.

stylolite /stī-lol'īt or stī'lə-līt/ (*geol*) *n* an irregular suture-like boundary creating columnar formations in some limestones and evaporites, *usu* independent of the bedding planes, and probably formed by pressure-controlled solution followed by redeposition. [Gr *stȳlos* pillar, and *lithos* stone]
■ **styloli'tic** *adj*.

stylometry /stī-lom'ə-tri/ *n* a method of studying literary style and development by means of statistical analysis. [Gr *stȳlos* a style, and *metron* a measure]

stylopized or **-s-** /stī'lo-pīzd/ *adj* (of eg bees) infested with a strepsipterous parasite of the *Stylops* or a similar genus.

stylopodium /stī-lō-pō'di-əm/ (*bot*) *n* the swollen disc-shaped or conical base of the style in umbelliferous plants. [Gr *stȳlos* pillar (as if style), and *podion*, dimin of *pous, podos* foot]

stylus /stī'ləs/ *n* (*pl* **styli** /stī'lī/ or **sty'luses**) the cutting needle used in making gramophone records; a durable needle (eg sapphire- or diamond-tipped) for replaying a disc recording; a digital pen (qv under **digit**); same as **style** in the sense of the writing instrument or similar. [Ety as for **style**]
❑ **stylus pen** *n* a tool for entering data into a mobile electronic device by writing on a screen.

styme or **stime** /stīm/ (*Scot*) *n* a glimmer or glimpse (of light); a tiny amount, jot, particle, etc. ◆ *vi* to peer. [Origin obscure]
■ **stymie**, **stimie** or **stimy** /stī'mi/ *n* a purblind person (*Scot*); a situation on the putting green, once difficult to overcome, in which an opponent's ball blocks the way to the hole, the rules now allowing the obstructing ball to be lifted and its position marked (*golf*); hence, a situation from which it is difficult or impossible to proceed. ◆ *vt* (*pat* and *pap* **sty'mied**) to put in such a situation (also **lay someone a stymie**); to frustrate, thwart, prevent, obstruct, block, stop.

styptic /stip'tik/ *adj* drawing together; astringent; checking bleeding, haemostatic. ◆ *n* a styptic agent. [Gr *stȳptikos*, from *stȳphein* to contract]
■ **styp'sis** *n* the use, action, etc of a styptic or styptics. **styp'tical** *adj*. **stypticity** /-tis'i-ti/ *n*.
❑ **styptic pencil** *n* a healing agent for minor cuts, *esp* sustained during shaving.

styrax /stī'raks/ *n* any tropical or subtropical styracaceous tree or shrub of the genus *Styrax*, eg *S. officinalis* (see **storax**). [Gr]
■ **styraca'ceous** *adj* of, related or belonging to the storax family Styracaceae, chiefly American and Asian trees and shrubs with leathery, alternate leaves and often fragrant, bell-shaped white flowers.

styre see **stir**[1].

styrene /stī'rēn or stē'rēn/ *n* an unsaturated hydrocarbon obtained from essential oils (such as the balsam storax) and coal tar, forming thermoplastics (**styrene resins**) on polymerization. [Gr *styrax*; cf **storax**]

Styrofoam® /stī'rə-fōm/ (also without *cap*) *n* a type of expanded plastic made from polystyrene.

SU *abbrev* : strontium unit.

suable /sū' or soo'ə-bl/ *adj* that may be sued (also **sue'able**).
■ **suabil'ity** or **sueabil'ity** *n*. **su'ably** *adv*.

suasion /swā'zhən/ *n* persuasion. [L *suāsiō, -ōnis*, from *suādēre* to advise]
■ **sua'sible** /-si-bl/ *adj*. **sua'sive** /-siv/ *adj*. **sua'sively** *adv*. **sua'siveness** *n*. **sua'sory** *adj*.

suave /swäv (formerly swāv)/ *adj* (of a person, *esp* a man) polite, sophisticated and smoothly affable, *esp* superficially so; smooth, bland. [Fr, from L *suāvis* sweet, agreeable]
■ **suave'ly** *adv*. **suavity** /swäv'i-ti/ *n*.

suaveolent /swə-vē'ə-lənt/ (*rare*) *adj* fragrant. [L *suāveolēns, -entis*, from *suāvē* sweetly, and *olēns* smelling]

sub /sub/ (*inf*) *n* a subordinate; a subaltern; a subeditor; a sublieutenant; a subsidiary; a subway; a subscription (also **subs**); a subscriber; a substitute; a submarine; subsistence money, hence a loan, an advance payment. ◆ *vi* (**subb'ing**; **subbed**) (*inf*) to act as a sub; to work as a substitute; to work as a newspaper subeditor; to subcontract. ◆ *vt* (*inf*) to subedit; to subcontract; to lend (money). [Short form]
■ **subb'ing** *n* (*inf*) the advancing of part of the wages while the work is going on.

sub. *abbrev* : subject.

sub- /sub- or səb-/ pfx (1) under, underneath, underlying, below, at the bottom of; (2) subordinate, subsidiary, secondary; (3) part of, a subdivision of; (4) almost, partially, nearly, somewhat imperfectly, bordering on, deviating slightly from; (5) secretly, covertly; (6) in smaller proportion (chem); (7) in the style of but inferior to, as in sub-Chaplin, sub-Beethoven (inf). [L sub under, near; in composition, in some degree, secretly]

> Words formed using the prefix **sub-** are listed as separate entries in the main word list or, if their meaning is self-evident, at the foot of the page.

subacid /sub-as'id/ adj somewhat or moderately acid or sour (lit and fig). [**sub-** (4)]
■ **subacid'ity** or **subac'idness** n. **subac'idly** adv.

subact /sub-akt'/ vt to work up (as in cultivation, the process of digestion, etc); to subdue. [L subactus, pap of subigere, from sub under, and agere to drive, do]
■ **subac'tion** /-shən/ n.

subacute /sub-ə-kūt'/ adj slightly or moderately acute; (of a disease) not acute but progressing more rapidly than chronic (med). [**sub-** (4)]
■ **subacute'ly** adv.

subadar see under **subah**.

subadult /sub-ad'ult or sub-ə-dult'/ adj (usu of an animal) fully or almost fully grown but not yet having developed all the adult characteristics; adolescent. ◆ n an individual at subadult stage. [**sub-** (4)]

subaerial /sub-ā-(ē)'ri-əl/ adj in the open air; occurring on the land at or near the earth's surface, as opposed to underground or under water. [**sub-** (1)]
■ **subaē'rially** adv.

subah /soo'bä/ n a province of the Mogul empire; a subahdar. [Hindi and Pers]
■ **su'bahdar** or **su'badar** n orig the governor of a subah; a native officer in an Indian regiment corresponding to a captain. **subahdar'y** or **su'bahship** n the office of subahdar.

subalpine /sub-al'pīn/ adj bordering on the alpine; at the foot of or on the lower slopes of the Alps; (of a plant) growing just below the tree line in mountainous regions. [**sub-** (4) and (1)]

subaltern /sub'əl-tərn (N Am, except in logic, usu sub-öl'tərn)/ adj (of military officers) under the rank of captain; particular (logic); being at once a genus and a species of a higher genus (logic); ranked successively (rare); subordinate, of inferior status; occupied by, or having the status of, a vassal (archaic). ◆ n a subaltern officer; a proposition differing from another in quantity alone (both being affirmative or both negative, but one universal, the other particular) (logic); a subordinate. [L subalternus, from sub under, and alter another]
■ **subalter'nant** n (logic) a universal in relation to the subaltern particular. **subalter'nate** n (logic) a particular proposition in relation to the subaltern universal. ◆ adj subservient, lesser in status, etc; intermediate between alternate and opposite (bot). **subalternation** /sub-öl-tər-nā'shən/ n the relation between a universal and particular of the same quality. **subalter'nity** n subordinate position.

subapical /sub-ā'pi-kəl or -ap'i-/ adj below the apex. [**sub-** (1)]

subapostolic /sub-a-pə-stol'ik/ adj of the time just after that of the apostles. [**sub-** (4)]

subaquatic /sub-ə-kwat'ik/ adj under water (also **subā'queous**); partially aquatic (zool and bot). [**sub-** (1) and (4)]
■ **suba'qua** or **sub-a'qua** adj of or relating to underwater sport.

subarachnoid /sub-ə-rak'noid/ (anat) adj below the arachnoid membrane; of, relating to or occurring in the space between the arachnoid membrane and the pia meninges of the brain. [**sub-** (1)]

subarcuate /sub-är'kū-āt/ adj somewhat arched; with two or more arches under a main arch (archit). [**sub-** (4) and (1)]
■ **subarcūa'tion** n.

subarrhation or **subarration** /sub-ə-rā'shən/ n an ancient mode of betrothal in which a ring or gift, esp of money, was bestowed by the

man upon the woman. [L subarr(h)ātiō, -ōnis, from sub under, and arr(h)a earnest-money]

subassembly /sub-ə-sem'bli/ (engineering) n an assembled unit that may be incorporated with others in a more complex assembly. [**sub-** (2)]
■ **subassem'ble** vt.

subastral /sub-as'trəl/ adj beneath the stars, terrestrial. [**sub-** (1)]

subatom /sub-at'əm/ n a constituent part of an atom. [**sub-** (3)]
■ **subatom'ic** adj relating to particles constituting the atom or processes that occur within the atom or at less than atomic level. **subatom'ics** n sing the study of these particles and processes.

subaudition /sub-ö-dish'ən/ (esp grammar) n a sense understood or implied without being expressed. [**sub-** (5)]

subbase /sub'bās/ n the lowest part of a base (archit); a division of a military base. [**sub-** (1) and (3)]
■ **subbasal** /sub'bās'əl/ adj near or below the base.

subbie /sub'ē/ (inf) n a subcontractor, esp one working for a main contractor in the construction industry (also **subby**).

Subbuteo® /sə-boo'ti-ō also su-, -bū'/ n a version of table football in which individual toy players mounted on hemispherical bases are flicked with the fingers.

subcalibre or (N Am) **subcaliber** /sub-kal'i-bər/ adj (of ammunition) of a calibre less than the firearm or barrel used to fire it. [**sub-** (4)]

subcarrier /sub-kar'i-ər/ (telecom) n a modulated frequency used to modulate (with others) a main carrier wave. [**sub-** (2)]

subcartilaginous /sub-kär-ti-laj'i-nəs/ adj composed partly of cartilage; situated under a cartilage. [**sub-** (4) and (1)]

subcellular /sub-sel'ū-lər/ (biol) adj occurring within a cell; smaller than a cell. [**sub-** (3) and (6)]

subception see **subliminal perception** under **subliminal**.

subchanter /sub'chän'tər/ n a precentor's deputy; an officer or lay member of a cathedral who assists in chanting the litany. [**sub-** (2)]

subclavian /sub-klā'vi-ən/ (anat) adj and n (any of the arteries, nerves, etc) situated or passing under the clavicle. [**sub-** (1) and **clavicle**]
■ **subclavic'ular** adj.

subclimax /sub-klī'maks/ (ecology) n a relatively stable plant community or system at some stage of a succession preceding climax. [**sub-** (4)]

subclinical /sub-klin'i-kəl/ adj (of a disease) not sufficiently developed to be detectable by usual clinical methods. [**sub-** (4)]

subcompact /sub-kom'pakt/ (N Am) n a small car, such as a sports car. [**sub-** (2)]

subconscious /sub-kon'shəs/ adj dimly conscious; distant from the focus of attention but capable of being consciously recalled; (of memories, motives, intentions, thoughts, etc) of which the individual is only dimly aware but which exert an influence on his or her behaviour. ◆ n the subconscious mind or activities. [**sub-** (4)]
■ **subcon'sciously** adv. **subcon'sciousness** n.

subcontinent /sub-kon'ti-nənt/ n a large portion of a continent with a character of its own (a term formerly applied to South Africa, later to India); a large landmass not large enough or distinct enough to be called a continent. [**sub-** (2), (4) and (1)]
■ **subcontinent'al** adj.
■ **Indian subcontinent** the area covered by India, Pakistan, Bangladesh, Bhutan and Nepal.

subcontract /sub-kon'trakt/ n a contract subordinate to another contract, as for the subletting of work. ◆ vi /-kən-trakt'/ to let out or undertake work under a subcontract. ◆ vt to engage one or more parties as subcontractor(s) to carry out (work forming all or part of an original contract); to undertake (work) under a subcontract. [**sub-** (2)]
■ **subcontract'ing** n. **subcontract'or** n.

subcontrary /sub-kon'trə-ri/ (logic) adj (of a particular proposition in relation to another differing only in quality) such that at least one must be true. ◆ n a subcontrary proposition. [**sub-** (4)]
■ **subcontrarī'ety** n.

Some words formed with the prefix **sub-**; the numbers in brackets refer to the numbered senses in the entry for **sub-**.

sub'abbot n (2).	suba'gent n (2).	subarbor'eal adj (1), (4).
subabdom'inal adj (1).	subagg'regate n and adj (6).	subarboresc'ent adj (1), (4).
subac'etate n (6).	subaggrega'tion n (6).	subarc'tic adj (4).
subac'rid adj (4).	subballi'ance n (2).	sub'area n (2), (3).
subadmin'istrative adj (2).	suballoca'tion n (3).	subar'id adj (4).
subadmin'istrator n (2).	subang'ular adj (4).	sub'article n (2), (3).
subaff'luent adj (4).	subantarc'tic adj (4).	subassocia'tion n (2).
suba'gency n (2).	subappear'ance n (2).	subatmospher'ic adj (1), (4).

■ words derived from main entry word; ▫ compound words; ▪ idioms and phrasal verbs

subcostal /sub-kos'təl/ adj near or under a rib or the ribs; behind or near the costa. ◆ n the subcostal nervure or vein of an insect's wing (also **subcost'a**). [**sub-** (1)]

subcritical /sub-krit'i-kl/ adj of insufficient mass to sustain a chain reaction (phys); below the critical temperature for hardening metals. [**sub-** (1)]

subculture /sub'kul-chər/ n a social, ethnic or economic group with a particular character of its own within a larger culture or society; a culture (eg of a microorganism) derived from a pre-existing one. [**sub-** (2) and (3)]
■ **subcul'tural** adj.

subcutaneous /sub-kū-tā'ni-əs/ adj beneath or just under the skin. [**sub-** (1)]
■ **subcuta'neously** adv.

subdeacon /sub-dē'kən/ n a member of the order of the ministry next below that of deacon, preparing the vessels, etc at the Eucharist. [**sub-** (2)]
■ **subdea'conry** n. **subdea'conship** n.

subdelirious /sub-di-lir'i-əs or -lē'ri-əs or -də-/ adj mildly or intermittently delirious. [**sub-** (4)]
■ **subdelir'ium** n.

subdew an obsolete form of **subdue**.

subdirectory /sub'dī-rek-tə-ri/ (comput) n a directory that is contained within another. [**sub-** (3)]

subdivide /sub-di-vīd'/ vt and vi to divide into smaller divisions; to divide again. [**sub-** (3)]
■ **subdivid'er** n. **subdivisible** /-viz'/ adj. **subdivision** /-vizh'ən/ n. **subdivis'ional** adj. **subdivi'sive** adj.

sub divo /sub dī'vō, sūb dē'vō or -wō/ or **sub Jove** /jō've, yō've or -we/ (L) adv under the sky; in the open air.

subdolous /sub'dō-ləs/ (rare) adj crafty. [L pfx sub-, in sense of somewhat, and dolus a wile]

subdominant /sub-dom'i-nənt/ n the fourth degree of the diatonic scale, eg F in the scale of C (music); something that is partially or not quite dominant. ◆ adj not quite ranking as dominant; partially dominant. [**sub-** (1) and (4)]

subduce /sub-dūs'/ vt (obs) to withdraw. [L sub, and dūcere, ductum to lead, take]
■ **subduct** /-dukt'/ vt to withdraw, take away (now rare); to abstract or take away secretly or surreptitiously (rare); to lift up; to cause subduction. ◆ vi to take something away (now rare); to undergo subduction. **subduc'tion** n a withdrawal, subtraction (now rare); the action or process of one part of the earth's crust moving underneath another. ❏ **subduction zone** n the Benioff zone.

subdue (Spenser **subdew**) /sub-dū'/ vt to overcome, conquer; to overpower; to subject; to make (a person or animal) submissive; to bring (land) under cultivation; to allay; to reduce the intensity, degree, etc of; to quieten; to tone down; to achieve (Spenser). [OFr souduire, from L subdūcere; see **subduce**]
■ **subdu'able** adj. **subdu'al** n. **subdued'** adj toned down; quiet, restrained; dejected, in low spirits; passive. **subdued'ly** (or /-dū'id-li/) adv. **subdued'ness** n. **subdue'ment** n. **subdu'er** n.

subduple /sub-dū'pl or sub'dū-pl/ adj in the ratio of one to two. [LL subduplus]
■ **subdu'plicate** adj (of a ratio) expressed as the ratio of square roots.

subdural /sub-dū'rəl or -doo'rəl/ (anat) adj below the dura mater; of, relating to or occurring in the space between the dura mater and the arachnoid membrane of the brain. [**sub-** (1)]

subedar same as **subahdar** (see under **subah**).

subedit /sub-ed'it/ vt to select and edit material for (a newspaper); also, to assist in editing. [**sub-** (2)]
■ **subed'itor** n. **subeditorial** /-tōr' or -tör'/ adj. **subed'itorship** n.

subentire /sub-en-tīr'/ (bot) adj (of a leaf or other flat plant member) with very faintly indented margin. [**sub-** (4)]

suber /sū'bər/ (bot and chem) n the bark of the cork tree; cork. [L sūber, -eris the cork oak]

■ **su'berate** n a salt of suberic acid. **subē'reous** or **suberic** /-ber'ik/ adj of cork (**suberic acid** an acid, HOOC(CH$_2$)$_6$COOH, obtained by the action of nitric acid on cork). **su'berin** n the complex of fatty substances that form the chemical basis of cork tissue making it waterproof and resistant to decay. **suberīzā'tion** or **-s-** n the deposition of suberin in the cell walls of cork. **su'berize** or **-ise** vt to deposit suberin in (cell walls) thus forming cork. **su'berose** or **su'berous** adj like or having the appearance of cork.

subfamily /sub'fa-mi-li/ (bot and zool) n a taxonomic division of a family, of one or more genera. [**sub-** (3)]

subfeu /sub'fū/ (hist) n a feu granted to a vassal. [**sub-** (2)]
■ **subfeu** vt to make a subinfeudation of. **subfeudā'tion** n subinfeudation. **subfeud'atory** adj.

subfloor /sub'flōr or -flör/ n a rough floor forming the foundation for the finished floor. [**sub-** (1)]

subframe /sub'frām/ n the frame on which the coachwork of a motor car is built (cf **chassis**); a frame built into a wall to which a door or window frame is fixed. [**sub-** (1)]

subfusc or, less commonly, **subfusk** /sub'fusk or sub-fusk'/ adj dusky; sombre. ◆ n dark, formal clothes worn in combination with the academic gown, esp at Oxford University. [L subfuscus dark brown, from sub under, and fuscus tawny]
■ **subfusc'ous** adj (rare).

subgenus /sub-jē'nəs/ (bot and zool) n (pl **subgenera** /-jen'ə-rə/ or **subge'nuses**) a taxonomic division of a genus. [**sub-** (3)]
■ **subgener'ic** adj. **subgener'ically** adv.

subglacial /sub-glā'si-əl or -glā'shəl/ adj at the base or bottom of a glacier. [**sub-** (1)]
■ **subgla'cially** adv.

subgrade /sub'grād/ n levelled ground under the foundations of a road or a railway. [**sub-** (1)]

subgum /sub-gum'/ n and adj (of) a Chinese-style dish consisting of mixed vegetables, and sometimes diced meat or seafood. [Chin (Cantonese) sháp kám, literally, mixture]

subha see **sabha**.

subhastation /sub-ha-stā'shən/ (obs or hist) n sale by public auction. [L sub under, and hasta a lance (set up by the Romans as a sign that an auction was to be held)]

subhedral /sub-hē'drəl/ (geol) adj showing some traces of crystal form. [**sub-** (4)]

subhuman /sub-hū'mən/ adj less than human, not quite human; of or designating animals that are below the human race in evolutionary development. [**sub-** (4)]

subhumid /sub-hū'mid/ adj (of a climate) too wet for xerophytic vegetation but not wet enough for tree growth. [**sub-** (4)]

subimago /sub-i-mā'gō/ n (pl **subimagines** /-i-mā'jin-ēz or -gin-/ or **subimā'gōs**) a stage in the life history of a mayfly, emerging from the last aquatic nymph already winged but before the last moult. [**sub-** (4)]
■ **subima'ginal** adj.

subincision /sub-in-sizh'ən/ n the formation of an opening into the urethra by incision of the underside of the penis, as a puberty rite practised by some tribal peoples. [**sub-** (1)]
■ **subincise'** vt to perform subincision upon.

subindicate /sub-in'di-kāt/ (obs) vt to hint. [**sub-** (4)]
■ **subindicā'tion** n. **subindic'ative** adj.

subinfeudation /sub-in-fū-dā'shən/ n the granting of land by a feudal tenant or vassal to a subtenant who became his vassal; the tenure so granted or established. [**sub-** (2)]
■ **subinfeu'date** vt and vi. **subinfeud'atory** adj and n.

subintelligitur /sub-in-te-lij'i-tər or sūb-in-te-lig'i-tŭr/ n an implication that is understood without necessarily being stated (also **subintellec'tion** or **subintell'igence**). [L, literally, it is more or less understood, from sub in the sense of covertly, and intelligere to understand]

subintrant /sub-in'trənt/ (med) adj (of fevers) with paroxysms succeeding close upon one another. [**sub-** (4)]

---

subau'dible adj (1).	**subcab'inet** n (1).	**sub'cellar** n (1).
subaud'io adj (4).	**subcan'tor** n (2).	**subcent'ral** adj (1), (4).
subau'ral adj (4).	**subcap'sular** adj (4).	**sub'chapter** n (2), (3).
subauric'ular adj (1).	**subcar'dinal** n (2).	**sub'charter** n (2).
subav'erage adj (1).	**sub'caste** n (3).	**sub'chelate** adj (6).
subax'illary adj (1).	**subcat'egory** n (3).	**sub'chief** n (2).
subbase'ment n (1).	**subcau'dal** adj (1).	**sub'chloride** n (6).
sub'branch n (2), (3).	**subcav'ity** n (1).	**sub'chord** n (1).
sub'breed n (3).	**subceil'ing** n (1).	**sub'circuit** n (2).
sub'bureau n (2).	**subceles'tial** adj (1).	**subciviliza'tion** or **subcivilisa'tion** n (4).

---

subintroduce /sub-in-trō-dūs'/ vt to bring in surreptitiously or subtly. [**sub-** (5)]

subinvolution /sub-in-və-lū'shən or -loo'/ (med) n partial or complete failure of the uterus to return to its normal size in the six weeks following childbirth. [**sub-** (4)]

subirrigation /sub-i-ri-gā'shən/ n irrigation by underground pipes; irrigation from beneath. [**sub-** (1)]
■ **subirr'igate** vt.

subitize or **-ise** /sub'i-tīz/ (psychol) vt to perceive or be capable of perceiving (the number of items in a group) at a glance without actually counting. ◆ vi (of the number of items in a group) to be perceived in this way. [L subitus sudden, and **-ize**]

subito /soo'bi-tō/ (music) adv suddenly; immediately; in haste. [Ital]

subj. abbrev : subject; subjective; subjunctive.

subjacent /sub-jā'sənt/ adj underlying; (of a rock mass) having no perceptible base, bottomless (geol). [L subjacēns, -entis, from sub under, and jacēre to lie]

subject /sub'jekt or -jikt/ adj (often with to) under rule, government, jurisdiction, or control; owing allegiance; under obligation; subordinate; subservient; dependent; liable; exposed; prone, disposed; cognizable; dependent upon condition or contingency; underlying; spread out below (obs). ◆ adv conditionally (with to). ◆ n a person who is subject; a person who is under, or who owes allegiance to, a sovereign, a state, a feudal superior, etc; a citizen; a body of such persons (Shakesp); a thing over which a legal right is exercised; a piece of property (Scot); a substance (obs); something having inherent attributes; a thing existing independently; the mind regarded as the thinking power (as opposed to the object about which it thinks); that of which something is predicated, or the term denoting it (logic); that part of a sentence or clause denoting the person or thing about which something is said (grammar); a topic; a matter of discourse, thought, or study; a department of study; a theme; a person or thing on which any operation is performed; a person or thing that is treated or handled; matter for any action or operation; a ground; a sufferer from disease, a patient; a dead body for dissection (anat); a person peculiarly sensitive to hypnotic influence; the person or thing that an artist or photographer seeks to represent or express; a picture representing action and incident; a theme or phrase around which a movement of music is built. ◆ vt /səb-jekt'/ to make subject; to make liable; to subordinate; to submit; to subdue; to lay open. [L subjectus thrown under, from sub under, and jacere to throw]
■ **subject'ed** adj made subject; subjacent (obs). **subject'ify** vt to make subjective. **subjec'tion** n. **subject'ive** adj relating to the subject; derived from, expressive of or existing in one's own consciousness; personal, individual; influenced by or derived from personal taste or opinion and lacking impartiality or objectivity; nominative (grammar); introspective. ◆ n (grammar) the subjective case. **subject'ively** adv. **subject'iveness** n. **subject'ivism** n (philos) a term used loosely to denote any view, statement, etc in which the truth of the statement, etc depends or is founded on the mental state or reactions of the individual making it, and not on objective reasoning. **subject'ivist** n and adj. **subjectivist'ic** adj. **subjectivist'ically** adv. **subjectiv'ity** n. **subjectiviza'tion** or **-s-** n. **subject'ivize** or **-ise** vt. **sub'jectless** adj. **sub'jectship** n the state of being subject.
◻ **subject catalogue** n in a library, a catalogue of books arranged according to subjects dealt with. **subject heading** n. **subjective idealism** n (philos) a view that what is perceived exists only when and because it is perceived, subjectivism. **subject matter** n the subject, theme or topic. **sub'ject-ob'ject** n (philos) the immediate object of cognition, or the thought itself. **sub'ject-super'ior** n a superior who is himself the subject of a sovereign.

subjoin /sub-join'/ vt (formal) to add at the end or afterwards, to append. [**sub-** in addition, and **join**]
■ **subjoin'der** n (Lamb) a remark following on another. **subjunc'tion** n the act or fact of subjoining.

sub Jove see **sub divo**.

sub judice /sub joo'di-sē or sūb ū'di-ke/ (formal or law) adj under (judicial) consideration; before, but not yet decided by, a judge or court (and therefore not able to be discussed or reported). [L]

subjugate /sub'joo-gāt/ vt to bring under the yoke; to bring under power or domination; to make subservient; to conquer. [L subjugāre, -ātum, from sub under, and jugum a yoke]
■ **subjugā'tion** n. **sub'jugātor** n.

subjunction see under **subjoin**.

subjunctive /səb-jungk'tiv/ adj subjoined, added to something; (of a verb) in a mood or form expressing condition, hypothesis, or contingency (grammar). ◆ n the subjunctive mood; a subjunctive form; a verb in the subjunctive mood (eg if I were you, far be it from me, etc). [L subjunctīvus, from sub, and jungere, to join]
■ **subjunct'ively** adv.

subkingdom /sub'king-dəm/ (bot and zool) n a taxonomic division of a kingdom; a phylum. [**sub-** (2)]

Sublapsarian /sub-lap-sā'ri-ən/ (also without cap) n a believer in Sublapsarianism (also adj). [L sub in some degree, and lāpsus a fall]
■ **Sublapsā'rianism** n a doctrine of moderate Calvinists, that God permitted the fall of Adam without preordaining it.

sublate /sub-lāt'/ vt to deny, contradict (logic); to resolve in a higher all-embracing unity by combining thesis and antithesis in a synthesis (philos); to remove (obs). [L sublātum, used as supine of tollere to take away, from sub- in sense of away, and lātum]
■ **sublā'tion** n.

sublease /sub'lēs/ n an underlease or lease by a tenant to another. ◆ vt and vi /sub-lēs'/ to lease property on which one holds a lease. [**sub-** (2)]
■ **sublessee'** n the holder of a sublease. **subless'or** n a person who or organization that grants a sublease.

sublet /sub-let'/ vt and vi (pat and pap **sublet'**) to sublease. ◆ n /sub'let/ a subletting. [**sub-** (2)]
■ **sublett'er** n. **sublett'ing** n.

sublieutenant /sub-lef-ten'ənt or (US) -loo-/ n a naval officer ranking below a lieutenant but with an army lieutenant (formerly **mate**, or **passed midshipman**). [**sub-** (2)]

sublime /sə-blīm'/ adj exalted, lofty; majestic; supreme; of the highest or noblest nature; awakening feelings of awe and veneration; raised up, lifted on high (archaic); of proud or supercilious aspect or bearing (literary); just under the skin (anat). ◆ n that which is sublime; a pinnacle of achievement, surpassing excellence, the lofty or grand, in thought, arrangement or style; the supreme degree. ◆ vt to raise up, exalt; to transmute into something higher; to object to or obtain by sublimation; to deposit as a sublimate; to purify by (or as if by) sublimation. ◆ vi to undergo sublimation. [L sublimis in a high position, exalted, from sublimāre, -ātum to exalt; origin unknown]
■ **sublīm'able** adj. **sublimate** /sub'lim-āt/ vt to elevate; to sublime; to purify by sublimation; to transmute into something higher; to direct unconsciously (a primitive impulse such as an aggressive or sexual impulse) into a higher or more socially acceptable action; to direct into a higher channel. ◆ n /-mət/ (chem) a product of sublimation, esp a corrosive sublimate. ◆ adj /-mət/ sublimed or sublimated. **sub'limated** adj. **sublimā'tion** n the change from solid to vapour without passing through the liquid state, usu with subsequent change back to solid (chem); purification by this process; a sublimate; elevation; ecstasy; the acme, height; transmutation into something higher; the unconscious diversion towards higher aims or more socially acceptable actions of the energy derived from an instinct which is denied gratification, such as an aggressive or sexual impulse. **sublimed** /səb-blīmd'/ adj. **sublime'ly** adv. **sublime'ness** n. **sublīm'ing** n and adj. **sublimity** /səb-lim'/ n loftiness; elevation; grandeur; nobleness of nature, thought, execution; the emotion of awe and veneration; that which evokes it; the summit, height, acme. **sub'limize** or **-ise** vt (rare) to make sublime; to exalt; to purify, refine.

subliminal /sub-lim'i-nəl or sə-blim'/ adj beneath the threshold of consciousness, subconscious; (of stimuli, images, etc) of insufficient intensity or duration to produce a response or register in the conscious

---

Some words formed with the prefix **sub-**; the numbers in brackets refer to the numbered senses in the entry for **sub-**.

subciv'ilized or **subciv'ilised** adj (4).	**subcommun'ity** n (3).	**subcrā'nial** adj (1).
sub'claim n (2).	**subcontig'uous** adj (4).	**sub'crust** n (1).
sub'class n (3).	**subcontin'uous** adj (4).	**subcrust'al** adj (1).
sub'clause n (2).	**sub'cool** adj (1).	**subdean'** adj (2).
subcommiss'ion n (2), (3).	**subcor'date** adj (4).	**subdean'ery** n (2).
subcommiss'ioner n (2), (3).	**subcor'tex** n (1), (4).	**subdeca'nal** adj (2).
subcommitt'ee n (2), (3).	**subcort'ical** adj (1), (4).	**subder'mal** adj (1).

---

mind. ◆ *n* a subliminal message, image, stimulus, etc. [L *sub* under, and *līmen, -inis* threshold]

■ **sublim'inally** *adv*.

❑ **subliminal advertising** *n* the insertion of subliminal images into the run of a cinema film, television programme, etc in order to exert subconscious influences on the viewer. **subliminal perception** *n* (*behaviourism*) a controversial hypothesis that suggests that external stimuli presented below the level of conscious awareness may influence or affect behaviour (also called **subcep'tion**).

sublinear /*sub-lin'i-ər*/ *adj* under the line; nearly linear (*bot*). [**sub-** (1) and (4)]

■ **sublinea'tion** *n* underlining.

sublingual /*sub-ling'gwəl*/ *adj* under the tongue. [**sub-** (1)]

sublittoral /*sub-lit'ə-rəl*/ *adj* growing, living or occurring near but not on the shore, whether on land or at sea; of or relating to the zone of the sea between the lowest mark of ordinary tides and the edge of the continental shelf. ◆ *n* a sublittoral zone. [**sub-** (4)]

sublunary /*sub-loo'nə-ri*/, also **sublunar** /*-loo'nər*/ *adj* under the moon; earthly; of this world; between (the orbit of) the moon and the earth, under the moon's influence. [**sub-** (1)]

sublunate /*sub-loo'nāt*/ *adj* approaching, or nearly in, the form of a crescent. [**sub-** (4)]

subluxation /*sub-luk-sā'shən*/ (*med*) *n* partial dislocation or displacement, eg of a bone in a joint or tooth in its socket. [**sub-** (4)]

submachine-gun /*sub-mə-shēn'gun*/ *n* a light machine-gun, *usu* one fired from the hip or shoulder. [**sub-** (4)]

subman /*sub'man*/ *n* an animal not quite a man; a primitive or subnormal type of human being. [**sub-** (4)]

submarginal /*sub-mär'ji-nəl*/ *adj* near the margin; below the minimum necessary; (of land) that cannot be farmed profitably. [**sub-** (4)]

submarine /*sub'mə-rēn* or *sub-mə-rēn'*/ *adj* under the sea; under the surface of or on the bed of the sea. ◆ *n* a submersible vessel, *esp* for warfare; a submarine organism or dweller; a submarine sandwich (qv below). ◆ *vt* to attack by submarine. ◆ *vi* (of the occupant of a vehicle) to be subjected to the submarine effect. [**sub-** (1)]

■ **submarin'er** (or /*-mar'in-*/) *n* a member of the crew of a submarine. ❑ **submarine canyon** *n* (*geol*) a trench on the continental shelf, sometimes with tributaries. **submarine effect** *n* one in which the occupant of a vehicle simultaneously moves forward and slides out from under the seat belt, *esp* during a collision, rendering him or her vulnerable to an increased risk of injury. **submarine sandwich** *n* a large sandwich made with a bread roll long, thin and rounded enough to suggest the shape of a submarine.

submaxillary /*sub-maks'i-lə-ri* or *-mak-sil'ə-*/ *adj* of or under the lower jaw. ◆ *n* a nerve, artery, etc situated below the lower jaw. [**sub-** (1)]

submediant /*sub-mē'di-ənt*/ (*music*) *n* the sixth degree of the diatonic scale, eg A in the scale of C major. [**sub-** (1)]

submental /*sub-men'təl*/ *adj* below the chin; of the submentum. [L *sub* under, and *mentum* chin]

■ **subment'um** *n* the basal part of the lower lip in insects.

submerge /*səb-mûrj'*/ *vt* to put under the surface of liquid; to sink; to cover over with liquid; to overwhelm; to conceal, suppress. ◆ *vi* to sink under the surface of liquid. [L *submergere, -mersum,* from *sub* under, and *mergere* to plunge]

■ **submerged'** *adj* sunk; entirely under the surface of liquid; growing under water, submersed; obscured, concealed; swamped. **submerge'ment** *n* (*rare*). **submerg'ence** *n* submersion. **submergibil'ity** *n*. **submerg'ible** *adj* submersible. **submerse** /*-mûrs'*/ *vt* to submerge. **submersed'** *adj* (*bot*) growing (almost) entirely under water. **submersibil'ity** *n*. **submers'ible** *adj* capable of being submerged at will. ◆ *n* a submersible boat. **submer'sion** /*-shən*/ *n* the act of submerging; the state or fact of being submerged.

submicron /*sub-mī'kron*/ *n* a particle visible by ultramicroscope but not by the ordinary microscope (50–2000 angstrom units). [**sub-** (1)]

subminiature /*sub-min'i-chər* or *-min'ə-, min'i-ə-*/ *adj* smaller than miniature; (of a camera) of a very small size, for taking photographs on 16mm film. ◆ *n* a subminiature camera or component. [**sub-** (1)]

submit /*sub-mit'*/ *vt* (**submitt'ing**; **submitt'ed**) (often with *to*) to yield, resign; to subordinate; to subject; to offer, lodge or refer for decision, consideration, sanction, arbitration, etc; to put forward in respectful (eg legal) debate; to lower, lay down (*obs*). ◆ *vi* to yield; to surrender; to be subjected to; to be resigned; to consent. [L *sub* beneath, and *mittere, missum* to send]

■ **submiss'** *adj* (*archaic*) submissive; subdued, low-toned. **submiss'ible** *adj*. **submission** /*-mish'ən*/ *n* an act of submitting; a reference, or agreement to refer, to arbitration; a view, plan, contribution, etc submitted; resignedness, submissiveness; a surrender; a confession (*Shakesp*). **submiss'ive** *adj* willing or ready to submit; yielding. **submiss'ively** *adv*. **submiss'iveness** *n*. **submiss'ly** *adv* (*archaic*). **submiss'ness** *n* (*archaic*). **submitt'ed** *adj*. **submitt'er** *n*. **submitt'ing** *n* and *adj*.

submontane /*sub-mon'tān*/ *adj* under or at the foot of a mountain range. [**sub-** (1)]

submucosa /*sub-mū-kō'zə*/ *n* (pl **submucosae** /*-sē*/) the connective tissue underlying a mucous membrane. [**sub-** (1)]

■ **submuco'sal** or **submū'cous** *adj*.

submultiple /*sub-mul'ti-pl*/ (*maths*) *n* a number that will divide another number exactly without a remainder, an aliquot part, a factor. [LL *submultiplus*]

submunition /*sub-mū-nish'ən*/ *n* any of a number of smaller independent weapons or warheads contained within a larger weapon or warhead. [**sub-** (2) and (3)]

subnascent /*sub-nas'ənt* or *-nā'sənt*/ *adj* growing beneath (*obs*); growing up from beneath. [L *subnāscēns, -entis*]

subneural /*sub-nū'rəl*/ (*anat*) *adj* beneath a main neural axis or cord in the nervous system. [**sub-** (1)]

subniveal /*sub-niv'i-əl*/ *adj* under snow (also **subniv'ean**). [**sub-** (1), and L *nix, nivis* snow]

subnormal /*sub-nör'məl*/ *adj* less than normal; (of a person) having intellectual powers that fall below a given point on a standardized intelligence test; (of a person) having intellectual powers so underdeveloped that he or she is not capable of looking after him- or herself. ◆ *n* (*geom*) the projection of the normal on the axis. [**sub-** (4) and (1)]

■ **subnormal'ity** *n*.

subnuclear /*sub-nū'kli-ər*/ (*phys*) *adj* referring to particles within the nucleus of an atom; smaller than the nucleus of an atom. [**sub-** (3)]

suboccipital /*sub-ok-sip'i-təl*/ (*anat*) *adj* below or behind the occiput, or the occipital lobe. [**sub-** (1)]

suboctave /*sub-ok'tiv*/ *n* the octave below; (also **suboctave coupler**) an organ coupler that gives an octave below. [**sub-** (1)]

suboctuple /*sub-ok-tū'pl* or *sub-ok'tū-pl*/ *adj* in the ratio of one to eight. [LL *suboctuplus*]

suboperculum /*sub-o-pûr'kū-ləm* or *-ō-*/ *n* (in fishes) a bone below and partly behind the gill cover. [**sub-** (1)]

■ **suboper'cular** *adj*.

suboptimal /*sub-op'ti-məl*/ *adj* not of the highest standard; not satisfactory. [**sub-** (2)]

suborbital /*sub-ör'bi-təl*/ *adj* below the orbit of the eye (*anat*); of less than a complete orbit. [**sub-** (1)]

subordinary /*sub-ör'di-nə-ri*/ (*heraldry*) *n* a less honourable armorial charge. [**sub-** (2)]

subordinate /*sub-ör'di-nāt* or *-nit*/ *adj* lower in order, rank, nature, power, importance, etc; dependent; under the orders or authority of another person; submissive (*obs*); lower in a series of successive divisions; underlying. ◆ *n* a person who or thing that is subordinate or ranked lower; a person who works under another. ◆ *vt* /*-nāt*/ to place in a lower order; to consider of less value; to subject. [LL *subordinātus,* from *sub-* under, and *ordināre* to ordain]

■ **subor'dinacy** *n* subordination. **subor'dinately** *adv*. **subor'dinateness** *n*. **subordina'tion** *n* arrangement in a series of

---

Some words formed with the prefix **sub-**; the numbers in brackets refer to the numbered senses in the entry for **sub-**.

subdia'conal *adj* (2).	**subequato'rial** *adj* (4).	**sub'genre** *n* (3).
subdia'conate *n* (2).	**suberect'** *adj* (4).	**subglobose'** *adj* (4).
subdi'alect *n* (3).	**subfacto'rial** *n* (2).	**subglob'ular** *adj* (4).
subdis'trict *n* (3).	**subfer'tile** *adj* (4).	**sub'goal** *n* (3).
sub'dorsal *adj* (1), (4).	**subfertil'ity** *n* (4).	**sub'group** *n* (3).
subeconom'ic *adj* (1).	**sub'field** *n* (3).	**subharmon'ic** *n* and *adj* (3).
sube'qual *adj* (4).	**sub'freezing** *adj* (1).	**sub'head** or **sub'heading** *n* (2).

---

successive orders; the disposition of successive recessed arches in an archway (*archit*); the act of subordinating or placing in a lower order; the state of being subordinate; inferiority of rank or position; submission and obedience to authority. **subordinā'tionism** *n* the doctrine according to which the second and third Persons of the Trinity are subordinate to the first. **subordinā'tionist** *n*. **subor'dinātive** *adj*.

□ **subordinate clause** *n* (*grammar*) a clause which cannot function as a separate sentence in its own right, but performs an adjectival, adverbial or nominal function. **subordinated debt** same as **mezzanine finance** (see under **mezzanine**). **subordinating conjunction** *n* (*grammar*) a conjunction which introduces a subordinate clause.

suborn /sə- or su-börn'/ *vt* to bribe or procure to commit perjury or other unlawful or wrongful act; to prepare, provide, or achieve by stealthy means. [L *sub-* in the sense of secret, and *ornāre* to equip]
■ **subornā'tion** /sub-ör-/ *n*. **suborn'er** /səb-/ *n*.

subpanation /sub-pan-ā'shən/ (*rare*) *n* the doctrine that the body and blood of Christ are locally and materially present in the Eucharist under the form of bread and wine. [L *sub* under, and *pānis* bread]

subplot /sub'plot/ *n* a subsidiary plot coinciding with the main action in a play or story. [**sub-** (2)]

subpoena /sub- or sə-pē'nə/ *n* a writ commanding attendance (eg of a witness) or submission (eg of a document) as evidence in court. ◆ *vt* (pat and pap **subpoe'na'd** or **subpoe'naed**) to serve with such a writ. [L, under a penalty]

subpopulation /sub-pop-ū-lā'shən/ *n* a subdivision of a statistical population. [**sub-** (3)]

sub-prime /sub-prīm'/ (*finance*) *adj* (of a loan) made to a person whose creditworthiness is in doubt. [**sub-** (2)]

subreference /sub' or sub-ref'(ə-)rəns/ *n* an incomplete or surreptitious reference; an appeal by a veiled understanding. [**sub-** (5)]

subreption /sub-rep'shən/ (*law*, *obs*) *n* procuring an advantage or benefit by misrepresentation or concealment of the truth, *esp* an ecclesiastical benefit, or (*Scots law*) a gift of escheat (cf **obreption**). [L *subreptiō, -ōnis*, from *sub-* secretly, and *rapere* to snatch; cf **surreptitious**]
■ **subreptitious** /-tish'əs/ *adj* obtained by subreption; surreptitious. **subrep'tive** *adj* surreptitious; arising out of obscure and unconscious suggestions of experience (*philos*).

subrogate /sub'rō-gāt or -rə-/ *vt* to substitute; to put in place of another party as successor to that party's rights (*law*). [See ety for **surrogate**]
■ **subrogā'tion** *n*.

sub rosa /sub rō'zə or sŭb ro'zä/ (L) literally, under the rose (a traditional symbol of secrecy); hence, privately, confidentially.

subroutine /sub'roo-tēn/ *n* a self-contained part of a complete computer program which performs a specific task and which can be called into use at any time throughout the running of the main program. [**sub-** (2)]

subs see **sub**.

subsacral /sub-sā'krəl or -sak'rəl/ *adj* below (in humans in front of) the sacrum. [**sub-** (1)]

subscapular /sub-skap'ū-lər/ *adj* below (in humans in front of) the shoulder-blade. ◆ *n* a subscapular vessel or nerve. [**sub-** (1)]

subscribe /səb-skrīb'/ *vi* to contribute money; to put one's name down as a purchaser or donor; to make periodical payments by arrangement; (*usu* with *to*) to sign one's name; to assent, agree; to make acknowledgement; to undertake to answer; to submit (*Shakesp*). ◆ *vt* to sign, *orig* and *esp* at the bottom; to write beneath (*archaic*); to profess to be (by signing); to declare assent to; to make a signed promise of payment for or regular contributions to; to set down, declare, in writing (*Shakesp*); to give up by signing (*Shakesp*). [L *subscrībere*, from *sub* beneath, below, and *scrībere* to write]

■ **subscrīb'able** *adj*. **subscrībed'** *adj*. **subscrīb'er** *n*. **subscrīb'ing** *n* and *adj*. **subscript** /sub'skript/ *adj* and *n* (a character) written or printed beneath the normal line of script or type, *esp* in chemistry, mathematics, etc (eg the number 2 in H₂O). **subscrip'tion** *n* an act of subscribing; that which is subscribed; a membership fee; a contribution to a fund, society, etc; a method of sale to subscribers; a raising of money from subscribers; advance ordering, *esp* of a book or magazine before publication; an advance order, *esp* for a book or magazine before publication; a signature; assent, sanction, endorsement; submission (*Shakesp*). **subscrip'tive** *adj*.

□ **subscriber set** *n* (*comput*) a modem. **subscriber station** *n* (*comput*) a connection for transmission of data linking an outside location with a central office. **subscriber trunk dialling** *n* a dialling system in which subscribers in exchanges in many countries of the world can dial each other directly (*abbrev* **STD**). **subscription concert** *n* one of a series of concerts for which tickets are sold as a batch in advance. **subscription library** *n* a lending library run commercially and funded by members' subscriptions. **subscription price** *n* (*stock exchange*) the price at which members of the public may subscribe for shares. **subscription television** *n* pay television.

subsea /sub'sē/ *adj* occurring, used, etc under the surface of the sea. [**sub-** (1)]

subsecive /sub'si-siv/ (*obs* or *rare*) *adj* remaining over; spare. [L *subsecīvus*, from *sub* after, and *secāre* to cut]

subsellium /sub-sel'i-əm/ *n* (pl **subsell'ia**) a seat in a Roman amphitheatre; a misericord. [L, a low bench, from *sub* below, and *sella* seat]

subsensible /sub-sen'si-bl/ *adj* below the range of sense. [**sub-** (4)]

subsequence[1] see under **subsequent**.

subsequence[2] /sub'sē'kwəns/ *n* a sequence (*esp maths*) that forms part of another sequence. [**sub-** (3)]

subsequent /sub'si-kwənt or -sə-/ *adj* following or coming after; (of a stream, river, etc) flowing approximately at right angles to the original slope of the land, *usu* along the line of a fault, distinguished from *consequent* and *obsequent*. [L *subsequēns, -entis*, prp of *subsequī*, from *sub* under, after, and *sequī* to follow]
■ **sub'sequence** *n*. **subsequential** /-kwen'shl/ *adj* subsequent. **sub'sequently** *adv*.
■ **subsequent to** after.

subsere /sub'sēr/ (*ecology*) *n* a secondary sere occurring when a sere has been interrupted. [**sub-** (3)]

subserve /sub-sûrv'/ *vt* to help forward. ◆ *vi* to help in a subordinate way; to be subordinate (*obs*). [L *subservīre*, from *sub* under, and *servīre* to serve]
■ **subser'vience** or **subser'viency** *n*. **subser'vient** *adj* obsequious; slavish; subserving; serving to promote, instrumental; subject, subordinate. ◆ *n* a subservient person or thing. **subser'viently** *adv*.

subset /sub'set/ *n* a set that forms part of a larger set, *specif* a set *x* is a subset of *y* if and only if *x* is an element of *y* (*maths*); a functionally or structurally different population of cells within a single cell type (*immunol*); short for subscriber set (*comput*). [**sub-** (3)]

subshrub /sub'shrub/ *n* a low-growing shrub. [**sub-** (4)]
■ **sub'shrubby** *adj*.

subside /səb-sīd'/ *vi* to settle, sink down; to fall into a state of quiet or calm; to diminish in intensity, amount, extent, etc, to become less. [L *subsīdere*, from *sub* down, and *sīdere* to settle]
■ **subsidence** /sub'si-dəns, often səb-sī'dəns/ or (*rare*) **sub'sidency** (or /-sī'/) *n* the process of subsiding, settling, or sinking.

subsidy /sub'si-di/ *n* aid in the form of money; a grant of public money in aid of some enterprise, industry, etc, or to support or keep down the price of a commodity, or from one state to another; a special parliamentary grant of money to the king (*hist*); a payment exacted by a king or feudal lord (*hist*); assistance (*obs*). [L *subsidium*, orig troops stationed behind in reserve, aid, from *sub* under, and *sīdere* to settle]
■ **subsid'iarily** *adv*. **subsidiar'ity** *n* the state or quality of being (a) subsidiary; the concept of a central governing body permitting its

---

Some words formed with the prefix **sub-**; the numbers in brackets refer to the numbered senses in the entry for **sub-**.

subin'dustry *n* (3).	**sublibra'rian** *n* (2).	**submol'ecule** *n* (3).
subinsinua'tion *n* (4), (5).	**subman'ager** *n* (2).	**subnat'ural** *adj* (4).
subinspec'tor *n* (2).	**submandib'ular** *adj* (1).	**subocean'ic** *adj* (1).
subinspec'torship *n* (2).	**sub'matrix** *n* (3).	**suboc'ular** *adj* (1).
sublan'ceolate *adj* (4).	**submicromin'iature** *adj* (4).	**sub'office** *n* (2), (3).
sub'language *n* (3).	**submicroscop'ic** *adj* (4).	**sub'officer** *n* (2), (3).
suble'thal *adj* (4).	**submin'iaturize** or **submin'iaturise** *vt* (4).	**sub'order** *n* (3).

---

member states, branches, etc to take decisions on issues best dealt with at local or subsidiary level. **subsid'iary** *adj* furnishing a subsidy, help, or additional supplies; aiding; subordinate; relating to or depending on subsidies. ◆ *n* someone who or something which aids or supplies; an assistant; a subordinate; a subsidiary company. **sub'sidize** or **-ise** *vt* to provide with a subsidy, grant, or regular allowance; to purchase the aid of, to buy over.
□ **subsidiary company** *n* one of which another company holds most of the shares. **subsidiary troops** *n pl* mercenaries.

subsist /səb-sist'/ *vi* to have existence (often with *in*); to have the means of living (often with *on*); to remain, continue; to consist or be inherent; to hold out, stand fast (*Milton*). [L *subsistere* to stand still, from *sub* under, and *sistere* to stand]
■ **subsist'ence** *n* the state of being subsistent; real being; the means of supporting life; livelihood. ◆ *adj* (used eg of an allowance, wage) providing the bare necessities of living. **subsist'ent** *adj* subsisting; having real being; inherent. **subsistential** /*sub-sis-ten'shl*/ *adj*.
□ **subsistence allowance** see **subsistence money** below. **subsistence farming** *n* farming in which land will yield just enough to support the farmer and his or her dependents, leaving little or nothing to be sold. **subsistence level** *n* the level of income which will purchase bare necessities only. **subsistence money** or **allowance** *n* a portion of wages paid in advance for immediate needs, colloquially known as a **sub**; a special allowance for exceptional circumstances. **subsistence wage** *n* one fixed at subsistence level.

subsizar /sub-sī'zər/ *n* a Cambridge undergraduate (now only at certain colleges) ranking below a sizar. [**sub-** (1)]

subsoil /sub'soil/ *n* a layer of broken or partly weathered rock underlying the soil, *esp* that part below the layer normally used in cultivation. ◆ *vt* to turn up or loosen the subsoil of. [**sub-** (1)]
■ **sub'soiler** *n* a plough for subsoiling. **sub'soiling** *n* ploughing the subsoil.

subsolar /sub-sō'lər/ *adj* directly under the sun, as a point on the earth's surface where the sun is vertically overhead. [**sub-** (1)]

subsong /sub'song/ *n* a low-volume, often unstructured, song produced by certain songbirds before the full song of the breeding season. [**sub-** (4)]

subsonic /sub-son'ik/ *adj* having, or (capable of) travelling at, a speed slower than that of sound. [**sub-** (4)]

sub specie /sub spē'shi-ē or sŭb spek'i-ā/ (L) *adv* under the appearance or aspect (of).
■ **sub specie aeternitatis** /ē-tûr-ni-tāt'is or ī-ter-ni-tät'is/ (seen) under the aspect of eternity (*Spinoza*); hence, as it essentially is.

subst. *abbrev* : substantive (*grammar*); substitute.

substage /sub'stāj/ *n* apparatus under the stage of a microscope; a division of a stage (*esp geol*). [**sub-** (1) and (3)]

substance /sub'stəns/ *n* something in which qualities or attributes exist, the existence to which qualities belong; that which makes anything what it is; the principal part; gist; subject matter; body; matter, material; a kind of matter, *esp* one of definite chemical nature; amount (*Shakesp*); wealth, property; solidity, body; solid worth; foundation, ground; marijuana or other illegal drug (*euphem*). [L *substantia* substance, essence, property, from *sub* under, and *stāre* to stand]
■ **substantial** /səb-stan'shl/ *adj* of or having substance; being a substance; essential; actually existing; real; corporeal, material; solid; stable; solidly based; durable; enduring; firm, stout, strong; considerable in amount; bulky; well-to-do, wealthy, influential; of firm, solid or sound value. **substan'tialism** *n* the theory that there is a real existence or substratum underlying phenomena. **substan'tialist** *n*. **substantiality** /-shi-al'i-ti/ *n*. **substan'tialize** or **-ise** *vt* to give reality to. **substan'tially** *adv*. **substan'tialness** *n*. **substan'tiate** /-shi-āt or -si-āt/ *vt* to make substantial; to embody; to prove or confirm. **substantiā'tion** *n*. **substantival** /sub-stən-tī'vl/ *adj* of, or of the nature of, a substantive. **substantiv'ally** *adv*. **sub'stantive** /-tiv/ *adj* relating to substance; expressing existence; real; of real, independent importance; substantival; (of dyes) taking effect without a mordant; definite and permanent; considerable in amount. ◆ *n* (*grammar*) a noun or noun-like item. **sub'stantively** *adv*. **sub'stantiveness** *n*. **substantiv'ity** *n* substantiality; affinity for a dyestuff. **sub'stantivize** or **-ise** (or /-stan'/) *vt* to turn into a noun.
□ **substance abuse** *n* (*euphem*) a general term for the inappropriate use of substances such as alcohol, solvents, drugs, etc, often leading to dependency or other harmful effects. **substance P** *n* a peptide neurotransmitter, present in nerve cells and intestinal tissue, that induces vasodilation and contraction of intestinal smooth muscle.
■ **in substance** in general; in the most important aspects.

substation /sub'stā-shən/ *n* a subordinate station, *esp* a switching, transforming, or converting electrical station intermediate between the generating station and the low-tension distribution network. [**sub-** (2)]

substellar /sub-stel'ər/ *adj* directly under a star, applied eg to a point on the earth's surface where the star is vertically overhead; under the influence of a star. [**sub-** (1)]

substitute /sub'sti-tūt/ *n* one put in place of another; a thing used instead of another; a deputy; a proxy (*Shakesp*); an heir (*law*); a person entitled to receive a hereditary peerage if no male heir is produced. ◆ *vt* to use instead of, or put in place of, another (often with *for*); to appoint as deputy; to nominate in remainder. ◆ *vi* (*orig US*) to act as substitute. [L *substituere, -ūtum*, from *sub* under, and *statuere* to set]
■ **substit'uent** *n* something that may be, or is, substituted, *esp* one atom or radical replacing another in a molecule (also *adj*). **substitūtabil'ity** *n*. **substitū'table** *adj*. **sub'stituted** *adj*. **substitū'tion** *n* the act of substituting; the condition of being a substitute; the substituting of one atom or radical for another without breaking up the molecule (*chem*); the replacement of one idea by another, as a form of defence mechanism (*psychiatry*); the replacement of one kind of metrical foot by another, eg for emphasis (*prosody*); a rule of inference in which an expression replaces a variable throughout a theorem (*maths*); delegation (*Shakesp*). **substitū'tional** or **substitū'tionary** *adj*. **substitū'tionally** *adv*. **sub'stitūtive** *adj*. **sub'stitutively** *adv*. **substitutiv'ity** *n*.
□ **substitution product** *n* a substance obtained by substitution of so many equivalents for certain atoms or groups.

substract /səb-strakt'/ *vt* (now *non-standard*) to subtract. [LL *substrahere, substractum*, for L *subtrahere*, after the model of **abstract**]
■ **substrac'tion** *n* (now *non-standard*). **substrac'tor** *n* (*Shakesp*) a detractor.

substrata, substrate, etc see **substratum**.

substratosphere /sub-strat'ō-sfēr/ *n* the region of the atmosphere below the stratosphere and over $3\frac{1}{2}$ miles above the earth. [**sub-** (4)]

substratum /sub-strä'təm or -strā'/ *n* (*pl* **substra'ta**) a basis, foundation, ground; the material in which a plant grows or on which an animal moves or rests; an underlying layer, *esp* of rock or soil. [L *substernere, -strātum*, from *sub* under, and *sternere* to spread]
■ **substra'tal** or **substra'tive** *adj*. **sub'strate** *n* a substratum; a base; a medium on which an organism can grow (*biol*); a solid object to which a plant, such as seaweed, is attached; a body of material on or in which integrated circuits or circuit elements are fabricated (*electronics*); the substance or substances on which an enzyme can act; the substances used by a plant in respiration (*bot*).

substruct /sub-strukt'/ *vt* to build beneath, lay as a foundation. [**sub-** (1)]
■ **substruc'tion** *n*. **substruc'tural** *adj*. **sub'structure** *n* an understructure; a foundation, a supporting structure.

substyle /sub'stīl/ *n* the straight line on which the style of a dial is erected. [**sub-** (1)]
■ **sub'stylar** (or /-stī'/) *adj*.

Some words formed with the prefix **sub-**; the numbers in brackets refer to the numbered senses in the entry for **sub-**.

subor'dinal *adj* (4).	**sub-post'master** *n* (3).	**sub'prior** *n* (2).
subo'vate *adj* (4).	**sub-post'mistress** *n* (3).	**subpri'oress** *n* (2).
subox'ide *n* (6).	**sub-post'office** *n* (3).	**sub'program** *n* (2), (3).
subpar'allel *adj* (4).	**subpo'tent** *adj* (4).	**subre'gion** *n* (3).
sub'phrenic *adj* (1).	**subpre'fect** *n* (2).	**subre'gional** *adj* (3).
subphy'lum *n* (3).	**subpre'fecture** *n* (2).	**sub'ring** *n* (2).
subpol'ar *adj* (4).	**subprin'cipal** *n* (2).	**sub-Sahar'an** *adj* (1).

---

subsultive /sub-sul′tiv/ or **subsultory** /-tə-ri/ adj (rare) moving by sudden leaps or starts; twitching. [L subsultāre to jump, hop, from sub up, and salīre to leap]
■ **subsult′orily** adv. **subsult′us** n (med) an abnormal convulsive or twitching movement, usu of the muscles.

subsume /sub-sūm′/ vt to take in under a more comprehensive term or proposition; to include in something larger; to take over (official jargon). [L sub under, and sūmere to take]
■ **subsum′able** adj. **subsumption** /səb-sump′shən/ n. **subsump′tive** adj.

subtack /sub′tak′/ n a sublease in Scotland. [**sub-** (2)]
■ **sub′tack′sman** n a holder (of land) by subtack.

subtalar /sub-tā′lər/ adj below the ankle-bone. [**sub-** (1)]

subtangent /sub-tan′jənt/ (geom) n (of a curve) the projection of the tangent on the axis. [**sub-** (1)]

subteen /sub′tēn or -tēn′/ (chiefly N Am) n and adj (of or for) a child younger than thirteen years. [**sub-** (1)]

subtemperate /sub-tem′pə-rət or (rare) -rāt/ adj slightly colder than temperate, cold-temperate. [**sub-** (4)]

subtend /səb-tend′/ vt to be opposite to (as a hypotenuse is to a right-angle) or to extend under (as a chord does an arc) (geom); to be situated immediately below (as a leaf is to a bud in its axil) (bot). [L sub under, and tendere, tentum or tēnsum to stretch]
■ **subtense′** n a subtending line. ◆ adj placed so as to subtend an angle, as a rod or bar used as a distance base in tacheometry.

subter- /sub-tər-/ combining form signifying under, as in subterhuman, subterjacent. [L]

subterfuge /sub′tər-fūj/ n an evasive device, as used in discussion or argument; action taken, or manoeuvres made, to evade, conceal or obscure; a refuge (obs). [L subter under, and fugere to take flight]

subternatural /sub-tər-nach′(ə-)rəl/ adj below that which is considered natural, less than natural. [L subter under, and **natural**]

subterranean /sub-tə-rā′ni-ən/ adj underground; operating underground; hidden, working, etc, in secret. ◆ n a person who or thing that is subterranean. [L sub under, and terra the earth]
■ **sub′terrane** or **sub′terrain** n an underground chamber, room or dwelling. **subterrā′neous** adj underground. **subterrā′neously** adv. **subterrene′** adj underground. ◆ n an underground dwelling; the underworld. **subterres′trial** adj and n (a person or thing) existing underground.

subtext /sub′tekst/ n an underlying theme, esp in literature; a footnote (obs). [**sub-** (1)]

subthreshold /sub-thresh′(h)ōld/ (psychol) adj not sufficient to produce a specified response; subliminal. [**sub-** (1)]

subtil and **subtile** archaic forms of **subtle**.

subtitle /sub′tī-tl/ n (in a book, etc) an additional or second title; a half-title; a repetition of the title at the head of the text; (usu in pl) wording superimposed on a film or television picture, eg a printed translation at the foot of the screen of dialogue that is in a language foreign to the viewers or other descriptive text similarly displayed (cf **supertitle**). ◆ vt to provide with a subtitle or subtitles. [**sub-** (2)]

subtle /sut′l/ adj tenuous, slight; elusive, impalpable; showing or calling for fine discrimination; delicate, refined; overrefined or overrefining, rarefied; abstruse; crafty, artful; insidious, devious; ticklish, tricky (Shakesp). [OFr soutil and its source L subtīlis, from sub under, and tēla a web]
■ **subtīlīzā′tion** or **-s-** /sut-/ n. **subtilize** or **-ise** /sut′/ vt to rarefy, refine; to make subtle. ◆ vi to refine, use subtlety. **subt′leness** or **subt′lety** n the state or quality of being subtle; a subtle trick or refinement; an ornamental device in sugar (obs; cookery). **subt′ly** adv.

subtonic /sub-ton′ik/ (music) n the seventh degree of the diatonic scale, the leading note. [**sub-** (1)]

subtopia /sub-tō′pi-ə/ (derog) n an area of sprawling housing estates spreading into the countryside, in which suburban dwellers enjoy some aspects of rural living while clinging to urban amenities. [Coined in the 1950s by British architect I Nairn (1930–83); from **suburb** and **Utopia**]
■ **subto′pian** adj.

subtract /səb-trakt′/ vt to withdraw, remove; to withhold; to take from another quantity so as to find the difference (maths). [L sub- (in the sense of away), and trahēre, tractum to draw]
■ **subtract′er** n (comput) a device performing subtraction using digital signals. **subtrac′tion** n withdrawal, removal; withholding, esp in violation of a right; the operation of finding the difference between two quantities by taking one from the other (maths). **subtract′ive** adj indicating, tending towards or of the nature of subtraction; negative. **subtract′or** n a light filter to eliminate a particular colour.
□ **subtractive process** n (image technol) the basis of all modern colour photography and colour printing, in which the red, green and blue components of a subject are reproduced as separate images in complementary or subtractive colours, ie cyan, magenta and yellow, which are superimposed to produce the final print.

subtrahend /sub′trə-hend/ (maths) n that which is to be subtracted (cf **minuend**). [L sub- away, and trahendus requiring to be drawn (gerundive of trahēre to draw)]

subtriplicate /sub-trip′li-kit or -kāt/ adj expressed by the cube root. [LL subtriplus in the ratio of one to three]

subtrist /sub-trist′/ (archaic) adj somewhat sad. [L subtrīstis, from sub in some degree, and trīstis sad]

subtropical /sub-trop′i-kl/ or **subtropic** /-trop′ik/ adj specif of, from or characteristic of those areas (the **subtropics**) lying between the Tropic of Cancer and 40° N and the Tropic of Capricorn and 40° S, esp the climatic conditions of these areas; (loosely) of, having or resembling near-tropical climate. [**sub-** (4)]
■ **subtrop′ically** adv.

subtrude /sub-trood′/ vi to push in stealthily. [L sub- in sense of secretly, and trūdere to thrust]

subucula /sub-ū′kū-lə or sūb-oo′kū-la/ n in ancient Rome, a man's undergarment or shirt; in the early English Church, a kind of cassock worn under the alb. [L subūcula, from sub under, and the root of induere to put on, and exuere to take off]

subulate /sū′bū-lāt or -lət/ (biol, esp bot) adj long, narrow and tapering to a point, awl-shaped. [L sūbula an awl]

subumbrella /sub-um-brel′ə/ n the undersurface of a jellyfish's umbrella. [**sub-** (1)]
■ **subumbrell′ar** adj.

subungulate /sub-ung′gū-lət/ n and adj (a member) of the **Subungulā′ta**, a classification of animals which are related to, but whose evolution diverged from, the Ungulata before the development of the hoof, consisting of four orders incl the elephants, hyraxes, sea cows and aardvark. [**sub-** (4)]

suburb /sub′ûrb/ n a district or community adjoining a town or city, esp one having relatively low-density housing and open space as characteristic features; (in pl) the outskirts of a town; outskirts generally. ◆ adj suburban; characteristic of the suburbs. [L suburbium, from sub under, near, and urbs a city]
■ **suburban** /səb-ûr′bən/ adj situated or living in the suburbs; typical of the suburbs; without the good qualities either of town or country; provincial, narrow in outlook; cosily traditional or unadventurous in tastes, as in the stereotypical suburbanite. ◆ n someone living in a suburb. **subur′banism** n the state of being suburban. **subur′banite** n a person who lives in the suburbs. **suburbanity** /sub-ər-ban′i-ti/ n suburban quality; suburbanism; a suburban place. **suburbanizā′tion** or **-s-** n. **subur′banize** or **-ise** vt to make suburban. **subur′bia** n (often used pejoratively) the suburban world. **suburbicā′rian** adj being near the city, esp of the dioceses and churches of the cardinal bishops in the suburbs of Rome.

subvention /səb-ven′shən/ n a grant of money in aid, eg public money or an ex gratia payment from one company in a group to another.

Some words formed with the prefix **sub-**; the numbers in brackets refer to the numbered senses in the entry for **sub-**.

subsam′ple n and vt (3).	**sub′species** n (3).	**sub′surface** adj (1).
sub′schema n (3).	**subspecif′ic** adj (3).	**sub′system** n (2).
sub′section n (3).	**subspecif′ically** adv (3).	**sub′task** n (2).
subser′ies n (3).	**subspi′nous** adj (4).	**sub′tenancy** n (2).
sub′sessile adj (4).	**substan′dard** adj (1), (2).	**subten′ant** n (2).
sub′set n (3).	**sub′state** n (2), (3).	**subten′ure** n (2).
subspecial′ity n (2).	**subster′nal** adj (1).	**subter′minal** adj (4).

■ words derived from main entry word; □ compound words; ■ idioms and phrasal verbs

[L *subventiō*, *-ōnis* a coming to help, from *sub* from below, and *venīre*, *ventum* to come]
■ **subven'tionary** *adj.*

sub verbo see **sub voce**.

subvert /səb-vûrt'/ *vt* to overthrow, overturn, ruin (eg principles, a political system, etc); to pervert or corrupt (a person). [L *sub* under, and *vertere*, *versum* to turn]
■ **subver'sal** *n.* **subverse'** *vt* (*pap* in *Spenser* **subverst'**; *obs*). **subver'sion** *n* overthrow, ruin; perversion, corruption. **subver'sive** or, less commonly, **subver'sionary** *adj* tending to overthrow or subvert. ◆ *n* a subversive person, *esp* politically. **subvert'er** *n.*

subviral /sub-vī'rəl/ *adj* referring to, or caused by, a structural part of a virus. [**sub-** (3)]

subvocal /sub-vō'kəl/ *adj* (of words) formed in speech order in the mind with or without accompanying (inaudible) movements of the speech organs. [**sub-** (1)]
■ **subvō'calize** or **-ise** *vi* and *vt.*

sub voce /sub vō'sē, sŭb vō'ke or wō'/ or **sub verbo** /vûr'bō or wûr'/ (*L*) literally, under the voice or word, used in giving references in dictionaries, etc (*abbrev* **sv**).

subway /sub'wā/ *n* a tunnel for pedestrians; an underground passage for water pipes, gas-pipes, sewers, etc; an underground railway. [**sub-** (1)]

subwoofer /sub'wŭ-fər/ *n* a loudspeaker for reproducing the lowest frequencies. [**sub-** (1)]

subzero /sub-zē'rō/ *adj* less than zero, *esp* of temperature. [**sub-** (1)]

succade /su-kād'/ *n* fruit or vegetable candied or in syrup. [Anglo-Fr *sukade*, perh from L *succus* juice]

succah see **sukkah**.

succedaneum /suk-si-dā'ni-əm/ *n* (*pl* **succeda'nea** /-ni-ə/) (*esp med*) something, *esp* a drug, that can act as a substitute for something else. [L, neuter of *succēdāneus*, from *succēdere* to come after]
■ **succedā'neous** *adj* (*esp med*) serving as a substitute.

succeed /sək-sēd'/ *vt* to come after, follow; to follow up or in order; to take the place of (*esp* in office, title, or possession); to inherit (*Shakesp*); to cause to succeed (*obs*). ◆ *vi* to follow in order; to take the place of another (often with *to*); to devolve, pass in succession (*Shakesp*); to turn out (*archaic*); to turn out well; to prosper; to obtain one's wish or accomplish what is attempted; to avail, be successful (with *in*); to approach (*obs*). [OFr *succeder*, from L *succēdere*, *-cēssum*, from *sub-* in sense of near, next after, and *cēdere* to go]
■ **succeed'er** *n* someone who is successful; a successor. **succeed'ing** *adj.* **success** /sək-ses'/ *n* an act of succeeding; the state of having succeeded; upshot (*obs*); prosperous progress, achievement, or termination; prosperity; attainment of wealth, influence or acclaim; a successful person, book, affair, etc; sequence (*obs*); succession (*obs*). **success'antly** *adv* (*Shakesp*) in succession. **success'ful** *adj* resulting in success; achieving, having achieved, or having, the desired effect or outcome; prosperous, flourishing. **success'fully** *adv* with success; with promise of success (*Shakesp*). **success'fulness** *n.* **succession** /-sesh'ən/ *n* a coming after or following; a coming into another's place; a sequence in time or place; law, recognized mode, right, order or turn, of succeeding one to another; (in Roman and Scots law) the taking of property by one person in place of another; rotation of crops; heirs collectively; posterity; a set of strata which represents an unbroken chronological sequence (*geol*); in an ecological community, the sequence of changes as one set of species succeeds another. **success'ional** *adj.* **success'ionally** *adv.* **success'ionist** *n* a believer in the necessity of Apostolic succession. **success'ionless** *adj.* **successive** /sək-ses'iv or (*Shakesp*) suk'/ *adj* coming in succession or in order; hereditary (*obs*). **success'ively** *adv.* **success'iveness** *n.* **success'less** *adj.* **success'lessly** *adv.* **success'lessness** *n.* **success'or** *n* a person who, or thing which, succeeds or comes after; a person appointed to succeed. **success'orship** *n.*
□ **succession duty** *n* a tax formerly imposed on succession to property, varying with the degree of relationship. **succession**

house *n* a forcing-house in a graded series, in which plants are moved on from one to the next. **succession states** *n pl* states resulting from the break-up of previously existing countries, such as those established after the break-up of the Austro-Hungarian empire. **success story** *n* (the record of) a person's, company's, etc rise to prosperity, fame, etc.
■ **in succession** following one another, one after another. **plant succession** a series of vegetation types following one another in the same region.

succentor /sək-sen'tər/ *n* a subordinate cantor; a bass soloist in a choir. [L *succentor*, from *succinere*, from *sub* under, and *canere* to sing]

succès /sük-se'/ (*Fr*) *n* success.
□ **succès de scandale** /də skā-dal/ *n* success of a book, dramatic entertainment, due not to merit but to its connection with or reference to a topical scandal. **succès d'estime** /des-tēm/ *n* a success of esteem or approval; success with more honour than profit. **succès fou** /foo/ *n* extraordinary success.

success, etc see under **succeed**.

succi see **succus**.

succinate see under **succinic**.

succinct /sək- or *suk-singkt'*/ *adj* brief and precise, concise; girded up (*archaic* and *poetic*); close-fitting (*archaic* and *poetic*). [L *succinctus*, from *sub* up, and *cingere* to gird]
■ **succinct'ly** *adv.* **succinct'ness** *n.* **succincto'rium** or **succinct'ory** *n* a band embroidered with an Agnus Dei, worn hanging from the girdle by the Pope on some occasions.

succinic /suk-sin'ik/ *adj* of, relating to or derived from amber. [L *succinum* amber]
■ **suc'cinate** *n* a salt of succinic acid. **suc'cinite** *n* amber, *esp* a variety from which succinic acid was originally obtained. **suc'cinyl** *n* either of two chemical groups of succinic acid.
□ **succinic acid** *n* a dibasic acid, $C_4H_6O_4$, occurring in plant resins such as amber, in various animal tissues, etc (also called **butanediō'ic acid**). **succinylchō'line** *n* a synthetic compound used medicinally as a muscle relaxant.

succise /suk'sīs/ (*bot*) *adj* (of leaves, etc) ending abruptly below, as if cut off. [L *succisus* cut below]

succor a N American spelling of **succour**.

succory /suk'ə-ri/ *n* another name for **chicory**.

succose see under **succus**.

succotash /suk'ō-tash/ *n* a stew of green Indian corn and beans and sometimes pork. [Narragansett *msiquatash*]

Succoth same as **Sukkoth**.

succour or (*N Am*) **succor** /suk'ər/ *vt* to aid in distress; to relieve. ◆ *n* aid; relief. [Anglo-Fr *socorre*, from L *succurrere* to run to help, from *sub* up, and *currere* to run]
■ **succ'ourable** *adj.* **succ'ourer** *n.* **succ'ourless** *adj.*

succous see under **succus**.

succubous /suk'ū-bus/ (*bot*) *adj* having the lower leaf-margin overlapping the leaf below. [L *sub* under, and *cubāre* to lie]

succubus /suk'ū-bəs/, also **succuba** /-bə/ *n* (*pl* **succ'ubuses** or **succ'ubī**, also **succ'ubae** /-bē/ or **succ'ubas**) a devil supposed to assume a female body and have sex with men in their sleep (cf **incubus**); a strumpet (*archaic*). [L *succuba* a whore, from *sub* under, and *cubāre* to lie]
■ **succ'ubine** *adj.*

succulent /suk'ū-lənt/ *adj* juicy; sappy; tasty; juicy and fleshy, or (loosely) merely fleshy (*bot*). ◆ *n* a plant, such as a cactus, that stores water in its stem and leaves. [L *sūculentus*, from *sūcus* juice]
■ **succ'ulence** or **succ'ulency** *n.* **succ'ulently** *adv.*
□ **succ'ulent-house** *n* a building where succulents are grown.

succumb /sə-kum'/ *vi* to give way or sink under pressure, difficulty, temptation, etc (often with *to*); to yield; to die. [L *sub* under, and *cumbere* to lie down]

succursal /su-kûr'sl/ *adj* subsidiary, *usu* applied to a religious establishment; branch. ◆ *n* a branch or subsidiary establishment

---

Some words formed with the prefix **sub-**; the numbers in brackets refer to the numbered senses in the entry for **sub-**.

sub'tidal *adj* (4).	**sub'tribe** *n* (3).	**subver'tebral** *adj* (1).
subtor'rid *adj* (4).	**sub'type** *n* (3).	**subver'tical** *adj* (4).
sub'total *n* and *vt* (3).	**subu'nit** *n* (3).	**subvit'reous** *adj* (4).
subtreas'urer *n* (2).	**subur'sine** *adj* (4).	**subwar'den** *n* (2).
subtreas'ury *n* (2).	**subvari'ety** *n* (3).	**sub'zonal** *adj* (1).
subtriang'ular *adj* (4).	**sub'vassal** *n* (2).	**sub'zone** *n* (3).

(often as Fr fem **succursale** /sük-ür-sal/). [Fr, from L *succurrere* to succour]

succus /suk'əs/ n (pl **succi** /suk'sī/) juice; any fluid secretion from a plant or animal, eg from a gland; extracted juice. [L *sūcus, succus* juice]

■ **succ'ose** or **succ'ous** adj.

succuss /su-kus'/ vt to shake up. [L *succutere, succussum* to toss up, from *sub* up, and *quatere* to shake]

■ **succussā'tion** n a shaking up, violent shaking; the trotting of a horse (obs). **succussion** /-ush'ən/ n an act or instance of shaking; a method of diagnosis in which a patient is shaken to detect the presence of an abnormal quantity of fluid in a body cavity, eg the pleural cavity (med); the splashing sound made by such fluid when the patient moves suddenly or is deliberately shaken. **succuss'ive** adj.

such /such/ adj of that kind, a similar kind, or the same kind (often followed by as or by a clause beginning with that); so characterized; of what kind; what (exclamatorily); so great; mentioned earlier; some particular but unspecified. ◆ adv so (preceding the indefinite article, if any). ◆ pronoun such a person, persons, thing, or things; the before-mentioned; that. [OE *swilc*; cognate with Gothic *swaleiks*; cf **so¹** and **like¹**]

■ **such'like** adj of such a kind. ◆ pronoun suchlike persons or things (or person or thing). **such'ness** n (archaic) quality. **such'wise** adv in such a manner.

❑ **such'-and-such** adj this or that, some, some or other (before the indefinite article, if any). ◆ pronoun such-and-such a person.

■ **as such** as it is described; in a particular capacity. **such as** for example. **such as it is** being what it is (and no better). **such that** in such a way, to such an extent, etc that.

suck /suk/ vt to draw into the mouth by producing a partial vacuum with the lips and tongue; to draw (milk or some other liquid) from with the mouth; to apply to or hold, roll about or squeeze in the mouth; to draw or render by suction; to absorb, draw in; to extract; to imbibe; to drain, exhaust. ◆ vi to draw in with the mouth; to suck milk from the breast; to draw in or up by suction; to make a noise of sucking; to draw in air as a dry pump; to draw in; to be repellent or contemptible (sl, orig US). ◆ n an act or spell of sucking; milk drawn from the breast; suction; a short drink, esp a dram of spirits (old sl). [OE *sūcan, sūgan*; Ger *saugen*, Du *zuigen*, Swed *suga*; cf L *sūgere*]

■ **sucked** adj. **suck'er** n a person who, or thing which, sucks; a sucking-pig, new-born whale, or other unweaned animal; a suckerfish; an American freshwater fish related to the carps, that feeds by sucking up small animals from the bottom; a sucking or adhesive organ; a device that adheres, draws water, etc by suction, such as a pump piston; a sweet or lollipop (inf); a shoot rising from an underground stem or root and developing into a new plant; a new shoot; a parasite, toady or sponge; a hard drinker (old sl); a gullible person, one taken advantage of (inf); a person who is drawn to, or who has a weakness for, a specified thing (inf); any person or thing (N Am inf). ◆ vt to strip off superfluous shoots from; to dupe, make a sucker of (esp US). ◆ vi (of a plant) to develop suckers. **suck'ered** adj having suckers. **suck'ing** n and adj.

❑ **suck'erfish** or **sucking fish** n the remora or any other fish with an adhesive disc, eg a lumpsucker. **suck'er-punch** n (US sl) a quick, surprise punch, esp from behind. ◆ vt (US sl) to give (someone) a sudden unexpected punch. **suck'-hole, suck''ole** or **suck'-holer** n (Aust sl) an ingratiating, servile, fawning, obsequious person. **suck-in'** n (sl, orig US) a disconcerting disappointment. **sucking bottle** n a milk bottle for infants. **sucking fish** see suckerfish above. **sucking louse** n a bloodsucking wingless insect of the order Anoplura. **suck'ing-pig** n a young milk-fed pig. **suck'-up** n (sl, orig US) an obsequious person.

■ **be a sucker for** (inf) to be unable to resist. **suck face** (chiefly US sl) to kiss. **suck in** to absorb; to engulf; to take in, deceive (sl). **suck off** (sl) to perform fellatio or cunnilingus on. **sucks!** or **sucks to you!** an expression of derision, contempt, etc. **suck up to** (inf) to flatter, be ingratiatingly nice to.

sucken /suk'n/ (Scots law; obs) n the district or population thirled to a mill; thirlage; an area of jurisdiction or field of operation. [**soken** (see **soc**)]

■ **suck'ener** n a tenant under the sucken or thirlage system.

sucket /suk'it/ an obsolete form of **succade.**

❑ **sucket spoon** or **fork** n an old table implement, spoon at one end, fork at the other.

suckle /suk'l/ vt to feed by allowing to suck milk from the breast or other mamma. ◆ vi to take milk in this way. [Prob back-formation from **suckling**]

■ **suck'ler** n an animal that suckles; a suckling. **suck'lers** n pl (dialect) heads of clover.

suckling /suk'ling/ n an unweaned child or animal; the act of giving suck; clover, also honeysuckle (dialect). ◆ adj giving suck; putting to suck; sucking.

sucralfate /soo'krəl-fāt/ n a drug used in the treatment of peptic ulcers.

sucre /soo'krā/ n the standard monetary unit of Ecuador (100 centavos). [Antonio José de Sucre (1795–1830), S American soldier-patriot]

sucrose /soo' or sū'krōs/ n a disaccharide carbohydrate ($C_{12}H_{22}O_{11}$), occurring in beet, sugar cane and other plants; sugar, cane sugar (inf). [Fr *sucre* sugar]

■ **su'cralose** n an artificial sweetener made from sucrose. **su'crase** same as **invertase** (see under **invert**). **sucrier** /sü-kri-ā/ n (Fr) a table vessel for sugar, usu of porcelain, etc.

suction /suk'shən/ n the act or power of sucking or of drawing or adhesion by reducing pressure of air; the removal of unwanted material, liquid or semi-liquid, from the body using a syringe, hollow needle or mechanical pump (med). [L *sūgere, suctum*; related to **suck**]

■ **sucto'rial** adj (zool) (adapted for) sucking or adhering. **sucto'rian** n and adj (zool) (a member) of the **Sucto'ria**, a subclass of Ciliata.

❑ **suction lipectomy** n a technique used in cosmetic surgery in which unwanted fat is removed through a suction instrument inserted through a small skin incision. **suction pump** n a pump for raising fluids by suction. **suction** (or **suctional**) **stop** n (phonetics) a stop consonant in which the contact of the articulating organs is followed by an inrush of air, a click or implosive.

sucurujú /soo-koo-roo-zhoo'/ n a local name in S America for the anaconda.

SUD abbrev : Sudan (IVR).

sud see **suds.**

sudamina /soo- or sū-dam'i-nə/ (pathol) n pl (sing **sudamen** /-dā'mən/) whitish vesicles due to retention of sweat in the sweat ducts or upper layers of skin. [L *sūdāmen*, pl *sūdāmina*, from *sūdāre* to sweat]

■ **sudam'inal** adj.

Sudanese /soo-də-nēz'* or soo'/ n (pl **Sudanese**) a native or inhabitant of *Sudan*, a republic of NE Africa, or of the region south of the Sahara and Libyan deserts. ◆ adj of or relating to Sudan or its inhabitants.

■ **Sudan'ic** n a group of languages spoken in Sudan. ◆ adj of or relating to these languages; of or relating to Sudan.

❑ **Sudan grass** n a sorghum, *Sorghum vulgare sudanensis*, grown for hay and fodder.

sudate /sū'dāt or soo'/ (rare) vi to sweat. [L *sūdāre, -ātum* to sweat]

■ **suda'rium** or **su'dary** /-də-ri/ n a cloth for wiping sweat, esp the veil or handkerchief of St Veronica, believed to have retained miraculously the image of Christ's face. **suda'tion** n sweating; sweat; a watery exudation from plants. **sudatorium** /-də-tö'ri-əm/ n a hot room (such as in an ancient Roman bathhouse) which induces sweating. **su'datory** /-tə-ri/ n a sudatorium; a drug which induces sweating. ◆ adj of sweat; inducing sweating.

sudd /sud/ n a mass of vegetation floating on water in NE Africa, particularly on the White Nile where it may obstruct navigation; a temporary dam. [Ar, obstruction]

sudden /sud'n/ adj without warning or apparent preparation; unexpected; hasty; abrupt; prompt; swift in action or production; glancing quickly; improvised. ◆ adv suddenly. [Anglo-Fr *sodain*, from L *subitāneus* sudden, from *subitus* approaching stealthily, from *subīre, -itum*, from *sub* in the sense of 'secretly', and *īre* to go]

■ **sudd'enly** adv. **sudd'enness** or (Scot; rare) **sudd'enty** n.

❑ **sudden death** n (sport) an extended period of play to settle a tied contest, ending when one of the contestants scores. **sudden infant death syndrome** see **cot death** under **cot¹**. **sudden oak death** n a destructive disease of oak trees caused by the fungus *Phytophthora ramorum*. **sudden unexplained death syndrome** n a mysterious condition, particularly affecting young men of SE Asian origin, in which sudden death occurs from unknown causes, and usu without previous symptoms of illness (abbrev **SUDS**).

■ **all of a sudden** all at once, suddenly.

sudder /sud'ər/ (Anglo-Ind) adj chief, supreme. ◆ n a supreme court. [Ar *çadr* chief]

Sudeck's atrophy /soo'deks at'rə-fi/ n local osteoporosis that develops rapidly in a hand or foot as a result of injury, infection, etc. [PHM Sudeck (1866–1938), German surgeon]

sudoku /sū-dō'koo/ n a type of puzzle in which numbers must be entered into a square grid in such a way that no number is repeated in any row, column or internal square. [Jap *su* number, and *doku* singular]

sudor /sū'dör, soo'* or -dər/ (med) n sweat. [L *sūdor, -ōris* sweat]

■ **su'doral** *adj*. **sudorif'erous** *adj* inducing or secreting sweat. **sudorif'ic** *adj* causing sweat. ◆ *n* a diaphoretic. **sudorip'arous** *adj* secreting sweat. **su'dorous** *adj* sweaty.

Sudra /soo'dra/ (*Anglo-Ind*) *n* a member of the fourth and lowest of the great Hindu castes. [Sans *śūdra*]

SUDS *abbrev*: sudden unexplained death syndrome (see under **sudden**).

suds /sudz/ *n pl* froth of soapy water (rarely in *sing* **sud**); beer (*N Am inf*). ◆ *vt* to wash in soap suds, to lather. ◆ *vi* (*N Am*) to lather, form suds. [Prob from MDu *sudse* marsh, swamp; connected with **seethe, sodden**]

■ **sud'ser** *n* (*press sl*) a soap opera. **sud'sy** *adj*.

sue /sū or soo/ (*Spenser* **sew**) *vt* (**su'ing; sued**) to prosecute at law; to petition for, apply for; to court (*archaic*); to follow, pursue (*obs*). ◆ *vi* to make legal claim; to make application; to entreat; to be a wooer (*Shakesp*); to do service (*obs*). [OFr *suir* (Fr *suivre*), from L *sequī*, *secūtus* to follow]

■ **sueabil'ity** *n* same as **suability** (see under **suable**). **sue'able** *adj* same as **suable**. **su'er** *n*. **su'ing** *n* and *adj*.

■ **standing to sue** (*law*) the right to bring a case to court.

suede or **suède** /swād (Fr sü-ed')/ *n* undressed kidskin or other leather with a soft unglazed nap finish, used eg for gloves and shoe uppers; the colour of undressed kidskin, a light beige. ◆ *adj* made of suede; of the colour of suede. ◆ *vt* to give a suede finish to (leather or cloth). [Fr (*gants de*) *Suède*, (gloves of) Sweden]

■ **suedette'** *n* a fabric made with a velvet-like nap resembling suede.

suet /sū'it or soo'it/ *n* a solid fatty tissue, accumulating around the kidneys and omentum of the ox, sheep, etc. [OFr *seu* (Fr *suif*), from L *sēbum* fat]

■ **su'ety** (also **su'etty**) *adj* of or resembling suet; (of a person's face or complexion) fatty and having a pallor resembling suet.

❑ **suet pudding** *n* a boiled pudding, savoury or sweet, made with suet.

suffect /suf'ekt/ *adj* (of a Roman consul or his office) additional, ie elected during the official year. [L *suffectus*, pap of *sufficere* to substitute]

suffer /suf'ər/ *vt* to undergo; to endure; to tolerate; to be affected by; to permit (*Bible* and *archaic*); to inflict pain on (*Shakesp*). ◆ *vi* to feel or undergo pain, grief, privation, etc; to sustain loss or disadvantage; to be injured; to undergo a punishment or penalty, such as death or martyrdom; to be the object of an action. [L *sufferre* to sustain, from *sub* in the sense of 'up from underneath', and *ferre* to carry]

■ **suff'erable** *adj*. **suff'erableness** *n*. **suff'erably** *adv*. **suff'erance** *n* tacit or unwilling assent; toleration; capacity to endure pain, injury, etc; suffering (*archaic*); patient endurance (*archaic*). **suff'erer** *n*. **suff'ering** *n* and *adj*.

■ **on sufferance** tolerated with reluctance. **suffer fools gladly** to be tolerant of other people's stupidity.

suffete /suf'ēt/ *n* one of the chief administrative officials of ancient Carthage. [L *sūfes*, *-etis*, from a Punic word]

suffice /sə-fīs'/ *vi* to be enough; to be competent or adequate. ◆ *vt* to satisfy. [Through Fr, from L *sufficere* to suffice, from *sub* below, and *facere* to make]

■ **suffīc'er** *n*. **sufficience** /sə-fish'əns/ *n* (*archaic*) sufficiency; capacity; ability; competence; sustenance. **sufficiency** /sə-fish' əns-i/ *n* the state of being sufficient; a sufficient quantity or supply; means enough for a comfortable living; adequate ability, competence, capacity (*obs* or *archaic*). **suffic'ient** *adj* adequate for the purpose; sufficing; effective; being a sufficient condition (*logic*); competent (*archaic*). ◆ *n* a sufficient quantity, enough. **suffic'iently** *adv*. **suffic'ing** *adj*. **suffic'ingness** *n*. **suffisance** /suf' i-zəns/ *n* (*obs*) sufficiency; satisfaction; enjoyment.

❑ **sufficient condition** *n* (*logic*) a condition or proposition whose existence assures the truth of, or leads to the occurrence of, a further condition.

■ **suffice it to say** let it be enough to say.

suffigance /suf' i-gans/ (*Shakesp, Much Ado About Nothing*) *n* Dogberry's blunder for **suffisance** (qv under **suffice**).

suffisance see under **suffice**.

suffix /suf'iks/ *n* an affix attached to the end of a root, stem or word (*grammar*); an index placed after and below a symbol, such as *n* in x_n (*maths*). ◆ *vt* (also /sə-fiks'/) to add as a suffix; to subjoin. [L *suffīxus*, from *sub* under, and *fīgere* to fix]

■ **suff'ixal** *adj*. **suffixā'tion** or **suffix'ion** *n*.

sufflate /sə-flāt'/ (*archaic*) *vt* and *vi* to inflate. [L *sufflāre*]

■ **sufflā'tion** *n*.

suffocate /suf'ə-kāt/ *vt* and *vi* to choke by stopping or obstructing the passage of air to the lungs; to stifle, eg in hot, airless conditions; to oppress or feel oppressed. ◆ *adj* (*Shakesp*) suffocated. [From pap of L *suffōcāre*, from *sub* under, and *faucēs* the throat]

■ **suff'ocating** *n* and *adj*. **suff'ocatingly** *adv*. **suffocā'tion** *n*. **suff'ocative** *adj* tending to suffocate.

Suffolk /suf'ək/ *n* an English breed of large, well-muscled, blackfaced sheep without horns. [From the English county]

❑ **Suffolk punch** see **punch**[3].

suffragan /suf'rə-gən/ *n* an assistant bishop; any bishop in relation to his metropolitan. ◆ *adj* acting as a suffragan. [LL *suffrāgāneus* assistant, supporting, from L *suffrāgium* a vote]

■ **suff'raganship** *n*.

suffrage /suf'rij/ *n* the right or power to vote; a vote; a supporting opinion, sanction; a prayer, *esp* for the dead, or in a litany. [L *suffrāgium* a vote]

■ **suffragette** /suf-rə-jet'/ *n* (*hist*; an improperly formed word) a woman (in the late 19c and early 20c) who sought, sometimes by extreme methods, to obtain voting rights for women. **suffraget'tism** *n*. **suff'ragism** *n*. **suff'ragist** *n* a believer in the right (eg of women) to vote.

suffruticose /sə-froo'ti-kōs/ (*bot*) *adj* herbaceous with a woody persistent stem-base (also **suffrutes'cent**). [L *sub* under, and *frutex*, *-icis* a shrub]

suffumigate /sə-fū'mi-gāt/ *vt* to fumigate from below. [L *sub*, and *fūmigāre*]

■ **suffumigā'tion** *n*.

suffuse /sə-fūz'/ *vt* to spread over or through, or cover, eg with a liquid or a tint; to permeate. ◆ *adj* /sə-fūs'/ (*bot*) spread out on the substratum. [L *sub* underneath, and *fundere*, *fūsum* to pour]

■ **suffū'sion** /-zhən/ *n*. **suffū'sive** /-siv/ *adj*.

Sufi or **Sofi** /soo'fē/ *n* (*pl* **Su'fis** or **So'fis**) an adherent of various Muslim orders or groups that aspire to a state of union with God through mystical contemplation, a Muslim mystic. [Ar *çūfī*, prob man of wool, from *çuf* coarse wool (as worn by ascetics)]

■ **Su'fic** or **Sufist'ic** *adj*. **Su'fism** or **So'fism** *n*.

sugar /shŭg'ər/ *n* a sweet substance (sucrose or cane sugar, $C_{12}H_{22}O_{11}$) obtained chiefly from cane and beet; extended to any water-soluble, crystalline monosaccharide or oligosaccharide, eg fructose, lactose, glucose, etc; a measure (eg a lump, teaspoonful) of sugar; money (*sl*); a term of endearment (*inf*); flattery (*sl*); heroin or LSD (*sl*). ◆ *adj* made with or of sugar; sweet (*Shakesp*). ◆ *vt* to sprinkle, coat, mix, or sweeten with sugar. [OFr (Fr) *sucre*, from Ar *sukkar*, from Sans *sharkarā*; the *g* unexplained; cf **saccharin**]

■ **sug'ared** *adj* sweetened or coated with sugar; sugary. **sug'ariness** *n*. **sug'aring** *n* sweetening with sugar; coating trees with sugar as a method of collecting insects; formation of sugar or syrup by boiling maple sap (also **sugaring off**; *N Am*); removing body hair by applying a sticky sugar paste which is then peeled away. **sug'arless** *adj*. **sug'ary** *adj* like sugar in taste or appearance; having or containing much sugar; cloyingly sweet, sickly, over-sentimental.

❑ **sugarally** or **sugarallie** /-al'i/ *n* (*Scot*) liquorice. **sugar apple** *n* the sweetsop fruit. **sug'ar-baker** *n* (*obs*) a sugar refiner; also a confectioner. **sugar basin** or **bowl** *n* a small basin for holding sugar at table. **sugar bean** *n* the lima bean. **sugar beet** *n* any variety of common beet, *esp* the variety *Rapa*, grown for sugar. **sugar bird** *n* either of two S African birds of the genus *Promerops* that suck nectar from flowers. **sugar bowl** see **sugar basin** above. **sugar bush** *n* (*US*) an area of woodland with a preponderance of sugar maples. **sugar candy** *n* sugar in large crystals (also **rock candy**); a sweet, confection (*US*). **sug'arcane** or **sugar cane** *n* a tall woody grass (*Saccharum officinarum*) of tropical and semitropical regions, cultivated in the West Indies, the southern USA, Australia, and elsewhere, one of the chief sources of sugar. **sugar charcoal** *n* a pure form of charcoal obtained from sucrose. **sug'arcoat** *vt* to coat with sugar; to disguise (something unpleasant) with a superficial attractiveness. **sugar-coat'ed** *adj*. **sug'ar-cube** or **-lump** *n* a small square block of sugar. **sugar daddy** *n* (*inf*) a wealthy, elderly or middle-aged man who lavishes money or gifts on a young woman or young homosexual man, *usu* in return for sexual favours or companionship. **sugar diabetes** *n* diabetes mellitus. **sugar foot** *n* a dance step used in tap, jazz, line dancing, etc. **sug'ar-free** *adj* containing no sugar. **sugar glider** *n* an Australian possum, *Petaurus breviceps*, with winglike flaps of skin enabling it to make long gliding jumps between trees. **sugar grass** *n* sweet sorghum. **sugar gum** *n* a eucalyptus, *Eucalyptus cladocalyx*, with sweet-tasting foliage. **sug'arhouse** *n* a factory, etc where sugar or maple sugar syrup is made. **sugar kelp** *n* a type of kelp, *Laminaria saccharina*, a source of mannitol (also called **sea belt**). **sug'arloaf** *n* a loaf or hard mass of refined sugar, *usu* more or less conical (see also **loaf sugar** under **loaf**[1]); a hill, hat, or other object of similar form. **sugar-lump** see **sugar-cube** above. **sugar maple** *n* a N American maple (*Acer saccharum* or related species) from whose sap maple syrup or maple sugar is made. **sugar mill** *n* a machine for pressing out the juice of the sugar cane. **sugar mimic** *n* any substance, either occurring naturally or developed synthetically, which mimics certain sugars in plant or animal cells. **sugar mite** *n* a mite infesting unrefined sugar. **sugar of lead** *n* lead acetate, sweet and poisonous, used as a mordant for dyeing and printing textiles, and as a drier for paints and varnishes. **sugar palm** *n* a palm (of various species) yielding sugar. **sugar pea** *n* a sugar snap pea. **sugar pine** *n* a tall W American pine (*Pinus lambertiana*) with sugary heartwood. **sug'arplum** *n* a small round boiled sweet; something pleasing, such as a compliment; a term of endearment. **sug'ar-refi'ner** *n*. **sug'ar-refi'nery** *n*. **sug'ar-refi'ning** *n*. **sugar sifter** *n* a container for sugar with a perforated top, enabling the sugar to be sprinkled. **sugar snap pea** or **sugar snap** *n* a variety of pea cultivated by crossing a mangetout with another pea. **sugar soap** *n* an alkaline cleansing or stripping preparation for paint surfaces. **sugar tongs** *n pl* small tongs for lifting sugar-lumps at table.

■ **heavy sugar** (*sl*) big money. **sugar the pill** to compensate somewhat for an unpleasant prospect, unwelcome imposition, etc.

suggest /sə-jest'/ or (*US*) səg-jest'/ *vt* to introduce indirectly to the thoughts; to call up in the mind; to put forward (a plan, hypothesis, thought, etc); to give an impression of; to tempt (*Shakesp*); to insinuate (*Shakesp*); to influence hypnotically. ◆ *vi* to make suggestions. [L *suggerere*, -*gestum*, from *sub* under, and *gerere* to carry]

■ **suggest'er** *n*. **suggestibil'ity** *n*. **suggest'ible** *adj* capable of being suggested, or of being influenced by suggestion, *esp* hypnotic. **suggest'ion** /-yən/ *n* a process or act of suggesting; a hint; a proposal; an indecent proposal; incitement, temptation; information without oath, not being pleadable (*law*); a false or underhand representation (*obs*); communication of belief or impulse to a hypnotized person. **suggest'ionism** *n* treatment by suggestion; the theory that hypnotic effects are entirely due to the action of suggestion. **suggest'ionist** *n*. **suggestioniza'tion** or -**s**- *n*. **suggest'ionize** or -**ise** *vt* to subject to suggestion. **suggest'ive** *adj* containing a hint; tending to suggest or evoke, evocative; awaking the mind; stimulating; relating to hypnotic suggestion; tending to awake indecent mental images or thoughts (*inf*; *euphem*). **suggest'ively** *adv*. **suggest'iveness** *n*.

sugging see under **sug**.

sugo /soo'gō/ *n* (in Italian cookery) sauce [Ital]

suhur /sə-hûr'/ *n* another name for **sehri**.

sui /soo'ī, soo'ē or sū'ē/ (*L*) of himself, herself, itself.
■ **sui generis** /jen'ər-is or ge'ne-ris/ of its own kind, the only one of its kind. **sui juris** /jŭr'is or ūr'/ having full legal capacity to act; (in Roman law) having the rights of a freeman.

suicide /sū'i-sīd or soo'/ *n* the act of killing oneself intentionally; a person who kills himself or herself intentionally. Cf **parasuicide**. ◆ *adj* relating to or involving suicide, as in *suicide mission*. [L *suī* of himself, and *caedere* to kill]

■ **suici'dal** *adj*. **suici'dally** *adv*. **suicidol'ogist** *n*. **suicidol'ogy** *n* the study of suicide.

❑ **suicide bomber** *n* a person who aims to detonate explosives in a terrorist attack knowing that self-destruction will ensue. **suicide pact** *n* an agreement between (*usu* two) people to kill themselves together. **suicide watch** *n* round-the-clock surveillance of a prisoner thought likely to attempt suicide.

■ **commit suicide** to kill oneself.

suid /sū'id or soo'/ *n* any member of the pig family Suidae, *incl* wild pigs such as the wild boar and warthog of the Old World, and domestic pigs of the genus *Sus*. [L *sūs*, *suis* pig, adj *suillus*, *suilla*, *suillum*]

■ **suid'ian** *adj* and *n*. **su'illine** *adj*.

suint /soo'int or swint/ *n* perspiration of sheep that dries in the wool and which consists of fatty matter and potassium salts. [Fr, from *suer* to sweat, from L *sūdāre*]

suit /sūt or soot/ *n* the process or act of suing; an action at law; courtship; a petition; a series or set; a sequence; a set of cards of the same denomination, in the pack or in one player's hand; a number of articles made to be worn together, eg a set of clothes or armour; matching trousers (or skirt) and jacket, sometimes with a waistcoat; such an outfit for a specified occasion or purpose; a business manager or accounts executive (as contrasted with ordinary workers or creative individuals) (*inf*); (used contemptuously) a bureaucratic functionary or administrative official (*inf*); pursuit (*obs*); a suite (*obs*). ◆ *vt* to provide or furnish; to fall in with the requirements of; to fit; to become, look attractive on; to please; to attire (*obs*). ◆ *vi* to agree; to match or be fitting. [Fr *suite*; cf **sue** and **suite**]

■ **suitabil'ity** *n*. **suit'able** *adj* that suits; fitting; agreeing; adequate. **suit'ableness** *n*. **suit'ably** *adv*. **suit'ed** *adj* wearing a suit; dressed, clothed; matched, appropriate; belonging to the same suit (*poker*). **suit'ing** *n* (sometimes in *pl*) cloth suitable for making suits. **suit'or** *n* a person who sues; a petitioner; a man seeking the love of a woman, or her hand in marriage. ◆ *vi* (*archaic*) to be or act as a suitor. **suit'ress** *n* (*rare*) a female suitor.

❑ **suit'case** *n* a portable oblong travelling case for carrying suits, clothes, etc.

■ **follow suit** to play a card of the suit led; to do the same. **strong suit** something one is specially good at. **suit yourself** do what you like.

suite /swēt/ *n* a train of followers or attendants; a set, as of furniture or rooms; a sequence of instrumental movements, *usu* dance tunes, in related keys; a related set of programs (*comput*); a sequel. [Fr, from a LL form of L *secūta*, fem pap of *sequī* to follow]

suitor, suitress see under **suit**.

suivante /swē'vənt/ *n* a waiting-woman or lady's maid; a confidential maid. [Fr]

suivez /swē-vā'/ (*music*) follow (the solo part, a direction to accompanist(s)). [Fr]

sujee see **soogee**.

suk, sukh see **souk**.

sukiyaki /soo-kē-yä'kē or sŭ-kē'-ä-kē/ *n* a Japanese dish of thinly-sliced meat (*usu* beef), vegetables, soya sauce, etc, cooked quickly together, often at the table. [Jap]

sukkah or **succah** /suk'ä or sŭk'ə/ *n* a hut or shelter roofed with branches, used by the orthodox Jews as temporary living accommodation during the festival of Sukkoth. [Heb, hut, tabernacle; see also **Sukkoth**]

Sukkoth /suk'əth, suk'ət or sŭk'əs/ or **Sukkot** /suk'ət/ *n* an eight-day Jewish harvest festival beginning on the 15th day of Tishri and commemorating the wanderings of the ancient Israelites in the wilderness, the Feast of Tabernacles (also **Succ'oth**). [Heb pl *sukkōth* huts, tents]

sulcus /sul'kəs/ *n* (pl **sul'ci** /-sī/) a groove, furrow or fissure; a groove or furrow between two convolutions of the brain (*anat*). [L *sulcus* a furrow]

■ **sul'cal** /-kl/ *adj* of a sulcus; grooved; furrowed. **sul'calize** or -**ise** *vt* to furrow. **sul'cate** or **sul'cated** *adj* furrowed, grooved; with parallel longitudinal furrows. **sulca'tion** *n*.

sulf- see **sulph-**.

sulfa US spelling of **sulpha**.

sulfadoxine /sul-fə-dok'sin/ *n* a drug used in combination with other drugs in the treatment of malaria.

sulfate, sulfide, etc US spellings of **sulphate, sulphide**, etc.

sulfo- see **sulph-**.

sulk /sulk/ *vi* to be sullen, silent or aloof, *esp* out of petty resentment or bad temper. ◆ *n* someone who sulks; (often in *pl*) a fit of sulking. [Prob from the root seen in OE *āseolcan* to slack, be slow, pap *āsolcen*]

■ **sulk'ily** *adv*. **sulk'iness** *n*. **sulk'y** *adj* sullen; inclined to sulk. ◆ *n* a light two-wheeled horse-drawn vehicle for one person.

sullage /sul'ij/ *n* filth; refuse, sewage; scum; scoria; silt. [Perh connected with **sully**]

sullen /sul'ən/ *adj* gloomily angry and silent; malignant, baleful; dull, dismal. ◆ *adv* sullenly. [Appar through an OFr derivative from L *sōlus* alone]

■ **sull'enly** *adv*. **sull'enness** *n*.

sully /sul'i/ *vt* (**sull'ying**; **sull'ied**) to soil; to tarnish; to mar or stain; to pollute or defile. ◆ *vi* (*archaic*) to be or become soiled. ◆ *n* a spot; tarnish. [OE *sylian* to defile, from *sol* mud; or from OFr *souiller* to soil]

sulph- /sulf-/ or **sulpho-** /sul-fō-/, also (chiefly *US*) **sulf-** or **sulfo-** *pfx* denoting sulphur.

sulpha or (*US*) **sulfa** /sul'fə/ *adj* of a class of synthetic antibacterial drugs, the sulphonamides. ◆ *n* any drug of this class. [*sulph*anilamide]

sulphacetamide or (*US*) **sulfacetamide** /sul-fə-sē'ta-mīd/ *n* a sulphonamide used in eye drops against conjunctivitis, etc. [*sulpha*, *cet*yl and *amide*]

sulphadiazine or (*US*) **sulfadiazine** /sul-fə-dī'ə-zēn or -zin/ *n* a sulphonamide, $C_{10}H_{10}N_4O_2S$, used, *usu* in combination with an antibiotic, in the treatment of pneumonia, meningitis, etc. [*sulpha* and *diazine*]

sulphadimidine /sul-fə-dim'i-dēn/ *n* a sulphonamide used in treating bacterial infections in humans and animals. [*sulpha*-, *di*- and *pyrimidine*]

sulphamethoxazole or **sulfamethoxazole** /sul-fə-meth-ok'sə-zōl/ n a sulphonamide, $C_{10}H_{11}N_3O_3S$, used with trimethoprim in the combination drug co-trimoxazole, to treat various infections such as bronchitis, pneumonia, etc. [*sulpha*, *methyl* and *isoxazole*]

sulphanilamide or (*US*) **sulfanilamide** /sul-fə-nil'a-mīd/ n a white crystalline compound, $C_6H_8N_2O_2S$, formerly used as an antibacterial drug. [*sulpha*, *anil*ine and *amide*]

sulphatase or (*US*) **sulfatase** /sul'fə-tāz/ n any of a group of enzymes found in microorganisms and animal tissue that help to break down sulphuric acid esters.

sulphate or (*US*) **sulfate** /sul'fāt/ n a salt of sulphuric acid. ◆ vt to form a deposit of lead sulphate on; to treat or impregnate with sulphur or a sulphate. ◆ vi to become sulphated. [Fr, from New L *sulfātum*] ■ **sulphatic** /-at'ik/ adj. **sulphā'tion** or (*US*) **sulfā'tion** n.

sulphathiazole or (*US*) **sulfathiazole** /sul-fə-thī'ə-zōl/ n a sulphonamide formerly used in human medicine against staphylococcal infection (now only used in veterinary medicine). [*sulpha* and *thiazole*]

sulphhydryl or (*US*) **sulfhydryl** /sulf-(h)ī'dril/ n a chemical group, SH, characteristic of sulphur-containing compounds and present in certain proteins, coenzymes, etc. [*sulph-* and *hydryl*]

sulphide or (*US*) **sulfide** /sul'fīd/ n a compound of an element or radical with sulphur; a salt of hydrosulphuric acid. [**-ide**]

sulphinpyrazone or **sulfinpyrazone** /sul-fin-pī'rə-zōn/ n a drug used to treat gout.

sulphinyl or (*US*) **sulfinyl** /sul'fə-nil/ n the bivalent chemical group, SO.

sulphite or (*US*) **sulfite** /sul'fīt/ n a salt of sulphurous acid. [**-ite** (4)] ❑ **sulphite pulp** n in paper-making, wood chips treated with calcium or magnesium acid sulphite.

sulpho- see **sulph-**.

sulphone or (*US*) **sulfone** /sul'fōn/ n any of a class of substances consisting of two organic radicals combined with SO_2. [Ger *Sulfon*] ■ **sulphon'amide** or (*US*) **sulfon'amide** n an amide of a sulphonic acid, any of a group of drugs with antibacterial action. **sul'phonate** or (*US*) **sul'fonate** n a salt or ester derived from a sulphonic acid. ◆ vt to convert (*esp* an aliphatic or aromatic compound) into a sulphonic acid by treating with sulphuric acid; to introduce the sulphonic group, SO_2OH, into (an organic compound). **sulphona'tion** or (*US*) **sulfona'tion** n. **sul'phonyl** or (*US*) **sul'fonyl** n a bivalent sulphone group SO_2, also called **sulphuryl**; a compound containing this group. ❑ **sulphon'ic** (or *US* **sulfon'ic**) **acid** n any of a group of organic acids containing the group SO_2OH, used in the manufacture of phenols, dyes, etc.

sulphonium or (*US*) **sulfonium** /sul-fō'ni-əm/ n the positively charged group SH_3, its salts or derivatives. [**sulph-** and sfx *-onium*, as in *ammonium*]

sulphonylurea /sul-fō-nil-yoo-rē'ə/ n a synthetic compound used to reduce the level of glucose in the blood in diabetes mellitus. [**sulphonyl** and **urea**]

sulphur or (*US*) **sulfur** /sul'fər/ n a yellow, very brittle, fusible and inflammable nonmetallic element (symbol **S**; atomic no 16) occurring in nature uncombined, as metal sulphides such as galena and pyrite, or as sulphur-containing compounds, used in the manufacture of sulphuric acid, in vulcanization of rubber and as a constituent of certain drugs; the colour of sulphur, a bright yellow. ◆ adj composed of sulphur. ◆ vt to treat or fumigate with sulphur. [L *sulphur*, *sulfur*, *sulpur*, *-uris*] ■ **sul'phurate** /-fū-rāt/ vt to combine with, or subject to the action of, sulphur. **sulphura'tion** n. **sul'phurator** /-fū'ri-əs/ adj sulphury; sulphur-yellow. **sulphu'reously** adv. **sulphu'reousness** n. **sul'phuret** /-fū-ret/ n (*obs*) a sulphide. ◆ vt (**sul'phuretting** or (*esp US*) **-eting**; **sul'phuretted** or (*esp US*) **-eted**) to impregnate, treat or combine with sulphur. **sul'phuretted** adj combined with sulphur. **sulphu'ric** adj containing sulphur in relatively high valency (cf **sulphurous**). **sulphuriza'tion** or **-s-** n. **sul'phurize** or **-ise** vt to sulphurate. **sul'phurous** /-fūr- or -fər-/ adj relating to, resembling or containing sulphur; containing sulphur in relatively low valency (*chem*) /-fū'rəs/; of or relating to hellfire, infernal, satanic; fiery; blasphemous. **sulphury** /sul'fər-i/ adj like sulphur. ❑ **sulphur bacteria** n pl bacteria that liberate sulphur from hydrogen sulphide, etc and ultimately form sulphuric acid. **sul'phur-bottom** n the blue whale (from the yellowish spots on its underside). **sulphur dioxide** n a pungent, colourless, non-flammable gas, SO_2, formed when sulphur burns, a major pollutant when discharged into the atmosphere in waste from industrial processes and used in the manufacture of sulphuric acid, in bleaching, disinfecting and

preserving. **sulphuretted hydrogen** n hydrogen sulphide. **sulphuric acid** n oil of vitriol, a very corrosive acid, H_2SO_4, an important heavy chemical used extensively in industry. **sulphurous acid** n an unstable acid, H_2SO_3, used as a food preservative and bleaching agent. **sul'phur-root** or **sul'phurwort** n an umbelliferous plant (various species of *Peucedanum*) akin to parsnip, with yellow flowers and juice. **sulphur trioxide** n a corrosive substance, SO_3, the anhydride of sulphuric acid. **sulphur tuft** n a poisonous fungus (*Hypholoma fasciculare*) with a yellowish cap.

sultan /sul'tən/ n a Muslim ruler, *esp* (*hist*) the former head of the Ottoman Empire; a despot; a small white (*orig* Turkish) variety of domestic fowl with feathered legs and feet. [Ar *sultān*] ■ **sultana** /sul- or səl-tä'nə/ n a small, pale, seedless raisin; a sultan's wife or concubine; a sultan's mother, sister or daughter; a fiddle strung with wires in pairs. **sul'tanate** n the rank or office of sultan; the territory ruled over by a sultan. **sul'taness** n. **sultanic** /sul-tan'ik/ adj. **sul'tanship** n. ■ **sweet sultan** a name given to two annual species of *Centaurea*, C. *moschata* and C. *suaveolens*.

sultry /sul'tri/ adj humid and oppressive, sweltering; hot with anger; passionate, voluptuous; (of language) lurid, verging on the indecent, indelicate (*old sl*). [**swelter**] ■ **sul'trily** adv. **sul'triness** n.

Sulu /soo'loo/ n a member of a Muslim people of the *Sulu* Archipelago in the SW Philippines; their Malayan language. ◆ adj of or relating to the Sulus or their language.

sulu /soo'loo/ n a length of cloth worn in Fiji, etc as a sarong. [Fijian]

sum¹ /sum/ n the total, whole; the aggregate, whole amount; the result of addition; an amount; a quantity of money; a problem in addition, or in arithmetic generally; chief points; the substance or result; summation; height, culmination, completion. ◆ vt (**summ'ing**; **summed**) (often with *up*) to add, make up the total of; to be an epitome of, exemplify; to summarize; to reckon up, form an estimate of; to complete the development of, bring to perfection (*obs*). ◆ vi (with *up*) to summarize or make a summing-up; to express fully and concisely; to do sums. [OFr *summe*, from L *summa*, from *summus* highest] ■ **sum'less** adj not to be summed or counted; incalculable. **sum'mand** (or /-and'/) n an addend; a part of a sum. **summation** n see separate entry. **summed** adj. **summ'er** n. **summ'ing** n and adj. ❑ **summing-up'** n a recapitulation or review of the leading points, *esp* a judge's summary survey of the evidence given to a jury before it withdraws to consider its verdict. **sum total** n a complete or final sum. ■ **in sum** in short; to sum up. **sum and substance** the gist; the essence. **the sum of things** the public weal; the universe.

sum² /sŭm/ n (pl **sumy** /sŭ'mi/) the standard monetary unit of Uzbekistan (100 tiyin).

sumac or **sumach** /soo', shoo' or sŭ'mak/ n any tree or shrub of the genus *Rhus*, *esp* R. *coriaria*; the leaves and shoots used in dyeing; the dried ground berries of R. *coriaria* used as a spice in Middle-Eastern cookery. [Fr *sumac* or LL *sumach*, from Ar *summāq*]

sumatra /sŭ-mä'trə/ n a short, violent squall in or near the Straits of Malacca in Indonesia, coming from the island of *Sumatra*.

Sumatran /sŭ-mä'trən/ adj of Sumatra, a mountainous island in W Indonesia, its inhabitants or their language. ◆ n a native or inhabitant of Sumatra; the language of Sumatra. ❑ **Sumatran rhinoceros** n an Asian two-horned rhinoceros whose young are covered in thick brown hair.

Sumerian /soo- or sū-mē'ri-ən, also -mä'ri-ən/ adj of or relating to the ancient civilization, people, language, etc of the region of *Sumer* in southern Babylonia (fl 3500BC). ◆ n a native of Sumer; the language or its cuneiform script.

summa /sum'ə/ n (pl **summ'ae** /-ē/) a treatise giving a summary of a whole subject. [L *summa* sum] ■ **summar** /sum'ər/ adj (*Scot*) summary. **summ'ist** n a writer of summae; an epitomist. ❑ **Summar Roll** n a list of cases requiring dispatch.

summa cum laude /sum'ə kum lö'dē or sŭm'ä kŭm low'dā/ adv and adj with greatest distinction. [L]

summand see under **sum¹**.

summar see under **summa**.

summary /sum'ə-ri/ n an abstract, abridgement or compendium; a shortened form of a story or report, etc summing up the main points. ◆ adj condensed; short; brief; compendious; done by a short method; without unnecessary formalities or delay, without further application to the court. [L *summārium*, from *summa* sum]

■ **summ'arily** adv. **summ'ariness** n. **summ'arist** n someone who summarizes. **summ'arize** or **-ise** vt to present in a summary or briefly. **summ'arizer** or **-s-** n.

❑ **summary offence** n (law) one which is tried by a magistrate.

summat /sum'ət/ a dialect form of **something, somewhat** (see under **some**).

summate /sum'āt/ vt to add together. [Back-formation from **summation**]

summation /su-mā'shən/ n the process of finding the sum, addition; accumulation; an aggregate; a summing-up, summary. [Med L summātio, from summare to sum up, from L summa sum]

■ **summa'tional** adj. **summ'ative** adj additive.

summer[1] /sum'ər/ n the warm season of the year, lasting approximately from June to August in the northern hemisphere and from December to February in the southern hemisphere; in the astronomical year, the period of time between the summer solstice and the autumnal equinox; a spell of warm weather (see **Indian summer** under **Indian, St Luke's summer** and **St Martin's summer** under **saint**); a year (poetic); a time of peak maturity, heyday. ◆ adj of, for or occurring in summer. ◆ vi to pass the summer. ◆ vt to keep through the summer. [OE sumer, sumor; Du zomer, Ger Sommer]

■ **summ'ering** n. **summ'erlike** adj. **summ'erly** adj warm and bright like summer. **summ'ery** adj like summer; suitable for summer.

❑ **summer cypress** n another name for **kochia**. **summ'erhouse** n a small building in a garden for sitting in in good weather; a summer residence. **summer pudding** n a pudding made of seasonal soft fruit and bread. **summer savory** see **savory**. **summer school** n a course of study held during the summer. **summer season** n summer regarded as the busiest time of year for holidays and businesses connected with them, esp hotels. **summ'er-seeming** adj (Shakesp) perhaps hot and transient, like summer. **summer solstice** n the solstice that occurs around 21 June in the northern hemisphere (December in the southern). **summer stock** n (US) a summer season of plays presented by a repertory company; summer theatres collectively. **summ'ertide** n (archaic or poetic) the summer season. **summ'ertime** n the summer season. **summer time** n time adopted in the summer (for daylight-saving purposes), usu one hour in advance of the standard local time. **summ'er-weight** adj (of clothes) light enough to be worn in summer. **summ'erwood** n wood with smaller and thicker-walled cells than springwood, formed late in the growing season.

summer[2] /sum'ər/ n a great horizontal beam or lintel, esp supporting a floor or roof (also **summ'er-tree**); a pack-horse, a sumpter (obs). [See **sumpter**]

summer[3] see under **sum**[1].

summersault, summerset same as **somersault**.

summist see under **summa**.

summit /sum'it/ n the highest point or degree; the top, apex; a summit conference. [OFr sommette, somet (Fr sommet), dimin of som, from L summum highest]

■ **summ'ital** adj. **summiteer'** n a participant in summit conferences. **summ'itless** adj. **summ'itry** n the practice or technique of holding summit conferences.

❑ **summit conference, talks** or **meeting** n a conference between heads of states; sometimes extended to mean a conference between heads of lesser organizations. **summ'it-level** n the highest level.

summon /sum'ən/ vt to call up, forth, or together; to call upon to appear (eg in court) or to do something; to rouse, gather (eg strength or energy). [OFr somoner, from L summonēre, from subsecretly, and monēre to warn; sense partly from OE somnian to assemble]

■ **summ'onable** adj. **summ'oner** n someone who summons; an officer who serves summonses; an apparitor. **summ'ons** n (pl **summ'onses**) a summoning or an authoritative call; a call to appear (esp in court); a call to surrender. ◆ vt to serve with a summons.

summum bonum /sum'əm bō'nəm or sŭm'ŭm bon'ŭm/ (L) n the chief good (as the ultimate ethical objective).

summum genus /sum'əm jē'nəs or sŭm'ŭm gen'ŭs/ n the highest division in a classification; a genus that cannot be categorized under a higher genus (logic). [New L]

sumo /soo'mō/ n (pl **su'mos**) a traditional Japanese sport, a form of wrestling, in which the aim is to force the opponent out of the ring or causes him or her to touch the ground within it with any part of the body other than the soles of the feet. [Jap sumō]

■ **sumotō'ri** n (pl **sumotō'ri** or **sumotō'ris**) a sumo wrestler.

sump /sump/ n a bog, pool, puddle (now dialect); a pit or depression into which liquid drains, such as the lowest point of a mine into which

water drains, a depression into which seawater drains at a salt work; a reservoir for liquid esp the lower part of the crankcase in an internal-combustion engine serving as a receptacle for oil. [Du somp; Ger Sumpf]

sumph /sumf/ (Scot) n a stupid person, a simpleton; a surly, sullen person. [Origin unknown]

■ **sumph'ish** adj. **sumph'ishness** n.

sumpit /sum'pit/ or **sumpitan** /sum'pi-tan/ n a Malay blowpipe made from a hollow cane and used for shooting (esp poisonous) arrows. [Malay]

sumpter /sum(p)'tər/ (archaic) n a packhorse or mule (also **sumpter horse**). [OFr sommetier, a packhorse driver, from Gr sagma a pack, saddlebag, sattein to pack]

sumptuary /sump'tū-ə-ri or sum'tū-ə-ri/ adj relating to or regulating expense; relating to the control or moderation of extravagance. [L sumptuārius, from sumptus cost]

sumptuous /sum(p)'tū-əs/ adj costly; magnificently luxurious. [L sūmptus cost, from sūmere, sūmptum to take]

■ **sumptuos'ity** n. **sump'tūously** adv. **sump'tūousness** n.

Sun. abbrev: Sunday.

sun /sun/ n the star which is the gravitational centre around which the planets, etc revolve, and the source of light and heat to our planetary system (often with cap); its heat and light; the position of this star or the time when it is visible in the sky; sunshine; any star around which planets, etc revolve; a representation of the sun, often with a human face; a person or thing likened to the sun, eg in splendour, glory, as the central body in a system, etc; a year, or a day (archaic and poetic); sunrise; sunset. ◆ vt (**sunn'ing; sunned**) to expose to the sun's rays; to warm, etc in sunshine. ◆ vi to be exposed or expose oneself to the sun's rays; to bask in sunshine. [OE sunne; ON sunna, OHGer sunnô]

■ **sun'less** adj. **sun'lessness** n. **sun'like** adj. **sunned** adj exposed to the sun or sunshine. **sunn'ies** n pl (inf) sunglasses. **sunn'ily** adv. **sunn'iness** n. **sunn'y** adj of, from, like or lighted, coloured or warmed by the sun; genial; cheerful. **sun'ward** adj and adv towards the sun. **sun'wards** adv. **sun'wise** adv in the direction of the sun's apparent revolution.

❑ **sun-and-plan'et** adj geared so that one wheel moves round another. **sun animalcule** n a heliozoan. **sun'bake** vi (Aust) to sunbathe (also n). **sun'baked** adj baked or dried by the heat of the sun. **sun'bath** n a period of sunbathing. **sun'bathe** vi to expose the body to the sun's rays, esp in order to tan the skin (also n). **sun'bather** /-bādh-/ n. **sun'bathing** n. **sun'beam** n a shaft of sunlight. **sun'beamed** adj. **sun'beamy** adj. **sun bear** n a small black bear (Helarctos malayanus) of forest areas of SE Asia, with a crescent-shaped yellowish-white patch at the front of its neck. **sun'beat** or **sun'beaten** adj continually exposed to the sun. **sun'bed** n a unit consisting of a couch with sunlamps for obtaining an artificial suntan; a sunlounger. **sun'belt** n a region with a warm, sunny climate, a preferred place to live; a favoured area generally; (often with cap; also **Sun Belt**) the Southern states of the USA. **sun'berry** n a dark-red edible fruit, a hybrid resulting from a cross between a blackberry and a raspberry; the plant producing this fruit. **sun'bird** n any of the Nectariniidae, a family of small, often brightly-coloured, tropical birds related to honeyeaters and superficially like hummingbirds. **sun bittern** n a S American wading bird (Eurypyga helias) with brilliant many-coloured markings. **sun'blind** n a shade or awning for a window. **sun'-blind** adj blinded by the sun. **sun'-blink** n (Scot) a gleam of sunshine. **sun'block** n a sunscreen that completely protects the skin from the sun's ultraviolet rays. **sun bonnet** n a light bonnet projecting beyond the face at the top and sides to provide protection from the sun. **sun'bow** n a bow or arc of rainbow-like colours that is made by the sun shining through spray or mist, eg of a waterfall. **sun'bright** adj bright as the sun. **sun'burn** n reddening of the skin and tenderness caused by excessive exposure to the sun's ultraviolet rays; tanning of the skin. ◆ vt to burn or tan by exposure to the sun. ◆ vi to become sunburned. **sun'burned** or **sun'burnt** adj. **sun'burst** n a strong outburst of sunlight; something, eg a jewel or ornament, resembling the rayed sun. **sun'-clad** adj clothed in radiant light. **sun crack** n a crack formed in clayey ground as it dries in the sun, often preserved in rocks. **sun cream** n a cream sunscreen that promotes a suntan. **sun cult** n worship of a sun-god or of the sun. **sun'-cured** adj cured in the sun. **sun dance** n a Native American ceremonial dance, performed in honour of the sun. **sun deck** or **sun'deck** n the upper deck of a passenger ship that is exposed to the sun; a roof, balcony or terrace used for sunbathing. **sun'dew** n an insectivorous bog-plant (genus Drosera). **sun'dial** n a device for telling the time by a shadow cast by the gnomon on a graduated flat surface. **sun disc** or (esp N Am) **sun disk** n the visible disc of the sun; a winged disc, an ancient Egyptian symbol of the sun-god. **sun'dog** n a mock sun or parhelion. **sun'down** n sunset; a woman's broad-brimmed hat (US inf). ◆ vi (of a person with dementia) to enter into a state of increased agitation towards the end of the day. **sun'downer** *n* in Australia, a loafer or tramp who arrives at a place in time for a meal and lodging, but too late to do any work in exchange; a government official who practises a profession after hours (*US*); an alcoholic drink taken after sunset. **sun'drenched** *adj* exposed to long periods of hot sunshine. **sun'dress** *n* a low-cut dress, leaving the arms, shoulders and back exposed to the sun. **sun'-dried** *adj* dried in the sun. **sun'drops** *n sing* an American evening primrose of the genus *Oenothera*, with flowers that open at or around sunrise. **sun'-expelling** *adj* (*Shakesp*) keeping off the sun. **sun'fast** *adj* (chiefly *N Am*) (of dye, fabric or garment colour) not fading in the sunlight. **sun'fish** *n* any of various N American perch-like fishes of the family Centrarchidae, eg the largemouth bass, smallmouth bass and pumpkinseed, all having rounded, often brightly-coloured bodies and differing from the perches in that they build nests and care for their young; any large marine fish of the family Molidae, *esp Mola mola*, of temperate and tropical seas, having a deep almost oval body and teeth fused to form a sharp beak. **sun'flower** *n* a composite plant (genus *Helianthus*) or its large head with yellow rays and edible seeds from which an oil is extracted. **sun'gazer** *n* an African lizard (*Cordylus giganteus*) given to basking in the sun. **sun'glass** *n* a burning-glass. **sun'glasses** *n pl* dark-lensed spectacles used to protect the eyes against strong sunlight. **sun'glow** *n* the glow in the sky before sunrise and after sunset. **sun'-god** *n* a god personifying or concerned with the sun. **sun'grebe** *n* a tropical diving bird of the Heliornithidae family. **sun'hat** *n* a hat with a brim to shade the face. **sun'-kissed** *adj* warmed, tanned or ripened by the sun. **sun'lamp** *n* a lamp that gives out ultraviolet rays, used curatively or to induce artificial suntan; a lamp producing a very bright light, used in film-making. **sun'light** *n* the light of the sun. **sun'lit** *adj* lighted by the sun. **sun lounge** or (*US*) **sun parlor** *n* a room with large windows, or a glass wall, to admit the maximum sunlight. **sun'lounger** *n* a long, *usu* folding, seat for sunbathing. **sun myth** *n* a solar myth (qv). **sunny side** *n* a pleasant or cheerful part or point of view; the better side; an age less than one specified, as *on the sunny side of fifty* (see also below). **sun parlor** see **sun lounge** above. **sun picture** or **print** *n* (*obs*) a photograph. **sun'proof** *adj*. **sun protection factor** *n* the effectiveness of a sunscreen in protecting the skin from the sun's ultraviolet rays, *usu* indicated by a number on a rising scale (*abbrev* SPF). **sun'ray** *n* a sunbeam, ray of sunshine. **sunray pleats** *n pl* tapering knife pleats giving a flared effect to skirts, etc. **sun'rise** or **sun'rising** *n* the rising or first appearance of the sun above the horizon; the time or colour-effects of this rising; the east. **sunrise industry** *n* a new and rapidly growing industry, often based on electronics. **sun'roof** or **sunshine roof** *n* a section in a car roof that can be slid open to admit light and air. **sun room** *n* a sun lounge. **sun'screen** *n* a lotion, cream, etc that prevents sunburn by screening the skin from ultraviolet rays. **sun'set** or **sun'setting** *n* the setting or going down of the sun; the time or phenomenon of this; the west; a decline (*fig*). **sunset clause** *n* a clause in a law, contract, etc that stipulates that the agreement will become invalid after a certain period of time. **sun'shade** *n* a parasol; an awning. **sun'shine** *n* bright sunlight; brightness; prosperity; geniality; an informal term of address, often used in a gently scolding or ironic tone. ♦ *adj* sunshiny; fair-weather. **sunshine recorder** *n* an instrument for recording duration of sunshine. **sunshine roof** see **sunroof** above. **sun'shiny** *adj* bright with sunshine; pleasant; bright like the sun; genial. **sun'spot** *n* a relatively dark patch on the surface of the sun; a place with a very warm sunny climate. **sun spurge** *n* a spurge (*Euphorbia helioscopia*) supposed to turn with the sun, a common weed. **sun'stone** *n* aventurine feldspar. **sun'stroke** *n* a medical condition of general collapse caused by prolonged exposure to intense sunlight, which can result in delirium, convulsions and coma. **sun'struck** *adj* affected with sunstroke. **sun'suit** *n* a child's outfit for playing in the sun, leaving most of the body exposed. **sun'tan** *n* a browning of the skin as a result of exposure to the sun; (in *pl*) a light-coloured military uniform for summer wear (*US*). **sun'tanned** *adj*. **sun'trap** *n* a sheltered, sunny place. **sun'up** *n* sunrise. **sun visor** *n*. **sun worship** *n* adoration or deification of the sun. **sun worshipper** or **sun'worshipper** *n* an adherent of sun worship; a person who spends long periods of time sunbathing. ■ **a place in the sun** a place or opportunity for good living or attaining prosperity. **a touch of the sun** mild sunburn; mild sunstroke. **between** (in *Shakesp* **'twixt**) **sun and sun** or **from sun to sun** between sunrise and sunset. **catch the sun** to be sunburnt. **have been in the sunshine** or **have the sun in one's eyes** to be drunk. **sunny side up** (*inf*) (of an egg) fried on one side only, so that the yolk is visible. **take the sun** to ascertain the sun's meridian altitude; to walk or laze in the sun. **under the sun** on earth.

sundae /*sun'dā* or -*di*/ *n* an ice-cream with syrup or crushed fruit; a mixed nougat or confection. [Perh **Sunday**]

sundari /*sun'də-rē*/ *n* a S Asian sterculiaceous timber tree of the genus *Heritiera* (also **sun'dra**, **sun'dri** or **sun'der**). [Sans *sundarī*]

Sunday /*sun'dā* or -*di*/ *n* the first day of the week, dedicated in ancient times to the sun, regarded as the Sabbath by most Christians; a newspaper published on Sundays. [OE *sunnan dæg*, transl of L *diēs sōlis* day of the sun]
■ **Sun'days** *adv* on Sundays.
❑ **Sunday best** *n* one's best clothes. **Sunday driver** *n* someone who drives a car at weekends only, hence an unpractised and incompetent driver. **Sun'day-go-to-meeting** *adj* appropriate to Sunday and churchgoing. **Sunday painters** *n pl* people who paint seriously but in their spare time. **Sunday punch** *n* (*N Am inf*) a powerful punch intended to knock out one's opponent (also *fig*). **Sunday saint** *n* someone whose religion or morality is confined to Sundays. **Sunday school** *n* a school for religious (*orig* general) instruction for children on Sunday.
■ **a month of Sundays** a long time.

sunder¹ /*sun'dər*/ (*archaic* and *poetic*) *vt* and *vi* to separate; to part. [OE *syndrian* to separate, *sundor* separate; ON *sundr* asunder]
■ **sun'derance** *n*. **sun'dered** *adj*. **sun'derer** *n*. **sun'dering** *n* and *adj*. **sun'derment** *n*.
■ **in sunder** (*Bible*) asunder.

sunder² see **sundari**.

sundew, sundial, etc see under **sun**.

sundra, sundri see **sundari**.

sundry /*sun'dri*/ *adj* separate; more than one or two; several; miscellaneous, various; varied (*Shakesp*). [OE *syndrig*; cf **sunder¹**]
■ **sun'dries** *n pl* sundry things; miscellaneous small things, *esp* things of low or little value.
■ **all and sundry** all collectively and individually.

sunfast, sunfish, sunflower see under **sun**.

Sung /*sŭng*/ or **Song** /*song*/ *n* a Chinese dynasty (960–1279). ♦ *adj* of the dynasty, or its culture, including its pottery.

sung /*sung*/ see **sing¹**.

sungar see **sangar**.

sungazer...to...**sunhat** see under **sun**.

suni /*soo'ni*/ *n* a small SE African antelope (*Neotragus moschatus*). [Bantu]

sunk¹ /*sungk*/, **sunken** /*sung'kn*/ see **sink**.

sunk² /*sungk*/ (*Scot*) *n* a turf seat; a pad; a bank; an overweight person. [Origin unknown]
■ **sunk'ie** *n* a little stool.

sunket /*sung'kit*/ (*Scot*) *n* (*usu* in *pl*) a dainty or delicacy. [From *sumquhat*, Scot form of **somewhat**]

sunlamp...to...**sun myth** see under **sun**.

sunn /*sun*/ *n* a leguminous tropical shrub (*Crotalaria juncea*) that yields a tough fibre used in rope-making, etc; this fibre (also **sunn hemp**). [Hindi *san*]

Sunna or **Sunnah** /*sŭn'ə* or *sun'ə*/ *n* the traditional root of Muslim law, based on biographical stories about Mohammed, constituting a secondary source of revelation to that which is written down in the Koran. [Ar *sunnah*]
■ **Sunn'i** /-*ē*/ *n* one of the two main branches of Islam, accepting the authority of the Sunna (cf **Shia**); a member of this (also **Sunn'ite** or **Sonn'ite**). **Sunn'ism** *n* the teachings and beliefs of orthodox Muslims.

sunny...to...**sun worshipper** see under **sun**.

suo jure /*soo'ō jŭr'ē* or *sū'ō yoo'rē*/ (*esp law*) *adv* in one's own right. [L]

suo loco /*soo'ō lō'kō* or *sū'ō lok'ō*/ (*esp law*) *adv* in one's (or its) rightful place. [L]

Suomi /*soo'ö-mi*/ *n* Finland or the Finnish language. ♦ *n pl* the Finns.
■ **Suo'mic** or **Suo'mish** *adj*.

suovetaurilia /*sū-o-vi-tö-ril'i-ə* or *sū-o-we-tow-rē'li-a*/ *n pl* a Roman sacrifice of a sheep, a pig, and an ox. [L *sūs* pig, *ovis* sheep, and *taurus* ox]

sup /*sup*/ *vt* (**supp'ing**; **supped**) to take (a liquid) into the mouth, to drink; to eat with a spoon (*Scot*); to provide supper for (*Shakesp*). ♦ *vi* to eat the evening meal (*archaic*); to sip (*Bible*). ♦ *n* a small mouthful, as of a liquid; alcoholic drink (*dialect*). [OE *sūpan*; ON *sūpa*, Ger *saufen* to drink; partly from OFr *soper*, *souper* (Fr *souper*) to take supper]

sup. *abbrev*: superfine; superior; superlative (also **superl.**); supine; supplement; *supra* (L), above; supreme.

supawn see **suppawn**.

Sup. Ct. *abbrev*: Superior Court; Supreme Court.

supe see **super²**.

super¹ /sooˈpər or sūˈpər/ adj of superior quality; exceptionally good; delightful. ◆ n something of superior quality or grade, such as a grade of petrol. ◆ interj (inf) good!, lovely!, smashing! [L, above]

super² /sooˈpər or sūˈpər/ an informal short form of superfine, superintendent and supernumerary, esp a supernumerary actor (also **supe**).

super- /soo-pər- or sū-pər-/ pfx denoting: (1) above or over; (2) beyond, exceeding, exceedingly, surpassing all others; (3) of greater size, strength, extent, power, quantity, etc; (4) in addition, extra; (5) in greater proportion (chem). [L super above; cf **over**, Gr hyper]

> Words formed using the prefix **super-** are listed as separate entries in the main word list or, if their meaning is self-evident, at the foot of the page.

superable see under **superate**.

superabound /soo- or sū-pər-ə-bowndˈ/ vi to be more, very, or excessively abundant. [**super-** (2)]
■ **superabunˈdance** n. **superabundˈant** adj. **superabundˈantly** adv.

superadd /soo- or sū-pər-adˈ/ vt to add over and above. [L superaddere, from super and addere]
■ **superaddiˈtion** n. **superaddiˈtional** adj.

superalloy /soo- or sū-pər-alˈoi/ n an alloy that has good stability at 600°C to 1000°C. [**super-** (3)]

superaltar /soo- or sū-pər-ölˈtər/ n a slab of stone used as a portable altar to be laid on the top of an unconsecrated altar; a structure over an altar. [**super-** (1)]

superannuate /soo- or sū-pər-anˈū-āt/ vt to set aside or cause to retire on account of age; to pension off. ◆ adj /-ət/ (rare) superannuated. ◆ n /-ət/ (rare) a superannuated person. [L super above, and annus year]
■ **superannˈuable** adj. **superannˈūated** adj involving a pension; pensioned off; so old as to be unfit for use, obsolete. **superannūāˈtion** n the act or state of superannuating; a pension; a regular contribution paid by an employee towards a pension.

superate /soo- or sūˈpə-rāt/ vt (obs) to overcome, outdo, or surmount. [L superāre to go over, surmount]
■ **suˈperable** adj capable of being overcome, outdone, surmountable. **suˈperably** adv. **superāˈtion** n.

superb /soo- or sū-pûrbˈ/ adj magnificent; gorgeous; triumphantly effective; supremely excellent (inf); proud, haughty (obs). [L superbus proud]
■ **superbˈity** n (rare). **superbˈly** adv. **superbˈness** n.

super bantamweight see **bantamweight** under **bantam**.

superbike /sooˈ or sūˈpər-bīk/ n a very powerful motorcycle. [**super-** (2)]

Super Bowl® /sooˈpər bōl/ n the annual championship game of the US National Football League, played between the respective champions of the National Football Conference and the American Football Conference.

superbug /sooˈ or sūˈpər-bug/ n a strain of bacteria that is resistant to antibiotics. [**super-** (3)]

supercalender /soo- or sū-pər-kalˈən-dər/ vt to give a high polish to (paper, cloth, etc) by calendering. ◆ n a machine for this. [**super-** (3)]
■ **supercalˈendered** adj.

supercargo /soo- or sū-pər-kärˈgō/ n (pl **supercarˈgoes**) a person in a ship placed in charge of the cargo and superintending all commercial transactions of the voyage. [**super-** (1)]
■ **supercarˈgoship** n.

supercharge /soo- or sū-pər-chärjˈ/ vt to fill to excess; to charge above the normal; to add pressure to; /sooˈ or sūˈ/ to fit with a supercharger; to charge exorbitantly, overcharge; to place as an overcharge (heraldry). ◆ n /sooˈ or sūˈ/ an excessive, exorbitant, or greater than normal charge; a charge borne upon an ordinary or other charge (heraldry). [**super-** (2)]
■ **suˈpercharger** n a device for increasing the pressure, and hence the power output, in an internal-combustion engine.

superciliary /soo- or sū-pər-silˈi-ə-ri or -yə-ri/ adj of, on or near the eyebrow; marked above the eye. ◆ n a superciliary ridge or mark. [L supercilium, from super above, and cilium eyelid]

supercilious /soo- or sū-pər-silˈi-əs/ adj disdainfully superior in manner; overbearing (obs); superciliary (rare). [Ety as for **superciliary**]
■ **supercilˈiously** adv. **supercilˈiousness** n.

superclass /sooˈ or sūˈpər-kläs/ (biol) n a taxonomic category that consists of a number of related classes between a class and a subphylum or phylum. [**super-** (3)]

supercluster /sooˈ or sūˈpər-klus-tər/ (astron) n a large cluster of galaxies. [**super-** (3)]

supercoil /sooˈ or sūˈpər-koil/ n a complex coil formed by intertwining strands of protein or DNA. [**super-** (3)]
■ **suˈpercoiled** adj.

supercold /sooˈ or sūˈpər-kōld/ same as **cryogenic** (see under **cryo-**).

supercollider /sooˈ or sūˈpər-kə-lī-dər/ n an extremely powerful particle accelerator. [**super-** (3)]

supercolumnar /soo- or sū-pər-kə-lumˈnər/ (archit) adj above a column or colonnade; with one colonnade above another. [**super-** (1)]
■ **supercolumniāˈtion** n.

supercomputer /sooˈ or sūˈpər-kəm-pū-tər/ n a powerful computer which can perform a large number of mathematical calculations very quickly. [**super-** (3)]

superconduct /soo- or sū-pər-kən-duktˈ/ vi to conduct electricity without resistance. [**super-** (3)]
■ **superconducˈtive** adj. **superconductivˈity** n complete loss of electrical resistance shown by certain pure metals and alloys at temperatures approaching absolute zero and by certain ceramics at higher temperatures. **superconducˈtor** n a substance having superconductivity.

supercontinent /sooˈ or sūˈpər-kon-ti-nənt or -konˈ/ n any of the vast land-masses from which the continents were originally formed. [**super-** (3)]

supercool /soo- or sū-pər-koolˈ/ vt to cool (a liquid) below normal freezing point without freezing or crystallization occurring. ◆ vi to become supercooled. ◆ adj (inf; esp N Am) (of a person) extremely calm, unflappable, imperturbable; having admirable or excellent qualities to a supreme degree. [**super-** (2)]

supercritical /soo- or sū-pər-kritˈi-k(ə)l/ adj of or relating to an assembly of fissile material for which the multiplication factor is greater than unity (nuclear phys); (of an aerofoil, aircraft's wing) moving slower than sound while the surrounding air moves faster than sound, hence permitting increased lift and speed. [**super-** (2)]

superdelegate /soo- or sūˈpər-del-i-gət/ (US politics) n a delegate to an electoral college who is not mandated to vote for a particular candidate. [**super-** (3)]

superdense /soo- or sū-pər-densˈ/ (astron) adj extremely dense. [**super-** (2)]
❑ **superdense theory** n big-bang theory.

superdominant /soo- or sū-pər-domˈi-nənt/ (music) n the submediant.

super-duper /sooˈpər-dooˈpər/ (inf) adj superlatively fine or great; marvellous. [Reduplication of **super¹**]

superego /soo- or sū-pər-ēˈgō, or -egˈō/ (psychol) n the strong unconscious inhibitory mechanism which criticizes the ego and causes it pain and distress when it accepts unworthy impulses from the id. [**super-** (1)]

Super 8® /sooˈ or sūˈpər āt/ n a variety of 8mm film used in cine cameras and for home film-making.

superelevation /soo- or sū-pər-el-ə-vāˈshən/ n excess in height; the difference in height between the opposite sides of a road or railway on a curve. [**super-** (2) and (1)]

supereminent /soo- or sū-pər-emˈi-nənt/ adj of a degree of eminence or excellence surpassing all others. [**super-** (2)]
■ **superemˈinence** n. **superemˈinently** adv.

supererogation /soo- or sū-pər-er-ə-gāˈshən/ n doing more than is required. [L super above, and ērogāre, -ātum to pay out]

superabsorbˈent adj (2).	suˈperbrain n (3).	supercelestˈial adj (1), (2).
superacˈtive adj (2).	suˈperbrat n (2).	supercleanˈ adj (2).
superacuteˈ adj (3).	superbrightˈ adj (2).	superconˈfidence n (2).
superambiˈtious adj (2).	suˈpercar n (3).	superconˈfident adj (2).
superboldˈ adj (3).	supercauˈtious adj (2).	supercrimˈinal n and adj (3).

Some words formed with the prefix **super-**; the numbers in brackets refer to the numbered senses in the entry for **super-**.

■ words derived from main entry word; ❑ compound words; ■ idioms and phrasal verbs

■ **superer'ogate** vi (obs). **supererogatory** /-ə-rog'ə-tər-i/, also (rare) **supererogant** /-er'ō-gənt/ or **supererogative** /-ə-rog'ə-tiv/ adj.

■ **works of supererogation** (RC) works which, not absolutely required of each individual for salvation, may be done for the sake of greater perfection, affording the church a store of surplus merit, to eke out the deficient merit of others.

superette /soo- or sū-pə-ret'/ (orig Aust and N Am) n a small local supermarket. [supermarket, and dimin sfx -ette]

superfamily /soo' or sū'pər-fam-i-li/ n a taxonomic group of related families between a suborder or order and a family. [**super-** (3)]

superfatted /soo- or sū-pər-fat'id/ adj (of soap) having an excess of fat, so that there is no free alkali. [**super-** (5)]

super featherweight see **featherweight** under **feather**.

superfecta /soo- or sū-pər-fek'tə/ (N Am) n a type of bet (eg on a horserace) in which the better must select the first four finishers in the correct order. [**super-** (3) and **perfecta**]

superfecundation /soo- or sū-pər-fē-kən-dā'shən or -fek-ən-/ n fertilization of two or more eggs produced at the same time by successive depositions of sperm, often from different males; fertilization of a large number of eggs. [**super-** (3)]

superfetation /soo- or sū-pər-fē-tā'shən/ n fertilization of a second ovum some time after the start of a pregnancy, resulting in two fetuses of different age in the same uterus, normal in some animals and believed by some to have occurred in women; superabundant production or accumulation. [L superfētāre, from pfx super- over, and fētus a fetus]

■ **superfē'tate** vi.

superficial /soo- or sū-pər-fish'(ə)l/ adj of, on or near the surface; not thorough or careful; not deep or profound; lacking sincerity or richness of personality, esp being concerned only with outward appearances. ◆ n that which is, or those who are, superficial; (in pl) surface characteristics. [LL superficiālis, from L superficiēs; see next entry]

■ **superficiality** /-fish-i-al'i-ti/ n. **superfic'ialize** or **-ise** vt to make superficial. ◆ vi to deal superficially. **superfic'ially** adv. **superfic'ialness** n.

superficies /soo- or sū-pər-fish'i-ēz/ n (pl **superfic'ies**) a surface, that which has length and breadth but no thickness (geom); a bounding or outer surface; a surface layer; a surface area; external features, appearance. [L superficiēs, from super, and facies face]

superfine /soo' or sū'pər-fīn/ or -fīn'/ adj of specially fine size or quality (short form **super**); excessively fastidious or proper. [**super-** (2)]

■ **su'perfineness** n.

superfit /soo' or sū'pər-fit or -fit'/ adj (of a person) extremely or exceptionally fit. [**super-** (2)]

superfluid /soo- or sū-pər-floo'id/ adj relating to, or demonstrating, superfluidity. [**super-** (3)]

■ **superfluid'ity** n a phenomenon observed in a form of helium (helium II), obtained below 2.19K, in which internal friction is negligible.

superfluous /soo- or sū-pûr'floo-əs/ adj above what is enough; redundant; unnecessary. [L superfluus overflowing, from super, and fluere to flow]

■ **superfluity** /-floo'/ n the state of being superfluous; a thing that is superfluous; superabundance. **super'fluously** adv. **super'fluousness** n superfluity. **su'perflux** n (Shakesp) superfluity.

super flyweight see **flyweight** under **fly**.

superfoetation same as **superfetation**.

superfrontal /soo- or sū-pər-frun'tl/ n a covering hanging over the upper edge of an altar frontal. [**super-** (1)]

superfuse /soo- or sū-pər-fyooz'/ vt to pour over (something else) (obs); to supercool. [**super-** (1) and (2)]

■ **superfu'sion** n.

super G /soo'pər jē/ (skiing) n a competitive event similar to giant slalom but skied over a longer distance with greater intervals between the gates. [super- in the sense of 'greater', and giant (slalom)]

supergene /soo' or sū'pər-jēn/ n a cluster of genes along a chromosome that may act as a unit in meiosis but may have unrelated functions. [**super-** (3)]

supergiant /soo' or sū'pər-jī-ənt or -jī'ənt/ n a very bright star of enormous size and low density, such as Betelgeuse and Antares. [**super-** (3)]

superglacial /soo- or sū-pər-glā'si-əl or -glā'shəl/ adj occurring or originating on the surface of a glacier. [**super-** (1)]

superglue /soo' or sū'pər-gloo/ n a very strong and quick-acting impact adhesive. ◆ vt and vi to stick with superglue. [**super-** (3)]

supergrass /soo' or sū'pər-gräs/ (sl) n a police informer who has given information leading to the arrest of a great number of criminals. [**super-** (2)]

supergravity /soo- or sū-pər-grav'i-ti/ n a supersymmetrical theory of gravitation. [**super-** (3)]

supergroup /soo' or sū'pər-groop/ n a rock or pop group made up of artists who are all famous in their own right; an internationally successful rock or pop group. [**super-** (2)]

superheat /soo- or sū-pər-hēt'/ vt to heat to excess; to heat (steam, etc) above the temperature of saturation; to heat (a liquid) above normal boiling point without vaporization. ◆ n the state of being superheated; the amount of superheating. [**super-** (2)]

■ **superheat'er** n.

superheavy /soo- or sū-pər-hev'i/ adj having an atomic number or weight heavier than the heaviest known. ◆ n a superheavy element. [**super-** (2)]

superhelix /soo' or sū'pər-hē-liks/ n a supercoil. [**super-** (3)]

superhero /soo' or sū'pər-hē-rō/ n any of various comic-book heroes with supernormal or superhuman powers. [**super-** (2)]

superheterodyne /soo- or sū-per-het'(ə-)rə-dīn/ adj of a type of radio or TV reception in which the incoming signal is mixed with a locally generated signal giving output of a signal of carrier frequency, but containing all the original modulation, which is then amplified and demodulated. ◆ n a superheterodyne receiver. [**super-** (3)]

superhigh frequency see **frequency** under **frequent**.

superhighway /soo' or sū'pər-hī-wā/ n a wide road for fast motor-traffic; a motorway, expressway (N Am); see **information superhighway** under **inform¹** (comput). [**super-** (3)]

superhive /soo' or sū'pər-hīv/ n a detachable upper compartment of a beehive. [**super-** (1)]

superhuman /soo- or sū-pər-hū'mən/ adj above man; greater than, or exceeding, the power, strength, capability, etc of man; more or higher than human. [**super-** (1) and (2)]

■ **superhūman'ity** n. **superhū'manize** or **-ise** vt. **superhū'manly** adv.

superhumeral /soo- or sū-pər-hū'mə-rəl/ n any ecclesiastical vestment worn on the shoulders. [**super-** (1)]

superimpose /soo- or sū-pər-im-pōz'/ vt to set on the top of something else; to place one over another; to establish in superaddition. [**super-** (1)]

■ **superimposed'** adj. **superimposi'tion** n.

superincumbent /soo- or sū-pər-in-kum'bənt/ adj resting on the top; overlying; overhanging; exerted from above. [**super-** (1)]

■ **superincum'bence** or **superincum'bency** n. **superincum'bently** adv.

superinduce /soo- or sū-pər-in-dūs'/ vt to bring in over and above, or in supersession of, something else; to superadd. [**super-** (1)]

■ **superinduce'ment** or **superinduc'tion** n.

superinfection /soo- or sū-pər-in-fek'shən/ n an infection arising during and in addition to another infection and caused by a different (or a different variety of the same) microorganism. [**super-** (4)]

■ **superinfect'** vt.

superintend /soo- or sū-pər-in-tend'/ vt to supervise; to exercise supervision over; to control or manage. [Church L superintendēre; see **super-** (1) and **intend**]

■ **superinten'dency** n the office or district of a superintendent; the act or process of superintending (also **superintend'ence**).

superdaint'y adj (2).	**superexc'ellent** adj (2).	**superjum'bo** n and adj (3).
superessen'tial adj (2).	**su'perfast** adj (2).	**superord'inary** adj (1), (2).
superev'ident adj (2).	**su'perfood** n (2).	**superpa'triot** n (2).
superexalt' vt (2).	**su'pergun** n (3).	**superpa'triotism** n (2).
superexaltā'tion n (2).	**superher'oine** n (2).	**superpol'ymer** n (3).
superexc'ellence n (2).	**superimpor'tant** adj (2).	**superpraise'** vt (2).

superinten'dent *n* a person who superintends; a police officer above a chief inspector; the head of a police department (*US*); an overseer; the head of a Sunday school; (in some Protestant churches) a clergyman having the oversight of the clergy of a district; (in the RSPCA) a rank between commander and chief inspector; the administrator of a local school system (*US*); the caretaker of a building (*N Am*). ♦ *adj* superintending. **superinten'dentship** *n*. **superintend'ing** *adj*.

superior /*soo-* or *sū-pē'ri-ər*/ *adj* upper; higher in nature, place, rank, or excellence; better (with *to*); surpassing others; beyond the influence, rising above (with *to*); supercilious or uppish; very worthy and highly respectable (often *patronizing*); of wider application, generic; set above the level of the line (*printing*); (of an ovary) inserted on the receptacle above the other parts (*bot*); (of other parts) seeming to arise above the ovary (*bot*). ♦ *n* a person or thing superior to others; the head of a religious house, order, etc; the feudal lord of a vassal (*hist*); a person to whom feu-duty was paid (*Scots law; obs*). [L, compar of *superus* on high, from *super* above]
■ **supe'rioress** *n* the head of a nunnery. **superiority** /-*or'i-ti*/ *n* the quality or state of being superior; pre-eminence; advantage; the right which the superior enjoyed in the land held by the vassal (*Scots law; obs*). **supe'riorly** *adv* in a superior manner or position. **supe'riorship** *n*.
□ **superior conjunction** *n* a conjunction of Venus or Mercury with the sun when the sun lies between the planet and the earth. **superior court** *n* a court intermediate between an inferior court (eg a magistrate's or district court) and a high court. **superiority complex** *n* (*psychol*) overvaluation of one's worth, often affected to cover a sense of inferiority. **superior planets** *n pl* those more distant from the sun than the earth is.

superjacent /*soo-* or *sū-pər-jā'sənt*/ *adj* lying above. [L *super*, and *jacēns, -entis*, prp of *jacēre* to lie]

superjet /*soo'* or *sū'pər-jet*/ *n* a supersonic jet aircraft. [*supersonic and jet*]

superl. *abbrev* : superlative.

superlative /*soo-* or *sū-pûr'lə-tiv*/ *adj* raised above others or to the highest degree; superior to all others; most eminent; expressing the highest degree (*grammar*). ♦ *n* the superlative or highest degree (*grammar*); an adjective or adverb in the superlative degree; any word or phrase of exaggeration. [L *superlātīvus*, from *super*, and *lātus* carried]
■ **super'latively** *adv*. **super'lativeness** *n*.

super lightweight see **lightweight** under **light²**.

superloo /*soo'* or *sū'pər-loo*/ (*inf*) *n* a type of public lavatory offering a greater number of facilities and a high level of luxury, or one which is fully automated, self-cleaning, etc. [**super-** (3)]

superluminal /*soo-, sū-pər-loo'mi-nəl* or *-lū-*/ *adj* faster than the speed of light; travelling, or able to travel, at such speed. [**super-** (2)]

superlunar /*soo-* or *sū-pər-loo'nər*/ or **superlunary** /*-loo'nə-rē*/ *adj* above the moon; not of this world, celestial. [**super-** (1)]

superman /*soo'* or *sū'pər-man*/ *n* an ideal man; a man with exceptional strength or ability; a fictional character with superhuman powers. [**super-** (2)]

supermarket /*soo'* or *sū'pər-mär-kit*/ *n* a large, mainly self-service, retail store selling food and other household goods (sometimes shortened to **su'permart**). [**super-** (3)]

supermassive /*soo-* or *sū-pər-mas'iv*/ (*astron*) *adj* (of stars) having an extremely high mass, extremely heavy. [**super-** (2)]

supermax /*soo'* or *sū'pər-maks*/ (*US*) *adj* (of a prison) designed to house the most dangerous prisoners. [**super-** (2) and *maximum security*]

super middleweight see **middleweight** under **middle**.

supermini /*soo'* or *sū'pər-mi-ni*/ *n* a car in a range between a mini-car and a small saloon. [**super-** (3)]

supermodel /*soo'* or *sū'pər-mo-dl*/ *n* an extremely glamorous and successful female fashion model. [**super-** (3)]

supermundane /*soo-* or *sū-pər-mun'dān* or *-dān'*/ *adj* above worldly things. [**super-** (1)]

supernaculum /*soo-* or *sū-pər-nak'ū-ləm*/ (*old sl*) *adv* to the last drop. ♦ *n* liquor of the best kind; anything excellent of its kind; a drinking of alcohol in a single draught; a full glass, a bumper. [Sham L *super naculum* on the nail, from L *super*, and Ger *Nagel* nail; from the old custom of turning the glass up to show that no more is left than will stand on the thumbnail]
■ **supernac'ular** *adj*.

supernal /*soo-* or *sū-pûr'nl*/ (*poetic*) *adj* on high; celestial; of a higher world; exalted; topmost. [L *supernus*, from *super*]
■ **super'nally** *adv*.

supernatant /*soo-* or *sū-pər-nā'tənt*/ *adj* floating or swimming above; (of a liquid) overlying a sediment. ♦ *n* a supernatant liquid. [L *supernatāns, -antis*, from *super*, and *natāre* to swim, float]

supernational, **supernationalism** see **supranational** under **supra-**.

supernatural /*soo-, sū-pər-nach'ə-rəl* or *-nat'yə-*/ *adj* above or beyond nature; not according to the laws of nature; miraculous; magical; spiritual; occult. ♦ *n* that which is supernatural; a supernatural being. [**super-** (1)]
■ **supernat'uralism** *n* supernatural character or agency; the belief in the influence of the supernatural in the world. **supernat'uralist** *n* a believer in the supernatural. ♦ *adj* of or relating to the supernatural. **supernaturalist'ic** *adj*. **supernat'uralize** or **-ise** *vt* to bring into the supernatural sphere. **supernat'urally** *adv*. **supernat'uralness** *n*. **su'pernature** *n* the supernatural.

supernormal /*soo-* or *sū-pər-nör'məl*/ *adj* beyond what is normal; in greater number, amount, concentration, etc than the normal. [**super-** (1) and (2)]
■ **supernormal'ity** *n*. **supernor'mally** *adv*.

supernova /*soo'* or *sū'pər-nō-və*/ *n* (pl **supernō'vae** /*-vē*/ or **supernō'vas**) a very brilliant nova resulting from an explosion which blows the star's material into space, leaving an expanding cloud of gas. [L *super-* above, and **nova**]

supernumerary /*soo-* or *sū-pər-nū'mə-rə-ri*/ *adj* over and above the stated, usual, normal or necessary number. ♦ *n* a supernumerary person or thing; an actor without speaking parts. [LL *supernumerārius*, from L *super*, and *numerus* number]

supernurse /*soo'* or *sū'pər-nûrs*/ *n* a highly experienced nurse paid to remain in the field of direct patient care rather than seek promotion to a management post. [**super-** (2)]

superoctave /*soo'*, *sū'pər-ok-tiv*/ *n* an organ coupler giving an octave higher; an organ stop two octaves above the basic pitch. [**super-** (1)]

superorder /*soo'* or *sū'pər-ör-dər*/ (*biol*) *n* a taxonomic category of related orders between an order and a subclass or sometimes class. [**super-** (1)]
■ **superord'inal** *adj* relating to a superorder.

superordinate /*soo-* or *sū-pər-ör'di-nət* or *-nit*/ *adj* superior in rank or condition; in the relation of superordination. ♦ *n* a superior in rank or condition. ♦ *vt* /-*āt*/ to make superordinate. [**super-** (1) and (2)]
■ **superordinā'tion** *n* (*logic*) the relation of a universal proposition to a particular proposition in the same terms.

superorganic /*soo-* or *sū-pər-ör-gan'ik*/ *adj* above or beyond the organic, psychical; relating to a higher organization, social. [**super-** (1) and (2)]
■ **superorg'anism** *n* a highly organized social community perceptible as a single organism (eg a colony of bees).

superovulation /*soo-* or *sū-pər-ov-ū-lā'shən*/ *n* the production of a larger number of ova than usual, eg under stimulus of injected hormones. [**super-** (3)]
■ **superov'ulate** *vi*.

superoxide /*soo-* or *sū-pər-ok'sīd*/ *n* any of various oxides having two oxygen atoms. [**super-** (5)]

superphosphate /*soo-* or *sū-pər-fos'fāt*/ *n* an acid phosphate; a mixture of calcium sulphate and calcium acid phosphate chiefly used as a fertilizer. [**super-** (5)]

superphylum /*soo'* or *sū'pər-fī-ləm*/ (*biol*) *n* a taxonomic category of related phyla between a phylum and a kingdom. [**super-** (3)]

Some words formed with the prefix **super-**; the numbers in brackets refer to the numbered senses in the entry for **super-**.

superrefine' *vt* (4).	**supersales'man** *n* (3).	**supersen'sitiveness** *n* (2).
superrefined' *adj* (4).	**su'persalt** *n* (5).	**supersen'sory** *adj* (2).
superrich' *adj* (2).	**superscreen'** *n* and *adj* (1), (3).	**supersen'sual** *adj* (2), (3).
supersafe' *adj* (2).	**su'persell** *n* (3).	**su'persharp** *adj* (2).
supersafe'ty *n* (2).	**supersen'sitive** *adj* (2).	**su'persleuth** *n* (2).

---

superphysical /soo- or sū-pər-fiz'i-kəl/ adj beyond or above the physical world, its laws or phenomena. [**super-** (1)]

superplastic /soo', sū'pər-plas'tik or -pläs'/ adj and n (a metal or alloy) that is extremely pliable, or capable of being moulded without fracturing, at high temperatures. [**super-** (2)]
■ **superplastic'ity** n.

superplus /soo' or sū'pər-plus/ (obs) n a surplus.

superpose /soo- or sū-pər-pōz'/ vt to bring, or suppose to be brought, into coincidence (geom); to place vertically over or on something else. [**super-** (1)]
■ **superpos'able** adj. **superposed'** adj. **superposi'tion** n an act of superposing; the state of being superposed; that which is above anything.

superpower /soo' or sū'pər-pow(-ə)r/ n a very powerful state, often applied to the USA and formerly to the USSR. [**super-** (2) and (3)]

superrealism /soo- or sū-pər-rē'ə-li-zm/ n (in art) a style that transcends realism; surrealism; photorealism. [**super-** (1) and (2)]
■ **superre'alist** n and adj.

super-royal /soo' or sū'pər-roi'əl/ adj (of paper-size) larger than royal. [**super**[1] and **royal**]

supersaturate /soo- or sū-pər-sat'ū-rāt or -sach'ə-rāt/ vt to saturate beyond the normal point; to increase the concentration of beyond saturation. [**super-** (2) and (3)]
■ **supersat'ūrated** adj. **supersaturā'tion** n.

supersaver /soo' or sū'pər-sā-vər/ n anything offered at a specially reduced price, esp a bus, rail or airplane fare. [**super-** (2)]

superscalar /soo' or sū'pər-skā-lər/ (comput) adj (of a processor) able to perform more than one instruction simultaneously. [**super-** (3)]

superscribe /soo- or sū-pər-skrīb'/ vt to write or engrave above, on the top or on the outside of something; to address (eg a letter); to sign at the top. [L super above, and scrībere, scrīptum to write]
■ **su'perscript** /-skript/ adj written above; superior (printing). ◆ n the superscription, address (archaic); a superior character (printing). **superscrip'tion** n the act of superscribing; that which is superscribed.

supersede /soo- or sū-pər-sēd'/ vt to set aside, discard; to set aside in favour of another, supplant; to come or put in the place of, to replace; to desist or refrain from (obs); to override (obs). ◆ vi (obs) to refrain, desist. [L supersedēre to sit above, refrain from, from super above, and sedēre, sessum to sit]
■ **supersē'deas** /-di-as/ n (law; hist) a writ to stay proceedings, or to suspend the powers of an officer (from the use of the Latin 2nd pers sing present subjunctive, you are to desist). **supersē'dence** n. **supersē'der** n. **supersedere** /-si-dē'ri or soo-per-se-dā're/ n a private agreement among creditors, under a trust-deed, to supersede or sist diligence for a certain period (Scots law); an order of court granting protection to a debtor. **supersē'dure** n. **supersession** /-sesh'ən/ n.

supersensible /soo- or sū-pər-sen'si-b(ə)l/ adj beyond the reach, or outside the realm, of the senses. [**super-** (1) and (2)]
■ **supersen'sibly** adv.

superserviceable /soo- or sū-pər-sûr'vi-sə-b(ə)l/ adj officious. [**super-** (2)]
■ **superserv'iceably** adv.

supersession see under **supersede**.

supersize /soo' or sū'pər-sīz/ vt to increase greatly in size; to replace with a larger version. [**super-** (3) and (4)]

supersonic /soo- or sū-pər-son'ik/ adj above the audible limit; too high-pitched for human hearing (ultrasonic); faster than the speed of sound; travelling, or capable of travelling, at such a speed. ◆ n a supersonic wave; (in pl) the study of such waves. [L super above, and sonus sound]
■ **superson'ically** adv.
❑ **supersonic boom** n a shock wave produced by an object moving supersonically. **supersonic-combustion ramjet** see **scramjet**.

supersound /soo' or sū'pər-sownd/ n sound vibrations too rapid to be audible. [**super-** (1) and (2)]

superstar /soo' or sū'pər-stär/ n an extremely popular and successful star of the cinema, popular music, etc.
■ **superstar'dom** n.

superstate /soo' or sū'pər-stāt/ n a state or organization having governing power over subordinate states. [**super-** (3)]

superstition /soo- or sū-pər-stish'ən/ n false worship or religion; an ignorant and irrational belief in supernatural agency, omens, divination, sorcery, etc; a deep-rooted but unfounded general belief; a rite or practice proceeding from superstitious belief or fear (obs). [L superstitiō, -ōnis]
■ **superstit'ious** adj. **superstit'iously** adv. **superstit'iousness** n.

superstore /soo' or sū'pər-stör/ n a large supermarket, which usually sells many different goods in addition to food. [**super-** (3)]

superstring theory see **string theory** under **string**.

superstructure /soo' or sū'pər-struk-chər/ n the part of a building above the foundations, or of a ship above the main deck; any thing or concept based or founded on another. [**super-** (1)]
■ **superstruct'** vt to build on something else as a foundation. **superstruc'tion** n. **superstruct'ive** adj. **superstruct'ural** adj.

supersubtle (or obs **supersubtile**) /soo- or sū-pər-sut'l/ adj excessively subtle; extremely subtle. [**super-** (2)]
■ **supersub'tlety** n.

supersymmetry /soo- or sū-pər-sim'i-tri/ (particle phys) n a theory that attempts to link all four fundamental forces, and postulates that each force emerged separately during the expansion of the very early universe. [**super-** (3)]
■ **supersymmet'rical** adj.

supertanker /soo' or sū'pər-tang-kər/ n a large tanker, esp one used for transporting crude oil. [**super-** (3)]

supertaster /soo- or sū'pər-tās-tə/ n a person who is able to experience an exceptionally wide range of taste sensations. [**super-** (3)]

supertax /soo' or sū'pər-taks/ n an extra or additional tax on large incomes (term not in official use). [**super-** (4)]

superteacher /soo' or sū'pər-tē-chər/ (inf) n same as **advanced skills teacher** (see under **advance**). [**super-** (2)]

superterranean /soo- or sū-pər-tə-rā'ni-ən/ adj living or situated on the earth's surface. [**super-** (1)]

superterrestrial /soo- or sū-pər-ti-res'tri-əl or -tə-/ adj above the earth; above worldly things. [**super-** (1)]

supertitle /soo- or sū'pər-tī-tl/ n a surtitle. [**super-** (1)]

supertonic /soo'pər- or sū'pər-to-nik/ (music) n the second degree of the diatonic scale, eg D in the scale of C. [**super-** (1)]

supertwist /soo- or sū-pər-twist'/ n a technique of twisting light rays, used to improve the quality of LCDs. [**super-** (2)]

superuser /soo' or sū'pər-ūz-ər/ (comput) n a special facility used by a systems administrator, giving unrestricted access to a system.

supervene /soo- or sū-pər-vēn'/ vi to come in addition, or closely after, esp so as to cause a change. [L super above, and venīre, ventum to come]
■ **supervēn'ience** n. **supervēn'ient** adj supervening. **supervention** /-ven'shən/ n.

supervise /soo' or sū'pər-vīz/ vt to oversee, manage or direct the operation of; to watch over, control. ◆ vi (Shakesp) to read over. ◆ n (Shakesp) reading over. [L super over, and vidēre, visum to see]
■ **supervī'sal** n (rare). **supervisee** /-vīz-ē'/ n a person who is supervised. **supervision** /-vizh'ən/ n the act of supervising; inspection; control. **supervisor** /-vī'zər (also soo' or sū')/ n a person who supervises; an overseer; an inspector; an elected local government official (US); a spectator (Shakesp). **supervī'sorship** n. **supervi'sory** adj relating to, or having, supervision.
❑ **supervision order** n a court order placing a child or young person who is the subject of care proceedings under the supervision of a named probation officer or social worker.

supervolute /soo' or sū'pər-vo-lūt', or -loot'/ (bot) adj convolute. [**super-** (2)]

Some words formed with the prefix **super-**; the numbers in brackets refer to the numbered senses in the entry for **super-**.

su'persoft adj (2).	**superstra'tum** n (1).	**supervir'ulent** adj (2).
supersophis'ticated adj (2).	**su'perstrong** adj (2).	**su'perweapon** n (3).
superspe'cies n (3).	**supersubstan'tial** adj (2).	**su'pertough** adj (2).
su'perspeed n (3).	**su'persweet** adj (2).	**su'pertram** n (3).
su'perspy n (2).	**su'perthin** adj (2).	**su'perunion** n (3).

---

superwaif /soo' or sū'pər-wāf/ (inf) n an extremely thin and childlike young fashion model. [**super-** (3)]

super welterweight see **welterweight**.

superwoman /soo' or sū'pər-wŭ-mən/ n an exceptionally strong, talented or energetic woman, esp one who successfully combines a career with bringing up children and household duties; a fictional woman with superhuman powers. [**super-** (2)]

supine /soo', sū'pīn or -pīn'/ adj lying on the back; leaning backward, inclined, sloping; negligently inert; indolent; passive. ♦ n /soo' or su'/ a Latin verbal noun in -tum (**first supine**, an old accusative) or -tū (**second supine**, an old locative), poss as formed from the stem of the passive participle; the English infinitive with to. [L supīnus supine; related to sub under, and super over]
■ **su'pinate** /-pin-āt/ vt to place (the hand) palm upward or forward, opp to **pronate**. **supinā'tion** n the placing or holding of the palm of the hand upward or forward. **su'pinator** n a muscle that extends from the elbow to the shaft of the radius that supinates the forearm and hand. **supine'ly** adv. **supine'ness** n.

suplex /soo'pleks/ n a wrestling hold in which the opponent is grasped around the waist from behind and thrown. [L supplex, -icis supplicant]

supp. or **suppl.** abbrev : supplement.

suppawn or **supawn** /sə-pön'/ n a kind of porridge made with maize flour boiled in water. [Natick (see under **Algonquian**) saupáun softened]

suppeago /sə-pē'gō/ see **serpigo**.

suppedaneum /sə-pə-dā'ni-əm/ n (pl **suppedā'nea** /-ni-ə/) a support under the foot of a crucified person. [L, footstool, from neuter of suppedaneus beneath the foot]

supper /sup'ər/ n a light meal eaten in the evening; a late-night snack taken in addition to and later than the main evening meal. ♦ vt (archaic) to provide with supper. [OFr soper (Fr souper)]
■ **supp'erless** adj.
❑ **supper cloth** n a tablecloth, larger than a teacloth, on which supper is served. **supp'ertime** n the time at which supper is usually eaten.

supping see **sup**.

supplant /sə-plänt'/ vt to oust; to supersede; to dispossess and take the place of; to overthrow, to lay low (Milton); to uproot (Shakesp). [L supplantāre to trip up, from sub under, and planta the sole]
■ **supplantation** /sup-lən-tā'shən/ n. **supplant'er** n.

supple[1] /sup'l/ adj pliant; lithe; yielding; fawning (archaic). ♦ vt (rare) to make supple; to make soft or compliant. ♦ vi (rare) to become supple. [Fr souple, from L supplex bending the knees, from sub under, and plicāre to fold]
■ **supp'lely** or **supp'ly** adv. **supp'leness** n.
❑ **supp'lejack** n any of various tropical shrubs with pliant or twining stems; a pliant cane.

supple[2] /sūp'l/ a Scots form of **swipple** (see also **souple**[2]).

supplement /sup'li-mənt/ n that which supplies a deficiency or fills a need; that which completes or brings closer to completion; an extra part added (later) to a publication, giving further information or listing corrections to earlier mistakes; a special part of a newspaper or periodical accompanying an ordinary part; an additional charge; the quantity by which an angle or an arc falls short of 180° or a semicircle. ♦ vt /-ment', also sup'li-mənt/ to supply or fill up; to add to. [L supplēmentum a filling up, supplēre to fill up]
■ **supplement'al** or **supplement'ary** adj and n (something) added to supply what is needed; (something that is) additional. **supplement'ally** or **supplement'arily** adv. **supplementā'tion** n. **supp'lementer** n. **supplé'tion** n a supplement; the adding of a word to supply a missing form of a conjugation, etc, such as went for the past tense of to go (grammar). **supplé'tive** or **supp'letory** adj supplemental.
❑ **supplementary angle** n either of a pair of angles whose sum is 180°. **supplementary benefit** n a state allowance paid each week to those with low incomes in order to bring them up to a certain established level (now called **income support** in the UK).

supplial see under **supply**[1].

suppliance see under **suppliant**[1] and **supply**[1].

suppliant[1] /sup'li-ənt/ adj supplicating; asking earnestly; entreating. ♦ n a humble petitioner. [Fr suppliant, prp of supplier, from L supplicāre; see **supplicant**]
■ **supp'liance** n supplication. **supp'liantly** adv.

suppliant[2], **supplier** see under **supply**[1].

supplicant /sup'li-kənt/ adj supplicating; asking submissively. ♦ n a person who supplicates or entreats earnestly. [L supplicāre, -ātum, from supplex; see **supple**[1]]
■ **supp'licat** n (in English universities) a petition. **supp'licate** vt and vi to entreat earnestly; to petition; to pray. **supp'licating** adj. **supp'licatingly** adv. **supplicā'tion** n an act of supplicating; an

earnest or humble petition; (in ancient Rome) a solemn service or day decreed for giving formal thanks to the gods for victory, etc; earnest prayer or entreaty, esp in liturgies, a litany petition for some special blessing. **supp'licatory** adj containing supplication or entreaty; humble. **supplicā'vit** n formerly, a writ issued by the King's Bench or Chancery for taking the surety of the peace against a person.

supply[1] /sə-plī'/ vt (**supply'ing**; **supplied**') to make good; to satisfy; to provide, furnish; to fill, occupy (as a substitute); to serve instead of; to supplement (obs); to reinforce, help (obs); to fill up a deficiency in (obs). ♦ n an act of supplying; that which is supplied or which supplies a need; an amount provided or in hand; the available amount of a commodity; an amount of food or money provided (used generally in pl); a source of water, electricity, etc; a parliamentary grant for expenses of government; a person who takes another's duty temporarily, a substitute, esp a teacher. [OFr suppleier, supplier (Fr suppléer), from L supplēre to fill up]
■ **supplī'al** n the act of supplying. **supplī'ance** n (Shakesp) supplying, something to fill up time, pastime, gratification. **supplī'ant** adj (Shakesp) supplementary, reinforcing. **supplī'er** n. **supply'ment** n (Shakesp) replenishment, supplementing.
❑ **supply chain** n (business) the succession of processes and transactions that takes place before a product reaches the final consumer. **supply curve** n (econ) a graph showing the quantity of a product that producers will offer for sale at different prices. **supply day** n in the House of Commons, a day in which backbenchers debate and vote on government expenditure. **supply'-side economics** n sing the theory that economic activity is a function of the supply of money, and that the level of economic activity may be regulated by increasing or reducing the money supply by devices such as taxation. **supply'-sider** n an advocate of supply-side economics.
■ **Commissioners of Supply** a former administrative and rating authority in Scotland, superseded by the County Council. **in short supply** see under **short**.

supply[2] see under **supple**[1].

support /sə-pōrt' or -pört'/ vt to bear the weight of; to hold up; to endure; to sustain; to maintain; to keep going; to corroborate; to make good; to uphold; to back up; to second; to contend for; to represent in acting; to maintain a loyal interest in the fortunes of (esp a sporting team), usu by regular attendance at matches; to perform as an introduction to (the main performer in a musical concert); to supply with means of living; to show an interest in the activities of, eg by attendance at meetings, etc; to nourish; to strengthen; to allow the use of (a particular program, language, etc) (comput). ♦ n the act or fact of supporting or upholding; a person who or thing that supports, sustains, or maintains; maintenance; backing; a prop; a body of supporters; an actor playing a subordinate part with a star. [L supportāre, from sub up, and portāre to bear]
■ **support'able** adj capable of being held up, carried, sustained, or maintained. **support'ableness** n. **support'ably** adv. **support'ance** n (Shakesp) support. **support'er** n a person who or thing that supports; an adherent; a defender; a person who attends matches and watches with interest the fortunes of a team; the supporting act or acts at a pop concert; a figure on each side of the escutcheon (heraldry). **support'ing** n and adj. **support'ive** adj. **support'less** adj. **support'ment** n (rare). **support'ress** n (rare). **support'ure** n (rare).
❑ **support area** see **support level** below. **support group** n a group of people who come together regularly to support each other in some common difficulty. **support hose**, **stockings** or **tights** n pl elasticated hose. **supporting act**, **film** or **programme** n a film, films, acts, etc accompanying the main film or star performance in a variety show. **support level** or **area** n (on the stock market) the price level below which a commodity does not decline, as it then becomes an investment proposition. **support stockings**, **support tights** see **support hose** above. **support worker** n a worker, esp in health care, who carries out various tasks under the supervision of registered practitioners.

suppose /sə-pōz'/ vt to incline to believe; to conceive, imagine, guess; to assume provisionally or for argument's sake; to imply, presuppose; (esp in passive) to expect in accordance with rules or conventions; to expect (Milton); to believe (Shakesp); to place underneath (obs); to substitute fraudulently (obs). ♦ n a supposition; an instance of supposing or saying 'suppose'; expectation (Shakesp). ♦ conj if; what if; even if (Scot). [Fr supposer, from pfx sup- (sub-), and poser; see **pose**[1], and cf **compose**, **dispose**, etc]
■ **suppo'sable** adj. **suppo'sably** adv. **suppo'sal** n supposition; a notion (Shakesp); a proposal (obs). **supposed** /-pōzd' (also -pō'zid)/ adj generally believed to be (often implying doubt or disagreement on the part of the speaker); assumed; conjectured; feigned (Shakesp); supposititious (obs); placed below, or having a note below, the fundamental of the chord (music). **suppo'sedly** adv according to

supposition. **suppo'ser** n. **suppo'sing** n the action of the verb. ◆conj if; what if; how about.
■ **supposed to** expected, intended or required to.

supposes /sə-pō'ziz/ (Shakesp, Taming of the Shrew V.1.104) n pl perhaps substitutes, or substitutions, or suppositions. See repeated play on the word in Shakespeare's source, Gascoigne's Supposes (and its original, Ariosto's I Suppositi).

supposition /sup-ə-zish'ən/ n an act of supposing; that which is supposed; an assumption; a presumption, opinion. [L suppōnere, -positum to set under, substitute, from sub, and pōnere to put]
■ **supposi'tional** adj hypothetical; conjectural; supposed. **supposi'tionally** adv. **supposi'tionary** adj suppositional. **supposi'tious** /-zi'shəs/ adj (rare) suppositional; usu a non-standard form of **supposititious**. **supposititious** /sə-poz-i-tish'əs/ adj secretly and cunningly substituted for another; spurious; suppositional. **supposi'tiously** adv. **supposi'tiousness** n. **suppos'itive** /-i-tiv/ adj suppositional.

suppository /sə-poz'i-t(ə-)ri/ n a medicated plug inserted in the rectum, vagina or urethra, and left to melt. [L suppositōrium; see ety for **supposition**]

suppress /sə-pres'/ vt to crush, put down; to subdue; to hold back, esp from publication, circulation, divulgation, expression or development; to check, stop, restrain; to hold in; to moderate; to leave out; to hold or press down (Spenser); to ravish (Spenser). [L supprimere, suppressum, from sub under, and premere to press]
■ **suppress'ant** n a substance, eg a drug, that suppresses rather than eliminates (also adj). **suppressed'** adj. **suppress'edly** adv. **suppress'ible** adj. **suppression** /-presh'/ n an act of suppressing; stoppage; concealment. **suppress'ive** adj tending to suppress; subduing. **suppress'or** n a person who suppresses anything; a device for suppressing anything, eg the echo of one's own voice on a telephone, electrical interference with television reception.
□ **suppressor cell** or **suppressor T-cell** n a lymphocyte capable of suppressing antibody production. **suppressor grid** n (electronics) a grid between the anode and screen of a pentode valve to repel secondary electrons back to the anode. **suppressor mutation** n (biol) a base change which suppresses the effect of mutations elsewhere.

suppurate /sup'ū-rāt/ vi to gather or discharge pus. [L sub under, and pūs, pūris pus]
■ **suppurā'tion** n. **supp'urative** adj causing suppuration. ◆n a suppurative agent.

Supr. abbrev : Supreme.

supra /soo'/ or /sū'prə/ adv above, esp referring to an earlier passage in a text. [L]

supra- /soo-/ or /sū-prə-/ pfx signifying above.
■ **supra-axill'ary** adj arising above an axil. **suprachias'mic** adj (anat) above the chiasm (esp in **suprachiasmic nucleus** a small area in the hypothalamus thought to regulate the biological clock). **supraciliary** /-sil'/ adj above the eyebrow. **supracost'al** adj above or on a rib. **supracrust'al** adj (of rocks) on or near the surface, above the earth's crust. **Supralapsarian** /-laps-ā'ri-ən/ n (L lāpsus fall) one of a class of Calvinists who make the decree of election and predestination to precede the Creation and the Fall, opp to Sublapsarian (also adj). **Supralapsa'rianism** n. **supralu'nar** adj beyond the moon; very lofty. **supramolec'ular** adj. **supramol'ecule** n a cluster of molecules, usu created artificially. **supramun'dane** adj above the world. **supranat'ional** adj overriding national sovereignty; in or belonging to more than one nation (also, less commonly, **supernational**). **supranat'ionalism** (also, less commonly, **supernationalism**) n. **supraor'bital** adj above the orbit of the eye. **suprapu'bic** adj above the pubic bone. **suprarē'nal** adj above the kidneys (**suprarenal capsules** or **glands** the adrenal glands; **suprarenal extract** an extract from these whose components are used in the treatment of haemorrhage, Addison's disease, etc). **suprasegmen'tal** adj (phonetics) representing or continuing through two or more speech sounds. **suprasens'ible** adj above the reach of the senses. **supratemp'oral** adj transcending time; of the upper part of the temples or temporal region.

supreme /sū-/ or /soo-prēm'/ adj highest; greatest; most excellent. ◆n the highest point; the highest authority. [L suprēmus, superl of superus high, from super above]
■ **suprem'acism** n (belief in) the supremacy of one particular group of people. **suprem'acist** n a believer in or supporter of supremacism. **supremacy** /-prem'ə-si/ n the state of being supreme; supreme position or power. **Suprematism** /sū-prem'ə-tizm/ n (also without cap) an extreme form of cubism using very simple geometrical shapes. **Suprem'atist** n and adj (also without cap). **supremely** /-prēm'/ adv.

supreme'ness or **supremity** /-prem'/ n. **suprē'mum** n (maths) the least upper bound (cf **infimum**; abbrev **sup**).
□ **Supreme Being** n a superior deity; God. **Supreme Court** n in the USA, the highest Federal court having jurisdiction over all lower courts; elsewhere, the highest court of a nation or state; in England and Wales, a court consisting of the Crown Court, High Court and Court of Appeal (in full **Supreme Court of Judicature**). **supreme sacrifice** n the giving up of one's life. **Supreme Soviet** n the legislature of the former USSR, consisting of two bodies, the Council of the Union, in which each deputy represented so many of the population, and the Council of Nationalities, in which each deputy represented one of the Republics or other distinct regions within the USSR.

suprême or **supreme** /sū-prem', sū- or soo-prēm'/ n a rich cream sauce; a dish of meat, esp breast of chicken, served in this sauce. [Fr]

supremo /sū- or soo-prē'mō/ n (pl supre'mos) a supreme head; a leader with unlimited powers. [Sp, from L suprēmus highest]

Supt abbrev : Superintendent.

suq see **souk**.

sur /sūr/ (Fr) prep on, above.
■ **sur le tapis** /lə ta-pē/ literally, on the carpet (as a table cover), hence, under discussion, the subject of talk. **sur place** /plas/ on the spot.

sur- /sûr-/ pfx signifying over, above, beyond. [Fr, from L super]

sura¹ or **surah** /soo'rə/ n a chapter of the Koran. [Ar sūra, sūrah step]

sura² /soo'rə/ n fermented palm sap. [Sans surā]

suraddition /sûr-ə-dish'ən/ (Shakesp) n an additional title or designation. [**sur-**]

surah¹ /sū' or soo'rə/ n a soft twilled silk or artificial fabric (also adj). [Poss from Surat in India]

surah² see **sura¹**.

sural /sū'r(ə)l/ adj relating to the calf of the leg. [L sūra the calf]

suramin /soo'rə-min/ n a drug formerly administered, usu by slow intravenous injection, in the treatment of trypanosomiasis.

surance /shoo'rəns/ (Shakesp) n assurance.

surat /soo-rat' or soo'/ n coarse uncoloured cotton; anything that is of inferior quality (old sl). [Surat, in India]

surbahar /sär-bə-här'/ n an Indian stringed instrument, larger than a sitar. [Bengali]

surbase /sûr'bās/ (archit) n a cornice or series of mouldings above the base of a pedestal, etc. [**sur-**]
■ **surbased** /-bāst'/ adj of an arch, lower than half the span. **surbase'ment** n.

surbate /sûr-bāt' or (Spenser) sûr'/ vt (pap **surbat'ed** or (Spenser) **surbet'**) to bruise (the hooves or feet) with walking, make footsore. [OFr surbatu excessively beaten, but with the meaning of Fr solbatu]

surbed /sûr-bed'/ (obs) vt to set on edge (applied to a stone with reference to the grain; masonry). [**sur-**]

surbet see **surbate**.

surcease /sûr-sēs'/ (archaic) vi to cease. ◆vt to desist or refrain from; to end, put a stop to. ◆n cessation. [OFr sursis, pap of surseoir, from L supersedēre to refrain from; cf **supersede**; spelling influenced by **cease**]

surcharge /sûr'chärj or -chärj'/ n an overcharge; an extra charge; an excessive load; an overloaded condition; an amount not passed by an auditor, which must be refunded; a new valuation or cancel-mark printed on or over a stamp; that part of a bank of earth, or its depth, lying above the top of a retaining wall. ◆vt to exact a surcharge from; to overcharge; to overload; to overburden; to overstock; to saturate; to print over the original printing; to disallow; to charge with overwhelming force (Spenser). [**sur-**]
■ **sur'charged** adj. **sur'chargement** n. **sur'charger** n.

surcingle /sûr'sing-gl/ n a girth or strap for holding a saddle on an animal's back; the girdle of a cassock. ◆vt to gird, fasten, or thrash with a surcingle. [OFr surcengle, from L super, and cingulum a belt]

surcoat /sûr'kōt/ n a medieval outer garment, usu sleeveless, often with heraldic devices, worn by men and women over armour or ordinary dress; an undershirt or waistcoat (esp Scot). [OFr surcote, surcot, from sur over, and cote garment]

surculus /sûr'kū-ləs/ (bot) n a sucker. [L sūrculus a twig]
■ **sur'culose** adj having or producing suckers.

surd /sûrd/ adj unable to be expressed in rational numbers (maths); voiceless (phonetics); deaf (obs); senseless (obs). ◆n an irrational quantity, esp an irrational root or a sum of irrational roots (maths); a

voiceless consonant (*phonetics*); someone who is deaf to persuasion, rational argument, etc. [L *surdus* deaf]
■ **surd'ity** *n* deafness.

sure[1] /*shoor*/ *adj* secure; safe; fit to be depended on; unerring; stable; bound in alliance (*esp* by betrothal or marriage; *obs*); certain; assured; confident beyond doubt; without other possibility. ◆ *interj* (*inf*) certainly, undoubtedly, yes. ◆ *adv* (now chiefly *Irish* or *N Am*, except in combination and in conventional phrases) surely. [OFr *sur, seur* (Fr *sûr*), from L *sēcūrus* ; see **secure**]
■ **sure'ly** *adv* firmly; confidently; safely; certainly; assuredly; as it would seem (often *ironic*). **sure'ness** *n.* **sure'ty** *n* certainty; safeguard; legal security against loss; a person who becomes legally responsible for another's liabilities; a sponsor. ◆ *vt* (*Shakesp*) to be security for. **sure'tyship** *n*.
❑ **sure-enough'** *adj* (*US*) genuine, real. **sure'-fire** *adj* (*inf*) infallible. **sure'footed** *adj* not liable to stumble, nimble; confident (*fig*). **surefoot'edly** *adv.* **surefoot'edness** *n.* **sure thing** *n* a certain success. ◆ *interj* without doubt, certainly.
■ **be sure** do not omit. **for sure** certainly; of a certainty. **make sure** see under **make**[1]. **stand surety for** to act as guarantor for. **sure enough** no doubt; in very fact; accordingly; there's no denying. **to be sure** certainly; I admit.

sure[2] an old spelling of **sewer** (see under **sew**[2]).

Sûreté /*sür-tā'*/ (*Fr*) *n* the French criminal investigation department.

surety see under **sure**[1].

SURF /*sûrf*/ (*nuclear eng*) *abbrev* : spent unreprocessed fuel.

surf /*sûrf*/ *n* surging water or waves rushing up a sloping beach; sea foam; an act of surfing. ◆ *vi* to bathe in or ride on surf. ◆ *vt* to browse through (television channels, the Internet, etc) with no fixed destination in mind. [Origin obscure]
■ **surf'er** *n* a person who goes surfing; a person who browses on the Internet. **surf'ie** *n* (*Aust inf*) a young, *usu* unemployed, person who spends a great deal of time surfing. **surf'ing** *n* the sport of riding breaking waves on a surfboard or in a surf canoe; any similar sport using a surfboard, such as snow surfing, sky surfing, etc. **surf'y** *adj*.
❑ **surf'-bather** *n.* **surf'-bathing** *n* bathing in surf. **surf'bird** *n* an American Pacific shorebird (*Aphriza virgata*) related to sandpipers. **surf'board** *n* a long narrow board used in surfing. **surf'boarding** *n.* **surf boat** *n* a boat for use in surf. **surf canoe** *n* a slalom canoe or a kayak used for surfing. **surf'caster** *n.* **surf'casting** *n* fishing from the shore by casting into surf. **surf duck** *n* the scoter. **surf'fish** *n* any fish of a W American viviparous perchoid family, Embiotocidae, that inhabit coastal waters (also called **surfperch**). **surf'man** *n* a man skilful in handling boats in surf. **surf' 'n'turf** *n* a dish in which seafood and meat are served together. **surf'perch** see **surffish** above. **surf'-riding** *n* riding on a surfboard.

surface /*sûr'fis*/ *n* the outer boundary or face of anything; the outside or upper layer; a flat, two-dimensional geometric figure that has length and breadth but no thickness; an area; the outer appearance, character or texture; an aerofoil. ◆ *adj* of, on, or near a surface; superficial. ◆ *vt* to apply a surface or finish to. ◆ *vi* to bring or rise to the surface; to be exposed or revealed, to become apparent; to regain consciousness (*inf*); to get out of bed (*inf*). [Fr, from *sur*, from L *super*, and *face*, from L *faciēs* face]
■ **sur'faced** *adj* having this or that kind of surface. **sur'facer** *n* a person or thing that smooths or levels a surface. **sur'facing** *n* giving a surface to anything; material for a surface layer; washing surface deposits for gold.
❑ **sur'face-active** *adj* able to alter the surface tension of liquids (see also **surfactant**). **surface activity** *n* the alteration to the surface tension of liquids due to superactive substances. **sur'face-craft** *n* a floating, not submersible, craft. **surface mail** *n* mail sent otherwise than by air. **sur'faceman** *n* a workman who keeps a railway bed in repair. **surface noise** *n* the noise produced by the friction of a stylus on a record. **surface plate** *n* (*engineering*) a rigid cast-iron plate whose surface is accurately scraped flat, used eg to test the flatness of other surfaces. **surface structure** *n* (*linguistics*) the formal structure of sentences, *esp* when broken down into their constituent parts. **surface tension** *n* that property in virtue of which a liquid surface behaves like a stretched elastic membrane, clinging to the sides of a container. **surface-to-air'** *adj* (of a missile, etc) travelling from a base on the ground to a target in the air (also *adv*). **surface-to-sur'face** *adj* and *adv*. **sur'face-vessel** *n.* **surface water** *n* water lying on the surface of a road, etc; drainage water. **surface wind** *n* (*meteorol*) the wind at a standard height of 10m (33ft) above ground. **surface worker** *n* a person engaged in any of the ancillary jobs in a coalmine not done underground.
■ **scratch the surface** to deal only superficially with an issue or problem.

surfactant /*sər-fak'tənt*/ *n* a substance, eg a detergent, which reduces surface tension; a wetting agent; a substance secreted by the

pneumocytes lining the alveoli of the lungs that prevents the walls of the alveoli from sticking together; a substance administered as a substitute for this, eg to premature babies whose lungs are not fully developed. [*surface-active agent*]

surfeit /*sûr'fit*/ *n* overfulness; gorging; gluttony; excess; an excessive meal; sickness or satiety caused by overeating or overdrinking. ◆ *vt* to feed or fill to satiety or disgust. ◆ *vi* to indulge to excess, *esp* in food and drink (*archaic*); to suffer from excess (*obs*). [OFr *surfait* excess, from L *super* above, and *facere* to make]
■ **sur'feited** *adj.* **sur'feiter** *n.* **sur'feiting** *n* and *adj*.

surficial /*sûr-fish'l*/ (*geol*) *adj* superficial, subaerial. [**surface**, altered in analogy with *superficial*]

surg. *abbrev* : surgeon; surgery; surgical.

surge[1] /*sûrj*/ *n* an uprush, boiling or tumultuous movement of liquid; a sudden powerful movement of a crowd; a sudden increase, *esp* of power; a great wave; a swell; a sudden oscillation; a jerk on a rope; (of spacecraft) movement in the direction of travel. ◆ *vi* to well up; to heave tumultuously; to slip back; to jerk. ◆ *vt* to send in surges; to slack suddenly. [L *surgere* to rise]
■ **surge'ful** *adj.* **surge'less** *adj.* **sur'gent** *adj.* **sur'ging** *n* and *adj.* **sur'gy** *adj*.

surge[2] an old spelling (*Shakesp*) of **cerge**.

surgeon /*sûr'jən*/ *n* a person who treats injuries or diseases by manual operations; an army or naval doctor; a ship's doctor; a surgeonfish. [Anglo-Fr *surgien* ; see **chirurgeon**]
■ **sur'geoncy** or **sur'geonship** *n* the office or employment of a surgeon in the army or navy. **sur'gery** *n* the art and practice of a surgeon; a doctor's or dentist's consulting room; a doctor's or dentist's time of consultation; a set, *usu* regular, time when a member of parliament, local councillor, etc is available to his or her constituents for consultation. **sur'gical** *adj* of, relating to, or used in surgery; (of a garment or appliance) designed to correct a physical deformity; incisive; precise. **sur'gically** *adv*.
❑ **sur'geonfish** *n* any member of the family Acanthuridae, tropical fishes having razor-sharp spines on their tails, *incl* the tangs and unicorn fishes. **surgeon general** *n* the senior officer in the medical branch of the service (*milit*); the head of the public health service (*US*). **surgeon's knot** *n* a knot like a reef knot but with a double turn in the first part (used in ligaturing a cut artery). **surgical boot** or **shoe** *n* a boot or shoe designed to correct deformities of the foot. **surgical neck** *n* (*anat*) the constriction of the shaft of the humerus below the head, a frequent site of fractures. **surgical shock** see **shock**[1]. **surgical spirit** *n* methylated spirit with small amounts of castor oil and oil of wintergreen.

surgy see under **surge**[1].

suricate /*sū'-* or *soo'ri-kāt*/ *n* a S African animal of the civet family, the slender-tailed meerkat. [From Du *surikat*; of uncertain origin]

Suriname or **Surinam** /*sū-* or *soo-ri-nam'*, also *sū'* or *soo'*/ *n* a republic, *orig* a Dutch colony, in S America.
■ **Surinam'er** *n* a native or citizen of Suriname. **Surinam'ese** *adj* of or relating to Suriname or its people.
❑ **Surinam poison** *n* fish-poison obtained from a S American papilionaceous plant, *Tephrosia*. **Surinam toad** *n* a S American amphibian that hatches its eggs in pits in its back.

surjection /*sûr-jek'shən*/ (*maths*) *n* a mapping function in which all the elements in one set correspond to all the elements in another set (cf **injection**). [**sur-** and L *jacēre* to throw]

surloin same as **sirloin**.

surly /*sûr'li*/ *adj* morose; gruff and grumpy; rough and gloomy; haughty (*Shakesp*); refractory. ◆ *adv* (*Shakesp*) surlily. [From obs *sirly* haughty, from **sir** and **like**[1]]
■ **sur'lily** *adv.* **sur'liness** *n*.

surmaster /*sûr'mä-stər*/ (*archaic*) *n* the second master or deputy head in a school (also *fem* **sur'mistress**). [**sur-**]

surmise /*sər-mīz'*/ *vt* to imagine; to suspect; to conjecture, guess. ◆ *n* a suspicion; a conjecture; an allegation (*obs*). [OFr, from *surmettre* to accuse, from L *super* upon, and *mittere* to send]
■ **surmis'able** *adj.* **surmis'al** *n.* **surmis'er** *n.* **surmis'ing** *n* and *adj*.

surmistress see **surmaster**.

surmount /*sər-mownt'*/ *vt* to mount above; to be on or go to the top of; to surpass; to get the better of, overcome. [OFr *surmunter* (Fr *surmonter*), from LL *supermontāre* ; see **mount**[1]]
■ **surmount'able** *adj.* **surmount'ed** *adj* surpassed; overcome; higher than half the span (*archit*); having another figure laid over (*heraldry*). **surmount'er** *n.* **surmount'ing** *n* and *adj*.

surmullet /*sər-mul'it*/ *n* a species of red mullet, admired by the Romans for its colour changes as it died. [Fr *surmullet*]

surname /sûr'nām/ n a family name; an additional name (*archaic*). ◆ vt to name by a surname. [On the analogy of Fr *surnom*, from Eng **name** and L *nōmen, -inis*]
■ **surnom'inal** adj.

surpass /sər-päs'/ vt to go or be beyond; to exceed; to excel. [Fr *surpasser*, from *sur-*, and *passer* to pass]
■ **surpass'able** adj. **surpass'ing** adj passing beyond others; excellent in a high degree. ◆ adv (*obs* or *poetic*) so as to exceed all others; in a most excellent manner. **surpass'ingly** adv. **surpass'ingness** n.

surplice /sûr'plis/ n a white linen vestment worn over the cassock. [Fr *surplis*, from LL *superpellicium* an overgarment, from *pellis* skin]
■ **sur'pliced** adj wearing a surplice.

surplus /sûr'pləs/ n that which is left over; a remainder; excess over what is required; excess of revenue over expenditure. ◆ adj left over; in excess of requirements. [Fr, from LL *superplūs*, from *super*, and *plūs* more]
■ **sur'plusage** n surplus; superfluity.

surprise /sər-prīz'/ n a catching, or being caught, unawares; the emotion caused by anything sudden or contrary to expectation; anything that causes or is intended to cause this emotion. ◆ adj catching, or intended to catch, unawares. ◆ vt to come upon suddenly or unawares; to capture by an unexpected assault; to lead or bring unawares, betray (with *into*); to strike with wonder or astonishment; to confuse; to seize (*obs*). ◆ vi (*formal*) to cause surprise. [OFr (Fr) fem pap of *surprendre*, from L *super*, and *prehendere* to catch]
■ **surpris'al** n an act of surprising. **surprised'** adj. **surpris'edly** adv. **surpris'er** n. **surpris'ing** n and adj. **surpris'ingly** adv. **surpris'ingness** n.
■ **much** (or **greatly**, etc) **to one's surprise** causing one great surprise. **surprise, surprise** an ironic exclamation of surprise.

surquedry /sûr'kwi-dri/ or **surquedy** /-di/ (*obs*) n arrogance. [OFr *surcuiderie*, from *surcuidier*, from L *super* above, and *cōgitāre, -ātum* to think]

surra /soo'rə/ (*vet*) n a trypanosome disease of the blood in horses, etc. [Marathi *sūra* wheezing]

surrealism /sə-rē'ə-li-zm/ n a movement in art and literature, begun in France around 1919, that sought to resolve the contradictory conditions of dream and reality into an absolute reality by various techniques, thus escaping the dominance of reason and conscious control. [Fr *surréalisme*, from *sur* above, and *réalisme* realism]
■ **surre'al** adj of or relating to surrealism; dreamlike, bizarre. **surre'alist** adj and n. **surrealist'ic** adj. **surrealist'ically** adv.

surrebut /sur-i-but'/ (*law*) vi to reply to a defendant's rebutter. [**sur-**]
■ **surrebutt'al** n a plaintiff's evidence or presentation of evidence, in response to a defendant's rebuttal. **surrebutt'er** n the plaintiff's reply, in common law pleading, to a defendant's rebutter.

surreined /sū'rānd/ adj overridden. [Appar **sur-** and **rein¹**]

surrejoin /sur-i-join'/ (*law*) vt and vi to reply to a defendant's rejoinder. [**sur-**]
■ **surrejoind'er** n a plaintiff's reply to a defendant's rejoinder.

surrender /sə-ren'dər/ vt to deliver over; to relinquish; to yield up; to resign. ◆ vi to yield oneself up; to yield. ◆ n the act of surrendering. [Anglo-Fr *surrender*, OFr *surrendre*, from *sur-*, and *rendre*; see **render**]
■ **surrenderee'** n a person to whom a legal surrender is made. **surren'derer** n. **surren'deror** n (*law*) a person who makes a surrender. **surren'dry** n (*obs*) a surrender.
□ **surrender value** n the amount to be paid to an insured person who surrenders his or her policy.

surreptitious /sur-əp-tish'əs/ adj done by stealth or fraud; stealthy. [See **subreption**]
■ **surrepti'tiously** adv.

surrey /sur'i/ (*US*) n a light four-wheeled horse-drawn vehicle for four, usu with two seats. [Developed from a vehicle used in *Surrey*]

sur-reyn'd a Shakespearean spelling of **surreined**.

surrogate /sur'ō-git/ or /-gāt/ n a substitute; a deputy, *esp* of an ecclesiastical judge; a deputy of a bishop who grants marriage licences; (in some US states) a judge of probate; a person or thing standing, eg in a dream, for another person or thing, or a person who fills the role of another in one's emotional life (eg *mother surrogate*; see also **surrogate mother** below). [L *surrogāre, -ātum*, from *sub* in the place of, and *rogāre* to ask]
■ **surr'ogacy** n the state of being a surrogate; use of a surrogate, *esp* of a surrogate mother. **surr'ogateship** n. **surroga'tion** n subrogation. **surroga'tum** n a substitute (*obs*); something that stands in place of something else, eg a price instead of the thing itself (*Scots law*).

□ **surrogate mother** n a woman who bears a baby for another (*esp* childless) couple, after either (artificial) insemination by the male or implantation of an embryo from the female; a woman who fills the role of mother to children she did not bear. **surrogate motherhood** n.

surround /sə-rownd'/ vt to go or extend all around; to encompass, environ; to encircle; to be the background situation to, or make up the context or environment of; to maintain around (oneself) a following of people or collection of things; to make a circuit of (*rare*); to overflow (*obs*). ◆ n an act of surrounding (*esp* hunted animals); a border, *esp* the floor or floor-covering around a carpet; an ornamental structure fitted around (eg an open fire). [OFr *suronder*, from L *superundāre* to overflow, from *super*, and *unda* wave; confused with **round¹**]
■ **surround'ing** adj encompassing; neighbouring. ◆ n an encompassing; (in *pl*) the environment, things round about.
□ **surround sound** n any form of stereophonic sound reproduction using three or more speakers to give an effect of sound coming from all directions.

surroyal /sə-roi'əl/ n any tine of a stag's horn above the royal. [**sur-**]

surtarbrand see **surturbrand**.

surtax /sûr'taks/ n an additional tax; tax payable on incomes above a certain high level (term not in official use in this sense). ◆ vt to tax additionally; to charge surtax. [**sur-**]

surtitle /sûr'tī-tl/ n a printed translation of the libretto of an opera in a language foreign to the audience, projected above the proscenium arch. ◆ vt to provide with surtitles. [**sur-**]

surtout /sər-too'/ or /-toot'/ n a close-bodied 19c frock-coat; an overcoat (*obs*); a lady's hood (*obs*); a raised portion of the parapet of a work at the angles, to protect from enfilade fire (*fortif*). [Fr, from LL *supertōtus* an outer garment, from L *super*, and *tōtus* all]

surturbrand or **surtarbrand** /sûr'tər-brand/ n lignite found interbedded with lavas in Iceland. [Icel *surtarbrandr*, from *Surtar*, genitive of *Surtr* name of a fire-giant, and *brandr* brand]

surveillance /sər-vā'ləns or -lyəns/ n a watch kept over someone or something, *esp* over a criminal (and his or her activities) by the police; vigilant supervision; superintendence. [Fr, from *surveiller*, from *sur*, and *veiller* to watch, from L *vigilāre*]
■ **surveil** or **surveille** /-vāl'/ vt (back-formation; *US*) to observe, keep under surveillance. **surveill'ant** n.
□ **surveillance radar** n a plan-position indicator radar showing the position of aircraft within an air-traffic control area.

survew, survewe Spenserian spellings of **surview**.

survey /sər-vā'/ vt to view comprehensively and extensively; to examine in detail; to examine (a building) in order to assess structural soundness or determine value; to measure (land heights and distances in an area) for mapping purposes; to canvass and assess (opinions, etc); to perceive, spy (*Shakesp*). ◆ n /sûr'vā or -vā'/ a general view, or a statement of its results; an inspection; collection of data for mapping; an organization or body of people for that purpose; superintendence. [OFr *surveoir*, from L *super* over, and *vidēre* to see]
■ **survey'al** n. **survey'ance** n. **survey'ing** n. **survey'or** n an overseer; a measurer of land; an inspector of buildings, their structure, state of repair, etc; an inspector of roads, of weights and measures, of customs duties, etc). **survey'orship** n.

surview /sər-vū'/ vt to survey, look over; to command a view of. [**sur-**]

survive /sər-vīv'/ vt to live or exist after or in spite of; to outlive. ◆ vi to remain alive or in existence. [Fr *survivre*, from L *super* beyond, and *vīvere* to live]
■ **survivabil'ity** n. **survi'vable** adj. **survi'val** n a surviving or living after; anything that continues to exist after others of its kind have disappeared, or after the time to which it naturally belongs. ◆ adj (*esp* of standard equipment) designed to help one to survive exposure to extreme cold or other dangerous conditions. **survi'valism** n. **survi'valist** n a person who takes measures to ensure their own survival after a catastrophic event, or measures for their own personal protection from attack, robbery, etc (also adj). **survi'vance** n survival; succession or right to succeed on surviving the present holder. **survi'ving** adj. **survi'vor** n one that survives; a person who is able to overcome adversity, *esp* through resourcefulness and determination. **survi'vorship** n.
□ **survival bag** n a large plastic or foil bag in which a climber seeks emergency protection against exposure. **survival curve** n (*radiol*) a curve showing the percentage of organisms surviving at different times after subjection to a large radiation dose. **survivor guilt** n a sense of having done wrong by surviving an event that proved fatal for others.

■ **survival of the fittest** the longer average life of the best adapted members of a (*esp* animal) community in the struggle for existence, and the consequent transmission of healthy or otherwise favourable characteristics to later generations.

Surya /soor'yə/ *n* the Hindu sun-god. [Sans]

Sus. (*Bible*) *abbrev* : (the Apocryphal Book of) Susanna.

sus or **suss** /sus/ (*sl*) *n* a suspect; suspicion; suspicious behaviour, eg loitering with intent. ◆ *vt* (**suss'ing**; **sussed**) to arrest for suspicious behaviour; see also separate entry **suss**. [**suspect** or **suspicion**]
❑ **sus** (or **suss**) **laws** *n pl* laws allowing a person to be arrested on suspicion of having committed a crime.

susceptible /sə-sep'ti-bl/ *adj* (*usu* with *to*) open to, admitting of; suffering readily (from), prone (to); capable of receiving; impressionable, easily influenced or persuaded; easily affected by emotion (*esp* amatory). [L *suscipere, susceptum* to take up, from *sus-* (*subs-*) up, and *capere* to take]
■ **suscep'tance** *n* (*phys*) the imaginary part of the admittance. **susceptibil'ity** *n* the state or quality of being susceptible; (in *pl*) feelings; sensibilities. **suscep'tibleness** *n*. **suscep'tibly** *adv*. **suscep'tive** *adj* capable of receiving or admitting; readily admitting. **suscep'tiveness** *n*. **susceptiv'ity** /sus-/ *n*. **suscep'tor** *n* (*obs*) a sponsor. **suscip'ient** *n* a recipient, *esp* of a sacrament. ◆ *adj* receiving.

suscipient see under **susceptible**.

suscitate /sus'i-tāt/ *vt* to excite, rouse. [L *suscitāre, -ātum*, from *sus-* (*subs-*) under, and *citāre* to arouse]
■ **suscitā'tion** *n*.

sushi /soo'shi/ *n* a Japanese dish of small cakes of cold vinegared rice topped with fish, vegetables, egg, etc. [Jap]

suslik /sus'lik/ or /sūs'lik/ *n* a ground squirrel, a chipmunk. [Russ]

suspect /sə-spekt'/ *vt* to mistrust; to imagine to be guilty; to doubt; to be ready to believe, but without sufficient evidence; to incline to believe the existence, presence, or agency of; to have an inkling of; to conjecture. ◆ *vi* to imagine guilt, to be suspicious. ◆ *n* /sus'pekt/ a person suspected; /səs-pekt'/ suspicion (*archaic*). ◆ *adj* /sus'pekt/ suspected; thought to be untrue or unreliable; dubious. [L *suspicere, suspectum* to look at secretly or askance, from *su-* (*sub-*), and *specere* to look]
■ **suspect'able** *adj*. **suspect'ed** *adj*. **suspect'edly** *adv*. **suspect'edness** *n*. **suspect'ful** *adj* suspicious. **sus'pectless** *adj* unsuspicious; unsuspected.

suspend /səs-pend'/ *vt* to hang; to make to depend; to keep from falling; to put or hold in a state of suspense or suspension; to make to stop for a time; to defer; to defer or stay (eg a sentence) (*law*); to debar from any privilege, office, emolument, etc, for a time; to sustain into a following chord, producing discord (*music*); to hold in an indeterminate state. [L *suspendere, -pēnsum*, from pfx *sus-* (*subs-*), and *pendere* to hang]
■ **suspen'ded** *adj*. **suspend'er** *n* someone or something that suspends; a strap to support a sock or stocking; (in *pl*) braces for trousers (*N Am*).
❑ **suspended animation** *n* temporary slowing down to an absolute minimum of the body's principal functions, eg in hibernation. **suspended sentence** *n* a sentence of imprisonment not served unless the offender commits another crime. **suspen'der-belt** *n* a woman's undergarment with stocking suspenders attached.
■ **suspend payment** publicly to stop paying debts from insolvency.

suspense /səs-pens'/ *n* intermission; cessation; deferring (eg of judgement); a state or atmosphere of nervous or excited uncertainty; indecision. ◆ *adj* in suspense; (*Milton* **suspens'** or **suspence'**) suspended, held back. [Ety as for **suspend**]
■ **suspense'ful** *adj*. **suspens'er** *n* something, eg a film or book, that is filled with suspense. **suspensibil'ity** *n*. **suspen'sible** *adj*. **suspen'sion** /-shən/ *n* an act of suspending; interruption; delay; temporary debarment from office or privilege; a temporary or conditional withholding; holding a note from a chord into the next chord (*music*); a discord so produced (*music*); a mixture of a fluid with dense particles which are prevented from settling by viscosity and impact of molecules (*chem*); (in a motor vehicle or railway carriage) the system of springs, etc supporting the chassis on the axles. **suspen'sive** *adj*. **suspen'sively** *adv*. **suspen'soid** *n* (*chem*) a colloid dispersed with difficulty, yielding an unstable solution that cannot be reformed after coagulation. **suspen'sor** *n* a chain of cells to which a plant embryo is fixed (*bot*); a suspensory bandage. **suspensorial** /sus-pen-sō'ri-əl/ or /-sö'/ *adj*. **suspenso'rium** *n* that which holds up a part, *esp* the arrangement joining the lower jaw to the cranium in vertebrates below mammals. **suspen'sory** *adj* suspending; having the power or effect of delaying or staying; of the suspensorium. ◆ *n* a suspensorium.
❑ **suspense account** *n* an account in which items are entered which cannot at once be placed in an ordinary account. **suspension bridge** *n* a bridge with a roadway hanging on cables, which are themselves *usu* suspended from heavier cables stretched between elevated piers. **suspension building** *n* building round a concrete core and from the top downward but sometimes attached directly to the piers. **suspension culture** *n* (*biol*) a method of culturing large quantities of cells by keeping them in vessels continually stirred and aerated.

suspercollate /sus-pər-koľāt/ (*facetious*) *vt* to hang. [*sus. per col.*, abbrev of L *suspendātur per collum* let him be hanged by the neck]

suspicion /sə-spish'ən/ *n* the act of suspecting; the state of being suspected; the imagining of something without evidence or on slender evidence; an inkling; mistrust; a slight quantity, minute trace, eg of spirits (*inf*); ground for suspicion (*Shakesp*). ◆ *vt* (*dialect* and *US dialect*) to suspect. [L *suspīciō, -ōnis*; see **suspect**]
■ **suspi'cionless** *adj*. **suspi'cious** *adj* full of suspicion; showing suspicion; inclined to suspect; giving ground for suspicion; liable to suspicion, doubtful. **suspi'ciously** *adv*. **suspi'ciousness** *n*.
■ **above** (or **beyond**) **suspicion** too honest, virtuous, etc to be suspected of a crime or fault. **on suspicion** (**of**) suspected (of). **under suspicion** suspected.

suspire /səs-pīr'/ (*archaic* or *poetic*) *vi* to sigh; to breathe. ◆ *vt* to breathe forth. [L *suspīrāre*, from *su-* (*sub-*), and *spīrāre* to breathe]
■ **suspiration** /sus-pə-rā'shən/ *n* sighing. **suspirious** /səs-pir'i-əs/ *adj* breathing labouredly; sighing.

suss or **sus** /sus/ (*sl*) *vt* (often with *out*) to investigate; to find out, discover; to suspect. ◆ *n* knowledge, awareness; see also separate entry **sus**. [**sus**]
■ **sussed** *adj* well-informed, in the know.

sussarara same as **siserary**.

sustain /səs-tān'/ *vt* to hold up; to bear; to support; to provide for; to maintain; to sanction; to keep going; to keep up; to support the life of; to prolong; to suffer, undergo. ◆ *n* a sustained musical note; the facility of an instrument to sustain a note; means of sustenance (*Milton*). [L *sustinēre*, from pfx *sus-* (*subs-*), and *tenēre* to hold; partly through OFr *sustenir* [Fr *soutenir*)]
■ **sustainabil'ity** *n* that which is capable of being sustained; in ecology, the amount or degree to which the earth's resources may be exploited without damage to the environment. **sustain'able** *adj* able to be sustained; involving the long-term use of resources that do not damage the environment. **sustained'** *adj*. **sustain'edly** *adv*. **sustain'er** *n* a person who, or thing that, sustains; the main motor in a rocket, continuing with it throughout its flight (cf **booster**). **sustain'ing** *n* and *adj*. **sustain'ment** *n* an act of sustaining; sustenance. **sustenance** /sus'ti-nəns/ *n* that which sustains; maintenance; nourishment. **sustentac'ular** *adj* supporting. **sustentac'ulum** *n* a supporting part or structure. **sus'tentāte** *vt* to sustain. **sustentā'tion** *n*. **sustentative** /sus'tən-tā-tiv or sus-ten'tə-tiv/ *adj* sustaining. **sus'tentātor** *n* a sustaining part or structure. **susten'tion** *n* the act of sustaining. **susten'tive** *adj*. **sus'tinent** *adj* sustaining.
❑ **sustained yield** *n* the amount of a natural resource that can be harvested or removed regularly without long-term depletion of the resource. **sustaining pedal** *n* a pedal on a piano which sustains the note(s) played by allowing the strings to continue vibrating.

sustenance, sustentacular, sustentation, sustinent, etc see under **sustain**.

Susu /soo'soo/ *n* a people of W Africa, living mainly in Mali, Guinea and Sierra Leone; a member of this people; their language.

susu or **sou-sou** /soo'soo/ *n* (*esp* in the West Indies) a savings scheme in which members make regular deposits and take it in turns to receive the total amount collected. [Yoruba]

susurrus /sū- or soo-sur'əs/ (*poetic*) *n* a murmuring; a whisper; a rustling. [L]
■ **susurr'ant** *adj*. **su'surrate** *vi*. **susurrā'tion** *n*.

sutile /sū', soo'tīl or -til/ (*rare*) *adj* done by stitching. [L *sūtilis*, from *suere* to sew]

sutler /sut'lər/ (*hist*) *n* a person who sells liquor or provisions to soldiers in camp or garrison; a camp-hawker. [Du *zoetelaar* (earlier *soeteler*)]
■ **sut'lery** *n* a sutler's work or stall. **sutt'le** *vi* to trade as a sutler.

sutor /sū', soo'tör or -tər/ (*archaic*) *n* a cobbler. [**souter**; or directly from L *sūtor, -ōris* cobbler]
■ **suto'rial** or **suto'rian** *adj* relating to cobbling or to sewing.

sutra /soo'trə/ *n* (in Sanskrit literature) an aphoristic rule or book of aphorisms on ritual, grammar, metre, philosophy, etc; (in Buddhist sacred literature) any of a group of writings including the sermons of Buddha and other doctrinal works. [Sans *sūtra* thread]

suttee or **sati** /sut'ē or sut-ē'/ n an Indian widow who burned herself on her husband's funeral pyre; the Hindu custom of so doing. [Sans satī a true wife]
■ **suttee'ism** n.

suttle[1] /sut'l/ (obs) adj light (esp of weight when tare is subtracted). [**subtle**]

suttle[2] /sut'l/ (Milton) adj subtle. [**subtle**]
■ **sutt'letie** n subtlety. **sutt'ly** adv.

suttle[3] see under **sutler**.

suture /sū', soo'chər or -tūr/ n a seam; a stitching; the stitching of a wound; the thread, etc for this; a junction or meeting of margins, esp of bones or of carpels; a line of dehiscence; a line of union. ◆ vt to stitch up. [L sūtūra a seam, from suere to sew]
■ **su'tural** adj. **su'turally** adv. **sutura'tion** n. **su'tured** adj.

suum cuique /soo'əm kwē'kwe or -kwā/ (L) to each his own.

SUV abbrev : sport utility vehicle.

suversed /sū-vûrst'/ (obs; maths) adj versed of the supplement. [From the contraction sup. (meaning 'supplement') versed]

suzerain /soo'zə-rān or sū'/ n a feudal lord; supreme or paramount ruler; a state having supremacy over another. ◆ adj paramount. [Fr, formed in imitation of souverain from sus- over, from L sūsum (for sūrsum, subvorsum)]
■ **su'zerainty** n the position or power of a suzerain.

SV abbrev : Sancta Virgo (L), Holy Virgin; Sanctitas Vestra (L), Your Holiness.

Sv symbol : sievert (SI unit).

sv or **s.v.** abbrev : sub verbo (L), under the word; sub voce (L), under that heading.

svarabhakti /svä-rä-bäk'tē/ n development of a vowel between consonants. [Sans svara vowel, and bhakti separation]

Svarga see **Swarga**.

svastika /svas'ti-kə/ see **swastika**.

svelte /svelt/ adj attractively slim; slender and graceful; lissom, lithe; (in art) free, easy, light and bold. [Fr]

Svengali /sven-gä'lē/ n a person who exerts total mental control over another, usu for evil ends. [Name of the evil hypnotist in George du Maurier's novel Trilby (1894)]

SVGA (comput) abbrev : super video graphics array, a video graphics adapter.

SVQ abbrev : Scottish Vocational Qualification.

SW abbrev : short wave; small women or women's (clothing size); south-west; south-western.

SWA abbrev : South-West Africa (Namibia).

swab /swob/ n a bit of cotton wool or the like for mopping up blood or discharges, applying antiseptics, cleaning a patient's mouth, or taking a specimen of a bodily secretion for examination; a specimen so taken; a mop for cleaning or drying floors or decks; a brush for wetting foundry moulds; a sponge or the like for cleaning the bore of a firearm; a naval officer's epaulette (old sl); a lubber or clumsy fellow (old sl); in an old form of whist, a card entitling its holder to a share of the stakes. ◆ vt (**swabb'ing**; **swabbed**) to absorb or mop with a swab. [Du zwabber swabber]
■ **swabb'er** n a person who uses a swab; a mop for cleaning ovens; a swab in whist as formerly played; (in pl) whist so played (also **whisk and swabbers**). **swabb'y** n (US sl) a seaman, esp a new recruit.

swack /swak or swäk/ (Scot) adj pliant; nimble. [Cf LGer swak, Du zwak; Ger schwach weak]

swad /swod/ (dialect) n a country lout; a soldier. [Perh Scand, or from **squad**, **squaddy**]
■ **swadd'y** n a soldier, esp a militiaman.

swaddle /swod'l/ vt to swathe; to bandage; to wrap (an infant) tightly in strips of cloth, as was formerly done to soothe or prevent over-exertion; to thrash, beat soundly (obs). ◆ n swaddling-clothes; a bandage. [OE swæthel, swethel bandage; cf **swathe**[1]]
■ **swadd'ler** n (Anglo-Irish inf) a Methodist or Protestant in general.
□ **swadd'ling-band** or **swadd'ling-clothes** n (Bible) a strip or strips of cloth for swaddling an infant.

swaddy see under **swad**.

Swadeshi /swə- or swä-dā'shē/ (hist) n a pre-Independence Indian nationalist movement, promoting home industries and boycott of foreign, esp British, goods; a product made in India. ◆ adj denoting this movement or these products. [Bengali, own country]
■ **Swade'shism** n.

swag /swag/ n a festoon; a curtain or length of material hung in folds, esp at a window; a subsidence, as of ground over a mine; a depression; a bundle of possessions carried by someone travelling on foot (esp Aust); a journey made carrying such a bundle; plunder (sl). ◆ vi (**swagg'ing**; **swagged**) to sway; to sag; (often with it) to travel around carrying a bundle, as a vagrant or in search of work (Aust sl). [Related to **sway**; prob Scand]
■ **swagg'ie** n (Aust sl) a swagman.
□ **swag'-bellied** adj having a pendulous belly. **swag'-belly** n a pendulous belly; someone whose belly swags. **swag'man** n (Aust) a man who carries his swag about with him, esp in search of work. **swag'shop** n (sl) a place where cheap and trashy goods are sold. **swags'man** n a swagman; a burglar's accomplice who carries the plunder (sl).

swage[1] /swāj/ n a grooved or moulded border (obs); any of several tools including a tool in two grooved parts, for shaping metal. ◆ vt to shape with a swage; to reduce the cross-section of a rod or tube, eg by forcing it through a tapered aperture between two grooved dies. [OFr souage]
□ **swage block** n a block with various holes, grooves, etc, for use in metalworking.

swage[2] /swāj/ (Milton) vt to assuage. [Anglo-Fr suagier, from L suāvis, mild or aphetic for **assuage**]

swagger /swag'ər/ vi to walk with a blustering or overweening air of superiority and self-confidence; to brag noisily or ostentatiously; to behave arrogantly. ◆ vt to do, bring or render by swaggering. ◆ n a swaggering gait, manner, mien or behaviour. ◆ adj (inf) ostentatiously fashionable; smart. [**swag**]
■ **swagg'erer** n. **swagg'ering** n and adj. **swagg'eringly** adv.
□ **swagger cane** or **stick** n a short military cane. **swagger coat** n a coat that flares loosely from the shoulders.

Swahili /swä-hē'li/ n the people of Zanzibar and the opposite coast; one of them; loosely, their language (Kiswahili), a Bantu tongue modified by Arabic, spoken in Kenya, Tanzania and other parts of E Africa. [Ar sawāhil, pl sāhil coast, with sfx]

swain /swān/ (poetic, often ironic; also archaic) n a young man; a peasant or rustic; a lover or suitor. [ON sveinn young man, servant; OE swān]
■ **swain'ing** n love-making. **swain'ish** adj boorish. **swain'ishness** n boorishness.

swale[1] /swāl/ (dialect) n a shady spot; shade; a sunken or marshy place. [Cf ON svalr cool]
■ **swāl'y** adj.

swale[2] /swāl/ vi to sway.

swale[3] see **sweal**.

Swaledale /swāl'dāl/ n a hardy breed of long-woolled sheep orig reared in Swaledale, N Yorkshire.

swaling see **sweal**.

SWALK /swölk or swalk/ abbrev : sealed with a loving kiss (written on the back of an envelope containing a love letter).

swallet see under **swallow**[1].

swallow[1] /swol'ō/ vt to take into the stomach through the gullet by a muscular movement of the throat; to engulf or subsume (often with up); to take in; to accept, sit down under (eg an affront); to stifle or repress (eg tears or one's pride); to believe credulously. ◆ vi to perform the action of swallowing something. ◆ n an abyss; a swallow hole; a throat; an act of swallowing; a gulp; a quantity swallowed at once; capacity for swallowing; the aperture in a block, between the sheave and frame, through which the rope runs (naut). [OE swelgan (verb), geswelg (noun); cf Ger schwelgen]
■ **swall'et** n a swallow hole. **swall'ower** n.
□ **swallow hole** n a funnel or fissure through which surface water passes underground, esp in limestone (also called **sink hole**).
■ **swallow one's pride** to humble oneself.

swallow[2] /swol'ō/ n a small long-winged migratory bird (Hirundo rustica), with a forked tail, that catches insects on the wing; any bird of its genus or family; extended to various unrelated birds of similar form or habits. [OE swalwe, swealwe; Ger Schwalbe]
□ **swall'ow-dive** n a dive during which one's arms are outstretched to the sides (also vi). **swall'owtail** n a forked tail; a long-tailed dress coat; a butterfly of the family Papilionidae with prolongations of the hind wings; a barbed arrow; a pennon; a swallowtailed bird (eg the hummingbird and the kite). **swall'owtailed** adj with a forked and pointed tail. **swall'ow-wort** n an asclepiad (Cynanchum or Vincetoxicum), from the swallowtailed appearance of its paired pods; hence any asclepiad; the greater celandine (qv under **celandine**).

swam /swam/ pat (and Shakesp, etc, pap) of **swim**.

swami /swä'mē/ n a Hindu idol; a Hindu religious instructor, esp (often with cap) as a form of address; a mystic. [Hindi svāmī lord, master]

swamp /swomp/ n a tract of wet, spongy (in the USA often tree-clad) land; low waterlogged ground. ◆ vt to cause to sink or become stuck in a swamp (also fig); to cause (eg a boat) to fill with water; to overwhelm, inundate. ◆ vi to become swamped. ◆ adj of, or of the nature of, swamp; living or growing in swamps. [Perh from LGer; prob related to OE swamm mushroom, Ger Schwamm sponge, fungus]
■ **swamp'er** n (US) a person who lives or works in the swamps. **swamp'iness** n. **swamp'y** adj.
❑ **swamp boat** n a flat-bottomed boat with a raised aeroplane engine for travelling over swamps. **swamp cypress** n a deciduous conifer, Taxodium, of swamps in the southern USA. **swamp fever** n leptospirosis; a viral disease of horses (also called **equine infectious anaemia**); malaria (US). **swamp gas** n marsh gas. **swamp'land** n. **swamp oak** n any of the various trees of the genus Casuarina.

swan /swon/ n any species of Cygnus, a genus of large, graceful, stately, long-necked aquatic birds; one of these birds. ◆ vi (inf) to swim, move, glide, etc like a swan; to swan about (see below). [OE swan; Ger Schwan, Du zwaan]
■ **swan'like** adj. **swann'ery** n a place where swans are kept or bred. **swann'ing** n (inf). **swann'y** adj swanlike.
❑ **swan dive** n (N Am) a swallow-dive. **swan'-goose** n the Chinese goose (qv); the coscoroba swan (Coscoroba coscoroba) of S America. **swan'herd** n someone who tends swans. **swan'-hopping** n (non-standard) swan-upping. **swan'-maiden** n (in Germanic folklore) a maiden who can become a swan by putting on her feather-garment. **swan'-mark** n the notch made on the swan's upper mandible, as a mark of ownership. **swan'-mussel** n a large freshwater mussel. **swan neck** n an S-shaped bend or piece. **swans'-down** or **swans'down** n the under-plumage of a swan; a soft woollen or mixed cloth; a thick cotton with a soft nap on one side. **swan'-shot** n a shot of large size, like buckshot. **swan'skin** or **swan'-skin** n the unplucked skin of a swan; a soft, nappy, fine-twilled fabric. **swan'song** or **swan song** n the fabled song of a swan just before its death; a writer's or musician's last work; one's last work or final appearance. **swan'-upping** n an annual expedition up the Thames for the marking of young swans belonging to the Dyers' and Vintners' Companies (those belonging to the crown being unmarked) (see **up** vt).
■ **swan about** or **around** (inf) to move about aimlessly, or gracefully. **swan in** or **up** (inf) to arrive, either aimlessly or gracefully. **swan off** (inf) to wander off, or depart, in a nonchalant, relaxed or oblivious manner.

Swanee whistle /swon'i (h)wis'l/ (also without cap) n a musical instrument, a kind of whistle in which sliding notes are produced by moving a plunger in and out. [Swanee, variant of Suwannee, a river in SE USA]

swang /swang/ (Wordsworth) a rare pat of **swing**.

swanherd see under **swan**.

swank /swangk/ n (inf) ostentation; pretentiousness; a person who swanks. ◆ vi (inf) to show off; to swot (archaic). ◆ adj smart, swanky (inf); slender, pliant (Scot); agile (Scot). [Cf OE swancor pliant, MHGer swanken to sway]
■ **swank'er** n. **swankey, swankie** n see **swanky** below. **swank'ing** adj strapping, vigorous and strong; showing off (inf); showy (inf). **swank'y** adj (inf) ostentatiously smart. ◆ n (also (Scot) **swank'ey, swank'ie**) an active, smart, vigorous person; poor thin beer or any sloppy drink, even sweetened water and vinegar.
❑ **swank'pot** n (inf) a swanker.

swap or **swop** /swop/ vt (**swapp'ing** or **swopp'ing**; **swapped** or **swopped**, also (formerly) **swapt** or **swopt**) to barter; to give in exchange; to exchange; to strike (as a bargain); to strike, hit (obs); to slam, plump, slap down (dialect); to reap (corn, etc) close to the ground (dialect). ◆ vi to barter; to exchange one for another, carry out a mutual exchange; to smite (obs); to flop (rare). ◆ n an exchange; something which is exchanged or offered in exchange; an exchange (of a sum of money) at different rates (finance); a blow, stroke (obs). ◆ adv (dialect) suddenly. [ME swappen; perh imit; or connected with **sweep** or **swoop**]
■ **swapp'er** or **swopp'er** n a person who swaps; a very big thing, a whopper (old sl). **swapp'ing** or **swopp'ing** n and adj.
❑ **swap file** n (comput) an area of the hard disk of a computer into which any information not immediately required may be moved, thus maximizing the available memory. **swap line** n (econ) a lending arrangement between central banks. **swap meet** n a gathering at which collectors, dealers, etc trade or barter. **swap option** n (finance) a right to exchange a sum of money at different rates on or before a certain date. **swap'-shop** n a shop, meeting, etc where goods are exchanged for other goods or services rather than for money.

SWAPO /swä'pō/ abbrev : South-West Africa People's Organization.

swaption /swop'shən/ (finance) n a swap option (see under **swap**).

swaraj /swä-räj'/ (Ind hist) n self-government, independence, Home Rule. [Sans svarājya, from sva own, and rājya rule]
■ **swaraj'ism** n formerly, the policy of Indian political independence. **swaraj'ist** n an advocate of this.

sward /swörd/ (usu poetic) n (also **swarth**) the grassy surface of land; green turf. ◆ vt (usu in passive) to cover with sward. [OE sweard skin, rind; Du zwoord, Ger Schwarte]
■ **sward'ed** or **sward'y** adj covered with sward.

sware /swār/ archaic pat of **swear**.

swarf¹ /swörf/ n grit from an axle, etc; stone or metal grindings, filings, turnings, etc. [ON svarf file-dust]

swarf² /swörf/ or **swerf** /swûrf/ (Scot) n a swoon. ◆ vi (also **swarve** /swärv/ or **swerve** /swûrv/) to faint.

Swarga or **Svarga**, also (Southey) **Swerga** /swär'gä or swur'gə/ n heaven; Indra's paradise. [Sans Svarga]

swarm¹ /swörm/ n a body of bees going off to found a new community; a throng of insects or other small animals; a throng (of people, or of inanimate objects), esp one on the move, eg a mass of meteorites travelling through space; a colony, offshoot. ◆ vi to go off in a swarm; to occur or come in swarms; to abound, teem. ◆ vt to cause to swarm; to throng (chiefly US except in passive). [OE swearm; Ger Schwarm]
■ **swarm'er** n. **swarm'ing** n and adj.
❑ **swarm'-spore** or **-cell** n a free-swimming, generally ciliated, asexual reproductive body (bot); an active germ produced by sporulation in Protozoa (zool).

swarm² /swörm/ vt and vi to climb (eg a pole or tree) by clasping with arms and legs. [Origin unknown]

swart /swört/ or **swarth** /swörth/ adj (archaic or dialect) black; dusky; blackening, hence, malignant, baleful. [OE sweart; ON svartr, Ger schwarz black]
■ **swart'ness** n. **swart'y** adj (obs).
❑ **swart'-back** n (ON svartbakr) the great black-backed gull. **swart star** n (Milton) appar the Dogstar, in reference to its appearance in the summer, when the sun darkens the skin.

swarth /swörth/ same as **sward**, **swart** or (Shakesp) **swath¹**.

swarthy /swör'dhi/ adj dark-complexioned; blackish. [swart]
■ **swar'thily** adv. **swar'thiness** n.

swarty see under **swart**.

swarve see **swarf²**.

swash¹ /swosh/ n slush; pig-wash; a wash of liquid, eg of water over a beach; the action or sound of splashing liquid; a dash; a heavy blow; a clashing or dashing sound; a swashbuckler (archaic); swaggering (archaic). ◆ adv with a splash, heavy blow, or with a clashing or dashing sound. ◆ vt and vi to dash; to splash; to clash. [Imit]
■ **swash'er** n (Shakesp) a blusterer. **swash'ing** n and adj slashing, crushing; blustering. **swash'y** adj slushy.
❑ **swash'buckler** n a person who clashes a sword on a buckler; hence, a bully, a blusterer; a swaggering dare-devil; a film, novel, etc featuring the exploits of a swaggering hero. **swash'buckling** adj of or resembling a swashbuckler; adventurous, exciting.

swash² /swosh/ n (obs) a piece of turner's work with mouldings oblique to the axis; a flourish on a letter. ◆ adj (printing) (of letters) ornamental italic, with decorative strokes that end in a flourish, used only at the beginning or end of a word. [Origin unknown]
❑ **swash plate** n (engineering) a disc set obliquely on a revolving axis. **swash'work** n turner's work cut obliquely.

swastika /swos'ti-ka/, also **svastika** /svas'-/ n an ancient and worldwide symbol, a Greek cross with arms bent at a right angle, esp clockwise (see also **fylfot**), emblematic of the sun, good luck, anti-semitism or Nazism (see also **gammadion**). [Sans svastika, from svasti wellbeing, from su good, and asti he is]

SWAT /swot/ abbrev : Special Weapons and Tactics, a US police unit used against highly armed criminals, employing military-style weapons and tactics.

swat¹ /swot/ vt to hit smartly or heavily. ◆ n a sharp or heavy blow; a swatter. [squat]
■ **swatt'er** n an instrument consisting of a flexible shaft with a wide, flat, flaplike head, with which to swat flies.

swat² see **swot**.

swat³ /swot or swöt/ (Scot and Spenser) pat of **sweat**.

swatch /swoch/ n a sample, esp of cloth, or of carpet, wallpaper, etc. [Origin unknown]
❑ **swatch'book** n a collection of swatches bound together into book form.

swath¹ /swöth or swoth/ or **swathe** /swädh/ n a band of mown ground or of grass or corn cut by the scythe or mowing machine, or ready for these; a broad band; the sweep of a scythe or mowing-machine.

■ words derived from main entry word; ❑ compound words; ■ idioms and phrasal verbs

◆ *vt* (**swathe**; *Can*) to cut and leave (grain) lying in swathes to ripen on the ground. [OE *swæth* and *swathu* track; Du *zwade*]

■ **swathy** /swōth'i/ or *swādh'i/ adj.

■ **cut a swath(e) through** to destroy and kill many of; to devastate.

swath² /swoth/ (*Shakesp*) *n* same as **swathe¹**.

swathe¹ /swādh/ *vt* to bind round, envelop; to bandage. ◆*n* a bandage; a wrapping. [OE *swathian*]

❑ **swath'ing-clothes** *n pl* (*Shakesp*; or another reading, **swath'ling-** or **swoth'ling-clouts**) swaddling-clothes.

swathe², **swathy** see **swath¹**.

swats /swots/ (*Scot*) *n* new ale. [OE *swatan* (pl) beer]

swatter¹ /swot'ər or swat'ər/ (*dialect*) *vi* to squatter; to splash or spill about. [Cf **squatter**]

swatter² see under **swat¹**.

sway /swā/ *vt* to cause to move swingingly or sweepingly from side to side, *usu* slowly; to cause to lean or incline; to divert; to influence by power or moral force; to wield (*archaic*); to govern, hold sway (*archaic*); to control (*archaic*); to have a preponderating influence upon (*archaic*); (*usu with up*) to hoist (*naut*). ◆ *vi* to swing; to oscillate; to swerve; to incline to one side; to have preponderating weight or influence; to rule (*archaic or poetic*); to proceed, bend one's course (*Shakesp*); to advance in hostility (*Spenser*). ◆*n* directing force or influence; preponderance, dominance; rule, supremacy; a swinging or sweeping motion; a motion to and fro or back and forth; a swerve; a rotation (*Shakesp*); (in thatching) a hazel lath laid horizontally to hold down the straw or reed. [Perh from a lost OE word, or the corresponding ON *sveigja* to bend, swing; prob partly from LGer *swājen* (Ger *schweien*) to swing]

■ **swayed** *adj* (eg of a horse) bent down in the back. **sway'er** *n*. **sway'ing** *n* and *adj*.

❑ **sway'back** *n* an abnormal downward curvature of the spine of an animal, *esp* a horse; a nervous disease of lambs causing difficulty in walking or standing. ◆ *adj* (eg of a horse) swayed. **sway'backed** *adj*.

■ **hold sway (over)** to have power, authority (over).

swayl, **swayling** see **sweal**.

Swazi /swä'zē/ *n* a people inhabiting *Swaziland* and parts of the Eastern Transvaal of South Africa; a member of this people; its Bantu language. [*Mswati*, a 19c king of this people]

swazzle or **swozzle** /swoz'l/ *n* an instrument consisting of two convex pieces of metal with a tape stretched between them, placed in the mouth to make the voice of Mr Punch in a Punch and Judy show. [Perh from Ger *schwätzen* to chatter, tattle]

sweal, **sweel** /swēl/, **swale** or **swayl** /swāl/ (*dialect*) *vt* to scorch; to singe; to roast in the skin; to burn off (eg heather and gorse, or soot in a chimney); to cause (a candle) to gutter; to waste away. ◆ *vi* to be burning hot; (of a candle) to gutter. [OE *swǣlan* (vt), *swelan* (vi) to burn]

■ **sweal'ing**, **swal'ing** or **swayl'ing** *n* and *adj*.

swear /swār/ *vi* (pat **swore** /swōr or swor/, *archaic* **sware**; *pap* **sworn** /swōrn or swōrn/ or *archaic* and *non-standard* **swōre**) to take or utter an oath; to utter indecent or blasphemous language; to utter imprecations; (eg of a cat) to utter defiant noises (*inf*); to give evidence on oath (*rare*). ◆ *vt* to assert, promise, agree to, confirm or value, on oath; to assert loudly or boldly; to invoke (*Shakesp*); to administer an oath to; to put on oath; to bind by oath; (now *usu* **swear in**) to admit to office by an oath; to bring, put or render by swearing. ◆*n* an expression that is formally an oath or a curse, or bad language generally (*inf*); a bout of swearing, bad language (*inf*); an oath (*archaic*). [OE *swerian*; Du *zweren*, Ger *schwören*]

■ **swear'er** *n* and *adj*. **swear'y** *adj* (*inf*) relating to, containing or inclined to use swear-words. **sworn** *adj* attested; bound by oath; having taken an oath; devoted, inveterate, confirmed, as if by oath.

❑ **swear'-word** *n* a word that is considered bad language.

■ **swear at** to hurl oaths and curses at; to be very incongruous with, *esp* in colour (*inf*). **swear blind** (*inf*) to assert emphatically. **swear by** to invoke as witness to an oath; to put complete confidence in. **swear in** to inaugurate by oath. **swear off** to renounce, promise to give up. **swear to** to affirm or identify on oath.

sweard /swērd/ (*Spenser*) *n* same as **sword**.

sweat /swet/ *n* the moisture excreted by the skin; moisture exuding or seeming to exude from anything; a state, fit or process of exuding sweat; exercise or treatment inducing sweat; sweating sickness (*obs*); labour; long, hard work; drudgery; fidgety anxiety; a soldier (*sl*); (in *pl*) a sweatsuit or sweatpants (*inf*, *esp* N Am). ◆ *vi* (pat and pap **sweat'ed** (or **sweat**)) to give out sweat or moisture; to do difficult, strenuous work (*inf*); to toil, drudge for poor wages; to exude; to become coated with moisture; to worry, be anxious (*inf*); to suffer penalty, smart (*obs*). ◆ *vt* to exude as, or like, sweat; to cause to sweat;

to heat (fruit, meat, etc) slowly so as to extract the juices (*cookery*); to squeeze money or extortionate interest from; to exact the utmost from; to wring evidence or confession from (*US sl*); to extract undue gains from, eg by removing gold from a coin; to compel to do hard work for meagre wages; to unite by the partial fusion of metal surfaces; to wet or soil with sweat; to worry over (*US inf*). [OE *swǣtan* to sweat; cf Ger *schweissen*; the OE noun was *swāt*]

■ **sweat'ed** *adj*. **sweat'er** *n* a person who or animal, etc that sweats; a cause of sweating, eg a diaphoretic medicine; a (heavy) jersey for leisurewear, intervals in exercise, etc (*orig* one for reducing weight by sweating); someone who sweats coins or workers; a London street ruffian in Queen Anne's time who prodded and threatened passers-by with his sword. **sweat'iness** *n*. **sweat'ing** *n* and *adj*. **sweat'y** *adj*.

❑ **sweat band** *n* the leather or similar band inside a man's hat; a band worn to absorb perspiration from the forehead; an absorbent wristlet worn by eg tennis players to prevent sweat running down to their hands. **sweat cooling** *n* (*aeronautics*) cooling a component by evaporating fluid through a porous layer. **sweated labour** *n* hard work obtained by exploitation. **sweat'er-girl** *n* (*inf*) a woman with a large bust, *usu* one wearing a tight-fitting sweater. **sweat gland** *n* any of the glands producing sweat. **sweating sickness** *n* an epidemic disorder (*usu* fatal) which ravaged Europe and *esp* England in the 15c and 16c, a violent inflammatory fever, with a fetid perspiration over the whole body. **sweating system** *n* the practice of working poor people at starvation wages, for long hours, at home or in unhealthy rooms. **sweat'pants** *n pl* (*esp* US) trousers of (*usu* thick) cotton material, with drawstring or elasticated waist and cuffs, as worn by athletes when warming up or after exercise or as leisurewear. **sweat'-shirt** or **sweat'shirt** *n* a long-sleeved knitted cotton sweater, *usu* fleecy on the inside. **sweat shop** *n* a factory or shop using sweated labour. **sweat'suit** or **sweat suit** *n* a loose-fitting suit consisting of sweater and trousers, *usu* close-fitting at wrist and ankle, worn by athletes, etc.

■ **in a cold sweat** (*fig*) in a state of terror or anxiety. **no sweat** (*inf*) words used to signify assent, or indicating that something will present no problems. **sweat blood** to work or worry extremely hard. **sweat it out** (*inf*) to endure, live through a time of danger, etc.

sweath-band /swēth'band/ (*Spenser*) *n* a swaddling-band. [**swathe¹**]

Swede /swēd/ *n* a native or citizen of *Sweden* in N Europe; (without *cap*) a Swedish turnip, a large buff-flowered, glaucous-leaved kind with yellow flesh.

■ **Swed'ish** *adj* of or relating to Sweden, its people or language. ◆*n* the Scandinavian language of Sweden; (as *pl*) the natives or people of Sweden.

❑ **Swedish massage** *n* a system of massage developed in Sweden that incorporates active exercising of muscles and joints.

Swedenborgian /swē-dn-bör'ji-ən/ *n* a follower of Emanuel *Swedenborg*, a Swedish religious teacher (1688–1772), who claimed to be in direct contact with the spiritual world, and whose followers founded the New Jerusalem Church (also *adj*).

■ **Swedenbor'gianism** *n*.

swee or **swey** /swē/ (*Scot*) *n* a sway, swerve or lurch; a children's swing; the horizontal iron bar which could be swung over an old fireplace, on which cooking vessels were hung. ◆ *vt* and *vi* to sway; to swing. [**sway**]

sweel see **sweal**.

sweeney todd /swē'ni tod/ or **sweeney** *n* rhyming slang for **flying squad** in the British police force, *esp* in London (see under **fly**).

sweeny /swē'ni/ (*vet*) *n* atrophy of the shoulder muscles of a horse, eg following nerve injury. [OE *swindan* to pine away, disappear]

sweep /swēp/ *vi* (pat and pap **swept**) to pass swiftly or forcibly, *esp* with a swinging movement or in a curve; to move with trailing or flowing drapery, hence with pomp, indignation, etc; to extend in a long curve; to range systematically or searchingly; to play a sweep stroke (*cricket*); to row with sweeps. ◆ *vt* to pass something brushingly over; to elicit by so doing (*poetic*); to pass brushingly; to wipe, clean, move or remove with a broom; to carry along or off with a long brushing stroke, swiftly and/or with force; to wipe out or remove at a stroke (often with *away* or *up*); to perform with a sweeping movement; to trail with a curving movement; to drag as with a net or rope; to search; to describe, generate or swing through (eg a curve, angle or area); to range or move over exploratively or searchingly; to play a sweep stroke at (*cricket*); to row with sweeps. ◆*n* an act of sweeping; a sweeping movement, swing; an onrush, surge; impetus; a clearance; range, compass; a curved stair; a curved drive in front of a building; that which is swept, sweepings; a sweepstake; a search; a pump-handle; a long oar; a sail of a windmill; a wire drag used in searching for shoals, mines, etc; a chimney-sweep; a cricket stroke in which the batter goes down on one knee to play the ball to the legside with a horizontal bat; a periodic survey of the audience ratings of television stations, used in fixing rates for advertising (*N Am*); a blackguard (*old sl*); sweepback (*aeronautics*). [Prob from a lost OE word related to *swāpan* to sweep, and *geswǣpe* sweepings; cf **soop** and **swoop**]

■ **sweep'er** *n* a person who, or thing which, sweeps; (in association football) a defensive player with no marking responsibility who assists the other defenders; (in cricket) a fielder positioned on the boundary in front of square to stop balls hit through the infield. **sweep'ing** *n* the action of the verb in any sense; (*usu* in *pl*) things collected by sweeping, rubbish. ◆ *adj* performing the action of sweeping in any sense; of wide scope, wholesale, indiscriminate. **sweep'ingly** *adv*. **sweep'ingness** *n*. **sweep'y** *adj* swaying, sweeping, curving.

□ **sweep'back** *n* (*aeronautics*) the angle at which an aeroplane wing is set back relatively to the axis. **sweep hand** or **sweep second hand** *n* a hand on a clock or watch that indicates seconds. **sweep'-net** or **-seine** *n* a long net paid out in a curve and dragged ashore; an insect net with a handle. **sweep'-saw** *n* a turning-saw (qv under **turn**). **sweep'stake** or **sweep'stakes** *n* a method of gambling by which participators' stakes are pooled, numbers, horses, etc assigned by lot, and prize(s) awarded accordingly on decision of event; such a prize, race, etc. **sweep'-washer** *n* a person who recovers gold or silver from the sweepings of refineries. **swept'back** *adj* sweptwing. **swept'wing** *adj* (of an aircraft, etc) having wings that are swept back.

■ **make a clean sweep** (**of**) to clear out completely; to win all the awards, prizes, etc. **sweep the board** see under **board**.

sweer or **sweir** /swēr/ (*Scot*) *adj* (also **sweered**, **sweert** or **sweirt**) slothful; loth. [OE *swǣr*, *swǣre* heavy, grievous, sluggish; cf Ger *schwer*]

■ **sweir'ness** *n*.

sweet /swēt/ *adj* having one of the fundamental varieties of taste, that of sugar, honey, ripe fruits (distinguished from *salt*, *acid* or *sour*, *bitter*, *dry*); sugary; pleasing to the taste, senses or feelings; fragrant; clear and tuneful; smoothly running; easy, free from harshness, benign; (of water) fresh, not salt; (of milk) fresh, not tainted; (of wine, ale, etc) not dry or bitter, retaining a sugary or fruity flavour; wholesome; gracious; amiable; mild, soft, gentle; delightful, charming (*inf*); all right, satisfactory (*Aust inf*); dear, beloved (*archaic*); ingratiating, often insipidly; cloying or sickly in taste, smell, etc; more or less enamoured (with *on* or *upon*; *inf*). ◆ *adv* sweetly. ◆ *n* that which is sweet; a sweet dish (pudding, fruit, etc) as a course; a sweetmeat, confection, *esp* a boiled sweet (see under **boil**[1]); (a form of address used to) a beloved person; (in *pl*) wines and cordials sweetened with syrup. ◆ *vt* (now *rare*) to sweeten. [OE *swēte*; Ger *süss*, Gr *hēdys*, L *suāvis*, Sans *svādu* sweet]

■ **sweet'en** *vt* to make sweet; to mitigate something unpleasant; to pacify, make (a person) agreeable (often with *up*). **sweet'ener** *n* a substance that sweetens, *esp* one not containing sugar; a person who sweetens; a bribe (*inf*). **sweet'ening** *n*. **sweet'ie** or **sweet'y** *n* a sweetmeat, item of confectionery; a sweetheart (*inf*); (**sweetie**; often with *cap*) a large, seedless citrus fruit with greenish-yellow skin, its pulp sweeter than that of the grapefruit. **sweet'ing** *n* a sweet apple; a darling (*archaic*). **sweet'ish** *adj*. **sweet'ishness** *n*. **sweet'ly** *adv*. **sweet'ness** *n*. **sweety** *n* see **sweetie** above.

□ **sweet alyssum** see under **alyssum**. **sweet'-and-sour'** *adj* cooked with sugar and vinegar or lemon juice; (in Oriental cookery) having a seasoning of sugar, vinegar, soy sauce, etc. **sweet'-and-twen'ty** *adj* both fair and young (after *Shakesp*, who perhaps meant only sweet indeed; see also **and twenty** under **twenty**). **sweet bay** *n* the laurel (*Laurus nobilis*); a kind of magnolia (*US*). **sweet'bread** *n* the pancreas (*stomach sweetbread*), or sometimes the thymus (*neck sweetbread*), *esp* as a food. **sweet'brier** or **sweet'briar** *n* a wild rose with fragrant foliage (*Rosa rubiginosa*). **sweet chestnut** see **chestnut**. **sweet cicely** *n* an aromatic umbelliferous plant (*Myrrhis odorata*). **sweet'corn** *n* a sweet variety of maize; the yellow kernels of this, eaten as a vegetable. **sweet Fanny Adams** see under **Fanny Adams**. **sweetfish** see **ayu**. **sweet flag** *n* an aromatic araceous pond-plant (*Acorus calamus*). **sweet gale** *n* bog myrtle, a low-growing aromatic shrub found in bogs. **sweet gas** *n* hydrocarbon gas without sulphur compounds. **sweet gum** *n* the N American liquidambar; its aromatic resin. **sweet'heart** *n* a lover or beloved. ◆ *vt* and *vi* to court. **sweetheart agreement**, **contract**, etc *n* an agreement between a trade union and an employer that excessively favours the employer, and is often concluded without the consent of higher-ranking trade union officials. **sweetheart ivy** see **shield ivy** under **shield**. **sweetheart neckline** *n* a low heart-shaped neckline on a woman's garment. **sweet'ie-pie** *n* (*inf*) a term of endearment. **sweet'ie-wife** *n* (*Scot*) a woman who sells sweets; (*esp* of an effeminate man) a gossip, scandalmonger. **sweet'lips** or **sweet'lip** *n* *sing* any of several fish of the grunt family with large fleshy lips. **sweet'meal** *adj* (of biscuits) made of wholemeal and sweetened. **sweet'meat** *n* any confection made wholly or chiefly of sugar; any sweet food (*obs*). **sweet nothings** see under **nothing**. **sweet'-oil** *n* olive oil; rape-oil; any oil of mild pleasant taste. **sweet pea** *n* a S European papilionaceous garden plant (*Lathyrus odoratus*)

with bright-coloured fragrant flowers. **sweet pepper** see under **pepper**. **sweet potato** *n* batata, a tropical and subtropical twining plant (*Ipomoea batatas*) of the convolvulus family; its large sweetish edible tuber. **sweet-sa'voured** *adj* having a sweet smell. **sweet-scent'ed** *adj* having a sweet smell. **sweet'sop** *n* a tropical American evergreen (*Annona squamosa*); its pulpy fruit. **sweet spot** *n* (*sport*) the spot on a golf club, tennis or squash racket, etc where, for best effect and control, the ball should ideally make contact. **sweet'-stuff** *n* confectionery; sweetheart (*inf*, as a term of address). **sweet sultan** see under **sultan**. **sweet talk** *n* flattery, persuasion. **sweet'-talk** *vt* (*inf*) to coax, flatter, persuade. **sweet-tem'pered** *adj* having a mild, amiable disposition. **sweet-toothed'** *adj* fond of sweet things. **sweet'water** *n* a very sweet white grape. **sweet'-water** *adj* freshwater. **sweet william** *n* a garden pink (*Dianthus barbatus*) with bearded petals. **sweet willow** *n* any of various trees, eg bay-leaved sweet willow (*Salix pentandra*); sweet gale. **sweet'wood** *n* a name for various S American and West Indian lauraceous trees. **sweet'-wort** *n* (in beer-making) sweet-flavoured wort, before the addition of hops.

■ **a sweet tooth** a fondness for sweet things. **keep someone sweet** to ensure that someone remains well-disposed towards one. **sweetness and light** an appearance of mildness, reasonableness, etc.

sweir, **sweirt**, etc see **sweer**.

swelchie /swel'hhi/ (*Orkney*) *n* a whirlpool; a tidal race. [ON *svelgr*, cf **swallow**[1]]

swell /swel/ *vi* (pat **swelled**; pap **swelled** or **swollen** /swōln or swōl'ən/, sometimes **swoln**) to expand; to increase in volume; to be inflated; to bulge out; to grow louder; to rise into waves; to heave; to well up; to rise and fall in loudness; to be bombastic; to be elated or dilated with emotion; to give a feeling of expansion or welling up. ◆ *vt* to augment; to expand; to dilate; to fill full; to louden; to elate. ◆ *n* the act, power, habit or condition of swelling; distension; a heaving; a bulge; an enlargement (*rare*); a loudening; a device in an organ for gradually varying loudness; a crescendo followed by a diminuendo (*music*); an area of gently rising ground, an incline; a dandy, a fashionable or finely dressed person (*sl*); a member of the governing class, a bigwig, an adept (*sl*). ◆ *adj* (*sl*, *esp US*) a vague word of commendation (as being of, of the nature of, or befitting a swell). [OE *swellan*; Ger *schwellen*]

■ **swell'dom** *n* (*sl*) the fashionable world. **swelled** *adj*. **swell'er** *n*. **swell'ing** *adj* and *n*. **swell'ingly** *adv*. **swell'ish** *adj* (*sl*) foppish, dandified. **swollen** /swōl'ən/ *adj*.

□ **swell box** *n* (in an organ) a chamber containing a set of pipes or reeds, which is opened or closed by the swell. **swelled head** *n* self-conceit, *esp* in someone carried away by success. **swelled-head'ed**, **swell-head'ed** or **swollen-head'ed** *adj* conceited. **swell'-mob** *n* (*obs sl*) well-dressed pickpockets collectively. **swell-mobs'man** *n* (*obs sl*). **swell organ** *n* the pipes enclosed in the swell box.

swelt /swelt/ *vi* (pat **swelt'ed** or (*Spenser*) **swelt**) to die (*obs* or *dialect*); to faint (*Spenser*, *obs Scot*); to swelter (*obs*); to pass like a fever (*Spenser*). [OE *sweltan* to die]

■ **swelt'er** *vi* to endure great heat; to sweat copiously or feel faint or oppressed by heat; to exude (in *passive*; *archaic*). ◆ *vt* to overpower, as with heat; to exude (*archaic*; *Shakesp*). ◆ *n* a sweltering; a sweating; sweltered venom (*archaic*). **swelt'ered** *adj*. **swelt'ering** *n* and *adj*. **swelt'ry** *adj* sultry; oppressive or oppressed with heat.

swept /swept/ pat and pap of **sweep**.

□ **sweptback**, **sweptwing** see under **sweep**.

swerf see **swarf**[2].

Swerga see **Swarga**.

swerve[1] /swûrv/ *vi* to turn aside; to deviate, *esp* to change course suddenly; to give way, shrink (*Milton*); to swarm, scramble (*Dryden*). ◆ *vt* to deflect; to cause (a ball) to swerve in the air. ◆ *n* a turning aside; a (sudden) deviation; a deflection; the act or trick of making the ball swerve in the air (*cricket*). [ME; the OE *sweorfan* to rub, file, scour, is not known to have had this sense]

■ **swerve'less** *adj* unswerving. **swerv'er** *n*. **swerv'ing** *n* and *adj*.

swerve[2] see **swarf**[2].

sweven /swev'n/ (*obs*) *n* a dream. [OE *swefn*]

swey see **swee**.

SWG or **swg** *abbrev*: standard wire gauge, (a measure in) the UK scale of standard wire thicknesses.

swidden /swid'ən/ (*agric*) *n* an area of land made cultivable by cutting or burning off the vegetative cover. [ON *svithin*, pap of *svitha* to burn]

swift[1] /swift/ *adj* fleet; rapid; speedy; prompt. ◆ *adv* swiftly. ◆ *n* a bird (*Apus apus* or *Cypselus apus*) superficially like a swallow but structurally nearer the hummingbirds and goatsuckers; any bird of its genus or family; the common newt (now *dialect*); a reel for winding yarn; the main cylinder of a carding machine; a rapid (obs). [OE swift, from same root as **swoop**]

■ **swift'let** n a species of swift (genus Collocalia), the builder of edible nests. **swift'ly** adv. **swift'ness** n.

□ **swift'-foot** or **-footed** adj. **swift fox** n a small fox (Vulpes velox) of the N American plains. **swift'-winged** adj.

swift² /swift/ (naut) vt to tighten with a rope. [Prob Scand or LGer]

■ **swift'er** n a rope used to tighten or keep a thing in its place.

Swiftian /swif'ti-ən/ adj of, or in the style of, the (esp satirical) writings of Jonathan Swift (1667–1745), Anglo-Irish writer and cleric.

swig¹ /swig/ n a deep draught of (esp alcoholic) drink; toast and ale (archaic); a wassail (Oxford University). ◆ vt (**swigg'ing**; **swigged**) to take a swig or swigs of or from. ◆ vi to drink, take swigs. [Origin unknown]

■ **swigg'er** n.

swig² /swig/ n (naut) a pulley with ropes not parallel. ◆ vt to tighten by hauling at right angles (naut); to castrate (eg a ram) by ligature. [Prob connected with **swag**]

swill /swil/ vt or vi to rinse (often with out); to dash water over or around; to wash; to drink greedily or in quantity. ◆ n a large draught of liquor; hogwash. [OE swilian to wash]

■ **swill'er** n. **swill'ing** n and adj.

□ **swill'-tub** n a tub for hogwash.

swim /swim/ vi (**swimm'ing**; **swam** /swam/ or old **swum**; **swum** (Shakesp, etc, **swam**)) to propel oneself in water (or other liquid); to float; to come to the surface; to travel or be conveyed by water; to be suffused; to be immersed or steeped; to glide smoothly; to be dizzy. ◆ vt to pass or cross by swimming; to cover (a distance) by swimming; to cause to swim or float; to test for witchcraft by immersion (hist). ◆ n an act, performance or spell of swimming; any motion like swimming; the general movement or current of affairs; a dizzy state; a crossing-place for swimmers (dialect); a place where many fishes swim; the air-bladder of a fish (obs). [OE swimman; Ger schwimmen]

■ **swimm'able** adj capable of being swum. **swimm'er** n. **swimm'eret** n a crustacean's abdominal appendage used in swimming. **swimm'ing** n and adj. **swimm'ingly** adv in a gliding manner as if swimming; smoothly, successfully (inf). **swimm'ingness** n the state of swimming; a melting look, tearfulness. **swimm'y** adj inclined to dizziness.

□ **swim bladder** n a fish's air-bladder. **swimm'ing-bath** n (also in pl) an indoor swimming-pool. **swimm'ing-bell** n a medusoid modified as a swimming organ. **swimming costume** n a swimsuit. **swimming hole** n a natural pool or lake suitable for swimming in. **swimm'ing-pond** n. **swimm'ing-pool** n an artificial pool for swimming in. **swim'suit** n a garment worn for swimming; now esp a one-piece woman's garment of stretch fabric, covering the torso only. **swim'wear** n (in shops, fashion magazines, etc) garments worn for swimming.

■ **in the swim** in the main current (of affairs, business, etc). **swim with** (or **against**) **the stream** or **tide** to conform to (or go against) normal behaviour, opinions, etc.

swindge (Shakesp and Milton) same as **swinge¹**.

□ **swindge'-buckler** (Shakesp) same as **swinge-buckler** (see under **swinge¹**).

swindle /swin'dl/ vt and vi to cheat. ◆ n a fraud; anything not really what it appears to be. [Ger Schwindler a giddy-minded person, swindler, from schwindeln to be giddy]

■ **swin'dler** n a cheat. **swin'dling** n and adj.

swine /swīn/ n (pl **swine**) a pig; a term of strong abuse; a sensual person (archaic). [OE swīn a pig; Ger Schwein, L (adj) suīnus, from sūs, Gr hȳs]

■ **swine'hood** n the status of a swine. **swin'ery** n a place where pigs are kept; swinishness; swine collectively. **swin'ish** adj of or like swine; sensual (archaic); filthy; voracious; beastly. **swin'ishly** adv. **swin'ishness** n.

□ **swine'-drunk** adj (Shakesp) extremely drunk. **swine fever** n hog-cholera, a highly contagious disease of pigs due to a virus. **swine'-fish** n the wolffish. **swine flu** n a highly contagious strain of influenza that affects pigs and can be transmitted to, and between, humans. **swine'herd** n (archaic) a person who herds pigs. **swine'-keeping** n. **swine'-pox** n a form of chickenpox; a viral skin disease of pigs. **swine's cress** n a cruciferous weed of waste places (Senebiera or Coronopus); applied to various other plants. **swine's succory** n a small plant (genus Arnoseris) related to chicory. **swine'stone** n stinkstone. **swine'-sty** n (archaic or dialect) a pig-sty. **swine vesicular disease** n a highly contagious viral disease of pigs, causing sores on the skin of the feet, legs and mouth.

Swing /swing/ (hist) n a fictitious captain in whose name rick-burners sent threatening letters to users of threshing mills about 1830–33; the movement, operations or methods of the rick-burners.

■ **swing'ism** n.

swing /swing/ vi (pat **swung** or (rare) **swang**; pap **swung**) to sway or wave to and fro, as a body hanging freely; to amuse oneself on a swing; to oscillate; to hang; to be hanged; to sweep, wheel, sway; to swerve; to move with a swaying gait; (of a ship) to turn round (eg to test the compass); to attract, excite or be perfectly appropriate to place or mood (inf); (of a person) to be thoroughly responsive (to jazz, any of the arts or any aspect of living) (inf); to be lively or up-to-date (inf); to take part in sexual activity on an uncommitted basis (inf). ◆ vt to cause to swing; to set swinging; to control; to sway; to hurl, whirl; to brandish (eg a weapon); to transport in suspension (eg an object suspended from a crane); to move in a sweep; (of a bell) to sound or send out (sound) by swinging; to indicate by an oscillation; to impart swing to; to perform as swing-music; to fix up so as to hang freely; to influence the result of (eg a doubtful election, decision, etc) in favour of an individual or party; to arrange, fix (inf). ◆ n an act, manner, etc or spell of swinging; oscillating, waving, sweeping; motion to and fro; a shift from one position, etc to a markedly different one (lit and fig); the sweep or compass of a swinging body; the sweep of a golf club, bat, or the like; a punch delivered with a swing of the arm; sway; scope, free indulgence; impetus; vigorous sweeping rhythm; big-band jazz music with strong rhythm and improvisations, as played in the 1930s and 1940s (also **swing'-music**); a suspended seat or carriage for the amusement of swinging; a reversal of fortune; the movement of voters from one party to another as compared with the previous election; the act or trick of making the ball swerve in the air (cricket). [OE swingan; Ger schwingen]

■ **swing'er** /swing'ər/ n a person or thing that swings; a ball bowled so as to swerve in the air (cricket); a badly centred gramophone record; a lively and up-to-date person (inf); a person engaging freely in sexual activity, usu in groups (inf); either of the middle pair in a team of six horses; a Hindu devotee who swings from hooks in his flesh. **swinging** /swing'ing/ n the act of moving to and fro in suspension, esp as a pastime; hanging (inf); the practice of unrestrained sexual activity, esp in groups, swapping partners, etc (inf); hanging by hooks, as by a Hindu devotee. ◆ adj swaying; turning; with a swing; having a free easy motion; with it, fully alive to, and appreciative of, the most recent trends and fashions in living (inf); up-to-date (inf); lively (inf); sexually promiscuous, esp indulging in partner-swapping or group sex (inf). **swing'ingly** adv. **swingom'eter** n a device which shows the direction and extent of the current swing of the counted votes in an election. **swing'y** adj (inf) having swing.

□ **swing'arm** n the part of a motorcycle chassis to which the rear wheel is attached. **swing'-back** n a reaction; a camera back that can be tilted. **swing'beat** n a type of dance music influenced by hip-hop, rap music, and rhythm and blues. **swing'bin** n a rubbish bin with a lid that opens when pushed and swings shut. **swing'boat** n a boat-shaped swinging carriage for fairs, etc. **swing bridge** n a bridge that may be opened by swinging it to one side. **swing'-by** n the passing of a spacecraft near a planet in order to use its gravitational field to change course. **swing door** n a door (usu one of a pair) that opens either way and swings shut by itself. **swing'-handle** n a usu semicircular or arched handle, as on a pail or some kettles, so attached at both ends that it can swing to one side. **swing'ing-boom** n (naut) the spar that stretches the foot of a lower studding-sail. **swing'ing-post** n the post to which a gate is hung. **swing-music** see **swing** (n) above. **swing'-plough** n a plough without a fore-wheel under the beam. **swing'-shelf** n a hanging shelf. **swing shift** n (US) the work shift between the day and night shifts (eg from mid-afternoon until midnight); the workers allocated to this shift; the workers employed to take irregular shifts over a seven-day week to enable other workers to work a regular five-day week. **swing'-stock** n an upright timber, with a blunt upper edge for swingling flax on (also **swing'ing-block**). **swing'-swang** n a complete (to and fro) oscillation. **swingtail cargo aircraft** n an aircraft with tail that swings aside to give access to the full cross-section of the fuselage for rapid loading and unloading of cargo. **swing'tree** n a whippletree. **swing vote** n (US) a casting vote; a vote that determines the outcome of a ballot. **swing'-wheel** n the wheel that drives a clock pendulum. **swing'-wing** (**aircraft**) n variable-geometry aircraft.

■ **get** (**back**) **into the swing of things** to become (re-)accustomed to a routine. **in full swing** in fully active operation; in mid-career. **swing by** to arrive or visit casually, often on the way elsewhere. **swings and roundabouts** a situation in which advantages and disadvantages cancel each other out. **swing the lead** see under **lead²**.

swinge¹ /swinj/ vt (prp **swinge'ing**) to beat (archaic or dialect); to chastise (obs); to lash, sway, flourish (obs). [ME swenge, from OE swengan to shake, causative of swingan to swing]

■ **swinge'ing** *adj* (*inf*) great, huge, thumping; severe, drastic. **swinge'ingly** *adv*. **swinger** /swinj'ər/ *n* (*inf*; *archaic* and *rare*) any great or astonishing person or thing; a bold lie, a whopper.
❑ **swinge'-buckler** *n* (*obs*) a swashbuckler.

swinge² /swinj/ (*Spenser*) *vt* same as **singe**.

swingism see under **Swing**.

swingle /swing'gl/ *n* a scutching tool; the swipple of a flail. ◆ *vt* to scutch. [Cf OE *swingell* stroke, scourge, rod, and MDu *swinghel*]
■ **swing'ling** *n*.
❑ **swing'le-bar** or **swing'letree** *n* a whippletree; a swing-stock. **swing'le-hand** *n* a scutching tool. **swing'ling-stock** *n* a swing-stock.

swingometer see under **swing**.

swinish, etc see under **swine**.

swink /swingk/ (*archaic*) *vi* to toil. ◆ *n* toil. [OE *swinc* (noun), *swincan* (verb)]
■ **swinked** (*Milton* **swink't**) *adj* toilworn, fatigued.

swipe /swīp/ *vt* to purloin, steal (*inf*); to strike with a swipe; to pass (a credit card etc) through an electronic reading terminal (see also **wipe**); to gulp (*archaic sl*). ◆ *vi* to make a swipe; to sweep for old anchors. ◆ *n* a sweeping stroke; a swath (*archaic*). [OE *swipian* to beat]
■ **swip'er** *n*. **swipes** *n* (*sl*) bad or spoilt beer; small beer. **swip'ey** *adj* (*rare*) fuddled with malt liquor.
❑ **swipe card** *n* a credit card, charge card, etc with a magnetic strip suitable for swiping through a terminal.

swipple /swip'l/ *n* a swingle or striking part of a flail. [Cf **swipe** and **sweep**]

swire /swīr/ *n* a neck (*obs*); (in place names) a hollow between two hills. [OE *swēora* (Scot and N Eng *swīra*) neck]

swirl /swûrl/ *n* an eddy; a whirl; a curl. ◆ *vt* to whirl; to wind. ◆ *vi* to eddy; to whirl; to spin. [Orig Scot; cf Norw dialect *svirla*]
■ **swirl'y** *adj*.
❑ **swirl vanes** *n pl* (*aeronautics*) vanes that cause a swirling motion in the air entering a gas-turbine combustion chamber.

swish¹ /swish/ *n* a prolonged and rushing sibilant sound, such as is produced by branches being swept to and fro by the wind, or by fabric brushing along the ground; a movement producing such a sound; a dashing spray; a cane or birch; a male homosexual, *esp* if effeminate (*US derog inf*). ◆ *vt* to whisk with a swish; to flog, thrash. ◆ *vi* to make or go with a swish. ◆ *adv* with a swish. [Imit]
■ **swish'er** *n*. **swish'ing** *n* and *adj*. **swish'y** *adj*.

swish² /swish/ (*inf*) *adj* smart, stylish. [Origin unknown]

Swiss /swis/ *adj* of or relating to Switzerland or its people. ◆ *n* (pl **Swiss** (formerly **Swiss'es**)) a native or citizen of Switzerland; the High German dialect spoken by most of the Swiss. [Fr *Suisse*, OHGer *swīz*]
■ **Swit'zer** *n* (*archaic*) a Swiss; a Swiss (or other) mercenary or member of a bodyguard.
❑ **Swiss army knife** *n* a pocket knife with a blade and various other tools that all fold into the handle. **Swiss ball** *n* a large inflatable plastic ball used in various fitness exercises. **Swiss chard** see under **chard**. **Swiss cheese plant** *n* a tropical climbing plant (*Monstera deliciosa*) with large, thick, perforated leaves, often grown as a house plant. **Swiss Guards** *n pl* a body of Swiss mercenaries in the French guards from 1616, wiped out in the Revolution; the Pope's bodyguard. **Swiss roll** *n* a thin cake of sponge rolled up with jam, cream, etc; a flexible floating pier.

swissing /swis'ing/ *n* ordinary calendering of cloth. [Origin unknown]

switch /swich/ (*Shakesp* **swits** /swits/) *n* a device for making, breaking or changing an electric circuit; a changeover (*esp* in cards to another suit, led or called); *orig* a long flexible twig; a tapering riding whip; a rod, cane; an application of a switch; a brushing blow; a whisk, jerk; a tool for beating eggs or cream; a tress, *usu* false; the tuft of an animal's tail; a movable rail for shunting; a switchboard; a turn of a switch. ◆ *vt* to exchange; to strike with a switch; to drive with, or as if with, a switch; to whisk, jerk, lash; to beat up, whip (eg an egg or cream); to prune; to shunt; to divert; to turn (off, on, or to another circuit); to race (a horse) under the name of another horse. ◆ *vi* to change over; to use a switch; to turn aside; to whisk. [Earlier *swits* (Shakespeare), *switz*; prob from Du or LGer]
■ **switch'able** *adj*. **switch'er** *n*. **switch'ing** *n*. **switch'y** *adj*.
❑ **switch'back** *n orig* a zigzag mountain railway on which the train shunted back at each stage; an up-and-down track on which cars rise by the momentum gained in coming down; an up-and-down road (also *fig*). **switch'blade** or **switchblade knife** *n* a flick-knife. **switch'board** *n* a board or frame bearing apparatus for making or breaking an electric current or circuit; a board for connecting telephones. **switch'gear** *n* the apparatus that controls the switches in the electric circuits of a power station or a motor vehicle. **switch'grass** *n* a N American grass

(*Panicum virgatum*). **switch hit** *n* (*cricket*) an attacking shot played by a batsman who has reversed his or her stance as the bowler delivers the ball. **switch hitter** *n* a baseball player who is able to bat right-handed or left-handed; a bisexual (*N Am sl*). **switch'man** *n* a pointsman. **switch'-over** *n* the action of the verb; a changeover. **switch'-plant** *n* a plant with long slim green shoots, the leaves reduced or sparse. **switch selling** *n* the practice of arousing the interest of a prospective buyer by offering a low-priced article, then describing the shortcomings of the cheap article and trying to sell the customer a more expensive one.
■ **switched on** aware of and responsive to all that is most up-to-date (*inf*); under the influence of drugs (*old inf*). **switch off** to turn off (an electrical device); to cease paying attention. **switch on** to turn on (an electrical device); to assume (false emotion, insincere charm, etc) at will.

switchel /swich'əl/ (*N Am*) *n* treacle-beer, a drink of molasses and water, etc; (in Newfoundland) cold tea. [Origin unknown]

swith /swith/ (*obs*) *adv* quickly; at once. ◆ *interj* away. [OE *swīthe* very]

swither /swidh'ər/ (*Scot*) *vi* to be undecided. ◆ *n* indecision; a flurry. [Poss OE *swethrian* to subside]

swits see **switch**.

Switzer see under **Swiss**.

swive /swīv/ (*archaic*) *vt* to make love to, have sexual intercourse with (a female). [Appar OE *swifan*, see **swivel**]

swivel /swiv'(ə)l/ *n* a ring or link that turns round on a pin or neck; a swivel-gun. ◆ *vt* and *vi* (**swiv'elling**; **swiv'elled**) to turn (as if) on a pin or pivot. [OE *swīfan* to move quickly, to turn round]
❑ **swiv'elblock** *n* a block on which a swivel is mounted. **swiv'el-chair** *n* a chair with a seat that swivels round. **swiv'el-eye** *n* (*inf*) a squint-eye. **swiv'el-gun** *n* a gun that turns on a pivot. **swiv'el-hook** *n* a hook secured to anything by means of a swivel.

swivet /swiv'it/ (*dialect*) *n* a state of nervous agitation. [Origin unknown]

swiz /swiz/ or **swizzle** /swiz'l/ (*inf*) *n* a fraud; a great disappointment. ◆ *vt* to defraud, cheat. [Poss **swindle**]

swizzle¹ /swiz'l/ (*inf* and *dialect*) *n* a mixed or compounded drink containing rum or other spirit. ◆ *vi* to drink to excess. ◆ *vt* to mix or swirl, as with a swizzle-stick. [Origin unknown]
❑ **swizzle'-stick** *n* a stick or whisk used to stir a drink.

swizzle² see **swiz**.

SWL (*Brit*) *abbrev* : safe working load (for eg a derrick).

swob, swobber, etc same as **swab, swabber**, etc.

swollen, swoln see **swell**.

swoon /swoon/, also (*archaic* and *poetic*) **sound** /sownd/, **swoun** /swown/ or **swound** /swownd/ *n* a fainting fit; a sleep (*Spenser*). ◆ *vi* to faint; to be languorous, give a feeling of fainting (*poetic*); to subside (*poetic*). [Prob from ME *iswowen*, from OE *geswōgen* (pap; other parts unknown) in a swoon, wrongly analysed as *in swoon*]
■ **swooned** *adj* in a swoon. **swoon'ing** *n* and *adj*. **swoon'ingly** *adv*.

swoop /swoop/ *vi* to come down with a sweeping rush; to rush suddenly; to sweep along (*obs*). ◆ *vt* (*obs*) to pounce on, snatch with a sweep, *esp* on the wing. ◆ *n* an act of swooping; a sudden onslaught. [Appar OE *swāpan* to sweep; perh infl by **soop**]
❑ **swoop'stake-like** see under **soop**.
■ **at one fell swoop** (*Shakesp*, *Macbeth* IV.3.218) by one terrible blow; (also **in** or **with**) by one complete decisive action; suddenly.

swoosh /swŭsh or swoosh/ *n* a noise of or resembling a rush of air, water, etc. ◆ *vi* to make this noise. [Prob imit, or from **swish¹** and **swoop**]

swop, swopper, swopping, swopt see **swap**.

sword /sörd or sōrd/ *n* a weapon with a long blade, sharp on one or both edges, for cutting or thrusting; a blade or flat rod resembling a sword; a swordfish's snout; destruction or death by the sword or by war; war; military force; the emblem of vengeance or justice, or of authority and power; (in *pl*) a suit in the tarot pack. ◆ *vi* (*archaic*) to wield a sword. [OE *sweord*; Ger *Schwert*]
■ **sword'er** *n* (*archaic*) a gladiator; an assassin, a cut-throat; a swordsman. **sword'less** *adj*. **sword'like** *adj*.
❑ **sword'-and-buck'ler** *adj* fought or armed with sword and buckler. **sword'-and-san'dal** *adj* of or relating to a genre of film depicting swashbuckling events in the ancient world. **sword'-and-sor'cery** *adj* of or relating to a genre of fiction generally set in a milieu in which no firearms exist and magic is used. **sword'-arm, -hand** *n* the arm, and hand, that wield the sword. **sword'-bayonet** *n* a bayonet shaped somewhat like a sword, and used as one. **sword'-bean** *n* an Indian papilionaceous plant (genus *Canavalia*) with long sword-shaped edible pods; its seed. **sword'-bearer** *n* a public officer who carries the

sword of state. **sword'-belt** *n* a belt from which the sword is hung. **sword'bill** *n* a S American hummingbird with a bill longer than its body. **sword'-blade** *n* the blade of a sword. **sword'-breaker** *n* an old weapon for grasping and breaking an adversary's sword. **sword'-cane** or **-stick** *n* a hollow cane or stick containing a sword. **sword'craft** *n* swordsmanship; military power. **sword'-cut** *n* a cut with the edge of a sword; a wound or scar so produced. **sword dance** *n* a dance performed sword in hand or among or over swords. **sword'-dollar** *n* (*hist*) a Scottish silver coin of James VI, worth 30s Scots (2s 6d English), with a sword on the reverse. **sword fern** *n* a fern with long sword-shaped fronds. **sword'fish** *n* a large fish (*Xiphias* or other genus of the family Xiphiidae) with upper jaw compressed and prolonged as a stabbing weapon. **sword grass** *n* a name for many plants with sword-shaped leaves. **sword'-guard** *n* the part of a sword-hilt that protects the bearer's hand. **sword-hand** see **sword-arm** above. **sword knot** *n* a ribbon tied to the hilt of a sword. **sword'-law** *n* government by the sword. **sword lily** *n* the gladiolus. **sword'man** *n* a swordsman; a fighting man. **sword'play** *n* fencing. **sword'player** *n*. **sword'proof** *adj* capable of resisting the blow or thrust of a sword. **sword'-rack** *n* a rack for holding swords. **sword'-shaped** *adj*. **sword side** same as **spear side** (see under **spear**). **swords'man** or **swords'woman** *n* a person who is skilled in the use of a sword. **swords'manship** *n*. **sword-stick** see **sword-cane** above. **sword'-swallower** *n* a performer who inserts the blade of a sword inside his or her throat. **sword'tail** *n* a small Central American freshwater Cyprinodont fish with a swordlike tail-lobe.
■ **cross swords with** see under **cross**. **put to the sword** (of armies, etc) to kill (prisoners, etc) by the sword; to defeat utterly. **the sword of Damocles** /dam'ə-klēz/ the visible prospect of imminent calamity (from *Damocles*, the Syracuse courtier, forced to sit through a feast with a sword suspended over his head by a single hair).

swore, sworn see **swear**.

SWOT (*marketing*) *abbrev* : strengths, weaknesses, opportunities and *t*hreats (considered in the analysis of a product).

swot or **swat** /swot/ (*sl*) *vt* and *vi* (**swott'ing** or **swatt'ing**; **swott'ed** or **swatt'ed**) to study hard. ◆ *n* hard study; a person who swots. [**sweat**]
■ **swott'er** or **swatt'er** *n*. **swott'ing** or **swatt'ing** *n*. **swott'y** or **swatt'y** *adj*.

swothling-clouts see **swathing-clothes** under **swathe¹**.

swoun, swound archaic or poetic forms of **swoon**. —The forms **swoune, swownd** and **swowne** are used by Spenser.

swounds, 'swounds same as **zounds**.

swozzle see **swazzle**.

SWP *abbrev* : Socialist Workers' Party.

SWRI *abbrev* : Scottish Women's Rural Institute.

swum /swum/ *pap* and old-fashioned *pat* of **swim**.

swung /swung/ *pat* and *pap* of **swing**.
❑ **swung dash** *n* (*printing*) the sign B used to represent a word that has already been printed.

swy /swī/ (*Aust sl*) *n* the Australian game of two-up (also **swy game** or **swy'-up**); a two-year prison sentence. [Ger *zwei* two]

SY *abbrev* : Seychelles (IVR).

sy- see **syn-**.

Syalon® /sī'ə-lon/ *n* a hard, strong, light, ceramic material for use in high-temperature environments, eg gas turbines and car engines. [*si*licon, *al*umina, *oxy-* *n*itrides (its components)]

Sybarite /sib'ə-rīt/ *n* an inhabitant of *Sybaris*, a Greek city in ancient Italy, on the Gulf of Tarentum, noted for luxury; a person devoted to luxury. ◆ *adj* of or relating to the Sybarites; devoted to luxury.
■ **Sybaritic** /-rit'ik/ or **Sybarit'ical** *adj*. **Sybarit'ish** *adj*. **Sybarit'ism** *n*. —All words also without *cap*.

sybbe see **sib**.

sybil same as **sibyl**.

sybo, syboe or **sybow** /sī'bō or sī'bi/ (*Scot*) *n* (*pl* **sy'boes** or **sy'bows**) a cibol; a young or spring onion. [**cibol**]

sybotic /sī-bot'ik/ (*rare*) *adj* relating to a swineherd. [Gr *sybōtēs* swineherd, from *sȳs* swine, and *boskein* to feed, tend]
■ **sybotism** /sib'ə-tizm/ *n*.

sycamine /sik'ə-mīn/ (*Bible*) *n* the mulberry tree. [Gr *sȳkaminos*, of Semitic origin, infl by *sȳkon* a fig]

sycamore /sik'ə-mōr or -mör/ *n* a tree of the maple family (*Acer pseudoplatanus*) called in Scotland the plane (formerly **syc'omore**); a kind of fig tree (*Ficus sycomorus*; also **sycomore** or **sycomore fig**); (in the USA) any true plane (genus *Platanus*). [Gr *sȳkomoros*, from *sȳkon* a fig, and *moron* black mulberry]

syce, sice or **saice** /sīs/ (*esp Ind*) *n* a groom, mounted attendant; a chauffeur. [Ar *sā'is*]

sycee /sī-sē'/ *n* silver ingots used as Chinese money (also **sycee silver**). [Chin (Cantonese) *sai si*]

sycomore see **sycamore**.

syconium /sī-kō'ni-əm/ (*bot*) *n* a multiple fruit in which the true fruits (the pips) are enclosed in a hollow fleshy receptacle, eg the fig. [Gr *sȳkon* a fig]

sycophant /sik'ō-fənt or sik'ə-, also *-fant*/ *n* a servile flatterer; a common informer (*Gr hist*). [Gr *sȳkophantēs* an informer, swindler, confidential agent, from *sȳkon* a fig, and *phainein* to show; variously but unsatisfactorily explained]
■ **syc'ophancy** *n* the behaviour of a sycophant; obsequious flattery; servility; mean tale-bearing (*Gr hist*). **sycophantic** /-fant'ik/ or (*obs*) **sycophant'ical** *adj*. **sycophant'ically** *adv*. **syc'ophantish** (or /-fant'ish/) *adj*. **syc'ophantishly** *adv*. **syc'ophantize** or **-ise** *vi* to play the sycophant. **syc'ophantry** *n* the arts of the sycophant.

sycosis /sī-kō'sis/ (*med*) *n* inflammation of the hair follicles, *esp* of the beard. [Gr *sȳkōsis* a fig-shaped ulcer, from *sȳkon* a fig]

Sydenham's chorea /sid'ə-nəmz ko-rē'ə/ *n* a neurological disorder that occurs in the course of acute rheumatic fever, involving irregular involuntary movements of the limbs and face. [Thomas *Sydenham* (1624–89), English physician]

Sydneysider /sid'ni-sī-dər/ *n* a person who comes from or is resident in *Sydney*, Australia, or the surrounding area.

sye /sī/ (now *dialect*) *vt* to strain. ◆ *n* a sieve; a milk-strainer. [OE *sīon, sēon* to strain]

syen a Shakespearean spelling of **scion**.

syenite /sī'ə-nīt/ *n* a coarse-grained plutonic rock composed of orthoclase and a ferromagnesian mineral, *usu* hornblende. [L *syēnītēs* (*lapis*) a hornblende granite (not syenite) found at Aswan (Gr *Syēnē*) in Egypt]
■ **syenitic** /-it'ik/ *adj* relating to *Syene* in Egypt; relating to syenite.

SYHA *abbrev* : Scottish Youth Hostels Association.

syke see **sike¹**.

syker /sik'ər/ (*Spenser*) *adv* surely. [**sicker**]

syl. *abbrev* : syllable; syllabus.

syl- see **syn-**.

syllable /sil'ə-bl/ *n* a segment of speech uttered by a (more or less) single effort of the voice, forming a spoken word or part of a word; (loosely, *usu* with a *neg*) a single sound or word, a murmur. ◆ *vt* to express by syllables, utter articulately. [L *syllaba*, from Gr *syllabē*, from *syn* with, and *lab-*, root of *lambanein* to take; *-le* as in principle, participle]
■ **syll'abary** *n* a (system of writing composed of a) set of symbols representing syllables (also **syllabā'rium**). **syllabic** /sil-ab'ik/ *adj* of or constituting a syllable or syllables; syllable by syllable; based on a fixed number of syllables. **syllab'ical** *adj* (*obs*) syllabic. **syllab'ically** *adv*. **syllab'icate** *vt* to syllabify. **syllabicā'tion** *n* syllabification. **syllabicity** /-is'i-ti/ *n*. **syllab'ics** *n pl* verse patterned not by stresses but by syllables. **syllabificā'tion** *n* pronunciation as a syllable; division into syllables. **syllab'ify** *vt* to divide into syllables. **syll'abism** *n* use of a syllabary; division into syllables. **syll'abize** or **-ise** *vt* to form or divide into syllables; to sing to syllables. **syll'abled** *adj* having (in compounds, so many) syllables.
❑ **syllabic verse** or **metre** *n* syllabics.
■ **in words of one syllable** (*inf*) very simply, bluntly.

syllabub or (*rare*) **sillabub** /sil'ə-bub/ *n* a dish of cream curdled (eg with wine), flavoured and frothed up; anything frothy or insubstantial. [Origin obscure]

syllabus /sil'ə-bəs/ *n* (*pl* **syll'abuses** or **syll'abi** /-bī/) an abstract or programme, eg of a series of lectures or a course of studies; either of two catalogues of doctrinal positions or practices condemned by the Roman Catholic Church (produced in 1864 and 1907). [Orig a misprint for L *sittybas*, accusative plural of *sittyba*, Gr *sittybā* a book-label]

syllepsis /si-lep'sis/ *n* (*pl* **syllep'ses** /-sēz/) a figure in rhetoric by which a word does duty in a sentence in the same syntactical relation to two or more words but has a different sense in relation to each. [Gr *syllēpsis* a taking together, from *syn* together, and the root of *lambanein* to take]
■ **syllep'tic** or **syllep'tical** *adj*. **syllep'tically** *adv*.

sylloge /sil'ə-jē/ *n* a collection or summary. [Gr *syllogē*]

syllogism /sil'ə-ji-zm/ *n* a logical argument in three propositions, two premises and a conclusion that follows necessarily from them; deductive reasoning; a clever, subtle or specious argument.

[Gr *syllogismos*, from *syllogizesthai*, from *syn* together, and *logizesthai* to reckon, from *logos* speech, reason]

■ **syllogistic** /-*jist'ik*/ *adj* of, relating to or consisting of syllogisms (also **syllogist'ical**). ◆ *n* (often *pl*) the branch of logic concerned with syllogisms. **syllogist'ically** *adv*. **syllogization** or **-s-** /-*jī-zā'shan*/ *n*. **syll'ogize** or **-ise** *vi* to reason by syllogisms. ◆ *vt* to deduce syllogistically. **syll'ogizer** or **-s-** *n*.

sylph /*silf*/ *n* a spirit of the air; a sylphlike being; a slim person; a kind of hummingbird. [Coined by Paracelsus]
■ **sylph'id** or **sylph'ide** *n* a little sylph (also *adj*). **sylph'idine** *adj* (*Meredith*). **sylph'ine, sylph'ish, sylph'like** *adj* slim and graceful. **sylph'y** *adj*.

sylvan /*sil'van*/ *adj* (*literary* and *poetic*) of woods or woodland; wooded, tree-lined; romantically rural, arcadian. ◆ *n* a wood-god; a forest-dweller. [L *silva* (sometimes *sylva*) wood]
■ **sylvat'ic** *adj*. **sylves'trian** *adj*. **sylvicul'tural** *adj*. **syl'viculture** *n* forestry. —All these words are often found spelt with *i*.

sylvaner /*sil-vä'nər*/ (often with *cap*) *n* a German grape, used in making white wine; wine made from this grape. [Ger]

sylvanite /*sil'və-nīt*/ *n* a mineral, telluride of gold and silver. [*Transylvania* (part of modern Romania), where it is found]

sylvia /*sil'vi-ə*/ *n* any warbler of the genus *Sylvia*, which gives its name to the warbler family **Sylviidae**. [L *silva* a wood]
■ **syl'viine** *adj*.

Sylvian /*sil'vi-ən*/ *adj* of *Sylvius*, ie either the French anatomist Jacques Dubois (1478–1555), or Franz de la Boë (1614–72), the Dutch-German iatrochemist.
❑ **Sylvian fissure** *n* (*anat*) a deep lateral fissure in the cerebrum, discovered apparently by the latter.

sylviculture, etc see under **sylvan**.

sylvine /*sil'vēn*/ or **sylvite** /*sil'vīt*/ *n* native potassium chloride, a source of potash. [Formerly called digestive salt of *Sylvius* (see **Sylvian**)]
■ **syl'vinite** /-*vin-īt*/ *n* a rock composed of sylvine and rock salt.

sym. *abbrev* : symbol; symmetrical; symphony; symptom.

sym- see **syn-**.

symar same as **cymar**.

symbiosis /*sim-bi-ō'sis* or *-bī-*/ *n* a mutually beneficial partnership between organisms of different kinds, *esp* where one lives on or within the other (*biol*); a mutually beneficial relationship between two people or bodies of people. [Gr *syn* together, and *bios* livelihood]
■ **sym'bion** or **sym'biont** /-*bi-ont*/ *n* an organism living in symbiosis. **symbiotic** /-*bi-ot'ik*/ *adj*. **symbiot'ically** *adv*.

symbol /*sim'b(ə)l*/ *n* an emblem; a sign used to represent something; that which by custom or convention represents something else; a type (*obs*); a creed, compendium of doctrine, or a typical religious rite, such as the Eucharist (*theol*); an object or act representing an unconscious or repressed conflict (*psychol*). ◆ *vt* to symbolize. [Gr *symbolon* a token, from *syn* together, and *ballein* to throw]
■ **symbolic** /-*bol'ik*/ or **symbol'ical** *adj*. **symbol'ically** *adv*. **symbol'icalness** *n*. **symbol'ics** *n sing* the study of creeds. **sym'bolism** *n* representation by symbols or signs; a system of symbols; use of symbols; use of symbols in literature or art; (often with *cap*) a late-19c movement in art and poetry that treated the actual as an expression of something underlying; symbolics. **sym'bolist** *n* and *adj*. **symbolist'ic** or **symbolist'ical** *adj*. **symbolizā'tion** or **-s-** *n*. **sym'bolize** or **-ise** *vt* to be symbolic of; to represent by symbols; to combine (*obs*); to formulate in a creed. ◆ *vi* (*obs*) to agree. **sym'bolizer** or **-s-** *n*. **sym'bolled** *adj* symbolized; bearing symbols. **symbolog'raphy** *n* symbolic writing or representation. **symbol'ogy** *n* (for **symbolol'ogy**) the study or use of symbols. **symbolol'atry** *n* (Gr *latreiā* worship) undue veneration for symbols.
❑ **symbol grocer**, etc *n* (*marketing*) a member of an independent group (**symbol group**) of retail grocers, etc who join together to obtain improved discounts and prices from suppliers, and display a common symbol or logo on their shops, packaging, etc. **symbolic interactionism** *n* the sociological theory that stresses the importance of the subjective understanding of language and gesture in social behaviour. **symbolic logic** *n* a branch of logic which uses symbols instead of terms, propositions, etc in order to clarify reasoning.

symbole an old spelling of **cymbal**.

symitar, symitare obsolete spellings of **scimitar**.

symmetallism or (*US*) **symmetalism** /*si-met'ə-li-zm*/ *n* a monetary system in which an alloy of two or more metals in a fixed proportion is used as the standard of currency; advocacy of this system. [Gr *syn-* together, and **metal**]

■ **symmetallic** /-*mi-tal'ik*/ *adj*.

symmetry /*sim'i-tri*/ *n* exact correspondence of parts on either side of a straight line or plane, or about a centre or axis; balance or due proportion; beauty of form; disposition of parts, eg the method of arrangement of constituent parts of the animal body; the quality of remaining unchanged despite transformations in the surrounding environment or structure (*phys*). [Gr *symmetriā*, from *syn* together, and *metron* a measure]
■ **symm'etral** *adj* of symmetry. **symmetrian** /*si-met'ri-ən*/ *n* a person who studies or theorizes on the due proportions of things. **symmet'ric** or **symmet'rical** *adj* having symmetry; actinomorphic (*bot* and *zool*). **symmet'rically** *adv*. **symmet'ricalness** *n*. **symmetrizā'tion** or **-s-** *n*. **symm'etrize** or **-ise** *vt* to make symmetrical. **symmetrophō'bia** *n* (Gr *phobos* fear) fear or dislike of symmetry.

sympathectomy /*sim-pə-thek'tə-mi*/ (*surg*) *n* excision of part of a sympathetic nerve. [From **sympathetic**, and Gr *ektomē* excision]

sympathin /*sim'pə-thin*/ (*biochem*) *n* a substance, secreted by sympathetic nerve-endings, which constricts and dilates blood vessels. [From **sympathetic**]

sympathique /*sẽ-pa-tēk'*/ (*Fr*) *adj* to one's taste, congenial, evoking a sense of affinity or harmony.

sympathy /*sim'pə-thi*/ *n* community of feeling; power of entering into another's feelings or mind; harmonious understanding; compassion, pity; affinity or correlation whereby one thing responds to the action of another or to action upon another; agreement; (often in *pl*) a feeling of agreement or support, or an expression of this. [Gr *sympatheia*, from *syn* with, and *pathos* suffering]
■ **sympathet'ic** *adj* feeling, inclined to or expressing sympathy; in sympathy; acting or done in sympathy; induced by sympathy (as sounds in a resonating body); congenial; compassionate; of the sympathetic nervous system (see below); (a Gallicism) able to awake sympathy. **sympathet'ical** *adj* (*obs*) sympathetic. **sympathet'ically** *adv*. **sym'pathize** or **-ise** *vi* to be in sympathy; to feel with or for another; to be compassionate; to be in accord, correspond. ◆ *vt* (*Shakesp*) to be in sympathy, accord or harmony with; to combine harmoniously; to represent or understand sympathetically; *perh* to affect all alike. **sym'pathizer** or **-s-** *n*. **sympatholyt'ic** *adj* (*med*) inhibiting the action of the sympathetic nervous system. ◆ *n* a drug which has this effect. **sympathomimet'ic** *adj* (*pharmacol*) mimicking the action of the sympathetic nervous system. ◆ *n* a drug which does this.
❑ **sympathetic ink** see under **ink**. **sympathetic magic** *n* magic depending upon a supposed sympathy, eg between a person and his or her name or portrait, between rainfall and libations. **sympathetic nervous system** *n* a system of nerves supplying the involuntary muscles and glands, *esp* those originating from the cervical, thoracic and lumbar regions of the spinal cord; sometimes also including those from the brain and the sacral region (the **parasympathetic nervous system**). **sympathetic string** *n* a string on a musical instrument that is not struck itself, but resonates with strings that are actually bowed or plucked. **sympathy** (or **sympathetic**) **strike** *n* a strike in support of other workers, not in furtherance of the strikers' own claims.
■ **in sympathy** (**with**) in agreement (with), in support (of).

sympatric /*sim-pat'rik*/ (*biol*) *adj* (eg of species) of, occurring in, or from the same geographical region, or overlapping regions, but which do not interbreed (cf **allopatric**). [**sym-**, Gr *patrā* fatherland, with sfx *-ic*]

sympetalous /*sim-pet'ə-las*/ (*bot*) *adj* having the petals united. [Gr *syn* together, and *petalon* leaf]
■ **Sympet'alae** /-*lē*/ *n pl* a main division of dicotyledons, typically having united petals.

symphile /*sim'fīl*/ (*zool*) *n* an animal of another kind kept as a guest or domestic animal in an ants' or termites' nest. [Gr *symphiliā* mutual friendship, from *syn* together, and *philos* a friend]
■ **sym'philism** /-*fil-izm*/ or **sym'phily** *n*. **sym'philous** *adj*.

symphony /*sim'fə-ni*/ *n* harmony, *esp* of sound; an orchestral composition on a great scale in sonata form (*music*); an instrumental portion of a primarily vocal work (*archaic*); a symphony orchestra; an *obs* name for various musical instruments (bagpipe, drum, hurdy-gurdy, virginal). [Gr *symphōniā* harmony, orchestra, from *syn* together, and *phōnē* a sound]
■ **symphonic** /*sim-fon'ik*/ *adj*. **symphō'nion** *n* a combination of piano and harmonium. **symphonious** /-*fō'ni-əs*/ *adj* agreeing or harmonizing in sound; accordant; harmonious. **sym'phonist** *n* a composer or (rarely) performer of symphonies.
❑ **symphonic poem** *n* a large orchestral composition in programme music with the movements run together. **symphony orchestra** *n* a large orchestra comprising strings, woodwind, brass and percussion, capable of performing symphonies.

■ words derived from main entry word; ❑ compound words; ■ idioms and phrasal verbs

Symphyla /sim'fi-lə/ n a class or order of arthropods linking the bristle-tails with the centipedes. [Gr *symphylos* of the same race, from *syn* with, and *phylē*, *phylon* a race, clan]
■ **sym'phylous** *adj*.

symphysis /sim'fi-sis/ n the union or growing together of parts, concrescence (*zool*); union of bones by fusion, cartilage or ligament (*anat*); a place of junction of parts (*bot* and *zool*). [Gr *symphysis*, from *syn* with, and *phyein* to grow]
■ **symphyseal** or **symphysial** /sim-fiz'i-əl/ *adj*. **symphyseot'omy** or **symphysiot'omy** n (Gr *tomē* a cut; *surg*) the operation of cutting through the pubic symphysis. **symphytic** /-fit'ik/ *adj* by fusion. **Sym'phytum** n the comfrey genus of the borage family, *perh* from its supposed virtue of closing wounds or healing fractures.

sympiesometer /sim-pi-i-zom'i-tər or -som'/ n a barometer with a gas instead of a vacuum; an instrument for measuring the pressure of a current. [Gr *sympiesis* a pressing together, from *syn* with, *piezein* to press, and *metron* a measure]

symplast /sim'plāst or -plast/ (*bot*) n the continuous network of protoplasts, linked by plasmodesmata, bounded by the cell membrane. [**sym-** and **-plast** (from Gr *plastos* formed, from *plassein* to form)]

symploce /sim'plō-sē/ (*rhetoric*) n the repetition of a word at the beginning and another at the end of successive clauses. [Gr *symplokē* an interweaving, from *syn* with, and *plekein* to weave]

sympodium /sim-pō'di-əm/ (*bot*) n (pl **sympo'dia**) a stem involved in sympodial growth. [Gr *syn* together, and *pous*, *podos* foot]
■ **sympo'dial** *adj*. **sympo'dially** *adv*.
□ **sympodial growth** n a pattern of growth in which a shoot ceases to grow and one or more of the lateral buds next to the apical bud grow(s) out and repeat(s) the pattern.

symposium /sim-pō'zi-əm/ n (pl **sympo'sia**) a conference; a collection of views on one topic; a meeting for (*orig* philosophical) conversation; a drinking party (*hist*). [Latinized from Gr *symposion*, from *syn* together, and *posis* drinking]
■ **sympo'siac** or **sympo'sial** *adj*. **sympo'siarch** /-ärk/ n (Gr *archos* leader) the master, director, etc of the feast or conference. **sympo'siast** n a person who takes part in a symposium.

symptom /sim(p)'təm/ n a subjective indication of a disease, ie something experienced by the patient, not outwardly visible (*med*); any abnormal sensation, or emotional expression or thought, accompanying disease or disorder of body or mind (*med*); (loosely) any objective evidence of disease or bodily disorder; a characteristic sign or indication of the existence of a state. [Gr *symptōma*, *symptōsis*, from *syn* with, and root of *piptein* to fall]
■ **symptomat'ic** or (*rare*) **symptomat'ical** *adj*. **symptomat'ically** *adv*. **symp'tomatize** or **-ise** *vt* to symptomize. **symptomatol'ogy** the study of symptoms; the symptoms of a patient or a disease taken as a whole. **symp'tomize** or **-ise** *vt* to be a symptom of. **symptomolog'ical** *adj*. **symptō'sis** n wasting; emaciation. **symptotic** /-tot'ik/ *adj*.

syn. *abbrev* : synonym; synthetic.

syn- /sin-/, **sy-** /si-/, **syl-** /sil-/, **sym-** /sim-/ or **sys-** /sis-/ *pfx* signifying together, with. [Gr *syn* with]

synadelphite /sin-ə-del'fīt/ (*mineralogy*) n a manganese aluminium arsenate. [Gr *syn* with, and *adelphos* brother, as found along with similar minerals]

synaeresis /sin-ē'rə-sis/ n the running together of two vowels into one or into a diphthong (*phonetics*); the spontaneous expulsion of liquid from a gel (*chem*). [Gr *syn* together, and *hairesis* taking, from *haireein* to take]

synaesthesia /sin-ēs- or sin-is-thē'zi-ə or -zh(y)ə/ n sensation produced at a point different from the point of stimulation; a sensation of another kind suggested by one experienced (eg in colour hearing). [Gr *syn* together, and *aisthēsis* sensation]
■ **syn'aesthete** n a person who experiences such sensations. **synaesthet'ic** *adj*.

synagogue /sin'ə-gog/ n an assembly of Jews for worship and for instruction in the Torah; a Jewish place of worship. [Gr *synagōgē*, from *syn* together, and *agōgē* a bringing, from *agein* to lead]
■ **syn'agogal** /-gō-gl/ or **synagog'ical** /-gog'* or *-goj'i-kl/ *adj*.

synaloepha /sin-ə-lē'fə/ (*grammar*) n the melting of a final vowel or diphthong into the initial vowel or diphthong of the next word. [Latinized from Gr *synaloiphē*, from *synaleiphein* to coalesce, smear together, from *syn* together, and *aleiphein* to anoint]

synandrium /sin-an'dri-əm/ (*bot*) n a mass of united stamens. [Gr *syn* together, and *anēr* a man (male)]
■ **synan'drous** *adj* having united stamens.

synangium /sin-an'ji-əm/ n an arterial trunk (*anat*); a group of united sporangia (found in Marattiaceae) (*bot*). [Gr *syn* together, and *angeion* a vessel]

synantherous /sin-an'thə-rəs/ (*bot*) *adj* syngenesious. [Gr *syn*, and **anther**]

synanthesis /sin-an-thē'sis/ (*bot*) n simultaneous ripening of stamens and stigmas. [Gr *syn* together, and *anthēsis* flowering, from *anthos* a flower]
■ **synanthet'ic** *adj*. **synan'thic** *adj* showing synanthy. **synan'thous** *adj* synanthic; flowering and leafing simultaneously. **synan'thy** n abnormal fusion of flowers.

synaphea or **synapheia** /sin-ə-fē'ə/ (*prosody*) n metrical continuity between verses in a system, so that they can be scanned as one verse, as in anapaestics, with possibility of elision at the end of a line. [Gr *synapheia*, from *syn* together, and *haph-*, root of *haptein* to join]

synaposematic /sin-a-pə-sē-mat'ik/ (*zool*) *adj* having a warning coloration common to a number of dangerous species in the same region. [Gr *syn* together, and **aposematic**]
■ **synaposematism** /-sē'mə-tizm/ n.

synapse see under **synapsis**.

synapsid /si-nap'sid/ n a member of the **Synap'sida**, a class of mammal-like reptiles of the Carboniferous, Permian and Triassic periods having a single pair of lateral temporal openings in the skull (also *adj*). [New L *Synapsida*, from Gr *syn* together, and *apsis* arch or vault]

synapsis /sin-ap'sis/ n (pl **synaps'es** /-ēz/) the pairing of chromosomes of paternal and maternal origin before meiosis (*biol*); a synapse (*med*). [Gr *synapsis* contact, junction, from *syn* together, and *haptein* to fasten]
■ **synapse** /sīn'aps or sin'/ n (*med*) an interlacing or enveloping connection of one nerve-cell with another. **synapt'ase** n emulsin. **synapte** /sin-ap'tē/ n in the Greek Church, a litany. **synapt'ic** *adj*.

synarchy /sin'ər-ki/ n joint sovereignty. [Gr *synarchiā*, from *syn* with, and *archein* to rule]

synarthrosis /sin-är-thrō'sis/ (*anat*) n (pl **synarthro'ses** /-sēz/) immovable articulation. [Gr *synarthrōsis*, from *syn* together, and *arthron* a joint; also *arthrōdiā* a flattish joint]
■ **synarthro'dial** *adj*. **synarthro'dially** *adv*.

synastry /sin-as'tri/ (*astrol*) n a coincidence of stellar influences; comparison of the horoscopes of two or more people. [Gr *syn* together, and *astron* a star]

synaxis /si-nak'sis/ n in the early Church, meeting for worship, *esp* for the Eucharist. [Gr *synaxis* a bringing together, from *syn* together, and *agein* to lead]
■ **synaxā'rion** n (*Gr church*) a lection containing an account of a saint's life.

synbiotic /sin-bī-ot'ik/ n a substance that contains a probiotic and a prebiotic that supports it. [Gr *syn* together]

sync or **synch** /singk/ n, vi and vt short for **synchronization** and **synchronize** (see under **synchronal**).
■ **in sync** (or **synch**) synchronized; running together correctly, sharing a common rhythm, time, pattern, etc; matching, harmonious. **out of sync** (or **synch**) not synchronized; having different and jarring rhythms; (loosely) ill-matched (with *with*).

syncarp /sin'kärp/ (*bot*) n a compound fruit formed from two or more carpels, of one or more than one flower. [Gr *syn* together, and *karpos* a fruit]
■ **syncarpous** /sin-kär'pəs/ *adj* of or having united carpels. **syn'carpy** n.

syncategorematic /sin-kat-i-go-ri-mat'ik/ (*linguistics*) *adj* not able to form a term without other words. [Gr *synkatēgorēmatikos*, from *syn* with, and *katēgorēma* predicate]
■ **syncategoremat'ically** *adv*.

synch see **sync**.

synchondrosis /sing-kon-drō'sis/ (*anat*) n (pl **synchondro'ses** /-sēz/) connection of bones by cartilage. [Gr *synchondrōsis*, from *syn* with, and *chondros* a cartilage]

synchoresis /sing-kō-rē'sis/ (*rhetoric*) n a concession, *esp* one made for the sake of a more effective retort. [Gr *synchōrēsis*, from *synchōreein* to agree, yield ground, from *syn* with, and *chōros* space]

synchro /sing'krō/ see **synchronized swimming** under **synchronal**.

synchrocyclotron /sing-krō-sī'klō-tron/ see **accelerator** under **accelerate**.

synchroflash /sing'krō-flash/ (*photog*) n a mechanism which synchronizes the opening of a camera shutter with the peak of brilliance of a flash bulb. [*synchronized flash*]

synchromesh /sing'krō-mesh/ *adj* of a gear in which the speeds of the driving and driven members are automatically synchronized before coupling, so as to avoid shock and noise in gear-changing. ◆ *n* such a gear. [*synchronized mesh*]

synchronal /*sing'krə-nəl*/ *adj* coinciding in time. [Gr *syn* together, and *chronos* time]

■ **synchronic** /-*kron'ik*/ or **synchron'ical** *adj* synchronous; concerned with the study of a subject (*esp* a language) at a particular period, without considering the past or the future, *opp* to *diachronic*. **synchron'ically** *adv*. **synchronicity** /-*is'i-ti*/ *n* coincidence of events that appear to be related but are not. **synch'ronism** *n* coincidence in time; simultaneity; keeping time together; occurrence of similar phrases at the same time; exhibition of contemporary history in one scheme; the bringing together of different parts of a story (occurring at different times) in one picture or work of art. **synchronis'tic** or (*rare*) **synchronis'tical** *adj*. **synchronis'tically** *adv*. **synchronizā'tion** or **-s-** *n*. **syn'chronize** or **-ise** *vi* to coincide or agree in time. ◆ *vt* to cause to coincide or agree in time; to time together or to a standard; to represent or identify as contemporary; to enable (an electronic device) to be updated with changes made to another device; to make (the soundtrack of a film) exactly simultaneous with the picture (*TV and film*). **synch'ronizer** or **-s-** *n* that which, or someone who, synchronizes; a synchroscope; a unit for maintaining synchronism when transmitting data between two devices (*comput*). **synchronol'ogy** *n* chronological arrangement side by side. **synch'ronous** *adj* simultaneous; contemporary; keeping time together. **synch'ronously** *adv*. **synch'ronousness** *n*. **synch'rony** *n* simultaneity. ❑ **synchronized swimming** (also *inf* **synchro swimming** or **synch'ro**) *n* a sport in which a swimmer or group of swimmers performs a sequence of gymnastic and balletic movements in time to music. **synchronous motor** *n* an electric motor whose speed is exactly proportional to the frequency of the supply current. **synchronous orbit** *n* geostationary orbit. **synchronous transmission** *n* (*comput*) transmission of data along communication lines at a fixed rate and in a continuous string.

synchroscope /*sin'krō-skōp*/ (*elec eng*) *n* an instrument which indicates the difference in frequency between two AC supplies. [*synchro*nism, and **-scope**]

synchrotron /*sing'krō-tron*/ (*phys*) *n* a type of very high-energy particle accelerator. [Gr *syn* together, *chronos* time, and *electron*] ❑ **synchrotron radiation** *n* electromagnetic radiation emitted by charged particles passing through magnetic fields, produced in the form of a very intense polarized beam, with important uses for analysing the structure and behaviour of substances.

synchysis /*sing'ki-sis*/ *n* confusion of meaning due to unusual arrangement (*rhetoric*); fluidity of the vitreous humour of the eye (*pathol*). [Gr, from *syn* together, with, and *cheein* to pour]

synclastic /*sin-klas'tik*/ (*geom*) *adj* having the same kind of curvature in all directions. [Gr *syn* together, and *klastos* broken]

syncline /*sin'klīn*/ (*geol*) *n* a fold in which the beds dip downwards towards the axis. [Gr *syn* together, and *klīnein* to cause to lean] ■ **synclin'al** *adj* of or like a syncline. ◆ *n* a syncline. **synclinorium** /-*kli-nō'ri-əm* or -*nō'*/ *n* (*pl* **synclino'ria**) a great synclinal structure carrying minor flexures.

Syncom /*sin'kom*/ *n* one of a series of communication satellites in a synchronous orbit. [*synchronous communications satellite*]

syncope /*sing'kə-pi*/ *n* the elision of a letter or syllable from the middle of a word; a fainting fit caused by a sudden fall of blood pressure in the brain (*med*); a cutting short (*rare*); syncopation (*obs*). [Gr *synkopē* a cutting up, cutting short, syncope, from *syn* together, and *koptein* to cut off] ■ **sync'opal** *adj* of syncope. **sync'opate** *vt* to shorten by cutting out the middle (of a word); to alter the rhythm of (music, etc) temporarily by transferring the accent to a normally unaccented beat. **sync'opated** *adj*. **syncopa'tion** *n*. **sync'opātor** *n*. **syncopic** /*sing-kop'ik*/ *adj*. **syncopt'ic** *adj*.

syncretism /*sin*(*g*)*'kri-ti-zm*/ *n* reconciliation of, or attempt to reconcile, different systems of belief, *esp* of different forms of Christianity, by German Lutheran Georg Calixtus (1586–1656); fusion or blending of religions, as by identification of gods, taking over of observances, or selection of whatever seems best in each (*usu derog*); illogical compromise in religion; the fusion of *orig* distinct inflectional forms of a word (*linguistics*). [Gr *synkrētismos* a confederation (orig appar of *Cretan* communities)] ■ **syncretic** /*sin-krē'tik* or *sing-*/ *adj*. **syn'cretist** *n*. **syncretis'tic** *adj*. **syncretize** or **-ise** /*sing'kri-tīz*/ *vt* and *vi*.

syncytium /*sin-sit'i-əm*/ (*biol*) *n* (*pl* **syncyt'ia**) a multinucleate cell; a tissue without distinguishable cell membranes. [Gr *syn* together, and *kytos* a vessel] ■ **syncyt'ial** *adj*.

synd or **sind** /*sīnd*/ (*Scot and N Eng*) *vt* (*esp* with *out*) to rinse; to wash out or down. ◆ *n* (also (*Burns*) **syne**) a rinsing; a washing down with liquor. [Origin obscure] ■ **synd'ings** or **sind'ings** *n pl*.

synd. *abbrev* : syndicate.

syndactyl /*sin-dak'til*/ (*zool*) *adj* having fused digits, as do many birds and lower mammals. [Gr *syn* together, and *daktylos* finger, toe] ■ **syndac'tylism** *n*. **syndac'tylous** *adj*. **syndac'tyly** *n*.

synderesis see **synteresis**.

syndesis /*sin'di-sis*/ *n* (*obs*) a binding; synapsis (*biol*). [Gr *syndesis*, from *syn* together, and *deein* to bind] ■ **syndetic** /-*det'ik*/ or **syndet'ical** *adj* connective; of a construction in which clauses are connected by conjunctions (*grammar*). **syndet'ically** *adv*.

syndesmosis /*sin-des-mō'sis* or -*dez-*/ (*zool*) *n* (*pl* **syndesmo'ses** /-*sēz*/) the connection of bones by ligaments. [Gr *syndesmos*, from *syn* together, and *desmos* a bond] ■ **syndesmotic** /-*mot'ik*/ *adj*.

syndet /*sin'det*/ *n* synthetic *det*ergent.

syndetic, etc see under **syndesis**.

syndic /*sin'dik*/ *n* a person chosen to transact business for others, *esp* the accredited legal representative of a corporation, society or company; a member of a committee of the Senate of Cambridge University; (at various times and places) a magistrate or mayor; (in ancient Greece) an advocate, delegate or judge. [Gr *syndikos*, from *syn* with, and *dikē* justice] ■ **syn'dical** *adj* **syndical chamber** or **union** a French trade union). **syn'dicalism** *n* a development of trade unionism which originated in France, aiming at putting the means of production in the hands of unions of workers. **syn'dicalist** *n* and *adj*. **syndicalist'ic** *adj*. **syn'dicate** /-*di-kət*/ *n* a body of people chosen to watch the interests of a company, or to manage a bankrupt's property; a combination of people for some common purpose or interest; an association of business people or companies to undertake a project requiring a large amount of capital; an association of criminals who organize and control illegal operations; a combined group of newspapers; a body of syndics; a council; the office of a syndic. ◆ *vt* /-*kāt*/ to control, effect, or publish by means of a syndicate; to sell (eg an article) for simultaneous publication in a number of newspapers or periodicals; to sell radio or TV programmes for broadcasting by many different radio or TV stations; to join in a syndicate; to judge, censure (*obs*). ◆ *vi* to join in a syndicate. **syndicā'tion** *n*. **syn'dicātor** *n*.

syndrome /*sin'drōm*/ (or formerly *sin'drə-mi* or -*mē*, *sin'drō-mi* or -*mē*/) *n* concurrence, *esp* (*pathol*) of symptoms; a characteristic pattern or group of symptoms; a pattern or group of actions, feelings, observed happenings, etc characteristic of a particular problem or condition. [Gr *syndromē*] ■ **syndromic** /-*drom'ik*/ *adj*.

syndyasmian /*sin-di-az'mi-ən* or -*dī-*/ (*anthrop*) *adj* pairing, applied to a form of family founded on a loose temporary marriage. [Gr *syndyasmos* coupling]

syne[1] /*sīn*/ (*Scot*) *adv* then, next; afterwards, later; ago, since (as in *auld lang syne*). [**sithen**]

syne[2] see **synd**.

synecdoche /*sin-ek'də-kē* or -*ki*/ (*rhetoric*) *n* a figure of speech in which a part is used to refer to the whole, or vice versa, as in *wiser heads* used to mean wiser people. [Gr *synekdochē*, from *syn* together, and *ekdechesthai* to receive] ■ **synecdochic** /-*dok'ik*/ or **synecdoch'ical** *adj*. **synecdoch'ically** *adv*. **synec'dochism** *n* use of synecdoche; use of part for the whole in sympathetic magic.

synechia /*sin-e-kī'ə* or *sin-ē'ki-ə*/ (*pathol*) *n* abnormal adhesion, *esp* of the iris to the cornea or to the lens. [Gr *synecheia* continuity, from *syn* together, and *echein* to hold]

synecology /*sin-ē-kol'ə-ji*/ *n* the ecological study of communities of plants or animals. [Gr *syn* together, (**syn-**) and **ecology**] ■ **synecolog'ic** or **synecolog'ical** *adj*. **synecolog'ically** *adv*. **synecol'ogist** *n*.

synecphonesis /*sin-ek-fō-nē'sis*/ (*phonetics*) *n* synizesis. [Gr *syn* together, and *ekphōnēsis* pronunciation, from *ek* out, and *phōnē* voice, utterance]

synectics /*sin-ek'tiks*/ *n sing* the study of processes leading to invention, with the end aim of solving practical problems, *esp* by a **synectics group**, a miscellaneous group of people of imagination and ability but varied interests. [Gr *synektikos* fit for holding together] ■ **synec'tic** *adj*. **synec'tically** *adv*.

---

synedrion /sin-ed'ri-on or -ən/, also **synedrium** /-əm/ n (pl **syned'ria**) a judicial assembly; (specif) a sanhedrin. [Gr syn together, and hedrā seat]
■ **syned'rial** adj.

syneidesis /sin-ī-dē'sis/ (theol) n conscience as passing judgement on past acts, opp to synteresis. [Gr syneidēsis conscience, from syn with, together, and eidenai to know]

syneresis same as **synaeresis**.

synergy /sin'ər-ji/ n combined or co-ordinated action; synergism. [Gr synergiā co-operation, from syn together, and ergon work]
■ **synergetic** /-jet'ik/ or **syner'gic** adj working together. **syner'gid** n (bot) either of the two cells in the embryo-sac that seem to guide the pollen tube. **synergism** /sin' or -ûr'/ n the doctrine (ascribed to Melanchthon) that the human will and the Divine Spirit are two efficient agents that co-operate in regeneration (theol); increased effect of two substances, esp drugs, obtained by using them together; (more generally) the working together of a number of individuals for greater effect. **syn'ergist** (or /-ûr'/) n a substance which increases the effect of another (eg pesticide); a muscle, etc that acts with another. **synergist'ic** adj. **synergist'ically** adv. **syn'ergize** or **-ise** vi to act as a synergist (with another substance).

synesis /sin'ə-sis/ n syntax having regard to meaning rather than grammatical form. [Gr, sense]

synfuel /sin'fū-əl/ n any type of fuel synthesized from a fossil fuel. [synthetic and fuel]

syngamy /sing'gə-mi/ (biol) n free interbreeding; union of gametes. [Gr syn together, and gamos marriage]
■ **syngamic** /sin-gam'ik/ or **syngamous** /sing'gə-məs/ adj.

syngas /sin'gas/ n a mixture of hydrogen and carbon monoxide, from which various hydrocarbons (eg methanol and gasoline) can be synthesized. [synthesis and gas]

syngeneic /sin-ji-nē'ik or -nā'ik/ (immunol) adj genetically identical. [Gr syngeneia kinship]

syngenesis /sin-jen'i-sis/ n (biol) reproduction by fusion of male and female elements, the offspring being derived from both parents. [Gr syn together, and genesis formation, generation]
■ **Syngenesia** /sin-ji-nē'si-ə/ n pl in the Linnaean system, a class of plants with syngenesious stamens, corresponding to the Compositae. **syngene'sious** adj (bot) having the anthers united in a tube around the style, as in Compositae. **syngenetic** /-net'ik/ adj of or by syngenesis; (of minerals) formed contemporaneously with the enclosing rock.

syngnathous /sin(g)'gna-thəs/, also **sing'nath-/** (zool) adj (of certain fish) having the jaws fused to form a tubular structure. [Gr syn together, and gnathos jaw]
■ **Syngnathidae** /sin- or sing-gnath'i-dē, also sing-nath'/ n pl the pipefish family.

syngraph /sing'graf/ (rare) n a writing, eg a contract, signed by both or all of the parties to it. [Gr syn together, and graphein to write]

synkaryon /sin-kar'i-ən/ (biol) n a cell nucleus formed by the fusion of two separate nuclei, or (as in fungal hypha) a pair of nuclei in close association. [Gr syn together, and karyon kernel]

synod /sin'əd/ n an ecclesiastical council; a Presbyterian church court intermediate between presbytery and the General Assembly; the supreme court of the former United Presbyterian Church; an administrative district of the United Reformed Church; conjunction (astrol; obs). [Gr synodos a meeting, conjunction, from syn together, and hodos a way]
■ **syn'odal** adj of, of the nature of, or done in a synod. ♦ n a payment made by a clergyman on the occasion of a synod, or at a visitation. **synodic** /-od'ik/ or **synod'ical** adj synodal; relating to conjunction (astron); from conjunction to conjunction (see **synodic month** under **month**). **synod'ically** adv.
□ **synodic period** n (astron) the time between two successive conjunctions of a heavenly body with the sun. **syn'odsman** n a lay member of a synod.
■ **General Synod of the Church of England** the governing body of the Church of England, composed of the Houses of Bishops, Clergy and Laity.

synoecete /sin-ē'sēt/ or **synoekete** /-kēt/ n a guest tolerated with indifference in an ants' or termites' nest. [Gr synoikia a living together, community, synoiketēs a house-fellow, synoikizein to unite in one community, from syn with, and oikeein to dwell]
■ **synoeciosis** /-si-ō'sis/ n the rhetorical figure of coupling opposites. **synoecious** /-ē'shəs/ or **synoicous** /-oi'kəs/ adj (bot) having antheridia and archegonia in the same group. **synoe'cism** n union of communities or cities. **syn'oecize** or **-ise** /-ē-sīz/ vt and vi to unite in one community or city state. **synoecology** /-kol'ə-ji/ n same as **synecology**.

synonym /sin'ə-nim/ n a word having the same meaning as another in the same language (usu very nearly the same meaning); a word or term used as an alternative to another of the same meaning; a systematic name to which another is preferred as valid (biol). [Gr synōnymon, from syn with, and onoma a name]
■ **synonymatic** /sin-on-i-mat'ik/, **synonym'ic** or **synonym'ical** adj of, consisting of, relating to, etc synonyms. **synonym'icon** n a dictionary of synonyms. **synon'ymist** n a person who studies synonyms, or the different names of plants and animals. **synonym'ity** n the fact or quality of being synonymous. **synon'ymize** or **-ise** vt to be synonymous with, or a synonym for; to give, or analyse, the synonyms of (rare); (loosely) to exemplify, embody (inf). **synon'ymous** adj having the same meaning; closely associated. **synon'ymously** adv. **synon'ymousness** n. **synon'ymy** n the fact of being synonymous; the rhetorical use of synonyms; a list of synonyms.

synop. abbrev : synopsis.

synopsis /sin-op'sis/ n (pl **synop'sēs**) a general view; a summary or outline (esp of a book). [Gr synopsis, from syn with, together, and opsis a view]
■ **synop'size** or **-ise** vt to make a synopsis of. **synop'tic** or **synop'tical** adj affording or taking a general view of the whole. **synop'tically** adv. **synop'tist** n one of the writers of the Synoptic Gospels. **synoptis'tic** adj.
□ **Synoptic Gospels** n pl those of Matthew, Mark and Luke, which can readily be said to have been written from a common point of view.

synostosis /sin-o-stō'sis/ (anat) n (pl **synosto'ses** /-sēz/) complete union of bones. [Gr syn with, together, and osteon bone]

synovia /sin-ō'vi-ə/ n (physiol) a viscous, glair-like lubricating fluid in the joints and in the tendon sheaths and capsular ligaments surrounding joints. [Appar an arbitrary coinage of Paracelsus, who applied it more generally]
■ **syno'vial** adj. **synovitic** /-vit'ik/ adj relating to synovitis. **synovī'tis** n (med) inflammation of a synovial membrane.
□ **synovial membrane** n (anat) a membrane of connective tissue that lines tendon sheaths and capsular ligaments and secretes synovia.

synroc /sin'rok/ n a type of synthetic rock developed especially to fuse with radioactive waste and remain stable over geological time, for burial deep underground. [synthetic rock]

syntactic, **syntagma**, etc see under **syntax**.

syntan /sin'tan/ n a synthetic tanning agent.

syntax /sin'taks/ n grammatical structure in sentences; one of the classes in some Roman Catholic schools; systematic order or arrangement of elements; a set of rules for combining the elements of a programming language into permitted constructions (comput). [Gr syntaxis, from syn together, and tassein to put in order]
■ **syntac'tic** or **syntac'tical** adj. **syntac'tically** adv. **syntag'ma** or (rare) **syntagm** /sin'tam/ n (pl **syntag'mata** or (rare) **syn'tagms**) a systematic body, system or group; a word or words constituting a syntactic unit (linguistics). **syntagmat'ic** adj. **syntag'matite** n a kind of hornblende.

syntectic, **syntectical** see under **syntexis**.

syntenosis /sin-tə-nō'sis/ (zool) n (pl **syntenoses** /-nō'sēz/) the connection of bones by tendons. [Gr syn with, and tenōn a sinew]

synteresis /sin-ti-rē'sis/ (theol) n conscience as a guide to future action, opp to syneidesis (also (from the later Greek pronunciation) **synderē'sis**). [Gr syntērēsis observation, from syn with, and tēreein to watch over]

syntexis /sin-tek'sis/ n (rare) liquefaction; melting; wasting. [Gr syntēxis, from syn with, and tēkein to melt]
■ **syntec'tic** or **syntec'tical** adj (obs).

synth /sinth/ n short for synthesizer (also adj).

synthase /sin'thāz/ n an enzyme that catalyses a particular synthesis. [synthesis and -ase]

synthesis /sin'thi-sis or -thə-/ n (pl **syn'theses** /-sēz/) building up; putting together; making a whole out of parts; the combination of separate elements of thought into a whole; reasoning from principles to a conclusion, opp to analysis; the indication of grammatical relationships by inflection rather than word order or function. [Gr synthesis, from syn with, together, and thesis a placing]
■ **syn'thesist** n someone who makes a synthesis. **syn'thesize** or **-ise** vt to put together in synthesis; to form by synthesis. **syn'thesīzer** or **-s-** n a person who, or thing which, synthesizes; a computerized instrument for generating sounds, often beyond the range of conventional instruments, used esp in making electronic music. **synthetic** /-thet'/ adj (also **synthet'ical**) relating to, consisting in, or formed by, synthesis; artificially produced but of similar nature to, not a mere substitute for, the natural product; artificial; not sincere, sham (inf). ♦ n a synthetic substance. **synthet'ically** adv. **synthet'icism** n

the principles of synthesis, a synthetic system. **syn'thetize** or **-ise** vt to synthesize. **syn'thetizer** or **-s-**, or **syn'thetist** n.

❑ **synthesis gas** n see separate entry **syngas**. **synthetic aperture radar** n a radar system that produces finely detailed images, an increased antenna aperture being obtained by integrating individual readings from the same area as the aircraft or spacecraft moves over it (abbrev **SAR**). **synthetic drug** n a drug made in the laboratory, whether one occurring naturally or an artificial one. **synthetic languages** n pl those that use inflectional forms instead of word order, prepositions, etc to express syntactical relationships. **synthetic philosophy** n Herbert Spencer's system, a fusion, as he thought, of the different sciences into a whole. **synthetic phonics** n sing (educ) a variation on the phonic method (qv) that encourages learners to form words by blending sounds together. **synthetic resin** see under **resin**.

synthon /sin'thon/ (chem) n (within a molecule to be synthesized) a constituent part which can be readily used in the synthesis process. [synthetic and ion]

synthronus /sin'thrə-nəs/ (church hist or Gr church) n the seat of the bishop and his presbyters, behind the altar. [Gr syn together, and thronos a throne]

syntony /sin'tə-ni/ n (elec eng; old) tuning, or agreement in resonance frequency, of radio apparatus. [Gr syn together, and tonos tone]

■ **syntonic** /sin-ton'ik/ adj tuned together (music); showing a normal emotional response to one's environment (psychol). **syn'tonin** n (biol) a substance similar to fibrin, found in muscle. **syn'tonize** or **-ise** vt (elec) to adjust to agree in frequency. **syn'tonous** adj (music) syntonic.

sype same as **sipe**[1].

sypher /sī'fər/ (carpentry) vt to lay (the chamfered edge of a plank) over that of another to make a flush surface. [Variant of **cipher**]

syphilis /sif'i-lis/ (med and pathol) n a contagious venereal disease due to infection with a micro-organism Spirochaeta pallida (Treponema pallidum). [Title of Fracastoro's Latin poem (1530), whose hero Syphilus is infected]

■ **syphilit'ic** adj affected with, caused by, or relating to syphilis. ◆ n a person suffering from syphilis. **syphiliza'tion** or **-s-** n. **syph'ilize** or **-ise** vt to inoculate or infect with syphilis. **syph'iloid** adj like syphilis. **syphilol'ogist** n. **syphilol'ogy** n the study of syphilis. **syphilō'ma** n a syphilitic tumour. **syphilophō'bia** n a morbid dread of syphilis.

syphon same as **siphon**.

SYR abbrev : Syria (IVR).

Syrah /sē-rä'/ n a red wine grape; (also without cap) wine made from this. [The ancient Persian City of Shiraz, where the grape is supposed to have originated]

syren same as **siren**.

Syriac /sir'i-ak/ n the ancient Aramaic dialect of Syria; a modern form of this dialect still spoken in the Middle East and in the USA. ◆ adj of or relating to this dialect.

■ **Syr'iacism** /-ə-sizm/, **Syr'ianism**, **Syr'iasm** or (rare) **Syr'ism** n a Syriac idiom. **Syr'ian** adj of or relating to Syria, a republic in the Middle East, or its people. ◆ n a native or citizen of Syria. **Syr'iarch** /-ärk/ n (hist) the chief priest in Roman Syria. **Syrophoenicia** /sī-rō-fi-nish'yə/ n (hist) a Roman province between Lebanon and the coast. **Syrophoeni'cian** n and adj.

syringa /si-ring'gə/ n orig (and still popularly) the mock orange; the lilac; (with cap) after Linnaeus, the generic name of the lilac. [New L, from Gr syrinx (from its stems being used for pipes; see ety for **syrinx**)]

syringe /si-rinj'/ n an instrument for injecting or extracting fluids. ◆ vt and vi to clean, spray or inject with a syringe. [Ety as for **syrinx**]

syringeal...to...**syringotomy** see under **syrinx**.

syrinx /sir'ingks/ n (pl **syringes** /-in'jēz/ or **syr'inxes**) Pan-pipes; the vocal organ of birds; a fistula or fistulous opening (pathol); a rock-cut tunnel, as in Egyptian tombs (archaeol). [Gr sȳrinx, -ingos Pan-pipes, channel, tube]

■ **syringeal** /-in'ji-əl/ adj. **syringitis** /-jī'tis/ n (med) inflammation of the Eustachian tube. **syringomyelia** /si-ring-gō-mī-ē'li-ə/ n (Gr myelos marrow; pathol) a chronic, progressive disease of the spinal cord, causing paralysis and loss of sensitivity to pain and temperature. **syringotomy** /sir-ing-got'ə-mi/ n (surg) cutting of a fistula.

syrlye an old form (Spenser) of **surly**.

Syrophoenicia, **Syrophoenician** see under **Syriac**.

Syrphus /sûr'fəs/ n a genus of wasp-like flies that hover and dart, giving the name to the family **Syr'phidae** /-fi-dē/. [Gr syrphos gnat]

■ **syr'phid** n and adj.

syrtis /sûr'tis/ (Milton) n (pl **syr'tes** /-tēz/) a patch or area of quicksand. [L Syrtēs, Gr Syrtides (sing of each Syrtis), name of two sandy bays of N Africa, from Gr sȳrein to draw, sweep along]

syrup, also (esp US) **sirup** /sir'əp/ n a saturated solution of sugar boiled to prevent fermentation; any thick sweet liquid; a sugar-flavoured liquid medicine; cloying sweetness (inf); a wig (from syrup of figs; Cockney rhyming sl). ◆ vt to make into syrup; to cover, fill, etc with syrup. [Fr sirop, from Ar sharāb; cf **shrub**[2] and **sherbet**]

■ **syr'upy** adj.

■ **golden syrup** the uncrystallizable part left over from the manufacture of crystallized sugar, a golden-yellow, clear syrup used in baking, etc.

sys- see **syn-**.

sysop /sis'op/ (comput) n short for **system operator**, a person responsible for the orderly running of a computer system, often dealing with primary support and problem-solving.

syssarcosis /sis-är-kō'sis/ (zool and anat) n (pl **syssarcoses** /-kō'sēz/) the connection of one bone with another by intervening muscle. [Gr syn together, and sarx flesh]

syssitia /si-sit'i-ə or -sish'/ n the ancient Spartan custom of eating the main meal together in public. [Gr syssītiā, from syn together, and sītos food]

systaltic /sis-tal'tik/ adj alternately contracting and dilating, pulsatory. [Gr systaltikos depressing; cf **systole**]

system /sis'tim or -təm/ n anything formed of parts placed together or adjusted into a regular and connected whole; a set of things considered as a connected whole; a group of heavenly bodies moving mainly under the influence of their mutual attraction (astron); a set of bodily organs of similar composition or concurring in function; the bodily organism; a geological period, a subdivision of the Palaeozoic, Mesozoic and Cenozoic eras; a plan of action; a method of procedure; a method of organization; an organized set of computer components (hardware) which interact to allow the processing of data; the operating procedures and computer hardware and software required to process data in a given application; methodicalness; a systematic treatise; (with the, often with cap) society seen as a soulless and monolithic organization thwarting individual effort; a group of (Greek) verses; a body of doctrine; a theory of the universe; a full and connected view of some department of knowledge; an explanatory hypothesis; a scheme of classification; a manner of crystallization. [Gr systēma, from sy-, syn- together, and the root of histanai to set]

■ **systemat'ic** or **systemat'ical** adj relating to, consisting of, for the purpose of, observing, or according to system; methodical; habitual; intentional. **systemat'ically** adv. **systematician** /-ə-tish'ən/ n. **systemat'ics** n sing the science of classification; the study of classification of living things in accordance with their natural relationships. **sys'tematism** n. **sys'tematist** n. **systematīzā'tion** or **-s-** or **systemīzā'tion** or **-s-** n. **sys'tematize** or **-ise**, **sys'temize** or **-ise** vt to reduce to a system. **sys'tematizer** or **-s-** n. **systematol'ogy** n. **sys'temed** adj. **systemic** /-tem'ik/ adj relating to the bodily system or to a system of bodily organs; affecting the body as a whole; (of a pesticide, etc) spreading through all the tissues, without harming the plant but making it toxic to the insect, etc; (of a herbicide) spreading through all the tissues of a plant and killing it. **sys'temless** adj without system; not exhibiting organic structure.

❑ **systematic desensitization** n a form of behaviour therapy used esp in the treatment of phobias, in which fear is reduced by exposing the sufferer to the feared object in the presence of a stimulus that inhibits the fear. **system building** n building using standardized factory-produced components. **sys'tem-built** adj. **sys'tem-maker** or **-monger** n someone unduly fond of constructing systems. **system operator** see **sysop**. **systems analysis** n. **systems analyst** n a person who analyses the operation of a scientific, commercial, industrial, etc procedure, usu with a computer, in order to plan more efficient methods, better use of equipment, or the introduction of computers into the operation. **systems engineering** n a branch of engineering that uses information theory and systems analysis to design integrated systems. **systems flowchart** n (comput) a flowchart designed to analyse the operation of a computing system with a view to improving it. **systems program** n (comput) a software program which controls the operation of a computer system (cf **applications program** under **apply**). **systems software** n (comput) a set of programs used to run the operating system of a computer, making it usable and controlling its performance.

systole /sis'to-lē or -tə-lē/ n rhythmical contraction, esp of the heart, opp to diastole (physiol); collapse of the nucleus in mitosis; the shortening of a long syllable (grammar). [Gr systolē, from syn together, and stellein to place]

■ words derived from main entry word; ❑ compound words; ■ idioms and phrasal verbs

■ **systolic** /-tol'ik/ adj.

systyle /sis'tīl/ (archit) adj having columns two diameters apart. ◆ n such an arrangement; a building or part constructed in this way. [Gr systýlos, from sy-, syn- together, and stýlos a column]

sythe (Spenser) see **sith²**.

syver or **siver** /sī'vər/ (Scot) n a drain; a grating over a drain. [Perh a form of **sewer** (see **sew²**)]

syzygy /siz'i-ji/ n (pl **syz'ygies**) conjunction or opposition; the period of new or full moon (astron); a dipody (classical prosody). [Gr syzygīa union, coupling, from sy-, syn- with, together, and zygon a yoke]

■ **syzyg'ial** adj.

Szekely /sek'ə-li/ n a member of a Hungarian-speaking ethnic group living mainly in Transylvania, Romania (also **Szekel** /sek'l/ or **Szekler** /sek'lər/). [Hung sékel to reside]

Tt

a b c d e f g h i j k l m n o p q r s t u v w x y z

Times New Roman Designed by Stanley Morison and Victor Lardent in 1931. UK.

T or **t** /tē/ n the twentieth letter in the modern English alphabet, nineteenth in the Roman, its sound *usu* a voiceless alveolar stop produced with the tip of the tongue in contact with teeth, gums or palate; anything shaped like the letter T (also **tee**).

☐ **T'-band'age** n a bandage composed of two strips fashioned in the shape of the letter T. **T'-bar** n a metal bar with cross-section in the shape of the letter T; a type of ski-lift (also **T'-bar lift**). **T'-bone** n a bone shaped like a T, *esp* in a large steak cut from the sirloin of beef. **T'-cart** n a four-wheeled, horse-drawn carriage, *usu* used for pleasure-trips, with a T-shaped body. **T'-cloth** n a type of plain cotton, *orig* made for export to India and China and stamped with a T. **T'-cross** n a tau cross. **T'-junction** n a road junction in the shape of a T. **T'-plate** n a T-shaped plate, eg for strengthening a joint in a wooden framework. **T'-rail** n a rail with T-shaped cross-section. **T'-shaped** adj. **T'-shirt** see under **tee**[1]. **T'-square** n a T-shaped ruler. **T'-strap** n a T-shaped strap on a shoe. **T-zone** n the roughly T-shaped area of the face comprising forehead, nose and chin.

■ **marked with a T** branded as thief. **to a T** with perfect exactness.

T or **T.** *abbrev* : tenor (*music*); tera-; Thailand (IVR).

☐ **T'-cell** n a type of lymphocyte involved in cellular immunity that matures (in mammals) in the *t*hymus gland, eg a *cytotoxic T-cell* able to kill virus-infected cells. **T'-commerce** n the use of television as a medium for commercial transactions such as shopping and banking. **T'-group** n (*psychol*) (sensitivity-*t*raining *group*) an encounter group whose purpose is to improve the communication skills of individual members by discussion and analysis of the roles that they each adopt habitually in their dealings with others. **T'-lymphocyte** n a T-cell.

T *symbol* : (as a medieval Roman numeral) 160; surface tension; tesla (SI unit); tritium (*chem*).

T̄ *symbol* : (medieval Roman numeral) 160000.

t or **t.** *abbrev* : tare (see **tare**[2]); temperature; tense; ton(s); transitive; troy (weight).

t *symbol* : time.

t- or **t'** an obsolete shortened form of **to** before a vowel, as in *t*advance (*Spenser*); N Eng dialect form of **the**.

't a shortened form of **it**.

TA *abbrev* : Territorial Army.

Ta (*chem*) *symbol* : tantalum.

ta /tä/ (*inf*) *interj* thank you. [Imit of baby talk]

Taal /täl/ (*archaic*) n (with *the*) Afrikaans or Cape Dutch. [Du, speech]

TAB *abbrev* : Totalizator Agency Board, the off-course betting statutory authority (*Aust* and *NZ*); typhoid-paratyphoid A and B (vaccine).

tab[1] /tab/ n a small tag, flap or strap attached to something; a loop for hanging something up by, etc; a loop for drawing a stage curtain; hence, a stage curtain; the insignia distinguishing a staff officer, on the collar of his or her uniform (*milit*); a small auxiliary aerofoil on eg a rudder or aileron, which helps control the aircraft in flight; a cigarette (*N Eng sl*); a ring pull (*N Am*); the bill, tally, cost, check (chiefly *N Am*). ◆ vt (**tabb'ing**; **tabbed**) to fix a tab to. [Ety doubtful]

■ **tabbed** adj.

■ **keep tabs on** see under **keep**. **pick up the tab** (chiefly *N Am inf*) to pay the bill.

tab[2] /tab/ n short for (typewriter) **tabulator** (see under **tabular**). ◆ vt short for **tabulate** under **tabular**. ◆ vi (*comput*) to move to the next tab stop.

☐ **tab character** n (*comput*) a control character that causes movement to the next tab stop. **tab key** n (*comput*) a key that inserts the tab character. **tab stop** n (*comput*) a point reached, eg by a cursor, when the tab key is pressed.

tab[3] /tab/ n short for **tablet**; a pill or drug, *esp* Ecstasy or a small square of paper containing LSD.

Tabanus /tə-bā'nəs/ n the gadfly genus. [L *tabānus*]

■ **tabanid** /tə-bā'nid/ n any member of this bloodsucking genus, or of its family **Tabanidae** /tə-ban'i-dē/, *incl* eg the horsefly.

tabard, also formerly **taberd** /tab'ərd or -ärd/ n a medieval peasant's overcoat (*hist*); a knight's sleeveless or short-sleeved coat (*hist*); a herald's coat or tunic bearing a coat of arms; a woman's outer garment, a sleeveless tunic. [OFr *tabart*]

■ **tab'erdar** n a scholar of Queen's College, Oxford, from the gowns they wore, now applied to the holders of some scholarships at that college.

tabaret /tab'ə-ret/ n an upholsterer's silk fabric, with alternate stripes of watered and satin surface. [Orig tradename, prob formed from **tabby**]

Tabasco® /tə-bas'kō/ n a hot pepper sauce. [*Tabasco* state in Mexico]

tabasheer or **tabashir** /tab-ə-shēr'/ n a siliceous substance sometimes found in crude form in hollows of bamboos (also prepared by chemical processes) and used in Eastern medicine. [Hindi, Pers, Ar *tabāshīr*]

tabbinet see under **tabby**.

tabbouleh or **tabouli** /ta-boo'le/ n a Mediterranean salad introduced from Lebanon, made with cracked wheat, tomatoes, cucumber, mint, parsley, lemon juice and olive oil. [Ar *tabbūla*]

tabby /tab'i/ n a coarse waved or watered silk fabric; an artificial stone; a tabby-cat; a gossiping, interfering woman (*inf*); a girl or woman (*obs Aust sl*). ◆ adj brindled. ◆ vt (**tabb'ying**; **tabb'ied**) to water (silk, etc) or cause to look wavy. [Fr *tabis*, appar from '*Attābiy*, a quarter in Baghdad where it was made]

■ **tabb'inet** or **tab'inet** n a more delicate kind of tabby resembling damask, used for window curtains. **tabb'yhood** n (*obs*) the condition of being an old maid.

☐ **tabby cat** n a brindled cat, *esp* a greyish or brownish cat with dark stripes; sometimes (*perh* from *Tabitha*) a female cat; an old maid; a spiteful gossiping woman.

tabefaction /tab-i-fak'shən/ (*pathol*; *rare*) n wasting away, emaciation. [L *tābēs* wasting away, and *facere* to do]

■ **tab'efy** vt and vi.

tabellion /tə-bel'yən/ n an official scrivener in the Roman Empire and elsewhere. [LL *tabelliō, -ōnis*, from L *tabella* tablet, dimin of *tabula* a board]

taberdar see under **tabard**.

tabernacle /tab'ər-na-kl/ n a tent or movable hut; the tent carried by the Jews through the desert, used as a temple and to house the Ark of the Covenant (*hist*); the human body as the temporary abode of the soul; a place of worship, *esp* temporary or dissenting; a receptacle for the pyx (*RC*); a canopied niche or seat (*relig*); a canopy; a reliquary; a socket for a mast (*naut*). ◆ vi to sojourn. ◆ vt to put or enshrine in a tabernacle. [L *tabernāculum*, dimin of *taberna* a hut]

■ **tab'ernacled** adj. **tabernacular** /-nak'ū-lər/ adj.

☐ **tab'ernacle-work** n ornamental work over niches, stalls, etc, with canopies and pinnacles, or any work in which this forms a characteristic feature.

■ **Feast of Tabernacles** (also called **Feast of Ingathering** or **Sukkoth**) a Jewish harvest festival, commemorating the sojourn in tents in the wilderness.

tabes /tā'bēz/ (*pathol*) n wasting away; tabes dorsalis. See also **tabefaction**, **tabefy**. [L *tābēs, -is*]

■ **tabescence** /tə-bes'əns/ n wasting; shrivelling. **tabesc'ent** adj. **tabetic** /-bet'ik/ or **tab'id** adj. **tabet'ic** n.

☐ **tabes dorsalis** /dor-sā'lis/ n a complication of syphilis, appearing many years after infection, in which degeneration of the spinal cord causes muscular inco-ordination, severe pains in the trunk and legs and incontinence (also called **locomotor ataxia**). **tābōparē'sis** n an effect of syphilitic infection of the nervous system in which there are symptoms of tabes dorsalis and general paresis.

tabi /tab'i/ n (pl **tab'i**) a sock, worn with Japanese sandals, with a thick sole and a division for the big toe. [Jap]

■ words derived from main entry word; ☐ compound words; ■ idioms and phrasal verbs

tabinet
1583
tacahout

tabinet same as **tabbinet** (see under **tabby**).

tabla /*tab'lə* or *-lä*/ *n* an Indian percussion instrument, a pair of small drums played with the hands. [Hindi]

tablanette /*tab-lə-net'*/ *n* a variant of the card game casino. [Perh from Fr *table nette* clean table]

tablature /*tab'lə-chər*/ *n* an old notation for lute music, etc, with a line for each string and letters or figures to indicate the stopping, used with modifications for other instruments; a tablet; a painting, picture, pictorial representation or work. [L *tabula* a board]

table /*tā'bl*/ *n* an article of furniture consisting of a flat top on legs, a pillar or trestles, for use at meals, work, play, for holding things, etc (often in combination, as in *worktable*, *gaming-table*, etc); a flat surface, such as a plateau; a slab or board; a layer; a compact scheme of numerical information, words, facts, etc, *usu* in columns; (in *pl*) a collection of these for reference; a syllabus or index; a condensed statement; a slab with or for an inscription; a slab inscribed with laws; (in *pl*) a code of law (eg the *Twelve Tables of ancient Rome*); a writing tablet (*esp* in the *obs* phrase *a pair of tables*); supply of food, entertainment; the company at a table; the soundboard of a violin, guitar or similar instrument; a string-course (*archit*); a panel; a board for painting on; a picture; a broad flat surface on a cut gem; a tabular crystal; a board for a game, eg chess; each half of a folding board; (in *pl*) a backgammon board, or the game itself (*obs*); a quadrangular space on the palm of the hand (*Shakesp*); a flat gravestone supported on pillars; a board or committee; a dispensing of the communion; a projecting part of a scarfed joint. ◆ *adj* of, for, like or relating to a table or meals. ◆ *vt* to put forward (a bill, order, proposal, etc) for discussion in parliament or some formal meeting; to postpone discussion of (a bill, etc) for some time or indefinitely (*N Am*); to tabulate; to lay on the table; to pay down; to board. ◆ *vi* to board. [Partly OE *tabule*, *tabele*, partly OFr (and Fr) *table*, both from L *tabula* a board]

■ **tabled** /*tā'bld*/ *adj* flat-topped; having a smooth sloping surface of dressed stone; having a table or tables. **ta'bleful** *n* as much as a table will hold. **ta'blewise** *adj* and *adv* in the form or in the manner of a table; (of the communion table) not altarwise. **ta'bling** *n* tabulation; the presenting of a bill, order, proposal, etc for discussion; playing at tables or backgammon; board; provision of tables; scarfing; a broad hem on the skirt of a sail to reinforce it.

❑ **table beer** *n* light beer for common use. **table book** *n* a book of writing tablets, memorandum book or notebook; an ornamental book intended to lie on a table; a book of tables. **ta'blecloth** *n* a cloth for covering a table, *esp* at meals. **table cover** *n* a cloth for covering a table, *esp* at other than meal-times. **ta'ble-cut** *adj* (of gems) cut with a flat top. **ta'ble-dancer** *n* a striptease dancer who performs on a table in front of individual clients at a club. **ta'ble-dancing** *n*. **table d'hôte** /*tä-bl'-dōt*/ *n* (*pl* **tables d'hôte** /*tä-bl'-dōt*/) (Fr, host's table) a meal at a fixed price (as at a hotel). ◆ *adj* (of a meal) charged at a fixed price. **table football** *n* a version of football played on a table with small metal, etc players *usu* suspended on rods, which are turned and spun to strike the ball. **table game** *n* a board game. **table knife** *n* a knife for cutting one's meat, etc with at the table. **ta'bleland** *n* an extensive region of elevated land with a flat or undulating surface; a plateau. **table leaf** *n* an extension to a table top, hinged, drawn out or inserted. **table licence** *n* a licence to serve alcoholic drinks with meals only. **table linen** *n* linen tablecloths, napkins, etc. **table maid** *n* a woman who sets the table and waits. **table manners** *n pl* social behaviour at the table during meals. **table mat** *n* a mat placed under dishes on a table. **table money** *n* an allowance (*esp* in the services) for official entertainment; a restaurateur's euphemism for cover-charge. **table music** *n* music in parts that can be read by performers at each side of a table. **table napkin** *n* a cloth (or paper substitute) used during a meal to protect the clothes and to wipe fingers and lips. **ta'ble-rapping** *n* knocking or tapping sounds on a table, attributed by spiritualists to the spirits of the dead attempting to communicate with the living. **table salt** *n* fine salt suitable for adding as a seasoning to food. **table skittles** *n sing* a game in which a suspended ball is swung to knock down pegs set up on a board. **ta'blespoon** *n* one of the largest spoons used for measuring and serving food. **ta'blespoonful** *n* (*pl* **ta'blespoonfuls**) as much as will fill a tablespoon. **ta'ble-sport** *n* (*Shakesp*) the butt of the company at table. **table talk** *n* familiar conversation, as at the table, during and after meals. **table tennis** *n* a game like lawn tennis played on a table using hollow balls of Celluloid or similar light material. **table top** *n* the top of a table; a flat top; a piece of equipment small or portable enough to be used on a table, desk, etc. **ta'ble-topped** *adj*. **ta'ble-turning** *n* movements of tables (or other objects) attributed by spiritualists to the agency of spirits, and by the sceptical to collective involuntary muscular action; the practice of turning tables (see **turn the tables** below). **ta'bleware** *n* dishes, spoons, knives, forks, etc for table use. **table water** *n* a mineral water suitable for drinking with a meal. **table wine** *n* an ordinary wine *usu* drunk with a meal. **ta'ble-work** *n* (*printing*) the setting of type for tables, columns of figures, etc.

■ **at table** at a meal. **fence the tables** see under **fence**. **lay on the table** to table (a bill, etc; see *vt* above). **Lord's table** see under **lord**. **turn the tables** to bring about a complete reversal of circumstances, from the idea of players at backgammon changing sides. **under the table** not above-board, illicit; hopelessly drunk (*inf*).

tableau /*tab'lō* or *ta-blō'*/ *n* (*pl* **tableaux** /*tab'lōz*/) a picture or vivid pictorial impression; a suddenly created dramatic situation; a tableau vivant; a moment or scene in which the action is 'frozen' for dramatic effect (*theatre*). [Fr dimin of *table*]

❑ **tableau curtains** *n pl* theatre curtains drawn back and up, to give a draped effect when opened. **tableau vivant** *n* (*pl* **tableaux vivants** /*tä-blō-vē-vä*/) a 'living picture', a motionless representation, often of some famous scene from history, by living people in costume.

tablet /*tab'lit*/ *n* a small, flattish slab, eg of soap; a small flat cake of any solid material, *esp* medicinal; a device that converts the movement of a specially adapted pen or mouse into digital or analog signals, allowing graphic designs to be displayed on a screen (*comput*); a small personal computer with a touch screen as an input device; a slab or stiff sheet for making notes on; a pad of writing paper (*orig US*); a panel, *esp* inscribed or for inscription; an inscribed plate hung up in fulfilment of a vow; a brittle confection of sugar, butter and condensed milk, made in slabs (*Scot*). ◆ *vt* to provide with, inscribe on, or make into, a tablet. [OFr *tablete*, dimin of *table*]

tablier /*tab'li-ā*/ (*hist*) *n* an apron; part of a girl's or woman's dress resembling an apron; an overall buttoning behind. [Fr]

tabloid /*tab'loid*/ *n* a newspaper of small format, measuring *approx* 30 × 40cm (about 12 × 16in), *usu* rather informal or sensationalistic in style and with many photographs; anything in a concentrated form, a summary. ◆ *adj* of, for, or in the form of, tabloid newspapers; (of eg television programmes) designed to appeal to a mass audience; concentrated. [From *Tabloid*, trademark for a medicine in tablet form] ■ **tabloidizā'tion** or **-s-** *n*. **tab'loidize** or **-ise** *vt* to apply the sensationalist values of a tabloid newspaper to (a news medium or story). **tab'loidy** *adj* (*inf*).

taboggan see **toboggan**.

taboo or **tabu** /*tə-boo'*/ *adj* subject to taboo; forbidden, *esp* because holy or unclean. ◆ *n* (*pl* **taboos'** or **tabus'**) any recognized or general prohibition, interdict, restraint, ban, exclusion or ostracism; *orig* a Polynesian (or other) system of prohibitions connected with things considered holy or unclean; any one of these prohibitions. ◆ *vt* (**taboo'ing** or **tabu'ing**; **tabooed'** or **tabued'**) to place under taboo; to forbid approach to or use of. [Tongan *tabu* (pronounced /*tä'boo*/) holy, unclean]

tabor or **tabour** /*tā'bər*/ *n* a small drum like a tambourine without jingles, *usu* played with a stick held in one hand, to accompany a pipe held in the other (*hist*); a taborer. ◆ *vi* and *vt* to play on a tabor; to beat or drum. [OFr *tabour*; an Oriental word]

■ **tā'borer** (*Spenser* **taberere** /*ta-brēr'*/) *n* a person who beats the tabor. **taborin** or **tabourin** /*tab'ə-rin* or *-rēn*/ *n* a small drum longer in body than the tabor, used in a similar way. **tabouret** or in *US* **taboret** /*tab'ə-ret* or *tä-boo-rā*/ *n* a low stool, *orig* drum-shaped; an embroidery frame, a tambour. **tabret** /*tab'rit*/ (*hist*) a small tabor.

Taborite /*tā'bə-rīt*/ *n* a Hussite of Žižka's party, opposed to the Calixtines or Utraquists (also *adj*). [*Tabor* in Bohemia, founded by them as headquarters].

tabouli see **tabbouleh**.

tabour, **tabourin**, etc and **tabret** see **tabor**.

tabu see **taboo**.

tabula /*tab'ū-lə*, *tab'ū-la*/ *n* (*pl* **tab'ulae** /*-lē*, *-lī*/) a writing tablet; an altar frontal (*relig*); a flattened structure; a horizontal partition in corals. [L, writing table]

■ **tab'ulate** *adj* having tabulae.

❑ **tabula rasa** /*tab'ū-la rä'zə* or *tab'ū-la rä'sa*/ *n* (*pl* **tabulae** /*-lē*, *-lī*/ **rasae** /*-sē*, *-sī*/) a smoothed or blank tablet; a clean slate (*lit* and *fig*); a mind not yet influenced by outside impressions and experience.

tabular /*tab'ū-lər*/ *adj* of, in the form of, like or according to, a table or tablet; laminated; platy; horizontally flattened. [L *tabula* table]

■ **tabularīzā'tion** or **-s-** *n*. **tab'ularize** or **-ise** *vt* to tabulate. **tab'ularly** *adv*. **tab'ulate** *vt* to reduce to or lay out in the form of a table or synopsis. ◆ *adj* tabular. **tabulā'tion** *n*. **tab'ulātor** *n* a person or machine that tabulates data; a device in a typewriter that sets and then finds automatically the margins, etc needed in tabular work; a machine that prints lists or tables of data from punched cards, etc, onto continuous paper (*comput*; *old*). **tab'ulatory** /*-lə-tə-ri*/ *adj*.

❑ **tabular spar** *n* another name for **wollastonite**.

tabun /*tä-boon'*/ (also with *cap*) *n* an organic phosphorus compound, $C_5H_{11}N_2O_2P$, which can be used as a nerve gas. [Ger]

tacahout /*tak'ə-howt*/ *n* a gall on the tamarisk, a source of gallic acid. [From Berber]

tacamahac /tak'ə-mə-hak/, also **tacmahack** /tak'mə-hak/ n a gum-resin yielded by several tropical trees; the balsam poplar, or its resin. [From Nahuatl]

TACAN, **Tacan** or **tacan** /tak'an/ n an electronic system of air navigation that gives an aircraft a direct reading of distance and bearing from a ground-based transmitter. [tactical air navigation]

tac-au-tac /tak'ō-tak'/ (fencing) n the parry combined with the riposte; also a series of close attacks and parries between fencers of equal skill. [Fr]

tace[1] /tā'sē or ta'kā/ imperative be silent. [L tacē, imperative, tacet, 3rd pers sing pr indic, of tacēre to be silent]
■ **tacet** /tā'set or ta'ket/ vi (music) is silent (marked on a score as an instruction for a particular singer or instrument).
■ **tace is Latin for a candle** a phrase understood as requesting or promising silence.

tace[2] see **tasse**.

tach or **tache** /tach/ (Bible) n a fastening or clasp. [OFr tache, cf **tack**[1] and **attach**]

tache[1] /tash/ (inf) n short for **moustache**.

tache[2] same as **tach**.

tacheometer /tak-i-om'i-tər/ n a surveying instrument for rapid measurement of points on a survey, such as distance, elevation, etc. [Fr tachéomètre, from Gr tache-, oblique stem of tachys swift, and of tachos speed, and -mètre -meter]
■ **tacheomet'ric** or **tacheomet'rical** adj. **tacheom'etry** n.

tachinid /tak'i-nid/ n any dipterous bristly fly of the family **Tachinidae** whose larvae are parasites of other insects and are therefore useful as a biological control of insect pests (also adj). [New L Tachina genus name, from Gr tachinos swift, from tachos swiftness]

tachism /tash'i-zm/ or (Fr) **tachisme** /ta-shē'zm'/ n a mid-20c movement in abstract painting characterized by irregular splotches and dabs of colour apparently applied at random for dramatic or emotional effect rather than to represent or express. [Fr tache blob (of paint)]
■ **tach'ist** or **tachiste** /-shēst/ n and adj.

tachistoscope /tə-kis'tə-skōp/ n an instrument that flashes visual images, sentences, etc onto a screen for brief, exactly measured intervals of time, used eg to test speed of perception and comprehension, and to increase reading speed. [Gr tachistos, superl of tachys swift, and -**scope**]
■ **tachistoscop'ic** adj. **tachistoscop'ically** adv.

tacho /tak'ō/ (inf) n (pl **tach'os**) a tachograph or tachometer.

tacho- /tak-ō-, -ə-, -o-/ combining form denoting speed. [Gr tachos speed]
■ **tach'ogram** n a record made by a tachograph. **tach'ograph** n a recording tachometer; a tachogram; an instrument fitted to commercial vehicles to record mileage, speed, number and location of stops, etc. **tachom'eter** n a device showing speed of rotation; an instrument for measuring the velocity of machines or currents. **tachomet'ric** or **tachomet'rical** adj. **tachom'etry** n.

tachy- /tak-i-/ combining form denoting fast, rapid. [Gr tachys swift]
■ **tachycar'dia** n abnormal rapidity of heartbeat. **tach'ygraph**, **tachyg'rapher** or **tachyg'raphist** n a shorthand writer, a stenographer or practitioner of tachygraphy. **tachygraph'ic** or **tachygraph'ical** adj. **tachyg'raphy** n shorthand, esp that used by the ancient Greeks and Romans; the abbreviated form of Greek and Latin found in medieval manuscripts. **tach'ylyte** n (also **tach'ylite**; Gr lytos melted, because easily fused; mineralogy) a black opaque glass occurring as a thin selvage to intrusive basalt. **tachylytic** or **tachylitic** /-lit'ik/ adj. **tachym'eter** n a tacheometer (qv). **tachymet'ric** or **tachymet'rical** adj. **tachym'etry** n. **tachyphasia** /-fā'zi-ə/ or **tachyphrasia** /-frā'zi-ə/ n (Gr phasis utterance, phrasis speed) abnormally rapid or voluble speech. **tachyphylaxis** /-fi-lak'sis/ n (Gr phylax a guard) rapid build-up of tolerance to the effects of a drug. **tachypnoea** or (US) **tachypnea** /-ip-nē'ə/ n (Gr -pnoia breathing) abnormally rapid respiration.

tachyon /tak'i-on/ (phys) n a theoretical elementary particle moving faster than light. [Gr tachys swift, and **-on**]

tacit /tas'it/ adj unspoken; understood or implied without being expressed directly; silent. [L tacitus silent, unspoken, unspeaking, from tacēre to be silent]
■ **tac'itly** adv. **tac'itness** n.

taciturn /tas'i-tûrn/ adj disinclined to speak, uncommunicative, reticent. [L taciturnus, from tacitus silent, unspoken or unspeaking]
■ **taciturn'ity** n. **tac'iturnly** adv.

tack[1] /tak/ n a short, sharp nail with a broad head; a drawing pin (N Am); a long loose temporary stitch; a fastening strip; a rope or other fastening for the lower windward corner of a sail (naut); the corner itself (naut); the course of a sailing ship with respect to the side of the

sail against which the wind is blowing (naut); an alternate course in zigzag to take advantage of wind blowing from the side when sailing to windward (naut); a course of action; a direction taken in argument, thinking, etc; a change of policy, a strategical move; something tacked on; stickiness. ◆ vt to attach or fasten, esp in a loose, hasty or impermanent manner, eg by tacks or long loose stitches; to append or affix (with on); to change the course of (a sailing ship) by a tack (naut); to steer (a sailing ship) by tacking. ◆ vi to change the course or tack of a ship by shifting the position of the sails (naut); to zigzag; to shift one's position, to veer; to change one's position or behaviour, often abruptly. [OFr taque, doublet of tache (see **tach**)]
■ **tacked** adj. **tack'er** n. **tack'et** n (Scot and dialect) a hobnail. **tack'ety** adj. **tack'ily** adv. **tack'iness** n. **tack'ing** n proceeding by tacks (naut); fastening; fastening by tacks; introducing into a bill (esp a money bill) provisions beyond its natural scope (politics). **tack'y** adj (**tack'ier**; **tack'iest**) slightly sticky.
□ **tacked'-on** adj. **tack hammer** n a light hammer for driving in tacks. **tack'-weld** vt and vi to join (pieces of metal) with several welds placed some distance apart. **tack'-welding** n.
■ **change tack** to change course, take a new direction. **on the right** (or **wrong**) **tack** following the right (or wrong) course of action, train of thought, etc.

tack[2] /tak/ n riding harness, saddles, bridles, etc. [**tackle**]
□ **tack room** n a room in or near a stable where tack is kept.

tack[3] /tak/ n food generally, fare, esp of the bread kind, such as hard tack (ship biscuit), soft tack (loaves). [Origin uncertain]

tack[4] /tak/ n the sound of a sharp tap. [Imit]

tack[5] see under **tacky**[1].

tack[6] /tak/ (Scot) n a tenure; a lease; a leased tenement; a spell; a take or catch. [See **tak** and **take**]
□ **tacks'man** n (Scot) a lessee; in the Scottish Highlands, a person who holds a lease and sublets.

tack[7] /tak/ (dialect) n any distinctive flavour, smack.

tacker, **tacket**, **tackety** see under **tack**[1].

tackiness see under **tack**[1] and **tacky**[1].

tacking see under **tack**[1].

tackle /tak'l/ n the ropes, rigging, etc of a ship (naut) /tāk'l/; tools, gear, weapons, equipment (for sports, etc); ropes, etc for raising heavy weights; a pulley; the act of gripping; an act of tackling (football); a player positioned on the outside of a guard on the line of scrimmage (American football); (also **wedding tackle**) the male genitalia (vulgar sl). ◆ vt to seize or take hold of; to grapple with; to come to grips with; to begin to deal in earnest with; to confront, encounter, challenge; to harness. ◆ vt and vi (rugby) to seize and stop or (football) intercept (a player who has possession of the ball) in an effort to get the ball away. [Cf LGer takel]
■ **tackled** /tak'ld/ adj fitted with harness or tackle; made of ropes (Shakesp). **tack'ler** n. **tack'ling** n furniture or apparatus belonging to the masts, yards, etc, of a ship; harness for drawing a carriage; tackle or instruments; grappling.

tacky[1] /tak'i/ (inf) adj (**tack'ier**; **tack'iest**) (orig US) shabby; sleazy; vulgar, gaudy, in bad taste. ◆ n (US) a poor ill-conditioned horse or person. [Origin uncertain]
■ **tack** n (back-formation) a shabby, vulgar or gaudy object or collection of objects; sleaze; bad taste. **tack'ily** adv. **tack'iness** n.

tacky[2] see under **tack**[1].

tacky[3] /tak'i/ (S Afr sl) n (pl **tack'ies**) a tennis shoe, plimsoll. [Perh from **tack**[1]]

tacmahack see **tacamahac**.

taco /tä'kō or tak'ō/ n (pl **ta'cos**) in Mexican cooking, a very thin rolled pancake with a meat filling, usu fried crisp. [Mex Sp]

taconite /tak'ə-nīt/ n a sedimentary rock containing enough iron to make it a low-grade iron ore. [Taconic Mountains in NE USA]

tacrine /tak'rēn/ n a drug used in the treatment of Alzheimer's disease.

tacrolimus /tə-krō'li-məs/ n a drug used in the treatment of atopic eczema and to prevent the rejection of organs after transplantation.

tact /takt/ n adroitness in managing the feelings of persons dealt with; fine perception in seeing and doing exactly what is best in the circumstances; the stroke in keeping time (music). [L tactus, -ūs, from tangere, tactum to touch]
■ **tact'ful** adj. **tact'fully** adv. **tact'fulness** n. **tact'less** adj. **tact'lessly** adv. **tact'lessness** n.

Tactel® /tak'tel/ n a soft, lightweight fabric used in sportswear. [L tactus, pap of tangere to touch]

tactic /tak'tik/ or **tactical** /tak'ti-kəl/ adj relating to taxis or tactism, or to tactics; (**tactical**) skilful, adroit, calculated; (**tactical**) of weapons, bombing, etc) used to support military or naval operations. ◆ n (**tactic**) a system, or a piece, of tactics. [Gr *taktikos* fit for arranging, from *taktos* ordered, verbal adj of *tassein* to arrange]

■ **tac'tically** *adv.* **tactician** /-*tish'ən*/ *n* a person skilled in tactics. **tactic'ity** *n* (*chem*) the stereochemical arrangement of units in the main chain of a polymer. **tac'tics** *n sing* the science or art of manoeuvring in presence of the enemy. ◆ *n pl* the means adopted to achieve an end; purposeful procedure. **tac'tism** *n* (*biol*) taxis.

❏ **tactical voting** *n* the practice of voting for a political party one does not support in order to prevent the election of a party one is even more opposed to.

tactile /*tak'tīl*/ *adj* perceptible by touch; relating to the sense of touch; concerned with perception by touch; suggestive of touch. [L *tactilis*, from *tangere, tactum* to touch]

■ **tactil'ist** /-*i-list*/ *n* a painter who aims at tactile effects. **tactil'ity** *n*.

taction /*tak'shən*/ (*rare*) *n* contact, touch. [L *tactiō, -ōnis*, from *tangere, tactum* to touch]

tactual /*tak'tū-əl*/ *adj* relating to or derived from the sense of touch. [L *tactus, -ūs* touch, from *tangere, tactum* to touch]

■ **tactual'ity** *n* tactual quality. **tact'ually** *adv.*

tad /*tad*/ (*inf, esp N Am*) *n* a small amount; a little lad. [Short for **tadpole**]

taddie /*tad'i*/ (*Aust inf*) a tadpole.

Tadjik see **Tajik**.

tadpole /*tad'pōl*/ *n* the larva of a toad or frog, or (rarely) of an ascidian. [OE *tāde* toad, and **poll**[1] (head)]

■ **Tadpole and Taper** political hacks, from characters in Disraeli's *Coningsby*.

Tadzhik see **Tajik**.

tae /*tā*/ a Scots form of **toe, to** and **too** (meaning 'also'), also in the phrase *the tae* for *that ae*, the one (adjectivally). [See **tone**[2] and **tother**]

Tae-Bo® /*tā'bō* or *tī'bō*/ *n* an exercise system that combines the techniques of tae kwon do with aerobics and dance routines. [Korean *tae* kick, and **boxing**]

taedium an obsolete spelling of **tedium**.

❏ **taedium vitae** /*tē'di-əm vī'tē* or *tī'di-ŭm vē'tī* or *wē'tī*/ *n* (L) weariness of life.

tae kwon do /*tī* or *tā kwon dō'* or -*kwon'dō*/ *n* a Korean martial art, similar to karate. [Korean *tae* kick, *kwon* fist, and *do* method]

tael /*tāl*/ *n* Chinese *liang* or ounce, about 38g (1.3oz); a money of account (not normally a coin) in China, *orig* a tael weight of pure silver. [Port, from Malay *tail* weight]

❏ **tael bar** *n* a gold bullion measure used in the Far East (1, 5 or 10 tael weight).

ta'en /*tān*/ a contraction of **taken**.

taenia or (*US*) **tenia** /*tē'ni-ə*/ *n* (*pl* **tae'niae** /-*ni-ē*/ or **tae'nias**) a ribbon or headband; the band above the architrave of the Doric order (*archit*); a ribbon-like structure; any member of the tapeworm genus *Taenia*. [L, from Gr *tainia* a band]

■ **taen'iacide** /-*sīd*/ *n* a substance that destroys tapeworms. **taen'iafuge** /-*fūj*/ *n* a substance, eg a drug, for expelling tapeworms from the body. **taenī'asis** *n* infestation with tapeworms. **tae'niate** or **tae'nioid** *adj* like a ribbon or a tapeworm.

TAFE /*tāf*/ *abbrev*: Technical and Further Education.

tafferel see **taffrail**.

taffeta /*taf'i-tə*/ or **taffetas** /*taf'i-tas*/ *n* a thin glossy silk fabric; loosely applied to various similar or mixed fabrics. ◆ *adj* (also **taffety** /*taf'i-ti*/) made of taffeta; florid, over-dainty (*Shakesp*). [Through Fr or LL from Pers *tāftah* woven, from *tāftan* to twist]

taffrail /*taf'rāl*/, also **tafferel** /-*ə-rəl*/ *n* the rail round the stern of a ship; the upper part of a ship's stern timbers. [Du *tafereel* a panel, from *tafel* a table]

Taffy /*taf'i*/ (*sl, often offensive*) *n* a Welshman. [From *Dafydd*, Welsh form of David]

taffy /*taf'i*/ *n* toffee (*N Am*); flattery, blarney (*US inf*).

tafia or **taffia** /*taf'i-ə*/ *n* a type of rum. [Perh a W Ind name, but cf Malay *tāfiā*]

tag[1] /*tag*/ *n* a tab; a label, *esp* a tie-on label; an identifying mark or sign; a symbol or signature used by a graffiti-writer, eg as a message, means of identification, etc (*sl*); a device used for electronic tagging (qv); a label or marker giving summarized information, descriptions, attributes, etc which apply to the text following (or if one of a pair, also preceding) it (*comput*); the metal or plastic point of a lace; any small thing tacked or attached to another; a flap, or a loose or flapping end; a flap of a slashed garment; a shred; a stray, matted or dirty lock, eg of a sheep's wool; the tip of an animal's tail; the tail end; a trite (*esp* Latin) quotation; a moral to a story; the closing words of a play, etc, *usu* addressed to the audience; a refrain; a vehicle licence plate (*US*);

a parking ticket (*US*); the rabble, the common people (*obs*); anything mean; a piece of brightly-coloured wire, fabric, etc tied to the end of the body of an artificial fly (*angling*); (in *pl*) a footman's shoulder-knot. ◆ *vt* (**tagg'ing; tagged**) to put a tag or tags on; to attach as a tag; to put a signature or similar mark on (*sl*); to mark (text) with tags (*comput*); to apply a hashtag to (an item posted on a social media site); to fit with an electronic tag; to tack, fasten, append; to remove tags from; to dog or follow closely; to give (a driver or vehicle) a parking ticket (*US*); to replace an atom in (a molecule or compound) by a radioactive isotope, for the purpose of identification. ◆ *vi* to make tags, to string words or ideas together; to go behind as a follower (with *on* or *along*). [Origin obscure]

■ **taggee** *n* a person wearing an electronic tag. **tagg'er** *n*. **tagg'ers** *n pl* thin sheet iron or sheet steel coated with tin. **tagg'ing** *n*. **tagg'y** *adj* (of eg wool) matted into tags. **tag'less** *adj*.

❏ **tag day** *n* (*N Am*) a flag day. **tag end** *n* (*esp N Am*) the fag end, tail end. **tagged atom** *n* a radioactive isotopic atom of a tracer element. **tag line** *n* (*esp N Am*) a punchline; a watchword, slogan. **tag question** *n* an interrogative clause (eg *can't you?*) added to the end of a statement to invite agreement (also **question tag**). **tag'rag** *n* the rabble (*old*); a fluttering rag, a tatter. ◆ *adj* vulgar (*old*); ragged. **tag tail** *n* a worm with a tail like a tag.

■ **tag along** (with *with*) to follow, accompany or trail after someone, *esp* when uninvited. **tag rag and bobtail** rag-tag and bobtail.

tag[2] /*tag*/ *n* the children's game of tig; the act of putting out a runner by touching him or her with the ball or the hand holding the ball (*baseball*). ◆ *vt* (**tagg'ing; tagged**) to tig; to put out (a runner) by a tag (*baseball*). [Ety doubtful]

❏ **tag team** *n* a pair of tag wrestlers; a pair of people working together (chiefly *N Am*). **tag wrestling** *n* a contest between two teams of two wrestlers, in which only one wrestler from each team is in the ring at any one time and may be replaced by the wrestler outside the ring after touching the latter's hand.

Tagálog or **Tagalog** /*tə-gä'log*/ *n* a people of the Philippine Islands; their Austronesian language. ◆ *adj* of or relating to the Tagálog or their language.

tagetes /*tə-jē'tēz*/ *n* (*pl* **tagē'tes**) a plant of the Mexican and S American *Tagetes* genus of composites with yellow and orange flowers, *incl* the French marigold and African marigold. [L *Tagēs*, an Etruscan god]

tagine or **tajine** /*ta-zhēn'*/ *n* a conical clay pot used in N African cooking; any stew cooked in such a pot. [Fr dimin of **taj**]

Tagliacotian see **Taliacotian**.

tagliarini or **taglierini** /*täl-yə-rē'ni*/ *n* pasta cut into flat, very thin strips. [Ital]

tagliatelle /*tal-yə-tel'*i, *tä-lya-tel'ä*/ *n* pasta made in long ribbons. [Ital]

taglioni /*tal-yō'nē*/ *n* an early-19c overcoat. [Named after a family of Italian ballet dancers]

tagma /*tag'mə*/ (*zool*) *n* (*pl* **tag'mata**) any of the distinct regions of the body in arthropods and other animals with segmented bodies, eg, in insects, the head, thorax or abdomen. [Gr, a grouping or arrangement, from *tassein* to arrange]

tagmeme /*tag'mēm*/ (*linguistics*) *n* any of the positions in the structure of a sentence into which a certain class of grammatical items can fit. [Gr *tagma* arrangement, order]

■ **tagme'mic** *adj.* **tagme'mics** *n sing* the analysis of the grammar of a language based on the arrangement or positions of the spoken elements.

taguan /*tag'wan* or *tä'gwän*/ *n* a large East Indian flying squirrel. [Tagálog]

taha /*tä'hä*/ *n* a S African weaver bird. [Zulu *taka*]

tahini /*tə-hē'nē*/ or **tahina** /-*na*/ *n* an oily paste made of crushed sesame seeds. [Ar, from *ṭaḥana* to grind]

Tahitian /*tä-hē'shən*/ *adj* of or relating to *Tahiti* in the S Pacific, its inhabitants or their language. ◆ *n* a native or inhabitant of Tahiti; the Polynesian language of Tahiti.

tahr or **tehr** /*tär*/ *n* a beardless Himalayan wild goat (*Hemitragus jemlahicus*) that frequents forest peaks. [Appar its name in the W Himalayas, confused with Nepali *thār*; see **thar**]

tahsil, tahsildar see **tehsil**.

TAI *abbrev*: *Temps Atomique Internationale* (*Fr*), International Atomic Time.

Tai or **T'ai** same as **Thai**.

tai /*tī*/ *n* a Japanese sea bream. [Jap]

taiaha /*tī'ə-hä*/ *n* a Maori weapon in the form of a carved staff, now held during ceremonial public speaking. [Maori]

t'ai chi /*tī chē'*/ or **t'ai chi ch'uan** /*chwän'*/ *n* a Chinese system of exercise and self-defence in which good use of co-ordination and balance allows effort to be minimized. [Chin *tài* greatest, *jí* extreme, and *quán* fist]

Taig /*tāg*/ (*offensive sl*) *n* (in Northern Ireland) a Catholic. [Variant of *Teague*, orig used as nickname for any Irishman]

taiga /*tī'gə*/ *n* marshy pine forest spreading across much of subarctic N America and Eurasia, with tundra to the north and steppe to the south. [Russ *taiga*]

taigle /*tā'gl*/ (*Scot*) *vt* to entangle or hinder. ◆ *vi* to linger or loiter; to trudge. [Cf Swed (Bornholm) *taggla* to disorder]

taiko or **daiko** /*tī'kō*/ *n* (*pl* **tai'ko, taikos, dai'ko** or **dai'kos**) a large Japanese drum. [Jap]

taikonaut /*tī'kə-nöt*/ *n* an astronaut in the Chinese space programme. [Chin *tàikōng* outer space, and Gr *nautēs* a sailor]

tail¹ /*tāl*/ *n* the posterior extremity of an animal, *usu* a slender prolongation beyond the anus; a bird's train of feathers; a fish's caudal fin; anything of similar appearance, position, etc; the back, lower, rear, latter, downstream, weaker or inferior part or prolongation of anything, often *opp* to *head*; the rear, stabilizing part of an aircraft, *incl* tailplane, fin and control surfaces, or of a rocket, missile, etc; the stem of a note in written music; a downward extension of a letter; a retinue, suite; a queue; a train; anything long and trailing or hanging, such as a catkin, the luminous train of a comet or long curl or braid of hair; (*usu* in *pl*) the reverse of a coin; (in *pl*) the depleted uranium produced during enrichment (*nuclear eng*); the end of a shoal sloping into deeper water; the weaker batsmen at the end of a team's batting order (*cricket*); (often in *pl*) the skirts of a garment (*old*); (in *pl*) a tail coat; (in *pl*) evening dress, *incl* a tail coat; in Turkey, a horse-tail, formerly a mark of rank; a person engaged to follow and keep a constant watch on someone (*inf*); the route or course taken by someone running away (*inf*); the margin at the bottom of the page, or the bottom edge of the page (*printing*); the buttocks, backside (*inf*); the female genitalia or the penis (*sl*); sexual intercourse (*sl*); a woman (*offensive sl*). ◆ *vt* to provide with a tail; to be a tail to; to remove the tail or stalk from; to grip or drag by the tail; to join end to end; to insert or incorporate the end of (a tile, brick, timber, etc) into a wall or other support; to herd (*Aust*); to follow closely, shadow. ◆ *vi* to taper (often with *off* or *away*); to lessen or deteriorate slowly (with *off* or *away*); to straggle; to show the tail. [OE *tægl, tægel*; Gothic *tagl* hair]
■ **tailed** *adj* having a tail (of a specific kind); with the tail removed. **tail'ing** *n* the inner covered end of a projecting brick or stone in a wall (*building*); a winter sport in which a tail-like string of luges is drawn along by a horse-sleigh; (in *pl*) refuse, dregs; (in *pl*) the rejected or washed away portion of an ore (*mining*); (in *pl*) poor quality grain or flour; (in *pl*) the higher boiling fraction in a distillation process. **tail'less** *adj* having no tail. **tail'-like** *adj*.
❑ **tail'back** *n* a line of traffic stretching back from anything obstructing or slowing down traffic flow; the running back positioned furthest away from the line of scrimmage (*American football*). **tail'board** *n* a movable board at the back of a cart, wagon or lorry. **tail'bone** *n* the coccyx. **tail boom** *n* a longitudinal strut supporting the tail of an aeroplane. **tail coat** *n* a man's formal coat, cut away at the front and with narrow tails at the back. **tail covert** *n* any of a bird's covert feathers covering the base of its tail feathers. **tail end** *n* the fag end, final and/or inferior part; (in *pl*) inferior corn sorted out from better; something that comes at the end. **tail-end Charlie** *n* (*inf*) a person who comes at the end. **tail-en'der** *n* (*inf*) someone or something coming at the end. **tail feather** *n* one of the rectrices or stiff rudder-feathers of a bird's tail, used in steering; a feather on a bird's back forming a train, as in the peacock. **tail fly** *n* (*angling*) the fly at the end of the leader. **tail'gate** *n* lower gate of a lock; a tailboard (*N Am*); a door at the back of a car that opens upwards on hinges at its top edge; a jazz style of playing *esp* the trombone. ◆ *vt* and *vi* (*sl*) to drive dangerously close behind (another vehicle). ◆ *vi* (*N Am*) to picnic around the boot of one's car, *esp* outside a stadium before a sports match. **tail'gater** *n* a person who tailgates. **tail lamp** or **tail light** *n* (*esp N Am*) a *usu* red light carried at the back of a train, tram, car or other vehicle. **tail'piece** *n* a piece at the tail or end; an engraving, design, etc occupying the bottom of a page, eg at the end of a chapter; a strip of ebony, etc to which the ends of the strings are attached in a fiddle. **tail'pipe** *n* the exhaust pipe of a car (*orig US*); the suction-pipe in a pump. ◆ *vt* to tie a tin can or similar object to the tail of (a dog) to frighten or annoy it (the precise force of 'pipe' being unknown). **tail'plane** *n* a horizontal aerofoil on the tail of an aircraft. **tail'race** *n* the channel in which water runs away below a millwheel, or from a hydraulically-operated machine, etc. **tail rhyme** or **tailed rhyme** *n* a verse form in which two or more rhymed lines are followed by a shorter line that does not rhyme with the others. **tail rope** *n* a rope attached to the rear part of anything. **tail rotor** *n* (on a helicopter) a small rear propeller designed to counteract the torque of the main rotor. **tail'skid** *n* a support under the tail of an aeroplane on the ground; (in a motor vehicle) a skid starting with the rear wheels. **tail'spin** *n* a spiral dive of an aeroplane; an uncontrolled downward

spiral; a state of panic or frenzy (*inf*). **tail'stock** *n* a slidable casting mounted on a lathe, aligned with the headstock, used to support the free end of the piece being worked on. **tail'wheel** *n* a wheel at the rear of a vehicle, *esp* that under the rear end of an aircraft. **tail wind** *n* a wind blowing in the same direction as one is travelling in.
■ **a bit** (or **piece**) **of tail** (*offensive sl*) a woman. **not make head or tail of** to make no sense of. **on someone's tail** following someone very closely. **tail off** to become gradually less or fewer. **tail of the eye** the outer corner of the eye; the margin of the field of vision. **the tail wagging the dog** (*inf*) a situation in which the less important element or factor controls or influences the more important. **turn tail** to turn round (and run off). **twist the lion's tail** to irritate Britain. **with one's tail up** perky, in good humour. **with the tail between the legs** in a state of dejection after chastisement or humiliation, like a beaten cur.

tail² /*tāl*/ (*law*) *n* limitation of inheritance to certain heirs. ◆ *adj* limited. [Fr *taille* cutting]
❑ **tail male** *n* limitation to male heirs.
■ **in tail** subject to such a limitation.

tailard see **tailor²**.

taileron /*tā'lə-ron*/ (*aeronautics*) *n* either part of a two-piece tailplane whose two halves can operate either together or differentially. [**tail¹** and **aileron**]

taille /*tī*/ (*hist*) *n* (*pl* **tailles** /*tī*/) a tax levied by a French king or overlord on his subjects, or on lands held from or under him. [Fr, from OFr *taillier* to cut or shape]

tailleur /*ta-yûr'*/ *n* a woman's tailored suit. [Fr]

taillie see **tailzie**.

tailor¹ /*tā'lər*/ *n* a person whose business is to cut out and make outer garments, *esp* for men (*fem* **tail'oress**); any of several fish, *incl* the bluefish and the Australian skipjack (*Teninodon saltator*); a teller stroke (*bellringing*; *esp dialect*). ◆ *vi* to work as a tailor. ◆ *vt* to make clothes for; to fit with clothes; to fashion by tailor's work; to make or adapt so as to fit a special need exactly. [Anglo-Fr *taillour* (Fr *tailleur*), from LL *tāliātor, -ōris*, from *tāliāre* to cut]
■ **tail'ored** *adj* tailor-made; wearing well-tailored clothes; well cared for. **tail'oring** *n*.
❑ **tail'orbird** *n* any Asian warbler of the genus *Orthotomus* (*esp O. sutorius*) that sews leaves together to form a nest. **tail'or-made** *adj* made by a tailor to fit a particular person; exactly adapted (for a purpose). ◆ *n* a tailor-made garment; a factory-made cigarette, not one rolled by hand (*inf*). **tail'ormake** *vt* (*orig* and *esp US*) to make especially to suit a particular purpose or person, etc. **tailor's chalk** *n* a small piece of French chalk used by tailors and dressmakers to mark the position of seams, darts, etc on cloth. **tailor's tack** *n* a long loose stitch used eg to hold fabric to a pattern during cutting, or to mark the position of seams, darts, etc prior to fitting.

tailor² /*tā'lər*/ (*Shakesp, Midsummer Night's Dream* II.1.54) *interj* variously explained as referring to a tumble backwards, *opp* to *header*, to the tailor-like squatting position that results, or as the obsolete **tailard**, a person with a tail.

tailzie, tailye or **taillie** /*tāl'yi, tā'li*/ (*law*) *n* Scots forms of **tail²**; entail.

Taino /*tī'nō*/ *n* (*pl* **Tai'nos** or collectively **Tai'no**) a member of an extinct Indian tribe of the West Indies; the language spoken by this people. ◆ *adj* of or relating to the Taino or their language.

taint /*tānt*/ *n* a stain or blemish; pollution; infection; a tinge of some evil quality; a contaminating or corrupting influence; a latent or incipient defect or corruption; attaint (*obs*); a hit in tilting (*obs*); tint, tinge (*obs*). ◆ *vt* to affect or imbue with anything objectionable; to contaminate or infect; to impart a taint to, to tarnish; to attaint (*obs*); to touch in tilting (*obs*); to tint, tinge (*obs*). ◆ *vi* to become infected or rotten; to go bad; to weaken, wilt, wither. [Partly aphetic for **attaint**; partly OFr *taint* (Fr *teint*), from L *tinctus, -ūs*, from *tingere, tinctum* to wet, dye]
■ **taint'ed** *adj*. **taint'less** *adj*. **taint'lessly** *adv*. **taint'ure** *n* defilement.
❑ **taint'-worm** *n* (*Milton*) a worm supposed to infect cattle.

'taint /*tānt*/ (*sl* or *non-standard*) contraction of **it is not**.

taipan¹ /*tī'pan*/ *n* a large venomous Australian snake, *Oxyuranus scutellatus*. [Aboriginal name]

taipan² /*tī'pan*/ *n* a foreigner living in China and head of a foreign business there. [Chin (Cantonese)]

T'ai-p'ing /*tī-ping'*/ *n* the new order that Hong Xiquan sought to found in central and N China; a participator in his rebellion (1851–65). [Chin *tài píng* great peace or great harmony]

taira see **tayra**.

taisch or **taish** /*tīsh*/ *n* (in the Scottish Highlands) an apparition or voice, *esp* of someone about to die; second-sight. [Gaelic *taibhis, taibhse* apparition]

tait¹ same as **tate**.

tait² /tāt/ (*Aust*) *n* the honey possum (genus *Tarsipes*). [Aboriginal name]

taiver see **taver¹,²**.

taivert see under **taver²**.

Taiwanese /tī-wə-nēz'/ *adj* of or relating to the island of *Taiwan* or its people. ◆ *n* (*pl* **Taiwanese'**) a native of Taiwan.

taj /täj/ *n* a crown; a dervish's tall conical cap. [Ar and Pers *tāj* crown]

Tajik, **Tadjik** or **Tadzhik** /taj'ik/ *n* a people of an Iranian race living in Tajikistan and other central Asian countries; a member of this people; its dialect, resembling Farsi. ◆ *adj* of or relating to the Tajiks or their dialect. [Pers, a Persian]

tak /tak or täk/ a Scots form of **take**.

taka /tä'kə/ *n* the standard monetary unit of Bangladesh (100 poisha). [Bengali]

takahe /tä'kə-hē/ *n* a large flightless bird (*Notornis* or *Porphyrio mantelli*) of the rail family with brilliant blue-green plumage, a heavy pink bill and a large red shield on its forehead, thought to be extinct until 1948 when a small population was discovered in the South Island of New Zealand. [Maori]

takamaka /tak'ə-mak-ə/ same as **tacamahac**.

take /tāk/ *vt* (*pat* **took**, *pap* **tā'ken**) to lay hold of; to get into one's possession; to seize, catch, capture; to captivate; to receive or come to have willingly or by an act of one's own; to pay for, buy or rent; to appropriate; to assume, adopt; to consider as an example; to accept; to receive; to admit; to submerge (*Scot*); to have normally assigned to one; to find out, come upon, surprise, detect; to swallow or inhale; to eat or drink, often habitually; to apply to oneself; to obtain; to engage, secure; to seek and receive; to have recourse to; to make use of; to deal with or react to in a specified way; to teach (a subject or class); to attend a course in; to undertake (a course) or attend (a regular class) in some subject; to visit; to call for, necessitate, use up; to remove; to cause to go; to subtract; to convey; to carry with one; to escort; to detract; to derive; to understand; to apprehend; (with *it*) to assume, suppose; to mistake; to conceive or think of; to accept as true; to tolerate or endure; to ascertain; to observe or measure; to ascertain something from; to execute, perform; to set down; to portray; to photograph; to charge oneself with; to declare solemnly; to strike; to come upon and affect; to bewitch or charm; to blight; to put an end to (someone's, or one's own, life); to cheat, swindle or deceive (*inf*); to deliver, give (*obs*); to have sexual intercourse with (*archaic*); to betake. ◆ *vi* to have the intended effect; to be effective, to work; (of plants, *esp* grafted buds) to begin to grow shoots (cf **strike**); to please the public; to betake oneself, begin; (of a fish) to bite; to make a capture or acquisition; to be capable of being taken; to become, fall, eg ill (*inf*); to freeze (*N Am*); to cast a spell (*Shakesp*). ◆ *n* an act of taking, or of catching (eg the ball in rugby, etc); a person's opinion or perspective on a particular situation, concept, etc; a capture; quantity taken on one occasion; the amount of money taken, eg from a business enterprise, admission charges, etc; the amount of film (eg one scene) photographed, music recorded, etc at any one time; the amount of copy set up by a printer at one time; a sign on the body (eg a rash) that a vaccine has been successful; a successful tissue graft. [Late OE *tacan* (pat *tōc*) to touch, take, from ON *taka* (pat *tōk*; pap *tekinn*)]

■ **take'able** or **tā'kable** *adj*. **tā'ken** *adj* (with *with*; *inf*) impressed or attracted by. **tā'ker** *n*. **tā'king** *n* the action of the verb in any sense; (*usu* in *pl*) that which is taken; receipts; plight (*Spenser*); bewitchment, malignant influence (*Shakesp*); agitation, perplexity (*inf*). ◆ *adj* captivating; alluring; infectious, catching. **tā'kingly** *adv*. **tā'kingness** *n*. **tā'ky** *adj* (*old inf*) attractive.

❑ **take'away** *adj* (of cooked food) sold for consumption away from the place of sale; (of a restaurant) selling such food. ◆ *n* such a restaurant; a takeaway meal. **take'-down** *n* a humiliation. ◆ *adj* capable of being disassembled quickly. **take-home pay** *n* pay after deduction of tax, etc. **take'-in** *n* a deception, fraud or disappointment of hopes. **take'-leave** *n* leave-taking. **take'-off** *n* a burlesque mimicking; the place, act or mode of leaving the ground for a jump, dive or flight (also *fig*); a drawback. **take-off rocket** *n* (*aeronautics*) a rocket used to assist the acceleration of an aircraft at take-off. **take'out** *adj* (*N Am*) takeaway. ◆ *adj* and *n* (*bridge*) (of or designating) a conventional bid asking one's partner to bid a different suit. **take'over** *n* the acquirement of control of a business by purchase of a majority of its shares (also *adj*). **take'-up** *n* the fact, or an instance, of taking up (ie using or accepting, or picking up). **take-up rate** *n* the number of people, as a percentage of the total number eligible, who claim a benefit to which they are entitled or who accept an offer. **tāking-off'** *n* removal, assassination.

■ Many phrases with **take** are given below; others are covered in the entries for their other elements: **for the taking** readily available to be taken (advantage of). **have what it takes** to possess the requisite skills, qualities, etc. **on the take** engaged in small-scale dishonest making of

profit. **take after** to resemble (eg a parent) in appearance or characteristics. **take against** to take a dislike to; to oppose. **take apart** to separate into component parts; to defeat convincingly (*inf*); to criticize or scold severely (*sl*). **take away** to subtract; to carry somewhere else, remove; to detract (from). **take back** to retract, withdraw; to carry back (mentally) in time; to return to an original position; to regain possession of; to move (text) to the previous line (*printing*). **take down** to go above in class; to demolish, pull down or dismantle; to take to pieces; to report or write down to dictation; (of a man) to escort (a lady) to the dining room; (also, more *usu*, **take down a peg**) to humiliate to some degree; to reduce; to lower. **take effect** to come off, succeed; to come into force. **take five** (or **ten**) (*inf*) to take a short break of five (or ten) minutes. **take for** to suppose to be, *esp* wrongly. **take fright** see under **fright**. **take heed** to be careful; to pay attention. **take in** to enclose; to comprise; to annex; to grasp, realize or understand; to accept as true; to cheat; to subscribe for, buy regularly; to receive into one's home, eg as a guest or lodger; to accept (work, eg washing) for doing in one's own home for payment; to tighten, contract, make smaller; to furl; to admit; to subdue; to visit (a place) or go to (a show, etc) *esp* as part of an itinerary or plan (*esp US*); (of a man) to conduct (a lady) to the dining room (*hist*). **take in hand** to undertake; to undertake to reform, help or guide (someone). **take into one's head** to be seized with a notion. **take in vain** to use (eg God's name) with unsuitable levity. **take it** to assume; to endure punishment or bad luck without giving way or collapsing under the strain (*inf*). **take it from me** you can believe me, believe me when I say. **take it from there** to deal with a situation appropriately, at whatever point it falls to one to do so. **take it or leave it** to accept something with all its disadvantages, or else do without it. **take it out of** to exhaust the strength or energy of; to exact the utmost from. **take it out on** to make (an innocent person or object) suffer for one's anger or frustration; to vent one's bad temper, anger, etc on. **take me with you** (*Shakesp*) let me understand what you mean. **take notice** to observe; to show that observation is made; (with *of*) to remark upon. **take off** to remove, detach; to mimic; to leave the ground for a jump or flight; to begin a rapid improvement, expansion, or surge in popularity; to depart or set out (*inf*); to swallow. **take on** to receive aboard; to agree to do, to undertake; to assume or acquire; to take into employment; to be very upset or distraught (*inf*); to accept a challenge from (*esp* a stronger opponent); (of ideas, etc) to gain acceptance. **take out** to remove from within; to extract; to go out with, escort; to obtain (eg a licence) on application; to receive an equivalent for; to copy (*Shakesp*); to kill, destroy or defeat (*sl*); to bid a different suit from (one's partner) (*bridge*). **take over** to receive by transfer; to convey across; to assume control of; to move (text) to the following line (*printing*). **take someone out of himself** or **herself** to make someone forget his or her problems or worries. **take someone up on** to accept someone's offer or challenge with respect to; to challenge someone over (a statement, point, etc). **take to** to make for, take oneself off to; to adapt oneself to; to become fond of, to begin to do regularly as a habit. **take to pieces** to separate into component parts. **take to task** to call to account, reprove. **take to wife** (*archaic*) to marry. **take up** to lift, raise or collect; to pick up for use; to absorb; to accept (an offer); to adopt the practice, study, etc, of, begin to go in for; to begin to patronize, seek to advance; to become interested in and begin to do; to discuss with; to shorten (a garment); to engross, occupy or fill fully; to interrupt sharply; to arrest; to resume; to take in hand; to buy up; to settle, compound (a quarrel) (*Shakesp*); to reprove (*Shakesp*); to cope with (*Shakesp*); to obtain on credit (*Shakesp*); (*usu* in passive) to interest, please (with *about* or *with*); to borrow; to secure, fasten. **take upon oneself** to assume; to presume; to take responsibility for; to undertake; to feign, make believe (*Shakesp*). **take up with** to begin to associate with, form a connection with.

takhi or **taki** /tak'i/ *n* a rare wild horse (*Equus przewalskii*) native to the Mongolian steppes, with a reddish-brown coat, stiff black mane and white muzzle. [Native Mongolian name]

takin /tä'kin or tä-kēn'/ *n* a large horned, hoofed mammal (*Budorcas taxicolor*) of the Himalayas, China, etc, related to the goats and antelopes. [Tibetan]

tala¹ /tä'lə/ *n* (*pl* **ta'la** or **ta'las**) the standard monetary unit of Samoa (100 sene). [Samoan]

tala² /tä'la/ *n* a traditional rhythmic pattern in Indian music. [Sans, hand-clapping]

talak see **talaq**.

talant and **talaunt** Spenserian forms of **talon**.

talapoin /tal'ə-poin/ *n* (a title of respect for) a Buddhist monk, *esp* of Pegu, Myanmar (Burma); a small green W African guenon monkey (*Cercopithecus talapoin*). [Port *talapão*, from Old Peguan *tala pói* my lord]

talaq or **talak** /ta-läk'/ *n* (under Islamic law) a form of divorce. [Ar *talāq* divorce]

talar, **talaria** see under **talus**[1].

talayot /tä-lä'yot/ (*archaeol*) *n* a prehistoric *usu* unchambered stone monument of the Balearic Islands. [Balearic Sp for Sp *atalaya* an outlook, from Ar *al talā'i* the vanguard]

talbot /töl'bət/ *n* a breed of broad-mouthed large-eared hound, *usu* white, now extinct. [Poss from the *Talbot* family]

talbotype /töl'bə-tīp/ *n* calotype, invented by William Henry Fox *Talbot* (1800–77).

talc /talk/ *n* talcum powder; a very soft, pliable, greasy, silvery-white, foliated, granular or compact mineral, acid magnesium silicate, found in magnesium-rich rocks and dolomitic limestones. ◆ *vt* (**talc'ing** /talk'/ or **talck'ing**; **talc'ed** /talkt/ or **talck'ed**) to apply or treat with talc. [Fr *talc* or LL *talcum*, from Ar *talq*, from Pers *talk*]
■ **talc'ose**, **talc'ous**, **talc'y** /talk'/ or **talck'y** *adj*. **talc'um** *n* talc.
❑ **talc schist** *n* a schistose rock composed essentially of talc, with accessory minerals. **talcum powder** *n* purified powdered talc, *usu* perfumed, applied to the skin to absorb moisture.

tale /tāl/ *n* a narrative, story; an act of telling; a false story; a mere story; (in *pl*) things told idly or to get others into trouble; number, total (*archaic*); reckoning (*archaic*); discourse, talk (*obs*). [OE *talu* story, number; Ger *Zahl* number]
■ **tale'ful** *adj* full of stories.
❑ **tale'bearer** *n* someone who gossips idly or maliciously passes on (*esp* discreditable) information about others, *esp* to someone in authority. **tale'bearing** *n* and *adj*. **tale'-teller** *n* a teller of stories, narrator; a talebearer. **tale'-telling** *n*.
■ **be in a** (or **one**) **tale** (*archaic*) to be in full agreement. **old wives' tale** a superstitious or misleading story, explanation or precept; any extraordinary tale that makes demands on one's credulity. **tell a tale** to disclose something important. **tell one's** (or **its**) **own tale** to speak for oneself or itself. **tell tales** to gossip or pass on (discreditable) information about others, to be a talebearer. **tell tales out of school** to reveal confidential matters.

talea /tä'li-ə/ (*music*) *n* (*pl* **taleae** /tä'li-ē/) a recurring rhythmic pattern in isorhythmic medieval motets. [L, literally stick or cutting]

talegalla /tal-i-gal'ə/ *n* the brush turkey, *Talegalla* (or *Alectura*) *lathami*. [Malagasy *talèva* the purple coot, and L *gallus* a cock]

Taleggio /tä-led'jō/ *n* a semi-soft cow's milk cheese from *Taleggio* in the Lombardy region of Italy.

talent[1] /tal'ənt/ *n* any natural or special gift; special aptitude or ability; eminent ability short of genius; people possessing special ability; young girls or young men, *esp* attractive, handsome, etc (*sl*); disposition; *orig* an ancient unit of weight and of money equal to 60 minas or 6000 drachmas, or about 38kg (Aeginetan talent), 25kg (Euboic), 26kg (Attic) of gold or silver; hence (from the parable in Bible, Matthew 25.14–30) faculty. [L *talentum*, from Gr *talanton* a balance, a talent]
■ **tal'ented** *adj* possessing talent or aptitude. **tal'entless** *adj*.
❑ **talent scout** or **talent spotter** *n* someone whose business is to discover and recruit talented people, *esp* in entertainment and sport. **tal'ent-spot** *vi* and *vt*.

talent[2] an old form (Shakesp, *Walter Scott*, now *dialect*) of **talon**.

taler see **thaler**.

tales /tā'lēz/ (*orig pl; law*) *n* the filling up, from those who are present, of a deficiency in the number of jurors. [From the phrase *tālēs de circumstantibus* such of the bystanders; *tālēs*, pl of L *tālis* such]
❑ **talesman** /tā'lēz-mən or tālz'mən/ *n* a bystander chosen to make up a deficiency in a jury.
■ **pray a tales** to plead that the number of jurors be completed in this way.

tali see **talus**[1].

Taliacotian or **Tagliacotian** /tal-yə-kō'shən/ *adj* relating to the Italian surgeon Gasparo *Tagliacozzi* or *Taliacotius* (1546–99), or his rhinoplastic operation.

Talib /tal'ib/ *n* a member of the **Taliban** or **Taleban** /tal'i-bän/, an Islamic fundamentalist group ruling Afghanistan from 1996 to 2001. [Ar *tālib* seeker]

taligrade /tal'i-grād/ (*zool*) *adj* walking on the outside of the feet. [L *talus* ankle, and *gradus* step]

talion /tal'i-ən/ (*legal hist*) *n* like for like; retaliation. [L *tāliō, -ōnis* like punishment, from *tālis* such]
■ **talion'ic** *adj*.

talipes /tal'i-pēz/ *n* club foot. [L *tālus* ankle, and *pēs* foot]
■ **tal'iped** /-ped/ *adj* having a club foot (also *n*).

talipot or **talipat** /tal'i-pot, -pat, -put/ *n* an E Asian palm (genus *Corypha*) with large, hand-shaped leaves. [Sinhalese *talapata*, from Sans *tālī* palmyra palm, and *pattra* leaf]

talisman /tal'is-mən or -iz-/ *n* (*pl* **tal'ismans**) an object supposed to be endued with magical powers and able to protect, bring good fortune, etc to the possessor; an amulet or charm. [Ar *tilsam*, from Gr *telesma* payment, certificate, later completion, rite, consecrated object, from *teleein* to complete, fulfil, consecrate]
■ **talismanic** /-man'ik/ or **talisman'ical** *adj*.

talk /tök/ *vi* to speak, to express or communicate in spoken words; to converse; to have a discussion (often with *about*); to give a talk or lecture; to chat or gossip; to be able to speak; to speak indiscreetly; to divulge secrets, part with (*esp* incriminating) information, eg to the police (*inf*); to speak pompously or bombastically; (of eg money, wealth, etc) to have influence, be effective (*inf*). ◆ *vt* to utter; to speak about; to mean, have in mind, as in *we're talking millions here* (*inf*; *esp US*); to speak in (a language); to bring or render by talking. ◆ *n* conversation; discussion; gossip or rumour; mention of possibility or proposal; a general theme, eg of gossip or a conversation; utterance; pompous or bombastic speech (*inf*); a short informal address; (in *pl*) detailed and extended discussions; a particular way of speaking. [ME *talken*, frequentative of **tell**]
■ **talkabil'ity** *n*. **talk'able** *adj* easy to converse with; to be talked about. **talk'athon** *n* (*inf*, *orig US*) a long-drawn-out discussion, debate, talking session, etc. **talk'ative** *adj* chatty, given to much talking. **talk'atively** *adv*. **talk'ativeness** *n*. **talk'er** *n*. **talk'ie** *n* (*old inf*; commonly in *pl*) a cinema film in which moving pictures are accompanied by sound. **talk'ing** *n* and *adj*. **talk'y** *adj* talkative.
❑ **talk'back** *n* a two-way radio system; a phone-in (*Aust* and *NZ*). **talk'ee-talk'ee** or **talk'y-talk'y** *n* a corrupt dialect; chatter; a little harangue. **talk'fest** *n* (*inf*; *esp N Am*) an informal meeting for, *usu* extensive, discussion. **talk'-in** (a gathering for the purpose of) an informal yet intensive discussion. **talking book** *n* a recording of a reading of a book, *esp* for use by the blind. **talking head** *n* a person talking on television, viewed in close-up, contrasted with programmes with more action. **talking machine** *n* a machine to produce imitation speech. **talking point** *n* a matter of or for talk. **talking shop** *n* (*inf*) a meeting or a place for discussion, as opposed to decision or action (also **talk shop**). **talk'ing-to** *n* a reproof, ticking-off. **talk radio** *n* radio programming based around conversations and interviews rather than music. **talkshow** see **chat show** under **chat**[1]. **talk'time** *n* the total amount of time available to the user of a telephone to make calls. **talk'-you-down** *n* an apparatus by means of which instructions are given to aircraft pilots to help them to land.
■ **know what one is talking about** (*inf*) to be an expert. **look who's talking** (*ironic*) you're a fine one to be saying that. **now you're talking** (*inf*) now you are saying something I want to hear, or something important or to the point. **talk about...!** (*inf*) what a perfect instance of...! **talk against time** to keep on talking merely to fill up time, as often happens in parliament. **talk at** to address remarks to indirectly; to talk to incessantly, without waiting for a response; to address pompously. **talk back** to reply impudently; to reply on a two-way radio system. **talk big** to talk boastfully or over-confidently. **talk down** to speak or argue more loudly or aggressively than, and so silence; to talk as though to people inferior to oneself in intellect or education; to denigrate, make little of; to bring (an aircraft) to a landing by radioed instructions from the ground (**talk-down system** the apparatus and procedures for doing this). **talking of** apropos of, now that mention has been made of. **talk into** (or **out of**) to persuade to do (or not to do). **talk out** to defeat (a parliamentary bill or motion) by going on speaking until it is too late to vote on it; to resolve (a difference of opinion) by thorough discussion. **talk over** to persuade, convince; to discuss, consider together. **talk round** to talk of all sorts of related matters without tackling (the subject at issue); to bring to one's way of thinking by talking persuasively. **talk shop** see under **shop**. **talk smack** see under **smack**. **talk tall** to boast. **talk the hindlegs off a donkey** see under **donkey**. **talk through** to explain a process by talking about each part of it in a logical sequence. **talk to** to address; to rebuke. **talk trash** see under **trash**[1]. **talk turkey** see under **turkey**. **talk up** to speak boldly; to praise, *esp* to arouse interest in; to make much of. **you can't** (or **can**) **talk** (*inf*) you are in no position to criticize or disagree.

tall /töl/ *adj* high in stature, *esp* higher than average; long, *esp* in a vertical direction; lofty; (*usu* of a person) of a stated height, as in *six feet tall*; great, remarkable; (of talk) bombastic, inflated in style; hardly to be believed (as in *tall tale*); doughty, stout (*obs*). [Appar OE *getæl* prompt]
■ **tall'ish** *adj*. **tall'ness** *n*.
❑ **tall'boy** *n* a high chest of drawers, one portion superimposed on another or on a dressing-table; a glass with a long stem; a long narrow top for a smoky chimney. **tall copy** *n* a book with ample margins above and below. **tall hat** *n* a top hat. **tall order** see under **order**. **tall poppy syndrome** *n* (*Aust inf*) the tendency or desire to cut any successful or prominent person down to size. **tall ship** *n* a square-rigged ship.
■ **a tall man of his hands** a deft worker; a sturdy fighter. **talk tall** and **walk tall** see under **talk** and **walk**[1].

---

tallage /tal'ij/ n a tax levied by the Norman and Angevin kings on their demesne lands and towns, or by a feudal lord on his tenants (*hist*); an aid, toll or rate. ♦ vt to levy a tax upon. [OFr *taillage*, from *tailler* to cut or to tax]
■ **tall'iable** adj subject to tallage. **tall'iate** vt to lay a tallage upon.

tallat, **tallet** or **tallot** /tal'ət/ (*W Eng*) n a loft. [Welsh *taflod*, from LL *tabulāta* flooring]

tallent /tal'ənt/ (*Shakesp*) n *perh* wealth, abundance, or *perh* golden tresses. [**talent**[1]]

tallet see **tallat**.

talliable and **talliate** see under **tallage**.

tallier see under **tally**.

tallith /tal'ith/ n (pl **tall'iths** or **tall'ithim** /-thim/) the Jewish prayer shawl. [Heb *tallīth*]

tall oil /täl'oil/ n an oily liquid which is a by-product of chemical wood pulp, used in the manufacture of paints, linoleums, soaps, etc. [Swed *tallolja*, from *tall* pine, and *olja* oil]

tallot see **tallat**.

tallow /tal'ō/ n fat, grease; rendered fat, *esp* of cattle and sheep, used eg for making soap and candles; any coarse, hard fat. ♦ adj of, for or like tallow. ♦ vt to grease with tallow; to produce tallow. [ME *talgh*; cf Ger *Talg*]
■ **tall'owish** adj. **tall'owy** adj.
❑ **tallow candle** n a candle made of tallow. **tallow catch** n (*Shakesp*) *perh* a receptacle for tallow, or a lump (keech) of tallow. **tallow chandler** n a dealer in tallow candles, etc. **tallow dip** n a candle made by dipping a wick in tallow. **tallow face** n (*Shakesp*) a person with a pasty yellow face. **tall'ow-faced** adj. **tallow tree** n any of various trees (eg *Sapium, Pentadesma, Aleurites*) yielding a thick oil or vegetable tallow, or a substance capable of making candles. **tallow wood** n a large eucalyptus tree (*Eucalyptus microcorys*), found in coastal regions of Australia, yielding hard greasy timber.

tally /tal'i/ n (pl **tall'ies**) a score or account, *esp* one kept by notches or marks; a mark made in recording or scoring an account; credit, tick; a full number or total score; a number taken as a unit in computation; a stick notched to mark numbers or keep accounts; half of such a stick split across the notches, serving as receipt or record (*hist*); a corresponding part, a counterpart; a distinguishing mark; a label; a plant-label; a tag. ♦ adv (*old sl*) in concubinage. ♦ vt (**tall'ying**; **tall'ied**) to keep score, count, calculate or mark down by tally; to mark or provide with a label or tally; to notch or mark as a tally; to reckon; to match, adapt. ♦ vi to correspond, match, agree; to deal on credit. [Anglo-Fr *tallie*, from L *tālea* a stick]
■ **tall'ier** n.
❑ **tally clerk** n a checker of ships' cargoes against a list. **tall'yman** or **tall'ywoman** n a person who keeps a tallyshop; a salesman for a tallyshop; someone who keeps a tally; someone who lives with another person without marriage (*old sl*). **tall'yshop** n a shop where goods are sold on credit to be paid for by instalments, the seller having one account book which tallies with the buyer's. **tally system** or **trade** n a method of dealing on credit for payment by instalments. **tall'ywhacker** n (*vulgar sl*) the penis.
■ **live tally** (*old sl*) to cohabit without marriage.

tally-ho /tal-i-hō'/ interj the huntsman's cry signifying that a fox has been sighted. ♦ n (pl **tally-hos'**) a cry of tally-ho; a four-in-hand coach. ♦ vt (**tally-ho'ing**; **tally-ho'd** or **tally-ho'ed**) to greet with tally-ho. ♦ vi to call tally-ho. [Cf Fr *taïaut*]

talma /tal'mə/ n a loose cloak or cape. [FJ *Talma* (1763–1826), French actor]

Talmud /tal'mŭd/ or -mud/ (also without *cap*) n the fundamental code of Jewish civil and canon law, the *Mishnah* and the *Gemara*. [Heb *talmūd* instruction, from *lāmad* to learn]
■ **Talmud'ic** or **Talmud'ical** adj. **Tal'mudism** n. **Tal'mudist** n a scholar of the Talmud. **Talmudist'ic** adj.

talon /tal'ən/ n a hooked claw or finger; an ogee moulding (*archit*); the part of the bolt of a lock that the key presses on when it is turned; cards remaining after the deal, the stock; a detachable printed part of a form or certificate, *esp* of bearer bonds entitling the holder to apply for a new sheet of coupons (*stock exchange*). [Fr *talon*, from LL *tālō, -ōnis*, from L *tālus* the heel]
■ **tal'oned** adj.

Talpa /tal'pə/ n the mole genus of the family **Tal'pidae** /-pi-dē/; (without *cap*) an encysted tumour on the head, a wen. [L, a mole]

taluk /tä-look'/, **taluka** or **talooka** /tä-loo'kə/ (*Ind*) n a hereditary estate; a subdivision of a district for revenue purposes, a collectorate. [Hindi *ta'alluq* estate]
■ **taluk'dar** n holder of a taluk.

talus[1] /tā'ləs/ n (pl **tā'lī**) the ankle-bone or astragalus. [L *tālus* ankle]

■ **tā'lar** n a robe reaching the ankles. **talaria** /tə-lā'ri-ə/ n pl winged sandals, or wings on the ankles, as of Hermes in Greek mythology.

talus[2] /tā'ləs/ n (pl **tāl'uses**) the sloping part of a work (*fortif*); a scree formed from frost-shattered rocks (*geol*); a slope (*archaic*). [Fr, from LL *talutium* a slope]

talweg same as **thalweg**.

TAM *abbrev* : television audience measurement.

tam see **Tam o' Shanter**.

tamale /tä-mä'li/ n a highly seasoned Mexican dish of meat, chilli sauce and maize dough wrapped *usu* in a corn husk and steamed or baked (also **tamal**'). [Sp *tamal* (pl *tamales*), from Nahuatl *tamalli*]

tamandua /tä-män'dū-ä or -dwä'/ n a S American anteater smaller than the antbear (also **tamandu**'). [Port *tamanduá*, from Sp *tamándoa*, from Tupí *tamanduà*]
■ **tamanoir** /tä-mä-nwär'/ n (Carib *tamanoa*, same root as *tamanduà*) the great antbear.

tamanu /tä'mä-noo/ n a lofty gamboge tree of the East Indies and Pacific Islands, its trunk yielding tacamahac. [E Ind]

tamara /tam'ə-rə or tə-mä'rə/ n a mixture of cinnamon, cloves, coriander, etc. [Hindi, spice]

tamarack /tam'ə-rak/ n (the wood of) the American or black larch. [Native American]

tamarau, **tamarao** /tam'ə-row/ or **timarau** /tim'ə-row/ n a small wild buffalo (*Bubalus* (or *Anoa*) *mindorensis*) native to Mindoro in the Philippines, with thick brown hair and short horns. [Tagálog]

tamari /ta-mä'ri/ n a concentrated sauce made of soya beans and salt. [Jap]

tamarillo /tam-ə-ril'ō/ n (pl **tamarill'os**) same as **tree tomato** (see under **tree**).

tamarin /tam'ə-rin/ n any small Central and S American monkey of the genera *Leontocebus* and *Leontideus*, related to the marmosets. [Fr, from Carib]

tamarind /tam'ə-rind/ n a large tropical caesalpiniaceous tree (*Tamarindus indica*) that bears yellow flowers and long brown seed pods; its wood; its pod, filled with a pleasant, slightly acid, sweet, reddish-black pulp used in making drinks and medicines. [Ar *tamr-Hindī* date of India]

tamarisk /tam'ə-risk/ n a plant of the genus *Tamarix* giving name to a family (**Tamaricā'ceae** /-ri-kā'si-ē/) of xerophytic plants with slender branches and pink and white flowers, one species a naturalized shrub of S English seashores. [L *tamariscus, tamarix*]

tamasha /tə-mä'shä/ (*Ind*) n an entertainment, show; fuss. [Ar and Pers *tamāshā*]

tambac see **tombac**.

tambala /tam-bä'lə/ n (pl **tamba'la** or **tamba'las**) a monetary unit in Malawi, $\frac{1}{100}$ of a kwacha. [Nyanja, literally, cockerel]

tamber /tam'bər/ n anglicized form of **timbre**.

tambour /tam'boor/ n a drum of any of various types, eg the bass drum, or a single-headed tambourine-like instrument, *usu* without jingles; a circular embroidery frame for keeping the fabric being worked taut; a rich gold and silver embroidery; embroidery done on a tambour; a cylindrical stone forming part of a column or the centre of a Corinthian capital (*archit*); the drum of a recording instrument; a vestibule in a church porch, etc; palisading to defend a gate, etc; a flexible top (eg of a desk) or front (eg of a cabinet) made of narrow strips of wood fixed closely together on canvas, the whole sliding in grooves; a sloping buttress or projection for deflecting a ball in eg real tennis and fives. ♦ vt to embroider on a tambour. ♦ vi to do tambour-work. [Fr *tambour* drum; Pers *tanbūr*, and Ar *tunbūr* tamboura]
■ **tambour'a** n an Eastern stringed instrument, used to produce a drone (also **tambura**). **tambourin** /tä-boo-rĕ̃/ n a Provençal dance or dance tune with drone bass; a long, narrow drum used *esp* to accompany this. **tambourine** /tam-bə-rēn'/ n a shallow single-headed drum with jingles fitted round its rim, played on by beating or tapping with the hand (also (*Spenser*) **tam'burin**). **tambourin'ist** n.

tambura see **tamboura** under **tambour**.

tame /tām/ adj having lost native wildness and shyness; cultivated; domesticated; (of land, crops, etc) improved by cultivation (*US*); gentle; spiritless; without vigour; dull, flat, uninspiring; wonted, accustomed (*Shakesp*). ♦ vt to make tame or domestic; to make gentle; to subdue; to reclaim. ♦ vi to become tame. [OE *tam*; Ger *zahm*; Gr *damaein*, L *domāre* to tame]
■ **tamabil'ity** or **tameabil'ity** n. **tam'able** or **tame'able** adj. **tam'ableness** or **tame'ableness** n. **tame'less** adj. **tame'lessness** n. **tame'ly** adv. **tame'ness** n. **tam'er** n. **tam'ing** n.
❑ **tame cat** n (*US*) a person who is happy to be completely dominated by another. **tame cheater** see under **cheat**[1].

Tamiflu® /tam'i-floo/ n a proprietary name for the antiviral drug oseltamivir.

Tamil /tam'il/ n a member of a people of SE India and N, E, and central Sri Lanka; the language of this people. ◆ *adj* of the Tamils or their language.
■ **Tamil'ian**, **Tamil'ic** or **Tamūl'ic** *adj*.
❑ **Tamil tiger** n a member of a Sri Lankan guerrilla organization seeking independence for the Tamils.

tamin or **tamine** /tam'in/ n a thin worsted fabric, with a highly glazed finish. [Fr *étamine* ; cf **stammel**]

tamis /tam'is/ n same as **tammy²**. [Fr]
■ **tamise** /tä-mēz'/ n a name for various thin woollen fabrics.

Tammany Hall /tam'ə-ni höl/ n a Democratic political society, notorious for its corrupt influence in New York city politics in the 19c (also **Tamm'any**); the building it met in, leased to the Democratic party of New York. [Native American chief, *Tammanend*, who is said to have signed the treaty with Penn]
■ **Tamm'any** *adj*. **Tamm'anyism** n. **Tamm'anyite** n.

tammar /tam'ər/ n a small scrub wallaby (*Macropus eugenii*) native to S and SW Australia. [From an Aboriginal language]

Tammie Norie /tam'i nō'ri/ (*Scot*) n the puffin.

Tammuz /tam'ooz or -ŭz/ n a Babylonian, Sumerian and Assyrian sun-god, identified with Adonis (also called **Thammuz**); the tenth month of the Jewish civil year, fourth of the ecclesiastical.

tammy¹ /tam'i/ n a Tam o' Shanter.

tammy² /tam'i/ n a strainer; a glazed woollen or mixed fabric. [Appar same as **tamis**, or perh **tamin**]

Tam o' Shanter /tam ə-shan'tər/ n the hero of Burns's poem of the same name; a cap with broad circular flat top (*inf* **tam** or **tamm'y**).

tamoxifen /tə-mok'si- or ta-mok'si-fen/ n a drug that inhibits the effect of oestrogen, used *esp* in the treatment of infertility and advanced breast cancer, and now also thought to have useful preventive effects in certain women at relatively high risk of developing breast cancer.

tamp /tamp/ vt to stop up (a shot hole) with earth, etc after the explosive has been introduced; to ram down so as to consolidate (eg ballast on a railway track); to pack round. [Perh back-formation from *tampin*, variant of **tampion**]
■ **tamp'er** n a person or thing that tamps; an instrument for pressing down tobacco in a pipe; a casting round the core of a nuclear weapon to delay expansion and act as a neutron reflector. **tamp'ing** n the act of filling up a hole for blasting; the material used.
■ **tamp down** (*inf*) to bend the thumb over the neck of a guitar and hold down (one or more bass strings) with it.

tamper¹ /tam'pər/ vi (*usu* with *with*) to interfere unwarrantably or damagingly; to meddle; to work, contrive or practise; to have secret or corrupt dealings. ◆ *vt* (*obs*) to temper (eg clay). [A by-form of **temper**]
■ **tam'perer** n. **tam'pering** n.
❑ **tamper-ev'ident** *adj* (of packaging) designed in such a way that it is obvious when it has been tampered with. **tamp'er-proof** *adj* (of locks, etc) that cannot be tampered with. **tamper-resist'ant** *adj*.

tamper², **tamping** see under **tamp**.

Tampico /tam-pē'kō/ n a port in Mexico.
❑ **Tampico fibre** n istle.

tampion /tam'pi-ən/ or **tompion** /tom'pi-ən/ n a plug, *esp* a protective plug placed in the muzzle of a gun when not in use. [Fr *tampon*, from *tapon* a plug of cloth]

tampon /tam'pon/ n a plug of cotton or other absorbent material inserted into a wound or orifice to control haemorrhage, etc or into the vagina to absorb menstrual flow; an inking-pad; a two-headed drumstick. ◆ *vt* to plug with a tampon. [A reintroduction from Fr; see ety for **tampion**]
■ **tamponade'** /-nād'/ or **tam'ponage** n surgical use of a tampon.

tam-tam /tum'tum or tam'tam/ n a gong, *esp* one used in an orchestra; *esp* formerly, a tom-tom. [**tom-tom**]

Tamulic see under **Tamil**.

tamworth /tam'wərth or -wûrth/ (also with *cap*) n a breed of long-bodied pigs with golden-red hair. [*Tamworth* in Staffordshire, where the breed originated]

tan¹ /tan/ n a suntan; a tawny brown colour; a lightish brown colour, beige (*US*); oak bark or other material used for tanning; spent bark. ◆ *adj* tawny or (*US*) beige. ◆ *vt* (**tann'ing**; **tanned**) to convert into leather by steeping in vegetable solutions containing tannin, or mineral salts, or synthesized chemicals; to treat with tan or tannin; to make brown, suntanned or tawny; to beat (*inf*). ◆ *vi* to become tanned. [OE *tannian* (found in pap *getanned*), *tannere* tanner; also OFr *tan*, from Breton *tann* oak]
■ **tan'ling** n (*Shakesp*) someone tanned by the sun. **tann'able** *adj*. **tann'age** n tanning; that which is tanned. **tann'ate** n a salt of tannic

acid. **tanned** *adj*. **tann'er** n a person whose job is to tan animal hide; a lotion for the promotion of a suntan. **tann'ery** n a place where hides, etc are tanned. **tann'ic** *adj* of, relating to or produced by tan or tannin. **tann'in** n a colourless, amorphous, bitter substance derived from gallnuts, sumach, many barks and other vegetable matter, used in tanning and dyeing, and occurring in wines (*esp* red), giving a distinctive flavour. **tann'ing** n the art or practice of tanning or converting skins and hides into leather (also *adj*). **tann'ish** *adj*.
❑ **tan balls** n pl tanner's used bark pressed into lumps for fuel. **tan'bark** n any bark good for tanning. **tan bed** n (*hortic*) a bark-bed. **tan'-coloured** *adj*. **tan liquor**, **ooze** or **pickle** n an aqueous extract of tanbark. **tannic acid** n tannin. **tan pit** or **vat** n a vat in which hides are steeped with tan. **tan ride** n a riding track laid with tan. **tan'yard** n a tannery, or a part of it.
■ **flowers of tan** a slime fungus on tanbark.

tan² /tan/ (*maths*) n a conventional short form for **tangent**.

tana¹ /tä'nə/ n a military or police station in India (also **ta'nna**, **ta'nnah**, **tha'na**, **tha'nah**, **tha'nna** or **tha'nnah**). [Hindi *thānā*, *thāna*]
■ **ta'nadar** or **tha'nadar** n an officer in charge of a tana.

tana² /tä'nə/ n a mainly terrestrial tree shrew (*Lyonogale tana*) of Sumatra and Borneo. [Malay (*tūpai*) *tāna* ground (squirrel)]

Tanach /tan'ahh/ n the three divisions of the Jewish Old Testament, comprising the Law, Prophets and Hagiographa, taken as a whole. [Vocalization of the Heb acronym *TNK*, *torah* law, *nebhī'īm* prophets, and *kethūbhīm* (other) writings]

tanager /tan'ə-jər/ n any passerine bird of the S American subfamily Thraupinae, closely related to the buntings, the males having brightly-coloured plumage. [Tupí *tangará*]
■ **Tan'agra** n a genus of this subfamily. **tan'agrine** *adj*.

tanagra /tan'ə-grə/ n a terracotta figurine made in the town of *Tanagra* in ancient Boeotia.

Tanaiste /tö'nish-tā/ n the deputy prime minister of the Republic of Ireland. [Ir, second, next, deputy; cf **tanist**]

tanalized or **-s-** /tan'ə-līzd/ (*building*) *adj* (of timber) treated with **Tan'alith®**, a proprietary preservative.

tandem /tan'dəm/ n a bicycle, tricycle, etc for two people, one behind the other; an arrangement of two things, one placed behind the other, *orig* of two horses harnessed singly one behind the other; a vehicle with such a team of horses. ◆ *adj* arranged with one behind the other. ◆ *adv* one behind the other; in the position of horses harnessed singly one behind the other. [Punning application of L *tandem* at length]
■ **tan'demwise** *adv*.
❑ **tandem roller** n a road roller with front and back rollers of *approx* the same diameter.
■ **in tandem** with one behind the other; together or in conjunction.

T&G same as **TGWU**

tandoori /tan- or tun-doo'ri/ n a type of Indian cooking in which meat, vegetables, etc are baked over charcoal in a clay oven. ◆ *adj* (of food) baked over charcoal in a clay oven. [Hindi *tandoor* a clay oven]
■ **tandoor'** n a clay oven.

tane¹ or **ta'ne** obsolete spellings (*Spenser* and *Shakesp*, etc) of **ta'en**.

tane² /tān/ (*Scot*) pronoun one (**the tane** for *that ane*, the one). [See **tae**, **tone²**, **tother**]

T'ang or **Tang** /tang/ n a Chinese dynasty (618–907AD). ◆ *adj* of this dynasty, its period or its poetry and art, *esp* pottery, etc. [Chin *Táng*]

tang¹ /tang/ n a biting, characteristic or extraneous flavour, aftertaste or smell; a smack, tinge or hint; pungency; a projecting piece or shank; a point, sting or spike; part of a tool that goes into the haft; a prong; a barb; a sea surgeon. [ON *tange* point, tang]
■ **tanged** /tangd/ *adj* with a tang; barbed. **tangy** /tang'i/ *adj* (**tang'ier**; **tang'iest**) having a fresh or sharp taste or smell (also *fig*).

tang² /tang/ n a ringing sound; a twang. ◆ *vt* to cause to ring; to utter ringingly (*Shakesp*). ◆ *vi* to ring. [Imit; influenced by next word]

tang³ /tang/ n coarse seaweed. [Cf Norw and Dan *tang*]

tanga /tang'gə/ n a brief string-like bikini; (women's or men's) briefs consisting of a waistband and a triangle of fabric at front and back, so that the hips are left exposed at either side. [Port, from Kimbundu (SW Afr language) *ntanga* loincloth]

tangelo /tan'ji-lō/ n (pl **tan'gelos**) a hybrid between *tangerine* orange and *pomelo*. [Portmanteau word]

tangent /tan'jənt/ n a line that touches a curve; the limiting case of a secant when the two points of intersection coincide (*maths*); one of the six trigonometrical functions of an angle, the ratio of the side of a right-angled triangle opposite the given angle to the side opposite the other acute angle (*abbrev* **tan**); the striking-pin of a clavichord. ◆ *adj* of or involving a tangent; touching without intersecting. [L *tangens, -entis*, prp of *tangere* to touch]

■ **tan'gency** /-jən-si/ *n* fact of being tangent; a contact or touching. **tangential** /-jen'shəl/ *adj* of a tangent; in the direction of a tangent; peripheral, incidental, irrelevant (*fig*). **tangentiality** /tan-jen-shi-al'i-ti/ *n*. **tangen'tially** or **tangen'tally** *adv* in the direction of a tangent. □ **tangent galvanometer** *n* a galvanometer with a vertical circular coil and a horizontal magnetic needle, which measures a current passed through it by assessing the magnetic field produced which deflects the needle.

■ **at a tangent** in the direction of the tangent; in a divergent train of thought or action; in continuation in the momentary direction instead of following the general course.

tangerine /tan'jə-rēn/ or -rēn'/ *n* a mandarin orange, *esp* a small, flattish, loose-skinned variety; the tree bearing this; the colour of this fruit, a reddish orange; (with *cap*) a native of *Tangier* on the coast of Morocco. ◆ *adj* tangerine-coloured or -flavoured; (with *cap*) of Tangier.

tanghin /tang'gin/ *n* a Madagascan poison, formerly used to test the guilt of someone suspected of a crime; the apocynaceous tree yielding it. [Malagasy *tangèna*]
■ **tangh'inin** *n* its active principle.

tangi /tang'i/ *n* a Maori ceremony of mourning, a funeral. [Maori *tangihanga*]

tangible /tan'ji-bl/ *adj* perceptible by the touch; capable of being possessed or realized; material, corporeal. ◆ *n* (*usu pl*) a tangible thing or asset, ie physical property as opposed to goodwill. [L *tangibilis*, from *tangere* to touch]
■ **tangibil'ity** or **tan'gibleness** *n*. **tan'gibly** *adv*.

tangie /tang'i/ *n* an Orcadian water spirit, appearing as a seahorse, or man covered with seaweed. [From **tang³**]

tangle¹ /tang'gl/ *vt* to form into, involve in, or cover with, a confused interwoven mass; to entangle; to hamper or trap (*inf*). ◆ *vi* to become tangled; (with *with*) to become involved in conflict or argument (*inf*); (with *with*) to embrace (*inf*). ◆ *n* a tangled mass or condition; a perplexity or complication; a naturalist's dredge consisting of bundles of frayed rope or similar material; involved relations, conflict, argument. [Appar from earlier *tagle*; see **taigle**]
■ **tang'led** *adj*. **tang'lement** *n*. **tang'ler** *n*. **tang'lesome** *adj*. **tang'ling** *n* and *adj*. **tang'lingly** *adv*. **tang'ly** *adj* tangled; inclined to tangle.
□ **tang'lefoot** *n* (*N Am*) whisky, intoxicating drink. **tangle net** *n* a long net, anchored to the seabed at both ends. **tangle'-netter** *n* a fishing-boat using a tangle net.

tangle² /tang'gl/ *n* coarse seaweed, *esp* the edible Laminaria. [Appar connected with ON *thöngull* Laminaria stalk, from *thang* bladderwrack]
■ **tang'ly** *adj*.
□ **tang'le-picker** *n* the turnstone (qv under **turn**). **tan'gleweed** *n* tangle.

tangle³ /tang'gl/ (*Scot*) *n* any tall and limp person or thing; an icicle. ◆ *adj* long and limp. [Origin obscure]
■ **tang'ly** *adj*.

Tango or **tango** /tang'gō/ *n* (in international radio communication) a code word for the letter *t*.

tango /tang'gō/ *n* (*pl* **tan'gos**) a ballroom dance or dance tune in 4–4 time, of Argentinian origin, characterized by long steps and pauses. ◆ *vi* (**tang'oing**; **tang'oed**) to dance the tango. [Sp, a Black S American festival or dance]
■ **tang'oist** *n*.

tangram /tan'gram/ *n* a Chinese puzzle, a square cut into seven pieces that will fit together in various ways. [Origin obscure]

tangun /tang'gun/ *n* the Tibetan piebald pony. [Hindi *tāghan*, from Tibetan *rtanān*]

tangy see under **tang¹**.

tanh /tansh, than or tan-āch'/ *abbrev*: hyperbolic *tangent* (see **hyperbolic functions** under **hyper-**).

tanist /tan'ist/ (*hist*) *n* a Celtic chief's heir elect. [Ir *tánaiste*, Gaelic *tànaiste* heir, successor]
■ **tan'istry** *n* the system of succession by a previously elected member of the family.

taniwha /tan'i-fä/ *n* a mythical Maori monster, *usu* a water monster. [Maori]

tank /tangk/ *n* a large basin or cistern; a reservoir of water, oil, etc; an armoured, enclosed, armed vehicle moving on caterpillar wheels; a receptacle for developing solutions (*photog*); the amount held in a tank, a tankful; a police or prison cell (*US sl*); a pool, pond, reservoir (*Ind, NZ* and *Aust*); a pond (*US*). ◆ *vt* to store in a tank; to plunge into a tank; to defeat, thrash (*sl*). ◆ *vi* to drink heavily (with *up*; *sl*); to refuel (often with *up*; *inf*); to travel (*esp* to drive) at great speed or relentlessly; to fail, *esp* at great cost (*US inf*); to lose or drop points,

games, etc deliberately (*tennis sl*). [Port *tanque*, from L *stagnum* a pool]
■ **tank'age** *n* storing in tanks; charge for such storage; the capacity of a tank or tanks; residue from tanks; a fertilizer derived from the dried residues of animal carcases. **tanked** *adj* (*sl*; often with *up*) drunk. **tank'er** *n* a ship or heavy vehicle that carries liquids, *esp* oil in bulk; an aircraft that refuels others. ◆ *vt* to transport in a tanker. **tank'ful** *n* (*pl* **tank'fuls**). **tank'ing** *n* a defeat, a thrashing (*sl*); waterproof material included in an underground structure to prevent infiltration of subsoil water (*building, civil eng*). **tank'less** *adj*.
□ **tank'buster** *n* (*milit sl*) a jet aircraft designed to attack and destroy tanks. **tank'busting** *n*. **tank car** or **wagon** *n* a railway wagon for carrying oil or other liquid in a large tank. **tank engine** *n* a locomotive that incorporates its own tanks for carrying water and coal (without the need for a tender). **tank farm** *n* an area with tanks for storing oil. **tank'-farmer** *n*. **tank'-farming** *n* hydroponics. **tank furnace** *n* (*glass-making*) a furnace consisting of a large 'box' of refractory material, which can hold up to 200 tonnes of glass. **tank top** *n* a sleeveless pullover, *usu* with a low round neckline, worn over a shirt, etc. **tank trap** *n* an obstacle large enough to stop a military tank.
■ **tanked up** (*inf*) having drunk a large amount of alcohol.

tanka¹ /tang'kə/ or *täng'kä*/ (also with *cap*) *n* the boat-dwelling population of Canton, inhabiting **tanka boats** (also **tan'kia**). [Chin]

tanka² /tang'kə/ *n* (*pl* **tan'ka** or **tan'kas**) a waka, a Japanese poem of five lines and 31 syllables, the first and third lines having five syllables and the others seven. [Jap *tan* short, and *ka* verse]

tankard /tang'kərd/ *n* a large mug-like vessel, *usu* with a handle and sometimes a hinged lid, used *esp* for drinking beer from; the amount contained in a tankard. [Cf MDu *tanckaert*]
■ **cool-tankard** see under **cool**.

tankia see **tanka¹**.

tankini /tang-kē'ni/ *n* a garment that combines a *tank* top with a bik*ini* bottom.

tanky /tang'ki/ (*sl*) *n* a hard-line communist, a strict follower of Marxism-Leninism. [Perh from **tank**, because of hard-line communist reluctance to condemn Soviet intervention (using *tanks*) in Afghanistan in 1979]

tanling see under **tan¹**.

tanna see **tana¹**.

tannable, **tannage** see under **tan¹**.

tannah see **tana¹**.

tannate, **tanned** see under **tan¹**.

tanner¹ /tan'ər/ (*old sl*) *n* a sixpence.

tanner², **tannery**, **tannic**, **tannin**, etc see under **tan¹**.

Tannoy® /tan'oi/ *n* a sound-reproducing and amplifying system. ◆ *vt* (without *cap*) to call by, use, or make a sound by, Tannoy. [**tantalum** and **alloy**]

tanrec see **tenrec**.

tansy /tan'zi/ *n* a bitter, aromatic roadside composite plant (*Tanacetum vulgare*) with small heads of tubular yellow flowers, the leaves having formerly been used in cookery and medicine; extended to other plants, such as ragwort, silverweed and yarrow; a pudding or cake flavoured with tansy, eaten at Easter. [OFr *tanasie*, through LL from Gr *athanasiā* immortality]
■ **like a tansy** exactly right.

tantalate see under **tantalum**.

Tantalean, Tantalian, Tantalic see under **Tantalus**.

tantalic, tantalite, tantalous see under **tantalum**.

tantalize or **-ise** /tan'tə-līz/ *vt* to torment by presenting something desirable but keeping it out of reach; to entice or provoke frustratingly; to torture or tease laboriously into unnatural form (*obs*). [**Tantalus**]
■ **tan'talism** *n* the punishment of Tantalus; a tormenting. **tantalīzā'tion** or **-s-** *n*. **tan'talizer** or **-s-** *n*. **tan'talizing** or **-s-** *n* and *adj*. **tan'talizingly** or **-s-** *adv*.

tantalum /tan'tə-ləm/ *n* an acid-resistant metallic element (symbol **Ta**; atomic no 73), useful for electronic and surgical parts. [**Tantalus**, from its inability to absorb water]
■ **tan'talate** *n* a salt of tantalic acid. **tantal'ic** *adj* of or containing tantalum, *esp* in a higher valency. **tan'talite** *n* a black mineral, the main ore from which tantalum is derived. **tan'talous** *adj* of or containing trivalent tantalum.
□ **tantalic acid** *n* an acid ($HTaO_3$) that forms salts or tantalates. **tantalum lamp** *n* an electric lamp with tantalum filament.

Tantalus /tan'tə-ləs/ *n* a son of Zeus punished in Tartarus (for revealing secrets of the gods) by having to stand in water that ebbed when he attempted to drink, overhung by grapes that drew back when he reached for them; (without *cap*) a case in which alcohol decanters are visible but locked up; (without *cap*) any bird of the wood-ibis genus *Tantalus*.

■ **Tantā'lean**, **Tantā'lian** or **Tantalic** /-tal'ik/ *adj* of Tantalus.
□ **Tan'talus-cup** *n* a philosophical toy, with a siphon within the figure of a man whose chin is on a level with its bend.

tantamount /tan'tə-mownt/ *adj* (with *to*) amounting to as much or to the same; equivalent; equal in value or meaning. [Anglo-Fr *tant amunter* to amount to as much]

tantara /tan-tä'rä or tan'tə-rə/ *n* a blast on the trumpet or horn (also **tantara'ra**). [Imit]

tanti /tan'tī or tan'tē/ (*archaic*) *adj* worthwhile. [L, of so much worth; genitive of *tantum*, neuter of *tantus* so much]

tantivy /tan-tiv'i/ (*rare* or *archaic*) *adv* at full gallop; headlong. ◆ *n* a hunting cry; a rapid rush; a nickname for a Tory High Churchman (*hist*). ◆ *adj* headlong; High Church Tory (*hist*). ◆ *interj* expressive of galloping or (later) expressive of the sound of the hunting-horn. [Imit]

tant mieux /tä myø'/ (*Fr*) so much the better.

tanto /tan'tō/ (*Ital*; *music*) *adv* so much, too much. [L *tantum* so much]

tantony see **Anthony**.

tanto uberior /tan'tō ū-bē'ri-ər or oo-be'ri-or/ (*L*) so much the richer.

tant pis /tä pē'/ (*Fr*) so much the worse.

Tantra or **tantra** /tan' or tun'trə/ *n* any of a number of Hindu and Buddhist writings giving religious teaching and ritual instructions (including the use of incantations, diagrams, etc); the teaching of the Tantras. [Sans *tantra* thread, fundamental doctrine]
■ **Tan'tric** or **tan'tric** *adj*. **Tan'trism** *n* the teaching of the Tantras. **Tan'trist** *n*.

tantrum /tan'trəm/ *n* a sudden fit of childish, uncontrolled bad temper or rage. [Origin unknown]

Tantum ergo /tan'təm ûr'gō or tan'tŭm er'gō/ the fifth stanza of the Latin hymn 'Pange, lingua, gloriosi corporis mysterium', written for the office of the Festival of Corpus Christi, which St Thomas Aquinas drew up in 1263. [From its opening words]

Tanzanian /tan-zə-nē'ən/ *adj* of or relating to the E African republic of *Tanzania* or its inhabitants. ◆ *n* a native or inhabitant of Tanzania.

Tao /tä'ō, tow or dow/ *n* (in Taoism) the absolute entity which is the source of all existence and change; (in Confucianism and some other philosophies) the way to be followed, right or proper conduct. [Chin *dào* way, path]

Taoiseach /tē'shohh/ *n* the prime minister of the Republic of Ireland. [Ir, chief, leader]

Taoism /tä'ō-izm, tow'izm or dow'izm/ *n* the philosophical system set forth in the *Tao Te Ching* (ascribed to the legendary Chinese philosopher Lao-tzu, *perh* born 604BC), and other works; a religious system combining Taoist philosophy with magic and superstition and the worship of many gods. [**Tao**]
■ **Ta'oist** *n* and *adj*. **Taoist'ic** *adj*.

taonga /tä-ong'ə/ *n* (in Maori culture) anything highly prized. [Maori]

tap¹ /tap/ *n* a gentle knock or its sound; a protective piece on a shoe heel; a shoe sole (*dialect*); a metal piece attached to the sole and heel of a shoe for tap-dancing; tap-dancing; (in *pl*) a signal (*esp* a bugle-call) for putting lights out, also used at military funerals (*orig US milit*); (in *pl*; in the Guide movement) a song sung at the end of a meeting or round a campfire. ◆ *vt* and *vi* (**tapp'ing**; **tapped**) to knock gently. ◆ *vi* to walk making a tapping sound; to tap-dance. ◆ *vt* to provide or repair with a tap. [OFr *taper*]
■ **tapp'able** *adj*. **tapp'er** *n* a person who taps; a person who attaches soles and heels to shoes; an instrument or part that taps; a decoherer (qv). **tapp'ing** *n* and *adj*.
□ **tap'-dance** *n* and *vi*. **tap'-dancer** *n*. **tap'-dancing** *n* dancing characterized by rhythmical striking of dancer's tapped shoes on the floor. **tap'-in** *n* a simple shot from a short distance into an undefended goal (*football*); an act of striking the ball in the air with the hand, so that it goes into the basket (*basketball*); a very short, light putt required to put the ball into the hole (*golf*). **tap kick** or **tap penalty** *n* (*rugby*) a light kick which starts play from a penalty, with the same team keeping possession of the ball. **tap shoe** *n* a tapped shoe for tap-dancing.
■ **tap up** (*inf*) to make a covert approach to a potential employee.

tap² /tap/ *n* a hole or short pipe with a valve for running off a fluid; a peg or stopper on a barrel, etc; a taproom; any particular alcoholic drink drawn through a tap; the withdrawal of liquid from a place, *esp* from a body cavity; a screw for cutting an internal thread; a taproot; a device, which when attached to a telephone line, enables, eg the police, security forces, etc secretly to listen to conversations; an instance of tapping a telephone wire; (often in *pl*) tap stock. ◆ *vt* (**tapp'ing**; **tapped**) to pierce, so as to let out fluid; to broach; to draw off; to draw upon, *esp* for the first time (*fig*); to attach a receiver to (a telephone line) in order secretly to overhear conversations; to

eavesdrop on (a conversation) by this means; to get supplies, information, etc from; to get money from (*sl*); to supply with a tap; to cut a screw-thread. ◆ *vi* to act as a tapster. [OE *tæppa* tap, *tæppestre* (female) tapster; Du *tap*, Ger *Zapfen* tap]
■ **tapp'able** *adj*. **tapp'er** *n* someone who taps trees, etc; a milking machine. **tapp'ing** *n* the act or art of drawing out or running off a fluid; an operation for removal of liquid from the body. **tap'ster** *n* a person who draws alcoholic drinks, a barperson.
□ **tap bolt** *n* a screwed-in bolt. **tap cinder** *n* slag produced in a puddling furnace. **tap'-dressing** *n* well dressing. **tap'house** *n* a tavern. **tap issue** *n* tap stocks. **tap'lash** *n* poor or weak alcohol, *esp* stale beer; the dregs from a cask. **tap'room** *n* a room where beer is served from the tap or cask. **tap'root** *n* a strong main root growing down vertically. **tap stock** *n* government bonds, etc to which the public can subscribe at any time. **tap water** *n* water from a household tap.
■ **on tap** kept in cask, *opp* to *bottled*; continuously and readily available (*fig*); on schedule (*N Am*). **tap into** (*comput*) to gain unauthorized access to (a company's computer system, files, etc).

tap³ /tap/ *n* a Scots form of **top**.
■ **tapp'it** *adj* crested.
□ **tappit hen** *n* a crested hen; a drinking vessel with a knob on the lid, of capacity variously stated at 1, 3 or 6 imperial quarts; a wine-bottle size equivalent to *approx* three standard bottles, 2.27 litres, used *esp* for port. **taps'man** *n* a servant in overall charge of others; chief of a company of drovers.
■ **take one's tap in one's lap** (*Scot*) to bundle up (one's flax or tow for the distaff) and go home.

tap⁴ /tap/ *n* an Indian malarial fever. [Pers]

tapa¹ or **tappa** /tä'pə/ *n* paper mulberry bark; a fabric made from this. [Polynesian]

tapa² /tä'pa or tap'a/ *n* (*pl* **ta'pas**) (*usu* in *pl*) a light savoury snack or appetizer, *esp* one based on Mediterranean, *esp* Spanish, foods and cooking techniques. [Sp]
□ **tapas bar** *n* a bar where tapas are served along with alcoholic drinks.

tapaculo /tä-pä-koo'lō/ or **tapacolo** /tä-pä-kō'lō/ *n* (*pl* **tapacu'los** or **tapaco'los**) a small S American passerine bird (family Rhinocryptidae) with a tilted tail. [Sp *tapaculo*, from *tapa* cover (imperative), and *culo* posterior]

tapadera /tä-pä-dā'rə/ or **tapadero** /tä-pä-dā'rō/ *n* (*pl* **tapader'as** and **tapader'os**) the leather guard in front of a Mexican stirrup. [Sp, lid, cover, from *tapar* to cover]

tape /tāp/ *n* material woven in long narrow bands; a strip of such material, used for tying up, connecting, sticking, etc; a strip of material stretched across the track at the winning-line of a race; a ribbon of paper printed by a recording instrument, as in telegraphy; a flexible band that guides the sheets (*printing*); a tape measure; magnetic tape; a tape recording or cassette; alcoholic drink (*sl*). ◆ *vt* to provide, fasten, bind or measure with a tape; to tape-record; to get the range or measure of; to deal out, or use, sparingly (*Scot*). ◆ *vi* to tape-record. [OE *tæppe* tape, fillet]
■ **tape'able** *adj*. **tape'less** *adj*. **tape'like** *adj*. **tā'pen** *adj* (*rare*) made of tape. **tā'per** *n* a person who works with tapes. **tā'pist** *n* a red-tapist.
□ **tape deck** *n* a machine for recording sound on tape and playing tape-recorded sound through a separate amplifier as part of a hi-fi system; a tape drive. **tape drive**, **deck** or **transport** *n* (*comput*) a mechanism within a computer or peripheral device which moves magnetic tape across the recording and playback heads. **tape echo** see **tape slap** below. **tape grass** *n* any plant of the genus *Vallisneria*. **tape'line** or **tape measure** *n* a flexible measuring strip of tape, steel or other material. **tape loop** *n* a length of magnetic tape or film with the ends joined together to form an endless strip, allowing a recording to be continuously repeated. **tape'-lure** *vt*. **tape luring** *n* the luring and subsequent capture of a seabird by playing tape recordings of its call from beaches and cliffs. **tape machine** *n* a telegraphic instrument by which messages received are automatically printed on a tape; a tape recorder. **tape punch** *n* (*comput*) a device once used for encoding data by punching holes in paper tape. **tape reader** *n* a device that senses data recorded on paper or magnetic tape and converts it into a form suitable for computer processing. **tape'-record** *vt* to record (sound) using a tape recorder. **tape recorder** *n* an instrument for recording sound on magnetic tape and subsequently reproducing the sound. **tape'-recording** *n* the act or process of recording sound on magnetic tape; (**tape recording**) a magnetic tape on which sound has been recorded; the sound so recorded. **tape'script** *n* a tape-recorded reading of a complete text. **tape slap** or **tape echo** *n* the delaying of the repeat of a sound by adjusting the time lapse between the recording and playback heads on a tape recorder; videotape instability caused as the tape makes and breaks contact with the heads on the drum (*image technol*). **tape streamer** *n* (*comput*) a device using magnetic tape to back up data. **tape'-tied** *adj* tied up with tape;

■ words derived from main entry word; □ compound words; ■ idioms and phrasal verbs

bound with, or by, red tape (see under **red**[1]). **tape transport** see **tape drive** above. **tape'worm** *n* a ribbon-shaped segmented parasitic worm, any cestode, but *esp* of *Taenia* or related genus.

■ **breast the tape** in winning a foot-race, to pass through or break with one's chest the tape stretched across the track at the winning-line. **have something** or **someone taped** to have a thorough understanding of something or someone. **magnetic tape** see under **magnet. red tape** see under **red**[1].

tapenade /*tap-ə-näd*'/ *n* a paste made from capers, anchovies and black olives, seasoned with olive oil and lemon juice, used in French (*esp* Provençal) cooking. [Provençal *tapéo* capers]

taper /*tā'pər*/ *n* a long thin waxed wick or spill; a feeble light; lengthwise diminution in width; gradual leaving off; a wax candle (*obs*). ◆ *adj* tapering. ◆ *vi* to become gradually smaller towards one end; to diminish slowly in size, quantity or importance (with *off*). ◆ *vt* to make to taper. [OE *tapor*]

■ **tā'pered** *adj* tapering; lighted by tapers (*literary*). **tā'perer** *n* a person who carries a taper. **tā'pering** *n* and *adj*. **tā'peringly** *adv*. **tā'perness** *n*. **tā'perwise** *adv*.

◻ **taper pin** *n* (*engineering*) a pin, used as a fastener, very slightly tapered to act as a wedge. **taper roller bearing** *n* (*engineering*) a roller bearing able to sustain end thrust by the use of tapered rollers.

tapestry /*tap'i-stri*/ *n* an ornamental textile used for the covering of walls and furniture, etc, and for curtains, made by passing coloured threads or wools through a fixed-warp fabric; a picture or design made of this; a machine-made imitation of this; anything like a tapestry in being intricate and with many closely-interwoven elements (*fig*). ◆ *adj* of tapestry (*Milton* **tap'stry**). ◆ *vt* (**tap'estrying**; **tap'estried**) to hang with tapestry; to work or represent in tapestry. [Fr *tapisserie*, from *tapis* a carpet, from LL *tapētium*, from Gr *tapētion*, dimin of *tapēs*, *-ētos*, prob of Iranian origin]

■ **tap'estried** *adj*.

◻ **tapestry moth** *n* a moth of the Tineidae family (*Trichophaga tapetzella*), with brown, white-tipped forewings.

tapet /*tap'it*/ (*Spenser*) *n* a piece of tapestry. [L *tapēte*, perh through OE *tæppet*]

tapeti /*tap'ə-ti*/ *n* a species of rabbit (*Sylvilagus brasiliensis*) found in Central and S America, the Brazilian rabbit. [Tupí]

tapetum /*tə-pē'təm*/ *n* (*pl* **tapē'ta**) a layer of cells surrounding spore mother cells (*bot*); the light-reflecting pigmentary layer of the retina (*zool*). [L *tapētum*, from Gr *tapēs*, *-ētos* carpet]

■ **tapē'tal** *adj*.

taphephobia or **taphophobia** /*taf-ə-fō'bi-ə*/ *n* morbid fear of being buried alive. [Gr *taphē* burial, *taphos* grave, and **phobia**]

taphonomy /*tə-fon'ə-mi*/ *n* the study or science of how plants and animals die, decay and become buried, fossil or fossilized. [Gr *taphos* grave, and **-nomy**]

■ **taphonom'ic** or **taphonom'ical** *adj*. **taphon'omist** *n* an expert or specialist in taphonomy.

taphrogenesis /*taf-rō-jen'ə-sis*/ (*geol*) *n* vertical movements of the earth's crust resulting in the formation of major faults and rift valleys. [Gr *taphros* pit, and **genesis**]

tapioca /*tap-i-ō'kə*/ *n* a farinaceous substance made by heating cassava; extended to a kind of sago and a preparation of potato starch; a pudding made from tapioca. [Tupí-Guaraní *tipyoca*, from *tipi* juice, and *ok* to squeeze out]

■ **pearl-tapioca** see under **pearl**[1].

tapir /*tā'pər* or *tā'pēr*/ *n* a large odd-toed hoofed mammal with a short flexible proboscis, several species of which are found in S America, Malaya, etc. [Tupí *tapira*]

■ **tā'piroid** *adj*.

tapis /*tä'pē*, also *tap'is*/ (*obs*) *n* a covering, hanging, etc of tapestry or the like. [Fr]

■ **on the tapis** on the table; under consideration.

tapist see under **tape**.

tapotement /*tə-pōt'mənt*, *tä-pot-mä'*/ *n* the use of light taps in massage. [Fr]

tappa see **tapa**[1].

tappet /*tap'it*/ *n* a projection that transmits motion from one part of a machine to another by tapping, *esp* in an internal-combustion engine from the camshaft to the valves. [**tap**[1]]

◻ **tapp'et-loom, -motion, -ring, -rod**, etc *n*.

tappice /*tap'is*/ *vi* to lie low. ◆ *vt* to hide. [Fr *tapir*, *tapiss-*]

tappit, tappit hen, tapsman see under **tap**[3].

tapsalteerie /*tap-sl-tē'ri*/ or **tapsieteerie** /*tap-si-tē'ri*/ *adv*, *adj* and *n* Scots forms of **topsy-turvy**.

tapstry /*tap'stri*/ (*Milton*) see **tapestry**.

tapu /*tä'poo*/ same as **taboo**. [Maori]

taqueria /*tak-ə-rē'ə*/ *n* a Mexican restaurant that serves mainly tacos. [Mex Sp; see **taco**]

tar[1] /*tär*/ *n* a dark, viscous mixture obtained by destructive distillation of wood, coal, peat, etc; a natural bituminous substance of similar appearance (mineral tar). ◆ *vt* (**tarr'ing**; **tarred**) to smear, coat or treat, with tar. [OE *teru*, *teoro*; Ger *Teer* (from LGer), and Du *teer*]

■ **tarriness** /*tär'i-nis*/ *n*. **tarr'ing** *n* and *adj*. **tarr'y** /*tär'i*/ *adj* of, like, covered or soiled with tar.

◻ **tar baby** *n* (*chiefly US*) an intractable problem which embroils those who try to solve it. **tar box** *n* a shepherd's box for tar as ointment for sheep; a shepherd. **tar'boy** *n* a person who, during the shearing of sheep, puts tar or antiseptic on cuts. **tar brush** *n* a brush for applying tar. **tar heel** *n* (*US sl*) a North Carolinian. **tar'mac** *vt* (**tar'macking**; **tar'macked**) to surface with tarmacadam. **tarmacad'am** or **tar'mac** *n* (also **Tarmac**® in *US*) a road surfacing of broken stone covered or mixed with tar; (**tar'mac**) the runways of an airport. **tar paper** *n* heavy paper treated with tar, used as a building material. **tar pit** *n* (*geol*) an outcrop where natural bitumen occurs. **tarry breeks** *n sing* (*Scot*) a sailor. **tarr'y-fingered** *adj* thievish. **tar sand** *n* a deposit of sand or sandstone saturated with bitumen, from which petroleum can be extracted. **tar seal** *n* (*NZ*) a tarmacadam surface on a road; a road so surfaced. **tar'-seal** *vt* to seal the surface of (a road) by covering with tarmacadam. **tar spot** *n* a black spot of Rhytisma. **tar water** *n* a cold infusion of tar in water, once popular as a medicine. **tar'weed** *n* a name for various heavy-scented American composites.

■ **tar and feather** to smear with tar and then cover with feathers as a punishment. **tarred with the same brush** or **stick** having the same defects. **touch of the tar brush** (*offensive*) a certain amount of eg African blood resulting in darkish skin.

tar[2] /*tär*/ (*inf*) *n* a sailor. [Perh for **tarpaulin**]

tar[3] (*Shakesp* **tarre**) /*tär*/ *vt* to set on, incite to fight. [Connected with OE *tergan* to worry]

tara /*tä'rə*/ *n* a variety of bracken found in New Zealand and Tasmania, with an edible rhizome (also **tara fern**). [Perh a native Tasmanian name]

taradiddle see **tarradiddle**.

tarakihi /*ta-rə-kē'hē*, *-kē'ē*/ or **terakihi** /*te-rə-*/ *n* a morwong. [Maori]

taramasalata or **taramosalata** /*tar-ə-mə-sə-lä'tə*/ *n* a Greek dish, a pink creamy paste made of grey mullet or smoked cod's roe with olive oil and garlic. [Mod Gr, from *taramas* preserved roe, and *salata* salad]

tarantara see **taratantara**.

tarantas or **tarantass** /*tä-rən-täs'*/ *n* a four-wheeled, horse-drawn Russian vehicle mounted on horizontal flexible poles. [Russ *tarantas*]

tarantella /*tar-ən-tel'ə*/ *n* a lively Neapolitan dance (in triplets for one couple), once thought a remedy for tarantism; a tune for it. [*Taranto*, in S Italy]

■ **tar'antism** *n* (*med hist*) an epidemic dancing mania *esp* prevalent in S Italy from 15c to 17c, popularly thought to be caused by the tarantula bite.

tarantula /*tə-ran'tū-lə*/ *n* a large venomous S European hairy wolf spider (*Lycosa tarantula*), once supposed to cause tarantism; any of various large hairy spiders of the family Theraphosidae, whose bite is painful but not generally venomous to man; (in America) applied to large venomous spiders of the bird-catching family (Aviculariidae); (in Africa) a biting but non-venomous solpugid; (in Australia) applied to several large harmless laterigrade spiders, *esp* the huntsman spider; (with *cap*) a genus of pedipalps. [Med L *tarantula*, from Ital *tarantola*, from Gr *Taras*, *-antos* Tarentum, Taranto]

◻ **tarantula juice** *n* (*US*) bad whisky.

taratantara /*tä-rə-tan'tə-rə* or *-tan-tä'rə*/, also **tarantara** /*tə-ran'tə-rə*/ *n* the sound of a trumpet or trumpet fanfare (also *interj*, *adj*, *adv*, *vt* and *vi*). [Imit]

taraxacum /*tə-rak'sə-kəm*/ *n* a plant of the dandelion genus *Taraxacum*; its root and rootstock, a tonic laxative. [Appar from Ar *tarakhshaqōq*, from Pers *talkh chakōk*, assimilated to Gr *taraxis* disturbance]

tarboggin see **toboggan**.

tarboosh, tarboush or **tarbush** /*tär-boosh'*/ *n* a fez, a hat worn by Muslim men, sometimes as the base of a turban. [Ar *tarbūsh*]

tarcel see **tercel**.

Tardenoisian /*tär-di-noi'zi-ən*/ (*archaeol*) *adj* belonging to a stage of culture represented by flint implements found at *Tardenois*, Aisne, France, transitional between Palaeolithic and Neolithic.

tardigrade /*tär'di-grād*/ *adj* slow-paced; of or relating to the Tardigrada. ◆ *n* a member of the Tardigrada. [L *tardus* slow, and *gradī* to step]

■ **Tardigrā'da** *n pl* a class of arthropods found in water, ditches, etc, the bear-animalcules; formerly the sloths.

Tardis /tär'dis/ n an object that is more spacious inside than it would appear to be when viewed from the outside. [From the time-travel device used in the BBC television series *Dr Who*, explained as an acronym for Time And Relative Dimensions In Space]

tardy /tär'di/ adj (**tar'dier; tar'diest**) slow; sluggish; behindhand; too long delayed; late; caught at fault (*obs*). ◆ vt (*Shakesp*) to retard. ◆ n (*N Am*) a person who arrives late, *esp* to school. [Fr *tardif*, from L *tardus* slow]
■ **tar'dily** adv. **tar'diness** n. **tar'dive** /-div/ adj late in development.
❏ **tardive dyskinesia** n (*med*) a condition caused by long-term use of some tranquillizers, characterized by loss of muscle control leading to eg involuntary facial and head movements and excessive salivating. **tar'dy-gaited** adj (*archaic*) slow-paced.

tare¹ /tär/ n a vetch of various kinds, *esp* of the lentil-like group; a weed, *prob* darnel (*Bible*). [Origin obscure]

tare² /tär/ n the weight of a vessel, wrapping or container, which subtracted from the gross weight gives the net weight; an allowance made for this; the weight of an empty vehicle, without cargo, passengers, fuel, etc. ◆ vt to ascertain or allow for the tare of. [Fr, from Sp *tara*, from Ar *tarhah* thrown away]
■ **tar'ing** n the calculating of a tare.

tare³ /tär/ an archaic *pat* of **tear²**.

targa top /tär'gə top/ n a removable hard roof on a car, which fits into the boot when not in use. [Orig used on the Porsche 911 *Targa*]
■ **targa-topp'ed** adj.

targe¹ /tärj/ n a shield, *esp* a light shield. [OFr *targe*, from ON *targe* shield]

targe² /tärj/ (*Scot*) vt to cross-examine; to supervise strictly; to reprimand; to thrash. [Origin unknown]

target /tär'git/ n a round or shield-like mark to shoot at for practice or competition; an object aimed at (also *fig*); a butt or focus (eg of unkind remarks or actions); a result to be aimed at; a shooting score; a neck and breast of lamb; a small buckler or round shield (*hist*); a surface on which electrons impinge at high velocity, such as the fluorescent screen of a cathode-ray tube; a plate in a television camera tube on which external scenes are focused and scanned by an electron beam; a reflecting object which returns radiated pulse energy to the receiver of a radar system (*radar*); a sight on a levelling staff; an American railway signal. ◆ adj chosen as a target, aimed at. ◆ vt to aim; to aim at; to make, or identify as, a focus, target or victim. [OFr *targuete*; cf **targe¹**]
■ **tar'getable** adj able to be aimed, or aimed at. **tar'geted** adj selected as a target, aimed at; provided with a shield (*hist*). **targeteer'** n (*hist*) a person armed with a shield, a peltast.
❏ **target acquisition** see under **acquire**. **target area** n an area containing a target, or which is a target, eg of missiles. **target cell** n an antigen-bearing cell which is the target of attack by lymphocytes or a specific antibody (*immunol*); (in haematology) an abnormally shaped red blood cell with a central stained area seen in blood films. **target language** n the language into which a text is to be translated; the foreign language being learned by a student. **target man** n (*football*) a tall forward player to whom high passes can be made. **target practice** n repeated shooting at a target to improve one's aim.
■ **on target** on the correct course for a target; on schedule.

Targum /tär-goom'* or *tär'gəm/ n (pl **Targums**) any Aramaic version or paraphrase of the Old Testament. [Chaldean *targūm* interpretation]
■ **Targumic** /tär-goo'mik, -gū'mik or -gum'ik/ or **Targum'ical** adj. **Targum'ist** n a writer of a Targum; a person who studies the Targums. **Targumist'ic** adj.

tariff /tar'if/ n a list or set of customs duties; a customs duty levied on particular goods (eg at a hotel); (a list of) standard rates charged for a service, eg electricity or insurance; a menu; a scale of penalties established by law for sentencing those convicted of certain crimes. ◆ vt to set a tariff on. [Ital *tariffa*, from Ar *ta'rīf* explanation, from *'arafa* to explain]
■ **tariffica'tion** n the fixing of a tariff; conversion (eg of import restrictions) into a tariff. **tar'iffless** adj.
❏ **tariff reformer** n a person who favoured the early 20c movement for **Tariff Reform** or Protection, as opposed to Free Trade. **tariff wall** n a barrier to the flow of imports made by high rates of customs duties.

taring see under **tare²**.

tarlatan /tär'lə-tən/ n an open, stiff, transparent muslin. [Fr *tarlatane*; origin doubtful]

tarmac, tarmacadam see under **tar¹**.

tarn /tärn/ n a small mountain lake. [ON *tjörn*]

tarnal /tär'nl/ and **tarnation** /tär-nā'shən/ (chiefly N Am sl) adj and adv softened forms of **eternal** and **damnation**, *appar* influenced by each other.
■ **tar'nally** adv.

tarnish /tär'nish/ vt to dull, discolour, render iridescent, diminish the lustre of, etc by exposure to the air, etc; to sully or impair. ◆ vi to become dull; to lose lustre. ◆ n loss of lustre; a surface discoloration or iridescence on metal or mineral; a stain or blemish; a film of oxide, sulphide, etc. [Fr *ternir, terniss-*, from *terne* dull, wan; poss Gmc]
■ **tar'nishable** adj. **tar'nished** adj. **tar'nisher** n.

taro /tä'rō/ n (pl **ta'ros**) a plant (genus *Colocasia*) of the arum family, widely cultivated in the islands of the Pacific for its edible rootstock (also called **eddo**). [Polynesian]

tarot /tar'ō/ n (formerly also **taroc** or **tarok** /tar'ok/) a card of a type originating in Italy with an allegorical picture; a set, traditionally consisting of 78 such cards, used in card games and *esp* fortune-telling; (*usu* in *pl*) a game played with tarots together with cards of the ordinary suits. [Fr *tarot*, from Ital *tarocco*]

TARP /tärp/ (*US*) abbrev : Troubled Assets Relief Program.

tarp /tärp/ short for **tarpaulin**.

tarpan /tär'pan/ n a small wild horse of the steppes of S European Russia, long extinct but now somewhat restored by selective breeding and introduced into Poland, not identical with the takhi. [Tatar]

tarpaulin /tär-pö'lin/, also **tarpauling** /-ling/ n strong linen or hempen cloth waterproofed, *esp* with tar; a sheet of it; a sailor's waterproof hat; a sailor (*inf*); a sea-bred officer (*obs*). ◆ adj made of tarpaulin; relating to a sailor or sea-bred officer (*obs*). [Appar **tar¹** and **palling**, from **pall¹**]

Tarpeian /tär-pē'ən/ adj of Tarpeia, according to legend a Roman officer's daughter who betrayed the Capitol at Rome to the Sabines and was buried beneath the **Tarpeian Rock** on the Capitoline Hill, from which traitors were thrown.

tarpon /tär'pon/ n a very large fish (*Tarpon* or *Megalops*) related to the herring, popular with anglers on the Florida and Gulf coasts. [Origin unknown]

tarradiddle or **taradiddle** /tar-ə-did'l or *tar'ə-/ n a fib, a lie; nonsense. [Appar founded on **diddle¹**]

tarragon /tar'ə-gən/ n an aromatic herb (genus *Artemisia*), whose leaves are used for flavouring vinegar, sauces, etc. [Ar *tarkhūn*, perh from Gr *drakōn* a dragon]

Tarragona /tar-ə-gō'nə/ n a strong dry red Spanish wine used in blending or as a substitute for port. [Province in Catalonia]

tarras¹ /tar'əs/ n Spenserian for **terrace**.

tarras² see **trass**.

tarre¹ see **tar³**.

tarre² a Spenserian form of **tar¹**.

tarriance, tarrier, tarrow see under **tarry¹**.

tarrock /tar'ək/ n a seabird of various kinds (applied to different ones in different areas). [Origin obscure]

tarry¹ /tar'i/ vi (**tarr'ying; tarr'ied**) to linger; to loiter; to delay; to stay behind; to sojourn; to wait. ◆ vt (*archaic*) to await. ◆ n (*archaic*) delay; sojourn, stay. [History obscure; the form agrees with OE *tergan* to irritate, the meaning with OFr *tarier*]
■ **tarr'iance** n (*archaic*) tarrying; delay; waiting; a sojourn. **tarr'ier** n a person who tarries or delays. **tarr'ow** /tar'ō/ vi (*Scot*) to hesitate; to be unwilling.

tarry² /tä'ri/ see under **tar¹**.

tarsal¹, tarsel /tär'sl/ see **tercel**.

tarsal², tarsalgia see under **tarsus**.

tarsia /tär'si-ə or *tär-sē'ä/ n intarsia (qv) (also **tar'sia-work**). [Ital]

tarsier /tär'si-ər/ n a lemuroid monkey (genus *Tarsius*) of the East Indies, nocturnal, tree-dwelling, with large eyes and long tarsal bones. [Fr, from *tarre tarsus*]
■ **tar'sioid** adj like the tarsier; of the tarsier genus *Tarsius*.

Tarsipes /tär'si-pēz/ n the genus represented by the honey possum, a long-snouted Australian honey-sucking phalanger with feet like a tarsier. [New L *tarsus* tarsus, and L *pēs* foot]
■ **tar'siped** n a marsupial of the genus *Tarsipes*.

tarsus /tär'səs/ n (pl **tar'sī**) the bones forming part of the foot to which the leg is articulated; (in birds) sometimes applied to the tarsometatarsus; (in insects) the five-jointed foot; a plate of connective tissue at the edge of the eyelid. [Gr *tarsos* the flat of the foot]
■ **tar'sal** adj relating to the tarsus or ankle. ◆ n a bone of the tarsus. **tarsalgia** /-sal'ji-ə/ n pain in the instep. **tarsometatar'sal** adj. **tarsometatar'sus** n a bird's shank-bone, the combined metatarsals and distal tarsals.

tart¹ /tärt/ adj sharp; biting; caustic. [OE *teart*]
■ **tart'ish** adj. **tart'ly** adv. **tart'ness** n.

tart² /tärt/ *n* a dish of pastry distinguished from a pie either by being uncovered or by having a sweet, not savoury, filling; a girl (*offensive sl*); a prostitute (*derog sl*); someone who repeatedly changes allegiance or affiliation (*sl*). [OFr *tarte*]

■ **tart'iness** *n*. **tart'let** *n* a small tart. **tart'y** *adj* (**tart'ier**; **tart'iest**) (*sl*) like a tart; vulgar, cheaply and blatantly provocative (*esp* of a woman or woman's clothing, etc).

■ **tart up** (*inf*) to make more showy or striking, *esp* in a superficial, meretricious or inartistic way; to smarten up (**tart'ed-up** *adj*).

Tartan® /tär'tən/ *n* a material used to lay tracks for athletic events, usable in all weathers.

tartan¹ /tär'tən/ *n* a woollen (or other) checked material; any of a large variety of checked patterns, as worn by Highland clans of Scotland, each the distinctive mark of an individual clan. ◆ *adj* of tartan; checked in tartan; Scottish, *esp* referring to self-consciously Scottish artefacts or attitudes (*derog*). [Poss from MFr *tiretaine* linsey-woolsey]

■ **tartanā'lia** or **tar'tanry** *n* (*derog*) artefacts, imagery, etc that are self-consciously Scottish. **tar'taned** *adj* clad in tartan.

❑ **Tartan Army** *n* (*inf*) the supporters of Scotland's national football team, *esp* when travelling abroad. **Tartan tax** *n* (*inf*) a tax over and above standard UK taxes, raised in Scotland by a Scottish parliament.

tartan² /tär'tən/ *n* a Mediterranean vessel with a lateen sail (also **tartane** /tär-tän'/). [Fr *tartane*, poss from Ar *tarīdah* a small ship]

tartana /tär-tä'nə/ *n* a little covered wagon. [Sp]

Tartar¹ /tär'tər/ *n* a Tatar; the Turkic language spoken by the Tatars; (*without cap*) a formidable, rough, unmanageable or ferocious person; (*without cap*) a person who unexpectedly turns the tables on his or her assailant. ◆ *adj* of or relating to the Tatars or their language. [See **Tatar**]

■ **Tartarian** /-tā'ri-ən/ *n* and *adj* Tartar, Tatar. **Tartaric** /-tar'ik/ *adj* of the Tartars. **Tar'tarly** *adj* like a Tartar; (*without cap*) ferocious. **Tar'tary** *n* Tatary (qv under **Tatar**).

❑ **Tartarian lamb** *n* barometz.

Tartar² see **Tartarus**.

tartar /tär'tər/ *n* recrystallized and partially purified argol, chiefly acid potassium tartrate (with calcium tartrate, etc); a deposit of calcium phosphate and other matter on the teeth. [LL *tartarum*, perh from Ar]

■ **tartareous** /-tā'ri-əs/ *adj* of or like tartar; with rough crumbly surface (*bot*). **tartaric** /tär-tar'ik/ *adj* of or derived from tartar (**tartaric acid**, $C_4H_6O_6$, prepared from argol or found naturally in plants and fruit). **tartariza'tion** or **-s-** *n*. **tar'tarize** or **-ise** *vt* to treat, mix or combine with tartar. **tar'trate** *n* a salt of tartaric acid. **tar'trazine** /-zēn/ *n* a yellow dye used in textiles, food and drugs.

❑ **tartar emetic** *n* a compound of potassium, antimony, carbon, hydrogen and oxygen, used in dyeing and in medicine.

■ **cream of tartar** purified argol, used in baking powder, etc.

Tartare see **Tartarus**.

tartare¹ /tär-tär'/ *adj* (of fish) served raw, *usu* in small cakes.

■ **steak tartare** see under **steak**.

tartare² /tär-tär'/ *n* (also **tartare sauce** or **tartar** /tär'tər/ **sauce**) a mayonnaise dressing with chopped pickles, olives, capers, etc added, *usu* served with fish. [Fr *sauce tartare*, from **Tartar¹**]

tartareous, tartaric see under **tartar**.

Tartarie see **Tartarus**.

tartarize see under **tartar**.

Tartarus /tär'tə-rəs/ *n* in Homer, a deep and sunless abyss, as far below Hades as earth is below heaven; a place for the punishment of evil-doers in Hades; hell. —Also (*Spenser* and *Shakesp*) **Tar'tar**, and (*Spenser*) **Tar'tare**, **Tar'tarie** and **Tar'tary**. [L, from Gr *Tartaros*]

■ **Tartarean** /-tā'ri-ən/ *adj*.

Tartary see under **Tartar¹** and **Tartarus**.

tarte tatin /tärt ta-t ɛ̃'/ (*Fr*) *n* a fruit (*usu* apple) pie cooked with a covering of caramelized pastry and turned upside down on a serving dish. [Named after a Mlle *Tatin*, who first made it]

tartine /tär-tēn'/ (*Fr*) *n* a slice of bread with butter or jam.

tartrate, tartrazine see under **tartar**.

Tartuffe or **Tartufe** /tär-tüf', -toof'/ *n* a hypocritical person who pretends to be deeply religious. [From the title character in Molière's *Tartuffe* (1664)]

■ **Tartuff'ery** or **Tartuff'erie** *n*. **Tartuff'ian**, **Tartuf'ian**, **Tartuff'ish** or **Tartuf'ish** *adj*. **Tartuff'ism** or **Tartuf'ism** *n*.

tartuffe /tär-toof'/ *n* a sweet truffle. [Fr]

tartufo /tär-too'fō/ *n* (*pl* **tartu'fos**) a ball-shaped dessert of ice cream or light mousse-like chocolate. [Ital, truffle]

tarty see under **tart²**.

tarwhine /tär'(h)wīn/ *n* an Australian sea bream. [From an Aboriginal language]

Tarzan /tär'zan/ *n* a man of great strength and agility. [From the hero of stories by Edgar Rice Burroughs (1875–1950)]

Tas. *abbrev* : Tasmania.

tasar /tus'ər/ same as **tusser**.

tasbih /taz'bē/ same as **sabha**.

taseometer /tas-i-om'i-tər/ *n* an instrument for measuring strains in a structure. [Gr *tasis*, *-eōs* a stretching, and *metron* measure]

taser /lā'zər/ *n* a weapon used to induce temporary paralysis in its target by firing barbs wired to an electrical source. ◆ *vt* to use such a weapon on (someone).

tash¹ /täsh/ (*Scot*) *vt* to soil; to blemish; to disfigure; to disarray. [Fr *tacher*]

tash² /tash/ (*inf*) *n* short for **moustache**.

Tashi Lama /tash'i lä'mə/ *n* another name for **Panchen Lama**. [*Tashi*, the name of the monastery of which this lama is the head]

tasimeter /tə-sim'i-tər/ *n* an instrument for measuring changes in pressure, etc by variations in electrical conductivity. [Gr *tasis* a stretch, and *metron* measure]

■ **tasimet'ric** *adj*.

task /täsk or task/ *n* a piece or amount of work set or undertaken (sometimes an *esp* burdensome, difficult or unpleasant one); a single piece of work to be processed (*comput*). ◆ *vt* to burden with heavy or difficult work; to put (a person's skills or capacity) fully or severely to the test; to assign a task or (eg military) mission to; to allocate as a task; to tax (*Shakesp*). [OFr *tasque* (Fr *tâche*), from LL *tasca*, *taxa*, from L *taxāre* to rate]

■ **task'er** *n* a person who imposes or performs a task; a person who does piecework. **task'ing** *n* taskwork.

❑ **task'bar** *n* an area on a computer screen that displays details of all programs currently running. **task force** or **task group** *n* a group formed by selection from different branches of the armed services to carry out a specific task; a similar group within the police force; a working party (qv under **work**) for a civilian purpose. **task-o'riented** *adj* measuring success in terms of completion of tasks. **task'master** *n* (also *fem* **task'mistress**) a person who allots tasks *esp* involving hard, regular or continuous work. **task swapping** or **task switching** *n* (*comput*) an operation whereby control can be swapped between two or more application programs, either on a command from the user or by the operating system. **task'work** *n* work done as a task, or by the job.

■ **take (someone) to task** to rebuke (someone).

taslet see under **tasse**.

TASM *abbrev* : tactical air-to-surface missile.

Tasmanian /tas- or taz-mā'ni-ən/ *adj* of *Tasmania*, island state of Australia discovered in 1642 by Abel Janszoon *Tasman*. ◆ *n* a native or citizen of Tasmania.

❑ **Tasmanian devil** *n* a small ferocious marsupial of the Tasmanian dasyure family, *Sarcophilus harrisii*. **Tasmanian myrtle** *n* a Tasmanian and Victorian evergreen beech. **Tasmanian wolf** (or **tiger**) *n* the thylacine, a striped wolflike dasyure of Tasmania, perhaps extant in remote areas, perhaps extinct.

TASS /tas/ *abbrev* : *Telegrafnoye Agentstvo Sovietskovo Soyuza* (*Russ*), telegraph agency of the former Soviet Union (replaced in 1992 by **ITAR-Tass**).

tass¹ /täs/ (*dialect*) *n* a mow, a heap. [OFr *tas*, poss from Du]

tass² /tas/ *n* a drinking cup; a small alcoholic drink. [Fr *tasse*, from Ar *tāss* cup]

■ **tass'ie** *n* (*Scot*) a small cup.

tassa /ta'sə/ *n* a large Indian kettledrum, worn hanging round the neck. [Hindi]

tasse, **tasset** or **tace** /tas/ *n* (in plate armour) one of a series of overlapping pieces forming a kind of skirt. [OFr *tasse*, *tasselet*, *tassete*]

■ **tas'let** or **tass'et** *n* a tasse.

tassel¹ /tas'l/ *n* an ornamental hanging tuft of threads; an inflorescence of similar appearance, *esp* of maize; a ribbon bookmark; a clasp or fastening (*Shakesp*); a gold or silver plate on a vestment. ◆ *vt* (**tass'elling** or (*US*) **tass'eling**; **tass'elled** or (*US*) **tass'eled**) to provide with tassels; to remove the tassels from. ◆ *vi* (eg of maize) to form tassels, flower. [OFr *tassel*; origin doubtful]

■ **tass'elled** *adj*. **tass'elling** *n*. **tass'elly** *adj*.

tassel² see **torsel**.

tassel³ or **tassell**, **tassell-gent** or **tassel-gentle** see under **tercel**.

tasset see under **tasse**.

Tassie /taz'i/ (*Aust inf*) *n* Tasmania.

tassie see under **tass²**.

taste /tāst/ n the act of tasting; the particular sensation caused by a substance on the tongue; the sense by which we perceive the flavour of a thing; the quality or flavour of anything; a small portion; an experience; discernment of, or accordance with, what is socially right or acceptable; the faculty by which the mind perceives the beautiful or elegant; fine perception; choice, predilection, liking; the act of testing (obs). ◆ vt to try, or to perceive, by the sense located in the tongue and palate; to try or test by eating or drinking a small amount; to eat or drink a small amount of; to partake of; to experience, perceive; to try, test (obs); to relish, enjoy (archaic); to enjoy carnally (Shakesp); to give a flavour to (rare). ◆ vi to try or perceive by the mouth; to have a flavour (with of); to act as taster. [OFr taster (Fr tâter), as if from a LL frequentative of L taxāre to touch, handle, estimate, from tangere to touch]
■ **tāst'able** adj. **tāst'ed** adj having a taste. **taste'ful** adj full of taste; having a pleasant or a high relish; showing good taste. **taste'fully** adv. **taste'fulness** n. **taste'less** adj without taste; without good taste; insipid. **taste'lessly** adv. **taste'lessness** n. **tāst'er** n someone skilful in distinguishing flavours by the taste; someone employed to test the innocuousness of food by tasting it before serving it to his or her master or mistress (hist); any implement or device used to obtain samples for tasting; a publisher's reader (inf); an extract or sample (inf). **tāst'ily** adv. **tāst'iness** n. **tāst'ing** n the action of the verb; an event at which wine, cheese, etc is sampled. **tāst'y** adj (**tāst'ier**; **tāst'iest**) savoury, appetizing; interesting, attractive (sl); tasteful (inf).
❑ **taste bud** n a group of cells on the tongue sensitive to taste (also **taste bulb**).
■ **good taste** intuitive feeling for what is aesthetically or socially right. **to one's taste** to one's liking, agreeable to one.

tastevin /tāst' or tast'vẽ/ n a small shallow cup used for testing by observation the colour, clarity, etc of wine. [Fr]

-tastic /-tas-tik/ combining form denoting something 'fantastic' in terms of the thing specified in the word's first element, eg poptastic, rocktastic. [Fanciful formation from fantastic]

tat¹ or **tatt** /tat/ n pretentious odds and ends of little real value, eg in an antique shop; tawdry or shabby articles esp clothes; a rag, esp an old one. ◆ vt to touch up. [tatter]
■ **tatt'ily** adv. **tatt'iness** n. **tatt'y** adj (**tatt'ier**; **tatt'iest**) cheap, of poor quality; untidy; shabby; (of clothes or ornament) fussy; precious, and often bogus.

tat² or **tatt** /tat/ vt to make by tatting. ◆ vi to make tatting. [Origin uncertain]
■ **tatt'ing** n knotted lace edging made by hand with a shuttle from sewing-thread; the act or process of making this.

tat³ /tät/ n E Indian hempen matting. [Hindi tāt]

tat⁴ /tat/ n see **tattoo³**.

tat⁵ /tat/ n a tap. ◆ vt to touch, tap; to flog. [Cf **tap¹**, and see **tit²**]

tat⁶ see **tit for tat** under **tit²**.

ta-ta /tä-tä'/ (childish and inf) interj goodbye.

tatami /ta-tä'mi/ n a type of mat, of a standard size, made from rice stalks, used as a floor-covering in Japanese houses. [Jap]

Tatar /tä'tər/ n orig a member of any of certain Tungusic tribes in Chinese Tartary; extended to any of the Mongol, Turkish and other warriors who swept over Asia and Europe; loosely, one of the mixed inhabitants of Tartary, Siberia and the Russian steppes, incl Kazan Tartars, Crim Tartars, Kipchaks, Kalmucks, etc; any of the languages spoken by the Tatars, belonging to the Turkic group of languages; a speaker of a Turkic language. ◆ adj of or relating to the Tatars or their languages. [Turk and Pers Tatar; association with Gr Tartaros hell, seems to have suggested the form Tartar]
■ **Tatarian** /tä-tä'ri-ən/ or **Tataric** /-tar'ik/ adj of the Tatars; of the Turkic group of languages. **Ta'tary** or **Tar'tary** n (hist) a name given from the 14c by W European peoples to a vast, ill-defined area of E Europe and Asia, inhabited by Tatars.

tate or **tait** /tāt/ (Scot) n a small portion, pinch, tuft.

tater /tā'tər/ n an informal form of **potato** (also **tā'tie**).

tath /täth/ (dialect) n cattle dung; coarse tufted grass that grows where it has fallen. ◆ vt to manure. ◆ vi to drop dung. [ON tath]

tatler see under **tattle**.

tatou /tat'oo or ta-too'/ n an armadillo, esp the giant armadillo. [Tupí tatú]

tatouay /tat'oo-ā/ n a large armadillo (Cabassous unicinctus) of tropical S America. [Sp tatuay, from Guaraní tatu armadillo, and ai lazy, worthless]

TATP abbrev: triacetone triperoxide, a powerful explosive.

tatt¹, **tattily**, **tattiness**, **tatty** see **tat¹**.

tatt² see **tat²**.

tatter /tat'ər/ n (usu in pl) a torn shred; a loose hanging rag. ◆ vt to tear to tatters. ◆ vi to fall into tatters. [Cf Icel töturr]
■ **tatt'ered** adj. **tatt'ery** adj ragged.
■ **in tatters** ragged; ruined.

tatterdemalion /tat-ər-di-mā'lyən/ or **tatterdemallion** /-mal'yən/ n a tattered person, a ragamuffin. ◆ adj ragged, tattered, scarecrowlike. [From tattered or tatter, with termination of uncertain formation]

Tattersall's or **Tattersalls** /tat'ər-sölz/ n a famous London horse-market and haunt of racing-men, founded 1766 by Richard Tattersall (1724–95); an enclosure at a racecourse, offering cheaper admission than the Members' Enclosure (inf **Tatts**); a sweepstake or lottery agency with headquarters at Melbourne, Australia (inf **Tatts**).
■ **Tatt'ersall** n (a fabric with) a pattern of checks like that of the horse-blankets orig used at Tattersall's horse-market (also **Tattersall check**).

tattie /tat'i/ n a Scots form of **potato**.
❑ **tatt'ie-bogle** n a scarecrow. **tatt'ie-claw** n potato soup. **tatt'ie-lifting** or **-howk'ing** n the potato harvest. **tatt'ie-shaw** n the part of a potato plant above the ground.

tatting see under **tat²**.

tattle /tat'l/ n idle talk, chatter; gossip. ◆ vi to talk idly, chatter; to gossip, tell tales or secrets. ◆ vt to tell, give away, in tattle. [Used by Caxton to translate MDu tatelen; imit]
■ **tatt'ler** n (formerly **tat'ler**) an indiscreet talker; a chatterer, a gossip; any (esp American) bird of the Totaninae family, members of which have a loud cry. **tatt'ling** n and adj chattering; tale-telling. **tatt'lingly** adv.
❑ **tatt'letale** n (chiefly N Am) a telltale. ◆ vi to tell tales.

tattoo¹ /ta-, tə-too'/, earlier **tatu** /tə-too'/ and **tattow** /-tow'/ n a design marked on the skin by pricking in indelible dyes. ◆ vt (pat and pap **tattooed'**) to mark (the skin) in this way; to produce (a design) in this way. [Tahitian ta'tau, Marquesan ta'tu]
■ **tattoo'er** or **tattoo'ist** n.

tattoo² /ta- or tə-too'/ n a beat of drum or other signal calling soldiers to quarters; a drumming; a military entertainment, with marching, displays of prowess, etc, held at night. [Du taptoe, from tap tap (of a barrel), and toe to, in the sense of shut]
■ **the devil's tattoo** drumming with the fingers on a table, etc, absent-mindedly or impatiently.

tattoo³ /tut'oo/ n a native-bred Indian pony (short form **tat**). [Hindi tattū]

tattow see **tattoo¹**.

Tatts see **Tattersall's**.

tatty¹ see under **tat¹** and **taut²**.

tatty² /tat'i/ n an Indian mat of bamboo, cuscus-grass roots, etc, esp one kept wet in a doorway or window to cool the air. [Hindi ṭaṭṭī]

tatu see **tattoo¹**.

tau /tow/ n the nineteenth letter (T, τ) of the Greek alphabet, corresponding to T; a tau cross; as a numeral τ' = 300, ͵τ = 300000; a tau particle. [Gr tau, of Semitic origin]
❑ **tau cross** n a T-shaped cross, St Anthony's cross. **tau neutrino** n (phys) a neutrino of the kind associated with the decay of tau particles. **tau particle** n (phys) a lepton of mass 3600 times greater than that of an electron. **tau staff** n a staff with a crosspiece at the top like a crutch.

taube /tow'bə/ n a German monoplane with recurved wings (1914–18 war). [Ger, dove]

taught¹ /töt/ pat and pap of **teach**.

taught² see **taut¹**.

tauld /töld/ a Scots form of **told** (pat and pap).

taunt¹ /tönt/ vt to goad or provoke in a wounding way; to censure or reproach sarcastically or contemptuously. ◆ vi to gibe. ◆ n a wounding gibe; an object of taunts (Bible). [Poss OFr tanter, from L tentāre to tempt; or Fr tant pour tant tit for tat]
■ **taunt'er** n. **taunt'ing** n and adj. **taunt'ingly** adv.

taunt² /tönt/ (naut) adj (esp of the masts of ships) very tall. [Origin unknown]

taupe /tōp/ adj and n (of) a brownish-grey colour. [Fr, mole, from L talpa]

taupie see **tawpie**.

Taurean see under **Taurus¹**.

taurean /tö'rē-ən or tö-rē'ən/ or **tauric** /tö'rik/ adj of or relating to a bull. [L taurus bull]

tauriform /tö'ri-förm/ adj having the form of a bull. [L taurus bull, and -form]

taurine¹ /tö'rīn/ adj of a bull; bull-like. [L taurīnus, from taurus bull]

taurine[2] /tö'rēn/ n a neutral crystalline compound occurring esp in invertebrates. [L taurus bull (because discovered in the bile of cattle), and **-ine**[1]]

tauro- /tö-rō-, -rə-, -ro-/ combining form denoting a bull. [L taurus and Gr tauros bull]

■ **taurobō'lium** n (Gr taurobolion, from bolē a throw or stroke) the sacrifice of a bull, eg as in the ancient Phrygian cult of Cybele; an artistic representation of this. **tauromachian** /-mā'ki-ən/ adj. **tauromachy** /-rom'ə-ki/ n (Gr tauromachiā, from machē fight) bullfighting; a bullfight. **tauromor'phous** adj (Gr morphē form) bull-shaped.

Taurus[1] /tö'rəs or tow'rŭs/ n the Bull, a constellation giving its name to, and formerly coinciding with, a sign of the zodiac (astron); the second sign of the zodiac, between Aries and Gemini (astrol); a person born between 21 April and 20 May, under the sign of Taurus (astrol; pl **Tau'rus** or **Tau'ruses**). [L taurus and Gr tauros bull]

■ **Tau'rean** (or /-rē'ən/) n and adj (relating to or characteristic of) a person born under the sign of Taurus.

Taurus[2] /tö'rəs/ (stock exchange) abbrev: transfer and automated registration of uncertified stock, a computerized system of share settlement, without the need for share certificates, abandoned March 1993.

taut[1] (obs **taught**) /töt/ adj tightly drawn; tense; (of a ship) in good condition. [Prob connected with **tow**[1] and **tight**[1]]

■ **taut'en** vt and vi to tighten. **taut'ly** adv. **taut'ness** n.

taut[2] or **tawt** /töt/ (Scot) vt and vi to mat, tangle. [Cf OE tætteca rag]

■ **taut'it** adj. **tawt'ie** or **tatt'y** adj.

taut- /töt-/ or **tauto-** /tö-tō-, tö-tə- or tö-to-/ combining form denoting the same. [Gr tauto, for to auto the same]

■ **taut'ochrone** /-krōn/ n (Gr chronos time) a curve such that a particle travelling along it under gravity reaches a fixed point in the same time, no matter where it starts. **tautoch'ronism** n. **tautoch'ronous** adj. **tautolog'ic** /-loj'/ or **tautolog'ical** adj. **tautolog'ically** adv. **tautol'ogism** n. **tautol'ogist** n. **tautol'ogize** or **-ise** vi to use tautology. **tautol'ogous** /-ə-gəs/ adj tautological. **tautol'ogously** adv. **tautol'ogy** n (Gr tautologia, from tautologos saying the same thing, from legein to say) use of words, esp as an error of style, that repeat something already implied in the same statement, etc, as in all at once she suddenly remembered; a statement that is necessarily always true (logic). **taut'omer** n (chem) (Gr meros part) a readily interconvertible isomer. **tautomer'ic** adj. **tautom'erism** n. **tautomet'ric** or **tautomet'rical** adj exactly corresponding in arrangement of syllables. **taut'onym** n (Gr onyma name) in a biological nomenclature, a taxonomic name in which the specific name repeats the generic. **tauton'ymous** adj. **tauton'ymy** n. **tautophon'ic** or **tautophon'ical** adj. **tautoph'ony** n (Gr phōnē sound) repetition of a sound.

tautog /tö-tog'/ n a labroid fish (Tautoga onitis) of the N American Atlantic coast. [Narraganset tautauog]

tav /täv/ n the twenty-second letter of the Hebrew alphabet. [Heb]

tava or **tavah** /tä'və/ same as **tawa**[2].

Tavel /tä-vel'/ n a rosé wine produced near Tavel, in S France.

taver[1] or **taiver** /tā'vər/ (Scot) n (often in pl) a shred, tatter. [Cf Norw and Dan tave]

taver[2] or **taiver** /tā'vər/ (Scot) vi to wander about aimlessly; to rave. [Cf Norw tava to toil, fumble]

■ **ta'vert** or **tai'vert** adj muddled; fuddled; bewildered; stupid.

tavern /tav'ərn/ (usu archaic or literary) n a public house or inn. [OFr (Fr) taverne, from L taberna shed, stall, tavern, from the root of tabula a board]

■ **tav'erner** n a publican.

taverna /tə-vûr'nə/ n in Greece, a type of guesthouse with a bar, popular as holiday accommodation; a Greek restaurant. [Adopted into Mod Gr; see tavern]

TAVR abbrev: Territorial and Army Volunteer Reserve (replaced in 1979 by **TA**).

taw[1] /tö/ vt to prepare (skins) for white leather by soaking, salting, stretching and paring; to flog (obs). ◆ n (obs) tawed leather; a thong or whip. [OE tawian to prepare; Du touwen to curry; OHGer zawjan to make, prepare]

■ **taw'er** n a maker of white leather. **taw'ery** n a place where skins are dressed. **taw'ie** adj (Scot) tractable. **taw'ing** n.

taw[2] /tö/ n a large or choice marble; a game of marbles; the line shot from at marbles. [Origin unknown]

tawa[1] /tä'wə/ n an evergreen tree (Beilschmiedia tawa) of the Lauraceae family, with slender branches and graceful foliage, bearing a damsonlike fruit, native to New Zealand. [Maori]

tawa[2] /tä'wə/ n a griddle used in Indian cookery (also **tava** or **tavah**). [Hindi and Punjabi tava griddle, frying-pan]

tawdry /tö'dri/ adj (**taw'drier**; **taw'driest**) showy without taste or worth; gaudily adorned. ◆ n trumpery; a tawdry lace (obs). [St Audrey (ie Æthelthrȳth, daughter of Anna, king of East Anglia), who thought a tumour in her throat a punishment for having worn jewelled necklaces]

■ **taw'drily** adv. **taw'driness** n.

❑ **tawdry lace** n (obs) a woman's silk necktie (in Spenser a waistbelt) such as was sold at St Audrey's Fair at Ely (17 October); gaudy adornment.

tawer, tawery, tawie see under **taw**[1].

tawny, also **tawney** /tö'ni/ adj and n (of) a brownish-yellow or -orange colour. ◆ n a port of a rich brownish-orange colour. [Fr tanné, pap of tanner to tan]

■ **taw'niness** n.

❑ **tawny eagle** n a tawny-coloured eagle of Africa and Asia (Aquila rapax). **tawny owl** n a tawny-coloured European owl (Strix aluco).

tawpie or **taupie** /tö'pi/ (Scot) n a clumsy, heedless or inefficient girl. [Cf Norw taap a halfwit]

taws or **tawse** /töz/ (esp Scot) n sing or n pl a leather strap, usu cut into strips at the end, for corporal punishment. [Poss pl of **taw**[1]]

tawt, tawtie see **taut**[2].

tax /taks/ vt to levy a tax on (people, businesses, incomes or goods); to pay tax on (a car, etc); to register or enrol for fiscal purposes (Bible: Luke 2.1–5); to make heavy demands on; to accuse, charge (usu with with); to assess (costs) (law); to examine (accounts) in order to allow or disallow items. ◆ n a contribution to revenue exacted by the state from individuals or businesses; a burden, drain or strain (with on or upon); a charge, accusation (obs). [Fr taxe a tax, from L taxāre to handle, value, charge]

■ **taxabil'ity** n. **tax'able** adj. **tax'ably** adv. **taxā'tion** n. **tax'ative** adj taxing; of taxing. **taxed** adj. **tax'er** n (also **tax'or**). **tax'ing** n imposition of taxes; the practice of mugging a person for his or her fashionable footwear (street sl; orig US); censure, satire (obs). ◆ adj demanding; onerous. **tax'less** adj.

❑ **tax allowance** n a sum which is deducted from total income to arrive at taxable income. **tax avoidance** n steps taken within the law to minimize one's taxable income. **tax break** n (inf) an opportunity legally available for reducing one's tax obligations. **tax cart** or **taxed cart** n (hist) a light spring-cart (orig paying a lower tax, later none). **tax collector** n. **tax credit** n a sum that may be set against liability for tax. **tax-deduct'ible** adj (of expenses, etc) that may be deducted from one's income before it is assessed for tax. **tax disc** n a paper disc displayed on a motor vehicle's windscreen to show that the road tax has been paid for a given period. **tax evasion** n illegal evasion of payment of tax. **tax-exempt'** adj not liable to taxation. **tax exile** n a person living abroad so as not to pay high taxes. **tax farmer** n (esp hist) a tax gatherer who pays a fixed sum for the right to collect taxes, retaining the revenue as income. **tax-free'** adj and adv without payment of tax. **tax gatherer** n. **tax haven** n a country or state where taxes are comparatively low. **tax holiday** n a period during which a government makes tax concessions available to business, eg to encourage exports. **taxing master** n an officer of a court of law who examines bills of costs. **tax loss** n a loss that can be offset against taxable future profits. **tax'man** n (inf) a tax collector; tax collectors collectively. **tax'payer** n a person who pays tax or taxes; a person who is liable to taxation; a building put up for the express purpose of earning money to pay tax on the land (US). **tax'-paying** adj. **tax point** n the date on which value-added tax becomes payable. **tax relief** n the cancelling of part of the income tax due. **tax reserve certificate** n a government receipt for money deposited that may later be used, with certain advantages, for payment of tax. **tax return** n a yearly statement of one's income, from which the amount due in tax is calculated. **tax shelter** n a financial arrangement made in order to pay the minimum taxation. **tax'-sheltered** adj of or produced by a tax shelter; of or involving investments legally exempt from tax. **tax threshold** n the level of income at which tax starts to be payable.

taxa see **taxon**.

Taxaceae, taxaceous see **Taxus**.

taxameter see **taximeter**.

taxeme /tak'sēm/ n (linguistics) any element of language that can affect the meaning of an utterance. [Gr taxis order, and -eme (after phoneme)]

taxes /tak'siz/ plural of **tax** or /tak'sēz/ plural of **taxis**.

taxi /tak'si/ n (pl **tax'is** or **tax'ies**) a motor car, usu fitted with a taximeter, licensed to carry passengers on request to a specified destination (also **tax'icab**); any other vehicle available for hire, such as a boat or small aircraft. ◆ vi (prp **tax'ying** or **tax'iing**; pat and pap **tax'ied**; 3rd pers sing pres indicative **tax'ies**) to travel by taxi; (of an aeroplane) to run along the ground, or (of a seaplane) over the surface of water, before take-off or after landing, at low speed under its own power. ♦ *vt* to run (an aeroplane) along the ground in this way; to send or convey by taxi. [Shortening of *taximeter cab*]

❑ **taxi dancer** *n* a person, *usu* a woman, hirable as a partner, dance by dance, in a dance hall. **tax'i-driver** *n*. **tax'iman** *n* a taxi-driver. **taxi rank** or (*US*) **taxi stand** *n* a place where taxis congregate for hiring. **taxi track** or **tax'iway** *n* (at an airport or aerodrome) a specially prepared track used for ground movement of aircraft, eg from runways to terminals, etc.

taxiarch see under **taxis**.

taxidermy /*tak'si-dûr-mi*/ *n* the art of preparing, stuffing and mounting the skins of animals and birds so that they present a lifelike appearance. [Gr *taxis* arrangement, and *derma* a skin]

■ **taxider'mal** or **taxider'mic** *adj*. **tax'idermist** *n*. **tax'idermize** or **-ise** *vt*.

taximeter /*tak'si-mē-tər* or *tak-sim'i-tər*/ (*obs* **taxameter**) *n* an instrument attached to a cab for indicating (distance travelled and) fare due. [Fr *taxe* price, and **-meter**]

taxis /*tak'sis*/ *n* (*pl* **tax'ēs**) return to position of displaced parts by means of manipulation only (*surg*); movement of a whole organism, eg a bacterium in response to stimulus (*biol*); arrangement or order; a division of an ancient Greek army (in Athens the contingent from a phyle). [Gr, from *tassein* to arrange]

■ **tax'iarch** /*-i-ärk*/ *n* the commander of an ancient Greek taxis.

Taxol® see under **Taxus**.

taxon /*tak'sən* or *tak'son*/ *n* (*pl* **tax'a**) a biological category, a taxonomic group (eg *species*) or its name. [Back-formation from *taxonomy*]

taxonomy /*tak-son'ə-mi*/ *n* classification or its principles; classification of plants or animals, *incl* the study of means by which formation of species, etc takes place. [Gr *taxis* order, and *-nomia* distribution]

■ **taxon'omer** *n* a taxonomist. **taxonom'ic** or **taxonom'ical** *adj*. **taxonom'ically** *adv*. **taxon'omist** *n*.

taxor see **taxer** under **tax**.

Taxus /*tak'səs*/ *n* the yew genus of conifers, giving name to the family **Taxā'ceae** /*-si-ē*/. [L *taxus* yew]

■ **taxā'ceous** *adj* of, relating to or belonging to the Taxaceae. **Taxō'dium** *n* (Gr *eidos* form) the swamp-cypress genus. **Tax'ol**® *n* a drug, *orig* made from the bark of the Pacific yew, used in the treatment of cancer. **Taxotere**® /*tak'sō-tēr*/ *n* a semi-synthetic form of Taxol®, made from clippings from the European yew.

tay /*tā*/ (dialect, esp Irish) *n* tea.

tayassuid /*tä-yə-soo'id*/ *n* any member of the peccary family **Tayassuidae** of New World pigs. [From *tayassu* (the common peccary), from Tupí *tayau*]

tayberry /*tā'bə-ri*/ *n* a hybrid plant, a blackberry crossed with a raspberry; the fruit of this plant. [*Tayside* in Scotland, where it was first produced]

tayra or **taira** /*tī'rə*/ *n* a large S American member (*Eira barbara*) of the weasel family. [Tupí *taira*]

Tay-Sachs disease /*tā-saks' di-zēz'*/ *n* a congenital disorder, prevalent in Ashkenazi Jews, caused by a faulty gene, in which progressive degeneration of nerve cells in the brain and spinal cord causes mental retardation, blindness, paralysis and *usu* an early death in childhood (also called **amaurotic familial idiocy**). [W *Tay* (1843–1927), British doctor and B *Sachs* (1858–1944), US neurologist]

tazza /*tat'sə*/ *n* (*pl* **taz'ze** /*-sā*/ or **taz'zas**) a shallow cup mounted on a circular foot; a saucer-shaped bowl. [Ital, cup; cf **tass**²]

TB *abbrev*: terabyte(s) (also **Tb**); torpedo boat; tubercle bacillus; tuberculosis.

Tb (*chem*) *symbol*: terbium.

tba *abbrev*: to be advised (or announced).

tbc *abbrev*: to be confirmed.

tbsp *abbrev*: tablespoon(ful) (*pl* **tbsps**).

TBT *abbrev*: tributyltin.

TBTF *abbrev*: too big to fail.

Tc (*chem*) *symbol*: technetium.

TCA *abbrev*: tricarboxylic acid.

TCAS /*tē'kas*/ *abbrev*: Traffic Alert and Collision Avoidance System, used to warn pilots of potential midair collisions.

TCD *abbrev*: Trinity College, Dublin.

TCH *abbrev*: Chad (ie *Tchad*; IVR).

tchick /*chik* or *ch'*/ *n* a sound made by pressing the tongue against the roof of the mouth and then drawing back one side, as in urging a horse on. ♦ *vi* to make such a sound. [Imit]

tchoukball /*tchook'böl*/ *n* a game, invented in the 1970s, in which the object is to prevent the ball (thrown by the opposing team against a

highly sprung net) from landing when it rebounds, physical contact with other players being against the rules. [Imit of the sound of the ball hitting the net]

TCM *abbrev*: traditional Chinese medicine; Trinity College of Music, London.

TCP *abbrev*: Transmission (or Transport) Control Protocol (*comput*); *t*richloro*p*henylmethyliodosalicyl, a proprietary germicide.

TCP/IP (*comput*) *abbrev*: Transmission Control Protocol/Internet Protocol.

TD *abbrev*: *Teachta Dála*, Deputy to the Dáil; technical drawing; Territorial Decoration.

TDMA *abbrev*: Time Division Multiple Access, a digital transmission system used in personal communication devices such as mobile phones.

Te (*chem*) *symbol*: tellurium.

te see **ti**¹.

tea /*tē*, formerly *tā*/ *n* a tree (*Camellia sinensis*, family Theaceae) cultivated in China, Assam, etc; its dried and prepared leaves, buds and shoots; a beverage made by infusing the leaves in boiling water; extended to any of various substitutes (see **Labrador tea** under **Labrador**, **Paraguay tea** under **Paraguayan**, etc); the leaves of any plant infused as a beverage; more rarely, a similar preparation of animal origin (eg *beef tea*); a cup of tea; an afternoon meal or light refreshment at which tea is generally served; a cooked meal taken in the early evening, high tea (*Brit*); marijuana (old US *sl*). ♦ *vi* (**tea'ing**; **teaed** or **tea'd**) (*inf*) to take tea. ♦ *vt* (*inf*) to provide tea for. [S Chinese *te*, the common form being *chá* or *ts'a*]

❑ **tea bag** or **tea'bag** *n* a bag containing tea leaves for infusion. **tea ball** *n* chiefly in USA, a perforated metal ball-shaped container to hold the tea leaves for infusion. **tea'berry** *n* wintergreen; a wintergreen berry. **tea biscuit** *n* any of various kinds of sweetish biscuits, often eaten with tea. **tea'board** *n* a tea tray. **tea bread** *n* light sweet bread or buns to be eaten with tea. **tea break** *n* a break for tea or other refreshment during the working day. **tea caddy** or **tea canister** *n* an airtight container for holding tea. **tea'cake** *n* a glazed currant bun, *usu* eaten toasted. **tea ceremony** *n* in Japan, the ceremonial making and serving of tea. **tea chest** *n* a tall wooden container with a metal lining, in which tea is packed for transporting. **tea clipper** *n* (*hist*) a fast sailing-ship in the tea trade. **tea cloth** *n* a small tablecloth; a tea towel, a drying-up cloth. **tea cosy** *n* a thick cover for a teapot to keep the tea hot. **tea'cup** *n* a *usu* medium-sized bowl-shaped cup designed for drinking tea out of; a teacupful. **tea'cupful** *n* (*pl* **tea'cupfuls**) the amount held by a teacup, about 140ml (5floz). **tea dance** *n* a thé dansant. **tea'-dealer** *n* a buyer and seller of tea. **tea dish** *n* an old name for a teacup. **tea drinker** *n*. **tea equipage** *n* apparatus for making and serving tea with all that accompanies it. **tea fight** *n* (*inf*) a tea party. **tea garden** *n* a plantation of tea; an open-air restaurant for tea and other refreshments. **tea gown** *n* a loose gown formerly worn at afternoon tea at home. **tea house** *n* a restaurant in China, Japan, or other eastern countries where tea, etc is served. **tea kettle** *n* a kettle for boiling water for tea. **tea lady** *n* a woman who makes and serves tea in an office or factory. **tea lead** *n* lead with a little tin for lining tea chests. **tea leaf** *n* a leaf of tea; (*usu* in *pl*) a small piece of such a leaf, *esp* when it has been used in making tea; a thief (*rhyming sl*). **tea'light** *n* a small round candle, sometimes scented, in a metal or plastic case, used decoratively or in warming devices. **tea meeting** *n* a public social meeting at which tea is drunk. **tea party** *n* a social gathering at which tea is served; the people present; (with *cap*) a political movement in the USA advocating low taxation and government spending. **tea plant** *n*. **tea plantation** *n*. **tea planter** *n* the owner or cultivator of a tea plantation. **tea'pot** *n* a spouted vessel for pouring out tea. **tea room** *n* a restaurant where tea and light refreshments are served; a room used for refreshment and informal conversation by the staff or members of an establishment; a small shop selling a variety of perishable goods, cigarettes, newspapers, etc (*S Afr*). **tea rose** *n* a hybrid rose, derived from *Rosa odorata*, with a scent resembling that of tea. **tea service** or **tea set** *n* a set of utensils for serving tea. **tea shop** *n* a shop where tea is sold; a restaurant in which teas are served. **Teas'made**® *n* small machine with an alarm clock or timer which makes tea, *usu* by the pot, at a preset time. **tea'spoon** *n* a small spoon used with a teacup; the amount held by a teaspoon, used eg as a measure in cookery. **tea'spoonful** *n* (*pl* **tea'spoonfuls**). **tea'-strainer** *n* a small strainer to catch tea leaves when pouring tea. **tea table** *n* a table at which tea is drunk; the company at tea. **tea taster** *n* an expert who judges tea by tasting it. **tea'-tasting** *n*. **tea things** *n pl* the tea pot, cups, etc. **tea'time** *n* the time in the afternoon or early evening when tea is taken (also *adj*). **tea towel** *n* a cloth for drying crockery, kitchen utensils, etc. **tea tray** *n* a tray for carrying tea things. **tea tree** *n* the common tea plant or shrub; a name of Australian plants of the Myrtaceae family (*Melaleuca*, *Leptospermum*; also called **manuka**), the leaves of which were formerly used to make a type of tea; an African solanaceous shrub (genus *Lycium*) said to have been labelled by mistake. **tea trolley** or (*N Am*) **tea wagon** *n* a small tiered table on wheels from which afternoon tea, etc is served. **tea urn** *n* a large closed urn with a tap, often also a heating device, for making tea in quantity.

■ **another cup of tea** a very different thing. **black tea** tea which has been fermented between rolling and firing (heating with charcoal in a sieve). **green tea** tea which is fired immediately after rolling. **high tea** an early-evening meal with tea and eg meat, eggs, fish, or a savoury dish. (**not**) **for all the tea in China** (not) for any reward whatever. **one's cup of tea** (*inf*) what is to one's taste or appeals to one. **Russian tea** tea with lemon and no milk *usu* served in a glass. **tea and sympathy** (*inf*) hospitality and kind words offered to someone in trouble, as being the only, albeit *usu* inadequate, help one can give.

teach /tēch/ *vt* (*pat* and *pap* **taught** /töt/) to impart knowledge or art to; to impart the knowledge or art of; to guide the studies of; to exhibit so as to impress upon the mind; to show; to direct; to accustom; to counsel; to be an object lesson to (someone) to do or not to do something in future; to force home the desirability or undesirability of (particular conduct, etc) to. ◆ *vi* to impart knowledge or give instruction as one's profession. [OE *tǣcan* to show, teach; cf Ger *zeigen* to show; Gr *deiknynai* to show]

■ **teachabil'ity** *n*. **teach'able** *adj* capable of being taught; willing and quick to learn, responsive to teaching. **teach'ableness** *n*. **teach'er** *n* a person whose profession, or whose talent, is the ability to impart knowledge, practical skill, or understanding. **teach'erless** *adj*. **teach'erly** *adj*. **teach'ership** *n*. **teach'ing** *n* the act, practice or profession of giving instruction; doctrine; instruction. ◆ *adj* occupied with giving instruction; instructive. **teach'less** *adj* (*archaic*) incapable of being taught.

❑ **teacher-gov'ernor** *n* a teacher who has also been elected to his or her school's board of governors. **teach'-in** *n* a long public debate consisting of a succession of speeches by well-informed persons holding different views on a matter of general importance, *usu* with discussion, etc. **teaching aid** *n* any object or device used by a teacher to help to explain or illustrate a subject. **teaching fellow** *n* a postgraduate student who receives tuition, accommodation, etc in return for teaching duties. **teaching hospital** *n* a hospital in which medical students are trained. **teaching machine** *n* any mechanical device capable of presenting an instructional programme. **teaching practice** *n* a trainee teacher's temporary period of teaching in a school, *usu* under supervision.

■ **teach school** (*N Am*) to be a teacher in a school. **teach** (**someone**) **a lesson** to bring home to (someone) his or her folly. **that'll teach you**, **him**, etc (*inf*) that (unpleasant experience) will teach you, him, etc to behave better, be more careful, etc next time.

teachie obsolete form of **tetchy**.

tead or **teade** /tēd/ (*Spenser*) *n* a torch. [L *taeda*]

teagle /tē'gl/ (*dialect*) *n* a hoist or lift; a baited line for catching birds. ◆ *vt* to hoist or catch with a teagle. [Prob a form of **tackle**]

Teague /tēg/ *n* an old nickname for an Irishman. [*Tadhg*, an Irish name, Thady]

teak /tēk/ *n* a verbenaceous tree (*Tectona grandis*) of India, Malaya, etc; its hard and durable wood; the yellowish-brown colour of its wood; any of several trees or their wood, resembling, or used as a substitute for, teak. [Malayalam *tēkka*]

■ **African teak** an African euphorbiaceous tree, *Oldfieldia africana*. **bastard teak** dhak. **white teak** a Flindersia.

teal /tēl/ *n* (*pl* **teals** or **teal**) any of several kinds of small freshwater duck, *esp Anas crecca*, with variegated plumage and a distinctive chestnut and green head in the male; a dark greenish-blue colour. ◆ *adj* having this colour. [ME *tēle*, prob from OE; cf Du *teling*, *taling*]

team /tēm/ *n* a set of people constituting one side in a competitive game, a side; a set of people working in combination; a set of animals harnessed together; a set of animals with the vehicle to which they are harnessed, an equipage, a turn-out; a stock of animals; a string of flying ducks, geese, etc; a brood, a litter (*obs* or *dialect*); a chain, *esp* for hauling a plough, etc (*dialect*). ◆ *vt* to join together in order to make a team or co-operative effort (with *with*); to match (clothes, etc; often with *with*); to harness (animals) in a team, to yoke; to draw or convey with a team (*N Am*). ◆ *vi* to drive a team. [OE *tēam* childbearing, brood, team; in related languages a bridle, rope, draught of a net; cf OE *tēon* to draw]

■ **teamed** (*Spenser* **tem'ed** and **teem'ed**) *adj* harnessed in a team. **team'er** *n* a teamster. **team'ing** *n* driving a team; work apportioned to a team; transport by team; removal of excavated material from cutting to bank. **team'ster** *n* a person who drives a team; a truck-driver (*US*). **team'wise** *adv* harnessed together.

❑ **team effort** *n* a co-operative endeavour, teamwork. **team game** *n* an *esp* outdoor game played by *usu* two teams in opposition. **team'mate** *n* a fellow member of a team. **team player** *n* a person who works well as a member of a team, *esp* in business. **team spirit** *n* the spirit of willingness to co-operate with others and work, etc as (a member of) a team. **team teaching** *n* instruction given by two or more teachers organized as a team, rather than by individual teachers in individual classes. **team'work** *n* work done by organized division of labour; co-operation, pulling together, regard to success of the enterprise as a whole rather than personal exploits or achievement.

■ **team up with** to join forces with.

Tean see Teian.

teapoy /tē'poi/ *n* a small table with a three-legged or four-legged base; (by confusion with **tea**) a tea-caddy. [Hindi *tīn*, *tīr-* three, and Pers *pāi* foot]

tear¹ /tēr/ *n* a drop of liquid secreted by the lachrymal gland that moistens and cleans the eye, or overflows from it as a manifestation of emotion, *esp* sorrow; an exuding drop; a blob, bead, pear-shaped drop; a small flaw or cavity, as in glass. ◆ *vi* (*pat* **teared**) (*chiefly US*; of the eyes) to fill with tears (also **tear up**). [OE *tēar*; Gothic *tagr*; Gr *dakry*]

■ **tear'ful** *adj* brimming with, ready to shed, or shedding, tears, crying; inclined to cry, lachrymose; emotion-filled, producing tears. **tear'fully** *adv*. **tear'fulness** *n*. **tear'less** *adj* shedding no tears, dry-eyed; sorrowless. **tear'y** *adj* tearful.

❑ **tear bag** *n* the lachrymal gland; the tear pit. **tear bottle** *n* (*archaeol*) a small bottle once thought to contain mourners' tears. **tear drop** *n* a tear; anything having a similar shape. **tear duct** *n* the opening at the inner corner of the eye by which tears drain into the nose, the lachrymal duct. **tear'-falling** *adj* (*Shakesp*) shedding tears. **tear gas** *n* a gas or volatile substance that blinds temporarily by provoking tears. **tear'-gas** *vt* to use tear gas on. **tear gland** *n* the lachrymal gland. **tear'-jerker** *n* an extravagantly sentimental song, book, film, etc, inviting pity, grief, sorrow. **tear'-jerking** *adj*. **tear pit** *n* (in deer) a gland below the eye secreting a waxy substance. **tear shell** *n* a shell that disperses tear gas. **tear smoke** *n* a lachrymatory vapour that, as opposed to tear gas, is visible. **tear'-stained** *adj* (of the face or cheeks) streaked with tracks left by tears.

■ **bored to tears** bored beyond endurance. **in tears** weeping. **without tears** by an easy or painless method.

tear² /tār/ *vt* (*pat* **tore** /tör or tōr/, *archaic* **tare**; *pap* **torn** /törn or tōrn/) to draw apart or separate with violence; to rend, rip, lacerate; to cause pain, bitterness, etc to; to make (a hole, rent, etc) by tearing. ◆ *vi* to move or act with violence; to rush, move very quickly; to rage; to become torn. ◆ *n* an act of tearing; a rent or hole torn in something; a rush (*sl*); a spree. [OE *teran*; cf Ger *zehren*]

■ **tear'able** *adj*. **tear'er** *n* someone or something that tears; a boisterous person (*sl*). **tear'ing** *adj* great, terrible, rushing.

❑ **tear'away** *n* a reckless and *usu* violent young person. ◆ *adj* impetuous, reckless; of or relating to a tearaway. **tear'sheet** *n* a page, eg in a magazine, perforated to facilitate its removal for reference, etc *esp* one demonstrating the work of a fashion model, photographer, etc. **tear strip** *n* a narrow perforated strip on a paper or card wrapper which can be pulled away to facilitate opening (also **tear'-off strip**). **tear webbing** *n* webbing in which two adhering layers form a fold that will tear apart so as to lessen the violence of a sudden strain.

■ **tear a** (or **the**) **cat** (*obs*) to rant. **tear and wear** see **wear and tear** under **wear¹**. **tear apart** (*inf*) to criticize vehemently or destructively; to search (eg a room) thoroughly; to cause severe distress to. **tear a strip off** (**someone**) or **tear** (**someone**) **off a strip** (*inf*) to reprimand (someone). **tear away** to remove by tearing; to remove (oneself) reluctantly. **tear down** to demolish violently. **tear into** to attack physically or verbally; to scold furiously. **tear off** to remove by tearing; to depart hurriedly; to compose or produce hurriedly. **tear one's hair** formerly, to be reduced by grief or rage to tearing out handfuls of one's hair; to reach an extreme pitch of frenzy and frustration. **tear up** to remove violently from a fixed state; to pull to pieces. **that's torn it!** see under **torn**.

tease /tēz/ *vt* to make fun of, to disconcert for one's own amusement; to plague, irritate, *esp* playfully, mischievously or unkindly; to arouse sexual desire in (someone) but refuse to satisfy it; to tantalize; to subject to banter; to open out the fibres of; to comb or card (wool, etc); to scratch (cloth) with teasels, so as to raise a nap; to raise a nap on; to back-comb (the hair). ◆ *n* a person given to teasing; an act of teasing. [OE *tǣsan* to card]

■ **teas'er** *n* any person who teases; a tricky question; a riddle, conundrum; an introductory, appetite-whetting advertisement; a male horse used to arouse a mare's interest before the selected stallion is put to her. **teas'ing** *n* and *adj*. **teas'ingly** *adv*.

■ **tease out** to open out the fibres of; to clarify (an obscure point) by discussion, etc.

teasel, also **teazel** or **teazle** /tē'zl/ *n* a plant of the genus *Dipsacus*, *esp D. fullonum*, with prickly flowers; its dried flower-head, with hooked bracts used in raising a nap on cloth; an artificial substitute for its head. ◆ *vt* (**teas'elling** or (*US*) **teas'eling**, etc; **teas'elled** or (*US*)

teas'eled, etc) to raise a nap on with the teasel. [OE *tǣsel*, from *tǣsan*; see **tease**]
■ **teas'eller** or **teas'eler** *n*. **teas'elling** or **teas'eling** *n*.

teat /tēt/ *n* the small protuberance through which the mammalian young suck the milk; a similarly-shaped piece of rubber through which milk is sucked from a baby's or young animal's feeding bottle; a nipple. [OE *titt*, *tit*; influenced by OFr *tete* (Fr *tette*)]
■ **teat'ed** *adj* having a teat or teats.

teaze an obsolete spelling of **tease**.

teazel and **teazle** see **teasel**.

tebbad /teb'ad/ *n* a sandstorm. [Cf Pers *tab* fever, and *bād* wind]

Tebeth /teb'eth/ *n* the tenth month of the Jewish ecclesiastical, and fourth of the secular, year, parts of December and January (also **Tebet** or **Tevet** /*tev-et'*/). [Heb *Tēbēth*]

Tebilize® or **-ise** /teb'i-līz/ *vt* to treat (cotton and linen fabrics) by a finishing process that prevents shrinking and creasing.

TEC or **Tec** *abbrev* : Training and Enterprise Council (now replaced by **LSC**).

'tec /tek/ (*inf*) *n* a detective.

tech /tek/ (*inf*) *n* a technical college.

tech. *abbrev* : technical; technology.

techie /tek'i/ (*sl*) *n* a devotee of or expert in (some aspect of) technology. [Short form]

techily, **techiness** see under **tetchy**.

techMARK® /tek'märk/ *n* a Stock Exchange market featuring new technology companies.

technetium /tek-nē'shi-əm/ *n* a chemical element (symbol **Tc**; atomic no 43), the first element to be produced artificially. [Gr *technētos* artificial, from *technē* art]

technic /tek'nik/ *n* technology; (often in *pl*) technicality, technique. [Gr *technikos*, from *technē* art, skill]
■ **technician** /-nish'ən/ *n* a person skilled in a practical or mechanical art; a person who does the practical work in a laboratory, etc. **tech'nicism** *n* (too great) an emphasis on or concern with practical results or method. **tech'nicist** *n* a technician. **tech'nicize** or **-ise** *vt* to render technical or technological. **tech'nics** *n pl* technical details or procedure. ◆ *n sing* technology; the study of industry.

technical /tek'ni-k(ə)l/ *adj* relating to a practical or mechanical art or applied science; industrial; belonging to, or in the language of, a particular art, department of knowledge or skill, or profession; so called in strict legal or technical language; being so by virtue of a strict application or interpretation of the rules; caused by a mechanical problem or failure; of or relating to a market whose prices are influenced by internal factors (such as supply and demand) rather than external ones (such as general economic conditions) (*finance*). ◆ *n* a technical foul; (in *pl*) technical details, *esp* when used to predict fluctuations in share prices (*inf*); (*usu* in *pl*) a large civilian vehicle fitted with heavy artillery. [Gr *technikos* (see **technic**), and sfx *-al*]
■ **technical'ity** *n* a technical term of expression; a technical point, a point of strictly correct procedure, etc; the state of being technical. **tech'nically** *adv*. **tech'nicalness** *n*.
❏ **technical area** *n* (*football*) an area beside the pitch inside which non-playing members of a team must remain during a match. **technical chemistry** *n* industrial chemistry. **technical college** *n* a college of further education that specializes in technical subjects, such as industrial skills, secretarial work, etc. **technical drawing** *n* the drawing of plans, machinery, etc done with precision using compasses, rulers, etc; a drawing done for industry or business. **technical foul** *n* (*sport*) a foul that does not involve physical contact. **technical hitch** *n* a mechanical fault that brings a broadcast, etc, to a temporary halt. **technical knockout** *n* (*boxing*) a defeat on the referee's decision that the losing contestant, though not actually knocked out, is unable to continue the fight. **technical sergeant** *n* in the US Marine Corps or Air Force, a noncommissioned officer ranking below a master sergeant. **technical support** *n* help and advice given to registered users of a piece of computer software or hardware by its providers; the provider of such advice.

Technicolor® /tek'ni-kul-ər/ *n* a process of colour photography in motion pictures in which films of the same scene, using different filters, are projected simultaneously.
■ **tech'nicolour** *adj* (modelled on above) in exaggeratedly bright colours; garishly romanticized. **tech'nicoloured** *adj*.
❏ **technicolour yawn** *n* (*sl*) vomit, in reference to its variegated appearance.

technique /tek-nēk'/ *n* a skilled procedure or method; a knack or trick of doing something; proficiency, refinement, in artistic performance. [Fr, from Gr *technikos*; see **technic**]

techno /tek'nō/ *n* a type of fast, repetitive electronic dance music.

techno- /tek-nō-, tek-nə- or tek-no-/ *combining form* denoting: craft, art, eg *technography*; technical, technological or technology, eg *technophobia*, *technomania*. [Gr *technē* art, skill]
■ **tech'nobabble** *n* (*inf*) technical jargon, specialized words, acronyms and abbreviations used to describe modern technology, *esp* computer hardware and software. **technoc'racy** *n* government or management by technical experts; a state, etc, so governed; a body of technical experts in political control. **tech'nocrat** *n* a member of a technocracy; a believer in technocracy. **technocrat'ic** *adj*. **tech'nofear** *n* (*inf*) technophobia. **technog'raphy** *n* the study and description of the arts, crafts and sciences in their historical and geographical contexts. **tech'nojunkie** *n* (*inf*) someone who is obsessed with technology. **technomā'nia** *n* a mania for technology. **technomā'niac** *n*. **tech'nomusic** *n* same as **techno**. **tech'nophile** *n* a person who likes and promotes technology. **technophil'ia** *n*. **technophil'ic** *adj*. **tech'nophobe** *n* a person who fears and dislikes technology. **technophō'bia** *n*. **technophō'bic** *adj* and *n*. **tech'nopole** *n* a place where high-technology industries are concentrated. **technop'olis** *n* a society ruled by technology; a geographical area where projects in technological research and development are concentrated. **technopol'itan** *n* and *adj*. **tech'nopop** *n* pop music using synthesizers and other electronic equipment. **tech'nospeak** *n* (*inf*) technical jargon, technobabble. **tech'nostress** *n* stress resulting from over-involvement with computers. **tech'nostructure** *n* the people in control of technology in a society.

technology /tek-nol'ə-ji/ *n* the practice of any or all of the applied sciences that have practical value and/or industrial use; technical methods in a particular area of industry or art; technical nomenclature; technical means and skills characteristic of a particular civilization, group or period. [Gr *technē* art, skill, and **-logy**]
■ **technolog'ical** *adj*. **technolog'ically** *adv*. **technol'ogist** *n* a person skilled in technology and its applications.
❏ **technological fix** or **technological optimum** *n* (often used pejoratively) the reliance on technological developments to solve human problems. **technology park** *n* a science park.

techy see **tetchy**.

teckel /tek'l/ *n* a dachshund. [Ger]

tectibranch /tek'ti-brangk/ (*zool*) *n* any member of the **Tectibranchiā'ta**, opisthobranch molluscs with gill covered by the mantle, *incl* eg the sea slugs. [L *tegere*, *tēctum* to cover, and *branchiae* gills]
■ **tectibranch'iate** *n* and *adj*.

tectiform /tek'ti-förm/ *adj* roof-like; roofing. [L *tēctum* a roof, and *förma* shape]

tectonic /tek-ton'ik/ *adj* relating to building; relating to structural changes in the earth's crust caused by upheavals and other movements within it (*geol*). [Gr *tektōn* a builder]
■ **tecton'ically** *adv*. **tecton'ics** *n sing* building as an art; structural geology (see also **plate tectonics** under **plate**). ◆ *n pl* the constructive arts; structural features.
❏ **tectonic plate** *n* (*geol*) one of several rigid plates forming the earth's crust, continually shifting slightly in relation one to another.

tectorial /tek-tō'ri-əl or -tö'ri-əl/ (*anat*) *adj* covering. [L *tectōrius*, from *tegere*, *tectum* to cover]
❏ **tectorial membrane** *n* the membrane covering the organ of Corti in the inner ear.

tectrix /tek'triks/ *n* (*pl* **tec'trices** /-sēz or -trī'sēz/) a feather covering the quill bases on a bird's wings and tail (also called **covert**). [L *tectrix*, *-īcis*, fem of *tector*, *-ōris* a coverer, from *tegere* to cover]
■ **tectricial** /-trish'l/ *adj*.

tectum /tek'təm/ (*anat*) *n* the roof of the midbrain. [L *tectum* roof, canopy]

Ted /ted/ (*inf*; also without *cap*) *n* a Teddy boy or girl.

ted /ted/ *vt* (**tedd'ing**; **tedd'ed**) to spread (new-mown grass) for drying. [Prob from a lost OE *teddan*; cf Icel *tethja* to manure]
■ **tedd'er** *n* a person who teds; an implement for tedding.

teddy[1] /ted'i/ *n* (in full **teddy bear**) a furry, stuffed toy bear. [Named after US President Theodore (*Teddy*) Roosevelt (1858–1919), well-known as a bear hunter]

teddy[2] /ted'i/ *n* a one-piece undergarment for a woman, combining panties and chemise (also **tedd'ie**). [Perh a use of **teddy**[1]]

Teddy boy /ted'i boi/ *n* an unruly adolescent, *orig* in the 1950s, affecting a dandyish style of dress reminiscent of Edward VII's time (also *fem* **Teddy girl**). [*Edward*]

Te Deum /tē dē'əm or tā dā'ŭm/ *n* a famous Latin hymn of the Western Church, expressing praise and thanksgiving; a musical setting of it. [From its first words, *Tē Deum laudāmus* thee, God, we praise]

■ words derived from main entry word; ❏ compound words; ■ idioms and phrasal verbs

tedium or (*obs*) **taedium** /*tē'di-əm*/ *n* the quality of being tiresome or wearisome, *usu* because long-drawn-out or slow in progress; monotony; irksomeness; boredom. [L *taedium*, from *taedēre* to weary]
■ **tedios'ity** *n.* **te'dious** *adj* tiresomely long; long-winded; monotonous; boring. **te'diously** *adv.* **te'diousness** *n.* **te'disome** or **te'diousome** *adj* (*Scot*). **te'dy** *adj* (*Walter Scott*).

TED spread /*ted spred*/ (*finance*) *n* a measure of the difference between the value of three-month US Treasury bills and three-month Eurodollar futures contracts.

tee[1] /*tē*/ *n* the twentieth letter of the modern English alphabet (T or t); a T-shaped object or mark; (*inf*) a tee shirt.
❏ **tee shirt** or **T'-shirt** *n* a slip-on shirt, typically of knitted cotton, with short sleeves and no collar or buttons, shaped like a letter T when laid flat. **tee'-square** see under **T**.
■ **to a tee** exactly, to a perfection.

tee[2] /*tē*/ *n* a small plastic or wooden support for the ball, with a concave top, used when it is first played at each hole (*golf*); the strip of ground (also **teeing ground** or **area**) where this is done; a plastic support from which a dead ball may be kicked in rugby and American football; the mark aimed at in quoits or curling. ◆ *vt* and *vi* (**tee'ing**; **teed** or **tee'd**) (often with *up*) to place (the golf ball) on the tee. [False sing from orig form *teaz*, itself of uncertain origin]
❏ **tee box** *n* (*golf*) a box containing sand for filling divots made on the tee; the teeing ground. **tee marker** *n* (*golf*) a coloured marker on the ground indicating the forward limit of the teeing ground. **tee'-off** *n* (*golf*) the strip of ground where tees are placed and where play begins at each hole; the act of hitting the golf ball from the tee to begin play at a hole (also **teeing-off'**). **tee shot** *n* (*golf*) the first stroke at a hole.
■ **tee off** to start play with a shot from the tee (*golf*); generally, to start proceedings, make the opening move, etc (*inf*); to annoy (*inf*). **tee up** to prepare (oneself or something) (with *for*).

tee[3] /*tē*/ *n* the umbrella-shaped finial of a dagoba. [Burmese *h'ti* umbrella]

tee-hee or **te-hee** /*tē'hē'*/ *interj* expressing derision or merriment. ◆ *n* a laugh, titter. ◆ *vi* (**tee-hee'ing**; **tee-heed'**) to titter. [Written representation of a titter or snigger]

teel see **til**.

teem[1] /*tēm*/ *vi* to be full, abound (with *with*); to abound, be plentiful; to bear or be fruitful; to be pregnant (*obs*). ◆ *vt* (*obs*) to bring forth (young). [OE *tīeman*, from *tēam*; see **team**]
■ **teem'ful** *adj.* **teem'ing** *adj* swarming, overrun (with *with*); full of creatures, people, etc, crowded; plentiful, copious, present in vast numbers. **teem'less** *adj* (*rare*) barren.

teem[2] /*tēm*/ *vi* to pour, fall in torrents (with *down*); to flow copiously. ◆ *vt* to pour, empty. [ON *tœma* to empty; cf **toom**]
■ **teem'er** *n.*

teemed (*Spenser*) see under **team**.

teen[1] /*tēn*/ *n* any number or year of age, etc, from *thirteen* to *nineteen* (*usu* in *pl*); a teenager (*inf*). ◆ *adj* belonging to people in their teens, teenage. [OE sfx *-tīene*, from *tēn* ten]
■ **teen'age** *adj* in the teens; of or appropriate to someone in the teens. **teen'aged** *adj.*
❏ **teen'ager** *n* a person from thirteen to nineteen years old inclusive. **tee'ny-bopper** *n* (*inf*) a young teenager, *esp* a girl, who follows enthusiastically the latest trends in pop music, clothes, etc.

teen[2], **teene** or **tene** /*tēn*/ (*archaic*) *n* injury; affliction; grief; anger; pains. [OE *tēona*, injury, anger, grief]

teend see **tind**.

teene[1] /*tēn*/ (*Spenser*) *vt appar* to allot.

teene[2] see **teen**[2].

teeny /*tē'ni*/ (*inf*) *adj* tiny (also (often *facetious*) **teen'sy** /*tēn'zi*/, **teensy-weensy** /*-wēn'zi*/, **teen'tsy** /*tēn'tsi*/, **teen'ty** /*tēn'ti*/ and **teen'y-ween'y** /*-wē'ni*/).

teepee see **tepee**.

teer /*tēr*/ (*technical* or *dialect*) *vt* to plaster; to daub; to spread. [OFr *terer*, from *terre* earth]

tee shirt see under **tee**[1].

Teeswater /*tēz'wö-tər*/ *n* a breed of large hornless sheep with long-fibred fleece, developed in the Tees valley in the NE of England. [District of County Durham]

tee-tee[1] /*tē'tē'*/ (*inf*) *adj* teetotal. ◆ *n* teetotaller. [The abbrev **TT**]

tee-tee[2] same as **titi**[1].

teeter /*tē'tər*/ *vi* to sway as if about to fall, wobble; to move unsteadily; to vacillate, hesitate, waver; to see-saw (*N Am*). ◆ *vt* to cause to teeter. ◆ *n* a see-saw (*N Am*). [ME *titeren* to totter]
❏ **teet'er-board** *n* a see-saw; (also **teet'er-tott'er**) a board which throws one into the air when someone else jumps on the opposite end of it.

teeth /*tēth*/ plural of **tooth**.

teethe /*tēdh*/ *vi* to develop or cut (*esp* milk) teeth. ◆ *vt* to provide with teeth. [From **teeth**, pl of **tooth**]
■ **teething** /*tēdh'ing*/ *n* and *adj*.
❏ **teething ring** *n* a ring of plastic, bone, etc for a baby to chew on when teething. **teething troubles** *n pl* pain and irritation caused by the cutting of teeth; (also **teething problems**) mechanical difficulties encountered on first using a new machine, etc or in the early stages of any undertaking.

teetotal /*tē-tō't(ə)l*/ *adj* abstaining totally from alcoholic drink; out-and-out, complete (*dialect*). ◆ *n* a total abstainer; a principle, movement or pledge of total abstinence (*rare*). [*Teetotally* prob established first as a facetious or emphatic reduplicative form of *totally*; *teetotal* subsequently used in a speech by Richard Turner of Preston in 1833 advocating abstinence]
■ **teetō'talism** *n.* **teetō'taller** *n* a total abstainer from alcoholic drink. **teetō'tally** *adv*.

teetotum /*tē-tō'təm*/ (*hist*) *n* (*pl* **teeto'tums**) a small spinning top inscribed with letters, or a gambling game played with it, decided by the letter that came uppermost, T standing for (L) *tōtum*, all, ie take all the stakes; any small top twirled by the fingers. [Orig T *totum*, ie a *totum* (= this kind of top) with a T on one face]

tef or **teff** /*tef*/ *n* an Ethiopian cereal grass, *Eragrostis tef*. [Amharic *tēf*]

tefillin or **tephillin** /*tə-fē'lin*/ (*Judaism*) *n pl* (*sing* **tefill'ah** or **tephill'ah** /*-fē'lə*/) phylacteries, or the texts quoted on them. [Heb, from *tephillāh* prayer]

TEFL /*tef'l*/ *abbrev* : Teaching English as a Foreign Language.

Teflon® /*tef'lon*/ *n* a trademark for polytetrafluoroethylene, as used eg to coat the inside of cooking pans to render them non-stick. ◆ *adj* (*facetious, orig US*; *specif* of politicians, statesmen, etc) to whom the blame for incompetence, dubious dealings, etc somehow fails to adhere, attaching itself instead to others.

teg or **tegg** /*teg*/ *n* a sheep (or *obs* a doe) in its second year; the fleece of a sheep in its second year. [Perh Scand]

tegmen /*teg'mən*/ *n* (*pl* **teg'mina**) a covering; the inner coat of a seed covering (*bot*); the leathery forewing in *Orthoptera*, the cockroaches and related insects. [L *tegere* to cover]
■ **tegmental** /*-men'təl*/ *adj.* **tegment'um** *n* (*pl* **tegment'a**) a scale protecting a bud.

teguexin /*te-gwek'sin*/ *n* a large black-and-yellow S American lizard, *Tupinambis teguexin* (also called **tegu** /*teg'ū*/). [Aztec *tecoixin*]

tegula /*teg'ū-lə*/ *n* (*pl* **teg'ūlae** /*-lē*/) a scale at the base of the forewing in some insects; a flat roofing-tile. [L *tegula* a tile, from *tegere* to cover]
■ **teg'ūlar** *adj* of, like or overlapping like tiles or slates. **teg'ūlarly** *adv*. **teg'ūlāted** *adj* composed of plates overlapping like tiles.

tegument /*teg'ū-mənt*/ *n* the skin or other natural covering of an animal or plant body, an integument. [L *tegumentum*, a covering, from *tegere* to cover]
■ **tegūment'al** or **tegūment'ary** *adj*.

te-hee see **tee-hee**.

tehr /*tār*/ same as **tahr**.

tehsil or **tahsil** /*tə-sēl'* or *tahh-sēl'*/ *n* in India, a division of a district for revenue and certain other purposes. [Hindi *tahsīl*, from Ar]
■ **tehsildar'** or **tahsildar'** *n* an officer of a tehsil.

Teian or **Tean** /*tē'ən*/ *adj* of Teos in ancient Ionia, or of the poet Anacreon, a native of Teos. [Gr *Tēïos* Teian, from *Teōs* Teos]

teichopsia /*tī-kop'si-ə*/ *n* temporary blurring of vision, or partial blindness, with the appearance of a multi-coloured zigzag of light before the eye, accompanying migraine. [Gr *teichos* wall, and *opsis* sight]

te igitur /*tē ij'i-tər* or *tā ig'i-tŭr*/ *n* the first paragraph of the canon of the mass; a service-book on which oaths were taken. [L *tē igitur*, thee therefore (the first words)]

teil /*tēl*/ *n* the linden or lime tree. [OFr *teil*, from L *tilia*]
❏ **teil tree** *n* the lime; the terebinth (*Bible*).

tein /*tā'in*/ *n* (*pl* **te'in** or **te'ins**) a monetary unit in Kazakhstan, $\frac{1}{100}$ of a tenge.

teind /*tēnd*/ *n* in Scotland, a tithe. ◆ *vt* to assess or take a tithe on. [A form of **tenth**, **tithe**]

teinoscope /*tī'nə-skōp*/ (*obs*) *n* a combination of prisms which magnify or diminish the linear dimensions of objects while at the same time correcting chromatic aberration. [Gr *teinein* to stretch, and **-scope**]

teknonymy /*tek-non'i-mi*/ *n* the naming of the parent from the child. [Gr *teknon* a child, and *onyma*, *onoma* a name]
■ **teknon'ymous** *adj*.

tektite /*tek'tīt*/ *n* a type of small glassy stone, of uncertain and perhaps extraterrestrial origin, found in certain areas of the earth (*incl* Australia, where it is known as **australite**). [Gr *tēktos* molten]

tel see **tell²**.

tel. *abbrev*: telephone number.

tel- see **tele-**.

tela /tē'lə or tā'lä/ n (pl **tē'lae** /-lē or tā'lī/) a web, weblike structure or tissue. [L *tēla*]
■ **tē'lary** *adj* web-spinning.

telaesthesia or (US) **telesthesia** /tel-ēs-thē'z(h)i-ə, -zhyə/ n an abnormal impression, eg of perception of objects or occurrences beyond the normal range of the senses. [**tele-** (1), and Gr *aisthēsiā* sensation]
■ **telaesthetic** or (US) **telesthetic** /-thet'ik/ adj.

telamon /tel'ə-mən/ (archit) n (pl **telamones** /-mō'nēz/) a man's figure used as a supporting pillar. [Gr mythological hero, *Telamōn*, from *tlēnai* to endure, bear]

telangiectasis /tel-an-ji-ek'tə-sis/ or **telangiectasia** /-tā'z(h)i-ə, -tā'zhyə/ (pathol) n dilatation of the small arteries or capillaries. [Gr *telos* end, *angeion* a vessel, and *ektasis* extension]
■ **telangiectatic** /-ek-tat'ik/ adj.

telary see under **tela**.

Telautograph® /tel-ö'tə-gräf/ n a telegraph for reproducing the movement of a pen or pencil and so transmitting writings or drawings; one for transmission of images by electric scanning. [**tele-** (1), **auto-** and **-graph**]
■ **telautographic** /-graf'ik/ adj. **telautography** /-tog'rə-fi/ n.

telco /tel'kō/ (finance) n (pl **tel'cos**) a telecommunications company.

teld /teld/ (Spenser) pat and pap of **tell**.

tele /tel'i/ n an informal form of **television**.

tele- /tel-i-/ (also **tel-** /tel-/) combining form denoting: (1) far, distant, over a distance; (2) television; (3) telephone. [Gr *tēle* far]

tele-ad /tel'i-ad/ n a classified advertisement submitted to a newspaper, etc by telephone. [**tele-** (3) and **advertisement**]

telearchics see **telecontrol**. [**tele-** (1), and Gr *archein* to rule]

telebanking /tel'i-bang-king/ n an electronic banking service accessed by telephone. [**tele-** (1)]

telebridge /tel'i-brij/ n a television broadcast of a discussion between studio audiences in different countries linked by satellite. [**tele-** (1)]

telecamera /tel'i-kam(-ə)-rə/ n a television camera (see under **camera**).

telecast /tel'i-käst/ n a television broadcast. ◆ vt and vi (**tel'ecasting**; **tel'ecast** or **tel'ecasted**) to transmit by television.
■ **tel'ecaster** n.

telecentre /tel'i-sen-tə/ n a telecottage. [**tele-** (1)]

telechir /tel'i-kēr/ n a type of robot controlled by telecommand by an operator who has feedback from electronic sensors, eg television cameras. [**tele-** (1), and Gr *cheir* hand]
■ **telechir'ic** adj.

telecine /tel-i-sin'i/ n transmission of filmed material by television; the equipment required for this. [**tele-** (2) and **cine-**]

telecom /tel'i-kom/ or **telecoms** /-komz/ n sing short for **telecommunication** or **telecommunications**.

telecommand /tel'i-kə-mänd/ n the operation of machinery by remote electronic control. [**tele-** (1)]

telecommunication /tel-i-kə-mū-ni-kā'shən/ n communication of information, in verbal, written, coded or pictorial form, by telephone, radio, television, fax, radar, etc. [**tele-** (1)]
■ **telecommunica'tions** n sing the science of technology of such communication.

telecommute /tel-i-kə-mūt'/ vi to work at home, communicating with the office by telephone, computer link, etc. [**tele-** (3)]
■ **telecommū'ter** n. **telecommū'ting** n.

teleconference /tel', tel-i-kon'f(ə-)rəns/ n a meeting between people physically separated but linked by video, audio and/or computer facilities. [**tele-** (1)]
■ **telecon'ferencing** n the practice of holding such conferences, or the technology involved.

telecontrol /tel-i-kon-trōl' or -kən-/ n control of mechanical devices remotely, either by radio (as of ships and aircraft), by sound waves, or by beams of light (also **telearchics** /-ark'/). [**tele-** (1)]

teleconverter /tel-i-kən-vûr'tər/ (image technol) n a supplementary lens system for converting a camera lens to a greater focal length. [**tele-** (1)]

telecottage /tel'i-kot-ij/ n a building or room in a rural area with electronic equipment, services, etc for teleworking, often shared by a number of local residents. [**tele-** (1)]
■ **tel'ecottaging** n.

teledildonics /tel-i-dil-don'iks/ n sing sexual activity available through computer networks or by means of virtual reality; cybersex. [**tele-** (1), **dildo** and **-ics**]

teledu /tel'ə-doo/ n a small short-tailed carnivorous Indonesian mammal (*Mydaus javanensis*), which can give off a strong, offensive odour, the stinking badger of Java or stinkard. [Javanese]

telefax /tel'i-faks/ n (also **telefacsim'ile**) fax, a facsimile of a document. ◆ vt to send (a copy of a document) by fax machine. [**tele-** (3)]

téléférique /tā-lā-fā-rēk'/ (Fr) n a light aerial cable-car, esp one electrically propelled.

telefilm /tel'i-film/ n a motion picture made specially for subsequent television transmission. [**tele-** (2)]

telega /te-leg'ə or tel-yeg'ə/ n a four-wheeled Russian wagon, without springs. [Russ]

telegenic /tel-i-jen'ik/ adj having a presence, appearance and manner suitable for television. [**tele-** (2); modelled on **photogenic**]

telegnosis /tel-i-nō'sis or -ig-nō'sis/ n the knowledge of events taking place far away, not obtained in any normal way. [**tele-** (1), and **-gnosis**]
■ **telegnos'tic** adj.

telegony /ti-leg'ə-ni/ n the (imaginary) transmitted influence of a previous mate on the offspring of a female by a later mate. [**tele-** (1), and Gr *gonos* begetting]
■ **telegon'ic** or **teleg'onous** adj.

telegram /tel'i-gram/ n a message sent by telegraph and usu presented in printed form (in UK since 1981 only available for international messages). [**tele-** (1), and **-gram**]
■ **telegrammat'ic** or **telegramm'ic** adj of or like a telegram.

telegraph /tel'i-gräf/ n a combination of apparatus for transmitting information to a distance, now almost exclusively by electrical impulses; a telegraph board; used as the name of a newspaper; a message sent by telegraph (obs). ◆ vt to convey or announce by telegraph; to send a message by telegraph to (a person or place); to signal; to give a premature indication of something to come. ◆ vi to signal; to send a telegram. [**tele-** (1) and **-graph**]
■ **telegrapher** /ti-leg'rə-fər/ n a telegraphist. **telegraphese** /ti-leg-rə-fēz'/ n (facetious) the jargon or contracted style of language used in telegrams. **telegraphic** /-graf'ik/ adj. **telegraph'ically** adv. **teleg'raphist** n a person who works a telegraph. **teleg'raphy** n the science or art of constructing or using telegraphs.
□ **telegraph board** n a scoreboard or information board that can be read at a distance, used at matches, athletics meetings, races, etc. **telegraph cable** n a cable containing wires for transmitting telegraphic messages. **telegraphic address** n a shortened address registered for use in telegraphing. **telegraph plant** n an Indian papilionaceous plant (*Desmodium gyrans*) whose leaves jerk spontaneously in different directions, like semaphore arms. **telegraph pole** n a pole supporting telegraph wires. **telegraph wire** n a wire for carrying telegraphic messages.

Telegu see **Telugu**.

telejournalist /tel-i-jûr'nə-list/ n a journalist working in television. [**tele-** (2)]
■ **telejourn'alism** n.

telekinesis /tel-i-ki-nē'sis, -kī-/ n the production of motion at a distance by willpower or thought alone. [**tele-** (1), and **kinesis**]
■ **telekinetic** /-net'ik/ adj.

telemark /tel'i-märk/ n (in skiing) a sudden turn on the outer ski, first practised at *Telemark* in Norway; (in ballroom dancing) a step incorporating a heel pivot. ◆ vi to execute a telemark.

telemarketing see **teleselling**.

telematics /tel-i-mat'iks/ n sing the transmission of computerized information over long distances. [**tele-** (1), and *informatics*]
■ **telemat'ic** adj.

telemedicine /tel'i-med-sin/ n the use of telecommunications technology to transmit medical advice, diagnoses, etc. [**tele-** (1)]

Telemessage® /tel'i-mes-ij/ n a message sent by telex or telephone, superseding the telegram. [**tele-** (1)]

telemeter /ti-lem'i-tər/ n an instrument for measuring distances (surveying); a photographer's rangefinder; an instrument for measuring an electrical or other quantity and signalling the measurement to a distant point (also called **radiotelem'eter**). ◆ vt to record and signal by telemeter. [**tele-** (1), and **-meter**]
■ **telemetric** /tel-i-met'rik/ adj. **telem'etry** n.

telencephalon /tel-en-sef'ə-lon/ (zool) n part of the forebrain in vertebrates, comprising the cerebral hemispheres, the olfactory lobes and the olfactory bulbs. [Gr *telos* end, and **encephalon**]
■ **telencephal'ic** adj.

■ words derived from main entry word; □ compound words; ■ idioms and phrasal verbs

teleo-¹ /tel-i-ō-, -ə- or -o-/ *combining form* denoting perfect, complete. [Gr *teleios* perfect, complete]

teleo-² /tel-i-ō-, -ə-, -o- or tē-/ *combining form* denoting end, purpose. [Gr *telos, teleos* end]

teleology /tel-i-ol'ə-ji or tē-li-/ *n* the doctrine of the final causes of things; interpretation of phenomena in terms of their purpose rather than possible causes. [**teleo-²**, and **-logy**]
■ **teleologic** /-ə-loj'ik/ or **teleolog'ical** *adj*. **teleolog'ically** *adv*. **teleol'ogism** *n*. **teleol'ogist** *n*.

teleonomy /tel-i-on'ə-mi or tē-li-/ *n* the characteristic of being governed by an overall purpose. [**teleo-²**, and **-nomy**]
■ **teleonom'ic** *adj*.

Teleosaurus /tel-i-ə-sö'rəs/ *n* a Jurassic genus of fossil crocodiles. [**teleo-¹**, and Gr *sauros* a lizard]
■ **tel'eosaur** *n* an animal of this genus. **teleosau'rian** *adj* and *n*.

Teleostei /tel-i-os'ti-ī/ *n pl* the bony fishes with well-developed bones. [**teleo-¹**, and Gr *osteon* bone]
■ **tel'eost** or **teleos'tean** *n* and *adj*.

Teleostomi /tel-i-os'tə-mī/ *n pl* fishes with membrane bones in the skull, jaws, etc, all ordinary fishes except the sharks and rays. [**teleo-¹**, and Gr *stoma* mouth]
■ **tel'eostome** /-stōm/ *n*. **teleos'tomous** *adj*.

telepathy /ti-lep'ə-thi/ *n* communication between mind and mind otherwise than through the known channels of the senses. [**tele-** (1), and Gr *pathos* feeling]
■ **telepath** /tel'i-path/ *n* a telepathic subject. ◆ *vt* and *vi* to communicate by telepathy. **telepath'ic** *adj*. **telepath'ically** *adv*. **telep'athist** *n* a person who believes in or practises telepathy. **telep'athize** or **-ise** *vt* to affect or act upon through telepathy. ◆ *vi* to communicate or become aware through telepathy.

telepheme /tel'i-fēm/ *n* a telephone message. [**tele-** (3), and Gr *phēmē* a saying]

téléphérique same as **téléférique**.

telephone /tel'i-fōn/ *n* an instrument for reproducing sound at a distance, *esp* by means of electricity; *specif* an instrument with a microphone and a receiver mounted on a handset, for transmitting speech; the system of communication which uses these instruments. ◆ *vt* to contact and speak to by telephone; to convey (a message, etc) by telephone. ◆ *vi* to make a telephone call. [**tele-** (1), and Gr *phōnē* a sound]
■ **tel'ephoner** *n*. **telephonic** /-fon'ik/ *adj*. **telephon'ically** *adv*. **telephonist** /ti-lef'ə-nist/ *n* a person who operates a switchboard or works as an operator in a telephone exchange. **teleph'ony** *n* telephonic communication.
❑ **telephone answering machine** *n* an answerphone. **telephone banking** *n* telebanking. **telephone book** or **directory** *n* a book listing the names, addresses and numbers of telephone subscribers. **telephone box**, **booth** or **kiosk** *n* a *usu* enclosed place with a telephone for public use. **telephone exchange** *n* a central office where telephone lines are connected. **telephone number** *n* a number that identifies a particular telephone and is dialled to make connections with it; (often in *pl*) a very large number or amount (*esp* of money; *inf*). **telephone-tapping** see **tap²**.

telephoto /tel-i-fō'tō/ *adj* a shortening of **telephotographic**. ◆ *n* (*pl* **telephō'tos**) a telephoto lens; a photograph taken using such a lens. ❑ **telephoto lens** *n* a lens of long focal length for obtaining large images of distant objects.

telephotography /tel-i-fə-tog'rə-fi/ *n* photography of distant objects by means of suitable lenses; phototelegraphy (*non-standard*). [**tele-** (1)]
■ **telepho'tograph** *n*. **telephotograph'ic** *adj*.

telepic /tel'i-pik/ *n* a film made to be shown on television. [**tele-** (2)]

teleplay /tel'i-plā/ *n* a play written to be performed on television. [**tele-** (2)]

telepoint /tel'i-point/ *n* a device located in eg a public place that activates any portable cordless telephones being carried within a certain radius of it, enabling those carrying them to make calls. [**tele-** (3)]

teleport /tel'i-pört/ (*psychol*) *vt* to move by telekinesis. [**tele-** (1)]
■ **teleportā'tion** *n*.

telepresence /tel'i-prez-əns/ *n* the use of virtual reality to create the illusion of being at a different or imaginary location. [**tele-** (1)]

teleprinter /tel'i-prin-tər/ *n* a telegraph transmitter with typewriter keyboard. [**tele-** (1)]

teleprocessing /tel-i-prō'se-sing/ *n* the use of a computer to process data transmitted from distant points. [**tele-** (1)]

Teleprompter® /tel'i-promp-tər/ *n* a device located out of view of the audience by which a television speaker or actor sees a projection of what he or she is to say. [**tele-** (2)]

teleradium unit see **radium bomb** under **radium**.

telerecording /tel-i-ri-kör'ding/ *n* recording for broadcasting by television; a television transmission from a recording. [**tele-** (2)]
■ **telerecord'** *vt*.

telergy /tel'ər-ji/ *n* a physical force assumed to be at work in telepathy. [**tele-** (1), and Gr *ergon* work]
■ **teler'gic** /-ûr'jik/ *adj* working at a distance, as in telepathy. **teler'gically** *adv*.

telesale see under **teleselling**.

telescience /tel'i-sī-əns/ (*astronautics*) *n* the performing of scientific experiments at a distance, controlled remotely by the experimenter. [**tele-** (1)]

telescope /tel'i-skōp/ *n* an optical instrument for viewing objects at a distance; a radio telescope (qv). ◆ *vt* to drive or slide one into another like the movable joints of a telescope; to compress, shorten, make smaller, etc; to compact, crush. ◆ *vi* to collapse part within part, like a telescope; to be compressed or compacted. [**tele-** (1), and **-scope**]
■ **telescopic** /-skop'ik/ or **telescop'ical** *adj* of, performed by, or like a telescope; seen only by a telescope; sliding, or arranged, like the joints of a telescope; capable of retraction and protrusion. **telescop'ically** *adv*. **telescop'iform** *adj*. **telescopist** /ti-les'kə-pist/ *n* a person who uses a telescope. **Telescōp'ium** *n* (*astron*) the Telescope, a small southern constellation between the constellations of *Ara* and *Corona Austrinus*. **teles'copy** *n* the art of constructing or of using the telescope.
❑ **telescopic shaft** *n* (*engineering*) an assembly of one or more tubes and a solid rod sliding one within the other to provide a shaft of variable length. **telescopic sight** *n* a telescope on a gun used as a sight.

telescreen /tel'i-skrēn/ *n* a television screen. [**tele-** (2)]

teleselling /tel'i-sel-ing/ *n* the selling of goods or services by using the telephone to seek customers (also called **telemark'eting** or **tel'esales**). [**tele-** (3)]
■ **tel'esale** *n* a sale made on the telephone.

teleseme /tel'i-sēm/ *n* a signalling apparatus with an indicator. [**tele-** (1), and Gr *sēma* a sign]

teleservices /tel'i-sûr-vi-siz or -səz/ *n pl* information, etc services available to users of teletext and viewdata systems. [**tele-** (2)]

teleshopping /tel'i-shop-ing/ *n* an electronic shopping service accessed by a telephone or computer link. [**tele-** (1)]

telesis /tel'i-sis/ *n* the activity of making use of natural and social processes for the achievement of a particular purpose. [Gr, fulfilment, from *teleein* to accomplish, fulfil, from *telos* end, purpose]

telesm /tel'e-zm/ *n* a talisman. [Gr *telesma*; see **talisman**]
■ **telesmat'ic** or **telesmat'ical** *adj*. **telesmat'ically** *adv*.

telesoftware /tel-i-soft'wär/ (*comput*) *n* software that is transmitted to users by means of a teletext or viewdata system. [**tele-** (2)]

telespectroscope /tel-i-spek'trə-skōp/ *n* a combination of a telescope and a spectroscope, used for observing and analysing the radiation given off by celestial objects. [**tele-** (1), and **spectroscope**]

telestereoscope /tel-i-ster'i-ə-skōp/ *n* a binocular optical instrument used for viewing distant objects stereoscopically. [**tele-** (1), and **stereoscope**]

telesthesia see **telaesthesia**.

telestic /ti-les'tik/ *adj* relating to religious rituals of initiation. [Gr *telestikos*, from Gr *teleein* to fulfil, consummate, initiate, perform, from *telos* end, rite, etc]

telestrator /tel'i-strā-tər/ *n* a device that enables a television presenter to superimpose diagrams, writing, etc on the screen during a broadcast. [**tele-** and illus*trator*]

teletex /tel'i-teks/ *n* a means of transmitting written data, similar in principle to telex, but using more modern, high-speed electronic apparatus. [**tele-** (1), and **text**]

teletext /tel'i-tekst/ *n* a computer-based information-retrieval system that allows current, regularly updated, news and information in the form of text and graphics to be transmitted by television companies in the form of coded pulses that can be decoded by a special adapter for viewing on a page-by-page basis on a conventional television. [**tele-** (2)]

telethon /tel'ə-thon/ (*orig US*) *n* a very long television programme, *esp* one seeking to raise money for a charity, or support for eg a political candidate. [*tele*vision mara*thon*]

teletron /tel'i-tron/ *n* a cathode-ray tube for synthesis of television images. [**tele-** (2), and **-tron**]

Teletype® /tel'i-tīp/ n a type of teleprinter; a message sent by Teletype. ◆ vt to send (a message) by Teletype. ◆ vi to operate a Teletype. [**tele-** (1), and **type**]
❑ **Teletype'setter**® n an obsolete telegraphic machine that delivered its message as a perforated roll used to actuate a typesetting machine. **teletype'writer** n (US) a teleprinter.

teleutospore /te-, ti-lū'tō-spōr or -spör/ n a thick-walled winter spore of the rust fungi, producing a promycelium on germination. [Gr teleutē completion, and sporā seed]

televangelist /tel-i-van'ji-list/ n (esp in US) an evangelical, esp fundamentalist, preacher with a regular slot on television. [**tele-** (2), and **evangelist**]
■ **televangel'ical** adj. **televan'gelism** n.

televérité /tel-i-ver'i-tā/ n the televising of scenes from actual life in order to convey a heightened realism (see also **cinéma vérité** under **cinema**). [**tele-** (2); modelled on **cinéma vérité**]

television /tel-i-vizh'ən or tel'i-vi-zhən/ n the transmission by radio waves, and reproduction on a screen, of visual images, usu accompanied by sound; (also **television set**) an apparatus incorporating a screen, for receiving these; television broadcasting in general; those occupations concerned with television broadcasting (abbrev **TV**). [**tele-** (1)]
■ **tel'eview** vt and vi to view by television. **tel'eviewer** n a television watcher. **tel'eviewing** n and adj. **tel'evise** /tel'i-vīz/ vt and vi to transmit by television. **tel'eviser** n. **televi'sional** or **televi'sionary** adj of or relating to television. **televi'sor** n a receiver for television. **televi'sual** adj relating to television; suitable for televising, telegenic. **televis'ually** adv.
❑ **television tube** n a cathode-ray tube for the reproduction of television images.

teleworker /tel'i-wûr-kər/ n a telecommuter. [**tele-** (3)]
■ **tel'ework** vi. **tel'eworking** n.

telewriter /tel-i-rī'tər/ n a telegraph instrument that reproduces handwriting. [**tele-** (1)]

telex /tel'eks/ n an international telegraphic service whereby subscribers hire the use of teleprinters; a teleprinter used in this service; a message transferred by this service. ◆ vt and vi to send (someone) (a message) by telex. [teleprinter and exchange]

telfer, etc see **telpher**.

telic see under **telos**.

teliospore /tē'li-ə-spōr/ same as **teleutospore**. [**telium**, and **spore**]

telium /tē'li-əm/ n (pl **tē'lia**) the cluster of spore cases of the rust fungi, producing teleutospores. [New L, from Gr teleios finished]
■ **tē'lial** adj.

tell[1] /tel/ vt (pat and pap **tōld**, (Scot) **teld**, **tell'd** or **telt**) to utter, to express in words; to narrate; to disclose or make known; to inform; to discern or distinguish (with from); to explain; to order, direct, instruct; to assure; to count (votes); to count out (archaic); to bid (goodbye; US). ◆ vi to give an account (with of); to have an effect (with on); to have weight; to make an effective story; to give an indication, be evidence (with of); to give away secrets; to play the informer; to know definitely; to have an influence or be evidence (with against). ◆ n (esp in card games) an unconscious tic or other physical betrayal of one's thoughts or intentions. [OE tellan ; ON telja, Ger zählen to number]
■ **tell'able** adj capable of being told; fit to tell. **tell'er** n a person who tells or narrates; a person who counts votes; a clerk whose duty it is to receive and pay money, esp in a bank; an automatic cash dispenser (chiefly N Am); one of the strokes made by a church bell ringing a funeral knell (also, esp dialect, **tailor**). **tell'ership** n. **tell'ing** adj effective; significant, meaningful. ◆ n numbering; narration; instruction, orders. **tell'ingly** adv.
❑ **telling-off'** n a reprimand. **tell'tale** n a person who reports the private concerns or misdeeds of others; a tattler (bird); anything revealing or betraying; any of several indicators or monitors; a recording clock; a strip of material outside the playing area at the foot of the front wall of a squash court, which makes a distinctive sound when hit; one of the lengths of wool sewn or tied on a yacht's sail to indicate airflow (naut). ◆ adj blabbing; revealing, betraying; indicating.
■ **as far as one can tell** judging from information available so far. **I tell you** or **I'm telling you** I assure you, I insist. **take a telling** to do as one is asked without having to be told again. **tell apart** to distinguish between. **tell a tale** to be revealing. **tell me about it!** (inf) I know exactly what you mean. **tell me another** (inf) used to express disbelief. **tell off** to reprimand (inf); to count off and detach on some special duty. **tell on** (inf) to betray, inform on or give away secrets about. **tell the time** to read the time on a clock or watch. **there's no telling** one cannot possibly know or predict. **you're telling me** (interj; inf) I know that only too well.

tell[2] or **tel** /tel/ n in Arab lands, a hill or ancient mound formed from the accumulated debris from earlier mud or wattle habitations. [Ar tall]

tellar, **teller** same as **tiller**[2].

tellen see **tellin**.

teller see **tellar** and under **tell**[1].

Tellima /tel'i-mə/ n a genus of hardy herbaceous perennials of the saxifrage family. [New L]

tellin or **tellen** /tel'in/ n any bivalve mollusc of the Tellina genus, with thin, delicate shells tinted yellow or pink, living in estuaries. [New L Tellina, the name of the genus, from tellinē a shellfish]
■ **tell'inoid** adj.

Tellus /tel'əs/ n the Roman earth goddess; (also without cap) the earth. [L Tellūs, -ūris]
■ **tell'ūral** adj relating to the earth. **tell'ūrate** n a salt of telluric acid. **tell'ūretted** adj combined with tellurium. **tellū'rian** adj terrestrial. ◆ n an inhabitant of the earth; a tellurion. **tellū'ric** adj of or from the earth; of tellurium in higher valency (chem). **tell'ūride** n a compound of tellurium with another element or radical. **tellū'rion** or **tellū'rian** n an apparatus representing the earth and sun, demonstrating the occurrence of day, night, the seasons, etc. **tell'ūrite** n native oxide of tellurium (mineralogy); a salt of tellurous acid (chem). **tellū'rium** n a rare silvery metalloid element (symbol **Te**; atomic no 52) appar so named by Martin Klaproth (in 1798) as the counterpart of his previous discovery of uranium. **tell'ūrize** or **-ise** vt to combine with tellurium. **tellūrom'eter** n an electronic instrument used to measure survey lines by measurement of the time required for a radar signal to echo back. **tell'ūrous** adj of tellurium in lower valency.
❑ **telluric acid** n a white crystalline acid (H_2TeO_4) produced when tellurium is oxidized by hydrogen peroxide. **tellurous acid** n a weak, unstable acid (H_2TeO_3) containing tetravalent tellurium.

telly /tel'i/ (inf) n television.

telnet /tel'net/ n (also with cap) a system of remote access to computers by means of telecommunications. [**tele-** (1) and **network**]

telocentric /tel-ə-sen'trik/ (genetics) adj (of a chromosome) having the centromere at one end of the chromosome. [Gr telos end, and kentron centre]

telomere /tel'ə-mēr/ (genetics) n the structure which terminates the arm of a chromosome, protecting the chromosome against gene loss and decay. [Gr telos end, and meros part]
■ **telom'erase** n an enzyme, found in some cancer cells, that negates the actions of telomeres and enables rapid cell division.

telophase /tel'ō-fāz/ n in mitosis, the stage of reconstruction of nuclei after separation of daughter chromosomes. [Gr telos completion, and phasis phase]
■ **telopha'sic** adj.

telos /tel'os/ n (pl **tel'oi**) aim, purpose, ultimate end. [Gr telos end, purpose]
■ **tel'ic** adj expressing purpose; purposive.

telpher /tel'fər/ n a system of automatic electric transport, esp using cars or containers suspended from overhead cables; a car or carrier in such a system (also **tel'fer**). ◆ adj relating to a system of telpherage. ◆ vt to transport by means of a telpher system. [Irreg coined by 19c British inventor Fleeming Jenkin, from Gr tēle far, and phoros bearing, from pherein to bear]
■ **tel'pherage**, also **tel'ferage** n any system of automatic electric transport, a telpher; an electric ropeway or cableway system; overhead traction in general. **tel'pheric** or **tel'feric** adj.
❑ **tel'pherline** n. **tel'pherman** n. **tel'pherway** n.

telson /tel'sən/ (zool) n the terminal or hindmost segment of a crustacean or arachnid. [Gr telson a headland in ploughing; cf telos end]

Telstar /tel'stär/ n a satellite launched on 10 July 1962, used to relay television pictures and telephone conversations across the Atlantic.

telt /telt/ (Scot) pat and pap of **tell**[1].

Telugu /tel'ŭ-goo or tel'ə-goo/, also **Telegu** /tel'ə-goo/ n (pl **Tel'ugus**, **Tel'ugu**, etc) a Dravidian language of SE India; one of the people speaking it. ◆ adj of or relating to (the) Telugu.

TEM (phys) abbrev : transmission electron microscope.

Temazepam /tə-mā'zi-pam or -maz'i-/ (also without cap) n a drug used to treat insomnia, also used as a sedative before operations.

temblor /tem'blör/ (esp US) n (pl **tem'blors** or **temblores** /-blör'āz/) an earthquake or earth tremor. [Am Sp, from Sp tremblar to tremble, shake]

teme an obsolete spelling of **team**.

temenos /tem'ə-nos/ n (pl **tem'ene**) a place dedicated to a god, a sacred precinct. [Gr, shrine, from temnein to cut off]

■ words derived from main entry word; ❑ compound words; ■ idioms and phrasal verbs

temerity /tə-, ti-mer'i-ti/ n rashness; unreasonable contempt for danger. [L *temeritās, -ātis*, and *temerārius*, from *temere* by chance, rashly]
■ **temerarious** /tem-ə-rā'ri-əs/ adj (*rare* or *literary*) rash, reckless. **temerā'riously** adv. **tem'erous** adj rash. **tem'erously** adv.

Temne /tem'ni/ or /tim'ni/ n (pl **Tem'nes** or **Tem'ne**) a member of a people of N Sierra Leone; the language of this people. ♦ adj of or relating to the Temne or their language.

temozolomide /tem-ō-zol'ə-mīd/ n a drug that interferes with DNA synthesis, used in the treatment of brain tumours.

temp /temp/ (*inf*) n a temporarily-employed secretarial or other office worker. ♦ vi to work as a temp. [**temporary**]

temp. abbrev : temperature; temporal; temporary; *tempore* (*L*), in the time of.

Tempe /tem'pē/ n the valley of the Peneus in Thessaly, praised by the ancient poets for its unsurpassed beauty; hence, any place of choice beauty. [Gr *Tempē* (*Tempea*)]
■ **Tempē'an** adj.

tempeh /tem'pā/ n a high-protein food prepared by incubating soya beans with a fungus to bring about fermentation, made *esp* in Japan and Indonesia. [Indonesian *tempe*]

temper /tem'pər/ n temperament, disposition; a habitual or transitory frame of mind; mood; composure; self-control; uncontrolled anger; a fit of ill-humour or rage; the hardness, elasticity, etc of a metal; proper mixture or balance of different or contrasting qualities; constitution of the body; lime or other substance used to neutralize the acidity of cane juice. ♦ vt to modify by blending or adding a lesser ingredient; to moderate, soften; to harden (steel) by heating to red heat and quenching, or, after this, to heat moderately and cool slowly, or to perform both these actions; to adjust, attune; to tune; to tune the notes on (a piano or other keyboard instruments) so that the intervals between them are correct, or to adjust the pitch of the notes of (a scale) (*music*); to mix in proper proportions; to bring to a favourable state of mind. ♦ vi to become tempered; to tamper, meddle (*Shakesp*); to soften (*Shakesp*). [L *temperāre* to temper, restrain, moderate, mix, partly through OE *temprian* to moderate]
■ **temperabil'ity** n. **tem'perable** adj capable of being tempered. **tem'pered** adj having a certain specified disposition or temper; (of eg steel) brought to a certain temper; tuned or adjusted to some mean, or to equal, temperament (*music*). ♦ adj combining form possessing, or showing, a specified disposition of temper, as in *ill-tempered, bad-tempered, sweet-tempered*, etc. **tem'perer** n. **tem'pering** n and adj. ■ **out of temper** irritable, peevish.

tempera /tem'pə-rə/ (*art*) n an emulsion, *esp* made with egg yolk, used as a medium for powdered pigments; the paint so produced; the technique of painting with this paint; distemper. [Ital, from L *temperāre* to mix proportionately]

temperalitie /tem-pə-ral'i-ti/ (*Shakesp, 2 Henry IV* II.4.23) n Mistress Quickly's elaboration of temper, frame of mind.

temperament /tem'prə-mənt/ n disposition, personality, *esp* with regard to emotional make-up; high excitability, nervous instability, and sensitiveness; an adjustment made to the intervals between notes on a keyboard to allow modulation to any key (*music*); any of the recognized types of physical and mental make-up, believed to be controlled by the humours, ie choleric or bilious, sanguine, melancholy, phlegmatic (*obs physiol*); combination or predominance of humour (*obs physiol*); state with respect to combination or predominance of qualities (*obs*); proportioned mixture; climate (*obs*); internal constitution or state; tempering (*archaic*); compromise (*archaic*). [L *temperamentum* the mixing of things in proper proportion]
■ **temperament'al** adj relating to temperament; of a volatile, excitable temperament, given to extreme swings of mood; (of a machine, etc) working erratically, unreliable. **temperament'ally** adv. **temperament'ful** adj.
■ **equal temperament** (*music*) a tuning adjustment by which the octave on a keyboard is divided into twelve equal intervals.

temperance /tem'pə-rəns/ n moderation, *esp* in the indulgence of the natural appetites and passions, or, in a narrower sense, moderation in the use of alcohol, and even entire abstinence from it. ♦ adj advocating or consistent with temperance in or abstinence from alcoholic drinks. [L *temperantia* sobriety, moderation]
❏ **temperance hotel** n (*hist*) one at which no alcohol is supplied.

temperate /tem'pə-rət/ adj moderate; self-restrained, *esp* in appetites and passions; abstemious; moderate in temperature, neither very hot nor very cold. ♦ vt (*obs* or *rare*) to temper; to moderate; to restrain. [L *temperātus*, pap of *temperāre* to restrain, modify]
■ **tem'perately** adv. **tem'perateness** n. **tem'perative** adj having a moderating influence.
❏ **temperate phage** n (*biol*) a bacteriophage that integrates its genome into that of its host, where it lies dormant for many generations. **temperate zones** n pl the parts of the earth of moderate temperature between the tropics and the polar circles.

temperature /tem'prə-chər/ n degree of hotness of a body, etc or medium (eg air, water) ascertainable by means of a thermometer; a body temperature above normal, fever; condition determining interchange of heat between bodies; the degree of warmth or friendliness in an interchange or relationship; the degree of enthusiasm, excitement or animation generated during debate; tempering; tempered condition; mixture; constitution; proportion. [L *temperātūra* appropriate measure, proportion]
❏ **temperature coefficient** n (*biol*) the ratio of the rate of any reaction or process at a given temperature to the rate at a temperature 10°C lower (also **Q₁₀**). **temperature-humidity index** n an index measuring temperature and humidity with regard to human discomfort. **temperature inversion** n (*meteorol*) anomalous increase in temperature with height in the troposphere. **temperature-sensitive mutant** n (*biol*) a mutant organism able to grow at one temperature (the *permissive temperature*) but unable to do so at another (the *restrictive temperature*).
■ **absolute temperature** see under **absolute**. **have a temperature** to have a raised body temperature, a fever. **take someone's temperature** to use a thermometer to ascertain someone's body temperature, as part of diagnosis.

tempest /tem'pist/ n a violent windstorm; a violent commotion or agitation. ♦ vt (*Milton*) to stir violently. [OFr *tempeste*, from a LL form of L *tempestās* a season, tempest, from *tempus* time]
■ **tempestive** /-pest'iv/ adj timely; seasonable. **tempest'ūous** adj stormy, windy, turbulent; wild, passionate. **tempest'ūously** adv. **tempest'ūousness** n.
❏ **tem'pest-beaten, tem'pest-tossed** or **tem'pest-tost** adj (*Shakesp*) driven about by storms.

tempi see **tempo**.

Templar /tem'plər/ n a member of a religious and military order (**Knights Templar** or **Knights Templars**) founded in 1119 for the protection of the Holy Sepulchre and pilgrims going there, extinguished 1307–14; (also without *cap*) a student or lawyer, living or with chambers, in the Temple, London; a member of a US order of Freemasons; see also under **good**. [Med L *templārius* of the temple]

templar see under **temple¹**.

template /tem'plit/ or /-plāt/ or **templet** n a thin plate cut to the shape required, used as a guide in cutting wood, metal, etc; a pattern cut in card or plastic for shaping pieces of cloth for patchwork; any model from which others form, are produced, etc; a mould shaped to a required outline from which to execute moulding; a timber or small beam used to spread the load in a wall; the coded instructions for the formation of a further molecule carried by a molecule of DNA, etc (*biochem*). [Earlier form was *templet*, perh a Fr dimin of L *templum* a small timber]

temple¹ /tem'pl/ n a building or place dedicated to, or regarded as the house of, a god; a place of worship; in France, a Protestant church; (with *cap*) the headquarters of the Knights Templar on or near the site of Solomon's temple in Jerusalem; (with *cap*) in London, two inns of court (**Inner** and **Middle Temple**) on the site once occupied by the Knights Templar, with the Knights' church; a synagogue, *esp* of Reform or Conservative Judaism (*N Am*); a building or place thought of as the centre of an activity or interest. [L *templum*]
■ **tem'plar** adj of a temple. **tem'pled** adj.

temple² /tem'pl/ n the flat portion of either side of the head above the cheekbone. [OFr, from L *tempus, -oris*]

temple³ /tem'pl/ n a pair of rollers fitted to the sides of a loom to keep the cloth at full width and suitably tensioned as it is woven. [ME, from L *templum* a small timber]

templet see **template**.

tempo /tem'pō/ (*music*) n (pl **tem'pos** or **tem'pi** /-pē/) time; speed, rate. [Ital]

tempolabile /tem-pō-lā'bīl/ (*chem*) adj tending to change with time. [*tempus, -oris* time, and *lābilis*, from *lābī* to slip]

temporal¹ /tem'pə-rəl/ adj relating to time; relating to time in this life or world, opp to *eternal*; worldly, secular, or civil, opp to *spiritual, sacred* or *ecclesiastical*; relating to tense or the expression of time (*grammar*); lasting for a short time. [L *temporālis*, from *tempus, -oris* time]
■ **temporality** /-al'i-ti/ n the state or fact of being temporal; that which relates to temporal welfare; (*usu* in pl) secular possessions, revenues of an ecclesiastic proceeding from lands, tithes, etc. **tem'porally** adv. **tem'poralness** n. **tem'poralty** n the laity; lay peers; (*usu* pl) worldly possessions.

temporal² /tem'pə-rəl/ (*anat*) adj relating to or close to the temples on either side of the head. ♦ n a bone, muscle or scale in that position. [L *tempus, -oris*; see **temple²**]

❑ **temporal lobe** *n* a lobe at the side of each cerebral hemisphere by the temple, concerned with hearing and speech.

temporaneous /tem-pə-rā'ni-əs/ (*obs*) *adj* lasting only a relatively short time, temporary; relating to time, temporal. [L *temporāneus* opportune, timely, from *tempus, -oris* time]

temporary /tem'pə-rə-ri/ *adj* lasting for a time only; transient; impermanent; provisional. ◆ *n* (*pl* **tem'poraries**) a person employed temporarily (see also **temp**). [L *temporārius* lasting briefly, from *tempus, -oris* time]
■ **tem'porarily** *adv*. **tem'porariness** *n*.
❑ **temporary hardness** *n* hardness of water due to the presence of mineral salts, which are precipitated as carbonates by boiling.

tempore /tem'pə-rē, tem'po-re/ (L) in the time of.

temporize or **-ise** /tem'pə-rīz/ *vi* to comply with the demands of the moment, yield to circumstances; to use delaying tactics, behave so as to gain time. [Fr *temporiser*, from L *tempus, -oris* time]
■ **temporizā'tion** or **-s-** *n*. **tem'porizer** or **-s-** *n*. **tem'porizing** or **-s-** *n* and *adj*. **tem'porizingly** or **-s-** *adv*.

temporomandibular /tem-pə-rō-man-dib'ū-lər/ (*anat*) *adj* relating to the joint that connects the lower jawbone to the skull. [**temporal²** and **mandible**]

tempt /tempt/ *vt* to try or tend to persuade, *esp* to do wrong; to entice or invite; to dispose, incline; to attract; to make trial of, test the virtue of (*archaic, Bible* or *literary*). [OFr *tempter*, from L *tentāre*, an intensive of *tendere* to stretch]
■ **temptabil'ity** *n*. **temp'table** *adj*. **temp'tableness** *n*. **temptā'tion** *n* the act of tempting; the state of being tempted; that which tempts; enticement to do wrong; trial. **temptā'tious** *adj* (*rare*) seductive. **temp'ter** *n* (also *fem* **temp'tress**) a person or being who tempts. **temp'ting** *n*. ◆ *adj* attractive, enticing. **temp'tingly** *adv*. **temp'tingness** *n*.
■ **the Tempter** the Devil. **tempt fate** (or **providence**) to risk causing something undesirable, *esp* by foolhardy actions.

'tempt or **tempt** aphetic for **attempt**.

tempura /tem'pu̅-rə/ *n* a Japanese dish of seafood or vegetables deep-fried in batter. [Jap, from Port *tempero* seasoning]

tempus fugit /tem'pəs fū'jit* or *tem'pu̅s foo'git/ (L) time flies.

temse or **tems** /tems, temz/ (now *dialect*) *n* a sieve, strainer. ◆ *vt* (**tems'ing; temsed**) to sift. [OE *temesian* to sift; cf Du *tems*]

temulence /tem'u̅-ləns/ (*rare*) *n* intoxication (also **tem'ulency**). [L *tēmulentus* drunk]
■ **tem'ulent** *adj*. **tem'ulently** *adv*.

ten /ten/ *n* the cardinal number next above nine; a symbol representing that number (10, x, etc); a set of ten things or people; a score of ten points, strokes, tricks, etc; an article of a size denoted by 10; a playing card with ten pips; used indefinitely, a large number; the tenth hour after midnight or midday; the age of ten years. ◆ *adj* of the number ten; ten years old. [OE (Anglian) *tēn, tēne* (WSax *tīen, tīene*); Ger *zehn*, Welsh *deg*, L *decem*, Gr *deka*, Sans *dasa*]
■ **ten'fold** *adj* and *adv* in ten divisions; ten times as much. **tenn'er** *n* (*inf*) a ten-pound note; a ten-dollar bill; ten years. **tenth** *adj* the last of ten; next after the ninth; equal to one of ten equal parts. ◆ *n* a tenth part; a tenth part of the annual profit of a church living; a person or thing in tenth position; an octave and a third (*music*); a note at that interval (*music*). ◆ *adv* in tenth position; as the tenth point, etc. **tenth'ly** *adv*.
❑ **Ten Commandments** see under **command**. **ten'-foot** *adj* measuring ten feet. **ten-gallon hat** *n* (*US*) a cowboy's broad-brimmed hat. **ten-minute rule** *n* a parliamentary procedure by which a member makes a short speech (lasting no more than ten minutes) requesting permission to introduce a bill. **ten'pence** *n* an amount in money equal to ten pennies. **ten'penny** *adj* offered for, or sold at, tenpence. **tenpenny nail** *n* formerly, a nail sold at tenpence a hundred; a large nail. **ten'pin** *n* one of the target pins in tenpin bowling. **tenpin bowling** or **ten'pins** *n* a game like skittles, in which the aim is to knock down ten target pins standing at the end of a long lane by rolling a heavy ball at them. **ten-point'er** *n* a stag with ten points or tines. **ten'-pound** *adj* weighing, worth, sold or offered for, ten pounds. **ten-pound'er** *n* something weighing or worth ten pounds; any of a family (Elopidae) of marine or freshwater bony fishes; a person who was a voter by virtue of occupying property worth ten pounds a year (*hist*). **ten'-score** *adj* two hundred. **tenth'-rate** *adj* of very poor quality.
■ **long ten** the ten of trumps in catch-the-ten. **ten to one** in all probability.

ten. (*music*) *abbrev* : tenuto.

tenable /ten'ə-bl/ or (*archaic*) tē'nə-/ *adj* capable of being retained, kept or defended. [Fr *tenable*, from *tenir* to hold]
■ **tenabil'ity** or **ten'ableness** *n*.

tenace /ten'ās, -is/ (*cards*) *n* the combination in one hand of the cards next above and next below a high card held by the other side. [Sp *tenaza* pincers]

tenacious /ti-nā'shəs/ *adj* retentive; (with *of*) holding fast to; clinging; sticking firmly; cohesive; tough; stubborn, obdurate, determined. [L *tenāx, -ācis*, from *tenēre* to hold]
■ **tenā'ciously** *adv*. **tenā'ciousness** or **tenacity** /-nas'i-ti/ *n*.

tenaculum /ti-nak'ū-ləm/ *n* (*pl* **tenac'ula** /-lə/) a surgical hook or forceps for picking up blood vessels; a band of muscle or fibrous tissue that holds, eg an organ, in place (*anat*). [L *tenāculum* holder, pincers]

tenaille /ti-nāl'/ (*fortif*) *n* an outwork in the main ditch in front of the curtain (also **tenail'**). [Fr, from L *tenāculum* pincers, from *tenēre* to hold]
■ **tenaillon** /ti-nal'yən/ *n* a work to strengthen the side of a small ravelin.

tenant /ten'ənt/ *n* a person who occupies property owned by another, in return for rent, service, etc; a person who has, on certain conditions, temporary possession of any place; an occupant; someone who possesses land or property by private ownership (*law*). ◆ *vt* to hold as a tenant; to occupy. ◆ *vi* to dwell. [Fr *tenant*, prp of *tenir*, from L *tenēre* to hold]
■ **ten'ancy** *n* a temporary occupation or holding of land or property by a tenant; time of such holding; the property held by a tenant; possession by private ownership. **ten'antable** *adj* fit to be tenanted; in a state of repair suitable for a tenant. **ten'antless** *adj*. **ten'antry** *n* the state or time of being a tenant; a set or body of tenants, *esp* of the same landlord. **ten'antship** *n*.
❑ **tenant-at-will** *n* a tenant who holds property only so long as the proprietor wills. **tenant farmer** *n* a farmer who rents a farm. **tenant-in-chief'** *n* a tenant holding lands directly from the sovereign. **tenant right** *n* the right of a tenant, *esp* that of a customary tenant, to sit continuously at a reasonable rent, the right to receive compensation for his or her interest from the incoming tenant, and for all permanent or unexhausted improvements from the landlord. **tenants' association** *n* an organization of tenants, eg on a housing estate, who work to improve housing conditions, amenities, etc on that estate. **tenants' charter** *n* a document listing the legal rights of local-authority and housing-association tenants, *incl* right of tenancy.

Tencel® /ten'sel/ *n* a man-made fibre processed from wood pulp.

tench /tench or tensh/ *n* a dark bronze-green to brown freshwater fish (*Tinca tinca*) of the carp family, its mouth bearing a pair of short barbels used in sensing prey. [OFr *tenche* (Fr *tanche*), from L *tinca*]

tend¹ /tend/ *vt* to attend to, take care of; to mind; to watch over or stand by and perform services for or connected with; to minister to, wait upon; to escort (*Shakesp*). ◆ *vi* to pay attention (with *to*, *esp US*); to wait on, attend to (with *on, upon*; *old*); to attend, hearken (*Shakesp*); to be in waiting or readiness (*Shakesp*); to wait, attend (*Shakesp*). [Aphetic for **attend**]
■ **ten'dance** *n* tending; expectation (*Spenser*); attendants collectively (*Shakesp*). **ten'ded** *adj*. **ten'der** *n* a person who tends; a small craft that attends a larger; a carriage attached to a locomotive to carry fuel and water.
■ **tend out on** (*US*) to attend or attend to.

tend² /tend/ *vi* to be apt or prone (to do something); to move or incline in some direction; to be directed to any end or purpose; to conduce. [L *tendere* and Fr *tendre* to stretch]
■ **ten'dence** or **tendenz** /ten-dents'/ *n* (*Ger*) tendency (*esp* in composition, tendentious). **ten'dency** *n* a trend, drift, inclination; proneness; a faction within a particular political movement. **tenden'tious**, also **tenden'tial** or **tenden'cious** *adj* purposely tending or angled; with an object; biased, *esp* towards controversy. **tenden'tiously** *adv*. **tenden'tiousness** *n*.

tender¹ /ten'dər/ *adj* soft, delicate, fragile; easily chewed, not tough; easily impressed or injured; not hardy; gentle; youthful; vulnerable; sensitive, *esp* to pain or sorrow; painful when touched or pressed; requiring gentle or tactful handling; easily moved to pity, love, etc; careful not to hurt; kind, sympathetic, considerate, careful (with *of*; *archaic*); pathetic; expressive of, of the nature of, or arousing the softer passions; compassionate, loving, affectionate; (of porcelain) soft-paste; scrupulous, chary; beloved (*Shakesp*); (of a ship) apt to lean over under sail. ◆ *vt* (*obs* or *dialect*) to cherish; to value, have respect to; to make tender; to treat with tenderness (*Shakesp*); to feel tenderness for (*Shakesp*). ◆ *n* care, regard, concern (*Shakesp*); tender feeling, fondness (now *usu* in Fr form **tendre** /tädr'/). [Fr *tendre*, from L *tener*]
■ **ten'derize** or **-ise** *vt* to break down the connective tissue of (meat) so as to make it tender, either by pounding or by applying a chemical or marinade. **ten'derizer** or **-s-** *n* a pounding instrument or a substance that tenderizes meat. **ten'derling** *n* a person coddled too much, an effeminate person; one of the first horns of a deer. **ten'derly** *adv*. **ten'derness** *n*.

❑ **ten'der-dying** adj (Shakesp) dying young. **ten'derfoot** n (pl **ten'derfoots** or **ten'derfeet**) (orig and esp N Am) a person not yet hardened to life in the prairie, mining-camp, etc; a newcomer; a greenhorn, beginner; formerly, a boy scout or girl guide who has passed only the first tests. **tender-heart'ed** adj compassionate, easily touched or moved. **tender-heart'edly** adv. **tender-heart'edness** n. **tender-heft'ed** adj (Shakesp) perh set in a tender bodily 'haft' or frame. **ten'derloin** n the tenderest part of the loin of beef, pork, etc, close to the lumbar vertebrae; a district where bribes to the police and other forms of corruption are extremely common (N Am sl). **tenderstem broccoli** n broccolini.

tender² /ten'dər/ vt to offer for acceptance, esp to offer in payment; to proffer. ◆ vi to make a tender. ◆ n an offer or proposal, esp one in writing offering to provide a particular service for a particular price; the paper containing it; the thing offered; a formal offer to save the consequences of non-payment or non-performance (law); a formal offer of a sum of money to settle a court case (Scots law). [Fr tendre to stretch, reach out]
■ **ten'derer** n. **ten'dering** n.
■ **legal tender** see under **legal. put out to tender** to invite tenders for a particular job.

tender³ see under **tend¹**.

tendon /ten'dən/ n a cord, band or sheet of fibrous tissue attaching a muscle to a bone or other structure. [LL tendō, -inis or -ōnis, appar from Gr tenōn, -ontos sinew, tendon; cf teinein to stretch; d suggested by L tendere]
■ **tendinitis** or **tendonitis** /-ī'tis/ n inflammation of a tendon. **ten'dinous** adj.

tendovaginitis see **tenovaginitis**.

tendre see **tender¹**.

tendril /ten'dril/ n a plant's coiling threadlike climbing organ (leaf, leaflet or shoot); anything resembling a tendril, such as a curl of hair. [Ety doubtful; cf Fr tendrillon shoot]
■ **ten'drillar** or **ten'drillous** adj. **ten'drilled** adj.

tendron /ten'drən/ n a shoot, sprout; (in pl) cartilages of the ribs. [Fr]

tene see **teen²**.

tenebrae /ten'i-brē, ten'e-brī/ (RC; also with cap) n pl matins and lauds of the following day sung on the Wednesday, Thursday and Friday of Holy Week, when candles are extinguished one by one at the end of each psalm with the final psalm being sung in darkness. [L, darkness]

tenebrio /ti-neb'ri-ō/ n (pl teneb'rios) a night spirit; a night prowler; (with cap) the mealworm genus of beetles, giving name to the family **Tenebrionidae** /-on'i-dē/. [L tenebriō a person who lurks in the dark, from tenebrae darkness]

tenebrious see **tenebrose**.

tenebrism /ten'ə-bri-zm/ (art) n the 17c Italian and Spanish naturalist school of painting, esp of Caravaggio, characterized by large expanses of shadow. [L tenebrae darkness]
■ **ten'ebrist** n and adj.

tenebrose /ten'i-brōz/, **tenebrious** /tə-neb'ri-əs/ or **tenebrous** /ten'i-brəs/ adj dark, gloomy. [L tenebrae darkness]
■ **teneb'rity** or **tenebros'ity** n.

tenement /ten'i-mənt/ n a dwelling or habitation, or part of it, used by one family; one of a set of apartments in one building, each occupied by a separate family; a building divided into dwellings for a number of families (Scot and US); a holding, by any tenure; anything held, or that may be held, by a tenant. [LL tenementum, from L tenēre to hold]
■ **tenemental** /-ment'l/ adj. **tenement'ary** adj.
❑ **tenement building** n. **tenement house** n.

tenendum /ti-nen'dəm/ n (in a deed) the clause in which the tenure of the land is defined and limited. [L neuter of tenendus, gerundive of tenēre to hold]

tenesmus /ti-nes'məs or -nez'məs/ (med) n a continuous or frequently recurring desire to defecate, with painful and ineffectual straining to empty the bowels. [Latinized from Gr teinesmos, from teinein to strain]

tenet /ten'it (also tē'nit)/ n any opinion, principle or doctrine which a person holds or maintains as true. [L tenet, (he) holds, from tenēre to hold]

tenfold see under **ten**.

tenge /teng'gä/ n (pl teng'e or teng'es) the standard monetary unit of Kazakhstan (100 tein); a monetary unit in Turkmenistan, $\frac{1}{100}$ of a manat.

Tengku see **Tunku**.

tenia, tenioid, etc variant spellings of **taenia, taenioid**, etc.

Tenn. abbrev : Tennessee (US state).

tennantite /ten'ən-tīt/ n a mineral composed of sulphur, arsenic and copper, usu with iron. [Smithson Tennant (1761–1815), English chemist]

tenné /ten'ā/ (heraldry) adj and n (of) an orange-brown colour (also **tenn'y**). [Obs Fr; cf **tawny**]

tenner see under **ten**.

tennis /ten'is/ n a game played by hitting a small ball over a net with a racket, if possible in such a way as to prevent its return, usu now referring to **lawn tennis**, played by one or two a side on a grass, clay or hard court, but formerly to an ancient game played (orig using the palms of the hands) in a specially constructed building or enclosed court, and distinguished from lawn tennis, which was derived from it, as **close, court, real** (ie genuine, original), or (in Australia from the late 19c) **royal tennis**. [Prob Fr tenez, (Anglo-Fr tenetz) imperative of tenir to take, receive]
❑ **tennis elbow** n an inflamed condition of the muscle that extends the wrist, at the point where it arises at the elbow, caused by over-exercise.
■ **short tennis** see under **short**.

tenno /ten'ō/ n (pl tenn'o or tenn'os) the formal title of the emperor of Japan, esp in his former capacity as a divine leader. [Jap]

tenny see **tenné**.

tenon /ten'ən/ n a projection at the end of a piece of wood, etc, inserted into the socket or mortise of another, to hold the two together. ◆ vt to fix or fit with a tenon; to cut a tenon in (a piece of wood). [Fr tenon, from tenir to hold, from L tenēre]
■ **ten'oner** n.
❑ **tenon saw** n a thin backsaw for tenons, etc.

tenor (obs or old **tenour**) /ten'ər/ n the adult male voice intermediate between baritone and alto; in early polyphonic music, the part maintaining the melody, often assigned, in counterpoint singing, to this voice; a person who sings tenor; the part next above the bass in a vocal quartet; an instrument, eg the viola or recorder, of corresponding range; the largest and lowest-pitched bell in a full peal; continuity of state; general run or course; the value of a banknote or bill (hist); the proportion of ore mineral in an ore; general purport, drift; the subject referred to by a metaphor; the exact wording of a document (law); an exact transcript of a document (law); the time required for a bill of exchange or promissory note to become due for payment (finance). ◆ adj of the tenor range. [L tenor a course followed or held to, from tenēre to hold]
■ **ten'orist** n a person who plays a tenor instrument. **tenoroon'** n an obsolete tenor bassoon.
❑ **tenor clef** n (music) the clef on which middle C is placed on the fourth line of the stave. **tenor cor** n the mellophone (see under **mellow**). **tenor drum** n a snareless drum intermediate between a side drum and a bass drum, used esp in military bands.

tenorite /ten'ə-rīt/ n melaconite, black copper ore (CuO), found in volcanic regions (orig on Vesuvius) and copper veins. [G Tenore, President of the Naples Academy, 1841]

tenorrhaphy /ti-nor'ə-fi/ (med) n the repairing of a split or torn tendon by sutures. [Gr tenōn tendon, and raphē suture]

tenosynovitis /ten-ō-sī-nə-vī'tis/ (med) n painful inflammation and swelling of a tendon, associated with repetitive movements. [Gr tenōn tendon, and **synovitis**]

tenotomy /tə-not'ə-mi/ n surgical cutting of a tendon. [Gr tenōn tendon, and tomē a cut]
■ **tenot'omist** n.

tenour see **tenor**.

tenovaginitis /ten-ō-va-ji-nī'tis/ or **tendovaginitis** /ten-dō-/ n inflammation or thickening of the fibrous wall of the sheath surrounding a tendon, esp in the hand. [Gr tenōn or L tendō tendon, and **vaginitis**]

tenpence, etc see under **ten**.

tenrec /ten'rek/ or **tanrec** /tan'rek/ n a large Madagascan insectivore of the **Tenrecidae** /-res'i-dē/ family (esp Tenrec ecaudatus) similar to the hedgehog. [Malagasy t(r)àndraka]

TENS abbrev : transcutaneous electrical nerve stimulation (see under **transcutaneous**).

tense¹ /tens/ n time in grammar, the form of a verb to indicate the time of the action. [OFr tens (Fr temps), from L tempus time]
■ **tense'less** adj.

tense² /tens/ adj stretched tight; strained or producing strain; rigid; pronounced with the tongue tightened or narrowed (phonetics). ◆ vt and vi to make or become tense. [L tensus, pap of tendere to stretch]
■ **tense'ly** adv. **tense'ness** n state of being tense. **tensibil'ity** n. **tens'ible** adj capable of being stretched. **tens'ile** /-sīl or (esp US) -sil or -səl/ adj tensile; of or relating to stretching. **tensility** /-sil'i-ti/ n. **tensim'eter** n an instrument for measuring vapour pressure. **tensiom'eter** n an instrument for measuring tension, tensile strength, the moisture content of soil. **tensiom'etry** n the branch of physics relating to tension, tensile strength, etc. **tension** /ten'shən/ n

tenson 1608 **tera-**

stretching; a pulling strain; stretched or strained state; strain generally; formerly, pressure in gases or vapours; electromotive force; a state of barely suppressed emotion, such as excitement, anxiety or hostility; a feeling of strain with resultant symptoms (*psychol*); strained relations between persons; opposition between conflicting ideas or forces; a device for regulating the tautness of a string, thread in a sewing machine, etc; the looseness with which a person knits. ◆ *vt* to subject to tension. **ten'sional** *adj*. **ten'sionally** *adv*. **ten'sionless** *adj*. **tens'ity** *n* tenseness. **tens'ive** *adj* giving the sensation of tenseness or stiffness. **tens'or** *n* a muscle that tightens a part (*anat*); a mathematical or physical entity represented by components which depend in a special way on the choice of a co-ordinate system. **tensorial** /-sö'ri-əl/ *adj*.
□ **tensile strength** *n* the strength of a material when being stretched, expressed as the greatest stress it can resist before breaking. **tensile test** *n* (*engineering*) a test performed on a metal or other material to determine its tensile characteristics. **tension rod** *n* a structural member subjected to tensile stress only.

tenson /ten'sn/, also **tenzon** /-zn/ *n* a competition in verse between two troubadours before a court of love; a subdivision of the piece of verse so composed. [Fr, from L *tensio*, *-ōnis* a struggle]

tensor see under **tense²**.

tent¹ /tent/ *n* a portable shelter of canvas or other cloth stretched on poles and attached to the ground by pegs; anything resembling a tent, eg (*med*) an enclosure within which to regulate the oxygen supply to a patient; a temporary field pulpit; a common shelter spun by a company of caterpillars. ◆ *vi* to camp in a tent; to camp temporarily. ◆ *vt* to cover or shelter (as if) with a tent; to lodge in tents. [Fr *tente*, from L *tendere*, *tentum* to stretch]
■ **tent'age** *n* tents collectively; material for making tents. **ten'ted** *adj* covered with tents; formed like a tent; (of a settlement or camp) dwelling in tents. **tent'er** *n* someone who lives in a tent. **tent'ful** *n* as many as a tent will hold. **tent'ing** *n*. ◆ *adj* (*Keats*) having the form of a tent. **tent'less** *adj*. **tent'wise** *adv*.
□ **tent bed** *n* a camp bed, a bed with a canopy hanging from a central point. **tent caterpillar** *n* any of several caterpillars that build communal shelters in trees. **tent cloth** *n* cloth suitable for tents. **tent coat**, **tent dress**, etc *n* a coat, dress, etc shaped like a circular tent, narrow at the shoulders and wide at the hem. **tent'-fly** *n* a flap forming a door to a tent; a subsidiary outer roof to a tent. **tent'-guy** *n* a stay or guy rope for a tent. **tent'maker** *n*. **tent peg** or **tent pin** *n* a strong notched peg driven into the ground to fasten a tent. **tent'-pegging** *n* the sport of riding at full speed and trying to bear off a tent peg on the point of a lance. **tent pole** *n* a pole to support a tent. **tent'-preaching** *n* open-air preaching. **tent rope** *n* a rope for securing a tent to a peg.
■ **big tent** see under **big¹**.

tent² /tent/ *n* a plug or roll of soft material for dilating a wound or keeping open an orifice (*med*); a probe (*obs*). ◆ *vt* to dilate or keep open with a tent (*med*); to probe (*obs*). [Fr *tente*, from L *tentāre* to try]

tent³ /tent/ *n* a deep-red Spanish wine. [Sp *tinto*, from L *tinctus*, pap of *tingere* to dye]

tent⁴ /tent/ (*Scot*) *n* heed. ◆ *vt* to take heed or notice of, attend to. [Aphetic for **attent** and **intent**]
■ **tent'er** *n* a person who tends, *esp* to a machine. **tent'ie** or **tent'y** *adj* wary, attentive.

tent⁵ /tent/ *n* (*obs*) an embroidery or tapestry frame. [Origin obscure, perh related to **tent¹**; cf ME *tent* to stretch, **tenter¹**, and L *tendere*, *tentum*]
□ **tent stitch** *n* an embroidery stitch made in parallel series diagonally to the canvas threads; tent-work. **tent'-work** *n* work in tent stitch.

tentacle /ten'tə-kl/ *n* (also **tentaculum** /-tak'ū-ləm/ (*pl* **tentac'ūla**)) a slender flexible organ, *esp* in invertebrates, for feeling, grasping, etc; any sensitive filament in insectivorous plants used in the capture of prey, eg the gland-tipped leaf hairs of the sundew plant; anything resembling a tentacle, *esp* in its ability to grasp or feel. [L *tentāre* to feel]
■ **ten'tacled** *adj*. **tentac'ūlar** *adj*. **tentac'ūlate** *adj*. **tentacūlif'erous** *adj*. **tentac'ūlite** *n* (*palaeontol*) a ringed conical Silurian and Devonian fossil, *appar* a pteropod. **tentac'ūloid** *adj*.

tentation /ten-tā'shən/ *n* an old form of **temptation**; a method of adjusting by a succession of trials (*mech*). [L *tentātiō*, *-ōnis*, from *tentāre* to test]

tentative /ten'tə-tiv/ *adj* done or made provisionally and experimentally; cautious, hesitant, diffident. ◆ *n* an experimental attempt. [L *tentāre* to try]
■ **ten'tatively** *adv*. **ten'tativeness** *n*.

tenter¹ /ten'tər/ *n* a frame for stretching cloth, *esp* so that it retains its shape while drying; a tenterhook; a hook. ◆ *vt* to stretch on hooks. [Appar connected with Fr *tenture* hangings, and L *tendere* to stretch]

□ **ten'terhook** *n* a sharp, hooked nail to fasten cloth to a tenter; a hook.
■ **on tenterhooks** in impatient suspense.

tenter² see under **tent¹,⁴**.

tenth see under **ten**.

tentie see under **tent⁴**.

tentigo /ten-tī'gō/ *n* priapism; morbid lasciviousness. [L *tentīgō*, *-inis*, from *tendere* to stretch]
■ **tentiginous** /-tij'i-nəs/ *adj*.

tentorium /ten-tō'ri-əm, -tō'/ *n* (*pl* **tento'ria**) a sheet of the dura mater stretched between the cerebrum and the cerebellum (*anat*); the internal chitinous skeleton of an insect's head. [L *tentōrium* a tent, from *tendere* to stretch]
■ **tento'rial** *adj*.

tenty see under **tent⁴**.

tenue /tə-nü'/ *n* bearing, carriage; manner of dress. [Fr]

tenuirostral /ten-ū-i-ros'trəl/ *adj* (of a bird) slender-billed. [L *tenuis* thin, and *rōstrum* bill]

tenuis /ten'ū-is, ten'ŭ-is/ *n* (*pl* **ten'ues** /-ēz, ās/) an unaspirated voiceless stop consonant, such as *k*, *p* or *t*. [L, thin]

tenuity see under **tenuous**.

tenuous /ten'ū-əs/ or (*rare*) **tenuious** /-ū'i-əs/ *adj* thin; slender; slight; insubstantial; rarefied. [L *tenuis* thin; cf *tendere* to stretch]
■ **tenū'ity** or **ten'uousness** *n*. **ten'uously** *adv*.

tenure¹ /ten'yər/ *n* holding, occupation; time of holding; the holding of an appointment in a university or college for an assured length of time after a period of probation; conditions on which property is held; a tenant's rights, duties, etc. [Anglo-Fr *tenure*, from *tenir* to hold]
■ **ten'urable** *adj* (of a university post) giving tenure. **ten'ured** *adj* (of *esp* a university lecturer) having tenure. **tenūr'ial** *adj*. **tenūr'ially** *adv*.
□ **tenure track** *n* (chiefly N Am) a career path, *usu* in higher education, with a guarantee of tenure after a given number of years' service or probationary period.

tenure² a Shakespearean form of **tenor**.

tenuto /te-noo'tō/ (*music*) *adj* and *adv* sustained. ◆ *n* (*pl* **tenu'tos** or **tenu'ti** /-tē/) a sustained note or chord. [Ital, pap of *tenere* to hold]

tenzon see **tenson**.

teocalli /tē-ō-kal'i, tē-ə-kal'i or tä-ō-kal'yi/ *n* a Mexican pyramid temple. [Nahuatl, from *teotl* god, and *calli* house]

teosinte /tē-ō-sin'ti/ *n* a tall grass (*Euchlaena mexicana*), related to maize, a native of the southern USA and Mexico, often used as a fodder crop. [Nahuatl, from *teotl* god, and *centli* ear of corn]

tepal /tē'pəl or tep'əl/ (*bot*) *n* one of the subdivisions of a perianth that is not clearly differentiated into a calyx and a corolla. [Fr *tépale*, changed from *pétale* petal, influenced by *sépale* sepal]

tepee, **teepee**, or **tipi** /tē'pē or ti-pē'/ *n* a Native American tent formed of skins, etc, stretched over a frame of converging poles. [Sioux *tīpī* dwelling]

tepefy /tep'i-fī/ *vt* and *vi* (**tep'efying; tep'efied**) to make or become tepid. [L *tepefacere*, from *tepēre* to be tepid, and *facere* to make]
■ **tepefac'tion** *n*.

tephigram /tē'fi-gram/ *n* (*meteorol*) a diagram on which information about vertical variation of atmospheric conditions is plotted. [*t*, for temperature, *phi*, former symbol for entropy, and **-gram**]

tephillin see **tefillin**.

tephra /tef'rə/ *n* ash and debris ejected by a volcano. [Gr *tephrā* ashes]

tephrite /tef'rīt/ *n* a fine-grained basaltic rock containing a feldspathoid as well as feldspar, but no olivine. [Gr *tephrā* ashes, *tephros* ash-coloured]
■ **tephritic** /-rit'ik/ *adj*. **teph'roite** /-rō-īt/ *n* an ashy-grey or reddish silicate of manganese. **teph'romancy** *n* (see **-mancy**) divination by ashes, *esp* those left after a sacrifice.

tepid /tep'id/ *adj* moderately warm, lukewarm; lacking enthusiasm, half-hearted. [L *tepidus*, from *tepēre* to be warm]
■ **tepidā'rium** (or /-dä'ri-ūm/) *n* (*pl* **tepidā'ria**) a warm room between the cold and hot rooms of a Roman bath. **tepid'ity** or **tep'idness** *n*. **tep'idly** *adv*.

tequila or **tequilla** /tə-kē'lə/ *n* a Mexican alcoholic drink made from an agave plant (*Agave tequilana*). [From a district of Mexico]
□ **Tequila Sunrise** *n* a multicoloured cocktail containing tequila, grenadine and orange juice.

Ter. *abbrev* : Terrace (in street names); Territory.

ter- /tûr-/ *combining form* thrice, three, threefold. [L, thrice]

tera- /ter-ə-/ *combining form* denoting 10^{12}, or loosely (*comput*) 2^{40}. [Gr *teras*, *-atos* monster]

■ words derived from main entry word; □ compound words; ■ idioms and phrasal verbs

■ **ter'abyte** n (comput) a unit of storage capacity equal to 10^{12} or (loosely) 2^{40} bytes. **ter'aflop** n (comput) a unit of processing speed equal to 10^{12} floating-point operations per second. ◆ adj able to perform at this speed, as in teraflop chip.

terai /tə-rī'/ n a wide-brimmed double-crowned ventilated felt hat, first worn in the Terai (Taráí), India.

terakihi see **tarakihi**.

teraph /ter'əf/ n (pl **ter'aphim**; also used as sing) in ancient Jewish religion and divination, an image of some sort, such as a household deity. [Heb]

teras /ter'əs/ (biol and pathol) n (pl **ter'ata**) a monstrosity. [Gr teras, -atos monster]
■ **ter'atism** n a monster; a malformed person or animal, esp in the fetal stage.

terato- /ter-ə-tō-, -tə- or -to-/ combining form denoting monster, congenital malformation. [Gr teras, -atos monster]
■ **terat'ogen** /-jen/ n an agent that raises the incidence of congenital malformation. **teratogen'esis** n abnormal growth, esp as a result of exposure of the fetus to a teratogen. **teratogen'ic** adj producing monsters; causing abnormal growth (in a fetus). **teratog'eny** /-toj'i-ni/ n the production of monsters. **teratolog'ic** or **teratolog'ical** adj. **teratol'ogist** n. **teratol'ogy** n the study of biological malformations or abnormal growths; a collection of tales and myths about fantastic monsters.

teratoid /ter'ə-toid/ (biol) adj monstrous. [Gr teras, -atos monster]

teratoma /ter-ə-tō'mə/ (med) n (pl **teratō'mata** or **teratō'mas**) a tumour consisting of tissue not normally found at that site, occurring esp in the testis or ovary. [Gr teras, -atos monster]
■ **teratō'matous** adj.

terbium /tûr'bi-əm/ n a rare metallic element (symbol **Tb**; atomic no 65) found in certain yttrium minerals. [Ytterby, Sweden, where it was discovered]
■ **ter'bic** adj.

terce /tûrs/ n one of the hours of the Divine Office, orig held at the third hour of the day (9am) (also **tierce**; RC); (before 1964) a widow's right, where she had no conventional provision, to a life-rent of a third of the husband's heritable property (Scots law). [See **tierce**]

tercel /tûr'səl/, **tiercel** /tēr'səl/, **tarcel**, **tarsal**, **tarsel** /tär'səl/, **tassel** or **tassell** /tas'əl/ n a male hawk. [OFr tercel, from L tertius third, perh as being one-third smaller than the female, or from the belief that the male hawk hatched from the last egg of three]
■ **terc'elet** or **tierc'elet** n a tercel.
❑ **ter'cel-gent'le** (Walter Scott), **tass'el-gentle** (Shakesp) or **tass'ell-gent** (Spenser) n a male peregrine falcon. **ter'cel-jerkin** n a male gerfalcon.

tercentenary /tûr-sən-tē'nə-ri or tûr-sen-ten'ə-ri/ adj of or relating to three hundred years, or to a 300th anniversary or the celebrations for it. ◆ n a 300th anniversary, or the celebrations for it. [L ter thrice, and **centenary**]
■ **tercentennial** /tûr-sen-ten'yəl/ adj of 300 years. ◆ n a 300th anniversary.

tercet /tûr'sit/ (prosody) n a group of three lines that rhyme together or are associated by rhyme with an adjacent set of three (also **tiercet**). [Ital terzetto]

tercio /tûr'si-ō, -shi-ō/ (Walter Scott **tertia**), (hist) n (pl **ter'cios**) an infantry regiment, orig Spanish. [Sp]

terebene /ter'i-bēn/ n a light-yellow disinfectant liquid, a mixture of hydrocarbons made from oil of turpentine, used as a solvent for paint. [terebinth, and sfx -ene]

terebinth /ter'i-binth/ n the turpentine tree (Pistacia terebinthus; family Anacardiaceae) yielding turpentine. [Gr terebinthos]
■ **terebinth'ine** adj of or relating to the terebinth; of, relating to or resembling turpentine.

terebra /ter'i-brə/ n (pl **ter'ebras** or **ter'ebrae** /-ē/) a Roman contrivance for boring walls (hist); a boring instrument or organ; a piercing ovipositor (biol); (with cap) a genus of gastropods with auger-shaped shell. [L terebra]
■ **ter'ebrant** adj boring; having a piercing ovipositor. ◆ n (facetious) a bore. **ter'ebrate** vt and vi to bore. ◆ adj /-brət/ having scattered perforations; (eg of insects) having a boring organ, such as a sting. **terebrā'tion** n. **terebrat'ula** n (pl **terebrat'ulas** or **terebrat'ulae** /-lē/) a member of Terebratula, the lamp-shell genus of brachiopods, with perforated beak.

teredo /te-rē'dō/ n (pl **terē'dos** or **terē'dines** /-di-nēz/) a member of the shipworm genus of molluscs Teredo, a bivalvular mollusc that bores into wooden ships. [L terēdō, -inis, from Gr terēdōn, -onos a boring worm, from root of teirein to wear away]

terefa or **terefah** /tə-rā-fä', -rä'/ same as **tref**.

terek /ter'ik/ n a sandpiper (Xenus cinereus) found at the river Terek (Russia) and elsewhere (also **Terek sandpiper**).

Terentian /tə-ren'sh(y)ən/ adj relating to or associated with the Roman comic poet Terence, Publius Terentius Afer (fl 165BC).

terephthalic acid /ter-əf-thal'ik as'id/ n a chemical widely used in the manufacture of synthetic, esp polyester, fibres. [terebene, and phthalic]

teres /ter'ēz/ (anat) n either of two muscles of the shoulder blade, **teres major** and **teres minor**, that rotate the arm inwards and outwards respectively. [L terēs smooth]

terete /tə-rēt', ter'ēt/ (biol) adj smooth and cylindrical. [L teres, teretis smooth, from terere to rub]

terf and **terfe** Milton's spellings of **turf**.

terfenadine /tûr-fen'ə-dēn/ n an antihistamine drug used in the treatment of hay fever.

tergite /tûr'jīt/ n the backplate of a somite. [**tergum**]

tergiversate /tûr'ji-vər-sāt/ vi to turn one's back; to desert, change sides; to shuffle, shift, use evasions. [L tergum the back, and versārī to turn]
■ **tergiversā'tion** n. **ter'giversātor** n. **tergiver'satory** adj.

tergum /tûr'gəm/ n (pl **ter'ga**) the back of an arthropod; the thickened dorsal plate of an arthropod segment. [L, back]
■ **ter'gal** adj.

teriyaki /ter-i-yä'ki/ n and adj in Japanese cookery, (a dish of meat or shellfish) marinated in a soy sauce and grilled or broiled. [Jap teri sunshine, and yaki roast, broiled]

term /tûrm/ n an end; the normal duration of a pregnancy, or its completion; any limited period; the time for which anything lasts; a division of the academic or school year, alternating with holiday; a period of sittings (law); (in pl) conditions, stipulations; (in pl) charge, fee; a quantity added to or subtracted from others in an expression (maths); an item in a series; either of the two quantities in a ratio (maths); that which may be a subject or predicate of a proposition (logic); a word used in a specially understood or defined sense; an expression generally; (in pl) language generally; a limit, boundary (archaic); a term day; (in pl) a footing, relation; (in pl) respect (Shakesp); a bust in continuity with its pedestal (art and archaeol). ◆ vt to call, designate. [Fr terme a limit, from L terminus a boundary]
■ **term'er** n a person who came to town during a law term (hist); a termor (obs). **term'less** adj endless; inexpressible (Shakesp); unconditional. **term'ly** adj and adv. ◆ n a publication appearing once a term. **term'or** or (obs) **term'er** n a person who holds an estate for a term of years or for life.
❑ **term assurance** n a usu cheap form of life insurance which pays out only if the insured dies within the period specified. **term day** n a day of the year fixed for some purpose, such as payment of rent, the beginning or end of a tenancy, hiring of servants, household removals. **term of art** n a term having a special meaning in a certain art, craft, etc, a technical term. **term of years** n an interest or estate in land for a fixed period. **terms of reference** see under **refer**. **terms of trade** n pl relation between export and import prices in national accounts. **term'-time** n and adj.
■ **bring to terms** to compel to the acceptance of conditions. **come to terms** to come to an agreement; to submit. **come to terms with** to find a way of living with (some personal trouble or difficulty). **eat one's terms** see under **eat**. **in terms** in so many words, explicitly; engaged in negotiations. **in terms of** having or using as unit; in the language peculiar to; in respect of, with regard to. **keep a term** to give the regular attendance during a period of study. **long'-** or **short'-termer** a person serving respectively a long or short prison sentence. **make terms** to reach an agreement. **on speaking terms** friendly enough to speak to each other; well enough acquainted to speak. **on terms** in friendly relations; on an equal footing. **stand upon terms** to insist upon conditions.

termagant /tûr'mə-gənt/ n a brawling, scolding woman. ◆ adj scolding, shrewish; brawling. [ME Termagan or Tervagant, a supposed Muslim idol, represented in the old plays and moralities as having a violent character]
■ **ter'magancy** n. **ter'magantly** adv.

termer see under **term**.

Termes /tûr'mēz/ n a genus of termites. [L termes, -itis a woodworm]

terminable /tûr'mi-nə-bl/ adj that may come or be brought to an end. [L termināre to limit, from terminus limit, boundary]
■ **terminabil'ity** n. **ter'minableness** n. **ter'minably** adv.

terminal /tûr'mi-nəl/ adj of, at, forming or marking, an end, boundary or terminus; final; (of a diseased condition) representing the final stages of a fatal illness; (of a disease) ending in death; suffering from a terminal illness; extreme, acute (inf); on the terminal market; of a term; occurring every term. ◆ n an end; an ending; a rail or bus terminus; an arrival and departure building for travellers by air; the storage base and distribution centre for raw material, eg at the head of an oil pipeline; a free end in an open electric circuit; a device linked to a computer and at a distance from it, by which the computer can be operated (also **terminal unit**); a patient with a terminal illness. [L *terminālis*, from *terminus* limit, boundary]

■ **ter'minally** *adv*.

□ **terminal guidance** *n* a system for guiding sub-units of a missile warhead towards multiple targets near the end of the missile's flight. **terminal illness** *n* a fatal disease in its final stages. **terminal market** *n* (*finance*) the central market in London for dealing in general commodities. **terminal platform** *n* (*oil*) an offshore platform used as a base for pumping oil or gas ashore. **terminal unit** see **terminal** (*n*) above. **terminal velocity** *n* the speed of an object on impact with a target; the greatest speed attained by an object falling or fired through a fluid.

Terminalia /tûr-mi-nā'li-ə/ *n pl* an annual Roman festival in honour of the god Terminus. ♦ *n sing* the myrobalan genus of Combretaceae. [**terminus**]

terminate /tûr'mi-nāt/ *vt* to bring to an end; to end (a pregnancy) before its term. ♦ *vi* to come to an end; (of eg a word) to end (with *in*). [L *termināre* to set a limit to]

■ **termina'tion** *n* the act of terminating; an end or terminating part; ending or result; the ending of a pregnancy before term (*med*). **termina'tional** *adj*. **ter'minative** *adj* tending to terminate or determine; expressive of completion; definitive; absolute. **ter'minatively** *adv*. **ter'minator** *n* someone or something that terminates; the boundary between the illuminated and dark portions of the moon or of a planet. **ter'minatory** *adj*.

□ **terminate and stay resident** see **TSR**. **terminator gene** *n* a gene inserted into some crops to prevent them producing fertile seeds.

terminer /tûr'mi-nər/ (*law*; *obs*) *n* the act of determining. [L *termināre* to set a limit to]

termini see **terminus**.

terminism /tûr'mi-ni-zm/ *n* nominalism (*philos*); the doctrine that there is a time limit for the repentance and operation of grace (*theol*). [L *termināre* to set a limit to]

■ **ter'minist** *n*.

terminology /tûr-mi-nol'ə-ji/ *n* nomenclature; the set of terms used in any art, science, etc; the study of correct terms. [Med L *terminus* term]

■ **terminolog'ical** *adj*. **terminolog'ically** *adv*. **terminol'ogist** *n*.

□ **terminological inexactitude** *n* (*facetious*) a lie.

terminus /tûr'mi-nəs/ *n* (*pl* **ter'mini** /-nī/ or **ter'minuses**) an end, limit; an end point of a bus or railway route; a station at such a point; a finishing point or goal; a starting-point; a boundary stone; a bust ending in a pedestal (*art* and *archit*); (with *cap*) the Roman god of boundaries. [L, boundary, limit]

□ **terminus ad quem** /ad kwem/ *n* (*L*) the end or limit to which; a finishing point; point of destination. **terminus ante quem** /an'ti/ *n* (*L*) the end limit of a period of time; the established time or date before which the event in question must have occurred. **terminus a quo** /ä kwō/ *n* (*L*) the end or limit from which; a starting point. **terminus post quem** /pōst/ *n* (*L*) the starting point, earliest point, or a period of time; the established time or date after which the event in question must have occurred.

termite /tûr'mīt/ *n* a so-called white ant, a pale-coloured insect of the order Isoptera, some species feeding on wood and damaging trees, buildings, etc. [L *termes, termitis* a woodworm]

■ **termitarium** /tûr-mi-tā'ri-əm/ or **ter'mitary** /-tə-ri/ *n* a nest or mound of termites.

termless, termly, termor see under **term**.

tern[1] /tûrn/ *n* a long-winged aquatic bird of the subfamily Sterninae, related to the gulls but *usu* smaller and with a long forked tail. [Cf ON *therna*; OE *stearn, tearn*]

tern[2] /tûrn/ *n* a three, set of three; a prize for drawing three winning numbers; a three-masted schooner. [L *ternī* three each, from *trēs* three]

■ **ter'nal** *adj* threefold. **ter'nary** *adj* in threes; consisting of three components; based on three; to the base three (*maths*); of a third order. ♦ *n* (*obs*) a triad. **ter'nate** *adj* consisting of three leaflets (*bot*); grouped in threes. **ter'nately** *adv*. **ter'nion** *n* a triad; a section of paper for a book containing three double leaves or twelve pages.

□ **ternary form** *n* (*music*) a structure in which a first subject is followed by a second and then a repetition of the first.

terne /tûrn/ *n* an alloy, chiefly of lead and tin, known as **terne metal**; sheet iron or steel coated with this alloy (also **terne plate**). ♦ *vt* to cover with terne metal. [Fr *terne* dull]

ternion see under **tern**[2].

Ternstroemiaceae /tûrn-strē-mi-ā'shi-ē/ *n pl* the Theaceae or tea family of plants. [From a genus *Ternstroemia*, named after Christopher *Ternström*, Swedish naturalist]

terotechnology /ter-ō-tek-nol'ə-ji/ *n* the application of managerial, financial, engineering and other skills to extend the operational life of, and increase the efficiency of, equipment and machinery. [Gr *tereein* to watch, observe, and **technology**]

terpene /tûr'pēn/ (*chem*) *n* any one of a group of hydrocarbons with a composition $(C_5H_8)_n$ found in the essential oils of some plants, *esp* conifers. [From *terpentin*, old form of **turpentine**]

■ **ter'penoid** *n* any of a group of substances having a structure like that of terpene. **terpin'eol** /tûr-pin'i-ol/ *n* a terpene alcohol used extensively as a perfume base.

Terpsichore /tərp-sik'ə-rē/ *n* the Muse of choral song and dance. [Gr *Terpsichorē*, from *terpsis* delight, from *terpein* to enjoy, and *choros* dance]

■ **terpsichorē'an** *adj* of or relating to dancing (also **terpsichorē'al**). ♦ *n* a dancer.

Terr. *abbrev*: Terrace (in street names); Territory.

terra /ter'ə/ *n* (*pl* **terr'ae** /-ē/) the Latin and Italian word for earth, used eg in legal contexts; any area of higher land on the moon's surface.

■ **terraqueous** /te-rā'kwi-əs/ *adj* (L *aqua* water) of land and water. **terra'rium** *n* (*pl* **terrār'iums** or **terrāria**) a vivarium for land animals or (*usu* in the form of a large, often sealed, bottle or jar) for plants.

□ **terra alba** /al'bə/ *n* (L, white) any of various white, earthlike substances such as gypsum, kaolin, pipeclay, etc. **terracott'a** *n* (Ital *cotta*, from L *cocta* (fem) baked) an unglazed earthenware made from a mixture of clay and sand, used for statues, etc, and *esp* formerly, as an ornamental building material for facings, etc; an object of art made of it; its deep reddish-brown colour. ♦ *adj* made of terracotta; deep reddish-brown. **terra firma** /fûr'mə/ *n* the mainland, solid earth; dry land (*inf*). **ter'raform** *vt* to alter the atmosphere and ecology of (a planet) artificially, so as to make plant, animal and human life viable there. **ter'raforming** *n*. **terra ignota** /ig-nō'tə/ or **terra incognita** /in-kog'ni-tə/ *n* (L *ignota* (fem) strange, unfamiliar, and *incognita* (fem) unknown) an unexplored or unknown country or region. **terra-japon'ica** *n* pale catechu or gambier. **terramara** /te-rə-mä'rə/ *n* (*pl* **-re** /-rā/; Ital dialect for *terra marna* marl-earth) a dark earthy deposit formed under prehistoric pile-dwellings in Italy (also **terramare** /te-rə-mä'ri, te-rə-mär/). **terra nullius** *n* (L, nobody's land) land that is not part of the sovereign territory of any country. **terra rossa** /te-rə-ros'ə/ *n* (Ital *rossa* (fem) red) a ferruginous red earth, the residue of the weathering of limestone. **terra sigillata** /sij-i-lä'tə, sig-i-lä'tə/ *n* (L, sealed earth) a reddish-brown astringent clay found eg on the islands of Lemnos and Samos; earthenware pottery made from it; Samian ware.

terrace /ter'is/ *n* a raised level bank or walk; a level stretch along the side or top of a slope; ground or a structure that rises stepwise; a connected row of *usu* identical houses, properly one overlooking a slope; a raised paved area alongside a house; a gallery open at the side; a balcony; a flat rooftop; (*usu* in *pl*) the open areas rising in tiers around a football stadium, where spectators stand; a defective spot in marble. ♦ *vt* to form into a terrace or terraces. [Fr *terrasse*, from Ital *terrazza*, from LL *terrācea* an earthen mound, from L *terra* the earth]

■ **terr'aced** *adj* in terraces. **terracette** /-set'/ *n* a small terrace on a slope resulting from soil creep or erosion (also called **sheeptrack**). **terr'acing** *n*.

□ **terraced** (or **terrace**) **house** *n* one of the houses forming a terrace.

terracotta see under **terra**.

terrae filius /ter'ē fil'i-əs, ter'ī fē'li-ŭs/ (*L*) a son of the soil; a person of humble birth.

terra firma, terraform, terra ignota see under **terra**.

terrain[1] /tə-, te-rān' or ter'ān/ *n* ground, a tract, regarded as a field of view or of operations, or as having some sort of unity or prevailing character. [Fr, from a LL form of *terrēnum* terrene]

□ **terrain park** *n* a landscaped area of snow in which snowboarders and skiers can perform manoeuvres.

terrain[2] see **terrane**.

terra incognita, terra-Japonica, terramara, terramare see under **terra**.

Terramycin® /ter-ə-mī'sin/ *n* oxytetracycline, an antibiotic effective against a wide range of bacteria and some Rickettsiae viruses, and protozoan parasites. [L *terra* the earth, and Gr *mykēs* fungus]

Terran /ter'ən/ *n* a term sometimes used in science fiction for an inhabitant of the planet earth (also *adj*). [L *terra* earth]

terrane /ter'ān/ (*geol*) *n* a rock formation, or series of connected formations (also **terrain**). [See **terrain**[1]]

terra nullius see under **terra**.

terrapin /ter'ə-pin/ *n* any of various webfooted pond or river turtles of the family Emydidae (also called **water tortoise**); (**Terrapin**®) a temporary prefabricated building. [Of Algonquian origin]

terraqueous, terrarium, terra rossa see under **terra**.

---

terras see **trass**.

terra sigillata see under **terra**.

terrazzo /te-rat'sō, -raz'ō/ n (pl **terrazz'os**) a mosaic covering (sometimes precast) for concrete floors, consisting of marble or other chips set in cement and then polished (also called **Venetian mosaic**). [Ital, terrace, balcony]

terreen an older spelling of **tureen**.

terrella /ter-el'ə/ n a magnetic model of the earth. [A Mod dimin of L *terra* the earth]

terremotive /ter-i-mō'tiv/ adj seismic. [L *terrae motus* earthquake]

terrene /ti-rēn'/ or /ter'ēn/ adj of the earth; earthly, worldly; mundane; earthy; terrestrial. ◆ n the world; a region, terrain. [L *terrēnus*, from *terra* the earth]
■ **terrene'ly** adv.

terreplein /tār'plān, ter-plē'/ (fortif) n orig the talus on the inner side of a rampart; the top of a rampart, or space behind the parapet, where guns are mounted. [Fr, from L *terra* earth, and *plēnus* full]

terrestrial /tə-, te-, ti-res'tri-əl/ adj of, or existing on, the earth; earthly, worldly; living or growing on land or on the ground (*esp* as opposed to the sea or air); representing the earth; (of a planet) like the earth in size or form; signifying signals sent by a land transmitter as distinct from a satellite (*TV*). ◆ n an inhabitant of the earth; a man of the world, layman (*Shakesp*). [L *terrestris*, from *terra* the earth]
■ **terres'trially** adv.
❑ **terrestrial magnetism** n the magnetic properties exhibited within, on and outside the earth's surface. **terrestrial poles** n pl (*geol*) the two points diametrically opposite on the earth's surface (cf **magnetic poles**). **terrestrial radiation** n (*meteorol*) the loss of the earth's heat by radiation to the sky, resulting in dew and hoarfrost. **terrestrial telescope** n a telescope giving an erect image, used for viewing over distances on the earth's surface rather than astronomically.

terret or **territ** /ter'it/, also **torret** /tor'/ or **turret** /tur'/ n a swivel-ring; a ring for fastening a chain to, eg on a dog's collar; either of the two rings or loops on a harness through which driving reins pass. [OFr *toret*, dimin of *tor, tour* a round]

terre verte /ter vert'/ n green earth (see under **green¹**). [Fr]

terrible /ter'i-bl/ adj inspiring fear, terror or awe; awful; dreadful; very bad; pronounced, extreme, notable (*inf*). ◆ n a terrible thing. [L *terribilis*, from *terrēre* to frighten]
■ **terribil'ity** n (*rare*). **terr'ibleness** n. **terr'ibly** adv in a terrible manner; very (*inf*).

terricolous /te-rik'ə-ləs/ adj living in or on the soil. [L *terricola* a dweller upon earth, from *terra* earth, and *colere* to inhabit]
■ **terr'icole** /-i-kōl/ n a land animal or plant; a burrower. ◆ adj living on land; burrowing.

terrier¹ /ter'i-ər/ n a small dog of various breeds, orig one that would follow burrowing animals underground; a keen, eager person; (*punningly*) a territorial soldier; a person who hunts after criminals. [OFr, (*chien*) *terrier* earth (dog), from LL *terrārius* (adj), from *terra* land]

terrier² /ter'i-ər/ (*hist*) n a register or roll of a landed estate; an inventory; a rent-roll. [OFr, from LL *terrārius* (adj), from *terra* land]

terrific /tə-rif'ik/ adj prodigious, very great, large or intense (*inf*); marvellous, excellent (*inf*); very good, enjoyable, attractive, etc (*inf*); frightening, terrifying; dreadful. [L *terrificus* frightful]
■ **terrif'ically** adv.

terrify /ter'i-fī/ vt (**terr'ifying; terr'ified**) to cause terror in; to frighten badly. [L *terrificāre*, from *terrēre* to terrify, and *facere* to make]
■ **terr'ifier** n. **terr'ifying** adj. **terr'ifyingly** adv.

terrigenous /te-rij'i-nəs/ adj earthborn; derived from the land. [L *terrigenus*, from *terra* earth, and *gignere* to produce]
❑ **terrigenous sediments** n pl sediment derived from the erosion of land deposited either on land or in the sea.

terrine /tə-rēn'/ n a casserole, etc, orig of earthenware; a dish of meat or fish, etc, cooked in it, *esp* pâté; an earthenware jar sold containing a table delicacy; a tureen. [Fr; see **tureen**]

territ see **terret**.

territory /ter'ə- or ter'i-tə-ri, -tri/ n possessions in land; the whole, or a portion, of the land belonging to a state; (also with *cap*) part of a confederation with an organized government but not yet admitted to statehood; (also with *cap*) a dependency; a region; a jurisdiction; a field of activity; domain; an area in which an agent, commercial traveller, etc works; an area that an animal or bird treats as its own; the area defended by a team or player (*sport*). [L *territōrium*, domain of a town, perh not orig connected with *terra*]
■ **territo'rial** adj constituting, concerned with or relating to territory; limited or restricted to a particular territory; (*esp* of an animal, bird, etc) inclined to establish its own stretch of territory and defend it. ◆ n a soldier in the Territorial Army. **territo'rialism** n a social system in which the landowning class is dominant; organization on a territorial

basis; the theory of church government according to which the civil power is supreme over the church; territoriality. **territō'rialist** n. **territorial'ity** n territorial status; an animal's or bird's tendency to establish and defend its own territory. **territorializā'tion** or **-s-** n. **territo'rialize** or **-ise** vt to make a territory of; to make territorial; to put on a territorial basis; to enlarge (a country) by adding more territory. **territo'rially** adv. **terr'itoried** adj having territory.
❑ **Territorial Army** n the name (1920–67, and from 1979) of the voluntary military force organized on a territorial basis, founded in 1908 as the **Territorial Force**, and known (1967–79) as the **Territorial and Army Volunteer Reserve**. **territorial imperative** n the need, in vertebrate animals, to occupy and defend a particular area. **territorial waters** n pl that part of the sea reckoned as part of the adjacent state, *orig* within a three-mile limit.

terroir /ter-wär'/ (*Fr*) n the distinctive quality imparted to a wine by the climate and soil in which its grapes are grown.

terror /ter'ər/ n extreme fear; a time of, or government by, terrorism; a person or thing causing extreme fear or dread; a mischievous or troublesome person (*esp* a child), a rogue (*inf*). [L *terror*, from *terrēre* to frighten]
■ **terr'orful** adj. **terr'orism** n an organized system of violence and intimidation, *esp* for political ends; the state of fear and submission caused by this. **terr'orist** n and adj. **terrorist'ic** adj. **terrorizā'tion** or **-s-** n. **terr'orize** or **-ise** vt to terrify; to subject to terrorism. **terr'orizer** or **-s-** n. **terr'orless** adj.
❑ **terror novel** n a novel full of supernatural horrors. **terr'or-stricken** or **terr'or-struck** adj smitten with terror.
■ **King of Terrors** death. **Reign of Terror** or **the Terror** the period (April 1793 to July 1794) of repression and persecution in the French Revolution when thousands went to the guillotine.

terry /ter'i/ n a pile fabric with uncut looped pile, used *esp* for towelling; one of the loops; a baby's towelling nappy. ◆ adj made of terry. [Origin unknown]

tersanctus /tûr-sangk'təs or tûr-sang'təs/ n the Sanctus (qv). [L *ter* thrice, and **Sanctus**]

terse /tûrs/ adj compact, concise, succinct; crisply brief; abrupt, brusque; smooth, clean-cut (*obs*). [L *tersus*, pap of *tergēre, tersum* to rub clean]
■ **terse'ly** adv. **terse'ness** n. **tersion** /tûr'shən/ n wiping.

tertia see **tercio**.

tertial /tûr'sh(ə)l/ adj (*ornithol*) of or designating the third rank among flight-feathers of a wing. ◆ n a tertiary flight-feather. [L *tertiālis, tertiānus, tertiārius*, from *tertius* third]
■ **ter'tian** /-shən/ adj occurring every other day (ie on the *third* day, reckoning both first and last days). ◆ n a fever with paroxysms every other day. **ter'tiary** /-shər-i/ adj of the third degree, order or formation; tertial (*ornithol*); (with *cap*) of or belonging to the earlier period of the Cenozoic era, between 65 and 1.8 million years ago (*geol*); ranking above secondary (*esp* of education); (of an industry) providing services rather than production or extraction. ◆ n the Tertiary period; (without *cap*) a member of a third order of a monastic order, a layman who may continue to live an ordinary life in the world; a tertiary feather; that which is tertiary.
❑ **tertiary amines** n pl (*chem*) amines in which the nitrogen atom is attached to three groups. **tertiary college** n a college, *esp* one with vocational courses, for the teaching of sixth-form-level students. **tertiary colours** n pl colours resulting from the mixing of two secondary colours, eg olive produced by mixing orange and green.

tertium quid /tûr'sh(i-)əm kwid or ter'ti-ūm/ (*L*) a third unknown thing related to two specific known things; something intermediate between opposites; the third person in the eternal triangle. [Literally, some third thing]

tertius /tûr'shyəs, -shəs, ter'ti-ūs/ (*L*) adj and n third (person).
❑ **tertius gaudens** /gö'denz, gow'dens/ or **gaudet** /gö'det, gow'/ n the third person (who) takes advantage from a dispute between others.

terts /tûrts/ n sing tetrachlor(o)ethylene.

tervalent /tûr-vā'lənt or tûr'və-lənt/ (*chem*) adj having a valency of three, trivalent. [L *ter* thrice, and **-valent**]

Terylene® /ter'i-lēn/ n a synthetic fabric of polyester fibres, light, strong and crease-resistant.

terza rima /ter'tsə rē'mə/ n (pl **terze rime** /ter'tsä rē'mä/) an Italian verse form in triplets, in which the middle line of each triplet rhymes with the first and third lines of the next with an odd line to end off the canto. [Ital, third rhyme]

terzetta /ter-tset'ə/ n a tercet (qv). [Ital]
■ **terzett'o** n (pl **terzett'os** or **terzett'i** /-ē/) a trio.

TES abbrev: Times Educational Supplement.

teschenite /tesh'ə-nīt/ n a coarse-grained basic igneous rock composed essentially of plagioclase and augite, *usu* with much analcime. [Found near *Teschen* in Silesia]

TESL (often /tes'əl/) *abbrev*: Teaching (of) English as a Second Language.

tesla /tes'lə/ n a derived SI unit, the unit of magnetic flux density (symbol **T**), equal to one weber per square metre. [N *Tesla* (1856–1943), Croatian-born US inventor]
  ❑ **tesla coil** n (*elec eng*) a simple source of high voltage oscillations for rough testing of vacuums and gas (by discharge colour) in vacuum systems.

TESOL /tē'sol/ *abbrev*: Teaching (of) English to Speakers of Other Languages.

TESSA /tes'ə/ *abbrev*: (from 1991 to 1999) Tax-Exempt Special Savings Account.

tessara- or **tessera-** /tes-ə-rə-/ *combining form* denoting four, as in **tess'araglot**, in four languages. [Gr *tessares* four]
  ■ **tess'eract** n (Gr *aktis* ray) a figure of a cube within a cube.

tessella /te-sel'ə/ n (*pl* **tessell'ae** /-ē, -ī/) a little tessera. [L *tessella*, dimin of *tessera*; see ety for **tessera**]
  ■ **tess'ellar** *adj.* **tessellate** /tes'i-lāt/ *vt* to pave with tesserae; to mark like a mosaic. ◆ *vi* (of a number of identical shapes) to fit together exactly, leaving no spaces. ◆ *adj* marked out in little squarish areas. **tess'ellated** *adj.* **tessella'tion** n the act of tessellating; the form of tessellated work; an example of tessellated work.

tessera /tes'ə-rə/ n (*pl* **tess'erae** /-ē, -ī/) one of the small pieces of which a mosaic is made; a token or ticket made *usu* of wood or bone (*ancient hist*); a password. See also **tessara-**. [L *tessera* a die, small cube, from Gr *tessares* four]
  ■ **tess'eral** *adj* of tesserae; cubic, isometric (*crystallog*).

tesseract see under **tessara-**.

tessitura /tes-i-too'rə/ n the ordinary range of pitch of a voice or a piece of vocal music. [Ital, texture]

Test. *abbrev*: Testament.

test¹ /test/ n any critical trial; a means of trial, a standard for trial, judgement or comparison; a written examination, *esp* a short one; anything used to distinguish or detect substances, a reagent (*chem*); a pot or cupel in which metals are tried and refined; any trial; a trial of fitness for admission, eg to an examination; an oath or other evidence of religious belief required as a condition of office or exercise of rights; a test match. ◆ *vt* to put to proof; to try or examine critically; to examine using a reagent (*chem*); to assay and refine (metal). ◆ *vi* to achieve a stated result in a test. [Orig a pot for treating metals, from OFr *test*, from L *testum* an earthen pot, a potsherd, related to *testa* a shell]
  ■ **testabil'ity** n. **test'able** *adj.* **testee'** n a person who undergoes a test. **test'er** n a person who tests or thing used for testing. **test'ing** n the act of subjecting to a test. ◆ *adj* mentally taxing; troublesome, difficult; of or for a test.
  ❑ **Test Acts** n pl acts meant to secure that none but members of the established religion shall hold office; *esp* an English act of 1673 designed to exclude Roman Catholics from public office. **test ban** n the banning (by mutual agreement between nations (**test-ban treaty**)) of the testing of any or all nuclear weapons. **test bed** n an iron framework on which a machine is placed for testing; anything with a similar purpose (also *fig*). **test card** see **test pattern** below. **test case** n a law case that acts as a precedent and may settle similar questions about the same point of law in the future. **test drive** n a trial drive of a motor vehicle, *usu* with a view to purchasing the vehicle if it is satisfactory; extended to a trial of any piece of equipment or machinery (*inf*). **test'-drive** *vt.* **test flight** n a trial flight of a new aeroplane. **test'-fly** *vt.* **test'-market** *vt* to offer (a product) for sale in order to test demand, popularity, etc. **test match** n an international sports match (*esp* in cricket), *usu* forming part of a series. **test paper** n a bibulous paper saturated with some substance that changes colour when exposed to certain chemicals; a paper or questions to test fitness for a more serious examination. **test pattern, card** or **chart** n (*image technol*) a transmitted chart with lines and details to indicate particular characteristics of a transmission system, used in TV for general testing purposes. **test pilot** n a pilot whose work is testing new aircraft by flying them. **test tube** n a glass cylinder closed at one end, used in chemistry, bacteriology, etc. **test-tube baby** n *esp* formerly, a child born as the result of artificial insemination, now *usu* one born from an ovum implanted in the womb after fertilization in a laboratory.

test² /test/ (*zool* and *bot*) a testa (qv). [See ety for **testa**]

test³ /test/ *vt* to attest legally and date; to authenticate by a testing clause. [L *testārī* to testify, witness, pap (neuter) *testātum*; partly through OFr *tester* to bequeath, partly aphetic for **attest**]
  ■ **test'acy** /-ə-si/ n the state of being testate. **test'āte** *adj* having made and left a valid will. ◆ n a person who dies testate. **testā'tion** n a

witnessing; a giving by will. **testā'tor**, *fem* **testā'trix** n a person who leaves a valid will at death. **testā'tum** n one of the clauses of an English deed, enumerating the operative words of transfer, statement of consideration, money, etc.
  ❑ **testing clause** n (in a Scots deed) the last clause which recounts when and where the parties signed the deed, before what witnesses, by whose hand it was written, etc.

testa /tes'tə/ n (*pl* **tes'tae** /-tē/) a hard shell (*zool*); a seed-coat, derived from the ovule integuments (*bot*). [L *testa* a shell, related to *testum* an earthen pot, a potsherd]
  ■ **testaceous** /-ā'shəs/ *adj* of or having a hard shell; brick-red.

testament /tes'tə-mənt/ n that which testifies, or in which an attestation is made; the solemn declaration in writing of one's will; a will; a writing or decree appointing an executor, by the testator (**tes'tament-testament'ar**) or by a court (**tes'tament-dā'tive**) (*Scots law*); (with *cap*) either of the main two divisions (**Old Testament** and **New Testament**) of the Bible (a transl of Gr *diathēkē* disposition, compact, covenant); a covenant between God and man, either that with Moses (as expressed in the *Old Testament*), or that instituted by Christ (as expressed in the *New Testament*); (with *cap*) a copy of the New Testament. [L *testāmentum*]
  ■ **testament'al, testament'ar** (*Scots law*) or **testamen'tary** *adj* relating to a testament or will; bequeathed or done by will. **testamen'tarily** *adv*.

testamur /te-stā'mür/ n a certificate of having passed an examination. [L *testāmur*, 1st pers pl of *testārī* to testify, witness]

testate, etc see under **test³**.

teste /tes'ti, -te/ (L) (so-and-so being) witness, on the testimony of (so-and-so). [Ablative of *testis* witness, in ablative absolute construction]

testee see under **test¹**.

tester¹ /tes'tər/ n a canopy or its support, or both, *esp* over a bed. [OFr *testre*, the vertical part of a bed behind the head, and *testiere*, a head-covering, from *teste* (Fr *tête*) head, from L *testa* an earthen pot, the skull]

tester² /tes'tər/ or **testern** /tes'tərn/ (*archaic*) n a sixpence. [See **teston**]
  ■ **tes'tern** *vt* (*Shakesp*) to present or reward with a sixpence.

tester³ see under **test¹**.

testes see **testis**.

Testicardines /tes-ti-kär'di-nēz/ n pl a class of brachiopods with hinged shell and arm skeleton. [L *testa* shell, and *cardo, -inis* hinge]

testicle /tes'ti-kl/ n a male reproductive gland producing spermatozoa and testosterone, *usu* one of a pair enclosed in the scrotum of mammals. [L *testiculus*, dimin of *testis* witness (eg of virility), testicle]
  ■ **testic'ūlar** *adj* of or like a testicle. **testic'ūlate** /-lət/ or **testic'ūlated** *adj* like a testicle, egg in shape.

testify /tes'ti-fī/ *vi* (**tes'tifying**; **tes'tified**) to bear witness; to make a solemn declaration; to protest or declare a charge (with *against*); to give evidence (eg in a court of law). ◆ *vt* to bear witness to; to be evidence of; to affirm or declare solemnly or on oath; to proclaim, declare. [L *testificārī*, from *testis* a witness, and *facere* to make]
  ■ **testif'icate** n (*Scots law*) a solemn written assertion. **testifica'tion** n the act of testifying or of bearing witness. **testif'icātor** n. **testif'icatory** *adj.* **tes'tified** *adj.* **tes'tifier** n.

testimony /tes'ti-mə-ni/ n evidence; evidence given by a witness, *esp* orally, under oath (*law*); declaration to prove some fact; proof; the two tables of the law on which the Ten Commandments are inscribed (*Bible*); the Ark of the Covenant containing these (*Bible*); divine law; a solemn protestation. ◆ *vt* (*Shakesp*) to test, prove or judge by evidence. [L *testimōnium*, from *testārī* to witness]
  ■ **testi'mōnial** *adj* of, affording or of the nature of testimony. ◆ n a written attestation; a writing or certificate bearing testimony to a person's character or abilities or to a product's quality; a gift or memorial as a token of respect, *esp* one presented or taking place in public; (in full **testimonial match**) a sports match played in order to raise money for a player nearing retirement. **testimō'nialize** or **-ise** *vt* to present with a testimonial.

testis /tes'tis/ n (*pl* **tes'tes** /-tēz/) (a more formal word for) a testicle; a rounded body like it. [L, a witness (eg of virility), hence a testicle]

teston /tes'tən/ n a name for various silver coins, *orig* bearing a king's or duke's head; a Henry VIII shilling; later, a sixpence. [Obs Fr *teston*, Port *testão*, Ital *testone*, from Ital *testa* head]
  ■ **testoon'** n a Portuguese or Italian teston.

testosterone /te-stos'tə-rōn/ n the chief male sex hormone, a steroid secreted by the testes. [*testo-* (combining form for *testis*), ster*ol*, and chem sfx *-one*]

testrill or **testril** /tes'tril/ (*obs*) n a sixpence. [**tester²**]

testudo /te-stū'dō/ n (*pl* **testū'dōs** or **testū'dinēs**) a wheeled shelter used by Roman soldiers under attack from above; a similar shelter made by joining shields; a vaulted roof; an ancient lyre, said to have been first made of a tortoiseshell; (with *cap*) the genus comprising the typical land tortoises. [L *testūdō*, *-inis* tortoise]

■ **testū'dinal**, **testū'dinary** or **testūdin'eous** *adj* like a tortoise, tortoiseshell, or a testudo.

testy /tes'ti/ *adj* (**tes'tier**; **tes'tiest**) irritable; (of remarks, etc) showing touchiness or irritability. [OFr *testif* headstrong, from *teste* (Fr *tête*) head, from L *testa* pot]

■ **tes'tily** *adv*. **tes'tiness** *n*.

Tet /tet/ *n* the Vietnamese lunar new year festival. [Viet]

tetanus /tet'ə-nəs/ *n* a disease due to a bacillus, marked by painful tonic spasms of the muscles of the jaw and other parts; the state of prolonged contraction of a muscle under quickly repeated stimuli. [L, from Gr *tetanos*, from *teinein* to stretch]

■ **tet'anal** *adj*. **tetanic** /ti-tan'ik/ *adj* of, occurring in or causing tetanus or the spasms characteristic of tetanus. ◆ *n* a tetanus-causing agent. **tetan'ically** *adv*. **tetanīza'tion** or **-s-** *n*. **tet'anize** or **-ise** *vt* to produce tetanus or tetanic spasms in. **tet'anoid** *adj*. **tet'any** *n* heightened excitability of the motor nerves resulting in painful muscular cramps, associated with lower than normal levels of calcium in the blood.

tetartohedral /ti-tär-tō-hē'drəl/ (*crystallog*) *adj* having one-fourth the number of faces required for full symmetry. [Gr *tetartos* fourth, and *hedrā* seat]

tetchy or **techy** /tech'i/ *adj* (**tetch'ier** or **tech'ier**; **tetch'iest** or **tech'iest**) irritable. [Perh from obs *tecche*, *tetch*, *tache* blemish, defect, from OFr *tache* spot]

■ **tetch'ily** or **tech'ily** *adv*. **tetch'iness** or **tech'iness** *n*.

tête[1] /tet/ (Fr) *n* a head.

□ **tête-à-tête** /-*a*-tet' or *tāt-a-tāt'*/ *n* (*pl* **tête-à-têtes**, **têtes-à-têtes**) a private confidential interview; an S-shaped sofa for two, bringing sitters face to face. ◆ *adj* confidential, secret. ◆ *adv* in private conversation; face to face. **tête-bêche** /-besh'/ *adv* (Fr *bêche*, from obs *béchevet* double-headed) head to tail; (of a postage stamp) printed in an inverted position in relation to its neighbour. **tête-de-pont** /-*d*ə-*p*ɔ̃'/ *n* bridgehead. **tête folle** /fol'/ *n* (Fr *folle* fem of *fou* mad) a scatterbrain.

tête[2] /tet/ (*obs*) *n* an elaborately dressed head of hair; a headdress. [Fr]

teth /tāt/ *n* the ninth letter of the Hebrew alphabet. [Heb]

tether /tedh'ər/ *n* a rope or chain for confining an animal within certain limits; the extent of one's knowledge, endurance, authority, etc. ◆ *vt* to confine with a tether; to restrain within certain limits. [Appar ON *tjōthr*]

■ **at the end of one's tether** desperate, having no further strength, patience, resources, etc.

Tethys /tē'this, teth'is/ *n* a sea nymph, wife of Oceanus; a sea that extended in Mesozoic times from Mexico across the middle Atlantic and the Mediterranean into the centre of Asia (*geol*); the third natural satellite of Saturn. [Gr *Tēthys*]

TETRA /tet'rə/ *abbrev* : *T*errestrial *T*runked *R*adio, a European standard for mobile communications used by the emergency services.

tetra- or **tetr-** /tet-r(ə)-, ti-tr(a)-/ *combining form* denoting four. [Gr *tetra-*, combining form of *tettares*, *tessares* four]

■ **tetraba'sic** *adj* (*chem*) capable of reacting with four equivalents of an acid; (of acids) having four replaceable hydrogen atoms. **tetrabasicity** /tet-rə-bā-sis'i-ti/ *n*. **Tetrabranchia** or **Tetrabranchiata** /-brang'ki-ə, -ki-ā'tə/ *n pl* (Gr *branchia* gills) a former order of the nautilus subclass of cephalopods, with four gills. **tetrabranch'iate** *adj* four-gilled. ◆ *n* any mollusc belonging to the Tetrabranchia. **tetrachlo'ride** *n* any compound with four chlorine atoms per molecule. **tetrachloroeth'ylene** or **tetrachloreth'ylene** *n* $C_2H_2Cl_4$, a liquid used in dry-cleaning, as a solvent, etc (also called **tetrachloreth'ane**). **tetrachlorōme'thane** *n* carbon tetrachloride. **tet'rachord** /-körd/ *n* (Gr *chordē* string) a four-stringed instrument; a series of four sounds, forming a scale of two tones and a half. **tetrachord'al** *adj*. **tetrachot'omous** *adj*. **tetrachotomy** /-kot'ə-mi/ *n* (Gr *tetracha* in four parts, and *-tomia* a cutting) division in fours. **tetrac'id** *adj* having four replaceable hydrogen atoms; capable of replacing four hydrogen atoms of an acid. **tetract** /tet'rakt/ *adj* (Gr *aktīs*, *-īnos* ray) four-rayed. ◆ *n* a four-rayed sponge spicule. **tetract'inal** (or */-ī'nəl/*) or **tetrac'tine** *adj*. **Tetractinell'ida** *n pl* an order of sponges in which some of the spicules are four-rayed. **tetracyclic** /-sī'klik/ *adj* (Gr *kyklos* ring, wheel) of, in or with four whorls or rings; (of a compound) having four fused hydrocarbon rings in its molecular structure (*chem*). **tetracy'cline** *n* a crystalline antibiotic used to treat a wide range of infections, *esp* of the respiratory and urinary tracts. **tetrad** /tet'rad/ *n* a group of four; an atom, radical or element having a combining power of four (*chem*). **tet'rad** or **tetrad'ic** *adj*. **tetradactyl** /-dak'til/ *adj* (Gr *daktylos* digit; *zool*) four-fingered; four-toed. ◆ *n* a four-toed animal. **tetradac'tylous** *adj* having four fingers or toes. **tetradac'tyly** *n* the condition of being

tetradactylous. **tet'radite** *n* a person who attaches mystic properties to the number four; a believer in a godhead of four persons. **tet'radrachm** /-dram/ *n* an ancient Greek coin worth four drachmas. **tetradymite** /ti-trad'i-mīt/ *n* (Gr *tetradymos* fourfold) a grey metallic mineral, an ore of tellurium, Bi_2Te_2S. **Tetradynamia** /-di-nā'mi-ə/ *n pl* (in Linnaeus's system) a class corresponding to the Cruciferae. **tetradynamous** /-din'ə-məs/ *adj* (Gr *dynamis* power) having four long stamens in pairs and two short, as in the Cruciferae. **tetraethyl** /-ēth'īl, -e'thil/ *adj* having four ethyl groups, as **tetraethyl lead** or **lead tetraethyl**, $Pb(C_2H_5)_4$, a compound formerly added to petrol as an antiknock agent. **tetrafluoroeth'ylene** *n* a dense colourless gas that is polymerized to make polytetrafluoroethylene. **tet'ragon** /-gon, -gon/ *n* (see **-gon**) a plane figure of four angles and four sides. **tetragonal** /-rag'ə-nəl/ *adj* having the form of a tetragon; referable to three axes at right angles, two of them equal (*crystallog*). **tetrag'onally** *adv*. **tetrag'onous** (*bot*) *adj* with four angles and convex faces. **tet'ragram** /-gram/ *n* (Gr *gramma* a letter) a word or inscription of four letters; (also with *cap*) the tetragrammaton; a (complete) quadrilateral (*geom*). **tetragramm'aton** *n* (also with *cap*) vocalized as the name YaHWeH, JeHoVaH, etc, as written with four Hebrew letters, regarded as a mystic symbol; any other sacred word of four letters, as the Latin *Deus*. **Tetragynia** /-jin'i-ə/ *n pl* (see **gyn-**) (in the Linnaean system) an order of plants (in various classes) with four pistils. **tetragyn'ian** or **tetragynous** /-raj'i-nəs/ *adj*. **tetrahē'dral** *adj* of, relating to, like or in the form of a tetrahedron. **tetrahē'drally** *adv*. **tetrahē'drite** *n* grey copper ore, sulphide of copper and antimony often occurring in tetrahedral crystals. **tetrahedron** /-hē'drən/ *n* (*pl* **tetrahē'drons** or **tetrahē'dra** /-drə/) (Gr *hedrā* a base) a solid figure or body with four plane faces; (in full, **regular tetrahedron**) a tetrahedron whose surfaces are equilateral triangles. **tetrahydrocann'abinol** *n* the main intoxicant substance in marijuana. **tetrahydrofō'late** *n* folic acid, vitamin B₇. **tetrahydrogestrinone** /-jest'ri-nōn/ *n* a synthetic steroid, illegally used as a performance-enhancing drug by some athletes (*abbrev* **THG**). **tetrakishexahē'dron** *n* (Gr *tetrakis* four times) a figure formed by erecting equal pyramids on all the faces of a cube. **tetral'ogy** *n* (Gr *tetralogiā*) (in ancient Greece) a group of four dramas, *usu* three tragic and one satyric; any series of four related dramatic or operatic works or stories. **tetram'eral** *adj* four-parted. **tetram'erism** *n* division into four parts. **tetram'erous** *adj* (Gr *meros* part) having four parts, or parts in fours. **tetrameter** /ti-tram'i-tər/ *n* (Gr *metron* measure) a line of a verse of four measures (dipodies or feet). **Tet'ramorph** *n* a pictorial representation of the symbolic attributes of the four evangelists combined in a single figure. **tetramor'phic** *adj* (see **morphic**) having four forms. **Tetran'dria** *n pl* (in Linnaeus's classification) a class of plants with four stamens. **tetran'drian** *adj*. **tetran'drous** *adj* (Gr *anēr*, *andros* man; in the sense of male) having four stamens. **tetrapla** /tet'rə-plə/ *n* (Gr neuter *pl* of *tetraploos* fourfold) an edition of four parallel texts, *esp* Origen's of the Old Testament. **tetraplē'gia** *n* quadriplegia. **tetraplē'gic** *adj*. **tetraploid** /tet'rə-ploid/ *adj* (Gr *tetraploos* fourfold, and *eidos* form) of cells, nuclei or organisms, having four times the haploid (twice the normal) number of chromosomes. ◆ *n* a tetraploid organism, cell or nucleus. **tet'raploidy** *n* the condition of being tetraploid. **tet'rapod** /-pod/ *n* (Gr *tetrapous* four-footed, from *pous*, *podos* foot) a four-footed animal; any vertebrate above the fishes; a reinforced-concrete block laid against a sea wall to break the force of the waves; a structure with four supporting arms at 120° to each other radiating from a central point, three arms supporting the structure at any one time, with the fourth vertical. ◆ *adj* (of an animal or structure) having four feet. **tetrapod'ic** *adj* (of verse) having four metrical feet. **tetrapodous** /-trap'/ *adj*. **tetrap'ody** *n* a group of four metrical feet. **tetrapolis** /ti-trap'o-lis/ *n* (Gr *polis* a city) a group of four towns. **tetrapol'itan** *adj* (**Tetrapolitan Confession** the Confession which the four cities of Strasburg, Constance, Memmingen and Lindau presented to the Diet of Augsburg (11 July 1530), and, properly speaking, the first Confession of the Reformed Church). **tetrap'teran** /-rən/ or **tetrap'terous** *adj* (see **-pteran**, **-pterous** under **ptero-**) four-winged. **tetraptote** /tet'rap-tōt/ *n* (Gr *ptōsis* a case) a noun with only four cases. **tetrarch** /tet'rärk or tē'trärk/ *n* (Gr *archē* rule, origin; *hist*) under the Romans, the ruler of the fourth part of a province; a subordinate prince; the commander of a subdivision of a Greek phalanx; one of four joint rulers. ◆ *adj* (*bot*; also **tetrarch'ical**) having four xylem strands. **tetrarch'ic** *adj*. **tet'rarchy** *n* the office, rank, period of office or jurisdiction of a tetrarch; the fourth part of a province (also **tet'rarchate**); the condition of being tetrarch (*bot*). **tetrasemic** /-sē'mik/ *adj* (Gr *sēma* a sign; *prosody*) equivalent to four short syllables, as is a dactyl, anapaest or spondee. **tetrasporangium** /-spə-ran'ji-əm/ *n* the sporangium in which tetraspores are formed. **tet'raspore** /-spōr, -spör/ *n* (Gr *sporā* seed) an asexual spore formed in groups of four in red seaweeds. **tetrasporic** /-spor'ik/ or **tetrasporous** /ti-tras'pə-rəs or tet-rə-spō'rəs, -spö'/ *adj*. **tet'rastich** /-stik/ *n* (Gr *stichos* a row) a stanza or set of four lines. **tetrastichal** /ti-tras'ti-kl/ or **tetrastichic** /tet-rə-stik'ik/ *adj* of (the nature of) tetrastichs. **tetras'tichous** *adj* (*bot*) in four rows. **tet'rastyle** /-stīl/ *n* (Gr *stȳlos* a column) a building or portico with four columns supporting a ceiling in front; a group of four pillars. ◆ *adj* having four columns. **tetrasyllabic** /-ab'ik/ or **tetrasyllab'ical** *adj*. **tetrasyllable** /-sil'ə-bl/ *n* a word of four syllables. **tet'ratheism** /-thē-izm/ *n* (Gr *theos* god) the belief in four elements in the Godhead, ie the three persons of the Trinity and a divine essence out of which each of these originates. **tetrathlon** /te-trath'lən/ *n* (Gr *athlon* contest) a four-event sporting contest. **tetratom'ic** *adj* having or composed of four atoms to a molecule. **tetravalent** /ti-trav'ə-lənt, tet-rə-vā'lənt/ *n* quadrivalent. **tetraxon** /ti-trak'son/ *n* (Gr *axōn, -onos* an axis) a sponge spicule with four axes. **tetrode** /tet'rōd/ *n* (Gr *hodos* a way) a thermionic valve with four electrodes. **tetrox'ide** *n* an oxide with four atoms of oxygen in the molecule. **tetryl** /tet'ril/ *n* a yellow crystalline explosive compound used as a detonator.

tetra¹ /tet'rə/ *n* any of various species of tropical freshwater fish of the family Characidae. [Short form of *Tetragonopterus*, former name of the genus]

tetra² /tet'rə/ *n* a plant mentioned by Spenser (*The Faerie Queene* II.7.52.4).

tetri /tet'rē/ *n* (*pl* **tet'ri**) a monetary unit in Georgia, $\frac{1}{100}$ of a lari.

tetrodotoxin /tet-rə-dō-tok'sin/ or **tetrotoxin** /tet-rō-tok'sin/ *n* a deadly nerve poison ($C_{11}H_{17}N_3O_3$) found in a species of Japanese puffer fish. [New L *Tetrodon* (from Gr *tetra-* four-, and *odous, odontos* tooth) a genus of puffer fish, and **toxin**]

tetronal /tet'rə-nəl/ *n* a hypnotic and sedative drug, no longer used because of its high toxicity.

tetroxide, tetryl see under **tetra-**.

tetter /tet'ər/ *n* a skin eruption, eg eczema. ◆ *vt* to affect with a tetter. [OE *teter*]
■ **tett'erous** *adj*.

tettix /tet'iks/ *n* a cicada; a cicada-shaped ornament for the hair (*ancient Greece*). [Gr]

teuch or **teugh** /tūhh/ *adj* a Scots form of **tough**.

teuchat (*Scot*) see under **tewit**.

teuchter /tūhh'tər/ (*Scot; derog*) *n* a term originally used by Lowland Scots for a Highlander, *esp* a Gaelic-speaker; any unsophisticated country person. [Origin uncertain]

Teucrian /tū'kri-ən/ *n* and *adj* (a) Trojan. [Gr *Teukros* Teucer, first king of Troy]

Teut. *abbrev* : Teutonic.

Teuton /tū'tən/ or *-ton/ n* any speaker of a Germanic language; a member of an ancient Germanic tribe from Jutland (*hist*); (*popularly*) a German. ◆ *adj* Teutonic. [L *Teutonēs*, from the root of OE *thēod* people, nation; cf **Dutch**, Ger *deutsch*]
■ **Teutonic** /-ton'ik/ *adj* Germanic, ie of the linguistic family that includes English, German, Dutch and the Scandinavian languages; of the Teutons; (*popularly*) German in any sense. ◆ *n* the parent language of the Teutons, primitive Germanic. **Teuton'ically** *adv*. **Teuton'icism** /-i-sizm/ or **Teu'tonism** *n* a Germanism; belief in or enthusiasm for the Teutons; the study of Germanic philology and culture. **Teu'tonist** *n*. **Teutonīzā'tion** or **-s-** *n*. **Teu'tonize** or **-ise** *vt* and *vi* to make or become Teutonic, Germanic or German.
□ **Teutonic Knights** *n pl* a military-religious order founded in 1191–98 to tend wounded Christians and to fight unbelievers, active first (during the Third Crusade) in Palestine and later against the Prussians and Lithuanians.

Tevet see **Tebeth**.

tew /tū/ (*obs* or *dialect*) *vt* to work up; to taw. ◆ *vi* to toil, hustle. ◆ *n* worry; excitement. [Cf **taw¹**]

tewart same as **tuart**.

tewel /tū'əl/ *n* the rectum or anus, *esp* of a horse (*dialect*); a flue (*obs*); a tuyère (*dialect*). [OFr *tuel* (Fr *tuyau*) tube]

tewit /tē'wit/ or **tewhit** /tē'hwit, -wit/ (*Scot* **teuchat** /tūhh'ət/) (*dialect*) *n* a lapwing. [Imit]

Tex. *abbrev* : Texas (US state).

Texas /tek'səs/ *n* a state of the USA (*abbrev* **TX** or **Tex.**); (*without cap*) an upper structure on a river-steamer.
■ **Tex'an** *n* and *adj* (a native or inhabitant) of Texas.
□ **Texas fever** *n* a protozoal disease of cattle transmitted by ticks. **Texas hold 'em** *n* a variety of the game of poker in which players attempt to form the best hand from two personal cards and five community cards (short form **hold 'em**). **Texas Rangers** *n pl* Texas state police, formed in the 19c. **Texas scramble** *n* a golf match in which all of the players hit each shot from the same place, the best ball determining the location of the next shot. **Texas tower** *n* a radar tower built offshore as part of an early warning system. **Texas wedge** *n* (*golf sl*) a putter used to play a stroke from off the green.

Texel /tek'səl/ *n* a breed of sheep, originating in Holland and first imported in quantity to Britain for breeding purposes in 1974. [*Texel*, one of the Friesian islands of the Netherlands]

Tex-Mex /teks'meks'/ (*US*) *adj* being an Americanized version of some aspect of Mexican culture or cuisine. [*Texas*, and *Mexico*]

text /tekst/ *n* the actual words of a book, poem, etc, in their original form or any form they have been transmitted in or transmuted into; a book of such words; words set to music; the main body of matter in a book, distinguished from notes, commentary or other subsidiary matter; the exact wording of a book or piece of writing as opposed to a translation, paraphrase or revision; words or a piece of writing displayed on a screen (*comput*); a text message; matter commented on; a short passage from the Bible taken as the subject of a sermon, quoted in authority, displayed as a motto, etc; a theme; a textbook; (in *pl*) books for study; the Bible (*Shakesp*); a copybook heading; text-hand. ◆ *vt* and *vi* to send a text message (to). [Med L *textus* text, from L *textus* structure, texture, from *texere, textum* to weave]
■ **tex'ter** *n*. **tex'ting** *n*. **text'ism** *n* the language, or a particular usage, characteristic of text messages. **text'less** *adj*.
□ **text'book** *n* a book containing the main principles of a subject. ◆ *adj* (of an operation, example, etc) exactly as planned, in perfect accordance with theory or calculation. **text'bookish** *adj*. **text editor** *n* (*comput*) a program or series of programs that allows text to be entered and edited on-screen. **text'-hand** *n* a large hand in writing, *orig* one suitable for the text of a manuscript book. **text'-man** *n* a quoter of texts; a textualist. **text message** *n* a short message, often using abbreviations, typed and sent by means of a mobile phone. **text messaging** *n*. **text mining** *n* (*comput*) the application of the principles of data mining (qv) to large amounts of written text. **text'phone** *n* a telephone specially adapted to convert text into spoken messages and vice versa. **text processing** *n* (*comput*) the handling of text by computer, eg converting it from one page format to another. **text'speak** *n* the style of language commonly used in text messages, including abbreviations, truncations, use of numbers, etc.

textile /tek'stīl or (*US*) -stil/ *n* a woven fabric; fibre, yarn, etc suitable for weaving into fabric; any cloth or fabric. ◆ *adj* woven or capable of being woven; of or relating to the manufacture of woven fabric. [L *textilis*, from *texere, textum* to weave]
■ **texto'rial** *adj* (*archaic*) relating to weaving.

textonym /teks'tə-nim/ (*inf*) *n* one of several words that may be keyed into a mobile phone by pressing the same sequence of buttons. [**text** and **synonym**]

textual /tek'stū-əl/ *adj* relating to, or contained in, the text; serving for a text. [Med L *textuālis*, from *texere, textum* to weave]
■ **tex'tualism** *n* (too) strict adherence to a text, *esp* that of the Bible; textual criticism, *esp* of the Bible. **tex'tualist** *n* a person learned in, or a strict adherer to, the text, *esp* of the Bible; a literal interpreter; a quoter of texts. **tex'tually** *adv*. **tex'tuary** *n* a textualist.
□ **textual criticism** *n* critical study directed towards determining the true reading of a text.

texture /tek'styər or teks'chər/ *n* the quality of a material as conveyed to the touch, for example its roughness, smoothness, etc; the general structure, appearance and feel of something; the general quality, character or tenor of something; structural impression resulting from the way that the different elements are combined or interrelated to form a whole, as in music, art, etc; the manner of weaving or connecting (*archaic*); anything woven, a web (*archaic*); disposition of the parts of a body. ◆ *vt* to give a certain texture to, texturize; to weave. [L *textūra* web, from *texere, textum* to weave]
■ **tex'tural** *adj* relating to, in the matter of, texture. **textur'ally** *adv*. **tex'tured** *adj*. **tex'tureless** *adj*. **tex'turize** or **-ise** *vt* to give a particular texture to (food, fabric), to texture.
□ **texturized vegetable protein** *n* a vegetable substance, *usu* made from soya beans, prepared to resemble meat in appearance and taste (*abbrev* **TVP**).

textus receptus /tek'stəs rə-sep'təs, tek'stŭs re-kep'tŭs/ (*L*) the received text (of the Greek New Testament).

TFT screen /tē-ef-tē' skrēn/ *n* a thin film transistor screen, giving good display, used in laptop computers.

TG *abbrev* : Togo (IVR); transformational grammar.

TGV *abbrev* : Train à Grande Vitesse (qv).

TGWU *abbrev* : Transport and General Workers' Union (now part of Unite).

Th (*chem*) *symbol* : thorium.

Th. *abbrev* : Thursday.

th- (*obs*) or **th'** (*archaic* or *dialect*) forms of **the**, *esp* before a vowel, as in *Spenser* **thelement**, the element, **thelf**, the elf, **thother**, the other.

-th¹ *sfx* forming nouns (1) from verbs, denoting action or process (*growth*); (2) from adjectives, denoting abstract qualities (*filth, width*). [OE *-thu, -tho, -th*]

■ words derived from main entry word; □ compound words; ■ idioms and phrasal verbs

-th² or **-eth** *sfx* forming ordinal numbers and fractions from cardinal numbers greater than, or ending in a number greater than, three. [OE *-tha*, *-the*]

thack /thak/ *n* a Scots form of **thatch**.
■ **under thack and rape** safely secured under thatch and rope, snug generally.

thae /dhā/ (*Scot*) *demonstrative pronoun* and *demonstrative adj* those. [OE *thā*; see **tho¹**]

thagi see under **thug**.

Thai /tī, tä'ē/ *adj* of or relating to the kingdom of *Thailand* (formerly Siam) in SE Asia. ◆ *n* a native of Thailand (also **Thai'lander**); the language of Thailand.
❏ **Thai boxing** *n* a form of boxing practised in Thailand, using gloved fists, feet, knees and elbows. **Thai massage** *n* a form of massage, originating in Thailand, in which hands, feet, elbows and knees are used to remove energy blockages.

thaim /dhām/ Scots form of **them**.

thairm /thārm/ (*Scot*) *n* an intestine; catgut, a musical string. [OE *tharm*, *thearm*]

thalamencephalon /thal-ə-men-sef'ə-lon/ (*anat*) *n* an older name for **diencephalon**; that part of the diencephalon *incl* the pineal gland and thalamus. [**thalamus** and **encephalon**]
■ **thalamencephal'ic** *adj*.

thalamus /thal'ə-mas/ *n* (*pl* **thal'ami** /-mī/ or *-mē*/) (in ancient Greece) an inner room, chamber; the receptacle of a flower (*bot*); part of the midbrain where the optic nerve emerges (also, *esp* formerly, **optic thalamus**; *anat*). [Gr *thalamos* an inner room, bedroom]
■ **thal'amic** (or /tha-lam'ik/) *adj* of the thalamus. **Thalamiflorae** /-i-flō'rē, -flō'/ *n pl* (L *flōs*, *flōris* flower) in some systems, a subclass of dicotyledons with petals free and stamens hypogynous. **thalamiflo'ral** *adj*.

thalassian /tha-las'i-ən/ *adj* marine. ◆ *n* a sea turtle. [Gr *thalassa*, *thalatta* sea]
■ **thalassaemia** or **thalassemia** /thal-ə-sē'mi-ə/ *n* a hereditary disorder of the blood causing anaemia, sometimes fatal in children. **thalassae'mic** or **thalassē'mic** *adj*. **thalass'ic** *adj* marine; of the seas, *esp* those which are small or inland. **thalassoc'racy** or **thalattoc'racy** *n* (Gr *kratos* power) sovereignty of the seas. **thalassog'rapher** *n*. **thalassograph'ic** *adj*. **thalassog'raphy** *n* the science of the sea. **thalassother'apy** *n* therapy, said to bring harmony to and detoxify the body, rid one of stress, etc, involving the application of mud and seaweed, seawater baths and massage.

thale cress /thāl kres/ *n* a cruciferous wall plant with small white flowers (*Sisymbrium thalianum*). [Johann *Thal* (1542–83), German physician]

thaler or **taler** /tä'lər/ *n* an obsolete German silver coin. [Ger; cf **dollar**]

thali /tä'li/ *n* (*pl* **tha'lis**) (in Indian cookery) a set meal of a variety of curry dishes with rice or chapatis; a metal plate for serving Indian food. [Hindi]

Thalia /thə-lī'ə/ (*Gr myth*) *n* the Muse of comedy and pastoral poetry; one of the Graces. [Gr *Thaleia*, *Thaliā*, from *thallein* to bloom]
■ **thalī'an** *adj*.

thalictrum /thə-lik'trəm/ *n* a plant of the meadow-rue genus *Thalictrum*. [Gr *thaliktron*, from *thallein* to bloom]

thalidomide /thə-lid'ə-mīd, tha-/ *n* a non-barbiturate sedative drug, withdrawn in 1961 because found to cause malformation in the fetus if taken during pregnancy.

thalli see **thallus**.

thallium /thal'i-əm/ *n* a soft, highly toxic white leadlike metallic element (symbol **Tl**; atomic no 81) discovered in 1861. [Gr *thallos* a young shoot, from the bright-green line in its spectrum]
■ **thall'ic** *adj* of or containing trivalent thallium. **thall'ous** *adj* of or containing univalent thallium.

Thallophyta, **thallophyte** see under **thallus**.

thallus /thal'əs/ *n* (*pl* **thall'uses** or **thall'ī**) a plant body not differentiated into leaf, stem and root. [Gr *thallos* a young shoot]
■ **thall'iform** *adj*. **thall'ine** *adj*. **thall'oid** *adj*. **Thallophy'ta** *n pl* (Gr *phyton* plant) the lowest main division of the plant kingdom, lacking true stems, roots and leaves, *incl* bacteria, fungi and algae. **thall'ophyte** *n* any plant belonging to the Thallophyta. **thallophy'tic** *adj*.

thalweg or **talweg** /tä'veg, -vähh/ (*geol*) *n* the longitudinal profile of the bottom of a river bed; the middle of a main navigable waterway, acting as a boundary between states. [Ger, from *Thal* (now *Tal*) valley, and *Weg* way]

Thammuz /tam'ooz, -ŭz/ (*Milton*) same as **Tammuz**.

than¹ /dhan, dhən/ *conj* used after a comparative, actual or felt, to introduce that which is in the lower degree; used after adverbs such as *rather* to introduce the *usu* less desirable or rejected option in a statement of alternatives; except, other than. ◆ *prep* (popularly, and in some authors, eg Shelley) in comparison with (*esp* with *whom*, as in Milton). [OE *thonne*, *thanne*, *thænne* than, orig then]

than² /dhan, dhən/ an obsolete or dialect form of **then¹**.

thana or **thanah**, and **thanadar** see **tana¹**.

thanage see under **thane**.

thanatism /than'ə-ti-zm/ *n* belief that the soul dies with the body. [Gr *thanatos* death]
■ **than'atist** *n*.

thanato- /than-ə-tō-, -tə-, -to-/ or **thanat-** /than-ət-/ *combining form* denoting death. [Gr *thanatos* death]
■ **thanatognomon'ic** *adj* (see **gnomonic** under **gnomon**) indicating or characteristic of death. **thanatog'raphy** *n* a narrative of a death. **than'atoid** *adj* apparently dead; deathly; deadly. **thanatol'ogy** *n* the scientific study of death and the customs and practices associated with it; care or psychological therapy for the dying. **thanatophō'bia** *n* a morbid dread of death. **thanatop'sis** *n* a view of, or reflection upon, death. **thanatō'sis** *n* gangrene.

thane /thān/ *n* (in Anglo-Saxon England) king's companion, a person who held land by service, hence a noble of lower rank than eorl or ealdorman; a hereditary (not military) tenant of the Crown, often a clan chief (*Scot hist*). See also **thegn**. [OE *thegn* servant, follower, courtier, nobleman; cf ON *thegn* a man, warrior, Ger *Degen* a soldier, servant, Gr *teknon* child]
■ **thā'nage**, **thane'dom**, **thane'hood** or **thane'ship** *n*.

thang /thang/ *n* a non-standard form of **thing**. [Imit of southern US pronunciation]

thank /thangk/ *n* (*usu* in *pl*) gratitude; an expression of gratitude. ◆ *vt* to express gratitude to; to blame or hold responsible. [OE *thanc*, *thonc*; cognate with Ger *Dank*; from the root of **think¹**]
■ **thankee** *interj* see **thank you** below. **thank'er** *n*. **thank'ful** *adj* grateful; gladly relieved. **thank'fully** *adv* gratefully, with a thankful feeling; one feels thankful (that); (of eg words) expressing gratitude. **thank'fulness** *n*. **thank'ing** *n* (*usu* in *pl*; *Shakesp*) thanks. **thank'less** *adj* unthankful; not expressing thanks for favours; bringing no thanks, appreciation, pleasure or profit. **thank'lessly** *adv*. **thank'lessness** *n*. **thanks** *interj* see **thank you** below. **thank'worthily** *adv*. **thank'worthiness** *n*. **thank'worthy** *adj* worthy of or deserving thanks.
❏ **thank'-offering** *n* an offering made to express thanks. **thanks'giver** *n*. **thanks'giving** *n* the act of giving thanks; a public acknowledgement of divine goodness and mercy; (with *cap*) a day (**Thanksgiving Day**) set apart for this, *esp* that in the USA since the time of the Pilgrim Fathers, now fixed as the fourth Thursday of November, or that in Canada, fixed as the second Monday in October; a form of giving thanks, a grace, that form preceding the last two prayers of morning or evening prayer or of the litany, the *General Thanksgiving*. ◆ *adj* serving to give thanks. **thank'you** *adj* expressing gratitude. ◆ *n* anything expressing gratitude, *esp* a gift. **thank'-you-ma'am** *n* (*US*) a ridge or hollow in a road that causes those who drive over it to bob their heads.
■ **be thankit** (*Scot*) thank God. **have** (**only**) **oneself to thank for** to be the cause of (one's own misfortune). **I'll thank you**, **him**, etc **to** used, *usu* in anger, to introduce a request or command. **no thanks to** not owing to, implying that gratitude is far from being due. **thank God** (or **thank goodness**, **thank heavens**, etc) an expression of relief. **thank one's lucky stars** see under **star¹**. **thanks be** thank God. **thanks to** owing to. **thank you**, **thanks** or (*old*) **thank'ee** elliptical forms of earlier *thanks be to you*, *I thank you* and similar expressions, conventional expressions of gratitude. **thank you** (or **thanks**) **for nothing** (*inf*) an expression implying that no gratitude is due at all.

thanna or **thannah** see **tana¹**.

thar /tär/ *n* the serow, a Himalayan goat like an antelope; by confusion applied to the tahr. [Nepali (Indic language of Nepal) *thār*]

tharborough see **farborough**.

Thargelia /thär-gē'li-ə or -jē'/ *n pl* an ancient Athenian festival, in honour of Apollo, in the month of *Thargēliōn* (May-June).

that /dhat/ *demonstrative pronoun* and *demonstrative adj* (*pl* **those**) used in pointing out a person or thing; indicating the thing, person, idea, event, etc (already) mentioned, specified or understood; the former (of two); the more distant, removed or less obvious (of two); not this but the other (as in contrast); the one to be indicated or defined; the person spoken to on the telephone; such (*obs*); often indicating an accompanying snap of the fingers (as *I don't care that*, *It wants that*). ◆ *relative pronoun* (*sing* and *pl*) /dhət, dhat/ who, whom, or which (*esp* when defining or limiting, not merely linking on an addition). ◆ *adv* /dhat/ to the degree or extent shown or understood; at which (often omitted); to such a degree or extent, so (*inf* or *dialect*). ◆ *conj* /*dhət*, *dhat*/ used to introduce a noun clause, an adverbial clause showing purpose, reason, result or consequence, or an expression of a wish in the subjunctive; because (*Shakesp*). [OE *thæt*, neuter demonstrative pronoun cognate with Ger *das*, *dass*; Gr *to*, Sans *tad*; see **the**]

■ **that'away** *adv* (*N Am dialect*, or *facetious*) in that direction; in that way. **that'ness** *n* the quality of being a definite thing, that.

■ **all that** (*inf*) (*usu* with a negative) very. **and (all) that** (*inf*) and all the rest of that sort of thing, used as a summary way of dismissing what is vaguely thought of. **(and) that's that** (and) that is the end of that matter; no more of that. **at that** at that point; moreover (*inf*); nevertheless (*inf*). **(just) like that** straight away, without effort; without further ado. **that's more like it** that is better, that is more like what is required.

thatch /*thach*/ *vt* to cover or roof with straw, reeds, heather, palm-leaves, or any similar material. ◆ *vi* to do thatching. ◆ *n* a covering or covering material of straw, reeds, heather, palm-leaves, etc; a roof or covering formed from such material; thick hair; a condition of grass in which a mat of dead vegetative fibre builds up, inhibiting the penetration of air to, and the growth of, the roots. [OE *thæc* covering, thatch, and *theccan* to cover; cognate with Ger *decken*, L *tegere*, Gr *stegein* to cover]

■ **thatched** (or *old* **thatcht**) *adj*. **thatch'er** *n*. **thatch'ing** *n* the act or art of covering with thatch; materials used for thatching; the development of thatch in grass. **thatch'less** *adj*.

❑ **thatch'-board** *n* a building-board made of straw.

Thatcherism /*thach'ə-ri-zm*/ *n* the policies and style of government associated with Margaret *Thatcher*, British prime minister 1979–90.

■ **Thatch'erite** *adj* of, relating to or representing the policies of Margaret Thatcher and her associates (also *n*).

thaumasite /*thö'mə-sīt*/ *n* a mineral, hydrated silicate, carbonate and sulphate of calcium. [Gr *thaumasios* wonderful]

thaumato- /*thö-mə-to-*/ or **thaumat-** /*thö-mat-*/ *combining form* denoting wonder or miracle. [Gr *thaumat*(o)-, from *thauma*, *-atos* wonder]

■ **thau'matin** *n* a sweetener extracted from a W African fruit, *Thaumatococcus daniellii*, 2000 to 4000 times sweeter than sucrose. **thaumatogeny** /*-toj'*/ *n* the doctrine of the miraculous origination of life. **thaumatog'raphy** *n* description of natural wonders. **thaumatol'atry** *n* (see **-latry**) wonder-worship. **thaumatol'ogy** *n* the study of, or a written study on, miracles. **thau'matrope** *n* (Gr *thauma* wonder, and *tropos* a turning) an optical toy in which pictures on both sides of a card are seen to combine when the card is rotated rapidly. **thaumaturge** /*thö'mə-tûrj*/ *n* (Gr *thaumatourgos* wonder-worker, from *ergon* work) a wonder-worker, magician. **thaumatur'gic** or **thaumatur'gical** *adj*. **thaumatur'gics** *n pl* the performance of magic tricks using sleight-of-hand, etc. **thaumatur'gism** *n*. **thaumatur'gist** *n*. **thaumaturgus** /*-tûr'gəs*/ *n* a wonder-worker, a thaumaturge; a worker of miracles, applied eg to certain saints. **thau'maturgy** *n* the performing of miracles.

thaw /*thö*/ *vi* (of ice, etc) to melt or grow liquid; to become so warm as to melt ice; to become less cold, stiff or reserved in manner. ◆ *vt* to cause to melt. ◆ *n* the melting of ice or snow by heat; the change of weather that causes it; an increase in relaxation, a lessening of control; an increase in friendliness of manner. [OE *thawian*]

■ **thaw'er** *n* an ice-melting agent or apparatus. **thaw'ing** *n* and *adj*. **thaw'less** *adj*. **thaw'y** *adj* inclined to thaw.

■ **thaw out** to return from frozen to normal condition.

THC *abbrev*: tetrahydrocannabinol.

ThD *abbrev*: *Theologiae Doctor* (*New L*), Doctor of Theology.

the¹ /*dhē* (emphatic), *dhə* or *dhi*, *dhē*/ (before vowels) *demonstrative adj* called the definite article, used to refer to a particular person or thing, or a group of things, already mentioned, implied or known; used to refer to a unique person or thing; used before a singular noun to refer to all the members of that group or class; used before a singular noun to denote a species; used before certain titles and proper names; used before an adjective or noun describing an identified person; used after a preposition to refer to a unit of time, quantity, etc; used before a noun denoting a profession or activity; (*usu* stressed) the best (*inf*); my, our (*inf* or *facetious*); used instead of the pfx *to-*, this (*Scot*; as **the day** today, **the night** tonight, **the morn** tomorrow, **the morn's morn** tomorrow morning, **the year** this year). [OE *the* (supplanting *se*), masc of *thæt* that]

the² /*dhə*/ *adv* (with comparatives) (by) how much; (by) so much; used before superlative adjectives and adverbs to indicate an amount beyond all others. [OE *thy* by that, by that much, the instrumental case of the definite article]

Thea /*thē'ə*/ *n* the tea genus of evergreen plants (sometimes *incl Camellia*), giving name to the family **Theā'ceae** /*-ā'si-ē*/, related to the Guttíferae. [From the root of **tea**, but taken as if from Gr *theā* goddess]

■ **theā'ceous** *adj*.

theandric /*thē-an'drik*/ *adj* divine and human at the same time. [Gr *theos* a god, and *anēr*, *andros* man]

theanthropic /*thē-ən-throp'ik*/ *adj* simultaneously divine and human; embodying deity in human forms. [Gr *theos* a god, and *anthrōpos* man]

■ **thean'thropism** or **thean'thropy** *n* the ascribing of human qualities to deity, or divine qualities to man; a doctrine of union of divine and human. **thean'thropist** *n*.

thearchy /*thē'ärk-i*, *-ər-ki*/ *n* rule or government by a god or gods, theocracy; a body of divine rulers. [Gr *theos* a god, and *archein* to rule]

■ **thear'chic** *adj*.

Theatine /*thē'ə-tīn*/ *n* a member of a Roman Catholic religious brotherhood founded in 1524 by Giovanni Pietro Carafa, bishop of Chieti (L *Theāte*), afterwards Pope Paul IV, and others, or of a sisterhood modelled on it (also *adj*).

theatre or (*N Am*) **theater** /*thē'ə-tar*/ *n* a structure, *orig* in the open air, for drama or other spectacles; a cinema (chiefly *N Am* and *Aust*); any natural land formation backed by a curving hillside or rising by steps like seats of a theatre; a building or room, *usu* with tiered seats, which is adapted for lectures, anatomical or surgical demonstrations, etc; an operating theatre; a scene of action, field of operations; (with *the*) the social unit comprising actors, theatre companies, producers, etc, or its characteristic environment and conditions; an audience, house; (with *the*) plays or a specified group of plays, collectively; the writing and production of plays; material or method judged by its suitability for a dramatic presentation. [Gr *theātron*, from *theaesthai* to see]

■ **the'atral** *adj*. **theat'rical** (or *rare* **theat'ric**) *adj* relating or suitable to, or savouring of, the stage, actors or acting; stagy; histrionic, melodramatic, exaggerated; aiming at or producing dramatic effects; of, in or for the cinema (*esp N Am*). **theat'ricalism** or **theatrical'ity** *n* staginess, artificiality. **theatricalīzā'tion** or **-s-** *n*. **theat'ricalize** or **-ise** *vt* to adapt to dramatic representation; to make stagy. ◆ *vi* to act; to attend the theatre. **theat'rically** *adv*. **theat'ricalness** *n*. **theat'ricals** *n pl* dramatic performances; theatrical affairs, properties or people. **theat'ricism** *n* theatricality, affectation, staginess. **theat'ricize** or **-ise** /*-sīz*/ *vi* to play a part. **theat'rics** *n sing* the staging of plays, etc, or the art of doing this; histrionics. **theatromā'nia** *n* a craze for play-going. **theat'rophone** *n* (*hist*) a telephone connecting callers to a theatre so they can listen to a live performance there.

❑ **the'atre-goer** *n* a person who regularly goes to the theatre. **theatre-in-the-round'** *n* (*pl* **theatres-in-the-round'**) a theatre with a central stage and the audience on all sides; the style of staging plays in such a theatre. **theatre of cruelty** *n* a branch of drama, based on the theories of Antonin Artaud (1896–1948), intended to induce in the audience a feeling of suffering and an awareness of the presence of evil. **theatre of fact** *n* a branch of drama using material closely based on real happenings. **theatre of the absurd** *n* a branch of drama dealing with fantastic deliberately unreal situations, in reaction against the tragedy and irrationality of life. **theatre organ** *n* a cinema-organ. **theatre sister** *n* a sister in charge of the nursing team in an operating theatre. **theatre weapons** *n pl* weapons for use in a theatre of war (as opposed to intercontinental or strategic weapons), applied *esp* to nuclear weapons.

theave /*thēv*/ (*dialect*) *n* a young ewe, *esp* in its first year.

thebaine /*thē'bā-ēn*, *-īn*, *thē'bə-ēn*/ *n* a poisonous alkaloid ($C_{19}H_{21}NO_3$) obtained from opium. [New L *thebaia* opium, as prepared at **Thebes**, Egypt; chem sfx *-ine*]

thebe /*thā'bā*/ *n* (*pl* **the'be**) a Botswanan monetary unit, $\frac{1}{100}$ of a pula. [Tswana, literally, shield]

Thebes /*thēbz*/ *n* a city of ancient Boeotia, in Greece; a city of ancient Egypt. [Gr *Thēbai* Thebes]

■ **Thebaic** /*thē-bā'ik*/ *adj* of Egyptian Thebes; of opium (as an Egyptian product). **Thebaid** /*thē'bā-id*/ *n* a poem on the Seven against Thebes (such as that by Statius); the district of Thebes (Egyptian or Greek). **Thē'ban** *adj* of Thebes. ◆ *n* a native of Thebes; a Boeotian.

❑ **Theban year** *n* the Egyptian year of $365\frac{1}{4}$ days.

theca /*thē'kə*/ *n* (*pl* **thē'cae** /*-sē*/) a sheath, case or sac (*zool*); a spore-case (*bot*); a lobe or loculus of an anther (*bot*). [Latinized from Gr *thēkē* case, sheath]

■ **thē'cal** *adj* of a theca. **thē'cate** *adj* having a theca.

Thecla /*thek'lə*/ *n* the hair-streak genus of butterflies. [New L]

thecodont /*thek'ə-dont* or *thē'kə-dont*/ *n* an extinct reptile of the Triassic period, having teeth set in sockets. ◆ *adj* (of mammals) having teeth set in sockets. [Gr *thēkē* case, and *odous*, *odontis* a tooth]

■ words derived from main entry word; ❑ compound words; ■ idioms and phrasal verbs

thé dansant /tä dä-sä'/ (Fr) n (pl **thés dansants**) a dance held in the afternoon at which tea is served.

thee¹ /dhē/ (formal, church, dialect or archaic) pronoun the dative and accusative form of **thou¹**; the nominative form of **thou¹**, used esp formerly by Quakers. ◆ vt to use thee in speaking to (someone). ◆ vi to use thee. [OE thē the]

thee² /thē/ (Spenser) vi to prosper, to thrive. [OE thēon; cf Ger gedeihen]

theek /thēk/ a Scots form of **thatch** (v).

theft /theft/ n (an) act of thieving; a thing stolen. [OE thēofth, thīefth, from thēof thief]
  ■ **theft'ūous** adj thievish. **theft'ūously** adv.
  ❑ **theft'boot** or **theft'-bote** n illegal compounding of a theft.

thegither /dhə-gidh'ər/ a Scots form of **together**.

thegn /thān/ (hist) n the older form of **thane**.

theine /thē'īn, -in/ n an alkaloid found in tea, identical with caffeine. [Thea]
  ■ **thē'ic** n a person who drinks too much tea or who suffers from theism. **thē'ism** n an unhealthy condition resulting from too much tea-drinking.

their /dhār, dhər/ pronoun and possessive adj of or belonging to them; his or her (a use unacceptable to some; see **they**). [ON theirra, superseding OE thǣra, genitive pl of the definite article]
  ■ **theirs** pronoun (the one or ones) belonging to them.

theism¹ /thē'i-zm/ n belief in the existence of God with or without a belief in a special revelation. [Gr theos God]
  ■ **thē'ist** n. **thēist'ic** or **thēist'ical** adj.

theism² see under **theine**.

thelement, thelf see **th-**.

Thelemite /thel'ə-mīt/ n a monk of Rabelais's imaginary abbey of Thélème, of an order whose rule was 'Do as you like' (also adj). [Gr thelēma will]

thelytoky /thi-lit'ə-ki/ n parthenogenetic production of female offspring only. [Gr thēlys female, and tokos birth]
  ■ **thelyt'okous** adj.

them /dhem, dhəm/ pronoun the dative and accusative form of **they**; themselves (archaic, inf or US dialect); a dialect or non-standard form of **those**. [ON theim or OE (Anglian) thæm (dative)]
  ■ **them and us** (inf) any of various pairs of groups in society, such as management and workforce, considered to be in opposition to each other.

theme /thēm/ n a subject set or proposed for discussion, or spoken or written about; a recurrent idea in literature or art; subject, a short melody developed with variations or otherwise (music); the stem of a word without its inflections; a thesis, a brief essay or exercise; a ground for action; an administrative division of the Byzantine empire. ◆ adj planned around or having a certain subject. ◆ vt to decorate or equip (a pub, restaurant, etc) in keeping with a certain subject, eg seafaring or the Wild West. [Gr thema, -atos, from root of tithenai to place, set; partly through OFr tesme]
  ■ **thē'ma** (or /them'ə/) n (pl **them'ata**) a theme. **thematic** /thi-mat'ik/ adj of or relating to a theme; (of philately) concerned with collection of sets showing flowers, or birds, etc; (of a vowel) not forming part of the root of a word, nor part of any inflection or suffix (as the vowel o in cytoplasm); (of a word) forming the major constituent of a sentence (linguistics). ◆ n a thematic vowel. **themat'ically** adv. **themed** adj having or planned around a single unifying subject or theme. **theme'less** adj.
  ❑ **thematic catalogue** n (music) a catalogue giving the names, etc of works and also their opening themes. **theme park** n a large area with displays, fairground, rides, etc, all devoted to or based on one subject. **theme song** or **theme tune** n a melody that is repeated often in a musical drama, film, or radio or television series, and is associated with a certain character, idea, emotion, etc; a signature tune; a person's characteristic, often repeated, complaint, etc.

Themis /them'is/ n the Greek goddess of law and justice. [Gr Themis]

themselves /dhəm-selvz'/ pronoun pl of **himself**, **herself** and **itself**; himself or herself (a use unacceptable to some; see **they**). [**them** and **self**]
  ■ **themself'** pronoun (inf; unrecognized in standard English) introduced as a sing pronoun to avoid **himself** or **herself** when the sex of the person is unspecified.

then¹ /dhen, dhən/ adv at that time; afterward, after that; immediately; at another time; further, again; on the other hand, at the same time; for that reason, therefore; in that case; used to continue a narrative after a break or digression; used esp at the end of the questions that ask for an explanation, opinion, etc or that ask for or assume agreement. ◆ adj being at that time. ◆ n that time. [OE thonne, thanne, thænne]
  ❑ **then'about** or **then'abouts** adv about that time.
  ■ **by then** by that time. **then and there** at once and on the spot.

then² /dhən/ (Spenser, etc) conj same as **than¹**.

thenar /thē'när/ (anat) n the palm; the ball of the thumb; the sole. ◆ adj of or relating to the thenar. [Gr thenar, -aros]

thenardite /thi-när'dīt/ (mineralogy) n an anhydrous form of sodium sulphate. [Baron Louis-Jacques Thenard (1777–1857), French chemist]

thence /dhens/ adv from that place; from those premises; from that time; from that cause, for that reason. [ME thennes, from thenne (OE thanon thence), with adverbial genitive ending; cf **hence**, **whence**]
  ❑ **thence'forth** or **thencefor'ward** adv from that time forward; from that place onward.

theo- /thē-ō-, -ə- or -o-/ combining form denoting god. [Gr theos a god]
  ■ **Theobroma** /-brō'mə/ n (Gr brōma food) the chocolate or cocoa genus. **theobrō'mine** /-mēn, -mīn, -min/ n an alkaloid obtained from the chocolate seed, used in medicine. **theocen'tric** adj having god as its centre. **theocracy** /thē-ok'rə-si/ n (Gr theokratiā, from krateein to rule) that constitution of a state in which God, or a god, is regarded as the sole sovereign, and the laws of the realm as divine commands rather than human ordinances, the priesthood necessarily becoming the officers of the invisible ruler; the state governed in this way. **theocrasy** /thē-ok'rə-si, thē-ō-krā'si/ n (Gr krāsis a mixing) a mixture of religions; the identification or equating of one god with another or others; a mystic union of the soul with God reached through profound contemplation. **theocrat** /thē'ə-krat/ n a divine or deified ruler. **theocrat'ic** or **theocrat'ical** adj. **theocrat'ically** adv. **theodicean** /thē-od-i-sē'ən/ n and adj (a person) practising theodicy. **theod'icy** n (Gr dikē justice) a vindication of the justice of God in establishing a world in which evil exists. **theogonic** /thē-ə-gon'ik/ or **theogon'ical** adj of or relating to theogony or a theogony. **theog'onist** n a writer on theogony. **theogony** /thē-og'ə-ni/ n (Gr theogoniā, from -gonia begetting, generation) the birth and genealogy of the gods; an account of this, eg in poetry. **theolinguis'tics** n sing the study of the language of religious theory and practice. **theologaster** /-gas'tər/ n a shallow theologian. **theol'ogate** /-gət/ n a seminary for Roman Catholic priests. **theol'oger** /-jər/ n (sometimes derog) a theologian. **theologian** /thē-ə-lō'jyən/ n a student of, or a person well versed, in theology, esp (in Roman Catholic usage) a theological lecturer attached to a cathedral or collegiate church. **theologic** /thē-ə-loj'ik/ or **theolog'ical** adj (**theological virtues** faith, hope and charity). **theolog'ically** adv. **theol'ogist** n (rare) a theologian. **theol'ogize** or **-ise** vt to render theological, to treat theologically. ◆ vi to discourse, speculate, etc, on theology. **theol'ogizer** or **-s-** n. **theologoumenon** /thē-ə-lə-goo'mə-non/ n (pl **theologou'mena**) (Gr, from theologein to talk about God) a theological statement that is not agreed to be a divine revelation or an inspired doctrine. **thē'ologue** /-log/ n a theologian (rare); a theological student (US). **theology** /thē-ol'ə-ji/ n (Gr theologiā, from logos discourse) the study of God, religion and revelation; a system of theological doctrine; a system of principles, esp one rigidly adhered to. **theomachist** /thē-om'ə-kist/ n. **theom'achy** n (Gr theomachiā, from machē a battle) war among or against the gods, as (in Greek mythology) by the Titans and giants; opposition to the divine will. **theomancy** /thē'ə-man-si/ n (Gr theomanteiā spirit of prophecy, from manteiā divination) divination by means of oracles, or of persons directly inspired immediately by some divinity. **theomania** /-mā'ni-ə/ n (see **mania**) religious madness; belief that one is a god oneself. **theomā'niac** n. **theoman'tic** adj of or relating to theomancy. **theomorphic** /-mör'fik/ adj (Gr theomorphos of divine form, from morphē form) having the form or likeness of a god; in the image of God. **theomor'phism** n. **theon'omous** adj. **theon'omy** n (Gr nomos law) government or rule by God; the state of being so ruled. **Theopaschite** /-pas'kīt/ n (Gr paschein to suffer) a Monophysite, believing that God had suffered and been crucified. **Theopaschitic** /-kit'ik/ adj. **Theopas'chitism** /-ki-tizm/ n. **theopathet'ic** adj of or relating to theopathy. **theopathy** /thē-op'ə-thi/ n (Gr pathos experience, emotion) a religious emotion aroused by meditation about God. **theophagous** /thē-of'ə-gəs/ adj. **theoph'agy** /-ji/ n (Gr phagein to eat) the sacramental eating of a god. **theophanic** /thē-ə-fan'ik/ adj. **theophany** /thē-of'ə-ni/ n (Gr theophaneiā a vision of God, exhibition of gods' statues, from phainein to show) a manifestation or appearance of deity to man. **theophilanthrop'ic** adj. **theophilan'thropism** n. **theophilan'thropist** n. **theophilanthropy** /-fi-lan'thrə-pi/ n (Fr théophilanthropie love to God and man; cf **philanthropy**) a deistical system of religion drawn up under the French Directory in 1796, and designed to take the place of Christianity. **theophobia** /-fō'bi-ə/ n (see **phobia**) extreme fear of God; hatred of God. **theophō'biac** or **theophobist** /-of'ə-bist/ n. **theophor'ic** adj derived from or bearing the name of a god. **theopneust** /thē'op-nūst/ or **theopneu'stic** adj (Gr theopneustos, from pneustos inspired, from pneein to breathe)

divinely inspired. **theopneust'y** *n* divine inspiration. **theosoph** /*thē'ə-sof*/, **theos'opher** or **theos'ophist** *n* someone who practises or believes in theosophy. **theosoph'ic** or **theosoph'ical** *adj.* **theosoph'ically** *adv.* **theos'ophism** *n* theosophical tenets. **theosophist'ical** *adj* theosophical; sophistical in theology. **theos'ophize** or **-ise** *vi* to practise theosophy. **theosophy** /*thē-os'ə-fi*/ *n* (Gr *theosophos* wise in things of God, from *sophos* wise) divine wisdom; immediate divine illumination or inspiration claimed to be possessed by specially gifted people, along with abnormal control over natural forces; the system of doctrine expounded by the **Theosophical Society**, a religious body founded by Mme Blavatsky and others in 1875, whose doctrines include belief in karma and reincarnation. **theotechnic** /*-tek'nik*/ *adj.* **theotech'ny** *n* (Gr *technē* art) the employment of gods as the machinery or moving forces of a poem. **theotokos** /*thē-ot'ə-kos*/ *n* (Gr *theotokos*, from *-tokos* having given birth to, from *tiktein* to give birth to) the mother of God, a title of the Virgin Mary repudiated by Nestorius, accepted by the Council of Ephesus.

Theobroma...to...**theocrat** see under **theo-**.

Theocritean /*thē-o-kri-tē'ən*/ *adj* after the manner of *Theocritus* (3c BC), the greatest of Greek pastoral poets; pastoral, idyllic.

theodicy, etc see under **theo-**.

theodolite /*thē-od'ə-līt*/ *n* a surveying instrument for measuring horizontal and vertical angles, consisting of a small telescope able to move both horizontally and vertically. [Ety unknown]
■ **theodolit'ic** *adj.*

theogony, etc see under **theo-**.

theol. *abbrev* : theologian; theological; theology.

theologaster...to...**theophoric** see under **theo-**.

theophylline /*thē-ə-fil'ēn, -īn, -in*/ (*chem*) *n* an isomer of theobromine found in tea, used in medicine. [**Thea**, and Gr *phyllon* leaf]

theopneust, etc see under **theo-**.

theorbo /*thē-ör'bō*/ *n* (*pl* **theorb'os**) a large double-necked bass lute, the second neck carrying bass strings. [Ital *tiorba*]
■ **theorb'ist** *n*.

theorem /*thē'ə-rəm*/ *n* a demonstrable or established but not self-evident principle; a proposition to be proved. [Gr *theōrēma, -atos* spectacle, speculation, theorem, from *theōreein* to be a spectator, to view]
■ **theoremat'ic** or **theoremat'ical** *adj.* **theoremat'ically** *adv.* **theorematist** /*-rem'ə-tist*/ *n*.

theory /*thē'ə-ri*/ *n* an explanation or system of anything; an exposition of the abstract principles of a science or art; an idea or explanation that has not yet been proved, a conjecture; speculation as opposed to practice; an ideal, hypothetical or abstract situation, *esp* in the phrase *in theory*; ideal, hypothetical or abstract reasoning. [Gr *theōriā* view, theory, from *theōreein* to be a spectator, to view]
■ **theoret'ic** or **theoret'ical** *adj* based on, or relating, according, or given to, theory; not practical; speculative. **theoret'ic** *n* (*usu* in *pl*) the speculative aspects of a science. **theoret'ically** *adv.* **theoretician** /*-ə-tish'ən*/ *n* a person who is concerned chiefly with the theoretical aspect of a subject. **the'oric** or **the'orique** *n* (*Shakesp*) theory, speculation. **the'orist** *n* a theorizer; a person given to theory and speculation, to the invention of theories; a person who is expert in the abstract principles of a subject. **theoriza'tion** or **-s-** *n*. **the'orize** or **-ise** *vi* to form a theory; to form opinions solely by theories; to speculate. **the'orizer** or **-s-** *n*.
❑ **theoretical plate** *n* (*chem eng*) a concept, used in distillation design, of a plate in which the vapour and liquid leaving the plate are in equilibrium with each other. **the'ory-laden** *adj* (of a term, concept, etc) meaningful only within the context of a particular theory, and implying acceptance of that theory. **theory of everything** *n* (*phys*) a comprehensive theory, yet to be satisfactorily formulated, that is believed will explain all known physical phenomena in quantum terms, possible candidates for the designation being the twistor theory and string theory (*abbrev* **TOE**).

theosoph...to...**theotokos** see under **theo-**.

theow /*thā'ow*/ (*hist*) *n* a slave. [OE *thēow*]

theralite /*thē'rə-līt*/ *n* a holocrystalline igneous rock composed essentially of plagioclase, nepheline and augite. [Gr *thēraein* to hunt, seek after, and *lithos* stone, so called because its discovery was expected]

Therapeutae /*ther-ə-pū'tē, ther-a-pū'tī*/ *n pl* a traditional ascetic sect, allied to the Essenes, living chiefly near Alexandria in the 1c AD. [L, from Gr *therapeutai* servants, ministers]

therapeutic /*ther-ə-pū'tik*/ *adj* relating to the healing arts; of or relating to the curing of disease, curative; contributing towards or performed to improve health or general wellbeing. [Gr *therapeutēs* servant, worshipper, medical attendant, from *therapeuein* to take care of, to heal]
■ **therapeu'tically** *adv.* **therapeu'tics** *n sing* that part of medicine concerned with the treatment and cure of diseases. **therapeu'tist** *n* a person skilled in therapeutics.

therapsid /*thə-rap'sid*/ *n* a member of the **Therap'sida**, an order of extinct reptiles of the Permian and Triassic periods, showing many mammal-like features and thought to be the ancestors of the mammals (also *adj*). [New L *Therapsida*, from Gr *thēr* wild beast, and *apsis* arch or vault, so called because of the temporal arch of the skull]

therapy /*ther'ə-pi*/ *n* the treatment of physical or mental diseases and disorders by means other than surgery; treatment used to combat a disease or an abnormal condition; therapeutics; curative power. [Gr *therapeiā* service, treatment, from *therapeuein* to take care of, to heal]
■ **ther'apist** *n* a person who practises therapy of a particular kind.

Theravada /*ther-ə-vä'də*/ *n* the doctrines of the Hinayana Buddhists. [Pali, doctrine of the elders]
■ **Theravad'in** *adj.*

there /*dhār*/ *adv* in that place; at that point; to that place; in that respect; (also /*dhr*/) used without any meaning of its own to allow the subject to follow the predicate, and also in corresponding interrogative sentences, etc; used without any meaning to draw or attract attention or for emphasis. ◆*n* that place. ◆*interj* expressing reassurance, sympathy, satisfaction, approval, encouragement, finality, accompanying a blow, to comfort, etc. [OE *thær* ; related to **the**, **that**, etc]
■ **there'ness** *n* the property of having relative situation or existence. ❑ **there'about** or **there'abouts** (also /*-bowts'*/) *adv* about or near that place; near that number, quantity, degree, or time. **thereaft'er** *adv* after or according to that; accordingly. **thereagainst'** *adv* against that. **thereamong'** *adv* among that or those. **thereanent'** *adv* (*Scot*) concerning that matter. **thereat'** *adv* at that point, place or occurrence; on that account. **there'away** *adv* in that direction; thereabout. **therebeside'** *adv* beside that. **thereby'** *adv* beside that; about that amount; by that means; in consequence of that. **therefor'** *adv* (*law*) for that. **therefore** /*dher'fər*/ *adv* for that reason; consequently. **therefrom'** *adv* (*formal*) from that. **therein'** *adv* (*formal*) in or into that or it; indoors (*Scot*). **thereinaft'er** *adv* (*formal*) later or from that point in the same document. **thereinbefore'** *adv* (*formal*) earlier or up to that point in the same document. **therein'to** *adv* (*formal*) into that place, thing, matter, etc. **thereof'** *adv* (*formal*) of that; from that. **thereon'** *adv* (*old*) on that. **thereout'** *adv* (*old*) out of that; out of doors (*Scot*). **therethrough'** *adv* (*old*) through that; by that means. **thereto'** or **thereun'to** *adv* (*formal*) to that; in addition. **there'tofore** *adv* (*formal*) before that time. **thereun'der** *adv* (*formal*) under that. **thereunto'** *adv* (*old*) to that. **thereupon'** *adv* upon that; immediately; in consequence of that (*Shakesp*). **therewith'** *adv* with that; thereupon; for that reason (*old*). **there'withal** *adv* (*old*) with that; immediately after; in addition. **therewithin'** *adv* (*old*) within that.
■ **all there** (*inf*) of normal intelligence. **be there** (often with *for*) to be available or on hand to give someone emotional support. **have been there before** (*sl*) to have been in the same, *esp* unpleasant, situation before. **so there** an expression of triumph, defiance, derision, finality, etc. **there and then** forthwith; immediately. **there it is** that is the situation (and nothing can be done about it). **there or thereabouts** somewhere near. **there you are** used to express triumph when something one predicted would occur does occur, or resignation over something that cannot be changed; used to accompany the action of handing something expected or requested to someone. **there you go** (*inf*) used with the same force as **there you are** above, both as a comment and as an accompaniment to the gesture of handing or passing.

theremin /*ther'ə-min*/ *n* an electronic musical instrument played by moving the hands around two antennae to vary pitch and volume. [Leon *Theremin* (1896–1993), its Russian inventor]

theriac /*thē'ri-ak*/ or **theriaca** /*thē-rī'ə-kə*/ (*archaic*) *n* an antidote to venomous bites, etc. [Gr *thēriakē*, from *thērion* a wild beast, esp a poisonous snake]
■ **therī'acal** *adj.*

therian /*thē'ri-ən*/ (*zool*) *adj* of or belonging to the **Thēr'ia** subclass of mammals, comprising marsupials and placentals, and their extinct ancestors. ◆ *n* a therian animal. [Gr *thērion* wild animal]

therio- or before a vowel **theri-** /*thē-ri(-ō)-*, (*-ə*)-, (*-o*)-/, or **thero-** /*thē-rō-, -rə-, -ro-*/ or before a vowel **ther-** /*thēr-*/ *combining form* denoting beast, mammal. [Gr *thēr* and *thērion* a wild beast]
■ **therianthrop'ic** *adj* (Gr *anthrōpos* man) combining human and animal forms (of eg certain gods, mythical figures); of or relating to therianthropic gods or figures. **therian'thropism** *n* the representation or worship of therianthropic forms or gods. **Theriodontia** /*-ə-don'shyə, -ti-ə*/ *n pl* (Gr *odous, odontos* a tooth) an extinct order of reptiles with teeth like mammals. **theriol'atry** *n* (see **-latry**) animal-worship. **ther'iomorph** *n* (see **-morph**) an animal form in art. **Theriomor'pha**

---

or **Theromor'pha** *n pl* an extinct order of reptiles with affinities with the labyrinthodont Amphibia and mammals. **theriomorph'ic** *adj* (*esp* of gods) having an animal-like form; of theriomorphism. **theriomorph'ism** *n* belief in or worship of gods of the form of animals. **theriomorphō'sis** (or */-mör'/*) *n* transformation into a beast. **theriomor'phous** *adj* beastlike; mammal-like; of the Theriomorpha. **therol'ogy** *n* the study of mammals. **ther'opod** *n* (see **-pod**) any dinosaur of the **Therop'oda**, bipedal, carnivorous, saurischian dinosaurs.

therm */thûrm/* *n* 100000 British thermal units (used as a unit in reckoning payment for gas); a bathing establishment, public bath or hot bath (often in *pl*; *archaic*). [Gr *thermē* heat]
■ **therm'ic** or **therm'ical** *adj* of or by heat. **therm'ically** *adv*.
◻ **thermic lance** *n* a cutting instrument consisting of a steel tube containing metal rods which, with the help of oxygen, are raised to an intense heat.

thermae */thûr'mē/* *n pl* hot springs or baths, *esp* in ancient Greece or Rome. [L, from Gr *thermai*, pl of *thermē* heat]

thermal */thûr'məl/* *adj* relating to, caused by or producing heat; warm; (of clothes) designed to prevent the loss of body heat. ◆ *n* an ascending current of warm air, used eg by birds and gliders to gain height; (in *pl*) clothes, *esp* underclothes, designed to retain heat. [Fr *thermal*, from Gr *thermē* heat]
■ **thermaliza'tion** or **-s-** *n*. **ther'malize** or **-ise** *vt* to reduce the kinetic energy and speed of (fast neutrons) in a nuclear reactor. ◆ *vi* to undergo thermalization. **therm'ally** *adv*.
◻ **thermal agitation** *n* (*phys*) the random movements of free electrons in a conductor, caused by thermal energy and producing noise signals which may be noticeable in some circumstances. **thermal barrier** *n* heat barrier. **thermal capacity** *n* (*phys*) the amount of heat required to raise the temperature of a system through one degree. **thermal conductivity** *n* (*phys*) a measure of the rate of flow of thermal energy through a material in the presence of a temperature gradient. **thermal conductor** *n* a material that allows the flow of heat through it by conduction. **thermal diffusion** *n* (*phys*) a process in which a temperature gradient in a mixture of fluids tends to establish a concentration gradient. **thermal dissociation** *n* the splitting of certain molecules into simpler molecules by heat, followed by recombination on cooling. **thermal efficiency** *n* (*engineering*) (of a heat engine) the ratio of the work done by the engine to the mechanical equivalent of the heat supplied in the steam or fuel. **thermal imaging** *n* the visualization of objects, substances, etc by detecting and processing the infrared energy they emit, used in medical thermography and to locate bodies underground. **thermal neutron** *n* (*phys*) a neutron of very low speed and hence very low energy, responsible for various types of nuclear reaction, *incl* fission. **thermal noise** *n* (*electronics*) noise arising from random movements of electrons in conductors and semiconductors, limiting the sensitivity of electronic amplifiers and detectors. **thermal printer** *n* (*comput*) an old form of dot matrix printer using heated pins to fix images on heat-sensitive paper. **thermal reactor** *n* a nuclear reactor in which fission is induced mainly by low-energy neutrons. **thermal shock** *n* stress, often resulting in fracture, occurring when a body is subjected to sudden changes in temperature. **thermal signature** *n* the characteristic appearance of a substance or object when viewed with thermal-imaging equipment. **thermal springs** *n pl* natural springs of hot water.

Thermalite® */thûr'mə-līt/* *n* a manufactured material for building blocks, of light density and high insulation value. [**thermal** and **-ite**]

Thermidor */thûr-mi-dör'/* *n* the eleventh month of the French Revolutionary calendar, 19 July–17 August. ◆ *adj* (*cookery*; without cap and postpositive, in *lobster thermidor*) denoting a method of preparation, the flesh being mixed with a cream sauce seasoned with mustard, and served in the shell. [Gr *thermē* heat, and *dōron* gift]
■ **Thermido'rian** *n* a participator in the fall of Robespierre.

thermion */thûr'mi-ən/* *n* an electrically-charged particle, an electron or ion, emitted by an incandescent body. [Gr *thermē* heat, and **ion**]
■ **thermion'ic** *adj* of or relating to thermions. **thermion'ics** *n sing* the science of thermions and thermionic emissions.
◻ **thermionic emission** *n* the emission of electrons from incandescent solids or liquids. **thermionic valve** or **tube** *n* a vacuum tube containing a heated cathode from which electrons are emitted, an anode for collecting some or all of these electrons and, generally, additional electrodes for controlling their flow to the anode.

thermistor */thûr-mis'tər/* (*elec eng*) *n* a semiconductor, a mixture of certain oxides with finely divided copper, of which the resistance is very sensitive to change of temperature. [*therm*al res*istor*]

thermite */thûr'mīt/* or **Thermit**® */thûr'mit/* *n* a mixture of aluminium powder with oxide of metal (*esp* iron), which when ignited produces great heat, used for local heating, welding and in some incendiary bombs. [Ger *Thermit*, from Gr *thermē* heat]

thermo- */thûr-mō-, -mə-* or *-mo-/* *combining form* denoting heat. [Gr *thermos* hot, *thermē* heat, *thermotēs* heat]
■ **thermo-bal'ance** *n* a balance for weighing bodies at high temperatures. **thermobaric** */-bar'ik/* *adj* (of a weapon) using a combination of heat and pressure to create a blast more powerful than that of conventional weapons. **thermochem'ical** *adj*. **thermochem'ically** *adv*. **thermochem'ist** *n*. **thermochem'istry** *n* the study of heat changes accompanying chemical action. **therm'ocline** *n* (in lakes) a region of rapidly changing temperature, found between the epilimnion and the hypolimnion. **therm'ocouple** *n* a pair of different metals in contact giving a thermoelectric current. **thermodū'ric** *adj* resistant to heat. **thermodynam'ic** or **thermodynam'ical** *adj*. **thermodynam'ically** *adv*. **thermodynam'ics** *n sing* the science of the relation of heat to mechanical and other forms of energy. **thermoelec'tric** or **thermoelec'trical** *adj*. **thermoelec'trically** *adv*. **thermoelectric'ity** *n* electricity developed by bodies at different temperatures, *esp* between a junction of dissimilar metals and another part of a circuit. **therm'oform** *n* a three-dimensional representation, or a relief, of a painting in an art gallery, designed to help visitors (*esp* those who are blind) to appreciate the tactile qualities, perspective, etc of the painting. **thermogenesis** */-jen'/* *n* production of heat, *esp* in the body by physiological processes. **thermogenet'ic** or **thermogen'ic** *adj*. **therm'ogram** *n* a thermograph record of temperature. **therm'ograph** *n* a self-registering thermometer; the photographic apparatus used in the process of thermography. **thermog'rapher** *n*. **thermograph'ic** *adj*. **thermog'raphy** *n* any process of writing, photographing, etc involving the use of heat; a method of producing embossed text, using a heating process (*printing*); the production of an image on film or a screen using an infrared camera; an image of heat emission from the patient's body used in medical diagnosis, eg for detecting tumours. **thermohā'line** *adj* (*meteorol*) involving both temperature and salinity. **thermolā'bile** *adj* readily decomposed by heat. **thermol'ogy** *n* the science of heat. **thermoluminesc'ence** *n* release of light by heating previously irradiated material, used in archaeological dating. **thermoluminesc'ent** *adj*. **thermol'ysis** *n* (see **lysis**) dissociation or dissolution by heat; loss of body heat. **thermolyt'ic** *adj*. **thermometer** */-om'i-tər/* *n* an instrument for measuring temperature depending on any of several properties of a substance that vary linearly with change of temperature, *esp* a graduated sealed tube containing mercury or alcohol. **thermometric** */-ə-met'rik/* or **thermomet'rical** *adj*. **thermomet'rically** *adv*. **thermomet'rograph** *n* a self-registering thermometer, a thermograph. **thermom'etry** *n* the branch of physics dealing with the measurement of temperature and the design of thermometers, etc. **therm'onasty** *n* nastic movement in response to heat or temperature change. **thermonuc'lear** *adj* exhibiting or dealing with the fusion of nuclei as seen in a **thermonuclear reaction**, a power reaction produced by the fusion of nuclei at extremely high temperatures, as in the interior of stars and some nuclear weapons; relating to the use of such reactions as a source of power or force. **therm'ophile** */-fīl/*, **therm'ophil**, **thermophil'ic** or **thermoph'ilous** *adj* (of eg bacteria, plants) requiring, or thriving best in, high temperatures. **therm'ophile** or **therm'ophil** *n* a bacterium, plant, etc, that requires, or thrives best in, high temperatures. **thermoph'yllous** *adj* (Gr *phyllon* a leaf) (*bot*) having leaves only in the warmer part of the year, deciduous. **therm'opile** */-pīl/* *n* an apparatus, *usu* consisting of thermocouples, for the direct conversion of heat into electrical energy. **thermoplast'ic** *adj* becoming plastic when heated and hardening again when cooled. ◆ *n* any resin that can be melted and cooled repeatedly without appreciable change in properties. **thermoplastic'ity** *n*. **therm'oscope** *n* an instrument for detecting changes of temperature. **thermoscop'ic** *adj* indicating, or sensitive to, temperature changes. **thermoscop'ically** *adv*. **thermosett'ing** *adj* (of eg resin or plastic) setting permanently, after melting and moulding. **thermosiph'on** *n* (*engineering*) a method of circulating a cooling liquid through a system by using the slight difference in density between the hot and cool parts. **therm'osphere** *n* the region of the earth's atmosphere above the mesosphere, in which the temperature rises steadily with height. **thermosta'ble** *adj* not readily decomposed by heating. **therm'ostat** *n* a device for keeping temperature steady. **thermostat'ic** *adj*. **thermostat'ically** *adv*. **thermotact'ic** or **thermotax'ic** *adj* of or showing thermotaxis. **thermotax'is** *n* a movement of an organism towards a position of higher or lower temperature. **thermother'apy** *n* (*med*) the treatment of a part of the body by heat. **thermot'ic** or **thermot'ical** *adj* of or due to heat. **thermot'ics** *n sing* the science of heat. **thermotol'erant** *adj* (*bot*) able to endure high temperatures but not growing well under such conditions. **thermotrop'ic** *adj* bending towards or away from a heat source. ◆ *n* a thermotropic plant. **thermot'ropism** *n* (Gr *tropos* turning) the tendency of a plant to grow towards, or bend away from, a source of heat.

Thermos® */thûr'məs* or *-mos/* *n* a brand of vacuum flask (also **Thermos**® **flask**). [Gr *thermos* hot]

-thermy /-*thûr-mi*/ *combining form* denoting heat, heat generation. [New L -*thermia*, from Gr *thermē* heat]
■ **-thermic** or **-thermal** *adj combining form*.

thero- see **therio-**.

theroid /*thē'roid*/ *adj* of, relating to or like a beast or wild animal. [Gr *thēr* wild animal, and **-oid**]

Thersitic /*thər-sit'ik*/ or **Thersitical** /-*kəl*/ (also without *cap*) *adj* abusively critical. [*Thersītēs*, a character in Homer's *Iliad*, who was forever vilifying the Greek leaders]

thesaurus /*thi-sö'rəs*/ *n* (*pl* **thesau'ri** /-*rī*/ or **thesau'ruses**) a storehouse of knowledge, *esp* of words, quotations, etc, a dictionary; a book with systematically arranged lists of words and their synonyms, antonyms, etc, a word-finder; a treasury. [L, from Gr *thēsauros*]

these /*dhēz*/ *demonstrative adj* and *demonstrative pronoun* plural of **this**. [OE *thæs*, a by-form of *thās*, pl of *thēs*, *thēos*, *this*, this; cf **those**]

thesis /*thē'sis*/ or (*prosody*, *music*) /*thes'is*/ *n* (*pl* **the'ses** /-*sēz*/) a long dissertation, *esp* one based on original research and presented for a doctorate; a subject dealt with in this way; a position or that which is set down or advanced for argument; an essay on a theme; a downbeat in a bar or metrical foot (*classical prosody* and *music*); hence, the strong position in a bar or foot; understood by the Romans as the weak position; used in English in both senses, *opp* to *arsis*. [Gr *thesis*, from the root of *tithenai* to put, set]
■ **thetic** /*thet'ik*/ or **thet'ical** *adj* positively asserting; bearing the thesis (*classical prosody* and *music*). **thet'ically** *adv*.
❑ **thesis novel** *n* a roman à thèse (see under **roman**).

Thesmophoria /*thes-mə-fö'ri-ə* or *-fö'ri-ə*/ *n pl* in ancient Greece, a married women's festival in honour of Demeter *Thesmophoros* (lawgiving). [Gr *thesmophoria*]

thesmothete /*thes'mə-thēt*/ *n* a lawgiver, *esp* one of the six junior archons in ancient Athens. [Gr *thesmothetēs*, from *thesmos* law, and *thetēs* a placer, setter]

thesp /*thesp*/ (*inf*) *n* an actor. [From **Thespian**]

Thespian /*thes'pi-ən*/ (also without *cap*) *adj* relating to tragedy or to drama in general; tragic. ◆ *n* a tragic actor; an actor (*facetious*). [*Thespis*, regarded as the founder of Greek tragedy]

Thess. (*Bible*) *abbrev* : (the Letters to the) Thessalonians.

theta /*thē'tə*, *thā'tə*/ *n* the eighth (*orig* ninth) letter of the Greek alphabet (Θ, θ) transliterated *th*, its sound an aspirated *t*, but in modern Greek like English *th*; as a Greek numeral θ' = 9, ‚θ = 9000; a mark of condemnation (from the θ for *thanatos* death, used in balloting). [Gr *thēta*; Semitic]

thetch /*thech*/ (*Spenser*) *vi* to thatch. [OE *theccan*]

thete /*thēt*/ (*Gr hist*) *n* orig a serf; a poor freeman in Athens under Solon's constitution. [Gr *thēs*, *thētos*]

thether see **thither**.

thetic see under **thesis**.

theurgy /*thē'ər-ji*/ *n* magic or miracles by the agency of good spirits; miraculous divine action; the beneficial magical science of the Egyptian Neoplatonists. [Gr *theourgiā*, from *theos* a god, and *ergon* work]
■ **theur'gic** or **theur'gical** *adj*. **the'urgist** *n*.

thew /*thū*/ (*literary*) *n* (used chiefly in *pl* **thews** or **thewes**) custom; trait; manner; moral quality; bodily quality, muscle or strength. [OE *thēaw* manner]
■ **thewed** *adj* mannered (*Spenser*); muscular. **thew'less** *adj* (see also **thowless**). **thew'y** *adj* muscular, strong.

they /*dhā*/ *pronoun nominative pl* used as plural of **he**, **she**, **it**[1]; people in general, some; used, with a plural verb, instead of **he** or **she**, where the antecedent is a singular common-gender word such as *someone* or *person* (but unacceptable to some, *esp* in written English); people in authority. [ME *thei*, from ON *theirr*, which supplanted *hi* (OE *hīe*)]
❑ **they'd** *n* a contraction of **they had** or **they would**. **they'll** *n* a contraction of **they will** or **they shall**. **they're** *n* a contraction of **they are**. **they've** *n* a contraction of **they have**.

THG *abbrev* : tetrahydrogestrinone.

THI *abbrev* : temperature-humidity index.

thi- see **thio-**.

thiamine /*thī'ə-mēn*, -*min*/ or **thiamin** /*thī'ə-min*/ *n* vitamin B$_1$, found in seeds, grains, beans and liver, a deficiency of which causes beriberi (also called **aneurin**). [Gr *theion* sulphur, and **amine**]

thiasus /*thī'ə-səs*/ *n* a group of worshippers collected together to sing and dance in praise of a god, *esp* Bacchus. [Gr *thiasos*]

thiazide /*thī'ə-zīd*/ *n* any of a group of drugs used as diuretics and to treat hypertension. [*thio*-, *azo*-, *oxide*]

thiazine /*thī'ə-zēn*/ (*chem*) *n* any of several organic compounds containing four carbon atoms, one sulphur and one nitrogen atom.

thiazole /*thī'ə-zōl*/ (*chem*) *n* a colourless, highly volatile liquid (C$_3$H$_3$NS) closely resembling pyridine.

Thibet see **Tibet**.

thible /*thib'l*, *thī'bl*/ or **thivel** /*thiv'l*, *thī'vl*/ (*Scot* and *N Eng*) *n* a stick for stirring porridge. [Origin unknown]

thick[1] /*thik*/ *adj* having a great (or specified) distance in measurement from surface to surface in the lesser dimension; broad; deep; dense; viscous; firm or dense in consistency, close-set or packed; crowded; made of thick or warm material; very friendly, intimate, in close confidence (*inf*); abundant; frequent, in quick succession; heavily or completely covered or occupied; foggy; opaque; dull; stupid; gross; husky, muffled; indistinctly articulate; (of an accent) strong, marked; excessive, unfair, approaching the intolerable (*inf*). ◆ *n* the thickest part of anything; the midst; a stupid person (*sl*); a thicket (*Spenser*). ◆ *adv* thickly; closely; frequently; fast; to a great (or specified) depth. ◆ *vt* and *vi* (*Spenser*, *Shakesp*) to make or become thick. [OE *thicce*; Ger *dick*]
■ **thick'en** *vt* and *vi* to make or become thick or thicker. ◆ *vi* to become more complicated. **thick'ener** *n*. **thick'ening** a making or becoming thicker; a thickened part or area; material or a substance added to something (*esp* liquid) to thicken it. **thick'et** *n* (OE *thiccet*) a dense mass of trees or shrubs. **thick'eted** *adj*. **thick'ety** *adj*. **thick'ie** or **thick'y** *n* (*sl*) a stupid person. **thick'ish** *adj* somewhat thick. **thick'ly** *adv*. **thick'ness** *n* the state or quality of being thick; the degree to which something is thick; the space between outer surfaces; the thick part of something; a layer. **thick'o** *n* (*pl* **thick'os** or **thick'oes**) (*sl*) a stupid person.
❑ **thick-and-thin'** *adj* unwavering in devotion to party or principle. **thick'-com'ing** *adj* (*Shakesp*) coming close upon one another. **thick ear** *n* (*inf*) a swollen ear, *usu* a result of a blow administered as punishment. **thick'-eyed** *adj* dim-sighted. **thick film** *n* (*electronics*) film deposited by screen-printing or a similar process. **thick'-grown** *adj* (*Shakesp*). **thick'head** *n* a stupid person, a blockhead; any bird of an Australian family (Pachycephalidae) related to flycatchers and shrikes. **thickhead'ed** *adj* having a thick head or skull; stupid; having a feeling of numbness, paralysis and often pain in the head often accompanying eg a cold or a hangover. **thickhead'edness** *n*. **thick knee** *n* the stone curlew. **thick'-lipped** *adj* (*Shakesp*). **thick'-lips** *n* (*Shakesp*) a black person. **thick'-pleached** *adj* (*Shakesp*) closely interwoven. **thick'-ribbed** *adj* (*Shakesp*). **thick'set** *adj* having a short thick body; closely set or planted. ◆ *n* a thicket; a stout cotton. **thick'-sight'ed** *adj* (*Shakesp*) dim-sighted. **thick'skin** *n* a blockhead. **thick-skinned'** *adj* having a thick skin; insensitive; indifferent to criticism or insult. **thick'-skull** *n* a blockhead. **thick-skulled'** *adj* having a thick skull; stupid; dull, slow to learn, doltish. **thick'-sown** *adj* planted closely; close-set. **thick''un** *n* (*hist sl*) a sovereign; a crown. **thick-witt'ed** *adj* dull, slow to learn, doltish. **thick-witt'edly** *adv*. **thick-witt'edness** *n*.
■ **a bit thick** (*inf*) more than one can reasonably be expected to put up with. **as thick as a plank** or **as thick as two short planks** very stupid. **as thick as thieves** very friendly. **in the thick of** in the middle of, extremely busy or occupied with. **lay it on thick** to praise something extravagantly; to exaggerate. **thick and fast** frequently and in large numbers. **through thick and thin** in spite of all obstacles; without any wavering.

thick[2], **thicky** see **thilk**.

thief /*thēf*/ *n* (*pl* **thieves** /*thēvz*/) someone who takes unlawfully what is not his or her own, *esp* by stealth; a flaw in a candlewick that causes guttering. [OE *thēof*; cf Ger *Dieb*]
■ **thief'like** *adj* and *adv*.
❑ **thief'-catcher** or **-taker** *n* a person whose business is to arrest thieves; a detective. **thieves' kitchen** *n* a haunt of thieves and other criminals.

thieve /*thēv*/ *vi* to practise theft; to steal. ◆ *vt* to steal (something). [OE *thēofian* to thieve, and *thēof* thief]
■ **thiev'ery** *n* an act or the practice of thieving; what is thieved. **thiev'ing** *n* and *adj*. **thiev'ish** *adj* given to, or like, theft; thieflike; furtive; infested by thieves (*Shakesp*). **thiev'ishly** *adv*. **thiev'ishness** *n*.

thig /*thig*/ (*Scot*) *vi* (*pat* and *pap* **thigg'it**) to beg; to live on alms. ◆ *vt* to beg; to get by begging. [ON *thiggja*; cf OE *thicgan* to take]
■ **thigg'er** *n*. **thigg'ing** *n*.
■ **thigging and sorning** extortionate begging and sponging.

thigh /*thī*/ *n* the thick fleshy part of the leg from the knee to the hip; a corresponding part in animals. [OE *thēoh* (Anglian *thēh*); ON *thjō*; OHGer *dioh*]
❑ **thigh bone** *n* the bone of the leg between the hip joint and the knee, the femur. **thigh boot** *n* a tall boot covering the thigh.

thigmotaxis /*thig-mə-tak'sis*/ (*biol*) *n* the movement of an organism towards or away from a solid object, in response to contact with it. [Gr *thigma*, -*atos* touch, and *taxis*, from *tassein* to arrange]
■ **thigmotac'tic** *adj*. **thigmotac'tically** *adv*.

thigmotropism /thig-mot'rə-pi-zm, -mə-trō'/ (biol) n the turning of an organism (or part of it) towards or away from an object in response to the stimulus of touch. [Gr thigma, -atos touch, and tropos a turning]
■ **thigmotropic** /-mə-trop'ik/ adj.

thilk /dhilk/ (dialect) adj and pronoun (also (SW Eng) **thick** /dhik/ or **thicky** /dhik'i/) the same, that same; this. [the ilk]

thill¹ /thil/ n the shaft of a cart or carriage. [Poss OE thille board, plank]
■ **thill'er** n a thill-horse.
□ **thill'-horse** n a shaft-horse, or the last of a team.

thill² /thil/ (dialect) n underclay or floor of a coal seam; a bed of fireclay. [Origin unknown]

thimble /thim'bl/ n a (metal, ceramic, plastic, etc) protective cover for the finger, used in sewing; any object of similar form; a metal ring with a grooved or concave outer edge fitted into a rope ring, etc to prevent chafing (naut); a thimbleful. ◆ vi to use a thimble. ◆ vt to use a thimble on. [OE thŷmel thumb covering, from thūma thumb]
■ **thim'bleful** n (pl **thim'blefuls**) as much as a thimble will hold; a small quantity.
□ **thimble case** n. **thim'blerig** n a sleight-of-hand trick in which the performer conceals, or pretends to conceal, a pea or small ball under one of three thimble-like cups. ◆ vi to cheat by such means. ◆ vt (**thimb'lerigging**; **thimb'lerigged**) to manipulate in this or a similar way. **thimb'lerigger** n. **thim'blerigging** n. **thimb'leweed** n any of several plants with a thimble-shaped head, esp the N American Anemone riparia or Anemone virginiana.

thimerosal /thī-mer'ə-səl/ (pharmacol) n a cream-coloured, crystalline, water-soluble powder, used eg on the skin to treat minor abrasions.

thin /thin/ adj (**thinn'er**; **thinn'est**) having little thickness; slim; lean; narrow; freely mobile; watery; dilute, lacking viscosity; of little density; rarefied; not closely packed, covered or occupied; sparse; made of thin material; slight; flimsy; lacking in body or solidity; meagre; poor; tinkling; travelling on too flat a trajectory (golf). ◆ n that which is thin. ◆ adv thinly. ◆ vt (**thinn'ing**; **thinned**) to make thin or thinner; to make less close, crowded or dense (with away, out, etc); to hit (the ball) too near the top so that it travels parallel to the ground, but only just above it, thus not travelling very far (golf). ◆ vi to grow or become thin or thinner. [OE thynne; Ger dünn; ON thunnr]
■ **thin'ly** adv. **thinn'er** n a person or thing that thins, esp (often in pl, sometimes treated as sing) a diluent for paint. **thin'ness** n. **thinn'ing** n and adj. **thinn'ings** n pl seedlings removed from a forest, etc to improve the growth of remaining plants. **thinn'ish** adj somewhat thin. □ **thin'-belly** adj (Shakesp) narrow in the belly. **thin'-faced** adj (Shakesp). **thin'-film** adj (electronics) made by chemical or physical vapour deposition or electrolysis, typically no more than a few micrometres thick. **thin-skinned'** adj having thin skin; sensitive; irritable. **thin-skinned'ness** n. **thin'-sown** adj sparsely sown. **thin'-spun** adj drawn out fine. **thin''un** n (hist sl) a half sovereign. **thin-walled'** adj.
■ **a thin time** a time of hardship, misery, etc. **into** (or **out of**) **thin air** into (or out of) nothing or nothingness. **thin blue line** a line of policemen drawn up to quell crowd violence, etc (coined in imitation of **thin red line** below). **thin on the ground** present in very small, inadequate quality or numbers. **thin on top** balding. **thin red line** a designation for the British Army (orig used in reports of the Crimean campaign, when uniforms were still red) conveying an image of indomitability against heavy odds.

thine /dhīn/ (formal, church, dialect or archaic) pronoun genitive of **thou¹**, used predicatively or absolutely, belonging to thee; thy people; that which belongs to thee; adjectivally, esp before a vowel or h, thy. [OE thīn]

thing /thing/ n a matter, affair, problem, point; a circumstance; a fact; an event, happening, action; an entity; that which exists or can be thought of; an inanimate object; a quality; a living creature (esp in pity, tolerant affection, kindly reproach); a possession; that which is wanted or is appropriate (inf); a slight obsession or phobia (inf); a typical example; an unaccountable liking or dislike (inf); (in pl) clothes, esp a woman's additional outdoor garments; (in pl) utensils, esp for the table; (in pl) personal belongings; an aim; (in pl) affairs in general; property (law); a piece of writing, composition, etc; an assembly, parliament, court, council (hist). [OE and ON thing parliament, object, etc; Norw, Swed, Dan ting parliament; Ger Ding thing]
■ **thing'amy**, **thing'ummy**, **thing'amybob**, **thing'amyjig**, **thing'umabob**, **thing'umajig**, **thing'umbob**, **thing'ummybob** or **thing'ummyjig** n (inf) what-d'you-call-him, -her, -it; what's-his-name, etc (used when one cannot or will not recall the name). **thing'iness** or **thing'liness** n reality, objectivity; a materialistic or matter-of-fact turn of mind. **thing'ness** n the character or fact of being a thing; reality. **thing'y** adj real; actual; objective; matter-of-fact. ◆ n thingumajig.
□ **thing-in-itself'** n (in the philosophy of Kant) a noumenon, the German Ding an sich.

■ **a good thing** a fortunate circumstance. **and things** and other (similar) things. **a stupid** (or **wise**, etc) **thing to do** a stupid (or wise, etc) action. **be all things to all men** to meet each person on his or her own ground, accommodate oneself to his or her circumstances and outlook (Bible, 1 Corinthians 9.22); (loosely and disparagingly) to keep changing one's opinions, etc, so as to suit one's company. **be on to a good thing** (inf) to be in a particularly profitable position, job, etc. **do one's** (**own**) **thing** (inf) to behave as is natural to or characteristic of oneself; to do something in which one specializes. **do the handsome thing by** to treat generously. **do things to** to affect in some good or bad way. **for one thing… for another** (**thing**) expressions used in enumerating reasons. **have a good thing going** (inf) to be established in a particularly profitable position, etc. **hear things** to hear imaginary noises, voices, etc. **know a thing or two** (inf) to be shrewd. **make a good thing of it** to reap a good advantage from. **make a thing of** to make an issue, point of controversy, etc of; to fuss about. **no such thing** something very different; no, not at all. **not a thing** (inf) nothing. **not quite the thing** (old inf) not in very good health (see also **the thing** below). (**now**) **there's a thing** (inf) that surprises me. **one of those things** a happening one cannot account for or do anything to prevent. **see things** to see something that is not really there. **the thing** or **the done thing** that which is conventional, fashionable, approved, right or desirable.

think¹ /thingk/ vt (pat and pap **thought** /thöt/) to form, conceive or revolve in the mind; to have as a thought; to imagine; to judge; to believe or consider; to expect or intend; to purpose, design; to remember or recollect; to bring into a particular condition by thinking; to believe to exist (Milton). ◆ vi to exercise the mind (often with about, of, or (archaic) on, upon); to revolve ideas in the mind; to judge; to be of an opinion; to consider; to call to mind, recollect; to conceive or hit on a thought; to aspire or form designs (with of or about); to be capable of thinking and reflecting. ◆ n (inf) a spell of thinking; a thought. [OE thencan]
■ **think'able** adj capable of being thought; conceivably possible. **think'er** n a person who thinks, esp someone with a powerful mind; a horse that takes care of itself in a race and therefore does not try hard enough (horse-racing). **think'ing** n an opinion or judgement; the process of thought. ◆ adj using or capable of rational thought. **think'ingly** adv.
□ **think'-in** n (inf) a meeting to discuss ideas, thoughts on a subject, etc. **think piece** n an article in a newspaper or magazine expressing the writer's thoughts or opinion on a particular subject. **think tank** n a person or a group of people, usu expert in some field, regarded as a source of ideas and solutions to problems.

■ **have another think coming** (inf) to be wrong in what one thinks (about future events or actions). **I don't think** I disbelieve; a warning that what was said was ironical (inf). **I shouldn't** (or **wouldn't**) **think of** I would not under any conditions. **just think of it** or **to think of it** an expression of surprise, disapproval, longing, etc. **put on one's thinking-cap** to devote some time to thinking about some problem. **think again** to (be forced to) change one's opinion. **think aloud** to utter one's thoughts unintentionally. **think back to** to bring to one's mind the memory of (a past event, etc). **think better of** to change one's mind about (doing something) on reflection; to feel more approval for. **think for** (archaic) to expect. **think little** (or **much, well**) **of** to have a poor (or high) opinion of. **think long** (archaic) to yearn; to weary (from deferred hopes or boredom). **think nothing of** not to consider difficult, exceptional, etc; not to hesitate in (doing). **think nothing of it** it does not matter, it is not important. **think on one's feet** to solve problems as they arise during an activity. **think out** to devise, project completely; to solve by a process of thought. **think over** to reconsider at leisure. **think shame** to be ashamed. **think through** to solve by a process of thought; to project and consider all the possible consequences, problems, etc relating to (some course of action). **think twice** (often with about) to hesitate (before doing something); to decide not to do something. **think up** to find by thinking, devise or concoct.

think² /thingk/ vi (pat **thought** /thöt/) (impers, archaic with dative pronoun prefixed, as in methinks; otherwise obs) to seem. [OE thyncan to seem]

thio- or **thi-** /thī(-ō)-, (-ə)-/ combining form denoting sulphur; indicating in chemistry a compound theoretically derived from another by substituting an atom or more of sulphur for oxygen. [Gr theion sulphur]
■ **thi'o-acid** n an acid analogous in constitution to an oxyacid, sulphur taking the place of oxygen. **thioal'cohol** n mercaptan. **thiobacill'us** n any of several rod-shaped bacteria, genus Thiobacillus, that live in soil, sewage, etc and that derive energy from the oxidation of sulphur or sulphur compounds (**Thiobacillus ferrooxidans** a thiobacillus that, in the presence of water, converts copper sulphide ores into copper sulphate (see **bacterial leaching** under **leach¹**)). **thiobarbit'urate** n a salt of **thiobarbitu'ric acid** ($C_4H_4N_2O_2S$) similar in effect to a barbiturate. **thiocar'bamide** n thiourea. **thiocy'anate** n a

salt of **thiocyan'ic acid** (HSCN). **thiodiglycol** /-*dī-glī'kol*/ *n* a chemical compound soluble in eg water and alcohol used eg as an industrial cleaning agent, and also as an ingredient of mustard gas and nerve gas. **thio-e'ther** *n* a compound in which the ether oxygen has been replaced by sulphur. **thī'ol** (or /-*ōl*/) *n* mercaptan. **thī'onyl** *adj* containing the group -SO. **thiopent'one** or (*N Am*) **thiopent'al** *n* see **Pentothal**®. **thi'ophen** /-*fen*/ or **thi'ophene** /-*fēn*/ *n* a five-membered heterocyclic compound with sulphur. **thi'ophil** *adj* (of eg bacteria) having an affinity for sulphur and its compounds. **thi'o-salt** *n* a salt of a thio-acid. **thiosul'phate** *n* a salt of **thiosulphuric acid** ($H_2S_2O_3$), used in photographic fixing; hypo. **thiouracil** /*thī-ō-ū'rə-sil*/ *n* a derivative of thiourea that interferes with the synthesis of thyroid hormone. **thiourea** /*thī-ō-ū'ri-ə*/ *n* urea with its oxygen replaced by sulphur, a bitter crystalline substance that inhibits thyroid activity and is used in organic synthesis and as a reagent for bismuth (also called **thiocarbamide**).

thir /*dhir*/ (*Scot*) *demonstrative pronoun* and *demonstrative adj* these. [Origin obscure]

thiram /*thī'ram*/ *n* a fungicide. [*thiourea* and *carbamic*]

third /*thûrd*/ *adj* the last of three; next after the second in time, place, order, rank, etc; equal to one of three equal parts. ◆ *n* one of three equal parts; a person or thing in third position; an interval of two (conventionally called three) diatonic degrees (*music*); a note separated from another by this interval (*music*); third gear; (also **third class**) an honours degree of the third, and *usu* lowest, class. ◆ *adv* in the third place; as the third point. ◆ *vt* to divide by three; to support after the seconder. [OE *thridda*; cf Ger *dritte*, Gr *tritos*, L *tertius*]
■ **third'ing** *n* a third part. **third'ly** *adv* in the third place; as the third point.
❑ **Third Age** *n* those people aged over 60 (in some cases over 50) collectively seen as a distinct group within society, with opportunities (eg for travel and education), special needs, and a positive contribution to make to society in general. **Third-A'ger** *n*. **third class** *n* the class (of degree, hotel accommodation, travel, etc) next below second class. **third-class'** *adj* and *adv*. **third degree** see under **degree**. **third dimension** *n* depth, thickness; the dimension of depth, distinguishing a solid object from a two-dimensional or planar object. **third-dimen'sional** *adj*. **third estate** see under **estate**. **third eye** *n* (*inf*) the pineal gland; an organ supposed to enable extrasensory perception. **third eyelid** *n* the nictitating membrane (qv under **nictate**). **third force** *n* a group (eg in a political party) following a middle or uncommitted course between contending extremes. **third gear** *n* the gear which is one faster than second, and *usu* one lower than top, in a gearbox. **third gender** *n* (*anthrop*) a class of people who identify themselves as neither male nor female. **third-gender** *adj*. **third'-generation** *adj* (also **3G**) relating to communications technology providing more advanced services than WAP technology. **third-hand'** *adj*. **Third International** see under **international**. **third man** *n* (*cricket*) a fielder, or a fielding position, near the boundary on the offside behind the slips. **Third market** *n* (*stock exchange, esp US*) trade in listed stocks done otherwise than on the Stock Exchange; the market where such trade is done. **third order** *n* the lay members affiliated to a monastic order, who continue to live an ordinary life in the world. **third party** *n* a person other than the principal people involved (eg in the agreement between the insured and insurer). **third'-party** *adj*. **third person** see under **person**. **third'-programme** *adj* highbrow, in allusion to the Third Programme (1946–70) of the BBC. **third rail** *n* a rail carrying electricity to an electrically-powered train; a highly controversial topic that politicians choose not to discuss. **third-rail system** *n* (*elec eng*) a system of electric traction supply by which current is fed to the tractor from an insulated conductor rail running parallel with the track. **third'-rate** *adj* of the third rank, class, order, etc; of poor quality. **third reading** *n* (in a legislative assembly) in Britain the consideration of committee reports on a bill; in the USA the final consideration of a bill. **Third Reich** see under **Reich**. **third sector** *n* the part of a country's economy made up of charities, voluntary groups, non-profit-making organizations, etc. **thirds'man** *n* a mediator. **third stream** *n* a style of music having features of both jazz and classical music. **third'-stream** *adj*. **third wave** *n* the age of information technology regarded as successor to the agrarian and industrial ages. **third way** *n* (*esp* in politics) a hitherto unconsidered alternative to two prevailing systems. **third wheel** *n* (*inf*) a person in a group of three whose presence is unwanted by the other two. **Third World** *n* the developing countries of Africa, Asia and Latin America, not aligned politically with the large power blocks. **Third-Worl'der** *n* a person living in or from the Third World; a believer in or supporter of Third-Worldism. **Third-Worl'dism** *n* an ideology which supports and encourages the development of the Third World.
■ **Picardy third** tierce de Picardie.

thirdborough /*thûrd'bə-rə*/ (*hist*) *n* an under-constable. [Supposed to be from OE *frithborh* a surety for peace (see under **frith**²)]

thirl¹ /*thûrl*/ (*dialect*) *n* a hole; an opening; a short passage between two headings in a mine. ◆ *vt* to pierce; to thrill. ◆ *vi* to vibrate, tingle, thrill. [OE *thyrel* hole, from *thurh* through; cf **thrill**]

thirl² /*thûrl*/ *n* a serf, a form of **thrall** (*rare*); thirlage. ◆ *vt* to bind or subject; to enslave; to confine, restrict. [Esp Scot, variant of *thrill* to enslave, variant of **thrall**]
■ **thirl'age** *n* a form of servitude by which the grain produced on certain lands had to be ground (or at least paid for) at a certain mill.

thirst /*thûrst*/ *n* the discomfort caused by lack of drink; vehement desire for drink; eager desire or craving for anything. ◆ *vi* to feel thirst. [OE *thurst* (noun), *thyrstan* (verb); cf Ger *Durst*, *dürsten*, L *torrēre* to dry]
■ **thirst'er** *n*. **thirst'ful** *adj*. **thirst'ily** *adv*. **thirst'iness** *n*. **thirst'less** *adj*. **thirst'y** *adj* (**thirst'ier**; **thirst'iest**) suffering from thirst; dry; parched; causing thirst; vehemently desiring.

thirteen /*thûr'tēn* or *-tēn'*/ *n* and *adj* three and ten. [OE *thrēotīene*, *-tēne*; see **three** and **ten**]
■ **thir'teenth** (or /*-tēnth'*/) *adj* last of thirteen; next after the twelfth; equal to one of thirteen equal parts. ◆ *n* a thirteenth part; a person or thing in thirteenth position. **thirteenth'ly** *adv*.

thirty /*thûr'ti*/ *n* and *adj* three times ten. [OE *thrītig*, from *thrēo* three, and sfx *-tig*, denoting ten]
■ **thir'ties** *n pl* the numbers from 30 to 39; the years so numbered in life or any century; a range of temperatures from thirty to just under forty degrees. **thir'tieth** *adj* last of thirty; next after the twenty-ninth; equal to one of thirty equal parts. ◆ *n* a thirtieth part; a person or thing in thirtieth position. **thir'tyfold** *adj* and *adv*. **thir'tyish** *adj* somewhere about the age of thirty.
❑ **Thirty-nine Articles** *n pl* the set of doctrines of the Church of England, formally accepted by those taking orders. **thirty-second note** *n* (*N Am; music*) a demisemiquaver. **thir'tysomething** *n* (*inf*) the ages between 30 and 39; a person aged between 30 and 39, *esp* when considered as part of a social group of similarly aged people with specific desires, aims and needs. ◆ *adj* (*inf*) of, being or for a person aged between 30 and 39. **thirty-two-bit** or **32-bit** *adj* (*comput*) denoting a processor handling data consisting of 32 binary digits. **thirty-two'mo** *adj* (for *tricesimo secundo*, 32mo) of a book, in sheets folded to give 32 leaves (64 pages). ◆ *n* (*pl* **thirty-two'mos**) a book constructed in this way.

this /*dhis*/ *demonstrative pronoun* (*pl* **these**) denoting a person, animal, thing or idea near, topical, already mentioned or about to be mentioned, or otherwise understood from the context; a person, animal or thing which is nearby, *esp* which is closer to the speaker than something else (often designated by *that*); (up to and including) the present time or place; the place where the speaker is; an action, event or circumstance; (when telephoning) the person speaking, or the person spoken to. ◆ *adj* (*pl* **these**) being the person, animal or thing just mentioned, about to be mentioned, or otherwise understood from the context; being the person, animal or thing which is nearby, *esp* closer than something else; relating to today, or time in the recent past ending today; used sometimes almost with the force of an indefinite or definite article, eg for emphasis or in narrative, as in *I saw this big bright object in the sky* (*inf*). ◆ *adv* to this (extreme) degree or extent, with adjectives or adverbs *esp* of quantity, eg *this high*, *far*, etc, or (*inf*) with others, eg *this difficult*, *well*, etc; thus (*Shakesp*). [OE, neuter of *thēs*, *thēos*, *this* (instrumental *thīs*, *thȳs*; nominative pl *thās*, *thāes*)]
■ **this'ness** *n* the quality of being this, not something else, haecceity.
■ **this and that** or **this, that and the other** various minor unspecified objects, actions, etc. **this here** (*inf*) an emphatic form of this. **with this** at that, thereupon.

thistle /*this'l*/ *n* a prickly composite plant (*Carduus*, *Cnicus*, *Onopordon*, etc) with pink, white, yellow but *usu* purple flower-heads, the national emblem of Scotland. [OE *thistel*]
■ **this'tly** *adj* like a thistle; overgrown with thistles.
❑ **thistle butterfly** *n* the painted lady, *Vanessa cardui*. **this'tledown** *n* the tufted feathery parachutes of thistle seeds.
■ **Order of the Thistle** a Scottish order of knighthood.

thither /*dhidh'ər*/ (*Spenser* often **thether**; *literary*, *formal* or *archaic*) *adv* to that place; to that end. ◆ *adv* on the far side. [OE *thider*]
■ **thith'erward** or **thith'erwards** *adv* toward that place.

thivel see **thible**.

thixotropy /*thik-sot'rə-pi*/ *n* (*chem*, *engineering*, *paint technol*, etc) the property (of gels) of showing a temporary reduction in viscosity when shaken or stirred. [Gr *thixis* action of touching, and *tropos* a turn]
■ **thix'otrope** *n* a thixotropic substance. **thixotropic** /*-trop'ik*/ *adj* of or showing, thixotropy; (of paints) non-drip.

thlipsis /*thlip'sis*/ *n* constriction; compression. [Gr *thlīpsis*, from *thlībein* to press]

tho¹ /*dhō*/ (*Spenser*) *demonstrative adj* those. [OE *thā*, pl of *se*, *sēo*, *thæt* that]

tho² /dhō/ (*Spenser*) *adv* then. [OE (and ON) *thā*]

tho' (*US* or *poetic*) same as **though**.

thoft /thoft/ (*dialect*) *n* a rowing-bench. [OE *thofte*]

thole¹ /thōl/ *n* (also **thole pin**) a pin in the side of a boat to keep the oar in place; a peg. [OE *thol*; Du *dol*, ON *thollr*]

thole² /thōl/ (chiefly *Scot*) *vt* and *vi* to endure; to suffer. [OE *tholian* to suffer; Gothic *thulan*, ON *thola*; OHGer *dolén*, Ger *Geduld* patience, *dulden* to suffer, L *tollere*, Gr *tolmaein*]

tholus /thō'ləs/ *n* (*pl* **thō'li** /-lī/) a round building, dome, cupola, or tomb, *esp* a dome-shaped tomb from the Mycenaean period (also **tholos** /thol'os/ (*pl* **thol'oi**)). [Gr *tholos*]
■ **tholobate** /thol'ə-bāt/ *n* (from Gr *-batēs* someone or something that goes, from *bainein* to go) the substructure of a dome or cupola.

Thomism /tō'mi-zm/ *n* the theological and philosophical doctrines of *Thomas* Aquinas (born *prob* 1225; died 1274).
■ **Thō'mist** *n* and *adj*. **Thōmist'ic** or **Thōmist'ical** *adj*.

Thompson submachine-gun /tom(p)'sən sub-mə-shēn'gun/ *n* a tommy gun (also **Thompson gun**).

thon /dhon/ and **thonder** /-dər/ unexplained modern Scots forms of **yon** and **yonder** *prob* influenced by **this** and **that**.

-thon see **-athon**.

thong /thong/ *n* a strap; a strip; the lash of a whip or crop; a sandal held on by a thong between the toes, a flip-flop (*N Am, Aust* and *NZ*); a garment, eg for wear on the beach, consisting of a narrow band of material running between the legs and attached to a cord round the waist. [OE *thwang*]
■ **thonged** *adj* having a thong or thongs.

Thor /thōr/ *n* the Scandinavian thunder god, Old English Thunor. [ON *Thōrr*]

thoraces, thoracic see **thorax**.

thoraco- /thō-rə-kō-, -kə-, -ko-* or *thö-/, or **thorac-** /-rəs-, -rək-/ *combining form* denoting thorax. [Gr *thōrāx, -ākos* breastplate, chest]
■ **thoracentesis** or **thoracocentesis** /-sen-tē'sis/ *n* (Gr *kentēsis*, from *kentein* to prick) surgery performed to draw off fluid from the pleural cavity, *usu* using a hollow needle inserted through the wall of the chest. **tho'racoplasty** *n* (Gr *plassein* to form) surgery to collapse a diseased lung by removing selected portions of the ribs. **tho'racoscope** *n* an instrument for examining the pleura covering the lung and the chest wall. **thoracos'tomy** *n* (see **-stomy**) the construction of an artificial opening in the chest, *usu* to draw off fluid or release a build-up of air. **thoracot'omy** *n* (see **-tomy**) an incision into the wall of the chest, to draw pus from the pleural cavity or lung.

Thorah see **Torah**.

thorax /thō'raks, thö'/ *n* (*pl* **tho'raxes** or **tho'races** /-sēz/) the part of the body between the head and abdomen, in man the chest, in insects the division that bears legs and wings (*zool*); a corslet or breastplate (*ancient Greece*). [Gr *thōrāx, -ākos*]
■ **thoracic** /-ras'ik/ or **tho'racal** /-rə-kl/ *adj*.
□ **thoracic duct** *n* the main trunk of the vessels conveying lymph in the body.

thoria /thō'ri-ə, thö'/ *n* the oxide of thorium. [**thorium**]

thorite /thō'rīt, thö'/ *n* a radioactive mineral, thorium silicate, in which thorium was first discovered by Berzelius. [**thorium**]

thorium /thō'ri-əm, thö'/ *n* a radioactive metallic element (symbol **Th**; atomic no 90) resembling aluminium, used eg as a source of nuclear power. [**Thor**]

thorn /thörn/ *n* a sharp hard part of the leaf, stem or root of a plant; an animal spine; anything prickly; a spiny plant; a thorn-bearing tree or shrub, *esp* the hawthorn; the wood of such a tree or shrub; the Old English and Old Norse letter Þ (th). ♦ *vt* to set with thorns; to prick. [OE *thorn*; ON *thorn*, Ger *Dorn*]
■ **thorned** *adj*. **thorn'iness** *n*. **thorn'less** *adj*. **thorn'set** *adj* set or beset with thorns. **thorn'y** *adj* (**thorn'ier**; **thorn'iest**) full of thorns; prickly; troublesome, difficult; harassing.
□ **thorn apple** *n* a poisonous plant (*Datura stramonium*, or related species) of the potato family, with a prickly capsule; a haw. **thorn'back** *n* the roker, a ray (*Raja clavata*) with large-based thorns in its back. **thorn'bill** *n* any of several Australian warblers of the genus *Acanthiza*; any of several S American hummingbirds with thornlike bills, *esp* of the genera *Chalcostigma* and *Ramphomicron*. **thorn'bird** *n* any of several tropical birds of the genus *Phacellodomus* that construct large globe-shaped nests. **thorn'bush** *n* any thorny shrub, *esp* hawthorn. **thorn'hedge** *n* a hedge of hawthorn. **thorn moth** *n* any of various woodland moths. **thorn'proof** *adj*. **thorn'proofs** *n pl* trousers made *usu* from thick brushed cotton, typically worn for country pursuits. **thorn'tree** *n* a thorny tree, *esp* a hawthorn. **thorny devil** *n* the Australian moloch lizard.
■ **thorn in the flesh** any cause of constant irritation (from Bible, 2 Corinthians 12.7).

thoron /thō'ron, thö'/ *n* the radioactive isotope of radon given off by the decomposition of thorium. [**thorium**]

thorough /thur'ə, also (*N Am*) thur'ō/ *adj* passing or carried through, or to the end; complete; entire; out-and-out; (of a person) assiduous and scrupulous in completing work and attending to every detail; (of a task, etc) done with great care and attention to detail. ♦ *prep* (*obs*) through. ♦ *n* that which goes through, a passage; (also with *cap*) the blind and obstinately tyrannical policy of Strafford and Laud in administering civil and ecclesiastical affairs without regard to opposite convictions (*hist*). [The longer form of **through**]
■ **thor'oughly** *adv*. **thor'oughness** *n*.
□ **thorough bass** *n* (*music*) (*esp* in baroque music) a bass part underlying a piece, *usu* with figures to indicate the chords, and *usu* played on a keyboard instrument; (loosely) harmony; a deep bass (*non-standard*). **thor'oughbrace** *n* (*US*) a leather band supporting the body of certain types of carriage; a stagecoach. **thor'oughbraced** *adj*. **thor'oughbred** *adj* thoroughly or completely bred or trained; (of a horse) bred from a dam and sire of the best blood, and having the qualities supposed to depend on such breeding; pure-bred; (with *cap*) relating to the Thoroughbred breed of horses; high-spirited. ♦ *n* an animal (*esp* a horse) of pure blood; (with *cap*) a racehorse of a breed descended from any of three Arabian stallions of the early 18c whose ideal gait is the gallop. **thor'oughfare** *n* a passage or way through; a road open at both ends; a public way or street; right of passing through. **thor'oughgoing** *adj* going through or to the end; going all lengths; complete; out-and-out. **thor'oughgoingly** *adv*. **thor'oughgoingness** *n*. **thor'ough-paced** *adj* (of a horse) thoroughly or perfectly trained in all paces; complete. **thor'oughpin** *n* (*vet*) inflammation of a horse's hock joint. **thor'oughwax** or **thor'ow-wax** *n* the plant hare's-ear, from the stem seeming to *wax* (ie grow) through the leaves.
■ **post-vintage thoroughbred** a car built between 1 January 1931 and 31 December 1941.

thorp or **thorpe** /thörp/ (*archaic*; found eg in place names) *n* a hamlet; a village. [OE *thorp, throp*; ON *thorp*, Gothic *thaurp*, Ger *Dorf*]

those /dhōz/ *demonstrative pronoun* and *adj* plural of **that**. [OE *thās*, pl of *thēs* this]

Thoth /thōth, thoth/ *n* the ancient Egyptian ibis-headed god of art, science, etc. [Gr *Thōth*, from Egyp *Tehuti*]

thother see **th-**.

thou¹ /dhow/ (*formal, church, dialect* or *archaic*) *pronoun* the nominative of the second person singular pronoun, now largely superseded by **you**. ♦ *vt* (*pat* and *pap* **thou'd**) to apply the pronoun *thou* to. —See also **thee**, **thine** and **thy**. [OE *thū*; Gothic *thu*, Doric Gr *ty*, L *tū*, Sans *tvam*]

thou² /thow/ *n* (*pl* **thou** or **thous**) one-thousandth of an inch. ♦ *n* and *adj* (*inf*) thousand or thousandth.

though /dhō/ *conj* admitting; allowing; if or even if; notwithstanding that. ♦ *adv* nevertheless; however. [ON *thauh, thō*; OE *thēah, thēh*, Ger *doch*]
■ **as though** as if.

thought¹ /thöt/ *n* the act or process of thinking; mind; consciousness; the faculty or power of reasoning; serious and careful consideration, deliberation; (often in *pl*) that which one thinks; a notion, idea, fancy; consideration, opinion, meditation; design, care, considerateness; purpose, intention; the intellectual ideas that are typical of a particular place, time, group, etc; resolution; a very slight amount, a hint or trace; grief, anxiety (*obs*). [OE (ge)*thōht*]
■ **thought'ed** *adj* having thoughts. **thought'en** *adj* (*Shakesp*) firm in belief, assured. **thought'ful** *adj* full of thought; engaged in or fond of meditation, pensive; attentive; considerate; expressive of or favourable to meditation. **thought'fully** *adv*. **thought'fulness** *n*. **thought'less** *adj* inconsiderate; unthinking; incapable of thinking; showing a lack of careful or serious thought; carefree; careless; inattentive. **thought'lessly** *adv*. **thought'lessness** *n*.
□ **thought'cast** *n* a mode of thought. **thought disorder** *n* extremely irrational thought and conversation, a characteristic of schizophrenia. **thought-ex'ecuting** *adj* carrying out the wishes of someone, *esp* a master (*old*); *perh* acting with the speed of thought (*Shakesp*). **thought process** *n* a train of thought; a manner of thinking. **thought'-reader** *n*. **thought'-reading** *n* discerning what is passing in another's mind by any means other than the ordinary and obvious, mind-reading. **thought'-sick** *adj* (*Shakesp*) sick with the thought. **thought transference** *n* telepathy. **thought wave** *n* a wavelike progress of a thought among a crowd or the public; a sudden accession of thought in the mind; an impulse in some hypothetical medium assumed to explain telepathy.
■ **in thought** thinking, reflecting. **on second thoughts** on reconsideration. **take thought** to think things over; to conceive a purpose; to be anxious or troubled (*obs*). **upon** (or **with**) **a thought** (*Shakesp*) in a moment; with the speed of thought.

thought² /thöt/ pat and pap of **think¹** and pat of **think²**. [OE *thōhte*, past tense, (ge)*thōht*, past participle]

thous /dhowz/ a Scot and N Eng contracted form of *thou is*, thou art (*Spenser*) and of *thou sal*, thou shalt.

thousand /thow'zənd/ n (pl **thousands** or, in the first sense given, **thousand**) ten hundred; anything having one thousand parts, etc; (in *pl*) an unspecified, very large number. ◆ adj being a thousand in number. [OE *thūsend*; Ger *tausend*, Gothic *thūsundi*]
■ **thou'sandfold** adj, adv and n a thousand times as much. **thou'sandth** adj last of a thousand, or in an equivalent position in a greater number; equal to one of a thousand equal parts. ◆ n a thousandth part; a person or thing in thousandth position.
❑ **Thousand Island dressing** n a salad dressing made with mayonnaise, and flavoured with chopped gherkins, pimentos, etc. **thou'sand-legs** n a centipede or millipede. **thousand-pound'** adj weighing, costing, priced at a thousand pounds. **thou'sand-year** adj lasting or coming once in a thousand years.
■ **a thousand and one** (*inf*) very many; an overwhelming number. **one in** (or **of**) **a thousand** anything exceedingly rare or excellent.

thowel and **thowl** obsolete forms of **thole¹**.

thowless /thow'lis/ (*Scot*) adj pithless; listless; inert. [Appar **thewless**]

thrae /thrā/ another form of Scots **frae**.

thrall /thröl/ n (*literary* or *archaic*) a slave, serf; slavery, servitude, subjugation; a stand for barrels, pans, etc. ◆ adj (*archaic*) enslaved. ◆ vt to enslave. [OE *thrǣ*, from ON *thrǣll*]
■ **thral'dom** or (*esp N Am*) **thrall'dom** n slavery; bondage.
■ **in thrall** in a state of rapt absorption or immobility, under some powerful influence.

thrang /thrang/ a Scots form of **throng**.

thrapple /thrap'l/ a Scots form of **thropple**.

thrash¹ /thrash/ vt (with *out*) to discuss exhaustively, or arrive at by debate; to beat soundly or severely; to defeat thoroughly. ◆ vi to lash out, beat about, in anger, panic, etc; to move the legs up and down in swimming; to force one's way, *esp* against the wind or tide (*naut*); to thresh. ◆ n an act of thrashing or threshing; a party (*inf*); thrash metal (*sl*). [Orig a dialect form of **thresh¹**]
■ **thrash'er** n a thresher-shark, a large, long-tailed shark; someone or something that thrashes; a thresher. **thrash'ing** n beating; excessive inefficient activity, eg of a hard disk (*comput*); threshing. ◆ adj beating; threshing.
❑ **thrash'ing-floor**, **thrash'ing-machine**, **thrash'ing-mill** n same as **threshing floor**, etc under **thresh¹**. **thrash metal** n a type of very fast, loud rock music, often with violent themes.

thrash² /thrash/ or **thresh** /thresh/ (*Scot*) n a rush (plant). [Obscurely connected with **rush²**]

thrasher¹ /thrash'ər/ or **thresher** /thresh'ər/ n any of several American birds of the mockingbird family (Mimidae). [Perh Eng dialect *thresher* thrush]

thrasher² see under **thrash¹**.

thrasonic /thrə-, thrā-son'ik/ or **thrasonical** /-i-kl/ adj boastful, bragging. [*Thrasōn*, the bragging soldier, a stock character in Greek New Comedy, or *Thrasō* in Terence's *Eunuchus*]
■ **thrason'ically** adv.

thrave /thrāv/ or **threave** /thrēv/ (*dialect*) n two stooks of (*usu*) twelve sheaves each; two dozen; a good number. [Scand; cf Icel *threfi*, Dan *trave*]

thraw /thrö/ a Scots form of **throw¹** with some old senses preserved; also of **throe**, with senses overlapping **throw¹**. vt (pat **threw**; pap **thrawn**) to turn; to twist; to wring; to distort; to wrest; to cross, thwart. ◆ vi to turn; to twist; to writhe; to sway; to go counter; to be perverse. ◆ adj twisted; distorted; wry. ◆ n a twist; a fit of perversity; a throe.
■ **thrawn** adj twisted; wry, crooked; stubborn, perverse.
■ **dead thraw** the agony of death. **heads and thraws** side by side, the head of the one by the feet of another.

thrawart or **thraward** /thrö'ərt/ (*Scot*) adj froward, obstinate; crooked. [ME *fraward*; see **froward**; perh influenced by **thraw**; cf **thrae**]

thrawn see under **thraw**.

thread /thred/ n a very thin line of any substance, *esp* linen or cotton, twisted or drawn out; several strands of yarn twisted together for sewing; a filament; a fibre; (in *pl*) clothes (*sl*); the prominent spiral part of a screw; a continuous connecting element in a story, argument, etc; a thin seam of coal or vein of ore; a series of postings on an Internet message board, each concerning the same subject. ◆ vt to pass a thread through; to string on a thread; to pass through, make (one's way) through (a narrow way, a crowd, obstacles, etc); to fit or supply with a thread. ◆ vi (of boiling syrup) to form a fine strand when poured. ◆ adj made of linen or cotton thread. [OE *thrǣd*; cf **throw¹**, **thraw**]

■ **thread'en** adj (*Shakesp*) made of thread. **thread'er** n. **thread'iness** n. **thread'like** adj. **thread'y** adj (**thread'ier**; **thread'iest**) like thread or threads; slender; containing or consisting of thread; (of the pulse) barely perceptible (*med*).
❑ **thread'bare** adj worn to the bare thread; having the nap worn off; poor or meagre; shabby; hackneyed; used until its novelty or interest is gone. **thread'bareness** n. **thread'-cell** n (in jellyfishes, etc) a stinging cell that throws out a stinging thread. **thread count** n a measure of the coarseness or fineness of fabric, corresponding to the total number of warp and weft threads in one square inch. **thread'fin** n any small, spiny-finned tropical fish of the family Polynemidae, with five threads on its pectoral fins. **thread'-lace** n lace made of linen thread. **thread'maker** n. **thread mark** n a coloured thread incorporated in banknotes to make counterfeiting difficult. **thread'-paper** n a piece of thin soft paper for wrapping up a skein of thread. **thread vein** n a very fine vein on the surface of the skin, *esp* on the face. **thread'worm** n any member of the Nematoda, a phylum of more or less threadlike worms, many of which are parasitic, *esp Oxyuris vermicularis*, parasitic in the human rectum.
■ **hang by a thread** see under **hang**. **thread and thrum** all, the good and bad together. **thread of life** (*Gr myth*) the thread imagined to be spun and cut by the Fates.

Threadneedle Street /thred'nē-dl strēt/ n a street in the city of London.
■ **Old Lady** (or **Woman**) **of Threadneedle Street** the Bank of England.

threap or **threep** /thrēp/ (*Scot* and *N Eng* dialect) vt (pat and pap **threap'it** or **threep'it**) to rebuke; to maintain persistently; to insist on; to urge, to press eagerly; to contradict. ◆ vi to dispute. ◆ n stubborn insistence or assertion; accusation; a traditional belief. [OE *thrēapian* to rebuke]

threat /thret/ n a declaration or indication of an intention to inflict harm, punish or hurt; an appearance of impending evil; a source of danger (with *to*). ◆ vt and vi (*Shakesp*, *Milton*, *Byron*, etc) to threaten. [OE *thrēat* (noun), *thrēatian* (verb), *thrēatnian* (verb); cf Ger *verdriessen* to tremble, L *trūdere* to thrust]
■ **threat'en** vt to offer a threat of, or against; to intimidate by threats; to seem to impend over; to indicate danger of, or to, to portend. ◆ vi to use threats; to give warning that something is likely to happen; to portend evil. **threat'ened** adj. **threat'ener** n. **threat'ening** n. ◆ adj menacing; portending danger or evil; (of the sky) heavily clouded over, promising rain, stormy weather, etc. **threat'eningly** adv. **threat'ful** adj menacing.

threave see **thrave**.

three /thrē/ n the cardinal number next above two; a symbol representing that number (3, iii, etc); a set of three things or people; a score of three points, strokes, tricks, etc; an article of a size denoted by 3; a playing card with three pips; the third hour after midnight or midday; the age of three years. ◆ adj of the number three; three years old. [OE *thrēo*, fem and neuter of *thrī*; Gothic *threis*, Ger *drei*, L *trēs*, *trēs*, *tria*, Gr *treis*, *treis*, *tria*, Sans *tri*]
■ **three'ness** n the state of being three. **three'some** n a group of three people; a game or dance for three. ◆ adj for three; triple.
❑ **three balls** n pl the pawnbroker's sign. **three-bott'le** adj able to drink three bottles of wine at a sitting. **three'-card** adj played with three cards. **three-card trick** n a card-sharp's play in which the victim is invited to bet on which of three cards, turned face down and deftly manipulated, is the queen (also called **find the lady**). **three-cen'tred** adj (of an arch) composed of circular arcs with three different centres. **three cheers** n pl three shouts of 'hurrah', to show approval, etc (also *fig*). **three'-cleft** adj cut halfway down into three lobes. **three'-colour** adj involving or using three colours as primaries. **three-colour process** n the method of producing colour pictures from the three primary originals (yellow, red and blue) prepared by photography. **three-cor'nered** adj triangular in form or section; having three competitors or three members. **three-day event**, **three-day eventer** see under **event**. **three'-deck** adj. **three-deck'er** n a ship with three decks or guns on three decks; a building or structure with three floors or tiers; a pulpit with three levels; a three-volume novel; a double sandwich, with two layers of filling and three layers of bread; any other thing with three layers, levels, etc. ◆ adj having three decks or layers. **three-dimen'sional** adj having, or seeming to have, three dimensions; giving the effect of being seen or heard in an environment of three dimensions (shortened to **three-D** or **3-D**); (of, eg a literary work) developed in detail and thus realistic. **three'-dimensional'ity** n. **three-far'thing** adj. **three-far'things** n sing a silver coin issued under Queen Elizabeth I, distinguished from a penny by a rose behind the queen's head. **three'fold** adj and adv in three parts; (by) three times as much. **three'foldness** n. **three'-foot** adj measuring or having three feet. **three-four'** adj (*music*) with three crotchets to the bar. **three-four'** or **three-four time** n the time signature ($\frac{3}{4}$) indicating three crochets to the bar. **three-halfpence** /thrē-hā'pəns/ n an old penny

and a halfpenny; a coin of that value. **three-halfpenny** /thrē-hāp'ni/ adj. **three-half'pennyworth** or **threeha'porth** /thrē-hāp'ərth/ n an amount of something costing one old penny and a halfpenny. **three'-handed** adj having three hands; played by three players. **three-jaw chuck** n (engineering) a scroll chuck (qv) with three jaws for holding cylindrical workpieces, materials or tools. **three'-leaved** (or **three'-leafed**) adj having three leaves or leaflets; having leaves in threes. **three'-legged** /-legd, -leg'id/ adj having three legs; (of a race) run by pairs of runners, each with a leg tied to his or her partner's adjacent one. **three-line whip** see under **whip**. **three'-man** adj (Shakesp) worked or performed by three men. **three-mast'ed** adj. **three-mast'er** n a ship with three masts. **three-mile limit** n (in international law) the outer limit of the territorial waters around a state, extending to three nautical miles. **three'-monthly** n and adj quarterly. **three'-nooked** adj (Shakesp) three-cornered. **three'-pair** or **three'-pair-of-stairs** adj on a third floor. ◆ n a room so situated. **three'-part** adj composed in three parts or for three voices. **three-part'ed** adj consisting of three parts; parted in three; divided into three nearly to the base. **three'-parts** adv to the extent of three-quarters. **threepence** /threp', thrip', thrup'əns/ n money, or a coin, of the value of three old pence. **threepenny** /threp', thrip', thrup'ni or -ə-ni/ adj sold or offered at threepence; of little worth; mean, vulgar. ◆ n a coin of the value of threepence (also **threepenny bit** or **piece**). **threepennyworth** or **threepenn'orth** /thrē-pen'i-wərth, thrē-pen'ərth/, also (chiefly Scot) **threep'enceworth** n an amount of something costing threepence. **three-per-cents'** n pl bonds or other securities paying three per cent interest, esp a portion of the consolidated debt of Great Britain. **three'-phase** adj (elec eng) (of an electric supply system) in which the alternating potentials on the three wires differ in phase from each other by 120°. **three'-piece** adj comprising three parts, three matching pieces, etc. ◆ n anything with three matching pieces, esp a suite of furniture. **three'-pile** adj having loops of three threads. ◆ n (Shakesp) the finest kind of velvet. **three'-piled** adj three-pile; piled three-high. **three'-ply** adj having three layers or strands. ◆ n any material with three layers or strands. **three-point landing** n (aeronautics) a landing with all three wheels touching the ground at the same moment, a perfect landing. **three-point turn** n the process of turning a vehicle round to face in the opposite direction by moving it forward, reversing, then moving forward again, turning the steering-wheel appropriately. **three'-pound** adj costing or weighing three pounds. **three-pound'er** n a thing that weighs three pounds; a gun that shoots a three-pound ball. **three'-pricker** n (RAF sl) a three-point landing; anything right or perfect. **three-quar'ter** adj and adv to the amount of three-fourths; (adj) being three quarters of the normal size or length (used of beds, coats, etc). ◆ n a three-quarter back. **three-quarter back** n (rugby) a player between halfbacks and full back. **three-quarter face** n an aspect between full face and profile. **three-quar'ter-length** adj (of a coat, sleeve, etc) being three quarters of the full length. **three quarters** n (a part equal to) three fourths of a whole; the greater part of something. **three-ring circus** n a circus with three rings in which simultaneous separate performances are given; a showy or extravagant event (fig); a confusing or bewildering scene or situation. **three'score** n and adj sixty. **three-sid'ed** adj having three sides. **three-speed gear** n a gear-changing device with three gear positions. **three'-square** adj having an equilateral triangle as a cross-section. **three-star'** adj (esp of a hotel) of a quality or rank denoted by three in a four- or five-star grading system; of or being a lieutenant-general (US). **three'-suit'ed** adj (Shakesp) allowed three suits of clothes a year as a serving-man. **three'-volume** adj in three volumes. **three'-way** adj giving connection in three directions from a centre; involving three people or things. **three-went way** n (dialect) a place where three roads meet. **three-wheel'er** n a vehicle having three wheels, esp a motor vehicle with two rear wheels and a single front wheel. ■ **the three R's** see under **R**. **the Three Wise Men** see under **magus**. **threescore and ten** seventy. **three times three** three cheers repeated three times.

threep see **threap**.

threepeat /thrē'pēt/ (N Am inf) n the achievement of a feat, esp the winning of a sporting trophy, on three consecutive occasions. ◆ vi to achieve a threepeat. [**three** and **repeat**]

threequel /thrē'kwəl/ n a film, play, book, etc that is a sequel to a first sequel.

thremmatology /threm-ə-tol'ə-ji/ n the science of breeding domestic animals and plants. [Gr thremma, -atos a nurseling, and logos discourse]

threnody /thren'ə-di, thrē'nə/ or **threnode** /-ōd/ n an ode or song of lamentation, esp for the dead (also (Shakesp) **threne** /thrēn/ or **thren'os**). [Gr thrēnōidiā, from thrēnos a lament, and ōidē song] ■ **threnet'ic** or **threnet'ical** adj. **threnō'dial** or **threnodic** /-od'/ adj. **thren'odist** n.

threonine /thrē'ə-nēn/ n an amino acid essential for bodily growth and health, present in certain proteins. [Gr erythro- red, by rearrangement, with -n- and -ine]

thresh[1] /thresh/ vt to beat out, subject to beating out, by trampling, flail or machinery; to thrash. ◆ vi to thresh corn, to separate the grain from the husks and straw; to thrash. ◆ n an act of threshing. [OE therscan; cf Ger derschen to thresh; see **thrash**[1]] ■ **thresh'el** n a flail; a flail-like weapon, a spiky ball on the end of a chain. **thresh'er** n a person who threshes; a flail; a threshing-machine or a beating part of it; (also **thresh'er-shark**) a large, long-tailed shark of the genus Alopias, especially Alopias vulpinus. **thresh'ing** n and adj. ❑ **thresher whale** n a grampus. **threshing floor** n a surface on which grain is threshed. **threshing machine** or **mill** n one for threshing corn, etc.

thresh[2] see **thrash**[2].

thresher see **thrasher**[1] and **thresh**[1].

threshold /thresh'ōld, -hōld/ n the sill of a house door; the place or point of entering; the outset; the limit of consciousness; the point at which a stimulus begins to bring a response, as in threshold of pain, etc; the smallest dose of radiation that will produce a specified result; the point, stage, level, etc, at which something will happen, become true, etc; (in a pay agreement, etc) a point in the rise of the cost of living at which a wage-increase is prescribed. ◆ adj at or constituting a threshold. [OE therscold, therscwald, threscold, appar from therscan to thrash, thresh, in its older sense of trample, tread] ❑ **threshold dose** n (radiol) the smallest dose of radiation that will produce a specified result. **threshold lighting** or **lights** n a line of lights across the ends of a runway or landing area to indicate the usable limits. ■ **threshold of audibility** or **sound** the minimum intensity or pressure of sound wave which the normal human listener can just detect at any given frequency.

thretty /thret'i/ a dialect form of **thirty**.

threw /throo/ pat of **throw**[1].

thrice /thrīs/ (formal) adv three times; three times as much; highly, greatly (archaic). [ME thriës, from OE thrīwa, thrīga thrice, from thrī three, with adverbial genitive ending -es]

thrid /thrid/ (Spenser) n a thread. ◆ vt (obs) to thread. [thread]

thridace /thrid'əs/ n inspissated lettuce juice used eg as a sedative. [Gr thridax lettuce]

thrift /thrift/ n frugality; economy; the sea pink (genus Armeria), a seaside and alpine plant of the Plumbaginaceae family; a savings and loan association similar in function to a building society (US finance); the state of thriving (rare or old); prosperity (archaic); increase of wealth (archaic); gain (archaic); profitable occupation (dialect); savings (archaic). [**thrive**] ■ **thrift'ily** adv. **thrift'iness** n. **thrift'less** adj not thrifty; extravagant; not thriving (rare or old). **thrift'lessly** adv. **thrift'lessness** n. **thrift'y** adj (**thrift'ier**; **thrift'iest**) showing thrift or economy; thriving by frugality; prosperous, in good condition (US). ❑ **thrift shop** or **store** n (chiefly US) a shop, usu run on behalf of a charity, that sells second-hand clothes and other articles.

thrill /thril/ vt to affect with a strong glow or tingle of sense or emotion, now esp a feeling of excitement or extreme pleasure; to pierce (archaic). ◆ vi to pass tinglingly; to quiver; to feel a sharp, shivering sensation; (of something sharp) to pierce or penetrate (with through) (archaic). ◆ n a sudden feeling of excitement or extreme pleasure; something causing such a feeling; a tingle; a shivering feeling or emotion; a tremor or vibration palpable at the surface of the body, esp in valvular disease of the heart (med). [OE thyrlian to bore, from thyrel a hole; Ger drillen to drill a hole] ■ **thrill'ant** adj (Spenser) piercing. **thrilled** adj excited; delighted. **thrill'er** n a sensational or exciting story, esp one about crime and detection; any person or thing that thrills. **thrill'ing** adj. **thrill'ingly** adv. **thrill'ingness** n. **thrill'y** adj.

thrimsa see **thrymsa**.

thrips /thrips/ n (pl **thrips** or **thrip'ses**) any insect of the order Thysanoptera, esp a minute black insect of the genus Thrips, common in flowers; popularly extended to leaf-hoppers, and to other small insects. [Gr thrīps, thrīpos a woodworm]

thrissel or **thristle** /thris'l, thrus'l/ Scots forms of **thistle**. [Poss influenced by thrist to thrust]

thrist /thrist/ and **thristy** /thris'ti/ old forms (Spenser) of **thirst** (n and v) and **thirsty**.

thrive /thrīv/ vi (pat **thrōve** or **thrīved**; pap **thriven** /thriv'n/ or **thrīved**) to grow; to grow healthily and vigorously; to get on, do well; to be successful, flourish; to increase in goods. [ON thrīfa to grasp]

■ **thrīve'less** *adj* not thriving or prospering. **thriven** /thriv'n/ *adj* grown, developed; successful. **thrī'ver** *n.* **thrī'ving** *n* and *adj.* **thrī'vingly** *adv* (*rare*). **thrī'vingness** *n.*

thro' or **thro** /throo/ same as **through**.

throat /thrōt/ *n* the passage leading from the back of the mouth; the forepart of the neck, in which the gullet and windpipe are located; voice; a sore throat (*inf*); a narrow entrance, aperture or passage; the narrow part, eg of a vase; a corolla (*bot*); a groove under a coping; the end of a gaff next to the mast (*naut*). [OE *throte*; cf **throttle**]

■ **throat'ed** *adj* with a throat. **throat'ily** *adv.* **throat'iness** *n.* **throat'y** *adj* (**throat'ier**; **throat'iest**) sounding as from the throat, guttural; hoarse; croaking; deep or full-throated; having a rather sore throat (*inf*); full or loose-skinned about the throat; potent in swallowing.

❑ **throat'band, -strap, -lash** or **-latch** *n* a band about the throat, eg holding a horse's bridle in place. **throat'-full** *adj* full to the throat. **throat microphone** *n* one held directly against the speaker's throat and actuated by vibrations of the larynx. **throat'wort** *n* the nettle-leaved bellflower (*Campanula trachelium*) once reputed good for throat ailments; the giant bellflower (*C. latifolium*).

■ **be at someone's throat** or **at each other's throats** (*inf*) to be engaged in a fierce, bitter argument with someone or with each other. **cut one's (own) throat** to commit suicide by cutting (*usu*) the jugular vein; to pursue some course ruinous to one's interests. **give someone the lie in his** or **her throat** to accuse someone to his or her face of uttering a lie. **have by the throat** to have at one's mercy. **jump down someone's throat** see under **jump**[1]. **sore throat** an inflamed and painful condition of the tonsils and neighbouring parts. **stick in one's throat** to be more than one can bear, accept or manage. **thrust (or ram) down someone's throat** to force (eg one's own opinion) upon someone insistently.

throb /throb/ *vi* (**throbb'ing**; **throbbed**) to beat strongly, as the heart or pulse does, *esp* in response to some emotion, stimulus, etc; (of an injured or sore part of the body) to be affected by rhythmic waves of pain; (of an engine, etc) to produce a deep regular sound. ◆ *n* a beat or strong pulsation. [ME *throbben*; poss connected with L *trepidus* trembling]

■ **throbb'ing** *n* and *adj.* **throbb'ingly** *adv.* **throb'less** *adj.*

throe /thrō/, earlier (*Shakesp, Spenser*) **throw** or **throwe** /thrō/, or (*Scot*) **thraw** /thrö/ *n* a spasm; a paroxysm; a pang or pain, *esp* a birth-pang. ◆ *vt* to subject to pangs. ◆ *vi* to suffer pangs. [ME *thrahes, throwes, thrawes*; perh there have been cross-influences between OE *thrawu* pang, *thrāg* paroxysm, *thrōwian* to suffer, *thrāwan* to twist, throw; see also **thraw**]

■ **in the throes** in the struggle (of), struggling (with); in the thick (of); in travail.

thrombin /throm'bin/ *n* an enzyme that causes the blood to clot. [*thromb*us and *-in*]

thrombo- /throm-bō-, -bə-/ (*med*) *combining form* denoting a blood clot. [Gr *thrombos* a clot]

■ **throm'bocyte** *n* (Gr *kytos* vessel, hollow) a platelet. **thrombocytopē'nia** *n* (Gr *penia* poverty) an abnormal decrease in the number of platelets in the blood, causing haemorrhage. **thromboem'bolism** *n* a blockage of a blood vessel caused by an embolus carried by the bloodstream from its point of origin. **thrombokī'nase** *n* an enzyme active in the clotting of blood; thromboplastin. **thrombol'ysis** (also /-bə-lī'sis/) *n* the dissolving of blood clots. **thrombolyt'ic** *adj* (of a drug) dissolving clots in the blood. ◆ *n* a thrombolytic drug. **thrombophil'ia** *n* an abnormal tendency to develop blood clots. **thrombophlebī'tis** *n* inflammation of a vein accompanied by formation of a thrombus. **thromboplas'tin** *n* a substance, found *esp* in platelets, which participates in the clotting of blood.

thrombose /throm-bōz'/ *vt* to cause thrombosis in. ◆ *vi* to be affected with thrombosis. [Back-formation from **thrombosis**]

thrombosis /throm-bō'sis/ *n* (*pl* **thrombō'sēs**) clotting of blood in a vessel during life; a coronary thrombosis. [Gr *thrombōsis* curdling, from *thrombos* a clot]

■ **thrombot'ic** *adj.*

thrombus /throm'bəs/ *n* (*pl* **throm'bī**) a clot of blood in a living vessel, obstructing circulation. [Gr *thrombōs* a clot]

throne /thrōn/ *n* a monarch's, pope's, or bishop's chair of state; kingship; the power or duty of a monarch, etc; a lavatory (*inf*); an angel of the third of the nine orders of angels. ◆ *vt* to enthrone; to exalt. ◆ *vi* to sit in state, to sit on a throne. [Gr *thronos* a seat]

■ **throned** *adj.* **throne'less** *adj.*

❑ **throne room** *n* a room in a palace or great house containing a throne, used for holding audiences.

■ **power behind the throne** a person or group of people who exercise power or influence without having the formal authority to do so.

throng /throng/ *n* a crowd; a great multitude; crowding. ◆ *vt* to crowd (a place); to press or jostle; to press hard (*Shakesp*). ◆ *vi* to move or gather in a crowd. ◆ *adj* (*inf*) crowded; busy; intimate. [OE *gethrang*, from *thringan* to press]

■ **thronged** *adj* packed, crowded; (with *up*) overpowered (*Shakesp*). **throng'ful** *adj* thronged. **throng'ing** *n* and *adj.*

thropple /throp'l/ or (*Scot*) **thrapple** /thrap'l/ *n* the throat; the windpipe, *esp* of an animal. ◆ *vt* to throttle; to strangle. [Poss OE *throtbolla* windpipe, gullet, from *throte* throat, and *bolla* boll]

throstle /thros'l/ *n* the song thrush; (in full **throstle frame**) a machine for drawing, twisting and winding fibres (from its sound). [OE *throstle*; Ger *Drossel*, L *turdus* thrush]

❑ **thros'tle-cock** *n* a male song thrush or (*dialect*) mistle-thrush.

throttle /throt'l/ *n* (in full **throttle valve**) a valve regulating the supply of steam or of gas and air in an engine; (in full **throttle lever**) a lever that opens and closes a throttle valve; the throat or windpipe (now *dialect*). ◆ *vt* to choke by pressure on the windpipe; to strangle; to suppress or silence; to check the flow of; to cut down the supply of steam, or of gas and air, to or in, by means of a throttle. ◆ *vi* to breathe hard, as when nearly suffocated. [Appar dimin of **throat**]

■ **thrott'ler** *n.* **thrott'ling** *n* and *adj.*

❑ **throttle pipe** *n* the vertical pipe between the throttle valve and the dry-pipe of a locomotive.

■ **at full throttle** at full speed. **throttle back** or **down** to slow down by closing the throttle (also *fig*).

through /throo/ *prep* from end to end, side to side, or boundary to boundary of, by way of the interior; from place to place within; everywhere within; by way of; along the passage of; clear of; among; from beginning to end of; up to and including, to or until the end of (*N Am*); by means of; in consequence of. ◆ *adv* from one end or side to the other; from beginning to end; all the way; clear; into a position of having passed; in connection or communication all the way. ◆ *adj* passing, or serving for passage, all the way without interruption; having completed or come to the end; (in telephoning) connected (*inf*). [OE *thurh*; Ger *durch*]

■ **through'ly** *adv* same as **thoroughly** (see under **thorough**) (*obs*); far through (*archaic*). **throughout'** *prep* in, into, through or during the whole of. ◆ *adv* in every part; everywhere; during the whole time.

❑ **through ball** *n* (*football*) a ball passed forward between defenders. **through bolt** *n* a bolt that passes through from side to side of what it fastens. **through bridge** *n* (*civil eng*) a bridge in which the track is carried by the lower strings. **through-compōs'ed** *adj* (*music*) (of a song) having different music for each verse. **through'fare** (*Shakesp*) same as **thoroughfare** (see under **thorough**). **through'-ganging** *adj* (*Scot*) thoroughgoing. **through'-going** (*Scot* **through'gaun** /-gön/) *n* a scolding. ◆ *adj* passing through; active, energetic. **through'-other** *adv* (*Scot*) in indiscriminate mixture; higgledy-piggledy, in disorder. ◆ *adj* (*Scot*) confusedly mixed; without orderliness. **through pass** same as **through ball** above. **through'put** *n* the amount of material, etc, put through a process. **through'-stone** *n* (*building*) a bonder or bondstone in building; see also separate entry. **through ticket** *n* a ticket for the whole of a journey that is made up of several parts. **through'-ticketing** *n* an arrangement whereby passengers can use a through ticket to travel over more than one railway network. **through traffic** *n* the traffic between two centres at a distance from each other; traffic passing straight through an area, as opposed to that travelling within the area. **through train** *n* a train that goes the whole length of a long route. **through'way** or **thru'way** *n* (*N Am*) a motorway.

■ **be through** (*N Am*) to have done (with *with*); to be finished; to have no future (as); to have no more to do (with *with*). **through and through** through the whole thickness; completely; in every point. **through the day** or **through the night** (*Scot*) in the daytime or in the night-time.

through-stone /throohh', throhh'stōn/ or **through-stane** /-stän/ (*Scot*) *n* a horizontal tombstone on pillars (see also **through-stone** under **through**). [OE *thrūh* sarcophagus, and **stone**]

throve /thrōv/ *pat* of **thrive**.

throw[1] /thrō/ *vt* (*pat* **threw** /throo/; *pap* **thrown** /thrōn/) to cast, hurl, fling through the air; to project; to emit; to cause (one's voice) to appear to come from elsewhere; to cause to be in some place or condition, *esp* suddenly; to render suddenly; to put; to put on or take off (clothes, etc) quickly, carelessly or violently (with *off, on, onto*); to execute, perform; to have or suffer (eg a fit or tantrum); to give (a party); to bemuse, perplex, disconcert; to move (a switch) so as to connect or disconnect; to form (pottery) on a wheel; to turn with a lathe; to wind or twist (yarn) together; (of a horse) to dislodge (its rider) from the saddle; (of a horse) to lose (a shoe); to cast (one's opponent) to the ground (*wrestling, judo*); to deliver (a punch) (*boxing*); to bowl (a ball) bending illegally and straightening the arm during delivery (*cricket*); to play (a card); to make a cast of dice amounting to; to cast (dice); to lose (a contest) deliberately, *esp* in return for a bribe (*inf*); to defeat, get the better of, or discomfit; (of an animal) to give birth to; to produce. ◆ *vi* to cast or hurl; to cast dice; to lay about one (*Spenser*). ◆ *n* an act of throwing; a cast, *esp* of dice or a fishing-line; the distance to which anything may be thrown; a woollen wrap or small rug (*esp N Am*); (also **throw'over**) a piece of fabric spread over a piece of furniture, *esp* a bed or sofa, to improve its appearance or protect it; an article, item, turn, go, occasion, etc (*inf*); a risky venture (*inf*); the vertical displacement of a particular rock, vein or stratum due to a fault (cf **lateral shift**; *geol*); a deflection caused by a sudden fluctuation (*phys*); amplitude of movement (*phys*); a blow (*Spenser*). [OE *thrāwan* to turn, to twist; Ger *drehen* to twist; see also **thraw**, **throe**] ■ **throw'er** *n*. **throw'ing** *n* and *adj*. **thrown** *adj* twisted; cast, flung. **throw'ster** *n* a person who twists silk thread into yarn; a gambler. □ **throw'away** *n* an advertisement brochure or handbill freely distributed to the public (*N Am*); a contest without serious competition; a line, or a joke, that an actor purposely delivers casually or without emphasis, often for the sake of realism. ◆ *adj* (of manner or technique) casual, without attempt at dramatic effect; ridiculously cheap, as if being thrown away; intended to be discarded or not recovered after use. **throw'back** *n* a reversion (eg to an earlier developmental type); a person, plant, etc showing characteristics of an earlier developmental type; a setback. **throw'-down** *n* a home-made firework, *esp* one that makes a noise when dropped on the ground. **throw'-in** *n* an act of throwing in; a throw to put the ball back into play (*football, basketball*, etc). **throwing stick** *n* a grooved stick for giving a spear greater leverage when thrown; a throw stick. **throwing table** *n* a potter's wheel. **thrown silk** *n* organzine. **throw'-out** *n* an act of throwing out; a rejected thing. **throw'over** see **throw** (*n*) above. **throw rug** *n* a small rug, decorative rather than utilitarian. **throw stick** *n* a weapon thrown whirling from the hand, such as the boomerang. **throw weight** *n* the maximum weight that can be lifted by a ballistic missile, *incl* the weight of the warhead(s) and guidance systems, but not the weight of the rocket itself.

■ **throw about** or **throw around** to spend (money) extravagantly or recklessly; to throw carelessly in different directions; (**throw about**) to cast about or try expedients (*Spenser*). **throw a fit** (*inf*) to have a fit, behave wildly. **throw away** to reject, toss aside; to squander; to fail to take advantage of; to discard (a card); (of an actor) to speak (lines) deliberately without emphasis; to bestow or expend on something unworthy. **throw back** to retort, to refuse; to delay or hinder the progress of; to force (someone) to rely (on something); to revert to some ancestral character. **throw** (**caution**, etc) **to the winds** see under **wind**[1]. **throw down** to demolish. **throw down the gauntlet** see under **gauntlet**[1]. **throw in** to interject; to throw (a football) back into play from the side of the pitch; to add as an extra at no extra cost. **throw in one's lot** see under **lot**. **throw in the towel** or **throw in one's hand** see under **hand**. **throw mud at** see under **mud**. **throw off** to divest oneself of; to disengage or release oneself from; to tell or compose in an offhand way; to perplex or disconcert. **throw on** to put on hastily. **throw oneself at** to make a determined and obvious attempt to captivate. **throw oneself into** to engage heartily in. **throw oneself on** or **upon** to attack, assault; to entrust oneself to the power of. **throw open** to cause to swing wide open; to make freely accessible. **throw out** to cast out; to reject; to expel; to emit; to utter casually; to cause to project; to build (a projecting extension); to cause to be misaligned; to disconcert or distract; to dismiss (a batsman) by throwing the ball at, and hitting, the wicket (*cricket*); to put (the batter) out by throwing the ball to a fielder to prevent the batter from reaching a base (*baseball*); to distance, leave behind. **throw over** to discard, desert or jilt. **throw together** to put together in a hurry; to bring into contact by chance. **throw up** to erect hastily; to show prominently, to reveal; to give up, to resign; to vomit (*inf*). **throw up one's hands** to raise one's hands as an expression of exasperation, despair, horror, etc. **throw up** (**something**) **against someone** to reproach someone with (something). **throw up the sponge** see under **sponge**.

throw[2] */thrō/* (*Spenser*) *n* a while. [OE *thrāg, thrāh*]

throw[3], **throwe** see **throe**.

thru (*esp N Am*) an informal or commercial spelling of **through**, alone or in compounds.

thrum[1] */thrum/* *vt* and *vi* (**thrumm'ing**; **thrummed**) to strum rhythmically and monotonously; to hum, drone or repeat monotonously; to drum with the fingers. ◆ *n* an act or the sound of monotonous strumming; a purring (*dialect*). [Imit] ■ **thrumm'er** *n*. **thrumm'ing** *n* and *adj*. **thrumm'ingly** *adv*.

thrum[2] */thrum/* *n* the end of a weaver's thread; any loose thread or fringe; bits of coarse yarn. ◆ *adj* made of or having thrums. ◆ *vt* (**thrumm'ing**; **thrummed**) to furnish, cover or fringe with thrums. [OE *thrum* (found in combination); Ger *Trumm*] ■ **thrumm'y** *adj* made of, or like, thrums. □ **thrum cap** *n* a cap made of thrums or of coarse, shaggy cloth. **thrum'-eyed** *adj* (*esp* of primulas) short-styled with the stamens in the throat of the corolla, *opp* to **pin-eyed**. **thrummed hat** *n* (*Shakesp*) a hat made of, fringed with, or covered with thrums.

thruppence or **thruppenny** informal variants of **threepence**, **threepenny** (see under **three**).

thrush[1] */thrush/* *n* any member of the Turdidae family of songbirds, *esp* those of the genus *Turdus*, particularly those species having a spotted breast, eg the song thrush (*T. philomelos*) and missel-thrush (*T. viscivorus*); applied to other birds more or less similar, such as some of the babblers. [OE *thrysce*]

thrush[2] */thrush/* *n* a disease, *esp* of children, causing fungous blisters in the mouth and throat; a similar fungal disease affecting the vagina; an inflammation in the frog of a horse's foot. [Cf Dan and Norw *troske*, Swed *torsk* thrush]

thrust[1] */thrust/* *vt* (*pat* and *pap* **thrust**) to push, *esp* with sudden force or violence; to impose or inflict (something on someone); to force; to push one's way; to stab, pierce; to intrude (oneself). ◆ *vi* to make a lunge (with *at*); to force one's way (with *into, past, through*, etc). ◆ *n* a sudden or violent push; a pushing force; a stab; pertinacity, determination, drive; the chief message, gist or direction of an argument, etc; the force produced by a jet or rocket engine that drives an aircraft forward, or the measurement of this; the horizontal force on the abutment of an arch; a thrust plane. [ON *thrȳsta* to press] ■ **thrust'er** *n* a person or thing that thrusts; a small rocket engine used as a booster rocket, or to correct course or altitude; an auxiliary propeller on a ship that may be operated athwartships. **thrust'ing** *n* and *adj*. □ **thrust bearing** *n* (*engineering*) a shaft bearing designed to take an axial load. **thrust hoe** *n* a hoe worked by pushing. **thrust plane** *n* (*geol*) a plane along which a block of lower rocks has overridden higher rocks almost horizontally, a reversed fault of very low hade. **thrust stage** *n* a stage that extends into the auditorium.

thrust[2] */thrust/* (*Spenser*) *vi* to thirst. ◆ *n* thirst.

thrutch */thruch/* (*dialect*) *vt* to thrust, press, shove; to crush, squeeze. ◆ *vi* to make one's way by great effort. ◆ *n* an instance of thrutching. [OE *thrycc(e)an*]

thruway a N American spelling of **throughway**.

thrymsa or **thrimsa** */thrim'zə, -sə/* *n* an Anglo-Saxon gold coin, or its value. [OE, genitive pl of *trymes, trimes*, a coin representing the Roman *tremis*, a third of an aureus; influenced by *thri* three]

Thu. *abbrev* : Thursday.

thud */thud/* *n* a dull sound as of a heavy body falling softly. ◆ *vi* (**thudd'ing**; **thudd'ed**) to make a thud; to fall with a thud. ◆ *vt* to beat. [Perh OE *thyddan* to strike] ■ **thudd'ing** *adj*. **thudd'ingly** *adv*.

thug */thug/* *n* a violent ruffian; a cut-throat; (properly */t'hug/*) a member of a religious fraternity in India that murdered stealthily by strangling or poisoning with datura, extirpated 1826–35 (*hist*). [Hindi *thag* cheat] ■ **thuggee**[1], **thagi**[1] or **thugg'ism** *n* the practices of the Indian thugs. **thugg'ery** *n* thuggism; ruffianly or violent behaviour. **thugg'ish** *adj*. **thugg'o** *n* (*pl* **thugg'os**) (*inf*) a ruffian or thug.

thuja */thoo'jə, -yə/* or **thuya** */thoo'yə/* *n* an evergreen tree of the arbor vitae genus *Thuja*, with small, scalelike leaves. [Gr *thyia* a kind of juniper]

Thule */thū'lē/* *n* an island six days north of Orkney discovered by Pytheas (4c BC), variously identified as Shetland, Iceland, Norway, Jutland; hence (*usu* **ultima Thule**) the extreme limit, northernmost land. [L *Thūlē*, from Gr *Thoulē* (understood by PT Cleve (1840–1905, Swedish chemist) as Scandinavia)] ■ **thu'lia** *n* thulium oxide. **thu'lite** *n* a red zoisite found in Norway. **thu'lium** *n* a soft metallic element (symbol **Tm**; atomic no 69) of the lanthanide series.

thumb */thum/* *n* the short, thick digit, consisting of two phalanges, on the radial side of the human hand; the part of a glove that covers it; the corresponding digit in other animals, or that of the hind foot, *esp* when opposable; a thumb's breadth, an inch. ◆ *vt* to play, spread, press, touch, wear or smudge with the thumb; to read intensively; to turn (the pages of a book, etc) rapidly with the thumb (also *vi* with *through*); to signal to with the thumb; to hit (in the eye) with the thumb (*boxing*); to handle awkwardly. [OE *thūma*; Ger *Daumen*] ■ **thumbed** *adj* having thumbs; marked by the thumb, worn. **thumb'ikins** or **thumb'kins** *n pl* (*Scot*) the thumbscrew. **thumb'less** *adj*. **thumb'like** *adj*. **thumb'ling** *n* a pygmy. **thumb'y** *adj* grubby with thumb marks; like thumbs, clumsy, awkward. □ **thumb hole** *n* a hole to insert the thumb in. **thumb index** *n* one arranged as indentations on the outer margins of the pages of books, to facilitate quick reference to a particular place. **thumb-in'dex** *vt* to provide with a thumb index. **thumb knot** *n* an overhand knot. **thumb latch** *n* a latch worked by pressure of the thumb. **thumb mark** *n* a mark left by the thumb, eg on a book; a thumbprint. **thumb'-marked** *adj*. **thumb'nail** *n* the nail of the thumb; a sketch (more *usu* **thumb'nail sketch**) as small as a thumbnail; a miniature version of a graphic image (*comput*). ◆ *adj* brief, concise. **thumb'nut** *n* a butterfly nut. **thumb piano** *n* an mbira (qv). **thumb'piece** *n* a piece that is pressed by the thumb or receives the thumb. **thumb'pot** *n* a very small flowerpot. **thumb'print** *n* an impression of the markings of the

thumb, taken as a means of identification. **thumb ring** *n* a ring worn on the thumb (*Shakesp*); a ring to protect an archer's thumb. **thumb'screw** *n* an old instrument of torture for compressing the thumb by means of a screw; a type of screw with a raised head, able to be turned using the thumb and forefinger. **thumbs-down, thumbs-up** see **thumbs down** and **thumbs up** below. **thumb'stall** *n* a covering or sheath for the thumb. **thumb'tack** *n* (*N Am*) a drawing pin.
■ **be all (fingers and) thumbs, one's fingers are all thumbs** or **have one's fingers all thumbs** to be awkward and fumbling. **bite one's thumb** to make a sign threatening revenge. **keep one's thumb on** to keep secret. **rule of thumb** a rough-and-ready practical method, found by experience to be convenient. **thumb a lift** or **ride** (*inf*) to beg a lift from passing motorists by signalling from the side of the road with the thumb. **thumb one's nose** to cock a snook (*lit* and *fig*) (see under **snook²**). **thumbs down** a sign indicating disapproval, prohibition, failure, etc (also *fig*; see also **pollice verso**; **thumbs-down**' *n*). **thumbs up** a sign indicating approval, success, hope of, or wishes for, success, etc (also *fig*; **thumbs-up**' *n*). **under one's thumb** under one's domination.

Thummim see **Urim and Thummim**.

thump /*thump*/ *n* a dull heavy blow (*esp* with the hand) or its sound. ◆ *vt* to beat with dull heavy blows; to play (a tune), *esp* on a piano, by pounding heavily on the keys (with *out*); to trounce. ◆ *vi* to throb or beat violently; to deliver dull heavy blows (with *at*, *on*, etc); to move with heavy, pounding steps (with *along*, *around*, etc). [Prob imit]
■ **thump'er** *n* someone or something that thumps; anything very big, a big lie, etc (*inf*). **thump'ing** *adj* (*inf*) unusually big (often as an intensifier). **thump'ingly** *adv*.

thunbergia /*thŭn-bûr'ji-ə, toon-ber'gi-ə*/ *n* any plant of the *Thunbergia* genus of evergreen climbing plants of the acanthus family (Acanthaceae). [Carl *Thunberg* (1743–1828), Swedish botanist]

thunder /*thun'dər*/ *n* the deep rumbling sound after a flash of lightning, caused by the disturbance by electricity of atmospheric gases; any loud noise; a thunderbolt; vehement denunciation. ◆ *vi* (*usu* with *it* as the subject) to make the noise of thunder; to make a noise like thunder; to move very heavily and *usu* quickly; to inveigh or denounce with vehemence (with *against*, etc). ◆ *vt* to utter with noise or violent denunciation; to deal or inflict (blows, etc) like thunder. [OE *thunor* thunder, *Thunor* the thunder god, Thor; Ger *Donner* thunder, L *tonāre* to thunder; cf **Thor, Thursday**]
■ **thun'derer** *n* a thunder god, Zeus, Thor, etc; a thundering denunciator, inveigher, orator, journalist or periodical, especially *The Times* or its leader-writer; a person who operates stage thunder; a bull-roarer. **thun'dering** *adj* discharging thunder; unusually big, tremendous (*inf*). ◆ *adv* used as an intensifier. **thun'deringly** *adv*. **thun'derless** *adj*. **thun'derlike** *adj* (*Shakesp*). **thun'derous** or **thun'drous** *adj* like, threatening, or suggesting thunder. **thun'derously** *adv*. **thun'derousness** *n*. **thun'dery** *adj* indicative of thunder, or accompanied by it.
❑ **thun'der-and-light'ning** *adj* in glaring colours. ◆ *n* a glaringly coloured woollen cloth. **thun'der-bearer** *n* (*Shakesp*) Jove. **thun'derbird** *n* a huge mythical bird thought by some Native American peoples to cause thunder and lightning; a representation of such a bird. **thun'derbolt** *n* a clap of thunder accompanied by a flash of lightning; a popularly imagined material body seen as lightning; a stone identified with it, such as a belemnite, a stone axe; anything sudden and overwhelming; a missile of the thunder god; a fulmination; a violent and irresistible destroyer or hero. **thun'derbox** *n* (*sl*) a chamberpot enclosed in a box or stool; any primitive or portable toilet. **thun'derclap** *n* a sudden crash of thunder; anything unexpected and alarming. **thun'dercloud** *n* a cloud charged with electricity; a black or livid threatening appearance. **thun'der-dart** *n* a thunderbolt. **thun'der-darter** or **thun'der-master** *n* (both *Shakesp*) Jove. **thun'der-drive** *vt* (*Spenser*) to drive with thunderbolts. **thun'deregg** *n* (*Aust* and *US*) an agate-filled cavity within a rock mass, or a fossil, supposed to have been flung to earth by lightning. **thun'derflash** *n* a container, such as a blank shell, filled with explosive powder, which makes a flash and a loud explosion when detonated. **thunder god** *n* a god that wields thunder. **thun'derhead** *n* a distinctively rounded mass of cumulus cloud projecting above the general cloud mass, *usu* the precursor of a storm. **thunder peal** *n* a resounding noise of thunder. **thunder sheet** *n* a large sheet of tin-plate shaken to produce the sound of thunder or similar noises as a theatrical, etc sound-effect. **thun'dershower** *n* a shower accompanied with thunder, or a short heavy shower from a thundercloud. **thun'derstone** *n* (*Shakesp*) a thunderbolt. **thun'derstorm** *n* continued discharges of electricity from the clouds, producing lightning and thunder, generally with heavy rain. **thun'derstrike** *vt* to strike with, or as if with, lightning. **thun'derstroke** *n* (*Shakesp*) a stroke or blast by lightning. **thun'derstruck** *adj* (also **thun'derstricken**) struck by lightning; struck dumb with astonishment, amazed, shocked.
■ **steal someone's thunder** see under **steal¹**.

Thur. or **Thurs.** *abbrev*: Thursday.

Thurberesque /*thûr-bə-resk*'/ *adj* similar in style, etc to the work of James *Thurber* (1894–1961), US writer and cartoonist.

thurible /*thū'ri-bl*/ *n* a censer. [L *t(h)ūs, t(h)ūris* frankincense, from Gr *thyos* a sacrifice; cf **thyme**]
■ **thū'rifer** *n* an acolyte who carries the thurible during a religious ceremony. **thurif'erous** *adj* incense-bearing. **thurificā'tion** *n*. **thū'rify** *vt* to cense. **thus** /*thus, thūs*/ *n* frankincense.

Thursday /*thûrz'dā* or *-di*/ *n* the fifth day of the week. [OE *Thunres dæg* the day of Thunor, the English thunder god; ON *Thōrsdagr* Thor's day]
■ **Thurs'days** *adv* on Thursdays.

thus¹ /*dhus*/ *adv* in this or that manner, in the way mentioned or demonstrated; to this degree or extent; accordingly, therefore. [OE *thus*]
■ **thus'ly** *adv* (often *facetious*) in this manner. **thus'ness** *n* (*usu facetious*) the state of being thus. **thus'wise** *adv* in this manner.
■ **thus far** so far, until now.

thus² see under **thurible**.

thuya see **thuja**.

thwack /*thwak*/ *vt* to whack, strike loudly, *esp* with something flat. ◆ *n* a loud whack. [Perh **whack**, or OE *thaccian* to smack]
■ **thwack'er** *n*. **thwack'ing** *n* and *adj*.

thwaite /*thwāt*/ *n* a piece of reclaimed wasteland (now only found in place names). [ON *thveit*]

thwart /*thwört*/ *vt* to oppose; to frustrate; to balk; to cross; to cross the path of; to obstruct; to set crosswise; to plough crosswise. ◆ *vi* to cross; to conflict. ◆ *n* frustration; hindrance; a rower's bench placed across a boat. ◆ *adv* crosswise; from side to side. ◆ *adj* crosswise, transverse; cross, adverse; cross, perverse, cross-grained. ◆ *prep* (*obs*) across, athwart. [ON *thvert*, neuter of *thverr* perverse]
■ **thwar'ted** *adj* prevented, frustrated. **thwar'tedly** *adv*. **thwar'ter** *n*. **thwar'ting** *n* and *adj*. **thwar'tingly** *adv* perversely. **thwart'ly** *adv*. **thwart'ship** or **thwart'ships** *adv* across the ship. **thwart'ship** *adj*. **thwart'ways** *adv*. **thwart'wise** *adv* and *adj*.

thy /*dhī*/ (*formal, church, dialect* or *archaic*) possessive pronoun or *adj* of thee (cf **thine**). [**thine**]

Thyestean or **Thyestian** /*thī-es'ti-ən, -ə-stē'ən*/ *adj* of *Thyestes*, who was made to eat his own sons (*Gr myth*); cannibal.

thyine /*thī'in*/ *adj* of a tree supposed to be sandarach (Bible, Revelation 18.12). [Gr *thyinos*, from *thyon, thyā* thyine tree]

thylacine /*thī'lə-sēn, -sīn, -sin*/ *n* the so-called Tasmanian wolf (qv). [Gr *thylakos* pouch]

thylakoid /*thī'lə-koid*/ (*bot*) *n* one of the many plate-like discs that make up the grana of chloroplasts. [Gr *thylakos* sac]

thylose, thylosis see **tylosis**.

thyme /*tīm*/ *n* any member of the labiate genus *Thymus*, low half-shrubby plants with two-lipped corolla and calyx and four diverging stamens, *esp* the fragrant garden thyme (*T. vulgaris*) and wild thyme (*T. serpyllum*). [Fr *thym*, from L *thymum*, from Gr *thymon*, from *thyein* to burn a sacrifice]
■ **thymol** /*thī'mol*/ *n* an antiseptic phenol obtained from oil of thyme by distillation. **thymy** /*tī'mi*/ *adj* like, smelling of or abounding in thyme.
■ **basil thyme** a kind of calamint. **lemon thyme** a species of thyme (*T. citriodorus*) with a lemony flavour and scent. **oil of thyme** a fragrant essential oil obtained from garden and other thymes. **water thyme** Canadian pondweed.

thymectomy see under **thymus**.

thymelaeaceous /*thim-ə-li-ā'shəs*/ *adj* of the **Thymelaeā'ceae** /*-si-ē*/, the family of trees and shrubs with simple leaves and tough bark to which *Daphne* (spurge laurel) belongs. [Gr *thymelaiā*, supposed to be a species of *Daphne*, from *thymos* thyme, and *elaiā* olive]

thymic, thymidine, thymine, thymocyte see under **thymus**.

thymol see under **thyme**.

thymus /*thī'məs*/ (*anat*) *n* (*pl* **thy'muses** or **thy'mī**) a ductless gland near the root of the neck, producing white blood cells at early ages but vestigial in adult humans, that of veal and lamb being called *neck sweetbread*. [Gr *thymos* thymus gland]
■ **thymec'tomy** *n* surgical removal of the thymus. **thy'mic** *adj* of or relating to the thymus. **thy'midine** /*-dēn*/ *n* a nucleoside of thymine, found in DNA. **thymine** /*thī'mēn*/ *n* one of the four bases in deoxyribonucleic acids (DNA), in close association with adenine. **thy'mocyte** *n* a lymphocyte found in the thymus.
❑ **thymus-derived cells** *n pl* (*immunol*) lymphocytes derived from the thymus.

thymy see under **thyme**.

---

thyratron /thī'rə-tron/ (*electronics*) *n* a gas-filled valve with heated cathode, able to carry very high currents, *orig* a trademark for one containing mercury vapour. [Gr *thyrā* door]
- **thyristor** /thī-ris'tər/ *n* (*thyratron* and trans*istor*) a thyratron-like solid-state semiconductor device.

thyro- /thī-rō-, -rə-/ or **thyreo-** /-ri-ō-, -ə-/ or **thyr-** /thīr-/ *combining form* denoting thyroid. [**thyroid, thyreoid**]
- **thyrotoxicō'sis** *n* hyperthyroidism; hyperthyroidism with goitre and exophthalmia, Graves' disease. **thyrotrō'pin** or **thyrotrō'phin** *n* a hormone, produced in the anterior lobe of the pituitary gland, which stimulates the thyroid gland. **thyrox'in** or **thyrox'ine** *n* an iodine compound, the hormone forming the active principle of the thyroid gland; a synthetic form of this, used to treat underactivity of the thyroid gland.

thyroid /thī'roid/, more correctly but less commonly **thyreoid** /-ri-oid/ *adj* relating to the thyroid gland or the thyroid cartilage; shield-shaped. ◆ *n* the thyroid gland, a ductless gland in the neck which secretes thyroxin, whose overactivity may lead to exophthalmic goitre and swelling of the eyeballs, and whose malfunction may lead to cretinism; the principal cartilage of the larynx, forming the Adam's apple. [Gr *thyreoeidēs* shield-shaped, the thyroid cartilage, from *thyreos* a (door-shaped) shield, from *thyrā* a door, and *eidos* form]
- **thyroidec'tomy** *n* the surgical removal of the thyroid gland. **thyroidī'tis** *n* inflammation of the thyroid gland.
- **thyroid-stimulating hormone** *n* thyrotropin.

Thyrostraca /thī-ros'trə-kə/ *n pl* the cirripedes. [Gr *thyrā* door, valve, and *ostrakon* shell]

thyrsus /thûr'səs/ *n* (*pl* **thyr'si** /-sī/) the wand of Bacchus, a staff wreathed with ivy; a dense panicle broadest in the middle, eg in the lilac and grape (*bot*); *esp* one whose lateral branches are cymose. [Gr *thyrsos*]
- **thyrse** /thûrs/ *n* (*pl* **thyr'ses**) a thyrsus. **thyr'soid** or **thyr'soidal** *adj* having the form of a thyrsus.

Thysanoptera /this-ə-nop'tə-rə/ *n pl* an order of insects with fringed wings, some of which are serious pests to fruit, such as thrips. [Gr *thysanos* fringe, tassel, and *pteron* a wing]
- **thysanop'terous** *adj*.

Thysanura /this-ə-nū'rə/ *n pl* the bristletails, an order of small wingless insects with abdominal appendages. [Gr *thysanos* a fringe, tassel, and *ourā* a tail]
- **thysanū'ran** *n* and *adj* (a member) of this order. **thysanū'rous** *adj*.

thyself /dhī-self'/ (*formal, church, dialect* or *archaic*) *pronoun* emphatic for (and *usu* in apposition to) **thou**[1] or **thee**[1]; reflexive for **thee**[1]. [**thee**[1] altered to **thy**), and **self**]

Ti (*chem*) *symbol*: titanium.

ti[1], also **te** /tē/ (*music*) *n* the seventh note of the scale in sol-fa notation, a substitute for *si*, to avoid the initial sound of *so* (*sol*). [See **Aretinian**]

ti[2] /tē/ *n* a small Pacific tree of the genus *Cordyline, esp C. terminalis*, with edible roots, whose sword-shaped leaves are used for thatching and fodder; sometimes also applied (wrongly) to the Australian **tea tree**. [Polynesian]

TIA *abbrev*: transient ischaemic attack, a temporary disturbance of bodily functions caused by interruption of the blood supply to the brain.

Tia Maria® /tē'ə mə-rē'ə/ *n* a coffee-flavoured liqueur. [Sp, aunt Maria]

tian /tyan/ *n* a light gratin baked in an earthenware dish. [Provençal, a shallow dish]

tiara /ti-ä'rə/ *n* a richly jewelled semicircular head-ornament worn by women; the Jewish high-priest's mitre; the Pope's triple crown; the papal office; the high ornamental headdress of the ancient Persian kings. [Gr *tiārā*]
- **tiar** /tī'ər, tīr/ *n* (*poetic*) a tiara. **tia'ra'd** or **tia'raed** *adj* wearing a tiara.

Tib /tib/ *n* used as a typical woman's name (*Shakesp*); the ace of trumps in the game of gleek (*obs; Walter Scott*). [*Isabella*]
- **Tib'-cat** *n* a she-cat. **Tib's** or **Tibb's Eve** see under **saint**.

Tibert /tib'ərt, tī'bərt/ *n* the cat in *Reynard the Fox*; in *Shakesp* identified with Tibalt.

Tibet or **Thibet** /ti-bet'/ *n* an autonomous region in W China, with the Himalayas in the south; (**thibet**) a woollen fabric generally printed in colours; a heavy goat's-hair fabric used instead of fur (also **Tibet cloth**).
- **Tibet'an** (or /tib'/) *adj* belonging to or characteristic of Tibet. ◆ *n* the language of Tibet, of the Sino-Tibetan family of languages; a native of Tibet.
- **Tibetan terrier** *n* a breed of dog (not in fact a terrier) with a soft, woolly coat.

tibia /tib'i-ə/ *n* (*pl* **tib'ias** or **tib'iae** /-i-ē/) (*anat* and *zool*) the shinbone, the thicker of the two bones of the leg below the knee in humans; the

corresponding bone in other vertebrates; the tibiotarsus in birds; the fourth joint of an insect's leg; an ancient flute or pipe. [L *tībia* shinbone, flute]
- **tib'ial** *adj*. **tibiotarsus** /tib-i-ə-tär'səs/ *n* (*pl* **tibiotar'si** /-sī/) (in birds) a bone formed by the fusion of the tibia and some of the tarsals.

tibouchina /ti-bə-kī'nə, -kē'/ *n* a plant of the *Tibouchina* genus of shrubs and herbs (family Melastomaceae) with purple flowers. [From a native name in Guiana]

tic /tik/ *n* a convulsive (*esp* nervous) twitching of certain muscles, *esp* of the face; an involuntary habitual response (*fig*). [Fr; cf **tick**[5]]
- **tic douloureux** /dol-ə-roo', tēk doo-loo-rə/ *n* a disorder of the fifth cranial nerve causing paroxysms of pain in the face and forehead.

tical /ti-käl', tik'l/ *n* an obsolete Siamese silver coin, about equal to a rupee, replaced by the baht in 1928; a unit of weight formerly used in Siam (Thailand), *approx* 14 g ($\frac{1}{2}$ oz). [Port *tical*]

ticca /tik'ə/ (*Ind*) *adj* hired. [Hindi *thīkā* hire]

tice /tīs/ *vt* (*Shakesp*) to entice. ◆ *n* an enticement (*Shakesp*); a ball played as a decoy to tempt one's opponent (*croquet*). [Aphetic for **entice**, or from OFr *atisier*]

tich, tichy see **titch**.

tichorrhine /tī'kə-rīn/ *adj* having an ossified nasal septum, as the fossil woolly rhinoceros. [Gr *teichos* wall, and *rhīs, rhīnos* nose]

tick[1] /tik/ *n* the sound of a watch, clock, etc; a beat; a moment (*inf*); a small mark (✓) used to indicate or mark off anything as checked, dealt with, required, correct, etc; a light tap or pat (*obs*); the game of tig. ◆ *vi* to make a sound like a mechanical clock; to beat time; to work, be operated; to tap, pat (*obs*; **tick and toy** to dally). ◆ *vt* to mark with a tick (sometimes with *off*); to measure, record, indicate (eg time) by a ticking sound (sometimes with *out*); to dot. [ME *tek*; cf Du *tik*, LGer *tikk*; prob imit]
- **ticked** *adj* ticked off; speckled. **tick'er** *n* anything that ticks, *esp* a telegraph instrument that prints signals on a tape, or (*sl*) a watch; the heart (*sl*). **tick'ing** *n* and *adj*.
- **tick box** *n* a box on a printed form or computer screen into which a tick may be inserted to show that something has been checked, dealt with, agreed to, etc. **ticker tape** *n* paper ribbon on which a ticker prints; anything similar, such as a streamer (**ticker-tape welcome**, etc, a welcome, etc, *esp* in New York, in which ticker tape, confetti, etc is thrown (through the streets) during the progress of a celebrity). **ticking-off'** *n* (*sl*) a reprimand. **tick'-tack** *n* ticking of a clock, etc; (also **tic'-tac**) bookmakers' telegraphy by arm signals; see also **trick-track**. ◆ *adv* with recurring ticking. **tick-tack-toe'**, **tick-tack-too'** or **tic-tac-to'** *n* (*N Am*) noughts and crosses. **tick-tick'** *n* a ticking; /tik'tik/ a child's word for a watch. **tick-tock'** *n* a ticking, as of a big clock; a tapping; /tik'tok/ a child's word for a clock. ◆ *vi* (of a clock) to tick.
- **in two ticks** in a moment. **make** (**someone** or **something**) **tick** (*inf*) to cause to operate or function; to be the driving force behind; to cause to behave, think, etc in a certain way. **tick all the (right) boxes** (*inf*) to fulfil all requirements. **tick away** (of time, life, etc) to pass away with the regularity of the ticking of a clock. **tick down** (of time) to move inexorably towards a deadline. **ticked off** (*US sl*) annoyed, angry. **tick off** to mark with a tick; to reprimand (*sl*). **tick over** (of an engine) to run gently, disconnected from the transmission (**tick'-over** *n*); (of a person) to lead an inactive, uneventful existence; to function, operate, *esp* at a low level of activity (*fig*). **tick up** (*chiefly N Am*) to increase.

tick[2] /tik/ *n* any of the larger bloodsucking mites of the Acarina order; applied also to the sheep-ked and similar degenerate bloodsucking Diptera parasitic on cattle and horses, etc; a small and *usu* objectionable person (*inf*). [OE *ticia* (perh for *tīca* or *ticca*); Du *teek*, Ger *Zecke*]
- **tick bird** *n* the oxpecker. **tick fever** *n* Rocky Mountain spotted fever or any similar disease transmitted by ticks; East Coast fever; Texas fever. **tick trefoil** *n* any of a genus (*Desmodium*) of leguminous plants with clusters of small purple flowers and jointed prickly pods.

tick[3] /tik/ *n* the cover of a mattress; ticking. [L *thēca*, from Gr *thēkē* a case; see **theca**]
- **tick'en** or **tick'ing** *n* the strong cloth of which ticks are made.

tick[4] /tik/ (*sl*) *n* credit, delayed payment, *esp* in the phrase *on tick*; trust. ◆ *vi* to get or give credit. [**ticket**]
- **tick shop** *n* a shop where goods are given on credit.

tick[5] /tik/ *n* crib-biting; a whimsy. [**tic**]

ticket /tik'it/ *n* a card, slip, or (formerly) placard bearing a notice or serving as a token of any right or debt, eg for admission, travel by public transport, penalty for some offence (*esp* motoring), etc; a tag or label, *esp* one showing the price, size, etc of the item to which it is attached; a certificate (*sl*); discharge from the army (*sl*); a licence or permit, *esp* one allowing work as a ship's master or pilot (*inf*); a list of candidates put forward by a party for election (*N Am*); any or all of the principles associated with a particular political party, *esp* as a basis for its election to government (*N Am*); a visiting card (*obs*). ◆ *vt* to label, to designate for a particular use; to issue a ticket to. [OFr *estiquet*(*te*), from *estiquer* to stick, from OLGer *stekan*; cf **stick²**]

■ **tick'etless** *adj*.

❏ **ticket agent** *n* an agent who sells tickets on behalf of a theatre, or a railway, etc. **ticket collector** *n*. **ticket day** *n* the day before settling-day on the Stock Exchange, when notes of transactions completed are received. **tick'et-holder** *n* a person possessing a ticket, eg for a concert or other event. **ticket office** *n* a place where tickets are sold. **ticket of leave** *n* formerly, a licence to leave prison before expiry of sentence, but with certain restrictions on one. **ticket-of-leave man** *n*. **ticket porter** *n* a licensed porter; a railway porter who collects tickets. **ticket punch** *n* an instrument for punching holes in tickets. **ticket tout** see under **tout¹**. **ticket writer** *n* an expert in lettering who writes placards for shop windows, etc. **tick'et-writing** *n*.

■ **be tickets** (*S Afr sl*) to be the end. **have tickets on oneself** (*Aust* and *NZ sl*) to be conceited. **straight ticket** all the nominees of a political party, and no others. **that's** (**just**) **the ticket** (*inf*) that's exactly the right thing or the thing to be done.

tickety-boo or **tickettyboo** /tik-i-ti-boo'/ (*inf*) *adj* fine, satisfactory. [Ety uncertain]

tickey or **ticky** /tik'i/ (*S Afr*) *n* a former South African coin, a threepenny-bit; now used of a decimal coin of small denomination. [Origin uncertain]

tickle /tik'l/ *vt* to excite with a pleasant thrill; to produce a disturbing feeling in (someone) by a light touch, *usu* tending to excite involuntary laughter, accompanied by attempts to wriggle free; to amuse (*inf*); to please (*inf*); to perplex; to touch lightly, *esp* when catching fish using the hands; to beat. ◆ *vi* to be the site of a tickling or itching feeling; to tingle (*Spenser*). ◆ *adj* unstable, in unstable equilibrium, delicately set, insecure (*Spenser, Shakesp*); ticklish, nice (*obs* or *dialect*). ◆ *n* an act or feeling of tickling; a slight touch, eg (*cricket*) of the ball with the bat. [Perh a frequentative of **tick¹**; perh by metathesis from **kittle**]

■ **tick'ler** *n* someone or something that tickles; a puzzle, a difficult problem (*inf*); a feather-brush; a poker; a cane; a device for reminding; a dram of spirits. **tick'ling** *n* and *adj*. **tick'lish** *adj* easily tickled; difficult, needing careful attention, treatment, etc; unstable, precarious; easily affected; nice; critical. **tick'lishly** *adv*. **tick'lishness** *n*. **tick'ly** *adj* tickling; easily tickled.

❏ **tick'le-brain** *n* (*Shakesp*) strong liquor. **tickler file** *n* (*esp N Am*) a file containing memoranda, short notes, etc, to remind the user of facts, things to be done, etc.

■ **tickle pink** or **tickle to death** (*inf*) to please or amuse very much. **tickle the ivories** see under **ivory**.

tick-tack-toe, **tick-tack-too** see under **tick¹**.

ticky see **tickey**.

ticky-tacky /tik'i-tak-i/ (*US inf*) *n* cheap material. *adj* of inferior quality. [Reduplicated form of **tacky¹**]

Tico /tē'kō/ (*US* and *Central American*) *n* (*pl* **Ti'cos**) a native or inhabitant of Costa Rica. ◆ *adj* of or relating to Costa Rica or its inhabitants. [Perh from Sp Am sfx *-itico*, used to form diminutives]

tic-tac same as **tick-tack** (see under **tick¹**).

tic-tac-to see under **tick¹**.

tid /tid/ (*Scot*) *n* fit time or condition; a mood.

tid or **t.i.d.** *abbrev* : (in prescriptions) *ter in die* (*L*), three times a day.

tidal see under **tide¹**.

tidbit same as **titbit**.

tiddle¹ /tid'l/ *vi* a child's word for urinate (also *n*). [Cf **widdle**]

tiddle² /tid'l/ *vi* to potter, trifle. [Origin uncertain]

tiddled see under **tiddly¹**.

tiddledywink see **tiddlywink**.

tiddler /tid'lər/ *n* a small fish, eg a minnow or a stickleback; any very small person or thing. [Perh **tittlebat**, **tiddly²** or **tiddy²**]

tiddley¹ /tid'li/ (*naval inf*) *adj* smart and trim (also **tidd'ly**). [Perh **tiddly²** or **tidy**]

tiddley² see under **tiddly¹,²**.

tiddly¹, also **tiddley** /tid'li/ (*sl*) *adj* (**tidd'lier**; **tidd'liest**) slightly drunk. ◆ *n* alcoholic drink. [Earlier *titley*]

■ **tidd'led** *adj* (*inf*) slightly drunk.

■ **on the tiddly** (*sl*) drunk.

tiddly² /tid'li/ (*inf* or *dialect*) *adj* (**tidd'lier**; **tidd'liest**) small, tiny (also **tidd'ley**). [Perh a childish form of **little**; cf **tiddy²**]

tiddlywink /tid'li-wingk/ *n* (also **tiddledywink** /tid'l-di-/) any of the discs used in **tiddlywinks**, or **tiddledywinks**, a game in which one attempts to flip a small disc into a cup by pressing its edge with a bigger one; an unlicensed pawnshop or beer house (*sl*).

tiddy¹ /tid'i/ (*Walter Scott*) *n* the four of trumps in the game of gleek.

tiddy² /tid'i/ (*dialect*) *adj* very small. [Origin uncertain]

tide¹ /tīd/ *n* ebb and flow, *esp* of the sea twice daily, caused by the gravitational pull of the sun and moon; a time of ebbing, of flowing, or both; a sudden access or flood of feeling, etc; a time or season (*archaic* or *poetic*); a festival (*archaic* or *poetic*); opportunity (*archaic*); a trend; sea-water (*poetic*); a flow; a river, river water, or current (*poetic*); floodtide. ◆ *combining form* (*archaic* or *poetic*) denoting a time or season (*usu* attached to a church festival, as in *Christmas-tide*, *Easter-tide*). ◆ *vt* (*esp fig*) to carry by, or as if by, the tide; to effect by means of the tide. ◆ *vi* to run like the tides; to make one's way by taking advantage of the tides, to be carried by the tide (also *vt* with *it*). [OE *tīd*; Du *tijd*, Ger *Zeit*]

■ **tīd'al** *adj* of, depending on or regulated by the tide; flowing and ebbing. **tīd'ally** *adv*. **tide'less** *adj*.

❏ **tidal basin** *n* a basin or dock that fills at high tide. **tidal flow** *n* the regulated movement of traffic in both directions along a multi-laned road, the numbers of lanes for travel in each direction being governed by the amount of traffic travelling in that direction. **tidal power** *n* (the generation of electricity by harnessing) the energy of tidal flows. **tidal wave** *n* a huge wave caused by the tides; improperly, a huge wave started by an earthquake and running on with its own momentum (see **tsunami**); a widespread demonstration of public opinion, feeling, etc; the tidewave. **tide gate** *n* a gate that admits water at floodtide and retains it at ebb. **tide gauge** *n* an instrument for registering the state of the tide continuously. **tide'land** *n* (*N Am*) land that is submerged at high tide. **tide lock** *n* a lock by which ships may pass out or in at all times of the tide. **tide'mark** *n* a line on the shore made by the tide at the water's highest point; a marker indicating the highest point reached by the tide; a mark of the limit of washing (*joc*; *fig*). **tide'mill** *n* a mill with a water wheel moved by tidewater. **tide race** *n* a swift tidal current. **tide rip** *n* disturbed sea due to currents; a tidal wave. **tides'man** *n* a customs officer who waited the arrival of ships (*orig* coming in with the tide). **tide table** *n* a table of times of high tide. **tide'waiter** *n* a tidesman; a person who waits to see how things go before acting. **tide'waitership** *n*. **tide'water** *n* water brought by the tide; river water affected by the tide (*US*); coastal land, seaboard (*US*). **tide'wave** *n* the tide regarded as a wave passing round the earth. **tide'way** *n* a track followed by the tide, *esp* a channel through which there is a strong current or tide.

■ **tide over** to carry (someone) over, or (*old*) to get over (a critical or difficult period).

tide² /tīd/ (*archaic*) *vi* to happen. [OE (ge)*tīdan*; cf **betide**]

tide³ Spenser's spelling of **tied**.

tidings /tī'dingz/ (*esp literary*) *n pl* news. [Late OE *tīdung*, from OE *tīdan* to tide, happen, or from ON *tīthindi* events, tidings]

tidivate same as **titivate**.

tidy /tī'di/ *adj* (**tī'dier**; **tī'diest**) trim; orderly; neat; fairly good or big, considerable (*inf*); seasonable (*obs*); in good condition or order (*dialect*); plump (*dialect*); comely (*dialect*); shapely (*dialect*). ◆ *n* a receptacle for odd scraps; a cover for a chair-back (*esp US*); an act of tidying. ◆ *vt* (**tī'dying**; **tī'died**) to make neat and tidy; to clear away for the sake of tidiness. [**tide¹**; cf Ger *zeitig*]

■ **tī'dily** *adv*. **tī'diness** *n*.

tie¹ /tī/ *vt* (**ty'ing**; **tied** /tīd/) to bind; to fasten; to knot; to make (a knot, etc); to restrict, restrain; to unite; to mark (two notes of the same pitch) with a curved line indicating that they are to be played as a single sustained, not repeated, note (*music*); to perform in this way (*music*); to limit; to oblige; to equal in competition, etc; to subject to bonds; to confirm (*Shakesp*); to ligature; to make (an artificial fly for angling). ◆ *vi* (of a garment, etc) to be fastened with a knot, ribbon, etc; to be equal in votes, score, etc; (of dogs) to linger on the scent. ◆ *n* a knot, bow, etc; a bond; a string, ribbon, etc, for tying; a band of material passed under the collar of a shirt, etc and tied under the chin, *esp* one having one end wider than the other, tied to hang down the shirt front with the wider end overlying the narrower, worn *esp* by men, or as part of a uniform; a shoe tied with a lace (*US*); a structural member sustaining only a tension; a railway sleeper (*N Am*); a restraint; an obligation; a mode of tying; an equality in score, votes, etc; a match, *esp* one at any stage of a tournament in which the losers are eliminated; a curved line drawn over notes of the same pitch to be performed as one, sustained not repeated (*music*); a tie-wig (*obs*). [OE *tēah* band, string, *tīgan* to tie]

■ **tied** *adj* having been tied; having a draw or equality as a result; (of a public house or garage) denoting one whose tenant is obliged to get his or her supplies from one particular brewer or distiller, or oil- and petrol-producer; (of a house, cottage, etc) denoting one whose tenant may occupy the premises only as long as he or she is employed by the owner; (of a loan or aid) conditional on money being spent on goods and services provided by the lender. **tie'less** *adj*. **tī'er** *n* a person who ties; a child's apron (*US*).

❏ **tie'back** *n* a length of fabric or ribbon used to tie a curtain to one side. **tie beam** *n* a beam connecting the lower ends of rafters to prevent them from moving apart. **tie'-break** *n* a number of points played at the end of a tied set to decide the winner (*tennis*); generally, a situation in a contest when a tiebreaker is required to decide the winner. **tie'breaker** *n* a tie-break; any game(s), question(s) or competition(s) intended to break a tie and decide a winner. **tie clip** or **clasp** *n* an ornamental clip which attaches one's tie to one's shirt. **tie'-dye** or **tie-dye'ing** *n* a method of hand-dyeing textiles in which patterns are produced by binding or knotting parts of the fabric so as to resist the dye (also **tie'-and-dye'**). **tie'-dyed** *adj*. **tie'-in** *n* a connection; something, *esp* a book, that ties in with, is connected or promoted with something else, eg a film or TV programme; the practice of selling an item on condition that additional items are purchased (chiefly *N Am*). **tie line** *n* a telephone line used solely for connecting two private branch exchanges (also **interswitchboard line**). **tie'-neck** *n* a collar terminating in two long pieces that can be tied in a bow, etc under the chin. ◆ *adj* (of a blouse, etc) having a tie-neck. **tie'pin** *n* an ornamental pin for securing one's tie to one's shirt. **tie rod** *n* a rod, eg in a vehicle, that prevents parts from moving apart. **tie'tac** or **tie'tack** *n* a tie clip. **tie'-up** *n* a stand-still; an entanglement; a connection; a business association; tape for tying a bookbinding or portfolio; a building for tying up cattle overnight (*US*); an animal tied up for a bait; a mooring. **tie'-wig** *n* a wig tied with ribbon at the back. ■ **fit to be tied** (*inf*) extremely angry. **tie down** to fix (*lit* and *fig*); to bind by conditions, etc. **tie in with** or **tie up with** to agree with; to be closely associated with; to be linked with, as eg a book containing the story of, or a story concerning the characters in, a popular film or TV series. **tie up** to parcel up with string; to tie so as to remain up, hanging, etc; to tether, secure or bind by tying; to moor; to keep occupied; to invest, make illiquid (funds, etc); to secure against squandering, alienation, etc, or restrict the use of, by conditions.

tie² see **tye¹**.

tie³ see **tye²**.

tier /tēr/ *n* a row, level, rank, or layer, *esp* one of several placed one above another; a row of guns; a mountain range (*Tasmania*). ◆ *combining form* denoting an object or system that has a specified number of tiers, as in *three-tier*. ◆ *vt* and *vi* to pile or be piled in tiers. [OFr *tire* sequence]
■ **tiered** *adj* and *combining form*.

tierce /tērs/ *n* one-third of a pipe (of wine), *approx* 35 British or 42 US gallons; a cask or vessel of that capacity; a third (*obs*); /tûrs/ a sequence of three cards of the same suit; a third (*music*); the note two octaves and a third above a given note (*music*); an organ stop producing such a note; a parrying position, or the corresponding thrust (*fencing*); one of the hours of the Divine Office, terce. [OFr *tiers*, *tierce*, from L *tertia* (*pars*)]
■ **tiercé** /tēr'si/ *adj* (Fr, divided into three parts; *heraldry*) (of the surface of a shield) divided into three equal parts, each of a different metal or colour (also **tierced**). ◆ *n* (in horse-racing) a system of betting by which the first, second and third horses must be named in the right order, or a race for which this system obtains. **tier'ceron** /-sə-ron/ *n* (*archit*) (in vaulting) a subordinate rib springing from the intersection of two other ribs.
❑ **tierce de Picardie** /tyers' də pē-kar-dē'/ *n* (*music*) a major third closing a piece otherwise in a minor key.

tiercel, tiercelet see **tercel**.

tierceron see under **tierce**.

tiercet same as **tercet**.

tiers état /tyer-zā-tä'/ (Fr hist) *n* the third estate, or commons. [Fr]

TIFF (*comput*) *abbrev* : tagged-image file format, a standard graphics file format.

tiff¹ /tif/, also (*esp Scot*) **tift** /tift/ *n* a slight quarrel; a display of irritation, a pet, huff. ◆ *vi* to be in a huff; to squabble. [Prob imit]

tiff² /tif/, also (*Scot* and *dialect*) **tift** /tift/ *n* stale, sour, or thin liquor; a sip; a dram. ◆ *vi* to sip; to drink; to lunch. [Perh orig slang]
■ **tiff'ing** *n* sipping; (also **tiff'in**; *esp* as used by the British Raj in colonial India) lunch, a light meal.

tiff³ /tif/ (*obs*) *vt* and *vi* to dress, trick out. [OFr *tiffer* (Fr *atiffer*), to adorn]

Tiffany /tif'ə-ni/ *adj* denoting objects designed or produced by CL *Tiffany* (1812–1902), founder of the New York jeweller's, Tiffany and Co., or (*esp*) his son LC Tiffany (1848–1933), Art Nouveau glassmaker and designer.
❑ **Tiffany glass** *n* another name for **favrile**. **Tiffany lamp** *n* a lamp with a distinctive umbrella-shaped shade made of favrile.

tiffany /tif'ə-ni/ *n* a silk-like gauze. ◆ *adj* of tiffany; transparent. [Gr *theophaneia* theophany, or *diaphaneia* transparency]

tiffin see **tiffing** under **tiff²**.

tifosi /ti-fō'zē/ (*Ital*) *n pl* (*sing* **tifo'sō**) fans, devotees, *esp* of some sport. [*tifo* typhus, fanaticism]

tift see **tiff¹,²**.

tig¹ /tig/ *n* a touch; a twitch; a game in which someone who is 'it' chases the others, the person he or she touches then becoming 'it'. ◆ *vt* (**tigg'ing; tigged'**) to touch, *esp* in the game of tig. [Poss a form of **tick¹**]

tig² /tig/ *n* an old drinking cup with two or more handles. [Origin unknown]

tige /tēzh/ *n* (*archit*) the shaft of a column. [Fr, from L *tibia* a pipe]

tiger /tī'gər/, *fem* **tigress** /tī'gris/ *n* a fierce, yellowish, black-striped Asiatic animal, one of the two largest cats (*Panthera tigris*); the leopard (*S Afr*); the jaguar (*American tiger*) (*US*); the puma (*red tiger*); a ferocious or bloodthirsty person; a flashy vulgarian; a formidable opponent or competitor; a boy in livery *usu* perched behind a vehicle; a yell to supplement a cheer (*US*); a tiger beetle, tiger moth, tiger shark, tiger lily, etc. ◆ *adj* (of an economy) having the potential, sometimes achieved and not always retained, for performing vigorously, *orig* applied to the economies of some countries in E Asia. [Fr *tigre*, from L *tigris*, from Gr *tigris*, prob from Zend]
■ **ti'gerish** or **ti'grish** *adj* like a tiger in manner, *esp* fierce-tempered; flashy. **ti'gerishly** or **ti'grishly** *adv*. **ti'gerishness** or **ti'grishness** *n*. **ti'gerism** *n* swagger. **ti'gerly** *adj*. **ti'gery, ti'grine** /-grīn/ or **ti'groid** *adj* like a tiger.
❑ **tiger badge** *n* a proficiency badge awarded by the Himalayan Club to Sherpas. **Tiger balm®** *n* a soothing mentholated ointment. **tiger beetle** *n* any flesh-eating beetle of the Cicindelidae, found mainly in warm, dry regions. **tiger cat** *n* a general name for a middle-sized striped or spotted wildcat, such as the margay, ocelot, serval, etc. **tiger country** *n* (*golf sl*) dense rough. **tiger eye** or **tiger's eye** *n* a golden-brown striped pseudomorph of quartz after crocidolite, used eg in jewellery; a pottery glaze resembling this. **tiger fish** *n* a large game fish of African rivers, *Hydrocyenus goliath*. **tiger flower** *n* a Mexican iridaceous plant (genus *Tigridia*) with purple, yellow or white streaked flowers. **ti'ger-foot'ed** *adj* (*Shakesp*) fiercely swift. **tiger lily** *n* a lily with black-spotted orange flowers. **tiger moth** *n* any one of the Arctiidae family of moths, with long and *usu* brightly-coloured wings. **tiger nut** *n* the edible rhizome of *Cyperus esculentus*, a European sedge; the chufa (*US*). **tiger prawn** *n* a large edible prawn, marked with dark stripes. **tiger shark** *n* a voracious striped shark of the Indian Ocean (*Galeocerdo cuvieri*), a tiger prawn. **tiger shrimp** *n* a tiger prawn. **tiger snake** *n* the most deadly of Australian snakes (*Notechis scutatus*), brown with black crossbands. **tiger tail** *n* a type of fast-growing hybrid worm. **tiger team** *n* (*US*) a group of counter-intelligence agents who test the security of military bases; a group of computer hackers who are employed to test the secureness of a computer system. **tiger wolf** *n* the spotted hyena; the thylacine. **ti'gerwood** *n* any of several showy black-striped woods used in cabinetmaking. **tiger worm** *n* another name for brandling.

tiggywinkle /tig'i-wing-k(ə)l/ (*inf*) *n* a hedgehog. [Appar coined by Beatrix Potter (1866–1943), English children's author, perh from dialect *tig* little pig]

tight¹ /tīt/ *adj* close; compact; close-fitting; too close-fitting; cramped; (of a schedule, timetable, etc) allowing little space, time or opportunity for deviation from plan; (of a situation) difficult or dangerous; (of a contest) closely fought; (of style) concise; taut, not slack; (of eg control) very firm, strict; precise; under control; firmly fixed; impervious, not leaky, proof; trim; neat; snug; competent; hampered or characterized by lack of money; (of money or a commodity) scarce, hard to obtain; unwilling to part with money, miserly (*inf*); intoxicated (*inf*); (of a person, muscle, etc) showing tension, taut, not relaxed (*inf*); (of a team of people) working or performing well together, well-co-ordinated; denoting play in set scrums and line-outs (*rugby*). ◆ *adv* tightly; soundly. ◆ *n* (*rugby*) tight play. ◆ *combining form* signifying proof against or impervious to the thing specified. [Earlier *thight*, appar from an older form of ON *thēttr*, influenced by various Eng words of similar meaning; cf Ger *dicht*]
■ **tight'en** *vt* and *vi* (sometimes with *up*) to make or grow tight or tighter. **tight'ener** *n* a person or thing that tightens; a tensor (*anat*); a heavy meal (*sl*). **tight'ish** *adj*. **tight'ishly** *adv*. **tight'ly** *adv*. **tight'ness** *n*. **tights** *n pl* a close-fitting garment, often made of nylon, covering the lower part of the body and the legs *esp* as worn by women and girls as an alternative to stockings; close-fitting men's breeches (*hist*).
❑ **tight arse** or (*N Am*) **tight ass** *n* (*sl*) a mean, tight-fisted person; an excessively conservative or repressed person. **tight end** *n* (*American football*) a player who is positioned at the outside of the offensive line. **tight'-fisted** *adj* (*inf*) stingy. **tight-head prop** *n* (*rugby*) the prop forward on the right of the front row of the scrum in either team. **tight junction** *n* (*biol*) a junction between epithelial cells where the membranes are in close contact, with no intervening intercellular space. **tight-knit'** or **tightly-knit'** *adj* close-knit; closely integrated; tightly organized. **tight-lace'** *vt* and *vi* (of clothing) to tie tightly, so compressing the waist. **tight-laced'** or **tight'-lace** *adj* strait-laced.

tight-lā'cer *n*. **tight-lā'cing** *n* compression of the waist by tight clothes. **tight'-lipped** *adj* uncommunicative. **tight'rope** *n* a taut rope or wire on which feats of balancing and acrobatics are performed; a middle course between dangerous or undesirable alternatives (*fig*). **tight'wad** *n* (*inf*; *esp N Am*) a skinflint, miser. **tight'y-whit'ies** *n pl* (*US inf*) men's brief underpants.
■ **a tight corner** or **spot** a difficult situation. **run a tight ship** to be in control of an efficient, well-run organization or group. **tighten the screws** to increase pressure (*esp* on someone to do something).

tight² /tīt/ (*Spenser*) *pat* and *pap* of **tie¹**.

tight³ see **tite**.

tigon /tī'gon, -gən/ *n* the offspring of a tiger and a lioness (also **tī'glon**). [*tiger* and *lion*]

tigress, tigrine or **tigroid, tigrish** see **tiger**.

Tigrinya /ti-grēn'yə/ *n* an Afro-Asiatic language spoken in Eritrea and N Ethiopia. [*Tigray*, province of Ethiopia]

tika /tē'kə/ *n* a red mark or pendant on the forehead of Hindu women, originally of religious significance but now also worn for ornament (also **tilak** /til'uk/). [Hindi]

tike same as **tyke**.

tiki /tik'ē/ *n* an image, often in the form of a large wooden or small greenstone ornament, representing an ancestor, the smaller form being worn in some Polynesian cultures as an amulet or charm; a similar ornament or statue representing a Polynesian god. [Maori]
❑ **tiki bar** *n* in USA, a bar selling Polynesian food and drinks.

tikka /tik'ə/ or /tē'kə/ (*Ind cookery*) *adj* denoting a dish of meat or vegetables marinated in yoghurt and spices and cooked in a clay oven, eg *chicken tikka, lamb tikka*. [Hindi *tikka*]

til /til, tēl/ *n* sesame (also **teel**). [Hindi *til*, from Sans *tila*]
❑ **til oil** *n*. **til seed** *n*.

tilak see **tika**.

tilapia /ti-lap'i-ə, -lā'/ *n* any member of an African freshwater genus (*Tilapia*) of edible cichlid fishes. [New L]

tilbury /til'bə-ri/ *n* a light, open, two-wheeled, horse-drawn carriage seating two people. [Said to be so named from its first maker]

tilde /til'dā, -di, -də, tild/ *n* the diacritical sign used over *n* in Spanish to indicate the sound /ny/, as in *cañon*, and over *a* and *o* in Portuguese to indicate nasalization. [Sp, from L *titulus* a title]

tile /tīl/ *n* a slab of baked clay (or a substitute) for covering roofs, floors, etc; a tube-shaped piece of baked clay used in pipes for drains; a piece in the board game of mah-jong; tiling, a tiled area; a hat (*sl*); a top hat (*Scot*). ◆ *vt* to cover with tiles; to drain by means of tiles; to arrange (windows) on the screen so that they do not overlap (*comput*); to secure against intrusion by placing a person at the door; to bind to secrecy. [OE *tigele*, from L *tēgula*, from *tegere* to cover]
■ **tiled** *adj* covered with tiles; imbricated; (of fish) sun-dried (*Walter Scott*). **til'er**, also **tyl'er** *n* a maker or layer of tiles; a freemasons' doorkeeper. **til'ery** *n* a place where tiles are made. **til'ing** *n* an area covered with tiles; tiles collectively; the act of laying tiles.
❑ **tile hat** *n* (*Scot*) a top hat. **tile'-hung** *adj* (of a wall) covered with flat roofing tiles as protection against the weather. **tile'-red** *adj* and *n* (of) a brownish-red, the colour of baked tiles. **tile stone** *n* a flat stone used for roofing, *esp* a thin-bedded sandstone.
■ **Dutch tiles** enamelled earthenware tiles, *usu* decorated in blue, with scriptural subjects, etc, for chimney-pieces, etc. **have a tile loose** (*sl*) to be a little mad. **hung tiles** tiles hung vertically, covering a wall. **on the tiles** (*inf*) enjoying a lively period of drinking, dancing, etc.

tilefish /tīl'fish/ *n* an American Atlantic food-fish noted for the sudden changes in its numbers. [Appar from its generic name, Lopholatilus, and perh its tile-like spotted pattern]

tiler, tilery see under **tile**.

Tilia /til'i-ə/ *n* the lime or linden genus of flowering trees and shrubs, giving name to the family **Tiliā'ceae** /-si-ē/, related to the mallows. [L *tilia* lime-tree]
■ **tiliā'ceous** *adj* belonging to the family.

tiling see under **tile**.

till¹ /til/ *prep* up to the time of; to, towards (*Scot*); to (with the infinitive) (*Scot*). ◆ *conj* up to the time when. [OE (Northumbrian) *til*, from ON *til*; cf OE *till* a fixed point, Ger *Ziel* end, goal]

till² /til/ *n* a drawer or receptacle for money in or behind a counter; a compartment or drawer in a chest, cabinet, etc (*obs*). [Cf ME *tillen* to draw, OE *fortyllan* to draw aside, seduce]

till³ /til/ *vt* to work (land), cultivate; to set (*obs* or *dialect*). [OE *tilian* to aim at, till, from *till* limit; see ety for **till¹**]
■ **till'able** *adj* arable. **till'age** *n* the act or practice of tilling; husbandry; tilled land. **till'er** *n* a cultivator. **till'ing** *n*.

till⁴ /til/ *n* a stiff impervious clay (*orig Scot*); boulder clay (*geol*); shale (*mining*). [Cf **thill²**]
■ **till'ite** *n* indurated till. **till'y** *adj*.

tillandsia /ti-land'zi-ə/ *n* any plant of the mainly epiphytic tropical American genus *Tillandsia* of the pineapple family. [Elias *Tillands* (died 1693), Finno-Swedish botanist]

tiller¹ /til'ər/ *n* the handle or lever for turning a rudder. [ME *tillen* to draw (see **till²**), or OFr *telier* crossbow stock, from LL *tēlārium* a weaver's beam, from L *tēla* a web]
■ **till'erless** *adj*.
❑ **till'er-chain** or **-rope** *n* the chain or rope connecting the tiller with the steering-wheel.

tiller² /til'ər/, **teller** or **tellar** /tel'ər/ *n* a sapling; a shoot from a tree stump; a sucker from the base of a stem; a side-shoot from the base as in corn, etc. ◆ *vi* to form tillers. [OE *telgor* shoot, twig]

tiller³ see under **till³**.

tillite, tilly see under **till⁴**.

tilly-vally /til'i-val'i/ or **tilly-fally** /-fal'i/ (*Shakesp*) *interj* expressing impatience at what has been said (also **till'ey-vall'ey**).

tilt¹ /tilt/ *vi* to lean, heel over; to slope; (of a ship) to pitch; to slant, *esp* in a vertical plane; to joust, ride and thrust with a spear; to charge, attack (with *at*; *lit* or *fig*); to take part in a contest (with *with*); to criticize (with *at*); to thrust. ◆ *vt* to incline, slant; to tip out, by tilting; to move by tilting; to forge using a tilt hammer. ◆ *n* an act of tilting; a condition of being tilted; a slope; a joust, a charge against an opponent with a lance; an encounter, attack, etc; a dispute; a duel; a thrust; a tilt yard. [OE *tealt* tottering]
■ **tilt'able** *adj*. **tilt'er** *n*. **tilt'ing** *n*.
❑ **tilt** or **tilting fillet** *n* (*building*) a triangular roofing timber used at eaves to tilt the undereaves course of slates, etc to close off the front edge. **tilt hammer** *n* a heavy pivoted hammer lifted by a cam, used in forging. **tilting train** *n* a train with a tilting mechanism that enables it to travel at high speed on a standard track. **tilt yard** *n* (*hist*) a place for tilting, jousting.
■ **full tilt** at full speed, headlong.

tilt² /tilt/ *n* a cover, awning, for a wagon, boat, etc; a tent; a hut. ◆ *vt* to cover with a tilt. [OE *teld*; cf Ger *Zelt*]
■ **tilt'ed** *adj*.
❑ **tilt'-boat** *n* a large rowing boat with a tilt. **tilt'-rotor** *n* a large retractable propeller on the wing of an aircraft that enables vertical take-off and landing; an aircraft fitted with such propellers.

tilth /tilth/ *n* cultivation; cultivated land; the depth of soil turned up in cultivation. [From **till³**]

TIM *abbrev*: traditional Indian medicine (see **ayurveda**).

Tim. (*Bible*) *abbrev*: (the Letters to) Timothy.

timarau see **tamarau**.

timariot /ti-mä'ri-ot/ (*hist*) *n* a Turkish feudal militiaman. [Fr, from Turk *timār*]

timbal or **tymbal** /tim'bl/ (*archaic*) *n* a kettledrum. [Fr *timbale*; see **atabal**; appar influenced by L *tympanum*]
■ **timbale** /tẽ-bal', tam'bal, tim'bl/ *n* a dish of meat, fish, etc cooked in a cup-shaped mould or shell; a mould (of pastry) for such a dish.

timber /tim'bər/ *n* wood suitable for building or carpentry, whether growing or cut; standing trees of oak, ash, elm, or (locally by custom) other kinds suitable for timber, forming part of an inheritance (*Eng law*); material generally; a beam or large piece of wood in a framework, of eg a house, ship, etc; familiarly, a wooden object or part; (in *pl*) cricket stumps (*inf*); a wooden leg; wood (*dialect*); woodland, forest-land (*N Am*). ◆ *adj* of timber; wooden; wooden in tone, unmusical (*Scot*). ◆ *vt* to provide or cover with timber or beams; to build (*obs*). ◆ *interj* a warning given when a tree being felled is about to fall. [OE *timber* building, wood, *timbrian* to build; Ger *Zimmer* room]
■ **tim'bered** *adj* built, constructed, *esp* of wood; provided with timber; shored up with timber; (of country) wooded; *appar* massive (*Spenser*). **tim'bering** *n* timber collectively; work in timber.
❑ **tim'berhead** *n* the top of a ship's timber rising above the deck and used as a bollard; a bollard placed in a similar position. **timber hitch** see under **hitch**. **tim'berland** *n* (*N Am*) land covered with trees used for timber. **timber line** *n* the upper limit of timber trees on the mountains, etc. **tim'berman** *n* a person responsible for the timbers in a mine; a person who works with timber; any of various longicorn beetles of the genus *Acanthocinus*, whose larvae live in fallen trees. **tim'ber-mare** see under **horse**. **tim'ber-toes** *n sing* a person with a wooden leg. **timber tree** *n* a tree suitable or grown for timber. **timber wolf** *n* an American variety of the common wolf, the grey wolf. **tim'beryard** *n* a yard or place where timber is stored or sold.
■ **half-timbered** see under **half**.

---

timbó /tim-bō'/ n (pl **timbós'**) a S American sapindaceous climbing plant (*Paullinia pinnata*); a fish-poison and insecticide obtained from its bark. [Guaraní]

timbre /tē'br', tim'bər, tam'bər/ n the quality of a sound, tone-colour, as opposed to pitch and loudness. [OFr, bell, from L *tympanum* a drum]

timbrel /tim'brəl/ (*hist, esp Bible*) n an Oriental tabor or tambourine. [OFr *timbre*, from L *tympanum* drum]
■ **tim'brel'd** adj (*Milton*) sung to the timbrel.

timbrology /tim-brol'ə-ji/, **timbromania** /-brō-mā'ni-ə/ and **timbrophily** /-brof'i-li/ n old-fashioned words for stamp-collecting. [Fr *timbre* postage-stamp]
■ **timbrol'ogist**, **timbromā'niac** and **timbroph'ilist** n.

Timbuktu or **Timbuctoo** /tim-buk-too'/ n any distant place. [*Timbuktu*, a town in Mali on the River Niger]

time /tīm/ n a concept arising from change experienced and observed, expressed by past, present and future, and often measured by the amount of turning of the earth on its axis; a quantity measured by the angle through which the earth turns on its axis; (with *cap*) any of the clock-settings used as standard times in the various time zones, as in *Pacific Time, Central European Time*, etc; a moment at which, or stretch of existence during which, things happen; season; the due, appointed, suitable or usual occasion of occurrence; the hour of death or of birth or coming into existence; a spell, interval, period; the actual occasion or period of being something or somewhere, eg apprenticeship, residence, prison sentence, student days, life, etc; (a given period in) the existence of the world; leisure or opportunity long enough for a purpose; a spell of exciting, *usu* pleasurable, experience; the duration, or shortest duration, of performance, as in a race; rhythm, tempo (*music*); the duration of a note (*music*); rate of speed; a unit of duration in metre, a mora (*prosody*); an occasion; an occasion regarded as one of a recurring series; one of a number of multiplied instances; generalized as an indication of multiplication (eg *3 times* = multiplied by 3); (the rate of) payment for work by the hour, day, etc; back pay (also **back time**); a reckoning of time; an interval; past existence; an allotted period, *esp* its completion, as in boxing rounds, permitted drinking hours, etc; the call, bell, whistle, buzzer or other signal announcing this; (in *pl*) the contemporary, obtaining conditions; (in *pl*; with *cap*) often the name of a newspaper; (with *cap*) a personification of time, a bald-headed old man with a forelock, a beard, a scythe, and often an hourglass. ◆ vt to arrange, fix or choose a time for; to mark, measure, adjust or observe the rhythm or time of; to ascertain the time taken by; to regulate the time of. ◆ vi to keep or beat time. ◆ adj of or relating to time; reckoned by time; timed; of or for a future time. ◆ interj indicating that time is up, or that action is now forbidden or permitted. [OE *tīma*; ON *tīmī*]
■ **timed** adj. **time'less** adj independent of time; unconnected with the passage of time; eternal, unaffected by time; untimely (*archaic*); premature (*Shakesp*); ill-timed; failing to keep time or rhythm. **time'lessly** adv. **time'lessness** n. **time'liness** n. **time'ly** adj (**time'lier; time'liest**) coming or occurring at a suitable or the correct time; well-timed; in good time, early; seasonable; temporal (*obs*); of the time of day (*Spenser*); in time, keeping time (*Spenser*). ◆ adv (*archaic*) early, soon; in due time or in good time. **timeous** or **timous** /tī'məs/ adj (*chiefly Scot*) in good time; seasonable. **time'ously** or **ti'mously** adv in good time. **tī'mer** n a person or thing that times anything; a clocklike device which sets something off or switches something on or off at a preset time; (in combination) signifying a person who belongs to, works for, etc, a specified time. **ti'ming** n fixing, choosing, adjusting, ascertaining, or recording of times; (the co-ordination of) departure and arrival times; co-ordination in time; (in an internal-combustion engine) the regulation of the valve-operating mechanism so that the valves open and close in correct relation to the crank. **ti'mist** n a timeserver (*obs*); a person who keeps in time; a person who times his or her movements.
❑ **time-and-motion study** n an investigation of the motions performed and time taken in industrial, etc, work with a view to increased proficiency and thus production. **time ball** n a ball mounted on a vertical pole, eg on top of a high building, that drops at a regular point in each day as an indication of mean time. **time bargain** n a contract to buy or sell at a certain time in the future. **time'-barred** adj disallowed because out of legal time limits. **time-beguil'ing** adj making time seem to pass quickly. **time-bett'ering** adj (*Shakesp*) in which times are growing better. **time-bewast'ed** adj (*Shakesp*) spent by time. **time bill** n a timetable. **time bomb** n a bomb that is exploded by a time-fuse; a routine actuated at a particular time or date which destroys data held in a computer program. **time capsule** n a capsule containing objects, etc, representative of the current time, buried in the ground or set in the foundations of a building for discovery at a future date. **time'card** n a card for use with a time clock. **time charter** n a hire agreement valid for a specified period of time. **time clock** n a clocklike apparatus that stamps on cards the time of arrival and

departure of eg office or factory workers. **time code** n a track separate from the main one on a video or audio tape, on which time is recorded digitally, to help editing. **time constant** n (*elec eng*) the time required by the output of a measuring system to change by 63% when a step change in the detected signal occurs. **time'-consum'ing** adj requiring much, or too much time; wasting time. **time deposit** n a bank deposit from which withdrawals may be made only after a certain time or with due notice. **time dilation** n (*phys*) the principle, a consequence of the special theory of relativity, that the time interval between two events appears to be larger when they occur in a reference frame which is moving relative to the observer's reference frame than when they occur at rest relative to the observer. **time division multiplex** n (*telecom*) a form of multiplex (qv) in which each signal is sent as a series of pulses, the gaps between which allow other pulses to be interleaved. **time'-expired** adj having completed a term of enlistment. **time exposure** n (*photog*) an exposure for a relatively long time (*usu* seconds) in comparison with one called instantaneous. **time'frame** n a limited or restricted period of time, eg as allotted for an event. **time fuse** n a fuse preset to act at a definite time. **time gun** n a gun fired to indicate a certain hour. **time'-honoured** adj (of a custom) honoured or respected on account of antiquity. **time immemorial** n the distant past no longer remembered; time before legal memory, fixed by statute as before 1189 (*law*). **time'keeper** n a clock, watch or other instrument that measures time; a person who keeps account of workers' hours; an employee thought of in terms of his or her punctuality; a person who beats or observes time. **time'keeping** n. **time'-killer** n a person or thing that kills time (see **kill**[1]). **time'-killing** n and adj. **time lag** n the interval of delay between two connected events or phenomena. **time'-lapse** adj of or relating to **time-lapse photography**, a method of recording and condensing long or slow processes by taking a large number of photographs at regular intervals, the film made from these being projected at normal speed. **time limit** n a time within which something has to be done. **time'line** n a period of time regarded or represented in a linear way; a deadline. **time loan** n a loan repayable by a specified date. **timely-part'ed** adj (*Shakesp*) having died at a natural time. **time machine** n a hypothetical machine by which one may travel to the future or past, through time. **time out** n a short break during a sporting contest for rest, discussion of tactics, substitution of a player, etc; any similar short suspension of activity; a cancellation action or automatic logoff that takes place if the user does not input data or a command within a given time, or if a computer fails to make contact with a peripheral device (eg a printer) within a given time (*comput*). **time'pass** n and adj (*Ind*) (something) done to pass spare time or relieve boredom. **time'piece** n a piece of machinery for keeping time, *esp* one that does not strike but is bigger than a watch. **time'-pleaser** n (*Shakesp*) a timeserver. **time-poor** adj short of time. **time'-release** or **timed'-release** adj slow-release. **time'-saving** n and adj. **time'scale** n the time envisaged for the carrying out of (the stages of) a project; a statement of the times of occurrence, completion, etc of a series of processes, stages, etc. **time series** n (*stats*) a set of observations taken sequentially over time. **time'-served** adj (of a craftsman) having completed his or her apprenticeship, fully trained. **time'server** n a person who cynically or servilely suits his or her opinions to the times or those in authority for the time. **time'-service** n. **time'-serving** n and adj. **time'share** n the time-sharing of property, etc; such a property. ◆ adj (of a property) owned on the basis of time-sharing. **time'-sharer** n. **time'-sharing** n a scheme by which a person buys the right to use a holiday home for the same specified period of time each year for a specified number of years; a means of providing multi-access to a computer with each user in turn allowed a time slice of the central processor. **time sheet** n a record of the time worked by a person. **time signal** n an indication of the exact time given by radio or otherwise from an observatory. **time signature** n (*music*) an indication of rhythm (in the form of two figures placed one over the other, the top one representing the number of beats to the bar, and the bottom, the length of the beat) at the beginning of a line or wherever there is a change. **time slice** n (*comput*) a predetermined maximum length of time during which each program is allowed to run. **time slot** n a particular period of time in the day or week allocated to a certain radio or television programme; a particular period assigned to a certain purpose, etc. **time spirit** n the genius of the age. **time'stamp** n a record of the time of an event or transaction, automatically created by and stored on a computer. ◆ vt (of a computer) to add a record of the time of an event or transaction to (data). **time switch** n one working automatically at a set time. **time'table** n a table of times, eg of classes, events, trains, etc. ◆ vt to insert into a timetable; to plan, divide into sessions, etc, according to a timetable. **time'-thrust** n (*fencing; obs*) a stop hit (qv). **time trial** n an event, *esp* in cycling, in which competitors set off one at a time, and attempt to cover a set distance in the shortest time. **time'-trialling** n. **time unit** n. **time warp** n (in science fiction, etc) a hypothetical distortion in the time continuum, allowing one to pass from the present to the past or future, or to stand still in the present. **time'-work** n work paid for by the hour or the day, *opp* to *piecework*.

time'-worker n. **time'-worn** adj worn or decayed by time. **time zone** n one of 24 longitudinal divisions of the globe, each 15° wide, having a standard time throughout its area; a similar zone adapted to a particular country.

■ **about time** none too soon. **against time** with the aim or necessity of finishing by a certain time. **ahead of one's time** having ideas, etc too advanced or progressive to be acceptable at the time. **ahead of time** earlier than expected. **all in good time** in due course; soon enough. **all the time** continuously, constantly. **apparent time** time according to the real sun, ie sundial time without regard to the equation of time. **astronomical time** a form of mean solar time (qv below), using a twenty-four-hour day beginning at mean noon (in general use for nautical almanacs before 1925). **at one time** formerly; simultaneously. **at the same time** simultaneously; notwithstanding. **at the time** at the time stated or under consideration. **at times** at distant intervals; occasionally. **before one's time** ahead of one's time (see above). **behind the times** not abreast of changes. **behind time** late. **between times** in the intervals. **by times** betimes. **common time** (music) time with two beats or a multiple of two beats to a bar or other measure (**compound common time** where each beat is of three quavers or crotchets). **do time** (sl) to serve a sentence of imprisonment. **for a time** for a while; temporarily. **for the time being** at the present time or the actual time in question. **from time to time** now and then. **gain time** to provide oneself with more time to do something (eg by delaying something else). **half the time** (inf) as often as not, frequently. **have a good time** to enjoy oneself. **have a time of it** (inf) to experience problems, difficulties, etc. **have little** (or **no**) **time for** to have little (or no) interest in or patience with. **in good time** quite early enough; with some time to spare; indeed (ironic; obs). **in one's own** (or **own good**) **time** at a time, rate, etc of one's own choosing. **in one's own time** in one's spare time, when not at work. **in one's time** at some past time in one's life, esp when one was at one's peak. **in the nick of time** see under **nick**[1]. **in time** after a lapse of time; early enough; eventually; keeping rhythm. **keep time** to run accurately, like a clock (also **keep good time**); to move or perform in the same rhythm; to record times of workers, etc. **know the time of day** to know the state of affairs, what is going on; to know what one is about, or the best way of doing something. **local time** time reckoned from the local meridian. **lose time** (of eg a clock) to run down; to fall behindhand; to let time pass without full advantage. **make good time** to make speedy progress on a journey. **make time** to regain lost time; to find an opportunity. **mark time** see under **mark**[1]. **mean solar time** time reckoned not by the actual but by the mean position of the sun. **not before time** rather tardily; none too soon; about time too! **no time** or **no time at all** a very short time. **on** (or **upon**) **a time** once; at a time in the past (usu imaginary). **on time** punctual, in accordance with time limits; punctually. **out of time** not keeping rhythm; too late (law). **pass the time of day** to chat unhurriedly and casually. **sidereal time** the portion of a sidereal day that has elapsed since the transit of the first point of Aries. **solar time** time reckoned by the sun, real or mean. **standard time** a system of time adopted for a wide area instead of local time, usu Greenwich Mean Time or a time differing from it by a whole number of hours. **summer time** see under **summer**[1]. **take one's time** (inf) not to hurry, to dawdle. **take Time by the forelock** to seize an opportunity before it is too late. **take time off** (or US **out**) to find time to do something, or time for an activity. **the time of one's life** a very enjoyable time. **time about** (chiefly Scot) in turns, alternately. **time after time** repeatedly. **time and again** repeatedly. **time and a half** a rate of pay equivalent to one and a half times the usual rate, offered eg for overtime. **time of day** the time by the clock; the point of time reached; a greeting, salutation. **time out** (comput) (of a computer) to enter an automatic logoff command (eg from a printer) if data or a command is not input within a given time. **time out of mind** during the whole time within human memory, from time immemorial. **time was** there once was a time (when). **time-zone disease** or **fatigue** jet lag. **triple time** (music) three beats, or three times three beats, to a bar or other measure. **up to time** punctual, punctually; not later than the due time. **what time** (poetic) when.

timenoguy /tim'ə-no-gi/ n a rope stretched from place to place in a ship, esp one to prevent the fore-sheet fouling (naut); a makeshift; a what's-its-name. [Origin obscure, perh Fr timon (see **timon**) and **guy**[1]]

timid /tim'id/ adj inclined to fear or alarm; lacking courage; faint-hearted; shy. [L timidus timid, timor, -ōris fear, from timēre to fear]
■ **timid'ity** n. **tim'idly** adv. **tim'idness** n. **tim'orous** /-ə-rəs/ adj very timid. **tim'orously** adv. **tim'orousness** n. **tim'orsome** adj (dialect) easily frightened.

timing, timist see under **time**.

timocracy /tī-mok'rə-si/ n a form of government in which property is a qualification for office; a form of government in which ambition or desire of honour is a guiding principle. [Gr tīmokratiā, from tīmē honour, and krateein to rule]
■ **timocratic** /-ō-krat'ik/ or **timocrat'ical** adj.

Timon /tī'mən/ n a famous Athenian misanthrope (5c BC) celebrated by Aristophanes, Lucian, Plutarch and Shakespeare; hence, a misanthrope.
■ **Tī'monism** n. **Tī'monist** n. **Tī'monize** or **-ise** vi to play the misanthrope.

timon /tī'mən/ (obs) n a helm. [Fr, from L tēmō, -ōnis a beam]
■ **timoneer'** n a helmsman.

Timorese /tē-mö-rēz'/ adj of or relating to the island of Timor or its people. ◆ n (pl **Timorese'**) a native or citizen of Timor.

timorous, etc see under **timid**.

timothy /tim'ə-thi/ n (in full **timothy grass**) cat's-tail grass (Phleum pratense), a perennial grass used as fodder and pasture. [Timothy Hanson, who promoted its cultivation in America about 1720]

timous same as **timeous** (see under **time**).

timpano or **tympano** /tim'pə-nō/ n (pl **tim'pani** or **tym'pani** /-nē/, often (inf) shortened to **timps**) an orchestral kettledrum. [Ital; see **tympanum**]
■ **timp'anist** or **tymp'anist** n a person who plays timpani.

tim-whiskey or **tim-whisky** /tim'(h)wis'ki/ n a whisky (gig).

tin /tin/ n a silvery-white easily fusible malleable metallic element (symbol **Sn**; atomic no 50); a usu airtight container or vessel of tin or tin-plate, a can, etc; a tinful; a rectangular loaf of bread; a strip of tin along the lower boundary of the playable area of the front wall of a squash court; money (sl). ◆ adj made of tin or tin-plate or (inf) of corrugated iron; paltry (inf). ◆ vt (**tinn'ing**; **tinned**) to coat or overlay with tin or tinfoil; to cover thinly with solder before soldering; to pack (eg food) in tins for preservation. [OE tin; ON tin, Ger Zinn]
■ **tin'ful** n (pl **tin'fuls**). **tinned** adj coated with tin; preserved in a tin. **tinn'er** n a tinsmith; a tin-miner; a canner. **tinn'ily** adv. **tinn'iness** n. **tinn'ing** n covering with tin; tin mining. **tinn'y** adj (**tinn'ier**; **tinn'iest**) like tin; (of sound) thin and metallic, not rounded and resonant; (of metal goods) cheaply and flimsily made; lucky (Aust and NZ inf). ◆ n (sl; also **tinn'ie**) a mug made of tin-plate; a can of beer (chiefly Aust and NZ).
❑ **tin can** n a metal container for preserving food, esp an empty one. **tin fish** n (naut sl) a torpedo. **tin'foil** n tin or (now) tin-lead alloy (or aluminium) in thin sheets, eg for wrapping foodstuffs. **tin god** n an overbearing, dictatorial person; someone or something misguidedly revered. **tin hat** n (inf) a military steel helmet. **tin'horn** n (orig and esp US) a flashy, small-time gambler; a pretentious but worthless person. ◆ adj pretentious but inferior. **tin lizzie** n (old inf, chiefly N Am) an old or decrepit motor car, esp a Model T Ford. **tin'man** n a worker in tin; a dresser of tin ore; a dealer in tinware. **tin'-opener** n an instrument for cutting open tins of food, etc. **Tin Pan Alley** n orig a nickname for 28th Street, New York, the centre of the song-publishing district; the popular-music-publishing district of a city; the realm of popular-music production. **tin'plate** n thin sheet iron or steel coated with tin (also adj). ◆ vt to coat with tinplate. **tin'pot** n a pot of or for tin or tinplate. ◆ adj paltry, rubbishy. **tin'smith** n a worker in tin. **tin'snips** n pl a pair of hand-shears for cutting sheet metal, esp tin plate. **tin soldier** n a toy soldier made of metal; someone who enjoys playing at being a soldier. **tin'stone** n cassiterite, a brown tin dioxide. **tin'-streamer** n a person who washes tin from alluvial deposits. **tin'-streaming** n. **tin'tack** n a tack coated with tin. **tin terne** same as **terne**. **tin'type** n a ferrotype. **tin'ware** n articles made of tin. **tin whistle** n a cheap six-holed metal flageolet. **tin works** n a place where tin is prepared for use.
■ **put the tin hat** (or **lid**) **on** to finish off, bring to an end, suppress.

Tina or **tina** /tē'nə/ (drug sl) n methamphetamine in its crystal form. [Short form of the name Christina, a pun on crystal]

Tina /tē'na/ abbrev: there is no alternative.

tinaja /ti-nahh'a/ n a very large full-bellied earthenware jar, used (esp for storing and maturing wine) in Spain. [Sp]

tinamou /tin'ə-moo/ n a S American partridge-like bird (genus Tinamus) of or related to the Ratitae. [Fr, from Galibi (Ind language of Fr Guiana) tinamu]

tincal /ting'kəl/ n crude borax. [Malay tingkal]

tinchel /ting'hhyəl, ting'kəl/ n a circle of men who close in round a herd of deer. [Gaelic timchioll a circuit]

tinct /tingkt/ n a tint; a tinge; the alchemist's elixir (Shakesp). ◆ adj (Spenser) tinged. ◆ vt (obs) to tint, tinge, dye; to imbue; to subject to transmutation. [L tingere, tinctum to dye; cf **tint**[1], **tinge**]
■ **tinctō'rial** adj of or relating to dyeing; giving colour. **tinct'ure** n a tinge or shade of colour; a colouring matter; a metal, colour, or fur (heraldry); a quality or slight taste added to anything; an alcoholic solution of a drug (med); a usu small alcoholic drink (inf); a principle extracted in solution (old chem); the transmuting elixir or philosopher's stone (alchemy). ◆ vt to tinge; to imbue.

tind /tind, tīnd/ (now dialect), **teend** /tēnd/ (Herrick), or **tine** /tīn/ (Milton) vt and vi (pat and pap **tind'ed** or **tined**, also (Spenser) **tind**,

tynd or **tynde**) to kindle. [OE *tendan*, and prob a lost collateral form; cf **tinder**]

tindal /tin'dəl/ n a petty officer of lascars. [Malayalam *tandal*]

tinder /tin'dər/ n dry inflammable matter, *esp* that used for kindling fire from a spark. [OE *tynder*; ON *tundr*, Ger *Zunder*; OE *tendan*, Ger *zünden* to kindle]
■ **tin'der-like** adj (*Shakesp*) inflammable as tinder. **tin'dery** adj like tinder; easily angered.
□ **tin'derbox** n a box for tinder, and *usu* flint and steel; a person, thing or situation that is (potentially) explosive.

tine[1] /tīn/ n a spike or point, eg of a fork, harrow or deer's horn. [OE *tind*]
■ **tīned** adj.

tine[2] or **tyne** /tīn/ (*Scot*) vt (*pat* and *pap* **tint** /tint/ or (*Spenser*) **tyned**) to lose. ◆ vi to be lost; to be painful (*Spenser*); to perish (*Spenser*). ◆ n (*Spenser*) teen, affliction. [ON *tȳna* to destroy, lose, perish; cf **teen**[2]]
■ **tinsel** /tin'sl/ n (*Scot*) loss.

tine[3] /tīn/ (*dialect*) vt to shut; to enclose. [OE *tȳnan* to surround; cf **town**]

tine[4] /tīn/ (*dialect*) n a wild vetch or tare.

tine[5] or **tyne** /tīn/ (*Shakesp*) adj tiny (always preceded by little).

tine[6] see **tind**.

tinea /tin'i-ə/ n ringworm; any of several skin diseases caused by fungi, such as **tinea pedis**, athlete's foot; (with *cap*) the clothes moth genus, giving its name to the **Tineidae** /ti-nē'i-dē/, a large family of small moths. [L *tinea* moth, bookworm, etc]
■ **tin'eal** adj of, relating to or of the nature of tinea. **tineid** /tin-ē'id/ adj of or relating to the Tineidae family or *Tinea* genus. ◆ n an individual tineid moth.

ting /ting/ vt and vi to ring. ◆ n the sound of a small bell. [Imit]
□ **ting'-a-ling** n a ringing or tinkling (also *adv*).

tinge /tinj/ vt (*prp* **tin'ging** or **tinge'ing**) to tint or colour; to suffuse; to impart a slight modification or trace to. ◆ vi to take on a tinge. ◆ n a slight colouring, modification or trace. [L *tingere*, *tinctum*; connected with Gr *tengein* to wet, to stain]

tingle[1] /ting'gl/ vi to feel or be the site of a thrilling or slight stinging sensation; to thrill; to throb; to ring; to vibrate. ◆ vt to cause to tingle; to ring. ◆ n a tingling sensation. [ME *tinglen*, a variant of *tinklen*]
■ **ting'ler** n a stinging blow. **ting'ling** n and adj. **ting'lish** adj thrilling. **ting'ly** (**ting'lier**; **ting'liest**) adj tingling.

tingle[2] /ting'gl/ n a small tack or nail; a clip of lead; a patch over a leak in a boat's planking. [Cf Ger *Zingel*]

tinguaite /ting'gwə-īt/ n a fine-grained igneous rock composed essentially of feldspar, nepheline and aegirine. [*Tingua* Mountains in Brazil]

tinhorn see under **tin**.

tinier, etc see **tiny**.

tink /tingk/ n a clear high-pitched short bell-like sound; a chime of rhyme; a tinker (*Scot derog*); a quarrelsome, vulgar person (*Scot derog*). ◆ vt and vi to sound in this way; to tinker. [ME *tinken* to tink]

tinker /ting'kər/ n an itinerant mender of kettles, pans, etc; a botcher or bungler; a rascal (*inf*); a member of a group of Travelling People, a Gypsy (*esp Scot* and *Irish*; *derog*); a slight, temporary or unskilful patching-up. ◆ vt (*archaic*) to repair, *esp* ineffectually. ◆ vi to do a tinker's work; (often with *with*) to potter, fiddle, meddle, in trivial, ineffectual ways. [ME *tinkere* pert, connected with *tinken* to tink]
■ **tink'erer** n. **tink'ering** n.
■ **not give a tinker's curse** or **damn** (*sl*) not to care in the slightest.

tinkle /ting'k(ə)l/ vi to make small, bell-like sounds; to jingle; to clink repeatedly or continuously; (*esp* of water) to go with tinkling sounds; (used *esp* to or by children) to urinate; to tingle; to make empty sounds or mere sound. ◆ vt to cause to tinkle; to ring. ◆ n a sound of tinkling; a telephone call (*inf*); (used *esp* to or by children) an act of urinating. [ME *tinken* to tink; imit]
■ **tink'ler** n a small bell; a tinker, gypsy or vagrant (*Scot derog*). **tink'ling** n and adj. **tink'lingly** adv. **tink'ly** adj.
■ **give someone a tinkle** (*inf*) to call someone on the telephone.

tinnie, **tinny** see under **tin**.

tinnitus /ti-nī'təs, tin'i-təs/ n a medical condition in which there is constant ringing or other noise in the ears. [L *tinnītus*, -ūs a jingling, from *tinnīre* to ring]

tinsel[1] /tin's(ə)l/ n thin glittering metallic sheets or spangles, used eg to decorate Christmas trees; yarn or fabric with interwoven metallic, glittery threads; anything showy but of little value. ◆ adj of or like tinsel; gaudy. ◆ vt (**tin'selling** or (*US*) **tin'seling**; **tin'selled** or (*US*) **tin'seled**) to adorn with, or as if with, tinsel; to make glittering or gaudy. [OFr *estincelle*, from L *scintilla* a spark]

■ **tin'selled** adj. **tin'selly** adj like tinsel, gaudy, showy. **tin'selry** n glittering and tawdry material. **tin'sey** n and adj (*obs dialect*) tinsel.
□ **tinsel-slipp'er'd** adj (*Milton*) wearing glittering footwear. **Tin'seltown** n (*inf*) Hollywood.

tinsel[2] see under **tine**[2].

tinsey see under **tinsel**[1].

tint[1] /tint/ n a colour, shade; a slight tinge distinct from the principal colour; a hue mixed with white; a series of parallel lines or rows of dots in engraving, producing a uniform shading; a faint colour forming a background; hair dye which *usu* washes out after a few weeks. ◆ vt to colour slightly, to give a tint to; to tinge. ◆ vi to take on a tint. [L *tinctus*; cf **tinct**, **tinge**]
■ **tint'ed** adj. **tint'er** n a person or thing that tints. **tint'iness** n. **tint'ing** n. **tint'less** adj. **Tintom'eter**® n a name for a colorimeter. **tin'ty** adj unevenly tinted.
□ **tint block** n a block for printing a background. **tint tool** n an implement for producing a tint by parallel lines or rows of dots.

tint[2] /tint/ see **tine**[2].

tintinnabulate /tin-ti-nab'ū-lāt/ vi (*esp* of bells) to ring. [L *tintinnabulum* a bell, from *tintinnāre* to jingle, reduplicated from *tinnīre* to jingle]
■ **tintinnab'ulant**, **tintinnab'ular** or **tintinnab'ulary** adj ringing. **tintinnabulā'tion** n bellringing. **tintinnab'ulous** adj. **tintinnab'ulum** n (*pl* **tintinnab'ula**) a *usu* high-pitched bell; a bell-rattle.

tiny /tī'ni/ adj (**ti'nier**; **ti'niest**) very small. ◆ n (*usu* in *pl*) a small child. [Cf **tine**[5]]
■ **ti'nily** adv. **ti'niness** n.

-tion /-shən/ sfx forming nouns denoting action, condition, result or process. [From OFr, from L *-tiō*, *-tiōnis*]

tip[1] /tip/ n a slender, often tapering extremity; a small piece forming an end; the furthest part; a leafbud on tea. ◆ vt (**tip'ping**; **tipped** or **tipt**) to put a tip on; to be the tip of; to remove the tip from; to add colour to the tips of (the hair of a person or animal); (with *in*) to attach (a page) to the inside edge of another page. [Cf ON *typpa* to tip, Du, Norw, Dan *tip*, Ger (dimin) *Zipfel*]
■ **tip'less** adj. **tipped** or **tipt** adj. **tipp'ing** n the action of the verb. ◆ adj (*sl*) topping, ripping, excellent. **tipp'y** adj (*sl*) in the height of fashion; smart.
□ **tip'-tilted** adj (*Tennyson*) of the nose, turned up at the tip.
■ **on the tip of one's tongue** almost, but not (yet) quite, remembered; on the very point of being spoken. **tip of the iceberg** see under **ice**.

tip[2] /tip/ vt (**tipp'ing**; **tipped**) to throw down; to upset or overturn; to tilt; to shoot, dump, empty (out) by tilting; to toss (off). ◆ vi to topple (over); to tilt. ◆ n a tilt; a place for tipping rubbish, coal, etc; a dump; an extremely untidy place (*inf*); a staithe or shoot; a tram for speedy transference of coal. [ME *type*; origin obscure]
■ **tipp'able** adj. **tipp'er** n a person or thing that tips; a lorry or truck, the body of which can be tipped up for unloading (also *adj*). **tipp'ing** n. **tipp'y** adj inclined or likely to tip, eg because of being top-heavy.
□ **tip'-cart** n a cart emptied by being tilted up. **tip'cat** n a short piece of wood that is pointed at both ends; a game in which the cat is struck with a cat-stick and made to flip up. **tip'-cheese** n (*Dickens*) appar, tipcat. **tipping point** n the point in a process at which an irreversible momentum is reached. **tip'-up** adj constructed so as to be able to be tilted.
■ **tip (it) down** to rain heavily. **tip off liquor** to turn up the glass, bottle, etc until quite empty. **tip one's hat** to raise, tilt or touch the brim of one's hat as a polite greeting. **tip the balance** or **tip the scale** (or **scales**) to make something more, or less, favourable to someone; to be the deciding factor in a result. **tip the scale** or **scales** to depress one end of the scales; to weigh (with *at*).

tip[3] /tip/ vt (**tipp'ing**; **tipped**) to give, hand, pass, convey; to give a tip to; to indicate. ◆ vi to give tips. ◆ n a gift of money in return for services, in excess of any charges, a gratuity; a hint or piece of special, *usu* inside information supposed to be useful (eg in betting, examinations, etc); a helpful or casual piece of advice; a trick or dodge. [Orig rogues' cant]
■ **tipp'er** n a person giving the tip specified, as in *a generous tipper*. **tipp'ing** n. **tip'ster** n a person who makes a living by providing tips, *esp* about horses on which to bet.
□ **tip'-off** n (*pl* **tip'-offs**) a hint, warning, a piece of secret information (eg about a crime) (see also under **tip**[4]). **tip sheet** n a leaflet offering advice; a newspaper containing tips on likely movements in financial markets.
■ **tip off** to give a tip-off to. **tip someone the wink** to convey a secret hint.

tip[4] /tip/ vt (**tipp'ing**; **tipped**) to strike lightly but definitely; to hit glancingly. ◆ n a tap; a glancing blow. [Cf Du and Ger *tippen*, Swed *tippa* to tip]
■ **tipp'ing** n a way of articulating with the tongue to give staccato effects on the flute, trumpet, etc.

❑ **tip-and-run'** n an informal kind of cricket in which the batsmen must run if they hit the ball. ◆ adj denoting a raid in which the raiders make off at once. **tip'-off** n (pl **tip'-offs**) the opening jump ball in a game of basketball (see also under **tip³**). ■ **tip off** to begin a game of basketball.

tipi see **tepee**.

tipper¹ /tip'ər/ n a kind of ale. [Thomas *Tipper*, who brewed it in Sussex]

tipper² see under **tip²,³**.

tippet /tip'it/ n a long band of cloth or fur, eg (hist) on a hanging part of a garment; a shoulder cape, esp of fur; an animal's ruff of hair or feathers; an ecclesiastical scarf; the hangman's rope (obs, facetious); a moth's patagium. [Prob **tip¹**]

Tipp-Ex® or (non-standard) **Tippex** /tip'eks/ n correcting fluid, usu white, for covering over mistakes in typing or writing. ◆ vt (often with out) to cover over with correcting fluid. [Formed from Ger *tippen* to type, and L *ex* out]

tipple¹ /tip'l/ vt and vi to drink alcohol constantly in small quantities; to booze, esp habitually. ◆ n an alcoholic drink. [Cf Norw dialect *tipla* to drip slowly]
■ **tipp'ler** n.
❑ **tipp'ling-house** n.

tipple² /tip'l/ n a device that overturns freight cars, mine trucks, etc to unload their contents; a place where this is done; an area where coal is cleaned and loaded into freight cars, trucks, etc in a mine. [From **tip²**]
■ **tipp'ler** n a person who works at a tipple, esp in a mine.

tippy see under **tip¹,²**.

tippy-toe (US) a variant of **tiptoe**.

tipstaff /tip'stäf/ n (pl **tip'staffs** or **tip'staves** /-stāvz/) a staff tipped with metal; an officer who carries it, a sheriff's officer. [**tip¹** and **staff¹**]

tipster see under **tip³**.

tipsy /tip'si/ adj (**tip'sier**; **tip'siest**) partially or slightly intoxicated; askew, awry, esp as if slightly intoxicated. [Prob from **tip²**]
■ **tip'sify** vt to make drunk. **tip'sily** adv. **tip'siness** n.
❑ **tipsy cake** n a cake made of pastry and almonds, with wine.

tipt see under **tip¹**.

tiptoe /tip'tō/ n the end of the toe or toes, more often merely the toes. ◆ adv on tiptoe (lit or fig), through excitement, expectation, etc. ◆ vi (**tip'toeing**; **tip'toed**) to walk on tiptoe, to go lightly and stealthily. [**tip¹** and **toe**]
■ **on tiptoe** on the tips of one's toes, as if trying to be quiet or stealthy; eagerly or excitedly expecting.

tiptop /tip-top'/ n the extreme top; the height of excellence. ◆ adj of the highest excellence (also adv). [**tip¹** and **top¹**]

Tiptronic® **transmission** /tip-tron'ik tranz-mish'ən/ n an electronic automatic transmission system that allows the driver to select an individual gear by a manually operated switch.

tipula /tip'ū-lə/ n any fly of the daddy-long-legs genus of flies *Tipula*, giving its name to the family **Tipū'lidae**. [L *tippula* a water spider]

TIR abbrev : *Transports Internationaux Routiers* (Fr), International Road Transport, an international system enabling the rapid passage of goods through customs at intermediate points in a journey.

tirade /ti-rād', tī-rād', tē-räd'/ n a long vehement or angry harangue; a string of invectives; a laisse (prosody); a run between two notes (music). [Fr, from Ital *tirata*, from *tirare* to pull]

tirage à part /tē-räzh a pär'/ (Fr) n an offprint or article reprinted separately from a periodical.

tirailleur /tē-rä-yœr'/ n a skirmisher, sharpshooter. [Fr]

tiramisu /ti-rə-mi-soo'/ n a dessert made with pieces of sponge soaked in coffee and marsala, layered with mascarpone and chocolate. [Ital, literally, pull me up]

tirasse /ti-ras'/ n a device for coupling pedals in an organ. [Fr, from *tirer* to pull]

tire¹ /tīr/ vi to become weary; to have one's energy exhausted; to have one's interest or patience exhausted or worn down. ◆ vt to make weary; to exhaust the energy of; to bore; to wear out. [Appar OE *tēorian* to be tired]
■ **tired** adj exhausted, fatigued; wearied, bored (with of); showing deterioration through time or usage, eg limp, grubby, played out. **tired'ly** adv. **tired'ness** n. **tire'less** adj untiring. **tire'lessly** adv. **tire'lessness** n. **tire'ling** n a tired animal (also adj). **tire'some** adj fatiguing; wearisome; boring; tedious; (loosely) irritating, troublesome, irksome (inf). **tire'somely** adv. **tire'someness** n. **tir'ing** adj.
■ **tired and emotional** (inf, joc, euphem) drunk. **tire down** to hunt to exhaustion.

tire² /tīr/ n a metal hoop to bind a wheel; an obs or N Am spelling of **tyre**. ◆ vt to put a tire on. [Archaic *tire* a headdress, from ME, aphetic for **attire**]
■ **tired** adj. **tire'less** adj. **tir'ing** n.

tire³ /tīr/ (archaic) n equipment, furniture (Shakesp); attire, apparel; a headdress; a pinafore (US). ◆ vt to attire; to dress (eg the head). [Aphetic for **attire**]
■ **tir'ing** n.
❑ **tire'-val'iant** n (Shakesp) a kind of fanciful headdress. **tire'-woman** n a lady's-maid. **tir'ing-glass** n a mirror. **tir'ing-house** or **-room** n a theatre dressing-room. **tir'ing-woman** n a tire-woman.

tire⁴ /tīr/ (Spenser) n a train; a tier of guns. [Variant of **tier**]

tire⁵ /tīr/ n a volley; a broadside. [Fr *tir*]

tire⁶ /tīr/ (Shakesp) vi to tear and tug or feed greedily, like a bird of prey; to be intent, occupy oneself, feed one's thoughts or desires. [OFr *tirer* to pull]
■ **tir'ing** n (in falconry) a bony or tough portion of meat given to a bird to pull at for exercise.

tired see under **tire¹,²**.

tirl¹ /tirl/ (Scot) vt and vi to turn; to whirl; to rattle. ◆ n a turnstile or the like. [**trill²**]
❑ **tirlie-wir'lie** n a twirl. ◆ adj twirled; intricate. **tirl'ing-pin** n the pin of a door-latch, rattled to seek admission (obs); now usu taken to mean a risp.

tirl² /tirl/ (Scot) vt to strip. [Cf **tirr**]

Tir nan-Og or **Tir-na-nOg** /tēr-nan-nōg'/ n the Irish Elysium. [Ir, land of the young]

tiro or **tyro** /tī'rō/ n (pl **ti'ros**, **ti'roes**, **tyros**, **ty'roes** or **tyrones** /tī-rō'nēz/) a beginner; a novice. [L *tīrō* (LL *tȳrō*), -*ōnis* a recruit, *tīrōcinium* a first campaign]
■ **tirocinium** /-sin'i-əm/ n early training; first experience.

Tirolese, etc see **Tyrolese**.

Tironensian, also **Tyronensian** /tī-rō-nen'si-ən/ n a Benedictine of a congregation founded (1109) at *Tiron* (Thiron, near Nogent-le-Rotrou), absorbed (in 1627) by that of St Maur (also adj).

Tironian /tī-rō'ni-ən/ adj of Tiro, Cicero's amanuensis, or of shorthand writing (**Tironian notes**) ascribed to him.
❑ **Tironian sign** n an ampersand.

Tiros /tī'rōs/ n the name given to one of a series of satellites transmitting meteorological information to the earth from observation of the clouds. [From *t*elevision *i*nfra-*r*ed *o*bservation *s*atellite]

tirr /tir/ (Scot) vt and vi to strip. [ME *tirve* ; origin unknown]

tirra-lirra or **tirra-lyra** /tir-ə-lir'ə/ n and interj an old refrain, ascribed by Shakespeare to the lark.

tirrit /tir'it/ (Shakesp, 2 Henry IV II.4.195) n Mistress Quickly's word for alarm, fright.

tirrivee or **tirrivie** /tir'i-vi, -vē'/ (Scot) n a tantrum or fit of passion; a commotion.

'tis /tiz/ a contraction of **it is**.

tisane /ti-zan'/ n an infusion of eg herbs or flowers. [See **ptisan**]

Tishah b'Ab or **Tisha be'Ab** /tish'ə bə-ab/ n (in the Jewish calendar) the ninth day of the month of Ab, observed as a fast-day to commemorate the destruction of the first and second temples in Jerusalem (also **Tishah B'Av**, **Tisha Be'Av**, **Tisha Baav** or **Tisha Bov**). [Heb, ninth in Ab]

Tishri /tish'ri/ same as **Tisri**.

tisick /tiz'ik/ (Shakesp) n a cough. [**phthisic**]

Tisiphone /ti-sif'ə-nē/ (Gr myth) n one of the Furies. [Gr *Tīsiphonē*, from *tisis* retribution, and *phonos* murder]

'tisn't /tiz'nt/ a contraction of **it is not**.

Tisri /tiz'ri/ or **Tishri** /tish'ri/ n (in the Jewish calendar) the first month of the Jewish civil year, seventh of the ecclesiastical, usu part of September and October.

tissue /tish'oo, -ū, tis'ū/ n a collection of cells with a similar structure and particular function in an animal or plant (such as *muscle tissue*) (biol); tissue paper; a piece of soft, absorbent paper used as a disposable handkerchief, etc; anything woven, esp a rich or gauzy fabric interwoven with gold or silver thread; a complex accumulation (of lies, nonsense, etc); paper coated with gelatine and pigment (photog). ◆ vt to weave or interweave, esp with gold or silver thread; to clothe, cover or decorate with tissue or tissue paper; to variegate. [Fr *tissu* woven, pap of *titre* (OFr *tistre*), from L *texere* to weave]
❑ **tissue culture** n the growing of detached pieces of animal or plant tissue in nutritive fluids; a piece so grown. **tissue engineering** n the creation of new body parts for transplantation, etc. **tissue-equivalent material** n (radiol) phantom material. **tissue paper** n a thin, soft, semitransparent paper used for tracing, wrapping delicate or

breakable objects, decoration, etc (said *orig* to have been put between folds of tissue). **tissue plasminogen activator** *n* (*med*) an anti-clotting enzyme occurring naturally in the blood, manufactured genetically as a drug and used to dissolve blood clots. **tissue-specific antigen** *n* (*immunol*) an antigen present in a certain tissue but not found in other tissues. **tiss'ue-typing** *n* the determination of body tissue types, eg to ensure compatibility between the donor and the recipient in transplant surgery.

tiswas or **tizwas** /*tiz'woz*/ (*inf*) *n* a tizzy, flap, state of excitement, commotion. [Ety unknown; connected with **tizzy, tizz**]

Tit. (*Bible*) *abbrev* : (The Letter to) Titus.

tit¹ /*tit*/ *n* any of various kinds of small songbirds of the family Paridae (the titmice), of several genera, *esp* (formerly) those of the genus *Parus*; a small, inferior, worthless or worn-out horse; a nag; a girl, young woman (*derog*). [Icel *tittr* titmouse]

tit² /*tit*/ *n* (*dialect*) a tap. [A variant of **tip⁴**]
■ **tit for tat** an eye for an eye (a tip for a tap), retaliation in kind (**tit-for-tat'** *adj*); a hat, *usu* shortened to **tit'fer** (*Cockney rhyming sl*).

tit³ /*tit*/ *n* a variant of **teat**; a nipple (*inf*); (*usu* in *pl*) a female breast (*inf*); a contemptible person (*sl*).
■ **titt'ish** *adj*.
□ **tit tape** *n* (*inf*) double-sided adhesive tape used to secure the position of the breasts so that a revealing outfit does not reveal everything.
■ **get on one's tits** (*vulgar sl*) to be a source of extreme irritation.

tit⁴ /*tit*/ (chiefly *Scot*) *n* a twitch; a tug. ◆ *vt* and *vi* to tug.

tit⁵ see **tite**.

Titan /*tī'tən*/ (*Gr myth*) *n* a son, daughter or other descendant of Uranus and Gaea; one of the elder gods and goddesses overthrown by Zeus; the name of one of them, Hyperion; Helios, the sun god; the sun personified; Prometheus; Saturn's largest satellite (*astron*); (without *cap*) anything gigantic; (without *cap*) a person of great intellect but not the highest inspiration. ◆ *adj* (also without *cap*) Titanic. [Gr *Tītān*]
■ **Tītanesque** /*-esk'*/ *adj*. **Tī'taness** *n* a female Titan. **Titania** /*tī-tā'ni-ə, ti-tā'ni-ə*/ *n* the queen of fairyland, wife of Oberon; a satellite of Uranus (*astron*). **Titā'nian** *adj*. **Titanic** or **titanic** /*tī-* or *ti-tan'ik*/ *adj* of or like the Titans, *esp* in being of enormous size or strength; requiring unusual strength or effort. **Titan'ically** or **titan'ically** *adv*. **Tītā'nis** *n* (also without *cap*) an ostrich-like prehistoric N American bird. **Tī'tanism** *n* (also without *cap*) the spirit of revolt against the universe, the established order, authority, convention. **Titanomachy** /*-om'ə-ki*/ *n* (Gr *machē* fight; *Gr myth*) the war of the Titans against the Olympian gods. **Tītanosau'rus** *n* a gigantic Cretaceous dinosaur. **Tītanothē'rium** *n* a huge rhinoceros-like American Oligocene fossil ungulate.
□ **Titan arum** *n* an extremely large flowering plant, *Amorphophallus titanum*, which is native to Indonesia and blooms only very infrequently to produce short-lived, foul-smelling flowers.

Titanic see under **Titan**.

titanic see under **Titan** and **titanium**.

titanium /*ti-, tī-tā'ni-əm*/ *n* a strong, light and corrosion-resistant metallic element (symbol **Ti**; atomic no 22) found in ilmenite, sphene, rutile, etc, and used in aircraft manufacture. [Gr *Tītān* Titan, on the analogy of **uranium**]
■ **titanate** /*tī'tə-nāt*/ *n* a salt of titanic acid. ◆ *adj* (of a mineral) containing titanate. **tītanic** /*-tan'ik*/ *adj* of or containing quadrivalent titanium (**titanic acid** H_2TiO_3; **titanic iron** ilmenite). **tītanif'erous** *adj* containing titanium. **tī'tanite** *n* sphene, a brown, green or yellow monoclinic mineral, calcium silicate and titanate. **tī'tanous** *adj* of or containing trivalent titanium.
□ **titanium dioxide** *n* a pure white powder (TiO_2) of high opacity occurring naturally used *esp* as a pigment. **titanium white** *n* titanium dioxide used as pigment.

titbit /*tit'bit*/ or (*esp* N Am) **tidbit** /*tid'*/ *n* a choice delicacy or item. [Origin uncertain]

titch or **tich** /*tich*/ (*inf*) *n* a very small person; often used with *cap* as a nickname. [From the music-hall artist Harry Relph (1867–1928), known as Little *Tich*]
■ **titch'y** or **tich'y** *adj*.

tite, tyte, tight /*tīt*/, **tit** /*tit*/ or **titely**, etc /*-li*/ (*obs*) *adv* promptly; at once. [Cf ON *tītt* often]

titer see **titration** under **titrate**.

titfer /*tit'fər*/ see **tit for tat** under **tit²**.

tithe, tythe /*tīdh*/ *n* a tenth part, an indefinitely small part; the tenth of the produce of land and stock taken *orig* as a tax for church purposes; rent charged in lieu of this; any levy or fee of one-tenth. ◆ *adj* tenth. ◆ *vt* to take a tithe of or from; to pay a tithe on; to decimate (*obs*). ◆ *vi* to pay a tithe. [OE *tēotha* tenth; cf **tenth, teind**]

■ **tith'able** *adj* subject to the payment of tithes. **tithed** *adj*. **tith'er** *n* a person who collects tithes. **tith'ing** *n* a tithe; exaction or payment of tithes; a district containing ten householders, each responsible for the behaviour of the rest (*hist*).
□ **tithe barn** *n* formerly a barn for storing the tithe in corn paid by a parish. **tithe'-free** *adj* exempt from paying tithes. **tithe'-gatherer** *n*. **tithe'-paying** *adj*. **tithe'-pig** *n* one pig out of ten paid as a tithe. **tithe'-proctor** *n* a collector of tithes. **tith'ingman** *n* (*hist*) the chief man of a tithing.

titi¹ or **tee-tee** /*tē'tē*/ *n* a small S American monkey of the genus *Callicebus* with a long, non-prehensile tail.

titi² /*tē'tē*/ *n* a shrub or small tree of the family Cyrillaceae, native to the southern USA, *esp Cliftonia monophylla*, which has glossy leaves and clusters of fragrant white flowers. [Ety uncertain]

Titian or **titian** /*tish'ən, -yən*/ *n* (in full **Titian red**) a striking red colour used by the Venetian painter *Titian* (Tiziano Vecellio, c.1490–1576) *esp* for hair. ◆ *adj* (chiefly of hair) red-gold, or (loosely) any other shade of red or reddish-brown.
■ **Titianesque** /*-esk'*/ *adj* in the manner of Titian, a combination of the richest surface and colour.

titillate /*tit'i-lāt*/ *vt* to stimulate gently, *esp* in a sexual way; to tickle. [L *titillāre, -ātum*]
■ **tit'illāting** *adj*. **tit'illātingly** *adv*. **titillā'tion** *n*. **tit'illātive** *adj*. **tit'illātor** *n*.

titivate, tittivate /*tit'i-vāt*/ or **tidivate** /*tid'*/ (*sl*) *vi* and *vt* to smarten up or put the finishing touches to (eg one's appearance). [Poss coined from **tidy**]
■ **titivā'tion, tittivā'tion** or **tidivā'tion** *n*.

titlark /*tit'lärk*/ *n* any bird of the pipit family, *esp* the meadow pipit. [**tit¹** and **lark¹**]

title /*tī'tl*/ *n* the distinctive name of a book, poem, tale, picture, etc; a chapter-heading; a title-page; a book or publication, as an item in a catalogue (*publishing jargon*); (often in *pl*) a caption giving credits at the end of a film or television programme; a subtitle; an appellation of rank or distinction or a formal designation; an inscription or descriptive placard; a section of a law-book; a championship (*sport*); a right to possession or ownership (*law*); a basis of a claim (*law*); the evidence supporting a claim or right; a title deed (*law*); a fixed sphere of work, source of maintenance, or a certificate of this, required as a condition for ordination (*relig*); a cardinal-priest's parish in Rome. ◆ *vt* to designate; to give or attach a title to. [OE *titul* or *titul* and OFr *title* (Fr *titre*), from L *titulus*]
■ **ti'tled** *adj* having a title, *esp* an appellation of rank or nobility. **ti'tleless** *adj* untitled; nameless (*Shakesp*). **ti'tler** *n* a writer of titles; a claimant (*obs*). **ti'tling** *n* the giving or attaching of a title; titles, captions, etc collectively.
□ **title bar** *n* (*comput*) the narrow horizontal block at the top of a window showing the program and document name. **title deed** *n* a document that proves right to possession. **ti'tle-holder** *n* a person holding a title, *esp* legal, or a championship in some sport. **title leaf** *n* the leaf containing the title of a book. **title page** *n* the page of a book containing its title and the author's (and often publisher's) name. **title poem** *n* the poem which gives its title to a book. **title role** *n* the character in a play, film, etc after whom the work is named. **title sheet** *n* the first sheet of a book as printed, containing title, abbreviated or short title, etc. **title track** *n* the song which gives its title to a record album.

titling /*tit'ling*/ *n* a small stockfish; the meadow pipit (*esp Scot*); the hedge sparrow. [Norw dialect *titling* small stockfish; ON *titlingr* sparrow; cf **tit¹**]

titmouse /*tit'mows*/ (*Spenser* **titmose** /*-mōs*/) *n* (*pl* **titmice** /*tit'mīs*/) a tit, any of various kinds of small active acrobatic bird of several genera, *esp*, formerly, of the genus *Parus*. [**tit¹** and ME *mose* titmouse, from OE *māse*; Ger *Meise*; confused with **mouse**]

Titoism /*tē'tō-izm*/ *n* the variant of communism as practised by Marshal *Tito* (1892–1980) in the former Yugoslavia, adhering to international communism but not at the sacrifice of national independence.
■ **Ti'toist** *n* and *adj*.

titoki /*ti-tok'i, tē'*/ *n* a New Zealand tree with reddish paniculate flowers. [Maori]

titrate /*tī'trāt, tī-trāt'*/ (*chem*) *vt* to measure the strength of (a solution) by titration. [Fr *titre* standard]
■ **titrā'table** *adj*. **titrā'tion** *n* the addition of a solution from a graduated vessel to a known volume of a second solution until the chemical reaction is just completed, the knowledge of the volume of liquid added (the **titre** or (*US*) **titer**; /*tī'tər* or *tē'tər*/) and of the concentration of one of the solutions enabling that of the other to be calculated.

ti tree same as **ti²**.

---

titter¹ /tit'ər/ vi to giggle, snicker or laugh furtively or restrainedly. ♦ n a stifled laugh. [Cf Swed dialect *tittra*]
■ **titt'erer** n. **titt'ering** n and adj. **titt'eringly** adv.

titter² /tit'ər/ vi to totter, sway. [ON *titra* to shake]

tittivate see **titivate**.

tittle¹ /tit'l/ n a dot, stroke, accent, vowel point, contraction or punctuation mark; the smallest part. [OFr *title*, from L *titulus* a title]

tittle² /tit'l/ (dialect) vt and vi to whisper; to tattle.
□ **titt'le-tatt'le** n idle, empty talk, rumour. ♦ vi to talk idly, esp in relaying rumours or gossip. **titt'le-tatt'ler** n. **titt'le-tatt'ling** n.

tittlebat /tit'l-bat/ n a childish form of **stickleback**.

tittup or **titup** /tit'əp/ vi (**titt'upping** or **tit'upping**, or (US) **titt'uping** or **tit'uping**; **titt'upped** or **tit'upped**, or (US) **titt'uped** or **tit'uped**) to prance, skip about gaily. ♦ n a light springy step, a canter. [Imit]
■ **titt'upy** or **tit'upy** adj jolly, lively; unsteady.

titty¹ /tit'i/ (sl or used by children) n a teat; the breast. [Dimin of **tit³** or **teat**]

titty² /tit'i/ (Scot) n a sister.

titubate /tit'ū-bāt/ vi to stagger, stumble. [L *titubāre, -ātum* to stagger]
■ **tit'ūbancy** n staggering. **tit'ūbant** adj. **titūbā'tion** n (med) staggering; unsteadiness; a tremor (esp of the head), often a symptom of a cerebral or spinal disease.

titular /tit'ū-lər/ adj of or relating to title; in name or title only; nominal; having the title without the duties of an office; (of a church) giving a title to a cardinal or bishop. ♦ n a titled person; someone who enjoys the title of an office, without actual possession; a person invested with a title in virtue of which he or she holds a benefice, whether or not he or she performs its duties; the holy personage, entity, etc from which a church takes its name (eg Corpus Christi), as opposed to *patron* if it takes its name from a saint or angel (RC). [L *titulus*]
■ **titularity** /-ar'i-ti/ n. **tit'ularly** adv. **tit'ulary** adj titular. ♦ n a person holding a title.
□ **titular bishop** n (RC) a bishop without a diocese, taking his title from a place where there is no longer a bishop's see (before 1882 bishop *in partibus infidelium*). **titular of the teinds** or **tithes** n a layman invested with church lands after the Reformation in Scotland.

titule /tit'ūl/ n and vt same as **title**. [L *titulus*]

titup see **tittup**.

Tiv /tiv/ n (a member of) a people living in SE Nigeria; the language of this people. ♦ adj of or relating to the Tiv or their language.

TiVo® /tē'vō/ n a system for making digital recordings of television programmes on a hard disk. ♦ vt (**Ti'voing**; **Ti'voed**) (inf) to record (a programme) using this system.

Tiw /tē'w/ or **Tiu** /tē'oo/ n the old English war god. [OE *Tīw*; cf **Tuesday, Tyr**]

tix /tiks/ (inf) n pl tickets.

tiyin or **tyiyn** /tē'yin/ n (pl **ti'yin**, **ti'yins**, **ty'iyn** or **ty'iyns**) a monetary unit in Kazakhstan, Kyrgyzstan and Uzbekistan, one hundredth of the standard unit of currency.

tizwas see **tiswas**.

tizzy /tiz'i/ n a state of agitation, nervousness, confusion or dither for little reason (also **tizz**; sl); a sixpence (old sl). [Ety unknown]

TJ abbrev : Tajikistan (IVR).

tjanting /chan'ting/ n a small tool consisting of a long bamboo handle with a small copper or brass bowl at one end, used for applying hot wax to cloth to form patterns in batik. [Indonesian word]

TKO (boxing) abbrev : technical knockout.

Tl (chem) symbol : thallium.

TLA (comput) abbrev : Three-Letter Acronym (sometimes used to mean one that is longer or often one that is confusing).

TLC (facetious) abbrev : tender loving care.

Tlingit /tlin'git/ n (a member of) a native N American people living in parts of Alaska and British Columbia; the language spoken by this people. ♦ adj of or relating to this people, their language or culture. [Tlingit, person]

TLS abbrev : Times Literary Supplement.

TM abbrev : transcendental meditation; Turkmenistan (IVR).

Tm (chem) symbol : thulium.

tmesis /tmē'sis/ (grammar) n (pl **tmē'sēs**) the separation or splitting up of a word into parts by one or more intervening words. [Gr *tmēsis*, from *temnein* to cut]

TMI (inf) abbrev : too much information, an expression of boredom or disgust at information offered.

TMS abbrev : transcranial magnetic stimulation, a technique for investigating and treating neurological conditions.

TMT abbrev : technology, media and telecommunications.

TN abbrev : Tennessee (US state); tradename; Tunisia (IVR).

TNF abbrev : tumour necrosis factor, a protein that destroys tumours.

TNT abbrev : trinitrotoluene or trinitrotoluol.

TO abbrev : Tax Officer; telegraph office; Transport Officer; turn over.

to /too, tŭ, tə/ prep serving as sign of the infinitive (which is sometimes understood) and forming a substitute for the dative case; used to introduce the indirect object of a verb; in the direction of; as far as; all the way in the direction of; until; into the condition of; towards; beside; near; at; in contact with, close against; before, before the hour of; answering, by way of response or reaction; for; of; with the object or result of; against; in accordance, comparison, proportion or relation with; in honour of, or expressing good wishes for; along with, in addition. ♦ adv in one direction, forward; in or into a required or fixed position, contact, closed or fastened condition. [OE *tō*; Ger *zu*, Gothic *du*; Gr sfx *-de*]
■ **to and fro** alternately this way and that. **toing and froing** going backwards and forwards in an agitated way, or without achieving anything (also fig).

toad /tōd/ n a toothless tailless amphibian (family Bufonidae) with a warty skin that walks or crawls instead of jumping like the frog, esp one belonging to the *Bufo* or related genus; any of several similar amphibians belonging to different families; a hateful or contemptible person or animal; bufo (alchemy). [OE *tāde, tādige, tādie*]
■ **toad'y** n a sycophant, an obsequious flatterer; a toadfish (Aust inf). ♦ vt and vi (**toad'ying**; **toad'ied**) to fawn on and flatter like a sycophant. **toad'yish** adj. **toad'yism** n.
□ **toad'-eater** n (archaic) a toady, a fawning sycophant, orig a mountebank's assistant, whose duty was to swallow, or pretend to swallow, toads. **toad'-eating** n sycophancy. ♦ adj sycophantic. **toad'fish** n any of several toadlike fish of the Batrachoidiae family, with wide mouths, large heads and tapering bodies. **toad'flax** n any species of *Linaria*, a genus closely related to the snapdragon, with flaxlike leaves. **toad-in-the-hole'** n a dish orig of beef, now usu sausage meat, cooked in batter. **toad'rush** or **toad'grass** n a low rush (*Juncus bufonius*) with mostly solitary flowers. **toad spit** or **toad spittle** n cuckoo-spit. **toad'-spotted** adj thickly stained or spotted like a toad. **toad'stone** n a stone formerly believed to be found in a toad's head, and valued as an amulet; a basalt lava found in Carboniferous limestone in Derbyshire (so called perhaps because of its toadlike markings, but possibly from German *totes Gestein* dead stone, from the lead-miner's point of view). **toad'stool** n any of several spore-producing, poisonous, umbrella-shaped fungi; any capped fungi incl the edible mushroom and poisonous toadstool (old rare).

toast /tōst/ vt to brown (esp bread) by exposing it to direct heat, eg under a grill; to half-melt (eg cheese) in this way; to warm, by exposing to heat; to dry and parch; to drink to (someone's health, success, etc). ♦ vi to drink toasts; (of esp bread) to become brown or be suitable for browning by exposing to direct heat; to become warm by being exposed to heat. ♦ n slices of bread toasted on both sides; the person (orig a woman) or thing drunk to, as the most admired and celebrated for the moment; a call to drink to an admired person or thing; a wish for someone's continued health; a piece of spiced toasted bread put in alcohol (archaic). [OFr *toster*, from L *tostus* roasted, pap of *torrēre*; some senses of the verb and noun reflect the idea that a woman's name (ie as the person whose health is being drunk) would flavour the wine like spiced toast]
■ **toast'ed** adj. **toast'er** n an electric device, usu with a timer, for toasting bread; a person who toasts; a toasting fork; that which can be toasted. **toast'ie** n (inf) a toasted sandwich. **toast'ing** n. ♦ adj (inf) hot. **toast'y** adj (**toast'ier**; **toast'iest**) resembling toast; cosily warm. ♦ n same as **toastie** above.
□ **toasting fork** or **toasting iron** n a long-handled fork for toasting bread; a sword (facetious). **toast'master** or **toast'mistress** n a person who announces toasts, introduces speakers, at a dinner. **toast rack** n a stand with partitions for slices of toast.
■ **have been had on toast** to have been swindled. **have someone on toast** (inf) to be in a dominant position over someone, to have someone at one's mercy. **on toast** served on a slice of toast.

toaze /tōz/ (Shakesp) see under **toze**.

Tob. (Bible) abbrev : (the Apocryphal Book of) Tobit.

tobacco /tə-bak'ō/ n (pl **tobacc'os** or **tobacc'oes**) (in full **tobacco plant**) any American solanaceous plant of the genus *Nicotiana*, especially *N. tabacum*, with narcotic leaves; its prepared leaves used for smoking, chewing, or snuff. [Sp *tabaco*, from Haitian]
■ **tobaccanā'lian** n a smoker (facetious, after *bacchanalian*). **tobacc'onist** n a seller or manufacturer of tobacco and cigarettes; a smoker (obs).
□ **tobacc'o-heart** n (old) a functional disorder of the heart due to excessive use of tobacco. **tobacco mosaic virus** n a virus causing mosaic disease in tobacco. **tobacco pipe** n a pipe for smoking

---

■ words derived from main entry word; □ compound words; ■ idioms and phrasal verbs

tobacco. **tobacco pouch** *n* a pouch for holding tobacco. **tobacc'o-stopper** *n* an instrument for pressing down the tobacco in a pipe.

Tobagonian /tə-bā-gō'ni-ən/ *adj* of or relating to the island of *Tobago* in the West Indies. ◆ *n* a native of Tobago.

to-be /tū- or tə-bē'/ *adj* signifying something in the future, yet to become (now *usu combining form* as in *bride-to-be*). ◆ *n* the future.

Tobin tax /tō'bin taks/ (*econ*) *n* a proposed tax on foreign exchange transactions, intended to deter short-term currency speculation. [James Tobin (1918–2002), US economist]

Tobit /tō'bit/ *n* an apocryphal Old Testament book, containing the story of *Tobit*.

toboggan /tə-bog'ən/ *n* a long narrow flat sledge that curves up at the front, used on snow and ice. ◆ *vi* (**tobogg'aning**; **tobogg'aned**) to slide, coast or travel on, or as if on, a toboggan (also (*earlier*) **tobogg'in**, **tabogg'an** or **tarbogg'in**). [Micmac *tobākun*]
■ **tobogg'aner** *n*. **tobogg'aning** *n*. **tobogg'anist** *n*.

to-break /tū- or tə-brāk'/ (*obs*) *vt* (*pat* (*Bible, Bunyan*) **to-brake'** (*usu* printed *to brake*); *pap* **to-bro'ken**) to break in pieces. [OE *tōbrecan*, from pfx *tō-* asunder, and *brecan* to break]

to-bruise /tə-brooz'/ (*obs*) *vt* (*pap* (*Spenser*) **to-brusd'**) to bruise severely; to break up. [OE *tō-brȳsan*]

Toby /tō'bi/ *n* a beer mug or other vessel shaped like a man wearing a three-cornered hat (also **To'by-jug**; also without *cap*); Punch's dog.

toby /tō'bi/ *n* the road (*criminal sl*); robbery on the road; a stop-cock in a gas or water main under the road (*Scot*); the cover protecting it (*Scot*). [Shelta *tōbar*]
■ **high toby** highway robbery on horseback. **low toby** robbery by a highwayman on foot.

TOC *abbrev*: train operating company.

toc or **tock** /tok/ *n* telecommunications code for signalling the letter *t*.
□ **toc emma** /em'ə/ *n* (emma, signallers' code for *m*; *milit sl*) a trench mortar. **Toc H** /āch/ *n* (signallers' code for *h*) a society formed after World War I to promote comradeship and Christian fellowship, from its first meetings at *Talbot House*, at Poperinghe in Belgium.

toccata /to-kä'tə/ (*music*) *n* a musical work intended primarily to display the performer's touch, or in which he or she seems to try the touch of an instrument in a series of runs and chords before breaking into a fugue; (loosely) a sort of fantasia or overture. [Ital, from *toccare* to touch]
■ **toccatel'la** or **toccatina** /-tē'nə/ *n* a short toccata.

toc emma, **Toc H** see under **toc**.

Tocharian or **Tokharian** /to-kä'ri-ən, -kā'/ *n* (also **Tocha'rish** or **Tokha'rish**) an extinct Indo-European language, related to Latin and Celtic, preserved in manuscripts discovered in the 20c in Chinese Turkestan, and divided into two dialects, **Tocharian A** and **Tocharian B**; a member of the people speaking this language, living in central Asia until c.800AD. ◆ *adj* of or relating to this language or its speakers. [Gr *Tocharoi*, a people supposed to be its speakers on the strength of the Uigur (language of Chinese Turkestan) name *Tochri*]

tocher /tohh'ər/ (*Scot*) *n* a dowry. ◆ *vt* to dower. [Ir *tochar*, Gaelic *tochradh*]
■ **toch'erless** *adj*.
□ **toch'er-good** *n* property given as tocher.

tock[1] /tok/ *n* the sound made by a clock or watch, like a tick but deeper and more resonant. ◆ *vi* (of a clock, etc) to make such a sound. [Prob imit]
□ **tick-tock** see under **tick**[1].

tock[2] see **toc**.

toco or **toko** /tō'kō/ (*sl*) *n* (*pl* **to'cos** or **to'kos**) punishment. [Origin uncertain; Gr *tokos* interest, and Hindi *thōkō*, from *thoknā* to thrash, have been suggested]

tocology or **tokology** /to-kol'ə-ji/ *n* obstetrics. [Gr *tokos* birth, offspring, and *logos* discourse]

tocopherol /to-kof'ə-rol/ *n* vitamin E, a group of fat-soluble substances found in wheatgerm, egg yolk, green leafy vegetables, etc, whose deficiency causes sterility in some species. [Gr *tokos* birth, offspring, *pherein* to bring, bear, and **-ol**[1]]

tocsin /tok'sin/ *n* an alarm-bell, or the ringing of it. [Fr *tocsin*, from Provencal *tocasenh*, from *tocar* to touch, strike, and *senh*, from L *signum* sign (LL bell)]

tod[1] /tod/ (*Scot*) *n* a fox; a sly person. [Origin unknown]
□ **Tod-low'rie** *n* a nickname for a fox, (ie Laurence) Reynard.

tod[2] (*Spenser* **todde**) /tod/ *n* a bush, *esp* of ivy; an old wool weight, about 28lb; a load. ◆ *vi* to yield a tod. ◆ *vt* to yield a tod for.

tod[3] /tod/ *n* one's own, *esp* in the phrase *on one's tod*. [Rhyming slang *Tod Sloan* own]

today /tū-, tə-dā'/ *n* this day; the present times. ◆ *adv* on or during the present day; nowadays. [OE *tōdæg(e)*]

todde see **tod**[2].

toddle /tod'l/ *vi* to walk with short feeble steps, as a young child does; to saunter (*inf*); (with *off*) to go, depart (*facetious*). ◆ *n* a toddling gait; an aimless stroll (*inf*); a toddling child. [Orig Scot and N Eng dialect]
■ **todd'ler** *n* a person who toddles, *esp* a young child learning to walk. ◆ *adj* of or for a toddler. **todd'lerhood** *n*. **todd'ling** *adj*.

toddy /tod'i/ *n* the fermented sap of various palm trees; a mixture of spirits, sugar and hot water. [Hindi *tāṛī*, from *tāṛ* a palm tree, prob of Dravidian origin]
□ **toddy cat** *n* the palm civet. **todd'y-ladle** *n* a small ladle for mixing or serving toddy. **todd'y-palm** *n* coconut, palmyra or other species of palm yielding toddy. **todd'y-stick** *n* a stick used in mixing toddy.

todger /toj'ər/ (*sl*) *n* the penis.

to-do /tə-, tū-doo'/ *n* (*pl* **to-dos**) a bustle; a stir; a commotion.
□ **to-do list** *n* a list of tasks to be done.

tody /tō'di/ *n* a small West Indian insectivorous bird of the genus *Todus*, including the *green sparrow*, *green hummingbird*, etc, related to the kingfishers. [L *todus* a small bird of some kind]

TOE (*phys*) *abbrev*: theory of everything.

toe /tō/ *n* one of the five small projecting members at the front of the human foot; the corresponding part of other animals; the front of a hoof; the corresponding part of a shoe, sock, etc, covering the toes; the corresponding part of the head of a golf club, hockey stick, etc; the lowest part of the front of anything, *esp* if it projects. ◆ *vt* (**toe'ing**; **toed**) to stand with the toes against (eg a starting-line); to provide (eg a sock or stocking) with a toe; to mend the toe of (a sock, etc); to kick; to strike with the toe of a club; to nail obliquely through the foot; to perform with the toe. ◆ *vi* to walk with the toes pointing in a particular direction. [OE *tā* (pl *tān*); ON *tā*, Ger *Zehe*]
■ **toed** /tōd/ *adj* having toes (of a specified kind or number; also *combining form*); nailed obliquely.
□ **toe'cap** *n* a (*usu* steel) cap covering the toe of a shoe or boot. **toe'clip** *n* an attachment to a bicycle pedal that holds the toe and thus the foot, firm. **toe'-curling** *adj* see **make one's toes curl** below. **toe dance** *n* a dance performed on tiptoes. **toe'-dance** *vi*. **toe'hold** *n* a place to anchor the toes in; a first established position, an initial position or advantage; a hold in which the opponent's toes are grasped and the foot is bent back or twisted (*wrestling*). **toe'-in** *n* a slight forward convergence given to the planes of a vehicle's front wheels to promote steering stability and equalize tyre-wear. **toe jump** *n* (*ice skating*) a jump executed by pushing off with the toe of one's free foot. **toe loop** *n* (*ice skating*) a toe jump and a loop performed in combination. **toe'nail** *n* a nail covering the upper surface of a human or animal toe; an obliquely driven nail. ◆ *vt* to join (eg two pieces of wood) by driving nails obliquely. **toe'-piece** *n*. **toe poke** *n* (*football*) a shot struck at full stretch with the end of the foot.
■ **big** or **great toe** the largest of the toes. **little toe** the smallest of the toes. **make one's toes curl** (*inf*) to make one feel exquisite pleasure or extreme disgust (**toe'-curling** *adj*). **on one's toes** poised for a quick start, alert, eager. **take to one's toes** to run away. **toe the line** to stand with toes against a marked line, eg when starting a race; to conform. **toe to toe** (*fig*) in close, direct confrontation (**toe-to-toe** *adj*). **tread on someone's toes** to offend someone. **turn up one's toes** (*inf*) to die.

toea /tō'ä or tō'ə/ *n* a monetary unit of Papua New Guinea, $\frac{1}{100}$ of a kina. [Native name]

toerag /tō'rag/ (*sl*) *n* a beggar, tramp (also **toeragg'er**); generally, a ruffian or rascal; a despicable person. [Prob from the strips of rag used by tramps to wrap around their toes in place of socks]

toetoe see **toitoi**.

toey /tō'i/ (*Aust* and *NZ sl*) *adj* nervous, restless, on edge, irritable; in a state of keen anticipation; sexually aroused.

to-fall /too'föl/ (*archaic*) *n* a beginning, incidence. [**to** and **fall**]

toff /tof/ (*sl*) *n* a person of the upper classes, *esp* wealthy and smartly dressed; a good sort. [Perh **tuft**]
■ **toff'ish** *adj*. **toff'ishness** *n*. **toff'y** *adj*.

toffee or **toffy** /tof'i/ *n* (a piece of) a hard-baked chewy sweet, made of sugar and butter (earlier and US **taff'y**). [Ety unknown]
□ **toffee apple** *n* a toffee-coated apple on a stick. **toff'ee-nose** or **toff'ee-nosed** *adj* (*sl*) supercilious, conceited, snobbish.
■ **for toffee** (*inf*) (always with a *neg*) at all, as in *he can't dance for toffee*.

tofore /tū-, tə-fōr', -för'/ *adv* (*Shakesp*), *prep* and *conj* (*obs*) before. [OE *tōforan* (prep)]

toft /toft/ *n* a homestead (*hist*); a hillock (*dialect*). [Late OE *toft*, from ON *topt, tupt, toft*]

tofu /tō'foo/ *n* unfermented soy bean curd, having a pale, creamy colour and a bland flavour. [Jap, from Chin *dòu fǔ* rotten beans]

tog[1] /*tog*/ (*sl*) *n* (*usu* in *pl*) a garment, an item of clothing; a swimming costume (*Aust, NZ* and *Irish*). ◆ *vt* (**togg'ing; togged**) to dress. [Prob ult L *toga* a robe]

■ **togg'ery** *n* clothes.

■ **long'-togs** (*naut*) shore clothes. **tog up** or **out** to dress (oneself) *esp* in one's best clothes.

tog[2] /*tog*/ *n* a unit of measurement of thermal insulation as a property of textile fabrics used eg for quilts. [Appar an invention, perh connected with **tog**[1]]

❑ **tog rating** or **value** *n* the amount of thermal insulation provided by a fabric, measured in togs.

toga /tō'gə/ *n* the outer garment of a Roman citizen, a long piece of cloth wound round and draped over the body (also (*obs*) **toge** /*tōg*/). [L *toga*; cf *tegere* to cover; **thatch**]

■ **tō'ga'd, tō'gaed, tō'gate, tō'gated** or **toged** /*tōgd*/ *adj* (*Shakesp*). ❑ **toga praetexta** /*prē-, prī-teks'tə, -tə*/ *n* a toga with a deep border of purple, worn by boys, magistrates, etc. **toga virilis** /*vir-ī'lis, wir-ē'lis*/ *n* a toga put on at a boy's coming of age.

together /tə-, tŭ-gedh'ər/ *adv* with someone or something else, in company; in or into one place; at the same time; so as to be in contact, joined or united; by action with one or more other people; continuously; into a proper or suitable order or state of being organized (*inf*). ◆ *adj* (*inf*) well-organized, mentally composed, emotionally stable, etc. [OE *tōgædere*, from *tō* to, and *geador* together]

■ **togeth'erness** *n* unity; closeness; a sense of unity or affection from being with other people.

■ **get** or **put it** (**all**) **together** (*inf*) to perform something successfully, get something right; to become well-organized, stable, etc; to establish a good relationship (with).

toggery see under **tog**[1].

toggle /*tog'l*/ *n* a crosspiece on a rope, chain, rod, etc, to prevent slipping through a hole, or to allow the rope, etc to be twisted; a short bar acting as a button, passed through a loop for fastening a garment; an appliance for transmitting force at right angles to its direction; a switch or a keyboard command which turns a particular feature (eg bold type or read-only mode) on or off (*comput*). ◆ *vt* to hold or provide with a toggle; to fix fast; (with *on, off*) to turn (a particular feature, eg bold type) on or off using a toggle switch or a keyboard command (*comput*). ◆ *vi* (*comput*) (with *between*) to move between (different features, modes, files, etc) using a toggle switch or keyboard command. [Appar connected with **tug** and **tow**[1]]

❑ **toggle iron** *n* a harpoon with a toggle instead of barbs. **toggle joint** *n* an elbow or knee joint; a mechanism consisting of two levers hinged together, force applied to straighten the hinge producing a considerable force along the levers. **toggle switch** *n* a switch which, in a circuit having two stable or quasi-stable states, produces a transition from one to the other (*telecom* and *electronics*); a switch or button on a computer keyboard used to turn a particular feature (eg bold type) on or off (*comput*).

Togolese /tog-ə-lēz'/ *adj* of or relating to *Togo* in W Africa, or its inhabitants. ◆ *n* a person born in, or a naturalized inhabitant of, Togo.

togs see **tog**[1].

togue /*tōg*/ *n* the Great Lake char (or trout), a gigantic salmonid of N America. [From a Native American name]

toheroa /tō-ə-rō'ə/ *n* an edible shellfish found at low tide buried in sandy beaches in New Zealand; a soup made from it. [Maori]

toho /tō-hō'/ *interj* a call to pointers or setters to stop.

tohu bohu /tō'hoo bō'hoo/ *n* chaos. [Heb *thōhū wa-bhōhū* emptiness and desolation (Bible, Genesis 1.2)]

tohunga /to'hŭng-ə, to-hŭng'ə/ (*NZ*) *n* a Maori priest, a wise man with healing powers. [Maori]

toil[1] /*toil*/ *vi* to struggle hard; to work long and hard; to make one's way forwards or progress with great difficulty or effort. ◆ *vt* (*archaic* or *dialect*) to effect or work out with toil; to subject to toil. ◆ *n* a struggle; hard or exhausting labour; contention (*obs*). [Anglo-Fr *toiler* (Fr *touillier*) said to be from L *tudiculāre* to stir]

■ **toiled** *adj*. **toil'er** *n*. **toil'ful** *adj*. **toil'ing** *n* and *adj*. **toil'less** *adj*. **toil'some** *adj* involving toil, laborious; toiling; owing to toil (*Spenser* **toyl'som** or **toyle'some**). **toil'somely** *adv*. **toil'someness** *n*. ❑ **toil'worn** *adj* worn, weary with toil.

toil[2] /*toil*/ (*usu* in *pl*, often *fig*) *n* a net; a snare or trap. [OFr *toile*, from L *tēla* web]

toile /*twäl*/ *n* a thin cotton or linen dress material; a sample of a garment made in cheap material so that alterations may be made before the garment is made up in the correct material. [Fr, from L *tēla* web]

toilet /*toi'lit*/ or *-lət*/ *n* a bowl-like receptacle for the body's waste matter, with a water supply for washing this into a sewer; a dressing-room, bathroom, or lavatory; the act or process of dressing; the whole dress and appearance of a person, any particular costume; the cleansing and dressing of a wound; a dressing-table with a mirror; a toilet table; the articles used in dressing; a toilet cover; a cloth for the shoulder during hairdressing (*archaic*). ◆ *vt* to take to the toilet or otherwise assist with toilet procedures. [Fr *toilette*, dimin of *toile*, from L *tēla* web]

■ **toil'eted** *adj* (*archaic*) dressed. **toil'etry** *n* (*pl* **toil'etries**) (*usu* in *pl*) any article, preparation or cosmetic used in washing and dressing oneself.

❑ **toilet bag** *n* a waterproof bag for holding toiletries. **toilet cloth** or **cover** *n* a dressing-table cover. **toilet glass** *n* a mirror set on the dressing-table. **toilet paper** or **tissue** *n* thin, absorbent paper for wiping oneself after defecation or urination. **toilet roll** *n* a roll of toilet paper. **toilet service** or **set** *n* the utensils (eg brushes, combs, etc) used in dressing. **toilet soap** *n* soap for personal use. **toilet table** *n* a dressing-table. **toilet training** *n* the training of children to control bladder and bowels and to use the lavatory. **toilet water** *n* a lightly perfumed liquid similar to cologne.

toilette /*twä-let'*/ *n* the act of washing and dressing oneself. [Fr, dimin of *toile*, from L *tēla* web]

toilinet or **toilinette** /*toi-, twä-li-net'*/ *n* a kind of woollen cloth, silk and cotton warp with woollen weft, used for waistcoats. [Prob from Fr *toile* linen, cloth, and *-et, -ette*, from *satinet, satinette, sarsanet*, etc]

toing and froing see under **to**.

toise /*toiz*/ *n* an old French lineal measure equivalent to 6.395ft (very nearly 2m). [Fr, from L *tendere, tēnsum* to stretch]

toiseach or **toisech** /tō'shəhh/ (*hist*) *n* a Celtic noble of ancient times ranking below a mormaor. [Gaelic]

toison /*twa-zõ'*/ (*Fr*) *n* a fleece.

❑ **toison d'or** /*dor'*/ *n* the golden fleece.

toitoi or **toetoe** /*toi'toi*/ *n* any of several tall reedlike grasses native to New Zealand, *esp* those of the genus *Arundo*, and *esp A. conspicua*. [Maori]

tokamak /tō'kə-mak/ (*nuclear eng*) *n* in fusion, a toroidal apparatus in which plasma is contained by means of two magnetic fields, a strong toroidal field and a weaker poloidal field generated by an intense electric current through the plasma (also *adj*). [Russ, acronym from *to*roidalnaya *ka*mera s *ma*gnitnym polem (toroidal chamber with a magnetic field)]

Tokay /tō-kā'/ (also without *cap*) *n* a sweetish and heavy wine with an aromatic flavour, produced at *Tokay* (Tokaj) in Hungary; the grape used to produce this wine.

tokay /tō-kā'/ *n* a gecko (*Gekko gecko*), native to the Malay archipelago and SE Asia. [Malay]

toke /*tōk*/ (*sl*) *n* a puff on a cigarette (*esp* one containing marijuana). ◆ *vi* to take a toke. [Poss short for **token**]

■ **tok'er** *n*.

token /tō'k(ə)n/ *n* a mark, sign or distinctive feature (of something); a symbol; a portent; an indication; something providing evidence; a plague-spot (*obs*); anything serving as evidence of authenticity, proof or a guarantee; anything serving as a reminder or souvenir, a keepsake; a voucher worth a stated amount of money which can be exchanged for goods of the same value; a small coin-like piece of metal or plastic which is used instead of money, eg in slot machines; a unit of computer code representing a word or character used in a program (see **lexical analysis** under **lexicon**); (in Presbyterian churches) a metal voucher admitting to communion (superseded by the communion card); a measure of hand-press work, *usu* 250 pulls. ◆ *adj* serving as a symbol; done or given as a token and therefore of no real value, nominal. ◆ *vt* to be a warning or sign of, to betoken. [OE *tācen*; Ger *Zeichen* a mark]

■ **tō'ken'd** *adj* (*Shakesp*) indicated by plague-spots. **tō'kenism** *n* the principle or practice of doing something on a single occasion or with minimum effort, in order to create the impression that a law, code or precept is being properly complied with, eg employing one black person or one woman to give the impression of being committed to equal opportunities. **tokenist'ic** *adj*.

❑ **token money** *n* money worth more than its intrinsic value as metal; private tokens. **token ring** *n* (*comput*) a form of network in which a token or signal controls access to the network. **token vote** *n* a parliamentary vote of money in which the amount stipulated forms a basis for discussion and is not meant to be binding.

■ **by the same token** in addition, in corroboration, by the way. **in token of** as a symbol of. **more by token** see under **more**[1]. **the Lord's tokens** (*Shakesp*) plague-spots.

Tokharian, Tokharish see **Tocharian**.

toko see **toco**.

tokology see **tocology**.

tokoloshe /tok-o-losh'i/ *n* (in Bantu folklore) a hairy malevolent dwarflike creature with supernatural powers. [Zulu *tikoloshe*]

Tok Pisin /tok piz'in or pis'in/ *n* Melanesian pidgin, as spoken in Papua New Guinea. [*talk pidgin*]

tola /tō'lə/ *n* an Indian unit of weight equivalent to 180 grains troy (11.66 grammes). [Hindi, from Sans *tulā* weight]

tolar /tol'är/ *n* a former unit of currency in Slovenia, replaced by the euro. [Slovene; cf **dollar**]

tolbooth see under **toll**².

tolbutamide /tol-bū'tə-mīd/ *n* a drug administered orally in the treatment of diabetes. [*tol*uyl, *but*yric acid, and **amide**]

told /tōld/ *pat* and *pap* of **tell**¹.

tole¹ /tōl/ *n* painted, lacquered or Japanned tinware, popular in the 18c and 19c. [Fr *tôle* sheet metal, from a dialect word for table]
■ **tole'ware** *n* articles made of tole collectively.

tole² or **toll** /tōl/ *vt* (now *US* and *dialect*) to lure, decoy. [ME *tollen*, from root of OE *(for)tyllan*; see **till**²]
■ **tol'ing** or **toll'ing** *n* (*US*) the use of toll bait; a method of decoying ducks, etc, by exciting their curiosity.
□ **toll bait** *n* (*US*) chopped bait thrown to attract fish.

Toledo /tə- or tō-lē'dō/ *n* (*pl* **Tole'dos**) a tapering sword or sword-blade made in *Toledo*, Spain.

tolerate /tol'ə-rāt/ *vt* to endure, *esp* with patience or forebearance, to put up with; to treat fairly, to accept (a person with different religious, political, etc beliefs or opinions); to allow to be done or to exist, to permit; to be able to resist the (harmful) effects of (a drug). [L *tolerāre*, -*ātum*, from *tollere* to lift up]
■ **tolerabil'ity** *n*. **tol'erable** *adj* endurable; passable; fairly good. **tol'erableness** *n*. **tol'erably** *adv*. **tol'erance** *n* the ability to resist or endure pain or hardship; the disposition, ability or willingness to be fair towards and accepting of different religious, political, etc beliefs and opinions; the ability to tolerate and hence no longer benefit from the effects of a drug after prolonged use; the permissible range of variation in values when measuring. **tol'erant** *adj* tolerating the beliefs, opinions, etc of others; enduring; capable of enduring (eg unfavourable conditions, a parasite, a drug) without showing serious effects (*biol* and *med*); indulgent, permissive; favouring toleration. **tol'erantly** *adv*. **tolerā'tion** *n* the act of tolerating; the allowance of what is not approved; the freedom of a minority to hold and express political or religious opinions that differ from those of the majority. **tolerā'tionism** *n*. **tolerā'tionist** *n*. **tol'erātor** *n*.
□ **tolerance dose** *n* (*med*) the maximum dose during radiotherapy that can be permitted to a specific tissue to minimize damage to an adjacent tissue.

toll¹ /tōl/ *vi* to sound, as a large bell does, *esp* with slow, measured strokes. ◆ *vt* to cause (a bell) to sound with slow, measured strokes; to sound, strike, signal, announce, summon, send, etc by tolling; to toll for the death of. ◆ *n* an act of tolling; the slow, measured sound of a bell tolling. [Prob **tole**²]
■ **toll'er** *n*.

toll² /tōl/ *n* a tax for the privilege of using a bridge or road, selling goods in a market, etc; a portion of grain kept by a miller in payment for grinding; a place where there is or was or might have been a building for collecting road tolls or tollbar, a road junction (*Scot*); the cost in damage, injury or lives; a toll call. ◆ *vi* to take or pay tolls. ◆ *vt* to take toll of; to take as a toll. [OE *toll*; cf Du *tol*, Ger *Zoll*; supposed to be from LL *tolōneum*, from Gr *telōnion* customs, from *telos* fulfilment, tax, etc; by some connected with **tell**, **tale**]
■ **toll'able** *adj* subject to toll. **toll'age** *n* payment of toll; the right to charge a toll; the amount paid as toll. **toll'er** *n* a person who collects a toll. **tolsel** /tōl'sel/, **tolzey** /-zi/ or **tolsey** /tol'si/ *n* local names for a tolbooth or exchange (*appar* from OE *seld* seat, or *sæl* hall).
□ **tolbooth** or **tollbooth** /tōl', tol'booth, -boodh, also (*Scot*) -bəth/ *n* an office where tolls are or were collected; a town hall (*Scot*); a prison (*Scot*); often a building combining a town hall and a prison (*Scot*). **toll bar** *n* a movable bar across a road, etc, to stop travellers liable to pay a toll. **toll'bridge** or **toll'gate** *n* a bridge or gate where tolls are collected. **toll call** *n* a short-distance telephone trunk call; a long-distance telephone call at a charge above the local rate (*N Am*); a long-distance telephone call to a place outside a free-dialling area (*NZ*). **toll'dish** *n* a dish for measuring the toll of grain in a mill. **toll-free'** *adj* and *adv*. **toll'-gatherer** *n* a person who collects a toll, eg at a tollbridge or tollgate; a person who collects taxes. **toll'house** *n* a house at a tollbridge, tollgate, etc used by the collector of tolls. **toll'man** *n* a person who collects tolls; a person who collects taxes. **toll'way** *n* (*N Am*) a highway on which tolls are charged.
■ **take (a) toll of** or **take its toll on** to inflict loss, hardship, pain, etc, on; to have a deleterious effect on.

toll³ /tōl/ (*law*; *hist*) *vt* to bar; to take away the right of. [Anglo-Fr *toller*, from L *tollere* to take away]

toll⁴ see **tole**².

tolley /tol'i/ *n* (in the game of marbles) a marble fired at others to drive them from the central ring. [Perh from **taw**² and **alley**²]

tolsel, tolsey see under **toll**².

tolt /tōlt/ *n* an old English writ removing a court-baron cause to a county court. [Anglo-Fr *tolte*, from LL *tolta*, from L *tollere* to take away]

Toltec /tol'tek/ *n* a member of a central Native American people who lived in Mexico until overrun by the Aztecs; the language spoken by this people. ◆ *adj* of or relating to the Toltecs or their language. [Nahuatl *tōltēcah*, *pl* of *tōltēcatl* person from *Tula* (the capital of the Toltec civilization)]
■ **Tol'tecan** *adj*.

tolter /tol'tər/ (*dialect*) *vi* to flounder about.

Tolu or **tolu** /tō-loo'/ *n* (in full **balsam of Tolu**) a balsam yielded by the S American papilionaceous tree *Myro-xylon toluifera* or *M. balsamum*, used in medicine and perfumery. [From Santiago de *Tolú* in Colombia]

toluate /tol'ū-āt/ (*chem*) *n* any salt or ester of toluic acid. [**Tolu** and chem sfx -*ate*]

toluene /tol'ū-ēn/ or **toluol** /tol'ū-ol/ (*chem*) *n* methyl benzene, a colourless flammable liquid ($C_6H_5CH_3$) used as a solvent and in the manufacture of other organic chemicals and explosives. [**Tolu** and chem sfx -*ene*]

toluic /tol-ū'ik/ (*chem*) *adj* of or containing toluene or toluic acid. [*tol*uene and chem sfx -*ic*]
□ **toluic acid** *n* any of four isomeric acids derived from toluene, all having the formula $CH_3C_6H_4COOH$.

toluidine /tol-ū'i-dēn/ (*chem*) *n* an amine ($CH_3C_6H_4NH_2$) derived from toluene, used in making dyes (also **methylaminoben'zene**). [*tol*uene and chem sfxs -*ide* and -*ine*]

tolzey see under **toll**².

tom¹ /tom/ *n* a male of various animals, *esp* a cat; a name for a big bell; a prostitute (*police* and *criminal sl*); (with *cap*) an Uncle Tom (*US sl*). ◆ *vi* (**tomm'ing**; **tommed**) to work as a prostitute (*police* and *criminal sl*). [Short form of *Thomas*]
□ **Tom and Jerry** *n* hot rum and eggs, spiced and sweetened. **tom'cat** *n* a male cat. **Tom Collins** see under **Collins**¹. **Tom-nodd'y** *n* the puffin; a fool. **Tom'-trot** *n* a kind of toffee.
■ **Long Tom** a long gun, *esp* one carried amidships on a swivelling carriage. **Old Tom** gin. **Tom, Dick, and/or Harry** anybody; people in general (also (*old*) **Tom and Tib**). **Tom o' Bedlam** formerly, a madman let out of an asylum with a licence to beg. **Tom Tiddler's ground** a place where wealth is to be had for the picking up; debatable land; no-man's-land (from a children's game so called). **Uncle Tom** see under **uncle**.

tom² see **tomfoolery** under **tomfool**.

tom. *abbrev*: *tomus* (L), tome or volume.

tomahawk /tom'ə-hök/ *n* a Native American war-axe; a hatchet (*Aust*). ◆ *vt* to attack or kill with a tomahawk; to hack, cut up or slate. [Virginian Ind *tämähāk*]

tomalley /to-mal'i/ *n* American lobster fat ('liver'), eaten as a delicacy; extended to tamale (qv). [Perh Carib]

toman /tō-män'/ *n* a myriad, or ten thousand; a former Persian gold coin worth 10000 dinars. [Pers *tumān*]

tomatillo /tom-ə-tēl'yō, tom-ə-tē'ō/ *n* (*pl* **tomati'lloes** or **tomati'llos**) a plant, *Physalis ixocarpa*, of the nightshade family with yellow flowers and sticky edible berries, native to Mexico; a berry from this plant, much used in Mexican cooking. [Sp, dimin of *tomate* tomato]

tomato /tə-mä'tō or (*N Am*) -mā'/ *n* (*pl* **toma'toes**) a S American plant (*Lycopersicum esculentum* or *Solanum lycopersicum*) related to the potato, formerly called the love apple; its glossy red or yellow pulpy edible fruit. [Sp *tomate*, from Mex *tomatl*]
■ **toma'toey** *adj*.
■ **gooseberry tomato** or **strawberry tomato** the Cape gooseberry.

tomb /toom/ *n* any place serving as a grave; a *usu* underground vault for the disposal of dead bodies; a sepulchral monument; (with *the*) death. ◆ *vt* to entomb; to bury. [OFr (Fr) *tombe*, from L *tumba*, from Gr *tymbos*]
■ **tombic** /toom'ik, -bik/ *adj*. **tomb'less** *adj*.
□ **tomb'stone** *n* a memorial stone over a tomb. **tomb'stoning** *n* an extreme sport in which participants dive into water from a cliff.

tombac, tombak /tom'bak/ or **tambac** /tam'bak/ *n* an alloy of either copper with a little zinc or copper and arsenic, used for making cheap jewellery. [Fr *tombac*, from Malay *tambaga* copper]

tomboc /tom'bok/ *n* a Javanese long-handled weapon. [Javanese]

tombola /tom-bō'lə, tom'/ n a kind of lottery in which winning tickets are drawn from a revolving drum (at a fête, etc); a type of bingo, played *esp* in the armed services. [Ital, from *tombolare* to tumble]

tombolo /tom'bə-lō/ n (pl **tom'bolos**) a bar of sand or gravel connecting an island with another or with the mainland. [Ital, from L *tumulus* mound]

tomboy /tom'boi/ n a high-spirited romping girl; a girl with boyish looks, dress, habits, etc; formerly, a hoyden; an immodest woman (*Shakesp*). [From the name *Tom* and **boy**]
■ **tom'boyish** adj. **tom'boyishly** adv. **tom'boyishness** n.

tome /tōm/ n a large, *usu* scholarly, book or volume. [Fr, from L *tomus*, from Gr *tomos*, from *temnein* to cut]

-tome /-tōm/ combining form denoting: an instrument for cutting; a segment. [Gr *tomē* a cutting, from *temnein* to cut]

tomentum /tō-men'təm/ n (pl **tomen'ta**) a matted cottony down on leaves and stems, etc (*bot*); the deep layer of the pia mater, composed of many minute blood vessels (*anat*). [L]
■ **tomentose** /tō-mən-tōs', tō-men'tōs/ or **tomen'tous** adj.

tomfool /tom-fool'/ n a great fool; a trifling person (*archaic*). ◆ adj extremely foolish. ◆ vi to play the fool. [From the name *Tom*]
■ **tomfool'ery** n foolish behaviour; nonsense, rubbish; buffoonery; trifles, ornaments; jewellery, *esp* stolen jewellery (often shortened to **tom**; *rhyming sl*). **tomfool'ishness** n.

tomium /tō'mi-əm/ n the cutting edge of a bird's bill. [Latinized from Gr *tomeion* a knife-edge, from *temnein* to cut]
■ **tō'mial** adj.

tommy /tom'i/ n (sometimes with *cap*) a private in the British Army; a penny roll, bread; food; a tommy shop; the truck system. ◆ vt to oppress by the truck system. [From the name *Thomas*]
❑ **Tommy Atkins** n a generic name for the private in the British Army. **tommy bar** n a rod used as a lever for turning a tubular spanner or the like. **tommy gun** n a light submachine-gun (after its American inventor, General JT *Thompson*). **tomm'yrot** n absolute nonsense. **tommy shop** n a truck shop.
■ **soft tommy** soft bread, as opposed to hardtack or sea-biscuit.

tomography /tə- or tō-mog'rə-fi/ n any scanning technique used to obtain a detailed image of a particular section or plane, of or within a solid structure or body, *esp* (*med*) the use of X-rays or ultrasound waves to produce an image, for diagnostic purposes, of a chosen section at a particular plane within the body. [Gr *tomos* slice, and *graphein* to draw]
■ **tom'ogram** n a radiogram or other visual record produced by tomography. **tom'ograph** n a machine for producing tomograms. **tomograph'ic** adj.
■ **positron emission tomography** (*med*) a technique used to evaluate brain function by measuring the emission (by active brain cells) of radioactive particles injected into the patient (*abbrev* PET).

tomorrow /tə-, tŭ-mor'ō/ n the day after today; the future. ◆ adv on the day after today; in the future. [OE *tō morgen*]

tompion[1] see **tampion**.

tompion[2] /tom'pi-ən/ (*obs*) n a watch of the kind made by Thomas Tompion (1639–1713).

tompon same as **tampon**.

Tom Thumb /tom thum/ n a dwarf or midget; a dwarf variety of a plant. [*Tom Thumb* the tiny hero of several folk tales]

tomtit /tom'tit/ n the blue tit or other species of tit. [From the name *Tom* and **tit**[1]]

tom-tom /tom'tom/, also (*esp* formerly) **tam-tam** /tam'tam/ or **tum-tum** /tum'tum/ n a Native American or oriental drum played with the hands; a similar drum used in jazz-bands, etc; any primitive drum or substitute; (*esp* formerly) a Chinese gong, tam-tam. ◆ vi (**tom'-tomming**; **tom'-tommed**) to beat on or play a tom-tom. [Hindi *tam-tam*, imit]

-tomy /-tə-mi/ combining form denoting surgical incision into an organ. [Gr *-tomia* the operation of cutting, from *tomē* a cut, from *temnein* to cut]

ton[1] /tun/ n (in full **long ton**) a unit of weight equivalent to 20cwt (2240lb or 1016kg); (in full **short ton**) a unit of weight equivalent to 2000lb (907.2kg, N Am); (in full **metric ton**, also **tonne**) a unit of weight equal to 1000kg (*approx* 2204.6lb); (in full **displacement ton**) a unit used to measure the amount of water a ship displaces, equal to 2240lb or 35 cubic feet of sea water; (in full **register ton**) a unit (*orig* a *tun* of wine) used to measure a ship's internal capacity, equal to 100 cubic feet; (in full **freight ton**) a unit for measuring the space taken up by cargo, equal to 40 cubic feet; 100 (*inf*); a score, total, etc of 100 (*inf*); 100mph (preceded by *a* or *the*; *sl*); a great weight (*inf*); (in *pl*) many, a great amount (*inf*). See also **tonnage**. [OE *tunne* a vat, tub; see **tun**]

■ **-tonner** combining form denoting a vehicle, vessel, etc weighing a specified number of tons or having a specified amount of tonnage; a load of a specified number of tons.
❑ **ton'-up** adj (*sl*) (*orig* of a motorcyclist) travelling or having travelled at more than 100mph; fond of travelling at fast speed; noisy and reckless. ◆ n a speed of 100mph; a person who habitually travels this fast.

ton[2] /tõ/ n fashion; people of fashion. [Fr]
■ **tonish** or **tonnish** /ton'ish/ adj modish, having ton. **ton'ishly** or **tonn'ishly** adv. **ton'ishness** or **tonn'ishness** n.

tonal /tō'nəl/ adj of or relating to tone or tonality; according to key; (of a fugue) having an answer written in the same key but with different melodic invervals. [Med L *tonālis*, from L *tonus*, from Gr *tonos* pitch, tension]
■ **tōnal'itive** adj of tonality. **tōnal'ity** n the melodic and harmonic relationships between the tones of a scale or musical system (*music*); a particular scale, a key (*music*); the scheme of colours, shades and tones in a painting. **tōn'ally** adv.

tonalite /tō'nə-līt/ n a coarse-grained igneous rock, quartz-mica-diorite, found at Monte *Tonale*, Tyrol.
■ **tonalitic** /-lit'ik/ adj.

tonalitive, tonality see under **tonal**.

to-name /too'nām/ n a byname, nickname; an additional name used to distinguish persons whose names are alike. [OE *tōnama*, from pfx *tō-* in addition to, and *nama* name]

tonant /tō'nənt/ adj thundering. [L *tonāns*, *-antis*, prp of *tonāre* to thunder]

tondo /ton'dō/ n (pl **ton'di** /-dē/ or **ton'dos**) a circular painting or circular carving in relief. [Ital short for *rotondo* round, from L *rotundus*]
■ **tondi'no** /-dē'nō/ n (pl **tondi'ni** /-nē/ or **tondi'nos**) a circular or semicircular moulding (*archit*); a small tondo.

tone[1] /tōn/ n the character of a sound; the quality of sound; accent; intonation; vocal inflection, rise or fall in pitch, *esp* as expressing feeling, mood, etc; rising, falling intonation or pitch, etc used as a way of distinguishing words, eg in Mandarin Chinese (*linguistics*); a musical sound of definite pitch; a major second, one of the larger intervals between successive notes in the scale, as between C and D (*music*); a Gregorian psalm-tune; vocal expression; bodily firmness, elasticity, or tension, *esp* in muscles; the general or prevailing character, quality or style (eg of a piece of writing, speech, etc); a generally high quality, style, character, etc, *esp* in the phrase *lower the tone*; mood; temper; harmony or general effect of colours; depth or brilliance of colour; a tint or shade. ◆ vt to give tone or the desired tone to; to alter the tone of; to give (a photograph) a softer or otherwise altered colour using a chemical solution (*photog*); to intone (*archaic*). ◆ vi to take a tone; to harmonize (with *in* or *with*). [Gr *tonos* pitch, tension, partly through Fr *ton* and L *tonus*]
■ **toned** adj having a tone (in compounds); braced up; treated to give tone; slightly tinted; (of the body, muscles, etc) kept firm through exercise. **tone'less** adj soundless; expressionless; dull; relaxed; listless. **tone'lessly** adv. **tone'lessness** n. **ton'er** n a person or thing that tones; a cosmetic lotion for toning the skin; a hair preparation used for toning or tinting; fine powdered pigment used in xerography; a chemical solution used to soften, etc colours or tones in photographic work. **tōn'ey** or **tōn'y** adj (*sl*) high-toned; fashionable. **tōn'ing** n and adj.
❑ **tone arm** n the movable arm that carries an electric pick-up on a record player; (*orig*) that part of a gramophone connecting the soundbox to the horn. **tone cluster** n (*music*) a group of adjacent notes played simultaneously. **tone colour** n timbre. **tone control** n a manual control in a radio set which adjusts the relative amplitude of high, medium and low frequencies. **tone'-deaf** adj unable to appreciate or distinguish differences in musical pitch. **tone'-deaf'ness** n. **tone dialling** n a telephone dialling system in which digits are transmitted as a combination of tones. **tone language** n a language (eg Chinese) in which difference of intonation distinguishes words of different meaning that would otherwise sound the same. **tone'pad** n an electronic device similar to a remote control handset for a television, video, etc, which allows data to be input into a central computer from a distance, *usu* via a telephone link. **tone picture** n a piece of descriptive music. **tone poem** n a piece of programme music, not divided into movements, conveying or translating a poetic idea or literary theme. **tone row** n (in serial music) the basic set of notes in the chosen order. **toning table** n a machine with parts that can move to exercise a variety of muscles of the person lying on it.
■ **tone down** to make or become lower in tone; to moderate; to soften, to harmonize the colours of (eg a painting) as to light and shade. **tone up** to make or become stronger in tone; to make or become intensified; to make or become healthier, stronger, more vigorous.

■ words derived from main entry word; ❑ compound words; ■ idioms and phrasal verbs

tone² /tōn/ (obs or dialect) pronoun and adj the one. [that one; cf **tother**]

toneme /tō'nēm/ (linguistics) n (in a tone language) a phoneme which can be distinguished from another only by its particular intonation. [**tone¹** and phoneme]
■ **tone'mic** adj.

tonetic /tō-net'ik/ (linguistics) adj of or relating to linguistic tones, tone languages or intonation. [**tone¹** and phonetic]
■ **tonet'ically** adv.

toney see under **tone¹**.

tong¹ /tong/ n a Chinese guild or secret society, particularly one associated with organized crime. [Chin (Cantonese)]
■ **tong'ster** n (inf) a member of a tong.

tong² /tong/ (orig and esp US) vt to hold, pick up, manipulate, curl (hair), etc using tongs. ◆ vi to use tongs. [**tongs**]

Tonga /tong'gə/ n a people of southern Africa living mainly in Zambia, Zimbabwe and Mozambique; any of the Bantu languages of this people. ◆ adj of or relating to the Tonga or their language.

tonga¹ /tong'gə/ n a light two-wheeled Indian vehicle. [Hindi tāngā]

tonga² /tong'gə/ n a Fijian toothache remedy made from an aroid root (genus Epipremnum). [Arbitrary invention]

tonga-bean see **tonka-bean**.

Tongan /tong'gən/ n a native or inhabitant of the Kingdom of Tonga in the SW Pacific; the Polynesian language spoken in Tonga. ◆ adj of or relating to Tonga, its inhabitants, or their language.

tongs /tongz/ n pl a gripping and lifting instrument, consisting of two legs joined by a pivot, hinge, or spring; curling tongs. [OE tang, tange; ON töng, Ger Zange]
□ **tong-test ammeter** n (elec eng) an AC ammeter and current transformer combination whose iron core can be opened and closed round a cable.

tongue /tung/ n the fleshy organ in the mouth, used in tasting, swallowing and speech; the tongue of an ox, etc, as food; the rasping organ in molluscs; the power of speech; the manner of speaking; a language; speech; discourse; voice; utterance; anything like a tongue in shape; a point of land; a bell clapper; the reed of a musical instrument; a flap in the opening of a shoe or boot; the catch of a buckle; the pointer of a balance; any narrow projection; a langue or language (qv) of a religious or military order; a vote (Shakesp). ◆ vt to utter; to lick; to touch with the tongue; to provide with a tongue; to talk, prate (with it); to produce or play by tonguing (music); to pronounce (dialect); to articulate; to attack with words (Shakesp). ◆ vi to give tongue; to stick out; to practise tonguing (music). [OE tunge; ON tunga, Ger Zunge the tongue; L lingua (from dingua)]
■ **tongued** adj having a tongue; played by tonguing (music). **tongue'less** adj having no tongue; unspoken of (Shakesp). **tongue'let** n a little tongue. **tongue'like** adj. **tongue'ster** n a babbler. **tongu'ing** n (music) articulation to separate the notes in playing wind instruments (see also **flutter**).
□ **tongue-and-groove'** n a system of joining boards by fitting a projection along the side of one into a groove in the next; these boards. **tongue-doubt'ie** adj (ie **doughty**; Milton) bragging. **tongue-in-cheek'** adj and adv with ironic, insincere or humorous intention. **tongue'-lashing** n a severe verbal reprimand. **tongue'-tacked** adj tongue-tied. **tongue'-tie** n (med) a congenital condition in which the tongue's mobility is impeded by an abnormally short frenum. **tongue'-tied** adj unable to speak out, esp because of fear or embarrassment; affected with tongue-tie. **tongue'-twister** n a formula or sequence of words difficult to pronounce without blundering. **tongue'-work** n babble, chatter. **tongue worm** n a tongue-shaped parasite, Linguatula serrata, occurring in the nasal passages of dogs, foxes and wolves.
■ **give tongue** to give utterance, to voice; to give voice as hounds on a scent do. **hold one's tongue** see under **hold¹**. **lose one's tongue** to become speechless from emotion. **on the tip of one's tongue** see under **tip¹**. **speaking in tongues** or **gift of tongues** glossolalia or xenoglossia. **with one's tongue hanging out** (inf) eagerly. **with (one's) tongue in (one's) cheek** tongue-in-cheek (adv).

tonic /ton'ik/ adj relating to tone or tones; producing tension, eg of the muscles; giving tone and vigour to the system (med); giving or increasing strength; of or being the first note of a scale (music); of or relating to the main or primary stress on a word. ◆ n a medicine that invigorates and strengthens; any person or thing that enlivens or invigorates; the first note of a scale, a keynote (music); a key or chord based on the keynote (music); tonic water; a stressed syllable in a word. [Gr tonikos relating to stretching or tones]
■ **tonicity** /ton-is'i-ti/ n the property or condition of having tone; mode of reaction to stimulus; the healthy elasticity of muscular fibres when at rest.

□ **tonic accent** n emphasis given to a particular syllable through a change in pitch. **tonic sol-fa** n (music) a system of notation and teaching devised by Sarah Glover (1785–1867) and developed by John Curwen (1816–80), using modified sol-fa syllables and their initial letters for the notes of the scale with doh (see **doh¹**) as the keynote for the major keys and lah (see **la¹**) for the minor, and dividing the bar by colons, dots and inverted commas. **tonic spasm** n (med) a prolonged uniform muscular spasm, opp to clonic spasm or clonus. **tonic water** n aerated quinine water.

tonight /tə-, tŭ-nīt'/ n this night; the night of the present day. ◆ adv on this night or the night of today; last night (obs; Shakesp). [OE tō niht]

tonish see under **ton²**.

tonite /tō'nīt/ n a blasting explosive made from guncotton and barium nitrate. [L tonāre to thunder]

tonk¹ /tongk/ (inf) vt to strike; to defeat; to hit (a cricket ball) hard; to hit (a ball) with a flat, wooden sound, or with an unenergetic or casual stroke. [Imit]
■ **tonk'er** n.

tonk² /tongk/ (Aust sl) n the penis; a homosexual; an effeminate, weak or ineffectual person. [Ety unknown]

tonka-bean /tong'kə-bēn'/ n (also **tonga-bean** /tong'gə-/, **tonquin-bean** /tong'kēn-/) the coumarin-scented seed of a large papilionaceous tree (genus Dipteryx) of Guiana, used for flavouring snuff, etc; the tree from which it comes. [Local name]

tonker see under **tonk¹**.

tonlet /tun'lət/ n one of a set of overlapping strips that make up the skirt on a suit of armour; a skirt of armour. [MFr tonnel a short skirt; also Fr tonnelet, dimin of tonneau a cask, barrel (similarly made up of strips)]

tonnag /tō'nag/ n a shawl with a shaped neck and side fastening. [Gaelic]

tonnage /tun'ij/ n the cargo- or freight-carrying capacity of a ship measured in tons (orig in tuns of wine); the weight of a cargo or freight on a ship; the total cargo-carrying capacity of a country's merchant shipping, measured in tons; a duty on ships, based on their cargo-carrying capacity; a duty on cargo charged per ton; a tax of so much a tun on imported wines (sometimes **tunnage**; hist). See also **ton¹**. [See **ton¹**, **tun**]
■ **gross tonnage** the total space capable of carrying cargo in a ship, measured in register tons. **net register tonnage** gross tonnage less deducted spaces (qv under **deduce**).

tonne /tun, ton/ n the preferred name for a **metric ton**, a unit of weight equal to 1000 kilograms (2204.62lb, or 0.984 ton). [Fr]

tonneau /ton'ō/ n (pl **tonn'eaus** or **tonn'eaux** /-nō, -nōz/) the rear part of a (usu open) motorcar body in which passengers sit, orig opening at the back; (in full **tonneau cover**) a detachable cover to protect the rear passenger seats in an open car when not in use; a tonne. [Fr, cask, tun]

tonnell obsolete form of **tunnel**.

-tonner see under **ton¹**.

tonnish see under **ton²**.

tonometer /tō-nom'ə-tər/ n a device for determining the frequencies of tones, esp one consisting of tuning forks (music); an instrument for measuring fluid pressure (eg within the eyeball), blood pressure or vapour pressure. [Gr tonos pitch, tension, and metron measure]
■ **tonom'etry** n.

tonoplast /tō'nə-plast/ (bot) n the membrane around a vacuole in a plant cell. [Gr tonos tone, and **-plast**]

tonquin-bean see **tonka-bean**.

tonsil /ton'sl, -sīl/ n either of two lymph glands on either side of the root of the tongue in vertebrates (zool); any mass of lymphatic tissue (anat). [L tōnsillae (pl)]
■ **ton'sillar** or **ton'sillary** adj. **tonsillec'tomy** n surgical removal of one or both of the tonsils (also **tonsilec'tomy**). **tonsillit'ic** adj. **tonsillī'tis** n inflammation of the tonsils (also **tonsilī'tis**). **tonsillot'omy** n an incision into, usu followed by complete or partial removal of, a tonsil (also **tonsilot'omy**).
□ **tonsil tennis** or **hockey** n (sl) passionate kissing, esp French kissing (qv).

tonsor /ton'sər/ n a barber. [L tōnsor barber, tōnsūra a shearing, from tondēre, tōnsum to clip]
■ **tonso'rial** adj (usu facetious) of or relating to hairdressing or barbering. **ton'sure** /-shər/ n the act or mode of clipping the hair, or of shaving the head; (in the Roman Catholic and Eastern Churches) the shaving or cutting of part of the hair of the head (typically that on the crown) on entering the priesthood or a monastic order; the shaven part; the state of being shaven. ◆ vt to give a tonsure to. **ton'sured** adj (of eg a priest) having the crown of the head shaven; shaven; bald; clipped.

tontine /ton'tēn, ton-tēn'/ n an annuity scheme in which several subscribers share a common fund, with their individual benefits increasing as members die until only one member is left alive and receives everything or until a specified date at which the proceeds are divided amongst the survivors (also adj). [Lorenzo *Tonti*, a Neapolitan who devised the scheme in 1653]
■ **tontin'er** n.

tonus /tō'nəs/ (*med*) n the normal elasticity of healthy muscle at rest, tonicity; atonic spasm. [New L, from L *tonus*, from Gr *tonos* pitch, tension]

Tony /tō'ni/ n (pl **Tonys** or **Tonies**) (in the USA) an award for meritorious work in the theatre. [*Antoinette* Perry (died 1946), US actress]

tony¹ /tō'ni/ (*obs sl*) n a simpleton. [*Antony*]

tony² see under **tone**¹.

too /too/ adv as well, in addition, also, likewise; to a greater extent than is required, desirable or suitable; so much as to be incompatible with a condition; extremely; used to enforce eg a command (*inf*). [Stressed form of **to**]
□ **too'-too** or **too too** adj (*inf*) exquisite; extravagantly and affectedly sentimental, gushing. ◆ adv all too; quite too.
■ **none too** hardly, barely; not very. **too much** more than is reasonable, tolerable, tolerated, etc; also used as an interjection expressing approval, amazement, etc (*sl*, chiefly *US*).

tooart same as **tuart**.

toodle-oo /too'd(ə-)loo'/ or **toodle-pip** /-pip'/ (*old inf*) interj goodbye. [Perh imit of a motorcar horn, or from Fr (à) *toute à l'heure* see you later]

took /took/ pat and obsolete pap of **take**.

tool /tool/ n a working instrument, *esp* one used by hand; the cutting part of a machine tool; someone who is used as the mere instrument of another; (*esp in pl*) anything necessary to the pursuit of a particular activity; any of several devices used to impress a design on a book cover; an impressed design on a book cover; a weapon, *esp* a gun (*sl*); the penis (*vulgar sl*); a fool (*sl*); a despicable person (*sl*); a utility, feature or function available as part of eg a word processing package or database (*comput*). ◆ vt to shape or finish with a tool; to mark with a tool, *esp* to ornament or imprint designs upon (a book cover), or to chisel the face of (stone); to supply with tools, *esp* with machine tools for a particular purpose (also **tool up**); to drive (a car or other vehicle) *esp* smoothly and skilfully, and *usu* at moderate speed (*sl*); to carry or draw in a vehicle. ◆ vi to work with a tool; to provide tools (also **tool up**); to travel (along) in a vehicle, *esp* smoothly and skilfully, and *usu* at moderate speed; (of a vehicle, draught animal) to travel (along, etc) in this way. [OE *tōl*]
■ **tool'er** n. **tool'ing** n workmanship done with a tool, eg on stonework or a book cover; the provision and setting up of tools for eg a machining process.
□ **tool'bag** (or **tool'box**) n a bag (or box) for carrying and storing tools. **tool'bar** n (*comput*) a bar with a list of utilities, features, functions, etc which appears at the top of an application window. **tool'house** n a shed or outhouse for keeping tools in. **tool'kit** n a set of tools. **tool'maker** n a craftsman who makes or repairs tools, *esp* machine tools. **tool'making** n. **tool'man** n a man who works with tools or in a toolroom. **tool post** n a rigid device holding the cutting tool on a lathe or other machine. **tool'pusher** n the supervisor of drilling operations at an oil well. **tool'room** n that part of a factory occupied by toolmakers. **tool shed** n. **tool steel** n steel suitable for making tools, hard enough and tough enough to keep a cutting edge. **tool'tip** n (*comput*) a box containing supplementary information which appears onscreen when a particular utility, feature, function, etc is used.
■ **tooled up** (*sl*) carrying a weapon, *esp* a gun.

toom /toom, tüm, tim/ (now only *Scot*) adj empty. ◆ n a rubbish tip. ◆ vt to empty. [OE *tōm* clear]

toon¹ /toon/ n an Indian tree (*Cedrela toona*), of the mahogany family, with aromatic red wood used for furniture, carving, etc and astringent bark. [Hindi *tūn*]

toon², **toun** /toon/ (*Scot*) n same as **town**.

toon³ /toon/ n a slang word for **tune** or **cartoon**.

toonie /too'ni/ (*Can inf*) n a Canadian two-dollar coin. [Modelled on **loonie**]

toorie or **tourie** /too'ri/ (*Scot*) n a small heap; a knob of hair; a tuft or bobble on a bonnet, or (also **toorie bonnet**) the bonnet itself. [Dimin of *toor*, Scot for **tower**]

toot¹ or **tout** /toot/ vi to make short sharp sounds, eg on a flute or horn. ◆ vt to blow (eg a horn, etc) so as to give short sharp sounds; to inhale (a drug, *usu* cocaine) (chiefly *US sl*). ◆ n a blast, *esp* as of a horn; a drinking binge (*N Am sl*); a quantity of a drug (*esp* cocaine) for inhaling (chiefly *US sl*); an act of inhaling a drug (*esp* cocaine); a toilet (*Aust sl*). [Prob imit]
■ **toot'er** n a person who toots, or the instrument used.

toot² /toot/ vi to pry, peer, peep about (*Spenser*); to be prominent (*obs*). ◆ n a hill on which a lookout is posted (*SW Eng*); a lookout place (*obs*). [OE *tōtian* to stick out, peep out]
■ **toot'er** n.

toot³ see **tut**¹.

tooth /tooth/ n (pl **teeth** /tēth/) one of the hard bonelike enamel-coated structures embedded in the jawbones, used for biting and chewing; a hard projection of similar function in invertebrates; taste, relish or appetite; a toothlike projection, prong, cog, jag, as on the margin of a leaf, on a comb, saw or wheel; (in *pl*) force, sufficient power to be effective. ◆ vt to provide with teeth; to cut into teeth. ◆ vi (of cogwheels) to interlock. [OE *tōth* (pl *tēth*); Gothic *tunthus*, L *dēns, dentis*, Gr *odous, odontos*, Sans *danta*]
■ **toothed** /tootht, toodhd/ adj having teeth; dentate. **tooth'ful** adj full of teeth; toothsome. ◆ n a small drink of spirits, etc. **tooth'ily** adv. **tooth'iness** n. **tooth'less** adj lacking teeth; powerless or ineffective. **tooth'like** adj. **tooth'some** adj appetizing, tasty; attractive, pleasant, agreeable. **tooth'somely** adv. **tooth'someness** n. **tooth'y** adj (**tooth'ier; tooth'iest**) with prominent teeth; toothsome; biting (*Scot*).
□ **tooth'ache** n an ache or pain in a tooth. **toothache tree** n the prickly ash (genus *Xanthoxylum*), so-called because its leaves and bark were used formerly to make a concoction to relieve toothache. **tooth'-billed pigeon** same as **manumea**. **tooth'brush** n a brush for cleaning the teeth. **toothbrush moustache** n a small stiff moustache. **tooth'comb** n a fine-tooth(ed) comb (qv under **fine**¹). **tooth'-drawer** n (*Shakesp*) an extractor of teeth. **tooth'-drawing** n and adj. **toothed whale** n any whale of the suborder Odontoceti, with a single blowhole and simple teeth. **tooth fairy** n (*orig US*) a fairy who substitutes a coin for a milk tooth placed under a child's pillow. **tooth'fish** n any food fish of the southern hemisphere genus *Dissostichus*. **tooth'-ornament** n dogtooth. **tooth'paste** (or **tooth powder**) n a paste (or powder) used with a toothbrush to clean the teeth. **tooth'pick** n an instrument for picking shreds of food from between the teeth; a Bowie knife (*US sl*). **tooth'-picker** n (*Shakesp*) a toothpick; someone or something that picks teeth, eg the bird trochilus. **tooth'shell** n the tusk shell, *Dentalium*. **tooth'wash** n a liquid preparation for cleansing the teeth. **tooth'wort** n a pale fleshy plant (*Lathraea squamaria*) of the broomrape family, parasitic on tree-roots, with toothlike scale-leaves; the cruciferous coralroot (*Cardamine*, or *Dentaria*, *bulbifera*).
■ **a colt's tooth** an addiction to youthful pleasures. **armed to the teeth** armed as completely as possible, from top to toe. **a sweet tooth** a taste for sweet things. **by the skin of one's teeth** see under **skin**. **cast, throw** or **fling in someone's teeth** to fling at someone as a taunt or reproach. **cut one's eye teeth** to cease to be a child; to become shrewd. **get one's teeth into** to tackle, deal with, vigorously, eagerly, etc. **in** or **to someone's teeth** to someone's face; in direct affront. **in spite of someone's teeth** or **in the teeth of** in direct opposition to. **lie through one's teeth** to lie brazenly. **long in the tooth** elderly, like a horse whose gums are receding with age. **set one's teeth on edge** see under **edge**. **take the teeth out of** to render harmless or powerless. **through clenched teeth** reluctantly. **tooth and nail** with all possible vigour and fury.

tootle /too'tl/ vi to make feeble sounds, as on the flute; to go casually along, *esp* by car (*inf*). ◆ n a soft sound on the flute, etc; a casual trip, a drive (*inf*). [Frequentative of **toot**¹]

toots¹ see **tut**¹.

toots² /toots/ or **tootsy** /tūt'si/ (*inf, esp US*) n sweetheart. [Ety obscure]

tootsie, tootsy or **tootsy-wootsy** /tūt'si (-wūt'si)/ n jocular or childish words for a foot or toe. [Perh a childish pronunciation of **foot**]

top¹ /top/ n the highest or uppermost part or place; the highest or most important position (eg in a profession, company, salary scale, scale of authority or privilege, etc); the person occupying this position; the upper edge or surface; a lid or cover; a garment for the upper part of a person's (*esp* a woman's or child's) body; the highest or loudest degree of pitch; (in *pl*; with *the*) the very best person or thing (*inf*); top gear; (*esp in pl*) the part of a root vegetable that is above the ground; a handful or bundle of flax, wool, etc, for spinning; a circus tent (*sl*; **big top** the main tent); a topsail; a small platform at the head of the lower mast; a crest or tuft (*naut*); a trench parapet; a top boot (*esp in pl*); topspin; the earliest part (as in the Irish greeting *top of the morning*); (in *pl*) in oil-refining, the first part of a volatile mixture to come off in the distillation process; a stroke that hits the upper part of the ball (*golf*). ◆ adj highest; best; most important, able, etc; very good (*inf*). ◆ vt (**topp'ing; topped**) to cover on the top; to tip; to rise above; to surpass; to reach the top of; to surmount; to be on or at the top of; to take off the top of; to hit (the ball) on the upper part, so that it only travels a short distance along the ground (*golf*); to kill (*sl*); (eg of a male animal) to cover (*Shakesp*). ◆ vi to finish up, round off (with *off* or *up*). [OE *top*; Ger *Zopf*]
■ **top'full** adj (*Shakesp*) full to the top or brim. **top'less** adj without a top; (of women's clothing) leaving the breasts uncovered; (of a

woman) with bare breasts; (of a place, entertainment, etc) that features women with bare breasts; without superior (*Shakesp*). **top'lessness** *n*. **top'most** /-*mōst*, -*məst*/ *adj* uppermost; highest. **topped** *adj*. **topp'er** *n* a person or thing that tops in any sense; a person who excels at anything, a good sort (*inf*); a top hat (*inf*). **topp'ing** *n* the act of a person or thing that tops; (in *pl*) pieces cut from the top; a sauce or dressing to go over food. ◆ *adj* surpassing, pre-eminent; excellent (*old sl*); arrogant (*US*). **topp'ingly** *adv*. **topp'y** *adj* (*inf*) (of audio reproduction) dominated by high-frequency sounds; (of prices, etc) at the highest level known or expected. **tops** *adj* (*inf*) best, excellent. ◆ *adv* (*inf*) at most, as a maximum.
◻ **top banana** see under **banana**. **top boot** *n* a knee-length boot with a showy band of leather round the top. **top'-booted** *adj* wearing top boots. **top brass** see under **brass**. **top'coat** *n* an overcoat; an outer coat of paint. **top dead centre** *n* (of a reciprocating engine or pump) the piston position at the beginning of the outstroke, ie when the crank pin is nearest to the cylinder (also **inner dead centre**). **top dog** *n* (*inf*) the winner, leader or dominant person. **top-down'** *adj* organized or controlled from the top, by the most important or powerful people involved. **top drawer** *n* the highest level, *esp* of society (**out of the top drawer**, belonging to this social rank). **top-draw'er** *adj*. **top'-dress** *vt*. **top dressing** *n* manure or fertilizer applied to the surface of soil and not dug in; the application of it; any superficial covering or treatment (*fig*). **top'-end** *adj* best or most expensive. **top'-flight** *adj* excellent, superior, of the highest class or quality. **topgallant** /*tə*-, *topgal'ənt*/ *adj* above the topmast and topsail and below the royal mast. ◆ *n* a topgallant mast or sail, or the topgallant rigging. **top gear** *n* the highest gear in a motor vehicle or on a bicycle. **top hamper** *n* unnecessary weight on a ship's upper deck. **top hat** *n* a man's tall cylindrical hat with a narrow brim, made of silk plush. ◆ *adj* (with *hyphen*) upper class; designed to benefit high executives, or the rich, as in *top-hat budget*, *top-hat* (*insurance*) *policy*. **top-heav'ily** *adv*. **top-heav'iness** *n*. **top-heav'y** *adj* having the upper part too heavy or large for the lower; (eg of an organization or company) with too many administrative staff or executives; (of a company) overcapitalized; tipsy. **top-hole'** *adj* (*old sl*) excellent, first-class (also *interj*). **top'knot** *n* a crest, tuft of hair, often a piece of added hair, or knot of ribbons, etc, on the top of the head; the head (*sl*); a small fish (of several species) related to the turbot. **top'knotted** *adj*. **top'-level** *adj* at the highest level; involving people from this level. **top'line** *adj* important enough to be mentioned in a headline. ◆ *vi* to feature in a headline; to star, appear as the principal performer. **toplin'er** *n* a person who is topline; a principal performer, a star. **top'loftical** or **top'lofty** *adj* (*facetious*) high and mighty, haughty; stuck-up. **top'loftily** *adv*. **top'loftiness** *n*. **top'maker** *n* a person who supplies combed wool for spinning. **top'making** *n*. **top'man** *n* a seaman stationed in the topgallant or topsail rigging; a top-sawyer. **top'mast** /-*mast*, -*mäst*/ *n* the second mast, or that immediately above the lower mast. **top'minnow** *n* a small, surface-feeding, soft-rayed fish belonging to any of various species, either viviparous (of the family Cyprinodontidae) or egg-laying (of the family Poeciliidae) (also called **mosquito fish**; see also **killifish** under **kill²**). **top-notch'** *adj* (*inf*) excellent, first-rate. **top-notch'er** *n*. **topped crude** *n* crude oil after some of its lighter constituents have been removed by distillation. **topping lift** *n* (*naut*) tackle running from the masthead for raising booms. **topp'ing-out** see **top out** below. **top'-proud** *adj* (*Shakesp*) proud in the highest degree. **top quark** *n* (*phys*) a particle believed to be one of the fundamental constituents of nuclear matter. **top'sail** /-*sl*, -*säl*/ *n* a sail across the topmast. **top-saw'yer** *n* the upper sawyer in a sawpit; a superior, a person of importance (*inf*). **top secret** *adj* profoundly secret and of the highest importance. **top'-shelf** *adj* (of a publication) too explicitly pornographic to be displayed for sale at eye level; of the latest design (*Aust*). **top'side** *n* the upper part; the outer part of a round of beef; a lean cut of beef from the rump; the part of an oil rig, etc above the deck; (also in *pl*) the part of the outer surface of a vessel above the waterline. ◆ *adv* on or towards the top. **top-slice'** *vt* to subtract a sum of money from (a fund) before any other transactions are made, *usu* to finance a specific project. **tops'man** *n* a head drover, a foreman (*Scot*); a hangman (*sl*). **top'soil** *n* the upper part or surface of the soil. **top'soiling** *n* removal of the topsoil. **top'spin** *n* spin imparted to a ball by hitting it sharply on the upper half with a forward and upward stroke to make it travel higher, further, or more quickly; extra, not always reliable or well-attested, information (*press sl*). **top stone** *n* a stone placed on the top, or forming the top. **top table** *n* the place assigned to the most important people at a meeting or banquet. **top'-up** *n* an amount added to bring something back up to a reasonable or the original level. **top-up, topping-up** see also **top up** below. **top-up loan** *n* a loan to bring a mortgage, grant, etc up to the required amount.
■ **at the top of one's voice** at one's loudest. **from top to toe** completely; from head to foot. **go over the top** to go over the front of a trench and attack the enemy; to take sudden action after hesitation; to exceed the bounds of reason, decorum, etc. **in the top flight** in the highest class. **off the top of one's head** without previous thought or

preparation. **on top of** in control; in addition to. **on top of the world** near the north pole; on a high mountain; exuberant, in the very best of spirits. **over the top** (*inf*) too far, extreme, to an excess, to, at or of an unreasonable or unnecessary degree. **the tops** (*inf*) the very best. **top and tail** to wash (a baby's) face and buttocks; to prepare (fruit or vegetables, eg carrots) by removing the top and bottom parts. **top off** to finish decoratively or memorably. **top one's part** (*theatre*) to excel in playing one's part. **top out** to finish (a building) by putting on the top or highest course; (of eg prices) to reach the highest level (and go no further) (**topp'ing-out** *n*). **top the bill** to be the most important attraction in a programme of entertainment, etc. **top up** to fill up, eg with fuel oil, alcohol; to bring (eg a wage) up to a generally accepted or satisfactory level (**top'-up** or **topp'ing-up** *n*); (of a ship's yards) to place at an angle to the deck (*naut*).

top² /*top*/ *n* a toy that can be set spinning on its pointed base (also called **spinning top**); a grooved cone held back between the strands in rope-making; a marine gastropod with a pearly flattish-based conical shell (also called **top'-shell**). [Appar late OE *top* (but the meaning is doubtful)]
■ **sleep like a top** to sleep very soundly.

toparch /*top'ärk*/ *n* the ruler of a district. [Gr *toparchēs*, from *topos* a place, and *archein* to rule]
■ **top'archy** *n* a toparch's territory.

topaz /*tō'paz*/ *n* a precious stone, silicate of aluminium and fluorine, yellowish, bluish or colourless; a variety of orange and tangerine hybrid; (loosely) a shade of dark yellow; a S American hummingbird of the genus *Topaza*. ◆ *adj* of a dark yellow colour. [Gr *topazos* a green gem]
■ **tō'pazine** *adj*. **topaz'olite** *n* a yellowish or greenish garnet.
■ **oriental topaz** a yellow corundum.

tope¹ /*tōp*/ *vi* to drink hard regularly. ◆ *interj* (*obs*) used in drinking to someone's health. [Poss Fr *toper* to accept a wager]
■ **tō'per** *n* a drunkard.

tope² /*tōp*/ *n* a dome-shaped shrine for Buddhist relics. [Hindi *top*, from Sans *stūpa* a heap]

tope³ /*tōp*/ *n* any of various small sharks, *esp Galeorhinus galeus*. [Said to be Cornish]

tope⁴ /*tōp*/ *n* in (E) India, a grove (eg of mangoes), a plantation. [Tamil *tōppu*, from Telugu *topu*]

topectomy /*to-*, *tə-pek'tə-mi*/ (*med*; now *obs*) *n* the excision of a part of the cerebral cortex as treatment for certain mental illnesses. [Gr *topos* place, *ek* from, and **-tomy**]

topee see **topi¹**.

topek same as **tupik**.

Tophet /*tō'fet*/ *n* an ancient place of human sacrifice near Jerusalem, the valley of Hinnom or part of it, later a place of refuse disposal; hence Hell. [Heb *tōpheth*]

tophus /*tō'fəs*/ (*med*) *n* (*pl* **tō'phi** /-*fī*/) a gouty deposit, a hard nodule formed of sodium biurate crystals in soft body tissue. [L *tōphus*, *tōfus* porous stone, tufa]
■ **topha'ceous** *adj*.

topi¹ or **topee** /*tō-pē'*, *tō'pē*/ *n* a hat, *esp* a sola hat, pith helmet, worn *esp* in India. [Hindi *topī* hat (perh from Port *topo* top)]
◻ **to'pi-wallah** *n* (*old*) a European in India.

topi² /*tō'pi*/ *n* a large African antelope (*Damaliscus korrigum*) with curved horns and long muzzle. [Appar from a native word]

topiary /*tō'pi-ə-ri* or *tō'pyə-ri*/ *n* a branch of gardening, the clipping of trees into imitative and fantastic shapes; an example of this; mural decoration in fanciful landscape. [L *topiārius*, from *topia* (*pl*), landscape, landscape gardening, from Gr *topos* a place]
■ **topiā'rian** *adj*. **tō'piarist** *n*.

topic /*top'ik*/ *n* a general consideration suitable for argument; a subject or theme of discourse or argument; a matter; a head under which a rhetorician might look up matter for discourse. [Gr *topikos* relating to place or to commonplaces, *ta topika* the general principles of argument, from *topos* a place]
■ **top'ical** *adj* of or relating to current affairs; local; relating to a topic or subject; affecting only part of the body (*med*). **topical'ity** *n* the quality of being topical; an item or subject possessing this. **top'ically** *adv*.
◻ **topic sentence** *n* the sentence in a paragraph that expresses the main idea of the paragraph.

to-pinch a false emendation of some Shakespearean editors (*Merry Wives of Windsor* IV.4.56), for *to pinch*, the second of two infinitives having *to* where the first is without *to*.

topo /*top'ō*/ (*mountaineering*) *n* a diagram showing the route of a rock climb. [Short for *topographical map*]

topography /*to-pog'rə-fi*/ *n* the detailed study, description or features of a limited area, district, etc; the detailed study or description of external features of the body with reference to those underneath. [Gr *topographiā*, from *topos* a place, and *graphein* to describe]

■ **topog'rapher** *n*. **topographic** /*top-ə-graf'ik*/ or **topograph'ical** *adj*. **topograph'ically** *adv*.

topoi see **topos**.

topology /*to-pol'ə-ji*/ *n* the topographical study of a particular place; topographical anatomy; a branch of geometry concerned with those properties of a figure which remain unchanged even when the figure is bent, stretched, etc; the study of those properties of sets of points (eg geometrical figures) that are invariant under one-to-one continuous transformations (*maths*); the interconnection, organization, etc of computers within a network. [Gr *topos* a place, and *logos* a discourse]

■ **topolog'ic** or **topolog'ical** *adj*. **topolog'ically** *adv*. **topol'ogist** *n*.

toponym /*top'ə-nim*/ *n* a place name; a descriptive place name, *usu* derived from a geographical feature; a name derived from a place name, eg a place of origin. [Gr *topos* place, and *onyma* (*onoma*) name]

■ **topon'ymal**, **toponymic** /*-ə-nim'ik*/ or **toponym'ical** *adj*. **toponymy** /*top-on'i-mi*/ *n* the study of place names (also *n sing* **toponym'ics**); the nomenclature of regions of the body.

topophilia /*top-ə-fil'-i-ə*/ *n* great affection for a particular place. [Gr *topos* place, and *phileein* to love]

topos /*top'os*/ *n* (*pl* **top'oi** /*-oi, -ē*/) a stock theme, topic or expression in literature or rhetoric. [Gr, literally, a place]

topotype /*top'ə-tīp*/ (*zool*) *n* a specimen collected in the same locality as the original specimen of the same species. [Gr *topos* a place, and **type**]

topped, **topping**, etc see under **top**[1].

topple /*top'l*/ *vi* to overbalance and fall headlong; to threaten to fall from top-heaviness; to totter. ◆ *vt* to cause to topple. [**top**[1]]

topsy-turvy /*top'si-tûr'vi*/ *adv* bottom upwards; in confusion. ◆ *adj* turned upside down; confused. ◆ *n* confusion. ◆ *vt* to turn upside down. —Also, as *adv*, *adj*, *n* **top'side-tur'v(e)y** or (*Scot*) **tap'salteer'ie**. [**top**[1], **so**[1], **set**, and **side** are only conjectures]

■ **topsy-turvificā'tion** *n* a turning upside down. **topsy-tur'vily** *adv*. **topsy-tur'viness** *n*. **topsy-tur'vydom** *n*.

toque /*tōk*/ *n* a woman's close-fitting brimless or nearly brimless hat; a 16c form of cap or turban (*hist*); a hair-pad (*obs*); a chef's tall white hat; /*took*/ a woolly hat (*Can*); a macaque, *Macacus pileatus*, of Sri Lanka. [Fr]

toquilla /*tə-kē'yə*/ *n* (a fibre obtained from the leaves of) a S American palm-like tree, *Carludovica palmata*. [Sp, dimin of *toca* toque]

tor or **torr** /*tör*/ *n* a hill, a rocky height. [OE *torr* tor, from L *turris* tower, or perh from Celtic]

Torah or **Thorah** /*tō'*, *tö'rə*/ (*Judaism*) *n* the Mosaic Law; the book of the law, the Pentateuch; a scroll containing this. [Heb *Tōrāh*]

toran /*tō'*, *tö'rən*/ or **torana** /*-rən-ə*/ *n* (in India) a type of arched gateway; a garland of flowers or leaves hung between two points; a richly embroidered hanging hung above the doorway to the main room of a house. [Hindi]

torbanite /*tör'bə-nīt*/ *n* a shale, almost a coal, once mined for oil at *Torbane* Hill, Bathgate, Scotland.

torbernite /*tör'bər-nīt*/ *n* a bright-green radioactive hydrous phosphate of copper and uranium. [*Torbern* Bergmann (1735–84), Swed chemist]

torc see **torque**.

torch /*törch*/ *n* a piece of wood or inflammable material dipped in tallow or wax and lighted, carried or mounted on a wall, etc to give light; a large candle; a small, battery-powered portable electric lamp; an appliance producing a hot flame for welding, burning, etc; a source of enlightenment, guidance, etc; an arsonist (*US sl*); a glowing flower or inflorescence, eg mullein; a tall cactaceous plant. ◆ *vt* to light with a torch or torches; to set alight deliberately (*sl, esp US*); to sing (a torch song) (*rare; US*). [Fr *torche*, from L *torquēre, tortum* to twist]

■ **torch'er** *n* (*Shakesp*) a light-giver. **torch'ing** *n* (*sl, esp US*) the act of setting something alight, *esp* deliberately.

❑ **torch'bearer** *n* a person who carries a torch; a leading, prominent figure in a cause, etc (*fig*). **torch'-dance** *n*. **torch'light** *n*. **torch'-lily** *n* the red-hot poker (*Kniphofia* or *Tritoma*). **torch'-race** *n* (*hist*) a race in which the runners carried torches and passed them to others. **torch singer** *n*. **torch song** *n* a popular song of the 1930s giving lugubrious expression to the pangs of unrequited love; a sentimental or melancholy love song. **torch'-staff** *n* (*pl* **torch'-staves**) (*Shakesp*) a staff for carrying a torch. **torch'-thistle** *n* a cereus. **torch'wood** *n* any of several resinous woods suitable for making torches; any tree yielding such wood, *esp Amyris balsamifera*, native to Florida and the West Indies.

■ **carry the** (or **a**) **torch** (**for**) to suffer unrequited love (for). **put to the torch** to burn down.

torchère /*tor-sher'*/ (*Fr*) *n* a tall ornamental candlestick or lampstand.

torchier or **torchière** /*tor-shēr'* or (*Fr*) *tor-shyer'*/ (*Fr*) *n* a floor lamp consisting of a bowl for reflecting light upwards mounted on a tall stand.

torchon /*tör-shõ*/ *n* (*Fr*) a duster or dishcloth; (in full **torchon lace**) peasants' bobbin lace of loose texture and geometrical design, or a machine-made imitation; (in full **torchon paper**) a rough paper for watercolour drawing. [Fr, from *torcher* to wipe]

torcular /*tör'kū-lər*/ *n* a tourniquet. [L *torcular, -āris* a press for wine or oil]

tordion /*tor-di-ōn'*, *tor'di-ən*/ *n* a dance similar to, but less spirited than, a galliard, *esp* common in the 15c and 16c. [Fr, from OFr *tourdion*, from Fr *tordre* to twist]

tore[1] /*tōr, tör*/ *pat* and obsolete *pap* of **tear**[2].

tore[2] see under **torus**.

toreador /*tor'i-ə-dör*/ *n* a bullfighter, *esp* on horseback. [Sp, from *toro* bull, from L *taurus* bull]

■ **torero** /*tor-ā'rō*/ *n* (*pl* **tore'ros**) a bullfighter on foot.

❑ **toreador pants** *n pl* tight-fitting calf-length trousers for women (resembling those worn by toreadors).

to-rend /*tə-, tŭ-rend'*/ (*obs*) *vt* (*pap* (*Spenser*) **to-rent'**) to rend in pieces.

toreutic /*tö-rū'tik, -roo'*/ *adj* (of metal) chased or embossed. [Gr *toreutikos, -ē, -on*, from *toreuein* to bore]

■ **toreu'tics** *n sing* artistic work in metal, producing by chasing and embossing.

torgoch /*tör'gohh*/ *n* the red-bellied char. [Welsh]

tori, **toric** see **torus**.

torii /*tö'rē-ē*/ *n* (*pl* **tor'ii**) a Japanese Shinto temple gateway. [Jap]

torment /*tör'ment*/ *n* physical or mental pain or suffering; a cause of this; torture (*archaic*); an instrument of torture (*archaic*). [L *tormentum*, from *torquēre* to twist]

■ **torment** /*-ment'*/ *vt* to cause extreme pain or suffering to; to distress; to afflict; to pester or tease; to harass; to torture (*archaic*); to agitate, stir violently; to distort, force violently. **tormen'ted** *adj*. **torment'edly** *adv*. **torment'ing** *n* and *adj*. **tormen'tingly** *adv*. **tormen'tor** or **tormen'ter** *n* a person or thing that torments; a torturer, an executioner (*Bible*); a long meat-fork; a wing in the first groove of a stage, screened from the audience eg by a curtain.

tormentil /*tör'men-til*/ *n* a four-petalled potentilla with bright yellow flowers and an astringent woody root, growing on heaths. [OFr *tormentille*, from Med L *tormentilla*, from L *tormentum* torment, in reference to its use as an analgesic]

tormentum /*tör-men'təm*/ (*hist*) *n* (*pl* **torment'a** or **torment'ums**) a Roman machine for hurling missiles. [L, from *torquēre* to twist]

tormina /*tör'mi-nə*/ *n pl* gripes. [L, from *torquēre* to twist]

■ **tor'minal** or **tor'minous** *adj*.

torn /*törn, tōrn*/ *pap* of **tear**[2].

❑ **torn'-down** *adj* (*US*) unruly.

■ **that's torn it!** (*inf*) an expression of annoyance indicating that something has spoilt one's plans, etc.

tornado /*tör-nā'dō*/ *n* (*pl* **tornā'does** or **tornā'dos**) (*orig*) a violent tropical Atlantic thunderstorm, occurring eg off the W coast of Africa; a very violent whirling windstorm characterized by a long, funnel-shaped cloud, affecting a narrow strip of country; (loosely) a hurricane. [Prob Sp *tronada* thunderstorm, altered as if from Sp *tornada* turning]

■ **tornade'** *n* (*poetic*). **tornadic** /*-nad'ik*/ *adj*.

toroid, **toroidal** see under **torus**.

Toronto blessing /*tə-ron'tō bles'ing*/ (*Christianity*) *n* a form of behaviour involving weeping, fainting, and other highly emotional or hysterical reactions attributed to the action of the Holy Spirit. [*Toronto*, Canada, where it originated in the 1980s]

torose /*tö'rōs*/ or **torous** /*tö'rəs*/ *adj* cylindrical with swelling or bulges at intervals (*bot*); swelling, bulging, knobby. [L *torōsus* bulging, full of muscle]

torpedo /*tör-pē'dō*/ *n* (*pl* **torpē'does** or **torpē'dos**) a self-propelled submarine weapon (*usu* cigar-shaped), carrying a charge that explodes on impact, launched from aircraft, ships or submarines; a bomb, cartridge, case of explosives, or detonator of various kinds, used in warfare, in boring, as a fog signal, firework, etc (chiefly *N Am*); a member of the genus *Torpedo* of cartilaginous fishes, related to the skates and rays, with organs on the head that give an electric shock, giving name to the family **Torpedinidae** /*-pə-din'i-dē*/. ◆ *vt* to attack, strike, destroy, by torpedo; to wreck (eg a plan). [L *torpēdō, -inis* numbness, the torpedo (fish), from *torpēre* to be stiff]

■ **torpe'dinous** *adj* numbing. **torpe'doer** *n*. **torpe'doist** *n*.

❏ **torpedo boat** *n* a small swift warship discharging torpedoes. **torpe'do-boat destroyer** *n* a swifter, more powerful, type of torpedo boat *orig* used to destroy ordinary torpedo boats. **torpedo boom** *n* a spar for carrying a torpedo, projecting from a boat or anchored in a channel. **torpedo net** *n* a steel net hung round a ship to intercept torpedoes. **torpedo tube** *n* a tube from which torpedoes are discharged.

torpefy /tör'pi-fī/ *vt* (**tor'pefying**; **tor'pefied**) to make numb or torpid, to paralyse. [L *torpefacere* to make numb, and *torpescēre* to grow numb, from *torpēre* to be numb]
■ **torpesc'ence** *n* the process of becoming numb or torpid. **torpesc'ent** *adj* becoming numb or torpid.

torpid /tör'pid/ *adj* numb; lethargic; having lost the power of motion and feeling; sluggish; (of a hibernating animal) dormant. ◆ *n* (at Oxford University) a second boat of a college, or its crew; (in *pl*) the Lent term races of eight-oared clinker-built boats. [L *torpidus, torpor,* from *torpēre* to be numb]
■ **torpid'ity** *n*. **tor'pidly** *adv*. **tor'pidness** *n*. **tor'pitude** *n*. **tor'por** *n* numbness; inactivity; dullness; stupidity. **torporif'ic** *adj*.

torquate /tör'kwāt/ or **torquated** /-id/ (*zool*) *adj* with a distinctive ring (eg of feathers or a different colour) round the neck. [L *torquātus* wearing a necklace, from *torquēs, -is* a necklace]

torque /törk/ *n* the measure of the turning effect of a tangential force; a force or system of forces causing or tending to cause rotation or torsion; a necklace or armband in the form of a twisted metal band (also **torc**). [L *torquēre* to twist; *torquēs, -is* a necklace]
■ **torqued** /törkt/ *adj* twisted.
❏ **torque converter** *n* (*mech*) a device that acts as an infinitely variable gear. **torque meter** *n*. **torque spanner** *n* (*engineering*) a spanner with a special attachment allowing a preset force to be applied when tightening a nut on a bolt. **torque wrench** *n* a wrench with a gauge indicating the torque applied.

torr¹ see **tor**.

torr² /tör/ (*phys*) *n* a unit used in expressing very low pressures, $\frac{1}{760}$ of a standard atmosphere, equal to one millimetre of mercury or 133.3Nm⁻². [E Torricelli; see **Torricellian**]

torrefy /tor'i-fī/ *vt* (**tor'refying**; **tor'refied**) to scorch or parch; to dry or roast (ore, drugs, etc) with intense heat. [L *torrēre* to parch, roast, and *facere* to make]
■ **torrefac'tion** *n*.

torrent /tor'ənt/ *n* a rushing stream; a variable mountain stream; an abounding, strong or turbulent flow. ◆ *adj* rushing in a stream. [L *torrēns, -entis* boiling, prp of *torrēre* to dry]
■ **torrential** /-en'shl/ *adj*. **torrentiality** /-en-shi-al'i-ti/ *n*. **torren'tially** *adv*. **torrent'uous** *adj*.
❏ **torr'ent-bow** *n* a bow of prismatic colours formed by the spray of a torrent.

torret /tor'it/ see **terret**.

Torricellian /tor-i-chel'i-ən/ *adj* relating to or associated with the Italian mathematician Evangelista *Torricelli* (1608–47) who discovered in 1643 the principle of the barometer.
❏ **Torricellian tube** *n* a barometer in which mercury rises and falls in a vacuum. **Torricellian vacuum** *n* the vacuum in this type of barometer.

torrid /tor'id/ *adj* scorching or parching; extremely hot; dried with heat; intensely passionate, emotional, etc. [L *torridus,* from *torrēre* to parch, roast]
■ **torrid'ity** or **torr'idness** *n*. **torr'idly** *adv*.
❏ **torrid zone** *n* the zone between the tropics.

Torridonian /tor-i-dō'ni-ən/ (*geol*) *n* and *adj* Precambrian of the NW Highlands of Scotland, as around Loch *Torridon*.

torse¹ /törs/ *n* a heraldic wreath. [Fr, from L *torquēre* to twist]
■ **torsade** /-sād'/ *n* an ornament like a twisted cord, eg on a hat.

torse² see **torso**.

torsel /tör'sl/ *n* a plate in a brick wall to support the end of a beam (also **tassel**). [L *taxillus* a die, Ital *tassello,* Fr *tasseau*]

torsi see **torso**.

torsion /tör'shən/ *n* twisting; a twist; the strain produced by twisting; the force with which a thread or wire tends to return when twisted; the checking of a haemorrhage by twisting the cut end of the artery (*surg*). [L *torsiō, -ōnis,* from *torquēre, tortum* to twist]
■ **torsibility** /-si-bil'i-ti/ *n* the ability to be twisted or subjected to torsion; the degree to which twisting or torsion can be recovered from. **tor'siograph** *n* an instrument for measuring and recording the frequency and amplitude of torsional vibrations in a shaft. **tor'sional** *adj*. **tor'sionally** *adv*. **tor'sive** *adj* twisted spirally.
❏ **torsion balance** *n* an instrument for measuring very minute forces by a horizontal needle suspended by a very fine filament. **torsion bar**

n a metal bar which absorbs force by twisting, used *esp* in vehicle suspension. **torsion meter** *n* a torque meter.

torsk /törsk/ *n* a N Atlantic fish (*Brosme brosme*) of the cod family, with a long single dorsal fin. [Swed, Norw, Dan *torsk,* from ON *thorskr*; cf Ger *Dorsch* haddock]

torso /tör'sō/ *n* (*pl* **tor'sos** or (*rare*) **tor'si** /-sē/) the trunk of a statue or human body, without head or limbs (also (*Fr*) **torse**); anything incomplete or unfinished. [Ital, stalk, core, torso, from L *thyrsus,* from Gr *thyrsos*]

tort /tört/ *n* wrong, injury (*Spenser*); any wrong, not arising out of contract, for which an action for compensation or damages may be brought (*law*). [Fr, from LL *tortum,* from L *torquēre, tortum* to twist]
■ **tortious** /tör'shəs/ *adj* wrongful; of the nature of a tort (*law*). **tor'tiously** *adv*.
❏ **tort'feasor** /-fē-zər/ *n* (*law*) a person guilty of tort.

torte /tör'tə, tört/ *n* (*pl* **tor'ten, tor'tes** /-ez/ or **tortes** /törts/) a rich sweet cake or pastry, Austrian in origin, often garnished or filled with fruit, nuts, cream, chocolate, etc. [Ger, perh from LL *torta* a round loaf]

tortelli /tör-tel'i/ *n pl* small pasta parcels stuffed with meat, cheese or vegetables. [Ital, ult from LL *torta* a round loaf of bread]

tortellini /tör-tə-lē'ni/ *n pl* small round pasta cases filled with a savoury, *usu* meat, filling and seasoning and boiled in water. [Ital, dimin of **tortelli**]

tortfeasor see under **tort**.

torticollis /tör-ti-kol'is/ (*pathol*) *n* wryneck. [LL, from L *tortus* twisted, and *collum* neck]

tortile /tör'tīl/ *adj* twisted; wreathed; coiled. [L *tortilis, tortīvus,* from *torquēre* to twist]
■ **tortility** /-til'/ *n*. **tor'tive** *adj* (*Shakesp*) turned awry.

tortilla /tör-tē(l)'ya, -yə/ *n* (in Mexican cooking) a round flat cake of unleavened bread made from maize or wheat flour and cooked on a griddle, *usu* eaten hot with a filling; (in Spanish cooking) a thick omelette made mainly of potato and egg. [Sp, dimin of *torta* cake]

tortillon /tör-tē-yõ'/ *n* a pencil for softening hard lines or blending edges, a stump. [OFr *tortiller* to twist]

tortious see under **tort**.

tortive see under **tortile**.

tortoise /tör'təs, -toiz or -tois/ *n* any land or freshwater (rarely marine) chelonian of the family Testudinidae, with a dome-shaped leathery shell (now, in Britain, *usu* restricted to land forms); a testudo (*milit*). [LL *tortuca*]
❏ **tortoise beetle** *n* any of various beetles (Cassidinae) of the family Chrysomelidae which resemble the tortoise, having broad, often brightly-coloured or metallic wing-covers; (*specif*) a green leaf-beetle (*Cassida viridis*). **tortoise plant** *n* elephant's-foot. **tortoiseshell** /tör'tə-shel/ *n* the shell of a tortoise; a translucent mottled material, the horny plates (*esp* of the back) of the hawksbill turtle; a similar synthetic material; a tortoiseshell butterfly or cat. ◆ *adj* made of, or mottled like, tortoiseshell. **tortoiseshell butterfly** *n* any of several species of butterfly with orange or reddish wings marked with black and yellow, edged with blue, etc, *esp Aglais urticae* (small tortoiseshell), and *Nymphalis polychlorus* (large tortoiseshell). **tortoiseshell cat** *n* a domestic cat (nearly always female) mottled in yellow and black.

tortoni /tör-tō'nē/ *n* a rich ice cream flavoured with dessert or fortified wine and containing chopped fruit, nuts, etc. [Ital, perh from an Italian café owner in Paris in the 18c]

tortrix /tör'triks/ *n* (*pl* **tortrices** /-trī'sēz/) a member of the *Tortrix* genus of moths belonging to the **Tortricidae** /-tris'i-dē/, a large family of small moths whose caterpillars spin silken webs drawing leaves, flowers, etc into a rolled-up protective covering around themselves. [Invented L, twister]
■ **tortrī'cid** *n* any moth of the Tortricidae family (also *adj*).

tortuous /tör'tū-əs/ *adj* full of twistings and windings; devious; far from straightforward, circuitous. [L *tortuōsus,* from *torquēre, tortum* to twist]
■ **tortuos'ity** *n*. **tor'tuously** *adv*. **tor'tuousness** *n*.

torture /tör'chər/ *n* the infliction of severe pain *esp* as a means of punishment or persuasion; extreme physical or mental pain; a cause of this; anguish. ◆ *vt* to subject to torture; to subject to extreme pain; to exact by torture; to distort violently. [Fr, from L *tortūra* torment, from *torquēre, tortum* to twist]
■ **tor'tured** *adj* suffering or entailing torture or anguish; fraught with worries or difficulties, painful (*inf*); violently distorted. **tor'turedly** *adv*. **tor'turer** *n*. **tor'turesome** *adj*. **tor'turing** *n* and *adj*. **tor'turingly** *adv*. **tor'turous** *adj* causing torture or violent distortion.

toruffled /tə-, tŭ-ruf'ld/ (*archaic*) *adj* (*Milton* **to ruffl'd**) ruffled up. [Pfx *to-,* intens, and **ruffle¹**]

torula /tō'rū-lə/ n (pl **tor'ulae** /-lē/) a yeastlike microorganism of the genus *Torula*; a commercially produced yeast used in food and medicine. [New L, from L *torus* a bulge, swelling]
■ **tor'ūlin** n a vitamin in yeast. **torūlō'sis** n infection with a member of the *Torula* genus affecting the nervous system.

torulose /tō'rū-lōz/ (*bot*) adj with small swellings at intervals. [L *torus* a bulge, swelling]

torulus /tō'rū-ləs/ (*zool*) n (pl **tor'ūlī**) the socket of an insect's antenna. [Dimin of L *torus* a bulge, swelling]

torus /tō', tō'rəs/ n (pl **to'rī**) a large moulding, semicircular or nearly so in section, common at the base of a column (*archit*); a figure generated by the revolution of a circle or other conic section about a straight line in its own plane (*geom*); the receptacle of a flower (*bot*); a ridge or prominence (*zool, anat*); a ring-shaped discharge-tube. [L *torus* a bulge, swelling, bed, torus moulding]
■ **tore** /tōr, tōr/ n (*archit* and *geom*) a torus. **toric** /tor', tōr', tōr'/ adj of or having the form of a torus or a part of a torus. **toroid** /tor', tōr', tōr'/ adj shaped like an anchor-ring. ◆ n a coil or transformer of that shape. **toroid'al** adj.

Tory /tō', tō'ri/ n a Conservative (*Brit politics*); a bigoted or extreme Conservative; a member of the English political party who opposed the exclusion of James II from the monarchy in the 17c (*hist*); (in Ireland) a Roman Catholic, *esp* an outlaw or robber, who preyed on English settlers in the 17c (*hist*); a person who sided with the British in the Revolution (*US hist*). ◆ adj Conservative. [Ir *toiridhe* a pursuer, robber; first applied to the Tories in Ireland; next, about 1680, to the most hot-headed asserters of the royal prerogative]
■ **Tō'rify** or **Tō'ryfy** vt to infect with Tory principles. **Tō'ryish** adj. **Tō'ryism** n the principles of the Tories.

tosa /tō'zə/ n (in full **Japanese tosa**) a heavily built, smooth-haired dog, the adult of which weighs *approx* 7 stone, bred for fighting. [Jap]

tose see **toze**.

tosh¹ /tosh/ (*sl*) n bosh, twaddle.
■ **tosh'y** adj.

tosh² /tosh/ (*Scot*) adj neat, trim; comfortable, friendly, intimate. ◆ adv in a neat and tidy manner. ◆ vt to trim.

tosh³ /tosh/ (*sl*) n (used as a form of address) friend, chum.

toshach /tō'shəhh, tosh'əhh/ n a phonetic rendering of **toiseach**.

tosher /tosh'ər/ (*university sl*) n a non-collegiate student. [From **unattached**]

toss /tos/ vt (*pat* and *pap* **tossed** /tost/, or rarely **tost**; *infinitive* (*Spenser*) **toss'en**) to throw up in the air; to throw lightly and carelessly (with *away, aside, out*, etc); to fling, jerk (eg the head), eg as a sign of impatience; to roll about or throw from side to side or to and fro, *esp* repeatedly and violently; to throw (a coin) into the air to make a decision, etc based on the side which falls upwards; to settle a dispute with (someone) by doing this; (of a horse) to throw (its rider); (of a bull, etc) to throw (a person, etc) into the air with its horns; to coat (food) by mixing it gently with a dressing; to discuss or consider, *esp* in an informal or light-hearted way; to agitate; to turn the leaves of (*obs*); to tilt in drinking; to drink. ◆ vi to be tossed; to be in violent commotion; to be rolled or thrown about from side to side or to and fro, *esp* repeatedly and violently; to fling; to toss up a coin. ◆ n an act of throwing upward; a throwing up or back of the head; confusion, commotion; the act of tossing a coin; a fall from a horse. [Origin unknown]
■ **toss'er** n a person or thing that tosses; an unpleasant or despicable person (*vulgar sl*). **toss'ily** adv pertly. **toss'ing** n and adj. **toss'y** adj pert, contemptuous.
❑ **toss'pot** n (*sl*) a toper, a drunkard (*old*); an incompetent, unpleasant or foolish person (*prob* by confusion with **tosser** above); a jocular or hearty term of address, *usu* to a man (*Aust*). **toss'-up** n the throwing up of a coin to decide anything; an even chance or risk.
■ **argue the toss** to dispute a decision. **not give a toss** (*sl*) to have no concern whatever (about). **toss and turn** be wakeful, restless and fidgety in bed. **toss off** to perform or produce quickly or cursorily; to drink off in a single draught; to remark casually; to masturbate (*vulgar sl*). **toss out** (*old*) to dress smartly, fancily. **toss up** to toss a coin; to cook and serve up hastily.

tostada /to-stä'də/ n a tortilla fried until crisp and served with a savoury topping of eg beans, minced meat and vegetables. [Sp Am, from Sp *tostar* to toast]

tot¹ /tot/ n anything little, *esp* a young child, a drinking cup, or a dram. [Cf Icel *tottr* a dwarf]
■ **tott'ie** or **tott'y** n (*dimin*) a very small child; sexually attractive young people collectively (*sl*). ◆ adj (*dialect*) very small.

tot² /tot/ vt and vi (**tott'ing**; **tott'ed**) to add or mount up or total (also **tot up**). ◆ n an addition of a long column. [**total**]
❑ **totting-up'** n adding up; the cumulation of certain motoring offences, eventually resulting in disqualification.

tot³ /tot/ (*sl*) n a bone; anything retrieved from a dustbin, rubbish heap, etc. [Origin uncertain]
■ **tott'er** n a person who searches through dustbins and rubbish heaps for reusable or saleable items; a rag-and-bone-man, scrap dealer. **tott'ing** n retrieval of reusable or saleable objects from refuse.

total /tō't(ə)l/ adj whole; complete, absolute; including all; co-ordinating everything towards one end. ◆ n the whole; the entire amount. ◆ vt (**tō'talling**; **tō'talled**) to bring to a total, add up; to amount to; to kill or destroy completely (chiefly *N Am sl*). ◆ vi (with *to, up to*) to amount to. [LL *tōtālis*, from L *tōtus* whole]
■ **totalitarian** /tō-tal-i-tā'ri-ən/ adj of, relating to, or characteristic of, a form of government that includes control of everything under one authority, and allows no opposition. ◆ n a person in favour of such a government. **totalità'rianism** n. **totality** /tō-tal'i-ti/ n the condition or fact of being total; an entirety; completeness; the whole; the period during an eclipse when the eclipse is total (*astron*). **tōtalizā'tion** or **-s-** n. **tō'talizātor** or **-s-**, or **tō'talizer** or **-s-** n a system of betting in which the total amount staked (minus tax, etc) is divided among the winners in proportion to the size of their stake; an automatic betting-machine, the *pari-mutuel*. **tō'talize** or **-ise** vt to find the sum of; to bring to a total. ◆ vi to use a totalizator. **tō'tally** adv.
❑ **total abstainer** n a person who abstains altogether from all forms of alcohol. **total allergy syndrome** n a condition in which a person suffers from a collection of symptoms attributable to accumulated allergies to substances encountered in the modern environment. **total body burden** n (*radiol*) the summation of all radioactive materials contained in any person; the maximum total amount of radioactive material any person may be permitted to contain. **total depravity** n the theological doctrine that man is totally corrupt and completely dependent on God for spiritual regeneration. **total eclipse** n an eclipse in which the eclipsed body appears to be completely hidden. **total football** n a style of football where all players, including defenders, can be involved in attack. **total heat** n enthalpy. **total internal reflection** n (*phys*) the complete reflection of a light ray at the boundary of a medium with a lower refractive index. **total parenteral nutrition** n (*med*) hyperalimentation, the supply of essential nutrients intravenously to patients incapable of ingesting food normally (*abbrev* **TPN**). **total quality management** n a system of management that aims at continuously improving the quality of goods and services while reducing costs (*abbrev* **TQM**). **total recall** see **recall**. **total theatre** n dramatic entertainment comprising in one performance all or most of the following: acting, dancing, gymnastic feats, singing and instrumental music of various kinds, elaborate costumes and other visual effects, sometimes poetry. **total war** see under **war¹**.

totanus /tot'ə-nəs/ n the redshank (*Tringa totanus*), a member of the Tringidae subfamily of sandpipers, with toes webbed at the base. [Ital *totano* squid, from its habit of feeding on small crustaceans and invertebrates]

totaquine /tō'tə-kwēn, -kwin/ n a drug containing alkaloids derived from cinchona bark and quinine, formerly used as an antimalarial. [New L *tōtaquina*, from L *totus* whole, and Sp *quina* cinchona bark]

totara /tō'tə-rə/ n a large coniferous New Zealand tree, a variety of *Podocarpus*, valued for its hard reddish timber. [Maori]

Tote® /tōt/ n a form of totalizator.

tote¹ /tōt/ (*orig US*) vt to carry. ◆ n a burden. [Origin unknown]
❑ **tote bag** n a large bag for shopping, etc.

tote² /tōt/ (*sl*) vt to add (with *up*). [**total**]

to-tear /tə-, tŭ-tār'/ vt (*pap* (*Spenser*) **to-torne'**) to tear in pieces. [Pfx *to-* asunder, and **tear²**]

totem /tō'təm/ n (*esp* in Native American society) any species of living or inanimate thing regarded, and often venerated, as an outward symbol of an existing intimate unseen relation, often adopted as an emblem or symbol of a family, clan or tribe; any outward symbol given undue respect. [From Algonquin]
■ **totemic** /-tem'ik/ adj. **tō'temism** n the use of totems as the foundation of a social system of obligation and restriction; the rituals, customs and taboos associated with this. **tō'temist** n an individual or group designated by a totem. **totemist'ic** adj.
❑ **totem pole** n a pole carved and painted with totemic symbols, set up by indigenous peoples in the north-west of N America, eg as a tribal symbol; a hierarchical system (*inf*).

totes /tōts/ (*sl*) adv totally.

tother or **t'other** /tudh'ər/ (*dialect* or *humorous*) pronoun and adj the other. [*that other*; cf **tone²** and Scot **tae**, **tane²**]
■ **tell tother from which** tell one from another.

totidem verbis /tō-tī'dəm vûr'bis, tot'i-dem ver', wer'bēs/ (L) in just so many words.

totient /tō'shənt/ n the number of totitives of a number. [L *totiēs* so many]

---

toties quoties /tō'shi-ēz kwō'shi-ēz, tot'i-ās kwot'i-ās/ (L) as often as; on each occasion.

totipalmate /tō-ti-pal'mit or -māt/ (ornithol) adj (of birds) having all four toes fully webbed. [L tōtus entire, and **palmate**]
■ **totipalmā'tion** n.

totipotent /tō-tip'ə-tənt/ (zool) adj capable of development into a complete organ or embryo; capable of differentiation. [L totus entire, and **potent¹**]
■ **tōtipo'tency** n.

totitive /tot'i-tiv/ n a number less than another and prime to it. [L tot so many]

toto caelo /tō'tō sē', kī'lō/ (L) literally, by the whole heavens; diametrically opposed.

to-torne see **to-tear**.

totter¹ /tot'ər/ vi to stand or walk unsteadily; to sway; to waver; to rock; to threaten to fall; to reel; to be on the verge of ruin. ◆n a tottering movement. [Cf Norw dialect tutra, totra to quiver, Swed dialect tuttra]
■ **tott'erer** n. **tott'ering** n and adj. **tott'eringly** adv. **tott'ery** adj shaky.

totter² see under **tot³**.

tottered /tot'ərd/ adj a variant of **tattered** (Shakesp); later (from association with **totter¹**) ruinous.
■ **tott'ring** adj (Shakesp) hanging in rags.

tottie see under **tot¹**.

totting see under **tot²,³**.

totty¹ /tot'i/ adj unsteady; dazed; tipsy. [Cf **totter**]

totty² see under **tot¹**.

toucan /too'kən, -kan, -kän/ n any of various large tropical American fruit-eating birds of the family Rhamphastidae, with large brightly-coloured beaks. [Fr, from Tupí tucana]
■ **tou'canet** n a smaller kind of toucan.
□ **toucan crossing** n a form of road crossing with sensors that detect the approach of cyclists and pedestrians.

touch /tuch/ vt to come or be in contact with; to cause to be in contact; to feel or tap lightly, esp with the hand; to get at; to reach as far as; to attain; to equal, rival or compare with; to make a light application to; to begin to eat, eat a little of; to make use of; to affect, esp injuriously; to hit, wound or injure; to disturb or harm (usu with neg); to cope or deal with; to impress; to affect with emotion, esp pity; to have to do with; to concern; to strike home to; to mark or modify by light strokes; to tinge; to extract money from (with for; inf); to make some reference to, say something about esp in passing; to meet without cutting, or meet tangentially (geom); to play (eg an instrument or melody) (music); to call at (eg a port); to cause to touch the ground behind the try-line (commonly with down; rugby); to test as with a touchstone; to receive, draw, pocket; to bribe (obs); to cheat (sl). ◆ vi to be or come in contact; to make a passing call at a port; to verge; to make some mention or reference (with on or upon); to have reference. ◆n the sense by which nature, texture and quality of objects can be perceived through physical contact with the hands, feet, skin, lips, etc; the particular texture and qualities as perceived through such contact; an act of touching or the sense of being touched; a feeling; a slight application, modification, stroke; a small quantity; a slight attack of illness; a tinge; a trace; a smack; ability, skill; a trait; a little; a slight hit, wound, blemish or reproach; the manner or nicety of producing tone on (now esp) a keyed instrument; the instrument's response; a characteristic manner, style or trait; a stroke of art; the relation of communication, sympathy, harmony; communication, contact; a game in which one has to pursue and touch others; the area outside the field of play (football, etc); a test, eg with a touchstone; a touchstone; a black marble or similar monumental stone (obs); an official stamp of fineness on gold, etc; fineness; stamp (fig); theft (sl); a sum got by theft or by touching (sl); a person from whom money can be obtained by touching (sl); that which will find buyers at such and such a price (sl). [OFr tuchier (Fr toucher); origin doubtful]
■ **touch'able** adj capable of being touched; fit to be touched. **touch'ableness** n. **touched** adj having been touched; affected with emotion, esp pity; slightly unsound mentally. **touch'er** n. **touch'ily** adv. **touch'iness** n. **touch'ing** n. ◆adj affecting; moving; pathetic. ◆prep concerning. **touch'ingly** adv. **touch'ingness** n. **touch'less** adj without a sense of touch; intangible; not involving physical contact. **touch'y** adj (**touch'ier**; **touch'iest**) over-sensitive; irascible; risky, requiring careful handling or caution (esp US).
□ **touch and go** n a narrow escape; a critical or precariously balanced situation. ◆adj precarious; off-hand. **touch'back** n (American football) a play in which the ball is dead on or behind a team's own goal line, having been put across the line by an opponent but actually put down by a member of that team. **touch'-box** n a tinderbox for a matchlock. **touch'down** n touching of the ball to the ground by a player behind the try-line (rugby); the possession of the ball by a player behind the opponents' goal line (American football); (of air- or spacecraft) the act of alighting. **touch football** n football in which tackling is replaced by touching. **touch hole** n the small hole of a cannon through which the fire is communicated to the charge. **touch'-in-goal** n (rugby) the areas at each end of the pitch behind the try-lines and outside the touchlines. **touch judge** n (rugby) an official who marks when and where the ball goes into touch. **touch'line** n either of the lines marking the side boundary in football, etc. **touch mark** n the maker's official stamp on pewter. **touch'-me-not** n any of various plants of the genus Impatiens, having seed-pods which, when ripe, spring open at a touch; lupus; a forbidden topic. ◆adj stand-offish. **touch-me-not'ishness** n. **touchpad** n (comput) a small portable input device, operated by touching different areas on its surface (also **trackpad**). **touch'paper** n paper steeped in saltpetre for firing gunpowder, fireworks, etc. **touch'-piece** n a coin or medal formerly given by a king to those he touched for king's evil. **touch'-plate** n a plate bearing the pewterers' official stamp. **touch rugby** or **rugger** n a modified form of rugby in which touching takes the place of tackling. **touch screen** n (comput) a screen that doubles as an input device, and is operated by being touched. **touch'-screen** adj. **touch'stone** n Lydian stone, a highly siliceous (usu black) stone or other stone for testing gold or silver by the colour of the mark each makes on it; any criterion. **touch therapy** n a therapy, such as massage, laying-on of hands, reflexology or aromatherapy, involving physical contact. **touch'tone** adj (of telephones) having push buttons (rather than a dial) that cause distinct tones to sound at the exchange. ◆n (**Touchtone**®) telephone equipment using this system. **touch'-type** vt and vi to type without looking at the keys of the typewriter. **touch'-typing** n. **touch'-typist** n. **touch'-up** n the act or process of renovating or making minor improvements; an instance of this. **touch'wood** n decayed wood that can be used as tinder. **touchy-feel'y** adj (inf) involving emotion and personal contact as distinct from intellectual activity.
■ **an easy** (or **a soft**) **touch** (inf) a person or institution easily persuaded, esp to lend money. **in** (or **out of**) **touch** in (or out of) communication or direct relations. **near touch** a close shave. **touch base** (**with**) (chiefly N Am inf) to make personal contact with. **touch down** (of an air or spacecraft) to land; to ground the ball behind the opposing team's goal line (rugby). **touch off** to trigger, to cause to begin (also fig). **touch up** to improve by a series of small touches; to stimulate (eg a horse) by a light blow; to caress, touch or molest sexually. **touch wood** or (N Am) **knock on wood** or **knock wood** to touch something wooden as a superstitious act to guard against bad luck (also used as an interjection to accompany the gesture or as a substitute for it).

touché /too'shā, too-shā'/ interj claiming or acknowledging a hit in fencing, or a point scored in argument, etc. [Fr, touched, scored against]

tough /tuf/ adj stiff and dense; tenacious; hard to cut, chew, break up or penetrate; resistant; viscous, sticky; capable of or requiring strenuous effort and endurance; unyielding, resolute; intractable; robust; laborious; refractory; criminal, violent; unlucky, unfortunate (inf). ◆n a rough or aggressive person, esp a criminal or hooligan (also **tough guy**). ◆interj (inf) tough luck. ◆adv (inf) violently, aggressively. [OE tōh]
■ **tough'en** vt or vi to make or become tough. **tough'ener** n. **tough'ening** n and adj. **tough'ie** n (inf) a tough person, difficult or intractable problem, etc. **tough'ish** adj rather tough. **tough'ly** adv. **tough'ness** n.
□ **tough love** n the practice of keeping a loved one who has an addiction on a strict regime of abstinence while at the same time showing them love, care, sympathy, etc. **tough luck** see under **luck**. **tough-mind'ed** adj hard-headed, determined, not influenced by sentiment, etc. **tough-mind'edness** n.
■ **get tough with** (inf) to deal with (more) severely, sternly. **tough out** or **tough it out** (inf) to withstand; to endure stoically or defiantly.

touk see **tuck²**.

toun /toon/ n a Scots spelling of **town**.

toupee /too-pē', -pā', too'/, also **toupet** /too-pā', too'pā/ n a wig or hairpiece worn to disguise baldness; a wig with a topknot (hist). [Fr toupet]
■ **toupeed'** or (/too'/) adj wearing a toupee.

tour /toor/ n a round; a prolonged journey from place to place, eg for pleasure, or to give entertainment as a performer, or to give lectures, play matches, etc; a pleasure trip or outing; a shift or turn of work; a period of military or diplomatic service in a particular place (also **tour of duty**); a border of false hair (hist). ◆vi to make a tour, go on tour. ◆vt to make a tour through or of; to tour with (a play, etc). [Fr; see **turn**]

■ **tour'er** *n* a touring car; a tourist. **tour'ing** *n* and *adj*. **tour'ism** *n* the activities of tourists and those who cater for them, *esp* when regarded as an industry. **tour'ist** *n* a person who travels for pleasure, *esp* a sightseeing traveller; a member of a sports team travelling *usu* abroad to play a series of matches. **touris'tic** *adj*. **touris'tically** *adv*. **tour'isty** *adj* (*derog*) designed for, or full of, tourists.

□ **touring car** *n* a large motor car, with ample room for passengers and luggage. **tourist class** *n* the cheapest class of accommodation on a boat or aeroplane. **tourist information office** *n* a place where tourists can obtain information about local places of interest, accommodation, etc. **tourist route** *n* a route that avoids motorways and main roads and takes tourists to places of interest. **Tourist Trophy** *n* the prize awarded to the winner of an annual motorcycle race on the Isle of Man. **tour operator** *n* a person or firm organizing (*esp* package-tour) holidays.

■ **Grand Tour** a journey through W Europe, once fashionable as completing a youth's education.

touraco same as **turaco**.

tourbillion /toor-bil'yən/ or **tourbillon** /toor-bē-yɔ̃'/ *n* a swirl; a vortex; a whirlwind; a whirling firework; a whirling or revolving mechanism or system. [Fr *tourbillon* whirlwind, from L *turbō*, *-inis*]

tour de force /toor də förs'/ (Fr) *n* (*pl* **tours de force**) a feat of strength or skill; an outstanding effort or performance.

tour d'horizon /toor dor-ē-zɔ̃'/ (Fr) *n* (*pl* **tours d'horizon**) a general survey, review.

Tourette's syndrome /tū-rets' sin'drōm/ (*med*) *n* a disorder characterized by a variety of facial tics, muscular jerks and involuntary behaviour, sometimes involving compulsive imitation of others and use of offensive language (also **Tourette syndrome**). [Gilles de la *Tourette* (1857–1904), French physician]

tourie see **toorie**.

tourism, tourist, etc see under **tour**.

tourmaline /toor'mə-lēn/ *n* a beautiful mineral of complex and varying composition, *usu* black (schorl) or blackish, strongly pyro-electric and pleochroic. [Fr, from Sinhalese *tòramalli* carnelian]

tournament /tūr', tör', toor'nə-mənt/ *n* a series of games to determine a winner or winning team by elimination; a military and athletic display; a military sport of the Middle Ages in which combatants engaged mainly on horseback, either in troops or singly (as in jousts), with spear and sword. [OFr *tournoiement*, from *torner*, from L *tornāre* to turn]

tournedos /toor'nə-dō/ *n* (*pl* **tour'nedos** /-dōz/) a small round thick beef fillet. [Fr]

tourney /toor', tûr', tör'ni/ *n* a medieval tournament; a modern sporting tournament (chiefly *N Am*). ◆ *vi* to take part in a tournament. [OFr *tornoi*, from *torner*, from L *tornāre* to turn]

■ **tour'neyer** *n*.

tourniquet /tör' or toor'ni-ket, -kā/ *n* any appliance for compressing an artery to stop bleeding; a turnstile (*rare*). [Fr, from L *tornāre* to turn]

tournure /toor-nür'/ *n* contour, the characteristic turn of line; a bustle or pad worn at the waist. [Fr]

touse, touze, towse or **towze** /towz/ *vt* to haul, to pull about; to dishevel, rumple, tumble; to worry; to rack (*obs*); to tease out (*obs*). ◆ *vi* to touse each other; to be toused; to tussle; to rummage. ◆ *n* a tousing. [Prob from a lost OE word answering to Ger *zausen*]

■ **tous'er** or **tows'er** *n* someone who touses; (with *cap*) a common name for a big dog. **tous'ing** *n* and *adj*. **tousle** or **touzle** /towz'l or (*Scot*) *tooz'l*/ *vt* to disarrange, to tumble; to dishevel. ◆ *vi* to tussle; to touse things. ◆ *n* a tousled mass. **tous'led** *adj* tangled, dishevelled. **tousy, touzy, towsy** or **towzy** /towz'i or (*Scot*) *tooz'i*/ *adj* shaggy, unkempt, tousled; rough.

□ **tousy tea** *n* (*Scot*) high tea.

tous-les-mois /too-lā-mwä'/ *n* a West Indian plant (*Canna edulis*) with bright-red flowers, cultivated for the edible starch of its rhizome; its rhizome. [Fr, every month, but perh really from a native name]

toustie /too'sti/ (Walter Scott) *adj* irascible. [Perh a mixture of **testy** and **tout²**]

tout¹ /towt/ *vi* to solicit for custom in an obtrusive, aggressive or brazen way; to spy on racehorses in training. ◆ *vt* to watch or spy on; to advertise, praise or recommend strongly. ◆ *n* a person who touts; someone who hangs about racing-stables, etc, to pick up profitable information; someone who buys up numbers of tickets for a popular sporting event, etc and sells them at a large profit (also **ticket tout**). [Appar related to **toot¹**]

■ **tout'er** *n*.

tout² or **towt** /towt/ (Scot) *vi* to pout. ◆ *n* a pet, a fit of the sulks; a sudden illness.

■ **tout'ie** *adj* petulant.

tout³ /too/ (Fr) *adj* all; every; whole. ◆ *adv* quite; entirely.

tout à fait /too ta fe'/ entirely; wholly. **tout au contraire** /too tō kɔ̃-trer'/ quite the contrary. **tout à vous** /too ta voo'/ wholly yours; yours truly. **tout court** /koor'/ quite brief(ly), without preface, simply. **tout de même** /da mem'/ all the same; nevertheless. **tout de suite** /toot swēt', tood/ at once, immediately. **tout ensemble** see under **ensemble**. **tout le monde** /lə mɔ̃d'/ all the world, everybody.

tout⁴ see **toot¹**.

touze, touzle see **touse**.

tovarish /to-vä'rish/ *n* comrade (also **tova'risch** or **tova'rich**). [Russ *tovarishch*]

tow¹ /tō or (*Scot*) *tow*/ *vt* to pull (eg another car, caravan, etc) behind one with a rope or cable; to pull along. ◆ *vi* to proceed by being towed. ◆ *n* the condition of being towed; an act of towing; a tow rope; that which is towed; a rope, *esp* a bell-rope or a hangman's rope (*Scot*). [OE *togian* to drag]

■ **tow'able** *adj*. **tow'age** *n* an act of towing; the condition of being towed; a fee for towing. **tow'er** *n*. **tow'ing** *n* and *adj*.

□ **tow bar** *n* a metal bar or frame used for towing trailers, etc. **tow boat** *n* a tug. **tow'ing-bitts** *n pl* upright timbers projecting above eg a ship's deck for fastening towlines to. **tow'-iron** *n* a toggle iron used in whaling. **tow'line, tow rope** or **towing rope** *n* a line, rope or cable used in towing. **tow net** or **towing net** *n* a dragnet for collecting specimens, objects of natural history, etc. **tow'path** or **towing path** *n* a path beside a canal or river for horses towing barges. **tow'plane** *n* an aircraft that tows gliders. **tow truck** *n* (*N Am*) a breakdown truck, *esp* one able to tow another vehicle.

■ **have** (or **take**) **in tow** to tow (another vehicle, vessel, etc); to take along with one, to be accompanied by; to have or assume charge of. **on tow** (of vehicles) or **under tow** (of vessels) being towed.

tow² /tō/ *n* prepared fibres of flax, hemp or jute; *esp* separated shorter fibres; fibres of synthetic fabric, eg rayon. ◆ *adj* of or like tow. [OE *tow-* (in compounds), related to ON *tō* wool]

■ **tow'y** *adj*.

□ **tow'-coloured** *adj* (of hair) very fair, flax-coloured. **tow'-head** *n* a person with light-coloured or tousled hair. **tow'-headed** *adj*.

toward /tə-wörd', twörd, törd/ *prep* towards. ◆ *adv* in the direction facing one, inward. ◆ *adj* (*archaic*) or (*dialect*) approaching; at hand; impending; getting on; on hand; favourable; well-disposed; apt; ready to do or learn; on the left or near side. [OE *tōweard*, adj, adv, prep, from *tō* to, and sfx *-ward*]

■ **toward'liness** *n*. **toward'ly** *adj* (*archaic*) favourable; promising; well-disposed; tractable. ◆ *adv* (*archaic*) in a favourable or promising manner. **toward'ness** *n*. **towards** /tə-wördz', tū-wördz', twördz, tördz, tördz/ *prep* in the direction of; in relation or regard to; with a tendency to; for, as a help or contribution, to; near, a little short of.

towel /tow'əl or towl/ *n* a piece of absorbent cloth or paper for drying the body; a tea towel; a sanitary towel; formerly, a cloth for various purposes, eg a table-napkin, an altar-cloth. ◆ *vt* (**tow'elling** or (*N Am*) **tow'eling; tow'elled** or (*N Am*) **tow'eled**) to dry or rub (eg oneself) with a towel; to cudgel (*obs sl*); to thrash (*sl*). [OFr *toaille*, from Gmc; cf OHGer *dwahila*, from *dwahan*, *twahan*, OE *thwēan* to wash]

■ **tow'elling** *n* a rubbing with a towel; an absorbent fabric used for towels, bathrobes, etc; a thrashing (*sl*).

□ **tow'el-gourd** *n* the loofah. **tow'elhead** *n* (*sl*, *usu derog*) a person who wears a turban or headcloth. **tow'el-horse, tow'el-rack** or **tow'el-rail** *n* a frame or rail for hanging towels on.

■ **a lead towel** (*obs sl*) a bullet. **an oaken towel** (*obs sl*) a cudgel. **throw in the towel** see under **throw¹**.

tower /towr, tow'ər/ *n* a tall building, standing alone or forming part of another, eg a church; a fortress, castle, with or consisting of a tower; a place of defence or retreat; a medieval war machine consisting of a tall movable structure, which allowed access to a castle's ramparts from outside (*hist*); a control tower; a floor-standing unit housing a computer (*comput*); (*esp* in the 17c) a woman's high headdress; the high flight of a bird. ◆ *vi* to rise into the air (above); to be or stand very high or tall; to be superior; (of eg a hawk) to soar up high so as to swoop on quarry. ◆ *vt* (Milton) to rise aloft into. [OFr *tur*, from L *turris* a tower]

■ **tow'ered** *adj*. **tow'ering** *adj* very tall, elevated; (eg of anger, rage) very violent or intense. **tow'eringly** *adv*. **tow'erless** *adj*. **tow'ery** *adj* having towers; very tall.

□ **tower block** *n* a tall building containing offices or residential flats. **tower captain** *n* the leader of a group of bellringers. **tower mill** see **smock mill** under **smock**. **tow'er-shell** *n* a gastropod (genus *Turritella*) with an elongated many-whorled spiral shell, or its shell.

■ **tower of strength** a stable, reliable person. **tower over** to be considerably taller than; to be markedly superior to.

towhee /tow'hē, tō'hē/ *n* any of various N American buntings of the genera *Pipilo* and *Chlorura*, including the chewink. [Imit]

towmont, towmond or **towmon** /tow'mən(t), -ən(d)/ (*Scot* and *N Eng*) *n* forms of **twelvemonth**.

■ words derived from main entry word; □ compound words; ■ idioms and phrasal verbs

town /town/ n an urban area bigger or less rural than a village, with some level of local government and defined boundaries; the principal town of a district, esp (in SE England) London; an urban community; the permanent residents of a town, esp as opposed to the members of its university; the business or shopping centre; urban communities generically; a municipal or political division of a county (which may include villages and towns in the ordinary sense), a township (N Am); orig, an enclosure (obs); /tŭn/ a farmstead or similar group of houses (Scot). ◆ adj of a town; urban. [OE tūn an enclosure, town; ON tūn enclosure, Ger Zaun hedge]
■ **townee'** or **tow'nie** n (often derog) an inhabitant of a town, not a member of the university or a country-dweller. **town'ish** adj characteristic of town as opposed to country. **town'less** adj. **town'ling** n a town dweller. **town'ly** adj townish. **town'ship** n an urban settlement inhabited by poor black people (S Afr); a subdivision of a county or province (N Am); an administrative district (N Am); a thirty-six square mile block of public land (N Am); a site for a town (Aust); a small settlement (Aust); the territory or district of a town; the corporation of a town; a village, a community or local division; a parish (hist); a farm in joint tenancy (Scot); the people living in a township. **town'y** n an inhabitant of a town; a fellow inhabitant. ◆ adj townish.
❑ **town clerk** n (in Britain until 1974) the secretary and legal adviser of a town; the official responsible for town records (US). **town council** n the elected governing body in a town. **town councillor** n. **town crier** n (hist) an official who makes public proclamations in a town. **town dweller** n. **town end** n the end of the main street. **town (or towns) gas** n usu a mixture of coal gas and carburetted water gas, made and supplied for domestic or industrial use (now largely superseded by natural gas). **town hall** n a building for the official business of a town, usu with public rooms; a townhouse. **town'house** n (chiefly Scot) a town hall. **town house** n a house in town belonging to the owner of another in the country; a fashionable, usu terraced urban house, esp typically with a garage on the ground floor and living room above. **town'land** n (chiefly hist) the land forming a manor; (in Ireland) a sub-parochial land division, or a township; (in Scotland) the enclosure round a farm. **town meeting** n (in New England) a meeting of the voters of a town, esp to transact public business. **town planner** n. **town planning** n the deliberate designing of the building and growth of towns to avoid haphazard and speculative building. **town's'-bairn** n (Scot) a native of a town, esp one's own. **town'scape** n a portion of a town which the eye can view at once; a picture of it; the design or building of all or part of a town◆ vt and vi to design or build a town or part of a town. **town'scaping** n. **towns'folk** n pl the people of a town. **town'skip** n (Dickens) a city urchin. **towns'man** or **towns'woman** n an inhabitant or fellow inhabitant of a town. **towns'people** n pl townsfolk. **town talk** n the general talk of a town; the subject of common conversation.
■ **go to town** (inf) to act, behave or perform enthusiastically, with thoroughness, without restraint. **on the town** out to amuse oneself in town. **take to town** (sl) to mystify. **town and gown** the general community of a place and the members of its university respectively.

to-worne /tə-wörn', -wörn'/ adj (Spenser) worn-out. [Pfx to-, intens, and **worn**]

tow-rag a mistaken spelling of **toerag**.

towse, **towsy** see **touse**.

towt see **tout²**.

towy see under **tow²**.

towze, **towzy** see **touse**.

tox- /toks-/, **toxi-** /tok-si-/, **toxico-** /tok-si-kō-/, or **toxo-** /tok-sō-, tok-sə- or tok-so-/ combining form denoting poison, poisonous. [Gr toxikon (pharmakon) (poison) for the bow, from toxon bow]

toxaemia or (N Am) **toxemia** /tok-sē'mi-ə/ n blood poisoning; a condition in late pregnancy characterized by a sudden rise in blood pressure. [**tox-** and Gr haima blood]
■ **toxaem'ic** or (N Am) **toxe'mic** adj.

toxaphene /tok'sə-fēn/ (chem) n chlorinated camphene used as an insecticide. [**tox-** and camphene]

toxic /tok'sik/ adj of poison; poisonous; poisoned; caused by poison; damaging (inf); (of a financial asset) liable to cause a loss. [Gr toxon a bow, toxikos for the bow, toxikon arrow-poison]
■ **tox'ical** adj. **tox'ically** adv. **tox'icant** adj poisonous. ◆ n a poisonous substance. **toxicā'tion** or **toxicity** /-is'-/ n the state of being toxic; the degree to which a substance is toxic. **toxicolog'ic** or **toxicolog'ical** adj. **toxicolog'ically** adv. **toxicol'ogist** n. **toxicol'ogy** n the science or study of poisons and their antidotes.
❑ **toxic bank** same as **bad bank** (see under **bad**). **toxic shock syndrome** n a potentially fatal condition characterized by high fever, vomiting, and diarrhoea, sometimes occurring in menstruating women using tampons, and attributed to a toxin apparently associated with staphylococcal infection.

toxicogenic /tok-si-kō-jen'ik/ adj producing toxic substances and poisons; caused by a toxin. [**toxico-**, and Gr -genēs born]

toxicogenomics /tok-si-kō-ji-nō'miks/ or **toxicogenetics** /-ji-net'iks/ n sing the study of the effect of an individual's genetic constitution on the body's response to toxins. [**toxico-** and **gene**]

toxicomania /tok-si-kō-mā'ni-ə/ n a morbid craving for poisons. [**toxico-**, and **mania**]

toxicophagous /tok-si-kof'ə-gəs/ or **toxiphagous** /tok-sif'ə-gəs/ adj poison-eating. [**toxico-**, and Gr phagein to eat]

toxicophobia /tok-si-kō-fō'bi-ə/ or **toxiphobia** /tok-si-fō'bi-ə/ n morbid fear of poisoning. [**toxico-**, and Gr phobein to fear]
■ **toxiphō'biac** n and adj.

toxin /tok'sin/ n a ptomaine; a specific poison of organic origin, esp one stimulating the production of antibodies. [toxic and **-in**]

toxocara /tok-sə-kä'rə/ n any of various parasitic worms found in the intestines of dogs and cats and known to cause disease (**toxocarī'asis**) and eye damage in humans. [**toxo-**, and Gr kara head]
■ **toxocar'al** adj.

toxoid /tok'soid/ n a toxin that has been treated to remove its toxic properties without destroying its ability to stimulate production of antibodies. [toxin and **-oid**]

toxophilite /tok-sof'i-līt/ n a lover of archery; an archer. ◆ adj of or relating to archery. [Gr toxon a bow, and phileein to love]
■ **toxophilit'ic** adj. **toxoph'ily** n love of archery; archery.

toxoplasmosis /tok-sō-plaz-mō'sis/ n an infection of animals (esp the domestic cat) and humans by microorganisms, prob protozoa, of the genus Toxoplasma, causing eg spontaneous abortion in pregnant women. [**toxo-**, and **plasma**]
■ **toxoplas'mic** adj.

toy /toi/ n a plaything, esp for a child; a trifle; anything, esp a gadget, intended or thought of as for amusement, appearances or pleasure rather than practical use; a matter of no importance or thing of little value; a dwarf breed; a jest, idle tale (archaic); a trivial dance tune, or the like (archaic); a whim, crotchet; an old woman's cap with side flaps (Scot); amorous sport (archaic). ◆ adj made in imitation of something else as a plaything; of, for or being a dwarf breed. ◆ vi (usu with with) to play with in an idle way and without really being interested; to sport; to flirt or amuse oneself amorously (with). [Poss Du tuig tools; Ger Zeug stuff]
■ **toy'er** n. **toy'ing** n and adj. **toy'ish** adj given to toying or trifling; playful; wanton (obs). **toy'ishly** adv. **toy'ishness** n. **toy'less** adj. **toy'like** adj. **toy'some** adj sportive; playful; whimsical; disposed to toy; wanton (obs).
❑ **toy boy** n (sometimes derog) the young male lover of a much older woman. **toy dog** n a very small pet dog. **toy'man** or fem **toy'woman** n a seller of toys. **toy'shop** n a shop where toys are sold. **toy soldier** n a miniature model of a soldier; a soldier (derog sl).
■ **throw one's toys out of the pram** (sl) to have a tantrum.

toylsom, **toylesome** see **toilsome** under **toil¹**.

toyon /toi'on/ n a large evergreen shrub or tree of the rose family, with white flowers and red berries. [Mex Sp tollon]

toze or **tose** (Shakesp **toaze**) /tōz/ vt to tease out, card, comb; to draw out, elicit. [ME tosen, related to **tease**]

tozie /tō'zi/ (Walter Scott) n a shawl made from a goat's inner coat.

tp abbrev : township; troop.

t-pa abbrev : tissue plasminogen activator (see under **tissue**).

TPI abbrev : tax and prices index.

TPIM /tē'pim/ abbrev : Terrorism Prevention and Investigation Measure.

TPN abbrev : total parenteral nutrition.

Tpr abbrev : Trooper.

tpr abbrev : teleprinter.

TPWS abbrev : Train Protection and Warning System.

TQM abbrev : total quality management.

TR abbrev : Turkey (IVR).

tr. abbrev : transactions; transitive; translator; transpose; trustee.

tra- /tra-/ pfx signifying : across; beyond; through. [Ety as for **trans-**]

trabeate /trab'i-, trā'bi-āt/ or **trabeated** /-tid/ (archit) adj built of horizontal beams, not arches and vaults. [L trabs, trabis beam]
■ **trabeā'tion** n an entablature; a combination of beams in a structure.

trabecula /trə-bek'ū-lə/ (anat and bot) n (pl **trabec'ūlae** /-lē/) a cell, row of cells, band, or rodlike structure running across a cavity or forming an internal support to an organ. [L, dimin of trabs, trabis beam]
■ **trabec'ūlar**, **trabec'ūlate** or **trabec'ūlated** adj having trabeculae; transversely barred.

tracasserie /tra-kas(-ə)-rē/ (Fr) n turmoil.

trace[1] /trās/ n an indication, mark of what is or has been; a vestige; a small quantity that can just be detected; a track; a footprint; a beaten path (US); a tracing; a line marked by a recording instrument; a line or lines on the screen of a cathode-ray tube forming the display; a way of checking the logic of a program by causing the variables, etc to be printed out during execution (comput); a mental or neural change caused by learning; an amount of rain- or snowfall that is too small to be measured; an intersection with or projection on a surface; a way, course (Spenser); the ground-plan of a work (fortif). ◆ vt to track; to follow step by step; to detect; to discover the whereabouts of; to follow or mark the outline of (eg a design), esp mechanically or on a translucent paper; to outline, delineate, plan or write; to follow to its origins or source (usu with back); to produce as tracery; to cover with tracery; to take one's way along or through (eg a path), traverse. ◆ vi to be traceable or datable (usu with back); to proceed (archaic); to walk (archaic); to move (archaic); to tread a measure (obs). [Fr trace, from L tractus, pap of trahere to draw]

■ **traceabil'ity** n. **trace'able** adj that may be traced. **trace'ableness** n. **trace'ably** adv. **trace'less** adj. **trace'lessly** adv. **trā'cer** n a person who traces; an instrument for tracing; a probe for tracing a nerve, etc; a device by which a projectile leaves a detectable trail, usu of smoke; a projectile equipped with this; (also **tracer element**) a radioactive isotope introduced into the body to study physiological, etc processes by tracking the radiation it produces. **trā'ceried** adj. **trā'cery** n an ornamental, fine, decorative pattern; ornamental openwork in Gothic architecture, esp in the upper part of windows. **trā'cing** n the act of someone who traces; a drawing copied mechanically or on translucent paper laid over the original; an instrumental record.

❑ **trace element** n a micronutrient, a substance (such as zinc, copper, molybdenum, etc) whose presence in the soil or food in minute quantities is necessary for plant and animal growth. **trace fossil** n the fossilized tracks, burrows, etc of an organism (but not the organism itself). **tracer bullet** n. **tracer shell** n. **tracing paper** n translucent paper for tracing on.

trace[2] /trās/ n (usu in pl) a rope, chain or strap attached to an animal's collar or breast-strap for drawing a vehicle; a bar for transmitting motion; the vascular tissue branching from the cylinder to pass into a leaf or branch (bot); a short piece of wire, gut or nylon connecting the hook to the fishing-line (angling). ◆ vt to harness in traces. [OFr trays, trais, pl of trait draught; cf **trait**]

■ **trā'cer** n a trace-horse; a person (orig a boy) who tends a trace-horse.
❑ **trace'-horse** n a horse that pulls a vehicle using traces.
■ **kick over the traces** see under **kick**.

traceur /tra-sœr/ (Fr) n a person who participates in free running (qv under **free**). [Literally, tracer]

trachea /trə-kē'ə, trā'/ n (pl **trachē'ae** /-ē/) a passage strengthened by cartilaginous rings that carries air from the larynx to the bronchi, the windpipe; the air-tube in air-breathing arthropods; a conducting tube in xylem (bot). [Med L trāchēa for L trāchīa, from Gr trācheia (artēriā) rough (artery)]

■ **trachē'al** adj. **Trāchea'ria** n pl usu small arachnids such as mites and ticks, with tracheae, but no lung-books. **trāchea'rian** n and adj. **trā'cheary** adj breathing through tracheae (zool); relating to tracheae or tracheids (bot). ◆ n a tracheary animal. **Trāchea'ta** n pl arthropods with tracheae. **trā'cheate** or **trā'cheated** adj having a trachea. **tracheid** or **tracheide** /trə-kē'īd, -id, trak'i-/ n a long tubelike but closed cell in xylem. **tracheitis** /trak-i-ī'tis/ n inflammation of the trachea. **trachī'tis** n a non-standard form of **tracheitis**.

trachelate /trak'ə-lāt/ adj having a neck. [Gr trachēlos neck]

tracheo- /trak-i-ō- or trak-i-o-/ combining form denoting the trachea. [Ety as for **trachea**]
■ **tra'cheophyte** n (bot) a plant with a vascular system of xylem and phloem. **tracheos'copy** n inspection of the trachea. **tracheos'tomy** n surgical formation of a temporary or permanent opening into the trachea. **tracheot'omy** n an incision into the trachea, usu to relieve an obstruction.

trachinus /tra-kī'nəs/ n a member of the weever genus of fishes Trachinus, giving name to the family **Trachinidae** /-kin'i-dē/. [LL trachina, said to be a local name of a fish]

trachitis see under **trachea**.

trachoma /tra-kō'mə/ n a contagious disease of the eye, characterized by hard pustules on the inner surface of the eyelids. [Gr trāchōma]
■ **trachomatous** /-kom'ə-təs, -kō'mə-təs/ adj.

trachypterus /tra-kip'tə-rəs/ n a member of the dealfish genus Trachypterus, giving name to the ribbonfish family **Trachypteridae** /-ter'i-dē/. [Gr trāchys rough, and pteron fin]

trachyte /trak'īt/ n a fine-grained intermediate igneous rock, usu with little or no quartz, consisting largely of alkali-feldspars (eg sanidine)

and a small amount of coloured silicates (eg hornblende or mica). [Gr trāchys rough]
■ **trachytic** /trə-kit'ik/ adj. **trach'ytoid** adj.

tracing see under **trace**[1].

track[1] /trak/ n a mark or trail left; a beaten path or road; a made path; a sequence or course of thoughts or actions; the predetermined line of travel of an aircraft; a line of motion or travel; a course, usu oval-shaped, on which races are run; a railway line, the rails and the space between; the groove cut in a gramophone record by the recording instrument; one out of several items recorded on a disc or tape; one of several areas or paths on magnetic recording equipment (eg magnetic tape) receiving information from a single input channel; a film's soundtrack; any of several more or less demanding courses of study designed to meet the respective needs of students divided into groups according to ability (US); a plastic or metal rod from which curtains, lights, etc can be suspended; the endless band on which the wheels of a caterpillar vehicle run (**tracked** adj equipped with such metal bands); (in a factory, etc) a conveyor carrying goods in process of manufacture; track and field events collectively (N Am); the distance between a pair of wheels measured as the distance between their respective points of contact with the ground; a path followed by a particle, esp when rendered visible in photographic emulsion by cloud chamber, bubble chamber or spark chamber; (usu in pl) a red mark on the skin caused by using intravenous drugs (sl). ◆ vt to follow the track of; to find by so doing; to traverse; to beat, tread (a path, etc); to follow the progress of; to follow the movement of (a satellite, spacecraft, etc) by radar, etc, and record its positions; (of a stylus or laser beam) to read information from (a vinyl record, CD, etc); to follow or move in relation to (a moving object) while filming it; to leave dirty marks on (a floor) (with on or up; N Am); to make dirty marks on eg a floor with (snow, mud, etc) (N Am). ◆ vi to follow a trail; to make one's way (inf); to run in alignment, esp (of gramophone needles) to follow the grooves; (of a camera or camera operator) to follow or move in relation to a moving object being filmed; to move a dolly camera in a defined path while taking a shot (**tracking shot**). [Fr trac; prob Gmc; cf **track**[2]]

■ **track'able** adj. **track'age** n provision of railway tracks. **track'er** n a person or thing that tracks; an investment fund that aims to follow a stock market index. **track'ie** (inf) adj (of a garment) originally constituting part of a tracksuit. ◆ n (in pl) a tracksuit. **track'ing** n the action of the verb; excessive leakage current between two insulated points due eg to moisture (elec eng); disposition of the tone arm on a gramophone so that the stylus remains correctly positioned in the groove; the addition of prerecorded music to a motion picture instead of using specially-commissioned music; the division of study courses or students into tracks (qv above) (US). **track'less** adj without a path; untrodden; leaving no trace; running without rails. **track'lessly** adv. **track'lessness** n.

❑ **track and field** n athletic events collectively, incl running and hurdling races (**track events**), and jumping and throwing competitions (**field events**). **track'-and-field'** adj. **track'ball** or **track'erball** n (comput) a spherical ball that can be rotated with the palm of the hand causing the cursor to move across the screen. **track'bed** n the foundations of a railway track. **tracker dog** n one used for tracking, esp in police searches. **track event** n see **track and field** above. **tracking station** n a station with radar and radio equipment allowing it to track spacecraft, aircraft and satellites through the atmosphere or space. **track'layer** n a tracklaying vehicle; a trackman (N Am). **track'laying** adj (of a vehicle) having caterpillar tracks. **track'man** n (N Am) a platelayer. **track'pad** n same as **touchpad** (see under **touch**). **track record** n a record of past performance, orig that of an athlete, now generally that of any individual, company, etc. **track rod** n a rod connecting the front wheels of a vehicle, ensuring alignment and accurate steering. **track shoe** n a lightweight spiked running shoe worn by athletes. **track'suit** n a loose warm suit intended to be worn by athletes when warming up or training, but sometimes worn by others in an error of judgement. **track'-walker** n a person who has charge of a railway track. **track'way** n a beaten track; an ancient road.

■ **across the tracks** or **the wrong side of the tracks** (inf) a slum or other socially disadvantaged area. **cover one's tracks** to take measures to prevent discovery of one's actions, motives, etc. **in one's tracks** just where one stands. **keep** (or **lose**) **track of** keep (or fail to keep) oneself informed about. **make tracks** (inf) to make off; to go quickly. **make tracks for** (inf) to go towards. **off the beaten track** away from frequented roads; out of the usual, not normal or conventional (fig). **off the track** off course, in the wrong direction. **on the right** (or **wrong**) **track** pursuing a correct (or mistaken) course. **track down** to find after intensive search.

track[2] /trak/ vt to tow. ◆ vi to travel by towing. [See **trek**]
■ **track'age** n towing. **track'er** n a person who tows; a tug; a pulling part in the action of any organ.

■ words derived from main entry word; ❑ compound words; ■ idioms and phrasal verbs

❑ **track'-boat** *n* a towed boat. **track'road** *n* a towpath. **track'-scout** *n* a trekschuit.

tracklement /*trak'l-mənt*/ (*dialect*) *n* a condiment, accompaniment, etc, to food. [Ety uncertain]

tract¹ /*trakt*/ *n* a stretch or extent of space or time; a region, area; a region of the body occupied by a particular system (eg *the digestive tract*); a trace, track (*Shakesp, Spenser*); (also **tract'us**) a psalm sung in the Mass in Lent instead of the Alleluia (*perh* as drawn out, *perh* as sung at a stretch without answers). ◆ *vt* (*Spenser*) to trace, track. [L *tractus, -ūs* drawing, dragging, from *trahere, tractāre* to draw, pull]

tract² /*trakt*/ *n* a tractate; a pamphlet or leaflet, *esp* political or religious. [ME *tracte*, appar shortening of Med L *tractātus* tractate, from L *tractāre* to handle]
■ **tractā'rian** *n* a writer of tracts, *esp* (with *cap*) of the *Tracts for the Times* (Oxford, 1833–41), namely Pusey, Newman, Keble, Hurrell Froude, etc. ◆ *adj* of or relating to a tractarian or the Tractarian. **Tractār'ianism** *n* the system of religious opinion promulgated in these, its main aim being to assert the authority and dignity of the Anglican Church, the *Oxford Movement*. **tract'ate** *n* a treatise, a tract. **tractā'tor** *n* a tractarian.

tractable /*trak'tə-bl*/ *adj* easily drawn, managed or taught; docile; malleable. [L *tractābilis*, from *tractāre* to draw, handle]
■ **tractabil'ity** or **tract'ableness** *n*. **tract'ably** *adv*.

tractile /*trak'tīl*/ *adj* ductile, capable of being drawn out. [Ety as for **tract¹**]
■ **tractility** /*-il'*/ *n*.

traction /*trak'shən*/ *n* the act of drawing or pulling or state of being drawn or pulled; the pulling on a muscle, organ, etc, by means, eg of weights, to correct an abnormal condition (*med*); the grip of a wheel, tyre, etc on the surface on which it moves; the propulsion of vehicles. [Med L *tractio*, from *tractus*; see also ety for **tract¹**]
■ **trac'tional** *adj*. **tract'ive** *adj* pulling.
❑ **traction engine** *n* a locomotive for hauling heavy loads over roads, fields, etc. **traction load** *n* (*geol*) that part of the solid material carried by a river which is rolled along the river bed. **tractive force** *n* the pull that a locomotive, etc engine is capable of exerting at the drawbar; the force necessary to detach the armature from an excited electromagnet.

tractor /*trak'tər*/ *n* a motor vehicle used for hauling trailers, agricultural implements, etc; the short front section of an articulated lorry, containing the engine and driver's cab; a traction engine; an aircraft with a screw propeller in front; a screw propeller mounted in front on an aircraft; a motorized plough; (in *pl*) bars of different metals which, drawn over diseased parts of the body, were supposed to give relief (*hist*). [LL, that which draws, from *trahere, tractāre* to draw, pull]
■ **tractorā'tion** *n* (*hist*) the use of metal bars to give relief to diseased parts of the body.
❑ **tractor feed** *n* a device for feeding and advancing continuous stationery through the platen of a typewriter, printer, etc by use of a toothed wheel or sprocket and perforation in the paper.

tractrix /*trak'triks*/ (*maths*) *n* (*pl* **tractrices** /*trak-trī'sēz*/) a curve such that the intercept of a tangent by a fixed straight line is constant. [New L, from *trahere, tractāre* to draw, pull]

trad /*trad*/ or **trad jazz** /*jaz*/ *n* a shortened form of *traditional jazz*, a style of early 20c jazz which originated in New Orleans, characterized by improvisation against a regular rhythmical background (also *adj*).

trade /*trād*/ *n* an occupation, way of livelihood, *esp* skilled but not learned; shopkeeping; commerce, *esp* as opposed to a profession; buying and selling; people engaged in a specific occupation, *esp* the liquor trade or the book trade; customers, clientele; commercial customers as opposed to the public in general; business at a particular time or for a particular market; a craft, *esp* requiring training; a deal; commodities, *esp* for barter; a practice; (in *pl*) the trade winds; a track, trail, treading (*Spenser*); a way of traffic; resort (*Shakesp*); a way, a course (*obs*); rubbish (*dialect*); medicine. ◆ *vi* to have dealings (with *with*); to engage in commerce (often with *in*); to deal; to traffic; to buy and sell; to take goods to a place (with *to*); to reckon, count, presume (with *on*), *esp* unscrupulously; to tread, go (*obs*); to resort, *esp* for commerce; to ply; to occupy oneself (*obs*). ◆ *vt* to exchange (*esp* commercially), to barter; to buy and sell; to exchange (eg one thing for another, blows, etc); to tread (*obs*). [Prob LGer *trade* ; related to **tread**]
■ **trade'able** or **trad'able** *adj*. **trād'ed** *adj* (*Shakesp*) versed, practised. **trade'ful** *adj* (*Spenser*) busy in traffic. **trade'less** *adj*. **trād'er** *n* a person who trades; a trading ship; a member of the Stock Exchange trading privately and not for clients (*US*). **trād'ing** *n* and *adj*.
❑ **trade barrier** *n* anything that prevents or hinders international trade, eg tariffs and quotas. **trade board** *n* (*hist*) a council for settling disputes, consisting of representatives of both employers and employees in a trade. **trade'craft** *n* skill or expertise in the practice of a trade, *esp* that of espionage. **trade cycle** *n* the recurring series of conditions in trade from prosperity to depression and back to

prosperity. **trade deficit** see **trade gap** below. **trade discount** *n* a discount offered to others in the same trade; a discount given to professional users or re-sellers of a product. **traded option** *n* (*stock exchange*) an option that can itself be bought and sold. **trade edition** *n* a standard edition of a book rather than a de luxe or bookclub edition. **trade'-fallen** (*Shakesp* **trade'-falne**) *adj* unsuccessful in trade, bankrupt. **trade gap** or **trade deficit** *n* the amount by which a country's visible imports exceed its visible exports in value. **trade'-in** *n* that which is given in part payment. **trade journal** *n* a periodical containing information and comment on a particular trade. **trade-last'** *n* (*old US*) a compliment paid to someone which one offers to tell that person in exchange for a compliment heard about oneself. **trade'mark** or **trade mark** *n* any name or distinctive device warranting goods for sale as the production of any individual or firm; a distinguishing characteristic or feature (*fig*). ◆ *vt* to label with a trademark; to register as a trademark. **trade'marked** *adj*. **trade'name** *n* a name serving as a trademark; a name in use in the trade; the name under which a company trades. **trade'-off** *n* the giving up of one thing in return for another, *usu* as an act of compromise. **trade-off study** *n* (*aeronautics, space technol*) a logical evaluation, during the preliminary design process, of the pros and cons of alternative approaches and/or parameters which leads to the choice of the preferred ones. **trade paper** *n* a trade journal. **trade paperback** *n* a trade edition (qv above) of a paperback book. **trade plate** *n* a temporary number plate attached to a vehicle by dealers, etc prior to its being registered. **trade price** *n* the price at which goods are sold to members of the same trade, or by wholesale to retail dealers. **trade route** *n* a route followed by caravans or trading ships. **trade sale** *n* an auction sale of goods by producers, etc, to persons in the trade. **trade school** *n* a school teaching mainly skilled crafts. **trade secret** *n* a secret and successful formula, process, technique, etc known only to one manufacturer. **trades'folk** *n pl* tradespeople. **trades'man** or **trades'woman** *n* a shopkeeper; a skilled worker; a mechanic. **trades'manlike** *adj*. **trades'people** *n pl* people engaged in trade; shopkeepers; mechanics; skilled workers. **trades union** *n* an association of trade unions, as in the *Trades Union Congress*. **trade union** *n* an organized association of workers of an industry for the protection of their common interests. **trade unionism** *n* the system, principles and practices of trade unions. **trade unionist** *n* a member of a trade union. **trade'-weighted** *adj* (*econ*) (of exchange rates) weighted according to the significance of the trade carried on with the various countries listed. **trade wind** *n* a wind blowing toward the thermal equator and deflected westward by the eastward rotation of the earth. **trading estate** *n* an industrial or commercial estate. **trading post** *n* a store, etc established in an *esp* remote, thinly-populated or hostile area. **trading stamp** *n* a stamp given by the retailer to a purchaser of goods which, when a specified number have been collected, may be exchanged without payment for articles provided by the trading stamp firm.
■ **Board of Trade** see under **board. trade down** or **up** to deal in lower grade, cheaper or higher grade, dearer goods; to buy a smaller (or larger) house, etc than one sells. **trade in** to give in part payment. **trade off** to exchange, *esp* as a compromise. **trade on** to count on or take advantage of, *esp* unscrupulously.

tradescantia /*tra-di-skan'shi-ə* or *-ti-ə*/ *n* any plant of the American *Tradescantia* (spiderwort) genus, with attractive, often variegated foliage. [John *Tradescant* (c.1567–1637), English gardener, naturalist and traveller]

tradition /*trə-dish'ən*/ *n* the, *esp* oral, passing from generation to generation of tales, beliefs, practices, etc; a tale, belief or practice thus handed down; a collection of these belonging to a specific family, people, country, etc; a long-established belief, practice or custom; anything bound up with or continuing in the life of a family, community, etc; religious teaching, doctrine or laws based on (*usu* early) oral tradition, *esp* (often with *cap*) in Christianity, the teaching of Christ and the Apostles not found in Scripture, in Judaism, the laws believed to have been given to Moses by God, and in Islam, the words and deeds of Mohammed; the continuous development of principles, etc of a body of eg literature, music; a handing over (*law*). [L *trāditiō, -ōnis, trāditor, -ōris*, from *trādere* to give up, from *trāns* over, and *dare* to give]
■ **tradi'tional** or (*rare*) **tradi'tionary** *adj*. **tradi'tionalism** *n* (often excessive) adherence to or belief in tradition; the belief that religious knowledge and moral truth are obtained through divine revelation and are handed down and preserved by tradition. **tradi'tionalist** *n* and *adj*. **traditionalis'tic** *adj*. **traditional'ity** *n*. **tradi'tionally** or (*rare*) **tradi'tionarily** *adv*. **tradi'tioner** or **tradi'tionist** *n* a person who adheres to tradition. **tradi'tionless** *adj*. **traditive** /*trad'i-tiv*/ *adj* traditional. **trad'itor** *n* (*pl* **trad'itors** or **traditores** /*-tō'rāz*/) a traitor, betrayer (*obs*); a person who under persecution gave up sacred books or objects or the names of his or her coreligionists, *esp* a Christian under Roman persecution (*hist*).

❑ **traditional Chinese medicine** *n* a system of medicine developed in China, in which good health is seen as the harmonious balance of the yin and yang, achieved through acupuncture, massage, exercise, herbalism, or diet, and through control of the relationships between the five elements, earth, water, fire, metal (or air) and wood, considered to be associated with specific bodily organs (see **ko cycle, sheng cycle, wu cycle**). **traditional jazz** see **trad**. **traditional option** *n* (*stock exchange*) an option which, once purchased, cannot be exchanged.

traduce /trə-dūs'/ or (*US*) -*doos*' / *vt* to calumniate, to malign; to defame; to translate (*obs*); to propagate or transmit (*obs*). [L *trādūcere, trāductum*, from *trāns* across, and *dūcere* to bring]
■ **traduce'ment** *n*. **tradū'cer** *n*. **Tradū'cian** /-*shi-ən*/ *n* and *adj* (a person) believing that children receive a soul as well as or concomitantly with their body from their parents through natural generation. **Tradū'cianism** *n*. **Tradū'cianist** *n*. **Tradūcianis'tic** *adj*. **tradū'cible** *adj*. **tradū'cing** *n* and *adj*. **tradū'cingly** *adv*. **traduction** /-*duk'shən*/ *n*. **traduc'tive** *adj* transmitted.

traffic /traf'ik/ *n* vehicles, pedestrians, etc collectively, using a thoroughfare; similar movement at sea or in the air; the transportation of goods and people on a railway, air or sea route, etc; the goods or people transported along a route; dishonest or illegal trading; commerce, trade; dealings or communication between groups or individuals; a passing to and fro; the volume of messages transmitted through a communications system; a trading voyage (*obs*); commodities (*obs*). ◆ *vi* (**traff'icking; traff'icked**) to trade; to trade, *esp* dishonestly or illegally (with *in*); to intrigue. ◆ *vt* to trade in or barter; to use, pass to and fro on (a highway, etc). [From a Romance language; cf Fr *trafic*, Ital *traffico*, Sp *tráfico*; origin obscure]
■ **traff'icātor** *n* formerly, a movable pointer raised or lowered by the driver of a vehicle to warn of a change of direction. **traff'icker** *n* a dealer in (*esp* illegal) goods. **traff'icking** *n* and *adj*. **traff'icless** *adj*.
❑ **traff'ic-calming** *n* control of vehicular traffic in built-up, *esp* residential, areas by the use of various devices designed to reduce speed and volume, eg sleeping policemen, ramps, etc. **traffic circle** *n* (*N Am*) a road intersection where traffic circulates in one direction only, a roundabout. **traffic cone** *n* a plastic cone used for guiding diverted traffic. **traffic cop** *n* (*inf, esp US*) a policeman supervising road traffic. **traffic island** *n* a raised section in the centre of a road to separate lanes, guide traffic, etc. **traffic jam** *n* congestion, and resultant stoppage, of traffic, eg at a busy junction. **traffic lights** or **traffic signals** *n pl* coloured lights to regulate street traffic, *esp* at intersections. **traffic manager** *n* the manager of the traffic on a railway, etc. **traffic pattern** *n* the disposition of aircraft in the skies around an airport. **traffic police** *n pl* police whose duty is to deal with motoring offences and ensure smooth traffic flow. **traffic returns** *n pl* statistics of passengers and goods carried by a transportation service and money received in return. **traffic warden** *n* an official controlling road traffic, *esp* the parking of vehicles.

tragacanth /trag'ə-kanth/ *n* a gum (also **gum tragacanth**) used in pharmacy and as a vehicle for dye in calico-printing, obtained from several spiny shrubs of the genus *Astragalus*; the plant yielding it. [Gr *tragakantha*, from *tragos* goat, and *akantha* thorn]

tragedy /traj'i-di/ *n* a type of drama dealing with tragic events and often involving the fall of an honourable, worthy and important protagonist, often with elevated action and language; a play of this type; the art of such drama; any piece of literature, music, etc ending with disaster for the protagonist; a disaster, any sad story or turn of events; any event involving death or killing (*press*). [L *tragoedia*, from Gr *tragōidia* tragedy, appar literally goat-song, from *tragos* a he-goat, and *ōidē* song (variously explained)]
■ **tragedian** /trə-jē'di-ən/ *n* a writer or (*usu*) an actor of tragedy. **tragedienne** /trə-jē-di-en'/ or (*Fr*) **tragédienne** /trä-zhā-di-en/ *n* an actress of tragic roles.

tragelaph /trag', traj'i-laf/ *n* a fabulous animal, part goat, part stag; any spiral-horned African antelope of the genus *Tragelaphus*. [Gr *tragelaphos*, from *tragos* a goat, and *elaphos* a deer]
■ **tragel'aphine** *adj*.

tragi see **tragus**.

tragic /traj'ik/, also **tragical** /-i-kl/ *adj* extremely sad or distressing, disastrous; relating to or of the nature of tragedy. [L *tragicos*, from Gr *tragōidiā* tragedy; see ety for **tragedy**]
■ **trag'ically** *adv*. **trag'icalness** *n*.
❑ **tragic flaw** *n* another name for **hamartia**. **tragic hero** or **heroine** *n* the protagonist of a tragedy, classically provoking both pity and fear in the audience. **tragic irony** *n* a form of irony, *orig* in Greek tragedy, in which the tragic, prophetic meaning of the words is known to the audience but not the character speaking.

tragicomedy /tra-ji-kom'i-di/ *n* a play or story in which grave and comic scenes or themes are blended; a comedy that threatens to be a

tragedy; such plays as a genre; any event having both tragic and comic elements. [LL *tragicōmedia*; see etys for **tragedy** and **comedy**]
■ **tragicom'ic** or **tragicom'ical** *adj*. **tragicom'ically** *adv*.

tragopan /trag'ō-pan/ *n* a brilliantly-coloured Asiatic pheasant with horny process on the bill. [Gr *tragopān* hornbill, from *tragos* goat, and *Pān* the god Pan]

tragus /trā'gəs/ *n* (*pl* **trā'gi** /-*jī*/) a small fleshy prominence at the entrance of the external ear; any of the hairs growing in the outer ear, *esp* from this part. [Gr *tragos* goat, tragus]
■ **tragule** /trag'ūl/ *n* a chevrotain. **trag'uline** /-*īn*/ *adj*.

trahison /tra-ē-zõ'/ (*Fr*) *n* treason; treachery.
❑ **trahison des clercs** /dā kler'/ *n* the treason of intellectuals, the entry of academics into politics.

traik /trāk/ (*Scot*) *vi* to make one's way wearily or with effort; to stray; to get lost; to gad; to decline in health. ◆ *n* a loss, *esp* of sheep; the mutton of sheep that have died of disease or accident. [**trek**]
■ **traik'it** *adj* worn-out.
■ **traik after** to dangle after.

trail[1] /trāl/ *vt* to draw along behind or near the surface; to drag wearily; to drag along; to lag behind; to track, follow or hunt; to make (a path or track) through; to advertise (a forthcoming programme, etc) by trailer; to carry (a weapon) with the butt near the ground, or horizontally; to lead on; to quiz (*inf*); to cover with a trailing ornament. ◆ *vi* to be drawn out in length; (of eg a garment) to hang, float, or drag loosely behind; (of eg a plant) to sprawl over the ground or a support; to straggle or lag; to drag oneself along; to tail off (with *away* or *off*); to move with slow sweeping motion or with dragging drapery; to be losing in a game or competition. ◆ *n* a track or series of marks left by a person, animal, etc moving over a surface; a track or scent, eg of hunted game; a beaten path in the wilds; a path or route; anything drawn out in length or dragging behind; a train or tail; an act or manner of trailing; a television or cinema trailer; the track of a star on a stationary photographic plate; the part of a gun-carriage resting on the ground behind; the distance between the point at which a steered wheel meets the ground and that at which the intersection of a swivel-pin axis meets the ground (*motoring*). [Ety doubtful; OE *træglian* to pluck, pull, and OFr *trailler* to tow, perh from L *tragula* sledge, dragnet, are possibilities]
■ **trail'able** *adj*. **trail'er** *n* a person who trails; a tracker; a creeping plant; an *esp* two-wheeled cart, towed or dragged by a car, bicycle or tractor; the rear section of an articulated lorry; a house on wheels, a caravan (*N Am*); a short film or broadcast advertising a forthcoming entertainment on television or in the cinema; the blank piece of film at the end of a reel. ◆ *vt* to advertise (a programme, etc) by trailer. **trail'ing** *adj*. **trail'ingly** *adv*. **trail'less** *adj*.
❑ **trail bike** *n* a motorcycle suitable for riding over rough ground and tracks. **trail'blazer** *n* a pioneer; a person or thing that leads the way in anything. **trail'blazing** *adj* and *n*. **trailer park** *n* (*N Am*) an area reserved for mobile homes. **trailer trash** *n* (*US derog*) poor and uneducated people, typically living in trailer parks. **trailer truck** *n* (*US*) an articulated lorry. **trailing arbutus** see **arbutus**. **trailing edge** *n* the rear edge of a wing, aerofoil or propeller; the falling portion of a pulse signal (*telecom*). **trailing vortex** *n* (*aeronautics*) the vortex passing from the tips of the main surfaces of an aircraft and extending downstream and behind it. **trail mix** *n* a mixture of pieces of dried fruit (eg bananas, dates, pineapple, apricots, etc) nuts and seeds eaten as a snack, *orig* by hikers. **trail'-net** *n* a dragnet.
■ **trail a pike** (*obs*) to serve as a soldier. **trail away** or **off** (*esp* of a sound) to become fainter. **trail one's coat** to invite a quarrel.

trail[2] /trāl/ *n* an apheretic form of **entrail**.

trailbaston /trāl'ba-stən/ (*hist*) *n* a ruffian or brigand in 14c England. [Anglo-Fr *traille-baston*, from OFr *traille*, imperative of *trailler* to trail, and *baston* cudgel]

train[1] /trān/ *vt* to instruct and discipline, *esp* in a particular skill; to cause (a plant, etc) to grow in the desired manner; to prepare for a specific purpose (*esp* a competition) by instruction, practice, diet, exercise or otherwise; to bring up; to direct, aim (as a gun or telescope); to draw along (*archaic*); to allure (*obs*); to draw on (*obs*). ◆ *vi* (*Spenser* **trayne**) to undergo instruction, *esp* in a particular skill; to prepare oneself by instruction, exercise, diet or otherwise; to be under drill; to travel by rail; to trail, drag (*rare*). ◆ *n* a string of railway carriages or wagons with a locomotive or other means of propulsion; that which is dragged along or follows behind; a tail; tail feathers or trailing back-feathers; the part of a dress that trails; a retinue; a series; a sequence; a number of things, animals, etc in a string or succession; a process; a line of combustible material to fire an explosive charge; a set of wheels acting on each other, for transmitting motion; artillery and other equipment for a siege or battle; a lure; a thing dragged on the ground to make a scent; a sledge (*Can*). [Mainly OFr *trainer, trahiner* (Fr *traîner*) to drag (nouns *train, traîne*); partly with overlap of meanings, from OFr *traîne* guile]

■ **trainabil'ity** n. **train'able** adj. **trained** adj having received training; discerning, experienced; (of a plant, tree, etc) made to grow in a specified manner or place; having a train. **trainee'** n a person who is under training. **trainee'ship** n the period of being a trainee; the position of or maintenance provided for a trainee. **train'er** n a person who prepares athletes for competion, horses for a race, or the like; any machine or device used in training, esp an aeroplane with duplicated controls for training pilots; (usu in pl) a soft running shoe, usu laced, with a thick sole, used in training or for general casual wear (also **training shoe**). **train'ing** n the process of instructing in a skill, etc; practical education in any profession, art or handicraft; a course of diet and exercise for developing physical strength, endurance or dexterity. **train'less** adj.
❑ **train'band** n (hist) a band of citizens from the 16c to 18c trained to bear arms. **train'-bearer** n a person who holds up the train of a robe or gown. **trainer pants** or (US) **training pants** n pl thick cotton briefs with extra padding, used to help toilet-train young children. **train ferry** n a ferry that conveys railway trains. **Training Agency** n an organization established in 1989 to train and retrain adult workers and operate the Youth Training Scheme. **training college** n former name for a college of education. **training ship** n a ship in which young people are trained for the sea. **training shoe** see **trainer** above. **training wheels** n pl (N Am) a supplementary set of wheels attached to a child's bicycle, stabilizers. **train mile** n a unit of railway traffic, a run of one mile by one train. **train'spotter** n a person who collects locomotive or carriage numbers as a hobby; a person who takes a detailed or obsessive interest in a (usu trivial) subject (inf). **train'spotting** n.
■ **in train** in progress. **in training** undergoing training; physically fit. **out of training** no longer physically fit. **train down** to reduce one's body weight through diet and exercise in order to be fit for a particular sporting event. **train fine** to bring body or mind to a high pitch of efficiency.

train² /trān/ n (usu **train'-oil**) whale oil extracted from the blubber by boiling. [Du traen (now traan) tear, exudation]

Train à Grande Vitesse /trĕ-nä grä vi-tes'/ (Fr) n a French high-speed passenger train (abbrev **TGV**).

traipse or **trapes** /trāps/ vi to trail; to trudge; to gad; to go in a slatternly way. ◆ n a long tiring walk; a slattern. [Origin unknown]
■ **traips'ing** or **trapes'ing** n and adj. **trape** vi to traipse.

trait /trāt, trā/ n a characteristic or distinguishing feature; a stroke, touch. [Fr, from L trahere, tractum to draw]

traitor /trā'tər/ n a betrayer; a person who commits treason. [Fr traître, from L trāditor, from trādere to give up]
■ **trai'torhood, trai'torism** or **trai'torship** n. **trai'torly** adj (Shakesp). **trai'torous** adj treacherous. **trai'torously** adv. **trai'torousness** n betrayal; treason. **trai'tress** n a female traitor.

traject /trə-jekt'/ vt to take across (obs); to transmit or transport (archaic). ◆ n /traj'ikt/ a crossing; a ferry; a transference, transmission (rare). [L trājicere, -jectum, from trāns across, and jacere to throw]
■ **trajec'tion** /-shən/ n a crossing; a transmission; a transposition; a passage (obs). **trajectory** /traj'ik-tər-i, trə-jekt'ər-i/ n the path described by a body under the action of given forces, esp the curved path of a projectile; a curve that cuts a system of curves or surfaces at a constant angle (geom).

tra-la /trä'lä'/ interj used to express joy, pleasure, etc, or when humming a song.

tram¹ /tram/ n an electrically-powered public vehicle running on rails in the road (also **tram'car** or **tramway car**); a truck used in mines; a tramway; a shaft of a barrow or cart. [Cf LGer traam beam, shaft, etc]
❑ **tram conductor** n. **tram'line** n the track on which a tram runs; the route a tram takes; (in pl) the lines marking the sides of a tennis or badminton court and the lines parallel to them inside the court; (in pl) a rigid set of principles. **tram'lined** adj (inf) running, or as if running, in tramlines, very straight, rigid and inflexible. **tram'road** n a track with sunken wooden, stone or metal rails (legally one not running along a road). **tram'-stop** n a stopping-place for tramcars. **tram'way** n a track or system of tracks with sunken rails along a road; a tramcar system; a tramroad (esp US).

tram² /tram/ n silk yarn for weft, of two or more strands. [Fr trame, from L trāma weft]

tram³ /tram/ see under **trammel**.

tram⁴ /tram/ n a device for adjusting or aligning a piece of machinery. ◆ vt (**tramm'ing; tramm'ed**) to adjust or align using a tram. [A short form of **trammel**]

trammel /tram'l/ n anything that confines or hinders (usu in pl); a net whose inner fine-meshed layer is carried by the fish through the coarse-meshed outer layer, and encloses it in a pocket; a fowling-net; a hobble; shackles for making a horse amble; an instrument for drawing an ellipse consisting of a metal or wooden beam with two adjustable pegs (also **tram**); a beam compass; a series of adjustable

rings or hooks suspended from a crossbeam in the chimney, for hanging kettles, cooking pots, etc above a fireplace; (in pl) a tress. ◆ vt (**tramm'elling; tramm'elled**) to shackle; to confine; to impede or hinder; to entangle, esp in a trammel. [OFr tramail a net, from LL tramacula, from L trēs three, and macula a mesh]
■ **tramm'eller** n.
❑ **trammel net** n a trammel.

tramontane /tra-mon'tān/ adj beyond the mountains (esp the Alps from Rome); foreign; uncivilized. ◆ n an inhabitant of a region beyond the mountains; a foreigner; a barbarian. [Ital tramontana, from L trāns beyond, and mōns, montis a mountain]
■ **tramontana** /trä-mon-tä'na/ n (in Italy) a cold north wind.

tramp /tramp/ vi to tread, esp heavily or noisily; to walk; to go on a walking tour or long walk; to hike in the bush (NZ); to live as a vagrant; to go in a tramp steamer. ◆ vt to traverse on foot, esp wearily; to trample; to tread in a tub in washing clothes (Scot). ◆ n a journey on foot; the sound of heavy footsteps or horses hooves; a vagrant; a cargo boat with no fixed route (also **tramp steamer**); a prostitute, an immoral woman (sl); a plate of iron worn on the sole for pressing a spade or for giving a foothold on ice; the footrest of a spade. ◆ adv with tramping noise. [ME trampen; cf Ger trampen]
■ **tramp'er** n. **tramp'ing** n. **tramp'ish** adj.
❑ **tramp element** n (engineering) any of the noble metals (eg copper) present in steel scrap which are difficult to remove by refining; metal contaminating a structure, such as uranium on nuclear reactor pipework (nuclear eng). **tramp metal** n (engineering) stray metal pieces accidentally entrained in food or other processed materials, which must be removed before the material leaves the process.

trampet or **trampette** /tram-pet'/ n a small trampoline used for springing off, in gymnastic vaulting. [Dimin of **trampoline**]

trample /tram'pl/ vt to tread roughly under foot; to press down by treading; to treat with pride, to insult. ◆ vi (usu with on or upon) to tread roughly or in contempt; to tread forcibly and rapidly. ◆ n the sound or an act of trampling. [Frequentative of **tramp**]
■ **tramp'ler** n. **tramp'ling** n and adj.

trampoline /tram'pə-lin, -lēn or -lēn'/, also **trampolin** /-lin/ n a framework supporting a piece of canvas, stretched and attached by springs, for acrobats, gymnasts, diving learners, etc, to jump, somersault, etc on. ◆ vi to jump, turn somersaults, etc on a trampoline. [Ital trampolino springboard]
■ **tram'poliner** or **tram'polinist** n.

tran- /tran-/ pfx signifying: across; beyond; through. [L trans across, beyond]

trance¹ /träns/ n a dazed, abstracted, ecstatic or exalted state; a deep sleeplike state, profound and prolonged; catalepsy; a state of being apparently unaware of one's surroundings, as claimed by mediums; short for **trance music** below. ◆ vt to throw into a trance; to entrance (poetic). [Fr transe, from transir, from L trānsīre to go across, in LL, to die]
■ **tranced** /tränst, trän'sid/ adv in a trance. **tranc'edly** adv. **trance'like** adj. **tranc'ey** adj (of music, etc) creating a hypnotic effect. ❑ **tranced-out'** adj in a quasi-hypnotic state following prolonged listening to trance music. **trance music** n a type of repetitive electronic dance music.

trance² or **transe** /träns/ (Scot) n a through passage.

tranche /tränsh/ n a slice; a block, portion, esp of money or of an issue of shares. [Fr, slice, from trancher to cut]

tranchet /trä'shā/ n a shoemaker's paring knife; a neolithic or mesolithic flint with a chisel-shaped end (archaeol). [Fr, from trancher to cut]

tranect /tran'ekt/ (Shakesp) n a ferry. [As if L trāns across, and nectere to join; but supposed to be a misprint for **traject**]

trangam /trang'gəm/ n a showy, worthless article or knick-knack. [Origin unknown]

trangle /trang'gl/ (heraldry) n a diminutive of the fesse. [Obs Fr]

trankum /trang'kəm/ (Walter Scott) n a trinket. [**trinket**]

trannie or **tranny** /tran'i/ (inf) n a transistor radio; (usu **trannie**) a transvestite. [Short form]

tranquil /trang'kwil/ adj calm; peaceful. [L tranquillus]
■ **tranquill'ity** or (N Am) **tranquil'ity** n. **tranquilliza'tion** or **-s-**, or (N Am) **tranquiliza'tion** n. **tranq'uillize** or **-ise**, or (N Am) **tranq'uilize** vt to make tranquil or immobile, esp by sedation. **tranquilli'zer** or **-s-**, or (N Am) **tranquil'i'zer** n that which tranquillizes; a sedative drug. **tranquilli'zingly** or **-s-**, or (N Am) **tranquili'zingly** adv. **tran'quilly** adv. **tran'quilness** n.

trans /tranz/ (inf) adj transgender. ◆ n a transgender person.

trans. abbrev : transitive; translated; translation.

trans- /tranz-, tränz-, trənz-, trans-, träns-, trəns-/ pfx (also **tran-, tra-**) signifying: across; beyond; through; (of an isomer) having two identical groups of atoms on opposite sides of a bond (*chem*); having a higher atomic number. [L *trans* across, beyond]

transact /tranz-akt', tränz-, trənz-, -s-/ *vt* to conduct (business, etc), negotiate (a deal, etc); to perform; to deal with (*archaic*). ◆ *vi* to negotiate; to have to do. [L *transactum*, pap of *transigere*, from *agere* to carry on]

■ **transac'tion** *n* the act of transacting; an agreement; a piece of business performed; (*pl*) the reports or publications of certain learned societies. **transac'tional** *adj*. **transac'tionally** *adv*. **transac'tor** *n*.
❑ **transactional analysis** *n* (*psychol*) a form of psychotherapy based on the concept of three 'ego-states' of child, adult and parent existing in any one personality, and aimed at adjusting the balance between them, *esp* so as to improve the patient's interpersonal relations. **transaction processing** *n* (*comput*) the use of an online computer to interrogate or update files in real time.

transactinide /tranz-ak'ti-nīd/ (*chem*) *adj* of or relating to elements with atomic numbers higher than the actinide series. ◆ *n* such an element. [**trans-**]

transalpine /tranz-al'pīn, tränz-/ *adj* beyond the *Alps* (*orig* from Rome); crossing the Alps. ◆ *n* an inhabitant of a region or country beyond the Alps. [L *transalpīnus*, from *Alpae* Alps]

transaminase /tranz-am'i-nāz/ (*biol*) *n* an enzyme that converts keto acids to amino acids. [**trans-**, *amino* and **-ase**]
■ **transamina'tion** *n*.

transandine /tranz-an'dīn, tränz-, trənz-/, *also* **transandean** /-dē'ən or -an'di-ən/ *adj* beyond, or crossing, the *Andes*. [**trans-**]

transatlantic /tranz-ət-lan'tik, tränz-/ *adj* beyond, from or belonging to the other side of the *Atlantic* Ocean; crossing the Atlantic. [**trans-**]

transaxle /tranz'ak-s(ə)l/ (*engineering*) *n* (in a motor vehicle) a driving axle and differential gearbox forming an integral unit. [*transmission axle*]

transcalent /tranz-kā'lənt, tränz-/ *adj* pervious to or allowing the passage of heat. [**trans-**, and L *calēns*, -*entis*, from *calēre* to be hot]
■ **transcal'ency** *n*.

transcaucasian /tranz-kö-kā'zhən, tränz-/ *adj* across or beyond the *Caucasus* mountains in Georgia, Armenia and Azerbaijan; (with *cap*; *also n*) of or relating to the region or the people of *Transcaucasia*, south of the Caucasus mountains. [**trans-**]

transceiver /tran-sē'vər, tränz-/ *n* a piece of radio equipment (eg a walkie-talkie) whose circuitry permits both transmission and reception. [*transmitter* and *receiver*]

transcend /tran-send', tränz-/ *vt* to pass or lie beyond the range or limit of (human understanding, etc); to rise above; to surmount; to surpass; to exceed. [L *transcendere*, from *scandere* to climb]
■ **transcend'ence** or **transcend'ency** *n*. **transcend'ent** *adj* transcending; superior or supreme in excellence; surpassing others; as applicable to *being*, relating to the absolute, transcending all limitation; as applicable to *knowledge*, relating to what transcends experience, being given *a priori*; beyond human knowledge or consciousness; abstrusely speculative, fantastic. **transcenden'tal** *adj* transcending; going beyond usual human knowledge or experience; supereminent, excelling, surpassing others; concerned with what is independent of experience; supernatural or mystical; vague; (of a function) not capable of being produced or expressed algebraically (*maths*). ◆ *n* (*maths*) a transcendental number. **transcenden'talism** *n* the investigation of what is *a priori* in human knowledge, or independent of experience; that which is vague and illusive in philosophy; the state of being transcendental; transcendental language; the American reaction against Puritan prejudices, humdrum orthodoxy, old-fashioned metaphysics, materialistic philistinism, and materialism, particularly associated with the poet and critic Ralph Waldo Emerson (1803–82). **transcenden'talist** *n* and *adj*. **transcendental'ity** *n*. **transcenden'talize** or **-ise** *vt*. **transcenden'tally** *adv*. **transcend'ently** *adv*. **transcend'entness** *n*.
❑ **transcendental function** *n* (*maths*) any function that cannot be defined by a finite number of algebraic operations. **transcendental meditation** *n* a system of meditation designed to promote spiritual wellbeing and a relaxed state of consciousness through silent repetition of a mantra. **transcendental number** *n* (*maths*) a number that is not a root of any algebraic equation with integral coefficients.

transcode /trans-kōd', träns-, -z-/ (*comput*) *vt* to convert (data) from one digital format to another. [**trans-**]

transcontinental /tranz-kon-ti-nen't(ə)l, tränz-/ *adj* extending or passing across or belonging to the farther side of a *continent*. ◆ *n* a transcontinental train or railway. [**trans-**]
■ **transcontinen'tally** *adv*.

transcribe /tran-skrīb', tränz-/ *vt* to write over from one book into another; to copy; to write out (notes, etc) in full; to transliterate; to arrange (a composition) for an instrument, voice or combination other than that for which it was composed (*music*); to record for future

broadcasting or the like; to broadcast a transcription of; to transfer (information) from one type of storage system to another (*comput*); to make a phonetic or phonemic transcription of (speech, sounds, etc; *linguistics*); to cause to undergo transcription (qv below; *genetics*). [L *transcrībere, -scrīptum*]
■ **transcrīb'able** *adj*. **transcrīb'er** *n*. **transcript** /tran'skript, trän'/ *n* a written or printed copy, *esp* a legal or official copy of (sometimes secret) proceedings, testimony, etc; any copy; a length of RNA with its sequence copied by base pairing from a DNA template, or of DNA copied from an RNA template (*genetics, biochem*); an official copy of a school pupil's educational report (*N Am*). **transcrip'tion** *n* the act of transcribing; any transcribed text; the natural process by which a molecule of RNA is copied by base pairing from a DNA template carrying the necessary genetic information (*genetics*). **transcrip'tional** *adj*. **transcrip'tionally** *adv*. **transcrip'tive** *adj*. **transcrip'tively** *adv*.

transcriptase /tran-skrip'tāz, trän-/ (*genetics*) *n* the enzyme that brings about transcription (see also **reverse transcriptase** under **reverse**). [*transcript*ion and **-ase**]

transcutaneous /trans-kū-tā'ni-əs, träns-/ *adj* passing or entering through the skin. [**trans-**]
❑ **transcutaneous electrical nerve stimulation** *n* a method of pain relief in which electrodes are placed on the skin near the source of pain and a small electric current passed through, effective eg in childbirth (*abbrev* **TENS**).

transdermal /tranz- or trans-dûr'məl/ *adj* absorbed or injected through the skin. [**trans-**]

transducer /trans-dū'sər, träns-, -z- or (*US*) -doos'ər/ *n* a device that transfers power from one system to another in the same or in a different form. [L *transdūcere, -ductum* to lead across]
■ **transduc'tion** *n* transfer, *esp* transfer of genetic material from one bacterial cell to another by bacteriophage. **transduc'tor** *n* an arrangement of windings on a laminated core or cores, part of a device for amplifying current.

transe same as **trance²**.

transect /tran-sekt', trän-/ *vt* to cut across transversely. ◆ *n* /tran'sekt, trän'/ a sample belt of vegetation marked off for study. [**trans-** and **sect²**]
■ **transect'ion** *n*.

transenna /tran-sen'ə/ *n* a screen enclosing a shrine. [L *trānsenna* trellis, latticework]

transept /tran'sept, trän-/ (*archit*) *n* part of a church at right angles to the nave, or of another building to the main structure; either wing of such a part where it runs right across. [L *saeptum* (used in *pl*) fence, enclosure]
■ **transept'al** *adj* of a transept. **transept'ate** *adj* divided by transverse septa.

transeunt /tran'zi-ənt, trän', -si-/ see **transient**.

transexual see **transsexual**.

transf. *abbrev*: transfer; transferred; transference.

transfard /trans-färd'/ (*Spenser*) transferred (*pat*).

trans fatty acid /tranz fat'i as'id/ (*chem*) *n* a fatty acid containing one or more trans-isomeric double bonds, formed during partial hydrogenation of vegetable oils. [**trans-**]
■ **trans fat** *n* a trans fatty acid; an unsaturated fat containing trans fatty acids.

transfection /trans-fek'shən, träns-/ (*biol*) *n* the introduction of DNA isolated from a cell or virus into another cell. [*transfer* and *infection*]
■ **transfect'** *vt* to cause transfection in (a cell).

transfer /trans-fûr' or träns-/ *vt* (**transferr'ing; transferred'**) to carry or bring over; to convey or move from one place, person, ownership, object, group, school, football club, etc, to another; to change over; to convey (eg a design) to another surface. ◆ *vi* to change over, *esp* (*US*) from one railway, train or station, to another; to move from one school, football club, etc to another. ◆ *n* /trans' or träns'/ the act of transferring; a design to be conveyed from one surface to another; conveyance from one person, place, etc, to another; a person who or thing that is transferred or is to be transferred (eg a football player); a transfer ticket (*esp N Am*); the passing of property or some other right to another person (*law*); any document attesting to this (*law*). [L *trānsferre*, from *ferre* to carry]
■ **transferabil'ity**, *also* **transferrabil'ity** or **transferribil'ity** *n*. **transferable, transferrable** or **transferrible** /trans' or träns', or -fûr'/ *adj*. **transferee'** *n* the person to whom a thing is transferred; a person who is transferred. **trans'ference** *n* the act of transferring or conveying; passage from place to place; unconscious transferring of one's hopes, desires, fears, etc, from one person or object to another (*psychol*). **transferen'tial** *adj*. **transferr'al** *n* an act of transferring. **transferr'er** or (*law*) **trans'feror** *n* a person who transfers.
❑ **transferable vote** *n* a vote which, if the candidate voted for should be out of the running, is to be transferred to another as second or

subsequent choice. **transfer book** *n* a register of the transfer of property, shares, etc. **transfer day** *n* a day for registering transfer of bank-stock and government funds at the Bank of England. **transfer fee** *n* a fee paid by one club in return for a transferred player. **transfer list** *n* a list of footballers available for transfer to another club. **transfer machine** *n* (*engineering*) a machine in which a workpiece or assembly passes automatically through a number of stations, undergoing one or more production processes at each. **transfer paper** *n* a specially coated paper used for transferring impressions with copying presses, etc. **transfer payment** *n* money received through transfer from the state or other body, eg a pension, not reckoned when calculating national income. **Transfer Procedure test** *n* (in N Ireland) a test taken by primary school pupils, the results of which are taken into account when allocating places in grammar schools. **transfer RNA** *n* (*biochem*) RNA in the form of a small molecule that links messenger RNA and protein synthesis, a loop on one end of the molecule binding to a specific codon of the mRNA, the other end binding to the corresponding amino acid (*abbrev* **tRNA**). **transfer ticket** *n* a ticket for a journey to be resumed on another route.

transferase /*trans*'*fə-rāz*/ (*biol*) *n* an enzyme that catalyses the transfer of chemical groups between compounds. [**transfer** and **-ase**]

transferrin /*trans-fer*'*in*, *träns-*/ (*biochem*) *n* a protein in the blood that transports iron. [**trans-** and L *ferrum* iron]

transfigure /*trans-fig*'*ər*, *träns-*, *tranz-*/ *vt* to change the appearance or form of; to glorify. [L *trānsfigūrāre*, from *figūra* form]
■ **transfiguration** /*-ə-*, *-ū-rā*'*shən*/ *n* a transformation or glorification in appearance or form; (with *cap*) the glorification of Christ's appearance before three of his disciples (from Bible, Matthew 17.2); (with *cap*) the Christian festival celebrating this on 6 August. **transfig**'**urement** *n*.

transfinite /*trans-fī*'*nīt*, *träns-*/ *adj* surpassing what is finite; (of a cardinal or ordinal number) surpassing all finite numbers (*maths*). [**trans-**]

transfix /*trans-fiks*', *träns-*/ *vt* to paralyse with sudden emotion, horror or shock; to pierce through; to cut through (a limb), as in amputation (*med*). [L *trānsfīgere*, *-fīxum*, from *fīgere* to fix]
■ **transfixion** /*-fik*'*shən*/ *n*.

transform /*trans-förm*', *träns-*/ *vt* to change the shape of; to change *esp* radically or thoroughly to another form, appearance, substance or character; to change the form of (an algebraic expression or geometrical figure) (*maths*); to change the voltage of (an alternating current) using a transformer. ◆ *vi* to be changed in form or substance. ◆ *n* /*träns*'/ an expression or figure derived from another (*maths*); any of a group of linguistic constructions related in some way through the application of transformational rules; (in digital computers) a process that alters the form of information without changing its meaning. [L *trānsförmāre*, from *förma* form]
■ **transform**'**able** *adj*. **transformā**'**tion** *n* the act of transforming; a change of form, constitution or substance; metamorphosis (*zool*); transmutation; (in full **transformation scene**) a sudden, dramatic change of scene, *esp* a scene on the stage that changes in presence of the audience or in which the characters of the pantomime were transformed into those of the harlequinade; change from one linguistic transform to another of the group; (also **transformational rule**) any of a number of grammatical rules converting the deep structure of a sentence into its surface structure (*linguistics*); reflection, rotation, translation or dilatation (*geom*); the alteration of the bacterial or eukaryotic cell genotype following the uptake of purified DNA (*biol*); the alteration of cells in tissue-culture so that they behave like cancer cells (*biol*); a transformed person (*Shakesp*); false hair, a wig (*archaic*). **transformā**'**tional** *adj*. **transformā**'**tionally** *adv*. **transform**'**ative** *adj*. **transformed**' *adj*. **transform**'**er** *n* someone or something that transforms; an apparatus for changing the voltage of an alternating electric current. **transform**'**ing** *n* and *adj*. **transform**'**ism** *n* the theory of the mutability of species, the theory of evolution. **transform**'**ist** *n*. **transformis**'**tic** *adj*.
❑ **transformational grammar** *n* a method of studying or describing a language by stating which elements or structures can be derived from or related to others by transformation; a grammatical description that includes transformational rules.
■ **conformal transformation** (*maths*) a change of shape that still preserves a one-to-one matching of points in the original surface with points in the new surface, as in map making.

transfuse /*trans-fūz*', *träns-*/ *vt* to pour out into another vessel; to transfer (eg blood) to another's veins; to treat (a patient, etc) by transfusion; to cause to pass, enter or diffuse through; to imbue; to instil; to cause to be imbibed. [L *trānsfundere*, from *fundere*, *fūsum* to pour]
■ **transfū**'**ser** *n*. **transfū**'**sible** or **transfū**'**sable** *adj*. **transfū**'**sion** /*-zhən*/ *n* transfusing, *esp* of blood into a patient. **transfū**'**sionist** *n* a doctor who performs transfusions. **transfū**'**sive** /*-siv*/ *adj* tending to or having power to transfuse. **transfū**'**sively** *adv*.

transgender /*tranz-* or *trans-jen*'*dər*/ *adj* of or relating to individuals who do not identify entirely with the gender into which they were born, *incl* transsexuals and transvestites (also **transgen**'**dered**). [**trans-**]

transgenic /*tranz-* or *trans-jen*'*ik*/ (*bot* and *zool*) *adj* (of animals or plants) containing genetic material introduced from another species by techniques of genetic manipulation. ◆ *n* a transgenic animal or plant. [**trans-**]
■ **trans**'**gene** *n* a piece of genetic material transferred between species. **transgen**'**esis** *n* the creation of transgenic animals or plants. **transgen**'**ics** *n sing* the branch of science dealing with this.

transgress /*trans-gres*', *träns-*, *-z-*/ *vt* to pass beyond the limit of or set by; to overstep, exceed; to infringe; (of the sea) to flood over (the land). ◆ *vi* to offend by violating a law; to sin. [L *trānsgredī*, *-gressum*, from *gradī*, *gressum* to step]
■ **transgression** /*-gresh*'*ən*/ *n* an overstepping; an infringement; sin. **transgress**'**ional** *adj*. **transgressive** /*-gres*'*iv*/ *adj*. **transgress**'**ively** *adv*. **transgress**'**or** *n*.

tranship or **transship** /*tran(s)-ship*', *trän(s)-*, *trən-*/ *vt* to transfer from one ship or other form of transport to another. ◆ *vi* to change ship, etc. [**tran-**, **trans-**]
■ **tranship**'**ment** or **transship**'**ment** *n*. **transhipp**'**er** or **transshipp**'**er** *n*. **transhipp**'**ing** or **transshipp**'**ing** *n*.

transhume /*trans-(h)ūm*', *träns-*, *-z-*/ *vt* and *vi* to transfer or pass from summer to winter or from winter to summer pastures. [Sp *trashumar*, from L *trāns* across, beyond, and *humus* ground]
■ **transhu**'**mance** *n*. **transhu**'**mant** *adj*.

transience, **transiency** see under **transient**.

transient /*tran*'*zi-ənt*, *trän*', *-si-*/ *adj* passing; of short duration, impermanent; making, or for people making, only a short stay; passing (*music*); (of a mental process) producing an effect outside the mind (also **transeunt**; *philos*). ◆ *n* a temporary resident, worker, etc; a brief alteration in a waveform, etc, as a sudden surge of voltage or current (*phys*). [L *trānsiēns*, *-euntis*, from prp of *trānsīre* to cross, from *īre*, *itum* to go]
■ **tran**'**sience** or **tran**'**siency** *n*. **tran**'**siently** *adv*. **tran**'**sientness** *n*.

transilient /*tran-sil*'*i-ənt*, *trän-*, *trən-*/ *adj* leaping or passing across. [L *trānsilīre*, from *salīre* to leap]
■ **transil**'**iency** *n*.

transilluminate /*tranz-i-lū*'*mi-nāt*, *tränz-*, *-s-*, *-loo*'/ (*med*) *vt* to pass a strong light through, *esp* for the purposes of examination. [**trans-**]
■ **transilluminā**'**tion** *n*.

transire /*tranz-ī*'*ri*, *tränz-*, *-s-*, *träns-ē*'*re*/ *n* customs warrant for clearing goods, cargo, etc. [L *trānsīre*; *cf* **transient**]

transisthmian /*tranz-is(th)*'*mi-ən*, *tränz-*, *-s-*/ *adj* across an isthmus. [**trans-**]

transistor /*tranz-ist*'*ər*, *tränz-*, *-s-*/ *n* a three-electrode semiconductor device, able to perform many functions of multi-electrode valves; an amplifier with crystal and two cat's whiskers; a transistor radio. [*transfer* and *resistor*]
■ **transistorizā**'**tion** or **-s-** *n*. **transist**'**orize** or **-ise** *vt* to fit with or convert to use transistors.
❑ **transistor radio** *n* a small portable radio.

transit /*tran*'*zit*, *trän*', *-sit*/ *n* the conveyance or passage of things or people over, across or through a distance; a route; passenger transport (*esp US*); the apparent passage of a heavenly body over the meridian (*astron*); the apparent passage of a smaller planet, etc over the disc of a greater (*astron*); the passage of a planet across some particular region or point on the zodiac (*astrol*); a transit circle, transit instrument, or transit theodolite. ◆ *vi* to pass across. ◆ *vt* to pass across; to reverse. [L *trānsitus*, *-ūs*, from *īre*, *itum*, to go]
■ **trans**'**itable** *adj*.
❑ **transit camp** *n* a camp where eg refugees, immigrants, soldiers, etc are temporarily accommodated before travelling on to a further destination. **transit circle** *n* a transit instrument with a graduated circle for declinations. **transit duty** *n* a duty chargeable on goods passing through a country. **transit instrument** *n* a telescope mounted in the meridian and turned on a fixed east and west axis. **transit lounge** *n* a lounge for transit passengers at an airport. **transit passenger** *n* a passenger stopping briefly at an airport between flights. **transit theodolite** *n* (*surveying*) one whose telescope can be reversed. **transit trade** *n* the trade of carrying foreign goods through a country. **transit visa** *n* one allowing only transit through a country and not residence.
■ **in transit** (of goods, etc) in the process of being transported from one place to another.

transition /*tran-*, *trän-sizh*'*ən*, *-zish*'*ən*, *-sish*'*ən*/ *n* passage from one place, state, stage, style or subject to another; a change of key, *esp* a brief or abrupt one (*music*); the specific passage from Romanesque or Norman to Gothic (*archit*); a change in the structure of an atomic nucleus, accompanied by photon emission or absorption. ◆ *adj* transitional. ◆ *vi* to undergo a transition. [L *trānsitiō, -ōnis,* from *trānsitus*; see ety for **transit**]

■ **transi'tional** *adj* relating to transition. ◆ *n* (*archit*) transition. **transi'tionally** *adv.* **transi'tionary** *adj.*

❑ **transition element** or **transition metal** *n* (*phys*) one of a group with an incomplete inner electron shell, characterized by the ability to form coloured complexes. **transition point** *n* (*chem*) the temperature and pressure at which a crystalline form of a substance is converted into a solid form, ie that at which they can both exist in equilibrium. **transition temperature** *n* (*phys*) the temperature at which some critical change occurs, as in magnetism and superconductivity.

transitive /*tran'si-tiv, trän', -zi-*/ *adj* passing over; having the power of passing; (of a verb) taking a direct object (*grammar*); denoting a relation in which if the first element bears a relation to the second, and the second bears the same relation to a third, then the first bears the same relation to the third (*logic*). [LL *trānsitīvus,* from L *trānsitus*; see ety for **transit**]

■ **trans'itively** *adv.* **trans'itiveness** *n.* **transitiv'ity** *n.*

transitory /*tran'si-t(ə)ri, trän', -zi-*/ *adj* lasting or appearing for a short time; going or passing away; vanishing quickly. [LL *trānsitōrius,* from L *trānsitus*; see ety for **transit**]

■ **trans'itorily** *adv.* **trans'itoriness** *n.*

❑ **transitory action** *n* (*law*) an action that can be brought in any country no matter where the action originated.

translate /*trans-lāt', träns-, trəns-, -z-*/ *vt* to render into another language; to express in another artistic medium; to put in plainer terms, explain; to interpret the significance or meaning of (an action, behaviour, etc); to transfer (a cleric) from one ecclesiastical office to another; to remove or transfer to another place; to remove to heaven, *esp* without death; to transform or convert (often with *into*); to perform a translation on (*mech, maths*); to use the genetic information stored in RNA in the specification of the peptide sequence of a protein or polypeptide (*biol*); to enrapture; to renovate, make new from old. ◆ *vi* to practise translation; to be translatable; to be transformed or converted (with *into*). [L *trānslātum,* used as supine of *trānsferre*; see **transfer**]

■ **translātabil'ity** *n.* **translā'table** *adj.* **translā'tion** *n* the act of translating; rendering into another language; a version; removal to another place, see, ecclesiastical office, etc; motion, change of place, such that every point moves in the same direction at the same speed; similar change of place of a geometrical figure; an algebraic function obtained by adding the same constant to each value of the variable in a given function, thus moving the graph of this function (or moving the rectangular axes parallel to themselves) while preserving its shape; the automatic retransmission of a telegraphic message; the process by which genetic information stored in RNA causes a protein or polypeptide to be synthesized to a particular peptide sequence (*biol*); the working up of new things from old materials. **translā'tional** *adj.* **translā'tionally** *adv.* **translā'tive** *adj* (*grammar*) denoting, as in Finnish, 'turning into'. ◆ *n* the translative case. **translā'tor** *n* a person or machine that translates from one language into another; a program that converts another program from one language to another, *usu* into machine code (*comput*); a relay transmitter. **translātor'ial** *adj.* **trans'latory** (also /*-lā'*/) *adj* of or relating to direct onward motion without rotation.

transleithan /*tranz-lī't(h)ən, tränz-, -s-*/ *adj* beyond the river *Leitha,* once in part the boundary between Austria and Hungary; hence, Hungarian. [**trans-**]

transliterate /*tranz-lit'ə-rāt, tränz-, -s-*/ *vt* to write (a word) in letters of another alphabet or language. [**trans-** and L *littera* letter]

■ **transliterā'tion** *n.* **translit'erātor** *n.*

translocation /*tranz-lō-kā'shən, tränz-, -s-*/ *n* transference from place to place, *esp* of materials within the body of a plant; the transfer of a portion of a chromosome to another part of the same chromosome or to a different chromosome, without (**balanced translocation**) or with (**unbalanced translocation**) loss of genetic material (*genetics*). [**trans-** and L *locus* place]

■ **translocate'** *vt.*

translucent /*tranz-loo'sənt, tränz-, -s-, -lū'*/ *adj* shining through; imperfectly transparent; clear. [L *trānslūcēns, -entis,* from *lūcēre* to shine, from *lūx, lūcis* light]

■ **translu'cence** or **translu'cency** *n.* **translu'cently** *adv.* **translu'cid** *adj* translucent. **translucid'ity** *n.*

translunar /*tranz-loo'nər, tränz-, -s-*/ *adj* of or relating to the region beyond the moon's orbit round the earth. [**trans-**]

■ **translun'ary** /*tranz'*/ *adj* beyond the moon; visionary; celestial rather than earthly.

transmanche /*tranz-mäsh', träz-mäsh'*/ (*Fr*) *adj* of, for or relating to the tunnel under the English Channel. [Fr, from L *trans* across, and la *Manche* the English Channel]

transmarine /*tranz-mə-rēn', tränz-, -s-*/ *adj* across or beyond the sea. [L *trānsmarīnus,* from *mare* sea]

transmew /*tranz-mū', tränz-, -s-*/ (*Spenser*) *vt* to transmute. [OFr *transmuer,* from L *transmūtāre*; see **transmute**]

transmigrate /*tranz'mī-grāt, tränz', -s-, -grāt'*/ *vi* to move to another place of abode or state; (of the soul) to pass into another body at death. ◆ *vt* to cause to transmigrate. [L *trānsmigrāre, -ātum,* from *migrāre* to migrate]

■ **trans'mīgrant** (or /*-mī'*/) *n* a person who transmigrates; a migrant passing through a country on the way to another in which he or she means to settle. ◆ *adj* passing through; transmigrating. **transmīgrā'tion** *n.* **transmīgrā'tional** *adj.* **transmīgrā'tionism** *n* belief in the transmigration of souls. **transmīgrā'tionist** *n* a believer or advocate of this. **trans'mīgrātive** (or /*-mī'grə-tiv/*) *adj.* **trans'mīgrātor** *n.* **transmī'gratory** /*-grə-tər-i*/ *adj.*

transmissible, transmission, etc see under **transmit**.

transmit /*tranz-mit', tränz-, -s-*/ *vt* (**transmitt'ing; transmitt'ed**) to send on; to pass on; to hand on; to communicate; to hand down to posterity; to send out or broadcast (radio signals, programmes, etc); to transfer (eg power from one part of a machine to another); to allow the passage of, act as a medium for (heat, energy, light, sound, etc). ◆ *vi* to send out a radio signal, etc. [L *transmittere, -missum,* from *mittere, missum* to send]

■ **transmissibil'ity** *n.* **transmiss'ible** *adj* (also **transmitt'able,** or, less correctly **transmitt'ible**). **transmission** /*-mish'ən/* *n* the process of transmitting or state of being transmitted; that which is transmitted; a programme, message, etc sent out by radio, etc; the system of interdependent parts in a motor vehicle, by which power is transferred from the engine to the wheels; transmittance (*phys*). **transmiss'ional** *adj.* **transmiss'ive** *adj* having the quality of transmitting or of being transmitted. **transmiss'ively** *adv.* **transmiss'iveness** or **transmissiv'ity** *n* (*phys*) a measure of the ability of a material or medium to transmit radiation. **transmitt'al** *n.* **transmitt'ance** *n* the act of transmitting; the ratio of energy transmitted by a body to that incident on it (*phys*). **transmitt'er** *n* a person or thing that transmits; apparatus for producing, modulating and sending out anything, eg signals, messages, etc; a neurotransmitter.

❑ **transmission coefficient** *n* (*phys*) the probability of penetration of a nucleus by a particle striking it. **transmission electron microscope** *n* (*phys*) an electron microscope that produces a two-dimensional image because electrons undergo different scattering and energy loss according to the material they pass through. **transmission line** *n* (*elec eng*) any conductor used to transmit electric or electromagnetic energy, eg a power line or telephone line.

transmogrify /*tranz-mog'ri-fī, tränz-, -s-*/ (*inf, facetious*) *vt* (**transmog'rifying; transmog'rified**) to transform or transmute, *esp* bizarrely. [Appar pseudo-L]

■ **transmogrificā'tion** *n.*

transmontane /*tranz-mon'tān, tränz-, -s-*/ *adj* another form of **tramontane**.

transmove /*tranz-moov', tränz-, -s-*/ (*Spenser*) *vt* to transmute. [Appar for **transmew,** remodelled on **move**]

transmundane /*tranz-mun'dān, tränz-* or *-dān'*/ *adj* not belonging to this world, out of, beyond, this world. [LL *transmundanus,* from *mundus* world]

transmute /*tranz-mūt', tränz-, -s-*/ *vt* to change to another form or substance; to change (base metals) into gold or silver (*alchemy*). [L *trānsmūtāre,* from *mūtāre* to change]

■ **transmūtabil'ity** *n.* **transmū'table** *adj.* **transmū'tableness** *n.* **transmū'tably** *adv.* **transmūtā'tion** *n* a changing into a different form, nature or substance, *esp* that of one chemical element into another; the process supposed to change base metals into gold or silver (*alchemy*); (in full **atomic transmutation**) the change of one type of atom to another as a result of nuclear radiation (*phys*); the transformation of one species into another (*biol*). **transmūtā'tional** *adj.* **transmūtā'tionist** *n* and *adj.* **transmū'tative** *adj* serving or tending to transmute. **transmū'ter** *n.*

transnational /*tranz-nash'(ə-)nəl, tränz-, -s-*/ *adj* transcending national boundaries, concerning more than one nation. ◆ *n* a transnational company. [**trans-**]

transoceanic /*tranz-ō-shi-an'ik, tränz-, -s-*/ *adj* crossing the ocean; across or on the other side of the ocean. [**trans-**]

transom /*tran'səm*/ *n* a structure dividing a window horizontally; a lintel; (also **transom window**) a small window over the lintel of a door or window; a crosspiece; a crossbeam; any of several

crossbeams used to strengthen the stern of a vessel. [OFr *traversin*, from *traverse* crosspiece]
■ **tran'somed** *adj*.

transonic, transonics see under **trans-sonic**.

transpacific /*trans-pə-sif'ik, träns-*/ *adj* crossing the Pacific; beyond or on the other side of the Pacific. [**trans-**]

transpadane /*trans'pə-dān, träns-, -z-, -pā'dān*/ *adj* beyond or from beyond the Po (viewed from Rome). [L *Padus* the Po]

transparent /*trans-pā'rənt, träns-, trəns-, -z-, -par'ənt*/ *adj* able to be seen through, clear; pellucid; pervious to rays; denoting software that has been modified and through which the user accesses other software without being aware of its presence; easily detected, understood; obvious, evident; ingenuous, frank; shining through (*Shakesp*). [Med L *trānspārēns, -entis*, from L *pārēre* to appear]
■ **transpar'ency** *n* the quality of being transparent (also **transpar'ence**); that which is transparent; a picture, photograph, design or device visible, or to be viewed, by transmitted light, eg through a slide projector, a slide; Thackeray's humorous translation of the German title *Durchlaucht*. **transpar'ently** *adv*. **transpar'entness** *n*.

transpersonal /*trans-pûr'sə-nəl, träns-*/ *adj* going beyond or transcending the individual personality; denoting a form of psychology or psychotherapy that utilizes mystical, psychical or spiritual experience as a means of increasing human potential. [**trans-**]

transpicuous /*tran-spik'ū-əs, trän-, trən-*/ *adj* transparent. [L *trānspicere* to see through, from *specere* to look]
■ **transpic'ūously** *adv*.

transpierce /*trans-pērs', träns-*/ *vt* to pierce through; to permeate. [**trans-**]

transpire /*tran-spīr', trän-*/ *vi* to become known, come to light; (loosely) to happen; to prove to be the case; to exhale; to give off water vapour (as plants do) or waste material through the skin (as some animals do). ◆ *vt* to give off as vapour; to exhale; to emit through the skin. [L *trāns* through, and *spīrāre* to breathe]
■ **transpir'able** *adj*. **transpiration** /*tran-spi-rā'shən*/ *n* the act or process of transpiring; exhalation through the skin; (in plants) emission of water vapour through the stomata, etc. **transpir'atory** *adj*.

transplant /*trans-plänt', träns-, -z-/* *vt* to remove (a plant) from the ground where it grows and plant in another place; to transfer (eg an organ or tissue) surgically from one person or animal to another, or to another part of the same; to remove and establish elsewhere. ◆ *vi* to tolerate or withstand transplanting. ◆ *n* /*trans', träns'*/ an act of removing a part or organ from its normal position and grafting it into another position in the same individual or into another individual; the organ, tissue, etc transplanted; the act of transplanting a plant; a plant that has been transplanted. [LL *trānsplantāre*, from L *plantāre* to plant]
■ **transplan'table** *adj*. **transplantā'tion** *n*. **transplan'ter** *n*. **transplan'ting** *n*.

transponder /*tranz-pon'dər, tränz-, -s-/* *n* a radio or radar device that, on receiving a signal, transmits a signal of its own. [*trans*mitter res*ponder*]

transpontine /*trans-pon'tīn, träns-, -z-/* *adj* across or on the other side of a bridge; on the Surrey side of the Thames, hence, from the type of theatrical productions there in the 19c, melodramatic (*old*). [L *trāns* across, and *pōns, pontis* a bridge]

transport /*trans-pōrt', -pört', träns-, -z-/* *vt* to carry, convey or remove from one place to another; to send overseas to a penal colony (*hist*); to carry away by strong emotion; to throw into an ecstasy; to translate (eg a minister); to put to death (*Shakesp*); perh to carry off (as by the fairies) (*Shakesp*). ◆ *n* /*trans', träns'*/ carriage or conveyance of goods or people from one place to another; the management of or arrangements for such conveyance; means of conveyance for getting from place to place; the conveyance of troops and their equipment; a ship, aircraft, etc, for this purpose; ecstasy, or any strong emotion; someone who has been transported or sentenced to transportation (*hist*). [L *trānsportāre*, from *portāre* to carry]
■ **transportabil'ity** *n*. **transport'able** *adj* able to be transported; (eg of an offence) liable, or rendering liable, to transportation (*hist*). **transport'al** *n*. **transport'ance** *n* (*Shakesp*) conveyance, transport. **transportā'tion** *n* removal; the act of transporting or process of being transported; removal of offenders to penal colonies overseas (*hist*); the transporting of goods or people; means or system of transport; tickets or passes for transport. **transport'ed** *adj*. **transport'edly** *adv*. **transport'edness** *n*. **transport'er** *n* someone or something that transports, *esp* a large vehicle for carrying heavy goods. **transport'ing** *n* and *adj*. **transport'ingly** *adv*. **transport'ive** *adj* tending or having power to transport.
❑ **transport café** *n* a roadside café catering mainly for long-distance lorry drivers. **transporter bridge** *n* a bridge for transporting vehicles, consisting of a movable platform suspended from a girder. **transport**

rider *n* (*S Afr*; *hist*) a carrier transporting goods by wagon. **transport ship** *n* a ship used for carrying troops, stores, etc.

transpose /*trans-pōz', träns-, -z-/* *vt* to transfer; to turn, alter; to change the order or position of, interchange; to write, perform or render in another key (*music*); to transfer (a term) from one side of an equation to the other, with a corresponding reversal of sign (*maths*); to interchange the rows and columns of (a matrix) (*maths*); to transform (*Shakesp*). ◆ *n* (*maths*) a matrix resulting from rows and columns being interchanged. [Fr *transposer*; see **pose**[1]]
■ **transpōsabil'ity** *n*. **transpōs'able** *adj*. **transpōs'al** *n* a change of place or order. **transpos'ase** *n* (*genetics*) an enzyme that brings about the transposition of a sequence of DNA within a chromosome or between chromosomes. **transpōs'er** *n*. **transpōs'ing** *n* and *adj*. **transposition** /*-pō-, -pə-zish'ən*/ *n* the act or process of transposing; material that is transposed. **transposi'tional** *adj*. **transpositive** /*-poz'*/ *adj*.
❑ **transposable element** *n* (*genetics*) a transposon. **transposing instrument** *n* an instrument which, by a mechanical device, transposes music into another key; an instrument, eg a horn, for which music is written in a different key from the key that instrument actually produces.

transposon /*trans-pō'zon, träns-/* (*genetics*) *n* a sequence of DNA capable of moving to different sites in a chromosome or to a different chromosome, with a subsequent change in the genetic make-up of the cell. [*transposition* and *-on*]

transputer /*tranz-, trans-pū'tər, träns-/* (*comput*) *n* a chip capable of all the functions of a microprocessor, *incl* memory, and able to process in parallel rather than sequentially. [*transistor* and com*puter*]

transsexual, transexual or **trans-sexual** /*tran(z)- or trän(z)-sek'sū-əl* or *-shoo-al*, / *n* a person anatomically of one sex but having a strong desire to adopt the physical characteristics and role of a member of the opposite sex; a person who has had medical and surgical treatment to alter the external sexual features so that they resemble those of the opposite sex. ◆ *adj* of or relating to transsexuals. [**trans-**]
■ **trans(s)ex'ualism** *n*. **trans(s)exual'ity** *n*.

trans-shape /*trans-shāp', träns-, -z-/* (*Shakesp*) *vt* to transform.

trans-ship, transship same as **tranship**.

trans-sonic /*trans-son'ik, träns-/* *adj* relating to the range of speeds close to, or equalling, that of sound (also **transonic** /*tran-, tränson'ik/*). [L *sonus* sound]
■ **trans-son'ics** or **transon'ics** *n sing* the study of such speeds.
❑ **trans-sonic** (or **transonic**) **barrier** *n* the sound barrier.

transubstantiate /*tran-səb-stan'shi-āt, trän-/* *vt* and *vi* to change to another substance. [L *substantia* substance]
■ **transubstan'tial** *adj*. **transubstan'tially** *adv*. **transubstantiā'tion** *n* a change into another substance; the doctrine that, or the mystical process by which, in the consecration of the elements of the Eucharist, the whole substance of the bread and wine is converted into Christ's body and blood, only the appearances of bread and wine remaining (*Christianity, esp RC*; cf **consubstantiation**). **transubstantiā'tionalist** or **transubstantiā'tionist** *n* a person who believes in transubstantiation (also **transubstan'tiātor**).

transude /*tran-sūd', trän-, -zūd'/* *vi* and *vt* to ooze out, eg through pores. [L *sūdāre* to sweat]
■ **tran'sūdate'** *n* a substance that transudes or has been transuded, eg a fluid that passes through a membrane or the walls of a blood vessel. **transūdā'tion** *n*. **transū'datory** *adj*.

transume /*tran-sūm', trän-, -zūm'/* *vt* (*obs*) to transcribe officially. [L *trān(s)sūmere* to transcribe, from *sūmere* to take]
■ **transumpt** /*-sumt'/* *n* a copy of a legal document. **transumption** /*-sum'shən*/ *n* transcription; metaphor; transference or translation. **transumptive** /*-sump'tiv/* *adj*.

transuranic /*trans-ū-ran'ik, träns-, -z-/* *adj* (of an element) having an atomic number greater than that of *uranium* (also **transurā'nian** or **transurā'nium**). [**trans-**]

Transvaal daisy /*tranz'väl dā'zi* (or *tränz', träns'*)/ *n* a flower (*Gerbera jamesonii*) native to South Africa, cultivated for its large brightly-coloured petals. [*Transvaal*, former province of South Africa]

transvalue /*trans-val'ū, träns-, -z-/* *vt* to re-estimate the value of, *esp* on a basis differing from the accepted standards. [**trans-**]
■ **transvaluā'tion** *n*. **transval'uer** *n*.

transverse[1] /*tranz'vûrs, tränz', -vûrs'/* *adj* set, sent, lying, etc crosswise. ◆ *adv* crosswise. ◆ *n* anything set crosswise. ◆ *vt* /*-vûrs'/* to cross; to thwart; to reverse; to transform. [L *trānsversus*, from *vertere, versum* to turn]
■ **transvers'al** *adj* transverse. ◆ *n* a line cutting a set of lines. **transversal'ity** *n*. **transvers'ally** *adv*. **transverse'ly** *adv*. **transver'sion** *n*.
❑ **transverse colon** *n* (*anat*) the part of the colon lying across the abdominal cavity. **transverse flute** see under **flute**. **transverse**

fracture n (med) a fracture caused by an impact at right angles to the bone. **transverse wave** n (phys) a wave motion in which the disturbance of the medium occurs at right angles to the direction of wave propagation.

■ **by transverse** (Spenser) awry.

transverse² /tranz-vûrs', tränz-/ vt to turn from prose into verse. [A pun in Buckingham's comedy The Rehearsal (1671)]
■ **transver'sion** /-shən/ n.

transvest /tranz-vest', tränz-/ vt and vi to dress oneself in the clothes of another person, esp of the opposite sex. [**trans-**, and L vestis, from vestīre, vestītum to dress; cf **travesty**]
■ **transvest'ic** adj. **transvest'ism** n. **transvest'ist** n. **transvestite** /-vest'īt/ adj and n (of or relating to) a person who gets psychological gratification from wearing clothes typically worn by the opposite sex. **transvest'itism** n.

tranter /tran'tər/ (dialect) n a hawker; a carrier. [Cf LL trāvetārius]
■ **trant** vt and vi (back-formation) to hawk.

trap¹ /trap/ n any enclosure or mechanical device, usu baited, for catching animals, etc; a snare, gin; a hidden danger; a plan or trick for surprising a person into speech, action, or for catching someone unawares; a pitfall; a trapdoor; a door in a loft, allowing pigeons to enter but not leave; a ventilating door in a mine; a lock; a bend in a pipe, esp a drainpipe, to stop the passage of air or foul gases; a light carriage; a device for throwing up or releasing a ball or clay pigeons; a box-like stall from which a greyhound is released at the beginning of a race; the mouth (sl); a person who catches offenders (sl); (in pl) a police officer (obs Aust sl); trickery (sl); a bunker (golf); (in pl) drums or other percussion instruments (jazz). ◆ vt (**trapp'ing**; **trapped**) to catch in a trap; to catch (a person) out with a plan or trick; to provide with a trap or traps; to control (a ball) so that it stops dead (football). ◆ vi to act as a trapper. [OE trappe, from træppe, treppe]
■ **trap'like** adj. **trapp'er** n a person who traps animals for their fur; a person, orig a boy, who minds a mine trap; a horse for a trap. **trapp'iness** n. **trapp'ing** n and adj. **trapp'y** adj full of traps, treacherous.
□ **trap'ball** n an old game played with a ball, bat, and trap. **trap'door** n a door set in a floor, stage or ceiling, esp one flush with its surface. **trapdoor spider** n one that makes a lair in the ground and covers it with a hinged door composed of earth and silk. **trap'fall** n a trapdoor that gives way beneath the feet; a pitfall. **trap'line** n (N Am) a series of animal traps. **trap'shooter** n. **trap'shooting** n clay-pigeon shooting. **trap stick** n a bat for trapball.

trap² /trap/ (geol; in full **traprock**) n any dark fine-grained columnar igneous rock (lying often in steps or terraces), esp basalt. [Swed trapp, from trappa a stair]
■ **trapp'ean** (or /-ē'/) adj.

trap³ /trap/ n a fault (mining); a ladder leading to a loft (Scot); a flight of steps (Scot). [Cf Du trap step; cf ety for **trap²**]
□ **trap'-cut** adj (of gems) cut in steps, step-cut. **trap'-ladder, trap'-stair** n.

trap⁴ /trap/ n (in pl) personal luggage or belongings; a horsecloth (obs). ◆ vt (**trapp'ing**; **trapped**) to caparison, deck with trappings. [Appar connected with Fr drap, Sp and Port trapo, LL drappus (trapus) cloth]
■ **trapped** adj bedecked with trappings. **trapp'er** n (hist) a covering, either protective for use in battle or decorative, worn by a horse. **trapp'ings** n pl characteristic accompaniments, adornments, paraphernalia (of office, etc); ornaments, esp ceremonial harnesses, etc for horses; gay, colourful clothes.

trapan a variant spelling of **trepan²**.

trape, trapes see **traipse**.

trapeze /trə-pēz'/ n a swinglike apparatus used by acrobats, consisting of one or more crossbars suspended between two ropes; a device attached by a line to the masthead of a light sailing boat, allowing a crew member to sit almost completely out of the boat. ◆ vi to perform or go on a trapeze. [From Fr, special use of trapèze; see ety for **trapezium**]

trapezium /trə-pē'zi-əm/ n (pl **trapē'zia** or **trapē'ziums**) orig any quadrilateral that is not a parallelogram; one with one (and only one) pair of parallel sides (Brit); one with no sides parallel (N Am); a bone of the wrist articulating with the thumb metacarpal. [Latinized from Gr trapezion, dimin of trapeza a table; literally four-legged, from tetra-four, and peza a foot]
■ **trapē'zial** adj of or relating to a trapezium. **trapē'ziform** adj having the form of a trapezium. **trapē'zius** n (pl **trapē'ziuses** or **trapē'zii** /-zi-ī/) (either of two triangular halves of) a large, flat, quadrilateral-shaped muscle extending up the thoracic spine to the neck, and across the back of the shoulders, that draws the head and shoulders back (also **trapezius muscle**). **trapēzohē'dral** adj. **trapēzohē'dron** n (pl **trapēzohē'dra** or **trapēzohē'drons**) a solid figure whose faces are trapezia or trapezoids. **trapezoid** /trap'i-zoid, trə-pē'zoid/ n a quadrilateral with no sides parallel; one with two sides parallel (N

Am); a bone of the wrist next to the trapezium. ◆ adj like a trapezium; of or relating to a trapezoid. **trapezoid'al** adj.

trappean see under **trap²**.

trappings see under **trap⁴**.

Trappist /trap'ist/ n a Cistercian monk of the reformed rule established by De Rancé (1626–1700), abbot of La Trappe in Normandy, noted for its austerity and rule of silence (also adj).
■ **Trapp'istine** /-tēn, -tin/ n a nun of an affiliated order.

trapunto /trə-pun'tō, -poon'/ n an Italian type of quilting done by stitching the design through two layers of fabric, and inserting wadding between the threads of the back layer. [Ital, quilting]

trash¹ /trash/ n anything worthless or of poor quality; scraps; rubbish, refuse (esp N Am); a receptacle for rubbish (N Am); nonsense; paltry stuff; worthless people; (also called (**poor**) **white trash**) poor whites, esp in the Southern USA (US); a worthless person (Shakesp); broken twigs, hedge-cuttings, splinters; dry sugarcane refuse, used eg as fuel; inferior or ephemeral rock music. ◆ vt to remove the outer leaves and branches from (sugarcane); to lop the tops from; to discard, reject, expose or criticize as worthless; to wreck or vandalize (chiefly N Am inf). [Prob Scand; cf Norw dialect trask trash, ON tros fallen twigs]
■ **trashed** adj (sl) drunk. **trash'ery** n trash, rubbish. **trash'ily** adv. **trash'iness** n. **trash'trie** n (Scot) trash. **trash'y** adj (**trash'ier**; **trash'iest**) like trash; worthless, of poor quality.
□ **trash'can** n (chiefly US) a receptacle for refuse. **trash farming** n a method of cultivation in arid regions of N America in which waste plant material from crops, etc is left on or near the surface of the soil to inhibit erosion and enrich the soil. **trash'man** n (N Am) a dustman, refuse collector.
■ **talk trash** (N Am) to make abusive or disparaging remarks (**trash talking** n).

trash² /trash/ vt to check (Shakesp); to restrain with a leash (obs or dialect). ◆ n (dialect) a leash or other restraint. [Origin obscure]

trash³ /trash/ vt to wear out, to harass. ◆ vi to trudge. [Cf Swed traska, Norw traske]

trashtrie see under **trash¹**.

trass /tras/ n an earthy volcanic tuff used as a hydraulic cement (also **tarras'** or **terras'**). [Du tras]

trastuzumab /tra-stoo'zū-mab/ n a therapeutic antibody used in the treatment of advanced breast cancer. [tras (arbitrary syllable), tumour, zu (denoting a humanized antibody), and monoclonal antibody]

trattoria /trät-tö-rē'ə, tra-tə-rē'ə/ n (pl **trattō'rias** or **trattō'rie** /-rē-ā/) an Italian restaurant (short form **trat** or **tratt**). [Ital, from trattore restaurateur, from Fr traiteur]

trauchle /trä' or trö'hhl/ (Scot) vt to bedraggle; to weary or overburden with drudgery or plodding. ◆ vi to drudge; to trail along. ◆ n a troublesome task; drudgery. [Cf Flem tragelen to go heavily]

trauma /trö'mə, trow'mə/ n (pl **trau'mas** or **trau'mata**) a wound; an injury (med); an emotional shock that may be the origin of a neurosis (psychiatry); the state or condition caused by a physical or emotional shock. [Gr trauma, -atos a wound]
■ **traumatic** /-mat'ik/ adj relating to, resulting from, or causing wounds; of or causing a lasting emotional shock; (loosely) frightening, unpleasant. **traumat'ically** adv. **trau'matism** /-mə-tizm/ n a condition caused by a wound, shock; an injury or wound. **traumatizā'tion** or **-s-** n. **trau'matize** or **-ise** vt to inflict a mental or physical trauma on; (loosely) to distress, upset, shock. **trau'matized** or **-s-** adj. **trau'matizing** or **-s-** adj and n. **traumatolog'ical** adj. **traumatol'ogy** n the study of wounds and of the effects of injuries. **traumatonas'ty** n a nastic movement after wounding.
□ **trauma centre** n (orig US) a centre or hospital specifically for the treatment of trauma victims.

travail¹ /trav'āl, -əl/ (literary or archaic) n excessive labour; toil; labour in childbirth; travel (obs). ◆ vi to labour; to suffer the pains of childbirth; to travel (obs). [OFr (and Fr) travail]
■ **trav'ailed** adj toilworn; wearied; experienced; having been in travail.
□ **travail pain** n. **travail pang** n.

travail² see **travois**.

trave /trāv/ (obs or dialect) n a beam or shaft (eg of a cart); a frame in which to shoe a fractious horse. [OFr trave beam, from L trabs]

travel /trav'l/ vi (**trav'elling** or (N Am) **trav'eling**; **trav'elled** or (N Am) **trav'eled**) to journey; to be capable of withstanding a journey; to go; to go round as a salesman soliciting orders; to go on circuit; to move along a course; to go with impetus; to pass; to move; to walk (dialect); to travail (obs). ◆ vt to journey over or through; to conduct or send on a journey (archaic). ◆ n journeying; impetus; power of going; range of movement; passage; (in pl) an account of journeys; travail (obs). [Later variant of **travail¹**]

■ **trav'elled** or (*N Am*) **trav'eled** *adj* having made journeys; experienced; (of a road, etc) beaten, frequented; (of rocks, earth, etc) transported, not in its original place. **trav'eller** or (*N Am*) **trav'eler** *n* a person who travels or has travelled; a wayfarer; (with *cap*) one of the Travelling People; a salesman who travels for a company (*old*); a ring that slides along a rope or spar; a piece of mechanism that moves on a gantry, etc. **trav'elling** or (*N Am*) **trav'eling** *n* the act of going on a journey or journeys; the offence of carrying the ball too far without dribbling (*basketball*). ◆ *adj* engaged in a journey; moving from place to place as part of one's occupation, peripatetic. **travelogue** or (*N Am*) **travelog** /*trav'ə-log*/ *n* a talk, lecture, article, or film on travel.
❑ **travel agency** *n* an agency that provides information, brochures, tickets, etc, relating to travel. **travel agent** *n* a person who runs or works in a travel agency; a travel agency. **traveller's cheque** *n* a cheque that can be cashed at any foreign branch or specified agent of the bank issuing it. **traveller's joy** *n* a climbing plant, *Clematis vitalba*, sometimes called old man's beard. **traveller's tale** *n* an amazing account, *esp* an untrue one, about what one professes to have seen abroad. **traveller's tree** *n* a Madagascan tree (genus *Ravenala*) of the banana family with great leaves on two sides only, accumulating water in the leaf-bases. **Travelling Folk** or **People**, etc *n pl* the name by which itinerant people often call themselves, in preference to Gypsies or tinkers. **travelling rug** *n* a thick blanket for keeping travellers, spectators, etc warm or for sitting on outdoors. **travelling-wave tube** *n* a device used in communications for increasing signal power, amplification being produced by interaction between a wave of radio frequency travelling on a wire helix and an electron beam travelling at roughly the same velocity inside the helix. **trav'el-sick** *adj* suffering from travel sickness. **travel sickness** *n* nausea experienced, as a result of motion, by a passenger in a car, ship, aircraft, etc. **trav'el-soiled**, **trav'el-stained** or **trav'el-tainted** *adj* (*Shakesp*) showing the marks of travel.

travelator another spelling of **travolator**.

traverse /*trav'ûrs* or *trə-vûrs'*/ *adj* cross; oblique. ◆ *n* a crossing or passage across; a straight length in a zigzag course; a passage across the face of a rock (*mountaineering*); the zigzag course of a sailing vessel tacking (*naut*); a survey by measuring straight lines from point to point and the angles between (*surveying*); anything set or lying across, a crosspiece, etc; an obstruction; a parapet; adversity; a curtain, screen, partition (*obs*); a barrier (*obs*); a gallery from one side of a large building to another, a screened-off compartment; a denial or contradiction, *esp* (*law*) the formal denial of a fact alleged by the other side; an opposing, counteracting movement (*fencing*); the movement of the barrel of a large gun to one side. ◆ *vt* (also /*-vûrs'*/) to cross; to pass through, across, or over; to move about over; to pass over by traverse; to survey (a road, etc) by traverse; to examine, consider (a subject, problem, etc) carefully; to oppose; to thwart; to dispute; to deny, contradict (*esp law*); to turn sideways; to direct a gun to the right or left. ◆ *vi* to make a traverse; to move to the side. [Fr *travers*, *traverse*, *traverser*, from L *trāns*, and *vertere*, *versum* to turn]
■ **trav'ersable** *adj*. **travers'al** *n* the action of traversing. **trav'ersed** *adj* crossed, passed over; set crosswise (*Shakesp*). **trav'erser** *n* a person who traverses; a platform for shifting wagons and carriages sideways. **trav'ersing** *n* and *adj*.
❑ **traversing bridge** *n* one that can be withdrawn horizontally.

travertine /*trav'ər-tēn*, *-tēn*, *-tin*/ *n* a pale limestone deposited from solution, eg from springs (also **travertin**). [Ital *travertino*, from L *tīburtīnus* (*lapis*) stone of Tibur (now Tivoli) in Italy]

travesty /*trav'i-sti* or *trav'ə-sti*/ *n* burlesque, parody; a ridiculously inadequate representation (of something); disguise, *esp* of a man as a woman or vice versa. ◆ *vt* (**trav'estying**; **trav'estied**) to burlesque; to disguise. [Fr *travesti*, pap of *travestir* to disguise, from L *trāns*, and *vestīre* to clothe; cf **transvest**]

travis see **treviss**.

travois /*trä-voi'*/ or **travail** /*trä-vä'i*/ *n* (*pl* **travois** /*trä-voiz'*/ or **travails** /*trä-vä'iz*/) a kind of sledge used by native peoples in N America, a pair of trailing poles attached to each side of the saddle, joined by a board or net. [Can Fr pronunciation of Fr *travail*]

travolator /*trav'ō-lā-tər*/ or **travelator** /*trav'l-*/ *n* a moving footpath for the conveyance of pedestrians. [From stem of **travel**; modelled on **escalator**]

trawl /*tröl*/ *n* an open-mouthed bag-net for dragging along the seabed; a trawl-line (qv below); an act of trawling. ◆ *vt* and *vi* to catch or fish with a trawl or (*Scot* and *US*) a seine-net. ◆ *vt* to look for something (eg a suitable person for a post, etc) by gathering suggestions from various sources (with *for*; strictly, a meaning developed from **troll**[2]); to fish (an area) using a trawl net; to search over, comb, investigate thoroughly, in order to gather information. [Cf **trail**[1] and MDu *traghel* dragnet]
■ **traw'ler** *n* a trawling vessel; a person who trawls. **traw'ling** *n*.

❑ **trawl'erman** *n* a person who mans a trawler. **trawl'-fish** *n* fish caught with a trawl. **trawl'-line** *n* a buoyed line with baited hooks at intervals. **trawl'-net** *n* a trawl.

T-ray /*tē'rā*/ *n* an electromagnetic ray in the terahertz frequency range.

tray[1] /*trā*/ *n* a flat board, etc with a low rim, used for holding or carrying articles (such as crockery, etc); a tray of food, *esp* instead of a meal at table. [OE *trīg*, *trēg* board]
■ **tray'ful** *n* (*pl* **tray'fuls**).
❑ **tray'bake** *n* a cake, pie, confection, etc baked in a shallow rectangular container before division into portions. **tray cloth** *n* a cloth for covering a tray. **tray'mobile** *n* (*Aust*) a household trolley, for serving tea, etc.

tray[2] /*trā*/ or **traybit** /*trā'bit*/ see **trey**.
❑ **tray'-trip** *n* (*Shakesp*) a game played with dice.

trayne see **train**[1].

treacher or **treachour** /*trech'ər*/ *n* (*obs*; also **treach'erer**) a deceiver by trickery; a betrayer; a traitor. [OFr *trecheor*, *trecheur* deceiver, from *trechier* to trick; cf **trick**]

treacherous /*trech'ə-rəs*/ *adj* ready to betray; not to be trusted; misleadingly inviting in appearance. [OFr *trecheros*, *trecherie*, from *trecheur* (see **treacher**) and *trechier* to trick]
■ **treach'erously** *adv*. **treach'erousness** *n*. **treach'ery** *n* betrayal; readiness to betray; falseness; treason. **treach'etour** *n* (*Spenser*) a deceiver; a traitor.

treacle /*trē'kl*/ *n* the dark, viscous uncrystallizable syrup obtained in refining sugar (also called **black treacle**); molasses, the drainings of crude sugar; golden syrup; blandishments, *esp* when suggestive of the cloying and nauseating taste and thickness of treacle; intolerable sentimentality; *orig* an antidote or prophylactic against bites, poisons, etc. ◆ *vt* to dose or smear with treacle. ◆ *vi* to treacle trees in order to collect moths. [OFr *triacle*, from Gr *thēriakē* (*antidotos*) (an antidote to the bites) of beasts, from *thērion* a wild beast]
■ **trea'cliness** *n*. **trea'cly** *adj* of or like treacle; thick and sweet; unctuously blandishing; intolerably sentimental.
❑ **treacle mustard** *n* the cruciferous plant, *Erysimum cheiranthoides*.

tread /*tred*/ *vi* (*pat* **trod**; *pap* **trodd'en** or **trod**) to set the foot down; to step; to walk; to trample; (of a male bird) to copulate. ◆ *vt* to walk on; to press with the foot, eg in threshing or pressing grapes; to trample, crush with the feet; to beat or form (a path, etc); to perform by treading, dance; (of a male bird) to copulate with; to oppress (*fig*). ◆ *n* the act or manner of treading; a step or tramp; a thing or part trodden on, eg on a step; the part that touches the ground, eg on a shoe or a wheel; (the thickness of) the moulded ridged rubber surface of a pneumatic tyre, which has contact with the road; a footprint; a track; the distance between wheels or pedals; the cicatricula, or the chalaza, of an egg; business, trade (see also ety below) (*Scot*). [OE *tredan*; Ger *treten*; ON *trotha*; cf **trade**]
■ **tread'er** *n*. **tread'ing** *n*. **tread'le** or **tredd'le** *n* a foot-lever for working a machine; a pedal; the chalaza of an egg (once thought to be derived from the cock) (*dialect*). ◆ *vi* to work a treadle. **tread'ler** *n*. **tread'ling** *n*.
❑ **tread'mill** *n* a machine with a continuously moving surface of adjustable speed used for exercising on by running or walking; a cylinder turned by treading on boards on its outside, as formerly by prisoners; a mill so worked; routine drudgery. **tread'wheel** *n* a wheel or cylinder turned by treading outside or inside; a treadmill.
■ **tread** (or **walk**) **on air** to feel exhilarated. **tread the boards** to act on stage. **tread water** to float upright by an action as if of climbing a ladder; to hold back temporarily from making progress (*fig*).

treague /*trēg*/ (*Spenser*) *n* a truce. [LL *tregua*, *treuga*, from Gothic *triggwa* treaty]

treas. *abbrev*: treasurer.

treason /*trē'zn*/ *n* betraying or attempting to overthrow one's government, country or sovereign; treachery; disloyalty. [Anglo-Fr *tresun*, OFr *traïson* (Fr *trahison*), from *traïr* (*trahir*), from L *tradere* to betray]
■ **trea'sonable** *adj* relating to, consisting of or involving treason. **trea'sonableness** *n*. **trea'sonably** *adv*. **trea'sonous** *adj*.
❑ **treason felony** *n* any of several offences that ceased to be considered to be a full-blown act of treason in the mid-19c.
■ **constructive treason** anything that may be interpreted as equivalent to actual treason by leading naturally to it. **high treason** any of several offences against the state or the sovereign. **misprision of treason** knowledge of treason and concealment thereof. **petty treason** (*hist*) the murder of a husband by a wife, a master by a servant, etc.

treasure /*trezh'ər*/ *n* wealth stored up; riches; anything much valued; a valued, indispensable helper, friend, etc; a term of endearment. ◆ *vt* to hoard up; to collect for future use; to value greatly; to enrich (*obs*). [OFr *tresor* (Fr *trésor*), from L *thēsaurus*, from Gr *thēsauros*]

■ **treas'urer** n a person who is in charge of a treasure or treasury; a person who is in charge of collected funds. **treas'urership** n.

treas'ury n a place where treasure is deposited; a store or collection of valued items; (often with cap) a department of a government that has charge of the finances; the income or funds of a state, government, etc; mistakenly applied to a beehive tomb in Mycenaean Greece. □ **treas'ure-chest** n a box for keeping articles of value. **treas'ure-city** n a city for stores, etc. **treas'ure-house** n a house for holding treasures; a treasury; a store of valuable things. **treasure hunt** n a hunt for treasure; a game in which competitors attempt to win a prize by being first to complete a course indicated by clues that have to be solved. **treas'ure-trove** n (trové, pap of Anglo-Fr trover to find) ownerless objects of intrinsic or historical value found hidden (in England gold and silver only), property of the crown; a collection of treasured things. **Treasury bench** n the front bench on the Speaker's right in the House of Commons, occupied by the members of the government. **Treasury bill** n a security entitling the holder to a stated amount to be paid from the Consolidated Fund at a specified date. **Treasury bond** n a bond issued by the US treasury. **treasury note** n a note issued by a government that is accepted as legal tender. **treasury tag** n a short piece of cord with a metal tag at each end, for holding papers together.

treat /trēt/ vt to deal with; to handle; to discuss; to behave towards; to act upon; to deal with the case of; to deal with (illness or a sick person) by applying remedies; to subject to a process; to stand a drink or other gratification to. ◆ vi to negotiate; to deal (with of); to stand treat. ◆ n a free entertainment, pleasure excursion or feast; a turn or act of providing and paying; a source of great gratification; negotiation, parley (Spenser). [OFr traitier, from L tractāre to manage, from trahere, tractum to draw]

■ **treatabil'ity** n. **treat'able** adj able to be treated; tractable, moderate (obs). **treat'er** n. **treat'ing** n. **treat'ise** /-iz, -is/ n a written composition, esp one treating a subject formally or systematically. **treat'ment** n the act or manner, or an instance, of treating; management; behaviour to anyone; a draft of a screenplay, including camera angles, descriptions of sets, etc (cinematog). ■ **Dutch treat** see under **Dutch. go down a treat** to be received very well. **stand treat** see under **stand. the (full) treatment** (inf) the appropriate method (in every detail) of dealing, whether ceremoniously or punitively, with a particular type of person, case, etc.

treaty /trē'ti/ n negotiation; a formal agreement, esp between states; any of several formal agreements between the Canadian government and local tribes whereby the so-called **treaty Indians** gave up their lands (apart from allocated reserves) and received an annual payment of **treaty money**; entreaty (Shakesp). [Anglo-Fr treté, OFr traité, from Med L tractātus, from L tractāre (see ety of **treat**)] □ **treaty port** n a port, esp in China, etc, opened by treaty to foreign trade.

treble /treb'l/ adj triple; threefold; in the treble (music); high-pitched. ◆ n that which is triple or threefold; three times as much; the highest part, soprano, now esp applied to boys' voices (music); a treble singer, voice, instrument, string, sound, etc; high-frequency sound as output from an amplifier, etc; the narrow inner ring on a dartboard, or a hit on this; a bet involving three horse-races, the stake and winnings from the first being bet on the second, and those from the second on the third; the winning of three championships, cups, titles, etc in one season (sport). ◆ vt and vi to make or become three times as much or many. [OFr, from L triplus; see **triple**] ■ **treb'leness** n. **treb'ly** adv. □ **treble chance** n a mode of competing in football pools by choosing a number of matches from the fixture list with the aim of including eight score draws among the selection. **treble clef** n (music) the clef in which the G immediately above middle C is placed on the second line of the stave. **treb'le-dated** adj living three times as long as man.

trebuchet /treb'ū-shet, trā-bü-shā'/ (hist) n a medieval engine of war for launching stones, etc. [OFr]

trecento /trā-chen'tō/ n and adj 14th-century (in Italian art, etc). [Ital, three (for thirteen) hundred] ■ **trecen'tist** n an author or artist of this period.

treck same as **trek** (vi and n).

tre corde /trā kor'dā/ (music) a direction to piano players to release the soft pedal. [Ital, three strings]

treddle same as **treadle** (see under **tread**).

tredrille or **tredille** /tra-d(r)il'/ n a card game for three. [Modelled on **quadrille²**, from L trēs three]

tree /trē/ n a large plant with a single branched woody trunk (sometimes loosely applied); timber; a wooden structure or part of various kinds; a saddle-tree; a boot- or shoe-tree; a branching figure or structure, such as an arborescent aggregate of crystals (eg lead tree), a branching stand (eg ring-tree, mug-tree), a pedigree, a branching diagram; a gallows (archaic); a cross for crucifixion (archaic). ◆ vt (tree'ing; treed) to drive into a tree, to corner (also fig); to form on a tree. ◆ vi to take refuge in a tree. ◆ adj wooden. ◆ combining form denoting: inhabiting, frequenting or growing on trees; taking the form of a tree; dendritic. [OE trēow, trēo; cf Gr drȳs oak, and dory spear; Sans dru tree]

■ **tree'less** adj. **tree'lessness** n. **tree'like** adj. **tree'ship** n existence as a tree.

□ **tree bicycle** n a mechanical device used for climbing trees. **tree burial** n disposal of the dead in the branches of trees. **tree calf** n a light-brown calf bookbinding with a branching tree design. **tree creeper** n any small northern hemisphere bird of the family Certhiidae that runs up tree trunks in search of insects. **tree diagram** n a diagram in which different possible outcomes are presented as branches of a tree. **tree farm** n a commercially-managed forest or woodland area. **tree fern** n a large, tropical fern with a tall woody trunk. **tree frog** n an arboreal amphibian, esp one of the family Hylidae, more akin to toads than to frogs. **tree heath** another name for **brier². tree hopper** n any of the homopterous leaping insects of the family Membracidae. **tree house** n a house built in a tree, esp as a playhouse. **tree'-hugger** n (inf, usu derog) an environmentalist. **tree'-hugging** n. **tree kangaroo** n a tree-climbing kangaroo (genus Dendrolagus). **tree lily** n a xerophytic treelike plant of the Brazilian campos (genus Vellozia). **tree line** same as **timber line** (see under **timber**). **tree'-lined** adj (of roads, etc) having trees along either side. **tree mallow** n Lavatera arbarca, a treelike plant of the Malvaceae family, having reddish-purple flowers. **tree moss** n moss or lichen growing on a tree; a moss like a tiny tree in shape. **treenail** or **trenail** /trē'nāl, tren'l/ n a long wooden pin or nail to fasten the planks of a ship to the timbers. **tree of heaven** n ailanthus. **tree of lead** n Saturn's tree (qv). **tree of life** n arbor vitae; a tree in the Garden of Eden whose fruit gave everlasting life (Bible, Genesis 2.9). **tree of silver** or **Diana's tree** n an arborescent deposit of silver. **tree onion** n a variety of onion with bulbs instead of flowers. **tree peony** n a shrub (Paeonia suffruticosa, also called **moutan**) of the family Ranunculaceae, native to China and Tibet, with pale pink flowers, from which many garden varieties have been developed. **tree rings** n pl annual rings. **tree shrew** n a squirrel-shrew, any insectivorous mammal of the East Indian family Tupaiidae, squirrel-like animals related to shrews. **tree snake** n a tree-dwelling snake. **tree sparrow** n a small European bird (Passer montanus) of the sparrow family; a N American finch, Spizella arborea. **tree stump** n. **tree surgeon** n a person who treats and preserves diseased or damaged trees by filling cavities, amputating branches, etc. **tree surgery** n. **tree toad** n a tree frog. **tree tomato** n the tamarillo, a S American solanaceous shrub (Cyphomandra betacea or C. crassifolia) or its tomato-like fruit. **tree'top** n the top of a tree. **tree trunk** n. **tree worship** n. **tree worshipper** n.

■ **at the top of the tree** in the highest position in eg a profession. **family tree** pedigree. **out of one's tree** (sl) crazy. **the tree of knowledge (of good and evil)** the tree in the Garden of Eden which bore the forbidden fruit eaten by Adam and Eve (Bible, Genesis 2.17). **up a tree** (sl, esp N Am) in difficulties (cf **up a gum tree** under **gum²**).

treen /trē'ən/ adj of a tree (Spenser); wooden. ◆ n (usu pl) small articles made of wood, esp eating and drinking utensils (**treen'ware**) of past times; the art of craft of making treenware. [See ety for **tree** and sfx -en]

tref, treif /trāf/ or **trefa** /trā'fə/ (Judaism) adj forbidden as food, not kosher. [Heb terēphāh torn flesh, from taraph to tear]

trefoil /trē'foil, tref'oil/ n a three-lobed form, ornament or aperture, as in tracery or heraldry; a leaf of three leaflets; a trifoliate plant, esp of the clover genus (Trifolium). [Anglo-Fr trifoil, from L trifolium, from trēs three, and folium a leaf] ■ **tre'foiled** adj. ■ **bird's-foot trefoil** see under **bird. hare's-foot trefoil** see under **hare**.

tregetour /trej'ə-tər/ (archaic) n a juggler; a trickster; a deceiver. [OFr tresgetour, from tresgeter, from L trāns, and jactāre to throw]

trehala /tri-hä'lə/ n Turkish manna, a sweet substance obtained from the cocoons of a type of beetle. [Turk tīqālah] ■ **tre'halose** n a disaccharide sugar that occurs naturally in honey, mushrooms, seafood, etc.

treille /trāl/ n a trellis. [Fr, from L trichila a bower] ■ **treill'age** n trelliswork; a trellis. **treill'aged** adj.

trek /trek/ vi (trekk'ing; trekked) to make a long hard journey, usu on foot; to tramp and camp, dragging one's equipment; to migrate; to journey by ox-wagon (S Afr). ◆ vt to drag. ◆ n a journey or stage; a migration. [Du trekken to draw] ■ **trekk'er** n. **Trekk'ie** or **Trekk'er** n an enthusiast of the US television and film franchise Star Trek. □ **trek'-ox** n. **trek'schuit** /-s'hhoit, -skoit/ n a towed canal boat.

trellis /trel'is/ n a structure of crossbarred or latticework. ◆ vt to provide with a trellis; to train on a trellis. [OFr *treliz*, from L *trilīx, -īcis* woven with triple thread, modified by association with **treille**]
■ **trell'ised** adj.
❑ **trellis window** n a lattice window. **trellis work** n latticework.

trema /trē'mə/ n an orifice; a diaeresis, two dots placed as a mark of separate pronunciation over a vowel-letter. [Gr *trēma, -atos* a hole]
■ **trematic** /tri-mat'ik/ adj (*zool*) of the gill slits. **trematode** /trem'ə-tōd/ n any member of the **Tremato'da**, a class of parasitic, unsegmented flatworms with adhesive suckers. **trem'atoid** n and adj.

tremble /trem'bl/ vi to shake, eg from fear, cold, or weakness; to quiver; to vibrate; to pass tremulously. ◆ vt to set trembling. ◆ n the act of trembling; tremulousness; a tremulous state; (in *pl*) an unwholesome trembling; (in *pl; specif*) a condition of muscular weakness and trembling in cattle and sheep caused by eating certain plants, *esp* white snakeroot (*Eupatorium rugosum*), also a name for milk sickness (qv) in humans. [OFr (Fr) *trembler*, from L *tremulus* trembling, from *tremere* to shake]
■ **tremblant** /trem'blənt/ adj (of jewellery) having the stones set on springs, so as to give a trembling effect. **trem'blement** n. **trem'bler** n a person, animal or thing that trembles; any of a number of West Indian birds of the family Mimidae; a vibrating device that makes and breaks a circuit (*elec*); an earthquake (*inf*). ◆ adj (of jewellery) tremblant. **trem'bling** n and adj. **trem'blingly** adv. **trem'bly** (**trem'blier**; **trem'bliest**) adj tremulous.
❑ **trembling poplar** n the aspen.

Tremella /tri-mel'ə/ n a genus of gelatinous fungi, such as witches' meat, found on decaying wood, etc. [L *tremulus* quivering]

tremendous /tri-men'dəs/ adj awe-inspiring, dreadful; huge, extraordinarily great (*inf*); prodigious, extraordinary, very good (*sl*). [L *tremendus* to be trembled at]
■ **tremen'dously** adv. **tremen'dousness** n.

trémie or **tremie** /trā-mē', trem'i/ n a hopper-like device for laying concrete under water. [Fr, hopper, from L *trimodia* a three-peck measure]

tremolando, tremolant see under **tremolo**.

tremolite /trem'ə-līt/ n a calcium-magnesium amphibole, *usu* in long prisms or fibres, pale or colourless. [From the Val *Tremola* in the Alps, where the mineral found is not true tremolite]
■ **tremolitic** /-lit'ik/ adj.

tremolo /trem'ō-lō or trem'ə-lō/ (*music*) n (*pl* **trem'olos**) a tremulous effect as by a rapid succession of the same note or of two notes at least a third apart; a tremulant. ◆ adj having a tremolo effect. [Ital]
■ **tremolan'do** adj and adv played with a tremolo effect. ◆ n (*pl* **tremolan'di** or **tremolan'dos**) a tremolando passage or movement. **trem'olant** n and adj tremolo.
❑ **tremolo arm** n a metal lever attached to the bridge of an electric guitar for producing a tremolo effect.

tremor /trem'ər/ n a quiver; a quavering; a thrill; an involuntary agitation; a vibration. ◆ vi to quiver. [L *tremor, -ōris*]
■ **trem'orless** adj.

tremulous /trem'ū-ləs/ adj trembling; quivering; timorous, nervous. [L *tremulus* trembling, and LL *tremulāre, -ātum* to tremble]
■ **trem'ūlant** adj tremulous. ◆ n a device in an organ or electronic instrument for producing a tremolo effect. **trem'ūlate** vi and vt. **trem'ūlously** adv. **trem'ūlousness** n.

trenail see under **tree**.

trench /trench, trensh/ n a long, narrow, deep cut in the earth; a protective ditch dug in warfare, with the excavated earth used as a parapet; a long, narrow steep-sided depression in an ocean floor, *esp* one running parallel to a continent; a deep furrow or wrinkle in the skin. ◆ vi to make trenches; to dig deep with spade or plough; to encroach; to border, verge. ◆ vt to cut; to make trenches in; to put in a trench; to provide with a trench; to entrench; to divert by a trench (*Shakesp*). [OFr *trenche* cut (Fr *tranche* slice), and *trencher* (Fr *trancher* to cut, to slice) to cut, prob from L *truncāre* (see **truncate**)]
■ **trench'ancy** n causticity. **trench'ant** (*Spenser* **trench'and**) adj cutting; incisive, forthright; sharply defined, distinct. **trench'antly** adv. **trench'er** n.
❑ **trench coat** n a short waterproof coat with belt, for men or women. **trench fever** n an infectious disease causing pain in joints and muscles, prevalent among soldiers living in trenches, caused by a *Rickettsia* and transmitted by lice. **trench foot** or **feet** n a diseased condition of the feet caused by long exposure to cold and wet, *esp* affecting soldiers in trench warfare. **trench knife** n a knife with double-sided blade, used by patrols in the Trenches. **trench mortar** n a small mortar that throws large shells short distances, useful in trench warfare. **trench mouth** n a bacterial infection that causes the gums to become ulcerated and swollen, prevalent among soldiers in trench warfare. **trench plough** n a plough for ploughing more deeply than

usual. ◆ vt to plough with a trench plough. **trench warfare** n warfare in which each side entrenches itself in lines facing the enemy.
■ **the Trenches** (also without *cap*) the protective ditches dug for the infantry on the Western Front in World War I, or the Western Front itself.

trenchard see under **trencher¹**.

trencher¹ /tren'chər, -shər/ n a plate or platter (*old*); a board. [Anglo-Fr *trenchour* (Fr *tranchoir*), from *trencher* to cut]
■ **trenchard** /tren'shərd/ n the word used at St Andrews University for a trencher cap.
❑ **trencher cap** n a college cap, mortarboard. **tren'cher-fed** adj (of foxhounds) kept each by his owner, not in a pack. **tren'cher-friend** or **-knight** n (both *Shakesp*) a person who frequents the table of another, a parasite. **tren'cherman** n a hearty eater; a trencher-friend.

trencher² see under **trench**.

trend /trend/ vi to turn, wind; to read messages from (a person) on a social media site; to have a tendency or prevailing direction; to be currently popular. ◆ n general tendency; a bend (*dialect*). [OE *trendan*]
■ **trend'ily** adv. **trend'iness** n. **tren'dy** adj (**tren'dier**; **tren'diest**) (*inf*) in the forefront of fashion in any sphere. ◆ n (*usu derog*) a trendy person. **trend'yism** n.
❑ **trend'setter** n someone who helps to give a new direction to fashion. **trend'setting** n and adj.

trendle-tail see under **trundle**.

trenise /trə-nēz'/ n the fourth movement of a quadrille (also **la trenise**). [Fr]

trental /tren'tl/ n a series of thirty requiem masses. [LL *trentāle*, from L *trīgintā* thirty]

trente-et-quarante /trãt-ā-ka-rãt'/ n the card game rouge-et-noir. [Fr, thirty and forty]

trepan¹ /tri-pan'/ n an obsolete circular saw for perforating the skull; a tool for boring shafts. ◆ vt (**trepann'ing; trepanned'**) to remove a piece of the skull from (*surg*); to cut a cylindrical disc from; to cut an annular groove in. [Fr *trépan*, from LL *trepanum*, from Gr *trȳpanon*, from *trȳpaein* to bore]
■ **trepanation** /trep-ə-nā'shən/ n. **trepann'er** n. **trepann'ing** n and adj.

trepan² /tri-pan'/ (*archaic*) n a decoy; a snare; an entrapping. ◆ vt (**trepann'ing; trepanned'**) to ensnare; to lure. [Earlier *trapan*; prob connected with **trap¹**]
■ **trepann'er** n. **trepann'ing** n and adj.

trepang /tri-pang'/ n a sea cucumber, a holothurian eaten by the Chinese. [Malay *trīpang*]

trephine /tri-fēn', -fīn'/ (*surg*) n a refined form of trepan. ◆ vt to operate on, perforate, or remove a circular section from (eg the skull or cornea) with the trephine. [Earlier *trafine*, from L *trēs fīnēs* three ends, modified by **trepan¹**]
■ **trephination** /tref-i-nā'shən/ n. **trephin'er** n a surgeon who uses a trephine. **trephin'ing** n.

trepidation /trep-i-dā'shən/ n alarmed agitation; trembling; a libration of the celestial sphere assumed to explain a supposed oscillation of the ecliptic (*old astron; Milton*). [L *trepidāre, -ātum* to hurry with alarm, from *trepidus* restless]
■ **trep'id** adj (*rare*) quaking. **trep'idant** adj. **trepid'atory** adj.

treponema /trep-ə-nē'mə/ or **treponeme** /trep'ə-nēm/ n (*pl* **treponē'mata, treponē'mas** or **trep'onemes**) a bacterium of the genus *Treponema* of spirochaetes, one of which, *T. pallidum*, causes syphilis. [Gr *trepein* to turn, and *nēma* thread]

très /tre, trez/ (*inf*) adv very. [Fr]

trespass /tres'pəs or (*US*) -pas/ vi to interfere with another's person or property; to enter unlawfully upon another's land; to encroach (on); to intrude (with on); to sin (*church*). ◆ n an act of trespassing; any injury to another's person or property; a sin (*church*). [OFr *trespasser*, from L *trāns*, and *passus* a step]
■ **tres'passer** n.

tress¹ /tres/ n a plait or braid of the hair of the head; a long lock, braided or not. ◆ vt to form into tresses. [Fr *tresse*, from LL *tricia*, perh from Gr *tricha* threefold, from *treis* three]
■ **tressed** adj braided; in tresses; having tresses. ◆ *combining form* denoting having tresses of a specified kind. **tress'y** adj having or like tresses.

tress², tressel see **trestle**.

tressure /tresh'ər/ (*heraldry*) n a subordinary, half the breadth of the orle, and *usu* borne double, and flowered and counter-flowered with fleurs-de-lis. [Fr, from *tresser* to plait]
■ **tress'ured** adj.

trest see under **trestle**.

trestle, also **tressel** /tres'l/ n a support composed of a horizontal beam on sloping legs; a braced framework. [OFr *trestel* (Fr *tréteau*) and *treste*, *trestre*, from L *trānstrum* crossbeam]
- **tress** or **trest** /trest/ n (*obs* or *dialect*) a trestle.
- ▫ **trestle bridge** n one resting on trestlework. **trestle table** n one made of boards laid on trestles. **trest'letree** n (*naut*) either of a pair of horizontal pieces fixed on opposite sides of a masthead to support the topmast. **trest'lework** n a braced framework.

tret /tret/ (*hist*) n an allowance to purchasers of 4lb on every 104lb for waste. [Poss Anglo-Fr *tret* pull, turn of the scale, or Fr *traite* transport, both from *traire* to draw, from L *trahere*, *tractum*]

trevally /tri-val'i/ (*Aust* and *NZ*) n any horse-mackerel of the genus *Caranx*. [Prob a modification of **cavally**]

treviss or **trevis** /trev'is/ or **travis** /trav'is, trā'vis/ n a stall partition; a stall. [Variants of **traverse**]

trew an old spelling of **true**.

trews /trooz/ n pl (*orig sing*) trousers, *esp* of tartan cloth. [Ir *trius*, Gaelic *triubhas*; cf **trouse**, **trousers**]
- ▫ **trews'man** n a wearer of trews.

trey /trā/ n the three in cards and dice; a set of three; the third tine of a deer's horn (in full **trey-ant'ler**, **-tine**; also **tray** or **trez** /trā, trāz/); a threepenny bit (also **trey'bit**, **tray** or **tray'bit**; *sl*); anything with a value of three (*US sl*). [OFr *treis*, *trei*, from L *trēs* three]

trez see **trey**.

TRH *abbrev*: Their Royal Highnesses.

tri- /trī-, tri-/ *combining form* denoting three, threefold. [L *trēs*, *tria*, and Gr *treis*, *tria*]

triable see under **try**.

triacid /trī-as'id/ (*chem*) adj having three replaceable hydrogen atoms; capable of replacing three hydrogen atoms of an acid. [**tri-**]

triaconter /trī-ə-kon'tər/ n an ancient Greek ship, perhaps with thirty men to each group of oars. [Gr *triākontērēs*, from *triākonta* thirty]

triact /trī'akt/ (*zool*) adj three-rayed. [**tri-**, and Gr *aktīs*, *-īnos* ray]
- ▪ **triact'inal** /-i-nal or -ī'nal/ or **triact'ine** /-in/ adj.

triad /trī'ad, -əd/ n a group, set, or union of three; (in Welsh literature) a group of three sayings, stories, etc, about related subjects; a group of three lines or stanzas in different metres; a chord of three notes, *esp* the common chord (*music*); an atom, element, or radical with a valency of three (*chem*); (with *cap*) any of many Chinese secret societies (*orig* so named from their use of the triangle in their rituals), some founded in the 17c to resist the Manchu regime, some now associated with criminal activities, *esp* heroin trading. ◆ adj (also **trīad'ic**) in the form of or relating to a triad. [L *trias*, from Gr *trias*, *triados*, from *treis* three]
- ▪ **trī'adist** n a composer of triads.

triadelphous /trī-ə-del'fəs/ (*bot*) adj with three bundles of stamens. [**tri-** and Gr *adelphos* a brother]

triage see under **try**.

Trial /tri-al'/ (*Fr*) n a tenor with special aptitude for comedy parts, often noted more for his acting than for his vocalism. [Antoine *Trial* (1736–95), French tenor renowned for his comedy roles at the Opéra-Comique in Paris]

trial¹ /trī'əl/ n a trying; examination by a test; a test of the efficacy, safety, etc, of a new product, *esp* a drug before it is marketed, or in order to gain official approval for its general use; examination by a court to determine a question of law or fact, *esp* the guilt or innocence of a prisoner; (often in *pl*) examination, sometimes merely formal, of a candidate; (often in *pl*) a competition, *esp* to select members of a major team; a competition comprising various tests, for sheepdogs or horses; a competition to test vehicles in difficult conditions; suffering; temptation; an attempt; a piece used as a test; a troublesome thing, a nuisance. ◆ adj done, taken, etc, for the sake of trial. ◆ vt (**tri'alling**; **tri'alled**) to test (*esp* a new product). [Anglo-Fr, from *trier* to try]
- ▪ **tri'alist** or **tri'allist** n a person taking part in a trial or test; a competitor or player under consideration for a place in a major team (*sport*).
- ▫ **trial balance** n (*bookkeeping*) in the double-entry system, a listing of all the balances in a ledger to check that the total of credit balances is equal to the total of debit balances. **trial balloon** n a ballon d'essai. **trial court** n the first court where the facts of a case are decided; a court where cases are tried, as opposed to an appeal court (chiefly N Am). **tri'al-day** n (*Shakesp*) day of trial. **tri'al-fire** n (*Shakesp*) a fire for trying or proving. **trial marriage** n for a couple intending matrimony, a period of living together with a view to testing their compatibility. **trial run** n a test drive in a motor vehicle to ascertain its efficiency; any introductory test, rehearsal, etc. **trial trip** n an experimental trip of a new vessel, to test its sailing-powers, etc. **tri'alware** same as **shareware** (see under **share¹**).

- **by trial and error** by trying out several methods and discarding those which prove unsuccessful. **on trial** undergoing proceedings in a court of law; on probation, as an experiment; subject to a prospective purchase proving satisfactory. **stand trial** to undergo trial in a court of law. **trial of strength** a contest to find out who is the stronger (or strongest); a struggle between two irreconcilable parties, prolonged until one of them weakens.

trial² /trī'əl/ adj threefold, trinal; expressing or representing three things (*grammar*). ◆ n a grammatical form expressing or representing three things. [Modelled on **dual**, from L *trēs*, *tria* three]
- ▪ **tri'alism** n the doctrine of the existence of body, soul and spirit in man; a scheme for turning the Dual Monarchy into a triple (Austria, Hungary, and a South Slav state; *hist*). **tri'alist** n. **trīality** /-al'i-ti/ n.

trialogue /trī'ə-log/ n a conversation between three people. [On false analogy of **dialogue**, as if *dia-* meant two]

triandrous /trī-an'drəs/ (*bot*) adj with three stamens. [**tri-** and Gr *anēr*, *andros* a man, male]
- ▪ **Trian'dria** n pl (in Linnaeus's classification) a class of plants with three stamens. **trian'drian** adj.

triangle /trī'ang-gl (also *-ang'*)/ n a plane figure with three angles and three sides (*maths*); part of the surface of a sphere bounded by three arcs of great circles (*spherical triangle*); any mark or thing of that shape; a musical instrument of percussion, formed of a steel rod bent in triangle-form, open at one angle; a tripod, *esp* for a pulley for raising weights, or formerly (*usu* in *pl*) for binding soldiers to for flogging. [L *triangulum*, from *angulus* an angle]
- ▪ **tri'angled** adj. **triang'ular** adj having three angles; (of a number) any of the series of numbers 0, 1, 3, 6, 10, 15, etc, the series being formed by adding 1, 2, 3, 4, 5, consecutively to consecutive members of the series; involving three persons or parties. **triangular'ity** n. **triang'ularly** adv. **triang'ulate** vt to survey by means of a series of triangles. ◆ adj with, marked with or made up of triangles; triangular. **triang'ulately** adv. **triangula'tion** n the act or process of triangulating, eg for map-making; the series of triangles so used.
- ▫ **triangulation point** same as **trigonometrical point** (see under **trigonometry**).
- ▪ **the eternal triangle** an emotional situation involving two men and a woman or two women and a man.

triapsidal /trī-ap'si-d(ə)l/ adj with three apses (also **triaps'al**). [**tri-**]

triarch¹ /trī'ärk/ (*bot*) adj having three xylem strands in the stele. [**tri-** and Gr *archē* origin]

triarch² see under **triarchy**.

triarchy /trī'är-ki/ n government by three people; a state governed by a triumvirate; a state divided into three parts each having its own ruler; one of three such parts. [Gr *triarchiā*, from *archē* rule]
- ▪ **trī'arch** n a ruler of a triarchy, a member of a triumvirate.

Triassic /trī-as'ik/ (*geol*) adj of or belonging to a period of the Mesozoic era, between 250 and 200 million years ago. ◆ n (also **Trias** /trī'əs/) the Triassic period or system. [Gr *trias* triad, from its threefold subdivision in Germany into Bunter, Muschelkalk and Keuper]

triathlon /trī-ath'lon/ n a sporting contest consisting of three events held without a break between each, *usu* swimming, cycling and running. [**tri-** and Gr *athlon* a contest]
- ▪ **triath'lete** n.

triatic /trī-at'ik/ or **triatic stay** /stā/ (*naut*) n a rope joining adjacent mastheads to which tackle is attached; each of a pair of stays joining the tops of direction-finding masts diagonally and supporting from their points of intersection a vertical aerial. [Origin obscure]

triatomic /trī-ə-tom'ik/ adj consisting of three atoms; having three replaceable atoms or groups; trivalent. [**tri-**]
- ▪ **triatom'ically** adv.

triaxial /trī-ak'si-əl/, also **triaxon** /-ak'son/ adj having three axes. ◆ n a triaxial sponge spicule. [**tri-**, L *axis* axle, and Gr *axōn*]

triazine /trī'ə-zēn, trī-az'ēn/ (*chem*) n any of various compounds containing three 6-membered heterocyclic rings, each of which contains nitrogen, often used in herbicides. [**tri-** and **azine**]

triazole /trī'ə-zol, trī-az'ol, -zōl/ (*chem*) n any of various compounds containing three 5-membered heterocyclic rings, each of which contains nitrogen, often used in fungicides. [**tri-** and **azole**]

tribade /trib'ad/ n a female homosexual, a lesbian. [Fr, through L *tribas*, *-adis*, from Gr *tribas*, *-ados*, from *tribein* to rub]
- ▪ **tribad'ic** adj. **trib'adism** or **trib'ady** n lesbian masturbation simulating heterosexual intercourse in the missionary position.

tribal, etc see under **tribe**.

tri-band /trī'band/ adj (of a mobile phone) capable of operating on three frequency bands (900 MHz, 1800 MHz and 1900 MHz). [**tri-**]

tribasic /trī-bā'sik/ (*chem*) adj capable of reacting with three equivalents of an acid; (of acids) having three replaceable hydrogen atoms. [**tri-**, and **base**]

▪ words derived from main entry word; ▫ compound words; ▪ idioms and phrasal verbs

tribble /trib'l/ n a horizontal frame with wires stretched across it for drying paper. [Origin unknown]

tribe /trīb/ n a division of a pre-industrial nation or people for political purposes; a set of people theoretically of common descent; an aggregate of families, forming a community; a race; a breed; a class or set of people; (loosely) a classificatory division. [L *tribus*, *-ūs* one of the divisions of the ancient Roman people, conjecturally originally three in number, and hence perh related to L *trēs*, *tria* three]
■ **trī'bal** adj. **trī'balism** n the existence of tribes as a social phenomenon; (loyalty to) the conventions, etc, of one's tribe. **trī'balist** n. **trī'balistic** adj. **trī'bally** adv. **tribe'less** adj. **tribes'man** or **tribes'woman** n. **tribes'people** n pl.

triblet /trib'lit/ n a tapering mandrel on which rings, nuts, etc, are forged. [Fr *triboulet*]

tribo- /trī-bo-, trib-ō-, trī-bō or tri-bo-/ combining form denoting rubbing or friction. [Gr *tribein* to rub]
■ **triboelec'tric** adj. **triboelectric'ity** n electricity generated by friction. **tribol'ogist** n. **tribol'ogy** n the study of interacting surfaces in relative motion and of related subjects and practices. **triboluminescence** /-es'əns/ n emission of light caused by friction. **triboluminesˈcent** adj. **tribomˈeter** n a sled-like apparatus for measuring sliding friction.

tribrach /trī'brak/ (prosody) n a foot of three short syllables. [Gr *tribrachys*, from *brachys* short]
■ **tribrach'ic** adj.

tribromo- or **tribrom-** /trī-brōm(-ō)-/ combining form denoting (a compound) having three atoms of bromine, esp replacing hydrogen.

tribulation /trib-ū-lā'shən/ n severe affliction; the cause of this; the state of being in pawn (obs sl); a rowdy gang (Shakesp). [L *trībulāre*, *-ātum* to afflict, from *trībulum* a sledge for separating grain from chaff by rubbing, from *terere* to rub]

tribune /trib'ūn/ n a senior officer in a Roman legion; a magistrate elected by the plebeians in ancient Rome to defend their rights; a champion of popular rights; in this and the following sense, sometimes used as the title of a newspaper; a platform for speaking from; a raised area or stand; bishop's stall or throne. [L *tribūnus* tribune, and *tribūnāl* tribunal, from *tribus* a tribe]
■ **tribunal** /trib-, trīb-ū'nl, also (Spenser) trib'/ n a court of justice or arbitration; a body appointed to adjudicate in some matter or to enquire into some disputed question; a seat or bench in a court from which judgement is pronounced, a judgement-seat; a confessional. ♦ adj of, of the nature of or authorized by a tribunal. **trib'unate** or **trib'uneship** n the office of tribune. **Trib'unism** n. **Trib'unite** n a member of the Tribune Group. **tribunitial** or **tribunicial** /-ish'l/ or **tribunitian** or **tribunician** /-ish'ən/ adj.
□ **Tribune Group** n a left-wing group within the British Parliamentary Labour Party.

tribute /trib'ūt/ n a payment in acknowledgment of subjection (hist); an act, gift, words or other expression of approbation; (loosely) a testimony, a credit (to); a percentage of ore or its value received (or paid to the owners) by a miner. [L *tribūtum*, from *tribuere* to assign]
■ **trib'utarily** adv. **trib'utariness** n. **trib'utary** adj paying tribute; contributing; paid in tribute. ♦ n a payer of tribute; a stream that runs into another. **trib'uter** n a miner paid by tribute.
□ **tribute band** n a pop group that mimics the appearance and music of a famous group. **tribute money** n money paid as tribute.

tributyltin /trī-bū'til-tin/ n any of several organic compounds added to paint to prevent the growth of algae and other organisms on the hulls of ships, now believed to cause abnormalities in some marine creatures (abbrev **TBT**).

tricameral /trī'kam-ə-rəl, -kam'/ adj having three chambers. [**tri-** and L *camera* chamber]

tricar /trī'kär/ n a motor-tricycle with a passenger's seat or luggage carrier in front; a three-wheeled car. [**tri-**]

tricarboxylic /trī-kär-bok-sil'ik/ adj (of an acid) having three carboxyl groups in each molecule. [**tri-**]
□ **tricarboxylic acid cycle** n another name for **Krebs cycle**.

tricarpellary /trī-kär'pə-lər-i or -pel'ər-i/ (bot) adj of or with three carpels. [**tri-**]

trice /trīs/ vt (naut) to haul; to haul and make fast. ♦ n a moment (as if the time of a single tug); a pulley (obs). [MDu *trisen* (Du *trijsen*) to hoist]

tricentenary /trī-sen-tē'nə-ri or -ten'ə-ri/ n same as **tercentenary**.

tricephalous /trī-sef'ə-ləs/ adj three-headed. [Gr *trikephalos*, from *kephalē* a head]

triceps /trī'seps/ n (pl **trī'cepses** or **trī'ceps**) (anat) a muscle with three separately arising heads, esp the muscle at the back of the upper arm that straightens the elbow. ♦ adj three-headed. [L *trīceps*, *-cipitis*, from *caput* head]

triceratops /trī-ser'ə-tops/ n an ornithischian, quadrupedal, herbivorous dinosaur of the Cretaceous period, having a horn over each eye and one on its nose. [**tri-** and Gr *keras*, *keratos* horn, and *ōps* face]

tricerion /trī-sē'ri-on/ (Gr church) n a three-branched candlestick. [Late Gr, from Gr *kēros* wax]

trich- /trik-/ or **tricho-** /-ō-, -o-/ combining form denoting hair. [Gr *thrix*, genitive *trichos*]

trichiasis /trik-ī'ə-sis/ (med) n the turning in of hairs around an orifice, esp of eyelashes so that they rub against the eye; the presence of hairlike filaments in the urine. [LL, from Gr *thrix*, *trichos* hair]

trichina /trik'i-nə, tri-kī'nə/ or **trichinella** /trik-i-nel'ə/ n (pl **trichin(ell)ae** /-ē/ or **trichin(ell)as** a member of the genus *Trichinella* of nematode worms parasitic in rat, pig, and man, the adult in the small intestine, the larva encysted in muscle. [Gr *trichinos* of hair, from *thrix*, *trichos* hair]
■ **trichiniasis** /trik-i-nī'ə-sis/ or **trichinō'sis** n a disease caused by trichinae. **trichinīzā'tion** or **-s-** n infestation with trichinae. **trich'inize**, **-s-** or **trich'inose** /-nōs/ vt to infest with trichinae. **trichinot'ic** or **trich'inous** adj relating to trichinosis.

trichite /trik'īt/ n a hairlike crystallite. [Gr *thrix*, *trichos* hair]
■ **trichitic** /-it'ik/ adj.

Trichiurus /trik-i-ū'rəs or -oo'rəs/ n a genus of hair-tails, giving name to the family **Trichiu'ridae**, related to mackerels and tunnies. [**trich-** and Gr *oura* tail]

trichloro- or **trichlor-** /trī-klōr(-ō)-, -klōr(-ō)-/ combining form denoting (a compound) having three atoms of chlorine, esp replacing hydrogen.
■ **trichloroē'thane** n a chlorinated solvent used widely in industry as a cleaner for electrical equipment. **trichloroethylene** or **trichlorethylene** /trī-klōr(-ō)-eth'i-lēn, -klōr-/ n an ethylene derivative, used as a solvent, in paint manufacture, and as an analgesic and anaesthetic (inf short form **trike** /trīk/). **trichloromē'thane** n chloroform.

tricho- see **trich-**.

trichobacteria /trik-ō-bak-tē'ri-ə/ n pl filamentous bacteria. [**tricho-**]

trichocyst /trik'ə-sist/ n (in some Ciliophora) a minute hairlike body lying in the subcuticular layer of protoplasm. [**tricho-**]

trichogyne /trik'ō-jīn, -jin/ n in red seaweeds, and some fungi, a threadlike prolongation of the female organ. [**tricho-** and Gr *gynē* woman, female]

trichoid /trik'oid/ adj hairlike. [Gr *trichoeidēs*]

trichology /trik-ol'ə-ji/ n the scientific study of hair and its disorders. [Gr *thrix*, *trichos* a hair]
■ **tricholog'ical** adj. **trichol'ogist** n a person skilled in trichology; a name appropriated by hairdressers.

trichome /trik'ōm, trī'kōm/ n a plant hair or outgrowth from the epidermis. [Gr *trichōma* a growth of hair]

trichomonad /trik-ə-mon'ad/ n a parasitic protozoan of the genus **Trichomonas** /tri-kom'- or -kə-mon'/. [**tricho-** and Gr *monas*, *-ados* a unit]
■ **trichomon'al** adj. **trichomoni'asis** /-mon-ī'/ n a sexually transmitted disease caused by trichomonads, found in human beings and in animals.

trichophyton /trik-of'i-tən or trik-ə-fī'ton/ n any fungus of the genus *Trichophyton*, causing ringworm. [**tricho-** and Gr *phyton* plant]
■ **trichophytō'sis** n ringworm caused by *Trichophyton*.

Trichoptera /trik-op'tə-rə/ n pl an order of insects with hairy wings, caddis flies. [**tricho-** and Gr *pteron* wing]
■ **trichop'teran** n and adj (an insect) of the Trichoptera. **trichop'terist** n someone who studies the caddis flies. **trichop'terous** adj.

trichord /trī'körd/ adj three-stringed; with three strings to one note. ♦ n a three-stringed instrument; a triad. [Gr *trichordos*, from *chordē* a string]

trichosis /tri-kō'sis/ n arrangement, distribution, or diseased condition of hair. [Gr *trichōsis* hairiness]

trichotillomania /trik-ō-til-ō-mā'ni-ə/ n a neurosis in which the patient pulls out tufts of his or her own hair. [**tricho-**, Gr *tillein* to pull, and **mania**]

trichotomous /trī-kot'ə-məs/ adj divided into three; forking in threes. [Gr *tricha* threefold, from *treis* three, and *tomē* a cutting, from *temnein* to cut]
■ **trichot'omize** or **-ise** vt and vi to divide in three or threes. **trichot'omously** adv. **trichot'omy** n trichotomous division or forking.

trichroic /trī-krō'ik/ adj (esp of crystals) having or exhibiting three colours, esp when viewed along different axes. [Gr *trichroos* three-coloured]
■ **trī'chroism** n.

trichromatic /trī-krō-mat'ik/ *adj* characterized by three colours; having normal colour vision. [Gr *trichrōmatos*, from *chrōma* colour]
■ **trichro'mat** *n* someone who has normal colour vision. **trichrō'matism** *n*. **tri'chrome** *adj* trichromatic. **trichrō'mic** *adj* trichromatic. ◆ *n* a trichromat.

trichronous /trī'kro-nəs/ *adj* trisemic. [Gr *trichronos*, from *chronos* time]

trick /trik/ *n* an artifice; a deceitful device; a deception; a prank; a performance aimed at astonishing, puzzling, or amusing; an expedient or knack; a characteristic habit, mannerism or trait; a spell or turn, *esp* at the helm; a round of play at cards; the cards so played and taken by the winner, forming a unit in scoring; a trinket or toy; a watch (*sl*); an outline sketch (*heraldry*); the customer of a prostitute (*sl*). ◆ *vt* to deceive, to cheat; to beguile; to dress or decorate fancily (with *out*); to trim; to sketch in outline. ◆ *adj* of the nature of, or for the purpose or performance of, a trick; unreliable, defective (*US inf*); adroit and trim (*obs*). [OFr *trique*, Scot and N Eng form of *triche* deceit; perh in part of other origin]
■ **trick'er** *n*. **trick'ery** *n* the act or practice of playing tricks; artifice; stratagem; imposition. **trick'ily** *adv*. **trick'iness** *n*. **trick'ing** *n* and *adj*. **trick'ish** *adj* tricky. **trick'ishly** *adv*. **trick'ishness** *n*. **trick'less** *adj*. **trick'sily** *adv*. **trick'siness** *n*. **trick'some** *adj*. **trick'ster** *n* a cheat; someone who practises trickery. **trick'stering** *n* playing the trickster. **tricks'y** *adj* (**tricks'ier**; **tricks'iest**) given to pranks, mischievous; tricky, crafty; dressed or adorned smartly (*obs*). **trick'y** *adj* (**trick'ier**; **trick'iest**) ticklish, difficult to handle; complicated; addicted to trickery; clever in tricks.
❑ **trick cyclist** *n* an acrobat who performs tricks on a unicycle or cycle; a psychiatrist (*sl*).
■ **do the trick** to bring something about. **how's tricks?** (*sl*) how are you? **trick or treat** (*esp N Am*) the (children's) practice of dressing up to visit neighbouring houses at Hallowe'en, and threatening to play a trick unless a treat is produced. **turn a trick** (*sl*, *esp US*) (of a prostitute) to have sex with a client. **up to** (**one's**) **tricks** misbehaving.

trickle¹ /trik'l/ *vi* to run or pass in drops or in a small irregular stream. ◆ *vt* to emit in a trickle. ◆ *n* a succession of drops; a sparse intermittent rivulet; a drop (*obs*). [ME *triklen*, prob for *striklen*, frequentative of **strike**]
■ **trick'let** *n* a little trickle. **trick'ling** *n* and *adj*. **trick'ly** *adj* trickling.
❑ **trick'le-charge** *vt* to charge (a battery) over a long period at a low rate. **trickle charger** *n*. **trick'le-down** *n* (*orig* and *esp US*) filtration of benefits, *esp* money, downwards through the social community. ◆ *adj* of or relating to the idea that economic benefits received by advantaged sectors, eg large companies, ultimately filter down to benefit the less well-off.

trickle² /trik'l/ (*Spenser*) *adj* ticklish, precarious (another reading is **tickle**). [Prob derived from **trick**]

trick-track /trik'trak/ *n* a form of backgammon in which pegs as well as pieces are used (also **tric'-trac** or **tick'-tack**). [Fr *tric trac*; imit of the sound made by the pieces]

triclinic /trī-klin'ik/ (*mineralogy*) *adj* of the crystal system in which three unequal axes are obliquely inclined to each other. [Gr *treis* three, and *klīnein* to bend]

triclinium /trī-klin'i-əm/ (*ancient Rome*) *n* (*pl* **triclin'ia**) a couch running round three sides of a table for reclining on at meals; a dining room. [L *triclīnium*, from Gr *triklīnion*, from Gr *treis* three, and *klīnē* a couch]

triclosan /trī'klə-zan/ *n* an antimicrobial agent used in toiletries and cleaning products.

tricolour or (*US*) **tricolor** /trik'ə-lər/ or /trī'kul-ər/ *adj* three-coloured. ◆ *n* /trī'/ a three-coloured flag, *esp* that of France /trē-kol- or/. [L *tricolor* and Fr *tricolore*]
■ **trī'coloured** *adj*.

triconsonantal /trī-kon-sə-nan'tl/ *adj* having three consonants (also **triconsonan'tic**). [**tri-**]

tricorn or **tricorne** /trī'körn/ *adj* three-horned; three-cornered. ◆ *n* a three-cornered hat with the brims turned up. [L *tricornis* three-horned, from *cornū* a horn]

tricorporate /trī-kör'pə-rāt, -rit/ or **tricorporated** /-id/ (*esp heraldry*) *adj* three-bodied (with one head). [**tri-** and L *corpus*, *corporis* body]

tricostate /trī-kos'tāt/ *adj* three-ribbed. [**tri-** and L *costa* rib]

tricot /trē'kō/ *n* a hand-knitted woollen fabric, or imitation of this; a soft, slightly-ribbed cloth for women's garments. [Fr *tricot* knitting]
■ **tricoteuse** /trē-kot-øz/ *n* (literally, a woman who knits) in the French Revolution, one of the women who enthusiastically attended public meetings and executions, knitting as they sat; a 19c two-tiered worktable for knitters.

tricrotic /trī-krot'ik/ *adj* (in measuring an arterial pulse) having three waves to one beat of the pulse; triple-beating. [**tri-** and Gr *krotos* a beat]
■ **tri'crotism** *n*. **tri'crotous** *adj*.

tric-trac see **trick-track**.

tricuspid or **tricuspidate** /trī-kus'pid, -pi-dāt/ *adj* having three cusps or points. [L *tricuspis*, *-idis*, from *cuspis* a point]

tricycle /trī'si-kl/ *n* (short form **trike**) a three-wheeled cycle; a light three-wheeled car formerly used by disabled people. ◆ *vi* to ride a tricycle. [**tri-** and Gr *kyklos* circle, wheel]
■ **tri'cycler** *n*. **tricyclic** /trī-sī'klik/ *adj* having three whorls or rings; (of a chemical compound) having three rings in its molecular structure, some compounds of this type being used as antidepressant drugs. **tri'cycling** /-si-/ *n*. **tri'cyclist** *n*.
❑ **tricycle undercarriage** or **landing gear** *n* an aircraft's undercarriage or landing gear, which has three wheels.

tridacna /trī-dak'nə/ *n* any clam of the genus *Tridacna*, giant clams of the Indian Ocean, the largest known bivalves (more than 200kg). [Gr *tridaknos* eaten at three bites (applied to a big oyster), from *daknein* to bite]

tridactyl or **tridactylous** /trī-dak'til, -əs/ *adj* three-toed; three-fingered. [**tri-** and Gr *daktylos* finger, toe]

tridarn /trē'därn/ *n* a Welsh dresser having three tiers or stages. [Welsh]

tride an obsolete spelling (*Spenser*, *Shakesp*) of **tried** (see under **try**).

trident /trī'dənt/ *n* a three-pronged spear, *esp* that of the sea-god Poseidon or Neptune (*classical myth*); anything of similar shape; (with *cap*) a type of ballistic missile fired from a nuclear submarine. [L *tridēns*, *-dentis*, from *dēns* tooth]
■ **tri'dent**, **tridental** /-dent'/ or **trident'āte** *adj* three-pronged. **tridented** /trī-dent'id/ *adj* three-pronged; /trī'dənt-id/ having a trident.

Tridentine /trī-, tri-den'tīn/ (*hist* or *RC*) *adj* of Trent in S Tyrol, or the Council (1545–63) held there. ◆ *n* a native of Trent; a person who accepts the decrees of the Council, an orthodox Roman Catholic. [L *Tridentum* Trent]

tridimensional /trī-dī-men'shə-nəl/ *adj* having three dimensions. [**tri-**]

tridominium /trī-dō-min'i-əm/ *n* threefold rule. [**tri-** and L *dominium* lordship]

triduan see under **triduum**.

triduum /trid'ū-əm or trī'dū-/ (*esp RC*) *n* a space of three days; a period of prayer or religious celebration lasting three days. [L *trīduum*, from *diēs* day]
■ **trid'ūan** *adj* lasting three days.

tridymite /trid'i-mīt/ (*mineralogy*) *n* an orthorhombic form of silica, in hexagonal scales, often combined in threes. [Gr *tridymos* threefold]

trie an obsolete spelling of **try**.

triecious see **trioecious**.

tried see under **try**.

triene /trī'ēn/ *n* any chemical compound containing three double bonds. [**tri-**]

triennial /trī-en'yəl or -i-əl/ *adj* continuing for three years; happening every third year. ◆ *n* a period of three years; an event happening every third year. [L *triennis*, from *annus* a year]
■ **trienn'ially** *adv*. **trienn'ium** *n* (*pl* **trienn'iums** or **trienn'ia**) a period of three years.

trier see under **try**.

trierarch /trī'ə-rärk/ (*Gr hist*) *n* the commander of a trireme; a person required (alone or with others) to fit out a trireme. [Gr *triērarchos*, from *triērēs* a trireme, and *archein* to rule]
■ **tri'erarchal** *adj*. **tri'erarchy** *n* the office of trierarch; the obligation of fitting out ships.

trieteric /trī-i-ter'ik/ *adj* biennial. [Gr *trietērikos*, from *trietēris* a biennial festival, from *treis* three, and *etos* a year (inclusive reckoning being applied)]

triethyl /trī-ē'thīl or -eth'il/ *adj* having three ethyl groups. [**tri-**]
■ **triethylamine** /-ə-mēn'/ *n* an oily liquid corresponding to ammonia with ethyl replacing all the hydrogen.

trifacial /trī-fā'shl/ *adj* threefold and relating to the face. [**tri-** and **facial**]
❑ **trifacial nerve** *n* the trigeminal nerve.

trifarious /trī-fā'ri-əs/ *adj* arranged in three rows; facing three ways. [L *trifārius*]

trifecta /trī-fek'tə/ (*Aust*; *horse-racing*) *n* same as **triple**. [**tri-** and *perfecta*]

triff /trif/ (*sl*) *adj* terrific, excellent, highly enjoyable or attractive (also **triff'ic**). [Contraction of **terrific**]

triffid /trif'id/ n a monstrous (fictional) stinging plant, mobile and rapidly multiplying, of invasive habit and malign intent. [From John Wyndham's science-fiction novel *The Day of the Triffids* (1951)]
■ **triffid'ian** or **triff'idy** adj in the nature of or reminiscent of a triffid or triffids.

trifid /trif'id, trī'fid/ adj split or divided into three parts (*bot*, etc); (of a spoon) having a three-pointed decorative top to its handle. [L *trifidus* cleft into three parts, from *findere* to split]

trifle /trī'fl/ n anything of little importance or value; a small amount; a dessert of sponge cake soaked with sherry and covered with jam or fruit, topped with custard and whipped cream; a kind of pewter or articles made from it. ◆ vi (often with *with*) to occupy oneself desultorily; to play, toy, amuse oneself; to behave without seriousness or respect; to meddle irresponsibly. ◆ vt to spend, pass or waste (*esp* time) idly; to render trivial in comparison (*Shakesp*). [OFr *trufle* mockery, deception]
■ **tri'fler** n. **tri'fling** adj of small value, importance, or amount; trivial. **tri'flingly** adv. **tri'flingness** n.
■ **a trifle** slightly.

trifocal /trī-fō'kəl/ adj (of a spectacle lens) giving separately near, intermediate, and far vision. [**tri-**]
■ **trifo'cals** n pl spectacles with such lenses.

trifoliate /trī-fō'li-āt/ adj having three leaves or leaflets. [L *trifolium*, from *folium* leaf]
■ **trīfo'lium** n any plant of the clover or trefoil genus *Trifolium*. **trifoly** /trif'ə-li/ n (*Browning*) trefoil.

triforium /trī-fō'ri-əm, -fō'/ (*archit*) n (*pl* **trifo'ria**) a gallery, storey, or arcade over an aisle. [Anglo-L; ety obscure]

triform /trī'förm/ or **triformed** adj having a triple form. [L *triförmis*, from *förma* form]

trifurcate /trī'fər-kāt/ or -*fûr*'/ adj three-forked. ◆ vi and vt to divide into three branches. [L *trifurcus*, from *furca* a fork]
■ **tri'furcated** (or /-*fûr*'/) adj. **trifurcā'tion** n.

trig[1] /trig/ (*inf*) n trigonometry. ◆ adj trigonometric or trigonometrical.
□ **trig point** n trigonometrical point.

trig[2] /trig/ adj trim, neat (chiefly *Scot*); tight, sound. ◆ vt (**trigg'ing**; **trigg'ed**) to make trig; to block or hold back with a wedge; to stuff (*obs* except *dialect*). ◆ n a block or wedge to stop a wheel. [ON *tryggr* faithful, secure; cf **true**]
■ **trig'ly** adv. **trig'ness** n.
■ **trig out** to dress or decorate.

trigamy /trig'ə-mi/ n the having of three legal or supposed wives or husbands at once; a third marriage (*church law*). [Gr *trigamos* thrice married, from *gamos* marriage]
■ **trig'amist** n a person who has committed trigamy. **trig'amous** adj of the nature of, involving or living in trigamy.

trigeminal /trī-jem'i-n(ə)l/ adj threefold; three-branched. [L *trigeminus* born three at a birth, from *geminus* born at the same birth]
■ **trigem'inus** n the trigeminal nerve.
□ **trigeminal nerve** n (*anat*) a facial nerve having three branches, supplying the eye, nose, skin, scalp and muscles of mastication (also called **trifacial nerve**). **trigeminal neuralgia** n (*med*) another term for **tic douloureux** under **tic**.

trigger /trig'ər/ n a lever that releases a catch so as to fire a gun or set a mechanism going; anything that starts a train of actions. ◆ vt (often with *off*) to set in action. ◆ adj applied to something activated by or acting as a trigger. [Du *trekker*, from *trekken* to pull]
□ **trigger finger** n the finger used to pull the trigger on a gun, ie the forefinger of the dominant hand; a condition in which a finger is subject to involuntary muscular spasm, *esp* where it cannot be straightened when unclenching the fist (*med*). **trigg'erfish** n a fish of the family Balistidae, having on the first dorsal fin a large front spine which can be locked upright by a second smaller spine. **trigger-happ'iness** n. **trigg'er-happy** adj over-ready to shoot (*lit* and *fig*); irresponsibly willing to take the risk of beginning a fight or a war. **trigg'erman** n a gangster's bodyguard; the man who actually fires a shot. **trigger point** n one of a number of specific points or sites on the body at which acupuncture, heat, injection or massage may be applied to treat (sometimes remote) pain.

triglot /trī'glot/ adj able to speak three languages, trilingual; using or written in three languages. ◆ n a person who speaks three languages; a book written in three languages. [**tri-** and Gr *glötta* tongue]

triglyceride /trī-glis'ə-rīd/ (*chem*) n any of a group of commonly occurring fats, those fatty acid esters of glycerol in which all three hydroxyl groups have had their hydrogen atoms replaced by acid radicals. [**tri-**]

triglyph /trī'glif/ (*archit*) n a three-grooved tablet in the Doric frieze. [Gr *triglyphos*, from *glyphein* to carve]
■ **triglyph'ic** adj.

trigon /trī'gon/ n a triangle; (in ancient Greece or Rome) a type of lyre or harp; a set of three signs 120° apart, the zodiac being divided into four trigons, *watery* (consisting of Cancer, Scorpio and Pisces), *earthly* (Taurus, Virgo and Capricorn), *airy* (Gemini, Libra and Aquarius) and *fiery* (Aries, Leo and Sagittarius; *astrol*). [Gr *trigönon*, from *gönia* an angle]
■ **trigonal** /trig'ə-nl/ adj of a trigon; triangular; trigonous; bounded by three planes; (of symmetry about an axis) such that a rotation through 120° gives the same figure. **trig'onally** adv. **trigonic** /trī-gon'ik/ adj of a trigon; triangular. **trigonous** /trig'ə-nəs/ adj (*esp bot*) triangular in section, or nearly so.

trigonometry /trig-ə-nom'i-tri/ n the branch of mathematics that deals with the relations between the sides and angles of triangles. [Gr *trigönon* a triangle, and *metron* a measure]
■ **trigonom'eter** n a person skilled in or occupied with trigonometry; an instrument for solving triangles. **trigonometric** /-nə-met'rik/ or **trigonomet'rical** adj. **trigonomet'rically** adv.
□ **trigonometrical point** n (*geog*, etc) in triangulation, a fixed point whose position as vertex of a triangle is calculated astronomically (often shortened to **trig point**). **trigonometric function** and **trigonometric ratio** n any function of an angle that is defined by the relationship between the angles and sides of a right-angled triangle.

trigram /trī'gram/ n an inscription of three letters; a figure of three lines. [**tri-** and Gr *gramma* a letter]
■ **trigrammat'ic** or **trigramm'ic** adj.

trigraph /trī'gräf/ n a combination of three letters for one sound. [**tri-** and Gr *graphe* a writing]

Trigynia /trī-jin'i-ə/ n pl in the Linnaean system, an order of plants (in various classes) with three pistils. [**tri-** and Gr *gyne* a woman, female]
■ **trigyn'ian** or **trigynous** /trij'i-nəs/ adj.

trihedral /trī-hed'rəl, -hē'drəl/ (*geom*, etc) adj having three faces. ◆ n (also **trīhēd'ron**) a figure with a trihedral aspect, formed by three planes meeting at a point. [**tri-** and Gr *hedrā* a seat]

trihybrid /trī-hī'brid/ n a hybrid differing from its parents in three independently heritable characteristics (also adj). [**tri-**]

trihydric /trī-hī'drik/ (*chem*) adj having three hydroxyl groups. [**tri-**]

triiodothyronine /trī-ī-ə-dō-thī'rə-nēn/ n a hormone containing iodine, secreted by the thyroid gland.

tri-jet /trī'jet/ n an aircraft having three jet engines. [**tri-**]

trike[1] /trīk/ n trichloroethylene (see under **trichloro-**).

trike[2] /trīk/ (*inf*) n short form of **tricycle**.

trilateral /trī-lat'ə-rəl/ adj three-sided; of or having three parties or participants. ◆ n a triangle. [**tri-** and L *latus, lateris* side]
■ **trilat'eralism** n. **trilat'eralist** n. **trilat'erally** adv. **trilatera'tion** n a technique involving the measurement of selected sides of a triangulation network, for map-making, surveying, etc.

trilby /tril'bi/ n (*pl* **tril'bies** or **tril'bys**) a soft felt hat with an indented crown and narrow brim (also **trilby hat**); (in *pl*) feet (*sl*). [From George du Maurier's novel, *Trilby* (1894)]

trild (*Spenser*) see **trill**[2].

trilemma /trī-, trī-lem'ə/ n a form of argument or a situation differing from a dilemma in that there is a choice of three instead of two. [Modelled on **dilemma**]

Trilene® /trī'lēn/ n trichlorethylene.

trilinear /trī-lin'i-ər/ adj consisting of, having or referred to three lines. [**tri-** and L *līnea* line]
■ **trilin'eate** adj marked with three lines.

trilingual /trī-ling'gwəl/ adj in or using three languages, *esp* as native or habitual languages. [**tri-** and L *lingua* tongue]
■ **triling'ualism** n.

triliteral /trī-lit'ə-rəl/ adj consisting of three letters. [**tri-** and L *littera* a letter]
■ **trilit'eralism** n the characteristic (as in Semitic languages) of having roots consisting of three consonants.

trilith /trī'lith/ or **trilithon** /trī-lith'on, trī'li-thon, trī'li-thon/ n a form of megalithic monument consisting of two upright stones supporting another lying crosswise. [**tri-** and Gr *lithos* stone]
■ **trīlith'ic** adj.

trill[1] /tril/ n a trillo; a tremulous sound; a run or roulade of birdsong; a consonant sound produced by vibration. ◆ vt and vi to play, sing, pronounce or sound with a trill. [Ital *trillo*; imit]
■ **trill'o** n (*pl* **trill'oes**) (*music*) a rapid alternation of two notes a tone or semitone apart, commonly ending with a turn.

trill[2] /tril/ vt and vi (*pat* **trilled** (*Spenser* **trild**)) to twirl, roll, trundle; to pour in a fine stream. [Cf Norw and Swed *trilla* to roll]

trilling /tril'ing/ n a threefold compound of crystals; one child of triplets. [**tri-** and **-ling**[1]; cf Dan and Swed *trilling*; Ger *Drilling*]

trillion /tril′yən/ n the cube of ten thousand (10^{12}); (esp formerly, in Britain) the cube of a million (10^{18}); (loosely; esp in pl) an enormous number (inf). ◆ adj being a trillion in number. [Fr, from L trias three, and **million**]
■ **trill′ionth** adj and n.

trillium /tril′i-əm/ n a three-leaved trimerous plant of the Trillium genus of the lily family. [L trēs three]

trillo see under **trill**[1].

trilobe /trī′lōb/ n something that has three lobes (also adj). [**tri-** and Gr lobos lobe]
■ **trilobate** /trī′ or -lō′/, **tri′lobated** or **trī′lobed** adj having three lobes. **trilobite** /trī′lō-bīt or tril′ə-bīt/ n any fossil arthropod of the Palaeozoic order **Trilobi′ta**, with broad head-shield and body longitudinally furrowed into three lobes. **trilobitic** /-bit′ik/ adj.

trilocular /trī-lok′ū-lər/ (esp bot) adj three-celled. [**tri-** and L loculus]

trilogy /tril′ə-ji/ n any group of three works, such as novels, plays, etc; a group of three related Greek tragedies, orig performed together; a triad. [Gr trilogiā, from logos discourse]

trim /trim/ vt (**trimm′ing**; **trimmed**) to put in due condition; to fit out; to make ready for sailing; to adjust the balance of (a boat, submarine or aircraft); to dress, arrange; to set in order; to decorate (clothes, etc) eg with ribbons, lace, contrasting edging, etc; to make tidy or neat; to clip into shape; to make compact; to reduce the size of, by removing excess; to smooth; to rebuke sharply; to thrash; to cheat (sl); to adjust the inclination of a plane to the horizontal. ◆ vi to balance; to balance or fluctuate between parties, be a trimmer; to adjust one's behaviour as expediency dictates. ◆ adj in good order; neat; tidy; well-kept; clean-cut; slim. ◆ adv trimly. ◆ n condition for sailing or flight; balance; condition, order; a fit, trim condition; humour, disposition, temper, way; array; fittings; the colour scheme and chrome parts on the outside of a car, etc, or the upholstery, door-handles, etc inside it; decorative additions to clothes, eg contrasting edging, etc; an act of trimming; window-dressing (US); parts trimmed off; adjustment of an aircraft's controls to achieve stability in a desired condition of flight. [OE trymman, trymian to strengthen, set in order, from trum firm]
■ **trim′ly** adv. **trimm′er** n someone who or something that trims; a person who fluctuates between parties, adjusting his or her opinions, etc to match his or her changing loyalties; a timeserver; a scold; anything trouncing or redoubtable; a small horizontal beam on a floor into which the ends of joists are framed; a variable capacitor of small capacitance used to take up discrepancies between self and stray capacitances in a circuit (elec eng); a float bearing a baited hook and line, used in fishing for pike; a trimming tab; something fine, excellent, approved of (Aust and NZ inf). **trimm′ing** n making trim; balancing; clipping; a sharp rebuke; (usu in pl) ornamental additions; (in pl) accessories; (in pl) sauces and other accompaniments for a dish; (in pl) fittings; (in pl) parts trimmed off. ◆ adj that trims. **trimm′ingly** adv. **trim′ness** n.
❑ **trimming tab** or **trim′tab** n a tab or aerofoil on an aircraft or boat, that can be adjusted in mid-passage to trim the craft. **trim size** n (printing) the size of a book once its pages are trimmed.
■ **trim one's sails** to rule one's conduct, principles, etc, to accord with prevailing circumstances.

trimaran /trī′mə-ran/ n a boat with three hulls. [**tri-** and cata*maran*]

trimer /trī′mər/ (chem) n a substance in which molecules are formed from three molecules of a monomer. [**tri-** and Gr meros part]
■ **trimer′ic** adj (chem) having the same empirical formula but a relative molecular mass three times as great. **trim′erous** /trim′ə-rəs/ adj (bot) having three parts, or parts in three.

trimester /tri-mes′tər, trī-/ n three months; an academic term. [L trimēstris of three months, from mēnsis a month]
■ **trimes′trial** adj.

trimeter /trim′i-tər/ (prosody) n a line of verse of three measures (dipodies or feet). [Gr trimetros, from metron measure]
■ **trim′eter**, **trimetric** or **trimetrical** /trī-met′rik, -l/ adj consisting of three measures, esp iambic.

trimethyl /trī-mē′thīl or -meth′il/ (chem) adj containing three methyl radicals in combination. [**tri-**]
■ **trimeth′ylamine** /-ə-mēn/ n a gas, $(CH_3)_3N$, obtainable from herring-brine, corresponding to ammonia with methyl replacing all the hydrogen. **trimeth′ylene** /-ēn/ n cyclopropane.

trimetric see under **trimeter**.

Trimetrogon /trī-met′rə-gon/ n and adj applied to a technique of aerial photography using three cameras, which increases the range and detail of the coverage. [**tri-** and metrogon a type of camera lens]

trimix /trī′miks/ n a mixture of nitrogen, helium and oxygen, used by deep-sea divers. [**tri-** and **mix**]

trimonthly /trī-munth′li/ adj every three months. [**tri-**]

trimorphism /trī-mör′fi-zm/ n occurrence of three forms in the same species (biol); the property of crystallizing in three forms (chem). [**tri-** and Gr morphē form]
■ **trimor′phic** or **trimor′phous** adj.

trimtab see under **trim**.

Trimurti /tri-moor′ti/ n the Hindu trinity, Brahma, Vishnu, and Siva. [Sans tri three, and mūrti shape]

Trin. abbrev : Trinity.

trin see under **trine**[1].

Trinacrian /tri-, trī-nā′kri-ən/ adj Sicilian; (without cap) three-pointed; with three extremities. [L, from Gr Trīnakriā Sicily, from trinax, -akos a three-pronged mattock, or thrīnax a trident]
■ **trinacriform** /trin-ak′ri-förm/ adj three-pronged.

trinal, trinary see under **trine**[1].

trindle /trin′dl/ n one of several thin pieces of wood, etc, which hold the spine of a book flat while the front edge is trimmed; a wheel, esp of a barrow. ◆ vt and vi to roll, to trundle. [**trundle**]
❑ **trin′dle-tail** n a trundle-tail.

trine[1] /trīn/ adj threefold; (of the aspect between two planets) 120° apart (astrol); hence, benign (astrol). ◆ n a triad; the aspect of two planets, as seen from the earth, distant from each other one-third of the zodiac or 120° (astrol); a triplet. ◆ vt to join in trine aspect. [L trīnus, from trēs, tria three]
■ **trin** /trin/ n a triplet (by birth). **trinal** /trī′nl/ or **trī′nary** adj.

trine[2] /trīn/ vi to go. [Scand]
■ **trine to the** (**nubbing**) **cheat** (sl) to go the gallows.

tringle /tring′gl/ n a curtain rod. [Fr]

Trinidadian /tri-ni-dad′i-ən, -dā′di-ən/ adj of or relating to the island of Trinidad in the West Indies. ◆ n a native of Trinidad.

triniscope /trī′ni-skōp/ n a cathode-ray tube for colour television. [L trīnus triple, and Gr skopeein to view]

trinitro- /trī-nī-trō-/ combining form denoting (a compound) having three nitro-groups (NO_2), esp replacing hydrogen. [**tri-**]
■ **trini′trate** n a nitrate with three nitrate groups in the molecule. **trini′trin** n glyceryl trinitrate or nitroglycerine, used to treat angina pectoris. **trinitroben′zene** n $C_6H_3(NO_2)_3$, corresponding to benzene C_6H_6. **trinitrophe′nol** n a similar derivative of phenol, esp picric acid. **trinitrotol′uene** or **trinitrotol′uol** n a high explosive (commonly called **TNT**), a trinitro-derivative of toluene.

trinity /trin′i-ti/ n threefoldness; three in one; a triad; esp (with cap) the triune God of orthodox Christians (Father, Son and Holy Ghost); (with cap) any symbolical representation of the trinity; (with cap) Trinity Sunday; (with cap) Trinity term. [L trīnitās, -ātis, from trīnus threefold]
■ **Trinitā′rian** adj of, in relation to or believing in the Trinity; of the Trinitarians. ◆ n someone who adheres to the doctrine of the Trinity; a member of a religious order founded at Rome in 1198 to redeem Christian captives from the Muslims (also called **Mathurins** and **Redemptionists**); a member of Trinity College (eg in Cambridge or Dublin). **Trinitā′rianism** n.
❑ **Trinity Brethren** n pl the members of Trinity House. **Trinity House** n a lighthouse and pilot authority for England, Wales and the Channel Islands, orig chartered at Deptford in 1514. **Trinity Sunday** n the Sunday after Whitsunday. **Trinity term** n one of the terms of the English lawcourts beginning after Trinity Sunday (now **Trinity law sittings**); the university term beginning after Trinity Sunday.

trinket /tring′kit/ n a small ornament or piece of jewellery; any paltry object; a despised religious observance (hist); a delicacy (obs). ◆ vi (obs) to have secret or underhand dealings (with). [Poss OFr trenquet small knife]
■ **trink′eter** n (obs) an intriguer. **trink′eting** n. **trink′etry** n trinkets collectively.

trinkum /tring′kəm/, also **trinkum-trankum** /tring′kəm-trang′kəm/ same as **trankum**.

trinomial /trī-nō′mi-əl/ adj consisting of three terms (for genus, species and subspecies or variety; biol); consisting of three terms connected by the plus or minus sign (maths). ◆ n a trinomial name or expression. [Modelled on **binomial**]
■ **trino′mialism** n (biol) the system of naming by three terms. **trino′mialist** n.

trio /trē′ō/ n (pl **tri′os**) a set of three; a composition for, or combination of, three performers (music); the second section of a minuet, scherzo, or march (said to have been originally for three instruments), followed by a repetition of the first section (music); (in piquet) three cards of the same rank. [Ital]
❑ **trio sonata** n a sonata for three parts, often played either by four instruments (ie with an additional harpsichord accompaniment) or by eg an organ alone.

triode /trī′ōd/ adj with three electrodes. ◆ n a three-electrode valve; a three-terminal semiconductor. [**tri-** and Gr hodos a path, way]

■ words derived from main entry word; ❑ compound words; ■ idioms and phrasal verbs

Triodion /trī-ō'di-on/ (Gr church) n a service-book for the ten weeks before Easter. [Mod Gr triódion, from ōdē hymn]

trioecious or **triecious** /trī-ē'shəs/ (bot) adj (of an order of plants) having male, female, and hermaphrodite flowers on different individuals. [**tri-** and Gr oikos house]

triolet /trī'ō-lit, trē'ō-lā, -let/ n an eight-lined poem rhymed ab aa abab, lines 4 and 7 repeating 1, and 8 repeating 2. [Fr]

triones /trī-ō'nēz/ n pl the seven stars of the Plough. [L triōnēs plough-oxen]

trionym /trī'ə-nim/ n a trinomial. [Gr triōnymos, from onyma (onoma) name]
- **trionymal** /-on'i-məl/ adj.

trior see trier under **try**.

triose /trī'ōz, trī'ōs/ n the simplest monosaccharide, containing three carbon atoms in the molecule.

trioxide /trī-ok'sīd/ (chem) n a compound with three atoms of oxygen. [**tri-**]

trip¹ /trip/ vi (**tripp'ing**; **tripped**) to move with short, light steps or skips; to stumble or catch one's foot; to make a slip in accuracy, virtue, etc (often with up); to tip up, tilt; to make an excursion; to experience the hallucinatory effects of LSD or similar drug (also **trip out**; sl). ◆ vt to cause to stumble or fall by catching the foot (often with up); to catch in a fault; to dance trippingly; to trip or dance upon; to release (an anchor) from the seabed, by a long rope; to release or operate (a switch or piece of machinery) by striking; to tilt up. ◆ n a light, short step or skip; a catching of the foot, a stumble; a slip or lapse; a single journey, one way or to and fro; the distance of a race (horse-racing); a pleasure excursion, jaunt; a specially arranged journey at a cheap fare; a group of people on an excursion; a striking part that releases a catch; a hallucinatory experience under the influence of a drug such as LSD, or (loosely) a quantity of a drug that will produce such an experience (sl); any stimulating experience (good or bad) (sl). [OFr triper; of Gmc origin; cf OE treppan to tread, Ger trappe(l)n, Du trippen, trappen, trippelen, Swed trippa]
- **tripp'ant** adj (heraldry) tripping, with right foot raised. **tripp'er** n someone who trips; an excursionist, esp of the disturbing kind (often derog); a device that when struck, passed over, etc, operates a switch. **tripp'erish** or **tripp'ery** adj of, like or reminiscent of the vulgar or noisy tripper. **tripp'ing** n and adj. **tripp'ingly** adv. **tripp'y** adj (**tripp'ier**; **tripp'iest**) (sl) hallucinatory; in the style of trip hop (qv below).
- ❑ **trip hammer** n a tilt hammer. **trip'-hook** n (Browning) some kind of instrument of torture. **trip hop** n a type of dance music developed from hip-hop and adding psychedelic and dub effects. **trip meter** or **recorder** n an instrument in a vehicle that can be reset to record distance travelled eg on a specific trip. **trip switch** n a circuit breaker. **trip'wire** n a wire which releases some mechanism when pulled, eg by being tripped over.
- ■ **trip out** to stop (a machine) working by disconnecting it, esp automatically; (of a machine) to become disconnected and therefore stop working. **trip the light fantastic** (joc) to dance.

trip² /trip/ n a small flock of sheep, wildfowl, etc. [Perh related to **troop**]

tripartite /trī-pär'tīt/ adj in three parts; split in three nearly to the base (bot); relating to three parties. [L tripartītus, from partīrī to divide, from pars a part]
- ■ **tripar'titely** adv. **tripar'tism** n an established system of dialogue between three related groups, specif government, employers, and unions, for mutually acceptable planning and follow-up; division into three parts, esp political parties (rare). **tripartition** /-tish'ən/ n.

tripe /trīp/ n parts of the compound stomach of a ruminant, prepared as food, ie the paunch or rumen (**plain tripe**), and the smaller reticulum (**honeycomb tripe**); rubbish, poor stuff (inf); claptrap (inf); entrails (archaic). [OFr (Fr) tripe; origin obscure]
- ■ **trīp'ery** n a place for the preparation or sale of tripe. **trip'ey** or **trip'y** adj (inf) rubbishy, worthless.
- ❑ **tripe de roche** /trēp də rosh'/ n (Fr) rock-tripe. **tripe'hound** n (sl) a newspaper reporter; a dog (Aust). **tripe'-man**, **tripe'-wife** or **tripe'-woman** n a dresser or seller of tripe. **tripe'-shop** n. **tripe'-visag'd** adj (Shakesp) with a face like tripe.

tripedal /trip'-, trī'pi-dl, trī-pē'dl/ adj three-footed. [**tri-** and L pēs, pedis foot]

tripersonal /trī-pûr'sə-nəl/ adj consisting of three persons. [**tri-**]
- ■ **triper'sonalism** n belief in the Trinity. **triper'sonalist** n a believer in the Trinity. **tripersonal'ity** n.

tripetalous /trī-pet'ə-ləs/ adj three-petalled. [**tri-** and Gr petalon leaf]

tripey see under **tripe**.

triphenyl- /trī-fē'nil-/ (chem) combining form denoting (a compound) containing three phenyl radicals. [**tri-**]

- ■ **triphenylamine** /-ə-mēn/ n a crystalline compound corresponding to ammonia with all the hydrogen replaced by phenyl. **triphenylmē'thane** n a crystalline solid used in the preparation of dyes.

triphibious /trī-fib'i-əs/ adj (esp of military operations) taking place on land, in the water and in the air. [**tri-** and -phibious; modelled on **amphibious** with wrong word division]

triphone /trī'fōn/ n a shorthand sign representing a triphthongal sound. [**tri-** and Gr phōnē sound]

triphthong /trif'thong, trip'-/ n a combination of three vowel sounds in one syllable (phonetics); (loosely) a trigraph. [**tri-** and Gr phthongos sound]
- ■ **triphthongal** /-thong'gl/ adj.

triphyllous /trī-fil'əs/ (bot) adj three-leaved. [**tri-** and Gr phyllon a leaf]

Triphysite /trif'i-zīt, -sīt/ n a believer in the existence of three natures in Christ (human, divine, and a third resulting from the union of these). [**tri-** and Gr physis nature]

tripinnate /trī-pin'āt, -it/ adj pinnate with the pinnae themselves pinnate, and their pinnae again pinnate. [**tri-**]

Tripitaka /trip-i-tä'kə, -pit'ə-kə/ (also without cap) n the whole body of the northern Buddhist canonical writings, comprising the sutras, or discourses of the Buddha for the laity, Vinaya, or discipline for the order, and Abhidharma, or metaphysics. [Pali, literally, three baskets]

triplane /trī'plān/ n an aeroplane with three sets of wings, one above another. [**tri-**]

triple /trip'l/ adj threefold; consisting of three; three times as much; third (Shakesp). ◆ n a quantity three times as much; a thing (eg a star) that is triple; a peal of bells interchanging in three sets of two; a betting system requiring that the horses which finish first, second and third in a race are selected in correct order. ◆ vt and vi to treble. [Fr, from L triplus, from Gr triploos (triplous); and L triplex]
- ■ **trip'leness** n. **trip'let** n three of a kind, or three united; three lines rhyming together; a group of three notes occupying the time of two, indicated by a slur and the figure 3 (music); one of three (people or animals) born at one birth; a state in which there are two unpaired electrons (chem); a cycle for three riders. **trip'lex** adj triple. ◆ n a building divided into three flats (N Am); triple time (Shakesp). **triplicate** /trip'li-kit/ adj threefold; made thrice as much; equal to the cube of the quantity (old maths). ◆ n a third copy or thing corresponding to two others of the same kind; the third power or cube (old maths). ◆ vt /trip'li-kāt/ to make threefold. **triplica'tion** n the act of triplicating; a reply to a duplication. **triplicity** /trip-lis'i-ti/ n tripleness; a triad; a trigon (astrol). **trip'ling** n a making triple; a triplet, trilling or trin. **triply** /trip'li/ adv. ◆ n /trip-plī'/ (Scots law) a pursuer's reply to a defender's duply. ◆ vt and vi to reply to a duply.
- ❑ **Triple Alliance** n the league of England, Sweden, and the Netherlands formed against France in 1668; the alliance of Britain, France, and Holland against Spain in 1717; the alliance between Germany, Austria, and Italy, 1883–1915, counterbalanced by the **Triple Entente**, a friendly understanding (developing into an alliance) between Britain, France, and Russia. **triple bond** n (chem) a covalent bond between two atoms involving the sharing of three pairs of electrons. **triple crown** n the Pope's tiara; a victory in each race of the triple event in the same season (horse-racing); a victory by England, Scotland, Wales or Ireland in all three matches against the others in the series played each season (rugby, etc). **trip'le-crowned** adj having three crowns or a triple crown, as the Pope. **triple event** n (horse-racing) the Two Thousand Guineas, St Leger, and Derby. **triple glazing** n glazing formed by three layers of glass with the optimum air-space between each layer for insulation or soundproofing. **triple harp** n a Welsh harp. **trip'le-head'ed** adj three-headed. **triple jump** n an athletic event, formerly called the hop, skip and jump, the object of which is to cover the longest possible distance; a jump incorporating three aerial turns (ice skating). **trip'le-jump** vi to perform a triple jump. **trip'le-jumper** n. **triple play** n (baseball) a play putting out three runners. **triple point** n the temperature and pressure at which solid, liquid, and gaseous phases of a substance can coexist, esp triple point of water, 273.16K and $610N/m^{-2}$. **Triple sec** n a clear orange-flavoured liqueur. **triple time** n musical time or rhythm of three beats, or of three times three beats, in a bar. **triple-tongue'** vi (music) to produce a staccato sound by rapid articulation when playing fast passages in groups of three on a wind instrument. **triple-tongu'ing** n. **trip'le-turned** adj (Shakesp) three times faithless. **triple whammy** see **whammy** under **wham**. **triple witching** (**hour**) n (stock exchange) the final hour of certain periods of trading, when three kinds of future and option contracts expire and the market is exposed to extreme volatility (cf **double witching** (**hour**) under **double**). **Triplex**® **glass** n a combination of glass and mica in three layers. **triplicate-ternate** see under **triternate**.
- ■ **in triplicate** in three exact copies.

triploblastic /trip-lō-blas'tik/ adj having three types of tissue in the body, ie with a mesoderm between the ectoderm and endoderm. [Gr *triploos* triple, and *blastos* bud]

triploid /trip'loid/ (*biol*) adj having three times the haploid number of chromosomes. ◆ *n* an organism or cell of this kind. [Gr *triploos* triple]
■ **trip'loidy** *n* the state of being triploid.

triply see under **triple**.

tripod /trī'pod, trip'od/ *n* anything on three feet or legs, *esp* a stand for an instrument; the stool on which the priestess at Delphi sat to deliver an oracle. ◆ adj three-legged. [Gr *tripous, tripodos*, from *pous, podos* foot]
■ **tripodal** /trip'əd-əl/ adj. **tripody** /trip'ə-di/ *n* a line of verse or group of three feet.

tripoli /trip'ə-li/ *n* diatomite. [Orig brought from *Tripoli* in Libya]

tripos /trī'pos/ *n* any of the honours examinations for the BA degree at Cambridge; any of the recognized courses leading to the BA at Cambridge; the list of successful candidates in it; a tripod (*obs*). [L, three-legged stool; prob from the stool on which candidates used to sit while performing oral examinations]

trippant, tripper, tripping, etc see under **trip**[1].

trippet /trip'it/ *n* a trivet; (in a machine) a piece that projects in order to strike another part of the mechanism regularly. [Cf **trivet** and OFr *trepied*]

tripple /trip'l/ (*S Afr*) *n* a horse's ambling canter, between a fast walk and a slow trot (also *vi*). [Du *trippelen*]
■ **tripp'ler** *n*.

tripsis /trip'sis/ *n* pulverization; shampooing; massage. [Gr *tripsis*, from *tribein* to rub]

triptan /trip'tan/ *n* any of a family of drugs used for the acute treatment of migraine attacks. [5-hydroxy*trypt*oph*an* agonist]

triptane /trip'tān/ *n* trimethyl butane, a powerful aviation fuel. [*tri*methyl *butane*, with *b* altered to *p*]

tripterous /trip'tə-rəs/ (*bot*) adj three-winged. [Gr *tripteros*, from *pteron* wing]

triptote /trip'tōt/ adj used in three cases only. ◆ *n* a triptote word. [Gr *triptōtos*, from *ptōsis* a case, falling]

triptych /trip'tik/ *n* a set of three tablets, painted panels, etc, hinged together as one work of art. [Gr *triptychos* threefold, from *ptyx, ptychos* a fold, from *ptyssein* to fold]

triptyque /trēp-tēk'/ (*Fr*) *n* an international pass for a motor-car. [*triptych* (because divided in three sections)]

tripudium /tri-pū'di-əm, tri-pŭd'i-ŭm/ *n* an ancient Roman religious dance in triple time, or dance generally; divination from the hopping of birds feeding, or from the dropping of scraps from their bills. [L *tripudium*, prob from *trēs* three, and *pēs, pedis* foot]
■ **tripu'diary** adj. **tripu'diate** *vi* to dance for joy; to exult; to stamp. **tripudiā'tion** *n*.

tripy see under **tripe**.

triquetra /trī-kwet'rə/ *n* (*pl* **triquet'rae** /-rē/) an ornament consisting of three interlaced arcs, common in early art in N Europe. [L *triquetrus* triangular, from *trēs* three]
■ **triquet'ral** or **triquet'rous** adj triangular; three-edged with concave faces (*bot*). **triquet'rously** adv. **triquet'rum** *n* (*pl* **triquet'ra**) a Wormian bone.

triradiate /trī-rā'di-āt/ adj three-rayed (also **trirā'dial**). [**tri-**]

trireme /trī'rēm/ *n* an ancient Greek galley, *esp* a war-galley, with three banks of rowers. [L *trirēmis*, from *rēmus* an oar]

trisaccharide /trī-sak'ə-rīd/ *n* a sugar that hydrolyses into three molecules of simple sugars. [**tri-**]

trisagion /tri-sag'i-on/ *n* an ancient hymn consisting of the words 'O Holy God, holy and mighty, holy and immortal, have mercy on us'; loosely, the Tersanctus. [Gr *tris* thrice, and *hagios* holy]

trisect /trī-sekt'/ *vt* to cut or divide into three (*usu* equal) parts. [**tri-** and L *secāre, sectum* to cut]
■ **trisec'tion** /-shən/ *n*. **trisect'or** *n* a person who trisects; *esp* a person who thinks he or she can trisect an angle by Euclidean methods (ie using straight-edge and compasses) which has been proved to be impossible; a line that trisects. **trisect'rix** *n* a curve of polar equation $r = 1 + 2\cos\theta$, by which an angle can be trisected.

triseme /trī'sēm/ (*prosody*) adj equal to three short syllables. ◆ *n* a trisemic foot, the tribrach, iamb or trochee. [Gr *trisēmos*, from *sēma* a sign]
■ **trisē'mic** adj.

trishaw /trī'shö/ *n* a three-wheeled light vehicle pedalled by a driver behind the passenger seat. [**tri-** and *rickshaw*]

triskaidekaphobia or **triskaidecaphobia** /tris-kī-de-kə-fō'bi-ə/ *n* fear of the number thirteen. [Gr *tr(e)iskaideka* thirteen, and **phobia**]
■ **triskaidek'aphobe** *n* a person who suffers from triskaidekaphobia.

triskele /tris'kēl/ or **triskelion** /-kel'i-on/ *n* (*pl* **tris'keles** or **triskel'ia**) a figure consisting of three radiating curves or legs, as in the arms of the Isle of Man. [**tri-** and Gr *skelos* a leg]

Trismegistus /tris-mi-gis'təs, -mə-/ adj thrice greatest, an epithet of Thoth, the Egyptian moon god. [Latinized from Gr *trismegistos*]

trismus /triz'məs/ *n* (*med*) tetanic spasm of the muscles of mastication, causing difficulty in opening the mouth. [Latinized from Gr *trismos* a creaking, grating, from *trizein* to grate, gnash]

trisoctahedron /tris-ok-tə-hē'dron/ *n* (*pl* **trisoctahē'drons** or **trisoctahē'dra**) a solid with twenty-four faces, three for every face of an octahedron. [Gr *tris* thrice, and **octahedron**]

trisomic /trī-sō'mik/ adj designating an otherwise normal diploid organism in which one chromosome type is represented three times instead of twice. [**tri-**]
■ **tri'sōme** *n* a chromosome that occurs three times in a cell instead of twice; a trisomic individual. **trisō'mic** adj. **tri'sōmy** *n* a trisomic condition, *esp* **tri'sōmy-21**, associated with Down's syndrome.

trist or **triste** /trist/ (*archaic*) adj sorrowful; dismal. [Fr *triste*, from L *tristis* sad]
■ **tristesse'** *n* sorrow, grief, melancholy. **trist'ful** adj (*Shakesp*).

tristearin /trī-stē'ə-rin/ *n* another name for **stearin** (see under **stear-**).

tristich /tris'tik/ *n* (*pl* **tris'tichs** /-tiks/) a group of three lines of verse. [Gr *tristichiā* a triple row, from *stichos* a row]
■ **tristich'ic** adj. **tris'tichous** adj (*biol*) in or having three rows.

tristimulus values /trī-stim'ū-ləs val'ūz/ *n pl* amounts of each of three colour primaries that must be combined to form an objective colour match with a sample. [**tri-**]

trisula /tri-soo'lə/ *n* the trident of Siva (also **trisul'**). [Sans *trisūla*]

trisulcate /trī-sul'kāt/ adj having three forks or furrows. [L *trisulcus*, from *sulcus* a furrow]

trisulphide /trī-sul'fīd/ *n* a sulphide with three atoms of sulphur to the molecule. [**tri-**]

trisyllable /tri-sil'ə-bl, also *trī-*/ *n* a word or metrical foot of three syllables. [**tri-**]
■ **trisyllabic** /-ab'ik/ or **trisyllabical** adj. **trisyllab'ically** adv.

tritagonist /tri-tag'ə-nist/ *n* the third actor in importance in ancient Greek drama. [Gr *tritagōnistēs*, from *tritos* third, and *agōnistēs* an actor]

tritanopia /trī-tə-nō'pi-ə/ *n* inability to distinguish the colour blue. [Gr *tritos* a third, and New L *anopia* blindness, ie blindness to a third of the spectrum]
■ **trī'tanope** *n*. **trītanop'ic** adj.

trite[1] /trīt/ adj worn; worn-out; well-trodden; used until novelty and interest are lost; hackneyed. [L *trītus* rubbed, pap of *terere* to rub]
■ **trite'ly** adv. **trite'ness** *n*.

trite[2] /trī'tē/ (*Gr music*) *n* the third string of the lyre or tone of the tetrachord, reckoned downwards. [Gr *tritē* (fem) third]

triternate /trī-tûr'nāt/ adj thrice ternate, ie ternate with each division ternate, and each again ternate (also **trip'licate-ter'nate**). [**tri-**]

tritheism /trī'thē-izm/ *n* belief in three Gods; belief that the Father, Son and Holy Ghost are actually different beings. [**tri-** and Gr *theos* a god]
■ **tri'theist** *n*. **tritheis'tic** or **tritheis'tical** adj.

trithionic /trī-thī-on'ik/ adj containing three sulphur atoms (**trithionic acid**, $H_2S_3O_6$). [**tri-** and Gr *theion* sulphur]
■ **trithionate** /trī-thī'ən-āt/ *n* a salt of trithionic acid.

tritiate see under **tritium**.

tritical /trit'i-kl/ adj trite, common. [Formed from **trite**[1] in imitation of **critical**, etc]
■ **trit'ically** adv. **trit'icalness** or **trit'icism** *n* triteness.

Triticum /trit'i-kəm/ *n* the wheat genus of grasses. [L *trīticum* wheat, from *terere, trītum* to rub]
■ **trit'icale** *n* a hybrid cereal grass, a cross between wheat and rye, grown as a food crop. **triticeous** /-ish'əs/ adj wheatlike.

tritium /trish'i-əm, trit'/ (*chem*) *n* an isotope of hydrogen of triple mass. [New L, from Gr *tritos* third]
■ **tritiate** /trish'i-āt, trit'i-āt/ *vt* to replace normal hydrogen atoms in (a compound) by tritium. **tritiā'tion** *n*. **trit'ide** *n* a compound of tritium with another element or radical. **triton** /trī'tən/ *n* the nucleus of tritium, composed of one proton and two neutrons.

Tritoma /trit'ə-mə, -ō-, wrongly trī-tō'mə/ *n* a synonym of *Kniphofia*. [Gr *tritomos* thrice cut, from *tomē* a cut (from the splitting capsule)]

Triton /trī'tən/ *n* a minor Greek sea god, son of Poseidon and Amphitrite, represented with a dolphin's tail, and sometimes horse's forelegs, blowing a conch (*Gr myth*); (in *pl*) the attendants of

Poseidon; applied to a sailor or a ship (*fig*); a genus of large gastropods with shells that can be used like conchs; a disused generic name for newts; the larger of the two satellites of the planet Neptune, the other being Nereid. [Gr *Trītōn, -ōnos*]

triton see under **tritium**.

tritone /trī'tōn/ (*music*) *n* an augmented fourth, an interval of three whole tones. [Gr *tritonos*, from *tonos* tone]

tritonia /trī-tō'ni-ə/ *n* a plant of the genus *Tritonia* of iridaceous S African plants, sometimes called montbretia.

tritubercular /trī-tū-bûr'kū-lər/ *adj* having three tubercles or cusps (also **trituber'culate**). [**tri-**]
■ **trituber'culism, trituber'culy** *n*.

triturate /trit'ū-rāt/ *vt* to rub or grind to a fine powder. ◆ *n* the fine powder thus obtained. [LL *trītūrāre, -ātum*, from L *terere* to rub]
■ **tritura'tion** *n*. **trit'urātor** *n*.

triumph /trī'əmf/ *n* complete or notable victory or achievement; exultation for success; in ancient Rome, a solemn procession in honour of a victorious general; a pageant; festivity (*obs*); pomp, observance (*obs*); a captive led in triumph (*Milton*); a trump (*cards*; *obs*). ◆ *vi* to celebrate a victory with pomp; to rejoice for victory; to obtain victory, prevail (often with *over*); to exult, insult (often with *over*); to show in glory (*Shakesp*). ◆ *vt* (*Milton*) to triumph over. [L *triumphus*; related to Gr *thriambos* a hymn to Bacchus]
■ **triumphal** /trī-umf'l/ *adj* relating to triumph; used in celebrating victory. ◆ *n* (*Milton*) a token of victory. **triumph'alism** *n* an attitude of righteous pride and self-congratulation in the defeat of an opponent. **triumph'alist** *adj* and *n*. **triumph'ant** *adj* celebrating or having achieved a triumph; exultant; transcendent in glory (*Shakesp*); triumphal (*Shakesp*). **triumph'antly** *adv*. **tri'umpher** *n*. **triumph'ery** (*Shakesp*) see under **triumvir**. **tri'umphing** *n* and *adj*.
◻ **triumphal arch** *n* an arch erected in connection with the triumph of a Roman general; any decorative arch in public rejoicings, etc.
■ **church triumphant** see under **church**.

triumvir /trī-um'vər, trē-ŭm'vir/ *n* (*pl* **trium'virī** or **trium'virs**) each of three men in the same office or government; each of three sharing supreme power. [L *triumvir*, from the genitive *pl trium virōrum* of three men]
■ **trium'viral** *adj*. **trium'virate** (*obs* **trium'viry**; *Shakesp* **trium'phery**) *n* an association of three men in office or government, or for any political ends, *specif* that of Pompey, Crassus and Caesar (60BC), and that of Octavian (Augustus), Mark Antony and Lepidus (43BC); the rank or office of triumvir; any trio or triad.

triune /trī'ūn/ *adj* three in one. ◆ *n* a trinity in unity. [L *trēs, tria* three, and *ūnus* one]
■ **triū'nity** *n*.

trivalent /trī-vā'lənt, triv'ə-lənt/ (*chem*) *adj* having a valency of three. [**tri-** and **-valent**]
■ **trivā'lence** (or /triv'əl-/) or **trivā'lency** (or /triv'əl-/ *n*).

trivalve /trī'valv/ *adj* having three valves. ◆ *n* an animal, seed, etc with three valves. [**tri-** and L *valva* a door-leaf]
■ **tri'valved** or **trival'vūlar** *adj*.

trivet /triv'it/ *n* a tripod, *esp* one for a pot or kettle; a bracket with three projections for fixing on the top bar of a grate; a low stand for a hot food container, teapot, etc at table; a three-legged pot; a *usu* metal plate placed in a pressure cooker to raise the food to be cooked off the bottom of the vessel. [OE *trefet*, appar from L *tripēs, tripedis*, from *pēs* a foot]
■ **right as a trivet** perfectly right (from its stability).

trivia /triv'i-ə/ *n pl* trifles, trivialities, unimportant details. [L *trivium* a place where three ways meet, from *trēs* three, and *via* a way]
■ **trivial** /triv'i-əl/ *adj* of little importance; trifling; frivolous; of the trivium; to be found anywhere; vernacular (*biol*); (of a name) specific, *opp* to *generic* (*biol*); with value zero (*maths*). **triv'ialism** *n* a trivial matter or remark. **triviality** /-al'i-ti/ *n* the state or quality of being trivial; that which is trivial, a trifle. **trivializa'tion** or **-s-** *n*. **triv'ialize** or **-ise** *vi* to make trivial or unimportant. **triv'ially** *adv*. **triv'ialness** *n*. **triv'ium** *n* in medieval schools, the group of liberal arts first studied, comprising grammar, rhetoric and logic; the three anterior radii of an echinoderm (*zool*).

tri-weekly /trī-wēk'li/ *adj* occurring or appearing once in three weeks or three times a week. ◆ *adv* once in three weeks; three times a week. ◆ *n* a periodical appearing three times a week or every three weeks. [**tri-**]

-trix /-triks/ *sfx* (*pl* **-trixes** or **-trices** /-trī-sēz, -tri-siz/) denoting a feminine agent. [L]

trizone /trī'zōn/ *n* a unit or country formed of three zones, *specif* the area of West Germany comprised in the British, French and American zones of occupation after World War II (also called **Trizōn'ia**). [**tri-** and **zone**]
■ **trizō'nal** *adj*.

tRNA *abbrev*: transfer RNA.

troad or **troade** (*Spenser*) see **trod**[1].

troat /trōt/ *vi* (of a buck) to bellow (also *n*). [OFr *trout, trut*, interjection used to urge on animals]

trocar /trō'kär/ *n* a surgical perforator with a three-sided cutting point used for inserting a cannula, to drain off or introduce liquid, etc; sometimes, a cannula. [Fr *trocart*, from *trois* three, and *carre* side]

trochaic see under **trochee**.

trochal see under **trochus**.

trochanter /trō-kan'tər/ *n* a rough eminence on the thigh bone to which muscles are attached (*anat*); the second segment of an insect's leg (*zool*). [Gr *trochantēr*, from *trechein* to run]
■ **trochanteric** /-ter'ik/ *adj*.

troche and **trocheameter** see under **trochus**.

trochee /trō'kē/ (*prosody*) *n* a foot of two syllables, a long followed by a short; in English, etc, a stressed followed by an unstressed syllable. [Gr *trochaios* (*pous*) running or tripping (foot), from *trochos* a running, from *trechein* to run]
■ **trochaic** /-kā'ik/ *adj*. ◆ *n* (a) trochaic verse.

Trochelminthes and **Trochidae** see under **trochus**.

trochilus /trok'i-ləs/ *n* a concave moulding; the crocodile bird; any bird of the hummingbird genus *Trochilus*, giving its name to the hummingbird family **Trochil'idae**. [Gr *trochilos* a crocodile bird, a wren, a pulley sheaf, from *trechein* to run]
■ **trochil'ic** *adj* relating to rotatory motion.

trochiscus, trochisk and **trochite** see under **trochus**.

trochlea /trok'li-ə/ (*zool*) *n* (*pl* **troch'leae** /-li-ē/) any pulley-like structure, *esp* a foramen through which a tendon passes. [L *trochlea*, from Gr *trochiliā* a pulley]
■ **troch'lear** *adj*.
◻ **trochlear nerve** *n* the fourth cranial nerve.

trochoid, etc see under **trochus**.

trochus /trō'kəs/ *n* a wheel or hoop (*ancient Greece*); the inner ring of cilia in a rotifer; (with *cap*) the top genus of molluscs. [Gr *trochos* a wheel, from *trechein* to run]
■ **tro'chal** *adj* wheel-like. **troche** /trōk, trōsh* or *trōch/ *n* a round medicinal tablet. **Trochelminthes** /trōk-el-min'thēz/ *n pl* (Gr *helmins, helminthos* worm) the rotifer phylum of animals. **Troch'idae** *n pl* the top family of molluscs. **trochisc'us** or **troch'isk** *n* a troche. **troch'ite** *n* an encrinite joint. **troch'oid** *n* the curve traced by a fixed point, not on the circumference, in the plane of a rolling circle. ◆ *adj* wheel-like; like a Trochus; trochoidal. **trochoid'al** *adj* of the nature of a trochoid. **trochom'eter** or (*non-standard*) **trocheam'eter** *n* a hodometer. **troch'ophore** or **troch'osphere** *n* a free-swimming, pelagic larval form of many invertebrates. **troch'otron** *n* trochoidal magne*tron*, a high-frequency counting tube that deflects a beam onto radially disposed electrodes.

trock (*Scot*) see **truck**[2].

trocken /trok'(ə)n/ (*Ger*) *adj* (of wine) dry.

troctolite /trok'tə-līt/ *n* troutstone, a coarse-grained basic igneous rock composed of feldspar spotted with olivine. [Gr *trōktēs* a kind of sea-fish, from *trōgein* to gnaw, nibble, and *lithos* stone]

trod[1] /trod/ (*Spenser* **troad, troade** or **trode** /trōd/) (*obs*) *n* a track; path; footing. [OE *trod, trodu* track, trace; cf **tread**]
■ **hot trod** (*Walter Scott*) the pursuit of mosstroopers.

trod[2], and **trodden** see **tread**.

trode see **trod**[1].

troelie and **troely** see **troolie**.

trog /trog/ (*inf*) *vi* (**trogg'ing**; **trogged**) to walk, *usu* heavily and wearily. [Poss from **trudge** and **slog**]

troggs /trogz/ (*Scot*) *n* and *interj* troth.

troglodyte /trog'lə-dīt/ *n* a cave-dweller; an anthropoid ape (*obs* and *non-standard*). ◆ *adj* of or relating to cave-dwellers. [Gr *trōglodytēs*, from *trōglē* a hole, and *dyein* to get into]
■ **Troglodytes** /-lod'i-tēz/ *n* the wren genus. **troglodytic** /-dit'ik/ or **troglodyt'ical** *adj* cave-dwelling. **trog'lodytism** /-dīt-izm/ *n*.

trogon /trō'gon/ *n* any member of a family (**Trogon'idae**) of tropical and *esp* S American birds (*incl* the quetzal), with brilliantly-coloured plumage and backward-facing first and second toes. [Appar Gr *trōgōn* nibbling]

Troic /trō'ik/ *adj* Trojan. [Gr *Trōikos*]

troika /troi'kə/ *n* a Russian vehicle drawn by three horses abreast; a team of three horses abreast; a team of three people, etc, acting equally as leaders, a triumvirate; (with *cap*) a group forming the leadership of the European Union, consisting of the current and future holders of the Presidency, the European Commission and the Secretary General. [Russ, from *troe* a set of three]

troilism /troi'li-zm/ n sexual activity between three people (of two sexes). [Origin uncertain; perh Fr trois three, influenced by **dualism**]
■ **troi'list** n.

troilite /trō'i-līt/ n native ferrous sulphide, found in meteorites. [Dominico Troili, who observed it in the 18c]

troisième âge /trwä-zyem äzh'/ (Fr) n Third Age (see under **third**).

Trojan /trō'jən/ adj of Troy. ◆ n a citizen or inhabitant of Troy; a boon companion; a courageous, trusty or hard-working person; a good sort of person; a Trojan horse (see below; comput). [L Trōjānus, from Trōja Troy]
❑ **Trojan horse** n the gigantic wooden horse inside which the Greeks are said to have entered Troy; a person or organization, placed within a country, group, etc with the purpose of destroying it; a program containing hidden instructions so that, while it appears to carry out a useful function, it actually destroys or corrupts data (comput).

troke (Scot) see **truck²**.

troll¹ /trōl or trol/ (Norse myth) n an evil-tempered ugly dwarf (or, earlier, giant). [ON]

troll² /trōl or trol/ vt to fish for, or in, with a spinning or otherwise moving bait; to roll (obs); to trundle (archaic); to spin (archaic); to circulate, pass around the table (archaic); (Milton **troule**) to move nimbly, wag (the tongue); to utter fluently, set rolling off the tongue (obs); to sing the parts (eg a catch or round) in succession (archaic); to allure (obs). ◆ vi to fish with revolving or trailing bait (see also **trawl**); to roll (obs); to move or run about (obs); to sing a catch; to stroll, ramble (obs). ◆ n a lure for trolling; an instance of moving round, repetition; a round song; trolling. [Cf OFr troller (Fr trôler) to quest, Ger trollen to roll]
■ **troll'er** n. **troll'ing** n and adj.
❑ **troll'ing-bait** or **troll'ing-spoon** n a metallic revolving lure used in trolling.

troll³ /trol/ (comput sl) vi to make a conscious attempt to provoke controversy or disagreement on the Internet. ◆ vt to deliberately try to offend or abuse (someone) by means of an online posting. ◆ n an instance of this; a person who trolls. [Influenced by **troll¹** and **troll²**]

trolley¹ /trol'i/ n (also **troll'y** (pl **troll'ies**)) a basket, tray or table (or set of tiered trays) on castors or wheels, used for transporting goods, luggage, shopping, etc, or for serving food and drink; a bogie; a bed on wheels used for transporting hospital patients; a pulley, receptacle or car travelling on an overhead wire or rail; a trolley wheel; a tramcar (N Am). ◆ vt to convey by trolley. ◆ vi to travel by trolley. [Prob **troll²**]
■ **troll'eyed** adj (sl) drunk.
❑ **troll'eybus** n a bus that receives power by a trolley wheel from a pair of overhead wires. **trolley car** n (N Am) a tramcar so driven. **trolley dolly** n (sl) a female flight attendant. **trolley man** n a man who works a trolley or on a trolley. **trolley table** n a tiered trolley for a dining room. **trolley wheel** n a grooved wheel by which a bus, tramcar, etc receives current from an overhead wire.
■ **off one's trolley** (sl) daft, crazy.

trolley² or **trolly** /trol'i/ n (pl **troll'eys** or **troll'ies**) lace with the pattern outlined with thicker thread or a flat border. [Cf Flem tralje trellis]

trollius /trol'i-əs/ n a perennial plant of the genus Trollius, family Ranunculaceae, with orange or yellow globular flowers. [New L, appar from Ger Trollblume, from trollen to roll]

trollop /trol'əp/ n a slatternly or untidy woman; a shameless or promiscuous woman; a prostitute. ◆ vi (Scot) to draggle; to go, dress or work in a slovenly way. [Perh **troll²**]
■ **trollopee'** n (hist) a woman's loose dress worn in the 18c. **troll'oping**, **troll'opish** or **troll'opy** adj.

Trollopean or **Trollopian** /tro-lə-pē'ən or trə-lō'pē-ən/ adj of or in the style of the novels of Anthony Trollope (1815–82). ◆ n an admirer or student of his novels.

trolly see **trolley¹,²**.

tromba marina /trom'bə mə-rē'nə/ n an obsolete viol, generally one-stringed, with an irregular bridge, played in harmonics, giving a trumpet-like tone. [Ital, marine (speaking-)trumpet]

trombiculid /trom-bik'ū-lid/ adj of or relating to any of the mite family (**Trombiculidae**). ◆ n a trombiculid mite or harvest bug (qv).

trombone /trom-bōn'/ n a brass instrument, consisting of a tube bent twice on itself, with a slide, played in orchestras and brass bands. [Ital; augmentative of tromba trumpet]
■ **trombōn'ist** n.

tromino /trom'i-nō/ n (pl **trom'inos** or **trom'inoes**) a flat shape made up of three identical squares placed edge to edge. [**tri-** and (on a false analogy) **domino**]

trommel /trom'əl/ n a revolving cylindrical sieve for cleaning or sizing minerals. [Ger Trommel drum]

tromometer /tro-mom'i-tər/ n an instrument for measuring slight earthquake shocks. [Gr tromos a trembling, and metron a measure]
■ **tromomet'ric** adj.

tromp /tromp/ (esp US) vi to tramp or trample. [Variant of **tramp**, perh influenced by **stomp**]

trompe or **tromp** /tromp/ n an apparatus for producing a blast of air in a furnace by means of falling water. [Fr]

trompe l'œil /trõp lœy'/ (Fr) n (pl **trompe l'œils** /trõp lœ-y'/) literally, 'something that deceives the eye'; appearance of reality achieved by use of minute, often trivial, details or of other effects in painting, architecture, etc.

tron /tron/ or **trone** /trōn/ (chiefly Scot) n a public weighing-machine, used also as a place of punishment; the market-place; a system of weights used at the tron. [OFr trone, from L trutina, from Gr trȳtanē a pair of scales]

-tron /-tron/ sfx signifying agent or instrument, particularly: (1) thermionic valve, eg klystron, (2) elementary particle, eg positron, (3) particle accelerator, eg cyclotron. [Gr]

trona /trō'nə/ n a native combination of acid and normal sodium carbonate. [Swed, from Ar trōn for natrūn; see **natron**]

tronc /trongk or (Fr) trõ/ n a collection of tips to be divided out later, eg among waiters; the system by which this is done. [Fr, collecting box]

trone see **tron**.

troolie, **troelie** or **troely** /troo'li/ n the bussu palm; its leaf. [Tupí tururi]

troop /troop/ n a body of soldiers; (in pl) military forces; a band of people; a flock, herd or swarm of animals; (esp in pl) a great number; a division of a cavalry squadron; a group of (Boy) Scout patrols; a troupe; the command of a troop of horses; a drum signal for assembling. ◆ vi to pass in a body or in rapid succession; to be off; to assemble (archaic); to consort (archaic). ◆ vt to cause to troop; to receive and carry ceremonially along the ranks (as in troop the colour or colours). [Fr troupe, from LL troppus; poss Gmc]
■ **troop'er** n a private cavalry soldier (proverbially a swearer); a private soldier in armoured (tank) units; a mounted policeman (US and Aust); a state police officer (US); a cavalry horse; a troopship.
❑ **troop carrier** n a motor vehicle, ship or aeroplane for carrying troops. **troop horse** n a cavalry horse. **troop'ship** n a ship for transporting troops.

troopial same as **troupial**.

trop- see **tropo-**.

tropaeolum /tro-pē'ə-ləm/ n (pl **tropae'ola** or **tropae'olums**) the Indian cress and canary-creeper genus, S American trailing or climbing plants constituting a family **Tropaeolā'ceae** related to the geraniums, esp the garden nasturtium. [Gr tropaion a trophy (from the shield-shaped leaves and helmet-like flowers)]
■ **tropae'olin** n any of a group of dyes of complex structure.

troparion /tro-pā'ri-on or -ar'/ (Gr church) n (pl **tropar'ia**) a stanza or short hymn. [Dimin of Gr tropos trope]

trope /trōp/ n a figure of speech, properly one in which a word or expression is used in other than its literal sense, eg metaphor, metonymy, synecdoche or irony; a short cadence peculiar to Gregorian melodies; a phrase formerly interpolated in different parts of the mass. ◆ vt to provide with tropes. [Gr tropos a turn, from trepein to turn]
■ **trop'ical** adj. **trop'ist** n a user of tropes; someone who understands the Bible as having a figurative significance. **tropolog'ic** or **tropolog'ical** adj. **tropolog'ically** adv. **tropol'ogy** n figurative language; a moral interpretation of the Bible.

-trope /-trōp/ combining form denoting a tendency towards or affinity for, as in heliotrope. [Gr tropos a turn]
■ **-tropic** adj combining form. **-tropism** n combining form.

troph- /trof- or trəf-/, **tropho-** /-ō- or -o-/, **-troph-** /-trof-/ or **-trophy** /-trə-fi/ combining form denoting nutrition. [Gr trophē food, trophos a feeder, from trephein to feed]
■ **trophallac'tic** or **trophobīot'ic** adj. **trophallax'is** (Gr allaxis exchange) or **trophobīō'sis** (Gr biōsis way of life) n mutual exchange of nutriment in symbiosis. **trophesial** /-ē'zi-əl, -shl/ adj relating to trophesy. **troph'esy** or **trophoneurō'sis** n a state of deranged nutrition owing to disorder of the trophic action of the nerves. **trophi** /trō'fī/ n pl the mouth-parts of an insect; the teeth of the pharynx of a rotifer. **troph'ic** adj relating to nutrition (**trophic level** a division of an ecosystem consisting of all organisms whose food is obtained from plants by the same number of intermediate steps; **trophic structure** a feature of an ecosystem, measured and described in terms of standing crop per unit area or energy fixed per unit area per unit time). **troph'oblast** n the differentiated outer layer of epiblast in a segmenting mammalian ovum. **trophoblast'ic** adj. **trophol'ogy** n the study of nutrition. **troph'oplasm** n protoplasm which is mainly

concerned with nutrition. **trophotact'ic** or **trophotrop'ic** *adj*. **trophotax'is** and **trophot'ropism** *n* chemotaxis and chemotropism where the stimulating substance is food. **trophozo'ite** *n* in *Protozoa*, the trophic phase of the adult, which generally reproduces by schizogony.

Trophonian /trō-fō'ni-ən/ *adj* of the deified *Trophōnius* (Gr *Trophōnios*) or the cave in Boeotia where he delivered oracles and conferred solemnizing mystic experiences.

trophy /trō'fi/ *n* a memorial of victory, *orig* arms or other spoils set up on the spot; displayed spoils, such as skulls and antlers; a piece of plate or suchlike awarded as a prize; a memorial of success, glory, etc; an ornamental group of weapons, flags, etc, or a representation of such. ◆ *vt* (**trō'phying**; **trō'phied**) (*poetic*) to set with trophies; to confer trophies on. [Fr *trophée*, from L *trophaeum* (classical *tropaeum*), from Gr *tropaion*, from *tropē* a turning, from *trepein* to turn]
■ **trō'phied** *adj*.
❑ **trophy wife** *n* a young wife regarded as a status symbol for her (older) husband.

tropic /trop'ik/ *n* an imaginary circle on the celestial sphere about $23\frac{1}{2}°$ N (**tropic of Cancer**) or S (**tropic of Capricorn**) of the equator, where the sun turns on reaching its greatest declination north or south; a corresponding circle on the terrestrial globe; (in *pl*) the part of the earth between the tropics of Cancer and Capricorn; a turning point or limit. ◆ *adj* of or relating to the sun's turning; of the tropics; of or of the nature of a tropism (*biol*). [Gr *tropos* a turning]
■ **trop'ical** *adj* of or relating to a tropic or the tropics; found in or characteristic of the tropics; fervidly hot; luxuriant; of the nature of a trope, figurative. **trop'ically** *adv*.
❑ **tropical month** see under **month**. **tropical year** see under **year**. **trop'icbird** *n* a tropical seabird *Phaethon* with long tail feathers.

-tropic see under **-trope**.

tropism /trō'pi-zm/ (*biol*) *n* orientation in response to stimulus; a general term for helio*tropism*, geo*tropism*, etc. [Gr *tropos* a turning]
■ **tropistic** /trop-ist'ik/ *adj* of tropism.

-tropism see under **-trope**.

tropist see under **trope**.

tropo- /trō-pō-, trop-o-, -ō- or -ə-/, also **trop-** /trōp-, trop-/ *combining form* denoting: turning; change; tropism. [Gr *tropos* a turning]
■ **tropomy'osin** *n* (*biol*) a filamentous protein which controls the interaction of actin and myosin in muscle fibres, and hence muscle contraction. **trop'opause** *n* (Gr *pausis* a ceasing) the boundary between troposphere and stratosphere. **tropoph'ilous** *adj* tropophytic. **trop'ophyte** /-fīt/ *n* (Gr *phyton* plant) a plant adapted to alterations of moisture and drought. **tropophytic** /-fit'ik/ *adj*. **trop'oscatter** *n* the propagation of radio waves by using irregularities in the troposphere to scatter the signals beamed up by means of high-powered UHF transmitters and parabolic antennas. **trop'osphere** *n* the lowest layer of the atmosphere in which temperature falls as height increases. **tropospher'ic** *adj*.

tropologic, etc see under **trope**.

troppo[1] /trop'ō/ (*Ital*) *adv* in music, too much; excessively.

troppo[2] /trop'ō/ (*Aust inf*) *adj* driven insane by exposure to tropical heat. [From **tropical**]

trossers /tros'ərz/ *n* an obsolete form of **trousers**.

Trot /trot/ (*inf*; *derog*) *n* and *adj* short for **Trotskyist** or **Trotskyite**.

trot[1] /trot/ *n* a pace between walking and running (of a horse, with legs moving together diagonally); an act or spell of trotting; continual activity in moving about; a toddling child (*inf*); a trotline (*angling*); any of the single lines attached to a trotline; a crib, literal translation (*US sl*). ◆ *vi* (**trott'ing**; **trott'ed**) to go, ride or drive at a trot; to jog; to bustle about; to fish using a baited hook which travels downstream just above the bottom. ◆ *vt* to cause to trot; to conduct around; to bring out for exhibition; to draw out so as to make a butt of (*usu* with *out*); to jog on one's knee; to trot upon; to execute at a trot. [OFr *trot* (noun), *troter* (verb); perh Gmc; cf OHGer *trottôn*, Eng **tread**]
■ **trott'er** *n* a person or thing that trots; a horse trained to trot in harness racing; a foot, *esp* of a sheep or pig. **trott'ing** *n* the action of the verb; harness racing.
❑ **trot'line** *n* (*angling*) a long line across a waterway to which shorter lines with baited hooks are attached.
■ **on the trot** (*inf*) in succession, without a break; busy, bustling about. **the trots** (*sl*) diarrhoea. **trot out** to exhibit the paces of; to bring forward, adduce, produce for show, *esp* repeatedly or without much thought or effort; to go out with, court (*archaic*).

trot[2] /trot/ (*Shakesp*) *n* an old woman, a crone. [Anglo-Fr *trote*]

trot-cozy or **trot-cosey** /trot'kō'zi/ (*Walter Scott*) *n* a riding hood. [Appar **trot**[1] (Jamieson's *Dictionary of the Scottish Language* says **throat**) and **cosy**]

troth /trōth, troth/ (*formal* or *archaic*) *n* faith, fidelity. ◆ *vt* (*Shakesp*) to betroth. ◆ *interj* in truth. [Variant of **truth**]
■ **troth'ful** *adj*. **troth'less** *adj*.
❑ **troth'plight** *n* a plighting of troth, betrothal. ◆ *vt* (*archaic*) to betroth. ◆ *adj* (*Shakesp*) betrothed (also **troth'plighted**). **troth ring** *n* a betrothal ring.

Trotskyism /trot'ski-i-zm/ *n* the form of Communism associated with Leon *Trotsky* (pseudonym of Lev Davidovich Bronstein, 1879–1940), who advocated worldwide revolution.
■ **Trot'skyist** or **Trot'skyite** *n* and *adj*.

trottoir /trot-wär'/ (*Fr*) *n* a pavement. [Fr, from *trotter* to trot]

trotyl /trō'til/ *n* trinitrotoluene. [trinitro*tol*uene, and **-yl**]

troubadour /troo'bə-door, -dōr or -dör/ *n* any of a class of mostly aristocratic poets composing lyrics on courtly love, who first appeared in Provence, and flourished from the 11c to the 13c; a poet or singer (*usu* one whose theme is love). [Fr, from Provençal *trobador*, from *trobar* (Fr *trouver*) to find]

trouble /rub'l/ *vt* to agitate; to disturb; to muddy; to make turbid; to molest; to afflict; to annoy; to busy or engage overmuch; to put to inconvenience. ◆ *vi* to take pains; to put oneself to inconvenience; to be troublesome (*obs*). ◆ *n* disturbance; affliction; distress; a scrape; travail; anything amiss; disease; uneasiness; exertion; the taking of pains; a cause of trouble. [OFr *trubler* (Fr *troubler*) from a LL frequentative of L *turbāre* to disturb, from *turba* a crowd]
■ **troub'led** /rub'ld/ *adj*. **troub'ledly** *adv*. **troub'ler** *n*. **troub'lesome** *adj* causing or giving trouble or inconvenience; vexatious; importunate. **troub'lesomely** *adv*. **troub'lesomeness** *n*. **troub'ling** *n* and *adj*. **troub'lous** *adj* (*archaic* or *poetic*) full of trouble or disorder; agitated; tumultuous; disturbing. **troub'lously** *adv*. **troub'lousness** *n*.
❑ **troub'lefree** *adj* easy, not beset with problems. **troub'le-house**, **troub'le-state**, **troub'le-town** or **troub'le-world** *n* (*archaic* or *poetic*) someone who disturbs the peace of a house, state, etc. **troub'lemaker** *n* someone who disturbs the peace and (*usu*) incites others to do so. **troub'le-mirth** *n* a killjoy. **troub'leshoot** *vt*. **troub'leshooter** *n* an expert detector and mender of any trouble, mechanical or other. **troub'leshooting** *n* and *adj*. **trouble spot** *n* a place where trouble, *esp* social or political unrest, occurs.
■ **ask** or **look for** or (*US*) **borrow trouble** to behave in such a way as to bring trouble on oneself. **I'll trouble you** to please. **in trouble** (*euphem*) pregnant (when unmarried). **take** (**the**) **trouble** to make an effort. **the Troubles** periods of civil unrest in Northern Ireland in the years 1919–23 and 1969–98. **trouble and strife** (*rhyming sl*) wife. **trouble someone for** to ask someone to provide, pass, etc.

trough /trof/ *n* a long narrow vessel for watering or feeding animals; a vessel for kneading, brewing, washing, tanning or various domestic and industrial purposes; a vessel for liquid over which gases are collected (*pneumatic trough*); a channel, gutter or conduit; a long narrow depression; a hollow between wave crests; a low point (*fig*); an elongated area of low atmospheric pressure, *usu* extending from a depression and marking a change of air-mass (*meteorol*). [OE *trog*; Ger *Trog*]
❑ **trough fault** *n* (*geol*) a pair of parallel faults with downthrow between them. **trough shell** *n* a lamellibranch with a somewhat triangular shell thought to resemble a kneading-trough (genus *Mactra*).
■ **troughing and peaking** ranging between low and high points or levels.

troule (*Milton*) see **troll**[2].

trou-madame same as **troll-my-dame**.

trounce[1] /trowns/ *vt* to punish, beat, rebuke or censure severely; to indict (*dialect*); to harass (*obs*). [Origin obscure]
■ **trounc'er** *n*. **trounc'ing** *n*.

trounce[2] /trowns/ (*dialect* or *archaic*) *vi* to skip, prance, move briskly. ◆ *vt* to whisk off, make to skip. [Origin obscure]

troupe /troop/ *n* a company, *esp* of theatrical performers. ◆ *vi* to travel about as a member of a theatrical troupe. [Fr; see **troop**]
■ **troup'er** *n* a member of a theatrical troupe; an experienced, hard-working and loyal person, *esp* an actor.

troupial or **troopial** /troo'pi-əl/ *n* a bird (*Icterus icterus*) famous for its song; any bird of the Icteridae. [Fr *troupiale*, from *troupe* troop]

trouse /trooz, trowz/ (*archaic*) *n* Irish close-fitting breeches; trews. [See **trews**]
■ **trous'es** *n pl* (*sl*) trousers.

trousers /trow'zərz/, (*obs*) **trossers** /tros'ərz/ or (*Shakesp*) **strossers** /stros'/ *n pl* a garment worn on the lower part of the body with a loose tubular branch for each leg; (as *sing*, **trou'ser**) a pair or style of these; any other garment of similar form, such as pantalettes; long breeches. [See **trews**]
■ **trou'ser** *vt* (*sl*) to appropriate (money, etc), to pocket. ◆ *combining form* forming nouns, as in *trouser-leg*, *trouser-pocket*, *trouser-stretcher*. **trou'sered** *adj* wearing trousers. **trou'sering** *n* (*usu* in *pl*) material for trousers.

❑ **trouser suit** *n* a woman's suit, consisting of a jacket and trousers. ■ **all mouth and no trousers** (*inf*) given to making boasts that are not backed up by one's actions. (**caught**) **with one's trousers down** (taken) unawares. **wear the trousers** (used *esp* of a wife) to be the dominant partner in a marriage.

trousseau /troo'sō/ *n* (*pl* **trou'sseaux** or **trou'sseaus** /-sōz/) the clothes (and sometimes household linen, etc) collected by a bride for her marriage; a bundle (*archaic* and *rare*). [Fr, dimin of *trousse* bundle]

trout /trowt/ *n* (*pl* **trout** or (*rare*) **trouts**) a freshwater fish (*Salmo trutta*) of the salmon genus, much sought after by anglers; extended to various fishes related to or superficially resembling this; an unpleasant, interfering old person, *esp* a woman. [OE *truht*, from L *tructa*, *tructus*, from Gr *trōktēs* a sea-fish with sharp teeth, from *trōgein* to gnaw, nibble]
■ **trout'er** *n* a person who fishes for trout. **trout'ful** *adj* full of trout. **trout'ing** *adj* and *n* trout-fishing. **trout'less** *adj*. **trout'let** or **trout'ling** *n* a little trout. **trout'y** *adj*.
❑ **trout basket** *n* an osier or willow creel for carrying trout. **trout'-coloured** *adj* speckled like a trout; white, with spots of black, bay or sorrel. **trout farm** *n* a place where trout are reared artificially. **trout rod** *n* a fishing-rod for trout. **trout spoon** *n* a small revolving spoon used as a lure for trout. **trout'stone** *n* troctolite. **trout stream** *n* a stream in which trout are caught.

trouvaille /troo-vä'ē/ *n* a fortunate find. [Fr]

trouvère /troo-ver'/ or **trouveur** /troo-vær'/ *n* any of the medieval narrative or epic poets of N France. [Fr]

trove /trōv/ a shortened form of **treasure-trove** (see under **treasure**).

trover /trō'vər/ (*law*) *n* orig, finding and keeping; hence, formerly, a legal action brought to recover goods, or damages in their place, from a person to whom they do not belong. [OFr *trover* (Fr *trouver*) to find]

trow[1] /trō/ (*archaic*) *vt* to trust; to believe (often elliptically for *I trow* or *trow you?*). [OE *trēowan* (*trēowian*, *trūwian*); ON *trūa*, Ger *trauen*]

trow[2] /trow/ (*Shetland* and *Orkney*) *n* a form of **troll**[1].

trow[3] /trow/ (*dialect*) *n* any of various small boats or barges, *usu* flat-bottomed. [**trough**]

trowel /trow'əl/ *n* a flat or scoop-shaped tool with a short handle, for plastering, gardening, etc. ◆ *vt* (**trow'elling**; **trow'elled**) to dress, apply or move with or as if with a trowel. [OFr *truelle*, from LL *truella* (L *trulla*, dimin of *trua* a ladle)]
■ **trow'eller** *n*.
■ **lay it on with a trowel** to spread something thickly; to say grossly flattering things.

trowsers /trow'zərz/ (*archaic*) *n* a variant spelling of **trousers**.

troy /troi/ *adj* and *n* (relating to) a system of weights used for precious stones and metals, the pound (no longer in legal use) of 5760 grains being divided into 12 ounces of 20 pennyweight. [*Troyes*, in France]

Troyan /troi'ən/ (*Shakesp* and *Spenser*) *adj* Trojan.

truant /troo'ənt/ *n* someone who, idly or without excuse, absents himself or herself from school (also *fig*); an idler (*archaic*); a vagrant (*obs*); a vague term of reproach (*obs*). ◆ *adj* absent without excuse. ◆ *vi* to play truant. [OFr *truant* (Fr *truand*), prob from Celtic]
■ **tru'ancy**, **tru'antry** or **tru'antship** *n*.
■ **play truant** to stay away from school without permission or good reason.

Trubenize® or **Trubenise** /troo'bə-nīz/ *vt* to stiffen (a fabric) by binding together two layers by an intermediate layer of cellulose acetate.

trucage or **truquage** /trü-käzh'/ (*Fr*) *n* the faking of works of art.
■ **truqueur** /trü-kœr'/ *n* a faker of works of art.

truce /troos/ *n* a suspension of hostilities; a respite. [ME *trewes*, *treowes*, pl of *trewe*, from OE *trēow* truth, pledge, treaty; cf **true**]
■ **truce'less** *adj*. **trucial** /troo'shl, -syəl, -shi-əl/ *adj* bound by a truce.
❑ **truce'-breaker** *n*. **Truce of God** *n* a cessation of war, decreed by the Church, more or less observed, *esp* in the 11c and 12c, in France, Italy, England, etc, from Saturday (afterwards from Wednesday) evening to Monday morning, also during Advent and Lent and on certain holy days. **Trucial States** *n pl* former name (until 1971) for the United Arab Emirates on the S coast of the Persian Gulf, so called from being in treaty with Britain.

truchman /truch'mən/ (*obs*) *n* (*pl* **truch'men** or **truchmans**) an interpreter. [Ar *turjamān*; cf **dragoman**]

truck[1] /truk/ *n* an open railway wagon for goods; a trolley; a bogie; a low flat barrow; a small two-wheeled barrow with a turned-up front; a steerable axle on a skateboard; a motor vehicle of heavier construction than a car, designed for the transportation of commodities, or often a specific commodity; a lorry (chiefly *N Am*); a small or solid wheel; a cap at the top of a mast or flagstaff; a jazz dance, *orig* and *esp* of the 1930s, using a rhythmic strutting walk (*US sl*). ◆ *vi* to work as a truck driver (chiefly *N Am*); to dance the truck (see *n* above) (*US sl*); to walk in an affectedly lounging style with loping strides, the body laid back from the hips (*US sl*). ◆ *vt* to convey by truck; to put on a truck. [L *trochus* a wheel, from Gr *trochos*, from *trechein* to run]
■ **truck'age** *n* carriage by truck; charge for carriage by truck; supply of trucks. **truck'er** or **truck'man** *n* (chiefly *N Am*) a lorry driver. **truck'ie** *n* (*Aust* and *NZ inf*) a lorry driver. **truck'ing** *n*.
❑ **truck'load** *n* the amount carried in a truck; (*usu* in *pl*) large quantities (of) (*inf*). **truck stop** *n* (*N Am*) a transport café.

truck[2] /truk/ *vt* (also (*Scot*) **trock** /trok/ or **troke** /trōk/) to exchange; to barter; to pay in goods. ◆ *vi* to traffic; to have dealings; to barter; to bargain; to potter about; to do nothing (*sl*); to move along, make progress generally (*sl*); to persevere (*sl*). ◆ *n* exchange of goods; barter; payment in goods; (*Scot* **trock** or **troke**) dealings, intercourse; a small job, chore; small goods (*inf*); rubbish (*inf*); fresh vegetables, market-garden produce (*esp US*). [OFr *troquer* to truck; Sp *trocar* to barter, Ital *truccare* to truck]
■ **truck'age** *n* barter. **truck'er** *n* someone who trucks; a market-gardener (*US*). **truck'ing** *n*.
❑ **truck'-farm** *n* (*US*) a market-garden. **truck'-farmer** *n*. **truck'-farming** *n*. **truck shop** *n* (*hist*) a shop operated by employers in which their workers were obliged to buy goods. **truck system** *n* the practice of paying workers in goods instead of money, forbidden by the Truck Acts, 1831, etc.
■ **have no truck with** (*inf*) to have nothing to do with.

truckle /truk'l/ *n* a pulley-wheel; a castor (*obs*); a truckle bed; a barrel-shaped cheese. ◆ *vt* to move on rollers. ◆ *vi* to sleep in a truckle bed; to behave with servility (*usu* with *to*). [Gr *trochileiā*, *-liā*, etc a pulley, from *trochos* a wheel]
■ **truck'ler** *n*. **truck'ling** *n* and *adj*.
❑ **truckle bed** *n* a low bed that may be wheeled under another.

truculent /truk'ū-lənt/ *adj* aggressive and discourteous; very fierce (*archaic*); cruel (*archaic*). [L *truculentus*, from *trux* wild, fierce]
■ **truc'ulence** or **truc'ulency** *n*. **truc'ulently** *adv*.

trudge /truj/ *vi* to walk with labour or effort; to plod doggedly. ◆ *vt* to plod wearily or doggedly along, over, etc. ◆ *n* a heavy or weary walk; a trudger. [Origin obscure]
■ **trudg'er** *n* a person who trudges. **trudg'ing** *n* and *adj*.

trudgen (incorrectly **trudgeon**) /truj'ən/ *n* a swimming stroke in which each hand alternately is raised above the surface, thrust forward, and pulled back through the water (also *adj*). [John *Trudgen* (1852–1902), English swimmer who popularized the stroke in Britain]

true /troo/ *adj* genuine; properly so called; typical; conformable; accurately adjusted or in tune; straight or flat; agreeing with fact; actual; absolute; corrected; accurate; exact; right; rightful; honest; sincere; truthful; faithful; constant; trusty. ◆ *adv* truly; faithfully; honestly; in accurate adjustment; dead in tune; after the ancestral type. ◆ *vt* to adjust accurately. ◆ *n* that which is true, truth; accurate adjustment. [OE *trēowe*; ON *tryggr*, Ger *treu*]
■ **true'ness** *n*. **tru'ly** *adv*.
❑ **true bill** *n* (*law*; *N Am* or *hist*) a bill of indictment endorsed, after investigation, by a grand jury, as containing a case for the court. **true blue** see under **blue**[1]. **true'-born** *adj* of genuine birth; pure-bred; true to the qualities of the breed; legitimate. **true'-bred** *adj* pure-bred; typical; of good breeding. **true'-devot'ed** *adj* (*Shakesp*) full of honest zeal. **true'-dispos'ing** *adj* (*Shakesp*) just. **true-heart'ed** *adj* sincere; faithful. **true-heart'edness** *n*. **true'-life** *adj* taken from or comparable to real life. **true'love** *n* someone truly or really beloved; a sweetheart; a faithful lover; a true-love knot; a quatrefoil; a four-leaved clover (also **true'-love grass**; *obs*); herb Paris. **true-love knot** or **true'-lov'er's knot** *n* an ornamental or symbolic knot or interlaced design, as a two-looped bow or a knot with two interlaced loops. **true'man** *n* (*archaic*) an honest man. **true north** *n* the direction of the north pole, *opp* to *magnetic north*. **true'penny** *n* (*Shakesp*) an honest fellow. **true rib** see under **rib**[1]. **true-seem'ing** *adj* (*Spenser*) seeming (falsely or truly) to be true. **true time** *n* the time according to the position of the sun, *opp* to *mean time*. **true-type font** *n* (*comput*) a standard for scalable typefaces and fonts.
■ **out of true** not straight, not properly balanced, adjusted or calibrated.

truffle /truf'l, trūf'l/ *n* any fungus of the genus *Tuber* or the family Tuberaceae; its underground edible fructification; a rich confection made with chocolate, butter, etc, *usu* shaped into balls. [OFr *truffle* (Fr *truffe*); poss from L *tūber* lump, swelling]
■ **truff'led** *adj* cooked, stuffed or dressed, with truffles. **truff'ling** *n* the action of gathering truffles.
❑ **truffle dog** or **truffle pig** *n* a dog or pig trained to find truffles.

trug /trug/ (*dialect*) *n* a shallow wooden basket with a handle, used for carrying flowers or fruit. [Prob OE *trog* boat-shaped]

■ words derived from main entry word; ❑ compound words; ■ idioms and phrasal verbs

truism /troo'i-zm/ n a self-evident truth; a commonplace or trite statement. [**true**]
■ **truist'ic** adj.

trull /trul/ (archaic) n a prostitute. [Cf Ger Trolle]

Trullan /trul'ən/ adj held in the domed hall of the palace at Constantinople, applied to the Sixth Ecumenical Council (680–1) and esp to the Council of 692, which was not accepted by the Western Church. [LL trullus a dome, from L trulla a ladle]

truly see under **true**.

trumeau /troo-mō'/ n (pl **trumeaux** /-mōz'/) a piece of wall or pillar between two openings. [Fr]

trump[1] /trump/ n a card of a suit that ranks higher than any card of any other suit; ruff, an old card game like whist; a good, trusty person (inf). ◆ vt to play a trump card upon instead of following suit; to take (a trick, etc) in this way (also fig); of an Oxford University college, to gain (a student) by trumping. ◆ vi to play trumps on another suit. [**triumph**]
■ **trump'ing** at Oxford University, the system whereby colleges may offer an award and a place (which must be accepted) to other colleges' gifted applicants, so ensuring a more even spread of talented students among the colleges.
❑ **trump card** n (in some card games) the card turned up to determine the trump suit; any card of that suit; an advantageous or successful expedient.
■ **no'-trump'er** a hand suitable for no-trumps. **no'-trumps** a declaration in bridge and whist whereby no suit is more powerful than the rest (**no'-trump** adj). **turn** (or **come**) **up trumps** to behave in a very helpful or generous way, esp unexpectedly.

trump[2] /trump/ (archaic or poetic) n a trumpet; a blast; an act of breaking wind from the anus (sl); a Jew's-harp (now Scot). ◆ vt and vi to trumpet; to break wind from the anus (sl). [OFr trompe]
❑ **trump marine** n the tromba marina.
■ **the last trump** (relig) the trumpet blast to waken the dead on Judgement Day.

trump[3] /trump/ (obs) vt to deceive. [Fr tromper to deceive]
■ **trump'ery** n showy and worthless stuff; rubbish; ritual foolery. ◆ adj showy but worthless.

trump[4] /trump/ n (obs) an obstruction cast in one's way. ◆ vt to cast as an obstruction (obs); to allege (obs); to concoct and put forward unscrupulously (with up). [**trump**[1] affected by, or partly from, **trump**[3]]
❑ **trumped'-up** adj invented, false.

trumpet /trum'pit/ n an orchestral, military and signalling brass instrument of powerful and brilliant tone, in its present form a narrow tube bent twice upon itself, with cupped mouthpiece and flaring bell, giving, by action of the lips and breath pressure, harmonics of its fundamental, the scale filled up by use of crooks, slides, or valves; applied to other instruments more or less resembling this; a speaking-trumpet; an ear-trumpet; a trumpet-shaped object, such as a flared bell or horn, a corolla or corona; a sound of, or as if of, a trumpet; a trumpeter; an organ reed stop of trumpet-like tone. ◆ vt to sound or play on a trumpet or with trumpet-like sound; to proclaim, celebrate, summon, denounce, expel, etc by trumpet. ◆ vi to sound a trumpet; to make a sound like a trumpet. [Fr trompette, dimin of trompe trump]
■ **trum'peted** adj sounded on a trumpet; loudly extolled; having a trumpet; funnel-shaped. **trum'peter** n a person who plays or sounds the trumpet; a person who proclaims, praises or denounces; a loud-voiced crane-like S American bird (genus Psophia); a trumpeter swan; a kind of domestic pigeon; a large Australian and New Zealand food-fish (genus Latris) or other fish that trumpets when caught. **trum'peting** n and adj.
❑ **trumpet call** n a conventional phrase or passage played on the trumpet as a signal; any call to action. **trumpeter swan** n a black-billed American swan (Cygnus buccinator), the largest of the world's swans. **trum'petfish** n the snipefish or bellows-fish (Centriscus or Macrorhamphosus), a long-snouted fish related to the pipefish; a flutemouth, a sea fish with a tubular muzzle. **trumpet flower** n a name for various bignoniaceous, solanaceous and other plants with large trumpet-shaped flowers. **trumpet major** n a head trumpeter in a regiment. **trumpet marine** n the tromba marina. **trum'pet-shaped** adj like the bell of a trumpet. **trumpet shell** n a shell of the genus Triton. **trumpet tone** n the sound of a trumpet; a loud voice. **trum'pet-tongued** adj (Shakesp) proclaiming loud as a trumpet. **trumpet tree** or **trumpet wood** n a S American tree of the genus Cecropia whose hollow branches are used as trumpets by native peoples.
■ **blow one's own trumpet** to sound one's own praises. **feast of trumpets** another name for **Rosh Hashanah**.

truncal see under **trunk**.

truncate /trung-kāt'/ vt to cut short; to lop; to delete those digits of a number that are not considered to be significant (maths); to maim; to replace (an edge or corner where similar faces meet) by a symmetrically placed face (crystallog). [L truncāre, -ātum, from truncus (cf **trunk**)]

■ **trunc'ate** or **trunc'ated** adj appearing as if squared off at the tip; ending in a transverse line or plane, esp one parallel to the base. **trunc'ately** adv. **truncā'tion** n.
❑ **truncation error** n (maths) one caused by operating with a truncated number or numbers.

truncheon /trun'shən, -chən/ n a cudgel or baton carried by a police officer; a staff of authority; a broken or cut piece; a length for grafting or planting; a broken spear; a spear-shaft; a short staff; a cudgel (archaic). ◆ vt to carve (an eel); to beat with a truncheon. [OFr tronchon (Fr troncon), from tronc; see **trunk**]
■ **trun'cheoned** adj provided with a truncheon; armed with a lance. **trun'cheoner** n (Shakesp) a person armed with a truncheon.

trundle /trun'dl/ vt and vi to wheel, esp heavily or clumsily; to roll; to twirl; to spin (archaic); to bowl along. ◆ n the act or process of trundling; a little wheel, castor; a roller; a hoop; a truck (obs); a trundle bed; a spool of golden thread (heraldry). [OE trendel]
■ **trun'dler** n.
❑ **trundle bed** n (N Am) a truckle bed. **trun'dle-tail**, **tren'dle-tail** or **trin'dle-tail** n a curly-tailed dog.

trunk /trungk/ n the stem of a tree; the body of an animal apart from head and limbs; the body generally; a main line of road, railway, telephone, etc; a junction circuit between telephone exchanges (US); the main body of anything; the shaft of a column; the body of a pedestal; a chest or box, esp for travelling or for storing things; a box for fish; a box-like channel, trough, shaft, conduit or chute; a tube; a speaking tube; a telescope (obs); a pea-shooter (obs); a large hollow piston; a proboscis; same as **bus** (comput); (in pl) the game of trou-madame; (in pl) trunk hose, also breeches, esp those worn on the stage over tights; (in pl) pants worn for sports, swimming, etc; the luggage compartment of a car, the boot (N Am). [Fr tronc and L truncus a stock, a torso, from truncus maimed; with associations of Fr trompe a trump, a proboscis]
■ **trunc'al** adj relating to the trunk; principal. **trunked** adj having a trunk; truncated, beheaded (Spenser); relating to radio trunking. **trunk'ful** n (pl **trunk'fuls**) as much as will fill a trunk. **trunk'ing** n casing; a system of sharing a number of radio channels among a number of users of mobile (eg car) radio communication systems, the users being able to use any channel which is free at any given time. **trunk'less** adj.
❑ **trunk call** n the former name for a long-distance telephone call, involving connection between two centres, a **national call**. **trunk dialling** n the dialling of trunk telephone calls directly, connections not being made by an operator. **trunk'fish** n the coffer-fish. **trunk hose** or **trunk breeches** n pl full breeches reaching from waist to mid-thigh, worn in the 16c and early 17c. **trunk line** n the main line of a railway, canal, gas or oil pipeline, telephone system, etc. **trunk'-mail** n (obs) a travelling trunk. **trunk maker** n a maker of travelling trunks. **trunk road** n a main road, esp one administered by central authority. **trunk'sleeve** n (Shakesp) a puffed sleeve. **trunk'work** n (Shakesp) clandestine visiting in a trunk.

trunnel /trun'l/ n a variant spelling of **treenail**.

trunnion /trun'yən/ n either of a pair of side projections on which anything (eg formerly a big gun) is pivoted to move in a vertical plane; a stick, club (Walter Scott). [Fr trognon stump]
■ **trunn'ioned** adj provided with trunnions.

truquage and **truqueur** see **trucage**.

truss /trus/ n a framed structure for supporting a weight; a surgical appliance for retaining a reduced hernia; a bundle, esp of hay or straw, or a block cut from a stack (esp 56lb of old hay, 60lb of new, 36lb of straw); an attachment for holding a yard to the mast; a tuft of flowers or fruit at the top of the main stalk or stem; a corbel (archit); a close-fitting coat or (in pl) breeches (hist). ◆ vt to bundle up; to muffle up; to tuck up; to lace up, tie the points of (hist); to string up, hang (obs); to fix for cooking, as with a skewer; to catch in the talons, esp in the air, and carry off (falconry); to provide with a truss. ◆ vi to pack up; to make off. [Fr trousse (noun), trousser (verb)]
■ **trussed** adj. **truss'er** n. **truss'ing** n.
❑ **truss beam** n a wooden beam strengthened by a steel tie rod; a steel framework acting as a beam.

trust /trust/ n worthiness of being relied on; fidelity; confidence in the truth of anything; confident expectation; a resting on the integrity, friendship, etc of another; faith; hope; credit (esp sale on credit or on promise to pay); ground of confidence; that which is given or received in confidence; charge; responsibility; anything felt to impose moral obligations; an arrangement by which property is handed to or vested in a person, to use and dispose of it for the benefit of another; an estate so managed for another; an arrangement for the control of several companies under one direction, to cheapen expenses, regulate production, beat down competition, and so obtain a maximum return; a hospital trust (qv). ◆ adj held in trust. ◆ vt to place trust in; to believe; to expect confidently; to hope; to give credit to; to commit to trust. ◆ vi to have trust; to rely (with to). [ON traust trust; Ger Trost consolation]

■ **trust'able** adj. **trustee'** n a person to whom anything is entrusted; someone to whom the management of a property is committed in trust for the benefit of others. **trustee'ship** n the state of being or action of a trustee; a trust territory. **trust'er** n. **trust'ful** adj trusting. **trust'fully** adv. **trust'fulness** n. **trust'ily** adv. **trust'iness** n. **trust'ing** adj confiding. **trust'ingly** adv. **trust'ingness** n. **trust'less** adj not to be trusted, untrustworthy; distrustful. **trust'lessness** n. **trust'worthily** adv. **trust'worthiness** n. **trust'worthy** adj worthy of trust or confidence; trusty. **trust'y** adj (**trust'ier**, **trust'iest**) to be trusted; deserving confidence; faithful; honest; strong; firm; involving trust (Shakesp). ◆ n a person who can be trusted; a well-behaved prisoner, often granted special privileges; a greatcoat (Irish).
❑ **trust** or **trustee account** n a savings account administered by a trustee, the balance of which can be left to a beneficiary. **trust'buster** n (US and inf) a person who works for or achieves the break-up of business trusts, eg by legislation. **trust company** or **corporation** n a commercial enterprise formed to act as a trustee. **trust deed** n a deed conveying property to a trustee. **trust estate** n an estate held by trustees. **trust fund** n a fund of money, etc, held in trust. **trust hospital** n a hospital managed by a hospital trust (qv). **trust house** n a hotel or tavern owned by a trust company, not privately or by liquor manufacturers. **trust** or **trustee stock** n that in which a trustee may legally invest trust funds without being personally liable if it should depreciate in value. **trust territory** n a territory ruled by an administering country under supervision of the Trusteeship Council of the United Nations (also **trusteeship**).
■ **active** or **special trust** a trust in which the trustee's power of management depends upon his or her having the right of actual possession. **breach of trust** a violation of duty by a trustee, etc. **in trust** as a charge, for safekeeping, for management as a trustee. **investment trust** an organization that invests its stockholders' money and distributes the net return among them. **on trust** on credit; (accepted) without question. **Public Trustee** a government officer (and his or her department) empowered to act for the state as trustee, executor, etc. **split investment trust** see **split capital trust** under **split**. **trustee in bankruptcy** a person, usu an accountant, appointed (by the court) to administer the affairs of a bankrupt and to realize assets for the benefit of creditors. **trustee savings bank** a savings bank statutorily controlled under trustees and having its general fund guaranteed by the state. **unit trust** a type of investment trust in which given amounts of different securities form a unit, choice of a number of differently constituted units being available.

trustafarian /trus-tə-fä'ri-ən/ n an affluent young person who adopts a bohemian lifestyle and unkempt appearance (also adj). [trust fund and Rastafarian]

truth /trooth/ n faithfulness; constancy; veracity; agreement with reality; fact of being true; actuality; accuracy of adjustment or conformity; (in the fine arts) a faithful adherence to nature; that which is true or according to the facts of the case; that which one believes to be true; the true state of things, the facts; a true statement; an established fact; true belief; known facts, knowledge. [OE trēowth, from trēowe, trīewe true]
■ **truth'ful** adj habitually or actually telling what one believes to be true; put forward in good faith as what one believes to be true; conveying the truth. **truth'fully** adv. **truth'fulness** n. **truth'iness** n (rare) truth; truthfulness; (inf) the quality of having an air of the truth without necessarily a close connection to it. **truth'iness** n (inf) the quality of having an air of the truth without necessarily a close connection to it. **truth'less** adj. **truth'lessness** n. **truth'like** adj. **truth'y** adj (rare) true; truthful.
❑ **truth condition** n (logic) the circumstances that must be satisfied for a statement to be true. **truth drug** or **truth serum** n any of various drugs, such as scopolamine or thiopentone sodium, which make subjects under questioning less wary in their replies. **truth function** n (logic) a function that determines whether or not a complex sentence is true depending on the truth values of the component parts of the sentence. **truth table** n a Boolean logic table in which the binary digits 0 and 1 are assigned values either 'true' or 'false'; a similar table giving the outputs from all combinations of input (electronics). **truth'-teller** n. **truth'-telling** adj. **truth value** n (logic) the truth or falsity of a statement.
■ **God's** (**honest**) **truth** a thing or statement absolutely true. **in truth** truly, in fact. **moment of truth** see under **moment**. **of a truth** (Bible) truly. **tell the truth** to speak truthfully, not to lie.

try /trī/ vt (**try'ing**; **tried**) to attempt, endeavour (usu with to); to test; to prove by testing (Shakesp); to use, treat or resort to experimentally; to put to the test; to strain; to annoy, irritate, afflict; to experience, undergo (Milton); to examine critically; (of a judge) to examine and decide the truth, justice, guilt or innocence; (of a lawyer) to conduct in court (US); to separate out (obs); to sift (obs); to render; to extract (obs); to refine (obs); to purify (obs). ◆ vi to make an effort; (Spenser **trie**) to turn out, prove; to lie to, keep one's head to the wind (naut; Shakesp). ◆ n a trial; effort; in rugby, the score of four points (Rugby

League) or five points (Rugby Union) gained by a player who succeeds in placing the ball with his hand over the opposition's try-line; in American football, an attempt to gain a further point or points after scoring a touchdown. ◆ adj (Spenser **trye**) choice, purified. [OFr trier to pick out]
■ **tri'able** adj subject to legal trial; that can be tried. **tri'age** n sorting out; in war, etc, the selection for treatment of those casualties most likely to survive; allocation of resources to where they will have the most effect, rather than to where the need is most urgent or severe; broken coffee beans. **tri'al** n see separate entry. **tried** /trīd/ adj proved good by test. **tri'er** n a person who tries in any sense; a test; (formerly also **tri'or**) someone appointed to decide on a challenge to a juror, or a peer who is a juror in the trial of a peer; (also **try'er**) someone who is assiduous in trying to win. **try'ing** n. ◆ adj making trial or proof; adapted to try; searching, severe; testing; distressing; causing strain. **try'ingly** adv.
❑ **try house** n a place in which oil is extracted from blubber, etc. **trying plane** n a long plane for smoothing the surface of long boards. **try'-line** n (rugby) a line at either end of the pitch behind which a team must touch down the ball to score a try, a goal line. **try'-on** n an act of trying on a garment; an attempt at imposition by audacity (sl). **try'-out** n a test performance. **trysail** /trī'sl/ n a reduced sail used by small craft, instead of the mainsail, in a storm; a small fore-and-aft sail set with a boom and gaff. **try square** n a tool used in carpentry to check right angles.
■ **try and** (inf) try to. **try back** to revert, hark back. **try for** make an attempt to reach or gain. **try it on** (inf) to attempt to do something risky or audacious to see how far one can go unscathed. **try on** to put on (a garment, etc) for trial. **try out** to test (see also **try-out** above).

Trygon /trī'gon/ n the stingray genus. [Gr trȳgōn a stingray]

tryp /trip/ n short form of **trypanosome**.

trypaflavine /trip-ə-flä'vēn/ n acriflavine.

trypan blue /trip'ən, trip'an or tri-pan' bloo/ n a dye obtained from iodine used as a biological stain. [Short form of **trypanocidal**]

trypanosome /trip'ə-nə-sōm/ n a flagellate protozoan (genus Trypanosoma of various species, family **Trypanosomat'idae**) parasitic in the blood of vertebrates. [Gr trȳpanon a borer, from trȳpaein to bore, and sōma body]
■ **trypanocidal** /-sī'dl/ adj. **tryp'anocide** /-sīd/ n (L caedere to kill) a drug that kills trypanosomes. **trypanoso'mal** or **trypanosomic** /-som'ik/ adj. **trypanosomiasis** /-sō-mī'ə-sis/ n disease caused by a trypanosome, esp sleeping sickness.

trypsin /trip'sin/ (biol) n an enzyme secreted by the pancreas. [Gr trīpsis rubbing (as first obtained by rubbing down the pancreas with glycerine), or trȳein to wear out; modelled on **pepsin**]
■ **trypsin'ogen** n the inactive substance from which trypsin is formed in the duodenum. **tryp'tic** adj. **tryptophan** /trip'tō-fan/ or **tryptophane** /-fān/ n an essential amino acid obtained eg by the cleavage of casein by pancreatic enzymes.

trysail see under **try**.

tryst /trist or (Scot) trīst/ (archaic; formerly chiefly Scot) n an appointment to meet; appointed place of meeting; a cattle-fair. ◆ vt to make an appointment with. ◆ vi to agree to meet. [OFr triste a hunter's station]
■ **tryst'er** n.
❑ **tryst'ing-day** n. **tryst'ing-place**, **tryst'ing-stile**, **tryst'ing-tree** n.
■ **bide tryst** to wait for a person at the appointed place and time.

Tsabian see **Sabian**.

tsaddik and **tsaddiq** see **zaddik**.

tsamba /tsam'bə/ n a Tibetan barley dish. [Tibetan]

tsar or **czar**, also (rare) **tzar** /zär, tsär/ (hist) n the title of the emperors of Russia and of the kings of Bulgaria; a great potentate or despot; a person appointed as an authority or adjudicator on some subject, eg a language tsar. [Russ tsar', etc, from L Caesar, Caesar]
■ **tsar'dom** or **czar'dom** n. **tsar'evich** or **tsar'evitch**, **czar'evich** or **czar'evitch** n (Russ /tsär-ye'vĕch/) a son of a tsar. **tsarev'na** or **czarev'na** a daughter of a tsar; a wife of a tsarevitch. **tsarina** or **czarina** /-ē'nə/ (not a Russian form), **tsarit'sa** or **czarit'sa** n a Russian empress. **tsar'ism** or **czar'ism** n the government of the Russian tsars; absolutism. **tsar'ist** or **czar'ist** n an upholder of tsarism (also adj). **tsesar'evich**, **cesar'evich**, **tsesar'evitch**, **cesar'evitch**, **tsesar'ewich**, **cesar'ewich**, or **tsesar'ewitch**, **cesar'ewitch** /-ə-vich or (Russ) -ye'vĕch/ n the eldest son of a tsar; heir to the tsardom. **tsesarev'na** or **cesarev'na** n the wife of a tsar's eldest son.

tschernosem see **chernozem**.

TSE abbrev: transmissible spongiform encephalopathy.

tsessebe /tses'ə-bi/ (S Afr) n the sassaby. [Tswana tsésébe]

tsetse, **tzetse** or **tzetze** /tset'si/ n (also **tsetse fly**, **tzetse fly** or **tzetze fly**) a small fly of the African genus Glossina (esp G. palpalis and G.

morsitans) that transmits trypanosome parasites and causes sleeping sickness and nagana (**tsetse-fly disease**). [Tswana]

TSH *abbrev* : thyroid-stimulating hormone.

Tshi /*chē* or *chwē*/ *n* same as **Twi**.

T-shirt see under **tee¹**.

tsigane see **tzigany**.

TSO *abbrev* : town sub-office.

tsotsi /*tsot'si*/ *n* (*S Afr*) a member of a black African street gang, a young hooligan or thug. [Origin uncertain; perh from Nguni *ukutsotsa* to wear exaggerated dress]
□ **tsotsi suit** *n* a zoot suit.

tsouris see **tsuris**.

TSP *abbrev* : textured soya protein.

tsp *abbrev* : teaspoonful (*pl* **tsps**).

TSR (*comput*) *abbrev* : Terminate and Stay Resident, used of a program that remains in memory.

TSS *abbrev* : toxic shock syndrome.

tsuba /*tsoo'bə*/ *n* a metal plate at the top of a Japanese scabbard, serving as a sword guard, often highly ornamental. [Jap]

Tsuga /*tsoo'gə*/ *n* the hemlock spruce genus. [Jap *tsuga* larch]

tsunami /*tsoo-nä'mē*/ *n* a very swiftly travelling sea wave that attains great height, caused by an undersea earthquake or similar disturbance. [Jap *tsu* harbour, and *nami* wave]

tsuris or **tsouris** /*tsoo'ris*/ (*Yiddish*) *n* grief, trouble, woe. [Yiddish *tsures*, *tsores*, pl of *tsure*, *tsore* trouble, from Heb]

tsutsugamushi disease /*tsoo-tsoo-gə-moo'shi di-zēz'*/ *n* any of various rickettsial diseases, *incl* scrub typhus. [Jap *tsutsuga* illness, and *mushi* insect]

tsutsumu /*tsoo-tsoo'moo*/ *n* the Japanese art of wrapping articles in a harmonious way. [Jap, to wrap]

Tswana /*tswä'nə* or *swä'nə*/ *n* (*pl* **Tswan'a** or **Tswan'as**) an African people living mainly around Botswana; a member of this people; their language, of the Bantu family. ◆ *adj* of or relating to the Tswana or their language.

TT *abbrev* : teetotal(-ler); Tourist Trophy; Trinidad and Tobago (IVR); tuberculin tested.

TTFN (*inf*) *abbrev* : ta-ta for now.

TTL (*photog*) *abbrev* : through the lens, a system of metering light in cameras.

TTP *abbrev* : trusted third party.

TTS (*comput*) *abbrev* : text-to-speech.

TU *abbrev* : trade union.

Tu. or **Tues.** *abbrev* : Tuesday.

tuan¹ /*too-än'*/ *n* sir; lord, master; a title of respect in the Malay Archipelago and Indonesia. [Malay]

tuan² /*too'ən*/ *n* the brush-tailed phascogale or wambenger, an Australian arboreal marsupial (*Phascogale tapoatafa*). [Aboriginal native name]

Tuanku /*tŭ-äng'koo*/ (*Malay*) *n* majesty, highness (as a title or form of address).

Tuareg /*twä'reg*/ *n* a nomadic Berber of the Sahara; the language of the Tuaregs. ◆ *adj* of or relating to the Tuaregs or their language. [Ar *tawāriq*]

tuart, **tooart** /*too'ərt*/ or **tewart** /*tŭ'*/ *n* a strong-timbered eucalyptus (*Eucalyptus gomphocephala*). [From an Aboriginal language]

tuatara /*too-a-tä'rə*/ *n* a New Zealand lizard-like reptile (genus *Sphenodon* or *Hatteria*), the sole survivor of the class Rhynchocephalia. [Maori, spine on the back]

tuath /*too'ə*/ (*Irish hist*) *n* a people; an ancient territorial division. [Ir *tūath*]

tub /*tub*/ *n* an open container, *orig* of wooden staves and hoops, later also of metal, plastic, etc; a small cask or carton for food, etc, *usu* plastic or cardboard; anything like a tub; a tubful; a pulpit (*facetious*); a clumsy ship or boat; a bath, bathtub (*esp N Am*); a pit-shaft casing; a bucket, box or vehicle for bringing up coal from the mine; a tubfish. ◆ *vt* to set, bathe or treat in a tub; to line with a tub. ◆ *vi* to take a bath. [Cf LGer *tubbe*]
■ **tubb'able** *adj* able to be washed in a tub. **tubb'er** *n*. **tubb'iness** *n*. **tubb'ing** *n* the art of, or material for, making tubs; mine-shaft lining; rowing in clumsy boats; the taking of baths. **tubb'ish** *adj* round and fat. **tubb'y** *adj* (**tubb'ier**; **tubb'iest**) sounding like an empty tub; dull in sound; plump, round like a tub. **tub'ful** *n* (*pl* **tub'fuls**) as much as a tub will hold.
□ **tub'fast** *n* (*Shakesp*) treatment of venereal disease by fasting and sweating in a hot tub. **tub'fish** *n* the sapphirine (or other) gurnard.

tub'-thump *vi*. **tub'-thump'er** *n* a declamatory or ranting preacher or public speaker. **tub'-thumping** *n* and *adj*.

tuba /*tū'bə*, *too'bə*/ *n* (*pl* **tu'bas** or (L) **tu'bae** /*-bē*, *-bī*/) a straight trumpet (*ancient Rome*); the bombardon (**bass tuba**) or (sometimes) other low-pitched brass instrument of the saxhorn class; a powerful organ reed stop; a tube (*anat*). [L and Ital *tuba*]

tube /*tūb*/ *n* a pipe; any long hollow body; a telescope or other optical instrument (also **optic tube**; *archaic*); a collapsible cylinder from which material in the form of paste or viscous liquid can be squeezed out; a thermionic valve (*N Am*); an underground railway running through tube-shaped tunnels, *specif* (with *cap*; with *the*) the London Underground (*inf*); the united part of calyx, corolla, etc (*bot*); any vessel in a plant or animal body; an aircraft (*sl*); a television set (*sl*); a can or bottle of beer (*Aust sl*); an extremely stupid person (*sl*). ◆ *vt* to provide with, fit with or enclose in a tube; to insert a tube in the neck of (a horse) to help breathing. ◆ *vi* to travel by tube. [Fr, from L *tubus* a pipe; also (as in *Fallopian* and *Eustachian tubes*) from L *tuba* a trumpet (see **tuba**)]
■ **tub'age** *n* insertion of a tube. **tub'al**, **tub'ar** or **tub'ate** *adj* tubular. **tubec'tomy** *n* (*med*) surgical cutting or removal of the Fallopian tubes. **tubed** /*tūbd*/ *adj*. **tube'ful** *n* (*pl* **tube'fuls**). **tube'less** *adj*. **tube'like** *adj*. **tub'er** *n* a participant in the sport of tubing (see below). **tubic'olar** or **tubic'olous** *adj* inhabiting a tube. **tub'icole** *n* a tubicolous animal or plant (also *adj*). **tubiflo'rous** *adj* having tubular flowers. **tub'iform** *adj* shaped like a tube. **tub'ing** *n* the act of making or supplying tubes; the activity of travelling through water or snow in an inflated inner tube; tubes collectively; material for tubes. **tub'oplasty** *n* (*med*) surgical repair of a Fallopian tube. **tub'ular** *adj* having the form of a tube; made of or with tubes; having a sound like that made by the passage of air through a tube. **Tubūlā'ria** *n* a genus of Hydrozoa. **tubūlā'rian** *adj* and *n*. **tubūlar'ity** *n*. **tub'ūlate** *vt* to form into a tube; to provide with a tube. ◆ *adj* tubular. **tub'ūlated** *adj*. **tubūlā'tion** *n*. **tub'ūlature** *n*. **tub'ūle** *n* a small tube. **Tubūliflo'rae** *n pl* a section of the Compositae with tubular disc flowers. **tubūliflo'ral** or **tubūliflo'rous** *adj*. **tub'ulin** *n* (*biol*) a globular protein which forms the basic unit for the contraction of microtubules. **tub'ūlous** *adj* tubular.
□ **tubal ligation** *n* the placing of a clip or ligature round a loop in each of the Fallopian tubes as a means of sterilization. **tube foot** *n* in echinoderms, a tube protruding through a pore, used in locomotion and respiration. **tubeless tyre** or **tire** see under **tyre**. **tube'nose** *n* any seabird of the order Procellariiformes, characterized by having extended tubular nostrils (also called **petrel**). **tube skirt** *n* a close-fitting, straight skirt. **tube well** *n* a pipe used to obtain water from beneath the ground, with perforations just above its sharp point. **tube worm** *n* a worm that makes a tube to inhabit. **tubular bells** *n pl* an orchestral musical instrument in the percussion section, consisting of a number of metal tubes suspended in a frame, giving the sound of bells when struck.
■ **to go down the tubes** (*sl*) to fail dismally, to be ruined.

tuber¹ /*tū'bər*/ *n* a swelling, *usu* underground, in a plant, where reserves are stored up, formed either in the stem (as in the potato, Jerusalem artichoke, etc), or sometimes in the root (as in the dahlia); a lump; a rounded swelling (*pathol*); a knob; a protuberance; (with *cap*) the truffle genus of fungi, giving its name to the **Tuberā'ceae**, saprophytic Ascomycetes, many with edible underground fructifications. [L *tūber* a swelling, from root of L *tumēre* to swell]
■ **tuberā'ceous** *adj*. **tuberif'erous** *adj*. **tu'beriform** *adj*. **tuberose** /*tū'bə-rōs*, *-rōz*/ *adj* tuberous. ◆ *n* /*tū'bə-rōs*, *-rōz*; often, by false association with **tube** and **rose¹**, *tūb'rōz*/ a Mexican amaryllid (*Polianthes tuberosa*) grown for its fragrant creamy-white flowers, propagated by tubers. **tuberosity** /*-ros'i-ti*/ *n*. **tub'erous** *adj* having tubers; of the nature of, or like, a tuber; knobbed.
□ **tuberous root** *n* a fleshy root resembling a tuber but not having buds or eyes.

tuber² see under **tube**.

tubercle /*tū'bər-k(ə)l*/ *n* a small tuber, protuberance or swelling; a nodule; a nodule or diseased growth in the lung or elsewhere, in cases of tuberculosis (*pathol*). [L *tūberculum*, dimin of *tūber*]
■ **tu'bercled** *adj* having tubercles. **tubercular** /*-bûr'*/ *adj* nodular; having tubercles; affected by or suffering from tuberculosis. ◆ *n* someone suffering from tuberculosis. **tuber'culate** or **tuber'culated** *adj* having or covered with tubercles. **tuberculā'tion** *n*. **tu'bercule** *n* a tubercle. **tuber'culin** *n* a preparation from a culture of tubercle bacillus used for testing for tuberculosis. **tuberculizā'tion** or **-s-** *n*. **tuber'culize** or **-ise** *vt* to infect with tuberculosis. **tuberculo'ma** *n* a slow-growing, circumscribed tuberculous lesion. **tuber'culose** or **tuber'culosed** *adj* tuberculous; tuberculated. **tuberculō'sis** *n* consumption or phthisis, a disease caused by the **tubercle bacillus** (*Bacillus tuberculosis*), characterized by development of tubercles. **tuber'culous** *adj* of or affected by tuberculosis; tuberculated (now *rare*). **tuber'culum** *n* a tubercle.

◻ **tubercle bacillus** see **tuberculosis** above. **tuber'culin-tested** *adj* applied to milk from cows that have been tested for and certified free from tuberculous infection.

tuberose see under **tuber¹**.

tubfast see under **tub**.

tubicolar see under **tube**.

tubifex /*tū'bi-feks*/ *n* an oligochaete worm of the genus *Tubifex*, *usu* living in riverbeds or lake-beds. [New L]

tubiform, **tubing**, **tubular**, etc see under **tube**.

Tubigrip® /*tū'bi-grip*/ *n* a tubular elastic bandage for use on an ankle, knee, etc.

TUC *abbrev* : Trades Union Congress.

tuchun /*too-chün'*, *doo-jün'*/ *n* a Chinese military governor. [Chin]

tuck¹ /*tuk*/ *vt* to draw or thrust in or together; to stuff, cram; to fold under; to gather or gird up (often with *up*); to contract (with *up*); to enclose by pressing clothes closely around or under (*usu* with *in*); to put tucks in; to put or stow away; to full, dress, or put on tenters; to hamper; to eat (with *in*; *inf*); to hang (with *up*; *sl*). ◆ *vi* to make an onslaught upon food (*usu* with *in* or *into*). ◆ *n* an act of tucking; a pleat or fold, now one stitched down; in some sports, eg skiing, a position with the knees tucked close to the chest; the gathering of the bottom planks of a ship at the stern (*naut*); eatables, *esp* delicacies (*inf*). [OE *tūcian* to disturb, afflict; cf Ger *zucken* to twitch]
■ **tuck'er** *n* someone who or something that tucks; a piece of cloth tucked or drawn over the bodice of a low-cut dress; a fuller; food (chiefly *Aust* and *NZ sl*). ◆ *vt* (*sl*) to tire exceedingly (often with *out*). ◻ **tuck box** *n* (*inf*) a box of or for tuck, *esp* at a boarding school. **tuck'erbag** or **tuck'erbox** *n* (*Aust* and *NZ*) a bag or box, for carrying food in. **tuck'-in** *n* (*inf*) a hearty feed. ◆ *adj* contrived for tucking in an edge. **tuck'-mill** or **tuck'ing-mill** *n* a fulling-mill. **tuck'-out** *n* (*inf*) a tuck-in. **tuck shop** *n* (*orig school sl*) a confectioner's or a pastrycook's shop; now *esp* such a shop or anything similar on school premises.

tuck² /*tuk*/, *Scot* **touk** /*tŭk*/ (*dialect*) *n* a stroke, tap or beat, *esp* of a drum (also *vi* and *vt*). [ONFr *toker*, *toquer* (Fr *toucher*) to touch]

tuck³ /*tuk*/ (*Shakesp*) *n* a rapier. [Fr *estoc*, from Ger *Stock* stick]

tuckahoe /*tuk'ə-hō*/ *n* an edible but tasteless underground fungus of the southern USA; the edible rootstock of several American aroids; an inhabitant of eastern Virginia (*old US inf*). [Algonquian *ptuckweoo*]

tucket /*tuk'it*/ (*archaic*) *n* a flourish on a trumpet. [Cf **tuck²** and Ital *toccata* a touch]

tucutuco /*too-kŭ-too'kō*/ or **tucotuco** /*too-kō-too'kō*/ *n* (*pl* **tucutu'cos** or **tucotu'cos**) a S American rodent of mole-like habits (genus *Ctenomys*). [Imit, from its cry]

'tude /*tood*/ (*US sl*) *n* a short form of **attitude** in the sense of insolent manner.

Tudor /*tū'dər*/ *adj* relating to the Welsh family of *Tudor*, the time when it held the English throne (1485–1603), or the style of architecture (Late Perpendicular) that prevailed then.
■ **Tudorbē'than** *adj* in imitation of Tudor or Elizabethan style. **Tudoresque'** *adj*. ◻ **Tudor flower** *n* a trefoil ornament frequent in Tudor architecture. **Tudor rose** *n* a red and white rose (combining those of Lancaster and York) adopted as a badge by Henry VII. **Tu'dor-style** *adj* Tudoresque.

Tue. or **Tues.** *abbrev* : Tuesday.

Tuesday /*tūz'dā* or *-di*/ *n* the third day of the week. [OE *Tīwes dæg* the day of *Tīw*, the god of war, corresponding to L *diēs Martis* the day of Mars]
■ **Tues'days** *adv* on Tuesdays.

tufa /*too'fə*, *tū'fə*/ *n* calc-sinter (often *calcareous tufa*); tuff or other porous rock (*obs*). [Ital *tufa*, a variant of *tufo*, from L *tōfus* a soft stone]
■ **tufā'ceous** *adj*.

tuff /*tuf*, *tŭf*/ *n* a rock composed of fine volcanic fragments and dust; tufa or other porous rock (*obs*). [Fr *tuf*, *tuffe*, from Ital *tufo*; see **tufa**]
■ **tuffā'ceous** *adj*.

tuffe /*tuf*/ *n* (*Shakesp*) same as **tuft**.
■ **tuff'et** *n* a tuft; a tussock; a mound.

tuft /*tuft*/ *n* a bunched cluster; a clump; a crest; a separate lock of hair; any of the cut or uncut loops of wool, etc forming the pile of a carpet or rug; a goatee or imperial beard; a small tassel; a gold tassel formerly worn on a nobleman's cap in the English universities; hence, a titled undergraduate; a person of social consequence. ◆ *vt* to separate into tufts; to make or decorate with tufts; to beat (the ground) in deer-hunting; to dislodge (game). [Supposed to be from OFr *tuffe* (Fr *touffe*), from L *tūfa* crest, from Gmc (cf OLGer *top* top); but there are difficulties]
■ **tuft'ed** *adj* having or made of tufts; having many short crowded branches all arising at or near the same level (*bot*); (of birds) with a tuft

or crest of feathers on the head. **tuft'er** *n* a hound that drives deer out of cover. **tuft'ing** *n*. **tuft'y** *adj*. ◻ **tufted duck** *n* a freshwater European duck, the male of which has a drooping black crest. **tuft'-hunter** *n* a toady. **tuft'-hunting** *n*.

tug /*tug*/ *vt* (**tugg'ing**; **tugged**) to pull forcibly; to haul; to tow; to drag. ◆ *vi* to pull forcibly; to strive; to toil. ◆ *n* a forcible or jerking pull; a hard struggle; a rope or chain for pulling; a name for various parts of harness, such as a trace or a loop to receive a shaft; a tugboat; an aeroplane towing a glider. [ME *toggen*, intensive, from root of OE *tēon*; cf **tow¹**]
■ **tugg'er** *n* a person who tugs. **tugg'ing** *n* and *adj*. **tugg'ingly** *adv*. ◻ **tug'boat** *n* a towing vessel. **tug-of-love'** *n* a dispute over the guardianship of a child, eg between divorced parents, or natural and foster parents (also *adj*). **tug-of-war'** *n* a laborious contest; a contest in which opposing teams tug at a rope and strive to pull one another over a line.

tugra or **tughra** /*too'grə*/ (*hist*) *n* the ornamental monogram of the Turkish Sultan, used on coins and documents, etc. [Turk *tura*, *tuğra*]

tugrik or **tughrik** /*too'grēk*/ *n* the standard monetary unit of Mongolia (100 mongos). [Mongolian]

tui /*too'ē*/ *n* a New Zealand honey guide, *Prosthemadera novaeseelandiae*, with glossy blue-black plumage with tufts of white at the neck, the parson-bird. [Maori]

tuille /*twēl*/ *n* in plate armour, a steel plate hanging below the tasses; (also **tuile**) a very thin, crisp biscuit moulded into a curved shape, often eaten with desserts. [Fr, from L *tēgula* a tile]
■ **tuillette'** *n* (*dimin*).

tuilyie or **tuilzie** /*tūl'i*, *tūl'yi*/ (*Scot*; *obs*) *n* a fight, brawl, tussle. ◆ *vi* to struggle. [OFr *tooil* (noun), *toillier* (verb)]

tui na /*twe na*/ *n* a Chinese therapeutic massage system in which vigorous hand movements are used (also **tui'na**). [Chin, from *tūi* push, and *nā* take hold]

tuism /*tū'i-zm*/ *n* apostrophe; reference to, or regard to the interests of, a second person. [L *tū* thou]

tuition /*tū-ish'ən*/ *n* teaching, instruction; the fee levied or paid for teaching or instruction (chiefly *N Am*); guardianship (*obs*). [L *tuitiō*, *-ōnis*, from *tuērī*, *tuitus* to watch over]
■ **tui'tional** or **tui'tionary** *adj*.

tuk tuk /*tuk'tuk*/ *n* in Thailand, a motorized rickshaw. [Imit of the engine sound]

tularaemia or (*US*) **tularemia** /*too-lə-rē'mi-ə*/ *n* a disease of rodents caused by a bacterium (*Bacterium tularense* or *Pasteurella tularensis*) transmitted to humans either by insects or directly, causing fever, etc. [*Tulare* county, California, where it was first discovered, and Gr *haima* blood]
■ **tularae'mic** or **tulare'mic** *adj*.

tulban see **turban**.

tulchan /*tul'hhən*/ *n* a calf's skin set beside a cow to make her give milk freely. [Gaelic *tul(a)chan* a hillock]
◻ **tulchan bishop** *n* (*Scot hist*) a titular bishop appointed to transmit most of the revenues of a diocese to the nobles (1572).

tule /*too'lā*/ *n* a large American bulrush (genus *Scirpus*). [Sp, from Nahuatl *tollin*]

tulip /*tū'lip*/ *n* any plant or flower of the bulbous genus *Tulipa*, with showy, *usu* solitary, flowers; a showy person. [OFr *tulipe*, *tulippe*, *tulipan*, from Turk *tulbend* turban]
■ **tulipant'** *n* (*obs*) a turban. **tulipomā'nia** *n* a craze for tulip-growing. ◻ **tu'lip-eared** *adj* prick-eared, as a dog. **tulip poplar** *n* the tulip tree. **tulip root** *n* a disease affecting the stem of oats. **tulip tree** *n* a N American timber tree (genus *Liriodendron*) of the magnolia family with tulip-like flowers. **tu'lipwood** *n* its wood.
■ **African tulip tree** a tree of the genus *Spathodea*, of the family Bignoniaceae.

tulle /*tool*, *tūl*, *tül*/ *n* a delicate thin silk network fabric that was popularly used, *esp* in the 19c, for making veils, hats, etc. [Fr; from *Tulle*, in the department of Corrèze]

Tullian /*tul'i-ən*/ *adj* of or like *Tully*, ie Marcus *Tullius* Cicero; Ciceronian.

tulwar /*tul'wär*/ *n* an Indian sabre, *esp* the curved sabre used by the Sikhs. [Hindi *talwār*]

tum see **tummy**.

tumble /*tum'bl*/ *vi* to roll, wallow, toss about; to perform as a dancer or acrobat; to turn over in flight or fall; to fall headlong, floundering or revolving; to collapse, fall in a heap; to rush confusedly and hastily; to come by chance (*usu* with *on*); to comprehend (often with *to*; *inf*). ◆ *vt* to send tumbling or headlong; to overthrow; to bundle from one place to another; to jumble; to throw about; to disorder, rumple; to tumble-dry. ◆ *n* act of tumbling; a fall; a somersault; a tumbled condition or mass; an act of sexual intercourse (*sl*). [Frequentative from OE *tumbian*; cf Ger *tummeln*]

■ **tum'bler** *n* a person who tumbles; an acrobat; a large drinking-glass or tall cup, formerly one that could not stand; a tumblerful; a tumbrel; a toy weighted to rock and right itself; a pigeon that turns back-somersaults in the air; a dog that performed antics in catching rabbits (*obs*); a revolving barrel or cage; part of a lock that holds the bolt in place, until it is moved by the key; part of a firearm lock that receives the thrust of the mainspring and forces the hammer forward; a member of a gang of London ruffians in the early 18c who set women on their heads (*hist*); a tumble-drier (see below); a machine consisting of a revolving drum in which (gem)stones are polished (also **tumbling barrel** or **tumbling box**). **tum'blerful** *n* (*pl* **tum'blerfuls**) as much as will fill a tumbler. **tum'bling** *n* and *adj*.

□ **tumblebug** or **tumbledung** *n* (*N Am*) a dung beetle (from its activity of rolling pellets of dung). **tumble car** or **tumble cart** *n* a vehicle with wheels and axle in one piece. **tum'bledown** *adj* dilapidated, threatening to fall. **tum'ble-drī'er** or **tumb'le-dry'er** *n* a machine that dries (clothes, etc) by tumbling them in a strong current of hot air (also **tum'bler-drī'er** or **tum'bler-dry'er**). **tum'ble-dry** *vt* and *vi* to dry (clothes, etc) in a tumble-drier. **tum'blehome** *n* the inward curvature of the upper part of the sides of a ship. **tum'bler-switch** *n* a switch that is turned over to put electric current off or on. **tum'bleweed** *n* a type of plant that snaps off above the root, curls into a ball, and is blown about in the wind. **tumbling barrel**, **tumbling box** see **tumbler** above.

■ **take a tumble to oneself** (*inf*) to assess one's situation critically and improve it. **tumble in** or **home** (of a ship's sides) to incline inward above the extreme breadth; to fit, as a piece of timber into other work; to go to bed. **tumble over** to toss about carelessly, to upset; to fall over. **tumble up** to get out of bed; to throw into confusion; to scurry up on deck.

tumbrel /*tum'brəl*/ or **tumbril** /*tum'bril*/ *n* an old instrument of punishment, a pillory or cucking stool (*obs*); a cart, *esp* for dung, that tips over backwards to empty its load; a two-wheeled military cart (*archaic*); the name given to the carts that conveyed victims to the guillotine during the French Revolution. [OFr *tomberel* (Fr *tombereau*), from *tomber* to fall]

tumefy /*tū'mi-fī*/ *vi* and *vt* (**tu'mefying**; **tu'mefīed**) to swell. [L *tumefacere, tumescere, tumidus*, from *tumēre* to swell, and *facere* to make]

■ **tumefacient** /*tū-mi-fā'shənt*/ *adj*. **tumefac'tion** *n*. **tumesce'** *vi* and *vt* to (cause to) swell, to tumefy; to (cause to) have an erection (*facetious*). **tumescence** /*tū-mes'əns*/ *n* a tendency to swell; a swelling. **tumesc'ent** *adj* (becoming) swollen. **tumesc'ently** *adv*. **tu'mid** *adj* swollen or enlarged; inflated; falsely sublime; bombastic. **tumid'ity** *n*. **tu'midly** *adv*. **tu'midness** *n*.

tummy /*tum'i*/ (*inf* or *childish*) *n* a stomach. Also **tum** or **tum'-tum**.
□ **tummy ache** *n* stomach ache. **tummy button** *n* a navel. **tummy tuck** *n* (*inf*) an abdominoplasty.

tumour or (*US*) **tumor** /*tū'mər*/ *n* swelling; turgidity; an abnormal swelling or enlargement, now *esp* a new growth of cells in the body without inflammation. [L *tumor*, from *tumēre* to swell]

■ **tumorigen'esis** *n* (Gr *genesis* creation) the causing or production of tumours. **tumorigen'ic** or **tumorgen'ic** *adj* causing or producing tumours. **tumorigenic'ity** or **tumorgenic'ity** *n*. **tu'morous** *adj*.

tump[1] /*tump*/ (*dialect*) *n* a hillock, mound or barrow; a clump. ◆ *vt* to make a mound around. [Origin unknown]
■ **tump'y** *adj* (**tump'ier**; **tump'iest**) hummocky.

tump[2] /*tump*/ (*N Am*) *vt* to drag. [Prob from Algonquian]
□ **tump'line** *n* a strap across the forehead or chest for carrying burdens or hauling.

tumphy /*tum'fi*/ (*Scot*) *n* a blockhead; coaly fireclay.

tumshie /*tum'shi*/ *n* (*Scot*, often *humorous*) a turnip.

tum-tum[1] see **tom-tom**.

tum-tum[2] see **tummy**.

tumular, **tumulary** and **tumuli** see **tumulus**.

tumult /*tū'mult, -məlt*/ *n* violent commotion, *usu* with uproar; a riot; a state of violent and confused emotion. ◆ *vi* (Milton) to make a tumult. ◆ *vt* (*archaic*) to put in tumult. [L *tumultus, -ūs*, from *tumēre* to swell]

■ **tumultūary** /*-mult'*/ *adj* acted or acting in tumult; haphazard; chaotic; tumultuous. **tumult'ūate** *vi* (*archaic*) to make a tumult. ◆ *vt* (*archaic*) to disturb with tumult; to make a tumult in. **tumultūā'tion** *n* (*archaic*). **tumult'ūous** *adj* full of tumult; disorderly; agitated; noisy. **tumult'ūously** *adv*. **tumult'ūousness** *n*.

tumulus /*tū'mū-ləs, tūm'ū-lŭs*/ *n* (*pl* **tu'muli** /*-lī, -lē*/) a burial mound, a barrow. [L, from *tumēre* to swell]
■ **tū'mūlar** or **tū'mūlary** *adj*.

tun /*tun*/ *n* a large cask; an obsolete liquid measure equivalent to 216 gallons of ale, or 252 of wine; a ton (*obs*); a barrel-like state adopted by certain cryptobionts in extremely dry conditions (*biol*). ◆ *vt* (**tunn'ing**; **tunned**) to put in a tun. [OE *tunne*; cf **ton**[1]]

■ **tunn'age** *n* see **tonnage**. **tunn'ing** *n*.
□ **tun'bellied** *adj*. **tun'belly** *n* a pot-belly. **tun'-dish** *n* (*Shakesp*) a wooden funnel.

tuna[1] /*tū'nə, too'nə*/ *n* (*pl* **tu'na** or **tu'nas**) (also **tuna fish, tunn'y** or **tunny fish**) any large scombroid marine fish of the genus *Thunnus*; its flesh as food. [Am Sp, from Sp *atún*, from Ar *tún*, from L *tunnus*, from Gr *thynnos*]

tuna[2] /*too'nə, tū'nə*/ *n* a prickly pear (plant or fruit). [Haitian]

tuna[3] /*tūn'ə*/ *n* a New Zealand eel. [Maori]

tunable see under **tune**.

tund /*tund*/ (*archaic*) *vt* and *vi* to beat, thump. [L *tundere*]

tundra /*tun', tun'drə*/ *n* an Arctic plain with permanently frozen subsoil, and lichens, mosses and dwarfed vegetation. [Lapp]

tundun see **turndun**.

tune /*tūn*/ *n* a melody or air; melodiousness; tone; accurate adjustment in pitch or frequency; harmonious adjustment (*fig*); frame of mind, temper; a song (*inf*). ◆ *vt* to adjust the tones of; to put in condition for producing tones in tune; to put in smooth working order; to synchronize; to adjust (a radio, TV, video recorder, etc) so as to produce the optimum response to an incoming signal; to put in accord, bring to a desired state; to begin to play or sing (*archaic*); to start the singing of (*archaic*); to utter, express or celebrate in music (*archaic*). ◆ *vi* to give forth musical sound. [A form of **tone**[1]]

■ **tūn'able** or **tune'able** *adj* tuneful; in tune. **tun'ableness** *n*. **tun'ably** *adv*. **tuned** /*tūnd*/ *adj*. **tune'ful** *adj* full of tune; melodious; musical. **tune'fully** *adv*. **tune'fulness** *n*. **tune'less** *adj* without tune; not melodious or tuneful; unmusical; without sense of tune; silent (*poetic*). **tune'lessly** *adv*. **tune'lessness** *n*. **tun'er** *n* a person who tunes instruments, engines, etc; someone who makes music, or sings; an apparatus for receiving radio signals; a knob, dial, etc by which a radio or television is adjusted to different wavelengths; in organs, an adjustable flap for altering the pitch of the tone. **tun'ing** *n*. **tun'y** *adj* (**tun'ier**; **tun'iest**) tuneful, *esp* in a superficial, obvious way.

□ **tuner amplifier** *n* a piece of hi-fi equipment incorporating a radio receiver and an amplifier which can also be used with a record player, tape deck, etc. **tune'smith** *n* (*facetious*) a songwriter or composer of light music. **tuning fork** *n* a two-pronged instrument giving a sound of known pitch or vibration. **tuning key** or **tuning hammer** *n* a key for turning wrest pins. **tuning peg** or **tuning pin** *n* a peg on a musical instrument around which the end of a string is wound and by which it is tuned.

■ **call the tune** see **pay the piper** under **pipe**[1]. **change one's tune** or **sing another tune** to alter one's attitude, or way of talking. **in tune** true in pitch; in accord (*fig*). **out of tune** not true in pitch; not agreeing (*fig*). **to the tune of** to the amount of. **tune in** to adjust a radio for reception of a specific station, programme, etc (often with *to*). **tune one's pipes** see under **pipe**[1]. **tune out** to adjust (a radio, etc) so as to eliminate (a sound, frequency, etc); to ignore. **tune up** to put instruments into tune for beginning; of engines, etc, to (be) put into smooth working order; to begin to perform, strike up (**tune'-up** *n*).

tung oil /*tung oil*/ *n* wood oil obtained from seeds of the **tung tree** or **Chinese varnish tree** (*Aleurites fordii* or other species). [Chin *tóng*]

tungsten /*tung'stən*/ *n* a rare metallic element (symbol **W**; atomic no 74) chiefly obtained from wolframite, used for making lamp filaments and tungsten carbide (also known as **wolfram**). [Swed, literally heavy stone, from *tung* heavy, and *sten* stone]

■ **tung'state** *n* a salt of **tung'stic acid** (H_2WO_4). **tung'stite** *n* a hydrated oxide of tungsten.

□ **tungsten carbide** *n* a very hard material used for the cutting tips of metal working tools. **tungsten-halogen lamp** *n* a compact high-intensity light source (a development of the basic **tungsten lamp**), in which the casing is filled with halogen, used for car-lamps, cine projectors, etc. **tungsten steel** *n* a type of hard steel containing varying amounts of tungsten and traces of carbon, used in tools, etc.

Tungus /*tŭng'gŭs* or *tŭng-gŭs'*, *-gooz'*/ *n* (*pl* **Tungus** or **Tunguses**) a member of an E Siberian people and race, of the type often called Mongol; their language. ◆ *adj* of or relating to the Tungus or their language. [Russ *Tunguz*]

■ **Tungus'ic** *n* the family of Ural-Altaic languages that includes Tungus and Manchu. ◆ *adj* of or relating to (speakers of) these languages (also **Tungus'ian**).

tunic /*tū'nik*/ *n* a Roman shirtlike undergarment; applied also to the Greek chiton, and to various similar garments, *usu* a sort of gown or blouse; a close-fitting soldier's or police officer's jacket; a tunicle; an investing layer, membrane or integument (*biol*). [L *tunica*]

■ **Tunicā'ta** *n pl* the Urochordata, a subphylum of the Chordata, including the ascidians (the sea squirts). **tu'nicate** *n* a member of the Tunicata. **tu'nicate** or **tu'nicated** *adj* (*bot* and *zool*) having a tunic; formed in concentric coats; of the Tunicata. **tu'nicin** /*-ni-sin*/ *n* a gelatinous substance in the testae of tunicates. **tu'nicked** *adj.* **tu'nicle** *n* a little tunic; an ecclesiastical vestment like a dalmatic, worn by a subdeacon or a bishop at mass.

Tunisian /tū-niz'i-ən/ *adj* of or relating to the Republic of *Tunisia* in N Africa, or its people. ◆ *n* a native or citizen of Tunisia.

Tunker /tung'kər/ *n* see **Dunker**.

Tunku /tŭng'koo/ or **Tengku** /teng'koo/ (*Malay*) *n* prince, raja.

tunnage see **tonnage**.

tunnel /tun'l/ *n* a passage cut underground; any tubular passage; an animal's burrow, in earth, wood, etc; a tunnel net; a flue, chimney; (with *cap*) the tunnel under the English Channel connecting England and France; see also **snake**. ◆ *vt* (**tunn'elling** or (*US*) **tunn'eling**; **tunn'elled** or (*US*) **tunn'eled**) to make a passage or passages through; to hollow out; to catch in a tunnel net. ◆ *vi* to make a tunnel; to pass through, or as if through, a tunnel. [OFr *ton(n)el* (Fr *tonneau*) cask, and *tonnelle* vault, tunnel net, dimin of *tonne* cask]

■ **tunn'eller** or (*US*) **tunn'eler** *n*. **tunn'elling** *n* and *adj*. ❑ **tunnel diode** *n* (*electronics*) a junction diode, used as a low noise amplifier, oscillator or very low power microwave, in which electrons bypass the potential energy barrier by a phenomenon known in wave mechanics as **tunn'elling**. **tunnel net** *n* a funnel-shaped net. **tunnel of love** *n* a fairground ride consisting of a trip through a darkened tunnel by boat or train, used traditionally by courting couples. **tunnel vault** same as **barrel vault** (see under **barrel**). **tunnel vision** *n* a medical condition in which one is unable to see objects other than those straight ahead; single-minded concentration on one's own pursuits or viewpoints to the total exclusion of those of others.

tunny /tun'i/ *n* a tuna, *esp Thunnus thynnus* (also **tunny fish**). [L *tunnus*, from Gr *thynnos*]

tuny see under **tune**.

tup /tup/ *n* a ram; a paving rammer; a pile-driving monkey; the striking-face of a steam hammer. ◆ *vt* (**tupp'ing**; **tupped**) (of a ram) to copulate with (a ewe); to put to the ram. ◆ *vi* of sheep, to copulate. [Origin unknown]

Tupaia /tū-pī'ə/ *n* a genus of insectivores, giving its name to the tree-shrew family **Tupai'idae**. [Malay *tūpai* (*tānah* ground) squirrel]

TUPE /tū'pē/ *abbrev* : Transfer of Undertakings (Protection of Employment) Regulations, a set of rules protecting workers in a business which is transferred to another owner.

tupek see **tupik**.

tupelo /too'pə-lō/ *n* (*pl* **tu'pelos**) an American gum-tree (genus *Nyssa*). [From Creek]

Tupí or **Tupi** /too-pē', too'pē/ *n* a S American of a group of peoples inhabiting the Atlantic coast and the Amazon basin; their language, serving as a lingua franca. ◆ *adj* of or relating to the Tupís or their language.
■ **Tupi'an** *adj* and *n*.

tupik /tū'pik/ or **tupek** /-pek/ *n* an Inuit animal-skin tent. [Inuit]

tuple /tū'pl/ (*comput*) *n* a set of data that relates to, and may not be separated from, an object in a database. [Sfx *-tuple* denoting a set, as in *quintuple*]

tuppence and **tuppenny** informal forms of **twopence** and **twopenny**.

Tupperware® /tup'ər-wār/ *n* a range of plastic storage containers, *esp* for food. [US company name *Tupper* and **ware**[1]]

tuptowing see **typto**.

tuque /tūk/ (*obs*) *n* a Canadian cap made by tucking in one tapered end of a long cylindrical bag, closed at both ends. [Fr *toque*]

tu quoque /tū kwō'kwē, too kwok'we/ (*L*) *interj* you too, you're another.

turacin /tū'rə-sin/ *n* the soluble red pigment of turaco feathers, containing copper and porphyrin, unique in the animal kingdom. [*turaco* and *-in*]

turaco or **touraco** /too'rə-kō, -kō'/ *n* (*pl* **tu'racos** or **tou'racos**) any of various African arboreal birds of the family Musophagidae, of the genus *Tauraco* and related genera, with glossy, brightly-coloured plumage and short, stout bills. [Perh a W African name]

turacoverdin /too-rə-kō-vûr'din/ *n* an iron-based pigment in turaco feathers, the only pure green pigment found in birds. [**turaco** and *verdin*, from Fr *verd* green]

Turanian /tū-rā'ni-ən/ (*philology*; *obs*) *adj* of Asiatic languages, neither Iranian nor Semitic; latterly almost the same as Ural-Altaic. ◆ *n* a speaker of one of these languages. [Pers *Turān* not Iran, applied to those parts of the Sassanian Persian empire beyond the Oxus]

turban /tûr'bən/ *n* a head-covering, *esp* as worn by Muslim or Sikh men, consisting of a long sash wound round the head or round a cap; a woman's headdress similar to this. —Also found in obsolete forms

tulipant[1] and **tul'ban**; in Shakespeare spelt **tur'band** or **tur'bond**, in Spenser spelt **turribant'**, and in Milton **tur'bant**. [Turk *tulbend*, from Pers *dulband*; cf **tulip**]
■ **tur'baned** *adj* wearing a turban.

turbary /tûr'bə-ri/ *n* the right to take peat from another's ground; a place where peat is dug. [LL *turbāria*, from *turba* turf; of Gmc origin; see **turf**]

Turbellaria /tûr-bə-lā'ri-ə/ *n pl* a class of ciliated flatworms. [L *turbellae* a disturbance]
■ **turbellā'rian** *n* and *adj*.

turbid /tûr'bid/ *adj* disordered; muddy; thick. [L *turbidus*, from *turba* tumult]
■ **turbidim'eter** *n* a device for determining the surface area of a powder by measuring the light-scattering properties of a fluid suspension. **tur'bidite** *n* the sediment deposited by a turbidity current. **turbid'ity** *n*. **tur'bidly** *adv*. **tur'bidness** *n*.
❑ **turbidity current** *n* a volume of sediment-carrying water that flows violently down a slope under water.

turbine /tûr'bīn or tûr'bin/ *n* a rotary motor in which a wheel or drum with curved vanes is driven by reaction or impact or both by a fluid (water in the **water turbine**, steam in the **steam turbine**, expanding hot air in the **gas turbine**) admitted to it and allowed to escape. [Fr, from L *turbō*, *-inis* a whirl, a spinning-top]
■ **tur'binal** *adj* turbinate. ◆ *n* a scroll-like bone of the nose. **tur'binate** *n* a turbinal; a turbinate shell. **tur'binate** or **tur'binated** *adj* shaped like a top or inverted cone; spirally coiled; scroll-like; turbinal. **turbinā'tion** *n*. **tur'bined** *adj* having or driven by a turbine or turbines.
❑ **turbine pump** *n* a device for raising water by the inverted action of a turbine wheel. **turbine steamer** *n* a ship driven by a steam turbine.

turbines plural of **turbine** and **turbo**[2].

turbit /tûr'bit/ *n* a domestic pigeon having white body, coloured wings, and short beak. [Ety doubtful]

turbith see **turpeth**.

turbo[1] /tûr'bō/ *n* (*pl* **tur'bos**) short form of **turbocar** and **turbocharger**.

turbo[2] /tûr'bō/ *n* (*pl* **turbines** /tûr'bi-nēz/) a member of the tropical genus *Turbo* of turbinate wide-mouthed gastropods, large specimens of which are often used as ornaments. [L *turbō*, *-inis* a whirl, a spinning-top]

turbo- /tûr'bō-/ *combining form* signifying having, connected to or driven by a turbine. [Ety as **turbine**]
■ **tur'bocar** or **turbo car** *n* a car propelled by a turbocharged engine. **tur'bocharge** *vt* to fit with a turbocharger. **tur'bocharged** *adj*. **tur'bocharger** *n* a turbine operated by the exhaust gases of an engine, thereby boosting its power. **tur'bocharging** *n*. **turbo-elec'tric** *adj* using a form of electric drive in which turbine-driven generators supply electric power to motors coupled to propeller, axle shafts, etc. **tur'bofan** *n* a gas-turbine aero-engine in which part of the power developed is used to drive a fan which blows air out with the exhaust and so increases thrust (also **turbofan engine** or **ducted fan**); an aircraft powered by this kind of engine. **turbogen'erator** *n* a generator of electric power, driven by a steam turbine. **tur'bojet** *n* (an aeroplane powered by) an internal-combustion aero-engine in which the gas energy produced by a turbine-driven compressor is directed through a nozzle to produce thrust. **tur'boprop** *n* (an aeroplane powered by) a jet-engine in which the turbine is coupled to a propeller. **turbo-ram'-jet** *n* an engine consisting of a turbojet mounted within the duct of a ram jet. **turbosu'percharger** *n* an aero-engine supercharger operated by a turbine driven by the exhaust gases of the engine.

turbond (*Shakesp*) see **turban**.

turbot /tûr'bət/ *n* a large flatfish (*Psetta maxima*) with bony tubercles; its flesh (as a highly valued food); extended to various more or less similar fishes. [OFr *turbot*]

turbulent /tûr'bū-lənt/ *adj* tumultuous, violently disturbed; in violent commotion; producing commotion; stormy; (of fluid) showing turbulence; insubordinate, unruly; having an exciting, disturbing effect. [L *turbulentus*, from *turba* a turmoil]
■ **tur'bulātor** *n* a device which creates turbulence, eg in order to mix or disperse fluids; a device fitted to a ship's funnel to assist the dispersal of smoke, fumes, etc. **tur'bulence** *n* disturbed state (also, *esp* formerly, **tur'bulency**); unruly character or action; irregular eddying motion of particles in a fluid; irregular movement of large volumes of air (also **atmospheric turbulence**). **tur'bulently** *adv*.
❑ **turbulent flow** *n* (*phys*) fluid flow in which the particle motion at any point varies rapidly in magnitude and direction, giving rise to high drag.

Turco /tûr'kō/ (*inf*) *n* (*pl* **Tur'cos**) an Algerian infantryman in the French service. [Ital, a Turk]

Turcoman same as **Turkoman**.

Turcophil /tûr'kō-fil/ or **Turcophile** /-fīl/ n and adj (someone who is) friendly to the Turks. [Gr *Tourkos* Turk]
■ **Turcophilism** /-kof'il-izm/ n. **Tur'cophobe** n and adj (someone who is) fearful of the Turks. **Turcophō'bia** n.

turcopole /tûr'kō-pōl/ n a light-armed soldier of the Knights of St John of Jerusalem. [Mod Gr *Tourkopoulon* a Turkish boy]
■ **tur'copolier** /-pō-lēr/ n a turcopole commander, always an Englishman.

turd /tûrd/ n a lump of dung; a despicable person (*vulgar sl*). [OE *tord*]

turdion /tûr-di-ōn', tûr'di-ən/ same as **tordion**.

turducken /tûr-duk'ən/ n a dish, eaten *esp* at Thanksgiving dinners in the USA, consisting of a deboned turkey stuffed with a deboned duck that has itself been stuffed with a deboned chicken. [*turkey*, *duck* and *chicken*]

Turdus /tûr'dəs/ n the thrush genus. [L]
■ **tur'dine** /tûr'dīn, -din/ adj of, resembling or belonging to a thrush or the thrushes. **tur'doid** adj thrush-like.

tureen /tə-rēn', tū-rēn'/ n a large dish for holding soup, vegetables, etc at table. [Fr *terrine*, from L *terra* earth]

turf /tûrf/ n (*pl* **turfs**, sometimes **turves**) the surface of land matted with the roots of grass, etc; a slab of turf cut off; a sod; a slab of peat; territory, area of operation or influence, patch (*sl*); horse-racing, the race-course, the racing world. ◆ vt to cover with turf. [OE *turf*; ON *torf*]
■ **turfed** adj. **tur'fen** adj (*archaic*). **tur'finess** n. **tur'fing** n. **tur'fite** n (*sl*) someone devoted to horse-racing (also **turf'man**; chiefly *US*). **tur'fy** adj (**tur'fier**; **tur'fiest**) of, like or covered in turf; relating to horse-racing.
❑ **turf accountant** n (*euphem*) a bookmaker. **turf'-clad** adj covered with turf. **turf drain** n one covered with turf. **turfing iron** n an implement for cutting turf. **turf spade** n a long narrow spade for digging turf. **turf war** n a dispute over the right to operate within a particular territory.
■ **turf out** (*inf*) to throw out forcibly, to eject.

turgent /tûr'jənt/ adj (*obs*) turgid. [L *turgēre* to swell]
■ **tur'gently** adv (*obs*). **turgescence** /-jes'əns/ n the act or process of swelling up; swollenness; distension of cells and tissues with water. **turgesc'ency** n. **turgesc'ent** adj swelling; growing big. **tur'gid** adj swollen; extended beyond the natural size; dilated; inflated; pompous; bombastic; firm and tense by distension with water (*bot*). **turgid'ity** or **tur'gidness** n. **tur'gidly** adv. **turgor** /tûr'gör/ n the state of being full, the normal condition of the capillaries; balance of osmotic pressure and elasticity of cell wall (*bot*).

Turing machine /tū'ring mə-shēn'/ n a hypothetical computer, able to perform an infinite number of calculations. [First described by AM Turing (1912–54), British mathematician]

Turing test /tū'ring test/ n a test that provides a widely-accepted standard of artificial intelligence, stating that a computer is intelligent if a user is unable to tell which of two terminals is connected to the computer and which is relaying messages from another human being. [Ety as for **Turing machine**]

turion /tū'ri-ən/ (*bot*) n an underground bud, growing upward into a new stem. [L *turiō, -ōnis* a shoot]

Turk /tûrk/ n a native or citizen of *Turkey*; a Muslim of the former Ottoman Empire; any speaker of a Turkic language; a Muslim (*obs*); anyone with qualities ascribed to Turks, *esp* an unmanageable unruly person (*derog*); a Turkish horse; a Turkish ship. ◆ adj Turkish.
■ **Turkess** /tûrk'es/ n (*rare*) a Turkish woman. **Turki** /toor'kē/ adj of the Turkish as distinguished from the Tatar branch of Turko-Tatar languages. ◆ n a Turki speaker or language. **Turk'ic** or **Turko-Ta'tar** adj and n (of) that branch of the Ural-Altaic languages to which Turkish belongs. **Turk'icize** or **-ise** vt. **Turk'ify** vt. **Turk'ish** adj of Turkey, its people, or their language; Turkic. ◆ n the language of the Turkish people. **Turk'man** or **Turk'men** n and adj same as **Turkoman**.
❑ **Turkey carpet** or **Turkish carpet** n a soft thick kind of carpet with a distinctive bright pattern. **Turkey hone** n novaculite. **Turkey merchant** n one trading with the Near East. **Turkey oak** n an oak tree (*Quercus cerris*) of W and S Europe. **Turkey red** n (cotton coloured with) a fine durable red dye, obtained from madder, but now mostly chemically. **Turkey stone** n Turkey hone; the turquoise (*rare*). **Turkish bath** n a kind of hot-air bath in which the client is sweated, rubbed down, massaged, and gradually cooled. **Turkish coffee** n (a cup of) strong black coffee served with the grounds. **Turkish delight** n a gelatinous confection, *orig* and *esp* Turkish, variously flavoured and coloured, and coated with powdered sugar. **Turkish manna** n trehala. **Turkish towel** n a loose-piled terry towel. **Turk's cap** or **Turk's cap lily** n the martagon lily (*Lilium martagon*), from the appearance of the rolled-back petals of the nodding flower. **Turk's head** n a kind of knot; a long broom; a figure set up for practice in swordsmanship.

■ **Grand Turk** (*hist*) the Ottoman Sultan. **turn Turk** to become Muslim; to be completely reversed. **Young Turk** see under **young**.

turkey /tûr'ki/ n formerly, a guinea-fowl (thought to have come from *Turkey*); now, an American genus (*Meleagris*) of the pheasant family; a domestic breed of that genus; its flesh as food (in *US* also a substitute); extended to various big birds, such as bustard, ibis and megapode; a play, film, etc that is a complete failure (*sl*, chiefly *N Am*); a fool, a slow or inept person (*sl*).
❑ **turkey brown** n an angler's name for the mayfly *Paraleptophlebia submarginata*, or an artificial imitation of it. **turkey buzzard** or **vulture** n an American vulture, *Cathartes aura*. **turkey cock** n a male guinea-fowl (*obs*); a male turkey; a strutting, pompous, arrogant blusterer. **turkey hen** n a guinea-hen (*obs*); a female turkey. **turkey oak** n an American species of oak tree (*Quercus laevis*). **turk'ey-shoot** n (*sl, esp US*) a battle involving large-scale killing or destruction of easy targets (*milit*); anything easily won or accomplished. **turkey trot** n a kind of ragtime dance.
■ **cold turkey** see under **cold**. **talk turkey** (chiefly *N Am*) to talk bluntly; to talk business.

Turki see under **Turk**.

turkis and **turkies** see **turquoise**.

Turkoman or **Turcoman** /tûr'kō-man/, also **Turkman** /tûrk'man/ and **Turkmen** /turk'mən/ n a member of any of the Turkic peoples living mainly in *Turkmenistan* and NE Iran (*pl* **Tur'komans**, **Tur'comans**, **Turk'mans**, **Turk'men** or **Turk'mens**); their Turkic language. ◆ adj of or relating to the Turkomans or their language.
■ **Turkmē'nian** adj.

turlough /tûr'lohh/ (*Irish*) n a pond that dries up in summer. [Ir *turloch*]

turm or (*Milton*) **turme** /tûrm/ n a troop. [L *turma*]

turmeric /tûr'mə-rik/ n a plant (*Curcuma longa*) of the ginger family; its rootstock, or a powder made from it, used in making curry powder and as a dye. [Earlier *tarmaret*; cf Fr *terre-mérite*, as if from L *terra merita* deserved earth; origin unknown]
❑ **turmeric paper** n a chemical test paper impregnated with turmeric, changed from yellow to brown by alkali.

turmoil /tûr'moil/ or (*Shakesp*) -moil' / n commotion; disquiet; tumult. ◆ vt (formerly /-moil' /) (*archaic*) to harass with commotion; to toss about. ◆ vi (*dialect*) to toil. [Origin unknown]

turn /tûrn/ vi to revolve; to rotate, to spin, whirl; to move round; to hinge; to depend; to issue; to change or reverse direction or tendency; to return; to deviate; to direct oneself, face (with *to* or *towards*); to shape one's course; to take oneself; to direct one's attention; to change sides, religion or mode of life; to be fickle; to change; to be transformed or converted (often with *into*); to become; to result, prove or lead in the issue; to be shaped on the lathe; to become sour; to change colour; to become giddy; to be nauseated; to bend back, become turned; to tack, beat to windward (*naut*). ◆ vt to rotate; to move round; to change the direction of; to deflect; to bend; to bend back the edge of; to reverse; to pass round or beyond; to perform by turning; to wind; to set outside-in, or remake in that form; to set upside down; to direct; to point; to apply; to send, drive, set; to pour or tumble out; to employ in circulation, pass through one's hands; to translate; to change; to make (milk, cream, etc) sour; to nauseate; to make giddy; to infatuate; to transfer, hand over; to convert, make; to make the subject of (with *to* or *into*); to render; to put by turning; to return, give back; to form in a lathe; to shape; to round off, fashion; to pass, become (a certain age, hour, etc); to cause or persuade (an enemy agent) to work for one's own side. ◆ n act, occasion or place of turning; new direction or tendency; a twist; a winding; a complete revolution; a bend; a single traversing of a beat or course; a short walk (or ride or drive); a fit of illness or emotion, *esp* an emotional shock, jar or feeling of faintness; an embellishment in which the principal note is preceded by that next above and followed by that next below (or vice versa in the **inverted turn**), the whole ending (and sometimes beginning) with the principal note (*music*); turning point; a culmination; a time or moment of change; the halfway point on an eighteen-hole golf course, at which the players turn to begin the return nine holes; a crisis; a spell; a recurring opportunity or spell in rotation or alternation; rotation; a trick; a performer's act or the performer; a shift; a bout; fashion; manner; cast of mind; aptitude; bent; occasion, exigency; a vicissitude; a characteristic quality or effect; act of kindness or malice; an inverted type serving for a temporarily missing letter; a complete financial transaction, covering the buying and selling of a commodity, etc; the difference between the bid and offer price of shares (*stock exchange*); (also **turn card**) the fourth community card dealt in some forms of poker. [OE *turnian, tyrnan*, and perh partly OFr *torner* (Fr *tourner*); all from L *tornāre* to turn in a lathe, from *tornus* a turner's wheel, from Gr *tornos* lathe, compasses]
■ **turned** adj fashioned; wrought in a lathe; beyond the age (now *usu* without *of*); reversed; outside-in; (*esp* of printing type) upside down; soured. **turn'er** n someone or something that turns; a person who uses

a lathe; a member of a gymnastic club (*US*, from *Ger*). **turn'ery** *n* the art of turning in a lathe; turner's work; a turner's shop. **turn'ing** *n* rotation; reversal; a bend; the act of making a turn; a winding; deviation; a place where a road strikes off; a shaping, *esp* the art of shaping wood, metal, etc, into forms having a curved (generally circular or oval) transverse section, and also of engraving figures composed of curved lines upon a smooth surface, by means of a turning lathe; (in *pl*) the shavings from the lathe; in pottery, the shaping of a vase, etc; conversion, transformation.

□ **turn'about** or **turn'around** *n* a turning to face the opposite direction; a reversal in opinion, policy, course of action, etc. **turn'again** *n* (*archaic*) a refrain. **turnaround** see **turnabout** above and **turnround** below. **turn'back** *n* a folded-back part; a person who retreats from or abandons an enterprise. **turn'-back** *adj* (able to be) folded back. **turn'broach** *n* a turnspit. **turn'buckle** *n* a coupling with screw-threads for adjusting tension. **turn'coat** *n* a renegade to one's principles or party. **turn'cock** *n* a valve which by turning regulates waterflow; an official who turns off and on the water for the mains, etc. **turn'-down** *adj* folded down. ◆ *n* a turn-down part; a turn-down collar; a turning down, rejection. **turn-in** see **turn in** below. **turning circle** *n* the smallest possible circle in which a vehicle can turn round. **turning lathe** *n*. **turning point** *n* the point at which anything turns in its course; a maximum or minimum point on a graph; a critical point. **turn'ing-saw** *n* a sweep-saw, a thin-bladed saw held taut in a frame, used for cutting in curves. **turn'key** *n* an under-jailer; a turncock; (a contract for) a job in which the contractor is to complete the entire operation, leaving the building, plant, etc ready for use (also *adj*). ◆ *adj* (*comput*) designed and ready for immediate use by the purchaser, as in **turnkey system** or **package** (*comput*) a computer system complete with hardware and software, *usu* designed, installed, tested and maintained by the supplier and ready for immediate use by the purchaser. **turn'off** or **turn'-off** *n* a smaller road leading from a main one; see also **turn off** below. **turn-on** see **turn on** below. **turn'out** *n* a muster or assembly; the number of people attending a meeting or voting in an election; a coming on duty; a call to come on duty; a getting out of bed; a place in a road where a vehicle can be turned round (*N Am*); a siding, passing place, or turning place (*archaic*); a movable tapered rail for changing to another track; a carriage and its horses, a team; output; get-up, outfit (of clothes); a display (of goods, equipment, etc); a strike (*archaic*); a striker (*archaic*). **turn'over** *n* a turning over; a transference; a part folded over; a newspaper article begun on the front page and continued overleaf; a small pie made by folding over the crust; a small shawl (*archaic*); an apprentice transferred to a new employer to complete the apprenticeship (*dialect*); the total amount of money changing hands in a business; the number of employees starting or finishing employment at a particular place of work over a given period; the money value of total sales over a period; (in sports such as rugby and American football) loss of possession of the ball by a team, due to error or breach of a rule. ◆ *adj* folded over, or made to fold over. **turnover tax** *n* a tax paid every time goods change hands during manufacture and marketing. **turn'-penny** *n* (*archaic*) someone who is eager for profit. **turn'pike** *n* a spiked barrier (*hist*); a turnstile (*obs*); a tollgate or road with a tollgate (*hist*); a motorway on which tolls are paid (*US*); a spiral stair (also **turnpike stair**; *Scot*). **turnpike man** *n* (*hist*) a tollgate keeper. **turnpike road** *n* a road on which there are or were tollgates; a main road. **turn'round** or **turn'around** *n* a turning round; the whole process of a ship, aircraft, etc docking or landing, unloading, taking on cargo, passengers or both, and setting off again; generally, the whole process of dealing with something and passing it on to the next stage; a complete reversal of direction. **turn'-screw** *n* (*archaic*) a screwdriver. **turn'skin** *n* (*archaic*) a werewolf. **turn'spit** *n* a person who turns a spit; a long-bodied, short-legged dog employed to drive a wheel by which roasting-spits were turned; a spit, roasting jack. **turn'stile** *n* a revolving frame that allows one person to pass at a time. **turn'stone** *n* a bird (genus *Arenaria*), related to the plover and sandpiper, that turns over pebbles on the beach in search of food. **turn'table** *n* a rotating table, platform, disc or pair of rings, one rotating within another, used for turning a locomotive, carrying a record on a record player, cementing a microscope slide, turning a camera, etc. **turntable ladder** *n* a rotatable ladder mounted on a fire engine. **turn'tablist** *n* a performer who uses the turntable of a record player to create innovative sounds. **turn'-up** (or /*tûrn-up'*/) *n* a disturbance; a thing or part that is turned up, *esp* the cuff at the bottom of a trouser-leg; an unexpected or fortuitous result or occurrence; a piece of good luck. ◆ *adj* turned up.

■ **a good** (or **bad**) **turn** a helpful service (or a disservice). **at every turn** everywhere; incessantly. **by turns** one after another; at intervals. **in one's turn** when it is one's occasion, opportunity, duty, etc. **in turn** one after another, in succession. **not turn a hair** to be quite undisturbed or unaffected. **on the turn** at the turning point, changing; on the point of turning sour. **serve its** or **one's turn** to answer the purpose; to do well enough. **speak** or **talk out of turn** to say something indiscreet or tactless. **take a turn** to go for a stroll; to have a

go (*inf*). (**take**) **a turn for the better** (or **worse**) (to make) an improvement (or a deterioration). **take one's turn** or **take turns** to participate in rotation. **to a turn** exactly, perfectly (as if of the spit). **turn about** to face round to the opposite direction; to spin, rotate. **turn about** or **turn and turn about** alternately; in rotation. **turn adrift** to unmoor and let float away; to cast off. **turn again** to turn back; to revert. **turn against** to use to the injury of; to render hostile to; to rebel against. **turn an enemy's flank**, **line** or **position** to manoeuvre so as to attack in the rear; to outwit. **turn an honest penny** see under **penny**. **turn around** see **turn round** below. **turn aside** to avert; to deviate; to avert the face. **turn away** to dismiss from service, to discharge; to avert, to turn or look in another direction; to deviate, to depart; to refuse admittance to; to reject, send away. **turn back** to cause to retreat; to return; to fold back. **turn colour** to change colour. **turn down** to bend, double, or fold down; to invert; to lower (a light, volume on a radio, etc); to reject. **turn forth** to expel. **turn in** to bend inward; to enter; to register (a score); to surrender, hand over voluntarily (**turn'-in** *n*); to go to bed (*inf*). **turn in on oneself** to become introverted. **turn into** to become by a process of change. **turn it up** or **in** stop (saying) it (*imperative*; *inf*). **turn King's** or **Queen's evidence** see under **evident**. **turn loose** to set at liberty. **turn of events** course or direction of events. **turn off** to deviate; to dismiss; to divert; to complete, achieve by labour; to shut or switch off; to make (someone) lose interest or enthusiasm, to bore, be disliked by or distasteful to (**turn'-off** *n*; *sl*); to give in marriage (*archaic*); to hang (*obs sl*). **turn of speed** a burst of speed. **turn of the century** or **year** the period of the end of one century or year and the beginning of the next. **turn on** to set running (eg the flow of water); to set in operation by switching on (also *fig*); to depend on; to turn towards and attack (physically or verbally); to give (a person) a sense of heightened awareness and vitality, as do hallucinogenic drugs (*sl*); to rouse the interest of, excite, *esp* sexually (**turn'-on** *n*; *sl*). **turn one's back on** to abandon or reject. **turn one's hand to** to apply oneself to. **turn out** to bend outwards; to drive out, to expel; to remove the contents of; to dress, groom, take care of the appearance of; to put (cattle, etc) to pasture; to produce and put forth; to prove in the result; to muster; to go on strike; to switch off (a light); to get out of bed (*inf*); to go out of doors (*inf*). **turn over** to roll over; to set the other way up; to change sides; to hand over, pass on; to change the function of; to handle or do business to the amount of; to examine by turning the pages; to ponder; to rob (*sl*); to start up (an engine). **turn round** or **around** of a ship, aircraft, etc, to arrive, unload, reload and leave again; to reverse the course or direction of; to reverse the fortunes of (*fig*). **turn tail** see under **tail[1]**. **turn someone round one's little finger** same as **twist someone round one's little finger** (see under **finger**). **turn someone's head** or **brain** to make someone giddy; to infatuate with success. **turn the other cheek** to accept harm, violence, etc without defending oneself. **turn the scale** to decide, determine. **turn the stomach** to nauseate. **turn the tables** see under **table**. **turn to** to have recourse to; to point to; to result in; to change or be changed into; to set to work. **turn turtle** see under **turtle[1]**. **turn up** to point upwards; to fold upwards; to come or bring to light; to arrive or appear (by chance); to set face up; to invert; to grub up; to disturb; to strengthen or increase (eg the level of light, radio volume, etc); to refer to, look up; to disgust (*inf*). **turn-up for the book** or **books** a totally unexpected (*usu* pleasant) occurrence. **turn upon** to cast back upon, retort; to hinge on.

Turnbull's blue /*tûrn'bəlz bloo*/ *n* ferrous ferricyanide (or *poss* ferric ferrocyanide). [*Turnbull*, a Glasgow manufacturing chemist (18c), not the discoverer]

turndun /*tûrn'dʌn*/ or **tundun** /*tun'*/ *n* an Australian bull-roarer. [From an Aboriginal language]

turner[1] /*tûr'nər*/ *n* a 17c Scots bodle. [Origin doubtful; cf Fr *tournois* coined at *Tours*]

turner[2] see under **turn**.

Turneresque /*tûr-nə-resk'*/, also **Turnerian** /*-nē'ri-ən*/ *adj* resembling the work of the painter JMW *Turner* (1775–1851).

turnip /*tûr'nip*/ *n* the swollen edible root of *Brassica rapa* or (*Swedish turnip* or *swede*) of *Brassica rutabaga*, cruciferous biennials with respectively white and yellowish flesh; the root as food; the plant producing it; extended to more or less similar roots and plants, such as the American papilionaceous *prairie turnip* (*Psoralea esculenta*); a large old-fashioned watch (*old sl*); a dunderhead. ◆ *vt* to plant with turnips; to feed on turnips. [See **neep**; the first part may be from **turn** or Fr *tour*, implying roundness]

■ **tur'nipy** *adj*.

□ **turnip cabbage** same as **kohlrabi**. **turnip flea** *n* a leaping beetle that eats young turnip and cabbage plants. **turnip fly** *n* a fly whose maggots burrow in turnip roots; the turnip flea. **turnip greens** *n pl* turnip tops, *esp* as a vegetable. **turnip lantern** *n* a lantern made (*esp* traditionally at Hallowe'en) by scooping out the flesh of a swede. **turnip moth** *n* a noctuid moth (*Agrotis segetum*), the larvae of which feed on root crops and brassica stems. **turnip top** *n* the green sprout of a turnip in its second year, used as a vegetable.

turnkey...to...**turnskin** see under **turn**.

turnsole /tûrn'sōl/ *n* a plant whose flowers are supposed to face the sun, as heliotrope or the euphorbiaceous *Chrozophora tinctoria*; a deep-purple dye obtained from the latter; litmus. [Fr *tournesol*, from L *tornāre* (see **turn**), and *sōl* the sun]

turnspit...to...**turntable** see under **turn**.

turpentine /tûr'pən-tīn/ *n* a viscous resin, *orig* that of the terebinth tree (*Chian turpentine*), now generally of conifers; popularly, oil of turpentine; a tree that yields turpentine, *esp* the terebinth. ◆ *vt* to treat or smear with turpentine. [OFr *terbentine*, from L *terebinthina* (*rēsīna*) terebinth (resin); see **terebinth**]

■ **tur'pentīny** *adj*.

□ **turpentine tree** *n* a small Mediterranean tree (genus *Pitacia*) that yields a turpentine, the terebinth tree.

■ **oil** or **spirit of turpentine** (*inf* **turps**) an oil distilled from turpentine.

turpeth /tûr'pəth/ or **turbith** /-bith/ *n* an Oriental plant (genus *Ipomoea*) or its cathartic root. [LL *turpethum*, *turbithum*, from Pers and Ar *turbed*, *turbid*]

□ **turpeth mineral** *n* basic mercuric sulphate.

turpitude /tûr'pi-tūd/ *n* baseness; depravity; vileness. [L *turpitūdō*, from *turpis* base]

turps see under **turpentine**.

turquoise /tûr'kwäz, -k(w)oiz, -kwöz/, formerly **turkis** (Milton and Tennyson), **turkies** (Shakesp) /tûr'kiz, -kis/ *n* a massive opaque sky-blue to pale green mineral or gemstone, a hydrous basic aluminium phosphate, found in Persia; the colour of this stone. ◆ *adj* of turquoise; of the colour of turquoise. [OFr *turkeis* (later Fr *turquoise*) Turkish, as first brought through *Turkey* or from *Turkestan*]

□ **tur'quoise-blue'** *n* and *adj* turquoise. **tur'quoise-green'** *n* and *adj* pale bluish green.

■ **bone** or **fossil turquoise** odontolite.

turret[1] /tur'it/ *n* a small tower, *usu* attached to a building, often containing a spiral stair; a structure, often revolving, carrying a gun; part of a lathe that holds the cutting tool. [OFr *touret*, dimin of *tur*; see **tower**]

■ **turr'eted** *adj* having turrets; formed like a tower or a long spiral.

□ **turret clock** *n* a clock for a tower; a large clock with movement quite separate from the dials. **turret gun** *n* one for use in a revolving turret. **turret lathe** *n* a lathe having a number of tools carried on a turret mounted on a saddle which slides on the lathe bed. **turret ship** *n* a warship with gun turrets.

turret[2] same as **terret**.

turribant see **turban**.

turriculate /tu-rik'ū-lāt/ or **turriculated** /-lā-tid/ *adj* turreted; formed in a long spiral. [L *turris* a tower; dimin *turricula*]

■ **Turritell'a** *n* the tower-shell genus of gastropods.

turtle[1] /tûr'tl/ *n* any marine reptile of the order Chelonia; *esp* in USA, also a terrestrial chelonian; sometimes a freshwater chelonian; the edible flesh of a turtle, *esp* the green turtle; turtle soup; a drawing device that converts information from a computer into pictures, *orig* a device (**floor turtle**) with a pen or pens, that could be made to move across a flat surface with paper, etc on it, now often simulated by graphics on a screen (**screen turtle**) (*comput*). ◆ *vi* to hunt or catch turtles. [Fr *tortue*, Sp *tortuga* or Port *tartaruga* tortoise, assimilated to **turtle**[2], all from LL *tortuca*]

■ **tur'tler** *n* a hunter of turtles. **tur'tling** *n* the hunting of turtles.

□ **tur'tleback** *n* anything arched like a turtle's back, *esp* a structure over a ship's bows or stern. **turtle graphics** *n pl* (*comput*) drawing by means of a screen turtle. **tur'tleneck** *n* (a garment having) a high close-fitting neckline. **tur'tle-necked** *adj*. **tur'tleshell** *n* the shell of the hawk's-bill turtle, commonly called tortoise shell. **turtle soup** *n* a soup made from the flesh, fat, and gelatinous tissue of the female green turtle (*Chelone mydas*). **tur'tle-stone** *n* a septarium.

■ **mock turtle** a soup made of calf's head or other meat in lieu of turtle meat. **turn turtle** to render a turtle helpless by turning it on its back; to turn bottom up, capsize.

turtle[2] /tûr'tl/ *n* (*archaic*) a turtledove; a constant or demonstrative lover. [OE *turtla*, *turtle*, from L *turtur*; cf Ger *Turtel*, Fr *tourtereau*, *tourterelle*]

□ **tur'tledove** *n* any dove of the genus *Turtur* or *Streptopelia*, a favourite cage-bird, a type of conjugal affection and constancy; the mourning dove (*US*).

turves see **turf**.

Tuscan /tus'kən/ *adj* of Tuscany in Central Italy; Doric as modified by the Romans, with unfluted columns, and without triglyphs (*archit*). ◆ *n* classical Italian as spoken in Tuscany; a native or inhabitant of Tuscany; an ancient Etruscan. [L *Tuscānus* Etruscan]

□ **Tuscan kale** same as **cavolo nero**.

Tuscarora /tus-kə-rö'rə/ *n* (a member of) a Native American people forming part of the Iroquois; the extinct Iroquoian language of this people. ◆ *adj* of or relating to the Tuscarora or their language. [Iroquois]

tusche /tüsh/ *n* a substance used in lithography for drawing the design which then does not take up the printing medium. [Ger *tuschen* to touch up (with paint, etc)]

tush[1] /tush/ (*archaic*) *interj* pshaw; pooh. ◆ *vi* to say 'tush'.

■ **tush'ery** *n* word coined by RL Stevenson meaning (a style of period novel, etc using) would-be archaic language.

tush[2] /tŭsh/ or **toosh** (*sl*; chiefly *US*) *n* the bottom, buttocks (also **tush'ie** or **tush'y**). [Corrupted shortening of Yiddish *tokhes*]

tush[3] /tush/ (*Shakesp*) *n* a tusk (*archaic*); a small stunted tusk; a horse's canine tooth. [OE *tŭsc*; cf **tusk**[1]]

tushkar and **tushker** see **tuskar**.

tusk[1] /tusk/ *n* a long protruding tooth; a tush; a sharp projection. ◆ *vt* to pierce with the tusks. [OE *tūx* (*tūsc*); cf **tush**[3]]

■ **tusked** or **tusk'y** *adj*. **tusk'er** *n* a boar, elephant, etc with tusks. **tusk'ing** *n* (*archit*) the stubs of walling stones left projecting from a wall for bonding later with another wall or building. **tusk'less** *adj*.

□ **tusk shell** *n* the mollusc *Dentalium* or its shell.

tusk[2] same as **torsk**.

tuskar or **tusker** /tus'kər/, **tushkar** or **tushker** /tush'kər/ or **twiscar** /twis'kər/ (*Orkney* and *Shetland*) *n* a peat-spade. [ON *torfskeri*, from *torf* turf, and *skera* to cut]

tusky see under **tusk**[1].

tussac grass see under **tussock**.

tussah /tus'ə/ or **tusseh** /-e/ *n* non-standard forms of **tusser**.

tusser, **tussore** or **tasar** /tus'ər/ *n* a fawn-coloured silk from wild Indian silkworms (also **tusser silk**); the silkworm that produces tusser; its colour; a dress made of it. [Hindi *tasar* shuttle, from Sans *tasara* silkworm]

tussie mussie /tus'i-mus'i/ *n* a small bunch of flowers, a posy.

tussis /tus'is/ (*med*) *n* a cough. [L]

■ **tuss'al** or **tuss'ive** *adj* of, relating to, or caused by a cough.

tussle /tus'l/ *n* a sharp struggle. ◆ *vi* to struggle. [Frequentative of **touse**; cf **tousle**]

tussock /tus'ək/ *n* a tuft; a bunchy clump of grass, rushes, etc; tussock grass; a tussock moth. [Origin obscure]

■ **tuss'ocky** *adj*.

□ **tussock grass** or **tussac grass** *n* any of several tall-growing grasses of the southern hemisphere with a great number of stems sprouting from a central point. **tussock moth** *n* any moth of the family Lymantriidae (related to Lasiocampidae), from the tufts of hair on the caterpillars.

tussore same as **tusser**.

tut[1] /tut/ *interj* an exclamation of rebuke, mild disapprobation, impatience, etc (also **tut-tut'**; *Scot* **toot**, **toots** or **tuts**). ◆ *vi* (**tutt'ing**, **tutt'ed**) to say 'tut' (also **tut-tut'**).

■ **tutt'ing** or **tut-tutt'ing** *n*.

tut[2] /tut/ (*dialect*) *n* work paid by measurement or piece. ◆ *vi* (**tutt'ing**, **tutt'ed**) to do such work. [Origin unknown]

□ **tut'work** *n*. **tut'worker** *n*. **tut'workman** or **tut'man** *n*.

tutania /tū-tā'ni-ə/ *n* a kind of Britannia metal. [W *Tutin* (c.1780), its maker or inventor]

tutee see under **tutor**.

tutelage /tū'ti-lij/ *n* guardianship; state of being under a guardian; tuition. [L *tūtēla* guard, from *tūtārī* to guard, from *tuērī* to look to]

■ **tu'telar** or **tu'telary** *adj* protecting; having the charge of a person or place; belonging or relating to a guardian. ◆ *n* a guardian spirit, god, or saint.

tutenag /tū'ti-nag/ *n* an alloy of zinc, copper, etc; loosely, zinc. [Marathi *tuttināg*]

tutiorism /tū'ti-ə-ri-zm/ *n* in Roman Catholic moral theology, the doctrine that in a case of doubt between right and wrong one should take the safer course, ie the one in verbal accordance with the law. [L *tūtior*, *-ōris* safer, comparative of *tūtus* safe]

■ **tū'tiorist** *n* and *adj*.

tutor /tū'tər/ *n* a private instructor or coach; a person who helps a boy or girl with lessons; a college officer who has supervision of an undergraduate; a college teacher who instructs by conference with a small group of students; an instruction book; a guardian; a guardian of the person and estate of a boy under fourteen, or girl under twelve (*Scots law*). ◆ *vt* to act as tutor to; to instruct; to coach; to control; to discipline. [L *tūtor*, *-ōris* a guardian, from *tuērī* to look to]

■ **tutee'** *n* a person who is tutored. **tu'torage** *n* tutorship; tutoring; charge for tutoring; tutelage (*obs*). **tu'toress** or **tu'tress** *n* (*archaic*;

also *obs* **tu'trix**) a female tutor. **tutorial** /tū-tō'ri-əl or -tö'/ *adj* of a tutor. ◆ *n* a study meeting between one or more students and a college tutor; a lesson to be worked through by a learner at his or her own pace. **tuto'rially** *adv*. **tu'toring** *n*. **tu'torism** *n*. **tu'torize** or **-ise** *vt* and *vi*. **tu'torship** *n*.

tuts (*Scot*) see **tut¹**.

tutsan /tut'sən/ *n* parkleaves, a species of St John's wort (*Hypericum androsaemum*) once regarded as a panacea. [OFr *toutesaine*, from *tout*, from L *tōtus* all, and *sain*, from L *sānus* sound]

Tutsi /tŭt'si/ *n* a member of a Bantu people mainly living in Rwanda and Burundi. ◆ *adj* of or relating to this people. [Bantu]

tutti /tŭt'(t)ē/ (*music*) *adv* and *adj* (with) all (performers). ◆ *n* (*pl* **tutt'is**) a passage for the whole orchestra or choir, or its rendering. [Ital, *pl* of *tutto*, from L *tōtus* all]

tutti-frutti /toot'(t)ē-froot'(t)ē/ *n* a confection, *esp* ice-cream, flavoured with different kinds of fruit. [Ital, all fruits]

tut-tut /tut-tut'/ same as **tut¹**.

tutty /tut'i/ *n* crude zinc oxide. [OFr *tutie*, from LL *tutia*, from Ar *tūtiyā*]

tutu¹ /too'too/ *n* a ballerina's short, stiff, spreading skirt. [Fr]

tutu² /too'too/ *n* any of several New Zealand shrubs of the genus *Coriaria*, having poisonous black berries. [Maori]

Tuvaluan /too-və-loo'ən/ *adj* of or relating to the island group of *Tuvalu* in the SW Pacific, its people or their language. ◆ *n* a native or citizen of Tuvalu; the language of Tuvalu.

tu-whit tu-whoo /tŭ-(h)wit' tŭ-(h)woo'/ *n* an owl's hoot.
■ **tu-whoo'** *vi* to hoot.

tux /tuks/ (*inf*; *orig US* and *Aust*) *n* short for **tuxedo**.

tuxedo /tuk-sē'dō/ (*orig US*) *n* (*pl* **tuxe'dos** or **tuxe'does**) a dinner jacket; an evening suit with a dinner jacket. [Orig worn by the residents of *Tuxedo* Park, New York]

tuyère see **twyer**.

tuzz /tuz/ (*Dryden*) *n* a tuft.
❏ **tuzz'i-muzzy** or **tuzz'y-muzzy** *n* (*obs*) same as **tussie mussie**.

TV *abbrev* : television; transvestite (*inf*).
❏ **TV dinner** *n* a (*usu* pre-processed and easily prepared) meal for eating from a tray, etc while watching TV. **TV game** *n* an electronic game, played on a television. **TV movie** *n* a film made specifically for TV rather than cinema screening.

TVEI *abbrev* : Technical and Vocational Education Initiative, a national scheme, complementary to the National Curriculum, intended to give school students more job-orientated and technological courses.

TVP *abbrev* : textured vegetable protein.

twa /twä, twö, twä/, also **twae** or **tway** /twä/ *adj* and *n* Scots forms of **two**.
■ **twa'fald** /-föld/ *adj* and *adv* twofold; bent double. **twa'some** *n* and *adj* see **twosome** under **two**.
❏ **twa'-loft'ed** *adj* two-storied.

twaddle /twod'l/ *n* senseless or tedious uninteresting talk; a talker of twaddle (*obs*). ◆ *vi* to talk twaddle. [Perh **twattle**]
■ **twadd'ler** *n*. **twadd'ling** *n* and *adj*. **twadd'ly** *adj*.

twain /twān/ (*archaic*) *adj* two. ◆ *n* a couple, pair. [OE *twēgen* (*masc*) two]
■ **in twain** asunder.

twaite /twāt/ *n* one of the British species of shad (also **twaite shad**). [Origin unknown]

twal /twöl, twäl/ *adj* and *n* a Scots form of **twelve**.
■ **twal'hours** /-oorz/ *n* a noonday meal or refreshment. **twal'penny** or **twal'pennies** *n* (*hist*) a shilling in old Scots money, an old penny sterling.

twang¹ /twang/ *n* the sound of a plucked string; a nasal tone; a twinge (*dialect*); a local intonation (*inf*). ◆ *vt* and *vi* to sound with a twang. [Imit]
■ **twang'ing** *n* and *adj*. **twang'ingly** *adv*. **twangle** /twang'gl/ *n* a slack or jangly twanging. ◆ *vt* and *vi* to sound with a twangle. **twang'ling** /-gling/ *n* and *adj*. **twang'lingly** /-gling-li/ *adv*. **twangy** /twang'i/ *adj*. **twank** *n* (*dialect*) a short twang; a slap.

twang² /twang/ (*dialect*) *n* a sharp flavour; an aftertaste; a smack, suggestion. [**tang³** affected by **twang¹**]

twankay /twang'kā/ *n* a kind of green tea; gin (*sl*). [*Tong-ke* or Tun-chi in China]

'twas /twoz, twəz/ (*archaic* or *dialect*) a contraction of **it was**.

twat /twat, twot/ *n* the female genitals (*vulgar sl*); mistakenly, part of a nun's dress (*Browning*); a coarse general term of reproach (*sl*). ◆ *vt* (*sl*) to strike viciously. [Origin obscure]

twattle /twot'l/ *n* chatter; babble; twaddle. ◆ *vt* and *vi* to babble. [Perh connected with **tattle**]
■ **twatt'ler** *n*. **twatt'ling** *n* and *adj*.

tway /twä/ *adj* and *n* a form of **twain** (*Spenser*); a form of **twain** or **twa** (*Scot*).
❏ **tway'blade** *n* an orchid (genus *Listera*) with small green flowers and one pair of leaves; also an American orchid (genus *Liparis*).

tweak /twēk/ *vt* to twitch, to pull; to pull or twist with sudden jerks; to fine-tune (eg a mechanism); to rewrite or alter (editorial or author's copy) (*press sl*). ◆ *vi* (*inf*) to be in a state of irritation and paranoia as a result of sleep deprivation due to prolonged use of amphetamines. ◆ *n* a sharp pinch or twitch; a fine-tuning adjustment, a slight modification designed to improve anything; rewriting or alteration of copy (*press sl*); agitation, perplexity (*obs*). [Appar connected with **twitch¹**]
■ **tweak'er** *n*. **tweak'ing** *n*.

twee /twē/ (*inf*) *adj* small and sweet; affectedly or sentimentally pretty or quaint. [*tweet* for 'sweet', and later *tiny* and *wee*]
■ **twee'ly** *adv*. **twee'ness** *n*.

tweed /twēd/ *n* a rough woollen cloth much used for men's suits; (in *pl*) clothes of tweed. [Said to be from a misreading of **tweel**, the cloth being made in the Tweed basin; or a shortening of *tweeled* (twilled)]
■ **tweed'ily** *adv*. **tweed'iness** *n*. **tweed'y** *adj* (**tweed'ier**; **tweed'iest**) of or resembling tweed; of a predominantly upper-class, hearty, outdoor type.

tweedle /twē'dl/ *vi* to play casually (on an instrument), strum, tootle; (of a bird) to pipe or whistle; to swindle, con (*sl*). ◆ *vt* to pipe into acquiescence; to wheedle. [Prob imit, influenced by **wheedle**]
■ **tweedledee'** *n* (*Burns*) a fiddler. ◆ *vi* to tweedle. **tweed'ler** *n* (*sl*) a con man; a stolen vehicle sold as though legitimate.
■ **Tweedledee and Tweedledum** two almost indistinguishable characters or things (*orig* the proverbial names of two rival musicians).

tweedy see under **tweed**.

tweel /twēl/ a Scots form of **twill¹**.

'tween a contraction of **between**.
■ **tween'er** *n* (*US sl*) a person or thing that falls between two categories. **tween'y** *n* (*inf*) a between-maid.
❏ **'tween'-deck** *adj* lodging between decks. **'tween'decks** *n* (*naut*) the space between two decks of a vessel. ◆ *adv* in or into this area.

tweenager /twēn'ā-jər/ (*inf*) *n* a child who, although not yet a teenager, has already developed an interest in fashion, pop music, and exasperating his or her parents. [**between** and **teenager**]
■ **tween'age** *adj*.

tweer¹ see **twyer**.

tweer² see **twire¹**.

tweet /twēt/ or **tweet-tweet** /twēt'twēt'/ *n* the note of a small bird. ◆ *vt* and *vi* to chirp as a small bird does; (sometimes with *cap*) to post a comment on *Twitter*, a social networking website. [Imit]
■ **tweet'er** *n* a loudspeaker used in high-fidelity sound reproduction for the higher frequencies (also *inf* **top tweet**).

tweezers /twē'zərz/ *n pl* small pincers for pulling out hairs, etc. [Obs *tweeze* a surgeon's case of instruments, from Fr *étui*]
■ **tweeze** *vt* (*esp US*) to grasp or pluck with or as if with tweezers.
❏ **tweezer case** *n* an étui.

twelfth /twelfth/ *adj* last of twelve; immediately following the eleventh in order, position, etc; equal to one of twelve equal parts. ◆ *n* a twelfth part; a person or thing in twelfth position; a tone eleven (conventionally twelve) diatonic degrees above or below a given tone (*music*); an octave and a fifth. [OE *twelfta*, from *twelf*]
■ **twelfth'ly** *adv* in the twelfth place.
❏ **Twelfth cake** *n* an ornamental cake traditionally eaten on Twelfth Night. **Twelfth Day** *n* the twelfth day after Christmas, Epiphany, 6 January. **twelfth man** *n* (*cricket*) a player selected beyond the necessary eleven to play if required as a substitute fielder. **Twelfth Night** *n* the night of 5 January, the eve of Twelfth Day; also the evening of Twelfth Day, 6 January. **Twelfth'tide** *n* the season of Epiphany.
■ **the glorious Twelfth** 12 August, opening day of the grouse-shooting season.

twelve /twelv/ *n* the cardinal number next above eleven; a symbol representing that number (12, xii, etc); a set of twelve things or people; a score of twelve points, strokes, tricks, etc; an article of a size denoted by 12; (in *pl*) duodecimo; (**12**) a certificate designating a film passed as suitable only for people of twelve years and over; the hour of midnight or midday; the age of twelve years. ◆ *adj* of the number twelve; twelve years old. [OE *twelf* (Ger *zwölf* and Gothic *twa-lif*) ie prob two left; see **eleven**]

■ **twelve'fold** *adj* and *adv*. **twelve'mo** *n* (*pl* **twelve'mos**) duodecimo, written **12mo**.

□ **twelve-hour clock** *n* a method of reckoning time by two successive periods of twelve hours, beginning again at 1 after 12 noon. **twelve'month** *n* a year. **twelve'-penny** *adj* shilling. **twelve score** *n* two hundred and forty (yards). **twelve'-step** *adj* (*chiefly US*) relating to a process of recovery from addiction that involves twelve stages. **Twelve Tables** *n pl* the earliest code of Roman law, civil, criminal and religious, made by the decemvirs in 451–449BC. **twelve'-tone** or **twelve'-note** *adj* relating to music based on a pattern formed from the twelve notes of the chromatic scale, *esp* as developed by Arnold Schönberg (1874–1951) and his pupils (**twelve-tone row** or **twelve-note row** being the basic pattern of notes; see also **series** and **serial**).

■ **the Twelve** (*Bible*) the twelve apostles.

twenty /*twen'ti*/ *n* and *adj* twice ten; an indefinite number of. ◆ *n* a twenty-pound note; an old English division of infantry. [OE *twēntig*, prob from *twēgen* twain, and sfx *-tig* (Gothic *tigjus*) ten; Ger *zwanzig*]

■ **twen'ties** *n pl* the numbers twenty to twenty-nine; the years so numbered in life or any century; a range of temperatures from twenty to just less than thirty degrees. **twen'tieth** *adj* next after the nineteenth; last of twenty; equal to one of twenty equal parts. ◆ *n* a twentieth part; a person or thing in twentieth position. **twen'tyfold** *n*, *adj* and *adv* twenty times as many or much. **twen'tyish** *adj* about twenty.

□ **twenty-five'** *n* a line on a hockey pitch (and formerly on a rugby pitch) twenty-five yards from the goal-line. **twenty-four'** *n* a sheet folded into twenty-four leaves (forty-eight pages); a form arranged for printing it. **twen'ty-four-hour'** *adj* available at all times of day; (of an illness, etc) lasting a relatively short time. **twenty-four-hour clock** *n* a method of reckoning time by successive periods of twenty-four hours, continuing the sequence with 13 after 12 noon. **twenty-four'mo** *n* (written **24mo**) a book made up of sheets folded in twenty-four leaves (forty-eight pages). ◆ *adj* having twenty-four leaves to the sheet. **twen'ty-four-sev'en** (*usu* written **24–7**) *adv* (*inf*) all the time, twenty-four hours a day and seven days a week. **twenty-one'** *n* (*cards*) pontoon. **twen'ty-twen'ty** *adj* (also **20/20**) (of human vision) normal, also (*inf*) sharp, clear; (written **twenty20**) denoting a fast-paced form of cricket in which each side can bat for a maximum of 20 overs. **twenty-two'** *n* a line on a rugby pitch twenty-two metres from the goal-line.

■ **and twenty** (*Shakesp*) supposed to be a mere intensive, as in *good even and twenty* or *sweet and twenty* (see under **sweet**).

'twere a contraction of **it were**.

twerk /*twûrk*/ (*sl*) *vi* to thrust the hips up and down from a squatting position. [Perh **twist** and **jerk**]

■ **twerk'ing** *n*.

twerp /*twûrp*/ (*sl*) *n* a silly and/or contemptible person. [Origin uncertain; a connection with one TW Earp, once president of the Oxford University Union, has been suggested]

Twi, also **Tshi** /*ch(w)ē, twē*/ *n* a dialect, and also a literary language, of Ghana; a member of a people speaking this language (also *adj*).

twi- or **twy-** /*twī-*/ *pfx* two; double. [OE pfx *twi-*]

■ **twi'fold** or **twy'fold** *adj* twofold. **twi'forked** or **twy'forked** *adj* bifurcate. **twi'formed** or **twy'formed** *adj* having two forms. **twi'-natured** or **twy'-natured** *adj* of double nature.

twibill /*twī'bil*/ *n* a double-headed axe. [OE *twibill*, from **twi-** and **bill³**]

twice /*twīs*/ *adv* two times; doubly; for a second time. [Late OE *twiges*, from *twiga, twiwa, tuwa* twice, with adverbial genitive ending]

■ **twi'cer** *n* a person who is both compositor and pressman; someone who habitually goes to church twice on Sunday (*church sl*).

□ **twice'-born** *adj* born twice, *esp* applied as an epithet of the god Bacchus; of high Hindu caste; regenerate (*theol*). **twice'-laid** *adj* made of old yarns twisted together again. **twice'-told** *adj* counted twice; told twice; hackneyed.

■ **at twice** in two stages or operations. **twice over** twice (emphatically).

twichild /*twī'chīld*/ (now *dialect*) *n* a person in his or her second childhood. [**twi-**]

twiddle /*twid'l*/ *vt* to twirl idly; to finger idly, play with; to rotate. ◆ *vi* to twirl; to trifle with something. ◆ *n* a twirl; a curly mark, ornament. [Prob suggested by **twirl**, **twist** and **fiddle**]

■ **twidd'ler** *n*. **twidd'ling** *n* and *adj*. **twidd'ly** *adj*.

□ **twidd'ling-line** *n* formerly, a line for steadying the steering-wheel; a string for setting the compass card to play freely.

■ **twiddle one's thumbs** to rotate the thumbs around each other; to be idle (*fig*).

twier see **twyer**.

twig¹ /*twig*/ *n* a small thin shoot or branch; a divining rod. ◆ *adj* made of twigs. ◆ *vt* (**twigg'ing**; **twigged**) to birch, switch. [OE *twig*; cf Ger *Zweig*]

■ **twigged** *adj*. **twigg'en** *adj* (*Shakesp*) covered with or made of wickerwork. **twigg'y** *adj*. **twig'let** *n* a small twig. **twig'some** *adj*.

twig² /*twig*/ (*inf*) *vt* and *vi* (**twigg'ing**; **twigged**) to observe, perceive; to realize, comprehend (*esp* suddenly); to understand. [Poss Ir *tuigim* discern; cf Gaelic *tuig* understand]

twig³ /*twig*/ (*sl*) *n* fettle; fashion; recognizable condition. ◆ *vi* to act vigorously. [Origin obscure]

■ **twigg'er** *n* (*obs*) a vigorous breeder; a wanton.

twight /*twīt*/ *vt* (*Spenser*) for **twit²**.

twigloo /*twig'loo*/ (*inf, usu derog*) *n* a makeshift shelter made from branches, *esp* one set up in a tree during an environmental protest. [**twig¹** and **igloo**]

twilight /*twī'līt*/ *n* the faint light after sunset or before sunrise; this time of day; dim light or partial darkness; a period of decay following a period of success, vigour, greatness, etc. ◆ *adj* of or at twilight; *specif* of work, educational classes, etc, taking place after normal daytime hours, between late afternoon and early evening; faintly illuminated; obscure, indefinite; partial, transitional. ◆ *vt* to illuminate faintly. [**twi-** and **light**]

■ **twī'lighted** or **twī'lit** *adj*.

□ **twilight of the Gods** see ety for **Ragnarök**. **twilight sleep** *n* partial anaesthesia, eg in childbirth, by the use of drugs. **twilight zone** *n* a dilapidated, decaying area of a city or town typically situated between the main business and commercial area and the suburbs; the lowest depth of an ocean to which light can penetrate; any area or state transitional or indefinite in character; a place of supernatural and frighteningly unpredictable happenings (*inf*).

twill¹ /*twil*/, or (*Scot*) **tweel** /*twēl*/ *n* a woven fabric showing diagonal lines, the weft yarns having been worked over and under two or more warp yarns; the appearance so produced. ◆ *vt* to weave with a twill. [OE *twilic*]

■ **cavalry twill** a strong woollen twill used *esp* for trousers.

twill² /*twil*/ a dialect form of **quill¹**.

'twill (*archaic* or *dialect*) a contraction of **it will**.

twilled /*twil'id*/ (*Shakesp*) *adj* prob, protected against floods by plaited osiers (the word so used still at Stratford); according to some, ridged like twilled cloth; or reedy, from an alleged *obs* word *twill* a reed.

twilly /*twil'i*/ *n* a willowing-machine (see also **willy¹**). [**willow**]

twilt /*twilt*/ a dialect form of **quilt**.

twin¹ /*twin*/ *n* either of two born at a single birth; one very like, or closely associated with, another; a counterpart; (in *pl* with *cap* and *the*) Gemini; a pair of twins or pair generally (*obs*); a combination of two crystals symmetrically united about a plane that is a possible face of each or an axis that is a possible edge of each, or of more than two by repetition. ◆ *adj* twofold, double; born two at one birth; forming one, or consisting of both, of two identical or very similar parts or counterparts; very like another. ◆ *vt* (**twinn'ing**; **twinned**) to couple together, or to produce, like a twin or twins. ◆ *vi* to be born at the same birth; to give birth to twins at one birth; to be paired or suited. [OE *getwinn* (noun) twin, *twinn* (adj) double; cf **twi-**]

■ **twin'er** *n* (*de la Mare*) a double limerick. **twin'ling** *n* (now *dialect*) a twin. **twinned** *adj* produced at one birth; constituting a twin; paired, matched. **twinn'ing** *n*. **twin'ship** *n* the condition or relation of a twin or twins.

□ **twin axis** *n* the axis of symmetry of a twin crystal. **twin bed** *n* either of a matching pair of single beds. **twin-bedd'ed** *adj*. **twin birth** *n* a birth of twins; a twin; a pair of twins. **twin'-born** *adj* born at the same birth. **twin brother** *n* a brother born at the same birth. **twin-cam'** *adj* (of an engine) having two camshafts. **twin** (or **twinned**) **crystal** *n* (*crystallog, mineralogy*) a crystal composed of two or more individuals in a systematic crystallographic orientation with respect to one another. **twin-en'gined** *adj* (chiefly of an aircraft) having a pair of engines. **twin'flower** *n* a N American plant of the genus *Linnaea* having paired flowers. **twin-lens'** *adj* (of a camera) having two identical sets of lenses. **twin paradox** *n* a phenomenon suggested by the theory of relativity which imagines a scenario in which one of a pair of twins lives in the normal way, while the other twin is sent out in a spaceship travelling at great speeds, with the effect that the travelling twin eventually returns younger than the other twin. **twin plane** *n* the plane of symmetry of a twin crystal. **twin'-screw** *adj* (of a ship) with two propellers on separate shafts. **twin'set** *n* a cardigan and jumper made more or less to match. **twin sister** *n* a sister born at the same birth. **twin town** *n* a town paired with another foreign town of similar size for the purpose of social, cultural and commercial exchanges. **twin'-track** *adj* consisting of or split between two simultaneous, complementary or reciprocal elements, activities, jobs, etc. **twin'-tub** *n* a type of washing machine with separate drums for washing and spin-drying (also *adj*).

twin² /twin/ or **twine** /twīn/ (*obs* and *Scot*) *vt* and *vi* to separate; to part. ◆ *vt* to deprive. [**twin¹**]

twine¹ /twīn/ *n* a twisted cord; string or strong thread; a coil; a twist; a twisted stem or the like; an act of twisting or clasping. ◆ *vt* to wind; to coil; to wreathe; to twist; to twist together; to encircle; to make by twisting. ◆ *vi* to wind; to coil; to twist; to make turns; to rise or grow in spirals; to wriggle. [OE *twīn* double or twisted thread, linen thread; cf Du *twijn*]
■ **twīned** *adj*. **twī'ner** *n* a person or thing that twines; a twining plant. **twī'ning** *n* and *adj*. **twī'ningly** *adv*. **twī'ny** *adj*.
❏ **twining plant** *n* one that climbs by twining its stem round a support.

twine² /twīn/ *n* a variant of **twin²**.

twiner¹ see under **twin¹**.

twiner² see under **twine¹**.

twinge /twinj/ *vt* to tweak or pinch; to affect with a momentary pain. ◆ *vi* to feel or give a momentary pain. ◆ *n* a tweak, a pinch; a sudden short shooting pain; a brief pang. [OE *twengan* to pinch]

twi-night /twī'nīt/ (*N Am*) *adj* denoting a set of two baseball games, the first played in the late afternoon and the second in the evening of the same day. [*twi*light and **night**]
■ **twi'-nighter** *n*.

twink /twingk/ *vi* to blink; to twinkle. ◆ *n* a twinkling, a moment. [Root of **twinkle**]

twinkie /twing'ki/ (*N Am inf*) *n* a stereotypically brainless person, a bimbo; an attractive young male homosexual. [From a brand of sponge cake]

twinkle /twing'kl/ *vi* to blink; to quiver the eyelid; to shine by flashes; to glitter; to sparkle; to flicker, vibrate. ◆ *vt* to guide by twinkling. ◆ *n* a blink; a wink; a glitter; a quiver; a flicker; a sparkle; a twinkling; a dance step. [OE *twinclian*]
■ **twink'ler** *n*. **twink'ling** *n* a quick motion of the eye; the time occupied by a wink; an instant; the scintillation of the fixed stars. ◆ *adj* scintillating; quivering; blinking (*obs*). **twink'ly** *adj*.
❏ **twink'letoes** *n sing* (*inf*) a person who displays exceptionally agile footwork.
■ **in the twinkle** or **twinkling of an eye** in an instant.

twinter /twin'tər/ (*Scot*) *adj* two years old. ◆ *n* a two-year-old sheep or other animal. [OE *twiwintre* two-winter]

twire¹ /twīr/ or **tweer** /twēr/ (*Shakesp*) *vi* to peer. ◆ *n* (*obs*) a glance, leer. [Cf MHGer *zwieren* to peer]

twire² see **twyer**.

twirl /twûrl/ *vt* and *vi* to spin; to whirl; to twist; to coil. ◆ *n* a twist; a spin; a whirl; a whorl; a curly figure. [Connection with OE *thwiril* churn handle, whisk, doubtful]
■ **twirl'er** *n*. **twirl'y** *adj*.
■ **twirl one's thumbs** to twiddle one's thumbs.

twirp an alternative spelling of **twerp**.

twiscar see **tuskar**.

twist /twist/ *vt* to twine; to unite or form by winding together; to form from several threads; to wind spirally; to form into a spiral; to wring; to wrest; to distort; to force, pull out of natural shape, position, etc; to entangle; to impart a spin to; to force round; to eat heartily (often with *down*; *old sl*); to pervert, warp; to swindle (*inf*). ◆ *vi* to twine; to coil; to move spirally or tortuously; to turn aside; to revolve; to writhe; to dance the twist; in the card game vingt-et-un (pontoon), to deal or receive a card face upwards. ◆ *n* that which is twisted or formed by twisting; a cord; a strand; thread; silk thread; warp yarn; a twisted part; torsion; an act or manner of twisting; a contortion; a wrench; a wresting; a turning aside; a spin, screw, or break; a distortion; a perverted bent or set; an unexpected event or change of direction (*lit* and *fig*); a tangle; a twisted roll of tobacco or bread; a small curled piece of lemon, etc flavouring a drink; a spiral ornament in the stem of a glass; a twig (*obs*); the fork of the body (*obs*); a mixed drink (*sl*); a good appetite (*sl*). [OE *twist* rope (found in the compound *mæst-twist* a stay)]
■ **twist'able** *adj*. **twist'ed** *adj*. **twist'er** *n* someone or something that twists; someone who dances the twist; a sophistical, slippery, shuffling or dishonest person; a ball sent with a twist; a tornado (*N Am inf*). **twist'ing** *n* and *adj*. **twist'y** *adj*.
❏ **twist drill** *n* a drill for metal having one or more deep helical grooves round the body. **twisted pair** *n* (*comput* and *telecom*) a pair of electrically-insulated wires twisted together to form a single cable to improve signal transmission. **twist grip** *n* a control operated by twisting, eg the throttle on a motorcycle. **twist'-off** *adj* (of a lid, top, etc) able to be removed by twisting, and so not requiring a special opening device.

■ **round the twist** (*inf*) crazy, mad. **the twist** a dance which became popular in 1962, in which the dancer constantly twists the body. **twist someone round one's little finger** see under **finger**. **twist someone's arm** to persuade someone, *esp* forcefully.

twistor /twis'tər/ (*maths* and *phys*) *n* one of a number of complex variables representing the space-time co-ordinates, retaining their relevant symmetries.
❏ **twistor theory** *n* (*phys*) a theory, a candidate for the so-called 'theory of everything', that attempts to describe the structure of space as eight-dimensional, using complex numbers and particle spin, and with twistors as its building blocks.

twit¹ /twit/ (*sl*) *n* a fool. [Prob **twit²**]

twit² /twit/ *vt* (**twitt'ing**; **twitt'ed**) to upbraid; to taunt. ◆ *n* a reproach. [OE *ætwītan* to reproach, from *æt* against, and *wītan* to reproach]
■ **twitt'er** *vt* (*Fielding*) to twit. **twitt'ing** *n* and *adj*. **twitt'ingly** *adv*.

twitch¹ /twich/ *vt* to jerk; to pluck; to snatch; to steal; to pinch or tweak. ◆ *vi* to jerk; to move spasmodically; to carp, sneer. ◆ *n* a sudden, quick pull; a spasmodic contraction of the muscles; a twinge; a noose; the sudden tapering of a vein of ore. [Related to OE *twiccian* to pluck; Ger *zwicken*]
■ **twitch'er** *n* someone or something that twitches; a birdwatcher who tries to spot as many rare species as possible (*inf*). **twitch'ily** *adv*. **twitch'ing** *n* and *adj*. **twitch'y** *adj* (**twitch'ier**; **twitch'iest**) that twitches; jerky; inclined to twitch; on edge, nervous (*inf*).

twitch² /twich/ and **twitch grass** forms of **quitch¹** and **quitch grass** (see also **couch²** and **couch grass**).

twite /twīt/ *n* the mountain linnet, *Acanthis flavirostris*, a N European finch with streaked brown plumage. [From its note]

twitten /twit'n/ (*dialect*) *n* a narrow lane between two walls or hedges (also **twitt'ing**). [Perh related to LGer *twiete* alley, lane]

twitter¹ /twit'ər/ *n* a tremulous chirping; a flutter of the nerves; (with *cap*) a website on which people can post short comments about their activities, feelings, etc. ◆ *vi* to make a succession of small tremulous noises; to palpitate. ◆ *vt* to chirp out; to twiddle. [Imit; cf Ger *zwitschern*]
■ **twitterati** /-ä'tē/ *n pl* (modelled on *literati*; *inf*) influential commentators who use the Twitter website. **twitt'erer** *n*. **twitt'ering** *n* and *adj*. **twitt'eringly** *adv*. **twitt'ery** *adj*. **Twit'tersphere** or **Twit'terverse** *n* (*inf*) the community of Twitter users.

twitter² /twit'ər/ or **twitter-bone** /-bōn/ *n* an excrescence on a horse's hoof. [A form of **quitter**]
❏ **twitt'er-boned** *adj*.

twitter³ and **twitting¹** see under **twit²**.

twitting² see **twitten**.

'twixt a contraction of **betwixt**.

twizzle /twiz'(ə)l/ *vt* and *vi* to twirl, spin. ◆ *n* a twist or turn. [Prob formed under influence of **twist** and **twirl**]

two /tōō/ *n* the cardinal number next above one; a symbol representing that number (2, ii, etc); a pair; a score of two points, strokes, tricks, etc; an article of a size denoted by 2; a deuce, a playing card with two pips; a two-cylinder engine or car; the second hour after midnight or midday; the age of two years. ◆ *adj* of the number two; two years old. [OE *twā* (fem and neuter) two (masc *twēgen*); Ger *zwei*, Gothic *twai*; Gr *dyo*, L *duo*, Sans *dva*, Gaelic *dà*]
■ **two'er** *n* (*inf*) anything that counts as or for two, or scores two. **two'fold** *adj* and *adv* in two divisions; twice as much; (*esp Scot* **twafald** /twä, twö-föld/) in a doubled-up position. **two'foldness** *n*. **two'ness** *n* the state of being two; duality. **two'some** (*Scot* **twa'some**) *n* a group of two; a tête-à-tête; a game between two players (*golf*). ◆ *adj* consisting of two; performed by two.
❏ **two'-bit** *adj* (*N Am*) cheap, paltry. **two bits** *n pl* (*N Am*) twenty-five cents, a quarter. **two'-bottle** *adj* able to drink two bottles of wine at a sitting. **two-by-four'** *n* (a piece of) timber measuring four inches by two inches in cross-section (somewhat less when dressed). **two'-decker** *n* a ship with two decks or with guns on two decks; a bus or tram-car carrying passengers on a roofed top. **two'-digit** *adj* in double figures. **two'-dimensional** *adj* having length and breadth but no depth; having little depth or substance (*fig*). **two-dimensional'ity** *n* the property of having length and breadth but no depth. **two'-edged** *adj* having two cutting edges; capable of being turned against the user; having advantages and disadvantages. **two'-eyed** *adj* having two eyes (**two-eyed steak** (*sl*) a bloater). **two'-faced** *adj* having two faces; double-dealing, false. **two'-fisted** *adj* clumsy; capable of fighting with both fists; holding the racket with both hands (*tennis*). **two'-foot** *adj* measuring, or with, two feet. **two'-footed** *adj* having two feet;

capable of kicking and controlling the ball equally well with either foot (*football*, etc). **two'-for-his-heels** *n* (*old*) a rascal or knave (from the score for turning up a knave in cribbage). **two'-forked** *adj* having two prongs or branches. **two'-four** *adj* and *adv* (*music*) with two crotchets to the bar. **two'-hand** *adj* (*Shakesp*) for two hands. **two'-handed** *adj* with or for two hands; for two persons; ambidextrous; strapping. **two-hand'edly** *adv*. **two-hand'er** *n* anything designed for, written for or requiring both hands or two people (eg actors). **two'-headed** *adj* having two heads; directed by two authorities. **two'-horse** *adj* for two horses (**two-horse race** any contest in which only two of the participants have a genuine chance of winning). **two'-inch** *adj* measuring two inches. **two'-leaved** or **two'-leafed** *adj* with two leaves or leaflets; with leaves in twos. **two'-legged** *adj* with two legs. **two'-line** *adj* (*printing*) having double depth of body. **two'-lipped** *adj* having two lips; bilabiate. **two'-masted** *adj* having two masts. **two'-mast'er** *n* a two-masted ship. **two'-pair** or **two'-pair-of-stairs** *adj* on a second floor. ◆ *n* a room so situated. **two'-part** *adj* composed in two parts or for two voices. **two'-parted** *adj* bipartite; divided into two nearly to the base. **twopence** /tup'əns/ or (decimalized currency) **two pence** /too pens/ *n* the sum of two pennies; a coin worth two pence. **two'pence-coloured** *adj* see under **penny**. **twopenny** /tup'ni/ *adj* sold, offered at or worth twopence; cheap, worthless. ◆ *n* ale sold at twopence a quart; in leapfrog, the head. **twopenny-halfpenny** /tup'ni-hāp'ni/ or **twopence-halfpenny** *adj* paltry, petty. **two-penn'yworth** or **two-penn'orth** /too-pen'ərth/, also (chiefly *Scot*) **twopenceworth** /tup'/ *n* an amount worth twopence; one's own contribution to a debate. **two'-phase** *adj* (of an electrical circuit, device, etc) employing two phases whose voltages are displaced from one another by ninety electrical degrees. **two'-piece** *n* anything consisting of two separate parts, pieces or members (also *adj*). **two'-ply** *adj* having two layers, or consisting of two strands; woven double. ◆ *n* wool or yarn consisting of two strands twisted together. **two-power standard** *n* (*hist*) the principle that the strength of the British Navy must never be less than the combined strength of the navies of any two other powers. **two'-roomed** *adj*. **two'-score** *n* and *adj* forty. **two'seater** *n* a vehicle or aeroplane seated for two; a sofa for two. **two'-sid'ed** *adj* having two surfaces, aspects or parties; facing two ways; double-faced; having the two sides different. **two-sid'edness** *n*. **two-speed gear** *n* a gear-changing contrivance with two possibilities. **two-start thread** see **double-threaded screw** under **double. two'-step** *n* a gliding dance in duple time; a tune for it. ◆ *vi* to dance the two-step. **two'-storeyed** or **two'-stor'ey** *adj*. **two'stroke** *adj* (of an engine cycle) consisting of two piston strokes; relating to or designed for such an engine. ◆ *n* an engine working in such a way. **two'-time** *vt* and *vi* to deceive, *esp* to be unfaithful to a spouse or partner; to double-cross. **two'-timer** *n* a person who deceives or double-crosses. **two'-timing** *adj* and *n*. **two'-tone** *adj* having two colours or two shades of the same colour; (of eg a car horn) having two notes. **two'-up** *n* (in NZ and Australia) a game in which two coins are tossed and bets made on both falling heads up or both tails up. **two-up, two-down** *n* and *adj* (a small, traditionally built terraced house) having two bedrooms upstairs and two reception rooms downstairs. **two'-way** *adj* permitting passage along either of two ways *esp* in opposite directions; able to receive and send signals (*radio*); of communication between two persons, groups, etc, in which both participate equally; involving shared responsibility; able to be used in two ways; having a double mode of variation or two dimensions (*maths*). **two-way mirror** *n* one functioning as a mirror on one side and able to be seen through on the other. **two'-wheeled** *adj* having two wheels. **two-wheel'er** *n* a vehicle with two wheels, *esp* a motor-cycle, or formerly a hansom cab. **two'-year-old** *adj*. ◆ *n* a child, colt, etc aged two. — **be two** to be at variance. **in two** asunder, so as to form two pieces. **in two twos** or **two ticks** (*sl*) in a moment. **put two and two together** see under **put**[1]. **that makes two of us** (*inf*) the same thing applies to me. **two by two** in pairs. **two or three** a few.

TWOC /twok/ *abbrev* : taking without owner's consent, the technical name for the offence of breaking into a vehicle and driving it away. ■ **twocc'er** or **twock'er** *n* (*sl*) a person who commits this offence. **twocc'ing** or **twock'ing** *n* (*sl*).

'twould /twŭd/ (*archaic* or *dialect*) a contraction of **it would**.

twp /tŭp/ (*Welsh*) *adj* dim-witted, stupid. [Welsh]

twy- see **twi-**.

twyer, twyere, tweer, twier, twire or **tuyère** /twēr, also twīr, twē-yer'/ *n* a nozzle for a blast of air. [Fr *tuyère*]

TX *abbrev* : Texas (US state).

Tyburn /tī'bərn/ *n* the historic place of execution in London. ❑ **Ty'burn-ticket** *n* a certificate of exemption from certain parochial offices formerly granted to the prosecutor of a felon to conviction. **Ty'burn-tippet** *n* a halter. **Ty'burn-tree** *n* the gallows.

Tyche /tī'kē/ (*Gr myth*) *n* the goddess of fortune. [Gr *tychē* chance] ■ **ty'chism** *n* a theory that accepts pure chance.

Tychonic /tī-kon'ik/ *adj* relating to the Danish astronomer, *Tycho Brahe* (1546–1601), or his system.

tycoon /tī-koon'/ *n* a business magnate; *orig* the title by which the Shoguns of Japan were known to foreigners. [Jap *taikun* great prince, from Old Chin *dà* great, and *jūn* prince] ■ **tycoon'ate** *n* the shogunate. **tycoon'ery** *n*.

tyde a Spenserian spelling of **tied**, *pat* and *pap* of **tie**[1].

tye[1] or **tie** /tī/ *n* an inclined trough for washing ore. ◆ *vt* to wash in a tye. [OE *tēag* case, chest]

tye[2] or **tie** /tī/ (*dialect*) *n* an area of common land or pasture. [OE *tēag*, perh same as **tye**[1]; cf ON *teigr* strip of land]

tyg same as **tig**[2].

tying /tī'ing/ *prp* of **tie**[1].

tiyin see **tiyin**.

tyke or **tike** /tīk/ (chiefly *Scot* and *N Eng*) *n* a dog; a cur; a rough-mannered person; a small child, *esp* a cheeky or naughty one (*inf*); a Yorkshireman; a Roman Catholic (*old Aust* and *NZ derog sl*). [ON *tík* bitch] ■ **tyk'ish** *adj*.

tylectomy /tī-lek'tə-mi/ *n* the same as lumpectomy. [Gr *tylē* lump, and *ektomē* cutting out]

tyler see under **tile**.

Tylopoda /tī-lop'ə-də/ *n pl* a section of the ungulates with padded toes, comprising camels and llamas. [Gr *tylos* a knob, callus, and *pous, podos* a foot] ■ **ty'lopod** *n* and *adj*.

tylosis /tī-lō'sis/ *n* (*pl* **tylo'sēs**) an ingrowth from a neighbouring cell through a pit into a vessel (also, *perh orig*, **thylose** /thī'lōs/, or **thylosis** /thī-lō'sis/; *pl* **thylo'sēs**; *perh* from Gr *thylakos* a pocket; *bot*); an inflammation of the eyelids; a callosity. [Gr *tylos* a knob, callus] ■ **tylote** /tī'lōt/ *n* a cylindrical sponge spicule, knobbed at both ends.

tymbal same as **timbal**.

tymp /timp/ *n* the plate of a blast-furnace opening. [**tympan**]

tympan /tim'pən/ *n* any drum-like instrument (*archaic*); a tympanum; an ancient Irish stringed instrument played with a bow (Ir *tiompan*); a frame covered with parchment or cloth, on which sheets are placed for printing (*printing*); material placed between the platen and the paper to give an even impression (*printing*). [OFr, or as for **tympanum**]

tympana see **tympanum**.

tympanal see under **tympanum**.

tympani see **tympano**.

tympanic...to...**tympanitis** see under **tympanum**.

tympano /tim'pə-nō/ *n* (*pl* **tym'pani** /-ē/) a variant of **timpano**.

tympanum /tim'pə-nəm/ *n* (*pl* **tym'pana** or **tym'panums**) a drum; a drumhead; the middle ear; the membrane separating it from the outer ear, the drum (also called the **tympanic membrane**); in insects, a vibratory membrane in various parts of the body, serving as an eardrum; in birds, the resonating sac of the syrinx; an air-sac in the neck in grouse, etc; the recessed face of a pediment (*archit*); a space between a lintel and an arch over it (*archit*); a carving on this area (*archit*); an early type of wheel for scooping up water. [L *tympanum*, from Gr *tympanon, typanon* a kettledrum, from *typtein* to strike] ■ **tym'panal** *adj* (*anat* and *zool*) of or relating to the tympanum. **tympanic** /-pan'ik/ *adj* of or like a drum or tympanum; tympanitic. ◆ *n* (*anat*) a bone of the ear, supporting the drum-membrane. **tym'paniform** (or /-pan'/) *adj* drum-shaped; drum-like. **tym'panist** *n* a drummer, now *esp* (also **tim'panist**) a player of the timpani. **tympanī'tes** *n* flatulent distension of the belly. **tympanitic** /-it'ik/ *adj* of or affected with tympanites. **tympanī'tis** *n* (*med*) inflammation of the membrane of the ear. **tym'pany** *n* any swelling, *esp* of the abdomen; tympanites; a blowing up as with pride; a drum (*rare*).

tynd, tyn'd, tyned, tynde or **tyne** (also *Scot*), (*Spenser* and *Shakesp*) see **tind** and **tine**[2,5].

Tynwald /tin'wold/ *n* the parliament of the Isle of Man. [ON *thing-vǫllr*, from *thing* assembly, and *vǫllr* field]

typ or **typo** *abbrev* : typographer; typography.

type /tīp/ *n* a mark or stamp; the device on a coin or medal; a distinguishing mark; insignia; a designation; an emblem; a foreshadowing; an anticipation; an exemplar; a model or pattern; a kind; the general character of a class; that which well exemplifies the characteristics of a group; a person of well-marked characteristics; (loosely and derogatorily) a person; a simple chemical compound representative of the structure of more complex compounds; the actual specimen on which the description of a new species or genus is based (also called **type specimen**) (*biol*); a rectangular piece of metal or of wood on one end of which is cast or engraved a character, sign, etc used in printing; printing types collectively, letter; print; lettering. ◆ *adj* serving as a type. ◆ *vt* to prefigure, foreshadow, symbolize (*theol*); to be the type of; to determine the type of (*med*); to exemplify; to typewrite; to print (*rare*). ◆ *vi* to typewrite. [L *typus*, from Gr *typos* blow, mark, stamp, model, from *typtein* to strike]

■ **ty'pal** or **typic** /*tip'*/ *adj* typical. **typing** /*tīp'ing*/ *n*. **typist** /*tīp'ist*/ *n* a person who uses a typewriter; someone whose occupation is typewriting.

❑ **type'bar** *n* a line of type cast in one piece; in a typewriter, each of the levers on the ends of which are the types. **type'-body** *n* a measurement of breadth of shank for a size of type. **type case** *n* a tray with compartments for storing printing types. **type'cast** *vt* (**type'casting**; **type'cast**) to cast (someone) in a role that accords with what he or she is by nature; to cast continually for the same kind of part. **type'cast** *adj*. **type cutter** *n* someone who engraves dies for printing types. **type cylinder** *n* the cylinder of a rotary printing machine on which plates are fastened for printing. **type'face** *n* the printing surface of a type; any of a variety of styles in which it is cut; a complete range of type cut in a particular style. **type founder** *n* someone who founds or casts printers' type. **type founding** *n*. **type foundry** *n* the genus that gives its name to its family. **type'-high** *adj* and *adv* of or at the standard type height (*approx* 0.918in; 23.317mm), measured in the direction of the shank; (of a woodcut, etc) at the height required for printing. **type holder** *n* a bookbinder's pallet or holder for use in hand-stamping. **type locality** *n* the area in which a genus or a geological formation occurs most typically or in which it was classified. **type metal** *n* metal used for making types; an alloy of lead with antimony and tin, and sometimes copper. **type'script** *n* typewritten matter or copy; type in imitation of handwriting or of typewriting. ◆ *adj* typewritten. **type'set** *vt*. **type'setter** *n* a compositor; a machine for setting type. **type'setting** *n*. **type species** *n* a species taken as the one to which the generic name is primarily attached. **type specimen** *n* a holotype. **type'write** *vt* and *vi* to print or copy with a typewriter. **type'writer** *n* a machine, *usu* with a keyboard, for printing as a substitute for handwriting; a typist (*rare*). **type'writing** *n*. **type'written** *adj*.

-type /*-tīp*/ *sfx* of the same type as, resembling (eg *pampas-type grass*; *esp inf*). ◆ *combining form* denoting printing type. [**type**]

Typha /*tī'fə*/ (*bot*) *n* the reed-mace genus, giving its name to a family of monocotyledons, **Typhā'ceae**. [Gr *typhē* reed-mace]

■ **typhā'ceous** *adj*.

typhlitis /*tif-lī'tis*/ (*med*) *n* inflammation of the blind-gut. [Gr *typhlos* blind]

■ **typhlitic** /*-lit'ik*/ *adj*. **typhlol'ogy** *n* the study of blindness and the care of blind people.

Typhoeus /*tī-fō'yəs*, *tī-fē'əs*/ *n* a monster of Greek mythology buried under Etna. [Gr *Typhōeus*]

■ **Typhoean** /*tī-fō'yən*, *tī-fē'ən*/ *adj*.

typhoid /*tī'foid*/ *adj* like typhus. ◆ *n* (for **typhoid fever**) enteric fever caused by the bacillus *Salmonella typhi*, long confused with typhus, on account of the characteristic rash of rose-coloured spots. [Gr *typhōdēs* delirious, from *typhos* a fever, and *eidos* likeness; cf **typhus**]

■ **typhoid'al** *adj*.

Typhon /*tī'fon*, *-fən*/ *n* son of Typhoeus, later identified with him, father of dangerous winds (*Gr myth*); (without *cap*) a whirlwind (*obs*).

■ **Typhonian** /*-fō'ni-ən*/ or **Typhonic** /*-fon'ik*/ *adj* (also without *cap*).

typhoon /*tī-foon'*/ *n* a violent cyclonic storm of the China seas and W Pacific area. [Gr *Typhōn* Typhon, *typhōn* a whirlwind; but partly also from Port *tufâo*, from Ar, Pers, Hindi *tūfān* a hurricane (perh itself from Gr), and partly from Chin *tài fēng* a great wind]

typhus /*tī'fəs*/ *n* a dangerous fever transmitted by lice harbouring a Rickettsia and marked by the eruption of red spots. [Latinized from Gr *typhos* fever, stupor, delusion; cf *typhein* to smoke]

■ **ty'phoid** *adj* see separate entry. **ty'phous** *adj*.

typical /*tip'i-kəl*/ *adj* relating to, or constituting, a type; emblematic; figurative; characteristic; representative; typographical (*rare*). [Med L *typicālis*, from L *typicus*]

■ **typical'ity** *n*. **typ'ically** *adv*. **typ'icalness** *n*.

typify /*tip'i-fī*/ *vt* (**typ'ifying**; **typ'ifīed**) to make or be a type of; to exemplify or symbolize. [L *typus* (see **type**) and sfx *-fy* (ult from L *facere* to make)]

■ **typificā'tion** *n*. **typ'ifier** *n*.

typist, etc see under **type**.

typo¹ /*tī'po*/ (*inf*) *n* (*pl* **ty'pos**) a typographical error, a literal.

typo² see **typ.**

typography /*tī-pog'rə-fi*/ *n* the art or style of printing, or of using type effectively. [New L *typographia* (equivalent to **type** and **-graphy**)]

■ **typog'rapher** *n* a compositor; a person engaged in or skilled in typography; a beetle that bores letter-like tunnels in the bark of pine and other trees. **typograph'ia** *n pl* matter relating to printers and printing. **typograph'ic** or **typograph'ical** *adj*. **typograph'ically** *adv*. **typog'raphist** *n* a person who studies or is knowledgeable in the history or art of printing.

typology /*tī-pol'ə-ji*/ *n* the study of types and their succession in biology, archaeology, etc; the doctrine that things in the New Testament are foreshadowed symbolically in the Old. [Gr *typos* type, and **-logy**]

■ **typolog'ical** *adj*. **typol'ogist** *n*.

typomania /*tī-pō-* or *tī-pə-mā'ni-ə*/ *n* an irrational desire to have one's work published; a craze for searching the Old Testament for portents of the New Testament. [Gr *typos* type, and **mania**]

typto /*tip'tō*/ *vi* (*prp* (*Walter Scott*) **tup'towing**) to conjugate the Greek verb *typtō*, I strike; to work at Greek grammar.

Tyr /*tir*, *tür*/ *n* the old Norse war god. [ON *Tȳr*; OE *Tīw*; cf **Tuesday**]

Tyr *abbrev* : tyrosine.

tyramine /*tī'rə-mēn*/ *n* a colourless crystalline amine found in cheese, ergot, mistletoe and decayed animal tissue or derived from phenol, similar in action to adrenaline. [*tyrosine* and *amine*]

tyrannosaur /*tī-* or *ti-ran'ə-sör*/ or **tyrannosaurus** /*-sö'rəs*/ *n* a large bipedal carnivorous lizard-hipped dinosaur of the carnosaur group of theropods, common during the Cretaceous period. [New L *Tyrannosaurus*, from Gr *tyrannos* and *dinosaur*]

tyrant /*tī'rənt*/, *obs* **tyran** /*tī'rən*/ *n* a ruler who uses power arbitrarily and oppressively; an oppressor; a bully; in the *orig* Greek sense, an absolute ruler, or one whose power has not been constitutionally arrived at; a tyrant bird. [Gr *tyrannos*, partly through OFr *tirant* (Fr *tyran*) and L *tyrannus*]

■ **ty'ran**, **tyranne**, **ty'rant** *vt* and *vi* (*obs*). **tyr'anness** *n* (*archaic*) a female tyrant. **tyrannic** /*ti-ran'ik* (sometimes *tī-*)/ or **tyrann'ical** *adj*. **tyrann'ically** *adv*. **tyrann'icalness** *n*. **tyrannici'dal** *adj*. **tyrann'icide** *n* the killing or the killer of a tyrant. **Tyrann'idae** *n pl* the tyrant bird family. **tyrannis** /*ti-ran'is*/ *n* (Gr) a regime illegally set up. **tyrannize** or **-ise** /*tir'*/ *vi* to act as a tyrant; *esp* to rule with oppressive severity. ◆ *vt* to act the tyrant to. **tyrannous** /*tir'*/ *adj* despotic; domineering; overpowering; oppressive. **tyr'annously** *adv*. **tyranny** /*tir'*/ *n* absolute or illegally established power; the government or authority of a tyrant; absolute power cruelly administered; oppression; cruelty; harshness.

❑ **tyrant bird** or **tyrant flycatcher** *n* any member of an American family of birds related to the pittas and cotingas.

tyre /*tīr*/ *n* a variant spelling of **tire²**; a rubber cushion or tube round a wheel rim. [See **tire²**]

■ **tyred** *adj*. **tyre'less** *adj*.

❑ **tyre chains** *n pl* a circular apparatus of metal links fitted to the wheels of a car to provide traction in icy conditions. **tyre gauge** *n* a device for measuring the air pressure in a pneumatic tyre.

■ **tubeless tyre** a pneumatic tyre that has no inner tube, and, being self-sealing, deflates only slowly when punctured.

Tyrian /*tir'i-ən*/ *adj* of Tyre; red or purple, like the dye formerly prepared at the ancient Mediterranean port of Tyre. ◆ *n* a native of Tyre.

❑ **Tyrian cynosure** *n* the north star, a guide to Tyrian mariners.

tyro see **tiro**.

tyroglyphid /*ti-rog'li-fid*/ *n* a mite of the genus *Tyroglyphus*, including the cheesemite and the flour-mite. [Gr *tyros* cheese, and *glyphein* to carve]

Tyrolese or **Tirolese** /*tir-ə-lēz'*/ *adj* relating to the mountainous W Austrian province of *Tyrol* (*Tirol*), or to its people. ◆ *n* a native of Tyrol; the dialect of German spoken in this area.

■ **Tyrolē'an** or **Tirolē'an** (or /*tir-ō'li-ən*/) *n* and *adj*. **Tyrolienne** or **Tirolienne** /*ti-rō-li-en'*/ *n* a Tyrolese peasants' dance, song or tune with yodelling.

Tyronensian see **Tironensian**.

tyrones see **tiro**.

tyrosine /*tī'rō-sēn*/ *n* an amino acid formed by decomposition of proteins, first obtained from cheese. [Gr *tyros* cheese]

■ **ty'rosinase** *n* an enzyme found in plants and animals that works as a catalyst in the conversion of tyrosine to melanin.

Tyrrhenian /*ti-rē'ni-ən*/ *n* and *adj* Etruscan (also **Tyrrhēne'**). [Gr *Tyrrhēnia* Etruria]

❑ **Tyrrhenian Sea** *n* that part of the Mediterranean between Tuscany and Sardinia and Corsica.

Tyrtaean /tər-tē'ən/ adj of or relating to Tyrtaeus (Gr Tyrtaios), a Greek martial poet of the 7c BC.

tystie /tī'sti/ (Orkney and Shetland) n the black guillemot. [Scand; cf ON theist]

tyte see tite.

tythe see tithe.

tzaddi /tsä'dē/ same as **sadhe**.

tzaddik and **tzaddiq** see **zaddik**.

tzar see tsar.

tzatziki /tsat-sē'ki/ n a Greek dish made of yoghurt and finely sliced or chopped cucumber, flavoured with garlic, mint, etc, eaten as a dip. [Mod Gr]

tzetse, **tzetze** see **tsetse**.

tzigany /tsig'ä-ni, -ə-ni, -ny'/, also **tsigane** or **tzigane** /tsi-gän'/ n a Hungarian gypsy (also adj). [Hung cigány gypsy; cf Ital zingano, zingaro, Ger Zigeuner]

tzimmes /tsim'is/ n (pl **tzimm'es**) a sweetened stew or casserole of vegetables, fruit and sometimes meat. [Yiddish]

Uu

a b c d e f g h i j k l m n o p q r s t u v w x y z

Univers Designed by Adrian Frutiger in 1957. Switzerland.

U¹ or **u** /ū/ n the twenty-first letter in the modern English alphabet, with various sounds, as in rule, put, but, and the diphthongal sound that serves as the name of the letter; anything shaped like the letter U. —U derived from V, a form of Y which the Romans borrowed from the Greeks. From V, the lapidary and capital form, the uncial and cursive forms U and u were developed, with V (used until modern times initially) gradually becoming appropriated as the symbol for the consonant sound (see **V**) and the medial form u as the symbol for the vowel.
□ **U'-bend** n an air-trap in the form of a U-shaped bend in a pipe. **U'-bolt, U'-trap, U'-tube** n a bolt, drain-trap and tube bent like the letter U. **U'-shaped** adj. **U'-turn** n a turn made by a vehicle which reverses its direction of travel, crossing into the flow of traffic on the other side of the road; any reversal of direction (fig).

U² /oo/ n a Burmese title of respect, prefaced to a man's name. [Burmese]

U³ /ū/ (inf) adj (of words, behaviour, etc) as used by or found among the upper classes, hence socially acceptable; upper-class, opp to non-U. [**upper-class**]

U or **U.** abbrev: unionist; united; universal, (a certificate designating) a film that people of any age are allowed to see; university.

U (chem) symbol: uranium.

UA abbrev: Ukraine (IVR).

UAE abbrev: United Arab Emirates (also IVR).

uakari or **ouakari** /wa-kä'ri/ n any of various short-tailed, long-haired S American monkeys of the genus Cacajao (family Cebidae), related to the saki. [Tupí]

UAR abbrev: formerly, United Arab Republic.

UART (comput) abbrev: Universal Asynchronous Receiver/ Transmitter, a computer component that manages serial communication.

UAV abbrev: unmanned aerial vehicle.

uber- /oo-bər-/ or (Ger) **Über-** /ü-bər-/ pfx denoting: an exceptional type; an archetypal example. [On the model of **Übermensch**]

Übermensch /ü'bər-mensh/ (Ger) n a superman.

uberous /ū'bə-rəs/ (rare) adj yielding an abundance of milk; abounding. [L über udder, fruitfulness]
■ **u'berty** n fruitfulness; abundant productiveness.

uberrima fides /ū-ber'i-mə fī'dēz or oo-be-rē'ma fi'dās/ (L) complete faith.

uberty see under **uberous**.

UB40 abbrev: unemployment benefit (form) 40, a registration card formerly issued by the Department of Employment and held by an unemployed person.

ubiety /ū-bī'i-ti/ n the state of being in a definite place; location. [L ubi where]

ubique /ū-bī'kwē or ŭ-bē'kwe/ (L) adv everywhere.

ubiquinone /ū-bik'wi-nōn/ (biochem) n a quinone involved in the transfer of electrons during cell respiration. [L ubíque everywhere, and **quinone**]

ubiquity /ū-bik'wi-ti/ n existence everywhere at the same time; omnipresence. [L ubíque everywhere, from ubi where]
■ **ubiquá'rian** adj found everywhere; ubiquitous. **ubiquitá'rian** n and adj (someone) believing that Christ's body is everywhere, in the Eucharist as elsewhere. **ubiq'uitary** adj being everywhere at once. **ubiq'uitin** n (biochem) a widely distributed polypeptide that is involved in many cell processes. **ubiq'uitous** adj to be found everywhere. **ubiq'uitously** adv.

ubi supra /ū'bī soo'prə or ŭb'ē soo'prä/ (L) where mentioned above.

U-boat /ū'bōt or (Ger) oo'/ n a German submarine. [Ger Unterseeboot]

UBR abbrev: Uniform Business Rate.

ubuntu /ŭ-bŭn'tŭ/ (S Afr) n a quality of humanity and compassion. [Xhosa]

UC abbrev: University College.

uc (printing) abbrev: upper-case, ie capital.

UCAR abbrev: formerly, Union of Central African Republics.

UCAS /ū'kas/ abbrev: Universities and Colleges Admissions Service.

UCATT /ū'kat/ abbrev: Union of Construction, Allied Trades and Technicians.

UCCA /uk'ə/ abbrev: Universities Central Council on Admissions (now replaced by **UCAS**).

UCI abbrev: Union Cycliste Internationale (Fr), International Cycling Union.

uckers /uk'ərz/ n a form of the game ludo, played in the Royal Navy. [Origin uncertain]

UCU abbrev: University and College Union.

UDA abbrev: Ulster Defence Association.

udal /ū'dl/ (Orkney and Shetland) adj without feudal superior, allodial.
♦ n an estate so held. [ON ōthal]
■ **u'daller** n a holder of such an estate.

UDC abbrev: Universal Decimal Classification.

udder /ud'ər/ n the organ containing the mammary glands of the cow, mare, etc, having more than one teat; a dug or teat (rare). [OE ūder; Ger Euter, L über, Gr outhar]
■ **udd'ered** adj. **udd'erful** adj with full udder. **udd'erless** adj unsuckled.

UDF abbrev: United Democratic Front, a former organization of anti-apartheid groups in South Africa.

UDHR abbrev: Universal Declaration of Human Rights.

UDI abbrev: Unilateral Declaration of Independence.

UDM abbrev: Union of Democratic Mineworkers.

udo /oo'dō/ (bot) n (pl **u'dos**) a Japanese species of Aralia with edible shoots. [Jap]

udometer /ū-dom'i-tər/ n a name for a rain gauge, never included in the official glossary of British meteorological terms. [Through Fr, from L ūdus wet, and **-meter**]
■ **udomet'ric** adj.

udon /oo'don/ n in Japanese cookery, a thick noodle made from wheat flour. [Jap]

UDR abbrev: Ulster Defence Regiment (now replaced by the Royal Irish Regiment).

uds /udz/ (archaic) interj in oaths, for **God's**, or for **God save** (as in uds my life).

UDT abbrev: United Dominions Trust.

UEFA /ū-ā'fə or ū-ē'fə/ abbrev: Union of European Football Associations.

uey /ū'i/ (Aust inf; usu fig) n a U-turn, as in do a uey.

UF abbrev: United Free Church (of Scotland).

UFC abbrev: Universities Funding Council (now replaced by **HEFCE** (see **HEFC**)); Ultimate Fighting Championship.

UFF abbrev: Ulster Freedom Fighters.

UFO or **ufo** /ū-ef-ō' or ū'fō/ (inf) n (pl **UFOs'** or **u'fos**) an unidentified flying object, such as a flying saucer.
■ **ufol'ogist** n. **ufology** /ū-fol'ə-ji/ n the study of UFOs.

ug see under **ugly**.

Ugandan /ū-gan'dən/ adj of or relating to the Republic of Uganda in E Africa, or its inhabitants. ♦ n a native or citizen of Uganda.

■ words derived from main entry word; □ compound words; ■ idioms and phrasal verbs

Ugg® **boots** /ug boots/ (orig Aust) n pl women's flat-heeled sheepskin boots with a wool lining. [Origin uncertain]

ugh /uhh, ug, ŭh or ŭh/ interj an exclamation of repugnance. ◆ n (old) used as a representation of a cough or grunt.

Ugli® /ug'li/ n a name given to a citrus fruit which is believed to be a cross between a grapefruit and a tangerine; the plant producing this fruit. [ugly; from the fruit's unprepossessing appearance]

ugly /ug'li/ adj offensive to the sight or other sense, or to refined taste or moral feeling; ill-natured; threatening; disquieting; suggesting suspicion of evil; frightful, horrible (obs). ◆ n an ugly person (inf); a shade attached to a lady's hat (mid-19c). ◆ vt (rare) to make ugly. [ON uggligr frightful, uggr fear]
■ **ug** vt (pat and pap **ugged**) (obs or dialect in all meanings) to arouse loathing in; to loathe. ◆ vi to feel loathing. **uglifica'tion** n. **ug'lify** vt to make ugly. **ug'lily** adv. **ug'liness** n. **ug'some** adj (obs) disgusting; hideous. **ug'someness** n (obs).
❑ **ugly customer** n a dangerous antagonist. **ugly duckling** n a despised or overlooked member of a family or group who later proves the most successful, attractive, etc. **ugly man** n (obs) an actual garrotter, distinguished from his confederates.

Ugrian /ū'gri-ən or oo'/ adj and n (of or relating to) that division of the Finno-Ugrian languages and peoples that includes the Magyars, Ostyaks and Voguls (also **U'gric**). [Russ Ugri the Ugrian peoples]
❑ **U'gro-Finn'ic** adj Finno-Ugrian.

UHF (radio) abbrev: ultra-high frequency (see **frequency** under **frequent**).

uh-huh /u'hu or m'hm/ interj a sound used in place of 'yes'.

uhlan /oo'län or ū'/ (hist) n a light cavalryman in semi-oriental uniform; a Prussian lancer. [Ger Uhlan, from Pol ulan, orig a light Tatar horseman, from Turk oġlan a young man]

UHT abbrev: ultra-heat-treated; ultra-high temperature.

uh-uh /u'u/ interj a sound used in place of 'no' or to express disagreement.

uhuru /oo-hoo'roo/ n (esp in E Africa) freedom (eg from slavery); national independence. [Swahili, from huru free]

uillean(n) pipes /il'(y)ən pīps/ n pl Irish bagpipes, worked by squeezing bellows under the arm (also **union pipes**). [Ir piob uilleann; piob pipe, and uilleann, genitive sing of uille elbow]

uintaite or **uintahite** /ū-in'tä-īt/ n a natural tarlike asphalt found in the Uinta valley, Utah (also **gilsonite** /gil'sən-īt/).
■ **uint'athēre** n any animal of the genus **Uintathē'rium**, gigantic Eocene fossil ungulates from Uinta County, Wyoming.

uitlander /æ'it-, āt' or ā'it-lan-dər/ (S Afr; chiefly hist) n a foreigner (orig a British person in the Transvaal or Orange Free State). [Afrik, outlander, foreigner, from Du uit out, and land land]

ujamaa /oo-jə-mä'/ n in Tanzania, a form of village community based on collective ownership and work-sharing, resembling the Israeli kibbutz; a policy of collectivism followed in Tanzania in the mid-20c. [Swahili, brotherhood]

UJD abbrev: Utriusque Juris Doctor (L), Doctor of both Laws (Canon and Civil).

UK abbrev: United Kingdom.

UKADGE abbrev: United Kingdom Air Defence Ground Environment (now replaced by **UK ASACS**).

UKAEA abbrev: United Kingdom Atomic Energy Authority.

UK ASACS abbrev: United Kingdom Air Surveillance and Control System.

ukase /ū-kāz' or -kās'/ n an edict with force of law in Tsarist Russia; an edict with bearing on existing legislation issued by the Presidium of the Supreme Soviet and subject to later ratification by the Supreme Soviet; any arbitrary decree from any source. [Russ ukaz]

uke /ūk/ (inf) n a ukulele.

ukelele a common spelling of **ukulele**.

UKIP /ū'kip/ abbrev: United Kingdom Independence Party.

ukiyo-e /oo-kē'(y)ō-ā/ n a Japanese style of painting and print-making flourishing between the 17c and 19c, typically depicting scenes from everyday life. [Jap, world, life picture]

Ukrainian /ū-krā'ni-ən or oo-krī'ni-ən/ n a native or citizen of the republic of (the) Ukraine, formerly part of the Soviet Union; the language of this people. ◆ adj of or relating to the Ukrainians or their language.

ukulele /ū-kə-lā'li or ŭ-kŭ-lā'lä/ n a small, usu four-stringed, guitar, popularized in Hawaii, although orig Portuguese. [Hawaiian, jumping flea]

ULA or **ula** (comput) abbrev: uncommitted logic array.

ULCC abbrev: ultra-large crude carrier, a tanker over 320000 dead-weight tons.

ulcer /ul'sər/ n an open sore, on the skin or mucous membrane, often discharging pus; a continuing source of evil, pain or corruption, an unsound element. ◆ vt and vi to ulcerate. [L ulcus, ulceris; cf Gr helkos]
■ **ul'cerate** vi to form an ulcer. ◆ vt to cause an ulcer in; to affect with insidious corruption. **ulcerā'tion** n. **ul'cerātive** adj. **ul'cered** adj. **ul'cerous** adj. **ul'cerously** adv. **ul'cerousness** n.
❑ **ulcerative colitis** n (med) chronic ulceration of the colon. **ulcerative dermal necrosis** n a fungal disease of salmon.

ule or **hule** /oo'lā/ n a Central American rubber tree (genus Castilloa); its crude rubber. [Sp hule, from Nahuatl ulli]

-ule /-ūl/ n sfx indicating a diminutive form, as in globule, module. [L -ulus]

ulema /oo'li-mə/ n the body of professional theologians, expounders of the law, in a Muslim country; a member of such a body. [Ar 'ulema, pl of 'ālim learned]

-ulent /-ū-lənt/ adj sfx denoting a copious amount, as in fraudulent, purulent. [L -ulentus]

ulex /ū'leks/ n (pl **ū'lexes** or **ulices** /ū'li-sēz/) any plant of the gorse genus Ulex. [L ulex, -icis a kind of rosemary or the like]

ULF abbrev: ultra-low frequency.

ulicon, ulichon and **ulikon** /oo'li-kən/ same as **eulachon**.

uliginose or **uliginous** /ū-lij'i-nəs/ adj slimy; oozy; swampy; growing in swampy places. [L ūlīginōsus, from ūlīgō, -inis moisture]

ulitis /ū-lī'tis/ n inflammation of the gums, gingivitis. [Gr oula gums, and -itis]

ullage /ul'ij/ n the quantity by which a vessel is holding less than its full capacity, or sometimes the amount left in the vessel; loss by evaporation or leakage; dregs (sl). ◆ vt to reckon the ullage of; to affect with ullage; to fill up; to draw off a little from. [Anglo-Fr ulliage, OFr eullage, from œiller to fill up]
■ **ull'ing** n the making good of ullage.

Ulmus /ul'məs/ n the elm genus, giving name to the family **Ulmā'ceae**, related to the nettles. [L ulmus elm]
■ **ulmā'ceous** adj of or like an elm; of its family. **ul'min** n a gummy exudation from elms and other trees.

ulna /ul'nə/ n (pl **ul'nae** /-nē/) the inner and larger of the two bones of the forearm; the corresponding bone in an animal's foreleg or a bird's wing (zool). [L ulna elbow, arm; cf **ell**[1], and Gr ōlenē forearm]
■ **ul'nar** adj. **ulnā'rē** n (pl **ulnā'ria**) the bone of the carpus opposite the ulna.

ulosis /ū-lō'sis/ (med) n the formation of a scar. [Gr oulōsis, from oulē a scar]

Ulothrix /ū'lō-thriks/ n a genus of filamentous algae, giving name to the **Ulotrichales** /ū-lot-ri-kā'lēz/, an order of multicellular uninucleate green algae, marine and freshwater. [Gr oulos woolly, and thrix, trichos hair]
■ **ulotrichous** /ū-lot'ri-kəs/ adj woolly-haired. **ulot'richy** /-ki/ n woolly-hairedness.

ulster /ul'stər/ n a long loose overcoat, first made in Ulster, Northern Ireland.
■ **ul'stered** adj wearing an ulster. **ulsterette'** n a light ulster.
❑ **Ul'sterman, Ul'sterwoman** n a native or inhabitant of Ulster.

ult. abbrev: ultimate; ultimately; see also **ultimo** under **ultimate**.

ulterior /ul-tē'ri-ər/ adj (of eg a motive) beyond what is stated or apparent; on the further side; beyond; in the future; remoter. [L ulterior, from ultrā (adv and prep), uls (prep) beyond]
■ **ultē'riorly** adv.

ultima /ul'ti-mə/ n the last syllable of a word. [L, fem of ultimus last]
❑ **ultima ratio** /ul'ti-mə rä'shē-ō or ŭl'ti-ma rä'ti-ō/ n (L) the last argument. **ultima ratio regum** /rē'gəm or rä'gŭm/ n (L) the last argument of kings; once inscribed on French cannon.

ultimate /ul'ti-māt, -mət or -mit/ adj furthest; last; final; fundamental; maximum; most important; greatest; limiting. ◆ n a final point; a fundamental; the greatest (or otherwise most extreme) thing achievable or conceivable of its sort (inf). [L ultimus last]
■ **ul'timacy** /-mə-si/ n. **ul'timately** adv finally. **ultimā'tum** n (pl **ultimā'ta** or **ultimā'tums**) final terms; a last offer or demand; a last word; a final point; something fundamental. **ul'timo** adj in the last (month) (abbrev **ult.** or **ulto.**). **ultimogeniture** /-jen'/ n (law) succession of the youngest, as in borough-English (qv), opp to primogeniture.
❑ **ultimate fighting** n a competitive sport in which two opponents fight each other without protective gear, subject to only minimal rules on the types of blow permissible (also called **extreme fighting**). **ultimate load** n (aeronautics) the maximum load that a structure is designed to withstand without a failure. **ultimate tensile stress** n (engineering) the highest load applied to a metal in the course of a tensile test, divided by the original cross-sectional area.
■ **the ultimate deterrent** nuclear weapons.

ultima Thule see **Thule**.

ultimus haeres /ul'ti-məs hē'rēz or ŭl'ti-mŭs hī'räs/ (*L*) in law, the crown or the state, which succeeds to the property of those who die intestate or without next of kin.

ultion /ul'shən/ (*obs*) *n* revenge; avengement. [L *ultiō*, *-ōnis*]

ulto. *abbrev* : ultimo (see under **ultimate**).

Ultonian /ul-tō'ni-ən/ *adj* of Ulster. ◆*n* an Ulsterman or -woman. [LL *Ultōnia* Ulster; OIr *Ult-*, stem of *Ulaid* Ulster]

ultra- /ul-trə-/ *pfx* signifying: (1) beyond in place or position (as in *ultra-Neptunian*); (2) beyond the limit, range, etc, of (as in *ultramicroscopic*); (3) beyond the ordinary, or excessive(ly) (as in *ultra-careful, ultra-modern*). [L *ultrā* beyond]
  ■ **ul'tra** *adj* extreme, *esp* in royalism, fashion, or religious or political opinion. ◆*n* an extremist. **ultraism** /ul'trə-izm/ *n* (an) extreme principle, opinion, or measure; an attempt to pass beyond the limits of the known. **ul'traist** *n*.

ultrabasic /ul-trə-bā'sik/ (*petrology*) *adj* extremely basic, very poor in silica. [**ultra-** (3)]

ultracentrifuge /ul-trə-sen'tri-fūj/ *n* a very high-speed type of centrifuge. ◆*vt* to subject to the action of an ultracentrifuge. [**ultra-** (2)]
  ■ **ultracentrif'ugal** (or /-fū'gəl/) *adj*. **ultracentrifugation** /-gā'shən/ *n*.

ultra-distance /ul-trə-dis'təns/ (*athletics*) *adj* denoting a distance greater than 30 miles, *esp* as part of a competition, eg a race run over several days. [**ultra-** (3)]

ultrafiche /ul'trə-fēsh/ *n* a sheet of microfilm the same size as a microfiche but with a greater number of microcopied records on it. [**ultra-** (3)]

ultrafilter /ul'trə-fil-tər/ (*biol* and *chem*) *n* an extremely fine filter which retains particles as fine as large molecules. ◆*vt* to pass through an ultrafilter. [**ultra-** (2)]
  ■ **ultrafil'trate** *n* a substance that has passed through an ultrafilter. **ultrafiltra'tion** *n* the separation of particles by filtration, under suction or pressure.

ultra-heat-treated /ul-trə-hēt-trē'tid/ *adj* (of milk, etc) sterilized by exposing to very high temperatures, increasing shelf life (*abbrev* **UHT**). [**ultra-** (3)]

ultra-high /ul-trə-hī'/ *adj* very high. [**ultra-** (3)]
  ❑ **ultra-high frequency** see **frequency** under **frequent**.

ultraism, ultraist see under **ultra-**.

ultramarathon /ul'trə-mar-ə-thən/ *n* a long-distance race that is longer than a marathon. [**ultra-** (2)]

ultramarine /ul-trə-mə-rēn'/ *adj* overseas; from overseas; deep blue. ◆*n* a deep blue pigment, *orig* made from lapis-lazuli brought from beyond the sea; its colour. [L *ultrāmarīnus*, from *ultrā* beyond, and *mare* sea]

ultramicro- /ul-trə-mī-krō-/ *pfx* signifying smaller than, or dealing with smaller quantities than, **micro-**, eg **ultramicrochem'istry** chemistry dealing with minute quantities, sometimes no greater than one-millionth of a gram.

ultramicroscope /ul-trə-mī'krə-skōp/ *n* a microscope with strong illumination from the side, whereby the presence of ultramicroscopic objects can be observed through the scattering of light from them. [**ultra-** (2)]
  ■ **ultramicroscopic** /-skop'ik/ *adj* too small to be visible under the ordinary microscope; relating to ultramicroscopy. **ultramicroscopy** /-kros'kə-pi/ *n*.

ultramicrotome /ul-trə-mī'krə-tōm/ *n* a microtome for cutting ultra-thin sections for examination with the electron microscope. [**ultra-** (2)]
  ■ **ultramicrotomy** /-ot'ə-mi/ *n*.

ultramontane /ul-trə-mon'tān/ *adj* beyond the mountains (*esp* the Alps); *orig* used in Italy of the French, Germans, etc; afterwards applied by the northern nations to the Italians; of or relating to a faction within the Roman Catholic Church which is extreme in favouring the Pope's supremacy. ◆*n* a person who lives beyond the mountains, *esp* south of the Alps; a member of the ultramontane faction within the Roman Catholic Church. [Med L *ultrāmontānus*, from L *ultrā* beyond, and *mons, montis* a mountain]
  ■ **ultramon'tanism** /-tən-izm/ *n*. **ultramon'tanist** *n*.

ultramundane /ul-trə-mun'dān or -dān'/ *adj* beyond the world, or beyond the limits of our solar system. [LL *ultrāmundānus*, from L *ultrā* beyond, and *mundus* world]

ultra-rapid /ul-trə-rap'id/ *adj* of a motion-picture film, exposed at much greater speed than that at which it is to be exhibited, giving a slow-motion picture. [**ultra-** (3)]

ultrared /ul-trə-red'/ (*obs*) *adj* infra-red. [**ultra-** (1)]

ultrasensual /ul-trə-sen'sū-əl or -shŭ-əl/ *adj* beyond the reach of the senses. [**ultra-** (2)]

ultrashort /ul-trə-shört'/ *adj* (of electromagnetic waves) of less than ten metres' wavelength. [**ultra-** (3)]

ultrasonic /ul-trə-son'ik/ *adj* relating to, or (of an instrument or process) using sound waves of too high a frequency to be audible to the human ear. [**ultra-** (2)]
  ■ **ultrason'ically** *adv*. **ultrason'ics** *n sing* the study of such vibrations, used medically for diagnostic and therapeutic purposes. **ultrasonography** /-sən-og'rə-fi/ *n* the directing of ultrasonic waves through body tissues to detect abnormalities, eg in a fetus.
  ❑ **ultrasonic communication** *n* underwater communication using ultrasonic waves.

ultrasound /ul'trə-sownd/ *n* sound waves or vibrations too rapid to be audible, useful *esp* in medical diagnosis (see also **ultrasonic**). [**ultra-** (2)]

ultrastructure /ul'trə-struk-chər/ (*biol*) *n* the ultimate structure of protoplasm at a lower level than can be examined in the light microscope. [**ultra-** (2)]

ultra-tropical /ul-trə-trop'i-kəl/ *adj* beyond the tropics; hotter than the tropics. [**ultra-** (1) and (3)]

ultraviolet /ul-trə-vī'ə-lit/ (*phys*) *adj* beyond the violet end of the visible spectrum, of wavelength between *approx* 400 and 10 nanometres; relating to, or using, radiations of wavelengths less than those of visible light. [**ultra-** (1)]
  ❑ **ultraviolet spectroscopy** *n* (*chem*) the study of material by its absorption of ultraviolet radiation. **ultraviolet star** *n* one of a class of invisible stars giving out intense ultraviolet radiation.

ultra vires /ul'trə vī'rēz or ŭl'trä wē'räs/ (*L*) beyond one's powers or authority.

ultra-virtuous /ul-trə-vûr'tū-əs/ *adj* prudish. [**ultra-** (3)]

ultroneous /ul-trō'ni-əs/ *adj* spontaneous, voluntary. [L *ultrōneus*, from *ultrō* spontaneously]
  ■ **ultrō'neously** *adv*. **ultrō'neousness** *n*.

ululate /ūl'ū-lāt, also ul'/ *vi* to hoot or screech. [L *ululāre, -ātum* to hoot]
  ■ **ul'ulant** *adj*. **ululā'tion** *n* howling, wailing.

ulva /ul'və/ (*bot*) *n* a kind of edible seaweed. [L *ulva* sedge]

ulyie and **ulzie** /ŭl'yi or ŭl'i/ obsolete Scots forms of **oil**.

um /əm or um/ *interj* used by speakers when momentarily hesitating or in doubt.
  ❑ **um and ah** to hesitate, *esp* when speaking.

umami /oo-mä'mi/ *n* a savoury, satisfying taste, like that of monosodium glutamate. ◆*adj* having such a taste. [Jap, savoury flavour]

Umayyad /oo'mī-yad/ or **Omayyad** /ō'mī-yad/ *n* any member of the earlier (661–750) of the two great dynasties of caliphs, descendants of *Umayya*, a distant relative of Mohammed. ◆*adj* of or relating to this dynasty.

umbel /um'bəl/ (*bot*) *n* a flat-topped inflorescence in which the flower-stalks all spring from about the same point in an axis (which in a **compound umbel** is grouped in the same way with other axes). [L *umbella* a sunshade, dimin of *umbra* a shade]
  ■ **um'bellar** (or /-bel'/) *adj*. **um'bellate** or **um'bellated** *adj* constituting an umbel; having umbels. **um'bellately** *adv*. **umbellifer** /um-bel'i-fər/ *n* any plant of the Umbelliferae family, with umbels and divided leaves. **Umbellif'erae** *n pl* the carrot and hemlock family of plants with (*usu* compound) umbels, schizocarpic fruit, leaves with sheathing bases. **umbellif'erous** *adj*. **um'bellule** *n* a partial umbel.

umber¹ /um'bər/ *n* a brown earthy mineral (hydrated oxides of iron and manganese) used as a pigment. ◆*vt* to colour with umber. ◆*adj* brown like umber. [Ital *terra d'ombra* shadow earth, or possibly *Umbrian* earth]
  ■ **um'bered** or **um'bery** *adj*.
  ❑ **um'ber-bird** *n* the umbrette.
  ■ **burnt umber** umber heated to give a dark reddish-brown colour. **raw umber** untreated umber, a yellowish-brown colour.

umber² /um'bər/ *n* the grayling. [L *umbra*]

umbilicus /um-bil'i-kəs or um-bi-lī'kəs/ *n* the navel; a depression at the axial base of a spiral shell; a small depression. [L *umbilīcus* the navel; Gr *omphalos*]
  ■ **umbilical** /-bil' (sometimes -bi-lī')/ *adj* relating to the umbilicus or the umbilical cord. **umbil'icate** *adj* navel-like; having a depression like a navel. **umbilica'tion** *n*.
  ❑ **umbilical cord** *n* a long flexible tube connecting the fetus to the placenta, the navel-string; an electrical cable or other servicing line attached to a rocket vehicle or spacecraft during preparations for launch; the lifeline outside a vehicle in space by which astronauts receive air and communicate with the vehicle; any similar connection of fundamental importance.

umbles /um'blz/ n pl entrails (liver, heart, etc), esp of a deer (also **hum'bles** or **num'bles**). [OFr nombles, from lomble loin, from L lumbulus, dimin of lumbus loin]
  □ **um'ble-pie'**, **hum'ble-pie'** or **num'ble-pie'** n a pie made from the umbles of a deer.

umbo /um'bō/ n (pl **umbō'nēs** or **um'bos**) the central boss of a shield; a knob; the protuberant oldest part of a bivalve shell; a knob on a toadstool cap; a projection on the inner surface of the eardrum where the malleus is attached. [L umbō, -ōnis]
  ■ **um'bonal** /-bən-əl/ adj. **um'bonate** adj (bot) having a central boss. **umbonā'tion** n.

umbra /um'brə/ n (pl **um'brae** /-brē/ or **um'bras**) a shadow; the darker part of the shadow or dark inner cone projected in an eclipse (astron); the darker part of a sunspot; a shade or ghost; an uninvited guest who comes with an invited one. [L umbra shade, shadow, dimin umbrāculum, adj umbrātilis]
  ■ **umbraculate** /um-brak'ū-lāt or -lət/ adj overshadowed by an umbraculum. **umbrac'uliform** adj umbrella-shaped. **umbrac'ulum** n an umbrella-shaped structure. **um'bral** adj of an umbra. **um'brāted** adj (heraldry) faintly traced. **umbratic** /-brat'/ (rare), **umbrat'ical**, **umbratile** /um'brə-tīl or -til/ or **umbratilous** /-brat'i-ləs/ adj shadowy; shaded; shade-giving; indoor; secluded. **umbrif'erous** adj shade-giving. **umbrose** /-brōs'/ adj shade-giving; dusky. **um'brous** adj shaded.

umbrage /um'brij/ n offence, esp in the phrases give and take umbrage ; suspicion of injury; shade, shadow, or something that casts a shadow (archaic or poetic); a shelter (obs); a shadowy appearance (rare); a pretext, colour (obs); an inkling (obs). ◆ vt to shade; to offend (rare). [Fr ombrage, from L umbrāticum (neuter adj), from umbra a shadow]
  ■ **umbrā'geous** adj shady or forming a shade. **umbrā'geously** adv. **umbrā'geousness** n.

umbral...to...**umbratilous** see under **umbra**.

umbre /um'bər/ see **umbrette**.

umbrel see **umbriere**.

umbrella /um-brel'ə/ n (also (obs) **ombrell'a** or **umbrell'o**) a dome-shaped canopy of light fabric mounted on a stick, carried or set up as a protection against rain or sun, that can be collapsed and furled when not in use; anything of similar form, eg a jellyfish disc; a protection; (something, eg an agency, that provides) a general cover or representation; a cover of fighter aircraft for ground forces (milit). ◆ adj broadly embracing or including a number or a variety of things. [Ital ombrella, ombrello, from ombra a shade, from L umbra]
  ■ **umbrell'aed** or **umbrell'a'd** adj with an umbrella.
  □ **umbrell'a-ant** n the sauba ant. **umbrella bird** n any of a number of birds of the Cotinga genus with umbrella-like crest and a lappet attached to the throat or breast. **umbrella fir** n a Japanese conifer with radiating tufts of needles. **umbrella group**, **organization**, etc n a group of representatives of small parties, clubs, etc, which acts for all of them where they have common interests. **umbrella pine** same as **stone pine** (see under **stone**). **umbrella plant** n an African sedge with umbrella-like clusters of slender leaves, a common houseplant. **umbrella stand** n a rack or receptacle for closed umbrellas and walking-sticks. **umbrella tree** n any of various trees or shrubs whose leaves or branches grow in an umbrella-like formation, esp a small N American magnolia.

umbrere see **umbriere**.

umbrette /um-bret'/ n the hammerhead (Scopus umbretta), a brown African bird related to the storks, remarkable for its huge nest (also **um'bre** /-bər/ or **umber-bird**). [Fr ombrette, from ombre umber]

Umbrian /um'bri-ən/ adj of Umbria, in central Italy. ◆ n a native of Umbria; an Indo-European language related to Oscan.

umbriere /um'bri-ēr/ (Spenser) n a visor (also **um'brere**, **um'bril** or **um'brel**). [OFr ombriere, ombrel shade]

umbriferous, **umbrose**, **umbrous** see under **umbra**.

umbril see **umbriere**.

umiak, **oomiak**, **oomiac** or **oomiack** /oo'mi-ak or -myak/ n an open boat, made of wood and stretched skins, usu crewed by women. [Inuit]

UMIST /ū'mist/ abbrev : University of Manchester Institute of Science and Technology.

umlaut /ŭm'lowt/ n a vowel change in Germanic languages brought about by a vowel or semivowel (esp i or j, usu now lost) in the following syllable; the diacritical sign ("), dots placed over a vowel, indicating such a modification. ◆ vt to modify (a vowel) with an umlaut. [Ger, from um around, and Laut sound]

umma or **ummah** /ŭm'ə/ n the body of Muslim believers considered as one community. [Ar, people, community]

ump /ump/ (inf) n short for **umpire**.

umph /hmh, hm or mf/ same as **humph**[1].

umpire /um'pīr/ n an impartial person chosen to supervise the game, enforce the rules, and decide disputes (cricket, etc); a third person called in to decide a dispute or a deadlock; an arbitrator. ◆ vi and vt to act as an umpire (in or for). [ME noumpere, oumper, from OFr nomper, from non- not, and per, pair peer, equal]
  ■ **um'pirage** or **um'pireship** n.

umpteen /um(p)'tēn/ or **umpty** /um(p)'ti/ (inf) adj an indefinitely large number. [Umpty in Morse, a dash, from its sound on a telegraph key]
  ■ **ump'teenth** or **ump'tieth** adj latest or last of many.

umquhile or **umwhile** /um'hwīl/ (archaic, chiefly Scot) adv and adj (at) one time, former(ly). [OE ymb(e) hwīle about or at a time]

umra or **umrah** /ŭm'rə/ n the lesser Muslim pilgrimage to Mecca. [Ar 'umrah visit]

UMTS abbrev : Universal Mobile Telecommunications System, a third-generation mobile communications system.

umwhile see **umquhile**.

UN abbrev : United Nations.

un or **'un** /un or ən/ (dialect) pronoun and n for **one**; also for **him**. [OE accusative hine]

Words formed using the prefix un- are listed in the following entry or, if their meaning is self-evident, at the foot of the page; other words spelt with un- (such as uncle and union) follow in the main word list. Words formed using the prefix under- are listed in a separate entry. The words listed include the most common words with un- but the prefix is living and many other words using it may be formed.

---

un- /un-/ pfx (1) meaning 'not' (in many cases, the resultant word is more than a mere negation and has a positive force, as in unkind, which usu means 'cruel' rather than just 'not kind'); (2) indicating a reversal of process, removal or deprivation; (3) merely emphasizing reversal or deprivation already expressed by the simple word, as in unbare or unloose ; sometimes (in Shakesp and Milton) added to a present participle with a passive meaning. The meaning is often ambiguous, esp in participial adjectives. [Partly OE un-, negative; cf Ger un-, L in-, Gr an- or a-; partly OE on- (or un-), the unstressed form of and-; cf Ger ent-, Gr anti against]
  ■ **unaba'ted** adj not made less in degree. **una'ble** adj not able; not having sufficient strength, power or skill (to do); weak, incompetent (archaic); ineffectual (archaic). **unaccent'ed** adj without accent or stress in pronunciation; not marked with an accent. **unaccomm'odated** adj unprovided. **unaccomm'odating** adj not compliant. **unaccom'panied** adj not accompanied, escorted or attended; having no instrumental accompaniment (music). **unaccom'plished** adj not achieved; lacking accomplishments. **unaccom'plishment** n the fact of not being achieved. **unaccountabil'ity** n. **unaccount'able** adj difficult or impossible to explain; not answerable (to a higher authority); (of a person) puzzling

---

Some words formed with the prefix un-; the numbers in brackets refer to the numbered senses in the entry for **un-**.

unabashed' adj (1).	**unaccept'ance** n (1).	**unaddressed'** adj (1).
unabbrēv'iated adj (1).	**unaccred'ited** adj (1).	**unadjust'ed** adj (1).
unabol'ished adj (1).	**unaccūs'able** adj (1).	**unadmīred'** adj (1).
unabridged' adj (1).	**unaccūs'ably** adv (1).	**unadmīr'ing** adj (1).
unab'rogated adj (1).	**unaccūsed'** adj (1).	**unadmitt'ed** adj (1).
unacadem'ic adj (1).	**unachiev'able** adj (1).	**unadmon'ished** adj (1).
unaccen'tūated adj (1).	**unāch'ing** adj (1).	**unadōred'** adj (1).
unaccept'able adj (1).	**unac'tuated** adj (1).	**unadorned'** adj (1).
unaccept'ableness n (1).	**unadapt'able** adj (1).	**unadvent'urous** (Milton **unadvent'rous**)
unaccept'able adj (1).	**unadapt'ed** adj (1).	adj (1).

in character. **unaccount'ableness** *n.* **unaccount'ably** *adv* inexplicably. **unaccount'ed-for** *adj* unexplained; missing without explanation; not included in an account. **unaccus'tomed** *adj* not usual or customary; not used (with *to*). **unaccus'tomedness** *n.* **unacknowl'edged** *adj* not acknowledged, recognized, confessed or noticed. **unacquaint'ance** *n* lack of acquaintance (often with *with*). **unacquaint'ed** (*Scot* **unacquaint'**) *adj* not on terms of acquaintance (with *with*); ignorant of (with *with*, or (*Swift*) *in*); uninformed; unknown (*obs*); unusual (*Spenser*). **unacquaint'edness** *n.* **unact'able** *adj* unfit for the stage. **unact'ed** *adj* not performed. **unac'tive** *adj* inactive. **unadop'ted** *adj* not adopted (**unadopted road** a road for the repairing, maintenance, etc, of which the Local Authority is not responsible). **unadul'terāte** or **unadul'terated** *adj* unmixed, pure or genuine; sheer, absolute. **unadvīs'able** *adj* inadvisable; not prepared to accept advice. **unadvīs'ableness** *n.* **unadvīs'ably** *adv.* **unadvīsed'** *adj* not advised; without advice; not prudent or discreet; ill-judged; inadvertent (*Spenser*). **unadvīs'edly** *adv.* **unadvīs'edness** *n.* **unaffect'ed** *adj* not affected or influenced; untouched by emotion; without affection; not assumed; plain; real; sincere. **unaffect'edly** *adv.* **unaffect'edness** *n.* **unaffect'ing** *adj.* **unagree'able** *adj* disagreeable (with *to*); inconsistent (with *with*); discordant. **unāk'ing** *adj* (*Shakesp*) unaching. **unā'lienable** *adj* inalienable. **unā'lienably** *adv.* **unaligned'** *adj* non-aligned. **unalive'** *adj* not fully aware of (with *to*); lacking in vitality. **unallayed'** *adj* unmixed, unqualified; not diminished, unquenched. **unallied'** *adj* not related; without allies. **unalloyed'** *adj* not alloyed or mixed, pure (*lit* and *fig*). **un-Amer'ican** *adj* not in accordance with American character, ideas, feeling or traditions; disloyal, against American interests. **un-Amer'icanize** or **-ise** *vt* to make un-American. **unanch'or** *vt* to loose from anchorage. ◆ *vi* to become loose or unattached; to weigh anchor. **unaneled** or (*Shakesp*) **unnaneld** /*un-ə-nēld'*/ *adj* without extreme unction. **unan'imated** *adj* not alive; not animated or lively; not actuated (with *by*). **unannealed'** *adj* not annealed (but see also **unaneled** above). **unan'swerable** *adj* impossible to answer; not to be refuted, conclusive. **unan'swerableness** *n.* **unan'swerably** *adv.* **unan'swered** *adj* not answered; unrequited. **unappeal'able** *adj* not allowing or being capable of an appeal to a higher court, conclusive, final. **unapplaus'ive** *adj* not applauding. **unappoint'ed** *adj* not appointed;

not equipped. **unapprehend'ed** *adj* not understood; not arrested. **unapprehen'sible** *adj.* **unapprehen'sive** *adj* without fear; without understanding. **unapprehen'siveness** *n.* **unapprised'** *adj* not informed. **unapproach'able** *adj* out of reach, inaccessible; stand-offish; inaccessible to advances or intimacy; beyond rivalry. **unapproach'ableness** *n.* **unapproach'ably** *adv.* **unapproached'** *adj.* **unapprō'priate** *adj* unappropriated; inappropriate. **unapprō'priated** *adj* not taken possession of; not applied to some purpose; not granted to any person, corporation, etc. **unapproved'** *adj* unproved; unsanctioned; not approved of; untested (*obs*). **unapprov'ing** *adj.* **unapprov'ingly** *adv.* **unapt'** *adj* unfitted; unsuitable; not readily inclined or accustomed (with *to*); lacking in aptitude, slow. **unapt'ly** *adv.* **unapt'ness** *n.* **unar'gūable** *adj* that cannot be argued; irrefutable. **unar'gūably** *adv.* **unar'gued** *adj* (*Milton*) undisputed; not debated. **unarm'** *vt* to help (someone) to take off armour; to strip (oneself) of armour; to deprive of arms, to disarm; to make harmless. ◆ *vi* to take off one's armour. **unarmed'** *adj* without weapons; defenceless; unprotected; unaided or without accessory apparatus; without arms or similar limbs or appendages. **unar'moured** *adj* without armour or armour-plating. **unart'ful** *adj* artless, genuine; inartistic; unskilful. **unart'fully** *adv.* **unartic'ūlate** *adj* not articulate. **unartic'ūlated** *adj* not jointed; not in distinct syllables; not expressed. **unartist'ic** *adj* not coming within the sphere of art; not concerned with art; inartistic. **unasked'** *adj* not asked; not asked for; uninvited; (with *for*) unsought. **unassayed'** *adj* not attempted; untested. **unassumed'** *adj.* **unassum'ing** *adj* making no assumption; unpretentious, modest. **unassum'ingly** *adv.* **unassum'ingness** *n.* **unassured'** *adj* uncertain (of); doubtfully recognized (*Spenser*); insecure; lacking in self-assurance, diffident; not insured against loss. **unatōn'able** *adj* that cannot be atoned for; irreconcilable (*archaic*). **unattached'** *adj* not attached; detached; not arrested; not belonging to a club, party, college, diocese, department, regiment, etc; not married; having no romantic and/or sexual attachment to a particular person. **unattaint'ed** *adj* not legally attainted; unstained; not blemished by partiality (*Shakesp*). **unattempt'ed** *adj* not attempted; not made the subject of an attempt or attack. **unattend'ed** *adj* not accompanied or attended; not listened to or paid attention; not attended to (*archaic*). **unatten'tive** *adj* inattentive (the latter being the preferred form). **unaugment'ed** *adj* not augmented;

Some words formed with the prefix **un-**; the numbers in brackets refer to the numbered senses in the entry for **un-**.

unad'vertised *adj* (1).	**unanx'ious** *adj* (1).	**unassist'edly** *adv* (1).
unaffil'iated *adj* (1).	**unapologet'ic** *adj* (1).	**unassist'ing** *adj* (1).
unafraid' *adj* (1).	**unapostol'ic** or **unapostol'ical** *adj* (1).	**unassō'ciated** *adj* (1).
unaid'able *adj* (1).	**unapostol'ically** *adv* (1).	**unassuage'able** *adj* (1).
unaid'ed *adj* (1).	**unappalled'** *adj* (1).	**unassuaged'** *adj* (1).
unaimed' *adj* (1).	**unappar'el** *vt* (2).	**unatōned'** *adj* (1).
unaired' *adj* (1).	**unappar'elled** *adj* (1).	**unattain'able** *adj* (1).
unalike' *adj* (1).	**unappar'ent** *adj* (1).	**unattain'ableness** *n* (1).
unallott'ed *adj* (1).	**unappeal'ing** *adj* (1).	**unattain'ably** *adv* (1).
unallow'able *adj* (1).	**unappeas'able** *adj* (1).	**unattend'ing** *adj* (1).
unalterabil'ity *n* (1).	**unappeased'** *adj* (1).	**unattest'ed** *adj* (1).
unal'terable *adj* (1).	**unapp'etizing** or **unapp'etising** *adj* (1).	**unattīred'** *adj* (1).
unal'terableness *n* (1).	**unapplic'able** *adj* (1).	**unattract'ive** *adj* (1).
unal'terably *adv* (1).	**unapplied'** *adj* (1).	**unattract'ively** *adv* (1).
unal'tered *adj* (1).	**unapprē'ciated** *adj* (1).	**unattract'iveness** *n* (1).
unal'tering *adj* (1).	**unapprē'ciative** *adj* (1).	**unattrib'uted** *adj* (1).
unamazed' *adj* (1).	**unaris'en** *adj* (1).	**unauthen'tic** *adj* (1).
unambig'ūous *adj* (1).	**unarranged'** *adj* (1).	**unauthen'ticated** *adj* (1).
unambig'ūously *adv* (1).	**unartifi'cial** *adj* (1).	**unauthen'ticity** *n* (1).
unambi'tious *adj* (1).	**unartifi'cially** *adv* (1).	**unauthor'itative** *adj* (1).
unambi'tiously *adv* (1).	**unart'istlike** *adj* (1).	**unau'thorized** or **unau'thorised** *adj* (1).
uname'nable *adj* (1).	**unascend'able** or **unascend'ible** *adj* (1).	**unavailabil'ity** *n* (1).
unamend'able *adj* (1).	**unascend'ed** *adj* (1).	**unavenged'** *adj* (1).
unamend'ed *adj* (1).	**unascertain'able** *adj* (1).	**unavert'able** or (*rare*) **unavert'ible** *adj* (1).
unamerced' *adj* (1).	**unascertained'** *adj* (1).	
unāmiabil'ity *n* (1).	**unashamed'** *adj* (1).	**unavowed'** *adj* (1).
unā'miable *adj* (1).	**unasham'edly** *adv* (1).	**unavow'edly** *adv* (1).
unā'miableness *n* (1).	**unas'pirated** *adj* (1).	**unawāk'ened** *adj* (1).
unamū'sable *adj* (1).	**unaspīr'ing** *adj* (1).	**unawāk'ening** *adj* (1).
unamūsed' *adj* (1).	**unaspīr'ingly** *adv* (1).	**unawed'** *adj* (1).
unamū'sing *adj* (1).	**unaspīr'ingness** *n* (1).	**unbaff'led** *adj* (1).
unamū'singly *adv* (1).	**unassail'able** *adj* (1).	**unbail'able** *adj* (1).
unanalys'able or **unanalyz'able** *adj* (1).	**unassailed'** *adj* (1).	**unbait'ed** *adj* (1).
unan'alysed or **unan'alyzed** *adj* (1).	**unasser'tive** *adj* (1).	**unband'ed** *adj* (1).
unanalyt'ic or **unanalyt'ical** *adj* (1).	**unassīgn'able** *adj* (1).	**unbaptize'** or **baptise'** *vt* (2).
unanch'ored *adj* (1).	**unassīgned'** *adj* (1).	**unbaptized'** or **unbaptised'** *adj* (1).
unann'otated *adj* (1).	**unassim'ilable** *adj* (1).	**unbar'bered** *adj* (1).
unannounced' *adj* (1).	**unassim'ilated** *adj* (1).	**unbarred'** *adj* (1).
unantic'ipāted *adj* (1).	**unassist'ed** *adj* (1).	**unbarr'icade** *vt* (2).

■ words derived from main entry word; �□ compound words; ■ idioms and phrasal verbs without the augment (*grammar*). **unauspi'cious** *adj* (*Shakesp*) inauspicious. **unavail'able** *adj* not available; of no avail (*archaic*). **unavail'ableness** *n*. **unavail'ably** *adv*. **unavail'ing** *adj* of no avail or effect, useless. **unavoidabil'ity** *n*. **unavoid'able** *adj* not to be avoided; inevitable; not voidable (*law*). **unavoid'ableness** *n*. **unavoid'ably** *adv*. **unavoid'ed** *adj* not avoided; unavoidable, inevitable (*Shakesp*). **unaware'** *adj* not aware; unwary (*Shelley*). ◆ *adv* unawares. **unaware'ness** *n*. **unawares'** *adv* without being, or making, aware; without being perceived; unexpectedly. ◆ *n* in the phrase **at unawares** unexpectedly, at a sudden disadvantage. **unbacked'** *adj* without a back; without backing or backers; unaided; not moved back; riderless; never yet ridden. **unbag'** *vt* to let out of a bag. **unbaked'** *adj* not baked; immature. **unbal'ance** *n* lack of balance. ◆ *vt* to throw off balance; to derange. **unbal'anced** *adj* not in a state of equilibrium; without a counterpoise or compensation; without mental balance, erratic or deranged; (of eg a view or judgement) not giving due weight to all features of the situation; not adjusted so as to show the difference between debit and credit columns (*bookkeeping*). **unball'asted** *adj* without ballast; unsteady, unstable, flighty. **unbanked'** *adj* not deposited in, provided with, or having, a bank. **unbar'** *vt* to remove a bar from or of; to unfasten. ◆ *vi* to become unbarred. **unbarbed'** *adj* without barb; without bard, caparison or armour (so *prob* in *Shakesp, Coriolanus* III.2.99); uncropped, untrimmed. **unbare'** *vt* to bare, lay bare. **unbark'** *vt* to strip of bark. **unbarked'** *adj* not deprived of bark; deprived of bark. **unbash'ful** *adj* free from bashfulness; shameless (*Shakesp*). **unba'ted** *adj* undiminished; unblunted (*Shakesp*). **unbathed'** *adj* not washed in a bath (**bath¹**); /*un-bādhd¹*/ not soaked or bathed (**bathe**). **unbe'** *vt* (*obs*) to cause not to be. ◆ *vi* (*Hardy*) to cease to be, or be non-existent. **unbear'** *vt* to free from the bearing rein. **unbear'able** *adj* intolerable. **unbear'ableness** *n*. **unbear'ably** *adv*. **unbear'ing** *adj* barren. **unbea'vered** *adj* without a beaver or hat (*archaic*); having the beaver of the helmet open (*hist*). **unbecom'ing** *adj* unsuitable; not suited to the wearer, or not showing her or him to advantage; (of behaviour, etc) not befitting, unseemly (with *to* or *in*, or, *archaic*, without preposition or with *of*). ◆ *n* the transition from existence to non-existence. **unbecom'ingly** *adv*. **unbecom'ingness** *n*. **unbed'** *vt* to rouse, remove or dislodge from a bed. **unbedd'ed** *adj* unstratified; not put to bed. **unbedinned'** *adj* (*Leigh Hunt*) not made noisy.

unbeget' *vt* to undo the begetting of. **unbegged'** *adj* (of a person) not entreated; not begged for. **unbeginn'ing** *adj* without beginning. **unbegot'** or **unbegott'en** *adj* not yet begotten; existing independent of any generating cause. **unbeguile'** *vt* to undeceive. **unbeguiled'** *adj* not deceived. **unbegun'** *adj* not yet begun; without beginning. **unbehol'den** *adj* unseen; under no obligation of gratitude. **unbe'ing** *adj* non-existent. ◆ *n* non-existence. **unbeknown'** or **unbeknownst'** *adj* unknown. ◆ *adv* (with *to*) without the knowledge of, unobserved by. **un'belief'** (or /-*lēf¹*/) *n* disbelief, or withholding of belief, *esp* in accepted religion. **unbeliev'able** *adj* incredible; (loosely) astonishing, remarkable. **unbeliev'ably** *adv*. **unbelieve'** *vt* and *vi* to disbelieve; to refrain from believing; to cease to believe. **unbelieved'** *adj*. **unbeliev'er** *n* a person who does not believe, *esp* in the prevailing religion; a habitually incredulous person. **unbeliev'ing** *adj*. **unbeliev'ingly** *adv*. **unbelt'** *vt* to undo the belt of (a garment). **unbelt'ed** *adj* without a belt; freed from a belt. **unbend'** *vt* to relax (eg a bow) from a bending tension; to straighten; to undo, unfasten (*naut*); to relax (the mind); to allow a frown, etc, to disappear from (the brow, etc). ◆ *vi* to become relaxed; to behave with freedom from stiffness, to be affable. **unbend'able** *adj*. **unbend'ed** *adj*. **unbend'ing** *adj* not bending; unyielding; resolute. ◆ *n* a relaxing. **unbend'ingly** *adv*. **unbend'ingness** *n*. **unbent'** *adj* not bent; relaxed; not overcome or vanquished. **unbeseem'** *vt* to be unbecoming or unsuitable to; to fail to fulfil (*Byron*). **unbeseem'ing** *adj*. **unbeseem'ingly** *adv*. **unbespeak'** *vt* to cancel an order for. **unbi'as** *vt* to free from bias. **unbi'ased** *adj* (sometimes **unbi'assed**). **unbi'asedly** or **unbi'assedly** *adv*. **unbi'asedness** or **unbi'assedness** *n*. **unbib'lical** *adj* contrary to or unwarranted by the Bible. **unbid'** *adj* unbidden; not bid; not prayed for (*Spenser*). **unbidd'en** *adj* not bid or commanded; uninvited; spontaneous. **unbind'** *vt* to remove a band from; to loose; to set free. **unbind'ing** *n* the removal of a band or bond; a loosing; a setting free. ◆ *adj* loosening; not binding. **unbirth'day** *adj* and *n* (*Lewis Carroll*) (relating to) a day other than one's birthday. **unbish'op** *vt* to deprive of the status of bishop. **unbitt'** *vt* (*naut*) to take off from the bitts. **unbitt'ed** *adj* without a bit; unbridled. **unblenched'** (or (*Milton*) /*un¹*/) *adj* unflinching; unstained. **unblench'ing** *adj* unflinching. **unbless'** *vt* to withhold happiness from; to deprive of blessing. **unblessed'** or **unblest'** *adj*. **unbless'edness** *n*. **unblind'** *adj* not blind. ◆ *vt* to free

---

---

from blindness or from blindfolding. **unblind'ed** adj. **unblink'ing** adj without blinking; not wavering; not showing emotion, esp fear. **unblink'ingly** adv. **unblowed'** (Shakesp), **unblown'** (or /un'/) adj not blown; still in the bud, not yet having bloomed. **unblush'ing** adj not blushing; without shame; impudent. **unblush'ingly** adv. **unbod'ied** adj disembodied; not having a body or a form. **unbo'ding** adj not expecting. **unbolt'** vt to draw back a bolt from. ◆ vi to become unbolted; to explain, expound (Shakesp). **unbolt'ed** adj unfastened by withdrawing a bolt; not fastened by bolts; not separated by bolting or sifting; coarse. **unbonn'et** vt to remove the bonnet from. ◆ vi to uncover the head. **unbonn'eted** adj bareheaded; in Shakesp, Othello I.2.25, according to some, without taking off the cap, on equal terms. **unbooked'** adj not entered in a book; unreserved; not literary. **unbook'ish** adj unlearned; not given to or depending on reading; not savouring of books. **unborn'** adj not yet born; non-existent; without beginning. **unborr'owed** adj not borrowed; original. **unbo'som** vt to pour out, tell freely (what is in the mind); to reveal to the eye; (reflexive) to unburden (oneself) confide freely (also vi). **unbo'somer** n. **unbott'omed** adj bottomless; having no foundation or support; not founded (with in or on). **unbought'** adj obtained without buying; not bribed. **unbound'** adj not bound; loose; without binding (also pat and pap of **unbind**, freed from bonds). **unbound'ed** adj not limited; boundless; having no check or control. **unbound'edly** adv. **unbound'edness** n. **unbowed'** adj not bowed or bent; not vanquished or overcome, free. **unbox'** vt to remove from a box or crate. **unbrace'** vt to undo the braces, points or bands of; to loose or relax. **unbraced'** (Spenser **unbräste**') adj not braced; with clothing unfastened; (of a drum) with tension released; relaxed (lit and fig). **unbraid'ed** adj not plaited; untarnished, unfaded (Shakesp). **unbrand'ed** adj without a brand name; not branded. **unbreath'able** adj not fit for breathing. **unbreathed'** adj out of breath; not out of breath; not breathed; not even whispered; not exercised or practised (Shakesp). **unbreathed'-on** untouched by breath, esp the breath of detraction. **unbreath'ing** adj not breathing. **unbred'** adj ill-bred; untrained; not yet born (Shakesp). **unbreech'** vt to remove the breeches, breech or breeching from. **unbreeched'** adj wearing no breeches. **unbrī'dle** vt to free from the bridle; to free from (usu politic) restraint. **unbrī'dled** adj not bridled; unrestrained. **unbrī'dledness** n. **un-Brit'ish** adj not in accordance with British character or traditions.

unbrizzed adj see **unbruised** below. **unbroke'** adj (archaic) unbroken. **unbrō'ken** adj not broken; (of a record) not surpassed; uninterrupted; not thrown into disorder; not variegated; not infringed. **unbrō'kenly** adv. **unbrō'kenness** n. **unbruised'** (Shakesp **un'brused**; Walter Scott **unbrizzed**') adj not bruised or crushed. **unbuck'le** vt to unfasten the buckle(s) of; to unfasten. ◆ vi to undo the buckle(s) of a garment, etc; to unbend (fig). **unbudd'ed** adj not yet in bud; not yet having emerged from the bud. **unbuild'** vt to demolish, pull down. **unbuilt'** (or /un'/) adj not built; not built upon. **unbuilt'-on** adj. **unbun'dle** vi and vt to price and sell separately the constituents of a larger package of products or services; to divide (a business corporation) into separate companies. **unbun'dler** n. **unbun'dling** n. **unbur'den**, (archaic) **unbur'then** vt to free from a burden; to discharge, cast off (eg a burden); (reflexive) to tell one's secrets or anxieties freely, unbosom (oneself). **unbur'dened**, (archaic) **unbur'thened** adj not burdened; relieved of a burden. **unburr'ow** vt and vi to bring or come out of a burrow. **unbur'y** vt to disinter. **unbutt'on** vt to undo the buttons of. ◆ vi to undo one's buttons; to unbend and tell one's thoughts. **unbutt'oned** adj without a button; with buttons undone; in a relaxed confidential state; unrestrained. **uncage'** vt. **uncaged'** adj released from a cage; not confined. **uncalled'** adj not called or summoned; not invited; not called up for payment. **uncalled'-for** adj (or, predicatively, **uncalled for**) not required, unnecessary; unprovoked; offensively or aggressively gratuitous. **uncann'ily** adv. **uncann'iness** n. **uncann'y** adj weird, supernatural; (of eg skill) much greater than one would expect from an ordinary human being; unsafe to associate with; unpleasantly severe (Scot); unsafe (Scot). **uncap'** vt to remove a cap from (eg a container); to remove an upper limit from. ◆ vi to take off one's cap. **uncā'pable** adj (Shakesp) incapable. **uncape'** vi (Shakesp) prob a misprint for **uncope**; explained by some as to uncouple hounds, to unkennel a fox, etc. **uncapped'** adj not having been selected to play for a team, esp a national team; (in cricket) not having been awarded the cap given to regular members of a county side. **uncared'-for** adj (or, predicatively, **uncared for**) neglected; showing signs of neglect. **uncare'ful** adj careless; carefree. **uncar'ing** adj without anxiety, concern or caution; not caring about (Burns). **uncase'** vt to take out of a case; to lay bare; to flay (obs); to undress (Shakesp). ◆ vi (Shakesp) to strip. **uncaused'** adj without any precedent cause, self-existent.

Some words formed with the prefix **un-**; the numbers in brackets refer to the numbered senses in the entry for **un-**.

unclass'y adj (1).
unclear' adj (1).
uncleared' adj (1).
unclear'ly adv (1).
unclear'ness n (1).
unclench' vt and vi (2).
unclimb'able adj (1).
unclimbed' adj (1).
unclipped' or **unclipt'** adj (1).
unclōven' adj (1).
unclub'able or **unclubb'able** adj (1).
unclutt'ered adj (1).
uncoat'ed adj (1).
uncollect'ed adj (1).
uncol'oured adj (1).
uncombed' adj (1).
uncommend'able adj (1).
uncommend'ably adv (1).
uncommend'ed adj (1).
uncommer'cial adj (1).
uncommū'nicable adj (1).
uncommū'nicated adj (1).
uncommū'nicative adj (1).
uncommū'nicativeness n (1).
uncommū'ted adj (1).
uncompact'ed adj (1).
uncompass'ionate adj (1).
uncompelled' adj (1).
uncom'pensated adj (1).
uncompet'itive adj (1).
uncomplain'ing adj (1).
uncomplain'ingly adv (1).
uncomplais'ant adj (1).
uncomplais'antly adv (1).
uncomplē'ted adj (1).
uncomplī'ant adj (1).
uncomply'ing adj (1).
uncomprehend'ed adj (1).
uncomprehend'ing adj (1).

unconceal'able adj (1).
unconcealed' adj (1).
unconceal'ing adj (1).
unconcert'ed adj (1).
unconcil'iatory adj (1).
unconfed'erated adj (1).
unconfessed' adj (1).
uncon'fident adj (1).
unconfused' adj (1).
unconfus'edly adv (1).
uncongē'nial adj (1).
uncongēnial'ity n (1).
unconject'ured adj (1).
unconnect'ed adj (1).
unconq'uerable adj (1).
unconq'uerableness n (1).
unconq'uerably adv (1).
unconq'uered adj (1).
unconscien'tious adj (1).
unconscien'tiously adv (1).
unconscien'tiousness n (1).
unconsent'ing adj (1).
unconsoled' adj (1).
unconsol'idated adj (1).
unconstitū'tional adj (1).
unconstitūtional'ity n (1).
unconstitū'tionally adv (1).
unconsumed' adj (1).
uncon'summated adj (1).
uncontain'able adj (1).
uncontam'inated adj (1).
uncon'templated adj (1).
unconten'tious adj (1).
uncontradict'ed adj (1).
uncontrived' adj (1).
uncontrover'sial adj (1).
unconvers'ant adj (1).
unconvert'ed adj (1).
unconvert'ible adj (1).

unconvict'ed adj (1).
unconvinced' adj (1).
unconvinc'ing adj (1).
uncooked' adj (1).
unco-op'erative or **uncoop'erative** adj (1).
unco-op'eratively or **uncoop'eratively** adv (1).
uncoquett'ish adj (1).
uncor'dial adj (1).
uncork' vt (2).
uncorrect'ed adj (1).
uncorrob'orated adj (1).
uncor'seted adj (1).
uncount'able adj (1).
uncount'ed adj (1).
uncourt'liness n (1).
uncourt'ly adj (1).
uncrate' vt (2).
uncropped' adj (1).
uncross'able adj (1).
uncrow'ded adj (1).
uncrump'le vt (2).
uncrush'able adj (1).
uncrystallīz'able or **uncrystallīs'able** adj (1).
uncrys'tallized or **uncrys'tallised** adj (1).
uncuck'olded adj (1).
unculled' adj (1).
uncult'ivable or **uncultivāt'able** adj (1).
uncult'ivated adj (1).
uncum'bered adj (1).
uncurb'able adj (1).
uncurbed' adj (1).
uncurd'led adj (1).
uncured' adj (1).
uncurr'ent adj (1).
uncurtailed' adj (1).
uncurved' adj (1).

■ words derived from main entry word; ❑ compound words; ■ idioms and phrasal verbs

unceas'ing *adj* ceaseless; never-ending. **unceas'ingly** *adv*. **unceremō'nious** *adj* informal; off-hand. **unceremō'niously** *adv*. **unceremō'niousness** *n*. **uncer'tain** *adj* not certain (with *of* or *about*); not definitely known or decided; subject to doubt or question (**in no uncertain terms** unambiguously); not to be depended upon; subject to vicissitude; hesitant, lacking confidence. **uncer'tainly** *adv*. **uncer'tainness** *n*. **uncer'tainty** *n* (**uncertainty principle** the principle that there is a limit (a) to the precision with which the position and momentum of a particle can be simultaneously known and (b) to the knowledge of the energy of a particle when it is measured for a finite time (also called **indeterminacy principle** or **Heisenberg('s) (uncertainty) principle**)). **uncer'tified** *adj* not assured, attested or guaranteed. **uncess'ant** *adj* (*Milton*) incessant. **unchain'** *vt* to release from a chain; to remove a chain from; to let loose. **unchained'** *adj*. **unchan'cy** *adj* (*Scot*) unlucky; ill-omened; dangerous; ticklish. **uncharge'** *vt* to unload; to acquit (*Shakesp*). **uncharged'** *adj* not charged; not attacked (*Shakesp*). **unchar'ity** *n* lack of charity. **uncharm'** *vt* to free from a spell; to destroy the magical power of. **uncharmed'** *adj* not affected by a spell; not charmed. **unchar'ming** *adj* not charming or attractive. **unchar'nel** *vt* to take from a charnel. **unchart'ed** *adj* (*lit* and *fig*) not mapped in detail; not shown in a chart; not yet examined, investigated or visited. **unchart'ered** *adj* not holding a charter; unauthorized. **unchas'tity** *n* lack or breach of chastity. **uncheck'** *vt* (*Shakesp*) to fail to check. **uncheck'able** *adj*. **unchecked'** *adj* not checked or verified; not restrained; not marked with a tick (*N Am*); (of a square in a crossword puzzle) holding a letter that forms part of one word-solution only; not contradicted (*Shakesp*). **unchild'** *vt* (*Shakesp*) to make childless; to change from being a child. **unchild'like** *adj*. **unchris'om** *adj* (*Lamb*) unchristened. **unchrist'en** *vt* to annul the christening of; to deprive of a name; to unchristianize (*Milton*). **unchrist'ened** *adj* unbaptized; without a name. **unchris'tian** *adj* against the spirit of Christianity; non-Christian (*rare*); uncharitable; unreasonable, outrageous (*inf*). ◆ *vt* (*obs*) to unchristianize. **unchris'tianize** or **-ise** *vt* to cause to change from the Christian faith or character. **unchris'tianlike** *adj*. **unchris'tianly** *adv*. ◆ *adj* unchristianlike. **unchurch'** *vt* to deprive of church membership or of the possession of a church; to take the status of a church from. **unci'pher** *vt* (*obs*) to decipher. **uncir'cumcised** *adj* not circumcised; gentile; unpurified (*fig*). **uncircumcis'ion** *n*

uncircumcised condition; the uncircumcised, the gentiles (*Bible*). **unciv'il** *adj* discourteous; unseemly; against the civic good; not civilized (*Spenser*). **unciv'ilized** or **-s-** *adj* not civilized; away from civilized communities; rough, impolite. **unciv'illy** *adv*. **unclasp'** *vt* to loose from a clasp; to relax from clasping; to open. ◆ *vi* to close in a clasp. **unclassed'** *adj* without class divisions; unclassified; not placed in a class. **unclass'ifīable** (or /-fī'/) *adj* that cannot be classified. **unclass'ified** *adj* not classified; (of a road) minor, not classified as a motorway, A-road or B-road; (of information) not given a special security classification. **unclean** /-klēn'/ *adj* not clean; foul; ceremonially impure; lewd. **uncleaned'** *adj* not cleaned. **uncleanliness** /-klen'/ *n*. **uncleanly** /-klen'/ *adj* not clean in habits or person. ◆ *adv* /-klēn'/ not done or performed cleanly. **uncleanness** /-klēn'nis/ *n*. **uncleansed** /-klenzd'/ *adj*. **uncler'ical** *adj* not characteristic of, or befitting, a clergyman. **unclew'** *vt* (*archaic*) to unwind, unfold or undo. **uncloak'** *vt* to divest of a cloak; to show up. ◆ *vi* to take one's cloak off. **unclog'** *vt* to free from a clog or obstruction. **unclogged'** *adj* not clogged. **unclois'ter** *vt* to free or remove from the cloister. **unclois'tered** *adj* not cloistered; without a cloister; freed or taken from a cloister. **unclose** /un-klōz'/ *vt* and *vi* to open. ◆ *adj* /-klōs'/ not close. **unclosed** /un-klōzd'/ *adj* not closed; unenclosed; opened. **unclothe'** *vt* to take the clothes off; to divest of covering. **unclothed'** *adj*. **uncloud'** *vt* and *vi* to clear of clouds or obscurity. **uncloud'ed** *adj* free from clouds, obscurity or gloom; calm. **uncloud'edness** *n*. **uncloud'y** *adj*. **unclutch'** *vt* to release from a clutch. **uncock'** *vt* to let down the hammer of (a gun); to spread out from a haycock. **uncoff'ined** *adj* not put into a coffin; removed from a coffin. **uncoil'** *vt* and *vi* to unwind. **uncoined'** *adj* not coined; (*Shakesp* **uncoyned**) variously explained, but *prob* meaning 'natural', 'not artificial or counterfeit'. **uncolt'** *vt* (*Shakesp*, punning on Falstaff's use of *colt* to cheat, *1 Henry IV* II.2.38) to deprive of a horse. **uncomatable** or **uncomeatable** /un-kum-at'ə-bl/ *adj* inaccessible; out of reach. **uncombine'** *vt* and *vi* (*Dickens*) to separate. **uncome'liness** *n*. **uncome'ly** *adj* not comely; indecent; unseemly. **uncom'fortable** *adj* feeling, involving or causing discomfort or unease. **uncom'fortableness** *n*. **uncom'fortably** *adv*. **uncom'forted** *adj*. **uncom'fy** *adj* (*inf*) uncomfortable. **uncommitt'ed** *adj* not pledged to support any party, policy or action; impartial; not committed (**uncommitted logic array** (*comput*) a microchip whose logic circuits

---

Some words formed with the prefix **un-**; the numbers in brackets refer to the numbered senses in the entry for **un-**.

undam' *vt* (2).	**undescend'ible** or **undescend'able** *adj*	**undissolved'** *adj* (1).
undam'aged *adj* (1).	(1).	**undissol'ving** *adj* (1).
undammed' *adj* (1), (2).	**undescried'** *adj* (1).	**undistilled'** *adj* (1).
undamned' *adj* (1).	**undespair'ing** *adj* (1).	**undistort'ed** *adj* (1).
undamped' *adj* (1).	**undespair'ingly** *adv* (1).	**undistract'ed** *adj* (1).
undaunt'able *adj* (1).	**undespoiled'** *adj* (1).	**undistract'edly** *adv* (1).
undealt' *adj* (1).	**undestroyed'** *adj* (1).	**undistract'edness** *n* (1).
undear' *adj* (1).	**undetect'able** *adj* (1).	**undistract'ing** *adj* (1).
undebarred' *adj* (1).	**undetect'ed** *adj* (1).	**undisturbed'** *adj* (1).
undebased' *adj* (1).	**undē'viating** *adj* (1).	**undistur'bedly** *adv* (1).
undebauched' *adj* (1).	**undē'viatingly** *adv* (1).	**undistur'bing** *adj* (1).
undecayed' *adj* (1).	**undevout'** *adj* (1).	**undivers'ified** *adj* (1).
undecīd'able *adj* (1).	**undiagnosed'** *adj* (1).	**undivine'** *adj* (1).
undeclared' *adj* (1).	**undigest'ed** *adj* (1).	**undivorced'** *adj* (1).
undecompōs'able *adj* (1).	**undilut'ed** *adj* (1).	**undivulged'** *adj* (1).
undecomposed' *adj* (1).	**undimin'ishable** *adj* (1).	**undoc'umented** *adj* (1).
undec'orated *adj* (1).	**undimin'ished** *adj* (1).	**undoomed'** *adj* (1).
undefaced' *adj* (1).	**undimmed'** *adj* (1).	**undrain'able** *adj* (1).
undefeat'ed *adj* (1).	**undint'ed** *adj* (1).	**undrained'** *adj* (1).
undefend'ed *adj* (1).	**undiplomat'ic** *adj* (1).	**undramat'ic** *adj* (1).
undefiled' *adj* (1).	**undirect'ed** *adj* (1).	**undread'ed** *adj* (1).
undelayed' *adj* (1).	**undisappoint'ing** *adj* (1).	**undread'ing** *adj* (1).
undelay'ing *adj* (1).	**undisclosed'** *adj* (1).	**undream'ing** *adj* (1).
undelect'able *adj* (1).	**undiscom'fited** *adj* (1).	**undried'** *adj* (1).
undel'egated *adj* (1).	**undiscord'ant** *adj* (1).	**undrilled'** *adj* (1).
undelib'erate *adj* (1).	**undiscour'aged** *adj* (1).	**undrink'able** *adj* (1).
undeliv'erable *adj* (1).	**undiscov'erable** *adj* (1).	**undrive'able** *adj* (1).
undeliv'ered *adj* (1).	**undiscov'erably** *adv* (1).	**undriv'en** *adj* (1).
undelud'ed *adj* (1).	**undiscov'ered** *adj* (1).	**undroop'ing** *adj* (1).
undemand'ing *adj* (1).	**undiscuss'able** or **undiscuss'ible** *adj* (1).	**undrowned'** *adj* (1).
undemocrat'ic *adj* (1).	**undishon'oured** *adj* (1).	**undrunk'** *adj* (1).
undemon'strable *adj* (1).	**undismant'led** *adj* (1).	**undubbed'** *adj* (1).
undemon'strative *adj* (1).	**undismayed'** *adj* (1).	**undug'** *adj* (1).
undemon'strativeness *n* (1).	**undisor'dered** *adj* (1).	**undulled'** *adj* (1).
undeplored' *adj* (1).	**undispatched'** *adj* (1).	**uneat'able** *adj* (1).
undepraved' *adj* (1).	**undispensed'** *adj* (1).	**uneat'ableness** *n* (1).
undeprē'ciated *adj* (1).	**undispūt'ed** *adj* (1).	**uneat'en** *adj* (1).
undepressed' *adj* (1).	**undispūt'edly** *adv* (1).	**uneclipsed'** *adj* (1).
undeprived' *adj* (1).	**undissō'ciated** *adj* (1).	**uned'ucable** *adj* (1).

---

are left unconnected during manufacture and completed later to the customer's specification (*abbrev* **ULA** or **ula**)). **uncomm'on** *adj* not common; unusual; remarkably great; strange. ◆ *adv* (*old sl*) remarkably, very. **uncomm'only** *adv* rarely (*esp* in *not uncommonly*, frequently); in an unusually great degree. **uncomm'onness** *n*. **uncom'panied** *adj* unaccompanied. **uncompan'ionable** *adj* unsociable. **uncompan'ioned** *adj* without a companion or an equal. **uncom'plicated** *adj* straightforward, not made difficult by the variety of factors involved; (of a person) simple in character and outlook. **uncompliment'ary** *adj* not at all complimentary, derogatory. **uncompō'sable** *adj* incapable of being composed or reconciled. **uncompound'ed** *adj* not compounded, unmixed; not worsened or intensified. **uncomprehen'sive** *adj* not comprehensive; incomprehensible (*Shakesp*). **uncom'promising** *adj* refusing to compromise; unyielding; out-and-out. **uncom'promisingly** *adv*. **uncom'promisingness** *n*. **unconceiv'able** *adj* inconceivable. **unconceiv'ableness** *n*. **unconceiv'ably** *adv*. **unconceived'** *adj*. **unconcern'** *n* lack of concern or anxiety; indifference. **unconcerned'** *adj* not concerned, not involved (in); impartial; uninterested; indifferent; untroubled, carelessly secure; sober, unaffected by liquor (*obs*). **unconcern'edly** *adv*. **unconcern'edness** *n*. **unconcern'ing** *adj*. **unconcern'ment** *n*. **unconclu'sive** *adj* inconclusive. **unconcoct'ed** *adj* not digested; crude; not elaborated or finished (*fig*). **uncondi'tional** *adj* not conditional; absolute, unlimited. **unconditional'ity** *n*. **uncondi'tionally** *adv*. **uncondi'tionalness** *n*. **uncondi'tioned** *adj* not subject to condition or limitation; infinite, absolute, unknowable; (of a person, response, etc) not conditioned by learning or experience (**unconditioned stimulus** one provoking an unconditioned response); not put into the required state. **unconfī'nable** *adj* not to be confined; unbounded (*Shakesp*). **unconfine'** *vt* to release from restraint; to divulge (*Keats*). **unconfined'** *adj* not confined; not restricted; unlimited; set free. **unconfī'nedly** *adv*. **unconfirmed'** *adj* not confirmed; not yet having received confirmation; uncorroborated; not yet firm or strong; ignorant (*Shakesp*). **unconform'** *adj* (*Milton*) unlike. **unconformabil'ity** *n* the state or the quality of being unconformable; an unconformity in stratification (*geol*). **unconform'able** *adj* not conforming (to eg *hist*, the practices of the Church of England); unwilling to conform; showing an unconformability (*geol*). **unconform'ableness** *n*.

unconform'ably *adv*. **unconform'ing** *adj* not conforming. **unconform'ity** *n* lack of conformity (*archaic*); nonconformity (*obs*); a substantial break in the succession of stratified sedimentary rocks, following a period of non-deposition (*geol*). **uncongeal'** *vt* and *vi* to thaw, melt. **uncon'jugal** *adj* (*Milton*) not suited to, or fitting in, marriage. **unconjunc'tive** *adj* (*Milton*) impossible to be joined. **unconni'ving** *adj* (*Milton*) refusing indulgence. **uncon'scionable** *adj* (of a person) unscrupulous; not conformable to conscience; outrageous, unthinkable, inordinate. **uncon'scionableness** *n*. **uncon'scionably** *adv*. **uncon'scious** *adj* without consciousness; unaware (with *of*); present within one but unrecognized; not self-conscious. ◆ *n* (with *the*) the deepest, inaccessible level of the psyche in which repressed impulses and memories are present in dynamic state. **uncon'sciously** *adv*. **uncon'sciousness** *n*. **uncon'secrate** *vt* to deprive of the character or state of consecration. ◆ *adj* unconsecrated. **uncon'secrated** *adj* not consecrated. **unconsentā'neous** *adj* (*Thomas Love Peacock*) not in agreement. **unconsid'ered** *adj* not valued or esteemed; done without considering. **unconsid'ering** *adj*. **uncon'stant** *adj* (*Shakesp*) inconstant. **unconstrain'able** *adj*. **unconstrained'** *adj*. **unconstrain'edly** *adv*. **unconstraint'** *n* absence of constraint. **uncontemned'** *adj* (*Shakesp*) not despised. **uncontest'able** *adj* incontestable. **uncontest'ed** *adj*. **uncontrōll'able** *adj* not capable of being controlled; absolute, not controlled (*archaic*); indisputable (*obs*). **uncontrōll'ableness** *n*. **uncontrōll'ably** *adv*. **uncontrolled'** *adj* not controlled; not disputed (*obs*). **uncontrōll'edly** *adv*. **uncontrovert'ed** *adj* not disputed. **uncontrovert'ible** *adj*. **unconven'tional** *adj* not conventional; free in one's ways. **unconventional'ity** *n*. **unconvers'able** *adj* not able or not disposed to converse freely. **uncool'** *adj* (*derog inf*) not sophisticated or smart, old-fashioned; not relaxed or calm. **unco-or'dinated** or **uncoor'dinated** *adj* not co-ordinated; having clumsy movements, as if muscles were not co-ordinated. **uncope'** *vt* to unmuzzle, or unsew the mouth of (a ferret; cf **uncape** above). **uncord'** *vt* to free (eg a trunk) from cords. **uncorrupt'** *adj* incorrupt. **uncorrupt'ed** *adj*. **uncost'ly** *adj* inexpensive. **uncoun'selled** *adj* not given advice; not advised. **uncoup'le** *vt* to undo the coupling of; to release. ◆ *vi* to become detached; to uncouple hounds. **uncoup'led** *adj* not married; detached. **uncour'teous** *adj* discourteous. **uncouth** /*un-kooth'*/ *adj*

---

uned'ucated *adj* (1).	**unespied'** *adj* (1).	**unexplored'** *adj* (1).
uneffaced' *adj* (1).	**unessayed'** *adj* (1).	**unexposed'** *adj* (1).
uneffect'ed *adj* (1).	**uneth'ical** *adj* (1).	**unexpressed'** *adj* (1).
unelab'orate *adj* (1).	**unevangel'ical** *adj* (1).	**unexpress'ible** *adj* (1).
unelab'orated *adj* (1).	**unē'ven** *adj* (1).	**unex'purgated** *adj* (1).
unelat'ed *adj* (1).	**unē'venly** *adv* (1).	**unexten'ded** *adj* (1).
unelect'able *adj* (1).	**unē'venness** *n* (1).	**unexten'uated** *adj* (1).
unelect'ed *adj* (1).	**unevent'ful** *adj* (1).	**unexting'uishable** *adj* (1).
unelect'rified *adj* (1).	**unevent'fully** *adv* (1).	**unexting'uishably** *adv* (1).
unembarr'assed *adj* (1).	**unev'idenced** *adj* (1).	**unexting'uished** *adj* (1).
unembell'ished *adj* (1).	**unexact'ing** *adj* (1).	**unextreme'** *adj* (1).
unembitt'ered *adj* (1).	**unexagg'erated** *adj* (1).	**unfa'dable** *adj* (1).
unembod'ied *adj* (1).	**unexalt'ed** *adj* (1).	**unfa'ded** *adj* (1).
unemphat'ic *adj* (1).	**unexam'ined** *adj* (1).	**unfa'ding** *adj* (1).
unemp'tied *adj* (1).	**unex'cavated** *adj* (1).	**unfa'dingly** *adv* (1).
unenclosed' *adj* (1).	**unexcelled'** *adj* (1).	**unfa'dingness** *n* (1).
unencumb'ered *adj* (1).	**unexcī'table** *adj* (1).	**unfall'en** *adj* (1).
unendang'ered *adj* (1).	**unexcī'ted** *adj* (1).	**unfal'tering** *adj* (1).
unendowed' *adj* (1).	**unexcī'ting** *adj* (1).	**unfal'teringly** *adv* (1).
unendūr'able *adj* (1).	**unexclu'ded** *adj* (1).	**unfamed'** *adj* (1).
unendūr'ably *adv* (1).	**unexclu'sive** *adj* (1).	**unfamil'iar** *adj* (1).
unengaged' *adj* (1).	**unexclu'sively** *adv* (1).	**unfamiliar'ity** *n* (1).
unenjoy'able *adj* (1).	**unexem'plified** *adj* (1).	**unfamil'iarly** *adv* (1).
unenlight'ened *adj* (1).	**unex'ercised** *adj* (1).	**unfanned'** *adj* (1).
unenquīr'ing *adj* (1).	**unexhaus'ted** *adj* (1).	**unfastid'ious** *adj* (1).
unenriched' *adj* (1).	**unexpan'ded** *adj* (1).	**unfault'y** *adj* (1).
unenslaved' *adj* (1).	**unexpec'tant** *adj* (1).	**unfa'vourable** *adj* (1).
unentailed' *adj* (1).	**unexpec'ted** *adj* (1).	**unfa'vourableness** *n* (1).
unen'tered *adj* (1).	**unexpec'tedly** *adv* (1).	**unfa'vourably** *adv* (1).
unen'terprising *adj* (1).	**unexpec'tedness** *n* (1).	**unfeas'ible** *adj* (1).
unentertained' *adj* (1).	**unexpen'sive** *adj* (1).	**unfeath'ered** *adj* (1).
unentertain'ing *adj* (1).	**unexpen'sively** *adv* (1).	**unfed'** *adj* (1).
unenthralled' *adj* (1).	**unexpē'rienced** *adj* (1).	**unfelled'** *adj* (1).
unenthusiast'ic *adj* (1).	**unex'piated** *adj* (1).	**unfem'inine** *adj* (1).
unentīt'led *adj* (1).	**unexpired'** *adj* (1).	**unfenced'** *adj* (1).
uneq'uable *adj* (1).	**unexplain'able** *adj* (1).	**unferment'ed** *adj* (1).
unerā'sable *adj* (1).	**unexplained'** *adj* (1).	**unfer'tilized** or **unfer'tilised** *adj* (1).
unescāp'able *adj* (1).	**unexplō'ded** *adj* (1).	**unfeued'** *adj* (1).
unescort'ed *adj* (1).	**unexploit'ed** *adj* (1).	**unfig'ured** *adj* (1).

(OE *uncūth* unknown or strange, from *un-*, and *cūth*, known) awkward, ungraceful, uncultured, *esp* in manners or language; strange and wild or unattractive; unfamiliar (*archaic*); unknown (*obs*); see also separate entry **unco**. **uncouth'ly** *adv*. **uncouth'ness** *n*. **uncov'enanted** *adj* not promised or bound by covenant; not included in a covenant; not having subscribed to the Solemn League and Covenant of 1643. **uncov'er** *vt* to remove the cover of; to lay open; to expose; to drive out of cover. ◆ *vi* to take off one's hat or other head covering. **uncov'ered** *adj*. **uncowl'** *vt* to withdraw the cowl from. **uncowled'** *adj*. **uncoyned** *adj* see **uncoined** above. **uncreate'** *vt* to deprive of existence. **uncrea'ted** *adj* not (yet) created; not produced by creation (*Milton*). **uncreat'edness** *n*. **uncrea'ting** *adj*. **uncred'ible** *adj* (*obs*) incredible. **uncred'itable** *adj* (*obs*) discreditable. **uncred'ited** *adj* not acknowledged. **uncrit'ical** *adj* not critical, without discrimination; not in accordance with the principles of criticism. **uncrit'ically** *adv*. **uncross'** *vt* to change or move from a crossed position. **uncrossed'** *adj* not crossed; not passed over, marked with a cross, thwarted, etc; not marked off as paid (*Shakesp*). **uncrown'** *vt* to dethrone; to remove the crown from. **uncrowned'** *adj* not crowned; not yet formally crowned; possessing kingly power without the actual title (**uncrowned king** or **queen** (*facetious*) a man or woman having supreme influence, or commanding the highest respect, within a particular group); unfulfilled. **uncrudd'ed** *adj* (*Spenser*) uncurdled. **uncul'tured** *adj* not cultured; not cultivated. **uncūr'able** *adj* (*Shakesp*) incurable. **uncū'rious** *adj* incurious; not strange. **uncurl'** *vt* and *vi* to take or come out of a curl, twist or roll. **uncurled'** *adj* not curled; unrolled or uncoiled. **uncurl'ing** *adj*. **uncurse'** *vt* to free from a curse, unsay a curse upon. **uncur'tain** *vt* to remove a curtain from. **uncur'tained** *adj* curtainless. **uncus'tomed** *adj* (of goods) on which customs duty is unpaid, or not payable; unaccustomed (*archaic*); not customary (*archaic*). **uncut'** *adj* not cut; not shaped by cutting; not abridged; (of a book) (bibliographically) with margins not cut down by the binder (even though opened with a paper-cutter), (*popularly*) unopened; (of illegal drugs) not adulterated. **undashed'** *adj* undismayed. **undāt'ed** *adj* with no date marked or assigned; unending. **undaunt'ed** *adj* not daunted; bold, intrepid. **undaunt'edly** *adv*. **undaunt'edness** *n*. **undawn'ing** *adj* not yet dawning or showing light. **undazz'le** *vi* (*Tennyson*) to recover from a dazed state. **undazz'led** *adj* not dazzled. **undead'** *adj* (of a ghost, vampire, etc) dead but not at rest. ◆ *n* (with *the*) such spirits. **undeaf'** *vt* (*Shakesp*) to free from deafness. **undeceiv'able** *adj* incapable of being deceived; incapable of deceiving (*obs*). **undeceive'** *vt* to free from a mistaken belief, reveal the truth to. **undeceived'** *adj* not deceived; set free from a delusion. **undē'cent** *adj* indecent (*dialect*); unfitting (*archaic*); unhandsome (*obs*). **undecīd'ed** *adj* not decided or settled; uncertain, irresolute. **undecīd'edly** *adv*. **undecī'pherable** *adj* indecipherable. **undecī'sive** *adj* indecisive. **undeck'** *vt* to divest of ornaments. **undecked'** *adj* not adorned; having no deck. **undeclīn'ing** *adj* unbowed, unsubmissive. **undeed'ed** *adj* (*Shakesp*) unused in any action. **undefied'** (or *Spenser* **undefide'**) *adj* not defied or challenged. **undefīn'able** *adj*. **undefined'** *adj* not defined; indefinite. **undē'ify** *vt* to deprive of the nature or honour of a god. **undelete'** *vt* (*comput*) to restore (text or a file that has been deleted). **undelight'** *n* lack of delight. **undelight'ed** *adj*. **undelight'ful** *adj*. **undenī'able** *adj* not to be denied, indisputable; not to be refused; obviously true; unexceptionable, excellent (*old*). **undenī'ableness** *n*. **undenī'ably** *adv* certainly, one cannot deny it. **undenominā'tional** *adj* not confined to or favouring any particular sect. **undenominā'tionalism** *n*. **undepend'able** *adj* not to be depended upon. **undepen'dableness** *n*. **undepen'ding** *adj* (*obs*) independent. **undescen'ded** *adj* (of the testes) remaining in the abdominal cavity, failing to move down into the scrotum. **undescrī'bable** *adj* indescribable. **undescribed'** *adj*. **un'desert** *n* lack of merit, unworthiness. **undeserve'** *vt* to fail or cease to deserve. **undeserved'** *adj* not deserved. **undeser'vedly** *adv*. **undeser'vedness** *n*. **undeser'ver** *n* (*Shakesp*) someone who is not deserving or worthy. **undeser'ving** *adj*. **undeser'vingly** *adv*. **undesigned'** *adj*. **undesign'edly** *adv*. **undesign'edness** *n*. **undesign'ing** *adj* not designing; artless; straightforward; sincere. **undesirabil'ity** *n*. **undesīr'able** *adj* not to be wished for; not sexually desirable. ◆ *n* an undesirable or objectionable person or thing. **undesīr'ableness** *n*. **undesīr'ably** *adv*. **undesired'** *adj*. **undesīr'ing** *adj*. **undesīr'ous** *adj*. **undeter'minable** *adj* indeterminable. **undeter'minate** *adj* indeterminate. **undeter'minateness** *n*. **undeterminā'tion** *n*. **undeter'mined** *adj* not settled, not fixed; not ascertained; not limited. **undeterred'** *adj* not discouraged or prevented (from). **undevel'oped** *adj* not developed; (of land) not built on or used for public works. **undid'** *vt pat* of **undo**. **undiff'erenced** *adj* (*heraldry*) without a

---

unfil'ial *adj* (1).
unfil'ially *adv* (1).
unfill'able *adj* (1).
unfilled' *adj* (1).
unfilmed' *adj* (1).
unfil'tered *adj* (1).
unfired' *adj* (1).
unfirm' *adj* (1).
unfished' *adj* (1).
unflagg'ing *adj* (1).
unflagg'ingly *adv* (1).
unflatt'ering *adj* (1).
unflatt'eringly *adv* (1).
unflā'voured *adj* (1).
unflawed' *adj* (1).
unflinch'ing *adj* (1).
unflinch'ingly *adv* (1).
unfloored' *adj* (1).
unflus'tered *adj* (1).
unfō'cused or **unfō'cussed** *adj* (1).
unforbid' (*Milton*) or **unforbidd'en** *adj* (1).
unford'able *adj* (1).
unforeknow'able *adj* (1).
unforeknown' *adj* (1).
unforesee'able *adj* (1).
unforesee'ing *adj* (1).
unforeseen' *adj* (1).
unforetold' *adj* (1).
unforewarned' *adj* (1).
unfor'feited *adj* (1).
unforged' *adj* (1).
unforgett'able *adj* (1).
unforgett'ably *adv* (1).
unforgiv'able *adj* (1).
unforgiv'en *adj* (1).
unforgiv'eness *n* (1).
unforgiv'ing *adj* (1).
unforgiv'ingness *n* (1).

unforgott'en (*archaic* **unforgot'**) *adj* (1).
unfor'matted *adj* (1).
unfor'midable *adj* (1).
unform'ulated *adj* (1).
unforsā'ken *adj* (1).
unforthcom'ing *adj* (1).
unfor'tified *adj* (1).
unfossilif'erous *adj* (1).
unfoss'ilized or **unfoss'ilised** *adj* (1).
unfos'tered *adj* (1).
unfran'chised *adj* (1).
unfranked' *adj* (1).
unfrē'quent *adj* (1).
unfrequen'ted *adj* (1).
unfrequent'edness *n* (1).
unfrē'quently *adv* (1).
unfright'ened *adj* (1).
unfrō'zen *adj* (1).
unfruc'tuous *adj* (1).
unfruit'ful *adj* (1).
unfruit'fully *adv* (1).
unfruit'fulness *n* (1).
unfū'elled *adj* (1).
unfulfilled' *adj* (1).
unfunn'y *adj* (1).
unfurred' *adj* (1).
unfurr'owed *adj* (1).
ungag' *vt* (2).
ungainsaid' *adj* (1).
ungainsay'able *adj* (1).
ungall'ant *adj* (1).
ungall'antly *adv* (1).
ungar'bled *adj* (1).
ungar'mented *adj* (1).
ungar'nered *adj* (1).
ungar'nished *adj* (1).
ungar'tered *adj* (1).
ungath'ered *adj* (1).
ungauged' *adj* (1).

ungen'erous *adj* (1).
ungen'erously *adv* (1).
ungenteel' *adj* (1).
ungenteel'ly *adv* (1).
ungen'uine *adj* (1).
ungen'uineness *n* (1).
ungift'ed *adj* (1).
ungild' *vt* (2).
ungild'ed *adj* (1).
ungilt' *adj* (1).
ungiv'ing *adj* (1).
unglad' *adj* (1).
unglam'orous *adj* (1).
unglazed' *adj* (1).
unglossed' *adj* (1).
unglove' *vt* (2).
ungloved' *adj* (1).
ungraced' *adj* (1).
ungrace'ful *adj* (1).
ungrace'fully *adv* (1).
ungrace'fulness *n* (1).
ungrammat'ic or **ungrammat'ical** *adj* (1).
ungrammat'ically *adv* (1).
ungrasp'able *adj* (1).
ungrat'ified *adj* (1).
ungrav'ly (*Shakesp*) *adj* (1).
ungroomed' *adj* (1).
ungrown' *adj* (1).
ungrudged' *adj* (1).
ungrudg'ing *adj* (1).
ungrudg'ingly *adv* (1).
unguer'doned *adj* (1).
unguessed' *adj* (1).
unguid'ed *adj* (1).
unguil'ty *adj* (1).
ungyve' *vt* (2).
ungyved' *adj* (1).
unhab'itable *adj* (1).
unhabit'uated *adj* (1).

---

modification to distinguish a cadet from the main line. **undifferen'tiated** *adj* not differentiated. **undight** /*un-dīt'*/ *vt* (*pat* and *pap* **undight'**) (*Spenser*) to undo, take off, doff. ◆ *adj* unadorned; not dressed, (of hair) loose (*Spenser*, etc). **undig'nified** *adj*. **undig'nify** *vt* to deprive of dignity. **undipped'** *adj* not dipped; unbaptized. **undiscerned'** *adj* unobserved, unperceived. **undiscern'edly** *adv*. **undiscern'ible** *adj*. **undiscern'ibly** *adv*. **undiscern'ing** *adj* showing lack of discernment or discrimination. ◆ *n* lack of discernment. **undischarged'** *adj* not paid or settled; (of eg an obligation) not carried out; not released from debt or other liability; (of a gun) not fired. **undisc'iplinable** *adj*. **undisc'ipline** *n* lack of discipline. **undisc'iplined** *adj* untrained; unruly. **undiscord'ing** *adj* (*Milton*) not discordant. **undiscrim'inating** *adj* not making distinctions; not showing critical taste or ability. **undiscussed'** *adj* not discussed; unsettled (*obs*). **undisguis'able** *adj*. **undisguised'** *adj* not disguised; frank, open. **undisguis'edly** *adv*. **undisposed'** *adj* not disposed (*usu* with *-of*); disinclined (*Shakesp*); disinclined (to do, or with *to*). **undissem'bled** *adj* unfeigned; undisguised, unconcealed. **undistemp'ered** *adj* not deranged, disturbed, ruffled or in unhealthy condition. **undistinc'tive** *adj* not distinctive; not distinguishing clearly. **undisting'uishable** *adj* indistinguishable. **undisting'uishableness** *n*. **undisting'uishably** *adv*. **undisting'uished** *adj* not distinguished or observed; not marked out by conspicuous qualities, not famous; not having an air of distinction. **undisting'uishing** *adj* not discriminating. **undistrib'uted** *adj* not distributed (**undistributed middle** the fallacy of reasoning without distributing the middle term, ie without making it universal, in at least one premise). **undivert'ed** *adj* not turned away; not amused. **undivert'ing** *adj*. **undivest'ed** *adj* (*Richardson*) detached. **undivest'edly** *adv*. **undivid'able** *adj* indivisible. **undivī'ded** *adj* not divided; (of one's attention to something) wholly concentrated, not distracted. **undivī'dedly** *adv*. **undivī'dedness** *n*. **undo** *vt* (*pat* **undid'**; *pap* **undone** /*un-dun'*/ (see also below)) /*un-doo'*/ to reverse the doing of; to cancel or annul; to bring to nothing; to unfasten by unbolting, etc; to open; to unbutton, untie, etc; to unravel; to solve (a problem or riddle) (*archaic*); to bring ruin on (*archaic*); to seduce (*archaic*); to prevent the happening or being of (*Shakesp*). ◆ *vi* to come undone; to reverse what has been done. **undock'** *vt* to take (a ship) out of dock; to release (a spacecraft) from its coupling with another spacecraft, station, etc in space. ◆ *vi* to become undocked. **undocked'** *adj* not docked or cut short. **undoc'tored** *adj* without a doctor's degree; not patched up, tampered with or sophisticated. **undoer** /*un-doo'ər*/ *n* someone who undoes; someone who ruins; a seducer (*archaic*). **undo'ing** *n* the reversal of what has been done; unfastening; opening; ruin or cause of ruin. **undomes'tic** *adj* not domestic; not content with, adapted to, or relating to, home life; unhomelike (*Coleridge*). **undomes'ticate** *vt* to make undomestic; to untame.

undomes'ticated *adj* not domesticated; not tamed; emancipated from mere domestic interests. **undone** /*un-dun'*/ *adj* not done; annulled; brought to naught; unfastened (**come undone** to become unfastened or detached; to go wrong); opened; ruined; seduced (*archaic*). **undoub'le** *vt* and *vi* to unfold, open out. **undoubt'able** *adj* indubitable. **undoubt'ed** *adj* not doubted; unquestioned; certainly genuine or such as is represented; indubitable. **undoubt'edly** *adv* without doubt, certainly. **undoubt'ful** *adj*. **undoubt'ing** *adj*. **undoubt'ingly** *adv*. **undraped'** *adj* without drapery; nude. **undraw'** *vt* and *vi* to draw back. **undreamed'** or **undreamt'** *adj* (often with *-of*) not imagined even in a dream. **undress'** *vt* to remove the clothes or dressing from. ◆ *vi* to take off one's clothes. ◆ *n* scanty or incomplete dress; ordinary, informal dress; uniform for ordinary occasions. ◆ *adj* not requiring formal dress. **undressed'** *adj* not dressed; not set in order, or made trim, or treated or prepared for use, etc; divested of clothes (**get undressed** to take one's clothes off). **undress'ing** *n*. **undross'y** *adj* (*Pope*) pure. **undue** *adj* not due or owing; unjustifiable; inappropriate; excessive (**undue influence** (*law*) a strong influence over another person which might impede the exercise of that person's free will). **undū'ly** *adv* unjustifiably; more than is right or reasonable, excessively; wrongfully (*archaic*). **undū'teous** *adj* (*poetic*) undutiful. **undū'tiful** *adj*. **undū'tifully** *adv*. **undū'tifulness** *n*. **undyed'** *adj* not dyed. **undy'ing** *adj* not dying, immortal; unceasing. **undy'ingly** *adv*. **undy'ingness** *n*. **uneared'** *adj* not eared; untilled (*Shakesp*). **unearned'** *adj* not earned by work (**unearned income** income, eg dividends, that is not remuneration for work done; **unearned increment** increase in value of land independent of owner's labour or expenditure); (of something pleasant or unpleasant) unmerited. **unearth'** *vt* to dig up, disinter; to bring out of obscurity, bring to light; to expel from a burrow. **unearthed'** *adj* not connected to earth electrically; dug up, brought to light, etc. **unearth'liness** *n*. **unearth'ly** *adj* celestial; weird, ghostly; unconscionable, absurd (*esp* of an early hour). **unease'** *n* lack of ease; discomfort; apprehension. **uneas'ily** *adv*. **uneas'iness** *n*. **uneas'y** *adj* not at ease; disquieted; apprehensive; showing troubled restlessness (*lit* and *fig*); uncomfortable, unsettling; difficult to do or accomplish (now *rare*); (of roads, etc) difficult because of physical obstacles (*obs*). **uneath** /*un-ēth'*/ *adj* (OE *unēathe*; see **eath**; *archaic*) difficult; distressing. ◆ *adv* (*archaic*; also **uneth'**, **uneathes'** or **unnethes'**) with difficulty; in hardship; hardly, scarcely; almost (*Spenser*). **uneconom'ic** *adj* not in accordance with sound economics. **uneconom'ical** *adj* not economical. **unedge'** *vt* to blunt. **uned'ifying** *adj* not instructing or uplifting morally or aesthetically; morally degrading or degraded. **uned'ited** *adj* never edited, never before published. **unemo'tional** *adj*. **unemo'tionally** *adv*. **unemo'tioned** *adj* impassive. **unemploy'able** *adj* not fit for employment. **unemployed'** *adj* out of work; not put to use or profit; for or relating to those who are out of

---

Some words formed with the prefix **un-**; the numbers in brackets refer to the numbered senses in the entry for **un-**.

unhacked' *adj* (1).	**unheed'ingly** *adv* (1).	**unīdentifī'able** *adj* (1).
unhack'neyed *adj* (1).	**unheed'y** *adj* (1).	**unīdent'ified** *adj* (1).
unhailed' *adj* (1).	**unhelped'** *adj* (1).	**unidiomat'ic** *adj* (1).
unhall'ow *vt* (2).	**unhelp'ful** *adj* (1).	**unidiomat'ically** *adv* (1).
unhall'owed *adj* (1).	**unher'alded** *adj* (1).	**unillumed'** *adj* (1).
unhamp'ered *adj* (1).	**unherō'ic** or **unherō'ical** *adj* (1).	**unillu'minated** *adj* (1).
unhand'selled *adj* (1).	**unherō'ically** *adv* (1).	**unillu'minating** *adj* (1).
unhang' *vt* (2).	**unhewn'** *adj* (1).	**unillu'mined** *adj* (1).
unhanged' *adj* (1).	**unhidd'en** *adj* (1).	**unill'ustrated** *adj* (1).
unhar'dened *adj* (1).	**unhind'ered** *adj* (1).	**unimbued'** *adj* (1).
unhar'dy *adj* (1).	**unhired'** *adj* (1).	**unimmor'tal** (*Milton*) *adj* (1).
unharmed' *adj* (1).	**unhitch'** *vt* (2).	**unimpaired'** *adj* (1).
unharm'ful *adj* (1).	**unhome'like** *adj* (1).	**unimpart'ed** *adj* (1).
unharm'fully *adv* (1).	**unhome'ly** *adj* (1).	**unimpēd'ed** *adj* (1).
unharm'ing *adj* (1).	**unhon'oured** *adj* (1).	**unimpēd'edly** *adv* (1).
unharmo'nious *adj* (1).	**unhood'** *vt* (2).	**unimplored'** *adj* (1).
unhar'vested *adj* (1).	**unhood'ed** *adj* (1), (2).	**unimport'ance** *n* (1).
unhast'ing *adj* (1).	**unhook'** *vt* (2).	**unimport'ant** *adj* (1).
unhast'y *adj* (1).	**unhū'man** *adj* (1).	**unimpreg'nāted** *adj* (1).
unhaunt'ed *adj* (1).	**unhū'manize** or **unhū'manise** *vt* (2).	**unimpressed'** *adj* (1).
unhaz'arded *adj* (1).	**unhum'bled** *adj* (1).	**unimpress'ible** *adj* (1).
unhaz'ardous *adj* (1).	**unhunt'ed** *adj* (1).	**unimpress'ionable** *adj* (1).
unheal'able *adj* (1).	**unhurr'ied** *adj* (1).	**unimpress'ive** *adj* (1).
unhealed' *adj* (1).	**unhurr'iedly** *adv* (1).	**unimpris'oned** *adj* (1), (2).
unheat'ed *adj* (1).	**unhurr'ying** *adj* (1).	**unimpugn'able** *adj* (1).
unhedged' *adj* (1).	**unhurt'** *adj* (1).	**uninaug'urated** *adj* (1).
unheed'ed *adj* (1).	**unhurt'ful** *adj* (1).	**unincit'ed** *adj* (1).
unheed'edly *adv* (1).	**unhurt'fully** *adv* (1).	**uninclosed'** *adj* (1).
unheed'ful *adj* (1).	**unhurt'fulness** *n* (1).	**unincor'porated** *adj* (1).
unheed'fully *adv* (1).	**unhygien'ic** *adj* (1).	**uninfect'ed** *adj* (1).
unheed'ing *adj* (1).	**unhy'phenated** *adj* (1).	**uninflamed'** *adj* (1).

■ words derived from main entry word; ❑ compound words; ▨ idioms and phrasal verbs work. ◆ *n* (with *the*) the number of people out of work in a given period. **unemploy'ment** *n* (**unemployment benefit** formerly a weekly payment supplied under the national insurance scheme to an unemployed person, replaced by Jobseeker's Allowance in 1996). **unenchant'ed** (*Milton* **uninchant'ed**) *adj* not under an enchantment. **unendeared'** (*Milton* **unindeared'**) *adj* not made precious. **unend'ing** *adj* endless; everlasting; never ceasing, incessant; thorough-going (*Carlyle*). **unend'ingly** *adv*. **unend'ingness** *n*. **unenforce'able** *adj* that cannot be (*esp* legally) enforced. **unenforced'** *adj*. **un-Eng'lish** *adj* not English in character. **un-Eng'lished** *adj* not translated into English. **unen'viable** *adj* not to be envied; (of a task, etc) not exciting envy. **unen'viably** *adv*. **unen'vied** *adj*. **unen'vious** *adj*. **unen'vying** *adj*. **unë'qual** *adj* not equal; not or adequate or equal (with *to*); varying, not uniform; (of an agreement, etc) not evenly balanced, eg with regard to concessions made or advantages gained; inadequate (*obs*); unjust (*obs*); excessive (*obs*). ◆ *adv* (*Shakesp*) in an unequal manner. ◆ *n* someone who is not equal in rank, ability, etc. **unë'qualled** *adj* without an equal. **unë'qually** *adv*. **uneq'uitable** *adj* inequitable. **unequiv'ocal** *adj* unambiguous; explicit; clear and emphatic. **unequiv'ocally** *adv*. **unerr'ing** *adj* making no error, infallible; not, or never, missing the mark (*lit and fig*). **unerr'ingly** *adv*. **unerr'ingness** *n*. **uness'ence** *vt* (*Lamb*) to deprive of essence or being. **unessen'tial** *adj* not of the essence; inessential, not necessary, not important; without being, immaterial (*Milton*, etc). **unestab'lished** *adj* not established; not on the establishment or permanent staff. **uneth** *adj* see **uneath** above. **unexam'pled** *adj* unprecedented, without like or parallel. **unexcep'tionable** *adj* not liable to objection or criticism; exactly right, excellent; without exception (*Ruskin*). **unexcep'tionableness** *n*. **unexcep'tionably** *adv*. **unexcep'tional** *adj* not admitting or forming an exception; run-of-the-mill; unexceptionable. **unexcep'tionally** *adv*. **unex'ecuted** *adj* not executed; not brought into action (*Shakesp*). **unexpë'rient** *adj* (*Shakesp*) inexperienced. **unexpress'ive** *adj* not expressive; inexpressible, beyond the power of description (*Shakesp, Milton*). **unexpug'nable** *adj* inexpugnable. **unextinct'** *adj* (*fig*) not extinguished or dead. **uneyed'** *adj* unseen, unobserved. **unfa'bled** *adj* not fabled, real. **un'fact** *n* a fact that must not be acknowledged, or a falsehood that must pass as fact, *esp* in international politics. **unfail'ing** *adj* never failing or giving up; infallible; constant; certain; inexhaustible. **unfail'ingly** *adv*. **unfair'** *adj* inequitable, unjust; involving deception or fraud and leading to undue advantage over business rival(s); not fair, ugly. ◆ *vt* (*Shakesp*) to deprive of beauty. **unfair'ly** *adv*. **unfair'ness** *n*. **unfaith'** *n* lack of faith or trust. **unfaith'ful** *adj* not faithful, violating trust; breaking faith with one's husband, wife or lover, *usu* by having sexual intercourse with someone else; not true to the original; not of the approved religion. **unfaith'fully** *adv*. **unfaith'fulness** *n*. **unfall'ible** *adj* (*Shakesp*)

infallible. **unfanc'ied** *adj* not thought likely to win or do well. **unfash'ionable** *adj* not fashionable; shapeless (*Shakesp*); incapable of being fashioned (*obs*). **unfash'ionableness** *n*. **unfash'ionably** *adv*. **unfash'ioned** *adj* not formed; not shaped; not made polished, elegant, etc (*obs*). **unfasten** /*un-fäs'n*/ *vt* to release from a fastening; to unfix (*Shakesp*). ◆ *vi* to become loose or open. **unfas'tened** *adj* released from fastening; not fastened. **unfa'thered** *adj* without a father or acknowledged father; deprived of a father; of unknown source, origin, etc. **unfa'therly** *adj* unbefitting a father. **unfath'omable** *adj* not able to be fathomed (*lit and fig*). **unfath'omableness** *n*. **unfath'omably** *adv*. **unfath'omed** *adj* not sounded, of unknown depth; of unascertained meaning (*fig*). **unfā'vourite** or (*US*) **unfā'vorite** *n* and *adj* (something) most disliked. **unfazed'** *adj* not perturbed. **unfeared'** *adj* not feared; unafraid (*obs*). **unfear'ful** *adj* not afraid. **unfear'fully** *adv*. **unfear'ing** *adj*. **unfeat'ured** *adj* without marked or well-formed features (*lit and fig*). **unfeed'** *adj* not retained by a fee; unpaid. **unfeel'ing** *adj* without physical sensation; without kind or sympathetic feelings; hard-hearted. **unfeel'ingly** *adv*. **unfeel'ingness** *n*. **unfeigned'** *adj* not feigned, real; not feigning, sincere. **unfeign'edly** *adv*. **unfeign'edness** *n*. **unfeign'ing** *adj*. **unfell'owed** *adj* unmatched. **unfelt'** *adj* not felt; intangible (*Shakesp*). **unfett'er** *vt* to free from fetters. **unfett'ered** *adj* unrestrained. **unfeu'dal** *adj* not marked by social attitudes and assumptions like those under the feudal system. **unfeud'alize** or **-ise** *vt* to defeudalize. **unfiled'** *adj* not rubbed with a file (**file²**), unpolished (*Spenser* **unfilde'**); undefiled (**file³**; now *dialect*); not placed on a file (**file¹**). **unfill'eted** *adj* not bound with a fillet; not boned. **unfil'terable** or **unfil'trable** *adj* unable to pass through a filter (or an ordinary filter). **unfine'** *adj* not fine. **unfin'ished** *adj*. **unfin'ishing** *n* (*Milton*) the leaving unfinished. **unfit'** *adj* not fit; not fitting or suitable; not in fit condition; not meeting required standards. ◆ *n* an unfit person. ◆ *vt* to make unfit; to render or cause to be unsuitable (with *for*); to disqualify. **unfit'ly** *adv* unsuitably, inappropriately. **unfit'ness** *n*. **unfitt'ed** *adj* not provided (with *with*); without fittings; not made to fit, or tested for fit; not adapted, qualified, or having the ability (to do, or with *for*). **unfitt'edness** *n*. **unfitt'ing** *adj* unsuitable; unbecoming, indecorous. **unfitt'ingly** *adv*. **unfix'** *vt* to unfasten, detach; to unsettle (*fig*). ◆ *vi* to become loose. **unfixed'** *adj*. **unfix'edness** or **unfix'ity** *n*. **unflappabil'ity** *n*. **unflapp'able** *adj* (*inf*) imperturbable, never agitated or alarmed. **unflapp'ably** *adv*. **unfledged'** *adj* not yet fledged; undeveloped or inexperienced; of early youth. **unflesh'** *vt* to remove the flesh from. **unfleshed'** *adj* deprived of flesh, reduced to a skeleton; not fleshed, not having tasted blood, uninitiated. **unflesh'ly** *adj* spiritual; incorporeal; not carnal. **unflush'** *vi* (*Matthew Arnold*) to lose a flush of colour. **unfold'** *vt* to open the folds of (**fold¹**); to spread out; to tell; to disclose, make known; to reveal, display; to let out from a sheep-fold (**fold²**). ◆ *vi* to

---

Some words formed with the prefix **un-**; the numbers in brackets refer to the numbered senses in the entry for **un-**.

uninflamm'able *adj* (1).	**unintermitt'edly** *adv* (1).	**unlä'dylike** *adj* (1).
uninflāt'ed *adj* (1).	**unintermitt'ing** *adj* (1).	**unlament'ed** *adj* (1).
uninflect'ed *adj* (1).	**unintermitt'ingly** *adv* (1).	**unleased'** *adj* (1).
unin'fluenced *adj* (1).	**uninter'pretable** *adj* (1).	**unleav'ened** *adj* (1).
uninfluen'tial *adj* (1).	**uninterrup'ted** *adj* (1).	**unleis'ured** *adj* (1).
uninhab'itable *adj* (1).	**uninterrup'tedly** *adv* (1).	**unleis'urely** *adj* (1).
uninhab'ited *adj* (1).	**unintox'icating** *adj* (1).	**unlet'** *adj* (1).
uninhib'ited *adj* (1).	**unintroduced'** *adj* (1).	**unlib'erated** *adj* (1).
unini'tiated *adj* (1).	**uninured'** *adj* (1).	**unlibid'inous** (*Milton*) *adj* (1).
unin'jured *adj* (1).	**uninven'tive** *adj* (1).	**unlife'like** *adj* (1).
uninquīr'ing *adj* (1).	**uninvest'ed** *adj* (1).	**unlight'ed** *adj* (1).
uninquis'itive *adj* (1).	**uninvest'igated** *adj* (1).	**unlight'ened** *adj* (1).
uninscribed' *adj* (1).	**uninvid'ious** *adj* (1).	**unlim'ited** *adj* (1).
uninspired' *adj* (1).	**uninvī'ted** *adj* (1).	**unlim'itedly** *adv* (1).
uninspīr'ing *adj* (1).	**uninvī'ting** *adj* (1).	**unlim'itedness** *n* (1).
uninstruct'ed *adj* (1).	**uninvolved'** *adj* (1).	**unlin'eal** *adj* (1).
uninstruct'ive *adj* (1).	**unī'roned** *adj* (1).	**unliq'uefied** *adj* (1).
unin'sulated *adj* (1).	**unjä'ded** *adj* (1).	**unliq'uidated** *adj* (1).
uninsū'rable *adj* (1).	**unjaun'diced** *adj* (1).	**unlist'enable** *adj* (1).
uninsured' *adj* (1).	**unjeal'ous** *adj* (1).	**unlit'** *adj* (1).
unin'tegrated *adj* (1).	**unjoy'ful** *adj* (1).	**unlit'erary** *adj* (1).
unintellect'ual *adj* (1).	**unjoy'ous** *adj* (1).	**unliv'able** or **unlive'able** *adj* (1).
unintell'igent *adj* (1).	**unjust'** *adj* (1).	**unlive'liness** *n* (1).
unintelligibil'ity *n* (1).	**unjus'tifiable** *adj* (1).	**unlive'ly** *adj* (1).
unintell'igible *adj* (1).	**unjus'tifiably** *adv* (1).	**unlopped'** *adj* (1).
unintell'igibly *adv* (1).	**unjus'tified** *adj* (1).	**unlos'able** *adj* (1).
unintend'ed *adj* (1).	**unjust'ly** *adv* (1).	**unlost'** *adj* (1).
uninten'tional *adj* (1).	**unjust'ness** *n* (1).	**unlove'liness** *n* (1).
unintentional'ity *n* (1).	**unkill'able** *adj* (1).	**unlove'ly** *adj* (1).
uninten'tionally *adv* (1).	**unlä'belled** *adj* (1).	**unluxur'iant** *adj* (1).
unintermitt'ed *adj* (1).	**unlabō'rious** *adj* (1).	**unluxur'ious** *adj* (1).

---

open out, spread open to the view (*lit* and *fig*). **unfold'ed** *adj* not folded; opened out from a folded state; not enclosed in a sheep-fold. **unfold'er** *n*. **unfold'ing** *n* and *adj* opening out from folds; disclosing; letting out from a sheep-fold. ◆ *adj* (of a star; *Shakesp*) showing the time for unfolding sheep. **unfoll'ow** *vt* to decline to receive messages from (a person who is posting on a social media site). **unfool'** *vt* to undo the fooling of; to undeceive. **unfoot'ed** *adj* untrodden. **unforced'** *adj* natural, not strained or artificial; not compelled (**unforced error** in sport, a mistake arising from one's own poor play rather than the superior play of an opponent). **unfor'cedly** *adv*. **unfor'cible** *adj* incapable of being forced or (*Milton*) enforced; without strength (*obs*). **unforebōd'ing** *adj* not giving or feeling foreboding. **unfore'skinned** *adj* (*Milton*) circumcised. **unfor'ested** *adj* not wooded; not reckoned as deer forest; deforested. **unform'** *vt* to unmake. **unfor'mal** *adj* informal. **unfor'malized** or **-s-** *adj* not made formal. **unformed'** *adj* unmade, uncreated; formless, unshaped; immature, undeveloped. **unfor'tunate** *adj* unlucky; regrettable; of ill omen; (*esp* formerly) living by prostitution. ◆ *n* an unfortunate person. **unfor'tunately** *adv* in an unlucky way; by bad luck; I'm sorry to say. **unfor'tunateness** *n*. **unfor'tune** *n* (*archaic*). **unfor'tuned** *adj*. **unfought'** (*archaic* **unfought'en** *adj*). **unfound'** *adj* not found. **unfound'ed** *adj* not founded; without foundation, baseless; without bottom, bottomless (*Milton*). **unfound'edly** *adv*. **unframed'** *adj* not formed or fashioned (*lit* and *fig*); not set in a frame. **unfraught'** *adj* not fraught or charged. ◆ *vt* to unload or discharge. **unfree'** *adj* not free; in servitude; not having the freedom of a corporation (*obs*). **unfreed'** *adj*. **unfree'man** *n* (*obs*) someone who does not have the freedom of a corporation. **unfreeze'** *vt* and *vi* to thaw; to (allow to) progress, move, etc after a temporary restriction or stoppage. ◆ *vt* to free (prices, wages, funds) from the control imposed by a government, etc. **unfrett'ed** *adj* not eaten away or rubbed; not annoyed or worried. **unfriend'** *n* a person who is not a friend. ◆ *vt* same as **defriend**. **unfriend'ed** *adj* not provided with or supported by friends. **unfriend'edness** *n*. **unfriend'lily** *adv*. **unfriend'liness** *n*. **unfriend'ly** *adj* ill-disposed; somewhat hostile. ◆ *adv* (*old*) unkindly. **unfriend'ship** *n* (*archaic*) unfriendliness. **unfright'ed** *adj* (*archaic*) not frightened. **unfrock'** *vt* to strip of a frock or gown; to depose from priesthood; to remove from a comparable position in another sphere of activity. **unfrocked'** *adj*. **unfumed'** *adj* not fumigated. ◆ *adj* (*Milton*) undistilled. **unfund'ed** *adj* (of a public debt, etc) not funded, floating, in the form of exchequer bills and bonds, to be paid up at certain dates. **unfurl'** *vt* to release from being rolled up; to unfold or display. ◆ *vi* to spread open. **unfur'nish** *vt* to deprive of men, defences, furniture; to deprive (*Shakesp*). **unfur'nished** *adj* not furnished; unsupplied. **unfuss'y** *adj* not over-elaborate. **ungain'** *adj* (*obs, archaic* or *dialect*; from **gain²**) indirect; inconvenient; unpleasant; ungainly, awkward; unskilled. **ungain'ful** *adj*. **ungain'liness** *n*. **ungain'ly** *adj* awkward, clumsy, uncouth. ◆ *adv* (*rare*)

awkwardly. **ungalled'** *adj* not made painful by rubbing; not irritated or inflamed (*fig*). **ungazed'** *adj* not gazed (with *at* or *upon*). **ungear'** *vt* to disconnect (a part of a system of moving parts) (also *fig*); to unharness (*archaic*). **ungeared'** *adj* (*econ*) of a business, etc, having no borrowing in its capital structure, financed entirely by equity capital. **ungē'nial** *adj* not sympathetically cheerful; not comfortably warm, raw; not congenial; not favourable to natural growth. **ungen'itured** *adj* (*Shakesp*) without means of generation, or not produced by ordinary generation. **ungentil'ity** *n*. **ungen'tle** *adj* not gentle; not of gentle birth; not of or befitting the gentle. **ungen'tlemanlike** *adj* and *adv* not like or befitting a gentleman. **ungen'tlemanliness** *n*. **ungen'tlemanly** *adj* unbecoming a gentleman; not gentlemanlike. ◆ *adv* in an ungentlemanly manner. **ungen'tleness** *n*. **ungent'ly** *adv*. **ungermane** /-*jər-mān'*/ *adj* irrelevant. **unget'** *vt* to deny the begetting of; to disown. **ungetat'able** or **unget-at'-able** *adj* (*inf*) inaccessible. **unghost'ly** *adj* not pertaining to or like a ghost; not spiritual. **ungird'** *vt* to free from a girdle or band; to undo the fastening of and take off. **ungirt'** or **ungird'ed** *adj* not girt; freed from a girdle; not tightened up, not strengthened for action (*fig*). **ungirth'** *vt* to remove a girth from; to free from a girth. **ungirthed'** *adj*. **unglue'** *vt* to loosen or detach (something glued). ◆ *vi* (*rare*) to become loose or detached. **unglued'** *adj* no longer held or fixed together by glue (**become** or **come unglued** to go awry, become confused, come apart). **ungod'** *vt* to divest of divinity; to make godless. **ungod'like** *adj*. **ungod'lily** *adv* in an ungodly manner. **ungod'liness** *n*. **ungod'ly** *adj* not godly; outrageous, unconscionable (*inf*). **ungored'** *adj* (*Shakesp* **ungord'**; another reading **ungorg'd'**) unwounded. **ungorged'** *adj* not gorged or sated. **ungott'en** *adj* not got or acquired; unbegotten. **ungov'ernable** *adj* uncontrollable; unruly. **ungov'ernableness** *n*. **ungov'ernably** *adv*. **ungov'erned** *adj*. **ungown'** *vt* to deprive or divest of a gown; to unfrock. **ungowned'** *adj* not wearing a gown; deprived of one's gown. **ungrā'cious** *adj* without grace; graceless; ungraceful; lacking in courtesy, affability or urbanity; behaving with a bad grace; unmannerly; making offensive or disagreeable. **ungrā'ciously** *adv*. **ungrā'ciousness** *n*. **ungrād'ed** *adj* not classified in grades; not adjusted to easy gradients. **ungrassed'** *adj* not grown with grass, without grass growing. **ungrate'ful** *adj* not feeling gratitude; disagreeable, irksome; not repaying one's labour, thankless. **ungrate'fully** *adv*. **ungrate'fulness** *n*. **ungrazed'** *adj* not grazed; (of land) not grazed by livestock. **ungreen'** *adj* harmful to, or lacking consideration for, the environment. **unground'** *adj* not ground. **unground'ed** *adj* not based (with *in*); without basis, unreal or false; without sound fundamental instruction. **unground'edly** *adv*. **unground'edness** *n*. **unguard'** *vt* to make or leave unguarded. **unguard'ed** *adj* without guard; unprotected; unscreened; incautious; inadvertent. **unguard'edly** *adv*. **unguard'edness** *n*. **ungum'** *vt* to free from gum or gummed condition. **ungummed'** *adj* not gummed; freed from gum or

---

Some words formed with the prefix **un-**; the numbers in brackets refer to the numbered senses in the entry for **un-**.

unmacad'amized or **unmacad'amised** *adj* (1).
unmaimed' *adj* (1).
unmaintain'able *adj* (1).
unmaintained' *adj* (1).
unmali'cious *adj* (1).
unmalleabil'ity *n* (1).
unmall'eable *adj* (1).
unman'acle *vt* (2).
unman'acled *adj* (1), (2).
unman'ageable *adj* (1).
unman'ageableness *n* (1).
unman'ageably *adv* (1).
unman'aged *adj* (1).
unmapped' *adj* (1).
unmas'culine *adj* (1).
unmā'ted *adj* (1).
unmater'nal *adj* (1).
unmathemat'ical *adj* (1).
unmatric'ulated *adj* (1).
unmatured' *adj* (1).
unmechan'ical (*archaic* **unmechan'ic**) *adj* (1).
unmeek' *adj* (1).
unmell'owed *adj* (1).
unmelo'dious *adj* (1).
unmelt'ed *adj* (1).
unmem'orable *adj* (1).
unmer'cenary *adj* (1).
unmer'chantable *adj* (1).
unmet'alled *adj* (1).

unmetaphor'ical *adj* (1).
unmetaphys'ical *adj* (1).
unmethod'ical *adj* (1).
unmeth'odized or **unmeth'odised** *adj* (1).
unmet'rical *adj* (1).
unmil'itary *adj* (1).
unmilked' *adj* (1).
unmilled' *adj* (1).
unmin'gled *adj* (1).
unministē'rial *adj* (1).
unmirac'ulous *adj* (1).
unmī'ry *adj* (1).
unmissed' *adj* (1).
unmistāk'able or **unmistake'able** *adj* (1).
unmistāk'ably or **unmistake'ably** *adv* (1).
unmistrust'ful *adj* (1).
unmixed' *adj* (1).
unmix'edly *adv* (1).
unmod'ernized or **unmod'ernised** *adj* (1).
unmod'ifiable *adj* (1).
unmod'ifiableness *n* (1).
unmod'ified *adj* (1).
unmod'ulated *adj* (1).
unmois'tened *adj* (1).
unmolest'ed *adj* (1).
unmort'gaged *adj* (1).
unmort'ified *adj* (1).
unmourned' *adj* (1).
unmown' *adj* (1).

unmuni'tioned *adj* (1).
unmur'muring *adj* (1).
unmur'muringly *adv* (1).
unmūs'ical *adj* (1).
unmūs'ically *adv* (1).
unmūtilated' *adj* (1).
unneed'ed *adj* (1).
unneed'ful *adj* (1).
unneed'fully *adv* (1).
unnō'ted *adj* (1).
unnō'ticeable *adj* (1).
unnō'ticed *adj* (1).
unnō'ticing *adj* (1).
unnour'ished *adj* (1).
unnour'ishing *adj* (1).
unobjec'tionable *adj* (1).
unobjec'tionably *adv* (1).
unobnox'ious *adj* (1).
unobscured' *adj* (1).
unobstruc'ted *adj* (1).
unobstruc'tive *adj* (1).
unobtain'able *adj* (1).
unobtained' *adj* (1).
unobtru'sive *adj* (1).
unobtru'sively *adv* (1).
unobtru'siveness *n* (1).
unob'vious *adj* (1).
unocc'upied *adj* (1).
unoff'ered *adj* (1).
unoff'icered *adj* (1).
unoiled' *adj* (1).

■ words derived from main entry word; □ compound words; ▪ idioms and phrasal verbs gumming (**come ungummed** (*sl;* of a plan) to go amiss). **unhā'ble** *adj* an obsolete form of **unable**. **unhair'** *vt* to deprive of hair. ◆ *vi* to become free from hair. **unhaired'** *adj* freed from hair. **unhalsed** /*un-hōst*/ *adj* (*Walter Scott*) unsaluted. **unhand'** *vt* to take the hands off; to let go. **unhand'ily** *adv* awkwardly. **unhand'iness** *n*. **unhan'dled** *adj* not handled or managed; not broken in. **unhand'some** *adj* not handsome; unseemly; ungenerous; ungracious; unskilful in action (*obs*); clumsy, inconvenient (*obs*). **unhand'somely** *adv*. **unhand'someness** *n*. **unhand'y** *adj* awkward, not skilful; not convenient. **unhapp'ily** *adv* in an unhappy manner; unfortunately, regrettably, I'm sorry to say; unsuccessfully; unfavourably (*Shakesp*); shrewdly (*Shakesp*); maliciously (*obs*). **unhapp'iness** *n*. **unhapp'y** *adj* bringing misfortune; not fortunate; miserable; infelicitous, inapt; mischievous (*obs*). ◆ *vt* (*Shakesp*) to make unhappy or unfortunate. **unhar'bour** *vt* to dislodge from shelter. **unhar'boured** *adj* without a shelter; dislodged from shelter. **unhar'ness** *vt* to take the harness or the armour off. **unhar'nessed** *adj* not in, or freed from, harness or armour. **unhasp'** *vt* to unfasten by undoing a hasp. **unhat'** *vi* to take off the hat as a sign of respect. **unhatched'** (*Shakesp* **unhatch'd**) *adj* not out of the egg; not developed; not shaded; unhacked. **unhatt'ed** *adj* hatless. **unhatt'ing** *n* lifting of the hat. **unhead'** *vt* to take the head from. **unheal'** *vt* see **unhele** below. **unhealth'** *n* ill-health. **unhealth'ful** *adj*. **unhealth'fully** *adv*. **unhealth'fulness** *n*. **unheal'thily** *adv*. **unheal'thiness** *n*. **unheal'thy** *adj* not healthy; morbid; unfavourable to health; dangerous (*inf*). **unheard'** *adj* not heard; not granted a hearing; (*usu* **unheard'-of**) not heard of, unknown to fame; unprecedented (in *Shakesp, King John* V.2.133, understood by some as unhaired or beardless). **unhearse'** *vt* (used by Spenser in the *pat* **unherst'**) *appar* to remove from a hearse or a stand for candles at a funeral. **unhearsed'** *adj* without a hearse. **unheart'** *vt* (*Shakesp*) to dishearten. **unheed'ily** *adv* unheedfully. **unhele'** or **unheal'** *vt* (*Spenser*) to uncover, disclose. **unhelm'** *vt* to divest of helmet. **unhelmed'** or **unhel'meted** *adj* without or divested of helm or helmet. **unhelp'able** *adj* incapable of receiving help. **unheppen** /*un-ep'n*/ *adj* (ON *heppinn* dexterous; *Yorks, Lincs, Tennyson*) clumsy. **unherst'** *vt* (*pat*) see **unhearse** above. **unhes'itating** *adj* not hesitating or doubting; prompt; ready. **unhes'itatingly** *adv*. **unhide'bound** *adj* (*Milton*) not having a skin confining the body. **unhinge'** *vt* to take from the hinges; to derange. **unhinged'** *adj*. **unhinge'ment** *n*. **unhip'** *adj* (*sl*) square, not trendy. **unhistor'ic** *adj* not historic. **unhistor'ical** *adj* not mentioned in history; not in accordance with history; not important historically; not having actually existed or happened. **unhive'** *vt* to drive from a hive. **unhoard'** *vt* to take from a hoard. **unhō'lily** *adv*. **unhō'liness** *n*. **unhōl'pen** *adj* (*archaic*) not helped. **unhō'ly** *adj* not holy; very wicked; unnatural; unconscionable, outrageous, unearthly (*inf*).

unhon'est *adj* (*obs*) unseemly, indecent, dishonourable; immoral; dishonest. **unhoop'** *vt* to remove hoops from. **unhoped'** *adj* beyond what was expected with hope (now **unhoped'-for**; *archaic*); unexpected (*obs*). **unhope'ful** *adj*. **unhope'fully** *adv*. **unhorse'** *vt* to dislodge or throw from a horse; to take a horse or horses from. **unhos'pitable** *adj* (now *usu* **inhospitable**). **unhouse'** *vt* to deprive of or drive from a house or shelter. **unhoused'** *adj* houseless; deprived of a house. **unhous'elled** (*Shakesp* **unhouzz'led**) *adj* not having received the sacrament. **unhung'** *adj* not hung; without hangings; unhanged. **unhus'banded** *adj* uncultivated; without a husband. **unhusk'** *vt* to strip the husk from. **unīdē'a'd** *adj* without ideas; with unfurnished mind. **unīdē'al** *adj* not ideal; not idealistic; without ideals; conveying no idea (*obs*); without ideas (*obs*). **unīdē'alism** *n*. **unīdēalist'ic** *adj*. **unimag'inable** *adj*. **unimag'inableness** *n*. **unimag'inably** *adv*. **unimag'inative** *adj* not imaginative, prosaic. **unimag'inatively** *adv*. **unimag'inativeness** *n*. **unimag'ined** *adj*. **unimpass'ioned** *adj* not impassioned, calm, tranquil. **unimpeach'able** *adj* not to be impeached; not liable to be accused; free from fault; blameless. **unimpeached'** *adj*. **unim'portuned** (or /-*tūnd'*, -*choond'*/, often -*pör'*/) *adj* not persistently begged (to do something). **unimposed'** *adj*. **unimpōs'ing** *adj* unimpressive; not burdensome (*obs*). **unimproved'** *adj* not made better; not cultivated, cleared or built upon; not put to use. **uninchant'ed** *adj* unenchanted. **unincum'bered** *adj* unencumbered. **unindeared'** *adj* unendeared. **unin'dexed** *adj* not containing an index; not index-linked. **uninforce'able** *adj* unenforceable. **uninforced'** *adj* unenforced. **uninform'ative** *adj*. **uninformed'** *adj* not having received information; untaught; uneducated; not imbued with life or activity (*archaic*). **uninform'ing** *adj*. **uninstall'** (*comput*) *vt* to remove (a program) from a system or storage device. ◆ *n* the process of removing software programs in such a way that the remaining programs function correctly. **unin'terested** *adj* not personally concerned; not taking an interest. **unin'teresting** *adj*. **unin'terestingly** *adv*. **unī'onized** or **-s-** *adj* not ionized. **un-Islam'ic** *adj* against the spirit, beliefs or traditions of Islam. **unjoint'** *vt* to disjoint. **unjoint'ed** *adj* disjointed, incoherent; without joints. **unked, unket** and **unkid** /*ŭngk'id*/ or *ungk'id*, -*it*/ *adj* (*N and W Eng*) forms of **uncouth** strange, uncomfortable, lonely, eerie. **unkempt'** *adj* (see **kemb**) uncombed; scruffy; unpolished, rough. **unkenned'** or **unkent'** *adj* unknown. **unkenn'el** *vt* to dislodge (a fox) from a hole; to let out from a kennel. **unkept'** *adj* not kept; untended. **unket** and **unkid** *adj* see **unked** above. **unkīnd'** *adj* lacking in kindness; cruel; unnaturally wicked (*obs*). **unkin'dled** *adj* not kindled. **unkīnd'liness** *n* lack of kindliness. **unkīnd'ly** *adj* unnatural; not kind. ◆ *adv* in an unkindly manner; cruelly; unnaturally (*Milton*); against right feeling (*Shakesp*). **unkīnd'ness** *n* lack of kindness or affection; cruelty; ill-feeling; a flock of ravens (*obs*). **unking'** *vt* to deprive of kingship or of a king.

Some words formed with the prefix **un-**; the numbers in brackets refer to the numbered senses in the entry for **un-**.

unopposed' *adj* (1).	**unpā'tented** *adj* (1).	**unperplexed'** *adj* (1).
unoppress'ive *adj* (1).	**unpathed'** *adj* (1).	**unper'secuted** *adj* (1).
unordained' *adj* (1).	**unpathet'ic** *adj* (1).	**unpersuād'able** *adj* (1).
unor'ganized or **unor'ganised** *adj* (1).	**unpath'wayed** *adj* (1).	**unpersuād'ableness** *n* (1).
unornamen'tal *adj* (1).	**unpatriot'ic** *adj* (1).	**unpersuād'ed** *adj* (1).
unor'namented *adj* (1).	**unpatriot'ically** *adv* (1).	**unpersuās'ive** *adj* (1).
unor'thodox *adj* (1).	**unpat'ronized** or **unpat'ronised** *adj* (1).	**unperturbed'** *adj* (1).
unor'thodoxly *adv* (1).	**unpeace'able** *adj* (1).	**unphilosoph'ic** or **unphilosoph'ical** *adj*
unor'thodoxy *n* (1).	**unpeace'ableness** *n* (1).	(1).
unoss'ified *adj* (1).	**unpeace'ful** *adj* (1).	**unphilosoph'ically** *adv* (1).
unostentā'tious *adj* (1).	**unpeace'fully** *adv* (1).	**unphonet'ic** *adj* (1).
unostentā'tiously *adv* (1).	**unped'igreed** *adj* (1).	**unpierced'** *adj* (1).
unostentā'tiousness *n* (1).	**unpeg'** *vt* (2).	**unpī'loted** *adj* (1).
unovercome' *adj* (1).	**unpen'sioned** *adj* (1).	**unpinned'** *adj* (1), (2).
unoverthrown' *adj* (1).	**unpepp'ered** *adj* (1).	**unpit'ied** *adj* (1).
unox'idized or **unox'idised** *adj* (1).	**unperceiv'able** *adj* (1).	**unpit'iful** *adj* (1).
unpac'ified *adj* (1).	**unperceiv'ably** *adv* (1).	**unpit'ifully** *adv* (1).
unpaid' *adj* (1).	**unperceived'** *adj* (1).	**unpit'ifulness** *n* (1).
unpained' *adj* (1).	**unperceiv'edly** *adv* (1).	**unpit'ying** *adj* (1).
unpain'ful *adj* (1).	**unpercep'tive** *adj* (1).	**unpit'yingly** *adv* (1).
unpal'sied *adj* (1).	**unper'forated** *adj* (1).	**unplagued'** *adj* (1).
unpam'pered *adj* (1).	**unperformed'** *adj* (1).	**unplait'** *vt* (2).
unpar'donable *adj* (1).	**unperform'ing** *adj* (1).	**unplait'ed** *adj* (1), (2).
unpar'donableness *n* (1).	**unper'fumed** *adj* (1).	**unplanked'** *adj* (1).
unpar'donably *adv* (1).	**unper'ilous** *adj* (1).	**unplanned'** *adj* (1).
unpar'doned *adj* (1).	**unper'ishable** *adj* (1).	**unplant'ed** *adj* (1).
unpar'doning *adj* (1).	**unper'ished** *adj* (1).	**unplast'ered** *adj* (1).
unpar'tial *adj* (1).	**unper'ishing** *adj* (1).	**unplay'able** *adj* (1).
unpas'teurized or **unpas'teurised** *adj* (1).	**unper'jured** *adj* (1).	**unplayed'** *adj* (1).
unpas'toral *adj* (1).	**unper'petrated** *adj* (1).	**unpleat'ed** *adj* (1).
unpas'tured *adj* (1).	**unperplex'** *vt* (2).	

---

fāte; fär; mē; fûr; mīne; mōte; för; mūte; pŭt; dhen (then); *el'ə-mənt* (element) • For other sounds see detailed chart of pronunciation

unking'like *adj*. **unking'ly** *adj* unbecoming a king; unlike a king. **unkiss'** *vt* (*Shakesp*) to annul by means of a kiss. **unkissed'** *adj* not kissed. **unknelled** /*un-neld*'/ *adj* without tolling. **unknight** /*un-nīt*'/ *vt* to divest of knighthood. **unknight'ed** *adj* not knighted. **unknight'liness** *n*. **unknightly** /*un-nīt'li*/ *adj* unlike or unbecoming to a knight. ◆ *adv* in an unknightly manner. **unknit** /*un-nit*'/ *vt* to undo the knitting of; to untie; to smooth out (the eyebrows) from a frown; to relax. ◆ *vi* to become unknitted. ◆ *adj* loose, not closely compacted or united. **unknot** /*un-not*'/ *vt* to free from knots; to untie. **unknowable** /*un-nō'ə-bl*/ *adj* incapable of being known. ◆ *n* an unknowable thing; the first or original cause; that which is cognizable only in its relations. **unknow'ableness** *n*. **unknow'ing** *adj* ignorant, unaware; unwitting; unknown (with *to*; *dialect*); ignorant (with *or*; *archaic*); not knowing (*archaic* or *poetic*). **unknow'ingly** *adv*. **unknow'ingness** *n*. **unknown** /*un-nōn*'/ *adj* not known. ◆ *n* an unknown person or quantity; (with *the*) that which is unknown. **unknown'ness** *n*. **unlā'boured** *adj* showing no traces of labour; unworked; unrestrained, easy; natural, not contrived or forced. **unlā'bouring** *adj*. **unlace'** *vt* to free from being laced; to undo the lacing of; to carve (*esp a rabbit*) (*obs*); to undo, destroy (*Shakesp*). **unlade'** *vt* to unload. **unlā'den** *adj* not laden. **unlā'ding** *n*. **unlaid'** *adj* not laid. **unlash'** *vt* (*naut*) to loose the lashings of. **unlast** or **unlaste** /*un-läst*' or *-läst*'/ *vt* Spenserian *pat* and *pap* of **unlace**. **unlatch'** *vt* to lift the latch of. **un'law** *n* breach of law (*archaic*); a fine, penalty (*Scots law*; *obs*). ◆ *vt* /*-lö*'/ to annul, repeal; to fine (*obs*). **unlaw'ful** *adj* forbidden by law; illegitimate; illicit; acting illegally (**unlawful assembly** a meeting of three or more people that is considered likely to cause a breach of the peace or endanger the public). **unlaw'fully** *adv*. **unlaw'fulness** *n*. **unlay'** *vt* (*naut*) to untwist. **unlead** /*un-led*'/ *vt* (*printing*) to take the lead or leads from. **unlead'ed** *adj* not covered or decorated, etc with lead; (of petrol) with no added lead; (of type) without leading (*printing*). **unleal'** *adj* (*archaic*) unfaithful. **unlearn'** *vt* to undo the process of learning; to rid one's mind of, eliminate habit(s) of. **unlearned** /*-lûr'nid*, also (*poetic*) *-lûrnd*'/ *adj* having no learning; uneducated; /*-lûrnd*'/ not learnt, got up or acquired; eliminated by unlearning. **unlear'nedly** *adv*. **unlear'nedness** *n*. **unlearnt** /*-lûrnt*'/ *adj* not learnt; eliminated by unlearning. **unleash'** *vt* to free from a leash, let go; to release (*lit* and *fig*). **unled'** *adj* not led, without guidance. **unless'oned** *adj* not instructed. **unlett'able** *adj* (of a building) that cannot be let, *usu* because it is in unfit condition. **unlett'ered** *adj* unlearned; illiterate; without lettering. **unlī'censed** *adj* without a licence; unauthorized. **unlich** /*un-lich*'/ *adj* (*Spenser*) unlike. **unlicked'** *adj* not licked; not licked into shape. **unlid'** *vt* to uncover, open. **unlidd'ed** *adj* lidless. **unlight'some** *adj* (*Milton*) without light. **unlik'able** or **unlike'able** *adj* not likable. **unlike'** *adj* and *adv* (tending to become a *prep*) not like; different (from); unlikely (*Spenser* and *Shakesp*). ◆ *n* someone who or something that is unlike.

unlike'lihood or **unlike'liness** *n* improbability. **unlike'ly** *adj* not likely; improbable; unpromising (*obs*); unprepossessing (*obs* or *dialect*); unsuitable (*obs*). ◆ *adv* in an unlikely manner, improbably. **unlike'ness** *n* lack of resemblance. **unlim'ber** *vt* to remove (a gun) from its limber ready for use. **unlime'** *vt* to free from lime. **unlimed'** *adj* not limed. **unline'** *vt* to remove the lining from. **unlined'** *adj* without lines or lining. **unlink'** *vt* to undo the linking or links of. ◆ *vi* to become unlinked. **unlinked'** *adj* not linked. **unliq'uored** *adj* (*Milton*) not in liquor, sober. **unlist'ed** *adj* not entered in a list; (of a telephone number) not listed in a directory, ex-directory (*N Am*); (of companies and securities) not quoted on the Stock Exchange's official list (**unlisted securities market** a market trading in shares of smaller companies not listed on the Stock Exchange and not subject to the rules governing listed securities). **unlis'tened** *adj* not listened to (also **unlis'tened-to**; *poetic*). **unlis'tening** *adj*. **unlive** /*un-liv*'/ *vt* to undo the living of; to live in the contrary manner to; to live down; /*un-līv*'/ to deprive of life (*Shakesp*). **unlived'-in** *adj* not lived in. **unliv'ing** *adj*. **unload'** *vt* to take the load or charge from; to discharge; to disburden; to remove as a load; to get rid of; to dump. ◆ *vi* to discharge freight. **unload'ed** *adj* not loaded; discharged. **unload'er** *n*. **unload'ing** *n*. **unlocā'ted** *adj* not located; not surveyed or marked off (*US*). **unlock'** *vt* to undo the locking of; to free from being locked up; to let loose; to open, make accessible, or disclose. ◆ *vi* to become unlocked. **unlock'able** *adj*. **unlocked'** *adj*. **unlog'ical** *adj* not logical; illogical. **unlooked'** *adj* not looked (with *at* or *into*). **unlooked'-for** *adj* unexpected. **unloose'** (or more *usu*) **unloos'en** *vt* to loosen, unfasten, detach; to set free (also *fig*); (**unloose**) to discharge (a debt, etc) (*Scot*). **unlord'** *vt* to strip of the dignity of a lord. **unlor'ded** *adj* deprived of, or not raised to, the rank of lord; not lorded over, without a lord. **unlord'ly** *adj*. **unlov'able** or **unlove'able** *adj*. **unlove'** *vt* to cease to love; not to love. ◆ *n* /*un*'/ absence of love. **unloved'** *adj*. **unlov'erlike** *adj*. **unlov'ing** *adj*. **unlov'ingly** *adv*. **unlov'ingness** *n*. **unluck'ily** *adv* in an unlucky way; by bad luck; I'm sorry to say, unfortunately. **unluck'iness** *n*. **unluck'y** *adj* unfortunate; ill-omened; bringing bad luck; not praiseworthy (*archaic*). **unmade** *adj* not made or not yet made; self-existent; subjected to unmaking. **unmade-up'** *adj* not made up; not a made road (qv); (of a person) not wearing make-up. **unmaid'enly** *adj* unbecoming a maiden; not like a maiden. **unmail'able** *adj* (*US*) incapable of being transmitted or delivered by post. **unmailed'** *adj* not clad in mail (*hist*; **mail**[2]); not sent by post (**mail**[1]). **unmā'kable** *adj*. **unmake'** *vt* to undo the making of; to undo, ruin. **unmā'king** *n*. **unman'** *vt* to deprive of the nature, attributes and powers of humanity, manhood or maleness; to deprive of fortitude; to deprive of men. **unman'fully** *adv*. **unman'like** *adj*. **unman'liness** *n*. **unman'ly** *adj* not becoming a man; unworthy of a noble mind; base; cowardly. **unmanned'** *adj* without a crew; without a garrison; without inhabitants; untamed (*esp* of a hawk); deprived of fortitude.

Some words formed with the prefix **un-**; the numbers in brackets refer to the numbered senses in the entry for **un-**.

unpledged' *adj* (1).	**unprej'udiced** *adj* (1).	**unprohib'ited** *adj* (1).
unplī'able *adj* (1).	**unpreocc'upied** *adj* (1).	**unprojec'ted** *adj* (1).
unplī'ably *adv* (1).	**unprescribed'** *adj* (1).	**unprolif'ic** *adj* (1).
unplī'ant *adj* (1).	**unpressed'** *adj* (1).	**unprom'ised** *adj* (1)
unploughed' *adj* (1).	**unpresum'ing** *adj* (1).	**unprom'ising** *adj* (1).
unplucked' *adj* (1).	**unpresump'tuous** *adj* (1).	**unprom'isingly** *adv* (1).
unplug' *vt* (2).	**unpreten'tiousness** *n* (1).	**unpromp'ted** *adj* (1).
unpoet'ic or **unpoet'ical** *adj* (1).	**unprett'iness** *n* (1).	**unpronounce'able** *adj* (1).
unpoet'ically *adv* (1).	**unprett'y** *adj* (1).	**unpronounced'** *adj* (1).
unpoet'icalness *n* (1).	**unprimed'** *adj* (1).	**unprop'** *vt* (2).
unpoised' *adj* (1).	**unprince'ly** *adj* (1).	**unprop'ertied** *adj* (1).
unpolariz'able or **unpolarīs'able** *adj* (1).	**unpris'on** *vt* (2).	**unprophet'ic** or **unprophet'ical** *adj* (1).
unpo'larized or **unpo'larised** *adj* (1).	**unpris'oned** *adj* (1), (2).	**unpropi'tious** *adj* (1).
unpoliced' *adj* (1).	**unpriv'ileged** *adj* (1).	**unpropi'tiously** *adv* (1).
unpol'ish *vt* (2).	**unprō'cessed** *adj* (1).	**unpropi'tiousness** *n* (1).
unpol'ishable *adj* (1).	**unproclaimed'** *adj* (1).	**unproposed'** *adj* (1).
unpol'ished *adj* (1).	**unprocūr'able** *adj* (1).	**unpropped'** *adj* (1).
unpol'itic *adj* (1).	**unproduced'** *adj* (1).	**unpros'perous** *adj* (1).
unpolit'ical *adj* (1).	**unproduc'tive** *adj* (1).	**unpros'perously** *adv* (1).
unpollut'ed *adj* (1).	**unproduc'tively** *adv* (1).	**unpros'perousness** *n* (1).
unpop'ular *adj* (1).	**unproduc'tiveness** *n* (1).	**unprotest'ing** *adj* (1).
unpop'ularity *n* (1).	**unproductiv'ity** *n* (1).	**unprov'able** *adj* (1).
unpop'ularly *adv* (1).	**unprofaned'** *adj* (1).	**unproved'** *adj* (1).
unpop'ulated *adj* (1).	**unprofitabil'ity** *n* (1).	**unprō'ven** *adj* (1).
unpop'ulous *adj* (1).	**unprof'itable** *adj* (1).	**unprovis'ioned** *adj* (1).
unposed' *adj* (1).	**unprof'itableness** *n* (1).	**unprovoc'ative** *adj* (1).
unpow'dered *adj* (1).	**unprof'itably** *adv* (1).	**unpruned'** *adj* (1).
unprac'tical *adj* (1).	**unprof'iting** *adj* (1).	**unpub'lished** *adj* (1).
unpractical'ity *n* (1).	**unprogress'ive** *adj* (1).	**unpuck'ered** *adj* (1).
unprac'tically *adv* (1).	**unprogress'ively** *adv* (1).	**unpulled'** *adj* (1).
unprecise' *adj* (1).	**unprogress'iveness** *n* (1).	**unpunct'ual** *adj* (1).

■ words derived from main entry word; ❑ compound words; ▪ idioms and phrasal verbs

unmann'ered *adj* unmannerly, bad-mannered; not affected or pretentious, free from mannerism. **unmann'erliness** *n.* **unmann'erly** *adj* not mannerly; ill-bred. ◆ *adv* in an unmannerly manner. **unman'tle** *vt* to divest of a mantle; to dismantle (*rare*). ◆ *vi* to take off one's mantle. **unmanufac'tured** *adj* in a raw state. **unmanured'** *adj* not manured; untilled (*obs*). **unmarked'** *adj* bearing no mark; not noticed. **unmar'ketable** *adj* not suitable for the market, not saleable. **unmarred'** (*Spenser* **unmard'**) *adj* not marred. **unmarr'iable** (*obs*), **unmarr'iageable** *adj*. **unmarr'iageableness** *n.* **unmarr'ied** *adj* not married, *usu* never having been married; freed from marriage. **unmarr'y** *vt* to dissolve the marriage of. ◆ *vi* to dissolve one's marriage. **unmask'** *vt* to take a mask or a disguise from; to discover the identity of (eg a thief; *fig*); to reveal the place of (a gun, battery) by firing; to expose, show up. ◆ *vi* to take off a mask. **unmasked'** *adj* not wearing a mask; undisguised; divested of mask or disguise; (of eg identity) revealed. **unmask'er** *n.* **unmask'ing** *n.* **unmas'tered** *adj* uncontrolled; not overcome; without a master. **unmatch'able** *adj*. **unmatched'** *adj* matchless; unequalled. **unmatē'rial** *adj* not composed of matter. **unmatē'rialized** or **-s-** *adj*. **unmean'ing** *adj* meaningless; purposeless; expressionless. **unmean'ingly** *adv*. **unmean'ingness** *n.* **unmeant** /un-ment'/ *adj*. **unmeas'urable** *adj* immeasurable; too great to measure; inordinate; not capable of being measured. **unmeas'urably** *adv*. **unmeas'ured** *adj*. **unmech'anize** or **-ise** *vt* (*Sterne*) to disorganize. **unmech'anized** or **-s-** *adj* disorganized; not mechanized. **unmedicinable** /un-med'sin-ə-bl/ *adj* incurable; unable to cure. **unmed'itated** *adj* not meditated, unpremeditated. **unmeet'** *adj* not meet, unfit. **unmeet'ly** *adv*. **unmeet'ness** *n.* **unmen'tionable** *adj* not fit to be mentioned. **unmen'tionableness** *n.* **unmen'tionables** *n pl* a 19c would-be humorous name for trousers (also **inexpressibles**); now *usu* humorously used for articles of underclothing. **unmen'tioned** *adj*. **unmer'ciful** *adj* merciless; excessively and unpleasantly great. **unmer'cifully** *adv*. **unmer'cifulness** *n.* **unmer'itable** *adj* (*Shakesp*) undeserving. **unmer'ited** *adj*. **unmer'itedly** *adv*. **unmer'iting** *adj*. **unmet'** *adj* not met; (of a payment, need, etc) not satisfied. **unmē'ted** *adj* not meted or measured. **unmew'** *vt* to free, to release as if from a mew or cage. **unmind'ed** *adj* unheeded. **unmind'ful** *adj* not keeping in mind, regardless (of). **unmind'fully** *adv*. **unmind'fulness** *n.* **unmiss'able** *adj* too good to be missed; impossible to miss. **unmit'igable** *adj* that cannot be mitigated. **unmit'igably** *adv*. **unmit'igated** *adj* not mitigated; unqualified, utter. **unmit'igatedly** *adv*. **unmoaned'** *adj* not lamented. **unmō'dish** *adj* unfashionable. **unmon'eyed** or **unmon'ied** *adj* without money; not rich. **unmoor'** *vt* to loose from moorings. ◆ *vi* to cast off moorings. **unmor'al** *adj* having no relation to morality; amoral. **unmoral'ity** *n* detachment from questions of morality. **unmor'alized** or **-s-** *adj* not moralized upon; having no moral attached; without morality. **unmor'alizing** or **-s-** *adj*.

unmor'tised *adj* disjoined from a mortise (*lit* and *fig*). **un-Mosā'ic** *adj* not of or according to *Moses* or the Mosaic law. **unmoth'ered** *adj* without a mother; deprived of a mother. **unmoth'erly** *adj*. **unmō'tivated** *adj* having no motive; lacking incentive. **unmō'tived** *adj* without motive; without an artistic motive. **unmould'** *vt* to change or destroy the form of. **unmould'ed** *adj* not moulded. **unmount'** *vt* to remove from mountings or mount; to dismount. ◆ *vi* to dismount. **unmount'ed** *adj* not mounted. **unmov'able** or **unmove'able** *adj* immovable; not movable. **unmov'ably** or **unmove'ably** *adv*. **unmoved'** *adj* firm, not moved; not persuaded; not touched by emotion, calm. **unmov'edly** *adv*. **unmov'ing** *adj*. **unmuff'le** *vt* to take a muffle, muffling or covering from. ◆ *vi* to throw off mufflings. **unmuzz'le** *vt* to take a muzzle off (*lit* and *fig*). **unmuzz'led** *adj*. **unmuzz'ling** *n.* **unnail'** /un-nāl'/ *vt* to free from nails or from being nailed. **unnamable** or **unnameable** /un-nā'mə-bl/ *adj* impossible to name; not to be named. **unnamed** /un-nāmd'/ *adj*. **unnaneld** *adj* Shakespearean spelling of **unaneled**. **unnative** /un-nā'tiv/ *adj* not native. **unnatural** /un-nat'ū-rəl/ *adj* not according to nature; without natural affection; monstrous, heinous; (of a sexual act, vice, etc) considered not only immoral but also unacceptably indecent or abnormal; affected, insincere. **unnat'uralize** or **-ise** *vt* to make unnatural; to divest of nationality. **unnat'uralized** or **-s-** *adj* not naturalized. **unnat'urally** *adv* in an unnatural or improbable way (*esp* in the phrase **not unnaturally** of course, naturally). **unnat'uralness** *n.* **unnavigable** /un-nav'/ *adj* impossible to navigate. **unnav'igated** *adj* not yet navigated. **unnecessarily** /un-nes'/ *adv*. **unnec'essariness** *n.* **unnec'essary** *adj* not necessary. **unneighboured** /un-nā'bərd/ *adj* without neighbours. **unneigh'bourliness** *n.* **unneigh'bourly** *adj* not neighbourly, friendly or social. ◆ *adv* in an unneighbourly manner. **unnerve** /un-nûrv'/ *vt* to deprive of nerve, strength or vigour; to weaken; to disconcert. **unnerved'** *adj*. **unnerv'ing** *adj*. **unnest** /un-nest'/ *vt* to turn out of a nest (*lit* and *fig*). **unnethes** *adv see* **uneath**. **unnett'ed** *adj* not enclosed in a net. **unnō'ble** *adj* not noble; ignoble (*Spenser* and *Shakesp*). ◆ *vt* to deprive of nobility. **unnumbered** /un-num'bərd/ *adj* not counted, too many to be numbered; not marked or provided with a number. **unnurtured** /un-nûr'chərd/ *adj* not nurtured or educated; ill-bred. **unoaked'** *adj* (of wine) not fermented in an oak barrel. **unobē'dient** *adj* disobedient. **unobeyed'** *adj* (*Milton*). **unobserv'able** *adj*. **unobser'vance** *n* failure to observe rules, etc; failure to notice; lack of observing power; inattention. **unobser'vant** *adj*. **unobserved'** *adj*. **unobserv'edly** *adv*. **unobser'ving** *adj*. **unoffend'ed** *adj*. **unoffend'ing** *adj*. **unoffen'sive** *adj* inoffensive. **unoffi'cial** *adj* not official. **unoffi'cially** *adv*. **unoffi'cious** *adj* not officious. **unoften** /un-of'n/ *adv* (*rare*) seldom (*usu* as *not unoften*). **unō'pened** *adj* not opened; (of a book) not having the leaves cut apart. **unop'erative** *adj* inoperative. **unor'der** *vt* to countermand. **unor'dered** *adj* disordered; unarranged, not ordered or commanded.

Some words formed with the prefix **un-**; the numbers in brackets refer to the numbered senses in the entry for **un-**.

unpunctual'ity *n* (1).
unpunct'uated *adj* (1).
unpun'ishable *adj* (1).
unpun'ishably *adv* (1).
unpun'ished *adj* (1).
unpur'chasable or **unpur'chaseable** *adj* (1).
unpur'chased *adj* (1).
unpurged' *adj* (1).
unpū'rified *adj* (1).
unpur'posed *adj* (1).
unpursued' *adj* (1).
unqual'ifiable *adj* (1).
unqual'ified *adj* (1).
unqual'ifiedly *adv* (1).
unqual'ifiedness *n* (1).
unqual'ify *vt* (2).
unquanti'fied *adj* (1).
unquant'ized or **unquant'ised** *adj* (1).
unquarr'ied *adj* (1).
unqueen'like *adj* (1).
unqueen'ly *adj* (1).
unquelled' *adj* (1).
unquench'able *adj* (1).
unquench'ably *adv* (1).
unquenched' *adj* (1).
unquick'ened *adj* (1).
unraced' *adj* (1).
unraised' *adj* (1).
unran'somed *adj* (1).
unrat'ed *adj* (1).

unrat'ified *adj* (1).
unrav'ished *adj* (1).
unreach'able *adj* (1).
unreached' *adj* (1).
unreac'tive *adj* (1).
unreaped' *adj* (1).
unrebuked' *adj* (1).
unrecap'turable *adj* (1).
unreceipt'ed *adj* (1).
unreceived' *adj* (1).
unrecep'tive *adj* (1).
unrecip'rocated *adj* (1).
unreck'onable *adj* (1).
unreck'oned *adj* (1).
unreclaim'able *adj* (1).
unreclaim'ably *adv* (1).
unreclaimed' *adj* (1).
unrecogniz'able or **unrecognīs'able** *adj* (1).
unrecogniz'ably or **unrecognīs'ably** *adv* (1).
unrec'ognized or **unrec'ognised** *adj* (1).
unrec'ognizing or **unrec'ognising** *adj* (1).
unrecollect'ed *adj* (1).
unrecommend'able *adj* (1).
unrecommend'ed *adj* (1).
unrec'ompensed *adj* (1).
unreconcil'able *adj* (1).
unreconcil'ableness *n* (1).

unreconcil'ably *adv* (1).
unrec'onciled *adj* (1).
unrecord'ed *adj* (1).
unrecount'ed *adj* (1).
unrecov'erable *adj* (1).
unrecov'erably *adv* (1).
unrecov'ered *adj* (1).
unrect'ified *adj* (1).
unreduced' *adj* (1).
unredūc'ible *adj* (1).
unreel' *vt* and *vi* (1).
unrefined' *adj* (1).
unreflect'ed *adj* (1).
unreflect'ing *adj* (1).
unreflect'ingly *adv* (1).
unreflect'ive *adj* (1).
unreform'able *adj* (1).
unreformed' *adj* (1).
unrefract'ed *adj* (1).
unrefreshed' *adj* (1).
unrefresh'ing *adj* (1).
unrefū'ted *adj* (1).
unregard'ed *adj* (1).
unregard'ing *adj* (1).
unreg'imented *adj* (1).
unreg'istered *adj* (1).
unreg'ulated *adj* (1).
unrehearsed' *adj* (1).
unrejoiced' *adj* (1).
unrejoic'ing *adj* (1).
unrelāt'ed *adj* (1).

---

fāte; fär; mē; fûr; mīne; mōte; för; mūte; pūt; dhen (then); *el'ə-mənt* (element) • For other sounds see detailed chart of pronunciation

unor'derly *adj* not orderly. **unor'dinary** *adj* not ordinary. **unorig'inal** *adj* not original; without origin or birth (*Milton*). **unoriginality** /-*al'*/ *n*. **unorig'inate** or **unorig'inated** *adj* not originated. **unowed'** *adj* not owed or due; unowned (*Shakesp*). **unowned'** *adj* unavowed, unacknowledged; ownerless; /*un-ō'nid*/ lost (*Milton*). **unpaced'** *adj* (*athletics, cycling,* etc) without the assistance of a pace-setter. **unpack'** *vt* to remove packed articles from (a case, etc); to take out of a suitcase or other packed container; to remove from packing materials; to open; to analyse something by examining each of its constituent parts; to unzip (*comput*); to remove a pack from (a pack animal). ◆ *vi* to do unpacking. **unpacked'** *adj* subjected to unpacking; /*un'pakt*/ not packed. **unpack'er** *n*. **unpack'ing** *n*. **unpaged'** *adj* without numbering of pages. **unpaint'** *vt* to free from paint; to paint out, obliterate by painting over. **unpaint'able** *adj*. **unpaint'ed** *adj* not painted. **unpaired'** *adj* not paired; not forming one of a pair. **unpal'atable** *adj* unpleasant to taste, distasteful, disagreeable (*lit* and *fig*). **unpal'atably** *adv*. **unpan'el** *vt* (*obs*; also **unpann'el**; from **panel** (*n*), a saddle) to unsaddle. **unpan'elled** *adj* not panelled. **unpanged'** *adj* without pangs. **unpā'per** *vt* to remove paper from. **unpā'pered** *adj* not papered. **unpar'adise** *vt* to turn out of Paradise; to make no longer a paradise. **unpar'agoned** *adj* unmatched. **unpar'allel** *adj* not parallel. **unpar'alleled** *adj* without parallel or equal. **unpared'** *adj* (of fruit) not having the skin removed; (of nails) not cut. **unparent'al** *adj* not befitting a parent. **unpā'rented** *adj* without parent or acknowledged parent, or parental care. **unparliament'ary** *adj* contrary to the usages of Parliament. ◆ *adv* not such as may be spoken, or (of language) used, in Parliament. **unpass'able** *adj* impassable; (of money) not current. **unpass'ableness** *n*. **unpass'ionate** or **unpass'ioned** *adj* without passions; calm; dispassionate. **unpatt'erned** *adj* unexampled, unequalled; without a pattern. **unpaved'** *adj* without pavement; gelded (*Shakesp*). **unpavil'ioned** *adj* without a canopy. **unpay'** *vt* to make good, undo, do away with by payment. **unpay'able** *adj*. **unpeeled'** *adj* not peeled; in *Shakesp, Love's Labours Lost* II.1.88, (according to some) stripped, desolate (others think it a misprint for **unpeopled** below (without servants) (the folio reading)). **unpeer'able** *adj* not to be matched. **unpeered'** *adj* unequalled. **unpen'** *vt* to let out from a pen or enclosure. **unpenned'** *adj* unwritten (**pen**[1]); unconfined, let loose (**pen**[2]). **unpenn'ied** *adj* without pennies. **unpent'** *adj* not penned in. **unpeo'ple** *vt* to empty of people. **unpeo'pled** *adj* uninhabited; without servants; depopulated. **unperch'** *vt* to drive from a perch. **unper'fect** *adj* (now *rare*) imperfect; unskilled. **unperfec'ted** *adj*. **unperfec'tion** *n* (*obs*). **unper'fectly** *adv* (*obs*). **unper'fectness** *n* (*rare*). **un'person** *n* an individual whose existence is officially denied, ignored, or deleted from record, eg a person who has been politically superseded. ◆ *vt* /-*pûr'*/ to make (someone) into an unperson. **unpervert'** *vt* to reconvert (a person who has abandoned a doctrine assumed to be true). **unpervert'ed** *adj* not perverted. **unpick'** *vt* to pick loose, undo by picking. **unpick'able** *adj* impossible to pick; able to be unpicked. **unpicked'** *adj* not gathered; not selected; not having had unwanted material removed by picking; picked loose. **unpill'ared** *adj* stripped of pillars; without pillars. **unpin'** *vt* to free from pins or pinning; to unfasten the dress of by removing pins. **unpinked'** or **unpinkt'** *adj* (*Shakesp*) not pinked, not ornamental with punched holes. **unplace'** *vt* to displace. **unplaced'** *adj* not assigned to or set in a place; not inducted to a church; not appointed to an office; not among the first three (horses) in a race. **unplained'** *adj* (*Spenser*) not lamented. **unplau'sible** *adj* implausible. **unplau'sibly** *adv*. **unplau'sive** *adj* not approving. **unpleas'ant** *adj* not pleasant; disagreeable. **unpleas'antly** *adv*. **unpleas'antness** *n* the state or quality of being unpleasant, disagreeableness; a disagreeable incident; disagreement involving open hostility. **unpleas'antry** *n* lack of pleasantness; any unpleasant occurrence, any discomfort. **unpleased'** *adj*. **unpleas'ing** *adj* not pleasing; displeasing. **unpleas'ingly** *adv*. **unpleas'urable** *adj*. **unpleas'urably** *adv*. **unplugged'** *adj* and *adv* (performed) using acoustic rather than electronically amplified instruments. **unplumb'** *vt* to remove the lead from. **unplumbed'** *adj* unsounded; unfathomed; without plumbing. **unplume'** *vt* to strip of feathers or plumes (often *fig*). **unpoint'ed** *adj* not pointed; without point or points; with joints uncemented. **unpoi'son** *vt* to rid of poison, cure of poisoning. **unpoi'soned** *adj* not poisoned. **unpol'icied** *adj* without formal political organization; impolitic. **unpolite'** *adj* impolite; unpolished (*obs*); inelegant (*obs*). **unpolite'ly** *adv*. **unpolite'ness** *n*. **unpolled'** *adj* not polled; not having voted. **unpope'** *vt* to deprive (a pope) of office. **unpor'tioned** *adj* without a portion. **unpossessed'** *adj* not possessed; not in possession; unprejudiced (*obs*). **unpossess'ing** *adj* (*Shakesp*); without possessions. **unposs'ible** *adj* (*Shakesp; dialect*) impossible. **unpost'ed** *adj* not posted, in any sense; not posted up; without a post. **unpō'table** *adj* undrinkable, unfit to drink. **unprac'ticable** *adj* (formerly common) impracticable. **unprac'tised** *adj* having little or no practice or experience, inexpert; not carried out in practice; not yet familiar through practice (*obs*). **unprac'tisedness** *n*. **unpraise'** *vt* to dispraise; to deprive of praise. **unpraised'** *adj* not praised. **unpraise'worthy** *adj*. **unpray'** *vt* to revoke the praying of. **unpreach'** *vi* and *vt* to recant in preaching; to undo the preaching of. **unpreach'ing** *adj* not preaching. **unprec'edented** /-*pres'*/ or -*prēs'*/ *adj* not warranted by judicial, etc, precedent; of which there has been no previous instance. **unprec'edentedly** *adv*. **unpredict'** *vi* (*Milton*) to revoke what has been predicted. **unpredictabil'ity** *n*. **unpredict'able** *adj* that cannot be foretold; (of a person or thing) liable to behave in a way that cannot be predicted. **unpredict'ably** *adv*. **unpreferred'** *adj* without preferment or advancement. **unpreg'nant** *adj* (*Shakesp*) slow-witted, unready, ineffective; not quickened by a

---

Some words formed with the prefix **un-**; the numbers in brackets refer to the numbered senses in the entry for **un-**.

unrel'ative *adj* (1).	**unrepī'ning** *adj* (1).	**unrestraint'** *n* (1).
unrelaxed' *adj* (1).	**unrepī'ningly** *adv* (1).	**unrestric'ted** *adj* (1).
unreleased' *adj* (1).	**unreplace'able** *adj* (1).	**unrestric'tedly** *adv* (1).
unreliev'able *adj* (1).	**unreplen'ished** *adj* (1).	**unretard'ed** *adj* (1).
unrelieved' *adj* (1).	**unreport'able** *adj* (1).	**unretent'ive** *adj* (1).
unreliev'edly *adv* (1).	**unreport'ed** *adj* (1).	**unretouched'** *adj* (1).
unrel'ished *adj* (1).	**unrepose'ful** *adj* (1).	**unreturn'able** *adj* (1).
unreluc'tant *adj* (1).	**unrepōs'ing** *adj* (1).	**unreturned'** *adj* (1).
unremain'ing *adj* (1).	**unrepresent'ative** *adj* (1).	**unreturn'ing** *adj* (1).
unremark'able *adj* (1).	**unrepresent'ed** *adj* (1).	**unreturn'ingly** *adv* (1).
unremarked' *adj* (1).	**unrepriev'able** *adj* (1).	**unreveal'able** *adj* (1).
unrem'edied *adj* (1).	**unreprieved'** *adj* (1).	**unrevealed'** *adj* (1).
unremem'bered *adj* (1).	**unrep'rimanded** *adj* (1).	**unreveal'ing** *adj* (1).
unremem'bering *adj* (1).	**unreproached'** *adj* (1).	**unrevenged'** *adj* (1).
unremūn'erative *adj* (1).	**unreproach'ful** *adj* (1).	**unrevenge'ful** *adj* (1).
unren'dered *adj* (1).	**unreproach'ing** *adj* (1).	**unreversed'** *adj* (1).
unrenewed' *adj* (1).	**unreprodūc'ible** *adj* (1).	**unrevised'** *adj* (1).
unrenowned' *adj* (1).	**unrepug'nant** *adj* (1).	**unrevoked'** *adj* (1).
unrent' *adj* (1).	**unrepuls'able** *adj* (1).	**unrewar'ded** *adj* (1).
unrepaid' *adj* (1).	**unreq'uisite** *adj* (1).	**unrewar'dedly** *adv* (1).
unrepair' *n* (1).	**unrescind'ed** *adj* (1).	**unrewar'ding** *adj* (1).
unrepair'able *adj* (1).	**unresent'ed** *adj* (1).	**unrhyth'mical** *adj* (1).
unrepaired' *adj* (1).	**unresent'ful** *adj* (1).	**unrhyth'mically** *adv* (1).
unrepeal'able *adj* (1).	**unresent'ing** *adj* (1).	**unribbed'** *adj* (1).
unrepealed' *adj* (1).	**unrespon'sive** *adj* (1).	**unrid'able** or **unride'able** *adj* (1).
unrepelled' *adj* (1).	**unrespon'sively** *adv* (1).	**unridd'en** *adj* (1).
unrepen'tance *n* (1).	**unrespon'siveness** *n* (1).	**unrī'fled** *adj* (1).
unrepen'tant *adj* (1).	**unrestored'** *adj* (1).	**unringed'** *adj* (1).
unrepen'ted *adj* (1).	**unrestrain'able** *adj* (1).	**unripe'** *adj* (1).
unrepen'ting *adj* (1).	**unrestrained'** *adj* (1).	**unrī'pened** *adj* (1).
unrepen'tingly *adv* (1).	**unrestrain'edly** *adv* (1).	**unripe'ness** *n* (1).

■ words derived from main entry word; ❑ compound words; ◼ idioms and phrasal verbs lively sense (with *of*). **unprelat'ical** *adj* unbecoming in or to a prelate; not episcopal. **unpremed'itable** *adj* not to be foreseen. **unpremed'itated** *adj* not studied or purposed beforehand. **unpremed'itatedly** *adv*. **unpremed'itatedness** *n*. **unpremeditā'tion** *n*. unpreparedness. **unprepare'** *vt* to make unprepared. **unprepared'** *adj* not prepared or ready; not prepared for death; without preparation. **unprepā'redly** *adv*. **unprepā'redness** *n*. **unprepossessed'** *adj* not prepossessed or prejudiced. **unprepossess'ing** *adj* not predisposing others in one's favour, unpleasing. **unpresent'able** *adj* not fit to be seen. **unpretend'ing** *adj* not pretending or making pretence; modest. **unpreten'dingly** *adv*. **unpreten'tious** *adj* not pretentious; modest. **unprevail'ing** *adj* unavailing. **unpreven'table** *adj*. **unpreven'tableness** *n*. **unpreven'ted** *adj* not prevented or obviated; not anticipated or preceded (*obs*). **unpriced'** *adj* having no fixed or stated price; beyond price, priceless. **unpriest'** *vt* to divest of priesthood. **unpriest'ly** *adj* unbecoming, unlike or not of the nature of, a priest. **unprin'cipled** *adj* without good principles; not based on or in accordance with principles; not restrained by conscience; profligate; uninstructed (*Milton*). **unprint'able** *adj* not fit to be printed. **unprint'ed** *adj*. **unprīz'able** *adj* (*Shakesp*) worthless; beyond price. **unprized'** *adj* not prized. **unprocē'dūral** *adj* not in accordance with established or accepted procedures. **unprofessed'** *adj*. **unprofess'ional** *adj* not of a profession or the profession in question; beyond the limits of one's profession; unbecoming to a member of a particular profession. **unprofess'ionally** *adv*. **unprof'ited** *adj* without profit or advantage. **unprop'er** *adj* improper; common, not one's own (*Shakesp*). **unprop'erly** *adv*. **unpropor'tionable** *adj* out of due proportion. **unpropor'tionably** *adv*. **unpropor'tionate** *adj* out of due proportion. **unpropor'tionately** *adv*. **unpropor'tioned** *adj* not proportioned. **unprotec'ted** *adj* having no protection; (of sexual intercourse) done without the use of a condom. **unprotec'tedness** *n*. **unprot'estantize** or **-ise** *vt* to transform from Protestantism; to strip of Protestant character. **unprotest'ed** *adj* not objected to or protested against. **unprovide'** *vt* (*Shakesp*) to unfurnish, to deprive of what is necessary. **unprovī'ded** *adj* not furnished, provided, or provided for (also **unprovī'ded-for**). **unprovī'dedly** *adv*. **unprov'ident** *adj* (*Shakesp*) improvident. **un'provoke** *vt* (*Shakesp*) to counteract provocation of. **unprovoked'** *adj* not provoked; uncalled-for. **unprovō'kedly** *adv*. **unprovō'king** *adj*. **unpurse'** *vt* to relax (the lips) from pursing; to disburse. **unpurveyed'** (*Spenser* **unpurvaide'**) *adj* not purveyed; not provided with (with *of* ; *Spenser*); unprovided or unprepared (*obs*). **unputdown'able** *adj* (*inf*) of a book, too absorbing to be set aside, compelling one to read to the end without interruption. **unqual'itied** or **unqual'ited** *adj* (*Shakesp*) bereft of qualities. **unqueen'** *vt* to deprive of the rank of a queen; in beekeeping, to deprive (a beehive) of a queen bee. **unqueened'** *adj*. **unques'tionable** *adj* not to be questioned, certain, beyond doubt;

averse to conversation, or *perh* impatient of question (*Shakesp*). **unques'tionably** *adv* in such a way as to be unquestionable; certainly, without doubt. **unques'tioned** *adj* not called in question; not subjected to questioning; not examined. **unques'tioning** *adj*. **unquī'et** *adj* disturbed; restless; uneasy. ◆ *vt* to disquiet. **unquī'etly** *adv*. **unquī'etness** *n*. **unquōt'able** *adj* unsuitable or unfit for quotation. **unquote'** *vi* to close a quotation; to mark the end of a quoted passage with superscript comma or commas, used as an interjection to indicate that a quotation is finished. **unquot'ed** *adj* (of a company) not quoted on the Stock Exchange list. **unracked'** *adj* (of liquor) not drawn off from the lees; not stretched on the rack; not strained. **unrake'** *vt* to uncover by raking. **unraked'** *adj* not raked; uncovered by raking; (of a fire) not banked up. **unrav'el** *vt* to disentangle; to unknit. ◆ *vi* to become disentangled. **unrav'elled** *adj*. **unrav'eller** *n*. **unrav'elling** *n*. **unrav'elment** *n*. **unrā'zored** *adj* unshaven. **unread** /un-red'/ *adj* not informed by reading; not perused. **unreadable** /un-rēd'ə-bl/ *adj* indecipherable; too dull or badly written to be read. **unread'ableness** *n*. **unreadily** /-red'/ *adv*. **unread'iness** *n*. **unread'y** *adj* not ready, prepared or prompt; hesitating, holding back; undressed or not dressed (*Shakesp*, etc; **make unready** (*obs*) to undress); (earlier **unredy**) uncounselled or unwise, redeless (*obs*; from **rede**). **unrē'al** *adj* not real or like reality; incredible; illusory; amazing, unbelievable (*inf*); a general expression of appreciation or admiration (*sl*, *orig US*). **unrē'alism** *n*. **unrealist'ic** *adj* not like reality; unreasonable or impracticable. **unreal'ity** *n* absence or lack of reality or existence; an unreal thing. **unrealī'zable** or **-s-** *adj* impossible. **unrē'alize** or **-ise** *vt* to divest of reality. **unrē'alized** or **-s-** *adj*. **unrē'ally** *adv*. **unrēa'son** *n* lack of reason or reasonableness; nonsense; injustice (*obs*); see also **abbot of unreason** under **abbot**. **unrea'sonable** *adj* not agreeable to reason; exceeding the bounds of reason, immoderate; not influenced by reason. **unrea'sonableness** *n*. **unrea'sonably** *adv*. **unrea'soned** *adj* not argued or thought out. **unrea'soning** *adj* not reasoning; showing lack of reason, irrational. **unrea'soningly** *adv*. **unreave'** *vt* (from dialect *reeve* or *reave* to wind or unwind) to unweave (*Spenser*); to unwind (*dialect*). **unrebā'ted** *adj* unblunted; undulled; without rebate. **unrecall'able** *adj*. **unrecalled'** *adj*. **unrecall'ing** *adj* (*Shakesp*; *Milton*) impossible to undo, not to be recalled. **unrecked'** *adj* not regarded or cared about. **unreconcil'iable** *adj* (*Shakesp*) unreconcilable. **unreconstruct'ed** *adj* not reconstructed or rebuilt; not accepting the current situation or opinions; not adjusted or reconciled to reconstruction (*US hist*). **unrecūr'ing** *adj* (*Shakesp*) incurable. **unred'** *adj* (*Spenser*) for **unread** above (unrecounted, untold). **unredeem'able** *adj*. **unredeemed'** *adj* not redeemed, *esp* spiritually or from pawn; without compensatory quality or circumstance, hence unmitigated, unrelieved. **unredressed'** or **unredrest'** *adj* not redressed; without redress or

---

Some words formed with the prefix **un-**; the numbers in brackets refer to the numbered senses in the entry for **un-**.

unris'en *adj* (1).	**unsatir'ical** *adj* (1).	**unsecta'rianism** *n* (1).
unrī'valled *adj* (1).	**unsatisfac'tion** *n* (1).	**unsec'ular** *adj* (1).
unriv'en *adj* (1).	**unsatisfac'torily** *adv* (1).	**unseduced'** *adj* (1).
unroad'worthy *adj* (1).	**unsatisfac'toriness** *n* (1).	**unsegment'ed** *adj* (1).
unrō'manized or **unrō'manised** *adj* (1).	**unsatisfac'tory** *adj* (1).	**unseg'regated** *adj* (1).
unroman'tic or **unroman'tical** *adj* (1).	**unsat'isfiable** *adj* (1).	**unselec'tive** *adj* (1).
unroman'tically *adv* (1).	**unsat'isfied** *adj* (1).	**unselfcon'scious** *adj* (1).
unros'ined *adj* (1).	**unsat'isfiedness** *n* (1).	**unselfcon'sciously** *adv* (1).
unrott'ed *adj* (1).	**unsat'isfying** *adj* (1).	**unselfcon'sciousness** *n* (1).
unrott'en *adj* (1).	**unsat'isfyingness** *n* (1).	**unsell'able** *adj* (1).
unrouged' *adj* (1).	**unsatura'tion** *n* (1).	**unsensā'tional** *adj* (1).
unround' *adj* (1) and *vt* (2).	**unsaved'** *adj* (1).	**unsens'itive** *adj* (1).
unroused' *adj* (1).	**unscarred'** *adj* (1).	**unsens'itized** or **unsens'itised** *adj* (1).
unroy'al *adj* (1).	**unscar'y** *adj* (1).	**unsent'** *adj* (1).
unroy'ally *adv* (1).	**unscent'ed** *adj* (1).	**unsent'enced** *adj* (1).
unrubbed' *adj* (1).	**unsched'uled** *adj* (1).	**unsentimen'tal** *adj* (1).
unrum'pled *adj* (1).	**unschol'arlike** *adj* (1).	**unsep'arable** (*Shakesp*) *adj* (1).
unsalabil'ity or **unsaleabil'ity** *n* (1).	**unschol'arly** *adj* (1).	**unsep'arated** *adj* (1).
unsal'able or **unsale'able** *adj* (1).	**unschooled'** *adj* (1).	**unsep'ulchred** *adj* (1).
unsal'aried *adj* (1).	**unscientif'ic** *adj* (1).	**unsē'rious** *adj* (1).
unsalt'ed *adj* (1).	**unscientif'ically** *adv* (1).	**unser'viceable** *adj* (1).
unsalu'ted *adj* (1).	**unscorched'** *adj* (1).	**unsev'ered** *adj* (1).
unsal'vageable *adj* (1).	**unscoured'** *adj* (1).	**unsex'ist** *adj* (1).
unsanc'tioned *adj* (1).	**unscratched'** *adj* (1).	**unsex'ual** *adj* (1).
unsan'dalled *adj* (1).	**unscru'tinized** or **unscru'tinised** *adj* (1).	**unsex'y** *adj* (1).
unsapped' *adj* (1).	**unsculp'tured** *adj* (1).	**unshā'ded** *adj* (1).
unsashed' *adj* (1).	**unscythed'** *adj* (1).	**unshak'able** or **unshake'able** *adj* (1).
unsāt'ed *adj* (1).	**unsea'worthiness** *n* (1).	**unshak'ably** or **unshake'ably** *adv* (1).
unsā'tiate or **unsā'tiated** *adj* (1).	**unsea'worthy** *adj* (1).	**unshaked'** (*Shakesp*) *adj* (1).
unsā'tiating *adj* (1).	**unsec'onded** *adj* (1).	**unshāk'en** *adj* (1).
unsāt'ing *adj* (1).	**unsecta'rian** *adj* (1).	**unshāk'enly** *adv* (1).

---

possibility of escape (*Spenser*). **unredy** *adj* see **unready** above. **unreeve'** *vt* to withdraw from being reeved. **unregen'eracy** *n*. **unregen'erate** *adj* not regenerate; unrepentant, refusing to be reformed. **unregen'erated** *adj*. **unrein'** *vt* to relax the rein of, give rein to. **unreined'** *adj* unchecked. **unrelen'ting** *adj*. **unrelen'tingly** *adv*. **unrelen'tingness** *n*. **unrelen'tor** *n* (*Keats*) someone who does not relent. **unrelīabil'ity** *n* (see note at **rely**). **unrelī'able** *adj* not to be relied upon. **unrelī'ableness** *n*. **unrelig'ious** *adj* not connected with religion; not religious without being necessarily contrary or hostile to religion; irreligious. **unremitt'ed** *adj*. **unremitt'edly** *adv*. **unremitt'ent** *adj*. **unremitt'ently** *adv*. **unremitt'ing** *adj* not remitting or relaxing; continued; incessant. **unremitt'ingly** *adv*. **unremitt'ingness** *n*. **unremorse'ful** *adj* feeling no remorse. **unremorse'fully** *adv*. **unremorse'less** *adj* (*obs*) remorseless. **unremov'able** *adj* not removable; immovable, fixed, constant (*obs*). **unremoved'** *adj* not removed; fixed, unshaken (*obs*). **unrepeat'able** *adj* not repeatable; indecent, gross; that cannot be done, etc again. **unrepeat'ed** *adj*. **unreprov'able** *adj*. **unreproved'** (or /-*proo'vid*/) *adj* not reproved; not liable to reproof, blameless (*Spenser* and *Milton*). **unreprov'ing** *adj*. **unrequired'** *adj* unasked; unasked-for; unnecessary. **unrequit'ed** *adj* not reciprocated or returned. **unrequīt'edly** *adv*. **unreserve'** *n* absence of reserve. **unreserved'** *adj* not reserved; without reserve or reservation; unrestricted, unqualified. **unreser'vedly** *adv*. **unreser'vedness** *n*. **unresist'ed** *adj*. **unresist'ible** *adj* (*rare*) irresistible. **unresist'ing** *adj*. **unresis'tingly** *adv*. **unresolv'able** *adj*. **unresolved'** *adj* not resolved, determined, settled or solved; irresolute; undecided; not separated into its constituent parts. **unresol'vedness** *n* irresolution. **unrespect'ed** *adj*. **unrespect'ive** *adj* indiscriminate; inattentive, unthinking (*Shakesp*); undiscriminating (*Shakesp*). **unres'pited** *adj* (*Milton*) without respite or pause. **unrest'** *n* lack of rest; disquiet; disturbance; discontent verging on insurrection. **unrest'ful** *adj* not restful; uneasy; full of unrest. **unrest'fulness** *n*. **unrest'ing** *adj*. **unrest'ingly** *adv*. **unrest'ingness** *n*. **unrev'erend** *adj* not reverend; not reverent, irreverent, unreverent (*Shakesp*). **unrev'erent** *adj* not reverent. **unrevert'ed** *adj* not turned back. **unrhymed'** *adj* not rhymed. **unrid'** *adj* (*archaic*) unridden. **unridd'le** *vt* to read the riddle of; to solve. **unridd'leable** *adj*. **unridd'ler** *n*. **unrig'** *vt* to strip of rigging or of clothes, etc. **unrigged'** *adj* without rigging; stripped of rigging. **unright'** *n* (*archaic*) wrong; unfairness, injustice. ◆*adj* (*archaic*) wrong. **unrigh'teous** *adj* sinful or unjust. **unrigh'teously** *adv*. **unrigh'teousness** *n*. **unright'ful** *adj*. **unright'fully** *adv*. **unright'fulness** *n*. **unrimed'** *adj* same as **unrhymed** above. **unrip'** *vt* to rip up or open; to strip, lay bare; to disclose. **unripped'** *adj* not ripped; ripped up or open. **unripp'ing** *n*. **unriv'et** *vt* to loose from being riveted; to detach (*fig*). **unrobe'** *vt* to strip of a robe, to undress. ◆ *vi* to take off a robe, *esp* of state. **unroll'** *vt* to open out from a rolled state; to strike off the roll (*Shakesp*). ◆ *vi* to

become unrolled. **unroof'** *vt* to strip the roof from. **unroofed'** *adj* not roofed; stripped of its roof. **unroost'** *vt* (*Shakesp*) to drive out of a roost. **unroot'** *vt* to tear up by the roots. **unroot'ed** *adj* without root; not uprooted (with *out*); rooted out. **unrope'** *vt* to loose from a rope. **unrough'** *adj* not rough; (*Shakesp* **unruffe'**) beardless. **unround'ed** *adj* not rounded; articulated with spread lips (*phonetics*). **unrude'** *adj* not rude; also (*obs, prob* by confusion from obsolete *unride*, from OE *ungerȳde* rough, from *gerȳde* smooth, easy) rude, uncouth. **unruff'able** *adj* (*Dickens*) imperturbable. **unruff'le** *vt* to restore or recover from ruffling. **unruff'led** *adj* smooth; calm; not disturbed or flustered. **unrule'** *n* anarchy. **unruled'** *adj* not governed; without ruled lines. **unrul'iment** *n* (*Spenser*) unruliness. **unrul'iness** *n*. **unrul'y** *adj* ungovernable; unmanageable; turbulent; stormy. **unsadd'le** *vt* to take the saddle from; to dislodge from the saddle. **unsadd'led** *adj*. **unsafe'** *adj* not safe or secure; (of a conclusion, conviction, etc) based on insufficient or suspect evidence; (of sexual intercourse) done without the use of a condom. **unsafe'ly** *adv*. **unsafe'ness** *n*. **unsafe'ty** *n*. **unsaid'** *adj* not said (see also **unsay** below). **unsailed'** *adj* unnavigated. **unsained'** *adj* unblessed. **unsaint'** *vt* to divest of saintliness or of the title of saint. **unsaint'liness** *n*. **unsaint'ly** *adj*. **unsanc'tified** *adj*. **unsanc'tify** *vt* to undo the sanctification of; to desecrate. **unsan'itary** *adj* without (regard to) sanitation, unhealthy. **unsā'table** *adj* (*Browning*) and **unsā'tiable** (now *rare*) insatiable. **unsat'urated** *adj* not saturated; containing a double or triple bond in the molecule, and thus susceptible to addition reactions (*chem*; **unsaturated fat** a vegetable or fish oil or fat (*usu* a liquid, eg olive oil or cod-liver oil) containing a high proportion of unsaturated fatty acids). **unsā'vourily** *adv*. **unsā'vouriness** *n*. **unsā'voury** *adj* not savoury, tasteless; unpleasant, disagreeable; offensive; disreputable. **unsay'** *vt* (*pat* and *pap* **unsaid'**) to retract. **unsay'able** *adj* that cannot be said. **unscabb'ard** *vt* to unsheathe. **unscāl'able** *adj* that cannot be climbed. **unscale'** *vt* to remove scales from. **unscaled'** *adj* unclimbed; cleared of scales; scaleless. **unscanned'** *adj* not scanned as verse; not scrutinized; (*Shakesp* **un'skan'd**) unconsidered. **unscathed'** *adj* not harmed or injured. **unscav'engered** *adj* (*Dickens*) not cleared of rubbish. **unscep'tred** *adj* without a sceptre; deposed. **unsciss'ored** *adj* not cut with scissors. **unscott'ified** *adj* deprived of Scottish qualities or characteristics. **unscram'ble** *vt* to decode from a scrambled state, or to restore to natural sound; to restore (something in which categories have been deliberately jumbled) to a system of classification and separation. **unscreened'** *adj* not screened; unsifted. **unscrew'** *vt* to loose from a state of being screwed; to open, loosen or detach by screwing. ◆ *vi* to be capable of being or becoming unscrewed. **unscrip'ted** *adj* not using a script; unrehearsed; (of comments, moves, etc) not planned, not in the script (*radio, TV*, etc). **unscrip'tural** *adj* not in accordance with, or not warranted by, the Bible. **unscrip'turally**

Some words formed with the prefix **un-**; the numbers in brackets refer to the numbered senses in the entry for **un-**.

unshared' *adj* (1).	**unskimmed'** *adj* (1).	**unsol'idly** *adv* (1).
unsharp'ened *adj* (1).	**unslain'** *adj* (1).	**unson'sy** (*Scot*) *adj* (1).
unshaved' *adj* (1).	**unslāk'able** or **unslāke'able** *adj* (1).	**unsoured'** *adj* (1).
unshā'ven *adj* (1).	**unslaked'** *adj* (1).	**unsown'** *adj* (1).
unshel'tered *adj* (1).	**unsleep'ing** *adj* (1).	**unspeak'ing** *adj* (1).
unshewn' (*archaic*) *adj* (1).	**unslept'-in** *adj* (1).	**unspe'cialized** or **unspe'cialised** *adj* (1).
unshield'ed *adj* (1).	**unsliced'** *adj* (1).	**unspecif'ic** *adj* (1).
unshift'ing *adj* (1).	**unslipp'ing** *adj* (1).	**unspec'ified** *adj* (1).
unshing'led *adj* (1).	**unslum'bering** *adj* (1).	**unspec'tacled** *adj* (1).
unshock'able *adj* (1).	**unslum'brous** *adj* (1).	**unspectac'ular** *adj* (1).
unshocked' *adj* (1).	**unslung'** *adj* (1).	**unspec'ulative** *adj* (1).
unshorn' *adj* (1).	**unsmart'** *adj* (1).	**unspilled'** *adj* (1).
unshot' *adj* (1).	**unsmiled'-on** *adj* (1).	**unspilt'** *adj* (1).
unshown' *adj* (1).	**unsmil'ing** *adj* (1).	**unspirit'ed** *adj* (1).
unshrink'able *adj* (1).	**unsmil'ingly** *adv* (1).	**unsplint'erable** *adj* (1).
unshrink'ing *adj* (1).	**unsmirched'** *adj* (1).	**unspoiled'** *adj* (1).
unshrink'ingly *adv* (1).	**unsmitt'en** *adj* (1).	**unspoilt'** *adj* (1).
unshrived' *adj* (1).	**unsmoth'erable** *adj* (1).	**unspoke'** (*Shakesp*) *adj* (1).
unshriv'en *adj* (1).	**unsnap'** *vt* (2).	**unspō'ken** *adj* (1).
unsick'er (*Scot*) *adj* (1).	**unsneck'** *vt* (2).	**unsport'ing** *adj* (1).
unsick'led *adj* (1).	**unsnuffed'** *adj* (1).	**unsports'manlike** *adj* (1).
unsighed'-for *adj* (1).	**unsoftened'** *adj* (1).	**unspott'ed** *adj* (1).
unsigh'ing *adj* (1).	**unsoftening'** *adj* (1).	**unspott'edness** *n* (1).
unsigned' *adj* (1).	**unsoiled'** *adj* (1).	**unsprink'led** *adj* (1).
unsink'able *adj* (1).	**unsol'aced** *adj* (1).	**unspun'** *adj* (1).
unsis'terliness *n* (1).	**unsōld'** *adj* (1).	**unsquared'** *adj* (1).
unsis'terly *adj* (1).	**unsōl'dierlike** *adj* (1).	**unstā'ble** *adj* (1).
unskil'ful *adj* (1).	**unsōl'dierly** *adj* (1).	**unstā'bleness** *n* (1).
unskil'fully *adv* (1).	**unsolic'itous** *adj* (1).	**unstaid'** *adj* (1).
unskil'fulness *n* (1).	**unsol'id** *adj* (1).	**unstaid'ness** *n* (1).
unskilled' *adj* (1).	**unsolid'ity** *n* (1).	**unstain'able** *adj* (1).

■ words derived from main entry word; ❑ compound words; ▪ idioms and phrasal verbs

adv. **unscru'pled** *adj* unscrupulous; not scrupled at. **unscru'pulous** *adj* without scruples or principles. **unscru'pulously** *adv.* **unscru'pulousness** *n.* **unseal'** *vt* to remove or break the seal of; to free from sealing or closure; to open (sometimes *prob* for **unseel** below). **unsealed'** *adj* not sealed; freed from a seal; opened. **unseam'** *vt* to undo a seam of; to rip open (*Shakesp*). **unseamed'** *adj* without seams. **unsearch'able** *adj* inscrutable, not possible to be searched into; mysterious. **unsearch'ableness** *n.* **unsearch'ably** *adv.* **unsearched'** *adj.* **unsea'son** *vt* (*Spenser*) to affect disagreeably. **unsea'sonable** *adj* not in season; ill-timed. **unsea'sonableness** *n.* **unsea'sonably** *adv.* **unsea'sonal** *adj* inappropriate for the season. **unsea'soned** *adj* without seasoning; not matured; not inured or habituated; unseasonable (*Shakesp*). **unseat'** *vt* to remove from a seat; to throw (a horse-rider); to oust from a parliamentary seat. **unseat'ed** *adj* not seated; ousted, thrown, removed from a seat. **unsē'cret** *adj* (*Shakesp*) failing to preserve secrecy. **unsecu'red** *adj* not secured or made safe; (of a loan or creditor) without security. **unsee'able** *adj* invisible. **unseed'ed** *adj* not seeded; (in tennis tournaments, etc) not placed in the draw of top players. **unsee'ing** *adj* not seeing; unobservant; without insight or understanding. **unseel'** *vt* (**seel**[1]) to unsew the eyes of, undo the seeling of. **unseem'ing** *n* (*Shakesp*) not seeming. ◆ *adj* (*obs*) unbecoming, unseemly. **unseem'liness** *n.* **unseem'ly** *adj* not seemly, becoming or decent; ill-looking. ◆ *adv* in an unseemly manner. **unseen'** *adj* not seen; invisible; not previously seen or prepared for; inexperienced, not well up (*obs*). ◆ *n* an unprepared passage for translation. **unseiz'able** *adj.* **unseized'** *adj* not seized; not taken or put in possession. **unsel'dom** *adv* not seldom (*lit* and *rare*); misused to mean seldom (as in *not unseldom*, frequently). **un'self** *n* altruism; impersonality. ◆ *vt* /-*self*'/ to divest of personality, individuality, selfhood or selfishness. **unself'ish** *adj* having or showing concern for others; generous. **unself'ishly** *adv.* **unself'ishness** *n.* **unsem'inar'd** or **unsem'inaried** *adj* (*Shakesp*) without means of generation, deprived of semen or seed. **unsense'** *vt* to deprive of sense or consciousness. **unsensed'** *adj* meaningless. **unsens'ible** *adj* (*obs* or *dialect*) insensible. **unsens'ibly** *adv* (*obs*) insensibly, imperceptibly; without sense. **unsens'ualize** or **-ise** *vt* to free from the dominion of the senses. **unset'** *vt* to undo the setting of. ◆ *adj* not set; not yet firm or solid; (of a jewel) not in a setting; unplanted. **unsett'le** *vt* to change from being settled; to make uncertain, unstable or restless; to unfix. ◆ *vi* to become unsettled. **unsett'led** *adj* not settled, fixed or determined; changeable; not having the dregs deposited; not yet inhabited and cultivated; turbulent, lawless. **unsett'ledly** *adv.* **unsett'ledness** *n.* **unsett'lement** *n.* **unsett'ling** *n* and *adj.* **unsew'** *vt* to undo the stitching of (a garment, etc). **unsewn'** (also **unsewed'**) *adj* not sewn (**unsewn binding** a bookbinding in which the gathered sections are held in place by a process other than sewing, *esp* perfect binding or

burst binding (qqv)). **unsex'** *vt* to divest of sex; to divest of the characteristics or of the qualities expected of one's own sex. **unsexed'** *adj* without the characteristics or qualities expected of one's sex. **unshack'le** *vt* to loose from shackles; to remove a shackle from. **unshack'led** *adj.* **unshad'ow** *vt* to clear of shadow; to reveal. **unshad'owable** *adj* impossible to shadow. **unshad'owed** *adj* not darkened. **unshale'** *vt* to shale or shell, strip the husk from; to reveal. **unshamed'** *adj* not ashamed; not put to shame. **unshape'** *vt* to deprive of shape; to undo, destroy or confound. **unshaped'** *adj.* **unshape'ly** *adj.* **unshāp'en** *adj.* **unsheathe'** *vt* to draw from the sheath; to uncover. **unsheathed'** *adj* drawn from the sheath; not sheathed. **unshed'** *adj* not shed; unparted (*Spenser*). **unshell'** *vt* to shell, remove the shell from. **unshent'** *adj* (*archaic*) uninjured; not disgraced. **unship'** *vt* to unload (cargo) from a ship or boat, etc; to remove from a fixed or allotted place (such as oars from the rowlocks); (of a horse) to unseat (the rider). ◆ *vi* to be capable of or undergo unshipping. **unshod'** *adj* shoeless; with shoe or shoes removed. **unshoe'** *vt* to strip of a shoe or shoes. **unshout'** (*Shakesp* **unshoot'**) *vt* to revoke the shouting of by a contrary shout. **unshowered** /*un-showrd'*/ *adj* not watered by showers. **unshroud'** *vt* to uncover. **unshrubbed'** *adj* (*Shakesp* **unshrubd'**) without shrubs. **unshunn'able** *adj.* **unshunned'** (*Shakesp* **unshun'd'**) *adj* inevitable. **unshut'** *vt*, *vi* and *adj* open. **unshutt'er** *vt* to open or remove the shutters of. **unsift'ed** *adj* not sifted; not critically examined; inexperienced. **unsight'ed** *adj* not seen (also *obs*, **unsight'**); (of a gun, etc) having no sights; fired without use of sights; prevented from seeing, *esp* by an obstruction; blind. **unsight'liness** *n.* **unsight'ly** *adj* displeasing to the eye; ugly. **unsin'ew** *vt* to take the strength from. **unsin'ewed** (*Shakesp* **unsinn'owed** *adj*). **unsis'tered** *adj* without a sister. **unsist'ing** *adj* (*Shakesp, Measure for Measure* IV.2.85) variously explained as unassisting, unresisting, insisting, unresting. **unsiz'able** or **unsize'able** *adj* (*obs*) extraordinarily big; too little, immature. **unsized'** *adj* not fitted, adjusted or sorted in respect of size; not treated with size. **unskan'd** *adj* (*Shakesp*) see **unscanned** above. **unskinned'** *adj* skinned; not skinned. **unsling'** *vt* (*pat* and *pap* **unslung'**) to free from slings or from being slung. **unsluice'** *vt* to let flow; to open the sluice of. **unsmoked'** *adj* not smoked; not cured by smoke. **unsmooth'** *adj.* ◆ *vt* to roughen; to wrinkle. **unsmoothed'** *adj.* **unsmote'** *adj* (*archaic*) unsmitten. **unsnarl'** *vt* to disentangle. **unsoaped'** *adj* not soaped; unwashed. **unsociabil'ity** *n.* **unsō'ciable** *adj* not wanting to associate with others. **unsō'ciableness** *n.* **unsō'ciably** *adv.* **unsō'cial** *adj* not social; not regarding or contributing to the good of society; not sociable; (of hours of work) not falling within the normal working day. **unsō'cialism** or **unsocial'ity** *n.* **unsō'cialized** or **-s-** *adj* not socialized, not aware of one's function in, or lacking attributes for living in, society. **unsō'cially** *adv.* **unsock'et** *vt* to take out of the socket. **unsod'** or **unsodd'en** *adj*

Some words formed with the prefix **un-**; the numbers in brackets refer to the numbered senses in the entry for **un-**.

unstained' *adj* (1).	**unsubmitt'ing** *adj* (1).	**unsustained'** *adj* (1).
unstamped' *adj* (1).	**unsubscribe'** *vi* and *vt* (2).	**unsustain'ing** *adj* (1).
unstates'manlike *adj* (1).	**unsubscribed'** *adj* (1).	**unswall'owed** *adj* (1).
unstead'fast *adj* (1).	**unsub'sidized** or **unsub'sidised** *adj* (1).	**unsweet'** *adj* (1).
unstead'fastly *adv* (1).	**unsubstan'tiated** *adj* (1).	**unsweet'ened** *adj* (1).
unstead'fastness *n* (1).	**unsubstantiā'tion** *n* (1).	**unswept'** *adj* (1).
unster'ile *adj* (1).	**unsubt'le** *adj* (1).	**unsympathet'ic** *adj* (1).
unster'ilized or **unster'ilised** *adj* (1).	**unsucc'oured** *adj* (1).	**unsympathet'ically** *adv* (1).
unstī'fled *adj* (1).	**unsucked'** *adj* (1).	**unsym'pathizing** or **unsym'pathising** *adj*
unstig'matized or **unstig'matised** *adj* (1).	**unsued'-for** or **unsued-to** *adj* (1).	(1).
unstilled' *adj* (1).	**unsull'ied** *adj* (1).	**unsym'pathy** *n* (1).
unstim'ulated *adj* (1).	**unsumm'oned** *adj* (1).	**unsystemat'ic** or **unsystemat'ical** *adj* (1).
unstint'ed *adj* (1).	**unsuper'fluous** (*Milton*) *adj* (1).	**unsystemat'ically** *adv* (1).
unstint'ing *adj* (1).	**unsu'pervised** *adj* (1).	**unsys'tematized** or **unsys'tematised** *adj*
unstirred' *adj* (1).	**unsupp'le** *adj* (1).	(1).
unstoop'ing *adj* (1).	**unsupp'leness** *n* (1).	**untailed'** *adj* (1).
unstrapped' *adj* (1).	**unsupplied'** *adj* (1).	**untā'ken** *adj* (1).
unstrat'ified *adj* (1).	**unsuppōs'able** *adj* (1).	**untal'ented** *adj* (1).
unstrength'ened *adj* (1).	**unsuppressed'** *adj* (1).	**untalked'-of** *adj* (1).
unstriped' *adj* (1).	**unsur'faced** *adj* (1).	**untan'gible** *adj* (1).
unstruck' *adj* (1).	**unsurmised'** *adj* (1).	**untanned'** *adj* (1).
unstruc'tured *adj* (1).	**unsurpass'able** *adj* (1).	**untaped'** *adj* (1).
unstuffed' (*Shakesp* **un'stuft**) *adj* (1).	**unsurpass'ably** *adv* (1).	**untapped'** *adj* (1).
unsubdū'able *adj* (1).	**unsurpassed'** *adj* (1).	**untar'nished** *adj* (1).
unsubdued' *adj* (1).	**unsurprised'** *adj* (1).	**untarred'** *adj* (1).
unsub'ject *adj* (1).	**unsurprī'sing** *adj* (1).	**untast'ed** *adj* (1).
unsubject'ed *adj* (1).	**unsurprī'singly** *adv* (1).	**untaste'ful** *adj* (1).
unsub'limated *adj* (1).	**unsurveyed'** *adj* (1).	**untear'able** *adj* (1).
unsublimed' *adj* (1).	**unsuscept'ible** *adj* (1).	**untech'nical** *adj* (1).
unsubmerged' *adj* (1).	**unsuspend'ed** *adj* (1).	**untell'able** *adj* (1).
unsubmiss'ive *adj* (1).	**unsustain'able** *adj* (1).	**untemp'ted** *adj* (1).

---

unboiled; not soaked or saturated. **unsoft'** adv (Spenser) not softly. **unsolder** /un-sod'ər or -sol'dər, -sōl', -sö' or -sö'/ vt to separate from being soldered. **unsol'emn** adj not solemn; informal. **unsolic'ited** adj not sought or invited; voluntary. **unsolv'able** adj impossible to solve. **unsolved'** adj not solved. **unsoote'** adj (Spenser) unsweet. **unsophis'ticate** (now rare) or **unsophis'ticated** adj genuine, unadulterated; unfalsified; free from artificiality; simple, basic; ingenuous; inexperienced in evil. **unsophis'ticatedness** n. **unsophistica'tion** n. **unsort'ed** adj not sorted or arranged; ill-chosen; unfitting, unsuitable. **unsought'** adj not sought or solicited. **unsoul'** vt to deprive of soul or spirit. **unsouled'** adj deprived of or not endowed with soul. **unsound'** adj unhealthy; injured or damaged; not firm or solid; ill-founded; unreliable. **unsound'able** adj unfathomable. **unsound'ed** adj not sounded, pronounced or made to sound; unfathomed, unplumbed. **unsound'ly** adv. **unsound'ness** n. **unsourced'** adj having no source, or no established or authenticated source. **unspar'** vt to withdraw a spar from. **unspared'** adj not spared; unstinted. **unspār'ing** adj not sparing, liberal, profuse; unmerciful. **unspār'ingly** adv. **unspār'ingness** n. **unspeak'** vt (Shakesp) to retract. **unspeak'able** adj unutterable; inexpressible, esp indescribably bad. **unspeak'ableness** n. **unspeak'ably** adv. **unsped'** adj (rare) without achievement or success; unaccomplished. **unspell'** vt to free from a spell. **unspent'** adj not spent. **unsphere'** vt to draw or remove from its sphere. **unspied'** (Spenser **unspide'**, Milton **unspi'd'**) adj unobserved. **unspir'itual** adj. **unspir'itualize** or **-ise** vt to deprive of spirituality. **unspir'itually** adv. **unsprung'** adj not sprung; without springs. **unstack'** vt to remove from a stack. **unstanch'able** or **unstaunch'able** adj. **unstanched'** or **unstaunched'** (or /un'/) adj not stanched; unsated (Shakesp); leaky, hence incontinent (Shakesp). **unstarch'** vt to free from starch. **unstarched'** adj not starched. **unstate'** vt (Shakesp) to deprive of state or dignity. **unstat'ed** adj not stated or declared. **unstat'ūtable** adj contrary to statute. **unstat'ūtably** adv. **unstayed'** adj not stayed or restrained; unsupported; unsteady (Spenser); without stays. **unstay'ing** adj without stop. **unstead'ily** adv. **unstead'iness** n. **unstead'y** adj. ◆ vt to make unsteady. **unsteel'** vt to soften, to disarm. **unstep'** vt to remove (esp a mast) from its place. **unsterc'orated** adj not manured. **unstick'** vt (pat and pap **unstuck'**) to free from sticking. ◆ vi to come off from the surface. ◆ adj detached, loosened from sticking (**come unstuck** of a plan, to go amiss). **unstitch'** vt to take out the stitches of. **unstock'** vt to deplete of stock; to remove the stock from; to launch (obs). **unstocked'** adj not stocked; without stock; not wearing a stock. **unstock'inged** adj not wearing a stocking or stockings. **unstop'** vt to free from being stopped; to draw out the stop or stopper of. **unstopp'able** adj not able to be stopped. **unstopp'ably** adv. **unstopped'** adj not stopped; (of a consonant) open; without a pause at the end of the line. **unstopp'er** vt to take the stopper from. **unstow'** vt to empty of contents; to take out of stowage. **unstrained'** adj not strained or purified by straining; not subjected to strain; not forced, natural. **unstrap'** vt to undo the straps of. **unstreamed'** adj (of schoolchildren) not divided into classes according to ability. **unstressed'** adj not subject to stress; not stressed or emphasized. **unstrī'ated** adj not striped. **unstring'** vt to take the strings from; to loose the strings of; to take from a string; to put out of tone; to disorganize. ◆ vi to loose the strings of one's purse. **unstringed'** adj not stringed, not provided with strings. **unstrip'** vt (now dialect) to strip. **unstripped'** adj not stripped. **unstrung'** adj with strings removed or slackened; not strung; relaxed; disorganized; unnerved. **unstuck** adj see unstick above. **unstud'ied** adj not studied; not having studied; without premeditation; unlaboured; spontaneous; natural, easy. **un'stuffy** adj (fig) not stodgy or strait-laced. **unsubstan'tial** adj not substantial, real, corporeal, solid or strong. **unsubstantial'ity** n. **unsubstan'tialize** or **-ise** vt. **unsucceed'ed** adj without a successor. **unsuccess'** n lack of success; failure. **unsuccess'ful** adj. **unsuccess'fully** adv. **unsuccess'fulness** n. **unsuccess'ive** adj not successive; not in or passing by succession. **unsuff'erable** adj (obs) insufferable. **unsuffi'cient** adj (obs) insufficient. **unsuit'** vt to make unsuitable. **unsuitabil'ity** n. **unsuit'able** adj. **unsuit'ableness** n. **unsuit'ably** adv. **unsuit'ed** adj not suited or adapted. **unsuit'ing** adj. **unsummed'** adj uncounted. **unsumm'ered** adj not possessing the characteristics of summer. **unsung'** adj not sung; not celebrated in song; not honoured, not given due recognition. **unsunned'** adj not exposed to the sun; not lighted, warmed or affected by the sun; not exposed to view. **unsunn'y** adj. **unsupport'able** adj insupportable; indefensible. **unsupport'ed** adj. **unsupport'edly** adv. **unsure** /un-shoor'/ adj insecure; precarious; uncertain; doubtful; not assured; untrustworthy. **unsured'** adj (Shakesp) not made sure. **unsurmount'able** adj insurmountable. **unsuspect'** adj (Milton) not subject to suspicion. **unsuspec'ted** adj not suspected; not known or supposed to exist. **unsuspec'tedly** adv. **unsuspec'tedness** n. **unsuspec'ting** adj not suspecting; innocent. **unsuspec'tingly** adv. **unsuspec'tingness** n. **unsuspi'cion** n absence of suspicion. **unsuspi'cious** adj not feeling or arousing suspicion. **unsuspi'ciously** adv. **unsuspi'ciousness** n. **unswadd'le** vt to unswathe. **unswathe'** vt to take swathings or bandages from. **unsway'able** adj (Shakesp). **unswayed'** (Shakesp **unswai'd'**) adj not wielded; not controlled; uninfluenced; not persuaded. **unswear'** vt to retract the swearing of. ◆ vi to recall an oath. **unswear'ing** n. **unswerv'ing** adj not swerving or deviating; steadfast. **unswerv'ingly** adv. **unsworn'** adj not confirmed, or not bound, by oath. **unsyll'abled** adj not syllabled; not articulated. **unsymmet'rical** adj. **unsymmet'rically** adv. **unsymm'etrized** or **-s-** adj. **unsymm'etry** n asymmetry. **untack'** vt to detach from tacking; to unharness. **untack'le** vt to strip of tackle; to free from tackle; to unharness. **untaint'ed** adj not tainted; unblemished; not attainted. **untaint'edly** adv. **untaint'edness** n. **untaint'ing** adj. **untām'able** or **untame'able** adj that cannot be tamed. **untam'ableness** or **untame'ableness** n. **untam'ably** or **untame'ably** adv. **untame'** adj not tame. ◆ vt to make untame, undo the taming of. **untamed'** adj not tamed; wild. **untamed'ness** n. **untang'le** vt to disentangle. **untang'led** adj. **untaught'** adj uninstructed; not taught or communicated by teaching; spontaneous, native or inborn. **untax'** vt to remit a tax on. **untaxed'** adj not taxed; not charged with any fault. **unteach'** vt to undo the teaching of. **unteach'able** adj not capable of being instructed; that cannot be imparted by teaching. **unteach'ableness** n. **unteam'** vt to unyoke. **untem'per** vt to destroy the temper of, deprive of suitable temper. **untem'pered** adj not tempered; not regulated. **untem'pering** adj (Shakesp) unconciliating. **untenabil'ity** n. **unten'able** (or /-tē'/) adj not tenable, not defensible. **unten'ableness** n untenability. **unten'ant** vt to deprive of a tenant; to dislodge. **unten'antable** adj. **unten'anted** adj not occupied. **untent'** vt to remove from a tent. **untent'ed** adj having no tents; (of a wound) unprobed, undressed or impossible to treat with a tent; unheeded

---

Some words formed with the prefix **un-**; the numbers in brackets refer to the numbered senses in the entry for **un-**.

untend'ed adj (1).	**untill'able** adj (1).	**untransformed'** adj (1).
untend'er adj (1).	**untilled'** adj (1).	**untranslatabil'ity** n (1).
unten'dered adj (1).	**untinc'tured** adj (1).	**untranslāt'able** adj (1).
unten'derly adv (1).	**untinged'** adj (1).	**untranslāt'ableness** n (1).
unter'minated adj (1).	**untīr'able** (Shakesp **untyre'able**) adj (1).	**untranslāt'ably** adv (1).
unterres'trial adj (1).	**untired'** adj (1).	**untranslāt'ed** adj (1).
unterr'ified adj (1).	**untīr'ing** adj (1).	**untransmīgrāt'ed** adj (1).
unterr'ifying adj (1).	**untīr'ingly** adv (1).	**untransmiss'ible** adj (1).
untest'ed adj (1).	**untoil'ing** adj (1).	**untransmitt'ed** adj (1).
unthanked' adj (1).	**untorment'ed** adj (1).	**untransmūt'able** adj (1).
unthank'ful adj (1).	**untorn'** adj (1).	**untransmūt'ed** adj (1).
unthank'fully adv (1).	**untor'tured** adj (1).	**untranspa'rent** adj (1).
unthank'fulness n (1).	**untracked'** adj (1).	**untrav'elled** adj (1).
untheolog'ical adj (1).	**untract'able** adj (1).	**untrav'ersable** adj (1).
unthick'ened adj (1).	**untract'ableness** n (1).	**untrav'ersed** adj (1).
unthor'ough adj (1).	**untrained'** adj (1).	**untrem'bling** adj (1).
unthreat'ened adj (1).	**untramm'elled** adj (1).	**untrem'blingly** adv (1).
unthreat'ening adj (1).	**untramp'led** adj (1).	**untremen'dous** adj (1).
untī'dily adv (1).	**untran'quil** adj (1).	**untrem'ulous** adj (1).
untī'diness n (1).	**untransfer'able** or **untransferr'able** adj (1).	**untrenched'** adj (1).
untī'dy adj (1) and vt (2).		**untres'passing** adj (1).

■ words derived from main entry word; ❑ compound words; ■ idioms and phrasal verbs

(Scot). **untent'y** adj (Scot) careless. **unteth'er** vt to release from a tether. **unteth'ered** adj not tethered. **unthatch'** vt to strip of thatch. **unthatched'** adj not thatched. **unthaw'** vt and vi to thaw. **unthawed'** adj not thawed. **unthink'** vt and vi to think to the contrary, reverse in thought. **unthinkabil'ity** n. **unthink'able** adj that cannot be thought; outside the realm of thought; beyond the power of thought; inconceivable; unimaginable; utterly impossible (often of things impending but too painful to think about). **unthink'ing** adj not thinking; thoughtless. **unthink'ingly** adv. **unthink'ingness** n. **unthought'ful** adj. **unthought'fully** adv. **unthought'fulness** n. **unthought'-of** adj. **unthread'** vt to take a thread from; to unweave; to loosen; to find one's way through. **unthread'ed** adj not threaded. **un'thrift** n unthriftiness; a prodigal; a spendthrift. ◆ adj prodigal. **unthrift'ily** adv. **unthrift'iness** n. **unthrift'y** adj not thrifty; wasteful; prodigal; not thriving; unprofitable. **unthrift'yhed** or **unthrift'yhead** n (Spenser) unthriftiness. **unthrone'** vt to dethrone. **untie'** vt to loose from being tied; to unbind; to solve, resolve. ◆ vi to come loose. **untied'** adj not tied; loosed; not loosed, still tied (Shakesp). **untile'** vt to strip of tiles. **untiled'** adj not tiled; stripped of tiles. **untim'bered** adj not strongly timbered (Shakesp); unwooded. **untime'liness** n. **untime'ly** adj not timely; before the time, premature; immature; unseasonable, ill-timed; inopportune. ◆ adv (archaic) at an unsuitable time; too early, prematurely; unseasonably; inopportunely. **untimeous** /un-tī'mas/ adj untimely. **untime'ously** adv. **untin'** vt to take the tin from. **untinned'** adj not tinned. **untī'tled** adj having no title; deprived of title; having no legal claim. **untoch'ered** adj (Scot) without tocher or dowry. **untogeth'er** adj (inf) unorganized; not mentally stable; not self-possessed. **untold'** (or /un'/) adj not counted; innumerable; not narrated; not communicated; not informed. **untomb'** vt to disentomb, remove from a tomb. **untombed'** adj not entombed. **untoned'** adj not toned; without tones. **untouch'able** adj impossible to touch; not to be equalled or touched. ◆ n someone whose excellence in some respect cannot be rivalled; (esp formerly) a Hindu of very low caste, a member of one of the scheduled castes. **untouched'** adj not touched; intact; unrivalled. **untoward** /un-ta-wörd'/ or un-tō'ərd/ adj inconvenient; unlucky; unfavourable; unfitting; not easily guided; froward; awkward. **untoward'liness** (or /un-tō'/) n. **untoward'ly** (or /un-tō'/) adv. ◆ adj untoward. **untoward'ness** (or /un-tō'/) n. **untrace'** vt to loose from traces. **untrace'able** adj impossible to trace. **untraced'** adj not traced or found. **untrā'ded** adj unfrequented, specif for trade (obs); unhackneyed (Shakesp). **untread'** vt (Shakesp) to tread back, to retrace. **untreas'ure** vt to despoil (of treasure). **untreat'able** adj that cannot be treated; intractable (obs). **untreat'ed** adj. **untressed'** adj not dressed or arranged in tresses. **untried'** adj not tried, tested, attempted, experienced or subjected to trial in court; (Shakesp **untride'**) prob not ventured upon, hence not noticed or dealt with. **untrim'** vt to deprive of trimming or trimness. **untrimmed'** adj not trimmed. **untrodd'en** or (archaic) **untrod'** adj not trodden upon; unfrequented. **untroub'led** adj not troubled or disturbed; not turbid. **untroub'ledly** adv. **untrue'** adj not true; false; not faithful; dishonest; inexact; not in accordance with a standard. ◆ adv (Shakesp) untruly, untruthfully. **untrue'ness** n. **untru'ism** n an untrue platitude. **untru'ly** adv falsely. **untruss'** vt to unpack; to unfasten; to untie (esp the points or laces on clothes; hist); to untie the points of (hist). **untrussed'** or **untrust'** adj not trussed; untied; with points untied (hist). **untruss'er** n. **untruss'ing** n. **untrust'** n distrust.

untrust'ful adj not trusting; not trustworthy; not to be trusted. **untrust'iness** n (obs). **untrust'worthily** adv. **untrust'worthiness** n. **untrust'worthy** adj not worthy of trust. **untrust'y** adj not trusty, not deserving trust. **untruth'** n falseness; falsity; that which is untrue; a lie; unfaithfulness. **untruth'ful** adj not truthful. **untruth'fully** adv. **untruth'fulness** n. **untuck'** vt to unfold or undo from being tucked up or in; to take out tucks from. **untucked'** adj not tucked up or in. **untuck'ered** adj not having a tucker on. **untūn'able** (also **untune'able**) adj harsh. **untūn'ableness** n. **untūn'ably** adv. **untune'** vt to put out of tune. **untuned'** adj not tuned; put out of tune. **untune'ful** adj not tuneful or melodious. **untune'fully** adv. **untune'fulness** n. **unturf'** vt to strip of turf. **unturn'** vt to turn backwards. **unturn'able** adj. **unturned'** adj not turned. **unturn'ing** adj. **untū'tored** adj untaught; uninstructed. **untwine'** vt and vi to untwist; to separate by untwisting. **untwist'** vt and vi to twist backwards so as to open out; to straighten out from a twist. **untwist'ed** adj not twisted; subjected to untwisting. **untwist'ing** n. **unty'pable** adj that cannot be defined as a particular type. **unused** /un-ūzd'/ adj not used; (also /un-ūst'/) unaccustomed; unusual (archaic). **unuseful** /-ūs'/ adj. **unuse'fully** adv. **unuse'fulness** n. **unūs'ual** adj not usual; uncommon; remarkable. **unūs'ually** adv more than usually; in an unusual way. **unūs'ualness** n. **unutt'erable** adj beyond utterance, inexpressible; not to be uttered. ◆ n an unutterable thing; (in pl) trousers (old sl). **unutt'erably** adv. **unutt'ered** adj. **unval'uable** adj not valuable, of little worth; invaluable, priceless (obs). **unval'ued** adj not prized or highly esteemed; without having a value assigned; invaluable, priceless (now rare). **unvar'nished** adj not varnished; not artfully embellished or sophisticated. **unveil'** vt (obs **unvail'** or **unvaile'**) to remove or set aside a veil from; to open to public view by the ceremonial removal of a covering; to disclose or reveal; to announce or introduce publicly for the first time. ◆ vi to remove one's veil; to become unveiled, to reveal oneself. **unveiled'** adj without a veil; with veil set aside or removed; unconcealed and undisguised. **unveil'er** n. **unveil'ing** n the ceremonial removal of a covering; the formal presentation of something new. **unvent'ed** adj not vented; without a vent. **unverā'cious** adj not truthful. **unverac'ity** n. **unversed'** adj not experienced or skilled; not put in verse. **unvir'tue** n lack of virtue. **unvir'tuous** adj. **unvir'tuously** adv. **unvis'itable** adj unfit to be visited; unsuitable for visiting; unable to visit (obs). **unvis'ited** adj. **unvīs'or** or **unvīz'ard** vt to remove or open the visor of. ◆ vi to unvisor oneself; to unmask. **unvoice'** vt to change to, or utter with, a voiceless sound. **unvoiced'** adj not spoken or expressed; without voice; (of a speech sound) voiceless, uttered with the breath rather than with vibration of the vocal cords (phonetics). **unvoic'ing** n change to a voiceless sound. **unvoy'ageable** adj not navigable, impassable. **unvul'gar** adj. **unvul'garize** or **-ise** vt to free from vulgarity. **unwaged'** adj not given wages; unpaid; unemployed; (with the) those who are not in paid employment. **unware'** adj (OE unwær) unwary (obs); unaware, without knowing (Spenser and Milton) unexpected (obs). ◆ adv unknowingly; unexpectedly. **unware'ly** adv unwarily (obs); suddenly, unexpectedly (Spenser). **unware'ness** n (archaic) unwariness. **unwares'** adv (archaic) unawares; unexpectedly, suddenly; unknowingly (Shakesp). **unwā'rily** adv. **unwā'riness** n. **unwarr'antable** adj not justifiable. **unwarr'antably** adv. **unwarr'anted** adj not justified or deserved. **unwarr'antedly** adv. **unwā'ry** adj not wary; not aware of danger; (Spenser **unwarie**)

Some words formed with the prefix **un-**; the numbers in brackets refer to the numbered senses in the entry for **un-**.

untum'bled adj (1).	**unvent'ilated** adj (1).	**unward'ed** adj (1).
untumult'uous adj (1).	**unver'ifiable** adj (1).	**unwar'like** adj (1).
untur'bid adj (1).	**unverifiabil'ity** n (1).	**unwarmed'** adj (1).
unty'ing n (1).	**unver'ified** adj (1).	**unwarned'** adj (1).
untyp'ical adj (1).	**unvett'ed** adj (1).	**unwarped'** adj (1).
ununderstand'able adj (1).	**unvī'able** adj (1).	**unwāst'ed** adj (1).
unuplift'ed adj (1).	**unviewed'** adj (1).	**unwāst'ing** adj (1).
unurged' adj (1).	**unvī'olated** adj (1).	**unwatched'** adj (1).
unū'sable adj (1).	**unvī'tal** adj (1).	**unwatch'ful** adj (1).
unū'sably adv (1).	**unvi'tiated** adj (1).	**unwatch'fully** adv (1).
unush'ered adj (1).	**unvit'ifiable** adj (1).	**unwatch'fulness** n (1).
unū'tilized or **unū'tilised** adj (1).	**unvit'rified** adj (1).	**unwā'vering** adj (1).
unvac'cinated adj (1).	**unvō'cal** adj (1).	**unwā'veringly** adv (1).
unvac'quishable adj (1).	**unvō'calized** or **unvō'calised** adj (1).	**unweak'ened** adj (1).
unvan'quished adj (1).	**unvul'nerable** (Shakesp) adj (1).	**unweaned'** adj (1).
unvā'riable adj (1).	**unwaked'** adj (1).	**unwear'able** adj (1).
unvā'ried adj (1).	**unwāk'ened** adj (1).	**unwea'riable** adj (1).
unvā'riegated adj (1).	**unwalled'** adj (1).	**unwea'riably** adv (1).
unvā'rying adj (1).	**unwand'ering** adj (1).	**unwea'ried** adj (1).
unvend'ible adj (1).	**unwant'ed** adj (1).	**unwea'riedly** adv (1).
unven'erable adj (1).		**unwea'ry** adj (1).

---

unexpected. **unwashed'** or (*Bible*) **unwash'en** *adj* (**the great unwashed** see under **great**). **unwatch'able** *adj* not watchable; too dull or poor in quality to be worth watching. **unwa'ter** *vt* to drain (*esp* a mine). **unwa'tered** *adj* freed from water; not watered. **unwa'tery** *adj*. **unwayed'** *adj* (*obs*) not accustomed to roads; (hence) intractable. **unweal'** *n* (*obs*) affliction, ill. **unweap'on** *vt* to disarm. **unweap'oned** *adj* unarmed; disarmed. **unweath'ered** *adj* not worn by the weather or atmospheric agencies. **unweave'** *vt* to undo from being woven. **unwedge'able** (*Shakesp* **unwedg'able**) *adj* unable to be split with wedges. **unweened'** *adj* (*archaic*) unexpected. **unweet'ing** *adj* (*archaic*) unwitting. **unweet'ingly** *adv* (*archaic*) unwittingly. **unweighed'** *adj* not weighed; not pondered; unguarded. **unweigh'ing** *adj* (*Shakesp*) thoughtless, inconsiderate. **unweight'ed** *adj* (of an estimate, average, etc) assigning equal value to all factors; (of a fishing lure) not attached to a weight. **unwell'** *adj* in poor health; mildly sick, indisposed. **unwell'ness** *n*. **unwept'** *adj* not wept for; (of tears) not shed. **unwhole'some** *adj* not wholesome; unsound; tainted in health, taste or morals. **unwhole'somely** *adv*. **unwhole'someness** *n*. **unwiel'dily** *adv*. **unwiel'diness** *n*. **unwiel'dy** (*Spenser*, etc **unwel'dy**) *adj* difficult to wield or move, from bulk or weakness; heavily awkward; unmanageable. **unwill'** *vt* to will the contrary of; to deprive of will. **unwilled'** *adj* not willed; involuntary. **unwill'ing** *adj* reluctant; done reluctantly; not willed, unintentional (*Shakesp*). **unwill'ingly** *adv*. **unwill'ingness** *n*. **unwind** /un-wīnd'/ *vt* (*pat* and *pap* **unwound** /un-wownd'/) to undo the winding of; to free from being wound; to wind down or off; to slacken; to relax (*inf*); to free oneself from an outstanding obligation to honour (a contract to buy or sell a commodity) (*finance*). ◆ *vi* to become unwound; to relax (*inf*). ◆ *adj* not wound; released from being wound. **unwind'ing** *n* and *adj* uncoiling. ◆ *adj* not winding. **unwire'** *vt* to take the wire from. **unwis'dom** *n* lack of wisdom; foolishness; injudiciousness. **unwise'** *adj* not wise; injudicious; foolish. **unwise'ly** *adv*. **unwise'ness** *n*. **unwish'** *vt* (*Shakesp*) to wish to be away, not to be, to be unfulfilled or to be undone. **unwished'** (or **unwished'-for**) *adj* not wished for. **unwish'ful** *adj*. **unwish'ing** *adj*. **unwist'** *adj* not known (*archaic*; *Spenser*, etc); unknowing (*Spenser*). **unwit'** *vt* (*Shakesp*) to deprive of wits. **unwitch'** *vt* to free from witchcraft. **unwithdraw'ing** *adj* liberal, lavish. **unwithhold'en** *adj* (*Coleridge*) not held back, not restrained. **unwithhold'ing** *adj* not holding back. **unwitt'ily** *adv*. **unwitt'ing** *adj* without knowing; unaware; not cognizant; unintentional. **unwitt'ingly** *adv*. **unwitt'ingness** *n*. **unwitt'y** *adj* foolish; without wit; unskilled (*archaic*). **unwive'** *vt* to deprive of a wife. **unwived'** *adj* without a wife. **unwo'man** *vt* to make unwomanly. **unwo'manliness** *n*. **unwo'manly** *adj* not befitting a woman; not such as a woman is expected to be. ◆ *adv* in an unwomanly manner. **unwont'** *adj* (now *rare*; *Spenser*, etc) or **unwont'ed** unaccustomed; unusual. **unwont'edly** *adv*. **unwont'edness** *n*. **unword'ed** *adj* speechless; not expressed in words. **unwork'** *vt* to undo. **unwork'able** *adj* not workable; impracticable. **unworked'** *adj* not shaped or moulded; not mined, not exploited. **unwork'ing** *adj*. **unwork'manlike** *adj* not like or worthy of a good workman. **unworld'liness** *n*. **unworld'ly** *adj* not of this world; spiritual; naive; above worldly or self-interested motives. **unwormed'** *adj* not worm-eaten; (of a dog) not having had the worm or lytta cut out from the tongue. **unworth'** *n* lack of worth. ◆ *adj* unworthy. **unwor'thily** *adv*. **unwor'thiness** *n*. **unwor'thy** *adj* not worthy; worthless; unbecoming; discreditable; undeserved. **unwound** *adj* see **unwind** above. **unwrap** /un-rap'/ *vt* to remove wrappings from; to unroll, unwind. ◆ *vi* to become unwrapped. **unwreaked** /un-rēkt'/ *adj* unrevenged. **unwreathe** /un-rēdh'/ *vt* to take out of a wreathed condition. **unwrink'le** *vt* and *vi* to smooth out from a wrinkled state. **unwrink'led** *adj* not wrinkled, smooth. **unwrite'** *vt* to undo the writing of. **unwrit'ing** *adj* not writing. **unwritt'en** *adj* not written or reduced to writing, oral; (of a rule, law, etc) traditional, generally accepted; containing no writing. **unwrought** /un-röt'/ *adj*

not done or worked; not fashioned, formed, composed or worked up; not mined; not tilled; undone, brought back to an original state. **unyeaned'** *adj* (*dialect*) unborn. **unyiel'ding** *adj* not yielding; stiff; obstinate. **unyiel'dingly** *adv*. **unyiel'dingness** *n*. **unyoke'** *vt* to loose from a yoke or harness; to set free; to disjoin. ◆ *vi* to unyoke an animal; to cease work. **unyoked'** *adj* not yoked or harnessed; freed from yoke or harness; unrestrained (*Shakesp*). **unzip'** *vt* to unfasten or open by undoing a zip; to decompress (data or files that have been compressed to save storage space) (*comput*). ◆ *vi* to become unfastened or open by the undoing of a zip. **unzoned'** *adj* not in or divided into zones; ungirt.

UNA *abbrev* : United Nations Association.

una corda /ū'nə kör'də or oo'nä kör'dä/ (*music*) one string (an indication to pianists to use the soft pedal). [Ital]

unalist /ū'nə-list/ (*relig*) *n* a holder of one benefice. [L *ūnus* one]

unanimous /ū-nan'i-məs/ *adj* of one mind; without anyone's dissenting. [L *ūnanimus*, from *ūnus* one, and *animus* mind]
■ **unanimity** /ū-nən-im'i-ti/ *n* agreement without anyone's dissenting. **unan'imously** *adv*.

unary /ū'nə-ri/ (*maths*) *adj* applied to or involving a single component. [L *unus* one]

unau /ū'nö or oo'now/ *n* the two-toed sloth. [Fr, from Tupí]

una voce /ū'nə vö'sē or oo'nä wō'ke/ (*L*) with one voice, by general consent.

unberufen /un'bə-roo-fən/ (*Ger*) *adj* not called for, used as an exclamation to avert the ill-luck that may possibly follow an over-confident or boastful statement.

uncate see under **uncus**.

unce /uns/ *n* Scots form of **ounce**[1].

uncial /un'shəl or -si-əl/ *adj* denoting, or executed in, a form of writing found in Greek and Latin manuscripts of the 3c to the 9c, using majuscule letters of rounded form; relating to an inch or an ounce. ◆ *n* an uncial letter; uncial writing; a manuscript written in uncials. [L *unciālis*, from *uncia* a twelfth; meaning with reference to lettering disputed, poss 'an inch high' or perh an error for *uncīnālis* hooked]

unciform, uncinate, etc see under **uncus**.

uncinariasis /un-sin-ə-rī'ə-sis/ *n* infestation of the small intestine by hookworm. [*Uncinaria*, a hookworm genus]

uncle /ung'kl/ *n* the brother of one's father or mother, or an aunt's husband, or a great-uncle (used with *cap* as a title, either before a man's first name or independently); used as a form of address to an elderly, *esp* black, man (chiefly *US*); a pawnbroker (*sl*); (with *cap*) a title sometimes used by children for male friends of their parents. ◆ *vt* to address as uncle. [OFr *uncle* (Fr *oncle*), from L *avunculus* a maternal uncle]
■ **un'cleship** *n* the state of being an uncle.
❑ **uncle** (or **Uncle**) **Dick** *adj* (*Cockney rhyming sl*) sick. **Uncle Sam** *n* the United States or its people. **Uncle Tom** *n* (*US derog*) a black American whose co-operative attitude to white people is thought to show disloyalty to black people (based on the hero of Harriet Beecher-Stowe's *Uncle Tom's Cabin* (1851–2)).
■ **cry** or **say uncle** (*US*) to surrender or admit defeat.

unco /ung'kə or -kō/ (*Scot*) *adj* strange, unusual; fearsome; remarkable; great. ◆ *n* (*pl* **un'cos**) a stranger; a piece of news; a remarkable thing. ◆ *adv* remarkably, very. [**uncouth**]
❑ **unco guid** /gid/ *n* the obtrusively rigorous in morals.

uncouth see under **un-**.

UNCTAD /ungk'tad/ *abbrev* : United Nations Conference on Trade and Development.

Some words formed with the prefix **un-**; the numbers in brackets refer to the numbered senses in the entry for **un-**.

unwea'rying *adj* (1).
unwea'ryingly *adv* (1).
unwebbed' *adj* (1).
unwed' *adj* (1).
unwedd'ed *adj* (1).
unweed'ed *adj* (1).
unwel'come *adj* (1).
unwel'comed *adj* (1).
unwel'comely *adj* (1).
unwel'comeness *n* (1).
unwel'coming *adj* (1).
unwet' *adj* (1).
unwett'ed *adj* (1).
unwhipped' (*obs* **unwhipt'**) *adj* (1).

unwhis'tleable *adj* (1).
unwife'like *adj* (1).
unwife'ly *adj* (1).
unwigged' *adj* (1).
unwil'ful *adj* (1).
unwinged' *adj* (1).
unwink'ing *adj* (1).
unwink'ingly *adv* (1).
unwinn'able *adj* (1).
unwinn'owed *adj* (1).
unwiped' *adj* (1).
unwith'ered *adj* (1).
unwith'ering *adj* (1).
unwithheld' *adj* (1).

unwithstood' *adj* (1).
unwit'nessed *adj* (1).
unwon' *adj* (1).
unwood'ed *adj* (1).
unwooed' *adj* (1).
unworn' *adj* (1).
unworr'ied *adj* (1).
unwor'shipful *adj* (1).
unwor'shipped *adj* (1).
unwound'able *adj* (1).
unwound'ed *adj* (1).
unwö'ven *adj* (1).
unwrit'able *adj* (1).
unwrung' *adj* (1).

■ words derived from main entry word; ❑ compound words; ■ idioms and phrasal verbs

unction /ungk'shən/ n an anointing; that which is used for anointing; ointment; that quality in language which raises emotion or devotion; warmth of address; religious glibness; divine or sanctifying grace; gusto. [L *unctiō, -ōnis* unction, besmearing, *ūnctum* fat]

■ **unctūos'ity** n unctuousness. **unc'tūous** adj oily; greasy; full of unction; offensively suave and smug. **unc'tūously** adv. **unc'tūousness** n.

■ **extreme unction** (*RC*) the sacrament of anointing a dying person with consecrated oil.

uncus /ung'kəs/ n (pl **unci** /un'sī/) a hook or hook-like process. [L *uncus* and *uncinus* hook]

■ **unc'ate** adj hooked. **unciform** /un'si-förm/ adj hook-shaped. **un'cinate** or **un'cinated** adj uncinform; hooked at the end. **unci'nus** n (pl **unci'nī**) (*zool*) a hooklet; a marginal tooth of a mollusc's radula; a hooked chaeta in annelids.

undated[1] /un'dā-tid/ or **undate** /un'dāt/ adj wavy. [L *unda* a wave]

undated[2] see under **un-**.

UNDCP abbrev : United Nations Drug Control Programme.

undé, unde see **undee**.

undecagon /un-dek'ə-gon/ n a plane figure of eleven angles and sides. [L *undecim* eleven, and *gōniā* an angle]

undecimal /un-des'i-məl/ adj based on the number eleven. [L *undecim* eleven, from *ūnus* one, and *decem* ten]

■ **undec'imole** n (*music*) a group of eleven notes in the time of eight.

undee, undée, undé or **unde** /un'dā/ (*heraldry*) adj wavy. [Fr *ondé*; cf *oundy*, *undate*]

under /un'dər/ prep beneath; below; in or to a position lower than that of, *esp* vertically lower; at the foot of; within, on the covered side of; short of; in or into subjection, subordination, obligation, liability, etc, to; in course of; in the state of; (of cultivated land) supporting a specified crop; by the authority or attestation of; in accordance with; in the aspect of; referred to the class, heading, name, etc, of; in the reign or administration of; within the influence of (a particular sign of the zodiac). ◆ adv in or to a lower (*esp* vertically lower) position; in or into a lower degree or condition; in or into subjection; in or into a covered, submerged or hidden state; in a state of unconsciousness (*inf*); below; under par (*golf*). ◆ adj lower; subordinate; falling short. [OE *under*; Gothic *undar*, ON *undir*, Ger *unter*, L *infrā*]

■ **un'derling** n a disparaging word for a subordinate; a weakling (*archaic*). **un'dermost** adj lowest; inmost. ◆ adv in or to the undermost place.

❑ **under-and-over** see **over-and-under** under **over**.

▦ **go, knock** or **snow under** see **go**[1], **knock, snow**[1]. **under age, arms, canvas**, etc see under **age, arm**[2], **canvas**, etc. **under starter's orders** see under **start**. **under-the-counter** see under **counter**[2]. **under the lee** to the leeward.

> Words formed from the preposition or adverb **under** are listed in the entry above, and those formed using the prefix **under-** are listed in the following entry or, if their meaning is self-evident, at the foot of the page; other words spelt with *under-* follow in the main word list.

under- /un-dər-/ pfx signifying: (1) below, beneath; (2) lower in physical position; (3) lower in rank, or subordinate; (4a) too little in quantity, too small, insufficient; (4b) in too small a degree, insufficiently; (5) not coming, or not allowed to come, to the surface or into the open.

■ **underachieve'** vi to achieve less than one's potential or less than expected, *esp* academically. **underachieve'ment** n. **underachiev'er** n. **underact'** vt and vi to make too little of (one's part, etc) in acting; to perform a part with little emphasis, for the sake of effect. **underac'tion** n subordinate action; less than normal or adequate action. **underact'or** n. **under-age'** adj (done, participated in, etc, by someone) not yet of full, or the required, age; immature. **underä'gent** n a subordinate agent. **un'derarm** adj and adv placed or held under the arm; relating to the armpit; with the arm kept below the shoulder. **underbear'** vt (*Shakesp*) to sustain; (*pap* **underborne'** *Shakesp*) perh to trim (on the lower part), perh to line or support by a foundation, perh to have sewn underneath or on strips of tinsel. **un'derbearer** n (*dialect*) someone who helps to carry a coffin. **underbear'ing** n. ◆ adj unassuming. **un'derbelly** n the undersurface of a body or of something suggesting a body; (also **soft underbelly**) the vulnerable part or spot; the hidden or little-known side of something. **underbid'** vt to offer a lower bid than; to offer at a price lower than that of; to outbid; to bid less than the value of (*bridge*). ◆ vi to bid unduly low. ◆ n (*bridge*) a bid too low to be valid, or less than the hand is worth. **underbidd'er** n someone who underbids; the next below the highest bidder. **un'derbite** n the (amount of) extension of the lower incisors beyond the upper when the mouth is closed. ◆ vt /-bīt'/ to bite insufficiently with acid, as in etching. **underbitt'en** adj. **un'derblanket** n a blanket of a warm material placed under, rather than over, a person in bed. **un'der-board** adv (*obs*) secretly, under the table, *opp* to *above board*. **un'derbody** n the underside of a motor vehicle; the underbelly. **un'der-bonnet** adj relating to the engine of a motor vehicle, generally to be found under the bonnet. **underborne** adj see **underbear** above. **un'derbough** n a lower branch. **un'der-boy** n a boy in the lower or more junior part of a school. **un'derbreath** n a subdued voice; rumour. **underbred'** adj of inferior breeding or manners; not pure-bred. **un'derbridge** n a bridge carrying a road or railway as opposed to a bridge over one. **un'derbrush** n undergrowth of brushwood or shrubs. ◆ vt to clear of underbrush. **underbuild'** vt to build under in support, to underpin; to build too little upon or in. **un'derbuilder** n a subordinate or assistant builder. **un'derburnt** adj insufficiently burnt. **un'derbush** n and vt same as **underbrush** above. **underbuy'** vt to buy less of than the amount required; to buy at less than the price paid by, or the value of. **un'dercard** n (*boxing*) a programme of matches supporting the main event. **un'dercarriage** n the supporting framework under the body of a carriage or vehicle; the landing gear of an aircraft, or its main part. **un'dercart** n (*inf*) an aircraft's landing gear, the undercarriage. **un'dercast** n an air-passage crossing under a road in a mine. **un'dercharge** n too small a charge. ◆ vt /-chärj'/ to charge too little, or too little for. **underclad'** adj not wearing enough clothes. **un'derclass** n a low, or the lowest, social class. **underclass'man** n (*US*) a sophomore or freshman. **un'derclay** n a bed of clay underlying a coal seam representing the soil in which the plants grew. **un'der-clerk** n a subordinate clerk. **un'der-clerk'ship** n. **un'dercliff** n a terrace of material that has fallen from a cliff. **un'derclothe** vt (*rare*) to provide with underclothing. **un'derclothed** adj provided with or wearing underclothing; /-klōdhd'/ underclad, not wearing enough clothing. **un'derclothes** n pl (also *sing* **un'derclothing**) clothes worn under others, *esp* those next to the skin. **underclub'** vi (*golf*) to hit a shot with a club that has too much loft to achieve the desired distance. **un'dercoat** n a coat worn under another; an underlayer of fur or hair, or of paint; an underskirt (*obs*). ◆ vt to paint with an undercoat. **undercook'** vt to cook insufficiently or to a lesser extent than usual. **un'dercool** vt to supercool; to cool insufficiently. **un'dercountenance** n (*Wordsworth*) that which underlies the superficial aspect of the face. **un'dercover** adj working or done in secret. ◆ adv in secret. **un'dercovert** n a covert of undergrowth. **un'dercrackers** n pl (*inf*) underpants. **un'der-craft** n (*Sterne*) a sly trick. **undercrest'** vt (*Shakesp*) to bear like a crest. **un'dercroft** n (cf Du *krocht* crypt) a crypt or vault. **un'dercurrent** n a current under the surface (*lit* and *fig*). ◆ adj running below or unseen. **undercut'** vt to cut under; to cut away under the surface, so as to leave part overhanging; to undermine; to strike with a heavy blow upward; to underbid; to offer at a lower price than; to apply backspin to. ◆ adj made so as to cut from the underside; done by undercutting; having the parts in relief cut under. ◆ n /un'/ the act or effect of cutting under; a blow dealt upward; the tenderloin, or fillet, or underside of a sirloin; a notch cut in a tree on the side to which it is intended to fall when felled. **un'derdamper** n (*music*) in a type of upright piano, a damper positioned below the hammers. **underdevel'op** vt. **underdevel'oped** adj insufficiently developed; (of a country) with resources inadequately used, having a low standard of living and education. **underdevel'opment** n. **underdo'** vt (*pat* **underdid'**; *pap* **underdone'**) to do, perform, act or *esp* cook insufficiently or inadequately. **underdo'er** n. **un'derdog** n the dog that gets the worst of it in a fight; anyone in adversity; a person dominated, or being or likely to be beaten, by another. **underdone'** adj done less than is necessary; insufficiently or slightly cooked.

Some words formed with the prefix **under-**; the numbers in brackets refer to the numbered senses in the entry for **under-**.

underbud'get vt and vi (4b).	**un'der-constable** n (3).	**un'derfloor** adj (1).
undercapitalizā'tion or	**un'derdeck** n (2).	**underfulfil'** vt (4b).
undercapitalisā'tion n (4a).	**undered'ucated** adj (4b).	**un'dergown** n (1).
undercap'italized or **undercap'italised**	**underem'phasize** or **underem'phasise**	**un'dergrown** adj (4b).
adj (4a).	vt (4b).	**un'der-hangman** n (3).
undercon'sciousness n (5).	**underfish'** vt (4b).	**underinsure'** vi and vt (4b).

underdrain' *vt* to drain by deep underground ditches. **un'derdraw'** *vt* to draw or describe with moderation or reticence or short of the truth; to cover the underside of with boards or lath and plaster. **un'derdrawing** *n* an outline drawing on a canvas, etc, done before paint is applied. **un'derdress** *n* underclothing; a dress or part of a dress worn or showing under another. ◆ *vt* and *vi* /-*dres*'/ to dress too plainly or simply. **underdressed'** *adj*. **un'derdrive** *n* a gear that transmits to the driving shaft a speed less than engine speed. **under-driv'en** *adj* driven from beneath. **un'derearth** *adj* underground. **underemployed'** *adj*. **underemploy'ment** *n* insufficient use (with *of*); the condition of having too large a part of the labour force unemployed; partial employment, or employment on work requiring less skill than the worker has. **un'der-espi'al** *n* (*Walter Scott*) a subordinate spy. **underes'timate** *vt* to estimate or value too low. ◆ *n* an estimate that falls short of the truth or true quantity. **underestima'tion** *n*. **underexpose'** *vt* to expose too little, *esp* (*photog*) to light. **underexpōs'ure** *n*. **underfeed'** *vt* and *vi* to give too little food. **underfed'** *adj* insufficiently fed. **un'derfelt** *n* an older term for an underlay, *usu* of felt. **underfin'ished** *adj* (of cattle and sheep) having too little finish (qv). **un'derfire'** *vt* to fire or bake insufficiently. **un'derflow** *n* an undercurrent; a condition in which a number to be stored is less than the smallest number that can be represented (*comput*). **underfoot'** *adv* beneath one's feet; in the way; in a downtrodden manner. ◆ *vt* to underpin. ◆ *adj* /*un*'/ downtrodden. **un'derframe** *n* a subframe. **underfund'** *vt* to provide with insufficient funds. **underfund'ing** *n*. **un'derfur** *n* short fur hidden by longer hairs. **un'dergarment** *n* any article of clothing worn under another, *esp* that worn next to the skin, underclothing. **undergird'** *vt* to brace with ropes under the bottom; to support (*fig*). **un'derglaze** *adj* applied or done before glazing (**underglaze painting** painting in a vitrifiable pigment before the glaze is applied). ◆ *n* a pigment, decoration, etc applied before glazing. **undergrad'uate** *n* a student who has not taken any degree (*inf* contraction **un'dergrad**). ◆ *adj* relating to such a student. **undergrad'uateship** *n*. **undergraduette'** *n* (*old inf*) a female undergraduate. **un'derground** *adj* under the surface of the ground; (of a railway) running through underground tunnels; secret; characterized by avant-gardism and experimentation, rejection of current trends or norms, appeal to a minority, anti-establishment tendencies, etc. ◆ *n* the underworld; an underground place; an underground railway; underlying ground; low ground; a secret resistance movement, or body of people; a group whose activities are partly concerned with resisting things they disapprove of in social, artistic and political life. ◆ *adv* /-*grownd*'/ beneath the surface of the earth; secretly; into hiding. **un'dergrove** *n* a grove of low trees under taller trees. **un'dergrowth** *n* low plants growing under taller ones, *esp* shrubs under trees; stunted growth. **underhand'** *adv* surreptitiously; with the hand kept below the elbow or shoulder. ◆ *adj* /*un*'/ surreptitious, secret; not straightforward; delivered underhand; unobtrusive (*Shakesp*). ◆ *n* /*un*'/ an underhand ball; (with *the*) a subordinate position. **underhan'ded** *adj* and *adv* underhand; short of workers. **underhan'dedly** *adv*. **underhan'dedness** *n*. **underhon'est** *adj* (*Shakesp*) not quite honest. **underhung'** (or /*un*'/) *adj* (of a lower jaw) protruding; having a protruding lower jaw; running on rollers on a rail below. **underinvest'ment** *n* insufficient investment. **under-jaw'** *n* the lower jaw. **un'derjawed** *adj* with a heavy or underhung under-jaw. **underkeep'** *vt* (*Spenser*) to keep under or in subjection. **underlaid** *adj* see **underlay** below. **underlain** *adj* see **underlie** below. **underlap'** *vt* to extend beneath and some way beyond the edge of. **underlay'** *vt* (*pat* and *pap* **underlaid'**) to support or provide with something laid under; to lay under; to put down, surpass (*Spenser*); often used erroneously for **underlie** below, of which it is the *pat*. ◆ *vi* (*mining*) to slope away from the vertical, to hade. ◆ *n* /*un*'/ something laid under, eg felt or rubber to help preserve a carpet, or (*printing*) a piece of paper, etc, pasted under to bring to type-height. **underlay'er** *n* someone who underlays; /*un*'/ a lower layer, substratum. **un'derlease** *n* a sublease. ◆ *vt* and *vi* /-*lēs*'/ to sublease. **underlet'** *vt* to let below the full value; (also *vi*) to sublet. **underlett'er** *n*. **underlett'ing** *n*. **underle'veraged** *adj* (of a business) having too small a debt to be fully efficient. **underlie'** *vt* (**underly'ing**; **underlay'**; **underlain'**) to lie beneath (*lit* and *fig*); to undergo; to be subject or liable to. ◆ *n* (*mining*) a hade, a slope away from the vertical. **underline'** *vt* to draw a line under; to stress. ◆ *n* /*un*'/ a caption, legend; a line drawn under a word. **un'derlinen** *n* (*archaic*) underclothing, properly of linen. **un'derling** *n* see at **under. un'derlip** *n* a lower lip. **un'derlooker** *n* a

mine manager's assistant. **underly'ing** *adj* lying beneath (*lit* and *fig*); fundamental; present though not immediately obvious. **un'derman** *n* an inferior; a subordinate; a man subjected to adverse conditions. ◆ *vt* /-*man*'/ to supply or man with too few workers. **undermanned'** *adj*. **undermast'ed** *adj* with too small masts. **undermen'tioned** *adj* mentioned underneath or hereafter. **undermine'** (*Spenser* **underminde'**) *vt* to dig beneath (eg a wall) in order to make it fall; to wash away or remove by burrowing, etc, the ground from under; to weaken gradually or insidiously; to intrigue against; to tamper with the fidelity of. **undermī'ner** *n*. **undermī'ning** *n*. **undernice'ness** *n* lack of niceness or delicacy. **un'dernote** *n* a subdued note; an undertone; a note added below. ◆ *vt* to note below. **un'dernoted** *adj*. **undernour'ished** *adj* living on less food than is necessary for satisfactory health and growth (also *fig*). **undernour'ishment** *n*. **underpaint'ing** *n* the first layer of painting, when the design is set out. **un'derpants** *n pl* an undergarment worn by men and boys, covering the body from the hips to the tops of the thighs. **un'derpass** *n* a road passing under another road or a railway, etc; a pedestrian tunnel passing below a road, railway, etc. **un'derpassion** *n* an underlying or subconscious passion. **un'derpay** *vt* and *vi* to pay less than required or deserved. **underpay'ment** *n*. **underpeep'** *vt* (*Shakesp*) to peep under. **underpeo'pled** *adj* not sufficiently populated. **underperform'** *vi* to do less well than expected or thought possible, etc (traditionally used in relation to the England football team). ◆ *vt* to do less well than. **underperform'ance** *n*. **underpin'** *vt* to support by building underneath, or to prop up (also *fig*); to corroborate. **underpinn'ing** *n*. **underplant'** *vt* to plant smaller plants in between (trees or taller plants). **underplay'** *vi* to play a low card while holding a higher of the same suit. ◆ *vt* to play down, understate. ◆ *vt* and *vi* to underact. ◆ *n* /*un*'/ (*cards*) the stratagem of underplaying. **un'derplot** *n* a subordinate plot in a play or tale; a secret scheme, a trick. **underpop'ulated** *adj* having too small a population, insufficient to exploit the land. **un'der-power** *n* (*Wordsworth*) an auxiliary power. **underpow'ered** *adj* insufficiently or not fully powered. **underpraise'** *vt* to praise below what is deserved. **underpriced'** *adj* having too low a price. **underpriv'ileged** *adj* not enjoying normal social and economic rights. ◆ *n* (with *the*) underprivileged people. **underprize'** *vt* (*obs* **underprise'**) to value too little; to underpraise (*Shakesp*). **underproduce'** *vt* and *vi*. **underproduc'tion** *n* too little production; production short of demand. **underproof'** *adj* (of alcohol) lower or weaker than proof. **underquote'** *vt* to offer at a price lower than. **underrate'** *vt* to rate too low. ◆ *n* /*un*'/ a price less than the worth. ◆ *adj* /*un*'/ (*Swift*) inferior. **under-representa'tion** *n* too little representation; less representation than one is entitled to. **under-represent'ed** *adj*. **un'der-ring** *vt* and *vi* to ring up (an amount or total) less than the actual price on a till. ◆ *n* an instance of under-ringing. **un'der-ripe'** *adj* not quite ripe. **un'der-roof** *n* (*Tennyson*) a roof under another. **underrun'** *vt* to run or pass beneath; to take aboard on one side (eg a cable, line, or net for examination, clearing or baiting) and put overboard on the other. ◆ *vi* to move under; to run on the underside. **underrunn'ing** *n*. **undersat'urated** *adj* (of igneous rocks) deficient in silica. **un'der-saw'yer** *n* a bottom-sawyer; an inferior, an unimportant person. **undersay'** *vt* (*obs; Spenser* **undersaye'**) to say in answer or contradiction. **un'der-school** *n* (*obs*) the lower or junior school. **underscore'** *vt* to underline. ◆ *n* /*un*'/ an underline. **un'derscrub** *n* brushwood. **undersea'** *adj* and *adv* below the surface of the sea. **underseal'** *vt* to coat exposed parts of the underside of (a motor vehicle) with a corrosion-resisting substance. ◆ *n* /*un*'/ a substance used to underseal vehicles. **underseal'ing** *n*. **un'der-secretary** *n* a secretary immediately under the principal secretary. **un'der-secretaryship** *n*. **un'derself** *n* the subconscious self. **undersell'** *vt* to sell below the price charged by; to sell too cheap. **undersell'er** *n*. **un'dersense** *n* a deeper sense; a secondary sense; a subconscious awareness. **underserved'** *adj* inadequately provided with services. **un'derset** *n* an undercurrent; a lower vein of ore; a set of underclothing. ◆ *vt* /-*set*'/ to set under; to prop; to sublet (*obs*). **undersexed'** *adj* having less than normal interest in sexual relations or sexual activity. **un'dershapen** *adj* (*Tennyson*) imperfectly formed. **un'dershirt** *n* (*N Am*) an undergarment worn under a shirt *usu* made of cotton jersey, a vest. **undershoot'** *vt* to fail to reach by falling short (also *fig*). ◆ *n* /*un*'/ (*aeronautics*) a falling short of the mark in landing. **un'dershorts** *n pl* (*N Am*) short underpants. **un'dershot** *adj* driven by water passing under; having the lower jaw projecting, underhung. **un'dershrub** *n* a shrubby plant or a low shrub. **un'derside** *n* the

---

Some words formed with the prefix **under-**; the numbers in brackets refer to the numbered senses in the entry for **under-**.

underinsured' *adj* (4b).	**un'dermeaning** *n* (5).	**underprepared'** *adj* (4b).
un'derkeeper *n* (3).	**un'dernamed** *adj* (1).	**underprop'** *vt* (1).
un'derking *n* (3).	**underpaid'** *adj* (4b).	**under-report'** *vt* (4b).
un'derkingdom *n* (3).	**un'derpart** *n* (1).	**un'der-shepherd** *n* (3).
un'dermanager *n* (3).	**underprepara'tion** *n* (4b).	**un'dersheriff** *n* (3).

■ words derived from main entry word; ❑ compound words; ■ idioms and phrasal verbs

lower or undersurface. **undersign'** *vt* to sign below. **un'dersigned** (or /-sīnd'/) *adj* whose signature is appended. **un'dersized** *adj* below the usual or desired size. **un'derskinker** *n* (*Shakesp*) an assistant tapster. **un'derskirt** *n* a petticoat; a foundation for a dress or skirt. **un'dersky** *n* (*poetic*) a lower sky. **underslung'** *adj* suspended, or supported, from above, or hung so as to extend below a part which, in another arrangement, it might be wholly above; (of a vehicle chassis) extending below the axles. **un'dersong** *n* (*archaic*) a burden or refrain, etc of song or of sound; an undertone less pleasant in quality (*fig*). **underspend'** *vi* and *vt* to spend less than one could or should of (eg a budget). ◆ *n* /un'/ the amount left unspent from an allocated budget, etc. **understaffed'** *adj* having too few members of staff. **understate'** *vt* to state more moderately than truth would allow or require; to state or describe, or to use artistically, without emphasis. **understät'ed** *adj* effective through simplicity, without embellishment or dramatic emphasis. **understate'ment** (or /un'/) *n*. **un'dersteer** *n* a tendency in a motor vehicle to follow a wider curve than the turning applied by the steering wheel should cause it to follow (also *vi*). **un'derstock** *n* (*archaic*) a stocking. ◆ *vt* /-stok'/ to supply with an insufficient amount of stock. **understood** *adj* see separate entry **understand**. **un'derstorey** or (*rare*) **un'derstory** *n* the smaller trees and bushes forming a lower level of cover beneath the tallest trees in a forest, etc. **un'derstrapper** *n* an inferior agent, an underling. **un'derstrapping** *adj* subordinate. **un'derstratum** *n* (*pl* **un'derstrata**) an underlayer. **un'derstudy** *vt* to study (a part), or to study the part of (an actor or other person) in order to take over in an emergency, or in due course (also *vi*). ◆ *n* someone who understudies. **undersubscribed'** *adj* (of a share issue, etc) not having enough people subscribing to it; having fewer applicants than there are places available. **un'derthings** *n pl* underclothes. **un'derthirst** *n* (*Wordsworth*) an underlying or subconscious thirst. **un'derthrust** *n* (*geol*) a fault in which one mass of rock is moved under another relatively static layer. **undertimed'** *adj* (of a photograph) underexposed. **un'dertint** *n* a subdued tint; a tint showing through. **un'dertone** *n* a subdued tone of voice, sound, colour, etc; a tone felt as if pervading, underlying, or perceptible through others, including (*fig*) an emotional tone; a difference tone (qv under **differ**); a low state of body. **un'dertoned** *adj* in an undertone; /-tond'/ lacking in tone. **un'dertow** /-tō/ *n* an undercurrent opposed to the surface current; the recoil or back-draught of a wave. **un'dertrick** *n* (*bridge*) a trick short of the number specified in the contract. **under-turn'key** *n* (*hist*) an assistant jailer. **undervaluä'tion** *n*. **underval'ue** *vt* to value below the real worth; to reduce the value of; to esteem too lightly; to rate as inferior (with *to*; *Shakesp*). ◆ *n* /un'/ a value or price under the real worth. **underval'uer** *n*. **undervest'** *n* an undershirt, or a similar garment for a woman. **un'derviewer** *n* an underlooker. **un'dervoice** *n* a subdued voice. **un'derwater** *n* underground water; undertow. ◆ *adj* (existing, acting, carried out, etc) below the surface of the water; below the waterline. ◆ *adv* /-wö'/ below the water. **un'derwear** *n* underclothing. **un'derweight** *n* shortness of weight; short weight. ◆ *adj* /-wät'/ short in weight; (of an investment fund) containing less than the optimum proportion of a certain type of asset. **underwhelm'** *vt* (*facetious*) to fail to impress. **un'derwing** *n* a wing covered by another, such as an insect's hindwing; a moth (*Catocala*, etc) with conspicuous hindwings. ◆ *adj* (of a bird or aircraft) under the wing (also *adv* /-wing'/). **underwire'** *vt* to provide shape to (a bra) by means of a thin strip of light metal, etc under each cup. ◆ *adj* (of a bra) having shaping provided in this way (also **underwired'**). ◆ *n* an underwire bra. **underwir'ing** *n*. **un'derwit** *n* inferior wit; a half-wit. **un'derwood** *n* undergrowth; a coppice. **underwork'** *vt* to undermine; to employ too little in work; to work for less than the wage of; to work secretly against (*obs*; *Shakesp pat* **underwrought'**). ◆ *vi* to do less work than is desirable. ◆ *n* /un'/ a substructure; underhand, inferior or subordinate work. **un'derworker** *n*. **un'der-work'man** *n*. **un'derworld** *n* the world beneath the heavens; the world, or a region, beneath the earth; the place of departed souls; the part of the world below the horizon; the antipodes; a submerged, hidden or secret region or sphere of life, *esp* one given to crime, profligacy or intrigue. **un'derwrite** *vt* to write (something) beneath; to subscribe to (a statement, etc); to accept the risk of insuring; to guarantee to take, or find others to take (certain shares, under certain conditions); to write too little about; (*reflexive*) to write below the level of which one is capable, not to do (oneself) justice; to sign one's name beneath (*obs*); to subscribe (one's name;

obs); to agree to (*Shakesp*). ◆ *vi* to practise as an underwriter. **un'derwriter** *n* someone who practises insurance business, *esp* in ships; someone who underwrites share issues, etc. **un'derwriting** *n*. **underwrought** *vt* see **underwork** above.

underachieve...to...**underflow** see under **under-**.

underfoot...to...**underglaze** see under **under-**.

undergo /un-dər-gō'/ *vt* (*pat* **underwent'**; *pap* **undergone'**) to be subjected to; to endure or suffer; to pass through, experience; to enjoy, partake of (*Shakesp*); to take in hand (*Shakesp*). [Late OE *undergān*, from *gān* to go]
■ **undergō'ing** *adj* (*Shakesp*) enduring.

undergraduate...to...**undermining** see under **under-**.

undern /un'dərn/ (*obs*) *n* the third hour, about nine in the morning; terce; the forenoon; the afternoon or early evening; a light meal. [OE *undern*]
■ **un'derntime** (*Spenser* **un'dertime**) *n* the time of the midday meal.

underneath /un-dər-nēth'/ *adv* and *prep* beneath, below in position; under the control of (*archaic*). ◆ *n* the under part or side. ◆ *adj* lower. [OE *underneothan*]

underniceness...to...**understaffed** see under **under-**.

understand /un-dər-stand'/ *vt* (*pat* and *pap* **understood'**, *archaic pap* **understand'ed**) to comprehend; to grasp with the mind; to be able to follow the working, logic, or meaning, etc, of; to take the meaning of (a sign or a person); to realize; to have a sympathetic, *usu* tacit, perception of the character and aims, etc, of (a person); to know the meaning of; to be expert in; to have knowledge or information (that), to have been informed; to assume, take to be true; to interpret (as), take to mean; to imply; to support; (*reflexive*) to know how to conduct (oneself) (*Shakesp*); to stand under (*Shakesp*). ◆ *vi* to have understanding; to comprehend. [OE *understandan*, from **under** and *standan* to stand]
■ **understand'able** *adj*. **understand'er** *n* someone who understands; a supporter (*Browning*); someone who stands in the pit of a theatre (*obs*). **understand'ing** *n* the act of comprehending; the power to understand; intellect; an informal agreement; an understood condition (eg *on the understanding that*); sympathetic or amicable agreement of minds; (in *pl*) feet, legs, shoes, boots (*old sl*). ◆ *adj* intelligent; discerning; sympathetic. **understand'ingly** *adv*. **understood'** *adj* (often *grammar*) implied but not expressed.
■ **understand each other** or **one another** to have reached an agreement, sometimes collusive.

understate...to...**undersubscribed** see under **under-**.

undertake /un-dər-tāk'/ *vt* (*pat* **undertook'**; *pap* **undertä'ken**, (*Shakesp*, etc) **undertä'en'**, (*Spenser*) **undertane'**) to pledge oneself (that); to take upon oneself; to take upon oneself (to deal with, manage or look after); to set about, engage in; to engage in contest with; to receive (*obs*); to perceive (*Spenser*); to assume (*Shakesp*); to be surety for (*Shakesp*). ◆ *vi* to promise (*archaic*; sometimes with *for*); to become a surety (with *for*); to conduct funerals (*inf*). [12c *undertaken* to entrap, from OE *under*, and late OE *tacan*; see **take**]
■ **undertä'kable** *adj*. **un'dertaker** *n* someone who manages funerals; someone who takes in hand an enterprise, task or encounter; a projector, entrepreneur; a contractor; a publisher (*obs*); a stage producer (*obs*); a compiler or editor (*obs*); a sponsor or surety (*obs*); a tax farmer (see under **tax**; *obs*); one of the Fife adventurers who tried to colonize the island of Lewis (c.1600); one of those who undertook to manage the House of Commons for the Stewart kings; one of the English and Scottish settlers on forfeited lands in Ireland. **un'dertaking** *n* that which is undertaken; any business or project engaged in; a task one sets oneself; the business of conducting funerals. ◆ *adj* enterprising, full of initiative.

underthings, **underthirst**, **underthrust** see under **under-**.

undertime see **underntime** under **undern**.

undertimed...to...**underwater** see under **under-**.

underway see under **way**[1] and **weigh**[2].

underwear...to...**underwrought** see under **under-**.

undies /un'diz/ or *-dēz/* (*inf*) *n pl* underpants. [**under**]

undine /un'dēn or un-dēn'/ (Ger *ŭn-dē'nə*) *n* according to Paracelsus, a water spirit that can obtain a human soul by bearing a child to a human husband. [L *unda* a wave]

Some words formed with the prefix **under-**; the numbers in brackets refer to the numbered senses in the entry for **under-**.

un'dersleeve *n* (1).	**un'derten'ancy** *n* (3).	**underutiliza'tion** or **underutilisa'tion** *n*
un'dersoil *n* (2).	**un'dertenant** *n* (3).	(4a).
un'dersupply *n* (4a)	**un'der-tu'nic** *n* (1).	**underū'tilize** or **underū'tilise** *vt* (4b).
and *vt* (4b).	**underuse'** *n* (4a)	**underū'tilized** or **underū'tilised**
un'dersurface *n* (1).	and *vt* (4b).	*adj* (4b).

❑ **un'dinism** *n* (*psychol*) a preoccupation with water, specifically with urine and the act of urination.

UNDP *abbrev* : United Nations Development Programme.

UNDRO *abbrev* : formerly, United Nations Disaster Relief Organization.

undulate /un'dū-lāt/ *vt* and *vi* to move like or in waves; to make or be wavy; to vibrate. ◆ *adj* (also **un'dulated**) wavy; with wavy margin, surface or markings. [L *undulātus* undulated, from *unda* a wave]

■ **un'dulancy** *n*. **un'dulant** *adj* undulating; rising and falling. **un'dulately** *adv*. **un'dulating** *adj*. **un'dulatingly** *adv*. **undulā'tion** *n* an undulating, a wavelike motion or form; waviness; a wave. **undulā'tionist** *n* someone who holds the undulatory theory of light. **un'dulatory** *adj* of the nature of undulation; undulating; wavy; referring light to waves in a medium. **undulatus** /-lā'tus/ *adj* (of a cloud formation) having a wave-like shape. **un'dulose** or **un'dulous** *adj* (both *rare*) undulating.

❑ **undulant fever** *n* Malta, Mediterranean, Neapolitan, or Rock fever, a remittent fever with swelling of the joints and enlarged spleen, caused by a bacterium (genus *Brucella*) transmitted by goat's (or cow's) milk.

UNECA *abbrev* : United Nations Economic Commission for Africa.

UNECE *abbrev* : United Nations Economic Commission for Europe.

UNEF /ū'nef/ *abbrev* : United Nations Emergency Force.

UNEP *abbrev* : United Nations Environment Programme.

UNESCAP *abbrev* : United Nations Economic and Social Commission for Asia and the Pacific.

UNESCO /ū-nes'kō/ *abbrev* : United Nations Educational, Scientific and Cultural Organization.

UNFPA *abbrev* : United Nations Population Fund (formerly known as United Nations Fund for Population Activities).

unguent /ung'gwənt/ *n* ointment. [L *unguentum*, from *unguere* to anoint]

■ **unguentā'rium** *n* a vessel for holding unguents. **ung'uentary** *adj* of or for unguents. ◆ *n* an unguentarium; a perfumer, a maker of or dealer in unguents.

unguis /ung'gwis/ *n* (*pl* **ung'ues** /-gwēz/) a claw or nail (*zool*); the claw of an insect's foot; the base of a petal (*bot*). [L *unguis* a nail]

■ **ung'ual** /-gwəl/ *adj* of or relating to the fingernails or toenails; of or bearing a claw. **unguiculate** /ung-gwik'ū-lāt/ or **unguic'ulated** *adj* clawed; clawlike. **unguiform** /ung'gwi-förm/ *adj*.

ungula /ung'gū-lə/ *n* (*pl* **ung'ulae** /-lē/) a hoof (*zool*); a section of a cylinder, cone, etc, cut off by a plane oblique to the base (*geom*). [L *ungula* claw, hoof, from *unguis* nail]

■ **ung'ulate** *adj* hoofed. ◆ *n* a term applied to several groups of superficially similar hoofed animals which are not necessarily closely related taxonomically, eg horses, cows, deer, tapirs. **unguled** /ung'gūld/ *adj* (*heraldry*) with claws or hoofs tinctured specially. **ung'uligrade** *adj* walking on hoofs.

UNHCR *abbrev* : United Nations High Commission (or Commissioner) for Refugees.

uni /ū'ni/ (*inf*) *n* university.

uni- /ū'ni-/ *combining form* denoting one. [L *ūnus* one; Gr *oine* ace (on dice); OE *ān* one]

■ **uniax'ial** *adj* having one axis, *esp* (*crystallog*) one optic axis or (*biol*) one main line of growth or unbranched axis. **uniax'ially** *adv*. **ū'nibrow** *n* a pair of eyebrows without a gap between them, appearing as a continuous growth of hair. **unicam'eral** *adj* (L *camera* vault; see **chamber**) having or consisting of only one chamber. **unicam'eralism** *n* the system or principle of having one legislative chamber. **unicam'eralist** *n*. **unicell'ular** *adj* of or having only one cell. **unicen'tral** *adj* having a single centre. **ū'nicolor, ū'nicolour, ū'nicoloured,** (or /-kul'/), **unicol'orate** or **unicol'orous** *adj* of one uniform colour. **ū'nicorn** *n* (L *cornū* a horn) a mythical animal mentioned by ancient Greek and Roman authors as a native of India, with a body like a horse and one straight horn; an unfortunate translation of the Hebrew *re'ēm* (Assyrian *rímu*) anticipated by the *monokerōs* of the Septuagint, variously understood as the rhinoceros, wild ox, or ox-antelope (*Bible*); applied to various animals with the appearance of a single horn, such as the narwhal (also **un'icorn-whale**), a moth (**un'icorn-moth**) whose caterpillar has a long process, an American Pacific gastropod (genus *Latirus*, etc) with a spine on the lip of the shell (**un'icorn-shell**); a team of two abreast and one in front, or a carriage drawn by it; an old Scottish gold coin bearing a unicorn, worth 18 shillings Scots; (with *cap*) one of the Scottish pursuivants. ◆ *adj* one-horned. ◆ *adv* with two abreast and one in front. **unicos'tate** *adj* (L *costa* rib) one-ribbed. **ū'nicycle** *n* an acrobat's one-wheeled cycle. **unidirec'tional** *adj* mainly or wholly in one direction. **unifil'ar** *adj* (L *fīlum* thread) with one thread. **uniflō'rous** *adj* (L *flōs, flōris* a flower) one-flowered. **unifo'liate** *adj* (L *folium* leaf; *bot*) with only one leaf; unifoliolate. **unifo'liolate** *adj*

(L *foliolum, dimin* of *folium* leaf; *bot*) having a single leaflet, but compound in structure. **unilā'biate** *adj* (L *labium* lip) one-lipped. **unilat'eral** *adj* (L *latus, lateris* side) one-sided; on one side; affecting or involving, etc, only one person or group, etc, out of several; produced with one side of the tongue only, as a Welsh *ll* (*phonetics*) (**Unilateral Declaration of Independence** one declared by a dependent state without the agreement of its protector). **unilat'eralism** *n*. **unilat'eralist** *n* someone who favours unilateral action, *esp* in abandoning or reducing production of nuclear weapons. **unilateral'ity** *n*. **unilat'erally** *adv*. **uniling'ual** *adj* (L *lingua* tongue) of, in or using, one tongue or language. **unilit'eral** *adj* (L *littera, lītera* letter) of, or involving, one letter or script. **unilō'bar** or **unilō'bed'** *adj* having one lobe. **unilob'ular** *adj* having one lobule. **uniloc'ular** *adj* having only one loculus or cavity. **unimolec'ular** *adj* monomolecular. **uninū'clear** *adj* with a single nucleus. **uninū'cleate** *adj*. **unip'arous** *adj* (L *parere* to bring forth) producing one at a birth. ◆ *adj* (*bot*) monochasial. **unipar'tite** *adj* not divided into parts. **u'niped** *adj* (see **-ped**) one-footed. ◆ *n* a one-footed person, animal or object. **uniper'sonal** *adj* existing as only one person. **uniplā'nar** *adj* lying in one plane. **ū'nipod** *n* (see **-pod**) a one-legged support, eg for a camera. **unipō'lar** *adj* of, from or using one pole; (of a nerve cell) having one process only; (of a psychiatric illness) characterized by either depressive or manic episodes but not both. **unipolar'ity** *n*. **unipō'tent** *adj* (*zool*) capable of forming only a single cell type. **u'niramous** *adj* (*zool*) having only one branch, as some Crustacean appendages (cf **biramous**). **unisē'rial** *adj* in one series or row. **unisē'rially** *adv*. **unisē'riate** *adj* uniserial. **unisē'riately** *adv*. **ū'nisex** *adj* (of a style, *esp* in clothes) adopted by both sexes; applicable to or usable by, etc, persons of either sex. **unisex'ual** *adj* of one sex only. **unisexual'ity** *n*. **unisex'ually** *adv*. **ū'nison** (or/-zən/) *n* (L *sonus* sound, *sonāre* to sound) identity of pitch; loosely, pitch differing by one or more octaves; a sound of the same pitch; complete agreement. ◆ *adj* in unison. **unis'onal** *adj*. **unis'onally** *adv*. **unis'onance** *n*. **unis'onant** *adj*. **unis'onous** *adj*. **univā'lence** (or /-iv'əl-/) or **univā'lency** (or /-iv'əl-/ *n*). **univā'lent** (or /-iv'əl-/) *adj* (*chem*) having a valency of one, capable of combining with one atom of hydrogen or its equivalent. ◆ *adj* and *n* (relating to) one of the single chromosomes that separate in the first meiotic division. **ū'nivalve** *adj* having one valve or shell only. ◆ *n* a shell of one valve only; a mollusc whose shell is composed of a single piece. **unival'vular** *adj*. **univā'riant** *adj* having one degree of freedom. **univā'riate** *adj* (of a distribution) having one variate only. **univol'tine** *adj* (Ital *volta* a turn, winding) of silkworms, having one brood a year.

Uniat /ū'ni-ət/ or **Uniate** /ū'ni-āt or -ət/ *n* a member of any community of Christians, *esp* in E Europe and Asia, that acknowledges the papal supremacy but which is allowed to retain its own customs and practices with regard to all else, ie clerical matrimony, communion in both kinds, church discipline, rites and liturgy. [Russ *uniyat*, from *uniya* union, from LL *ūniō, -ōnis*, from L *ūnus* one]

uniaxial, unicameral see under **uni-**.

UNICEF /ū'ni-sef/ *abbrev* : United Nations Children's Fund (formerly known as United Nations International Children's Emergency Fund).

unicellular...to...**unicentral** see under **uni-**.

unicity /ū-nis'i-ti/ *n* oneness; uniqueness. [L *ūnicus* unique]

Unicode /ū'ni-kōd/ *n* (*comput*) an international standard for representing symbols and characters in 16-bit codes, with space for all foreseeable languages and symbols. [**uni-** or **unique**]

unicolor...to...**unidirectional** see under **uni-**.

UNIDO /ū-nē'dō/ *abbrev* : United Nations Industrial Development Organization.

Unifil *abbrev* : United Nations Interim Force in Lebanon.

unifilar...to...**unifoliolate** see under **uni-**.

Uniform or **uniform** /ū'ni-förm/ *n* (in international radio communication) a code word for the letter *u*.

uniform /ū'ni-förm/ *adj* alike; alike all over, throughout, or at all times; unvarying; of a military or other uniform. ◆ *n* a distinctive garb for members of a body; a suit of it. ◆ *vt* to make uniform; to clothe in uniform. [L *ūniformis*, from *ūnus* one, and *fōrma* form]

■ **ū'niformed** *adj* wearing uniform. **uniformitā'rian** *n* and *adj*. **uniformitā'rianism** *n* the doctrine that geological changes were brought about not in the main by great convulsions but by such action as may be seen going on now. **uniformitā'rianist** *n*. **uniform'ity** *n* the state or fact of being uniform; agreement with a pattern or rule; sameness; likeness between parts. **ū'niformly** *adv*. **ū'niformness** *n*. ❑ **Uniform Business Rate** *n* (*finance*) a system of business rating introduced in 1990.

unify /ū'ni-fī/ *vt* (**u'nifying; u'nified**) to make into one; to consolidate. [LL *ūnificāre*, from L *ūnus* one, and *facere* to make]

■ **ū'nifiable** *adj*. **unif'ic** *adj* making one. **unificā'tion** *n*. **ū'nified** *adj*. **ū'nifier** *n*. **ū'nifying** *n* and *adj*.

❑ **Unification Church** see **Moonie**. **unified field** *n* an ultimate basis on which the physicist seeks to bring within a single theory the workings of all natural phenomena. **unified scale** *n* the scale of atomic and molecular weights based on the mass of the carbon-12 isotope of carbon being taken as 12 exactly.

unigeniture /ū-ni-jen'i-chər/ *n* the state or fact of being the only begotten. [LL *ūnigenitus* only-begotten]
■ **Unigen'itus** *n* (from its first word) a bull of Clement XI (1713) condemning 101 propositions of the Jansenist Quesnel.

unilabiate...to...**uninucleate** see under **uni-**.

Unio /ū'ni-ō/ *n* the pearl mussel genus of freshwater molluscs, giving name to the family **Unionidae** /ū-ni-on'i-dē/. [L *ūniō, -ōnis*, prob from *ūnus* one; cf **solitaire** as applied to a diamond set by itself]
■ **union** /ūn'yən/ *n* (*Shakesp*) a fine large pearl, a unique or single pearl.

union[1] /ū'nyən or ū'ni-ən/ *n* a uniting; the state of being united; the state of wedlock; a united whole; combination; a growing together in healing; general concord; the incorporation of states in a federation or in a single state; a single state (or sometimes a federation) formed in this way; an association or league, *esp* a trade union; a students' club; formerly, a combination of parishes for poor-law purposes; its workhouse or poorhouse; a connecting part for pipes, etc; a device emblematic of union shown on a flag; the same device used separately as a flag, such as the Union Jack; a textile fabric of more than one kind of fibre; the set formed from all the elements present in two (or more) sets (*maths*). [Fr *union*, from LL *ūniō, -ōnis*, from L *ūnus* one]
■ **ūn'ionism** *n* (also with *cap*). **ūn'ionist** *n* an advocate or supporter of or believer in union or trade unions; a member of a trade union; (with *cap*) an opponent of Irish Home Rule, *esp* a Liberal Unionist (see under **liberal**); hence, a Conservative; (with *cap*) a supporter of the federal union of the United States, *esp* at the time of the Civil War. ◆ *adj* of or relating to trade unions; (with *cap*) of or relating to Unionists. **ūnioniza'tion** or **-s-** *n*. **ūn'ionize** or **-ise** *vt* to recruit into a trade union; to organize the workforce of (a body, company or industry) into a trade union.
❑ **union catalogue** *n* a library catalogue combining, *usu* alphabetically, the contents of a number of catalogues or listing the contents of a number of libraries. **union flag** *n* a flag symbolizing union, *esp* the national flag of the United Kingdom, consisting of a union of the crosses of St George, St Andrew, and St Patrick, commonly called the **Union Jack**. **union language** *n* an artificial language formed from related dialects. **union list** *n* a list of materials available on a specific subject, in each case naming the library, and locating the material precisely in it. **union pipes** see **uillean(n) pipes**. **Union Shona** see **Shona**. **union shop** *n* a workplace in which employees must belong to a trade union. **union suit** *n* underwear in the form of combinations for man or boy. **union territory** *n* one of the administrative divisions that, along with states, make up the Republic of India.
■ **art union** an association aiming at promotion of an interest in the fine arts, *esp* by raffling pictures. **the Union** the legislative incorporation of England and Scotland in 1707, or of Ireland with both in 1801; the American Union or United States; the Union of South Africa (1910).

union[2] see under **Unio**.

unionized[1] or **-s-** /un-ī'ə-nīzd/ see under **un-**.

unionized[2] or **-s-** *pat* and *pap* of **unionize** (see under **union**[1]).

uniparous...to...**unipotent** see under **uni-**.

unique /ū-nēk'/ *adj* sole; without a like; often used loosely for unusual, pre-eminent; found solely in, belonging solely to, etc (with *to*). ◆ *n* anything that is unique. [Fr, from L *ūnicus*, from *ūnu*]
■ **unique'ly** *adv*. **unique'ness** *n*.

uniserial...to...**unisexual** see under **uni-**.

UNISON /ū'ni-sən/ *n* an amalgamated trade union for public service workers, formed in 1993 from COHSE, NALGO, and NUPE.

unison, etc see under **uni-**.

Unit. *abbrev*: Unitarian.

unit /ū'nit or yūn'it/ *n* one; a single thing or person; a single element, section or item, regarded as the lowest subdivision of a whole; a group of persons forming a subdivision of a larger body; a distinct part within a piece of electrically-powered equipment which has its own specific function; a single complete domestic fixture combining what are sometimes separate parts; a *usu* independently owned dwelling apartment, one of several into which a building is divided, a home unit (*Aust*); the least whole number; anything taken as one; a quantity by reference to which others are measured. ◆ *adj* of the character or value of a unit; individual. [Formed from **unity**, following eg *digit*]
■ **ū'nital** *adj*. **ū'nitary** *adj* relating to unity or to a unit; of the nature of a unit; integral; based on unity; (of local-government administration)

provided by a single body. **unitīzā'tion** or **-s-** *n*. **ū'nitize** or **-ise** *vt* to convert into unit trusts (*commerce*); to make into, or treat as, a unit.
❑ **unitary taxation** *n* (*US*) the system of taxing multinational companies on their worldwide income rather than merely that received within the area under the taxation authority's jurisdiction. **unit cell** *n* the smallest group of atoms, ions or molecules whose repetition at regular intervals produces the lattice of a crystal. **unit cost** *n* the cost per item of producing a product. **unit furniture** *n* furniture which may be bought as single items rather than as sets or suites. **u'nitholder** *n* someone holding a unit of securities in a unit trust. **u'nit-linked** *adj* (of a life-insurance policy or personal equity plan) having a return based on the value of a unit trust. **unit of account** *n* a monetary unit not necessarily corresponding to any actual denomination of currency and in certain cases of variable value, used as a basis of exchange or comparison or as a unit in accounting. **unit-pack'aging** *n* a method of packaging (pills, etc) in which the items are individually encased. **unit price** *n*. **unit-pri'cing** *n* a method of pricing foodstuffs, etc by showing the cost per agreed unit (eg kilogram or pound) as well as, or instead of, the overall price of the item. **unit trust** see under **trust**.

UNITA /ū-nē'tə/ *abbrev*: *União Nacional para a Independência Total de Angola* (*Port*), National Union for the Total Independence of Angola.

unitard /ū'ni-tärd/ *n* a *usu* close-fitting one-piece garment extending from the neck to the feet, worn chiefly by dancers, gymnasts, etc. [**uni-** and leo*tard*]

Unitarian /ū-ni-tā'ri-ən/ *n* someone who asserts the unity of the Godhead as opposed to the Trinity, ascribing divinity to God the Father only; a member or adherent of a non-credal church which stresses freedom of, and tolerance for differences in, religious beliefs; a monotheist generally; (without *cap*) a holder of some belief based on unity or union. ◆ *adj* of or relating to Unitarians or Unitarianism; (without *cap*) of or relating to unitarians or unitarianism. [Mod L *unitarius*, from *ūnitās* unity]
■ **Unitā'rianism** *n* (also without *cap*).

unite /ū-nīt'/ *vt* to make one; to join into one; to join; to combine; to clasp; to marry; to have in combination; to make to agree or adhere. ◆ *vi* to become one; to combine; to join; to grow or act together. ◆ *n* (also /ū'/) an English gold coin of James I, worth 20 shillings, later 22 shillings; (with *cap*) a British trade union comprising Amicus and TGWU. [L *ūnītus*, pap of *ūnīre* to unite, from *ūnus* one]
■ **unī'ted** *adj*. **unī'tedly** *adv*. **unī'tedness** *n*. **unī'ter** *n*. **unī'ting** *n* and *adj*. **unition** /ū-nish'ən/ *n* conjunction. **unitive** /ū'ni-tiv/ *adj* harmonizing, uniting. **u'nitively** *adv*.
❑ **United Brethren** see **Moravian**[1]. **United Free Church** see under **free**. **United Irishmen** *n pl* a radical political organization which, agitating for absolute emancipation, parliamentary reform and universal suffrage, caused the 1798 rising. **United Kingdom** (**of Great Britain and Northern Ireland**; or before 1922 **Ireland**) *n* the official title adopted in 1801 for the kingdom consisting of England and Wales, Scotland, and (Northern) Ireland. **United Nations** *n* (treated as *sing* or *pl*) an association of states formed in 1945 to promote peace and international security and co-operation, taking over many of the functions of the dissolved League of Nations. **United Presbyterian Church** see under **Presbyterian**. **United Provinces** *n pl* Holland, Zealand (Zeeland), Utrecht, Gelderland, Groningen, Friesland and Overyssel, united in 1579 under the Union of Utrecht. **United Reformed Church** *n* a church formed by the union in 1972 of the Presbyterian Church in England and the Congregational Church in England and Wales. **United States** *n sing* a federal union of states, *esp* that of (North) America.

unity /ū'ni-ti/ *n* oneness; the number one; the state or fact of being one or at one; that which has oneness; a single whole; the arrangement of all the parts to one purpose or effect; a unite (*Dickens*). [L *ūnitās, -ātis*, from *ūnus* one]
❑ **unity element** *n* (*maths*) an identity element for multiplication.
■ **the unities** (**of place, time and action**) the three canons of the classical drama, ie that the scenes should be at the same place, that all the events should be such as might happen within a single day, and that nothing should be admitted not directly relevant to the development of the plot.

Univ *abbrev*: Universalist; University.

univalence...to...**univariate** see under **uni-**.

universe /ū'ni-vûrs/ *n* the cosmos; the whole system of things; all that is; the world, everyone; a clearly demarcated domain or sphere. [L *ūniversum*, neuter singular of *ūniversus* whole, from *ūnus* one, and *vertere, versus* to turn]
■ **univers'al** *adj* of the universe; comprehending, affecting, or for use by the whole world or all people; without exception; comprising all the particulars; all-round; unlimited; wide-ranging and comprehensive; capable of being applied to a great variety of uses. ◆ *n* something that is universal; a universal proposition; a general term; a

universal concept. **Univer'salism** *n* the doctrine or belief of universal salvation, or the ultimate salvation of all mankind, and even of the fallen angels. **Univer'salist** *n* a believer in Universalism. ◆ *adj* of or relating to Universalists or Universalism. **universalis'tic** *adj*. **universality** /-*sal´*/ *n* the state or quality of being universal. **universalīza'tion** or **-s-** *n*. **univer'salize** or **-ise** *vt*. **univer'sally** *adv*. **univer'salness** *n*.

◻ **universal beam** *n* a beam made in a standard size. **universal coupling** same as **universal joint** below. **universal donor** *n* a person whose blood is of group O, which can therefore be transfused into persons of other blood groups. **universal grinder** *n* a versatile machine tool, able to perform external and internal cylindrical grinding, surface-grinding, etc. **universal indicator** *n* a mixture of chemical indicators that gives a definite colour change for each integral change in pH value over a wide range. **universal joint** *n* a joint capable of turning all ways. **universal quantifier** *n* (*logic*) a formal expression indicating that a statement is true for all members of a universe of discourse. **universal recipient** *n* a person whose blood is of group AB and who can therefore receive blood of most other groups. **universal set** same as **universe of discourse** below. **universal time** *n* mean solar time or Greenwich time, in which the value of the second is subject to irregularities which are due to characteristics of the earth's rotation. **universe of discourse** *n* (*logic*) all of the objects, ideas, etc that are expressed or implied in a discussion.

university /ū-ni-vûr´si-ti/ *n* an institution of higher learning with power to grant degrees, its body of teachers, students, graduates, etc, its college or colleges, or its buildings; a corporate body (*obs*). [L *ūniversitās*, *-ātis* a whole, in LL a corporation; see **universe**]

■ **universitā'rian** *adj*.

◻ **university of the air** *n* an earlier name for the **open university** (see under **open**).

univocal /ū-ni-vō´kl/ or /ū-niv´ə-kl/ *adj* of one voice; having one meaning only; unmistakable; unambiguous; of things of the same species (*obs*). ◆ *n* a word with only one meaning. [L *ūnivocus*, from *ūnus* one, and *vōx*, *vōcis* a voice]

■ **univō'cally** *adv*.

univoltine see under **uni-**.

Unix /ū´niks/ (*comput*) *n* a multiuser operating system for handling large amounts of data. [**uni-** and **-ics**]

unked, unkempt, unket, unkid see under **un-**.

unless /un-les´/ or /ən-les´/ *conj* (tending to pass into a *prep*) if not; except (when or if). [Earlier followed by *than* or *that* ; *on lesse than* on a less condition than]

UNMOVIC /un´mə-vik/ *abbrev* : United Nations Monitoring, Verification and Inspection Commission.

unneath /ə-nēth´/ (*dialect*) *prep* underneath. [Cf **aneath, underneath**]

unnil- /ū-nil-/ *pfx* denoting a chemical element with an atomic number between 100 and 109, eg *unnilquadium* is element 104 (rutherfordium). [Literally one-zero-, from L *ūnus* one, and *nīl* nothing]

UNO *abbrev* : United Nations Organization.

uno animo /ū´nō or oo´nō an´i-mō/ *adv* with one mind, with one accord. [L]

UNRRA *abbrev* : formerly, United Nations Relief and Rehabilitation Administration.

UNRWA /un´rə/ *abbrev* : United Nations Relief and Works Agency for Palestine Refugees in the Near East.

UNSCOM /un´skom/ *abbrev* : (formerly) United Nations Special Commission.

until /un-til´/ or /ən-til´/ *prep* and *conj* till. [Pfx *und-* as far as, and **till**[1]]

unto /un´too/ or -*tŭ*/ (*archaic* or *formal*) *prep* to. ◆ *conj* (*obs*) until. [Pfx *und-* as far as, and **to**]

unun- /ūn-ūn-/ *pfx* denoting a chemical element with an atomic number between 110 and 119, eg *ununquadium* is element 114. [Literally one-one-, from L *ūnus* one]

UOM *abbrev* : Union of Myanmar (formerly Burma).

UP *abbrev* : United Presbyterian; United Press.

up /up/ *adv* in, to or toward a higher place, level or state; aloft; on high; towards a centre (such as a capital, great town, or university); in residence, at school or college; northward; to windward; in or to a more erect position or more advanced stage of erection; out of bed; on horseback; in an excited state; in revolt; with (increased) vigour, intensity or loudness; afoot; amiss; into prominence, notice or consideration; forward for sale; in or into court; into custody; keeping or possession; away in a receptacle, place of storage or lodging (such as a sheath, purse or stable); ahead in scoring; into closed or compact state, together; to a total; in, near or towards arrival, overtaking or being abreast; as far as; all the way; to a standstill; at an end; to a finish; thoroughly, completely, fully; well-informed, versed.

—Also elliptically passing into use as a verb or interjection by omission of verbs such as *go, come, put,* etc, often followed by *with*. ◆ *adj* (*compar* **upp´er**; *superl* **upp'most** or **upp'ermost** see below) placed, going or directed up; top; risen; (of time) ended; having won (a stated number) more holes than an opponent (*golf*). ◆ *prep* in an ascent along, through or by; to or in a higher position on; to or in an inner or more remote part of; along against the current; along; up into (*N Am*). ◆ *n* a rise; a high place; a success, spell of prosperity; someone who is in prosperity. ◆ *vt* (**upp'ing**; **upped** /upt/) to drive upstream (as swans for owner marking); to lift or haul up; to raise, increase. ◆ *vi* (*inf*) to set up; to move up; to intervene boldly, start into activity or speech. [OE *ūp*, *upp* up, *uppe* above, *uppian* to rise; Ger *auf*]

■ **up'most** *adj* uppermost. **upp'er** *adj* (see above) higher; superior; higher in rank. ◆ *n* the part of a boot or shoe above the sole and welt; an upper tooth; a drug producing a stimulant or euphoric effect, or a pill containing such a drug (*sl*). **upp'ermost** *adj* (see above) highest; first to come into the mind. ◆ *adv* in the highest place, first. **upp'ing** *n* the action of **up** (*vt*) (see above). **upp'ish** *adj* assuming, pretentious, snobbish. **upp'ishly** *adv*. **upp'ishness** *n*. **upp'ity** *adj* uppish; difficult to control, resistant to persuasion. **up'ward** /-*wərd*/ *adv* (also **upwards**) from lower to higher; from outlet towards source; from modern to more ancient; in the upper part (**upward of** or **upwards of** more than; **and upwards** and higher, and more). ◆ *prep* upwards along. ◆ *adj* directed upward; ascending; placed high. ◆ *n* (*Shakesp*) top. **up'wardly** *adv*. **up'wardness** *n* a rising tendency; a state of being high.

◻ **up'-and-com'ing** *adj* alert and pushful; likely to succeed (in a career, etc). **up-and-down'** *adj* (see also **up and down** below) undulating; going or working both, or alternately, up and down; downright (*US*). ◆ *n* (*golf*; *inf*) an act of completing a hole from a position off the green by using one lofted shot and one putt. **up'-and-o'ver** *adj* (of a door, etc) raised to a horizontal position when opened (also **up'-o'ver**). **up'-and-un'der** *n* (*rugby*) a movement in which the ball is kicked high and forward, and the players rush to try to catch it. **up'-beat** *n* an unaccented beat, at which the conductor raises his baton; an optimistic note or mood; a promising development. ◆ *adj* (*inf*; **up'beat**) cheerful; optimistic. **up'bow** *n* (*music*) a movement of the bow from point towards nut over the strings. **up'-current** or **up'-draught** *n* a rising current of air. **upfront** see **up front** below. **up'land** *n* inland, hilly or high-lying country; upper or high land, as opposed to meadows, river-sides, etc (*N Am*). ◆ *adj* high-lying; remote; inland; rural; of the uplands. **upland cotton** *n* a variety of cotton (*Gossypium hirsutum*) orig grown in America. **up'lander** *n*. **upland'ish** *adj* (*obs*) rustic; rural; outlandish. **up'-line** *n* a railway line for upgoing trains (ie those going to, not from, eg a city). **upper atmosphere** *n* the region of the atmosphere above about 20 miles from the earth. **upp'er-brack'et** *adj* in an upper grouping in a list, etc. **upp'er-case** *adj* (*printing*) literally, kept in an upper case, capital as opposed to small (of letters). **upper chamber** same as **upper house** below. **upper class** or **classes** *n* the people of the highest social rank. **upp'er-class'** *adj*. **upper crust** *n* the top of a loaf; the aristocracy, or the upper class or classes in any society; the head (*sl*); a hat (*sl*). **upp'er-crust'** *adj* upper-class, aristocratic. **upp'ercut** *n* an upward short-arm blow. **upper hand** *n* mastery, advantage. **upper house** *n* in a bicameral legislature, the house that is the more restricted in membership, eg House of Lords, Senate of USA and other countries. **upper regions** *n pl* heaven; the heavens, the sky. **Upper Roger** *n* corruption of Hindi *Yuva-rājā*, young prince. **upper school** *n* the senior pupils in a secondary school. **upper storey** or (*esp in N Am*) **story** *n* any storey above the first floor; the brain (*sl*). **upper ten** (**thousand**) *n* the richest or most influential class. **upp'erworks** *n pl* the upper part of a structure (of a ship above the load-line); the head (*sl*). **upp'ing-block**, **upp'ing-stock** or **upp'ing-stone** *n* a mounting block. **up'side** *n* the upper side; a positive or favourable aspect. ◆ *adv* on the upper side. **upside down** or **up'side-down'** *adv* (earlier **up so down**; *Spenser* **up'sidowne'**) with the upper part undermost; in, or into, complete confusion. ◆ *adj* turned upside down. **upside-down cake** *n* a sponge cake baked with fruit at the bottom and turned upside down before it is served. **up'sides** *adv* on a par (with *with*); beside. **up'-train** *n* a railway train proceeding towards the chief terminus. **upward mobility** *n* the (desired) state of the **upwardly mobile**, those people moving (or attempting to move) to a higher social rank or position of greater status.

■ **be up in** to have a knowledge of. **have had it up to here** (*inf*) to have had as much as one can take, to be fed up (*usu* with a gesture towards the throat). **it is all up (with)** there is no hope (for). **not up** (*tennis*) called when the ball bounces twice before the player manages to hit it. **on one's uppers** with soles worn off one's shoes; very short of money. **on the up** (*cricket*) (of a stroke) played as the ball rises from its bounce. **on the up and up** in a state of continuous progress towards ever greater success; honest, on the level. **something is up** something is amiss, something unusual or unexpected is happening or has happened. **up against** face to face with, confronted with. **up**

against it in almost desperate straits. **up and doing** bestirring oneself. **up and down** to and fro; here and there through or about; throughout; vertically; out-and-out. **up and running** fully functional. **up at** attending, studying at (a university). **up close and personal** intimate or intimately. **up for** available for or undergoing (some process); willing to take part in (*inf*); standing as a candidate for. **up front** at the front; to the forefront; foremost; (of money) paid in advance; candidly, openly (**up-front'** or **upfront'** *adj*). **up oneself** (*sl*) smugly pleased with oneself. **ups and downs** undulations; vicissitudes. **up sticks** (*inf*) to move one's home, business, etc, decamp. **up to** as far up as; into the immediate neighbourhood or presence of; immersed or embedded as far as; about, meditating or engaged in doing (*inf*); capable of and ready for (*inf*); incumbent upon. **up to date** to the present time or time in question; containing all recent facts, statistics, etc; knowing the latest developments of fashion, usage, etc (**up'-to-date'** *adj*). **up top** (*inf*) in the head, in respect of intelligence. **up to speed** having reached the required speed; fully informed of the latest developments (*inf*); on the alert, ready for action (*inf*). **up to the minute** or **moment** right up to the present time (**up-to-the-min'ute** or **up-to-the-mo'ment** *adj*) very up-to-date. **up town** into town; in or to the residential part of a town (*N Am*). **up with** abreast of; even with; to take off or swallow; put, get, etc up (see under **up**), often as an exclamation of approbation and partisanship. **up yours** (*vulgar sl*) an expression of strong refusal, defiance, contempt, etc. **what's up?** (**with you?**, etc) what's the matter, what's wrong (with you, etc)?

> Words formed from the adverb or preposition **up** are listed in the entry above, and those formed using the prefix **up-** are listed in the following entry or, if their meaning is self-evident, at the foot of the page; other words spelt with *up-* follow in the main word list.

up- /*up-*/ *pfx* used with *adv*, *prep* and *adj* meanings of **up** (see previous article). Many of the compounds are archaic or poetic.

■ **up'-along** *adv* (*dialect*) up the road; homeward. **up-anch'or** *vi* to weigh anchor. **upbear'** *vt* to raise aloft; to hold up; to sustain. **upbind'** *vt* (*pap* **upbound'** (*Spenser* also **upbound'en**)) to bind up. **upblow'** *vt* and *vi* to blow up or upward; (of the wind) to spring up. **upblown'** (or /*up'*/) *adj* inflated. **upbraid** *vt* see separate entry. **upbrast'** *vt* (*Spenser*) *pat* of **upburst. upbray'** *vt* (*Spenser*) see separate entry. **up'break** *n* a break-up; an outbreak. ◆ *vt* /-*brāk*'/ to break up or open. ◆ *vi* to break out. **up'bringing** *n* bringing up, rearing, training, education. **upbrought'** *vt* (*Spenser*) *pap* of *obs* **upbring'** to bring up. **upbuild'** *vt* to build up. **upbuild'ing** (or /*up'*/) *n* building up; development; edification. **upbuoy'ance** *n* (*rare*) buoying up. **upburn'ing** *adj* flaming upwards. **up'burst** *n* a bursting upwards. ◆ *vt* and *vi* /-*bûrst*'/ to burst upwards. **upburst'ing** *adj*. **upby'** or **upbye'** *adv* (*Scot*) up the way, a little farther on or up; up there; at the big house. **up'cast** *n* an upward throw; an upthrow; material thrown up; an upward current of air from a mine; a shaft carrying it (**up'cast-shaft**); a chance, accident, fluke or, according to some, throw or final throw at bowls (*Shakesp*); a reproach (*Scot*); an upset (*Scot*). ◆ *adj* thrown or turned upward. ◆ *vt* /-*kāst*'/ to cast up. **upcatch'** *vt* (*pat* and *pap* **upcaught'**) to catch up. **up-Chann'el** *adv* along the English Channel from west to east (also *adj*). **upcheer'** *vt* (*pat* **upcheered'** or (*Spenser*) **upcheard'**) to encourage. **up'chuck** *vi* and *vt* (*N Am sl*) to vomit. **up'coast** *adj* along the coast. ◆ *adv* /-*kōst*'/ in or toward a position along the coast. **upcoil'** *vi* to coil upwards; to coil up. **up'come** *n* produce, outcome; outward appearance of promise (*Scot*; *obs*); decisive movement (*Scot*). **up'coming** *adj* forthcoming, approaching; likely to succeed. **up'-country** *n* the interior, inland part. ◆ *adj* of or in the interior. ◆ *adv* /-*kun*'/ in or to the interior. **up'cycle** *vt* to recycle (waste products) into something of a higher value than the original material. **update'** *vt* to bring up to date. ◆ *n* /*up'*/ the act of bringing up to date; an updated account or version; a report or bulletin that updates. **up'do** *n* a hairstyle in which long hair is gathered up and pinned to the top of the head. **up-end'** or **upend'** *vt* to set on end; to affect or alter greatly, turn upside down. ◆ *vi* to rise on end. **upfield'** *adv* in or to a position closer to the other end of a playing field. **up'flow** *n* an upward flowing. ◆ *vi* /-*flō*'/ to stream up. **upfoll'ow** *vt* (*Keats*) to follow. **up'gang** *n* (*Scot*) ascent. **upgath'er** *vt* to gather up or together. **upgrad'able** or **upgrade'able** *adj* (of a piece of equipment) able to be upgraded. **upgradabil'ity** or **upgradeabil'ity** *n*.

upgradā'tion *n*. **up'grade** *n* an upward slope or course; an improved upgraded piece of equipment. ◆ *adj* and *adv* uphill. ◆ *vt* /-*grād*'/ to raise in status, quality or value, etc; to improve (equipment or machinery) by replacing an old, out-of-date component with a new one. **upgrow'** *vi* (**upgrow'ing**; **upgrew'**; **upgrown'**) to grow up. **up'growing** *n* and *adj*. **up'grown** *adj*. **up'growth** *n* the process of growing up, development; that which grows up; a structure that has grown upward. **up'gush** *n* a rising surge. ◆ *vi* /-*gush*'/ to surge up. **up'gushing** *adj*. **up'hand** *adj* lifted by hand. **uphaud'** *vt* (*pap* **uphudd'en**) Scots form of **uphold**. **upheav'al** *n* a profound, thorough or revolutionary change or movement; any large-scale disturbance or disruption; the bodily elevation of tracts of country (*geol*); a heaving up. **upheave'** *vt* and *vi*. **upheld**, **uphild** see **uphold** below. **up'hill** *adj* ascending; difficult. ◆ *n* an ascent. ◆ *adv* /-*hil*'/ towards the top of a hill. **uphill'ward** *adv* (*Milton*). **uphoard'** *vt* (*Spenser, Shakesp* **uphoord'**) to hoard or heap up. **uphold'** *vt* (*pat* **upheld'**; *pap* **upheld'**, (*Spenser*) **uphild'**) to hold up; to sustain; to countenance; to defend, give support to; to keep in repair or good condition; (chiefly *Scot*, **uphaud'**) to maintain, warrant. **uphold'er** *n* a support or supporter; a dealer in second-hand clothes and furniture, etc (*obs*); a funeral undertaker (*obs*); an upholsterer (*obs*). **uphold'ing** *n* and *adj*. **upjet'** *vi* to spout up. **up'keep** *n* (the cost of) maintenance. **upknit'** *vt* to knit up; to bring together, reconcile, or perhaps conclude, explain or sum up (*Spenser*). **uplay'** *vt* to lay up, to hoard. **uplead'** /-*lēd*'/ *vt* (*pat* and *pap* **upled'**) to lead up. **uplean'** *vi* (*Spenser*) to rest one's weight. **uplift'** *vt* (*pap* **uplift'ed** or (*archaic*) **uplift'**) to lift up, raise; to elevate; to raise to a higher moral or spiritual level; to elate; to collect (eg a parcel or passenger) (*Scot, NZ*); draw (money) (*Scot*); to increase (eg an interim dividend) (*commerce*). ◆ *n* /*up'*/ a lifting up, raising; upheaval; elevation, *esp* moral or spiritual, or the feeling of it; an increase or mark-up (*commerce*). ◆ *adj* (of a brassière) designed to raise the breasts higher; providing uplift, eg of a moral or spiritual kind. **uplift'er** *n*. **uplift'ing** *n* and *adj*. **uplift'ingly** *adv*. **uplight'ed** *adj* lighted from below. **up'lighter** *n* a light-fitting that throws light upwards. **up'link** *n* a transmitter that sends signals up to a communications satellite. **up'linking** *n* and *adj*. **upload'** *vt* and *vi* to transmit (data from a computer) to a larger system. ◆ *n* /*up'*/ an act or the process of uploading; something uploaded. **uplock'** *vt* to lock up. **uplock'ed** *adj* (*Shakesp*). **uplook'** *vi* to look up. ◆ *n* /*up'*/ an upward look. **up'lying** *adj* upland, elevated. **up'make** *n* the action or mode of making up; constitution (*esp* mental or moral); galley proofs arranged in page form. **up'maker** *n*. **up'making** *n* filling up, *esp* between bilge-ways and ship's bottom before launching; arrangement of lines into columns or pages (*printing*). **up'manship** *n* same as **one-upmanship** (see under **one**). **upmar'ket** *adj* (of buying, selling or using) commodities relatively high in price, quality or prestige (also *adv*). ◆ *vt* to make (more) upmarket. **up-perch'ed** *adj* (*Keats*) perched aloft. **uppiled'** *adj* piled up. **up-pricked'** *adj* pricked up, erected. **up'-putting** *n* (*Scot*) lodging and entertainment. **upraise'** *vt* to raise or lift up; to exalt; to excite, arouse (*Milton*). **upraised'** *adj*. **uprate'** *vt* to upgrade; to increase the rate or size of. **uprear'** *vt* to raise up; to rear up. **upreared'** *adj*. **uprest** *n* see **uprist** below. **up'right** (also /*up'rīt*' or *up-rīt*'/) *adj* right or straight up; in an erect position (**upright piano** one with the wires in a vertical plane); habitually honourable or righteous; honest; just; supine (eg *lying upright*; *obs*). ◆ *n* /*up'rīt*/ an upright post, stone, stroke, etc; a vertical member of a structure; an upright piano; verticality; an elevation (*obs*); a basket-maker's tool. ◆ *vt* /*up'rīt*/ to set erect or right side up. ◆ *adv* /*up'rīt*, *up'rīt*' or *up-rīt*'/ vertically; honestly. **upright'eously** *adv* (*Shakesp*) with moral right. **up'rightly** *adv* in an upright manner; honestly; vertically. **up'right-man** *n* (*obs sl*) a sturdy beggar, leader of a gang. **up'rightness** *n*. **uprīs'al** *n*. **uprise'** (or /*up'*/) *n* rising. ◆ *vi* /-*rīz*'/ (*pat* **uprose'**; *pap* **upris'en**) to rise up, arise. **upris'ing** (or /*up'*/) *n* a rising up; a violent revolt against a ruling power. ◆ *adj* which rises up or is rising up. **uprist'** *n* (also (*Shelley*) **uprest'**) rising. ◆ *vi* (*Coleridge*; also (*Spenser*) **upryst'**) an old form of *upriseth*, mistakenly used for a *pat* or *pap* (or *perh* from a misunderstanding of the noun). **up'river** *adj* near the source of a river. ◆ *adv* /-*riv'ər*/ towards the source of a river. **up'roar** *n* see separate entry. **uproll'** *vt* and *vi* to roll up or close; to roll upward. **uproot'** *vt* to pull up by the roots; to destroy or eradicate (*fig*); to remove forcibly and completely (from eg native land). **uproot'al** *n* uprooting. **uproot'er** *n*. **uproot'ing** *n*. **uprose'** *vi* *pat* of

uprise. **up'rush** n a rising surge. ◆ vi /-rush'/ to surge up. **upryst** vi see **uprist** above. **up'scale** adj upmarket. ◆ vt to increase the scale of. **up'sell** vi and vt to persuade a customer to make a more expensive purchase than originally intended. **upset'** vt (pat and pap **upset'**) to overturn, capsize; to spill or tip out; to interfere with, defeat (a plan); to disconcert; to distress; to disorder (a bodily process or organ); to affect the health of (a person) temporarily; to thicken and shorten (metal, eg the end of a bar). ◆ vi to be upset. ◆ n /up'/ the action of upsetting or state of being upset; an upheaval or disturbance; an unexpected outcome. ◆ adj /-set'/ disturbed, anxious, unhappy; /up'/ (of a price) the lowest that will be accepted, at which bidding is started. **upsett'er** n. **upsett'ing** adj causing upset; conceited, assuming (Scot). ◆ n overturning; overthrow; metal-working to produce an increase in the size of part of a component (engineering); /up'/ presumption, overweening assumption (Scot). **upshoot'** vt and vi to shoot upward. ◆ n /up'/ an upshooting; that which shoots up; upshot (Shakesp). **up'shot** n the outcome, final result; the conclusion of an argument; the substance, the general effect; the final shot (archery); aim (Spenser); end (obs). ◆ adj /up'shot'/ shot upward (also pat and pap of **upshoot**). **up'sitting** n sitting up, esp after illness or childbirth (archaic); a reception of company on such an occasion (obs); sitting up at night as part of courtship (S Afr); listlessness (obs Scot). ◆ adj (obs Scot) listless. **upskill'** vi to improve one's skills. ◆ vt to improve the skills of. **upspeak'** vi (pat **upspoke'**, (archaic) **upspake'**) to begin to speak. **upspear'** vi (Cowper) (of grass) to shoot up straight like a spear. **upspring'** vi (pat **upsprang'**; pap **upsprung'**) to spring up; to come into being. ◆ n /up'/ (Shakesp) a lively dance (according to others, adj newly introduced). **up'stage** adv towards the back of the stage. ◆ adj towards the back of the stage; stand-offish, superior (sl). ◆ vt /-stāj'/ to treat in a supercilious manner; (of an actor) to move upstage and so force (another actor) to face away from the audience, putting him or her at a disadvantage; to divert interest or attention away from (a fellow actor) to oneself; generally, to outshine or draw attention away from (someone or something). **upstairs'** adv in or toward a higher storey, or (fig) position; in the head, mentally (inf). ◆ n the part of a building above the ground floor; (esp formerly) the upper part of a house, as opposed to the servants' quarters in the basement; its occupants, usu the householder and family. ◆ adj /up'/ (also **up'stair**) of or in an upper storey or flat. **upstand'** vi (pat **upstood'**) (Milton) to stand up. ◆ n (building) a turned-up edge on a horizontal or sloping plane where it adjoins a vertical plane. **upstand'ing** adj erect; on one's feet (Scot); straight and well-built; honest and respectable. **upstare'** vi to stare upward; (of hair) to stand up (Spenser, Shakesp). **upstar'ing** adj. **up'start** n someone who has suddenly risen to wealth, importance or power, a parvenu. ◆ adj newly or suddenly come into being; characteristic of a parvenu; pretentious and vulgar; new-fangled; standing on end (Spenser). ◆ vi /-stärt'/ to start up. **up'state** adj and adv (US) in, towards or pertaining to a part of a state away from, and usu to the north of, the principal city of the state. **upstay'** vt to sustain. **up'stream** (or /-strēm'/) adv against the current. ◆ adj further up the stream; going against the current; relating to any of the activities which precede production, eg exploration (oil); in any process or activity, denoting a previous stage. ◆ vi /-strēm'/ to stream up. **up'stroke** n an upward stroke; an upward line in writing. **upsurge** vi to surge up. ◆ n /up'/ a surging up, esp of emotion. **upsur'gence** n. **up-swarm'** vt (Shakesp) to send up in a swarm. **upsway'** vt to swing up. **upswept'** adj with an upward sweep or curve; (of hair) brushed upwards. **up'swing** n an upward swing; an economic recovery. **up'take** n the act of lifting up; a pipe or flue with upward current; the act of taking up; the extent to which this is done; understanding, mental apprehension (orig Scot; in Scot usu **up'tak**; **gleg in** or **at the uptak** quick to understand). ◆ vt /-tāk'/ to take up. **up'talk** or **up'talking** n (inf) the practice of speaking with a rising intonation at the end of each statement, as if one were asking a question. **uptear'** vt to pull up or out by the roots, from the base, etc. **up-tem'po** adj played or sung at a fast tempo. **upthrow'** vt to throw up. ◆ n /up'/ an upheaval, uplift; the amount of vertical displacement of the relatively raised strata at a fault (geol). **upthrust'** vt to thrust upward. ◆ n /up'/ a thrusting upwards. **upthun'der** vi (Coleridge) to send up a noise like thunder. **up'tick** n (chiefly N Am) an increase. **uptie'** vt to tie up; to conclude, to wind up (fig). **uptight'** adj (inf) tense, in a nervy state; angry, irritated; conventional, strait-laced. **up'till'** prep (obs and Scot) up to. **up'time** n the time during which

something, esp a computer, is operating. **up'torn** adj (also /up-torn'/ pap of **uptear**). **uptown'** adv or adj and n /up'/ (in or toward) the upper part or (US) the residential quarters of a town. **uptown'er** (or /up'/) n. **uptrain'** vt and vi (obs) to train up, educate. **up'trend** n upward tendency. **up'trilled** adj (Coleridge) trilled high. **up'turn** n an upheaval; a disturbance; a movement upward or towards improvement, a rise; an upturned part. **up'turned** adj. **upturn'ing** n and adj. **upvalua'tion** n. **upval'ue** vt to increase the value of. **upwell'ing** n a welling up; the rising to the surface of nutriment-bearing water from the depths of the ocean. **upwind** /up-wīnd'/ vt and vi (pat and pap **upwound'**) to wind up. ◆ adv /up-wind'/ (also **up-wind'**) against the wind. ◆ adj /up'/ (also **up'-wind**) going against the wind. **up'wrap** n (geol) an anticline. **upwrought'** vt (pap) wrought-up.

upadaisy same as **ups-a-daisy**.

upaithric /ū-pī'thrik/ adj hypaethral (qv). [Gr hypo beneath, and aithēr upper air, sky]

Upanishad or **Upanisad** /oo-pan'i-shad or oo-pä'ni-shäd/ n any of a number of Sanskrit theosophic or philosophical treatises. [Sans upa near, and ni-sad a sitting down]

upas /ū'pəs/ n (in full **u'pas-tree**) a fabulous Javanese tree that poisoned everything for miles around (myth); a Javanese tree (Antiaris toxicaria) of the mulberry family, yielding sap used as poison; the poison of its latex. [Malay, poison]

upbraid /up-brād'/ vt to reproach or chide; to adduce in reproach (against or to a person; obs). ◆ vi to utter reproaches. ◆ n (obs) reproach, reproof. [OE ūpbregdan]
■ **upbraid'er** n. **upbraid'ing** n and adj.

upbray /up-brā'/ (Spenser) vt to upbraid; to bring reproach on. ◆ n an upbraiding. [From upbrayd, obs pat of **upbraid**]

Up-Helly-Aa /up-hel'i-ä/ n a midwinter festival, representing an older Celtic fire festival, held on the last Tuesday of January in Lerwick, Shetland, and now including guisers (qv) and the ceremonial burning of a Viking ship. [**up** at an end, finished, and Scot haliday holiday, ie the end of the Yule holiday]

upholster /up-hōl'stər/ vt to provide with stuffing, springs, covers, etc; to cushion, be a cover to; to provide with curtains and carpets, etc. ◆ vi to do upholstery. ◆ n (obs) an upholsterer. [Back-formation from upholsterer, from upholder in obs sense (see under **up-**)]
■ **uphōl'sterer**, fem **uphōl'stress** n someone who makes or deals in furniture, beds, and curtains, etc.
❏ **uphōl'stery** n upholsterer's work or goods.

uphroe /ū'frō/ same as **euphroe**.

UPI abbrev : United Press International.

upmost see under **up**.

upo' /ə-pō'/ (archaic or dialect) prep upon. [From up of]

upon /ə-pon'/ prep on. ◆ adv thereon, on the surface (Shakesp); on the person (archaic); thereafter (Shakesp); close in approach (Shakesp). [ME, from **up** and **on**]

upper, uppermost see under **up**.

uproar /up'rōr or -rör/ n loud outcry, clamour; insurrection, tumult (now rare). [Du oproer, from op up, and roeren (Ger rühren, OE hrēran) to stir; modified by association with **roar**]
■ **uproar'** vt (Shakesp) to throw into uproar or confusion. ◆ vi to make an uproar. **uproar'ious** adj. **uproar'iously** adv. **uproar'iousness** n.

UPS (comput) abbrev : Uninterruptible Power Supply.

ups-a-daisy /ups'ə-dā'zi/ interj of encouragement eg when lifting a child or helping someone climb or to get up after falling.

upsey, upsee or **upsy** /up'si/ (obs) prep in the manner of. ◆ adv (in full upsey Dutch, English, or Friese /frēz/, in the German, English, or Frisian manner of drinking) deeply, heavily, heartily. ◆ n a carousal. ◆ interj a Bacchanalian exclamation. [Du op zijn, in his (ie the; 'manner' understood)]

upsilon /ūp-sī'lon, ūp-, ūp'si- or up'si-/ or **ypsilon** /ip-sī'lon or ip'si-/ n the twentieth letter of the Greek alphabet (Y, υ); as a numeral υ' = 400, ‚υ = 400000; a short-lived heavy subatomic particle

---

Some words formed with the prefix **up-**.

upheap' vt.	**uprouse'** vt.	**uptilt'** vt.
upheap'ing n.	**uprun'** vi.	**uptilt'ed** adj.
uphoist' vt.	**upsend'** vt.	**upwaft'** vt.
uphurl' vt.	**up'sweep** n.	**upwell'** vi.
upleap' vi.	**upswell'** vt and vi.	**upwhirl'** vt and vi.

---

produced when beryllium nuclei are bombarded with high-energy protons. [Gr, simple u]

upsy same as **upsey**.

upsy-daisy /up'si-dā-zi/ interj same as **ups-a-daisy**.

uptrain see under **up-**.

up-train see under **up**.

UPU abbrev : Universal Postal Union.

UPVC or **uPVC** abbrev : unplasticized polyvinyl chloride.

upward see under **up**.

ur /ûr/ interj used by speakers to fill a gap in speech, when hesitant.

ur- /oor-/ pfx primitive, original. [Ger]

urachus /ū'rə-kəs/ n a ligament connecting the bladder with the umbilicus. [Gr ourachos, the fetal structure from which it is formed]

uracil /ū'rə-sil/ (biochem) n a form of pyrimidine present in living tissue as a base of RNA. [urea and acetic]

uraemia or (US) **uremia** /ū-rē'mi-ə/ (med) n retention in the blood of waste materials normally excreted in urine. [Gr ouron urine, and haima blood]
■ **urae'mic** or (US) **ure'mic** adj.

uraeus /ū-rē'əs/ n the snake symbol on the headdress of Egyptian gods and kings. [Gr ouraios a kind of snake; prob Egyp]

Ural /ū'rəl/ n a river rising in the Urals and flowing through Kazakhstan to the Caspian Sea; (usu in pl) a mountain range running from the Arctic Ocean through Russia and Kazakhstan to the Caspian Sea.
■ **Uralian** /ū-rā'li-ən/ adj of the Ural Mountains (**Uralian emerald** a semi-precious green garnet); of or relating to Uralic. ◆ n Uralic. **Uralic** /ū-ral'ik/ n a language group comprising the Finno-Ugric and the Samoyed languages. ◆ adj Uralian. **ū'ralite** n an altered mineral, hornblende after augite. **uralitic** /-lit'ik/ adj. **uralītizā'tion** or **-s-** n. **ū'ralitize** or **-ise** vt to turn into uralite.
❑ **Ural-Altaic** /-al-tā'ik/ adj of the Ural and Altai Mountains; applied to a family of languages (Finno-Ugrian, Turko-Tatar, Mongolian, Manchu, Tungus, etc) and their speakers. ◆ n the Ural-Altaic family of languages.

urali same as **wourali**.

uranalysis see **urinalysis** under **urine**.

Urania /ū-rā'ni-ə/ (Gr myth) n the Muse of astronomy; a name for Aphrodite. [L, from Gr Ourania, from ouranos heaven]
■ **Ura'nian** adj.

Uranian see under **Urania** and **Uranus**.

uranic /ū-ran'ik/ adj of uranium in higher valency (chem); celestial (obs); of the palate. [From Gr ouranos heaven, roof of the mouth, palate]

uranide /ū'rə-nīd/ n a transuranic element. [uranium and chem sfx -ide]

uranin /ū'rə-nin/ (chem) n a sodium or potassium salt of fluorescein (from its fluorescence, like that of uranium glass). [uranium]

uraninite /ū-ran'i-nīt/ n a brownish to black crystalline mineral consisting mainly of uranium oxide, when massive known as pitchblende. [uranium]

uraniscus /ū-rə-nis'kəs/ n the roof of the mouth. [Gr ouraniskos]

uranism /ū'rə-ni-zm/ (rare) n homosexuality, esp male homosexuality. [Ger Uranismus, from Gr ouranious heavenly, esp as applied to Aphrodite]

uranite /ū'rə-nīt/ n autunite; torbernite. [uranium]
■ **uranit'ic** adj.

uranium /ū-rā'ni-əm/ n a radioactive metallic element (symbol U; atomic no 92) named by German chemist Martin Klaproth in 1789, after the recently discovered planet Uranus.
❑ **uranium glass** n a yellow fluorescent glass containing uranium compounds. **uranium hexafluoride** n a volatile compound of uranium with fluorine, used in the gaseous diffusion process for separating the uranium isotopes. **uranium-lead dating** n (geol) a method of determining the age in years of geological material, based on the known decay rate of uranium isotopes to lead isotopes.

urano- /ū-rə-nō-, -nə- or -no-/ combining form denoting: the sky, the heavens; the roof of the mouth, palate (med); uranium. [Gr ouranos heaven]
■ **uranog'rapher** n. **uranograph'ic** or **uranograph'ical** adj. **uranog'raphist** n. **uranog'raphy** n (see **-graphy**) descriptive astronomy and mapping, esp of the constellations. **uranol'ogy** n astronomy. **uranom'etry** n astronomical measurement. **ū'ranoplasty** n plastic surgery of the palate.

Uranoscopus /ū-rə-nos'ko-pəs/ n the star-gazer genus of fishes. [Gr ouranoskopos heaven-gazing]

uranous /ū'rə-nəs/ (chem) adj of uranium in lower valency. [uranium]

Uranus /ū'rə-nəs or ū-rā'nəs/ n an old Greek god, father of Kronos (Saturn) and the Titans (Gr myth); a planet discovered in 1781 by Sir William Herschel. [L, from Gr Ouranos]
■ **Urā'nian** adj (also without cap) heavenly; of the heavens; astronomical; of the god or planet Uranus.

uranyl /ū'rə-nil/ (chem) n the group UO_2. [uranium]
■ **ūranyl'ic** adj.

urao /oo-rä'ō/ n natron. [Sp urao, from Carib]

urari same as **wourali**.

urate /ū'rāt/ see under **uric**.

urban /ûr'bən/ adj of, situated in or belonging to a city or town; relating to a style of popular dance music influenced by rap. [L urbānus, from urbs a city]
■ **urbane** /ûr-bān'/ adj relating to or influenced by a city; civilized; elegant; refined; courteous; smooth-mannered. **urbane'ly** adv. **urbane'ness** n. **ur'banism** n (the study of) the urban way of life. **ur'banist** n. **urbanist'ic** adj relating to the planning and development of towns. **ur'banite** n a person who lives in a town or city. **urbanity** /-ban'i-ti/ n the quality of being urbane; (in pl) civilities; townishness; town-life. **urbaniza'tion** or **-s-** n. **ur'banize** or **-ise** vt to make (a district) townlike (as opposed to rural) in character. **urbanol'ogist** n someone who studies urban conditions. **urbanol'ogy** n.
❑ **urban district** n (hist) a thickly-populated district, a subdivision of a county, administered by an **Urban District Council**. **urban guerrilla** n a guerrilla engaged in terrorist activities in towns and cities. **urban legend** or **myth** n a story or anecdote of modern life, often untrue or apocryphal. **urban renewal** n (esp US) the clearing and/or redevelopment of slums, etc.

urbi et orbi /ûr'bi (or oor') et ör'bi/ (L) (of a papal blessing, addressed) to the city and to the world.

URC abbrev : United Reformed Church.

urceolus /ûr-sē'ə-ləs/ (zool and bot) n a pitcher-shaped structure, with contracted mouth, such as the sheath of some rotifers. [L urceolus, dimin of urceus a pitcher]
■ **ur'ceolate** adj having the form of an urceolus.

urchin /ûr'chin/ n a mischievous child, esp a boy, and esp when young and raggedly dressed; a child; a sea urchin; a hedgehog (archaic or dialect); a deformed person, a hunchback (obs or dialect); an elf or imp (obs). ◆ adj like, of the nature of or due to an urchin. [OFr herichon, heriçon (Fr hérisson), from L ēricius a hedgehog]
❑ **urchin cut** n a women's short, artfully rough hairstyle. **ur'chin-snout'ed** adj with a snout like a hedgehog.

urd /ûrd/ n an Indian plant (Phaseolus mungo) of the bean family, or its edible blackish seed (also **urd bean** or **black gram**). [Hindi]

urdé, **urdée**, **urdee**, or **urdy** /ûr'dā, -dē or -di/ (heraldry) adj pointed; having points. [Origin obscure]

Urdu /oor'doo or oor-doo'/ n a form of Hindustani incorporating many Persian and Arabic words, the official literary language of Pakistan. ◆ adj of or relating to this language. [Hindi urdū camp (language); cf **horde**]

ure¹ /ūr/ (obs) n use, practice, operation. [OFr uevre (Fr œuvre), from L opera work, service]

ure² /ūr/ (obs) n the urus, an extinct wild ox. [L ūrus]

ure³ /ûr/ (hist; Orkney and Shetland) n an eighth of a mark, or an area of land paying so much in feu-duty. [Cf Norw, Swed, Dan öre, from L aureus a gold solidus]

-ure /-ūr/ sfx forming nouns denoting: action, process or result; office or function. [L -ura]

urea /ū-rē'ə or ū'rē-ə/ n carbamide, $CO(NH_2)_2$, a substance found in mammalian urine, the chief form in which nitrogenous waste is excreted and the first natural product to be synthesized. [Gr ouron urine]
■ **ure'al** (or /ū'ri-əl/) or **ūre'ic** adj. **ureide** /ū'rē-īd/ n (chem) any of several organic compounds derived from urea; an acyl derivative of urea, such as urethan. **ū'ridine** n a pyrimidine nucleoside found in RNA and formed from uracil and ribose.
❑ **urea-formal'dehyde resin** n a resin produced by condensation of urea with formaldehyde. **urea resins** n pl thermosetting resins used eg in adhesive, made by heating urea and aldehyde, usu formaldehyde.

uredo /ū-rē'dō/ n (pl **uredines** /ū-rē'di-nēz/) rust in plants; a rust-fungus in its summer stage (also **ure'do-stage**); urticaria. [L ūrēdō, -inis blight, from ūrere to burn]
■ **Uredinā'lēs** n pl the Uredineae. **uredine** /ū'ri-dīn/ adj. **Uredineae** /ū-ri-din'i-ē/ n pl the rust-fungi, an order of parasitic Basidiomycetes. **uredin'ial** adj (US). **uredin'iospore** or **ure'diospore** n (US) a uredospore. **uredin'ium** or **ure'dium** n (pl **uredin'ia** or **ure'dia**) (US) a uredosorus. **ure'dinous** adj. **ure'doso'rus** /-sö' or -sö'/ n a pustule

producing and containing uredospores. **urē'dospore** *n* a spore produced by rust-fungi in the uredo-stage.

ureide see under **urea**.

uremia, **uremic** see **uraemia**, **uraemic**.

urena /ū-rē'nə/ *n* any plant of the tropical genus *Urena* of the mallow family, yielding a jute substitute. [Malayalam *uren*]

urent /ū'rənt/ *adj* burning, stinging. [L *ūrēns, -entis*, prp of *ūrere* to burn]

uresis /ū-rē'sis/ (*med*) *n* urination. [Gr *ourēsis*]

ureter /ū-rē'tər/ (*anat* and *zool*) *n* a duct that conveys urine from the kidneys to the bladder or cloaca. [Gr *ourētēr, -ēros*, from *ouron* urine]
■ **urē'teral** *adj*. **ureteric** /ū-ri-ter'ik/ *adj*. **urēterī'tis** *n* (*med*) inflammation of a ureter.

urethan or **urethane** /ū'ri-than, -thān* or *-than', -thān'/ *n* a crystalline ester, $NH_2COOC_2H_5$, prepared from urea and ethyl alcohol, used eg in pesticides and in polymerized form as a coating, plastic, adhesive etc, and formerly as an anaesthetic. [**urea**, **ethyl** and chem sfx *-ane*]

urethra /ū-rē'thrə/ (*anat* and *zool*) *n* (*pl* **urethras** or **urethrae** /-thrē/) the canal by which the urine is discharged from the bladder. [Gr *ourēthrā*, from *ouron* urine]
■ **urē'thral** *adj*. **urēthrit'ic** *adj*. **urēthrī'tis** *n* (*med*) inflammation of the urethra. **urē'throscope** *n* (*med*) an instrument for examining the urethra. **urēthrosco'pic** *adj*. **urēthros'copy** *n*.
■ **non-specific urethritis** (*med*) a disease resembling gonorrhoea, not associated with any identifiable virus.

uretic /ū-ret'ik/ *adj* relating to, or occurring in urine. [Gr *ourētikos*, from *ouron* urine]

urge /ûrj/ *vt* to put forward (an argument, etc; or in argument, with *that*); to incite; to allege earnestly; to advise strongly; to drive, impel; to press forward, *esp* with earnestness, or insistence (success, an enterprise, etc; *archaic*); to stimulate, excite (*archaic*); to hasten (*archaic*). ◆ *vi* to press; to be urgent or insistent; to push on. ◆ *n* an impulse; a prompting; a strong desire or drive. [L *urgēre*]
■ **ur'gence** *n* (*rare*). **ur'gency** *n*. **ur'gent** *adj* earnest, persistent; pressing; calling for immediate attention. **ur'gently** *adv*. **ur'ger** *n*. **ur'ging** *n* and *adj*.

URI *abbrev* : upper respiratory infection.

-uria /-ū-ri-ə/ *sfx* forming nouns denoting the presence of a substance in, or an abnormal condition of, the urine. [Mod L, from Gr *ouron* urine]
■ **-uric** *adj sfx*.

urial or **oorial** /oo'ri-əl/ *n* a Himalayan wild sheep. [Punjabi *hureāl*]

uric /ū'rik/ *adj* of, obtained from or present in urine. [Gr *ouron* urine]
■ **ū'rate** *n* a salt of uric acid. **ū'ricase** *n* an enzyme occurring in the liver and kidneys, which catalyses the oxidation of uric acid.
□ **uric acid** *n* an acid of the purine group, $C_5H_4N_4O_3$, present in urine and blood (also called **2,6,8-trihydroxypu'rine**).

Uriconian /ū-ri-kō'ni-ən/ *adj* of the Roman station *Uriconium* (*Viroconium*) on the site of Wroxeter in Shropshire; applied to the apparently Precambrian igneous rocks forming the Wrekin, etc.

uridine see under **urea**.

Urim and Thummim /ū'rim ənd thum'im/ *n pl* first mentioned in the Bible, Exodus 28.30, *appar* a pair of objects used as a kind of traditional oracle. [Heb *ūrīm* and *t(h)ummīm*]

urinal see under **urine**.

urinant /ū'ri-nənt/ (*heraldry*) *adj* diving, head downward. [L *ūrīnārī* to plunge]
■ **ū'rinātor** *n* a diver.

urine /ū'rin/ *n* the *usu* amber liquid produced by the kidneys, the chief means of excreting nitrogenous waste. ◆ *vi* (*obs*) to urinate. [L *ūrīna*; cf Gr *ouron*]
■ **ū'rinal** (or /-rī'/) *n* a sanitary fitting *usu* plumbed into a wall, for the use of men when urinating; a room or building having fixed receptacle(s) for use in urination; a vessel for urine, *esp* one for the use of an incontinent or bedridden person; a chamberpot (*archaic*). **urinal'ysis** *n* analysis of urine, eg to detect disease (also **uranal'ysis**). **ū'rinary** *adj* relating to or like urine, or the organs producing urine. ◆ *n* (*obs*) a reservoir for the collection of urine eg for manure; a urinal. **ū'rinate** *vi* to discharge urine. **urinā'tion** *n*. **ū'rinative** *adj*. **urinif'erous** *adj* conveying urine. **urinip'arous** *adj* producing urine. **urinogen'ital** *adj* relating jointly to urinary and genital functions or organs. **urinol'ogy**, **urinos'copy**, etc variant forms of **urology**, **uroscopy**, etc (see under **uro-¹**). **urinom'eter** *n* a hydrometer for urine. **ū'rinous** *adj* like or of the nature of urine (also **ū'rinose**).

urite /ū'rīt/ *n* an abdominal segment. [Gr *ourā* a tail]

URL (*comput*) *abbrev* : Uniform Resource Locator (the system of addresses for the World Wide Web).

urman /oor-män'/ *n* (swampy) pine forest. [Russ, from Tatar *ūrmān*]

urn /ûrn/ *n* a vase with rounded body, *usu* a narrowed mouth and often a foot; *esp* such a vase for ashes of the dead; hence, any repository for the dead (*esp poetic*); a monumental imitation of a burial-urn; a river-source (*poetic*); a vessel for water; a closed vessel with a tap and now *usu* with a heating device inside, for making tea or coffee in quantity; a moss-capsule (*bot*); an urn-shaped object; a ballot box; a container into which to put voting-tablets, etc (*Roman hist*, etc). ◆ *vt* to enclose in an urn. [L *urna*]
■ **urn'al** *adj*. **urned** *adj*. **urn'ful** *n* (*pl* **urn'fuls**) as much as an urn will hold.
□ **urn'field** *n* a late Bronze Age cemetery containing cinerary urns. ◆ *adj* of or relating to a people, culture, etc using this method of burial. **urn'-shaped** *adj* rounded with a narrowed mouth.

urning /ûr'ning/ (*rare*) *n* a (*esp* male) homosexual. [Ger, irregularly formed; cf **uranism**]

uro-¹ /ū-rō-, -rə- or *-ro-/ *combining form* denoting urine. [Gr *ouron* urine; cf L *ūrīna*]
■ **ū'rochrome** *n* the yellow pigment in urine. **urodynam'ics** *n sing* the study of urine flow. **urogen'ital** *adj* urinogenital. **urog'enous** *adj* producing, or produced in, urine; having a function in the production and excretion of urine. **urograph'ic** *adj*. **urog'raphy** *n* radiological examination of the urinary tract. **urokī'nase** (or /-kin'/) *n* an enzyme, found in human urine, which dissolves blood clots, used in the treatment of pulmonary embolisms. **urolag'nia** *n* sexual arousal caused by, or associated with, urination or urine. **ū'rolith** *n* (*med*) a calculus in the urine or the urinary tract. **urolithī'asis** *n* (*med*) the formation of uroliths; the condition caused by uroliths. **ūrolith'ic** *adj*. **urolog'ic** or **urolog'ical** *adj*. **urol'ogist** *n*. **urol'ogy** *n* the branch of medicine dealing with diseases and abnormalities of the urinary tract and their treatment; the scientific study of urine (*obs*). **uropoiē'sis** *n* formation of urine. **uroscop'ic** *adj*. **uros'copist** *n*. **uros'copy** *n* diagnostic examination of urine. **urō'sis** *n* disease of the urinary organs. **uros'tomy** *n* an artificial opening made in part of the urinary tract, with a passage constructed out through the skin or to another organ, allowing urine to be drained.

uro-² /ū-rō-, -rə- or *-ro-/ *combining form* denoting: tail; posterior part. [Gr *ourā* tail]
■ **uroboros** see **ouroboros**. **ū'rochord** /-körd/ *n* a notochord confined to the caudal region, as in larval ascidians; any member of the **Urochord'a** or **Urochorda'ta**, a subphylum of Chordata whose larvae have a urochord, ie ascidians and related forms. **urochor'dal** *adj*. **urochor'date** *adj* and *n*. **Urodē'la** *n pl* (Gr *dēlos* clear, plain) the (permanently) tailed Amphibia, eg newts and salamanders. **urodē'lan** or **ū'rodele** *n* and *adj*. **urodē'lous** *adj*. **ū'romere** *n* (Gr *meros* part) an abdominal segment of an arthropod. **ū'ropod** *n* an abdominal appendage of an arthropod, *esp* just before the telson. **ū'rosome** *n* (see **-some²**) the tail region. **urostege** /ū'rə-stēj/ or **urostegite** /ū-ros'ti-jīt/ *n* (Gr *stegē* roof, deck) a snake's ventral tail-plate. **urosthen'ic** *adj* (Gr *sthenos* strength) having a tail developed for propulsion. **ū'rostyle** *n* (Gr *stȳlos* column) a prolongation of the last vertebra in frogs, toads, etc.

uropygium /ū-rō-pij'i-əm/ *n* (in birds) the rump, which supports the tail feathers. [Gr *ouropȳgion* or *orropȳgion*, from *orros* the end of the sacrum, and *pȳgē* buttocks]
■ **uropyg'ial** *adj*.
□ **uropygial gland** *n* a gland at the base of the tail in most birds, which secretes oil used in preening.

Ursa /ûr'sə/ *n* the Latin name of two constellations, *Ursa Major* and *Ursa Minor*, the Great and the Little Bear. [L *ursus, ursa* bear]
■ **ur'sine** *adj* of a bear; bearlike. **Ur'sus** *n* the bear genus.

urson /ûr'sən/ *n* the Canadian porcupine. [Fr *ourson*, dimin of *ours*, from L *ursus* bear]

Ursuline /ûr'sū-lin or *-līn/ *adj* of or relating to St *Ursula*, *esp* of the teaching order of nuns founded by St Angela Merici of Brescia in 1537 (also *n*).

Ursus see under **Ursa**.

urtext /ûr'tekst/ *n* the earliest version of a text, from which extant texts are deemed to be derived; an edition of a musical score showing only the composer's own original work, not altered by subsequent editorial revision. [Ger, from *ur* original, and *Text*]

urtica /ûr-tī'kə or commonly *ûr'ti-kə/ *n* any plant of the nettle genus *Urtica*, giving name to the family **Urticaceae** /ûr-ti-kā'si-ē/, related to (or including) elms and mulberries. [L *urtīca* a nettle, from *ūrere* to burn]
■ **urtica'ceous** *adj* like or of the nature of a nettle; of the nettle family. **ur'ticant** *adj* stinging; irritating. **urticā'ria** *n* (*med*) nettle rash. **urticā'rial** *adj*. **urticā'rious** *adj*. **ur'ticate** *vt* to sting; to flog with nettles. **urticā'tion** *n*.

Uru. *abbrev* : Uruguay.

urubu /oo-roo-boo'/ *n* a S American vulture. [Tupí *urubú*]

Uruguayan /ū-rə-gwī'ən/ adj of or relating to the republic of *Uruguay* in S America, or its people. ◆ n a native or citizen of Uruguay.

urus /ū'rəs/ n (pl **urusēs**') the aurochs (qv).

urushiol /ŭ-roo'shi-ol/ n a poisonous and irritant oily liquid present in poison ivy and the lacquer tree. [Jap *urushi* lacquer, and **-ol²**]

urva /ûr'və/ n the crab-eating mongoose of SE Asia. [Nepali]

US abbrev : under-secretary; United Service(s); United States (of America).

U/S or **u/s** abbrev : unserviceable.

us /us/ or /uz/ pronoun the objective (dative and accusative) case of **we**; (in editorial and royal use) one, oneself; me (inf). [OE ūs]
■ **us'ward** adv toward us (also n as in to usward).

us abbrev : ut supra (L), as above.

USA abbrev : United States Army; United States of America (also IVR).

usable see under **use¹**.

USAF abbrev : United States Air Force.

usage /ū'zij/ or -sij/ n use; act or mode of using; treatment; practice; custom; the normal or acceptable speech patterns, vocabulary, etc of a language or dialect; interest on money (obs); (in pl, with the) four ceremonies in the celebration of the Eucharist, dispute about which caused a separation of the Nonjurors into two groups (hist). [OFr, from L ūsus use]
■ **ū'sager** n (hist) one of the Nonjurors who maintained 'the usages'. **ū'sance** n usage; interest, or lending at interest (Shakesp); time allowed for payment of foreign bills of exchange.

USAID abbrev : United States Agency for International Development.

USB (comput) abbrev : Universal Serial Bus, a fast versatile bus for communicating with peripheral devices.

USCL abbrev : United Society for Christian Literature.

USDAW /uz'dö/ abbrev : Union of Shop, Distributive and Allied Workers.

use¹ /ūz/ vt to put to some purpose; to avail oneself of; to employ habitually, to exercise; to treat or behave towards; to make use of (a person; see under **use²**); to take or consume (drugs or alcohol) regularly (sl; also vi); to habituate or accustom (old except in pap; see **used** below); to observe, practise, follow (archaic); to resort to (a place) (archaic); to behave, comport (oneself) (archaic). ◆ vi to be accustomed (to do, etc; chiefly in the past tense **used**, pronounced in this sense /ūst/; **usedn't** or **usen't** /ūs'nt/, for used not); to accustom oneself (with to) (Scot); to be in the habit of so doing (archaic); to resort (archaic). [Fr user, from LL ūsāre, from L ūtī, ūsus to use]
■ **ūs'able** or **ūse'able** adj. **ūs'ableness** or **ūse'ableness**, **ūsabil'ity** or **ūseabil'ity** n. **ūs'ably** or **ūse'ably** adv. **used** /ūzd/ adj already made use of; second-hand; experienced, expert (Scot); usual, customary (obs); /ūst/ accustomed, habituated (with to, or (old Scot) in or with). **ū'ser** n a person who uses; a person who takes drugs, a drug addict (inf); continual enjoyment of a right (cf **non-user**; Fr user); a right established by long use (law). □ **use-by date** n a date, indicated on a manufacturer's or distributor's label, after which goods, esp foods, are considered no longer fit for use (also fig). **used-up'** adj exhausted. **user-friend'ly** adj (of a computer or software item) designed to be easily understood and operable by non-specialists, guiding the user by means of clear instructions and menus, etc; (generally, of any product, etc) designed with the ease of the user in mind, deliberately not off-putting. **user interface** n the means of communication between a computer system and the user. **ū'sername** or **user ID** n the name or code by which a person or group is identified when gaining access to a computer network. ■ **I could use** (inf) I would feel better for, I want, need. **use up** to consume; to exhaust; to tire out.

use² /ūs/ n the act of using; the state or fact of being used; an advantageous purpose for which a thing can be used; the fact of serving a purpose; usefulness; employment causing wear; a need to use (with for); the manner of using; the power of using (eg tongue or limb); the habit of using; custom; ordinary experience (Shakesp); a distinctive form of public worship or service peculiar to a church or diocese, etc; the profit derived from property; (in pl) a form of equitable ownership peculiar to English law by which one person enjoys the profit of lands, etc, the legal title to which is vested in another in trust; interest for money (archaic; also fig in Shakesp). [L ūsus, from ūtī to use]
■ **use'ful** adj advantageous, serviceable (**useful** or **applied arts** those arts with a utilitarian purpose (eg weaving or pottery) as opposed to the fine arts (see under **art¹**)); competent, proficient (inf). **use'fully** adv. **use'fulness** n. **use'less** adj having no use; not answering any good purpose or the end proposed; weak, poor, ineffectual (often with at ; inf). **use'lessly** adv. **use'lessness** n.

□ **useful life** n (elec eng) the life that can be expected from a component before the chance of failure begins to increase (often fig). **useful load** n the maximum load of passengers or cargo that an aircraft can carry in addition to its own weight.
■ **have no use for** to have no need for; to have no liking for. **in use** in employment or practice. **make use of** to use, employ; to take the help, etc, of (a person) in obtaining an end with no intention of repaying him or her, to exploit. **of no use** useless. **of use** useful. **out of use** not being used or employed. **use and wont** the customary practice.

Usenet /ūz'net/ (comput) n a worldwide collection of newsgroups. [**use¹** and Internet]

USGA abbrev : United States Golf Association.

usher /ush'ər/ n a doorkeeper; someone who escorts people to seats in a hall, etc; an officer who introduces strangers or walks before a person of rank; a minor court official responsible for keeping order (Eng law); an under-teacher or assistant (hist). ◆ vt to conduct; to show (in or out); to introduce, lead up to (now usu with in). [Anglo-Fr usser, OFr ussier (Fr huissier), from L ostiārius a doorkeeper, from ostium a door]
■ **ush'eress** or **usherette'** n a female usher, esp in a theatre or cinema. **ush'ering** n. **ush'ership** n.

USIA abbrev : United States Information Agency (now replaced by **IIP**).

USM abbrev : Unlisted Securities Market.

USN abbrev : United States Navy.

usnea /us'ni-ə/ n any member of the Usnea genus of lichens, tree-moss. [Pers ushnah moss]

USO abbrev : United Service Organizations.

USP abbrev : (marketing) unique selling point (or proposition), a feature that differentiates a product or service from all its competitors.

USPG abbrev : United Society for the Propagation of the Gospel.

usque ad nauseam /us'kwi ad nö'zi-am or ŭs'kwe ad now'se-am/ (L) adv to the point of disgust.

usquebaugh /us'kwi-bö/ n whisky. [Ir and Gaelic uisgebeatha, from uisge water, and beatha life]

USS abbrev : United States Ship or Steamer.

USSR or (Russ) **CCCP** abbrev : Union of Soviet Socialist Republics.

Ustilago /us-ti-lā'gō/ n a genus of basidiomycetous fungi, of the family **Ustilaginaceae** /-laj-i-nā'si-ē/ and order **Ustilaginales** /-laj-i-nā'lēz/ or **Ustilagin'eae**, the smut-fungi. [L ustilāgō, -inis a kind of thistle]
■ **ustilagin'eous** or **ustilag'inous** adj.

usu. or **usu** abbrev : usually.

usual /ū'zhū-əl or -zhoo-/ adj occurring in ordinary use; common; customary. ◆ n (inf) one's normal health; one's habitual drink, etc. [L ūsuālis, from ūsus use]
■ **ū'sually** adv. **ū'sualness** n.
■ **as usual** as is or was usual. **the usual** (inf) the drink, etc one regularly orders or takes; anything one customarily experiences or does, eg menstruation.

usucapion /ū-zū-kā'pi-ən/ or **usucaption** /-kap'shən/ (Roman and Scots law) n the acquisition of property by long possession and enjoyment. [L ūsūcapere, from ūsus use, and capere, captum to take]
■ **usucā'pient** n a person who claims or holds by usucapion. **ū'sucapt** /-kapt/ vt to acquire by usucapion. **usucapt'ible** adj.

usufruct /ū'zū-frukt/ (Roman and Scots law) n the right to use and profit from another's property on the condition that it remains uninjured; life-rent. ◆ vt to hold in usufruct. [LL ūsūfrūctus, from L ūsus (et) frūctus use and enjoyment]
■ **usufruc'tūary** adj. ◆ n someone who has usufruct.

usure, usurer, etc see under **usury**.

usurp /ū-zûrp'/ vt to take possession of by force, without right, or unjustly; to assume (the authority or place, etc, of someone or something else); to take possession of (the mind); to take or borrow (a name or a word); to supplant (archaic). ◆ vi to practise usurpation; to encroach (with on or upon). [Fr usurper and L ūsūrpāre, perh from ūsus use, and rapere to seize]
■ **usurpā'tion** n. **usur'pative** or **usur'patory** adj. **usurpā'ture** n (poetic) usurpation. **usurped'** adj. **usur'pedly** adv. **usur'per** n. **usur'ping** n and adj. **usur'pingly** adv.

usury /ū'zhə-ri or -zū-/ n the taking of (now only iniquitous or illegal) interest on a loan; interest (archaic); moneylending (archaic). [LL ūsūria, L ūsūra, from ūtī, ūsus to use]
■ **ū'sure** n (obs) interest; usury. ◆ vi (obs) to practise usury. **ū'surer** n (also fem **ū'suress**) a moneylender (now usu at excessive rates of interest). **ū'suring** adj (Shakesp) taking or expecting usury. **usū'rious** adj. **usū'riously** adv. **usū'riousness** n. **ū'surous** adj (obs).

usus loquendi /ū'zəs lo-kwen'dī or oo'sŭs lo-kwen'dē/ (L) n current usage of speech.

USW *abbrev* : ultrashort waves; ultrasonic waves.

usw *abbrev* : *und so weiter* (*Ger*), and so forth.

usward see under **us** (*pronoun*).

UT *abbrev* : Universal Time; Utah (US state; also **Ut.**).

ut¹ /oot/ or /ut/ *n* a syllable representing the first note of the scale, now generally superseded by *doh*. [See **Aretinian** and **gamut**]

ut² /ut/ or /ŭt/ (*L*) *adv* and *conj* as.
■ **ut dictum** /dik'tɘm/ or -*tŭm*/ as said (*abbrev* **ut dict.**). **ut infra** /in'frä/ or /ēn'frä/ as below. **ut supra** /sū'prä, sŭ'prä/ or /soo'/ as above (*abbrev* **ut sup.**).

utas /ū'tɘs/ (*obs*) *n* the octave of a festival. [MFr *huitaves*, from OFr *outaves* (pl), from L *octāva* eight]

UTC *abbrev* : Universal Time, Co-ordinated (used in telecommunications for GMT).

ut dict. see **ut dictum** under **ut²**.

Ute /ūt/ or /ū'ti/ *n* (pl **Ute** /ū'te/ or **Utes** /ū'tes/) (a member of) a Native American people of Utah, Colorado and New Mexico; the Uto-Aztecan language of this people. ◆ *adj* of this people or their language. [Shortening of *Utah*]

ute see **utility**.

utensil /ū-ten'sil, formerly ū'ten-sil/ *n* any useful or ceremonial implement, tool or vessel. [OFr *utensile*, from L *ūtēnsilis* fit for use, from *ūtī* to use]

uterus /ū'tɘ-rɘs/ *n* (pl **ū'terī**) the womb. [L]
■ **uterec'tomy** *n* hysterectomy. **ū'terine** /-īn/ *adj* of, in or for the uterus; (of siblings) having the same mother but a different father. **uterī'tis** *n* inflammation of the womb. **ū'terogestā'tion** *n* gestation in the womb. **uterot'omy** *n* hysterotomy.

Utgard /ŭt'gärd/ (*Norse myth*) *n* the abode of the giants. [ON *ūt* out, and *garthr* garth, yard]

UTI *abbrev* : urinary tract infection.

utile /ū'tīl/ *adj* (with *to*) useful, profitable. [ME, from OFr, from L *ūtilis* useful, from *ūtī* to use]

utilitarian /ū-ti-li-tā'ri-ɘn/ *adj* consisting in, based upon or relating to utility or to utilitarianism; concerned with or based on usefulness alone, without regard to beauty and pleasantness, etc. ◆ *n* someone believing in utilitarianism; someone who looks to usefulness alone. [Jeremy Bentham's coinage from **utility**]
■ **utili'rianism** *n* the ethical theory which finds the basis of moral distinctions in the utility of actions, ie their fitness to produce happiness for the majority. **utilitā'rianize** or **-ise** *vt* to make to serve a utilitarian purpose.

utility /ū-til'i-ti/ *n* usefulness; the power to satisfy the wants of people in general (*philos*); a utility program (*comput*); a useful thing; a public utility, public service, or a company providing such (*esp US*); profit (*obs*); (*usu* in *pl*) stock or bond of public utility; a small pick-up truck (in full **utility truck** or **vehicle**; short form **ute**; *Aust* and *NZ*). ◆ *adj* produced or supplied primarily for usefulness; provided in order that the public may be supplied in spite of rise of prices; (of a breed of dog) originally bred to be useful, to serve a practical purpose. [L *ūtilitās* usefulness]
◻ **utility function** *n* (*econ*) a mathematical function relating goods and services to their utility to individuals. **utility man** *n* an actor playing several important parts; a person who can be used to fill any gap, do any job, etc; (also **utility player**) a player who can play in any of various positions as required (*sport*). **utility player** *n* a member of a sports team who can fill several different positions. **utility pole** *n* (*US*) a pole supporting power cables, telegraph wires, etc. **utility program** *n* (*comput*) a program in the system software designed to perform a commonplace task such as transferring data from one storage device to another or sorting a set of data. **utility room** *n* a room, *esp* in a private house, where things required for the work of running the house are kept, eg a washing machine.

utilize or **-ise** /ū'ti-līz/ *vt* to make use of, turn to use. [Fr *utiliser*, from *utile* useful, from L *ūtilis*, from *ūtī* to use]
■ **ū'tilizable** or **-s-** *adj*. **utilizā'tion** or **-s-** *n*. **ū'tilizer** or **-s-** *n*.
◻ **utilization factor** *n* (*elec eng*) the ratio of the luminous flux reaching a specified plane to the total flux emanating from an electric lamp.

ut infra see under **ut²**.

uti possidetis /ū'tī pos-i-dē'tis or ū'tē pos-i-dā'tis/ (*L*) *n* (in international law) the principle under which belligerents keep the territory or property they possess at the close of hostilities unless otherwise agreed. [L, as you possess]

utis /ū'tis/ (*Shakesp*) *n* clamour, din. [ME *ūthēs* hue and cry, appar from OE *ūt* out, and *hæs* hest]

utmost /ut'mōst or -mɘst/ *adj* outmost; last; in the greatest degree; extreme. ◆ *n* the limit; the extreme; the most or greatest possible; the

end (*Shakesp*). [OE *ūtemest*, with double superl sfx *-m-est* from *ūte* out]

Uto-Aztecan /ū'tō-az'te-kɘn/ *n* a large linguistic and geographic group of Native Americans, of central and western N America, including Shoshone, Hopi, Ute, Comanche and Nahuatl (Aztec); a person belonging to this group. ◆ *adj* of or relating to any of these peoples or their languages. [**Ute** and **Aztec**]

Utopia /ū-tō'pi-ɘ/ *n* an imaginary state described in Sir Thomas More's Latin political romance or satire *Utopia* (1516); (often without *cap*) any real or imaginary state or place believed to be ideal, perfect, excellent. [Literally 'no place', from Gr *ou* not, and *topos* a place; *Eutopia* (Gr *eu* well), 'ideal place' coined, poss by More himself, in a punning reference to *Utopia*]
■ **Utō'pian** *adj* (also without *cap*). ◆ *n* an inhabitant of Utopia; someone who imagines or believes in a Utopia; (often without *cap*) someone who advocates impracticable reforms or who expects an impossible state of perfection in society. **utō'pianism** *n*. **utō'pianize** or **-ise** *vt* and *vi*. **utō'pianizer** or **-s-** *n*. **utō'piast** *n*. **ū'topism** /-tɘp-izm/ *n*. **ū'topist** *n*.
◻ **utopian socialism** *n* a form of socialism based on the peaceful persuasion of capitalists to relinquish control of the means of production.

Utraquist /ū'trɘ-kwist/ *n* a Calixtine, or asserter of the right of the laity to communicate in both kinds (ie to take the wine as well as the bread) (also *adj*). [L *utrāque*, from *sub utrāque specie* under each kind]
■ **U'traquism** *n*.

utricle /ū'tri-kl/ *n* a little bag, bladder or cell (*biol*); a bladder-like envelope of some fruits (*bot*); a chamber in the inner ear (*zool*). [L *ūtriculus* a small bag, dimin of *ūter*, *ūtris* a bag, a bottle]
■ **ūtric'ular** *adj* like or having a utricle. **utriculā'ria** *n* any plant of the bladderwort genus *Utricularia* of Lentibulariaceae. **ūtric'ulus** *n* (pl **ūtric'ūlī**) a utricle.

ut sup. see **ut supra** under **ut²**.

utter¹ /ut'ɘr/ *vt* to speak, pronounce, give voice to; to put (money) in circulation; to (try to) pass off (a forged document, etc) as genuine or put (counterfeit money) into circulation (*law*); to offer for sale (*obs*); to put out, emit, *esp* with force (*lit* and *fig*; *archaic*). ◆ *vi* (*inf*) to make a remark or express an opinion. [ME *uttren*, from OE *ūt* out; and MDu *uteren* to announce]
■ **utt'erable** *adj*. **utt'erableness** *n*. **utt'erance** *n* an act of uttering; a thing uttered; a manner of or the power of speaking; the expression in speech, or in other sound, of a thought or emotion (eg **give utterance to**); a stretch of speech in some way isolated from, or independent of, what precedes and follows it (*linguistics*). **utt'erer** *n*. **utt'ering** *n* the circulation eg of counterfeit notes, etc. **utt'erless** *adj* that cannot be uttered in words.

utter² /ut'ɘr/ *adj* (superl **utt'erest**) extreme; total, absolute; out-and-out; outer (*archaic*). [OE *ūtor* outer, from *ūt* out]
■ **utt'erly** *adv*. **utt'ermost** *adj* and *n* utmost. **utt'erness** *n*.
◻ **utter barrister** *n* formerly, a barrister of rank next below a bencher; a person who pleads outside the bar, an ordinary barrister, not a king's or queen's counsel or a serjeant-at-law.

utterance¹ see under **utter¹**.

utterance² /ut'ɘ-rɘns/ *n* extremity, the bitter end (*Shakesp*); the utmost degree (*obs*); the utmost effort or force (*archaic*). [Fr *outrance*, from *outre*, from L *ultrā* beyond]

utu /oo'too/ (*Maori*) *n* settlement (whether monetary or in kind) of a debt; retribution, vengeance.

UU *abbrev* : Ulster Unionist.

UV or **uv** *abbrev* : ultraviolet.

UVA or **UV-A** *abbrev* : ultraviolet radiation with a range of 320–380 nanometres.

uva /ū'vɘ/ (*bot*) *n* a grape; a grapelike berry, one formed from a superior ovary. [L *ūva* grape]
◻ **u'va-ursi** /ûr'sī/ *n* (L *ursī* bear's) bearberry; an infusion of its leaves.

uvarovite /oo-vä'rɘ-vīt/ *n* a green garnet, essentially silicate of calcium and chromium. [Count SS *Uvarov* (1785–1855), Russian minister of education]

UVB or **UV-B** *abbrev* : ultraviolet radiation with a range of 280–320 nanometres.

UVC *abbrev* : ultraviolet radiation C (of very short wavelength).

uvea /ū'vi-ɘ/ (*zool*) *n* the posterior pigment-bearing layer of the iris of the eye; the iris, ciliary body and choroid. [Med L, from L *uva* grape]
■ **ū'veal** or **ū'veous** *adj* of the uvea. **ūvei'tic** *adj*. **uveitis** /ū-vi-ī'tis/ *n* inflammation of the iris, ciliary body and choroid.

UVF *abbrev* : Ulster Volunteer Force.

UVR *abbrev* : ultraviolet radiation.

uvula /ū'vū-lə or -vyŭ-/ (anat) n (pl ū'vulas or ū'vulae /-lē/) the fleshy conical body suspended from the palate over the back part of the tongue. [Dimin from L ūva grape]
■ ū'vular adj of or produced by vibration of the uvula. ◆ n a uvular consonant (eg the Parisian French r). ū'vularly adv. uvulī'tis n inflammation of the uvula.

UWB (telecom) abbrev : ultra-wideband.

UWIST /ū'wist/ abbrev : University of Wales Institute of Science and Technology (now replaced by the University of Cardiff).

UWT see NASUWT.

ux. abbrev : uxor (L), wife.

uxorial /uk-sō'ri-əl, -sö', -zō' or -zö'/ adj of a wife. [L uxor, -ōris a wife]
■ **uxor'ially** adv. **uxoricī'dal** adj. **uxo'ricide** /-sīd/ n a wife-killer; wife-killing. **uxorilo'cal** adj (of marriage) matrilocal. **uxo'rious** adj excessively or submissively fond of a wife. **uxo'riously** adv. **uxo'riousness** n.

UZ abbrev : Uzbekistan (IVR).

Uzbek /uz'bek/ or **Uzbeg** /uz'beg/ n a member of a Turkic people of central Asia; a native or citizen of Uzbekistan; the language of the Uzbeks and Uzbekistan. ◆ adj of or relating to the Uzbeks or their language.

Uzi /oo'zi/ n an Israeli submachine-gun. [Uziel Gal, Israeli army officer who designed it]

V v

V or **v** /vē/ n the twenty-second letter in the modern English alphabet, twentieth in the Roman, a differentiated form of U, its sound a voiced labiodental fricative; anything shaped like the letter V.
 ❑ **V'-neck** n the neck of a garment cut in a V-shape. **V'-necked** adj. **V'-shape** n. **V'-shaped** adj. **V'-sign** n a sign made with the index and middle fingers in the form of a V, with palm turned outwards in token of victory or peace, with palm inwards as a sign of contempt or derision. **V-6, V-8**, etc n an engine or car with 6, 8, etc cylinders arranged in a V-shape.

V abbrev : Vatican City (IVR); vatu (currency of Vanuatu; also **VT**).
 ❑ **V'-agents** n pl poisonous gases, less volatile than G-agents. **V'-chip** n (short for *viewer* or *violence*) a computer chip installed in a television receiver to control its use, *esp* to limit use by young viewers. **V'-day** n Victory day, *specif* VE day. **V1** and **V2** n see separate entry.

V symbol : (as a Roman numeral) 5; vanadium (*chem*); volt (SI unit).

V̄ symbol : (Roman numeral) 5000.

v abbrev : velocity; verb; verse; verso; versus; very; *vide* (L), see; volume.

VA abbrev : Vicar Apostolic; Vice-Admiral; (Royal Order of) Victoria and Albert; Virginia (US state; also **Va.**).

vac /vak/ (inf) n the (esp university) vacation; a vacuum cleaner. ◆ vt and vi (**vack'ing; vacked**) to clean with a vacuum cleaner.

vacant /vā'kənt/ adj empty; unoccupied; (of a period of time) not assigned to any activity, free; blankly incurious; unthinking; inane, vacuous. [L *vacāre*, -ātum to be empty; prp *vacāns*, -antis; 3rd pers pr indicative passive *vacātur*]
 ■ **vacance** /və-kans', -käns' or va'/ n (Scot) vacation. **vā'cancy** n emptiness; empty space; a gap; an unfilled post or situation; a room available (in a hotel, boarding house, etc); idleness, inactivity; emptiness of mind, inanity; blankness; (a period of) leisure (obs). **vā'cantly** adv. **vā'cantness** n. **vacate** /və-kāt' or (N Am) vā'kāt/ vt to stop occupying, leave empty; to empty out, unload; to quit; to annul, to make useless (obs). **vacā'tion** n a vacating; a voiding; the holidays, *esp* of schools, colleges, lawcourts; a holiday (esp N Am); leisure (obs); an intermission (obs). ◆ vi (esp N Am) to take a holiday. **vacā'tioner** or **vacā'tionist** n (N Am) a holidaymaker. **vacā'tionless** adj. **vacā'tur** n the act of annulling in law.
 ❑ **vacant possession** n (of property) (the state of being ready for) occupation immediately after purchase, the previous owner or occupier already having left.

vaccine /vak'sēn or -sin/ n any preparation containing dead or attenuated microorganisms, eg viruses or bacteria, used to confer immunity to a disease by inoculation; cowpox virus or lymph containing it, used for inoculation against smallpox (hist); a program intended to combat a computer virus. ◆ adj of, or derived from, the cow; of vaccinia; of vaccination. [L *vaccīnus*, from *vacca* a cow]
 ■ **vac'cinal** /-sin-/ adj of or due to vaccine or vaccination. **vac'cinate** vt to inoculate with a vaccine. **vaccinā'tion** n. **vac'cinātor** n. **vac'cinatory** adj. **vaccin'ia** n cowpox; (in humans) a mild or localized reaction to inoculation with the vaccinia virus against smallpox. **vaccin'ial** adj.

vaccinium /vak-sin'i-əm/ n any plant of the genus *Vaccinium* including cranberry, whortleberry, and cowberry, giving name to a family **Vacciniā'ceae**, or a division **Vaccinioid'eae** of Ericaceae. [L *vaccīnium* whortleberry]

vacherin /vash-rē'/ n a rich soft white cheese made from cow's milk; a dessert made with meringue, whipped cream and ice cream, named for its resemblance to the cheese. [Fr *vache* cow]

vacillate /vas'i-lāt/ vi to sway to and fro; to waver; to be unsteady. [L *vacillāre*, -ātum]
 ■ **vac'illant** adj vacillating. **vac'illāting** adj. **vac'illātingly** adv. **vacillā'tion** n. **vac'illatory** adj wavering.

vacked, vacking see **vac**.

vacuate /vak'ū-āt/ (obs) vt to empty; to evacuate; to annul. [L *vacuāre*, -atum to empty]
 ■ **vacūā'tion** n.

vacuity see under **vacuous**.

vacuole /vak'ū-ōl/ n a small cavity in a cell, containing air, fluid, etc. [Fr, little vacuum]
 ■ **vac'ūolar** adj of a vacuole. **vac'ūolate** or **vac'ūolated** adj having vacuoles. **vacūolā'tion** n. **vacūolīzā'tion** or **-s-** n formation of vacuoles.

vacuous /vak'ū-əs/ adj blank, expressionless; foolish, empty-headed; empty. [L *vacuus* empty]
 ■ **vacū'ity** n emptiness; space unoccupied; idleness, listlessness; vacancy of mind. **vac'ūously** adv. **vac'ūousness** n.

vacuum /vak'ū-əm, -ūm or -yūm/ n (pl **vac'ūums** or (not of the cleaner) **vac'ua** /-ū-ə/) a space completely empty of matter; a space from which air has been excluded as completely as possible; a space containing gas at a pressure lower than atmospheric; an emptiness or void left where something has ceased or been removed; a condition of isolation or insulation from outside forces and influences; a vacuum cleaner (inf). ◆ vt and vi to clean with a vacuum cleaner. ◆ adj relating to a vacuum; containing a vacuum; operating by means of a vacuum. [L, neuter of *vacuus* empty]
 ■ **vac'ūist** n a person who thinks there are empty spaces in nature.
 ❑ **vacuum brake** n a brake in the working of which suction by vacuum(s) supplements the pressure applied by the operator, *esp* a braking system of this type applied simultaneously throughout a train. **vac'ūum-clean** vt and vi. **vacuum cleaner** n an apparatus for removing dust by suction. **vacuum cleaning** n. **vacuum concrete** n concrete enclosed in special shuttering which enables suction to be applied to remove excess water. **vacuum flask** n an insulated flask for keeping substances hot or cold by means of a vacuum lining. **vacuum forming** n a method or process of shaping thermoplastic by applying suction to it when warmed and placed over a mould. **vacuum gauge** n a gauge used to measure pressures lower than atmospheric pressure. **vac'ūum-packed** adj sealed in a container from which most of the air has been removed. **vacuum printing frame** n a frame from which air can be exhausted to ensure close contact between the film image and plate. **vacuum pump** n a general term for apparatus which displaces gas against a pressure. **vacuum tube** n a sealed glass tube in which a vacuum has been made, eg a thermionic valve.
 ▪ **ultra-high vacuum** a very close approach to complete vacuum, important for certain work of scientists and technologists.

VAD abbrev : Voluntary Aid Detachment, an organization of volunteer nurses, *esp* in wartime.

vade /vād/ vi to fade (Shakesp); to pass away (Spenser); to depart (obs). [Partly a form of **fade¹**, partly from, or associated with, L *vādere* to go]

vade-mecum /vä'di-mē'kəm/ n a useful handbook that one carries about with one for constant reference, a pocket-companion. [L *vāde* go (imperative of *vādere*), and *mēcum* with me]

vadose /vā'dōs/ adj of or relating to underground water above the water table. [L *vadōsus* full of shallows, from *vadum* a shallow piece of water]

vae /vā/ same as **voe**.

vae victis /vē vik'tēs, vī or wī wik'/ (L) woe to the conquered.

vagabond /vag'ə-bond/ n a person who wanders without settled habitation; an idle wanderer; a vagrant; a scamp, a rascal (humorous). ◆ adj roving; without settled home; unsettled. ◆ vi to play the vagabond. [Fr *vagabond* and L *vagābundus*, from *vagārī* to wander]
 ■ **vag'abondage** n. **vag'abondish** adj. **vag'abondism** n. **vag'abondize** or **-ise** vi to wander like a vagabond.

vagal see under **vagus**.

vagary /vā'gə-ri or və-gā'ri/ n (pl **vagaries**) an unpredictable change; a devious excursion; a digression or rambling; a freakish prank. [Appar L *vagārī* to wander]
 ■ **vagā'rious** adj. **vagā'rish** adj.

▪ words derived from main entry word; ❑ compound words; ▪ idioms and phrasal verbs

vagi see **vagus**.

vagile /ˈvajˈīl/ or /-il/ adj having the ability to move about. [L vagus wandering]
■ **vagility** /-jilˈ/ n the quality of being vagile; hence the ability to succeed in the struggle for existence.

vagina /vəˈjīˈnə/ n (pl **vagiˈnas** or **vagiˈnae** /-nē/) the genital passage in women and girls and other female mammals, running from the neck of the womb to the external opening contained within the vulva; a sheath; a sheathing leaf-base. [L vāgīna sheath]
■ **vagiˈnal** (or /vajˈi-nəl/) adj. **vagiˈnally** adv. **vagˈinant** adj sheathing. **vagˈinate** /-nāt or nət/ or **vagˈināted** adj (bot) sheathed; having a sheath. **vaginicˈoline** or **vaginicˈolous** adj living in a sheath. **vaginisˈmus** n spasmodic contraction of the vagina. **vaginiˈtis** n inflammation of the vagina. **vaginˈūla** (or /-jīnˈ/) or **vagˈinule** n (pl **vaginˈūlae** /-lē/ or **vagˈinules**) a little sheath, esp one surrounding the base of a moss seta.

vagotomy see under **vagus**.

vagrant /ˈvāˈgrənt/ n a person who has no settled home or work; a tramp, wanderer. ◆ adj wandering, roving, travelling from place to place; having no settled dwelling; unsettled, inconstant; uncertain, erratic; (of plants) of straggling growth. [Perh Anglo-Fr wakerant of Gmc origin (cf walk), assimilated to L vagārī to wander]
■ **vāˈgrancy** n.

vagrom /ˈvāˈgrəm/ adj (Shakesp) Dogberry's perversion of **vagrant** (Much Ado About Nothing III.3.22).

vague /vāg/ adj lacking precision or sharpness of definition; indistinct; blurred; uncertain, indefinite; addicted to, or showing, haziness of thought. ◆ n (obs) a vague or indefinite state; an indefinite expanse. ◆ vi to be vague; to wander (Scot; now rare). [L vagus wandering, from vagārī to wander]
■ **vagueˈly** adv. **vagueˈness** n.

vagus /ˈvāˈgəs/ (anat) n (pl **vāˈgi** /-jī/) the tenth cranial nerve, concerned in regulating heartbeat, rhythm of breathing, etc. [L, wandering]
■ **vāˈgal** /-gəl/ adj. **vagotˈomy** n a surgical excision into the vagus, esp to reduce gastric secretion.

vahine /väˈhēˈnä/ n in Polynesia, a woman or wife. [Tahitian]

vail¹ an obsolete spelling of **veil**.

vail² /vāl/ (archaic) vt to lower, let down; to doff in salutation or submission. ◆ vi to lower a sail; to lift one's hat; to yield; to do homage (Shakesp); to go down; to abate. ◆ n (Shakesp) setting. [OFr valer, or aphetic for **avale**]

vail³ /vāl/ (archaic) vi and vt to profit, avail. ◆ n (usu in pl; also **vales**) a tip, perquisite, dole, or bribe. [OFr valoir to be worth]

vain /vān/ adj without real worth; futile; unavailing; thoughtless; empty-headed; pettily self-complacent; priding oneself inordinately on one's appearance, accomplishments or possessions; conceited; empty, devoid (obs). [Fr vain, from L vānus empty]
■ **vainˈesse** n (Spenser) vanity, futility. **vainˈly** adv. **vainˈness** n vanity.
■ **for vain** (Shakesp) in vain, vainly. **in vain** fruitlessly; to no end. **take in vain** to utter (esp God's name) with levity.

vainglory /vānˈglōˈri/ n vain or empty glory in one's own performances; idle boastfulness. ◆ vi to boast vainly. [OFr vaine gloire]
■ **vainglorious** /-glōˈ or -glōˈ/ adj given to, or proceeding from, vainglory. **vaingloˈriously** adv. **vaingloˈriousness** n.

vair /vār/ n a kind of squirrel fur, bluish-grey and white, represented heraldically by rows of blue and white shields or bells. [OFr, from L varius variegated]
■ **vairé** or **vairy** /ˈvāˈri/ adj charged or variegated with vair.

Vaishnava /ˈvīshˈnä-və or -nə-və/ n a worshipper of Vishnu (also adj). [Sans]

Vaisya /ˈvīsˈyä or vīshˈ/ or **Vaishya** /ˈvīshˈyä/ or n a member of the third caste among the Hindus. [Sans vaisya]

vaivode see **voivode**.

vajazzle /vəˈjazˈl/ (sl) vi to adorn the female pubic area with glittery spangles. n an instance of vajazzling. [**vagina** and **bedazzle**]

vakas /ˈväˈkäs/ n a kind of mantle worn by priests in the Armenian church. [Armenian]

vakil or **vakeel** /väˈkēlˈ/ n an Indian agent, representative, or pleader. [Hindi, from Ar vakīl]

valance, also **valence** /ˈvalˈəns/ n a hanging border of drapery, attached eg along the sides of a bed; a pelmet (N Am); a side panel on the side of a vehicle allowing access to the engine; a side panel on a vehicle or locomotive which partially covers a wheel or wheels and is designed to reduce drag or catch splashes. [Poss Anglo-Fr valer to descend]
■ **valˈanced** adj trimmed with a valance.

Valdenses see **Waldenses**.

vale¹ /vāl/ n a valley (chiefly poetic); the world (fig, as in vale of tears, earthly vale). [Fr val, from L vallis a vale]
■ **vale of years** old age.

vale² /ˈvāˈlē, väˈlä or wäˈ/ n and interj farewell (addressed to one person). [L vale, imperative of valēre to be well]
■ **valete** /-lēˈtē or -läˈtä/ interj and n (addressed to more than one person).

valediction /valˈi-dikˈshən/ (formal) n the act of bidding farewell; a farewell. [L vale farewell, and dīcere, dictum to say]
■ **valedictoˈrian** n (N Am) the speaker of a college valedictory address. **valedicˈtory** adj saying farewell; in the nature of a farewell; of or for a leave-taking. ◆ n (N Am) a farewell address given by a graduand.

valence¹ /ˈvāˈləns/ (chem) n valency (esp N Am); a chemical bond. [L valentia capacity, strength]

valence² see **valance**.

Valenciennes /valˈən-sēnzˈ, -si-enˈ or vä-lä-syenˈ/ n a kind of lace made at Valenciennes in France, the design being made at the same time as the ground and with the same thread.

valency /ˈvāˈlən-si/ n the combining power of an atom measured by the number of hydrogen (or equivalent) atoms that it can combine with or displace (chem); the capacity (expressed numerically) of a verb to combine dependent elements within a sentence (linguistics). [L valentia strength, capacity]
□ **valency** or **valence electrons** n pl those of the outermost shell of the atom, largely responsible for its chemical and physical properties.

-valent /-vā-lent or -və-lənt/ combining form denoting a stated valency, as in trivalent. [L valens, -entis, prp of valēre to be strong]

valentine /valˈən-tīn/ n a person chosen on St Valentine's day, 14 February, as one's sweetheart; an amatory or humorous card, message or gift sent, often anonymously, that day; (with cap) a British heavy tank of World War II. [L Valentīnus, name of two early saints]
■ **Saint Valˈentide** (Spenser) the season of St Valentine's Day.

Valentinian /valˈən-tinˈi-ən/ n a follower of the Gnostic Valentinus (died c.160AD). ◆ adj of or relating to the Valentinians.

valerian /vəˈlēˈri-ən/ n the plant allheal (Valeriana officinalis) or other plant of the genus, which gives name to the family **Valeriānaˈceae** /-si-ē/ related to the teasels; its rhizome and roots which have medicinal properties. [Perh from someone called Valerius, or from L valēre to be strong]
■ **valeriānaˈceous** adj of this family.
□ **valerianic** /-anˈik/ or **valeric** /-erˈik/ **acid** n a fatty acid $C_5H_{10}O_2$ (in several isomers).
■ **Greek valerian** Jacob's ladder. **red** or **spur valerian** a plant (genus Centranthus) related to valerian.

vales see **vail³**.

valet /ˈvalˈit or valˈā/ n a male servant who attends to a gentleman's clothes, dressing, grooming, etc. ◆ vt /valˈit/ to serve or attend to as valet; to clean esp the interior of (a car). [Fr]
■ **valˈeting** n.
□ **valet de chambre** /valˈā də shäbrˈ/ n an attendant; a footman. **valet de place** /valˈā də plasˈ/ n a person who serves as a guide, messenger, etc, esp for strangers. **valet parking** n (esp N Am) a service at a restaurant, airport, etc, whereby a patron's car is taken away to, and fetched back from, a parking place by an attendant.

valeta see **veleta**.

valetudinarian /valˈi-tū-di-nāˈri-ən/ adj relating to ill-health; sickly; weak; anxious and fanciful about one's own health. ◆ n a valetudinarian person. [L valētūdinārius, from valētūdō state of health, from valēre to be strong]
■ **valetūdināˈrianism** n. **valetūdˈinary** /-ə-ri/ adj and n valetudinarian.

valgus /ˈvalˈgəs/ (pathol) adj displaced from normal alignment so as to deviate away from the midline of the body (also **valˈgous** (rare)). ◆ n a valgus condition. [L, bow-legged]

Valhalla /valˈhalˈə/ (Norse myth) n the palace of bliss for the souls of slain heroes. [ON Valhöll, from valr the slain, and höll hall]

vali /väˈlēˈ/ n a governor, esp of a vilayet. [Turk]

valiant /valˈyənt/ adj brave; actively courageous; heroic; strong (obs). ◆ n (obs) a valiant person. [Fr vaillant, from L valēre to be strong]
■ **valˈiance** or **valˈiancy** n valour; a deed of valour. **valˈiantly** adv.

valid /valˈid/ adj sound; legally adequate, or efficacious; fulfilling all the necessary conditions; (in logic) well based, applicable; strong (archaic). [L validus, from valēre to be strong]
■ **valˈidate** vt to make valid; to ratify; to check (data) to ensure that it conforms to input rules and eg falls within an acceptable range (comput); to confirm, substantiate, verify. **validaˈtion** n the act of validating. **validˈity** n. **valˈidly** adv. **valˈidness** n.

valine /vā'lēn/ or /val'/ n an amino acid, $(CH_3)_2CH(NH_2)COOH$, essential to health and growth in humans and vertebrate animals. [From *val*eric acid]

valise /və-lēz'/ or (now *rare* except *US*) -ēs'/n an overnight travelling bag; a kitbag. [Fr; cf Ital *valigia*, Sp *valija*]

Valium® /val'i-əm or -yəm/ n a proprietary name for diazepam, a tranquillizer.
▫ **valium picnic** n (*sl*) a day on the New York Stock Exchange when business is slow.

Valkyrie /val'ki-ri, val-kī'ri, -kir'i or -kē'ri/ (*Norse myth*) n (*pl* **Valkyries** or **Valkyr'iur**) any one of the minor goddesses who conducted the slain from the battlefield to Valhalla. [ON *Valkyrja*, from *valr* the slain, and the root of *kjōsa* to choose; cf OE *Wælcyrige*, Ger *Walküre*]

vallar, vallary see under **vallum**.

vallecula /va-lek'ū-lə/ n (*pl* **vallec'ulae** /-lē/) a groove or furrow. [LL dimin of L *vallis* valley]
■ **vallec'ular** or **vallec'ulate** adj.

valley /val'i/ n (*pl* **vall'eys**) an elongated hollow between hills; a stretch of country watered by a river; a trough between ridges; the hollow between two roof-slopes, or between one and a wall. [OFr *valee* (Fr *vallée*), from *val*, from L *vallis* a valley]
▫ **valley fever** n coccidioidomycosis (*orig* discovered in the San Joaquin *Valley* in California). **Valley girl** n (*inf*; also without *cap*) a brash and fashion-conscious teenage girl (*orig* one from the San Fernando *Valley* in California).

Vallisneria /val-is-nē'ri-ə/ n a tropical and subtropical genus of submerged water plants of the frogbit family. [Antonio *Vallisnieri* (1661–1730), Italian naturalist]

vallum /val'əm/ (*archaeol*) n a rampart; a wall of sods, earth, or other material, *esp* of that thrown up from a ditch. [L]
■ **vall'ar** or **vall'ary** adj applied to an honorific garland bestowed in ancient Rome on the first to mount an enemy's rampart.

Valonia /və-lō'ni-ə/ n a genus of marine green algae, forming the family **Valoniā'cëae**.

valonia, vallonia or **valonea** /və-lō'ni-ə/ n a tanning material, acorns of a Levantine oak (**valonia oak**, *Quercus aegilops*) or similar species. [Ital *vallonea*, from Gr *balanos* an acorn]

valorize or **-ise** /val'ə-rīz/ vt to fix or stabilize the price of, *esp* by a policy imposed by a government or controlling body. [**valour** (in obs sense of 'value')]
■ **valorīzā'tion** or **-s-** n.

valour or (now *US*) **valor** /val'ər/ n intrepidity; courage; bravery; value, worth (*obs*). [OFr *valour*, from LL *valor*, *-ōris*, from L *valēre* to be strong]
■ **val'orous** adj intrepid; courageous. **val'orously** adv.

Valpolicella /val-pol-i-chel'a/ n a dry red wine of the *Valpolicella* district of the Veneto in NE Italy.

valproate /val'prō-āt/ n any salt of **val'proic acid** $(C_8H_{16}O_2)$, *esp* sodium valproate, used to treat epilepsy and bipolar disorder.

valse /väls/ n, vi and vt waltz. [Fr]

value /val'ū/ n worth; a fair equivalent; intrinsic worth or goodness; recognition of such worth; that which renders anything useful or estimable; the degree of this quality; relative worth; high worth; esteem; efficacy; excellence; price; precise meaning; relative duration (*music*); relation with reference to light and shade (*art*); the special determination of a quantity (*maths*); the exact amount of a variable quantity in a particular case; the sound represented by a written symbol (*phonetics*); (in *pl*) moral principles, standards, etc. ◆ vt to estimate the worth of; to rate at a price; to esteem; to prize. ◆ vt or vi (*Shakesp*) to be worth. [OFr *value*, fem pap of *valoir* to be worth, from L *valēre*]
■ **val'uable** adj having value or worth; of high value. ◆ n (*usu* in *pl*) a thing of value, a choice article. **val'uableness** n. **val'uably** adv. **val'uate** vt (*US*) to appraise, value or evaluate. **valuā'tion** n estimation of value; the price at which something is valued. **valuā'tional** adj. **val'uātor** n a person who makes valuations, an appraiser. **val'ued** adj with a value assigned; priced; highly esteemed; prized. **val'ueless** adj. **val'uer** n a valuator; a person who sets a high value.
▫ **valuable consideration** n (*law*) a consideration (qv under **consider**) having material or monetary value. **valuation roll** n a list of properties and their assessed values for local taxation purposes. **value added** n the difference between the overall cost of a manufacturing or marketing process and the final value of the goods. **value-add'ed tax** n a tax on the increase in price of a good or service as it passes along the supply chain (*abbrev* **VAT**). **value date** n the date on which obligations accepted in a financial transaction must be fulfilled. **value-free'** adj not subject to value judgement. **value judgement** n a personal estimate of merit in a particular respect.

■ **good value** full worth in exchange. **value in exchange** exchange value; the amount of other commodities for which a thing can be exchanged in the open market (*econ*). **value received** a phrase indicating that a bill of exchange, etc, has been accepted for a valuable consideration.

valuta /vä-lū'tə or -loo'/ n the comparative value of a currency; a standard of money. [Ital]

valvassor see **vavasour**.

valve /valv/ n a structure or device that regulates flow or passage or allows it in one direction only; one of the mechanical devices on almost all modern brass musical instruments, pressed down by the player so as to increase the length of the tube and thereby enable a full chromatic scale to be played; a rectifier (*elec*); (loosely) a thermionic device once commonly used in electronic apparatus as rectifier, amplifier, oscillator or otherwise (also (*US*) **tube**); a single piece forming part or the whole of a shell; one of the parts of a dry fruit separating in dehiscence; a leaf of a folding door (*archaic*). ◆ vt (*rare*) to fit with a valve or valves. ◆ vt and (*rare*) vi (often with *off*) to release gas through a valve (from eg a vacuum system, hot-air balloon, etc). [L *valva* a folding door]
■ **val'val** adj. **val'var** adj. **val'vate** adj with or having a valve or valves; meeting at the edges without overlapping (*bot*). **valved** adj. **valve'less** adj. **valve'let** n. **val'vūla** or **val'vule** n (*pl* **val'vūlae** /-lē/ or **val'vules**) a little valve. **val'vūlar** adj of or having a valvule or valve. **valvūlī'tis** n inflammation of a valve of the heart. **valvūlo**-*combining form* denoting valvule or valve.
▫ **valve bounce** n the unintended secondary opening of an engine valve due to inadequate rigidity of various parts in the valve gear. **valve gear** n the linkage by which the valves of an engine derive their motion and timing from the crankshaft rotation.

vambrace /vam'brās/ (*hist*) n armour for the forearm (also **vant'brace** or (*Milton*) **vant'brass**). [Anglo-Fr *vantbras* for *avant-bras* forearm]
■ **vam'braced** adj.

vamoose /və-moos'/ or **vamose** /-mōs'/ (*sl*) vi to depart, leave in a hurry. ◆ vt to leave. [Sp *vamos* let us go]

vamp[1] /vamp/ (*inf*) n a woman who attracts men sexually, then seduces and exploits them. ◆ vt to seduce and/or exploit (a man) in this way. [Short form of **vampire**]
■ **vamp'ish** adj.

vamp[2] /vamp/ n the part of a boot or shoe covering the front of the foot; anything patched up; a simple and uninspired improvised accompaniment (*music*). ◆ vt to provide with a vamp; to repair with a new vamp; to patch up; to give a new face to; to improvise inartistically (*music*). ◆ vi to improvise crude accompaniments; to trudge (now *dialect*). [OFr *avanpié*, from *avan* (Fr *avant*) before, and *pié* (Fr *pied*), from L *pēs*, *pedis* foot]
■ **vam'per** n. **vamp'ing** n and adj.

vampire /vam'pīr/ n in E European folklore, a dead person that leaves the grave to drink the blood of the living; a bloodsucker, a relentless extortionate parasite or blackmailer; a vampire bat; a stage trapdoor. ◆ vt to prey upon. [Some Slav languages have *vampir*]
■ **vampir'ic** adj. **vam'pirism** n belief in human vampires; the actions of a vampire. **vam'pirize** or **-ise** vi to play the vampire. ◆ vt (*lit* and *fig*) to suck the blood of.
▫ **vampire bat** n a bloodsucking Central and S American bat (eg *Desmodus* or *Diphylla*); applied to various bats wrongly supposed to be bloodsuckers (eg *Vampyrus*).

vamplate /vam'plāt/ n a guard for the hand on a lance. [Anglo-Fr *van* for *avant* before, and *plate* plate]

van[1] /van/ n a light vehicle used in transporting goods; a railway carriage or compartment for luggage, etc; a large covered wagon; a caravan. ◆ vt and vi (**vann'ing; vanned**) to send, convey, confine, travel, or tour in a van. [Short form of **caravan**]
■ **vann'er** n a horse suitable for a van.

van[2] /van/ n (also (*Shakesp*) **vant** or **vaunt**) short for **vanguard** (often *fig*, as in *in the van of fashion*).
■ **van'ward** adj and adv towards the van or front.

van[3] /van/ (*tennis*) n short for **advantage**.

van[4] /van/ n a shovel for testing ore; a test of ore by washing on a shovel; a winnowing basket or shovel; a wing; a windmill sail. ◆ vt to winnow or test with a van. [S Eng form of **fan**[1]; perh in part directly from L *vannus* or OFr *van*]
■ **vann'er** n one who vans; an ore-separator. **vann'ing** n and adj.

vanadium /və-nā'di-əm/ n a silvery metallic element (symbol **V**; atomic no 23). [Named by the Swedish chemist NG Sefström from ON *Vanadīs*, the goddess Freyja]
■ **vanadate** /van'ə-dāt/ n a salt of vanadic acid. **vanadic** /və-nad'ik/ adj of vanadium in higher valency. **van'adinite** (or /-nad'/) n a mineral, lead vanadate and chloride. **van'adous** adj of vanadium in lower valency.

■ words derived from main entry word; ▫ compound words; ■ idioms and phrasal verbs

Van Allen (radiation) belts /van al'ən (rā-di-ā'shən) belts/ n pl either of two rings of intense particle radiation surrounding the earth at a distance of above 1200 miles (1930km) from it. [JA *Van Allen* (1914–2006), American physicist]

vanaspati /və-näs'pə-ti/ n a vegetable oil used in Indian cookery. [Sans *vanas-pati* lord of plants]

vancomycin /vang-kō-mī'sin/ n an antibiotic drug obtained from the bacterium *Streptomyces orientalis*, used against bacteria that are resistant to other antibiotics.

V and A or **V&A** /vē-ənd-ā'/ (*inf*) the Victoria *and* Albert Museum, London.

vandal /van'dəl/ n a person who wantonly damages property; a person who destroys what is beautiful; (with *cap*) a member of a north-eastern Germanic people who overran Gaul, Spain, and N Africa, and sacked Rome in 455.
■ **Van'dal** *adj*. **Vandal'ic** *adj*. **van'dalism** *n*. **vandalis'tic** *adj*. **vandalīzā'tion** or **-s-** *n*. **van'dalize** or **-ise** *vt* to inflict wilful and senseless damage on (property, etc).

Van de Graaff generator /van də gräf jen'ə-rā-tər/ (*elec eng*) n a very high voltage electrostatic machine, using a high-speed belt to accumulate charge on the surface. [RJ *Van de Graaff* (1901–67), US physicist]

Van der Hum /van der hum/ n a South African liqueur flavoured with tangerines. [Perh from a personal name]

van der Waals' forces /van der wälz (or vælz) för'sis/ (*chem*) n pl weak attractive forces between molecules, or crystals. [JD *van der Waals* (1837–1923), Dutch scientist]

vandyke or **Vandyke** /van-dīk' or van'/ n a broad collar with the edge cut into deep points (also **Vandyke collar**); (something with) a deep-cut edging; a short pointed beard (also called **Vandyke beard**). ◆ *vt* and *vi* to notch or zigzag. [Sir Antony *Van Dyke* (or *Vandyke*) (1599–1641), painter, of whose portraits these features were characteristic]
■ **vandyked'** *adj*.
❑ **van'dyke brown** *n* a deep brown colour; a mixture of lampblack or other material and ochre.

vane /vān/ n a weathercock or revolving plate, or a streamer, serving to show how the wind blows; a heraldic or ornamental plate fixed on a pinnacle; a blade of a windmill, propeller, revolving fan, etc; a fin on a bomb or a paravane; a sight on an observing or surveying instrument; the web of a feather. [S Eng variant of **fane¹**]
■ **vaned** *adj* having a vane or vanes. **vane'less** *adj*.

vanessa /və-nes'ə/ n a butterfly of the red admiral genus *Vanessa*. [Perh for *Phanessa*, from Gr *Phānēs*, a mystic divinity]
■ **vaness'id** *n* and *adj*.

vang /vang/ (*naut*) n a guy-rope to steady a gaff. [A form of **fang**]

vanguard /van'gärd/ n the foremost of an army, etc; the forefront; those who lead the way or anticipate progress. [Fr *avant-garde*, from *avant* before, and *garde* guard]
■ **van'guardism** *n* the condition of being or practice of positioning oneself as or within the vanguard of a movement (*esp* political).

vanilla /və-nil'ə/ n a flavouring substance obtained from the pods of *Vanilla planifolia*, a Mexican climbing orchid, and other species; the plant yielding it. ◆ *adj* flavoured with vanilla or a substitute; ordinary, usual, plain (*orig comput sl*). [Sp *vainilla*, from *vaina*, from L *vāgīna* a sheath]
■ **vanill'in** *n* the aromatic essence of vanilla ($C_8H_8O_3$).

vanish /van'ish/ *vi* to disappear; to fade out; to cease to exist; to become zero (*maths*); to exhale, emanate (*Shakesp*). ◆ *vt* to cause to disappear. ◆ *n* a vanishing; a glide with which a sound ends. [Aphetic for **evanish**]
■ **van'isher** *n*. **van'ishing** *n* and *adj*. **van'ishingly** *adv*. **van'ishment** *n*.
❑ **vanishing cream** *n* cosmetic cream that, when rubbed over the skin, virtually disappears. **vanishing point** *n* the point at which parallel lines seen in perspective converge; the verge of disappearance of anything.

vanitas /van'i-tas/ n a 17c Dutch still-life painting in which motifs such as the hourglass, skull or candle feature as reminders of the transience and vanity of human life and aspirations; any painting of this genre. [L, vanity]

Vanitory® /van'i-tə-ri/ n (often without *cap*) a vanity unit (also **Vanitory unit**).

vanity /van'i-ti/ n the priding of oneself on one's personal appearance, accomplishments, etc; conceit; extravagance or ostentation; folly or futility; something vain; a dressing-table (*N Am*). [Fr *vanité*, from L *vānitās, -ātis*; see **vain**]
❑ **vanity bag**, **vanity box** or **vanity case** *n* a container for cosmetics and a small mirror, etc, carried by a woman. **Vanity Fair** *n* the world, or any place or society in it where people are wholly devoted to

vanity, triviality, and empty ostentation (from the fair at the town of Vanity, in Bunyan's *Pilgrim's Progress*). **vanity mirror** *n* a small mirror mounted on the back of a sun visor in a car. **vanity plate** *n* (*N Am*) a vehicle number plate purchased independently of a vehicle because of its distinctive combination of characters. **vanity publishing** *n* publication by the author, at his or her own expense. **vanity table** *n* a dressing-table. **vanity unit** *n* a unit consisting of a washbasin built into a dressing-table.

vanner, vanning, etc see **van¹,⁴**.

vanquish /vang'kwish/ *vt* to conquer; to overcome. ◆ *vi* to be victor. [Anglo-Fr *venquir, venquiss-* (Fr *vaincre*), from L *vincere* to conquer]
■ **vanq'uishable** *adj*. **vanq'uisher** *n*. **vanq'uishment** *n*.

Vansittartism /van-sit'ər-ti-zm/ *n* extreme anti-Germanism. [Lord *Vansittart* (1881–1957), British diplomat]

vant /vant/ (*Shakesp*) *n* see **van²**.

vantage /vän'tij/ *n* advantage; opportunity (*Shakesp*); excess, addition (*Shakesp*). ◆ *vi* (*Spenser*) to benefit, profit. [Anglo-Fr *vantage*; cf **advantage**]
■ **van'tageless** *adj*.
❑ **vantage ground** or **point** *n* a favourable or commanding position.

vantbrace, vantbrass see **vambrace**.

vanward see under **van²**.

vapid /vap'id/ *adj* insipid; dull; flat. [L *vapidus*]
■ **vapid'ity** *n*. **vap'idly** *adv*. **vap'idness** *n*.

vaporetto /va-po-ret'ō/ *n* (*pl* **vaporett'os** or **vaporett'i** /-ē/) a motorboat that serves as a water bus in Venice. [Ital, from *vapore* a steamboat]

vapour or (*esp US*) **vapor** /vā'pər/ *n* a substance in the form of a mist, fume, or smoke, *esp* one coming off from a solid or liquid; a gas below its critical temperature, liquefiable by pressure; water in the atmosphere; (in *pl*) exhalations supposed to arise in the stomach or elsewhere in the body, affecting the health (*old med*); (in *pl*, *usu* with *the*) low spirits, boredom, nervous disorder; anything insubstantial, vain, or transitory; a fanciful notion; a boast. ◆ *vi* to pass off in vapour; to emit vapour; to evaporate; to brag, make empty boasts; to swagger, show off. ◆ *vt* to convert into vapour; to affect with the vapours; to boast; to drive (*away*) by bluster. [L *vapor, -ōris*]
■ **vā'porable** *adj* capable of being turned to vapour. **vāporif'ic** *adj* vaporizing. **vā'poriform** *adj* existing in the form of vapour. **vāporim'eter** *n* an instrument for measuring vapour pressure or vapour. **vāporiz'able** or **-s-** *adj*. **vāporizā'tion** or **-s-** *n*. **vā'porize** or **-ise** *vt* to convert into vapour; to make disappear suddenly; to spray; to obliterate (*inf*). ◆ *vi* to become vapour. **vāporiz'er** or **-s-** *n* an apparatus for discharging liquid in a fine spray. **vāporos'ity** *n*. **vā'porous** *adj* of, in the form of, like, or full of vapour; vain; affected with the vapours; insubstantial; flimsy; vainly fanciful. **vā'porously** *adv*. **vā'porousness** *n*. **vā'poured** *adj* full of vapours; affected with the vapours. **vā'pourer** *n* a person who vapours; a moth (genus *Orgyia*) of the tussock family. **vā'pouring** *n* and *adj*. **vā'pouringly** *adv*. **vā'pourish** *adj* vapoury. **vā'pourishness** *n*. **vā'poury** *adj* full of vapour; affected with the vapours.
❑ **va'pour-bath** *n* a bath in vapour; a place or apparatus for the purpose. **vapour density** *n* the density of a gas or vapour relative to that of hydrogen at the same temperature and pressure. **vapour lock** *n* (*engineering*) the formation of vapour in a pipe carrying a volatile fluid, resulting in an interruption of the flow. **vapour pressure** *n* the pressure exerted by a vapour in contact with its liquid or solid form. **vapour trail** *n* a white trail of condensed vapour left by high-flying aircraft (also *US* **contrail**). **va'pourware** or (*esp US*) **va'porware** *n* (*comput sl*) software or hardware that is loudly heralded but not yet (and possibly never to be) available.

vapulate /vap'ū-lāt/ *vt* to flog. ◆ *vi* to be flogged. [L *vāpulāre, -ātum* to be flogged]
■ **vapūlā'tion** *n* a flogging.

vaquero /va- or vä-kā'rō/ (*US*) *n* (*pl* **vaque'ros**) a herdsman, cowboy. [Sp, from L *vacca* a cow]

VAR *abbrev*: value-added reseller (*esp* of computer equipment, offering aftersales service).

var. *abbrev*: variable; variant; variety.

vara /vä'rä/ *n* a Spanish-American linear measure, varying from 33 to 43 inches (c.84–110cm). [See **vare**]

varactor /var-ak'tər/ (*electronics*) *n* a two-electrode semiconductor device in which capacitance varies with voltage. [*varying* rea*ctor*]

varan /var'ən/ *n* a monitor lizard. [Ar *waran*]
■ **Var'anus** *n* the monitor genus, constituting the family **Varanidae** /-an'/.

Varangian /va-ran'ji-ən/ *n* a Scandinavian settler in what became Russia; a (*usu* Scandinavian) member of the bodyguard of the Eastern emperors; their Scandinavian language (*Walter Scott*). ◆ *adj* of or

fāte; fär; mē; fûr; mūne; mōte; för; mūte; pŭt; dhen (then); *el'ə-mənt* (element) • For other sounds see detailed chart of pronunciation relating to the Varangians or their language. [LL *Varangus*, from Late Gr *Barangos*, from ON *Væringi*]

vardy /vär'di/ *n* an obsolete or dialect variant of **verdict**.

vare /vär/ *n* a vara; a wand of authority. [Sp *vara* a rod, from L *vāra* a trestle, forked stick, from *vārus* crooked]

varec or **varech** /var'ek/ *n* kelp; wrack. [Fr; of Scand origin; cf **wrack²**, **wreck¹**]

varenicline /və-ren'i-klēn/ *n* a drug used in the treatment of nicotine addiction.

vareuse /vä-rœz'/ (*Southern US*) *n* a kind of loose jacket. [Fr]

vargueño /vär-gä'nyō/ *n* (*pl* **vargue'ños**) a cabinet or desk of a kind made at *Vargas* (Bargas) near Toledo in Spain.

variable /vä'ri-ə-bl* or *-ryə-bl*/ *adj* that may be varied; changeable; tending or liable to change or vary; showing variations; unsteady; quantitatively indeterminate (*maths*); changing in brightness (*astron*). ◆ *n* a quantity subject to continual increase or decrease (*maths*); an expression which may have any of a number of values (*maths*, *comput*); a symbol referring to a known semantic range, but unspecified as to exact meaning (*logic*); a shifting wind; a variable star. ■ **variabil'ity** *n*. **vä'riableness** *n*. **vä'riably** *adv*. □ **variable costs** *n pl* costs which, unlike fixed costs, vary with the level of production. **variable gear** see under **gear**. **variable-geometry aeroplane** *n* an aeroplane of varying wing, swept-back for flight, but at right angles for take-off and landing, so removing the need for long runways and high landing-speeds. **variable interest rate** *n* a rate of interest on a loan, etc, that varies with the market rate of interest. **variable-pitch propeller** *n* (*aeronautics*) a propeller with blades movable by mechanical means during rotation to optimize the pitch for different speeds and engine revs. **variable region** *n* (*immunol*) part of an immunoglobulin molecule which differs in amino acid sequence between different molecules. **variable star** *n* any star with a luminosity not constant with time. **va'riable-sweep'** *adj* (of an aircraft wing) of which the sweep-back may be varied, as on a variable-geometry aeroplane.

variae lectiones /vä'ri-ē lek-shi-ō'nēz or wa'ri-ī lek-ti-ō'nās/ (*L*) various readings.

variance /vä'ri-əns/ *n* variation; deviation; alteration; an exemption from normal building regulations (*N Am*); a discrepancy; the difference between budgeted and actual costs (*commerce*); a disagreement, dispute; the average of the squares of the deviations of a number of observations from the mean (*stats*). [OFr, from L *variāre* to vary] ■ **va'riant** *n* a different form of the same thing (*esp* a word); a different reading; a specimen slightly differing from a type or standard. ◆ *adj* changeful; varying; diversified; different; diverging from a type or standard. □ **variant Creutzfeldt-Jakob disease** see **Creutzfeldt-Jakob disease**. ■ **at variance** in disagreement, dissension or dispute (with); not in accordance (with).

variate /vä'ri-ət/ *n* any one of the observed values of a quantity (*stats*); the variable quantity that is being studied (*stats*); a variant. ◆ *vt and vi* to change, vary. [L *variātus*, pap of *variāre* to vary] ■ **varia'tion** *n* a varying; a change; continuous change; difference in structure or character among offspring of the same parents or among members of a related group; departure from the mean or usual character; the extent to which a thing varies; a variant; declination of the compass; an inequality in the moon's motion discovered by Tycho Brahe; a change in the elements of an orbit by the disturbing force of another body; transformation of a theme by means of new figures in counterpoint, florid treatment, changes in tempo, key, etc (*music*); a solo dance (*ballet*). **varia'tional** *adj*. **varia'tionist** *n* a composer of variations; a person who attaches importance to variation. **vä'riative** *adj* variational.

variceal see under **varix**.

varicella /var-i-sel'ə/ (*med*) *n* chickenpox. [Irreg dimin of **variola**] ■ **varicell'ar** *adj*. **varicell'oid** *adj* resembling varicella. **varicell'ous** *adj* relating to varicella.

varices plural of **varix**.

varicocele /var'i-kō-sēl/ (*pathol*) *n* an enlargement of the veins of the spermatic cord, or of those of the scrotum. [L *varix*, *varicis* varicose vein, and Gr *kēlē* tumour]

varicoloured /vä'ri-kul-ərd/ *adj* diversified in colour. [L *varius* various, and *color* colour]

varicose /var'i-kōs/ *adj* (of superficial veins, *esp* those of the leg) twisted and dilated so that they produce raised knots on the surface of the skin. [L *varicōsus*, from *varix* varicose vein] ■ **varicosity** /var-i-kos'i-ti/ *n* the state of being varicose; a distended place or vein. □ **varicose ulcer** *n* an ulcerating knot of varicose veins.

varicotomy see under **varix**.

Varidase® /vä'ri-dāz/ *n* the proprietary name of a drug used to liquefy, for draining away, clotted blood, thick pus, and dead tissue in deep infections.

varied, etc see **vary**.

variegate /vä'ri-(ə-)gāt/ *vt* to diversify, *esp* with colours in patches. [L *variegātus*, from *varius*; see **vary**] ■ **vä'riegated** *adj*. **vāriega'tion** *n*. **vä'riegātor** *n*.

variety /və-rī'ə-ti/ *n* (*pl* **varī'eties**) the quality of being various; diversity; difference; many-sidedness, versatility; a varied group or collection; a kind differing in minor features or points; a race not sufficiently distinct to be counted a species, a subspecies; an artificially bred strain; music-hall entertainment, a succession of varied turns. ◆ *adj* of, for, or performing in, music-hall entertainment. [L *varietās*, -*ātis*, from *varius* various] ■ **varī'etal** *adj* of or having the character of a variety (*biol*); (of wine) (named as being) from a single variety of grape. ◆ *n* such a wine. **varī'etally** *adv*. □ **variety meat** *n* offal (*US*); processed meat, sausage, etc (*orig US*).

varifocal /vä-ri-fō'kəl/ *adj* having variable focal lengths. [**variable**, after **bifocal**] ■ **varifō'cals** *n pl* spectacles with varifocal lenses, for a wide range of vision.

variform /var'i-förm/ *adj* of various forms. [L *varius*, and **-form**]

variola /və-rī'ə-la/ (*med*) *n* smallpox; sheep-pox. [LL *variola* pustule, pox, from L *varius* various, spotted] ■ **varī'olar** *adj*. **variolate** /vä'ri-ə-lāt/ *vt* to inoculate with smallpox virus. **vāriolā'tion** *n* inoculation with smallpox virus. **vä'riolātor** *n* a person who carries out variolation. **variole** /vä'ri-ōl/ *n* a pock-like marking; a spherule in variolite. **vä'riolite** *n* (Gr *lithos* stone) a fine-grained basic igneous rock with spherules of radiating feldspar resembling pock-marks. **varíolitic** /-lit'ik/ *adj* of or like variolite. **vä'rioloid** *adj* resembling smallpox. ◆ *n* modified smallpox occurring in the vaccinated or those who have already had the disease. **variolous** /və-rī'ō-las/ *adj* of, relating to, or suffering from, smallpox; covered with varioles.

variometer /vä-ri-om'ə-tər/ *n* an instrument for comparing magnetic forces; a variable inductor composed of two connected coils, one rotating inside the other (*electronics*); an instrument that indicates by a needle the rate of climb and descent (*aeronautics*). [L *varius* various, and **meter¹**]

variorum /vä-ri-ö'rəm/ *adj* (of an edition of a text) including the notes of earlier commentators or editors, or variant readings. ◆ *n* a variorum edition; a succession of changes (*joc*). [L *cum notis variorum* with the notes of various scholars]

various /vä'ri-əs/ *adj* varied, different; several; unlike each other; variegated; changeable, uncertain (*archaic*). [L *varius*; see **vary**] ■ **vä'riously** *adv*. **vä'riousness** *n*.

variscite /var'i-sīt/ *n* a greenish mineral, hydrated aluminium phosphate. [L *Variscia*, Vogtland, in Saxony]

varistor /və-ris'tər/ *n* a two-electrode semi-conductor used to short-circuit transient high voltages in delicate electronic devices. [*variable resistor*]

Varityper® /vä'ri-tī-pər/ *n* a typewriter-like machine which has changeable type. ■ **vä'ritypist** *n*.

varix /vä'riks or wa'riks/ *n* (*pl* **varices** /vä'ri-sēz or wa'ri-kās/) an abnormally dilated, lengthened, and tortuous vein, artery, or lymphatic vessel (*med*); dilatation of a blood vessel (*med*); a ridge marking a former position of the mouth of a shell (*zool*). [L] ■ **varicē'al** *adj* of or relating to a varix. **varicot'omy** *n* the surgical removal of a varix or a varicose vein.

var. lect. *abbrev*: *varia lectio* (*L*), a variant reading.

varlet /vär'lit/ (*archaic*) *n* an attendant; a municipal officer; a rascal, rogue, knave. [OFr *varlet*; cf **valet**] ■ **var'letess** *n* (*rare*) a female varlet. **var'letry** *n* (*Shakesp*) the rabble, the crowd. **varlett'o** *n* (*Shakesp, pseudo-Ital*) a varlet.

varmint or **varment** /vär'mint/ *n* old variants (now *dialect*, *esp US* or *sl*) of **vermin**; a troublesome or mischievous animal or person; (*perh* another word) a skilled amateur sportsman (*obs*). ◆ *adj* natty, dashing; sharp, cunning.

varna /vûr'nə or vär'nə/ *n* any of the four great Hindu castes. [Sans, colour]

varnish /vär'nish/ *n* a resinous solution used to coat and give a hard, glossy, *usu* transparent surface to woodwork, paintings, etc; any of several other preparations for giving a glossy surface to something, eg *nail varnish*; a gloss or glaze; a superficial lustre, a surface showiness, *esp* with the implication of underlying shoddiness or inadequacy; an application of varnish. ◆ *vt* to coat with varnish; to give a superficial lustre or sheen to. [Fr *vernis*; prob from Med L *veronix* sandarac]

■ **var'nisher** *n*. **var'nishing** *n*.

❏ **var'nishing-day** *n* a day before the opening of a picture exhibition when exhibitors may varnish or retouch their pictures after they have been hung. **varnish tree** *n* the tung tree or other tree whose resinous juice is used for varnishing or for lacquering.

varroa /*var'ō-ə*/ *n* (also with *cap*) an Asiatic mite (*Varroa jacobsoni*) which parasitizes and kills the honey bee; infection by this mite. [LL, after Publius Terentius *Varro* (c.82–37BC), Roman scholar who wrote on bee-keeping]

varsal /*vär'səl*/ (*non-standard*) *adj* universal.

varsity /*vär'si-ti*/ (*inf*; *usu sport*) *n* and *adj* university.

varsovienne /*vär-sō-vi-en'*/ *n* a dance imitated from the Polish mazurka; a tune for it. [Fr, fem of *Varsovien* from Varsovie, Warsaw]

vartabed /*vär'tə-bed*/ *n* a member of an Armenian order of clergy. [Armenian *vartabet*]

Varuna /*vu'rū-nä, var'* or *vär'*/ *n* an ancient Indian Vedic god of the heavens, later of the waters. [Sans; cf Gr *Ouranos*]

varus /*vä'rəs*/ (*pathol*) *adj* displaced from normal alignment so as to deviate towards the midline of the body. ◆ *n* a varus condition. [L *vārus* bent, knock-kneed]

varve /*värv*/ (*geol*) *n* a seasonal layer of sediment deposited in still water, used in establishing Ice Age chronology. ◆ *adj* (also **varved**) stratified in distinct layers of annual deposit. [Swed *varv* layer]

varvel, varvelled see **vervel, vervelled**.

vary /*vä'ri*/ *vt* (**vä'rying; vä'ried**) to make different; to diversify, modify; to alter or embellish (a melody) preserving its identity (*music*); to change to something else; to make of different kinds; to express in other words (*obs*). ◆ *vi* to alter or be altered; to be or become different; to change in succession; to deviate; to disagree; to be subject to continuous increase or decrease (*maths*). ◆ *n* a change. [ME, from (O)Fr *varier* or L *variāre*, from L *varius* various, diverse]

■ **vä'ried** *adj*. **vä'riedly** *adv*. **vä'rier** *n* a person who varies. **vä'rying** *n* and *adj*.

vas /*vas*/ (*anat*) *n* (*pl* **vasa** /*vä'sə*/) a vessel, tube or duct carrying liquid. [L *vās, vāsis* vessel]

■ **vä'sal** *adj*. **vasectomy** /*və-sek'tə-mi*/ *n* (Gr *ek* out, and *tomē* a cut) the excision of part or all of the vas deferens, *esp* in order to produce sterility. **vasiform** /*vä'zi-förm*/ *adj* duct-shaped; tubular; vase-shaped.

❏ **vas def'erens** /*def'ə-renz*/ *n* (*pl* **vä'sa deferen'tia** /*-shyə*/) the spermatic duct, carrying spermatozoa from the testis to the urethra.

vasculum /*vas'kū-ləm*/ *n* (*pl* **vas'culums** or **vas'cula**) a botanist's collecting case. [L *vāsculum*, dimin of *vās* a vessel]

■ **vas'cular** *adj* of, relating to, composed of, or provided with vessels conveying fluids, eg blood, sap. **vascular'ity** *n*. **vasculariza'tion** or **-s-** *n* the formation of blood vessels in an organ or tissue. **vas'cularize** or **-ise** *vt* to cause to become vascular. **vas'cularly** *adv*. **vas'culature** *n* a vascular system. **vas'culiform** *adj* shaped like a small vase. **vasculi'tis** *n* inflammation of a blood vessel.

❏ **vascular bundle** *n* a strand of **vascular tissue** in the higher plants, composed of xylem, phloem, and cambium. **vascular cryptogams** *n pl* the pteridophytes, or ferns or related plants. **vascular cylinder** *n* (*bot*) a stele. **vascular disease** *n* any of various diseased conditions of the blood vessels. **vascular plants** *n pl* seed-plants and pteridophytes (ferns).

vase /*väz*, or (*old*) *vöz*, or (*Brit* and *US*) *väz*, or (*US*) *väs*/ *n* a vessel, usually tall, round in section, and (now) ornamental, now used *esp* for holding cut flowers; the body of the Corinthian capital (*archit*). [Fr, from L *vās*]

vasectomy see under **vas**.

Vaseline® /*vas'i-lēn*/ *n* an ointment or lubricant consisting of petroleum jelly. ◆ *vt* to apply Vaseline to. [Ger *Wasser* water, and Gr *elaion* oil]

vasiform see under **vas**.

vaso- /*vä-zō-* or *-zə-*/ (*med*) *combining form* denoting a duct or vessel. [L *vās, vāsis* vessel]

■ **vasoac'tive** *adj* promoting the narrowing or expansion of blood vessels. **vasoconstric'tion** *n* narrowing of a blood vessel. **vasoconstric'tor** *n* a nerve or drug that causes vasoconstriction. **vasoconstric'tory** *adj*. **vasodilatā'tion** or **vasodilā'tion** *n* expansion of a blood vessel. **vasodilatā'tory** or **vasodilā'tory** *adj*. **vasodilā'tor** *n* a nerve or drug that causes vasodilatation. **vasodilā'tory** *adj*. **vasomō'tor** *adj* causing constriction or expansion of blood vessels. **vasopress'in** *n* a pituitary hormone (also prepared synthetically) that raises blood pressure, regulates kidney secretion, etc. **vasopress'or** *n* a substance that causes a rise of blood pressure (also *adj*). **vasovā'gal** *adj* relating to the effect of the vagus nerve on blood pressure and circulation.

vassail see **vessel**.

vassal /*vas'əl*/ *n* a dependant, retainer; a person or nation subject to another; a person holding land from a feudal superior in return for homage and loyalty (*hist*); a person holding land from a superior in return for the payment of feu-duty (*Scots law*; *obs*); a low wretch (*Shakesp*). ◆ *adj* in the relation or state of a vassal; subordinate; servile; of a vassal. ◆ *vt* to subject. [Fr, from LL *vassallus* servant, from Celtic; cf Breton *goaz* man, Welsh *gwas* boy, servant]

■ **vass'alage** *n* the state of being a vassal; dependence; subjection; a fee, fief; vassals collectively; prowess, or deeds of prowess (*obs*). **vass'aless** *n* a female vassal. **vass'alry** *n* vassals collectively.

vast /*väst*/ *adj* boundless; huge; exceedingly great; considerable, appreciable (*inf*). ◆ *n* an immense tract, a boundless or empty expanse of space or time; a huge quantity, vast amount (*dialect* or *inf*). [L *vastus* waste, desolate, huge; cf **waste**]

■ **vastid'ity, vast'itude** or **vast'ity** *n* vastness; a vast extent. **vast'ly** *adv*. **vast'ness** *n*. **vast'y** *adj* (*archaic*) vast.

■ **a vast many** (*obs*) a great many.

Vat or **VAT** /*vat* or *vē-ā-tē'*/ *n* (sometimes without *cap(s)*) a colloquial acronym for value-added tax.

■ **vat'able** or **VAT'able** /*vat'*/ *adj* (of goods, etc) liable to VAT. **Vat'man** or **VAT'man** *n* (sometimes without *cap(s)*) an employee of the Customs and Excise Board responsible for administering, assessing, collecting, etc value-added tax.

vat /*vat*/ *n* a large vessel or tank, *esp* for fermentation, dyeing, or tanning; a liquor containing a reduced, colourless, soluble form of insoluble dye (**vat dye**) in which textiles are soaked, in order afterwards to take up the colour through oxidation when exposed to the air. ◆ *vt* (**vatt'ing; vatt'ed**) to put, or treat, in a vat. [S Eng form of **fat²**, from OE *fæt*; cf Du *vat*, ON *fat*, Ger *Fass*]

■ **vat'ful** *n* (*pl* **vat'fuls**) as much as a vat will hold. **vatt'er** *n*.

vatic /*vat'ik*/ *adj* prophetic; oracular; inspired. [L *vātēs* a prophet]

■ **vat'icide** /*-sīd*/ *n* (see **-cide**) the killer or killing of a prophet. **vaticinal** /*-is'i-nl*/ *adj*. **vati'cinate** *vt* and *vi* (*esp ironic*) to prophesy. **vaticinā'tion** *n* prophecy. **vati'cinator** *n* a prophet.

Vatican /*vat'i-kən*/ *n* an assemblage of buildings on the Vatican Hill in Rome, including one of the Pope's palaces; the papal authority. [L *Mōns Vāticānus* the Vatican Hill]

■ **Vat'icanism** *n* the system of theology and ecclesiastical government based on absolute papal authority, ultramontanism. **Vat'icanist** *n*. **Vaticanol'ogist** *n* (*inf*) a person who studies Vatican affairs, history, etc.

❏ **Vatican City** *n* a small area on the Vatican Hill set up as an independent papal state in 1929. **Vatican Council** *n* the council that met in St Peter's (1869) and proclaimed papal infallibility (1870), or the similar council (**Vatican II**) held between 1962 and 1965.

vaticide, vaticinate, etc see under **vatic**.

vatu /*vä'too*/ *n* the standard monetary unit of Vanuatu (100 centimes).

vau /*wow*/ *n* the digamma (see **episemon**). [L, from Gr *wau*, from Semitic *wāw*]

vaudeville /*vō'də-vil* or *vö'də-vil*/ *n* variety entertainment; a play interspersed with dances and songs incidentally introduced and usually comic; *orig* a popular song with topical allusions. ◆ *adj* of or relating to vaudeville or a vaudeville. [From *vau* (*val*) *de Vire* the valley of the Vire, in Normandy, where such songs were composed in the 15c]

■ **vaudevill'ian** or **vaudevill'ean** *n* a performer or writer of vaudeville (also *adj*). **vau'devillist** *n* a composer of vaudeville.

Vaudois¹ /*vō-dwä'*/ *n* a native of the Swiss Canton Vaud (*pl* **Vaudois**); the dialect of French spoken in Vaud. ◆ *adj* of or relating to the Vaudois or their dialect. [Fr]

Vaudois² /*vō-dwä'*/ *n* and *adj* Waldensian. [Fr; same root as **Waldenses**]

vaudoo, vaudoux see **voodoo**.

vault¹ /*völt* or earlier *vöt*/ *n* an arched roof or ceiling; a chamber with an arched roof or ceiling, *esp* underground; a cellar; a wine cellar; a burial chamber; a fortified room for storing valuables in a bank, etc; a cavern; anything vaultlike such as the *vault of heaven*, or the *cranial vault* the dome of the skull. ◆ *vt* to shape as a vault; to roof with an arch or vault; to form vaults in. ◆ *vi* to curve in a vault. [OFr *vaute, vaulte, voute, volte* (Fr *voûte*), from L *volvere, volūtum* to roll]

■ **vaul'tage** *n* an arched cellar (*Shakesp*); a cavern; a range of vaults; vaulted work. **vaul'ted** *adj* arched; concave overhead; covered with an arch or vault. **vaul'ting** *n* vaulted work. **vaul'ty** *adj* (*Shakesp*) vaultlike.

vault² /*völt* or earlier *vöt*/ *vi* to leap, *esp* by springing initially onto one or both hands, or by using a pole, to get extra height; to achieve great heights of success, fame, etc. ◆ *vt* to spring or leap over, *esp* by this means; to cause (someone or something) to attain great success, etc. ◆ *n* an act of vaulting. [Appar OFr *volter* to leap]

■ **vault'er** *n*. **vault'ing** *n*. ◆ *adj* relating to or for vaulting; (of eg ambition) inordinate, overweening.

❑ **vault'ing-horse** *n* a piece of gymnastic apparatus for vaulting over. **vault'ing-house** *n* (*obs*) a brothel.

vaunce /vöns/ *vt* and *vi* (*prp* (*Spenser*) **vaunc'ing**) obsolete aphetic form of **advance**.

vaunt¹ /vönt/ or (*US*) vänt/ *vi* to boast; to behave boastfully or exultingly. ◆ *vt* to boast; to boast of; to make known by display (*Spenser*). ◆ *n* a boast; boastful behaviour. [OFr *vanter*, from LL *vānitāre*, from L *vānitās* vanity, from *vānus* vain; partly aphetic for **avaunt²**]

■ **vaunt'ed** *adj*. **vaunt'er** *n*. **vaunt'ery** *n* (*archaic*) vaunting. **vaunt'ful** *adj*. **vaunt'ing** *n* and *adj*. **vaunt'ingly** *adv*. **vaunt'y** *adj* (*esp Scot*).

vaunt² /vönt/ (*Shakesp*) *n* the first part. [Cf **van²**]

vauntage /vön'tij/ (*Spenser*) *n* same as **vantage**.

vaunt-courier /vönt-koo'ri-ər/ (*archaic*) *n* one sent in advance; a forerunner. [Fr *avant-coureur*]

vaurien /vō-ryē'/ (*Fr*) *n* a good-for-nothing.

vaut, vaute old forms of **vault¹,²**.

vav /väv/ *n* the sixth letter of the Hebrew alphabet. [Heb]

vavasour /vav'ə-soor/ or **valvassor** /val'və-sör/ *n* (in feudal society) a knight, noble, etc, with vassals under him, who is himself the vassal of a greater noble. [OFr, appar from LL *vassus vassōrum* vassal of vassals, from *vassus* vassal]

■ **vav'asory** *n* the tenure or the lands of a vavasour.

va-va-voom /va-va-vŭm'/ (*inf*) *n* the quality of being simultaneously sexy, stylish and exciting. [Imit of the sound of an accelerating sports car]

vaward /vö'ərd/ (*Shakesp*) *n* forefront. ◆ *adj* front. [A form of **vanguard**]

vawte an old form of **vault¹,²**.

VB (*comput*) *abbrev* : Visual Basic.

vb *abbrev* : verb.

VBIED *abbrev* : vehicle-borne improvised explosive device.

VC *abbrev* : vice-chancellor; Victoria Cross.

vCJD *abbrev* : variant Creutzfeldt-Jakob disease.

VCR *abbrev* : video cassette recorder.

VCT *abbrev* : venture capital trust.

VD *abbrev* : venereal disease.

VDQS *abbrev* : *vins délimités de qualité supérieure* (*Fr*), wines of superior quality from approved vineyards.

VDSL *abbrev* : Very High Speed Digital Subscriber Line.

VDU *abbrev* : visual display unit.

've /v/ a shortened form of **have**.

Veadar /vē'ə-där/ *n* an intercalary month in the Jewish calendar, following Adar in embolismic years. [Heb *ve* and]

veal /vēl/ *n* calf's flesh as food; a calf (*obs*). ◆ *adj* of veal. [OFr *veël* (Provençal *vedel*), from L *vitellus*, dimin of *vitulus*; cf Gr *italos* a calf]

■ **veal'er** *n* (*esp N Am, Aust and NZ*) a calf raised to provide veal. **veal'y** *adj* like veal or like a calf; immature.

veale /vēl/ (*Spenser*) same as **veil**.

Vectian /vek'ti-ən/ (*geol*) *adj* of or relating to the Isle of Wight or the geological formation of which it is a part. [L *Vectis* the Isle of Wight]

vector /vek'tər/ *n* a directed quantity, as a straight line in space, involving both its direction and magnitude (*maths*); a carrier of disease or infection; a phage or plasmid that is used in genetic engineering to transfer foreign DNA into a cell; the course of an aircraft, missile, etc; a one-dimensional sequence of elements within a matrix (*comput*); such a sequence having a single identifying code or symbol, *esp* one acting as an intermediate address (*comput*); a DNA molecule from eg a plasmid into which other DNA can be inserted and which can be used to transfer this DNA from one organism to another (*biol*). ◆ *vt* to direct (an aircraft in flight) to the required destination, *esp* by radio; to direct or change the direction of (*esp* the thrust of an aircraft engine). [L *vector*, -*ōris* bearer, carrier, from *vehere*, *vectum* to convey]

■ **vec'tograph** *n* a picture giving a three-dimensional effect when looked at through special spectacles. **vectorgraph'ics** *n sing* a method of drawing in which lines are drawn directly from co-ordinates calculated by a computer. **vectō'rial** *adj*. **vectō'rially** *adv*. **vec'toring** *n* (*comput*) the process of transferring control (in a program) to an intermediate vector. **vectoriza'tion** or -**s-** *n*. **vec'torize** or -**ise** *vt* (*maths, comput*). **vec'torscope** *n* an instrument that displays the phase and amplitude of an applied signal, eg of the chrominance signal in colour television.

❑ **vector product** *n* (*maths*) a vector that is the result of multiplying two other vectors.

VED *abbrev* : vehicle excise duty.

Veda /vā'də or vē'/ *n* (*pl* **Vedas**) any one of, or all of, four ancient holy books of the Hindus. [Sans *veda* knowledge; cf **wit²**, L *vidēre* to see, Gr *oida* I know]

■ **Vedan'ta** *n* (Sans *anta* end) a system of Hindu philosophy based on the Vedas. **Vedan'tic** *adj*. **Ve'dic** *adj* of or relating to the Vedas. ◆ *n* the old Sanskrit language of the Vedas. **Ve'dism** *n*. **Ve'dist** *n* a person learned in the Vedas.

vedalia /vi-dā'li-ə/ *n* an *orig* Australian ladybird, *Rodolia cardinalis*, introduced elsewhere to control insect pests.

VE day /vē-ē'dā/ *abbrev* : Victory in Europe day (8 May, the date of the Allied victory in 1945).

Vedda /ved'ə/ *n* (a member of) an aboriginal people of Sri Lanka.

■ **Vedd'oid** *adj* of, relating to, or resembling, the Veddas; of a S Asian race, dark-skinned and curly-haired, to which the Veddas belong. ◆ *n* a Vedda; a member of the Veddoid race.

vedette /vi- or və-det'/ *n* a mounted sentry stationed to watch an enemy; a small vessel (**vedette'-boat**) for a similar purpose; /və-det'/ a stage or film star. [Fr, from Ital *vedetta*, from *vedere*, from L *vidēre* to see]

Vedic, Vedism, Vedist see under **Veda**.

veduta /ve-doo'tə or -tä/ *n* (*pl* **vedu'te** /-tā/) a panoramic view of a town, etc. [Ital, a view]

■ **vedutis'ta** *n* (*pl* **vedutis'ti** /-tē/) a painter of vedute.

vee /vē/ *n* the twenty-second letter of the modern English alphabet (V or v); a mark or object shaped or angled like a V. ◆ *combining form* (also **V-**) shaped like the letter V, as in *vee-gutter, vee-joint*, etc.

vee-jay or **veejay** /vē'jā/ (*inf*) *n* a broadcaster who introduces and plays music videos. [Phonetic representation of *VJ*, abbrev for *video jockey*]

veena same as **vina**.

veep /vēp/ (*US inf*) *n* a vice-president. [**VP**]

veer¹ /vēr/ *vi* to change direction, *esp* (of the wind) clockwise; to shift round in direction or in mental attitude; to change course, *esp* away from the wind (*naut*); to turn, wind. ◆ *vt* to turn, shift; to turn away from the wind. ◆ *n* a shifting round. [Fr *virer*]

■ **veer'ing** *n* and *adj*. **veer'ingly** *adv*.

veer² /vēr/ (*naut*) *vt* to pay out (cable, etc); to slack. [MDu *vieren*]

veery /vē'ri/ *n* a small American migratory bird of the thrush family. [Prob imit]

veg¹ /vej/ (*inf*) *n* short for vegetable or vegetables.

veg² /vej/ (*inf*) *vi* (often with *out*) to laze about or engage in mindless activity, *esp* after exertion. [Shortened form of **vegetate**]

Vega /vē'gə/ *n* the first-magnitude star α Lyrae. [Ar *al wāqi'* (*al nasr*) the falling (vulture)]

vega /vā'gə/ *n* in Spain and S America, a low fertile plain; in Cuba, etc a tobacco-field. [Sp]

vegan /vē'gən/ (also with *cap*) *n* and *adj* (a person) using no animal produce at all. [From **vegetarian**]

■ **vegan'ic** *adj* relating to manuring with material which is purely vegetable organic. **vē'ganism** *n*.

vegeburger or **veggie-burger** /vej'i-bûr-gər/ *n* a hamburger-like creation prepared from vegetables rather than meat products. [**vegetable** or **veggie** and ham*burger*]

vegelate /vej'ə-lāt/ *n* chocolate made with vegetable fat as well as cocoa butter. [**vegetable** and **chocolate**]

Vegemite® /vej'i-mīt/ (*Aust*) *n* a strongly flavoured yeast extract used as a spread, etc.

vegetable /vej'(i-)tə-bl/ *n* a plant or part of one used for food, other than those considered to be fruits; a person who is scarcely able to function as a human, *esp* because of damage to the brain (*offensive*); a dull, uninteresting person (*derog inf*); an organism belonging to the plant kingdom. ◆ *adj* of, for, derived from, composed of or of the nature of vegetables. [L *vegetābilis* animating, from *vegetāre* to animate; cf **vigour**]

■ **veg'etably** *adv* in the manner of a vegetable.

❑ **vegetable butter** *n* any of several butter-like vegetable fats. **vegetable ivory** see under **ivory**. **vegetable kingdom** *n* that division of natural objects which consists of vegetables or plants. **vegetable marrow** *n* a variety of pumpkin cooked as a vegetable; the akee fruit. **vegetable mould** *n* mould consisting mostly of humus. **vegetable oil** *n* any of various oils extracted from plants, used eg in cooking. **vegetable oyster** *n* salsify. **vegetable parchment** *n* paper treated with dilute sulphuric acid. **vegetable sheep** *n* in New Zealand, a dense cushion of composite plants (*Raoulia, Haastia*) at a distance

---

■ words derived from main entry word; ❑ compound words; ■ idioms and phrasal verbs

resembling a sheep. **vegetable wax** *n* a wax secreted by various plants that protects their surface from moisture loss.

vegetal /vej'i-təl/ *adj* belonging to or characteristic of vegetables or plants in general; vegetative; of a level of life below the sensitive. ◆ *n* (*rare*) a plant, vegetable. [Med L *vegetālis*, from L *vegetāre* to animate]
☐ **vegetal pole** *n* (*zool*) the lower portion or pole of an ovum in which cleavage is slow owing to the presence of yolk.

vegetarian /vej-i-tā'ri-ən/ *n* a person who excludes meat and often fish and other animal products from their diet. ◆ *adj* of or relating to vegetarianism; (of food) suitable for vegetarians. [*veget*able and sfx *-arian*]
■ **vegetā'rianism** *n* the theory or practice of a vegetarian.

vegetate /vej'i-tāt/ *vi* to grow or live as, or like, a vegetable or plant; to increase vegetatively; to live an inactive, almost purely physical, or dull life. [L *vegetāre*, *vegetātum* to animate]
■ **veg'etant** *adj* vegetating. **veg'etāted** *adj* covered with vegetation. **veg'etāting** *n* and *adj*. **vegetā'tion** *n* the process of vegetating; vegetable growth; a plantlike growth; plants growing in the mass; a plant (*obs*). **vegetā'tional** *adj*. **veg'etātive** *adj* growing, as plants; producing growth in plants; concerned with the life of the individual rather than of the race (*biol*); by means of vegetative organs, not special reproductive structures (*biol*); relating to unconscious or involuntary bodily functions as resembling the process of vegetable growth (*biol*); without intellectual activity, unprogressive. **veg'etātively** *adv*. **veg'etātiveness** *n*.
☐ **vegetative nervous system** *n* the nervous system regulating involuntary bodily activity, as the secretion of the glands, the beating of the heart, etc. **vegetative organs** *n pl* leaves, stems, roots. **vegetative reproduction** *n* reproduction by detachment of part of the plant-body; budding.

vegete /vi-jēt'/ *adj* vigorous. [L *vegetus*, from *vegēre* to be vigorous]

vegetive /vej'i-tiv/ *n* (*Shakesp*) a vegetable. ◆ *adj* vegetative. [Back-formation from *vegetive* (see under **vegetate**)]

veggie or **vegie** /vej'i/ (*inf*) *n* and *adj* (a) vegetarian.
■ **vegg'ies** *n pl* vegetables.
☐ **veggie-burger** see **vegeburger**.

vehement /vē'(h)ə-mənt/ *adj* marked by, or evincing, an urgency and forcefulness born of strong conviction. [L *vehemēns*, *-entis* eager, ardent]
■ **vē'hemence** or (now *rare*) **vē'hemency** *n*. **vē'hemently** *adv*.

vehicle /vē'i-kl or -ə-/ *n* a means of conveyance or transmission, *esp* a structure with wheels in or on which people or things are transported by land; a medium, eg for the expressing or performing of something; a substance with which a medicine, a pigment, etc, is mixed for administration or application; (**space vehicle**) a structure for carrying burdens through air or space or (also **launch vehicle**) a rocket used to launch a spacecraft. [L *vehiculum*, from *vehere* to carry]
■ **vehicular** /vi-hik'ū-lər/ *adj*.
☐ **vehicle-actuated signal** see under **pad**[1]. **vehicle excise duty** *n* a tax payable on motor vehicles.

Vehm or **Fehm** /fām/ or **Vehmgericht** or **Fehmgericht** /fām'gə-rihht/ *n* (*pl* **Vehm'e**, **Fehm'e**, **Vehm'gerichte** or **Fehm'gerichte** /-ə/) a medieval German (*esp* Westphalian) court in which initiated persons held power from the emperor to try capital cases in public or in secret, their lower officers executing the guilty on the spot or where they could find them. —Forms without *-gericht* are also spelt without capitals. [Ger *Vehm*, *Fehm*, now *Feme* criminal court, and *Gericht* court, judgement]
■ **Vehm'ic**, **Vehm'ique** or **Fehm'ic** *adj*.

veil /vāl/ *n* a covering of fine fabric for the head, face, or both, for protection, concealment, adornment or ceremonial purpose, *esp* the white transparent one often worn by a bride; a nun's or novice's head-covering; a disguise or concealment; an obstruction of tone in singing; a velum; a humeral; a curtain, a covering (*archaic*). ◆ *vt* to cover with a veil; to conceal, disguise or obscure. ◆ *vi* to wear a veil. [OFr *veile* (Fr *voile*), from L *vēlum* a curtain, veil, sail]
■ **veiled** *adj*. **veil'ing** *n* the act of concealing with a veil; a veil; material for making veils. **veil'less** *adj* wanting a veil; uncovered. **veil'y** *adj* like a veil, diaphanous.
♦ **draw a veil over** to conceal discreetly; to refrain from mentioning. **Eucharistic** or **sacramental veils** linen or silk covers for Eucharistic vessels and elements. **take the veil** to become a nun.

veilleuse /vā-yœz'/ *n* a shaded night-lamp. [Fr, from *veiller* to watch]

vein /vān/ *n* one of the vessels or tubes that convey the blood back to the heart; (loosely) any blood vessel; one of the horny tubes forming the framework of an insect's wing; a vascular bundle forming a rib, *esp* a small rib, in a leaf; a small intrusion, or a seam of a different mineral running through a rock; a fissure or cavity; a streak in wood, stone, etc; a streak running through one's nature, a strain of character or ability; (a recurrent characteristic streak in) manner or style; a mood

or humour. ◆ *vt* to form veins or the appearance of veins in. [Fr *veine*, from L *vēna*. See **vena**]
■ **veined** *adj* having veins; streaked, variegated. **vein'ing** *n* formation or disposition of veins; streaking. **vein'let** *n*. **vein'ous** *adj* full of veins. **vein'y** *adj* veined; veinous.
☐ **vein'stone** or **vein'stuff** *n* gangue.

Vela /vē'lə/ *n* the Sail, a southern constellation, one of the divisions of Argo. [L, pl of *vēlum* sail]

vela see **velum**.

velamen /və-lā'mən/ *n* (*pl* **velā'mina**) a multi-layered sheath of dead cells on some aerial roots (*bot*); a velum (*anat*). [L, veil]

velar, velarium, velate, etc see under **velum**.

velatura /vel-ə-too'rə/ *n* a method of glazing a painting by rubbing with the hand. [Ital]

Velcro® /vel'krō/ *n* a nylon fastening material for clothes, etc consisting of two facing layers, the one composed of tiny hooks, the other of tiny loops, strips of which, attached one on either side of an opening, form a secure closure when pressed together. [Fr *velours croché* hooked velvet]

veld or (outside S Africa) **veldt** /felt or velt/ *n* in S Africa, open, unforested, or thinly-forested grass-country. [Du *veld* (formerly *veldt*) field]

veldschoen (*old*) or **veldskoen** /felt'skoon/ *n* same as **velskoen**.

vele /vēl/ (*Spenser*) *n* same as **veil**.

veleta or **valeta** /və-lē'tə/ *n* a dance or dance tune in quick waltz time (also **valē'ta**). [Sp, weathercock]

veliger see under **velum**.

velitation /vel-i-tā'shən/ *n* a skirmish. [L *vēlitātiō*, *-ōnis*, from *vēles*, *-itis* a light-armed soldier]

vell /vel/ *n* the fourth stomach of a calf, used in making rennet. [Origin unknown]

velleity /ve-lē'i-ti/ *n* volition in its lowest form; mere inclination. [LL *velleitās*, irregularly formed from L *velle* to wish]

vellenage /vel'ə-nāj/ (*Spenser*) same as **villeinage** (see under **villein**).

vellet /vel'it/ (*Spenser*) same as **velvet**.

vellicate /vel'i-kāt/ *vt* and *vi* to twitch. [L *vellicāre*, *-ātum* to pluck]
■ **vellicā'tion** *n*.

vellon /vel-yon'/ *n* billon; old Spanish copper money. [Sp *vellon*, from Fr *billon*]

Vellozia /ve-lō'zi-ə/ *n* the Brazilian tree-lily genus, giving name to an African and S American family **Velloziā'ceae**, related to the amaryllids. [José *Vellozo* (1742–1811), Brazilian botanist]

vellum /vel'əm/ *n* a fine kind of parchment prepared by lime-baths and burnishing from the skins of calves, kids, or lambs; a manuscript, etc printed or written on vellum; a superior quality of writing paper. ◆ *adj* made of, printed on, etc vellum. [OFr *velin*, from *vel* calf]

vellus hair /vel'əs hār/ *n* short fine unpigmented hair covering the human body. [L *vellus*, *-eris* fleece]

veloce /vā-lō'chā/ (*music*) *adj* and *adv* with great rapidity. [Ital]

velocimeter /vel-ə-sim'ə-tər/ *n* an instrument that measures velocity. [L *vēlōcitas*, and **-meter**]
■ **velocim'etry** *n*.

velocipede /vi-los'i-pēd/ *n* an early form of bicycle, *orig* one propelled by the feet on the ground; a swift-footed person (*obs*). ◆ *adj* swift of foot. ◆ *vi* to ride a velocipede. [Fr *vélocipède*, from L *vēlōx*, *-ōcis* swift, and *pēs*, *pedis* foot]
■ **velocipē'dean** or **velocipē'dian** *n* and *adj*. **veloc'ipēder** (or /-pēd'/) *n*. **velocipedestrian** /-pi-des'tri-ən/ *n* and *adj* (*obs*). **veloc'ipēdist** (or /-pēd'/) *n*.

velociraptor /vi-los'i-rap-tər/ *n* a small bipedal Cretaceous dinosaur with a long narrow head and a sickle-like claw on each hind foot. [Mod L, as for **velocipede** and **raptor**]

velocity /vi-los'i-ti/ *n* rate of motion (distance per unit of time) in a stated direction; (loosely) speed. [L *vēlōcitās*, *-ātis*, from *vēlōx* swift]
☐ **velocity-distance law** *n* (*astron*) the law that the more distant a nebula the greater is its speed of recession. **velocity of circulation** *n* (*econ*) the ratio between the value of a country's national product and the money supply within a specified time.

velodrome /vel'ə-drōm/ *n* a stadium containing a cycle-racing track. [Fr *vélodrome*]

velours or **velour** /və-loor'/ *n* a fabric with velvet-like pile (also *adj*); a polishing pad for silk hats. [Fr *velours*]
■ **veloutine** /vel-oo-tēn'/ *n* a velvety corded wool fabric. **velure** /və-loor' or -lūr'/ *n* (*Shakesp*) velvet; a velours. ◆ *vt* to dress (a hat) with a velours. **velutinous** /-loo' or -lū'/ *adj* velvety.

velouté or **velouté sauce** /və-loo-tā' (sös)/ n a smooth white sauce made with stock. [Fr, velvety]

velskoen /fel'skoon/ (S Afr) n a shoe made of rawhide. [Du vel skin, and schoen shoe]

velt-mareschal /velt'mär-shl/ (Walter Scott) n a field marshal. [Ger Feldmarschall]

velum /vē'ləm, vä' or wä'lŭm/ n (pl vē'la) an integument or membrane; the membrane joining the rim of a young toadstool with the stalk; the pendulous soft palate; a ciliated disc, a locomotor organ in some molluscan larvae; an in-turned rim in jellyfishes. [L vēlum veil, sail, vēlāmen, -āminis covering, vēlārium awning]
■ **vē'lar** adj of the velum; produced by the back of the tongue brought close to, or in contact with, the soft palate (phonetics). ◆ n a velar consonant, back consonant. **velar'ic** adj relating to a velar. **velā'rium** (L /vä-lä'ri-ŭm/) n (pl velā'ria) an awning over an auditorium; in Scyphozoa, the thin marginal region of the umbrella. **velarizā'tion** or **-s-** n. **ve'larize** or **-ise** vt to pronounce (a non-velar sound) with the back of the tongue brought close to the soft palate, esp through the influences of a vowel sound. **ve'larized** or **-s-** adj. **vē'late** or **vēlā'ted** adj having a velum. **vē'liger** /-jər/ n a mollusc larva with a velum.

velure, **velutinous** see under **velours**.

Velux® window /vē'luks win'dō/ n a brand of roof window.

velvet /vel'vit/ n a silk, cotton, etc fabric with a soft close-cut pile; any of various other velvety fabrics; the velvet-like covering of a growing antler; a velvety surface or skin; gains, winnings (sl). ◆ adj made of velvet; soft or smooth like velvet. [LL velvettum, related to L villus a tuft]
■ **vel'veret** n a cotton with a silk pile. **vel'veted** adj clad in velvet. **velveteen'** n a cotton, or mixed cotton and silk, fabric similar to velvet. **vel'vetiness** n. **vel'veting** n velvet material. **vel'vety** adj soft and smooth like velvet; deep and soft in colouring.
❑ **velvet ant** n a wasp of the family Mutillidae. **velvet duck** or **velvet scoter** n a species of duck, the male of which is black with white patches on the wing and under the eye. **velvet glove** n gentleness concealing strength (see **iron hand** under **iron**). **vel'vet-guards** n pl (Shakesp) velvet trimmings, applied metaphorically to the citizens who wore them. **vel'vet-leaf** n false pareira; tree-mallow. **vel'vet-pa'per** n flock-paper. **vel'vet-pile** n material with a soft nap.
■ **on velvet** in a safe or advantageous position; secure against losing, whatever happens. **the velvet revolution** the bloodless transition from communism to democracy in Czechoslovakia in 1989.

Ven. abbrev : Venerable.

vena /vē'nə/ (anat) n (pl ve'nae) a vein. [L, vein]
■ **vē'nal** adj venous. **venation** /vi-nā'shən/ n a system or arrangement of blood vessels or of the veins of a leaf or an insect's wing. **venā'tional** adj. **venesec'tion** or **venisec'tion** n surgical incision into a vein, phlebotomy; the opening of a vein so as to let blood as a remedial measure. **venograph'ic** or **venograph'ical** adj. **venog'raphy** n radiography of a vein after injection of a contrast medium.
❑ **vena cava** /kā'və/ n (pl vēnae cāvae /-nē and -vē/) either of the two major veins (the **superior** and **inferior vena cava**) taking venous blood to the heart. **vena contrac'ta** n the point of minimum cross-sectional area in a jet of fluid discharged from an orifice.

venal¹ /vē'nl/ adj open to bribery, able to be bought over; corruptly mercenary. [L vēnālis, from vēnum goods for sale; cf Gr ōnē purchase]
■ **venality** /-nal'i-ti/ n. **vē'nally** adv.

venal² see under **vena**.

venatic or **venatical** /vi-nat'ik or -i-kəl/ adj relating to hunting. [L vēnārī to hunt]
■ **venat'ically** adv. **venation** /vi-nā'shən/ n (rare) hunting; a hunt. **venā'tor** n a huntsman, hunter. **venatorial** /ven-ə-tō'ri-əl or -tō'/ adj.

venation see under **vena** and **venatic**.

vend /vend/ vt to sell or offer for sale, deal in, esp in a small way; to utter (perh altered from vent¹). ◆ n a sale; the amount sold. [Fr vendre or L vendere to sell, from vēnum dare to offer for sale]
■ **vendee'** n a buyer. **vender** n see **vendor** below. **vendibil'ity** n. **vend'ible** adj that may be sold, offered for sale, or readily sold. ◆ n a thing for sale; a possible object of trade. **ven'dibleness** n. **ven'dibly** adv. **venditā'tion** n (rare) offering for sale. **vendi'tion** n sale. **ven'dor** or **ven'der** n a seller (esp law); a vending machine.
❑ **vending machine** n a slot-machine dispensing esp food or cigarettes.

vendace, also **vendis** or **vendiss** /ven'dəs or -dis/ n a freshwater white fish (Coregonus albula) formerly found in lochs in SW Scotland and still found in lakes in NW England. [Poss OFr vendese, vendoise (Fr vandoise) dace]

vendange /vä-däzh' or van'danj/ n the grape harvest (also **vendage** /ven'dij/). [ME, from (O)Fr vendange ; see **vintage**]

Vendean /ven-dē'ən/ n an inhabitant of La Vendée, in France; one of those who there resisted the French Revolution. ◆ adj of or relating to the Vendeans.

vendee see under **vend**.

Vendémiaire /vä-dā-myer'/ n the first month in the French Revolutionary calendar, about 22 September to 21 October. [Fr, from L vīndēmia vintage, from vīnum wine, and dēmere to take away, from dē from, and emere to take]

vendetta /ven-det'ə/ n a blood-feud; any similarly prolonged, violent, etc feud or quarrel. [Ital, from L vindicta revenge, from vindicāre to claim]

vendeuse /vä-dœz'/ n a saleswoman. [Fr]

vendible, **venditation**, **vendition**, etc see under **vend**.

vendis, **vendiss** see **vendace**.

vendor see under **vend**.

vendue /ven-dū'/ (US) n a public auction sale. [Du vendu, from Fr vendue]

veneer /və-nēr'/ vt to overlay or face (coarse wood, etc) with a thin sheet of fine wood or other material; to disguise with superficial refinement. ◆ n a thin layer for veneering; a specious outward appearance of good quality, refinement, respectability, etc; a grass moth, from its markings (also **veneer'-moth**). [Formerly **fineer¹**, from Ger furniren, from OFr fornir (Fr fournir), Ital fornire to furnish]
■ **veneer'er** n. **veneer'ing** n.

venefic or **venefical** /vi-nef'ik or -i-kəl/, **veneficious** /ven-i-fish'əs/ or **veneficous** /vi-nef'i-kəs/ adj acting by poison or potions or by sorcery. [L venēficus, from venēnum poison, and facere to do]
■ **venef'ically**, **venefic'iously** or **venefic'ously** adv.

venepuncture or **venipuncture** /ven'i- or vē'ni-pungk-chər/ (med) n the puncturing of a vein with a hypodermic needle, to draw off a sample of blood or inject a drug. [L vēna a vein]

venerable /ven'(ə-)rə-bl/ adj worthy of reverence; hallowed by associations or age; aged-looking; an honorific prefix to the name of an archdeacon, or to a person in process of canonization. [L venerābilis worthy of reverence]
■ **ven'erableness** n. **ven'erably** adv.

venerate /ven'ə-rāt/ vt to treat with respect and awe. [L venerārī, -ātus]
■ **venerā'tion** n the act of venerating; the state of being venerated; awed respect. **ven'erātor** n.

venereal /vi-nē'ri-əl/ adj relating to sexual desire or intercourse; transmitted by sexual intercourse; relating to or affected by venereal disease. [L venereus, from Venus, Veneris the goddess of love]
■ **venē'rean** adj (obs) relating to Venus or her service, or to sexual desire or intercourse. ◆ n (obs) a person addicted to sexual gratification. **venē'reous** adj lustful; venereal; aphrodisiac.
❑ **venereal disease** n any of various contagious diseases characteristically transmitted by sexual intercourse.

venereology /vi-nē-ri-ol'ə-ji/ n the study of venereal diseases. [L venereus relating to sexual love, and **-ology**]
■ **venereolog'ical** adj. **venereol'ogist** n.

venerer see under **venery²**.

venery¹ /ven'ə-ri/ (archaic) n the pursuit of sexual gratification. [Med L veneria, from L Venus, Veneris the goddess of love]

venery² /ven'ə-ri/ (archaic) n hunting; game. [OFr venerie, from vener, from L vēnārī to hunt]
■ **ven'erer** n a gamekeeper; a hunter.

venesection see under **vena**.

Venetian /vi-nē'shən/ adj of Venice, a city and former republic in NE Italy. ◆ n a native or inhabitant of Venice; a Venetian blind. [L Venetiānus, from Venetia Venice]
■ **Vene'tianed** adj having Venetian blinds or shutters.
❑ **Venetian blind** n a window blind of horizontal slats adjustable to let in or keep out light. **Venetian glass** n very delicate glass made at Murano, near Venice. **Venetian mast** n a spirally banded pole for street decoration. **Venetian mosaic** see under **terrazzo**. **Venetian red** n ferric oxide as a pigment.

venewe /ven'ū/ or **veney** /ven'i/ Shakespearean forms of **venue**.

Venezuelan /ven-ə-zwä'lən/ adj of or relating to the Republic of Venezuela in S America, or its inhabitants. ◆ n a native or citizen of Venezuela.

venge /venj/ vt (Shakesp) to avenge. [OFr venger, from L vindicāre]
■ **venge'able** adj revengeful (Spenser); destructive (dialect); extraordinarily great (obs). **venge'ably** adv. **venge'ment** n (Spenser) vengeance, penal retribution. **ven'ger** n (Spenser) an avenger.

vengeance /ven'jəns/ n the inflicting of injury in punishment or revenge; retribution; harm, mischief (Shakesp); a curse (Shakesp). ◆ adv (Shakesp) extremely, exceedingly. [OFr, from venger to avenge, from L vindicāre]

■ words derived from main entry word; ❑ compound words; ■ idioms and phrasal verbs

■ **what a** (or **the**) **vengeance** used to intensify questions. **with a vengeance** (*orig*) with a curse; violently, thoroughly, exceedingly.

vengeful /venjˈfəl/ *adj* eager for revenge; vindictive; retributive, retaliatory. [**venge**]
■ **venge'fully** *adv*. **venge'fulness** *n*.

venial /vēˈni-əl/ *adj* pardonable; excusable; permissible (*Milton*). [L *veniālis* pardonable, from *venia* pardon]
■ **veniality** /-alˈi-ti/ *n*. **vē'nially** *adv*.
❏ **venial sin** *n* sin other than mortal.

Venice /venˈis/ *n* a city and former republic of NE Italy. ◆ *adj* (*archaic*) Venetian. [Fr *Venise*, from L *Venetia*]
❏ **Venice glass** *n* the former name for Venetian glass. **Venice gold** *n* (*Shakesp*) gold thread made in Venice. **Venice talc** *n* steatite. **Venice treacle** *n* (*archaic*) a supposed antidote for all poisons, of many ingredients. **Venice turpentine** *n* larch turpentine, formerly shipped from Venice.

venidium /ve-niˈdi-əm/ (*hortic*) *n* a plant native to S Africa, of the *Venidium* genus (family Compositae), having yellow or cream flowers. [New L, from L *vēna* vein]

venin /venˈin/ (*chem*) *n* any of various toxic substances in venom. [*venom* and **-in**]

venipuncture see **venepuncture**.

venire /ve-nīˈrē* or *we-nēˈre/ (in full **venire facias** /fāˈshi-as* or *faˈki-as/ *hist* and *US*) *n* a writ issued to a sheriff requiring him to cause a certain number of qualified persons to appear in court at a specified time so that jurors may be chosen from them; the persons so caused to appear. [L, make come]
❏ **venī'reman** *n* (*US*) a juror.

venison /venˈi-zn* or (*esp* in Scotland) *-i-sən/ *n* deer's flesh as food; any game animal, *esp* its flesh as food (*obs*). [Anglo-Fr *venison* (Fr *venaison*), from L *vēnātiō, -ōnis* hunting, from *vēnārī* to hunt]

venite /vi-nīˈti* or *we-nēˈte/ *n* Psalm 95, beginning *Venīte exultēmus O* come let us rejoice; a musical setting of this.

Venn diagram /ven dīˈə-gram/ (*maths*) *n* a diagram in which sets and their relationships are represented, by overlapping circles or other figures. [John *Venn* (1834–1923), English logician]

vennel /venˈl/ (*Scot*) *n* a lane. [Fr *venelle*, from L *vēna* a vein]

venogram /vēˈnə-gram/ *n* an image made by **venog'raphy**, the radiographic examination of veins after injection with a substance opaque to X-rays. [L *vēna* a vein]

venom /venˈəm/ *n* poisonous fluid secreted by certain snakes and various other creatures, introduced into the victim by a bite or sting; spite. ◆ *adj* (*Shakesp*) poisonous. ◆ *vi* (*obs*) to poison; to envenom. [OFr *venim* (Fr *venin*), from L *venēnum* poison]
■ **ven'omed** *adj* venomous; charged with poison, envenomed. **ven'omous** *adj* poisonous; having power to poison, *esp* by bite or sting; malignant, full of spite. **ven'omously** *adv*. **ven'omousness** *n*.
❏ **ven'om'd-mouth'd** *adj* (*Shakesp*) having a venomous mouth, slanderous.

venose /vēˈnōs* or *-nōsˈ/ *adj* veiny; veined; with very marked veins. [L *vēnōsus* veiny]

venous /vēˈnəs/ *adj* relating to, or contained in, veins; full of veins; (of blood) deoxygenated, and, in human beings, dark red in colour; veined. [L *vēna* vein, and **-ous**]
■ **venosity** /vē-nosˈi-ti/ *n* the state or quality of being venous, or of having or being like venous blood.

ven'son same as **venison**.

vent[1] /vent/ *n* an opening, aperture; an airhole; a touch hole for firing a cannon, etc; an outlet; a volcanic orifice; an animal's or bird's anus; a chimney flue (*Scot*); an outlet; an emission, discharge or escape, *esp* of gas, smoke or a liquid; an otter's rise to the surface for breath; the opening in a parachute canopy through which air escapes at a controlled rate. ◆ *vt* to give a vent or opening to; to let out, as at a vent; to allow to escape; to publish, utter (*archaic*); to discharge, emit, pour forth; to scent; to sniff at; to lift or open so as to admit air (*Spenser*). ◆ *vi* to have or find an outlet; to discharge smoke, to function as a chimney, draw (*Scot*); to sniff or snuff; (of a beaver or otter) to take breath or rise for breath. [Fr, from L *ventus* wind; partly Fr *éventer* to expose to air; associated with **vent**[2] and **vent**[3]]
■ **vent'age** or **vent'ige** *n* (*Shakesp*) a fingerhole, as in a flute; a small hole. **vent'ed** *adj*. **vent'er** *n* (*obs*) a person who utters or publishes. **vent'iduct** *n* (L *dūcere, ductum* to lead) a ventilating pipe or passage. **vent'ing** *n* and *adj*. **vent'less** *adj*.
❏ **vent'-hole** *n* a hole for admission or escape of air, fumes, etc, or to admit light. **vent'-peg** or **vent'-plug** *n* a plug for stopping the vent of a barrel. **vent'-pipe** *n* an escape-pipe, eg for steam or foul gases.
■ **give vent to** to allow to escape or break out; to give (*usu* violent) expression to (an emotion).

vent[2] /vent/ *n* a slit in a garment, *esp* in the back of a jacket; a crenel (*obs*). [Fr *fente*, from L *findere* to split; cf **fent**]

vent[3] /vent/ (*obs*) *n* a sale; a market. ◆ *vt* (*obs* or *dialect*) to sell. [OFr *vente*, from L *vendere, venditum* to sell]

ventail, (*Spenser*) **ventayle** or **ventaile** /venˈtāl/ *n* in medieval armour, the part of a helmet protecting the lower part of the face. [Fr *ventail*, OFr *ventaille*, ult from L *ventus* wind]

ventana /ven-täˈnä/ *n* a window. [Sp]

ventayle see **ventail**.

venter[1] /venˈtər/ (chiefly *zool* and *bot*) *n* the belly or abdomen; a womb or mother (*law*); a swelling or protuberance; a medial swelling; the dilated basal part of an archegonium; a shallow concave surface of a bone; the upper side or surface of a leaf, etc. [L *venter, -tris* belly, dimin *ventriculus*]
■ **ven'tral** *adj* of the belly; on the upper side or towards the axis (*bot*); on the side normally turned towards the ground, *opp* to *dorsal* or *neural* (*zool*). ◆ *n* a ventral fin. **ven'trally** *adv*. **ven'tricose** or (*rare*) **ven'tricous** *adj* distended or swollen in the middle, at the side, or round the base (*bot, zool*); having a prominent or swollen belly.
❏ **ventral fin** *n* either of the paired fins on the belly of a fish. **ventral tank** *n* (*aeronautics*) an auxiliary fuel tank, fixed or able to be jettisoned, mounted externally under the fuselage (also **belly tank**).

venter[2] /venˈtər/ an old form (*Milton*) of **venture**.

venter[3] see under **vent**[1].

ventiduct see under **vent**[1].

ventifact /venˈti-fakt/ (*geol*) *n* a stone shaped and/or polished by windblown sand. [L *ventus* wind, and art*ifact*]

ventige see under **vent**[1].

ventil /venˈtil/ (*music*) *n* a valve for giving sounds intermediate between the open harmonics in wind instruments; a valve in an organ for controlling the wind supply to various stops. [Ger, from LL *ventīle* shutter, sluice, from *ventus* wind]

ventilate /venˈti-lāt/ *vt* to open or expose to the free passage of air; to provide with duct(s) for circulating air or for escape of air; to cause (blood) to take up oxygen, by supply of air; to supply air to (lungs); to expose to examination and discussion, to make public; to fan, winnow, blow upon. [L *ventilāre, -ātum* to fan, wave, agitate, from *ventus* wind]
■ **ven'tilable** *adj*. **ventila'tion** *n*. **ven'tilative** *adj*. **ven'tilator** *n* a device for introducing fresh air; a machine that ventilates the lungs of a person whose respiratory system is not functioning adequately; a person, animal or object that causes ventilation. **ventilā'tory** *adj*.

venting see under **vent**[1].

ventose /ven-tōs'* or *ven'/ *adj* windy; flatulent; puffed up with conceit. [L *ventōsus*, from *ventus* wind]
■ **Ventôse** /vã-tōz/ *n* the sixth month of the French Revolutionary calendar, about 19 February to 20 March. **ventosity** /ven-tos'i-ti/ *n* windiness.

ventouse extraction /vã-tooz iks-trak'shən/ *n* a method of obstetric delivery using a vacuum suction cup on the crown of the baby's head. [Fr *ventouse* suction cup]

ventral, etc see under **venter**[1].

ventre /ven'tər/ an old form of **venture**.

ventre à terre /vã-tra-ter'/ (*Fr*) at high speed (literally, belly to the ground).

ventricle /ven'tri-kl/ (*anat*) *n* either of the two lower contractile chambers of the heart, the right ventricle receiving venous blood from the right atrium and pumping it into the pulmonary loop for oxygenation, the left receiving oxygenated blood from the left atrium and pumping it into the arterial system for circulation round the body; any of various other cavities in the body, eg one of the four main cavities of the brain; the stomach (*obs*); the womb (*Shakesp*). [L *ventriculus*, dimin of *venter* belly]
■ **ventric'ular** *adj* of or of the nature of a ventricle; abdominal. **ven'tricule** or **ventric'ūlus** *n* (*pl* **ven'tricules** or **ventric'ūlī**) a ventricle. **ventriculog'raphy** *n* (*med*) radiography of the heart or brain after the introduction of a contrast medium (in the latter case *usu* air) into the ventricle(s).
❏ **ventricular fibrillation** *n* unco-ordinated rapid electric activity of a heart ventricle.

ventricose see under **venter**[1].

ventricular...to...**ventriculography** see under **ventricle**.

ventriloquism /ven-tril'ə-kwi-zm/ *n* the art of speaking so as to give the illusion that the sound comes from some other source. [L *ventriloquus* a person who speaks by a spirit in the belly, from *venter* the belly, and *loquī* to speak]
■ **ventril'oqual** or **ventriloquial** /-lō'kwi-əl/ *adj*. **ventrilō'quially** *adv*. **ventril'oquist** *n*. **ventriloquis'tic** *adj*. **ventril'oquize** or **-ise** *vi*

to practise ventriloquism. **ventril'oquous** *adj*. **ventril'oquy** *n* ventriloquism.

ventring see under **venture**.

venture /ven'chər/ *n* an undertaking whose issue is uncertain or dangerous; a commercial enterprise or speculation with a risk of loss; something attempted; chance, luck, hazard (*archaic*); that which is put to hazard (*esp* goods sent by sea at the sender's risk); a prostitute (*Shakesp*). ◆ *vt* to expose to hazard; to risk; to take the risk of; to dare to put forward; to send on a venture. ◆ *vi* to make a venture; to run a risk; to dare; to dare to go. [For *a venture*, obs variant of **adventure**]
■ **ven'turer** *n*. **ven'turesome** *adj* inclined or willing to take risks; involving the taking of risk; risky. **ven'turesomely** *adv*. **ven'turesomeness** *n*. **ven'turing** (*Milton* **ven'tring**) *n* and *adj*. **ven'turingly** *adv*. **ven'turous** (*Spenser, Milton*, etc, **ven'trous** or **ven't'rous**) *adj* adventurous; daring. **ven'turously** *adv*. **ven'turousness** *n*.
❑ **venture capital** *n* money supplied by individual investors or business organizations for a new, *esp* speculative, business enterprise, also called **risk capital**. **venture capitalist** *n* such an investor. **venture capital trust** *n* an investment which, subject to certain conditions, has tax advantages (*abbrev* **VCT**). **Venture Scout, Venture Air Scout, Venture Sea Scout** *n* a male or female member of a senior branch of the Scout organization (for 16 to 20-year-olds), formerly called Rover (Scout).
■ **at a venture** at hazard, random.

Venturi /ven-tūr'i/ or **Venturi tube** /tūb/ (also without *cap*) *n* a tube or duct, wasp-waisted and expanding at the ends, used in measuring the flow rate of fluids, or as a means of regulating flow, or to provide suction. [GB *Venturi* (1746–1822), Italian physicist]

venue /ven'ū/ (*Shakesp* **venewe** or **veney**) *n* a meeting-place or rendezvous; the chosen location for a sports event, concert, etc; the place where a case is to be tried, or the district from which the jurors are drawn (*usu* the county in which the alleged offence was committed) (*law, hist*); a hit or thrust in fencing (*obs*); a bout or match (*obs*). [OFr *venue* arrival, from *venir*, from L *venīre* to come]
■ **change of venue** change of place of trial. **lay the venue** to specify the place where the trial is to be held.

venule /ven'ūl/ (*anat* and *zool*) *n* a branch of a vein in an insect's wing; any of the small-calibre blood vessels into which the capillaries empty, and which join up to form veins. [L *vēnula*, dimin of *vēna* vein]

Venus /vē'nəs/ *n* the goddess of love, *orig* of spring, patron of flower-gardens, later identified with the Greek Aphrodite (*Roman myth*); the most brilliant of the planets, second in order from the sun; copper (*alchemy*); an alluring grace, beauty (*obs*); venery (*obs*); (also without *cap*) a mollusc of a genus (*Venus*) of lamellibranch molluscs, including the quahog, or of related genera (**Ve'nus-shell'** a shell, or mollusc, of the genus). [L, *orig* personified from *venus, veneris* desire; related to *venerāri* to worship]
■ **Venusian** /ven-oo'zi-ən or ven-ū'/, less commonly **Venutian** /ven-oo'shi-ən or ven-ū'/ *n* and *adj* (in science fiction, an inhabitant) of the planet Venus.
❑ **Venus** (or **Venus's**) **flytrap** *n* an insectivorous plant with hinged leaves that snap shut on insects that land on them. **Venus's comb** *n* an umbelliferous plant (*Scandix pecten-Veneris*) with long-beaked fruits set like comb teeth. **Venus's flowerbasket** *n* a deep-sea sponge with a skeleton of glassy spicules. **Venus's girdle** *n* a ribbonlike gelatinous sea creature. **Venus's looking-glass** *n* a garden plant (genus *Specularia*) with small bright flowers.
■ **girdle of Venus** (*palmistry*) a line on the palm forming a semicircle from between the first and second to between the third and fourth fingers, apparently indicative of a hysterical and desponding temperament. **mount of Venus** the elevation at the base of the thumb; the mons Veneris or mons pubis (qqv).

venville /ven'vil/ *n* a form of tenure in parishes around Dartmoor that gives tenants certain rights to the use of land on Dartmoor. [Origin obscure]

Vera /vē'rə/ *n* a machine that records television pictures and sound on magnetic tape for almost immediate reproduction. [*v*ision *e*lectronic *r*ecording *a*pparatus]

veracious /və-rā'shəs/ *adj* truthful. [L *vērāx, -ācis*, from *vērus* true]
■ **verā'ciously** *adv*. **veracity** /-ras'i-ti/ *n* truthfulness.

veranda or **verandah** /və-ran'də/ *n* a roofed gallery, terrace, or open portico along the front or side of a building; a canopy sheltering the street in front of a shop (*NZ*). [Hindi *varaṇḍā*, prob from Port *varanda* a balcony]
■ **veran'da'd** or **veran'dahed** *adj* having a veranda.

verapamil /və-rap'ə-mil/ *n* a vasodilatory drug that inhibits the movement of calcium, used in treating heart arrhythmia and angina pectoris. [Coinage based on *valeric* acid and *nitrile*]

veratrum /və-rā'trəm/ *n* a plant of the white hellebore genus *Veratrum*. [L *vērātrum* hellebore]
■ **veratrin** or **veratrine** /ver'ə-trin or -trēn/ *n* an alkaloid or mixture of alkaloids obtained from white hellebore rhizomes, sabadilla, etc.

verb /vûrb/ (*grammar*) *n* a part of speech consisting of a word or group of words that signifies an action, experience, occurrence or state, in sentence analysis constituting or introducing the predicate. [L *verbum* word]
■ **verbal** *adj* see separate entry. **verb'id** *n* a non-finite part of a verb, such as a verbal noun or infinitive. **verbificā'tion** *n*. **verb'ify** *vt* to convert into a verb. **verb'less** *adj*.
❑ **verbal noun** *n* a form of a verb, eg infinitive or (*esp*) gerund, functioning as a noun. **verb phrase** *n* a phrase containing a verb and an object but not a subject.

verbal /vûr'bəl/ *adj* of, relating to or derived from a verb or verbs; of, in, of the nature of, in the matter of or concerned with words, or words rather than things; word for word, literal; oral; voluble; articulate. ◆ *n* a word, *esp* a noun, derived from a verb; (often in *pl*) an oral statement, *esp* an arrested suspect's confession of guilt, made to the police, or claimed by them to have been made (*sl*); (an) insult, (piece of) abuse or invective (*sl*); (*usu* in *pl*) fast talk, glib patter. ◆ *vt* (**verb'alling**; **verb'alled**) (*sl*) (of the police) to attribute a statement or admission to, or extract it from (a suspect, etc). [L *verbum* word]
■ **ver'balism** *n* an expression; wording; undue attention to words alone; literalism. **ver'balist** *n* a person skilled in words; a literalist; a person who is concerned with words alone. **verbal'ity** *n* the quality of being verbal or merely verbal; mere words. **verbalīzā'tion** or **-s-** *n*. **ver'balize** or **-ise** *vt* to turn into a verb; to put in words. ◆ *vi* to use too many words, be prolix. **ver'bally** *adv*. **verbā'rian** *n* a coiner of words. **verb'icide** /-sīd/ *n* and *adj* (the quality of) destroying the meaning of a word. **verbigerate** /-ij'ə-rāt/ *vi*. **verbigerā'tion** *n* the morbid and purposeless repetition of certain words and phrases at short intervals, eg as occurs in schizophrenia.
❑ **verbal inspiration** *n* dictation of every word of a book (*usu* the Bible) by God. **verbal note** *n* in diplomacy, an unsigned reminder of a neglected, though perhaps not urgent, matter.

Verbascum /vər-bas'kəm/ *n* the mullein genus. [L]

verbatim /vər-bā'tim or -ba'tim/ *adv* word for word, using exactly the same words (also *adj*); by word of mouth (*Shakesp*). [L]
■ **verbatim et literatim** /-ā'tim or -a'tim/ word for word and letter for letter.

verbena /vûr-bē'nə/ *n* a plant of the vervain genus *Verbena*, giving name to the family **Verbenaceae** /vûr-bi-nā'si-ē/, closely related to the labiates; any plant of similar appearance. [L *verbēna* a leafy twig, sacred bough]
■ **verbenā'ceous** *adj*.
❑ **verbe'na-oil** *n* an oil obtained from the related plant *Lippia citriodora* (called **lemon verbena**) or from lemon grass.

verberate /vûr'bə-rāt/ (*archaic*) *vt* to beat. [L *verberāre, -ātum* to scourge]
■ **verberā'tion** *n*.

verbiage /vûr'bi-ij or -əj/ *n* superfluity of words, verbosity, prolixity; wording (*rare*). [Fr, from OFr *verbier* to chatter]

verbicide see under **verbal**.

verbid, verbify see under **verb**.

verbigeration see under **verbal**.

verbose /vûr- or və-bōs'/ *adj* using or containing more words than are desirable; wordy. [L *verbōsus* prolix]
■ **verbose'ly** *adv*. **verbose'ness** or **verbosity** /-bos'/ *n*.

verboten /fer-bō'tən/ (*Ger*) *adj* forbidden.

verb. sap., verbum sap. or **verbum sat.** /vûrb or vûr'bəm/ *abbrev* : *verbum sapienti sat est* (L), a word is sufficient to the wise, no need for further explanation.

verdant /vûr'dənt/ *adj* (*esp* of landscape or vegetation) green; covered with fresh green vegetation; green, unsophisticated, raw and gullible. [OFr *verdeant, verdet*, ult from L *vindis* green]
■ **ver'dancy** *n*. **ver'dantly** *adv*. **ver'det** *n* copper acetate.

verd-antique /vûrd-an-tēk'/ (*obs Fr*) or **verde-antico** /ver'dā-än-tē'kō/ (*Ital*) *n* a breccia of serpentine containing calcite, etc. [Antique green; Fr now *vert*]
■ **oriental verd-antique** a green porphyry.

verdelho /vər-del'yū/ *n* (a white Madeira made from) a white grape grown *orig* in Madeira, now also in Portugal, Sicily, Australia and S Africa. [Port]

verderer or **verderor** /vûr'də-rər/ (hist) n an officer of the law responsible for order in the royal forests. [Anglo-Fr, from OFr verdier, from L viridis green]

verdet see under **verdant**.

verdict /vûr'dikt/ or formerly (Spenser, Milton) **verdit** /-dit/ n the decision of a jury at a trial; judicial decision or decision generally. [OFr verdit and LL vērēdictum, from L vērē truly, and dictum said] ■ **formal verdict** see under **formal**. **open verdict** see under **open**. **special verdict** a verdict in which specific facts are found and put on the record.

verdigris /vûr'di-grēs/ n basic cupric acetate; (popularly) the green coating of basic cupric carbonate that forms in the atmosphere on copper, brass, or bronze. ◆ vt to coat with verdigris. [OFr verd de Grece green of Greece]

verdin /vûr'din/ n a small yellow-headed tit, Auriparus flaviceps, from south-western N America. [Fr, yellowhammer]

verdit see **verdict**.

verdite /vûr'dīt/ n a S African green mica, used ornamentally in jewellery and architecture. [verdant and -**ite**]

verditer /vûr'di-tər/ (archaic) n a blue or green pigment, hydrated cupric carbonate. [OFr verd-de-terre earth green]

verdoy /vûr'doi/ (heraldry) adj charged with flowers, leaves, or vegetable charges, as a bordure. [Fr verdoyé, pap of verdoyer to become green]

verdure /vûr'dyər/ (chiefly poetic) n fresh greenness; greenery, green vegetation; fresh taste (obs); freshness (fig). [OFr, from verd (Fr vert), from L viridis green] ■ **ver'dured** adj clad with verdure. **ver'dureless** adj. **ver'durous** adj.

verecund /ver'i-kund/ adj modest. [L verēcundus]

Verein /fər-īn'/ (Ger) n union, association.

Verey light see **Very light**.

verge¹ /vûrj/ n a limit, boundary; a rim; the brink, extreme edge; the horizon (poetic); the edge of a roof projecting beyond the gable (archit); a grass edging to a road, etc; a rod or rodlike part; the spindle of the balance wheel in early clocks; a rod or staff of office; extent of jurisdiction, esp of the Lord High Steward of the royal household (hist); a precinct or pale; range or scope; jurisdiction. ◆ vt to edge. ◆ vi (with on) to border, be on the edge of; (with on) to come close to, nearly be (a state or condition). [L virga a rod; the area of jurisdiction of the holder of the office symbolized by the rod, hence, limit, boundary] ❑ **verge'-board** n a bargeboard. ■ **on the verge of** on the point of; on the brink of, very close to (a state, condition or situation).

verge² /vûrj/ vi to incline; to tend downward; to slope; to tend; to pass gradually, merge. [L vergere to bend] ■ **ver'gence** n (ophthalmol) the simultaneous motion of both eyes either inwards or outwards when changing focus. **ver'gency** n.

verger /vûr'jər/ n in various Episcopal churches, a church official who acts as attendant and caretaker; an official who, on ceremonial occasions, bears the verge or staff of office before a bishop or other dignitary. [**verge¹**] ■ **ver'gership** n.

Vergilian see **Virgilian**.

verglas /ver'glä/ n a film of ice on rock, etc. [Fr (verre glass, and glace ice), from OFr]

veridical /vi-rid'i-kl/ adj truthful; coinciding with fact; (of a dream or vision) corresponding exactly with what has happened or with what happens later; seemingly true to fact. [L vēridicus, from vērus true, and dīcere to say] ■ **veridicality** /-kal'i-ti/ n. **verid'ically** adv. **verid'icous** adj truthful.

verier, veriest see **very**.

verify /ver'i-fī/ vt (**ver'ifying**; **ver'ified**) to ascertain, confirm, check or test the truth or accuracy of; to assert or prove to be true; to testify to the truth of, support (a statement; law); to check (items of data input) for accuracy eg by having the same data keyed twice, by two separate operators, and then checked by computer for discrepancies (comput); to back up or support (Shakesp). [L vērus true, and facere to make] ■ **verifiabil'ity** n. **ver'ifiable** adj. **verificā'tion** n. **ver'ificātory** adj. **ver'ifier** n. ❑ **verification principle** n (in logical positivism) the principle that a statement is meaningful only if its truth or falsity can be established empirically.

verily see under **very**.

verisimilitude /ver-i-si-mil'i-tūd/ n the quality of seeming real or true, an appearance of truth or reality; a statement, etc that merely sounds true. [L vērīsimilitūdō, from vērus true, and similis like]

■ **verisim'ilar** adj. **verisim'ilarly** adv. **verisimil'ity** n (obs). **verisim'ilous** adj.

verism /vē'ri-zm or ver'i-zm/ n use of everyday contemporary material, including what is ugly or sordid, in the arts, esp in early 20c Italian opera (Ital **verismo** /vā-rēs'mō/); the theory supporting this. [Ital verismo from vero, from L vērus true] ■ **ver'ist** adj and n. **verist'ic** adj.

vérité see **cinéma vérité** under **cinema**.

verity /ver'i-ti/ n (pl **ver'ities**) truth; a truth, esp a basic or fundamental one; truthfulness; something that exists, a reality. [L vēritās, -ātis, from vērus true] ■ **ver'itable** adj true; genuine; real, actual; truly or justifiably so called. **ver'itableness** n. **ver'itably** adv. ■ **of a verity** (archaic) assuredly.

verjuice /vûr'joos/ n the juice of unripe fruit; sourness, tartness. ◆ adj sour. [Fr verjus, from vert (L viridis) green, and jus juice (L jūs broth)] ■ **ver'juiced** adj soured.

verkramp /fər-kramp'/ adj (used predicatively) in South Africa, narrow-minded, illiberal and rigidly conservative in attitude, esp towards black people and people of mixed race. [Afrik, restricted] ■ **verkrampte** /-kram(p)'tə/ adj (used attrib) and n (a person) of such rigidly conservative political attitudes.

verlig /fər-lihh'/ adj (used predicatively) in South Africa, liberal, politically enlightened, esp towards black people and people of mixed race. [Afrik, enlightened] ■ **verligte** /-lihh'tə/ adj (used attrib) and n (a person) of such enlightened and liberal political attitudes.

vermal see under **vermis**.

vermeil /vûr'mil or -māl/ n and adj bright-red, scarlet, vermilion; silver-gilt or gilt bronze. ◆ vt to colour with vermeil. —Also **ver'mil**, **ver'meille** or (Spenser) **ver'mell** or **ver'mily**. [OFr and Fr, from L vermiculus a little worm, kermes, dimin of vermis worm; cf **vermilion**]

vermes see **vermis**.

vermi- /vûr-mi-/ combining form denoting worm. [L vermis, a worm] ■ **ver'micidal** /vûr'mi-sī-dl/ adj. **ver'micide** n a worm-killing agent. **ver'miculture** n the farming of earthworms, esp as bait for fishing. **ver'miform** adj having the form of a worm (**vermiform appendix** (anat) the appendix, a worm-shaped process projecting from the lower end of the ascending colon). **vermifugal** /vər-mif'ū-gl/ adj expelling worms. **ver'mifuge** /-fūj/ n a drug that expels worms. **vermiv'orous** adj worm-eating.

vermian see under **vermis**.

vermicelli /vûr-mi-sel'i or -chel'i/ n a very slender type of spaghetti; (more usu **chocolate vermicelli**) short thin pieces of chocolate used for decoration of cakes, sweets, etc. [Ital, pl of vermicello, dimin of verme worm, from L vermis]

vermicidal, etc see under **vermi-**.

vermicular /vûr-mik'ū-lər/ adj of, of the nature of or like a worm; relating to or caused by intestinal worms (pathol); vermiculate (archit). [L vermiculus, dimin of vermis worm] ■ **vermic'ulate** /-lət/ or **vermic'ulated** adj bearing a decoration reminiscent of a mass of curly worms, rusticated (archit); worm-eaten. **vermiculā'tion** n rustication (archit); a worm-eaten condition; peristalsis of the intestines (physiol). **ver'micule** n a little worm. **vermic'ūlite** n an altered mica that curls before the blowpipe flame and expands greatly at high temperature, forming a water-absorbent substance used in seed-planting, and also used as insulating material. **vermic'ūlous** adj wormy.

vermiculture, vermiform, vermifugal, etc see under **vermi-**.

vermil, etc see **vermeil**.

vermilion /vər-mil'yən/ n a bright-red pigment, mercuric sulphide; its bright scarlet colour. ◆ adj bright scarlet. ◆ vt to colour vermilion. [OFr vermillon, from vermeil (see **vermeil**)]

vermin /vûr'min/ n a collective name for small animals, insects or birds that are troublesome or destructive to crops, game or domestic stock; obnoxious or despicable people. [Fr vermine, from L vermis a worm] ■ **ver'minate** vi to breed vermin. **verminā'tion** n. **ver'mined** adj infested with vermin. **ver'minous** or **ver'miny** adj infested with vermin; like vermin. ❑ **ver'min-killer** n.

vermis /vûr'mis/ n (pl **vermes** /-mēz/) a worm or wormlike structure, eg (anat) the **vermis cerebelli**, the central lobe of the cerebellum; (in pl; with cap) in old classifications, a subkingdom of animals, according to Linnaeus including all invertebrates except arthropods, later mainly flatworms, thread-worms and annelids. [L, worm] ■ **ver'mal** or **ver'mian** adj.

vermivorous see under **vermi-**.

vermouth /vûr'məth or vər-mooth'/ n a drink with white wine base, flavoured with wormwood or other aromatic herbs. [Fr, from Ger *Wermut(h)* wormwood (OE *wermōd*)]

vernacuiar /vər-nak'ū-lər/ adj (of language) indigenous, native, spoken by the people of the country or of one's own country; of, in, or using the vernacular language; of the jargon or idiom of a particular group; (of other things) native, local, endemic, *esp* of architecture or general style of building. ◆ *n* a native language or dialect; a class jargon; profane language (*facetious*); a vernacular style of building. [L *vernāculus*, from *verna* a home-born slave]
■ **vernac'ularism** n a vernacular expression or idiom; the use of the vernacular. **vernac'ularist** n a user of the vernacular. **vernacularity** /-lar'i-ti/ n. **vernaculariză'tion** or **-s-** n. **vernac'ularize** or **-ise** vt to make vernacular. **vernac'ularly** adv.

vernal /vûr'nəl/ adj of, happening or appearing in spring; springlike; fresh and youthful (*poetic*). [L *vērnālis* vernal, *vērnāre*, *-ātum* to sprout, from *vēr* spring]
■ **vernality** /-nal'i-ti/ n springlike quality; freshness. **vernalīză'tion** or **-s-** n. **ver'nalize** or **-ise** vt to make springlike; to freshen; to hasten the development of (seeds or seedlings) by treating them in various ways before planting, eg by subjecting them to a low temperature. **ver'nally** adv. **ver'nant** adj (*Milton*) flowering or sprouting in spring. **vernā'tion** n the arrangement of leaves in the vegetative bud (rarely that of the individual leaf).
□ **vernal grass** n an early-sprouting meadow grass (*Anthoxanthum odoratum*) that gives its scent of coumarin to hay.

Verner's law see under **law**[1].

vernicle /vûr'ni-kl/ n a cloth bearing an impression of the face of Christ, believed to have been miraculously impressed on it when St *Veronica* wiped his face; any representation of this; a medal or badge bearing it, worn by pilgrims who had been at Rome. [OFr *veronicle*, from L *veronica* St Veronica's cloth]

vernier /vûr'ni-ər/ n a short scale sliding on a graduated scale to give fractional readings; a small auxiliary device that enables a piece of apparatus to be adjusted very accurately (eg a **vernier condenser** a condenser of small capacitance connected in parallel with one of larger capacitance); a small rocket engine used to make the movement of a booster rocket, or of a ballistic missile, more precisely as required. ◆ *adj* of, relating to, or having a vernier. [P *Vernier* (1580–1637), French mathematician, who invented the scale]

vernis martin /ver-nē mär-tē'/ n (also with *caps*) a varnish used on 18c furniture, etc, in imitation of oriental lacquer. [Fr *vernis* varnish, and *Martin* surname of the French brothers who were noted as producers of such items]

vernissage /ver-nē-säzh'/ n varnishing-day (qv under **varnish**). [Fr, varnishing]

Veronal® or **veronal** /ver'ə-nal or -əl/ n barbitone.

veronica /və-ron'i-kə/ n any of several herbs and shrubs of the speedwell genus *Veronica*; (Sp /vā-rō'nē-kä/) in bullfighting) a movement with the cape supposedly reminiscent of St Veronica's in offering her handkerchief to Christ; a vernicle. [St *Veronica*]

véronique /vā-ro-nēk'/ (Fr) adj (used after the noun) served with white grapes, eg *sole véronique*. [Origin uncertain]

verquere /vər-k(w)ēr'/ n an obsolete form of backgammon (also (*Walter Scott*) **verquire'**). [Du *verkeeren* to turn round, to play at backgammon]

verrel /ver'l/ n old (now *dialect*) form of **ferrule**.

verrey, verry /ver'i/ same as **vairé** (see under **vair**).

verrine /və-rēn'/ n an appetizer or dessert consisting of layers of different foods presented in a glass. [Fr *verrine*, from *verre* glass]

verruca /və-roo'kə/ n (pl **verru'cae** /-sē or -kī/ or **verru'cas**) a wart, *esp* on the sole of the foot; a wartlike outgrowth. [L *verrūca* a wart]
■ **verru'ciform** /-si-förm/ adj wartlike. **verrucose** /ver' or -roo'/ or **verru'cous** (or /ver'/) adj warty. **verru'ga** n a fever with warty tumours, endemic in Peru (also (*pl*) **verru'gas**).

vers /ver/ (Fr) n verse.
■ **verset** /vûr'sət/ n a short organ interlude or prelude (*music*); a versicle; a little scrap of verse.
□ **vers de société** /də so-syä-tā/ n light witty verse. **vers d'occasion** /dok-az-yō/ n occasional verse, produced for a particular event. **vers libre** /lē'br'/ n free verse, hence **verslibrist** /ver-lē'brist/ or (Fr) **verslibriste** /ver-lē'brēst/ a writer of free verse.

versability /vûr-sə-bil'i-ti/ (*obs*) n aptness to be turned round. [L *versābilis*, from *versāre* to turn over]

versal[1] /vûr'səl or vär'səl/ (*obs inf*) adj whole; single, individual. [For **universal**]

versal[2] /vûr'səl/ n an ornamental letter at the beginning of a section, eg in an illuminated manuscript. [**verse**, and *-al*, noun-forming suffix]

versant[1] /vûr'sənt/ n the general slope of a mountain, or the area over which this extends. [Fr *versant*, from *verser* to turn over, from L *versāre*]

versant[2] /vûr'sənt/ adj versed, conversant; busied, concerned. [L *versāns*, *-antis*, prp of *versāre* to turn over, consider]

versatile /vûr'sə-tīl or (US) -təl/ adj turning easily from one thing to another; of many-sided ability; capable of many uses; turning freely; dangling, hanging freely, as an anther attached by the middle of the back (*bot*); capable of free movement, reversible, as the toes of some birds (*zool*); changeable; unsteady. [L *versātilis*, from *versāre*, frequentative of *vertere* to turn]
■ **ver'satilely** adv. **ver'satileness** or **versatility** /-til'i-ti/ n.

verse[1] /vûrs/ n poetry as opposed to prose; a line of metre; a metrical composition, form, or work; versification; a stanza; a short division of a chapter, *esp* of the Bible; a portion of an anthem to be performed by a single voice to each part; a versicle. ◆ *vt and vi* to versify. [OE *fers*, reinforced by Fr *vers*, both from L *versus*, *vorsus*, *-ūs* a line, row, verse, from *vertere* to turn]
■ **verse'let** n a little verse; a short poem. **ver'ser** n a writer of verse. **ver'sicle** n a little verse; in liturgy, the verse said by the officiant. **versic'ūlar** adj of or in verse. **ver'sing** n the composing of verse.
□ **verse'-maker** n. **verse'-making** n. **verse'-man** n (*archaic*) a writer of verse. **verse'-monger** n a scribbler of verses. **verse'-mongering** n. **verse'-smith** n a writer of verse.
■ **free verse** see under **free**.

verse[2] see under **versed**[1].

versed[1] /vûrst/ adj thoroughly acquainted, skilled (with *in*). [L *versātus*, pap of *versārī* to busy oneself]
■ **verse** vt to make conversant (with *in*).

versed[2] /vûrst/ (*maths*) adj turned, reversed. [L *versus*, pap of *vertere* to turn]
□ **versed sine** n a trigonometrical function of an angle, one minus the cosine (short form **versin** or **versine**).

verselet, verser see under **verse**[1].

verset see under **vers**.

versicle, etc see under **verse**[1].

versicoloured /vûr'si-kul-ərd/ adj diversely or changeably coloured. [L *versicolor*, *-ōris*, from *vertere*, *versum* to change, and *color* colour]

versiform /vûr'si-förm/ adj varying in form. [L *versus* turned, and **-form**]

versify /vûr'si-fī/ vi (**ver'sifying**; **ver'sified**) to compose verse. ◆ *vt* to tell or express in verse; to turn into verse. [OFr *versifier*, from L *versificāre*, from *versus* verse, and *facere* to make]
■ **versifica'tion** n the art or process of composing in verse or turning something into verse; the manner of construction, metrical pattern, etc of verse. **ver'sificātor** or **ver'sifier** n a maker of verses.

versin /vûr'sin/ or **versine** /vûr'sīn/ (*maths*) n short for **versed sine** (see under **versed**[2]).

version /vûr'shən or -zhən/ n a particular form in which something is embodied, as a particular way of telling a story; a variant; a turning (of something), now *esp* (*med*) a manual turning of the fetus shortly before birth to a head-first position; translation; a Latin prose (*Scot*). ◆ *vt* to make a new version of. [L *versiō*, *-ōnis*, from *vertere*, *versum* to turn]
■ **ver'sional** adj. **ver'sioner** or **ver'sionist** n the producer of a version.

verslibrist(e) see **vers libre** under **vers**.

verso /vûr'sō/ n (pl **ver'sos**) the back of a leaf of printed or manuscript material; a left-hand page of an open book (*printing*, etc); the reverse of a coin or medal. [L *versō* (*foliō*) turned leaf (ablative)]

verst /vûrst/ n a Russian measure of length, *approx* 1.07km (0.66 miles). [Russ *versta*]

versus /vûr'səs/ (*law, games*) prep against (*abbrev* **v** and **vs**). [L]

versute /vər-sūt'/ adj crafty, wily. [L *versūtus*]

vert[1] /vûrt/ n in forest law, all greenery in a forest that may serve as cover for deer; the right or power to cut green trees or wood (*archaic*); a green colour, represented by parallel lines sloping diagonally from dexter chief to sinister base (*heraldry*). [Fr *vert*, from L *viridis* green]

vert[2] /vûrt/ n a familiar shortening of **convert** (*esp* to Roman Catholicism) or (*hist*) **pervert**. ◆ *vi* to become a vert.

vert[3] /vûrt/ n (in skateboarding and snowboarding) a *vert*ical extension to a ramp, from which stunts are performed.

vertebra /vûr'ti-brə/ n (pl **ver'tebrae** /-brē/) any of the segments that compose the backbone. [L, from *vertere* to turn]
■ **ver'tebral** adj relating to vertebrae (**vertebral column** the spinal column). **ver'tebrally** adv. **ver'tebrate** adj backboned; of, belonging or relating to the vertebrates; articulated; firm of character. ◆ *n* a backboned animal, one belonging to the subphylum **Vertebrā'ta**,

including fishes, amphibians, reptiles, birds and mammals. **ver'tebrated** adj having a backbone; articulated like a backbone. **vertebra'tion** n vertebral structure; division into vertebrae or vertebra-like segments; backbone (fig).

vertex /vûr'teks/ n (pl **ver'texes** or **ver'tices** /-ti-sēz/) the top or summit; the zenith (astron); the crown of the head (anat); the point opposite the base (geom); the meeting-point of the lines bounding an angle; the intersection of a curve with its axis. [L vertex, verticis summit]
  ■ **vertic'ity** /-tis'i-ti/ n the power of turning.

vertical /vûr'ti-kl/ adj perpendicular to the plane of the horizon; of or at the vertex; in the direction of the axis (bot); comprising the various successive stages in the production of the same goods; in strata one above the other; (of a mechanism) in which one part is above another; denoting a balance sheet in which the components are arranged in the form of a list, in a single column (account). ◆ n a vertical line or position. [Fr vertical, from L vertex, verticis summit, from vertere to turn]
  ■ **verticality** /-kal'i-ti/ n. **ver'tically** adv. **ver'ticalness** n.
  ◻ **vertical angles** n pl opposite angles formed by intersecting lines. **vertical circle** n a great circle of the heavens passing through the zenith and the nadir. **vertical grouping** n in primary schools, the teaching of groups of children of various ages together (also called **family grouping**). **vertical integration** n (econ) the merging (or takeover) of one company with (or by) another involved in a different stage of production of the same thing. **vertically challenged** adj (in politically correct language) denoting a person of less than average height. **vertical scanning** n (TV) scanning in which the lines are vertical, not, as normally, horizontal. **vertical take-off** n (aeronautics) immediate take-off without preliminary run. **vertical thinking** n thinking by logical deduction, as opposed to lateral thinking (qv).

verticil /vûr'ti-sil/ (bot) n a whorl. [L verticillus, dimin of vertex]
  ■ **verticillas'ter** n (bot) an inflorescence so condensed as to look like a whorl. **verticillate** /vər-tis'i-lət/ or **vertic'illated** adj whorled. **verticill'ium** n a fungus some species of which cause plant disease.

vertigo /vûr'ti-gō/ n (pl **vertigos**, **vertigoes** or **vertigines** /-tij'i-nēz/) dizziness, giddiness; a whirling sensation experienced when the sense of balance is disturbed. [L vertīgō, vertiginis, from vertere to turn]
  ■ **vertiginous** /-tij'/ adj relating to vertigo; dizzy; giddy; whirling; producing dizziness, dizzying. **vertig'inously** adv. **vertig'inousness** n.

vertiport /vûr'ti-pört/ n an airport designed for vertical take-off and landing. [**vertical** and **airport**]

Vertoscope® /vûr'tō-skōp/ n a device in which any photographic negative can be viewed immediately as a positive. [L vertere to turn, and **-scope**]

vertu¹ /vər-too'/ n a variant of **virtu**.

vertu² or **vertue** /vûr'tū/ n old forms of **virtue**.
  ■ **ver'tuous** adj (Spenser) possessing virtue or power.

Verulamian /ver-ū-lā'mi-ən or ver-ū-/ adj of or relating to St Albans, or Francis Bacon, Baron Verulam, Viscount St Albans (1561–1626). [L Verulāmium, an ancient British city near the site of St Albans]

verumontanum /ver-ū-mon-tā'nəm/ (anat) n (pl **verumontā'na** or **verumontā'nums**) a ridge on the male urethra where the duct conveying prostatic fluid, sperm and other fluids enters it. [L veru spit, and montanus hilly]

vervain /vûr'vān/ n a wild verbena, long believed to have great magical and medicinal powers. [OFr verveine, from L verbēna]

verve /vûrv/ n gusto, spirit, animation, energy; enthusiasm that animates a poet or artist (archaic). [Fr]

vervel /vûr'vl/ or **varvel** /vär'-/ n a ring for a hawk's jess. [Fr vervelle]
  ■ **ver'velled** or **var'velled** adj.

verven /vûr'vən/ (Spenser) n vervain.

vervet /vûr'vit/ n an African guenon monkey. [Fr]

very /ver'i/ adv in a high degree, extremely; (used for emphasis with the superlative form of an adjective or with own or same) absolutely, quite, truly, as in my very own room, the very best quality, the very same day. ◆ adj used for emphasis, eg with the force of 'absolute' (the very top), precise, 'actual' (this very minute, her very words), 'most suitable' (the very tool), 'mere' (the very thought); true (archaic); used, chiefly formerly, in compar **ver'ier**, and also (more often) in superl **ver'iest**, most truly so called, merest. [Older verray, veray, from Anglo-Fr ver(r)ai (Fr vrai), from a derivative of L vērus true; cf Ger wahr]
  ■ **ver'ily** adv (church, formal or archaic) truly; really.
  ■ **in very deed** of a truth, certainly. **not very** far from, not at all, the opposite of. **the very thing** precisely what is wanted or needed. **very good** or **very well** used in compliance or assent. **very high frequency** (radio) a frequency between 30 and 300 megahertz (abbrev **VHF**). **very large scale integration** see **VLSI**. **very low**

frequency (radio) a frequency between 3 and 30 kilohertz (abbrev **VLF**). **Very Reverend** see under **revere**.

Very light or **Verey light** /ver'i līt or vē'ri/ n a signalling or illuminating coloured flare fired from a pistol (**Very pistol**). [Invented by Edward W Very (1847–1910), US naval officer]

VESA abbrev : Video Electronics Standards Association.

Vesak or **Wesak** /ves'äk/ n a Buddhist festival held in May to commemorate the birth, enlightenment and death of the Buddha. [Sans, from the month of vaisakha]

vesica /ves'i-kə or vi-sī'/ (anat) n (pl **vesicae** /ves'i-sē or vi-sī'/) a bladder, sac, esp the urinary bladder. [L vēsica bladder, blister]
  ■ **vesical** /ves'i-kl/ adj of or relating to a vesica. **ves'icant** adj blistering. ◆ n anything that causes blisters. **ves'icate** vt and vi to blister. **vesica'tion** n. **ves'icatory** (or /-ik'/) n and adj vesicant. **ves'icle** n (med and zool) a small globule, bladder, sac, blister, cavity, or swelling; a primary cavity of the vertebrate brain; a more or less spherical cavity in igneous rock caused by expansion of gases. **vesic'ūla** n (pl **vesic'ūlae** /-lē/) a vesicle. **vesic'ūlar** adj. **vesic'ūlate** vi to become vesicular. **vesic'ūlate** /-lət/ or **vesic'ūlated** adj. **vesiculā'tion** n formation of vesicles. **vesic'ūlose** adj.
  ◻ **vesica piscis** /pis'is/ n (L, fish's bladder) a halo in the form of two circular arcs each (properly) passing through the other's centre, enclosing the whole figure.

Vespa® /ves'pə/ n a brand of Italian-made motor scooter.

vespa /ves'pə/ n a common wasp of the genus Vespa, giving name to the family **Ves'pidae** /-dē/. [L vespa wasp]
  ■ **ves'piary** n (modelled on apiary) a wasps' nest. **ves'pine** adj of wasps; wasp-like. **ves'poid** adj wasp-like.

vesper /ves'pər/ n evening (poetic); (usu in pl) one of the hours of the Divine Office, orig held at sunset, also known as evening prayer (RC); (usu in pl) evensong, evening service generally; a vesper-bell; (with cap) Venus as the evening star, Hesperus. [L vesper; cf Gr hesperos]
  ■ **ves'peral** adj. **vespertil'ionid** n and adj (a member) of the widespread family **Vespertilionidae** of insect-eating bats. **vesperti'nal** or **ves'pertine** adj of or relating to the evening; happening, opening, appearing, active, or setting, in the evening.
  ◻ **ves'per-bell** n the bell that summons to vespers.

vespiary, **vespine**, **vespoid** see under **vespa**.

vessel /ves'l/ n a utensil for holding something; a craft or structure (usu large) for transport by water; an airship; a conducting tube for body fluids in animals, for water in plants; a person regarded as a receptacle, recipient, or embodiment (Bible, etc); vessels collectively, plate (Walter Scott **vessail** or **vassail**). [OFr vessel (Fr vaisseau), from L vāscellum, dimin of vās, vāsis a vessel]
  ■ **the weaker vessel** a woman (Bible, 1 Peter 3.7).

vest /vest/ n an undergarment for the top half of the body, an undershirt; a waistcoat (chiefly N Am); an additional facing to the front of a bodice; garb, dress (obs); a garment (obs); a robe (obs); a vestment (obs). ◆ vt to invest; to settle, secure, or put in fixed right of possession (law); to endow (law); to clothe, robe, put vestments on (archaic); to drape (an altar). ◆ vi (of a right, etc) to descend, devolve, or take effect. [L vestis]
  ■ **vest'ed** adj clad, robed, wearing vestments; not contingent or suspended, hence (law) already acquired. **vest'ing** n the act or fact of clothing, investing, securing legally, etc; material for waistcoats.
  ◻ **vested interest** n a particular interest in the continuance of an existing system, institution, etc, for personal reasons, often financial; an entitlement or interest under a will or trust that is not contingent or defeasible (Scots law); (in pl) interests already established; (in pl) the class of persons who have acquired rights or powers in any sphere of a country's activities. **vest pocket** n a waistcoat-pocket. **vest'-pocket** adj small enough to go into one (also fig).

vesta /ves'tə/ n (pl **ves'tas**) a wax-stemmed match; a short match with a wooden stem. [L Vesta, the Roman goddess of the hearth and household]

vestal /ves'təl/ adj (often with cap) relating or consecrated to the Roman goddess Vesta; of or like the vestal virgins; virgin; chaste. ◆ n one of the Roman patrician virgins consecrated to Vesta; a woman dedicated to celibacy, a nun; a virgin; a woman of spotless chastity. [L vestālis, from Vesta]
  ◻ **vestal virgin** n (hist) in ancient Rome, one of the patrician virgins consecrated to Vesta, who kept the sacred fire burning on her altar.

vestiary /ves'ti-ə-ri or -tyə-ri/ n a vestry, robing room, or cloakroom. ◆ adj of or relating to clothes. [L vestiārium; see **vestry**]

vestibule /ves'ti-būl/ n an entrance hall; a cavity serving as entrance to another, esp that of the inner ear (anat); part of a railway carriage connecting with and giving access to the next (N Am); a forecourt (ancient hist). ◆ vt to provide with a vestibule. [L vestibulum]

■ **vestib'ular** *adj.* **vestibuli'tis** *n* (*med*) inflammation of the labyrinth and cochlea of the inner ear, causing vertigo, ataxia and deafness. **vestib'ūlum** *n* (*anat*) a vestibule.

vestige /ves'tij/ *n* a trace; a surviving trace of what has almost disappeared; a footprint (*rare*); a scrap, shred, the least bit; a reduced and functionless structure, organ, etc, representing what was once useful and developed (also **vestig'ium**; *pl* **vestig'ia**; *biol*). [Fr, from L *vestīgium* footprint]
■ **vestig'ial** *adj.*

vestiment /ves'ti-mənt/ (*obs*) *n* vestment, garb, garment. [L *vestīmentum*]
■ **vestimental** /-men'tl/ or **vestiment'ary** *adj.*

vestiture /ves'ti-chər/ (*rare*) *n* investiture; clothes; covering, such as hair, feathers, scales. [LL *vestītūra*, from L *vestis*]

vestment /vest'mənt/ *n* a ceremonial garment, *esp* one worn in religious ceremonies; an official or state robe; a garment as covering. [L *vestīmentum*, from *vestīre* to clothe, *vestis* a garment]
■ **vestment'al** *adj.* **vest'mented** *adj.*

vestry /ves'tri/ *n* a room in a church in which vestments are kept and parochial meetings held; a small room attached to a church; in Anglican and Episcopalian parishes, a meeting of church members or their elected representatives; the group who meet thus for parish business; a robing room; a cloakroom; apparel (*obs*). [Prob through OFr, from L *vestiārium*, from *vestis* a garment]
■ **ves'tral** *adj.*
❑ **ves'try-clerk** *n* an officer chosen by the vestry to keep the parish accounts and books. **ves'tryman** or **ves'trywoman** *n* a member of a vestry. **ves'try-room** *n* a vestry; the meeting-place of a vestry.
■ **common vestry** an assembly of all the ratepayers. **select vestry** a board of representatives of the ratepayers.

vesture /ves'chər/ *n* garb, clothing (*archaic*); a garment (*archaic*); vegetation covering the soil (*law*). ◆ *vt* (*archaic*) to cover or clothe. [OFr, from LL *vestītūra*, from *vestis* garment]
■ **vest'ural** *adj.* **vest'ured** *adj.* **vest'urer** *n* a keeper of vestments.

Vesuvian /vi-soo'vi-ən, -sū'/ or *-zoo'/ adj* of or like the volcano *Vesuvius* in S Italy. ◆ *n* (without *cap*) a smoker's slow-burning match (*archaic*); vesuvianite.
■ **vesu'vianite** *n* the mineral idocrase, silicate of aluminium and calcium, found in blocks ejected by Vesuvius.

vet¹ /vet/ *n* a veterinary surgeon. ◆ *vt* (**vett'ing**; **vett'ed**) to treat, or examine, medically (an animal, or *facetiously*, a person); to examine (eg a document or candidate) thoroughly and critically (and pass as sound or correct).

vet² see **veteran**.

vetch /vech/ *n* any of various climbing plants of the pea family, *usu* with blue or purple flowers, often used as fodder. [ONFr *veche* (Fr *vesce*), from L *vicia*]
■ **vetch'ling** *n* any plant of the sweet pea genus (*Lathyrus*). **vetch'y** *adj* covered with vetches.
■ **bitter vetch** various species of the *Vicia* and *Lathyrus* genera. **kidney vetch** see under **kidney**. **milk vetch** a plant of the *Astragalus* genus.

veteran /vet'(ə-)rən/ *n* a person who has seen long service in any activity; an experienced soldier; an ex-serviceman or -woman (often shortened to **vet**; *N Am*). ◆ *adj* old, experienced; experienced in military service. [L *veterānus*, from *vetus, veteris* old]
❑ **veteran car** *n* an early motor car, *specif* one made before 1905. **Veterans Day** *n* 11 November, observed in the USA to commemorate former members of the armed forces.

veterinary /vet'(ə-)ri-n(ə)-ri/ *adj* concerned with the treatment of diseases of animals. ◆ *n* a person trained in the treatment of diseases of domestic animals (also **veterinary surgeon** and (*N Am*) **veterinā'rian**). [L *veterīnārius*, from *veterīnae* cattle, beasts of burden]

vetiver /vet'i-vər/ *n* cuscus grass and root. [Fr *vétiver*, from Tamil *veltivēru*]

vetkoek /fet'kŭk/ (*S Afr*) *n* a deep-fried cake, *usu* unsweetened, but otherwise similar to a doughnut. [Afrik, from Du *vet* fat, and *koek* cake]

veto /vē'tō/ *n* (*pl* **vetoes** /vē'tōz/) any authoritative prohibition; the power of rejecting or forbidding; the right to reject or forbid a proposed measure, *esp* in a legislative assembly or the UN Security Council. ◆ *vt* to reject by a veto; to withhold assent to; to forbid. [L *vetō* I forbid]
■ **local veto** see under **local**.

Vet. Surg. *abbrev*: Veterinary Surgeon.

vettura /vet-too'rə/ *n* in Italy, a carriage, cab, or car. [Ital, from L *vectūra* a carrying, from *vehere* to convey]
■ **vetturino** /-rē'nō/ *n* (*pl* **vetturi'ni** /-nē/) its driver or proprietor.

vex /veks/ *vt* to harass; to distress; to annoy; to trouble, agitate, annoy; to discuss to excess. ◆ *vi* (now *rare*) to grieve, fret. ◆ *n* (*Scot*) a grief. [Fr *vexer*, from L *vexāre* to shake, annoy]
■ **vexā'tion** *n* a vexing; the state or feeling of being vexed; a source of grief or annoyance. **vexā'tious** *adj* vexing; troublesome; (of a law action) brought on insufficient grounds, with the intention merely of annoying the defendant. **vexā'tiously** *adv.* **vexā'tiousness** *n.* **vex'atory** *adj.* **vexed** or (*obs*) **vext** /vekst/ *adj.* **vex'edly** *adv.* **vex'edness** *n.* **vex'er** *n.* **vex'ing** *n* and *adj.* **vex'ingly** *adv.* **vex'ingness** *n.*
❑ **vexed question** *n* a matter greatly debated.

vexata quaestio /vek-sä'tə kwēs'ti-ō or wek-sä'ta kwīs'ti-ō/ (L) *n* a disputed question.

vexillum /vek-sil'əm/ *n* (*pl* **vexill'a**) the series of barbs on the sides of the shaft of a feather (*zool*); a standard (*bot*); a Roman standard; a vexillation; a scarf on a pastoral staff. [L *vehere* to carry]
■ **vex'illary** *n* a standard-bearer; one of a company of Roman veterans serving under a special standard. ◆ *adj* of, relating to or under a vexillum. **vexillā'tion** *n* a company under one vexillum. **vexillol'ogist** *n.* **vexillol'ogy** *n* the study of flags.

vezir see **vizier**.

VF *abbrev* : video frequency; voice frequency.

VFM *abbrev* : value for money.

VG *abbrev* : Vicar-General.

vg *abbrev* : very good.

VGA *abbrev* : video graphics array, a computer monitor screen display system.

VHF *abbrev* : very high frequency.

VHS *abbrev* : video home system, a video cassette system for use in domestic video recorders.

VI *abbrev* : Vancouver Island; Vehicle Inspectorate; Virgin Islands.

vi *abbrev* : verb intransitive.

via¹ or **viâ** /vī'ə, vē'ə or wē'ä/ *prep* by way of; through. [L *viā*, ablative of *via* way]

via² /vī'ə, vē'ə or wē'a/ (L) *n* a way, road.
❑ **via crucis** /kroo'sis or -kis/ *n* the way of the Cross, the succession of stations of the Cross (see under **station**). **via dolorosa** /dol-ə-rō'sə or do-lō-rō'sa/ *n* the way to Calvary (literally, mournful way); an upsetting or daunting course of action. **via ferrata** /fe-rä'tə/ *n* a route onto a mountain, prepared with permanent ladders, bridges, etc. [Ital, iron way]. **Via Lactea** /lak'ti-ə or -te-a/ *n* the Milky Way. **via media** /mē'di-ə or me'di-a/ *n* a middle course. **via trita, via tuta** /trī'tə or trē'ta, tūt'ə or too'ta/ *n* a beaten path is a safe path.

via³ /vē'ə/ (*obs*) *interj* expressing incitement or dismissal. [Ital, from L *via* way]

viable /vī'ə-bl/ *adj* capable of living, surviving, germinating, or hatching; (of a plan or project) of such a kind that it has a prospect of success; practicable. [Fr, from *vie*, from L *vīta* life]
■ **viabil'ity** *n.*

viaduct /vī'ə-dukt/ *n* a structure carrying a road or railway over a valley, etc. [Modelled on **aqueduct**, from L *via* a way]

Viagra® /vī-ag'rə/ *n* a proprietary name for sildenafil citrate, a drug used in treating impotence.

vial /vī'əl/ *n* same as **phial**; a spirit-level.
■ **vī'alful** *n.* **vī'alled** *adj* put or contained in a vial.
■ **pour out vials of wrath** to inflict judgement (Bible, Revelation 16.1); to storm, rage.

vialone nano /vē-ə-lō'nä nan'ō/ *n* a type of rice with small round grains, used in making risotto. [Ital]

viameter /vī-am'i-tər/ (*archaic*) *n* a hodometer; a cyclometer. [L *via* road, and **-meter**]

viand /vī'ənd/ *n* (*formal*) an article of food; (*usu* in *pl*) food. [Fr *viande*, from L *vīvenda* food necessary for life, from *vīvere* to live]

viaticum /vī-at'ik-əm or wē-ä'ti-kŭm/ *n* (*pl* **viat'icums** or **viat'ica**) money, provisions, etc, for a journey; the Eucharist given to people in danger of dying (*RC church*). [L *viāticum*, from *via* way]
■ **viat'icals** *n pl* baggage.

viator /vī-ā'tər or wē-ä'tör/ *n* traveller, wayfarer. [L *viātor, -ōris*, from *via* a way]
■ **viatorial** /vī-ə-tö'ri-əl or -tö'/ *adj.*

vibes /vībz/ (*inf*) *n pl* feelings, sensations, etc experienced or communicated (also *n sing* **vibe**; shortening of **vibrations**). ◆ *n sing* or *n pl* informal shortening of **vibraphone**.
■ **vī'bist** *n* (*inf*) a person who plays the vibraphone.

vibex /vī'beks/ (*med*) *n* (*pl* **vibices** /vī- or vi-bī'sēz/) a streak under the skin due to the leakage of blood. [L *vībex, vībīcis* a weal]

vibra- variant of **vibro-**.

vibraculum /vī-brak'ū-ləm/ n (pl **vibrac'ula**) a long bristle, a modified zooid, in some Polyzoa (also **vibraculā'rium** (pl **vibraculā'ria**)). [Coined from L *vibrāre* to shake]

vibraharp see **vibraphone**.

Vibram® /ve'brəm or vī'/ n tough heavily-patterned rubber used, without nails, for the soles of climbing and walking boots. [*Vitale Bram*ani, its Italian inventor]
- **vibs** /vibz/ n pl (*inf*) shoes with Vibram soles.

vibrant /vī'brənt/ adj vibrating; thrilling; resonant; (of colours) very bright. [L *vibrans, -antis*, prp of *vibrāre* to vibrate]
- **vibrancy** /vī'brən-si/ n. **vī'brantly** adv.

vibraphone /vī'brə-fōn/ n an instrument having metal bars under which are electrically-operated resonators, played by striking the bars with small hammers (also called (*US*) **vī'braharp**). [L *vibrāre* to shake, and Gr *phōnē* voice]
- **vī'braphōnist** n.

vibrate /vī'brāt or -brāt'/ vi to shake, to tremble; to oscillate; to swing; to change to and fro, *esp* rapidly; to resound, ring; to tingle, thrill. ◆ vt to cause to vibrate; to give off (sound, light, etc) in vibrations; to measure by single vibrations; to brandish (*obs*). [L *vibrāre, -ātum* to tremble]
- **vī'bratile** /-brə-tīl/ or (*N Am*) -til or -təl/ adj vibratory; having or capable of vibratory motion. **vibratility** /-til'i-ti/ n. **vibrā'tion** n a vibrating; the state of being vibrated; tremulousness; quivering motion; a whole period or movement to and fro of anything vibrating; sometimes a half period or movement one way; (in *pl*, often **vibes**) feelings communicated from person to person (*inf*); (in *pl*, often **vibes**) feelings aroused in one by a person, place, etc (*inf*). **vibrā'tional** adj. **vibrā'tionless** adj. **vibratiuncle** /vī-brə-shi-ung'kl/ n a small vibration. **vī'brative** /-brə-tiv/ adj vibrating; consisting in vibrations; causing vibrations. **vi'brātor** n that which vibrates; a vibrating part in many appliances; a vibrating tool; a type of dildo that can be made to vibrate. **vibratory** /vī'brə-tər-i/ adj of, of the nature of, causing, or capable of, vibration.
- **vibrational energy** n (*chem*) energy due to the relative oscillation of two contiguous atoms in a molecule. **vibration white finger** see **white finger** under **white**.

vibrato /ve-brä'tō or vi-/ (*music*) n (pl **vibra'tos**) a throbbing effect, without perceptible change of pitch, in singing and in stringed and wind instrument playing, obtained by varying breath pressure or by the shaking movement of the finger on a string. [Ital]

vibrio /vib'ri-ō or vī'bri-o/ n (pl **vib'rios**) a bacterium of the genus *Vibrio*, with a slight spiral curve and *usu* one flagellum, eg that of cholera. [New L, from L *vibrāre* to shake]
- **vibriō'sis** n infection with these bacteria.

vibrissa /vī-bris'ə/ n (pl **vibriss'ae** /-ē/) a tactile bristle, such as a cat's whisker; a vaneless rictal feather; a bristle, hair, as in the nostril. [L, a hair in the nostril]

vibro- /vī-brō- or -bro-/ combining form denoting vibration. [L *vibrāre, -ātum* to tremble, shake]
- **vī'broflotation** n a process for compacting sand. **vī'brograph** or **vibrom'eter** n an instrument for recording vibrations.

vibronic /vī-bron'ik/ (*phys*) adj of, relating to, caused by, etc, electronic vibration. [*vibration*, and *electronic*]

vibs see under **Vibram**®.

viburnum /vī-bûr'nəm/ n any plant of the guelder-rose and wayfaring-tree genus (*Viburnum*) of Caprifoliaceae. [L *vīburnum* the wayfaring tree]

Vic. abbrev : Vicar; Vicarage; Victoria (Australian state).

vicar /vik'ər/ n a parson of a parish (who formerly received only the smaller tithes or a salary) (*C of E*); a bishop's deputy (*RC*); a person who holds authority as the delegate or substitute of another, *esp* in the performance of a religious function; a deputy or substitute. [OFr *vicaire*, from L *vicārius* substitute; see **vicarious** and **vice**³]
- **vic'arage** n the residence or benefice of a vicar. **vic'arate** n vicariate. **vic'aress** n an abbess's deputy; a vicar's wife (*obs*). **vicarial** /vī- or vi-kā'ri-əl/ adj delegated; of a vicar or vicars. **vicā'riate** adj delegated. ◆ n the office, authority, time of office, or sphere of a vicar, in any sense. **vic'arship** n the (time of) office of a vicar. **vic'ary** n (*obs*) a vicarship.
- **vicar-apostol'ic** n formerly, one to whom the Pope delegated some remote portion of his jurisdiction; (now *usu*) a titular bishop appointed to a country where there are no sees; a titular bishop exercising authority in a vacant see or during the bishop's incapacity. **vicar-cho'ral** n a cleric or layman appointed to sing in an English cathedral choir. **vic'ar-forane** /for-ān'/ n (a variant of **foreign**) a rural dean. **vicar-gen'eral** n an official performing the work of an archdeacon under the bishop (*RC*); a lay official representing the bishop, the chancellor of the diocese. **Vicar of Bray** n a person who changes allegiance to suit the times (from Simon Aleyn, vicar of *Bray*,

Berkshire, from 1540 to 1588). **Vicar** or (*obs*) **vicar-general of Christ** n (*RC*) the Pope, as representative of Christ on earth.

vicarious /vi-kā'ri-əs/ adj (loosely) not experienced personally but imagined through the experience of others; exercised, performed or suffered by one person or thing instead of another; filling the place of another. [L *vicarius*, from *vicis* a recurring turn, a role or function]
- **vicā'riously** adv. **vicā'riousness** n.
- **vicarious sacrifice** n the suffering and death of Christ held by orthodox Christians to be accepted by God in lieu of the punishment to which sinful humankind is liable.

vice¹ or (*N Am*) **vise** /vīs/ n a tool with movable jaws for gripping an object that is being worked on; a grip (*Shakesp*); a screw (*obs*); a winding stair or its newel (*obs*). ◆ vt to grip, force, jam or strain as with a vice. [OFr (and Fr) *vis* screw, from L *vītis* a vine]
- **vice'like** adj.

vice² /vīs/ n a blemish or fault; immorality, depravity; an immoral habit; a bad trick or habit, eg in a horse; (with *cap*) the personification of a vice in a morality play, *usu* a farcical part (*hist*); hence, a buffoon (*hist*). [OFr, from L *vitium* defect]
- **vice'less** adj.
- **vice ring** n a number of criminals acting together in running prostitution, etc. **vice squad** n a police squad whose task is to see that the laws dealing with gambling, prostitution, etc, are observed.

vice³ /vī'si, vī'sē or vīs/ prep in place of; in succession to. ◆ n /vīs/ place, stead (*rare*); short for **vice-president**, **vice-chancellor**, etc below (*inf*). ◆ combining form /vīs-/ in place of. [L ablative, in the turn or place, from *vicis* a turn]
- **vice-ad'miral** n a navy officer ranking next under an admiral. **vice-ad'miralty** n the office or jurisdiction of a vice-admiral. **vice-chair'** n a vice-chairman or vice-chairwoman. **vice-chair'man** or **vice-chair'woman** n a deputy chairman. **vice-chair'manship** n. **vice-cham'berlain** n the Lord Chamberlain's deputy and assistant. **vice-chan'cellor** n a person acting for a chancellor; (in certain British universities) the head of administration, the chancellor being titular head only. **vice-chan'cellorship** n. **vice-con'sul** n a consul's deputy; an official who acts as consul in a less important district. **vice-con'sulate** n. **vice-con'sulship** n. **vice-count'y** n part of a county divided for the purposes of recording plant species found in it. **vice'-dean** n a canon chosen to represent an absent dean. **vicegerency** /-jer' or -jēr'ən-si/ n. **vicegerent** /-jer' or -jēr'/ adj (L *vicem gerēns, -entis* wielding office) acting in place of another, having delegated authority. ◆ n a person ruling or acting in place of a superior. **vice-gov'ernor** n deputy governor. **vice'-king** n a person who acts in place of a king. **vice-mar'shal** n same as **air vice-marshal**. **vice-pres'idency** n. **vice-pres'ident** n a president's deputy or assistant; an officer next below the president (*abbrev* VP). **vice-presiden'tial** adj. **vice-princ'ipal** n assistant principal. **vice'-queen** n a female viceroy; a viceroy's wife, vicereine. **vice-re'gal** adj of a viceroy; of a governor-general (*Aust, NZ*). **vicere'gent** n properly, a substitute for a regent; often used mistakenly for vicegerent. **vicereine** /vīs-ren' or -rān'/ n a viceroy's wife; a female viceroy (*rare*). **vice'roy** n a governor acting in the name of the sovereign. **viceroy'alty** or **vice'royship** n.

vice anglais /vēs ã-gle'/ n the English vice, most often applied to flagellation or corporal punishment, but also to eg sodomy. [Fr]

vicenary /vis'i-nə-ri/ adj based on the number twenty. [L *vīcēnārius*, from *vīcēnī* twenty each, from *vīgintī* twenty]

vicennial /vī-sen'yəl/ adj lasting, or coming at the end of, twenty years; occurring every twenty years. [L *vīcennium*, from *vīciēs* twenty times, and *annus* a year]

vicesimal, etc see **vigesimal**.

vice versa /vī'si, vī'sē or vīs vûr'sə/ adv the other way round. [L, the position having been turned, from *vicis* position, and *verto, versum* to turn, change]

Vichyite /ve'shē-īt or vish'i-īt/ n an adherent of the French Government (1940–42) ruling the unoccupied part of France from *Vichy*, and collaborating with the Germans (also *adj*). [*Vichy*, town in central France]
- **vichyssois** /vē-shē-swä'/ or (*fem*) **vichyssoise** /-swäz'/ adj of the Vichyite government. **vichyssoise'** n a cream soup *usu* served chilled, with ingredients such as potatoes and leeks.
- **Vichy** (or **vichy**) **water** /vē'shē/ n mineral water from Vichy springs, containing sodium bicarbonate, etc, or a natural or artificial water resembling it (also **vichy**).

viciate see **vitiate**.

vicinage /vis'i-nij/ n a neighbourhood; the residents in such. [L *vīcīnus* neighbour, from *vīcus* street, village, district]
- **vic'inal** (or /-īn'əl/) adj neighbouring; local; denoting or relating to positions on adjacent carbon atoms in a molecule (*organic chem*); of crystal faces, very nearly in the plane of a normal face. **vicin'ity** n neighbourhood; nearness.

viciosity see **vitiosity** under **vitiate**.

vicious /vish'əs/ adj malignant, spiteful, cruel; bad-tempered; addicted to vice or bad habits; immoral, depraved; bad; faulty; (also **vit'ious**) impaired, nullified by a flaw, unlawful (law); mistaken (Shakesp); foul, impure, morbid (obs med, etc). [OFr vicieus, from L vitiōsus faulty, vicious]
■ **vic'iously** adv. **vic'iousness** n.
❑ **vicious circle** n reasoning in a circle, seeking to prove a proposition by means of a conclusion drawn from it; a process in which an evil is aggravated by its own consequences. **vicious intromission** see under **intromit**.

vicissitude /vi-sis'i-tūd/ n change; alternation; mutation; change of fortune (inf, for the worse). [L vicissitūdō, -tūdinis; see **vice**[3]]
■ **vicissitū'dinous** adj.

vicomte /vē-kõt'/ (Fr) n in France, a noble equal in rank to a viscount.
■ **vicomtesse** /-es/ n a noblewoman of this rank; the wife or widow of a vicomte.

victim /vik'tim/ n a living being offered as a sacrifice; a living being subjected to death, suffering, or ill-treatment; a prey; a sufferer. [L victima a beast for sacrifice]
■ **vic'timhood** n. **victimīzā'tion** or **-s-** n. **vic'timize** or **-ise** vt to make a victim of; to single out for oppressive treatment; to cheat. **vic'timizer** or **-s-** n. **vic'timless** adj (of crimes) involving no injured party, such as loitering, drunkenness, etc. **victimol'ogist** n. **victimol'ogy** n the behavioural study of victims of crime, to discover the psychological effects on them, and their role in its commission.

Victor or **victor** /vik'tər/ n (in international radio communication) a code word for the letter v.

victor /vik'tər/ n a winner or winning side in a contest of any kind. ◆ adj (archaic) victorious. [L victor, -ōris, from vincere, victum to conquer]
■ **vic'toress** (obs), **vic'tress** or **vic'trix** n a female victor. **victo'rious** /-tō' or -tö'/ adj having gained a victory; winning in a contest; of, with or marking victory. **victo'riously** adv. **victo'riousness** n. **victory** /vik'tər-i/ n a contest won; success against an opponent; (with cap) (a statue of) the Roman goddess Victoria or the Greek goddess Nike. **vic'toryless** adj.
❑ **victory roll** n an aerobatic manoeuvre performed by the pilot of a fighter aircraft returning from combat to celebrate or announce success, esp the shooting down of an enemy plane. **victory ship** n a successor to the liberty ship.

victoria /vik-tō'ri-ə or -tö'/ n a gigantic water lily of the Brazilian genus Victoria; a low, light, four-wheeled carriage with a folding hood; (also with cap) a large red and yellow oval plum (also **victoria plum**). [Victoria, queen of the United Kingdom (reigned 1837–1901)]
■ **Victo'rian** adj of, contemporary with or typical of the reign of Queen Victoria; strict but somewhat conventional in morals, with connotations of prudery, solemnity and sometimes hypocrisy; of or relating to the state (colony 1851–1901) of Victoria in Australia. ◆ n a contemporary of Queen Victoria; a person of Victorian morality or outlook; a native or inhabitant of Victoria. **Victoriana** /vik-tō-ri-ä'nə, -tö- or -ä'nə/ n pl (also without cap) bric-à-brac and other characteristic possessions or creations of the Victorian age. **Victo'rianism** n.
❑ **Victoria Cross** n the highest British military decoration awarded for outstanding bravery in battle, founded by Queen Victoria in 1856 and awarded in the form of a bronze Maltese cross. **Victoria Day** n Empire Day, a day on or near Queen Victoria's birthday (24 May), observed as a holiday in Canada.

victor ludorum /vik'tər loo-dö'rəm or vik'tör loo-dō'rŭm/ (L) n in school sports, etc, the most outstanding athlete.

victress, victrix see under **victor**.

Victrolla® /vik-trō'lə/ n an early variety of gramophone. [From the company producing it, Victor Talking Machine Co]

victual /vit'l/ n (usu in pl) food, esp food for humans; (in sing) grain crops, cut or ready for cutting (Scot). ◆ vt (**victualling** /vit'l-ing/; **victualled** /vit'ld/) to supply or store with provisions. ◆ vi to lay in victuals; (esp of animals) to feed. [OFr vitaille, from LL victuālia, from L victuālis, from victus food, from vivere, victum to live]
■ **vict'uallage** n provisions. **victualler** /vit'l-ər/ n a purveyor of provisions; a victualling-ship. **vict'ualless** adj.
❑ **vict'ualling-bill** n a customs document warranting the captain of an outward-bound vessel to ship bonded stores for the voyage. **vict'ualling-off'ice** or **vict'ualling-ship** n an office supplying, or a ship conveying, provisions to the navy. **vict'ualling-yard'** n a public establishment for the collection and supply of provisions to the navy.
■ **licensed victualler** see under **licence**.

vicuña /vi-koo'nyə/ n a wild species of the Vicugna genus, closely related to llamas, native to high grassland in the Andes Mountains of S America; (cloth made of) its fine soft wool, or an imitation. [Sp, from Quechua]

vid /vid/ (inf) n a video recording. [Short form of **video**]

vidame /vē-däm'/ n in French feudal jurisprudence, the deputy of a bishop in temporal affairs; a minor noble. [Fr, from LL vicedominus]

vide /vī'dē, vē' or wi'dā/ (L) see, consult, refer to.
■ **vide infra** /in'frə or ēn'frä/ see below. **vide supra** /sū'prə or sū'prä/ see above.

videlicet /vi-del'i-sit, vi- or wi-dā'li-ket/ (L) to wit, namely (abbrev **viz**).

videndum /vī-den'dəm, vi- or wi-den'dŭm/ (pl **videnda** /-də or -da/; L) thing(s) to be seen.

video /vid'i-ō/ n (pl **vid'eos**) a videocassette or videocassette recorder; video recording; television as a medium (US inf); the visual aspect or elements of TV, etc (cf **audio**). ◆ adj relating to the bandwidth and spectrum position of the signal arising from TV scanning, or to the signal, or to the resultant image, or to television; using, used for, relating to, etc, the system of video recording. ◆ vt and vi (**vid'eoing**; **vid'eoed**) to make a video recording (of). [Modelled on **audio**, from L vidēre to see]
■ **vid'eogram** n a commercial video film; a prerecorded video cassette or videodisc.
❑ **video camera** n a camera that records its (moving) film onto videotape. **video card** same as **graphics card** under **graph**. **video cassette** n a cassette containing videotape. **video cassette recorder** n a video recorder in which videocassettes are used. **videocon'ference** n. **videocon'ferencing** n live discussion between people in different places using electronically linked telephones and video screens. **video diary** n a video record of day-to-day events, esp one made by an individual with a camcorder. **vid'eodisc** (or **vid'eodisk**) n a compact disc on which visual images and sound are prerecorded for playing back on a CD player linked to hi-fi and TV. **vid'eofit** n a type of identikit picture put together on television. **video frequency** n a frequency in the range required for a video signal. **video game** n an electronically-operated game played on a visual display unit. **video grab** n a still picture created from a frame in a video recording. **video jockey** n a broadcaster who introduces and plays music videos. **video nasty** n a pornographic or horror video film. **video-on-demand'** n a system of access to video films by means of a cable link (abbrev **VOD**). **vid'eophone** or **videotel'ephone** n a telephone with accompanying means of transmitting a picture of each speaker. **video recorder** n a machine for recording and playing back television broadcasts or films made on videotape, using videotape or videodiscs. **vid'eosender** or **video sender** n a small TV transmitter that can be plugged into the back of a video recorder or satellite receiver and used to broadcast the signal received there to other TV sets in the same premises rather than connecting these by cable. **video signal** n that part of a TV signal which conveys all the information required for establishing the visual image. **vid'eotape** n magnetic tape for recording visual images (as well as sound), esp television programmes or film for later transmission. ◆ vt to record on videotape. **videotape recorder** n a tape recorder that records visual images on magnetic tape. **vid'eotex** or **vid'eotext** n a system used to display pages of information on a television screen, eg teletext or viewdata. **video tube** n a television tube. **video wall** n a bank of VDU screens used for display purposes, showing a series of different pictures, the same picture repeated, or a composite picture.

vidette a variant of **vedette**.

Vidicon® /vid'i-kon/ n a small television camera tube operating on the photoconducting principle. [Video icon(oscope)]

vidimus /vī'di-məs, vē' or wē'di-mŭs/ n an attested copy; an inspection, eg of accounts. [L vīdimus we have seen, from vidēre to see]

viduous /vid'ū-əs/ adj widowed; empty. [L vidua a widow, viduus deprived, bereaved]
■ **vid'uage** n widowhood; widows collectively. **vid'ual** adj. **vidū'ity** n widowhood.

vie /vī/ vi (**vy'ing**; **vied** /vīd/) to contend in rivalry; to make a vie (obs). ◆ vt (obs) to stake; to declare, bid (cards); to put forward in competition or emulation, or (Shakesp) repeatedly. ◆ n (obs) a bid, challenge, stake. [Fr envier, from L invītāre to challenge, invite]
■ **vī'er** n. **vy'ingly** adv.

vielle /vē-el'/ n a hurdy-gurdy, a stringed instrument played by a wheel; a medieval stringed and bowed instrument resembling a viol. [Fr]

Viennese /vē-e-nēz'/ adj of Vienna, the capital of Austria. ◆ n sing and n pl an inhabitant or the inhabitants of Vienna.
❑ **vienna** (or **Vienna**) **loaf** n a long, round-ended loaf of white bread. **vienna steak** n a meat rissole.

vi et armis /vī et är'mis, vē or wē et är'mēs/ (L) forcibly. [Literally, by force and arms]

Viet Cong or **Vietcong** /vē-et-kong'/ n a member of the South Vietnamese Communist guerrilla army in the Vietnam war (also adj). [Viet Viet Nam Cong San Vietnamese Communist]

■ words derived from main entry word; ❑ compound words; ■ idioms and phrasal verbs

Vietnam /vē-et-nam'/ n a war or conflict which sucks in to an ever-increasing extent, and then exhausts, the resources of an apparently overwhelmingly superior participant. [From the experience of the USA in the Vietnam war of the 1960s and 1970s]

Vietnamese /vē-et-nə-mēz'/ n (pl **Vietnamese**') a native or inhabitant, or the language, of Vietnam in SE Asia. ◆ adj of or relating to Vietnam, its people, or their language.

vieux jeu /vyoo zhoo' or (Fr) vyø zhø'/ adj old-fashioned; old hat. [Fr, literally, old game or joke]

view /vū/ n an act, possibility or opportunity of looking; range or field of sight; whole extent seen; a prospect, wide or distant extent seen; that which is seen; an inspection; appearance; an aspect or scene; the picture of a scene; general survey of a subject; mode of thinking of something; opinion; intention, purpose; expectation; (with cap) used in street names, etc. ◆ vt to see; to look at; to look at on television; to inspect (a house) as a prospective purchaser; to observe; to consider; to examine intellectually. ◆ vi to watch television. [Fr vue, from vu, pap of voir, from L vidēre to see]
■ **view'able** adj able to be seen; sufficiently interesting to be looked at or watched. **view'er** n a person who views; a television watcher; an apparatus used to project film for purposes of editing and cutting; a device with magnifying lens, etc, for viewing transparencies; an inspector, a person appointed to examine and report; a colliery superintendent. **view'ership** n the estimated number of viewers of a television programme. **view'iness** n the condition or quality of being viewy. **view'ing** n. **view'less** adj (poetic) invisible. **view'lessly** adv. **view'ly** adj (dialect) pleasing to look at. **view'y** adj showy; having views that are considered odd or fanciful by most.
❑ **view'data** n a communications system by which information can be received and requested via a telephone line and presented through a television or video display unit. **view'finder** n a camera attachment or part for determining the field of view. **view'-halloo'** n the huntsman's cry when the fox breaks cover (also interj). **view'phone** n another name for **videophone** (see under **video**). **view'point** n point of view; standpoint; a selected position for admiring scenery.
■ **dissolving views** pictures thrown on a screen and made to pass one into another. **in view** in sight; in mind; as an aim or prospect. **in view of** in a position to see or to be seen by; having regard to. **on view** open to general inspection. **take a dim view of** to regard unfavourably. **view away** to see (a hunted animal) breaking cover. **with a view to** having in mind; with the aim of.

vifda see **vivda**.

vig /vig/ n a short form of **vigorish**.

vigesimal /vī-jes'i-məl/ or **vicesimal** /vī-ses'i-məl/ adj based on the number twenty. [L vigēsimus (or vīcēsimus) twentieth, from vīgintī twenty]
■ **viges'imo-** (or **vices'imo-)quar'to** adj (printing) twenty-four-mo.

vigia /vi-jē'ə or vi-hhē'ä/ n a danger warning on a chart. [Sp vigía lookout, from L vigilia]

vigil /vij'il/ n watching, esp by night, usu on guard or in prayer; the eve of a holy day; a religious service by night; a keeping awake, wakefulness. [L vigilia, from vigil awake, watchful; cf vigēre to be lively]
■ **vig'ilance** n watchfulness; wakefulness; a guard, watch (Milton); a planned effort to uncover and punish corruption and bribery (Ind). **vig'ilant** adj watchful. **vigilante** /-an'ti/ n (orig US, from Sp) a member of an organization formed to look after the interests, threatened in some way, of a group, esp a self-appointed and unofficial policeman; a member of a vigilance committee. **vigilan'tism** n behaviour associated with vigilantes, esp militarism and bellicosity. **vig'ilantly** adv.
❑ **vigilance committee** n (US) an unauthorized body which, in the absence or inefficiency of regular government, exercises powers of arrest, punishment, etc; any self-appointed association for the compulsory improvement of local morals according to its own standards.

vigneron /vē-nyə-rō'/ n a vine-grower. [Fr]

vignette /vē-nyet'/ n a character sketch, a word picture; a small embellishment without a border, esp on a title-page or as a headpiece or tailpiece; a photographic portrait shading off around the head; the illustration on a banknote; orig a design of vine-leaves and tendrils. ◆ vt to make a vignette of. [Fr, from vigne, from L vīnea a vine, a vineyard]
■ **vignett'er** or **vignett'ist** n.

vigorish /vig'ə-rish/ (US sl) n a percentage of a gambler's winnings taken by the bookmaker, organizers of a game, etc; excessive interest charged on a loan. [Prob Yiddish, from Russ vȳigrȳsh profit, winnings]

vigoro /vig'ə-rō/ (Aust) n a 12-a-side game (played by women) having similarities to cricket and baseball. [Poss from **vigour**]

vigour or (N Am) **vigor** /vig'ər/ n active strength; vital power; healthy growth (in plants, etc); forcefulness; activity; energy; legal validity (now esp US law). [Anglo-Fr vigour (Fr vigueur), and L vigor, -ōris, from vigēre to be strong]
■ **vig'orous** adj. **vig'orously** adv. **vig'orousness** n.

vihara /vē-hä'rə/ n a Buddhist or Jain precinct, temple, or monastery. [Sans vihāra]

vihuela /vi-wä'lə/ n an old Spanish musical instrument, related to the guitar. [Sp]

viking /vī'king/ (also with cap) n any of the Scandinavian adventurers who raided, traded with, and settled in, many parts of Europe between the eighth and eleventh centuries; any aggressive sea-raider, a pirate. ◆ adj of or relating to vikings. [ON vīkingr, prob from OE wīcing pirate]
■ **vī'kingism** n.

vil. or **vill.** abbrev : village.

vilayet /vi-lä'yet/ (hist) n a province of the Ottoman empire. [Turk vilāyet, from Ar welāyeh]

vild or **vilde** /vīld/ adj an old variant (Spenser, Shakesp) of **vile**.
■ **vild'ly** adv. **vild'ness** n.

vile /vīl/ adj detestable, loathsome; foul; depraved; very bad; base; worthless, mean, paltry. ◆ adv (archaic) vilely. [OFr vil and L vīlis worthless]
■ **vile'ly** adv. **vile'ness** n. **vilifica'tion** /vil-/ n the act of vilifying; defamatory speech; abuse. **vilifier** /vil'/ n. **vilify** /vil'/ vt to make vile; to disparage; to defame. **vilipend** /vil'/ vt (L vīlipendere, from pendere to weigh) to despise, make light of; to disparage; to slander, vilify. ◆ vi to use vilification.

viliaco or **villiaco** /vil-yä'kō/, also **viliago** or (Shakesp) **villiago** /-gō/ (obs) n (pl **-oes** or **-os**) a coward (also (Walter Scott, prob erroneous) **villagio**). [Ital vigliacco, from L vīlis worthless]

vilification, etc see under **vile**.

vill /vil/ n a township, or feudal territorial unit (hist); a manor (hist); a village (poetic). [OFr ville farm, village (Fr, town), from L villa (see **villa**)]
■ **vill'ar** adj of a vill.

vill. see **vil**.

villa /vil'ə/ n orig, a country house or farmhouse with subsidiary buildings; a country seat, in Italy often a castle; a detached house of some size; a superior middle-class house; a holiday home, esp abroad. [L villa a country house, through Ital]
■ **vill'adom** n villas collectively; the villa-dwelling world. **villatic** /-at'ik/ adj (Milton) of or relating to a farmyard or village.
❑ **villa home** or **unit** n (Aust) a terraced, esp single-storey house, typically joined to the next house by a garage.

village /vil'ij/ n an assemblage of houses, shops, etc smaller than a town, usu in or close to the countryside; a small municipality (N Am); a residential complex temporarily housing participants at a particular event, esp the athletes and officials taking part in international games; the people of a village. ◆ adj of or dwelling in a village. [Fr village, L villāticus]
■ **vill'ager** n an inhabitant of a village. **villagery** /vil'ij-ri/ (Shakesp **villagree**) n villages collectively or perh village people. **villagiza'tion** or **-s-** n the organization of land, esp in Africa and Asia, so that it is under the control of villages (as opposed to nationalization); the removal of scattered groups of population into large new villages, esp in Africa and Asia.
❑ **village cart** see under **cart**. **village college** n a secondary school that also acts as an adult educational and recreational centre for a rural area (cf **community college**). **village idiot** n a person stigmatized as being the most stupid within a community (orig a village).
■ **the Village** Greenwich Village in New York.

villagio see **viliaco**.

villagree see under **village**.

villain /vil'ən/ n a violent, malevolent or unscrupulous evil-doer; the wicked enemy of the hero or heroine in a story or play; playfully, a wretch; a criminal (inf); (orig) a villein. ◆ adj villainous; low-born (archaic); base (obs). [OFr villain, from LL villānus, from L villa a country house]
■ **vill'ainage** or **vill'anage** n villeinage. **vill'ainess** n a female villain. **vill'ainous** or **vill'anous** adj of the nature of, like, or suited to a villain; detestable, vile. ◆ adv (Shakesp) villainously. **vill'ainously** or **vill'anously** adv. **vill'ainousness** or **vill'anousness** n. **vill'ainy** or **vill'any** n the act or (obs) the words of a villain; extreme wickedness; an atrocious crime; disgrace (obs). **vill'an** n a villein.

villanelle /vil-ə-nel'/ n a poem, on two rhymes, in five tercets and a quatrain, the first line repeated as sixth, twelfth, and eighteenth, the third as ninth, fifteenth, and last. [Fr, from Ital villanella, from villano rustic]

villanous(ly) see under **villain**.

Villanovan /vil-ə-nō'vən/ adj of an early Iron Age culture of which remains occur at *Villanova*, near Bologna.

villany see under **villain**.

villar see under **vill**.

villatic see under **villa**.

-ville /-vil/ (sl) combining form denoting a supposed world, milieu, etc, frequented by a specified type of person, or characterized by a specified quality, etc, as in *squaresville*, *dullsville*. [Sfx -*ville* in names of towns, esp in US, from Fr *ville* town]

villeggiatura /vi-lej-ə-too'rə/ n a stay in the country. [Ital]

villein /vil'ən or vil'in/ (hist) n orig appar a free villager; later (13c) a serf, free in relation to all but his lord, and not absolutely a slave; later a copyholder. [Anglo-Fr; cf **villain**]
  ■ **vill'einage** or **vill'enage** n a villein's tenure or status.

villenage see under **villein**.

villi, **villiform** see **villus**.

villiaco, **villiago** see **viliaco**.

villication /vil-i-kā'shən/ (Smollett) n appar intended as a Scots pronunciation of **vellication** (see under **vellicate**).

villus /vil'əs/ (bot and anat) n (pl **vill'i** /-ī/) a long soft hair; a hairlike process, esp one of the frond-like extensions of the lining of the small intestine. [L, wool]
  ■ **vill'iform** adj having the form of villi. **vill'ose** or **vill'ous** adj covered with or formed of villi; like the pile of velvet. **villos'ity** n.

vim /vim/ (inf) n energy, vigour. [Appar L *vim*, accusative of *vīs* force]

vimana /vi-män'ə/ n the central shrine of an Indian temple with pyramidal roof; a temple gate; a heavenly chariot, chariot of the gods. [Sans *vimāna*, literally, a marking out]

vimineous /vi-min'i-əs/ (bot) adj with long flexible shoots. [L *vīmineus*, from *vīmen*, -*inis* osier, switch]

Vimule® /vim'ūl/ adj and n (denoting) a type of contraceptive cap for the cervix with a two-tiered dome.

vin /vɛ̃/ (Fr) n wine.
  □ **vin blanc** /blã/ n white wine. **vin du** (or **de**) **pays** /dü or də pā-ē/ n country or local wine. **vin ordinaire** /ör-di-nār'/ n inexpensive table wine for ordinary use. **vin rosé** /rō'zä/ n rosé wine. **vin rouge** /roozh/ n red wine.
  ■ **les grands vins** wines from famous vineyards.

vina /vɛ'nə/ n an Indian stringed instrument with fretted fingerboard over two gourds. [Sans *vīṇā*]

vinaceous see under **vini-**.

vinaigrette /vi-nā-gret' or -ni-/ n a mixture of oil, vinegar, seasoning and herbs, used as a salad dressing (also **vinaigrette dressing** or **sauce**); a box or bottle for aromatic vinegar or smelling salts. ◆ adj (esp placed after its noun) of a dish, served with this dressing. [Fr, from *vinaigre* vinegar]

vinal, **Vinalia** see under **vini-**.

vinasse /vi-nas'/ n residue in alcoholic distillation, esp in beet-sugar-making, a source of potash salts. [Fr]

vinblastine /vin-blas'tēn/ n a drug derived from the Madagascar or rosy periwinkle (*Cantharanthus roseus*), used in the treatment of cancer, esp leukaemias and lymphomas. [Contraction of *vincaleucoblastine*, from **vinca** and **leucoblast**]

vinca /ving'kə/ n any plant of the periwinkle genus *Vinca*. [New L, from L *vinca pervinca*]

Vincentian /vin-sen'shən or -shyən/ adj relating to St *Vincent* de Paul (1576–1660) or to the charitable associations founded by him, or to St *Vincent* of Lérins (died 450), or other *Vincent*.

Vincent's angina /vin'sənts an-jī'nə/ n a bacterial infection of the tonsils, mouth and gums. [JK *Vincent* (1862–1950), French physician]

vincible /vin'si-bl/ adj that may be overcome. [L *vincibilis*, from *vincere*, *victum* to conquer]
  ■ **vincibil'ity** n.

vincristine /vin-kris'tēn/ n an alkaloid substance derived from the Madagascar or rosy periwinkle (*Catharanthus roseus*), used in the treatment of certain types of leukaemia. [New L *vinca* a periwinkle, and *crista* fold]

vinculum /ving'kū-ləm/ n (pl **vinc'ula**) a horizontal line placed above a part of an equation, etc, equivalent to brackets (maths); a tendinous band (anat); a bond. [L, from *vincīre* to bind]

vindaloo /vin-də-loo'/ n a type of very hot Indian curry. [Prob Port *vin(ho) d'alho* wine and garlic (sauce)]

vindemial /vin-dē'mi-əl/ (archaic) adj relating to the vintage. [L *vīndēmia* vintage; see **vintage**]
  ■ **vindē'miate** vi (archaic) to gather grapes or other fruit.

vindicate /vin'di-kāt/ vt to justify; to clear from criticism, etc; to defend with success; to make good a claim to; to lay claim to; to maintain (a point of view, cause, etc); to avenge (obs); to free (obs). [L *vindicāre*, -*ātum*]
  ■ **vindicability** /-kə-bil'i-ti/ n. **vin'dicable** adj. **vindica'tion** n act of vindicating; defence; justification; support. **vin'dicative** (or /vin-dik'ə-tiv/) adj vindicating; tending to vindicate; revengeful, vindictive (Shakesp). **vindic'ativeness** n vindictiveness. **vin'dicātor** n a person who vindicates (fem **vin'dicātress**). **vin'dicatorily** adv. **vin'dicatory** /-ə-tər-i or -ā-tər-i/ adj serving or tending to vindicate; punitive; retributive; avenging.

vindictive /vin-dik'tiv/ adj revengeful or spiteful; pursuing revenge; punitive (as in *vindictive damages*); retributive (as in *vindictive justice*). [L *vindicta* revenge; see **vindicate**]
  ■ **vindic'tively** adv. **vindic'tiveness** n.

vine /vīn/ n a woody climbing plant (*Vitis vinifera* or other of the genus) that produces grapes; a climbing or trailing stem or (US) plant (hortic); (**Vine**®) an application for posting video clips on the Twitter website. ◆ vt to remove vines from, eg vines and pods from (peas). [OFr *vine*, *vigne*, from L *vīnea* a vineyard, a vine, from *vīnum* wine; Gr *oinos* wine]
  ■ **vi'ner** n a vine-grower. **vinery** /vī'nə-ri/ n a hot-house for rearing vines; a vineyard (obs). **vī'ny** adj relating to, like, consisting of or bearing vines; entwining.
  □ **vine'-branch** n a branch of a vine; a Roman centurion's badge. **vine'-clad** adj covered with vines. **vine'-disease** n a disease affecting the vine. **vine'-dresser** n a person who trims and cultivates vines. **vine'-fretter** n a small insect that infests vines, esp Phylloxera or other greenfly. **vine fruit** n the fruit of the vine in any form, ie as grape or raisin, etc. **vine'-gall** n a gall on a vine, esp one made by a weevil. **vine'-leaf** n the leaf of a vine. **vine'-mildew** n a disease of vines due to the oidium stage of a mildew fungus, *Uncinula*. **vine'-prop** n a support for a vine. **vine'-rod** n a Roman centurion's badge. **vine'-stock** n the stock on which a vine of another kind is grafted. **vine tomato** n a variety of tomato grown on indeterminate vines and usu sold still attached to part of the vine. **vineyard** /vin'yərd or -yärd/ n a plantation of vines, esp grape-bearing vines; a particular sphere of labour, esp of an intellectual, academic or spiritual kind.
  ■ **dwell under one's vine and fig tree** to live at peace on one's own land.

vinegar /vin'i-gər/ n a condiment and pickling medium, a dilute impure acetic acid, made from beer, weak wine, etc; bad temper or mood; energy or vigour (N Am inf). ◆ vt to apply vinegar to. [Fr *vinaigre*, from *vin* (L *vīnum*) wine, and *aigre* sour (L *ācer* keen, sharp, pungent)]
  ■ **vinegarette'** n a vinaigrette, the container. **vin'egarish** adj sourish. **vin'egary** adj like or flavoured with vinegar; sour (also fig).
  □ **vin'egar-eel** n a minute threadworm that breeds in vinegar. **vin'egar-fly** n a fruit fly. **vin'egar-plant** n a bacterium causing acetic fermentation.

vinew /vin'ū/ vt and vi to make or become mouldy. ◆ n mouldiness. [OE *fynegian* to become mouldy, from *fynig* mouldy, from *fyne* mould]
  ■ **vin'ewed** adj mouldy; musty.

vingt-et-un /vɛ̃-tā-œ̃'/ or **vingt-un** /vɛ̃-tœ̃'/ n a card game with the aim of acquiring cards to the value of exactly (or the nearest below) twenty-one, pontoon. [Fr, twenty-one]

vinho verde /vē'nyō ver'de/ n a light, sharp, immature Portuguese wine. [Port, literally, green wine]

vini- or **vin-** /vin(-i)- or vīn(-i)-/ combining form denoting wine. [L *vīnum* wine]
  ■ **vīnā'ceous** adj wine-coloured. **vī'nal** adj of or due to wine. **Vīnā'lia** /vē-nä'li-ə/ n pl an ancient Roman wine festival celebrated on 23 April, when the previous year's vintage was tasted and offered to Jupiter; an ancient Roman vintage festival on 19 August. **vinicul'tural** /vin- or vīn-/ adj. **vin'iculture** n cultivation of the vine for wine-making, and often also the making of the wine. **vinicul'turist** n. **vinifica'tion** /vin-/ n the process of converting grape-juice, etc, into wine. **vin'ificātor** n a condensing device that collects the alcoholic vapour produced by fermentation. **vī'nolent** adj (obs) addicted to wine. **vinol'ogist** /vīn- or vin-/ n. **vinol'ogy** n the scientific study of vines, esp the grapevine. **vīnos'ity** n vinous character; the characteristic qualities of a particular wine; addiction to wine. **vī'nous** adj relating to wine; like wine; wine-coloured; caused by or indicative of wine.

vino /vē'nō/ (sl) n (pl **vi'nos**) wine. [Ital and Sp]

vinolent, **vinology**, **vinous**, etc see under **vini-**.

vin santo /vin san'tō/ n a sweet dessert wine from central Italy made from partially dried white grapes. [Ital, literally, holy wine]

vint[1] /vint/ n a card game like contract bridge. [Russ]

vint[2] see under **vintage**.

vintage /vin'tij/ n the gathering of grapes and preparation for wine-making; a season's yield of grapes or wine; the time of gathering grapes; wine, esp of a good year; the product of a particular period; a period of origin. ◆ adj relating to the grape vintage; (of wine) of a specified year and of good quality; generally (eg of a play by an author or of a period) among the (best and) most characteristic; out of date and no longer admired. ◆ vt to strip of grapes; to gather (grapes); to make (wine), esp of a good year. [Anglo-Fr vintage, OFr (Fr) vendange, from L vīndēmia, from vīnum wine, grapes, and dēmere to remove (from dē out of or away, and emere to take); modified by influence of **vintner**]
■ **vint** n and vt (back-formation from **vintage**). **vint'ager** n a worker at the vintage. **vint'aging** n.
❑ **vintage car** n an old-fashioned car (specif one built between 1919 and 1930). **vintage year** n one in which a particular product (usu wine) reaches an exceptionally high standard.
■ **post-vintage thoroughbred** see under **thorough**.

vintner /vint'nər/ n a person who sells wine. [OFr vinetier, from LL vīnetārius, from L vīnum wine]
■ **vint'ry** n a wine-store; a wine shop.

viny see under **vine**.

vinyasa yoga /vin-yä'sə yō'gə/ n a form of ashtanga yoga based on transitions through a series of poses. [Sans vinyāsa placement]

vinyl /vī'n(ə)l/ or -nil/ n an organic radical $CH_2=CH-$, the equivalent of a molecule of ethylene with a hydrogen atom removed; any vinyl polymer, plastic or resin, esp used in making wall coverings and gramophone records; gramophone records collectively (inf). ◆ adj of, consisting of, containing or made of vinyl. [L vīnum wine, and -yl]
■ **vinylidene** /vīn-il'i-dēn/ n the bivalent radical $CH_2C=$. **Vinylite** /vīn'il-īt/ n proprietary name for a series of vinyl resins.
❑ **vinyl resins, plastics** n pl thermoplastic resins, polymers or co-polymers of vinyl compounds, eg polymers of **vinyl chloride** (CH_2CHCl) a gaseous compound with various industrial applications, and **vinyl acetate**($CH_3COOCHCH_2$) a colourless liquid used to make polyvinyl acetate (see under **poly-**).

Viognier /vē-on'yä/ n a variety of white grape, orig from the Rhône valley in S France, used in making dry white wine; the wine made from this grape.

viol /vī'əl/ n any member of a class of stringed instruments, tuned in fourths and thirds, forerunners of the violin class, of which the double bass is perhaps the closest modern relative. [Partly **vielle**; partly Fr viole and Ital viola, dimin violino, augmentative violone, and its dimin violoncello; origin uncertain; cf LL vitula, and **fiddle**]
■ **viola** /vi-ō'lə/ n a stringed instrument, slightly bigger than the violin, tuned a fifth lower. **violer** /vī'ə-lər/ n a viol player; a fiddler. **violin** /vī-ə-lin' or vī'/ n the smallest of the modern orchestral stringed instruments, with four strings tuned in fifths (G, D, A, E), held under the chin and played with a bow; a violinist. **vī'olinist** (or /-lin'/) n a player on the violin. **violinist'ic** adj. **violinist'ically** adv. **violist** /vī'əl-ist/ n a player on the viol; /vē-ō'list/ a player on the viola. **violoncellist** /vē- or vī-ə-lan-chel'ist/ n a cello-player. **violoncell'o** n (pl **violoncell'os**) a bass instrument of the violin class, commonly called **cello**. **violone** /vē-ō-lō'nā or vī'ə-lōn/ n a double-bass viol, bigger than the viola da gamba, perhaps the ancestor of the modern double bass.
❑ **viola da braccio** /dä brät'chō/ n (Ital, viol for the arm) a tenor viol, held along the arm. **viola da gamba** /gäm'ba/ n (Ital, viol for the leg) a bass viol, resembling the cello. **viola d'amore** /dä-mō'rā/ n (Ital, of love) a tenor viol with sympathetic strings under the fingerboard. **viola da spalla** /späl'la/ n (Ital, for the shoulder) a bigger form of tenor viol. **vi'ol-de-gam'boys** n (Shakesp) the viola da gamba. **violin spider** n a very small brown and orange spotted spider of S America, whose bite can be fatal to humans.

viola[1] see under **viol**.

viola[2] /vī'ə-lə/ n any plant of the violet and pansy genus Viola, giving name to the family **Viola'ceae**, with spurred zygomorphic flowers. [L]
■ **violā'ceous** adj of the Violaceae; violet-coloured.

violate /vī'ə-lāt/ vt to fail to observe duly; to abuse; to rape or submit to sexual abuse of any kind; to profane; to do violence to (obs). ◆ adj violated; defiled. [L violāre, -ātum, from vīs strength]
■ **vī'olable** adj that may be violated. **vī'olably** adv. **vī'olāter** n. **violā'tion** n. **vī'olātive** adj causing, tending towards or involving violation. **vī'olātor** n.

viold (Milton) same as **vialled** (see under **vial**).

violent /vī'ə-lənt/ adj intensely forcible; impetuous and unrestrained in action; domineeringly vehement; due to violence; perverting or distorting the meaning, etc; expressing violence. ◆ vt (obs) to force. ◆ vi (Shakesp) to rage. [L violentus or violēns, -entis, from vīs]
■ **vi'olence** n the state or quality of being violent; excessive, unrestrained, or unjustifiable force; outrage; profanation; injury; distortion of the meaning, etc; rape. **vi'olently** adv.

■ **violent storm** n (meteorol) a wind of force 11 on the Beaufort scale, reaching speeds of 64 to 72mph.
■ **do violence to** to harm, ruin, distort.

violer see under **viol**.

violet /vī'ə-lit/ n any plant or flower of the genus Viola; extended to unrelated plants, such as **African violet** (see under **African**) or **water violet** (see under **water**); a bluish purple. ◆ adj bluish purple. [Fr violette, from L viola]
■ **shrinking violet** (facetious) a shy, hesitant person.

violin, violist, violoncello, etc see under **viol**.

VIP abbrev : vasoactive intestinal peptide; very important person.

viper /vī'pər/ n any of the small venomous snakes of the family **Viperidae** /vī-per'i-dē/, including the **common viper** or adder, Britain's only venomous snake; extended to some other snakes, eg the pit vipers and horned vipers; an ungrateful or treacherous, malignant person. [L vīpera, from vīvus living, and parere to bring forth]
■ **viperiform** /-per'/ adj resembling the viper. **vī'perine** /-pər-īn/ adj related to or resembling the viper. **vī'perish** adj venomous; spiteful; like a viper. **vī'perous** adj having the qualities of a viper; venomous; malignant. **vī'perously** adv.
❑ **viper's bugloss** n a stiff bristly boraginaceous plant (genus Echium) of dry places, with intensely blue flowers, once thought to be a remedy or prophylactic for snakebite. **viper's grass** n black salsify.

VIR abbrev : Victoria Imperatrix Regina (L), Victoria, Empress and Queen.

viraemia, viraemic see under **virus**.

virago /vi-rä'gō or vi-rā'gō/ n (pl **vira'goes** or **vira'gos**) a violent or bad-tempered woman; a heroic or manlike woman; an amazon. [L virāgō, virāginis, from vir a man]
■ **viraginian** /vi-rə-jin'i-ən/, **viraginous** /vi-raj'/ or **vira'goish** adj.

viral, etc see under **virus**.

viranda, virando (pl **viran'das** or **viran'dos**) obsolete forms of **veranda**.

vire see under **virement**.

virelay /vir'ə-lā/ n an old French lyric form in two-rhymed stanzas of short lines, linked by recurrent lines. [Fr virelai, appar from meaningless refrain vireli, but associated with virer to turn, and lai a song]

virement /vē-rə-mä' or vīr'mənt/ (account) n authorized transference of a surplus to balance a deficit under another heading; authorized redirection of funds for one purpose to a more urgent occasion. [Fr virement]
■ **vire** /vīr/ vt to transfer (funds) in this way.

viremia see under **virus**.

virent /vī'rənt/ adj verdant (archaic); fresh (obs); green (archaic). [L virēns, -entis, prp of virēre to be green; virēscēns, prp of virēscere to become green]
■ **virescence** /vir- or vīr-es'əns/ n. **viresc'ent** adj turning green; inclining to green; fresh; green; abnormally green.

vireo /vir'i-ō/ n (pl **vir'eos**) any American singing bird of the genus Vireo, the greenlets, giving name to the family **Vireonidae** /-on'i-dē/. [L vireō, -ōnis perh greenfinch]

vires see under **vis**.

virescence, virescent see under **virent**.

viretot /vir'i-tot/ (Walter Scott after Chaucer) n rush, dash, gad. [Origin obscure]

virga /vûr'gə/ (meteorol) n (also n pl) trails of water, drops, or ice particles coming from a cloud but not reaching the ground as precipitation. [L, a twig, streak in the sky]

virgate /vûr'gāt/ adj rodlike; twiggy. ◆ n an old land measure, commonly 30 acres. [L virga rod]

virge /vûrj/ n an obsolete Latinized spelling of **verge**[1].
■ **virg'er** n (obs except in certain cathedrals, esp St Paul's) verger.

Virgilian or **Vergilian** /vər-jil'i-ən/ adj of or in the manner of Virgil (Publius Vergilius Maro), the Roman poet (70–19BC).

virgin /vûr'jin/ n a person (esp a woman) who has had no sexual intercourse; a person who has no previous experience of a specified thing (facetious); a member of a religious order of women who have undertaken to remain virgins; a maiden; (usu with cap) a Madonna, a figure of the Virgin; (with cap and the) Virgo. ◆ adj in a state of virginity; of a virgin; maidenly; pure; chaste; undefiled; in the original condition, unattained, untouched, unexploited, never scaled, felled, captured, wrought, used, etc; never having previously undergone or been affected by the thing mentioned; (of esp olive oil) obtained at the first pressing; (of silver, etc) mined in a pure, unmixed state. ◆ vt (with it; Shakesp) to continue chaste. [Partly through Fr, from L virgō, virginis]

■ **vir'ginal** *adj* of or appropriate to a virgin or virginity; in a state of virginity; like a virgin; parthenogenetic. **vir'ginally** *adv*. **vir'ginhood** or **vir'ginity** *n* the state or fact of being a virgin. **vir'ginly** *adj* pure. ◆ *adv* chastely.

❑ **virgin birth** or **generation** *n* parthenogenesis. **Virgin Birth** *n* (*theol*) (the doctrine of) the birth of Christ, His mother being a virgin. **virg'in-born** *adj* born of a virgin. **virgin gold** *n* gold in the condition in which it is found. **virgin knot** *n* the fastening of a Greek or Roman woman's girdle, loosed at marriage. **virgin neutron** *n* a neutron which has not yet experienced a collision and therefore retains its energy at birth. **vir'gin's-bow'er** *n* traveller's-joy (*Clematis vitalba*). **virgin soil** *n* soil never previously tilled or cultivated; material as yet untried or unaffected.

■ **the Blessed Virgin** or **the Virgin** Mary the mother of Christ. **the Virgin Queen** Elizabeth I of England.

virginal¹, **virginhood**, etc see under **virgin**.

virginal² /*vûr'ji-nəl*/ *n* (often in *pl*; also **pair of virginals**) an old keyboard instrument like a small single-manual harpsichord. ◆ *vi* (*Shakesp*) to finger, as on a virginal. [Perh because it was played by young ladies (see **virgin** above), or perh from L *virga* rod, which formed part of the instrument's action]

Virginia /*vər-jin'yə*/ *n* a tobacco grown and manufactured in *Virginia*. [The US state, named after Elizabeth, the *Virgin* Queen]

■ **Virgin'ian** *adj*. ◆ *n* a native or citizen of Virginia. **virgin'ium** *n* (*chem*) a name proposed for the element of atomic no 87 (see **francium**).

❑ **Virginia creeper** *n* an American climbing plant closely related to the vine, bright-red in autumn. **Virginia stock** *n* a Mediterranean plant (*Malcolmia maritima*) with pink, violet or purple flowers.

virginiamycin /*vər-jin-yə-mī'sin*/ *n* an antibiotic obtained from a bacterium related to *Streptomyces virginiae*.

virginity, etc see under **virgin**.

Virgo /*vûr'gō*/ *n* the Virgin, a constellation giving its name to, and formerly coinciding with, a sign of the zodiac (*astron*); the sixth sign of the zodiac, between Leo and Libra (*astrol*); a person born between 24 August and 23 September, under the sign of Virgo (*astrol*; *pl* **Vir'gos**). [L]

■ **Virgō'an** *adj* and *n* (relating to or characteristic of) a person born under the sign of Virgo.

❑ **virgo intacta** /*in-tak'tə* or *-ta*/ *n* (L, untouched) a woman who has not had sexual intercourse.

virgule /*vûr'gūl*/ *n* a slanting line, an old form of comma, a solidus. [Fr, comma, from L *virgula*, dimin of *virga* a twig, rod]

■ **vir'gulate** *adj* shaped like a rod.

viricide, etc see under **virus**.

virid /*vir'id*/ *adj* green. [L *viridis* green, from *virēre* to be green]

■ **viridesc'ence** *n*. **viridesc'ent** *adj* greenish. **virid'ian** *n* a green pigment, hydrated chromium sesquioxide. **vir'idite** *n* an indeterminate green decomposition product in rocks. **virid'ity** *n* verdure; greenness.

virile /*vir'īl* or (*esp N Am*) *vir'il*/ *adj* having the qualities of a mature male human being; robustly masculine; manly; (of a man) sexually potent or with a particularly high sexual drive. [L *virīlis*, from *vir* a man; cf OE *wer* man]

■ **virilescence** /*vir-il-es'əns*/ *n* development of male character in the female. **virilesc'ent** *adj*. **vir'ilism** *n* (*med*) the presence of male sexual characteristics in a female. **viril'ity** *n* the state or quality of being a mature male; the power (*esp* sexual) of a mature male; manhood; masculinity; vigour, energy. **virilizā'tion** or **-s-** *n* the development of male sexual characteristics in the female. **vir'ilized** or **-s-** *adj*. **vir'ilizing** or **-s-** *adj*.

virino, **virion** see under **virus**.

virl /*vîrl*/ (now *Scot*) *n* see under **ferrule**.

virogene, **virology**, **virose**, etc see under **virus**.

virtu /*vûr-too'*/ *n* a love of the fine arts; a taste for curiosities; objects of art or antiquity collectively; worth, *esp* moral, in a person or thing. [Ital *virtù*, from L *virtūs*, -*ūtis* (see **virtue**)]

■ **article** (or **object**) **of virtu** an object of artistic or antiquarian interest, a curio.

virtual /*vûr'tū-əl* or *-chū-əl*/ *adj* in effect, though not in fact; not such in fact but capable of being considered as such for some purposes; relating to virtual reality; of interaction, connection, use, etc, via the Internet; having virtue or efficacy (*archaic*); virtuous (*obs*). [Med L *virtuālis*, from L *virtus* virtue]

■ **vir'tualism** *n* the doctrine of Christ's virtual presence in the Eucharist. **vir'tualist** *n*. **virtual'ity** *n* essential nature; potentiality; virtual reality. **virtualizā'tion** or **-s-** *n*. **vir'tualize** or **-ise** *vt* to recreate in virtual reality; to transform into an electronic medium. **vir'tually** *adv* in effect, though not in fact; (loosely) almost, nearly; in virtual reality; by computer.

❑ **virtual community** *n* a community or group of people dependent on computer communication with one another. **virtual image** see under **image**. **virtual machine** *n* (*comput*) a cross-platform environment for the consistent execution of a program or application. **virtual memory** *n* (*comput*) memory that appears to be internal but is actually transferred from or to a disk. **virtual pet** see **cyberpet**. **virtual reality** *n* a computer-simulated environment (used, eg for training astronauts, and for video games) which gives the operator the impression of actually being in the environment, interacting with it and causing things to happen, by means of goggles, a joystick, datagloves or other special equipment (*abbrev* **VR**).

virtue /*vûr'tū* or *-chū*/ *n* excellence; worth; moral excellence; inherent power; efficacy; the practice of duty; a good quality, *esp* moral; sexual purity; (loosely) virginity; one of the orders of the medieval celestial hierarchy; an accomplishment (*rare*); valour (now *rare*). [OFr *vertu* and L *virtus* bravery, moral excellence, from *vir* a man; cf Gr *hērōs*, Sans *vīra* a hero, OE *wer* man]

■ **vir'tueless** *adj*. **vir'tuous** *adj* having virtue; morally good; blameless; righteous; practising duty; according to moral law; chaste. **vir'tuously** *adv*. **vir'tuousness** *n*.

❑ **vir'tue-proof** (*Milton* vertue-) *adj* impregnable in virtue. **virtuous circle** *n* a process by which something good or beneficial is enhanced by its own consequences, *opp* to *vicious circle*.

■ **by** (or **in**) **virtue of** through the power, force, or efficacy of; because of; on account of. **make a virtue of necessity** to do as if from a sense of duty (or with a sense of duty called in for the occasion) something unpleasant one is forced to do. **seven principal virtues** faith, hope, charity, justice, prudence, temperance, and fortitude, the first three being the *theological*, the last four the *moral* virtues. **the cardinal virtues** see under **cardinal**.

virtuoso /*vûr-tū-ō'sō* or *-zō*/ *n* (*pl* **virtuō'sos** or **virtuō'si** /*-sē*/) a musician (or other artist) of the highest technical skill (also *adj*); a person with a good deal of knowledge of or interest in works of art, antiquities, curiosities and the like. [Ital, skilful, from L *virtus* virtue]

■ **virtuosa** /*-tū-ō'sa*/ *n* (*pl* **virtuō'se** /*-sā*/) a female virtuoso. **virtuose** /*-tū-ōs'*/ or **virtuō'sic** *adj* exhibiting the qualities of a virtuoso. **virtuosity** /*-os'*/ *n* exceptional technical skill in music or other fine art; the character of a virtuoso; interest in or knowledge of articles of virtu. **virtuō'soship** *n*.

virtute officii /*vər-tū'ti o-fis'i-ī* or *wir-too-te o-fik'i-ē*/ (L) by virtue of office.

virucidal, etc see under **virus**.

virulent /*vir'ū-lənt* or *-ū-*/ *adj* extremely infectious; highly poisonous or malignant; venomous; acrimonious. [L *vīrulentus*, from *vīrus* (see **virus**)]

■ **vir'ulence** or **vir'ulency** *n*. **vir'ulently** *adv*.

❑ **virulent phage** *n* a bacteriophage which always kills its host.

virus /*vī'rəs*/ *n* a pathogenic agent, *usu* a protein-coated particle of RNA or DNA, capable of increasing rapidly inside a living cell; an illness caused by a virus (*inf*); (**computer virus**) a piece of computer code inserted into an apparently innocent program in order to corrupt or destroy other data and unknowingly passed on from one user to another; the transmitted cause of infection; contagious or poisonous matter (as of ulcers, etc); venom; any corrupting influence. [L *vīrus* venom; Gr *īos*, Sans *viṣa* poison]

■ **viraemia** or (*US*) **viremia** /*vī-rē'mi-ə*/ *n* the presence of viruses in the bloodstream. **vīrae'mic** *adj*. **vī'ral** *adj* relating to or caused by a virus. ◆ *n* a sales promotion carried out through viral marketing (qv below). **vīrality** /*-al'i-ti*/ *n* the quality of spreading rapidly on the Internet. **vī'rally** *adv*. **vī'ricidal** (or /*vir'*/) *adj*. **vī'ricide** (or /*vir'*/) *n* a substance that destroys or eliminates a virus. **virino** /*vi-rē'nō*/ *n* a hypothetical organism formerly suggested as the cause of BSE, said to be a tiny piece of nucleic acid coated with protective protein taken from the host. **vī'rion** (or /*vir'*/) *n* a virus particle in its mature, infectious state. **vī'rogene** a virus-forming gene. **vī'roid** *n* a particle of RNA, uncoated by protein, that can cause some diseases in plants. **virolog'ical** *adj*. **virol'ogist** *n*. **virol'ogy** *n* the study of virus, viruses and virus diseases. **vī'rose** *adj* poisonous; foul. **virō'sis** *n* a disease caused by a virus. **vī'rous** *adj* virose. **vī'rucidal** *adj*. **vī'rucide** *n* same as **viricide** above.

❑ **viral marketing** *n* a marketing technique in which a company's customers are encouraged to spread knowledge or endorsement of a product by word of mouth or the Internet. **virus disease** *n* a disease caused by a virus.

Vis. *abbrev* : Viscount.

vis /*vis*, *vēs* or *wēs*/ (L) *n* (*pl* **vires** /*vī'rēz* or *wē'rāz*/) force, power.

❑ **vis a tergo** /*ā tûr'gō* or *ä ter'gō*/ *n* compulsion from behind. **vis comica** /*kom'ik-ə* or *kōm'ik-a*/ *n* comic power. **vis inertiae** /*in-ûr'shi-ē* or *in-ert'i-ī*/ *n* the power of inertia; passive resistance. **vis major** /*mā'jər* or *mä'yor*/ *n* superior force. **vis mortua** /*mör'tū-ə* or *mor'tū-a*/ *n* force of pressure, dead force. **vis viva** /*vī'və*, *vē'va* or *wē'wa*/ *n* living force, equal to the mass of a moving body multiplied by the square of its velocity.

visa /vē'zə/ or (archaic) **visé** /vē'zā/ n an authenticating endorsement on a passport, etc, allowing the holder to enter or leave the country issuing it. ◆ vt (pat and pap **vi'saed** or **vi'séed**) to put a visa on. [L vīsa, pap fem of vidēre to see, and Fr visé, pap masc of viser to examine]

visage /viz'ij/ n (literary) the face; an outward appearance (archaic). [Fr visage, from L vīsus look]
■ **vis'aged** adj. **visagiste** /vē-zazh-ēst'/ or **visagist** /viz'ə-jist/ n an expert in facial make-up.

vis-à-vis /vē-za-vē' or vi-za- or -zə-, -zä-/ adv face-to-face. ◆ prep face-to-face with; in relation to, with regard to. ◆ n a person who faces, or is opposite to, another; an opposite number; a light carriage with seats facing each other; an S-shaped couch. [Fr vis face (from L vīsus look), and à to]

Visc. abbrev : Viscount.

viscacha /vi-skä'chə/ n a S American burrowing rodent of heavy build (also **vizca'cha**, **bisca'cha** and **bizca'cha**). [Sp, from Quechua huiscacha]
■ **viscachera** /-chä'rə/ n a settlement of viscachas.

viscera, **visceral** and **viscerate** see viscus.

viscero- /vis-ə-rō-/ or **visceri-** /vis-ə-ri-/ combining form denoting of or relating to the internal organs. [L vīscus, pl vīscera bowel, entrail]
■ **visceröptō'sis** n (Gr ptōsis a falling) an abnormally low position of the intestines in the abdominal cavity. **viscerötōn'ia** n a pattern of temperament associated with the endomorphic body type, extravert, sociable and fond of bodily comforts. **viscerötōn'ic** adj.

viscid /vis'id/ adj semi-fluid, sticky, glutinous, viscous; (of a surface) clammy and covered with a sticky secretion (bot). [LL viscidus, from L viscum (see viscous)]
■ **viscid'ity** n. **viscin** /vis'in/ n the sticky substance present in the fruits of mistletoe.

visco- /vis-kō-/ combining form denoting viscous or viscosity- [See viscous]
■ **viscŏelas'tic** adj having both viscous and elastic properties. **viscoelastic'ity** n. **viscom'eter** or **viscōsim'eter** n an instrument for measuring viscosity. **viscōmet'ric**, **viscōsimet'rical**, **viscōsimet'ric** or **viscosimet'rical** adj. **viscom'etry** or **viscōsim'etry** n.

viscose /vis'kōs/ n the sodium salt of cellulose xanthate, used in the manufacture of **viscose rayon**. ◆ adj viscous. [Ety as for **viscous**]

viscosimeter see under visco-.

viscosity see under viscous.

viscount /vī'kownt/ n a British title of nobility next below an earl (first granted in 1440); the son or young brother of a count; an officer who acted as administrative deputy to an earl, a sheriff (hist); (esp with cap) a similar official in Jersey. [OFr visconte (Fr vicomte), from vis- (L vice in place of), and conte count, after LL vicecomes, from L comes a companion]
■ **vi'scountcy** or **vi'scountship** n a viscountcy. **viscountess** /vī'kownt-es/ n the wife or widow of a viscount; a woman holding a viscounty in her own right; a size of roofing slate, 18 × 10in (457 × 254mm). **vi'scounty** n the rank of a viscount; the jurisdiction of, or territory under, a viscount (hist); a viscount (obs).

viscous /vis'kəs/ adj resistant, or highly resistant, to flow owing to forces acting between the molecules; sticky; viscid. [LL viscōsus sticky, from L viscum bird-lime, mistletoe; cognate with Gr ixos mistletoe]
■ **viscos'ity** n the quality of being viscous. **vis'cousness** n.
❑ **viscous damping** n (phys) an opposing force proportional to velocity, eg that resulting from viscosity of oil. **viscous flow** n a type of fluid flow in which there is a continuous steady motion of the particles, the motion at a fixed point always remaining constant. **viscous water** n water thickened by addition of chemicals, used in fighting forest fires.

viscum /vis'kəm/ n bird-lime; (with cap) a genus of parasitic plants including the common mistletoe. [L]

viscus /vis'kəs/ (med and zool) n (pl **viscera** /vis'ər-ə/ in common general use, esp the abdominal organs) any one of the organs situated within the chest and the abdomen, heart, lungs, liver, etc. [L vīscus, pl vīscera]
■ **visc'eral** adj of or relating to the viscera; instinctive or intuitive, not cerebral or rational (inf); having to do with the more earthy feelings and emotions (inf). **visc'erate** vt to disembowel.

vise[1] N American spelling of vice[1].

vise[2] /vīz/ (obs) vt to advise; to look at. ◆ vi to look (with on); to consider (with on). [Partly **advise**; partly Fr viser, from L vidēre, vīsum to see]

visé, viséed see visa.

vishing /vish'ing/ (comput) n the practice of making VOIP telephone calls in an attempt to elicit confidential information for financial gain. [From voice phishing]

Vishnu /vish'noo/ (Hinduism) n the second god of the Hindu triad, believed to appear in many incarnations, regarded by some worshippers as the saviour. [Sans]
■ **Vish'nuism** n. **Vish'nuite** n and adj.

visible /viz'i-bl/ adj that may be seen; in sight; obvious; (of supplies of a commodity) actually in store, known to be available; relating to goods rather than services (econ); applied to indexing systems in which the edge of each card, etc (containing key information) is immediately visible, in order to make it easier to correct card, etc (commerce); ready or willing to receive a visitor or visitors. ◆ n a visible thing (often in pl). [Through OFr or direct from L vīsibilis, from vidēre; see vision]
■ **visibil'ity** n the state or quality of being visible, or perceivable by the eye; the clearness of the atmosphere; clarity and range of vision in the atmospheric conditions, seeing; a visible thing (usu in pl); a sight, showplace (obs); appearance (obs); the power of seeing, sight (obs). **vis'ibleness** n. **vis'ibly** adv.
❑ **Visible Church** n the body of professing Christians on earth at any specific moment. **visible exports** or **imports** see under **export** or **import**. **visible horizon** see under **horizon**. **visible means** n pl means or resources that are apparent to or ascertainable by others. **visible panty line** n the outline of women's underwear visible through tight-fitting outer clothes (abbrev **VPL**). **visible radiation** n electromagnetic radiation that can be detected by the eye, light. **visible speech** n a system of phonetic characters each of which suggests the configuration of the organs in producing the sound.

visie see under vision.

visier see vizier.

Visigoth /viz'i-goth/ (hist) n one of the Western Goths (as distinguished from the Ostrogoths or Eastern Goths) who formed settlements in the south of France and in Spain, their kingdom in the latter lasting into the 8c. [LL Visigothī, from Gmc word meaning perh noble Goths, perh west Goths]
■ **Visigoth'ic** adj.

visile /viz'īl or -il/ adj of or relating to sight; learning by means of visual images and recalling such images readily. ◆ n a person who learns and remembers best by visual images. [Modelled on **audile**, from L vidēre, vīsum to see]

visiogenic /viz-i-ō-jen'ik/ adj suitable artistically for television transmission. [Television and **-genic**]

vision /vizh'ən/ n the act of seeing; the faculty of sight; anything seen; television, esp as opposed to sound radio; the picture on a television screen; a look, glance; a vivid concept or mental picture; a person or scene of great beauty (sometimes ironically); a pleasing imaginative plan for, or anticipation of, future events; an apparition; a revelation, esp divine, in sleep or a trance (sometimes without article); the act or power of perceiving imaginative mental images; imaginative perception; foresight; mystical awareness of the supernatural. ◆ vt to see as a vision, to imagine; to present, or to call up, as in a vision. [Fr, from L visiō, visiōnis, from vidēre, vīsum to see; cf Gr idein, Eng wit]
■ **visie**, **viz'y** or **vizz'ie** n (Scot) /viz'i/ a close or careful look; aim; a sight on the muzzle of a gun. ◆ vt and vi (Scot) to look (at) closely; to aim. **vis'ional** adj of or relating to a vision; derived from a vision; visionary, not real; relating to sight. **vis'ionally** adv. **vis'ionariness** n. **vis'ionary** adj capable of seeing visions; apt to see visions; given to reverie or fantasy; showing or marked by imagination or foresight; out of touch with reality, unpractical; of the nature of, or seen in, a vision, visional; fanciful, not real; impracticable; characterized by visions or fantasy; relating to physical or mental vision. ◆ n a person who sees visions; a person who forms impracticable schemes; a person of imagination or foresight. **vis'ioned** adj inspired so as to see visions; seen in a vision; produced by or associated with a vision. **vis'ioner** n a visionary. **vis'ioning** n seeing visions. **vis'ionist** n a person who professes to be a visionary; a person who believes that the Biblical details of creation were revealed in vision. **vis'ionless** adj destitute of vision.
❑ **vision mix** n. **vision mixer** n a technician who blends or combines different camera shots in television or films; a piece of equipment for doing this. **vision thing** n (esp US) the need to take long-term objectives into account in formulating policy.
■ **beatific vision** see under **beatify**.

visiophone /viz'i-ə-fōn/ or -i-ō-/ n a videophone (qv under **video**). [vision and telephone]

visit /viz'it/ vt to pay a call upon, or to be in the habit of doing so; to go to for sight-seeing, recreation, or religious purposes; to go to stay with; to make a stay in, eg of migratory birds; (of a professional or his or her client, patient, etc) to go to see professionally; to examine or inspect (a place), esp officially; to come to, or to go to see, in order to give comfort or aid; to go to with intention of injuring; to inflict (punishment, etc) (with *on*); to punish (a person) (with *with*; *archaic*); to punish (eg wrongdoing) (*archaic*); (of an idea) to take temporary hold on the mind of; to afflict or trouble, eg with disease (*archaic*). ◆ *vi* to be in the habit of seeing or meeting each other at home; to make a visit or visits. ◆ *n* an act of visiting; a short stay; a sightseeing excursion; an official or a professional call; a chat (*N Am inf*). [Fr *visiter*, from L *visitāre*, frequentative of *visere* to go to see, visit, from *vidēre* to see]

■ **vis'itable** *adj* subject to official visitation; attractive to visitors. **vis'itant** *adj* paying visits, visiting. ◆ *n* a person who visits; a person who is a guest in the house of another; a supernatural visitor; a migratory bird; (with *cap*) one of an order of nuns founded by St Francis de Sales in 1610, also called **Salesians, Order** (or **Nuns**) **of the Visitation. visitā'tion** *n* the act of visiting; a long and wearisome visit; the right of a divorced parent to have access to a child or children who live with a former partner (*US*); a formal or official visit by a superior, *esp* ecclesiastical; an examination by authority; the act of a naval commander in boarding a merchant vessel of another state to ascertain her character and object; a visit of God, or of a good (or evil) supernatural being; a dispensation of divine favour or displeasure; a sore affliction; the operation of a destructive power, or an instance of it; an influence acting on the mind; an unusual and extensive influx of a species of animals into a region; (with *cap*) a Christian festival to commemorate the visit of the Virgin Mary to Elizabeth, observed by the Roman Catholic Church on 31 May. **visitā'tional** or **vis'itātive** *adj*. **vis'itātor** *n* an official visitor. **visitātō'rial** *adj*. **visitee'** *n* the person to whom a visit is paid. **vis'iting** *n* the act, or an instance, of paying a visit; a visitation, in the senses of divine dispensation, heavy affliction, or influence operating on the mind. ◆ *adj* that visits, often *opp* to *resident*; relating to visiting. **vis'itor** *n* (now rarely **vis'iter**; *fem* **vis'itress**) a person who visits, calls on, or makes a stay with another person; a person authorized to visit for purposes of inspection or supervision; a migratory bird. **visitō'rial** *adj*.

❑ **vis'iting-book** *n* a book recording the names of persons who have called or are to be called on; a visitors' book (*Thackeray*). **visiting card** *n* a small card bearing the name and address, or title, left in paying visits, and sometimes (*esp* formerly) sent as an act of courtesy or in token of sympathy. **vis'iting-day** *n* a day on which one is at home and ready to receive callers. **visiting fireman** *n* an important visitor who is to be lavishly entertained (*US inf*). **visiting hours** *n pl* the period during which hospital patients, etc are permitted to receive visitors. **visiting professor** *n* someone (*esp* a professor from another university) who is invited to teach in a university for a certain period. **visitor general** *n* (*hist*) a personal representative of the King of Spain appointed to investigate affairs, *esp* in Spanish America. **visitors' book** *n* a book in which visitors write their names and sometimes comments. **visitors' passport** *n* (also **British Visitors' Passport**) a simplified form of passport, discontinued in 1995, valid for one year for visits not exceeding three months to certain countries.

■ **visitation of the sick** an Anglican form of service for use by clergy visiting the sick. **visit with** (*N Am*) to visit; to be a guest with; to chat with.

visite /vi-zēt'/ *n* a woman's light short cloak worn in the mid 19c. [Fr]

visive /viz'iv/ (*rare*) *adj* of or relating to sight, visual; able to see; able to be seen. [LL *visivus*, from L *visus* sight]

visne /vē'ni/ (*law*) *n* a venue. [OFr *visné* neighbourhood, from L *vicīnus* neighbour]

visnomy /viz'nə-mi/ (*archaic* and *dialect*) *n* physiognomy (also **vis'nomie**). [Variant of **physiognomy**]

vison /vī'sən/ *n* the American mink. [Fr; origin unknown]

visor or **vizor** /vī'zər/ *n* a movable part of a helmet covering the face, or the upper part of the face, with holes or slits for the eyes and mouth; a mask or other means of disguise (*archaic*); the peak of a cap; a movable flap on a motor-car windscreen, used as a shade against the sun; a hood placed over a signal light; face, aspect, outward appearance (*obs*). ◆ *vt* to disguise or cover with a visor. [Anglo-Fr *viser* (Fr *visière*), from *vis* countenance]

■ **vis'ored** or **viz'ored** *adj*.
❑ **vis'or-mask** *n* a vizard-mask.

vista /vis'tə/ *n* (also (*obs*) **vis'to** (*pl* **vis'tos**)) a view or prospect, *esp* as seen through an avenue; an avenue or other long narrow opening or passage; the trees, etc that form the avenue; a mental view or vision extending far into the past or future, or into any subject engaging the thoughts. ◆ *vt* (*rare*) to make into, or see in, vistas. [Ital *vista* sight, view, from L *vidēre*, *vīsum* to see]

■ **vis'ta'd** or **vis'taed** /-tad/ *adj* having or forming a vista or vistas (*lit* and *fig*). **vis'tal** *adj*. **vis'taless** /-tə-les/ *adj*.

visual /vizh'ū-əl or viz'ū-əl/ *adj* of or relating to sight; concerned with seeing, or (*fig*) with mental vision; attained by, or received through, sight, now often as contrasted with a mechanical or other means of observation; of the nature of, or conveying, a mental vision; visible, having visibility; optic, as in *visual axis* (see **optic axis** under **optic**); of the eye (*poetic*); (of beams) coming from the eye (*obs*). ◆ *n* something visible; a rough sketch of the layout of an advertisement or design; (often in *pl*) a drawing, piece of film, etc, as distinct from the words or sound accompanying it. [LL *visuālis*, from L *vīsus* sight]

■ **vis'ualist** *n* a visualizer; a visile. **visual'ity** *n* (*Carlyle*) the quality or state of being visible to the mind; a mental picture. **visualizā'tion** or **-s-** *n* the act or process of visualizing, often used in distant healing. **vis'ualize** or **-ise** *vt* to make visible, externalise to the eye; to call up a clear visual image of. ◆ *vi* to call up a clear visual image; to become visible (*med*). **vis'ualīzer** or **-s-** *n*. **vis'ually** *adv*.

❑ **visual acuity** *n* the spatial resolving power of the eye. **visual aid** *n* a picture, photograph, film, diagram, etc, used as an aid to teaching. **visual arts** *n pl* painting, sculpture, films, etc as opposed to literature, music, etc. **Visual Basic** *n* (*comput*) a form of the programming language BASIC, widely used in creating graphics and software (*abbrev* **VB**). **visual display unit** *n* (*comput*) an older name for a cathode-ray tube which displays data, entered by keyboard or light pen, from a computer's memory (*abbrev* **VDU**). **visual field** see under **field**. **visually challenged** *adj* (in politically correct language) blind. **visual purple** see under **purple**.

visuo- /vizh-ū-ō- or viz-ū-ō-/ *combining form* denoting sight. [L *vīsus*]

■ **vis'uomotor** *adj* of or relating to the coordination of movement and vision in the brain.

vita /vī'tə, vē'* or wē'ta/ (*L*) *n* (*pl* **vi'tas** (or /vē'/)) life; a CV (also **vitae** /-et'ī or -tē/).

■ **vita patris** /-tä pat'ris/ in the father's lifetime.

Vitaceae see **Vitis**.

Vita glass® /vī'tə gläs/ *n* a type of glass that transmits ultraviolet rays.

vital /vī't(ə)l/ *adj* characteristic of life, or of living things; supporting or necessary to life; essential; extremely important; relating to life, birth, and death; fatal to life (*obs*); full of life, lively, energetic; being a manifestation of life (*biol*); life-giving, invigorating (*poetic*); animate, living (*archaic*); capable of living (*obs*). ◆ *n* (*pl*; rarely in *sing*) the interior organs essential for life; the part of any whole necessary for its existence (*obs*). [L *vītālis*, from *vīta* life, from *vīvere* to live; cognate with Gr *bios* life]

■ **vi'talism** *n* the doctrine that there is a vital force (qv below). **vi'talist** *n* a person who holds this doctrine. **vitalis'tic** *adj*. **vitalis'tically** *adv*. **vitality** /-tal'/ *n* (*pl* **vital'ities**) the state or quality of being vital; the quality of being fully or intensely alive; the capacity to endure and flourish; animation, liveliness; the principle of life, power of living; the state of being alive; a living or vital thing or quality. **vitalizā'tion** or **-s-** *n*. **vi'talize** or **-ise** *vt* to give life to; to stimulate activity in; to give vigour to; to make lifelike. **vi'talizer** or **-s-** *n*. **vi'talizing** or **-s-** *adj*. **vi'tally** *adv*. **vi'tascope** *n* an early form of motion-picture projector. **vi'tative** *adj* concerned with the preservation of life. **vi'tativeness** *n* love of life, assigned by the phrenologists to a protuberance under the ear.

❑ **vital air** *n* (*obs*) oxygen. **vital capacity** *n* the volume of air that can be expelled from the lungs after taking the deepest possible breath. **vital force** *n* the force on which the phenomena of life in animals and plants were thought to depend, distinct from chemical and mechanical forces operating in them. **vital functions** *n pl* the bodily functions that are essential to life, such as the circulation of the blood. **vital principle** *n* the principle (the *anima mundi*) which according to the doctrine of vitalism, gives life to all nature; a principle that directs all the actions and functions of living bodies. **vital signs** *n pl* (the level or rate of) breathing, heartbeat, etc. **vital spark** or **flame** *n* life or a trace of life; the principle of life in man. **vital stain** *n* (*bot, zool*) a stain that can be used on living cells without killing them. **vital statistics** *n pl* statistics dealing with the facts of population, ie births, deaths, etc; a woman's bust, waist and hip measurements (*inf*).

vitamin /vit'ə-min or (*esp N Am*) vī'tə-/, (*orig* **vitamine** /-mēn/) *n* any of numerous organic substances, 'accessory food factors', present in minute quantities in nutritive foods and essential for the health of animals, designated provisionally vitamin A, B_1, B_2, B_6, B_{12}, C, D, D_2, D_3, E, F (*obs*), G (another name for B_2; *esp N Am*), H, K, K_1, K_2, K_3, L, P (previously called X), PP (a vitamin effective against pellagra, as nicotinic acid) – later these were analysed and given names indicating something of their nature, such as: retinol; aneurin (thiamine), riboflavin, pantothenic acid, nicotinic acid (niacin), pyridoxine (adermin), cyanocobalamin, folic acid, pteroic acid; ascorbic acid; calciferol, *esp cholecalciferol* and *ergocalciferol*; tocopherol; linoleic and linolenic acid; biotin; phylloquinone (or phytonadione), menadione, menaquinone; bioflavonoid (citrin). [Coined in 1906 from L *vīta* life, and (inappropriately) **amine**]

■ **vi'taminize** or **-ise** *vt* to add vitamins to (a food).
❑ **vitamin B complex** *n* a group of vitamins formerly regarded as being a single vitamin.

vitascope, vitative, etc see under **vital**.

vite /vēt/ (*music*) *adv* quickly. [Fr]

vitellus /vi- or vī-tel'əs/ n (pl **vitell'ī**) the yolk of an egg. [L, a yolk; a transferred use of vitellus, from vitulus a calf]
■ **vit'ellary** adj relating to the vitellus; yellow like the yolk of an egg. **vitell'icle** n a yolk sac. **vitelligenous** /-ij'/ adj producing yolk. **vitell'in** n a phosphoprotein present in yolks of eggs. **vitell'ine** n a vitellus. ◆ adj vitellary.
❑ **vitelline membrane** n (zool) a protective membrane formed around a fertilized ovum to prevent the entry of further sperms.

vitex /vī'teks/ n any plant of the genus Vitex of trees or shrubs, chiefly tropical, of the family Verbenaceae, having a drupe with a four-celled stone, some species of which yield valuable timber. [L]

vitiate /vish'i-āt/ vt (also (obs) **vi'ciate**) to render faulty or defective; to spoil; to make impure; to deprave, corrupt, pervert, debase; to make ineffectual, invalid or inconclusive; to violate or rape (obs); to adulterate (obs). ◆ adj (archaic) vitiated. [L vitiāre, -ātum, from vitium (see vice²)]
■ **vi'tiable** adj. **vitia'tion** n. **vi'tiātor** n. **vitios'ity** (also **vicios'ity**) n the state or quality of being vicious, or (Scots law) faulty.

viticetum, viticide, viticulture, etc see under **Vitis**.

vitiligo /vit-i-lī'gō or -ə-lē'gō/ (med) n a skin abnormality in which irregular patches of the skin lose colour and turn white. [L vitilīgo a skin eruption]

vitiosity see under **vitiate**.

vitious see **vicious**.

Vitis /vī'tis/ n the grapevine genus of woody climbing plants of the family **Vitaceae** /vī-tā'sē-ē/ or Ampelidaceae. [L vītis a vine, from viēre to twist]
■ **viticetum** /vīt- or vit-i-sē'təm/ n a plantation of vines. **vit'icide** n a vine pest. **vitic'olous** adj living on vines. **viticul'tural** adj connected with vines or viticulture. **vit'iculture** n cultivation of the vine. **viticul'turist** n. **vitif'erous** adj bearing vines.

vitrage /vē-träzh' or vit'rij/ n (used also adjectivally) a kind of thin curtain for windows or glazed doors. [Fr, glass window]

vitrail /vit'rāl or vē-trä'ē/ n (pl **vitraux** /vē-trō' or vit'/) stained glass. [Fr]
■ **vitrailled** /vit'rāld/ adj. **vit'raillist** n a maker of glass, esp stained glass.

vitrain /vit'rān/ n a separable constituent of bright coal, of vitreous appearance. [L vitrum glass, and sfx -ain]

vitraux see **vitrail**.

Vitreosil® see under **vitreous**.

vitreous /vit'ri-əs/ adj glassy; relating to, consisting of or like glass; glass-green in colour; resembling glass in absence of crystalline structure, in lustre, etc (geol). [L vitrum glass]
■ **vitrect'omy** n a surgical operation to remove all or part of the vitreous humour. **Vit'reosil**® n vitreous silica used for apparatus which is subject to large temperature variations. **vitreos'ity** or **vit'reousness** n. **vitresc'ence** n. **vitresc'ent** adj tending to become glass; capable of being turned into glass. **vitrescibil'ity** n. **vitresc'ible** adj. **vit'reum** n the vitreous humour of the eye. **vit'ric** adj. **vit'rics** n pl glassy materials; glassware. ◆ n sing the study of glass and its manufacture. **vitrifac'tion** or **vitrifica'tion** n the act, process, or operation of vitrifying, or converting into glass; the state of being vitrified; a vitrified substance; (usu **vitrification**) a technique of IVF in which embryos are frozen quickly in liquid nitrogen. **vitrifac'ture** n the manufacture of glass. **vit'rifiable** adj. **vit'rified** adj. **vit'riform** adj having the form or appearance of glass. **vit'rify** vt and vi to make into or become glass or a glassy substance. **Vitri'na** n a genus of thin-shelled land molluscs, between slugs and true snails, the glass-snails. **vit'rine** /-rēn or -rin/ n a glass display case used to protect delicate articles, exhibit specimens, etc.
❑ **vitreous electricity** n an old name for positive electricity, because glass becomes positively charged when rubbed with silk. **vitreous enamel** n a glazed coating fused onto a steel surface for protection and/or decoration. **vitreous humour** n the jellylike substance filling the posterior chamber of the eye of a vertebrate, between the lens and the retina. **vitrified fort** n a hill fort in (esp) Scotland, in which the siliceous stone has been vitrified by fire, whether by intention or accident is uncertain.

vitriol /vit'ri-əl/ n same as **oil of vitriol** below; a hydrous sulphate of a metal, eg **blue**, **green** and **white vitriol**, respectively that of copper (cupric), iron (ferrous), and zinc; rancorous or caustic criticism, etc. [Fr, from LL vitriolum, from L vitreus of glass]
■ **vit'riolate** vt to convert into or treat with vitriol. **vitriola'tion** n. **vitriolic** /-ol'/ adj relating to, or having the qualities of, vitriol; biting, scathing, expressing intense ill-will. **vitrioliza'tion** or **-s-** n. **vit'riolize** or **-ise** vt to vitriolate; to injure with vitriol.
■ **elixir of vitriol** aromatic sulphuric acid (ie sulphuric acid mixed with certain other substances for use in medicine). **oil of vitriol** concentrated sulphuric acid (formerly prepared from green vitriol).

vitro- /vit-rō-/ combining form denoting glass. [L vitrum glass]

■ **Vit'rolite**® /-līt/ n a kind of opaque glass with a fire-finished surface.

vitro-di-trina /vit'rō-di-trē'nä/ n a Venetian white glass in which fine threads of cane form a lace-like pattern. [Ital, glass of lace]

Vitruvian /vi-troo'vi-ən/ adj of or in the style of Vitruvius Pollio, a Roman architect under the emperor Augustus; denoting a kind of convoluted scrollwork.

vitta /vit'ə/ n (pl **vitt'ae** /-ē/) a stripe of colour (bot and zool); a thin, elongated cavity containing oil, found in the pericarps of some fruits (bot). [L, a fillet or band for the head]
■ **vitt'ate** adj having vittae; striped lengthwise.

vittle or **vittles** /vit'l(z)/ a variant (esp dialect) form of **victual** or **victuals**.

vitular /vit'ū-lər/ adj relating to a calf or to calving. [L vitulus a calf]
■ **vituline** /vit'ū-līn/ adj relating to a calf or to veal.

vituperate /vi-tū'pə-rāt or vī-/ vt to attack with violently abusive criticism or disapproval. ◆ vi to use violently abusive language. [L vituperāre, -ātum, from vitium a fault, and parāre to set in order, prepare]
■ **vitū'perable** adj deserving vituperation. **vitūperā'tion** n. **vitū'perative** /-rət- or -rāt-/ adj containing vituperation; uttering, or prone to utter, abuse. **vitū'peratively** adv. **vitū'perātor** n. **vitū'peratory** adj vituperative.

Vitus see **St Vitus's dance** under **saint**.

viva¹ /vē'vä/ (Ital and Sp) interj long live.

viva² see **viva voce**.

vivace /vē-vä'che/ (music) adj and adv (superl **vivacis'simo**) lively; in a lively manner. [Ital]

vivacious /vi-vā'shəs or vī-/ adj lively, full of vitality; sprightly, sportive; long-lived, or tenacious of life (obs). [L vīvāx, vīvācis, from vīvere to live]
■ **vivā'ciously** adv. **vivā'ciousness** or **vivac'ity** n the state of being vivacious; vigour; animation; liveliness or sprightliness of temper or behaviour; a vivacious act or saying (rare); vitality (obs); tenacity of life, or longevity (archaic).

vivamente see under **vivo**.

vivandière /vē-vä-dyer'/ (hist) n in the French and some other Continental armies, a female attendant in a regiment, who sold spirits and provisions. [Fr, fem of vivandier, from Ital vivandiere a sutler, from assumed LL vivanda food]
■ **vivandier** /-dyä/ n a man who sold such provisions.

vivarium /vī-vā'ri-əm/ n (pl **vivā'ria** or **vivāriums**) an artificial enclosure for keeping or raising living animals, such as a park, fish pond, etc (also (archaic) **vī'vary**). [L vīvārium, from vīvus alive, from vīvere to live]

vivat /vī'vat or vē'vat/ (L) interj long live. ◆ n an expression of applause or enthusiastic approval.

viva voce /vī'və vō'sē or vō'chi/ adv by oral testimony. ◆ n (usu **viva** alone) an oral examination. ◆ vt (usu **viva**) to examine orally. [L]

vivda /viv'dä or vev'dä/ n in Shetland, meat hung and dried without salt (also **vif'da**). [Perh ON vöthvi muscle]

vive¹ /vīv/ (Scot and obs) adj lively, forcible; vivid. [Fr, or L vīvus alive]
■ **vive'ly** adv. **vīv'ency** n (rare) vitality.

vive² /vēv/ (Fr) interj long live.

viver¹ /vē'vər/ (obs and dialect) n a fish pond. [Anglo-Fr, from L vīvārium; see **vivarium**]

viver² /vī'vər/ (dialect) n a fibre, rootlet. [Variant of **fibre**]

Viverra /vi- or vī-ver'ə/ n the civet genus, giving name to the family **Viverr'idae** /-i-dē/, and the subfamily **Viverrinae** /-ī'nē/; (usu without cap) any of the Viverridae. [L viverra a ferret]
■ **viverr'id** n. **viverr'ine** adj of or like the ferret or the civet family.

vivers /vī'vərz or vē'vərz/ (Scot and literary) n pl food, eatables. [Fr vivres, from L vīvere to live]

vives /vīvz/ n sing a disease of horses, swelling of the submaxillary glands. [OFr avives, vives, from Sp avivas, from Ar addhība, from al the, and dhība she-wolf]

vivi- /vi-vi-/ combining form denoting alive, living. [L vīvus]
■ **vivip'arism** n viviparous reproduction. **viviparity** /viv-i-par'i-ti/ or **vivip'arousness** n the quality of being viviparous. **viviparous** /vī-vip'ə-rəs or vi-/ adj (L parere to produce) producing living young that have already reached an advanced stage of development before delivery, opp to **oviparous** (zool); germinating from a seed still on the parent plant (bot); producing bulbils or young plants in the flower clusters, etc (bot). **vivip'arously** adv. **vivip'ary** n viviparity in plants. **vivisect'** vt to practise vivisection on (also vi). **vivisection** /-sek'shən/ n (L sectiō the act of cutting, from secāre to cut) the act or practice, or an instance, of making surgical operations on living animals for

the purposes of physiological research or demonstration; merciless and minute examination or criticism. **vivisec'tional** *adj*. **vivisec'tionist** *n* a person who practises or defends vivisection. **vivisec'tive** *adj* practising vivisection. **vivisec'tor** *n* someone who practises vivisection. **vivisectō'rium** *n* a place for vivisection. **vivisepulture** /-sep'l-chər/ *n* (*rare*) burial alive.

vivianite /viv'yə-nīt/ *n* ferrous phosphate, blue by oxidation, often found coating fossil fishes and bones. [JG *Vivian* (1785–1855), English mineralogist, who first found it crystallized]

vivid /viv'id/ *adj* (of a colour) very bright; presenting a clear and striking picture; forming brilliant mental images; lively, intense; full of life, vigorous. [L *vīvidus*, from *vīvere* to live]
■ **viv'idly** *adv*. **viv'idness** or (*rare*) **vivid'ity** *n*. **vivif'ic** *adj* vivifying. **vivificā'tion** *n*. **viv'ifier** *n*. **viv'ify** *vt* to endue with life; to make vivid; to assimilate or convert into living tissue. **viv'ifying** *adj*.

viviparous, vivisection, etc see under **vivi-**.

vivo /vē'vō/ (*music*) *adj* lively. [Ital]
■ **vivamente** /vē-vä-men'tä/ *adv* in a lively manner.

vivres same as **vivers**.

vixen /vik's(ə)n/ *n* a female fox; a bad-tempered woman. [S Eng dialect form of *fixen*, from OE *fyxen*, fem of *fox*]
■ **vix'en, vix'enish** or **vix'enly** *adj* bad-tempered, snarling.

Viyella® /vī-el'ə/ *n* a fine soft woven fabric made of cotton and wool (also *adj*).

viz see **videlicet**.

vizament /viz'ə-mənt/ (*Shakesp*) *n* for **advisement** (see under **advise**).

vizard /viz'ərd/ (*obs*) *n* a mask. ◆ *vt* to mask; to disguise, conceal. [Variant of **visor**]
■ **viz'arded** *adj* masked; pretended.
□ **viz'ard-mask** *n* a mask; a masked woman; a prostitute.

vizcacha see **viscacha**.

vizier or **vizir** /vi-zēr', viz'yər or viz'i-ər/ *n* a minister or councillor of state in various Muslim states (also **visier', vezir'** or **wizier'**). [Ar *wazīr* a porter, from *wazara* to bear a burden]
■ **vizier'ate, vizir'ate, vizier'ship** or **vizir'ship** *n* the office of a vizier. **vizier'ial** or **vizir'ial** *adj*.
■ **Grand Vizier** in pre-Republican Turkey, the prime minister, and at one time also commander of the army.

vizor see **visor**.

vizsla /viz'lə or vizh'lə/ *n* a Hungarian breed of hunting dog with smooth red or rust-coloured coat. [*Vizsla*, a town in Hungary]

vizy, vizzie see **visie** under **vision**.

VJ *abbrev*: video jockey.

VJ day /vē-jā'dā/ *abbrev*: Victory over Japan day (15 August 1945, the date of the surrender of Japan to the Allies).

vl *abbrev*: *varia lectio* (L), variant reading (*pl* **vvll**).

Vlach /vlak or vlahh/ *n* one of a non-Slav people of SE Europe, found chiefly in Romania, a Wallachian. [OSlav *Vlachu*, from OHGer *walh* a foreigner, esp a Slav or a Latin]

VLCC *abbrev*: very large crude carrier, a tanker between 200000 and 320000 dead-weight tons.

VLCD *abbrev*: very low calorie diet.

VLE *abbrev*: virtual learning environment.

vlei /flā/ *n* (also **vly**) low-lying ground where a shallow lake forms in the wet season (*Afrik*); a swamp (local *US*). [Dialect Du, from Du *wallei* valley]

VLF *abbrev*: very low frequency.

vlog /vlog/ *n* a weblog consisting primarily or exclusively of moving images. [Short for *video log*; cf **blog**]
■ **vlogg'er** *n*. **vlogg'ing** *n*.

VLSI (*comput*) *abbrev*: very large scale integration, a technological process by which 100000 or more circuits are integrated onto a single silicon chip.

VMD *abbrev*: *Veterināriae Medicinae Doctor* (*L*), Doctor of Veterinary Medicine.

VMH *abbrev*: Victoria Medal of Honour.

VMI (*comput*) *abbrev*: Vertical Motion Index.

VN *abbrev*: Vietnam (IVR).

VO *abbrev*: Royal Victorian Order.

vo *abbrev*: verso.

voar /vōr or vör/ *n* in Orkney and Shetland, spring, seed time. [ON *vár* spring; cf **ware**³]

voc. *abbrev*: vocative.

vocab /vō'kab or və-kab'/ (*inf*) *n* vocabulary.

vocable /vō'kə-bl/ *n* that which is sounded with the voice, a word, or a single sound of a word; a term, name (*obs*). ◆ *adj* capable of being uttered. [L *vocābulum* a name or term, from *vōx, vōcis* voice]
■ **vocab'ular** /vō- or və-kab'/ *adj* of or concerning words. **vocabūlār'ian** *adj* of or relating to vocabulary. ◆ *n* a person much, or too much, concerned with words. **vocab'ularied** *adj*. **vocab'ulary** *n* a list of words explained in alphabetical order; a dictionary; any list of words; the words of a language; the words known to and used by eg a particular person; the words used in a (particular) science or art; the signs or symbols used in any non-verbal type of communication, eg in computer technology; a collection of forms used in an art or by a particular practitioner of an art. **vocab'ulist** *n* the maker of a vocabulary; a lexicographer.

vocal /vō'kəl/ *adj* having a voice; uttered by the voice; oral; sung, or for singing, *opp* to *instrumental*; resounding; talkative; outspoken; eloquent; concerned in the production of speech; of or relating to a vowel; having a vowel function; voiced. ◆ *n* (often in *pl*) singing, or that which is sung, *esp* in a piece of popular music. [L *vōcālis*, from *vōx, vōcis* voice]
■ **vōcalese'** *n* (*jazz*) a type of singing in which the singer improvises words to familiar instrumental solos. **vocal'ic** *adj* containing (*esp* many) vowels; of, relating to, or of the nature of a vowel or vowels. **vocalise** /vō-kə-lēz'/ *n* (*music*) a wordless composition or exercise for solo voice. **vō'calism** *n* exercise of the vocal organs; the art of using the voice in singing; a vocal sound; a system of vowels. **vō'calist** *n* a singer, *esp opp* to *instrumentalist*. **vōcal'ity** *n*. **vōcalizā'tion** or **-s-** *n*. **vō'calize** or **-ise** *vt* to form into voice, to articulate; to sing; to give expression to; to make vocal, endow with power of expression; to convert into a vowel; to utter with voice (*phonetics*); to insert the vowel points eg in Hebrew. ◆ *vi* to sing; to sing *esp* exercises on a vowel or vowels. **vō'calizer** or **-s-** *n*. **vō'cally** *adv*. **vō'calness** *n*. **vocicul'tūral** /vō-si-/ *adj* relating to voice-training. **vocūlar** /vok'/ *adj* (*rare*) vocal. **vocule** /vok'ūl/ *n* a slight vowel sound completing the articulation of certain consonants.
□ **vocal cords** *n pl* in air-breathing vertebrates, folds of the lining membrane of the larynx, by the vibration of the edges of which, under the influence of the breath, the voice is produced. **vocal music** *n* music produced by the human voice alone, *opp* to *instrumental music*. **vocal score** *n* a musical score showing the singing parts in full and the instrumental parts as a piano accompaniment.

vocalion /vō-kā'li-ən/ *n* a musical instrument resembling a harmonium, with broad reeds. [**vocal**, and sfx *-ion*, as in **accordion**]

vocation /vō-kā'shən/ *n* an occupation or profession demanding dedication and skill; a way of living or sphere of activity to which one has been called by God, or for which one has a special fitness or inclination; one's occupation, business, or profession; a calling by God to his service in special work or in a special position, or to a state of salvation; a fitness for God's or other specified work. [L *vocātiō, -ōnis*, from *vocāre* to call]
■ **vocā'tional** *adj* relating to, concerned with, or in preparation for a trade or occupation. **vocā'tionalism** *n* the giving of an important place in education to vocational training. **vocā'tionally** *adv*.

vocative /vok'ə-tiv/ *adj* relating to the act of calling; applied to the grammatical case used in some inflected languages in direct personal address. ◆ *n* the case of a word when a person or thing is addressed; a word in that case. [L *vocātīvus*, from *vocāre* to call]

voces see **vox**.

vocicultural see under **vocal**.

vociferate /vō-sif'ə-rāt/ *vi* to cry out with a loud voice, to bawl. ◆ *vt* to utter in a loud voice. [L *vōciferāt-*, pap stem of *vōciferāri*, from *vōx, vōcis* voice, and *ferre* to carry]
■ **vocif'erance** *n* clamour. **vocif'erant** *adj* clamorous. **vociferā'tion** *n* the act of vociferating; a violent or loud outcry. **vocif'erātor** *n*. **vociferos'ity** *n* (*rare*). **vocif'erous** *adj* making a loud outcry; noisy. **vocif'erously** *adv*. **vocif'erousness** *n*.

vocoder /vō-kō'dər/ *n* an electronic device, similar to a synthesizer, for producing synthetic speech. [*vocal codifier*]

vocular, vocule see under **vocal**.

VOD *abbrev*: video-on-demand.

vodcast /vod'käst/ *vt* and *vi* to publish (video images) on the Internet to be downloaded and played on a client device. ◆ *n* a film or video that is disseminated in this way. [**video** and **podcast**]
■ **vod'caster** *n*. **vod'casting** *n*.

voddy /vod'i/ (*inf*) *n* vodka.

vodka /vod'kə/ *n* a Russian spirit, properly distilled from rye, but sometimes from potatoes, etc. [Russ, dimin of *voda* water]

voe /vō/ *n* in Orkney and Shetland, a bay, creek. [ON *vágr* a creek]

voetganger /fŭt'hhäng-ər or fŭt'gäng-ər/ (*S Afr*) *n* a locust before its wings grow; a pedestrian; an infantryman. [Du *voet* foot, and *gang* walk]

voetsak /fŭt'sak/ (S Afr inf) interj used as an impolite term of dismissal. [Afrik, from Du voort seg ik away, I say]

voetstoots /fŭt'stoo(-ə)ts/ (S Afr) adj (of something sold) as it stands, with any defects it has, visible or not (also adv). [Afrik]

vogie /vō'gi/ (Scot) adj vain; merry. [Origin obscure]

vogue[1] /vōg/ n the mode or fashion at any particular time; a place in popular favour, or the period of it; popularity; the chief place in popular esteem (obs). ◆ adj in vogue, fashionable. ◆ vt (archaic or obs) to give vogue to, or to repute, reckon. [Fr vogue (orig the trim of a rowing vessel), from voguer to row, from Ital vogare; ety uncertain]
■ **vog'uey** or **vog'uish** adj.
❏ **vogue word** n a word much used at a particular time.

vogue[2] /vōg/ (inf, orig US) vi to perform to pop music a stylized dance imitative of the poses of fashion models. [From Vogue, the fashion magazine]
■ **vōg'uer** n. **vōg'uing** (or **vog'ueing**) n.

voice /vois/ n sound produced by the vocal organs of living beings, esp of human beings in speech or song; sound given out by anything; the faculty or power of speech or song; the ability to sing, esp well; a mode of utterance; the quality and range of musical sounds produced by a singer; a singer; a part for a singer, or one of the parts in an instrumental composition; utterance, expression; someone who speaks; sound uttered with resonance of the vocal cords (phonetics); a mode of inflecting verbs to indicate their relationship with the subject (grammar; see **active**, **passive**, and **middle**); an expressed wish or opinion; a vote, approval; a medium of expression; something said (obs); rumour, report, reputation (obs). ◆ vt to utter (rare); to give utterance or expression to; to regulate the tone of (music); to write the voice parts of; to utter with vibration of the vocal cords (phonetics); to endow with voice; to act as mouthpiece of (rare); to rumour or esp (in impers construction) to be rumoured or commonly stated (obs); to speak of (obs); to acclaim (obs); to nominate, appoint, elect (obs). [Anglo-Fr voiz, voice (Fr voix), from L vōx, vōcis; related to Gr epos a word]
■ **voiced** adj endowed with voice; having a voice of a specified kind; uttered with voice (phonetics). **voice'ful** adj having a voice; vocal (with with); full of sound. **voice'fulness** n. **voice'less** adj having no voice; speechless, silent; unspoken; failing to, or unable to, express one's opinion or desire, or to make this felt; having no vote; not voiced (phonetics). **voice'lessness** n. **voic'er** n. **voic'ing** n the regulation of the tone of organ pipes, ensuring proper power, pitch, and quality.
❏ **voice box** n the larynx. **voice mail** or **voice'mail** n (telecom) a system by which telephone messages can be stored in a central location and picked up by the addressee at their convenience. **voice'-mail** adj. **Voice of America** n an international broadcasting service funded by the US government. **voice'-over** n the background voice of an unseen narrator in a film, etc. **voice'print** n an electronically recorded visual representation of speech indicating frequency, amplitude and duration. **voice recognition** n the identification of a human speaker by a computer (which compares their voice with sounds stored in its memory) before it carries out an instruction, allows access, etc. **voice response** n output from a computer in the form of synthesized speech rather than a visual display. **voice synthesis** n the ability of a computer to produce simulated speech from sounds stored in its memory. **voice vote** n a vote judged on the relative strengths of the shouted ayes and noes.
■ **give voice to** to express. **in good voice** or **in voice** in good condition for singing or speaking. **in my voice** (Shakesp) in my name. **with one voice** unanimously.

void /void/ adj containing nothing, empty, deserted; unoccupied, unutilized; having no holder, vacant; devoid, destitute, free (with of); ineffectual, useless; not binding in law, null, invalid; worthless (obs). ◆ n an empty space; (with the) the expanse of space; emptiness; a lack, esp an emotional lack strongly felt; an unfilled space (archit); the total absence of cards of a particular suit (bridge, etc). ◆ vt to make vacant, to empty, clear; to empty (the bladder or bowels); to send out, discharge, emit; to make of no effect, to nullify; to send away, dismiss (obs); to remove, clear away (obs); to go away from, withdraw from, quit (obs); to avoid (obs); to lay aside, divest oneself of (obs). [OFr voide empty, from popular L vocitus, from vocitāre to empty, from vocuus, for L vacuus empty]
■ **void'able** adj that may be voided; (of a deed or transaction) valid or effective yet remaining open to legal challenge (law). **void'ance** n the act of voiding or emptying; the state of being void; (of a benefice) the fact or state of being vacant. **void'ed** adj (heraldry) (of a charge) having the inner part cut away and showing the tincture of the field. **void'ee** n (hist) wine and light food taken before going to bed, or before the departure of guests. **void'er** n (lit and fig) a person who empties or (hist) who clears a table; a tray for carrying away dirty dishes, crumbs, etc, or a tray, etc, for carrying sweetmeats (obs); a piece of armour covering an unprotected part of the body. **void'ing** n the act of voiding; that which is voided (often in pl). **void'ness** n.
❏ **void'ing-lobby** n (obs) an anteroom.

voilà /vwä-lä'/ interj behold; there you are. [Fr, behold, there is, there are]
❏ **voilà tout** /too/ n that is all.

voile /voil or vwäl/ n any of several kinds of thin semitransparent material. [Fr, veil]

VOIP /voip/ abbrev: Voice Over Internet Protocol, a telecommunications standard that enables spoken communication via the Internet.

voir dire /vwär dēr'/ (law) n an oath administered to a witness; an investigation, in the course of a trial, into the truth or admissibility of evidence about to be given. [OFr voir true, truth, and dire to say]

voisinage /voi'si-nij/ (obs) n neighbourhood, or the neighbourhood. [Fr]

voiture /vwä-tür'/ n a carriage. [Fr]
■ **voiturier** /vwä-tür-yā/ n the driver of a carriage or coach.

voivode /voi'vōd/ or **vaivode** /vä'vōd/ n orig, the leader of an army; later, in SE Europe, the title of the head of an administrative division, a provincial governor; a title of the former princes of Moldavia and Wallachia; in Turkey, an inferior administrative official. [Russ voevoda (Serb vojvoda, Pol wojewoda)]
■ **voi'vodeship** or **vai'vodeship** n.

voix céleste /vwä sā-lest'/ n an organ stop producing a soft, tremulous sound. [Fr, heavenly voice]

vol /vol/ (heraldry) n two wings displayed and conjoined in base. [Fr]

vol. abbrev: volume; voluntary; volunteer.

vola /vō'lə/ (anat) n (pl volae /vō'lē/) the hollow of the hand or foot. [L]
■ **vo'lar** adj relating to the palm or to the sole.

volable /vol'ə-bl/ (Shakesp) adj nimble-witted. [L volāre to fly]

volage /vō'läzh/ or **volageous** /vō-lä'jəs/ adj giddy, flighty, fickle. [Fr]

Volans /vol'ans or vō'lans/ n the Flying Fish, a southern constellation. [L prp of volāre to fly]

volant /vō'lənt/ adj flying; passing lightly through the air; flying or relating to flight (zool); nimble; represented as flying (heraldry); (of armed forces, etc) organized for rapid movement (obs). [L volāre to fly]
■ **volante** /vō-län'tā/ adj (music) moving lightly and rapidly. **vo'lary** n an aviary. **volat'ic** adj (now rare) flying about. **vol'ery** n a volary; a place for repair, etc, of aircraft.

volante[1] /vō-lan'tā/ n a two-wheeled covered vehicle with long shafts, with a chaise-body hung before the axle, and the horse, or one of the horses, being ridden by a postillion. [Sp]

volante[2] see under **volant**.

Volapük /vol', vōl'ə-pük, -puk or -pük'/ n an early international language invented about 1879 by the German priest Johann Schleyer. [Literally, world-speech, from vol world, and pük speak]
■ **Volapük'ist** n one versed in Volapük; one who advocates the adoption of Volapük.

volar see under **vola**.

volary, etc see under **volant**.

volatile /vol'ə-tīl or (N Am) -til or -təl/ adj evaporating very quickly; explosive; subject to sudden changes in emotional state; flighty, apt to change; (of stock markets, etc) showing rapid changes in prices; transient, short-lived, fleeting; denoting a type of memory (**volatile memory**) that does not retain information after the power supply is turned off, opp to non-volatile (comput); capable of flying; moving lightly and rapidly about. ◆ n a volatile substance; a creature capable of flying (obs). [L volātilis able to fly, fleeting, from volāre to fly]
■ **vol'atileness** or **volatility** /-til'/ n. **vol'atilizable** or **-s-** (or /-at'/) adj. **volatilīzā'tion** or **-s-** n. **vol'atilize** or **-ise** (or /-at'/) vt and vi to make or become volatile. ◆ vt to cause to evaporate; to make light, unsubstantial or delicate (fig).
❏ **volatile alkali** n (obs) ammonia. **volatile oils** see **essential oils** under **essence**.

vol-au-vent /vol'ō-vä/ n a kind of small pie of light puff pastry filled with meat, or fish, etc in a sauce. [Fr, literally flight in the wind]

volcano /vol-kā'nō/ n (pl volcan'oes) a centre of eruption of subterranean matter, typically a more or less conical hill or mountain, built of ash and lava, with a central crater and pipe; a state of affairs, emotional condition, etc, suggestive of a volcano because an upheaval or outburst seems imminent; a form of firework. [Ital volcano, from L Volcānus, Vulcānus Vulcan, god of fire]
■ **volca'nian** adj (Keats). **volcanic** /vol-kan'ik/ adj relating to, of the nature of, produced or caused by a volcano; characterized by the presence of volcanoes; given to sudden outbursts of emotion. **volcan'ically** adv. **volcanicity** /-kə-nis'i-ti/ n volcanic action or phenomena. **volcanism** and **volcanist** n (also with caps) see **vulcanism** and **Vulcanist** under **Vulcan**. **volcanizā'tion** or **-s-** n. **vol'canize** or **-ise** vt to subject to the action of volcanic heat.

vol'canized or **-s-** adj. **volcanolog'ical** adj. **volcanol'ogist** n a vulcanologist. **volcanol'ogy** n vulcanology.

❑ **volcanic ash** or **ashes** see under **ash**[1]. **volcanic bomb** see under **bomb**. **volcanic dust** n fine particles of powdered rock blown out from a volcano. **volcanic glass** n rock without a crystalline structure, as obsidian, pumice, etc, produced by rapid cooling of molten lava. **volcanic mud** or **sand** n volcanic ash that has been deposited under water and sorted and stratified. **volcanic rocks** n pl those formed by volcanic agency.

vole[1] /vōl/ n any of numerous blunt-nosed, short-eared, mouselike or ratlike rodents, including the so-called water rat and some fieldmice. [For vole-mouse, ie fieldmouse, of Scand origin]

vole[2] /vōl/ n in certain card games, (the winning of) all the tricks in one deal. ◆ vi to win all the tricks in one deal. [Fr, from L volāre to fly]
■ **go the vole** to risk all for great gain; to try everything.

volens /vō'lenz/ (law) n and adj (a person) consenting to a course of action which involves a risk of some sort (and therefore unable to sue if injury occurs). [Prp of L velle to be willing]
■ **volenti non fit injuria** /vō-len'ti nōn fit in-joo'ri-a/ no injury is done to a consenting party.

volente Deo /va-len'tē dē'ō, vō- or wō-len'te de'ō/ (L) God willing.

volery see under **volant**.

volet /vol'ā/ n one of the wings of a triptych picture; a short veil worn at the back of the head (hist). [OFr (Fr, a shutter), from L volāre to fly]

Volga-Baltaic /vol'gä-böl-tā'ik/ adj of or relating to the group of languages to which Estonian, Finnish and Lapp belong. [Volga river, and Baltic Sea]

volitant /vol'ə-tant/ adj flying; flitting; fluttering; moving about; able to fly. [L volitāre to flit, flutter]
■ **vol'itate** vi to flutter, fly. **volitā'tion** n flight; the power of flying. **volitā'tional** adj. **volitorial** /-tö'ri-/ adj having the power of flight.

volition /vō-lish'ən/ n the act of willing or choosing; the exercise of the will, or the result of this; the power of determining. [Fr, from LL volitiō, from L volō, pr indicative of velle to will, be willing]
■ **voli'tient** adj (rare) willing. **voli'tional** or **voli'tionary** adj. **voli'tionally** adv. **voli'tionless** adj. **vol'itive** adj of or relating to the will; originating in the will; willed, deliberate; expressing a wish (grammar). ◆ n a desiderative verb, etc.

volk /folk/ (S Afr) n a people, esp the Afrikaner people. [Du, people, nation]

Völkerwanderung /fœl'kər-van-də-rŭng/ (Ger) n the migration of Germanic and other peoples, chiefly in the 4c to 6c.

Volkskammer /folks'kam-ər/ n the parliament of the former German Democratic Republic. [Ger Volk people, and Kammer chamber]

Volkslied /folks'lēt/ n (pl **Volkslieder** /-lē-dər/) a German folk song. [Ger]

volksraad /folks'rät/ n a legislative assembly, esp (with cap) that of the Transvaal or the Orange Free State before 1900. [Du volk people, and raad council]

volley /vol'i/ n (pl **voll'eys**) a flight of missiles; the discharge of many weapons (esp small arms) at once; a round fired by every gun in a battery; an outburst of many words, etc at once; (in tennis, football, etc) a strike of the ball before it reaches the ground (a **half volley** is a strike of the ball immediately after it bounces); a ball struck in this way. ◆ vt to discharge in a volley; to return (a ball) before it bounces; to fire a volley or volleys at. ◆ vi to fly or be discharged in a volley; to sound or produce sounds like a volley; to roll, move or be emitted like a volley; to produce a volley in tennis, etc. [Fr volée a flight, from L volāre to fly]
■ **voll'eyed** adj. **voll'eyer** n.
❑ **voll'eyball** n a team game in which a large ball is volleyed by the hand over a high net; the ball used in the game.

volost /vō'lost/ n a division for local government in tsarist Russia (hist); a soviet of a rural district. [Russ]

volpino /vol-pē'nō/ n (pl **volpin'os**) a small Italian dog with long, straight hair and fox-like appearance. [Ital, foxy, from volpe fox, from L vulpēs]

volplane /vol'plän/ (aeronautics) vi to glide down to earth in an aeroplane with the engine shut off; to glide to earth. ◆ n a descent of this kind. [Fr vol plané, from vol flight, and plané, pap of planer to glide]

Volscian /vol'shən/ n one of the Volscī, an ancient Italian people incessantly at war with the Romans for 200 years previous to 338BC; their Italic language. ◆ adj of or relating to the Volsci or their language.

Volsungs /vol'soongz/ n pl a famous heroic race in old German legend, its founder Volsung being the grandson of Woden or Odin.

volt[1] /vōlt/ n a derived SI unit, the unit of electromotive force, electric potential, or potential difference (symbol **V**), equal to the potential difference across a conductor when one ampere of current in it dissipates one watt of power. [Alessandro Volta (1745–1827), Italian scientist]
■ **volta-** /vol-tə-/ combining form denoting voltaic, as in volta-electricity and volta-electric. **voltage** /volt' or vōlt'ij/ n electromotive force in volts; power, intensity (fig). **voltaic** /vol-tā'ik/ adj relating to Alessandro Volta, who constructed the first electrical battery, a **voltaic pile**, and established the science of current electricity; (of electricity) generated by chemical action; used in producing such electricity; of, relating to or caused by voltaic electricity. **vol'taism** n the branch of electricity concerning the production of an electric current from the chemical interaction of two immersed dissimilar metals. **voltameter** /vol-tam'i-tər/ n an instrument formerly used for measuring an electric current by means of the amount of metal deposited, or gas liberated, from an electrolyte in a given time by the passage of the current. **vōlt'meter** n an instrument for measuring electromotive force directly, calibrated in volts.
❑ **voltage divider** n a chain of impedances, most commonly resistors or capacitors, such that the voltage across one or more is an accurately known fraction of that applied to all. **voltaic cell** n a primary cell. **volt-amp'eres** n pl the product of actual voltage (in volts) and actual current (in amperes) in a circuit.

volt[2] or **volte** /volt/ n a sudden movement or leap to avoid a thrust (fencing); the gait of a horse going sideways round a centre; a track made by a horse executing this movement. ◆ vi to make a volt. [Fr volte, from Ital volta, from L volvere, volūtum to turn]
■ **vol'tage** n.

volta /vol'tə/ n (pl **vol'te** /-tā/) an old dance, the lavolta; turn, time (music). [Ital]

voltage see under **volt**[1,2].

voltaic see under **volt**[1].

Voltairian or **Voltairean** /vol-tār'i-ən/ adj relating to or associated with Voltaire (1694–1778), French poet, dramatist, historian, and sceptic. ◆ n a person who advocates the views and principles of Voltaire.
■ **Voltair'ianism**, **Voltair'eanism** or **Voltair'ism** n the spirit of Voltaire, ie a sceptical and sarcastic attitude, esp towards Christianity, or an instance of this, or adherence to his doctrines.

voltameter see under **volt**[1].

volte see **volt**[2], **volta**.

volte-face /volt-fäs'/ n a turning round; a sudden and complete change in opinion or in views expressed. [Fr]

voltigeur /vol-ti-zhœr'/ (hist) n in the French Army, one of a light-armed company of picked men for skirmishing. [Fr, from voltiger to flutter, vault]

voltinism /vol'tin-i-zm/ n breeding rhythm, brood frequency (esp of insects). [Ital volta]

voluble /vol'ū-bl/ adj fluent in speech; too fluent or glib; talkative, verbose; twining (bot); changeable (rare); easy to roll, revolving readily or smoothly (rare; Milton volubil); flowing smoothly. [L volūbilis, from volvere, volūtum to roll]
■ **volubil'ity** or **vol'ubleness** n. **vol'ubly** adv.

volucrine /vol'ū-krin or -krīn/ adj relating to birds, birdlike. [L volucris a bird, from volāre to fly]

volume /vol'ūm/ n quantity, bulk; cubic capacity; a large quantity; a quantity considered in terms of its bulk; fullness of tone; loudness, or the control for adjusting it on a radio, etc; a book, whether complete in itself or part of a larger work; a roll or scroll, which was the form of ancient books; a fixed amount of storage on a disk or tape (comput); anything (esp in the natural world) that may be studied like a book (archaic). ◆ vi (archaic) to swell, rise, roll. ◆ vt (archaic) to send out in volumes, or in great quantity; to make into or bind into a volume. ◆ adj of or concerned with large volumes or amounts. [Fr, from L volūmen, -inis a roll, from volvere, volūtum to roll]
■ **vol'umed** adj having the form of a volume or roll; bulky. ◆ combining form denoting consisting of (esp a specified number of) volumes. **volumenom'eter** or **volumom'eter** n an instrument for measuring the volume of a solid body by the quantity of fluid it displaces. **volu'meter** n an instrument for measuring the volumes of gases and liquids. **volumet'ric** or **volumet'rical** adj. **volumet'rically** adv. **volu'minal** adj relating to cubic capacity. **voluminos'ity** n extensiveness of writing. **volu'minous** adj bulky, filling much space; in many volumes; capable of filling many volumes; having written much, as an author; consisting of many coils, windings or folds. **volu'minously** adv. **volu'minousness** n. **vol'umist** n (rare) an author. **vol'umize** or **-ise** vt to give extra body to (hair). **vol'umizer** or **-s-** n.
❑ **volumetric analysis** n the estimation of the amount of a particular constituent present in a compound by determining the quantity of a

voluntary /vol'ən-tər-i or -tri/ adj spontaneous, free; done or made without compulsion or legal obligation; acting by choice, able to will; freely given, or supported by contributions freely given; done without expectation of payment or recompense of any kind, esp monetary; free from state control; proceeding from the will; designed, intentional; subject to the will; of or relating to voluntaryism. ◆ n a person who does anything of his or her own free will; a piece of music played at will; a voluntary or extempore composition of any kind; a piece of music played before, during, or after a church service; an unwarranted fall from a horse; an upholder of voluntaryism; a volunteer (obs). [L voluntārius, from voluntās choice, from volō, pres indicative of velle to will]
■ **vol'untarily** adv. **vol'untariness** n. **vol'untarism** n the philosophical doctrine that the will dominates the intellect; voluntaryism. **vol'untarist** n. **voluntaris'tic** adj. **vol'untaryism** n the principle or practice of reliance on voluntary action, not coercion; the principle or system of maintaining the church by voluntary offerings, instead of by the aid of the state; the principle or system of maintaining voluntary schools (qv below). **vol'untaryist** n. **vol'untātive** adj voluntary.
◻ **voluntary-aided school** n a state school partly funded by a local education authority and supported by a religious organization, which has a role in governing it. **voluntary chain** or **retailers** n a group of independent retailers who combine to buy their stock so as to increase profits. **voluntary-controlled school** n a state school funded and governed entirely by a local education authority. **voluntary muscle** n a muscle, or muscular tissue, that is controlled by the will. **voluntary school** n a school supported by voluntary subscriptions, in many cases controlled by a religious body. **voluntary sector** n the part of a country's economy made up of voluntary organizations. **Voluntary Service Overseas** n a British organization that promotes voluntary work, mainly by young people, in developing countries; the work itself (abbrev **VSO**).

volunteer /vol-ən-tēr'/ n a person who offers to do something voluntarily; a person who enters military service, of his or her own free choice; a soldier belonging to any body other than the regular army; someone who acts of his or her own free will, esp (law) in a transaction, without either legal obligation to do so or promise of remuneration; a person to whom property is transferred without their giving valuable consideration (law). ◆ adj consisting of or relating to volunteers; giving voluntary service; given voluntarily; (of a plant or plants) growing spontaneously, from seed not deliberately sown. ◆ vt to offer voluntarily to give, supply or perform; to give (information) unasked; to assign (a person, etc) to a task without consultation (inf). ◆ vi to offer to do something of one's own free will or without being asked; to enter military service voluntarily. [Fr volontaire, from L voluntārius]
■ **volunteer'ism** n (US) the use of volunteers in educational and social work in a community.

voluptuary /və-lup'tū-ə-ri/ n a person excessively fond of or devoted to bodily enjoyments or luxury, a sensualist. ◆ adj promoting or characterized by sensual pleasure. [LL voluptuārius, from L voluptās pleasure]

voluptuous /və-lup'tū-əs/ adj full of or suggestive of pleasure, esp sensuous; relating to, consisting of, derived from or ministering to sensual pleasure; shapely and sexually attractive; given to excess of pleasure, esp sensual. [L voluptuōsus, from voluptās pleasure]
■ **volup'tuously** adv. **volup'tuousness** or (obs) **voluptuos'ity** n.

Völuspa /vol-u-spa' or væl'oo-spa/ n one of the poems of the Elder Edda; (without cap) a sibyl or prophetess (a wrong use, found in Scott's Pirate). [ON Völuspā the song of the sibyl, from völva a wise woman]

volutation /vol-ū-tā'shən/ (rare or obs; lit and fig) n the action of rolling, turning, wallowing. [L volūtātiō, -ōnis, from volūtāre, from volvere, volūtum to roll]

volute /və-lūt' or vol'ūt/ n a spiral scroll used esp in Ionic capitals; a spiral form; a thing or part having such a shape; any marine shell of the genus Voluta or related genera, allied to the whelks, or the animal itself; a whorl of a spiral shell. ◆ adj rolled up in any direction, having a spiral form. [L volvere, volūtum to roll]
■ **volū'ted** adj in spiral form; having a volute or volutes. **vol'ūtin** n a substance found in granular form (**volutin granules**) in the cytoplasm of various cells, believed to contribute to the formation of chromatin. **volū'tion** n a revolving movement; a convolution; a whorl. **vol'ūtoid** adj like a volute.

volva /vol'və/ (bot) n a sheath enclosing the whole of the fruit body of some agarics. [L; see vulva]
■ **vol'vate** adj having a volva.

volve /volv/ (obs) vt and vi to turn over; to ponder. [L volvere]

volvox /vol'voks/ (bot) n any member of the genus Volvox of simple organisms found in ponds, canals, etc, commonly regarded as algae, consisting of green flagellate cells united by protoplasmic bridges in a hollow spherical colony. [New L, from L volvere]

volvulus /vol'vū-ləs/ (med) n the twisting of an abdominal viscus causing internal obstruction. [New L, from L volvere]

vom /vom/ (sl) vi (**vomm'ing**, **vommed**) to vomit. ◆ n an act of vomiting.

vomer /vō'mər/ (anat and zool) n a bone of the skull in most vertebrates, in humans a thin flat bone, shaped like a wedge or ploughshare, forming part of the middle partition of the nose. [L vōmer a ploughshare]
■ **vomerine** /vō' or vo'mə-rīn or -rin/ adj. **vomero-** combining form denoting the vomer, as in **vomeronas'al**, relating to the vomer and the nasal cavity.

vomica see under vomit.

vomit /vom'it/ vi (**vom'iting**; **vom'ited**) to throw up the contents of the stomach through the mouth, to spew; (of an emetic) to cause vomiting; to be ejected with violence. ◆ vt to spew; to throw out with violence; to cause to vomit. ◆ n the act of vomiting; matter ejected from the stomach; vile people or things; something that induces vomiting, an emetic. [L vomere, -itum to vomit; Gr emeein]
■ **vom'ica** n a cavity in the lung containing pus. **vom'iting** n. **vom'itive** adj causing vomiting. ◆ n an emetic. **vom'ito** n the worst form of yellow fever, usu accompanied by black vomit. **vom'itory** n an opening in a large building by which the crowd is let out (also, Roman hist, **vomitō'rium**); a vent (lit and fig); an emetic (archaic). ◆ adj emetic. **vomituri'tion** n violent retching. **vom'itus** n matter vomited.

V-1 /vē-wun'/ and **V-2** /vē-too'/ n respectively, a robot flying bomb and long-range rocket-powered missile, used by the Germans in World War II esp to bomb the southern part of England. [Ger Vergeltungswaffe retaliation weapon]

vongole /von'gə-lā/ n pl in Italian cookery, small clams. [Ital]

voodoo or **voudou** /voo'doo or -doo'/ n (also **vaudoux** or **vaudoo** /vō-doo'/) religious beliefs and practices of African origin found among the black peoples of the West Indies and Southern USA, formerly including serpent-worship, human sacrifice and cannibalism, but now largely confined to sorcery; any form of magic-working; a person who practises this kind of religious sorcery. ◆ adj of, relating to or carrying out voodoo practices. ◆ vt to bewitch by voodoo charms. [W Afr vodu a spirit]
■ **voo'dooism** (or /-doo'/) n voodoo practices or beliefs. **voo'dooist** (or /-doo'/) n. **voodooist'ic** adj.

voortrekker /fōr-trek'ər, foor' or vōr-/ n (usu with cap) one of the Dutch farmers from Cape Colony who took part in the Great Trek into the Transvaal in 1836 and following years; a member of an Afrikaner Scout-type youth movement; a pioneer. [Cape Du, from Du voor- before, and **trek**]

Vor or **VOR** /vōr/ n an American aid to aircraft navigation. [Very-High-Frequency Omni-Directional-Range]

vor /vōr/ (Shakesp, King Lear IV.6.247, in dialect passage) vt (perh) to warn.

voracious /və-rā'shəs, vō- or vō-/ adj eating greedily or in large quantities; taking in or engulfing a great deal; very eager, or insatiable; characterized by greediness (lit and fig). [L vorāx, vorācis, from vorāre to devour]
■ **vorā'ciously** adv. **voracity** /-ras'/ or **vorā'ciousness** n.

voraginous /vō-raj'i-nəs or vō-/ (obs or rare) adj relating to a whirlpool; voracious. [L vorāgo, from vorāre to devour]
■ **vorā'go** /-gō/ n (pl **vorā'goes**) a gulf.

vorant /vō'rənt or vō'/ (heraldry) adj devouring. [L vorāns, -antis, prp of vorāre to devour]

-vore /-vōr/ combining form denoting the eater of a specific sort of food, as in insectivore. [L -vorus (adj sfx), from vorāre to devour]
■ **-vorous** adj combining form.

vorpal /vōr'pəl/ adj a nonsense word coined by Lewis Carroll to describe a sword, later used to mean sharp-edged.

vortex /vōr'teks/ n (pl **vor'tices** /-ti-sēz/ or **vor'texes**) a whirling motion of a liquid, gas or fire forming a cavity in the centre, a whirlpool, an eddy, a whirlwind; a pursuit, way of life, situation, etc, that engulfs one irresistibly or remorselessly, taking up all one's attention or energies; according to a hypothesis of Descartes, etc, a rotary movement of atoms or particles of subtle matter round an axis, or the matter itself in rotation, such phenomena accounting for the formation of the universe and the relative motion of its parts. [L vortex, variant of vertex, -icis, from vortere, variant of vertere to turn]

■ **vor'tical** *adj* of or relating to a vortex; whirling. **vor'tically** *adv*. **vor'ticism** /-*tis-izm*'/ *n* a British movement in the arts, a development from futurism, blending cubism and expressionism, and emphasizing the complications of machinery that characterize modern life. **vor'ticist** *n* a person who supports or practises vorticism. **vortic'ity** *n* the amount of vortical motion in a fluid. **vor'ticose**, **vortic'ular** or **vortiginous** /-*ij*'/ *adj* vortical. ❑ **vortex street** *n* (*aerodynamics*) the regular procession of vortices forming behind a bluff or rectangle body in two parallel rows. **vortex theory** *n* a theory (by Kelvin) that the material atom consists of a vortically moving frictionless fluid.

vorticella /vör-ti-sel'ə/ *n* (*pl* **-ae** /-ē/) any organism of the genus *Vorticella* of ciliated protozoans belonging to the order Peritrichida, in which the cilia are restricted to a fringe round the mouth. [New L dimin, from L *vortex*]

Vosgian or **Vosgean** /vö'zhi-ən/ *adj* of or relating to the *Vosges* Mountains in E France.

votary /vö'tə-ri/ *n* (also *fem* **vō'taress** or **vō'tress**) a person dedicated by or as if by a vow to some service, worship or way of life; someone enthusiastically addicted to a pursuit, study, etc; a devoted worshipper or adherent. ◆ *adj* (*obs*) consecrated by, or of the nature of, vows; of the nature of a vow. [LL *vōtārius*, from L *vovēre*, *vōtum* to vow] ■ **vō'tarist** *n* a votary. **vot'ive** *adj* given, erected, etc, by vow; undertaken or observed in fulfilment of a vow; consisting of or expressing a vow or a wish; voluntary, not obligatory (*relig*, *esp RC*). ❑ **votive picture** or **tablet** *n* one dedicated in fulfilment of a vow.

vote /vöt/ *n* an expression of a wish or opinion in an authorized formal way; collective opinion, decision by a majority; a group of votes or voters collectively; a voter; the right to vote; a means by which a choice is expressed, such as a ballot; a ballot paper; the total number of votes cast; an earnest desire (*obs*). ◆ *vi* to express choice, *esp* at an election, by vote; to declare oneself in favour of, or against (with *for* or *against*), *esp* by vote; to give one's vote to a specified political party, on a particular occasion or habitually. ◆ *vt* to determine by vote; to grant by vote; to bring about (a specified result or change) by vote; to elect to an office; to declare by general consent, to pronounce, adjudge to be (*inf*); to propose, suggest (*inf*); to present for voting, to record the votes of (*US*). [L *vōtum* a wish, from *vovēre*, *vōtum* to vow] ■ **vote'less** *adj*. **vō'ter** *n*. ❑ **vote of confidence** *n* a vote that demonstrates support for a leader, government, etc. **vote of no confidence** *n* the legal method of forcing the resignation of a leader, government or governing body. **voting machine** *n* (*esp US*) a machine on which to register votes. ■ **split one's vote** or **votes** to divide one's votes among two or more candidates. **split the vote** to injure a cause by influencing a body of possible supporters to vote in some other way (**vote'-splitt'ing** *n*). **vote down** to defeat or suppress by vote, or by some other means. **vote in** to elect. **vote out** to dismiss from office by a vote. **vote straight** to give one's vote honestly. **vote with one's feet** to indicate one's dissatisfaction with a situation or conditions by leaving.

voteen /vö-tēn'/ (*Irish*) *n* a devotee. [Perh **devote**]

votive see under **votary**.

vouch /vowch/ *vi* to bear witness, or be surety (with *for*). ◆ *vt* to support by evidence; to testify (that); to be sponsor for (*rare*); to guarantee legal possession of (*Shakesp*); to vouchsafe, condescend to grant (*archaic*); to second, support (*Milton*); to call upon to witness, *esp* to a title to real estate (also **vouch to warrant**, **vouch to warranty**; *archaic*); to cite as authority (*obs*); to assert, declare (*obs*); to assert or guarantee to be true (*obs*). ◆ *n* an assertion; an attestation. [OFr *voucher*, *vocher* to call to defend, from L *vocāre* to call] ■ **vouchee'** *n* the person summoned to witness to a title to real estate; a person quoted as authority or appealed to as witness. **vouch'er** *n* (partly Anglo-Fr *voucher*, infinitive; partly sfx *-er*) a piece of evidence, or a written document serving as proof; a paper that confirms the truth of anything, such as a receipt, a certificate of correctness; a ticket, etc, substituting or exchangeable for cash or goods; a person who vouches or gives witness; the act of vouching to warrant (*obs law*).

vouchsafe /vowch-sāf'/, formerly also (*Milton*) **voutsafe** /vowt'sāf/ *vt* (**vouchsāf'ing**; **vouchsafed'**) to condescend to grant; to condescend to allow, to accept, or to engage in; to condescend, be graciously willing to tell, etc; to warrant safe, guarantee (*obs*). ◆ *vi* to condescend. [Orig two words, **vouch** and **safe**] ■ **vouchsafe'ment** *n*. **vouchsāf'ing** *n*.

voudou see **voodoo**.

vouge or **voulge** /voozh/ *n* a weapon carried by foot soldiers in the 14c, having a blade fixed on a long staff. [Fr]

voulu /voo-lü'/ (*Fr*) *adj* deliberate, studied.

voussoir /voo-swär'/ (*archit*) *n* one of the wedge-like stones that form part of an arch. ◆ *vt* to form with voussoirs. [Fr, through LL, from L *volūtus*, from *volvere* to roll]

voutsafe see **vouchsafe**.

Vouvray /voo'vrā/ *n* a dry white wine of the *Vouvray* district of the Loire Valley.

vow /vow/ *n* a voluntary promise made to God, or to a saint, or to a god or gods; a binding undertaking or resolve; a solemn or formal promise of fidelity or affection; a firm assertion; an earnest wish or prayer. ◆ *vt* to give or dedicate by solemn promise; to promise or threaten solemnly; to maintain solemnly. ◆ *vi* to make vows. [OFr *vou* (Fr *vœu*), from L *vōtum*, from *vovēre* to vow] ■ **vowed** *adj* devoted, confirmed, undertaken, etc, by vow, or as if by vow; bound by religious vows (*obs*). **vow'er** *n*. **vow'ess** *n* (*hist*) a woman who has taken a vow; a nun. ❑ **vow'-fellow** *n* (*Shakesp*) a person bound by the same vow. ■ **baptismal vows** the promises made at baptism by the person baptized, or by their sponsors or parents. **simple vow** a more limited, less permanent vow than a solemn vow. **solemn vow** a vow made on entering a religious order (such as those of poverty, obedience, and chastity), involving complete and irrevocable commitment.

vowel /vow'əl/ *n* a speech-sound produced by the unimpeded passage of the breath (modified by the vocal cords into voice) through the mouth, different vowel sounds being made by altering the form and position of the tongue and the lips; a letter (usually *a*, *e*, *i*, *o* or *u*) used alone or in combination to represent a vowel sound; (in *pl*) an IOU (*old sl*). ◆ *adj* of, representing or of the nature of a vowel. ◆ *vt* (also **vow'elize** or **-ise**) to insert vowel signs in (words written primarily with consonants only); to use as a vowel; to modify by vowel sounds; (**vowel**) to promise to pay, offer an IOU to (*old sl*). [Fr *voyelle*, from L *vōcālis*, from *vōx*, *vōcis* voice] ■ **vow'elled** *adj* having vowels, *esp* to a marked degree; having a vowel or vowels of a specified kind. **vow'elless** *adj* without vowels. **vow'elly** *adj* full of vowels. ❑ **vowel gradation** *n* ablaut. **vowel mutation** *n* umlaut. **vowel point** *n* a mark inserted, eg in Hebrew, to indicate a vowel. **vowel'-rhyme** *n* assonance.

vox /voks, vōks or wōks/ *n* (*pl* **voces** /vō'sēz, -kēs or wō'kās/) voice. [L *vōx*] ❑ **vox angelica** /an-jel'i-kə or an-gel'i-ka/, **vox caelestis** /sē-les'tis or kī-/ *n* voix céleste. **vox humana** /hū-mä'nə, hū-mä'nə or hoo-mä'na/ *n* in organ-building, a reed stop producing tones resembling those of the human voice. ■ **vox populi vox Dei** /pop'ū-lī, dē'ī, po'pŭ-lē, de'ē or dä'ē'/ the voice of the people is the voice of God, hence **vox populi** (often shortened to **vox pop**) public or popular opinion, **vox pop** now *esp* applied to brief street interviews with members of the public on radio or TV (also *adj*).

voxel /vok'səl/ (*comput*, *image technol*) *n* a point in a three-dimensional computer image, equivalent to a pixel in a two-dimensional image. [*vol*ume and *el*ement, after **pixel**]

voyage /voi'ij/ *n* a passage by water or by air to some place at a considerable distance; a round trip; a cruise; an account of such a journey; a journey of any kind (*archaic*); travel (*obs*); a military expedition (*obs*); an enterprise (*obs*). ◆ *vi* to make a voyage, cruise or journey. ◆ *vt* to traverse, pass over. [OFr *veage*, *voiage*, etc, from L *viāticum* (see **viaticum**)] ■ **voy'ageable** *adj* navigable. **voy'ager** *n*. **voyageur** /vwä-yä-zhœr'/ in Canada, a person who kept up communication by canoe between trading-posts; a boatman; a trapper.

voyeur /vwä-yœr'/ *n* a person who derives gratification from surreptitiously watching sexual acts or objects; a peeping Tom; a person who takes a morbid interest in sordid sights. [Fr, one who sees] ■ **voy'eurism** *n*. **voyeuris'tic** *adj*.

vozhd /vozhd/ *n* a supreme leader in Russia, often applied to Stalin. [Russ, chief]

VP *abbrev* : Vice-President.

VPL *abbrev* : visible panty line.

VPN *abbrev* : virtual private network, a secure computer network that contains links to a larger network.

VR *abbrev* : variant reading; *Victoria Regina* (*L*), Queen Victoria; virtual reality.

vraic /vrāk/ *n* a Channel Islands name for seaweed, used for fuel and manure. [Dialect Fr; see **varec**] ■ **vraick'er** *n* a gatherer of vraic. **vraick'ing** *n* the gathering of vraic.

vraisemblance /vrā- or vre-sä-bläs'/ *n* verisimilitude; a picture. [Fr *vrai* true, and *semblance* appearance]

VRAM (*comput*) *abbrev* : video random access memory.

V. Rev. *abbrev* : Very Reverend.

VRI *abbrev* : *Victoria Regina et Imperatrix* (*L*), Victoria, Queen and Empress.

■ words derived from main entry word; ❑ compound words; ■ idioms and phrasal verbs

VRML (*comput*) *abbrev*: Virtual Reality Modelling Language (*orig* Mark-up Language).

vroom /vroom or vrŭm/ (*inf*) *interj* denoting the sound of an engine revving or of a car travelling at high speed. ◆ *vi* to travel speedily. ◆ *vt* to rev (an engine).

vrouw or **vrow** /vrow or frow/ *n* (*esp* of Afrikaners in South Africa) a woman, goodwife, housewife. [Du]

VS *abbrev*: Veterinary Surgeon.

vs *abbrev*: versus (also **v**).

VSO *abbrev*: Voluntary Service Overseas.

VSOP *abbrev*: very special old pale, a grade of brandy.

VT *abbrev*: vatu (currency of Vanuatu; also **V**); Vermont (US state; also **Vt.**).

vt *abbrev*: verb transitive.

VTOL /vē'tol/ *n* a system enabling aircraft to land and take off vertically; an aircraft operating by this system. [Vertical *t*ake-off and *l*anding]

VTR *abbrev*: videotape recorder.

vug /vug/ *n* a Cornish miner's name for a cavity in a rock, *usu* lined with crystals.
  ■ **vugg'y** *adj*.

Vul. or **Vulg.** *abbrev*: Vulgate.

Vulcan /vul'kən/ *n* the god of fire and metal-working, identified with the Greek Hephaestus (*Roman myth*); a planet (*intramercurial planet*) once postulated between the sun and Mercury; (without *cap*) a blacksmith or an iron-worker (*poetic*). [L *Vulcānus*]
  ■ **Vulcanā'lia** *n* an ancient Roman festival in honour of Vulcan, held on 23 August. **Vulcā'nian** *adj* of, relating to, like, relating to, sprung from or made by Vulcan; (without *cap*) volcanic; (without *cap*) of a volcanic eruption that discharges gases and ash but little or no lava. **vulcanic** /-kan'ik/ *adj* volcanic; (with *cap*) of Vulcan. **vulcanicity** /-is'i-ti/ *n* volcanic action or phenomena, volcanicity. **vul'canism** *n* volcanic activity (also **vol'canism**); (with *cap*) the teaching of the Vulcanists. **Vul'canist** or **Vol'canist** *n* (*obs geol*) a Plutonist, a follower of James Hutton (1726–97), who asserted the geological importance of subterranean heat and the igneous origin of such rocks as basalt, *opp* to *Neptunist*; (without *cap*) a vulcanologist. **vul'canite** *n* the harder of the two kinds of vulcanized rubber, the softer kind being called *soft rubber*; a general name for any igneous rock of fine grain-size. **vulcanī'zable** or **-s-** *adj*. **vulcanīzā'tion** or **-s-** *n*. **vul'canize** or **-ise** *vt* to treat (rubber, etc) with sulphur or sulphur compounds, etc to improve its strength or otherwise modify its properties. ◆ *vi* to undergo such treatment. **vulcanolog'ical** or **volcanolog'ical** *adj*. **vulcanol'ogist** or **volcanol'ogist** *n*. **vulcanol'ogy** *n* the scientific study of volcanoes and volcanic phenomena.
  ❏ **vulcanized fibre** *n* a fibre obtained by treating paper pulp with zinc chloride solution, used for low-voltage insulation. **Vulcan's badge** *n* a cuckold's horns.

vulgar /vul'gər/ *adj* unrefined; (of language, etc) coarse; lacking in taste, manners, delicacy, etc; spiritually paltry, ignoble, debased, or pretentious; relating to the common people; plebeian; vernacular; public; common, usual, customary; common to all; prevalent; commonplace. ◆ *n* the common people; one of the unrefined, of the uneducated, or of those not in good society; the common language of a country, the vernacular; a class of inferior persons (*obs*). [L *vulgāris*, from *vulgus* the people]
  ■ **vulgā'rian** *n* a vulgar person; a rich unrefined person. ◆ *adj* of or relating to a vulgarian. **vul'garism** *n* a vulgar phrase; coarseness; an instance of this. **vulgarity** /-gar'/ *n*. **vulgarīzā'tion** or **-s-** *n*. **vul'garize** or **-ise** *vt* to make common or ordinary; to popularize (and therefore spoil to some extent); to make unrefined or coarse. **vul'garly** *adv*.
  ❏ **Vulgar era** *n* the Christian era. **vulgar fraction** *n* a fraction written in the usual way (one number above another, separated by a line), *opp* to *decimal fraction*. **Vulgar Latin** *n* any of the spoken varieties of Latin in the Common Era (as opposed to literary Classical Latin) *esp* when considered as the precursors of the Romance languages. **vulgar tongue** *n* the vernacular.

Vulgate /vul'gāt or -git/ *n* a Latin version of the Scriptures, made by St Jerome and others in the 4c, and later twice revised, so called from its common use in the Roman Catholic Church; (without *cap*) a comparable accepted text of any other book or author; commonly used or accepted speech. ◆ *adj* of or relating to the Vulgate; (without *cap*; of speech, etc) commonly used or accepted. [L *vulgāta* (*editio*) popular edition (of the Bible); see **vulgar**]

vulgo /vul'gō, vŭl' or wŭl'gō/ *adv* commonly, popularly. [L]

vulgus /vul'gəs/ *n* the common people; in some public schools, a short verse task in Latin. [L; see **vulgar**]

vulnerable /vul'n(ə)-rə-bl/ *adj* capable of being physically or emotionally wounded or injured; open to successful attack; capable of being persuaded or tempted; (in contract bridge, of a side that has won a game towards the rubber) liable to increased penalties (or bonuses) accordingly. [L *vulnerāre* to wound, from *vulnus*, *vulneris* a wound]
  ■ **vuln** /vuln/ *vt* (*heraldry*) to wound. **vulned** *adj* (*heraldry*). **vulnerabil'ity** or **vul'nerableness** *n*. **vul'nerary** *adj* relating to wounds; useful in healing wounds. ◆ *n* anything useful in curing wounds. **vul'nerate** *vt* (*obs*) to wound. **vulnerā'tion** *n* (*obs*).

Vulpes /vul'pēz/ *n* the genus of carnivorous animals that includes the common fox. [L *vulpēs* a fox]
  ■ **vul'picide** *n* the killing of a fox, except in hunting; a fox-killer. **vulpine** /vul'pīn or -pin/ *adj* of, relating to or like a fox; cunning. **vul'pinism** *n* craftiness.
  ❏ **vulpine opossum** or **phalanger** *n* the common bushy-tailed Australian opossum (*Trichosurus vulpecula*).

vulpinite /vul'pi-nīt/ *n* a granular scaly form of the mineral anhydrite. [*Vulpino* in Lombardy]

vulsella /vul-sel'ə/ *n* (*pl* **vulsell'ae** /-ē/) a forceps with toothed or clawed blades (also **vulsell'um** (*pl* **-a**)). [L]

vulture /vul'chər/ *n* any of a number of large rapacious birds of prey, feeding chiefly on carrion, belonging to the families Accipitridae (Old World) and Cathartidae (New World); someone who or something that resembles a vulture. ◆ *adj* of or resembling a vulture. [OFr *voutour*, *voltour*, etc (Fr *vautour*), from L *vulturius*, from *vultur*]
  ■ **vul'turine**, **vul'turish** or **vul'turous** *adj* of, relating to or like a vulture; rapacious. **vul'turism** *n* (*Carlyle*) rapacity. **vul'turn** /-tûrn/ *n* (*obs*) the Australian brush turkey.
  ❏ **vulture fund** *n* an investment based on mainly hostile bids for poorly-performing companies.

vulva /vul'və/ (*anat* and *zool*) *n* the external genitals of the female mammal, *esp* the orifice of the vagina. [L *vulva*, *volva* wrapping, womb]
  ■ **vul'val**, **vul'var** or **vul'vate** *adj*. **vul'viform** *adj* oval; like a cleft with projecting edges. **vulvī'tis** *n* (*med*) inflammation of the vulva. **vulvo-** *combining form* denoting the vulva, as **vul'vo-ū'terine**, relating to the vulva and the uterus.

vum /vum/ (*US dialect*) *vt* and *vi* a corruption of **vow**, in the phrase *I vum*.

vu quang ox /voo kwang oks/ or **bovid** /bō'vid/ same as **saola**.

vuvuzela /vŭ-vŭ-ze'lə/ *n* a large, *usu* plastic, trumpet-shaped horn, that produces a loud montone note. [poss Zulu; origin uncertain]

vv *abbrev*: verses; vice versa; volumes.

vvll see **vl**.

VW *abbrev*: Very Worshipful; Volkswagen.

Vw *abbrev*: View (in addresses, etc).

VX gas /vē-eks' gas/ *n* an organic compound developed as a lethal nerve gas.

vying /vī'ing/ *prp* of **vie**.

Ww

W or **w** /*dub'l-ū*/ *n* the twenty-third letter in the modern English alphabet, a 5c addition to the Roman alphabet, a doubled u or v used to express the voiced consonantal sound heard eg in English *way*, *weak*, *warrant*; anything shaped like the letter W. —W was regularly used in written English from the 13c, superseding the letter wyn (qv). In modern English *w* is found as a consonant and also as the second component in certain vowel and diphthong digraphs, ie those in *law*, *few*, *now*. The unvoiced form of the consonant is written *wh* (corresponding to OE *hw*), as in *what*, *when*, but most English people substitute the voiced sound in pronouncing words spelt *wh*, and Scottish speakers insist upon sounding *hw*. W is no longer pronounced in *write*, *two*, etc, or in *whole* (which represents a dialectal variation of OE *hāl*). OE *cw* has become *qu*, as in *queen*, from OE *cwēn*.

W or **W.** *abbrev*: weak (*phys*; in particle physics a **W particle** or **W boson** is a hypothetical positively or negatively charged subatomic particle of large mass, responsible in theory for weak interaction between particles); Welsh; West; Western; wicket(s) (*cricket*); women or women's; won (Korean currency).

W *symbol*: watt (SI unit); wolframium (*L*) (from *wolfram*, an earlier name), tungsten (*chem*).

w *abbrev*: week; weight; wide (*cricket*); width; wife; with.

WA *abbrev*: Washington (US state); West Africa; Western Australia.

wa' /*wö*/ a Scots form of **wall**.

WAAC or **Waac** /*wak*/ *n* the Women's Army Auxiliary Corps (founded 1917), or a member of it, now **WRAC**.

WAAF or **Waaf** /*waf*/ *n* the Women's Auxiliary Air Force (founded 1939), or a member, now **WRAF**.

wab /*wab*/ (*US derog sl*) *n* a Mexican immigrant. [Perh a corruption of *wetback*]

wabain see **ouabain**.

wabbit /*wab'it*/ (*Scot*) *adj* exhausted, tired out. [Scot *wobart* feeble]

wabble, **wabbler**, etc obsolete forms of **wobble**, **wobbler**, etc.

waboom see **wagenboom**.

wabster see **webster**.

wack¹ /*wak*/ (*US sl*) *n* an eccentric person. ◆ *adj* bad; extreme. [Poss back-formation from **wacky**]

wack² /*wak*/ (*dialect, esp Liverpool*) *n* (also **wack'er**) a familiar term of address for a companion, pal, mate. [Origin uncertain]

wacke /*wak'ə*/ *n* an old name for a decomposed basalt. [Ger, from OHGer *wagge* a pebble; cf **greywacke**]

wacko or **whacko** /*wak'ō*/ (*sl*) *adj* mad; eccentric. ◆ *n* (*pl* **wack'os** or **whack'os**) a deranged or eccentric person. [Cf **wacky**]

wacky /*wak'i*/ (*inf*) *adj* crazy. [Perh connected with *whack*, or with dialect *whacky* left-handed, a fool]
- **wack'ily** *adv*. **wack'iness** *n*.
- **wacky baccy** *n* (*inf*) cannabis.

wad¹ /*wod*/ *n* a pad of loose material such as hay, tow, etc, used for packing, etc; a disc of felt or paper (formerly a small plug of paper or tow, etc) to keep the charge in a gun; a sandwich, cake or bun (*sl*); a bundle eg of hay; a roll or bundle, eg of banknotes; a large quantity, *esp* of money (*sl*); a compact mass, often small; a lump of a soft substance (*rare*). ◆ *vt* (**wadd'ing**; **wadd'ed**) to form into a mass; to pad, stuff out; to stuff a wad into. [Origin uncertain; cf Swed *vadd* wadding; Ger *Watte*, Fr *ouate*]
- **wadd'ing** *n* a wad or the materials for wads; sheets of carded cotton for stuffing garments, etc; cotton wool.

wad², **wadd** or **wadt** /*wod*/ *n* an earthy ore of manganese, mainly hydrated oxide of manganese; plumbago or black lead (*dialect*). [Ety doubtful]

wad³ see **wed**.

WADA /*wä'də*/ *abbrev*: World Anti-Doping Agency.

waddle /*wod'l*/ *vi* to take short steps and sway from side to side in walking, as a duck does; to move in a way suggestive of this; to become a defaulter (*stock exchange sl*). ◆ *n* the act of waddling; a clumsy, rocking gait. [Frequentative of **wade**]
- **wadd'ler** *n*. **wadd'ling** *adj*.

waddy or **waddie** /*wod'i*/ *n* an Australian Aboriginal wooden club used in warfare; a cowboy; a walking-stick. ◆ *vt* to strike with a waddy. [Perh from Eng **wood¹**]

wade /*wād*/ *vi* to walk through a substance that yields with difficulty to the feet, *esp* water; (with *through*) to make one's way through laboriously; to go (*obs*). ◆ *vt* to cross by wading; to cause to cross thus. ◆ *n* the act of wading; a ford (*inf*). [OE *wadan* to go; Ger *waten*]
- **wā'dable** or **wade'able** *adj*. **wā'der** *n* someone who wades; a bird that wades in search of food, eg the snipe, sandpiper, etc, and sometimes larger birds such as the heron, etc; a high waterproof boot; (in *pl*) a waterproof garment for the feet, legs and lower body. **wā'ding** *n* and *adj*.
- **wade in** to make a very vigorous attack. **wade into** to tackle (eg a job) energetically; to attack or criticize fiercely.

wadi or **wady** /*wod'i*/ *n* the dry bed of a torrent; a river valley. [Ar *wādī*]

wadmal /*wod'*, *wäd'* or *wud'məl*/ (*hist*) *n* a thick or coarse woollen cloth, woven *esp* in Orkney and Shetland (also **wad'maal**, **wad'mol** or **wad'moll**). [ON *vathmāl*, from *vāth* cloth, and *māl* measure]

wadset or **wadsett** /*wod'set*/ (*Scot*) *n* a mortgage; something pledged or pawned. ◆ *vt* to mortgage; to pawn. [**wad**, Scot form of **wed**, and **set**]
- **wad'setter** *n* a mortgagee.

wadt see **wad²**.

wady see **wadi**.

wae /*wā*/ *n* (*Scot*, *Spenser*) woe. ◆ *adj* (*Scot*) sorrowful. [Dialect form of **woe**]
- **wae'ful** (sometimes **wae'fu'**) or **wae'some** *adj* (*Scot*) woeful, pitiful. **wae'ness** *n* sadness. **waesucks'** *interj* (*Scot*) alas.

Wafd /*woft*/ *n* a Nationalist party in Egypt founded in 1918, dissolved in 1953. [Ar *wafd* arrival, deputation]

wafer /*wā'fər*/ *n* a very thin crisp cake or biscuit baked in **wafer irons** or **wafer tongs**, formerly eaten with wine; a similar biscuit eaten with ice cream, etc; a thin round cake of unleavened bread, *usu* stamped with a cross, an Agnus Dei or the letters IHS, etc, used in the Eucharist; a leaf of adhesive material for sealing letters, etc; a piece of edible material used to enclose a medicinal powder, etc to be swallowed; a thin slice of silicon on which multiple chips are formed; a thin slice of anything. ◆ *vt* to close, fasten, stick (eg on a wall), with a wafer. [ONFr *waufre* (OFr and Fr *gaufre*), from MLGer *wafel* cake of wax]
- **wā'fery** *adj* like a wafer.
- **wafer cake** *n* a wafer. **wā'fer-thin** *adj* very thin, *usu* in the order of a few millimetres thick; (of the plot of fictional work, etc) not convincingly developed.

waff¹ /*waf* or *wöf*/ (*Scot*) *adj* wandering, stray; worthless, paltry; listless. ◆ *n* a worthless person. [Variant of **waif¹**]

waff² /*waf*/ *n* (*Scot*) a waving, or a slight, hasty motion; a signal; a quick light blow; a puff or blast; a sudden ailment; a faint, *usu* disagreeable odour; a glimpse; a ghost. ◆ *vt* and *vi* (*dialect* or *obs*) to wave, flap, flutter, wave away. [Noun from verb, which is a variant of **wave**]

waff³ /*waf*/ (*dialect*) *vi* to bark (also **waugh**). [Imit]

waffle¹ /*wof'l*/ *n* a kind of cake made from batter, baked in an iron utensil of hinged halves called a **waffle iron**. [Du *wafel* wafer]

waffle² /*wof'l*/ (*dialect*) *vi* to wave. [Frequentative of **waff²**]

waffle³ /*wof'l*/ (*inf*) *vi* to talk or write in an imprecise and wordy manner, to go on and on, to talk or write nonsense (often with *on*); to

---

waver, vacillate. ◆ *n* such talk or writing; vacillation. [Frequentative of **waff³**]
■ **waff'ler** *n*. **waff'ling** *n* and *adj*. **waff'ly** *adj*.

waft /*wäft, woft* or *waft*/ *vt* (*pat* and *pap* **waft'ed** (*Spenser* **weft**)) to bear, convey, transport or propel safely or lightly on the surface of or through a fluid medium such as air or water (*poetic*; also *fig*); to signal to, beckon (*perh* for **waff²**); to turn (one's eyes; *Shakesp*). ◆ *vi* to float, sail, pass through the air. ◆ *n* a scent or sound, or puff of smoke or vapour carried by the air; a rush of air (also *fig*); a slight taste, *esp* an unpleasant one; an act of wafting or waving; a waving movement; a passage across the sea or other water (*obs*); a flag or substitute hoisted as a signal, *esp* an ensign, stopped together at the head and middle portions, slightly rolled up lengthwise, and hoisted at different positions at the after part of a ship (also **weft** or **wheft**); the act of displaying such a signal. [From *obs* **wafter** a convoying vessel, prob from LGer or Du *wachter* guard]
■ **waft'age** *n* the act of wafting; transportation through air or across water. **waft'er** *n*. **waft'ing** *n*. **waft'ure** *n* (*Shakesp*; Rowe's emendation, *Julius Caesar*, II.1.246) the act of wafting or of waving; a waving motion; a beckoning; something wafted.

WAG *abbrev* : (West Africa) The Gambia (IVR); Writers and Artists Guild.

wag¹ /*wag*/ *vi* (**wagg'ing**; **wagged**) to move or be moved from side to side, or to shake to and fro, to oscillate; to move, or to move one's limbs; to move on, get on one's way (*archaic*); to play truant (*sl*); (of the tongue, chin, beard, etc) to move in light, gossiping or indiscreet talk; (of the world, etc, in the sense of human affairs) to go (in respect of good fortune and bad). ◆ *vt* to move, shake or wave to and fro or up and down; to move (the tongue, chin, etc) in chatter or indiscreet talk; to move (the head or *esp* the finger) so as to express reproof or derision, etc; to brandish (*obs*); (*usu* with *neg*) to move, stir (a limb, etc) (*obs*). ◆ *n* a shake; an act of wagging; ability to wag; truant (in **play the wag**); an amusing, mischievous person, a habitual joker, a wit (*perh* from obsolete **wag'halter**, someone who deserves hanging); a fellow (*obs*). [ME *waggen*, from same root as OE *wagian* to shake]
■ **wagg'ery** *n* mischievous merriment or jesting; an instance of this. **wagg'ish** *adj* amusing or mischievous. **wagg'ishly** *adv*. **wagg'ishness** *n*.
□ **wag'-at-the-wa''** or **wag'-at** (or **-by)-the-wall'** *n* (*Scot* and *N Eng*) a hanging clock with exposed pendulum and weights.

wag² /*wag*/ (*sl*) *n* a wife or girlfriend of a professional sportsman, *esp* one of group accompanying a travelling team. [Singular formed from WAGs, acronym for *Wives And Girlfriends*]

wage /*wāj*/ *vt* to engage in or carry on, *esp* war; (*esp* in *pap*) to pay wages to; to pledge, offer as a pledge (*obs*); to wager (*obs*); to hazard (*obs*); to hire for pay (*obs*); to bribe (*obs*); to let out for pay (*Spenser*). ◆ *vi* (*Shakesp*) to be equal in value; to contend, battle. ◆ *n* payment for services, *esp* a regular payment made by an employer to an (unskilled or semi-skilled) employee, or (*fig*) reward (both often **wages**, *pl* in form, but sometimes construed as *sing*); a gage or pledge (*obs*). [ME *wagen*, from ONFr *wagier* (OFr *gagier*) to pledge (through popular L from a Gmc word)]
■ **waged** *adj*. **wage'less** *adj* and *n pl*.
□ **wage differential** *n* the difference in the wages paid to different classes of workers (eg skilled and unskilled) in an industry, or to workers doing similar jobs in different industries or areas. **wage'-earner** *n* anyone who works for wages; the person who earns the money that supports, or money that helps to support, the household. **wage'-earning** *n*. **wage freeze** *n* a fixing of wages at a certain level for some time ahead. **wage fund**, **wages fund** or **wages-fund theory** *n* the former theory that there is at any given time in a country a determinate amount of capital available for the payment of labour, therefore the average wage depends on the proportion of this fund to the number of people who have to share in it. **wage packet** *n* a small envelope in which a worker's wages are issued; (loosely) one's wages. **wage plug** *n* (*old Aust inf*) a wage-earner or wage slave. **wage-push inflation** *n* inflation caused by wage increases. **wages council** *n* a body that settles wages, consisting of employers' and workers' representatives. **wage slave** *n* a person dependent on a (*usu* low) wage or salary. **wage slavery** *n*. **wage slip** or **wages slip** *n* a pay slip. **wage work** *n* work done for wages.
■ **living wage** see under **living**.

wagenboom /*vä'gən-bōm* or *-boom*/ or (*Afrik*) **waboom** /*vä'boom*/ *n* a S African tree (*Protea grandiflora*) whose wood is used in making wagon wheels. [Du, *wagon-tree*]

wager /*wā'jər*/ *n* something staked on an outcome not yet known; a bet; the act of making a bet; that on which bets are laid; a hazard (*rare*); a contest for a prize (*rare*); a pledge (*obs*); the act of giving a pledge (*obs*). ◆ *vt* to bet (money, etc) on the outcome of anything. ◆ *vi* to lay a wager, make a bet. [Anglo-Fr *wageure* a pledge, from ONFr *wagier* ; see **wage**]
■ **wā'gerer** *n*.

□ **wager boat** *n* a light boat for a race between single scullers. **wager of battle** *n* (*law*; *hist*) trial by combat, a usage which permitted the accused and accuser, in cases where direct evidence was lacking, to challenge each other to mortal combat. **wager of law** *n* (*hist*) compurgation, ie the act, by several witnesses, of swearing jointly to the character of a defendant or accused person, so as to clear him or her.

waggle /*wag'l*/ *vi* and *vt* to wag, *esp* in an unsteady manner. ◆ *n* an act or the action of waggling. [Frequentative of **wag¹**]
■ **wagg'ler** *n* a fisherman's long float, designed to indicate the slightest movement of the bait. **wagg'ly** *adj*.
□ **waggle dance** *n* (*animal behaviour*) the sequence of movements by which hive bees communicate the distance and location of new nest sites and food sources.

waggon, etc see **wagon**.

wagmoire /*wag'moir*/ (*Spenser*) *n* a quagmire.

wag-'n-bietjie see **wait-a-bit** under **wait¹**.

Wagnerian /*väg-nē'ri-ən*/ *adj* relating to or characterized by the ideas or style of Richard *Wagner* (1813–83), German composer of music dramas (qv); relating to Rudolf *Wagner* (1805–64), physiologist. ◆ *n* a follower or admirer of Richard Wagner.
■ **Wagneresque'** *adj*. **Wag'nerism** or **Wagne'rianism** *n* the artistic theory of Richard Wagner, its main object being the freeing of opera from traditional and conventional forms, and its only concern being the overall dramatic effect of the music. **Wag'nerist** or **Wag'nerite** *n* an adherent of Wagner's musical methods.

wagon or **waggon** /*wag'ən*/ *n* a four-wheeled vehicle, *esp* one for carrying heavy goods; an open railway truck or a closed railway van; a car, *esp* an estate car (*inf*); a movable piece of furniture with shelves (see **dinner-wagon** under **dinner**); a chariot (*obs*). ◆ *vt* to transport by wagon. ◆ *vi* to travel in a wagon. [Du *wagen*; cf OE *wægn*, Eng **wain**]
■ **wag'onage** *n* conveyance by wagon, or money paid for it; a collection of wagons (*Carlyle*). **wag'oner** or **wagg'oner** *n* someone who drives a wagon; a charioteer (*obs*). **wagonette'** *n* a kind of carriage with one or two seats crosswise in front, and two back seats arranged lengthways and facing inwards. **wag'onful** *n*.
□ **wagon box** or **bed** *n* the carrying part of a wagon. **wag'onload** *n* the load carried by a wagon; a great amount. **wagon lock** *n* a kind of iron shoe or other device placed on the rear wheel of a wagon to retard motion in going downhill. **wagon roof** or **vault** *n* a barrel vault. **wagon train** *n* a collection or service of army vehicles for the conveyance of ammunition, provisions, the sick, etc; a train of *usu* horse-drawn wagons used by pioneer settlers to travel into new territory (*hist*). **wag'onwright** *n* a maker of wagons.
■ **on** (or **off**) **the wagon** (*inf*) abstaining (or no longer abstaining) from alcohol. **the Wagon** the Plough, the seven brightest stars in the constellation Ursa Major. **the Wagoner** or **Waggoner** the constellation Auriga.

wagon-lit /*vä-gɔ̃-lē'* / *n* (*pl* **wagons-lit**, pronounced as *sing*; sometimes **wagon-lits**) a sleeping-carriage on a continental train. [Fr *wagon* (from Eng **wagon**), and *lit* bed]

wagtail /*wag'tāl*/ *n* any bird of the *Motacilla* and *Dendronanthus* genera, forming with the pipits the family Motacillidae, so named from their constant wagging of the tail; applied also to other birds, such as an American water thrush and an Australian flycatcher; contemptuously, a pert or obsequious person (*obs*); a harlot (*obs*).

wagyu /*wa'gyoo*/ *n* any of several breeds of Japanese beef cattle. [Jap *wa* beef, and *gyu* cattle]

Wahhabi, Wahabi or **Wahabee** /*wä-hä'bē*/ *n* a member of a sect of Muslims founded in Central Arabia about 1760 by Ibn Abd al-*Wahhab* (1691–1787), whose aim was to restore primitive Islam (also **Wahha'bite, Wahha'biite**, etc).
■ **Wahha'bism, Waha'bism, Wahha'biism** or **Waha'biism** *n* the doctrine and practices of the Wahhabis.

Wahiguru /*wä-hē-goo'roo*/ (*Sikhism*) *n* Wonderful Lord, a popular designation for God. [Hindi *wahi* great one, and *guru* teacher]

wahine /*wä-hē'ne*/ *n* a Maori woman. [Maori]

wahoo¹ /*wa-hoo'*/ *n* an ornamental shrub (genus *Euonymus* or *Evonymus*), with scarlet-coated seeds (also **burning bush**). [Dakota *wanhu*]

wahoo² /*wa-hoo'*/ *n* a Californian buckthorn (*Rhamnus purshiana*) which yields cascara sagrada; the winged elm, with hard-grained wood; also the rock elm. [Creek *ûhawhu*]

wahoo³ /*wa-hoo'*/ *n* a large fast-moving marine food and game fish, *Acanthocybium solandri*, related to the mackerel. [Origin unknown]

wah-wah /*wä'wä*/ (*music*) *n* the sound produced on a brass instrument by inserting and removing the mute, imitated on an electric guitar by varying the level of amplification. [Imit]

waid or **waide** old spellings of **weighed**, *pat* and *pap* of **weigh**[1], but in *Shakesp, Taming of the Shrew* III.2.52 probably for **swayed** (see **sway**).

waif[1] /wāf/ *n* a neglected, abandoned or orphaned child; a homeless wanderer; a fashionable young woman, *esp* a model, of extremely slender build (*inf*); a piece of property found ownerless, eg a strayed animal, or goods cast up by the tide (*Spenser* **waift** or **weft**; also *fig*); stolen goods abandoned by the thief (*obs*). ◆ *adj* (*Scot*) wandering, neglected. ◆ *vt* (*rare*; in *pap*) to cast up as a waif. [OFr *waif*; prob from Scand; cf ON *veif* any flapping or waving thing]
  ■ **waif'ish** *adj*. **waif'like** *adj*.
  ❑ **waif and stray** *n* strayed property (see *n* above). **waifs and strays** *n pl* homeless, destitute people.

waif[2] /wāf/ *n* a streak, puff, same as **waff**[2].

waift see **waif**[1].

wail /wāl/ *vi* to lament or express sorrow or pain audibly, *esp* with prolonged high-pitched mournful cries; to make a sound resembling such a cry; (of eyes) to weep (*Shakesp*). ◆ *vt* to bemoan; to grieve over. ◆ *n* the activity, or a spell, of wailing; a cry of woe; an animal cry or mechanical sound suggesting this. [ME *weilen, wailen*; cf ON *væla*]
  ■ **wail'er** *n*. **wail'ful** *adj* (*poetic*) sorrowful; expressing woe. **wail'ing** *n* and *adj*. **wail'ingly** *adv*.
  ❑ **Wailing Wall** *n* a wall in Jerusalem, 18m (59ft) high, a remnant of the western wall of the temple dating back to before the destruction of the city in 66AD, where Jews traditionally pray and from which they were excluded for a time.

wain /wān/ *n* a wagon, *esp* for hay or other agricultural produce (now *usu poetic*); a chariot (*obs*). ◆ *vt* (*obs*) to carry, convey. [OE *wægn, wægen, wæn*, from *wegen*, to carry; cf Du *wagen*, Ger *Wagen*, Eng **wagon**]
  ❑ **wain'wright** *n* a maker of wagons.
  ■ **the Lesser Wain** the constellation Ursa Minor, or the seven brightest stars in it. **the Wain** Charles's Wain; the Lesser Wain.

wainage /wā'nij/ (*hist*) *n* the team and implements necessary for the cultivation of land; land under cultivation. [ONFr *waaignage*, from OFr *gaaigner* to till, earn, gain]

wainscot /wān'skot, -skət or wen'/ *n* fine oak for panelling, etc; woodwork, *esp* panelled, on an interior wall; similar lining of other material; the lower part of an interior wall when lined with material different from that on the upper part; a collector's name for certain noctuid moths. ◆ *vt* (**wain'scoting** or **wain'scotting**; **wain'scoted** or **wain'scotted**) to line with, or as if with, boards or panels; to grain in imitation of oak. [Orig perh wood used for a partition in a wagon, from Du *wagen-schot*, oak-wood, from *wagen* wagon, or MDu *waeghe* wave (from the appearance of the grain of the wood), and *schot* partition]
  ■ **wain'scoting** or **wain'scotting** *n* the process of lining with boards or panels; materials for making a wainscot; wainscots collectively.
  ❑ **wainscot chair** *n* a heavy oak chair with a panelled back, seat, etc.

wainwright see under **wain**.

WAIS (*comput*) *abbrev*: wide area information server(s).

waist /wāst/ *n* the *usu* narrowest part of the human trunk, between the ribs and the hips; a narrow middle part of an insect; the part of a garment that lies round the waist of the body; a woman's blouse or bodice (*US*); any narrow middle part, eg of a musical instrument; the middle part of a ship; the middle (of the day or night) (*obs*); something that surrounds, a girdle (*obs*). [ME *wast*, from presumed OE *wæst* growth, size; cf Icel *vöxtr*, OE *wæstm* growth, Eng **wax**[2]]
  ■ **waist'ed** *adj* having a waist, often of specified type as in *high-waisted*. **waist'er** *n* a seaman stationed in the waist, performing menial duties, *esp* a greenhand on a whaler. **waist'less** *adj*.
  ❑ **waist anchor** *n* an anchor stowed in the waist of a ship. **waist apron** *n* an apron covering the body only from the waist down. **waist bag** *n* a small bag worn on a belt round the waist, a bum bag. **waist'band** *n* the strip of fabric in a garment that fits round the waist; a belt or sash. **waist'belt** *n* a belt for the waist. **waist'boat** *n* a boat carried in the waist of a vessel. **waist'cloth** *n* a loin cloth; (in *pl*) coloured cloths hung about a ship's waist as ceremonial decoration or to conceal the men in a naval action (*obs*). **waist'coat** /wās' or wāst'kōt, or (*archaic, now dialect*) wes'kət/ *n* a garment, plain or ornamental, reaching to or below the waist and now sleeveless, worn by men at different periods under doublet, coat, jacket, etc (and intended to be partly visible), and now often without any other garment over it; a woman's similar garment or front. **waistcoateer'** *n* (*obs*) a strumpet. **waist'coating** *n* material for men's waistcoats, *esp* of a fancy pattern. **waist'-deep** or **-high** *adj* deep or high enough to reach up to the waist. **waist'line** *n* a line thought of as marking the waist, but not fixed by anatomy in women's fashions; the measurement of a waist.

wait[1] /wāt/ *vi* to be or remain in expectation or readiness (with *for*); to be or remain in a place in readiness (also **wait about** or **around**); to

delay action; to be delayed; to remain temporarily undealt with; to be in attendance, or in readiness to carry out orders; to bring food to the table and clear away used dishes; to keep watch, be on guard (*Spenser* **waite**; *obs*); to be on the watch for someone, lie in ambush (*obs*). ◆ *vt* to postpone (eg a meal) for some purpose (*inf*); to watch, watch for, or lie in ambush for (*obs*); to be or remain in expectation of, await (*obs*); to attend on, attend or escort (*obs*). ◆ *n* the act or a period of waiting or of expecting; a delay; ambush (as in *lie in wait*); the period of attendance of a lord- or lady-in-waiting; (in *pl*) musicians employed by a town to play on ceremonial occasions (*hist*); (in *pl*) people who welcome in Christmas by playing or singing out of doors at night; a member of a Christmas band or town band of waits; a watchman, sentinel or spy (*obs*). [ONFr *waitier* (OFr *guaitier*, Fr *guetter*) to watch, attend; of Gmc origin; cf OHGer *wahta* (Ger *Wacht*) a watchman; cognate with OE *wacan* to watch]
  ■ **wait'er** *n* someone who waits; a man whose job is to wait, *esp* at table in a hotel or restaurant, etc; an attending servant (*obs*); a salver or tray; a dumb waiter; formerly, a uniformed attendant at the London Stock Exchange; a watchman (*obs*); a customs officer (*obs*). **wait'erage** *n* (*rare*) service. **wait'erhood** *n* (*rare*) or **wait'ering** the occupation of a waiter. **wait'ing** *n* the act or process of remaining in expectation, delaying, etc; attendance, service, eg in a restaurant. ◆ *adj* relating to, or suitable for waiting. **wait'ingly** *adv* (*rare*). **wait'ress** *n* a woman whose job is to wait at tables in a hotel or restaurant, etc. ◆ *vi* to work as a waitress. **wait'ressing** *n* the occupation of a waitress.
  ❑ **wait'-a-bit** (also often *adj*) a name given to various plants, *esp* S African (*Afrik* **wag-'n-bietjie** /vuhh''ə(n)-bē-kē/), with thorns that catch the clothing of passers-by. **wait'-a-while** *n* a wait-a-bit; an Australian wattle growing in dense thickets. **waiting list** or **wait list** *n* a list of people waiting, eg candidates awaiting a vacancy, etc. **wait'ing-maid** or **wait'ing-woman** *n* (*archaic*) a female attendant. **waiting room** *n* a room for the use of people waiting. **wait'ing-vassal** *n* (*obs*) an attendant. **wait list** see **waiting list** above. **wait'-list** *vt* to add the name of (a person) to a waiting list, *esp* for a seat on an aircraft. **wait-on** see **wait on** below. **wait'person** *n* (*US*) a waiter or waitress. **wait state** *n* (*comput*) the period of time that a microprocessor must wait while fetching data from a slower memory.
  ■ **lay wait** (*archaic*) to lie in wait. **lie in wait** to be in hiding ready to attack or surprise (*lit* and *fig*). **lords in waiting** certain officers in the Lord Chamberlain's department of the royal household. **minority waiter** (*Sheridan*) meaning uncertain (*perh* a waiter, or a tidewaiter, out of employment). **play a waiting game** to avoid action as far as possible in the hope of having an opportunity later to use one's energies with maximum effect. **wait attendance** (*Shakesp*) to remain in attendance. **wait for it!** (*inf*) an expression injected into a narrative to prepare listeners for something impressive. **wait off** (*racing*) to allow oneself to be temporarily outdistanced by other competitors, reserving one's energies for the final stretch. **wait on** to wait for (*inf*); to continue to wait (*Scot*); to be patient or wait (*Aust* and *NZ*); see **wait upon** below; (of a hawk) to circle or hover in the air above the falconer's head (*falconry*; **wait'-on** *n*). **wait table** to wait at table during a meal. **wait up** to stay out of bed waiting (with *for*); to slow down or wait (*US*). **wait upon** or **on** to call on, visit formally; to accompany; to attend and serve; to be connected with or follow as a consequence; to carry out the duties of (an office) (*Bible*); to gaze at, keep under observation (*obs*). **you wait!** (*inf*) an expression of warning.

wait[2] see **wit**[2].

Waitangi Day /wī-tung'i dā/ *n* 6 February, the national day of New Zealand.

waitress see under **wait**[1].

waive /wāv/ *vt* to give up voluntarily (eg a claim or a contention) (*law*); to refrain from claiming, demanding, taking or enforcing; to forgo; to evade, avoid (*archaic*); to defer, postpone; to leave out of consideration, disregard (*obs*); to put away, reject, abandon, forsake, vacate, or resign (*obs*); to declare (a woman) to be outside the protection of the law (the status of women in the eyes of the law being such that the term 'outlaw' was not applicable to them; *hist*); to abandon (stolen goods) (*obs*). [Anglo-Fr *weyver*, from OFr *guesver* to abandon; from same root as **waif**[1]]
  ■ **wai'ver** *n* the act, or an act, of waiving, or a written statement formally indicating this.

waivode /wā'vōd/ and **waiwode** /wā'wōd/ *n* variants of **voivode**.

waka[1] /wô'kə/ *n* a traditional Maori canoe, *usu* made of a hollowed tree trunk. [Maori]

waka[2] /wak'ə/ *n* a Japanese 31-syllable poem, a tanka, precursor of the haiku, used exclusively by members of the Japanese imperial family; a form of Japanese poetry derived from ancient ballads, lyrical in style. [Jap]

wakame /wak'ə-mä/ *n* an edible seaweed that can be soaked and used as a salad vegetable. [Jap]

wake[1] /wāk/ vi (pat **woke** or (archaic) **waked** /wākt/; pap **wo'ken** or (archaic) **waked**, (rare) **woke**) to be or remain awake, or active or vigilant; to keep watch or vigil, or pass the night in prayer; to hold a wake; to awake or be roused from sleep or from indifference, day-dreaming, etc (often with up); to become animated or lively; to be stirred up, aroused; to hold a late revel (obs). ◆ vt to rouse from sleep; to keep vigil over (obs or dialect); to excite, stir up (eg feelings, echoes); to disturb (eg the night or silence) with noise; to animate; to reanimate, revive. ◆ n the feast of the dedication of a church, formerly kept by watching all night; a festival; (usu in pl) an annual holiday esp in N England, as in Wakes Week (dialect); a watch or vigil beside a corpse, sometimes with revelry; the act or state of waking (obs except in sleep and/or wake, wake and/or dream); a serenade (James Hogg). [A combination of an OE strong verb wacan to be born, to awake, and an OE weak verb wacian to be awake, to watch; cf **watch**]
■ **wake'ful** adj not asleep; unable or indisposed to sleep; vigilant, watchful; waking; awakening or rousing (Milton). **wake'fully** adv. **wake'fulness** n. **wake'less** adj (of sleep) sound, undisturbed. **wā'ker** n someone who wakes. **wā'king** n. ◆ adj that wakes, keeps watch, or is vigilant; that rouses or becomes awake; passed, or experienced, in the waking state.
□ **wake'man** n (archaic) a watchman. **wake'rife** /-rīf or -rīf/ adj (Scot) wakeful; vigilant. **wake'-robin** n the cuckoo pint, Arum maculatum; the spotted orchis, Orchis maculata; applied to various other flowers, esp, in the USA, to any of the genus Trillium. **wake'-up** n (Aust inf) a wide-awake person, esp in **be a wake-up to** to be alert to. **wake'-up call** n a prearranged telephone call to inform someone that it is time to get up; something that makes people aware of an unsatisfactory, dangerous, or difficult situation (inf). **waking hours** n pl the period of the day during which one is normally awake.
■ **wake a** (or **the**) **night** to remain awake, or be up and about, all night. **wake to** or **wake up to** to become or make conscious of, alive to. **wake up and smell the coffee** (sl) to become aware of the reality of the situation.

wake[2] /wāk/ n the streak of smooth-looking or foamy water left in the track of a ship; disturbed air behind a flying body; a track on land (rare); a trail of light behind a moving body; the area behind someone or something passing through. [Of Scand origin; cf ON vök an ice hole, vökr moist]
□ **wake'board** n and vi. **wake'boarding** n a sport similar to water-skiing in which the participant is towed behind a motorboat while riding on a board like a short surfboard.
■ **in the wake of** close behind; immediately after (usu implying consequence).

waken[1] /wā'kən/ vi to be or become awake; to become active or lively; to remain awake, keep watch (obs). ◆ vt to rouse from sleep, unconsciousness or inaction; to excite, stir up, evoke. [OE wæcnan; cf ON vakna to awake]
■ **wā'kened** adj. **wā'kener** n someone who or something that wakens. **wā'kening** adj. ◆ n the act of waking; the revival of an action (Scots law).
■ **waken to** to make or become aware of.

waken[2] /wā'kən/ (Scot) adj waking, awake.

wakf see **waqf**.

wakiki /wä'kē-kē/ n shells formerly used as money in islands of the S Pacific. [Melanesian]

WAL abbrev: (West Africa) Sierra Leone (IVR).

Wal. abbrev: Walloon.

Walachian see **Wallachian**.

wald see **weld**[2].

Waldenses /wol-den'sēz/ n pl a Christian community of austere morality and devotion to the simplicity of the Gospel, orig followers of Peter Waldo, a merchant of Lyon and preacher in the second half of the 12c, having their chief centres in the Alpine regions of SE France and Piedmont (also **Valdenses** /val-/).
■ **Walden'sian** adj and n.

waldflute /wöld'floot/ n an organ flute stop sounding an octave above the basic pitch. [Formed after Ger Waldflöte, literally, forest flute]

waldgrave /wöld'grāv/ n in medieval Germany, a head forest-ranger; an old German title of nobility. [Ger Waldgraf, from Wald forest, and Graf count]
■ **waldgravine** /wöld'grä-vēn/ n the wife or widow of a waldgrave.

waldhorn /wöld'hörn or (Ger) valt'/ n a hunting-horn, a French horn without valves; an organ reed stop. [Ger]

waldo /wol'dō/ n (pl **wal'dos**) a mechanical gadget, esp a remote control device. [After a character created by American writer Robert Heinlein (1907–88)]

Waldorf salad /wöl'dörf sal'əd/ n a salad with apples, walnuts, celery and mayonnaise. [Waldorf-Astoria hotel in New York, where it was first served]

waldrapp /wöl'drap/ n the hermit ibis (Geronticus eremita) of N Africa and the Middle East, with black plumage, red face and a crest of feathers on the back of the head. [Ger Wald forest, and Rapp (variant of Rabe) crow]

Waldsterben /valt'shter-bən/ (ecology) n the dying-off of trees and other forest vegetation as a result of air pollution, observed since the 1970s (also without cap). [Ger, forest death, from Wald forest, and sterben to die]

wale[1] /wāl/ n same as **weal**[1], a ridge raised on the flesh by the stroke of a whip, etc; a ridge on the surface of cloth; texture; a vertical ridge in knitted fabrics; a horizontal timber used to bind together piles driven in a row; (in pl) planks all along the outer timbers on a ship's side, bends. ◆ vt to mark with wales; to make, provide or secure with wales. [OE walu; cf ON völr a rod]
□ **wale knot** see **wall knot** under **wall**.

wale[2] /wāl/ (Scot and N Eng) n the act of choosing; choice; the scope of choice; the pick or best. ◆ vt and vi to choose, pick. [ON val choice; Ger Wahl choice; from the root of **will**[1]]

waler /wā'lər/ (also with cap) n in India, a horse imported from New South Wales, or from Australia generally.

Walhalla /val-hal'ə/ n same as **Valhalla**.

wali /wä'lē/ n same as **vali**.

Walian /wä'li-ən/ adj of or relating to (North or South) Wales (as North Walian or South Walian). ◆ n a native or inhabitant of (North or South) Wales.

walise /perh wə-liz'/ (obs; Scot) n a variant of **valise**.

walk[1] /wök/ vi (of a biped) to move along on foot with alternate steps, the walker always having at least one foot on the ground; (of a quadruped) to move along in such a way that there are always at least two feet on the ground; to pace; to journey on foot; to ramble, go on foot for pleasure, exercise, etc; (of an inanimate object) to be in motion (obs); to make progress (naut); (of the tongue) to wag (obs); to make slow progress; to circulate, spread, be rife (obs); (of a ghost) to go restlessly about; to move; to behave in a certain way, follow a certain course; to move off, depart, withdraw; to conduct oneself, behave; to be in harmonious association (obs); to go to first base after receiving four balls (baseball); to leave the cricket pitch when dismissed, esp without waiting for the umpire to adjudicate on an appeal; (of an object) to disappear (usu with implications of unauthorized removal) (inf, esp facetious); to go free, esp from a court of law, without receiving any punishment (US). ◆ vt to pass through or over, perambulate, traverse; to follow or trace out on foot; to measure out by walking; to wear (eg through, to shreds) by walking; to go through (a dance) at a slow pace; to circulate (obs); to cause to walk, or to move as if walking; to lead or accompany by walking. ◆ n the action or an act of walking; a spell of walking, esp for pleasure or exercise; a perambulation in procession; a walking race; a gait; that in or through which one walks; a possible or suitable route or course for walking; a path or place for walking; a tree-bordered avenue; a place for animals, eg young hounds, to train or to exercise; a run for fowl; a place where a game cock is kept; high pasture-ground (obs); a division of a forest; a distance walked, or a distance as measured by the time taken to walk it; conduct; one's course of life, sphere of action or profession, esp in walk of life; the regular route of a postman, policeman, etc; a hawker's district or round; a hunting-ground (obs); (in pl) grounds or a park (obs); a flock of snipe or of wagtails. [ME walken, walkien to walk, to full, from OE wealcan to roll, toss, revolve, wealcian to roll up, curl; cognate with Ger walken to full cloth]
■ **walk'able** adj. **walk'er** n someone who walks or takes part in walking races; a colporteur or (dialect) a vagrant; a forester (hist); a person who trains and walks young hounds; any bird that walks rather than hops; a stick insect; any device which helps esp babies or elderly people to walk; a man of good social standing who accompanies a woman VIP on official engagements in the absence of her husband (US sl). ◆ interj (archaic sl; with cap; also **Hookey Walker**) an exclamation of incredulity. **walk'ing** n the verbal noun of walk; pedestrianism; the sport of racing using a walking rather than running gait; the condition of a surface from the point of view of someone who walks on it. ◆ adj that walks, or that moves as if walking; that oscillates; used in or for walking; performed by walking; worked by a person or animal who walks; in human form, as in walking dictionary, walking disaster.
□ **walk'about** adv on the move, as in go walkabout, esp temporarily back into the bush (of Australian Aborigines), or meeting the public on foot (of royalty, politicians, etc). ◆ n a wandering, a journey; a walk by royalty, etc in order to meet the public. **walk'-around'** n an old dance in which performers, often blackfaced minstrels, moved in a wide circular movement; a march in procession about the stage (theatre);

the music for either of these. **walk'-away** n (inf) an effortless victory. **walk'er-on'** n a performer who plays non-speaking roles. **walk'ie-talk'ie** or **walk'y-talk'y** n a portable transmitting and receiving radiotelephone. **walk'-in** n a person who enters premises to make enquiries or offer services without previously making contact; a theft committed by a walk-in thief. ◆ adj (of a thief) who gains entrance without breaking in; (of a cupboard, etc) big enough to walk into and move around in; (of a service, etc) available without requiring an appointment. **walking bass** n (jazz) a bass part in 4–4 rhythm using a simple repetitive tune moving up and down the octave. **walk'ing-beam** n a beam or oscillating lever for transmitting power, eg that actuating the cable in cable-drilling for oil. **walking bus** n a group of children who regularly walk between home and school together under adult supervision. **walking case** n a patient not confined to bed. **walking fern** n an American fern of the genus *Camptosorus*, whose frond tips take root when touching the ground. **walking fish** n any of various fishes, mainly Asiatic, that are able to move about on land. **walking frame** n a usu metal frame for giving an infirm person support while walking. **walking gentleman** or **lady** n an actor or actress playing very small non-speaking parts for which a good appearance is required. **walking leaf** n a leaf insect; another name for walking fern. **walk'ing-orders**, **walking papers** or **walk'ing-ticket** n pl (sl) dismissal. **walking part** n one in which the actor has nothing to say. **walking race** n a race in which competitors must walk rather than run. **walk'ing-stick**, **walk'ing-cane** or **walk'ing-staff** n a stick, cane or staff used for support in walking. **walking stick**, **walking straw** or **walking twig** n a stick insect. **walking toad** n a natterjack. **walking wounded** adj (of troops) wounded but not requiring stretchers, not bedridden. ◆ n pl such casualties; people handicapped by mental or emotional problems (inf). **walk'-mill** n a machine operated by the walking of a horse; see also **waulk**. **walk'-on** n a walking part. ◆ adj (of an air service or aeroplane) for which one does not have to purchase a ticket in advance, the seats being non-bookable; (of a part in a play, etc) non-speaking. **walk'out** n the act of walking out, usu to indicate disapproval; a sudden industrial strike. **walk'over** n a race where only one competitor appears, and has merely to cover the course to win; an easy or unopposed victory, usu in sport. **walk'-through** n a tentative practice, esp a rehearsal of a dramatic part without an audience, cameras, etc. **walk'-up** adj (chiefly N Am) reached by means of stairs; (of a building) with upper storeys accessible only by stairs; denoting spectators at a sports event who do not purchase tickets in advance. ◆ n a walk-up building, apartment, etc. **walk'way** n a road or path, etc constructed for pedestrians only; a country track for walkers. **walky-talky** see **walkie-talkie** above.
■ **charity walk** or **sponsored walk** an organized walk in aid of charity, each participator having obtained from a sponsor or sponsors an agreement to contribute money according to distance covered. **go walkies** (inf) (of a dog) to go for a walk; (of an inanimate object) to go missing, presumably stolen. **walk a tightrope** to follow a narrow and difficult route beset with dangers, as if on a tightrope. **walk away from** to outdistance or outdo easily; to have nothing more to do with; to emerge from (an accident, etc) with no or only minor injuries. **walk away with** to win (a prize, etc) with ease. **walk into** to collide or meet with unexpectedly; to involve oneself in (eg difficulties) esp without due circumspection; to enter without effort or opposition; to beat (archaic); to storm at (archaic); to eat a hearty quantity of (archaic). **walk it** to go on foot; to succeed, win easily (inf). **walk off** to leave; to depart; to get rid of (eg disagreeable feelings or effects) by walking. **walk off with** to steal; to win easily. **walk on** to walk ahead; to continue to walk; to have a walking part. **walk on air** to be exultant or light-hearted. **walk one's chalks** to quit, go away without ceremony. **walk out** to leave, esp as a gesture of disapproval; to strike. **walk out on** (inf) to desert, leave in the lurch. **walk out with** to go for walks with as a stage of courtship (also **walk with**; archaic). **walk over** to cross or traverse; to win an uncontested race; to have an easy victory or easy success (inf); to beat easily (inf); (also **walk all over**) to disregard the rights or feelings of (inf). **walk tall** (inf) to be proud, have self-respect. **walk the chalk** or **chalkmark** to walk along a chalked line as a test of sobriety; to keep a correct course in manners or morals. **walk the hospitals** or **wards** to be a student under clinical instruction at a general hospital or infirmary. **walk the plank** see under **plank**. **walk the streets** to wander about in search of work, or simply aimlessly; to be a prostitute.

walk², etc see **waulk**.

walkathon /wö'kə-thon/ n a long-distance walk, either as a race or in aid of charity. [walk and marathon]

Walkman® /wök'mən/ n a small portable MP3, CD or cassette player or radio with headphones, designed for personal use whilst walking, travelling, etc.

walkmill see under **waulk**.

Walkyrie /vol'ki-ri or -kir', also wol-, val- or wal-/ same as **Valkyrie**. [OE wælcyri(g)e]

wall /wöl/ n an erection of brick, stone, etc, for security or to enclose a space such as a piece of land; the side of a building or of a room; a very steep smooth rock face (mountaineering); (in pl) fortifications; any bounding or encasing surface suggestive of a wall, eg the membranous covering or lining of an organ of the body or of a plant or animal cell; the side next to the wall; a defence, means of security (fig); a psychological and physiological barrier to further effort, encountered eg by long-distance runners (fig); (in mah-jong) the arrangement of the tiles before the hands are drawn; one of the surfaces of rock enclosing the lode (mining). ◆ vt to enclose with, or as if with, a wall; to fortify with, or as if with, walls; to divide as if by a wall. ◆ combining form growing on, living in, for hanging on, or otherwise relating to a wall. [OE wall (WSax weall), from L vallum a rampart]
■ **walled** adj enclosed with a wall; fortified. **wall'er** n a builder of walls. **wall'ing** n walls collectively; materials for walls. **wall'-less** adj. □ **wall bars** n pl horizontal bars fixed to a wall, used by gymnasts. **wall'board** n building-board, board for lining walls, consisting of plaster or wood fibre compressed between layers of thick paper. **wall brown** n a brown butterfly with orange markings, *Lasiommata megera*. **wall'chart** n a chart of information, statistics, etc, displayed on a wall. **wall'climber** n (inf) a glass-walled elevator whose shaft is on the exterior wall of a building. **wall'covering** n wallpaper, or anything used in the same way. **wall'creeper** n a Eurasian songbird related to the nuthatch. **wall cress** n rockcress, or any species of *Arabis*. **walled garden** n a garden enclosed within high walls; a controlled secure environment, such as an Internet service with restrictions preventing those using it from accessing anything beyond its confines. **wall'eye** n see separate entry. **wall'-facing** n a facing for a wall. **wall'fish** n (dialect) a snail. **wall'flower** n a plant (*Cheiranthus cheiri*) with yellow, orange or orange-brown flowers, found esp on old walls; any of various cultivars of this, with various-coloured flowers; a person who remains a spectator at a dance, typically a woman who cannot obtain partners (inf); a yellowish-red colour (also **wallflower brown**). **wall fruit** n a fruit tree growing against a wall; its fruit. **wall game** n (also **Eton wall game**) a variety of football played at Eton against a wall ('at the wall' instead of 'in the field'). **wall gillyflower** n a wallflower. **wall knot** or (properly) **wale knot** n a nautical method of tying the strands at the end of a rope. **wall lizard** or **wall newt** n a common lizard living in the chinks of walls. **wall moss** n a yellow lichen; the common stonecrop. **wall mustard** or **wall rocket** n a yellow-flowered cruciferous plant (genus *Diplotaxis*) of walls, quarries, etc. **wall of death** n a fairground show in which a stunt-performer rides a motorcycle, at right angles to the ground, round the interior walls of a cylindrical enclosure. **wall painting** n the decoration of walls with ornamental painted designs; a work of art painted on a wall. **wall'paper** n paper, usu coloured or decorated, for pasting on the walls of a room; something of a bland or background nature, lacking originality or noteworthiness, etc (fig; inf); a background pattern on a computer screen. ◆ vt to cover with wallpaper. **wall pass** n (football) a one-two. **wall pepper** n the common stonecrop. **wall plate** n a horizontal piece of timber or of rolled steel on a wall, etc, to bear the ends of joists, etc. **wall rue** n a small fern growing on walls, etc, one of the spleenworts. **wall space** n space on a wall, eg on which to hang a picture. **Wall Street** n a street in New York, the chief financial centre in the United States; hence, American financial interests. **Wall'-Streeter** n a financier based in Wall Street. **wall'-to-wall'** adj (of carpets, etc) covering the entire floor; widespread, ubiquitous or uninterrupted (fig; inf). **wall tree** n a tree trained against a wall. **wall unit** n a piece of furniture attached to or standing against a wall. **wall'washer** n a light designed to give overall illumination to a wall or other vertical surface. **wall'wort** n a name applied to various plants growing on walls, eg pellitory (*Parietaria officinalis*), wall pepper, etc; see also separate entry.
■ **drive to the wall** to push to extremities. **go to the wall** (or obs **walls**) to be hard pressed; to be forced to give way; to fail, go under; to give precedence to something else. **hang by the wall** to remain unused. **off the wall** (US sl) off the cuff, unofficially, without preparation; unorthodox, strange. **push** or **thrust to the wall** to force to give way. **the wall** the right of taking the side of the road near the wall when encountering another person, as in the phrase give or take the wall. **turn one's face to the wall** to resign oneself to death or despair. **up the wall** (inf) mad, distracted. **wall a rope** to make a wall knot on the end of a rope. **walls have ears** see under **ear¹**. **wall up** to block with a wall; to entomb in or behind a wall. **with one's back to the wall** in desperate straits; at bay.

walla see **wallah**.

wallaba /wol'ə-bə/ n a caesalpiniaceous tree of northern S America, valuable for the medicinal properties of its resin and oil, and for its durable streaked reddish wood. [Native name]

wallaby /wol'ə-bi/ n any of a number of small marsupials of the family Macropodidae. [Aboriginal word wolabā]

■ **on the wallaby** or **on the wallaby track** (*inf*; *Aust*) travelling through the bush with one's swag, *esp* looking for work. **the Wallabies** the Australian national Rugby Union team.

Wallace's line /*wol*'*i-siz līn*/ *n* a line passing through the East Indian group of islands between Bali and Lombok, roughly separating the very different faunas of the Oriental region and the Australian region, or rather a transitional region. [Alfred Russel *Wallace* (1823–1913), naturalist]

Wallachian or **Walachian** /*wo-lā*'*ki-ən*/ *n* a Vlach. ◆ *adj* of or relating to the region of Romania which was formerly the principality of *Wal*(*l*)*achia*, or to the Vlach people.

wallah or **walla** /*wol*'*a* or *wol*'*ə*/ *n* (often as *combining form*) someone employed in, or concerned with, a specific type of work; someone who occupies an eminent position in an organization, etc. [Hindi *-wālā*, properly an adjectival suffix, in one sense comparable to L *-ārius* or Eng *-ar*, *-er*, *-or*]
■ **competition wallah** a member of the Indian Civil Service who obtained appointment by the competitive system instituted in 1856.

wallaroo /*wol-ə-roo*'/ *n* a large kangaroo, *Macropus robustus* (also called **euro**). [Aboriginal word *wolarū*]

wallet /*wol*'*it*/ *n* a small folding case for holding money, papers, etc, a pocketbook; a bag for tools; a bag for carrying necessaries on a journey; a bag with the opening at the middle and a pouch at each end; anything protuberant and hanging loosely (*Shakesp*). [ME *walet*, poss from *watel* a bag of woven material; cf **wattle**[1]]

walleye /*wol*'*ī*/ *n* an eye in which the iris is pale or whitish, particoloured or a different colour from the other, or in which the white part is large or noticeable (as in a divergent squint); glaucoma; any of various fishes, *esp* the pike-perch (*Stizostedion vitreum*; also **walleyed pike**) (*N Am*). [The adj *walleyed* is the earlier, representing ON *vagleygr*, of which the first element is perh connected with Mod Icel *vagl* a film over the eye, and the second is from *auga* eye]
❑ **wall'eyed** *adj* having pale irises, or a whitish or particoloured iris in one eye, or irises of different colours; having a divergent squint; having a staring, glazed or blank expression or (*fig*) appearance; glaring, fierce (*Shakesp*).

wallie see **wally**[1].

wallies see **wally**[2].

Walloon /*wə-* or *wo-loon*'/ *adj* of or relating to a French-speaking people living chiefly in S Belgium and adjacent parts of E France, or to their language. ◆ *n* a member of this people; their language, a dialect of French. [Fr *Wallon*; of Gmc origin, cognate with **Welsh**, **Wallachian**]

wallop /*wol*'*əp*/ *vt* to beat soundly, thrash; to strike with force. ◆ *vi* to move with noisy lumbering haste; to flounder; to gallop (*obs*); to bubble and boil (*perh* a different word); to flap about (*Scot*). ◆ *n* a plunging movement (*inf*); a heavy blow (*inf*); a powerful impression (*inf*); physical or financial power (*inf*); a gallop (*obs*); a flapping rag (*Scot*); beer (*sl*). ◆ *adv* with a wallop; heavily or noisily. [ONFr *waloper* (Fr *galoper*) relating to the obs verb sense above; cf **gallop**]
■ **wall'oper** *n* someone who or something that wallops; something enormous (*sl*); a policeman (*old Aust sl*). **wall'oping** *n* a sound thrashing. ◆ *adj* that wallops; enormous, bouncing, whopping (often as an intensifier; *inf*).
■ **wallop in a tow** or **tether** (*Scot*) to be hanged.

wallow[1] /*wol*'*ō*/ *vi* to roll about enjoyably in mud, etc, as an animal does; to immerse oneself (in emotion, etc); to flounder; (of a ship) to roll from side to side making little progress; in a bad sense, to live in filth or vice; to surge, heave, blow, well up, etc. ◆ *vt* (*obs*) to cause to wallow. ◆ *n* the act of wallowing; the place, or the filth, an animal wallows in; a hollow or depression suggestive of a wallowing-place; a rolling gait (*obs*); the swell of the sea (*poetic*). [OE *wealwian*, from L *volvere*]
■ **wall'ower** *n*. **wall'owing** *n*. ◆ *adj* that wallows; very rich (*sl*).

wallow[2] /*wol*'*ō*/ (*dialect*) *vi* to fade away. [OE *wealwian*]
■ **wall'owed** *adj* withered, faded.

wallsend /*wolz*'*end* or *wölz-end*'/ *n orig* coal dug at *Wallsend* (at the end of the Roman *Wall*) on Tyneside; later, coal of a certain quality and size.

wallwort /*wöl*'*wart*/ *n* dwarf elder (also called **Danewort**, **Dane's blood**, etc), a plant with an offensive smell and taste; see also under **wall**. [OE *wealhwyrt* from *wealh* a foreigner, or *wæelwyrt* (from the belief that it grew on battlefields, from *wæl* slaughter, and *wyrt* a root, a plant]

wally[1] or **wallie** /*wol*'*i*/ (*sl*; also with *cap*) *n* a stupid, inept or despised person; generally, a fool. [Ety uncertain; cf **wallydrag**; perh connected with the short form of the name *Walter*]

wally[2] /*wö*'*li* or *wal*'*i*/ (*Scot*) *adj* (also **wa'ly**) excellent, fine-looking, ample (a general term of commendation); made of china or glazed earthenware, etc; (of a tenement close) tiled. ◆ *adv* (*obs*) finely, well.

◆ *n* (*pl* **wall'ies**) an ornament; (in *pl*) finery; a showy trifle; china, glazed earthenware, etc, also (in *pl*) fragments of this used as children's playthings; (in *pl*) dentures (*sl*). [Ety uncertain; perh **wale**[2]]

wallydrag /*wol*'*i-drag*/ or **wallydraigle** /*wol*'*i-drā-gl*/ (*Scot*) *n* a person or animal that is feeble, worthless or slovenly; the youngest of a family. [Poss *waly*[2] and *drag*, *draigle* (Scot form of **draggle**)]

walnut /*wöl*'*nut*/ *n* a genus (*Juglans*) of beautiful trees, some yielding valuable furniture wood; one of these trees; their wood; the nut of the common or English walnut; walnut juice. ◆ *adj* made from walnutwood; light brown in colour. [OE *walhhnutu*, from *w*(*e*)*alh* foreigner, and *hnutu* a nut]
❑ **walnut juice** *n* juice from the husk of walnuts, used to stain the skin. **wal'nutwood** *n*.
■ **black walnut** a N American walnut, the timber of which is more valuable than that of the common walnut, though the fruit is inferior.

Walpurgis night /*val-pûr*'*gis nīt* or *-poor*'/ *n* the eve of the first of May, when witches, according to German popular superstition, rode on broomsticks and male goats to revel with their master the Devil, *esp* on the Brocken in the Harz Mountains. [So called because 1 May is the day of St *Walpurga*, abbess of Heidenheim, who died about 778]

walrus /*wöl*'*rəs* or *wol*'*rəs*/ *n* an aquatic, webfooted, carnivorous animal, related to the seals, having the upper canine teeth developed into enormous tusks (also called **morse** or, formerly, **seahorse**); a walrus moustache (*inf*). [Du *walrus*, *walros*, literally, whale horse; of Scand origin]
❑ **walrus moustache** *n* a thick moustache with long drooping ends.

Walter Mitty /*wol*' or *wöl*'*tər mit*'*i*/ *n* an ordinary person who indulges in escapist daydreams of fame, power, etc; an intrepid daydreamer. [From the hero of a short story by James Thurber (1894–1961), US writer]

Waltonian /*wol-tō*'*ni-ən*/ *adj* of or relating to Izaak *Walton* (1593–1683), who wrote *The Compleat Angler*. ◆ *n* a disciple of Walton; an angler.

walty /*wol*'*ti*/ (*naut*) *adj* inclined to lean or roll over. [Obs adj *walt* unsteady (from OE *wealt*, found only in *unwealt* steady), and sfx *-y*]

waltz /*wolts*, *wölts* or *wöls*/ *n orig* a German dance in triple time performed by couples with a rapid whirling motion; a slower circling dance, also in triple time; the music for either dance; a piece of instrumental music in 3–4 time (**concert waltz**). ◆ *vi* to dance a waltz; to move or trip lightly, to whirl (*inf*); to walk with arrogant assurance (*inf*); to progress with carefree ease (*inf*). ◆ *vt* to guide or partner in a waltz; to convey lightly and easily (*inf*). [Ger *Walzer* a waltz, from *walzen* to roll, dance]
■ **waltz'er** *n* someone who waltzes; a waltzing mouse; a type of fairground roundabout in which passengers are spun while revolving. **waltz'ing** *n*.
❑ **waltzing mouse** *n* a mouse of a breed that moves forward in small circles, rather than a straight line.
■ **waltz into** (*inf*) to storm at. **waltz Matilda** see under **Matilda**.

waly[1] see **wally**[2].

waly[2] /*wā*'*li*/ (*Scot*) *interj* alas. [**wellaway**]

wambenger /*wom-beng*'*ər*/ (*Aust*) *n* a small marsupial, same as **tuan**[2]. [From an Aboriginal language]

wame /*wām*/ (*dialect*) *n* (also (in 17c literature) **wem**, **wemb** and **weamb**) the womb or (more frequently) the belly; a protuberant part or a hollow enclosed part. [Variant of **womb**]
■ **wamed** *adj* having a wame (*usu* of a specified kind). **wame'ful** *n* a bellyful.

wammus see **wamus**.

wampee /*wom-pē*'/ *n* an edible Asiatic fruit (genus *Clausena*; family Rutaceae) about the size of a large grape, with a hard yellow rind. [Chin *hwáng pí*, literally, yellow skin]

wampish /*wom*'*pish*/ (*Walter Scott*) *vt* to brandish, flourish, wave about (also *vi*). [Origin uncertain]

wampum /*wom*'*pəm* or *wöm*'*pəm*/ (*hist*) *n* a shortened form of the Native American (Algonquian) name for beads made from shells, used as money, etc.
■ **wam'pumpeag** /*-pēg*/ *n* the word of which wampum is a shortened form, literally white string of beads.
❑ **wampum belt** *n* a belt consisting of shell beads so arranged as to convey a message or record a treaty, etc.

wampus see **wamus**.

wamus /*wöm*'*əs* or *wom*'*əs*/ (*US*; *old*) *n* a kind of cardigan or strong jacket buttoned at neck and wrists (also **wamm'us** or **wamp'us**). [Du *wammes*, from OFr *wambais* a military tunic orig worn under armour]

WAN (*comput*) *abbrev*: wide area network.

wan[1] /*won*/ *adj* lacking colour; pale and sickly; faint; dark, gloomy (*obs*). ◆ *n* (*rare*) wanness. ◆ *vt* and *vi* to make or to become wan. [OE *wann* dark, lurid; not found in other Gmc languages]

■ **wan'd** *adj* (*Shakesp, Antony and Cleopatra* II.1.21) *perh* for *pap* **wanned**. **wan'ly** *adv*. **wan'ness** *n*. **wann'ish** *adj* somewhat wan.

wan² /wan/ old *pat* of **win¹**; gained or took (*Spenser*).

wanchancy or **wanchancie** /won-chan'si/ (*Scot*) *adj* unlucky, dangerous or uncanny. [OE privative or negative pfx *wan-* (of Gmc origin; seen in Mod Du and in Eng **wanton**), **chance**, and sfx *-y*]

wand /wond/ *n* a rod of authority, a caduceus, a rod used by a fairy, magician, conjurer, conductor or diviner; *orig* something slender and supple, eg a twig, thin stem, branch or young shoot of a willow used in basket-making (now *poetic* and *dialect*); something slender and rigid, eg a light walking-cane (*obs*); a measuring rod; a mark in archery. [ON *vöndr* a shoot of a tree; Dan *vånd*]

wander /won'dər/ *vi* to ramble or move with no definite object, or with no fixed course, or by a roundabout way (*lit* and *fig*); to go astray, deviate from the right path or course, the subject of discussion, the object of attention, etc; to lose one's way (*inf*); to be incoherent in talk, disordered in mind, or delirious. ◆ *vt* to traverse; to lead astray, or to bewilder (*inf*). ◆ *n* a ramble, stroll. [OE *wandrian*; cf Ger *wandern*; related to **wend**, and to **wind²**]
■ **wan'dered** *adj* astray; incoherent; bewildered. **wan'derer** *n* a person or animal that wanders, *esp* habitually or from inclination; (with *cap*) a Covenanter who left his or her home to follow a dispossessed minister (*hist*). **wan'dering** *adj* and *n*. **wan'deringly** *adv*. □ **wandering albatross** *n* a large albatross, *Diomedea exulans*. **Wandering Jew** *n* a legendary Jew in the folklore *esp* of NW Europe who cannot die but must wander until the end of the world or until Christ's second coming, as a punishment for taunting Christ on the way to the Crucifixion, his name occurring variously as *Cartaphilus*, *Ahasuerus*, *Buttadeus*, etc. **wandering Jew** *n* any of several trailing or creeping plants, *esp* a species of *Tradescantia* (*T. fluminensis*) with variegated leaves. **wandering nerve** *n* the vagus, the tenth cranial nerve. **wandering sailor** *n* a popular trailing house plant, *Tradescantia blossfeldiana*, with leaves that are maroon on the underside. **wander plug** *n* an electrical plug on a flexible wire capable of being inserted in any appropriate socket. **wander year** *n* a year spent in travel to complete training or broaden experience before settling down to a trade or profession.

Wanderjahr /van'dər-yär/ (*Ger*) *n* (*pl* **Wanderjahre**) a year of journeymanship or travelling, a wander year.

wanderlust /won'dər-lust/ *n* an urge to travel or move from place to place. [Ger, wander-longing]

wanderoo /won-də-roo'/ *n* a name *usu* applied to the lion-tailed macaque, a native of the Malabar coast of India; properly, a langur of Sri Lanka. [Sinhalese *wanderu* monkey]

wandle /won'dl/ (*dialect*) *adj* supple, pliant, nimble (also **wanle** or **wannel**). [Ety uncertain]

wandoo /won'doo/ *n* a W Australian eucalyptus (*Eucalyptus redunca*) having white bark and durable brown wood. [From an Aboriginal language]

wane /wān/ *vi* (*esp* of the moon) to decrease in size, *opp* to **wax**; to decrease in volume (*obs*); to decline in power, prosperity, intensity, brightness, etc; to draw to a close. ◆ *n* gradual decrease or decline, as in *on the wane*, *in its wane*; the time when this is taking place; a defective edge or corner on a plank of wood. [OE *wanian*, *wonian* to lessen (ON *vana*), from *wana*, *wona* (also *wan*, *won*) deficient, lacking]
■ **waned** *adj* diminished; dying or dead. **wan'ey** or **wan'y** *adj*. **wan'ing** *adj* and *n*.

wang¹ /wang/ (*obs*) *n* the cheek; a wang tooth. [OE *wange*]
□ **wang tooth** *n* a molar.

wang² see **whang²**.

wangan and **wangun** see **wanigan**.

wangle /wang'gl/ (*inf*) *vt* to obtain or accomplish by craft; to manipulate or falsify. ◆ *vi* to get one's way by guile. ◆ *n* an exercise of such methods. [Origin uncertain]
■ **wang'ler** *n*. **wang'ling** *n*.

wanhope /won'hōp/ (*obs*) *n* despair. [OE privative or negative pfx *wan-* (see **wanchancy**), and **hope¹**]

wanigan /won'i-gən/ *n* (also **wan'gan** and **wan'gun**) in a lumber camp, a chest for supplies or a kind of houseboat for loggers and their supplies; also the pay office. [Algonquian]

wanion /won'yən/ (*Shakesp, Walter Scott*) *n* a word found in the phrases **with a** (**wild**) **wanion** with a vengeance, vehemently, and **with a** (**wild**) **wanion to him** bad luck to him, a curse on him. [Earlier (*in the*) *waniand* (in the) waning (of the moon), ie in an unlucky time]

wank /wangk/ (*vulgar sl*) *vi* (of a man) to masturbate. ◆ *vt* to masturbate (a man). ◆ *n* an act or instance of masturbation. [Origin unknown]
■ **wank'er** *n* someone who masturbates; a worthless, contemptible person. **wank'y** *adj* objectionable, contemptible.

Wankel engine /wang'kəl en'jin/ *n* a rotary automobile engine having an approximately triangular central rotor turning in a close-fitting oval-shaped chamber rather than conventional pistons and cylinders. [F *Wankel* (1902–88), the German engineer who invented it]

wankle /wong'kl/ (*dialect*) *adj* unstable, unsteady; changeable; not to be depended on. [OE *wancol*; of Gmc origin]

wanle and **wannel** see **wandle**.

wanly see under **wan¹**.

wanna /won'ə/ a spelling of **want to** representing colloquial pronunciation.

wannabe or **wannabee** /won'ə-bē/ (*inf*) *n* someone who aspires, *usu* ineffectually, to a particular lifestyle or image; a vain fantasist. [(*l*) *want to be*]

wanness see under **wan¹**.

wannion same as **wanion**.

wannish see under **wan¹**.

wanrestful /won-rest'fŭl or -fl/ (*Scot*) *adj* restless. [OE privative or negative pfx *wan-* (see **wanchancy**), and **restful**]

want¹ /wont/ *n* the state or fact of being without something or of having an insufficient quantity; absence or deficiency of necessities; poverty; (in *pl*) difficult or straitened circumstances (*obs*); a lack, deficiency; a blemish (*obs*); a defect, feebleness, in intelligence, as in *have a want* (*Scot*); (in *pl*) requirements or desires. ◆ *vt* to be destitute of or deficient in; to lack, be without (*Shakesp, Macbeth* III.6.8, *who cannot want, for who can want, the thought?*); to feel need of, desire; to require, need; to fall short of something by (a specified amount); to dispense with, do without (now *dialect*). ◆ *vi* to be deficient, entirely lacking (*archaic*); to be in need or destitution (*old*); to lack (with *for*; *old*). [ON *vant*, neuter of *vanr* lacking, and *vanta* to lack]
■ **want'age** *n* (*US*) deficiency, shortage. **want'ed** *adj* lacking; needed; desired; searched for, *esp* by the police. **want'er** *n* someone who wants. **want'ing** *adj* absent, missing, lacking; deficient (with *in*, or, *obs*, with *of*); failing to help, do justice to, come up to (with *to*; *old*); slow to (with *infinitive*; *obs*); below the desired or expected standard, in the phrase *found wanting*; mentally defective (*dialect*); poor, needy (*obs*). ◆ *prep* without, lacking, less.
□ **want ad** *n* (chiefly *US*) a small advertisement, *esp* in a newspaper, specifying goods, property, employment, etc required by the advertiser. **want'-wit** *n* a fool, someone lacking common sense (also *adj*).
■ **want in**, **out**, **up**, **down**, etc (*inf*) to want to get in, out, etc.

want² /wont/ (*dialect*) *n* a mole. [OE *wand*; cf Norw *vand*; prob same root as **wind²** and **wend**]
□ **want'-catcher** *n*. **want'hill** *n*.

wanthriven /won-thriv'n/ (*Scot*) *adj* stunted; ill-grown; emaciated. [Privative or negative pfx *wan-* (see **wanchancy**) and **thriven**]

wanton /won'tən/ *adj* thoughtlessly cruel; unprovoked, unjust, merciless; capricious (*archaic*); self-indulgent, given to luxury (*obs*); lascivious, or (*obs*) amorous; undisciplined, unruly, unmanageable (*obs*); immoral, licentious, lewd; insolent, arrogant, merciless in power or prosperity (*obs*); (of people) jovial (*obs*); (of animals and inanimate things) frisky, gay, moving freely or capriciously (*poetic*); growing luxuriantly (*poetic*); unrestrained, prodigal. ◆ *n* an immoral person, *esp* female; a trifler (*old*); a spoilt child or pampered, effeminate person (*obs*); a roguish, playful child, animal, etc (*obs*). ◆ *vi* to frolic; to play lasciviously or amorously; to idle, go idly; to trifle; to indulge oneself, run into excesses; to grow luxuriantly, ramble unchecked. ◆ *vt* to use wastefully, dissipate (also with *away*; *old*). [ME *wantowen*, from privative or negative pfx *wan-* (see **wanchancy**), and OE *togen*, pap of *tēon* to draw, lead, educate; cf Ger *ungezogen* ill-bred, rude]
■ **wan'tonize** or **-ise** *vi* (*archaic*) to play the wanton. **wan'tonly** *adv*. **wan'tonness** *n*.
■ **play the wanton** to trifle or (*obs*) to behave lewdly.

wanty /won'ti/ *n* a belt used to secure a load on a pack-horse's back (*obs*); the belly-band of a shaft-horse (*dialect*); a short rope, *esp* one used for binding hay on a cart (*dialect*). [**wame** and **tie¹**]

wanworth /won'wûrth/ (*Scot*) *n* a very low price; a bargain. [Privative or negative pfx *wan-* (see **wanchancy**), and **worth¹**]
■ **wanword'y** *adj* worthless; unworthy.

wanze /wonz/ (*obs*) *vi* to decrease, waste away. [OE *wansian*]

WAP *abbrev* : Wireless Application Protocol, a technology that enables the Internet to be accessed on a mobile phone.

wap¹ /wop/ *vt* (**wapp'ing**; **wapped**) to throw or pull quickly or roughly (*dialect*); to strike or drub (*inf*); to flap (*Scot*). ◆ *n* a smart blow; a shake or flap (*Scot*); a blast (*Scot*); a fight or quarrel (*Scot*). [Cf **whop**]

wap² /wop/ *vt* (*obs*) to wrap or bind. ◆ *n* (*dialect*) a turn of a string with which anything is tied; a bundle of hay. [Ety uncertain]

wapenshaw and **wapenschaw** see **wappenshaw**.

---

wapentake /wop'n-tāk/ (*esp hist*) *n* a name given in Yorkshire and certain other shires to a territorial division of the county similar to the *hundred* of southern counties. [Late OE *wǣpen(ge)tæc*, ON *vāpnatak*, literally, weapon-taking, assent at a meeting being signified by brandishing a weapon]

wapinshaw and **wapinschaw** see **wappenshaw**.

wapiti /wop'i-ti/ *n* a species (*Cervus canadensis*) of deer of large size, native to N America. [Algonquian]

wappend /wop'nd/ *adj* (*Shakesp, Timon of Athens* IV.3.38) *perh* for *wappered* (now *dialect*), fatigued, tired; *perh* meaning incontinent, unchaste, and connected with obsolete sense of **wap¹**, to copulate.

wappenshaw, wapenshaw, wapinshaw, wappenschaw, wapenschaw or **wapinschaw** /wop'n-shö or wap'/ *n* (also **weap'on-shaw** or **weap'on-schaw**) a periodical gathering of the people within an area for the purpose of seeing that each man was armed in accordance with his rank, and ready to take the field when required (*Scot hist*); a rifle-shooting competition (*S Afr*; equivalent to Du *wapenschouwing*). [Scot *wappen* weapon, and *schaw* show]
  ■ **wapp'enshawing**, etc *n* an older form, from which *wappenshaw* is a back-formation.

wapper /wop'ər/ (*dialect*) *vi* to blink; to move tremulously. [Cf Du *wapperen* to oscillate]
  ❑ **wapp'er-eyed** *adj* blinking. **wapp'er-jaw** *n* a projecting under-jaw. **wapp'er-jawed** *adj*.

waqf or **wakf** /wäkf/ (*Islam*) *n* the donation of land, property or money for charitable or pious purposes; such an endowment; (*with cap*) in Jerusalem the authority administering the holy sites. [Ar *waqf*]

War. *abbrev* : Warwickshire.

war¹ /wör/ *n* a state of conflict; a contest between states, or between parties within a state (**civil war**) carried on by arms; any long-continued struggle, often against or between impersonal forces (*fig*); fighting (*poetic*); open hostility; the profession of arms; an army, or war equipment (*rare; poetic*); a contest, conflict. ◆ *vi* (**warr'ing; warred**) to make war; to carry on war; to contend. ◆ *adj* of, characteristic of, resulting from, or relating to war. [Late OE and ONFr *werre* (OFr and Fr *guerre*), from OHGer *werra* quarrel]
  ■ **war'like** *adj* fond of war; bellicose; of or relating to war; martial, military; equipped for fighting (*obs*); intended for use in war (*obs*). **war'likeness** *n*.
  ❑ **war baby** *n* a baby born during a war, *esp* a serviceman's illegitimate child; any discreditable or troublesome result of war. **war'bird** *n* (*inf*) a vintage military aircraft. **war bonnet** *n* a headdress, often with long trailing chains of feathers, worn by members of certain Native American tribes. **war bride** *n* a soldier's bride, met as a result of wartime movements or postings. **war chest** *n* funds set aside to pay for a war, political campaign, etc. **war cloud** *n* a cloud of smoke and dust over a battlefield; a sign that war is threatening or impending (*fig*). **war correspondent** *n* a journalist or other person assigned to a war zone so as to give first-hand reports of events. **war crime** *n* a crime connected with war, *esp* one that violates the code of war. **war criminal** *n*. **war cry** *n* a cry used in battle for encouragement or as a signal; a slogan (*fig*). **war dance** *n* a dance engaged in by some peoples before going to war; a dance imitating the actions of a battle. **War Department** *n* the name borne 1784–1857 by what became the War Office, still used in speaking of property such as stores or land. **war'dog** *n* a dog used in war; an old warrior; a war hawk. **war drum** *n* a drum beaten as a summons to war, or during a battle; a rumbling or threat of impending war (*fig*). **war'fare** *n* (from *fare* (*n*)) the activity of engaging in, waging, or carrying on war; armed conflict; conflict, struggle or feuding of any kind. ◆ *vi* (*obs; lit* and *fig*) to wage war. **war'farer** *n*. **war'faring** *adj* and *n*. **war game** *n* a mock or imaginary battle or military exercise used to train personnel in tactics, a kriegspiel; a game, *esp* with detailed rules and using models, in which players enact historical or imaginary battles, etc. **war'-gamer** *n* a player of or participant in war games. **war gas** *n* (*chem*) any poisonous or irritant gaseous chemical substance used in warfare or riot control deliberately to harm or temporarily disable those exposed to it. **war god** or **goddess** *n* a deity who presides over war, assigning victory or defeat, etc. **war hawk** *n* someone eager for war. **war'head** *n* the section of a torpedo or other missile containing the explosive material. **war'horse** *n* a charger, a horse used in battle; an old warrior in any field of conflict; any standard, familiar, reliable, much-performed piece of music, play, etc. **war kettle** *n* among Native Americans, a kettle set on the fire as part of the ceremony of going to war. **war loan** *n* a loan raised to pay for a war. **war'lord** *n* (now *usu derog*) a commander or commander-in-chief, *esp* where and when the military power is great. **war machine** *n* a machine used in warfare; the combined technical and administrative military resources mobilized by a country, alliance, etc in order to engage in war. **war'man** *n* (*rare*) a warrior. **war memorial** *n* a monument erected to the memory of those (*esp* from a particular locality) who died in a war. **war'monger** *n* a mercenary soldier (*Spenser*); someone who

encourages war, *esp* for personal gain. **war'mongering** *n* and *adj*. **war neurosis** *n* a more accurate term for shellshock. **war note** *n* (*poetic*) a summons to war. **war of attrition** *n* a conflict in which both sides are worn down over a long period, with no decisive battles. **War Office** *n* a former department of the civil government, headed by the Secretary of State for War (since 1964 under the Ministry of Defence); the former premises of the department in Whitehall. **war of nerves** *n* systematic attempts to undermine morale by means of threats, rumours and counter-rumours, etc. **war paint** *n* paint applied to the face and body by primitive peoples, indicating that they are going to war; full dress, or finery, *esp* a woman's make-up (*inf*). **war'path** *n* among the Native Americans, the path followed on a military expedition, or the expedition itself (**on the warpath** engaged in conflict, in a mood for battle). **war'plane** *n* any aircraft designed or intended for use in warfare. **war'-proof** *n* (*rare*) a valour proved in war. ◆ *adj* able to withstand attack. **war'ship** *n* an armed vessel for use in war. **war song** *n* a song sung by men about to fight; a song celebrating brave deeds in war. **war'time** *n* a period during which a war is being fought. ◆ *adj* of, relating to or characteristic of a time of war. **war trial** *n* the trial of a person accused of war crimes. **war'-wast'ed** *adj* ravaged by war. **war'-wea'ried** or **-wea'ry** *adj* tired of or exhausted by war. **war whoop** *n* a cry uttered on going into battle. **war widow** *n* a woman whose husband has been killed in war. **war'wolf** *n* a medieval siege engine; a fierce warrior (*Walter Scott*); see also **werewolf**. **war'-worn** *adj* wearied, worn, wasted, ravaged or marked by war.
  ■ **carry the war into the enemy's camp** or **country** to take the offensive boldly (*lit* and *fig*). **civil war** see under **civil**. **cold war** see under **cold**. **declare war** (with *on* or *against*) to announce formally that one is about to begin hostilities; to set oneself to get rid of (*fig*). **go to the wars** (*archaic*) to go to fight in a foreign country. **go to war** to resort to armed conflict. **have been in the wars** (*fig*) to show signs of injury. **holy war** see under **holy**. **make** or **wage war** to carry on hostilities. **private war** warfare between people in their individual capacity, eg by duelling, family feuds, etc. **total war** war with every weapon at the combatant's disposal, sticking at nothing and sparing no one.

war² /wär or wör/ (*obs* except *dialect*; *Spenser* also **warre**; *Scot* and *N Eng* also **waur** /wör/) *adj* and *adv* (*superl* **warst** or **waurst**) worse. ◆ *vt* (**warr'ing** or **waur'ing**; **warred** or **waured**) (*Scot*) to defeat, worst; to excel. [ON *verre*]

waragi /war'ə-gi/ *n* a Ugandan alcoholic drink made from bananas. [Swahili *wargi*]

waratah /wor'ə-tä/ *n* any of a genus (*Telopea*) of Australian proteaceous shrubs with very showy flowers. [From an Aboriginal language]

warble¹ /wör'bl/ *vi* to sing in a vibrating treble or soprano, to trill (sometimes *facetious* or *derog*); to sing with elaborations such as runs and trills; to sing sweetly as birds do; to make or be produced as a sweet quavering sound; to yodel (*US*). ◆ *vt* to sing in a vibratory manner; to sing sweetly; to express or extol in poetry or song; to cause (eg a stringed instrument) to vibrate or sound musically. ◆ *n* the activity, or a spell, of warbling; a quavering modulation of the voice; a song. [ONFr *werbler* (OFr *guerbler*); of Gmc origin]
  ■ **war'bler** *n* someone who warbles; a songster; a singing-bird; any bird of the subfamily Sylviinae of the family Muscicapidae (willow warbler, reed warbler, whitethroat, blackcap, etc); any of numerous small, brightly-coloured American birds of the family Parulidae; a whistle used in infant classes, etc; (in bagpipe music) an ornamental group of grace notes. **war'bling** *n* and *adj*. **war'blingly** *adv*.

warble² /wör'bl/ *n* a small hard swelling on a horse's back, caused by the galling of the saddle, etc; a swelling caused by a warble fly or a botfly. [Ety uncertain]
  ❑ **warble fly** *n* any of several flies of the same family as botflies whose larvae cause painful swellings that spoil the hides of horses and cattle, etc.

warby /wör'bi/ (*Aust inf*) *adj* worn-out, decrepit, unattractive; unwell, unsteady. [Poss from Eng dialect *warbie* a maggot]

ward /wörd/ *vt* to parry or keep away (now *usu* **ward off**); to watch over, guard (*archaic*); to protect (with *from*; *archaic*); to enclose (eg machinery) in order to prevent accidents (*rare*); to place in a ward. ◆ *vi* to act on the defensive. ◆ *n* a room with several beds in a hospital, etc; the patients in a ward collectively; a division or department of a prison; the activity or a spell of watching or guarding; the state of being guarded; a lookout or watch; care, protection; guardianship; custody; (in feudal times) control of the lands of a minor; a minor or other person under a guardian; a body of guards; a guarded place, eg a courtyard of a castle (**inner** and **outer ward**); a means of protection, such as a bolt or bar; a part of a lock of special configuration to prevent its being turned by any except a particular key, or the part of the key of corresponding configuration; a defensive motion or position (*fencing*; also *fig*); a division of a county (*Scot* and *N Eng*); an administrative, electoral or other division of a town, etc; a division of an army (obs; as in van(t)ward (vanguard), middle ward and rearward (rearguard)). [OE weardian; cf Ger warten to wait, attend, take care of]

■ **ward'ed** adj (of a lock or key) having a ward or wards. **ward'er** n someone who guards or supervises; a prison officer in charge of prisoners in a jail; a staff or baton of authority (hist). ◆ vt to guard as a warder. **ward'ing** n and adj. **war'dress** n a female prison officer. **ward'ship** n the office of, or the state of being under, a guardian; protection, custody (fig); the state of being in guardianship (fig); in English feudal law, the guardianship that the feudal lord had of the land of his vassal while the latter was a minor.

□ **ward'corn** n (hist) a payment in corn in lieu of military service; misunderstood as the duty of keeping watch in order to give the alarm by blowing a horn. **ward in Chancery** n (hist) a minor under the protection of the Court of Chancery. **ward'mote** n a meeting of a ward, or of a court of a ward. **ward of court** n a minor or other person not of full legal capacity who has been placed under the protection of a court. **ward'room** n the mess room of the officers of a warship; the officers collectively.

-ward /-wərd or -wörd/ or **-wards** /-wərdz or -wördz/ sfx forming adjectives and adverbs with the sense of motion towards. [OE -weard (genitive -weardes), cognate with Ger -wärts; connected with OE weorthan to become and L vertere to turn]

warden¹ /wör'dən/ n someone who guards or keeps under supervision people, animals, buildings, precious objects, etc; a gatekeeper or sentinel (rare); a regent (hist); the governor of a town, district, etc (hist); a title of certain officers of the Crown; a member of certain governing bodies; a superintendent; the head of certain institutions, such as schools, colleges, hostels, etc; the officer in charge of a prison (N Am); a churchwarden; someone appointed for duties among the civil population in cases of fire or air-raids; (usu **traffic warden**) an official controlling traffic circulation and parking of motor vehicles. ◆ vt (rare) to guard as a warden. [ONFr wardein (OFr g(u)arden) guardian]

■ **ward'enry** n (rare) the office of, or district in the charge of, a warden; guardianship (Hardy). **ward'enship** n the office of warden. □ **Warden of the Cinque Ports** or **Lord Warden (of the Cinque Ports)** n the governor of the Cinque Ports, having the authority of an admiral and the power to hold a court of admiralty. **Wardens of the Marches** n pl officers formerly appointed to keep order in the marches or border districts of England and Scotland.

warden² /wör'dən/ n a kind of pear used esp in cooking. [Origin uncertain; perh from Anglo-Fr warder (Fr garder) to keep]

□ **warden pie** n a pie made of warden pears.

warder see under **ward**.

Wardian /wör'di-ən/ adj denoting a kind of glass case for transporting delicate ferns and other such plants or for growing them in indoors. [Nathaniel Bagshaw Ward (1791–1868), the inventor]

wardmote see under **ward**.

Wardour Street English /wör'dər strēt ing'glish/ n sham-antique diction as found in some historical novels. [Wardour Street, London, once noted for antique and imitation-antique furniture, now associated with the film industry]

wardress see under **ward**.

wardrobe /wör'drōb/ n a room or a piece of furniture for containing clothes or theatrical costumes; one's stock of clothes; the stock of costumes belonging to a theatrical company; bright or multicoloured decoration, eg that of flowers (fig and poetic; Milton **ward'rop**); a ship's complement of sails (naut); a department of a royal or noble household having charge of robes, clothes, jewels, etc. [ONFr wardrobe (OFr garderobe); see **guard** and **robe¹**]

■ **ward'rober** n (hist) a household official in charge of a royal or noble wardrobe. □ **wardrobe malfunction** n (facetious) the temporary failure of an item of clothing to do its job in covering a part of the body that it would be advisable to keep covered. **wardrobe mistress** or **master** n a person who looks after the theatrical costumes of a company or of an individual actor or actress. **wardrobe trunk** n a trunk in which clothing may be hung as in a wardrobe.

wardrop see **wardrobe**.

ware¹ /wār/ n (now usu in pl) articles of merchandise or produce collectively; an article of merchandise (rare); pottery, as in Delftware, Wedgwood ware; articles of fine workmanship, as in **Benares ware**, ornamental metalwork from India. ◆ combining form articles of a specified type or material, as in **hardware, earthenware**; used to denote categories of material used in computer processing, as in hardware, software, and various forms of software, as in shareware. [OE waru; cf Ger Ware]

□ **ware potatoes** n pl large potatoes sold to the public for consumption, as distinct from seed potatoes.

ware² /wār/ adj aware (archaic); wary, cautious (archaic; sometimes with of); prudent (archaic; esp in phrase ware and wise). ◆ vi and vt (archaic; usu in imperative) to beware, beware of; (in hunting) to avoid, refrain from riding over, etc (sometimes /wör/). [OE wær; cf ON varr; see **aware**]

■ **ware'less** adj (archaic) incautious; unaware (with of).

ware³ /wār/ (Scot and dialect) n springtime. [ON vār]

ware⁴ /wār/ (Scot and dialect) n (also **seaware**) seaweed. [OE wār; cf **ore²**]

ware⁵ /wār/ archaic pat of **wear¹**.

ware⁶ /wār/ (Scot) vt to spend. [ON verja to clothe, hence to invest; cf **wear¹**]

warehouse /wār'hows/ n a building or room for storing goods; a large, usu wholesale, shop; the music and dancing typical at a warehouse party (qv below) (pop culture). ◆ vt /-howz/ to deposit in a warehouse, esp a bonded warehouse; to store up (fig). [**ware¹** and **house**]

■ **ware'housing** n the act of depositing goods in a warehouse; the practice of covertly building up a block of company shares, using one or more front companies, etc, to obtain shares on behalf of the true purchaser (stock exchange). □ **warehouse club** n an establishment selling discounted goods to members. **ware'houseman** n a man who keeps, or is employed in, a warehouse or a wholesale store. **warehouse party** n an acid-house party held in a large unused building away from main residential areas. **warehousing system** n the plan of allowing importers of dutiable goods to store them in a government warehouse without payment of duties until ready to bring the goods into market.

wareless see under **ware²**.

warfare, etc see under **war¹**.

warfarin /wör'fə-rin/ n a crystalline insoluble substance ($C_{19}H_{16}O_4$) used as a rodenticide and medically (in the form of its sodium salt) as an anticoagulant. [Wisconsin Alumni Research Foundation (the patent owners) and coumarin]

warhable /wör-hā'bl/ (Spenser) adj fit for war. [**war¹** and **able**]

warhead, warhorse see under **war¹**.

warily, wariment, wariness, etc see under **wary**.

warison or **warrison** /wor'- or war'i-sən/ (obs) n wealth; reward or punishment; a note sounding the assault (Walter Scott, non-standard). [ONFr (OFr guarison), from warir to guard; cf **garrison**]

wark /wörk/ a Scots form of **work** (n).

warlike, etc see under **war¹**.

warling /wör'ling/ (obs) n someone disliked, in the proverb 'It is better to be an old man's darling than a young man's warling'. [Prob formed to rhyme with 'darling']

warlock /wör'lok/ n a wizard; a magician (Scot); a demon; a warrior who cannot be wounded with metals (Dryden, non-standard). [OE wǣrloga a breaker of an agreement, from wǣr a compact, and lēogan to lie; the ending -(c)k appears earliest in Scot]

■ **war'lockry** n sorcery.

warlord see under **war¹**.

warm /wörm/ adj having moderate heat; hot; imparting heat or a sensation of heat; retaining heat; affecting one (pleasantly or unpleasantly) as heat does (fig); (of work) making one hot, strenuous; harassing; characterized by danger or difficulty; passionate; vehement; angry; excited; ardent, enthusiastic; lively, glowing; kind-hearted; affectionate; amorous; indelicate (inf); comfortable, well-to-do (inf); (of a colour) containing red or, sometimes, yellow; esp in a game, close to discovery or attainment; (of a scent or trail) fresh; denoting a call on a potential customer or supporter made on the strength of a previous referral or contact already established (business or politics). ◆ vt to make warm or warmer; to interest; to excite; to impart brightness or a suggestion of life to; to beat (inf). ◆ vi to become warm or ardent; (with to) to begin to enjoy, approve of, feel enthusiastic about or fond of. ◆ n a beating (inf); an officer's thick overcoat (also **British warm**); a warm area or environment (inf); an act or instance of warming up or being warmed up (inf). ◆ adv warmly. [OE wearm; cf Ger warm]

■ **warmed** adj. **warm'er** n. **warm'ing** n the action of making or becoming warm; a beating (sl). **warm'ish** adj. **warm'ly** adv. **warm'ness** n. **warmth** n. □ **Warm'blood** n a breed of horse developed from pedigree bloodlines from native European mares for competition jumping and dressage; (also without cap) a horse of this type. **warm'-blood'ed** adj homothermous or idiothermous, ie having bodily temperature constantly maintained at a point usu above the environmental temperature; ardent, passionate. **warm'-blood'edness** n. **warm boot** n (comput) the rebooting of a machine without switching it off, eg when changing programs. **warm-boot'** vt. **warm'-down** n a period of gentle exercise after strenuous physical exertion. **warmed-o'ver** (*US*) or **warmed-up'** *adj* heated anew. **warm front** *n* (*meteorol*) the advancing front of a mass of warm air. **warm'-heart'ed** *adj* affectionate; hearty; sympathetic; generous. **warm'-heart'edly** *adv*. **warm'-heart'edness** *n*. **warming pan** *n* (*hist*) a covered pan with a long handle, for holding live coals to warm a bed; someone temporarily holding a post or position until the person intended for it is able to take it (*old*). **warm'-up** *n* a practice exercise before an event; a preliminary entertainment, etc intended to increase the excitement or enthusiasm of the audience.

■ **a warm reception** (*ironic*) display of hostility; a vigorous resistance or attack. **keep warm** to occupy (a post or position) for someone until he or she is ready to fill it. **warm down** to perform gentle exercises after strenuous physical exertion. **warm up** to make or become warm; to heat (already cooked food); to become lively or animated; to grow interested or eager; to limber up prior to an athletic event, contest, etc.

warman, **warmonger**, etc see under **war**[1].

warn[1] /wörn/ *vt* to give notice of danger or evil to; to notify in advance; to caution (with *against*); to admonish; to instruct, command; to summon; to bid or instruct to go or to keep away (with *off*, *away*, etc; *lit* and *fig*); to ban (someone) from all race meetings or from a particular course (with *off*; *horse-racing*); to forbid (*obs*). ◆ *vi* to give notice or warning (with *of*); (of a clock) to make a whirring sound before striking, to give warning. [OE *warnian*, *warenian* or *wearnian* to caution (cf Ger *warnen*) and perh in part *wiernan* to refuse, forbid]

■ **warn'er** *n*. **warn'ing** *n* a caution against danger, etc; something that gives this; an admonition; previous notice; notice to quit, of the termination of an engagement, etc; a summons, call; the sound accompanying the partial unlocking of the striking train in a clock, just before it strikes. ◆ *adj* giving a warning. **warn'ingly** *adv*.

❑ **warning coloration** *n* conspicuous or gaudy coloration on certain creatures, eg some stinging insects, that deters potential attackers. **warning triangle** *n* a fluorescent triangular sign that is placed at the roadside to warn other road users of a broken-down vehicle, an accident or other hazard.

warn[2] /wörn/ (*Shakesp* and *dialect*) *vt* to warrant.

warp /wörp/ *vt* to twist out of shape; to turn from the right course; to distort; to cause to contract or wrinkle (*Shakesp*); to pervert (eg the mind or character); to misinterpret or give a deliberately false meaning to; to arrange (threads) so as to form a warp; to entwine (*obs*); to move (a vessel) by hauling on ropes attached to posts on a wharf, etc; to improve (land) by flooding so that it is covered by a deposit of alluvial mud; to choke (eg a channel) with alluvial mud; in rope-making, to stretch into lengths for tarring; to cast, throw (*obs*); to lay (eggs) or to bring forth (young), *esp* prematurely (*dialect*). ◆ *vi* to be twisted out of shape; to become perverted or distorted (*fig*); to swerve; to move with effort, or on a zigzag course; (of cattle, sheep, etc) to miscarry. ◆ *n* the state or fact of being warped; the permanent distortion of a timber, etc; a mental twist or bias; the threads stretched out lengthways in a loom to be crossed by a woof (also *fig*); a twist, shift or displacement to a different or parallel position within a (*usu* conceptual) framework or scale, etc (as in *time warp*); a rope used in towing, one end being fastened to a fixed object; alluvial sediment; a reckoning of four (herrings, oysters, etc), thirty-three warps making a long hundred, and five long hundreds a mease or maze. [OE *weorpan*, *werpan* to throw, cast; cf Ger *werfen*, ON *verpa*]

■ **war'page** *n*. **warped** *adj* twisted by shrinking; distorted; perverted; covered or filled with a deposit of alluvial sediment. **war'per** *n*. **war'ping** *n*.

❑ **warp drive** *n* (in science fiction) an engine or power source that enables matter to be transported over thousands of light years in a few hours, supposedly achieved by the warping of space.

warpath see under **war**[1].

warragal, **warragle**, **warragul** see **warrigal**.

warran and **warrand** obsolete forms of **warrant**[1].

warrandice /wö'rən-dis/ (*Scot*; *archaic*) *n* a guarantee; a clause in a deed by which the grantor binds himself or herself to make good to the grantee the right conveyed. [Anglo-Fr *warandise*, *warantise*, from *warantir* to warrant]

warrant[1] /wor'ənt/ *vt* to authorize; to justify, be adequate grounds for; to guarantee to be as specified or alleged; to attest or guarantee the truth of, (*old inf*) equivalent to 'be sure', 'be convinced' and 'be bound' (also in phrases *I* (or *I'll*) *warrant you* and *I warrant me*); to predict or to presage (*obs*); to secure, or guarantee the possession of, to; to protect, defend, keep (*obs*); to give assurance against danger, etc (*rare*; with *against*, *from*). ◆ *n* someone or something that vouches, a guaranty; a pledge, assurance; a proof; that which authorizes; a writ for arresting a person or for carrying a judgement into execution, or for seizing or searching property; (in the services) an official certificate appointing the recipient to a rank inferior to a commissioned officer but superior to a non-commissioned officer; authorization;

justification; a written form authorizing the payment of money or certifying payment due, etc; a form of warehouse receipt for goods; a voucher (*obs*); a document issued to a stockholder permitting the purchase of further stock at a stated price; a defender (*obs*); a defence (*obs*). [OFr *warantir* (variant of *guarantir*); of Gmc origin]

■ **warr'antable** *adj* that may be permitted; justifiable; of good warrant, estimable (*obs*); of sufficient age to be hunted. **warr'antableness** *n*. **warr'antably** *adv*. **warr'anted** *adj*. **warrantee'** *n* the person to whom a warranty is given. **warr'anter** *n* someone who authorizes or guarantees; a warrantor. **warr'anting** *n*. **warr'antise** /-tīz/ *n* (*obs* or *archaic*) an act of guaranteeing; a guarantee; assurance; authorization. **warr'antor** *n* (*law*) someone who gives warranty; a warranter. **warr'anty** *n* (*law*) an act of warranting, *esp* in feudal times the covenant by which the grantor of land warranted the security of the title to the recipient (**general warranty** against the claims of all and every person; **special warranty** against the claims of the grantor, or others claiming through or by him or her); an undertaking or assurance expressed or implied in certain contracts; a guarantee, *usu* with an acceptance of responsibility for repairs during an initial period of use; authorization; justification; evidence.

❑ **warrant card** *n* a card carried by a police officer establishing his or her identity. **warrant of attachment** *n* a writ authorizing the seizure of property. **warrant of attorney** see under **attorn**. **warrant officer** *n* (in the services) an officer holding a warrant (see also **branch officer** under **branch**); a police officer whose duty it is to serve warrants. **warrant sale** *n* (*Scot*; *law*) a public auction of poinded or seized household goods and personal property, authorized by a sheriff for the recuperation of unpaid debt.

■ **of good warrant** (*obs*) esteemed, important. **of warrant** (*obs*) allowed, warranted; esteemed, important. **out of warrant** (*obs*) not allowed. **take warrant on oneself** (*archaic*) to make oneself responsible.

warrant[2] /wor'ənt/ or **warren** /wor'ən/ *n* (*mining*) underclay. [Perh a use of **warrant**[1]]

warray, also **warrey** /wö-rā'/ (*obs*) *vt* to make war on. ◆ *vi* to make war. [OFr *werreier* (variant of *guerreier*), from Gmc *werra* strife]

warre see **war**[2].

warred see under **war**[1,2].

warren[1] /wor'ən/ *n* a series of interconnected rabbit burrows; the rabbits living there; a densely populated dwelling or district; a maze of narrow passages; a piece of ground kept for breeding game, *esp* hares, rabbits, partridges, etc (**beasts** or **fowls of warren**; *hist*); the right of keeping or of hunting such game (*hist*). [Anglo-Fr *warenne* (OFr *garenne*), of Gmc origin]

■ **warr'ener** *n* the keeper or owner of a warren (*hist*); an inhabitant of a warren.

warren[2] see **warrant**[2].

warrey see **warray**.

warrigal /wor'i-gal* or *wor'ə-gl/ *n* the Australian wild dog, the dingo; a wild Australian horse. ◆ *adj* wild, savage. —Also **warr'agal**, **warr'agle** or **warr'agul**. [From an Aboriginal language]

warring see under **war**[1,2].

warrior /wor'i-ər/ *n* a skilled fighting man (in the early stages of civilization, or *poetic*); a veteran or distinguished fighter; a redoubtable person. [ME and ONFr *werreior*, from Gmc *werra* strife]

■ **warrioress'** *n* (*rare*) a female warrior.

warrison see **warison**.

Warsaw /wör'sö/ *n* the capital of Poland.

❑ **Warsaw Convention** *n* the set of rules agreed to at the international convention held in Warsaw in 1929, establishing, in principle and within limits, the liability of the airline or carrier for damage to passengers, baggage or cargo in international accidents. **Warsaw Pact** *n* an alliance of E European countries (including the Soviet Union, Bulgaria, Czechoslovakia, E Germany, Hungary, Poland and Romania) formed in 1955 and disbanded in 1991; the military treaty signed by these countries in Warsaw in 1955.

warship see under **war**[1].

warsle /wör'sl/ Scots form of **wrestle**.

warst see **war**[2].

wart /wört/ *n* a small hard excrescence on the skin caused by a virus; a small protuberance on a plant surface or on an animal's skin; an abusive term for a disliked person (*sl*). [OE *wearte*; Ger *Warze*; prob related to L *verrūca* wart]

■ **wart'ed** *adj*. **wart'less** *adj*. **wart'like** *adj*. **wart'y** *adj* like a wart; covered with warts.

❑ **wart'-biter** *n* (also **wart-biter cricket**) a large grasshopper native to S England, formerly prized by country people for its ability to bite off warts. **wart cress** *n* swine's cress. **wart'hog** or **wart hog** *n* any of a genus of wild hogs found in Africa, with large wartlike excrescences on their cheeks. **wart'weed** *n* a kind of spurge (its caustic juice thought to cure warts). **wart'wort** *n* any of a family of lichens having a warty thallus; a wartweed.

■ **warts and all** with blemishes or shortcomings frankly revealed or consciously taken into account.

wartime see under **war**[1].

warwolf see under **war**[1] and **werewolf**.

wary /wā'ri/ *adj* on one's guard against deception or danger; cautious; suspicious; circumspect; thrifty (*obs*). [**ware**[2]]

■ **war'ily** *adv*. **war'iment** *n* (*Spenser*) wariness. **war'iness** *n*.

■ **be wary of** to be cautious with regard to.

was /woz/ used as the *1st* and *3rd pers sing* of the *pat* of the verb **be**. [OE *wæs*, from *wesan* to be; see **wast**[1], **were**, **wert**]

wasabi /wə-sä'bi/ *n* the mountain hollyhock (*Wasabia japonica*); a pungent green paste made from this plant, used in Japanese cookery. [Jap]

wase /wāz/ (*dialect*) *n* a wisp of hay, straw, etc; a pad on the head to ease the pressure of a burden. [Gmc word; perh Scand]

wasegoose see **wayzgoose**.

Wash. *abbrev* : Washington (US state).

wash /wosh/ *vt* (*pap* **washed**, *archaic* **wash'en**) to cleanse, or to free from impurities, etc, with water or other liquid; to wet, moisten; (of an animal) to clean by licking; to flow over, past or against; to sweep along, down, etc; to form or erode by flowing over; to cover with a thin coat of metal or paint; to separate (ore, etc) from earth by means of water (*mining*); to launder (money, goods, etc) (*inf*). ◆ *vt* and *vi* (of water, etc) to have the property of cleansing. ◆ *vi* to clean oneself, clothes, etc with water; to wash clothes, etc as one's employment; to stand cleaning (with *well, badly*, etc); to be swept or carried by water; to stand the test, bear investigation (*inf*). ◆ *n* a washing; the process of washing; a collection of articles for washing or just having been washed; that with which anything is washed; a lotion; the break of waves on the shore; the sound of water breaking, lapping, etc; the rough water left behind by a boat, etc, or the disturbed air behind an aerofoil, etc (also *fig*); the shallow part of a river or arm of the sea; a marsh or fen; erosion by flowing water; alluvial matter; a liquor of fermented malt prior to distillation; waste liquor, refuse of food, etc, *esp* for giving to pigs; a watery mixture; a thin, tasteless drink; insipid discourse in speech or writing; a broad but thin layer of colour put on with a long sweep of the brush; a thin coat of paint, metal, etc; an outcome or situation in which there is no appreciable gain or loss (*US inf*); the blade of an oar; the material from which valuable minerals may be extracted by washing (*mining*). [OE *wæscan, wascan*; found in other Gmc languages eg OHGer *wascan* (Ger *waschen*); same root as **water**]

■ **washabil'ity** *n*. **wash'able** *adj* that may be washed without damage. **wash'er** *n* someone who washes; a washing machine; a facecloth (*Aust*); a ring, *usu* flat, of metal, rubber, etc, to keep joints or nuts secure, etc (*perh* a different word); hence derisively (in *pl*) small change (*sl*). ◆ *vt* to fit with a washer or washers. **wash'ery** *n* a washhouse (*archaic*); a place in which an industrial washing process takes place (eg of coal, ore or wool). **wash'iness** *n* the state of being watery; feebleness. **wash'ing** *n* the act of cleansing, wetting or coating, with liquid; clothes or other articles washed or to be washed; a thin coating; the action of breaking, lapping, etc (of waves, etc); (*usu* in *pl*) liquid that has been used to wash something, or matter separated or carried away by water or other liquid. ◆ *adj* that washes; used for washing; washable. **wash'y** *adj* watery; moist; thin; feeble; faded.

❑ **wash'-and-wear'** *adj* (of garments or fabrics) easily washed, quick-drying, and requiring no ironing. **wash'-away** *n* (*esp Aust*) the destruction of part of a road, railway, etc by flooding; the breach so caused; an erosion of the earth by the action of water; the channel so made. **wash'ball** *n* a ball of toilet-soap. **wash'basin**, **wash'bowl** or **washhand basin** *n* a basin to wash one's face and hands, etc in. **wash'board** *n* a corrugated metal board for rubbing clothes on in washing (also **wash'ing-board**), utilized as a percussion instrument in certain types of music, eg skiffle or Country and Western; a thin plank on a boat's gunwale to prevent the sea from breaking over; a skirting-board (*dialect*). **wash'-bott'le** or **wash'ing-bott'le** *n* a bottle containing liquid used for purifying gases; a bottle with tubes through the stopper, enabling a stream of cleansing liquid to be directed onto a chemical or a piece of apparatus. **wash'cloth** *n* a piece of cloth used in washing, *esp* a dishcloth; a facecloth or flannel (*N Am*). **wash'day** *n* a day (or the regular day) when one washes one's clothes and linen (also **wash'ing-day**). **wash'-dirt** *n* earth to be washed for gold. **wash drawing** *n* a drawing in pencil or pen and ink over which a transparent wash is applied by brush. **washed'-out** *adj* deprived of colour, *esp* by washing; deprived of energy or animation (*inf*). **washed'-up** *adj* deprived of energy or animation (*inf*); done for, at the end of one's resources (*sl*); unsuccessful (*sl*); finished (with *with*; *sl*). **washer-dri'er** or **-dry'er** *n* a combined washing machine and

drier. **wash'erman** or **wash'erwoman** *n* (*old*) a man or woman who washes clothes, *esp* for a living. **wash'-gild'ing** *n* a gilding made with an amalgam of gold from which the mercury is driven off by heat, leaving a coating of gold. **wash'house** or **wash'ing-house** *n* (*old*) a house or room for washing clothes in. **wash'-in** (or **-out**) *n* an increase (or decrease) in the angle of incidence, ie the angle between the chord of a wing and the wind relative to the aeroplane, in approaching the wing tip along the camber. **washing-blue** see under **blue**[1]. **washing line** *n* a clothes-line. **washing machine** *n* a machine for washing clothes. **washing powder** or **liquid** *n* a powdered or liquid preparation used in washing clothes. **washing-soda** see **soda**. **wash'ing-up** *n* the washing of dishes and cutlery after a meal; the crockery, cutlery, etc to be washed after use. **washing-up machine** *n* (*old*) a dishwasher. **wash'land** *n* an area of land periodically flooded by overflow water from a river, stream, or from the sea. **wash leather** *n* split sheepskin prepared with oil in imitation of chamois; a piece of this for washing windows; buff-leather for regimental belts. **wash'-out** or **wash'out** *n* an erosion of earth by the action of water; the hole or channel so made; an event spoilt or cancelled because of rain; a complete failure (*inf*); a useless person (*inf*); see also **wash-in** above. **wash'pot** *n* a vessel for washing one's hands, etc, or for boiling clothes in. **wash'rag** *n* (*N Am*) a facecloth, a flannel; a servant who washes dishes (*obs*). **wash'room** *n* a room containing lavatories and facilities for washing; a lavatory (chiefly *N Am*). **wash sale** *n* (*US*) the dishonest practice of buying and immediately re-selling large quantities of a stock at an inflated price, so as to create a false impression of strong market interest in it. **wash'stand** or **washhand stand** *n* (*old*) a piece of furniture for holding jug, basin and other requisites for washing oneself. **wash'tub** *n orig* a tub for washing clothes in; a washing machine. **wash'-up** *n* a washing-up; a washing-up place; anything cast up by the sea, etc; the washing of ore; a quantity of gold obtained by washing; an outcome or result (*Aust sl*); the period at the end of a parliament in which the government seeks to settle its unfinished business (*Brit*). **wash'wipe** *n* (in a motor vehicle) a mechanism for spraying the front or the rear windscreen with washing fluid, which is distributed and wiped off by the windscreen wiper.

■ **come out in the wash** (of a stain, etc) to disappear on washing; to become intelligible, work out satisfactorily (*fig*; *inf*). **wash away** (of flowing water) to carry off by force; to obliterate. **wash down** (of liquid) to carry downward; to wash from top to bottom; to help the swallowing or digestion of (a solid food) with a drink. **wash its face** (*sl*) (of an undertaking) to just pay its way. **wash one's hands of** to disclaim responsibility for. **wash out** to remove by washing; to wash free from dirt or soap, etc; (of colours or design) to disappear or become fainter as a result of washing; to rain off; to cancel (*inf*); to exhaust (*inf*; *esp* in *passive*); to bring the blade of an oar not cleanly out of the water (*rowing*). **wash up** to wash the dishes and cutlery after a meal; to wash one's hands and face (*esp US*); to sweep up onto the shore; to spoil (*inf*; *esp* in *passive*).

washeteria or **washateria** /wosh-ə-tē'ri-ə/ (*esp US*) *n* a launderette. [**wash** and sfx *-teria* from **cafeteria**]

washing /wosh'ing/ (*Shakesp, Romeo and Juliet* i.1.60) *adj* for **swashing** (see **swash**[1]).

Washingtonia /wosh-ing-tō'ni-ə/ *n* a genus of ornamental fan palms of California and Mexico; (also without *cap*) used as a name for the sequoia. [Named after George *Washington* (1732–99), first US President]

wasn't /woz'(ə)nt/ contracted form of **was not**.

WASP or **Wasp** /wosp/ (*US, usu derog*) *n* a White Anglo-Saxon *P*rotestant, supposedly representing the most privileged class in US society.

wasp /wosp/ *n* any of a large number of insects belonging to the order Hymenoptera and constituting many families, including the Vespidae, to which the common wasp (*Vespula vulgaris*) and the European hornet (*Vespa crabro*) belong, having black-and-yellow-striped bodies, and, in the case of the female, a stinging organ; a petulant and spiteful person. [OE *wæsp, wæps*; cf Ger *Wespe*, L *vespa*]

■ **was'pie** *n* (*old*) a ladies' corset which is laced or fitted tightly to draw the waist in; a similarly girdled belt. **was'pish** *adj* like a wasp; having a slender waist, like a wasp; quick to resent an injury; spiteful, virulent. **was'pishly** *adv*. **was'pishness** *n*. **wasp'-like** *adj*. **was'py** *adj* waspish.

❑ **was'pish-head'ed** *adj* (*Shakesp*) hot-headed, passionate. **wasp'nest**, **wasp's nest** or **wasps' nest** *n* the nest of a wasp or of a community of wasps; a place full of enemies or angry people (*fig*); circumstances in which one is assailed indignantly from all sides (*fig*). **wasp'-tongu'd** *adj* (*Shakesp, 1 Henry IV* I.3.236; 1st quarto **wasp'-stung**, others **wasp'-tongue**) having a biting tongue, shrewish. **wasp waist** *n* a very slender waist reminiscent of a wasp's, *esp* contrasting with more substantial proportions above and below it. **wasp'-waist'ed** *adj* slender-waisted; laced tightly.

■ words derived from main entry word; ❑ compound words; ■ idioms and phrasal verbs

wassail /wos'(ā)l or was'l/ (*hist*) *n* the salutation uttered in drinking a person's health; a liquor in which such healths were drunk, *esp* ale with roasted apples, sugar, nutmeg and toast; a festive occasion; revelry; a drinking bout; a drinking or festive song. ◆ *vi* to hold a wassail, to carouse; to sing good wishes, carols, etc from house to house at Christmas. ◆ *vt* to drink to or pour libations for (eg fruit trees) to ensure that they thrive. [ON *ves heill* 'be in health']
■ **wass'ailer** *n* someone who wassails; a reveller. **wass'ailing** *n*. **wass'ailry** *n*.
▫ **wassail bout** *n* a carouse. **wassail bowl** or **cup** *n* a bowl or cup used in wassailing.

Wassermann reaction /vas'ər-man rē-ak'shən/ or **test** /test/ *n* a test for syphilis made on the blood serum or cerebrospinal fluid. [A von *Wassermann* (1866–1925), German bacteriologist]

wast¹ /wost/ used (*archaic* or *dialect*) as *2nd pers sing pat* of the verb **be**. [See **was**]

wast², **wastfull**, **wastness** obsolete spellings of **waste**, **wasteful**, **wasteness**.

wast³ an obsolete spelling of **waist**.

waste /wāst/ *adj* rejected, superfluous; uncultivated, and at most sparsely inhabited; desolate; lying unused; unproductive; devastated, ruinous (*obs*); in a devastated condition, as in *lay waste*; empty, unoccupied; useless, vain (*obs*). ◆ *vt* to spend, use or occupy unprofitably; to use, consume or spend too lavishly; to use or bestow where due appreciation is lacking (often in *passive*); to fail to take advantage of; to treat as waste material; to injure (an estate or property) (*law*; *obs*); to devastate; to consume, wear out or impair gradually; to cause to decline, shrink physically, to enfeeble; to put an end to, kill (*obs* or *sl*); to impoverish (*obs*); to expend, spend, consume or pass (*obs*). ◆ *vi* to be diminished, used up or impaired by degrees; to lose strength or flesh or weight (often **waste away**); (of time) to be spent (*obs*); to be used to no, or little, purpose or effect; to be guilty of waste. ◆ *n* the act or process of wasting; superfluous, refuse or rejected material; too lavish, or useless, expenditure, or an example of it; squandering; consumption or expenditure (*obs*); a profusion (*archaic*); a waste pipe; gradual decay; destruction; loss; injury done to an estate or property by the tenant (*law*; *obs*); an uncultivated, unproductive or devastated region; a vast expanse, as of ocean or air; the darkness of midnight (*Shakesp*, *Hamlet* I.2.198, quartos 2, 3, 4; others have 'vast'); a disused working; (in *pl*) ravages (*obs*). [OFr *wast* (variant of *guast*), from L *vāstus* waste]
■ **wast'able** *adj*. **wāst'age** *n* loss by use or natural decay, etc; useless or unprofitable spending; loss, or amount of loss, through this; a devastated or ruined place (*Scot*); waste ground (*Scot*). **wāst'ed** *adj* unexploited or squandered; exhausted, worn-out; shrunken, emaciated; extremely drunk or high on drugs (*sl*; *esp US*). **waste'ful** *adj* causing waste; extravagant, over-lavish; causing devastation, consuming, destructive (*obs* or *rare*); causing wasting of the body (*rare*); lavish (*obs*); uninhabited, unfrequented, desolate (*poetic*); vain, profitless (*obs*). **waste'fully** *adv*. **waste'fulness** *n*. **waste'ness** *n* the state of being waste; a waste place (*obs*); devastation (*Bible*). **wast'er** *n* someone who or something that wastes; a spendthrift; a good-for-nothing (*inf*); used with uncertain significance to denote a class of thief (*hist*); an inferior article, *esp* one spoilt in the making; an animal that is not thriving, or that is not suitable for breeding purposes. ◆ *vt* (*Scot*) to use, spend extravagantly. **wāst'erful** *adj* (*Scot*) extravagant. **wāst'erfully** *adv*. **wāst'erfulness** *n*. **waste'rife** or **wast'rife** /-rif or -rīf/ *adj* (*Scot*) wasteful. ◆ *n* wastefulness. **wast'ery** or **wast'ry** *n* (*Scot*) prodigality. ◆ *adj* improvident. **wāst'ing** *n*. ◆ *adj* undergoing waste; destroying, devastating; (of an illness, etc) causing emaciation, destructive of body tissues, enfeebling. **wāst'rel** *n* a profligate, ne'er-do-well, idler; a waif (*old*); refuse (*obs*). ◆ *adj* spendthrift; (of an animal) feeble; waste, refuse (*obs*); going to waste (*obs*).
▫ **waste basket** (*N Am*), **waste bin**, **wastepaper basket** or **wastepaper bin** *n* a basket or bin for holding discarded paper and other rubbish. **waste book** *n* a day book or journal, or a rougher record preliminary to it. **waste disposal unit** *n* a system fitted to a kitchen sink for grinding down food waste so that it can be disposed of down the plug hole. **waste gate** *n* a gate for discharging surplus water from a dam, etc. **waste ground** or (*Can*) **waste'lot** *n* a piece of land lying unused in a built-up area. **waste'land** *n* a desolate, barren area; a culturally or intellectually empty place or time. **waste paper** *n* used paper no longer required for its original purpose; paper rejected as spoiled. **waste pipe** *n* a pipe for carrying off waste or surplus water. **waste product** *n* material produced in a process and discarded on the completion of that process. **wasting asset** *n* any asset (*esp* a natural resource, such as a mine) whose value decreases with its depletion and which cannot be replaced or renewed.
■ **go to waste** to be wasted. **grow to waste** (*obs*) (of a time) to come near an end. **in waste** (*obs*) to no effect, in vain. **lay waste** to devastate. **run to waste** (*orig* of liquids) to be wasted or lost.

wastel /wos'tl/ or **wastel bread** /bred/ (*hist*) *n* bread made from the finest flour. [OFr *wastel*, variant of *guastel*, *gastel* (Fr *gâteau* cake); of Gmc origin]

waster¹ /wā'stər/ (*hist*) *n* a wooden sword for practising fencing with; a cudgel; practice or play with a waster. [Ety uncertain]
■ **play at waster** or **wasters** to practise fencing.

waster² see under **waste**.

waster³ /wā'stər/ (*Scot*) *n* a four-pronged or five-pronged salmon-spear. [Earlier *wa(w)sper*, from **spear**, with spelling influenced by **leister**; ety otherwise obscure]

wasterife...to...**wastrel** see under **waste**.

wat¹ /wät/ *n* a Thai Buddhist temple or monastery. [Sans *vātā* enclosed ground]

wat² /wot/ (*obs*) *n* a hare. [Prob *Wat*, for Walter]

wat³ /wät/ (*Scot*) *adj* wet; drunken. [Variant of **wet**]

wat⁴ /wät/ Scots 1st person singular present tense form of **wit²**.

watap /wat'ap/ *n* fibre from conifer roots used by Native Americans for weaving or as sewing-thread. [Cree *watapiy*]

WATCH /woch/ *abbrev*: Women And The Church, an organization that aims to secure the ordination of women as bishops.

watch /woch/ *vt* to keep in view, to follow the motions of with the eyes; to observe the progress of, maintain an interest in, follow; to look at or observe attentively; (of a barrister) to attend the trial of (a case) on behalf of a client not directly involved in it; to have in one's care, to look after; to guard; to tend; to beware of danger to or from, to be on the alert to guard or guard against; to be on the alert to take advantage of (an opportunity, etc); to wait for (*obs*); to catch in an act (*Shakesp*); to keep (a hawk) from sleep, in order to tame it (*Shakesp*). ◆ *vi* to be on the alert; to look out (with *for*); to look with attention; to keep guard; (with *over*) to keep guard over; to remain awake; to keep vigil; to attend the sick by night (*old*). ◆ *n* a small timepiece for wearing on a strap round the wrist (also **wristwatch**), or carrying in a pocket; the state of being, or act of staying, awake (*old*); a religious vigil (*old* except in *watch night*); a vigil beside a corpse, a wake; a flock (of nightingales); a division of the night, of fixed length (*hist*); (in *pl*) the dark hours (of the night) (*poetic*); the state of remaining on the alert, being on the lookout or observing vigilantly; close observation; the activity of guarding, surveillance; the office or duty of keeping guard or of being a sentinel (**stand upon one's watch** (*Bible*) to fulfil the duty of watchman); the activity of lying in wait or in ambush; a watchman or body of watchmen; the body of men who, before the institution of a police force, patrolled the streets at night (*hist*); a sentinel, or the military guard of a place (*old*); in early 18c, a name applied to certain companies of irregular troops in the Scottish Highlands; a *usu* four-hour period of duty on deck (but see **dogwatch** under **dog¹**) (*naut*); those members (*usu* half) of a ship's officers and crew who are on duty at the same time (the *port* or (*orig*) *larboard watch* and the *starboard watch*); a sailor's or firefighter's turn or period of duty; something that measures or marks time or the passage of time, such as a marked candle, the cry of a watchman, a clock (*obs*); the dial of a clock (*obs*). ◆ *combining form* denoting vigilance exercised by a community over some aspect of the environment, *esp* as the professed brief of a television programme, as in *crimewatch*. [OE *wæcce* (noun), *wæccan*, *wacian* (verb); cognate with *wacan* to wake]
■ **watchabil'ity** *n*. **watch'able** *adj* that may be watched; (of an entertainment, *esp* a TV programme) having enjoyment or interest value (*inf*). **watch'er** *n* someone who watches; a name used for an angel or for a class of angels. **watch'ful** *adj* habitually on the alert or cautious; watching or observing carefully; wary; characterized by vigilance; requiring vigilance, or in which one must remain on the alert; wakeful (*archaic*); spent in watching (*archaic*). **watch'fully** *adv*. **watch'fulness** *n*. **watch'ing** *adj* (*naut*: of a buoy) fully afloat.
▫ **watch and ward** *n* the old custom of watching by night and by day in towns and cities; uninterrupted vigilance. **watch bill** *n* a list of the officers and crew of a ship, as divided into watches, with their respective stations. **watch'box** *n* a sentry box. **watch cap** *n* a close-fitting navy-blue cap worn by sailors in cold weather. **watch'case** *n* the outer case of a watch; a sentry box (*Shakesp*). **watch chain** *n* a chain for securing a watch to one's clothing. **watch clock** *n* a watchman's clock. **Watch Committee** *n* formerly, a committee of a local governing body exercising supervision over police services, etc. **watch crystal** see **watchglass** below. **watch'dog** *n* a dog kept to guard premises and property; any person or organization closely monitoring governmental or commercial operations, etc to guard against inefficiency and illegality (also *adj*). **watch fire** *n* a fire lit at night as a signal; a fire for the use of a watching party, sentinels, scouts, etc. **watch'glass** *n* a sandglass; a glass covering for the face of a watch (also **watch crystal**); a small curved glass dish used in laboratories to hold small quantities of a solution, etc. **watch'guard** *n* a chain or strap, etc used to attach a watch to one's clothing. **watch house** *n* a house in which a guard is placed; a police station or lock-

up (*old*). **watching brief** *n* instructions to a counsel to watch a legal case; (loosely) responsibility for observing developments, etc in a specific area. **watch key** *n* a key for winding a watch. **watch light** *n* a light used for watching or sitting up in the night. **watch list** *n* a list of countries, persons, etc whose activities are to be monitored, *esp* when thought to be potentially dangerous. **watch'maker** *n* a maker or repairer of watches. **watch'making** *n*. **watch'man** *n* a man who watches or guards a building (or, formerly, the streets of a city) at night. **watchman's clock** *n* a clock recording the times of a watchman's visits. **watch night** *n* (*relig*) in some Protestant churches, the night of Christmas Eve (24 December) or New Year's Eve (31 December); (also **watch-night service**) a service lasting through midnight held on these nights. **watch officer** *n* the officer in charge of the ship during a watch, also called **officer of the watch**. **watch'-out** *n* a lookout. **watch paper** *n* a round piece of paper, often decorated, formerly put inside the outer case of a watch to prevent rubbing. **watch pocket** *n* a small pocket for holding a watch. **watch'point** *n* a selected position for admiring scenery. **watch'spring** *n* the mainspring of a watch. **watch'strap** *n* a strap for fastening a watch round the wrist. **watch'tower** *n* a tower on which a sentinel is placed to look out for the approach of danger. **watch'word** *n* the password to be given to a watch or sentry (*obs*); any word used as a signal; a maxim, slogan or rallying-cry.

■ **Black Watch** the 42nd and 73rd Regiments, now the 3rd Battalion of the Royal Regiment of Scotland. **on one's watch** while one is in charge or responsible. **on the watch** vigilant, looking out (for danger, etc). **watch after** (*Thackeray*) to follow the movements of (with one's eyes). **watch in** to keep awake to welcome (the New Year). **watch it!** (*inf, esp admonitory*) be careful! **watch one's back** (*inf*) to be on the alert for treacherous moves against one. **watch one's step** to step with care; to act warily, be careful not to arouse opposition, give offence, etc (*inf*). **watch out** (*inf; orig US*) to look out, be careful. **watch over** to guard, take care of. **watch up** (*Thackeray*) to sit up at night.

watchet /woch'it/ (*archaic*) *n* a pale blue; a material of this colour; an angling fly. ♦ *adj* pale blue. [OFr *wachet*; perh orig a material]

wate see **wit²**.

water /wö'tər/ *n* (in a state of purity, at ordinary temperatures) a clear transparent colourless liquid, perfectly neutral in its reaction, and devoid of taste or smell; extended to the same substance (H_2O) in solid or gaseous state (ice or steam); any body of this (in varying degrees of impurity), such as an ocean, lake, river, etc; the surface of a body of water; (in *pl*) waves, moving water, a body of water; a river valley (*Scot*); the position of the tide, as in *high* or *low water*; one of the four elements recognized by early natural philosophers; a quantity of the liquid used in any one stage of a washing operation; a liquid resembling or containing water; mineral water (*usu* in *pl* if at a spa); saliva; (*usu* in *pl*) the amniotic fluid filling the space between the embryo and the amnion; applied to the fluids secreted by the body, tears, urine, sweat; rain; transparency, lustre, eg of a diamond; class, quality, excellence, *esp* in the phrase *of the first* or *purest water*; a wavy sheen on fabric, *esp* silk or satin; an increase in a company's stock issue without an increase in assets to back it up (*econ*). ♦ *vt* to wet, overflow or irrigate with water; to supply (a plant) with water; to give (an animal) water to drink; to dilute or adulterate with water; to soften by soaking (*obs*); (of a river, etc) to surround (a city, etc) (also **water about**; *obs*); to wet and press (eg silk) so as to give a wavy appearance to; to increase (the debt of a company) by issuing new stock without a corresponding increase in assets. ♦ *vi* to fill with, or shed, water; (of the mouth; also, *obs* and *Scot*, the teeth) to secrete saliva at the sight or thought of food, etc (*fig*) in anticipation of anything delightful; (of an animal) to drink; to take in water. ♦ *adj* relating to or used in the storage or distribution of water; worked by water; used, living or operating on or in water; by way of or across water; made with or formed by water. [OE *wæter*; cf Du *water*, Ger *Wasser*; cognate with Gr *hydōr*, L *ūdus* wet, *unda* a wave, Sans *udan* water]

■ **wa'terage** *n* conveyance (eg of cargo or passengers) by water; money paid for this. **wa'tered** *adj* (of eg silk) marked with a wavy pattern by watering; (of capital or stock) increased in nominal value without any corresponding increase in assets. **wa'terer** *n* someone who or something that waters; a vessel for dispensing water. **wa'teriness** *n*. **wa'tering** *n* the process of giving, irrigating, filling, etc with water; the act of drinking (*obs*); dilution with water; the art or process of giving fabric, etc a wavy, ornamental appearance; such an appearance. **wa'terish** *adj* resembling, abounding in or filled with water; dilute, thin, poor, insipid. **wa'terishness** *n*. **wa'terless** *adj*. **wa'tery** *adj* full of water; (of eyes) moist, secreting water noticeably; relating to, consisting of or containing water; like water; thin or transparent; tasteless; weak, vapid; (of the sky or sun) having a rainy appearance; associated with or controlling the sea, tides, rain, etc; (of the palate) watering, eager (*Shakesp, Troilus and Cressida* III.2.20).

❑ **water bag** *n* a bag for holding water; a camel's reticulum. **water bailiff** *n* a custom-house officer who inspects ships on reaching or

leaving port (*obs*); an official whose duty is to enforce bylaws relating to fishing, or to prevent poaching in protected waters (also, now *Scot*, **water bailie**). **water ballast** *n* water carried by a ship to balance or redress the change of draught due to consumption of fuel or provisions or discharge of cargo; water carried for purposes of stability. **water barometer** *n* a barometer in which water is substituted for mercury. **water barrel** or **water cask** *n* a barrel or cask for holding water. **water bath** *n* a bath composed of water; a vessel of water in which other vessels can be immersed, eg in chemical work. **water battery** *n* a voltaic battery in which the electrolyte is water; a battery nearly on a level with the water (*fortif*). **water bear** *n* the tardigrade, a tiny invertebrate. **Water Bearer** or **Water Carrier** *n* Aquarius. **water bed** *n* (a bed with) a rubber or plastic mattress filled with water. **water beetle** *n* any of a large number of beetles living on or in water, having fringed legs by means of which they swim easily. **water bellows** *n pl* or *n sing* a form of blower worked eg by a column of water falling through a vertical tube, formerly used to supply a blast for furnaces. **water bird** *n* a swimming or wading bird. **water birth** *n* a birth in which the mother is partially immersed in water in a birthing pool (qv under **birth¹**). **water biscuit** *n* a thin plain biscuit made with water. **water blink** *n* in Arctic regions, a patch of sky reflecting the colour, and hence indicating the presence, of open water; (in *pl*) the plant blinks (qv under **blink**). **water blister** *n* a blister containing watery fluid, not blood or pus. **water bloom** or **flowers** *n* large masses of algae, chiefly blue-green, which sometimes develop very suddenly in bodies of fresh water. **water boa** *n* the anaconda (*Eunectes murinus*). **wa'terboarding** *n* a form of water torture in which the victim is secured to a board, face upwards with the head inclined down, and has water poured over the face, nose and mouth. **water boatman** *n* any of a number of aquatic leathery-winged insects with hindlegs suggestive of oars. **wa'ter-borne** or **wa'terborne** *adj* floating on water; conveyed by water, *esp* in a boat; (of infection, etc) transmitted by means of water. **water bottle** *n* a leather, glass or plastic bottle for holding drinking water, carried eg by hikers. **water bouget** /boo'jət/ *n* (*hist*) a skin or leather bottle used to carry water, *usu* one of a pair hung on opposite ends of a yoke. **wa'ter-bound** *adj* detained by floods; (of a macadam road or road surfacing) formed of broken stone, rolled and covered with a thin layer of hoggin, which is watered in and binds the stones together. **water box** *n* a water jacket. **wa'ter-brain** *n* gid, a disease of sheep. **water brash** *n* pyrosis, a sudden gush into the mouth of acid fluids from the stomach, accompanied by a burning sensation (heartburn) in the gullet. **water break** *n* a stretch of water where the current is broken. **wa'ter-breather** *n* any creature that breathes by means of gills. **wa'ter-breathing** *adj*. **water brose** *n* (*Scot*) brose made of meal and water alone. **wa'terbuck** *n* any of several antelopes, *esp Cobus ellipsiprymnus*. **water buffalo** *n* the common domestic buffalo (genus *Bubalus*) of India, etc. **water bug** *n* any of a large variety of hemipterous insects, including water boatmen, etc, found in or beside ponds, etc. **water bull** *n* a mythical amphibious animal like a bull. **water bus** *n* a passenger-carrying boat plying a regular route across a lake, river, etc. **water butt** *n* a large barrel for collecting rainwater. **water cannon** *n* a high-pressure hosepipe used to disperse crowds. **wa'ter-carriage** *n* conveyance by water; facilities for it. **Water Carrier** see **Water Bearer** above. **water cart** *n* a cart for conveying water, *esp* for the purpose of watering streets or roads. **water cell** *n* one of several cells in a camel's stomach used for storing water. **water cement** *n* hydraulic cement. **water chestnut** *n* a water plant (*Trapa natans*, or other species) of or related to the Onagraceae; its edible seed; a Chinese sedge (*Eleocharis tuberosa*), or its edible tuber. **water chute** /shūt/ or /shoot/ *n* an artificial cascade or slope leading to water, down which people (sometimes in boats or toboggans) slide for sport. **water clerk** *n* (*old*) an employee of a ship's chandler, who sails about the harbour to seek custom from the ships about to dock. **water clock** *n* a clock that works by means of flowing water; a clepsydra. **water closet** *n* a lavatory of which the pan is flushed by water (*old*); a small room containing such a lavatory (*abbrev* **WC**). **water cock** *n* the kora, a large East Indian gallinule. **wa'tercolour** or (*US*) **wa'tercolor** *n* a pigment diluted with water and gum (or other substance) instead of oil; a painting in such a colour or colours. **wa'tercolourist** or (*US*) **wa'tercolorist** *n* a painter in watercolours. **wa'ter-cool** *vt* to cool (eg an engine) by means of water, *esp* circulating water. **wa'ter-cooled** *adj*. **water cooler** *n* a machine for cooling by means of water or for keeping water cool. **wa'ter-cooling** *adj* and *n*. **wa'ter-core** *n* (in an apple or other fruit) an abnormality consisting of water-soaked tissue, *esp* close to the core; (**water core**) (in founding) a hollow core through which water may be passed. **wa'tercourse** *n* a channel through which water flows or has flowed; an artificial water channel; a stream or river. **water cow** *n* a female water buffalo or water bull. **wa'tercraft** *n* a boat; (as *pl*) boats collectively; skill in swimming, etc, or in managing boats. **water crane** *n* an apparatus for supplying water from an elevated tank, *esp* to a locomotive tender; a hydraulic crane. **wa'tercress** *n* (often, *esp* formerly, in *pl*) a perennial cress (*Nasturtium officinale*) growing in watery places, used as a salad.

water culture n a method of cultivation, often an experimental means of determining the mineral requirements of a plant, the plant being grown with its roots dipping into solutions of known composition. **water cure** n medical treatment by means of water, hydrotherapy. **water cycle** n the cycle in which water from the sea evaporates into the atmosphere, later condenses and falls to earth as rain or snow, then evaporates directly back into the atmosphere or returns to the sea by rivers. **water deck** n a decorated canvas cover for a dragoon's saddle. **water deer** n a small Chinese musk deer of aquatic habits; in Africa, one of the chevrotains. **water diviner** n a person who, usu with the help of a divining rod, detects or tries to detect the presence of underground water. **water doctor** n a hydropathist; formerly, a doctor who divined diseases from the urine. **water dog** n any variety of dog (formerly a specific variety, a small poodle) valuable to sportsmen in hunting waterfowl on account of its aquatic habits; a water vole; an otter (obs); any of various other animals; an experienced sailor (inf); a good swimmer; a small irregular floating cloud supposed to indicate rain. **wa'ter-drinker** n a drinker of water; a teetotaller. **wa'terdrive** n the use of water pressure, either occurring naturally or by waterflood (qv below), to drive oil, gas, etc from a reservoir. **water drop** n a drop of water; a tear. **water dropwort** n a genus (Oenanthe) of umbelliferous plants, including the common water dropwort (Oenanthe fistulosa) and hemlock water dropwort, or water hemlock (Oenanthe crocata). **wa'tered-down** adj much diluted; reduced in vigour, modified, attenuated. **water elder** n the guelder rose. **water engine** n an engine for raising water; an engine worked by water; an engine for extinguishing fires (obs). **water equivalent** n thermal capacity, the product of the specific heat of a body and its mass. **wa'terfall** n a fall or perpendicular descent of a body of water, a cataract or cascade; a necktie (obs); a chignon (obs). **water fern** n any of the Hydropterideae or rhizocarps, water or marsh plants differing from ferns in the narrower sense in being heterosporous, classified in two families, Marsileaceae and Salviniaceae. **wa'ter-finder** n a water diviner. **water flag** n the yellow iris. **water flea** n the common name for any of numerous minute aquatic crustaceans; a daphnid. **water flood** n an inundation; (**wa'terflood**) the process or an instance of **wa'terflooding**, the practice, in oil, gas or petroleum production, of injecting water to maintain pressure in a reservoir and to drive the oil, etc towards the production wells. **water flow** n a current of water. **wa'ter-flowing** adj streaming. **water fly** n an aquatic insect; an insignificant, troublesome person (Shakesp). **wa'terfowl** n a fowl that frequents water; (as pl) swimming game birds collectively. **water frame** n a water-driven spinning-machine invented by Richard Arkwright in the 18c. **wa'terfront** n the buildings or part of a town along the edge of and facing the sea, a river, etc. **water gall** n (obs and dialect) a watery appearance in the sky accompanying a rainbow; a secondary rainbow. **water gap** n a gap in a mountain range containing a stream. **water gas** n a mixed gas obtained by passing steam (**blue water gas**) or steam and air (**semiwater gas**) over incandescent coke, or other source of carbon. **water gate** n a floodgate; a gate admitting to a river or other body of water; a street leading to the water (Scot); see also separate entry **Watergate**. **water gauge** or **gage** n an instrument for measuring the quantity or height of water; water pressure expressed in inches, in terms of the height of the head of water; an instrument for measuring differences in pressure (mining). **wa'ter-gilding** n wash-gilding. **water glass** n a water clock; an instrument for making observations beneath the surface of water; a glass vessel for containing water, eg one for holding plants; a finger bowl (obs); a tumbler; (**wa'terglass**) a concentrated and viscous solution of sodium or potassium silicate in water, used as adhesive, protective covering, etc, and (esp formerly) for preserving eggs. **water god** n a deity presiding over a tract of water. **water gong** n (music) the effect of dipping a vibrating gong into and raising it out of water to produce upward and downward glissandos. **water gruel** n gruel made with water; anything insipid. **water guard** n river, harbour or coast police. **water gun** n (esp N Am) a water pistol. **water hammer** n a wave of increased pressure travelling through water in a pipe caused by a sudden stoppage or change in the water flow; the concussion and noise so caused. **water head** n the source, eg of a stream; the region where this is found; a dammed-up body of water, or its quantity, height or pressure. **water heater** n an apparatus for heating domestic water. **water hemlock** n a poisonous plant, Cicuta virosa; any other plant of the same genus; water dropwort (qv above). **wa'terhen** n the gallinule or moorhen, or other bird of the rail genus. **water hole** n a pool in which water has collected, eg a spring in a desert or a pool in the dried-up course of a river. **water horse** n a water spirit like a horse; a kelpie. **water hyacinth** n a tropical floating aquatic plant (Eichhornia crassipes) with bluish flowers, that grows in thick masses in ponds, etc. **water ice** n sweetened fruit juice or purée diluted with water, frozen and served as a kind of ice cream, a sorbet. **wa'tering-call** n a cavalry trumpet signal to give water to horses. **watering can** or (US) **pot** n a vessel used for watering plants. **wa'tering-cap** n (obs) a cavalryman's fatigue cap. **watering hole** n a water hole, where animals go to drink; a place where humans seek

(esp alcoholic) refreshment, a pub (facetious). **wa'tering-house** n (obs) an inn or other place where horses are watered. **watering place** n a place where water may be obtained; a place to which people resort to drink mineral water, or for bathing, etc. **wa'tering-trough** n a trough from which horses and cattle drink; a trough between the rails containing water to be scooped up by locomotives. **water jacket** n a casing containing water placed round eg the cylinder block of an internal-combustion engine to keep it cool (also **water box**). **wa'ter-jet** adj operated by a jet of water. **water joint** n a joint in a pavement that is raised to prevent water lying in it; a joint in sheet metal roofing forming a channel for rainwater. **water jump** n a place where a jump across a stream, pool, ditch, etc, has to be made, eg in a steeplechase. **water key** n (music) in brass instruments, a sprung lever that allows drainage of accumulated moisture. **water leaf** n any plant of the genus Hydrophyllum or the family Hydrophyllaceae, N American herbs with sharply toothed leaves and cymose flowers; an ornament used in the capitals of columns, probably representing the leaf of some water plant (archit). **water lemon** n a species of passion flower, or its edible fruit. **water lens** n a simple lens formed by placing a few drops of water in a vessel, eg a small brass cell with blackened sides and a glass bottom. **water level** n the level formed by the surface of still water; an instrument in which water is used for establishing a horizontal line of sight; a waterline; a water table (geol); a slightly inclined road to carry off water (mining). **water lily** n a name commonly given to the different species of Nymphaea and Nuphar, and also to other members of the family Nymphaeaceae (the three British species are the white water lily Nymphaea alba, and the yellow water lilies Nuphar luteum and Nuphar minimum, the latter being rare). **wa'terline** n any of several lines on a ship to which it is submerged under different conditions of loading, eg the light waterline marking the depth when it is without cargo; any of certain lines on a vessel parallel with the water showing the contour of the hull at various heights (shipbuilding); the water level; the outline of a coast; a chain line in laid paper, one of the wider-spaced of the two sets of lines intersecting at right angles, visible by transmitted light (vertical in a folio or octavo page and horizontal in a quarto one). **wa'terlog** vt to make (a boat, etc) unmanageable by flooding with water; to saturate with water so as to make heavy, inert or unfit for use, or so as to impede life or growth (also fig). **wa'terlogged** adj. **water lot** n a piece or lot of ground that is under water. **water main** n a large subterranean pipe supplying water. **wa'terman** n a man who transports passengers in his boat, a boatman, a ferryman; a skilled oarsman; a person whose job is to supply water, eg (hist) to cab horses or coach horses; an imaginary being living in water. **wa'termanship** n oarsmanship. **wa'termark** n the line of the greatest height to which water has risen; a tidemark; a ship's waterline; a distinguishing mark in paper, a design visible by transmitted light, made by the mould or the dandy-roll. ◆ vt to mark with a watermark; to impress as a watermark. **water meadow** n a meadow kept fertile by flooding from a stream. **water measure** n (hist) a measurement used for goods such as coal, salt, etc sold on board ship, the bushel, etc being larger than the standard bushel, etc. **water measurer** n an aquatic insect of the genus Hydrometra, which walks on the surface of water preying on mosquito larvae, etc. **wa'termelon** n a plant (Citrullus vulgaris) of the cucumber family, of African origin, having a large, pulpy, pleasantly flavoured fruit; the fruit itself. **water meter** n an instrument for measuring the quantity of water passing through a particular outlet. **water milfoil** see under **milfoil**. **water mill** n a mill driven by water. **water moccasin** n a poisonous snake of the southern USA. **water mole** n the desman, a shrew-like aquatic animal; the duckbill or platypus. **water monkey** n a round, narrow-necked, porous earthenware jar for holding drinking water, cooled by evaporation and used in hot climates (also **monkey jar**). **water motor** n any water wheel or turbine, esp any small motor driven by water under pressure. **water mouse** n the water vole; any mouse of the genus Hydromys (Aust). **water music** n (hist) music performed, or composed for performance, during an excursion by water. **water nixie** n a nixie. **water nymph** n a nymph inhabiting water, esp a naiad of Greek mythology. **water of crystallization** or **hydration** n the water present in hydrated compounds, which, when crystallized from solution in water, retain a definite amount of water. **water of life** n spiritual refreshment; whisky, brandy, etc. **water on the brain** n hydrocephalus. **water on the knee** n an accumulation of serous fluid in the knee joint. **water opossum** n the yapok, an amphibious opossum of S America. **water ouzel** n the dipper, an aquatic songbird of the genus Cinclus. **water parsnip** n any plant of the aquatic umbelliferous genus Sium, esp the skirret. **wa'ter-parting** n a watershed or divide. **water pepper** n a very acrid persicaria (Polygonum hydropiper) of wet places. **water pipe** n a pipe for conveying water; a hookah. **water pistol** n a weapon or toy for shooting a jet of water or other liquid. **water plane** n a plane passing through any waterline of a ship; the plane of the surface of water; a canal on the level without locks (hist); a seaplane. **water plant** n a plant that grows in water. **water plantain** n a plant (Alisma plantago) having plantain-like leaves and clustered white or pink flowers; any other plant of the *Alisma* genus. **water plate** *n* a plate having a double bottom enclosing a space for hot water, used to keep food warm. **water poet** *n* a writer of doggerel verse (after John Taylor, 1580–1653, a writer of jingling verses, etc, who was for a time a Thames waterman and called himself 'the Water-poet'). **water polo** *n* an aquatic ball game played by swimmers, seven a side; a similar game played by contestants in canoes. **water pore** *n* (*bot*) a hydathode, a water-secreting organ; a madreporite, a sieve-like calcareous plate in certain echinoderms. **water pot** *n* a pot or vessel for holding water. **water potential** *n* (*bot*) a measure of the free energy of water in a solution, eg in a cell or soil sample, and hence of its tendency to move by diffusion, osmosis or in vapour form. **water power** *n* the power of water, employed to move machinery, etc; a flow or fall of water which may be so used. **wa'terpox** *n* (*rare*) varicella, ie chickenpox. **water privilege** *n* the right to the use of water, *esp* for driving machinery; a place where this right may be exercised. **wa'terproof** *adj* coated eg with rubber or plastic, so as to be impervious to water; so constructed as to exclude water. ◆ *n* a material or an outer garment made impervious to water. ◆ *vt and vi* to make or become impervious to water, *esp* through the process of coating with a solution. **wa'terproofing** *n* the process of making any substance impervious to water; the material with which this is done. **water pump** *n* a pump for raising water; the eye (*humorous*). **water purpie** *n* the plant brooklime. **wa'terquake** *n* a seismic disturbance affecting the sea. **water rail** *n* the common rail (*Rallus aquaticus*) of Europe, a long-beaked wading marsh bird. **water ram** *n* a hydraulic ram. **water rat** *n* the popular name of the water vole; the American muskrat; a pirate; a sailor or boatman. **water rate** *n* a rate or tax for the supply of water. **water reactor** *n* a water-cooled nuclear reactor. **wa'ter-repell'ent** *adj* (of a fabric, etc) treated so as not to absorb water. **wa'ter-resis'tant** *adj* (treated so as to be) resistant to penetration by water. **water rice** *n* see **zizania**. **water rug** *n* a kind of water dog, *perh* from **rug**[1] (*Shakesp*, *Macbeth* III.1.93). **water sail** *n* (*naut*) on square rigged ships, a fine-weather sail set below a lower studding-sail, almost touching the water. **water sapphire** *n* (translating Fr *saphir d'eau*) an intense blue variety of cordierite used as a gemstone. **water scorpion** *n* a long-legged water insect of the family Nepidae, which has a long breathing tube at the end of the abdomen and large forelegs for seizing and holding prey. **water seal** *n* a seal formed by water in a trap. **wa'tershed** *n* the line of high ground separating two river basins; a drainage or a catchment area (*non-standard*); a slope or structure down which water flows; a crucial point or dividing line between two phases, conditions; the time of the evening after which it is accepted that television programmes considered unsuitable for children may be broadcast, etc. **water shoot** *n* a channel for the overflow of water; a water chute. **wa'ter-shot** *adj* (*rare*) crossed by streams. **wa'terside** *n* the edge of a sea, lake, etc, a shore (also *adj*). **water sign** *n* any of the three signs of the zodiac (Cancer, Scorpio and Pisces) believed to have an affinity with water. **wa'ter-ski** *n* a water-planing ski used in **wa'ter-skiing**, the sport of being towed at speed on a ski or skis behind a motorboat. ◆ *vi* (**wa'ter-skiing; wa'ter-skied** or **wa'ter-ski'd**) to ride on water-skis. **wa'ter-skier** *n*. **water slide** *n* a slide, often lubricated with flowing water, that ends in a swimming pool. **wa'tersmeet** *n* the confluence of two streams. **water smoke** *n* water evaporating as visible mist. **water snail** *n* (*esp US*) a name for the Archimedean screw (qv). **water snake** *n* any of various kinds of snake (*esp* of genus *Natrix*) frequenting fresh water. **water softener** *n* a device or substance for removing the causes of hardness in water. **water soldier** *n* an aquatic plant (*Stratiotes aloides*) with sword-like leaves and white flowers reminiscent of plumes of feathers, common in lakes and ditches in the east of England. **wa'ter-soluble** *adj* soluble in water. **water souchy** /*soo'chi* or *soo'shi*/ *n* fish served in the water in which it is boiled (Du *waterzootje*, from *zootje* boiling). **water spaniel** *n* a spaniel bred to retrieve waterfowl, the **Irish water spaniel** having a liver-coloured coat. **water spider** *n* an aquatic spider, *esp Argyroneta aquatica*, which has an underwater bell-shaped web inflated with air carried down in bubbles. **water spirit** *n* a water sprite. **water splash** *n* a shallow stream running across a road. **water sports** *n pl* sports practised on or in the water; sexual arousal or gratification associated with urination (*inf*). **wa'terspout** *n* a pipe, etc from which water spouts; the spout of water; a torrential downpour of rain; a disturbance like a very small tornado, a revolving column of cloud, mist or spray. **water spring** *n* (*Bible*) a spring. **wa'ter-sprin'kle** *n* (*Spenser*) a spray of water; a sprinkle. **water sprite** *n* a sprite inhabiting water. **wa'terstanding** *adj* (*Shakesp*) brimming with tears. **water starwort** *n* a water plant, genus *Callitriche*. **water stick insect** *n* a slender twiglike water insect (*Ranatra linearis*), closely related to the water scorpion. **water strider** *n* any long-legged aquatic insect of the family Hydrobatidae. **water supply** *n* the obtaining and distribution of water, eg to a community; the amount of water thus distributed. **water table** *n* a moulding, *esp* in the string course of a building, designed to throw rainwater outwards so that it does not flow down the wall below (*archit*); the level below which fissures and pores in the strata are saturated with water (*geol*). **water tap** *n* a tap used for letting out

water. **water thermometer** *n* a thermometer filled with water instead of mercury, and used for showing the point at which water has its greatest density. **water thief** *n* (*Shakesp*) a pirate. **water thrush** *n* either of two species of American warbler (*Seiurus motacilla* or *S. noveboracensis*) with brownish backs and striped underparts, living near water. **water thyme** *n* the waterweed anacharis. **wa'tertight** *adj* so well-sealed as not to admit water or let it escape; (of an argument, etc) such that no flaw, weakness or source of misinterpretation can be found in it. **watertight compartment** *n* a section of a ship's hull or other underwater structure so formed that water cannot enter it from any other part; a part, *esp* of one's thoughts or beliefs, shut off from the influence of other parts. **wa'tertightness** *n*. **water tortoise** *n* a terrapin or other aquatic tortoise, eg *Pelomedusa subrufa*. **water torture** *n* torture using water, *esp* dripping it slowly onto the victim's forehead. **water tower** *n* a tower containing tanks in which water is stored so that it may be delivered at sufficient pressure for distribution to an area; a vertical pipe supplied with water under high pressure, used in firefighting. **water tube boiler** *n* a boiler consisting of a large number of closely-spaced water tubes connected to one or more drums, which act as water pockets and steam separators, giving rapid water circulation and quick steaming. **water tunnel** *n* (*aeronautics*) a tunnel in which water is circulated instead of air to obtain a visual representation of flow. **water twist** *n* a kind of cotton yarn, first made by the water frame; in spinning, more than the usual amount of twist. **water vapour** *n* water in gaseous form, *esp* when evaporation has occurred at a temperature below boiling point. **wa'ter-vas'cular** *adj* relating to vessels in certain invertebrates which contain a mixture of water and a nutritive fluid; in echinoderms, relating to the system of coelomic canals (**water-vascular system**) associated with the tube feet and supplying fluid for their movement. **water vine** *n* a name for various plants yielding a refreshing watery sap. **water violet** *n* a plant of the genus *Hottonia* of aquatic herbs with racemose flowers and crowded submerged leaves. **water vole** *n* a large British vole, *Arvicola amphibius*, commonly known as the water rat. **water wagon** *n* a wagon used to convey water; abstinence from alcohol, as in *be* or *go on the water wagon* (*inf*). **water wagtail** *n* a wagtail, *esp* the pied wagtail. **water wave** *n* a wave of water; a wave in the hair made by setting it when wet. **wa'ter-wave** *vt* to make such a wave in (hair). **wa'terway** *n* a series of pieces of timber, extending round a ship at the junction of the decks with the sides, having a groove connecting with the scuppers to carry off water; any channel for water; a stretch of navigable water; a route over, or by, water. **wa'terweed** *n* any plant with very small flowers and leaves growing in ponds, etc, *esp* anacharis. **water wheel** *n* a wheel moved by water, formerly used as a source of energy to drive machinery, etc; an engine for raising water. **water wings** *n pl* a winglike inflated device that fits across the chest, or a pair of inflatable armbands, for keeping a non-swimmer, *esp* a child learning to swim, afloat in water. **water witch** *n* a dowser. **water witching** *n* dowsing. **wa'terwork** *n* (*usu in pl*) any apparatus or plant by which water is supplied, eg to a town; (*usu in pl*) an ornamental fountain, cascade, etc (*obs*); fabric painted to look like and be used like tapestry (*hist*); (*usu in pl*) tear-shedding, weeping (*humorous*); (*usu in pl*) the urinary system (*euphem*). **wa'ter-worn** *adj* worn by the action of water. **water yam** *n* a plant with farinaceous rootstock, the lattice leaf.

■ **above water** out of difficulties, *esp* financial. **by water** using water transport, by ship, boat, etc. **cast someone's water** (*obs*) to examine someone's urine to aid in the diagnosis of disease. **high water** and **high-watermark** see under **high**[1]. **hold water** (of an argument, etc) to be correct or well-grounded, to bear examination. **in deep water** or **waters** in water too deep for safety; in trouble, difficulty or distress, *esp* of the financial kind. **keep one's head above water** to remain out of difficulty or trouble, *esp* to keep solvent. **like water** copiously; extravagantly, recklessly. **like water off a duck's back** (of a scolding, etc) having no effect, making no impression. **low water** and **low watermark** see under **low**[1]. **make a hole in the water** (*sl*) to drown oneself. **make the mouth water** to arouse a delightful feeling of anticipation or desire. **make water** (of a boat) to leak, take in water. **make** or **pass water** to urinate. **of the first** or **purest water** see **water** (*n*). **pour** or **throw cold water on** or **over** to discourage by one's indifference or dismissiveness. **pour oil on troubled waters** to take measures to calm down a stormy state of affairs, from the effect of pouring oil on rough water. **still waters run deep** a quiet exterior often conceals strong emotions, resolution, cunning, etc. **test the water** or **waters** to try to ascertain probable reaction or response before making a proposal, selling a product, etc. **under water** below the surface. **water down** (*lit and fig*) to dilute, make less strong, attenuate. **water under the bridge** experiences that are over and done with; past problems that have been forgotten or put down to experience.

Watergate /*wö'tar-gāt*/ *n* the US political scandal involving an attempted break-in at the Democratic Party headquarters (the *Watergate* building, Washington DC) in 1972 by agents employed by

---

■ words derived from main entry word; ▫ compound words; ■ idioms and phrasal verbs

President Richard Nixon's re-election organization, and the subsequent attempted cover-up by senior White House officials who had approved the break-in; hence any similar public scandal, *esp* one involving corruption, or misuse of power; see also **-gate**.

waterhen...to...**waterlog** see under **water**.

Waterloo /wö-tər-loo' or wö'/ *n* a final defeat. [*Waterloo*, near Brussels, where Napoleon was finally defeated in 1815]
◻ **Waterloo cracker** *n* (*obs*) a kind of firework.
■ **meet one's Waterloo** to be finally and decisively defeated.

waterman...to...**watery** see under **water**.

Watling Street /wot'ling strēt/ *n* one of the great Roman highways of Britain, running from near London through St Albans to Wroxeter; often extended at either end to include the roads to Dover and Chester; loosely applied to other Roman roads; the Milky Way (*obs*). [OE *Wæclinga stræt* the street of Wæcel's people (of whom nothing is known); the OE name of St Albans was *Wæclinga ceaster*]

wats see **wit²**.

watt /wot/ *n* a derived SI unit, the unit of power (symbol **W**), equal to a rate of working of one joule per second. [James *Watt* (1736–1819), Scottish engineer and inventor]
■ **watt'age** *n* an amount of power expressed in watts.
◻ **watt'-hour'** *n* a common unit of electrical energy, being the work done by one watt acting for one hour. **watt'meter** *n* an instrument containing a series (*current*) and a shunt (*voltage*) coil whose combined torque produces a deflection of the needle that is a direct measure of the circuit power in watts.

Watteau /wot'ō/ *adj* applied to articles or features of women's dress resembling those seen in the paintings of Antoine *Watteau* (1684–1721), as in **Watteau bodice**, one with a square opening at the neck and short sleeves.
■ **Watt'eauish** *adj*.

wattle¹ /wot'l/ *n* (collective *sing* or in *pl*) material for fences, roofs, etc, in the form of rods and branches, etc, either interwoven to form a network or loose; a hurdle (*dialect*); a twig or flexible rod (*dialect*); any of various Australian acacias; (*perh* a word of separate origin) the coloured fleshy excrescence under the throat of some birds, or a similar excrescence or process on any part of the head of a bird, fish, etc. ◆ *vt* to bind with wattle or twigs; to form by plaiting twigs. [OE *watul*, *watel*; origin uncertain]
■ **watt'led** *adj*. **watt'ling** *n* the act of making wattles by interweaving twigs, etc; wattlework, or the material for it.
◻ **wattle and daub** or (*rare*) **dab** *n* wattlework plastered with mud and used as a building material. **watt'lebark** *n* the bark of various acacias, used for tanning. **watt'lebird** *n* any of a number of honeyeaters of Australia that have ear wattles; a New Zealand songbird with wattles around its beak. **watt'lework** *n* wickerwork.

wattle² /wot'l/ (*hist*; *Orkney* and *Shetland*) *n* the obligation to entertain the foud on his annual journey, or a tax for which it was later commuted. [Perh Norw dialect *veitla*, from ON *veizla* entertainment]

Watusi /wə-too'si/ or **Watutsi** /-tŭt'si/ *n* the Tutsi people collectively; a lively dance popular in the 1960s. [Pl of **Tutsi**]

waucht see **waught**.

wauff variant of **waff¹,²**.

waugh¹ /wö/ *interj* expressing sorrow, anger, etc, *usu* attributed to Native Americans.

waugh² see **waff³**.

waught or **waucht** /wöhht/ (*Scot*) *n* a large draught. ◆ *vt* and *vi* to drink in large draughts. [Perh connected with **quaff¹**]

wauk and **waukmill** see **waulk**.

waukrife same as **wakerife** (see under **wake¹**).

waul¹ or **wawl** /wöl/ *vi* to cry like a cat or a baby (also *n*). [Imit]
■ **waul'ing** or **wawl'ing** *n* and *adj*.

waul² or **wawl** /wöl/ (*Scot*; *obs*) *vi* to roll the eyes; (of the eyes) to roll. [OE *wealwian* to roll, wallow]

waulk, walk or **wauk** /wök/ *vt* to full (cloth). [Orig the same verb as **walk¹**]
■ **waulk'er, walk'er** or **wauk'er** *n* a fuller of cloth.
◻ **waulk'ing-, walk'ing-** or **wauk'ing-song** *n* a song for singing while fulling cloth, *specif* one sung in Gaelic by Hebridean women, its beat setting or reflecting the work rhythm. **waulk'mill, walk'mill** or **wauk'mill** *n* a fulling-mill.

waur, waurst see **war²**.

WAV or **WAVE** /wāv/ (*comput*) *n* Waveform audio format, a standard audio file format.

wave /wāv/ *n* a ridge on the surface of a liquid, *esp* of the sea; a surge, consisting of vibrating particles of liquid, moving across the surface of a body of liquid such as the sea (**transverse wave**), the vibrations of the individual particles being at right angles to the line of advance; a

unit disturbance in any travelling system of vibrating particles such as a light wave (**transverse wave**) or a sound wave (**longitudinal wave**, the vibrations of the particles being in the direction of advance); an undulating or vibratory motion (eg as a signal), or sound; the sea, or other body of water (*poetic*); curved inequality of surface; a line or streak like a wave; an undulation; an undulating succession of curves in hair, or one of these; a movement of the raised hand expressing greeting, farewell, etc; a swell or increase, normally followed by a subsidence or decline; any movement suggestive of a surge, *esp* one of a series or progression. ◆ *vi* to move like a wave; to move backwards and forwards; to float or hover (*obs*); to flutter; to make a signal in this way; to move the raised hand in greeting, farewell, etc or as a signal or sign; to undulate; (of hair) to have a wave or waves, be full of waves; to waver, vacillate (*obs*). ◆ *vt* to move backwards and forwards; to brandish; to flutter; to waft or beckon; to express by a wave; to direct, signal an instruction to, by a wave; to raise into inequalities of surface; to give an undulating appearance to (hair). [OE *wafian* to wave; cf ON *vafra* to waver; noun also an alteration of ME *wage*, *wawe* flood, wave]
■ **waved** *adj* showing a wavelike form or outline; undulating; (of hair) artificially made to undulate; indented (*heraldry*); having on the margin a succession of curved segments or incisions. **wave'less** *adj*. **wave'let** *n* a little wave. **wave'like** *adj*. **wā'ving** *n* and *adj*.
◻ **wave'band** *n* (*radio*) a range of wavelengths occupied by transmission of a particular type. **wave energy** or **power** *n* energy or power derived, by some means of conversion, from the movement of sea waves. **wave equation** *n* (*phys*) a differential equation that describes the passage of harmonic waves through a medium. **wave farm** *n* a concentration at sea of machines that generate power from the movement of waves. **wave'form** or **wave'shape** *n* (*phys*) a graph showing variation of amplitude of electrical signal, or other wave, against time. **wave'front** *n* (*phys*) in a propagating vibratory disturbance, the continuous locus of points which are in the same phase of vibration. **wave function** *n* (*phys*) a mathematical equation representing the space and time variations in amplitude for a wave system. **wave'guide** *n* (*electronics*) a hollow metal conductor, *usu* rectangular, within which very high-frequency energy can be transmitted efficiently. **wave'length** *n* the distance between two successive similar points on an alternating wave, eg between successive maxima or between successive minima; the distance, measured radially from the source, between two successive points in free space at which an electromagnetic wave has the same phase; such a distance serving to identify radio waves from a particular transmitter (*radio*). **wave mechanics** *n sing* (*phys*) the part of quantum mechanics dealing with the wave aspect of the behaviour of radiations. **wave'meter** *n* an instrument for measuring wavelengths, directly or indirectly. **wave motion** *n* undulatory movement; motion in waves, or according to the same laws. **wave number** *n* (*phys*) in an electromagnetic wave, the reciprocal of the wavelength, ie the number of waves in unit distance. **wave offering** *n* an ancient Jewish custom of moving the hands in succession towards the four points of the compass in presenting certain offerings (cf **heave-offering** under **heave**). **wave-particle duality** *n* the circumstance that light and other electromagnetic radiation behave like a wave motion when being propagated and like particles when interacting with matter. **wave power** see **wave energy** above. **waveshape** see **waveform** above. **wave'table** *n* a collection of digitized samples of recorded sound stored as sound waves. **wave theory** *n* (*phys*) the theory, no longer widely held, that light or other radiation is transmitted only in the form of waves. **wave train** *n* a group of similar waves, of limited duration, produced by a single disturbance.
■ **make waves** to create a disturbance, make trouble. **on the same wavelength as** in tune with, having the same attitude of mind, background knowledge, etc. **wave aside** to dismiss (a suggestion, etc) as irrelevant or unimportant. **wave down** to signal to stop by waving. **wave off** to wave to (someone moving out of sight on departure) by way of farewell.

waveband...to...**wavelike** see under **wave**.

wavellite /wā'və-līt/ *n* hydrated phosphate of aluminium, occurring commonly in flattened globular aggregates, showing a strongly developed internal radiating structure. [Dr William *Wavel* or *Wavell* (died 1829), who discovered the mineral near Barnstaple]

wavemeter see under **wave**.

waver /wā'vər/ *vi* to move to and fro; to shake, be unsteady, be in danger of falling; to falter, show signs of giving way; to vacillate; to vary, change. [ON *vafra* to flicker]
■ **wā'verer** *n*. **wā'vering** *n* and *adj*. **wā'veringly** *adv* in a wavering or irresolute manner. **wā'veringness** *n*. **wā'very** or **wā'verous** *adj* unsteady.

WAVES or **waves** /wāvz/ *n pl* or *n sing* (*US*) the women's reserve of the US Navy. [*W*omen *A*ccepted for *V*oluntary *E*mergency *S*ervice]

waveshape see under **wave**.

wavetable see under **wave**.

wavey or **wavy** /wā'vi/ n the snow goose. [Cree]

waving see under **wave**.

wavy[1] /wā'vi/ adj (of hair) forming undulations, full of waves; (of a line, etc) describing a series of curves in alternating directions; like waves in shape or movement; curving, undulating; fluctuating. [**wave**]
■ **wā'vily** adv. **wā'viness** n the state or quality of being wavy.
❑ **Wavy Navy** n (old) the Royal Naval Volunteer Reserve, so called from the undulating gold braid on officers' sleeves.

wavy[2] see **wavey**.

waw (*Walter Scott*) or **wawe** (*Spenser*) /wö/ n a wave. [ME *wage*, *wawe* prob from a lost OE form akin to *wæg* wave]

wawl see **waul**[1,2].

wax[1] /waks/ n any of a class of substances of plant or animal origin, *usu* consisting of esters of monohydric alcohols, eg beeswax, $C_{30}H_{61}OCOC_{15}H_{31}$; any of certain hydrocarbons of mineral origin, eg ozokerite; any substance like a wax in some respect, such as ear wax or cerumen; sealing wax, prepared from shellac and turpentine; a resinous material used by shoemakers to rub their thread; a cosmetic treatment that uses hot wax to remove body hair; puddled clay (*mining*); a thick sugary substance made by boiling down the sap of the sugar maple, and cooling by exposure to the air; a person found to be readily impressionable or easily influenced; in *Shakesp, Timon of Athens* I.1.50, explanation uncertain (according to some, wax tablets; others have thought expansive growth, ie properly from **wax**[2]). ◆ vt to coat or treat with wax, *esp* so as to render waterproof; to smear, rub or (*obs*) join with wax; to remove hair from (a part of the body) by coating with wax which is left to dry and then peeled off. [OE *weax*; ON *vax*, Du *was*, Ger *Wachs*]
■ **waxed** adj (of a fabric or garment) made waterproof by being treated with wax. **wax'en** adj made of wax; like wax; easily impressed, penetrated, effaced. **wax'er** n someone or something that waxes. **wax'ily** adv. **wax'iness** n. **wax'ing** n. **wax'y** adj resembling wax in texture or appearance; soft; impressible; impressionable; pallid, pasty.
❑ **wax'berry** n the wax myrtle or its waxy-surfaced fruit. **wax'bill** n any of various small seed-eating birds of the weaver-finch family with coloured bills like sealing wax. **wax'-chandler** n a maker of, or dealer in, wax candles. **wax'cloth** n (old) another name for both oilcloth and linoleum. **wax doll** n a child's doll having the head and bust made of hardened beeswax. **waxed leather** n leather finished with a high wax polish on the flesh side. **wax end** or (better) **waxed end** n a strong thread having its end stiffened by shoemakers' wax, so as to go easily through the hole made by the awl. **wax flower** n an artificial flower made of wax; any of several plants, eg a white-flowered climbing plant of Madagascar, an epiphyte of Guyana, and plants of the genus *Eriostemon* of Australia. **wax insect** n an insect that secretes wax, eg any of several of the Coccidae, etc. **wax light** n a candle or taper made of wax. **wax moth** n a moth whose larvae are destructive to young bees. **wax myrtle** n the American candleberry tree. **wax painting** n encaustic (qv) painting. **wax palm** n either of two S American palms yielding wax. **wax paper** n paper spread with a thin coating of white wax and other materials. **wax plant** n any of several plants of the genus *Hoya*, *esp H. carnosa* of Australia and E Asia, an asclepiadaceous climbing plant, with clusters of waxy white or pink star-shaped flowers, and succulent leaves. **wax pocket** n in bees, a ventral abdominal pouch that secretes wax. **wax'-proofed** adj made waterproof with a coating of wax. **wax'-red** adj (*Shakesp*) bright-red like sealing wax. **wax tablet** n (*hist*) a wax-coated wooden writing tablet, for use with a stylus. **wax tree** n a tree from which wax is obtained, eg a Japanese sumac (*Rhus succedanea*), the wax myrtle, a privet (*Ligustrum lucidum*), etc. **wax'wing** n a member of a genus of passerine birds (*Bombycilla*) with small red horny appendages, resembling red sealing wax, on their wings. **wax'work** n work done in wax; a figure or object modelled in wax; (in pl) an exhibition of wax figures. **wax'worker** n. **waxy degeneration** n a morbid process by which the healthy tissue of various organs is transformed into a waxy albuminous substance.
■ **lost wax** see **cire perdue**. **wax up** (of a mare about to foal) to develop a sticky covering over the teats.

wax[2] /waks/ vi (pap (*archaic*) **wax'en**, also (*obs*) pat pl (as in *Shakesp, Midsummer Night's Dream* II.1.56) and *infinitive*) to grow or increase; (of the moon as it passes through its phases from new moon to full moon) to show, night by night, an increasing area of illuminated surface, *opp* to *wane*; to pass into another state, become, as in *wax lyrical*. [OE *weaxan*; ON *vaxa*, Ger *wachsen*, related to L *augēre*, Gr *auxanein*]
■ **wax and wane** to increase and decrease in alternating sequence.

wax[3] /waks/ (old inf) n a passion, a fit of anger. [Origin uncertain]
■ **wax'y** adj irate, incensed.

waxberry...to...**waxcloth** see under **wax**[1].

waxen see **wax**[1,2].

waxer...to...**waxwork** see under **wax**[1].

waxy see **wax**[1,3].

way[1] /wā/ n passage; a road, street, track; (with *cap*) used in street names; direction of motion; the correct or desired route or path; length of space, distance (also in pl (*inf, esp US*)); district; room or opportunity to advance; freedom of action, scope; manner of life; established routine; position, as in *wrong way up, other way round*, etc; condition, state; advance in life; normal or habitual course or conduct; (in pl) a characteristic feature of behaviour, an idiosyncrasy; manner, style; method; means; course; respect; will; progress, forward motion, as in *edge one's way, eat one's way through*, etc; progress or motion through the water, headway (*naut*); the direction of the weave, grain, etc; (in pl) the machined surfaces of the top of a lathe bed on which the carriage slides, shears (*engineering*); (in pl) the framework of timbers on which a ship slides when being launched. ◆ vi (*Spenser*) to journey. [OE *weg*; Ger *Weg*; related to Sans *vahati* he carries and to L *vehere* to carry, draw]
■ **way'less** adj without a path.
❑ **way baggage** n (US) baggage to be laid down at a way station. **way'bill** n a list of passengers and goods carried by a public vehicle; a document giving details regarding goods sent by rail or road vehicle, etc; a list of places to be visited on a journey. **way'board** or **weigh'board** n (*geol*) a thin stratum or seam separating thicker strata. **way'bread** n (OE *wegbræde*, from *brād* broad, flat; *dialect*) the common plantain. **way'fare** vi (*archaic*) to travel, *esp* on foot. ◆ n (*archaic*) travel, *esp* on foot. **way'farer** n a traveller, *esp* on foot. **way'faring** n and adj. **wayfaring tree** n *Viburnum lantana*, a large shrub with white flowers and berries that turn red and finally black, common in hedges. **way freight** n freight for a way station. **way'-going** n and adj (*Scot*) departing. **way'gone** adj exhausted by travelling. **waylay'** vt (**waylay'ing**; **waylaid'**) to lie in ambush for; to attack or seize on the way; to lie in wait for in order to converse with; to obstruct or intercept (*obs*). **waylay'er** n. **way'leave** n permission to pass over another's ground or property. **way'-maker** n a pioneer; a precursor. **way'mark** n a signpost; something that serves as a guide to a traveller. ◆ vt to mark out (a path, etc) with guideposts, signs, etc. **way of life** n the style or conditions in which a person lives; the living of one's life according to certain principles. **Way of the Cross** n a series of pictorial representations of the stages of Christ's progress to Calvary; devotions practised in connection with these stages. **way passenger** n one picked up or set down at a way station or an intermediate point on a coach or bus route. **way point** n a point for stopping, changing course, etc, on a journey. **way'post** n a guidepost. **ways and means** n pl resources; methods eg of raising money for the carrying on of government (**Committee of Ways and Means** the House of Commons sitting in the character of a committee to consider methods of raising money supplies; (in the USA) a permanent committee of the House of Representatives to which bills concerned with revenue are referred). **way'side** n the border of a way, path or highway (**fall by the wayside** to fail or give up in one's attempt to do something; to drop out). ◆ adj growing, situated or lying near the wayside. **way station** n (US) an intermediate station between principal stations. **way traffic** n (US) local traffic, as distinguished from through or express traffic. **way train** n (US) a train stopping at most of the stations on a line. **way warden** n a person appointed to supervise the upkeep of roads and footpaths in a district. **way'wiser** n an instrument for measuring distance travelled. **way'worn** adj worn out by travel.
■ **across** or **over the way** on the other side of the street, etc. **be by way of** to be supposed or alleged to be or be (doing, being, etc). **by** or **with someone's way of it** (*Scot*) according to someone's belief or assertion. **by the way** incidentally; while travelling; beside one's path. **by way of** travelling through, via; as if for the purpose of; in character of, as a substitute for. **come someone's way** to come within someone's experience or reach, to become attainable by someone. **come** or **go someone's way** to come or go in the same direction as someone. **divide three**, etc, **ways** to divide into three, etc portions. **get** or **have one's** or (**one's own**) **way** to get or do what one wants. **give way (to)** see under **give**[1]. **go all** or **the whole way (with)** (*inf*) to have sexual intercourse (with). **go one's own way** to act independently. **go one's way** to depart. **go out of the** (or **one's**) **way** to give oneself trouble; to make a special effort (to do something). **go someone's way** (of circumstances, etc) to favour someone. **go the way of all flesh** or **all the earth** to die. **have a way with** to be good at dealing with or managing (people, etc). **have a way with one** to have a fascinating personality or persuasive manner. **have it both ways** (*usu* with a *neg*) to benefit from two actions, situations, arguments, etc, each of which excludes the possibility, validity, etc of the other. **have it one's** (or **one's own**) **way** to do, think, etc what one pleases, with no regard for others' advice or opinions. **have one's way** to carry one's point, get what one wants. **have way** (*naut*) (of a vessel) to be in motion. **in a bad way** in a serious condition; very upset. **in a fair way to** likely to succeed in. **in a small** (or **big** or **large**) **way** on a petty (or a

large or grandiose) scale. **in a way** to some extent; from one point of view; in a state of agitation or distress (*old*). **in his**, etc **way** (or **own way**) as far as his, etc individual merits go, leaving aside the disadvantageous aspects. **in no way** not at all. **in the family way** see under **family**. **in the** (or **one's**) **way** in one's path, impeding one's progress, creating an obstruction; on the way. **in the way of** in a good position for effecting or attaining; in the habit of (*inf*); in respect of. **lead the way** to act as a guide or inspiration to others. **look the other way** to look away, sometimes deliberately in order not to see someone or something; to take no notice *esp* of something calling for attention. **lose the** (or **one's**) **way** to leave one's intended route by mistake and become lost. **make one's way** to move forward, sometimes with difficulty, to proceed; to make good progress, achieve success. **make way** to make room; to advance. **no two ways about it** that is certain, there is no doubt about it. **no way** (*inf*) under no circumstances, absolutely not. **one way and another** considering various aspects. **one way or the other** by any means possible. **on the** (or **one's**) **way** moving towards a destination or event; in progress; at a point on one's journey. **on the way out** becoming unpopular, unfashionable, etc. **out of the way** so as not to hinder or obstruct; away from main routes, remote (**out-of-the-way** *adj*); dealt with, finished with; in prison or dead and gone (*usu* with *neg*) out of the ordinary, unusual; lost, hidden (*Shakesp*). **put someone in the way of** to contrive to make available to someone. **take one's way** to set out, proceed; to follow one's own inclination or plan. **the Way** the Christian Religion (from Bible, Acts 9.2, etc). **under way** (of a vessel) in motion (also **underway**); progressing. **way to go** (*US inf*) an expression of praise or encouragement.

way² or **'way** /wā/ (*esp and orig US*) *adv* far; by a substantial distance or length of time; very, as in *way good* (*sl*). [Shortened from *away*]
❑ **way-out** *adj* (*inf*) excellent, very satisfying, exceptional; eccentric; unconventional, avant-garde, exotic; rapt, lost, carried away, *orig* in performing avant-garde jazz.
■ **way back** long ago; in the distant past; far into the past.

way³ /wā/ (*Spenser*) *vt* to weigh, esteem. [Variant of **weigh¹**]

way baggage...to...**waygone** see under **way¹**.

waygoose see **wayzgoose**.

wayless...to...**waymark** see under **way¹**.

wayment /wā-ment'/ (*Spenser*) *vt* and *vi* to lament, grieve. ◆ *n* lamentation, grief. [OFr *waimenter*, from *wai* alas]

way-out see under **way²**.

waypost see under **way¹**.

-ways /-wāz/ *sfx* forming adverbs and adjectives of direction and manner, as in *sideways*, *edgeways*. [**way¹**]

wayward /wā'wərd/ *adj* wilful; capricious; irregular. [For *awayward*, from *away* and **-ward**]
■ **way'wardly** *adv*. **way'wardness** *n*.

waywiser see under **way¹**.

waywode /wā'wōd/ *n* a variant of **voivode**.

wayworn see under **way¹**.

wayzgoose or **wasegoose** /wāz'goos/ *n* formerly, a printers' annual dinner or picnic (earlier **way'goose**). [Origin obscure]

waz or **wazz** /waz/ (*N Eng dialect*) *vi* to urinate. ◆ *n* an act of urinating. [Origin uncertain]

waza-ari /wä-zə-ä'ri/ *n* (in judo) a score of seven points or 'almost ippon', awarded for a throw or hold not quite worthy of a maximum score (ippon). [Jap]

wazir /wä-zēr'/ *n* a vizier. [Ar *wazīr*]

wazzock /waz'ək/ (*inf*) *n* a stupid or foolish person. [Origin unknown; perh connected with **waz**]

Wb *symbol*: weber (SI unit).

WBA *abbrev*: World Boxing Association.

WBC *abbrev*: World Boxing Council.

WBF *abbrev*: World Boxing Federation.

WBO *abbrev*: World Boxing Organization.

WC *abbrev*: water closet; West(ern) Central.

wc *abbrev*: water closet; without charge.

WCC *abbrev*: World Council of Churches.

W/Cdr *abbrev*: Wing-Commander.

WD *abbrev*: formerly, War Department; (Windward Islands) Dominica (IVR); Works Department.

w/d *abbrev*: wheel drive, as in *2-w/d* or *4-w/d*.

WDA *abbrev*: Welsh Development Agency.

we /wē/ *pronoun pl* of I; I and others; people in general; used for I by monarchs; also used by editors, etc; used when speaking patronizingly, *esp* to children, to mean 'you'. [OE *wē*; cognate with Gothic *weis*, Ger *wir*]

WEA *abbrev*: Workers' Educational Association.

weak /wēk/ *adj* lacking strength; not able to sustain a great weight; easily overcome; frail; having poor health; feeble; soft (*obs*); lacking moral or mental force; impressible, easily led; lacking artistic force; unconvincing; inconclusive; inconsiderable (*Shakesp*); having little of the important ingredient; (with *in*) deficient in respect of; (of a verb) inflected by regular syllabic addition rather than by change of main vowel; (of a Germanic noun or adjective) having inflections in *-n*; (of a sound or accent) having little force; (of a verse line) having the accent on a normally unstressed syllable; (of a syllable) unstressed; tending downward in price (*stock exchange*); (of an interaction between nuclear particles) having a decay time of *approx* 10^{-10} seconds. [ON *veikr*; related to OE *wāc* pliant, from *wīcan* to yield; Du *week*, Ger *weich*]
■ **weak'en** *vt* to make weaker; to reduce in strength or spirit. ◆ *vi* to grow weak or weaker; to become less resolute or determined, show signs of giving in. **weak'ener** *n*. **weak'ish** *adj*. **weak'liness** *n*. **weak'ling** *n* a weak or feeble creature. **weak'ly** *adv*. ◆ *adj* sickly; not robust; feeble. **weak'ness** *n* the state of being weak; a flaw, shortcoming; a liking or fondness (with *for*).
❑ **weaker sex** *n* (*usu facetious*) women. **weaker vessel** *n* a woman (from the Bible, 1 Peter 3.7). **weak'-eyed** *adj* having weak eyes or sight. **weak'fish** *n* any of a group of weak-mouthed food-fish of the genus *Cynoscion* (family Sciaenidae), *esp Cynoscion regalis*. **weak'-hand'ed** *adj* powerless. **weak'-head'ed** *adj* having a feeble intellect; easily affected by alcohol. **weak'-heart'ed** *adj* of weak spirit; soft-hearted. **weak'-hinged'** *adj* ill-balanced. **weak interaction** or **force** *n* (*phys*) an interaction between particles complete in about 10^{-10} seconds, such interactions involving neutrinos and antineutrinos and being responsible for radioactive β-ray decay. **weak'-kneed'** *adj* having weak knees or a feeling of faintness; weak-willed, feeble, pusillanimous. **weak'-kneed'ly** *adv*. **weak'-mind'ed** *adj* having feeble intelligence; having, or showing, lack of resolution; too easily convinced or persuaded by others. **weak'-mind'edly** *adv*. **weak'-mind'edness** *n*. **weak moment** *n* a moment when one is over-easily persuaded or tempted. **weak side** or **point** *n* that side or point in which a person is most easily influenced, most liable to temptation or most susceptible to error or attack. **weak'-sight'ed** *adj*. **weak sister** *n* (*inf*; *esp US*) a weak, unreliable member of a group. **weak'-spir'ited** *adj* cowardly. **weak'-will'ed** *adj* lacking strength of will, irresolute.

weal¹ /wēl/ *n* a raised streak left on the skin by a blow with a lash, etc. [Variant of **wale¹**]

weal² /wēl/ *n* the state of being well (*literary* or *archaic*); a sound or prosperous state; welfare; commonwealth (*obs*). [OE *wela*, *weola* wealth, bliss; related to **well¹**]
❑ **weal'-balanced** *adj* (*Shakesp, Measure for Measure* IV.3.96) *perh* kept in a state of just proportion by reasons of state, *perh* for well-balanced. **weals'man** *n* (*Shakesp*) a statesman.
■ **the public**, **general** or **common weal** the wellbeing, interest and prosperity of the country.

weal³ same as **weel¹**.

weald /wēld/ (*poetic*) *n* open country or wooded country. [OE (WSax) *weald* a forest, wold; cf **wold**]
■ **Weald'en** *adj* relating to the Weald; denoting a series of freshwater beds at the base of the Cretaceous, seen in the Weald (*geol*; also *n*).
■ **the Weald** a district, once forested, between the North and South Downs.

wealk'd see **welkt**.

wealth /welth/ *n* valuable possessions of any kind; riches; the condition of being rich; an abundance or plenitude (with *of*); prosperity, wellbeing (*archaic*). [ME *welthe*, from *wele*, from OE *wela* prosperity; see **weal²**]
■ **wealth'ily** *adv*. **wealth'iness** *n*. **wealth'y** *adj* rich; prosperous.
❑ **wealth tax** *n* a tax on personal property and capital.

weamb see **wame**.

wean¹ /wēn/ *vt* to accustom (a baby or young animal) to nourishment other than the mother's milk; to reconcile to doing without any accustomed thing, abstaining from a former habit, etc (with *from*). [OE *wenian* to accustom; ON *venja*, Ger *gewöhnen* to accustom, *entwöhnen* to disuse, wean]
■ **wean'el** *n* (*Spenser*) a weanling. **wean'er** *n* a young animal, *esp* a pig, that has recently been weaned. **wean'ling** *n* a child or animal newly weaned (also *adj*).
❑ **weaning brash** *n* a severe form of diarrhoea that sometimes occurs on weaning.

wean² /wān/ (*Scot*) *n* a child. [wee ane, ie little one]

weapon /wep'n/ *n* any instrument of offence or defence. [OE *wǣpen*; Gothic *wēpna* arms, Ger *Waffe*]

■ **weap'oned** adj. **weaponizā'tion** or **-s-** n. **weap'onize** or **-ise** vt to convert (a nuclear device, pathogen, etc) for use as a weapon. **weap'onless** adj having no weapons. **weap'onry** n weapons collectively; armament.

❑ **weapon of mass destruction** n a nuclear, biological or chemical weapon with the potential to kill large numbers of people. **weapon salve** n a salve supposed to cure a wound by being applied to the weapon that made it. **weap'ons-grade** adj (of fissile material) suitable for use in a nuclear weapon.

weapon-schaw, **weapon-shaw** see **wappenshaw**.

wear¹ /wār/ vt (pat **wore** /wōr/ or **wŏr**/, archaic **ware** /wār/; pap **worn** /wŏrn/ or **wŏrn**/) to be dressed in; to carry on the body; to arrange (one's clothes, etc) in a specified way; to display, show; (of eg the face) to exhibit (an expression, etc); to carry the burden of (one's age, years, experience, etc) eg lightly; (of a ship) to fly (a flag); to consume, waste or damage by use, time or exposure; to make or render by friction or constant use; to exhaust, to weary; to bring gradually (into a frame of mind, etc; old); to introduce (an idea) little by little (into someone's mind; old); to enable to last, endure (Scot) /wēr/; to spend (a period of time; poetic); to traverse (Spenser); to edge, guide or conduct, eg sheep into a fold (Scot); to tolerate, accept or believe (inf). ◆ vi to waste away by use or time; to be reduced or impaired little by little; (of time) to be spent or pass, esp tediously; to last under use; to resist the ravages of age; to stand the test of time; to be in fashion (Shakesp); to pass (into a next stage or phase); to become (obs); to go, move or progress slowly (Scot). ◆ n the act of wearing or state of being worn; reduction or impairment of by use or friction; durability; fitness for wearing; articles worn (usu in combination, as in menswear); fashion. [OE werian to wear; ON verja to clothe, Gothic wasian]

■ **wearabil'ity** n. **wear'able** adj fit to be worn; good for wearing. **wear'er** n. **wear'ing** adj made or designed for wear; exhausting; consuming. ◆ n the process of wasting by attrition or time; the fact of carrying on the body, or displaying, flying, etc; durability; the process of passing; that which is worn, clothes (obs). **wear'ingly** adv.

❑ **wear'ing-apparel** n (old) dress. **wearing course** n the upper layer of a bitumen or asphalt road or pavement. **wear iron** n an iron plate fitted in a mechanism to absorb wear due to friction.

■ **the worse for wear** showing signs of wear, worn; showing signs of exhaustion, intoxication, etc (inf). **wear and tear** or (rare) **tear and wear** damage by wear or use. **wear away** to impair or consume, or be reduced or impaired, by wear; to decay or fade out; to pass off. **wear down** to reduce or impair, or be reduced or impaired, by constant use or friction; to diminish or overcome (eg resistance) gradually by persistence. **wear off** to rub off by friction; to diminish by decay; to pass away by degrees. **wear on** (of time) to pass by, esp tediously. **wear out** to impair by use; to render or become useless through age, use or decay; to exhaust or consume; to harass or tire utterly. **wear thin** to become thin or threadbare through use; (of patience) to diminish with excessive calls on it; (of excuses) to become less convincing through over-use. **wear through** to develop a hole through friction or intensive use. **(win and) wear** to (win and) enjoy possession of (eg a wife; old).

wear² /wār/ (naut) vt and vi (pat and pap **wore**) to alter the course of (a ship) or (of a ship) to alter course by turning the stern to windward in a manoeuvre as opposed to tacking. [Origin uncertain; apparently unconnected with **veer¹**]

wear³ /wēr/ n another spelling of **weir¹**.

wear⁴ or **weir** /wēr/ (Scot) vt to guard; to ward off. [OE werian]

wearability, **wearable**, **wearer** see under **wear¹**.

weariful, **weariless**, **wearily**, **weariness** see under **weary¹**.

wearish /wē'rish/ adj tasteless, savourless, insipid (obs); feeble, withered, shrunk (dialect). [Late ME werische; cf **wersh**]

wearisome see under **weary¹**.

weary¹ /wē'ri/ adj having one's strength or patience exhausted; very tired; causing weariness; tiresome, tedious; puny (dialect). ◆ vt to make weary; to reduce the strength or patience of; to harass. ◆ vi to become weary or impatient; to long (with for; Scot). [OE wērig weary]

■ **wea'ried** adj tired. **wea'riful** adj (old) wearisome. **wea'rifully** adv. **wea'riless** adj (old) unwearying; incessant. **wear'ilessly** adv. **wea'rily** adv. **wea'riness** n. **wea'risome** adj causing weariness; tedious. **wea'risomely** adv. **wea'risomeness** n. **wear'ying** adj. **wear'yingly** adv.

❑ **Weary Willie** n (inf) a tramp or workshy person (old); a person habitually lackadaisical or deficient in energy or spirits.

■ **weary out** (old) to exhaust; to get tediously through (a period of time).

weary² /wē'ri/ (Scot) n a curse, as in weary on you, weary fall you. [**weary¹**, prob with some association with obs wary (OE wiergan) to curse]

weasand /wē'zənd/ (old or dialect) n the gullet; the windpipe; the throat. [OE wǣsand; OSax wāsend, OHGer weisant]

❑ **wea'sand-pipe** n (Spenser).

weasel /wē'zl/ n a small carnivore (Mustela nivalis) with long slender body, furtive and bloodthirsty, eating frogs, birds, mice, etc; any of various related species; a furtive, treacherous or sly person; a small amphibious military vehicle for carrying personnel or supplies. ◆ vi to equivocate; (with out of, on, round, etc) to extricate oneself from or circumvent (an obligation, etc), esp indefensibly (inf). [OE wesle]

■ **wea'seller** or **wea'seler** n. **wea'selly** adj.

❑ **weasel cat** n a civet-like animal of Borneo and Java, the linsang. **weasel coot** n the female or young male of the smew, a sea bird. **wea'sel-faced** adj with a lean sharp face. **weasel words** n pl (inf) words that make a statement evasive or misleading, orig (in sing) a word used illegitimately in conjunction with another word rendering it meaningless or sucking its meaning from it as a weasel sucks out the contents of an egg.

■ **weasel out** (inf) to evade obligation.

weather /wedh'ər/ n atmospheric conditions in terms of heat or cold, wetness, cloudiness, etc; type of atmospheric conditions; vicissitude of fortune; formerly, a storm or adverse weather; the direction in which the wind is blowing (naut); the angle the sail of a windmill makes with the perpendicular to its axis. ◆ vt to affect by exposing to the air; to put (a hawk) out of doors on a perch in fine weather (falconry); to sail to the windward of; to gain or pass (eg a cape); to come safely through (a storm or stormy situation); to shelter from (obs); to set (the sails of a windmill); to slope (a roof, etc; archit). ◆ vi to become discoloured, disintegrated, etc, by exposure; (of a hawk) to be weathered. ◆ adj (naut) toward the wind, windward. [OE weder; ON vedhr, Ger Wetter]

■ **weath'erable** adj. **weath'ered** adj having the surface altered in colour, form, texture or composition by the action of the elements (geol); seasoned by exposure to weather; made slightly sloping so as to throw off water (archit); (of boards or tiles) downward-sloping and overlapped so as to keep water out. **weath'ering** n the action of the elements in altering the form, colour, texture or composition of rocks (geol); seasoning by weather; a slight inclination given to the top of a cornice or moulding to prevent water from lodging on it (archit); the act of passing to windward of a coastal feature, obstacle or other vessel (naut); weather conditions (obs). **weath'erize** or **-ise** vt to make (a fabric) weatherproof. **weath'erliness** n. **weath'erly** adj (naut) making little leeway when close-hauled. **weath'ermost** adj (naut) furthest to windward. **weatherom'eter** n an instrument for determining the weather-resisting properties of paints or other surfaces.

❑ **weather anchor** n the anchor lying to windward. **weath'er-beaten** adj damaged, worn away or seasoned by the weather; (of someone's skin or face) tanned or lined from prolonged exposure. **weath'er-bitten** adj worn or defaced by exposure to the winds. **weath'erboard** n the windward side of a ship; a plank in the porthole, etc of a vessel placed so as to keep off rain, without preventing air from circulating; a sloping board fitted to the bottom of a door, window, etc to exclude rain; a board shaped so as to shed water from a building. ◆ vt to fit with such planks or boards. **weath'erboarding** n thin boards placed overlapping to keep out rain; the exterior covering of a wall or roof. **weath'er-bound** adj detained by bad weather. **weather bow** n the windward side of the bow. **weather box** see **weather house** below. **weather chart** n a weather map. **weath'ercloth** n a protecting tarpaulin on deck. **weath'ercock** n a vane in the form of a cock to show the direction of the wind; someone who changes his or her opinions, allegiance, etc easily and often. ◆ vt to serve as a weathercock for; to supply with a weathercock; (with it) to behave like a weathercock. **weath'er-driven** adj driven by winds or storms. **weather eye** n the eye considered as the means by which one forecasts the weather; an eye watchful for developments, as in keep one's weather eye open. **weath'er-fend** vt (Shakesp) to defend from the weather, to shelter. **weather forecast** n a forecast of the weather based on meteorological observations. **weather forecaster** n. **weather gage** or **gauge** n the position of a ship to the windward of another; advantage of position. **weather gall** (Scot **gaw**) n an imperfect rainbow or other supposed sign of coming weather. **weather glass** n a glass or instrument that indicates the changes of the weather; a barometer. **weath'er-headed** adj (Walter Scott) flighty. **weather helm** n a keeping of the helm somewhat to the weather side when a vessel shows a tendency to come into the wind. **weather house** or **weather box** n a toy house containing two figures, the emergence of one presaging dry weather, and of the other, rain. **weath'erman** or **weath'ergirl** n a person who prepares weather forecasts or delivers such forecasts on radio or television. **weather map** n a map indicating meteorological conditions over a large tract of country. **weather notation** n a system of abbreviation for meteorological phenomena. **weath'erproof** adj able to withstand rough weather. ◆ n weatherproof material or a weatherproof garment. ◆ vt to make weatherproof. **weather prophet** n someone who foretells weather; a device for foretelling the weather. **weather report** *n* loosely, a weather forecast. **weather roll** *n* the lurch of a vessel to windward when in the trough of the sea. **weather satellite** *n* a satellite used for the study of cloud formations and other meteorological conditions. **weather ship** *n* a ship engaged in meteorological work. **weather side** *n* the windward side. **weather sign** *n* a phenomenon indicating change of weather; any prognostic. **weather stain** *n* discoloration produced by exposure. **weather station** *n* a station where phenomena of weather are observed. **weather strip** or **weath'erstripping** *n* a thin piece of some material fixed along the edge of a window or door, to keep out wind and cold. **weather symbol** *n* a conventional sign used to indicate a meteorological phenomenon. **weather vane** *n* a vane showing the direction of the wind. **weather window** *n* a period of time in which the weather is suitable for a particular purpose, eg oil-drilling; any restricted period during which the opportunity should be seized for getting something done. **weath'er-wise** *adj* skilful in foreseeing the changes of the weather; quick to sense what turn events will take. ◆ *adv* with regard to weather conditions. **weath'er-worn** *adj* worn away or damaged by wind, storms, etc.

■ **above the weather** too high in the air to experience the weather conditions on the ground; not, or no longer, under the weather. **keep one's weather eye open** to be alert; to keep a sharp lookout. **keep** or **have the weather of** to be to the windward of; to have the advantage of. **make fair weather** (*Shakesp*) to be conciliatory, to use flattery (with *to* or *with*). **make good** or **bad weather of it** to behave well or badly in a storm (*lit* and *fig*). **make heavy weather of** to find excessive difficulty in. **stress of weather** violent and unfavourable winds. **under the weather** indisposed, seedy; drunk (*inf*). **weather along** to make headway against adverse weather. **weather a point** (*fig*) to gain an advantage or accomplish a purpose against opposition. **weather on** to gain on (another vessel) in a windward direction (*lit* and *fig*). **weather out** to hold out against or ride out (a storm or stormy situation) until the end. **weather the storm** to come safely through a period of difficulty, etc.

weave[1] /wēv/ *vt* (*pat* **wōve** or (*rare*) **weaved**; *pap* **wō'ven**; see also **wove**) to make (cloth, tapestry, basketwork, etc) by crossing threads, strands, strips, etc above and below one another; to interlace (eg threads in a loom to form cloth); to depict (figures, a story, etc) in woven work; to combine, mingle or work together into a whole; to introduce (an ingredient or element) subtly (into something); to construct, fabricate or contrive. ◆ *vi* to practise weaving. ◆ *n* the texture or structure of a woven fabric; a hairstyle in which artificial or human hair is interwoven with a person's own hair. [OE *wefan*; ON *vefa*, Ger *weben*; cognate with Gr *hyphē* a web, and *hyphainein* to weave]

■ **weav'er** *n* someone who weaves; any bird of a passerine family (Ploceidae) resembling the finches, so called from their remarkable woven nests. **weav'ing** *n* the act or art of making cloth or a 'web' by the intersecting of two distinct sets of fibres, threads or yarns, those passing longitudinally from end to end of the web forming the *warp*, those crossing and intersecting the warp at right angles forming the *weft*.

❑ **weaver bird** *n* a weaver or, less commonly, a weaver finch. **weaver finch** *n* any member of a family of small finch-like birds (Estrildidae) which includes the waxbills. **weaver's knot** or **hitch** *n* the sheet bend.

weave[2] /wēv/ *vi* (*pat* and *pap* **weaved**) to move to and fro; to wind in and out; to move back or forward with sinuous movements of the body (*boxing*); to fly a winding course (*aeronautics*). ◆ *vt* to move to and fro or up and down; to make a signal to by waving something. [ME *weve*; of uncertain origin]

■ **weav'ing** *n* and *adj*.

■ **get weaving** (*inf*) to get busy, get on the move.

weazand /wē'zənd/ *n* same as **weasand**.

weazen /wē'zn/ variant of **wizen**.

web /web/ *n* the fine structure of gossamer threads spun by a spider to entrap insects; that which is woven; a whole piece of cloth as woven in the loom; a kind of cloth or weave; a thin metal plate or sheet; (in paper-making) an endless wire mesh working on rollers; a large sheet or roll of paper; the skin between the toes of waterfowl, etc; in birds, the vexillum of a feather; any connective tissue (*anat*); the surface between the ribs of a vaulted roof (*archit*); a narrow connecting section between two stouter parts (*machinery*); (often with *cap*) the World Wide Web; a film over the eye (*obs*); anything like a cloth web in its complication or a spider's web in its flimsiness or power to entangle; a plot, snare, intrigue or fabrication. ◆ *adj* of or relating to the World Wide Web. ◆ *vt* to envelop or to connect with a web. ◆ *vi* to make or weave a web. [OE *webb*; ON *vefr*, Ger *Gewebe*; from root of **weave**[1]]

■ **webbed** *adj* having a web; (of the toes or fingers) partially joined together by a membrane of skin. **webb'ing** *n* a woven strip of hemp, used for belts, etc, for various purposes in upholstery, and as tapes conducting webs of paper in a printing machine; the condition of being palmate or hand-shaped, palmation (*zool*); the webs of webbed hands or feet. **webb'y** *adj*. **webifica'tion** *n*. **web'ify** *vt* (*inf*) to convert (data) into a form that can be published on the World Wide Web; to accommodate to the World Wide Web. **web'-like** *adj*.

❑ **web authoring** *n* the design and creation of pages on the World Wide Web. **web'cam** *n* a small digital video camera attached to a computer that can be used to send visual images across the Internet. **web'cast** *n* an audio or video programme that is broadcast live over the Internet. ◆ *vi* and *vt* to broadcast (a programme) live over the Internet. **web'chat** *n* communication in real time over the Internet. **web design** *n* the design and creation of websites. **web designer** *n*. **web'-fing'ered** *adj*. **web'foot** *n* a foot the toes of which are united with a web or membrane. **web'footed** *adj*. **web'head** *n* (*inf*) an enthusiastic user of the World Wide Web. **web'log** *n* a blog. **web'mail** *n* electronic mail accessed via the World Wide Web. **web'master** *n* a person who creates, manages or maintains a website. **web offset** *n* a method of offset printing using a reel of paper. **web page** *n* an electronic document on the World Wide Web, a component of a website, written in HTML and *usu* including additional scripts or graphics. **web'ring** *n* a set of websites, *usu* with a common theme, each of which can be accessed from another site in the group. **web'site** or **web site** *n* a location on the World Wide Web with content supplied and maintained by a single person or organization. **web spinner** *n* a mainly tropical insect which uses glands on its front legs to spin silk tunnels in which it lives. **web'-toed** *adj*. **web'wheel** *n* a wheel in which the rim, spokes and centre are formed from one single piece of material; a wheel with a web or plate instead of spokes. **web'worm** *n* (*US*) any of a number of caterpillars that spin webs in which they feed or rest. **web'zine** /-zēn/ *n* a journal available only on the World Wide Web.

■ **web and pin** or **pin and web** (*Shakesp*) see under **pin**.

weber /vā'bər or wē'bər/ *n* a derived SI unit, the unit of magnetic flux (symbol **Wb**), such that an electromotive force of one volt is induced in a circuit by a change in flux of one weber per second. [Wilhelm *Weber* (1804–91), German physicist]

webinar /web'i-när/ *n* a seminar conducted via the Internet. [**web** and **seminar**]

webisode /web'i-sōd/ *n* a short episode, *usu* of a TV show, first broadcast on the Internet. [**web** and **episode**]

webliography /web-li-og'rə-fi/ *n* a list of websites relating to a particular subject or person; a list of the websites referred to in writing a book, article, etc. [**web** and **bibliography** (see under **bibli-**)]

webster /web'stər/ (*obs*) *n* a weaver (also (*Scot*) **wab'ster**). [OE *webbestre* a female weaver, from *webban* to weave]

wecht /wehht/ (*Scot*) *n* an instrument for winnowing or for measuring grain. [Perh connected with **weigh**[1]]

Wed. *abbrev*: Wednesday.

wed /wed/ (*Scot* **wad** /wŏd/) *vt* (**wedd'ing**; **wedd'ed** or (*dialect*) **wed**; **wedd'ed** or (*dialect* and *poetic*) **wed**) to marry; to join in marriage; to unite closely; to wager (*obs*). ◆ *vi* to marry. ◆ *n* (*obs*; *Scot* **wad**) a pledge, security. [OE *weddian* to promise, to marry (Ger *wetten* to wager), from *wedd* a pledge; Gothic *wadi*, Ger *Wette* a bet]

■ **wedd'ed** *adj* married; of or relating to marriage; closely joined; persistently devoted. **wedd'ing** *n* marriage; marriage ceremony.

❑ **wedding anniversary** *n* the anniversary of one's wedding day. **wedding band** *n* (chiefly *N Am*) a wedding ring. **wedding bed** *n* the bridal bed. **wedding breakfast** *n* a meal served after a wedding. **wedding cake** *n* a highly decorated cake served at a wedding, and also divided among absent friends. **wedding cards** *n pl* cards announcing a wedding, sent to friends. **wedding day** *n* the day of marriage; its anniversary. **wedding dower** *n* a dowry. **wedding dress** *n* a bride's dress. **wedding favour** *n* a white rosette formerly worn by men at a wedding; a small gift given to guests at a wedding. **wedding finger** *n* the ring finger. **wedding garment** *n* a garment worn at a wedding. **wedding march** *n* music in march time played as the bride's party enters the church and at the close of a marriage ceremony. **wedding ring** *n* a *usu* plain, gold ring given by the groom to the bride at a wedding; a ring of the same or similar type given reciprocally by the bride to the groom. **wedding tackle** see **tackle**.

■ **penny-wedding** see under **penny**. **silver**, **ruby**, **golden** or **diamond wedding** or **wedding anniversary** the celebrations of the 25th, 40th, 50th and 60th anniversaries of a wedding respectively.

we'd /wēd/ a contraction of **we had** or **we would**.

Weddell seal /wed'əl sēl/ *n* a large brown seal of Antarctic waters (first described by James *Weddell*, Scottish navigator, 1787–1834), that winters under the ice.

wedder /wed'ər/ (*obs* or *dialect*, *esp Scot* and *N Eng*) a form of **wether** or **weather**.

wedding see **wed**.

wedeln /vāˈdəln/ (also with *cap*) *n* a style of downhill skiing in which the skis, kept parallel and close together, are swivelled rapidly from side to side. ◆ *n pl* such swivelling movements. ◆ *vi* (also with *cap*) to execute wedeln on a downhill run. [Ger, orig to wag one's tail]

wedge /wej/ *n* a piece of wood or metal, thick at one end and sloping to a thin edge at the other, used in splitting, or fixing tightly, etc; anything shaped more or less like a wedge, eg a formation of troops, the flying formation of geese and other wildfowl, a piece cut from a circular cake, a stroke in cuneiform characters or (*obs*) an ingot of gold or silver; any V-shaped sign used in notation or as a diacritic; an iron-headed golf club with a broad low-angled face, creating much loft; a stroke with such a club; a shoe in which the heel and sole together form a wedge with no gap under the instep (also **wedge-heeled shoe**). ◆ *vt* to force (open) or drive (apart) with, or as if with, a wedge; to thrust in tightly; to crowd closely; to fasten or fix with a wedge or wedges; to cleave with a wedge; to make into a wedge. ◆ *vi* to force one's way like a wedge; to become fixed or jammed by, or as if by, a wedge. [OE *wecg*; ON *veggr*, Ger dialect *weck* a wedge]
■ **wedged** *adj*. **wedge**'**-like** *adj*. **wedge**'**wise** *adv* in the manner of a wedge. **wedg**'**ie** *n* a wedge-heeled shoe (*inf*); a prank in which the victim's underpants are pulled up, causing uncomfortable constriction (*inf*). **wedg**'**ing** *n* a method of joining timbers. **wedg**'**y** *adj*.
❑ **wedge issue** *n* (*esp US politics*) a divisive issue, *esp* an emotive or controversial one. **wedge**'**-shaped** *adj* shaped like a wedge. **wedge**'**-tailed** *adj* having a tail in which the rectrices form the shape of a wedge, the central pair being longest, the outer pair shortest.
■ **drive a wedge between** to cause ill-feeling or division between. **the thin** or **small end of the wedge** a small beginning that is bound to be followed by a large or significant (and *usu* unwelcome) development. **the wedge** or **wooden wedge** formerly, the student lowest on the classical tripos list at Cambridge University (on the analogy of wooden spoon, from *Wedgwood*, a student at Christ's College, whose name was last on the first list, of 1824).

Wedgwood® /wejˈwŭd/ *n* pottery made by Josiah *Wedgwood* (1730–95) and his successors, including a distinctive type with cameo reliefs in white on a coloured ground (also **Wedgwood ware**).
❑ **Wedgwood blue** *n* a greyish-blue colour much used in Wedgwood pottery.

wedlock /wedˈlok/ *n* matrimony; the married state, *esp* in the phrase **born in** (or **out of**) **wedlock** ie legitimate (or illegitimate). [OE *wedlāc*, from *wedd* a pledge, and sfx *-lāc* implying action of some kind]
■ **break wedlock** (*old*) to commit adultery.

Wednesday /wenzˈ or wedˈnz-dā or -di/ *n* the fourth day of the week. [OE *Wōdnes dæg* the day of Woden, or Odin, the chief god]
■ **Wednes**'**days** *adv* on Wednesdays.

Weds. *abbrev* : Wednesday.

wee[1] /wē/ (*Scot*) *adj* little, tiny. ◆ *n* a short distance, a short time. [ME *we*, *wei* a bit, time or space, as in phrase *a little wei*]
❑ **Wee Free** *n* a member of the minority of the Free Church that refused to join with the United Presbyterian Church in 1900.

wee[2] /wē/ or **wee-wee** /wēˈwē/ *n* (*inf*; *esp childish*) the act of urinating; urine. ◆ *vi* (*pat* and *pap* **weed** or **wee**'**-weed**) to urinate. [Origin uncertain]

wee[3] /wē/ *interj* imitating the squeal of a young pig (also *vi* and *n*).

weed[1] /wēd/ *n* any useless plant of small growth; any plant growing where it is not wanted, *esp* amongst cultivated plants; any wild herb (often in combination, as in *bindweed, hogweed, knapweed*); a thick growth of wild herbs; a plant growing in fresh or salt water (*usu* in combination, as in *pondweed, seaweed, waterweed*); anything useless, troublesome or obnoxious; a worthless animal; a weak, ineffectual or unmanly man (*derog*); (often with *the*) tobacco or a cigar or cigarette (*inf*); marijuana (*sl*). ◆ *vt* to clear (a garden, etc) of weeds; to remove, uproot (weeds, etc) (often with *out*); to identify and remove (something or someone inferior, unwanted, etc) from a group or collection (*usu* with *out*). ◆ *vi* to uproot weeds. [OE *wēod* a herb]
■ **weed**'**ed** *adj*. **weed**'**er** *n*. **weed**'**ery** *n* a place full of weeds. **weedicide** /wēˈdi-sīd/ *n* a chemical weedkiller. **weed**'**iness** *n*. **weed**'**ing** *n* the task or process of clearing ground of weeds; what is weeded out. **weed**'**less** *adj* weed-like; full of weeds; lanky, ungainly or weakly in appearance; of insipid character.
❑ **weed**'**-grown** *adj* overgrown with weeds. **weed**'**ing-chisel**, **-forceps**, **-fork**, **-hook**, **-tongs**, etc *n* garden implements of varying forms for getting rid of weeds. **weed**'**killer** *n* a chemical preparation or other substance for killing weeds.

weed[2] /wēd/ *n* a garment, clothing or outfit (*archaic*); armour (*archaic*); (in *pl*) a widow's mourning apparel (also **widow's weeds**). [OE *wǣd*, *wēde* clothing; OHGer *wāt* cloth]
■ **weed**'**y** *adj* clad in widow's mourning.

weed[3] or **weid** /wēd/ (*Scot*) *n* any sudden illness, cold or relapse with febrile symptoms, *esp* in women after childbirth or nursing; a fever in

horses, etc. [From *wedenonfa*, from OE *wēden-* (in combination) mad, and Scot *onfa* **onfall**]

weed[4] see under **wee**[2].

week /wēk/ *n* the space of seven days, *esp* from Sunday to Saturday (inclusive); the working days of the week; (in *pl*) an indefinitely long period. [OE *wice*; Du *week*, Ger *Woche*]
■ **week**'**ly** *adj* coming, happening or done once a week. ◆ *adv* once a week; every week. ◆ *n* a publication appearing once a week.
❑ **week**'**day** *n* any day of the week except Sunday, and now *usu* also excluding Saturday. **week**'**end** (or *-end*'*/*) *n* the non-working period from Friday evening to Sunday evening (a **long weekend** *usu* incorporating Friday or Monday or both, or yet more liberally extended). ◆ *vi* to spend a weekend holiday. **weekend**'**er** *n*. **weekend**'**ing** *n*. **weekend warrior** *n* a member of a reserve force (*milit sl*); someone who is only intermittently active in a sport or pastime (*facetious*). **week**'**night** *n* the evening or night of a weekday.
■ **a prophetic week** (*Bible*) seven years. **a week of Sundays** (*inf*) seven weeks; a long time. **a week on Friday**, **Saturday**, etc the Friday, Saturday, etc after the next one. **a week** (or **two weeks**, etc) **today** one week (or two weeks, etc) from today. **Feast of Weeks** a Jewish festival seven weeks after the Passover (also **Shabuoth**, **Shavuot** or **Pentecost**). **Great Week**, **Holy Week** or **Passion Week** the week preceding Easter Sunday. **in by the week** (*obs*) trapped, caught. **this day week** a week from today. **week about** in alternate periods of seven days. **week in**, **week out** continuously without a break.

weeke /wēk/ (*Spenser*) *n* same as **wick**[1].

weel[1], **weil** or **wiel** (*Scot* and *N Eng*) /wēl/ *n* a whirlpool. [OE *wǣl*]

weel[2] /wēl/ *n* a trap or snare for fish (*dialect*); a bearing resembling this (*heraldry*). [OE *wile-* (in combination), from *wilige*; cf **willy**[1]]

weel[3] /wēl/ *adv* Scots form of **well**[1], as in **weel-faur'd**, **-far'd**, etc, well-favoured.

weeldlesse see under **wield**.

weem /wēm/ (*Scot*) *n* a subterranean dwelling. [Early Gaelic *uaim* cavern]

ween /wēn/ (*archaic* or *obs*) *vt* to think or fancy; to believe; to expect. ◆ *vi* (*Shakesp*) to imagine expectantly. [OE *wēnan*; cognate with *wēn* expectation, hope]

weenie or **weeny** /wēˈni/ (*US inf*) *n* a wiener sausage; a penis; a weak or ineffectual person.

weeny /wēˈni/ (*inf*; *esp childish*) *adj* very small, tiny. [*wee* and *tiny* or *teeny*]

weep /wēp/ *vi* (*pat* and *pap* **wept**) to express grief by shedding tears; to wail or lament; to drip, rain; to ooze; to leak; to exude; to droop or be pendent. ◆ *vt* to lament; to pour forth; to express while, or by, weeping; to exude. ◆ *n* a spell of weeping. [OE *wēpan*; related to *wēp* clamour; Gothic *wōpjan*]
■ **weep**'**er** *n* someone who weeps; a mourning figure carved on a tombstone; a hired mourner; a white border round the sleeve of a mourning dress; a crape hatband; a widow's crape veil; anything drooping or pendent; a weephole. **weep**'**ie** or **weep**'**y** *n* (*inf*) a highly emotional film, play or book. **weep**'**ily** *adv* (*inf*) tearfully. **weep**'**iness** *n*. **weep**'**ing** *n*. ◆ *adj* (of a tree or plant variety) having slender drooping branches. **weep**'**ingly** *adv*. **weep**'**y** *adj* tearful (*inf*); sentimental (*inf*); oozy (*dialect*). ◆ *n* see **weepie** above.
❑ **weep**'**hole** *n* a hole in a wall, etc to allow water to escape from behind it. **weeping ash** *n* a variety of the common European ash, with drooping branches. **weeping birch** *n* a variety of the white birch, with drooping branches. **Weeping Cross** or **weep**'**ing-cross** *n* (a former site of) a wayside cross where penitents might pray; in phrases such as **come home by Weeping Cross** to experience bitter regret, disappointment or failure. **weeping elm** *n* a variety of wych-elm, with drooping branches. **weep**'**ing-ripe** *adj* (*Shakesp*) ripe or ready for tears. **weeping rock** *n* a rock through which water percolates slowly. **weeping spring** *n* a spring from which water escapes slowly. **weeping willow** *n* an ornamental Chinese willow (*Salix babylonica*), with pendent branches.

weet[1] /wēt/ (*dialect* and *Spenser*) *adj*, *vt* and *n* a form of **wet**.

weet[2], **weete**, **weeten**, **weeting** see **wit**[2].

weetingly obsolete form of **wittingly**.

weetless obsolete form of **witless**.

weever /wēˈvər/ *n* a genus of fishes (*Trachinus*), of which two species are British, with sharp dorsal and opercular spines capable of inflicting serious wounds. [Prob OFr *wivre* serpent, weever, from L *vīpera*; cf **wyvern** and **viper**]

weevil /wēˈvl/ *n* a popular name for a large number of beetles (the group Rhynchophora, *esp* the family Curculionidae) with the anterior part of the head prolonged into a beak or proboscis, which, either in the larval or the adult form, damage fruit, nuts, grain, trees, etc; any insect injurious to stored grain, etc. [OE *wifel*]

■ **weev'illed**, **weev'iled**, **weev'illy** or **weev'ily** *adj* infested by weevils.

wee-wee see **wee²**.

wef *abbrev* : with effect from.

weft¹ /*weft*/ *n* the threads woven into and crossing the warp; the thread carried by the shuttle (also **woof** /*woof*/); a web; a film or cloud. ◆ *vi* (*rare*) to form a weft. [OE *weft*, *wefta* ; related to *wefan* ; see **weave¹**]

■ **weft'age** *n* texture.

weft² /*weft*/ (*Spenser*) *n* a waif, a castaway (also **wefte**). [Variant of **waif¹**]

weft³, also **wefte** /*weft*/ (*Spenser*) *pap* of **waive** and *pat* of **waft**.

Wehrmacht /*vār'mahht*/ *n* the German armed forces (1935–45). [Ger, from *Wehr* defence, and *Macht* force]

weid see **weed³**.

weigela /*wī'gi-lə* or *-geľ*/ *n* a plant of a genus (*Weigela*) of deciduous shrubs with large showy pink, purplish or white flowers. [CE von *Weigel* (1748–1831), German botanist]

weigh¹ /*wā*/ *vt* to find out the heaviness of; to be equal to in heaviness (as in *weigh 3 kilos*); to compare or counterbalance on or as if on scales (with *against* or *with*); to raise (a ship's anchor); to apportion or measure a specific weight of; to hold in the hand(s) in order to, or as if to, estimate the weight; to estimate the value of; to ponder in the mind, consider carefully; to consider worthy of notice; to keep evenly outspread (*Milton*). ◆ *vi* to have weight; to be considered of importance; to balance evenly (*Shakesp*); to have value (*Shakesp*); to press heavily (with *on*); to weigh anchor. [OE *wegan* to carry; Ger *wiegen* ; L *vehere* to carry]

■ **weigh'able** *adj* capable of being weighed. **weigh'age** *n* the rate paid for the weighing of goods. **weighed** *adj* experienced; considered, balanced. **weigh'er** *n* an official who weighs articles or tests weights. **weigh'ing** *n*.

□ **weigh'-bauk** *n* (*Scot*) the beam of a balance; (in *pl*) a pair of scales. **weigh'board** see **wayboard** under **way¹**. **weigh'bridge** *n* a machine for weighing vehicles with their loads. **weigh'-house** *n* a public building for weighing goods, ascertaining the tonnage of boats, etc. **weigh-in** see **weigh in** below. **weigh'ing-bottle** *n* (*chem*) a thin-walled cylindrical glass container with a tightly fitting lid, used for accurate weighing of hygroscopic and other materials. **weigh'ing-machine** *n* a machine or apparatus for weighing. **weigh-out** see **weigh out** below.

■ **weigh down** to force down; to depress or oppress; to preponderate over, outweigh. **weigh in** to ascertain one's weight before a boxing match or other sports competition, or after a horse race (**weigh'-in** *n*); to join in a project (*sl*). **weigh into** (*inf*) to attack. **weigh in with** to produce (a new argument, etc) in a discussion. **weigh off** (*sl*) to sentence (a criminal) *esp* to a term of imprisonment. **weigh out** to weigh and dispense in portions accordingly; to ascertain one's weight before a horse race (**weigh'-out** *n*). **weigh to the beam** (*Shakesp*) to outweigh completely. **weigh up** to force up (*lit* and *fig*); to consider carefully and assess the quality of (eg a person) (*inf*). **weigh with** to appear important to, to influence.

weigh² /*wā*/ *n* a variant of **way¹** in the phrase *under way*, through confusion with the phrase *weigh anchor*.

weight¹ /*wāt*/ *n* the heaviness of a thing, *esp* as determined by weighing; quantity as determined in this way; the force with which a body is attracted to the earth, measured by the product of the mass and the acceleration; a mass of metal adjusted to a standard and used for finding weight; a method of estimating, or a unit of, weight; the amount something ought to weigh; a standard amount that a boxer, etc, should weigh; (in *pl*) weightlifting or weight-training; scales (*Spenser*); a heavy object; anything heavy or oppressive; a ponderous mass; pressure; importance; power; impressiveness; preponderance or bulk (eg of evidence); the frequency of an item in a frequency distribution or a number indicating this. ◆ *vt* to make heavier; to attach or add a weight or weights to; to hold down in this way; to add substance or solidity to; to increase the weight of (a fabric) by adding chemicals; to assign a handicap weight to (a horse; also *fig*); to oppress, burden; to give (a law or administrative arrangement) a bias *against* or *in favour of* a certain group, etc; to assign greater value to (one factor) than to another; to attach numbers indicating their relative frequency to (items in a frequency distribution) (*stats*). [OE *wiht*]

■ **weigh'tily** *adv*. **weigh'tiness** *n*. **weight'ing** *n* a weighting allowance. **weight'less** *adj*. **weight'lessly** *adv*. **weight'lessness** *n* the condition of a freely falling body at the beginning of the fall when its inertia exactly balances the gravitational force, or that of a space traveller and his or her unpowered spacecraft in orbit beyond the earth's atmosphere. **weigh'ty** *adj* heavy; important; having great influence; being the fruit of judicious consideration and hence worthy of attention; worrying; severe (*Shakesp, Timon of Athens* III.5.102).

□ **weighted average** *n* (*stats*) the average reached when some factor of special importance relating to the variable is included in the calculation along with the frequency factor. **weighting allowance** *n* a salary differential to balance the higher cost of living in a particular area. **weight'lifter** *n*. **weight'lifting** *n* a sport in which competitors (attempt to) lift and hold above their heads a barbell made increasingly heavy as the competition progresses. **weight of metal** *n* (*rare* or *old*) the total weight of the projectiles thrown at one discharge from a ship's guns. **weight'-train** *vi*. **weight'-training** *n* physical training by means of a series of pulleys, levers, etc with adjustable weights, for building up individual muscle groups. **weight'-watcher** *n* a person, typically female, who is attempting to reduce weight by careful dieting, *esp* one who attends meetings of an association of people similarly engaged. **weight'-watching** *n*.

■ **by, in** or **with weight** (*Shakesp*) fully. **gain** (or **put on**) **weight** to increase one's body weight, get fatter. **lose weight** to decrease one's body weight, get thinner. **throw one's weight about** to over-exercise one's authority; to domineer. **throw one's weight behind** to give one's full support to. **worth one's weight in gold** exceptionally useful or helpful.

weight² /*wāt* or (*Scot*) *wehht*/ *n* same as **wecht**.

weil same as **weel¹**.

Weil's disease /*vīlz di-zēz'*/ *n* a severe type of jaundice caused by a spirochaete carried by the urine of rats. [HA *Weil* (1848–1916), German physician]

Weimar Republic /*vī'mär ri-pub'lik*/ *n* the federal republic in Germany that was founded in 1919 and lasted until 1933, its constitution having been established at *Weimar*.

■ **Weimaraner** /*vī-mə-rä'nər*, *wī-*, *vī'* or *wī'*/ *n* (any one of) a breed of grey short-haired gun dogs, *orig* developed at *Weimar*.

weir¹ or **wear** /*wēr*/ *n* a dam across a river; a fence of stakes set in a stream for catching fish. [OE *wer* an enclosure, related to *werian* to protect; cf Ger *Wehr* a dam, *wehren* to ward]

weir² another spelling of **wear⁴**.

weird /*wērd*/ *adj* unearthly, uncanny; peculiar, odd (*inf*); concerned with or controlling fate (*old*). ◆ *n* (*old* and *Scot*) fate; (with *cap*; in *pl*) the Fates; a witch; one's lot, *esp* if evil; a happening, *esp* uncanny; a tale of fate; a spell or charm. ◆ *vt* (*Scot*) to destine or doom; to hand over to as one's fate; to forewarn. [OE *wyrd* fate; related to *weorthan* to become; Ger *werden*]

■ **weird'ly** *adv*. **weird'ness** *n*. **weird'o** or **weird'ie** *n* (*pl* **weird'os** or **weird'ies**) (*inf*) an eccentric; someone unconventional in dress, etc.

■ **dree one's weird** see under **dree**. **the Weird Sisters** the Fates; applied by some also to the Norns, the Fates of Scandinavian mythology; the witches in Shakespeare's *Macbeth*. **weird out** (*sl*) to (cause to) feel uneasy or confused.

weise see **wise²**.

Weismannism /*vīs'ma-ni-zm*/ *n* the doctrine in biology of August *Weismann* (1834–1914), whose central teaching is that acquired characteristics are not transmitted.

weize see **wise²**.

weka /*we'kə*/ *n* any of the flightless rails of the genus *Ocydromus* or *Gallirallus* of New Zealand. [Maori, imit]

welaway see **wellaway**.

Welch and **welch** /*welsh*/ old forms of **Welsh** and **welsh**.

welcher see under **welsh**.

welcome /*wel'kəm*/ *adj* received with gladness; admitted willingly; causing gladness; free (to); (with *to*) free to take or enjoy (sometimes *ironic*). ◆ *n* the act of welcoming; a kindly reception; a reception. ◆ *vt* to greet; to receive with kindness or pleasure; to accept or undergo gladly. ◆ *interj* expressing pleasure, *esp* to guests on their arrival. [OE *wilcuma*, from *wil-* (*willa* will, pleasure), and *cuma* guest, with later alteration suggesting a connection with **well¹** and **come**, prob under the influence of eg OFr *bien venuz* ; cf ON *velkominn*]

■ **wel'comely** *adv*. **wel'comeness** *n*. **wel'comer** *n*. **wel'coming** *adj*. **wel'comingly** *adv*.

■ **bid a welcome** to receive with professions of kindness. **make someone welcome** to welcome someone, make someone feel welcome. **outstay one's welcome** to stay too long. **wear out one's welcome** to stay too long or visit too often. **you're welcome** it is (or was) no trouble, no thanks are needed.

weld¹ /*weld*/ *vt* to join (two pieces of metal) by fusing, forging or applying pressure, using any of several methods, eg raising the temperature at the joint by means of external heat or (**resistance welding**) of a heavy electric current or (**arc welding**) of an electric arc, or (**cold welding**) using pressure alone; to join closely. ◆ *vi* to undergo welding; to be capable of being welded. ◆ *n* a welded joint. [Same as obs or dialect verb *well*, meaning melt, weld; prob from *pap*]

■ **weldabil'ity** *n.* **weld'able** *adj.* **weld'er** or **weld'or** *n.* **weld'ing** *n* and *adj.* **weld'less** *adj* having no welds. **weld'ment** *n* the action or process of welding; a welded assembly.
❑ **welding rod** *n* filler metal in the form of a rod, *usu* coated with a flux.

weld² /weld/, or (*Scot*) **wald** /wäld/ *n* a scentless species of mignonette, also known as **dyer's rocket**, yielding a yellow dye; the dye itself. [Cf Ger *Wau*]

weld³ /weld/ (*obs* and *dialect*) *vt* a variant of **wield**.

Weldmesh® /weld'mesh/ *n* a type of fencing formed of two sets of parallel lengths of wire welded together at right angles to each other.

welfare /wel'fār/ *n* the state of faring or doing well; freedom from calamity, etc; enjoyment of health, etc; prosperity; financial support given to those in need; welfare work. [**well¹** and **fare**]
■ **wel'farism** *n* the social policies characteristic of a welfare state. **wel'farist** *n* and *adj.* **welfaris'tic** *adj.*
❑ **welfare state** *n* a social system or state in which the government undertakes to ensure the welfare of all who live in it, eg by paying benefits to the unemployed, old-age pensions, etc and by providing other social services. **welfare work** *n* efforts to improve conditions of living for a class, eg the very poor, or a group, eg employees or workers. **welfare worker** *n.*

welk¹ /welk/ (*obs*) *vi* and *vt* to wither or shrivel; to (cause to) wane or decline (also (*Spenser*) **welke**). [ME *welken*; cf Ger *welk* withered]

welk² see under **welkt**.

welkin /wel'kin/ *n* the sky or region of clouds. ♦*adj* (*Shakesp*) sky-blue. [OE *wolcnu*, plural of *wolcen* cloud, air, sky; Ger *Wolke* cloud]

welkt or **wealk'd** /welkt/ *adj* (*Shakesp*) twisted (in some modern editions written **whelk'd**). [**whelk¹**]
■ **welk** *vi* (*Walter Scott*, by inference from *Shakesp*) *appar* to twist about.

well¹ /wel/ *adj* (*compar* **bett'er**; *superl* **best**; *usu* predicative) in good condition; in good health; fortunate; advisable; satisfactory; comfortable. ♦*n* (*Spenser*) good health or fortune. ♦*adv* (*compar* **bett'er**; *superl* **best**) rightly; skilfully; thoroughly; intimately; favourably, successfully; abundantly; with some degree of luxury; with reason or propriety; conveniently; to a considerable extent; clearly; easily; very possibly; used as an intensifier, *esp* as *combining form* (eg (*Shakesp*) 'a well-accomplish'd youth' and (*sl*) 'well safe', ie absolutely reliable, 'well pleased', ie very pleased); so be it (said in assent; *archaic*). ♦*interj* expressing surprise, hesitation, resignation, etc, or introducing resumed narrative. [OE *wel*; cognate with Gothic *waila*, Ger *wohl*; from the root of **will¹**]
■ **well'ness** *n.*
❑ **well-acquaint'ed** *adj* having intimate personal knowledge, familiar (with *with*). **well-adjus'ted** *adj* emotionally and psychologically well-balanced. **well-advised'** *adj* prudent; in one's right mind (*Shakesp*). **well-affec'ted** *adj* well or favourably disposed (with *to* or *towards*); loyal. **well-aimed'** *adj.* **well-appoint'ed** *adj* well-equipped. **well-appoint'edness** *n.* **well-bal'anced** *adj* having the parts properly adjusted for smooth working; sane and sensible. **well-becom'ing** *adj* befitting, appropriate to; proper or suitable. **well-behaved'** *adj* behaving or acting in accordance with propriety or with requirements. **well'being** *n* welfare. **well-beloved** /-luvd/ or -luv'id/ *adj* very dear. **well-beseem'ing** *adj* befitting. **well-beseen'** *adj* (*obs*) showy in appearance. **well-born'** *adj* born of a good family, not of humble birth. **well-breathed** /-brēdhd/ or -bretht/ *adj* having strong lungs; exercised; not out of breath. **well-bred'** *adj* having polite manners and good breeding; of good stock. **well-built'** *adj* (of a building, a person, a garment, etc) of strong or well-proportioned make or form. **well-cho'sen** *adj* (now *esp* of words in a speech) carefully assembled, felicitously chosen. **well-condi'tioned** *adj* in good condition. **well-conduct'ed** *adj* properly managed; acting properly. **well-connec'ted** *adj* having friends or relatives in positions of importance or in the upper social strata. **well-cov'ered** *adj* plump. **well-defined'** *adj* clearly and precisely determined. **well-derived'** *adj* (*Shakesp*) of good stock or antecedents. **well-deserved'** *adj* properly merited or earned; condign. **well-desired'** *adj* (*Shakesp*) much sought after. **well-devel'oped** *adj* having developed to an advanced, elaborate, good, desirable, etc state. **well-direct'ed** *adj* skilfully aimed. **well-disposed'** *adj* well-placed or well arranged; inclined to be friendly (with *to* or *towards*); favourable; healthy (*obs*). **well'-doer** *n* someone who lives honourably or does good; someone who thrives and is prosperous (*dialect*). **well'-doing** *n* and *adj.* **well-done'** *adj* (of food, *esp* meat) thoroughly cooked (see also **well done** below). **well-dressed'** *adj* wearing stylish clothes. **well-earned'** *adj* thoroughly deserved. **well-ed'ucated** *adj* having had a good education. **well-endowed'** *adj* (*inf*, *facetious*) (of a man) having a large penis; (of a woman) having large breasts. **well-en'tered** *adj* (*Shakesp*) instructed, initiated. **well-famed'** *adj* (*Shakesp*) very famous. **well-fa'voured** or (*Scot*) **weel-faird** /wēl-färd'/, **weel-faur'd**, **weel-far'd** /-förd'/, **weel-far't** or **weel-faurt'**

/-fört/ *adj* good-looking. **well-fed'** *adj* plump; given nutritious food. **well-formed'** *adj* shapely, well-proportioned; correct according to the established rules of grammar (*linguistics*); corresponding or complying to set rules in a logical system. **well-found'** *adj* adequately provided, fully equipped; commendable (*obs*). **well-found'ed** *adj* built on secure foundations; based on solid evidence or sound reasoning. **well-giv'en** *adj* (*obs*) well-disposed. **well-got'ten** *adj* obtained honestly. **well-graced'** *adj* (*Shakesp*) popular. **well-groomed'** *adj* neat and smart in appearance. **well-ground'ed** *adj* thoroughly instructed in the fundamentals; firmly founded. **well-heeled'** *adj* prosperous, rich. **well-hung'** *adj* hung skilfully; (of meat) hung long enough to mature; (of a man) having sizeable genitals (*inf*). **well-informed'** *adj* having sound and sufficient information on a particular subject; full of varied information. **well-inten'tioned** *adj* having, or arising from, good intentions or purpose. **well-judged'** *adj* correctly calculated, judicious. **well-judg'ing** *adj.* **well-kept'** *adj* carefully looked after, kept in good condition or order. **well-knit'** *adj* (of a person) strongly built; closely and firmly connected, compact. **well-known'** *adj* fully known; celebrated; notorious. **well-li'king** *adj* (*archaic*) in good condition, plump (see also **liking** under **like²**). ♦*n* (*obs*) approbation, fondness. **well-lined'** *adj* with a good lining; full of money. **well-look'ing** *adj* good-looking. **well-made'** *adj* cleverly and competently made, produced, constructed, etc; (of a person or animal) strongly built; well-proportioned. **well-mann'ered** *adj* polite. **well-marked'** *adj* obvious, decided. **well-mean'ing** *adj* well-intentioned (though often unwise). **well-meant'** *adj* rightly or kindly intended (if often misguided). **well-mind'ed** *adj* favourably inclined; well-disposed. **well'-nigh** *adv* nearly, almost. **well-off'** *adj* moderately wealthy (see also **well off** below). **well-oiled'** *adj* drunk (*facetious*); smoothly mechanical from much practice. **well-ord'ered** *adj* correctly governed; properly arranged. **well-padd'ed** *adj* (*inf*) plump. **well-placed'** *adj* in a good position (for some purpose); in a position senior enough or intimate enough to gain information, etc. **well-pleas'ing** *adj* (*old*) acceptable. **well-plight'ed** *adj* folded, plaited or pleated well (see **plight¹**). **well-preserved'** *adj* in good condition, not decayed; looking youthful or younger than one's age. **well-propor'tioned** *adj* having correct or pleasing proportions. **well-read'** /-red'/ *adj* having read widely, well-informed on literature. **well-reg'ulated** *adj* well-ordered. **well-respect'ed** *adj* highly esteemed; given due consideration (*Shakesp, 1 Henry IV* IV.3.10). **well-round'ed** *adj* suitably curved; symmetrical; well constructed and complete; satisfactorily developed in all essentials. **well-seen'** *adj* (*archaic*) experienced, skilful. **well-set'** *adj* properly arranged, or well-placed; properly put together; firmly fixed; strongly built. **well-set-up'** *adj* (*inf*; of a person) well-built, shapely. **well-spent'** *adj* spent usefully or profitably. **well-spo'ken** *adj* ready, courteous, educated or refined in speech; spoken well or fittingly. **well-stacked'** *adj* (*inf*; of a woman) having large breasts (see also **stack¹**). **well-tem'pered** *adj* good-tempered; having a good bodily or mental constitution (*obs*); (of steel, mortar, etc) tempered satisfactorily; tuned in equal temperament (*music*). **well-thewed'** *adj* (*obs*) well-mannered, of good disposition; abounding in moral wisdom. **well-thought'-of** *adj* esteemed. **well-thought-out'** *adj* reasoned soundly and arranged with skill. **well-thumbed'** *adj* (of a book) showing marks of much handling or repeated use. **well-tim'bered** *adj* strongly built of wood; well-built; abounding in growing timber. **well-timed'** *adj* opportune, timely, judicious; keeping regular time; done at the right moment. **well-to-do'** or (*Scot* and *Shakesp*) **well-to-live'** *adj* prosperous, well-off. **well-travelled'** *adj* (of a person) having made many journeys; (of a route) much frequented. **well-tried'** *adj* tried often before, with satisfactory results. **well-trodd'en** *adj* frequently followed or walked along, much used or frequented. **well-turned'** *adj* accurately rounded; shapely; felicitously expressed. **well-uphol'stered** *adj* (*facetious*; of a person) plump, fat. **well-warr'anted** *adj* thoroughly justified. **well'-willer** *n* a well-wisher. **well'-wish** *n* (*rare*) an expression of good wishes. **well'-wished** *adj* (*Shakesp*) being the object of good wishes. **well'-wisher** *n* someone who is concerned for one's welfare. **well'-wishing** *adj* and *n.* **well woman** *n* a woman attending, and pronounced fit at, a **well-woman clinic**, set up to check women for gynaecological disorders and advise them on health matters. **well-won'** *adj* gained honestly or by hard endeavour. **well-worked-out'** *adj* thoroughly or logically planned or developed. **well-worn'** *adj* much worn; trite; becomingly worn (*rare*).

■ **all very well** an ironic phrase used to introduce an objection to what has gone before. **as well** in addition; also; equally satisfactorily. **as well as** in addition to; no less than. **be as well** (or **just as well**) to to be sensible to (do something). **do well** to prosper; to be wise (to do something). **just as well** fortunate, lucky. **leave** (or **let**) **well alone** not to interfere in a situation that can be tolerated as it is. **mean well** to have good intentions. **very well** a phrase signifying assent, sometimes ironic. **well and good** a phrase signifying acceptance of facts or a situation. **well and truly** completely, thoroughly. **well away** progressing rapidly; far away; drunk (*sl*). **well done** an expression of praise to someone who has accomplished something. **well enough** in a moderate but sufficient degree. **well in** (*inf*) on good or friendly terms (with *with*); prosperous (*Aust*). **well met** see under **meet¹**. **well now** or **well then** phrases used to preface questions, conclusions, comments, or requests for such, or other remarks. **well off** in satisfactory circumstances; moderately wealthy. **well out of** (*inf*) fortunate to be free of (something). **well up in** (*inf*) well versed in, well-acquainted with, knowledgeable on the subject of. **well, well** an expression of surprise. **wish someone well** to wish someone success or good fortune; to bear someone no ill will.

well² /wel/ *n* a lined shaft sunk in the earth from which a supply of water, oil, etc is obtained; a spring; a mineral spring; a source; an enclosure in a ship's hold round the pumps; a cockpit (*naut*); the vertical opening enclosed between the outer ends of the flights in a winding stair; a lift-shaft; a deep vertical space open to the sky within a block of tall buildings, admitting light and air; the open space in the middle of a courtroom; a cavity; a vessel serving as a reservoir, as in *inkwell*; an eddy. ◆ *vi* to issue forth, as water does from the earth (with *out*, *forth* or *up*). ◆ *vt* (*old*) to pour forth (with *out*, *forth* or *up*). [OE *wella*; cf *weallan* to boil, ON *vella* to boil]
■ **well'ing** *n* an outpouring.
□ **well boat** or **well smack** *n* a fishing-boat having a well for holding live fish. **well'-borer** *n* a person or machine employed in well-boring. **well'-boring** *n* sinking wells by drilling through rock. **well curb** *n* the stone ring built round the mouth of a well. **well deck** *n* a part of the upper deck of a ship enclosed fore and aft by the bulkheads supporting higher decks. **well drain** *n* a pit drawing the water from wet land. **well dressing** *n* the festal decoration of wells and springs, as in Derbyshire on Ascension Day, etc. **well'head** *n* the source of a spring; a fountainhead, origin or source; a spring in a marsh (*Scot*); the top of a well, or a structure built over it. **well hole** *n* a hole for a well of any kind; the shaft of a well; a shaft for machinery; the vertical opening up through the middle of a winding stair, enclosed by the ends of the flights. **well'house** or **well room** *n* a room built over a well. **well'-sinker** *n* someone employed in digging wells. **well'-sinking** *n*. **well'spring** *n* a fountain; any rich or bountiful source.
■ **the wells** any place where mineral wells are situated. **well over** to overflow.

we'll /wēl/ a contraction of **we will** or **we shall**.

welladay /wel'ə-dā/ (*archaic*) *interj* alas. [Alteration of **wellaway**]

wellanear /wel-ə-nēr'/ (*archaic*) *interj* alas. [Variation on **wellaway**]

wellaway or **welaway** /wel-ə-wā'/ (*archaic*) *interj* alas. [OE *weg la weg*, *wei la wei*, replacing *wa la wa* from *wa woe*]

wellie see **welly¹**.

wellington /wel'ing-tən/ or **wellington boot** /boot/ *n* a loose-fitting rubber or plastic waterproof boot covering the calf; a riding boot covering the knee in front but cut away behind (*hist*); a shorter closely-fitting boot, worn under the trousers (**half'-wellington**) (*hist*). [From boots worn by the Duke of *Wellington* (1769–1852)]

Wellingtonia /wel-ing-tō'ni-ə/ *n* a popular name for the genus *Sequoia* of giant conifers; (*without cap*) a tree of the genus. [Named after the Duke of *Wellington* (1769–1852)]

Wellsian /wel'zi-ən/ *adj* of, relating to or characteristic of HG *Wells* (1866–1946), historian and writer of stories and novels with scientific or social interest.

welly¹ or **wellie** /wel'i/ (*inf*) *n* a wellington of the loose rubber or plastic kind (also **well'y-boot** or **well'ie-boot**); (also **green welly**; often in *pl* and with *caps*) a student or other (young) person, typically of the landed class, whose noticeably preferred footwear is wellingtons, *esp* of a sturdy green variety, suggesting recent arrival from or imminent departure for a rural property (*orig university sl*; *derog*).
■ **give it** (**some**) **welly** or **wellie** (*sl*) to put one's foot down heavily on the accelerator; to put all one's efforts and energy into what one is doing.

welly² /wel'i/ (*dialect*) *adv* a corrupted form of **well-nigh**.

wels /wels/ *n* (*pl* **wels**) another name for the **sheatfish**. [Ger]

Welsh or (*obs*) **Welch** /welsh/ *adj* relating to *Wales* or its inhabitants. ◆ *n pl* the inhabitants of Wales. ◆ *n sing* their P-Celtic or Brythonic language, a development of the ancient British language, related to Cornish and Breton. [OE (Anglian and Kentish) *welisc*, from *wealh* foreigner, the Anglo-Saxons' word for Briton, Welshman, foreigner; from L *Volcae*, *orig* a Gaulish tribe]
■ **Welsh'ness** *n*.
□ **Welsh aunt** or **uncle** *n* (*dialect*) a first cousin of one's father or mother. **Welsh dresser** *n* a dresser *usu* with open shelves above cupboards and drawers. **Welsh harp** *n* a large harp with three rows of strings, two tuned in unison and in the diatonic scale, the third in the sharps and flats of the chromatic. **Welsh hook** *n* an old weapon, a billhook or something similar. **Welsh'man** or **Welsh'woman** *n* a native of Wales. **Welsh onion** *n* the cibol. **Welsh poppy** *n* a

European poppy (*Meconopsis cambrica*) with long slender stems and yellow flowers. **Welsh rabbit** or **Welsh rarebit** see **rarebit** under **rare¹**. **Welsh terrier** *n* a terrier with a rough black-and-tan coat.

welsh or (*obs*) **welch** /welsh/ *vi* to run off from a racecourse without settling or paying one's bets (*horse-racing*); (with *on*) to fail to pay (one's debts, *esp* in gambling); (with *on*) to avoid fulfilling (an obligation) or fail to keep one's promise to (a person). ◆ *vt* to cheat in such a way. [Of uncertain origin]
■ **welsh'er** or **welch'er** *n*.

Welsummer /wel'sum-ər/ *n* a breed of large poultry with golden plumage, prolific egg-layers. [After the Dutch village of *Welsum*, where it was first bred]

Welt /velt/ (*Ger*) *n* world.
□ **Weltanschauung** /velt'an-show-ūng/ *n* outlook on the world, world philosophy. **Weltgeist** /velt'gīst/ *n* the world spirit. **Weltpolitik** /velt'pol-i-tēk/ *n* world politics; the policy of taking a forceful part in international affairs. **Weltschmerz** /velt'shmerts/ *n* world sorrow; sympathy with universal misery; sadness for the human lot; world-weariness; thoroughgoing pessimism. **Weltstadt** /velt'shtat/ *n* a cosmopolitan city.

welt¹ /welt/ *n* a band, strip or ribbed border fastened to an edge to give strength or for ornament; a narrow strip of leather used in one method of sewing the upper to the sole of a shoe; a weal; a lash, blow. ◆ *vt* to fit with a welt; to lash, beat. [Origin obscure]

welt² /welt/ *vt* and *vi* to wither, dry. [Perh **welk¹**]

welter /wel'tər/ *vi* to roll or tumble about (*rare* or *dialect*); to wallow about in dirt or moral degradation, etc (*rare*); to be or lie soaked, eg in blood (*poetic*); to be sunk (with *in*); to roll or toss about in the waves; (of the sea) to roll or surge (*poetic*). ◆ *vt* (*rare*) to make (one's way) in a weltering manner. ◆ *n* a state of turmoil, agitation or confusion; a confused mass; a surging mass. [MDu *welteren*; cf OE *gewæltan* to roll]
■ **wel'tering** *adj*.

welterweight /wel'tər-wāt/ *n* a weight category, applied *esp* in boxing; a sportsperson of the specified weight for the category (eg in professional boxing above lightweight, **junior welterweight** or **super lightweight** (maximum 63.5kg/140lb), **welterweight** (maximum 67kg/147lb), and **super welterweight**, **light middleweight** or **junior middleweight** (maximum 70kg/154lb)); an unusually heavy weight, carried mostly in steeplechases and hurdle races. [Origin obscure]
□ **welter race** *n* a race in which such weights are carried. **welter stakes** *n pl* the stakes in a welter race.

Weltgeist...to...Weltstadt see under **Welt**.

welwitschia /wel-wich'i-ə/ *n* a plant of a SW African genus (*Welwitschia*) of one species, belonging to the Gnetaceae, with one pair of leaves that grow indefinitely. [F *Welwitsch* (1806–72), Austrian traveller]

wem or **wemb** see **wame**.

Wemyss ware /wēmz wār/ *n* a type of pottery originally produced between 1882 and 1930 in Kirkcaldy, Fife, named after the *Wemyss* family of Wemyss Castle, and characterized by lively colourful painted decoration, *esp* representing fruit and flowers.

wen¹ /wen/ *n* a sebaceous cyst, *esp* on the scalp; an enormous congested city as in *the great wen*, ie London. [OE *wen(n)* a swelling or a wart; Du *wen*; origin obscure]
■ **wenn'ish** or **wenn'y** *adj* wen-like.

wen² /wen/ *n* a former name for the runic and Old English letter wyn (qv).

wench /wench or wensh/ (*archaic* or *facetious*) *n* a girl or young woman; a servant girl; a child (*obs*); a mistress (*obs*); a prostitute, whore (*obs*). ◆ *vi* to frequent the company of prostitutes; to associate with girls (*Scot* **winch**); to go courting (*dialect*). [OE *wencel* a child]
■ **wench'er** *n* (*old*) a man who associates with prostitutes.

Wend /wend/ *n* a member of a branch of the Slavs that once occupied the north and east of Germany; a member of the Slavic population of Lusatia (part of Brandenburg, Saxony and Silesia) who still speak the Wendish language. [Ger *Wende*; origin obscure]
■ **Wend'ic** or **Wend'ish** *adj*. ◆ *n* the Wendish language.

wend /wend/ *vt* (*pat* and *pap* **wend'ed** or (*obs*) **went**, now used as *pat* of **go**) to turn (*obs*); to turn to the opposite tack (*naut*); to alter the course of (a person, or a person's thoughts; *obs*); (*reflexive*) to betake (oneself; *obs*); to change (*obs*). ◆ *vi* to turn (*obs*); to change (*obs*); to depart (*archaic*); to make one's way (*archaic*); to move, flow, wander (*archaic*). [OE *wendan*, a common Gmc verb]
■ **wend one's way** to make one's way, follow the road, *esp* in a leisurely fashion.

wendigo see **windigo**.

Wendy House® /wen'di hows/ *n* a structure of cloth or plastic sheeting, decorated to simulate a little house, stretched over a rigid frame, erected *usu* indoors for children to play in. [From the house built for *Wendy* in JM Barrie's *Peter Pan*]

Wenlock /wen'lok/ (*geol*) *adj* denoting a group or series of rocks of the Upper Silurian period consisting of limestone and shale and largely developed in the neighbourhood of *Wenlock* in Shropshire.

wennish and **wenny** see under **wen**[1].

Wensleydale /wenz'li-dāl/ *n* a breed of long-woolled sheep; a white crumbly variety of cheese. [*Wensleydale* in N Yorkshire]

went /went/ *orig pat* of **wend**, but now used as *pat* of **go**. *n* (*Spenser*) a path; a journey; a way; a course.

wentletrap /wen'tl-trap/ *n* any member of a genus (*Scala* or *Clathrus*) of gastropod molluscs, having a spiral shell with many deep whorls, crossed by elevated ribs. [Du *wenteltrap* (Ger *Wendeltreppe*) a winding staircase, a spiral shell]

wept /wept/ *pat* and *pap* of **weep**.

were /wûr/ the *pl* of **was**, used as *pat* (*pl*) and *past subjunctive* (*sing* and *pl*) of **be**. [OE *wǣron*, subjunctive *wǣre*; Ger *waren*, *wäre*]

we're /wēr/ contracted form of **we are**.

weren't /wûrnt/ contracted form of **were not**.

werewolf /wĕr'wŭlf or wār'-/ or **werwolf** /wûr'wŭlf/ *n* (*pl* **-wolves**) a person supposed to be able to change for a time into a wolf (*Scot* **war'wolf**); a member of an underground Nazi organization (also *adj*). [OE *werwulf*, from *wer* man, and *wulf* wolf]
■ **were'wolfish** or **wer'wolfish** *adj*. **were'wolfism** and **were'wolfery** *n* lycanthropy.

wergild /wûr'gild/ or **weregild** /wĕr'gild/ (*hist*) *n* among Teutonic peoples, a fine by which homicide and other heinous crimes against the person were expiated. [OE *wergield*, from *wer* man, and *gield* tribute, compensation, from *gieldan* to pay]

Wernerian /vûr-nē'ri-ən/ *adj* relating or according to the opinions or system of AG *Werner* (1750–1817), who attributed all geological phenomena to the action of water; Neptunian. ◆ *n* an upholder of Werner's theories.
■ **wer'nerite** *n* scapolite.

Wernicke's encephalopathy /vûr'ni-kəz (or wûr'ni-kəz) en-sef-ə-lop'ə-thi/ *n* a degenerative brain disease of haemorrhagic type caused by a deficiency of thiamine (vitamin B_1), in many cases the result of chronic alcoholism, characterized by paralysis of the eye muscles, double vision, nystagmus and impaired muscular control, frequently in association with Korsakoff's psychosis (qv). [Karl *Wernicke* (1848–1905), German neuropsychiatrist]

wersh /wersh or wûrsh/ (*Scot*) *adj* tasteless, insipid, unsalted; sour or bitter in taste; sickly, feeble; (of weather) raw. [**wearish**]

wert /wûrt/ used (*archaic* or *dialect*) as the *2nd pers sing* of the *past indicative* (for **wast**[1]) and *subjunctive* of **be**. [**were** and sfx -t]

Wertherian /vûr-tē'ri-ən/ *adj* relating to or resembling the character of *Werther* in Goethe's romance *The Sorrows of Young Werther*, ie morbidly sentimental.
■ **Wer'therism** *n*.

werwolf see **werewolf**.

Wesak same as **Vesak**.

wesand /wē'zənd/ *n* (*Spenser*) same as **weasand**.

Wesleyan /wez'li-ən or wes'li-ən/ *adj* relating to John *Wesley* (1703–91), or to Methodism, the name given to his system of religious doctrine and church organization, or to the Protestant denomination founded by him. ◆ *n* an adherent of Wesley or Methodism.
■ **Wes'leyanism** *n* Arminian Methodism, the doctrinal stance of the Wesleyan Methodists; their system of church organization.

Wessi /wes'i or ves'i/ (*inf*) *n* (*pl* **Wessis**) a citizen of the German Federal Republic (West Germany) before reunification in 1990. See also **Ossi**. [Ger abbrev of *Westdeutsch* West German]

west /west/ *n* the part of the sky where the sun sets at the equinoxes; one of the four cardinal points of the compass; (often with *cap* and *the*) the west part of the Earth or of a region, country or town; (with *cap* and *the*) the western countries of the world as distinct from the East or Orient; (with *cap* and *the*) in mid-to-late 20c politics, the countries of Europe and N America not under communist rule; (with *cap* and *the*) the western part of the USA, used relatively and vaguely, but *usu* the part to the west of the Appalachian Mountains, or to the west of the Mississippi or the Rocky Mountains (see also **Middle West** under **middle** and **Far West** under **far**); (with *cap*) the western part of the Roman Empire or Holy Roman Empire (*hist*); (*usu* with *cap*) in bridge, the player or position occupying the place designated 'west' on the table; the west wind (*poetic*). ◆ *adj* situated towards the west; forming the part that is towards the west; (of wind) blowing from the west. ◆ *adv* towards the west. ◆ *vi* (*archaic*) to move or turn west. [OE; cf L *vesper*]
■ **west'er** *n* a west wind or gale. ◆ *vi* to move or veer towards the west. **west'ering** *n* and *adj*. **west'erliness** *n*. **west'erly** *adj* situated in

the west; towards the west; (*esp* of the wind) coming from the west. ◆ *adv* on the west; towards the west; from the west. ◆ *n* a west wind. **west'ern** or (*obs* except in place names) **west'er** *adj* situated in the west or further to the west; coming from the west; towards the west; connected with the west; living in the west; (with *cap*) of, from or relating to the West. ◆ *n* a westerner; a film or novel set in the western United States, *esp* the former Wild West. **west'erner** *n* (sometimes with *cap*) a native or inhabitant of the west. **west'ernism** *n* a form of expression or characteristic peculiar to the west. **westerniza'tion** or **-s-** *n*. **west'ernize** or **-ise** *vt* to give a western character to. ◆ *vt* and *vi* to make or become like the people of Europe and America in customs, or like their institutions, practices or ideas. **west'ernmost**, **west'most** or (*obs*) **west'ermost** *adj* situated furthest west. **west'ing** *n* space or distance westward; departure westward; direction or course towards the west. **west'ward** *adv* towards the west (also *adj* and *n*). **west'wardly** *adv* and *adj*. **west'wards** *adv* westward.
□ **west'about** *adv* towards the west. **West Bank** *n* a territory to the west of the river Jordan and the Dead Sea, annexed by Israel from Jordan in 1967, a degree of autonomy being given to the majority Palestinian population in the 1990s. **West-Bank'er** *n* an inhabitant of the West Bank. **west'bound** *adj* travelling in a westward direction. **west'-by-north'** *n* the direction midway between west and west-north-west. **west'-by-south'** *n* the direction midway between west and west-south-west. **West Country** *n* the south-western part of England. **West-country whipping** *n* (*naut*) a rope-whipping method where a half knot is made alternately on each side, finished off with a reef knot. **West End** *n* the fashionable quarter in the west of London; a similar district in other large towns. **western blotting** *n* (*immunol*) see **immunoblot** under **immune**. **Western Church** *n* the Latin Church, having its doctrine and ritual from Rome, as distinguished from the Eastern or Greek Church. **Western Empire** *n* the western division of the later Roman Empire. **Western European Time** *n* one of the standard times used in Europe, being the same as Greenwich Mean Time (*abbrev* **WET**). **Western Front** *n* the belt of land, running SE from the coast of Belgium through Rheims to Verdun, which lay between the German and Allied Forces in World War I. **western hemisphere** *n* (also with *caps*) the hemisphere of the world containing the Americas. **western hemlock** *n* a large evergreen conifer of NW America (*Tsuga heterophylla*) with drooping foliage. **Western Isles** *n pl* the Hebrides. **western roll** *n* (*athletics*) a style of high-jumping, taking off from the inside foot and clearing the bar face downwards. **western saddle** *n* (sometimes with *cap*) a stock saddle as used by cowboys, with a high pommel behind, and wide leather leg-protecting flaps. **western swing** *n* a style of country music combined with elements of jazz, popular in the 1930s. **Western Wall** *n* the Wailing Wall (qv under **wail**). **West Highland** (**white**) **terrier** *n* a breed of small white terrier with a short stiff coat and small pointed ears. **West Indian**, **West Indies** see under **Indian**. **west'land** *n* the west (also *adj*). **west'lander** *n*. **West Lothian question** *n* in political devolution, the issue raised by the fact that a region with its own assembly might also have a voice in a national parliament on matters concerning other areas, whereas other regions have a voice only in the national parliament. **West Nile virus** *n* an arthropod-borne virus which is a cause of severe meningitis and encephalitis in humans. **west'-north-west'** *n* the direction midway between west and north-west (also *adj* and *adv*). **West Saxon** *n* a southern dialect of Old English, the chief literary dialect before the Norman Conquest. **West Side** *n* the western part of the city of New York. **west'-south-west'** *n* the direction midway between west and south-west (also *adj* and *adv*).
■ **go west** to go to the western states or western frontier; to go to America; to die (with reference to the setting sun, the Islands of the Blest, or Tyburn), or to be destroyed or completely dissipated. **westward ho!** to the west!, an old cry of London watermen travelling westwards.

Westie /wes'ti/ *n* a West Highland terrier.

westlin /wes'lin or west'lin/ (*Scot*) *adj* western.
■ **west'lins** *adv* to or in the west.

Westminster /west'min-stər/ *n* the British Parliament, from the London borough where the Houses of Parliament are situated; Westminster Hall, a court of justice; Westminster School, or a past or present pupil of it. ◆ *adj* denoting the presbyterian-dominated assembly of clerics and laymen convened by the English Long Parliament of 1643 to arrange a religious settlement to replace the Church of England, and the *Confession of Faith*, a statement of Calvinistic principles adopted by it.

Westphalian /west-fā'li-ən/ *adj* relating to *Westphalia*, a duchy, a kingdom, a province of Prussia and, since 1946, part of the German land of Nordrhein-Westfalen. ◆ *n* a native of Westphalia.

WET *abbrev* : Western European Time.

■ words derived from main entry word; □ compound words; ■ idioms and phrasal verbs

wet /wet/ adj (**wett'er**; **wett'est**) containing, soaked with or covered with water or other liquid; (of paint, washing, etc) not yet dried; rainy; bringing or foreboding moisture; suitable for rainy or watery conditions; tearful; grown in damp soil; (of a method) using liquid (*chem*, etc); (of natural gas) containing large amounts of liquid constituents; given to drinking, or tipsy (*sl*); allowing the sale of alcoholic drink; ineffectual or feeble (*inf*); crazily mistaken (*US sl*); in politics, moderately conservative (*derog*). ◆ n water, moisture, wetness; the rain; an act of wetting; a weak, ineffectual, wavering person (*inf*); a dram, a debauch; in politics, a moderate conservative (*derog*); a racing-car tyre designed for use in wet conditions. ◆ vt (**wett'ing**; **wet** or **wett'ed**) to make wet; to soak with water; to urinate, *esp* involuntarily, on or in; (*reflexive*) to make (oneself) wet by urinating inadvertently; to make (tea) by pouring water on the leaves (*dialect*); to celebrate by drinking (*sl*). [OE *wǣt* (noun and adj), *wǣtan* (verb); the short vowel is from the ME pat and pap of the verb] ■ **wet'ly** adv. **wet'ness** n. **wett'able** adj. **wett'ish** adj somewhat wet. □ **wet-and-dry-bulb thermometer** n a hygrometer consisting of two thermometers, one with a dry bulb, the other with the bulb kept moist. **wet-and-dry paper** n a stiff paper coated with powdered silicon carbide, like a fine sandpaper, used either wet or dry for smoothing surfaces. **wet assay** n the use of the processes of solution, flotation, or other liquid means to determine a given constituent in ores, metallurgical residues and alloys. **wet'back** n (*US inf*) someone illegally entering the USA from Mexico by wading or swimming the Rio Grande; an illegal immigrant generally. **wet bar** n (*US*) a bar from which to serve alcoholic drinks in a private house or hotel suite, equipped with a sink and running water. **wet bike** n a vehicle like a motorbike that travels over water on skis. **wet blanket** n (*inf*) a dismal person inclined to damp other peoples' spirits, a killjoy. **wet bob** n at Eton, a boy who goes in for rowing during the summer term (cf **dry bob**). **wet cell** n an electric cell with a liquid electrolyte. **wet dock** n a dock maintaining a level nearly uniform with that of high water. **wet dream** n an erotic dream resulting in ejaculation of semen. **wet fish** n fresh fish, as contrasted with frozen or dried fish. **wet'-fly** adj (*angling*) with the fly under water. **wet'land** n (also in *pl*) marshy land. **wet lease** n the leasing of aircraft complete with crew. **wet'-lease** vt. **wet'-look** adj made of a glossy material, *usu* PVC, which gives the appearance of being wet; (of hair) with the appearance of being wet from the application of a certain type of gel. **wet meter** n a gas meter in which the gas to be measured passes through water. **wet nurse** n a nurse who suckles a child for its mother. **wet'-nurse** vt to be a wet nurse to, to suckle (another woman's baby); to treat like a helpless child, to nanny. **wet pack** n the wrapping of a person in blankets or the like dampened with warm or cold water as a medical treatment; the dampened material used. **wet plate** n (*photog*) a plate coated with collodion and sensitized with a salt of silver. **wet room** n a completely tiled room containing an unenclosed shower unit, the water from which is carried away by a drain in the floor. **wet rot** n a form of decay in timber caused by certain fungi which develop in wood that is alternately wet and dry. **wet'-shod** (or *dialect* /wet'shod/) adj having wet shoes or feet. **wet'suit** n a suit for wearing in water, which allows water to pass through but retains body heat. **wetting** (or **wetting-out**) **agent** n any chemical that, added to a liquid, reduces its surface tension so that it is more readily spread over or absorbed by the materials it is applied to. **wet'ware** n (*comput sl*; *facetious*) the living human brain. ■ **wet behind the ears** very young, immature, gullible. **wet one's whistle** (*inf*) see under **whistle**. **wet out** to wet thoroughly (*old*); to cleanse (eg raw material in textile manufacture) by so doing. **wet the baby's head** (*inf*) to celebrate the baby's birth with (alcoholic) drinks. **wet the bed** to urinate accidentally in bed. **wet through** with one's clothes completely soaked.

weta /wet'ə/ n a large horned wingless grasshopper of New Zealand, its bite reported by some to be venomous. [Maori]

wether /wedh'ər/ n a castrated ram. [OE; cf Ger *Widder*]

wetted, **wetting**, **wettish** see **wet**.

WEU abbrev : Western European Union.

we've /wēv/ a contraction of **we have**.

wex and **wexe** obsolete forms of **wax**^1,2,3.

wey /wā/ n a measure or weight for dry goods differing with different commodities (eg, for salt, corn, etc 40 bushels). [Variant of **weigh**^1]

weyard and **weyward** obsolete spellings of **weird**, found in older editions of Shakespeare's *Macbeth*.

wezand obsolete form of **weasand**.

wf (*printing*) abbrev : wrong fount.

WFP abbrev : World Food Programme, a United Nations body.

WFTC abbrev : Working Families Tax Credit.

WFTU abbrev : World Federation of Trade Unions.

WG abbrev : (Windward Islands) Grenada (IVR).

wg abbrev : water gauge; wire gauge.

wha /hwä or hwö/ a Scots form of **who**.

whack /(h)wak/ (*inf*) vt to strike hard and smartly; to put or take with violence; to beat decisively; to parcel out, share; to murder (*esp criminal sl*). ◆ vi to strike; to settle accounts. ◆ n a blow; the sound of a blow; a share; an attempt. [Imit of the sound] ■ **whacked** adj (*inf*) exhausted. **whack'er** n (*inf*) something big of its kind; a blatant lie. **whack'ing** adj (*inf*) enormous (often as an intensifier). ◆ n a beating or thrashing. **whack'o** interj (*dated inf*) an expression of pleasure or enthusiasm. ■ **out of whack** (*inf*) out of order, not straight. **top** (or **full**) **whack** the highest price, wage, rate, etc. **whack off** (*vulgar sl*) to masturbate.

whacko^1 see **wacko**.

whacko^2 see under **whack**.

whacky /(h)wak'i/ adj same as **wacky**.

whaisle or **whaizle** /(h)wā'zl/ (*Scot*) vi to wheeze. [A form of **wheezle** (see under **wheeze**)]

whale^1 /(h)wāl/ n any of an order of cetaceous mammals, including the *toothed* whales, such as the sperm whales and the dolphins, and the *whalebone* whales, such as the right whales and the rorquals, in which the teeth are only rudimentary; a person with a large appetite (*inf*); something very large of its kind (*inf*); (with *cap*) the constellation Cetus. ◆ vi to hunt whales. [OE *hwæl*; cf ON *hvalr*, Ger *Walfisch*] ■ **whāl'er** n a whaleboat; a whaleman; something very large of its kind (*sl*); a tramp (*old Aust inf*). **whāl'ery** n whaling. **whāl'ing** adj concerned with or used in whale-catching. ◆ n the business of catching whales. □ **whale'back** n a turtleback; a kind of steamboat used on the Great Lakes to carry grain, etc having a rounded upper deck; a mound shaped like the back of a whale. **whale'boat** n a long, narrow boat sharp at both ends once used in the pursuit of whales; a similar boat carried on a large vessel as a life-boat. **whale'bone** n a light flexible substance consisting of the baleen plates of whales; an article made of this. ◆ adj made of whalebone. **whale calf** n (also **calf whale**) a young whale. **whale'-fisher** n. **whale'-fishery** n. **whale'-fishing** n. **whale'-head** n the shoebill (also **whale-headed stork**). **whale line** n strong rope used for harpoon lines in whale-fishing. **whale louse** n a genus (*Cyamus*) of amphipod Crustacea parasitic on the skin of cetaceans. **whale'man** n a person or ship employed in whale-fishing. **whale oil** n oil obtained from the blubber of a whale. **whale's bone** n (*obs*) ivory eg from the walrus. **whale's food** or **whale food** n small animals eaten by whales, *esp* the *Clio* genus of shell-less pteropods. **whale shark** n a huge but harmless shark of tropical seas. **whal'ing-gun** n a harpoon gun, a contrivance that fires a harpoon attached to a line. **whal'ing-master** n the captain of a whaler. **whal'ing-port** n a port where whalers are registered. ■ **bull** and **cow whale** an adult male and female whale respectively. **whale of a time** (*inf*) a hugely enjoyable time.

whale^2 /(h)wāl/ (*inf*) vt to thrash; to strike violently. [Perh **wale**^1; perh from *whalebone* whip] ■ **whāl'ing** n a thrashing. ◆ adj enormous (often as an intensifier).

whally /(h)wö'li/ (*Spenser*) adj walleyed; (of the eye) showing much white. [From **walleye**]

wham /(h)wam/ n a resounding noise caused by a hard blow (also interj). ◆ vi (**whamm'ing**; **whammed**) to crash or bang (with *into*, etc). ◆ vt to hit or bang. ◆ adv with a wham. [Imit] ■ **whamm'o** (or *wa-mō'* or *hwa-mō'*/) interj descriptive of violent impact. ◆ n impressive verve and energy. **whamm'y** n (*inf*, *orig US*) a malevolent spell or influence cast by someone's evil eye, such a spell cast by both eyes (ie a twofold spell) being a **double whammy**, and a threefold spell being a **triple whammy**; now, generally, a stunning blow, the winning punch (*inf*). ■ **put the whammy on** to put the evil eye on, cast an evil spell on. **wham bam thank you ma'am** (*vulgar sl*) quick impersonal sexual intercourse that brings speedy gratification to the male.

whample /hwöm'pl or hwam'pl/ (*Scot*) n a stroke or blow.

whanau /fä'now/ (*NZ*) n an extended family. [Maori]

whang^1 /(h)wang/ n a resounding noise; a blow. ◆ interj imitative of a resounding impact. ◆ vi to career or go headlong, with a resounding impact. ◆ vt to (cause to) hit with a whang. ◆ adv with a whang. [Imit]

whang^2 /(h)wang/ n a leather thong; a thick slice; (also **wang**) the penis (*vulgar sl*). ◆ vt to flog; to throw, push or pull violently; to cut in great slices. [*thwang*, obs form of **thong**]

whangee /(h)wang-gē'/ n any of several grasses of a genus (*Phyllostachys*) related to the bamboos, found in China and Japan; a cane made from the stem of one. [Prob Chin *huáng* yellow, and *li* bamboo]

whap, **whapped**, **whapping** see **whop**.

whare /(h)wor'i, hwär'ä or fär'ä/ (*NZ*) n a house. [Maori]

wharf /(h)wörf/ n (pl **wharfs** or **wharves**) a landing stage, built esp along the shore, for loading or unloading vessels; the bank of a river (*Shakesp*). ◆ vt to strengthen or secure by means of a wharf (*obs*); to place on, or bring to, a wharf. [Late OE *hwearf* bank, shore; related to *hweorfan* to turn]

■ **wharf'age** n the dues paid for using a wharf; accommodation for vessels at a wharf. **wharf'ie** n (*Aust* and *NZ inf*) someone who works at the shore; a wharf labourer. **wharf'ing** n material for making a wharf; wharfs. **wharfinger** /wör'fin-jər or hwör'fin-jər/ n the owner or keeper of a wharf.

◻ **wharf rat** n the common brown rat; someone who hangs about a wharf.

wharve see **whorl** (*spinning*).

wharves see **wharf**.

what /(h)wot/ interrog pronoun and adj neuter of **who**, used to form questions regarding identity, selection from an indefinite number, nature, value, etc (also used elliptically, as in *what did you say?*, *what do you think?*, *what is it?*). ◆ interrog pronoun (*obs*) who? ◆ relative pronoun and adj that which; such ... as; which (*dialect*); any or anything whatever; whoever (*Shakesp*). ◆ indefinite pronoun (or n) something; a portion, bit (*Spenser*); fare, in the phrase *such homely what* (*Spenser, Faerie Queene* VI.9.7.4). ◆ adv why? (*obs*); in what way, how? to what degree? ◆ conj as much as (*dialect*); that (as in **but what** that ... not). ◆ interj used in summoning, calling attention, expressing surprise, disapprobation, protest, etc. [OE *hwæt*, neuter of *hwā* who; Ger *was*, L *quod*]

■ **what'en** or **whatt'en** adj (from *whatkin* what kind; *dialect*) what; what kind of. **what'na** adj (from *whatkin* a) same as **whaten** above. **what'ness** n what a thing is; essence; quiddity.

◻ **what'abouts** n pl the things one is occupied about. **what'-d'you-call-it**, **-'em**, etc n a word substituted for the name of a thing or person in forgetfulness or contempt (also **what'-you-may-call-it**, etc). **whatev'er** or (*literary*) **whate'er** /wot-ār' or hwot-ār'/ pronoun anything that; no matter what; what? (*inf*). ◆ adj any or all that, no matter what. ◆ interj an expression intended to convey indifference. **what'-like** adj (*dialect*) of what kind, character or appearance. **what'not** see separate entry; see also **what not** below. **what's'-his-** (**her-, its-**, etc) **name** n (*inf*) someone or something indicated or understood whose name one cannot, or cannot be bothered to, recall (also **what'sit** and (*US*) **what'sis**). **what'so** adj (*archaic*) of whatever kind. ◆ pronoun whatever (*archaic*); whoever (*obs*); whosoever (*obs*). **whatsoev'er** or (*old*) **whatsoe'er** /wot-sō-ār' or hwot-sō-ār'/ adj and pronoun whatever. **whatsomev'er** adj and pronoun (*dialect*) whatsoever. **what-you-may-call-it** see **what-d'you-call-it** above.

■ **and what all** and so on, and suchlike things. **know what it is** to know what is involved in an action or experience; to have experienced or suffered it. **or whatever** (*inf*) or some such thing. **so what?** what of it? **what about** do you fancy (something, or doing something)?; what is your opinion of (someone or something)?; aren't you forgetting (someone or something)? **what an if** (*Shakesp*) what if, or though. **what else?** could anything else be the case? **what for** (*inf*) punishment, chastisement, as in *I'll give you what for!* **what ... for?** for what reason, or with what purpose in mind? (also *dialect* **what for...?**). **what for a** (*obs*) what kind of. **what have you** (*inf*) what not; anything else of the kind. **what ho** a loud hail or summons. **what if** what would it matter if? (also **what matter if**); what would happen if? **what ... like?** a common form of request for a description or opinion of something or someone, as in *what is she like?*, *what does this look, sound, like?* **what next?** what is to be done next?; what will happen next? (often said in despair or trepidation). **what not** (elliptical for 'what may I not say?') (and) other such things, (and) so forth; (and) anything and everything else (*old*). **what now?** what is the meaning of this latest interruption?; what is to be done now?; what's wrong now? **what of** what comes of or follows from?; what do you think of?; what is the news of? **what of it?** does it matter? (with the implication that it does not). **what's more** and, more importantly. **what's new?** see under **new**. **what's what** the true position of affairs; the proper, conventional or profitable way to behave or proceed; what really counts or matters. **what's with** (*inf; esp US*) what's the matter with?, what's up with?; what do you mean by (doing something)? **what the hell, the dickens, the devil**, etc (*inf*) whatever. **what then?** what would come of it?, what would be the consequence?; what happened after that? **what though** what does it matter though; notwithstanding the fact that. **what time** (*archaic*) at the very time when. **what with** because of, considering.

whaten, **whatten**, etc see under **what**.

whatevs /(h)wot-evz'/ (*sl*) interj expressing indifference. [Contraction of **whatever**]

Whatman paper® /(h)wot'mən pā'pər/ n fine-quality paper used for drawings, engravings, filtering, etc. [Name of manufacturing firm]

whatna see under **what**.

whatnot /(h)wot'not/ n a light piece of furniture with shelves for bric-à-brac, etc; a nondescript article. [**what** and **not**]

whatsis see **what's-his-name** under **what**.

whaup /hwöp or wop/ (*Scot*) n a curlew, sometimes *great whaup* as distinct from *little whaup*, the whimbrel. [Primarily imit; history uncertain]

whaur /(h)wör/ a Scots form of **where**.

wheal[1] variant of **weal**[1].

wheal[2] /(h)wēl/ n a Cornish name for a mine. [Cornish *hwel*]

whear or **wheare** obsolete spelling of **where**.

wheat /(h)wēt/ n any cereal grass of the genus *Triticum*, or its grain, from which a white or brown flour for bread, etc is produced (variously classified as **bearded, beardless** or **bald wheat**, according to the presence or absence of awns or beard; as **white, red** or **amber wheat** according to colour; and as **winter** or **spring wheat** according to whether it is a type normally sown in autumn or spring). [OE *hwǣte*; Ger *Weizen*; related to **white**; named from its colour]

■ **wheat'en** adj made of wheat; wholemeal; of the colour of ripe wheat. **wheat'y** adj tasting of wheat.

◻ **wheat berry** or **wheat corn** n the grain of wheat. **wheat bird** n the chaffinch. **wheat crop** n. **wheat ear** n an ear of wheat. **wheat-ear stitch** n a fancy stitch in embroidery. **wheat eel** n (also **wheat'worm**) a small nematode worm that makes its way up wheat stems to the ears; the disease it causes (also **ear-cockle**). **wheat'field** n. **wheat fly** n the name of several flies that destroy wheat, eg the Hessian fly. **wheat germ** n the vitamin-rich germ or embryo of wheat, part of a grain of wheat. **wheat'grass** n the young grass of wheat, the juice of which is valued for its nutritional qualities. **wheat'meal** n wheat flour with some of the bran and germ removed. **wheat midge** n a dipterous insect that lays its eggs in the flowers of wheat heads, and whose reddish larvae devour the kernels. **wheat mildew** n either of two fungus diseases of wheat. **wheat moth** n any of several small moths whose larvae devour stored wheat. **wheat sheaf** n a sheaf of wheat. **wheatworm** see **wheat eel** above.

■ **separate the wheat from the chaff** to identify (*esp* by some test) the superior members of any group.

wheatear /(h)wē'tēr/ n any of various songbirds of the genus *Oenanthe*, esp *O. oenanthe*, having a white rump. [Prob a corruption of *white arse*]

Wheatstone /(h)wēt'stən/ or **Wheatstone's bridge** /(h)wēt'stənz brij/ n an apparatus for measuring electrical resistance, much used, but not invented, by Sir Charles *Wheatstone* (1802–75).

whee /(h)wē/ interj an expression of delight, exuberance, etc.

wheech /(h)wēhh/ (*Scot*) vi to move rapidly with a whizzing sound; to dart; (with *through*) to do, deal with, etc rapidly. ◆ vt to carry, remove rapidly; to throw. ◆ n a rapid movement or throw; a whizzing sound. [Imit]

wheedle /(h)wē'dl/ vt and vi to entice by soft words, flatter, cajole; to obtain by coaxing (with *out of*); to cheat by cajolery (with *out of*); to winkle (with *out*). ◆ n a piece of wheedling; a person given to coaxing (*obs*). [Perh from OE *wǣdlian* (orig) to be in want, to beg]

■ **wheed'ler** n. **wheed'lesome** adj coaxing. **wheed'ling** n. **wheed'lingly** adv.

wheel /(h)wēl/ n a circular frame turning on an axle; a steering-wheel; a potter's wheel; a spinning-wheel; an old instrument of torture; a rotating firework; a bicycle or tricycle (*inf*); (in pl) personal transport (*inf*); the wheel by which a spit is turned (*Shakesp*); the wheel attributed to Fortune personified, the emblem of mutability; hence, the course of events; a celestial sphere (*obs*); a disc; a circular design; a circular motion; (in pl) the parts of a machine; the intricate workings of something; one or more short lines following a bob at the end of a stanza; a refrain; a dollar (*sl*). ◆ vt to cause (a body of troops) to turn or revolve, esp round an axis or pivot; to cause to move in a circular course; to put a wheel or wheels on; to form or treat on the wheel; to convey on wheels; to propel on wheels; to encircle (*Milton*); to make wheel-shaped (*rare*); (with *out, forward*, etc; *inf*) to bring out, forward, etc, to produce. ◆ vi to turn round or on an axis; to change direction; to change one's mind abruptly; to move in a circle; to reel, be giddy; to roll forward; to wander, roam (*Shakesp*); to travel in a wheeled vehicle; to ride a bicycle or tricycle (*inf*); to be provided with wheels on which to be propelled. [OE *hwēol*; ON *hjōl*]

■ **wheeled** adj having wheels; moving on wheels; (in combination) having a specified kind or number of wheels, as in *solid-wheeled*, *three-wheeled*; formed into a wheel (*rare*). **wheel'er** n someone who wheels; a cyclist (*inf*); a maker of wheels (*dialect*); (in combination) something that wheels, or that has a specified kind or number of wheels, as in *two-wheeler*; a wheelhorse. **wheel'ie** n (*inf*) a manoeuvre, eg on a bicycle, motorbike or skateboard, involving travelling for a short distance with the front wheel or wheels off the ground; a U-turn accomplished at speed with a loud skidding noise (*Aust*); a wheelie bin (*inf*). **wheel'ing** *n* the act of moving or conveying on wheels; a turning or circular movement; a rather coarse woollen yarn. **wheel'-less** *adj*. **wheel'y** *adj* like a wheel.

□ **wheel and axle** *n* one of the mechanical powers, in its primitive form a cylindrical axle, on which a wheel, concentric with the axle, is firmly fastened, the power being applied to the wheel, and the weight attached to the axle. **wheel animal** or **animalcule** *n* a tiny aquatic animal, a rotifer. **wheel'barrow** *n* a barrow with one wheel in front and two handles and legs behind; (loosely) any other handcart. **wheel'base** *n* the distance between the front and rear axles of a vehicle; the area enclosed by lines joining the points at which the wheels of a locomotive, etc touch the rails or the ground, or the length of this area. **wheel brace** *n* an implement for tightening and loosening the nuts that hold a wheel in position. **wheel carriage** *n* any kind of carriage moved on wheels. **wheel'chair** *n* a chair moving on wheels, *esp* a disabled person's chair. ♦ *adj* provided, designed, adapted or arranged for people confined to wheelchairs, as *wheelchair housing*, *wheelchair Olympics*, etc. **wheel clamp** *n* a device used by traffic authorities, etc to immobilize an illegally parked vehicle until it is removed after payment of a fine. **wheel'-clamp** *vt*. **wheel'-cut** *adj* (of glass) cut, or ground and polished, on a wheel. **wheel'-cutter** *n* a machine for cutting teeth on wheels. **wheel'er-deal'er** *n*. **wheel'er-deal'ing** *n* (*inf*; *orig US*) shrewd dealing or bargaining to one's maximum advantage in business, politics, etc, *esp* without regard for others' interests. **wheel'horse** *n* one of the horses next to the wheels in a team. **wheel'house** *n* a shelter in which a ship's steering-wheel is placed; a paddle box; a prehistoric wheel-shaped dwelling. **wheelie bin** *n* a large dustbin on wheels. **wheel lock** *n* (*hist*) (a gun having) a lock in which sparks are struck off a flint by a small steel wheel. **wheel'man** *n* a steersman (also **wheels'man**); a cyclist. **wheel of fortune** *n* Fortune's wheel (see *n* above); a gambling device. **wheel of life** *n* an optical toy giving an illusion of animation, a zoetrope. **wheel plough** *n* a plough running on wheels, or one the depth of whose furrow is regulated by a wheel. **wheel race** *n* the part of a channel in which the water wheel is fixed. **wheel spin** *n* rotation of the wheels of a vehicle without the purchase required for forward or backward movement. **wheel window** *n* a circular window with radiating tracery, a rose window. **wheel'work** *n* a combination of wheels and their connection in machinery. **wheel'wright** *n* a maker of wheels and wheeled carriages.

■ **at the wheel** driving a vehicle or steering a boat. **big wheel** a Ferris wheel; a person of importance or self-importance. **break a butterfly** (or **fly**, etc) **on the wheel** to inflict a punishment out of all proportion to the offence; to employ great exertions for insignificant ends. **go on wheels** to move swiftly, smoothly, and hence pleasantly. **left** (or **right**) **wheel** (a command to perform) a swing to the left (or right). **put a spoke in someone's wheel** see under **spoke²**. **put one's shoulder to the wheel** see under **shoulder**. **take the wheel** to take charge or control. **wheel and deal** (*inf*; *orig US*) to engage in wheeler-dealing. **wheeling and dealing** (*inf*; *orig US*) same as **wheeler-dealing** above. **wheels within wheels** said of a situation in which a complication of influences is at work.

wheen /(h)wēn/ (*Scot*) *n* a few. ♦ *adj* (*obs*) few. [OE *hwǣne*, from *hwoōn*, adv, a little]

■ **a wheen** a few; a good many; (used adverbially) a little.

wheenge see **whinge**.

wheeple /(h)wē'p̄l/ (*Scot*) *vi* to make a long-drawn-out cry such as that of the curlew; to whistle feebly (also *vt*). ♦ *n* a whistling noise. [Imit]

wheesh see **whish²**.

wheesht see **whisht**.

Wheeson /(h)wē'sun/ (*Shakesp, 2 Henry IV* II.1.85) *n* Whitsun.

wheeze /(h)wēz/ *vi* to breathe with a hissing sound; to breathe audibly or with difficulty. ♦ *vt* to utter with such a sound. ♦ *n* the act or sound of wheezing; a gag (*theatre sl*); a catchphrase (*sl*); a standard joke (*sl*); a cunning plan (*inf*). [Prob ON *hvæsa* to hiss]

■ **wheez'er** *n*. **wheez'ily** *adv*. **wheez'iness** *n*. **wheez'ing** *n*. **wheez'ingly** *adv*. **wheez'le** *vi* (*Scot*) to make wheezy sounds. **wheez'y** *adj*.

wheft see **waft**.

whelk¹ /(h)welk/ *n* a popular name for a number of marine gastropods, *esp* applied to species of the genus *Buccinum* common on the coasts of northern seas. [Wrong form of older *welk*, from OE *wiloc, weoluc*; origin obscure]

■ **whelked** *adj* ridged like a whelk. **whelk'y** *adj* knobby, rounded; formed in a shell (*Spenser, Virgil's Gnat*, 105).

whelk² /(h)welk/ *n* a pimple; by confusion with **wale¹**, the mark of a stripe on the body, a wrinkle, an inequality or protuberance. [Late OE (WSax) *hwylca*, from *hwelian* to suppurate]

whelk'd see **welkt**.

whelm /(h)welm/ (*archaic*) *vt* to turn (eg a hollow vessel) upside down, *esp* so as to cover something else (now *dialect*); to cover completely in such a way (*obs*), or with eg water, etc; to overturn, overthrow; to plunge deep; to submerge; to overpower; to overburden; to ruin, destroy; to pass over in such a way as to submerge. ♦ *n* the overwhelming surge of waves (*poetic*); a watercourse constructed from hollowed, inverted tree trunks. [ME *whelmen* to turn over]

whelp /(h)welp/ *n* a young dog, a puppy; the cub of a bear, wolf, lion or tiger (*archaic*); (contemptuously) a young man; a ridge running longitudinally on the barrel or drum of a capstan or windlass to control the cable; a sprocket on a wheel. ♦ *vi* and *vt* to bring forth (young). [OE *hwelp*; ON *hvelpr*]

whemmle /(h)wem'l/, **whomble**, **whommle** /(h)wom'l/ or **whummle** /(h)wum'l/ (*dialect*) *n* an overthrow, overturn; confusion. ♦ *vt* to overturn; to turn upside down; to throw into a state of disorder or agitation; to move from side to side; to cover eg with an inverted dish. ♦ *vi* to capsize. [By metathesis from **whelm**]

when /(h)wen/ *adv* (*interrog* and *relative*) and *conj* at what time?; at which time; at or after the time that; upon or after which; while; although; at which (or *relative pronoun*). ♦ *n* (the question of) the time at which something happened or is to happen. ♦ *interj* (*Shakesp*) an exclamation of impatience, like *what!* [OE *hwanne, hwonne* (Ger *wann, wenn*); from the stem of interrog pronoun *hwā* who]

□ **whenas'** *conj* (*archaic*) when; in as much as; whereas. **whenev'er** or (*literary*) **whene'er'** /*wen-ār'* or *hwen-ār'*/ *conj* at every time when; as soon as (*Scot*). **whensoev'er** or (*literary*) **whensoe'er** /*wen-sō-ār'* or *hwen-sō-ār'*/ *conj* at whatsoever time.

■ **or whenever** (*inf*) or at any comparable time. **say when** (*inf*) tell me when to stop, *specif* when pouring a drink. **seldom when** (*Shakesp*) seldom that.

whence /(h)wens/ *adv* and *conj* (also **from whence**) from what place; from which place?; from which things; wherefore. ♦ *n* a place of origin; a source. [ME *whennes, whannes*]

□ **whenceforth'** *adv* (*Spenser*) whence. **whencesoev'er** or **whencev'er** *conj* from whatsoever place, cause or source.

whenua /fen'oo-ə/ (*NZ*) *n* land. [Maori]

whe'r see **whether**.

where /(h)wār/ *adv* (*interrog* and *relative*) and *conj* at or to which place; at what place?; to what place?; from what source; to a, or the, place in or from which (*archaic*); in what circumstances or condition; at what point; whereas; wherever; (a or the place) in, at or to which (or *relative pronoun*). ♦ *n* (the question of) the location or destination of something. [OE *hwǣr, hwār*; from stem of **who**; cf **there**]

■ **where'ness** *n* the state of having place or position; position, situation.

□ **whereabout'** or **whereabouts'** *adv* and *conj* near what?; approximately where?; about which, about where; on what business (*Shakesp*). ♦ *n* /*wār'* or *hwār'*/ (*usu* **whereabouts**; *sing* or *pl*) one's (*esp* approximate) location. **whereaf'ter** *conj* after which. **whereagainst'** *adv* and *conj* (*archaic*) against which. **whereas'** *adv* and *conj* when in fact; but on the contrary; taking into consideration, in view of, the fact that; where (*obs*). **whereat'** *adv* and *conj* at which; at what? **whereby'** *adv* and *conj* by which. **wherefor'** *adv* and *conj* (*formal*) for which. **where'fore** /-*fər*/ *adv* and *conj* for which, or what, reason; why? ♦ *n* the cause. **wherefrom'** *adv* and *conj* (*archaic*) whence. **wherein'** *adv* and *conj* (*formal*) in which place or respect; in what? **whereinsoev'er** *adv* and *conj* (*archaic*) in whatsoever place or respect. **wherein'to** (or /-*in-too'*/) *adv* and *conj* (*archaic*) into which; into what? **whereof'** *adv* and *conj* (*formal*) of which; wherewith (*Shakesp*); of what? **whereon'** *adv* and *conj* (*archaic*) on which; on what? **whereout'** *adv* and *conj* (*archaic*) out of which. **wheresoev'er** or (*old*) **where'so** or **wheresoe'er** /*wār-sō-ār'* or *hwar-sō-ar'*/ *adv* and *conj* (*literary*) in or to whatsoever place; whencesoever (*archaic*). **wherethrough'** *adv* and *conj* (*archaic*) through which; through the agency of which. **whereto'** *adv* and *conj* (*formal*) to which; to what? **whereun'der** *adv* and *conj* (*formal*) under which. **whereuntil'** *adv* and *conj* (*Shakesp*) to what. ♦ *adv* and *conj* whereunto. **whereun'to** (or /-*un-too'*/) *adv* and *conj* (*archaic*) whereto; for what purpose? **whereupon'** *adv* and *conj* upon or in consequence of which; on what grounds (*Shakesp*). **wherev'er** or (*literary*) **where'er** /*war-ār'* or *hwār-ār'*/ *adv* and *conj* at whatever place. **wherewith'** *adv* and *conj* with which?; with what. **wherewithal** /*wār-wi-dhōl'* or *hwār-wi-dhōl'*/ *adv* and *conj* with which?; with what. ♦ *n* /*wār'* or *hwār'*/ the means.

■ **from where** whence; from the, or a, place where. **or wherever** (*inf*) or in (or towards) any comparable place. **see, look,** etc **where** behold. **tell someone where to get off** (*inf*) to tell someone that his or her behaviour will not be tolerated. **where away?** a query as to the direction of an object sighted by the lookout (*naut*); where are you going? (*dialect*). **where it is** (*inf*) the real situation, point or explanation. **where it's at** (*sl*) (the scene of) whatever is considered to

---

fāte; fär; mē; fûr; mīne; mōte; för; mūte; pŭt; dhen (then); el'ə-mənt (element) • For other sounds see detailed chart of pronunciation be the most important, exciting, trendy, etc. **where you are** (*inf*) what you are saying or getting at.

wherret see **whirret**.

wherry /(*h*)*wer′i*/ *n* (*pl* **wherr′ies**) a light shallow boat, sharp at both ends for speed; a kind of barge. [Ety dubious]
  ❑ **wherr′yman** *n* a man employed in a wherry, *esp* one who rows a wherry.

whet /(*h*)*wet*/ *vt* (**whett′ing**; **whett′ed**) to sharpen by rubbing; to make keen; to excite; to incite (*obs*); to preen (*obs*; *rare*). ◆ *n* an act of sharpening; sharpness; a time, occasion (*dialect*); an incitement or stimulus; something that sharpens the appetite; an appetizer. [OE *hwettan*, cognate with *hwæt* sharp; Ger *wetzen*]
  ■ **whett′er** *n*.
  ❑ **whet′-slate** *n* novaculite. **whet′stone** *n* a stone for sharpening edged instruments; a stimulant.
  ■ **whet on** or **forward** (*Shakesp*) to urge on.

whether /(*h*)*wedh′ər*/ (in *Shakesp* often scanned as one syllable; also spelt **whe′r**) *conj* introducing the first of two alternative words, phrases or clauses, the second being introduced by *or*, or (in the case of clauses) sometimes by *or whether*; introducing a single dependent question. ◆ *pronoun* (*interrog* and *relative*) (*archaic*) which (of two). [OE *hwæther*, from stem of *hwā* who, with the old compar sfx *-ther*; cognate with Gothic *hwathar*, Ger *weder*; also with L *uter*, Ionic Gr *koteros*, Sans *katara*]
  ■ **whether or no** (or **not**) whether so or not so; in any case, in any event.

whetstone, **whetted**, **whetter**, **whetting** see **whet**.

whew¹ or **wheugh** /*hū*, (*h*)*wū*/ *interj* expressing wonder, relief or dismay. ◆ *n* a whistling sound, *esp* one expressing astonishment. ◆ *vi* to utter such a sound. [Imit]

whew² /(*h*)*wū*/ (*dialect*) *vi* to bustle about. [Perh **whew¹**]

whewellite /*hū′ə-līt*/ *n* calcium oxalate. [Named after William *Whewell* (1794–1866)]

whey /(*h*)*wā*/ *n* the watery part of milk, separated from the curd, *esp* in making cheese. ◆ *adj* of or containing whey; like whey; whey-coloured. [OE *hwæg*; LGer *wey*]
  ■ **whey′ey** and **whey′ish** *adj* of whey; like whey. **whey′ishness** *n*.
  ❑ **whey′-face** *n* a pale or white face. **whey′-faced** *adj* pale, *esp* with terror. **whey tub** *n*.

which /(*h*)*wich*/ *interrog pronoun* and *adj* what (thing(s) or person(s)) of a number? ◆ *interrog pronoun* (*obs* or *dialect*) what? ◆ *interrog adj* (*obs*) of what sort or kind? ◆ *relative pronoun* (used chiefly in reference to things or ideas, etc rather than people) that; who or whom (*obs*); used after a comma to add a clause commenting on something, the antecedent sometimes being a circumstance or statement, and 'which' the equivalent of 'and that' or 'but that'. [OE *hwilc*, *hwelc*, from the stem of *hwā* who, and *līc* (from a word meaning body, form) like; Gothic *hweileiks*, Ger *welch*, *welcher*; L *qualis*; cf **such** and **each**]
  ❑ **whichev′er** or **whichsoev′er** *pronoun* and *adj* every one that; any one, no matter which.
  ■ **the which** (*archaic*) which. **which ... he** (*obs*) who. **which ... his** (*obs*) whose. **which is which?** which is the one and which is the other?

whicker /(*h*)*wik′ər*/ (*dialect*) *vi* to neigh; to bleat; to snigger, titter. ◆ *n* a neigh, bleat or titter. [Imit]

whid¹ /(*h*)*wid*/ (*Scot*) *n* a rapid noiseless movement. ◆ *vi* to move quickly, to whisk. [Perh connected with ON *hvitha* a squall, OE *hwitha* a breeze]
  ■ **whidd′er** *vi* to whiz.

whid² /(*h*)*wid*/ *n* a lie (*Scot*); a word (*obs sl*); a quarrel (*dialect*). ◆ *vi* (**whidd′ing**; **whidd′ed**) to lie. [Poss OE *cwide* a word, from *cwethan* to say]
  ■ **cut boon whids** to speak good words.

whidah see **whydah**.

whidder see under **whid¹**.

Whieldon /(*h*)*wēl′dən*/ *adj* denoting a type of pottery with a mottled underglaze in green, yellow and brown, made in the factory of Thomas *Whieldon* of Staffordshire (1719–95).

whiff¹ /(*h*)*wif*/ *n* a faint or brief smell, often an unpleasant one; a sudden puff of air or smoke from the mouth; a slight inhalation; a slight blast; a small amount, *esp* of something causing or associated with a transient sensation; a slight trace or suggestion; a discharge of shot; a cigarette (*sl*); a small cigar; a jiffy (*inf*); a failure to hit the ball, etc (*US*); a light kind of outrigger boat; a small signal flag (*naut*); a glimpse (*dialect*). ◆ *vt* to throw out in whiffs; to puff; to drive or convey by, or as if by, a whiff; to inhale, smell. ◆ *vi* to go out or off in a whiff; to move with, or as if with, a puff of air; to blow slightly; to aim at, and fail to hit, a ball, etc (*US*); to smell. [Prob partly ME *weffe*; imit]
  ■ **whiff′er** *n*. **whiff′y** *adj*.

whiff² /(*h*)*wif*/ *n* a fish related to the turbot. [Ety dubious]

whiff³ /(*h*)*wif*/ *vi* to fish with a hand line towed behind a boat. [Perh **whiff¹**]
  ■ **whiff′ing** *n*.

whiffet /(*h*)*wif′ət*/ *n* an insignificant person, a whippersnapper; a little dog. [**whiff¹**]

whiffle /(*h*)*wif′l*/ *vi* and *vt* to blow in puffs. ◆ *vi* to move as if blown by a puff; to talk idly; to make a slight whistling or puffing sound; to veer; to vacillate; to prevaricate. [Frequentative of **whiff¹**]
  ■ **whiff′led** *adj* (*sl*) drunk. **whiff′ler** *n* someone who whiffles; a swaggerer; a contemptible person. **whiff′lery** *n* levity; trifling. **whiff′ling** *n* and *adj*.

whiffler¹ /(*h*)*wif′lər*/ (*hist*) *n* an official who clears the way for a procession. [Perh *wifel* (*obs*) javelin, battle-axe; affected by **whiff¹** and **whiffle**]

whiffler² see under **whiffle**.

whiffletree /(*h*)*wif′l-trē*/ *n* same as **whippletree**.

whift /(*h*)*wift*/ (*obs* or *dialect*) *n* a slight puff or blast; a snatch of music or song; a small signal flag (*naut*). [Variant of **whiff¹**]

Whig /(*h*)*wig*/ (*hist*) *n* a name applied to members of one of the great English political parties, in the late 17c applied to those upholding popular rights and opposed to the King; after 1830 almost superseded by 'Liberal'; a Scottish Presbyterian, first so called in the middle of the 17c; one of those who in the colonial period were opposed to British rule (*US*); one of the party formed from the survivors of the old National Republican party and other elements, which disintegrated in the 1850s, first called by the name in 1834 (*US*). ◆ *adj* of, relating to or composed of Whigs. [Prob short for **whiggamore** a 17c Scottish Presbyterian rebel]
  ■ **Whigg′archy** *n* government by Whigs. **Whigg′ish** *adj*. **Whigg′ishly** *adv*. **Whigg′ism**, **Whigg′ery**, **Whigg′ishness** or **Whig′ship** *n* Whig principles.

whig¹ /(*h*)*wig*/ (*Scot*) *vi* (**whigg′ing**; **whigged**) to jog along. ◆ *vt* to urge forward. [Origin uncertain]

whig² /(*h*)*wig*/ (*dialect*) *n* sour milk; whey; buttermilk. ◆ *vt* and *vi* (**whigg′ing**; **whigged**) to curdle. [Prob related to **whey**]

whiggamore /(*h*)*wig′ə-mör*, *-mör*/ *n* one of the 7000 Western Covenanters who marched on Edinburgh in 1648, sealing the doom of Charles I; a Scottish Presbyterian, a Whig. [Origin disputed; most prob *whig* to urge forward, and *mere* mare]

Whiggery, etc see under **Whig**.

whigmaleerie or **whigmaleery** /(*h*)*wig-mə-lē′ri*/ (*Scot*) *n* a trinket or knick-knack; a fantastic ornamentation; a whim. [Origin uncertain]

while /(*h*)*wīl*/ *n* a space of time; time and trouble spent. ◆ *conj* (also **whilst** /*wīlst* or *hwīlst*/) during the time that; at the same time that; as long as; whereas; although; notwithstanding the admitted fact that; until (*Scot and N Eng dialect*). ◆ *prep* (*Shakesp*; *Scot and N Eng dialect*) until. ◆ *vt* to pass (time) in a leisurely or undemanding way (with *away*). [OE *hwīl*; Gothic *hweila*, Ger *Weile*]
  ■ **whiles** *conj* (*Bible*) while, at the same time that; until (*Shakesp*). ◆ *adv* (*Scot*) at times (*orig* genitive of OE *hwīl*).
  ❑ **while-ere** or **whilere** /*wī-lār′* or *hwī-lār′*/ *adv* (*archaic*) a little while ago, formerly. **whilev′er** *conj* (chiefly *Aust*) for as long as.
  ■ **all the while** during all the time (that). **in between whiles** during the intervals. **make it worth someone's while** (*inf*) to pay someone well for his or her trouble. **once** (or **every once**) **in a while** now and then. **the while** (*Shakesp*) at the present time, in the meantime. **the whilst** (*obs*) while; in the meantime. **worth** (**one's**) **while** worth taking time and trouble over.

whilk /(*h*)*wilk*/ *pronoun* obsolete and dialect form of **which**.

whilly /(*h*)*wil′i*/ (*Scot*) *vt* to wheedle, cajole. [Prob shortened from **whillywha**]

whillywha or **whillywhaw** /(*h*)*wil′i-(h*)*wö*/ (*Scot*) *vt* to coax, wheedle or cajole. ◆ *n* cajolery; a coaxing, insinuating person. ◆ *adj* smooth-tongued, wheedling. [Origin obscure; poss imit of equivocation]

whilom /(*h*)*wī′ləm*/ (*archaic*) *adv* formerly, once. ◆ *adj* former. [Orig dative plural of OE *hwīl* time]

whilst see **while**.

whim /(*h*)*wim*/ *n* a caprice; a fancy; a fantastic creation of brain or hand (*obs*); a whimsical person (*obs*); a vertical rope drum revolved by a horse, used for hoisting from shallow shafts. ◆ *vi* (**whimm′ing**; **whimmed**) (*obs*) (of the head) to turn round, swim; to be whimsical. ◆ *vt* to desire capriciously; to turn aside or put off by a whim (with *off*; *obs*). [Poss from **whim-wham**]
  ■ **whimm′y** *adj* full of whims.

whimberry /(*h*)*wim′bə-ri*/ *n* a localized name for the bilberry or whortleberry. [Assimilated form of **whinberry**]

■ words derived from main entry word; ❑ compound words; ■ idioms and phrasal verbs

whimbrel /(h)wim'brəl/ or **wimbrel** /wim'brəl/ *n* a species of small curlew. [Prob imit of bird's cry; dimin sfx *-rel*]

whimmy see under **whim**.

whimper /(h)wim'pər/ *vi* to cry feebly or plaintively. ◆ *vt* to utter plaintively or in a whimper. ◆ *n* a feebly plaintive cry. [Imit; cf Ger *wimmern*]

■ **whim'perer** *n*. **whim'pering** *n* and *adj*. **whim'peringly** *adv*.

whimple /(h)wim'pl/ *n* same as **wimple**.

whimsy or **whimsey** /(h)wim'zi/ *n* delicately fanciful behaviour; gentle fantasy; a whim or freak of fancy; something odd or quaint. ◆ *adj* full of whims, changeable; quaint, odd. [**whim**]

■ **whim'sical** *adj* full of whims; odd, fantastical; delicately fanciful; (loosely) expressing gently humorous tolerance. **whimsical'ity** or **whim'sicalness** *n*. **whim'sically** *adv*. **whim'sily** *adv*. **whim'siness** *n*.

whim-wham /(h)wim'(h)wam/ *n* a ridiculous notion; an odd device; a fanciful trifle. [Origin uncertain; cf ON *hvima* to have the eyes wandering]

whin¹ /(h)win/ *n* gorse, furze. [Prob Scand]

■ **whinn'y** *adj* abounding in whins.

❑ **whin'chat** *n* a bird that frequents whins, very similar in appearance, *esp* when it assumes its duller autumn plumage, to the stonechat, to which it is related.

whin² see **whinstone**.

whinberry /(h)win'bə-ri/ *n* an older form of **whimberry**. [Orig *winberry* or *wineberry*, from OE *winberige* grape]

whinchat see under **whin¹**.

whine /(h)wīn/ *vi* to utter a plaintive cry, whimper; to complain peevishly; to cry fretfully; to speak in a thin, ingratiating or servile tone; (of eg machinery) to make a continuous high-pitched noise. ◆ *vt* to express or utter in a whine; to say peevishly; to cause to make a whining noise. ◆ *n* a plaintive cry; a thin, ingratiating, nasal tone of utterance; a continuous shrill noise. [OE *hwīnan* to whine; ON *hvīna* to whistle through the air]

■ **whī'ner** *n*. **whī'niness** *n*. **whī'ning** *n* and *adj*. **whī'ningly** *adv*. **whī'ny** *adj*.

whinge /(h)winj/, also (*Scot*) **wheenge** /(h)wēnj/ (*inf*; *orig dialect*) *vi* to complain peevishly (also *Aust*); to whine; to cry fretfully. ◆ *n* a peevish complaint. [OE *hwinsian*, from root of *hwīnan*; see **whine**]

■ **whinge'ing** *adj* and *n*. **whinge'ingly** *adv*. **whing'er** *n*. **whing'y** *adj*.

whinger /(h)wing'ər/, also /(h)win'jər/ and /(h)wing'gər/ (*hist*) *n* a dirk or short sword. [Origin obscure; related to **whinyard**]

whiniard see **whinyard**.

whinid'st (*Shakesp*, *Troilus and Cressida* II.1.14) folio reading for which Johnson conjectured *vinewd'st* mouldy.

whinny¹ /(h)win'i/ *vi* (**whinn'ying**; **whinn'ied**) to neigh. ◆ *n* a neigh. [Imit]

whinny² see under **whin¹**.

whinstone /(h)win'stōn or -stən/ *n* (also **whin**) any hard and compact kind of rock, *usu* basalt or the like; a piece of this. [*whin* (origin obscure), and **stone**]

❑ **Whin Sill** *n* a sheet of intrusive quartz-dolerite or quartz-basalt exposed almost continuously for nearly 200 miles from the Farne Islands to Middleton-in-Teesdale.

whiny see under **whine**.

whinyard or **whiniard** /(h)win'yərd/ (*hist*) *n* a short sword or dirk. [Origin uncertain; related to **whinger**]

whip /(h)wip/ *n* a lash with a handle for punishing or driving; a stroke administered by a whip or similar implement; an act of whipping or a whipping motion; a driver, a coachman; someone who enforces the attendance and discipline of a political party; a call made on members of parliament to be in their places in readiness for an important division (called, according to the number of times the message is underlined as indication of urgency, **three-line whip**, etc; **five-line whip** is no longer used); a whipper-in, the person who manages the hounds; a simple form of hoisting apparatus, a small tackle consisting of a single rope and block; a preparation of whipped cream, eggs, etc; a whipping or overcasting; (also, more *usu*, **whip'-round**) a collection of cash contributions made hastily among a group of people; an individual share in money collected in equal amounts; an instant (*Scot*); an arm carrying a sail of a windmill; a long twig, slender branch or shoot; a fairground ride featuring cars that move with sudden jerks. ◆ *vt* (**whipp'ing**; **whipped** or (*old*) **whipt**) to strike with a lash; to drive, or force to move, with lashes; to punish with lashes, or (loosely) by spanking; to strike in a manner suggesting a lash; to lash with sarcasm; to lash (eg a crowd) into an emotional state; to defeat, outdo (*inf*); to stiffen (eg cream or egg whites) or make (eggs, etc) frothy, by rapid beating with a whisk or similar utensil; to keep (eg a party) together; to fly-fish; to overlay (eg one cord with another); to

bind round; to sew lightly; to overcast (eg a seam); to move quickly, snatch (with *up*, *away*, *out*, etc); to steal (*inf*); to prepare at short notice (with *up*; *inf*); to rouse (support, enthusiasm, etc; with *up*). ◆ *vi* to move nimbly; to move in the manner of a whiplash; to make a cast in fly-fishing. [ME *whippen*; cf Du *wippen* to shake]

■ **whip'less** *adj*. **whip'like** *adj*. **whipp'er** *n* someone who or something that whips; an official who inflicts the penalty of whipping. **whipp'iness** *n*. **whipp'ing** *n* the action of lashing; corporal punishment, *esp* with a whip or lash; a defeat; a binding of twine, eg at the end of a rope; material for binding in this way; overcasting. **whipp'y** *adj* whiplike; pliant; supple.

❑ **whip'-and-derr'y** *n* a hoisting apparatus consisting of a whip (qv above) and a derrick. **whip'bird** *n* the coachwhip-bird. **whip'cat** *n* (*old*) a tailor. **whip'cord** *n* cord for making whips; a fabric with a bold steep warp twill, used chiefly for dresses, suits and coats; a whiplike seaweed such as *Chorda filum* or *Chordaria flagelliformis*. ◆ *adj* (also **whip'cordy**) like whipcord. **whip graft** *n* a graft made by fitting a tongue cut on the scion to a slit cut slopingly in the stock. **whip'-graft** *vt*. **whip'-grafting** *n*. **whip hand** *n* the hand that holds the whip; the advantage. **whip handle** *n* the handle or stock of a whip; an advantage. **whip'jack** *n* (*old*) a whining beggar who pretended to be a sailor. **whip'lash** *n* the lash of a whip; something resembling or suggesting the lash of a whip or its action; (also **whiplash injury**) an injury to the neck caused by the sharp forwards-and-backwards wrenching it suffers in a vehicle collision. ◆ *vi* to move like a whiplash. **whipp'er-in** *n* an assistant to a huntsman, who controls the hounds; an official whose job is to enforce the discipline of a political party, a whip (*obs*); at any moment in a race, the horse in the last place (*sl*); a little or young insignificant but pretentious or irritating person. **whipping boy** *n* a boy educated along with a prince and punished for the royal pupil's faults (*hist*); anyone on whom falls the odium of, or blame and punishment for, the shortcomings of others. **whipp'ing-cheer** *n* (*obs*; *humorous*) flogging. **whipping cream** *n* cream with enough butterfat in it to allow it to be beaten stiff. **whipp'ing-post** *n* a post to which offenders are tied to be whipped; the punishment itself. **whipp'ing-top** (or **whip'-top**) *n* a top kept spinning by means of a whip. **whip-round** see *n* above. **whip'saw** *n* a narrow saw for dividing timber lengthways, *usu* set in a frame and often worked by two people. ◆ *vt* to cut with a whipsaw; to have the advantage of at every point, defeat at every turn (*sl*). **whip scorpion** *n* any arachnid of the order Uropygi, slightly resembling true scorpions but having no sting and *usu* having a whiplike appendage at the rear of the body. **whip snake** *n* any of various snakes resembling a whiplash, as *Masticophis flagellum* (the coachwhip snake) and species of *Philodryas*, etc. **whip socket** *n* a socket to hold the butt of a whip. **whip'staff** *n* a former steering device, a vertical wooden lever controlling a ship's rudder. **whip'stall** *n* (*aeronautics*) a stall as the result of which the nose of the aircraft whips forward and down. ◆ *vi* and *vt* to go, or put, into such a stall. **whip'stitch** *n* a small overcasting stitch; a hasty composition; a tailor; a kind of half-ploughing or raftering (*dialect*). ◆ *vt* and *vi* to sew (something) using a whipstitch. **whip'stock** *n* the rod or handle of a whip; in an oil well, a tapered steel wedge used to deflect the drill bit from a straight line. **whip'tail** or **whip'tailed** *adj* having a long, slender tail. **whip-top** see **whipping-top** above. **whip'worm** *n* a parasitic worm of the genus *Trichocephalus* or *Trichuris*, with posterior end thick and anterior long and thin, found as a parasite in human intestines.

■ **fair crack of the whip** a reasonable or fair chance given to one to do something properly. **whip and spur** with great haste. **whip in** to act as a whipper-in. **whip into shape** to get (a person or group) into a condition ready for action, etc by force or rigorous training; generally, to reshape vigorously to one's satisfaction. **whips of** (*Aust* and *NZ inf*) a large amount of. **whip the cat** (*old*) to practise small economies; to work by the day as a dressmaker, tailor, etc, going from house to house; to idle; to play a practical joke.

whippersnapper /(h)wip'ər-snap-ər/ (*old inf*) *n* a cheeky young lad; any lowly person who behaves impudently. [Perh jinglingly extended from *whip-snapper* a cracker of whips]

whippet /(h)wip'it/ *n* a breed of dog developed from a cross between a greyhound and spaniel or terrier; a racing-dog; a small speedy tank. [Partly **whip**, and partly obsolete *whippet* to move briskly]

■ **whipp'eting** *n* the training and racing of whippets.

whippletree /(h)wip'l-trē/ *n* the crosspiece of a carriage, plough, etc, which is made so as to swing on a pivot and to which the traces of a harnessed animal are fixed (often used in conjunction with a doubletree). [From **whip**]

whippoorwill /(h)wip'poor-wil or -wil' or -pər-/ *n* a species of nightjar native to N America. [Imit of its call]

whippy see under **whip**.

whipster /(h)wip'stər/ (*obs*) *n* a term of contempt formerly with various meanings, notably (*Shakesp*, *Othello* V.2.247) a whippersnapper. [**whip**]

whir see **whirr**.

whirl /(h)wûrl/ n a rapid turning; any of various devices that revolve rapidly, eg the whorl or flywheel of a spindle; another name for whorl in other senses; a brief trip (inf); a quick turn on the dance floor (inf); a round of intense activity; a giddy degree of emotion or excitement; a commotion or tumult; a circling or spiralling pattern. ◆ vi to revolve or circle rapidly; to move rapidly, esp in an agitated manner; to turn swiftly round or aside. ◆ vt to turn round rapidly; to carry or move rapidly, on or as if on wheels (often with away, off, etc); to throw violently. [ME whirlen, from ON hvirfla, frequentative of hverfa to turn round; Ger wirbeln]
■ **whirl'er** n. **whirl'ing** n and adj. **whirl'ingly** adv. **whirl'y** adj characterized by whirls or whirling.
□ **whirl'-about** n the act of whirling about; anything that turns round rapidly. **whirl'bat** (also **whorl'bat** and **hurl'bat**) n (obs) translating L caestus (see **cestus²**). **whirl'blast** n a whirling blast of wind. **whirl bone** n the round head of a bone turning in a socket; the knee-cap. **whirling dervish** n one of an order of Muslim devotees, founded in 1273, who dance or spin round as an aid to religious meditation (also **Mevlevi**). **whirl'ing-table** n a machine exhibiting the effects of centripetal and centrifugal forces (also **whirl'ing-machine**); a potter's wheel. **whirl'pool** n a circular current in a river or sea, produced by opposing tides, winds or currents; an eddy; a huge whale-like sea monster (obs). **whirlpool bath** same as **Jacuzzi®**. **whirl'wind** n a small rotating windstorm, which may extend upwards to a height of many hundred feet, a miniature cyclone; something that moves in a similarly rapid and usu destructive way. ◆ adj describing anything that develops rapidly or violently. **whirl'ybird** n (inf) a helicopter.
■ **give something a whirl** (inf) to try something out.

whirligig /(h)wûr'li-gig/ n a toy that spins or whirls round, eg a top or paper windmill; a merry-go-round; any device, etc that revolves rapidly; a dizzying round of activity or progression of events; an ancient instrument of punishment consisting of a pivoted wooden cage in which the prisoner was spun round; (also **whirligig beetle**) any water beetle of the family Gyrinidae (esp Gyrinus natator), from their habit of whirling round on the surface of ponds, etc. [**whirl** and obsolete gig whipping-top]

whirlybird see under **whirl**.

whirr or **whir** /(h)wûr/ n the sound of a rapid whirling or vibratory motion. ◆ vi (**whirr'ing; whirred**) to turn or spin with a humming noise; to fly or move with such a sound. ◆ vt to hurry away with, or as if with, a whirring or whizzing sound. ◆ adv with a whirr. [Imit; cf Dan hvirre to whirl]
■ **whirr'ing** n.

whirret /(h)wûr'it/ or **wherret** /(h)wer'-/ (obs) n a blow. ◆ vt to give a sharp blow to. [Poss imit]

whirry /(h)wûr'i/ (Scot) vi and vt to move rapidly. [Prob from **whirr**]

whirtle see **wortle**.

whish¹ /(h)wish/ (dialect) vi to move with the whizzing sound of rapid motion; to call 'whish'. ◆ vt to drive (animals, etc) with calls of 'whish'. ◆ n the rushing or swishing sound of rapid movement through the air, etc. ◆ interj imitative of a rushing sound or movement. [Imit]

whish² /(h)wish/ (dialect) interj (also Scot **wheesh** /hwēsh or wēsh/) calling for silence, hush! ◆ vt and vi to silence, fall silent or be silent. [Cf **hush**, **whisht**]

whisht /(h)wisht/, Scot **wheesht** /(h)wēsht/ (old or dialect) interj calling for silence, hush! ◆ n silence; a whisper. ◆ adj silent. ◆ vi and vt to keep silent. [Cf **whist²**, **hush**]
■ **hold one's whisht** or (Scot) **haud one's wheesht** to remain silent.

whisk¹ /(h)wisk/ vt to move quickly and lightly; to sweep rapidly; to beat (egg whites, cream, etc) with a quick, light movement. ◆ vi to move nimbly and rapidly. ◆ n a light rapid sweeping motion; a small hand-held utensil for beating or whisking eggs, etc; a small bundle or tuft of anything used as a brush; (also **fly whisk**) a flexible implement for swatting flies; a type of women's neckerchief or large collar worn in the later 17c (hist); a hairlike appendage, eg on an insect; a tuft; a panicle esp of millet; the common millet. [Orig Scot, related to ON visk wisp]
■ **whis'ker** n someone or something that whisks. **whis'king** adj moving briskly.
□ **whis'ky-fris'ky** adj flighty.

whisk² /(h)wisk/ n the earlier name for **whist¹**. [Said to be from **whisk¹**, from the rapid action of sweeping the cards off the table]

whisker¹ /(h)wis'kər/ n any of the long coarse sensory hairs growing round the mouth of a cat, mouse, etc; a coarse hair growing on a human face, usu a man's; (in pl) a man's moustache (esp formerly) or beard, esp the parts growing on the cheeks; a hair's breadth, a very narrow margin; a very thin strong fibre or filament made by growing a crystal, eg of silicon carbide, silicon nitride or sapphire; either of two

bars extending on each side of the bowsprit (naut). [Related to ON visk wisp]
■ **whis'kered** and **whis'kery** adj having whiskers.

whisker² see under **whisk¹**.

whisket /(h)wis'kit/ n variant of **wisket**.

Whiskey or **whiskey** /wis'ki/ n (in international radio communication) a code word for the letter w.

whisky¹ (Irish and US **whiskey**) /(h)wis'ki/ n as legally defined, a spirit obtained by distillation from a mash of cereal grains saccharified by the diastase of malt (see also **malt whisky** under **malt**); formerly applied also to a spirit obtained from potatoes, beetroot, or any starch-yielding material; a glass of any of such spirits. [Gaelic uisgebeatha, from uisge water, and beatha life; cf L vita life]
■ **whis'keyfied** or **whis'kified** adj intoxicated.
□ **Whisky Insurrection** n an outbreak against the excise regulations that occurred in W Pennsylvania in 1794. **whis'ky-liver** n cirrhosis of the liver, from too much whisky. **whisky mac** n a mixed drink of whisky and ginger wine. **whisky** (or **whiskey**) **sour** n a sour (qv) having whisky as its chief ingredient. **whisky toddy** n toddy having whisky as its chief ingredient.

whisky² or **whiskey** /(h)wis'ki/ n a light gig. [**whisk¹**]

whisky john /(h)wis'ki jon/ n the grey or Canada jay (also **whisky jack**). [From an Native American name of similar sound]

whisper /(h)wis'pər/ vi to speak by breathing rather than voicing one's words; to speak in a low voice; to speak covertly, spread rumours; to plot secretly; to make a rustling sound, or a sound like soft speech. ◆ vt to utter in a low voice or under the breath, or covertly, or by way of gossip. ◆ n a low hissing voice or sound; a sound uttered with the breath rather than the voice; voiceless speech with narrowed glottis (phonetics); a hissing or rustling sound; cautious or timorous speaking; a secret hint; a rumour. [OE hwisprian; Ger wispern, ON hviskra; related to **whistle**]
■ **whis'perer** n someone who whispers; a secret informer. **whis'pering** n and adj. **whis'peringly** adv in a whisper or low voice. **whis'perously** adv in a whisper. **whis'pery** adj.
□ **whispering campaign** n an attack by means of furtively spread rumours. **whispering gallery** or **dome** n a gallery or dome so constructed that a whisper or slight sound is carried to an unusual distance.

whiss /(h)wis/ vi to hiss, whistle, wheeze, etc. [Imit]

whist¹ /(h)wist/ n a card game played by two against two, in which the object is to take a majority of the thirteen tricks, each trick over six scoring one point. [**whisk²**; said to be assimilated to **whist¹** because of the silence during play]
□ **whist drive** n a progressive whist party. **whist'-player** n.
■ **dummy whist** whist played with a dummy hand. **long whist** a game of ten points. **short whist** a game of five points.

whist² /(h)wist/ interj hush; silence; be still. ◆ adj (archaic) hushed, silent; attentive. ◆ vi to become silent. ◆ vt (Spenser) to hush or silence. [Imit]

whistle /(h)wis'l/ vi to make a shrill sound by forcing the breath through the pursed lips or the teeth; to make this sound in derision, etc; to make this sound as a call or signal; (of a bird) to pipe, sing; to make a similar sound with a wind instrument or other device; (of eg the wind) to make a shrill sound; to whizz through the air; to become an informer (inf); to give a landlord information that leads to raising rent (Walter Scott). ◆ vt to perform, utter or express by whistling; to summon with a whistle (often with up); to send with a whistling sound. ◆ n an act of whistling; the sound made in whistling, or any similar sound; any of many devices producing a similar sound, eg one operated by steam on a railway locomotive or a kettle, or one blown by a referee to regulate play on the pitch; a simple wind instrument consisting of a wooden or metal pipe with finger holes; a summons; the throat (sl). [OE hwistlian]
■ **whis'tleable** adj. **whis'tled** adj (sl) drunk. **whis'tler** n someone or something that whistles; a whistling sound that descends in pitch, caused by the radiation produced by lightning flashes (radio); a large kind of marmot; a broken-winded horse; another name for the thickhead; a mythical bird whose whistle is fatal to the hearer (Spenser). **whis'tling** n. **whis'tlingly** adv.
□ **whis'tle-blower** n (inf) someone who blows the whistle on someone or something. **whis'tle-blowing** n and adj (inf). **whis'tle- (or whis'tled-)drunk** adj (obs) too drunk to whistle. **whistle fish** n a rockling. **whistle stop** n (inf) a small town or railway station, where trains stop only by signal; hence **whistle-stop speech** an electioneering speech made on tour (orig at railway stations), and **whistle-stop tour** orig such an electioneering tour, now any rapid tour involving brief stops at many places. **whis'tle-stop** vi (of a political candidate) to make an electioneering tour with many brief personal appearances. **whistling kettle** n a kettle whose spout is fitted with a device that gives a whistling sound when steam escapes

---

■ words derived from main entry word; □ compound words; ■ idioms and phrasal verbs

through it, indicating that the water in it is boiling. **whis'tling-shop** n (sl) somewhere such as a room in a prison, where liquor was sold without a licence. **whistling swan** n an American swan with a melodious whistling call.

■ **blow the whistle** (with on; inf) to expose or give information usu to the authorities about (illegal or underhand practices); to declare (something) illegal, underhand or otherwise unacceptable. **boatswain's whistle** (also **pipe, call**) a whistle of special shape used by a boatswain or boatswain's-mate to summon sailors to various duties. **go whistle** (Shakesp) to go to the devil. **pay for one's whistle** to pay highly for one's caprice (from Benjamin Franklin's story of a whistle he, as a boy, bought at an exorbitant price). **pigs and whistles** see under **pig²**. **wet one's whistle** (inf) to take an alcoholic drink. **whistle away** see **whistle off** below. **whistle down the wind** (from the practice of casting a hawk off down the wind when turning it loose) to abandon or let go; to talk to no purpose. **whistle for** to summon by whistling; to ask for or expect in vain (inf). **whistle for a wind** a superstitious practice of old sailors during a calm. **whistle in the dark** to do something to quell one's fear. **whistle in the wind** to make a futile attempt to achieve the impossible. **whistle off** or **whistle away** to send off or dismiss by, or as if by, a whistle (falconry); to turn loose; to abandon. **worth the whistle** worth the trouble of calling for.

Whit /(h)wit/ n Whitsuntide. ◆ adj of or belonging to Whitsuntide. ❑ **Whit Monday** n the Monday following Whitsunday. **Whit Sunday** n Whitsunday.

whit /(h)wit/ n the smallest particle imaginable; the least bit. [By-form of **wight¹** creature]

white /(h)wīt/ adj of the colour of snow, the colour that reflects the maximum and absorbs the minimum of light rays; snowy or snow-covered; (sometimes cap) belonging to one of the pale-skinned, specif European races; relating to or characteristic of these; abnormally pale, pallid, bloodless; colourless; (of eg a rabbit or mouse) albino; (of hair) lacking pigment, as in old age; (of the soul, etc) innocent, pure, unblemished, purified from sin (poetic); bright; (of steel) burnished; (of silver) unburnished; (of glass) transparent or colourless; (of a variety of anything, eg grapes) pale-coloured, as distinct from darker types; (of wine) made from white grapes or skinned black grapes; (of flour) having had the bran and wheat germ removed; (of bread) made with white flour; (of coffee or tea) with milk or cream added; clothed in white; relating to the Carmelite monks; in continental Europe, anti-revolutionary (politics); auspicious, favourable; reliable, honest, upright, honourable; (of a witch) not malevolent, using his or her power for good purposes; (of eg war) without bloodshed. ◆ n the colour of snow; white colouring matter, eg paint; white clothes, as in dressed in white; (often cap) a white person; (also **egg white**) the clear fluid surrounding the yolk of an egg, albumen; the white part of the eyeball surrounding the iris; white wine; a white butterfly; (usu with cap) in chess or draughts, the player with the white pieces; a white ball in snooker; (in pl) household linen, or white clothes worn eg for cricket or tennis; (in pl) leucorrhoea, a white discharge from the vagina; a member of a white political party. ◆ vt to make white. [OE hwīt; ON hvītr, Ger weiss]

■ **white'ly** adj (obs except Scot) whitish, pale. **whīt'en** vt to make white; to bleach; to free from guilt, or to make to appear guiltless. ◆ vi to become or turn white. **whīt'ener** n someone or something that whitens; artificial milk for coffee or tea. **white'ness** n. **whīt'ening** n the act or process of making or becoming white; a substance used to make white, whiting. **Whīt'ey** or **Whīt'y** n (inf, often derog; also without cap) a white person; white people as a race. **whīt'ing** n ground chalk free from stony matter and other impurities, extensively used as a size, colour, etc (also **whīte'ning, Spanish white** and, as the finest quality, **Paris white**). **whīt'ish** adj somewhat white. **whīt'ishness** n. **whīt'y** adj whitish. ◆ n (also with cap) see **Whitey** above.

❑ **white admiral** n any of a genus of butterflies of the same family as the red admiral (genus Vanessa), having white bands on the wings. **white ale** n (dialect) ale brewed or mixed with ingredients such as flour, eggs, etc that give it a whitish colour. **white ant** n a termite (order Isoptera). **white arm** n a sword, bayonet or lance, translating Fr arme blanche. **white arsenic** see **arsenic**. **white'bait** n the fry of various species of herring, sprat, etc. **white'bass** n a silvery food-fish of the American Great Lake region. **white'beam** n a small tree (Sorbus aria or Pyrus aria) with leaves white and downy on the underside. **white bear** n the polar bear. **white'beard** n an old man. **white'-bearded** adj. **white'-bellied** adj. **white'-billed** adj. **white birch** n any of several birch trees with white bark, such as the N American paper birch or the European silver birch. **white'board** n a board, used for teaching or presentation purposes, similar to a blackboard but with a white plastic surface for writing on using felt-tipped pens; any similar teaching device, esp (**interactive whiteboard**) a device that projects data from a computer onto a screen where it can be manipulated; a reserved area on a computer screen on which several users can write.

white bonnet n someone employed to bid at an auction to raise prices. **white book** n (in some countries) an official government publication bound in white. **white bottle** n bladder campion. **white boy** n a favourite boy, a white-headed boy. **White'boy** n a member of an association of Irish peasants first formed in County Tipperary about 1761 for the purpose of redressing grievances, who, wearing white shirts, committed agrarian outrages by night. **White'boyism** n (also without cap) the principles of the Whiteboys. **white brass** n an inferior alloy of copper and zinc. **white'-breasted** adj. **white bryony** see **bryony**. **white'cap** n the male redstart or other bird with light-coloured head; a crested wave; a member of a self-constituted vigilance committee who, under the guise of purifying the morals of the community, deal violently with persons of whom they disapprove (esp US hist). **white cedar** n either of two N American coniferous trees (Chamaecyparis thyoides and Thuja occidentalis); the wood of either of these trees. **white cell** or **white blood cell** n (biol) a colourless blood cell involved in the protection of the body from infection, a leucocyte. **white Christmas** n an occasion when snow falls on Christmas Day. **white clover** n a Eurasian clover (Trifolium repens) with white flowers, an important fodder plant. **white coal** n water power (Fr houille blanche). **white coat syndrome** n a syndrome in which hypertension is induced in a patient simply through being examined by a medical practitioner. **white'coat** n a wearer of a white coat, eg a hospital doctor or (esp hist) a soldier; a seal pup in its first furry white pelt. **white'-collar** adj relating to or designating the class of workers, such as clerks, etc, who are not engaged in manual labour. **white-collar crime** n crimes entailing intellectual effort (as distinct from violent crimes, larceny, etc) such as computer fraud, embezzlement, etc. **white copper** n a light-coloured alloy of copper. **white corpuscle** n a white blood cell, a leucocyte. **white'-crested** or **white'-crowned** adj (of birds) having a white crest or crown. **white crops** n pl grain crops such as barley, rye and wheat that lighten to a pale gold as they ripen. **white damp** n a poisonous mixture of gases with carbon monoxide predominating, occurring in coal mines. **whited sepulchre** n someone professedly righteous but inwardly wicked, a hypocrite (Bible, Matthew 23.27). **White Dwarf** n (also without caps) the name given to a class of small dim stars outside the normal spectral sequence, because their luminosities are extremely low for their spectral type, such stars being in the final stages of their evolution. **white elephant** see under **elephant**. **White Ensign** n a flag with a white field and St George's cross, with the Union Jack in the canton, until 1864 the flag of the White Squadron, now flown by the Royal Navy and the Royal Yacht Squadron. **white'-eye** n any bird of the genus Zosterops or of related genera of the family Zosteropidae, most species of which have a conspicuous ring of minute white feathers round the eye. **white-eyelid monkey** n any of the mangabeys, monkeys with white upper eyelids. **white'face** n white make-up, esp as worn by a traditional type of clown. **white'-faced** adj having a face pale with fear or from illness; wearing white make-up, eg as a clown; (of animals) having the face, or part of it, white; with white front (also **white'-fronted**). **white'-favoured** adj wearing white favours. **white feather** n a sign of cowardice, as in show the white feather. **white finger** n a loss of colour in the fingers caused by arterial spasms reducing the blood flow, often (**vibration white finger**) caused by prolonged use of vibrating machinery. **white fish** n a general name for such fish as the whiting, haddock, plaice, cod, sole, menhaden, etc; (**white'fish**) any species of Coregonus. **white flag** n an emblem of truce or surrender. **white flight** n the movement by white people out of neighbourhoods where non-white people have come to live. **white'fly** n any of several insect pests belonging to the family Aleurodidae. **white-footed mouse** n the deer mouse. **White Friar** n (also without caps) one of the Carmelite order of friars, so called from their white clothing. **white'-front'ed** adj see **white-faced** above. **white frost** n hoarfrost. **white gold** n gold alloyed with nickel or palladium to give it a white colour. **white goods** n pl refrigerators, washing machines, dish-washers, freezers and similar appliances, usu painted with white enamel; household linen. **white'-haired** adj having white hair; white-headed, darling. **Whitehall** see separate entry. **white'-hand'ed** adj having white hands or paws; having hands unstained with guilt. **white hass, hause** or **hawse** n (Scot) an oatmeal pudding made with sheep's gullet. **white'-hat hacker** n a computer hacker who tries to break into a system in order to test its security (cf **black-hat hacker**). **white'head** n the blue-winged snow goose; a breed of domestic pigeons; a pimple or pustule with a white top. **white'-headed** adj (of an animal) with a wholly or partly white head; having white or flaxen hair. **white-headed boy** n a favourite, a protégé. **white-headed eagle** n the N American bald eagle. **white'-heart** or **white-heart cherry** n a cultivated cherry, related to the gean, with soft, tender flesh and pale skin. **white heat** n the degree of heat at which metals, etc emit white light; an intense degree of emotion, passion, activity, keenness, etc. **white herring** n a fresh or uncured herring. **white hole** n a suggested source of the matter and energy observed flowing into the universe (cf **black hole**). **white honeysuckle** n an azalea known also as the clammy or swamp azalea. **white hope** n a person on whom hopes for success, honour, etc are grounded (also **great white hope**). **white horse** n a white-topped wave; a figure of a horse on a hillside, formed by removing the turf from the underlying chalk, the most famous being in Oxfordshire, at Uffington. **white-hot**′ adj heated to such a degree that white light is emitted; intensely emotional, passionate, etc. **White House** n the official residence in Washington of the President of the USA. **white hunter** n a white man who is a professional hunter of big game; a white man who acts as guide to hunting parties and safaris. **white iron** n pig iron or cast iron in which all the carbon is in chemical combination with the iron. **white knight** n (stock exchange) a person who rescues a company from an unwanted takeover bid (cf **white squire**). **white**′**-knuckle** adj (inf) giving rise to extreme anxiety, alarm or terror, esp in **white-knuckle ride** a fairground roller-coaster or any similarly terrifying ride. **white lady** n a spectral figure said to be associated with the fortunes of a family, as in some German castles; a cocktail made of gin, orange liqueur and lemon juice; methylated spirits as a drink, sometimes mixed with similar substances (old Aust sl). **white lead** n basic lead carbonate used in paint and putty. **white leather** n supple skins from deer, sheep and goats, tawed (ie soaked in alum, stretched and scraped) and kept in their natural colour, used for gloves, purses, etc. **white**′**-leg** n phlegmasia alba dolens, a form of phlebitis occurring after childbirth (also called **milk leg**). **white lie** n a forgivable lie, esp one told out of tactfulness. **white light** n light containing all wavelengths in the visible range at the same intensity (the term is used, however, to cover a wide range of intensity distribution in the spectrum). **white lime** n (obs) whitewash. **white line** n a longitudinal continuous or broken line painted on a highway as a line demarcation for traffic. **white**′**list** n a list of people, organizations, etc that are regarded with approval. ◆ vt to put on a whitelist. **white**′**-listed** adj having white stripes on a darker ground. **white**′**-livered** adj having a pale look (once thought to be caused by a white liver); cowardly. **white man** n a member of the white race; someone assumed to deal fairly with others (inf). **white man's burden** n (Kipling) the white man's (former) perceived obligation to govern and educate less civilized black peoples. **white matter** n (anat) pale-coloured fibrous nerve tissue in the brain and spinal cord. **white meat** n the flesh of poultry, rabbits, calves, etc; the lighter parts of the cooked flesh of poultry (eg the breast), as opposed to the darker meat of the leg; food made of milk, butter, eggs, etc. **white metal** n a tin-base alloy with over 50 per cent of tin; also, an alloy in which lead is the principal metal. **white meter** n a meter that records off-peak consumption of electricity. **white night** n a sleepless night; in northern latitudes, a summer night that never becomes completely dark. **white noise** n a noise in which there are a large number of frequencies of roughly equal intensity. **white**′**-out** n a phenomenon in snow-covered regions in fog or overcast conditions in which earth and sky merge in a single whiteness; a dense blizzard; see also **white out** below. **white paper** n (often with caps) a statement, printed on white paper, issued by government for the information of parliament. **white pepper** n light-coloured pepper made from peppercorns from which the dark outer husk has been removed. **white pine** n a N American conifer (Pinus strobus), valued for its light-coloured timber; the kahikatea. **white**′**pot** n a Devonshire dish of sliced rolls, milk, eggs, sugar, etc, baked. **white precipitate** n a white mercurial substance used in ointments for treating worm-infestations, etc. **white pudding** n an oatmeal and suet pudding in a sausage skin. **white pyrites** n pl marcasite. **white race** n one of the main divisions of mankind, distinguished generally by light complexion and certain types of hair and skull, also known as **Caucasian**. **white rat** n an albino strain of the brown rat, much used in laboratory experiments. **white rent** n (hist) the tinner's poll tax of eightpence to the Duke of Cornwall; rent paid in silver. **white rhinoceros** n a large African two-horned grazing rhinoceros, Ceratotherium simum (also **square-lipped rhinoceros**). **white rose** n (hist) in the Wars of the Roses, the emblem of the House of York. **white rot** n a disease of plants characterized by a white fungal growth. **white**′**-rumped** adj. **White Russian** n a Byelorussian; a cocktail consisting of vodka, Kahlúa and milk. **white sale** n a sale of linen goods at reduced prices. **white salt** n salt dried and calcined. **white sauce** n a sauce made with roux thinned with milk or stock eg from chicken or veal, and flavoured as desired. **white seam** n (Scot) plain needlework. **white**′**-seam** vi to do plain needlework. **white settler** n (derog) a usu wealthy outsider who moves into a district and makes use of its amenities without blending sympathetically into the local community. **white sheet** n (relig; hist) the clothing symbolically worn by a penitent. **white**′**-shoe** adj (sl; orig US) namby-pamby. **white slave** n a girl procured for prostitution purposes (esp when exported). **white slaver** n. **white slavery** n. **white**′**smith** n a worker in tinned or white iron; a tinsmith; a polisher or finisher of metals. **white spirit** n a petroleum distillate used as a substitute for turpentine in mixing paints, and in paint and varnish manufacture. **White Squadron** n one of three divisions of the British Navy in former times; white-painted vessels built in 1883 and following years as part of a strong US Navy. **white squall** n a sudden tropical whirlwind or windstorm heralded by little more than a choppiness of the sea or the appearance of a small white cloud. **white squire** n (stock exchange) a friendly party to whom a company chooses to transfer the bulk of its shares as a defence against a takeover move. **white stick** n a walking-stick used by a blind person to feel his or her way, painted white as an indication of the user's blindness. **white stuff** n (sl) heroin, morphine or cocaine. **white sugar** n refined sugar. **white-suprem**′**acist** n an advocate of **white supremacy** the philosophy or policy of giving dominance to white people on the grounds of their alleged superiority. **white**′**-tailed** adj. **white tea** n tea made from silvery-white buds and immature leaves that have not been fermented and retain a light colour. **white**′**thorn** n the common hawthorn. **white**′**throat** n either of two warblers of the same genus (Sylvia) as the blackcap, having white throat feathers; a species of American sparrow; any of several species of hummingbird. **white tie** n a white bow tie, part of formal evening dress; hence, formal evening dress. **white**′**-tie** adj. **white trash** n see **trash**[1]. **white van man** n (derog inf) the driver of a (typically white-coloured) commercial van, stereotypically an inconsiderate and aggressive driver. **white vitriol** n zinc sulphate. **white voice** n a singing voice of pure, neutral tone, expressing no emotion. **white**′**wall** adj (of pneumatic tyres) having a broad white band around the side walls (also n). **white**′**ware** n articles made of white porcelain, pottery or other ceramic material. **white**′**wash** n a mixture of lime and water, or whiting, size and water, used for coating walls; a wash for the skin; false colouring; statements made or measures taken to rehabilitate a reputation, cover up official misdemeanours, etc; a total defeat in a game, sporting contest, etc (inf); a glass of sherry after other wines; an act of whitewashing. ◆ vt to cover with whitewash; to give a fair appearance to; to take steps to clear the stain from (a reputation), cover up (an official misdemeanour) or rehabilitate (a person) in the public eye; to beat (an opponent) so decisively in a game that he or she fails to score at all (inf). **white**′**washer** n someone who whitewashes. **white water** n shoal water near the shore, breakers; the foaming water in rapids, etc (**white**′**-water** adj as in white-water canoeing, rafting, etc). **white wax** n bleached beeswax; Chinese wax. **white whale** n the beluga. **white**′**wing** n the velvet duck, or an American scoter closely related to it; the chaffinch. **white**′**-winged** adj. **white**′**wood** n a name applied to a large number of trees or their light-coloured timber, eg the American tulip tree, whitewood cedar (Tecoma, or Tabebuia, leucoxylon; Bignoniaceae), etc; unstained wood or wood prepared for staining (as in whitewood furniture). **whīt**′**ing-time** n (Shakesp) bleaching-time. **whīt**′**y-brown** adj white with a tinge of brown.

■ **bleed white** to drain completely of resources. **China white** a very pure variety of white lead (also **silver white** and **French white**). **mark with a white stone** see under **stone**. **white out** to delete (written or typed material) with (white) correcting fluid, over which a corrected version may be written; to omit or cover up (secret or sensitive material in a report, transcript, etc) so leaving blank spaces; to (cause to) lose definition in conditions of white-out (qv above); to subject (an audience) to a blinding glare or flash (theatre). **whiter than white** extremely white; very pure, very law-abiding.

Whitechapel /(h)wīt′chap-l/ n a lead from a one-card suit, straightforward leading out of winning cards, or other type of unskilful play (whist); the intentional pocketing of an opponent's ball (billiards). [Whitechapel in London]
□ **Whitechapel cart** see under **cart**.

Whitehall /(h)wīt′höl/ n a street with government offices, in London; the British government or its policy.

Whitey, **whitey** see under **white**.

whither[1] /(h)widh′ər/ adv and conj to what place?; in which direction?; towards what state?; to which place; (used relatively) to which; to what; whithersoever. [OE hwider, related to **who**]
■ **whith**′**erward** or **whith**′**erwards** adv in what direction, to what point.
□ **whithersoev**′**er** adv to whatsoever place.
■ **no whither** to no place.

whither[2] see **wuther**.

whiting[1] /(h)wī′ting/ n a small edible white-fleshed sea fish related to the cod; extended to various similar fishes, such as Merluccius bilinearis. [**white**]
□ **whiting pout** see **pout**[2].

whiting[2] see under **white**.

whitleather /(h)wit′ledh-ər/ n leather dressed with alum, white leather; the paxwax of the ox. [**white leather**]

Whitley Council /(h)wit′li kown′səl/ n a joint standing industrial council (national or local), composed of representatives of employers and workpeople in an organized trade, to consider and settle conditions of employment, etc (also called **industrial council**). [Recommended (1917) in the 'Whitley Report', the report of a Reconstruction Subcommittee presided over by Rt Hon JH Whitley]

■ words derived from main entry word; □ compound words; ■ idioms and phrasal verbs

whitling /(h)wit'ling/ n a kind of trout, probably a young bull trout. [**white**, and **-ling¹**]

whitlow /(h)wit'lō/ n a painful inflammation of a finger or toe, esp near the nail, paronychia. [Perh a corruption of *whick-flaw*, *quick-flaw* (cf **quick¹** and **flaw¹**) or of *whitflaw*, from **white** and **flaw¹**]
□ **whitlow grass** n any of several plants alleged to cure whitlows, eg a small British saxifrage (*Saxifraga tridactylites*), or a small crucifer (*Draba verna*); whitlow-wort. **whit'low-wort** n any of a number of plants of the genus *Paronychia*.

whitret see **whittret**.

whitster /(h)wit'stər/ (*archaic*) n a bleacher of clothes or cloth. [**white**, and female agent sfx -*ster*]

Whitsun /(h)wit'sən/ adj relating to or observed at Whitsuntide. ◆ n Whitsuntide. [**white** and **Sunday**]
□ **Whitsun ale** n a festival formerly held at Whitsuntide. **Whit'sunday** n the seventh Sunday after Easter, commemorating the day of Pentecost, when the converts in the primitive Church wore white robes; in Scotland, one of the term days (now fixed as 28 May) on which rents, annuities, etc are payable. **Whit'suntide** n the season of Pentecost, comprising **Whitsun week** or **Whit week**, the week beginning with Whitsunday.

whittawer /(h)wit'ö-ər/, also **whittaw** /(h)wit'ö/ n a saddler or harness-maker (*dialect*); a maker of white leather, a tawer (*hist* or *dialect*). [**white** and **tawer**]

whitter another spelling of **witter**.

whitterick see **whittret**.

whittie-whattie /(h)wit'i-(h)wot'i/ (*Scot*) vi to mutter, whisper; to shilly-shally. ◆ n vague language intended to deceive; a frivolous excuse. [Perh formed from **what**]

whittle¹ /(h)wit'l/ vt to pare or cut with a knife; to shape with a knife; to diminish gradually (often with *down*, *away*); to lessen the force or scope of (with *down*, *away*). ◆ vi to cut wood aimlessly; to peach, or to confess at the gallows (*obs sl*); to fret (*dialect*). ◆ n a clasp knife, sheath knife or other large knife. [ME *thwitel*, from OE *thwītan* to cut]
■ **whitt'ler** n. **whitt'ling** n.
■ **whittle away at** to pare or whittle; to reduce, curtail or circumscribe little by little.

whittle² /(h)wit'l/ (*dialect*) n a woollen shawl; a blanket. [OE *hwītel* a white mantle, from *hwīt* white]

whittret or **whitret** /(h)wit'rət/, (h)wut'rət/ or **whitterick** /(h)wit'(ə-)rik/ (*Scot*) n a weasel.

Whitworth /(h)wit'wərth/ (*engineering*) adj denoting the standard British pre-metric screw thread, cut with an inter-pitch angle of 55°, first proposed by Sir J *Whitworth* (1803–87) in 1841 and still common in the USA.

Whity, **whity** see under **white**.

whizz or **whiz** /(h)wiz/ vi (**whizz'ing**; **whizzed**) to fly through the air with or as if with a whistling noise; to move rapidly (*inf*); to make a hissing, rustling or sizzling noise (*dialect* or *old*); to urinate (*US sl*). ◆ vt to cause to whizz. ◆ n a person remarkably talented or skilful at something (*inf*); a hissing sound (also *interj*); a bargain, agreement (*US sl*); an act of urinating (*US sl*); amphetamine (*sl*). ◆ adv with a whizzing noise. [Imit; cf **wheeze**, **hiss**]
■ **whizz'er** n something that whizzes; a pickpocket (*sl*). **whizz'ing** n and adv. **whizz'ingly** adv. **whizz'o** or **whizz'y** adj (*inf*) excellent; impressive.
□ **whizz'-bang** or **whiz'bang** n a light shell of high velocity which is heard arriving shortly before exploding (*World War I sl*); a firework reminiscent of this. ◆ adj excellent; fast-paced. **whizz kid**, **whiz kid** or (suggesting influence by **wizard**) **wiz kid** n (*inf*) someone who achieves success rapidly and early, through ability, inventiveness, dynamism and ambition.

WHO abbrev : World Health Organization.

who /hoo/ pronoun (*interrog* and *relative*) (*objective case* **whom** (OE *hwām*, orig the dative of *hwā* who, in the 12c and 13c replaced the older accusative *hwone*); *possessive case* **whose** (ME *hwas*, from OE *hwæs*, genitive of *hwā*)) what person or people?; which person or people (replaceable by **that**); used after a comma to add a clause commenting on a person or people; he or she or they that, the person or people that, anyone that; whoever; of what name, standing, etc. [OE *hwā*; cognate with Gothic *hwas*, OHGer *hwer*, Ger *wer*; also with Sans *ka*, L *quis*]
□ **whoev'er**, **whosoev'er** or **who'so** pronoun (*objective case* **whom'ever** and **whomsoev'er**; *possessive case* **whosev'er** and **whosesoev'er**) (*archaic*) every one who; whatever person. **who's who** n a directory listing names and biographical details of prominent people.
■ **as who should say** (*Shakesp*) like someone saying. **know who's who** to know the position and influence of everyone. **the who** (*Shakesp*) who. **who but he** or **she**, etc who else?, he or she, etc only.

whoa /(h)wō/ interj stop.
□ **whoa-ho-ho'** or **-hoa'** interj (*obs*) used to hail a person from a distance.

who'd /hood/ contracted form of **who would** and **who had**.

whodunnit or **whodunit** /hoo-dun'it/ (*inf*) n a story or play concerned with the elucidation of a crime mystery. [**who** and **done** (non-standard past tense of **do**), and **it**]
■ **whodun'itry** or **whodunn'itry** n this genre of writing; over-zealous culprit-seeking.

whole /hōl/ adj not broken; undamaged; not broken up, or ground, or deprived of any part; containing the total amount, number, etc; complete; (of a sister or brother) full-blooded, related through both parents; as yet unworked (*mining*); from which no constituents have been removed, as in *whole blood*, *milk*, etc; processed as little as possible; sound in health (*archaic*); uninjured; restored to health; healed. ◆ n the entire thing; not less than, all (with *of*); something complete in itself, esp if an integrated system or combination of parts. ◆ adv completely, altogether; in one unbroken piece, as in *swallowed it whole*. [OE *hāl* healthy; ON *heill*, Ger *heil*; see **hale¹**]
■ **whole'ness** n. **whole'some** adj healthy in body, taste, morals or (*Shakesp*) condition; indicating health; conducive to bodily or spiritual health; remedial (*obs*); propitious (*Shakesp*); reasonable, sensible (*Shakesp*). **whole'somely** adv. **whole'someness** n. **who'lism** n an alteration of **holism**. **who'list** n. **wholist'ic** adj. **wholly** /hōl'li or hō'li/ adv completely, altogether.
□ **whole blood** n donor blood for use in transfusions, from which no constituents have been extracted. **whole-body monitor** n (*nuclear eng*) an assembly of large scintillation detectors, heavily shielded against background radiation, used to identify and measure the gamma radiation emitted by the human body. **whole cloth** n cloth in its full manufactured size (**cut out of whole cloth** (N Am inf) wholly fabricated, utterly false). **whole'-coloured** adj all of one colour. **whole'food** n food, unprocessed or processed as little as possible, produced without any artificial fertilizers or pesticides, etc. **whole'-foot'ed** adj (*inf*) unreserved. **whole'grain** adj (of bread, flour, etc) made from the complete grain, with no parts discarded during manufacture. **whole'heart'ed** adj hearty, generous, zealous and sincere. **whole'heart'edly** adv. **whole'-heart'edness** n. **whole'-hog** adj (*sl*) out-and-out, complete. **whole'-hogg'er** n someone who is inclined to go the whole hog. **whole'-hoofed** adj having an undivided hoof. **whole'-length** adj giving the whole figure; full-length. ◆ n a portrait or statue showing the whole figure. **whole-life insurance** n a life-insurance policy on which premiums are payable up to the death of the insured person. **whole'meal** n meal made from entire grains of wheat (also adj). **whole milk** n milk from which nothing has been extracted, as distinct from skimmed or semi-skimmed milk. **whole note** n (N Am) a semibreve. **whole number** n a unit, or a number composed of units, an integral number. **whole-plate** see under **plate**. **whole'sale** n sale of goods, usu by the whole piece or large quantity, to a retailer. ◆ adj buying and selling, or concerned with buying and selling, thus; extensive and indiscriminate. ◆ adv by wholesale; extensively and indiscriminately. ◆ vt to sell by wholesale. **whole'saler** n someone who sells by wholesale. **whole'-skinned** adj unhurt; safe in reputation. **whole'-souled'** adj wholehearted. **whole step** n (US) a whole tone. **whole'stitch** n (*lace-making*) a weaving stitch used to fill in a pattern, cloth stitch. **whole tone** n (*music*) an interval of two semitones. **whole'-tone scale** n (*music*) either of two scales produced by beginning on one of any two notes a chromatic semitone apart and ascending or descending in whole tones for an octave. **whole'wheat** adj wholemeal. **wholl'y-owned** adj describing a company all of whose shares are owned by another company.
■ **as a whole** in general; taken as a complete group, etc rather than as individuals. **go the whole hog** to do what one is doing thoroughly or completely; to commit oneself to anything unreservedly. **on** or **upon the whole** generally speaking; all things considered. **out of whole cloth** see **whole cloth** above. **with whole skin** safe, unscathed.

who'll /hool/ contracted form of **who will** and **who shall**.

wholly see under **whole**.

wholphin /wol'fin/ n the offspring of a *wh*ale and a *d*olphin.

whom, **whomever**, **whomsoever** see **who**.

whommle or **whomble** see **whemmle**.

whoobub /hoo'bub/ (*obs*) n see **hubbub**.

whoop /(h)woop or hoop/, also **hoop** /hoop/ n a loud eager cry; a Native American war cry; a form of hide-and-seek; /oop or hoop/ the long noisy inspiration heard in whooping cough. ◆ vi to give a loud cry of triumph, eagerness, scorn, etc; to hoot. ◆ vt to cheer or insult with shouts; to summon, or to urge on, by whooping. ◆ interj (*Shakesp*) ho! [OFr *houper* to shout]
■ **whoop'er** n someone who or something that whoops; a whooping swan or whooping crane (also **hoop'er**). **whoop'ing** n and adj.

❑ **whooper swan** *n* a swan (*Cygnus cygnus*) with a whooping call, common in N Europe and Asia. **whooping cough** or **hooping cough** *n* pertussis, an infectious and epidemic disease, mostly attacking children, characterized by catarrh of the respiratory tract with bouts of violent coughing that end in a long gasping inspiration. **whooping crane** *n* an American crane (*Grus americana*). **whooping swan** *n* a whooper swan.
■ **whoop it up** (*inf*) to indulge in noisy boisterous amusements or celebrations.

whoopee /(h)wŭ-pē'/ *interj* and *n* an exclamation of delight. [**whoop**]
❑ **whoopee cushion** /wŭ'pē or hwŭ'pē/ *n* a rubber cushion that makes a noise like the breaking of wind when sat on.
■ **make whoopee** /wŭ'pē or hwŭ'pē/ (*inf*) to indulge in hilarious fun or frivolity; to make love.

whoops /wŭps or woops/ *interj* an exclamation of surprise or concern made when one has a slight accident, makes an error, etc, or sees someone else do so. [Variant of **oops**]
■ **whoop'sie** *n* (*inf*) a mess, *specif* of the excretory kind, made by a baby, animal etc; an egregious error.

whoosh /(h)woosh, (h)wŭsh/ or **woosh** /woosh/ *n* the sound of, or like that of, something large passing rapidly through the air (also *interj*). ◆ *vi* and *vt* to move or cause to move with, or as if with, such a sound. ◆ *adv* with a whoosh. [Imit]

whoot obsolete variant of **hoot**.

whop or **whap** /(h)wop/ (*inf* or *dialect*) *vt* (**whopp'ing** or **whapp'ing**; **whopped** or **whapped**) to whip, thrash; to defeat or surpass; to throw or pull suddenly or violently. ◆ *vi* to fall, thump or move suddenly; to flop down. ◆ *n* a blow; a bump; the noise made by either of these. [Variant of **wap**¹; origin obscure, prob partly imit]
■ **whopp'er** *n* someone who or something that whops; anything very large; a lie. **whopp'ing** *adj* very large (often as an intensifier). ◆ *n* a thrashing.

whore /hōr or hör/ *n* a prostitute; any unchaste woman; an allegedly corrupt religious community or practice. ◆ *vi* to be, or associate with, a whore or whores. ◆ *vt* to make a whore of, debauch; to spend in whoring. [Late OE *hōre*, prob from ON *hōra* adulteress]
■ **whore'dom** *n* whoring; any illicit sexual intercourse; idolatry. **who'rish** *adj*. **who'rishly** *adv*. **who'rishness** *n*.
❑ **whore'house** *n* a brothel. **whore'master** *n* (*archaic*) a whoremonger. **whore'masterly** *adj* libidinous. **whore'mistress** *n* (*archaic*) a woman who runs a brothel. **whore'monger** *n* a lecher; a pander. **whore's bird** *n* a whore's child; used as a vulgar term of abuse. **whore's egg** *n* a sea-urchin. **whore'son** /-sən/ *n* (*archaic*) son of a whore; a bastard; a term of coarse contempt or familiarity. ◆ *adj* mean, scurvy.
■ **whore after** to pursue (an unworthy, dishonest or selfish goal).

whorl /(h)wörl or (h)wûrl/ *n* a group of similar members arising from the same level on a stem, and forming a circle around it (*bot*); a single turn in a spiral shell; a convolution, eg in the ear; a disc on the lower part of a spindle serving as a flywheel (also **wharve** /wörv or hwörv/; *spinning*); in a fingerprint, a ridge forming a complete circle; a type of fingerprint having such ridges. [Late ME *wharwyl*, etc, variants of **whirl**]
■ **whorled** *adj* having whorls; arranged in the form of a whorl or whorls.

whorlbat see **whirlbat** under **whirl**.

whortleberry /(h)wûr'tl-ber-i, also -bə-ri/ *n* a widely-spread heath plant with a dark blue edible berry, the bilberry, blaeberry or whimberry, sometimes contracted to **whort**; extended to certain other plants of the same genus (*Vaccinium*). [Orig a SW variant of **hurtleberry**]

who's /hooz/ contracted form of **who is** and **who has**.

whose /hooz/ *pronoun* the possessive case of **who** and also **which**.
❑ **whosesoever, whosever, whoso, whosoever** see under **who**.

whot /(h)wot/ (*Spenser*) *adj* variant of **hot**¹.

who've /hoov/ contracted form of **who have**.

Whovian /hoo'vi-ən/ (*inf*) *n* an enthusiast of the British television programme *Dr Who*.

whow /(h)wow/ (*Scot*) *interj* expressing deploration (often **eh whow** or **aich** /ăhh/ **whow**).

whummle see **whemmle**.

whunstane Scots form of **whinstone**.

whup /(h)wŭp/ (*sl*) *vt* (**whupp'ing**; **whupped**) to beat soundly or severely; to defeat thoroughly. [Scot dialect form of **whip**]
■ **whupp'ing** *n* a severe beating; a thorough defeat.

why /(h)wī/ *adv* and *conj* for what cause or reason?; wherefore; (used relatively) on account of which. ◆ *interj* expressing sudden realization or protest, or marking resumption after a question or a slight pause, or

(*Shakesp*) used to call a person. [OE *hwī, hwȳ*, instrumental case of *hwā* who, and *hwæt* what]
❑ **whyev'er** *adv* (*inf*) for whatever reason. **why'-not** *n* a challenge for reasons (*old*); a dilemma (**at a why-not** (*obs*) at a disadvantage).
■ **for why** (*archaic* and *dialect*) for what reason; because. **the whys and wherefores** all the reasons. **why, so** (*Shakesp*) so let it be.

whydah or **whidah** /(h)wī'də/ *n* (also **whidah bird** or **whydah bird**) any of a group of African birds belonging or related to the weaver finch family, with mostly black plumage; any of various birds of a related family (Ploceidae). [**widow bird**, from the widow's black clothing; spelling altered in the belief that the bird was named from *Whydah* (Ouidah) in Dahomey (now Benin)]

WI *abbrev* : West Indies; Wisconsin (US state); Women's Institute.

wibble /wib'l/ *vi* (often with *on*) to speak foolishly; to talk at length about inconsequential matters. [Poss from **witter** and **dribble**]

wicca /wik'ə/ *n* witchcraft, *esp* as a revived practice; (with *cap*) an organization or cult of people practising or involved in witchcraft. [Reuse of OE *wicca* a (male) witch]
■ **wicc'an** *n* a member of this cult, or a practiser of witchcraft (also *adj*).

wice /wīs/ (*Scot*) *adj* wise, canny; sane, rational. [**wise**]

wich see **wych**.

-wich see **wick**³.

wick¹ /wik/ *n* the twisted threads of cotton or other substance in a candle, lamp or lighter, which draw up the inflammable liquid to the flame; any strip of material that draws up liquid by capillary action. ◆ *vt* to draw up (liquid) in this way. [OE *wēoce, wēoc*; allied to Du *wick* a roll of lint, Ger *Wieche*]
■ **dip one's wick** (*vulgar sl*; of a man) to have sexual intercourse. **get on someone's wick** (*inf*) to irritate someone.

wick² /wik/ (*dialect*) *n* a creek. [ON *vīk* a bay]

wick³ /wik/ *n* a village or town (*dialect*); a farm (*dialect*); as *sfx* /-ik or -wik/ (also **-wich** /-ij, -ich or -wich/) in *Berwick, Greenwich*, etc. [OE *wīc*, prob an old Gmc borrowing from L *vīcus* a village]

wick⁴ /wik/ (*curling*) *vt* and *vi* to strike (a stone) in an oblique direction. [Perh OE *wīcan* to bend, yield, give way]

wick⁵ /wik/ (*obs* or *dialect*) *adj* wicked. [OE *wicca* wizard, *wicce* witch]

wick⁶ /wik/ (*N Eng dialect*) *adj* lively and energetic. [Variant of **quick**]

wicked /wik'id/ *adj* evil in principle or practice; sinful; ungodly; (of an animal) vicious; cruel; mischievous, spiteful; very bad, harmful, or offensive; roguish (*inf*); unlucky (*Shakesp*); excellent, admirable (*sl*). ◆ *n* a wicked person (*Bible*); (with *the*) wicked people. [ME *wicked, wikked*, prob from *wicke, wikke* wicked, from OE *wicca* wizard]
■ **wick'edly** *adv*. **wick'edness** *n*.
■ **the Wicked One** the Devil.

wicken see **quicken**¹.

wicker /wik'ər/ *n* a small pliant twig or osier; wickerwork. ◆ *adj* made of twigs or osiers; encased in wickerwork. [ME *wiker*, of Scand origin; cf OE *wīcan* to bend]
■ **wick'ered** *adj* made of wicker; covered with wickerwork.
❑ **wick'erwork** *n* basketwork of any kind.

wicket /wik'it/ *n* a small gate; a small door in or near a larger one; a grill or loophole (*obs*); an opening or a window with a grille, eg at a ticket office, bank, etc (*US*); (the following meanings all *cricket*) the upright arrangement of three stumps with two bails on top which the batsman defends against the bowling; a stump; the pitch, *esp* in respect of its condition; a batsman's stay at the wicket, or his joint stay there with another; a batsman's innings. [ONFr *wiket* (Fr *guichet*); of Gmc origin]
■ **wick'etless** *adj* (*cricket*) (of a bowler) not having dismissed a batsman.
❑ **wicket door** or **gate** *n* a wicket. **wick'etkeeper** *n* (*cricket*) the fieldsman who stands immediately behind the batsman's wicket and whose object is to stop balls missed by the batsman.
■ **get, take**, etc **a wicket** to bowl a batsman or have him dismissed in any way as a result of one's bowling. **keep wicket** to be the wicketkeeper. **over** (or **round**) **the wicket** (of bowling) delivered with the arm nearer (or farther away from) the wicket. **sticky wicket** see under **stick**². **throw down the wicket** (of a fielder) to break the wicket with a throw of the ball. **win by so many wickets** to win with so many wickets still to fall.

wickiup /wik'i-up/ *n* a Native American hut constructed with an oval frame and covered with grass or mats. [Fox (Native American language) *wikiyapi*]

wicky see **quicken**¹.

widdershins, widershins, etc variants of **withershins**.

■ words derived from main entry word; ❑ compound words; ■ idioms and phrasal verbs

widdle /wid'l/ (childish) vi to urinate. ◆ n urine; an act of urination. [Poss from **wee²** and **piddle**]

widdy¹ /wid'i/ (dialect) n a rope, esp one made of osiers; a halter for hanging. [Variant of **withy**]

widdy² /wid'i/ dialect form of **widow**.

wide /wīd/ adj extending far; having a considerable distance between the sides; broad; of a specified breadth; roomy; expanded or extended; opened as far as possible; far apart; far from the point aimed at, or (rare) place mentioned (with of); very different (with of; old); of large scope, including or considering much; astute, wily (sl); lax in morals (sl); broad, the reverse of narrow (phonetics). ◆ n wideness; a bowled ball that is judged by the umpire to be out of reach of the batsman (cricket); a penalty run allowed for this. ◆ adv (also **far and wide**) to a great distance, over a large region; at a distance (Spenser); far from the point aimed at, the subject under discussion, the truth, etc; far to one side (with of); so that there is a large space or distance between. ◆ combining form extending throughout a specified area, etc as in nationwide, countrywide, worldwide. [OE wīd; ON vīthr, Ger weit]

■ **wide'ly** adv. **wī'den** vt and vi to make or grow wide or wider; to throw open (Shakesp). **wī'dener** n someone who or something that widens; a kind of tool for widening something. **wide'ness** n. **wī'dish** adj.

□ **wide'-angle** adj (photog; of a lens) having an angle of view of 60° or more and a short focal length. **wide area network** n (comput) a computer network operating nationally or internationally, using telecommunications links, microwaves and satellites (abbrev **WAN**). **wide'awake** n a low wide-brimmed soft felt hat. **wide'-awake'ness** n the condition of being wide awake. **wide'band** adj another name for **broadband** (see under **broad**). **wide'body** or **wide'-bod'ied** adj (of aircraft) having a wide fuselage. **wide boy** n (inf) an astute or wily person, esp one prone to sharp practice. **wide'chapped** adj (Shakesp) open-mouthed. **wide'-eyed** adj showing great surprise; naive, credulous. **wide'-gab** n (Scot) the angler, a wide-mouthed fish. **wide-o'pen** adj (US) lax in enforcing laws and regulations. **wide'-rang'ing** adj covering a wide range of topics, interests, cases, etc. **wide receiver** n (American football) a member of the offense whose task is to catch passes and run with the ball. **wide'screen** adj denoting a cinema format in which the image is projected onto a wide curved screen to give the viewer a greater sense of actuality in the picture; denoting a television set with a picture-width-to-height ratio of 16:9, as opposed to the common standard of 4:3. ◆ n a widescreen television set. **wide'-spec'trum** adj (of an antibiotic, etc) effective against a wide range of micro-organisms. **wide'spread** adj extended or extending widely; found, operative, etc in many places. **wide'-stretched** adj (Shakesp) large. **wide'-watered** adj (eg Milton) bordered or covered by wide waters, having a great extent of water.

■ **to the wide** completely; utterly. **wide awake** fully awake; on the alert; keen and knowing (inf). **wide of** (Shakesp) indifferent to, far from observing. **wide of the mark** far out, astray from the truth. **wide open** opened wide; open to attack (inf); (of a contest, etc) having an uncertain or unpredictable outcome; same as **wide-open** above.

widgeon see **wigeon**.

widget /wij'it/ n a gadget; any small manufactured item or component; a device attached to the bottom of a can of beer that gives the beer a head like that on draught beer when it is poured; a single-purpose application that can be downloaded to a personal computer, mobile phone, or similar device (comput). [Ety obscure; perh an alteration of **gadget**]

widgie /wij'i/ (Aust and NZ) n an Australian Teddy girl of the 1950s, the female counterpart of a bodgie (qv). [Formed after **bodgie**]

widow /wid'ō/ n a woman whose husband is dead and who has not remarried; a woman whose husband spends much time away from her on some (esp sporting) pursuit, as in golf widow (inf); in the early Church, one of a special class of pious women; an extra hand in some card games; a short last line at the end of a paragraph that stands at the top of a page or column of print (printing). ◆ vt to leave (someone) a widow or widower; to strip of anything valued; to endow with a widow's right (Shakesp); to be a widow to (Shakesp). [OE widewe ; Ger Witwe, L vidua bereft of a husband, Sans vidhavā]

■ **wid'ower**, or (dialect) **wid'owman** n a man whose wife is dead. **wid'owerhood** n. **wid'owhood** n the state of being a widow (or sometimes a widower); a widow's right (Shakesp).

□ **widow bird** see **whydah**. **widow's bench** n (hist) a widow's share of her husband's estate besides her jointure. **widow's chamber** n the clothes and bedroom furniture of the widow of a London freeman, to which she was entitled. **widow's cruse** n a source of supply that never fails (from the story in the Bible, 1 Kings 17.10–16). **widow's man** n (naut) any of a number of fictitious persons formerly entered as a part of a ship's company in order that the pay allotted to them might be set aside for widows' pensions. **widow's mite** n a small offering generously given (Bible, Mark 12.42; see also **mite²**). **widow's peak** n

a point of hair over the forehead, like the cusped front of the widow's cap formerly worn. **widow's weeds** n pl the mourning clothes formerly worn by all widows. **widow wail** n a dwarf shrub (genus Cneorum) with pink scented flowers, native to Spain and S France; daphne or mezereon (Daphne mezereum).

■ **a widow bewitched** a woman deserted by or separated from her husband, a grass widow. **the Widow** Veuve (Fr, widow) Clicquot, a famous brand of champagne.

width /width/ n extent from side to side, breadth; wideness; the distance from side to side across a swimming-pool. [A 17c formation on the analogy of **breadth**, replacing **wideness**]

■ **width'ways** or **width'wise** adv in the direction of the width, across the width.

wiel same as **weel¹**.

wield /wēld/ vt to use, or lift ready to use (a tool, weapon, etc); to have or exert (power, authority, influence, etc); to use (eg one's pen, wit, etc) in the manner of a tool or weapon; to rule (obs); to possess, enjoy, gain (obs); to control, manage (eg lands; obs). [OE weldan (not recorded; WSax wealdan); Gothic waldan, Ger walten]

■ **wield'able** adj capable of being wielded. **wield'er** n. **wield'iness** n. **wield'less** (Spenser **weeldlesse**) adj unmanageable. **wield'y** adj easy to wield; manageable; dexterous, active (obs).

■ **wield the sceptre** to have supreme command or control.

wiener /wē'nər/ or (inf) **wienie** /wē'ni/ (N Am) n short for **wienerwurst** /wē'ner-wûrst/ a small smoked beef, pork or veal sausage. [Ger Wiener of Wien, ie Vienna]

□ **Wiener schnitzel** /vē'nər shnit'səl/ n a veal cutlet dressed with breadcrumbs and eggs. **Wiener Werkstätte** /vē'nər verk'shtet-ə/ n (Ger, Viennese workshops) an association of craftspeople and designers founded in Vienna in 1903 whose main influences were the English Arts and Crafts movement and Art Nouveau.

wife /wīf/ n (pl **wives**) a woman to whom someone is married; a married woman; a woman (archaic or dialect); (also **goodwife**) the mistress of a house, a hostess (obs); the passive or subservient partner in a homosexual relationship (sl). ◆ combining form denoting a woman engaged in some particular work or in the supply of a particular commodity, as in housewife, midwife, fishwife, alewife. [OE wīf ; ON vīf, Ger Weib]

■ **wife'hood** n the state of being a wife. **wife'less** adj without a wife. **wife'like** adj. **wife'liness** n. **wife'ly** adj. **wi'fey** n (inf) a patronizing way of referring to one's wife. **wī'fie** n (Scot inf) a woman.

□ **wife'-beater** n a man who physically abuses his wife; a vest worn without a shirt over it (N Am sl). **wife'-swapping** n (inf) a temporary exchange of sexual partners between married couples.

■ **take to wife** (archaic) to marry (a woman).

Wiffle® ball /wif'l böl/ n a light plastic ball with perforations that cause it to move erratically. [From **whiff¹** (in sense of fail to hit)]

Wi-Fi® /wī'fī/ n a method of transmitting data between computers without the use of wires, using high-frequency radio waves. [From wireless fidelity; modelled on **hi-fi**]

wig¹ /wig/ n an artificial covering of hair for the head worn to conceal baldness, to disguise the appearance or as part of stage costume, cosmetically, or for fashion's sake, as in the full-dress **full-bottomed wig** of Queen Anne's time, still worn in an official capacity by judges, and the smaller **tie-wig**, still represented by the judge's undress wig and the barrister's or advocate's frizzed wig; a judge (sl). [Short for **periwig**]

■ **wigged** adj wearing a wig. **wigg'ery** n false hair; excess of formality (Carlyle). **wig'less** adj without a wig. **wig'like** adj.

□ **wig block** n a block or shaped piece of wood for fitting a wig on. **wig'-maker** n a maker of wigs.

wig² /wig/ (inf) vt (**wigg'ing**; **wigged**) to scold. [**wig¹**]

■ **wigg'ing** n (inf) a scolding.

■ **wig out** (US sl) to go crazy, freak out.

wigan /wig'ən/ n a stiff canvas-like fabric for stiffening garments; a plain grey cloth for boot-linings, etc. [From the town of Wigan in NW England]

wigeon or (now rarely) **widgeon** /wij'ən/ n any of various ducks of the genus Anas, with long pointed wings and a wedge-shaped tail; in the UK, specif Anas penelope ; a fool (obs). [Of uncertain origin]

wigga see **wigger**.

wigged see **wig¹, ²**.

wigger /wig'ər/ or **wigga** /wig'ə/ (derog sl) n a white person who adopts elements of urban black culture. [From white nigger]

wiggery see under **wig¹**.

wigging see **wig²**.

wiggle /wig'l/ vi and vt to waggle, wriggle. ◆ n a wiggling motion. —Also (inf) **wigg'le-wagg'le**. [Frequentative of verb from which is derived dialect wig to wag; connected with MLGer wiggelen]

■ **wigg'ler** *n* someone who wriggles. **wigg'ly** *adj* wriggly; wavy, *esp* irregularly so.

❑ **wiggle room** *n* (*inf*) freedom and scope in which to act.

■ **get a wiggle on** (*sl*) to hurry.

wight[1] /wīt/ *n* a creature or a person (*archaic*, *dialect* or *ironic*); a supernatural being (*obs*). [OE *wiht* a creature, thing; Ger *Wicht*; cf **whit**]

wight[2] /wīt/ (*archaic* and *dialect*) *adj* swift, nimble; courageous, strong. [ON *vīgr* warlike, from *vīg* war (OE *wīg*)]

■ **wight'ly** *adv*.

wight[3] see **wite**[1].

Wigorn. *abbrev*: *Wigorniensis* (L), of Worcester.

wigwag /wig'wag/ *vi* to twist about; to signal by means of flags. ◆ *n* the act of wigwagging; a level crossing signal that gives its indication, with or without a red light, by swinging about a fixed axis. ◆ *adj* twisting. ◆ *adv* to and fro. [Dialect *wig* (from same root as **wiggle**) and **wag**[1]]

wigwam /wig'wam or wig'wom/ *n* a domed tent-like Native American dwelling made of arched poles covered with skins, bark or mats; often applied to the cone-shaped dwelling more correctly known as a tepee. [Abenaki and Massachuset *wikewam*]

wiki /wik'i/ *n* a type of computer software that enables any user of a website to edit and restructure its contents. [Coined by Ward Cunningham (born 1949), creator of the software, from Hawaiian *wiki wiki* very quick]

■ **wikial'ity** *n* (modelled on *reality*; *inf*) information that is assumed to be true because it appears in a wiki-based encyclopedia.

wilco /wil'kō/ *interj* (in signalling, telecommunications, etc) an *abbrev* of 'I *will* comply' (with instructions); used generally to signify compliance (*inf*).

wild[1] /wīld/ *adj* being in a state of nature, not tamed or cultivated; of an undomesticated or uncultivated kind; uncivilized, savage; desolate, rugged, inhospitable, uninhabitable or uninhabited; tempestuous; violent; fierce; passionate; frantically excited; unrestrained, uncontrolled, out of control; licentious; agitated; shy; distracted, distraught; furious; intensely enthusiastic, eager, keen (with *about*); strong and irrational; fantastic; crazy, impracticable; enjoyable, terrific (*sl*); disordered, dishevelled; unconsidered, rough, random, approximate; wide of the mark; fresh and natural; (with *cap*) applied to the extreme Evangelical party in the Church of Scotland (*hist*); (of a playing card) having any value desired. ◆ *adv* in a wild manner. ◆ *n* (also in *pl*) an uncultivated region; a wilderness or desert (also *fig*); an empty region of air or water (*poetic*); (in *sing*) a wild animal's or plant's natural environment or life in it. [OE *wilde*; common Gmc word]

■ **wīld'ing** *n* that which grows wild or without cultivation; a wild crab-apple; a garden plant self-sown, an escape; a wild animal; see **go wilding** below. ◆ *adj* uncultivated or wild. **wild'ish** *adj* somewhat wild. **wild'ly** *adv*. **wild'ness** *n*.

❑ **wild animals** *n pl* undomesticated animals. **wild ass** *n* any of several Asiatic or African asses, such as the onager, living naturally in a wild state. **wild birds** *n pl* birds not domesticated, *esp* those protected at certain seasons under the Acts of 1880 onwards. **wild boar** *n* a wild pig, *esp Sus scrofa*, from which most domestic pigs are derived. **wild'-born** *adj* born in the wild. **wild card** *n* a person allowed to compete in a sports event even though lacking the stipulated qualifications, etc; (the offering of) such a chance to compete; a character that can stand for any other character or group of characters in a file, etc (*comput*). **wild'cat** *n* an undomesticated species of cat (*Felis sylvestris*) native to Europe; any of various small wild animals of the cat family; the skins of these; a quick-tempered, fierce person; a speculative or unsound financial scheme (*US*); someone who takes part in such a scheme (*US*); an exploratory oil well (*US*). ◆ *adj* (of a business scheme, etc) haphazard, reckless, unsound financially; (of a strike) unauthorized by union officials; (of an oil well) exploratory (*US*). ◆ *vt* and *vi* (*US*) to drill an experimental well in an area of unknown productivity in search of oil, gas, ore, etc. **wild'catter** *n* (*US*). **wild cherry** *n* any uncultivated tree bearing cherries, such as the gean (*Prunus avium*), or its fruit. **wild child** *n* (*inf*) a young person who enjoys a hedonistic lifestyle. **wild dog** *n* any wild species of the dog genus or family, such as the dhole, the dingo, etc. **wild duck** see under **duck**[1]. **wild-eyed'** *adj* looking angrily distressed or distracted; (of an idea or plan) unrealistic, impracticable. **wild'fire** *n* a sweeping, destructive fire; a needfire; any of various inflammable materials used in warfare, such as Greek fire (*hist*) (**like wildfire** extremely fast); lightning without thunder; a disease of sheep; will-o'-the-wisp. **wild'fowl** *n* the birds of the duck tribe; game birds. **wild'fowler** *n*. **wild'fowling** *n* the pursuit of wildfowl. **wild ginger** *n* a N American plant (*Asarum canadense*) whose root is sometimes used as a substitute for ginger. **wild goose** *n* a wild or feral bird of the goose kind; a flighty or foolish person; (in *pl*, **Wild Geese**; *hist*) Irish Jacobites who migrated to the Continent after the abdication of James

II, *esp* those who joined the French army. **wild-goose chase** *n* a search that is doomed, *esp* for reasons unknown to the searcher, to be unsuccessful; *orig* a chase hither and thither of the follow-my-leader kind. **wild grape** *n* a grapevine (*Vitis* or *Muscadinia*) in the wild state, or its fruit; Coccoloba (see **grapetree** under **grape**[1]). **wild honey** *n* the honey of wild bees. **Wild Hunt** *n* in Germanic legend, a host of phantoms rushing along, accompanied by the shouting of huntsmen and the baying of dogs. **Wild Huntsman** *n* the leader of a Wild Hunt. **wild hyacinth** *n* (*esp Scot*) the bluebell, *Endymion* or *Scilla nonscriptus*. **wild indigo** *n* any of several plants of different genera belonging to the same family (Papilionaceae) as indigo, such as an American tumbleweed (*Baptisia tinctoria*). **wild'land** *n* land completely uncultivated. **wild'life** *n* wild animals, birds, etc collectively. **wildlife park** *n* a safari park containing native or non-native animals. **wild man** *n* someone uncivilized, a savage (*old*); a man of extreme or radical views in politics. **wild mare** *n* a seesaw; an instrument of punishment, the horse. **wild oat** *n* any of several tall perennial weeds related to the cultivated oat, eg *Avena fatua*. **wild olive** *n* the oleaster (qv). **wild rice** *n* see **zizania**. **wild service** *n* a tree, *Sorbus torminalis*, of the same genus as the service tree. **wild silk** *n* silk from wild silkworms; short-fibred silk imitating this. **wild thyme** see **thyme**. **wild track** *n* a soundtrack recorded independently of a photographic track, but used in editing. **wild type** *n* (*biol*) the form of a species typically occurring under natural breeding conditions, as distinct from mutant types. **wild water** *n* the foaming water in rapids, etc. **Wild West** *n* the western United States in the days of the first settlers, chiefly cattlemen and goldminers, before the establishment of law and order. **Wild-West Show** *n* a performance of roping or riding of steers, shooting, etc by (people dressed as) cowboys. **wild Williams** *n* (*dialect*) ragged Robin. **wild'wood** *n* wild uncultivated, or unfrequented, woodland (also *adj*).

■ **go wilding** (*US*) of a gang of youths, or as a member of such a gang, to attack violently, by beating, robbing and raping. **run wild** to take to loose living; to live or grow in freedom from constraint or control; to revert to the wild or uncultivated state. **sow one's wild oats** see under **oat**. **wild and woolly** unpolished; unrestrained; suggestive of the Wild West, lawless.

wild[2] /wīld/ obsolete variant of **weald** or **wield**.

wildcat see under **wild**[1].

wildebeest /wil'di-bēst, vil'də-bēst or vil'di-bäst/ (*S Afr*) *n* a gnu. [Du *wilde* wild, and *beest* ox]

wilder /wil'dər/ (*poetic*) *vt* to cause to stray; to bewilder. ◆ *vi* to wander wildly or widely. [Origin uncertain, perh formed from **wilderness**]

■ **wil'dered** *adj*. **wil'dering** *adj*. **wil'derment** *n*.

wilderness /wil'dər-nəs/ *n* a region uncultivated and uninhabited; a pathless, unfrequented or unexplored region; such a region deliberately preserved from the inroads of tourism; a desolate waste of any kind, eg an extent of open sea (*poetic*); a part of a garden or estate allowed to run wild, or cultivated in imitation of natural woodland; an overgrown tangle of weeds, etc; conditions of life, or a place, in which the spirit feels desolate; the situation of being without public office or influence, or of being forgotten by the public, after playing a leading role; the present world; a large confused or confusing assemblage; wildness (*obs*). [ME, from *wilderne* wild, wilderness, from OE *wilddēoren*, from *wild* wild, and *dēor* animal]

■ **crying in the wilderness** see under **cry**.

wildfowl, etc see under **wild**[1].

wildgrave /wīld'grāv/ (*obs*) *n* a waldgrave. [Ger *Wildgraf*, from *Wild* game, and *Graf* count]

wilding...to...wildness see under **wild**[1].

wile /wīl/ *n* a pleasing artifice; a trick; deceit (*rare*); (in *pl*) cajolery. ◆ *vt* to beguile, inveigle; to coax, cajole; to make to pass easily or pleasantly (with *away*; confused with **while**. [OE *wīl*; cf **guile**]

■ **wile'ful** *adj* full of wiles.

wilful or (*N Am*) **willful** /wil'fŭl/ *adj* self-willed, obstinate, headstrong; deliberate, intentional; willing (*Shakesp*). ◆ *adv* (*Shakesp*) wilfully. [**will**[1]]

■ **wil'fully** *adv*. **wil'fulness** *n*.

wilga /wil'gə/ (*Aust*) *n* a small white-flowered tree of the genus *Geijera*, able to withstand drought. [From an Aboriginal language]

Wilhelmine /vil'hal-mīn/ *adj* relating to Kaiser *Wilhelm* II of Germany (1888–1918) or his reign.

Wilhelmstrasse /vil'helm-shtra-sə/ *n* a street in Berlin; formerly, the German Foreign Office.

wili /vē'lē/ *n* in the ballet *Giselle* (based on a legendary theme from Heinrich Heine), the spirit of a maiden who dies before her wedding day. [Of Slav origin; cf Czech *víla* fairy]

wilily, **wiliness** see under **wily**.

wilja same as **wiltja**.

will[1] /wil/ v (2nd pers sing present indicative (with thou; archaic) **wilt**; 3rd pers **will**; pat **would** /wŭd/; 2nd pers sing (with thou; archaic) **wouldst**; no pap) used with an infinitive or absolutely: esp in 2nd and 3rd pers to form a future tense (**shall** often being used in 1st pers); in 1st pers to express intention or determination; to make requests, issue commands, or invite; to indicate capacity, as in the car will seat six; to suggest willingness or readiness on the part of someone or something, as in the car will not start; to express assumptions; to wish, desire or want, as in say what you will; to express resignation or frustration at events, another's perversity, etc. [OE wyllan, willan to wish, to be willing]

■ **will do** (inf) expressing readiness to do what is being asked of one.

will[2] /wil/ n the power or faculty of choosing or determining; the act of using this power; volition; choice or determination; pleasure, wish or desire; inclination, preference; lust; command; arbitrary disposal; (in combination) feeling towards others, as in goodwill or ill-will; the disposition of one's effects at death; the written document containing this. ◆ vt (pat and pap **willed**; 2nd pers present indicative **will'est**; 3rd pers **wills**) to decree; to seek to force, influence (oneself or another to perform a specified action) by silent exertion of the will; to dispose of by will, to bequeath; to wish, desire or want, as in what you will; to wish for (archaic); to command, order, require (obs). ◆ vi to exercise choice, choose, decree; to be willing. [OE willa will, determination, from which comes the weak verb willian]

■ **will'able** adj. **willed** adj having a will; voluntary; given or disposed of by will; brought under another's will, as in hypnotism; (in combination) having a will of a particular kind, as in weak-willed, strong-willed, etc. **will'er** n someone who wills. **will'-less** adj having no will of one's own. **will'-lessly** adv. **will'-lessness** n.

❑ **will'power** n the ability to control one's actions, emotions, impulses, etc. **will'-worship** n (Bible) worship after one's own will or fancy, superstitious observance without divine authority.

■ **at will** when or as one chooses. **a will of one's own** a strong, self-assertive will. **by my will** (Shakesp) voluntarily; with my consent. **conjoint** or **joint will** a testamentary act by two persons jointly in the same instrument. **have one's will** to obtain what one desires. **living will** see under **living**. **tenant at will** someone who holds lands only so long as the owner pleases. **with a will** heartily and energetically. **with the best will in the world** no matter how willing or persevering one is. **work one's will** to do whatever one chooses.

will[3] or **wull** /wil or wul/ (Scot) adj and adv at a loss; astray; bewildered. [ON villr astray; cf **wild**[1]]

willemite /wil'ə-mīt/ n orthosilicate of zinc, Zn_2SiO_4, white when pure but commonly red, brown, or green through the presence of manganese or iron, noteworthy as exhibiting an intense bright yellow fluorescence in ultraviolet light. [Willem (William) I of the Netherlands]

Willesden paper /wilz'dən pā'pər/ n a specially treated paper that keeps out wet and acts as a sound and heat insulator, placed under slates in roofing. [Willesden, orig place of manufacture]

willet /wil'it/ n a large N American wading bird (Catoptrophorus semipalmatus) of the sandpiper family, grey with black-and-white wings. [Imit]

willey see **willy**[1].

willful see **wilful**.

Williamite /wil'yə-mīt/ (hist) n during the political upheavals of 1688–9, a supporter of William of Orange (William III, 1688–1702). ◆ adj relating to or supporting the cause of William of Orange against the Jacobites (supporters of James II).

willie see **willy**[2].

willies /wil'iz/ (sl) n pl the creeps.

williewaught /wil'i-wöht/ (Scot) n a deep draught. [From misunderstanding of Burns, Auld Lang Syne 4.3, 'a right guid willie (or guid-willie) waught' (where 'guid willie' means 'good will'), a generous and friendly draught]

willing /wil'ing/ adj ready, glad or not disinclined (to do something); eager, co-operative; ready and prompt to act; voluntary; chosen; intentional (rare); of or relating to the will. [**will**[2]]

■ **will'ingly** adv. **will'ingness** n.

❑ **will'ing-heart'ed** adj heartily consenting. **willing horse** n a person or animal always prepared to work hard at any task.

williwaw /wil'i-wö/ n a gust of cold wind blowing seawards from a mountainous coast, eg in the Straits of Magellan; a sudden squall; a tumult or disturbance. [Origin uncertain]

will-o'-the-wisp /wil'ə-dhə-wisp'/ n (pl **wills-'o'-the-wisp** or **will'-o'-the-wisps'**) the ignis fatuus (qv); any elusive and deceptive person or thing. [Orig Will-with-the-wisp, from Will, short for William, and **wisp**]

willow /wil'ō/ n any tree or shrub of the genus Salix, having slender pliant branches; any of several plants resembling it; the wood of the willow; a cricket bat, traditionally made of willow; a willowing-machine. ◆ vt to clean in a willowing-machine. [OE welig; LGer wilge, Du wilg]

■ **will'owed** adj abounding with, or grown with, willows. **will'owish** adj like a willow; of the colour of willow leaves; slender and supple. **will'owy** adj abounding in willows; flexible; slender and graceful.

❑ **willow grouse** n a European species of grouse (Lagopus lagopus) with brown plumage. **will'owherb** n a perennial herb (Epilobium or Chamaenerion) of the evening primrose family (including rose-bay, bay willow, French or Persian willow) with willow-like leaves and seeds. **will'owing-machine** n a machine in which a spiked revolving cylinder, usu contained in a spiked box, loosens or cleans cotton, wool, rags for paper, etc. **willow pattern** n a blue design of Chinese character but English origin used on china from the late 18c onwards. **willow tit** n a small Eurasian dark-capped bird (Poecile montanus). **willow warbler** or **willow wren** n a small European sylviine bird (Phylloscopus trochilus). **willow weed** n one of various species of Polygonum or knotweed; the purple loosestrife.

willpower see under **will**[2].

willy[1] or **willey** /wil'i/ (dialect) n a willow basket; a willowing-machine. ◆ vt to clean in a willowing-machine. [OE wilige; related to **willow**]

willy[2] or **willie** /wil'i/ n a child's word for the penis.

willyard /wil'(y)ərd/ or **willyart** /wil'(y)ərt/ adj (Scot) wilful; shy. [**will**[3]]

willy-nilly /wil'i-nil'i/ adv willing or unwilling, whether one wishes or not; compulsorily, inevitably; haphazardly. ◆ adj having no choice; being so, or occurring, willy-nilly; vacillating (non-standard); haphazard. [**will**[1] and **nill**]

willy-willy /wil'i-wil'i/ (Aust) n a cyclone. [From an Aboriginal language]

Wilms' tumour /wilmz tū'mər/ (pathol) n a malignant kidney tumour usu occurring in early childhood, composed of embryonal structures. [M Wilms (1867–1918), German surgeon]

Wilson's disease /wil'sənz di-zēz'/ n a hereditary degenerative disease of the nervous system and liver, in which there is an accumulation of copper in the tissues. [Samuel Wilson (1878–1937), English neurologist]

wilt[1] /wilt/ vi (of flowers) to droop, become limp or wither, from heat or lack of water; to lose energy, to droop from fatigue or too much heat; to lose self-confidence or courage. ◆ vt to render limp, cause to droop or wither; to cause to lose spirit, self-confidence or courage. ◆ n the process of wilting; any of various diseases that cause wilting of plants. [Orig dialect; perh from **welk**[1]]

wilt[2] /wilt/ 2nd pers sing of **will**[1].

wiltja /wil'chə/ (Aust) n an Aboriginal shelter or hut. [From an Aboriginal language]

Wilton /wil'tən/ n (in full **Wilton carpet**) a carpet with a velvety cut-loop pile and a woven pattern, typically of a simple, three-colour kind, long made at Wilton, in Wiltshire.

Wilts. abbrev: Wiltshire.

wily /wī'li/ adj full of wiles, crafty, cunning, astute. [**wile**]

■ **wī'lily** adv. **wī'liness** n.

WiMAX /wī'maks/ abbrev: Worldwide Interoperability for Microwave Access, a technology for providing long-distance broadband Internet connections.

wimble[1] /wim'bl/ n an instrument for boring holes, turned by a handle; a gimlet; an auger; a kind of brace; an instrument for boring in soft ground. ◆ vt to bore through with a wimble. [Through ONFr, from MDu wimpel]

wimble[2] /wim'bl/ (Spenser) adj active, nimble. [Scot and N Eng word of Scand origin, now dialect]

wimbrel see **whimbrel**.

wimmin /wim'in/ n pl a variant spelling of **women**, used esp by feminist writers in order to omit the root 'men' from the word.

WIMP /wimp/ abbrev: weakly interacting massive particles (phys); windows, icons, mouse (or menus) and pointer (or printer or pull-down menus), a user-friendly computer interface.

wimp[1] /wimp/ (inf) n an ineffectual or pusillanimous person. [Orig US; variously explained]

■ **wim'pish** adj. **wim'pishly** adv. **wim'pishness** n. **wim'py** adj.

■ **wimp out** to lack the courage to do something.

wimp[2] /wimp/ n (old sl) a young woman. [Perh from **women**]

wimple /wim'pl/ or **whimple** /(h)wim'pl/ n a veil folded so as to cover the head and neck and closely frame the cheeks, a fashion of the Middle Ages that remained part of a nun's dress; a fold, wrinkle or ripple; a turn or bend; a crafty twist (Scot). ◆ vt to wrap in or hide with a wimple; to enwrap, enfold; to blindfold (Shakesp; in pap); to lay in folds. ◆ vi to meander; to ripple; to lie in folds (Spenser). [OE wimpel neck-covering; cf OHGer *wimpal* a light robe, Ger *Wimpel* a pennon, Fr *guimpe* a nun's veil, Eng *gimp* a thin cloth for trimming]

win[1] /win/ *vt* (**winn'ing**; **won** /wun/) to get by labour; to gain in contest; to secure; to achieve, effect; to reach; to be the victor in; to allure, persuade or prevail upon; to gain influence over; to obtain the favour of; to mine (an ore); to open up (a new portion of a coal seam). ◆ *vi* to gain the victory; to make one's way, betake oneself (*dialect*); to get oneself (into a desired place or state, etc). ◆ *n* (*inf*) a victory, success. [OE *winnan* to struggle, suffer; ON *vinna*, Ger *gewinnen* to win]
■ **win'less** *adj* without a win. **winnabil'ity** *n*. **winn'able** *adj*. **winn'er** *n* someone who or something that wins; something very good, impressive or successful (*inf*). **winn'ing** *n* the achieving of victory; (*usu* in *pl*) that which is won; a shaft or pit to open a bed of coal. ◆ *adj* that wins; of or relating to the achievement of victory; attractive, prepossessing; persuasive. **winn'ingly** *adv*. **winn'ingness** *n*.
❑ **winn'ing-gallery** *n* in real tennis, the gallery furthest away from the net at either end of the court, any shot played into this winning a point. **winning post** *n* a post marking the finishing point of a race-course. **win'-win' situation** *n* a situation in which one is bound to benefit or succeed; a situation in which all parties benefit.
■ **win by a head** or **short head** to win very narrowly. **win in a canter** to win easily. **win of** (*obs*) to get the better of. **win on** or **upon** to gain on; to get the better of; to obtain favour with or influence over. **win one's spurs** and **win one's worship** see under **spur** and **worship**. **win out** to get out; (also **win through**) to succeed or prevail, *esp* with a struggle (*inf*). **win over** or **round** to bring over to one's opinion or party. **you can't win** (*inf*) nothing you do will be satisfactory, find favour, etc.

win[2] /win/ (*Scot*) *vt* (**winn'ing**; **won** /wun/) to dry by exposure to the wind. [**win**[1] influenced by **wind**[1]]

win[3] or **winn** /win/ or **wing** /wing/ (*obs sl*) *n* a penny.

wince[1] /wins/ *vi* to shrink or start back; to make an involuntary movement, as in sudden pain; to register sudden mental pain or acute embarrassment; to kick (*obs* or *dialect*); to be restive, like a horse uneasy with its rider. ◆ *n* an involuntary start back or shrinking; a kick (*obs*). [Cf OFr *guinchir*, *ganchir* to wince, from a Gmc word; cf OHGer *wenkan* (Ger *wanken*) to wince]
■ **win'cer** *n*. **win'cing** *n* and *adj*. **win'cingly** *adv*.

wince[2] see **winch**[1].

wincey or **winsey** /win'si/ *n* a cloth, plain or twilled, *usu* with a linen or cotton warp and woollen filling. [Orig Scot, from **linsey-woolsey**]
■ **winceyette'** *n* a plain cotton cloth of light weight, raised slightly on both sides.

winch[1] /winch or winsh/ or **wince** /wins/ *n* a reel or roller; the crank of a wheel or axle; a powerful type of hauling or hoisting machine. ◆ *vt* to haul, hoist, etc using such a machine (with *up*, *in*, etc). [OE *wince*, from a Gmc and Indo-European root]
■ **winch'er** *n*.
❑ **winch'man** *n* someone who operates a winch or takes part in winching operations, eg aboard a helicopter.

winch[2] see **wench**.

Winchester /win'chəs-tər/ *adj* formerly used of various measures (eg 'Winchester bushel'), the standards of which were kept at *Winchester*. ◆ *n* (also *without cap*) a narrow-necked bottle for liquid chemicals, *orig* so called because it contained a 'Winchester quart' (*approx* 80 fluid ounces, or 2.25 litres).

Winchester® /win'chi-stər or -chə-/ *n orig* a tradename for a repeating rifle (**Winchester rifle**®) made by Oliver F *Winchester* (1810–80), American manufacturer; now a tradename for firearms, etc, produced by the makers of the rifle.

Winchester disk /win'chə-stər disk/ (*comput*) *n* same as **hard disk** (see under **hard**[1]). [After the *3030 Winchester rifle*, the IBM number of the disk being 3030]

wincopipe obsolete form of **wink-a-peep** (see under **wink**[1]).

wind[1] /wind or (*poetic*) wīnd/ *n* air in motion; a current of air, usually horizontal, either natural or produced by artificial means; any of the directions from which the wind may blow; breath; power of breathing; flatulence; conceit; empty, insignificant words; the wind instruments in an orchestra; their players; air impregnated with the scent of game or of a hunter or predator; a hint or suggestion, as of something secret; part of the body covering the stomach, a blow on which causes winding (*boxing sl*); a disease of sheep in which the inflamed intestines are distended by gases. ◆ *vt* (**wind'ing** or (of a horn) **wind'ing**; **wind'ed** or (of a horn) **wound** /wownd/) to perceive by the scent; to expose to wind; to drive or punch hard, so as to put out of breath; to allow to recover wind; to burp (a baby); /wīnd/ to sound or signal by blowing (*archaic*). [OE; related to ON *vindr*, Ger *Wind*, L *ventus*]
■ **wind'age** *n* the difference between the size of the bore of a gun and that of the ball or shell; the influence of the wind in deflecting a

missile, the amount of deflection due to wind, or the allowance made for it; air friction on a moving, *esp* revolving, part of a machine. **wind'er** *n* (*sl*) a blow that takes one's breath away; /wīnd'er/ someone who sounds a horn. **wind'ily** *adv*. **wind'iness** *n*. **wind'less** *adj* without wind. **wind'ward** *adj* relating to, or in, the direction from which the wind blows. ◆ *adv* towards the wind. ◆ *n* the windward side or quarter. **wind'wards** *adv*. **wind'y** *adj* like, characterized by or exposed to the wind; moved, played or produced by wind (*poetic*); controlling the winds (*poetic*); suffering from, producing or produced by flatulence; suggestive of wind, in being eg insubstantial, changeable, boastful, conceited or wordy; frightened, nervous (*inf*).
❑ **wind'bag** *n* a person of mere words, an excessively talkative person communicating little of interest or value (*inf*); the bellows of a bagpipe, or (*obs*) organ; the lungs or chest (*old facetious*); an inflated bag as a charm to procure a favourable wind. **wind'baggery** *n* (*inf*) the output of a windbag or empty talker. **wind band** *n* a musical ensemble made up of wind instruments. **wind'blow** *n* windthrow (qv below). **wind'blown** *adj* blown along or about by the wind; windswept. **wind'borne** *adj* (of pollen, seeds, etc) carried by the wind. **wind'bound** *adj* hindered from sailing by contrary wind. **wind'break** *n* something serving as a protection against the force of the wind, such as a fence or line of trees. **Wind'breaker**® *n* (*US*) a type of windproof jacket with elasticated cuffs and waistband. **wind'-broken** *adj* (of a horse) broken-winded. **wind'burn** *n* inflammation of the skin due to overexposure to the wind. **wind'burned** or **wind'burnt** *adj*. **wind'-changing** *adj* fickle. **wind chart** *n* a chart showing the direction of the wind. **wind'cheater** *n* a windproof jacket, an anorak; a close-knitted pullover. **wind chest** *n* the box or reservoir that supplies compressed air to the pipes or reeds of an organ. **wind chill** *n* the cooling effect that wind has as it blows on a surface; the combined chilling effect *esp* on a human body of low temperature, wind speed and relative humidity. **wind-chill factor** *n* a measurement of this. **wind chimes** *n pl* a hanging decoration composed of pieces of shell, metal, etc that tinkle against one another as the breeze catches them. **wind cone** *n* a sleeve floating from the top of a mast eg at an airport, its angle with the ground giving a rough conception of the velocity of the wind, and its angle in a horizontal plane the wind direction. **wind dispersal** *n* (*bot*) the dispersal of spores, seeds and fruits by the wind. **wind dropsy** *n* flatulent distension, tympanites. **wind egg** *n* an addled egg; a soft-shelled or imperfectly formed egg. **wind energy** *n* wind power (qv below). **wind'fall** *n* a piece of fruit blown off a tree by the wind; a sum of money that comes to one unexpectedly or suddenly, or any other piece of good fortune. **wind'fallen** *adj* blown down by wind. **windfall tax** *n* a tax levied on windfall profits, profits arising, *esp* suddenly and unexpectedly, as a result of events not directly connected with the company, etc concerned, such as changes in currency exchange rates. **wind farm** *n* a concentration of wind-driven electricity-generating turbines, *usu* sited on agricultural land. **wind'flower** *n* an anemone, *esp* the wood anemone. **wind furnace** *n* any form of furnace using the natural draught of a chimney without aid of a bellows. **wind'gall** *n* a puffy swelling around the fetlock joints of a horse. **wind gap** *n* a dried-up river valley in the mountains. **wind gauge** *n* an instrument for measuring the velocity of the wind; a gauge for measuring pressure of wind in an organ; an appliance fixed to a rifle by means of which the force of the wind is ascertained so that allowance may be made for it in sighting. **wind'gun** *n* an air-gun. **wind harp** *n* the aeolian harp (qv). **wind'hover** /-hov'ər or -huv'ər/ *n* the kestrel. **wind instrument** *n* a musical instrument sounded by means of a current of air, *esp* a woodwind or brass instrument sounded by the breath. **wind'jammer** *n* a large sailing vessel; a windproof jacket, a windcheater or anorak. **wind machine** *n* a machine that produces wind or the sound of wind (*theatre*, etc). **wind'mill** *n* a mill, eg for grinding grain, in which the motive power is the wind acting on a set of vanes or sails; a wind-driven set of vanes used to pump water, generate electricity, etc; any device that is caused to rotate by reason of its being carried through the air, and develops power (*aerodynamics*); a toy with a set of plastic or paper vanes mounted on a stick, that revolve in the wind. ◆ *vt* and *vi* (to cause) to move like the vanes of a windmill. **wind park** *n* a wind farm. **wind'pipe** *n* the passage running from the back of the throat to the lungs, through which air is drawn into and expelled from the lungs, the trachea. **wind power** *n* wind considered as an energy source, eg for the generation of electricity by means of windmills, etc. **wind'proof** *adj* (of garments or fabrics) resistant to or impenetrable by wind. **wind pump** *n* a windmill-driven pump. **wind rock** *n* the loosening effect on plant roots and tree roots of violent wind. **wind'-rode** *adj* (*naut*) riding at anchor with head to the wind. **wind rose** *n* a rosette-like diagram showing the relative strength and frequency of winds in a locality for given periods of the year. **wind'row** *n* hay raked together into a line to be made into cocks; a row of peats, etc, set up for drying. ◆ *vt* to arrange in windrows. **wind'sail** *n* (*naut*) a wide funnel of canvas used to convey a stream of air below deck; a vane of a windmill. **wind'screen** *n* the sheet of glass constituting the window

of a motor vehicle, *esp* the front window; a shelter against the wind. **wind'-shak'd** or **-shaken** *adj* agitated by the wind. **wind'shake** *n* a flaw in wood said to be due to the bending of the tree in the wind. **wind shear** *n* (*meteorol*) a sudden change in wind velocity at right angles (horizontally or vertically) to its direction; the rate of such change; conditions in which there are sudden changes of wind velocity and direction, constituting a danger to aircraft. **wind'shield** *n* a windscreen (*N Am*); a device to protect eg a microphone from the wind. **wind'ship** *n* a wind-powered ship, a sailing ship. **wind side** *n* the side exposed to the wind. **wind sleeve** or **wind'sock** *n* a wind cone. **wind'storm** *n* a storm consisting of very strong winds. **wind'-sucker** *n*. **wind'-sucking** *n* (in horses) a harmful habit of swallowing air, in many cases associated with crib-biting. **wind'surf** *vi* to ride on a sailboard. **wind'surfer** *n*. **wind'surfing** *n* (also called **sailboarding**) the sport of riding the waves on a sailboard. **wind'swept** *adj* exposed to, or swept by, the wind; dishevelled by the wind. **wind'-swift** *adj* swift as the wind. **wind synthesizer** *n* (*music*) a synthesizer designed with fingering like that of a wind instrument and played using the power of the player's breath, whose technique with the mouthpiece modulates the sound produced. **wind'throw** *n* the blowing-down of trees by the wind. **wind'tight** *adj* airtight. **wind tunnel** *n* an experimental apparatus for producing a uniform steady airstream past a model for aerodynamic investigation work. **wind turbine** *n* a wind-driven electricity generator, a tall slim structure with propeller-like vanes. **Windy City** *n* (*US inf*) Chicago.

■ **a capful of wind** a slight breeze. **before the wind** carried along by the wind. **between wind and water** that part of a ship's side which is first in, then out of, the water owing to the fluctuation of the waves; in a vulnerable or precarious place or position. **break wind** to release flatus from the anus. **cast** or **lay an anchor to windward** to make prudent provision for the future. **cast, fling** or **throw to the winds** to scatter or throw away recklessly; to abandon (restraint, prudence, caution, discretion, etc). **down the wind** moving with the wind; towards decay (*obs*). **fight windmills** to tilt at windmills (qv below). **get one's wind** to recover one's breath. **get the wind of** to get on the windward side of. **get** (or **have**) **the wind up** (*inf*) to become (or be) nervous, apprehensive, agitated. **get to windward of** to secure an advantage over. **get wind of** to get a hint or intimation of. **hang in the wind** to remain in suspense or uncertainty. **have the wind of** to be on the trail of. **how the wind blows** or **lies** the state of the wind; the position of affairs. **in the wind** astir, afoot. **in the wind's eye** or **in the teeth of the wind** right against the wind. **like the wind** rapidly. **on the windy side** (*Shakesp*) on the windward side, from which one cannot be attacked, hence safe, at an advantage. **put the wind up someone** (*inf*) to make someone apprehensive or agitated. **raise the wind** (*inf*) to raise the funds one needs. **sail close to** or **near the wind** to keep the boat's head so near to the wind as to fill but not shake the sails; to be in danger of transgressing an approved limit. **second wind** power of respiration recovered after breathlessness; the energy necessary for a renewal of effort. **sow the wind and reap the whirlwind** to act wrongly and receive a crushing retribution. **take the wind out of someone's sails** to deprive someone of an advantage, to frustrate or discomfit someone. **tilt at windmills** to struggle with imaginary opposition, from the story of Don Quixote who charged at windmills under the misapprehension that they were giants. **wind** or **winds of change** a pervasive influence bringing change, immortalized as a phrase by Harold Macmillan, speaking in 1960 of the inevitability of African independence, but previously used by Swinburne in his poem *Tiresias*.

wind² /*wīnd*/ *vt* (*prp* **wīnd'ing**; *pat* and *pap* **wound** /*wownd*/; chiefly *naut* **wind'ed**; *Burns* **win't**) to turn, to twist or coil; to (cause to) encircle or enfold; to coil the spring of (a watch, etc) or draw up the weights of (a clock) by turning a screw to start, or keep, it going; to make or direct (one's way) or (*archaic*) to traverse, by turning and twisting; to insinuate (oneself; *archaic*); to change the course of, deflect, control (*rare* or *obs*); to turn (a horse) to the left; to swing (a ship) round so as to head in another direction; to bring in, involve (*obs*), or to extricate, stealthily; to wind up or sum up (a discussion, etc; *archaic*); to weave (*Spenser*); to wield (*obs* or *dialect*); to haul or hoist, eg with a winch (*esp naut*). ◆ *vi* to turn round something (with *round*, etc); to twist; to move or go by turns and twists, or deviously; to meander; to go (*obs*); to writhe, wriggle (*obs* or *dialect*); to extricate oneself (with *out*; *obs*); to be twisted or warped (*dialect*); (of a horse) to turn to the left. ◆ *n* a turn, coil or twist; a turning; a twisted or warped condition. [OE *windan*; cf Ger *winden*, ON *vinda*, Gothic *windan*; cf **wend, wander**]

■ **wīnd'er** *n* someone who winds; an instrument for winding; a clock or watch key; an electrically driven winding engine for hoisting a cage or cages up a vertical mineshaft; the person who operates such an engine; a twisting plant; a triangular step at the turn of a stair or in a spiral staircase. **wind'ing** *adj* and *n*. **wind'ingly** *adv*. **wind'y** *adj*.

❑ **wind'-down** *n* a gradual slowing down towards the end of something. **winding engine** *n* a machine for hoisting. **winding sheet**

n a sheet for wrapping a corpse in; a shroud; the dripping grease that clings to the side of a candle (*dialect*). **winding stair** *n* a spiral stair constructed round a solid newel; a stair with an open well hole, constructed on a geometric (ie circular or elliptical) plan. **wind'ing-strips** *n pl* two pieces of wood with parallel edges, used for testing the trueness of timber, etc. **wind'-up** *n* the close, finish; an instance of winding up; a coiled position taken up by a pitcher before throwing the ball (*baseball*).

■ **turn the wind** (now *rare*) to go, move or cause to move from side to side or on a winding course. **wind down** to slow down and stop working; to relax or become quiet after a period of activity; to lose strength; to reduce the strength or scope of; to open (the window of a vehicle) by turning a handle. **wind up** to end up (*inf*); to bring or come to a conclusion; to adjust for final settlement; to terminate the activities of, liquidate (a commercial firm, etc); to excite or agitate (*esp* in *pap* **wound up**); to coil completely; to wind the spring or the mechanism of tightly; to close (the window of a vehicle) by turning a handle; to furl (*obs*); to tighten; to hoist, eg by a winch; to restore to harmony (*Shakesp*); to tease; to irritate, annoy or anger (*inf*). **wind up and down** (*obs*) to revolve in the mind.

windac see **windas**.

windage see under **wind¹**.

windas /*win'das*/ (*obs*) *n* a windlass; (*RL Stevenson* **wind'ac**) an instrument for bending a crossbow (*hist*). [Anglo-Fr *windas*; cf ON *vindáss*, from *vinda* to wind, and *áss* pole]

windbag...to...**windcheater** see under **wind¹**.

winded, winder see under **wind¹,²**.

windfall...to...**windhover** see under **wind¹**.

Windies /*win'dēz*/ (*cricket inf*) *n pl* the West *Indies*.

windigo /*win'di-gō*/ or **wendigo** /*wen'di-gō*/ *n* a mythical monster among some Native American tribes, which eats human flesh. [Ojibwa *wintiko*]

windily, windiness see under **wind¹**.

winding see under **wind¹,²**.

windjammer see under **wind¹**.

windlass¹ /*wind'las*/ *n* any of various modifications of the wheel and axle employing a revolving cylinder, used for hauling or hoisting; a windas for a crossbow (*hist*). ◆ *vi* to use a windlass. ◆ *vt* to hoist by means of a windlass. [Prob from **windas**]

windlass² /*wind'las*/ (*obs*) *n* a circuitous movement, *esp* to intercept game; an indirect, crafty action. ◆ *vi* to take a roundabout course. [Prob from *wanlace*, an earlier Anglo-Fr form, of unknown origin]

windle /*win'dl*/ *n* an appliance for winding yarn (also (*Scot*) **winn'le**). [**wind²**]

windless see under **wind¹**.

windlestraw /*win'dl-strö*/, also (*Scot*) **windlestrae** /*win'l-strā*/ *n* a thin dry stalk of grass; any of various long-stalked species of grass, eg rye grass; anything light or insubstantial; a lanky or feeble person. [OE *windelstrēaw*, from *windel* a woven basket, and *strēaw* straw]

windmill see under **wind¹**.

windock see **winnock**.

windore /*win'dör*/ or **-dör**/ (*Jonson*, etc; *obs*) *n* a form of **window**. [For *wind-door*, a popular derivation of **window**]

window /*win'dō*/ *n* an opening in the wall of a building, etc, to look out through, or to let in air and light; a wooden or metal frame fitted with panes of glass for placing in such an opening; the space immediately behind the opening; a windowpane; a glass-covered aperture eg at a theatre or railway station, at which one purchases one's ticket; any opening suggesting a window; (in *pl*) the eyes, or (*Shakesp*) the eyelids; (*esp* with *cap*) *orig* the codename for strips of metallic foil which, when scattered from aircraft deranged radar reception; a closed outcrop of strata lying beneath a thrust plane and exposed by denudation (*geol*); a weather window (qv); in various technical uses designating a part that is clear, free of a particular type of obstruction, etc; a gap in a schedule, etc available for some purpose; a chance to observe or experience something; a period of time when conditions are suitable for a particular activity and constitute an opportunity for it, as with **launch window** (planetary positions, weather conditions, etc, for the launch of a spacecraft), **re-entry window** (for the re-entry of a spacecraft), etc; a rectangular section of a screen which can be used independently of the rest of the screen (*comput*). ◆ *vt* to fit with windows; to make tears or holes in (*Shakesp*). [ME *windowe*, *windoge*, from ON *vindauga*, from *vindr* wind, and *auga* eye]

■ **win'dowed** *adj* having a window or windows, or openings or holes resembling these; placed in a window (*Shakesp*). **win'dowing** *n* (*comput*) the displaying in a window of an image or data from a file. **win'dowless** *adj* having no windows.

□ **window bar** *n* a wooden or iron bar between the panes of a window; a bar fitted into a window for security; (*Shakesp* **window-barne**, emended *bars*, *Timon of Athens* IV.3.116) latticework across a woman's stomacher. **window blind** *n* a blind or screen for a window. **window-bole** see **bole³**. **window box** *n* a box for growing plants in on a windowsill. **window curtain** *n* a curtain hung over a window, inside a room. **win'dow-dresser** *n*. **win'dow-dressing** *n* the arranging of goods in a shop window; the art of doing so effectively; the art or practice of giving something superficial appeal by skilful presentation. **window envelope** *n* an envelope with a transparent panel through which the address of the recipient on the enclosed letter can be read. **window frame** *n* a frame that surrounds a window. **window gardening** *n* the cultivation of plants indoors along a window ledge, or in boxes fitted on the outside sill. **window glass** *n* glass suitable or used for windows. **window ledge** *n* a windowsill. **win'dowpane** *n* a sheet of glass set in a window. **window sash** *n* a frame in which panes of glass are set. **window screen** *n* any ornamental device for filling the opening of a window. **window seat** *n* a seat in the recess of a window; a seat beside a window in a bus, aeroplane, etc. **win'dow-shop** *vi*. **win'dow-shopper** *n*. **win'dow-shopping** *n* the activity of looking at goods in shop windows as the next-best thing to buying them. **win'dowsill** *n* an interior or exterior ledge running along the bottom of a window. **window tax** *n* a tax levied on windows of houses (repealed 1851).

■ **out of** (or **out**) **the window** (*inf*) finished with, done for or abandoned.

Windows® /win'dōz/ *n* an operating environment for personal computers, providing a graphical user interface (qv under **graph**) and supporting peripheral devices.

windpipe, **windproof** see under **wind¹**.

windring /wīn'dring/ *adj* (*Shakesp*) *perh* for **winding** or **wandering**.

windrow see under **wind¹**.

winds see **winze²**.

windsail...to...**windship** see under **wind¹**.

Windsor /win'zər/ *adj* relating to the town of *Windsor*, in Berkshire.
□ **Windsor chair** *n* a chair with a solid wooden seat that has sockets into which the legs and the (*usu* slender spindle-shaped) uprights of the back are fitted. **Windsor knot** *n* a type of wide triangular knot used in tying a tie. **Windsor soap** *n* a kind of perfumed toilet soap (*usu* brown).

windsurf...to...**windwards** see under **wind¹**.

windy see under **wind¹,²**.

wine /wīn/ *n* an alcoholic drink made from the fermented juice of grapes or from other fruits or plants; a wine-drinking or wine party (*obs*); the rich dark-red colour of red wine. ◆ *adj* of, relating to or resembling wine; dark-red. ◆ *vt* to supply with wine; to treat or entertain with wine. ◆ *vi* to take wine. [OE *wīn*; Gothic *wein*, Ger *Wein*; all from L *vīnum*; cognate with Gr *oinos*]

■ **wī'nery** *n* (*orig US*) a place where wine is prepared. **wī'ny** or **wī'ney** *adj* tasting of or looking like wine; affected by wine-drinking, intoxicated (*obs*).
□ **wine bag** *n* a wineskin; a tippler. **wine bar** *n* a bar that specializes in serving wines and *usu* food. **wine'berry** *n* a grape (*obs*); a redcurrant, gooseberry or bilberry (*dialect*; see also **whinberry**); a raspberry (*Rubus phoenicolasius*) of China and Japan; the tutu, or another New Zealand tree, the makomako. **wine'bibber** *n* a continual drinker of wine; a drunkard. **wine'bibbing** *n*. **wine biscuit** *n* a biscuit *orig* intended to be served with wine. **wine bottle** *n* a glass bottle of a standard size for wine, holding 75cl (26⅔floz). **wine box** *n* a foil-lined cardboard carton of wine fitted with a tap for dispensing it. **wine cask** *n* a cask for holding wine. **wine cellar** *n* a cellar for storing wine; the wines stored there, or one's stock of wines generally. **wine'-coloured** *adj* of the colour of red wine. **wine cooler** *n* a receptacle for cooling wine in bottles about to be served at table. **wine funnel** *n* a type of funnel, *usu* made of silver or pewter, used for decanting wine from the bottle. **wine'glass** *n* a small glass used for drinking wine. **wine'glassful** *n*. **wine'-grower** *n* someone who cultivates a vineyard and makes wine. **wine'-growing** *n* and *adj*. **wine gum** *n* a type of gelatinous fruit-flavoured sweet. **wine lake** *n* a surplus of wine bought up by an economic community to prevent a fall in prices. **wine list** *n*. **wine measure** *n* an old English liquid measure, its gallon ⅚ of the gallon in beer measure. **wine merchant** *n* a dealer in wine, *esp* wholesale. **wine palm** *n* any palm yielding palm wine (eg *Borassus*, *Raphia*). **wine party** *n* a drinking party. **wine'press** *n* a machine in which grapes are pressed in the manufacture of wine. **wine'-sap** or **Wine'sap** *n* a variety of deep-red winter apple. **wine'skin** *n* a bag for holding wine, made out of a skin. **wine'-stone** *n* crude argol, the crust that forms on the walls of wine casks. **wine taster** *n* someone whose business is to sample wines. **wine tasting** *n* (a gathering for) sampling wines. **wine vat** or (*old*) **wine fat** *n* a vat in which grapes are pressed in wine-making. **wine vault** or **vaults** *n* a vaulted wine cellar; a place

where wine is tasted or drunk. **wine vinegar** *n* vinegar made from wine rather than malt. **wine waiter** *n* a waiter in charge of serving the wine in a restaurant, etc.

■ **in wine** (*archaic*) drunk, intoxicated. **red wine** see under **red¹**. **spirit of wine** alcohol. **white wine** see under **white**. **wine and dine** to partake of, or provide with, a meal accompanied by wine.

wing¹ /wing/ *n* one of the arm-like limbs of a bird or bat that are adapted for flying; an insect's similar flying-organ; an animal organ resembling a wing; any of various flat or projecting sections of a plant; one of the structures projecting from either side of an aircraft body, the plane of an aeroplane; flight; means of flying; anything resembling a wing; a fan or vane; (*usu* in *pl*) a sail; a part of a building projecting from the central or main section; (*usu* in *pl*) the area at each side of a stage where performers wait to enter, out of sight of the audience; a piece of stage scenery; any of the corner sections of a motor-vehicle body, forming covers for the wheels; a similar part of a carriage; a side piece projecting forward from the back of an armchair; one of the longer sides of crownworks or hornworks (*fortif*); the flank corps or division of an army on either side; the ships on either extremity of a fleet ranged in line; (a player on) either the extreme left or extreme right of the forward line in football, etc; either edge of a football, etc pitch; a section of a political party or other body, with its own distinct views and character; a group of several squadrons in the Royal Air Force; (in *pl*) a qualified pilot's badge; formerly, the badge of any member of an aircrew other than the pilot; a flock (of plovers); (*usu* in *pl*) means or power of rapid movement, a sudden access of speed; protection, as in *under someone's wing*. ◆ *vt* to provide or transport with wings; to lend speed to; to supply with side pieces; to bear in flight, to waft; to effect on wings; to traverse by flying; to wound in the wing; to wound superficially, *esp* in the arm or shoulder; to improvise one's way through (a speech or theatrical part that one has not fully rehearsed) (*inf*; see also **wing it** below). ◆ *vi* to soar on the wing; to move or travel with speed. [ON *væng* a wing]

■ **winged** /wingd/ or *wing'id*/ *adj* having wings; /wingd/ (of a stem) bearing the thin flattened bases of decurrent leaves, or (of a fruit or seed) having a flattened appendage; /wingd/ wounded in the wing, shoulder or arm; swift; lofty, sublime; (in **winged words**, rendering Homer's *epea pteroenta*) spoken, uttered, flying from one person to another; full of flying birds (*Milton*). **wing'edly** *adv* on or by wings. **wing'er** *n* a player in a position on the wing in football, etc; a pal, colleague or favourite (*milit sl*). ◆ *combining form* denoting a person belonging to a particular side of centre in a party, etc (as in *left-winger* or *right-winger*). **wing'less** *adj* without wings. **wing'let** *n* a small wing; a bastard wing (qv); a winglike appendage; a small vertical wing attached to the tip of an aeroplane wing to improve lift. **wing'like** *adj*. **wing'y** *adj* having, resembling or soaring on wings; lofty.
□ **wing'-and-wing** *adv* in the condition of a ship sailing before the wind with the foresail at one side and the mainsail at the other. **wing back** *n* (*football*) in formations using three central defenders, a player positioned on the flank with a more attacking role than a conventional full back. **wing'beat** *n* a beat or flap of a bird's or insect's wing. **wing case** *n* the horny case or cover over the wings of some insects, such as the beetles. **wing chair** *n* a high-backed armchair with forward-projecting lugs. **wing collar** *n* a man's stiff collar, worn upright with the points turned down. **wing commander** *n* a Royal Air Force officer of the rank below group captain, corresponding in rank to a naval commander or to a lieutenant-colonel. **winged bean** *n* a legume *orig* from SE Asia (*Psophocarpus tetragonolobus*), of special value for its high protein content. **winged bull** *n* a common form in Assyrian sculpture, symbolic of domination. **winged elm** *n* an elm tree of N America, its young branches having corky projections. **winged words** see **winged** above. **wing'-footed** *adj* having wings attached to the feet (*myth*, etc); fast-moving, swift (*poetic*); aliped (*zool*). **wing forward** *n* (*rugby*) one of the two outside players of the back row of the scrum, a flanker. **wing'-led** *adj* (*Shakesp*) *prob* led in wings or divisions. **wing loading** *n* (*aerodynamics*) the maximum flying weight of an aeroplane divided by the total area of the main planes, including the ailerons. **wing mirror** *n* a rear-view mirror projecting from the side of a vehicle. **wing nut** *n* a nut with flattened projections for easy turning by finger and thumb, a butterfly nut. **wing'over** *n* (*aerobatics*) a turning manoeuvre in which an aircraft is rolled onto its side and the nose is allowed to fall. **wing sheath** *n* a wing case. **wing shell** *n* a mollusc of the genus *Strombus*; a mollusc of genus *Malleus* or a related genus, or its shell; a wing snail. **wing shooting** *n* the act or practice of shooting flying birds. **wing shot** *n* a shot at a bird on the wing; a marksman who shoots birds in flight. **wing'-shot** *adj* shot in the wing, or while on the wing. **wing snail** *n* a swimming gastropod, the pteropod. **wing'span** or **wing'spread** *n* the distance from tip to tip of a bird's extended wings, or of the wings of an aircraft. **wing'suit** *n* a suit worn by skydivers for gliding when in free fall, with fabric between the legs and between the arms and body. **wing tip** *n* the extremity of a wing; (*US*; also **wing'tip**) a brogue shoe in which the toecap extends backwards and to the sides, suggesting the shape of a

bird with outstretched wings. **wing'-walker** *n* an acrobat who performs stunts on the wing of an airborne aeroplane. **wing'-walking** *n*.

▪ **birds of one wing** (*obs*) birds of the same kind. **flying wing** see under **fly**. **in the wings** (*inf*) waiting in reserve. **lend wings to** to give speed to. **make** or **take wing** to begin flight; to depart. **on a wing and a prayer** with no more than a slight hope of succeeding. **on** or **upon the wing** flying; in motion; departing. **on the wings of the wind** with the highest speed. **on wings** speedily. **spread** or **stretch one's wings** to explore one's potential. **under someone's wing** under someone's protection. **wing it** (*inf*) to extemporize in public speaking or ad-lib in a theatrical performance.

wing² see **win³**.

wingding /*wing'ding*/ (chiefly *N Am*) *n* a wild party; a lavish social function; a drug addict's seizure; a pretended seizure. [Origin uncertain]

winge /*winj*/ (*inf*) non-Scottish (*esp Aust*) variant of **whinge**.

winged, **winger**, **wingless**, **winglet**, **wingy** see under **wing¹**.

wink¹ /*wingk*/ *vi* to shut an eye briefly; to do this as a sign, hint or communication, eg to convey an amused understanding; to shut the eyes (*obs*); to blink; to seem not to see; to connive (*usu* with *at*); to flicker, twinkle. ◆ *vt* to close and open (an eye) quickly; to flicker; to express by flashlights. ◆ *n* the act of winking; a hint conveyed, or as if conveyed, by winking; a blink; a closing of the eyes for sleep, or a short spell of sleep, as in *forty winks*, *not sleep a wink*; a flicker; a very small time or distance. [OE *wincian*; Ger *winken*]

▪ **wink'er** *n* someone who winks; (*usu* in *pl*) a horse's blinker; an eye, eyelid or eyelash (*dialect* and *N Am inf*); the nictitating membrane of a bird's eye; a small bellows in an organ, regulated by a spring, controlling variations of wind pressure; either of the flashing direction indicators on a motor vehicle (*inf*). **wink'ing** *n* the act of giving a wink. ◆ *adj* (*Shakesp*) closed, or with eyes shut, or blind. **wink'ingly** *adv*.

❑ **wink'-a-peep** *n* (*dialect*) the scarlet pimpernel.

▪ **easy as winking** very easily indeed. **forty winks** see under **forty**. **like winking** (*sl*) very rapidly. **tip someone the wink** (*inf*) to give someone a useful hint.

wink² /*wingk*/ *n* one of the small coloured discs used in the game of tiddlywinks. [Short for **tiddlywink**]

winkle /*wing'kl*/ *n* a small edible snail-shaped shellfish, the periwinkle (see **periwinkle²**); the penis (*sl* or *childish*). ◆ *vt* (with *out*) to extract or force out little by little and with difficulty. [Short for **periwinkle²**]

▪ **wink'ler** *n* someone who or something that winkles out; a person who evicts tenants on behalf of the property owner (*inf*).

❑ **wink'le-pickers** *n pl* shoes with long pointed toes, *esp* popular in the early 1960s.

winn see **win³**.

winna /*win'ə* or *wun'ə*/ a Scots form of **will not**.

winnability, **winnable** see under **win¹**.

Winnebago /*win-ə-bā'gō*/ *n* (*pl* **Winnebā'go**, **Winnebā'gos** or **Winnebā'goes**) (a member of) a Native American people originally living in Wisconsin; the Siouan language of this people; (**Winnebago®**) a type of motorhome. ◆ *adj* of or relating to the Winnebago or their language.

winner...to...**winningness** see under **win¹**.

winnle see **windle**.

winnock /*win'ək*/ or **windock** /*win'dək*/ (*Scot*) *n* a window. [Scot development of ME *windoge*; see **window**; cf ety of **warlock**]

winnow /*win'ō*/ *vt* to separate the chaff from (grain) by blowing a current of air through it; to fan; to sift; to separate; to blow on; to waft; to diffuse; to set in motion (*Milton*); to flap, flutter (*rare*). ◆ *vi* to separate chaff from grain; to fly; to blow in gusts. ◆ *n* a fan for winnowing. [OE *windwian* to winnow, from *wind*; see **wind¹**]

▪ **winn'owed** *adj perh* wise (*Shakesp*). **winn'ower** *n*. **winn'owing** *n*.

❑ **winn'owing-fan** or **-machine** *n* a fan or machine for winnowing.

wino /*wī'nō*/ (*sl*) *n* (*pl* **wī'nos**) someone, *esp* a down-and-out, addicted to cheap wine. [**wine**]

winsey same as **wincey**.

winsome /*win'səm*/ *adj* charming, captivating, attractive; cheerful; pleasant. [OE *wynsum* pleasant, from *wyn* joy (Ger *Wonne*), and *-sum* (see **-some¹**)]

▪ **win'somely** *adv*. **win'someness** *n*.

win't (*Burns*) see **wind²**.

winter /*win'tər*/ *n* the cold season of the year, lasting approximately from December to February in the northern hemisphere and from June to August in the southern hemisphere; in the astronomical year, the period of time between the winter solstice and the vernal equinox; a year (*poetic*); any season of cheerlessness. ◆ *adj* of, for or occurring in winter; sown in autumn, as eg *winter wheat*, *winter crop*, etc. ◆ *vi* to

pass the winter somewhere, *esp* somewhere warm. ◆ *vt* to feed and keep through winter. [OE; cf ON *vetr*, Ger *Winter*; from the Indo-European root seen in **wet** and **water**]

▪ **win'tered** *adj* having seen many winters, aged (*obs*); exposed to winter; worn in winter (*Shakesp*). **win'terer** *n*. **winterizā'tion** or **-s-** *n*. **win'terize** or **-ise** *vt* (*esp N Am*) to make suitable for use under wintry conditions. **win'terless** *adj*. **win'terly** *adj* cheerless. **win'trily** *adv*. **win'triness** *n*. **win'try** or **win'tery** *adj* resembling, belonging to or characteristic of winter; stormy; cheerless, unfriendly, cold or hostile.

❑ **winter aconite** see under **aconite**. **winter apple** *n* an apple that keeps well in winter, or that does not ripen until winter. **win'ter-beaten** *adj* (*Spenser*) beaten or injured by the cold of winter. **win'terberry** *n* a name given to several shrubs of the genus *Ilex*, growing in the eastern parts of N America. **win'ter-bloom** *n* the witch-hazel; a species of azalea. **win'terbourne** *n* an intermittent spring of water, as found in the chalk districts. **winter bud** *n* a bud protected by scales in which next year's shoot passes the winter. **winter cherry** *n* any species of *Physalis*, *esp Physalis alkekengi*; its edible fruit; the balloon-vine, or its fruit. **win'ter-clad** *adj* warmly clad. **winter clover** *n* the partridgeberry. **winter cress** *n* a cruciferous plant (genus *Barbarea*) formerly cultivated for winter salad. **winter garden** *n* an ornamental garden of evergreens, etc, or a conservatory with flowers, for winter; (in *pl*; with *caps*) used sometimes as the name of a theatre, concert hall, etc. **win'tergreen** *n* a plant of the genus *Pyrola*, also of *Chimaphila*; a plant of the genus *Gaultheria*, whose oil (**oil of wintergreen**) is an aromatic stimulant, used in flavouring confectionery and in medicine (**chickweed wintergreen** either of two plants, *Trientalis europaea* or *Trientalis americana*, belonging to the Primulaceae, having white starlike flowers). **win'ter-ground** *vt* (*Shakesp, Cymbeline* IV.2.230) assumed to mean protect (a plant) from the inclemency of winter. **winter heliotrope** *n* a plant (*Petasites fragrans*) producing sweet-smelling lilac flowers in winter. **winter jasmine** *n* a shrub (*Jasminum nudiflorum*) which produces yellow flowers in winter. **win'terkill** *vt* (*N Am*) to kill (a plant or crop) by exposure to the winter's cold. **winter melon** *n* another name for casaba. **winter moth** *n* a moth (*Operophtera brumata*), the male of which emerges in winter. **winter quarters** *n pl* the quarters of an army during winter; a winter residence. **winter solstice** *n* the time of year when, in the northern hemisphere, the sun reaches its southernmost point, or, in the southern hemisphere, its northermost, respectively 21 December and 21 June; the point on the celestial sphere at which, in the northern hemisphere, the ecliptic is furthest south of the celestial equator, or in the southern hemisphere, furthest north (*astron*). **winter sports** *n pl* open-air sports practised on snow and ice, such as skiing, etc. **win'ter-sweet** *n* a Japanese shrub (*Chimonanthus praecox*) of the family Calycanthaceae whose fragrant yellow flowers appear before the leaves; another name for marjoram. **win'tertide** *n* (*archaic*) wintertime. **win'tertime** *n* the season of winter. **win'ter-weight** *adj* (of clothes) heavy enough or thick enough to be suitable for cold weather.

winter's bark /*win'tərz bärk*/ *n* a stimulant, aromatic and tonic bark, named after Captain *Winter*, who first brought it from the Strait of Magellan in 1579.

wintle /*win'tl*/ (*Scot*) *vi* to stagger. ◆ *n* a stagger. [Flem *windtelen*, from *winden* to wind]

Winton. *abbrev*: *Wintoniensis* (*L*), of Winchester.

wintriness, **wintry** see under **winter**.

winy see under **wine**.

winze¹ /*winz*/ (*Scot*) *n* a curse. [Flem *wensch*; from root of **wish¹**]

winze² /*winz*/ (*mining*) *n* a small ventilating shaft between two levels (also **winds**). [Perh **wind²**]

wipe /*wīp*/ *vt* to clean or dry by rubbing with a cloth, on a mat, etc; to remove by wiping (with *away*, *off*, *out*, *up*); to pass (eg a cloth) across something to clean or dry it, etc; to rub (a liquid, etc) onto a surface; to apply solder to (eg a joint between two lengths of lead piping) with a piece of cloth or leather); to strike (*inf*); to clear (magnetic tape) of its content or erase (the content) from magnetic tape; to pass (a credit or debit card, etc) through an electronic reading terminal (see also **swipe**); to eradicate or eliminate; to cancel, forget, scrub (*inf*); to reject (a person; *Aust*). ◆ *n* the act of cleaning by rubbing; a blow, a swipe; a brand, a scar (*Shakesp*); a sarcasm, a gibe (*obs*); a handkerchief (*old sl*); a piece of (*esp* specially treated) fabric or tissue for wiping and cleaning; a style of film editing in which the picture on the screen appears to be pushed or wiped off the screen by the following one. [OE *wīpian*; OHGer *wīfan* to wind round, *waif* bandage, Gothic *weipan* to crown]

▪ **wipe'able** *adj*. **wī'per** *n* someone who wipes, *esp* a cleaner in certain industrial jobs; something that wipes or is used for wiping; a mechanism attached to a rotating or oscillating part that causes forwards-and-backwards motion in another part (*weaving*); a cam or tappet; a moving arm or other conducting device for making a selected contact out of a number of possible connections (*elec*); (also **wind'screen-wiper**) a mechanical arm that swings to and fro across a windscreen to clear it of rain, etc. **wī'ping** *n* the act of cleaning, rubbing, erasing, etc; a thrashing.

❑ **wipe'-clean** *adj* (of a plastic, etc surface) easily cleaned by wiping. **wipeout** /wī'powt/ *n* a fall from a surfboard, skateboard or skis, etc, *esp* a spectacular one (*sl*); a complete failure or disaster (*inf*); the interruption of one radio signal by another, making reception impossible.

■ **wiped out** (*inf*) exhausted, weary, dead-beat; financially ruined. **wipe out** to obliterate, annihilate or abolish; to kill or murder (*inf*); to fall from a surfboard, skis, etc (*sl*). **wipe the floor with** see under **floor**.

WIPO /wī'pō/ *abbrev* : World Intellectual Property Organization.

wippen /wip'ən/ (*music*) *n* a part of the hammer mechanism in a piano, raised as the note is played. [Poss Ger *Wippe* seesaw or dialect *wippen* whippletree]

wire /wīr/ *n* metal drawn out to a narrow flexible strand or thread; a length of this for any of various purposes; a length of this *usu* enclosed in insulating material, used for carrying an electric current; (sometimes in *pl*) the cable connecting point with point in a telecommunications system; the telephone (*old inf*); a telegram or telegraph (*inf, esp US*); information (*sl, esp US*); a warning or tip-off (*sl, esp US*); a portable recording device (*sl, esp US*); a metallic string of a musical instrument; a metal knitting needle (*Scot*); a pickpocket (*sl*); a lash made of wire (*Shakesp*); a fence made of wire; a wire stretched over or across the starting and finishing line on a racetrack, hence *esp* the finishing line itself (*orig US*). ◆ *adj* formed of or using wire; running on wire; relating to wiredrawing. ◆ *vt* to bind, support, protect, snare or fit with wire; to supply (a building) with wires for carrying electricity; to connect up (an electrical apparatus) with wires, ready for use (with *up*); to supply (an area) with fibre-optic cables for the reception of cable television; to send a telegram to, or send (a message) by telegram; to place (a croquet ball) where a hoop hampers it. ◆ *vi* to send a telegram. [OE *wīr*; ON *vīrr* (combining form)]

■ **wired** *adj* supplied or secured with wire; (also **wired up**) taking drugs (*sl*); in a tense, nervous state (*sl*); connected to the Internet (*inf*). **wire'less** *adj* without, or lacking, a wire or wires; of or relating to telegraphy or telephony without wires. ◆ *n* (*old*) short for **wireless telegraphy** or **telephony**, signalling through space without the use of conducting wires between transmitter and receiver, by means of electromagnetic waves generated by high-frequency alternating currents; a receiving or transmitting set used for this purpose; a message or broadcast transmitted in this way (**wireless station** a station used for such transmission); broadcast programmes or broadcasting generally. ◆ *vt* and *vi* (*old*) to communicate by radio. **wī'rer** *n* someone who wires, or who uses wire, eg to snare animals. **wī'rily** *adv*. **wī'riness** *n*. **wī'ring** *n* the complex of wires in an electrical system or installation; the act of securing with, equipping with, or communicating by, wire. **wī'ry** *adj* made of or resembling wire; flexible and strong; (of hair) coarse and wavy; (of a person) of slight build but strong and agile.

❑ **wire bar** *n* (*metallurgy*) copper of a high purity cast into a tapered ingot and used to produce copper wire. **wire bird** *n* the St Helena plover, named from the wire grass that is its habitat. **wire bridge** *n* a suspension bridge. **wire brush** *n* a brush with wire bristles, for cleaning rust off metal, dirt off suede shoes, etc; a brush with long bristles which are scraped against drums or cymbals. **wire cloth** *n* closely-woven wire mesh. **wire'-dancer** *n* a performer on a tight wire. **wire'-dancing** *n*. **wired glass** *n* glass in which a wire mesh has been incorporated during rolling as a resistance against fire and explosion blast. **wire'draw** *vt* to draw into wire by pulling through successively smaller holes in a hard steel dieblock; to throttle a fluid by passing it through a small orifice, thus reducing the pressure; to draw or spin out to a great length; to strain the meaning of. **wire'drawer** *n*. **wire'drawing** *n*. **wire'drawn** *adj* spun out into needless fine distinctions. **wired wireless** *n* the transmission of signals by means of electromagnetic waves guided by conductors, the frequencies being of the same order as those used for radio communication. **wire fraud** *n* (*US law*) fraud committed by means of electronic communications. **wire gauge** *n* a disc or plate with graded indents representing standard sizes, in which to measure the diameter of wire; any system for designating the diameter of wires by means of a set of numbers; the diameter of a particular piece of wire. **wire gauze** *n* a kind of stiff close fabric made of fine wire. **wire glass** *n* glass reinforced with an embedded sheet or wire mesh. **wire grass** *n* a kind of fine meadow grass (*Poa compressa*); any of various other grasses with wiry stems. **wire guard** *n* a guard made of wire netting for placing in front of a fire. **wire'-guided** *adj* (of a missile) controlled by signals transmitted through fine wires which are connected to the control box and uncoiled during flight. **wire'-hair** *n* a wire-haired terrier. **wire'-haired** *adj* (of an animal) having a coat of rather rough, hard hair. **wire-haired terrier** *n* a fox terrier with this kind of coat. **wire'-heel** *n* in horses and cattle, a defect or disease of the foot. **wire line** *n* one of the close-set lines in laid paper, perpendicular to the waterlines or chain lines, visible by transmitted light. **wire'man** *n* a telegraph fitter or electrician

who installs or maintains wires; an expert at wiretapping (*inf*); a journalist sending wires for a telegraphic news agency (*inf*). **wire nail** *n* a common type of nail, round or elliptical in cross-section, cut from steel wire. **wire netting** *n* a texture of galvanized wire woven in the form of a net. **wire'photo** *n* a photograph sent over a wire circuit by electrical means. **wire'puller** *n* someone who exercises an influence felt but not seen; an intriguer or manipulator. **wire'pulling** *n*. **wire rope** *n* a rope made of twisted wire. **wire service** *n* (*chiefly N Am*) an agency that supplies news to radio or TV stations, newspapers, etc. **wire'-sewn** or **wire'-stitched** *adj* (of booklets, etc) stapled with wire rather than sewn with thread. **wire'-stringed** *adj*. **wire'stripper** *n* a tool for stripping the protective insulation from electrical wires. **wire'tap** *vt* to tap (a telephone) or the telephone of. **wire'tapper** *n*. **wire'tapping** *n*. **wire'-walker** *n* a wire-dancer. **wire'way** *n* an enclosed channel, duct or conduit for wires; channelling of wires thus. **wire wheel** *n* a wheel, *esp* on a sports car, etc, in which the rim is connected to the hub by wire spokes. **wire wool** *n* a mass of very fine wire for scouring. **wire'work** *n* the making of wire or of objects of wire; articles or fabric made of wire. **wire'worker** *n*. **wire'working** *n*. **wire'worm** *n* a hard-bodied wormlike larva of the click beetle, destructive to plant roots. **wire'wove** *adj* denoting a fine quality of writing paper (see **wove**).

■ **down to the wire** (*inf*) as far as the finishing post, up to the very last moment. **get one's wires crossed** (*inf*) to misunderstand or be confused about something. **give** (**someone**) **the wire** (*chiefly milit*) to give advance information. **pull the wires** to pull strings, exert an unseen influence. **under the wire** (*chiefly N Am inf*) at the last minute. **wire away** or **in** (*old inf*) to act or work with vigour. **wire into** (*old inf*) to eat vigorously and assiduously.

wirricow see **worricow**.

Wirtschaftswunder /virt'shafts-vŭn-dər/ (*Ger*) *n* an economic miracle, *specif* that of Germany's speedy recovery after the 1939–45 war.

Wis. *abbrev* : Wisconsin (US state).

wis /wis/, also **wist** /wist/, *Shakesp* **wish** /wish/ (all *pseudo-archaic*) *vt* to know; to believe. [Partly from misunderstanding of the adv **iwis** as *I wis*, partly a new present from the past tense **wist** (see **wit²**)]

wisard /wiz'ərd/ *n* an old spelling of **wizard**.

Wisc. *abbrev* : Wisconsin (US state).

Wisd. (*Bible*) *abbrev* : (the Apocryphal Book of) Wisdom of Solomon.

wisdom /wiz'dəm/ *n* the quality of being wise; judgement; the ability to make right use of knowledge; prudence, common sense; learning, knowledge; the weight of informed opinion; a wise discourse, saying or teaching, or wise sayings generally (*archaic*); skilfulness, speculation, spiritual perception (*Bible*); sanity (*Shakesp*); (with *cap*) the Apocryphal Book of the Wisdom of Solomon; (with *cap*) Jesus Christ (*theol*). [OE *wīsdōm*; from **wise** and **-dom**]

❑ **Wisdom literature** *n* writings of the ancient Middle East which consist of philosophical reflections on life or maxims and precepts about the right conduct of one's life; Jewish pre-Christian literature of this type as contained in the Book of Job, Proverbs, Ecclesiastes, Wisdom of Solomon, Ecclesiasticus, and certain Psalms, to which list some add the New Testament Epistle of James. **wisdom tooth** *n* any of four double back teeth cut after childhood, *usu* from the late teens.

■ **in his**, **her**, etc **wisdom** (*ironic*) for reasons best known to himself, herself, etc.

wise¹ /wīz/ *adj* having knowledge; learned; able to make good use of knowledge; judging rightly, prudent, sensible; astute, shrewd, sagacious; discreet; skilful, proficient (*obs*); dictated by wisdom; containing wisdom; pious, godly; skilled in magic (*dialect*); normal mentally (*dialect*). ◆ *combining form* knowing the ways of, as in *streetwise, worldly-wise*. [OE *wīs*; Ger *Weise*; from root of **wit²**]

■ **wise'-like** (or (*Scot*) /wĭs'līk/) *adj* sensible, judicious; decent; fitting; looking as if capable of playing one's part well. **wise'ling** *n* (*old*) someone who pretends to be wise. **wise'ly** *adv*. **wise'ness** *n*.

❑ **wise'crack** *n* a pungent retort or comment, a gibe or joke. ◆ *vi* to make wisecracks. **wise'cracker** *n*. **wise'cracking** *adj* making, or addicted to making, wisecracks. **wise guy** *n* a conceited, over-confident person; a smart alec; a member of the Mafia (*US inf*). **wise'-heart'ed** *adj* having wisdom; prudent. **wise man** *n* a sage or elder; a wizard, magician or seer (*dialect*). **wise woman** *n* a witch or seeress; a midwife (*Scot*).

■ **be** (or **get**) **wise to** (*inf*) to be or become aware of. **never**, **no**, **none** (or **not much** or **not any**) **the wiser** still in ignorance. **put someone wise** (*esp US inf*) to put someone in possession of essential information, make someone aware (with *to*). **the Wise Men** (**of the East**), **the Three Wise Men** the three Magi (in some traditions kings) who according to St Matthew's Gospel came to worship the baby Jesus at Bethlehem. **the wiser for** having learnt sense from (some salutary experience). **wise after the event** only too aware of how something could have been avoided, done better, etc, when it has

---

■ words derived from main entry word; ❑ compound words; ■ idioms and phrasal verbs

already occurred. **wise up** (*sl*) to make or become aware, informed, etc.

wise², **weise** or **weize** /wīz/ (*Scot*) *vt* to guide in a certain direction. [OE *wīsian*, from *wīs*; see **wise¹**]

wise³ /wīz/ (*archaic*) *n* way, manner, now chiefly in the phrases **in any wise** in any way, **in no wise** in no way, and **on this wise** in this way. ◆ *sfx* denoting direction or manner, as in *lengthwise, clockwise, likewise, otherwise*; meaning 'as regards', as in *money-wise, business-wise* (*inf*). [OE *wīse*; Ger *Weise*; related to **wise¹** and **wit²**; doublet of **guise**]

wiseacre /wīz'ā-kər/ *n* someone who unduly assumes an air of superior wisdom; a wise guy; a simpleton quite unconscious of being one. [MDu *wijssegger*, from OHGer *wīzago* a prophet]

wisecrack, wiseling, wisely, wiseness see under **wise¹**.

wisent /wē'zənt/ or /vē'-/ *n* another name for the European bison. [Ger]

wish¹ /wish/ *vt* to want or require, as in *anything you wish*, or (*dialect*) *wish a cup of tea*; to desire, *esp* vainly or helplessly, as in *wish you'd told me*; to express a desire for (luck, happiness, etc) to come to; to say (good afternoon, etc) to; (with a *neg* and *on*) to desire (something to be inflicted on), to invoke, as in *wouldn't wish it on my worst enemy*; to impose, inflict or foist (with *on*; *inf*); to bid or request; to hope (*archaic*); to recommend (*obs*); to bewitch (*dialect*); to greet, wish (someone) well (*S Afr*); to state (a wish) in superstitious hope of its being magically fulfilled. ◆ *vi* to have a desire (with *for*); to long (with *for*); to state a desire in superstitious hope of its being magically fulfilled. ◆ *n* a desire, longing; a thing desired; an expression of desire; (*usu* in *pl*) an expression of desire for good fortune for another; the stating of a desire in superstitious hope of its being magically fulfilled; a malediction (*obs*). [OE *wȳscan* to wish; Ger *wünschen*, Swed *önska*]
■ **wish'er** *n*. **wish'ful** *adj* having a wish or desire; eager; desirable, desired (*obs*). **wish'fully** *adv*. **wish'fulness** *n*. **wish'ing** *n* and *adj*.
❑ **wish'bone** or **wish'ing-bone** *n* the V-shaped bone formed by the fused clavicles of a bird's breast, by tradition pulled apart by two people in playful divination, the longer part indicating the first to be married or the one whose wish will be fulfilled; (**wish'bone**) a V-shaped member used in independent suspension systems (*motoring*). **wish fulfilment** *n* (*psychol*) the satisfaction of a desire in dreams, daydreams, etc. **wishful thinking** *n* (*psychol*) a type of thinking in which the individual substitutes the fantasy of the fulfilment of the wish for the actual achievement; a belief that a particular thing will happen, or is so, engendered by desire that it should happen, or be so; (loosely) thinking about and wishing for an event or turn of fortune that may not take place. **wish'ing-cap** *n* a cap by wearing which one obtains everything one wishes. **wishing stone**, **tree**, **well**, etc *n* a stone, tree, well, etc supposed to have the power of making a wish expressed at it come true. **wish list** *n* a mental list of desiderata.
■ **wish someone further** (*sl*) to wish someone was in some other place, not present. **wish someone joy of something** (*usu* ironic) to hope that the possession of something (*usu* that one is glad not to have, or glad to be rid of) will be of benefit to someone. **wish to God** to wish earnestly.

wish² see **wis**.

wish-wash /wish'wosh/ (*inf*) *n* anything wishy-washy.
■ **wish'y-wash'y** *adj* thin and weak; diluted; pale; feeble; of poor quality.

wisket /wis'kit/ (*dialect*) *n* a basket. [Scand, from the same root as **whisk¹**]

WISP /wisp/ *abbrev*: WAP Internet Service Provider.

wisp /wisp/ *n* a thin strand or band; a small bundle of straw or hay; a tuft, a shred; a small broom; a twisted bunch used as a torch; the will-o'-the-wisp; something slight or insubstantial; a flock (of snipe). ◆ *vt* to make into a wisp or bundle; to rub down with a wisp. ◆ *vi* to fall, drift or otherwise move in wisps or like a wisp. [Origin uncertain]
■ **wisp'ily** *adv*. **wisp'iness** *n*. **wisp'y** *adj* wisp-like, light and fine in texture; slight, flimsy, insubstantial.

wist /wist/ (*pseudo-archaic*) *vt* and *vi* to know. [See **wis, iwis, wit²**]

wistaria /wi-stā'ri-ə/ or more commonly **wisteria** /-stē'-/ *n* a plant of a genus (*Wistaria*) of papilionaceous plants native to E Asia and N America, some of the species among the most magnificent ornamental climbers, named after the American anatomist Caspar *Wistar* (1761–1818).

wistful /wist'fŭl/ or /-fl/ *adj* longing; yearning with little hope; pensive; intent (*obs*); earnest (*obs*). [Poss from *wistly* or its back-formation *wist* intent, with meaning altered through association with **wishful**]
■ **wist'fully** *adv*. **wist'fulness** *n*.

wistiti /wis'ti-ti/ *n* a marmoset. [Fr *ouistiti*; from its cry]

wistly /wist'li/ (*Shakesp*) *adv* longingly, earnestly. [Prob for *whistly* silently; see **whist²**]

wit¹ /wit/ *n* ingenuity; intelligence, sense (as in *have the wit to*); (*usu* in *pl*) any of the five bodily senses, or a mental faculty generally (*archaic*); the power of combining ideas with a pointed verbal effect; the product of this power; humour, wittiness; a person endowed with wit; the mind (*obs*); the understanding (*archaic*); imagination or invention (*archaic*); information, as in *to get wit of* (*obs*). [OE (*ge*)*wit*, from **wit²**]
■ **wit'less** *adj* lacking wit, wisdom or sense; without intellectual faculties (*obs*); out of one's mind; stupid, unintelligent; unaware, unconscious. **wit'lessly** *adv*. **wit'lessness** *n*. **wit'ling** *n* someone with little wit; a pretender to wit. **witt'ed** *adj* (*usu* as *combining form*) having wit or understanding (of a specified type, as in *quick-witted, slow-witted*). **witticism** /wit'i-sizm/ *n* a witty remark; a sentence or phrase affectedly witty; formerly, a gibe. **witt'ily** *adv*. **witt'iness** *n*. **witt'y** *adj* possessed of wit; amusing, droll; sarcastic; ingenious (*Bible*); wise, discreet, sensible (*obs*).
❑ **wit'-cracker** *n* someone who makes witty remarks in a crisp style. **wit'-monger** *n* a poor would-be wit. **wit'-snapper** *n* (*Shakesp*) someone who affects wit or repartee. **wit'wanton** *vt* (with *it*; *obs*) to indulge in irreverent wit.
■ **at one's wits'** (or **wit's**) **end** utterly perplexed; in a state of desperation. **have** (or **keep**) **one's wits about one** to be (or remain) alert and resourceful. **live by one's wits** to gain a livelihood by ingenious expedients rather than by honest labour. **scared out of one's wits** extremely scared. **the five wits** (*archaic*) the five senses.

wit² /wit/ *vt* and *vi* (*infinitive* **wit**, *Spenser, Shakesp* and others **weet** or **weete** /wēt/, *Spenser* **weet'en**, also **wot** /wot/; *Scot* **wat** /wöt/, **wite** or **wyte** /wīt/; *2nd pers sing* **wost** (**wott'est**); *3rd* **wot** (**wots, wott'eth**), *Scot* **wate, wait, wats**; *pl 1st, 2nd, 3rd* **wot**; *pat* **wist** (**wott'ed**); *prp* **witt'ing** or **weet'ing** (**wott'ing**); *pap* **wist**) (*archaic* except in legal use) to know; to be aware (with *of*); to recognize, discern; to know how. [OE *witan* to know (prt *wāt, wāst, wāt,* pl *witon*); *pat* *wiste*, or *wisse*, pl *wiston*, pap *wist*); Gothic *witan* to observe, Ger *wissen*; cf L *vidēre* to see; Gr *idein*]
■ **witt'ing** *n* (*obs* and *dialect*) knowledge; information. ◆ *adj* cognisant; conscious; deliberate. **witt'ingly** *adv* knowingly; by design.
■ **do to wit** to cause to know. **to wit** that is to say, namely (the OE gerund *tō witanne*).

witan /wit'an/ *n pl* members of the Anglo-Saxon council, the witenagemot (qv); the witenagemot itself. [Pl of OE *wita* a man of knowledge; cf **wit¹,²**]

witblits /vit'blits/ (*S Afr*) *n* a strong home-distilled alcoholic spirit. [Afrik *wit* white, and *blits* lightning]

witch¹ /wich/ *n* a person, *esp* a woman, supposed to have supernatural or magical power and knowledge *esp* through compact with the Devil or a minor evil spirit; a hag, crone; a dangerously or irresistibly fascinating woman (*inf*); a wizard (now *rare*); a flatfish, the craigfluke; (also **witch of Agnesi** /än-yā'zi/) a curve whose equation is $x^2y=4a^2(2a-y)$ (*maths*). ◆ *vt* to bewitch; to effect, change, transport, etc by means of witchcraft; to fascinate. ◆ *vi* to practise witchcraft or fascination. [ME *wicche* (both masc and fem), from OE *wicca* (masc), *wicce* (fem), wizard, witch, and verb *wiccian* to practise witchcraft; ety doubtful]
■ **witch'ery** *n* witchcraft; fascination. **witch'ing** *n* sorcery; enchantment. ◆ *adj* suited to witchcraft; weird; fascinating. **witch'ingly** *adv*. **witch'like** *adj*. **wit'chy** *adj* witchlike, suggestive of witches.
❑ **witch'craft** *n* the craft or practice of witches; the black art, sorcery; supernatural power. **witch doctor** *n* in tribal societies, a magician who detects witches and counteracts evil magical influences; someone who professes to heal by means of magic. **witch'-elm** *n* a less common spelling of **wych-elm**. **witches' brew** *n* (*fig*) a heady concoction of disparate elements, a confused or mysterious mixture. **witches' broom** *n* a dense tuft of poorly developed branches formed on a woody plant attacked by a parasite (chiefly fungi and mites). **witches' butter** *n* Nostoc and other gelatinous blue-green algae. **witches' meat** *n* Tremella. **witches' Sabbath** *n* a witches' midnight gathering (see also **Sabbath**). **witches' thimble** *n* a name for various plants with thimble-like flowers, eg the foxglove. **witch'-finder** *n* (*hist*) a person whose business was to detect witches; a witch doctor. **witch hunt** *n* (*orig US*) the searching out of political opponents for exposure on grounds of alleged disloyalty to the state, etc; any comparable hunting-down or persecution of a group or an individual alleged to be behaving in a dangerously heretical manner. **witching hour** *n* the hour when witches are supposed to stir into activity, midnight (see also **double witching (hour)** under **double**, **triple witching (hour)** under **triple**). **witch'knot** *n* a knot, *esp* in the hair, supposed to be tied by means of witchcraft. **witch'meal** *n* the inflammable pollen of the club moss, lycopodium. **witch'-ridden** *adj* ridden by witches. **witch's hat** *n* a tall black conical brimmed hat, the traditional wear of fairytale witches. **witch'-wife** *n* (*Scot*) a woman who practises witchcraft.

witch² see **wych**.

witchen /wich'ən/ n the mountain ash; the wych-elm. [**witch**[2]]

witchetty /wich'ə-ti/ n (also **witchetty grub**) any of the edible grubs of species of certain moths (genus *Cossus*) and of longicorn beetles. [From an Aboriginal language]

witch-hazel /wich'hā-zl/ n any of a number of trees, such as the wych-elm, the hornbeam, or a N American shrub (*Hamamelis virginiana*) a distillate of whose bark and leaves is dissolved in alcohol to make an astringent lotion; this lotion, used for treating bruises, etc. [**witch**[2]]

wite[1], **wyte** or **wight** /wīt/ vt (obs or Scot) to blame; to lay the blame on. ◆ n (now dialect) blame, reproach. [OE wītan to see, blame; related to **wit**[2]]
■ **wite'less** adj (now dialect) blameless.

wite[2] see **wit**[2].

witenagemot /wit'ə-nə-gə-mōt/, popularly wit-ə-nag'ə-mōt/ n the supreme council of England in Anglo-Saxon times, composed of the bishops, the ealdormen of shires, and a number of the king's friends and dependants. [OE witena, genitive pl of wita wise man, councillor, and gemōt meeting; cf **witan**, **wit**[1,2]]

witgat /vit'hhat/ or **witgatboom** /vit'hhat-bŭm/ n a S African evergreen tree (*Boscia albitrunca*) with pale bark, hard coarse-grained white wood, and edible roots used esp as a coffee substitute when roasted; any of various species of the genus *Boscia*. [Afrik, from wit white, gat hole, and boom tree]

with[1] /widh or with/ prep denoting nearness, association or connection; by, beside; among; on the side of; in the company of; in the possession or care of; having or containing; supplemented by (as in With the tip, it cost d10.50); possessing; characterized by; suffering from; affected by; in the same direction as; at the time of; at the same time or rate as (rise with the birds; Discretion increases with age); immediately after; in competition or contest against; in respect of, in regard of (What's wrong with it?); by, by means of, through; as a result of (shaking with fear); because of having (With her talents, she'll go far); in spite of having (With all his money he's still unhappy); using; denoting separation, from (dispense with); denoting manner (answered with a nod); denoting accompanying circumstances (fall asleep with the light on); in (the specified circumstances, as I can't go abroad with my mother so ill); expressing agreement, disagreement or comparison (correspond with, inconsistent with, compared with); featuring, starring; used in exclamations after adverbs (Down with the tyrant!); understanding (Are you with me?; inf); supporting (with you all the way). [OE with against; ON vith, Ger wider. It ousted the OE mid with (Ger mit)]
■ **feel** or **think with** to feel as, or be of the same opinion as. **in with** (inf) friendly with; enjoying the favour of. **what's with** see under **what**. **with it** (inf) following current trends in popular taste (**with'-it** adj). **with that** thereupon.

with[2] n see **withe**[1].

with[3] /with/ (building) n a partition between chimney flues (also **withe**). [Poss corruption of **width**]

withal /wi-dhöl'/ (literary or archaic) adv with all or the rest; besides; therewith; thereupon; nevertheless, for all that. ◆ prep an emphatic form of with, used after its object. [ME, from **with**[1] and **all**]

withdraw /widh-drö' or with-drö'/ vt (pat **withdrew** /-droo'/; pap **withdrawn**') to draw back or away; to take back or away; to cause (troops) to retire; to take (money, savings, etc) from deposit or investment; to remove (with from); to cancel or discontinue (a service, offer, etc); to deflect, turn aside (rare); to recall, retract, unsay. ◆ vi to retire; to go away; to back out of a contest or other activity; (with from) to stop oneself taking (a drug to which one is addicted); to become uncommunicative or unresponsive; to take back what one has said, or to recall a motion one has proposed. [Pfx with- against, back, and **draw**]
■ **withdraw'al** n an act or gradual process of withdrawing; retreat, esp if unforced; the removal of money from a bank account; the breaking of a drug addiction, with associated physical and psychological symptoms; a retreat into silence and self-absorption; (also **withdrawal method**) coitus interruptus, interruption of sexual intercourse before ejaculation of semen, as a means of contraception. **withdraw'er** n. **withdraw'ment** n (rare). **withdrawn'** adj (of a person, manner, etc) detached; uncommunicative, unresponsive, shy or reserved; introverted; (of a place) secluded; remote.
❑ **withdrawal symptom** n any of a number of symptoms such as pain, nausea or sweating, experienced by someone being deprived of a drug to which he or she is addicted. **withdraw'ing-room** n (archaic) a room used to retire into; a drawing room.

withe[1] or **with** /widh, with or wīdh/ n a flexible twig, esp of willow; a band of twisted twigs; a halter (obs); an elastic handle to a tool to save the hand from the shock of blows; a boom-iron. ◆ vt to bind with a withe or withes; to capture with a noose of withes. [OE withthe; ON vīthir, Ger Weide willow; cf **withy**[1]]
■ **with'y** adj made of withes; like withes, flexible, wiry and agile.

withe[2] see **with**[3].

wither /widh'ər/ vi to fade or become dry; to lose freshness; to languish, decline; to decay, waste. ◆ vt to cause to dry up, fade or decay; to blight, destroy; to humiliate, mortify or cause to feel unimportant or despicable; to dry (eg tea). [ME wederen to expose to weather]
■ **with'ered** adj dried, faded, shrivelled; (of a limb) stunted or shrivelled through illness or injury. **with'eredness** n. **with'ering** n. ◆ adj fading, becoming dry, etc, or causing to do so; used for drying or curing; blasting, blighting, scorching, destructive; snubbing, humiliating. **with'eringly** adv.
❑ **with'ering-floor** n the drying-floor of a malt-house.

witherite /widh'ə-rīt/ n the chief source of barium compounds, barium carbonate, occurring as orthorhombic crystals in pseudohexagonal pyramids. [Dr W Withering (1741–99), who first discriminated it from barytes (1784), and **-ite** (3)]

withers /widh'ərz/ n pl the ridge between the shoulder blades of a horse. [OE wither against, an extension of with against]
❑ **with'er-wrung** adj injured in the withers.
■ **wring someone's withers** to wound someone by a snub, etc; to cause someone anguish.

withershins /widh'ər-shinz or wid'ər-shinz/ (Scot) adv in the contrary direction, contrary to the course of the sun, opp to deasil; in the wrong way. [LGer weddersins; cf OE wither against, LGer sind direction, OE sīth journey]

withhault pseudo-archaic pat of **withhold**.

withhold /widh-hōld' or with-hōld'/ vt (pat and pap **withheld'** (archaic pap **withhold'en**)) to hold back, restrain; to keep back; to refuse to give; to keep in bondage or custody (obs). ◆ vi to refrain (with from or infinitive; obs); to postpone (Pope). [Pfx with- against, and **hold**]
■ **withhold'er** n. **withhold'ment** n.
❑ **withholding tax** n income tax deducted at source, incl tax levied by a country on dividends, etc paid to a non-resident.

within /wi-dhin' or wi-thin'/ prep inside; in the limits of; not going beyond; in less than (a certain time or distance, as in within the hour, within a hair's breadth of death); entered from; into; in or to the inner part of (archaic); on the inner side of (obs). ◆ adv inside; in the inner part; inwardly; in the mind, soul, heart; behind the scenes; at home (archaic); indoors; in or to an inner room (archaic); herein. [OE withinnan, from with against, with, and innan in]
■ **within land** (obs) inland. **within reach** so positioned as to be obtainable or attainable without much difficulty, effort or loss of time.

without /wi-dhowt' or wi-thowt'/ prep not having the company of; deprived of; not having; lacking; free from; not (behaving as expected or in a particular way), as in answered without smiling; not giving, showing, etc (complied without a murmur); not encountering (some expected circumstance), as in got there without anyone getting hurt; in neglect of (a usual procedure), as in imprisoned without trial; not using, not having the help of; if it had not been for (would have died without their help); outside or out of (archaic); outside the limits of (archaic); beyond (archaic). ◆ adv on the outside; outwardly; outside, not members of, a particular group or society; out of doors (archaic). ◆ conj (archaic or dialect) unless, except. [OE withūtan, from with against, and ūtan outside]
■ **without'en** prep (archaic) without.
❑ **without'-door** adj (Shakesp) outward.
■ **from without** from the outside. **without distinction** indiscriminately. **without doors** out of doors; outside the family, nation, etc; outside Parliament.

withstand /widh-stand' or with-stand'/ vt (pat and pap **withstood'**) to oppose, brave or resist; to hinder (obs). ◆ vi to stand one's ground, offer resistance. [OE withstandan, from with against; see **stand**]
■ **withstand'er** n.

withwind /with'wīnd/ or **withywind** /widh'i-wīnd/ (dialect) n bindweed, or other climbing plant. [OE withewinde; cf **withy**[1] and **wind**[2]]

withy[1] /widh'i/ n the osier willow; any willow; a flexible twig or branch, esp one used for binding. [OE wīthig willow; cf **widdy**[1], **withe**[1]]

withy[2] see under **withe**[1].

witless, **witling** see under **wit**[1].

witloof /wit'lōf/ n a kind of chicory with large leaves. [Du, literally, white leaf]

witness /wit'nis/ n someone who sees or has personal knowledge of an event, etc; someone who gives evidence; someone whose signature confirms the genuineness of a document, or of a signature already added; a remnant of original surface or scribed line, left during machining or hand-working to prove that a minimum quantity of material has been removed or an outline accurately preserved (engineering); (something that is) proof or evidence of anything;

knowledge brought in proof; testimony of a fact. ◆ *vt* to have direct knowledge of; (loosely) to see; (of a place or period) to be the scene or setting of; (of a person) to live through; to give testimony to; to attest; to act as legal witness of; to sign, to add one's signature in confirmation of the genuineness of (a document, another's signature, etc); to show; to evince (*archaic*). ◆ *vi* to give evidence; (with *to*) to confirm, attest to. [OE (*ge*)*witnes*, from (*ge*)*wit* ; see **wit¹**]

■ **wit'nesser** *n*.

❏ **witness box** or (*US*) **stand** *n* the enclosure in which a witness stands when giving evidence in a court of law.

■ **bear witness** to give or be evidence (*esp* with *to*). **with a witness** (*Shakesp*) with a vengeance. **witness** (**such and such**) let (such and such) serve as evidence.

witter /*wit'ər*/ or **whitter** /(*h*)*wit'ər*/ *vi* to talk or mutter peevishly or ineffectually (*esp* with *on*). [Ety doubtful]

witticism, wittily, wittiness see under **wit¹**.

witting see under **wit²**.

wittol /*wit'əl*/ (*archaic*) *n* a man who knows his wife's unfaithfulness, and accepts it. [ME *wetewold*; associated with **cuckold**, and perh from **witwall**, or from **wit²**]

■ **witt'olly** *adj* (*Shakesp*) like a wittol or contented cuckold.

witty see under **wit¹**.

witwall /*wit'wöl*/ (*dialect*) *n* the green woodpecker or the greater spotted woodpecker. [Cf Ger *Wittewal*, *Wiedewall*; cf also **woodwale**]

witwanton see under **wit¹**.

wive /*wīv*/ (*archaic*) *vt* to take for a wife; to provide with a wife; to become the wife of. ◆ *vi* to marry a wife. [OE *wīfian*, from *wīf* wife]

■ **wive'hood** *n* (*Spenser*) wifehood.

wivern same as **wyvern**.

wives /*wīvz*/ plural of **wife**.

wizard /*wiz'ərd*/ *n* a man who practises witchcraft or magic, a sorcerer or magician; someone who works wonders, an expert, a genius; a utility that facilitates a particular task, guiding the user step by step (*comput*); a wise man (*obs*). ◆ *adj* with magical powers (*old* or *poetic*); wonderful, delightful (*old inf*). [ME *wysar(d)*, from *wys* wise, and noun sfx *-ard*]

■ **wiz'ardly** *adj* like a wizard. **wiz'ardry** *n* sorcery, magic.

wizen /*wiz'n*/, also **weazen** /*wē'zn*/ *vt* and *vi* to make or become dry and shrivelled. ◆ *adj* (*old*) wizened. [OE *wisnian*, to wither; cognate with ON *visna* to wither]

■ **wiz'ened** *adj* dried up, thin, shrivelled, wrinkled.

❏ **wiz'en-faced** *adj* having a thin, shrivelled face.

wizier same as **vizier**.

wiz kid see under **whizz**.

WJEC *abbrev* : Welsh Joint Education Committee.

wk *abbrev* : week; work.

WL *abbrev* : (Windward Islands) St Lucia (IVR).

WLA *abbrev* : Women's Land Army (disbanded 1950).

WLTM *abbrev* : would like to meet (often seen in personal advertisements).

Wm *abbrev* : William.

WMD *abbrev* : weapon(s) of mass destruction.

WML (*comput*) *abbrev* : Wireless Mark-up Language.

WMO *abbrev* : World Meteorological Organization.

WNW *abbrev* : west-north-west.

WO *abbrev* : walkover; formerly, War Office; Warrant Officer.

wo older variant of **woe**, or **whoa**.

w/o *abbrev* : without.

woad /*wōd*/ *n* a genus (*Isatis*) of cruciferous plants, mostly natives of countries round the Mediterranean, a species of it, *Isatis tinctoria* or *dyer's woad*, yielding a permanent blue dye, largely superseded by indigo; the dye itself. [OE *wād*; Ger *Waid*]

■ **woad'ed** *adj* dyed blue with woad.

wobbegong /*wob'i-gong*/ *n* a carpet shark. [From an Aboriginal language]

wobble /*wob'l*/ *vi* to move unsteadily or uncertainly from side to side; to progress thus; to shake or rock, be unstable or unsteady; to quiver; (of the voice) to quaver, be unsteady; to vacillate, waver. ◆ *vt* to cause to wobble. ◆ *n* an unsteady, unequal motion or movement. [LGer *wabbeln*]

■ **wobb'ler** *n* someone or something that wobbles; a wobbly (*inf*). **wobb'liness** *n*. **wobb'ling** *n*. **wobb'ly** *adj* shaky; unsteady through illness; inclined to wobble. ◆ *n* (*inf*) a fit of nerves or anger.

❏ **wobble board** *n* a sheet of hardboard shaken to obtain certain sound effects.

■ **throw a wobbly** (*inf*) to have a fit of hysterics or a tantrum, or behave otherwise unnervingly.

wobegone see under **woe**.

wock an obsolete spelling of **wok**.

Woden or **Wodan** /*wō'dən*/ (*myth*) *n* the chief god of the ancient Germanic peoples. [OE *Wōden*; OHGer *Wuotan*; cf **Odin**]

■ **Wō'denism** *n* the worship of Woden.

wodge /*woj*/ (*inf*) *n* a large or roughly-cut portion; a lump, chunk or wad. [**wedge**]

woe or (*archaic*) **wo** /*wō*/ *n* grief (*archaic*); misery; (often in *pl*) a misfortune or calamity; a physical pain (*obs*); a curse (*obs*); (often **wō**, *pl* **wōs**) an exclamation of grief. ◆ *adj* (*archaic* and *dialect*) sad, wretched, sorry. [OE (interj) *wā*; Ger *Weh*; L *vae*; cf **wail**]

■ **woe'ful** or **wō'ful** *adj* sorrowful or afflicted; bringing misery or calamity; deplorable; wretched, paltry. **woe'fully** or **wō'fully** *adv*. **woe'fulness** or **wō'fulness** *n*. **woe'some** (*Scot* **wae'some**) *adj* woeful.

❏ **woe'begone** or **wō'begone** *adj* (see **bego**) beset with woe; dismal-looking, manifesting misery. **woe'-wea'ried** or **woe'-worn** *adj* wearied, worn with woe.

■ **in weal and woe** in prosperity and adversity. **woe betide** (*old* or *facetious*) misfortune will be (or may misfortune be) the lot of (whoever offends in some specified way). **woe is me** (*archaic*) unhappy that I am!; cursed am I. **woe unto** calamity will befall; may calamity befall. **woe worth the day** cursed be the day (see **worth²**).

wog¹ /*wog*/ (*offensive*) *n* any non-white foreigner, *orig* used only of Arabs. [Perh from **gollywog**; popularly thought to be an acronym, of which several expansions are propounded]

wog² /*wog*/ (*Aust inf*) *n* an insect or grub; a germ, bug, infection, illness. [Origin uncertain]

woggle /*wog'l*/ *n* the ring of leather, plastic or other material through which Scouts, etc thread their neckerchiefs. [Origin uncertain]

wo ha ho /*wō hä hō'*/ (*falconry*) *interj* a call for summoning a bird.

woiwode /*woi'wōd*/ a variant of **voivode**.

wok /*wok*/ *n* a hemispherical pan used in Chinese cookery. [Chin (Cantonese)]

woke, woken see **wake¹**.

wold /*wōld*/ *n* an open tract of country, now chiefly upland country. [OE (Anglian) *wald* forest, applied orig to wooded parts of the country; cf **weald**]

wolf /*wŭlf*/ *n* (*pl* **wolves** /*wŭlvz*/) the common name of certain predatory species of the genus *Canis* that hunt in packs, including the common wolf (*Canis lupus*), the grey or timber wolf, and the coyote; anything symbolically seen as a cruelly rapacious or ravenous creature; a greedy and cunning person; a tuberculous excrescence or cancerous growth (*obs*); a dissonance heard in a keyed instrument tuned by unequal temperament (*music*); an extraneous non-harmonic note made by the bow on a string of a violin, etc (*music*); a man who insatiably pursues and seduces women (*inf*). ◆ *vi* (also **wolve** /*wŭlv*/) to hunt for wolves. ◆ *vt* (often with *down* or *up*; *inf*) to devour ravenously. [OE *wulf*; Ger *Wolf*; L *vulpēs* fox, *lupus* wolf; Gr *lykos* wolf]

■ **wolf'er** or **wolv'er** *n* a hunter of wolves. **wolf'ing** or **wolv'ing** *n* the hunting of wolves for their skins. **wolf'ish** or **wolv'ish** *adj* like a wolf; rapacious; ravenous. **wolf'ishly** or **wolv'ishly** *adv*. **wolf'kin** and **wolf'ling** *n* a young wolf. **wolf'like** *adj*.

❏ **wolf'berry** *n* a N American shrub (*Symphoricarpus occidentalis*) of the honeysuckle family, with white berries, hairy leaves and pink flowers; another name for **goji**. **wolf cub** *n* a young wolf; (with *caps*) a member of the former Wolf Cubs (now Cub Scouts), a junior division of the Scout Association. **wolf dog** *n* a dog of a large breed formerly used in hunting wolves and guarding sheep from attack by wolves; (**wolf'-dog**) a cross between a wolf and a domestic dog. **wolf'fish** *n* (also **sea-wolf** and **catfish**) any genus of fierce and voracious salt-water fishes. **wolf'hound** *n* any of several breeds of large domestic dog, such as the Irish wolfhound, formerly used to hunt wolves. **wolf note** *n* (*music*) a wolf. **wolf pack** *n* a pack of wolves; a flotilla of submarines or group of aircraft sent out to attack enemy targets. **wolfs'bane** or **wolf's bane** *n* an aconite, *esp Aconitum lycoctonum*. **wolf's foot** or **wolf's claw** *n* the club moss (genus *Lycopodium*). **wolf'skin** *n* the skin or pelt of a wolf. **wolf's peach** *n* the tomato. **wolf spider** *n* any spider of the *Lycosa* genus, to which the true tarantula belongs, or of the family Lycosidae. **wolf tooth** *n* a small supernumerary premolar in a horse. **wolf whistle** *n* a two-note whistle uttered as a coarse expression of admiration, typically by a man at the sight of a woman. **wolf'-whistle** *vt* and *vi*.

■ **cry wolf** to give a false alarm, from the story of the boy who cried 'Wolf' when there was none, and was not believed when there was one. **have** (or **hold**) **a wolf by the ears** to be in a desperately difficult situation. **have a wolf in the stomach** to be ravenously hungry. **keep** the **wolf from the door** to keep away poverty or hunger. **see a wolf** to be tongue-tied (in allusion to an old superstition). **throw** or **fling to the wolves** to abandon to certain destruction. **wolf in sheep's clothing** someone who behind a kindly and inoffensive exterior is dangerous and unscrupulous.

Wolffian /wŭl'fi-ən or vol'fi-ən/ adj relating to, or associated with the German embryologist KF Wolff (1733–94); designating the renal organs in the embryo of vertebrates.
❑ **Wolffian body** n the organ of excretion in the embryo, the primitive kidney or mesonephros. **Wolffian duct** n the excretory duct of the mesonephros.

Wolfian[1] or **Wolffian** /wŭl'fi-ən or vol'fi-ən/ adj relating to the philosophy of Christian Wolf (1679–1754), who systematized and popularized the philosophy of Leibniz, and gave a strong impulse to that development of natural theology and rationalism.
■ **Wolf'ianism** n.

Wolfian[2] /wŭl'fi-ən or vol'fi-ən/ adj relating to, or associated with Friedrich August Wolf (1759–1824), applied esp to his theory that the Odyssey and Iliad consist of numerous ballads by a variety of minstrels, strung together in the course of time by editors.

wolfram /wŭl'frəm/ n (also **wolf'ramite**) a native compound of tungstate of iron and manganese; tungsten. [Ger; origin uncertain]

Wolf-Rayet star /wŭlf'rā'ət stär/ n one of a rare class of very hot stars, whose spectra are similar to those of novae, broad bright lines predominating, indicating violent motion in the stellar atmosphere. [CJE Wolf (1827–1918) and GAP Rayet (1839–1906), French astronomers]

wolfsbane, wolfskin see under **wolf**.

wollastonite /wŭl'ə-stə-nīt or wŭ-las'tə-nīt/ n a pyroxene of relatively simple composition, silicate of calcium, $CaSiO_3$, also called **tabular spar**. [WH Wollaston (1766–1828), English scientist]

wolly[1] /wol'i/ (sl) n a uniformed policeman, esp a raw young constable. [Ety uncertain; cf **wally**[1]]

wolly[2] /wol'i/ (Cockney sl) n a pickled olive or cucumber. [Origin uncertain; the street cry 'Oh! olives!' suggested]

Wolof /wō'lof/ n a people living near the Senegal River in W Africa; a member of this people; its language. ◆ adj of or relating to the Wolofs or their language.

wolve, wolver see **wolf**.

wolverine or **wolverene** /wŭl'və-rēn or wŭl-və-rēn'/ n a large solitary carnivorous mammal of the weasel family, found in forests in N America and Eurasia; its fur. [Extension of **wolf**]

wolves, wolving, wolvish see **wolf**.

woman /wŭm'ən/ n (pl **women** /wim'in/) an adult female of the human race; a wife (now dialect); a mistress or girlfriend; the female sex; women collectively; (with the) the natural urges specific to a woman; a man over-concerned with domestic niceties (derog); a female attendant (hist or archaic); a charwoman or daily domestic help (inf); the reverse or Britannia side of a coin. ◆ combining form denoting a woman of a specified occupation, skill or nationality, as in policewoman, markswoman, Manxwoman. ◆ adj female, as in woman doctor. ◆ vt to cause to act like a woman (obs); (with it) to play the part of a woman; to provide or staff with a woman or women; to call a person 'woman' abusively. [OE wimman, from wīfman, from wīf a woman, and man man, human being]
■ **wo'man'd** adj (Shakesp) accompanied by a woman. **wom'anfully** adv like a woman of spirit. **wom'anhood** n the state, character or qualities of a woman; womenkind. **wom'anish** adj (of a man, his behaviour or appearance) effeminate, unmanly; associated with women, feminine. **wom'anishly** adv. **wom'anishness** n. **wom'anism** n (US) feminism, esp when applied to African-American women. **wom'anist** n and adj. **wom'anize** or **-ise** vt and vi to make or become effeminate. ◆ vi (derog; of a man) to pursue women with a view to having casual affairs. **wom'anizer** or **-s-** n. **wom'ankind** n women generally, the female sex (also **wom'enkind**); a woman (obs). **wom'anless** adj. **wom'anlike** adj and adv. **wom'anliness** n. **wom'anly** adj like or becoming to a woman; feminine. ◆ adv in the manner of a woman.
❑ **wom'an-bod'y** n (Scot) a woman. **wom'an-born** adj born of woman. **wom'an-built** adj built by women. **wom'an-child** n (pl **wom'en-children**) a female child. **wom'an-grown** adj grown to womanhood. **wom'an-hater** n a man who hates women, a misogynist. **woman post** n (Shakesp) a female messenger. **wom'an-quell'er** n a killer of women. **wom'an-suffrage** n women's suffrage. **wom'an-tired** adj (tire[6]; Shakesp) hen-pecked. **wom'an-vested** adj wearing women's clothes. **wom'enfolk** or **wom'enfolks** n pl the women of a household, family or other community or group; women generally, womankind. **Women's Institute** n an organization for women esp of rural areas, with regular meetings for social and cultural activities, demonstrations of craftwork, etc. **women's liberation** n

(also with caps) a movement of active feminists forming part of the women's movement (inf contraction **women's lib**). **women's liberationist** n (inf contraction **women's libber**). **women's movement** n (also with caps) the movement amongst women to try to achieve equality with men, with regard to eg job opportunities, pay, legal status, etc. **women's rights** n pl equal rights with men sought by women. **women's studies** n sing an area of academic study incorporating elements of history, literature, etc, focusing on the achievements and experiences of women. **women's suffrage** n possession of the electoral franchise by women. **wom'enswear** n clothes for women.
■ **kept woman** a mistress. **play the woman** to give way to weakness. **the little woman** (facetious or patronizing) one's wife. **woman of letters** a scholar; a writer. **woman of the town** or **streets** a prostitute. **woman of the world** a woman of fashion or of worldly wisdom; a woman who knows and makes allowance for, or accepts, the ways of the world; a married woman (obs). **woman to woman** one woman to another as individuals in fight or talk; frank and confidential. **Women's Royal Voluntary Service** (from its formation in 1938 until 1966 the **Women's Voluntary Service**) a nationwide service assisting government departments, local authorities and other voluntary bodies in organizing and carrying out welfare and emergency work for the community.

womb /woom/ n the uterus, the organ in the female mammal in which the young develop after conception and stay until birth; the abdomen, the stomach or the bowels (obs); the place where anything is conceived, originated, developed or produced; any deep cavity; any warm, sheltering, enclosing environment. ◆ vt (Shakesp) to enclose. [OE wamb, womb; Ger Wamme paunch]
■ **wombed** adj. **womb'like** adj. **womb'y** adj (Shakesp) hollow, capacious.
❑ **womb'-leasing** n (inf) surrogate motherhood undertaken in return for a fee.

wombat /wom'bat/ n an animal belonging to any of several Australian species of heavy, short-legged, herbivorous, burrowing marsupials of the family Vombatidae. [From an Aboriginal language]

women see **woman**.

womera same as **woomera**.

womyn /wim'in/ n pl a spelling of **women** used by some feminist writers. [Altered to avoid the association with men]

won[1] /wun/ pat and pap of **win**[1,2].

won[2] /wun, wŭn or wŏn/ n (pl **won**) the standard monetary unit of North and South Korea (100 chon). [Korean wăn]

won[3] /wun or wŏn/ vi (pat **wonned**; pap **wont**) to dwell, abide (archaic and dialect); to be, or become, accustomed (obs). ◆ n (obs) a dwelling, an abode; habit, custom. [OE wunian, Du wonen, Ger wohnen to dwell]
■ **won'ing** or **wonn'ing** n the state of dwelling; a dwelling-place.
■ **did won** (Spenser) was accustomed.

wonder /wun'dər/ n the state of mind produced by something new, unexpected or extraordinary, amazement, awe or bafflement; admiration (obs); the quality of being strange, unexpected or awesome; a strange, astonishing or admirable thing or happening, a marvel; a prodigy; a miracle; a sweet friedcake, a cruller (US). ◆ adj and combining form notable for accomplishing marvels, as in wonder drug, wonderwoman, wonderboy. ◆ vi to feel wonder; to be surprised, as in shouldn't wonder if she won; to be amazed (with at); to speculate (with about); to feel doubt. ◆ vt to speculate, to ask oneself (with noun clause or direct quotation); used to introduce polite requests or inquiries. [OE wundor; Ger Wunder, ON undr]
■ **won'dered** or **wond'red** adj (obs) marvellous; having performed, or able to perform, wonders (Shakesp). **won'derer** n. **won'derful** adj causing wonder; strange, extraordinary; expressing vague commendation, admirable, splendid (inf). ◆ adv (archaic or dialect) wonderfully. **won'derfully** adv. **won'derfulness** n. **won'dering** n and adj. **won'deringly** adv. **won'derment** n awed surprise; an expression of wonder; a wonderful thing; the quality of being wonderful. **won'drous**, also (old) **won'derous** adj such as to cause wonder, wonderful, strange or awesome. ◆ adv (archaic) strangely, wonderfully; exceedingly. **won'drously** adv. **won'drousness** n.
❑ **Won'derbra**® n an underwired bra with side padding, designed to give uplift and a more conspicuous cleavage. **won'derland** n an imaginary place full of marvels, fairyland; a scene of strange unearthly beauty. **won'dermonger** n a wonder-worker; someone who talks garrulously of wonders, esp incredible ones. **won'dermongering** n. **won'der-struck** or **won'der-stricken** adj struck with wonder or astonishment, thunderstruck. **won'derwork** n a prodigy, miracle; thaumaturgy, the performing of miracles. **won'der-worker** n. **won'der-working** n and adj. **won'der-wounded** adj (Shakesp) wonder-stricken.

■ **bird of wonder** the phoenix. **do** or **work wonders** to achieve marvellous results. **for a wonder** by way of an unexpected but pleasant change. **nine days' wonder** something that astonishes everybody for the moment. **no** or **little** or **small wonder** it isn't surprising. **seven wonders of the world** see under **seven**. **to a wonder** (*archaic*) marvellously; extremely well. **wonders never** (or **will never) cease** (*inf*) an expression of surprise at some unexpected but welcome development.

wondred, wondrous see under **wonder**.

wonga /wong'gə/ (*sl*) *n* money. [Origin uncertain]

wonga-wonga /wong'ə-wong'ə or wong'gə-wong'ge/ *n* the large Australian white-faced pigeon (also **wong'a**); any of several varieties of hardy evergreen climbing vine of the family Bignoniaceae. [From an Aboriginal language]

wongi /wong'gi/ (*Aust inf*) *n* a talk, chat, conversation. ♦ *vi* (**wong'iing; wong'ied**) to converse, chat, talk. [From an Aboriginal language]

woning see under **won³**.

wonk /wongk/ (*sl, usu derog*) *n* a serious or studious person, *esp* one with an interest in a trivial or unfashionable subject. [Ety uncertain]

wonky /wong'ki/ (*inf*) *adj* unsound; shaky; amiss; awry. [Cf **wankle**] ■ **wonk'ily** *adv.* **wonk'iness** *n.*

wonned, wonning see **won³**.

wont commonly /wōnt, historically wunt/ *adj* (*literary* or *archaic*) used or accustomed. ♦ *n* (*literary* or *facetious*) habit. ♦ *vi* and *vt* to be or become, or cause to become, accustomed. [Orig pap of **won³**] ■ **wont'ed** *adj* accustomed, habituated; usual, customary. **wont'edness** *n.* **wont'less** *adj* (*archaic*) unaccustomed.

won't /wōnt/ will not. [Contracted form of ME *wol not*]

won ton /won ton/ (*Chinese cookery*) *n* a spicy dumpling containing minced pork, *esp* served in soup. [Chin (Cantonese) *wan tan* pastry]

WoO (*music*) *abbrev*: *Werke ohne Opuszahl* (*Ger*), works (by Beethoven) without an opus number (prefixed to assigned number).

woo /woo/ *vt* (*pat* and *pap* **wooed** /wood/) (of a man) to try to win the affection of, to court (a woman; *esp old*); to invite or court (eg destruction); to solicit eagerly, seek the support of (eg voters); to seek to gain (success, fame, etc). ♦ *vi* to go courting. [OE *wōgian* to woo; origin obscure] ■ **woo'able** *adj.* **woo'er** *n.* **woo'ing** *n* and *adj.* **woo'ingly** *adv.*

woobut see **woubit**.

wood¹ /wŭd/ *n* the hard substance composing the trunks and branches of trees and shrubs, xylem; trees cut or sawn, timber; a kind of timber or wood; firewood; (often in *pl*) a collection of more or less densely growing trees; a stretch of country supporting such growth; a tree (*obs*); the Cross (*obs*); the cask or barrel as storage for wine, etc, as distinguished from the bottle; a woodblock (*printing*); (commonly in *pl*) the woodwind instruments of an orchestra; a golf club with a bulky head, traditionally made of wood though now usually of metal, used for hitting the ball long distances; a bowl (*bowls*); the outer rim of a tennis racquet if, as traditionally, of wood; an idol made of wood; the pulpit (*old sl*). ♦ *adj* made of or using wood. ♦ *vt* (chiefly in *pap*) to cover with trees; to supply or load (a ship) with wood. ♦ *vi* to take in a supply of wood (sometimes with *up*). [OE *wudu*; cognate with ON *vithr* wood, OIr *fid* timber] ■ **wood'ed** *adj* covered with trees; supplied with wood. **wooden** *adj* see separate entry. **wood'less** *adj* without wood. **wood'lessness** *n.* **wood'sy** /wŭd-zi/ *adj* (*N Am inf*) characteristic of or relating to woods. **woody** *adj* see separate entry.

❑ **wood acid** *n* wood vinegar. **wood alcohol** *n* wood spirit. **wood anemone** *n* any anemone growing in woods, *esp Anemone nemorosa*, which has a single whorl of leaves and a white flower. **wood ant** *n* a large forest-dwelling ant; a termite infesting the wood of old buildings. **wood ash** *n* (often in *pl*) ash obtained by burning wood or plants, a source of potassium salts. **wood'block** *n* a die cut in relief on wood and ready to produce ink impressions; a woodcut. **wood'-borer** *n* any of a number of insect larvae, molluscs or Crustacea, that bore into wood. **wood'-boring** *adj.* **wood'-born** *adj* born in the woods. **wood'carver** *n.* **wood'carving** *n* the process of carving in wood; an object or decoration carved in wood. **wood'chat** *n* a species of shrike, with black-and-white plumage but a red-brown crown. **wood'chip** *n* a chip of wood; woodchip board or paper. **woodchip board** *n* reconstituted wooden board, chipboard. **woodchip paper** *n* paper for decorating walls, etc, incorporating chips of wood for texture. **wood coal** *n* coal like wood in texture, lignite or brown coal; charcoal. **wood'cock** *n* a genus (*Scolopax*) of birds related to the snipes, but bulkier in the body and shorter and stronger in the leg; a stupid person, a simpleton (*archaic*). **wood'cock's-head** *n* (*obs*) a tobacco pipe. **wood'craft** *n* skill in working or carving wood; skill in hunting and everything relating to life in the woods; forestry generally. **wood'cut** *n* a design for printing incised into the surface of a block of wood cut along the grain; an

impression taken from this. **wood'cutter** *n* someone who fells trees and cuts wood; a maker of woodcuts. **wood'cutting** *n.* **wood duck** *n* a N American duck (*Aix sponsa*) that nests in tree cavities, a popular game bird. **wood engraver** *n* a maker of wood engravings; any of certain beetles that make a pattern of furrows in the wood of trees. **wood engraving** *n* a design for printing, incised into the surface of a block of hard wood cut across the grain; an impression taken from this; the art of cutting such designs. **wood'-evil** *n* diarrhoea of herbivorous animals. **wood fibre** *n* a thick-walled, elongated, dead element found in wood, developed by the elongation and lignification of the wall of a single cell, differing from a tracheide in its inability to conduct water. **wood flour** or **wood'meal** *n* a fine powder, made from sawdust and wood waste, used as a filler in many industries, in the manufacture of guncotton and dynamite, and as an absorbent in surgical dressings. **wood'-fretter** *n* a wood-borer. **wood germander** *n Teucrium scorodonia*, which has racemes of yellow flowers. **wood'grouse** *n* the capercailzie. **wood hedgehog** *n* an edible fungus (*Hydnum repandum*) with spines under the cap. **wood'hole** *n* a place where wood is stored. **wood honey** *n* wild honey. **wood'horse** *n* a sawhorse. **wood'house** *n* a house or shed in which wood for fuel is deposited; a variant of **woodwose**. **wood hyacinth** *n* the wild hyacinth or English bluebell, of the genus *Endymion* (or *Scilla*). **wood ibis** *n* any bird of the genera *Mycteria* (or *Tantalus*) and *Ibis* of the subfamily Mycteriinae of storks. **wood'land** *n* (also in *pl*) land covered with wood (also *adj*). **wood'lander** *n* an inhabitant of woodland. **wood'lark** *n* a species of lark that perches on trees but sings chiefly on the wing. **wood lot** *n* a piece of land reserved entirely for the growing of timber. **wood'louse** *n* (*pl* **wood'lice**) any of numerous isopod crustaceans of family Oniscidae, found in damp places, under stones and bark, in woodwork, among moss, etc; a booklouse; a termite (*US*). **wood'man** *n* a man who fells trees for timber; a person with administrative responsibility for a forest (*hist*); a huntsman. **woodmeal** see **wood flour** above. **wood mite** *n* any of numerous small mites found in woods. **wood'mouse** *n* a type of fieldmouse, *Apodemus sylvaticus*, with large ears and a long tail. **wood naphtha** *n* wood spirit, methanol. **wood nightshade** another name for woody nightshade (qv under **woody**). **wood'note** *n* (*Milton*) a wild musical note, like that of a songbird. **wood nymph** *n* a nymph of the woods. **wood'-offering** *n* (*Bible*) wood burned on the altar. **wood oil** *n* gurjun balsam; tung oil; also various other oils obtained from trees. **wood opal** *n* a form of common opal which has replaced pieces of wood entombed as fossils in sediments, in some cases retaining the original structure. **wood owl** *n* the European brown or tawny owl, or other owl living in woods. **wood paper** *n* paper made from wood pulp. **wood'pecker** *n* any of a family (Picidae) of birds in the order Picariae, remarkable for modification of the skull and bill enabling the latter to be used to drill holes, and for the long flexible tongue, used to extract insects from crevices. **wood pigeon** *n* the ringdove, a common species of pigeon (*Columba palumbus*) living in woods; in New Zealand, the kuku (qv). **wood'pile** *n* a pile of wood, *esp* firewood. **wood pulp** *n* wood mechanically or chemically pulped for paper-making. **wood'rat** *n* another name for the **pack-rat** (see under **pack¹**). **wood'reeve** *n* the overseer of a wood. **wood'rush** *n* any plant of the genus *Luzula*, of the same family as the true rushes, growing in woods. **wood sage** *n* wood germander. **wood sandpiper** *n* a common European sandpiper. **wood sanicle** see **sanicle**. **wood'screw** *n* a tapered screw for fastening pieces of wood or wood and metal, etc. **wood'shed** *n* a shed for storing firewood (**something nasty in the woodshed** (*facetious*) an unpleasant or shocking experience from one's past, *esp* if kept hushed up); an intensive, *esp* private, practice or rehearsal (*music sl; orig US*). ♦ *vt* and *vi* to practise (a piece of music), *esp* intensively and alone. **wood'shedding** *n* such intensive practice; spontaneous barber-shop singing. **wood'shock** *n* a large N American marten with dark-brown fur. **wood'shrike** *n* the woodchat (qv above). **wood'skin** *n* a Native American canoe made of bark, or the bark itself. **woods'man** *n* someone familiar with the lore of the woods; a forester or woodcutter; a huntsman. **wood sorrel** *n* any plant of the genus *Oxalis*, *esp O. acetosella*, with trifoliate leaves and white or rose-tinted flowers, which yields potassium binoxalate, $KHC_2O_4.H_2O$. **wood spirit** *n* a spirit living among trees; methyl alcohol, wood naphtha or methanol. **wood'spite** *n* the green woodpecker. **wood stamp** *n* a stamp made of wood, as for stamping fabrics in colours. **wood'stone** *n* petrified wood. **wood sugar** *n* xylose. **wood swallow** *n* any of the fly-catching Artamidae, also called **swallow-shrikes**, the resemblance to shrikes being more fundamental than that to swallows. **wood tar** *n* a product of destructive distillation of wood, containing paraffins, naphthalene and phenols. **wood'thrush** *n* a thrush common in the woods of the eastern United States, with a reddish-brown head and back, olive rump, and spotted breast; locally in Britain, the missel thrush or the song thrush. **wood tick** *n* any tick of the family Ixodidae, the young of which are transferred to man and animals from bushes. **wood tin** *n* a botryoidal or reniform variety of the tin ore cassiterite showing a concentric structure of radiating brown, wood-like fibres. **wood**

vinegar *n* crude acetic acid obtained from wood, pyroligneous acid. **wood warbler** *n* a yellowish-green European warbler, *Phylloscopus sibilatrix*; any bird of the genera *Dendroica*, *Vermivora*, etc of the American family Parulidae. **wood'ward** *n* an officer who guards or has charge of the woods. **wood wasp** *n* a large hymenopterous insect (genus *Sirex*) that bores wood with its ovipositor, the horntail. **wood'wax** or **wood'waxen** *n* dyer's greenweed. **wood'wind** *n* any orchestral wind instrument other than the brass instruments, made, or formerly made, of wood, some now being made of metals such as silver, including the flute, oboe, bassoon, clarinet, etc; the section of an orchestra comprising these collectively. **wood wool** *n* fine wood shavings. **wood-wool slabs** *n pl* slabs made from long wood shavings with a cementing material, used for linings, partitions, etc. **wood'work** *n* the wooden parts of any structure (**crawl out of the woodwork** to put in an unwelcome appearance after a period of absence); carpentry or joinery; goalposts, etc (*football*, etc; *inf*). **wood'worker** *n* a craftsman or worker in wood. **wood'worm** *n* the larva of any of several beetles, that bores into wood; the diseased condition of wood affected by this creature. **wood wren** *n* the willow warbler (*Phylloscopus trochilus*); the wood warbler (*Phylloscopus sibilatrix*). **wood'yard** *n* a yard in which wood is cut and stored.
■ **Commissioners of Woods and Forests** a department (1810–1924) having charge of the Crown woods and forests. **not see the wood for the trees** to fail to grasp the whole because of the superabundance of, or one's over-concentration on, detail. **out of the wood** or **woods** out of difficulty or danger. **touch wood** see under **touch**.

wood² /wŭd/ (*Shakesp*; *Scot* **wud** /wud/) *adj* mad; fierce, furious. [OE *wōd*; ON *ōthr*, Ger *Wut* madness]
■ **wood'ness** *n*.

woodbine /wŭd'bīn/ or **woodbind** /wŭd'bīnd/ *n* the honeysuckle; applied also to other climbers, such as some kinds of ivy, the Virginia creeper, etc; *perh* bindweed (*Shakesp*); (also with *cap*) someone English, *esp* a soldier (*old Aust sl*; from the brand name of a popular and inexpensive cigarette). [OE *wudubind*, from *wudu* wood, and *bind* binding]

woodburytype /wŭd'bə-ri-tīp/ *n* a photomechanical process in which an exposed and developed bichromated film is forced into a metal plate by great pressure, and so forms a matrix for subsequent printing. [Named from the inventor]

woodchat, woodchip see under **wood¹**.

woodchuck /wŭd'chuk/ *n* a N American species of marmot (*Marmota monax*). [Corruption of a Native American name]

woodcock...to...**woodcutter** see under **wood¹**.

wooden /wŭd'ən/ *adj* made of or like wood; (of a golf club) having a head made of wood; hard; dull, insensible; heavy, stupid; lacking animation or grace of manner or execution, unnatural, inhibited; clumsy. [**wood¹**]
■ **wood'enly** *adv*. **wood'enness** *n* wooden quality; lack of spirit or expression.
❑ **wood'enhead** *n* (*inf*) a blockhead, stupid person. **woodenhead'ed** *adj* having a head made of wood; stupid. **woodenhead'edness** *n*. **wooden horse** *n* the Trojan horse (qv); a former instrument of punishment in the army (see **horse**); a ship (*archaic*). **wooden kimono** or **overcoat** *n* (*US sl*) a coffin. **wooden leg** *n* an artificial leg made of wood. **wooden pear** *n* an Australian tree whose pear-shaped seed vessels have a woody outside. **wooden spoon** *n* a spoon made of wood formerly presented to the person coming bottom in the mathematical tripos list at Cambridge; hence, a booby prize. **wooden tongue** *n* woody-tongue (qv under **woody**). **wooden entop** *n* (*derog sl*) a uniformed policeman; a guardsman. **wooden type** *n* large type cut in wood. **wooden walls** *n pl* (*literary*) warships (in allusion to Gr *xylinon teichos*, Herodotus 7.141).

wood-evil...to...**woodhouse** see under **wood¹**.

woodie /wŭd'i/ or *-ē/ (*Scot*) *n* the gallows. [**widdy¹**]

woodiness see under **woody**.

woodland...to...**woodreeve** see under **wood¹**.

woodruff /wŭd'ruf/ or (*obs*) **woodroof** /wŭd'rŭf/ *n* a plant of the genus *Asperula* of rubiaceous plants with whorled leaves and a funnel-shaped corolla, *esp* **sweet woodruff**, which has small white flowers and a pleasant scent. [OE *wuduroffe*, from *wudu* wood, with unexplained 2nd element]

Woodruff key /wŭd'ruf kē/ (*engineering*) *n* a key consisting of a segment of a disk, restrained in a shaft key-way milled by a cutter of the same radius, and fitting a normal key-way in the hub. [From the *Woodruff* Manufacturing Company of Hartford, Connecticut, where it was first manufactured in 1892]

woodrush...to...**woodshed** see under **wood¹**.

woodsia /wŭd'zi-ə/ *n* a fern of the genus *Woodsia* (family Polypodiaceae) of cool or mountainous regions, with tufted rhizomes. [James *Woods* (1776–1864), botanist]

woodskin...to...**woodstone** see under **wood¹**.

woodsy see under **wood¹**.

woodwale /wŭd'wāl/ *n* the woodpecker, *esp* the green woodpecker. [ME *wudewale*, from OE *wudu* wood, and an unexplained 2nd element; cf **witwall**]

woodwind...to...**woodworm** see under **wood¹**.

woodwose /wŭd'wōs/ or **woodhouse** /wŭd'hows/ (*obs* or *heraldry*) *n* a wild man of the woods, a figure sometimes found as a supporter in heraldry; a satyr, faun. [OE *wuduwāsa*, from *wudu* wood, with unexplained 2nd element]

woody /wŭd'i/ *adj* abounding with woods; inhabiting woods (*Spenser*); situated in a wood; relating to wood; consisting wholly or largely of wood; ligneous; like wood in texture, smell, taste, etc. [**wood¹**]
■ **wood'iness** *n*.
❑ **woody nightshade** *n* bittersweet (*Solanum dulcamara*), a purple-flowered climbing plant with poisonous red berries. **wood'y-tongue** *n* actinobacillosis, a chronic inflammation of cattle, rare in sheep and pigs, occasionally transmitted to man, due to infection, *usu* of the tongue, by the fungus *Actinobacillus ligniersi*.

woodyard see under **wood¹**.

wooer, wooing, etc see under **woo**.

woof¹ /woof/ *n* weft; thread for a weft; texture. [ME *oof*, with *w* added by association with **warp**, etc (*oof* being the normal development of OE *ōwef*, from *on* and *wefan* to weave)]
■ **woofed** /wooft or woof'id/ *adj* woven. **woof'y** *adj* dense in texture.

woof² /wŭf/ *n* (an approximate rendering of) the sound of a dog's bark.
♦ *vi* (of a dog) to bark; to imitate a dog's bark. [Imit]
■ **woof'er** *n* a large loudspeaker used to reproduce low-frequency sounds only (cf **tweeter**).

woof³ /wŭf/ (*N Eng*) *n* a catfish. [Origin obscure]

woofter /wŭf'tər/ (*sl*) *n* same as **poofter** (see **puff¹**).

woofy see under **woof¹**.

wool /wŭl/ *n* the fleece of sheep, goats, yaks, etc, a modified kind of hair of which the fibres are soft, fine and curly, with an imbricated surface that makes for felting; this spun into yarn or thread for knitting or weaving; fabric or clothing woven or knitted from such yarn; downy hair under the coat of any of various furry animals; short crisply-curling human hair, or (*facetious*) one's hair generally; short, thick human hair; any light, fleecy substance like wool, eg the fine soft fibres of some plants; any substance with a fibrous texture, resembling wool, eg steel wool, glass wool, wood wool. ♦ *adj* made of or relating to wool. [OE *wull*; Gothic *wulla*, Ger *Wolle*, L *vellus*]
■ **woolled** /wŭld/ *adj* bearing wool. **wool'-like** *adj*. **wool'ward** *adv* (*obs*) with wool next the skin, *esp* as a penance.
❑ **wool ball** *n* a ball of wool, such as is sometimes found in a sheep's stomach. **wool'-bearing** *adj* bearing or yielding wool. **wool card** or **wool comb** *n* a machine for **wool'-carding** or **wool'-combing**, separating the fibres of wool preparatory to spinning. **wool'-carder** or **wool'-comber** *n*. **wool church** *n* an English, *esp* East Anglian, church built or converted using funds accrued during the Tudor wool-trade boom, many seeming of inappropriate size and grandeur for their setting. **wool clip** *n* a crop of wool from a particular flock of sheep, *esp* that gathered in one season. **wool'-driver** *n* a buyer-up of wool. **wool'-dyed** *adj* dyed before spinning or weaving. **wool'fat** *n* lanolin. **wool'fell** *n* (*archaic*) the skin with the wool still on it. **wool'-gathering** *n* absent-minded dreaming. ♦ *adj* dreamy; absent-minded. **wool'-grower** *n* a breeder of sheep for the production of wool. **wool'-growing** *n*. **wool'man** *n* a dealer in wool. **wool mill** *n* a woollen mill. **wool oil** *n* any oil obtained from woolfat; an oil used to oil wool before spinning. **wool'pack** *n* the bag in which wool was formerly packed for sale, or the fabric of which it was made; a bale or bundle of wool, *esp* formerly weighing 240lb; cirro-cumulus cloud; the woolsack (*obs*). **wool'-packer** *n*. **wool'-picker** *n* a machine for cleaning wool. **wool'sack** *n* (also with *cap*) the seat of the speaker of the House of Lords, being a large square sack of wool covered with scarlet; the office of Lord Chancellor (*hist*). **wool shears** *n pl* shears used in shearing sheep. **wool'shed** *n* (*Aust* and *NZ*) a large shed for shearing sheep and baling wool. **wool'sorter** *n* a person who sorts wool according to quality, etc. **woolsorter's disease** *n* anthrax. **wool staple** *n* the fibre or pile of wool; a market where wool was sold. **wool'-stapler** *n* a dealer in wool; a woolsorter. **wool'-winder** *n* a person who packs fleeces. **wool'work** *n* needlework done in wool, *usu* in canvas, imitative of tapestry.
■ **against the wool** against the texture of the wool, the wrong way. **dye in the wool** to dye (wool) before spinning; see also **dye¹**. **great** or **much cry and little wool** much palaver and little result. **keep one's**

wool on (*inf*) to keep one's hair on, stay calm. **pull** or **draw the wool over someone's eyes** to hoodwink or deceive someone.

woold /woold/ *vt* to wind a rope or chain round. [Du *woelen*; Ger (*be*)*wuhlen*]
■ **woold'ed** *adj*. **woold'er** *n* a stick used in woolding a mast or yard; a pin in a ropemaker's top. **woold'ing** *n*.

woolen see **woollen**.

woolfat...to...**woolled** see under **wool**.

woollen or (*US*) **woolen** /wŭl'ən/ *adj* made of wool; relating to wool or the production of wool; covered or clad in wool; rustic, simple (*obs fig*). ◆ *n* a garment made of wool, *esp* a knitted one; a fabric made from wool. [**wool**]
❑ **wooll'en-draper** *n* a dealer in woollen goods. **wooll'en-drapery** *n*. **woollen mill** *n* a mill where wool is spun and woven into fabric.

woolly /wŭl'i/ *adj* made of or consisting of wool; resembling wool in texture or appearance; downy, fleecy; covered or clad in wool or a substance resembling it; (of language, thinking or argument) lacking clarity and logic; hazy, not firm, definite or distinct; (*esp* in *wild and woolly*) having the atmosphere or quality of the Wild West (*inf*). ◆ *n* (*pl* **wooll'ies**) (*inf*) a woollen garment, *esp* a knitted sweater, cardigan, etc; a sheep, *esp* before shearing (*Aust* and *US inf*). [**wool**]
■ **wooll'iness** *n*.
❑ **woolly aphis** *n* a plant louse (*Eriosoma lanigerum*), covered with hair resembling cotton wool, that infests *esp* apple trees. **wooll'yback** *n* (*inf*) a sheep; an unsophisticated person from out of town (*esp Liverpool dialect*). **woolly bear** *n* the hairy caterpillar of a number of moths, including the tiger moths; the larva of the carpet beetle. **wooll'ybutt** *n* (*Aust*) any of a number of eucalyptus trees, eg *Eucalyptus longifolia*, with fibrous bark. **wooll'y-haired** *adj* having thick soft curly hair; woolly-headed. **woolly-hand crab** *n* the mitten-crab (qv). **wooll'y-headed** *adj* having short, crisply-curling hair; woolly-minded. **woolly-min'ded** *adj* vague, illogical or muddled in thought. **woolly-min'dedness** *n*.

woolman...to...**woolsack** see under **wool**.

woolsey /wŭl'zi/ (*obs rare*) *n* a fabric composed of cotton and wool. [Shortened from **linsey-woolsey**]

woolshed...to...**woolwork** see under **wool**.

woomera /woo'mə-rə/, **womera** /wom'ə-rə/ or **woomerang** /woo'mə-rang/ (*Aust*) *n* a stick for launching a spear with greater force. [From an Aboriginal language]

woon /woon/ (*Spenser*) *vi* same as **won³**.

woopie /wŭp'i/ (also with *cap*) *n* a well-off older person, as a dismissive designation.

Woop Woop /woop woop/ (*Aust inf*) *n* a humorous name for a remote town or district. [Sham Aboriginal]

woorali, **woorara** see **wourali**.

woosel, **woosell** see **ouzel**.

woosh see **whoosh**.

woot or **woo't** /wŭt/, also **wot** /wot/ (*Shakesp*) wilt (thou)?

wootz /woots/ *n* steel made in India, from ancient times, by fusing iron with carbonaceous matter. [For *wook*, from Kanarese *ukku* steel]

woozy /woo'zi/ (*inf*) *adj* fuddled eg with drink or drugs, etc; dazed, dizzy; blurred, woolly, vague. [Origin obscure]
■ **wooz'ily** *adv*. **wooz'iness** *n*.

wop¹ /wop/ (*offensive sl*) *n* a member of a Mediterranean or Latin race, eg an Italian, *esp* as an immigrant or visitor. [Perh Ital (dialect) *guappo* swaggerer, from Sp *guapo* lady's man, pimp, ruffian]

wop² /wop/ *vt* (**wopp'ing**; **wopped**) variant of **whop**.

worcester /wŭs'tər/ *n* fine woollen material made at *Worcester* (*hist*); (with *cap*; in full **Worcester china**) fine china made there in the mid 18c.
❑ **worces'terberry** *n* a N American species of gooseberry (*Ribes divaricatum*), once thought to be a hybrid of the gooseberry and blackcurrant. **Worcester** (or **Worcestershire** /wŭs'tər-shər/) **sauce** *n* a pungent sauce *orig* made in Worcestershire.

Worcs. *abbrev*: Worcestershire.

word /wûrd/ *n* the smallest unit of language that can be used independently; such a unit represented in writing or printing, *usu* separated off by spaces; (in *pl*) language as a means of communication; a saying or expression; a brief conversation; a rumour; a hint; a signal or sign, as in *say the word*; a message, as in *send word*; one's solemn promise; one's expressed will or wishes; a declaration; news or information; a password; a watchword; a war cry; (in *pl*) verbal contention; (in *pl*) discussion in contrast to action; (in *pl*) the lyrics of a song, etc; (in *pl*) the text of an actor's part in a play; used as *combining form* after a letter, to mean 'that (*esp* unmentionable or taboo) word beginning with', eg *m-word* for 'marriage' (*inf*); a set of bits stored and transferred as a single unit of

meaning (*comput*). ◆ *vt* to express in (*esp* carefully chosen) words; to speak to, or of, in words (*obs*; *rare*); to flatter (*Shakesp*). ◆ *vi* (*obs*) to speak, talk. [OE; Gothic *waurd*, ON *orth*, Ger *Wort*; L *verbum* word, Gr *eirein* to say, speak]
■ **word'age** *n* words generally, *esp* text as opposed to pictures, etc; verbiage, wordiness; quantity of words, length of text; choice of words, wording. **word'ed** *adj* expressed in words. **word'ily** *adv*. **word'iness** *n* the quality of being wordy. **word'ing** *n* the process of expressing in words; choice of words, phrasing; speaking, utterance (*archaic*). **word'ish** *adj* (*obs*) verbose. **word'ishness** *n*. **word'less** *adj* unspoken; silent. **word'lessly** *adv*. **word'lessness** *n*. **word'y** *adj* using too many words to say something, long-winded, *esp* pompously so; conducted in words.
❑ **word association** *n* (*psychiatry*) the psychoanalytic practice of giving patients a word to which they have to respond with the first word that occurs to them, a technique believed to afford insights into the unconscious. **word bite** *n* (*inf*) any brief quotable item from a speech, etc, sounding as if it carries an important message. **word'-blind** *adj*. **word blindness** *n* the lack or loss of the ability to read, a non-technical name for both **alexia** and **dyslexia**. **word'book** *n* a book with a collection of words; a dictionary or vocabulary. **word'bound** *adj* unable to find expression in words; bound by a promise. **word'break** *n* (*printing*) the point of division in a word that runs onto the following line. **word'-building** *n* the formation of words from letters or from root words and affixes. **word class** *n* a set of words that all share a common grammatical property. **word'-deaf** *adj* affected by **word deafness**, inability to distinguish words, resulting from damage to the auditory part of the brain. **word'-finder** *n* a book designed as a tool for finding a required word; a thesaurus. **word'game** *n* any game or puzzle in which words have to be constructed, deciphered, etc. **word'lore** *n* information about the history, use, etc of words. **word memory** *n* the power of recalling words to the mind. **word order** *n* the sequence in which words are arranged in a sentence, relevant to the sense in many languages, including English. **word'-painter** *n*. **word'-painting** *n* the act or art of describing vividly in words. **word'-per'fect** *adj* having memorized (words to be repeated, recited, etc) exactly. **word picture** *n* a description in words that presents an object, scene, etc, to the mind as if in a picture. **word'play** *n* punning or witty repartee exploiting verbal ambiguity, etc. **word processing** *n* the arranging and storing of text with the aid of a word processor. **word processor** *n* any of several types of machine that perform electronically the tasks of typing, data-recording, dictating, transcribing, etc, *usu* incorporating screens for visual display. **word'-puzzler** *n* a person who engages in puzzles or games involving words. **word salad** *n* (*psychol*) a confused outpouring of speech consisting of real and non-existent words, typically occurring in severe cases of schizophrenia. **word'search** *n* a puzzle consisting of a grid filled with letters, within which various words are hidden. **word'smith** *n* an accomplished user of words (sometimes *ironic*); a coiner of words. **word'smithery** *n*. **word'-splitting** *n* hair-splitting, quibbling. **word square** *n* a square grid composed of a set of words that read the same down as they do across. **word wrapping** or **word wrap** *n* (*comput*) (on a screen) the automatic placing of a line feed between words so that any text placed beyond the right hand end of a line is moved to the start of the next line, wraparound.
■ **at a word** without more ado, at once; to be brief, in short (*obs*). **a word in someone's ear** a confidential conversation. **be as good as one's word** to keep one's promise. **break one's word** to fail to keep one's promise. **by word of mouth** orally, through the spoken word (**word'-of-mouth** *adj*). **eat one's words** to retract what one has said, or apologize for it, *usu* under compulsion. **fair words** (*archaic*) pleasant, conciliatory words, *usu* implying flattery or deceit. **get a word in edgeways** to interpose what one needs to say with difficulty into a conversation dominated by others or another. **have a word with** to speak to, *usu* for some specific purpose. **have no words for** to be at a loss to describe or express. **have words** to quarrel, dispute (with *with*). **in a** (or **one**) **word** in short, to sum up. **in other words** saying the same thing in a different way. **in so many words** explicitly; bluntly. **in word** in one's speech or professions only, in contrast to one's deeds. **keep one's word** to fulfil one's promise. **my word** or (*old*) **upon my word** a mild interjection expressing surprise, dismay, etc. **not the word for it** not a strong enough word to express or describe it. **of few** (or **many**) **words** taciturn (or verbose). **of one's word** (in *a man of his word*, etc) having a reputation for keeping one's promises. **on my word** on my honour, truly. **pass one's word** to make a promise. **put in a good word for** to make commendatory mention of (someone) in a quarter where it will do him or her good. **put words into someone's mouth** to attribute or supply to someone words that he or she did not, or does not intend to, use. **take someone at his** (or **her**) **word** to take someone's offer, etc literally. **take someone's word for it** to accept what someone says as true, when one has no means of knowing personally. **take** (or **take up**) **the word** to begin speaking or continue a discourse begun by someone

else. **take the words out of someone's mouth** to say exactly what someone else was about to say. **the last word** the closing remark in an argument, *esp* if having an appearance of conclusiveness; the conclusive statement; the ultimate authority; (also **the latest word**) the most up-to-date design or model, the most recent advance in something or a consummate example of it. **the Word (of God)** (*Christianity*) the Scriptures; the gospel message; the second person in the Trinity, the Logos. **too funny, stupid,** etc **for words** (*inf*) exceptionally funny, stupid, etc. **word for word** literally, verbatim. **words fail me** I am unable to express my feelings or reaction.

Wordsworthian /wûrdz-wûr'thi-ən/ *adj* relating to or associated with the poet William *Wordsworth* (1770–1850) or his style. ◆ *n* an admirer or imitator of Wordsworth.

wore /wōr/ or /wör/ *pat* of **wear**[1,2].

work /wûrk/ *n* physical or mental effort directed towards making or achieving something; employment; one's place of employment; tasks to be accomplished; that on which one is labouring, one's task or workpiece; the product of mental or physical labour, anything made or done; materials for accomplishing one's task; needlework, embroidery (*old*); a deed; doings; the result of action; the manner of performing or completing a task, quality of working, workmanship; (*usu* in *pl*) an action in its moral aspect, *esp* as tending to justification (*theol*); a literary, artistic, musical or dramatic composition or creation; a book; (as *combining form*) things made, or ornamentation executed, in the material or with the tools specified, as in *basketwork, woolwork, crewelwork*; (as *combining form*) the parts of a building, etc in a specified material, as in *brickwork, stonework, woodwork, paintwork*; (in *pl*) building or repair operations, as in *roadworks, clerk of works*; (in *pl*) a factory, workshop (as *adj* of a racing-car, entered officially in a race by the manufacturer); (in *pl*) walls, ramparts, trenches, etc (*fortif* or *archaeol*); (in *pl*) the mechanism or operating parts, eg of a watch; (in *pl*) the syringe and associated drug-injecting equipment (*drug sl*); the act of producing an effect by means of a force (*F*) whose point of application moves through a distance (*s*) in its own line of action, measured by the product of the force and the distance, so that $W=Fs$ (*phys*); the spin given to a ball by a bowler to cause it to break on pitching (*cricket*); (by confusion with OE *wærc*) ache, trouble, fuss (*dialect*). ◆ *adj* relating to, suitable for, etc work, as in *work clothes*. ◆ *vi* (*pat* and *pap* **worked** or (*archaic*) **wrought**) to exert oneself mentally or physically to achieve or attain anything, to toil, labour or study; to perform the tasks and duties involved in a job; to be occupied in business or labour; to be employed; to move, or make one's way, slowly and laboriously; to move or shift gradually out of position, as in *work loose*; (of a ship's timbers) to shift and gape through the action of wind and water; to be in action; to operate, function; to produce effects; to behave in the desired way when operated; to prove practicable; (of a craftsperson; with *in*) to fashion things in (a certain material); to ache, be painful (*dialect*); to ferment; (of eg features) to be agitated, move convulsively; to strain, labour; to sail in a course, *esp* to beat to windward (*naut*); to contrive, plan (*archaic*). ◆ *vt* to impose tasks on, to cause to labour; to put in motion or operate (a machine, etc); to shape or fashion (material or an artefact); to cultivate (land); to extract materials from (a mine); to knead or manipulate (dough); to cause to ferment; to sew or embroider (*old*); to cover (an area) as a sales representative, etc; to achieve (miracles, wonders, etc); to effect or seek to effect (one's revenge); to manipulate (a system, rules, etc) to one's advantage (*inf*); to influence, cajole or trick (*inf*); (*reflexive*) to get (oneself into an emotional state, rage, etc); to make (one's way); to cause to shift little by little, by persistent manipulation; to exercise (a part of the body); to purge (*dialect*); to solve by mathematical calculation (*N Am*); to earn (one's sea passage) by unpaid work on board; to finance (one's way through university, etc) by doing paid work. [OE *weorc*; ON *verk*, Ger *Werk*; further connected with Gr *ergon*]

■ **workabil'ity** or **work'ableness** *n*. **work'able** *adj* that may be worked; practicable. **work'ably** *adv*. **workaholic** /wûr-kə-hol'ik/ *n* and *adj* (a person) addicted to work (coined facetiously in imitation of *alcoholic*; see **-aholic**). **work'aholism** *n*. **worked** *adj* that has been treated or fashioned in some way; embroidered; ornamented. **work'er** *n* someone who works; a toiler; someone employed in manual work; an employee as opposed to an employer; (among social insects) one of a caste of sterile individuals that do all the work of the colony. **work'erist** *n* (*old*) a supporter of proletarian rights and values, *esp* (*derog*) one of upper or middle class (also *adj*). **work'ful** *adj* industrious. **work'ing** *n* the act or process of shaping, making, effecting, solving, fermenting, etc; an exposition of the process of calculation (*maths*, etc); manner of operating or functioning; (in *pl*) internal processes; endeavour (*obs*); (in *pl*) deeds (*obs*); mental or emotional activity (*obs*); contortion due to agitation; slow and laborious progress; (in *pl*) the parts of a mine, etc where work is, or has been, carried on. ◆ *adj* active; operational; labouring; having a job or employment; relating to labour, a job or employment; (of a period of time) devoted to, or denoting that part that is devoted to, work;

adequate for one's purposes, as in *working knowledge*; stirring the emotions (*obs*). **work'less** *adj* having no job, unemployed (also *n pl*). **work'some** *adj* (*Carlyle*) industrious.

❑ **work'aday** *adj* suitable for a work day, plain and practical; toiling; dull, prosaic. ◆ *n* (*obs* or *dialect*) a working day. **work'around** *n* (*comput*) a method used to circumvent, rather than fix, a problem or limitation in a system. **work'bag, work'basket** *n* respectively a bag and basket for holding materials for work, *esp* needlework. **work'bench** *n* a bench, often purpose-built, at which a craftsman, mechanic, etc works. **work'boat** *n* one used for work such as fishing, harbour maintenance, carrying industrial supplies, etc rather than for naval or passenger service. **work'book** *n* a book of exercises, often with spaces for the answers, to accompany another book; a record book of jobs undertaken, in progress or completed. **work'box** *n* a box for holding instruments or materials for work. **work camp** *n* a camp attended by *esp* young people who work voluntarily, and *usu* manually, on projects of benefit to the community. **work'day** *n* a day for work, a weekday. ◆ *adj* relating to a workday. **worker director** *n* a worker appointed to the board of a firm so as to represent its employees in policy-making discussions. **worker participation** *n* the involvement of workers in decision-making; see also **participate**. **worker priest** *n* a priest in the Roman Catholic Church who also works full-time or part-time in a secular job in order to understand better the problems of lay people. **workers' co-operative** *n* a business or other enterprise jointly owned and run by its members, who share the profits. **work ethic** *n* the general attitude of a group towards work, *esp* one (**Protestant work ethic**) that places a high moral value on (hard) work. **work experience** *n* a scheme by which school leavers work unpaid for a company or organization for a short time in order to gain experience of working life. **work'fare** *n* an unemployment benefit scheme under which recipients are required to do work of some kind, *usu* some kind of public service. **work'fellow** *n* someone engaged on the same job as oneself, a workmate. **work'flow** *n* the (rate of) progress in a particular task being carried out by a person, department, company, etc. **work'folk** or **work'folks** *n pl* workers. **work'force** *n* the number of workers engaged in a particular industry, factory, etc; the total number of workers potentially available. **work function** *n* (*phys*) the energy required to release a photoelectron from a cathode either by heating or irradiation. **work'girl** *n* a girl or young woman employed in manual labour. **work'group** *n* a group of computer users linked by means of a network. **work'-harden** *vt* (*engineering*) to harden and strengthen (metals) by working (*esp* cold-working) them, subjecting them to processes such as hammering and rolling. **work'-hardening** *n*. **work'horse** *n* a horse used in a labouring capacity rather than for recreation, racing, etc; a person, machine or anything else heavily depended on to do arduous work, give intensive service, etc. **work'house** *n* (*hist*) a house where any work or manufacture is carried on; a house of shelter for the poor, who are given work to do; a prison where petty offenders carry out physical labour (*US*). **work-in** see **work in** below. **work'ing-beam** *n* a walking-beam (qv under **walk**[1]). **working breakfast, lunch,** etc *n* one arranged as an alternative to a formal meeting, for the discussion of diplomatic or other business. **working capital** see under **capital**[1]. **working class** *n* (often in *pl*) the class in society that comprises manual workers and wage-earners. **work'ing-class** *adj*. **working day** *n* a day on which work is done; the period of actual work each day. **wor'king-day** *adj* laborious; plodding; ordinary. **working drawing** *n* a drawing of the details of the construction or assembly of something by which the builders are guided in their work. **working edge** *n* an edge of a piece of wood trued square with the working face to assist in truing the other surfaces square. **working face** *n* that face of a piece of wood which is first trued and then used as a basis for truing the other surfaces. **working girl** *n* (*inf*; *orig US*) a prostitute. **working hours** *n pl* the period of the day during which work is normally done, and offices, shops, etc are open. **working house** *n* (*obs*) a workshop. **working hypothesis** *n* an assumption on the basis of which to make plans or take action. **working lunch** see **working breakfast** above. **working majority** *n* a majority of sufficient size that the party in office would not expect to be defeated in any vote. **working man** or **woman** *n* a worker, *esp* a manual one. **working memory** *n* (*psychol*) that part of the memory that is contained in a person's consciousness at any particular time. **working model** *n* a model of a machine that can do, on a smaller scale, the same work as the machine. **working paper** *n* a paper produced as a basis for discussion, to report on progress made, etc, rather than as a final statement. **working** (or **work**) **party** *n* a group of people who carry out a specially assigned task; a group appointed to investigate a subject, such as methods of attaining maximum efficiency in an industry. **working week** or (*N Am*) **work'week** *n* that part of the week in which work is normally done, *esp* Monday to Friday; any week in which such work is done, as opposed eg to holidays. **work'load** *n* the amount of work assigned to an individual, machine, etc for completion within a certain time. **work'man** *n* a man who works, *esp* manually; a skilful artificer or craftsman. **work'manlike** *adj* like a workman; befitting a skilful

workman; well performed. **work'manly** adj befitting a skilful workman, workmanlike. ◆adv (old) in a workmanlike manner. **work'manship** n the skill of a workman; manner of making; the degree of expertise shown in making something, or of refinement of finish in the completed product; that which is made or produced by one's hands (also fig). **work'master** or **work'mistress** n an expert worker or craftsperson, overseer or employer. **work'mate** n a companion at work, a workfellow. **work of art** n a painting, sculpture or other production in the fine arts, esp one of high quality; anything constructed or composed with manifest skill. **workout** see **work out** below. **work'people** n pl people engaged in manual labour, workers. **work'piece** n a piece of work in progress, being manufactured; something on which a tool or machine is working. **work'place** n the office, factory, etc where one works. **work'room** n a room for working in. **works committee** or **council** n a body on which both employer and employees meet to handle labour relations within a business. **work shadowing** n the practice of shadowing a qualified worker as a means of gaining work experience. **work'-sharing** n job-sharing. **work'sheet** n a paper or form on which to detail work planned or performed; a sheet of paper used for making rough calculations or sketches; a paper with exercises to be completed by students. **work'shop** n a room or building where work is done; a group of people working on a creative or experimental project; such a project. ◆vt to hold a workshop in (an activity). **work'shy** adj hating or avoiding work, lazy (also n pl). **work'space** n a place where work is done; a location on a computer network where users can share files. **work'station** n (in an office or other workplace) a computer terminal having a keyboard, screen and processor, or the location of this; a computer with a high specification for eg computer aided design; (in a production line) a position at which a particular job is done (also as two words). **work study** n a time and motion study. **work'table** n a table on which work is done, esp, formerly, a small table used by ladies at their needlework. **work'top** n a surface designed for working on, fitted eg along the top of kitchen units, etc. **work'watcher** n (horse-racing; euphem) a tout. **work'wear** n overalls or other clothing for work, issued to factory workers, etc. **workweek** see **working week** above. **work'woman** n a woman who makes her living by manual labour. **work'y-day** adj and n (obs) workaday.
■ **a work of time** a change, achievement, etc requiring or brought about by time. **give someone the works** (sl) to give someone the full punitive, coercive, ceremonial, etc treatment considered appropriate to his or her case. **have one's work cut out** to have one's work prescribed; to be faced with a difficult task. **in working order** functioning properly. **make short work of** to accomplish, dispose of or consume speedily. **Ministry** (previously **Office**) **of Works** formerly, the body having the management and control of public works and buildings, the expenses of which are defrayed from public money. **out of work** without employment (**out'-of-work** adj and n pl unemployed (people)). **set to work** to employ in, or to engage energetically in, a piece of work. **Seven Works of Corporal Mercy** (RC) to feed the hungry, give drink to the thirsty, clothe the naked, visit prisoners, visit the sick, harbour strangers, bury the dead. **Seven Works of Spiritual Mercy** (RC) to convert sinners, instruct the ignorant, counsel the doubtful, console the afflicted, bear wrongs patiently, forgive injuries, pray for the living and the dead. **shoot the works** see under **shoot¹**. **the works** (inf) everything possible, available or going, the lot. **work at** to apply oneself to. **work back** (Aust) to work overtime. **work double tides** (naut) to work night and day. **work for** (or **against**) to exert oneself in support of (or in opposition to). **work in** to intermix; to introduce carefully and deliberately; to cause to penetrate; (of workers) to continue at work, esp by occupying the premises and taking over the running of the business, as a protest against proposed factory closure, dismissal, etc (**work'-in** n). **work into** to make way gradually into; to insinuate; to change or alter into. **work off** to separate and throw off; to get rid of by effort and exertion, or little by little; to repay (a debt, etc) with one's labour rather than with money; to print ready for circulation; to pass or palm off (inf); to dispose of by hanging (old sl). **work on** or **upon** to act or operate on; to try to perfect or improve; to use one's powers of persuasion on; to use (an assumption, hypothesis, etc) as a basis for planning, etc. **work out** to solve or calculate; to develop in detail, elaborate; to study fully (rare); to understand fully; to loosen or come out little by little; to turn out in the end; to reach a final (satisfactory) result; (of an athlete, etc) to train, exercise (**work'out** n); to effect by continued labour; to expiate, to discharge (a debt or obligation) with one's labour (old); to make by cutting, digging, etc (obs); to exhaust (a mine). **work over** to do or work at thoroughly or elaborately; to examine in detail; to beat up, thrash (sl; **work'-over** or **work'ing-over** n). **work through** to deal with (a problem, esp an emotional one) in one's own way, esp by absorption in it for some time. **work to rule** (of workers) to observe all the regulations scrupulously for the express purpose of slowing down work, as a form of industrial action (**work'-to-rule'** n). **work up** (often in pap) to excite, agitate or rouse; to create by slow degrees; to summon up (an appetite, enthusiasm, energy, etc);

to expand, elaborate; to use up (eg material); to give an irksome or needless task to (naut); to move upwards little by little; (with to) to reach or achieve, by effort and gradually.

world /wûrld/ n the earth; the earth and its inhabitants; the universe; the system of things; the present state of existence; any analogous state; any planet or heavenly body; public life or society; a sphere of interest or activity; environment; the public; the materialistically minded; mundane interests; a secular life; the course of life; one of the three kingdoms of nature; a class or division; a part, or a related group of parts, of the world, historically, sociologically or geographically speaking, as in Ancient World, Third World, Old World; a great deal, as in did her a world of good; a large quantity, as in a world of ills; time, as in world without end; the realm of possibility, as in nothing in the world; the ungodly (Bible). [OE woruld, world, weorold, orig meaning age or life of man, from wer man, and the root of **old**; ON veröld, OHGer weralt (Ger Welt)]
■ **world'ed** adj containing worlds. **world'ie** n (sl) something of world-class quality. **world'liness** n. **world'ling** n someone who is devoted to worldly pursuits and temporal possessions; a mortal (obs). **world'ly** adj relating to the world, esp as distinguished from the world to come; devoted to this life and its enjoyments; bent on gain; having knowledge and experience of the ways of the world; mortal (obs). ◆adv in a worldly manner. **world'wide** adj and adv (extending) over, or (found) everywhere in, the world.
❑ **World Bank** n the popular name of the International Bank for Reconstruction and Development, an agency of the United Nations set up in 1945 to make loans to poorer countries. **world'-beater** n (inf) a person, product, enterprise, etc that is supreme in its class. **world'-beating** adj. **world'-class** adj good enough to be classed with or compete with the best in the world. **World Court** n the popular name of the Permanent Court of International Justice (since 1946 the International Court of Justice) at the Hague, set up under the League of Nations in 1921 to settle or advise on disputes between states. **World Cup®** n a competition in some sport, notably football, between teams representing different countries, usu involving qualifying rounds and a final tournament. **world-fa'mous** adj known or renowned throughout the world. **world language** n a language either widely used internationally or designed for international use. **world line** n (phys) a curving line in space-time representing the path of a particle during its existence. **world'ly-mind'ed** adj having one's mind set on the present world, material possessions, etc. **world'ly-mind'edness** n. **worldly-wise'** adj having the wisdom of those experienced in, and affected by, the ways of the world, knowing, cynical. **world music** n popular folk music with its origins in non-western cultures, particularly African culture, esp as produced by non-Western artists. **world'-old** adj exceedingly ancient. **world power** n a state, group of states, etc, strong enough to make its influence felt in world politics. **world'scale** n the scale of freight rates for oil tankers. **World Series** n (baseball) a set of championship matches played annually between the winners of the major leagues. **world'-shaking** or **world'-shattering** adj (often ironic) devastatingly important. **world sheet** n (phys) the 2-dimensional space occupied by a string in its space-time history. **world'-view** n outlook on or attitude to the world or life. **World War** n a war of worldwide scope, esp the Great War of 1914–18 (First World War, World War I) and that of 1939–45 (Second World War, World War II). **world'-weariness** n. **world'-weary** or **world'-wearied** adj tired of the world, bored with life. **World Wide Web** n (comput) a network of Internet documents accessed by hypertext protocols.
■ **all the world** everybody; everything. (**all**) **the world and his wife** (inf) everybody; an ill-assorted assembly. **best** (or **worst**) **of both worlds** the advantage (or disadvantage) of both alternatives in a choice. **bring into the world** to give birth to; to attend the birth of, deliver. **carry the world before one** to pass through every obstacle to success. **come into the world** to be born. **come up** (or **down**) **in the world** to rise (or fall) in social status. **dead to the world** (inf) deeply asleep; in a drunken stupor. **First World** see under **first**. **for all the world** (inf) precisely or entirely (as if). **Fourth World** see under **fourth**. **go to the world** (Shakesp) to get married. **in another world** (inf) not in touch with reality. **in the world** used intensively, esp after an interrogative pronoun or adverb. **it's a small world** an indication of surprise, interest, etc at meeting someone in unexpected and unlikely circumstances. **man** (or **woman**) **of the world** someone experienced in the ways of the world. **next world** life after death. **not for the world** not for any reward, not under any circumstances. **not the end of the world** not a fatal setback. **on top of the world** (inf) in a state of great elation or happiness. **out of this world** wonderful, delightful, good beyond all experience. **Second World** see under **second¹**. **set the world on fire** to create a sensation, have spectacular success. **the New World** the western hemisphere, the Americas. **the Old World** the eastern hemisphere, comprising Europe, Africa and Asia. **the other world** the non-material sphere, the spiritual world. **the whole world** the sum of what is contained in the world. **the world is one's oyster** see under **oyster**. **the world over** throughout the world, worldwide.

the world's end the most distant point possible. **the world, the flesh and the devil** temptations of the kind that notoriously distract one from the path of virtue. **the world to come** the next world, the life after death. **think the world of** to be very fond of. **Third World** see under **third. worlds apart** as different as is possible. **world without end** eternally (**world'-without-end'** *adj*).

WORM /*wûrm*/ (*comput*) *abbrev*: write once read many times, denoting an optical disk whose contents can be written once by a computer but can be read many times.

worm /*wûrm*/ *n* a small long slender cylindrical animal without backbone or limbs, *esp* one of the classes Polychaeta and Oligochaeta, including the earthworm and marine worm; any superficially similar but unrelated animal, such as the flatworms (Platyhelminthes) and the roundworms (Nematoda); a grub; a maggot; a snake or a dragon (*archaic*); any creeping or crawling animal (*obs*); anything spiral; the thread of a screw; the lytta or vermiform cartilage of the tongue of a dog or other carnivorous mammal; a spiral pipe for condensation in distilling; anything that corrupts, gnaws or torments; remorse; a mean, grovelling or in any way contemptible creature; (in *pl*) any intestinal disease characterized by the presence of parasitic worms; any ailment supposed to be caused by a worm, eg toothache (*obs*); a tick or mite in the hand, etc, *esp* one alleged humorously to infest the hands of idlers (*obs*); a piece of software designed, like a virus, for sabotage, differing from a virus in being an independent program rather than a piece of coding, which, once inserted into a network, reproduces itself like a parasitic worm throughout it (*comput*); a graph displaying the progress of something, eg shifts in opinion, as a moving line. ◆ *vi* to seek for or catch worms; to move or make one's way like a worm, to squirm; to work slowly or secretly. ◆ *vt* to treat for or rid of worms; to cause to be eaten by worms; (*reflexive*) to work (oneself) slowly or secretly; to elicit by slow and indirect means (with *out* or *from*); to remove the lytta or vermiform cartilage from the tongue of; to fill the interstices in (a rope or cable) with spirally wound cord or packing (*orig naut*). [OE *wyrm* dragon, snake, creeping animal; cognate with Gothic *waurms* a serpent, ON *ormr*, Ger *Wurm*; also with L *vermis*]

■ **wormed** *adj* bored through or damaged by worms. **worm'er** *n*. **worm'ery** *n* a place, apparatus, etc in which worms are bred, eg as fishing bait. **worm'iness** *n*. **worm'like** *adj*. **worm'y** *adj* like a worm; grovelling; containing a worm; abounding in worms; relating to worms; dank-smelling; dismal, like the grave.

❑ **worm'cast** *n* a spiral heap of earth voided by an earthworm or lugworm as it burrows. **worm conveyor** *n* the Archimedean screw (qv). **worm'-eaten** *adj* eaten into by worms; old; worn-out. **worm'-eating** *adj* living habitually on worms. **worm fence** *n* a zigzag fence formed of stakes crossing at their ends. **worm fever** *n* a feverish condition in children ascribed to intestinal worms. **worm gear** *n* a gear connecting shafts whose axes are at right angles but do not intersect, consisting of a core carrying a single- or multi-start helical thread of special form (the *worm*), meshing in sliding contact with a concave-face gear-wheel (the *worm wheel*). **worm gearing** *n*. **worm grass** *n* pinkroot, any of several types of pink, whose roots are used as a vermifuge; a kind of stonecrop (*Sedum album*). **worm'hole** *n* the hole made by a woodworm, earthworm, etc; a hypothetical tunnel in space-time, serving as a short cut between widely distant parts of it (*phys*). **worm'holed** *adj* perforated by wormholes. **worm lizard** *n* a blind, limbless burrowing lizard of the family Amphisbaenidae. **worm powder** *n* a drug that expels intestinal worms, a vermifuge. **worm'seed** *n* any of a number of plants that (are said to) have anthelmintic properties, ie expel or destroy intestinal worms, such as certain species of *Artemisia* (eg *Artemisia santonica*), *Erysimum cheiranthoides* (**treacle wormseed** or **treacle mustard**), *Chenopodium anthelminticum*, etc; the drug santonica. **worm's eye view** *n* the view of events as seen from a low or humble position. **worm tube** *n* the twisted shell or tube produced by several marine worms. **worm wheel** see **worm gear** above.

■ **the worm may turn** the most abject of victims may be goaded into retaliating.

Wormian /*wûr'mi-ən*/ *adj* associated with the name of the Danish anatomist Olaus *Worm* (1588–1654), applied *esp* to the supernumerary bones developed in the sutures of the skull.

wormwood /*wûrm'wŭd*/ *n* the bitter plant *Artemisia absinthium*, formerly used as a vermifuge, with which absinthe is flavoured (see also **absinthe**); (a source of) acute chagrin or bitterness. [OE *wermōd* (Ger *Wermuth*) wormwood; of doubtful origin, but influenced by **worm** and **wood**[1]]

worn /*wŏrn* or *wörn*/ *pap* of **wear**[1]. *adj* that has been worn; showing effects of wear, or (*fig*) of work, worry, illness, age, etc; (of land) exhausted; hackneyed, trite.

❑ **worn'-out** *adj* extensively damaged or rendered useless by wear; (of expressions, language, etc) ineffective from overuse; wearied; exhausted; (of time) past, gone (*obs*).

worral or **worrel** /*wor'əl*/ *n* a monitor lizard. [Ar *waral* lizard]

worricow, worrycow or **wirricow** /*wur'i-kow*/ (*Scot*) *n* a hobgoblin; the Devil; anything frightful or grotesque. [**worry** (verb) and *cow* a hobgoblin]

worrit /*wur'it*/ *vt, vi* and *n* dialect form of **worry**.

worry /*wur'i*/ *vt* (**worr'ying**; **worr'ied**) to cause to be anxious; to harass; to pester; to tease; (of a dog, etc) to chase and bite; to tear with the teeth; to devour ravenously (*Scot*); to make, get, etc by persistent methods; to choke (*Scot*). ◆ *vi* to trouble oneself; to be unduly anxious; to fret. ◆ *n* trouble, perplexity; anxiety; a cause of this; a spell or bout of worrying; an act of biting and shaking by a dog, etc. [OE *wyrgan*, found in compound *āwyrgan* to harm; cf Du *worgen*, Ger *würgen* to strangle]

■ **worr'ied** *adj*. **worr'iedly** *adv*. **worr'ier** *n*. **worr'iment** *n* (*inf*; *esp N Am*) worry, anxiety; the cause of this. **worr'isome** *adj* (*old*) inclined to worry; causing worry, vexatious. **worr'isomely** *adv*. **worr'ying** *n* and *adj*. **worr'yingly** *adv*.

❑ **worry beads** *n pl* a string of beads serving as an object for the hands to play with, as a means of relieving mental tension, *esp* popular in Greece. **worr'yguts** and (*esp US*) **worr'ywart** /*wur'i-wört*/ *n* (*inf*) a person who worries unnecessarily or to excess.

■ **I should worry!** (*inf*; *ironic*) I'm the last person who should worry. **not to worry** or **no worries** (*inf*) there's no cause for alarm. **worry down** to swallow with a strong effort. **worry out** to find a solution to by intense or anxious effort.

worrycow see **worricow**.

worse /*wûrs*/ *adj* (used as *compar* of **bad** and **ill**) more bad; more ill; more grave, serious or acute; inferior in standard. ◆ *n* something worse, as in *worse was to come*. ◆ *adv* less well; more badly or severely. ◆ *vt* (*obs*) to worst. [OE *wyrsa* (Gothic *wairsiza*), formed with compar sfx from a Gmc root *wers*, found in Ger (*ver*)*wirren* to confuse, entangle]

■ **wors'en** *vi* and *vt* to grow or make worse. **worse'ness** *n*. **wors'er** *adj* and *adv* a redundant comparative of *worse*.

■ **could do worse than** would be well-advised to (do something). **for better or for worse** whatever may happen of good fortune or bad. **for the worse** to a worse state. **go by** or **with the worse** (*obs*) to lose, be defeated. **go from bad to worse** to get even worse, to deteriorate further. **have the worse** to be at a disadvantage; to be defeated. **none the worse for** not harmed by. **put to the worse** (*Bible*) to defeat. **the worse for** harmed or impaired by. **the worse for wear** worn or shabby from use; in a poor state of health, drunk (*inf*). **worse off** financially poorer.

worship /*wûr'ship*/ *n* adoration paid to a deity, etc; religious service; profound admiration and affection; glorification, exaltation, idolization; the act of revering or adoring; dignity, reputation, high standing (*archaic*); a position of honour (*obs*); (with *cap* preceded by *Your, His*, etc) a title of honour in addressing or referring to certain magistrates, etc. ◆ *vt* (**wor'shipping**; **wor'shipped**) to pay divine honours to; to adore or idolize; to glorify (something unworthy, eg money); to honour, respect, treat with signs of honour (*obs*). ◆ *vi* to perform acts of adoration; to take part in religious service. [OE *weorthscipe*, from *weorth, wurth* worth, and sfx *-scipe* -ship]

■ **wor'shipable** *adj* capable of being worshipped. **wor'shipful** *adj* worthy of worship or honour; used as a term of respect in addressing certain dignitaries, eg mayors; worshipping, adoring. **wor'shipfully** *adv*. **wor'shipfulness** *n*. **wor'shipless** *adj* without worship or worshippers. **wor'shipper** *n*.

■ **house** or **place of worship** a church or chapel, synagogue, mosque or temple. **win one's worship** (*obs*) to gain honour or fame.

worst /*wûrst*/ *adj* (used as *superl* of **bad** and **ill**) most bad, evil, unpleasant, etc; most grave, severe, acute or dire; most inferior, lowest in standard. ◆ *adv* most badly; most gravely, acutely or severely. ◆ *n* the most advanced degree of badness; the most bad, or least good, thing, part, state, effect or possibility. ◆ *vt* to get the better of in a contest; to defeat; to damage or make worse (*obs*). ◆ *vi* (*obs*) to grow worse. [OE *wyrst, wyrrest, wyrresta*, from the same source as **worse**] ❑ **worst case** *n* the most unfavourable circumstances possible. **worst'-case** *adj*.

■ **at** (or **at the**) **worst** in the worst possible circumstances, taking the most negative view possible. **at its**, etc **worst** in the worst state or severest degree. **do one's worst** to do one's utmost in evil or mischief; to produce one's worst possible effort, whether deliberately or not. **get the worst of it** or **come off worst** to be defeated in a contest, be the loser in a given situation; to produce one's worst possible effort, whether deliberately or not. **if the worst comes to the worst** if the worst or least desirable possibility occurs; if all else fails.

■ words derived from main entry word; ❑ compound words; ■ idioms and phrasal verbs

worsted¹ /wŭs'tid/ n *orig* a fine wool fabric; twisted thread or yarn spun out of long, combed wool; smooth, closely-woven material made from this; woollen yarn for ornamental needlework. ◆ *adj* made of worsted yarn. [*Worstead*, village near Norwich, England]
❑ **worst'ed-work** n needlework done with worsted.

worsted² /wûrs'tid/ *pat* and *pap* of **worst**.

wort¹ /wûrt/ n any herb or vegetable (now *rare* except as *combining form*); *specif* a plant of the cabbage kind (*obs*). [OE *wyrt* a root, herb; Ger *Wurz, Wurzel* a root]

wort² /wûrt/ n malt unfermented or in the process of fermentation (**sweet'wort**); such liquor boiled with hops (**hopped'-wort**); malt extract used as a medium for the culture of micro-organisms. [OE *wyrt*; cf Ger *Würze* spice; related to **wort¹**]

worth¹ /wûrth/ n value; price; an amount of something (the value of) which is expressed in money or otherwise, as in *a thousand pounds' worth of equipment, three days' worth of work*; that quality which renders a thing valuable; moral excellence; merit; importance; possessions (*obs*). ◆ *adj* equal in value to; having possessions to the value of; deserving, justifying, meriting, repaying or warranting (consideration, attention, the effort, the journey, taking some action, etc); valuable (*archaic*); worth while (*obs*). [OE *weorth, wurth* (Ger *Wert*) value]
■ **worth'ful** *adj* (*archaic*) honourable; meritorious; valuable. **worth'less** *adj* having no value, virtue, excellence, etc; useless; unworthy (*obs*). **worth'lessly** *adv*. **worth'lessness** n. **worthwhile'** *adj* such as to repay trouble and time spent on it (predicatively also, strictly, **worth while**; see **while**); good; estimable; useful, beneficial or rewarding.
■ **for all it's**, etc **worth** to the utmost. **for all one is worth** with all one's might or energy. **for what it is worth** a phrase implying that one is doubtful of the truth of what one has to report or unwilling to be responsible for its accuracy, or aware that one's proposal or suggestion may be of minimal worth. **well worth** amply repaying the effort of. **worth it** worth while.

worth² /wûrth/ *vi* to be, become, happen, as in the phrase **woe worth** woe be (to). [OE *weorthan* to become; cf Ger *werden*]

worthy /wûr'dhi/ *adj* having worth; valuable; estimable (*esp patronizing*); (with *of*) deserving; fit (to be or do something); deserving of (*archaic*); (with *of*) suited or appropriate to, in keeping with, proper for; of sufficient merit, fit, adequate, as in *a worthy successor*; of high social position (*obs*). ◆ *combining form* fit, in good condition for, as in *roadworthy*; deserving of, as in *trustworthy, noteworthy*. ◆ n (*pl* **wor'thies**) a person of eminent worth; a notability, *esp* local (sometimes *ironic*); anything of value, an excellence (*Shakesp*). ◆ *vt* (*obs*) to make worthy, to honour. [**worth¹**]
■ **wor'thily** *adv*. **wor'thiness** n.
■ **the nine worthies** a set of nine great heroes, *usu* listed as Hector, Alexander the Great, Julius Caesar, Joshua, David, Judas Maccabaeus, Arthur, Charlemagne, Godfrey of Bouillon. **worthiest of blood** (in questions of succession) male as opposed to female.

wortle /wûr'tl/ or **whirtle** /(h)wûr'tl/ n a perforated plate through which wire or tubing is drawn to make it thinner. [Ety uncertain]

wos see **woe**.

wosbird /wŏz'bûrd/ (*dialect*) n a variant of **whore's bird**.

wost see **wit²**.

wot¹, **wottest**, **wotteth**, etc see **wit²**.

wot² a facetious spelling of **what**.

wot³ see **woot**.

Wotan /wō'tan or vō'tan/ (*myth*) n the German name for the god Woden.

wotcher /woch'ər/, also **wotcha** /woch'ə/ (*sl*) *interj* a greeting, developed from *archaic* **what cheer?** how are you?

wotted, **wotting** see **wit²**.

would /wŭd/ (formerly, eg in *Spenser*, wōld) *auxiliary v* (*2nd pers sing archaic*; with *thou*) **wouldst** /wŭdst/) *pat* of **will¹**, used: in reported speech; to suggest willingness or readiness on the part of someone or something, as in *the car would not start*; to express probability and condition; to express lack of surprise or indicate frustration at events, another's perversity, etc; to formulate invitations, suggestions, offers, requests and desires. ◆ n the desired or intended, as distinct from *could*, or *should*. [OE *wolde*, pat of *wyllan* to wish, will]
❑ **would'-be** *adj* aspiring, or merely professing, to be; meant to be. ◆ n a vain pretender.
■ **would** (**that**), also **would to God** (or **to heaven**, etc) (**that**) (*literary* or *archaic*) used to express (*esp* vain) desires.

Woulfe bottle /wŭlf bot'l/ n a *usu* three-necked bottle used for purifying gases or dissolving them in suitable solvents. [Peter *Woulfe* (c.1727–1803), London chemist]

wound¹ /wownd/ *pat* and *pap* of **wind¹⁻²**.

wound² /woond/ n any open injury to living animal or plant tissue externally caused by eg cutting, piercing, striking, crushing, tearing or poisoning; a surgeon's incision; an injury caused to the pride, feelings, reputation, etc. ◆ *vi* and *vt* to make a wound (in), inflict a wound (on); to injure (feelings, etc). [OE *wund* (Ger *Wunde*, ON *und*); also OE *wund* wounded]
■ **wound'able** *adj* capable of being wounded. **wound'er** n. **wound'ily** *adv* (*archaic*) excessively. **wound'ing** n and *adj*. **wound'ingly** *adv*. **wound'less** *adj* unwounded; invulnerable (*obs*); harmless. **wound'y** *adj* and *adv* (*archaic*) excessive(ly).
❑ **wound tissue** n (*bot*) protective tissue that forms in response to wounding. **wound'wort** n any of several plants popularly held to have wound-healing properties, such as the kidney-vetch, and a number of plants of genus *Stachys* (**marsh** or **clown's woundwort**).

wourali or **woorali** /woo-rä'li/, **woorara** /woo-rä'rə/, **ourali** or **ourari** /oo-rä'ri/, **urali** /ŭ-rä'li/ or **urari** /oo-rä'ri/ n the plant yielding curare. [Carib variants of *kurari*; see **curare**]

wou-wou see **wow-wow**.

wove and **woven** *pat* and *pap* of **weave¹**.
❑ **wove paper** n paper with a fine, uniformly smooth surface, as distinct from laid paper (qv).

WOW *abbrev*: waiting on weather (*esp* in the oil industry).

wow¹ /wow/ *interj* (also **wowee'**) an exclamation of wonder, mingled with other emotions such as aversion, sorrow, admiration or pleasure (see **whow**). ◆ *vt* (*sl*) to impress (an audience, etc) considerably, to amaze, bowl over. ◆ n (*sl*) anything thrillingly good, successful, or according to one's wishes. [Perh orig Scot]
❑ **wow factor** n (*sl*) the quality of being impressive.

wow² /wow/ *vi* to howl. ◆ n a bark; a howl; rhythmic or arrhythmic changes in reproduced sound, fundamentally arising from fluctuations in speed, of comparatively long cycle, in the operation of either reproducer or recorder. [Imit]

wow³ /wow/ (*Spenser*) *vt* to woo.

wowf /wowf/ (*Scot*) *adj* crazy. [Origin unknown]

wowser /wow'zər/ (*esp Aust sl*) n a puritanical person who tries to interfere with the pleasures of others, a spoilsport; a teetotaller. [Origin uncertain]

wow-wow or **wou-wou** /wow'wow/ n the name for two types of gibbon found in Indonesia, the *silver gibbon* of Java and the *agile gibbon* of Sumatra. [Imit of its cry]

wox and **woxen** (*obs*) *pat* and *pap* of **wax²**.

WP *abbrev*: Warsaw Pact; (also **wp**) weather permitting; (also **wp**) word processing or word processor.

Wp *abbrev*: Worship or Worshipful.

wpb (*inf*) *abbrev*: wastepaper basket.

WPBSA *abbrev*: World Professional Billiards and Snooker Association (also known as World Snooker).

WPC *abbrev*: Woman Police Constable.

Wpfl *abbrev*: Worshipful.

wpm *abbrev*: words per minute.

WR *abbrev*: Western Region.

WRAAC *abbrev*: formerly, Women's Royal Australian Army Corps.

WRAAF *abbrev*: formerly, Women's Royal Australian Air Force.

WRAC /rak/ *abbrev*: formerly, Women's Royal Army Corps.

wrack¹ /rak/ n vengeance, punishment (*obs*); destruction, devastation (cf **rack²**); what remains after devastation, a remnant (in *Shakesp*, *Tempest* IV.1.156, an erroneous alteration of *rack*; see **rack⁶**). [OE *wræc*, from *wrecan* to drive; connected, and confused, with **wrack²**]
■ **wrack'ful** *adj* (*rare*) destructive.

wrack² /rak/ n a wreck (*dialect*); wreckage; seaweed cast ashore, or growing where it is exposed by the tide (*archaic*); any of the Fucaceae, the bladderwrack family of seaweeds. [MDu or MLGer *wrak*; cf **wrack¹**]

wrack³ /rak/ *vt* to torture, torment. [An erroneous spelling of **rack¹**]

WRAF /raf/ *abbrev*: Women's Royal Air Force.

wraith /rāth/ n a spectre; an apparition, *esp* of a living person; a person of spectral thinness and pallor. [Orig Scot; perh ON *vörthr* a guardian]
■ **wraith'like** *adj*.

wrangle /rang'gl/ *vi* to dispute noisily or peevishly; to argue, debate, dispute (*archaic*). ◆ *vt* to obtain, persuade or tire by, or spend (time) in, wrangling; to debate; to herd (cattle; *N Am*). ◆ n a noisy dispute; the activity of disputing, *esp* noisily (*rare*). [ME *wranglen*, a frequentative verb related to **wring**]
■ **wrang'ler** n someone who wrangles; a cattle-herder, a cowboy (*N Am*); (also **horse'-wrangler**) a horseman in charge of or escorting saddle horses or racers (*N Am*); a person in charge of animals used in making a film; a stubborn foe (*Shakesp*); at Cambridge University, a

student gaining first-class honours in the final mathematics examinations, the **senior wrangler** being the student with the highest marks and (formerly) the **second wrangler** the one in second place, and so on. **wrang'lership** n. **wrang'lesome** adj given to wrangling. **wrang'ling** n and adj.

WRANS abbrev : formerly, Women's Royal Australian Naval Service.

wrap¹ /rap/ vt (**wrapp'ing**; **wrapped**) to fold (something) round something; to enfold, envelop, clothe, cover or swathe (in something; often with up); to pack in paper for posting or presentation; to roll or fold together (old); to embrace (literary); to hide, obscure; to involve or entangle (obs); (with in) to absorb or engross; (with round) to crash (a vehicle) into (a tree, lamp post, etc; inf). ◆ vi to wind, twine or lap (with round, etc); (with up) to put on a wrap, cloak, etc; to dress warmly; to finish filming or recording (cinematog, TV). ◆ n a shawl or stole for the shoulders; an outdoor garment (old); a light dressing-gown or bathrobe; a protective covering or material for this, a wrapper, wrapping; a wraparound (printing); a single turn or fold round (old); (in pl) secrecy, concealment (inf); the completion of filming or recording, or the end of a session of filming or recording (cinematog, TV); a snack consisting of a flatbread, such as a tortilla, rolled around a filling; the flatbread itself; a bag containing a small quantity of a drug, esp heroin. [ME wrappen, also wlappen]
■ **wrapp'age** n the act of wrapping; covering; wrapping materials. **wrapp'er** n someone who or something that wraps; formerly, a loose outer garment for a woman; a loose paper book cover, a dust jacket; a paper band, eg put round a newspaper for posting; a paper or Cellophane cover for a sweet, packet, etc; a high quality tobacco leaf encasing a cigar. ◆ vt to cover with a wrapper. **wrapp'ing** n (often in pl) any of various types of cover, wrapper or packing material.
❑ **wrap'around** n a wraparound skirt, blouse, dress, etc (also **wrap'round**); on a visual display unit, the automatic division of input into lines, whereby a new line is started as the last character position on the previous line is occupied; (also **wrap'round**) a plate of flexible material, such as plastic, rubber or metal that wraps round a cylindrical plate (printing); (also **wrap'round**) a separately printed sheet that is wrapped round a gathering for binding (printing); (also **wrap'round**) a strip advertising a special offer, etc, wrapped round the dust cover of a book, etc. ◆ adj (of a blouse, skirt, dress, etc) designed so as to be wrapped round the body with one edge overlapping the other, and tied, tucked in, etc rather than fastened by a zip, row of buttons, etc (also **wrap'over** or **wrap'round**); (of a windscreen, bumper, etc) curving round from the front to the sides (also **wrap'round**); (of sunglasses) with a frame and lenses curving around the head from the front to the side. **wrap'over** n a wraparound skirt or other garment. **wrap party** n a party held to celebrate the completion of filming or recording (cinematog, TV). **wrapping paper** n paper, either strong and coarse, or decorative, for wrapping parcels. **wrap'ras'cal** n (humorous) a loose greatcoat worn in the 18c. **wraparound** see **wraparound** above.
■ **keep under wraps** (inf) to keep secret, conceal. **take the wraps off** (inf) to reveal, disclose. **wrapped up in** bound up in; comprised in; engrossed in, devoted to. **wrap up** (sl) to settle completely; to have completely in hand; to stop talking (often as imperative).

wrap² a non-standard form of **rap⁴**.

wrap³, **wrap up** see **rap⁵**.

wrapped and **wrapt** non-standard forms of **rapt**.

wrasse /ras/ n any of several brightly-coloured bony fishes of the family Labridae including many species on European and N African coasts. [Cornish wrach, related to Welsh gwrach old woman]

wrast obsolete Scot and N Eng form of **wrest** directly from Old Norse.

wrate obsolete and Scot pat of **write**.

wrath /röth, roth or (Scot) räth/ n violent anger; an instance, or fit, of anger (obs); divine indignation, the righteous anger of God; violence or severity (of eg a storm); ardour (Shakesp). ◆ adj (archaic) angry, wroth. ◆ vt and vi (obs) to make or become angry. [OE wrǣththu, from wrāth, adj; cf **wroth**]
■ **wrath'ful** adj very angry; springing from, expressing or characterized by wrath. **wrath'fully** adv. **wrath'fulness** n. **wrath'ily** adv. **wrath'iness** n. **wrath'less** adj. **wrath'y** adj (chiefly US) inclined to wrath; expressing or characterized by wrath; fierce, tempestuous.

wrawl /röl/ (Spenser) vi (of a cat) to caterwaul. [Imit]

wraxle /rak'sl/ (SW Eng dialect) vi to wrestle. [OE wraxlian; cf **wrestle**]
■ **wrax'ling** n.

wreak¹ /rēk/ vt (pat **wreaked**, archaic **wrōke**; pap **wreaked**, archaic **wrōk'en**, Spenser **wrōke** or **ywrōke**) to effect, bring about or cause (harm, havoc, damage, etc); to inflict (vengeance, one's revenge, etc; with on); to give expression, vent, free play to (anger, etc); (reflexive) of a feeling, quality, etc) to find expression or outlet for (itself); to bestow; to punish (obs); to harm (obs); to avenge (archaic); to take vengeance on (obs); to revenge (with of) (obs); to drive out (obs). ◆ n punishment,

vengeance (archaic); damage (obs). [OE wrecan to drive, push; ON reka to drive, pursue, avenge; Ger rächen; connected with L urgēre]
■ **wreak'er** n (archaic). **wreak'ful** adj revengeful; avenging. **wreak'less** adj unpunished.

wreak² /rēk/ (Spenser and Shakesp), also (Milton) **wreck** /rek/ variants of **reck**.

wreath /rēth/ n (pl **wreaths** /rēdhz/) a circlet or ring of flowers or foliage, eg for wearing on the head as a symbol of honour, or laying on a grave as a tribute; a circlet of other intertwined materials; a representation of such a circlet beneath a crest (heraldry); a carved representation of a wreath of foliage (archit); a single twist or coil in a helical object; a drift or curl of vapour or smoke; a snowdrift; a defect in glass. [OE writha; related to wrīthan to writhe]
■ **wreathe** /rēdh/ vt to form by twisting; to twist together; to form into a wreath; to twine about or encircle; to twist or contort (limbs); to cause (the face) to crease or pucker (in smiles); (of snow) to cover by drifting (Scot); to encircle, decorate, etc with a wreath or wreaths. ◆ vi to be interwoven; to twine; to twist; to form coils; (of snow) to form a drift or wreath (Scot); to turn (obs). **wreathed** /rēdhd or rēdh'id/ adj. **wreath'en** /rē'dhən/ adj (archaic pap) wreathed. **wreath'er** /rē'dhər/ n. **wreath'less** adj. **wreath'y** /rē'thi or rē'dhi/ adj.
❑ **wreathed string** n (building) the continuous curved outer string round the well hole of a wooden stair. **wreath filament** n a type of filament used in large gas-filled electric lamps, the filament wire being festooned from a horizontal supporting spider.

wreck¹ /rek/ n destruction; the act of wrecking or destroying; the destruction of a ship; a badly damaged ship; shipwrecked property; anything found underwater and brought ashore; the death of a large number of oceanic birds, eg during a storm; the remains of anything ruined; a person ruined mentally or physically; a dilapidated or unserviceable vessel or vehicle (inf). ◆ vt to destroy or disable; to cause the wreck of (a ship); to involve in a wreck; to cast up, eg on the shore; to ruin. ◆ vi to suffer wreck or ruin. [Anglo-Fr wrec, wrek, etc, of Scand origin; related to **wreak¹**]
■ **wreck'age** n the process of wrecking; wrecked material; a person whose life is, or people whose lives are, ruined. **wrecked** adj destroyed; rendered incapable by drink or drugs (sl). **wreck'er** n a person who purposely causes a wreck or who plunders wreckage; someone who criminally ruins anything; a person who (or machine that) demolishes or destroys; a person or ship employed in recovering disabled vessels or their cargo; a person, vehicle or train employed in removing wreckage; a vehicle equipped with a hoisting device, used to tow wrecked or disabled motor vehicles (US); a person who is employed in demolishing buildings, etc. **wreck'ful** adj (poetic) causing ruin. **wreck'ing** n and adj.
❑ **wreck buoy** n a buoy, usu green, marking the position of a wrecked vessel. **wreck commissioners** n pl a tribunal that inquires into shipping disasters. **wreck'fish** n the stone bass, a large perch of the Atlantic, Mediterranean and Tasman Sea, Polyprion americanus, having the reputation of frequenting wrecked ships. **wreck'ing ball** n a heavy metal globe suspended from a crane to be swung against a building in demolishing it. **wreck'master** n a person taking charge of a disabled ship or train and its cargo or freight.
■ **receivers of wrecks** wreckmasters.

wreck² see **wreak²**.

Wren /ren/ n a member of the WRNS.

wren /ren/ n a member of a genus (Troglodytes) of small songbirds, having very short and rounded wings, and a short tail carried erect, or of any of several related genera, together forming the family Troglodytidae; specif in the UK, Troglodytes troglodytes; extended to various very small birds, such as the **golden-crested wren** (goldcrest) and the **willow wren** (willow warbler). [OE wrenna, wrænna]
❑ **wren tit** n a Californian bird (Chamaea fasciata) resembling the wren and the titmouse.

wrench /rench or rensh/ vt to pull (something from someone or something) esp with a twisting or wringing action; to force or wrest violently; to shift with the help of a wrench; to sprain; to distort. ◆ vi to turn or twist suddenly or violently. ◆ n an act or instance of wrenching; a violent twist; a sprain; an instrument for turning nuts, etc, an adjustable spanner; a separation or change that is difficult to bear, or the pain of this; (in coursing) bringing the hare round at less than a right angle. [OE wrencan to deceive, twist, wrenc deceit, twisting; cf Ger renken to twist, Rank trick, intrigue]

wrenching /ren'shing/ (Shakesp) n for renching, from dialect verb rench to rinse.

wrest /rest/ vt to turn, twist, or (obs) screw; to twist, extract or take away, by force or unlawfully; to get by toil (eg a living from an unpromising environment); to twist from truth or natural meaning, to distort; to misinterpret; to pervert; to derive improperly (Spenser); to sprain (Scot). ◆ vi (Spenser) to force a way. ◆ n the act of wresting;

violent pulling and twisting; distortion; a wrench-like key for tuning a piano, etc (*archaic*). [OE *wrǣstan*; Dan *vriste*]

■ **wrest'er** *n*.

❑ **wrest block** or **wrest plank** *n* (in a piano, etc) the board fitted with the wrest pins. **wrest pin** *n* a pin round which the end of a wire (eg a piano wire) is wound, turned by the wrest.

wrestle /res'l/ *vi* to contend with another person by grappling, each trying to throw and then pinion the other; to struggle or tussle (with *with*); to apply oneself keenly to mastering something (with *with*); to pray earnestly (*with* God; *old*); to strive (*with* one's conscience, etc); to dispute, debate, argue, wrangle; to writhe, wriggle; to proceed laboriously. ◆ *vt* to contend with in wrestling; to push or force with a wriggling or wrestling motion; (with *out*) to go through, carry out, with a great struggle. ◆ *n* a bout, or the activity, of wrestling; a struggle. [OE *wrǣstan* to wrest]

■ **wrest'ler** *n*. **wrest'ling** *n* a sport or exercise in which two people struggle to throw and pin each other to the ground, governed by certain fixed rules; the activity of struggling, grappling, striving, contending, etc.

wretch /rech/ *n* a most miserable, unfortunate or pitiable person; a worthless or despicable person; a being, a creature (in pity or sometimes admiration); an exile or outcast (*obs*). ◆ *adj* (*Spenser*) wretched. [OE *wrecca* an outcast, from *wrecan*; see **wreak**[1]]

■ **wretched** /re'chid/ *adj* very miserable, distraught; unfortunate, pitiable; distressingly bad, pitiful; despicable; worthless; used to intensify, as in *wretched nuisance*, *bore*, etc. **wretch'edly** *adv*. **wretch'edness** *n*.

wrethe /rēth/ (*Spenser*) *vt* and *vi* same as **wreathe** (see under **wreath**).

WRI *abbrev*: Women's Rural Institute.

wrick or **rick** /rik/ *vt* to twist, sprain or strain. ◆ *n* a sprain or strain. [Related to LGer *wrikken* to turn]

wrier, **wriest** see **wry**.

wriggle /rig'l/ *vi* and *vt* to twist to and fro; to move, advance or make (one's way) sinuously or deviously. ◆ *vi* to use evasive tricks; (with *out of*) to evade or shirk (responsibilities, etc). ◆ *n* an act or the motion of wriggling; a sinuous or wavy marking, a turn or bend. [LGer *wriggeln*; cf Du *wriggelen* to wriggle]

■ **wrigg'ler** *n*. **wrigg'ling** *n*. **wrigg'ly** *adj*.

wright /rīt/ or (*Scot*) *rihht*/ *n* (*esp* as *combining form*) a maker, deviser or repairer (as in *shipwright*, *playwright*, *wainwright*, etc); a carpenter or joiner (*Scot*). [OE *wyrhta*, *wryhta*, related to *wyrht* a work, from *wyrcan* to work]

wring /ring/ *vt* (*pat* and *pap* **wrung**, *obs* **winged**) to twist; to expel moisture from (cloth, etc) by squeezing between rollers or twisting by hand; to force out (moisture) from cloth, etc by twisting; to force (eg tears) from someone, to extract *esp* with difficulty; to clasp and shake (someone's hand) fervently; to clasp or twist (the hands) together convulsively in grief or agitation; to break (the neck) of a bird, etc by twisting; (of a shoe) to pinch (*old*); to harrow or rend (the heart); to hurt or injure (*old*); to extort or exact (consent, admission or money) from someone; to bend or strain out of position; to distort; to wreathe, coil (*rare*). ◆ *vi* to twist or writhe (*rare*); to feel pain (*rare*). ◆ *n* an act or instance of wringing; a cider press, winepress or cheese press. [OE *wringan* to twist; Du *wringen*, Ger *ringen*]

■ **wring'er** *n* someone who wrings; a machine for forcing water from wet clothes (also **wring'ing-machine**). **wring'ing** *adj* soaking wet. ❑ **wring bolt** *n* (*naut*) a bolt with a ring or eye, used to secure a ship's planks against the frame until they are permanently fixed in place, a ringbolt. **wring staves** *n pl* (*sing* **wring staff**) strong pieces of wood used in applying wring bolts.

■ **wringing wet** so wet that water can be wrung out. **wring off** to force off by wringing. **wring out** to squeeze (moisture) out by twisting; to twist (a wet garment, cloth, etc) so as to expel the drops of liquid.

wrinkle[1] /ring'kl/ *n* a small crease or furrow on a surface; a crease or ridge in the skin (*esp* as a result of ageing); an unevenness; a minor problem or difficulty to be smoothed out. ◆ *vt* to contract into wrinkles or furrows; to make rough. ◆ *vi* to shrink into ridges. [History obscure; noun and verb may be back-formations from *adj* **wrinkled**]

■ **wrink'led** *adj*. **wrink'ly** *adj* full of wrinkles; liable to get wrinkled. ◆ *n* (*esp* in *pl*; *derog inf*) an elderly person.

wrinkle[2] /ring'kl/ (*inf*) *n* a tip, valuable hint; a handy dodge or trick; an idea, notion, suggestion. [Perh from OE *wrenc* a trick; perh same as **wrinkle**[1]]

wrist /rist/ *n* the joint by which the hand is connected to the forearm, the carpus; the part of the forearm where this joint is, or the part of a garment covering it; a corresponding part of an animal; a wrist pin. [OE; allied to *wrīthan* to twist; Ger *Rist*]

■ **wrist'let** *n* a band or strap for the wrist; a bracelet; a watch for wearing on the wrist (also **wristlet watch**); a handcuff (*sl*). **wrist'y** *adj* making extensive use of the wrist or wrists, as in a golf shot, etc.

❑ **wrist'band** *n* a band or part of a sleeve covering the wrist. **wrist drop** *n* inability to extend the hand, often caused by lead poisoning. **wrist pin** *n* a pin joining the end of a connecting rod to the end of a piston rod. **wrist shot** *n* (*sport*) a stroke made with a short backswing, using power mainly from the wrist. **wrist'watch** *n* a watch worn on a strap round the wrist.

■ **a slap** or **smack on the wrist** (*inf*) a slight but *usu* formal punishment or reprimand.

writ[1] /rit/ *n* a legal or formal document; a written document by which one is summoned or required to do, or refrain from doing, something (*law*); a writing (*rare*). [OE (*ge*)*writ*; ON *rit*, Gothic *writs*]

❑ **writ of execution** *n* (*law*) a written order for the execution of a judgement.

■ **Holy Writ** (also without *caps*) the Scriptures. **serve a writ on** (*law*) to deliver a summons to.

writ[2] /rit/ an archaic *pat* and *pap* of **write**.

❑ **writ large** *n* written in large letters, hence on a large scale or very obvious.

write /rīt/ *vt* (**wrīt'ing**; **wrōte**, (*archaic*) **writ** /rit/; **written** /rit'n/ (*archaic*) **writ**) to form (letters, symbols, numbers, words, sentences) with a pen, pencil, etc on a surface, *esp* paper; to express in writing; to compose, be the composer or author of; to inscribe, carve or engrave (a surface); to record, state or communicate in a letter, book, article, etc; to decree or foretell; to make out or fill in (a prescription, cheque, etc); to transfer (data) to a memory or storage device (*comput*); to display (a quality, condition, etc) all too clearly, as in *guilt written all over her face*; to communicate with by letter; to underwrite (an insurance policy). ◆ *vi* to perform or practise the art of writing; to be employed as a clerk; to compose articles, novels, etc; to work as an author; to compose or send a letter; to communicate with a person by letter. [OE *wrītan*, orig meaning to scratch; ON *rīta*]

■ **wrīt'able** *adj* capable of being expressed or described in writing; suitable for writing with. **wrīt'ative** *adj* (*rare*) inclined, or characterized by an inclination, to write. **wrīt'er** *n* someone who writes; a professional scribe or clerk; an ordinary legal practitioner in a Scottish country town; an author or his or her works; someone who paints lettering for signs; a seller (of options) (*stock exchange*). **wrīt'eress** *n* (*rare*) a female writer. **wrīt'erly** *adj* having or showing an accomplished literary style. **wrīt'ership** *n* the office of a writer. **wrīt'ing** *n* the act or activity of recording, expressing or communicating by inscribing words, letters, etc; that which is written; (often in *pl*) a literary production or composition; (in *pl*; with *cap*) the Old Testament books known as the Hagiographa (qv under **hagi-**; *relig*); handwriting, penmanship; the state of being written. **writt'en** *adj* reduced to or expressed in writing, *opp* to *oral*.

❑ **write'-back** *n* an amount restored to a company's accounts because the size of an earlier liability had been overestimated. **write-down** see **write down** below. **write'-in** *adj* (*N Am*) of or relating to a candidate not listed in the ballot paper, but whose name is written in by the voter. ◆ *n* such a candidate or vote. **write'-off** *n* a car so badly damaged that the cost of repair would exceed the car's value; a crashed aircraft (*RAF sl*); a total loss; see also **write off** below. **write'-once** *adj* denoting a storage medium in which the data can only be entered once, and then not changed or erased. **writer's block** *n* a temporary lack of enthusiasm and imagination that may prevent a writer from working. **writer's cramp** see under **cramp**. **Writer to the Signet** *n* a member of the oldest society of solicitors in Scotland, still active as a professional body, *orig* supervising the use of the Signet or royal seal required to be stamped on all summonses initiating actions in the Court of Session. **write-up** see **write up** below. **wrīt'ing-book** *n* a book of paper for practising penmanship. **writing case** *n* a portable case containing materials for writing. **writing desk** *n* a desk with a sloping top for writing on; a portable writing case. **wrīt'ing-ink** *n* ink suited for writing with. **wrīt'ing-master** *n* a master who teaches the art of penmanship; the yellow bunting. **writing pad** *n* a pad of writing paper. **writing paper** *n* paper finished with a smooth surface, for writing on. **wrīt'ing-school** *n* (*hist*) a school for penmanship. **writing table** *n* a table designed or used for writing on. **written law** *n* statute law as distinguished from common law.

■ **nothing to write home about** see under **home**. **write away** see **write off** below. **write down** to put down in written characters; to write in disparagement of; to write so as to be intelligible or attractive to people of lower intelligence or inferior taste; to reduce the book value of an asset (**write'-down** *n*). **write in** to write a letter to an organization, etc; (with *for*) to apply for or request in such a letter, send away for; to insert (extra matter) in writing into a document, etc; to add (the name of an extra candidate) to a ballot paper (*US*; **write'-in** *adj* and *n*). **write off** to cancel, *esp* in bookkeeping, to take (eg a bad debt) off the books; to regard or accept as an irredeemable loss; to destroy or damage irredeemably (a car, etc) (**write'-off** *n*); (*reflexive*) to get (oneself) killed (*RAF sl*); (also **write away**; with *for*) to apply for or request in a letter to an organization, etc; to compose (eg a letter) with fluent ease. **write out** to transcribe; to write in full; (*reflexive*) to exhaust one's mental resources by too much writing; to remove (a character or scene) from the script of a film, broadcast, etc. **write protect** (*comput*) protecting of data on disk from alteration or erasure, eg by software command or a mechanical device on the disk (**write-protect'** *adj* and *vt*). **write to** (*comput*) to record (data) onto a magnetic disk). **write up** to put a full description of in writing; to write a report or review of; to write in praise of, *esp* to praise above its merits; to bring the writing of (one's diary, etc) up to date; to increase the book value of an asset (**write'-up** *n*). **writing** (also, *esp US*, **handwriting**) **on the wall** a happening or sign foreshowing downfall and disaster (Bible, Daniel 5.5 *ff*). **written off** (of a car) damaged beyond reasonable repair; completely ruined; (of a person) killed (*RAF sl*); (of an aircraft) wrecked (*RAF sl*); see also **write off** above.

writhe /rīdh/ *vi* to move the body sinuously; to twist and contort oneself in agony; to feel acute shame or embarrassment (*inf*). ◆ *vt* to twist or coil; to intertwine (*obs*); to contort or distort (*obs*). ◆ *n* a twist or a contortion. [OE *wrīthan* to twist; ON *rītha*; cf **wreath, wrest, wrist**] ■ **writhen** or **wrythen** /rīdh'ən/ *adj* (*archaic*) twisted, convoluted, contorted. **wrīth'ing** *n* and *adj*. **wrīth'ingly** *adv*.

writhled /rith'ld/ (*archaic*) *adj* wrinkled, shrivelled. [Perh **writhe**]

writing, written, etc see under **write.**

wrizled /riz'ld/ (*Spenser*) *adj* wrinkled. [Perh **writhled**]

WRNS /renz/ *abbrev*: formerly, Women's Royal Naval Service.

wroath /rōth/ (*Shakesp*) *n* misfortune. [Prob from **ruth**]

wroke, wroken see **wreak**[1].

wrong /rong/ *adj* incorrect; erroneous; morally unacceptable, immoral, wicked, sinful; unacceptable according to some other recognized or imposed standard eg of taste or judgement; not that (thing or person) which is required, intended, advisable or suitable; amiss, unsatisfactory; defective, faulty; mistaken, misinformed; (of one side of a garment, fabric, etc) intended to be turned inward or under, not intended to be on view, under, inner, reverse; crooked, curved, twisted, bent (*obs*). ◆ *n* whatever is not right or just; any injury done to another; wrongdoing; damage, harm (*rare*). ◆ *adv* incorrectly; not in the right way, improperly, badly; away from the right direction, astray. ◆ *vt* to treat unjustly, do wrong to; to judge unfairly, impute fault to unjustly; to deprive of some right; to defraud; to dishonour; to seduce (*old*); to harm physically (*obs* and *Scot*); to impair, spoil (*obs*). [OE *wrang* a wrong; most prob ON *rangr* unjust; related to OE *wringan* to wring (like Fr *tort* from L *tortus* twisted)] ■ **wrong'er** *n* a person who wrongs another. **wrong'ful** *adj* wrong; unjust; unlawful; not legitimate; unjustly held (*Spenser*). **wrong'fully** *adv*. **wrong'fulness** *n*. **wrong'ly** *adv*. **wrong'ness** *n*. **wrong'ous** /rong'gəs or rong'əs/ *adj* (*old*) unjust, illegal, wrongful. **wrong'ously** *adv*.
□ **wrong'doer** *n* an offender or transgressor. **wrong'doing** *n* evil or illegal action or conduct. **wrong-foot'** *vt* to cause to be (physically or mentally) off balance, or at a disadvantage. **wrong-head'ed** *adj* obstinate and perverse, adhering stubbornly to wrong principles or policy. **wrong-head'edly** *adv*. **wrong-head'edness** *n*. **wrong-mind'ed** *adj* having erroneous views. **wrong number** *n* a telephone number with which a caller is connected in error, *esp* through misdialling; a call involving such a misconnection. **wrong'-timed'** *adj* (*old*) inopportune. **wrong''un** *n* (*inf*) a dishonest character, a rogue; a googly (*cricket*).
■ **do wrong** to act immorally or illegally. **do wrong to (someone)** or **do (someone) wrong** to treat (someone) unjustly; (with *oneself*) to be mistaken (*obs*). **get hold of the wrong end of the stick** to misunderstand something totally. **get in wrong with** (*inf*) to get on the wrong side of. **get off on the wrong foot** see under **foot**. **get on the wrong side of** to arouse dislike or antagonism in. **get out of bed on the wrong side** to get up in the morning in a bad mood. **get wrong** to misunderstand; to misinterpret (a person) as in (*inf*) **don't get me wrong**; to get the wrong answer to (a sum, puzzle, question, etc). **go down the wrong way** (of food) to enter the trachea instead of the oesophagus. **go wrong** (of plans, etc) to fail to go as intended; to make a mistake or mistakes; to stray morally; to stop functioning properly. **have wrong** (*obs*) to suffer injustice or injury. **in the wrong** holding an erroneous view or unjust position; guilty of error or injustice. **private wrong** a violation of the civil or personal rights of an individual. **public wrong** a crime that affects the community. **put in the wrong** to cause to appear in error, guilty of injustice, etc. **wrong in the head** (*inf*) mentally unbalanced, mad. **wrong side out** inside out. **wrong way round** or **up** respectively back to front and upside down.

wroot obsolete form of **root**[2] and **wrote**.

wrote /rōt/ *pat* of **write.**

wroth /rōth or roth/ (*literary* or *poetic*) *adj* wrathful; in commotion, stormy. [OE *wrāth* angry; cf ON *reithr*]

wrought /röt/ an archaic *pat* and *pap* of **work.** *adj* made, formed, fashioned or manufactured; decorated or ornamented; (of metal)

beaten into shape as distinct from being cast. [OE *worhte, geworht*, pat and pap of *wyrcan, wircan* to work]
□ **wrought iron** *n* malleable iron, iron containing only a very small amount of other elements, but containing slag in the form of particles elongated in one direction, more rust-resistant than steel and welding more easily. **wrought'-iron** *adj*. **wrought'-up** *adj* in an agitated condition, over-excited.

WRP *abbrev*: Workers' Revolutionary Party.

wrt *abbrev*: with respect (or regard) to.

wrung /rung/ *pat* and *pap* of **wring.**

WRVS *abbrev*: Women's Royal Voluntary Service.

wry /rī/ *adj* (**wry'er** or **wri'er**; **wry'est** or **wri'est**) (of a facial expression) with the features twisted into a grimace; (of a remark, sense of humour, etc) mocking, bitter, ironic or sardonic; twisted or turned to one side or in the wrong direction; perverse, cross, ill-natured (*old*). ◆ *n* (*rare*) distortion. ◆ *vi* to swerve, go astray (*obs*); to be deflected, undergo deflection (*obs*); to writhe (*obs*). ◆ *vt* to give a twist to, contort (*archaic*); to avert (the face, head, etc; *obs*); to pervert (*obs*). ◆ *adv* wryly. [OE *wrīgian* to strive, move, turn]
■ **wry'ly** *adv*. **wry'ness** *n*.
□ **wry'bill** *n* a New Zealand bird (*Anarhynchus frontalis*), related to the plovers, having a sideways-curving bill with which it gets food from under stones. **wry'-mouthed** *adj* having a crooked mouth; (of criticism, etc) mocking, bitter (*old*). **wry'neck** *n* a twisted position of the head on the neck due to spasm, with torsion of the cervical muscles, or to congenital injury to a neck muscle; a member of a genus of small birds (genus *Jynx*) related to the woodpecker, which twist round their heads strangely when surprised. **wry'-necked** *adj* having wryneck, or a twisted neck; denoting a kind of fife, either as having a twisted neck or played with the head on one side (*Shakesp*).
■ **make** or **pull a wry face** or **mouth** to pucker up the face or mouth in reaction to a bitter or astringent taste, or to pain, or to express disgust or distaste.

wrythen see under **writhe.**

WS *abbrev*: Western Samoa (IVR); Writer to the Signet.

WSW *abbrev*: west-south-west.

wt *abbrev*: weight.

WTF *abbrev*: what the fuck?

WTO *abbrev*: formerly, Warsaw Treaty Organization; World Tourism Organization; World Trade Organization.

Wu /woo/ *n* a group of Chinese dialects, spoken in the coastal provinces of Jiangsu and Zhejiang. [Chin]

wu cycle /woo sī'kl/ *n* in traditional Chinese medicine, the cycle in which balance is achieved through the interaction of the five basic elements (see also **ko cycle, sheng cycle**).

wud Scots form of **wood**[1,2].

wudu /wŭ'dŭ/ (*Islam*) *n* ritual washing before daily prayer; a room designated for this purpose. [Ar]

wulfenite /wŭl'fə-nīt/ *n* a molybdate of lead, $PbMoO_4$, occurring commonly as yellow crystals in veins with other lead ores. [FX von Wulfen (1728–1805), Austrian mineralogist]

wull[1] /wul/ (*Spenser* and *dialect*) *vi* same as **will**[1].

wull[2] see **will**[3].

wunderkind /vŭn'dər-kint/ *n* (*pl* **wun'derkinder** /-kin-dər/) a child prodigy; someone who achieves remarkable success early in life. [Ger, literally, wonder child]

wunner see **oner** under **one.**

wurley /wûr'li/ (*Aust*) *n* (*pl* **wur'leys** or **wur'lies**) an Aboriginal hut, traditionally made of branches, bark, leaves and plaited grass; a nest, *esp* a rat's nest. [From an Aboriginal language]

Würm /vürm/ *n* the fourth stage of glaciation in the Alps (also *adj*). [From a river of Upper Bavaria]
■ **Würm'ian** *adj*.

wurst /vŭrst or wûrst/ *n* a large German sausage of several types. [Ger, literally, something rolled; cf L *vertere* to turn]

wurtzite /wûrt'sīt/ *n* sulphide of zinc, ZnS, of the same composition as sphalerite, but crystallizing in the hexagonal system, in black hemimorphic pyramidal crystals. [CA *Wurtz* (1817–84), French chemist]

wus or **wuss** /wus/ (*S Wales dialect*) *n* a term used to address a companion, mate, pal. [Welsh *gwas* servant]

wushu, Wushu, wu shu or **Wu Shu** /woo'shoo/ *n* the Chinese martial arts, kung fu. [Chin, from *wŭ* military, and *shù* art]

wuss[1] /wŭs/ (chiefly *N Am sl*) *n* a weakling; an excessively timid person. [Origin uncertain]
■ **wuss'y** *n* and *adj*.

wuss[2] see **wus.**

■ words derived from main entry word; □ compound words; ■ idioms and phrasal verbs

wuther /wudh'ər/, also **whither** /(h)widh'ər/ (*dialect*) *vi* to move swiftly or with force; (of the wind) to make a roaring sound. ◆ *vt* to throw or beat violently. ◆ *n* a blow or blast, or the sound of these; a tremble. [From ON]

■ **wuth'ering** *adj* (of the wind) blowing strongly with a roaring sound; (of a place) characterized by windy weather of this kind.

wuxia /woo-shyä'/ *n* a Chinese genre of films featuring martial arts and fantasy sequences. [Chin *wǔshù* martial arts, and *xiá* chivalry]

wuzzle /wuz'l/ (*US*) *vt* to jumble.

WV *abbrev* : West Virginia (US state; also **W.Va.**); (Windward Islands) St Vincent and the Grenadines (IVR).

WWE *abbrev* : World Wrestling Entertainment.

WWF *abbrev* : Worldwide Fund for Nature (formerly World Wildlife Fund); World Wrestling Federation (now known as **WWE**).

WWI *abbrev* : World War I.

WWII *abbrev* : World War II.

WWW *abbrev* : World Wide Web.

WY *abbrev* : Wyoming (US state; also **Wy.**).

Wy *abbrev* : Way (in street names).

wyandotte /wī'ən-dot/ *n* (sometimes with *cap*) a medium-sized breed of the domestic fowl, of American origin. [From the name of a N American people]

wych, **wich** or **witch** /wich/ *n* and *combining form* a tree with pliant branches, such as the rowan. [OE *wice*, related to *wīcan* to give way] ❑ **wych'-alder** *n* any of a genus of N American shrubs related to the witch-hazel. **wych'-elm** *n* a common wild elm, also called **Scotch** elm or **witch-hazel**. **wych'-hazel** a less common spelling of **witch-hazel**.

Wyclifite or **Wycliffite** /wik'li-fīt/ *adj* relating to the English reformer and translator of the Bible, John *Wyclif* or *Wycliffe* (c.1329–84). ◆ *n* a follower of Wyclif; a Lollard.

wye /wī/ *n* the letter Y or anything shaped like it. ❑ **wye-level** see under **Y**.

Wykehamist /wik'ə-mist/ *n* a pupil or former pupil of Winchester College, which was founded by William of *Wykeham*, Bishop of Winchester (1324–1404).

wyliecoat /wī'li-kōt/ (*Scot*) *n* a flannel undervest or petticoat; a nightdress. [Unexplained first element, and prob **coat**]

wyn or **wynn** /win/ *n* a rune , having the value of modern English *w*, adopted into the Old English alphabet as Þ (also formerly **wen** /wen/). [(Initial letter of) OE *wynn* joy]

wynd /wīnd/ (*Scot*) *n* a narrow alley or lane in a town. [From the stem of **wind**²]

Wyo. *abbrev* : Wyoming (US state).

WYSIWYG or **wysiwyg** /wiz'i-wig/ (*comput*) *abbrev* : what you see (ie on the screen) *is* what you get (on the printout).

wyte see **wit**², **wite**¹.

wyvern /wī'vərn/ (*heraldry*) *n* a fictitious monster, winged and two-legged, combining characteristics of the dragon and the griffin. [ONFr *wivre* a viper, from L *vipera*]

X or **x** /eks/ n the twenty-fourth letter in the modern English alphabet, twenty-first in the Roman, taken from the Chalcidian alphabet, and of the same form, though perhaps not the same origin, as Ionic and classical Greek *chi* (X, χ; pronounced /k-h/, and later /hh/); anything shaped like the letter X. —X was used in Old English medially and finally as a variant for *cs*. In modern English, medially and finally, it has the value of /ks/, as in *extinct* and *axe*, and, medially only, of /gz/, as in *exist*, or /ksh/, as usu in *luxury*, or /gzh/, as in *luxurious*; at the beginning of a word it is usu pronounced /z/, or (rarely) /gz/.

X symbol : (as a Roman numeral) 10; (also **x** or x) the first variable, unknown or yet to be ascertained quantity or factor (*maths*, etc); Christ (see also **chi¹**), also used as an abbreviation, as in *Xmas* and *Xian* (Christian); a former category of cinema film to which persons under eighteen were not admitted (superseded by the designation **18**); used to indicate various other things, such as a choice on a ballot paper, an error on an examination paper, the signature of an illiterate person, etc, or a kiss.
□ **x'-axis** n (*maths*) in a graph, the horizontal axis along which the x-coordinate is plotted. Cf **y-axis**, **z-axis**. **X'-body** n (*bot*) an inclusion in a plant-cell suffering from a virus disease. **X'-chromosome** n a chromosome associated with sex-determination, in mammals occurring paired in the female zygote and cell, and alone in the male zygote and cell. **X'-craft** n (*hist*) a British midget submarine. **X'-factor** n that part of a serviceman's or servicewoman's pay intended as compensation for the disruptions and disadvantages of life in the armed forces; an indefinable quality that sets a person or thing apart (*inf*). **X'-generation** another term for **Generation X** (see under **generation**). **x'-height** n (*printing*) the height of a lower-case x, used as a measure of the height of a typeface. **X-inactivā'tion** n (*biol*) the inactivation of one or other X-chromosome in female mammalian cells, with repression of most of the genes on the chromosome. **X'-particle** n a meson. **X'-rated** adj of a film, in the former X category; graphically violent or sexually explicit in content, language, etc. **X-ray** see separate entry.

X̄ symbol : (Roman numeral) 10000.

x abbrev : ex (*L*, without), as in **xd**, ex dividend.

xanth- /zanth-/ or **xantho-** /zan-thō- or -tho-/ combining form denoting yellow. [Gr *xanthos* yellow]
■ **xan'than** /zan'than/ or **xan'tham** n (also **xanthan**, or **xantham**, **gum**) a substance used as a thickening agent in food preparation. **xan'thate** n a salt of xanthic acid. **xanthein** /zan'thē-in/ n a soluble yellow colouring matter present in flowers. **xanthene** /zan'thēn/ n a white crystalline compound of carbon, hydrogen and oxygen, from which are derived **xanthene dyestuffs**. **xan'thic** adj of a yellow tint, esp as a description of flowers (esp *bot*); relating to xanthin or xanthine; designating **xanthic acid**, any of a series of addition compounds of an alcohol with carbon disulphide, esp ethyl-xanthic acid. **xan'thin** n a name given to the insoluble yellow colouring matter found in various flowers; a yellow colouring matter obtained from madder; (usu **xan'thine**) a white substance, structurally related to uric acid, found in muscle tissue, the liver and other organs, urine, etc, which leaves a lemon-yellow residue when evaporated with nitric acid. **Xan'thium** n (Gr *xanthion* a plant used for dyeing the hair yellow) any of a small but widely-distributed genus of composite plants whose fruits bear hooked prickles very troublesome to sheep and other animals. **Xanthochroi** /zan-thok'rō-ī/ n pl (Gr *chroā* or *chroiā* skin) according to Huxley and other ethnologists, one of the five groups of human races, comprising those with fair hair and pale skin. **xanthochrō'ic** or **xan'thochroid** /-kroid/ adj (also used as n). **xanthochroism** /-thok'rō-izm/ n a condition in which all pigments other than yellows disappear, as in goldfish, or in which normal colouring is replaced by yellow. **xanthochrō'mia** n (*med*) any yellowish discoloration, esp of the cerebrospinal fluid. **xanthochroous** /-thok'rō-əs/ adj xanthochroic. **xanthoma**

/zan-thō'mə/ n (pl **xanthō'mas** or **xanthō'mata**) a yellow tumour composed of fibrous tissue and of cells containing cholesterol ester, occurring on the skin (eg in diabetes) or on the sheaths of tendons, or in any tissue of the body. **xanthō'matous** adj. **xanthomelanous** /zan-thō-mel'ə-nəs/ adj (Gr *melas, -anos* black) applied by Huxley to members of the human race with black hair and yellow or olive skins. **xanthophyll** /zan'thō-fil/ n any of the yellow pigments present in plants and egg yolk. **xanthop'sia** n the condition in which objects appear yellow to the observer, as in jaundice or after taking santonin. **xanthop'terin** or (*rare*) **xanthop'terine** /-in/ n a yellow pigment obtainable from the wings of yellow butterflies and the urine of mammals. **xanthous** /zan'thəs/ adj yellow. **xanthoxyl** /zan-thok'sil/ n (Gr *xylon* wood) a plant of the genus *Xanthoxylum* of the Rutaceae, comprising over one hundred species, of which many are found in Brazil and the West Indies; in particular, either of two species known respectively as the prickly-ash and Hercules club; the dried bark of either of these two species. **Xanthura** /-thū'rə/ or **Xanthoura** /-thoo'rə/ n (Gr *ourā* tail) the former name of a genus of yellow-tailed American jays, now *Cyanocorax*.

Xanthian /zan'thi-ən/ adj relating to *Xanthus*, the capital of ancient Lycia in Asia Minor.

xanthic, xanthin, Xanthium, xantho-, etc see **xanth-**.

Xantippe /zan-tip'i/ n a scolding or bad-tempered woman (also **Xanthippe** /-thip'i/ or (in older editions of Shakespeare) **Zan'tippe** or **Zen'tippe**). [*Xanthippē* the wife of Socrates]

X-body, X-chromosome and **X-craft** see under **X** (*symbol*).

xd abbrev : ex dividend, of a share price, etc, not including the next dividend to be paid.

Xe (*chem*) symbol : xenon.

xebec /zē'bek/ (*hist*) n a small three-masted ship used esp by the pirates of Algiers. [Fr *chebec*, influenced by the Spanish spelling; perh from Turkish or Arabic]

Xema /zē'mə/ n a genus or subgenus of gulls. [Arbitrarily invented by English zoologist William E Leach in 1819]

Xenarthra...to**...xenial** see under **xeno-**.

Xenical® /zen'i-kal/ n a proprietary name for the drug orlistat.

xenium see under **xeno-**.

xeno- /zen-ō-, zin-ō- or zē-no-/, or before a vowel **xen-** /zen-, zin- or zēn-/ combining form denoting: strange, foreign; a guest. [Gr *xenos* (noun) guest, host, stranger, (adj) strange, foreign]
■ **Xenar'thra** n (Gr *arthron* a joint) a group of American edentates, including anteaters, sloths and armadillos, the dorsolumbar vertebrae of which are jointed in an unusual manner. **xenar'thral** adj having additional facets on the dorsolumbar vertebrae. **xē'nia** n (*bot*) the direct influence of pollen upon endosperm (explained by double fertilization) or upon the mother-plant of the embryo. **xenial** /zē'ni-əl/ adj of or concerning hospitality or relations with guests. **xenium** /zē'ni-əm/ n (pl **xē'nia**) a present made to a guest or an ambassador; an offering, or a compulsory gift, to a ruler, the Church, etc. **xenobiotic** /-bī-ot'ik/ adj (*biol*, etc) denoting or relating to a substance foreign to or not rightly found in a body, biological system, etc. ◆ n a xenobiotic substance. **xen'ocryst** /-krist/ n (*geol*) a crystal or mineral grain which has been taken in by magma during its upward flow. **xenodochium** /zen-ō-do-kī'əm/ n (Gr *docheion* a receptacle) a building for the reception of strangers, eg a guest-house in a monastery. **xenogamy** /zen-og'ə-mi/ n (Gr *gamos* marriage; *bot*) cross-fertilization. **xenogeneic** /zen-ō-jen-ē'ik/ adj (Gr *genesis* birth) relating to grafted tissue derived from a species different from the recipient. **xenogen'esis** n the (imagined) generation of something altogether and permanently unlike the parent. **xenogenet'ic** adj. **xenogenous** /zi-noj'i-nəs/ adj due to an outside cause. **xenogloss'ia** n (Gr *glōssa* tongue) in psychical research, a person's knowledge of a language which he or she has never learned. **xen'ograft** n (*biol*) a graft from a member of a different species. **xen'olith** n a fragment of

---

■ words derived from main entry word; □ compound words; ■ idioms and phrasal verbs

rock of extraneous origin which has been incorporated in magma. **xenomania** /-mā'ni-ə/ n (Gr *maniā* madness) an inordinate attachment to foreign things. **xenomenia** /-mē'ni-ə/ n (Gr *mēniaia* menses) vicarious menstruation, in which, in the absence of normal menstruation, bleeding occurs at regular monthly intervals from other parts of the body (eg the nose). **xenomorphic** /-môr'fik/ adj (Gr *morphē* form; *geol*) a textural term applied to rock minerals which do not show their own characteristic shapes. **xen'ophile** n a person who likes foreigners or foreign things. **xen'ophobe** /-fōb/ n (Gr *phobos* fear) a person who fears or hates foreigners or foreign things. **xenophobia** /-fō'bi-ə/ or (*rare*) **xen'ophoby** n fear or hatred of foreigners and foreign things. **xenopho'bic** adj. **xenophya** /zen-of'i-ə/ n pl (Gr *xenophyēs* strange in shape or nature; *biol*) elements of a shell or skeleton not secreted by the organism itself. **xenoplas'tic** adj in experimental zoology, of a chimera in which transplant and host come from different species or genera. **Xen'opus** n a genus of African aquatic frogs (see **platanna**). **xenotime** /zen'ō-tīm/ n (Gr *xenos* strange, in error for *kenos* empty, vain, and *timē* honour, in reference to the fact that the mineral was at first thought to contain a new metal) yttrium phosphate, often containing small quantities of cerium, erbium and thorium, and an important source of these rare elements. **xē'notransplant** vt, vi and n. **xenotransplanta'tion** n the transplanting of an organ from an individual of one species into an individual of another species. **xenū'rine** adj. **Xenurus** /zē-nū'rəs/ n (Gr *ourā* tail) a genus of armadillos in which the tail is almost without plates.

xenon /zen'on or zē'non/ n a heavy gaseous element (symbol **Xe**; atomic no 54) of zero valency present in the atmosphere in the proportion of $1:17 \times 10^7$ by volume, and also a fission product. [Ety as for **xeno-**]
❑ **xenon lamp** n a high-pressure lamp, containing traces of xenon, used in film projectors, high-speed photography, etc.

xenurine and **Xenurus** see under **xeno-**.

xerafin or **xeraphin** /sher'ə-fēn/ n a former silver coin of Goa. [Port]

xeransis...to...**xerasia** see under **xero-**.

Xeres /hher'es/ (*obs*) n sherry. [Sp, wine of Jerez (formerly Xeres)]

xeric see under **xero-**.

xero- /zē-rō-/, or before a vowel **xer-** /zēr-/ combining form denoting dry. [Gr *xēros* dry]
■ **xeran'sis** n a drying-up. **xeranthemum** /-an'thi-məm/ n (Gr *anthemon* flower) any plant of the *Xeranthemum* genus of plants of S Europe, belonging to the thistle family; one species of these, also called **everlasting**. **xeran'tic** adj drying up. **xerarch** /zē'rärk/ adj (Gr *archē* beginning; *bot*) of a plant succession, starting on land where conditions are very dry. **xerasia** /zi-rā'si-ə/ n an abnormal or unhealthy dryness of the hair. **xē'ric** adj dry, lacking in moisture; xerophytic. **xerochasy** /zi-rok'ə-si/ n (*bot*, etc) dehiscence on drying. **xeroderma** /zē-rō-dûr'mə/ or **xeroder'mia** n (Gr *derma* skin) a disease characterized by abnormal dryness of the skin and by abnormal excessive growth of its horny layer, a mild form of ichthyosis (**xeroderma pigmentosum** /pig-men-tō'səm/ an inherited inability to repair DNA damage caused by exposure to ultraviolet light). **xerodermat'ic, xeroder'matous** or **xeroder'mic** adj. **xerograph'ic** adj. **xerog'raphy** n a non-chemical photographic process in which the plate is sensitized electrically and developed by dusting with electrically-charged fine powder. **xeroma** /-rō'-/ n (pl **xerō'mas** or **xerō'mata**) xerophthalmia. **xē'romorph** /-môrf/ n (Gr *morphē* form) a xerophyte. **xeromor'phic** or **xeromor'phous** adj of parts of a plant, protected against excessive loss of water by thick cuticles, coatings of hairs and similar structural features. **xerophagy** /zi-rof'ə-ji/ n (Gr *phagein* to eat) the eating of dry food, or of bread, vegetables and water, as a form of fast. **xē'rophile** n a xerophilous plant. **xerophilous** /-of'il-əs/ adj (Gr *philos* loving) of a plant, tolerant of a very dry habitat. **xeroph'ily** n adaptation to dry conditions. **xērophthalmia** /-of-thal'mi-ə/ n (Gr *ophthalmos* eye) a dry lustreless condition of the conjunctiva due to deficiency of vitamin A in the diet. **xē'rophyte** /-fīt/ n (Gr *phyton* plant) a plant able to inhabit places where the water supply is scanty, or where conditions, eg excess of salts, make it difficult to take in water. **xerophytic** /-fit'/ adj able to withstand drought. **xeroradiog'raphy** n X-ray photography by xerography. **xerō'sis** n abnormal dryness, eg of the skin, mouth, eyes, etc. **xerostoma** /-os'tom-ə/ or **xerostō'mia** n (Gr *stoma* mouth) excessive dryness of the mouth due to insufficient secretions. **xerotes** /zē'rō-tēz/ n xerosis. **xerotherm'ic** adj (of a region or climate) both dry and hot; (of an animal or plant) living in a xerothermic environment. **xerotic** /-rot'/ adj of bodily tissues, abnormally dry. **xerotripsis** /-trip'sis/ n (Gr *trīpsis*, from *trībein* to rub) dry friction.

Xerox® /zē'roks/ n a registered trademark used in respect of copying machines operating a xerographic method of reproduction; a copy so produced. ◆ vt to produce a copy by this method. [Ety as for **xero-**]

X-factor, x-height see under **X** (*symbol*).

Xhosa /kö- or kō'sə, -zə/ n (also **Xo'sa**) a group of Bantu-speaking peoples from the Cape district of South Africa; a member of one of these peoples; the language of these peoples. ◆ adj (also **Xho'san**) of or relating to these peoples or their language.

xi /zī, ksī or ksē/ n the fourteenth letter of the Greek alphabet (Ξ or ξ), corresponding to X; as a numeral ξ' = 60, ˏξ = 60000.

Xian short for **Christian** see also under **X** (*symbol*).

xiph- /zif-/ or **xipho-** /zif-o- or -ō-/ combining form denoting sword. [Gr *xiphos* a sword]
■ **xiphihumeralis** /-i-hū-mər-ā'lis/ n in vertebrates, a muscle leading from the xiphoid cartilage to the humerus. **xiphiplas'tral** adj and n. **xiphiplas'tron** n in chelonians, one of the plates forming the plastron, lying posterior to the hypoplastron. **xiphister'num** n a process at the lower end of the sternum. **xiph'oid** adj (*anat*) sword-shaped; relating to or designating the **xiphoid process** or xiphisternum (also, when cartilaginous, known as **xiphoid cartilage**). **xiphoid'al** adj. **xiphopagic** /-paj'ik/ or **xiphop'agous** adj. **xiphop'agus** n (Gr *pēgnynai* to fix or fasten together) conjoined twins joined in the region of the xiphoid cartilage. **xiphophyllous** /-ə-fil'əs/ adj (Gr *phyllon* leaf) with sword-shaped leaves. **Xiphosura** /-ō-sū'rə/ n (formed irregularly from Gr *ourā* tail) an order of Arthropoda of which the only survivors are the king crabs. **xiphosu'ran** adj and n.

Xiphias /zif'i-as/ n the common swordfish genus, from which the family **Xiphī'idae** is named. [Gr *xiphias* swordfish, from *xiphos* sword]

XL abbrev : extra large.

Xm abbrev : Christmas (see also **X** (*symbol*)).

Xmas /eks'məs or kris'məs/ n short form of **Christmas** (see also **X** (*symbol*)).

XML (*comput*) abbrev : extensible mark-up language.

XMS (*comput*) abbrev : extended memory system.

Xn abbrev : Christian (see also **X** (*symbol*)).

XNOR /eks-nôr'/ (*comput*) n a logic circuit that has two or more inputs and one output, the output signal being 1 if the inputs total an even number, and 0 if the inputs total an odd number (also adj). [exclusive *nor*]

xoanon /zō'ə-non/ n (pl **xō'ana**) a primitive statue, said to have fallen from heaven, *orig* of wood, later overlaid with ivory and gold. [Gr *xoanon*, from *xeein* to carve]

XOR /eks-ôr'/ (*comput*) n a logic circuit that has two or more inputs and one output, the output signal being 1 if the inputs total an odd number, and 0 if the inputs total an even number (also adj). [exclusive *or*]

Xosa see **Xhosa**.

XP abbrev : extreme programming.

X-particle see under **X** (*symbol*).

Xray or **xray** /eks'rā/ n (in international radio communication) a code word for the letter x.

X-ray /eks'rā/ n an electromagnetic ray of very short wavelength which can penetrate matter opaque to light-rays, produced when high-energy electrons impinge on matter, discovered by Röntgen in 1895 (also adj). ◆ n a photograph taken by X-rays. ◆ vt to photograph or treat by, or otherwise expose to, X-rays. [**X** (symbol) after its unknown nature on discovery; translated from original Ger term *X-Strahlen* (pl), *Strahl* a ray]
❑ **X-ray astronomy** n a branch of astronomy using satellites or rockets to detect and measure X-ray emissions from stars, etc. **X-ray crystallography** n the study of crystal structures as shown by their diffraction of X-rays. **X-ray diffraction** n the characteristic interference pattern produced by X-rays passing through a crystal structure. **X-ray micrography** n the preparation, and study through the microscope, of radiographs obtained by means of X-rays. **X-ray spectrum** n a wavelength or frequency diagram in which a series of lines indicate by their positions the energy of the X-rays emitted by a body as the result of electron bombardment. **X-ray telescope** n a telescope designed to investigate the emission of X-rays from stars, etc. **X-ray therapy** n the use of X-rays for medical treatment. **X-ray tube** n a tube enclosing a vacuum, in which X-rays are emitted from a metal target placed obliquely opposite to an incandescent cathode whose high-energy electrons impinge on the target.
■ **characteristic X-rays** secondary X-rays emitted when X-rays fall on matter, which contain monochromatic radiations that vary in wavelength according to the atoms from which they are scattered.

Xt abbrev : Christ (see also **X** (*symbol*)).

Xtian abbrev : Christian (see also **X** (*symbol*)).

xu /soo/ n (pl **xu**) a monetary unit in Vietnam, $\frac{1}{100}$ of a dong. [Viet, from Fr *sou* sou]

XXL abbrev : extra extra large.

xylo- /zī-lō-/, or before a vowel **xyl-** /zīl-/ *combining form* denoting wood. [Gr *xylon* wood]

■ **xylem** /zī'ləm/ *n* (*bot*) woody tissue in trees and plants, *usu* consisting of vessels, tracheides and fibres, all with lignified walls, with some more or less lignified parenchyma, concerned in the conduction of aqueous solutions, with storage and with mechanical support of the plant. **xy'lene** *n* C₆H₄(CH₃)₂, any of three dimethyl-benzenes, occurring in coal tar but not separable by fractional distillation. **xy'lenol** *n* a synthetic resin, (CH₃)₂C₆H₃OH, any of six monohydric phenols derived from xylenes. **xy'lic** *adj* relating to xylem; designating any of six acids, derivatives of xylene. **xy'litol** *n* a sweet crystalline alcohol obtained from xylose, that can be used as a sugar substitute. **xylobal'samum** *n* (Gr *balsamon* the balsam tree) the dried twigs, or the wood, of the balm of Gilead tree. **xy'locarp** *n* a hard and woody fruit, such as a coconut. **xylocarp'ous** *adj*. **xy'lochrome** *n* (Gr *chrōma* colour) a mixture of substances to which the colour of heartwood is due, including tannins, gums, and resins. **xy'logen** /-jen/ *n* xylem. **xylogenous** /-loj'ən-əs/ *adj* (*bot*) growing on wood. **xyl'ograph** *n* an impression or print from a wood block; an impression of the grain of wood for surface decoration. **xylog'rapher** *n*. **xylograph'ic** or **xylograph'ical** *adj*. **xylography** /zī-log'rə-fi/ *n* the art of engraving on wood. **xy'loid** *adj* woody, ligneous. **xyloidin** or **xyloidine** /zi-loi'din/ *n* (Gr *eidos* form, appearance) an explosive like gun-cotton, prepared by the action of strong nitric acid on starch or woody fibre such as pyroxylin, or a similar substance. **xy'lol** *n* (L *oleum* oil) xylene. **xylol'ogy** *n* the study of the structure of wood. **xylō'ma** *n* (*pl* **xylō'mas** or **xylō'mata**) in fungi, a sclerotium-like body which forms spores internally and does not put out branches which develop into sporophores. **xylom'eter** *n* an instrument for determining the specific gravity of wood. **xylon'ic** *adj* designating an acid obtained by oxidizing xylose. **xy'lonite** or **Xy'lonite**® *n* a non-thermosetting plastic of the nitrocellulose type. **xylophagan** /-lof'ə-gən/ *n* (Gr *phagein* to eat) one of the **Xyloph'aga**, a genus of boring bivalves. **xy'lophage** /-fāj/ *n* an insect larva, mollusc, etc that eats or bores into wood. **xylophagous** /-lof'ə-gəs/ *adj* wood-eating. **xyloph'ilous** *adj* fond of wood, living on wood. **xy'lophone** *n* (Gr *phōnē* voice) a musical instrument consisting of a graduated series of wooden bars, which are struck with wooden hammers; an instrument used to measure the elastic properties of wood. **xylophon'ic** *adj*. **xyloph'onist** *n*. **Xylopia** /-lō'pi-ə/ *n* (Gr *pikros* bitter) a genus of trees and shrubs of the custard apple family, natives of the tropics, chiefly in America. **xylopyrog'raphy** *n* designs engraved on wood with a hot poker; the act of making such designs. **xylorim'ba** *n* an extended xylophone combining the ranges of the *xylophone* and the m*arimba*. **xy'lose** *n* a pentose found in many plants, also known as **wood sugar** (C₅H₁₀O₅). **xylot'omous** *adj* (Gr *tomē* a cut) of insects, wood-boring or woodcutting. **xylotypograph'ic** *adj* relating to, or printed from, wooden type. **xylotypog'raphy** *n*. **xy'lyl** /-lil/ *n* any of the univalent radicals, C₈H₉, of the xylenes or their derivatives.

Xyris /zī'ris/ *n* a genus of sedge-like plants, *usu* with yellow flowers, of the family **Xyridaceae** /zir-i-dā'si-ē/ and order **Xyridales** /-dā'lēz/. [Gr *xyris* a kind of iris]

■ **xyrida'ceous** /-shəs/ *adj* of the Xyridaceae.

xyst see **xystus**.

xystus /zis'təs/ (*ancient hist*) *n* (*pl* **xys'tī**) (also **xys'tos** (*pl* **xys'toi**) and **xyst**) a covered portico used by athletes for their exercises; an open colonnade; a tree-planted walk. [L, from Gr *xystos* or *-on*, perh orig a cleared or raked place, from *xyein* to scrape; cf **xyster**]

XYY syndrome /eks-wī-wī' sin'drōm/ (*biol*) *n* a condition in which the human male has an extra Y-chromosome, resulting in reduced growth and sometimes minor behavioural abnormalities.

Y y

a b c d e f g h i j k l m n o p q r s t u v w x y z

Yearling Designed by Chank Diesel in 2001. USA.

Y or **y** /wī/ *n* the twenty-fifth letter in the modern English alphabet, twenty-second in the Roman, derived, as are also U and V, from Greek *upsilon* (Υ, υ); a YMCA or YWCA hostel (*N Am inf*); anything shaped like the letter Y. —Y is used to represent a consonant sound as in *year* (*y* = OE ȝ; ME ȝ, yogh), and the vowel and diphthongal sounds, /i/, as in *hymn* and *folly*; /ī/, as in *my* and *pyre*; /ə/, as in *satyr*; /û/, as in *myrrh*; it is also used in digraphs, such as *oy* instead of *oi* when word-final, eg in *toy*. Early printers used y as a substitute for thorn (Þ), which their founts lacked; hence it came to be so used in manuscripts and inscriptions, as in *yat* or *yᵗ* for *that*, or *ye* for *the* ; cf **ye²**.
□ **Y'-alloy** *n* an aluminium-based alloy of the duralumin type, containing copper 4%, magnesium 1.5%, silicon 0.7%, nickel 2%, iron 0.6%, and titanium 0.2%. **Y'-fronts** *n pl* underpants for men or boys, with a front seamed opening in the shape of an inverted Y. **Y'-level** *n* a type of engineers' level whose essential characteristic is the support of the telescope, namely, Y-shaped rests in which it may be rotated or reversed end-for-end (also called **wye'-level**). **Y'-moth** *n* any of a genus of destructive noctuid moths with a silvery Y-shaped mark on the forewings. **Y'-track** *n* a short track laid at right angles to a railway-line, connected with it by two switches resembling a Y, used for reversing engines.

Y or **Y.** *abbrev* : yen (Japanese currency); yotta-.

Y *symbol* : (as a medieval Roman numeral) 150; (also **y** or **y**) a variable, unknown or yet to be ascertained quantity or factor, used as distinct from and in addition to **X** (or **x** or **x**) (*maths*, etc); yttrium (*chem*).
□ **y'-axis** *n* (*maths*) in a graph, the vertical axis along which the y-coordinate is plotted. Cf **x-axis, z-axis. Y'-chromosome** *n* one of a pair of chromosomes associated with sex-determination in mammals (the other being the X-chromosome).

Y̅ *symbol* : (medieval Roman numeral) 150000.

y or **y.** *abbrev* : yard; year; yocto-.

y- /i-/ *pfx* derived from OE pfx ge- (ȝe-), *orig* a preposition meaning 'with', 'together', seen in OE nouns and adjectives, eg *geféra* companion, *getheaht* counsel, *gelīc* alike, and in verbs such as *gethēodan* to join together, *gerinnan* to congeal, but even in OE times often used with no very definite meaning; in primitive Germanic *gi-* imparted a perfective meaning to past participles; in OE (as ge-) and in ME (as ȝe-, y-, i-, etc) it was prefixed to past participles indiscriminately, and it was used freely in this way by Spenser and other archaizers.

-y¹ /-i/ *sfx* forming adjectives with the senses 'characterized by', 'full of', 'having the quality of' or 'inclined to', as in *icy*, *sandy*, *slangy*, *shiny*, etc. [OE *-ig*]

-y² /-i/ *sfx* forming nouns denoting: (1) a diminutive, or a term of affection, as in *doggy* or *daddy* ; (2) a person or thing having a certain specified characteristic, as in *fatty*. [Orig Scot *-ie* in names, etc]

-y³ /-i/ *sfx* forming nouns denoting a quality, state, action or entity, as in *fury*, *jealousy*, *subsidy*, etc. [OFr *-ie*, from L *-ia*]

yabber /yab'ər/ (*inf, orig Aust*) *n* talk, conversation, jabber. ♦ *vi* to talk or jabber. [Aboriginal word *yabba* language, perh modified by **jabber**]

yabby or **yabbie** /yab'i/ (*Aust*) *n* a small freshwater crayfish, often used as bait. [From an Aboriginal language]

ya-boo see **yah¹**.

yacca /yak'ə/ *n* either of two evergreens (*Podocarpus coriacea* or *Podocarpus purdieana*) of the West Indies; their wood. [Sp *yaca*, from Taino]

yacht /yot/ *n orig* a light fast sailing-vessel; a sailing, steam-powered, etc vessel elegantly fitted out for pleasure-trips or racing. ♦ *vi* to sail or race in a yacht. [Du *jacht* (formerly *jagt*), from *jagen* to chase; Ger *jagen* to hunt]
■ **yacht'er** *n* a person sailing a yacht. **yacht'ie** *n* (*inf* ; *esp Aust* and *NZ*) a yachtsman, yachtswoman or yachting enthusiast. **yacht'ing** *n* and *adj*.
□ **yacht'-built** *adj* built in the style of a yacht. **yacht club** *n* a club for yachtsmen and yachtswomen. **yachts'man** or **yachts'woman** *n* a

person who owns or sails a yacht. **yachts'manship** *n* the art of sailing a yacht.
■ **land'-yacht** or **sand'-yacht** a wheeled boat with sails, for running on land, *usu* along sea-beaches. **land'-yachting** or **sand'-yachting**.

yack or **yak** /yak/ (*sl*) *n* persistent, and often idle or stupid, talk. ♦ *vi* to talk persistently, *esp* in a foolish or gossiping manner. —Also **yack'ety-yack'**, **yak'ety-yak'** and **yak'ity-yak'**. [Imit]

yacker same as **yakka**.

yada yada yada or **yadda yadda yadda** /yad'ə yad'ə yad'ə/ (*US inf*) *n* tiresome, persistent or meaningless chatter. ♦ *adv* and so on. [Perh from Heb *yada* knowledge]

yaff /yaf/ (*Scot*) *vi* to bark like a snarling dog; to scold or nag. [Imit]

yaffle /yaf'l/ or (*dialect*) **yaffingale** /yaf'ing-gāl/ *n* the green woodpecker. [From its call; dialect form influenced by **nightingale¹**]

yag or **YAG** /yag/ *n* yttrium aluminium garnet, a heavy colourless artificial crystal used as a gemstone.

yager /yä'gər/ *n* same as **jäger**.

yagger /yag'ər/ (*Scot*) *n* a pedlar. [Variant of **jagger** (see under **jag²**)]

Yagi /yä'gi or yag'i/ *adj* denoting a type of highly directional television or radio astronomy aerial, with several elements in a close parallel arrangement, fixed at right angles to a central support that points in the direction of strongest reception. [Hidetsugu *Yagi* (1886–1976), Japanese electrical engineer]

yah¹ /yä/ *interj* an exclamation of derision, contemptuous defiance (also **ya(h)'-boo'** and **ya(h)-boo sucks'**) or disgust.

yah² /yä/ *adv* a variant of **yes**, *usu* attributed mockingly to an affected upper-class speaker. ♦ *n* (*sl*) an affected upper-class person.

Yahoo /yä'hoo or yä-hoo'/ *n* a name given by Swift in *Gulliver's Travels* to a class of animals which are human in form but which have the understanding and passions of brutes; (without *cap*) a brutal or boorish lout.

yahoo /yä-hoo' or yə-/ *interj* an exclamation of joy, excitement, etc. ♦ *n* (*cricket sl*) an exuberant attempt to hit the ball hard, often with disappointing results.

yahrzeit /yär'tsīt/ (also with *cap*) *n* in Judaism, an anniversary of a death, *esp* of a close relative. [Yiddish, anniversary time]

Yahweh or **Yahwe** /yä'wä/ *n* Jehovah (also **Yah've(h)**).
■ **Yah'wist** *n* Jehovist (also **Yah'vist**).

Yajurveda /yuj'ûr-vā-də or -ve-/ (*Hinduism*) *n* one of the four Vedas, the Veda of prayers. [Sans]

yak¹ /yak/ *n* a species of ox found in Tibet, and domesticated there, with a thick coat of long silky hair, the lower parts of which hang down almost to the ground. [Tibetan]

yak², **yakety-yak**, etc see **yack**.

yakhdan /yak'dän/ *n* a box used for carrying ice, strapped onto the back of an animal. [Pers *yakh* ice and *dān* box]

yakimono /ya-ki-mō'nō/ *n* in Japanese cookery, grilled food, a grilled dish. [Jap, from *yaki* grill, and *mono* thing]

yakitori /ya-ki-tō'ri or ya-ki-tö'ri/ *n* a Japanese dish of boneless chicken pieces, grilled on skewers and basted with a thick, sweet sauce (**yakitori sauce**) containing sake, mirin and soy sauce. [Jap, from *yaki* grill, and *tori* bird]

yakka /yak'ə/ (*Aust*) *n* work, *esp* of a physical nature (also **yacker** or **yakker**). [From an Aboriginal language of Queensland]

yakow /yak'ow/ *n* an animal crossbred from a male yak and a domestic cow. [**yak¹** and **cow¹**]

Yakut /yä-koot'/ *n* a member of a mixed Turkic people living in NE Siberia; their language. ♦ *adj* of or relating to this people or language.

yakuza /yə-koo'zə/ *n* (*pl* **yaku'za**) a Japanese gangster, typically involved in drug-dealing, gambling, extortion, gun-running or

fāte; fär; mē; fûr; mīne; mōte; för; mūte; pŭt; dhen (then); el'ə-mənt (element) • For other sounds see detailed chart of pronunciation prostitution. [Jap, from *ya* eight, *ku* nine, and *za* or *sa* three, this being the worst hand of cards in gambling]

yald see **yauld**.

Yale® /yāl/ or **Yale lock** /lok/ *n* a trademark for a type of cylinder lock operated by a flat key with a notched upper edge. [Linus *Yale* (1821–68), American locksmith]

yale /yāl/ *n* a mythical animal, depicted in heraldry as resembling a horse with tusks, horns and an elephant's tail. [L *ealē* an unidentified Ethiopian animal mentioned by Pliny]

y'all /yöl/ (*esp Southern US*) a contraction of **you-all** (see under **you**).

Y-alloy see under **Y** (*n*).

yam /yam/ *n* a large tuberous edible root like the potato, grown in tropical countries; any plant of the genus *Dioscorea*, some species of which yield these tubers; a variety of potato (*obs Scot*); a sweet potato (*Southern US*). [Port *inhame*]

Yama /yum'ə or yam'ə/ *n* the Hindu god of death. [Sans]

yamen /yä'men/ (*hist*) *n* the offices and residence of a mandarin. [Chin, from *ya* office, and *mén* gate]

yammer /yam'ər/ (*dialect and inf*) *vi* to lament or wail; to whine; to make an outcry; to talk loudly and at length; to express yearning. ◆ *n* a lamenting, wailing or whining sound; an outcry; lengthy loud talk. [OE *gēom(e)rian*, from *gēomor* sad; influenced in ME by Du *jammeren*]
 ■ **yamm'ering** *n* and *adj*.

yamulka /yä'məl-kə/ same as **yarmulka**.

yang¹ /yang/ (also with *cap*) *n* one of the two opposing and complementary principles of Chinese philosophy, religion, medicine, etc influencing destiny and governing nature, seen as the positive, masculine, light, warm, active element (cf **yin**¹). [Chin *yáng* masculine principle in nature, sun]

yang² /yang/ *n* any of various species of *Dipterocarpus*, all valuable timber trees. [Thai]

Yank /yangk/ (*inf*) *n* see **Yankee**¹.

yank /yangk/ *vt* (*inf*) to carry, move or pull with a jerk. ◆ *vi* to pull or jerk vigorously (*inf*); to move actively (*obs* or *dialect*). ◆ *n* a blow or slap (*Scot*); a strong jerk (*inf*). [Ety doubtful]
 ■ **yank'er** *n* (*Scot*) a rap; a big lie. **yank'ie** *n* (*Scot*) a scold; an impudent woman. **yank'ing** *adj* active (*Scot*); pulling, jerking (*inf*).

Yankee¹ /yang'ki/ *n* (also *inf* **Yank**) in America, a citizen of the New England States, or an inhabitant of the Northern United States, as opposed to the Southern; (also *inf* **Yank**) in British usage, generally an inhabitant of the United States; (also **Yankee bet**) a multiple bet on four horses in four races, consisting of six doubles, four trebles and one accumulator. ◆ *adj* of or relating to Yankees. [Prob Du *Jantje* Johnnie, or *Jan Kees* John Cheese, both said to be used by the Dutch settlers as nicknames for British settlers]
 ■ **Yank'eedom** *n* the land of Yankees; Yankees generally. **Yank'eefied** *adj*. **Yank'eeism** *n* Yankee characteristics.
 ❑ **Yankee bet** see above. **Yankee-Doo'dle** *n* a Yankee (from a popular song).

Yankee² or **yankee** /yang'ki/ *n* (in international radio communication) a code word for the letter *y*.

Yanomami /yan-ō-mä'mi/ *n* (*pl* **Yanoma'mi** or **Yanoma'mis**) (a member of) a people living in the rain forests of N Brazil and Venezuela who follow traditional lifestyles; the language of this people. —Also **Yanomamo** (*pl* **Yanoma'mo** or **Yanoma'mos**).

yanqui /yang'kē/ (*Sp*) *n* in Latin America, a N American, *esp* from the United States. [Sp form of **Yankee**¹]

yaourt see **yoghurt**.

yap /yap/ *vi* (**yapp'ing**; **yapped**) of eg a small dog, to bark sharply or constantly; to speak constantly, *esp* in a noisy or foolish manner (*inf*); to scold (*inf*). ◆ *n* a yelp; a cur (*dialect*); incessant, foolish chatter (*inf*); a fool or bumpkin (*US*); the mouth (*sl*). [Imit]
 ■ **yapp'er** *n* or **yap'ster** *n* a dog. **yap'py** *adj*.

yapok or **yapock** /yap'ək/ *n* the S American amphibious opossum (*Chironectes minimus*), which feeds on shrimps, etc. [From the river *Oyapok* in French Guiana]

yapon see **yaupon**.

yapp /yap/ *n* a type of limp binding in which the cover overlaps the edges of the book. [William *Yapp*, a 19c London bookseller]

yapper and **yapster** see under **yap**.

yappy¹ see under **yap**.

yappy² or **yappie** /yap'i/ (*inf*) *n* a young aspiring professional, or (more recently) young affluent parent. [Acronymic]

yaqona /yə-kō'nə/ *n* the Fijian name for kava (qv).

YAR *abbrev*: Yemen (IVR).

Yarborough /yär'b(ə-)rə/ *n* a hand containing no card above a nine. [From an Earl of *Yarborough*, said to have bet against its occurrence]

yard¹ /yärd/ *n* in English-speaking countries, a measure of 3 feet or 36 inches and equivalent to 0.9144 metre; a piece of material this length; a long beam on a mast for spreading square sails; a straight thin branch, a rod of authority, a stick for beating as punishment, or a rod for measuring (*obs*); the penis (*obs*). [OE *gyrd* or *gierd* a rod or measure; Du *garde*, Ger *Gerte*; connected with Gothic *gazds* a prickle or sting; and prob with L *hasta* a spear]
 ■ **yard'age** *n* the aggregate number of yards; the length, area or volume measured or estimated in linear, square or cubic yards; the cutting of coal at so much a yard.
 ❑ **yard'arm** *n* the outer tapering end of either half of a ship's yard. **yard'land** or **yard of land** *n* (*hist*) a measure of land, a virgate (30 acres). **yard'stick** or (*obs*) **yard'wand** *n* a stick 3 feet long; any standard of measurement (*fig*).
 ■ **by the yard** sold or measured in yard lengths; in large quantities (*fig*). **the whole nine yards** (*N Am sl*) the whole lot. **yard of ale**, etc a very long, narrow glass for beer, etc, or the amount it holds.

yard² /yärd/ *n* an enclosed place, *esp* near a building, often in compounds such as 'backyard', 'courtyard', 'farmyard' and 'prison-yard', or a place where any special work is carried on, as in 'brickyard', 'woodyard' and 'dockyard'; a garden. ◆ *vt* to enclose in a yard. [OE *geard* fence, dwelling, enclosure; Ger *Garten*; connected with L *hortus* and Gr *chortos*]
 ■ **yard'age** *n* the use of a yard, or the charge made for such.
 ❑ **yard'bird** *n* (*US sl*) a convict; a recruit; a soldier confined to camp or required to carry out some menial task as a punishment. **yard-long bean** *n* the asparagus bean. **yard'man** *n* a person in charge of a farmyard; a person employed in a marshalling yard in making up trains, etc; a person employed to do gardening and other outdoor tasks (*US*). **yard'-master** *n* a person in charge of a marshalling yard. **yard sale** *n* (*N Am*) a sale of second-hand goods, *usu* held in the owner's garden.
 ■ **the Yard** New Scotland Yard, the London Metropolitan Police headquarters.

yardang /yär'dang/ *n* a ridge formed by wind erosion from sand, silt, etc, *usu* lying parallel to the prevailing wind direction. [Turk, ablative of *yar* steep bank, precipice]

Yardie /yär'di/ (*sl*; *orig W Indies*) *n* a member of a West Indian gang or Mafia-like syndicate involved in drug-dealing and related crime (also *adj*). [Jamaican dialect *yard* a dwelling, home or (by Jamaicans abroad) Jamaica]
 ❑ **Yardie squad** *n* a special police squad set up to tackle Yardie activities.

yare /yär/ *adj* (*archaic and dialect*) ready, prepared; quick, brisk; easily handled, manageable. ◆ *interj* (*Shakesp*) quick. [OE *gearu* or *gearo*, ready, prompt; Du *gaar*, done, cooked sufficiently, Ger *gar* wholly]
 ■ **yare'ly** *adv* (*archaic and dialect*) promptly; skilfully.

yarfa see **yarpha**.

Yarg /yärg/ *n* a mild cow's milk cheese from Cornwall, wrapped in nettle leaves. [Reversed spelling of *Gray*, the surname of its original producers]

yarmulka or **yarmulke** /yär'məl-kə/ *n* the skullcap worn by Jewish males, *esp* during prayers or ceremonial occasions. [Yiddish, from Pol *yarmulka* small cap]

yarn /yärn/ *n* spun thread; one of the threads of a rope, or these collectively; a sailor's story, spun out to some length, and often having incredible elements; a story generally (*inf*). ◆ *vi* (*inf*) to tell stories. [OE *gearn* thread; ON *garn*, Ger *Garn*]
 ❑ **yarn'-dyed** *adj* (of material) dyed while in yarn form, before weaving.

yarpha or **yarfa** /yär'fə/ (*Scot*) *n* peaty soil in Shetland; clayey, sandy or fibrous peat; a peat bog. [ON *jörfi* gravel]

yarr /yär/ (*dialect*) *n* the corn spurrey, *Spergula arvensis*. [Cf Fris *jīr*]

yarraman /yar'ə-mən/ (*Aust*) *n* a horse. [From an Aboriginal language]

yarrow /yar'ō/ *n* a strong-scented plant, *Achillea millefolium*, or any similar species of milfoil. [OE *gearwe*; Ger *Garbe*]

yarta or **yarto** see **jarta**.

yashmak /yash'mak or -mak'/ *n* a double veil worn by some Muslim women in public, leaving only the eyes uncovered. [Ar *yashmaq*]

yatagan or **yataghan** /yat'ə-gan/ *n* a Turkish sword or long dagger, without a guard and *usu* curved. [Turk *yātāghan*]

yate /yāt/ (*Spenser*) *n* a gate. [Variant of **gate**¹]

yatter /yat'ər/ (*Scot*) *n* tiresome, irritatingly demanding or persistent chatter. ◆ *vi* to jabber incessantly. [Imit]
 ■ **yatt'ering** *n* and *adj*. **yatt'eringly** *adv*.

yaud /yöd or yäd/ (*Scot*) *n* a mare; an old mare; an old horse generally. [ON *jalda*. Cf **jade**²]

yauld or **yald** /yöld or yäld/ (Scot) adj active, nimble or strong. [Ety unknown]

yaup /yöp/ (Scot) adj hungry. [OE gēap shrewd]

yaupon /yö'pən/ n a bushy evergreen shrub (Ilex vomitoria) of the holly genus, native to the SE coasts of the USA, its leaves used to brew an emetic or purgative tea, the so-called 'black drink' of the Native Americans (also **yapon** /yö'/ or **yupon** /yoo'/). [Catawba]

yautia /yö'ti-ə/ n a tropical American aroid plant that yields an edible tuber; this tuber. [Am Sp, from Taino]

yaw /yö/ vi of a ship, to deviate temporarily from, or turn out of the line of, its course; to move unsteadily or zigzag (fig); of an aircraft, to deviate in a horizontal direction from the line of flight. ◆ vt to cause to deviate from course, cause to zigzag, etc. ◆ n a deviation from the course; the angular motion of an aircraft in a horizontal plane about the normally vertical axis. [Origin uncertain; cf ON jaga to move to and fro, eg as a door does on its hinges]

yawey see under **yaws**.

yawl[1] /yöl/ n a small fishing-boat; a small sailing-boat with a jigger and a shortened mainboom; a ship's small boat, generally with four or six oars (hist). [Du jol]

yawl[2] /yöl/ vi to howl. ◆ n a howl. [Variant of **yowl**]

yawn /yön/ vi to take a deep involuntary breath because of drowsiness, boredom, etc; to gape; to gape with astonishment (Shakesp); of eg a chasm, to be wide or wide open. ◆ vt to make or produce, or cause to be or become, by yawning; to utter with a yawn. ◆ n an involuntary deep breath caused by weariness or boredom; a boring event, person, etc (inf); a chasm or opening; dullness (Shelley). [OE gānian to yawn and geonian or ginian (combining form gīnan, pat gān), to gape widely; ON gīna to gape]
  ■ **yawn'er** n one who yawns; a boring thing (inf). **yawn'ing** adj gaping or wide open; drowsy; causing drowsiness or sleep (Shakesp). ◆ n the act of producing a yawn. **yawn'ingly** adv. **yawn'y** adj.

yawp /yöp/ (chiefly US) vi to utter or cry harshly or hoarsely and noisily; to yelp or bark. ◆ n a harsh, hoarse, etc cry. [Imit; cf **yap** and **yelp**]
  ■ **yawp'er** n.

yaws /yöz/ n a tropical epidemic and contagious disease of the skin (also known as **framboesia**, **button scurvy**, **verruga Peruviana**, **buba** or **boba**, etc). [Origin uncertain; perh Native American]
  ■ **yaw'ey** or **yaw'y** adj.

yay /yā/ interj an exclamation of joy, approbation, encouragement, etc. [Variant of **yes**]

Yb (chem) symbol : ytterbium.

ybet /i-bēt'/ an obsolete pap of **beat**.

yblent /i-blent'/ an obsolete pap of **blend**[2] and **blind**.

ybore /i-bör'/ an obsolete pap of **bear**[1].

ybound /i-bownd'/ and **ybounden** /i-bown'dən/ an obsolete pap of **bind**.

ybrent /i-brent'/ an obsolete pap of **burn**[1].

YC abbrev : Young Conservative(s).

Y-chromosome see under **Y** (symbol).

yclad /i-klad'/ and **ycled** /i-kled'/ obsolete forms of **clad**, pap of **clothe**.

ycleepe /i-klēp'/ (Spenser) vt to clepe. [Back-formation from **yclept**]

yclept /i-klept'/ and **ycleped** (or Milton **ycleap'd**) see **clepe**.

ycond /i-kond'/ an obsolete pap of **con**[2].

yd abbrev : yard (pl **yd** or **yds**).

ydrad /i-drad'/ or **ydred** /i-dred'/ obsolete pap of **dread**.

ye[1] /yē/ or **yi**/ (now archaic, dialect or poetic) pronoun the second person plural (sometimes singular) pronoun; cf **you**. Formerly, eg in the Authorized Version of the English Bible, ye was always used as a nominative, and you as a dative or accusative; later ye was sometimes used for all these cases. [ME ye, nominative; your, genitive; you, yow, dative and accusative pl, from OE gē, nominative; ēower, genitive; ēow, dative and accusative]

ye[2] /thē, thi/ or (reflecting the spelling) yē/ demonstrative adj an archaic spelling for 'the', arising from printers' use of y for the letter thorn, Þ. See **Y** (n).

yea /yā/ (archaic) adv yes, now esp in the phrase say yea or nay (for the former distinction between yea and yes, see the note at **yes**); indeed; indeed more than that. ◆ n (formal or archaic) an affirmative vote or voter. [OE gēa ; Du and Ger ja, ON jā ; cf **yes**]
  □ **yea'-sayer** n a person who agrees or assents, esp one who does so habitually and in a positive, enthusiastic manner.

yead, **yede** or **yeed** /yēd/ (Spenser) vi (pat **yod** /yod/ or **yode** /yōd/) to go or proceed. [OE ēode went, used as the pat of gān to go]

yeah /ye, yä or ye'ə/ (inf) adv yes.

yealdon /yel'dən/ (Walter Scott, as an imitation of Cumberland dialect) n same as **eldin**.

yealm see **yelm**.

yean /yēn/ (archaic and dialect) vt and vi esp of a sheep, to give birth to (young). [OE ge- (see **y-**) and eanian to give birth to (see **ean**)]
  ■ **yean'ling** n a lamb or a kid (also adj).

year /yēr or yûr/ n (pl **years** or, used adjectivally with a preceding numeral, **year**, eg a three-year period) the time taken by the earth to orbit the sun, approx 365 days 6 hours but varying slightly according to the method of measurement (see **anomalistic year**, **astronomical year**, etc below); the time taken by any specified planet to revolve round the sun or, eg in science fiction, round any star; the period of time beginning on 1 January and ending on 31 December, consisting of 365 days (except in a **leap year**, when one day is added to February, making the number 366), the present legal, civil or calendar year (see below); a space of twelve calendar months, or a period within each twelve-month space characterized by a particular activity, etc; students, etc as a group at the same stage of their education; (in pl) a period of time or a person's life; (in pl) a person's age; (in pl) old age (archaic or poetic); (in pl) a very long time. [OE gēar ; Ger Jahr, ON ār, Gr hōrā season]
  ■ **year'ling** n an animal a year old; a racehorse one year old, as calculated from 1 January of its year of foaling; a bond maturing after one year (finance). ◆ adj a year old; maturing after one year (finance). **year'ly** adj happening every year; lasting a year; for a year. ◆ adv once a year; from year to year. ◆ n a publication appearing, an event occurring, etc, once a year.
  □ **year'book** n a book published annually, reviewing the events of the past year. **year-end**' n the end of the (esp financial) year (also adj). **year'long** adj lasting a year. **year-on-year**' adj (econ) of figures, set against figures for the equivalent period in the previous year. **year'-round** adj existing, lasting, open, etc throughout the year.
  ■ **anomalistic year** a year as measured by the earth's time of passage from perihelion to perihelion, ie 365 days, 6 hours, 13 minutes, 49 seconds. **astronomical year** a year as measured by the time between two occurrences of the same equinox or solstice, ie the time taken for one complete mean apparent circuit of the ecliptic by the sun, ie 365 days, 5 hours, 48 minutes, 46 seconds (also called the **equinoctial**, **natural**, **solar** or **tropical year**). **calendar year** same as **legal year** below. **canicular year** the Sothic year (see under **Sothic**). **civil year** same as **legal year** below. **ecclesiastical year** the year as arranged in the ecclesiastical calendar, with the saints' days, festivals, etc. **embolismic year** a year of thirteen lunar months (384 days) occurring in a lunisolar calendar such as that of the Jews. **equinoctial year** see **astronomical year** above. **financial year** see under **finance**. **fiscal year** see under **fiscal**. **great year** see **Platonic year** below. **Hebrew year** a lunisolar year, of 12 or 13 months of 29 or 30 days, in every cycle of nineteen years the 6th, 8th, 11th, 14th, 17th and 19th having thirteen months instead of twelve. **Julian year** the year according to the Julian calendar (introduced by Julius Caesar, modified by Augustus; superseded by the Gregorian calendar), a period of $365\frac{1}{4}$ days, longer than an astronomical year by about 11 minutes (see also **style**). **leap year** see above. **legal year** the year by which dates are reckoned (it has begun on different dates at different periods in history, and for six centuries before 1752 it began in England on 25 March since when (earlier in Scotland) it has begun on 1 January). **lunar year** a period of twelve lunar months or 354 days. **natural year** see **astronomical year** above. **Platonic year** a cycle of years at the end of which the heavenly bodies were supposed to be again in the same place as at the Creation (also called **great** or **perfect year**). **sabbatical year** see under **Sabbath**. **sidereal year** the period required by the sun to move from a given star to the same star again, having a mean value of 365 days, 6 hours, 9 minutes, 9.6 seconds. **solar** or **tropical year** see **astronomical year** above. **the year dot** see under **dot**[1]. **the Year of Grace**, or **of our Lord** a formula used in stating any particular year since Christ's birth. **year in, year out** (happening, done, etc) every year; with monotonous regularity.

yeard and **yeard-hunger**, etc see **yird**.

yearn[1] /yûrn/ vi to express longing, eg by sound or appearance; to feel great desire; to feel compassion, tenderness or grief (also used impersonally, as 'it yearns me'; also **earn**; obs, Spenser and Shakesp). ◆ vt to desire strongly or feel longing for (also **earn**; obs); to express a desire for or ask for (obs); to cause to mourn (Shakesp). ◆ n a yearning. [OE geornan (WSax giernan) to desire; related to georn desirous, eager; cf Ger gern willingly]
  ■ **yearn'er** n. **yearn'ing** n and adj. **yearn'ingly** adv.

yearn[2] /yûrn/ (obs and dialect) vt to earn. [**earn**[1]]

yearn[3] see **earn**[2].

yeast /yēst/ n one of a group of simple unicellular fungi, with features making them highly suitable for genetic and biochemical studies, and

for use in brewing, baking, etc; the froth on beer (*obs*); spume or foam on water (*Shakesp*); leaven (*fig*). ◆ *vi* (*lit* and *fig*) to ferment or be covered with froth. [OE *gist* or *gyst*; Ger *Gäscht, Gischt*]
■ **yeast'iness** *n*. **yeast'like** *adj*. **yeast'y** *adj* like yeast; frothy or foamy; insubstantial.
❑ **yeast plant** *n* any of a group of tiny, one-celled fungi (genus *Saccharomyces*) that produce alcoholic fermentation in saccharine fluids. **yeast powder** *n* dry powdered yeast used in baking; baking powder.

yech /yehh, yuhh, yuk, yŭhh, etc/ *interj* an expression of distaste or disgust. [Imit; cf **yuck**[1] and **ugh**]

yede and **yeed** see **yead**.

yegg /yeg/ (*US*) *n* a burglar, *esp* a burglar of safes (also **yegg'man**). [Origin unknown]

yeld /yeld/ or **yell** /yel/ (*Scot*) *adj* barren; not giving milk; unproductive. [Late OE *gelde*; cf **geld**[1]]

yeldring /yeld'ring/ or **yeldrock** /yeld'rok/ *n* same as **yoldring**.

yelk see **yolk**[1].

yell[1] /yel/ *vi* to howl or cry out with a sharp noise; to scream in pain or terror. ◆ *vt* to utter with a yell. ◆ *n* a sharp cry or loud shout, whether of words or inarticulate sounds; a rhythmic cheer or chant, often including nonsense words or syllables, used eg to encourage sports teams, *esp* in N American colleges (*esp N Am*); an extremely funny person or thing, a scream (*old sl*). [OE (Anglian) *gellan*; Ger *gellen*; connected with OE *galan* to sing]
■ **yell'ing** *n*. **yell'och** /-əhh/ (*Scot*) *vi* to yell. ◆ *n* a yell.

yell[2] see **yeld**.

yellow /yel'ō/ *adj* of the colour of sulphur, egg yolk, gold, a ripe lemon, a primrose, etc; of Mongolic or Oriental race (Chinese, Japanese, etc) (now often considered *offensive*); of mixed black and white race (*US*); of skin, sallow, sickly-looking; cowardly (*inf*); sensational (*inf*). ◆ *n* the colour of the rainbow between the orange and the green or of sulphur, egg yolk, gold, a ripe lemon, a primrose, etc; any dye or pigment producing such a colour; a yolk; (in *pl*) peach-yellows (see **peach**[1]), or other plant disease in which the foliage turns yellow; (in *pl*) jaundice in horses, etc. ◆ *vt* and *vi* to make or become yellow. [OE *geolu*; Ger *gelb*; cognate with L *helvus* light bay]
■ **yell'owish** *adj* somewhat yellow. **yell'owishness** *n*. **yell'owness** *n* the quality or state of being yellow; jealousy (*obs*; *fig*). **yell'owy** *adj* yellowish.
❑ **yellow alert** *n* an alarm, etc one stage less serious than a red alert. **yellow-ammer** see **yellowhammer** below. **yellow archangel** *n* the dead-nettle archangel. **yell'owback** *n* a cheap, sensational novel, *specif* one with yellow board or paper covers, common in the 19c. **yell'ow-bellied** *adj* (*sl*) cowardly. **yell'ow-belly** *n* (*sl*) a coward. **yellow berries** *n pl* Persian berries, the fruit of various species of buckthorn. **yellow bile** see under **bile**. **yell'owbird** *n* any of various, *esp* N American, birds of a yellow colour such as the American goldfinch. **yell'ow-boy** *n* (*obs sl*) a gold coin; a mulatto or dark-skinned quadroon (*fem* **yell'ow-girl**). **yellow brick road** *n* a path to fame, wealth, etc. **yellow bunting** *n* the yellowhammer. **yell'owcake** *n* uranium oxide, obtained in the form of a yellow precipitate during the processing of uranium ore. **yellow card** *n* an official warning to a football, etc player (signalled by the showing of a yellow card), typically following an infringement; any similar warning, or a symbol of it (*fig*). **yellow centaury** same as **yellow-wort** below. **yellow dog** *n* a mongrel; a cur; a contemptible or cowardly person (also used adjectivally, *esp US*, as in **yellow-dog contract**, *orig* one requiring an employee not to be a member of a trade union, now, in a more general sense, one which gives acceptable advantages to an employee). **yellow earth** *n* yellow ochre. **yellow-eyed grass** *n* any plant of the genus *Xyris*, growing abundantly in the pine-barrens of the southern USA. **yellow fever** *n* an acute disease occurring in tropical America and W Africa, caused by infection with a virus transmitted to humans by the bite of a mosquito and characterized by high fever, acute nephritis, jaundice and haemorrhages. **yell'owfin** *n* a variety of tuna with yellow fins. **yellow flag** *n* a flag of a yellow colour, displayed by a vessel in quarantine or over a military hospital or ambulance. **yellow-girl** see **yellow-boy** above. **yell'owhammer** or (*obs*) **yell'ow-ammer** *n* a bunting (*Emberiza citrinella*), so named from the yellow colour of the male (also called **yellow bunting**). **yell'owhead** *n* a species of flycatcher (*Mohoua ochrocephala*) found in New Zealand. **yellow jack** *n* (*old*) yellow fever. **yellow jacket** *n* (*N Am*) a small common wasp or hornet (genus *Vespa*) with yellow and black markings. **yellow jersey** *n* (Fr *maillot jaune*) the jersey worn each day in the Tour de France cycle race by the overall leader in the race. **yell'owlegs** *n* a N American sandpiper with yellow legs. **yellow line** *n* a line of yellow paint, or other substance, on a road indicating parking restrictions. **yellow metal** *n* a brass consisting of sixty parts copper and forty parts zinc. **Yellow Pages**® *n* a telephone directory,

printed on yellow paper, which classifies participating subscribers alphabetically according to trades, professions, services, etc. **yellow pepper** see under **pepper**. **yellow peril** *n* (also with *caps*, *derog* or *facetious*) the supposed danger that the Oriental races, *esp* the Chinese, might overthrow the white or Western races and overrun the world; the Chinese or Japanese. **yellow poplar** *n* the American tulip tree, or its wood. **yellow press** *n* (also with *cap*) newspapers abounding in exaggerated, sensational articles. **yellow rattle** see under **rattle**. **yellow ribbon** *n* (*US*) a symbol of welcome for those returning home after having undergone some danger, *orig* a decoration on US cavalrymen's tunics, given to sweethearts as favours. **yell'ow-root** *n* golden-seal. **yellow rust** *n* a fungus damaging to wheat. **yellow snow** *n* snow sometimes observed in the Alps and in the Antarctic regions, coloured yellow by the growth on it of certain algae. **yellow soap** *n* common soap composed of tallow, resin and soda. **yellow spot** *n* the macula lutea, the small area at the centre of the retina in vertebrates at which vision is most distinct. **yellow streak** *n* a tendency to cowardly behaviour. **yell'owtail** *n* any of various sea fishes with yellow tail fins; a white tussock moth with a yellow-tipped abdomen. **yellow wash** *n* a lotion consisting of a mixture of mercuric chloride and lime water. **yell'ow-weed** *n* the common ragwort; goldenrod; weld (the plant) (*dialect*). **yell'ow-wood** *n* any of various woods that are light in colour, such as satinwood, or which yield yellow dye, such as *Cladrastis lutea* (American yellow-wood) of the southern USA; any of the trees that yield these woods; a tree, such as a sumach, that yields yellow dye from a part other than the wood. **yell'ow-wort** *n* an annual of the gentian family (also **yellow centaury**). **yell'ow-yite**, **yellow yoldring**, **yellow yorling** or **yellow-yow'ley** same as **yellowhammer** above.

yelm or **yealm** /yelm/ (*dialect*) *n* a bundle of straw laid straight, ready for thatching. ◆ *vt* to straighten and arrange (straw) for thatching. [OE *glim* a handful of reaped corn, a bundle]

yelp /yelp/ *vi* to utter a sharp cry or bark; to boast (*obs*). ◆ *n* a sharp cry or bark. [OE *gielpan* to boast or exult; ON *gjālpa* to yelp]
■ **yelp'er** *n*. **yelp'ing** *n* and *adj*.

yelt /yelt/ (*dialect*) *n* a young sow. [OE *gilte*, from MLGer *gelte* a spayed sow]

Yemeni /yem'ə-ni/ *adj* of or relating to the Republic of Yemen in the Arabian Peninsula or its inhabitants. ◆ *n* a native, citizen or inhabitant of Yemen.

yen[1] /yen/ *n* (*pl* **yen**) formerly a Japanese gold or silver coin; the standard monetary unit of Japan (100 sen). [Jap, from Chin *yuán* Chinese monetary unit]

yen[2] /yen/ (*inf*) *n* an intense desire, longing or urge. ◆ *vi* (**yenn'ing**; **yenned**) to desire or yearn. [Chin *yǐn* craving or addiction]

Yenglish see **Yinglish**.

yenta /yen'tə/ (*US*) *n* a gossip; a shrewish woman. [From the Yiddish personal name]

Yeo. *abbrev*: Yeomanry.

yeoman /yō'mən/ *n* (*pl* **yeo'men**) a gentleman serving in a royal or noble household, ranking between a sergeant and a groom (*hist*); after the 15c, a member of a class of small farmers, *usu* freeholders, the next grade below gentlemen (often serving as foot soldiers; *hist*); any small farmer or countryman above the grade of labourer; an assistant to an official; a member of the yeomanry cavalry or of the yeomen of the guard; a petty officer on a warship whose duties are clerical. [ME *yoman* or *yeman*; perh for *young man*]
■ **yeo'manly** *adj* of yeoman's rank; humble and honest; staunch; brave. ◆ *adv* staunchly or bravely. **yeo'manry** *n* the collective body of smaller freeholders; a cavalry volunteer force in Great Britain formed during the wars of the French Revolution, later mechanized as part of the Territorial Army.
❑ **yeoman** or **yeoman's service** *n* powerful aid, such as came from the yeomen in the English armies of early times. **Yeomen of the Guard** *n pl* a veteran company of picked soldiers, employed on special occasions in conjunction with the gentlemen-at-arms as the sovereign's bodyguard (constituted a corps in 1485 by Henry VII, and still wearing the costume of that period).

yep /yep/ (*esp N Am*) dialect and informal variant of **yes**.

yerba /yûr'bə/ *n* a herb, *esp* (also **yerba maté** or **yerba de maté**) Paraguay tea or maté (qv). [Sp, from L *herba*]

yerd and **yerd-hunger** see **yird**.

yerk /yûrk/ (all meanings now *dialect*) *vt* of a shoemaker, to draw (stitches) tight; to bind or tie with a jerk; to throw or thrust with a sudden, quick motion; to move with a jerk; to lash out with; to utter jerkily; to beat; to rouse or excite (*fig*). ◆ *vi* to draw tight, bind, strike, move or rise with a jerk; to kick; to engage in with energy or eagerness; to gibe or carp. [Origin obscure; earlier than **jerk**[1]]

yersinia /yər-sin'i-ə/ n (pl **yersin'ias** or **yersin'iae** /-i-ē/) a bacterium of the genus *Yersinia* spread by animals or birds, one of which (*Yersinia pestis*) causes plague and others **yersinio'sis**, an acute infection of the small intestine. [AEJ *Yersin* (1863–1943), French bacteriologist]

yes /yes/ adv a word of affirmation, agreement or consent; a word used to indicate that the speaker is present, or (often said interrogatively) to signal someone to act or to speak; a word used to express vehement satisfaction, joy, etc; in fact, indeed, or on the contrary (formerly used *esp* in answer to a negative question or to express disagreement with a previous negative statement, in contradistinction to *yea* which was used for simple agreement or affirmation until it became obsolete in the early 17c, its functions then being taken over by *yes*). ◆ n (pl **yess'es, yes'es** or **yes's**) a vote or answer of yes; a person who votes or answers yes. [OE *gēse* or *gīse*, from *gēa* or *gē* yea, and *sī* let it be] □ **yes-but'** n (*inf*) a qualified consent or agreement. **yes'-man** n (*inf*) someone who agrees with everything that is suggested; an obedient follower with no initiative.

yeshiva or **yeshivah** /yə-shē'və/ n (pl **yeshi'vas, yeshi'vahs, yeshi'vōt** or **yeshi'vōth**) a school for the study of the Jewish Scripture, the Talmud; a seminary for the training of rabbis; an orthodox Jewish elementary school. [Heb *yeshībhāh* a sitting]

yesk see **yex**.

yest and **yesty** obsolete forms of **yeast** and **yeasty**.

yester /yes'tər/ adj and *combining form* relating to yesterday; last. [OE *geostran* or *giestran* (always followed by *dæg*, etc); Ger *gestern*; cf L *hesternus*, Gr *chthes*]
■ **yes'tern** adj (*dialect* and *archaic*) yester. **yestreen'** adv (contraction of **yestereven**; *Scot* and *poetic*) yesterday evening.
□ **yes'terday** n the day immediately before today; (often in *pl*) the (recent) past. ◆ adv on the day immediately before today; formerly; in the (recent) past. **yestereve', yestere'ven, yestereve'ning, yestermorn', yestermorn'ing** n (*archaic, dialect* or *poetic*) yesterday evening, or morning. **yesternight'** n (*archaic, dialect* or *poetic*) last night. **yes'teryear** n (*orig* DG Rossetti) last year, or the past in general.

yet /yet/ adv in addition, besides; up to the present time; still; hitherto; at the same time; even; before the affair is finished. ◆ conj nevertheless; however. [OE *gīet*, *gīeta*; Ger *jetzt*]
■ **as yet** up to the time under consideration.

yeti /yet'i/ n the abominable snowman. [Tibetan *yeh-teh*]

yett /yet/ (*Scot*) n a gate or door. [Variant of **gate¹**]

yeuk see **yuke**.

yeve /yēv/ (*obs*) vt (pap (Spenser) **yeven** /yev'ən/) to give. [OE *giefan*; cf **give**]

yew /ū/ n any tree of the genus *Taxus* (family Taxaceae, itself a division of the group Coniferae) widely diffused over the northern parts of the world, with narrow lanceolate or linear leaves, *esp Taxus baccata* which yields an elastic wood good for bows; its wood; a bow made of its wood; yew twigs regarded as emblematic of grief (yew trees having traditionally been planted in graveyards throughout Europe). [OE *īw* or *ēow*; Ger *Eibe*]
■ **yew'en** adj (*archaic*) made of yew.
□ **yew tree** n.

yex /yeks/, also **yesk** /yesk/ (now *Scot* and *dialect*) vi to hiccup, belch or spit. ◆ n a hiccup, etc. [OE *geocsian* to sob]

Yezidi /ye'zi-di/ n a member of a sect in Armenia and the Caucasus who believe in a Supreme God but also pay respect to the Devil, believing him to have been reinstated as chief angel (called by them *Yazid*), and other minor gods (also **Yez'di, Yez'idee, Zez'idee**, etc).

yfere /i-fēr'/ (*obs*) adv together, in company. [See **fere¹** and **infere**]

Y-fronts see under **Y** (n).

Yggdrasil, Yggdrasill or **Ygdrasil** /ig'drə-sil/ (*Norse myth*) n the ash tree binding together heaven, earth and hell, and extending its branches over the whole world and above the heavens. [ON; perh from *Yggr* a surname of Odin, and *drasil* horse]

yglaunst /i-glönst'/ (*Spenser*) pap of **glance¹**.

ygo or **ygoe** /i-gō'/ (*Spenser*) pap of **go; ago**. [**go**]

YHA abbrev : Youth Hostels Association.

yibbles see **aiblins** under **able**.

yicker same as **yikker**.

Yiddish /yid'ish/ n a language spoken by Jews, based on medieval German dialects with Hebrew and Slavonic additions, *usu* written in the Hebrew alphabet. ◆ adj of or relating to Yiddish. [Ger *jüdisch* Jewish]
■ **Yid** n (*offensive*) a Jew. **Yidd'isher** adj in or relating to Yiddish; Jewish. ◆ n a Jew, a speaker of Yiddish. **Yidd'ishism** n an idiom or other speech characteristic derived from Yiddish.

yield /yēld/ vt to deliver, surrender, relinquish or resign; to grant or accord; to admit or concede; to give out; to furnish or afford; to produce; to pay or repay, or to reward (*obs*); to render as due or appropriate (*archaic*). ◆ vi to submit; to cease fighting or contesting; to give way under pressure; to give place; to concede; to give way (in traffic) (*N Am*). ◆ n an amount yielded; a product; the return of a financial investment, *usu* calculated with reference to the cost and dividend. [OE (WSax) *gieldan* to pay; OHGer *gelten*, ON *gjalda*]
■ **yield'able** adj that may be yielded; inclined to yield. **yield'ableness** n. **yield'er** n. **yield'ing** adj giving, or inclined to give, way; compliant. ◆ n a giving way; compliance. **yield'ingly** adv. **yield'ingness** n.
□ **yield point** n in iron and annealed steels, the stress at which a substantial amount of plastic deformation takes place suddenly. **yield strength** n in materials which do not exhibit a sudden plastic deformation under stress (cf **yield point** above), the level of stress at which a given amount of deformation takes place.
■ **yield up the ghost** (*archaic*) to give up the ghost (see under **ghost**).

yike /yīk/ or **yikes** /yīks/ (*inf*) interj expressing alarm or astonishment. ◆ n (*Aust*) an argument, fight.

yikker /yik'ər/ vi of an animal, to utter sharp little cries (also n). [Imit]

yill /yil/ n Scots form of **ale**.

yin¹ /yin/ (also with *cap*) n one of the two opposing and complementary principles of Chinese philosophy, religion, medicine, etc influencing destiny and governing nature, seen as the negative, feminine, dark, cold, passive element (cf **yang¹**). [Chin *yīn* feminine principle in nature, moon]

yin² /yin/ and **yince** /yins/ Scots forms of **one** and **once** generally written **ane** and **ance**.

yince-errand see under **errand**.

Yinglish, also **Yenglish** /ying'glish/ (*facetious, orig* US) n a mixture of Yiddish and English spoken by US Jews; a dialect of English containing a large number of Yiddishisms.

yip /yip/ vi *esp* of a dog, to give a short, sudden cry (also n). [Imit]

yippee /yi-pē'/ interj expressing delight, exultation, etc.

yipper see under **yips**.

yippie or **yippy** /yip'i/ n a member of a radical political group founded in 1967 with ideals based on those of the hippies. [From the *Youth International Party*]

yips /yips/ (*sport, esp* and *orig golf*) n pl (*usu* with *the*) a nervous twitching caused by tension before making a shot, etc.
■ **yipp'er** n a golfer, etc suffering from the yips.

yird /yûrd/ n (also **eard** /ûrd or erd/, **yeard** or **yerd**) a Scots form of **earth**. ◆ vt to bury. [**earth**]
□ **yird'-house, eard'-house**, etc n an earth-house (see under **earth**). **yird'-hunger, eard'-hunger**, etc n earth-hunger, a hunger for land; the hunger sometimes felt by persons approaching death; voracious hunger. **yird'-hungry, eard'-hungry**, etc adj.

yirk same as **yerk**.

yite /yīt/ (*dialect*) n the yellowhammer. [Origin obscure]

Yizkor /yiz'kər/ n a memorial prayer for deceased relatives. [Heb, literally, may he remember]

-yl /-il/ (*chem*) sfx forming nouns denoting a radical, eg *carbonyl, carboxyl*, etc. [Gr *hȳlē* matter]

ylang-ylang /ē'lang-ē'lang/ n a tree (*Cananga odoratum*) of the Malay Archipelago and Peninsula, the Philippines, etc; an essence (also **ylang-ylang oil**) distilled from its flowers. [Tagálog]

ylem /ī'lam/ n the original substance from which, according to some theories, the elements developed. [OFr *ilem*, from L *hȳlem*, accusative of *hȳlē*, from Gr *hȳlē* matter]

Y-level see under **Y** (n).

ylike (*Spenser*) same as **alike**.

ylke obsolete spelling of **ilk¹**.

YMCA abbrev : Young Men's Christian Association.

ymolt /i-mōlt'/ (*Spenser*) or **ymolten** /i-mōl'tən/ (*obs*) pap of **melt¹**.

Y-moth see under **Y** (n).

ympe and **ympt** (*Spenser*) same as **imp** and **imped**.

Yn abbrev : yen (Japanese currency).

ynambu /ē-nam-boo'/ n a very large tinamou. [Port *inambu*; of Tupi origin, related to **tinamou**]

Ynd (*Spenser*) same as **Ind**.

Yngling /ing'ling/ n a type of racing yacht with a heavy keel, sailed by a crew of three people. [Norw, youngster]

yo /yō/ interj calling for or accompanying effort, calling for attention or used in greeting, etc; used to indicate one's presence (eg at a roll-call), to acknowledge an order or request, etc (*inf, esp* US).
□ **yo-hō'** or **yo-hō-hō'** interj calling for attention; (also **yo-heave-hō'**) formerly, a sailors' chant while hauling on ropes.

---

yob /yob/ (*sl*) *n* a lout; a teenage loafer; a raw recruit. [Back-slang for **boy**]
■ **yobb'ery** *n* yobbish behaviour. **yobb'ish** *adj.* **yobb'ishly** *adv.* **yobb'ism** *n* yobbish behaviour. **yobb'o** *n* (*pl* **yobb'os** or **yobb'oes**) (*sl*) a yob.

yock see **yok**.

yocto- /yok-tō-/ *combining form* denoting 10^{-24}. [Altered from L *octo* eight (this being the eighth power of 10^{-3})]

yod[1] /yod/ *n* the tenth letter of the Hebrew alphabet. [Heb]

yod[2] or **yode** see **yead**.

yodel or **yodle**, also **jodel** /yō'dl/ (**yo'delling** or (*N Am*) **yo'deling**, etc; **yo'delled** or (*N Am*) **yo'deled**, etc) *vt* and *vi* to sing or shout, changing frequently from the ordinary voice to falsetto and back again. ◆ *n* a song or phrase sung, or a cry made, in this fashion. [Ger dialect *jodeln*]
■ **yō'deller**, **yō'dler** or (*N Am*) **yō'deler** *n*.

yoga /yō'gə/ *n* a system of Hindu philosophy showing the means of emancipating the soul from further reincarnations and uniting it with the supreme being; any of a number of systems of physical and mental disciplines based on this, such as hatha yoga (see below) or raja yoga (qv under **raj**); the practice of yogic exercises prescribed in such a system. [Sans, union]
■ **yō'gi** /-gē/ or **yō'gin** *n* (also *fem* **yōgi'ni**) a person who practises the yoga system, consisting in the withdrawal of the senses from external objects, the holding of special postures or asanas for long periods of time, etc. **yō'gic** *adj.* **yō'gism** *n*.
❑ **yogic flying** *n* in transcendental meditation, a form of levitation.
■ **hatha yoga** /hath'ə or hut'ə/ (Sans *haṭha* force) a form of yoga stressing the importance of physical exercises and positions and breathing-control in promoting physical and mental wellbeing.

Yogalates® /yō-gə-lä'tēz/ *n* an exercise system that combines elements of *yoga* and P*ilates*.

yogh /yohh/ *n* the Middle English letter ȝ, derived from Old English ȝ, representing especially *y* and *hh* sounds. [Origin uncertain, but appropriate as exemplifying the two chief sounds of the letter]

yoghurt, **yoghourt** or **yogurt** /yog'ərt or yō'gərt/ *n* a semi-liquid food made from fermented milk (also **yaourt** /yä'oort/). [Turk *yōghurt*]

yogi, **yogin**, etc see under **yoga**.

yohimbine /yo-him'bēn/ *n* an alkaloid obtained from the bark of *Corynanthe johimbe*, a W African rubiaceous tree. [Of Bantu origin]

yoicks /yoiks/ *interj* an old foxhunting cry.
■ **yoick** or **yoicks** *vi* or *vt* to make, or urge on by, this cry.

yojan /yō'jan/ or **yojana** /yō'ja-nə/ *n* an Indian measure of distance, *usu* about eight or nine miles. [Hindi *yojan*, from Sans *yojana* (distance covered in one) yoking]

yok or **yock** /yok/ (*theatre sl*) *n* a laugh (also *vi*). [Imit]

yoke /yōk/ *n* something that joins together; a frame of wood joining draught oxen at the necks; any similar frame, such as one for carrying pails; a part of a garment that fits the shoulders (or the hips); a period of work, eg from mealtime to mealtime (*dialect*); a mark of servitude; slavery; an oppressive burden; a bond or union; a pair or couple, eg of oxen; a set of current coils for deflecting the electron beam in a TV or VDU cathode-ray tube; part of a magnetic circuit not enclosed by a current-carrying coil; an object, a thing, a tool, etc (*Irish*). ◆ *vt* to put a yoke on; to join together; to attach a draught animal to; to enslave; to set to work (*fig*). ◆ *vi* to be joined; to go together; to set to work (*Scot*). [OE *geoc*; Ger *Joch*; L *jugum*, Gr *zygon*]
■ **yōk'ing** *n* (*dialect*) as much work as is done at one time.
❑ **yoke'-devil** *n* (*Shakesp*) a companion devil. **yoke'-fellow** or **yoke'-mate** *n* an associate, partner or fellow worker. **yoke'-toed** *adj* zygodactyl.

yokel /yō'kl/ *n* a country bumpkin. [Ety doubtful]
■ **yō'kelish** *adj.*

yokozuna /yō-kə-zoo'nə/ *n* in sumo wrestling, a grand champion. [Jap, from *yoko* across, and *tsuma* rope, from the garland orig presented to a champion]

yokul see **jokol**.

yold an obsolete *pat* and *pap* of **yield**.

yoldring /yōld'ring/ *n* a yellowhammer. [Variant of dialect *yowlring*, from OE *geolu*; see **yellowhammer** under **yellow**]

yolk[1] /yōk/ or (*obs* or *dialect*) **yelk** /yelk/ *n* the yellow part of the egg of a bird or reptile; the nutritive non-living material contained by an ovum. [OE *geolca*, from *geolu* yellow]
■ **yoiked** or **yolk'y** *adj* like yolk.
❑ **yolk sac** *n* (*zool*) the yolk-containing sac which is attached to the embryo by the **yolk stalk**, a short stalk by means of which yolk substance may pass into the alimentary canal of the embryo.

yolk[2] /yōk/ *n* wool oil, lanolin (cf **suint**). [OE *ēowocig* yolky]
■ **yolk'y** *adj.*

yolo *abbrev*: you only live once.

Yom Kippur /yom ki-poor' or kip'ər/ *n* the Day of Atonement, a Jewish fast-day. [Heb *yōm* day, and *kippūr* atonement]

yomp /yomp/ (*esp milit sl*) *vi* to carry heavy equipment on foot over difficult terrain; (loosely, often *facetious*) to walk or trek in a determined, dogged or laboured manner, *esp* heavily laden. ◆ *n* such a walk or trek. [Poss imit]

Yom Tob /yōm tōb/ or **Tov** /tōv/ *n* any Jewish religious festival. [Heb *yōm* day, and *tōbh* good]

yon /yon/ (now *poetic*, *Scot* or *dialect*) *adj* that; those; yonder. ◆ *pronoun* that; the thing you know of. ◆ *adv* yonder. [OE *geon* (adj, pronoun), *geond* (prep and adv), and ME *yonder*]
■ **yond** *prep* (*Scot usu* **yont**) across or through (*obs*); to, or in, a position beyond. ◆ *adj* and *pronoun* yon. ◆ *adv* yonder. **yon'der** *adv* to, or at, a distance but within view. ◆ *adj* that or those at a distance within view (actually or theoretically); (with *the*) farther, more distant. ◆ *pronoun* that one, yon. ◆ *n* (with *the*) the distance, distant places. **yon'derly** *adj* (*dialect*) mentally or emotionally distant, vague, absent-minded; mentally or physically weak or low (*archaic*).
■ **hither and yon**, or **yond** (*dialect*) hither and thither. **hither** (or **here**) **and yonder** hither and thither.

yond /yond/ (*Spenser*) *adj* furious, mad. [Said to be due to misunderstanding of a passage in an earlier writer; Chaucer's *Clerk's Tale* 1143 has been suggested, but 16c black-letter editions of Chaucer do not have the word in this line]

yonder see under **yon**.

yongthly same as **youngthly** (see under **young**).

yoni /yō'nē/ *n* the female genitals; a representation of these, the symbol under which the Hindu goddess Sakti is worshipped. [Sans]

yonker obsolete form of **younker**.

yonks /yongks/ (*inf*) *n pl* ages, a long time. [Poss years, months and weeks; or perh compressed from *donkey's years*]

yont see **yon**.

yoof /yoof/ (*inf*; *usu derog*) *n* youth, young people. ◆ *adj* (*esp* of magazines, TV or radio programmes, etc) relating to, specifically aimed at, pandering to, or dealing with topics (thought to be) of interest to modern youth. [**youth**, with *f* substituted for *th* as in certain forms of London speech]

yoo-hoo /yoo'hoo/ *interj* a call to attract someone's attention.

yoop /yoop/ *n* and *interj* (representing) a sobbing sound.

YOP /yop/ *abbrev*: Youth Opportunities Programme.

yore /yōr or yör/ (*obs* or *poetic*) *adv* long ago. ◆ *n* and *adj* (of or relating to) time long ago or long past. [OE *gēara* formerly; appar connected with *gēar* a year]
■ **days of yore** times past. **of yore** in times past.

yorker /yör'kər/ (*cricket*) *n* a ball bowled so as to pitch on the popping crease and pass under the bat. [Prob from *Yorkshire*, but history quite unknown]
■ **york** *vt* to bowl (or attempt to bowl) someone out with a yorker.

Yorkie /yör'ki/ (*inf*; also without *cap*) *n* a Yorkshire terrier.

Yorkish /yör'kish/ *adj* of, from or relating to the city of *York*; of or from the county of Yorkshire (*archaic*); supporting the House of York in the Wars of the Roses (*hist*).
■ **York'ist** *n* (*hist*) a supporter of the House of York (also *adj*). **York'shire** *adj* of or from the area comprising the historic county of Yorkshire in N England. ◆ *n* any of a breed of animal, *esp* pigs, originating in Yorkshire.
❑ **Yorkshire fog** *n* a tall grass, *Holcus lanatus*. **Yorkshire grit** *n* a grit from Yorkshire used for polishing. **Yorkshire pudding** *n* a pudding made of unsweetened batter, and baked along with meat or in meat dripping (*orig* under the spit so as to catch the drippings). **Yorkshire terrier** *n* a small long-haired kind of terrier.

Yorks. *abbrev*: Yorkshire.

Yoruba /yo'roo-bə or yō'-/ *n sing* and *n pl* a people of coastal W Africa; a member of this people; their language. ◆ *adj* of or relating to the Yoruba or their language.

yotta- /yot-ə-/ *combining form* denoting 10^{24}. [Altered from L *octo* eight (this being the eighth power of 10^3)]

you /ū/ *pronoun* the second person pronoun, *orig* only plural (cf **thou**[1]), now both singular and plural; (*indefinite pronoun*) anyone; the personality (or something in tune with the personality) of the person addressed (*inf*). [OE *ēow* (perh through a later form *eōw*), orig only dative and accusative; cf **ye**[1]]
❑ **you-all'** *pronoun* (*US*; *esp* Southern) you (*esp* in addressing two or more people). **you'-know-what'**, **you'-know-who'** *n* some unspecified but well-understood or well-known thing or person.

---

you'd /ūd or yŭd/ a contraction of **you had** or **you would**.

youk see **yuke**.

you'll /ūl or yŭl/ a contraction of **you will** or **you shall**.

young /yung/ adj (**younger** /yung'gər/; **youngest** /yung'gist/) born recently; in early life; in the first part of growth; youthful; vigorous; relating to youth; junior, the younger of two persons having the same name; inexperienced; newly arrived; miniature (inf). ◆ n the offspring of animals; (with the) those who are young. [OE geong; Ger jung; also connected with L juvenis, Sans yuvan young]

■ **youngish** /yung'ish or yung'gish/ adj fairly young. **young'ling** n (archaic) a young person or animal. ◆ adj youthful, young. **young'ly** adv (rare) in youth; in the manner of youth. **young'ness** n. **young'ster** n a young person, esp a young man, or (formerly) a lively young man; a child (inf). **youngth** n (Spenser) youth. **youngth'ly** adj (Spenser) youthful.

❑ **young adult offender** n (law) a lawbreaker aged between 18 and 21. **young blood** n a fresh accession of strength, personnel, ideas, etc. **Young England** n during the Corn-Laws struggle (1842–45), a small band of young Tory politicians who hated Free Trade and Radicalism, and professed a sentimental attachment to earlier forms of social life in England. **Young Britain, America**, etc n the rising generation in Britain, America, etc. **young'-eyed** adj (Shakesp) with the bright eyes of youth. **young fogy** or **fogey** n a young person with (esp vociferously proffered) conservative or reactionary opinions. **young fō'gyish** or **fō'geyish** adj. **young fustic** see under **fustic**. **young gun** n (inf) an enthusiastic and dynamic young person. **Young Ireland** n a group of Irish nationalists who broke away from O'Connell about 1844, because of his strong objection to the use of physical force. **Young Italy** n an association of Italian republican agitators, active about 1834, under the lead of Mazzini. **young lady** or **young man** n a girlfriend or boyfriend, a sweetheart. **young offender** n a lawbreaker aged between 10 and 21 (**young offender institution** an establishment, replacing the borstal, for the detention of young offenders who are given custodial sentences). **young person** n someone aged fourteen and over, but under eighteen (law); in Factory Acts, etc, a person who is under eighteen years of age but no longer a child. **Young Turk** n any of a body of Turkish reformers who brought about the revolution of 1908; (also without caps) a progressive, rebellious, impetuous, etc member of an organization.

■ **with young** (of an animal) pregnant.

youngberry /yung'ber-i or -bə-ri/ n a large reddish-black fruit, a cross between a variety of blackberry and a variety of dewberry. [BM Young, an early-20c US fruit-grower, and **berry**[1]]

Young modulus /yung mod'ū-ləs/ or **Young's modulus** /yungz/ n the coefficient of elasticity of stretching, ie for a stretched wire, the ratio of the stretching force per unit cross-sectional area to the elongation per unit length. [Thomas Young (1773–1829), English physicist]

younker /yung'kər/ n a young person (old); a young gentleman or knight (Spenser). [ODu jonckher (Du jonker), from jong heer young master or lord; Ger Junker]

your /yör or ūr/ pronoun (genitive pl) or possessive adj of or belonging to you; used to denote a person or thing of a particular well-known class or type, the typical or ordinary (usu implying some contempt; inf); of or relating to an unspecified person or people in general. [OE ēower, genitive of gē ye]

■ **yourn** pronoun (dialect) yours. **yours** pronoun (the one or ones) belonging to you; (used in correspondence) short for 'your letter'.
■ **you and yours** you and your family or property. **yours faithfully, sincerely, truly**, etc, **yours to command**, etc forms used conventionally in letters just before the signature. **yours truly** (inf) also sometimes used by a speaker to mean himself or herself.

you're /yör or ūr/ a contraction of **you are**.

yourself /ūr-self' or yör-/ pronoun (pl **yourselves'**) the emphatic form of **you**; in your real character; having command of your faculties; sane; in good form; the reflexive form of **you** (objective); often used colloquially and incorrectly instead of **you** (unreflexive second person singular).

yourt see **yurt**.

youse /ūz/ pronoun a dialect form of **you** used chiefly to address more than one person.

youth /ūth/ n the state of being young; early life, the period immediately following childhood; an early period of existence; a young person, esp a young man (pl **youths** /yoodhz/); young persons collectively; recentness, freshness (Shakesp). [OE geoguth, from geong young; Ger Jugend]

■ **youth'ful** adj relating to youth or early life; young; suitable to youth; fresh; buoyant, vigorous. **youth'fully** adv. **youth'fulness** n. **youth'head** or **youth'hood** n (obs) youth. **youth'ly** adj (Spenser) young, youthful (also adv). **youth'some** adj (obs) youthful. **youth'y** adj (Scot) young.

❑ **youth club** n a place or organization providing leisure activities for young people. **youth court** n a special court for the trial of young offenders. **youth credit** n a voucher issued to young people who are not in full-time education, exchangeable for training or part-time education. **youth custody** n a custodial sentence of between four and eighteen months passed on a person aged between 15 and 21. **youth hostel** n a hostel where hikers, etc who are members of the Youth Hostels Association or a related organization find inexpensive and simple accommodation. ◆ vi to stay in youth hostels. **youth hosteller** n. **youth leader** n a social worker who works with the young people of a particular community or area. **Youth Opportunities Programme** n a government-sponsored scheme introduced in 1978, giving work experience to unemployed young people, replaced in 1983 by the **Youth Training Scheme** a similar government-sponsored scheme to give training and job experience to unemployed school-leavers, which was itself phased out in the 1990s.

you've /ūv or yŭv/ a contraction of **you have**.

yow or **yowe** /yow/ (Scot and dialect) n a variant of **ewe**.

yowie[1] /yow'i/ (Scot) n a little ewe.

yowie[2] /yow'i/ (Aust folklore) n a tall, apelike monster of SE Australia. [Aboriginal word yuwi]

yowl /yowl/ vi (of eg a dog) to cry mournfully; to yell or bawl. ◆ n a cry of distress. [ME youlen; cf ON gaula to howl]

■ **yowl'ing** n a howling.

yowley same as **yoldring**.

yo-yo /yō'yō/ n a toy consisting of a reel wound with an attached length of string which is held in the hand while the reel is dropped to fall and rise under its own weight, similar to the 18c bandalore or quiz; any person or thing resembling a yo-yo in movement or ease of manipulation; an indecisive or useless person, a fool (sl; orig US). ◆ vi to operate a yo-yo; to move rapidly up and down; to fluctuate rapidly or be very unsettled. ◆ adj of or resembling a yo-yo; rising and falling, or fluctuating from one position or extreme to the other, esp rapidly or without due control (as in yo-yo economy, yo-yo dieting). [Manufacturer's trademark, appar from a Filipino word]

ypight /i-pīt'/ an obsolete pap of **pitch**[1].

yplast /i-pläst'/ an obsolete pap of **place**.

yplight /i-plīt'/ an obsolete pap of **plight**[1,2].

ypsilon /ip-sī'lon, -sē' or ip'si-/ (rare) n same as **upsilon**. [Ety as for **upsilon**]

■ **ypsiliform** /-sil'/ or **ypsiloid** /ip'sil-oid/ adj shaped like an upsilon.

yr abbrev : year; younger; your.

yrapt /i-rapt'/ (Spenser) same as **rapt**.

yravished /i-rav'i-shid/ (emendation of Shakespeare's iranyshed proposed by Edmond Malone) obsolete pat of **ravish**.

yrent /i-rent'/ an obsolete pap of **rend**.

yrivd /i-rīvd'/ an obsolete pap of **rive**.

yrs abbrev : years; yours.

ysame /i-sām'/ (Spenser) adv together. [Perh **in** and **same** (noun)]

yshend /i-shend'/ (Spenser) same as **shend**.

yslaked /i-slākt'/ obsolete pap of **slake**[1]; quenched or relaxed the energies of (Shakesp).

YT abbrev : Yukon Territory (Canada).

yt (obs) abbrev : that (see **Y** (n)).

ytd abbrev : year to date.

ythundered /i-thun'də-rid/ (Spenser) pap struck by a thunderbolt.

ytost /i-tost'/ (Spenser) pap of **toss**.

Y-track see under **Y** (n).

YTS abbrev : Youth Training Scheme.

ytterbium /i-tûr'bi-əm/ n a metallic element (symbol Yb; atomic no 70), a member of the rare-earth group; the name orig given to a substance later shown to consist of a mixture of this and lutetium. [From Ytterby, Sweden, where it was discovered]

■ **ytter'bia** n ytterbium oxide (Yb_2O_3).

yttrium /it'ri-əm/ n a metallic element (symbol Y; atomic no 39) in the third group of the periodic system, usu classed with the rare earths. [From Ytterby; see ety for **ytterbium**]

■ **ytt'ria** n its oxide (Y_2O_3), a yellowish-white powder. **ytt'ric** or **ytt'rious** adj. **yttrif'erous** adj.

❑ **ytt'roce'rite** n a rare mineral, usu violet in colour, found embedded in quartz, a fluoride of yttrium, cerium, etc. **yttro-col'umbite** or **yttro-tan'talite** n a brownish mineral found at Ytterby, a tantalate of yttrium, iron, calcium, etc.

Y2K /wī-too-kā'/ n and adj (of or relating to) the year 2000, esp in connection with the millennium bug (qv). [Year and 2K, symbol for two thousand]

yu /yū or ū/ n (also **yu'-stone**) precious jade (nephrite or jadeite). [Chin yù jade, yùshī jade-stone]

yuan /yū-än'/ n (pl **yuan**) the standard monetary unit of the People's Republic of China (100 fen) (also called **renminbi**). [Chin yuán]

yucca or **yuca** /yuk'ə/ n (usu **yuca**) cassava; any plant of the genus Yucca of plants of the family Liliaceae, native to Mexico, New Mexico, etc, some (such as Yucca gloriosa, the Spanish dagger) cultivated in gardens on account of their splendid appearance. [Of Carib origin]

yuck¹ or **yuk** /yuk/ (inf) n unpleasantly messy or disgusting material; sickly sweet sentimentality. ◆ interj expressing extreme distaste or disgust. [Imit]
■ **yucky** or **yukky** /yuk'i/ adj unpleasantly messy or disgusting; sickly sentimental.

yuck² see **yuke**.

yucker /yuk'ər/ n the American flicker or golden-winged woodpecker. [Imit of its note]

yucky¹ see under **yuck¹**.

yucky² see under **yuke**.

yuft /yuft/ n Russia leather. [Russ]

yuga /ū'gə/ n any of the four Hindu ages of the world (also **yug**). [Sans]

Yugoslav (also obs **Yugo-Slav**) /ū'gō-släv or -gə-, -släv'/ n a native, citizen or inhabitant of Yugoslavia in SE Europe; one of the southern group of Slavs consisting of Serbs, Croats and Slovenes; the Serbo-Croat language (see under **Serb**; rare). ◆ adj of or relating to the Yugoslavs. [Serbo-Croat jugo-, from jug the south, and Slav]
■ **Yugoslav'ian** and **Yugoslav'ic** adj and n. —Also (old) **Jugoslav**, **Jugo-Slav**, etc.

yuk and **yukky** see **yuck¹**.

yukata /ū-kat'ə/ n a light kimono, usu of printed cotton, worn as a bathrobe or housecoat. [Jap, from yu hot water, bath, and kata(bira) light kimono]

yuke /ūk/ or **yuck** /yuk/ (dialect) vi to itch. ◆ n itching; the itch. —Also spelt **youk**, **yeuk**, **euk** or **ewk**. [Same as **itch**; prob influenced by the MDu form jeuken]
■ **yuk'y** or **yuck'y** adj itchy.

yuko /ū'kō/ n a score worth five points, awarded in judo for a throw or hold not worthy of waza-ari. [Jap]

yulan /ū'lan/ n a Chinese magnolia, producing large white flowers. [Chin yùlán]

Yule /ūl/ (old or dialect) n the season or feast of Christmas (also **yule**). [OE gēol Yule, se ǣrra gēola December; ON jōl]
❏ **Yule log** n a chocolate cake shaped and decorated to resemble a log, eaten at Christmas-time; orig a log cut down in the forest, dragged to the house, and set alight in celebration of Christmas. **Yule'tide** n the time or season of Yule or Christmas (also **yule'tide**).

yum and **yummy** see **yum-yum**.

yump² see **yumpie**.

yumpie or **Yumpie** /yum'pi/, also **yump** /yump/ (inf) n one of the young upwardly-mobile people, an earlier designation for the people now known as yuppies.

yum-yum /yum'yum'/ or **yum** /yum/ (inf) interj expressing delight or pleasant anticipation, esp of delicious food. [Imit]
■ **yumm'y** interj yum-yum. ◆ adj delicious; attractive.
❏ **yummy mummy** n (inf) an attractive or glamorous mother.

yunx /yungks/ n a variant of **Jynx**.

yup /yup or yəp/ same as **yep**.

Yupik /ū'pik/ n sing and n pl a people inhabiting the W Alaskan coast and parts of Siberia, speaking an Eskimo-Aleut language; a member of this people; their language. ◆ adj of or relating to the Yupik or their language. [From the root of juk a person, the Yupik equivalent of inuk (see ety of **Inuit**)]

yupon see **yaupon**.

yuppie or **yuppy** /yup'i/ n (also with cap) a young urban professional (or upwardly-mobile person), a dismissive designation for the young city careerist. ◆ adj characteristic of, or reflecting the aspirations of, yuppies.
■ **yupp'iedom** n the state of being a yuppie; the world or circles which yuppies frequent. **yuppificā'tion** n. **yupp'ify** vt to adapt (esp a particular locality or a particular venue) to suit the taste of yuppies; to make popular with, typical of, or suitable for yuppies.
❏ **yuppie flu** n (inf) a derogatory name for chronic fatigue syndrome.

yurt or **yourt** /yûrt or ūrt/ n a light conical tent of skins etc, supported by posts, used by nomads in Siberia and Mongolia. [From Russ]

yuzu /ū'zoo/ n a small E Asian citrus tree (Citrus junos); its bitter-tasting fruit. [Jap]

YV abbrev : Venezuela (IVR).

YWCA abbrev : Young Women's Christian Association.

ywis see **iwis**.

ywroke see **wreak¹**.

■ words derived from main entry word; ❏ compound words; ■ idioms and phrasal verbs

Zz

Z or **z** /zed/ n the twenty-sixth and last letter in the modern English alphabet, twenty-third in the Roman, derived through the Greek *zeta* (Z, ζ), from *zayin*, the seventh letter of the Semitic alphabet; anything shaped like the letter Z, as in **Z'-bend** a series of sharp bends in a road. —Z is sounded as a voiced sibilant, either a voiced *s*, as in 'zeal', or a voiced *sh*, as in 'azure'. It is used in Scots to represent ME (the letter yogh), as in *capercailzie*, but now sometimes pronounced as a *z*, as in the English pronunciation of the Scottish family name *Menzies* /men'ziz/ (as opposed to the Scottish /ming'iz/). □ **z'-axis** n (*maths*) in a three-dimensional graph, the vertical axis at right angles to the x-axis and y-axis, along which the z-coordinate is plotted. **Z boson** same as **Z particle** below. **Z'-DNA** n a form of duplex DNA, in which purines and pyrimidines alternate in a strand, resulting in a left-handed helix. **Z'-list** adj (*inf*) belonging to the least important or famous group (of would-be celebrities, etc). **Z'-lister** n. **Z particle** n (*phys*) a subatomic particle that mediates weak interaction.

Z or **Z.** abbrev : Zambia (IVR); zetta-.

Z symbol : (as a medieval Roman numeral) 2000; (also **z** or *z*) the third variable, unknown or yet to be ascertained quantity or factor in a series, after X and Y (or **x, y** or *x, y*) (*maths*, etc).

Z symbol : atomic number (*chem*); impedance (*phys*).

Ž symbol : (medieval Roman numeral) 2 000 000.

z or **z.** abbrev : zenith; zepto-; zero; zone.

z symbol : used as a contraction-mark, as in *viz*, *oz*, etc.

ZA abbrev : South Africa (ie *Zuid Afrika* ; IVR).

za'atar /zä'tär/ n a mixture of herbs and spices, *incl* thyme, sesame and cumin, used in Middle Eastern cookery. [Ar, thyme]

zabaglione /zä-bäl-yō'ni/ n a frothy custard made from egg yolks, marsala and sugar (also **zabaione** /-bə-yō'ni/ or (*Fr*) **sabayon** /sa-bī-yõ/). [Ital]

zabeta /za-bē'ta/ (*Arab*) n a stated tariff.

Zabian /zā'bi-ən/ adj and n same as **Sabian**.

zabra /zä'brä/ (*hist*) n a small vessel used off the Spanish coast. [Sp]

zabtieh see **zaptieh**.

zack /zak/ (*old Aust sl*) n formerly a sixpenny, now a five-cent, piece.

zaddik, **tsaddik**, **tsaddiq**, **tzaddik** or **tzaddiq**, /tsad'ik/ n (*pl* **zaddikim**, etc or **zadd'iks**, etc) in Judaism, a Hasidic leader, or person of extraordinary piety. [Heb *saddīq* righteous or just]

Zadkiel /zad'ki-əl/ n the name assumed by Richard James Morrison (1794–1874), compiler of a popular astrological almanac.

zaffre or **zaffer** /zaf'ər/ n the impure oxide (used as a pigment) obtained by partially roasting cobalt ore previously mixed with two or three times its weight of fine sand. [Fr *zafre*, of Ar origin]

zaftig /zaf'tig/ or **zoftig** /zof'/ adj (of a woman) attractively full-figured. [Yiddish, from Ger *saftig* juicy]

zag /zag/ n a new line, or sharp change, of direction on a zigzag course (also *vi* (**zagg'ing**; **zagged**)). [-zag extracted from **zigzag**]

zaibatsu /zī-bat'soo/ n a large business or industrial group in Japan. [Jap *zai* wealth, and *batsu* clique]

zaire /zä-ēr'/ n (*pl* **zaire'**) the unit of currency formerly used in *Zaire* (now the Democratic Republic of Congo). ■ **Zairean** /-ē'ri-ən/ adj of or relating to Zaire. ◆ n a native or citizen of Zaire.

zaitech /zī'tek/ n the commercial practice of investing in financial markets to augment a company's normal business earnings. [Jap *zai* wealth, *teku* tech(nology)]

zakat /za-kät'/ n in Islam, a tax of 2½ per cent payable by Muslims on certain kinds of property, the money so raised being devoted to religious and charitable purposes. [Pers, from Ar *zakāh*]

zakuska /zä-koos'ka/ n (*pl* **zakuski** /-kē/) an hors-d'œuvre; a snack. [Russ]

zalambdodont /za-lam'dō-dont/ adj having molar teeth with V-shaped ridges, as some Insectivora do (also *n*). [Gr *za-* very, *lambda* the letter Λ (=L) and *odous*, *odontos* a tooth]

Zalophus /zal'ō-fəs/ n a genus of eared seals. [Gr *za-* (intensive), and *lophos* a crest]

zaman /zə-män'/ or **zamang** /zə-mäng'/ n the saman or rain tree. [Carib]

zamarra /thä-mä'rä/ or **zamarro** /-rō/ (*Sp*) n (*pl* **zamarr'as** or **zamarr'os**) a shepherd's sheepskin coat.

Zambian /zam'bi-ən/ adj of or relating to the republic of *Zambia* in central Africa. ◆ n a native or citizen of Zambia.

zambo /zam'bō/ n (*pl* **zam'bos**) same as **sambo¹**. [Sp; see **sambo¹**]

zambomba /thäm-bom'bä/ n a simple Spanish musical instrument, made by stretching a piece of parchment over a wide-mouthed jar and inserting a stick in it, sounded by rubbing the stick with the fingers. [Sp]

Zamboni® /zam-bō'ni/ n a proprietary name for a machine used to clean, resurface and smooth the ice at skating rinks, ice hockey arenas, etc. [Frank J *Zamboni* (1901–88), its American inventor]

zamboorak see **zumbooruk**.

zambuk or **zambuck** /zam'buk/ (*NZ* and *Aust inf*; also with *cap*) n a member of the St John's Ambulance Brigade, *esp* one on duty at a sporting event. [The proprietary name of an antiseptic ointment]

zamia /zā'mi-ə/ n a plant of the *Zamia* genus of palm-like trees or low shrubs of the family Cycadaceae, some species of which yield an edible starchy pith. [Named through misreading in Pliny *azaniae nuces*, pine cones that open on the tree, from Gr *azanein* or *azainein* to dry]

zamindar, **zamindari** and **zamindary** see **zemindar**.

zamouse /za-moos'/ n the short-horned buffalo of W Africa. [Ar *jāmūs*]

zampogna /tsam-pō'nyä/ n the Italian bagpipe. [Ital]

zampone /tsam-pō'nē/ n (*pl* **zampō'ni**) a stuffed pig's trotter, traditionally eaten at Christmas in Italy. [Ital, augmentative of *zampa* paw]

zanamivir /zä-nam'i-vēr/ n a drug used in the treatment of influenza.

zander /zan'dər/ or **sander** /san'/ n a species of pike-perch, *Stizostedion lucioperca*, a food-fish. [Ger]

zanella /zə-nel'ə/ n a mixed twilled fabric for covering umbrellas. [Origin uncertain]

zanja /thäng'hhä/ n in Latin America, an irrigating canal. [Am Sp, from Sp, ditch, trench] ■ **zanjero** /-hhä'rō/ n (*pl* **zanje'ros**) someone who superintends the distribution of water in irrigation canals.

Zantac® /zan'tak/ n a drug used in the treatment of ulcers.

zante /zan'tē/ n (also **zan'te-wood**) the wood of the European smoke tree, from *Zante*, one of the principal Ionian Islands; satinwood. ■ **Zan'tiot** /-ot/ or **Zan'tiote** /-ōt/ n a native or citizen of Zante. □ **Zante currant** the small seedless fruit of a Zante grape.

zantedeschia /zan-ti-des'ki-ə/ n a plant of the *Zantedeschia* genus of the arum family (Araceae), including *Zantedeschia aethiopica*, known as the calla lily. [Giovanni *Zantedeschi* (1773–1846), Italian botanist]

zanthoxyl same as **xanthoxyl** (see under **xanth-**).

Zantiot or **Zantiote** see under **zante**.

Zantippe see **Xantippe**.

ZANU /zä'noo/ abbrev : Zimbabwe African National Union (also **Za'nu**).

ZANU-PF abbrev : Zimbabwe African National Union-Patriotic Front.

zany /zā'ni/ adj clownish, amusingly eccentric (*inf*); of or relating to a zany; crazy. ◆ n someone who plays the fool (*inf*); an assistant clown

---

or buffoon (*hist*); a toady (*obs*); a simpleton (*dialect*). ◆ *vt* (*obs*) to play the zany to. [Fr *zani*, from Ital *zanni*, the Venetian form of *Gianni*, *Giovanni* John, a name given to comic servant characters in the commedia dell'arte]
■ **zā'niness** *n*. **zā'nyism** *n* the state of being, or the behaviour of, a buffoon.

zanze /zän'ze/ *n* an African musical instrument. [Ar *sanj* castanets or cymbals]

Zanzibari /zan-zi-bä'ri/ *n* a native or inhabitant of the island of Zanzibar in the Indian Ocean (also *adj*).

zap /zap/ (*inf*) *vt* (**zapp'ing**; **zapped**) to hit, strike, destroy, shoot, etc (*lit* and *fig*); to erase or correct (a fault) (*comput*); to cause to move or pass by quickly. ◆ *vi* to go speedily or suddenly (often with *off* or *along*); to keep changing television channels, using a remote-control device (*inf*). ◆ *n* vitality or force. ◆ *interj* expressing suddenness. [Imit]
■ **zapp'er** *n* (*inf*) a person who or thing that zaps, *esp* a remote-control device for a TV or video recorder or an electronic device for attracting and killing flying insects. **zapp'y** *adj* (*sl*) full of verve or punch, lively, energetic; speedy.
■ **zap** (**it**) **up** (*inf*) to make (things) livelier.

zapata /zə-pä'tə/ *adj* denoting a type of flowing moustache drooping down on each side of the mouth. [Emilio *Zapata* (1879–1919), Mexican revolutionary, who wore a moustache of this shape]

zapateado /thä-pä-te-ädh'ō/ *n* (*pl* **zapatead'os**) a lively Spanish dance for a solo performer, with a great deal of clicking and stamping of the heels. [Sp]

Zapatista /za-pa-tēs'tə/ *n* a member of the Zapatista National Liberation Army (Sp *Ejército Zapatista de Liberación Nacional*), a Mexican guerrilla movement fighting for the rights of the indigenous Maya people and greater democracy. [Emilio *Zapata* (1879–1919), Mexican revolutionary]

Zapodidae /za-pod'i-dē/ *n pl* the jumping mouse family. [Formed from Gr *za-* very, *pous*, *podos* foot, and sfx *-idae*]

Zaporogian /zä-pō-rō'ji-ən/ *adj* relating to or designating the Ukraine Cossacks dwelling near the Porogi or falls of the Dnieper. ◆ *n* a member of this people. [Russ *za* beyond, and *porogi* rapids]

Zapotec /zap'ə-tek/ *n* a member of a Native American people living in the Oaxaca area of Mexico, descendants of an advanced pre-Columbian civilization; the language of this people. ◆ *adj* of or relating to this people or their language. [Nahuatl *tzapotecatl* person from the place of the sapodilla]

zapotilla /zap-ō-til'ə/ *n* same as **sapodilla**.

zaptieh /zap'ti-e/ *n* a Turkish policeman (also **zap'tiah** or **zab'tieh**). [From Turk]

ZAPU /zä'poo/ *abbrev*: Zimbabwe African People's Union (also **Za'pu**).

zarape /sä-rä'pe/ *n* same as **serape**.

Zarathustrian /zar-ə-thoos'tri-ən/ *adj* and *n* (a) Zoroastrian. [*Zarathustra*, Avestan name for the founder of the religion]
■ **Zarathus'trianism** or **Zarathus'trism** *n* Zoroastrianism. **Zarathus'tric** *adj* and *n* Zoroastrian.

zaratite /zä'rə-tīt/ *n* a hydrous carbonate of nickel, found *usu* as an incrustation on chromite. [From the Spanish surname *Zárate*]

zareba, also **zareeba**, **zariba**, **zereba** or **zeriba** /zə-rē'bä/ *n* in Sudan, a stockade, thorn-hedge, etc protecting against wild animals or enemies; a fortified camp generally. [Ar *zarībah* a pen or enclosure for cattle]

zarf /zärf/ or **zurf** /zûrf/ *n* an ornamental holder for a hot coffee cup. [Ar *zarf* a vessel]

zari /zä'ri/ *n* a kind of embroidery using gold thread; the thread used in this. [Urdu, from Pers *zar* gold]

zarnich /zär'nik/ *n* a naturally occurring sulphide of arsenic, such as orpiment (arsenic trisulphide) or realgar (arsenic monosulphide) (also **zar'nec**). [Ar *zarnīkh*]

zarzuela /thär-thū-ā'lä or *-thwä'*/ *n* a traditional Spanish form of operetta or vaudeville; a Spanish fish and shellfish stew. [The royal residence of La *Zarzuela*, Madrid, where first performed]

zastruga /za-stroo'gä/ *n* (*pl* **zastru'gi** /-gē/) same as **sastruga**.

zati /zä'ti/ *n* the bonnet monkey.

zax a variant of **sax²**.

zayin /zä'yēn/ *n* the seventh letter of the Hebrew alphabet.

zazen /zä'zen/ *n* meditation practised in Zen Buddhism, *usu* in the lotus position. [Jap *za* sitting, and **Zen**]

z.B. *abbrev*: *zum Beispiel* (Ger), for example.

'zbud see **'sbodikins**.

Zea /zē'ə/ *n* a genus of cereals having monoecious flowers, the only species being *Zea mays*, maize; (without *cap*) the fresh styles and stigmas of this plant, formerly used as a diuretic. [Gr *zeā* or *zeia* one-seeded wheat]
■ **zē'atin** *n* a plant hormone that regulates growth, a type of cytokinin.

zeal /zēl/ *n* intense (sometimes fanatical) enthusiasm; activity arising from warm support or enthusiasm; strong feeling, such as love, anger, etc, or passionate ardour (*archaic*); a zealot (*obs*). [OFr *zele*, from L *zēlus*, from Gr *zēlos*, from *zeein* to boil]
■ **zeal'ant** or **zeal'ant** *n* (Bacon) a zealot. **zeal'ful** *adj*. **zeal'less** *adj*. **zealot** /zel'ət/ *n* an enthusiast; a fanatic; (with *cap*) a member of a militant Jewish sect vigorously opposing the Roman domination of Palestine until the ruin of Jerusalem in 70AD. **zealotism** /zel'/ *n* the character or actions of a zealot. **zealotry** /zel'/ *n*. **zealous** /zel'/ *adj* full of zeal; keenly engaged in, or ardent in support of, anything; devoted. **zealously** /zel'/ *adv*. **zealousness** /zel'/ *n*.

zeatin see under **Zea**.

zebec and **zebeck** variants of **xebec**.

zebra /zeb'rə or zē'brä/ *n* any of a group of striped animals of the genus *Equus*, all of which are peculiar to the African continent; (used, *esp* as *adj* in names, to denote) any animal, fish, plant or mineral having stripes reminiscent of a zebra's, such as the *zebra duiker* (a striped W African antelope), the *zebra finch* (see below), etc; a referee (having a striped shirt) in American football (*US sl*). [African]
■ **ze'brass** *n* the offspring of a male zebra and a female ass. **zē'brine** or **zē'broid** *adj*. **zebrinn'y** *n* (cf **hinny¹**) the offspring of a male horse and a female zebra. **ze'brule** or **ze'brula** *n* the offspring of a male zebra and a female horse.
❑ **zebra crossing** *n* a street crossing (marked with black-and-white stripes) where pedestrians have priority. **zebra finch** *n* an Australian weaver bird with black-and-white-striped markings. **zebra parakeet** *n* the budgerigar. **zebra plant** *n* a calathea with green and purple stripes in its leaves. **zebra spider** *n* any of several striped spiders of the Salticidae. **ze'brawood** *n* the hard and beautifully striped wood of a Guianan tree, *Connarus guianensis*; the tree itself; applied also to various other trees or their wood.

zebrina /ze-brī'nə/ *n* a trailing or creeping herbaceous plant of the Central American genus *Zebrina*, with pointed, ovate, striped leaves. [New L]

zebu /zē'bū or zē'boo/ *n* a humped domestic ox (*Bos indicus*) closely related to the common ox, found throughout the Indian subcontinent, China, the east coast of Africa, etc. [Fr *zebu*, the name taken by Buffon from the exhibitors of one at a French fair in 1752]

zebub /zē'bub/ *n* the zimb. [Ar (dialect) *zubāb* a fly]

zecchino /tsek-kē'nō/ *n* (*pl* **zecchi'nos** or **zecchi'ni** /-ē/) a former Italian gold coin (also called **zecchine** /zek'in/, **sequin**). [See **sequin**]

Zech. (*Bible*) *abbrev*: (the Book of) Zechariah.

Zechstein /zek'stīn/ (*geol*) *n* a deposit of calcareous rock, the higher of the two series into which the Permian system of Germany is divided. [Ger, from *Zeche* mine, and *Stein* stone]

zed /zed/, (US) **zee** /zē/ *n* the twenty-sixth letter of the modern English alphabet (Z or z); a bar of metal shaped like the letter Z. [Fr *zède*, from L and Gr *zēta*]

zedoary /zed'ō-ə-ri/ *n* certain species of *Curcuma*, native to the Indian subcontinent, China, etc, whose rootstocks are aromatic, bitter and pungent. [Through medieval L, from Ar *zedwār*]

zee /zē/ see **zed**.

Zeeman effect /zā'män i-fekt'/ (*phys*) *n* the splitting of a spectral line into several symmetrically disposed components which occurs when the source of light is placed in a strong magnetic field. [Dutch physicist Pieter *Zeeman* (1865–1943)]

zein /zē'in/ *n* a protein found in maize. [**Zea**]

zeitgeist /tsīt'gīst/ (also with *cap*) *n* the spirit of the age. [Ger]
■ **zeit'geisty** *adj*. [Ger]

Zeitvertreib /tsīt'fər-trīp/ (Ger) *n* a pastime.

zek /zek/ *n* an inmate of a prison or labour camp in the former USSR. [Russ slang, poss from abbrev *zk* for *zaklyuchënnyi* prisoner]

zel /zel/ *n* a form of Oriental cymbal. [Turk *zīl*]

Zelanian /zə-lā'ni-ən/ *adj* in zoogeography, of or relating to New Zealand.

zelant see under **zeal**.

zelophobia /zel-ō-fō'bi-ə/ *n* an irrational or morbid aversion to or fear of jealousy. [**zelotypia** and **phobia**]
■ **zelophō'bic** *adj* and *n*.

zeloso /ze-lō'sō/ (*music*) *adv* with fervour. [Ital]

zelotypia /zel-ō-tip'i-ə/ (*obs*) *n* jealousy; unhealthily excessive zeal in the carrying-out of any project or cause. [Gr *zēlotypiā* jealousy, from *zēlos* zeal, and *typtein* to strike]

zemindar /zem-in-där'/ or /zem'/ n (also **zamindar**) under the Mogul emperors of India, a tax farmer responsible for collecting revenue from land held in common by the cultivators; later, the actual native proprietor paying revenue direct, and not to any intermediate superior. [Hindi *zamīndār*, from Pers *zamīn* land, and *-dar* holder]

■ **zem'indari** or **zem'indary** n (also **zam'indari** or **zam'indary**) the jurisdiction of a zemindar; the system of land-tenure and taxation involving zemindars.

zemstvo /zems'tvō/ n (pl **zems'tvos** or **zems'tva**) in Russia, from 1864 until 1917, a district and provincial assembly to which the administration of certain of the affairs of the district and the province was committed. [Russ]

Zen /zen/ n an *orig* Japanese branch of Buddhism (with various sects) which holds that the truth is not in scriptures but in a person's own heart if they will only strive to find it by meditation and self-mastery (also *adj*). [Jap, from Chin *chán*, from Pali *jhāna* and Sans *dhyāna* religious contemplation]

■ **Zen'ic** *adj*. **Zen'ist** or **Zenn'ist** n.

zenana /ze-nä'nə/ n in India and Iran, etc, a part of a house in which women and girls are secluded, corresponding to the harem in Arabic-speaking Muslim countries. [Pers *zanāna*, from *zan* a woman]

□ **zenana mission** n a mission to women of the zenanas, necessarily conducted by women.

Zend /zend/ n the Avesta or Zend-Avesta; Avestan, the ancient East-Iranian Indo-European language in which the Zend-Avesta was orally preserved and finally written down, closely related to Vedic Sanskrit. [Pers *zend* or *zand* commentary]

□ **Zend-Aves'ta** n (properly meaning the Avesta with the commentary on it) the ancient sacred writings of the Parsees, including works of widely differing character and age, collected into their present canon under Shah-puhar or Shah-pur II (309–338AD).

zendik /zen'dik/ (*hist*) n in Middle-Eastern countries, an unbeliever in revealed religion, a heretic; someone who practises magic. [Ar *zendīq*]

Zener cards /zē'nər kärdz/ n pl a set of 25 cards, consisting of five sets of five, each set having one symbol, used in parapsychological experimentation. [Invented by KE *Zener* (1903–61), US psychologist]

Zener diode /zē'nər dī'ōd/ (*electronics*) n a type of semiconductor device, a diode whose sudden increase in reverse current makes it useful in voltage-limiting circuits. [CM *Zener* (1905–93), US physicist]

zenith /zen'ith or (N Am) zē'nith/ n the point on the celestial sphere vertically above the observer's head, one of the two poles of the horizon, the other being the nadir; the greatest height (*lit* and *fig*). [OFr *cenit* or *cenith*, ult from Ar *samt*, short for *samt-ar-ras*, literally, way or direction of the head]

■ **zen'ithal** *adj*.

□ **zenithal projection** n (*geog*) a type of map projection in which the plane of projection is tangential to the sphere. **zenith distance** n the angular distance of a heavenly body from the zenith. **zenith sector** n formerly, any of several instruments used for measuring zenith-distances.

Zeno's paradoxes /zē'nōz par'ə-dok-siz/ (*maths*) n pl four paradoxes designed to demonstrate that the supposition that motion actually occurs leads to logical dilemmas. [*Zeno* of Elea (c.490–c.420BC), Greek philosopher and mathematician]

Zentippe see **Xantippe**.

zeolite /zē'ō-līt/ n any of a large group of alumino-silicates of sodium, potassium, calcium and barium, containing very loosely held water which can be removed by heating and regained by exposure to a damp atmosphere. [Gr *zeein* to boil (in allusion to the fact that many swell up when heated with a blowpipe), and *lithos* a stone]

■ **zeolitic** /-lit'/ *adj*. **zeolit'iform** *adj*.

□ **zeolite process** n a water-softening process using zeolites (formerly zeolites occurring naturally, now synthetic ones).

Zeph. (*Bible*) *abbrev* : (Book of) Zephaniah.

zephyr /zef'ər/ n the west wind; a soft, gentle breeze (*poetic*); thin light worsted or woollen yarn; a shawl, jersey, or other garment made of such; any of various types of lightweight material, such as a gingham, a flannel with a silk warp, a thin woollen cloth, etc; anything very light and fine of its kind; (with *cap*) the god of the west wind. [Gr *Zephyros*, god of the west wind; related to *zophos* darkness, the west]

□ **zephyr lily** n a lily-like plant of the genus *Zephyranthes* (family Amaryllidaceae), *orig* from the warmer parts of N and S America.

zeppelin /zep'ə-lin/ (also with *cap*) n a dirigible, cigar-shaped airship of the type designed by the German aviation pioneer Count *Zeppelin* (c.1900).

zepto- /zep-tō-/ *combining form* denoting 10^{-21}. [Altered from L *septo* seven (this being the seventh power of 10^{-3})]

zerda /zûr'də/ n a fennec. [Ar *zardawa*]

zereba and **zeriba** see **zareba**.

Zernebock /zûr'nə-bok/ n Czerni Bog, an evil god of the Slavs, wrongly described by Scott in *Ivanhoe* as a god 'of the ancient Saxons'.

zero /zē'rō/ n (pl **zē'ros**) a cipher; nothing; the point from which the reckoning begins on scales, such as those of the barometer, etc; the lowest point (*fig*); zero hour; a worthless person (*inf*). ◆ *vt* (**zē'roing**; **zē'roed**) to set at or adjust to zero. ◆ *adj* having no measurable size, amount, etc; not any (*inf*). [Fr *zéro*, from Ar *sifr* ; cf **cipher**]

■ **zē'rōth** *adj* denoting a term in a series regarded as preceding the 'first' term.

□ **zero-base** (or **zero-based**) **budgeting** n a system in which the budget of an organization, department, etc is drawn up anew each year without reference to any previous budget. **zero-coupon bond** or **zero-dividend share** n (*stock exchange*) a bond, or share, that carries no interest, but has a redemption price higher than its issue price. **zero-emission vehicle** n a motor vehicle that does not emit polluting waste (*abbrev* **ZEV**). **zero fuel weight** n the weight of a loaded aircraft after all usable fuel has been consumed. **ze'ro-grazing** n a system of dairy farming in which the cattle are kept indoors and cut grass is brought to them, thus avoiding the wastage caused by conventional grazing. **zero hour** n the exact time (hour, minute and second) fixed for launching an attack or beginning an operation. **ze'ro-hour** or **ze'ro-hours contract** n an employment contract that requires a worker to be available at certain times but does not oblige the employer to offer him or her work. **zero option** n a proposal, *orig* made by President Reagan of the United States, to limit or abandon the deployment of (medium range) nuclear missiles if the opposing side does likewise; (loosely) a proposal to abandon or eliminate a particular range, category, division, etc. **ze'ro-point energy** n (*phys*) total energy at the absolute zero of temperature. **zero-power reactor** n a nuclear reactor, used for experimental purposes, in which there is no significant build-up of fission products and no cooling is required. **zē'ro-rate** *vt* to assess at a zero rate of value-added tax. **ze'ro-ra'ted** *adj* used of goods on which the purchaser pays no value-added tax and on which the seller can claim back any value-added tax already paid by him or her. **ze'ro-ra'ting** n. **ze'ro-sum** *adj* of a game, etc, in which the total cumulative gains equal the total cumulative losses. **zero tolerance** n total non-tolerance of something, *esp* a political or social wrong. **ze'ro-valent** *adj* (*chem*) incapable of combining with other atoms. **ze'ro-ze'ro** *adj* (*meteorol* and *aeronautics*) of conditions in which cloud ceiling and horizontal visibility are both zero. **zero-zero** (or sometimes **double zero**) **option** n a proposal which extends the zero option (qv above) to include also intermediate (300–600 mile) range missiles.

■ **absolute zero** see under **absolute**. **zero in** (**on**) (*inf*) to direct oneself straight towards (a target); to focus one's attention or energies on, as if on a target; to aim for or move towards.

zerumbet /zə-rum'bet or ze'/ n an E Asian plant of the ginger family. [Pers *zerunbād*]

zest /zest/ n enthusiasm; relish; piquancy; the thin outer layer of orange or lemon peel; orange or lemon peel, or the oil squeezed from it, used as a flavouring; anything that gives a relish. ◆ *vt* to give zest to. [Fr *zeste*, orig the woody thick skin quartering a walnut; origin obscure]

■ **zest'er** n a utensil scraped across the surface of an orange or lemon to remove the zest. **zest'ful** *adj*. **zest'fully** *adv*. **zest'fulness** n. **zest'y** *adj*.

ZETA or **Zeta** /zē'tə/ *abbrev* : zero-energy thermonuclear apparatus (formerly used in the study of controlled thermonuclear reactions), toroid in shape.

zeta¹ /zē'tə/ n the Greek z (Z, ζ); as a numeral ζ' = 7; ͵ζ = 7000.

zeta² /zē'tə/ (*hist*) n a small room or closet of some kind, as *perh* the sexton's room over a church porch. [Gr *diaita* a dwelling]

zetetic /ze-tet'ik/ *adj* proceeding by inquiry. ◆ n a search or investigation; a seeker, *specif* a Pyrrhonist. [Gr *zētētikos*, from *zēteein* to seek]

zetta- /zet-ə-/ *combining form* denoting 10^{21}. [Altered from L *septo* seven (this being the seventh power of 10^3)]

Zeuglodon /zū'glō-don/ n a genus of fossil whales, so named from the yoke-like double-rooted formation of their cheek teeth. [Gr *zeuglē* the strap or loop of the yoke, and *odous*, *-ontos* a tooth]

■ **zeug'lodont** *adj* and n. **Zeuglodon'tia** n pl a suborder of Cetacea, represented by the zeuglodonts.

zeugma /zūg' or zoog'mə/ n a figure of speech by which an adjective or verb is applied to two nouns, though strictly appropriate to only one of them. [Gr, from *zeugnynai* to yoke]

■ **zeugmat'ic** *adj*.

Zeus /zūs or zoos/ n the greatest of the ancient Greek gods, son of Kronos (Saturn) and Rhea, and consort of Hera, his supreme seat being Mount Olympus in Thessaly. [Gr]

Zeuxian /zūk' or zook'si-ən/ adj relating to Zeuxis, styled 'of Heraclea' and 'of Ephesus' (fl c.420–400BC), a Greek painter who excelled in accuracy of imitation of natural objects and in rendering types of sensuous beauty.

zeuxite /zūk'sīt/ n a ferriferous tourmaline. [Gr zeuxis joining, from zeugnynai to join]

ZEV abbrev : zero-emission vehicle.

zex /zeks/ (dialect) n a variant of **zax** or **sax**[2].

zeze /zā'zā/ n a stringed musical instrument resembling a zither, played in eastern and central Africa. [Swahili]

Zezidee see **Yezidi**.

zho /zhō/ n (also **zo**, **dso**, **dzho** or **dzo** /dzō/) a kind of hybrid domestic cattle found in parts of the Himalayas, said to be a cross between the male yak and the common horned cow; the male of this cross. [Tibetan mdzo].
■ **zhomo** /zhō'mō/ n (also **dsō'mo** or **jō'mo**) the female of this cross. **zō'bō** n (also **zō'bu** or **dsō'bō**) the male of this cross. —The plural of all spellings of all these words is formed by adding **-s**.

zhoosh /zhoosh/ (inf) vt (usu with up) to make more attractive. [Imit]

zibeline or **zibelline** /zib'ə-lin or -līn/ adj of or relating to the sable. ◆ n the fur of the sable; /zib'ə-lēn/ a soft woollen material with a lustrous pile. [Fr, from Ital zibellino, prob from Slav; cf **sable**[1]]

zibet /zib'it/ n an Asiatic civet. [Ital zibetto, from Ar zabād; cf **civet**]

zidovudine /zi-dō'vyū-dēn/ n the approved name of **AZT**. [From the chemical name, azidothymidine]

Ziegler catalyst /zē'glər kat'ə-list/ (chem) n a catalyst which induces specific steric orientation in polymer production. [Karl Ziegler (1898–1973), German chemist]

ziff /zif/ (old Aust and NZ sl) n a beard. [Ety unknown]

ziffius /zif'i-əs/ (Spenser) n a sea-monster, perh a swordfish. [Cf **Xiphias** and **Ziphius**]

ZIFT or **Zift** /zift/ abbrev : zygote intrafallopian transfer, a technique in which a fertilized egg is inserted into the recipient's fallopian tube.

zig /zig/ n a new line or sharp change of direction on a zigzag course (also vi (**zigg'ing**; **zigged**)). [zig- extracted from **zigzag**]

zigan /zi-gan'/ n a variant of **tzigany**.

ziganka /zi-gang'kə/ n a Russian country dance; the music for this, usu quick and with a drone bass. [Russ tsyganka a gypsy woman]

Zigeuner /tsi-goi'nər/ (Ger) n (pl **Zigeu'ner**) a gypsy.

ziggurat /zig'ŭ-rat/ n a temple-tower in ancient Mesopotamia, much like a pyramid in shape, consisting of a number of storeys each successive one of which was smaller than the one below it (also **zikkurat** /zik'/). [Assyrian ziqquratu a pinnacle, the top of a mountain]

zigzag /zig'zag/ n a short, sharp turning; a line, road, fence, moulding, etc with sharp angles to right and left alternately. ◆ adj having short, sharp alternate turns; bent from side to side alternately. ◆ vt (**zig'zagging**; **zig'zagged**) to form with short, alternate turns. ◆ vi to move forward making an alternation of short, sharp turns. ◆ adv with frequent sharp turns. [Fr zigzag; Ger Zickzack]
■ **zigzag'gery** n angular crookedness. **zig'zaggy** adj and adv zigzag. ❑ **zigzag stitch** n (sewing) a machine stitch worked in a zigzag line, used to prevent fraying, etc.

zikkurat same as **ziggurat**.

zilch /zilch/ (sl) n zero, nothing. [Origin unknown]

zillah or **zila** /zil'ə/ (hist) n an administrative district in British India. [Ar dīla (in Hindi pronunciation, zila) a rib, a side, a district]

zillion /zil'yən/ (inf) n an extremely large but unspecified number, many millions (analogous in formation and use to million and billion).
■ **zillionaire** /-ār'/ n a fabulously wealthy person. **zill'ionth** n and adj.

zimb /zimb/ n an Ethiopian dipterous insect, like the tsetse, harmful to cattle. [Amharic, a fly]

Zimbabwean /zim-bä'bwi-ən/ adj of or relating to the Republic of Zimbabwe in southern Africa. ◆ n a native or citizen of Zimbabwe.

zimbi /zim'bi/ n a kind of cowrie used as money. [Port zimbo; of African origin]

Zimmer® /zim'ər/ n (also **Zimmer®** frame) a metal frame held in front of one, used as an aid to walking. [Name of the original manufacturer]

zimocca /zi-mok'ə/ n a type of bath sponge. [New L]

zinc /zingk/ n a bluish-white metallic element (symbol **Zn**; atomic no 30) resistant to atmospheric corrosion, a constituent of several alloys (eg brass) and used in galvanizing, battery electrodes, etc (also adj). ◆ vt (**zincing** /zingk'ing/, **zinck'ing** or **zink'ing**; **zinced** /zingkt/, **zincked** or **zinked**) to coat with zinc. [Ger Zink; origin unknown]

■ **zincif'erous** /zingk-/ or **zinkif'erous** adj containing or producing zinc. **zincifica'tion**, **zinckifica'tion** or **zinkifica'tion** n the process of coating or impregnating an object with zinc. **zinc'ify**, **zinck'ify** or **zink'ify** vt to cover or impregnate with zinc. **zincite** /zingk'īt/ n a naturally occurring oxide of zinc, brittle, translucent and deep red. **zinco** /zing'kō/ n (pl **zinc'os**) a zincographic block or picture. **zinc'ode** n (obs) an anode. **zinc'ograph** n a plate or picture produced by zincography. **zincographer** /-kog'rə-fər/ n. **zincograph'ic** and **zincograph'ical** adj. **zincography** /-kog'rə-fi/ n an engraving process in which zinc is covered with wax and etched; any process in which designs for printing are made on zinc plates. **zinc'oid** adj like zinc. **zincol'ysis** n (obs) electrolysis. **zinc'ous** adj relating to or like zinc. **zinc'y**, **zinck'y** or **zink'y** adj relating to, containing, or looking like zinc.
❑ **zinc blende** n sphalerite, naturally occurring sulphide of zinc. **zinc'-bloom** n basic zinc carbonate, hydrozincite. **zinc colic** n a colic caused by the slow poisoning effect of zinc oxide. **zinc ointment** n a mixture of zinc oxide and a suitable ointment base (lanolin, petroleum jelly, etc). **zinc oxide** n a whitish solid, much used as a paint pigment in the rubber and other industries, and also medicinally as an antiseptic and astringent (also called **flowers of zinc**). **zinc white** n zinc oxide used as a pigment. **zinc'-worker** n.

Zincalo /zing'kə-lō/ n (pl **Zin'cali**) a Spanish gypsy (also fem **Zin'cala**). [Sp Romany name]

zindabad /zin'dä-bäd/ (Ind and Pak) interj long live. [Urdu]

zine /zēn/ (sl) n a magazine, esp one aimed at a special-interest group. ◆ combining form denoting a magazine on a particular subject or aimed at a particular group, as in fanzine, teen-zine.

zineb /zin'əb/ n an organic fungicide and insecticide sprayed on cereal grasses, fruit trees, etc. [Zinc ethylene bisdithiocarbamate, its chemical name]

Zinfandel or **zinfandel** /zin'fən-del/ n a black wine grape of California; the red or white dry wine produced from it. [Origin obscure]

zing /zing/ n a short shrill humming sound, such as that made by a bullet or vibrating string; zest, spirit, vitality, etc (inf). ◆ vi to move very swiftly, esp with a high-pitched hum. ◆ vt to make (something) zing; to criticize or scorn (US sl). [Imit]
■ **zing'er** n (inf; esp US) something or someone with zing, esp a sharp, lively quip, punchline or retort; an excellent person or thing; an astonishing turn of events. **zing'y** adj (inf) full of zest, etc.

Zingaro /zing'gə-rō/ (Ital) n (pl **Zing'ari**) a gypsy (also **Zing'ano**). [Cf **Zincalo** and **Zigeuner**]
■ **Zing'ara** n (pl **Zing'are**) a female gypsy (also **Zing'ana**).

zingel /tsing'əl or zing'əl/ n a fish of the Aspro genus of the perch family, esp Aspro zingel found in the Danube. [Ger]

zingiber /zin'ji-bər/ n any plant of the Zingiber genus (Zingiber officinale being the common ginger), belonging to the family **Zingiberaceae** /zin-ji-bə-rā'sē-ē/ of perennial aromatic tropical monocotyledonous herbs, with horizontal thickened rootstock and cone-like inflorescence. [L zingiber, from Gr zingiberis ginger]
■ **zingibera'ceous** or **zinzibera'ceous** adj.

zingy see under **zing**.

Zinjanthropus see **nutcracker man** under **nut**.

zinke /tsing'kə/ n an old wind instrument, the cornett. [Ger]

zinked, **zinkify**, etc see **zinc**.

zinkenite /zing'kə-nīt/ n a steel-grey mineral, essentially sulphide of lead and antimony. [JKL Zincken (1790–1862), a German mine director]

zinnia /zin'i-ə/ n any plant of the Zinnia genus of American composite plants, popular for their bright showy flowers. [From JG Zinn, German botanist (1727–59)]

zinziberaceous see under **zingiber**.

Zion /zī'ən/ n Jerusalem; the Israelite theocracy; the Jewish people; a place ruled over by God; the Christian Church; heaven. [Heb tsīyōn, orig the name of a part of one of the hills of Jerusalem]
■ **Zi'onism** n the movement which secured national privileges and territory in Palestine for the Jews and which now helps to maintain and develop the state of Israel; a religious movement in southern Africa in which traditional African beliefs are incorporated within Pentecostal Christianity. **Zi'onist** n a supporter of Zionism. **Zi'onward** adv heavenward.

zip[1] /zip/ n a zip fastener; energy, vigour (inf); the ping or sound of a bullet striking an object or whizzing through the air; a whizzing sound. ◆ vi and vt (**zipp'ing**; **zipped**) to fasten with a zip; to whizz; to be full of, act with, proceed with, or (usu **zip up**) infuse with, life and energy (inf); to compress (a file) into a standard format (comput). [Imit]

■ words derived from main entry word; ❑ compound words; ■ idioms and phrasal verbs

zipp'er *n* (*esp N Am*) a zip fastener. ♦ *vt* to fasten with a zipper. **zipp'ered** *adj* provided with a zip fastener. **zipp'y** *adj* (*inf*) quick, energetic or lively.
❑ **zip fastener** *n* a fastening device for clothes, etc, on which two sets of teeth can be opened or interlocked by pulling a slide along them. **zip'-front, zip'-neck, zip'top**, etc *adj* having the front-, neck- or top-opening, etc fastened with a zip. **zip gun** *n* (*N Am inf*) a home-made pistol powered by a spring or elastic band. **zip'lock** *adj* (*N Am*) of a plastic bag, having ridged strips at the opening which may be pressed together to interlock, so sealing the bag. ♦ *vt* to seal, *esp* by pressing together. **zip'-on, zip'-off, zip'-in**, etc *adj* able to be added, removed, inserted, etc by means of a zip. **zip'wire** or **zip'line** *n* a mechanism for travelling above the ground by holding a pulley that slides down a taut angled rope.

zip² /zip/ or **zippo** /zip'ō/ (*sl*; *orig US*) *n* nothing, zero.

zip code /zip' kōd/ (*US*) *n* the US postal code. [*zone improvement plan*]

Zip® **disk** /zip disk/ (*comput*) *n* a floppy disk with a very high capacity on which data is stored in compressed form using an independent specialized hard drive (**Zip®** **drive**).

Ziphius /zif'i-əs/ *n* a genus of whales, giving its name to the family **Ziphiidae**, the beaked whales. [Gr *xiphios* swordfish, from *xiphos* sword]

Zippo /zip'ō/ *n* a brand of cigarette lighter.

zircon /zûr'kən/ *n* a tetragonal mineral, zirconium silicate, of which jacinth and jargoon are varieties. [Ar *zarqūn*, from Pers *zargūn* gold-coloured; cf **jargoon**]
■ **zir'caloy** (also **Zir'coloy®**) *n* an alloy of zirconium with tin, chromium and nickel, widely used (*esp* in the nuclear power industry) for its heat- and corrosion-resistant properties. **zircoʹnia** *n* oxide of zirconium. **zirconic** /-kon'-/ *adj* of zirconium. **zircoʹnium** *n* a metallic element (symbol **Zr**; atomic no 40) highly resistant to corrosion.
■ **cubic zirconia** a synthetic stone used as a diamond substitute, produced from zirconia heated with any of various stabilizing metallic oxides.

zit /zit/ (*sl*; *orig N Am*) *n* a spot or pimple. [Origin obscure]

zite see **ziti**.

zither /zidh'ər or zith'ər/, also **zithern** /'ərn/ *n* a stringed instrument consisting of a wooden frame and flat soundbox with from twenty-nine to forty-two metal or sometimes gut strings, placed on a table or on the knees, some strings being played by a plectrum on the right thumb, others being played with the fingers; used generically for other instruments of this type and shape. [Ger *zither*]
■ **zith'erist** *n*.

ziti /zē'tē/ *n pl* a type of pasta shaped like large macaroni (also **zi'te**). [Ital, plural forms of *zito* and *zita*]

ziz see **zizz**.

zizania /zi- or zī-zā'ni-ə/ *n* any tall aquatic grass of the genus *Zizania*, also known as **wild, water, Indian** or **Canada rice** (ordinary cultivated rice belongs to the genus *Oryza*). [Gr *zizanion* darnel]

zizel /ziz'əl/ *n* the chipmunk. [Ger *Ziesel*]

zizyphus /ziz'i-fəs/ *n* a shrub or tree of the genus *Zizyphus* of the buckthorn family, the jujube trees. [L, jujube tree]

zizz or **ziz** /ziz/ (*inf*) *n* a nap or sleep (also *vi*). [Representation of z-z-z-z-, the conventional phoneticization of snoring used in strip cartoons, etc]

Zl *abbrev* : zloty.

zloty /zlot'i/ or /zwot'ü/ *n* (*pl* **zlot'y** or **zlot'ys**) the standard monetary unit of Poland (100 groszy). [Pol *zloty*, literally, golden]

Zn (*chem*) *symbol* : zinc.

zo see **zho**.

zo- see **zoo-**.

zoa see **zoon**.

Zoantharia /zō-an-thā'ri-ə/ *n pl* an order of Anthozoa, including sea-anemones and many corals, the members of which may be either solitary or colonial and possess either six, or more than eight, simple tentacles. [New L, from Gr *zōion* animal, and *anthos* flower]
■ **zoanthā'rian** *adj* and *n*.

zoanthropy /zō-an'thrə-pi/ *n* a form of mental delusion in which a person believes himself or herself to be an animal. [Gr *zōion* animal, and *anthrōpos* man]
■ **zōanthropic** /-throp'/ *adj*.

Zoanthus /zō-an'thəs/ *n* the typical genus of the **Zoan'thidae** /-ē/, a family of Anthozoa permanently attached by their bases and having no solid skeleton. [Gr *zōion* animal, and *anthos* flower]

zoarium /zō-ā'ri-əm/ *n* the zooids of a polyzoan colony collectively. [Gr *zōarion*, dimin of *zōion* animal]

zobo and **zobu** see **zho**.

zocco /zok'ō/ or **zoccolo** /-lō/ *n* (*pl* **zocc'os** or **zocc'ōlos**) a socle. [Ital *zocco, zoccolo*; see **socle**]

zodiac /zō'di-ak/ *n* an imaginary belt in the heavens, about 18° wide, through which the ecliptic passes centrally, and which forms the background of the motions of the sun, moon and planets. It is divided into twelve equal parts of 30° called **signs of the zodiac**, named from the constellations that once corresponded to them but no longer do so. The constellations, with the symbols of the corresponding signs, are as follows: Aries (*Ram*), ♈; Taurus (*Bull*), ♉; Gemini (*Twins*), ♊; Cancer (*Crab*), ♋; Leo (*Lion*), ♌; Virgo (*Virgin*), ♍; Libra (*Balance*), ♎; Scorpio (*Scorpion*), ♏; Sagittarius (*Archer*), ♐; Capricorn (*Goat*), ♑; Aquarius (*Water Bearer*), ♒; Pisces (*Fishes*), ♓; a set or diagram of these; a year (*obs*); a set of twelve, or a recurrent series or course (*fig*). [Fr *zodiaque*, from L *zōdiacus*, from Gr *zōidiakos* of figures, from *zōidion* a small carved or painted figure, from *zōion* an animal]
■ **zodī'acal** *adj*.
❑ **zodiacal light** *n* a faint illumination of the sky, lenticular in form and elongated in the direction of the ecliptic on either side of the sun, fading away at about 90° from it (best seen after sunset or before sunrise in the tropics).

zoea /zō-ē'ə/ *n* (*pl* **zoē'ae**, also **zoē'as**) a larval stage of certain decapod crustaceans, eg of crabs (also **zooea** /zō-ē'ə/). [Gr *zōē* life]
■ **zoē'al** or **zooē'al** *adj*. **zō'eform** *adj*.

zoechrome see **zoetrope**.

zoetic /zō-et'ik/ *adj* relating to life, vital. [Gr *zōē* life]

zoetrope /zō'i-trōp/ *n* the 'wheel of life', an instrument in which figures on the inside of a rotating cylinder are made visible through slots and provide an illusion of animated motion; (also **zō'echrome**) any of several early processes for colour cinematography, using rapidly repeated images of the selected colours in sequence on a screen, the synthesis arising from persistence of vision in the eye. [Gr *zōē* life, and *tropos* a turning]
■ **zoetropic** /-trop'ik/ *adj*.

zoftig see **zaftig**.

Zohar /zō'hăr/ *n* one of the most important cabbalistic texts, being an allegorical interpretation of the Pentateuch. [Heb, brightness, splendour]

zoiatria /zō-i-at'ri-ə/ or /zō-ī-ə-trī'ə/ or **zoiatrics** /zō-i-at'riks/ *n* veterinary surgery. [Gr *zōion* an animal, and *iātreiā* healing]

zoic /zō'ik/ *adj* relating to animals; of rocks, containing evidences of life, in the form of fossils (*geol*). [Gr *zōikos* of animals, from *zōion* an animal]

Zoilism /zō'i-li-zm/ *n* carping and unjust criticism.
■ **Zoil'ean** *adj* characteristic of *Zoilus*, a Greek grammarian who flourished in the time of Philip of Macedon, and criticized Homer with such asperity that his name became proverbial for a captious and malignant critic. **Zō'ilist** *n* a carping critic.

zoisite /zoi'sīt or zō'i-sīt/ *n* an orthorhombic mineral closely related to epidote. [Baron S *Zois* von Edelstein (1747–1819), Slovenian nobleman]

zoism /zō'i-zm/ *n* the doctrine that life originates from a specific vital principle. [Gr *zōē* life]
■ **zō'ist** *n* a person who maintains this theory.

Zolaism /zō'lä-i-zm/ *n* the literary principles and practice of the French novelist Émile *Zola* (1840–1902), who aimed at what he called 'naturalism' (qv).

Zöllner's lines /tsæl'nərz līnz/ *n pl* rows of parallel lines appearing to be not parallel through the optical effect of oblique lines intersecting them in something like a herringbone pattern (also **Zöllner's illusion** or **pattern**). [JKF *Zöllner* (1834–82), German physicist]

Zollverein /tsol'fər-īn/ *n* a customs union; a union of the German states, under the leadership of Prussia, to enable them to act as one state in their commercial relations with other countries (*hist*). [Ger *Zoll* duty, and *Verein* union]

zolpidem /zol'pi-dem/ *n* a drug used in the short-term treatment of insomnia.

zombie or **zombi** /zom'bi/ *n* a corpse reanimated by sorcery; the power supposed to enter such a body; a stupid or useless person; a very slow-moving, lethargic person; a computer that has been infected with a virus that allows it to be controlled by another user; (with *cap*) *orig* in W African voodooism, the python god; (with *cap*) in West Indian and American voodooism, the snake god. [Kongo (W African language) *zumbi* fetish, and *nzambi* god]
■ **zom'bify** *vt* to reduce to the state of a zombie. **zom'biism** *n* belief in a zombie, or practice of rites associated with this belief.

zomboruk see **zumbooruk**.

zona /zō'nə/ n (pl **zonae** /zō'nē/) a girdle or belt; an area, patch, strip or band (zool); a zone; a zona pellucida; herpes zoster. [L, girdle]
❑ **zona pellucida** /pe-loo'si-də/ n (zool) a thick, transparent membrane around the mature mammalian ovum.

zonal, **zonary**, etc see under **zone**.

zonda /son'də or zon'/ n a dry, hot, dusty wind blowing from the Andes across the Argentine pampas during July and August. [Sp; perh from a Native American language]

zone /zōn/ n any of the five great belts into which the surface of the earth is divided by the tropics and arctic and antarctic circles; any continuous tract with particular characteristics; a region; a group of strata characterized by a distinctive fauna or flora, and bearing the name of one fossil, called the **zonal index** (geol); a set of crystal faces all parallel to the same line (the **zonal** or **zone axis**); that part of the surface of a sphere between two parallel planes, intersecting the sphere (maths); a girdle, belt, or encircling band (chiefly poetic); an encircling stripe of different colour or substance. ◆ vt to surround with, or as with, a zone; to divide into, or assign to, zones; (esp with off) to mark as a zone. [L zōna, from Gr zōnē a girdle, from zōnnynai to gird]
■ **zō'nal** or **zō'nary** adj like a zone; arranged in zones; relating to a zone. **zō'nate** or **zō'nated** adj marked with zones, belted. **zonā'tion** n (bot) the formation of bands differentiated by colour or other characteristics, or the arrangement of such bands; the occurrence of vegetation in well-marked bands, each band having its characteristic dominant species. **zoned** adj having zones; wearing a zone. **zone'less** adj. **zō'ning** n division into zones; assignment according to zones. **zō'noid** adj like a zone. **Zonotrichia** /zō-nō-trik'i-ə/ n (Gr thrix, trichos hair) a genus of American sparrows, some with white or golden crowns. **zō'nula** n a small zone. **zō'nular** adj like a zone or zonule. **zon'ule** n a small zone or band. **zon'ulet** n (poetic) a small belt or girdle. **zonure** /zō'nūr/ n (Gr ourā tail) a lizard of the tropical African genus Zonurus of lizards whose tails are ringed with spiny scales, giving its name to the family **Zonu'ridae**.
❑ **zonal defence** n (football, etc) a method of defending in which a player patrols a particular area of the field rather than marking a specific opponent. **zone refining** n the purification of a solid by melting in a narrow band, concentrating the impurities at one end. **zone therapy** n a technique in which pressure or massage of certain surface areas or zones of the body is used to relieve pain in internal parts considered to be specifically related to particular zones. **zone'-ticket** n a railway ticket usable for a time between any stations of a group.
■ **in the zone** (inf) in a mental state that enables one to perform at the height of one's abilities. **zone out** (sl) to lose concentration or awareness of one's surroundings.

zonk /zongk/ (inf) n a sharp blow; the sound of a swift, sharp or firm impact. ◆ vt to hit sharply, or with a zonk; to blast. ◆ adv with a zonk. [Imit]
■ **zonked** /zongkt/, also **zonked out** adj (sl) utterly exhausted; in a deep sleep; intoxicated; under the influence of drugs.

zonula, **zonule**, **zonure**, etc see under **zone**.

zoo /zoo/ n a garden or park where animals are kept, studied and usu placed on show to the public; orig (with cap) the Zoological Gardens in London; a place, group of people, etc characterized by noise and unruly behaviour (fig; inf). [zoological garden]
❑ **zoo'keeper** n.

zoo- /zō-ō- or zō-o-/ or **zō-** /zō-/ combining form denoting (esp in zoological terms, etc) animal. [Gr zōion animal]
■ **zoobiotic** /zō-ō-bī-ot'ik/ adj (biol) parasitic on, or living in association with, an animal. **zooblast** /zō'ō-blast/ n (Gr blastos a germ; zool) a precursor animal cell. **zoocephalic** /-si-fal'ik/ adj animal-headed. **zōochem'ical** adj. **zōochem'istry** n the chemistry of the animal body. **zō'ochore** n. **zoochorous** /zō-ō-kör'əs/ adj (Gr chōreein to spread; bot) of spores or seeds, dispersed by animals. **zō'ochory** n (bot) the condition of being dispersed by animals. **zō'oculture** n (US) the domestication and control of animals. **zōocytium** /-sish'i-əm/ n (pl **zōocyt'ia**) (Gr kytos a hollow vessel; zool) a zoothecium. **zōoden'drium** n (zool) the branched stalk connecting the members of the colony in certain colonial Infusoria. **zooecium** /zō-ē'shi-əm/ n (pl **zooe'cia**) (Gr oikiā a house; zool) the body-wall or enclosing chamber of a polyzoan individual. **zō'ogamete** n a motile gamete. **zoogamous** /zō-og'ə-məs/ adj (Gr gamos marriage) relating to zoogamy. **zoog'amy** n sexual reproduction of animals. **zoogenic** /-jen'-/ or **zoog'enous** adj produced from animals. **zoogeny** /zō-oj'ə-ni/ n (Gr -geneia, sfx denoting production) the doctrine, or the process, of the origination of living beings. **zōogeog'rapher** n. **zōogeograph'ic** or **zōogeograph'ical** adj. **zōogeog'raphy** n the science of the distribution of animals on the surface of the globe. **zōogloea** /-glē'ə/ n (Gr gloiā glue; bacteriol) a mucilaginous mass of bacteria embedded in slimy material derived from swollen cell walls. **zōogloe'ic** adj. **zōogloe'oid** adj. **zōogonid'ium** n (pl **zōogonid'ia**) (bot and zool) a

swarm-spore. **zōog'onous** adj (zool) viviparous. **zoogony** /zō-og'ə-ni/ n (L -gonia, from Gr -goneia, sfx denoting origin or production) zoogeny. **zō'ograft** /-gräft/ n a piece of animal tissue grafted onto a human. **zō'ografting** n. **zō'ographer** or **zoog'raphist** n. **zōograph'ic** or **zōograph'ical** adj. **zoog'raphy** n the study or description of animals and their habits; the painting of animals. **zōol'ater** n (Gr latreiā worship) someone who worships animals. **zōolatrī'a** or **zōol'atry** n worship of animals. **zōol'atrous** adj. **zoolite** /zō'ō-līt/ n (Gr lithos a stone) a fossil animal (also **zō'olith**). **zōolith'ic** or **zōolit'ic** adj. **zōomagnet'ic** adj. **zōomag'netism** n animal magnetism. **zoomancy** /zō'ō-man-si/ n (Gr manteiā divination) divination by observation of animals. **zōōman'tic** adj. **zōōmet'ric** adj. **zōometry** /-om'ə-tri/ n (Gr metron a measure) comparative measurement of the parts of animals. **zō'omorph** /-mörf/ n (Gr morphē form) in art, a representation of an animal form; an image or symbol of a god, etc who is conceived as having an animal form. **zōomor'phic** adj relating to zoomorphism; representing animals in art. **zōomor'phism** n the representation, or the conception, of a god or a man in an animal form (also **zōomor'phy**). **zōon'ic** adj relating to animals. **zō'onite** n any of the segments of an articulated animal. **zōonit'ic** adj. **zōōnom'ic** adj. **zōon'omist** n. **zoonomy** /zō-on'ə-mi/ n (Gr nomos law) animal physiology (also **zōōnō'mia**). **zōopathol'ogy** n the study of disease in animals. **zōopathy** /zō-op'ə-thi/ n (Gr pathos suffering) animal pathology. **zōop'eral** adj. **zōop'erist** n. **zōop'ery** n (Gr peirā experiment) experimentation on animals. **Zoophaga** /zō-of'ə-gə/ n pl (Gr phagein to eat; zool) the carnivorous animals collectively. **zōoph'agan** n a carnivorous animal. **zōoph'agous** adj of or relating to the Zoophaga; feeding on animals. **zōoph'agy** n the practice of feeding on animals. **zō'ophile** /-fīl/ n (Gr philos loving) a zoophilist; a zoophilous plant (bot). **zōophil'ia**, **zōoph'ilism** or **zōoph'ily** n love of animals; erotic fondness for animals. **zoophilist** /zō-of'il-ist/ n a lover of animals; someone who has or suffers from zoophilia. **zōoph'ilous** adj loving animals; experiencing or suffering from zoophilia; pollinated by animals other than insects (bot); of insects, feeding on animals (zool). **zōophōb'ia** n (Gr phobos fear) abnormal fear of animals; fear of animal ghosts. **zōoph'obous** adj. **zōophoric** /-för'-/ adj. **zōophorus** /-of'ə-rəs/ n (Gr pherein to bear) a continuous frieze sculptured in relief with figures of people and animals. **zōophysiol'ogist** n. **zōophysiol'ogy** n animal physiology. **Zoophyta** /zō-of'it-ə/ n pl (Gr phyton plant) in older classifications, a group of invertebrates which lack the ability to move from place to place, such as sponges, corals, etc. **zō'ophyte** /-fīt/ n any plant supposed to resemble an animal (obs); any of numerous invertebrates resembling plants, such as sponges, corals, sea-anemones, etc, esp hydroid colonies of a branched form. **zōophytic** /-fit'/ or **zōophyt'ical** adj. **zōoph'ytoid** adj. **zōophytolog'ical** /-fīt-/ adj. **zōophytol'ogist** n. **zōophytol'ogy** n. **zōoplank'ton** n floating and drifting animal life. **zōoplas'tic** adj (Gr plassein to form) relating to **zō'oplasty**, the operation of transplanting living tissue from one of the lower animals to humans. **zōopsychol'ogy** n the psychology of the lower animals. **zōoscop'ic** adj. **zōoscopy** /-os'kop-i/ n (Gr skopeein to look at) a form of mental delusion in which one sees imaginary animals, esp snakes. **zō'osperm**, also **zōosper'mium** n (Gr sperma seed; biol) a spermatozoid; a zoospore. **zōospermat'ic** adj. **zōosporan'gium** n (bot) a sporangium in which zoospores are formed. **zō'ospore** n (Gr sporos a seed) a swarm-spore; an asexual reproductive cell that can swim by means of flagella. **zōospor'ic** or **zōos'porous** adj. **zō'otaxy** n (Gr taxis arrangement) the science of the classification of animals, systematic zoology. **zōotechnics** /-tek'niks/ or **zō'otechny** n (Gr technē art) the science of the breeding and domestication of animals. **zōothap'sis** n (pl **zōothap'sēs** /-sēz/) (Gr thaptein to bury) premature burial. **zōothē'cial** /-shi-əl/ adj. **zōothecium** /-thē'shi-əm or -si-/ n (pl **zōothē'cia**) (Gr thēkion casket, dimin of thēkē box; zool) the tubular sheath of certain social infusorians. **zōothē'ism** n the attribution of divine qualities to an animal. **zōotheis'tic** adj. **zōother'apy** n (Gr therapeiā treatment) veterinary therapeutics. **zō'othome** n (Gr thōmos heap; biol) a group of zooids, such as a mass of coral. **zōotom'ic** or **zōotom'ical** adj. **zōotom'ically** adv. **zōot'omist** n (Gr tomē a cut) someone who dissects the bodies of animals, an anatomist. **zōot'omy** n the dissection of animals; comparative anatomy. **zōotox'in** n a toxin produced by an animal such as a snake. **zō'otrope** n a zoetrope. **zōotrophic** /-trof'ik/ adj (Gr trophos food) relating to the nourishment of animals. **zōot'rophy** n. **zō'otype** n (zool) an animal serving as a type. **zōotypic** /-tip'ik/ adj.

zooea, **zooeal** see under **zoea**.

zooid /zō'oid/ (zool) n formerly, a free-moving cell, such as a sperm-cell; in alternation of generations, an individual of an asexually-produced form; usu, an individual forming part of a colonial organism. [**zoo-** and **-oid**]
■ **zōoid'al** adj.

zooks /zooks/ interj same as **gadzooks** (see under **gad²**).

zoolatry, etc see under **zoo-**.

■ words derived from main entry word; ❑ compound words; ■ idioms and phrasal verbs

zoology /zoo-ol'ə-ji or zō-ol'/ n the science of animal life, included along with botany in the science of biology; the animal life of a region, etc. [New L zoológia; see **zoo-** and **-logy**]
■ **zoological** /zoo-ō-loj'i-kl or zō-ō-/ adj relating to zoology. **zoolog'ically** adv. **zool'ogist** /zoo- or zō-/ n a specialist in or student of zoology.
◻ **zoological garden** or **park** n (old) a zoo.

zoom /zoom/ vi to move very quickly; to make a loud, deep, persistent buzzing noise; to move with this sound; to use the stored energy of the forward motion of an aircraft in order to gain height (aeronautics); to soar (fig); (often with in, out) to change focus rapidly, eg with a zoom lens; (usu with in) to enlarge a section of text, part of a diagram, a window, etc on a VDU screen, so as to make it easier to work on. ◆ vt to cause to zoom; to enlarge (a section of text, part of a diagram, a window, etc) on a VDU screen. ◆ n the act of zooming; a zooming noise. [Imit]
◻ **zoom lens** n a lens of variable focal length used, eg, for bringing television, cinematographic or cine-camera pictures from distance to close-up without moving the camera; a similar lens used in still cameras and in microscopes.

zoomagnetic...to...**zoomorphy** see under **zoo-**.

zoon /zō'on/ (zool) n (pl **zō'a** or **zō'ons**) a structurally unified individual creature, either the total product of a fertilized ovum or a group of zooids constituting a compound animal.
■ **zō'onal** adj like a zoon.

zoonic...to...**zoonomy** see under **zoo-**.

zoonosis /zō-ə-nō'sis or zō-on'ə-sis/ n (pl **zoonō'ses** /-sēz/) a disease of animals which can be transmitted to humans, such as rabies, etc; a disease due to animal parasites. [Gr zōïon an animal, and nosos disease]
■ **zoonot'ic** adj.

zoon politikon /zō'on po-lit'i-kon/ (Gr) n (said of a human being) a political animal.

zoopathology...to...**zootrophy** see under **zoo-**.

zoot suit /zoot soot or sūt/ n a flashy type of man's suit with padded shoulders, fitted waist, knee-length jacket, and trousers narrow at the ankles (introduced in the late 1940s). [Origin unknown; prob zoot coined to rhyme with **suit**]
■ **zoot'suiter** n someone who wears a zoot suit.

zootype, etc see under **zoo-**.

zopilote /sō-pi-lō'te or zō'pi-lōt/ n any of the smaller American vultures of the family Cathartidae, esp the turkey buzzard, or the urubu. [Mexican Sp, from Nahuatl pilotl]

zoppa /tsop'ə/ or (esp formerly) **zoppo** /tsop'ō/ (music) adj syncopated, usu in phrase alla zoppa, with syncopation. [Ital, limping]

Zorb® /zörb/ n a large inflatable ball containing a smaller ball within which a person is strapped and rolled around as a recreational activity.
■ **Zorb'ing** n.

zorgite /zör'gīt/ n a metallic copper-lead selenide, found at Zorge, in the Harz Mountains, Germany.

zori /zō'ri/ n (pl **zo'ris**) a Japanese sandal consisting of a flat sole with a thong between the toes. [Jap]

zoril, zorille, zorillo and **zorino** see under **zorro**.

Zoroastrianism /zor-ō-as'tri-ə-ni-zm/ n an ancient dualistic religion founded or reformed by Zoroaster (Gr Zoroastrēs, Avestan Zarathustra, c.630–553 BC), whose scriptures are the Zend-Avesta, and which is still adhered to by the Guebres in Iran and Parsees in India. [L Zōroastrēs, from Gr]
■ **Zoroas'trian** n and adj.

zorro /zor'ō or sor'ō/ n (pl **zorr'os**) a S American fox or fox-like wild dog. [Sp zorro or zorra fox, and dimin zorilla, zorillo (Fr zorille) skunk]
■ **zorilla** /zor-il'ə/ n an African skunk-like musteline animal (genus Zorilla) (also **zoril** or **zorille** /zor'il or -il'/). **zorillo** /sor-ē'yō or zor-il'ō/ n (pl **zorill'os**) a S American skunk. **zorino** /zor-ēn'ō/ n (pl **zorin'os**) a euphemism for skunk fur used to make garments.

zoster /zos'tər/ n an ancient Greek waistbelt for men; herpes zoster or shingles (med). [Gr zōstēr a girdle]

Zostera /zo-stē'rə/ n the eelgrass or grasswrack genus. [Gr zōstēr a kind of grasswrack]

Zouave /zū-äv' or zwäv/ (hist) n a soldier belonging to a body of French infantry, orig Algerians, wearing a quasi-Moorish uniform; any of a number of volunteer regiments, modelling themselves on the Zouaves, who fought on the side of the North in the American Civil War; a woman's short embroidered jacket. [From the Zouaoua, an Algerian tribe]

zouk /zook/ n a style of dance music, orig from the French Antilles, combining Latin American, African and Western disco rhythms. [Perh from W Ind creole zouk to enjoy oneself]

zounds /zowndz or zoondz/ (archaic) interj an exclamation of anger and astonishment. [A corruption of God's wounds]

zowie /zow'i/ (US) interj expressing surprise and pleasure. ◆ n (with cap) a former name for the slang in use among hippies.

ZPG abbrev : zero population growth.

Zr (chem) symbol : zirconium.

ZRE abbrev : Democratic Republic of Congo (formerly Zaire; IVR).

ZST abbrev : Zone Standard Time.

zucchetto, also **zuchetto** /tsŭ-ket'ō/ or **zuchetta** /-a/ n (pl **zucchett'os, zuchett'os** or **zuchett'as**) the skullcap worn by a Roman Catholic priest, etc, covering the tonsure. [Ital, dimin of zucca a gourd]

zucchini /zoo-kē'nē/ (esp N Am and Aust) n (pl **zucchi'ni** or **zucchi'nis**) a courgette. [Ital]

zufolo, also **zuffolo** /tsoo'fō-lō/ n (pl **zuf'oli** or **zuff'oli** /-ē/) a small flute or flageolet used in training songbirds. [Ital]

zugzwang /tsook' or tsoohh'tsväng/ n in chess, a blockade position in which any move is disadvantageous to the blockaded player. [Ger]

Zulu¹ /zoo'loo/ n a people of the Nguni branch of the Bantu family, inhabiting mainly Natal in S Africa; a member of this people; the Bantu language of the Zulus. ◆ adj relating to the Zulus, their language, etc; (without cap) in communications, used for zero. [Zulu amazulu people of heaven]
◻ **zulu time** n (telecom) Greenwich Mean Time.

Zulu² or **zulu** /zoo'loo/ n (in international radio communication) a code word for the letter z.

zulu /zoo'loo/ n a type of two-masted fishing-vessel formerly used in NE Scotland. [Said to have been introduced during the Zulu war of 1878–79]

Zumba® /zŭm'bə or zoom'bə/ n a system of exercises conducted to Latin-American and other dance music.

zum Beispiel /tsŭm bī'shpēl/ (Ger) for example (abbrev **z.B.**).

zumbooruk /zum'boo-ruk or -boo'/ n a small cannon mounted on a swivel, carried on the back of a camel (also **zum'booruck, zom'boruk** or **zam'boorak**). [Urdu, from Pers zambūrak; from zambūr bee]

Zuñi /zoo'nyē or soo'nyē/ or **Zuni** /zoo'nē/ n a member of a Pueblo Native American people traditionally living in large communal houses near the Zuñi river in W New Mexico; the language of the Zuñi. ◆ adj of or relating to the Zuñi or their language. [Am Sp, from Keresan (Native American language)]
■ **Zu'ñian** or **Zu'nian** adj and n.

zupa /zū'pə/ n a confederation of village communities governed by a **zū'pan**, in the early history of Serbia, etc. [Serbian]

zurf see **zarf**.

zuz /zooz/ n (pl **zuzim** or **zuzzim** /zoo-zēm'/) a silver coin of ancient Palestine. [Heb]

ZW abbrev : Zimbabwe (IVR).

zwanziger /tsvan'tsi-gər/ n an old Austrian silver coin, equivalent to twenty kreutzers. [Ger, from zwanzig twenty]

zwieback /tsvē'bäk or tswē'/ n biscuit rusk, or a sweet spiced bread toasted. [Ger]

Zwinglian /zwing'gli-ən or tsving'li-ən/ adj relating to the Swiss reformer Huldreich Zwingli (1484–1531), or his doctrines, esp his divergence from Luther in the doctrine of the Eucharist (Zwingli rejecting every form of local or corporeal presence, whether by transubstantiation, impanation or consubstantiation). ◆ n a follower of Zwingli.
■ **Zwing'lianism** n. **Zwing'lianist** n.

zwischenzug /zvish'ən-zoog or (Ger) tsvish'ən-tsook/ n in chess, an interim tactical move. [Ger, from zwischen between, and Zug move]

zwitterion /tsvit'ə-rī-ən/ (chem) n an ion carrying both a positive and a negative charge. [Ger Zwitter a hybrid, and **ion**]
■ **zwitterionic** /-ī-on'ik/ adj.

Zyban® /zī'ban/ n a proprietary name of a drug (bupropion) used in the treatment of nicotine addiction.

zydeco /zī'di-kō/ n a type of accordion-based popular dance music originating in Louisiana and partaking of French, Caribbean and blues influences. [Creole]

Zygaena /zī-jē'nə/ n the burnet moth genus, the typical genus of the family **Zygae'nidae**; the former name of the hammerhead genus of sharks, now called Sphyrna. [Gr zygaina a shark]
■ **zygae'nid, zygae'nine** or **zygae'noid** adj.

zygo- /zī-gō- or zig-ō-/, or before a vowel **zyg-** /zīg- or zig-/ *combining form* denoting a yoke, union or the presence of two similar things. [Gr *zygon* yoke]

■ **zy'gal** *adj* relating to a zygon; formed like a letter H. **zygan'trum** *n* (Gr *antron* a cave; *zool*) in snakes and some lizards, an additional vertebral articulation, consisting of a fossa on the posterior surface of the neural arch, into which the zygosphene fits. **zygapophyseal** or **zygapophysial** /-fiz'i-əl/ *adj.* **zygapophysis** /-pof'i-sis/ *n* (*pl* **zygapoph'ysēs**) (Gr *apophysis* process; *zool*) any of the yoke-pieces or articulations of the vertebrae. **zygobranchiate** /-brangk'i-āt/ *adj* (Gr *branchia* gills; *zool*) having paired, symmetrically placed, gills; belonging to the **Zygobranchiā'ta**, a division of the *Gastropoda*. **zy'gobranch** and **zygobranch'iate** *n* and *adj.* **zy'gocactus** *n* a cactus of the Brazilian genus *Zygocactus* of jointed, branching cacti with zygomorphic flowers, also known as the **Christmas cactus**. **zygocardiac** /-kär'di-ak/ *adj* (Gr *kardiā* heart; *zool*) a term used to describe certain paired lateral ossicles in the gastric mill of Crustacea. **zygodactyl** /-dak'til/ *adj* (Gr *daktylos* toe; *zool*) having two toes in front and two behind, as parrots have (also **zygodactyl'ic** or **zygodac'tylous**). **zygodac'tylism** *n.* **zy'godont** *adj* (Gr *odous, odontos* tooth) relating to molar teeth whose cusps are paired; possessing such molars. **zygomor'phic** or **zygomorphous** /-mör'fəs/ *adj* (Gr *morphē* form) yoke-shaped; designating flowers symmetrical about one plane only. **zygomor'phism** or **zy'gomorphy** *n.* **zygomycete'** *n* and *adj.* **Zygomycetes** /-mī-sē'tēz/ *n pl* (Gr *mykēs, mykētos* a mushroom) a group of fungi (moulds, etc), a division of the *Phycomycetes*, marked by the production of zygospores. **zygomycē'tous** *adj.* **zy'gon** *n* a connecting bar; an H-shaped fissure of the brain (*anat*). **Zygophyllaceae** /-fil-ā'sē-ē/ *n pl* (Gr *phyllon* a leaf) the bean caper family, desert and steppe plants related to the Rutaceae, the typical genus being **Zygophyll'um**. **zygophyllā'ceous** *adj.* **zy'gophyte** /-fīt/ *n* (Gr *phyton* a plant) a plant in which reproduction takes place by means of zygospores. **zygopleural** /-ploo'rəl/ *adj* (Gr *pleurā* side; *biol*) bilaterally symmetrical. **zy'gose** *adj* relating to zygosis. **zygosis** /-gō'sis/ *n* (*biol*) conjugation. **zy'gosphene** /-sfēn/ *n* (Gr *sphēn* wedge; *zool*) in snakes and some lizards, an additional vertebral articulation, consisting of a process on the anterior surface of the neural arch, which fits into the zygantrum. **zy'gospore** *n* (Gr *sporā* a seed; *bot*) a spore produced by the union of buds from two adjacent hyphae in the process of conjugation by which some fungi multiply (also **zy'gosperm**). **zy'gotene** /-tēn/ *n* (Gr *taenia* a band; *biol*) the second stage of the meiotic prophase, in which the chromatic threads approximate in pairs and become looped.

zygoma /zī-gō'mə or zi-/ (*anat*) *n* (*pl* **zygo'mas** or **zygo'mata**) the arch formed by the malar bone and the zygomatic process of the temporal bone of the skull. [New L, from Gr *zygōma*, from *zygon* yoke]

■ **zygomat'ic** *adj* relating to, or in the region of, the zygoma. ❑ **zygomatic arch** *n* the zygoma. **zygomatic bone** *n* the cheekbone. **zygomatic fossa** *n* the lower part of the fossa bridged over by the zygomatic arch. **zygomatic muscles** *n pl* two muscles, *major* and *minor*, extending from the zygomatic arch. **zygomatic process** *n* a projection of the temporal bone of the skull.

zygomorphic...to...**zygospore** see under **zygo-**.

zygote /zī'gōt or zig'/ *n* (*bot* and *zool*) the product of the union of two gametes; by extension, the individual developing from that product. [Gr *zygōtos* yoked, from *zygon* yoke]

■ **zygotic** /-got'/ *adj.*
❑ **zygotic number** *n* (*bot*) the diploid chromosome number.

zygotene see under **zygo-**.

zylonite a non-standard spelling of **xylonite**.

zymase /zī'māz or -mās/ *n* any of a group of enzymes inducing the alcoholic fermentation of carbohydrates. [Fr, from Gr *zȳmē* leaven, and **-ase**]

zyme /zīm/ *n* a ferment; a disease germ. [Gr *zȳmē* leaven, *zȳmōsis* fermentation]

■ **zy'mic** *adj* relating to fermentation. **zy'mite** *n* a priest who uses leavened bread in the Eucharist.

zymo- /zī-mō-/, or before a vowel **zym-** /zīm-/ *combining form* relating to fermentation. [Ety as for **zyme**]

■ **zy'mogen** *n* (*biol*) an inert precursor of many active proteins and degradative enzymes. **zymogen'ic** *adj.* **zy'moid** *adj* like a ferment. **zymolog'ic** or **zymolog'ical** *adj* relating to zymology. **zymol'ogist** *n* a specialist in zymology. **zymol'ogy** *n* the science of fermentation. **zymol'ysis** *n* the action of enzymes. **zymolyt'ic** *adj.* **zymom'eter** or **zymosim'eter** *n* an instrument for measuring the degree of fermentation. **zymō'sis** *n* fermentation; the course, process or condition, thought to be analogous to fermentation, constituting a zymotic disease. **zymotech'nic** or **zymotech'nical** *adj* producing and utilizing fermentation. **zymotech'nics** *n sing* the art of managing fermentation. **zymot'ic** *adj* relating to fermentation; of the nature of, relating to or causing an infectious disease. ◆ *n* an infectious disease. **zymot'ically** *adv.*

zymome /zī'mōm/ *n* an old name for the part of gluten insoluble in alcohol. [Gr *zȳmōma* a fermented mixture]

zymurgy /zī'mûr-ji/ *n* the branch of chemistry that deals with wine-making, brewing, distilling, and similar processes involving fermentation. [Gr *zȳmē* leaven, and *ergon* work]

Zyrian /zir'i-ən/ *n* a member of a people of NE Russia; their Finno-Ugric language. ◆ *adj* of or relating to the Zyrians or their language.

zythum /zī'thəm/ *n* a kind of beer made by the ancient Egyptians, highly commended by Diodorus Siculus, a writer of 1c BC. [Gr *zȳthos*]

Some first names

Masculine names are marked *m*, feminine names *f*.

Aaron *ā'rən, m* (*Heb*) lofty, mountaineer.

Abdul *ab-dŭl*, **Abd-al** *ab-däl, m* (*Ar*) combining element meaning 'servant of (the)', as, eg, in Abd-al-Rahman, servant of the Merciful (Allah).

Abigail *ab'i-gāl, f* (*Heb*) father rejoiced.–Dimins **Abby**, **Nabby**, **Gail**.

Abir *ä-bēr', f* (*Ar*) fragrance, perfume, aroma.

Abraham *ā'brə-həm,* **Abram** *ā'brəm, m* (*Heb*) *perh* father of a multitude, high father.–Dimins **Abe**, **Bram**.

Ada *ā'də, f prob* for Adelaide or other Germanic name beginning with *Adel-*, *Adal-* (noble).

Adam *ad'əm, m* (*Heb*) man, earth, red earth.

Adela *ad'i-lə,* **Adele** *-del', * **Adella** *-del'ə, f* (*Gmc*) noble.

Adelaide *ad'i-lād, f* from French *Adélaïde*, from German *Adelheid* (from *Adelheidis*), noble kind or sort.–Dimins **Addie**, **Addy**.

Adil, Adeel *ä-dēl', m* (*Ar*) fair, just.

Adnan *äd-nän', m* (*Ar*) of uncertain meaning, *perh* settler.

Adrian *ā'dri-ən, m* (*L*) of Adria (in Italy).–Fem **Adrianne** (*-an'*), **Adrienne** (*-en'*).

Afra *af'rə, f* a form of Aphra or (*L*) woman of Africa.

Agatha *ag'ə-thə, f* (*Gr*) good.–Dimin Aggie.

Agnes *ag'nis, f* (*Gr*) chaste.–Dimins **Aggie**, **Aggy**, **Annis**, **Annot**, **Nance**, **Nancy**, **Nessa**, **Nessie**, **Nesta**.

Ahmad *ähh'mäd,* **Ahmed** *ähh'med, m* (*Ar*) more commendable or praiseworthy.

Aidan, Aiden *ā'dən, m* (*Ir*) a diminutive form from *aodh*, fire.

Aileen *ā'lēn, ī'lēn, f* (Ir and Scot) *prob* a form of **Evelyn** and **Helen**, a variant of **Eileen**.

Ailie see **Eilidh**.

Ailish *ā'lish, f* (*Ir*) form of **Alice**.

Ailsa *āl'sə, f* from the Scottish island rock, *Ailsa* Craig.

Aine *ö'nyə, f* (*Ir*) radiance, brilliance; name of the fairy queen; also used as an Irish form of **Anne**.

Aisha, Ayesha, Aysha *ä'i-shə, f* (*Ar*) alive and prospering.

Aisling *ash'ling, f* (*Ir*) dream, vision.–Anglicized as **Ashling**.

Alan, Allan, Allen *al'ən, m* (*prob* Celtic) harmony.

Alannah, Alana *al-an'ə, al-a'nə, f perh* a feminine form of **Alan**, or from Irish form of endearment *a leanbh* oh child.

Alasdair, Alastair, Alistair, Alister *al'i-stər, m* (*Gaelic*) forms of **Alexander**.

Albert *al'bərt, m* (*Gmc*) nobly bright (famously noble).–Dimins **Al**, **Bert**, **Bertie**.–Fem **Albertina** (*-ē'na*), **Albertine** (*-ēn*).

Aled *al'id, m* from the name of a Welsh river.

Alexander *al-ig-zan'dər, -zän', m* (*Gr*) defender of men.– Dimins **Alec**, **Alex** (*-lik, -lix*), **Sandy**.–Fem **Alexandra**.– Dimins **Alex**, **Alexa**, **Sandra**, **Sandy**.

Alexei, Alexej *ə-lek'sā, m* Slavic forms of **Alexis**.

Alexis *ə-lek'sis, m* and *f* (*Gr*) helper.–Fem **Alexa**, **Alexia**.

Alfred *al'frid, m* (*Gmc*) elf counsel (good counsellor).–Dimins **Alf**, **Alfie**.

Algernon *al'jər-nən, m* (*OFr*) moustached.–Dimin **Algy**.

Ali *ä-lē', m* (*Ar*) sublime; *f* see **Alice**, **Alison**.

Alice *al'is,* **Alicia** *ə-lish'i-ə, -lis'i-ə, f* (*Gmc*) from Old French *Aliz* for *Adelheidis* (see **Adelaide**).–Dimins **Ali**, **Allie**, **Ally**, **Ellie**, **Elsie**. See also **Alison**.

Alison, Allison *al'i-sən, f* a Norman French pet form of **Alice**, latterly used *esp* in Scotland.–Dimins **Ailie**, **Ali**, **Elsie**.

Alistair see **Alasdair**.

Allan, Allen see **Alan**.

Allegra *ə-leg'rə, f* (Ital) cheerful, lively.

Alma *al'mə, f* (*L*) fostering, nourishing, loving.

Althea *al-thē'ə, al', f* (*Gr*) a healer, or wholesome.

Alun *al'ən, m* poss from the name of a Welsh river, but thought of as a variant of **Alan**.

Alwin, Alwyn *al'win, m* (*Gmc*) elf (good or noble) friend.

Amabel *am'ə-bel, f* (*L, amabilis*) lovable. See also **Mabel**.

Amanda *ə-man'də, f* (*L*) lovable.–Dimin **Mandy**.

Amber *am'bər, f* from the precious material.

Ambrose *am'brōz, m* (*Gr*) of the immortals, divine.

Amelia *ə-mē'li-ə, f* (*Gmc*) struggling , labour.–Dimin **Millie**.

Amin *a-mēn', m* (*Ar*) honest, reliable, trust worthy.–Fem **Amina** (*-mē'nə*).

Amrit *äm-rēt', m* (*Sans*) immortal.

Amy *ā'mi, f* (*Fr*) beloved.

Anaïs *an-ī-ēs, f* (Sp) derivative of **Ana** (**Anne**).

Anastasia *an-ə-stā'zhə, -zi-ə, f* (*Gr*) resurrection.–Dimin **Stacey**, **Stacy** (*stā'si*).

Andrew *an'droo, m* (*Gr*) manly.–Dimins **Andie**, **Andy**, **Drew** (*droo*).–Fem **Andrea** (*-dri-ə*), **Andrina** (*-drē'na*).

Aneurin, Aneirin *a-nā'rin, -nī ', -noi', m* (*Welsh*) of uncertain meaning, *perh* noble, seemly.–Dimin **Nye** (*nī*).

Angela *an'ji-lə, f,* **Angel** *ān'jəl, m* and *f* (*Gr*) angel, messenger.–Fem deriv **Angelica** (*-jel'ik-ə*).–Dimins **Angelina** (*an-ji-lē'nə, -lī'nə*), **Angie**, **Angy** (*an'ji*).

Angharad *an-gar'ad, -hhar'ad, f* (*Welsh*) much loved.

Angus *ang'gəs, m* (*Celtic*) *perh* one choice.–Dimin **Gus**.

Anil *ä-nēl', m* (*Sans*) wind, air.–Fem **Anila** (*-nē'lə*).

Anita see **Ann**.

Ann, Anne *an,* **Anna** *an'ə,* **Hannah** *han'ə, f* (*Heb*) God has favoured me.–Dimins **Anita** (*ə-nē'tə; Sp*), **Anneka**, **Annika** (*an'ə-kə; Swed*), **Annette** (*a-net'; Fr*), **Annie**, **Anushka** (*a-noo'shkə; Russ*), **Nan**, **Nance**, **Nancy**, **Nanette**, **Nina** (*nē'nə, nī'nə*), **Ninette** (*nē-net', ni-; Fr*).

Annabel, Annabelle *an'ə-bel,* **Annabella** *-bel'ə, f* poss an alteration of **Amabel**. –Dimins **Bel**, **Bell**, **Bella**, **Belle**.

Annis *an'is,* **Annot** *an'ət, f* diminutives of **Agnes**.

Anthea *an'thi-ə, f* (*Gr*) flowery.

Anthony *an'tə-ni,* (US) *an'thə-,* **Antony** *an'tə-ni, m* (*L*) from the Roman family name *Antonius*, of uncertain meaning. –Dimin **Tony** (*tō'ni*).–Fem **Antonia**.

Antoinette *an-twə-net', f* (*Fr*) a diminutive feminine of *Antoine*, French form of **Anthony**.

Anwar *än'wär, m* (*Ar*) brighter, clearer.

Aphra *Aphrah,* **Afra** *af'rə, f* (*Heb*) dust.

April *ā'pril, f* (*L*) from the name of the month.

Arabella *ar-ə-bel'ə, f* origin and meaning uncertain; *perh* an alteration of **Amabel**, or *perh* (*L orabilis*) easily entreated. –Dimins as for **Annabel**.

Archibald *är'chi-bld, -bōld, m* (*Gmc*) genuine and bold. –Dimins **Arch**, **Archie**, **Archy**. –See also **Gillespie**.

Areta *a-rē'tə,* **Aretha** *-thə, f* (*Gr*) virtue.

Ariadne *a-ri-ad'ni, f* (*Gr*) *perh* very holy.–Variants **Ariane** (*ar- i-än'; Fr*), **Arianne** (*-an'; Fr*), Arianna (*-an'ə; Ital*).

Arif *a'rēf, m* (*Ar*) acquainted, knowledgeable, knowing.

Arlene *är-len', f* (*Celtic*) pledge.

Arnold *är'nld, -nold, m* (*Gmc*) eagle ruler or power.

Arran *ar'ən, m* form of **Aaron** or (*Scot*) from the island of Arran.

Arthur *är'thər, m* (*Celtic*) *perh* bear, or (*Ir*) stone; or from a Roman family name *Artorius*.

Arun *ä-roon', m* (*Sans*) tawny red, like the dawn.–Fem **Aruna** (*-roo'nə*).

Asa *ā'sə, -zə, m* (*Heb*) healer.

Ashley, Ashleigh *ash'li, m* and *f* (*Gmc*) from the surname derived from a common place name, meaning ash wood.

Ashling see **Aisling**.

Ashraf *äsh'räf, m* (*Ar*) more honourable.

Ashton *ash'tən, m* (*OE*) 'ash-tree farmstead'.

Asif *a'sēf, a'zēf, m* (*Ar*) forgiveness.

Asma *äs'mə, f* (*Ar*) prestige.

Astrid *as'trid, f* (*Scand*) divinely beautiful.

Aubrey *ö'bri, m* (*Gmc*) elf rule; name of the Germanic king of the elves.–Dimin **Auberon**.

Audrey *ö'dri, f* (*Gmc*) noble power.

Augustine *ö'gəs-tēn, ö-gus'tin, m* (*L*) belonging to *Augustus*.

Augustus ŏ-gus'təs, *m* (*L*) venerable, exalted.–Dimins **Gus**, **Gussie**.–Fem **Augusta**.

Auriel, Auriol ör'i-əl, *f* derivatives of Latin *aurum*, gold.

Aurora ö-rö'rə, **Aurore** -rör', *f* (*L*) dawn.

Austin ö'stin, *m* a contraction of **Augustine**.

Ava ā'va, *f* of uncertain origin, *perh* Germanic, *perh* associated with Latin *avis*, bird.

Averil av'ə-ril, *m* and *f* (*Gmc*) *perh* like a boar in battle.

Avril av'ril, *m* and *f* (*Fr*) April.

Bailey bā'li, *m* (*Eng*) from the surname, itself sometimes given to someone who worked as a bailiff or lived near a bailey fortification.

Barbara bär'bə-rə, *f* (*Gr*) foreign woman.–Dimins **Bab**, **Babs**, **Babbie**, **Barbie**.

Barnabas bär'nə-bəs, **Barnaby** -bi, *m* (*Heb*) son of consolation.–Dimin **Barney**.

Barney bär'ni, *m* a diminutive of **Bernard**, **Barnabas**.

Barry bar'i, *m* (*Ir*) spear, or short for **Finbarr**, or from the surname and place name.–Dimins (*esp Aust*) **Baz**, **Bazza**.

Bartholomew bär-thol'ə-mū, *m* (*Heb*) son of **Talmi**.–Dimins **Bart**, **Bat**.

Basil baz'il, *m* (*Gr*) kingly.–Dimin **Baz**.

Beatrice bē'ə-tris, **Beatrix** -triks, bē-ā', *f* (*L*) making happy (*perh* an alteration of early Christian *Viatrix* (female voyager, pilgrim) by association with *beatus*, blessed).–Dimins **Bea**, **Bee**, **Beatty**, **Trix**, **Trixie**.

Becky bek'i, *f* a diminutive of **Rebecca**.

Belinda bə-lin'də, *f* of uncertain origin, *perh* Germanic, *perh* formed from Italian *bella*, beautiful.

Bell, Belle bel, **Bella** bel'ə, *f* see **Isabella**, **Annabel**, **Arabella**.

Benedict ben'i-dikt, **Benedick** -dik, *m* (*L*) blessed.

Benjamin ben'jə-min, *m* (*Heb*) son of the right hand (ie of good fortune).–Dimins **Ben**, **Benjie**, **Benjy**, **Benny**.

Berenice ber'i-nēs, **Bernice** bûr-nēs', *f* (*Gr*) from the Macedonian form of *Pherenike*, victory-bringer.

Bernard bûr'nərd, *m* (*Gmc*) strong as a bear.–Dimins **Bernie**, **Barney**.–Fem **Bernadette**.

Bert bûrt, **Bertie** bûr'ti, *m* diminutives of **Albert**, **Herbert** or other name ending in -**bert**, and of **Bertram** and (*f*) **Bertha**.

Bertha bûr'thə, *f* (*Gmc*) bright.–Dimins **Bert**, **Bertie**.

Bertram bûr'trəm, *m* (*Gmc*) bright raven.–Variant (or independent name meaning bright shield) **Bertrand** (bûr'trənd).–Dimins **Bertie**, **Bert**.

Beryl ber'il, *f* (*Gr*) from the precious stone.

Bess, Bessie, Beth see **Elizabeth**.

Bethany beth'ə-ni, *f* (*Biblical*) from the name of the village near Jerusalem.

Betsy, Bettina, Betty see **Elizabeth**.

Beverley bev'ər-li, *m* and *f* (*Gmc*) from the surname and place name, meaning meadow or stream of the beaver.

Bharat bä'rät, *m* (*Sans*) being maintained, an epithet of *Agni*, god of fire.–Fem **Bharati**.

Bianca bi-ang'kə, *f* the Italian form of **Blanche**.

Biddie, Biddy bid'i, *f* a diminutive of **Bridget**.

Bill bil, **Billy, Billie** bil'i, *m* diminutives of **William**.

Blair blār, *m* (*Gaelic*) from the surname, meaning 'plain or level field'.

Blaise blāz, *m* (*Fr*, from *L*) *perh* stuttering.

Blake blāk, *m* (*Eng*) from the surname, itself from Old English *blæc*, black, or *blāc*, pale, white, and given to people with either unusually dark or pale skin.

Blanche, Blanch blansh, *f* (*Fr*, from *Gmc*) white.

Bob see **Robert**.

Bobby see **Robert**.

Bonnie bon'i, *f* (*Scot*) pretty (used *esp* in US).

Boris bor'is, bö', *m* (*Russ perh Tatar*), small, but associated with *bor*, fight.

Bradley brad'lē, *m* from the surname, derived from the place name meaning 'broad clearing, meadow'. –Dimin **Brad**.

Bram see **Abraham**.

Brandon bran'dən, *m* from the surname, derived from the place name meaning 'hill covered with broom'; sometimes a variant of **Brendan**.

Brenda bren'də, *f perh* a feminine form of the Norse name **Brand**, brand or sword, or of Brendan.

Brendan bren'dən, *m* (*Ir*) meaning uncertain.

Brent brent, *m* from the surname, itself *orig* a place name.

Brett bret, *m* (*Eng*) from Latin *Brit(t)o*, Briton.

Brian, Bryan brī'ən, *m* (*Celtic*) meaning uncertain.

Bridget, Brigid, Brigit brij'it, **Bride** brīd, brē'jə, **Brīd** brēd, **Breda** brēd'ə *f* (*Celtic*) of uncertain meaning; name of a Celtic fire -goddess and an Irish saint.–Dimins **Biddie**, **Biddy**, **Bridie** (brī'di).

Briony, Bryony brī'ə-ni, *f* (*Eng*) from the plant name.

Brona bron'ə, **Bronach, Bronagh** bron'əhh, *f* (*Ir*) sorrowful.

Bronwen bron'win, *f* (*Welsh*) white breast.

Brooke brŭk, *f* (*Eng*) from the surname *Brook*, itself from the ordinary vocabulary word *brook*, meaning small stream.

Bruce broos, *m* from the surname, *orig* from Normandy, and the place name Brieuse.

Bruno broo'nō, *m* (*Gmc*) brown.

Bryan see **Brian**.

Brynmor brin'mör, *m* (*Welsh*) from the place name formed from *bryn*, hill and *mawr*, great.–Dimin **Bryn**.

Bryony see **Briony**.

Bunnie, Bunny bun'i, *m* and *f* (*Eng*) a pet name.

Bunty bun'ti, *f* (*Eng*) a pet name.

Caitlin kat'lin, kāt', -lēn', *f* (*Ir*) form of Catherine, anglicized as **Kathleen**.–Dimin **Cait**.

Caleb kā'leb, *m* (*Heb*) linked to the Hebrew word for 'dog' and thus representing loyalty or devotion.

Calum, Callum kal'əm, *m Gaelic* form of the saint's name Columba (*L*, dove).

Calvin kal'vin, *m* from the French surname, used in honour of the Protestant reformer and theologian John Calvin (1509–64).

Cameron kam'ə-ron, *m* (*Gaelic*) from the surname, *orig* meaning 'crooked nose'.

Camilla kə-mil'ə, *f* (*L*) *perh* a free -born attendant at a sacrifice ; in Virgil, name of a queen of the Volsci.

Campbell kam'bəl, *m* (*Gaelic*) from the surname, *orig* meaning 'crooked mouth'.

Candace, Candice kan'dis, *f* meaning uncertain; dynastic name of the queens of ancient Ethiopia. –Dimin **Candy**.

Candia kan'di-ə, *f* from the capital (now Heraklion) of Crete.

Candida kan'di-də, *f* (*L*) white.

Cara kä'rə, *f* (*L* and *Ital*) dear one.–Dimin **Carina** (kə-rē'nə).

Carl, Karl karl, *m* Germanic forms of Charles.–Fem **Carla, Karla** (kär'lə).–Fem derivs **Carleen, Carlene** (kär-lēn').–Dimins **Carlie, Carly**.

Carmel kär'məl (*Heb*), **Carmen** kär'men (*Sp*, altered by association with Latin *carmen*, a poem, song), *f* garden.

Carol kar'əl, *f perh* a diminutive of **Caroline**; *m* from *Carolus*, Latin form of **Charles**.–Fem derivs **Carola** (kar'ə-lə), **Carole** (kar'əl).

Caroline kar'ə-līn, **Carolyn** -lin, *f* derivatives of *Carolus*, Latin form of Charles.–Dimins **Caddie, Caro, Carrie, Lina** (lē'nə).

Carys kar'is, **Cerys** ker'is, *f* (*Welsh*) modern invention, from *car*, love.

Caspar kas'pər, *m* see **Jasper**.

Cassandra kə-san'drə, -sän', *f* (*Gr mythol*) a daughter of Priam of Troy, a prophetess whom no-one heeded.–Dimins **Cass, Cassie**.

Cathal, Cahal kä'həl, *m* (*Ir*) *perh* strong in battle.

Catherine, Catharine, Katharine, Katherine kath'ə-rin, kath'rin, **Kathryn** kath'rin, **Catherina** -ə-rē'nə, **Katrine** kat'rin, **Katerina** kat-ə-rē'nə, **Katrina** kə-trē'nə, *f* from Greek *Aikaterine*, of uncertain origin, later assimilated to *katharos*, pure.–Dimins **Cathie, Cathy, Kate, Katie, Katy, Katya** (*Russ*), **Kath, Kathie, Kathy, Kay, Kit, Kittie, Kitty**.

Catriona kə-trē'ə-nə, kat-ri-ō'nə, *f* the Gaelic form of **Catherine**.

Cecil ses'il, *m* (*L*) the Roman family name *Caecilius* (literally, blind).–Fem **Cecilia** (si-sil'yə, -sēl'yə), **Cecily** (ses'i-li), **Cicely** (sis'i-li).–Dimins **Cis, Cissy, Cissie**.

Cedric sed'rik, *m prob* a mistake of Sir Walter Scott's for *Cerdic* (name of the first king of the West Saxons).

Celia sē'li-ə, *f* feminine of the Roman family name *Caelius* (poss heavenly).

Celina si-lē'nə, *f* a variant of Selina or a derivative of **Celia**.

Ceri ker'i, *m* and *f* (*Welsh*) love, or (*f*) a diminutive of *Ceridwen* (*mythol*) goddess of poetic inspiration.

Cerys see Carys.

Chad *chad*, *m* (*Celtic*) battle; name of a Northumbrian saint.

Chaim *hhī'əm*, *m* (*Heb*) life.

Chandra *chän'drə*, *m* and f, **Chander** *chän'dər*, *m* (*Sans*) moon.

Chantal *shä-täl*, f from the French family name, itself a place name, used in honour of Saint Jeanne of Chantal.

Charity *char'i-ti*, f from the virtue.

Charles *chärlz*, *m* (*Gmc*) manly.–Dimins **Charlie**, **Charley**, **Chae**, **Chas**, **Chay** (*chä*) **Chic**, **Chick**, (*US*) **Chuck**.–Fem deriv **Charlene** (*shär'lēn*, *-lēn'*).

Charlotte *shär'lət*, f (*Fr*) diminutive of **Charles**.–Dimins **Charley**, **Lottie**.

Charmaine, Sharmaine *shär-mān'*, f prob a 20c invention.

Charmian *shär'mi-ən*, *chär'*, *kär'*, f (*Gr*) joy.

Chelsea, Chelsey *chel'si*, f from the London borough of Chelsea.

Cher, Chère *shär*, **Cherie, Sherry** *sher'i*, f (*Fr*) dear one.

Cherry *cher'i*, f from the fruit or blossom; also a variant of **Cherie**.– Deriv **Cheryl** (*cher'il*, *sher'il*), **Sheryl** (*sher'*).

Chloe *klō'i*, f (*Gr*) a green shoot, verdure.

Christabel *kris'tə-bel*, f (*Gr*) 'anointed' (or 'Christ ') and (*L*) 'fair '.

Christian *kris'ti-ən*, *-chən*, *m* and f, belonging to, follower of, Christ.–Dimins **Chris, Christie, Christy**.–Fem **Christiana** (*-ti-ä'nə*), **Christina** (*-tē'nə*), **Christine** (*kris'tēn* or *-tēn'*), (*Scot*) **Kirsteen** (*kûr'stēn*), **Kirstin**.–Dimins **Chris, Chrissie, Kirsty, Kirstie, Teenie, Tina** (*tē'nə*).

Christopher *kris'tə-fər*, *m* (*Gr*) carrying Christ.–Dimins **Chris**, (*Ir*) **Christy, Kit**.

Chrystal see **Crystal**.

Chuck *chuk*, *m* a diminutive of **Charles**.

Ciara, Ciaran see **Kieran**.

Cicely see **Cecil**.

Cindy, Sindy *sin'di*, f diminutives of **Cynthia, Lucinda**.

Cis, Cissy, Cissie see **Cecil**.

Clancy *klan'si*, *m perh* from the Irish surname *Mac- Fhlannchaidh*, or a diminutive of **Clarence**.

Clara *klä'rə*, **Clare, Claire** *klär*, f (*L*) bright.–Derivs **Clarice** (*klar'is*), **Clarinda** (*klə-rin'də*), **Clarissa** (*-ris'ə*).

Clarence *klar'əns*, *m* from the dukedom held by royal princes, from a place name.

Claud, Claude *klöd*, *m* (*L*) lame.–Fem **Claudia**.–Fem dimins **Claudette** (*klö-det'* ; *Fr*), **Claudine** (*-den'*; *Fr*).

Clement *klem'ənt*, *m* (*L*) mild, merciful.–Dimin **Clem**.–Fem **Clementina** (*-ē'nə*), **Clementine** (*-ēn*, *-īn*).

Cleopatra *kli-ə-pat'rə*, *-pä'*, f (*Gr*) glory of her father.–Dimin **Cleo** (*klē'ō*).

Clifford *klif'ərd*, *m* from the surname.

Clint *klint*, *m* diminutive of the surname **Clinton**.

Clive *klīv*, *m* from the surname, *orig* honouring Robert Clive of India (1725–74).

Clodagh *klō'də*, f (*Ir*) from the name of a river in Tipperary.

Clovis *klō'vis*, *m* a Latinization of Frankish *Chlodowig*, original form of **Louis, Lewis**.

Clyde *klīd*, *m* from the River *Clyde* in Scotland.

Colette *ko-let'*, f see **Nicholas**.

Colin *kol'in*, *kö'*, *m orig* a diminutive of **Nicholas**; also an anglicization of Gaelic *Cailean*, follower of Columba, or youth.

Colleen *ko-lēn'*, f (*Ir*) girl.

Colm, Colum *kol'əm*, *m* Irish forms of Latin *Columba*. See **Calum** and **Malcolm**.

Conor, Connor *kon'ər*, *m* (*Ir*) an anglicized form of *Conchobhar*, *perh* lover of hounds.

Conrad *kon'rad*, *m* (*Ger*) bold in counsel.

Constance *kon'stəns*, f (*L*) steadfast, or constancy.–Dimins **Con, Connie**.–Deriv **Constantine** (*kon'stən-tīn*), *m*.

Cora *kö'rə*, f poss (*Gr*) girl, used also as a diminutive eg of Spanish *Corazon*, heart.

Coral *kor'əl*, f from the precious material.

Cordelia *kör-dē'li-ə*, f perh (*L*) warm-hearted.

Corin *kor'in*, *m* (*L*) from *Quirinus*, a designation of *Romulus*, Rome's founder, of uncertain meaning.

Corinne *ko-rin'*, *-ren'*, **Corinna** *-rin'ə*, f (*Gr*) diminutive of *kore*, maiden.

Cornelia *kor-ne'li-ə*, f (*L*) feminine form of the Roman family name *Cornelius*, esp honouring the mother of reformers Tiberius and Gaius Gracchus.

Cosmo *koz'mō*, *m* (*Gr*) order.

Courtney *kört'ni*, *m* and f from the surname.

Craig *krāg*, *m* from the surname, itself from *Gaelic creag*, rock, found in place names.

Cressida *kres'i-də*, f (*Gr*) English form of *Chryseis*, accusative *Chryseida*, daughter of *Chryses*.

Crispin *kris'pin*, **Crispian** *-pi-ən*, *m* (*L*) from the Roman family name *Crispinus*, from *crispus*, curly-headed.

Crystal, Chrystal, Krystal, Krystle *kris'təl*, f crystal, the precious material, itself from Greek, ice.

Cuthbert *kuth'bərt*, *kudh'*, *m* (*OE*) well-known, bright.

Cynthia *sin'thi-ə*, f (*Gr*) of Mount Cynthus in Delos, an epithet of the goddess Artemis (Diana).–Dimins **Cindy, Sindy**.

Cyril *sir'il*, *m* (*Gr*) lordly.

Cyrus *sī'rəs*, *m* (*Pers*) of uncertain meaning.–Dimin **Cy**.

Dafydd *dav'idh*, *m* (*Welsh*) form of David.

Dai *dī*, *m* (*Welsh*) *perh orig* shining one, but taken as a diminutive of **Dafydd**.

Daisy *dā'zi*, f from the flower, also a pet form and punning translation of *Marguerite* (the French name for the flower).

Damian, Damien *dā'mi-ən*, **Damon** *-mən*, *m* (*Gr*) *perh* connected with *damaein*, to tame.

Dana *dā'nə* or *dä'nə*, *m* and f from the surname, or (f) a diminutive of **Daniela**.

Daniel *dan'yəl*, *m* (*Heb*) the Lord is judge.–Dimins **Dan, Danny**.– Fem **Daniela** (*-i-ā'lə*), **Daniella, Danielle** (*-el'*).

Daphne *daf'ni*, f (*Gr*) laurel.

Darcey *dä'si*, f (*Eng*) from the surname *Darcy*, itself derived from a Norman surname referring to the town of Arcy in France.

Darren *dar'ən*, *m* from the Irish surname.

David *dā'vid*, *m* (*Heb*) beloved.–Dimins **Dave, Davie, Davy**. –Fem **Davina** (*də-vē'nə*).

Dawn *dön*, f from the noun.

Dean *dēn*, *m* from the surname.

Deanna see **Diana**.

Deb, Debdan see **Dev, Devdan**.

Deborah *deb'ə-rə*, *di-bö'rə*, **Debra** *deb'rə*, f (*Heb*) bee.–Dimins **Deb, Debbie, Debby**.

Declan *dek'lən*, *m* (*Ir*) name of an Irish saint , of uncertain origin.

Dee *dē*, *m* and f from the surname, the river name, or a shortening of any name with the initial D.

Deepak, Deepika see **Dipak**.

Deirdre *dēr'dri*, f (*Ir*) meaning doubtful.

Del see **Derek**.

Delia *dē'li-ə*, f (*Gr*) of the island of Delos.

Della *del'ə*, f a diminutive of **Adela**, alteration of **Delia**, or a 19c invention.

Delroy *del'roi*, *m* variant of **Elroy**.

Delyth *del'ith*, f (*Welsh*) pretty.

Demelza *di-mel'zə*, f Cornish, from a local place name.

Denis, Dennis, Denys *den'is*, *m* (*Fr*) a medieval contraction of Latin *Dionysius*, belonging to Dionysus or Bacchus.–Dimins **Den, Denny**.–Fem **Denise** (*də-nēz'*).

Denzil *den'zil*, *m* from the Cornish surname, formerly *Denzell*, a local place name.

Derek, Derrick, Deryck *der'ik*, *m* (*Gmc*) a medieval form of *Theodoric*, ruler of the people.–Dimin **Del**.

Dermot see **Diarmid**.

Dervla *där'vlə*, f (*Ir*) anglicized form of *Dearbhla* or *Deirbhile*, of uncertain meaning.

Desiree *dä-zē'rā*, f (*Fr*, from *L*) longed-for.–Masc **Desire**.

Desmond *dez'mənd*, *m* (*Ir*) from the surname or the district.

Dev *dāv*, **Deb** *dāb*, *m* (*Sans*) god.

Devdan *dāv'dän*, **Debdan** *dāb'dän*, *m* (*Sans*) god-given.

Dewi *de'wi*, *m* (*Welsh*) form of **David**.

Dexter *dek'stə*, *m* from Old English *deag*, dye, and thus meaning 'dyer'.–Dimin **Dex**.

Diana *dī-an'ə*, **Dian** *dī-an'*, **Diane** *dē-an'*, *dī-an'*, **Dianne** *dē-an'*, *dī-an'*, **Deanne** *dē-an'*, **Deanna** *-an'ə*, f (*L*) the Roman goddess *Diana*.–Dimins **Di, Die** (*dī*).

Diarmid, Diarmuid, Diarmaid *dēr'məd*, *m* (*Celtic*) free from envy. –Anglicized as **Dermot**.

Dick, Dickie, Dickon see **Richard**.

Dilip *di-lēp'*, *m* (*Sans*) *perh* protector of Delhi.

Dilwyn *dil'in*, *m* (*Welsh*) steadfast and fair.

Dilys *dil'is*, f (*Welsh*) sure, constant, genuine.

Dinah *dī'nə, f (Heb)* judged, or dedicated.

Dionne *dē-on', f (Gr)* feminine, diminutive formed from *Dionysius* (see **Denis**).

Dipak, Deepak *dē'päk, m (Sans)* little lamp, or lamp -like.–Fem **Deepika** (*dē'pi-kə*).

Dirk *dûrk, m* Dutch form of **Derek**.

Dolina *do-le'nə, f (Scot)* formed from *Gaelic Dolag* (f), diminutive of **Donald**.

Dolly see **Dorothy**.

Dolores *də-lo'rez, f (Sp)* sorrows.–Dimin **Lola, Lolita**.

Dominic, Dominick *dom'i-nik, m (L)* Sunday.–Fem **Dominica** (*də-min'i-kə*).

Donald *don'əld, Donal dō'nəl, don', m (Celtic)* world chief.–Dimins **Don, Donnie**.

Donna *don'ə, f (Ital)* mistress, lady; sometimes used as feminine of **Donald**.

Dora *dö'rə, f prob* a diminutive of **Dorothy**; used also for **Theodora** and other names ending in *-dora*.

Doreen *dö'rēn, dö-rēn', f* a derivative of **Dora** or of **Dorothy**.

Doris *dor'is, f (Gr)* the name of a sea-nymph.

Dorothy *dor'ə-thi, Dorothea -thē'ə, f (Gr)* gift of God.–Dimins **Dolly, Dora, Dorrie, Do, Dot, Dottie**.

Dougal *doo'gəl, Dugald doo'gəld, m (Celtic)* dark stranger.

Douglas *dug'ləs, m (orig Scot)* from the surname, or the river. –Dimins **Doug** (*dug*), **Dougie, Duggie**.

Drew see **Andrew**.

Duane, Dwane *dwān, m (Ir)* from the surname *Dubhin*, from *dubh*, black.

Dudley *dud'li, m* from the surname.

Dugald see **Dougal**.

Dulcie *dul'si, f (L)* sweet ; a 19c invention.

Duncan *dung'kən, m (Celtic)* brown, brown warrior.

Dustin *dus'tin, m* from the surname.

Dylan *dil'ən, m (Welsh) perh* wave, the name of a sea god.

Dymphna *dimf'nə, Dympna dimp', f (Ir) prob* little fawn.

Eamonn, Eamunn *ā'mən, m* Irish form of **Edmund**.

Eartha *ûr'thə, f* from the noun 'earth'.

Edel *i-del', f (Ir) perh* darling.

Edgar *ed'gər, m (OE)* spearman.–Dimins **Ed, Eddie, Eddy, Ned, Neddie, Neddy**.

Edith *ē'dith, f (OE)* bringing riches in war.–Dimins **Edie, Edy**.

Edmund *ed'mənd, m (OE)* protector of riches.–Dimins **Ed, Eddie, Eddy, Ned, Neddie, Neddy**.

Edna *ed'nə, f* an anglicized form of Irish **Eithna**, or (*Heb*) pleasure, delight.

Edward *ed'wərd, m (OE)* rich guard.–Dimins **Ed, Eddie, Eddy, Ned, Neddie, Ted, Teddie, Teddy**.

Edwin *ed'win, m (OE)* prosperity or riches, friend.–Dimins as for **Edmund**.–Fem **Edwina** (*-wē'nə*).

Egon *ē'gon, m (Gmc) perh* sword- edge.

Eileen *ī'lēn, ī-lēn', f (Ir) prob* a form of **Evelyn**, also used for **Helen**. See also **Aileen**.

Eilidh *ā'li, f* Gaelic diminutive of **Alice** or **Helen**.–Anglicized as Ailie.

Eiluned, Eluned *i-lin'əd, f (Welsh)* idol, image.

Eirian *ī'ri-ən, f (Welsh)* fair, brilliant.

Eirlys *īr'lis, f (Welsh)* snowdrop.

Eithne, Ethne *eth'ni, Eithna, Ethna -nə, f (Ir)* from *aodhnait*, diminutive of *aodh*, fire. See also **Aidan**.

Elaine *i-lān', f* an Old French form of **Helen**; some suggest a Celtic origin, with meaning 'fawn'.

Eleanor, Eleanore, Elinor *el'i-nər, f perh* forms of **Helen**, or from a Germanic root meaning 'foreign'.–Dimins **Ella, Ellen, Nell, Nellie, Nelly, Nora**.

Elijah *eli'jə, m (Heb)* from Hebrew *Eliyahu*, God is Yah.

Elizabeth, Elisabeth *i-liz'ə-beth, f (Heb)* God is satisfaction. –Dimins **Bess, Bessie, Bessy, Bet, Beth, Betsy, Bettina, Betty, Eliza, Elsie, Libby, Lisa** (*lī 'zə, lē', lē'sə*), **Liza, Lise** (*lēz*), **Lisbet, Lisbeth, Lizbeth, Liz, Lizzie, Lisette** (*li-zet'*).

Ella *el'ə, f (Gmc)* all.–Also a diminutive of **Eleanor** and **Ellen** or of **Isabella** or other name ending in *-ella*.

Ellen *el'in, f* a form of **Helen**, also used for **Eleanor**.–Dimin **Ellie**.

Elliot, Elliott *el'iat, m (Eng)* from the surname, itself from an Old French version of *Elias*, the Greek translation of **Elijah**.

Ellis *el'is, m (Eng)* from the surname, itself from the Greek *Elias*,

the Greek translation of **Elijah**. Also associated with the Welsh *Elisud*, from *elus*, kind.

Elma *el'mə, f* a diminutive of **Wilhelmina**, or a combination of eg **Elizabeth Marjory, Elizabeth Mary**.

Eloise *el'ō-ēz, Eloisa el-ō-ē'zə, f (Gmc)* of uncertain derivation, *perh* from *Aloysius*, a Latin form of **Louis**.

Elroy *el'roi, m* variant of **Leroy**.

Elsie *el'si, f* a diminutive of **Elizabeth, Alison, Alice**.

Elspeth *el'spəth, Elspet el'spət, f (Scot)* forms of Elizabeth.

Elton *el'tən, m* from the surname.

Eluned see **Eiluned**.

Elvira *el-vē'rə or -vī 'rə, f (Sp) prob* of Germanic origin.

Eivis *el'vis, m (Ir) perh* from *Ailbhe*, the name of an Irish saint. –Fem **Elva**.

Elwyn *el'win, m (Welsh) perh* fair face.

Emerald *em'ə-rəld, f* from the precious stone.

Emily *em'i-li, em'li, f (L)* from the Roman family name *Aemilius*. –Dimin **Millie**.

Emlyn *em'lin, m (Welsh)* origin uncertain; Latin *Aemilianus*, a Roman family name, has been suggested.

Emma *em'ə, f (Gmc) orig* a diminutive of various names beginning *Ermin-, Irmin-*, an element denoting 'whole', 'universal'. –Dimins **Emm, Emmie, Emmy**.

Emmanuel *i-man'ū-əl, m (Heb)* God with us.–Dimin **Manny**.

Emmeline *em'i-lēn, f prob* a derivative of **Amelia**.

Emrys *em'ris, m* Welsh form of **Ambrose**.

Ena *ē'nə, f (Ir)* fire ; or a shortened form of **Eugenia** or other name of similar sound.

Enid *ē'nid, f (Welsh)* of uncertain origin.

Enoch *ē'nək, m (Heb) poss* consecrated, or teaching, skilled.

Eoin *ē'ən, ō'ən, m (Gaelic,* Ir) form of **John**.

Eric *er'ik, m (Gmc, ON Eirikr) perh* sole ruler.–Fem **Erica** (*er'i- kə*), associated with Greek *ereike*, Latin *erica*, heather.

Erin *er'in, ā'rin, f* Ireland, from Irish *Eirinn*, dative of Eire.

Ernest *ûr'nist, m (Gmc)* earnest.–Dimin **Ernie**.

Errol *er'əl, m* of obscure origin, *perh* from the Scottish place name, *perh* a variant of **Eryl**.

Eryl *er'il, m* and *f (Welsh)* watcher.

Esme, Esmé, Esmée *ez'mē, es-mā', m* and *f (Fr)* loved.

Esmond *ez'mənd, m (OE)* 'grace' and 'protection'.

Estelle *e-stel', f (OFr)* star.–Deriv **Estella** (*-stel'ə*).

Esther *es'tər, Hester hes'tər, f poss* Persian, 'star' or 'turtle'. –Dimins **Essie, Hetty**.

Ethan *ē'thən, m (Heb)* strong one, solid, enduring.

Ethel *eth'l, f (OE)* noble.

Ethne, Ethna see **Eithne**.

Euan see **Ewan**.

Eugene *ū'jēn, m (Gr)* well-born.–Dimin **Gene**.–Fem **Eugenia, Eugenie** (*ū-zhā'ni*).–Dimins **Ena, Gene**.

Eunice *ū'nis, f (Gr)* happy victory.

Euphemia *ū-fē'mi-ə, f (Gr)* of good report.–Dimins **Effie, Phemie**.

Eustace *ū'stas, m (Gr)* rich in corn (*eustachys*, confused with *eustathes*, stable).–Fem **Eustacia** (*ū-stā'si-ə, -shə*).

Eva *ē'və, Eve ēv, f (Heb)* life.–Dimin **Evie**.

Evadne *i-vad'ni, f (Gr mythol)* name (of uncertain meaning) of the wife of the Theban hero *Capaneus*, who threw herself on his funeral pyre.

Evan *ev'ən, m (Welsh)* an anglicization of *Iefan*, a form of **Ieuan**.

Evelyn *ēv'lin, ev'lin, ev'i-lin, f* partly diminutive of **Eve**, partly Germanic; (m) *prob* from the surname, derived from the female name.

Evonne *i-von', f* an alteration of **Yvonne**.

Ewan, Ewen, Euan *ū'ən, m (Ir* and *Gaelic)* anglicizations of **Eoghan**, of uncertain meaning. See also Owen.

Ezra *ez'rə, m (Heb)* help.

Fabian *fā'bi-ən, m (L)* from the Roman name *Fabianus*, itself derived from the family name *Fabius*.

Faisal, Faysal *fī'zäl, m (Ar)* judge, sword.

Faith *fāth, f* from the Christian virtue.

Fanny *fan'i, f* a diminutive of **Frances**.

Farah *fär'ə, f (Ar)* joy, happiness.

Farid, Fareed *fä-rēd' m (Ar)* unique, unequalled.–Fem **Farida, Fareeda** gem, pearl.

Faruq *fä-rook', m (Ar)* judge of right and wrong.

Fatima *fä'ti-mə, f (Ar)* chaste, motherly.

Fay, Faye *fā, f (OFr)* either fairy, or faith; also a shortening of **Faith**.

Faysal see **Faisal**.

Feargal *fûr'gəl, m (Ir) perh* man of courage.

Fedora *fi-dö'rə, f (esp US)* from *Feodora*, Russian form of **Theodora**.

Felicity *fi-lis'i-ti, f (L)* happiness.

Felix *fē'liks, m (L)* happy.–Fem **Felicia** *('-lish'i-ə, -lis-i-ə)*, **Felice** *('-lēs')*.

Fenella *fi-nel'ə, f* anglicization of *Gaelic Fionnghuala*, white shoulder.–*Ir* **Finola** *(fi-nō'lə)*, **Fionnuala** *(fi-noo'lə)*.–Dimins **Nola** *(nō'lə)*, **Nuala** *(noo'lə)*.

Ferdinand *fûr'di-nand, m (Gmc) perh* peace in bravery or *(Sp)* prepared for the journey.

Fergus *fûr'gəs, m (Gaelic)* an anglicization of *Fearghas, perh* manly vigour, or supremely choice.

Ffion *fē'on, f (Welsh)* rose -red, or the colour of foxgloves.

Finbar, Finbarr *fin'bär, m (Ir)* fairheaded one.

Fingal *fing'gəl, m (Gaelic)* an anglicization of *Fionnghall*, fair stranger.

Finlay, Finley *fin'li, m (Gaelic) prob* fair warrior.

Finn *fin*, **Fionn** *fyun, fūn, m* (Ir and *Gaelic*) fair.–Dimin **Fintan**.

Finola, Fionnuala see **Fenella**.

Fiona *fē-ō'nə, f* from *Gaelic fionn*, fair.

Flavia *flā'vi-ə, f (L)* feminine form of the Roman family name *Flavius*, derived from *flavus*, yellow, fair-haired.

Fleur *flûr, f (Fr)* flower.

Floella *flō-el'ə, f* combination of **Flo** and **Ella**.

Flora *flō'rə, f (L)* name of the Roman flower goddess.–Dimins **Flo**, **Florrie** *(flor'i)*.

Florence *flor'əns, f (L)* blooming; also, born in Florence.–Dimins **Flo**, **Florrie**, **Flossie**, **Floy**.

Floyd *floid, m prob* a variant of **Lloyd**.

Francesca *franches'ka, f (It)* from the Roman *Franciscus*, from the Latin meaning 'Frenchman'.

Francis *frän'sis, m (Fr)* French.–Fem **Frances** *(frän'sis)*.–Dimins **Fanny**, **Francie**, **Francine**, **Frankie**.

Frank *frangk, m* either *(Gmc)* a Frank, a Frenchman, or a diminutive of **Francis**.–Dimin **Frankie**.

Fraser, Frasier *frāz'ər, frāzh'ər, m* from the surname, *orig* Norman French de *Frisselle*, de *Fraseliere, perh* associated with *fraise*, strawberry.

Freda *frē'də, f* diminutive of **Winifred**, or a variant of **Frieda**.

Frederick, Frederic *fred'ə-rik, fred'rik, m (Gmc)* peaceful ruler. –Fem **Frederica** *(fred-ə-rē'kə)*.–Dimins (m and f) **Fred**, **Freddie**, **Freddy**.

Freya *frā'ə, f (ON)* the name of the goddess of love in Norse mythology.

Frieda *frē'də, f (Gmc)* peace.

Gabriel *gā'bri-əl, gab', m*, formerly also *f (Heb)* God is mighty, or man of God.–Fem **Gabrielle** *(gā'bri-əl, gab')*.–Dimins (*m* and *f*) **Gabi**, **Gabby**.

Gaenor see **Gaynor**.

Gaia, Gaea *gī'ə, f (Gr, mythol)* the goddess Earth.

Gail, Gale, Gayle *gāl, f orig* diminutive of **Abigail**.

Gamal see **Jamal**.

Gareth *gar'ith, m* Malory's remodelling of Old French *Gahariet, prob* from a Welsh name. ·

Garret *gar'it, m (esp Ir)* from the surname, itself a form of **Gerard** or **Gerald**.

Gary, Garry *gar'i, m* from the place name and surname, used also as a diminutive of **Gareth**.–Dimin **Gaz**.

Gauri *gö'ri, f (Sans)* white.

Gavin *gav'in, m (Welsh) perh* white hawk.

Gay, Gaye *gā, m* and *f (Eng)* cheerful.

Gaynor *gā'nər, f (Welsh)* a form of **Guinevere**.

Gaz see **Gary**.

Geeta see **Gita**.

Gemma, Jemma *jem'ə, f (Ital)* a gem.

Gene *jēn*, for **Eugene**, **Eugenia**.

Genevieve *jen'i-vēv, f (Fr, from Celtic)* of uncertain meaning.

Geoffrey, Jeffrey *jef'ri, m (OHGer) prob* a conflation of two names, *Gaufrid*, district peace (peaceful ruler), and *Walahfrid*, traveller peace (peaceful traveller).–Dimins **Geoff**, **Jeff**.

George *jörj, m (Gr)* farmer, husbandman.–Dimins **Geordie**, **Georgie**, **Georgy**.–Fem **Georgia** *(jör'jə)*, **Georgiana** *(-ji- ä'nə)*, **Georgette** *(-jet')*, **Georgina** *(-jē'nə)*.–Dimin **Georgie**.

Geraint *ge-rīnt', m (Welsh)* of uncertain origin.

Gerald *jer'əld, m (Gmc)* spear-wielding.–Fem **Geraldine** *(-ēn)*.

Gerard *jer'ärd, -ərd, jə-rärd', m (Gmc)* brave spearman.

Gerda *gûr'də, f (ON)* in Norse mythology, the name of the wife of the god Frey.

Germaine *jûr-mān', jər-, zher-men', f (Fr, from L)* German.

Gerrie, Gerry *jer'i, m* diminutive of **Gerald**, **Gerard**, or *(f)* of **Geraldine**.

Gertrude *gûr'trood, f (Gmc)* spearwoman, or strong as a spear.– Dimins **Gert**, **Gertie**, **Trudy**.

Gervase *jûr'vis, -vāz, m (Gmc) perh* a combination of 'spear ' and 'servant '.–Fem **Gervaise** *(jûr-vāz')*.

Ghislaine *gi-len'* or *giz-len', f (OFr) prob* an inflected form of **Giselle**.

Gideon *gid'i-ən, m (Heb)* hewer.

Gilbert *gil'bərt, m (Gmc)* bright pledge (famous or trusted pledger).–Dimin **Gil**.

Giles *jīlz, m (Fr, from Gr)* kid.

Gillespie *gi-les'pi, m (Gaelic)* servant of the bishop.–Anglicized by false etymology as **Archibald**.

Gillian *jil'i-ən, f orig* a variant of **Julian**.–Dimins **Gill**, **Gilly**.

Gina *jē'nə, f* diminutive of **Georgina** or **Regina**.

Ginny see **Virginia**.

Giselle *ji-zel', zhi-, f (Fr, from Gmc)* pledge.

Gita, Geeta *gē'tə, f (Sans)* song.

Gladys *glad'is, f* a simplified form of Welsh *Gwladys*, of uncertain origin.

Glen, Glenn *glen, m*, also *f*, from the surname, or directly from the *Gaelic* place -name element *gleann*, glen, valley.

Glenda *glen'də, f (Welsh)* a combination of *glan*, pure, and *da*, good.

Glenys *glen'is, f (Welsh)* pure, holy, clean.

Gloria *glō'ri-ə, glö', f (L)* glory.

Glyn *glin, m (Welsh)* valley.

Glynis *glin'is, f (Welsh) prob* pure, a variant of **Glenys**, but taken as a feminine of **Glyn**.

Gobind see **Govind**.

Godfrey *god'fri, m (Gmc)* God's peace.

Golda, Golde *gōl'də*, **Goldie** *gōl'di, f (Yiddish)* gold.

Gopal *gö'pal, m (Sans)* cowherd.

Gordon *gör'dən, m* from the Scottish surname.

Govind *gö'vind*, **Gobind** *gö'bind, m (Sans)* finder of cows.

Grace *grās, f (Fr)* grace, *orig esp* in its religious sense.–Dimin **Gracie**.

Graham, Grahame, Graeme *grā'əm, m* from the surname.

Gráinne, Granya *grä'nyə*, **Grania** *-ni-ə, f (Ir)* of uncertain origin, in Irish myth the name of the hero Finn's beloved.

Grant *gränt, m* from the surname, *orig* from the French *grand*, tall.

Gregory *greg'ə-ri, (Scot)* **Gregor** *greg'ər, m (Gr)* watcher.–Dimin **Greg**.

Greta *grē'tə, gre'tə, f* diminutive of **Margaret**.

Griselda, Grizelda *gri-zel'də, f (Gmc) perh* grey war, *perh* Christ war.–Dimin **Zelda**.

Gudrun *güd'rən, f (Gmc)* wise, or wily, in battle.

Guinevere *gwin'ə-vēr, f (OFr, from Welsh)* 'fair ' and 'soft '.

Gus *gus, m* a diminutive of **Angus** or **Augustus**.

Guy *gī, m (Gmc) perh* wood, *perh* wide.

Gwen *gwen, f (Welsh)* fair, white, blessed, or a diminutive of **Gwendolen** or **Gwenllian**.

Gwendolen *gwen'də-lin, f (Welsh)* white (second element obscure).–Dimins **Gwenda**, **Gwennie**.

Gwenllian *gwen'li-ən, f (Welsh) prob* fair-skinned.

Gwenyth *gwen'ith, f (Welsh)* a variant of **Gwyneth**.

Gwillym, Gwilym *gwil'im, m* Welsh forms of **William**.

Gwyn *gwin, m (Welsh)* white, fair.

Gwyneth *gwin'ith, f (Welsh)* blessed.

Hal *hal, m* a diminutive of **Henry**.

Haley see **Hayley**.

Hamish *hā'mish, m (Gaelic)* anglicization of *Sheumais*, vocative of *Seumas* (**James**).

Hamza, Hamzah *häm'zä*, *m* (*Ar*) *perh* strong , steadfast.

Hani *hä'ni*, *m* (*Ar*) glad, happy.–Fem **Haniyya** (*-në'ya*).

Hank *hangk*, *m* *orig* a back-formation from *Hankin*, a diminutive of **John**, now used as a diminutive of **Henry**.

Hannah *han'a*, *f* see **Ann**.

Hari *hä'ri*, *m* (*Sans*) an epithet of Vishnu or Krishna, literally yellowish brown.

Harley *hä'li* , *m* (*Eng*) from the surname, from Old English meaning 'from the hare meadow or hill'.

Harold *har'ald*, *m* (*Gmc*) army ruler.

Haroun, Harun *hä-roon'*, *m* (*Ar*) form of **Aaron**.

Harriet *har'i-at*, feminine form of **Henry**.–Dimin **Hatty**, **Hattie**.

Harrison *ha'risan*, *m* (*Eng*) from the surname, meaning 'son of Harry'.

Harry see **Henry**.

Harvey, Hervey *här'vi*, *m* (*Celtic*) from *Haerveu*, name of a Breton saint, *perh* worthy in battle; or from the surname.

Hasan, Hassan *hä'sän*, *m* (*Ar*) good, handsome.

Hattie, Hatty see **Harriet**, **Henry**.

Haydn, Hayden, Haydon *hä'dan*, *m* (*esp* in Welsh use) from the surnames, the first spelling honouring the composer.

Hayley, Haley *hä'li*, *f* from the surname.

Hazel *hä'zal*, *f* from the plant.

Heather *hedh'ar*, *f* from the plant. See also **Erica**.

Hector *hek'tar*, *m* (*Gr*) holding fast.

Heidi *hï'fidi*, *f* (*Ger*) diminutive of *Adelheid* (see **Adelaide**).

Helen *hel'an*, *-in*, **Helena** *hel'i-na*, *ha-lä'na*, *f* (*Gr*) bright.–Dimins **Lena** (*lë'na*), **Nell**, **Nellie**, **Nelly**.

Helga *hel'ga*, *f* (*Gmc, Norse*) holy.

Heloise *hel'ō-ëz*, *f* (*Fr*) form of **Eloise**.

Henry *hen'ri*, **Harry** *har'i*, *m* (*Gmc*) house ruler.–Dimin **Hal**.–Fem **Henrietta, Harriet**.–Dimins **Hattie, Hatty, Hetty**.

Herbert *hûr'bart*, *m* (*Gmc*) famous army or warrior.–Dimins **Bert**, **Bertie**, **Herbie**.

Hermia *hûr'mi-a*, **Hermione** *hûr-mï'a-në*, *f* (*Gr*) names derived from *Hermes* (the Greek god), the latter that of the daughter of Helen and Menelaus in Greek mythology.

Hervey see **Harvey**.

Hester see **Esther**.

Hetty *het'i*, *f* diminutive of **Hester** and **Henrietta**.

Hew see **Hugh**.

Hilary *hil'a-ri*, *m* and (more recently) *f* (*L*, from *Gr*) cheerful.

Hilda *hil'da*, *f* (*Gmc*) *orig* a short form of names containing the element *hild*, battle.

Hollie, Holly *hol'i*, *f* from the plant.

Homer *hō'mar*, *m* (*US*) from the name of the Greek poet.

Honor, Honour *on'ar*, **Honora** *ho-nö'ra*, **Onora** *o-nö'ra*, *f* (*L*) honour, honourable.–Dimins **Nora, Norah**, (*Ir*) **Noreen**.

Hope *hōp*, *m* and *f* (*Eng*) from the noun, *orig* as a Christian virtue.

Horace *hor'is*, *m* (*L*) from the Roman family name.

Horatius *Howard* howfiNrd, *m* from the surname, *perh* meaning high guardian.

Howel, Howell see **Hywel**.

Hubert *hü'bart*, *m* (*Gmc*) bright mind or spirit.

Hugh, Hew *hü*, **Hugo** *hü'gō*, *m* (*Gmc*) mind, spirit.–Dimins **Huey**, **Hughie**.

Humphrey, Humphry *hum'fri*, *m* (*Gmc*) *perh* peaceful warrior or bear.–Dimin **Humph**.

Husni *hŭs'ni*, *m* (*Ar*) variant of **Hussein**.

Hussein, Hussain, Husain, Husayn *hŭ-sän'*, *m* (*Ar*) a diminutive of **Hasan**.

Huw *hü*, *m* Welsh form of **Hugh**.

Hywel, Howel, Howell *how'al*, *m* (*Welsh*) eminent.

Iain, Ian *ë'an*, *m* (*Gaelic*) forms of **John**.

Ibrahim *ë'bra-hem*, *m* (*Ar*) form of **Abraham**.

Ida *ï'da*, *f* (*Gmc*) labour.

Idris *id'ris*, *m* (*Welsh*) fiery lord.

Ieuan, Ioan *y ï'an*, *m* (*Welsh*) form of **John**.

Ifor *ë'vor*, *m* (*Welsh*) of uncertain origin; anglicized as **Ivor**.

Ike see **Isaac**.

Ilana *i-lä'na*, *f* (*Heb*) tree.–Masc **Ilan** (*-lan'*).

Ilona *i-lō'na*, *f* (*Hung*) form of **Helen**.

Imelda *i-mel'da*, *f* (*Gmc*) *prob* a combination of words meaning 'whole' and 'battle'.

Imogen *im'-a-jan*, *f* *prob* a misprint for *Innogen* (Celtic, daughter, girl) in Shakespeare's *Cymbeline*.

Ina *ï'na*, *ë'na*, *f* *orig* a diminutive of any of several names ending in *-ina*.

Indira *in'di-ra*, *f* (*Sans*) an epithet of Lakshmi, wife of Vishnu, *prob* literally beauty.

Ines, Inez *ï'nez*, *ë'*, *f* (*Sp*) forms of **Agnes**.

Inga *ing'a*, *ing'ga*, **Inge** *ing'a*, *f* (*Scand, Ger*) *orig* a short form of names containing the god Ing's name, eg *Ingeborg*.

Ingrid *ing'grid*, *f* (*Scand*) a combination of 'Ing' (the Norse fertility god) and 'beautiful' or 'ride'.

Inigo *in'i-gō*, *m* (*Sp*) a form of the Roman family name *Ignatius* or *Egnatius*.

Iona *ï-ō'na*, *f* from the place name.

Ira *ï'ra*, *m* (*Heb*) watchful.

Irene *ï-rë'në*, also *ï'rën*, *ï-rën'*, **Irena** *i-rë'na*, *f* (*Gr*) peace.–Dimin **Rene** (*rë'ni*).

Iris *ï'ris*, *f* (*Gr*) rainbow, iris (plant).

Irma *ûr'ma*, *f* (*Gmc*) *orig* a short form of *Irmintrude* and other names beginning with the same element. See also **Emma**.

Isaac *ï'zak*, *m* (*Heb*) laugh.–Dimins **Ik, Ike, Iky**.

Isabella *iz-a-bel'a*, **Isabel, Isobel** *iz'a-bal*, *-bel*, or (*Gaelic*) **Iseabail, Iseabal, Ishbel** *ish'bal*, (*Scot*) **Isbel** *iz'bal*, *f* *orig* the Spanish form of **Elizabeth**.–Dimins **Bel, Bell, Belle, Bella, Ella, Ib, Ibby, Isa** (*ï'za*), **Tib, Tibbie, Tibby**.

Isaiah *ï-zï'a*, or *-zä'*, *m* (*Heb*) Jah (God) helps.

Iseult see **Isold**.

Isidore *iz'i-dör*, **Isadore, Isodore** *iz'a-*, *m* (*Gr*) *perh* gift of Isis.–Fem **Isidora, Isadora**.

Isla *ï'la*, *f* from the river name.

Ismail *ës'mä-ël*, *m* (*Ar*) form of the Biblical name *Ishmael*, from Hebrew *Yishma'el*, God will listen.

Isold, Isolde *i-zold'*, **Isolda** *-zol'da*, **Iseult** *-zült'*, *f perh* Celtic, fair.

Israel *iz'rä-al*, *m* (*Heb*) striving with God.

Ivan *ï'van*, *ë-vän'*, *m* (*Russ*) form of **John**.–Fem **Ivana** (*ë-vä'na*).

Ivo *ï'vo*, **Ivon** *ï'van*, *m* forms of **Yves**.

Ivor *ï'var*, *m* (*ON*) of uncertain meaning, *perh* bow-warrior.

Ivy *ï'vi*, *f* from the plant ; also (*m*; *Scot*) a diminutive of **Ivor**.

Jacinth, Jacinthe *ja-sinth'*, **Jacintha** *-sin'tha*, **Jacinta** *-sin'ta*, *f* forms of the flower name hyacinth (*Gr hyakinthos*, larkspur); also from the precious stone jacinth (*OFr jacinte*).

Jack, Jackie, Jacky *jak*, *m* *orig* a diminutive of **John**, from *Jankin*, its Middle English pet form. See also **Jake, Jock**.

Jackson *jak'san*, *m* (*Eng*) from the surname, meaning 'son of Jack'.

Jacob *jä'kab*, *m* (*Heb*) follower, supplanter, or deceiver.–Dimin **Jake**.

Jacqueline, Jaqueline *zhak'a-lën*, *jak'a-lin*, *-lën*, **Jackeline** *jak'a-lën*, *-lin*, **Jacquelyn** *jak'a-lin*, **Jacquetta** *ja-ket'a*, feminine derivatives of French *Jacques* (**James**). –Dimins **Jackie, Jacqui**.

Jade *jäd*, *f* from the precious stone.

Jaime, Jaimie *jä'mi*, *f* (*esp US, Can*) a respelling of **Jamie**, properly a Spanish form of **James**.

Jake *jäk*, *m* a form of **Jack** or a diminutive of **Jacob**.

Jamal *jä-mäl'*, **Gamal** *gä-mäl'*, *m* (*Ar*) beauty.

James *jämz*, *m* *orig* a form of **Jacob** through Latin *Jacobus* (later *Jacomus*, whence the forms with m).–Dimins **Jim, Jimmie, Jimmy, Jem, Jemmie, Jamie**.

Jamie *jä'mi*, *m* a diminutive of, or *f* (*esp US*) a feminine of, **James**.

Jamil *jä-mël'*, *m* (*Ar*) beautiful, graceful.–Fem **Jamila** (*-me'la*).

Jan *jan*, *f* a shortening of **Janet, Janice**.

Jancis *jan'sis*, *f* a blend of **Jan** and **Frances**.

Jane, Jayne *jän*, *orig* a feminine of **John**.–Dimins **Janey, Janie**.–See also **Jean, Joan, Joanna**.

Janet *jan'it*, *f* *orig* a diminutive of **Jane**.–Dimins **Jan**, (*Scot*) **Jess, Jessie, Jessy, Netta, Nettie, Nita** (*në'ta*).–Derivs **Janetta, Jannetta** (*ja-net'a*), **Janette** (*-net'*).

Janice, Janis *jan'is*, *f* *orig* a diminutive of **Jane**.

Janine *ja-nën'*, **Janina** *-në'na*, *f* derivatives of **Jan**, or from French *Jeannine*, diminutive of *Jeanne* (**Jane**).

Jared *jä'rid* or *jar'id*, *m* (*Heb*) descent.

Jarvis *jär'vis*, **Jervis** *jûr'*, *jär'*, *m* forms of **Gervase**.

Jasmine *jaz'min*, **Yasmin** *yaz'*, *f* (*Pers*) the flower jasmine.

Jason *jä'san*, *m* (*Gr*) *poss* a rendering of **Joshua**, or simply 'healer'.

Jasper *jas'pər*, Caspar kasfi, *m prob* Persian, treasure -bringer.

Jay *jā*, *m* and *f* a diminutive of names beginning with J, or (*OFr*) from the bird.

Jayden, Jaden *jā'dən*, *m* (*Eng*) of uncertain derivation.

Jean *jēn*, *f orig* a feminine of **John**.–Dimins **Jeanie**, **Jeannie**, **Jeanette, Jeannette** (*ji-net'* ; *Fr*).

Jeffrey *jef'ri*, *m* a form of **Geoffrey**.

Jem, Jemmie diminutives of **James**.

Jemima *ji-mī'mə*, *f* (*Heb*) meaning unknown (day, dove, pure, fortunate, have been suggested).

Jemma see **Gemma**.

Jennifer, Jenifer *jen'i-fər*, *f* the *orig* Cornish form of **Guinevere**.– Dimins **Jen**, **Jenna**, **Jennie**, **Jenny**.

Jenson *jen'sən*, *m* (*Scan*) from the surname, of Danish/Norwegian origin, meaning 'son of Jens'.

Jeremy *jer'i-mi*, *m* (*Heb*) Jah (God) is high, or heals, or founds.

Jerome *jer'ōm*, *ji-rōm'*, *m* (*Gr*) holy name.

Jerry *jer'i*, *m* diminutive of **Jeremy**, **Gerald**, **Gerard**, **Jerome**.

Jervis see **Jarvis**.

Jess *jes*, **Jessy**, **Jessie** *jes'i*, *f* diminutives of **Janet** (*esp Scot*), or of **Jessica** ; **Jess** (m) a shortening of **Jesse**.

Jesse *jes'i*, *m* (*Heb*) Jah (God) is.

Jessica *jes'i-kə*, *f* (appar Heb) *perh* Jah (God) is looking.

Jethro *jeth'r'*, *m* (*Heb*) superiority.

Jillian *jil'i-ən*, *f orig* a variant of **Julian**.–Dimin **Jill**.

Jim, Jimmie see **James**.

Jinny see **Virginia**.

Jo *jō*, *m* and *f* diminutive of **Joanna**, **Joseph**, **Josepha**, **Josephine**.

Joan *jōn*, *f orig* a contraction of Old French *Joanne* (see **Joanna**).–Dimins **Joanie**, **Joni**.

Joanna, Johanna *jō-an'ə*, **Joanne** *jō-anfi*, *f* respectively the Latin and Old French feminines of *Joannes*, *Johannes*, Latin forms of **John**.

Jocasta *jo-kas'tə*, *f* (*Gr mythol*) the mother and wife of Oedipus.

Jocelyn, Jocelin, Joscelin *jos'lin*, *-ə-lin*, *m* and *f perh* (*Gmc*) one of the Geats (a people of southern Sweden), or (*L*) connected with **Justin**.–Fem also **Joceline**.–Dimin **Joss**.

Jock *jok*, *m* (*Scot*) a form of **Jack**.–Dimin **Jockie**.

Jodie, Jodi, Jody *jō'di*, *f* diminutives of **Judith** or derivatives of **Jo**.

Joe, Joey *jō'i*, *m* and *f* diminutives of **Joseph**, **Josepha**, **Josephine**.

Joel *jō'əl*, *m* (*Heb*) Jah (God) is the Lord.–Fem **Joelle** (*jō-el'*), **Joely** (*jō'i-li*, *jō'li*).

John *jon*, *m* (*Heb*) poss Jah (God) is gracious.–Dimin **Johnnie**.– See also **Jack**.–Fem see **Jane**, **Jean**, **Joanna**.

Joleen, Jolene *jō'lēn*, *f* derivatives of **Jo**.

Jolyon *jō'li-ən*, *m* a variant of **Julian**.

Jon *jon*, *m* a diminutive of **Jonathan** or a variant of **John**. **Jonathan, Jonathon** *jon'ə-thən*, *m* (*Heb*) Jah (God) has given.

Joni see **Joan**.

Jonquil *jong'kwil*, *f* from the flower.

Jordan *jör'dən*, *m* either from the river, *orig* as the source of baptismal water, or, recently, from the surname.

Joseph *jō'zif*, *m* (*Heb*) Jah (God) increases.–Dimins **Jo**, **Joe**, **Joey**, **Jos** (jos).–Fem **Josepha** (*-zē'fə*, *-ze'fə*), **Josephine** (*jō'zi-fēn*).–Dimins **Jo**, **Joe**, **Josie**, **Jozy**.

Josette *jō-zet'*, *f* (*Fr*) a diminutive of **Josephine**.

Joshua *josh'ū-ə*, *m* (*Heb*) Jah (God) saves.–Dimin **Josh**.

Joss see **Jocelyn**.

Joy *joi*, *f* from the emotion, esp *orig* in a religious sense.

Joyce *jois*, f, formerly *m* (*Celtic*) lord.

Jude *jood*, *m* short form of *Judas* (for Hebrew *Judah*, *perh* 'praise'); also (f) a diminutive of **Judith**.

Judith *joo'dith*, *f* (*Heb*) Jewess.–Dimins **Judy**, **Judie**, **Jude**, **Jodie**.

Julia see **Julius**.

Julian *joo'lyən*, *-li-ən*, m, formerly also *f* (*L*) derived from, belonging to Julius.–Dimins **Jule**, **Jools**.–Fem **Juliana** (*-a'nə*).–Dimin **Julie**.

Julie *joo'li*, *f* the French form of **Julia** or a diminutive of **Julia** or **Juliana**.

Juliet *joo'li-et*, *f* English form of French *Juliette*, diminutive of **Julie**.

Julius *joo'li-əs*, *m* (*L*) a Roman family name, *perh* downy-bearded.–Dimin **Jule**.–Fem **Julia**.–Dimin **Julie**.

June *joon*, *f* (*L*) from the month.

Justin *jus'tin*, *m* (*L*) a derivative of *Justus*, just.–Fem **Justina** (*-tē'nə*, *-tī'nə*), **Justine** (*jus'tēn*).

Kai, Kaj *kī*, *m* (*Scan*) of uncertain meaning, *perh* from the Roman *Caius*.

Kamal *kä-mäl'*, *m* (*Ar*) perfect, complete.–Fem **Kamala** (*-ma'lə*).

Kanta *kän'tə*, *f* (*Sans*) beautiful, desired.

Karen, Karin *kä'rin*, *kar'in*, *kar'ən*, *f* respectively the Danish and Swedish forms of **Catherine**.

Karina, Karena *kə-rē'nə*, *f* variants of **Karin**, **Karen**, or of **Carina** (see **Cara**).

Karl, Karla see **Carl**.

Kasim see **Qasim**.

Kate, Katharine, Katrine, Katrina, Katya see **Catherine**.

Kathleen *kath'lēn*, *f* (*Ir*) *orig* an anglicization of **Caitlín**.–Dimin **Kath**.

Kay, Kaye *kā*, *f* a diminutive of names beginning with K, *esp* **Katharine**, or (*m*, *L*) a form of *Gaius*, *perh* joyful.

Kayden *kā'dən*, *m* (*Eng*) of uncertain derivation.

Kayla *kā'lə*, *f* (*Eng*) of uncertain derivation, *perh* from Kayleigh, itself *perh* from Irish O Caollaidhe, 'descendant of Caoladhe', derived from *caol*, 'slender'.

Keiron see **Kieran**.

Keith *kēth*, *m* from the surname or place name.

Kelly *kel'i*, *m* and *f* (*Ir*) from the surname.

Kelvin *kel'vin*, *m* (*Scot*) from the River *Kelvin*, flowing through Glasgow.

Kenneth *ken'ith*, *m* (*Gaelic*) handsome, or born of fire.–Dimins **Ken**, **Kennie**, **Kenny**.–Fem **Kenna**.

Kerry *ker'i*, *m* and *f* (*Ir*) from the name of the Irish county.

Kevin *kev'in*, **Kevan** *-ən*, *m* (*Ir*) fair.

Khadija *kä-dē'jə*, *f* (*Ar*) premature child.

Kian *kē'ən*, *m* (*Eng*) of uncertain derivation, sometimes linked with a Persian name meaning 'king' or 'realm'.

Kieran, Kieron, Ciaran *kē'ə-rən*, *m* (*Ir*) an Irish saint 's name, from *car*, dark.–Fem **Ciara**, **Kiera**, **Kyra** (*kē'ə-rə*).

Kilian, Killian *kil'i-ən*, *m* (*Ir*) name of several Irish saints, *perh* related to *cill*, church, cell, or *ceallach*, hermit.

Kim *kim*, *m* and *f* shortening (as in Kipling's *Kim*) of Irish **Kimball** (*kim'bəl*), *orig* a surname, or of **Kimberley**.

Kimberly, Kimberley *kim'bər-li*, f, *orig m*, from the S African town.

Kingsley *king'zli*, *m* from the surname.

Kiran *kē'ran*, *m* (*Sans*) beam of light, sunbeam.

Kirk *kûrk*, *m* from the surname.

Kirsty, Kirsteen see **Christian**.

Kit see **Christopher**, **Catherine**.

Kitty see **Catherine**.

Krishna *krish'nə*, *m* (*Sans*) dark , black.

Krystal, Krystle see **Crystal**.

Kumar *kŭ-mär'*, *m* (*Sans*) boy, prince.–Fem **Kumari** (*-mä'ri*).

Kurt *kûrt*, *m* (*Ger*) *orig* a diminutive of **Conrad**.

Kyle *kīl*, *m* (*Gaelic*) from the place name, *orig* from Gaelic *caol*, narrow.

Kylie *kī* fili, *f* (*orig Aust*) said to be an Aboriginal word for 'curl' or 'boomerang', *perh* used also as a variant of **Kelly**.

Kyra see **Kieran**.

Lacey *lā'si*, *f* (*Eng*) from the surname, originally Norman French referring to Lassy in Calvados.

Lachlan *lahh'lən*, *m* (*Gaelic*) warlike.–Dimin **Lachie**.

Lakshmi *lak'shmi*, *f* (*Sans*) the name of the goddess of good fortune or beauty, literally lucky sign.

Lal *läl*, *m* (*Sans*) darling boy, *orig* caress.–Fem **Lalita** (*lä-lē'tə*).

Lalage *lal'ə-jē*, *f* (*L*, from *Gr*) talkative.–Dimins **Lallie**, **Lally**, **Lala**, **Lalla**.

Lance *läns*, *m* (*Gmc*) land.–Dimins **Lancelot**, **Launcelot** (*-ə-lot*).

Lara *lä'rə*, *f* (Ital) explained as from *Larunda* (*Roman mythol*), a nymph, or *Larissa*, a Greek martyr.

Laraine, Larraine see **Lorraine**.

Larry see **Laurence**.

Laura *lö'rə*, *f* (*L*) laurel.–Dimins **Lauren** (thought of also as feminine of **Laurence**), **Lauretta**, **Laurie**, **Loretta**.

Laurel *lor'əl*, *f* from the tree, or *perh* used as a diminutive of **Laura**.

Laurence, Lawrence *lor'əns*, *m* (*L*) of Laurentum, a town in Italy. –Dimins **Larry**, **Laurie**, **Lawrie**.

Lavinia *lə-vin'i-ə*, *f* (*Roman mythol*) the name of Aeneas's second wife, of uncertain meaning.

Lea, Leah *lē'ə*, *f* (*Heb*) a cow.

Leanne, Lian, Lianne *lē-an'*, **Liane** *-än'*, **Liana** *-ä'nə*, **Lianna** *-an'ə*, *f perh* a form of French *Eliane* (from the Roman family name *Aelianus*), or a combination of **Lee** and **Anne**, or a diminutive of **Julian**.

Lee, Leigh *lē*, *m* and *f* from the surname.

Leila, Layla *lā'lə*, *lī'lə*, *f* (*Pers*) night.

Len, Lennie, Lenny see **Leonard**.

Lena see **Helen**, **Magdalen**.

Leo *lē'ō*, *m* (*L*) lion.–Fem **Leona** (*lē-ō'nə*), **Leonie** (*lē'ə-ni*).–Fem deriv **Leontine** (*lē'ən-ten*, *-tēn*), **Leontyne** (*-tīn*).

Leonard *len'ərd*, *m* (*Gmc*) strong as a lion.–Dimins **Len**, **Lennie**, **Lenny**.

Leonora *lē-ə-nö'rə*, *f* a form of **Eleanor**.

Leopold *lē'ə-pōld*, *m* (*Gmc*) people -bold (from a brave people).

Leroy *lə-roi'* or *lē'roi*, *m* from the surname, meaning servant of the king.

Leslie *m*, **Lesley** *f lez'li*, from the surname or place name.

Lester *les'tər*, *m* from the surname, *orig* a phonetic spelling of the place name Leicester.

Lettice *let'is*, **Letitia** *li-tish'ə*, *f* (*L*) gladness.–Dimins **Lettie**, **Letty**.

Lewis *loo'is*, **Louis** *loo'is*, *loo'i*, **Ludovic, Ludovick** *loo'də-vik*, *m* (*Gmc*) famous warrior.–Dimins **Lewie**, **Louie**, **Lew**.–Fem **Louisa** (*loo-ē'zə*), **Louise** (*-ēz'*).–Dimins **Lou**, **Louie**.

Lexi, Lexie *lek'si*, *f* (*Eng*) a diminutive of *Alexandra*. See **Alexander**.

Liam *lē'ə* m, *m* Irish form of **William**. **Lian, Liana, Lianne**, etc see **Leanne**.

Libby *lib'i*, *f* a diminutive of Elizabeth.

Lidya *lid'yə*, *f* (*Eng*) a variant of **Lydia**.

Lilian, Lillian *lil'i-ən*, (*Scot*) **Lilias, Lillias** *-əs*, *f prob orig* forms of **Elizabeth**, but associated with **Lily**.

Lily, Lilly *lil'i*, *f* from the flower.

Linda, Lynda *lin'də*, *f* of uncertain evolution, *perh orig* a diminutive of Germanic names ending in *-lind*, an element of disputed meaning, *perh* soft , gentle.–Dimin **Lindy**.

Lindsay, Lindsey *lind'zi*, **Lynsey** *lin'zi*, *m* and *f* from the surname.

Linnette, Linette, Linnet, Lynette *li-net'*, *f* (*Fr*) medieval French forms of Welsh Eluned.

Linus *lī'nəs*, *m* (*Gr mythol*) the name of a minstrel, of uncertain origin; also a New Testament name.

Lionel *lī'ə-nəl*, *m* (*L*) young lion.

Lisa, Lisbeth, Lise, Lisette, Liz, etc see **Elizabeth**.

Liv *lēv*, *f* (*Swed*) life.

Llewelyn *(h)le-wel'in*, *loo-el'in*, *m* (*Welsh*) meaning doubtful.

Lloyd *loid*, *m* (*Welsh*) grey.

Logan *lō'gən*, *m* (*Scot*) from the surname.

Lois *lō'is*, *f* (*Gr, Biblical*) of uncertain meaning.

Lola *lō'lə*, *f* a diminutive of **Dolores**.–Dimin **Lolita** (*lō-le'tə*).

Lorcan *lör'kən*, *m* (*Ir*) *perh* from *lorc*, fierce.–Formerly anglicized as **Laurence**.

Loretta *lo-ret'ə*, *f* a diminutive of **Laura**.

Lorna *lör'nə*, *f* popularized, if not invented, by R D Blackmore as the name of the heroine of his novel *Lorna Doone*.

Lorne *lörn*, *m* and *f* from the district in Argyll, used (*m*) as a masculine of **Lorna**.

Lorraine, Larraine, Laraine *lə-rān'*, *f* (*Fr*) from the region of France.

Lottie *lot'i*, *f* a diminutive of **Charlotte**.

Louis *m*, **Louisa, Louise** *f* see **Lewis**.

Lubna *loob'nə*, *f* (*Ar*) the storax tree.

Luca *look'ə*, *m* (*It*) Italian form of **Luke**.

Lucas *loo'kəs*, *m* from the surname, itself the Latin form (from Greek) of **Luke**.

Lucius *loo'si-əs*, *-shəs*, *m* (*L*) a Roman given name *prob* connected with *lux*, light.–Fem **Lucia** (*loo'si-ə*, *-shə*, (*Ital*) *-chē'ə*).–Derivs **Lucinda** (*loo'sin'də*), **Lucilla** (*-sil'ə*), **Lucille** (*-sēl'*).

Lucy *loo'si*, *f* anglicized form of Latin *Lucia* (see **Lucius**).

Ludovic, Ludovick see **Lewis**.

Luke *look*, *m* (*L*) of Lucania (in Italy).

Luther *loo'thər*, *m* from the German surname, honouring the religious reformer Martin *Luther* (1483–1586); *orig* a personal name, *perh* people's warrior.

Lydia *lid'i-ə*, *f* (*Gr*) Lydian woman.

Lynda see Linda.

Lynette see Linnette.

Lynn, Lynne *lin*, *f* diminutives of **Linda** or **Linnette**.

Mabel *mā'bl*, *f orig* an apheltic form of **Amabel**.

Madeleine, Madeline see **Magdalen**.

Madge *maj*, *f* a diminutive of **Margaret**.

Madhur *mäd'oor*, *f* (*Sans*) sweet.

Madison, Maddison *ma'disən*, *f* (*Eng*) from the surname, itself either derived from **Magdalen** or meaning 'son of Maud'.

Madoc *mad'ək*, *m* (*Welsh*) fortunate.

Madonna *mə-don'ə*, *f* (*Ital*) my lady, a title of the Virgin Mary.

Mae *mā*, *f* a variant of **May**.

Maeve, Maev *māv*, *f* (*Ir*) anglicizations of *Meadhbh*, name of a legendary queen of Connaught.

Mag *mag*, **Maggie** *mag'i*, *f* diminutives of **Margaret**.

Magdalen *mag'də-lin*, **Magdalene** *-lin*, *-len*, **Madeline** *mad'lin*, *-lēn*, *-lin*, *mad'ə-*, **Madeleine** *-len*, *-lēn*, *-lin*, *f* of Magdala on the Sea of Galilee.–Dimins **Lena** (*lē'nə*), **Magda**.

Magnus *mag'nəs*, *m* (*L*) great.

Mahmud *mähh'mood*, *m* (*Ar*) a form of **Muhammad**.

Máire *moi'rə*, **Máiri** *mä'ri*, *f* respectively Irish and Gaelic forms of **Mary**.

Mairead *mī'rad* (*Gaelic*), **Mairead** *mə-räd'* (*Ir*), *f* forms of **Margaret**.

Maisie *mā'zi*, *f orig* a diminutive of **Margaret**.

Malcolm *mal'kəm*, *möl'*, *m* (*Gaelic*) Columba's servant.

Mandy see **Amanda**.

Marcel *mär-sel'*, *m* (*Fr*, from *L*), a diminutive of **Marcus**.–Fem **Marcelle** (*-sel'*), **Marcella** (*-sel'ə*).

Marcia, Marsha *mär'shə*, *f* (*L*) from the Roman family name *Marcius*, derived from **Marcus**.

Marcus see **Mark**.

Margaret *mär'gə-rit*, *f* (*Gr*) pearl.–Dimins **Madge**, **Mag**, **Maggie**, **Margery**, **Marjory**, **Meg**, **Megan** (*meg'ən*; *Welsh*), **Meta** (*mē'tə*), **Maisie**, **Peg**, **Peggy**, **Greta**, **Rita**.

Margo *mär'gō*, *f* (*Fr*) *orig* a diminutive of *Marguerite* (**Margaret**).

Maria, Marie see **Mary**.

Marian, Marion *mar'i-ən*, *mä'ri-ən*, **Marianne** *mar-i-an'*, *f* (*Fr*) *orig* diminutives of **Mary**; used also for the combination **Mary Ann**.

Marigold *mar'i-gōld*, *f* from the flower.

Marilyn see **Mary**.

Marina *mə-rē 'nə*, *f* (*L*) *prob* from **Marcus**, but *usu* explained as from *marinus*, of the sea.

Marjory, Marjorie, Margery *mär'jə-ri*, *f orig* a diminutive of **Margaret**.

Mark *märk*, **Marcus** *mär'kəs*, *m* (*L*) a Roman given name *prob* derived from Mars (the god).

Marlene *mär'lēn*, *f* (*Ger*) a combination of **Maria** and **Magdalena**.

Marlon *mär'lon*, *m perh* a surname, or *perh* from French *Marc*, with diminutive suffix *-lon*.

Marsha see **Marcia**.

Martha *mär'thə*, *f* (*Aramaic*) lady, mistress.–Dimins **Mat**, **Mattie**, **Matty**, **Pat**, **Pattie**, **Patty**.

Martin, Martyn *mär'tin*, *m* (*L*) *prob* warlike, of Mars.–Fem **Martina** (*-tē'nə*), **Martine** (*-tēn'*).

Marvin *mär'vin* *m* a variant of **Mervyn**.

Mary *mā'ri*, **Maria** *mə-rī'ə*, *-rē'ə*, **Marie** *mä'ri*, *mə-rē'*, *f* (*Heb*) from the New Testament form (*Mariam*) of **Miriam**, of uncertain meaning.–Dimins **May**, **Moll**, **Molly**, **Mamie**, **Minnie**, **Poll**, **Polly**.–Deriv **Marilyn**.

Mason *mās'ən*, *m* (*Eng*) from the surname, originally given to people who worked with stone.

Mat, Matty see **Martha**, **Matilda**, **Matthew**.

Matilda, Mathilda *mə-til'də*, *f* (*Gmc*) mighty in battle.–Dimins **Mat**, **Matty**, **Maud**, **Maude**, **Patty**, **Tilly**, **Tilda**.

Matthew *math'ū*, **Matthias** *mə-thī'əs*, *m* (*Heb*) gift of Jah (God).–Dimin **Mat**.

Maud, Maude *möd*, *f orig* a diminutive of **Matilda** or **Magdalen**.

Maura *mö'rə*, *f* (*Celtic*) of uncertain origin, used in Ireland as a variant of **Mary**.

Maureen *mö'rēn, mŏ-rēn'*, *f* (*Ir*) an anglicization of *Máir|n*, a diminutive of *Máire* (**Mary**).–Dimin **Mo**.

Maurice, Morris *mor'is*, *m* (*L*) Moorish, dark-coloured.

Mavis *mā'vis*, *f* (from *OFr*) thrush.

Maximilian *mak-si-mil'yən*, *m* (*L*) a derivative of the Roman name *Maximus*, greatest.–Dimin **Max**, **Maxim**.

Maxine *mak'sēn*, *f* a 20c feminine of **Max**.

May *mā*, *f* partly a diminutive of **Mary**, partly from the month.– Dimin **Minnie**.

Maya *mī'yə*, *f* (*Eng*) perh of Greek or Roman origin, meaning 'nurse', or based on the Latin *mai*, 'great'. **Maia**, the name of the Roman goddess of spring, is a variant.

Meena, Mina *mē'nə*, *f* (*Sans*) fish.

Meg, Megan see **Margaret**.

Melanie *mel'ə-ni*, *f* (*Gr*) black.

Mélisande *mā-li-sānd*, *f* (*Fr*) form of **Millicent**.

Melissa *mə-lis'ə*, *f* (*Gr*) bee.

Melody *mel'ə-di*, *f* from the noun.

Melvin, Melvyn *mel'vin*, *m* from the surname, or a masculine of *Malvina*, from Macpherson's Ossianic poems.

Mercy *mûr'si*, *f* from the noun, *orig* esp as an attribute of God.

Meredith *mer'i-dith, mə-red'ith*, *m* and *f* (*Welsh*) an anglicization of *Maredudd*, of uncertain meaning , or from the surname.

Meriel, Merriel *mer'i-əl*, *f* forms of **Muriel**.

Merlin see **Myrddin**.

Mervyn *mûr'vin*, *m* (*Welsh*) of uncertain derivation.

Meryl *mer'il*, *f* poss a variant of **Meriel**.

Meta see **Margaret**.

Mia *mē'ə*, *f* an *orig* Scandinavian diminutive of **Maria**.

Michael *mī'kl*, *m* (*Heb*) who is like the Lord?–Dimins **Mick**, **Micky**, **Mike**.–Fem **Michaela** (*mi-kī'lə, -kā'*).

Michelle *mē-shel'*, *f* (*Fr*) a variant of *Michèle*, feminine of *Michel* (**Michael**).

Mildred *mil'drid*, *f* (*Gmc* ; *OE Mildthryth*) mild power, gentle and strong.–Dimin **Millie**.

Miles *mīlz*, *m* of uncertain origin, *perh* Slavonic 'merciful'.

Millicent *mil'i-sənt*, *f* (*Gmc*) hard-working, industrious.–Dimin **Millie**.

Millie *mil'i*, *f* a diminutive of **Mildred**, **Millicent**, **Amelia**, **Emily**.

Milton *mil'tən*, *m* from the surname, *esp* honouring the poet John Milton.

Minnie *min'i*, *f* a diminutive of **Mary**, **May**, or **Wilhelmina**.

Miranda *mi-ran'də*, *f* (*L*) to be admired or wondered at.

Miriam, Myriam *mir'i-əm*, *f* (*Heb*) perh wished-for child.

Mo see **Maureen**.

Moira, Moyra *moi'rə*, *f* (*Ir*) anglicizations of Irish *Maire* and Gaelic *Moire*, forms of **Mary**.

Moll, Molly *mol'i*, *f* orig diminutives of **Mary**.

Mona *mō'nə*, *f* (*Ir*) noble.

Monica *mon'i-kə*, *f* the name, possibly African, of St Augustine's mother.

Morag *mo'rag*, *f* (*Gaelic*) a diminutive of *Mor*, great.

Moray see **Murray**.

Mordecai *mör'di-kī*, *m* (*Pers*) follower of the god Marduk.

Morgan *mör'gən*, *m* (*Welsh*) variously thought to contain elements meaning 'sea', 'rim', 'great' and 'bright '; also from the surname.

Morna *mör'nə*, *f* (*Gaelic*) beloved.

Morris see **Maurice**.

Morven *mör'vən*, *f* (*Gaelic*) perh the Argyllshire district *Morvern* or 'great mountain'.

Morwenna *mör-wen'ə*, *f* (*Welsh* and *Cornish*) related to Welsh *morwyn*, maiden.

Moses *mō'zis*, **Moshe** *mosh'e*, *m* prob Egyptian rather than Hebrew, denoting child, born of, as in, eg, *Tuthmosis*, child of Thoth.

Muhammad, Mohammed *mŭ-häm'əd*, *m* (*Ar*) commendable, full of fine qualities.

Mungo *mung'gō*, *m* (*Gaelic*) amiable.

Murdo *mûr'dō*, **Murdoch** *mûr'dəhh, -dək*, *m* (*Gaelic*) seaman.

Muriel *mō'ri-əl*, *f* (*Celtic*) perh bright as the sea.

Murray, Moray *mur'i*, *m* from the surnames.

Mustafa *moo'stä-fä*, *m* (*Ar*) chosen, selected.

Myfanwy *mi-van'wi*, *f* (*Welsh*) perh my-banwy, my fine one.

Myles *mīlz*, *m* a variant of **Miles**.

Myra *mī'rə*, *f* an arbitrary invention; sometimes used as an anagram of **Mary** or a substitute for **Mairead**.

Myrddin *mûr'dhin* *m* (*Welsh*) thought to be related to the place name *Camarthen*.–Latinized form **Merlin**.

Myrna *mûr'nə*, *f* a variant of **Morna**.

Myrtle *mûr'tl*, *f* from the shrub.

Nabila *nä'bi-lə*, *f* (*Ar*) noble, honourable.

Nadia *nä'di-ə, nä'*, *f* from Russian *Nadya*, diminutive of *Nadezhda*, hope.

Nadine *nä'den, nä'*, *f* a French derivative of **Nadia**.

Nan *nan*, *f* diminutive of **Ann**.

Nance *nans*, **Nancy** *-si*, *f* orig diminutives of **Ann**, **Agnes**.

Nanette *nə-net'*, *f* a diminutive variation of **Nan**.

Naomi *na-ō'mi, -mī*, or *na'*, *f* (*Heb*) pleasant.

Nasim, Naseem, Nasseem *nas-ēm'*, *m* (*Ar*) fresh air, fresh.

Nasser *nas'ər*, *m* (*Ar*) victorious.

Nat *nat*, *m* a diminutive of **Nathaniel**, **Nathan**.

Natalie *nat'ə-li*, **Natalia** *-tä'li-ə*, *f* (*L*) (Christ's) birthday, Christmas.– Dimin **Natasha** (*nə-tash'ə*; *Russ*).

Nathan *nā'thən*, *m* (*Heb*) gift of God.–Dimin **Nat**.

Nathaniel *nə-than'yəl*, *m* (*Heb*) gift.–Dimin **Nat**.

Neal, Neale see **Neil**.

Ned *ned*, **Neddy**, **Neddie** *ned'i*, *m* diminutives of **Edward**, **Edgar**, **Edmund**, **Edwin**.

Neil, Neal, Neale, Niall *nēl*, *m* (*Ir*) perh champion.

Nell *nel*, **Nelly**, **Nellie** *nel'i*, *f* diminutives of **Helen**, **Ellen**, **Eleanor**.

Nerys *ner'is*, *f* (*Welsh*) perh based on *ner*, lord.

Netta *net'ə*, **Nettie**, **Netty** *net'i*, *f* diminutives of **Annette**, **Antoinette**, **Janet**, **Jeanette**.

Neville *nev'il*, *m* from the surname.

Ngaio *nī'ō*, *f* (*Maori*) from the name of a tree.

Niall *nēl* see **Neil**.

Niamh *nē'əv*, *f* (*Ir*) brightness; in Celtic mythology the daughter of the sea god Manannan.

Nicholas, Nicolas *nik'ə-ləs*, *m*, formerly also *f* (*Gr*) victory of the people.–Dimins (m) **Nick**, **Nicky**, **Colin**, **Colley**, **Nicol**, **Nichol**.–Fem **Nicola**, **Nichola** (*nik'ə-lə*), **Nicole** (*ni-kōl'*).–Dimins **Nicolette**, **Colette**, **Nicky**.

Nigel *nī'jil*, *m* anglicized form of *Nigellus*, Latinized form of **Neil**, but understood as diminutive of Latin *niger*, black.–Fem **Nigella** (*nī-jel'ə*).

Nina, əinette see **Ann**.

Ninian *nin'yə* n, *m* (*Celtic*) meaning unknown.

Noah *nō'ə*, *m* (*Heb*) rest, comfort.

Noam *nōm*, *m* (*Heb*) pleasantness.

Noel *nō'əl*, *m* and *f* (*Fr*, from Latin *natalis*) (Christ's) birthday, Christmas.–Fem also **Noele**, **Noelle** (*nō-el'*).

Nola see **Fenella**.

Nona *nō'nə*, *f* (*L*) ninth.

Nora, Norah *nö'rə*, *f* orig a diminutive of **Honora**, **Leonora**, **Eleanor**.–Deriv (*Ir*) **Noreen** (*-ren'*).

Norma *nör'mə*, *f* (*L*) a rule, precept ; used as a feminine of **Norman**.

Norman *nör'mən*, *m* (*Gmc*) Northman.

Nuala see **Fenella**.

Nye see **Aneurin**.

Odette *ō-det'*, *f* a diminutive of **Ottilie**.

Olga *ol'gə*, *f* (*Russ*, from *Norse*) holy.

Olive *ol'iv*, **Olivia** *ə-liv'i-ə*, *f* (*L*) olive.–Dimin **Livy** (*liv'i*).

Oliver *ol'i-vər*, *m* (*Fr*) olive-tree, or an alteration of *Olaf* or other Germanic name.–Dimin **Ollie**.

Olwen, Olwin, Olwyn, Olwyne *ol'wən*, *f* (*Welsh*) white track.

Omar *ō'mär*, **Umar** *oo'mär* *m* (*Ar*) flourishing.

Onora see **Honor**.

Oona, Oonagh *oo'nə* see **Una**.

Ophelia *ə-fē'li-ə, ō-*, *f* prob (*Gr*) help.

Oprah *op'rə, ō'* *f* a respelling of *Orpah*, prob (*Heb*) deer.

Orlando *ör-lan'dō*, *m* (*Ital*) form of **Roland**.

Orson *ör'sən*, *m* from the surname, itself *orig* a Norman French nickname, bear cub.

Osbert *oz'bərt*, *m* (*Gmc*) famous as a god.

Oscar *os'kər*, *m* of disputed origin, *perh* (*Gmc*) god-like spearsman or (*Ir* and *Gaelic*) champion.

Oswald *oz'wəld*, *m* (*Gmc*) godly ruler.–Dimins **Ozzie**, **Ozzy**.

Ottilie *ot'i-li*, f (*Gmc*) heritage.–Dimins **Odette** (*ŏ-det'*), **Ottoline**.

Owen *ō'ən*, m (*Welsh*) said to mean youth; (*Ir*) used as a substitute for *Eóghan* (see **Ewan**).

Paddy *pad'i*, m and f a diminutive of **Patrick**, **Patricia**.

Padma *päd'mä*, f (*Sans*) lotus.

Padraig, Padraic *pod'rəg, po(d)'rəc*, m Irish form of **Patrick**.

Page, Paige *pāj*, f (*esp US*) from the surname.

Paloma *pa-lō'mə*, f (*Sp*) dove.

Pamela *pam'i-lə*, f *prob* an invention (as *pa-mē'lə*) of Sir Philip Sidney's.–Dimins **Pam**, **Pammy**.

Pandora *pan-dö'rə*, f (*Gr*) every gift.

Pansy *pan'zi*, f (*Fr*) thought ; or from the name of the flower.

Parvati *pär'vä-ti*, f (*Sans*) an epithet of the wife of Shiva, literally 'of the mountain'.

Pascal *pas-käl*, m (*Fr*) Easter child.–Fem **Pascale**.

Pat *pat*, a diminutive of (m) **Patrick**, (f) **Patricia**, **Martha**.

Patience *pā'shəns*, f patience, *orig* in the sense of longsuffering.

Patrick *pat'rik*, m (*L*) nobleman, patrician.–Fem **Patricia** (*pə-trish'ə*).–Dimins **Pat**, **Paddy**, **Patsy**, **Patty**, **Tricia**, **Trisha**.

Paul *pöl*, m (*L*) little.–Fem **Paula** (*pö'lə*).–Derivs **Paulina** (*pö-lī 'nə, -lē'nə*), **Pauline** (*pö'lēn*).–Dimin **Paulette** (*-let'*).

Pearce *pērs*, m a variant of **Piers**, or from the surname.

Pearl *pûrl*, f from the gem.

Peg *peg*, **Peggy** *peg'i*, f diminutives of **Margaret**.

Penelope *pə-nel'ə-pi, pe-, pi-*, f (*Gr*) *perh* weaver.–Dimins **Pen**, **Penny**.

Percival, Perceval *pûr'si-vəl*, m (*Fr*) *perh* an alteration of **Peredur**.

Percy *pûr'si*, m from the surname.

Peredur *per'i-dər*, m (*Welsh*) *perh* hard steel; thought to be the original form of **Percival**.

Peregrine *per'i-grin*, m (*L*) wanderer, traveller, pilgrim.–Dimin **Perry**.

Peter *pē'tər*, m (*Gr*) rock.–Dimin **Pete** (*pēt*).

Petra *pet'rə*, f invented Latin feminine form of **Peter**.

Petula *pi-tū'lə*, f of uncertain origin, *perh* an invention based on the endearment 'pet '.

Philip, Phillip *fil'ip*, m (*Gr*) lover of horses.–Dimins **Phil**, **Pip**.–Fem **Philippa**.–Dimin **Pippa**.

Phoebe *fē'bi*, f (*Gr*) shining, a name of Artemis as moon-goddess.

Phyllis *fil'is*, f (*Gr*) foliage, leafy branch.–Variant **Phyllida** (*fil'i-də*).–Dimin **Phyl**.

Pia *pē'ə*, f (*L*) dutiful, loyal.

Pierce *pērs*, m a variant of **Piers**, or from the surname.

Piers *pērz*, m (*OFr*) the Middle English form of **Peter**.

Pip *pip*, m, and **Pippa** *pip'ə*, f diminutives of **Philip**.

Polly *pol'i*, f *orig* a variant of **Molly** as a diminutive of **Mary**.

Poppy *po'pi*, f (*Eng*) from the flower.

Primrose *prim'rōz*, f from the flower.

Priscilla *pri-sil'ə*, f (*L*) diminutive of the Roman name *Priscus*, meaning 'ancient '.

Priya *prē'yə*, f (*Sans*) dear, beloved.

Prudence *proo'dəns*, f from the virtue.–Dimin **Prue**.

Prunella *proo-nel'ə*, f (*L*) little plum.

Qasim, Kasim *kas'ēm*, m (*Ar*) sharer, distributor.

Queenie *kwē'ni*, f from queen.

Quintin *kwin'tin*, **Quinton** *-tən*, **Quentin** *kwen'*, m (*L*) fifth.

Rachel, Rachael *rā'chl*, f (*Heb*) ewe.–Dimins **Ray**, **Rae**, **Rach**.

Rae *rā*, f diminutive of **Rachel**, used (*esp Scot*) independently.–Deriv **Raelene** (*rā'lēn*).

Raine *rān*, f *poss* a respelling of French *reine*, queen, or from the surname.

Rajani *rä'jä-ni*, f (*Sans*) the dark one, night.

Rajesh *rä-jāsh'*, m (*Sans*) ruler of kings.

Rajiv *rä-jēv'*, m (*Sans*) lotus.

Rajni *räj'ni*, f (*Sans*) a contracted form of **Rajani**, or the feminine form of *raja*, king.

Ralph *ralf,räf*, m (*Gmc*) fearless adviser.

Ramesh *rä-māsh'*, m (*Sans*) an epithet of Vishnu, literally ruler of Lakshmi.

Rana *rä'nə*, m and f (*Ar*) beautiful object.

Ranald *ran'əld*, m (*Scot*) anglicization of *Raghnall*, Gaelic form of **Ronald**.

Randal, Randall *ran'dl*, **Randolf**, **Randolph** *ran'dolf*, m (*Gmc*) wolf-like shield.–Dimin **Randy**.

Ranulf, Ranulph *ran'əlf*, m either (*ON*) counsel-wolf, or a variant of **Randolph**.

Raquel *ra-kel'*, f (*Sp*) form of **Rachel**.

Ravi *rä'vi*, m (*Sans*) sun.

Ray *rā*, a diminutive of (m) **Raymond** or (f) **Rachel**, but also used independently.

Raymond *rā'mənd*, m (*Gmc*) wise protector.–Dimins **Ray**, **Rae**.

Raza *rä'zä*, **Reza** *rez'ä*, **Riza** *riz'ä*, m (*Ar*) contentment, approval.

Rebecca *ri-bek'ə*, f *perh* (*Heb*) noose.–Dimin **Becky**.

Regina *ri-jī'nə*, f (*L*) queen.–Dimin **Gina** (*jē'nə*).

Reginald *rej'i-nəld*, m (*Gmc*) wise ruler, from *Reginaldus*, Latin respelling of **Reynold**.–Dimins **Reg** (*rej*), **Reggie**.

Renata *ri-nä'tə*, f (*L*) born again.–See also **Rene**.

Rene see **Irene**.

René *ren'i, rə-nā'*, m (*Fr*) born again.–Fem **Renée**.

Reuben *roo'bən*, m (*Heb*) behold a son, or renewer.

Rex *reks*, m (*L*) king ; also a diminutive of **Reginald**.

Reynold *ren'əld*, m (*Gmc*) the original Norman form of **Reginald**.

Reza see **Raza**.

Rhian *rē-an'*, f (*Welsh*) maiden.

Rhiannon *rē-an'ən*, f (*Welsh*) goddess or nymph.

Rhoda *rō'da*, f (*Gr*) rose.

Rhona *rō'na*, f origin and meaning obscure, poss connected with **Rowena**.

Rhonda *ron'də*, f *prob* a combination of **Rhoda** and **Rhona**.

Rhys, Rees, Reece *rēs*, m (*Welsh*) *perh* impetuous man.

Ria *rē'ə*, f a diminutive of **Maria**.

Richard *rich'ərd*, m (*Gmc*) strong ruler.–Dimins **Dick**, **Dickie**, **Dicky**, **Dicken**, **Dickon**, **Rick**, **Ricky**, **Richie** (*rich'i*).

Riley *rī'li*, m (*Eng*) from the surname Riley, meaning 'rye meadow', or else from the Irish surname Reilly, itself of uncertain meaning.

Rita *rē'tə*, f *orig* a diminutive of **Margaret**.

Riza see **Raza**.

Roald *rōld*, m (*ON*) famous ruler.

Robert *rob'ərt*, m (*Gmc*) bright fame.–Dimins **Bert**, **Bertie**, **Bob**, **Bobbie**, **Bobby**, **Dob**, **Dobbin**, **Rob**, **Robbie**, (*Scot*) **Rab**, **Rabbie**.–Fem **Roberta** (*-bûr'tə*).

Robin *rob'in*, m and (also **Robyn**) f *orig* a diminutive of **Robert**.–Fem **Robina** (*ro-bē'nə*).

Roderick *rod'ə-rik*, m (*Gmc*) famous ruler.–Dimins **Rod**, **Roddy**.

Rodney *rod'ni*, m and f from the surname or place name.–Dimins **Rod**, **Roddy**.

Roger, Rodger *roj'er*, m (*Gmc*) famous spearman or warrior.

Roisin *ro-shēn'*, f (*Ir*) a diminutive of **Rose**.–Anglicized as **Rosheen**.

Roland, Rowland *rō'lənd*, m (*Gmc*) famed throughout the land.

Rolf *rolf*, m (*Gmc*) famous wolf.

Romy *rō'mi*, f a diminutive of **Rosemary** or (*Ger*) **Rosemarie**.

Rona *rō'nə*, f from the island name, derived from Gaelic *ron*, seal, but used as a variant of **Rhona**.

Ronald *ron'ə ld*, m (*ON*) wise ruler.

Ronan *rō'nən*, m (*Ir*) little seal.

Rory *rö'ri*, (*Ir*) **Ruaidhri**, (*Gaelic*) **Ruairidh**, **Ruaraidh**, **Ruairi** *roo'ə-ri*, m red.

Rosa, Rosabel, Rosalie see **Rose**.

Rosalind *roz'ə-lind*, f (*Gmc*) *perh* gentle horse, but associated with **Rose**.–Dimins **Ros**, **Roz**.

Rosamund, Rosamond *roz'ə-mənd*, f (*Gmc*) horse protection; reinterpreted as Latin *rosa munda*, fine rose, or *rosa mundi*, rose of the world.–Dimins **Ros**, **Roz**.

Rose *rōz*, **Rosa** *rō'zə*, f (*L*) rose, the flower ; also (*Gmc*) horse.–Derivs **Rosabel** (*roz'ə-bel*), **Rosalie** (*rō'zə-li, roz'* ; *L rosalia*, the hanging of rose garlands on tombs).–Dimins **Rosetta**, **Rosie**, **Rosina**.

Roseanna, Rosanna *rō-zan'ə*, **Roseanne** *-zan'*, **Rosemarie** *-mə-re*, f compounds of **Rose** with **Anna**, **Anne**, **Marie**.

Rosemary *rōz'mə-ri*, f from the plant ; also for **Rose Mary**.

Roshan *rö'shan*, f (*Pers*) splendid, shining , illustrious.

Rosheen *see* **Roisin**.

Rosie *rō'zi*, f a diminutive of **Rose** and **Rosemary**.

Rosina see **Rose**.

Ross *ros*, m from the surname and place name, *prob* from Gaelic *ros*, headland, peninsula.

Rowan *rō'ən, row'ən, m* from the Irish surname, derived from *ruadh*, red, or from the tree.

Rowena *rō-ē'nə, f perh* Geoffrey of Monmouth's mistake for Welsh *Rhonwen*, white skirt.

Rowland see **Roland**.

Roxane *rok-sän', **Roxanne** -san', **Roxana** -sä'nə, f (prob* Pers) *perh* dawn.

Roy *roi, m (Gaelic)* red.

Ruaidhri, Ruairidh see **Rory**.

Ruby *roo'bi, f* from the stone.–Deriv **Rubina** *(-bē'nə).*

Rudolf, Rudolph *roo'dolf, m (Gmc)* famous wolf, from *Rudolphus*, Latinized form of **Rolf**.–Dimin **Rudy**.

Rufus *roo'fəs, m (L)* red.

Rupert *roo'pərt, m (LGer)* form of **Robert**.

Rupinder *roo-pin'dər, m (Sans)* of the greatest beauty.

Rushdi *roosh'di, m (Ar)* good sense, maturity.

Russell *rus'əl, m* from the surname.

Ruth *rooth, f (Heb)* meaning obscure; associated with English *ruth*, pity.

Ryan *rī'ən, m* from the Irish surname.

Sabina *sə-bē'nə, **Sabine** -bēn', f (L)* woman of the Sabines, neighbours of newly founded Rome.

Sabrina *sə-brē'nə, f* the Latin name for the River Severn.

Sacha, Sasha *sash'ə, m* and *f (Russ)* diminutives of **Alexander** and **Alexandra**.

Sadie *sā'di, f* a diminutive of **Sarah**.

Saffron *saf'rən, f* from the flower, or the orange colour yielded by its stigmas.

Sal *sal, **Sally** sal'i, f* diminutives of **Sarah**.

Salim, Saleem *sä-lēm', m (Ar)* safe, secure.

Salome *sə-lō'mi, f (Heb)* perfect , or peace.

Samantha *sə-man'thə, f* of uncertain but *prob* American origin, *perh* devised as a feminine of **Samuel**.–Dimin **Sam**.

Samuel *sam'ū-əl, m (Heb)* heard by God, or name of God.–Dimins **Sam, Sammy**.

Sandra *san'drə, sän', f orig* Italian diminutive of **Alessandra**; used as a diminutive of **Alexandra**.

Sandy *san'di, m* a diminutive of **Alexander**.

Sanjay *sän'jā, m (Sans)* triumphant.

Sarah, Sara *sā'rə* or *sä'rə, f (Heb)* princess, queen.–Dimins **Sadie, Sal, Sally**.

Sasha see **Sacha**.

Saskia *sas'ki-ə, f (Du) poss* from an altered form of German *Sachs*, Saxon.

Saul *söl, m (Heb)* asked for.

Scarlett *skär'lit, f* from the surname.

Scott *skot, m* from the surname.

Seamas, Seamus *shä'məs, m (Ir)* forms of **James**.

Sean *shön, m (Ir)* form of **John**.

Sebastian *si-bas'ti-ən, m (Gr)* man of *Sebasteia* (in Pontus).

Selina *si-lē'nə, f poss* connected with **Celia**, but associated with Greek *selene*, moon.

Senga *seng'gə, f* backward spelling of **Agnes**, more likely from the Gaelic *seang* meaning slender.

Seonag *sho'nag, f (Gaelic)* form of **Joan**.

Seonaid *sho'nij, f (Gaelic)* form of **Janet**.

Seren *se'rən, f (Welsh)* star.

Serena *si-rē'nə, f (L)* calm, serene.–Deriv **Serenella** *(ser-ə-nel'ə)*

Seth *seth, m (Heb)* substitute, or compensation.

Seumas *shä'məs, m (Gaelic)* form of James.

Shakirah *sha-ke'rə, f prob* a feminine form of Arabic *Shakir*, grateful.

Shakuntala *sha-kun'ta-lə, f (Sans)* a derivative of *sakunta*, bird.

Shamus *sha'məs, m (Ir)* anglicization of **Seamas**.

Shane *shän, **Shaun, Shawn** shön, m (Ir)* anglicizations of **Sean**.

Shankar *shäng'kär, m (Sans)* bringer of happiness.

Shannon *sha'nən, f* from the name of the longest river in Ireland.

Sharif *shä-rēf', m (Ar)* honourable, distinguished.–Fem **Sharifa** *(-rē'fə)*.

Sharmaine see **Charmaine**.

Sharon *shä'rən, shar'ən, f (Heb)* a Biblical place name.

Shashi *shä-shē', f (Sans)* an epithet of the moon, literally having a hare.

Sheela *shē'lə, f* a variant of **Sheila**, or *(Sans)* conduct, character.

Sheena *shē'nə, f* an anglicization of **Síne, Sine**.

Sheila, Shelagh *shē'lə, f orig* anglicizations of *Síle*, Irish form of **Celia**.

Shelley *shel'i, m* from the surname, or (f) *perh* a variant of **Shirley**.

Sherry see **Cher**.

Sheryl *sher'il, f* a variant of **Cheryl** (see **Cherry**).

Shirley *shûr'li, f* (formerly m) from the surname or place name.

Shona *shō'nə, f (Gaelic) perh* ultimately a diminutive of **Catriona**, but thought of as an anglicization of *Seonaid* (**Janet**) or *Seonag* (**Joan**).

Shula *shoo'lə, f (Heb)* peace.

Sian *shän, f* Welsh form of **Jane**.

Sibyl, now **Sybil** *sib'il,* **Sibylla** *si-bil'ə, f (L)* from the noun *sibyl*, a female oracle.

Sidney, Sydney *sid'ni, m* and *f* from the surname.–Dimins **Sid, Syd**.

Sidony, Sidonie *sid'ə-ni, si-dō'ni, f* woman of Sidon.

Siegfried *sēg'frēd, m (Gmc)* peace after victory.

Sienna *si'ena, f (It)* from the town of Siena in Italy, or else referring to the orange-brown colour called burnt sienna.

Sigourney *si-gûr'ni, sig'ər-ni, f* from the surname.

Silas *sī'ləs, m (Gr)* a form of Latin *Silvanus*, of the woods.–Fem **Silvana**.

Silvester, Sylvester *sil-ves'tər, m (L)* of the woods.–Fem **Silvestra, Sylvestra**.

Silvia, Sylvia *sil'vi-ə, f (Roman mythol)* a name associated with *silva*, wood, and borne by the mother of Romulus and Remus, founders of Rome.

Simon *sī'mən, m (Heb) perh* the listener; *perh (Gr)* snub-nosed. –Dimin **Sim**.–Fem **Simone** *(-mōn')*.

Sindy see **Cindy**.

Sinéad *shi-näd', f (Ir)* form of **Janet**.

Síne, Sine *shē'nə, f* respectively Irish and Gaelic forms of **Jane**.

Siobhán *shə-von', f (Ir)* form of **Jane, Joan**.

Sión *shon, m* Welsh form of **John**.

Siri *sir'i, f* diminutive of Scandinavian *Sigrid*, beautiful victory.

Sita *sē'tə, f (Sans)* in Hindu tradition, the name of the goddess of agriculture, literally furrow.

Skye *skī, f (Eng)* from the Scottish place name.

Solomon *sol'ə-mən, m (Heb)* peaceable.–Dimins **Sol, Solly**.

Somhairle see **Sorley**.

Sonia, Sonya *son'yə, f (Russ) orig* a diminutive of **Sophia**.

Sonny, Sonnie *sə'ni, m (Heb)* diminutive of **Saul, Solomon** and other names.

Sophia, So'a *sə-fī'ə, -fē', **Sophie, Sofie, Sophy** sō'fi, f (Gr)* wisdom.

Sorcha *sor'ə-hhə, sör'kə, f (Ir)* bright.

Sorley, Somhairle *sör'li, m (Gaelic)* a form of Scandinavian *Somerled*, viking , literally summer wanderer.

Spencer *spen'sər, m* from the surname, *orig* from the Old French meaning 'dispenser of provisions'.

Stacey, Stacy see **Anastasia**.

Stanley *stan'li, m* from the surname or place name.–Dimin **Stan**.

Stella *stel'ə, f (L)* star. See also **Estelle**.

Stephen, Steven *stē'vən, m (Gr)* crown, wreath.–Dimins **Steve, Stevie**.–Fem **Stefanie, Stephanie** *(stef'ə-ni)*.–Dimin **Steph**.

Stewart, Steuart, Stuart *stū'ərt, m* from the surname.

St John *sin'jən, m* from the saint 's name.

Suhair *soo-här', f (Ar) perh* sleeplessness.

Suhayl *soo-hāl', m (Ar)* the star Canopus.

Summer *su'mə, f (Eng)* from the season.

Sunil *soo-nēl', m (Sans)* dark blue.

Surayya *sū-rā'yə, f (Ar)* the Pleiades.

Susan *soo'zən, sū'zən,* **Susanna, Susannah, Suzanna, Suzannah** *-zan'ə,* **Susanne, Suzanne** *-zan, f (Heb)* lily.–Dimins **Sue, Suke, Sukie, Suky, Susie, Susy, Suzy**.

Sybil see **Sibyl**.

Sydney see **Sidney**.

Sylvester, Sylvestra see **Silvester**.

Sylvia see **Silvia**.

Tabitha *tab'i-thə, f (Aramaic)* gazelle.

Taffy *taf'i, m* an anglicized form of *Dafydd*, the Welsh form of **David**.

Tamar *tam'är*, *f* (*Heb*) date palm.

Tamara *tǝ-mä'rǝ*, *f* (*Russ*) a Caucasian name, *perh* Tam (*Heb*) date palm.

Tammy, Tammie *tam'i*, *f* diminutives of **Tamara** and **Tamsin**.

Tamsin *tam'sin*, *f orig* a Cornish diminutive of **Thomasina**.

Tania, Tanya *tän'yǝ, tan'*, *f* diminutives of Russian *Tatiana*, from the Roman family name *Tatius*.

Tara *tä'rǝ*, *f* from the place name in County Meath, Ireland.

Tariq *tä'rēk*, *m* (*Ar*) night visitor.

Taylor *tā'lǝ*, *m* (*Eng*) from the surname, originally given to people working in tailoring.

Ted *ted*, **Teddy, Teddie** *-di*, *m* diminutives of **Edward**, **Theodore**.

Terence, Terrance *ter'ǝns*, *m* (*L*) the Roman family name *Terentius*.–Dimin **Terry**.

Teresa, Theresa *tǝ-rē'zǝ, -rä'zǝ*, **Theresia** *-zi-ǝ*, *f* (*Gr*); *perh* relating to the island *Thera*.–Dimins **Terry**, **Tessa**, **Tracy**.

Terry, Terri *ter'i*, *m* and *f* a diminutive of **Terence**, **Teresa** ; also (m) from the surname.

Tessa *tes'ǝ*, **Tess** *tes*, *f orig* diminutives of **Teresa**.

Thea *thē'ǝ*, *f* (*Gr*) goddess, or a diminutive of **Dorothea**.

Thelma *thel'mǝ*, *f poss* (*Gr*) will.

Theodore *thē'ǝ-dör*, *m* (*Gr*) gift of God.–Dimins **Theo**, **Teddy**. – Fem **Theodora** (*-dö'rǝ*).

Theresa, Theresia see **Teresa**.

Thomas *tom'ǝs*, *m* (*Heb*) twin.–Dimins **Tom**, **Tommy**, (*Scot*) **Tam**.–Fem **Thomasina, Tomasina** (*-sē'nǝ*).

Thora *thö'rǝ*, *f* (*Scand*) *perh* Thor's battle.

Tia *tē'ǝ*, *f* (*Eng*) diminutive of **Letitia** and other names.

Tiffany *tif'ǝ-ni*, *f* (*Gr*) from *theophania*, revelation of God.

Tilda *til'dǝ*, **Tilly** *til'i*, *f* diminutives of **Matilda**.

Timothy *tim'ǝ-thi*, *m* (*Gr*) honoured of God.–Dimins **Tim**, **Timmie**.

Tina *tē'nǝ*, *f* a diminutive of **Christina** (see **Christian**).

Toby *tō'bi*, **Tobias** *tǝ-bī'ǝs*, *m* (*Heb*) Jah (God) is good.

Tom, Tommy see **Thomas**.

Toni *f*, **Tony** *m*, *tō'ni* diminutives of **Antonia** and **Anthony** respectively.

Torquil *tör'kwil*, *m* (*Gaelic*, from *ON*) *perh* Thor's cauldron.

Tracy, Tracey *trā'si*, *f orig* a diminutive of **Teresa**, or (m) *perh* from the surname.

Trevor *trev'ǝr*, *m* from the surname.

Tricia, Trisha *trish'ǝ*, **Trish** *trish*, *f* diminutives of **Patricia**.

Trina *trē'nǝ*, *f* diminutive of **Catriona**.

Tristram *tris'trǝm*, **Tristan** *-tǝn*, *m* (*Celtic*) *perh* tumult.

Trix *triks*, **Trixie, Trixy** *trik'si*, *f* diminutives of **Beatrix**.

Trudy *troo'di*, *f orig* a diminutive of names ending in *-trude*, eg **Gertrude**.

Tudor *tū'dǝr*, *m* (*Welsh*) anglicized form of *Tudur*, people-ruler.

Tyler *tī'lǝ*, *m* (*Eng*) from the surname, originally given to people who tiled roofs.

Tyrone *ti-rōn'*, *m* (*Ir*) from the name of the Irish county.

Ulric *ul'rik, ŭl'*, *m* (*Gmc*) powerful as a wolf.–Fem **Ulrica** (*-rē'kǝ*).

Ultan *ul'tǝn, ŭl'*, *m* (*Ir*) Ulsterman.

Umar see **Omar**.

Una *ū'nǝ, oo'nǝ*, *f* (*Ir*) of uncertain meaning, interpreted as Latin 'one' (anglicized as **Oona** or **Oonagh**).

Unity *ū'ni-ti*, *f* from the noun.

Ursula *ûr'sū-lǝ*, *f* (*L*) little she-bear.

Valentine *val'ǝn-tīn*, *m* and *f* (*L*) healthy.–Dimin **Val**.

Valerie *val'ǝ-ri*, *f* (*L*) from the Roman family name *Valerius*.–Dimin **Val**.

Vanessa *vǝ-nes'ǝ*, *f* a name invented by Swift from *Esther Vanhomrigh*.

Vanora *vǝ-nö'rǝ*, *f* (*Scot*) form of **Guinevere**.

Vaughan *vön*, *m* (*Welsh*) small one.

Venetia *vǝ-ne'shǝ*, *f* (*L*) Venetian.

Vera *ve'rǝ*, *f* (*Russ*) faith, but understood as Latin 'true'.

Verity *ver'i-ti*, *f* (*L*) truth.

Vernon *vur'nǝn*, *m* from the surname.

Veronica *vi-ron'i-kǝ*, *f* (*Gr*) a form of **Berenice**, but seen as an anagrammatic form of Latin *vera icon*, true image.

Victor *vik'tǝr*, *m* (*L*) conqueror.–Dimin **Vic**.

Victoria *vik-tö'riǝ, -tö'*, *f* (*L*) victory.–Dimins **Tori**, **Tory**, **Vickie**, **Vicky**.

Vijay *vē'jä*, *m* (*Sans*) victory.–Fem **Vijaya** (*-jä-ǝ*).

Vikram *vē'kram*, *m* (*Sans*) valour.

Vinay *vē'nä*, *m* (*Sans*) modesty.–Fem **Vinaya** (*-nä-ǝ*).

Vincent *vin'sǝnt*, *m* (*L*) conquering.

Viola *vī'ǝ-lǝ*, **Violet** *-lit*, *f* (*L*) violet (the flower).

Virgil *vûr'jil*, *m* (*L*) from the Roman family name *Vergilius*, *esp* honouring the poet Publius Vergilius Maro.

Virginia *vǝr-jin'i-ǝ*, *f* (*L*) from the Roman family name *Virginius*.–Dimins **Ginny**, **Jinny** (*jin'i*).

Vita *vē'tǝ*, *f perh* (*L*) a feminine of the saint's name *Vitus*, or from *vita*, life; also a diminutive of **Victoria**.

Vivian, Vyvyan, Vyvian *viv'i-ǝn*, *m* and (*usu* Vivien) *f* (*L*) lively.–Dimin (*m* and *f*) **Viv**.

Waldo *wöl'dō*, *m* (*Gmc*) *orig* a short form of names beginning with *wald*, meaning 'the ruler '.

Walid *wä-lēd'*, *m* (*Ar*) newborn baby.

Walter *wöl'tǝr*, *m* (*Gmc*) army ruler.–Dimins **Wat** (*wot*), **Watty** (*wot'i*), **Wally** (*wol'i*), **Walt** (*wölt*).

Wanda *won'dǝ*, *f* (Gmc or Slavic) *perh* a Slavonic woman, a wanderer.

Wasim *wä-sēm'*, *m* (*Ar*) graceful, handsome.–Fem **Wasimah** (*-sē'mǝ*).

Wayne *wän*, *m* from the surname.

Wendy *wen'di*, *f* an invention of J M Barrie.

Wesley *wez'li*, wesfi, *m* from the surname, derived from the place name meaning 'west meadow'.–Dimin **Wes**.

Wilbur *wil'bǝr*, *m* (*Gmc*) bright resolve.

Wilfrid, Wilfred wilfifrid, *m* (*Gmc*) peacemaker.

Wilhelmina *wil-hǝl-mē'nǝ*, wil-Nl-, *f* (*Gmc*) a feminine formed from *Wilhelm* (German form of **William**).–Dimins **Elma**, **Wilma**, **Mina**, **Minnie**.

William *wil'yǝm*, *m* (*Gmc*) strong and resolute protector.–Dimins **Bill**, **Billie**, **Billy**, **Will**, **Willie**, **Wills**, **Willy**.

Willow *wi'lō*, *f* (*Eng*) tree.

Wilma see **Wilhelmina**.

Winifred *win'i-frid*, *f prob orig* Welsh 'holy reconciliation'.–Dimins **Win**, **Winnie**, **Freda** (*frē'dǝ*).

Winona, Wynona, Wenonah, *wi-nō'nǝ*, *f* (*Sioux*) first-born daughter.

Winston *win'stǝn*, *m* from the place name.

Woodrow *wŭd'rō*, *m* from the surname, derived from the place name meaning 'row of houses by a wood'.–Dimin **Woody** (*wŭd'i*).

Wyn *win*, *m* (*Welsh*) fair, white.

Wynne *win*, *m* (*OE*) from the surname, itself meaning 'friend'.

Xanthe *zan'thi*, *f* (*Gr*) fair, golden.

Xavier *zav'i-ǝr*, *m* (*Sp*) *prob* from a Basque place name.

Yasmin see **Jasmine**.

Yolanda *yō-lan'dǝ*, *f appar* a medieval form of *Violante*, a derivative of **Viola**.

Yousef, Youssef, Yusuf *yoo'sǝf*, *m* the Arabic form of Joseph; to increase (in power and influence); a Prophet 's name.

Yves *ēv*, *m* (*Fr*) from a Germanic source incorporating the element *iv-*, yew.–Fem dimin **Yvette** (*ē-vet'*).

Yvonne *ē-von'*, *f* (*Fr*) feminine formed from **Yvon**, inflected form of **Yves**.

Zachary *zak'ǝ-ri*, *m* (*Heb*) Jah (God) is renowned.–Dimins **Zach**, **Zack**.

Zahir, Zaheer *zä-hēr'*, *m* (*Ar*) radiant, flourishing.–Fem **Zahra** (*zä'rǝ*).

Zara *zä'rǝ*, *f* (*Ar*) *perh* flower, blossom, or bright as the dawn.

Zaynab, Zainab *zä'näb*, *f* (*Ar*) *perh* from the name of a fragrant plant.

Zelda see **Griselda**.

Zena *zē'nǝ*, *f perh* (*Pers*) a woman.

Zia *zē'ǝ*, *m* (*Ar*) light , splendour.

Zoe, Zoe, Zowie *zō'ē*, *f* (*Gr*) life.

Zola *zō'lǝ*, *f* from the Italian surname, or *perh* a derivative of **Zoe**.

Zubaida *zoo-ba'dǝ*, *f* (*Ar*) marigold.

Zuleika *zoo-le'kǝ, -lī'kǝ*, *f* (*Pers*) *perh* brilliance, beauty.

Phrases and quotations from foreign languages

Single foreign words, and certain phrases often used in an English context, are given in the main dictionary.

abiit, excessit, evasit, erupit (*L*) he is gone, he is off, he has escaped, he has broken away. —Cicero, *In Catilinam* II.i.1.

ab imo pectore (*L*) from the bottom of the heart.

à bon chat, bon rat (*Fr*) to a good cat, a good rat: well matched; set a thief to catch a thief.

ab ovo usque ad mala (*L*) from the egg to the apples: of a Roman banquet, from the beginning to the end.

ab uno disce omnes (*L*) from one learn all: from one example you may know or judge the rest.

abusus non tollit usum (*L*) abuse does not take away use: in law, the abuse of something, eg a right, does not render it invalid.

à chacun son métier (*Fr*) everyone to their own trade.

actum est de republica (*L*) it is all up with the state.

ad majorem Dei gloriam (*L*) for the greater glory of God. —the Jesuit motto.

ad hanc vocem (*L*) at this word (in a list or glossary).

ad hunc locum (*L*) at this place (in a text).

adios amigo (*Sp*) goodbye my friend.

ad vitam aut culpam (*L*) for life or till fault: of appointments, for life unless misconduct necessitates dismissal.

aide-toi, le ciel t'aidera (*Fr*) help yourself and heaven will help you.

à la guerre comme à la guerre (*Fr*) in war as in war: one must take things as they come.

alea jacta est see **jacta est alea**.

aliquid haeret (*L*) something sticks.

Allah il Allah a corruption of *Ar* lā ilāha illā'llāh.

alter ipse amicus (*L*) a friend is another self.

amare et sapere vix deo conceditur (*L*) to be in love and to be wise is scarce granted even to a god. — Laberius.

a mensa et toro (*L*) from bed and board.

annos vixit (*L*) he or she lived for…years.

à nos moutons see **revenons**.

à perte de vue (*Fr*) (reaching) out of sight; as far as the eye can see.

après moi (nous) le déluge (*Fr*) after me (us) the flood: what happens when I'm gone is none of my concern. — attributed to Madame de Pompadour and to Louis XV.

aquila non capit muscas (*L*) an eagle does not catch flies.

Arcades ambo (*L*) Arcadians both: two of the same stamp. —Virgil *Ecl.*, VII.4. —Rendered by Byron blackguards both, *Don Juan*, IV, xciii.

ariston men hydōr (*Gr*) water is best. —Pindar, *Olympian Odes* i.1.

ars est celare artem (*L*) true art is to conceal art.

ars gratia artis (*L*) art for art's sake.

ars longa, vita brevis (*L*) art is long, life is short. — Seneca, *De Brevitate Vitae*, 1. Cf **ho bios brachys**.

atra cura (*L*) black care.

at spes non fracta (*L*) but hope is not yet crushed.

au bout de son latin (*Fr*) at the end of his Latin: at the end of his knowledge, at his wits' end.

audentes fortuna juvat (*L*) fortune favours the daring. —Virgil, *Aen.*, X.284.

audi alteram partem (*L*) hear the other side. —St Augustine, *De Duabus Animabus*, XIV.2.

aufgeschoben ist nicht aufgehoben (*Ger*) put off is not given up.

aujourd'hui roi, demain rien (*Fr*) king today, nothing tomorrow.

auri sacra fames (*L*) accursed hunger for gold. — Virgil, *Aen.*, III.57.

au royaume des aveugles les borgnes sont rois (*Fr*) in the kingdom of the blind the one-eyed are kings. Cf **beati monoculi**.

aussitôt dit, aussitôt fait (*Fr*) no sooner said than done.

Austriae est imperare orbi universo (*L*) it is Austria's part to command the whole world (often AEIOU).

aut amat aut odit mulier, nihil est tertium (*L*) a woman either loves or hates, there is no third course. —Syrus, 42.

autant d'hommes (or **de têtes**), **autant d'avis** (*Fr*) so many men, so many minds. Cf **quot homines**.

aut Caesar aut nihil (or **nullus**) (*L*) either Caesar or nothing: all or nothing; either complete success or utter failure. —associated with Cesare Borgia (1476–1507).

aut insanit homo aut versus facit (*L*) either the man is mad or he is making verses. —Horace, *Sat.*, II.vii.117.

aut non tentaris aut perfice (*L*) either do not attempt or else achieve. —Ovid, *A.A.*, I.389.

aut regem aut fatuum nasci oportet (*L*) one should be born either king or fool. —proverb; quoted by Seneca.

aut vincere aut mori (*L*) to conquer or die.

aux grands maux les grands remèdes (*Fr*) to desperate evils desperate remedies.

ave, Caesar (or **imperator**), **morituri te salutant** (*L*) hail, Caesar, men doomed to die salute thee. —said by gladiators.

a verbis ad verbera (*L*) from words to blows.

à vieux comptes nouvelles disputes (*Fr*) old accounts breed new disputes.

avise la fin (*Fr*) consider the end. —motto of the Kennedy clan.

barba tenus sapientes (*L*) sages as far as the beard: with an appearance of wisdom only.

beati monoculi in regione caecorum (*L*) in the kingdom of the blind the one-eyed are kings. Cf **au royaume**.

bella, horrida bella (*L*) wars, horrid wars. —Virgil, *Aen.*, VI.86.

bellaque matribus detestata (*L*) and wars abhorred by mothers. —Horace, *Od.*, I.i.24–5.

belua multorum capitum (*L*) monster with many heads: the irrational mob. —Horace, *Epistolae*, I.i.76.

beneficium accipere libertatem est vendere (*L*) to accept a favour is to sell one's liberty. —Syrus, 49.

bene qui latuit bene vixit (*L*) he has lived well who has lived obscure. —Ovid, *Trist.*, III.iv.25.

bibere venenum in auro (*L*) to drink poison from a cup of gold.

bis dat qui cito dat (*L*) he gives twice who gives promptly. —proverb; by Bacon.

bis peccare in bello non licet (*L*) in war one may not blunder twice.

bis pueri senes (*L*) old men are twice boys.

Borgen macht Sorgen (*Ger*) borrowing makes sorrowing.

brevis esse laboro, obscurus fio (*L*) I labour to be brief, and I become obscure. —Horace, *A.P.*, 25–26.

briller par son absence (*Fr*) to be conspicuous by one's absence.

buen principio, la mitad es hecha (*Sp*) well begun is half-done.

cadit quaestio (*L*) the question drops: that is the end of the discussion, there is nothing more to discuss.

caeca invidia est (*L*) envy is blind. —Livy, xxxviii.49.

caelum non animum mutant qui trans mare currunt (*L*) they change their sky, not their mind, who scour across the sea. —Horace, *Epist.*, I.xi.27.

Caesar non supra grammaticos (*L*) Caesar has no authority over the grammarians.

ça ira (*Fr*) it will go. —refrain of a famous song of the French Revolution.

candida Pax (*L*) white-robed Peace. —Tibullus, I.x.45.

carpe diem, quam minimum credula postero (*L*) enjoy the present day, trust the least possible to the future. — Horace, *Od*, I.xi.8.

ça (or **cela**) **ne fait rien** (*Fr*) it doesn't matter.

ça (or **cela**) **saute aux yeux** (*Fr*) that leaps to the eyes: it is obvious or self-evident.

cedant arma togae (*L*) let arms yield to the gown: let military authority yield to civil. —Cicero, *De Officiis*, I.xxii.77, *in Pisonem*, xxx.73.

cela va sans dire (*Fr*) that goes without saying; of course.

celui qui veut, peut (*Fr*) who will, can.

ce monde est plein de fous (*Fr*) this world is full of madmen.

c'en est fait de lui (*Fr*) it is all up with him.

ce n'est que le premier pas qui coûte (*Fr*) see **il n'y a que**.

c'est égal (*Fr*) it's all one (to me); it makes no odds.

c'est le commencement de la fin (*Fr*) it is the beginning of the end. —attributed to Talleyrand.

c'est magnifique, mais ce n'est pas la guerre (*Fr*) it is magnificent, but it is not war. —said at Balaklava by a French general watching the charge of the Light Brigade.

c'est pire (or **plus**) **qu'un crime, c'est une faute** (*Fr*) it is worse than a crime, it is a blunder. —on the execution of the Duc d'Enghien; attributed to Talleyrand.

ceterum censeo (*L*) but I think. —said of persistent obstruction like that of Cato.

chacun à son goût (*Fr*) each to his own.

chapeaux bas (*Fr*) hats off.

cherchez la femme (*Fr*) look for the woman: there's a woman at the bottom of it. —Dumas *père*.

che sarà sarà (*Ital*) what will be will be.

chiesa libera in libero stato (*Ital*) a free church in a free state. —Cavour's ideal for Italy.

chi tace confessa (*Ital*) who keeps silence, confesses.

circulus in probando (*L*) arguing in a circle, using the conclusion as one of the arguments.

civis Romanus sum (*L*) I am a Roman citizen. — Cicero, *In Verrem*, VI.57.

como siempre (*Sp*) as always.

conscia mens recti (*L*) a mind conscious of rectitude. —Ovid, *Fast.*, IV.311. Cf **mens sibi**.

consensus facit legem (*L*) consent makes law or rule.

consuetudo pro lege servatur (*L*) custom is held as a law.

contraria contrariis curantur (*L*) opposites are cured by opposites.

corruptio optimi pessima (*L*) the corruption of the best is the worst of all.

coûte que coûte (*Fr*) cost what it may.

crambe repetita (*L*) cold cabbage warmed up again: tiresome repetition (of a story, etc). —Juvenal, VII.154.

cucullus non facit monachum (*L*) the cowl does not make the monk.

curiosa felicitas (*L*) studied felicity of expression: (loosely) curious felicity. —said by Petronius Arbiter, *Saturae* (*Satyricon*), 118, 5 of Horace's style.

damnosa haereditas (*L*) an inheritance of debts (*Roman law*); any hurtful inheritance. —Gaius, *Institutes*, ii.163.

damnum absque injuria (*L*) loss without legal injury.

das Ewig-Weibliche zieht uns hinan (*Ger*) the eternal feminine draws us upward. —Goethe, *Faust*, at end.

da multos annos (*L*) grant many years: a wish for long life, eg on the birthday of the person concerned.

data et accepta (*L*) expenditures and receipts.

de bene esse (*L*) as being good: in law, without prejudice; provisionally or conditionally.

decessit sine prole (*L*) died without issue.

decus et tutamen (*L*) an ornament and a safeguard. —Virgil, *Aen.*, V. 262; inscription round the edge of an English, Northern Irish or UK one-pound coin.

de die in diem (*L*) from day to day; daily.

de gustibus non est disputandum (*L*) there is no disputing about tastes.

de l'audace, encore de l'audace, et toujours de l'audace (*Fr*) to dare, still to dare, and ever to dare. —Danton's famous phrase.

delenda est Carthago (*L*) Carthage must be wiped out. —a saying constantly repeated by Cato.

de minimis non curat lex (*L*) the law does not concern itself about very small matters. —Bacon, Letter cclxxxii.

de mortuis nil nisi bonum (*L*) say nothing but good of the dead.

desipere in loco see **dulce**.

de te fabula narratur (*L*) the story is about you. —Horace, *Sat.*, I.i.69–70. See also **quid rides**.

Dichtung und Wahrheit (*Ger*) poetry and truth.

dictum de dicto (*L*) hearsay report.

dictum sapienti sat est (*L*) a word to the wise is enough (*usu* quoted as **verbum**). —Plautus, *Persa*, IV.vii.19.

diem perdidi (*L*) I have lost a day. —said by the Emperor Titus.

di grado in grado (*Ital*) by degrees.

dis aliter visum (*L*) the gods have adjudged otherwise. —Virgil, *Aen.*, II.428.

divide et impera (*L*) divide and rule.

docendo discimus (*L*) we learn by teaching.

doli capax (*L*) capable of committing a wrong (*opp* to *doli incapax*).

Domine, dirige nos (*L*) Lord, direct us. —the motto of London.

Dominus illuminatio mea (*L*) the Lord is my light.

domus et placens uxor (*L*) a home and a pleasing wife. —Horace, *Od.*, II.xiv.21–22.

dorer la pilule (*Fr*) to gild the pill.

dos moi pou stō kai tēn gēn kinēsō (*Gr*) give me where to stand, and I will move the earth. —attributed to Archimedes.

do ut des (*L*) I give that you may give.

dulce est desipere in loco (*L*) it is pleasant to play the fool on occasion. —Horace, *Od.*, IV.xii.28.

écrasez l'infâme (*Fr*) crush the vile thing. —Voltaire against the Roman Catholic Church of his time.

ego et rex meus (*L*) I and my king. —Cardinal Wolsey.

eheu fugaces. . . labuntur anni (*L*) alas! the fleeting years slip away. —Horace, *Od.*, II.xiv.1–2.

eile mit Weile (*Ger*) make speed with leisure.

ein Mal, kein Mal (*Ger*) just once counts nothing.

Ēli, Ēli, lama sabachthani (Matt. 27.46), **Eloi, Eloi, lamma sabachthani** (Mark 15.34) (*Gr* transliterations of *Aramaic*) my God, my god, why hast thou forsaken me?

epea pteroenta (*Gr*) winged words. —Homer (*Iliad*, 1.201, etc). See also Dictionary under **wing**[1].

ephphatha (*Aramaic*) be opened. — (Mark 7.34).

e pluribus unum (*L*) one out of many —before 1956 regarded as motto of the United States.

eppur si muove (*Ital*) and yet it does move. —attributed to Galileo, who recanted his theory that the earth moves round the sun.

ergo bibamus (*L*) therefore let us drink.

Erin go bragh (*Ir*) Erin forever.

errare est humanum (*L*) to err is human.

est modus in rebus (*L*) there is a mean in (all) things. —Horace, *Sat.*, I.i.106.

et tu, Brute (*L*) you too, Brutus. —Caesar's alleged exclamation when he saw Brutus amongst his assassins.

euphemeite (*Gr*) hush! —shouted at the start of a Greek drama.

eventus stultorum magister (*L*) the outcome is the schoolmaster of fools. —Livy, XXII,39.

exegi monumentum aere perennius (*L*) I have reared a monument more lasting than brass. —Horace, *Od.*, III.xxx.1.

exempla sunt odiosa (*L*) examples are hateful.

ex nihilo (or **nilo**) **nihil** (or **nil**) **fit** (*L*) out of nothing nothing comes.

ex pede Herculem (*L*) (we recognize) Hercules from his foot: to deduce the entirety of something from a small piece of it.

experientia docet stultos (*L*) experience teaches fools.

experto crede, or (Virgil, *Aen.*, XI.283) **credite** (*L*) trust one who has tried, or had experience.

expertus metuet, or **metuit** (*L*) he who has experienced it will fear (or fears). —Horace, *Epist.*, I.xviii.87.

ex ungue leonem (*L*) (judge, or infer) the lion from his claws.

fable convenue (*Fr*) fable agreed upon —Voltaire's name for history.

facile est inventis addere (*L*) it is easy to add to things invented already.

facilis descensus Averno, or **Averni** (*L*) descent to Avernus is easy: going to hell is easy (with the inference that returning is not). —Virgil, *Aen.*, VI.126.

facta non verba (*L*) deeds, not words.

factum est (*L*) it is done.

falsus in uno, falsus in omnibus (*L*) false in one thing, false in all.

fama nihil est celerius (*L*) nothing is swifter than rumour. —Livy.

fama semper vivat (*L*) may his (or her) fame live for ever.

far niente (*Ital*) doing nothing.

fas est et ab hoste doceri (*L*) it is right to learn even from an enemy. —Ovid, *Met.*, IV.428.

Fata obstant (*L*) the Fates oppose. —Virgil, *Aen.*, IV.440.

Fata viam invenient (*L*) the Fates will find out a way. —Virgil, *Aen.*, X.113.

felicitas multos habet amicos (*L*) prosperity has many friends.

fiat justitia, ruat caelum (*L*) let justice be done, though the heavens should fall.

fiat lux (*L*) let there be light.

fide, sed cui vide (*L*) trust, but take care in whom.

finem respice (*L*) see **respice finem**.

finis coronat opus (*L*) the end crowns the work.

fin mot de l'affaire (*Fr*) the bottom of the matter, the explanation.

flecti non frangi (*L*) to be bent, not broken.

forsan et haec olim meminisse juvabit (*L*) perhaps some day we shall like to remember even these things. —Virgil, *Aen.*, I.203.

Fors Clavigera (*L*) Fortune the club-bearer. —used as a title by Ruskin.

fortes Fortuna adjuvat (*L*) Fortune helps the brave. —Terence, *Phormio*, I.iv.26.

fortiter in re, suaviter in modo (*L*) see **suaviter**.

frangas, non flectes (*L*) you may break, you shall not bend.

fraus est celare fraudem (*L*) it is a fraud to conceal a fraud.

fugit hora (*L*) the hour flies. —Persius, V.153.

fulmen brutum (*L*) a harmless thunderbolt.

geflügelte Worte (*Ger*) winged words. See **epea**.

genus irritabile vatum (*L*) the irritable tribe of poets. —Horace, *Epist.*, II.ii.102.

giovine santo, diavolo vecchio (*Ital*) young saint, old devil.

gli assenti hanno torto (*Ital*) the absent are in the wrong.

gnōthi seauton (*Gr*) know thyself. —inscribed on the temple of Apollo at Delphi. See also **nosce teipsum**.

Gott mit uns (*Ger*) God with us. —Hohenzollern motto.

gradu diverso, via una (*L*) with different step on the one way.

gradus ad Parnassum (*L*) a step, or stairs, to Parnassus. —used as the name for a Latin or Greek poetical dictionary.

Graecum est: non legitur (*L*) this is Greek; it is not read. —placed against a Greek word in medieval MSS, a permission to skip the hard words.

gratia placendi (*L*) the delight of pleasing.

graviora manent (*L*) greater dangers remain: the worst is yet to come.

gravis ira regum est semper (*L*) the anger of kings is always serious.

grosse Seelen dulden still (*Ger*) great souls suffer in silence. —Schiller, *Don Carlos*, I.iv., end of scene.

gutta cavat lapidem (*L*) the drop wears away the stone. —Ovid, *Pont.*, IV.x.5.

habendum et tenendum (*L*) to have and to hold.

habent sua fata libelli (*L*) books have their destinies. —Maurus, *De Litteris, Syllabis et Metris*.

haec olim meminisse juvabit (*L*) see **forsan**.

Hannibal ad portas (*L*) Hannibal at the gates. —Cicero, *Philippica*, I.v.11.

heu pietas! heu prisca fides! (*L*) alas for piety! alas for the ancient faith! —Virgil, *Aen.*, VI.879.

hiatus valde deflendus (*L*) a gap deeply to be deplored.

hic finis fandi (*L*) here (was, or let there be) an end of the speaking.

hinc illae lacrimae (*L*) hence [came] those tears. —Terence, *Andria*, I.i.99; also Horace, *Epist.*, I.xix.41.

ho bios brachys, hē de technē makrē (*Gr*) life is short and art is long. —attributed to Hippocrates. Cf **ars longa**.

hoc age (*L*) this do.

hoc monumentum posuit (*L*) he or she erected this monument.

hoc saxum posuit (*L*) placed this stone.

hodie mihi, cras tibi (*L*) me today, you tomorrow.

hominis est errare (*L*) it belongs to man to err.

homo alieni juris (*L*) one under control of another.

homo sui juris (*L*) one who is his own master.

homo sum: humani nihil a me alienum puto (*L*) I am a man: I count nothing human indifferent to me. —Terence, *Heaut.*, I.i.25.

homo trium litterarum (*L*) man of three letters: ie *fur*, thief.

homo unius libri (*L*) a man of one book.

hon hoi theoi philousi apothnēskei neos (*Gr*) whom the gods love dies young. —Menander. Cf **quem di diligunt**.

honi soit qui mal y pense (*OFr*) the shame be his who thinks ill of it. —the motto of the Order of the Garter.

honneur et patrie (*Fr*) honour and fatherland. —the motto on the Légion d'Honneur.

honor virtutis praemium (*L*) honour is the reward of virtue.

hora fugit (*L*) the hour flies.

horas non numero nisi serenas (*L*) I number none but shining hours. —common on sundials.

horresco referens (*L*) I shudder in relating. —Virgil, *Aen.*, II.204.

horribile dictu (*L*) horrible to relate.

humanum est errare (*L*) to err is human.

hurtar para dar por Dios (*Sp*) to steal in order to give to God.

hypage Satana (*Gr*) away Satan. —Matt.4.10.

hypotheses non fingo (*L*) I do not frame hypotheses (ie unverifiable speculations). —Newton.

ich kann nicht anders (*Ger*) I can do no other: used by or of one who stands by his or her principles in the face of opposition. —from a speech by Martin Luther at the Diet of Worms, 1521.

Iesus Hominum Salvator (*L*) Jesus, Saviour of men.

ignorantia juris neminem excusat (*L*) ignorance of the law excuses nobody.

ignotum per ignotius (*L*) the unknown by the still more unknown.

i gran dolori sono muti (*Ital*) great griefs are mute.

il a inventé l'histoire (*Fr*) he has invented history. —said by Madame du Deffand, about Voltaire.

il a les défauts de ses qualités (*Fr*) he has the defects that answer to his good qualities.

il faut cultiver notre jardin (*Fr*) we must cultivate our garden: we must attend to our own affairs. —Voltaire, *Candide* xxx.

il faut souffrir pour être belle (*Fr*) it is necessary to suffer in order to be beautiful.

il gran rifiuto (*Ital*) the great refusal: the abdication of Pope Celestine V. —Dante, *Inferno*, III.60.

il n'y a pas à dire (*Fr*) there's no denying it.

il n'y a que le premier pas qui coûte (*Fr*) it is only the first step that counts. —Madame du Deffand on St Denis walking after decapitation.

ils ne passeront pas (*Fr*) they shall not pass: first used at Verdun in 1916.

ils n'ont rien appris ni rien oublié (*Fr*) they have learned nothing and forgotten nothing. —said of the French *Émigrés*, often of the Bourbons.

incidis in Scyllam cupiens vitare Charybdim (*L*) you fall into Scylla trying to avoid Charybdis. —Philip Gaultier de Lille.

incredulus odi (*L*) I hate and disbelieve. —Horace, *A.P.*, 188.

in meditatione fugae (*L*) in contemplation of flight.

integer vitae scelerisque purus (*L*) blameless in life and clear of offence. —Horace, *Od.*, I.xxii.1.

inter arma silent leges (*L*) amid wars laws are silent. —Cicero.

interdum stultus bene loquitur (*L*) sometimes a fool speaks aright.

invita Minerva (*L*) against the will of Minerva: uninspired. —Horace, *A.P.*, 385.

ira furor brevis est (*L*) rage is a brief madness. —Horace, *Epist.*, I.ii.62.

Italia irredenta (*Ital*) unredeemed Italy: the parts of Italy still under foreign domination after the war of 1866, ie South Tirol, etc.

j'accuse (*Fr*) I accuse: any publication that makes an accusation of intolerance, injustice, etc. —originally the title of a open letter from Emile Zola in connection with the Dreyfus case, published in *L'Aurore* (13 January 1898).

jacta est alea (*L*) the die is cast. —quoted as said by Caesar at the crossing of the Rubicon.

je n'en vois pas la nécessité (*Fr*) I don't see the necessity for that. —said by the Comte d'Argenson in reply to a man who pleaded, 'But one must live somehow'.

je pense donc je suis (*Fr*) I think therefore I am. —René Descartes, *Méditations metaphysiques*.

joci causa (*L*) for the joke.

j'y suis, j'y reste (*Fr*) here I am, here I stay. —said by General MacMahon after capturing the Malakoff fortress during the Crimean War and being told to leave it (it was mined).

kai ta leipomena, kai ta loipa (*Gr*) and the rest; and so on.

kat' exochēn (*Gr*) pre-eminently; *par excellence*.

keine Antwort ist auch eine Antwort (*Ger*) no answer is still an answer: silence gives consent.

Kirche, Küche, Kinder (*Ger*) church, kitchen, children. — said, eg during the Nazi period, to be the proper interests of a German woman.

laborare est orare (*L*) work is prayer.

labore et honore (*L*) by labour and honour.

labuntur et imputantur (*L*) [the moments] slip away and are laid to our account. —inscription on sundials. See also **pereunt et imputantur**.

la donna è mobile (*Ital*) woman is changeable.

la garde meurt et ne se rend pas (*Fr*) the guard dies, it does not surrender. —General Cambronne's reply when asked to surrender at the battle of Waterloo.

lā ilāha illā'llāh (*Ar*) there is no god but God.

l'appétit vient en mangeant (*Fr*) appetite comes as you eat: the more you have the more you want.

lasciate ogni speranza, voi ch'entrate (*Ital*) abandon all hope ye who enter. —Dante, *Inferno*. III.9. From the inscription over the gate of hell.

le coeur a ses raisons (que la raison ne connaît point) (*Fr*) the heart has its reasons (of which reason knows nothing). —Pascal, *Pensées*.

le génie n'est qu'une grande aptitude à la patience (*Fr*) genius is merely a great aptitude for patience. —attributed to Buffon.

le mieux est l'ennemi du bien (*Fr*) the best is the enemy of the good. —Voltaire, *Contes*, 'La Begueule', quoting an Italian proverb.

l'empire, c'est la paix (*Fr*) the empire means peace. —said by Louis Napoleon in 1852.

l'enfer c'est les autres (*Fr*) hell is other people. —Jean-Paul Sartre, *Huis Clos*.

les absents ont toujours tort (*Fr*) those absent are always wrong.

les jeux sont faits (*Fr*) in roulette, etc, the bets have been placed.

l'état, c'est moi (*Fr*) I am the state. —alleged to have been said by Louis XIV.

l'homme est un roseau pensant (*Fr*) man is a thinking reed —Pascal, *Pensées*.

liberté, égalité, fraternité (*Fr*) liberty, equality, fraternity. —a slogan of the French Revolution.

littera scripta manet (*L*) what is written down is permanent. See **vox audita**.

l'union fait la force (*Fr*) union makes strength.

lupus in fabula (*L*) the wolf in the fable: talk of the devil. —Terence, *Adelphi*, IV.i.21.

magna est veritas et praevalebit (or **praevalet**) (*L*) truth is great and will prevail.

magni nominis umbra (*L*) the mere shadow of a mighty name. —Lucan, I.135.

mea virtute me involvo (*L*) I wrap myself in my virtue. —Horace, *Od.*, III.xxix.54–55.

mēden agan (*Gr*) [let there be] nothing in excess.

medio tutissimus ibis (*L*) thou wilt go safest in the middle. —Ovid, *Met.*, II.137.

mega biblion, mega kakon (*Gr*) big book, great evil.

mē kinei Kamarinan (*Gr*) do not stir up Kamarina (a pestilent marsh in Sicily): let well alone.

mens sibi conscia recti (*L*) a mind conscious of rectitude. —Virgil, *Aen.*, I.604. Cf **conscia mens recti**.

mi casa es su casa (*Sp*) my house is your house: make yourself at home.

monstrum horrendum, informe, ingens (*L*) a frightful monster, ill-shapen, huge. —Virgil, *Aen.*, III.658.

morituri te salutant see **ave**.

natura abhorret vacuum (*L*) nature abhors a vacuum.

naviget Anticyram (*L*) let him sail to Anticyra: ie where hellebore could be had, to cure madness. —Horace, *Sat.*, II.iii.166.

nec cupias, nec metuas (*L*) neither desire nor fear.

ne cede malis (*L*) yield not to misfortune. —Virgil, *Aen.*, VI.95.

necessitas non habet legem (*L*) necessity has no law.

nec scire fas est omnia (*L*) it is not permitted to know all things. —Horace, *Od.*, IV.iv.22.

nemo me impune lacessit (*L*) no one provokes me with impunity. —the motto of the kings of Scotland and of the Order of the Thistle, and the inscription round the edge of a Scottish one-pound coin.

nemo repente fuit turpissimus (*L*) no one ever became utterly bad all at once. —Juvenal, II.83.

ne obliviscaris (*L*) do not forget.

neque semper arcum tendit Apollo (*L*) Apollo does not always bend his bow. —Horace, *Od.*, II.x.19–20.

ne quid nimis (*L*) [let there be] nothing in excess.

nescit vox missa reverti (*L*) a word published cannot be recalled. —Horace, *A.P.*, 390.

n'est-ce pas? (*Fr*) is it not so?

ne sutor ultra (or **supra**) **crepidam** (*L*) a cobbler should not criticize (a work of art) beyond (or above) the sandal: one should not criticize beyond one's sphere of knowledge. See also **ultracrepidate** in Dictionary.

ne temere (*L*) not rashly. —a papal decree of 1907 denying recognition to the marriage of a Catholic unless contracted before a priest.

nicht wahr ? (*Ger*) is it not true? isn't that so?

nisi Dominus frustra (*L*) except the Lord (keep the city, the watchman waketh but) in vain. —Psalm 127; the motto of Edinburgh.

nitor in adversum (*L*) I strive in opposition. —Ovid, *Met.*, II.72.

non est inventus (*L*) he has not been found: he has absconded.

non multa, sed multum (*L*) not many, but much.

non nobis, Domine (*L*) not unto us, O Lord. —Psalm 115.

non possumus (*L*) we cannot: a form of refusal.

non ut edam vivo sed ut vivam edo (*L*) I do not live to eat, but eat to live. —Quintilian.

nosce teipsum (*L*) know thyself. —a translation of **gnōthi seauton**.

nous avons changé tout cela (*Fr*) we have changed all that. —Molière, *Le Médecin malgré lui*, II.iv.

nous verrons (ce que nous verrons) (*Fr*) we shall see (what we shall see).

nulla nuova, buona nouva (*Ital*) no news is good news.

nunca más (*Sp*) never again.

nunc est bibendum (*L*) now is the time to drink. —Horace, *Od.*, I.xxxvii.1.

obscurum per obscurius (*L*) (explaining) the obscure by means of the more obscure.

odi et amo (*L*) I hate and I love: referring to the love–hate syndrome. —Catullus lxxxv.

odi profanum vulgus et arceo (*L*) I loathe and shun the profane rabble. —Horace, *Od.*, III.i.1.

O fortunatos nimium, sua si bona norint, agricolas (*L*) Oh too happy farmers, if they but knew their luck. — Virgil, *Georg.*, II.458.

ohe! jam satis (*L*) hold! enough now. —a common phrase.

ohne Hast, ohne Rast (*Ger*) without haste, without rest. —Goethe's motto.

olim meminisse juvabit see **forsan**.

omne ignotum pro magnifico (*L*) everything unknown is taken to be magnificent. —Tacitus, *Agricola* xxx, in a speech attributed to the British chieftain Calgacus.

omnem crede diem tibi diluxisse supremum (*L*) believe each day to have dawned as your last. — Horace, *Epist.*, I.iv.13.

omne tulit punctum qui miscuit utile dulci (*L*) he has carried every vote who has combined the useful with the pleasing. —Horace, *A.P.*, 343.

omne vivum ex ovo (*L*) every living thing comes from an egg. —attributed to Harvey.

omnia mutantur see **tempora mutantur**.

omnia vincit amor, et nos cedamus amori (*L*) love overcomes all things, let us too yield to love. —Virgil, *Ecl.*, X.69.

O si sic omnia! (*L*) Oh that he had done all things thus, or Oh that all things were thus!

O tempora! O mores! (*L*) O the times! O the manners! —occurs in Cicero's first speech against Catiline.

otium cum dignitate (*L*) dignified leisure.

ouk esti? (*Gr*) is it not so?

ovem lupo committere (*L*) to entrust the sheep to the wolf.

pace tua (*L*) by your leave.

pallida Mors aequo pulsat pede pauperum tabernas regumque turres (*L*) pale Death knocks with impartial foot at poor men's huts and kings' castles. — Horace, *Od.*, I.iv.13–14.

palmam qui meruit ferat (*L*) let him who has won the palm wear it. —Dr Jortin, *Lusus Poetici*, viii.20.

panem et circenses (*L*) bread and (Roman) circus-games: food and amusements at public expense. — Juvenal, X.81.

panta rhei (*Gr*) all things are in a flux. —a saying of Heraclitus.

parturiunt montes, nascetur ridiculus mus (*L*) the mountains are in labour, an absurd mouse will be born: a great effort for little reward. —Horace, *A.P.*, 139.

pas op (*Afrik*) look out.

pathēmata mathēmata (*Gr*) sufferings [are] lessons.

peccavi (*L*) I have sinned.

pereunt et imputantur (*L*) [the moments, hours] pass away and are reckoned to our account.

pleidiol wyf i'm gwlad (*Welsh*) loyal am I to my country. —inscription round the edge of a Welsh one-pound coin.

pleon hēmisy pantos (*Gr*) the half is more than the whole. —Hesiod, *Erga*, 40.

plus ça change, plus c'est la même chose (*Fr*) the more things change, the more they stay the same: no superficial or apparent change alters something's essential nature.

poeta nascitur, non fit (*L*) the poet is born, not made.

pollōn onomatōn mia morphē (*Gr*) one shape of many names. —Aeschylus, *Prometheus*, 210.

polyphloisboio thalassēs (*Gr*) of the much-sounding sea. —Homer, *Il.*, 1.34; also Hesiod, *Erga*, 648.

populus vult decipi, ergo decipiatur (*L*) the public wishes to be fooled, therefore let it be fooled. —ascribed to Cardinal Caraffa.

por favor (*Sp*) please.

post hoc, ergo propter hoc (*L*) after this, therefore because of this: a fallacious reasoning.

pour encourager les autres (*Fr*) to encourage the others —Voltaire, *Candide*, on the shooting of Admiral Byng.

purpureus pannus (*L*) a purple patch. —Horace, *A.P.*, 15–16.

que diable allait-il faire dans cette galère? (*Fr*) what the devil was he doing in that galley?: how did he get mixed up in that? —Molière, *Les Fourberies de Scapin*, II.vii.

quem di diligunt adolescens moritur (*L*) whom the gods love dies young. —Plautus's translation of **hon hoi theoi**…

quem Iuppiter vult perdere dementat prius, or **quem deus perdere vult, prius dementat** (*L*) whom Jupiter (a god) wishes to destroy, he first makes mad.

¿qué pasa? (*Sp*) what's up?

que sais-je (sçai-je)? (*Fr*) what do I know? —Montaigne's motto.

quicunque vult salvus esse (*L*) whosoever will be saved. —the beginning of the Athanasian creed.

quid rides? mutato nomine de te fabula narratur (*L*) why do you laugh? with change of name the story is about you. —Horace, *Sat.*, I.i.69–70.

quién sabe? (*Sp*) who knows?

quieta non movere (*L*) not to move things that are at rest: to let sleeping dogs lie.

quis custodiet ipsos custodes? (*L*) who will guard the guards themselves? —Juvenal, VI.347–8.

quis desiderio sit pudor aut modus tam cari capitis? (*L*) what shame or stint should there be in mourning for one so dear? —Horace, *Od.*, I.xxiv.1.

qui s'excuse s'accuse (*Fr*) he who excuses himself accuses himself.

qui tacet consentit (*L*) who keeps silence consents.

qui va là? (*Fr*) who goes there?

quocunque jeceris stabit (*L*) whithersoever you throw it, it will stand. —the motto of the Isle of Man.

quod ubique, quod semper, quod ab omnibus (*L*) what everywhere, what always, what by all (has been believed). —St Vincent of Lérin's definition of orthodoxy.

quot homines, tot sententiae (*L*) as many men, so many minds or opinions. —Terence, *Phormio*, II.iv.14 (or 1.454).

reculer pour mieux sauter (*Fr*) to draw back to take a better leap: to make a strategic retreat in preparation for a more effective attack.

redolet lucerna (*L*) it smells of the lamp: it shows signs of great elaboration or study.

re galantuomo (*Ital*) the honest king; king and gentleman. —said of Victor Emmanuel II.

religio loci (*L*) the religious spirit of the place. —Virgil, *Aen.*, VIII.349.

rem acu tetigisti (*L*) you have touched the thing with a needle, hit it exactly. —proverbial expression used by Plautus.

res ipsa loquitur (*L*) the thing speaks for itself: the accident as in itself evidence of negligence.

respice finem (*L*) look to the end. Playfully perverted into **respice funem**, beware of the (hangman's) rope.

retro me, satana (*L*) in Vulgate, **vade retro me, satana** get thee behind me, Satan: stop trying to tempt me. —Matt.16.23, Mark 8.33, Luke 4.8.

revenons à nos moutons (*Fr*) let us return to our sheep: ie our subject. —from the medieval farce *Maître Pathelin*.

rhododaktylos Eōs (*Gr*) rosy-fingered Dawn. —Homer, *Odyssey*, II.1.

Roma locuta, causa finita (*L*) Rome has spoken, the cause is ended.

ruat caelum see **fiat justitia**.

salus populi suprema lex esto (*L*) or (Cicero, *De Legibus*, III. iii) **suprema est lex** let the welfare of the people be the final law.

sans peur et sans reproche (*Fr*) without fear and without reproach: used to qualify le Chevalier Bayard.

sapere aude (*L*) dare to be wise. —Horace, *Epist.*, I.ii.40.

sartor resartus (*L*) the tailor retailored.

se non è vero, è ben trovato (*Ital*) if it is not true, it is cleverly invented.

sero venientibus ossa (*L*) the bones to the late-comers.

sic itur ad astra (*L*) such is the way to the stars. — Virgil, *Aen.*, IX.641.

sic transit gloria mundi (*L*) so passes away earthly glory.

si Dieu n'existait pas, il faudrait l'inventer (*Fr*) if God did not exist, it would be necessary to invent him. —Voltaire, *Epître sur les trois imposteurs*.

si jeunesse savait, si vieillesse pouvait (*Fr*) if youth but knew, if age but could.

s'il vous plaît (*Fr*) if you please.

similia similibus curantur (*L*) likes are cured by likes: a hair of the dog that bit one.

si monumentum requiris, circumspice (*L*) if you seek (his) monument, look round you. —inscription for the architect Christoper Wren's tomb in St Paul's.

simplex munditiis (*L*) elegant in simplicity. —Horace, *Od.*, I.v.5.

siste, viator (*L*) stop, traveller.

si vis pacem, para bellum (*L*) if you would have peace, be ready for war.

spero meliora (*L*) I hope for better things.

stet fortuna domus (*L*) may the fortune of the house last long.

sua si bona see **O fortunatos**.

suaviter in modo, fortiter in re (*L*) gentle in manner, resolute in deed.

suggestio falsi see **suppressio veri**.

sunt lacrimae rerum (*L*) there are tears for things (unhappy). —Virgil, *Aen.*, I.462.

suo motu (*L*) on one's own initiative.

suppressio veri suggestio falsi (*L*) suppression of truth is suggestion of the false. (In law, **suppressio veri** is passive, **suggestio falsi** active, misrepresentation.)

sursum corda (*L*) lift up your hearts.

surtout, pas de zèle (*Fr*) above all, no zeal. —Talleyrand's advice to foreign diplomats.

sutor ne ultra (or **supra**) **crepidam** see **ne sutor**.

tempora (*orig* **omnia**) **mutantur, nos et mutamur in illis** (*L*) the times (all things) change, and we with them.

tempus edax rerum (*L*) time, consumer of things. — Ovid, *Met.*, XV.234.

thalassa, thalassa! or **thalatta, thalatta!** (*Gr*) the sea, the sea!: the exulting cry of Xenophon's men on beholding the sea. —Xenophon, *Anabasis*, IV.7.

timeo Danaos et dona ferentes (*L*) I fear the Greeks, even when bringing gifts. —Virgil, *Aen.*, II.49.

tout est pour le mieux dans le meilleur des mondes possibles (*Fr*) all is for the best in the best of all possible worlds. —Voltaire, *Candide*.

tout comprendre c'est tout pardonner (*Fr*) to understand everything is to pardon everything.

toujours perdrix (*Fr*) partridge every day: too much of a good thing.

tria juncta in uno (*L*) three things in one.

ubi bene, ibi patria (*L*) where it goes well with me, there is my fatherland.

und so weiter or **usw** (*Ger*) and so forth.

vade in pace (*L*) go in peace.

vade retro me, satana see **retro**.

varium et mutabile semper femina (*L*) woman is ever a fickle and changeable thing. —Virgil, *Aen.*, IV.569.

vedi Napoli, e poi muori (*Ital*) see Naples, and die.

venceremos (*Sp*) we shall overcome.

veni Creator Spiritus (*L*) come, Creator Spirit. —the beginning of an early Latin hymn.

veritas odium parit (*L*) truth begets hatred. —Terence, *Andria*, I.i.41.

vestigia. . .nulla retrorsum (*L*) no footprints backwards (at the lion's den): sometimes used to mean no going back. —Horace, *Epist.*, I.i.74–75.

vigilate et orate (*L*) watch and pray.

virginibus puerisque (*L*) for maidens and boys. —Horace, *Od.*, III.i.4.

vita sine litteris mors est (*L*) life without literature is death.

vive la bagatelle (*quasi-Fr*) long live frivolity!

vive la différence (*Fr*) long live the difference! —usually referring to the difference between the sexes, but also applied to national, political, racial, or religious diversity.

vive ut vivas (*L*) live that you may live.

vivit post funera virtus (*L*) virtue lives beyond the grave.

vogue la galère! (*Fr*) row the boat: carry on regardless.

volto sciolto e pensieri stretti (*Ital*) open face, close thoughts.

vous l'avez voulu, George Dandin (*Fr*) you've only got yourself to blame. —Molière, *George Dandin*, Act I.

vox audita perit, littera scripta manet (*L*) the heard word is lost, the written letter abides.

Wein, Weib und Gesang (*Ger*) wine, women and song.

zonam perdidit (*L*) he has lost his money-belt: he is in needy circumstances.

zonam solvere (*L*) to loose the virgin zone: to marry.

Alphabets

The Greek alphabet

Letter		Name	Usual transliteration	Letter		Name	Usual transliteration
Α	α	alpha	a	Ν	ν	nū	n
Β	β	bēta	b	Ξ	ξ	xī	x
Γ	γ	gamma	g	Ο	ο	omicron	o
Δ	δ	delta	d	Π	π	pī	p
Ε	ε	epsīlon	e	Ρ	ρ	rhō	r
Ζ	ζ	zēta	z	Σ	σ ς	sigma	s
Η	η	ēta	ē	Τ	τ	tau	t
Θ	θ	thēta	th	Υ	υ	upsīlon	u or y
Ι	ι	iōta	i	Φ	φ	phī	ph
Κ	κ	kappa	k	Χ	χ	chī	kh or ch
Λ	λ	lambda	l	Ψ	ψ	psī	ps
Μ	μ	mū	m	Ω	ω	ōmega	ō

The Russian alphabet

Letter		Usual transliteration	Letter		Usual transliteration
А	а	a	С	с	s
Б	б	b	Т	т	t
В	в	v	У	у	u
Г	г	g	Ф	ф	f
Д	д	d	Х	х	kh
Е	е	e (ye)	Ц	ц	ts
Ё	ё	e (yö)	Ч	ч	ch
Ж	ж	zh	Ш	ш	sh
З	з	z	Щ	щ	shch (often pronounced rather as sh followed by consonantal y)
И	и	i (ē)			
Й	й	(consonantal y sound; only used as the second letter of a diphthong)	Ъ	ъ	(hard sign; used to separate in pronunciation a following palatalized vowel from a preceding consonant either palatalized or unpalatalized)
К	к	k	Ы	ы	i (a sound similar to i)
Л	л	l	Ь	ь	(soft sign; used after a consonant to indicate palatalization, a sound like consonantal y)
М	м	m			
Н	н	n			
О	о	o	Э	э	e (e)
П	п	p	Ю	ю	u (yoo)
Р	р	r	Я	я	ya (yä)

The Hebrew alphabet

Letter	Name	Usual transliteration	Letter	Name	Usual transliteration
א	aleph	'	ל	lamed	l
ב	beth	b	ם מ	mem	m
ג	gimel	g	ן נ	nun	n
ד	daleth	d	ס	samekh	s
ה	heh	h	ע	ayin	'
ו	vav	w	ף פ	peh	p, f
ז	zayin	z	ץ צ	sadhe	s
ח	cheth	h	ק	koph	q
ט	teth	t	ר	resh	r
י	yod	y, j	ש	sin	sh, s
ך כ	kaph	k	ת	tav	t

The Arabic alphabet

Letter	Name	Usual transliteration	Letter	Name	Usual transliteration
ا	'alif	'	ض	dad	d
ب	ba	b	ط	ta	t
ت	ta	t (palatalized)	ظ	za	z
ث	tha	th	ع	'ain	'
ج	jim	j	غ	ghain	gh
ح	ha	h (guttural)	ف	fa	f
خ	kha	kh	ق	qaf	q
د	dal	d (soft)	ك	kaf	k
ذ	dhal	dh	ل	lam	l
ر	ra	r	م	mim	m
ز	zain	z	ن	nun	n
س	sin	s	ه	ha	h
ش	shin	sh	و	waw	w
ص	sad	s	ي	ya	y

Roman numerals

I = 1   V = 5   X = 10   L = 50   C = 100   D = 500   M = 1000

From the above symbols the numbers are made up as follows:

I	=	1		L	=	50
II	=	2		LI	=	51
III	=	3		LII, etc	=	52, etc
IV (or IIII, eg on clocks)	=	4		LX	=	60
V	=	5		LXI	=	61
VI	=	6		LXII, etc	=	62, etc
VII	=	7		LXX	=	70
VIII	=	8		LXXI	=	71
IX	=	9		LXXII, etc	=	72, etc
X	=	10		LXXX	=	80
XI	=	11		LXXXI	=	81
XII	=	12		LXXXII, etc	=	82, etc
XIII	=	13		XC	=	90
XIV	=	14		XCI	=	91
XV	=	15		XCII, etc	=	92, etc
XVI	=	16		C	=	100
XVII	=	17		CC	=	200
XVIII	=	18		CCC	=	300
XIX	=	19		CCCC or CD	=	400
XX	=	20		D (or IƆ)	=	500
XXI	=	21		DC (or IƆC)	=	600
XXII, etc	=	22, etc		DCC (or IƆCC)	=	700
XXX	=	30		DCCC (or IƆCCC)	=	800
XXXI	=	31		CM (or DCCCC or IƆCCCC)	=	900
XXXII, etc	=	32, etc		M	=	1000
XL	=	40		MM	=	2000
XLI	=	41		$\bar{V}^3$ (or CIƆ)[1]	=	5000
XLII, etc	=	42, etc				

Other letters also were used as numerals in medieval times (see Dictionary). For additional information about medieval methods of writing numerals, see below.

1. The symbol Ɔ, known as the *apostrophus*, might be repeated one or more times after IƆ, each Ɔ making the number ten times greater, as IƆƆ = 5000, IƆƆƆ = 500000. A number of this type might be multiplied by two by adding (in front) as many C's as there were Ɔ's in the number, eg CCIƆƆ = 10000, CCCCIƆƆƆ = 1000000.

2. The symbols I, V, X, L, C, D, M are still used today. In the Middle Ages, and also in much later times, methods of writing numerals were common which are found neither in the Roman period nor in the present century. Some are noted below.

3. In the Middle Ages and later, a line was placed above a symbol representing a number 1000 times greater, as $\bar{X}$ = 10000. |X̄| and |X| were variant methods of expressing 1000000.

4. In the Middle Ages and later, and still in medical usage, numerals could be written lower case, and j was often substituted for final i.

5. In the Middle Ages and later, Ɔ appears with the same meaning as D, and there is sometimes a small version of the apostrophus. To take at random an example of the latter, the third volume of John Ray's *Historia Plantarum* is dated cIɔ Iɔ CCIV — that is 1704.

Chemical elements

Chemical elements with atomic numbers between 1 and 111 are given below.

Symbol	element	derived from	atomic no
Ac	actinium	Greek *aktis* = ray	89
Ag	silver	Old English *silfer*	47
Al	aluminium	Latin *alumen* = alum	13
Am	americium	America	95
Ar	argon	Greek *argon* = inactive	18
As	arsenic	Greek *arsenikon* = yellow orpiment	33
At	astatine	Greek *astatos* = unstable	85
Au	gold	Old English *gold*	79
B	boron	Arabic *buraq* = borax	5
Ba	barium	Greek *barys* = heavy	56
Be	beryllium	Greek *beryllos* = beryl	4
Bh	bohrium	Bohr, Danish physicist	107
Bi	bismuth	German (origin unknown)	83
Bk	berkelium	Berkeley, California	97
Br	bromine	Greek *bromos* = stink	35
C	carbon	Latin *carbo* = coal	6
Ca	calcium	Latin *calx* = lime	20
Cd	cadmium	Greek *kadmeia* = calamine	48
Ce	cerium	asteroid Ceres	58
Cf	californium	California	98
Cl	chlorine	Greek *chloros* = pale green	17
Cm	curium	Curie, French physicists	96
Co	cobalt	German *Kobold* = demon	27
Cr	chromium	Greek *chroma* = colour	24
Cs	caesium	Latin *caesius* = bluish-grey	55
Cu	copper	Cyprus	29
Db	dubnium	Dubna, Russia	105
Ds	darmstadtium	Darmstadt, Germany	110
Dy	dysprosium	Greek *dysprositos* = difficult to reach	66
Er	erbium	Ytterby, Sweden	68
Es	einsteinium	Einstein, US physicist	99
Eu	europium	Europe	63
F	fluorine	Latin *fluor* = flow	9
Fe	iron	Old English *iren*	26
Fm	fermium	Fermi, Italian physicist	100
Fr	francium	France	87
Ga	gallium	Latin *Gallia* = France, or *gallus* = cock	31
Gd	gadolinium	Gadolin, Finnish chemist	64
Ge	germanium	Germany	32
H	hydrogen	Greek *hydor* = water + *gennaein* = to produce	1
He	helium	Greek *helios* = sun	2
Hf	hafnium	Latin *Hafnia* = Copenhagen	72
Hg	mercury	Latin *Mercurius*	80
Ho	holmium	N Latin *Holmia* = Stockholm	67
Hs	hassium	Latin *Hassias* = Hesse	108
I	iodine	Greek *ioeides* = violet-coloured	53
In	indium	indigo lines in the spectrum	49
Ir	iridium	Latin *iris* = rainbow goddess	77
K	potassium	potash	19
Kr	krypton	Greek *kryptein* = hidden	36
La	lanthanum	Greek *lanthanein* = to escape notice	57
Li	lithium	Greek *lithos* = stone	3
Lr	lawrencium	Lawrence, US physicist	103
Lu	lutetium	Latin *Lutetia* = Paris	71
Md	mendelevium	Mendeleev, Russian scientist	101
Mg	magnesium	Magnesia, Thessaly, Greece	12
Mn	manganese	Latin *magnesia*	25
Mo	molybdenum	Greek *molybdos* = lead	42
Mt	meitnerium	Meitner, Austrian physicist	109
N	nitrogen	Greek *nitron* = sodium carbonate + *gennaein* = to produce soda	7
Na	sodium	soda	11
Nb	niobium	Niobe (Greek myth)	41
Nd	neodymium	Greek *neos* = new and *didymos* = twin	60
Ne	neon	Greek *neos* = new	10
Ni	nickel	German *Kupfernickel* = niccolite	28
No	nobelium	Nobel Institute	102
Np	neptunium	planet Neptune	93
O	oxygen	Greek *oxys* = acid + *gennaein* = to produce	8
Os	osmium	Greek *osme* = smell	76
P	phosphorus	Greek *phosphoros* = light-bearer	15
Pa	protactinium	Greek *protos* = first + actinium	91
Pb	lead	Old English *lead*	82
Pd	palladium	minor planet Pallas	46
Pm	promethium	Prometheus (Greek myth)	61
Po	polonium	Poland	84
Pr	praseodymium	Greek *prasios* = leek green and *didymos* = twin	59
Pt	platinum	Spanish *plata* = silver	78
Pu	plutonium	planet Pluto	94
Ra	radium	Latin *radius* = ray	88
Rb	rubidium	Latin *rubidus* = red	37
Re	rhenium	Latin *Rhenus* = the Rhine	75
Rf	rutherfordium	Rutherford, British physicist	104
Rg	roentgenium	Röntgen, German physicist	111
Rh	rhodium	Greek *rhodon* = rose	45
Rn	radon	radium	86
Ru	ruthenium	L Latin *Ruthenia* = Russia	44
S	sulphur	Latin *sulphur*	16
Sb	antimony	L Latin *antimonium*	51
Sc	scandium	Scandinavian	21
Se	selenium	Greek *selene* = moon	34
Sg	seaborgium	Seaborg, US physicist	106
Si	silicon	Latin *silex* = flint	14
Sm	samarium	Samarski, Russian engineer	62
Sn	tin	Old English *tin*	50
Sr	strontium	Strontian, Scotland	38
Ta	tantalum	Tantalus (Greek myth)	73
Tb	terbium	Ytterby, Sweden	65
Tc	technetium	Greek *technetos* = artificial	43
Te	tellurium	Latin *tellus* = earth	52
Th	thorium	Scandinavian god Thor	90
Ti	titanium	Greek *Titan* = Titan	22
Tl	thallium	Greek *thallos* = a young shoot	81
Tm	thulium	Latin *Thule* = a northern island	69
U	uranium	planet Uranus	92
V	vanadium	Old Norse *Vanadis* = goddess Freya	23
W	tungsten	Swedish *tungsten* = heavy stone	74
Xe	xenon	Greek *xenos* = stranger	54
Y	yttrium	Ytterby, Sweden	39
Yb	ytterbium	Ytterby, Sweden	70
Zn	zinc	German *zink*	30
Zr	zirconium	Persian *zargun* = gold-coloured	40

SI units

The International System (SI) of units has seven *base units*, two *supplementary units* (the radian and the steradian) and a variety of *derived units*. The seven physical quantities on which the system is based are listed in the table below.

Quantity	Unit	Symbol
length	metre	m
mass	kilogram	kg
time	second	s
electric current	ampere	A
temperature	kelvin	K
luminous intensity	candela	cd
amount of substance	mole	mol

The SI derived units for other physical quantities are formed from the base units. Thus, for example, force = mass × acceleration, and the unit of force, the newton, is equivalent to $kg\,m\,s^{-2}$. The two supplementary units and the principal derived units, together with some of the more important equivalents, are shown below.

Quantity	Unit	Symbol	Equivalent
plane angle	radian	rad	$(=180°/\pi)$
solid angle	steradian	sr	−
density	−	$kg\,m^{-3}$	−
velocity or speed	−	$m\,s^{-1}$	−
acceleration	−	$m\,s^{-2}$	−
momentum	−	$kg\,m\,s^{-1}$	−
moment of inertia	−	$kg\,m^{2}$	−
force	newton	N	$kg\,m\,s^{-2}$
pressure, stress	pascal	Pa	$N\,m^{-2}$
energy, work, heat	joule	J	$N\,m$
power	watt	W	$J\,s^{-1}$
dynamic viscosity	−	$N\,s\,m^{-2}$	$kg\,m^{-1}\,s^{-1}$
kinematic viscosity	−	$m^{2}\,s^{-1}$	−
frequency	hertz	Hz	s^{-1}
angular frequency	−	$rad\,s^{-1}$	$(=2\pi\,Hz)$
electric conductance	siemens	S	Ω^{-1}
electric charge	coulomb	C	$A\,s$
electric potential difference	volt	V	$W\,A^{-1}$
electric capacitance	farad	F	$C\,V^{-1}$
electric resistance	ohm	Ω	$V\,A^{-1}$
magnetic flux	weber	Wb	$V\,s$
magnetic flux density	tesla	T	$V\,s\,m^{-2}$
inductance	henry	H	$V\,s\,A^{-1}$
luminous flux	lumen	lm	$cd\,sr$
illuminance	lux	lx	$lm\,m^{-2}$
radioactivity	becquerel	Bq	s^{-1}
absorbed dose, ionizing radiation	gray	Gy	$J\,kg^{-1}$
radiation dose equivalent	sievert	Sv	$J\,kg^{-1}$
catalytic activity	katal	kat	$mol\,s^{-1}$

Beaufort scale

Beaufort number	m/sec	Windspeed kph	Windspeed mph	Wind name	Observable wind characteristics	Sea disturbance number	Average wave height m	Average wave height ft	Observable sea characteristics
0	1	<1	<1	Calm	Smoke rises vertically	0	0	0	Sea like a mirror
1	1	1–5	1–3	Light air	Wind direction shown by smoke drift, but not by wind vanes	0	0	0	Ripples like scales, without foam crests
2	2	6–11	4–7	Light breeze	Wind felt on face; leaves rustle; vanes moved by wind	1	0.3	0–1	More definite wavelets, but crests do not break
3	4	12–19	8–12	Gentle breeze	Leaves and small twigs in constant motion; wind extends light flag	2	0.3–0.6	1–2	Large wavelets; crests begin to break; scattered white horses
4	7	20–28	13–18	Moderate breeze	Raises dust, loose paper; small branches moved	3	0.6–1.2	2–4	Small waves become longer; fairly frequent white horses
5	10	29–38	19–24	Fresh breeze	Small trees in leaf begin to sway; crested wavelets on inland waters	4	1.2–2.4	4–8	Moderate waves with a more definite long form; many white horses; some spray possible
6	12	39–49	25–31	Strong breeze	Large branches in motion; difficult to use umbrellas; whistling heard in telegraph wires	5	2.4–4	8–13	Large waves form; more extensive white foam crests; some spray probable
7	15	50–61	32–38	Near gale	Whole trees in motion; inconvenience walking against wind	6	4–6	13–20	Sea heaps up; streaks of white foam blown along
8	18	62–74	39–46	Gale	Breaks twigs off trees; impedes progress	6	4–6	13–20	Moderately high waves of greater length; well-marked streaks of foam
9	20	75–88	47–54	Strong gale	Slight structural damage occurs	6	4–6	13–20	High waves; dense streaks of foam; sea begins to roll; spray affects visibility
10	26	89–102	55–63	Storm	Trees uprooted; considerable damage occurs	7	6–9	20–30	Very high waves with long overhanging crests; dense streaks of foam blown along; generally white appearance of surface; heavy rolling
11	30	103–117	64–72	Violent storm	Widespread damage	8	9–14	30–45	Exceptionally high waves; long white patches of foam; poor visibility; ships lost to view behind waves
12–17	⩾30	⩾118	⩾73	Hurricane		9	>14	>45	Air filled with foam and spray; sea completely white; very poor visibility

Mohs scale

The relative hardness of solids can be expressed using a scale of numbers from 1 to 10, each relating to a mineral (1 representing talc, 10 representing diamond). The method was devised by Friedrich Mohs (1773–1839), a German mineralogist. Sets of hardness pencils are used to test specimens to see which will scratch them; other useful instruments include: fingernail (2.5), copper coin (3.5), steel knife (5.5), glass (6.0).

Talc	1	Calcite	3	Apatite	5	Quartz	7	Corundum	9
Gypsum	2	Fluorite	4	Orthoclase	6	Topaz	8	Diamond	10

Earthquake severity measurement scales

Mercalli	Description	Richter
1	detected only by seismographs	<3
2	**feeble** just noticeable by some people	3–3.4
3	**slight** similar to passing of heavy lorries	3.5–4
4	**moderate** rocking of loose objects	4.1–4.4
5	**quite strong** felt by most people even when sleeping	4.5–4.8
6	**strong** trees rock and some structural damage is caused	4.9–5.4
7	**very strong** walls crack	5.5–6
8	**destructive** weak buildings collapse	6.1–6.5
9	**ruinous** houses collapse and ground pipes crack	6.6–7
10	**disastrous** landslides occur, ground cracks and buildings collapse	7.1–7.3
11	**very disastrous** few buildings remain standing	7.4–8.1
12	**catastrophic** ground rises and falls in waves	>8.1

Wine bottle sizes

Name	Capacity	
wine bottle	75 centilitres	standard size
flagon	1.13 litres or 2 pints	
magnum	1.5 litres	2 standard bottles
jeroboam	3 litres	4 standard bottles
rehoboam	4.5 litres	6 standard bottles
methuselah	6 litres	8 standard bottles
salmanazar	9 litres	12 standard bottles
balthazar	12 litres	16 standard bottles
nebuchadnezzar	15 litres	20 standard bottles

Wedding anniversaries

Traditional gift	Anniversary	Modern gift
Paper	1st	Clocks
Cotton	2nd	China
Leather	3rd	Crystal, glass
Fruit, flowers	4th	Appliances
Wood	5th	Silverware
Sugar, iron	6th	Wood
Copper, wool	7th	Desk sets
Bronze, pottery	8th	Linen, lace
Pottery, willow	9th	Leather
Tin, aluminium	10th	Diamond jewellery
Steel	11th	Fashion jewellery
Silk, linen	12th	Pearl
Lace	13th	Textiles, fur
Ivory	14th	Gold jewellery
Crystal	15th	Watches
China	20th	Platinum
Silver	25th	Silver
Pearl	30th	Diamond
Coral	35th	Jade
Ruby	40th	Ruby
Sapphire	45th	Sapphire
Gold	50th	Gold
Emerald	55th	Emerald
Diamond	60th	Diamond
Platinum	70th	Platinum

Mathematical symbols

+	plus; positive	⊥	perpendicular
−	minus; negative	∥	parallel
±	plus or minus; error margin	≅	congruent to
∓	minus or plus	∴	therefore
×	multiplied by	∵	because
•	multiplied by; scalar product of two vectors	∀	for all
		∃	there exists
÷ or /	divided by	{ }	set
=	equal to	⟨ ⟩	mean
≠	not equal to	∪	union
≡	defined as; identical to	∩	intersection
≈ or ≃	approximately equal to	⊂	is a subset of
:	ratio; such that	⊄	is not a subset of
⩾ or ≥	greater than or equal to	∂	partial derivative
>	greater than	∈	is an element of
≫	much greater than	∉	is not an element of
≯	not greater than	⇒	implies that
⩽ or ≤	less than or equal to	⇐	is implied by
<	less than	⇔	if and only if
≪	much less than	...	etc
≮	not less than	⋀	vector cross product
∝	directly proportional to	*	convolution
∞	infinity	○	composite function
→	approaches the limit	Δ	increment
√	square root	Σ	sum
!	factorial	∏	product
%	per cent	∇	del (differential operator)
′	first derivative; arcminutes; feet	∫	integral
″	second derivative; arcseconds; inches	∮	line integral around closed path
°	degrees	ℑ	imaginary part
∠	angle	ℜ	real part

Planets

Planet	Orbit period	Rotation period (d)	Equatorial diameter (km)	Mass (Earth=1)	Perihelion (AU)	Aphelion (AU)
Mercury	87.97 d	58.646	4878	0.06	0.31	0.47
Venus	224.70 d	243 R	12104	0.82	0.72	0.73
Earth	365.26 d	0.997	12756	1.00	0.98	1.02
Mars	686.98 d	1.026	6794	0.11	1.38	1.67
Jupiter	11.86 yr	0.410*	142800	317.83	4.95	5.45
Saturn	29.46 yr	0.426*	120536	95.17	9.01	10.07
Uranus	84.01 yr	~0.67 R	51118	14.50	18.28	20.09
Neptune	164.79 yr	~0.75	49492	17.20	29.8	30.32

R indicates retrograde motion
* Equatorial value
$1 AU = 1.496 \times 10^{11} m$

Major planetary satellites

Satellite	Year of discovery	Distance from planet (km)	Diameter (km)	Satellite	Year of discovery	Distance from planet (km)	Diameter (km)
Earth				Dione	1684	377000	1120
Moon	—	384000	3476	Rhea	1672	527000	1530
				Titan	1655	1222000	5150
Mars				Hyperion	1848	1481000	300
Phobos	1877	9380	27	Iapetus	1671	3560000	1460
Deimos	1877	23460	15				
				Uranus			
Jupiter				Miranda	1948	130000	470
Io	1610	422000	3630	Ariel	1851	191000	1160
Europa	1610	671000	3138	Umbriel	1851	266000	1170
Ganymede	1610	1070000	5260	Titania	1787	436000	1580
Callisto	1610	1883000	4800	Oberon	1787	583000	1520
Saturn				**Neptune**			
Mimas	1789	186000	390	Triton	1846	355000	2700
Enceladus	1789	238000	500	Nereid	1949	5515000	340
Tethys	1684	295000	1050	Proteus	1989	117600	400

The Word Lover's Ramble

Introducing the 11th edition of *Chambers* in 2008, the celebrated BBC interlocutor, Jeremy Paxman, recalled an old holiday-job boss of his accusing him of having *swallowed* a dictionary. It is a common enough charge directed at college types suddenly subordinate to plain-speaking men and women who've seen it all before. But if Jeremy had swallowed a dictionary (and one is usually enough for most people), I have been positively dining out on them. Let me explain.

Some time ago I took delivery of *16* Chambers dictionaries from the archive, stretching back to the first edition of 1872. Some, the early ones predominantly, I consumed whole, reading through the entries sequentially until my head began to spin. Others I picked at selectively, metaphorically riffling the bottom tray of the chocolate box before the top tray was empty, in search of the choicest nuggets – my personal favourite, for what it's worth, being the **glimmer gowk**, Tennyson's word for an owl.

The point of the exercise was to chart the evolution of our vocabulary, log some of the additions to it and, in the process, to see how it has been subtly and not so subtly amended over time to match the needs of successive generations. What follows is not an exhaustive survey but a personal selection of some of the more intriguing categories of words.

The box of chocolates that is *Chambers* is vast, comprising orange creams and nut clusters, pralines and caramels, champagne truffles and Turkish delight. And what a delight. Please feel free to tuck in.

Trevor Barnes, London, March 2014

The Word World of the 19th Century

To read the first edition of *Chambers's Etymological Dictionary of the English Language, edited by James Donald, F.R.G.S* is to step into a world the like of which we shall never see again: aeronautics: "the science or art of sailing in the air (as in a balloon)"; apartment: "a room"; casino: "a small house, a saloon for dancing"; catamaran: "a raft of three floating trees used by natives of India and Brazil"; chum: "a guest or chamber fellow, a comrade"; picnic: "an entertainment in the open air at which each person contributes something for the common table"; polytechnic: "comprehending many arts"; restaurant: "a house for refreshment or for restoring the strength when impaired by hunger or fatigue".

If it seems quaint ("neat; unusual; odd; whimsical") to our eyes and ears now remember that, at the moment of its publication in 1872, this was the modern world. The automatic dominance of the Classics as the only subject fit for study was being challenged and, as Donald remarked in his preface, "Great attention has been paid to the insertion of words in Natural History, Botany, Geology, Physics, Physiology, and other sciences which of late have become more commonly the subject of study in school."

Retaining something of its current meaning, homeopathy, for example, made an appearance as "a system of curing diseases by small quantities of those drugs which excite symptoms similar to those of the disease" while hypochondria, in contrast, was "a disease arising from the derangement of the digestive organs causing melancholy".

In a world that was decidedly non-PC (1993) a cretin was "one of a class of idiots found in deep valleys, especially among the Alps" and jesuitism was not only "principles and practices of the Jesuits" (a definition that still stands in the 13th edition) but also, helpfully, "cunning deceit" (which doesn't).

Moreover, words that exist today appear in a subtly different light: testicle: "that which testifies or shews manhood"; smart-money: "money required of a person that he may *smart* or be punished by its loss, for being set free from an unpleasant situation as military service"; steak: "a slice of meat (*esp* beef) that can be *stuck* on a sharp point before the fire"; tyro: "a recruit, beginner"; vandalism: "cruelty, hostility to arts or literature".

As the century drew to a close the editorship of the 1898 edition was in the hands of the Rev. Thomas Davidson, a clergyman who served with the Edinburgh firm of Chambers for 17 years before his death in 1923 at the age of 67. His aim was, in his own words, to satisfy the demands of "the plain man" and "the busy merchant" and to "include all the common terms of the arts and sciences of common life – of astronomy, physiology, and medicine as well as of photography, printing, golf, and heraldry".

His new edition included the high and the low or, as the clergyman that he was might have said, the sacred and the secular, the ancient and the modern. Antibarbarus and Arras sat alongside astrology and athleticism; cab ("short for cabriolet") sat alongside bus ("short for omnibus"). This was the world of spatter-dashes and hanky-panky ("jugglery and trickery"), of the duenna and the fugleman, of the poltroon, the rakehell, the drab and the pimp, of the sempster and the thurifer, of the grimalkin and the reremouse.

But it was also the world of Association Football, the auto-car, the cinematograph, journalism, the motor-car, Rugby Football, the savings bank and the saxophone. And, tellingly, of the new woman: "a name harmoniously applied to such modern women as rebel against the conventional restrictions of their sex; and ape men in their freedom, education, pursuits, amusements, clothing, manners, and sometimes morals".

With a twinkle in its eye Chambers was entering the Twentieth Century.

The Legacy of War

Over sixty years separate the world of the air raid (1933), the pillbox (1952) and ack-ack (1952) from that of the bioweapon, the IED and the cluster bomb. And while some words coined post 1914 have a strange sort of innocence about them (think Fritz, Jerry, Hun and Bosche for the German enemy) others in more recent editions have a deeply menacing feel (killing field, anti-personnel (mine), friendly fire, extraordinary rendition).

While the supplement to the 1933 edition listed for the first time World War ("esp the Great War of 14-18") by 1952 the phrase had been subdivided into two. This was, of course, entirely logical since the retronym First World War would have been a nonsense without the existence of World War 2.

Although the words air power, blighty, blimp, brass hat, bully beef, cushy, dixie, camouflage, counter-espionage, conscientious objector (or conchy), counter-attack, dug-out, No Man's Land, pacifist, Sam Browne, squarehead, Territorials, trench fever and whizzbang must have been in use much earlier it was the 1933 supplement that listed them for the first time.

And edition by edition words could subtly shift their meaning. In 1905, for example, shrapnel (accompanied by a helpful illustration) was "a shell filled with musket balls called after its inventor General Shrapnel (died 1842)" whereas by 1952 the word was used to describe "loose pieces from any shell".

A snapshot might be described in 1906 as "an instantaneous photograph" but by 1933 it had also come to mean "a quickly aimed shot". In 1906 a dugout was merely a "a boat made by hollowing out a tree" and lousy meant "literally swarming with lice" whereas by 1952 the former had also become "a rough shelter dug out of a slope or bank or in a trench" and the latter was popularly taken to be a synonym of "bad".

By this time, too, trench feet and duck board had been included along with demob and shellshock, this latter to describe "mental disturbance" itself replaced in time by post-traumatic stress disorder. Land-army: "a body of women organised for farm work in wartime" made an appearance in the 1952 edition together with flak ("anti aircraft fire or missiles from the German Flugabwehrkanone") and glasshouse: "military detention barracks (from one with a glass roof at Aldershot)".

In 1933 "a large bin or chest used for stowing various things, as coals" was enough to describe a bunker, although by 1952 "a bomb-proof shelter or fort" had been added as an extra, more martial definition.

Strangely enough as late as 1952 a booby trap was merely "a rude form of practical joke by which something is made to fall upon one entering a door or the like". After conflicts in Vietnam, Cyprus and elsewhere, however, editors had realised by 1968 that in wartime this "practical joke" could be used to more sinister effect and duly altered the entry to add "a harmless-looking object which on being touched sets off an explosion".

By 1952 commando had made it as "a unit of special service" and also (inaccurately) "one serving in such a unit". By 1977 it was accurate to describe a crack soldier as such – though by what etymological transmutation this elite squad had, by 2006 lent its name to the phrase to go commando: "(American slang) to forgo the wearing of underpants" remains uncertain.

By 1933 soldiers could get blotto or smoke a fag or a gasper to take their minds off things. But none of these temporary pleasures could completely shut out the ultimate taboo for the soldier in the field; death. Consequently they devised all sorts of words to keep it at bay. They could go west (1952) or snuff it (1977).

Anything, it seems, but die.

The End of Post-War Austerity

If you want to choose a year by which post-war belt-tightening and privation had officially come to an end, 1957 is as good a date as any to choose. In that year the Conservative Prime Minister, Harold Macmillan, told the British people they'd "never had it so good" and positively beamed as he invoked a blessed and contented isle enjoying "a state of prosperity such as we have never had in my lifetime – nor indeed in the history of this country."

Privileged background, Eton and Oxford education notwithstanding he was largely right. The welfare state (1952) promised social, financial and medical security "from cradle to grave", productivity was high, unemployment was low and the country had seen the end of the ration-book and the ration card: "a book, card of coupons or vouchers for rationed commodities".

Soldiers who had been demobbed donned their civvies and returned to civvy street to restart life, after the interruption of war, in a council house, perhaps, or a prefab. Across the land the contented nuclear family in suburbia could enjoy all that modern life had to offer in the way of comfort, consumer goods (1952) and opportunity.

True, there were existential worries. As Churchill had solemnly intoned, the Iron Curtain (1952) – joined by the Bamboo Curtain (1968) – had descended, separating the West from the countries of the Eastern Bloc and prompting the Cold War (1952) which would show no signs of thawing for 30 years and more.

Fear of the red (1952) menace reached hysterical proportions in America where McCarthyism (1968) took hold prompting witchhunts (1952) and blacklists (1906) of those suspected of harbouring Communist sympathies. Britain escaped the hysteria and instead had only to worry about that other minor threat to its way of life; the A bomb and H bomb (1968 supplement).

It was an era of swift social change. High culture was giving way to mass culture influenced by American fashions, films and music. Bill Haley's 1955 "Rock around the Clock" became an immediate hit ("surprising success",1952) and rock and roll was born, though it was only in 1968 that it found its way into the dictionary's supplement – along with anorak, aqualung, atomic, bebop, Big Brother, bobby dazzler, boogie woogie, bossa nova, bottle gas, bra, cha-cha(cha), flick knife, foam rubber, fruit machine, hit parade, housing estate, jazz age, lunatic fringe, meritocracy, moped, record-player, social security, and trick cyclist ("*sl*; psychiatrist").

In 1956 you could pay between five and fifteen shillings to see Osborne's "Look Back in Anger" at the Royal Court Theatre and watch as the old order was painfully giving birth to the new. You would, however, have to wait until 1968 before the phrase angry young man was officially recorded and until 1977 to realise you had been watching kitchen sink drama in which those of a less articulate disposition than its protagonist, Jimmy Porter, would have been labelled juvenile delinquents.

Mass culture was also increasingly youth culture. In 1933 the words teens existed to describe the years between 12 and 20 but teenager (or teener) would have to wait until 1952.

Similarly those who had been born during the baby boom of the 1950s would have to wait thirty years before Chambers informed them of the fact. In the meantime more change was afoot. Much more.

The 1960s; Culture and Counter-Culture

For most people living in Stoke-on-Trent, say, or for that matter in Bodmin, Prestatyn or Whitley Bay (in fact, anywhere outside London, or indeed anywhere more than roughly a mile away from the King's Road, Chelsea) the sixties didn't really "swing" until about 1971.

And just as it took time for all that excitement to reach parts of rural Norfolk and East Lothian, so it took time for the vocabulary of that not-so-innocent era to reach the pages of Chambers. Flower people made it to the 1977 edition; flower power was in by 1986. As for the love-in and granny glasses they take even longer – though the kaftan (or caftan: "Persian or Turkish vest") has a long history dating from 1883.

The time lag is perhaps best illustrated by the appearance, in the 1968 edition, of the beatnik who was, historically speaking, largely being replaced by the hippy who managed inclusion only by 1986. It was a fast-moving world with which lexicographers and printers were having a hard time keeping pace.

By now we had moved from the supersonic (1952) age to the space age and had our eyes fixed on the moon. Spaceship appeared in the 1952 edition but belonged more to science fiction (1977) than to reality. Sputnik (1968) changed that and the race into outer space was on. Then came spacecraft, space probe and space shuttle along with, of course, the spaceman (and spacewoman) invariably wearing spacesuits and later doing space-walks.

On planet earth meanwhile we were getting on with our everyday lives driving estate cars, perhaps staying in a motel (unlikely outside the US), playing pinball, or listening to an LP or and EP on our record player.

Such words, introduced into the 1968 supplement, gave a broad indication of what we were up to. Others included; bebop, battery (hens), bikini, bingo, bubble-car, bubble-gum, bulk buying, chi-chi, civil defence, common market, comprehensive school, coronary thrombosis, cover-charge, crew cut, discotheque ("a club for dancing to gramophone records", as opposed to night-club –"a club open between nightfall and morning for amusement or dissipation"). That year also saw the electric blanket, expense account, face-lift, facts of life, filling station, Free World, fuddy duddy, hi-fi, planned obsolescence, pony-tail, sound barrier, olde-worlde, straw poll, and sun-glasses.

Imagine these words as random objects in a time-capsule (1988) discovered centuries hence by aliens. Imagine, too, the head scratching as they sagely ponder the link between the bubble-car, bingo, and the pony-tail. Oh, not forgetting the abominable snowman which our extra-terrestrials (1986) would also have to factor into the mix.

1968 was the year the eleven plus exam and the GCE entered the dictionary – along with Oxbridge and the redbrick university at which institutions there would be sit-ins (though these did not merit inclusion until 1986).

Given the influence of designers like Mary Quant and the lure of Carnaby Street and the King's Road it is perhaps surprising that the mini-skirt does not get a mention until much later, circa 1977, when it is listed alongside those other two words that embarrassingly came to define a decade: groovy and psychedelic.

If you can remember the sixties, they say, you weren't there. What nobody has yet fathomed, however, is how many people would rather forget them.

Science and Technology

Printed in 1872, *Chambers's Etymological Dictionary of the English Language* was compiled at a pivotal time in British and world history. Manufacturing processes had been **revolutionized** over the preceding century with the development of **steam power** and machine tools. Hand production on a small scale had been replaced by **mass production** on an industrial scale and the resulting technological advances were affecting the lives of everyone.

Appearing in the aftermath of the **Industrial Revolution** (a phrase that was absent from editions as late as 1933) the dictionary reflected a society in change. Whether collaborators or competitors in the outside world, however, the agricultural and the industrial coexisted without comment or judgment within the pages of Chambers.

Thrash ("to beat out grain from the straw") had been included in the first edition (**thresh** was listed as the secondary spelling) but the **thrashing-machine** (invented by a Scottish engineer around 1784) would have to wait at least until 1898 for inclusion.

Alongside the **flail**, the **harrow**, the **ploughshare** and the **ploughboy** appeared the **steam-boat**, the **steam-ship**, the **steam-engine** and the **steamer** as technology powered on unstoppably.

Developments in the field of **electrical engineering** continued apace with practically a whole column devoted to it by 1898 (from **electricity** and **electrification** to **electro-chemistry** and **electro-statics**).

The appearance of **aeroplane** in the supplement to the 1933 edition took technology well and truly into the 20th century, though the accompanying definition as "a flying machine heavier than air with horizontal planes" has an archaic ring that a reader might easily assume owes more to the 19th.

That 1933 supplement also brought us **acid test**, **amplifier**, **arc lamp**, **botulism**, **brain-wave**, **central heating**, **concrete-steel**, **dictaphone**, **detectophone** ("a delicate secret telephone for eavesdropping"), **dry cell**, **exhaust**, **express delivery**, **finger-print**, **hydroplane**, **loud-speaker**, **photostat**, **plywood**, **radiotherapy**, **robot**, **talkies**, **transformer**, **transcontinental**, **vacuum cleaner** and **wireless telegraphy**.

As **pure science** continued in universities and private laboratories largely beyond the ken of ordinary people, **applied science** was bringing them inventions and **gadgets** (1933) that would transform their lives for good or ill.

Chief among these in the modern era was **nuclear** and **atomic energy**, both of which first appeared in Chambers in 1952. **Nuclear physics** and **nuclear reactor** also made an appearance and it was clear that the doors were opening to a brave new world of opportunity and danger, as **atomic bomb** and **atomic warfare** (listed in the same edition) hinted not too subtly.

Technology, however, had its pacific applications and as the 1950s gave way to the 1960s the pace of technological change quickened perceptibly. In 1968, for example, **video** accounted for five lines in the dictionary whereas by 1988 it covered thirty eight and included **video camera**, **videocassette**, **video recorder** and **videotape**.

1968 also introduced us to the **accelerator**, the **co-axial cable**, the **count-down**, **electronic music**, the **electric blanket**, the **electro-encephalograph**, the **fork-lift truck**, the **laser**, the **lie detector** and the **travelator**.

But then, in 1977, a one-syllable word appeared in the supplement and contained the potential to change everything. It was a familiar word that had appeared in every edition since that of 1872 but it now had an entirely new meaning. It was described as "a minute piece of silicon or other semi-conducting material, on which one or more microcircuits can be printed".

In the same edition **flying saucer** had also appeared, but whereas this belonged to **science fiction**, the **chip** belonged very much to science fact.

Words That Have Changed Their Meaning

Let's begin with a question that could come straight out of a Christmas cracker (in 1872 "a noisy firework or a hard biscuit", so at least some words retain some of their meanings). What do P Diddy, Jay-Z, Eminem and door knockers have in common? Answer; they're all rappers.

The 1872 edition of Chambers, assigned to rapper only one meaning; "one who raps; a doorknocker". In the 12th edition this definition is relegated to second place behind "a person who raps"; rap being "a rhythmic monologue delivered over a musical background".

The same sort of transformation has come over the word bingo which was, in 1933, a familiar name for brandy. In 1905 the verb to hang over meant merely "to project over". Hangover as a noun was not listed until 1952 when it denoted "the after effects of drink".

Words, as TS Eliot once wrote, "will not stay still". They are constantly evolving. Nervous in 1872 meant "sinewy, strong, vigorous"; buxom meant "obedient, gay, lively, vigorous" (we shall be returning to gay in a moment); nice meant *"ignorant, foolish;* foolishly particular, hard to please"; loo was "a game at cards" and a lavatory was "a place for laving or washing".

In 1883 sophisticated meant "not genuine, adulterated, impure"; terrific meant "creating or causing terror"; enthusiasm was "inspiration by a divine power"; to amuse was "to muse or meditate" and amusement was "deep thought."

Words have a habit of looking different in different ages and contexts. So while today a chemist might suggest ear drops to soften your ear-wax, in 1872 a jeweller would have been selling them in his shop. They were, you see, what we now call "ear rings". And to describe someone as abandoned was to describe that person as "very wicked".

Some words retained their archaic meanings well into the 20th century. As late as 1933, for example, aftermath was described as "a second crop of grass… a math or crop of grass coming after the first", sleazy meant "thin or flimsy" and a backlog was simply "a huge log at the back of the fire". In 1905, a chum was "a guest", and a chit was "a baby or lively young child".

In that same year kip gets several entries. It is variously; "(Scotch slang) to play truant", "the skin of a young animal", "a level or slight incline at the end of an underground way", or "a house of ill-fame". Nowhere is it described, as it is primarily today, as "(*sl*) a nap" – though the above meanings are listed in the 13th edition, too.

Some words have been co-opted to describe activities that simply did not exist years ago but which convey metaphorically something of the original. So broadcast in the modern-day, media sense has merely been lifted from its rural context where it meant "scattered or sown abroad by hand: dispersed widely." Similarly broadsheet: "a sheet of paper printed on one side". And for actors today to speak of an audition (originally simply "the sense of hearing; something heard") is for them to use the word in a sense that only slightly extends that earlier meaning.

Contrast those with words like mouse which has morphed from a small rodent into a moveable computer device, spam from a type of luncheon meat to unwanted email, chip from a small piece of wood or a fried potato to a silicon microcircuit, or, more troublingly, friend which used to be someone you knew and liked but which can now denote, in a social media setting, someone you've never even clapped eyes on. No matter, however, as these off-the-peg familiars can be instantly unfriended (2011) when either or both tire of the other.

Commentators on, or devotees of, modern fashions will frequently trawl the dictionary for a word that somehow seems to resonate with the fad in question, subsequently using it to denote something entirely unrelated. Thus punk, originally a strumpet or rotten wood used as tinder, became "a follower of punk rock, often recogniseable by the use of cheap utility articles, eg razor blades, plastic rubbish, bags safety pins, as clothes or decoration" and Goth, originally "one of an ancient Teutonic nation" became "a fan of Gothic music...characterised by...dark melancholy themes, severe black dress and white make-up".

Interestingly enough the troll, responsible for harassing people on the internet, has also retained his original definition, viz "(Norse myth) *n* an evil-tempered ugly dwarf". Strange, that.

And so we come to gay, which from the get-go meant "lively, bright, sportive, merry" and continued to do so well into the 20th century. The Chambers edition of 1914, for example, lists gay science as another phrase for "poetry" with not a mention of sexuality. In this latter context it is absent from the 1968 edition but makes it by 1977 as "homosexual" (gay liberation is listed by 1986). Today it is a word used by everyone from the Prime Minister to the Pope in a neutral sense that distinguishes it from camp and the usually-offensive queer, both of which were first included in the supplement to the 1968 edition.

Quite how "a nearly cylindrical fish" (mullet) can become a hairstyle, how a "tinker of earthenware" (mugger) can become a street attacker, or how the flesh of a cow (beef) can become a complaint remain matters of conjecture.

Words, like people, are nothing if not unpredictable.

Computing and Social Media

The **digital computer** first appeared in the supplement to the Chambers Dictionary of 1968, representing something of a technological milestone. **Computer** had been included in the main body of the text but only as "a calculator; a large machine carrying out calculations of several stages automatically".

A key word here is *large* as the early mechanical or **analogue** computers tended to be housed in large rooms occupying volumes of space unimaginable today. The invention of the **chip** changed all that, giving rise to **information science** and **modem** by 1977. Advances in the field of **nanotechnology** (Chambers 1993) have further accelerated the pace at which **computing** has developed and, by extension, the diversity of the vocabulary associated with it.

This is a world of **computerese, computer-aided learning, computer crime, computer dating, computer games, computer graphics, computer literacy** and the **computer virus** - and it is a world that is growing.

In 1993 **internet** made a tentative appearance (along with **internetting**: "an interconnection of computer networks") but by 1998 it had been accorded a full-scale entry including its diminutive **the Net** and the **Internet cafe** (also **cybercafe**).

The same edition also gave us for the first time the **Web**: "the World Wide Web (*comput*)". And that was that; an entry that was short and sweet and gave no indication of the size it would eventually become. Think **webcam, webcast, web design, weblog, webmail, webmaster, web page, website** and **webzine**. **Deep web** was added to the 11th edition, and **dark web** to the 13th.

The technology was swiftly harnessed by imaginative entrepreneurs to bring us **social networking** sites enabling "interaction between individuals for their mutual benefit, *esp* online". Preeminent among these perhaps is **Facebook** which merited an entry in the 12th edition. Twitter did not but **tweet** did. **Retweet** is included in this edition for the first time.

Also included in the 12th edition were **app, biocomputer, blook, cloud, cloud computing, cybersecurity, iPhone, mashup, microblogging, microbrowser, moderator, pay-per-click, tablet** and **widget**.

So now we all inhabit a world of **search engines** and **screen savers**, of **click streams** and **blogs**. As **netizens** all we can survey a landscape of **paywalls, emoticons, bytes** and **podcasts**. We can **reboot, surf, post, ping** and **programme**. Sure, we must beware the **cyberbully** and the **troll** (2002) but by and large we have all learnt to live with a creation that cannot be uninvented.

What next? This current edition lists for the first time **bashtag, big data, bitcoin, bitstream, bloggable, blogpost, click fraud, clickbait, clickjacking, hashtag, instagram, internet of things, netminder, Skype, touchless, trend, twitterati, Twittersphere, Twitterverse, webchat** and **wikiality**.

If you were born any time after the early 1980s many of the words used above belong not to what we once fondly called the "new technology" but to a computer era that is positively ancient now.

But should you conclude that this is a world only for the young, think again. We can all be **wired** well into our dotage. The 12th edition helpfully reassures us that we can become **silver surfers**. It *is* reassurance, of a sort.

Taboo and Swear Words

First a health warning. Do not continue reading if you are easily offended.

The words below are not occult, esoteric, arcane, or magical. On the contrary they are everyday. Sometimes depressingly so. You will have heard (if not uttered) most of them yourself and they are, of course, scattered throughout the very book you are holding.

But in isolation, listed, logged, categorized and repeated in myriad permutations these words have a critical mass that can offend, outrage and dismay. But they are, in the end, words belonging to the world all of us inhabit. Even if we do not use them ourselves, somebody else does (and has done repeatedly over time). It is the dictionary's job to record them dispassionately, offering the judgments of the lexicographer and etymologist but not the moralist.

A dictionary is not a prayer book, a hymn book or compilation of sacred writ. A sacred text, a text without profanity, belongs, you might say, to a linguistic Eden. A dictionary belongs to the fallen world and is situated well to the east where, like it or not, innocence and corruption co-exist.

And it is a place full of snares and temptations. You may, for example, be innocently looking up pricket ("a fallow dear buck in his second year") when inadvertently your eye strays to the previous entry. Likewise you may be checking that CUP really does stand for "Cambridge University Press" when you glance an entry higher. Perhaps you just want to be sure that fucus is the "bladderwrack genus of seaweeds" when something else catches your eye two or three lines up, or that shittim: (*Bible*; in full shittim wood, the wood of the shittah tree) is indeed "believed to be a species of acacia" when....

You can see where this is heading.

However in 1968 there was *no* entry separating fuchsite from fucus. Then by 1977 fuck had put in a discreet appearance ("old word, long taboo; all words, meanings still *vulg*"). The editors added, helpfully, fucked ("exhausted") as an adjective and fucking as a noun. Then it was on to the seaweed.

1986 saw fucker and (sweet) fuck-all. Fuckhead and fuckwit were in by 2003 along with fuck-me as an adjective ("as in fuck-me boots"). Fuck-up, fucker, fucking ("as an intensifier or meaningless qualification" synonymous with "very or to a great extent") were gradually added and with what the fuck, not give a fuck and fuck as an interjection expressing "displeasure, as in fuck him!" the entry was complete. For the time being.

Likewise in 1968 no word separated shirt from shittim until 1977 when shit, shite and bullshit intervened. The pace soon quickened; the shits (1986), shitty (1988), shithole, shit-hot, shit-stirrer (1993), shit-head and no shit (US slang) (1998), shitface, shit-faced, shit-scared, ape-shit (2003), in the shit, shit a brick (or bricks), up shit creek. They had really found their stride.

Arse entered the 1883 edition as nothing more than "an animal's behind" and remained so until achieving "vulgar" status in 1977 as "buttocks" generally. By 1986 arsehole, arse licker and arse around had made it as had, by 2003, get one's arse into gear and can't be arsed. In 2006 the curtain rose on arse bandit with the verb kick arse making its stage debut by 2008.

A similar upward curve can be seen with permutations of the words balls and cock. Make a balls of was there by 1977 and, as a noun meaning "nonsense", was in by 1986 along with balls-up. In 1988 balls reappeared as "guts and courage" and by 1993 featured as ball breaker, ball buster and by the balls.

Wank, and wanker ("a worthless, contemptible person") had been included by 1986, followed by wanky in 1993. We could go on but by now you get the idea.

There was no mention of arguably *the* most offensive word in the vocabulary of insult and offence – what is politely termed the "c" word – until 1977. Strangely, however, twat had been included since 1905 (still defined gnomically as "pudendum muliebre" into the late '70's). A "contemptible person" could still be described as a **yoni** (1905) but such was the unpopularity of Sanskrit on the building sites and shop floors of the day that it largely failed to gain traction.

But by 1977 Chambers pushed the boat out with both **cunnilingus** *and* **cunt** (**pussy** and **pussy-whipped** appeared post 1993) and with those perhaps the last taboo was broken. Widely used in film and intermittently used even on the BBC these days it, too, is being slowly absorbed despite its real ability, in certain circumstances, to shock.

Taboo or **tabu** appeared in the 1872 edition as "something held sacred or accursed; an institution among the Polynesians by which certain things are consecrated; prohibition or interdict".

As we have seen above, words denoting body parts and bodily functions which were once indeed **taboo** have been freed of commonly agreed restraints and, in the post-Satanic Verses era, it is perhaps to religion, especially Islam, that we will look as the last guardian of an orthodoxy we dare, even verbally, to cross at our peril.

But restraint *does* obtain and, just as we now no longer visit mental institutions to laugh at the afflicted we similarly refrain from using some words to denote aspects of our fellow human beings' lives and characteristics.

Indeed we would think more than twice before using the word **loony bin** (1952) to describe such mental institutions and a **loony** as one of its inmates. Similarly **cripple** and **spastic**, once freely used, are clearly signposted these days as "offensive", "derogatory" or "objectionable".

The same holds true for **chink**, **pikey**, **wop**, **spic(k)**, **kike**, **yid**, **gyppo**, and **paki** (though not, oddly, **Pak** which remains a neutral even affectionate term in the world of geopolitics). **Yid** as a contraction of **Yiddish** was not deemed offensive in 1968 but had become so by 1988. **Slant-eyed** likewise appeared without comment up until the late 80s but had become offensive by 1993.

As with the "c" word, the "n" word still retains its power to offend. By 1952 **nigger** was clearly judged "derogatory" leaving it, presumably, to the reader's judgment to decide whether deploying **nigger in the woodpile** (listed further below without qualification) during an address to, say, the board of governors would be appropriate. It is now agreed universally that it would not – even to the point that in America there have been reports that **niggard** and **niggardly**: "stingy" have themselves been proscribed even though the words come from a different etymological source and mean something quite different.

Some black activists have sought to reclaim the word just as some homosexual groups and academics have tried to rework the word **queer** as in "queer theory". As a result the 13th edition of Chambers described it as "usually derogatory". The thirteenth edition, however, upgraded nigger to taboo status, which it shares only with cunt and motherfucker (fuck having been downgraded from taboo in the same edition).

Queerdom and **queer-bashing** remain unequivocally derogatory as are **shirt lifter** (1993), **batty boy** (2003), **bull dyke** (2003), and **lez(z)**, **lezzie** (1986).

But, to repeat, the appearance of a word in Chambers (or indeed in any other dictionary) does not imply endorsement by the editors. As Thomas Davidson wrote in his 1905 preface, "The lexicographer is a 'harmless drudge' without prejudice, without passion."

We have considered but a handful of contentious words from the 620,000 words and more that Chambers lists. You have seen them dispassionately listed and has the sky fallen in or the world imploded?

Words indeed have power but only such power as we *let* them have. We would be wise to bear in mind the children's rhyme, "Sticks and stones will break my bones – but names will never hurt me." After all, on the occasions when words *do* hurt we can always reach for *other* words to defend ourselves.

Political Correctness

Consult the dictionary in 1988 and you will search in vain for it. Political animal, political prisoner, political science, yes, but not a sign of political correctness. No, you will have to wait at least until 1993 for it, along with its adjectival partner politically correct.

It is easy to malign the term and many have. The presiding geniusses of Chambers, however, James Donald and Thomas Davidson, the dictionary's first editors, would have done no such thing. They would merely have noted the terms without comment and left it to the reader to take a view as to whether or not it has "gone mad". The words may exist but there is, after all, no compunction to use them.

Blind, deaf, dumb, lame, crippled, spastic are all words attached to recognizable conditions (the last three passing rapidly out of popular use) but the addition of the definite article transforms mere adjectives into collective nouns shorn of humanity. An institute for *the* deaf, *the* dumb, *the* blind and even, until recently, *the* incurable is surely better replaced by blind *people*, deaf *people* and so on.

Similarly the disabled has become a phrase that many people have thought to replace with differently abled. It's longer, more cumbersome and not altogether elegant but perhaps what it lacks in concision it makes up for in consideration and empathy. For that reason our society has duly pressed it into service. And, to repeat, listing it obliges no one to use it.

Challenged and impaired belong in the same category – as in visually challenged, physically challenged, visually- and hearing impaired. Shellshock, after all, was a thoughtless and, more to the point, imprecise description of the mental disturbances caused by war. Calling it post traumatic stress may be less dramatic but it surely treats the condition with a sensitivity that those who have suffered the horror of battle deserve.

On a more mundane level what is really lost by referring to firefighters, police officers, spokespersons and chairs? At the very least you could say that it is only polite. Moreover the use of gender specific terms such as male model, male nurse and woman priest are surely unnecessary.

Euphemisms, as we know, can be precious, ridiculous and offensive. Who doesn't long for die (or even an honest slang term like kick the bucket) on hearing pass, pass on, depart? Who knows why toilet paper should have become toilet tissue, and retirement *home* anything but? Sometimes even Chambers cannot escape the trap. When it describes corrective training as "reformative imprisonment" it is hard to say which is the more evasive. And as for the termination/abortion debate we will all have our view.

In warfare we have been given collateral damage for "civilian casualties", sub-prime to describe a rotting hovel in Louisiana, and quantitative easing to put a respectable face on a financial wheeze few of us understand.

One suspects the editors of the 13th edition may be somewhat relieved that certain new euphemisms such as demised (used by HSBC for "sacked") or pushed with the head (used by Alan Pardew in place of "headbutted") do not seem to have caught on. But like Donald and Davidson and the editors since, if these words had merited inclusion they would merely have listed them and let *you* decide.

Jobs

An **accoucheur**: "a man who assists women at childbirth" (*feminine* **accoucheuse**) is the first occupation listed by the original 1872 edition and, typically for its time, refers to it preeminently as a job for man.

In the 1905 edition under **banker** we helpfully find the term **bankeress** while the word **clerk** (subdivided by 1933 into **clerkling**: "a young clerk") by 1952 offers the reader a **clerkess**. But essentially, in the words of the singer James Brown, "this is a man's world".

By 1977 we have equal opportunities with **lollipop man, woman**, and, later, **lady**. But we must wait until 1988 for the **dinnerlady** to appear – apparently one of the few jobs women alone can do. Another is **weathergirl** (a TV variation of the gender neutral **weather forecaster** which had appeared earlier).

What readers of the dictionary in 2172 will make of the **lollipopman/woman**, incidentally, is anyone's guess. Probably as much as we make today of that fringe occupation mentioned in 1883, the **Abraham-man**: "one of a class of sturdy beggars feigning lunacy. (From a ward in Bedlam, for the reception of idiots, called Abraham)".

In 1872 a **bouncer** is a "bully or a liar", a **clown** is "a ploughman" (from the Latin *colonus* 'a cultivator of the soil')", a **chapman** is "a dealer", a **drysalter** likewise is a "dealer in salted or dry meats or pickles; or in gums, dyes, drugs etc", and, by 1914, the **duffer** is "a dealer in sham goods".

The **fugleman** is "a soldier who stands before the company at drill", a **lifeguard** is "a guard of a prince or other dignitary", a **navvy** is a "labourer on internal canals for *navigation*", a **sempster** (presumably masculine) is the equivalent of "seamstress", and a **newsman** is "someone who delivers newspapers".

Over the next couple of editions we are introduced to the **limner** ("one who paints on paper"), the **doffer** ("a person who removes full bobbins from a machine") and the **sewer**: (an officer who set down and removed dishes at a feast").

We are, of course, given all the ancient occupations from **gladiator** (helpfully also **gladiatrix**), and **haruspex** ("in ancient Rome a person who foretold events from inspection of the entrails of animals"), **chamberlain**, **cupbearer**, and **brehon**: "a judge in medieval Ireland".

The 20th century brings us: the **postilion**; the **catchpole** ("a constable or sheriff's officer"); the **lamplighter**; the **gossoon** ("a boy servant in Ireland"); the Scots **orra man** (a farm worker kept to do any odd job that may occur); the **iceman**; and the **eggler** (surviving even into the 13th edition) who is, unsurprisingly, "a dealer in eggs". The **dust-man** of 1914 is a "scavenger".

The world changes post 1960 and, in America, the **soda jerk** performs a similar job with **soft drinks** as the **ale wife** did with alcohol over four generations earlier. We see the rise of the **typist** from the typing **pool** which seems to belong to those vanishing occupations like the **switchboard** operator, the **hot metal compositor**, and the **lift-boy,-girl,-man**.

And of course the dictionary brings us bang up to date, via the **deejay** or **DJ** and the **newscaster**, to the world of **public relations**, **human resources** and **big business** where the **head hunter**, the **programmer**, and the **spin doctor** reside.

In our leisure time we can hire a **personal shopper** (2011) to take the sweat out of all that buying, or a **personal trainer** to tell us to take more exercise and stop eating biscuits. We can go to a coffee shop where a **barista** will serve us coffee or to a bar where a **mixologist** will fix us a cocktail.

With all this choice, then, it is hardly surprising that in America you can buy the services of a **garbologist** (2011) to study "a society's waste materials in order to make deductions about the lifestyles of its people".

What will we think of next?

Scotticisms

Let's start with a couple of easy ones; **bairn** and **bonny**. Even the least informed **sassenach** (you'll find *that*, by the way, in the 13th edition of Chambers but, strangely, not in the 1st) will know the meaning of those two words. A "child", of course, in the first case; "beautiful", "handsome" and, erm, "gay" (1883), in the second.

But beyond that one noun and that one adjective how many Scottish words are widely known?

A **grimalkin**, for example? "An old cat". A **keeker**? "A black eye". A **mixter-maxter**? "A confused jumble". Or what about **clamjamphrie**? "Rubbish; nonsense; rabble". Or a **deoch-an-doruis**? "A parting drink".

If you thought only Britain and America were "divided by a common language" – a phrase variously (and, more than likely, erroneously) ascribed to Oscar Wilde, George Bernard Shaw and Winston Churchill – think again. Scotland, after all, is rather closer to England than America and the editors of the first Chambers dictionary, published in Edinburgh, were proud of their Scottish heritage.

The tradition continues to this day and the 13th edition is at pains to list alongside **karmic**, **kayac** and **kebab** words like **kebbie**: "a shepherd's crook", **kebbock**: "a cheese", and **keelie**: "a kestrel; an urban tough, *esp* from Glasgow".

A century and more before the appearance of the first edition many of the leading figures of the Scottish Enlightenment had serious reservations about the use of **Scotticisms** in their writings. David Hume, for example, is said to have avoided them in his philosophical work for fear of making them inaccessible to a wider audience and perhaps parochial when read alongside the work of his European contemporaries, Voltaire and Rousseau.

But James Donald and his successor, Thomas Davidson, took a different line and, as Davidson explained in his preface to the 1905 edition, his aim had been to include "all the common terms of the sciences and the arts of life...obsolete words imperishable in Spenser, Shakespeare, the Authorised Version of the Bible, and Milton; the Scotch words of Burns and Scott – of the heather if not the **kailyard** ["cabbage patch, kitchen garden"]; the slang words of Dickens and the man in the street".

It was a grand and commendably inclusive philosophy, and one that lends the dictionary such charm and surprise: A **glengarrie**, for instance, "a Highlander's cap of thick-milled woollen cloth"; **gleyed**: ("squint-eyed"); **gliff**: ("a fright, scare"); **glint**: ("to shine, gleam; to move quickly (Burns)"); a **glimmer-gowk**: ("an owl"); Alright, that last one is described "*dialect; Tennyson*" but what a word to ignore!

Some more: **hurdies** for "buttocks" (think "**hurdies** like a distant hill" from Burns's Ode To A Haggis); **bahookie** (also buttocks); **breeks** ("britches"); and **gant** ("to yawn"). A **beastie** ("a four-footed animal") is often usually **wee** ("small"), **sleekit** ("smooth, sleak; sly, cunning) and **tim'rous**, at least according to Burns in his Ode to a Mouse.

Puddock is "a toad or frog", **shoogle** is "to shake", **shoogly** is "wobbly", **gyre-carline** is "a witch", **stravaig** is "to wander about idly", **rammy**: is "a row, free-for-all fight", **scud** is "a state of nudity" (as in **in the scud**) and **brownie** is "a domestic spirit in the folklore of Scotland, represented as a good humoured, drudging goblin".

You can call someone "pale or ill-looking". Or you can say they're looking **peelie-wally**. You can call someone "daft" or you can call them **glaiket**. You can say you're feeling "mentally or physically exhausted" or that you're **puggled**. The church might say, as it did in 1898, that it was exacting a fine "as part of the discipline for the offence of fornication", or it could exact **buttock-mail**.

The difference? None in meaning. But in impact, the difference between talking in black and white and talking in **Technicolour**.

Americanisms

The 1872 edition includes the word Americanism but lists surprisingly few of them. Nouns like Bowie knife, Congress ("the federal legislature of the US") and wigwam appear but denote aspects of American life and culture in an almost anthropological way. Although the word skyscraper appears it means only "a sky-sail of a triangular shape" and we shall have to wait a few more editions until it is listed as "a lofty building of many storeys" (1933).

In the 1905 edition, however, Thomas Davidson acknowledges in his preface that he has consulted two American works, Funk and Wagnall's *Standard Dictionary* and the *Century Dictionary* of Professor Whitney. He now lists for the first time yankee, yank, yankeedom and Yankee-Doodle.

Things pick up over a quarter of a century later with the supplement to the 1933 edition listing; bootlegger, branche ("a tributary"), butt in, Charleston ("a modern dance characterised by spasmodic knee action"), cow-boy, jay walker, jazz, movies, rag-time, rough-house, talkies, teddy bear ("from Theodore Roosevelt, a famous hunter and President of the USA [1901–9], often called *Teddy*"), tepee, trash ("poor whites") and tuxedo.

Derringer, moonshine, railroad, supe ("a toady"), corn-ball, corn-cake and cow-catcher made it to the main dictionary that year but the influence of America began to be felt more keenly from the 1950s onwards.

The 1952 edition, for example, listed bourbon, cahoots, campus, cook-book, cookie, copy-book, corn-cracker ("a poor white"), corn whisky, chicken-feed, dame, drug-store, greenback, hobo, hot dog, jeep and wacky.

The popularity of American films, music and imported TV shows throughout the 50s and 60s ensured that, although many words became familiar to the British ear, not all were actually used in everyday speech. We might have known well enough that the garbageman was the dustman but we would have stopped well short of referring to him as such when complaining to the council about the mess he'd made outside our front door. Similarly we would never have referred to putting out the trash, or to putting stuff in the trash-can or garbage can.

The process by which certain words became the active currency of our everyday conversations and others didn't is a mysterious one. Why, for example, was it commonplace for us to refer to a cliff-hanger, the dog-house, an eager beaver or an egghead (US words in the 1968 supplement) yet to avoid funeral parlor and Bronx cheer in favour of "the undertakers" or the "raspberry"?

We frequently referred to Joe Soap, gobbledegook and the sixty four thousand dollar question but rarely (more likely, never) to a bohunk ("a Slav or Hungarian, *esp* an unskilled labourer"). And just as no American can say quid convincingly so, too, was it impossible for any English person to say limey (1968) and keep a straight face.

In 1968 a fair few of us would have been using malarkey, shindig, slush fund, big-time, shot-gun marriage and chopper (for helicopter) but no English person would have referred to a woman as a broad, a dog as a pooch or, by 1977, a diamond as a rock. Cracker barrel was borderline as also were grass-roots, grease-monkey, gripe, jerk and sad sack.

By 1977 we had been introduced to the caucus, the junkie and the stag-party which passed into popular use – unlike mad (borderline) as "furious with anger", the speak-easy and the realtor which even today has failed to replace "estate agent'.

As we have seen and will see, the worlds of technology, business and management are full of expressions minted across the Atlantic but in the end, it seems, certain words are just...well... *American* – and stay that way.

Brands and trademarks that have become everyday words

Dormobile (1993), flymo (1993) and portakabin (1986), of course. But who would have thought ping-pong (1906), muzak (1977), and kerosene (1883)? Not to mention styrofoam (1993), taser (1993), and granola (1993).

The stetson (1952), after all, is *the* broadbrimmed hat. The photo-fit (1977) is what *all* detectives seem to use to track down the villain. And photoshopping (2008) is what we do with our digital snaps now that photostatting (1977) them on the office copier feels rather dated these days.

One would assume that it would surely be every manufacturer's dream to name a product which then goes on to denote all subsequent variations and imitations of the original. At a stroke the makers (more likely their hired creatives) ensure that a crowded marketplace is dominated, at least in the popular consciousness, by one product; their own.

But, sellers, beware. Sometimes the trademarked product can be so darned catchy that manufacturers themselves suspect its overuse is siphoning off the uniqueness in which it invested so much (think intellectual property rights) in the first place. The Otis Elevator Company discovered this to its cost in 1950 when it failed to protect what it hoped was the trademarked status of its new product, the "Escalator". In a landmark court case at the time it had to accept that an escalator was simply a moving walkway – something Chambers had noted and duly reflected by 1952.

Would the "extruded plastic dingus" have fared quite so well as the renamed hula hoop? Would the "pluto platter" have brought the California-based toy company, Wham-O, quite so much kudos as the Frisbee that entered the Chambers Twentieth Century Dictionary supplement in 1977? It is surely pointless to enquire, as the Frisbee has popularly come to define all "plastic saucer-shaped disk(s) which can be made to skim through the air".

From the filofax (1988) to the yo-yo (1952), from aspirin (1933) to sellotape (1986), from the thermos (1914) to the cat's-eye (1986) the Chambers Dictionary has been hoovering up (1986) trademarked words that became the day-to-day expressions of many of their generic equivalents.

Before modern trademarking had gained such a foothold, kodak ("a small portable photographic camera") had come into use by 1905 and kola ("an aerated beverage") by 1914 – along with gobelin ("a tapestry") and glenlivet ("a good Scotch whisky from a valley in Banffshire"). Perspex and Terrylene had entered the dictionary by 1952 as had the Yale lock.

Following these, among many others, would be in 1977: the tannoy; in 1986: the jiffy bag and the lilo plus the zimmer frame, the ansaphone, formica, velcro, and the jacuzzi.

Astroturf and kleenex had made it by 1988 to be followed in 1993 by xerox, JCB, the stanley knife and Tipp-Ex.

In 1977 the dictionary had listed the word googol as "1 followed by 1,000 0s" and thereby anticipated after a fashion the appearance by 2006 of google as a verb. As the 21st century powered on the iPod made it into the 11th edition, the iPhone into the 12th, and the iPad into the 13th.

Food and Drink

From the first edition of Chambers in the late 19th century to this present edition in 2014 collop ("slice of meat") and curry have been constantly on the menu, as have haddock and ham and hash (unsurprisingly).

But *not* haggis.

It is the stuff of an H M Bateman cartoon. The scene: Edinburgh. The editorial offices of W and R Chambers, Limited. Bellowing executives in the foreground, a startled secretary dropping teacups in the background and centre stage a red-faced man surrounded by piles of dictionaries squirming in embarrassment. The caption: the lexicographer who omitted Scotland's most famous dish from the first edition! The oversight had been rectified by 1883 and haggis has never been removed. The fate of the lexicographer in question is unknown.

In fairness to him this may be a fanciful reading of events but the omission of this emblematic Scottish dish is a teasing linguistic conundrum which it may be prudent to pass over. So let us diplomatically move on.

Indeed let us console ourselves with gastronomic matters of a less contentious kind. In those distant times breakfast ("the breaking of a fast") was still "the first meal of the day". It was followed by lunch ("a *lump* of something eatable; a slight repast between breakfast and dinner". Dinner was: "the chief meal of the day: a feast".

In expectation of a feast a pie and a sandwich were still available, the latter defined as "two slices of bread with ham etc between (named after an *Earl of Sandwich*)". A salad in 1872 was "raw herbs cut up and seasoned with salt, vinegar etc." Vinaigrette existed but, even having directed the reader to look under vinegar, the dictionary unhelpfully eschewed a definition. By 1914 a definition was forthcoming: "a small box for holding aromatic vinegar". It remained so for over 60 years before it became by 1977 "a mixture of oil vinegar and seasoning used as a salad dressing." A long time to wait for those raw herbs to taste...well....tasty.

But even as early as 1872 the raw materials existed to make dishes as succulent as any we can experience today. Spices like cinnamon, cumin, garlic, nutmeg, turmeric were included alongside herbs like coriander, dill, parsley, rosemary, sage, thyme. There was saddle of mutton, a loin of this, a leg of that. You could accompany the dish with broccoli or samphire or you could combine them all in an olio: "a dish of different sorts of meat and vegetables boiled together". You could boil, broil, roast, fry or poach and round the meal off with a syllabub, a plumpudding or a posset. And if these native culinary traditions proved not to your taste the phrase ready-made existed prefiguring a style of cuisine (1883) that would become the norm by the mid 20th century. And by a process that mysteriously binds the acorn to the oak we can observe, through the pages of Chambers, the banquet (1872) morphing barely perceptibly into the TV dinner (1993).

Comestibles we think of as modern have a surprisingly long history. The lolly or lollypop dates from 1905 ("a coarse sweetmeat made with butter, flour, sugar, and treacle") while the doughnut ("sweetened dough fried in fat") dates from 1914. And the recent pub snack biltong: ("sundried lean meat") imported to counter the salted peanut and pork scratchings gets a mention as far back as 1933.

We shall have to wait until 1952 for the hot dog and the milkshake, and until 1977 for the pizza and wholefood. While we're doing so we can, by 1968, relax with a cuppa or an espresso (the same year incidentally that the daiquiri, black velvet and vegan food put in an appearance).

Camembert, the faggot ("internal organs of a pig mixed with bread and savoury herbs" – this is a dictionary, remember, not a restaurant menu), scrambled eggs, and tinned goods came to us in 1933. The cappuccino, the luncheon voucher, ravioli, and the Wimpy arrived in the 1968 supplement.

The 1872 edition had its stew but by 1883 it also had a French variant, the ragout. You only have to read Ode to A Haggis to realise that this was a dish of which Robert Burns was less than enamoured, but it was clearly catching on and providing the kind of gustatory sensation that mere "stew" could not altogether match.

Likewise the early edition had its soup and broth until 1905 when it was joined by consomme and "the Provencal kind of fish chowder", bouillabaise, adding something quite distinctive to the English vocabulary (and palate) in the process.

Meringue, pate, soufflé, casserole, daube, Blanquette, consommé, entrecote, escalope, brandade and fricassee followed in due course to be joined by the canapes and the amuses-bouches that caress our taste buds at soirees and in brasseries.

Germany and Eastern Europe brought us lager and pilsener with which we could wash down our sauerkraut and bratwurst. Japan provided us with sushi and the foodstuff that brightens everybody's Christmas, the satsuma, not to mention something no vegetarian or pescatarian (2011) could do without: tofu.

We have had pasta since 1977 but the varieties have continued to expand to include lasagne, fusilli, fettuccini, cannelloni, tagliatelli, linguini, and just plain spaghetti (1905). Orecchiette ("a pasta in the form of small concave discs") was added to the 11th edition, also joined by dashi ("a clear stock, usu flavoured with kelp, used in Japanese cookery"), dukkah ("a mixture of ground nuts with herbs and spices, used in Middle eastern cookery"), pad tha ("Thai-style dish of stir-fried rice noodles with seasoned shredded meat and vegetables, served with crushed peanuts"), pisco ("an alcoholic spirit distilled from grape wine") and rakija ("any of several alcoholic spirits distilled in the Balkans from fermented fruit juice, including raki and slivovitz").

And we haven't even travelled to India yet for our raita, pakora, chapati, naan and poppadums; to China for our pakchoi, chow mein or dim sum; to Spain for our tapas; to Russia for our blinis; or to Israel (and Golders Green) for our blintzes or matzot.

You can work up quite an appetite reading a dictionary.

Some Less than Objective Definitions

From the beginning the Chambers Dictionary has prided itself on balancing hard-headed information with a light-heartedness of touch. The inclusion of illustrations in the early books adds to the welcoming, **user-friendly** (1988) effect which, in its turn, is reinforced by the avuncular tone struck by Thomas Davidson in his prefaces.

It is immediately clear that Davidson wants to convey the excitement of words to the reader, inviting him or her to collude in the shared linguistic enterprise before them. In addressing the reader as an equal Davidson also drops his scholarly guard and provides an insight into the demands (and compromises) of his chosen discipline. "He must admit many words he would not himself use," he writes in 1905, "but which have been in use by his betters or are now current amongst his fellow-citizens whose speech he must needs understand." Then he offers this: "And it cannot be forgotten that Browning prepared himself for his trade as a poet by a study of Johnson's Dictionary," before adding mischievously, "– although it would perhaps have been better for his poetry if he had not."

It is perhaps this personal touch that sets Chambers apart from other dictionaries, that teasing sense of fun that is deployed from time to time to show that scholarship can be both educational *and* entertaining.

Below is a small selection of those entries that have the capacity to surprise and delight. It's fair to say the humour doesn't always survive the time-shift. But you get the idea.

ASBO a court order that places social restrictions on people with restricted social skills
  2006 edition

back-seat driver someone free of responsibility but full of advice
  supplement to 1952 edition

bafflegab the professional logorrhoea of many politicians, officials and salespeople, characterized by prolix abstract circumlocution and/or a profusion of abstruse technical terminology, used as a means of persuasion, pacification or obfuscation
  1988 edition

boy band a pop group, targeting mainly the teenage market, composed of young males chosen because they look good and can dance and sometimes even sing
  2003 edition

channel-surf to switch rapidly between different television channels in a forlorn attempt to find anything of interest
  2003 edition

charity begins at home usually an excuse for not allowing it to get abroad
  1901 edition

devil-dodger someone who attends churches of various kinds, to be on the safe side
  1952 edition

duvet day a day's absence from work arranged at short notice between an employee devoid of inspiration for a plausible excuse and an employer who has heard them all before
  2008 edition

éclair a cake, long in shape but short in duration, with cream filling and usually chocolate icing
  1952 edition

Havana cigar a fine quality of cigar, fondly supposed to be made at Havana
  1952 edition

kazoo a would-be musical instrument
  1988 edition

middle age between youth and old age, variously reckoned to suit the reckoner
1952 edition

mullet a hairstyle that is short at the front, long at the back, and ridiculous all round
2003 edition

nerd a clumsy, foolish, socially inept, feeble, unathletic, irritating or unprepossessing person, although often (eg in computers) knowledgeable
1998 edition

opinion what seems to one to be probably true
1952 edition

pink a person who is something of a socialist but hardly a red
1952 edition

regift to give (an unwanted present) as a gift to another person, in a process which is likely to continue almost indefinitely
2008 edition

road hog a swinishly selfish or boorishly reckless motorist or other user of the road
1952 edition

ski mask a knitted covering for the whole head except the eyes, worn for protection by skiers and bank robbers
2008 edition

tracksuit a loose warm suit intended to be worn by athletes when warming up or training, but sometimes worn by others in an error of judgement
2003 edition

vamp a featherless bird of prey
supplement to 1901 edition

wardrobe malfunction the temporary failure of an item of clothing to cover a part of the body that it would be advisable to keep covered
2008 edition

Sex and Sexuality

It is unlikely that men's and women's desires have changed that much over the 143 years since the Chambers dictionary first appeared. The social and sexual climate within which they have been expressing them, however, has changed beyond recognition. And the lifting of restrictions and taboos has led to a discernible increase in the vocabulary of sex and sexuality.

Were they alive today James Donald and Thomas Davidson, both devout Christians, would doubtless have had a view on the propriety or otherwise of the sexual revolution that has been underway since the 1960s. But as lexicographers and editors they would have left any moralising to one side, dispassionately listing words in current use and offering no personal judgment on any of them.

In those far off days there was an innocent simplicity surrounding this whole topic. Sex: "the distiction between male and female", sexual:"pertaining to sex", and sexuality:"state or quality of being sexual" accounted for a mere nine lines in 1872. The 12th edition had seventy-seven, listing words that would simply have baffled the early compilers.

One can just about see them wrestling manfully with sex aid, sex bomb, sex-change, sex kitten, sex offender, sexpot, sex shop, sex-starved, sex tourist and sex on legs but what they would have made of sex-and-shopping (a.k.a. shopping-and-fucking) simply defeats the imagination.

In their day it was more appropriate to devote the greater proportion of lines to love. By 1883, for example we had love-broker ("a third person who carries messages and arranges assignations between lovers"), love-letter, love-feast, love-knot, and lovelorn. Love-feat might need a bit of explaining these days ("the gallant act of a lover", since you ask) as would, without question, love-juice and love-shaft meaning, one hastens to add, "a concoction used to excite love" and "a dart of love from Cupid's bow" respectively.

Then, to make love to meant "to try to gain the affections of" and love-making meant "amorous courtship" not "sexual intercourse". It was taken as read that any physical intimacy would occur only between members of the opposite sex. As a result even as late as the 1933 edition there is no mention whatsoever of homosexuality. By 1952 homosexual is included as an adjective and homosexualist as a noun.

In that year the primary meaning of lesbian is given as an inhabitant of the Greek island of Lesbos and only secondarily as "homosexual". The order has been reversed in modern times. Bisexual as "hermaphrodite" is included in the 1952 edition while transvestite first puts in an appearance in the supplement to the 1968 edition.

For "amorous courtship" these days read slap and tickle, how's your father, rumpy pumpy or a leg-over (lesbians might prefer tribadism), while banging (1977 supplement), shagging, and bonking have taken over from "making love" in many popular contexts. Bonk is an interesting word which, though slang, can be used quite innocently (and certainly in contexts where fuck would be unacceptable). Its incorporation into the broadly uncontentious bonkbuster ("a novel, film etc featuring frequent and graphic scenes of sexual intercourse") is proof of that.

Gay has given rise to gay liberation and gay rights plus the more worrying gay-bashing and outright offensive gay plague. Gaydar, "the supposed ability of a person, esp a homosexual, to sense whether or not somebody else is homosexual" warrants an inclusion of its own in the 12th edition.

Today the sexual landscape is nothing if not inclusive and LGBT has been coined as an abbreviation for "lesbian, gay, bisexual and transgender".

If the 19th and 20th are anything to go by the 21st century will see even more added to the list.

Lifestyle and Leisure

Really, however did we manage before 1977? In 1968, if Chambers was the guide, none of us had a lifestyle. But magically, by the mid-1970s, we did.

For most of the chronology of humankind living has been more than enough to be getting on with; existing, surviving, subsisting, staying alive, drawing breath, getting by, or even (only latterly) making a living.

Between hunting, gathering and dodging the micro-organisms of whose existence we were blithely unaware we had precious little "spare" time. Our forebears may have celebrated Lammas or Beltane; they may have let their hair down at the summer solstice or later on high days and holy days, but for most of human history holidays in the way we talk of them today have simply not existed.

In 1872, however, the first edition of the dictionary allowed us to indulge in a hobby: "a favourite pursuit", which we could usefully slot into our lifestyle choices – though it would be 105 years before we knew that that was what we were doing.

What's more, the current edition introduces further possibilities. The bikini wax, for example, enabling women everywhere, since you ask, to vajazzle with the best of them.

Along with this exciting addition to the range of women's personal grooming options we can also add drinks like the appletini and the Long Island ice tea or foods like broccolini, cheesesteak, currywurst, and the cronut.

In this big society we can declutter, deep-clean, jibber-jabber or preach to the choir. We can screen grab, sext or take a selfie. We can play Wiffle ball or wear a onesie, twerk or photobomb. This is the world of the omnishambles and the one-trick pony, the payday loan and the Ponzi scheme. We can enjoy all the bounty the world has to offer from the Reuben sandwich to shale gas, from the traybake to slacklining.

Ever since the 1977 edition gave us cable television, flexitime, the blusher and the cagoule we have been indulging our lifestyle options with relish. In everything from the hairstyles we choose to sport (think beehive, bob and duck's arse) to the fashions we choose to wear, these lifestyle choices are plain to see. In that edition of '77, for example, the wet look was all the vogue. Or, if we preferred, we could wear the salopette, the tanga or the tank top. It was, however, the year of the bovver boy and the gang-bang, of Catch 22 and Dutch elm disease.

By the 12th edition the more foolhardy among us could go tombstoning, the more health conscious could become pescatarian or even, if a change in diet didn't prompt the longed-for weight loss, have a gastric band fitted. It was also the year we chose to forego the package holiday and enjoy a staycation.

But whether we are metrosexuals, fashionistas, shopaholics, ladettes or gold diggers enjoying a rave, a detox or a nip and tuck, the one thing we can't say any more is that we don't have choice.

OK, so these days we may have to put up with the zero hours contract, the fiscal cliff, kettling and fracking. But, hey, whatevs.

Business and Management

You will remember that the dictionary's second editor, the Rev Thomas Davidson, was very specific about the book's target audience. It was directed at both "the plain man who knows nothing and wishes to learn a little" and also at "the busy merchant (who) will find herein enough for the passing need of the moment, and perhaps, should occasion and taste cooperate, to whet his curiosity for further knowledge."

But the "busy merchant" in question would have had little time to study the dictionary in depth today because he would have been far *too* busy attending to the needs of his stakeholders, managing the bottom line, taking a conference call, worrying about the credit crunch, dealing with middle management or poring over his spreadsheets.

If our merchant had been only a half way successful businessman he would have been doing things for which no words existed in the late 19th century. He would, for example, have been constantly encouraging his staff in order to get the best out of them, showing them how they too could share in the success of the business. But he would have to wait until 1993 before he realised the importance of incentivizing his workforce.

Likewise he would have to have kept a close eye on how much he was earning and spending without ever realizing he was fretting over his cash flow (1977). And though his dream may have been to make big money that would not have been possible (in Chambers terms at least) until 1968. By that time he would have almost certainly grown the business and become a multinational (1977).

e-commerce was certainly a long way off (as, too, was mail order) but, working in a mixed economy, he would have known which of his products were money-spinners, which were loss-leaders, and which were duds. He would have already been task-oriented even though he would not have been informed of the fact until the 12th edition.

Similarly he would doubtless have been "cutting away, one by one, undesirable elements, eg particularly people, from (his) organization" without realising he was engaging in salami tactics or a salami strategy. It's a grand thing, education.

The current edition would have had even more wisdom to impart to his business. It would have told him that back-of-the-envelope calculations could come in very handy in his quest to make bajillions. It would have told him to prepare well in advance for Black Friday, to ensure his company was fit for purpose (by becoming a better man-manager), and, above all, warned him not to get mixed up in a Ponzi scheme.

He would have been advised of the pros and cons of issuing his staff with zero hours contracts and told to counsel them against slackerdom since if they were prepared to give sod all to the company a spot of gardening leave would be coming their way pdq (1993).

The business and management worlds have sometimes invented words from nothing but more often borrowed ordinary words and pressed them into service for different ends, drilling down, for example, outsourcing, whistleblowing, or number crunching.

And they are masters and mistresses of the art of transforming nouns into verbs; (to action, multiskill or multitask) and turning verbs into nouns (a big ask, a large spend or a quick build.)

How do they dream them up? Simple. Blue-sky thinking (2011).

Foreign Words

Some time in the mid 1980s, so the story goes, the then Secretary of State for Industry, Keith Joseph, found himself in Wales addressing a gathering of business types. Dismayed by their apparent lack of get-up-and-go and their unwillingness to embrace Thatcherism (1988) as warmly as he would have liked he berated them from the podium and, standing four-square before them, thundered, "Why! The Welsh don't even have a word for entrepreneur." To which, from the floor came the reply, "Neither do the English." But (and apologies for spoiling the admittedly rather good joke) they do. It is...ahem...entrepreneur.

You see, from the moment James Donald chose to include accoucheur, armada and assassin in his seminal 1872 edition it was clear that the Chambers Dictionary would have no qualms about including foreign words which, after a clear period of time, had embedded themselves in our "native" English vocabulary.

For what *is* our native tongue today but, at its core, an amalgam (from the Greek) of Anglo Saxon, Latin, Germanic, Norse, Norman and many other languages? It is part of a steady process of accretion that did not stop with the Norman Conquest. So let's take a look not at the pieces in a completed jigsaw (only dead languages can claim such fixity) but at some of the tiles (we could even say tessera) in an ever growing mosaic.

Let's begin with a lightning quiz and a brief canter from A to Z. Cover the page and list 26 foreign words alphabetically in quick succession.

You may have come up with;

abseil, blitz, cash (Tamil, since you ask), didgeridoo, ersatz, fandango, galleria, hara-kiri, imbroglio, jujitsu, klezmer, libretto, muesli, ninja, origami, poltergeist, quiche, riviera, soy, tsunami, umbra, vamoose, weltanschauung, xhosa, yo-yo (Tagalog, ditto), zeitgeist.

And they represent just the tip of a gigantic iceberg.

Who can resist an early morning cappuccino, perhaps a mid-morning bagel, a lunch-time pizza, an afternoon siesta, a lager at sundown, and a candle-lit supper a deux rounded off by petits fours and a schnapps? Sure, you might retire feeling like a zombie. But nothing a restorative ginseng and seltzer wouldn't cure the morning after.

Say it sotto voce but the Italians have swept the musical board. From andante to piano, from arpeggio to bel canto, from libretto to soprano – and all points in between.

But the French are up there in the medal table, too. We have them to thank for haute couture and Nouvelle Vague, for the femme fatale and the enfant terrible, and for culinary terms that include charcuterie, gateaux like the millefeuille and the madeleine, the casserole, the soufflé, and the aperitif. And these days what modern residence doesn't have its own en suite?

Japan has given us karaoke, kamikaze and the kimono; Scandinavia smorgasbord and the ombudsman; Germany the karabiner and the doppelganger; Tamil has produced candy and the cheroot; Hebrew the kibbutz; Yiddish the schnorrer and a touch of schmalz; Sanskrit the juggernaut and yoga; Hindi the sari and the Raj.

And in an arguably controversial move the 12th edition saw fit to introduce the Zulus' vuvuzela into the mix. Whether the editors were entirely compos mentis or just plain loco when they included this most irritating (and, one hopes, transient) of footballing accessories only time will tell.

But you surely can't fault their bona fides.

Words from Sport

The early editors had a bit of a soft spot for sport. In his 1898 preface Thomas Davidson included it among "the sciences and the arts of life", promising to devote space to "astronomy, physiology and medicine as well as...photography, printing, golf and heraldry". Golf and heraldry? An odd mix. But ours not to reason why.

Foot-ball had figured discreetly in the first edition of 1872 as "a large ball for *footing* or kicking about in sport; play with this ball" with not an inkling of the global phenomenon it was to become in the late 20th century. Cricket was likewise described bloodlessly in terms of its "11 persons, with 2 bats, a ball, and 2 wickets of 3 stumps or *staves* each" and was certainly not something you'd be inclined to cancel anything in order to watch. A test match it was not.

Tennis. "a game in which a ball is driven against a wall by rackets, and continually kept in motion" seems to be an entirely different game from its modern day equivalent. Golf and curling get a mention and seem largely unchanged though in this edition rugby does not appear at all.

By 1898, however, the popularity of some sports had clearly grown. We had Association Football ("game as formulated by the Football Association (1863))" and, by now, Rugby Football ("game according to the rules of the Rugby Football Union (1871))". Strangely enough drop goal first appears in the supplement to the 1933 edition leaving even the sporting ignoramus to wonder how they managed to play the game for so long without it.

That same year sees the puzzling inclusion of footballer leaving one similarly to wonder what players had been called hitherto. And with the addition, after a distance of a mere 35 years, of half time, linesman, league match, and offside one seriously has to question whether the beautiful game as played in those days bore any relation to what we see at Manchester United or Spurs today. Helpfully in that year five-a-side appeared – perhaps to take the pressure off the confusion.

By 1952 soccer has appeared as slang for association football and it is clearly well on the way to establishing itself as the national religion. From now on it is only a matter of time before it spawns a whole new vocabulary of referees, red cards, fouls, penalties, penalty shoot-outs, strikers, defenders, goalies and even soccer moms.

Olympiad and Olympic Games were included in the first edition of 1872 but until 1933 referred only to the four-yearly cycle of games in ancient Greece beginning in 776 BC. The 1933 edition referenced "the quadrennial international athletics contests held at various centres since 1896" and the way was clear for heats, time trials, decathlon, triathlon, pole vault, marathon, track and field, bronze, silver and gold medal.

The 1933 supplement also brought us golf's birdie and eagle, the fairway (what *had* it been called in the intervening years?) and the cricketing terms googly, leg before wicket, leg break. Winter Sports appeared that same year producing skiing, of course, skating – and, later, speed skating, bobsleigh which had appeared by 1952, the Norwegian slalom and downhill racer.

By 1968 a boxer could be afflicted with a cauliflower ear and we were introduced to water-skiing and the triple crown. Successive editions would introduce us to the slam dunk, grand slam, Grand National, and grandstand.

What Donald and Davidson would have made of the show off's desire to run naked across a pitch (to streak, 1977) we can only guess. Certainly the dictionary has come a long way from "golf and heraldry" listing all the major sports played the world over (and a few of the lesser ones like the current crop from the 13th edition, Wiffle ball and mixed martial arts , along with airball, athletic support, duathlete, duathlon).

And if all that sounds too tiring we can all retire to the sofa to work on our six-pack with a cold beer and a bag of crisps and, from 1993, relish our status as couch potatoes, content to cheer from the sidelines. Vuvuzela (2011) optional.

People who have lent their names to everyday words

Writers can be Pinteresque or Kafkaesque. They can be Shavian or Ciceronian. Orators and great leaders can be Jeffersonian or Churchillian while other, less lofty heads of state can be dismissed as Napoleons or little Hitlers.

But fame, notoriety and even great achievements are no guarantee in themselves of inclusion in the dictionary. No, that is the product of some mysterious alchemy by which Dickensian and Miltonian have been allotted duly descriptive lines while you will look in vain (at least in Chambers) for a corresponding adjective to memorialize the world view of Jane Austen, say, or Cervantes or Tolstoy.

In a less literary vein we have the Hungarians Laszlo Biro and Erno Rubik to thank for the ballpoint and the infuriating cube, while the Yorkshire show-jumper has bequeathed the world the Harvey Smith ("a V sign signifying derision") and the American film star the Mae West "an airman's inflatable life jacket used in World War II").

Macadamise made it into the first 1872 edition thanks to the work of John Loudon Macadam and soon became, courtesy of macadamisation in later volumes, the byword for metalled roads. That same year the Scottish chemist Charles Mackintosh achieved immortality with the inclusion of his "waterproof overcoat" and by 1898 the English chemist Sherard Cowper-Coles had lent his name to the verb sherardise ("to coat with zinc"). And as late as 1914 a fahrenheit was "a thermometer" after the 18th century German physicist Gabriel Fahrenheit.

By 1968 many more had made their way into Chambers; the French trapeze artist Jules Leotard with his "skintight garment worn by dancers, acrobats, etc", George Horace Gallup with his Gallup poll, and the artist William Heath Robinson whose name was routinely used to describe any "ridiculously complicated or elaborate mechanical contrivance".

From the world of fiction James's Thurber's Walter Mitty has become *the* "escapist daydreamer", Dickens's Scrooge the archetypal "miser", Sherlock the "detective", and Stevenson's Jekyll and Hyde the popular adjective describing "a split personality exemplifying good and evil".

To these we can add words like falstaffian, gargantuan, herculean, oedipal, micawberish, panglossian, pickwickian, pooterish to describe a spectrum of characteristics drawn from fictional creations that have lodged themselves into public speech and thus assured themselves a place in Chambers.

Are you a Shylock or a Romeo? A Fagin or a Man Friday? Ever tried to write a blurb? If so you will be invoking characters from entirely imagined worlds (this last, by the way, from the American humorist, Gelett Burgess, and his character Belinda Blurb). But if you wear Levi's, read braille or drive a diesel, and if you've ever tried to bowdlerise a book, or even lynch your boss you'll be invoking the names of real people who've left an indelible mark on the English language.

Axel Paulsen of Norway, Alois Lutz of Austria and Ullrich Salchow of Sweden, for example, have become immortalized among ice skaters for lending their names to specialized jumps. Likewise Dick Fosbury whose Fosbury Flop changed forever the way athletes approached the high jump.

And finally from the sublime to very nearly the ridiculous. The British theoretical physicist, Peter Higgs, must surely have reached higher than everyone when his Higgs boson achieved semi-divine status by being popularly dubbed the God particle (2014). Though the 15th century Mexican ruler, Montezuma the Second, can only boast (in the vulgar mind, that is) of having lent his name to Montezuma's revenge (1986) or "diarrhoea", aka, hilariously, the Aztec two-step (1993).

The World of Broadcasting

"Television?" the British journalist, C P Scott, is famously said to have wondered some time in the early 1930s. "The word is half Latin and half Greek. No good can come of it." As a classicist himself Scott knew, etymologically, whereof he spoke. But sociologically he was way off the mark.

A decade earlier Marconi et al had been developing the technology that would transform the world but it was only in 1933 that the supplement to the Chambers dictionary listed radio and wireless for the first time. By 1952 television and televise had been included and from then on words associated with the broadcast media were to proliferate unstoppably.

By that time, too, the word documentary had appeared blossoming into another hybrid, shockumentary, by the 12th edition ("a documentary film dealing with shocking subjects in a graphic way"). By 1988 the soap opera was now simply the soap enabling further transmogrifications like the docusoap to emerge.

But we are racing ahead of ourselves since, in the first instance, the British public had to be told what exactly it was that they were doing when staring at that box in the corner like meerkats eyeing a clock. As late as 1988, for example, a listener was simply "one who listens or hearkens", though by 1993 listenership ("the estimated number of listeners to a radio broadcast") had crept in. Until 1952 a viewer was merely "one who views" or, more surprisingly, "a colliery superintendent", a definition to which "a television watcher" had been added by 1968.

In that year things really got cracking and the supplement lists telecine, telefilm, telegenic ("ill-formed word"), teleprompter, telerecording, telescreen and, incidentally, Telstar ("a satellite launched on 10th July, 1962 used to relay television pictures across the Atlantic"). 1968 also saw the appearance for the first time of amplitude modulation (later AM), black comedy, compere, frequency modulation (later FM), hi-fi, monaural, quiz-master, typecast, video, videotape, weepie, wide-screen and zoom lens.

Technology aside, the content was soon starting to generate a vocabulary of its own as well, and by 1977 the talk-show, the chat-show, the phone-in, panel-games (the gameshow made it in 1998), the sitcom, the swingometer and even the Beeb had appeared – as had the word channel in any sense other than "groove or furrow". And, of course, as our TV sets now gave us two of these to choose from the word commercial duly appeared denoting the adverts.

Although we had been staring at it largely uncomprehendingly for years the test card had made an appearance in Chambers by 1993, not long before it was phased out. Not that it mattered much in all that time since most of us had been watching in monochrome anyway. The advent of colour, however, produced the retronym, black-and-white TV and has rendered "colour TV" tautologous.

And how the broadcast landscape has changed: cable television or cablevision, pay TV, pay-per-view, breakfast television, ratings, plasma screens, flat screens, telethons, terrestrial and satellite.

Not forgetting of course reality TV which had found its way into the 2003 edition – although there were tell-tale signs that real life had indeed been imitating art many years earlier.

In 1993 loadsamoney: "a grotesque character invented by H Enfield in 1988" had officially become a recognizably human type, having acquired, well, loads of money from the economic boom. And have we not all at one time or another had an attack of the lurgy which appeared in 1988 and denoted "a fictitious disease (invented and popularized by the cast of BBC's *The Goon Show*") Fictitious? Try telling that to the millions of us hoping for a duvet day: "a day's absence from work arranged at short notice between an employee devoid of inspiration for a plausible excuse and an employer who has heard them all before."

What has the world come to? Let's blame the TV for making square eyes of us all. No good can come of it.

Medicine

In Chambers terms the world became a much more dangerous place after 1998. Up until that point we had had no need to fear the superbug because no such organism technically existed. But in the closing years of the 20th century our eyes were first and finally opened to this terrible affliction. Help would be on hand ten years later, however, in the shape of the polypill. But it was a long time to wait.

On the plus side 1998 had brought us the smear test and introduced us to the body mass index (BMI) to help us keep a check on our obesity levels.

Medicine had come a long way since 1872 when the apothecary was "one who is licensed to dispense medicine and to act as a medical practitioner", licensed no doubt to dispense an anodyne ("a medicine that allays pain"). Back then surgeon was "one who cures external diseases by working or operating on them with the hand". Cancer existed but its definition, "an eating, spreading tumour or canker supposed to resemble a crab", suggested treatment of the condition was rudimentary, to say the least.

The pace of medical progress accelerated in the 20th century though, interestingly, as late as 1914, airspace was defined as "the cubic content of a room or hospital ward with reference to the respirable air within it", and euthanasia as "an easy mode of death".

1933 introduced us to adrenalin, botulism, blood-pressure, (hypertension appeared in 1952), blood test, change of life, contraception, fatty acids, first-aid, insulin, psycho-analysis, radiography, radiotherapy, sleeping sickness, vitamin and (rather late in the day) trench fever.

Parkinson's disease first put in an appearance in the supplement to the 1968 edition, the same year that saw the inclusion of athlete's foot, autism, cardiology, defence mechanism, kiss of life and neonatal.

The development of specialized diagnostic tools such as ultrasound, computerised axial tomography (which gave us the CAT scanner) and nuclear magnetic resonance (NMR) has improved our standards of healthcare. Improvements in our health service generally, however, have resulted in the unwelcome phenomenon of health tourism and the rise of the health tourist.

The English physician, Edward Jenner's pioneering work with smallpox in the late 18th century led to great advances in the field of immunology and coincided with the preparation of the first edition of the dictionary. As a result vaccinate: "to inoculate with the cowpox" and vaccination became pivotal medical terms entering our general vocabulary from the beginning.

Likewise Fleming's discovery of penicillin in 1928 added to our understanding of immunology eventually bringing words like antibiotic and its shadow side antibiotic resistance into circulation.

We were being encouraged to carry a donor card by 1977 and those concerned about appearance and ageing had another worrying phenomenon to factor into the mix; cellulite. That year produced the latest crop of medical terms including amniocentesis, anabolic steroids, brain death, community physician, cot death, life sciences and immunotherapy.

We would have to wait until 1993 for the body bag.

Religion

If you were an English person or a Scot in 1872 the chances are you were a Christian. Even if you were an atheist or an unbeliever it was more than likely that it was Christianity you *didn't* believe in. And you would have to wait the best part of a century before multi-faith services or interfaith dialogue became commonplace features of the religious landscape.

Ecumenical meaning "belonging to the entire Christian Church" first entered the dictionary in 1905 giving rise much later to the ecumenical movement. But any hopes that it will indeed bring "unity on all fundamental issues of belief, worship etc" in the near future belong more to the realm of wishful thinking than that of reality. For doctrinal (and other) differences abound, separating Catholicism from Protestantism, the established Church of England from the Free Churches, and the mainstream denominations from some of the smaller sects – the Wee Frees, "the minority of the Free Church that refused to join with the United Presbyterian Church in 1900", being among the smallest in Scotland.

Evangelical Christianity (and Evangelicalism) are joined by the charismatic movement in 1977 with the phenomenon known as the Toronto Blessing included in 1998. Born again makes an appearance as far back as 1883 but not the afterlife which is included by 1952.

The dictionary deals pretty comprehensively with the major world faiths referring from the first edition to Judaism, Hindu - or Hindooism, and Buddhism. Mohammedan, Mohammedism and Mohammedanise:"to convert to Mohammedism" are included but it was only by 1986 that the editors pointed out that "these words are felt to be offensive by many Muslims, who prefer Muslim, Islam, Islamic etc". The Sikh religion is perhaps the most obvious omission from the early volumes but by 1906 the word is included.

The old favourite antidisestablishmentarianism gets an honourable mention en route to Zoroastrianism several hundred thousand words later. Along the way we are introduced to gurdwara, mosque, synagogue, chapel, mandir, stupa, basilica, monastery, convent, meeting house and ashram (1977). Halacha and kosher are defined by 1905 but no mention of halal is made until 1952. Haram, perhaps surprisingly, has to wait until 2011 for inclusion.

Guru (or gooroo), avatar, priest, rabbi, imam, bodhisattva all feature in the text – along with religious concepts such as karma, nirvana, ayurveda, ahimsa, Shekinah and Sharia.

New age and new ager find their way into the dictionary by 1993 and the dictionary is happy to deal with concepts such as the astral body, the near death experience, feng shui, chi and the I ching.

The 1914 edition contained both the concept of supralapsarianism: a belief espoused by "one of a class of Calvinists who make the decree of election and predestination to precede the Creation and the Fall", and that of ultramontanism: a belief espoused by "a faction within the Roman Catholic Church which is extreme in favouring the Pope's supremacy". It is hard to imagine that either of these theological and philosophical ideas would be of immediate use to "the plain man" or the "busy merchant" but the fact that they have survived into the latest edition perhaps suggests otherwise.

The Environment

The **environment** had made it into Chambers by 1883 but denoted something rather different from what we now take it to mean. Then it meant "the act of environing; the state of being environed". Consulting the verb **environ** ("to surround or encompass") led you thus to conclude that it simply meant something that surrounds us all – which is partly, though by no means all, it means today.

By 1986 the word had begun to acquire its modern connotations; "external conditions influencing development or growth of people, animals or plants". However even before that, in the supplement to the 1977 edition, **environmentalism** ("concern about environment and its preservation from the effects of pollution etc") makes an appearance along with the **environmentalist**, and a new discipline is officially born.

Things **ecological** were absent from the 1933 edition but had made it by 1952 as "the study of organisms in relation to the environment". An **ecologist** thus emerges at around this time whose area of research is, naturally enough, the **ecosystem** (1977).

Given the newness of the discipline, however, it is interesting to note the relatively prompt appearance of one word that seems to introduce a sceptical tone into the proceedings and to suggest that this new philosophy is not being universally embraced with automatic gratitude; **econut** "(*slang*) a person showing extravagant concern for the effects of man's behaviour on the environment". The scepticism continued in a later edition (1986) with the addition of **ecofreak** (the slang this time described as *derog*).

By now several lines were devoted to the prefix **eco-**; **ecocide, ecospecies, ecosphere**. Fast forward (1988) to the 12th edition and we have **ecoclimate, ecofriendly, eco-labelling, ecoterrorism, eco-tourism, eco-village** and **ecowarrior**.

The movement was now becoming, linguistically and politically, well established, spawning a number of words we have come to take for granted. The importance of the **ozone layer** was highlighted in 1977 as were the potentially disastrous consequences of the **greenhouse effect** (and later of **greenhouse gas**). **Solar energy** put in an appearance, too, along with the **green pound, biological clock,** and **biomass**.

Green itself was acquiring political overtones ("concerned with care of the environment esp. as a political issue") by 1986 and has since given rise to such words as **green fund** and **green tax**, with the 12th edition even including the environmental pressure group, **Greenpeace**.

Factory farming had been introduced by 1977 and **acid rain** had begun to fall by 1986. In that year you would also find **biodegradable, biosphere,** and (the inevitable worm in the bud) **bioterrorism**.

Deforest put in an appearance in the 1905 edition and by 1952 **deforestation** as a generally accepted phenomenon had been included.

By 1993 we had become familiar with **biodiversity** and **renewable energy** (**renewables**, as a noun, describing collectively those energy sources derived from solar, wind and wave power) and we now took for granted **wind energy** and the **wind farm**.

The growing awareness of the environment as an important element of our social and political life was underlined in the 11th edition by the inclusion for the first time of **carbon credit, carbon footprint, food miles, biosafety** and **geo engineering** and, in the 12th edition, by **agflation, agroterrorism, biocomputer, carbon, capture, carbon storage,** and **carbon offsetting**.

Freega ("a person who expresses opposition to materialism and consumerism by retrieving and using discarded food, clothes etc") and **freecycle** (to recycle an unwanted product by giving it free to someone"), both words introduced in the last edition of Chambers, reminded us that there was something we could all do to conserve the earth's finite resources. This environment business was getting personal.

Society

Where to begin? Where to find the clues linking the society that we inhabit today to the one with which the earliest compilers of the Chambers Dictionary were familiar?

The questions are probably pointless since a dictionary is arguably the last place to look for patterns. All you will find are words listed promiscuously and with glorious abandon; the sacred next to the secular, the elevated next to the profane, the colloquial next to the technical. Words we use every day and words we shall probably never use in a lifetime.

Thus the supplement to the 1933 edition lists for the first time the bootlegger and the Boy Scout, the cave-man and the class-war, the crossword puzzle and the chiropractor. It lists speedway and cubism, feminism and sadism, the parka and the tuxedo not forgetting the Festschrift and the covering letter, co-education and eurythmics, the pogrom and the hairpin bend. If there is a pattern to be discerned you must admit it is mighty hard to discern it.

True, there are some fixed points. The croupier of 1872 ("he who watches the cards and collects the money") is recognizably the same figure today; the fanatic of 1872 ("extravagant in opinions esp on religious subjects") has not changed that much; and red tape of 1872 ("the red tape used in public, and esp government offices, for tying up documents etc and applied satirically to the intricate system of routine in vogue there") is what it always has been.

But most other things have altered - as they will do again and again until 2072 and beyond. The supplement to the 1968 edition, for example, saw fit to add, among others, words that subtly (and not so subtly) reflected our changing preoccupations, including; boiler suit, bikini, bonkers, bossa nova, bra, bubble car, bucket seat, piece of cake, cash and carry, the cha-cha(cha), cine camera, civil defence, comprehensive school, espresso, estate car, expense account, face-lift, fruit machine, lunatic fringe, method acting, national service, printed circuit, ravioli, red carpet, roller-coaster, social security, sugar daddy and yob ("teenage loafer").

What we wore, what we ate, the music we listened to, the values we espoused and even the way we thought (the intellectual and the intelligenstia were added in 1933) are logged within these pages and the results form not only a linguistic map of our evolving society but almost an archaeological record of our daily lives over a hundred years and more.

Flick further through the supplementary listings of 1977 and you encounter backpacking, buzz word, childminder, day centre, gazump, glue-sniffing, greenfield site, groupie, hang-gliding, hatchback, hit-man, Jobcentre, kneecapping, kung fu, pelican crossing, safari park, sheltered housing, sleeping policeman, tug of love and unsocial hours.

But how many more new words can one dictionary contain? The temptation could be to cull some to make way for others, to remove rare or archaic words like evoe ("*interj* expressing Bacchic frenzy"), fidibus ("a paper spill for lighting a pipe"), or Newgate frill/fringe ("a beard under the chin or jaw") in order to free up space for Arab Spring, bedroom tax, bitch-slap, Kindle or payday loan (new entries to the 13th edition). But the editors have valiantly resisted the temptation and pledged themselve to adding and not subtracting.

This treasury of rare, historical words, represents, after all, a continuous link with a vanished past and to purge them from the record is to rub out important elements of our shared history. And how might we feel if, in a hundred years time, an editor took a blue pencil to cage fighter, cougar, crotch rocket and cycling shorts? What if due diligence, fiscal cliff, fuck buddy and the grocer's apostrophe were to disappear? How would we react to losing jailbreak and jazz hands, legal high and lush, mini-me and M-theory? Wouldn't subsequent generations be the poorer for not having scrappage and screen grab before them? Not to mention Shabby Chic, shock and awe, silver bullet, Tea party and Trekkie, vinyasa yoga, X-factor and the zipwire.

To consign them to the bin would be like erasing hieroglyphs from the Rosetta Stone – not to mention causing mayhem for Scrabble players.

Slang

For over a hundred years a banana remained "a gigantic herbaceous plant or its nutritious fruit", bananas signifying two or more of the above-named nutritious fruits. In 1977, however, by some unfathomable linguistic transformation, it (or they) first entered the dictionary via the supplement and thus came formally to mean "mad" or "crazy" (as in to go bananas). Now you can also go ape, ape-shit, or ballistic. You can blow a fuse or a gasket or get your knickers in a twist.

Similarly in 1986 a dipstick was "a rod for measuring the depth of liquid in a sump". These days it means "a stupid or foolish person", as do dimwit, dingbat, fuckwit, dweeb, dope, dork, knucklehead, nitwit and numpty. You need make only a cursory examination of the 13th edition of Chambers to find many more.

In the process you will also unearth scores of words denoting the nitwit's opposite number in the grey matter department; the boffin (aka brains), and more words to describe people if they are too clever by half or clever-clever; a clever dick, for example, a clever clogs, a smart Alec, a smarty pants or a smartarse.

It is a characteristic of the human race that no sooner have we invented a word to describe something we invent another word to describe the same thing (a process without which poetry would not exist and the world would be a dull place indeed).

But not content with formal synonyms we will coin informal (usually shorter) words to connote even these. Telly, for instance, first appeared in 1968, helpfully halving the number of syllables we would need to use to describe the television set in the corner. The box (1977) went further still, halving even that.

Originally "a jargon of thieves and disreputable people" slang is now universally used by people of every socio-economic class who, in the supplement of 1968 were given licence by Chambers to get in a flap, belly-ache, go bonkers, feel cagey (or cheesed-off), drink a coke, date a chick, make a boob, take a gander or just waffle (in 1977 we could also rabbit on).

If we're courageous we've got balls, guts, bottle or grit. If we're sad we can be in the dumps or have a sour puss "face". The bonce, nut or napper denotes our head (the plural nuts referring to a quite different part of a man's anatomy), lugs our ears and beak, hooter or schnozz the nose.

And we have a plethora of words to choose from should we be in our cups or one over the eight. We could be sozzled, battered, bladdered, hammered or wrecked (if we're Scottish also puggled, blootered, guttered, wellied or stoatin'). And we might be pissed, variously, as a lord, newt, fart, skunk or rat. Quite what rats, skunks or newts have done to deserve this reputation has never been made clear.

In 1977 the verb to bomb was included for the first time to denote failing. Since then it's been joined by to nosedive or to go belly-up. And that same year saw a crop of new arrivals including come out (as gay etc), ego-trip, hassle, hype, nuke, nitty-gritty, raunchy, rip-off, skinflick, shades (sunglasses), spook, suss out, teeny-bopper, yucky, zonked and zilch.

The latest (13th) edition you're holding introduces jock itch, amazeballs and bunga bunga; boozehound and budgie smugglers; babelicious, chillax and twerk.

Rest assured that the 14th edition will bring you many more.